THE

PEOPLE'S STUDY BIBLE

King James Version

HAROLD LINDSELL, Ph.D., D.D.

GENERAL EDITOR

Tyndale House Publishers, Inc.
Wheaton, Illinois

The publisher gratefully acknowledges the use of
the following articles from other sources:

"Introduction to the Old Testament"
"Between the Testaments"
"Introduction to the New Testament"
"Introduction to the Gospels"
"The Bible: An Overview"
by William Kerr, from *Kerr's Handbook to the Bible;*
used by permission of the author

"The Bible" by F. F. Bruce
"Inspiration" by J. I. Packer
"English Versions of the Bible" by J. H. Skilton
from *New Bible Dictionary;* used by permission
of InterVarsity Press.

"Weights and Measures in the Bible" from *The Shaw Pocket Bible Handbook;* used by permission of
Harold Shaw Publishers.

"Old Testament Prophecies Fulfilled by the Messiah"
by Harold Willmington, from *The Visualized Bible;*
used by permission of Tyndale House Publishers, Inc.

"Guide to the Ancient Manuscripts" by Philip Comfort
from *Eight Translation New Testament;* used
by permission of the author.

"The Hebrew Calendar" from *New Bible Atlas:* used by
permission of InterVarsity Press.

THE PEOPLE'S STUDY BIBLE

First printing, October 1986

Appreciation is expressed to Zondervan Bible Publishers,
the Zondervan Corporation, for permission to use certain
material from The Harper Study Bible
(copyright 1964, 1965), edited by Harold Lindsell.

Library of Congress Catalog Card Number 86-050772
ISBN 0-8423-4764-X Cloth
ISBN 0-8423-4765-8 Black Bonded
ISBN 0-8423-4766-6 Burgundy Bonded

Printed in the United States of America

CONTENTS

NAMES AND ORDER OF THE
BOOKS OF THE BIBLE

THE OLD TESTAMENT

THE NEW TESTAMENT

ALPHABETICAL LIST OF THE
BOOKS OF THE BIBLE

THE OLD TESTAMENT

THE NEW TESTAMENT

CONTRIBUTORS

HAROLD LINDSELL, Ph.D., D.D. *General Editor*
Book Introductions, Outlines,
Key Thought Commentary, and
"The Bible, God's Inspired Word"

WILLIAM KERR, Th.D., S.T.D., D.D., LL.D.
"Introduction to the Old Testament,"
"Between the Testaments,"
"Introduction to the New Testament,"
"Introduction to the Gospels,"
and "The Bible: An Overview"

F. F. BRUCE, M.A., D.D., F.B.A.
"The Bible"

J. I. PACKER, M.A., D.Phil., D.D.
"Inspiration"

HAROLD WILLMINGTON, M.Div., D.Min.
"Old Testament Prophecies Fulfilled by Christ"

J. H. SKILTON, M.A., M.Div., Ph.D.
"English Versions of the Bible"

PHILIP COMFORT, M.A.
"Guide to the Ancient Manuscripts"

ACKNOWLEDGMENTS

My thanks and appreciation . . .

To Mark Taylor, president of Tyndale House Publishers and son of Kenneth and Margaret Taylor, my close friends for many years. He has enthusiastically supported the publication of *The People's Study Bible.*

To Wendell Hawley, Robert Bolinder, and Mark Carpenter for their help and encouragement.

To Virginia Muir for her supervision of the editorial process.

To Philip Comfort, project editor, who contributed many hours of valuable service and expertise in the editorial preparation of this material for publication.

To my wife, Marion, for her faithful encouragement during the years I have committed to this work.

Dr. Harold Lindsell
General Editor, *The People's Study Bible*

INTRODUCTION

THE BIBLE is the Word of God. God gave it to people for them to read, understand, believe, and obey. Every Christian should read the Bible and seek to understand it. Regular reading, accompanied by prayer, study, and the Holy Spirit's guidance, will produce stronger faith and obedience in each Christian's life.

The People's Study Bible is designed to help the reader gain a more thorough understanding of God's Word by bringing together as much useful information as can be contained in a single volume. The intention is to make that information immediately accessible to the reader. He can go on from there to peruse other excellent books that will provide more material in greater detail. But if he has neither access to other books nor time to study them, he will find enough in this study Bible to give him what he needs for Christian nurture, as well as more than a speaking acquaintance with Bible backgrounds, the great doctrines of the Christian faith, and explanatory material that ties all sixty-six books of Scripture into a unified whole.

A good plan to follow is to read one book of the Bible at a time (and the Bible should be read through at least once a year in its entirety). The introductory material to each book is important for a better understanding of the background, authorship, purpose, and characteristics of that book. All of the books have been outlined for study purposes. The outlines provide a structure for organizing thematic and chronological developments in the text. The notes in the *Key Thought Commentary* provide textual alternatives, explain difficult passages, enlarge upon important themes, and, most important, shed light on the key thought of the passage being discussed.

The *Key Theme Cross Reference* system indicates other scriptures that are relevant to the verse or verses being read. These cross references are thought-oriented, connecting the reader with verses that explain or develop the thought in the original verse. An asterisk (*) indicates the presence of a commentary note at the bottom of the page. The notes have been indexed by subject and appear at the end of the Bible in the *Index to Key Thought Commentary.* Almost any important biblical subject will be found in the index, with the Scripture reference. Thus, for example, the reader can locate information on such subjects as the new birth, justification, faith, sanctification, Christ's second coming, the virgin birth, etc. Many important notes are connected with the names of Bible characters such as Adam, Noah, Abraham, David, Elijah, Paul, and Jesus.

At the beginning of this volume the reader will find an extensive index called *The Key Topic Index.* This index, with more than 24,000 entries, is specifically designed to facilitate topical study. It lists significant aspects of each topic, with reference to the pertinent scriptures, with the page numbers.

The back of this volume contains several study aids. These include articles to help the reader gain a comprehensive view of the Bible, understand the Bible as a divinely inspired book, and learn about the ancient manuscripts and English translations of the Bible. And there are charts displaying a Bible Chronology, a Gospel Harmony, Parables of Christ, Miracles of Christ, and Messianic Prophecies. Other reference helps—Hebrew Calendar, Table of Weights and Measures, Concordance, Index to Proper Names, and Maps—should greatly help in Bible study.

In the notes I have frequently quoted Matthew Henry because he had deep spiritual insight and was able to apply the Bible to one's life. His commentary on the Bible is inexpensive and readily available. Every quotation from Matthew Henry is marked with an asterisk (*). Every quotation adapted from Dr. Kenneth Taylor's marginal notes in *The Living Bible* is marked with a dagger (†).

The reader should know that the notes present a variety of views on matters about which Christians have disagreed across the years. Thus, for example, neither an infant-baptism nor an anti-infant-baptism view is promoted, although information is available by way of explanation for both views. So also various notes present Calvinistic, Arminian, and Dispensational views. A variety of viewpoints about the millennium and the second advent are also given. Let us not be harsh or unkind toward those who hold views different from ours. So long as the differences do not have to do with the fundamentals of the Christian faith, we can allow for diversity, in a spirit of love. This does not mean that anyone needs to surrender personal convictions. Every Christian, as a priest of God, is entitled to search the Scriptures, trusting the guidance and enlightenment of the Holy Spirit.

The Bible alone is the infallible Word of God. Thus, I do not lay claim to infallibility for the outlines, the introductions, or the notes. However, they do fall within the boundaries of historic orthodoxy and reflect a commitment to such confessions as the Apostles' Creed. Any errors will be corrected in later printings. Furthermore, no English version, paraphrase, or translation is perfect. Only as they accurately reflect the languages in which the Scriptures were written can they be said to be faithful representations of the Word of God.

This book is dedicated to God for his glory. May he use it to help the reader understand his Word and grow in the knowledge of the Lord Jesus Christ.

Harold Lindsell
General Editor

ABBREVIATIONS USED IN THE NOTES

KJV	Authorized King James Version	*	Quotation from Matthew Henry's commentary on the Bible
NASB	New American Standard Bible	†	Adapted from Dr. Kenneth Taylor's notes in *The Living Bible*
NIV	New International Version	ff	The following verses
NJKV	New King James Version		
RSV	Revised Standard Version		
TEV	Today's English Version		
TLB	The Living Bible		

Abbreviations for Books in The Bible (in the order they appear)

OLD TESTAMENT

Genesis .... Gen
Exodus .... Exod
Leviticus .... Lev
Numbers .... Num
Deuteronomy .... Deut
Joshua .... Josh
Judges .... Judg
Ruth .... Ruth
1 Samuel .... 1 Sam
2 Samuel .... 2 Sam
1 Kings .... 1 Kings
2 Kings .... 2 Kings
1 Chronicles .... 1 Chron
2 Chronicles .... 2 Chron
Ezra .... Ezra
Nehemiah .... Neh
Esther .... Esther
Job .... Job
Psalms .... Ps
Proverbs .... Prov
Ecclesiastes .... Eccles
Song of Solomon .... Song of Sol
Isaiah .... Isa
Jeremiah .... Jer
Lamentations .... Lam
Ezekiel .... Ezek
Daniel .... Dan
Hosea .... Hos
Joel .... Joel
Amos .... Amos
Obadiah .... Obad
Jonah .... Jonah
Micah .... Mic
Nahum .... Nah
Habakkuk .... Hab
Zephaniah .... Zeph
Haggai .... Hag
Zechariah .... Zech
Malachi .... Mal

NEW TESTAMENT

Matthew .... Matt
Mark .... Mark
Luke .... Luke
John .... John
Acts of the Apostles .... Acts
Romans .... Rom
1 Corinthians .... 1 Cor
2 Corinthians .... 2 Cor
Galatians .... Gal
Ephesians .... Eph
Philippians .... Phil
Colossians .... Col
1 Thessalonians .... 1 Thess
2 Thessalonians .... 2 Thess
1 Timothy .... 1 Tim
2 Timothy .... 2 Tim
Titus .... Titus
Philemon .... Philem
Hebrews .... Heb
James .... James
1 Peter .... 1 Pet
2 Peter .... 2 Pet
1 John .... 1 John
2 John .... 2 John
3 John .... 3 John
Jude .... Jude
Revelation .... Rev

BOOK INTRODUCTION

It provides information on the background, authorship, purpose, and characteristics of the book.

Reading the introduction may lead you to other studies that can be done by using other portions of this study Bible. For example, you might want to study . . .

- the location of Ephesus; see Map, p.2272.
- the date of writing; see Chronology of the New Testament, p.2052.
- God being the author of Scripture; see "Inspiration," p.2003 and "The Bible, God's Inspired Word," p.1999.
- the omission of "at Ephesus" in certain ancient manuscripts; see "Guide to the Ancient Manuscripts," p.2044.
- various aspects of the church; see *The Key Topic Index*, p.52.
- the work and the person of the Holy Spirit; see *The Key Topic Index*, p.133.

THE EPISTLE OF PAUL THE APOSTLE TO THE

EPHESIANS

Authorship, date, and background Ephesians is one of the four "prison epistles" which include also Colossians, Philippians, and Philemon. Since Paul was in prison a number of times, the question arises, which of the many imprisonments was the locale from which these letters were sent to their destinations. Despite the difference of opinion, Rome is the most likely city, and the date of writing is A.D. 60–61. Two of the other most important questions have to do with the authorship of Ephesians and the destinations for which the letter was intended.

Liberal scholars almost without exception think Paul did not write Ephesians. Conservatives have always thought he did. The case for non-Pauline authorship is tenuous at best. The weight of evidence falls in favor of Pauline authorship. Perhaps the most important fact is that the letter itself claims to be Pauline, for the salutation says: "Paul, an apostle" (1:1). Thus, to say Paul did not write the letter is to disregard what the Bible itself says. If what is said is not true, then the same principle can be applied elsewhere with great damage. To suppose that someone else would claim to be Paul, however high his motive, given the fact that God is the author of Scripture, is hardly acceptable. The principle that what the Bible says is true must lead to the conclusion that Paul indeed was the author of the letter.

Some of the ancient manuscripts leave out the phrase "at Ephesus," which raises the question to whom the letter was addressed. A number of conservative scholars say it was an "encyclical letter," by which is meant a letter intended for more than a single person or place. It probably was sent to a number of churches in Asia which included Ephesus, of course. Tychicus was Paul's messenger who brought the letter from Rome to Asia (Ausia) (6:21). Aristarchus, Epaphras, Luke, and Demas, as well as Mark, were with Paul at the time of writing. The letter represents Paul's maturest thinking about the church. It also overlaps at points with Colossians, which was written during the same period.

Characteristics and content Ephesians comes at a point in time when many new churches have come into being. Paul, no doubt, has given great thought to the nature of the church and the churches, and under the guidance of the Holy Spirit he writes something unique. In this letter he talks about the church as a universal phenomenon, whereas in his other letters he has written to local congregations. Ephesians presents an overview of God's plan of the ages. Paul speaks about the purpose of God from before the beginning of the world, and the certainty that the divine intention will be realized through Jesus Christ via the apostles, prophets, and the apostle Paul himself.

Paul develops the doctrine of the church. He calls the church "his body," that is, the body of Christ (1:23). He also proclaims that it is the bride or wife of Christ (5:22ff.) and the dwelling place (temple) of the Holy Spirit (2:19–22). Christ is the head over the church and all believers are members of the body. This church includes believers of all ages, even those yet to come into it. Believers hear the good news that there is something beyond this earthly sphere. They are related to the "heavenly places" (as in 1:3, 2:6, and 3:10) both as a present relationship and with the sure guarantee of its eternal nature when Christ's people shall reign and rule with him forever. This view of the church in relation to the heavenlies finds its fullest disclosure in Ephesians as a mystery (secret plan) now made manifest.

Ephesians also treats the work of the Holy Spirit in the lives of believers by way of summation. Herein we learn that believers are "sealed with that holy spirit of promise" (1:13); that Jew and Gentile may come to God the Father through the Holy Spirit (2:18); that the Father would grant us "according to the riches of his glory, to be strengthened with might by his Spirit in the inner man" (3:16); that the revelation of God's plan of the ages has come to apostles and prophets by the Holy Spirit (3:5); that we ought to, and therefore can, "be filled with the Spirit" (5:18); that believers should pray "always with all prayer and supplication in the Spirit" (6:18); and that they are to be careful that they don't "grieve the holy Spirit of God" by the way they live (4:30).

In Ephesians, believers are marked off as members of the new humanity, a worldwide family of redeemed sons and daughters who have peace with God and should be at peace with each other and rejoice in and make use of the unfathomable riches they have in Jesus Christ.

THE PEOPLE'S STUDY BIBLE

Outline

I. Introduction (1:1, 2)
II. Doctrinal teaching (1:3—3:21)
III. Exhortations for the church (4:1—6:20)
IV. Conclusion (6:21-23)

I. INTRODUCTION (1:1, 2)

1 PAUL, an apostle of Jesus Christ by the will of God, to the saints
which are at Eph'e-sus, and to the faithful in Christ Jesus:
2 Grace *be* to you, and peace, from God our Father, and *from* the Lord
Jesus Christ.

II. DOCTRINAL TEACHING (1:3—3:21)

A. PRAISE TO THE TRIUNE GOD

3 Blessed *be* the God and Father of our Lord Jesus Christ, who hath
blessed us with all spiritual blessings in heavenly *places* in Christ:
4 According as he hath chosen us in him before the foundation of the
world, that we should be holy and without blame before him in love:
5 Having predestinated us unto the adoption of children by Jesus Christ
to himself, according to the good pleasure of his will,
6 To the praise of the glory of his grace, wherein he hath made us accepted
in the beloved.
7 In whom we have redemption through his blood, the forgiveness of sins,
according to the riches of his grace;
8 Wherein he hath abounded toward us in all wisdom and prudence;
9 Having made known unto us the mystery of his will, according to his
good pleasure which he hath purposed in himself:
10 That in the dispensation of the fulness of times he might gather
together in one all things in Christ, both which are in heaven, and which are
on earth; *even* in him:
11 In whom also we have obtained an inheritance, being predestinated
according to the purpose of him who worketh all things after the counsel of
his own will:
12 That we should be to the praise of his glory, who first trusted in Christ.
13 In whom ye also *trusted*, after that ye heard the word of truth, the
gospel of your salvation: in whom also after that ye believed, ye were sealed
with that holy Spirit of promise,

1:1 Rom 1:1; 1 Cor 1:1; 2 Cor 1:1; Col 1:2
1:2 Rom 1:7; Tit 1:4
☆**1:3** Ps 72:17; Eph 1:20; 2:6
☆**1:4** Lk 1:75; 2 Thess 2:13; 1 Pet 1:2, 20
1:5 Jn 1:12; Rom 8:15, 29; Gal 4:5; Eph 1:11
1:6 Isa 43:21; Mt 3:17; 17:5; Rom 3:24; Col 1:13
☆**1:7** 1 Cor 6:20; Col 1:14; Heb 9:12; Rev 5:9
1:9 Col 1:26, 27; 2:2
1:10 Mk 1:15; Gal 4:4; Col 1:20
1:11 Isa 46:10; Rom 9:11; Eph 3:11
1:12 Eph 1:6, 14; Jas 1:18
☆**1:13** 2 Cor 1:22; Eph 4:30; Col 1:5

1:3 *in heavenly places* (or "the heavenlies," from the Greek *hoi epouranioi*) is to be found in 1:20; 2:6; 3:10; 6:12 in the Greek. It is the place where Christ now reigns, his sacrifice having been accepted by the Father. In this spiritual realm believers enjoy every spiritual blessing. In this unseen but real world the Christian wages his warfare against the malign forces of Satan (6:12).
1:4 The doctrine of election is taught in the Scriptures. It is the outworking of God's power to effect what he chooses. The New Testament uses the term "elect" (*eklektoi*) variously. We are elected or chosen (1) to good works (2:10); (2) to become like Jesus (Rom. 8:29); (3) to obtain eternal glory (Rom. 8:21); and (4) to be adopted as sons and daughters of God (1:5). When it comes to salvation, theologians have argued about election. Some say that if only those who are elected are saved, then Christ's redemption was limited. Others reply that the call to salvation is universal, so that it is the divine intention to save all men; therefore, the redemption is potentially efficacious for all men, even when all men do not accept Christ. The Scriptures teach that election is according to God's sovereign purpose (Rom. 9:10-13; Eph. 1:11) and that it is related to God's foreknowledge (Rom. 8:29). Scripture does not explicitly say what it is in the divine foreknowledge that determines his elective choice. Scripture indicates that man is a free moral agent and that God sovereignly works out all things according to his own good pleasure.
1:7 Redemption includes the following: (1) the forgiveness of sins (1:7; Col. 1:14); (2) justification or right standing with God (Rom. 3:24); (3) adoption into the family of God (Gal. 4:4, 5); and (4) purification (Titus 2:14).
1:13 Whoever receives Jesus Christ as Savior is sealed by the Holy Spirit of God. This sealing guarantees that we are his and that we will secure the full

INTRODUCTORY OUTLINE

TEXTUAL OUTLINE

It provides a structure for organizing thematic developments in the text.

KEY THEME CROSS REFERENCES

These cross references are thought-oriented, connecting the reader with verses that explain or develop the thought in the original verse. You can use the references for studying similar themes throughout Scripture and for comparing the Old and New Testaments.

For example, note how often Colossians (Col) is cited. This is because Ephesians and Colossians share many of the same themes. You can also see how the ideas in Ephesians 1:3, 6, 11 are related to Psalm 72:17; Isaiah 43:21; 46:10.

An asterisk next to a cross reference indicates there is a comment on that verse.

KEY THOUGHT COMMENTARY

The commentary notes provide information on key phrases (for example, see explanation on *in heavenly places* in note to 1:3), significant theological terms (for example, see discussion on "election" in note on 1:4), and important biblical terms (for example, see details about "redemption" in note on 1:7).

KEY TOPIC INDEX

An index to all the key topics in the Bible arranged alphabetically with references and page numbers for every entry

The Key Topic Index provides an easy-to-use, alphabetical listing of all the important topics in the Bible. This includes major Bible themes, important Bible terms, key characters, significant places, and other topics important to Bible study. Each topic has been broken into several subheadings, each of which is followed by Scripture references and corresponding page numbers in *The People's Study Bible.*

Scripture references normally appear in canonical order (i.e., Genesis comes before Exodus and Exodus before Leviticus, etc.). Sometimes, Scripture references are not in canonical order because the passages so listed must be taken as a unit (e.g., this often occurs when a New Testament truth is typified in the Old Testament—the New Testament reference will immediately follow the Old Testament reference).

ADULTERY

AFFECTIONS, THE

AFFLICTION, PRAYER UNDER

AFFLICTIONS

AFFLICTIONS MADE BENEFICIAL

AFFLICTIONS OF THE WICKED, THE

AGRICULTURE

ALLIANCE AND SOCIETY WITH THE ENEMIES OF GOD

ALTARS

ALTAR OF BURNT-OFFERING, THE

ALTAR OF INCENSE

AMALEKITES, THE

AMUSEMENTS AND PLEASURES, WORLDLY

ANAKIM, THE

ANGELS

ANGER

ANGER OF GOD, THE

ANTICHRIST

APOSTATES

APOSTLES, THE

ARK OF THE COVENANT, THE

ARMIES

ARMS, MILITARY

ASTROLOGY

ASTRONOMY

ATONEMENT, THE

BACKSLIDING

BELIEVERS, NAMES AND TITLES OF

BLASPHEMY

Sometimes used in hunting ... Gen 27:3 ... 49
For shooting arrows ... 1 Chron 12:2 ... 681
Called the battle bow ... Zech 9:10 ... 1453
Zech 10:4 ... 1454

Those who used, called
—Bowmen ... Jer 4:29 ... 1170
—Archers ... 1 Sam 31:3 ... 500
Jer 51:3 ... 1246
Usually of steel ... 2 Sam 22:35 ... 546
Job 20:24 ... 850
Held in the left hand ... Ezek 39:3 ... 1327
Drawn with full force ... 2 Kings 9:24 ... 624
The Jews taught to use ... 2 Sam 1:18 ... 503
Used expertly by
—Lydians ... Jer 46:9 ... 1236
—Elamites ... Jer 49:35 ... 1243
—Philistines ... 1 Sam 31:2, 3 ... 500
—Sons of Reuben, Gad, and Manasseh ... 1 Chron 5:18 ... 669
—Benjamites ... 1 Chron 12:2 ... 681
2 Chron 14:8 ... 727

Given as a token of friendship ... 1 Sam 18:4 ... 477
Often furnished by the state ... 2 Chron 26:14 ... 746
Of the vanquished, broken and burned ... Ps 37:15 ... 904
Ezek 39:9 ... 1327

Illustrative
—Of strength and power ... Job 29:20 ... 858
—Of the tongue of the wicked ... Ps 11:2 ... 883
Jer 9:3 ... 1177
—(When deceitful,) of the hypocrite ... Ps 78:57 ... 942
Hos 7:16 ... 1383
—(When broken,) of the overthrow of power ... 1 Sam 2:4 ... 448
Jer 49:35 ... 1243
Hos 1:5 ... 1377
Hos 2:18 ... 1378

BRASS, OR COPPER

Dug out of the mountains ... Deut 8:9 ... 307
Purified by smelting ... Job 28:2 ... 857
Characterized by
—Strength ... Job 40:18 ... 872
—Hardness ... Lev 26:19 ... 213
—Yellow color ... Ezra 8:27 ... 780
—Fusibility ... Ezek 22:18, 20 ... 1297
—Sonorousness ... 1 Cor 13:1 ... 1802
Takes a high polish ... 2 Chron 4:16 ... 713
Ezek 1:7 ... 1263

Inferior in value to gold and silver ... Isa 60:17 ... 1153
Dan 2:32, 39 ... 1351
Antiquity of working in ... Gen 4:22 ... 10
Extensive commerce in ... Ezek 27:13 ... 1306
Rev 18:12 ... 1978
Working in, a trade ... Gen 4:22 ... 10
1 Kings 7:14 ... 566
2 Chron 24:12 ... 742
2 Tim 4:14 ... 1887
Canaan abounded in ... Deut 8:9 ... 307
Deut 33:25 ... 351
Taken in war,
—Often in great quantities ... Josh 22:8 ... 389
2 Sam 8:8 ... 516
2 Kings 25:13–16 ... 657
—Cleansed by fire ... Num 31:21–23 ... 280
—Generally consecrated to God ... Josh 6:19, 24 ... 362
2 Sam 8:10, 11 ... 516

Offerings of, for the tabernacle ... Exod 38:29 ... 161
Collected by David for the temple ... 1 Chron 22:3, 14 16 ... 696
1 Chron 29:2 ... 706
Offerings of, for the temple ... 1 Chron 29:6, 7 ... 707
Coined for money ... Matt 10:9 ... 1493
Mark 12:41 ... 1567

Made into
—Mirrors ... Exod 38:8 ... 160
—Gates ... Ps 107:16 ... 969
Isa 45:2 ... 1133
—Bars for gates ... 1 Kings 4:13 ... 561
—Fetters ... Judg 16:21 ... 427
2 Kings 25:7 ... 657
—Shields ... 1 Kings 14:27 ... 586
2 Chron 12:10 ... 725
—Helmets ... 1 Sam 17:5 ... 474
—Greaves for the legs ... 1 Sam 17:6 ... 474
—Household vessels ... Mark 7:4 ... 1553
—Sacred vessels ... Exod 27:3 ... 139
1 Kings 7:45 ... 568
—Altars ... Exod 27:2 ... 139
Exod 39:39 ... 163
—Sockets for pillars ... Exod 38:10, 11, 17 ... 160
—Lavers ... Exod 30:18 ... 146
1 Kings 7:38 ... 568
—Pillars ... 1 Kings 7:15, 16 ... 567
—Idols ... Dan 5:4 ... 1358
Rev 9:20 ... 1967
—Instruments of music ... 1 Chron 15:19 ... 686
Moses made the serpent of ... Num 21:9 ... 261
2 Kings 18:4 ... 642

Illustrative of
—Obstinate sinners ... Isa 48:4 ... 1137
Jer 6:28 ... 1173
—The decrees of God ... Zech 6:1 ... 1449
—The strength of firmness of Christ ... Dan 10:6 ... 1370
Rev 1:15 ... 1956
—Strength given to believers ... Jer 15:20 ... 1187
Mic 4:13 ... 1420
—Macedonian empire ... Dan 2:39 ... 1352
—Extreme drought ... Deut 28:23 ... 339
—The earth made barren ... Lev 26:19 ... 213

BREAD

Given by God ... Ruth 1:6 ... 439
Matt 6:11 ... 1486
Yielded by the earth ... Job 28:5 ... 857
Isa 55:10 ... 1147
Made of
—Wheat ... Exod 29:2 ... 143
Ps 81:16 ... 945
—Barley ... Judg 7:13 ... 409
John 6:9 ... 1656
—Beans, millet ... Ezek 4:9 ... 1267
—Manna (in the wilderness) ... Num 11:8 ... 242
Corn ground for making ... Isa 28:28 ... 1107
Was kneaded ... Gen 18:6 ... 30
Jer 7:18 ... 1175
Hos 7:4 ... 1382
Troughs used for kneading ... Exod 12:34 ... 114
Usually leavened ... Lev 23:17 ... 206
Matt 13:33 ... 1502

BREASTPLATE

BRIDE

BRIDEGROOM

BROOKS

BROTHER(S)

BURIAL

CALF OF GOLD

CALL OF GOD, THE

CALVES OF JEROBOAM

CAMEL, THE

CANAAN

CANAANITES, THE

CANDLESTICK

CAPTAIN(S)

CAPTIVITY

CARE, OVERMUCH

CHARACTER OF THE WICKED

CHERUBIM

CHILDREN

CHILDREN, GOOD

CHILDREN, WICKED

CHRIST, CHARACTER OF

CHRIST, HUMAN NATURE OF

CHRIST IS GOD

CHRIST, LIFE ON EARTH

CHRIST, THE HEAD OF THE CHURCH

CHRIST, THE HIGH PRIEST

CHRIST, THE SHEPHERD

CHRIST, NAMES AND TITLES OF

CHURCH, THE

CHURCH OF ISRAEL

CHURCH, TITLES AND NAMES OF

CIRCUMCISION

CITIES

CITIES OF REFUGE

CLEANSING, SPIRITUAL

CLOUDS

CLOUD OF GLORY

COMMANDMENTS, THE TEN

COMMERCE

COMMUNION OF SAINTS

COMMUNION OF THE LORD'S SUPPER

COMMUNION WITH GOD

COMPASSION AND SYMPATHY

COMPASSION AND SYMPATHY OF CHRIST, THE

CONDEMNATION

CONDUCT, CHRISTIAN

CONFESSING CHRIST

CONFESSION OF SIN

CONSCIENCE

CONTEMPT

CONTENTMENT

CONVERSION

COUNSELS AND PURPOSES OF GOD, THE

COURTS OF JUSTICE

DEACONS

DEAD, THE

DEATH, ETERNAL

DEATH, NATURAL

DEATH, SPIRITUAL

DECEIT

DEPRAVITY OF MAN

DESERT, JOURNEY OF ISRAEL THROUGH THE

DESERTS

DEVIL, NAMES OF TITLES OF

DEVOTEDNESS TO GOD

DIET OF THE JEWS, THE

DILIGENCE

DISCIPLINE OF THE CHURCH

DISEASES

DISOBEDIENCE TO GOD

DIVINATION

DIVISIONS

DIVORCE

DOCTRINES, FALSE

DOCTRINES OF THE GOSPEL, THE

DRINK OFFERING

DRUNKENNESS

EAGLE, THE

EARTHQUAKES

EDIFICATION

ENEMIES

ENTERTAINMENTS

ENVY

EPHOD, THE

EPHRAIM, TRIBE OF

ETERNAL

EUPHRATES, THE

EVENING, THE

FATHERLESS, THE

FAVOR OF GOD, THE

FEAR, GODLY

FEAR, UNHOLY

FEAST OF DEDICATION, THE

FEAST OF JUBILEE, THE

FEAST OF THE NEW MOON, THE

FEAST OF PENTECOST, THE

FEAST OF PURIM, OR LOTS, THE

FEAST OF SABBATICAL YEAR, THE

FEAST OF TABERNACLES, THE

FEAST OF THE PASSOVER, THE

FEASTS OF TRUMPETS, THE

FEASTS, THE ANNIVERSARY

FIRE

FIRSTBORN, THE

FIRST-FRUITS, THE

GARMENTS

GATES

GENEALOGIES

GENTILES

GIBEONITES

GIFT OF THE HOLY SPIRIT, THE

GIFTS OF GOD, THE

GIRDLES

GLORIFYING GOD

GLORY

GLORY OF GOD, THE

GOODNESS OF GOD, THE

GOSPEL, THE

GOVERNMENT

GRACE

HANDS, THE

HAPPINESS OF BELIEVERS IN THIS LIFE

HAPPINESS OF THE WICKED, THE

HATRED TO CHRIST

HEAD

HEART, CHARACTER OF THE UNRENEWED

HEATHEN, THE

HEEDFULNESS

HEIR

HELL

HERBS

HIGH PLACES

HIGH PRIEST, THE

HIGH-WAYS

HOLINESS OF GOD, THE

HOLY SPIRIT, NAMES AND TITLES OF

HOLY SPIRIT, THE COMFORTER, THE

HOLY SPIRIT, THE, IS GOD

HOLY SPIRIT, THE, PERSONALITY OF

HOLY SPIRIT, THE TEACHER, THE

HOLY LAND

HOLY OF HOLIES

HOMICIDE

HORNS

IGNORANCE OF GOD

INSECTS

INSPIRATION OF THE HOLY SPIRIT, THE

INTERCESSION

IRON

ISAAC

ISAIAH

ISHMAELITES, THE

ISRAELITES

see Jews

ISSACHAR, THE TRIBE OF

JACOB

JAMES

JEALOUSY

JEREMIAH

JERUSALEM

JOHN, THE APOSTLE

JOHN, THE BAPTIST

JORDAN, THE RIVER

JOSEPH

JOSHUA

JOY

JOY OF GOD OVER HIS PEOPLE, THE

JUDGES, EXTRAORDINARY

JUDGMENTS

JUDGMENT, THE

JUSTICE

JUSTICE OF GOD, THE

JUSTIFICATION BEFORE GOD

KISSING

KNOWLEDGE

LAMB, THE

LAMPS

LANGUAGE

LAVER OF BRASS

LAW OF GOD, THE

LAW OF MOSES, THE

LAWYER(S)

LETTERS

LEVIATHAN

LEVITES, THE

LIBERALITY

LIBERTY, CHRISTIAN

LIFE, ETERNAL

LIFE, NATURAL

LOVE TO GOD

LOVE TO MAN

LOVING-KINDNESS OF GOD, THE

LYING

MACEDONIAN EMPIRE, THE

MAGISTRATES

MANASSEH, THE TRIBE OF

MARTYRDOM

MARY

MASTERS

MATTHEW

MEASURES

MIRACLES OF CHRIST, THE

MIRACLES THROUGH EVIL AGENTS

MIRACLES WROUGHT THROUGH SERVANTS OF GOD

MIRACULOUS GIFTS OF THE HOLY SPIRIT

MISSIONARIES, ALL CHRISTIANS SHOULD BE AS

MISSIONARY-WORK BY MINISTERS

MORNING

MOSES

MOURNING

MULE, THE

MURDER

MURMURING

MUSIC

NIGHT

NILE, THE RIVER

NINEVEH

ONENESS

OPPRESSION

ORPHAN(S)

OSTRICH, THE

OWL, THE

PALACES

PALM TREE, THE

PARABLES

PARADISE

PARDON

PARENTS

PARTAKE

PASSOVER LAMB

PATIENCE

PATRIARCHAL GOVERNMENT

PEACE, SPIRITUAL

PHYSICIAN(S)

PILATE, PONTIUS

PILGRIMS AND STRANGERS

PILLARS

PLAGUE OR PESTILENCE, THE

POWER OF CHRIST, THE

POWER OF GOD, THE

POWER OF THE HOLY SPIRIT, THE

PRAISE

PRAYER

PRAYER, ANSWERS TO

PRAYER, INTERCESSORY

PRAYER, PRIVATE

PRAYER, PUBLIC

PRAYER, SOCIAL AND FAMILY

PREACHING

PRECIOUS STONES

PRECIOUSNESS OF CHRIST

PREDESTINATION

PRESENTS

PRESUMPTION

PRIDE

PRIESTHOOD

PRIESTS

PRISONS

PROPHECIES RESPECTING CHRIST

PROPHETS, FALSE

PROVIDENCE OF GOD, THE

PRUDENCE

PUBLICANS, THE

PSALM(S),

PUNISHMENT OF THE WICKED, THE

PUNISHMENTS

PURIFICATIONS OR BAPTISMS

RABBI (the title of a teacher or religious leader)

RAIN

RAINBOW

RANSOM

RAPE

RAVEN, THE

REAPING

REBELLION AGAINST GOD

RECHABITES

RECONCILIATION WITH GOD

REDEMPTION

RED HEIFER, THE

REMNANT

REPENTANCE

REPHAIM, OR GIANTS, THE

REPROBATE

REPROOF

REPTILES

RESURRECTION OF CHRIST, THE

REUBEN, THE TRIBE OF

REVIVAL(S) (SPIRITUAL)

REWARD OF BELIEVERS, THE

RICHES

RIGHTEOUSNESS IMPUTED

RIGHTEOUSNESS OF GOD, THE

RINGS

RIVERS

ROCKS

ROE, THE

ROMAN EMPIRE, THE

ROOT

SABBATH, THE

SACKCLOTH

SACRIFICES

SADDUCEES, THE

SALT

SALUTATIONS

SALVATION

SAMARIA, ANCIENT

SAMARIA, AT THE TIME OF CHRIST

SCORNING AND MOCKING

SCORPION, THE

SCRIBES

SCRIPTURES, THE

SEED

SEEKING GOD

SELF-DELUSION

SELF-DENIAL

SEXUAL RELATIONS

SICKNESS

SIDONIANS, THE

SIEGES

SILVER

SINCERITY

SIN OFFERING

SINS, NATIONAL

STONE(S)

STRANGERS IN ISRAEL

STRIFE

SUFFERING

SUICIDE

SUMMER

SUN, THE

SWEARING FALSELY

SWEARING, PROFANE

SWINE

TABERNACLE, THE

TAXES

TEACHERS

TEMPLE, THE FIRST

TESTIMONY

THANKSGIVING

TRESPASS OFFERING

TRIBES OF ISRAEL, THE

TRIBUTE

TRINITY, THE

TRUTH

TRUTH OF GOD, THE

TYPES OF CHRIST

TYRE

UNION WITH CHRIST

UNITY, AMONG GOD'S PEOPLE

UNITY OF GOD

VEIL

VEIL, THE SACRED

VINE, THE

VINEYARDS

VIRGIN(S)

VISIONS

VOWS

WAITING UPON GOD

WALLS

WAR

WARFARE OF BELIEVERS

WHIRLWIND

WICKED, NAMES AND TITLES OF

WICKED, THE, ARE COMPARED TO

WIDOWS

WILL, GOD'S

WILL, LAST TESTAMENT

WIND, THE

WINE

WINTER

WISDOM OF GOD, THE

WOMAN

WORD OF GOD

WORKS, GOOD

ZEBULUN, THE TRIBE OF

ZECHARIAH

ZION, MOUNT

INTRODUCTION TO THE OLD TESTAMENT

William Kerr

BOTH Jews and Christians believe the Old Testament is the inspired Word of God. The Jews, according to Paul, believed it to be "the oracles of God" (Rom. 3:2). For the Christian believer the character of the Old Testament is settled forever as the divinely inspired Word of God given under the infallible control of the Holy Spirit (Gal. 3:8; 2 Pet. 1:20, 21). This is so, because Christ—the central figure of the Old Testament—put his seal upon the Old Testament, which, in his day, as in ours, contained the same books from Genesis to Malachi, though the order of the books was different (Lk. 24:44ff).

In our English Bibles there are thirty-nine books arranged as follows: 17 historical books: Genesis—Esther; 5 poetical books: Job—Song of Solomon; 17 prophetic books: Isaiah—Malachi.

The Hebrew Bible in contrast numbers these same books as twenty-four. The classification is threefold: The Torah or Law—(5 books) Genesis—Deuteronomy; The Prophets or Nebiim—(8 books) Joshua, Judges, Samuel, Kings, Isaiah, Jeremiah, Ezekiel, the Twelve Minor Prophets; the Writings or Kethubim—(11 books) Psalms, Proverbs, Song of Solomon, Ruth, Lamentations, Ecclesiastes, Esther, Daniel, Ezra-Nehemiah, and Chronicles.

The idea of combining certain books in the Hebrew Bible was common. In the Hebrew canon 1 and 2 Samuel were counted as one, as were 1 and 2 Kings and 1 and 2 Chronicles. All twelve of the Minor Prophets were combined into one book—the reason for this was that they were so small (hence "Minor") that the Jews did not want to risk losing any.

This number of twenty-four books was further reduced to twenty-two by Josephus to make the books of the Old Testament correspond to the number of letters in the Hebrew alphabet. He accomplished this by attaching Ruth to Judges and Lamentations to Jeremiah.

The message of the Old Testament, regardless of the number and order of its books, is one, and the number of its books is identical with the King James Version today.

The central figure of the Old Testament, like that of the New, is the Messiah—Christ. Anticipated by the prophetic promises and represented symbolically in the sacrificial offerings, this Messiah would come to bring deliverance to his people. The very first redemptive promise indicated such deliverance: ". . . He (the Messiah) shall bruise his (the serpent's) head" (Gen. 3:15). From that promise on, through historical events, types, sacrificial offerings, judgments, and deliverances, God's people would learn much about this One who was to come. Thus the Old Testament story unfolds. It is a story of redemption—the story of a people who are to be holy unto their God. For the object of God's sovereign purpose in saving men was to have a society of redeemed people.

To accomplish this purpose, God began with his initial promise in Genesis 3:15. This was a promise of hope to Adam and Eve, whose relationship to God had been broken by their sin. But the pursuit of sin continued in man's history until the wickedness became so great that God had to destroy mankind in a flood—preserving only Noah and his family (Gen.7:1).

With Noah began God's covenantal relationship by which unilaterally he promised never to destroy man again by a great flood and sealed this Noahic Covenant by the symbol of a rainbow.

With the inauguration of the covenant relationship there came about a special and significant way by which God deals with man. And the most important covenant for all mankind was now made. This was the Abrahamic Covenant (Gen.12:1-3; 15:17, 18; 17:1, 2), which emphasized salvation by grace through the coming of One by whom all nations would be blessed. All of God's subsequent dealings redemptively would flow from this covenant and would come through the life and history of one nation— Israel.

God gave to this nation an affirmation that would set it apart from all other nations and would constitute its signal witness: "Hear, O Israel: The Lord our God is one Lord" (Deut. 6:4). This monotheistic proclamation was strongly implanted in the heart of every Israelite and today is the unifying factor in the heart of every Jew. Such an assertion, however, did not prevent Christ from dogmatically pronouncing that he is the Incarnation and full Revelation of that one God (John 10:29-38; 14:8-11; 17:21, 22).

The story of God's dealings with the nation Israel is the story of the Old Testament, a story whose climax was to be this coming of God manifest in human flesh (John 1:14-18). Thus in the Old Testament there are the divine dealings with Israel that prepared the world for that moment when the fullness of time was come, (and) God sent forth his Son, made of a woman, made under the law (Gal.4:4). Thus the Old Testament emphasizes God's *preparation* for the *Incarnation.*

The outline of the history of the Old Testament can be helpful in understanding this preparation:

I. Primal History—The Story of Origins. Genesis 1-11: The Creation to the Scattering of the Nations.

II. Patriarchal History—The Story of Israel's Founding Fathers. Genesis 12-50: The Call of Abraham to Joseph's Death.

III. Mosaic History—The Story of Israel's Wilderness Wanderings. Exodus-Deuteronomy: Deliverance from Egypt to the death of Moses.

IV. National History—The Story of Israel and the Promised Land. Joshua-Malachi: The Conquest of Canaan—to the Exile and Restoration.

The book of Malachi closes the Old Testament; the voice of God in divine revelation is silent. Israel awaits the advent of her Messiah—even Christ, God Incarnate.

THE OLD TESTAMENT

THE FIRST BOOK OF MOSES CALLED

GENESIS

Authorship, date, and background Genesis is the first of the five books in the Old Testament to which the title Pentateuch has been applied. They are also known as the Law or the Books of Moses. The Septuagint (the Greek translation of the Hebrew Old Testament, ca. 150 B.C.) translators used the name Genesis, which means "origin, beginning." The Hebrew title, *Bereshith,* is the first word in the text, meaning "in the beginning." Everything in Genesis predates the time of Moses, to whom the authorship of the Pentateuch has been attributed. This means that he secured his information from extant written materials or by oral transmission or by revelation from God or a combination of all. The source of his knowledge does not matter materially so long as we know that in the use of the materials the Holy Spirit enabled him to record only that which is true.

No verse in the Pentateuch names Moses directly as the author, but there are internal evidences favoring the Mosaic authorship as well as statements from the New Testament by Jesus and others which leads to this conclusion. In the Pentateuch itself (see here Ex 17:14; 24:4–7; 34:27; Num 33:1, 2; Deut 31:9–11) Moses was instructed by God to write down certain information. In addition, other books in the Old Testament speak of "the law of Moses" (1 Kgs 2:3; 2 Kgs 14:6), "the laws of Moses" (Ezra 6:18; Neh 13:1; etc.). Moreover, the New Testament refers again and again to the law of Moses in one form or another (see, for example, Mt 19:8; Mk 1:44; 10:4, 5; Lk 5:14; 16:31; 20:37; Acts 3:23; 13:39; 15:5ff.; 26:22; Rom 10:5, 19; 1 Cor 9:9; 2 Cor 3:15; Rev 15:3).

Liberal rationalist scholarship has vigorously objected to the Mosaic authorship of the Pentateuch. The Documentary Hypothesis of Wellhausen, the best known of these viewpoints, has been challenged both by liberal and conservative scholars. Most of the liberal scholars who hold to the non-Mosaic authorship of the Pentateuch accept the J E P D theory. Conservative scholars steadfastly hold to the Mosaic authorship of the first five books, attributing them to Moses even though there may have been minor editorial insertions and changes. The account of Moses' death may have been added by a later writer. And possibly later minor name changes may have been inserted to clarify for the reader what he might not otherwise have known. For example, in 14:14 the name of a city is given as Dan, whereas in Judges 18:29 it says that the city named Dan "had originally been called Laish."

Traditionally, the Jews and the church have always endorsed Mosaic authorship, and in view of the absence of sufficient evidence to undermine this tradition, believers can confidently accept the conclusion that Moses indeed authored these five books.

Characteristics and content The book of Genesis sets the scene for the entire Bible. Without it the reader would not know some of the most important happenings in the history of the world. Genesis tells us about the creation of the cosmos, the creation of man, the beginning of sin in the human race, the provision of God for redemption, the selection of one man through whose descendants salvation would be made possible, the person and nature of God, as well as about divine judgment and human responsibility. The first two chapters of Genesis speak of generation; chapters 3–11 deal with degeneration; chapters 12–50 have to do with regeneration.

Genesis is remarkably compact, encompassing long periods of time in a few sentences. It is written in a fascinating style which commands the interest of young and old alike. It is largely biographical, describing significant individuals who are essential participants of the story of redemption. From its earliest pages it points the way to salvation through the as yet unidentified descendant of Abraham, even Jesus Christ who is the Son of David. In the fall of Adam, the judgment of God on sin or disobedience may be seen. In the flood, the retributive justice of God is manifested. In the choice of Abraham, as the man through whom Messiah shall come, God's sovereign election is indicated.

Genesis recounts how the twelve patriarchs, from whom all of Israel would someday come, were fathered by Jacob, the grandson of Abraham. Despite sin and human error, the divine will is being worked out in the events which take place. The book tells us about some of the people of God who are unselfish, heroic, and faithful. Others are guilty of trickery, deception, fraud, and unfaithfulness. The characters are pictured as they really are, not as we wish they might have been. Perhaps most important of all, Genesis reveals that God chose to make himself known to men without which self-revelation the true knowledge of God would be impossible to attain. It is the story of God reaching down to sinful men, not of sinful men reaching up to God.

Outline

I. The story of creation (1:1—2:25)
II. Adam's sin and its consequences (3:1—5:32)
III. The sins of men and God's judgment (6:1—8:19)
IV. God's promise to Noah: a new beginning (8:20—11:26)
V. Abraham, the first patriarch (11:27—25:18)
VI. The patriarchs Isaac and Jacob (25:19—36:43)
VII. The story of Joseph's life (37:1—50:26)

1:1☆ Job 38:4; Ps 33:6; 89:11; 102:25; Prov 8:22–24; Isa 42:5; 48:13; Jn 1:1–3; Col 1:15, 16; Heb 1:10; 1 Jn 1:1
1:2☆ Job 26:13; Ps 104:30; Prov 3:19; Isa 45:18
1:3☆ Ps 33:9; 104:2; Isa 45:7; Jn 1:5; 2 Cor 4:6; 1 Jn 1:5
1:4, 5☆ Gen 8:22; Ps 74:16; Isa 45:7; Jer 33:20

I. THE STORY OF CREATION (1:1—2:25)

A. GOD BEGINS HIS CREATION

1 IN the beginning God created the heaven and the earth.
2 And the earth was without form, and void; and darkness *was* upon
the face of the deep. And the Spirit of God moved upon the face of the
waters.

B. THE SEVEN DAYS OF CREATION

1. Day One: The Light

3 And God said, Let there be light: and there was light.
4 And God saw the light, that *it was* good: and God divided the light from
the darkness.
5 And God called the light Day, and the darkness he called Night. And
the evening and the morning were the first day.

1:1 Monotheism, the belief in one God, has existed from time immemorial even in the earliest religions. This view is the opposite of the modern notion that the idea of God evolved from a primitive animism, to polytheism, to henotheism, to monotheism. The writings of Schmidt, Langdon, Petrie, and Zwemer strongly support primitive monotheism. Polytheism and lower views of God point to retrogression, explained by the advent of sin and the spiritual decline which followed. In Rom. 1:19–23 Paul summarizes the tragic devolution from monotheism.

1:2 *the earth was,* or, "the earth became . . ." "a shapeless, chaotic mass," or, "shapeless and void." *the face of the waters,* or, "over the cloud of darkness," or, "over the darkness and waters," or even, "over the dark gaseous mass." There is no "correct" way to translate these words.

1:3 The Genesis account of creation is only one of many extant records of the beginning. While there may be similarities to the biblical account, the other creation narratives are marked by polytheism, strange monsters, animal gods, impossible cosmology, and crude myths. The Babylonian and Assyrian stories are among the oldest and do no more than show that behind these accounts there was a creation. The Genesis account is unique in that it comes to men from God by revelation through the pen of the sacred writer inspired by the Holy Spirit. The basic question is whether matter is eternal or came into being sometime in the past. The biblical account makes it clear that God, who is spirit, created matter by the word of his power. He made all things, so that nothing was made without him, and in him all things hang together. Matter was created by God *ex nihilo,* i.e., "out of nothing." *God said, Let there be light.* Before the sun and moon were created, there was light. In his commentary on Genesis, John Calvin says: "It was proper that the light, by means of which the world was to be adorned with such excellent beauty, should be first created. . . . It did not, however, happen from inconsideration or by accident, that the light preceded the sun and the moon. To nothing are we more prone than to tie down the power of God to those instruments, the agency of which he employs. The sun and moon supply us with light and, according to our notions, we so include this power to give light to them, that if they were taken away from the world, it would seem impossible for any light to remain. Therefore, the Lord, by the very order of the creation, bears witness that he holds in his hand the light, which he is able to impart to us without the sun and moon." Note that in the New Jerusalem the sun and moon are not needed: "the Lamb is the light thereof" (Rev. 21:23).

1:5 *And the evening and the morning were the first day,* i.e., "together they formed the first day."† There are two views about the six days of creation: one holds that "days" were literal twenty-four-hour periods, the other that each "day" consisted of an extended period of time. It is true that the Hebrew word for day (*yom*) does not always mean a twenty-four-hour day, but generally it does. The long-day view is held by some

2. Day Two: The Sky and the Oceans

6¶And God said, Let there be a firmament in the midst of the waters, and
let it divide the waters from the waters.
7And God made the firmament, and divided the waters which *were* under
the firmament from the waters which *were* above the firmament: and it was
so.
8And God called the firmament Heaven. And the evening and the
morning were the second day.

☆1:6 Job 26:10; Ps 136:5, 6; Isa 40:22; Jer 10:12
☆1:7, 8 Job 38:3; Ps 148:4; Ps 150:1; Prov 8:28

3. Day Three: Dry Land and Plant Life

9¶And God said, Let the waters under the heaven be gathered together
unto one place, and let the dry *land* appear: and it was so.
10And God called the dry *land* Earth; and the gathering together of the
waters called he Seas: and God saw that *it was* good.
11And God said, Let the earth bring forth grass, the herb yielding seed,
and the fruit tree yielding fruit after his kind, whose seed *is* in itself, upon
the earth: and it was so.
12And the earth brought forth grass, *and* herb yielding seed after his kind,
and the tree yielding fruit, whose seed *was* in itself, after his kind: and God
saw that *it was* good.
13And the evening and the morning were the third day.

1:9 Job 26:7; Ps 24:1–2; 95:5; Prov 8:9; Jer 5:22; 2 Pet 3:5
1:10 Gen 1:4; Gen 1:12
1:11, 12 Gen 2:9; Ps 104:14–17; Mt 6:30; Lk 6:44; Heb 6:7

4. Day Four: Day and Night

14¶And God said, Let there be lights in the firmament of the heaven to
divide the day from the night; and let them be for signs, and for seasons,
and for days, and years:
15And let them be for lights in the firmament of the heaven to give light
upon the earth: and it was so.
16And God made two great lights; the greater light to rule the day, and
the lesser light to rule the night: *he made* the stars also.
17And God set them in the firmament of the heaven to give light upon the
earth,
18And to rule over the day and over the night, and to divide the light
from the darkness: and God saw that *it was* good.
19And the evening and the morning were the fourth day.

1:14, 15 Gen 8:22; Deut 4:19; Ps 74:16; 104:19
☆1:16 Ps 8:3; 19:1–6; Ps 136:7–9; 1 Cor 15:41; Rev 21:23
1:18 Jer 31:35

5. Day Five: Sea Life and Bird Life

20And God said, Let the waters bring forth abundantly the moving
creature that hath life, and fowl *that* may fly above the earth in the open
firmament of heaven.

1:20 Gen 8:17; Ps 104:24, 25; Ps 148:7

Christian scholars, but it suffers from some grave problems. If the seventh day was a long period of time, then 2:3, which speaks of the Sabbath—which can only be a twenty-four-hour day—becomes meaningless. Moreover, if man goes back millions of years, biblical chronology is seriously askew. In response to the claim of scientists that the earth is millions or billions of years old, some Christians assert that there is a gap between 1:1 and 1:2 (see *The Invisible War*, by Donald G. Barnhouse, Zondervan, 1965). In this view, the first creation was wrecked by Satan's fall; the six days were really a re-creation. The six-day view (twenty-four-hour days) appears to have fewer problems, especially in light of the fact that time in God's scale differs markedly from time in our scale, for "one day is with the Lord as a thousand years, and a thousand years as one day" (2 Pet. 3:8).

1:6 *let it divide the waters from the waters,* literally, "let there be a dome to divide the waters."

1:8 *And the evening and the morning were the second day,* i.e., "this all happened on the second day." So also for 1:13 (the third day); 1:19 (the fourth day); 1:23 (the fifth day); 1:31 (the sixth day).

1:16 *two great lights,* i.e., the sun and the moon. Since the creation of plants and other vegetation preceded this fourth-day creative act, we can see that God as light would make vegetation to grow and flower.

1:21, 22 Gen 6:20; 8:17, 19; 35:11; Lev 26:9

21 And God created great whales, and every living creature that moveth,
which the waters brought forth abundantly, after their kind, and every
winged fowl after his kind: and God saw that *it was* good.
22 And God blessed them, saying, Be fruitful, and multiply, and fill the
waters in the seas, and let fowl multiply in the earth.
23 And the evening and the morning were the fifth day.

6. Day Six: Animal Life and Man

24 ¶And God said, Let the earth bring forth the living creature after his
kind, cattle, and creeping thing, and beast of the earth after his kind: and it
was so.

1:25 Gen 2:19, 20; Job 12:7–9; Jer 27:5
1:26☆ Gen 5:1; 9:6; Ps 8:6–8; Eph 4:24; Col 3:10; Jas 3:9
1:27☆ Gen 2:21–25; Gen 5:2; Isa 43:7; Mt 19:4; 1 Cor 11:8, 9
1:28☆ Gen 1:22; 8:17; 17:16; Lev 26:9; Ps 128:3
1:29 Gen 9:3; Job 36:31; Ps 115:16; Ps 136:25; 145:15; Mt 6:11
1:30 Ps 104:14; Ps 147:9
1:31 Gen 2:18; Ps 19:1; 104:24; 1 Tim 4:4

25 And God made the beast of the earth after his kind, and cattle after
their kind, and every thing that creepeth upon the earth after his kind: and
God saw that *it was* good.
26 ¶And God said, Let us make man in our image, after our likeness: and
let them have dominion over the fish of the sea, and over the fowl of the air,
and over the cattle, and over all the earth, and over every creeping thing
that creepeth upon the earth.
27 So God created man in his *own* image, in the image of God created he
him; male and female created he them.
28 And God blessed them, and God said unto them, Be fruitful, and
multiply, and replenish the earth, and subdue it: and have dominion over
the fish of the sea, and over the fowl of the air, and over every living thing
that moveth upon the earth.
29 ¶And God said, Behold, I have given you every herb bearing seed,
which *is* upon the face of all the earth, and every tree, in the which *is* the
fruit of a tree yielding seed; to you it shall be for meat.
30 And to every beast of the earth, and to every fowl of the air, and to
every thing that creepeth upon the earth, wherein *there is* life, *I have given*
every green herb for meat: and it was so.
31 And God saw every thing that he had made, and, behold, *it was* very
good. And the evening and the morning were the sixth day.

7. Day Seven: God Rests on the Seventh Day

2:1 Gen 1:1; 1:10; Ex 20:11; Ps 136:5–9; Isa 42:5

2 THUS the heavens and the earth were finished, and all the host of
them.

1:22 *be fruitful,* i.e., they were to reproduce themselves. Thus we note that the creation of male and female existed before the coming of Adam and Eve. The sexes are God's order for all created things.
1:26 *let us make man.* Adam means "mankind" and Eve means "(she who gives) life." Because the names have such meanings, some have concluded that the Adam and Eve story is not real history. We must note, however, that all through the Bible, names are derived from words common to the speech of the people. Cain means "acquisition" and Abram means "father of height." Since these people were historical persons, it strengthens the case for the historicity of Adam and Eve.
1:27 The root question about the origin of man is: Was man immediately created by God or did he evolve from lower forms of vertebrate life over a long period of time? Those who hold to the six literal days of creation must necessarily say that Adam was created by God in a twenty-four-hour period. Others accept the theory of evolution—that inorganic matter became organic matter (life) and that man was derived from the organic by progressing from lower to higher forms of life. Many scientists have long since abandoned organic evolution, but it remains a popular myth. Paul Tournier quotes P. Lemoine, curator of the Paris Museum, who said: "Evolution is a kind of dogma in which its priests no longer believe, but which they preserve for the people. One must have the courage to say this" (Paul Tournier, *The Whole Person in a Broken World,* Harper and Row, 1977, p. 107).

The Hebrew word *bara* ("to create") is used here to describe the creation of the heaven and the earth (1:1), the creation of life (1:21), and the creation of human life (1:27). The entire human race has descended from Adam and Eve. This means, of course, that for the human race to grow, the sons of Adam married their sisters. When the race was fully developed, God no longer allowed this.
1:28 *have dominion.* This was part of God's cultural mandate. Man was to have charge of all creation, which would be subject to him. This could be for good or for evil.

2And on the seventh day God ended his work which he had made; and
he rested on the seventh day from all his work which he had made.
3And God blessed the seventh day, and sanctified it: because that in it he
had rested from all his work which God created and made.

☆2:2 Ex 31:17 Heb 4:4
2:3 Isa 56:2 58:13, 14

C. MAN AND HIS HABITATION

1. Adam Created and Placed in the Garden

4¶These *are* the generations of the heavens and of the earth when they
were created, in the day that the LORD God made the earth and the
heavens,
5And every plant of the field before it was in the earth, and every herb of
the field before it grew: for the LORD God had not caused it to rain upon
the earth, and *there was* not a man to till the ground.
6But there went up a mist from the earth, and watered the whole face of
the ground.
7And the LORD God formed man *of* the dust of the ground, and breathed
into his nostrils the breath of life; and man became a living soul.
8¶And the LORD God planted a garden eastward in Eden; and there he
put the man whom he had formed.
9And out of the ground made the LORD God to grow every tree that is
pleasant to the sight, and good for food; the tree of life also in the midst of
the garden, and the tree of knowledge of good and evil.
10And a river went out of Eden to water the garden; and from thence it
was parted, and became into four heads.
11The name of the first *is* Pi'son: that *is* it which compasseth the whole
land of Hav'i-lah, where *there is* gold;
12And the gold of that land *is* good: there *is* bdellium and the onyx stone.
13And the name of the second river *is* Gi'hon: the same *is* it that
compasseth the whole land of E-thi-o'pi-a.

☆2:4 Gen 1:3–31; 5:1; 6:9 Gen 10:1
☆2:5 Gen 1:12; 3:23
☆2:7 Gen 3:19, 23 Job 33:4 Ps 103:14 Ezek 37:5 Zech 12:1 Jn 20:22 1 Cor 15:45
☆2:8 Gen 3:23; 13:10 Isa 51:3 Ezek 28:13 Joel 2:3
2:9 Gen 3:22 Prov 3:18; 11:30 Ezek 47:12 Rev 2:7 22:2, 14
2:10 Rev 22:1, 17
☆2:11 Gen 25:18 1 Sam 15:7

2:2 *God ended his work,* i.e., "he rested on the seventh day." The Hebrew word used here is *shabath* ("to cease, rest"). Thus the seventh day was designated as *Shabbath,* the holy day of rest. It later was spelled "sabbath" from the Greek Septuagint. To assume that creation occurred without a supreme and divine being lying behind it smacks of the ridiculous. To suppose that accident, not design, lies behind the creation makes little sense. It is far simpler to believe what the Scriptures teach: God was present and at work in bringing everything into being. The complexity of living things would require chance selection of greater magnitude than the human mind can contemplate.

2:4 Many names for God appear in the Old Testament. Some are single; some are compound. Rationalist scholars suppose that the variety of names used in the Pentateuch means that the five books were written by several people. Conservatives hold that Moses himself used different names for God, or that his material came from different sources which used different names for God. Among the names used are: (1) *El, Eloah* (and its plural *Elohim*) which are translated "God" (implying the ruler over the entire universe), or "the Mighty One"; (2) *Yahweh,* the covenantal name for the God of Israel (*Jehovah* is an erroneous rendering), was regarded with such respect that Jews never uttered it. They substituted the word *Adonai* ("Lord") for it (in the RSV and KJV *Yahweh* is translated "LORD"); (3) *Adonai* ("Lord") emphasizes the sovereignty of God as king; (4) *Elyan* ("Most High"); and (5) *Shaddai* ("the Almighty"). In 2:4 the compound name *Yahweh Elohim* ("LORD God") appears: it refers to the mighty Creator who enters into covenant relationships with his creatures.

2:5 Rain did not occur until the time of the flood and thereafter. Some think that the tilting of the planet may account for rain.

2:7 *of the dust of the ground,* or, "from a lump of soil," or, "from clods in the soil," or, "from a clod of clay."

2:8 No one has been able to determine the precise location of the Garden of Eden. It seems to have been near the Tigris (*Hiddekel* in the KJV) and Euphrates Rivers where they were joined by the rivers Pishon and Gihon (which have never been identified). Tradition has it that Eden was south of Ur at a place known as *Eridu.* Eridu was excavated by British archeologists in 1918–1919, but this did not guarantee the certainty of the location of Eden. Albright holds the view that Pishon and Gihon may be the Blue and White Nile Rivers.

2:11, 12 *the whole land of Havilah,* located along the border of Babylonia.

2:14 Gen 15:18; Deut 1:7; Dan 10:4

14 And the name of the third river *is* Hid′de-kel: that *is* it which goeth toward the east of Assyria. And the fourth river *is* Eu-phra′tes.

2. Adam Forbidden to Eat the Fruit of the Tree of the Knowledge of Good and Evil

2:15 Gen 2:5, 8
2:16☆ Gen 2:9; 3:1, 2; Deut 30:15, 19, 20
2:17☆ Gen 3:1, 16, 17; Rom 5:2; 6:23; Jas 1:15

15 And the LORD God took the man, and put him into the garden of Eden to dress it and to keep it.
16 And the LORD God commanded the man, saying, Of every tree of the garden thou mayest freely eat:
17 But of the tree of the knowledge of good and evil, thou shalt not eat of it: for in the day that thou eatest thereof thou shalt surely die.

3. God Creates Eve

2:18 Gen 3:12; Prov 18:22
2:19☆ Gen 1:20–25; 6:20

18 ¶And the LORD God said, *It is* not good that the man should be alone; I will make him an help meet for him.
19 And out of the ground the LORD God formed every beast of the field, and every fowl of the air; and brought *them* unto Adam to see what he would call them: and whatsoever Adam called every living creature, that *was* the name thereof.
20 And Adam gave names to all cattle, and to the fowl of the air, and to every beast of the field; but for Adam there was not found an help meet for him.

2:22☆ 1 Cor 11:8; 1 Tim 2:13
2:23☆ Gen 29:14; Eph 5:28–30
2:24☆ Gen 24:58; Ps 45:10; Mal 2:15; Mt 19:5; 1 Cor 6:16; Eph 5:31
2:25 Gen 3:7, 10, 11

21 And the LORD God caused a deep sleep to fall upon Adam, and he slept: and he took one of his ribs, and closed up the flesh instead thereof;
22 And the rib, which the LORD God had taken from man, made he a woman, and brought her unto the man.
23 And Adam said, This *is* now bone of my bones, and flesh of my flesh: she shall be called Woman, because she was taken out of Man.
24 Therefore shall a man leave his father and his mother, and shall cleave unto his wife: and they shall be one flesh.
25 And they were both naked, the man and his wife, and were not ashamed.

2:16, 17 God made a covenant of works with Adam in the Garden of Eden. God gave Adam the right to eat of the fruit of the garden except for the fruit of the tree of the knowledge of good and evil. This single prohibition was the sign of Adam's perfect obedience. God warned Adam what the consequences would be if he broke the covenant by eating the fruit. Every covenant has a seal. The seal here was the tree of life. Adam broke the covenant by eating the fruit of the tree of the knowledge of good and evil. Death came for him and for the human race, since he was its federal head (Rom. 4:12, 18). Moreover, Adam was separated from the tree of life, lest he eat of it and live forever. The tree of life will become available to believers in the glory because of Christ's redemption (3:24; Rev. 22:2).

2:19 Adam is commanded to name birds and beasts. The mystery of the origin of language can be simply accounted for as stemming from God's creative activity. Later we are told that God confused the tongues of men so that even other languages sprang out of God's activity.

2:22 "The woman was *made of a rib out of the side of Adam;* not made out of his head to rule over him, nor out of his feet to be trampled upon by him, but out of his side to be equal with him, under his arm to be protected, and near his heart to be beloved."*

2:23 Eve (woman), like Adam, was made after the moral and spiritual image of God. Taken from Adam's side, Eve was to be a helpmeet, complementing man. She was made for Adam (1 Cor. 11:3), was subject to him (1 Cor. 11:3), and was to be his glory (1 Cor. 11:7). Eve was deceived by the serpent (3:1–6; 2 Cor. 11:3), but God had made no covenant with her. Adam deliberately disobeyed God and broke the covenant, meriting guilt and death.

2:24 God ordained and instituted marriage for the good of the human race. Woman was designed to complement man, and as partners they were to increase the human race (1:28; 2:18; 9:1). The New Testament expands our knowledge on the subject by teaching that (1) marriage is lawful and good (1 Cor. 7:2, 28; 1 Tim. 5:14); (2) marriage is an honorable estate (*timios* in Greek) (Heb. 13:4); (3) Christians should not marry unbelievers (2 Cor. 6:14–18), (4) marriage is for life, except for certain biblical reasons (Matt. 19:6ff; Rom. 7:2, 3). *they shall be one flesh,* i.e., "the two become one person."

II. ADAM'S SIN AND ITS CONSEQUENCES (3:1—5:32)

A. ADAM AND EVE EAT THE FORBIDDEN FRUIT

3 NOW the serpent was more subtil than any beast of the field which the
LORD God had made. And he said unto the woman, Yea, hath God
said, Ye shall not eat of every tree of the garden?
2 And the woman said unto the serpent, We may eat of the fruit of the
trees of the garden:
3 But of the fruit of the tree which *is* in the midst of the garden, God hath
said, Ye shall not eat of it, neither shall ye touch it, lest ye die.
4 And the serpent said unto the woman, Ye shall not surely die:
5 For God doth know that in the day ye eat thereof, then your eyes shall
be opened, and ye shall be as gods, knowing good and evil.
6 And when the woman saw that the tree *was* good for food, and that it
was pleasant to the eyes, and a tree to be desired to make *one* wise, she took
of the fruit thereof, and did eat, and gave also unto her husband with her;
and he did eat.
7 And the eyes of them both were opened, and they knew that they *were*
naked; and they sewed fig leaves together, and made themselves aprons.

B. GOD'S JUDGMENT

1. The Sin Uncovered

8 And they heard the voice of the LORD God walking in the garden in the
cool of the day: and Adam and his wife hid themselves from the presence of
the LORD God amongst the trees of the garden.
9 And the LORD God called unto Adam, and said unto him, Where *art*
thou?
10 And he said, I heard thy voice in the garden, and I was afraid, because
I *was* naked; and I hid myself.
11 And he said, Who told thee that thou *wast* naked? Hast thou eaten of
the tree, whereof I commanded thee that thou shouldest not eat?

3:1 1 Chron 21:1; Ezek 28:12–17; Mt 4:3, 6, 9; Rev 12:9; 20:2
☆**3:3** Gen 2:16; Ex 19:12
3:4 Jn 8:44; 2 Cor 2:11; 2 Cor 11:3
3:5 Gen 2:17; Gen 3:22; Ezek 28:2, 9; Mt 6:23; Acts 26:18
☆**3:6** Jer 7:23; 2 Cor 11:3; 1 Tim 2:14; Jas 1:14; 1 Jn 2:16
3:7 Isa 47:3; Lam 1:8; 2 Cor 5:2
3:8 Lev 26:12; Deut 23:14; Job 31:33; Ps 139:1–12; Jer 23:24; Rev 6:15–17
3:9 Gen 4:9; Gen 16:8
☆**3:10** Gen 2:25; Ex 3:6; Job 23:15; Ps 119–120; 1 Jn 3:20
3:11 Gen 4:10

3:2, 3 The seal of God's covenant with Adam was that Adam should refrain from eating the forbidden fruit. The sentence for disobeying God was twofold: (1) Adam would experience spiritual death, and would become corrupted and separated from his Creator; (2) physical death would result, although this sentence was not to be immediately carried out. Adam became mortal. The New Testament clearly teaches that both physical and spiritual death have been transmitted through Adam to the entire human race (Rom. 5:12–14).

3:6 Adam's sin consisted in disobeying God's express prohibition (3:6–12; Rom. 5:12–19). Satan provided the temptation (3:1–5, Rev. 12:9), but Adam acted voluntarily, by his own choice. Solicitation to sin does not, in itself, constitute guilt. As a consequence of his sin, Adam was condemned to temporal and eternal death (for which the gospel is the antidote), banished from the Garden of Eden, and promised labor and sorrow in this life. God also imposed the sentence of death upon all of Adam's descendants, since he was their federal representative. Theologians differ about the transmission of Adam's guilt to every infant. Some hold that every infant is born guilty before God by natural inheritance and lies under the wrath of God. Those dying in infancy are saved by the free application of Christ's merits to them. Some in the Reformed tradition say that elect infants who die in infancy are saved, but nonelect infants are lost.

Some theologians agree that all infants are born sinful but do not have personal guilt attached to them until they reach the age of accountability, at which time they consciously sin and become guilty. In this view, infants who die in infancy are saved because they have no guilt attached to them.

The first view (that infants are guilty from birth) is known under the term of federal headship—Adam, in God's covenant with him, was the representative of the entire human race; thus, all men sinned in Adam and were separated from God forever unless they come to him through faith in Jesus Christ.

3:10 *because I was naked.* Since Adam lived in innocence, nakedness was normal and provided no problems. Following his transgression Adam had a different understanding of nakedness, for it had become associated with man's fallen condition. Virtually all people cover themselves in part or in whole. A return to nakedness is a sign of increasing degeneracy.

3:12☆ Ex 32:21–24 Prov 28:13 Jas 1:13
3:13 Gen 4:10 44:15 2 Cor 11:3 1 Tim 2:14

12 And the man said, The woman whom thou gavest *to be* with me, she
gave me of the tree, and I did eat.
13 And the LORD God said unto the woman, What *is* this *that* thou hast
done? And the woman said, The serpent beguiled me, and I did eat.

2. God Curses the Serpent

3:14☆ Deut 28:15 Isa 65:25 Mic 7:17
3:15☆ Jn 8:44 Acts 13:10 Rom 16:20 Gal 4:4 Col 12:15 1 Jn 3:8–10 Rev 12:7

14 And the LORD God said unto the serpent, Because thou hast done this,
thou *art* cursed above all cattle, and above every beast of the field; upon thy
belly shalt thou go, and dust shalt thou eat all the days of thy life:
15 And I will put enmity between thee and the woman, and between thy
seed and her seed; it shall bruise thy head, and thou shalt bruise his heel.

3. God Punishes Eve

3:16 Gen 35:16 Isa 13:8 Jn 16:21 1 Cor 7:4; 11:3 Eph 5:22 1 Thess 5:3 Tit 2:5

16 Unto the woman he said, I will greatly multiply thy sorrow and thy
conception; in sorrow thou shalt bring forth children; and thy desire *shall*
be to thy husband, and he shall rule over thee.

4. God Curses Adam

3:17☆ Gen 5:29 Job 5:6, 7 Eccles 1:3 Isa 24:5 Rom 8:20–22
3:18☆ Prov 22:5 Heb 6:8
3:19 Gen 2:7 Ps 90:3; 104:29 Eccles 12:7 Rom 5:12 1 Cor 15:21, 22

17 And unto Adam he said, Because thou hast hearkened unto the voice of
thy wife, and hast eaten of the tree, of which I commanded thee, saying,
Thou shalt not eat of it: cursed *is* the ground for thy sake; in sorrow shalt
thou eat *of* it all the days of thy life;
18 Thorns also and thistles shall it bring forth to thee; and thou shalt eat
the herb of the field;
19 In the sweat of thy face shalt thou eat bread, till thou return unto the
ground; for out of it wast thou taken: for dust thou *art*, and unto dust shalt
thou return.

5. Adam Banished from the Garden

3:20☆ Acts 17:26 1 Tim 2:13

20 And Adam called his wife's name Eve; because she was the mother of
all living.

3:12 Adam blames God for giving him the woman who caused him to sin. And Eve in verse 13 pleads that she could not help herself. It was not her fault. The refusal to accept responsibility for our actions is commonplace today.

3:14 Subsequent to Adam's fall, God reordered life for Adam and his descendants as follows: (1) the serpent was cursed for his evil work; (2) the Redeemer was promised for the salvation of men; (3) womanhood was promised multiplied pain in childbirth and was placed in subjection to her husband; (4) the ground was cursed to produce thorns and thistles; (5) man was to eke out a living by the sweat of his brow; (6) physical death was to be the lot of all men (3:15–19).

3:15 Here God promises redemption to lost men through the coming of Jesus Christ the Redeemer. This age will witness the constant warfare between the offspring of the woman and the offspring of the serpent. Christ will ultimately defeat Satan and his seed. Satan will strike the heel of the Redeemer (Isa. 53:10 indicates that Christ's heel is bruised by the sovereign permissive will and all-wise plan of God the Father). Christ will bruise the head of the serpent. In the drama of redemption Satan prompted Cain to slay Abel, but God raised up Seth (4:25). Satan was foiled at the flood when God spared Noah and his family (chapters 6—9). Satan appeared to be victorious when Abraham and Sarah had no heir, but God miraculously intervened and Sarah gave birth to Isaac (21:1–8). Satan sought to have the infant Jesus slain but God prevented him from succeeding. Jesus resisted Satan's temptations in the wilderness. In the Garden of Gethsemane Satan was defeated again, and at Calvary Jesus struck the death blow to the enemy of men's souls and the victory was sealed by the resurrection of the Son of God from the grave.

3:17 *hearkened unto the voice of thy wife.* The influence of a wife—for good or for evil—cannot be over-estimated. Later, Abraham was to listen to the voice of Sarah and take Hagar to wife. Ishmael, the son of this relationship, was to become the father of the inveterate enemies of Israel. Both Adam and Abraham leave us an example that underscores the need for discretion when others try to influence our decisions.

3:18 Thorns and thistles may have existed outside of Eden before the fall. Death may have been present in the animal kingdom before Adam sinned.

3:20 *Eve* ("the life-giving one"). Many Hebrew names are based on puns. In this instance, the Hebrew word for Eve sounds similar to a Hebrew word that means "life-giving."

[21]Unto Adam also and to his wife did the LORD God make coats of skins,
and clothed them.
[22]¶And the LORD God said, Behold, the man is become as one of us, to
know good and evil: and now, lest he put forth his hand, and take also of
the tree of life, and eat, and live for ever:
[23]Therefore the LORD God sent him forth from the garden of Eden, to till
the ground from whence he was taken.
[24]So he drove out the man; and he placed at the east of the garden of
Eden Cher'u-bims, and a flaming sword which turned every way, to keep
the way of the tree of life.

3:21 Isa 61:10; 2 Cor 5:2, 3
☆3:22 Gen 1:26; 2:9; 11:6; Ps 22:26; Jn 6:48
3:23 Gen 2:5; 3:19
☆3:24 Ex 25:20; Num 22:23; 1 Sam 4:4; Heb 1:7; Rev 2:7; 22:2, 14

C. CAIN AND ABEL
1. Cain's and Abel's Offerings to God

4 AND Adam knew Eve his wife; and she conceived, and bare Cain, and
said, I have gotten a man from the LORD.
[2]And she again bare his brother Abel. And Abel was a keeper of sheep,
but Cain was a tiller of the ground.
[3]And in process of time it came to pass, that Cain brought of the fruit of
the ground an offering unto the LORD.
[4]And Abel, he also brought of the firstlings of his flock and of the fat
thereof. And the LORD had respect unto Abel and to his offering:
[5]But unto Cain and to his offering he had not respect. And Cain was very
wroth, and his countenance fell.
[6]And the LORD said unto Cain, Why art thou wroth? and why is thy
countenance fallen?
[7]If thou doest well, shalt thou not be accepted? and if thou doest not
well, sin lieth at the door. And unto thee *shall be* his desire, and thou shalt
rule over him.

☆4:1
4:2 Lk 11:50, 51
4:3 Lev 2:1; Num 18:12
☆4:4 Ex 13:12; Lev 3:15, 16; Num 18:17; Prov 3:9, 10; Ps 20:3; Heb 11:4
☆4:5 Mt 20:15
☆4:6 Isa 1:18–20; Mic 6:3–5
☆4:7 Num 32:23; Job 11:14, 15; Lk 11:35; Rom 6:12; Jas 1:15

2. Cain Murders Abel and Is Banished

[8]And Cain talked with Abel his brother: and it came to pass, when they
were in the field, that Cain rose up against Abel his brother, and slew him.
[9]¶And the LORD said unto Cain, Where *is* Abel thy brother? And he said,
I know not: *Am* I my brother's keeper?
[10]And he said, What hast thou done? the voice of thy brother's blood
crieth unto me from the ground.

4:8 2 Sam 14:6; Mt 23:35; Heb 12:24; 1 Jn 3:12; Jude 11
4:9 Gen 3:9; Ps 9:12; 10:13, 14
4:10 Num 35:33; Deut 21:1; Heb 12:24

3:22 *the tree of life.* Only two of the trees are mentioned by name. One is the tree of life. God did not forbid Adam to eat of that tree. Why he did not eat remains a mystery. He preferred the fruit of the one forbidden tree. It appears that eating of the tree of life would have gained Adam immortality, but certainly not the forgiveness of his sin.

3:24 *he drove out the man.* Adam had no choice. God displaced him from his original inheritance. Disobedience always has temporal consequences which should be thought of prior to the act. Nevertheless, the banishment was an act of God's mercy, for Adam and Eve would have lived forever alienated from their Creator. God would restore them by making reconciliation possible through the death of Jesus Christ.

4:1 *Adam knew his wife,* i.e., he had sexual relations with her. She conceived. Adam was aware of the fact that God is the Author of life. Eve's conception was a gift from God.

4:4, 5 Cain and Abel evidently knew that animal sacrifices were required by God. Cain offered the fruit of the ground while Abel offered the blood of an animal. Abel's sacrifice was accepted because it was a response of obedient faith. Heb. 11:4 states specifically that "Abel offered unto God a more excellent sacrifice than Cain." Righteous Abel was the first martyr for the faith (Matt. 23:35); he is listed as a hero of the faith in Heb. 11:4. Abel's death is favorably compared with Christ's death in Heb. 12:24.

4:6 *wroth,* i.e., angry. This is the first instance of human anger recorded in the Bible. Anger is neutral: it can be good or bad depending on the reason for the anger.

4:7 The same Hebrew word—*chattah*—is used for "sin" and "sin-offering." Under the old covenant, the one who offered the animal sacrifice placed his hand on the head of the victim, thus identifying himself with his sin-offering. This type was fulfilled in Christ, who became sin for us (2 Cor. 5:21) that we might become righteous through faith in him. (See note on 1 Pet. 2:24.)

4:11 Gen 3:14; Deut 27:15–26; Isa 26:21; Gal 3:10
4:12 Lev 26:20; Deut 28:15–24, 65; Hos 9:17
4:13☆
4:14 Gen 9:6; Job 15:22; Prov 14:32; 24:16; 28:1

11 And now *art* thou cursed from the earth, which hath opened her mouth
to receive thy brother's blood from thy hand;
12 When thou tillest the ground, it shall not henceforth yield unto thee her
strength; a fugitive and a vagabond shalt thou be in the earth.
13 And Cain said unto the LORD, My punishment *is* greater than I can
bear.
14 Behold, thou hast driven me out this day from the face of the earth; and
from thy face shall I be hid; and I shall be a fugitive and a vagabond in the
earth; and it shall come to pass, *that* every one that findeth me shall slay
me.

4:15 Ps 59:11; 79:12; Ezek 9:4; Rev 14:9

15 And the LORD said unto him, Therefore whosoever slayeth Cain,
vengeance shall be taken on him sevenfold. And the LORD set a mark upon
Cain, lest any finding him should kill him.

4:16☆ 2 Kgs 13:23; 24:20; Jer 23:39; 52:3

16 ¶And Cain went out from the presence of the LORD, and dwelt in the
land of Nod, on the east of Eden.

3. Cain's Children

4:17☆ Ps 49:11

17 And Cain knew his wife; and she conceived, and bare E'noch: and he
builded a city, and called the name of the city, after the name of his son,
E'noch.

4:18☆

18 And unto E'noch was born I'rad: and I'rad begat Me-hu'ja-el: and Me-
hu'ja-el begat Me-thu'sa-el: and Me-thu'sa-el begat La'mech.

4:19☆

19 ¶And La'mech took unto him two wives: the name of the one *was*
Adah, and the name of the other Zil'lah.
20 And Adah bare Ja'bal: he was the father of such as dwell in tents, and
of such as have cattle.

4:21☆

21 And his brother's name *was* Ju'bal: he was the father of all such as
handle the harp and organ.
22 And Zil'lah, she also bare Tu'bal–cain, an instructer of every artificer in
brass and iron: and the sister of Tu'bal–cain *was* Na'a-mah.

4:23 Lev 19:18; Deut. 32:35

23 And La'mech said unto his wives, Adah and Zil'lah, Hear my voice; ye
wives of La'mech, hearken unto my speech: for I have slain a man to my
wounding, and a young man to my hurt.
24 If Cain shall be avenged sevenfold, truly La'mech seventy and
sevenfold.

4:13 *my punishment is greater than I can bear.* If Cain had thought of the consequence of murder before the act, he might have restrained himself. To complain about the punishment a man deserves for a transgression, as Cain did, exposes the true depravity of his nature.

4:16 Cain and those in his line were impious and irreligious. They called themselves the sons of men. Seth and Enosh called themselves sons of God. From now on in the Scriptures there is a clear distinction between professors and profane. This distinction persists to this day.

4:17 In the 17th century Archbishop Ussher of England developed a scheme of Bible chronology which is still in use. But the modern carbon dating technique makes this chronology very suspect. Ussher's chronology was based on the judgment that Adam commenced his life around 4004 B.C. Many scholars allow for gaps in the chronologies that appear in Genesis 5 and 11. But the modern notion that man's long journey in history began millions of years ago does not fit the Bible pattern any more than the underlying evolutionary hypothesis which is part of this scheme. Man is a recent emergent and was created immediately and supernaturally by God.

4:18 *unto Enoch was born, i.e.,* . . . Enoch was the father of, or, "the ancestor of"; so also in the remainder of the verse.

4:19 *Lamech took unto him two wives.* This is the first instance of polygamy in the Scriptures. The words of Jesus indicate that it was not God's intention for a man to have more than one wife. To have more than one was a repudiation of the cultural mandate having to do with marriage. The "one flesh" principle is violated when a man has more than one wife (Matt. 19:3ff).

4:21 *harp and organ,* translated "lyre and pipe" in the NASB and RSV. This is the first of the musical instruments developed by man and mentioned in the Scriptures.

D. ADAM'S DESCENDANTS

1. Adam and Seth

25 ¶And Adam knew his wife again; and she bare a son, and called his
name Seth: For God, *said she*, hath appointed me another seed instead of
Abel, whom Cain slew.

4:25 Gen 4:8; 5:3 1 Chron 1:1 Lk 3:38

26 And to Seth, to him also there was born a son; and he called his name
Enos: then began men to call upon the name of the LORD.

☆**4:26** Gen 12:8 Deut 26:17 1 Kgs 18:24

5 THIS *is* the book of the generations of Adam. In the day that God
created man, in the likeness of God made he him;

☆**5:1** Gen 1:26; 6:9

2 Male and female created he them; and blessed them, and called their
name Adam, in the day when they were created.

5:2 Gen 1:27 Mk 10:6

3 ¶And Adam lived an hundred and thirty years, and begat *a son* in his
own likeness, after his image; and called his name Seth:

☆**5:3** Gen 4:25

4 And the days of Adam after he had begotten Seth were eight hundred
years: and he begat sons and daughters:

5:4 1 Chron 1:1

5 And all the days that Adam lived were nine hundred and thirty years:
and he died.

☆**5:5** Gen 3:19 Heb 9:27

2. Seth and Enos

6 And Seth lived an hundred and five years, and begat Enos:
7 And Seth lived after he begat Enos eight hundred and seven years, and
begat sons and daughters:
8 And all the days of Seth were nine hundred and twelve years: and he
died.

5:6 1 Chron 1:1 Lk 3:38
☆**5:7**

3. Enos and Cainan

9 ¶And Enos lived ninety years, and begat Ca-i'nan:
10 And Enos lived after he begat Ca-i'nan eight hundred and fifteen years,
and begat sons and daughters:
11 And all the days of Enos were nine hundred and five years: and he died.

5:9 1 Chron 1:1 Lk 3:37

4. Cainan and Mahalaleel

12 ¶And Ca-i'nan lived seventy years, and begat Ma-ha'la-le-el:
13 And Ca-i'nan lived after he begat Ma-ha'la-le-el eight hundred and
forty years, and begat sons and daughters:
14 And all the days of Ca-i'nan were nine hundred and ten years: and he
died.

5:12 1 Chron 1:1 Lk 3:37

5. Mahalaleel and Jared

15 ¶And Ma-ha'la-le-el lived sixty and five years, and begat Ja'red:
16 And Ma-ha'la-le-el lived after he begat Ja'red eight hundred and thirty
years, and begat sons and daughters:

4:26 *then began men to call upon the name of the* LORD, i.e., "this man was the first to invoke the name of Jehovah."†

5:1 *book of the generations of Adam,* i.e., a list or catalog of those descendants of Adam who were looking to the coming of Jesus Christ. It was not a list of all those of the seed of Adam, but only those related to the faith of Adam.

5:3 Better translated in the NASB: "When Adam lived one hundred and thirty years, he became the father of a son in his own likeness, according to his image, and named him Seth." So likewise in 5:6, 9, 15, 18, 21, 25, 28, and 32.

5:5 Adam lived for 930 years. Longevity was common at that time. Man's life expectancy was shortened so that by Abraham's time it was less than 200 years. Then in Psalm 90:10 we are told that "the days of our years are threescore and ten and if by reason of strength they be fourscore years . . ."

5:7 *other sons and daughters.* This refrain is repeated in verses 9, 13, 16, 19, 22, 26, and 30. Thus the population increased far more rapidly than some suppose. Moses, under the Spirit's guidance, did not mention all the descendants of each man mentioned in these verses.

17 And all the days of Ma-ha'la-le-el were eight hundred ninety and five years: and he died.

6. Jared and Enoch

5:18 1 Chron. 1:1 Lk 3:37 Jude 14

18 ¶And Ja'red lived an hundred sixty and two years, and he begat E'noch:

19 And Ja'red lived after he begat E'noch eight hundred years, and begat sons and daughters:

20 And all the days of Ja'red were nine hundred sixty and two years: and he died.

7. Enoch and Methuselah

5:22 Gen 6:9; 24:20; 48:15 Heb 11:5 Jude 14

5:24☆ 2 Kgs 2:11 Ps 49:5; 73:24

21 ¶And E'noch lived sixty and five years, and begat Me-thu'se-lah:

22 And E'noch walked with God after he begat Me-thu'se-lah three hundred years, and begat sons and daughters:

23 And all the days of E'noch were three hundred sixty and five years:

24 And E'noch walked with God: and he *was* not; for God took him.

8. Methuselah and Lamech

25 And Me-thu'se-lah lived an hundred eighty and seven years, and begat La'mech:

26 And Me-thu'se-lah lived after he begat La'mech seven hundred eighty and two years, and begat sons and daughters:

5:27☆

27 And all the days of Me-thu'se-lah were nine hundred sixty and nine years: and he died.

9. Lamech and Noah

5:28☆

5:29 Gen 3:17; 8:21 Rom 8:20

28 ¶And La'mech lived an hundred eighty and two years, and begat a son:

29 And he called his name Noah, saying, This *same* shall comfort us concerning our work and toil of our hands, because of the ground which the LORD hath cursed.

30 And La'mech lived after he begat Noah five hundred ninety and five years, and begat sons and daughters:

31 And all the days of La'mech were seven hundred seventy and seven years: and he died.

10. Noah and His Sons

5:32 Gen 7:6 Gen 9:18

32 And Noah was five hundred years old: and Noah begat Shem, Ham, and Ja'pheth.

5:24 *and he was not,* i.e., "Enoch was translated that he should not see death." This was a miracle, since Enoch never tasted physical death. The Bible records only one other translation—that of Elijah (2 Kings 2:11).

5:27 According to this scripture, Methuselah lived for 969 years. Three possible solutions have been advanced to explain this phenomenon. One is that physical conditions in the antediluvian age made such longevity possible. Man's life span has been reduced since the flood, according to this view. The second theory is that these age spans are figurative and must be reduced. The reduction-of-age theory does not work, however. If all of the ages were divided by ten, then Methuselah lived to be almost 100. But when the life span of his father Enoch is so reduced, we are faced with the fact that Enoch would have been six and a half years old when Methuselah was born. The third explanation is that the age span applies not to individuals but to families. But Heb. 11:5 speaks of the translation of Enoch as an individual and makes no mention of a family translation.

5:28 Lamech, the father of Noah, died five years before the flood. We can suppose that had he been alive he would have gone into the ark with his son.

III. THE SINS OF MEN AND GOD'S JUDGMENT (6:1—8:19)

A. THE POLLUTION OF THE WORLD

6 AND it came to pass, when men began to multiply on the face of the
earth, and daughters were born unto them,
2 That the sons of God saw the daughters of men that they *were* fair; and
they took them wives of all which they chose.
3 And the LORD said, My spirit shall not always strive with man, for that
he also *is* flesh: yet his days shall be an hundred and twenty years.
4 There were giants in the earth in those days; and also after that, when
the sons of God came in unto the daughters of men, and they bare *children*
to them, the same *became* mighty men which *were* of old, men of renown.
5 ¶And God saw that the wickedness of man *was* great in the earth, and
that every imagination of the thoughts of his heart *was* only evil continually.
6 And it repented the LORD that he had made man on the earth, and it
grieved him at his heart.
7 And the LORD said, I will destroy man whom I have created from the
face of the earth; both man, and beast, and the creeping thing, and the
fowls of the air; for it repenteth me that I have made them.
8 But Noah found grace in the eyes of the LORD.

B. RIGHTEOUS NOAH CHOSEN TO BUILD THE ARK

9 ¶These *are* the generations of Noah: Noah was a just man *and* perfect in
his generations, *and* Noah walked with God.
10 And Noah begat three sons, Shem, Ham, and Ja'pheth.
11 The earth also was corrupt before God, and the earth was filled with
violence.
12 And God looked upon the earth, and, behold, it was corrupt; for all
flesh had corrupted his way upon the earth.
13 And God said unto Noah, The end of all flesh is come before me; for
the earth is filled with violence through them; and, behold, I will destroy
them with the earth.
14 ¶Make thee an ark of gopher wood; rooms shalt thou make in the ark,
and shalt pitch it within and without with pitch.

☆**6:1** Gen 1:28
☆**6:2** 2 Pet 2:14
6:3 Num 11:17; Ps 78:39; Neh 9:30; Isa 63:10; 1 Pet 3:20
☆**6:4** Num 13:33
6:5 Gen 8:21; 18:20; Ps 14:2, 3
☆**6:6** Ex 32:14; Num 23:19; 1 Sam 15:29; 2 Sam 24:16; Jer 18:8; Amos 7:3, 6; Mal 3:6; Jas 1:7
6:7 Deut 29:19, 20
6:8 Ex 33:12; Prov 3:4
☆**6:9** a)Gen 2:4; 10:1; Job 1:1; b)Gen 7:1; Eccles 7:20; Ezek 14:14
6:10 1 Chron 1:5
6:11 Gen 13:13; Deut 31:29; Judg 2:19; Ezek 8:17
6:12 Gen 8:21; Ps 14:1–3; 53:2, 3; Rom 3–23
☆**6:13** Isa 34:1–4; Ezek 7:2, 3
☆**6:14** Ex 2:3

6:1, 2 *sons of God,* used here in the sense of God's created, supernatural beings, but no longer godly in character (6:3). Some commentators believe that the expression "sons of God" refers to the "godly line" of Seth, and "daughters of men" to women from the line of Cain.

6:4 This is a much disputed passage about which there are wide differences of opinion. J. O. Buswell says: ". . . there is nothing demonic or mythical in the entire passage. Moses is simply pointing out the fact that the mighty men of old, men of renown, were born of normal human marriage" (*The Zondervan Pictorial Encyclopedia of the Bible,* Zondervan, Vol. 4, p. 409). Then Buswell adds, "In a polytheistic world where mythological unions of gods and men were narrated, it is highly significant that Moses rejected the fanciful and degrading contemporary mythological speculations."

6:6 This verse is better translated in the NASB: "And the Lord was sorry that He had made man on the earth, and He was grieved in His heart." The word "repented" has a different connotation. The NIV says "The Lord was grieved. . . ."

6:9 Three expressions characterize the life of Noah: he was righteous, that is, he was redeemed and the righteousness of Christ was imputed to him; he was "perfect," that is, blameless; and he "walked with God." He was the prototype of the kind of people Christians ought to be in this generation.

6:13 *God said unto Noah.* God revealed to Noah what his intentions were in advance of the happening. The Scriptures do not tell us how God did this. God used different methods to make his will known; he was not limited to a single method of revelation.

6:14 Noah's ark was approximately 450 feet long by 75 feet wide, and was three-storied, with 15 feet between each story. Noah must have employed many people to assist him in the construction of the ark, which was made of gopher wood and covered with pitch. It has been estimated that it could have carried seventeen hundred animals. The ark is representative of Christ, who is the place of refuge for sinners who wish to be saved from the wrath to come (see 1 Pet. 3:20, 21).

15 And this *is the fashion* which thou shalt make it *of*: The length of the
ark *shall be* three hundred cubits, the breadth of it fifty cubits, and the
height of it thirty cubits.

6:16 Gen 7:16; 8:6

16 A window shalt thou make to the ark, and in a cubit shalt thou finish it
above; and the door of the ark shalt thou set in the side thereof; *with* lower,
second, and third *stories* shalt thou make it.

6:17☆ Gen 7:4, 21; Lev 26:28; Ps 29:10; Isa 54:9; 2 Pet 2:5

17 And, behold, I, even I, do bring a flood of waters upon the earth, to
destroy all flesh, wherein *is* the breath of life, from under heaven; *and* every
thing that *is* in the earth shall die.

6:18☆ Gen 9:9; 15:18; 17:21

18 But with thee will I establish my covenant; and thou shalt come into
the ark, thou, and thy sons, and thy wife, and thy sons' wives with thee.

6:19 Gen 7:14

19 And of every living thing of all flesh, two of every *sort* shalt thou bring
into the ark, to keep *them* alive with thee; they shall be male and female.

6:20 Gen 1:20–24

20 Of fowls after their kind, and of cattle after their kind, of every creeping
thing of the earth after his kind, two of every *sort* shall come unto thee, to
keep *them* alive.

6:21 Gen 1:29

21 And take thou unto thee of all food that is eaten, and thou shalt gather
it to thee; and it shall be for food for thee, and for them.

6:22☆ Gen 7:5; Ex 40:16

22 Thus did Noah; according to all that God commanded him, so did he.

C. GOD'S COMMAND TO FILL THE ARK

7:1 Gen 6:18; Job 5:19; Prov 11:8; Isa 26:20; Mt 24:38; Lk 17:26; Heb 11:17; 1 Pet 3:20

7 AND the LORD said unto Noah, Come thou and all thy house into the
ark; for thee have I seen righteous before me in this generation.

7:2 Lev 11:2–47; Deut 14:3–20; Ezek 44:23

2 Of every clean beast thou shalt take to thee by sevens, the male and his
female: and of beasts that *are* not clean by two, the male and his female.
3 Of fowls also of the air by sevens, the male and the female; to keep seed
alive upon the face of all the earth.

7:4☆ Gen 6:7, 13; 7:10, 12, 17

4 For yet seven days, and I will cause it to rain upon the earth forty days
and forty nights; and every living substance that I have made will I destroy
from off the face of the earth.

7:5 Gen 6:22

5 And Noah did according unto all that the LORD commanded him.

D. THE FLOOD BEGINS

7:6 Gen 5:32; 8:13

6 And Noah *was* six hundred years old when the flood of waters was upon
the earth.

7:7 Gen 6:18; 7:13

7 ¶And Noah went in, and his sons, and his wife, and his sons' wives with
him, into the ark, because of the waters of the flood.

7:8☆

8 Of clean beasts, and of beasts that *are* not clean, and of fowls, and of
every thing that creepeth upon the earth,
9 There went in two and two unto Noah into the ark, the male and the
female, as God had commanded Noah.

6:17 Three different views have emerged about the extent of the flood: (1) not all land was covered, and not all life died; (2) not all land was covered, but all life died; (3) all land was covered, and all life died. The last view is disliked especially by rationalist scholars. But there is a universal tradition about the flood among all peoples of the world. Recent evidence of a gigantic catyclysm in all parts of the world clearly suggests a universal flood.

6:18 God announces to Noah that he will make a covenant with him, but the details of that covenant are made known later in chapter 9.

6:22 Noah was obedient and did precisely what God told him to do. In 7:1 we are told: "for thee have I seen righteous before me." His righteousness was vindicated by his walk and fulfilled what James in his epistle indicates: we are saved by faith alone, yet saving faith is never alone; it is always accompanied by good works.

7:4 Until the time of the flood no rain had fallen on the planet earth. After this, rain became a constant factor. The earth got its water from what was stored up as moisture above the earth.

7:8 *of clean beasts, and of beasts that are not clean.* God had not yet told man which animals were good for food and which were not. Up to this point man may not have eaten animal flesh. Some Christians are vegetarians. The Scriptures nowhere enjoin us not to eat meat; neither do they command us to eat meat.

10 And it came to pass after seven days, that the waters of the flood were
upon the earth.
11 In the six hundredth year of Noah's life, in the second month, the
seventeenth day of the month, the same day were all the fountains of the
great deep broken up, and the windows of heaven were opened.
12 And the rain was upon the earth forty days and forty nights.
13 In the selfsame day entered Noah, and Shem, and Ham, and Ja'pheth,
the sons of Noah, and Noah's wife, and the three wives of his sons with
them, into the ark;
14 They, and every beast after his kind, and all the cattle after their kind,
and every creeping thing that creepeth upon the earth after his kind, and
every fowl after his kind, every bird of every sort.
15 And they went in unto Noah into the ark, two and two of all flesh,
wherein *is* the breath of life.
16 And they that went in, went in male and female of all flesh, as God had
commanded him: and the LORD shut him in.
17 And the flood was forty days upon the earth; and the waters increased,
and bare up the ark, and it was lift up above the earth.
18 And the waters prevailed, and were increased greatly upon the earth;
and the ark went upon the face of the waters.
19 And the waters prevailed exceedingly upon the earth; and all the high
hills, that *were* under the whole heaven, were covered.
20 Fifteen cubits upward did the waters prevail; and the mountains were
covered.
21 And all flesh died that moved upon the earth, both of fowl, and of
cattle, and of beast, and of every creeping thing that creepeth upon the
earth, and every man:
22 All in whose nostrils *was* the breath of life, of all that *was* in the dry
land, died.
23 And every living substance was destroyed which was upon the face of
the ground, both man, and cattle, and the creeping things, and the fowl of
the heaven; and they were destroyed from the earth: and Noah only
remained *alive*, and they that *were* with him in the ark.
24 And the waters prevailed upon the earth an hundred and fifty days.

7:10 Gen 7:4
☆7:11 Gen 8:2; Ps 78:23; Ezek 26:19; Mal 3:10
7:12 Gen 7:4, 17; 8:6; Ex 24:18; Deut 9:9; 1 Kgs 19:8; Mt 4:2
7:13 Gen 9:18; Heb 11:7; 1 Pet 3:20; 2 Pet 2:5
7:14 Gen 6:19, 20; 7:2, 3, 8, 9
7:15 Gen 6:19; 7:8
7:18 Ex 14:28; Ps 69:14, 15
7:19 Ps 46:2, 3; 2 Pet 3:6
7:20 Gen 8:4; Ps 104:6
7:21 Gen 6:7
☆7:23 Mt 24:37-39; 1 Pet 3:20; 2 Pet 2:5
7:24 Gen 7:11; 8:4

E. THE WATERS SUBSIDE

8 AND God remembered Noah, and every living thing, and all the cattle
that *was* with him in the ark: and God made a wind to pass over the
earth, and the waters asswaged;
2 The fountains also of the deep and the windows of heaven were stopped,
and the rain from heaven was restrained;
3 And the waters returned from off the earth continually: and after the
end of the hundred and fifty days the waters were abated.
4 And the ark rested in the seventh month, on the seventeenth day of the
month, upon the mountains of Ar'a-rat.

8:1 a)Gen 19:29; 30:22; Ex 2:24; Job 12:15; Isa 44:27; Jer 2:2; 2 Pet 2:5; b)Ex 14:21; Ps 104:7
☆8:2 Gen 7:11
☆8:3 Gen 7:24
☆8:4 Gen 7:11; Isa 37:38

7:11 It is apparent that man knew about the seasons of the year and had calendar months. There were months and days known to man. The divisions of the year may well have been included as part of God's revelation to man.
7:23 The effect of the flood did not extend to sea life, only to what lived on land, including birds and beasts.
8:2 *the windows of heaven were stopped.* The NASB has it that "the floodgates were closed, and the rain . . . was restrained." God was sovereignly doing what he pleased. He started the rain and stopped it when his purposes had been brought to pass.
8:3, 4 *the mountains of Ararat* constituted a range of mountains rising to a height of almost 17,000 feet above sea level. The ark probably rested on one of the lower mountains of this range, closer to sea level. The Babylonian flood epic says that the ark came to rest on Mount Nisir, east of the Tigris River.

8:5☆ [5]And the waters decreased continually until the tenth month: in the tenth
month, on the first *day* of the month, were the tops of the mountains seen.
8:6 Gen 6:16 [6]¶And it came to pass at the end of forty days, that Noah opened the
window of the ark which he had made:
8:7☆ Lev 11:15 Deut 14:14 1 Kgs 17:4 Lk 12:24 [7]And he sent forth a raven, which went forth to and fro, until the waters
were dried up from off the earth.
[8]Also he sent forth a dove from him, to see if the waters were abated
8:8 Isa 60:8 Hos 11:11 Mt 10:16 from off the face of the ground;
[9]But the dove found no rest for the sole of her foot, and she returned
unto him into the ark, for the waters *were* on the face of the whole earth:
then he put forth his hand, and took her, and pulled her in unto him into
the ark.
[10]And he stayed yet other seven days; and again he sent forth the dove
out of the ark;
[11]And the dove came in to him in the evening; and, lo, in her mouth *was*
an olive leaf pluckt off: so Noah knew that the waters were abated from off
the earth.
[12]And he stayed yet other seven days; and sent forth the dove; which
returned not again unto him any more.

F. LEAVING THE ARK FOR DRY LAND

8:13☆ Gen 7:11 [13]¶And it came to pass in the six hundredth and first year, in the first
month, the first *day* of the month, the waters were dried up from off the
earth: and Noah removed the covering of the ark, and looked, and, behold,
the face of the ground was dry.
[14]And in the second month, on the seven and twentieth day of the month,
was the earth dried.
8:15 Gen 6:13; 7:1 [15]¶And God spake unto Noah, saying,
8:16☆ [16]Go forth of the ark, thou, and thy wife, and thy sons, and thy sons'
wives with thee.
8:17 Gen 7:8, 14 [17]Bring forth with thee every living thing that *is* with thee, of all flesh,
both of fowl, and of cattle, and of every creeping thing that creepeth upon
the earth; that they may breed abundantly in the earth, and be fruitful, and
multiply upon the earth.
[18]And Noah went forth, and his sons, and his wife, and his sons' wives
with him:
8:19 Gen 7:2, 3, 8, 9 [19]Every beast, every creeping thing, and every fowl, *and* whatsoever
creepeth upon the earth, after their kinds, went forth out of the ark.

IV. GOD'S PROMISE TO NOAH: A NEW BEGINNING (8:20—11:26)

A. THE EARTH WILL NOT BE CURSED AGAIN

8:20☆ Gen 4:4; 12:7 13:18; 22:2 [20]¶And Noah builded an altar unto the LORD; and took of every clean
beast, and of every clean fowl, and offered burnt offerings on the altar.

8:5 *in the tenth month, on the first day of the month,* i.e., "three months later."†
8:7 *a raven, which went forth to and fro.* The raven apparently lighted from time to time upon carcasses of dead animals floating on the water. The dove, which Noah next dispatched, would not alight on such floating carrion, and was thus a good indication of the water level.
8:13 *in the 601st year, in the first month, the first day of the month,* i.e., "twenty-nine days after that."†
8:16 Noah went forth from the ark to a totally different world than had existed before. The planet had been affected by this catastrophe. The environment was less habitable; floods, earthquakes, and famine started to become commonplace.
8:20 *clean beast . . . clean fowl,* i.e., ritually approved by God.† *Noah . . . offered burnt offerings.* Animal sacrifices were already known to man as a means for obtaining atonement and forgiveness. God was pleased with what Noah did and promised that there never again would be a universal flood that would extinguish all life.

21And the LORD smelled a sweet savour; and the LORD said in his heart,
I will not again curse the ground any more for man's sake; for tne
imagination of man's heart *is* evil from his youth; neither will I again smite
any more every thing living, as I have done.
22While the earth remaineth, seedtime and harvest, and cold and heat,
and summer and winter, and day and night shall not cease.

8:21 Gen 3:17; 5:29 Lev 1:9 Isa 54:9
8:22 Gen 45:6 Ps 74:16, 17

B. MEN MAY EAT MEAT BUT NOT LIFE-BLOOD

9 AND God blessed Noah and his sons, and said unto them, Be fruitful,
and multiply, and replenish the earth.
2And the fear of you and the dread of you shall be upon every beast of
the earth, and upon every fowl of the air, upon all that moveth *upon* the
earth, and upon all the fishes of the sea; into your hand are they delivered.
3Every moving thing that liveth shall be meat for you; even as the green
herb have I given you all things.
4But flesh with the life thereof, *which is* the blood thereof, shall ye not eat.
5And surely your blood of your lives will I require; at the hand of every
beast will I require it, and at the hand of man; at the hand of every man's
brother will I require the life of man.
6Whoso sheddeth man's blood, by man shall his blood be shed: for in the
image of God made he man.
7And you, be ye fruitful, and multiply; bring forth abundantly in the
earth, and multiply therein.

☆**9:1** Gen 1:28; 9:7 24:60 Ps 128:3
9:2 Gen 1:26 Ps 8:6–8
9:3 Gen 1:29 Deut 12:15 14:3–21 Ps 104:14
9:4 Lev 3:17 7:26, 27; 17:10 Deut 12:16 Acts 15:29
9:5 Ex 21:12, 28, 29 Lev 19:17 Num 35:33
☆**9:6** Ex 20:13 Num 35:33
9:7 Gen 1:28; 8:17 9:1

C. GOD'S PROMISE AND THE RAINBOW SEAL

8¶And God spake unto Noah, and to his sons with him, saying,
9And I, behold, I establish my covenant with you, and with your seed
after you;
10And with every living creature that *is* with you, of the fowl, of the
cattle, and of every beast of the earth with you; from all that go out of the
ark, to every beast of the earth.
11And I will establish my covenant with you; neither shall all flesh be cut
off any more by the waters of a flood; neither shall there any more be a
flood to destroy the earth.
12And God said, This *is* the token of the covenant which I make between
me and you and every living creature that *is* with you, for perpetual
generations:
13I do set my bow in the cloud, and it shall be for a token of a covenant
between me and the earth.
14And it shall come to pass, when I bring a cloud over the earth, that the
bow shall be seen in the cloud:

9:8 Gen 8:15; 9:16
9:9 Gen 6:18 Isa 54:9 Ps 25:14
9:10 Gen 8:1 9:15, 16
9:11 Isa 54:9 2 Pet 3:6
9:12 Gen 17:11 Ex 12:13; 13:16 Mt 26:26–28
☆**9:13** Ezek 1:28

9:1 Following the flood, God made a covenant with Noah. The agreement specified that: (1) there would always be the seasons of the year with planting and harvest (8:22); (2) Noah and his family would replenish the earth (9:1); (3) law and government were to be reinstituted (9:1–6); (4) meat, except for the blood, and vegetables were to be given to man for food (9:3, 4); and (5) there would never again be a universal flood (9:15). God sealed the covenant with a rainbow (9:16, 17).

9:6 This verse commands capital punishment for murder. In Exodus 21:12–17 murder and other crimes worthy of capital punishment are spelled out by Moses. Nowhere in the Scriptures is capital punishment forbidden or the Old Testament commandment nullified. Paul recognizes that there are crimes for which capital punishment is the proper penalty and says he is willing to die if guilty of such crimes (Acts 25:11). Had capital punishment been repealed or set aside, Paul would have spoken quite differently.

9:13 *a covenant between me and the earth.* God made a covenant with Noah but he also made a covenant with the earth. God the creator is interested in his inanimate creation as well as in man. He determined to preserve the earth from the effects of the flood. Redemption was accomplished for the cosmos as well as for man. God's people should be careful about the way they use the earth on which they depend for sustenance.

9:15 Gen 6:18 8:21, 22 Deut 7:9
15 And I will remember my covenant, which *is* between me and you and
every living creature of all flesh; and the waters shall no more become a
flood to destroy all flesh.

9:16☆
16 And the bow shall be in the cloud; and I will look upon it, that I may
remember the everlasting covenant between God and every living creature
of all flesh that *is* upon the earth.

9:17☆
17 And God said unto Noah, This *is* the token of the covenant, which I
have established between me and all flesh that *is* upon the earth.

9:18☆ Gen 5:32 10:1, 32 1 Chron 1:4
18 ¶And the sons of Noah, that went forth of the ark, were Shem, and
Ham, and Ja′pheth: and Ham *is* the father of Canaan.
19 These *are* the three sons of Noah: and of them was the whole earth
overspread.

D. NOAH AND HIS CHILDREN

1. Canaan Cursed and Shem Blessed

9:20☆ Gen 5:29
20 And Noah began *to be an husbandman, and he planted a vineyard:*

9:21☆ Gen 19:32 Prov 20:1
21 And he drank of the wine, and was drunken; and he was uncovered
within his tent.

9:22 Gen 10:6 Prov 30:17 Heb 2:15
22 And Ham, the father of Canaan, saw the nakedness of his father, and
told his two brethren without.

9:23 Ex 20:12
23 And Shem and Ja′pheth took a garment, and laid *it* upon both their
shoulders, and went backward, and covered the nakedness of their father;
and their faces *were* backward, and they saw not their father's nakedness.

9:24 Deut 27:16
24 And Noah awoke from his wine, and knew what his younger son had
done unto him.

9:25☆ Judg 1:28
25 And he said, Cursed *be* Canaan; a servant of servants shall he be unto
his brethren.

9:26 Gen 14:20; 27:40
26 And he said, Blessed *be* the LORD God of Shem; and Canaan shall be
his servant.

9:27 Gen 10:2–5 Isa 66:19
27 God shall enlarge Ja′pheth, and he shall dwell in the tents of Shem; and
Canaan shall be his servant.
28 ¶And Noah lived after the flood three hundred and fifty years.

9:29 Gen 5:32; 7:11
29 And all the days of Noah were nine hundred and fifty years: and he
died.

9:16 *covenant between God and every living creature.* God made a covenant with Noah, and with the earth itself (see 9:13). Here God speaks of his covenant with all flesh. God is concerned for everything he created. Birds and animals are included in this everlasting covenant. Man should have a concern for all life, human and non-human, because all life comes as a gift from the Creator.

9:16, 17 God's covenants are always two-way streets. In them God obligates himself when he makes promises to men. Thus the Noahic covenant included a promise from God that never again would life be destroyed by a universal flood. The seal of this covenant was the rainbow. The new covenant has for its seal water baptism. Those who come to salvation by faith and are baptized receive the gift of eternal life and are made to be the children of God and heirs with Jesus in his kingdom.

9:18 *Ham is the father of Canaan.* Ham was not the ancestor of the Negro, as was once supposed.†

9:20, 21 God never reproved Noah for his drunkenness even though drunkenness is always reproved elsewhere. The phenomenon of fermentation probably began after the flood, not before. There is no instance of drunkenness recorded before the flood.

9:25 The Canaanites came from Canaan, who was the son of Ham, against whom Noah pronounced a curse. The myth that Ham was a Negro and that slavery and other restrictions against Negroes are of divine origin is untenable. Noah's curse was fulfilled when the Canaanites were overcome by the descendants of Shem and later by the Persians, Greeks, and Romans. Seven nations of people came from Canaan (Deut. 7:1) who were idolatrous, superstitious, and abominably wicked. Abraham roamed their land, and to him was the promise made to inherit Canaan. Centuries went by before Abraham's descendants occupied the land. When they entered their inheritance God commanded them: (1) to make no agreements with the Canaanites and show no mercy toward them (Deut. 7:2); (2) not to worship but to destroy their idols (Exod. 23:24; Deut. 7:5, 25); (3) not to follow their customs (Lev. 18:26, 27); (4) not to fear them (Deut. 7:17, 18; 31:7). When Israel sinned, God permitted a remnant to remain in Canaan for chastisement (Judg. 2:3, 21, 22; 3:1–4; 4:2; Num. 33:55).

2. The Sons of Japheth

10 NOW these *are* the generations of the sons of Noah, Shem, Ham,
and Ja′pheth: and unto them were sons born after the flood.
2 The sons of Ja′pheth; Go′mer, and Ma′gog, and Mad′a-i, and Ja′van,
and Tu′bal, and Me′shech, and Ti′ras.
3 And the sons of Go′mer; Ash′ke-naz, and Ri′phath, and To-gar′mah.
4 And the sons of Ja′van; E-li′shah, and Tarshish, Kit′tim, and Do′da-
nim.
5 By these were the isles of the Gentiles divided in their lands; every one
after his tongue, after their families, in their nations.

☆**10:1** Gen 6:9; 9:18; 1 Chron 1:4
10:2 1 Chron 1:5–7; Isa 66:19; Ezek 27:13; 38:2, 3, 6
10:3 Jer 51:27; Ezek 27:14
10:4 1 Chron 1:6, 7
☆**10:5**

3. The Sons of Ham

6 ¶And the sons of Ham; Cush, and Miz′ra-im, and Phut, and Canaan.
7 And the sons of Cush; Se′ba, and Hav′i-lah, and Sab′tah, and Ra′a-mah,
and Sab′te-cha: and the sons of Ra′a-mah; She′ba, and De′dan.
8 And Cush begat Nimrod: he began to be a mighty one in the earth.
9 He was a mighty hunter before the LORD: wherefore it is said, Even as
Nimrod the mighty hunter before the LORD.
10 And the beginning of his kingdom was Babel, and E′rech, and Ac′cad,
and Cal′neh, in the land of Shi′nar.
11 Out of that land went forth Asshur, and builded Nin′e-veh, and the city
Re-ho′both, and Ca′lah,
12 And Re′sen between Nin′e-veh and Ca′lah: the same *is* a great city.
13 And Miz′ra-im begat Lu′dim, and An′a-mim, and Le′ha-bim, and
Naph′tu-him,
14 And Path-ru′sim, and Cas′lu-him, (out of whom came Phi-lis′tim,) and
Caph′to-rim.
15 ¶And Canaan begat Si′don his firstborn, and Heth,
16 And the Jeb′u-site, and the Am′or-ite, and the Gir′ga-site,
17 And the Hi′vite, and the Ark′ite, and the Sin′ite,
18 And the Ar′vad-ite, and the Zem′a-rite, and the Ha′math-ite: and
afterward were the families of the Canaanites spread abroad.
19 And the border of the Canaanites was from Si′don, as thou comest to
Ge′rar, unto Ga′za; as thou goest, unto Sodom, and Go-mor′rah, and
Ad′mah, and Ze-bo′im, even unto La′sha.
20 These *are* the sons of Ham, after their families, after their tongues, in
their countries, *and* in their nations.

10:6 1 Chron 1:8, 9
10:7 Isa 43:3; Ezek 27:15, 20, 22
10:10 Gen 11:9
10:11 a)Mic 5:6; b)Num 4:22, 24; Ezra 4:2
10:13 1 Chron 1:11, 12; Jer 46:9
10:15 Gen 15:19–21; 23:3; 1 Chron 1:13; Jer 47:4
10:16 Gen 15:19–21
10:19 Gen 14:2, 3
☆**10:20**

4. The Sons of Shem

21 ¶Unto Shem also, the father of all the children of E′ber, the brother of
Ja′pheth the elder, even to him were *children* born.

10:1–32 After the flood, the human race descended from the children of Noah just as Noah's family had descended from Adam and Eve. In some instances the descendants must be understood by their political rather than their racial forebears. The Canaanites were Semites (sons of Shem) and are listed as sons of Ham (10:6), for prior to Israel's occupation of Canaan it had been under the control of the Hamites, the peoples of northeast Africa. If Lud refers to the Lydians of Asia Minor, they were racially Japhethites, not Shemites. Ancient archeological data have made probable identification fairly certain in many instances: *Madai* (10:2) are the Medes; *Javan* (10:2) are the Ionians or Greeks; *Ashkenaz* (10:3) probably refers to the Scythians; *Elishah* (10:3) is likely an ancient name for the people of Cyprus; *Tarshish* (10:3) is probably Spain or Sardinia; *Kittim* (10:3), the people of Cyprus; *Put,* Cyrenaica of North Africa; *Shinar,* Babylonia; *Caphtorim,* the Cretans; *Heth,* the Hittites; and *Sheba,* southwest Arabia, whose queen visited King Solomon.

10:5 *every one after his tongue,* i.e., his language. This verse does not mean that the sons of Noah spoke different languages. It looks forward, rather, to the event of the tower of Babel, which is soon to occur and out of which God will divide mankind into a variety of language groupings.

10:20 *their tongues.* See note to 10:5.

10:22 Gen 11:10–26; 2 Kgs 15:29; 1 Chron 1:17–23; Isa 66:19
10:23 Job 1:1; Jer 25:30
10:24 Lk 3:35

22 The children of Shem; E'lam, and Asshur, and Ar-phax'ad, and Lud,
and A'ram.
23 And the children of A'ram; Uz, and Hul, and Ge'ther, and Mash.
24 And Ar-phax'ad begat Sa'lah; and Sa'lah begat E'ber.
25 And unto E'ber were born two sons: the name of one *was* Pe'leg; for in
his days was the earth divided; and his brother's name *was* Jok'tan.
26 And Jok'tan begat Al-mo'dad, and She'leph, and Ha'zar-ma'veth, and
Je'rah,
27 And Ha-do'ram, and U'zal, and Dik'lah,
28 And O'bal, and A-bim'a-el, and She'ba,
29 And O'phir, and Hav'i-lah, and Jo'bab: all these *were* the sons of
Jok'tan.
30 And their dwelling was from Me'sha, as thou goest unto Se'phar a
mount of the east.
31 These *are* the sons of Shem, after their families, after their tongues, in
their lands, after their nations.

10:32 Gen 9:19; 10:1

32 These *are* the families of the sons of Noah, after their generations, in
their nations: and by these were the nations divided in the earth after the
flood.

E. THE TOWER OF CONFUSION (BABEL)

11:1☆
11:2☆ Gen 10:10; 14:1; Isa 11:11; Dan 1:2; Zech 5:11
11:3 Gen 14:10
11:4☆ 2 Sam 8:13; Ps 49:11–13
11:5☆ Gen 18:21; Ex 19:11
11:6☆ Gen 9:19; 11:1
11:7☆ Gen 1:26; 3:22; 10:5; Job 5:12
11:8☆ Gen 10:25, 32

11 AND the whole earth was of one language, and of one speech.
2 And it came to pass, as they journeyed from the east, that they
found a plain in the land of Shi'nar; and they dwelt there.
3 And they said one to another, Go to, let us make brick, and burn them
throughly. And they had brick for stone, and slime had they for morter.
4 And they said, Go to, let us build us a city and a tower, whose top *may*
reach unto heaven; and let us make us a name, lest we be scattered abroad
upon the face of the whole earth.
5 And the LORD came down to see the city and the tower, which the
children of men builded.
6 And the LORD said, Behold, the people *is* one, and they have all one
language; and this they begin to do: and now nothing will be restrained
from them, which they have imagined to do.
7 Go to, let us go down, and there confound their language, that they may
not understand one another's speech.
8 So the LORD scattered them abroad from thence upon the face of all the
earth: and they left off to build the city.

11:1 Before the flood, men spoke different languages. After the flood, all men spoke the same language. The period following the tower of Babel incident is anticipated in 10:5, 20, 31. When men at Babel sinned, God confused their languages; in so doing he made the advancement of wicked knowledge more difficult because of language barriers. Later, Pentecost was a sign of the reversal of the confusion. The time will come when language will no longer be a barrier in God's kingdom.
11:2 *the land of Shinar,* i.e., "the land of Babylon," located at the mouth of the Persian Gulf. *and they dwelt there,* i.e., "was soon thickly populated."†
11:4–9 The location of the tower of Babel is unknown. Birs Minrud, approximately seven miles from ancient Babylon, has been suggested as the site. Amran, which is within the city, is another. King Nebuchadnezzar spoke of the *Ziggurat Babili* ("Tower of Babylon"), which he restored after finding it in ruins. Bab-ili is from the Assyrian tongue and is the native name for the Greek Babylon. It means "Gate of God." It has nothing to do with the Hebrew word *balal,* which means "to confound." The Babel story finds its counterparts in ancient mythology, such as the Greek myth of the Titans who tried to climb to heaven. The biblical account is far older and is, of course, a historical fact which may have been influential in the formation of mythical tales elsewhere.
11:6 Language is the basis on which science feeds upon itself and grows. This was the beginning of an explosion of knowledge, nipped in the bud because of wrong motives and wrong use of the knowledge gained. Similarity with today's world is significant.
11:7 *let us.* The plural certainly suggests the triune personhood of God, who is one God in three persons—the Father, the Son, and the Holy Spirit.

9Therefore is the name of it called Babel; because the LORD did there confound the language of all the earth: and from thence did the LORD scatter them abroad upon the face of all the earth.

11:9 Gen 10:10 1 Cor 14:23

F. SHEM AND HIS DESCENDANTS

10¶These *are* the generations of Shem: Shem *was* an hundred years old, and begat Ar-phax'ad two years after the flood:
11And Shem lived after he begat Ar-phax'ad five hundred years, and begat sons and daughters.
12And Ar-phax'ad lived five and thirty years, and begat Sa'lah:
13And Ar-phax'ad lived after he begat Sa'lah four hundred and three years, and begat sons and daughters.
14And Sa'lah lived thirty years, and begat E'ber:
15And Sa'lah lived after he begat E'ber four hundred and three years, and begat sons and daughters.
16And E'ber lived four and thirty years, and begat Pe'leg:
17And E'ber lived after he begat Pe'leg four hundred and thirty years, and begat sons and daughters.
18And Pe'leg lived thirty years, and begat Re'u:
19And Pe'leg lived after he begat Re'u two hundred and nine years, and begat sons and daughters.
20And Re'u lived two and thirty years, and begat Se'rug:
21And Re'u lived after he begat Se'rug two hundred and seven years, and begat sons and daughters.
22And Se'rug lived thirty years, and begat Nahor:
23And Se'rug lived after he begat Nahor two hundred years, and begat sons and daughters.
24And Nahor lived nine and twenty years, and begat Te'rah:
25And Nahor lived after he begat Te'rah an hundred and nineteen years, and begat sons and daughters.
26And Te'rah lived seventy years, and begat Abram, Nahor, and Ha'ran.

11:10 Gen 10:22–25
☆11:12
☆11:13 1 Chron 1:17
11:24 Josh 24:2
11:26 Gen 22:20 1 Chron 1:26, 27

V. ABRAHAM, THE FIRST PATRIARCH (11:27—25:18)

A. ABRAHAM'S ANCESTORS

27¶Now these *are* the generations of Te'rah: Te'rah begat Abram, Nahor, and Ha'ran; and Ha'ran begat Lot.
28And Ha'ran died before his father Te'rah in the land of his nativity, in Ur of the Chal'dees.
29And Abram and Nahor took them wives: the name of Abram's wife *was Sa'rai; and the name of Nahor's wife,* Mil'cah, the daughter of Ha'ran, the father of Mil'cah, and the father of Is'cah.
30But Sa'rai was barren; she *had* no child.
31And Te'rah took Abram his son, and Lot the son of Ha'ran his son's son, and Sa'rai his daughter in law, his son Abram's wife; and they went

☆11:28
11:29 Gen 17:15 20:12; 22:20 31:53
11:30 Gen 15:2; 16:1 18:11; 25:21 1 Sam 1:5 Luke 1:7
11:31 Gen 27:43 Josh 24:2 Heb 11:8 Acts 7:2

11:12, 13 From here on, the life-span of men will decline sharply. The ages when men procreate will also be far younger than before. Noah (5:32) was five hundred years old when his wife had her three sons. In verses 12–26 the age of the fathers ranged from twenty-nine to thirty-five, except for Terah who was seventy.

11:28 Abram was not an uneducated, illiterate nomad. Archeological discoveries show that Ur of the Chaldees enjoyed an advanced culture, with libraries, schools, and temples. The people had textbooks on mathematics, religion, and politics, and used grammars, dictionaries, and encyclopedias. Egypt also had developed an advanced culture a thousand years before Abram's birth. Abram may have left written records for posterity which could have been used by Moses when he wrote the Pentateuch.

forth with them from Ur of the Chal'dees, to go into the land of Canaan;
and they came unto Ha'ran, and dwelt there.
11:32☆ [32]And the days of Te'rah were two hundred and five years: and Te'rah
died in Ha'ran.

B. ABRAHAM'S CALL BY GOD
1. God's Promise of a Great Nation

12:1☆ Gen 15:7 12 NOW the LORD had said unto Abram, Get thee out of thy country,
Acts 7:3 and from thy kindred, and from thy father's house, unto a land that
Heb 11:8 I will shew thee:
12:2☆ Gen 13:16 [2]And I will make of thee a great nation, and I will bless thee, and make
15:5; 17:5 18:18; 22:17 thy name great; and thou shalt be a blessing:
Zech 8:13 [3]And I will bless them that bless thee, and curse him that curseth thee:
12:3☆ Gen 22:18 and in thee shall all families of the earth be blessed.
26:4; 27:29
Ex 23:22
Acts 3:25 Gal 3:8

2. God's Promise of a Homeland: Canaan

12:4 Gen 11:26, 31 [4]So Abram departed, as the LORD had spoken unto him; and Lot went
with him: and Abram *was* seventy and five years old when he departed out
of Ha'ran.
[5]And Abram took Sa'rai his wife, and Lot his brother's son, and all their
substance that they had gathered, and the souls that they had gotten in
Ha'ran; and they went forth to go into the land of Canaan; and into the
land of Canaan they came.
12:6 Gen 33:18; 35:4 [6]¶And Abram passed through the land unto the place of Si'chem, unto
Deut 11:30 the plain of Mo'reh. And the Canaanite *was* then in the land.
12:7☆ Gen 13:15 [7]And the LORD appeared unto Abram, and said, Unto thy seed will I give
17:1; 18:1 Isa 41:8; 44:3 this land: and there builded he an altar unto the LORD, who appeared unto
Gal 3:16 him.
12:8 Gen 4:26; 8:20 [8]And he removed from thence unto a mountain on the east of Beth–el,
22:9 and pitched his tent, *having* Beth–el on the west, and Ha'i on the east: and
there he builded an altar unto the LORD, and called upon the name of the
LORD.
12:9☆ Gen 13:1; 20:1 [9]And Abram journeyed, going on still toward the south.

11:32 Terah died at the age of 205 years, Sarah at 127, Abraham at 175, Isaac at 180, Jacob at 147, and Joseph at 110. By the time of the monarchy David died at seventy. He was thirty when he began to reign and he reigned for forty years according to 2 Samuel 5:4. Thus the life span declined considerably from the days of Adam and of the patriarchs.

12:1 *Abram.* His name meant "father of height." He was renamed Abraham when God made his covenant with him. The name Abraham means "father of a multitude." From his loins came Isaac, Ishmael, and the descendants of his six sons born to Keturah, who became his wife after the death of Sarah. He was monogamous; yet a vast progeny can be traced back to him.

12:2 *thou shalt be a blessing,* or, "I will make your name so famous that it will be used to pronounce blessings on others."† The covenant God made with Abraham is mentioned several times in Genesis (13:14–17; chapters 15, 17, 18; 21:12; 22:16–18). God made certain promises to Abraham based upon his obedience or trust in God. The land of Palestine was promised to Abraham as was a posterity more numerous than the grains of sand on the seashore. God guaranteed Abraham a son and stated that, through Abraham, all the nations of the earth were to be blessed. Abraham believed God and it was counted unto him for righteousness.

12:3 *in thee shall all families of the earth be blessed,* or, "the nations will bless themselves because of you." There can be no doubt that 12:1–3 represents a unique disclosure of God's plan of salvation via missionary outreach. Paul clearly states that this scripture foresees the New Testament gospel. In Gal. 3:8, he writes: "And the scripture, foreseeing that God would justify the heathen through faith, preached before the gospel unto Abraham, saying, In thee shall all nations be blessed."

12:7 Abraham's altar implies animal sacrifice, common to the Semite peoples. This can undoubtedly be traced back to the earliest of all animal sacrifices—that of Abel, and the fact that, from the beginning, men knew that God had to be propitiated by blood sacrifice.

12:9 We now know that the Negeb was occupied during the time of Abraham (2100–1880 B.C.). He followed the trade route, which had water stations, from Mamre (Hebron) to Kadesh (later known as Kadesh-barnea). Jacob and Moses were also familiar with this route.

3. Abraham's Stay in Egypt

10 ¶And there was a famine in the land: and Abram went down into Egypt
to sojourn there; for the famine *was* grievous in the land.

12:10 Gen 26:1; 42:5

11 And it came to pass, when he was come near to enter into Egypt, that
he said unto Sa'rai his wife, Behold now, I know that thou *art* a fair woman
to look upon:

☆**12:11** Gen 26:7; 29:17

12 Therefore it shall come to pass, when the Egyptians shall see thee, that
they shall say, This *is* his wife: and they will kill me, but they will save thee
alive.

☆**12:12** Gen 20:11

13 Say, I pray thee, thou *art* my sister: that it may be well with me for thy
sake; and my soul shall live because of thee.

☆**12:13** Gen 20:2, 12

14 ¶And it came to pass, that, when Abram was come into Egypt, the
Egyptians beheld the woman that she *was* very fair.
15 The princes also of Pharaoh saw her, and commended her before
Pharaoh: and the woman was taken into Pharaoh's house.
16 And he entreated Abram well for her sake: and he had sheep, and oxen,
and he asses, and menservants, and maidservants, and she asses, and
camels.

12:16 Gen 13:2 20:14; 24:35

17 And the LORD plagued Pharaoh and his house with great plagues
because of Sa'rai Abram's wife.

12:17 1 Chron 16:21 Ps 105:14

18 And Pharaoh called Abram, and said, What *is* this *that* thou hast done
unto me? why didst thou not tell me that she *was* thy wife?

12:18 Gen 3:13; 4:10 20:9

19 Why saidst thou, She *is* my sister? so I might have taken her to me to
wife: now therefore behold thy wife, take *her*, and go thy way.
20 And Pharaoh commanded *his* men concerning him: and they sent him
away, and his wife, and all that he had.

C. THE SEPARATION OF ABRAHAM AND LOT

1. The Quarrel between Abraham's and Lot's Herdsmen

13 AND Abram went up out of Egypt, he, and his wife, and all that he
had, and Lot with him, into the south.

13:1 Gen 12:9; 20:1

2 And Abram *was* very rich in cattle, in silver, and in gold.

☆**13:2** Gen 12:16 20:14; 24:35

3 And he went on his journeys from the south even to Beth-el, unto the
place where his tent had been at the beginning, between Beth-el and Ha'i;

13:3 Gen 12:8; 28:19

4 Unto the place of the altar, which he had made there at the first: and
there Abram called on the name of the LORD.
5 ¶And Lot also, which went with Abram, had flocks, and herds, and
tents.

13:5 Gen 12:4, 5

6 And the land was not able to bear them, that they might dwell together:
for their substance was great, so that they could not dwell together.

13:6 Gen 36:6, 7

7 And there was a strife between the herdmen of Abram's cattle and the
herdmen of Lot's cattle: and the Canaanite and the Per'iz-zite dwelled then
in the land.

13:7 a)Gen 21:25 26:20 Ex 2:17 b)Gen 12:6 15:19–21

8 And Abram said unto Lot, Let there be no strife, I pray thee, between
me and thee, and between my herdmen and thy herdmen; for we *be*
brethren.

13:8 Prov 15:1, 18 20:3 Mt 5:9 Heb 12:14

12:11–13 Abraham faltered in his trust in God when he told Sarah to say she was his sister. By failing to tell the full truth, namely, that she was also his wife, he was walking by sight and not by faith. The consequences demonstrated that deceitfulness is never justified. Abraham was a man of faith, yet he was not perfect. The story shows that the end does not justify the means and that situational ethics are not acceptable to God. God's will must be done God's way.

13:2 *Abram . . . rich . . . in silver, and in gold.* From the earliest times men have prized silver and gold as precious. The record does not say how Abraham was able to gather so much wealth. Probably he traded cattle for silver and gold. In the Old Testament there is a definite relationship between fidelity to God and material benefits. God blessed the patriarch exceedingly and the surrounding people knew that God was his mentor.

13:9☆ Gen 20:15; 34:10

9 *Is* not the whole land before thee? separate thyself, I pray thee, from me: if *thou wilt take* the left hand, then I will go to the right; or if *thou depart* to the right hand, then I will go to the left.

2. Lot Chooses Sodom in the Jordan Valley

13:10☆ Gen 2:8; 14:2, 8; 19:22, 30; Deut 34:3

10 And Lot lifted up his eyes, and beheld all the plain of Jordan, that it *was* well watered every where, before the LORD destroyed Sodom and Gomor′rah, *even* as the garden of the LORD, like the land of Egypt, as thou comest unto Zo′ar.

11 Then Lot chose him all the plain of Jordan; and Lot journeyed east: and they separated themselves the one from the other.

13:12 Gen 14:2; 19:24

12 Abram dwelled in the land of Canaan, and Lot dwelled in the cities of the plain, and pitched *his* tent toward Sodom.

13:13☆ Gen 18:20; Deut 32:32; Isa 1:9; 3:9; Rom 9:29; 2 Pet 2:7

13 But the men of Sodom *were* wicked and sinners before the LORD exceedingly.

3. Abraham Chooses Hebron and Canaan

13:14 Gen 28:14; Deut 3:27; 34:1–4

14 ¶And the LORD said unto Abram, after that Lot was separated from him, Lift up now thine eyes, and look from the place where thou art northward, and southward, and eastward, and westward:

13:15 Gen 12:2, 7; 15:18; 17:7, 8

15 For all the land which thou seest, to thee will I give it, and to thy seed for ever.

13:16 Gen 15:5; 28:14; Num 23:10

16 And I will make thy seed as the dust of the earth: so that if a man can number the dust of the earth, *then* shall thy seed also be numbered.

13:17 Num 13:17–24

17 Arise, walk through the land in the length of it and in the breadth of it; for I will give it unto thee.

13:18 Gen 8:20; 12:7; 14:13; 18:1

18 Then Abram removed *his* tent, and came and dwelt in the plain of Mam′re, which *is* in Hebron, and built there an altar unto the LORD.

D. ABRAHAM RESCUES LOT

1. The Wars of the Kings

14:1 Gen 10:10; 11:2; 14:9; Jer 48:34; Dan 8:2; Acts 2:9
14:2 Gen 10:19; 13:10; 19:24; Deut 29:23
14:3 Num 34:12; Deut 3:17; Josh 3:16
14:4 Gen 14:1, 5, 9, 17
14:5 Gen 15:20; Deut 1:4; 2:10, 20; 3:11; Josh 13:19
14:6 Gen 21:21; 36:8, 20; Num 10:12

14 AND it came to pass in the days of Am′ra-phel king of Shi′nar, A′ri-och king of El′la-sar, Ched-or-la′o-mer king of E′lam, and Ti′dal king of nations;

2 *That these* made war with Be′ra king of Sodom, and with Bir′sha king of Go-mor′rah, Shi′nab king of Ad′mah, and Shem-e′ber king of Ze-boi′im, and the king of Be′la, which is Zo′ar.

3 All these were joined together in the vale of Sid′dim, which is the salt sea.

4 Twelve years they served Ched-or-la′o-mer, and in the thirteenth year they rebelled.

5 And in the fourteenth year came Ched-or-la′o-mer, and the kings that *were* with him, and smote the Reph′a-ims in Ash′te-roth Kar-na′im, and the Zu′zims in Ham, and the E′mims in Sha′veh Kir-i-a-tha′im,

6 And the Ho′rites in their mount Se′ir, unto El–pa′ran, which *is* by the wilderness.

13:9 Abraham's dependence was on God. He manifested this truth when he arranged for Lot to choose where he would go. Lot chose what was, humanly speaking, the more attractive place for his cattle. But with every rose there is a thorn; Lot's choice brought disaster to him and to his family.

13:10 *garden of the LORD*, i.e., "the garden of Eden."

13:13 Lot could not have been unaware of the fact that the people of Sodom were wicked. The text literally reads that they were "wicked and sinners exceedingly" (NASB). Why would any follower of God choose to reside among people like that?

7 And they returned, and came to En–mish′pat, which *is* Ka′desh, and
smote all the country of the Am′a-lek-ites, and also the Am′or-ites, that
dwelt in Haz′e-zon–ta′mar.
8 And there went out the king of Sodom, and the king of Go-mor′rah, and
the king of Ad′mah, and the king of Ze-boi′im, and the king of Be′la (the
same *is* Zo′ar;) and they joined battle with them in the vale of Sid′dim;
9 With Ched-or-la′o-mer the king of E′lam, and with Ti′dal king of
nations, and Am′ra-phel king of Shi′nar, and A′ri-och king of El′la-sar; four
kings with five.
10 And the vale of Sid′dim *was full of* slimepits; and the kings of Sodom
and Go-mor′rah fled, and fell there; and they that remained fled to the
mountain.
11 And they took all the goods of Sodom and Go-mor′rah, and all their
victuals, and went their way.
12 And they took Lot, Abram's brother's son, who dwelt in Sodom, and
his goods, and departed.
13 ¶And there came one that had escaped, and told Abram the Hebrew;
for he dwelt in the plain of Mam′re the Am′or-ite, brother of Esh′col, and
brother of Aner: and these *were* confederate with Abram.
14 And when Abram heard that his brother was taken captive, he armed
his trained *servants*, born in his own house, three hundred and eighteen, and
pursued *them* unto Dan.
15 And he divided himself against them, he and his servants, by night, and
smote them, and pursued them unto Ho′bah, which *is* on the left hand of
Damascus.
16 And he brought back all the goods, and also brought again his brother
Lot, and his goods, and the women also, and the people.

☆**14:7** Gen 16:14; 20:1; Num 13:26; Deut 1:19; 2 Chron 20:2
14:8 Gen 13:10; 14:2
☆**14:12** Gen 11:27; 13:6, 12
14:13 Gen 10:16; 13:18; 39:14
☆**14:14** Gen 12:5; Deut 34:1
14:15 Gen 15:2; 1 Kgs 15:8; Acts 9:2
14:16 Gen 14:12, 14

2. Abraham Pays a Tenth to Melchizedek

17 ¶And the king of Sodom went out to meet him after his return from the
slaughter of Ched-or-la′o-mer, and of the kings that *were* with him, at the
valley of Sha′veh, which *is* the king's dale.
18 And Mel-chiz′e-dek king of Salem brought forth bread and wine: and
he *was* the priest of the most high God.
19 And he blessed him, and said, Blessed *be* Abram of the most high God,
possessor of heaven and earth:
20 And blessed be the most high God, which hath delivered thine enemies
into thy hand. And he gave him tithes of all.

14:17 Gen 14:5; 2 Sam 18:18
☆**14:18** Ps 7:17; 50:14; 76:2; 110:4; Heb 5:6, 10; 7:1
14:19 Gen 27:25; 48:9; Mk 10:16
☆**14:20** Gen 9:26; 24:27; Ps 44:3; 72:17–19; Heb 7:4, 6

14:7 Glueck's findings indicate that these kings devastated the area from Transjordan down to Kadesh-barnea so that sedentary culture stopped ca. the 20th century B.C.

14:12 Lot's decision to settle in Sodom and Gomorrah was unwise. The Scriptures consistently warn about fraternization with unbelieving peoples. The Apostle Peter says that Lot "was a good man, sick of the terrible wickedness he saw around him day after day" (2 Pet. 2:8, TLB). Why he did not remove himself and his family from that rotten environment is not known. He smarted for his sin, was taken captive, delivered by Abraham, and was at last delivered from Sodom and Gomorrah when God destroyed them. Here we see the kindness and mercy of God displayed to a saved but backslidden Lot and his family. *Abram's brother's son,* i.e., "his nephew."

14:14 Abraham was not only wealthy; he had a large retinue of servants attached to him as well. We learn that they were instructed in the skills of warfare because when Abraham delivered Lot from captivity, it was accomplished by force. These military personnel were born in Abraham's house.

14:18 Melchizedek, whose name means "king of righteousness," was the king of Salem and a priest. The author of Hebrews presents him as a type of Christ and speaks of Christ's priesthood as springing from Melchizedek. Christ's priesthood preceded the Aaronic priesthood, was superior to it, and is eternal. (See Heb. 5:6ff.)

14:20 Tithing has a long history. This is the first instance in the Old Testament of a practice which is widely taught and practiced today. Abraham paid tithes to Melchizedek who, according to verse 18, "was the priest of the most high God." God had a priesthood before Aaron (see Heb. 7). In addition to Abraham and his family, there were other true believers who worshipped and served the living God. Abraham's tithing

3. Abraham Takes No Booty

21 And the king of Sodom said unto Abram, Give me the persons, and take the goods to thyself.

14:22☆ Gen 1:1

22 And Abram said to the king of Sodom, I have lift up mine hand unto the LORD, the most high God, the possessor of heaven and earth,

14:23 2 Kgs 5:16

23 That I will not *take* from a thread even to a shoelatchet, and that I will not take any thing that *is* thine, lest thou shouldest say, I have made Abram rich:

14:24 Gen 14:13

24 Save only that which the young men have eaten, and the portion of the men which went with me, Aner, Esh'col, and Mam're; let them take their portion.

E. GOD'S COVENANT WITH ABRAHAM

1. God Promises Abraham an Heir

15:1☆ Gen 21:17 26:24; 46:2 Num 12:6 Deut 33:29 Ps 3:3

15 AFTER these things the word of the LORD came unto Abram in a vision, saying, Fear not, Abram: I *am* thy shield, *and* thy exceeding great reward.

15:2☆

2 And Abram said, Lord GOD, what wilt thou give me, seeing I go childless, and the steward of my house *is* this E-li-e'zer of Damascus?

15:3 Gen 14:14

3 And Abram said, Behold, to me thou hast given no seed: and, lo, one born in my house is mine heir.

15:4 Gen 17:16 Gal 4:28

4 And, behold, the word of the LORD *came* unto him, saying, This shall not be thine heir; but he that shall come forth out of thine own bowels shall be thine heir.

15:5 Gen 12:2 22:17; 32:12 Rom 4:18

5 And he brought him forth abroad, and said, Look now toward heaven, and tell the stars, if thou be able to number them: and he said unto him, So shall thy seed be.

15:6☆ Ps 106:31 Rom 4:3 Gal 3:6 Jas 2:23

6 And he believed in the LORD; and he counted it to him for righteousness.

15:7 Gen 12:1; 13:15 Neh 9:7 Acts 7:2–4

2. Abraham Offers a Sacrifice

7 And he said unto him, I *am* the LORD that brought thee out of Ur of the Chal'dees, to give thee this land to inherit it.

15:8☆ Judg 6:17 Lk 1:18

8 And he said, Lord GOD, whereby shall I know that I shall inherit it?

---

practice was carried on by Jacob, for example, who at Bethel promised to tithe (Gen. 28:22). Jacob recognized what many Christians do not fully appreciate: what he gave to God was only a part of what God first had given to him.

14:22 *I have lift up my hand unto the LORD,* i.e., "I have solemnly promised." Oaths, covenants, or promises have been employed from earliest time, as evidenced here by Abraham's oath. God himself used oaths (Heb. 6:16, 17). Oaths were used in the Old Testament to (1) confirm covenants (26:28ff; 31:44, 53); (2) resolve controversies in courts of law (Exod. 22:11; Num. 5:19); and (3) guarantee the carrying out of promised acts (50:25). Followers of God have been forbidden to take oaths in the name of idols and created things (Josh. 23:7; Matt. 5:34–36; James 5:12). God used an oath to show his immutability (22:16; Num. 14:28; Heb. 6:17). Jesus taught that believers should do what they promise without making oaths; their pledged word should be all that is needed (Matt. 5:34–37).

15:1 God appeared to Abraham in a vision and spoke to him. Visions were not frequent and there is no reason to suppose that God cannot visit people in visions today, even though the revelation of God is complete in the Bible. If there should be any visions, they would not include further revelation, because nothing can be added to the Bible (see note to Psalm 89:19).

15:2, 3 The Nuzu tablets indicate that childless couples often adopted a slave who would care for them, give them a proper burial, then inherit their estate unless a son was born after the slave's adoption. In that event the slave heir was usually disinherited.

15:6 Under the Old Testament covenant, salvation was by grace through faith, just as under the new covenant. Abraham was saved the same way every believer is saved today. Indeed, Paul uses Abraham as a prime illustration of one who was justified by his faith, a new birth which occurred before his circumcision. Circumcision, then, was a seal that followed, not preceded, faith.

15:8ff Abraham heard the voice of God and his promise. He wanted to be sure that he was not mistaken so he asked for outward corroboratory evidence to certify the promise to him. The smoking furnace and the burning lamp (verse 17) supply Abraham with that evidence. What Abraham asked for is similar to the request of Gideon in Judges 6:36ff.

9 And he said unto him, Take me an heifer of three years old, and a she — **15:9** Lev 1:2
goat of three years old, and a ram of three years old, and a turtledove, and
a young pigeon.
10 And he took unto him all these, and divided them in the midst, and laid — ☆**15:10** Lev 1:17
each piece one against another: but the birds divided he not.
11 And when the fowls came down upon the carcases, Abram drove them
away.
12 And when the sun was going down, a deep sleep fell upon Abram; and, — **15:12** Gen 2:21; 28:11
lo, an horror of great darkness fell upon him. — 1 Sam 26:12
13 And he said unto Abram, Know of a surety that thy seed shall be a — ☆**15:13** Ex 12:40
stranger in a land *that is* not theirs, and shall serve them; and they shall — Acts 7:6
afflict them four hundred years; — Gal 3:17
14 And also that nation, whom they shall serve, will I judge: and afterward — **15:14** Ex 6:5
shall they come out with great substance.
15 And thou shalt go to thy fathers in peace; thou shalt be buried in a — **15:15** Gen 25:7, 8
good old age.
16 But in the fourth generation they shall come hither again: for the — ☆**15:16** Ex 33:2
iniquity of the Am'or-ites *is* not yet full.

3. God Promises Abraham a Land

17 And it came to pass, that, when the sun went down, and it was dark, — **15:17** Jer 34:18, 19
behold a smoking furnace, and a burning lamp that passed between those
pieces.
18 In the same day the LORD made a covenant with Abram, saying, Unto — ☆**15:18** Gen 13:15; 17:2
thy seed have I given this land, from the river of Egypt unto the great river, — Ex 23:31
the river Eu-phra'tes: — Num 34:1–15; Deut 1:7, 8
19 The Ken'ites, and the Ken'iz-zites, and the Kad'mon-ites, — **15:19** Num 24:21
20 And the Hittites, and the Per'iz-zites, and the Reph'a-ims, — **15:20** Gen 14:5
21 And the Am'or-ites, and the Canaanites, and the Gir'ga-shites, and the — **15:21** Gen 10:15
Jeb'u-sites. — Ex 23:23, 28

F. THE BIRTH OF ISHMAEL

1. Sarai Gives Hagar to Abraham

16 NOW Sa'rai Abram's wife bare him no children: and she had an — **16:1** Gen 11:30
handmaid, an Egyptian, whose name *was* Ha'gar. — 15:2; 21:9
2 And Sa'rai said unto Abram, Behold now, the LORD hath restrained me — Gal 4:24, 25
from bearing: I pray thee, go in unto my maid; it may be that I may obtain — ☆**16:2** Gen 30:3
children by her. And Abram hearkened to the voice of Sa'rai. — Ex 21:4

15:10 *divided them in the midst.* In 15:18 the Hebrew reads that God "cut a covenant" with Abraham. Cutting animals in half is related to that phrase. Data found at Qatna and Mari indicate that covenants were sealed by a ritual involving the cutting up of asses.

15:13 God revealed some of his descendants' future history to Abraham. The bondage in Egypt is set forth and its length (400 years) specified. This bondage was part of the divine plan for the numerical growth of the Hebrew race.

15:16 *fourth generation.* At that time it was a hundred years. Later on, with the decline in longevity, it became less. *the iniquity of the Amorites is not yet full,* i.e., "the wickedness of the Amorite nations living there now (implied) will not be ready for punishment until then."†

15:18 *river of Egypt,* i.e., "Wadi-el-Arish," at the southern border of Judah.†

16:2, 3 In 15:4 God promised Abram a son. When Sarai produced no heir, she gave Abram the slave girl Hagar, who gave birth to Ishmael. This was in accord with the custom of that age. Archeologists have discovered that, in some marriage contracts, a childless wife was obligated to furnish a substitute for her husband, since childlessness was considered tragic. It was wrong to send away the slave wife and her children. When Ishmael was born, Abraham was eighty-six years old (16:16). Ishmael was to be the progenitor of the Muslim peoples, who have challenged Jews and Christians alike across the centuries. God's promise to Abraham was fulfilled when Isaac was born. Abraham was then one hundred years old (21:5). There is a lesson to be learned from Abraham's experience. He and Sarai sought to shortcut God. They used the standards of the world to solve their problem, not the spiritual principles laid down by God. They did not understand that God's ways are not our ways, nor his thoughts our thoughts (Isa. 55:8, 9). They should have waited patiently for God to fulfill his covenant promise.

16:3☆ Gen 13:1 [3]And Sa′rai Abram's wife took Ha′gar her maid the Egyptian, after
Abram had dwelt ten years in the land of Canaan, and gave her to her
husband Abram to be his wife.
16:4 Gen 16:15 [4]¶And he went in unto Ha′gar, and she conceived: and when she saw that
she had conceived, her mistress was despised in her eyes.
16:5☆ Gen 31:53 [5]And Sa′rai said unto Abram, My wrong *be* upon thee: I have given my
maid into thy bosom; and when she saw that she had conceived, I was
despised in her eyes: the LORD judge between me and thee.
[6]But Abram said unto Sa′rai, Behold, thy maid *is* in thy hand; do to her
as it pleaseth thee. And when Sa′rai dealt hardly with her, she fled from her
face.

2. The Angel Brings God's Promise to Hagar

16:7☆ Gen 21:17 22:11 [7]¶And the angel of the LORD found her by a fountain of water in the
wilderness, by the fountain in the way to Shur.
16:8 Gen 3:9; 4:9 [8]And he said, Ha′gar, Sa′rai's maid, whence camest thou? and whither
wilt thou go? And she said, I flee from the face of my mistress Sa′rai.
16:9 Gen 21:12 Eccles 10:4 [9]And the angel of the LORD said unto her, Return to thy mistress, and
submit thyself under her hands.
Eph 6:5 Tit 2:9 [10]And the angel of the LORD said unto her, I will multiply thy seed
16:10 Gen 17:20 exceedingly, that it shall not be numbered for multitude.
16:11 Gen 16:15 Ex 3:7, 8 [11]And the angel of the LORD said unto her, Behold, thou *art* with child,
and shalt bear a son, and shalt call his name Ish′ma-el; because the LORD
hath heard thy affliction.
16:12 Gen 21:20 Job 39:5–8 [12]And he will be a wild man; his hand *will be* against every man, and
every man's hand against him; and he shall dwell in the presence of all his
brethren.
16:13 Gen 12:8; 32:30 [13]And she called the name of the LORD that spake unto her, Thou God
seest me: for she said, Have I also here looked after him that seeth me?
16:14☆ Gen 14:7 [14]Wherefore the well was called Be′er-la-hai′-roi; behold, *it is* between
Ka′desh and Be′red.

3. Ishmael Is Born

16:15☆ Gen 21:9; 25:12 [15]¶And Ha′gar bare Abram a son: and Abram called his son's name,
which Ha′gar bare, Ish′ma-el.
16:16 Gen 12:4; 16:3 [16]And Abram *was* fourscore and six years old, when Ha′gar bare Ish′ma-
el to Abram.

G. THE SIGN AND SEAL OF GOD'S COVENANT: ABRAHAM CIRCUMCISED

1. God's Restatement of His Covenant

17:1☆ a)Gen 12:7 16:16 b)Gen 28:3 35:11; 48:3 c)Gen 6:9 Deut 18:13 Mt 5:48
17 AND when Abram was ninety years old and nine, the LORD
appeared to Abram, and said unto him, I *am* the Almighty God;
walk before me, and be thou perfect.

16:5 Sarai experiences the contempt of Hagar who has borne a son for Abraham. Had she trusted God in the first place, this would not have happened. Implicitly, she seems to place the blame on Abraham rather than herself.

16:7 *angel of the LORD.* See note to Exodus 3:2.

16:14 The well of Beer–lahai–roi, located near Kadesh (called Kadesh–barnea in 32:8 and 34:4, as well as in Deuteronomy and Joshua), denotes how far Hagar had wandered in the wilderness. Isaac dwelt in this region (24:62; 25:11).

16:15 *Ishmael* which means "God (is) hearing." Abraham was eighty-six when the lad was born. God promised that Ishmael would beget twelve princes (Gen. 17:20), so from Abraham's loins came the twelve tribes of Ishmael and the twelve tribes of Israel, who have been inveterate enemies. Isaac and Ishmael met again at the funeral of their common father, Abraham (25:9).

17:1 *El Shaddai* ("God Almighty") comes from the Hebrew root word *shadad,* meaning "violent," or "irresistibly strong." Another interpretation has it as

2And I will make my covenant between me and thee, and will multiply
thee exceedingly.
3And Abram fell on his face: and God talked with him, saying,
4As for me, behold, my covenant *is* with thee, and thou shalt be a father
of many nations.
5Neither shall thy name any more be called Abram, but thy name shall
be Abraham; for a father of many nations have I made thee.
6And I will make thee exceeding fruitful, and I will make nations of thee,
and kings shall come out of thee.
7And I will establish my covenant between me and thee and thy seed
after thee in their generations for an everlasting covenant, to be a God unto
thee, and to thy seed after thee.
8And I will give unto thee, and to thy seed after thee, the land wherein
thou art a stranger, all the land of Canaan, for an everlasting possession;
and I will be their God.

17:2 Gen 13:16; 15:5; 17:2; 35:11
17:3 Gen 17:17; 18:2; Ex 3:6
17:5 Neh 9:7; Rom 4:17
17:6 Gen 35:11
17:7 Gen 12:7; 13:15; Lev 11:45; 26:12; Ps 105:8–11

2. The Sign and Seal of the Covenant

9¶And God said unto Abraham, Thou shalt keep my covenant therefore,
thou, and thy seed after thee in their generations.
10This *is* my covenant, which ye shall keep, between me and you and thy
seed after thee; Every man child among you shall be circumcised.
11And ye shall circumcise the flesh of your foreskin; and it shall be a
token of the covenant betwixt me and you.
12And he that is eight days old shall be circumcised among you, every
man child in your generations, he that is born in the house, or bought with
money of any stranger, which *is* not of thy seed.
13He that is born in thy house, and he that is bought with thy money,
must needs be circumcised: and my covenant shall be in your flesh for an
everlasting covenant.
14And the uncircumcised man child whose flesh of his foreskin is not
circumcised, that soul shall be cut off from his people; he hath broken my
covenant.

☆**17:9** Ex 19:5; 26:5; Ps 25:10
☆**17:10** Acts 7:8
17:11 Ex 12:48; Deut 10:16; Josh 5:3
17:12 Gen 21:4; Lev 12:3; Lk 1:59; 2:21; Phil 3:5
17:13 Ex 12:44
17:14 Ex 30:33; Lev 7:20

3. Sarai Will Be a Mother; Her Name Now Is Sarah

15¶And God said unto Abraham, As for Sa′rai thy wife, thou shalt not
call her name Sa′rai, but Sarah *shall* her name *be*.
16And I will bless her, and give thee a son also of her: yea, I will bless her,
and she shall be *a mother* of nations; kings of people shall be of her.

☆**17:15** Gen 17:5
17:16 Gen 18:10

"God of the mountain," because God appeared to Abraham on the mountain. Thus no nature worship or animism was implied. Abraham was ninety-nine years old when God appeared to him as *El Shaddai,* at a time when the birth of a son by Sarai seemed impossible. The Almighty stepped in and did the impossible. God changed Abram's name to Abraham (meaning "father of a multitude") and a year later Isaac was born. This Almighty God is also (1) eternal (1:1); (2) infinite and omnipresent (Ps. 139:7–10); (3) immutable (Mal. 3:6; Ps. 102:26, 27; James 1:17); (4) omniscient (Ps. 147:5; Acts 15:18; Ps. 139:1–6; Prov. 5:21); (5) holy (Isa. 6:3; Ps. 99:9); (6) just (Deut. 32:4; Rev. 15:3, 4); (7) love (1 John 4:8, 16). At Calvary, "Mercy and truth are met together; righteousness and peace have kissed each other" (Ps. 85:10).

17:9, 10 God instituted circumcision as the seal or sign of the covenant he had made with Abraham (17:11). Any failure to keep the seal meant that the individual was later cut off from the people of Israel. Moses reiterated the law of circumcision (Lev. 12; John 7:22, 23). Circumcision as a seal was abolished in the New Testament (Eph. 2:11–15; Col. 3:11); to insist on it is to become a legalist. Circumcision now is of the heart and not of the flesh, but even under the Abrahamic covenant it was useless unless accompanied by saving faith. Abraham himself was justified by faith (Rom. 3:30; Gal. 5:6; Rom. 2:25; 1 Cor. 7:19).

17:15 The promise to Abraham that Sarai would have a child was ratified by a change in her name, even as Abram became Abraham earlier. Sarai meant "my princess," which limited her honor to one family. But in Isaac Abraham's seed was to have greater signification. So God changed Sarai's name to Sarah ("princess"). Verse 16 says that she "also (i.e., in addition to being Isaac's mother) shall be a mother of nations, and kings of people shall be in her." Through her offspring the Messiah-king would come.

17:17 Gen 17:3; 18:13

17 Then Abraham fell upon his face, and laughed, and said in his heart,
Shall *a child* be born unto him that is an hundred years old? and shall
Sarah, that is ninety years old, bear?
18 And Abraham said unto God, O that Ish′ma-el might live before thee!

17:19 Gen 21:1, 2; 26:3–5

19 And God said, Sarah thy wife shall bear thee a son indeed; and thou
shalt call his name Isaac: and I will establish my covenant with him for an
everlasting covenant, *and* with his seed after him.

17:20 Gen 21:13; 25:16

20 And as for Ish′ma-el, I have heard thee: Behold, I have blessed him,
and will make him fruitful, and will multiply him exceedingly; twelve
princes shall he beget, and I will make him a great nation.

17:21 Gen 17:7, 19

21 But my covenant will I establish with Isaac, which Sarah shall bear
unto thee at this set time in the next year.

4. Abraham Is Circumcised; the Covenant Is Sealed

17:22 Gen 18:33; 35:13

22 And he left off talking with him, and God went up from Abraham.

17:23 Gen 14:14

23 ¶And Abraham took Ish′ma-el his son, and all that were born in his
house, and all that were bought with his money, every male among the men
of Abraham's house; and circumcised the flesh of their foreskin in the
selfsame day, as God had said unto him.

17:24 Gen 16:16; 17:1; Rom 4:11

24 And Abraham *was* ninety years old and nine, when he was circumcised
in the flesh of his foreskin.

17:25 Gen 16:16

25 And Ish′ma-el his son *was* thirteen years old, when he was circumcised
in the flesh of his foreskin.
26 In the selfsame day was Abraham circumcised, and Ish′ma-el his son.
27 And all the men of his house, born in the house, and bought with
money of the stranger, were circumcised with him.

H. SODOM AND GOMORRAH JUDGED; LOT RESCUED

1. The Heavenly Visitors

18:1 Gen 12:7; 13:18; Gen 14:13

18 AND the LORD appeared unto him in the plains of Mam′re: and he
sat in the tent door in the heat of the day;

18:2☆ Gen 19:1; 23:7; 33:3, 6, 7; Josh 5:13–15

2 And he lift up his eyes and looked, and, lo, three men stood by him: and
when he saw *them,* he ran to meet them from the tent door, and bowed
himself toward the ground,

18:3 Gen 19:2; 24:31

3 And said, My Lord, if now I have found favour in thy sight, pass not
away, I pray thee, from thy servant:
4 Let a little water, I pray you, be fetched, and wash your feet, and rest
yourselves under the tree:

18:5 Judg 6:18; 13:15, 16

5 And I will fetch a morsel of bread, and comfort ye your hearts; after
that ye shall pass on: for therefore are ye come to your servant. And they
said, So do, as thou hast said.
6 And Abraham hastened into the tent unto Sarah, and said, Make ready
quickly three measures of fine meal, knead *it,* and make cakes upon the
hearth.

18:7 Judg 13:15

7 And Abraham ran unto the herd, and fetcht a calf tender and good, and
gave *it* unto a young man; and he hasted to dress it.

18:18 Deut 32:14

8 And he took butter, and milk, and the calf which he had dressed, and set
it before them; and he stood by them under the tree, and they did eat.

18:2 *three men.* Apparently one was Yahweh (God) accompanied by two angels. Abraham said, "my Lord," not "my Lords," implying that he knew there was a difference between the Lord and the two angels. In 19:1 the two angels go to Sodom to destroy the city.

2. Sarah's Laughter

9¶And they said unto him, Where *is* Sarah thy wife? And he said, Behold,
in the tent.
10And he said, I will certainly return unto thee according to the time of **18:10**
life; and, lo, Sarah thy wife shall have a son. And Sarah heard *it* in the tent Gen 22:15 Judg 13:3
door, which *was* behind him. Rom 9:9
11Now Abraham and Sarah *were* old *and* well stricken in age; *and* it **18:11**
ceased to be with Sarah after the manner of women. Gen 17:17
12Therefore Sarah laughed within herself, saying, After I am waxed old ☆**18:12**
shall I have pleasure, my lord being old also? 1 Pet 3:6
13And the LORD said unto Abraham, Wherefore did Sarah laugh, saying,
Shall I of a surety bear a child, which am old?
14Is any thing too hard for the LORD? At the time appointed I will return ☆**18:14**
unto thee, according to the time of life, and Sarah shall have a son. Gen 18:10 Jer 32:17, 27
15Then Sarah denied, saying, I laughed not; for she was afraid. And he Lk 1:37
said, Nay; but thou didst laugh.

3. God Informs Abraham of Sodom's and Gomorrah's Destruction

16¶And the men rose up from thence, and looked toward Sodom: and **18:16**
Abraham went with them to bring them on the way. Gen 18:22; 19:1
17And the LORD said, Shall I hide from Abraham that thing which I do; ☆**18:17**
18Seeing that Abraham shall surely become a great and mighty nation, Gen 19:24 ☆**18:18**
and all the nations of the earth shall be blessed in him? Gen 12:2, 3 Gal 3:18
19For I know him, that he will command his children and his household ☆**18:19**
after him, and they shall keep the way of the LORD, to do justice and Neh 9:7
judgment; that the LORD may bring upon Abraham that which he hath
spoken of him.
20And the LORD said, Because the cry of Sodom and Go-mor′rah is great, **18:20**
and because their sin is very grievous; Gen 13:13 19:13
21I will go down now, and see whether they have done altogether **18:21**
according to the cry of it, which is come unto me; and if not, I will know. Gen 11:5 Ex 3:8

4. Abraham Pleads for Sodom

22And the men turned their faces from thence, and went toward Sodom: **18:22**
but Abraham stood yet before the LORD. Gen 18:16; 19:1
23¶And Abraham drew near, and said, Wilt thou also destroy the **18:23**
righteous with the wicked? Ex 23:7
24Peradventure there be fifty righteous within the city: wilt thou also
destroy and not spare the place for the fifty righteous that *are* therein? ☆**18:25**
25That be far from thee to do after this manner, to slay the righteous with Deut 1:16; 32:4 Ps 58:11

18:12–15 Sarah, like us, went through periods of doubt and disbelief. Sarah's laughter in her heart explains why God said to Abraham, "Is anything too hard for God? Next year, just as I told you, I will certainly see to it that Sarah has a son." 18:15 indicates: "But Sarah denied it. 'I didn't laugh,' she lied, for she was afraid."† Here God's purpose was not annulled at the disbelief of Sarah. The baby was born and Sarai's name was changed to Sarah, which means "princess."

18:17–19 These verses convey "God's friendly thoughts concerning Abraham, where we have his resolution to make known to Abraham his purpose concerning Sodom, with the reasons of it."* This was a soliloquy in which God was speaking his inner thoughts, intentions, and reasonings. It was given through the Holy Spirit's revelation to Moses, the author of the book.

18:25 God is love (1 John 4:8) but he is also just (Ps. 89:14; 145:17). The judgments of God are: (1) according to truth (Rev. 19:2); (2) universal and certain (Rom. 2:6); (3) impartial (Rom. 2:11); (4) based on the state of our hearts as well as our outward acts (Rom. 2:16; Luke 12:2, 3). Three major judgments of God are mentioned in Scripture: (1) the judgment of believers' sins which were taken care of at Calvary (John 5:24; Rom. 8:1); (2) the believers' judgment for rewards (2 Cor. 5:10; Rom. 14:10; 1 Cor. 3:10–15); and (3) the judgment of unbelievers at the great white throne (Rev. 20:11–15).

the wicked: and that the righteous should be as the wicked, that be far from
thee: Shall not the Judge of all the earth do right?
18:26 Isa 65:8 Jer 5:1 26 And the LORD said, If I find in Sodom fifty righteous within the city,
then I will spare all the place for their sakes.
18:27 Ezra 9:6 Isa 6:5 Lk 18:1 27 And Abraham answered and said, Behold now, I have taken upon me
to speak unto the Lord, which *am but* dust and ashes:
28 Peradventure there shall lack five of the fifty righteous: wilt thou
destroy all the city for *lack of* five? And he said, If I find there forty and
five, I will not destroy *it*.
29 And he spake unto him yet again, and said, Peradventure there shall be
forty found there. And he said, I will not do *it* for forty's sake.
18:30 Ex 32:32 30 And he said *unto him*, Oh let not the Lord be angry, and I will speak:
Peradventure there shall thirty be found there. And he said, I will not do *it*,
if I find thirty there.
31 And he said, Behold now, I have taken upon me to speak unto the
Lord: Peradventure there shall be twenty found there. And he said, I will
not destroy *it* for twenty's sake.
18:32☆ 32 And he said, Oh let not the Lord be angry, and I will speak yet but this
once: Peradventure ten shall be found there. And he said, I will not destroy
it for ten's sake.
18:33 Gen 17:22; 35:13 33 And the LORD went his way, as soon as he had left communing with
Abraham: and Abraham returned unto his place.

5. Two Angels Visit Lot

19:1☆ Gen 18:2 19 AND there came two angels to Sodom at even; and Lot sat in the
gate of Sodom; and Lot seeing *them* rose up to meet them; and he
bowed himself with his face toward the ground;
19:2 Gen 18:3 Lk 24:28 2 And he said, Behold now, my lords, turn in, I pray you, into your
servant's house, and tarry all night, and wash your feet, and ye shall rise up
early, and go on your ways. And they said, Nay; but we will abide in the
street all night.
19:3 Gen 18:6–8 3 And he pressed upon them greatly; and they turned in unto him, and
entered into his house; and he made them a feast, and did bake unleavened
bread, and they did eat.
19:4 Gen 13:13; 18:20 Prov 4:16 4 ¶But before they lay down, the men of the city, *even* the men of Sodom,
compassed the house round, both old and young, all the people from every
quarter:
19:5☆ Lev 18:22; 20:13 Judg 19:22 5 And they called unto Lot, and said unto him, Where *are* the men which
came in to thee this night? bring them out unto us, that we may know them.
6 And Lot went out at the door unto them, and shut the door after him,
7 And said, I pray you, brethren, do not so wickedly.
19:8 Deut 23:17 8 Behold now, I have two daughters which have not known man; let me,
I pray you, bring them out unto you, and do ye to them as *is* good in your

---

18:32 Abraham offered six petitions for Sodom. God said "yes" six times. He did not stop answering until Abraham stopped asking. This incident should encourage every Christian to expect God to answer prayer. In Sodom's case it is clear that the city's spiritual state was so awful that it did not contain even ten righteous men.

19:1 Abraham and Lot were both righteous men (15:6; 2 Pet. 2:7, 8), yet their world and life views differed greatly. Abraham had his eyes fixed on "that strong heavenly city whose designer and builder is God" (Heb. 11:10, TLB). Lot looked toward the secular city of man, his thoughts centering on the "here and now" without regard for eternity. He chose Sodom (13:5ff) and ended up bankrupt.

19:5 *that we may know them.* This was an incident in which the Sodomites wanted to have homosexual relations with these male strangers. It is reinforced by the fact that Lot offered his two daughters who "have not known men"—which could only have reference to sexual relations between a male and a female. The fact that he was willing to sacrifice his daughters indicates how seriously the people of those days took their responsibility of caring for the strangers who lodged in their homes as guests.

eyes: only unto these men do nothing; for therefore came they under the
shadow of my roof.
9 And they said, Stand back. And they said *again*, This one *fellow* came in
to sojourn, and he will needs be a judge: now will we deal worse with thee,
than with them. And they pressed sore upon the man, *even* Lot, and came
near to break the door.

19:9 Ex 2:14 Prov 9:7, 8

10 But the men put forth their hand, and pulled Lot into the house to
them, and shut to the door.

19:10 Gen 19:1

11 And they smote the men that *were* at the door of the house with
blindness, both small and great: so that they wearied themselves to find the
door.

19:11 Deut 28:28 2 Kgs 6:18 Acts 9:8

6. Lot Learns of the Doom of Sodom and Gomorrah

12 ¶And the men said unto Lot, Hast thou here any besides? son in law,
and thy sons, and thy daughters, and whatsoever thou hast in the city, bring
them out of this place:
13 For we will destroy this place, because the cry of them is waxen great
before the face of the LORD; and the LORD hath sent us to destroy it.
14 And Lot went out, and spake unto his sons in law, which married his
daughters, and said, Up, get you out of this place; for the LORD will destroy
this city. But he seemed as one that mocked unto his sons in law.

☆19:13 Gen 18:20 1 Chron 21:15 Jude 7
☆19:14 Ex 9:21 Jer 5:11, 12 43:1–3

7. Lot and His Family Flee to Zoar

15 ¶And when the morning arose, then the angels hastened Lot, saying,
Arise, take thy wife, and thy two daughters, which are here; lest thou be
consumed in the iniquity of the city.
16 And while he lingered, the men laid hold upon his hand, and upon the
hand of his wife, and upon the hand of his two daughters; the LORD being
merciful unto him: and they brought him forth, and set him without the
city.

19:16 Ps 119:60

17 ¶And it came to pass, when they had brought them forth abroad, that
he said, Escape for thy life; look not behind thee, neither stay thou in all the
plain; escape to the mountain, lest thou be consumed.
18 And Lot said unto them, Oh, not so, my Lord:
19 Behold now, thy servant hath found grace in thy sight, and thou hast
magnified thy mercy, which thou hast shewed unto me in saving my life;
and I cannot escape to the mountain, lest some evil take me, and I die:
20 Behold now, this city *is* near to flee unto, and it *is* a little one: Oh, let
me escape thither, (*is* it not a little one?) and my soul shall live.

☆19:17 Gen 13:10 19:26 1 Sam 19:11 Jer 48:6

21 And he said unto him, See, I have accepted thee concerning this thing
also, that I will not overthrow this city, for the which thou hast spoken.
22 Haste thee, escape thither; for I cannot do any thing till thou be come
thither. Therefore the name of the city was called Zo′ar.

19:21 Ps 102:17 145:19
☆19:22 Gen 13:10 19:30 Isa 15:5

19:13 *the LORD hath sent us to destroy it.* The incident tells us something about the power of angels, who exist to do the bidding of God. That same angelic power is available to the saints of God, for God has given his angels charge over us as ministering spirits (Heb. 1:14).

19:14 Lot was a true believer but suffered from severe family difficulties. His two daughters apparently were married to unbelievers who thought Lot was joking when he forecast the destruction of their city. They died as a consequence of their disbelief. Moreover, Lot's wife either disbelieved the angels who warned them not to look back or she was defiantly disobedient (19:26). Scripture everywhere declares that disbelief and defiance have their own rewards. Lot, as husband and father-in-law, could not save his wife and sons-in-law, however much he loved them.

19:17 *look not behind thee,* i.e., "do not look back." The admonition of the Scriptures is to forget those things which are behind, not to look back but rather to go forward (Phil. 3:13). Though we cannot change the past, we need not carry it with us into the future.

19:22 *Zoar,* meaning "little." Its exact location is now unknown, yet it must have been within walking distance of Sodom and Gomorrah.

8. God Destroys Sodom and Gomorrah

23 ¶The sun was risen upon the earth when Lot entered into Zo′ar.
19:24☆ Lk 17:29 2 Pet 2:6 Jude 7 — 24 Then the LORD rained upon Sodom and upon Go-mor′rah brimstone
and fire from the LORD out of heaven;
19:25 Deut 29:23 Isa 3:9; 13:19 Lam 4:6 2 Pet 2:6 — 25 And he overthrew those cities, and all the plain, and all the inhabitants
of the cities, and that which grew upon the ground.
19:26☆ Gen 19:17 Lk 17:32 — 26 ¶But his wife looked back from behind him, and she became a pillar of
salt.
19:27 Gen 18:22, 32 — 27 ¶And Abraham gat up early in the morning to the place where he stood
before the LORD:
19:28 Rev 9:2 — 28 And he looked toward Sodom and Go-mor′rah, and toward all the land
of the plain, and beheld, and, lo, the smoke of the country went up as the
smoke of a furnace.
19:29 Gen 8:1 Deut 7:8; 9:5 2 Pet 2:7, 8 — 29 ¶And it came to pass, when God destroyed the cities of the plain, that
God remembered Abraham, and sent Lot out of the midst of the overthrow,
when he overthrew the cities in the which Lot dwelt.

9. Lot's Daughters Sin: Moab and Ammon Born

19:30☆ Gen 13:10 1 Sam 22:1 1 Kgs 18:4 — 30 ¶And Lot went up out of Zo′ar, and dwelt in the mountain, and his two
daughters with him; for he feared to dwell in Zo′ar: and he dwelt in a cave,
he and his two daughters.
19:31 Gen 19:14 Gen 38:8, 9, 18 — 31 And the firstborn said unto the younger, Our father *is* old, and *there is*
not a man in the earth to come in unto us after the manner of all the earth:
19:32 Prov 23:31–33 Hab 2:15 — 32 Come, let us make our father drink wine, and we will lie with him, that
we may preserve seed of our father.
19:33 Gen 9:21 Lev 18:6 Prov 20:1 — 33 And they made their father drink wine that night: and the firstborn
went in, and lay with her father; and he perceived not when she lay down,
nor when she arose.
34 And it came to pass on the morrow, that the firstborn said unto the
younger, Behold, I lay yesternight with my father: let us make him drink
wine this night also; and go thou in, *and* lie with him, that we may preserve
seed of our father.
35 And they made their father drink wine that night also: and the younger
arose, and lay with him; and he perceived not when she lay down, nor when
she arose.
19:36☆ — 36 Thus were both the daughters of Lot with child by their father.
19:37☆ Gen 36:35 Ex 15:15 Num 21:29 Deut 2:9 Ruth 1:1 — 37 And the firstborn bare a son, and called his name Moab: the same *is*
the father of the Moabites unto this day.
19:38☆ Num 21:24 Deut 2:19 — 38 And the younger, she also bare a son, and called his name Ben-am′mi:
the same *is* the father of the children of Ammon unto this day.

19:24 Sodom and Gomorrah were located in the Valley of Siddom (or the Valley of the Dead Sea). The area was filled with bitumen pits (14:3, 10) and God probably sent an earthquake or lightning to destroy the two cities.

19:26 *his wife looked back . . . and became a pillar of salt.* This appeared to be a small sin, but it was a great one because Lot's wife had been expressly told not to look back. The punishment tells us something about the gravity of the sin, for the Scriptures say that the worse the sin is, the greater the penalty. Jesus specifically refers to Lot's wife in Luke 17:32 and cautions his hearers to remember her.

19:30 Lot lost everything in the destruction of Sodom and Gomorrah. At the time he left Abraham, he had much wealth; now he is seen living in a cave. His last estate was due to his mistaken decision to identify himself with the people of Sodom.

19:36 Moab and Ammon were born of incest. Had Lot spurned the alcohol offered by his daughters, he would not have cohabited with them. This verse marks the last we hear of Lot, and we do not know what became of him. We can hope he repented. Yet even in this case of incest, God used it to bring forth good and to glorify his name. Ruth was a Moabitess who married into the tribe of Judah and her name is listed in the genealogy of Jesus as an ancestress of the human Son of God.

19:37, 38 See notes on Ezekiel 25:2; 25:9, 10 for information on the Ammonites and Moabites.

I. ABRAHAM AND ABIMELECH
1. Abimelech Sins Ignorantly

20 AND Abraham journeyed from thence toward the south country,
and dwelled between Ka'desh and Shur, and sojourned in Ge'rar.
2 And Abraham said of Sarah his wife, She *is* my sister: and A-bim'e-lech
king of Ge'rar sent, and took Sarah.
3 But God came to A-bim'e-lech in a dream by night, and said to him,
Behold, thou *art but* a dead man, for the woman which thou hast taken; for
she *is* a man's wife.
4 But A-bim'e-lech had not come near her: and he said, Lord, wilt thou
slay also a righteous nation?
5 Said he not unto me, She *is* my sister? and she, even she herself said, He
is my brother: in the integrity of my heart and innocency of my hands have
I done this.
6 And God said unto him in a dream, Yea, I know that thou didst this in
the integrity of thy heart; for I also withheld thee from sinning against me:
therefore suffered I thee not to touch her.
7 Now therefore restore the man *his* wife; for he *is* a prophet, and he shall
pray for thee, and thou shalt live: and if thou restore *her* not, know thou
that thou shalt surely die, thou, and all that *are* thine.

20:1 Gen 13:1; 14:7 26:1
☆**20:2** Gen 12:13 20:12; 26:7
☆**20:3** Gen 28:12 31:24, 37:5
20:4 Gen 18:23–25
20:5 Gen 12:17 1 Kgs 9:4 Ps 7:8; 26:6
☆**20:6** Gen 15:1; 31:7 Ps 84:11
☆**20:7** Ex 7:1 1 Sam 7:5 Job 42:8

2. Abraham Prays and God Heals Abimelech

8 Therefore A-bim'e-lech rose early in the morning, and called all his
servants, and told all these things in their ears: and the men were sore
afraid.
9 Then A-bim'e-lech called Abraham, and said unto him, What hast thou
done unto us? and what have I offended thee, that thou hast brought on me
and on my kingdom a great sin? thou hast done deeds unto me that ought
not to be done.
10 And A-bim'e-lech said unto Abraham, What sawest thou, that thou
hast done this thing?
11 And Abraham said, Because I thought, Surely the fear of God *is* not in
this place; and they will slay me for my wife's sake.
12 And yet indeed *she is* my sister; she *is* the daughter of my father, but
not the daughter of my mother; and she became my wife.
13 And it came to pass, when God caused me to wander from my father's
house, that I said unto her, This *is* thy kindness which thou shalt shew unto
me; at every place whither we shall come, say of me, He *is* my brother.
14 And A-bim'e-lech took sheep, and oxen, and menservants, and
womenservants, and gave *them* unto Abraham, and restored him Sarah his
wife.
15 And A-bim'e-lech said, Behold, my land *is* before thee: dwell where it
pleaseth thee.

20:9 Gen 12:18
20:11 Gen 12:12 22:12; 42:18
20:13 Gen 11:31; 12:1
20:14 Gen 12:16
20:15 Gen 47:6

20:2 *she is my sister.* Abraham used this half-truth twice. He had not learned from his earlier experience that he could trust God in everything. So while he lied to protect himself, he opened the way for Sarah to commit adultery.
20:3 *she is a man's wife.* God chose to protect Abimelech, who was innocent of any wrongdoing, for he was unaware of Abraham's deceit.
20:6 God respected the integrity of Abimelech. He kept Abimelech from sinning in ignorance when Abraham failed to inform him that Sarah was his wife. We too can expect God to protect us in similar situations, when our hearts are right but we lack knowledge of the true facts.
20:7 God said that Abraham was a prophet and that Abraham's prayer for Abimelech's deliverance would be answered. Why God spoke this way is not clear. Perhaps since Abraham thought there was no fear of God in that place (verse 11), he needed to learn that God is concerned for unbelievers whose intentions are not evil and that he can deliver them in cases of this sort.

20:16 Gen 23:15
16 And unto Sarah he said, Behold, I have given thy brother a thousand
pieces of silver: behold, he *is* to thee a covering of the eyes, unto all that *are*
with thee, and with all *other:* thus she was reproved.

20:17☆ Num 12:13; 21:7
17 ¶So Abraham prayed unto God: and God healed A-bim′e-lech, and his
wife, and his maidservants; and they bare *children.*

20:18 Gen 12:17
18 For the LORD had fast closed up all the wombs of the house of A-bim′e-
lech, because of Sarah Abraham's wife.

J. THE BIRTH OF THE COVENANT CHILD ISAAC
1. Isaac Is Born and Circumcised

21:1☆ Gen 17:16, 21; 50:24
21 AND the LORD visited Sarah as he had said, and the LORD did
unto Sarah as he had spoken.

21:2 Gen 18:10; Gal 4:22, 28; Heb 11:11
2 For Sarah conceived, and bare Abraham a son in his old age, at the set
time of which God had spoken to him.

21:3 Gen 17:19
3 And Abraham called the name of his son that was born unto him, whom
Sarah bare to him, Isaac.

21:4 Gen 17:12; Acts 7:8
4 And Abraham circumcised his son Isaac being eight days old, as God
had commanded him.

21:5 Gen 17:1; Rom 4:19
5 And Abraham was an hundred years old, when his son Isaac was born
unto him.

21:6 Gen 18:12; Isa 54:1
6 ¶And Sarah said, God hath made me to laugh, *so that* all that hear will
laugh with me.

21:7 Gen 18:14; Lk 1:37
7 And she said, Who would have said unto Abraham, that Sarah should
have given children suck? for I have born *him* a son in his old age.

2. Ishmael and Hagar Banished

21:8 1 Sam 1:22
8 And the child grew, and was weaned: and Abraham made a great feast
the *same* day that Isaac was weaned.

21:9 Gal 4:29
9 ¶And Sarah saw the son of Ha′gar the Egyptian, which she had born
unto Abraham, mocking.

21:10 Gen 16:4, 5; Gal 4:30
10 Wherefore she said unto Abraham, Cast out this bondwoman and her
son: for the son of this bondwoman shall not be heir with my son, *even* with
Isaac.

21:11☆
11 And the thing was very grievous in Abraham's sight because of his son.

21:12☆ Rom 9:7; Heb 11:18
12 ¶And God said unto Abraham, Let it not be grievous in thy sight
because of the lad, and because of thy bondwoman; in all that Sarah hath
said unto thee, hearken unto her voice; for in Isaac shall thy seed be called.

21:13 Gen 16:10; 21:18; Gen 25:12–18
13 And also of the son of the bondwoman will I make a nation, because he
is thy seed.

21:14☆ Gen 16:7
14 And Abraham rose up early in the morning, and took bread, and a
bottle of water, and gave *it* unto Ha′gar, putting *it* on her shoulder, and the
child, and sent her away: and she departed, and wandered in the wilderness
of Be′er-she′ba.

20:17 *Abraham prayed to God.* Since Abraham was responsible for what had happened, it was proper that he should ask God to deliver the man and the family of the one he had wronged. The prayer would also afford him the opportunity to confess his own transgressions and find forgiveness.

21:1 *the LORD did unto Sarah as he had spoken.* Since Sarah was no longer fertile, God performed a miracle so she could become pregnant.

21:11 Apart from Abraham's personal hope to keep Ishmael near him, it was forbidden by the customary law of his day for a slave wife and her children to be ejected from their master's home. Sarah's jealousy must have been a trial for Abraham.

21:12 Sarah wanted Abraham to send Hagar and Ishmael away. God endorsed her judgment in that he intervened to command Abraham to follow her advice.

21:14 Since Ishmael was born when Abraham was eighty-six years old, he was by now a young teenager, not a baby. God protected Hagar and Ishmael and promised to make a nation out of the loins of Ishmael.

3. God Helps Hagar and Ishmael

15 And the water was spent in the bottle, and she cast the child under one
of the shrubs.
16 And she went, and sat her down over against *him* a good way off, as it **21:16** Jer 6:26
were a bowshot: for she said, Let me not see the death of the child. And she
sat over against *him,* and lift up her voice, and wept.
17 And God heard the voice of the lad; and the angel of God called to **21:17** Ex 3:7
Ha'gar out of heaven, and said unto her, What aileth thee, Ha'gar? fear not; Deut 26:7
for God hath heard the voice of the lad where he *is.* Ps 6:8
18 Arise, lift up the lad, and hold him in thine hand; for I will make him ☆**21:18** Gen 16:1–12;
a great nation. 25:12
19 And God opened her eyes, and she saw a well of water; and she went, **21:19** Isa 48:15
and filled the bottle with water, and gave the lad drink.
20 And God was with the lad; and he grew, and dwelt in the wilderness, ☆**21:20** Gen 28:15
and became an archer.
21 And he dwelt in the wilderness of Paran: and his mother took him a **21:21** Gen 14:6; 25:18
wife out of the land of Egypt.

K. THE DISPUTE BETWEEN ABRAHAM AND ABIMELECH

22 ¶And it came to pass at that time, that A-bim'e-lech and Phi'chol the ☆**21:22** Gen 26:26
chief captain of his host spake unto Abraham, saying, God *is* with thee in
all that thou doest:
23 Now therefore swear unto me here by God that thou wilt not deal **21:23** Gen 24:2
falsely with me, nor with my son, nor with my son's son: *but* according to
the kindness that I have done unto thee, thou shalt do unto me, and to the
land wherein thou hast sojourned.
24 And Abraham said, I will swear. **21:24** Gen 14:22
25 And Abraham reproved A-bim'e-lech because of a well of water, which **21:25** Gen 13:7; 26:15
A-bim'e-lech's servants had violently taken away.
26 And A-bim'e-lech said, I wot not who hath done this thing: neither
didst thou tell me, neither yet heard I *of it,* but to day.
27 And Abraham took sheep and oxen, and gave them unto A-bim'e-lech; **21:27** Gen 26:31
and both of them made a covenant. Prov 18:16
28 And Abraham set seven ewe lambs of the flock by themselves. 21:14
29 And A-bim'e-lech said unto Abraham, What *mean* these seven ewe
lambs which thou hast set by themselves?
30 And he said, For *these* seven ewe lambs shalt thou take of my hand, **21:30** Gen 31:44
that they may be a witness unto me, that I have digged this well.
31 Wherefore he called that place Be'er–she'ba; because there they sware ☆**21:31** Gen 21:14
both of them. 26:33
32 Thus they made a covenant at Be'er–she'ba: then A-bim'e-lech rose up, Josh 15:28
and Phi'chol the chief captain of his host, and they returned into the land of
the Philistines.

21:18 The expulsion of Hagar and Ishmael did not mean that the grace of God was withdrawn from two innocent people. God heard their cause and promised Hagar, "I will make Ishmael a great nation." The intention of God toward the descendants of Ishmael as well as toward the Gentiles is to save them from their sins and to give them the gift of everlasting life through Jesus Christ. That intention will continue to the end of the age by the free offer of salvation.

21:20 *and God was with the lad.* Abraham loved Ishmael and was sorry to send him and his mother away. God was understanding and used his divine power to protect Ishmael. Ishmael must have had some continuing contact with Abraham because he was present when Abraham was buried.

21:22 Abimelech was aware of how God promoted Abraham's material welfare. He sensed that God was with Abraham in all that he did. Thus he wanted to ally himself with Abraham in the interests of himself and of his family, then and for the future.

21:31 *Beer-sheba,* meaning, "Well of seven," or "Well of the oath."

21:33☆
1 Sam 22:6
31:13
Ps 90:2
Isa 9:6; 40:28
21:34
Gen 22:19

33¶And *Abraham* planted a grove in Be'er–she'ba, and called there on the name of the LORD, the everlasting God.

34And Abraham sojourned in the Philistines' land many days.

L. ABRAHAM'S OFFERING UP OF ISAAC

1. God Tests Abraham's Obedience

22:1☆
Ex 15:25; 16:4
Deut 8:2
Prov.17:3

22 AND it came to pass after these things, that God did tempt Abraham, and said unto him, Abraham: and he said, Behold, *here* I *am*.

22:2☆
2 Kgs 3:27
2 Chron 3:1
Jn 3:16

2And he said, Take now thy son, thine only *son* Isaac, whom thou lovest, and get thee into the land of Mo-ri'ah; and offer him there for a burnt offering upon one of the mountains which I will tell thee of.

22:3
Mt 10:37

3¶And Abraham rose up early in the morning, and saddled his ass, and took two of his young men with him, and Isaac his son, and clave the wood for the burnt offering, and rose up, and went unto the place of which God had told him.

4Then on the third day Abraham lifted up his eyes, and saw the place afar off.

5And Abraham said unto his young men, Abide ye here with the ass; and I and the lad will go yonder and worship, and come again to you.

6And Abraham took the wood of the burnt offering, and laid *it* upon Isaac his son; and he took the fire in his hand, and a knife; and they went both of them together.

22:7☆
Gen 8:20
Ex 29:38
Jn 1:29
Rev 13:7

7And Isaac spake unto Abraham his father, and said, My father: and he said, Here *am* I, my son. And he said, Behold the fire and the wood: but where *is* the lamb for a burnt offering?

22:8
Gen 18:14
Mt 19:26
1 Pet 1:19
Rev 5:6

8And Abraham said, My son, God will provide himself a lamb for a burnt offering: so they went both of them together.

2. God Substitutes a Ram for Isaac

22:9
Gen 12:7
Heb 11:17
Jas 2:21

9And they came to the place which God had told him of; and Abraham built an altar there, and laid the wood in order, and bound Isaac his son, and laid him on the altar upon the wood.

10And Abraham stretched forth his hand, and took the knife to slay his son.

22:11☆
Gen 16:7; 21:17
Ex 3:2

11And the angel of the LORD called unto him out of heaven, and said, Abraham, Abraham: and he said, Here *am* I.

21:33 *the everlasting God, El Olem* in the Hebrew, meaning *the God of eternity.*

22:1 *God did tempt Abraham,* i.e., God tested him. Abraham was an old man now. He had followed God for many years. Now that Isaac was a young man, God wanted to see whether Abraham loved Isaac more than he loved God. Abraham survived the test and left us an example. Is there anyone or anything we put in first place instead of Jesus the Lord? We too will be tested along this line.

22:2 Isaac is a type of Christ. He was an only son. His father offered him up as a sacrifice. Through Isaac came the descendants of Abraham. Abraham believed that if he offered Isaac as a sacrifice, God would raise Isaac from the dead (Heb. 11:17–19). Christ was an only Son who was offered and who was raised from the dead. 2 Chron. 3:1 speaks of David's building the Temple on Mt. Moriah, the site where Abraham was supposed to have offered Isaac. The account here speaks only of the *land* of Moriah, which was much more extensive than Mt. Moriah. Thus no one can be sure whether the place of sacrifice was the site where the Temple was later built.

22:7 Abraham had offered animal sacrifices before this. Isaac could not understand why his father had brought no lamb with him. How stunned Abraham must have been with the question! He spoke the language of faith when he said, "God will provide . . ." (22:8). He must have wondered whether God would ask him at last to do what God himself had forbidden—the taking of human life.

22:11 In 22:1 God calls Abraham by name once. Now he calls Abraham's name twice. Abraham responds immediately by saying, "Here am I." Had Abraham not been listening and had he not responded, he might have slain his only son.

12 And he said, Lay not thine hand upon the lad, neither do thou any
thing unto him: for now I know that thou fearest God, seeing thou hast not
withheld thy son, thine only *son* from me.

22:12 Heb 11:17

13 And Abraham lifted up his eyes, and looked, and behold behind *him* a
ram caught in a thicket by his horns: and Abraham went and took the ram,
and offered him up for a burnt offering in the stead of his son.

☆**22:13** Gen 8:20

14 And Abraham called the name of that place Je-ho'vah-ji'reh: as it is
said *to* this day, In the mount of the LORD it shall be seen.

☆**22:14**

3. God Promises to Bless Abraham Again

15 ¶And the angel of the LORD called unto Abraham out of heaven the
second time,

☆**22:15** Gen 22:11

16 And said, By myself have I sworn, saith the LORD, for because thou
hast done this thing, and hast not withheld thy son, thine only *son:*

22:16 49:13 Heb 6:13 Lk 1:73, 74

17 That in blessing I will bless thee, and in multiplying I will multiply thy
seed as the stars of the heaven, and as the sand which *is* upon the sea shore;
and thy seed shall possess the gate of his enemies;

22:17 Gen 12:12 13:16; 15:15 17:5

18 And in thy seed shall all the nations of the earth be blessed; because
thou hast obeyed my voice.

22:18 Gen 18:18 Acts 3:25 Gal 3:8, 16

19 So Abraham returned unto his young men, and they rose up and went
together to Be'er–she'ba; and Abraham dwelt at Be'er–she'ba.

22:19 Gen 21:31

20 ¶And it came to pass after these things, that it was told Abraham,
saying, Behold, Mil'cah, she hath also born children unto thy brother
Nahor;

22:20 Gen 11:29 31:53

21 Huz his firstborn, and Buz his brother, and Ke-mu'el the father of
A'ram,
22 And Che'sed, and Ha'zo, and Pil'dash, and Jid'laph, and Beth-u'el.
23 And Beth-u'el begat Rebekah: these eight Mil'cah did bear to Nahor,
Abraham's brother.

22:23 Gen 24:15

24 And his concubine, whose name *was* Reu'mah, she bare also Te'bah,
and Ga'ham, and Tha'hash, and Ma'a-chah.

☆**22:24**

M. SARAH'S DEATH AND BURIAL

23 AND Sarah was an hundred and seven and twenty years old: *these*
were the years of the life of Sarah.
2 And Sarah died in Kir'jath–ar'ba; the same *is* Hebron in the land of
Canaan: and Abraham came to mourn for Sarah, and to weep for her.

23:2 Josh 14:15 15:13; 21:11

3 ¶And Abraham stood up from before his dead, and spake unto the sons
of Heth, saying,

23:3 Gen 10:15

4 I *am* a stranger and a sojourner with you: give me a possession of a
buryingplace with you, that I may bury my dead out of my sight.

23:4 Lev 25:23 1 Chron 29:15 Ps 39:12 Heb 11:9

5 And the children of Heth answered Abraham, saying unto him,
6 Hear us, my lord: thou *art* a mighty prince among us: in the choice of
our sepulchres bury thy dead; none of us shall withhold from thee his
sepulchre, but that thou mayest bury thy dead.

23:6 Gen 13:2; 21:22

22:13 God's provision of the ram caught in the bush by its horn is a revelatory event. In his heart, Abraham believed that if he slew Isaac, God would raise him from the dead (see Heb. 11:19). But he still faced the problem of how God could command Isaac's death when killing was forbidden, and he could not reconcile the command with the promise of God that in Isaac his seed should be called. The deeper lesson is that God did not spare his only Son (Rom. 8:32), and as Abraham received Isaac back as though he had been slain, so Christ has been raised from the dead by the Father who gives all things to those who trust in Christ.

22:14 *Je-ho-vah-ji-reh,* which can be translated "The LORD will provide," or "the LORD will be seen."

22:15 *the angel of the LORD.* See note to Exod. 3:2.

22:24 *concubine,* (*pilegesh* in Hebrew) was a "half-wife." The status of a concubine was lesser than that of a full wife. Nowhere do the Scriptures endorse this sort of relationship. Technically, sexual relations with a concubine was adultery.

23:7 Gen 18:2; 19:1
7 And Abraham stood up, and bowed himself to the people of the land,
even to the children of Heth.

23:9☆ Gen 25:9
8 And he communed with them, saying, If it be your mind that I should
bury my dead out of my sight; hear me, and intreat for me to E'phron the
son of Zo'har,
9 That he may give me the cave of Mach-pe'lah, which he hath, which *is* in
the end of his field; for as much money as it is worth he shall give it me for
a possession of a buryingplace amongst you.

23:10 Ruth 4:11
10 And E'phron dwelt among the children of Heth: and E'phron the
Hittite answered Abraham in the audience of the children of Heth, *even* of
all that went in at the gate of his city, saying,
11 Nay, my lord, hear me: the field give I thee, and the cave that *is* therein,
I give it thee; in the presence of the sons of my people give I it thee: bury
thy dead.
12 And Abraham bowed down himself before the people of the land.

23:13 Gen 14:23; 2 Sam 24:24
13 And he spake unto E'phron in the audience of the people of the land,
saying, But if thou *wilt give it,* I pray thee, hear me: I will give thee money
for the field; take *it* of me, and I will bury my dead there.
14 And E'phron answered Abraham, saying unto him,

23:15 Ex 30:13
15 My lord, hearken unto me: the land *is worth* four hundred shekels of
silver; what *is* that betwixt me and thee? bury therefore thy dead.

23:16 Ezra 8:25; Jer 32:9
16 And Abraham hearkened unto E'phron; and Abraham weighed to
E'phron the silver, which he had named in the audience of the sons of Heth,
four hundred shekels of silver, current *money* with the merchant.

23:17☆ Gen 25:9; 49:29; 50:13
17 ¶And the field of E'phron, which *was* in Mach-pe'lah, which *was* before
Mam're, the field, and the cave which *was* therein, and all the trees that
were in the field, that *were* in all the borders round about, were made sure
18 Unto Abraham for a possession in the presence of the children of Heth,
before all that went in at the gate of his city.
19 And after this, Abraham buried Sarah his wife in the cave of the field of
Mach-pe'lah before Mam're: the same *is* Hebron in the land of Canaan.
20 And the field, and the cave that *is* therein, were made sure unto
Abraham for a possession of a buryingplace by the sons of Heth.

N. ISAAC MARRIES

1. Abraham Instructs His Servant to Find Isaac a Wife

24:1 Gen 12:2; 18:11; 24:35
24 AND Abraham was old, *and* well stricken in age: and the LORD
had blessed Abraham in all things.

24:2☆ Gen 47:29
2 And Abraham said unto his eldest servant of his house, that ruled over
all that he had, Put, I pray thee, thy hand under my thigh:

24:3☆ Gen 21:23; 26:34; 28:1
3 And I will make thee swear by the LORD, the God of heaven, and the
God of the earth, that thou shalt not take a wife unto my son of the
daughters of the Canaanites, among whom I dwell:

24:4 Gen 12:1
4 But thou shalt go unto my country, and to my kindred, and take a wife
unto my son Isaac.

23:9 *the cave of Mach-pe-lah.* Upon the death of Sarah, Abraham wanted to bury her in a cave owned by Ephron, the Hittite. The account is typical of the method employed in an age when bargaining was the normal procedure. Ephron in effect says to Abraham that he could have the cave for nothing. He did not mean that. When Abraham refuses the "gift," Ephron says it is worth four hundred shekels of silver but asks, "What is that betwixt me and thee? bury therefore your dead." Abraham does not haggle; he makes the purchase at the asking price. (See note on Acts 7:16 for the supposed discrepancy in the speech of Stephen regarding the cave of Machpelah and Ephron the Hittite.)

23:17, 18 Hittite real estate transactions included specific references to the trees on the land to be purchased.

24:2 *his eldest servant,* who undoubtedly was Eliezer, for in Genesis 15:2 Abraham speaks of Eliezer of Damascus as being his heir (if he had no seed).

24:3 *daughters of the Canaanites.* They were unbelievers. Abraham wanted Isaac to marry someone who was of the same faith. The New Testament contains similar injunctions (2 Cor. 6:14ff.).

5 And the servant said unto him, Peradventure the woman will not be
willing to follow me unto this land: must I needs bring thy son again unto
the land from whence thou camest?
6 And Abraham said unto him, Beware thou that thou bring not my son
thither again.
7 ¶The LORD God of heaven, which took me from my father's house, and
from the land of my kindred, and which spake unto me, and that sware
unto me, saying, Unto thy seed will I give this land; he shall send his angel
before thee, and thou shalt take a wife unto my son from thence.
8 And if the woman will not be willing to follow thee, then thou shalt be
clear from this my oath: only bring not my son thither again.
9 And the servant put his hand under the thigh of Abraham his master,
and sware to him concerning that matter.

☆**24:5** Gen 24:58
☆**24:7** Gen 12:7; 15:18 Gen 16:17; 22:11 Ex 23:20, 23
☆**24:9**

2. The Servant's Prayer for Help

10 ¶And the servant took ten camels of the camels of his master, and
departed; for all the goods of his master *were* in his hand: and he arose, and
went to Mes-o-po-ta′mi-a, unto the city of Nahor.
11 And he made his camels to kneel down without the city by a well of
water at the time of the evening, *even* the time that women go out to draw
water.
12 And he said, O LORD God of my master Abraham, I pray thee, send me
good speed this day, and shew kindness unto my master Abraham.
13 Behold, I stand *here* by the well of water; and the daughters of the men
of the city come out to draw water:
14 And let it come to pass, that the damsel to whom I shall say, Let down
thy pitcher, I pray thee, that I may drink; and she shall say, Drink, and I
will give thy camels drink also: *let the same be* she *that* thou hast appointed
for thy servant Isaac; and thereby shall I know that thou hast shewed
kindness unto my master.

☆**24:10** Gen 11:22 22:20 Deut 23:4
24:11 Gen 24:43
☆**24:12** Gen 24:27, 48
☆**24:14** a)Judg 6:17 1 Sam 14:9, 10 Prov 19:14 b)Gen 15:8 Ex 4:1–9

3. The Servant Meets Rebekah

15 ¶And it came to pass, before he had done speaking, that, behold,
Rebekah came out, who was born to Beth-u′el, son of Mil′cah, the wife of
Nahor, Abraham's brother, with her pitcher upon her shoulder.
16 And the damsel *was* very fair to look upon, a virgin, neither had any
man known her: and she went down to the well, and filled her pitcher, and
came up.
17 And the servant ran to meet her, and said, Let me, I pray thee, drink a
little water of thy pitcher.
18 And she said, Drink, my lord: and she hasted, and let down her pitcher
upon her hand, and gave him drink.

24:15 Gen 22:20–24 25:20
24:16 Gen 12:11 26:7; 29:17
24:17 1 Kgs 17:10 Jn 4:7

24:5 *bring thy son again unto the land.* Abraham forbade his servant to take Isaac back to the land from which he had come. He believed the covenant promise of God that Canaan was to be his offspring's residence in perpetuity. Isaac must remain in Canaan to await the fulfillment of the promise.
24:7 *he shall send his angel before thee.* Abraham herein expressed his confidence that God would guide his servant and prosper his journey. He knew about angels and understood their workings. This confidence was fulfilled, for God worked out every detail in the selection of Rebekah.
24:9 *put his hand under the thigh of Abraham his master, and sware to him,* i.e., "so the servant vowed." Putting a hand under the thigh was an ancient custom, a sign validating one's pledge.
24:10 *Mesopotamia,* or Iraq (Hebrew *Aram-naha-raim,* meaning "Aram of the Two Rivers"), was also called *Paddan-aram* (25:20; 28:2). *Nahor* was a town near Haran; its Hebrew spelling is slightly different from Nahor the brother of Abraham (24:15).
24:12–14 Abraham's servant prayed to the God of his master and asked him for a specific sign by which he would know the will of God in the selection of a wife for Isaac. God answered that prayer. Rebekah was God's choice for Isaac and they had a happy marriage. Had Isaac married a Canaanitish woman, the history of Israel might have been quite different.

24:19 Gen 24:14, 45, 46

19 And when she had done giving him drink, she said, I will draw *water* for thy camels also, until they have done drinking.

20 And she hasted, and emptied her pitcher into the trough, and ran again unto the well to draw *water,* and drew for all his camels.

24:21 2 Sam 7:18–20

21 And the man wondering at her held his peace, to wit whether the LORD had made his journey prosperous or not.

24:22 Gen 24:47

22 And it came to pass, as the camels had done drinking, that the man took a golden earring of half a shekel weight, and two bracelets for her hands of ten *shekels* weight of gold;

23 And said, Whose daughter *art* thou? tell me, I pray thee: is there room *in* thy father's house for us to lodge in?

24:24 Gen 24:15

24 And she said unto him, I *am* the daughter of Beth-u'el the son of Mil'cah, which she bare unto Nahor.

25 She said moreover unto him, We have both straw and provender enough, and room to lodge in.

24:26☆ Ex 4:31

26 And the man bowed down his head, and worshipped the LORD.

24:27 Gen 14:20 24:12, 48

27 And he said, Blessed *be* the LORD God of my master Abraham, who hath not left destitute my master of his mercy and his truth: I *being* in the way, the LORD led me to the house of my master's brethren.

24:28 Gen 29:12

28 And the damsel ran, and told *them of* her mother's house these things.

24:29 Gen 24:50 25:20; 29:5

29 ¶And Rebekah had a brother, and his name *was* Laban: and Laban ran out unto the man, unto the well.

24:30 Gen 24:22, 47

30 And it came to pass, when he saw the earring and bracelets upon his sister's hands, and when he heard the words of Rebekah his sister, saying, Thus spake the man unto me; that he came unto the man; and, behold, he stood by the camels at the well.

24:31 Gen 18:3–5 19:2

31 And he said, Come in, thou blessed of the LORD; wherefore standest thou without? for I have prepared the house, and room for the camels.

32 ¶And the man came into the house: and he ungirded his camels, and gave straw and provender for the camels, and water to wash his feet, and the men's feet that *were* with him.

33 And there was set *meat* before him to eat: but he said, I will not eat, until I have told mine errand. And he said, Speak on.

4. The Servant Asks for Rebekah's Hand for Isaac

24:34 Gen 24:2

34 And he said, I *am* Abraham's servant.

24:35 Gen 12:2; 13:2

35 And the LORD hath blessed my master greatly; and he is become great: and he hath given him flocks, and herds, and silver, and gold, and menservants, and maidservants, and camels, and asses.

24:36 Gen 21:1–7 25:5

36 And Sarah my master's wife bare a son to my master when she was old: and unto him hath he given all that he hath.

24:37 Gen 24:3; 28:1

37 And my master made me swear, saying, Thou shalt not take a wife to my son of the daughters of the Canaanites, in whose land I dwell:

38 But thou shalt go unto my father's house, and to my kindred, and take a wife unto my son.

39 And I said unto my master, Peradventure the woman will not follow me.

24:40 Gen 24:7

40 And he said unto me, The LORD, before whom I walk, will send his angel with thee, and prosper thy way; and thou shalt take a wife for my son of my kindred, and of my father's house:

24:26 Eliezer apparently was a true believer who worshipped God. In verse 27 he expresses his conviction that God has led him all the way. Eternity will reveal that at this time there were others, perhaps many, who had embraced the true faith.

41 Then shalt thou be clear from *this* my oath, when thou comest to my
kindred; and if they give not thee *one,* thou shalt be clear from my oath.
42 And I came this day unto the well, and said, O LORD God of my master ☆24:42–49
Abraham, if now thou do prosper my way which I go:
43 Behold, I stand by the well of water; and it shall come to pass, that
when the virgin cometh forth to draw *water,* and I say to her, Give me, I
pray thee, a little water of thy pitcher to drink;
44 And she say to me, Both drink thou, and I will also draw for thy
camels: *let* the same *be* the woman whom the LORD hath appointed out for
my master's son.
45 And before I had done speaking in mine heart, behold, Rebekah came ☆24:45
forth with her pitcher on her shoulder; and she went down unto the well, 1 Sam 1:13
and drew *water:* and I said unto her, Let me drink, I pray thee.
46 And she made haste, and let down her pitcher from her *shoulder,* and
said, Drink, and I will give thy camels drink also: so I drank, and she made
the camels drink also.
47 And I asked her, and said, Whose daughter *art* thou? And she said, The ☆24:47
daughter of Beth-u'el, Nahor's son, whom Mil'cah bare unto him: and I put Gen 24:23, 24
the earring upon her face, and the bracelets upon her hands.
48 And I bowed down my head, and worshipped the LORD, and blessed
the LORD God of my master Abraham, which had led me in the right way
to take my master's brother's daughter unto his son.
49 And now if ye will deal kindly and truly with my master, tell me: and ☆24:49
if not, tell me; that I may turn to the right hand, or to the left. Gen 32:10 47:29

5. The Servant Brings Rebekah to Isaac

50 Then Laban and Beth-u'el answered and said, The thing proceedeth 24:50 Ps 118:23
from the LORD: we cannot speak unto thee bad or good. Mt 21:42
51 Behold, Rebekah *is* before thee, take *her,* and go, and let her be thy 24:51
master's son's wife, as the LORD hath spoken. Gen 20:15
52 And it came to pass, that, when Abraham's servant heard their words, 24:52
he worshipped the LORD, *bowing himself* to the earth. Gen 24:26
53 And the servant brought forth jewels of silver, and jewels of gold, and ☆24:53
raiment, and gave *them* to Rebekah: he gave also to her brother and to her
mother precious things.
54 And they did eat and drink, he and the men that *were* with him, and 24:54
tarried all night; and they rose up in the morning, and he said, Send me Gen 28:6; 30:25
away unto my master.
55 And her brother and her mother said, Let the damsel abide with us *a* 24:55
few days, at the least ten; after that she shall go. Judg 19:4
56 And he said unto them, Hinder me not, seeing the LORD hath
prospered my way; send me away that I may go to my master.
57 And they said, We will call the damsel, and inquire at her mouth.
58 And they called Rebekah, and said unto her, Wilt thou go with this ☆24:58
man? And she said, I will go. Ps 45:10
59 And they sent away Rebekah their sister, and her nurse, and Abraham's 24:59
servant, and his men. Gen 35:8

24:42–49 Eliezer gives a clear account of what happened when he encountered Rebekah and expresses the conviction that it was all God's doing.

24:53 Abraham's servant gave costly presents to Rebekah and her family. This may have been a form of dowry certifying the integrity of Abraham, and assuring Rebekah's family that the wedding would take place.

24:58 There is no word that Rebekah's father was alive or involved in the wedding arrangements. Laban, her brother, plays a key role. Eliezer's desire to return in haste to Abraham with the bride is decided when Rebekah says she will go immediately. This was yet another sign of how God moved in her heart to make this possible.

24:60 Gen 17:16; 22:17; Dan 7:10

60 And they blessed Rebekah, and said unto her, Thou *art* our sister, be thou *the mother* of thousands of millions, and let thy seed possess the gate of those which hate them.

61 ¶And Rebekah arose, and her damsels, and they rode upon the camels, and followed the man: and the servant took Rebekah, and went his way.

6. Isaac and Rebekah Marry

24:62 Gen 16:14; 25:11

62 And Isaac came from the way of the well La-hai′-roi; for he dwelt in the south country.

24:63 Ps 119:15, 27, 47, 48

63 And Isaac went out to meditate in the field at the eventide: and he lifted up his eyes, and saw, and, behold, the camels *were* coming.

64 And Rebekah lifted up her eyes, and when she saw Isaac, she lighted off the camel.

24:65☆

65 For she *had* said unto the servant, What man *is* this that walketh in the field to meet us? And the servant *had* said, It *is* my master: therefore she took a vail, and covered herself.

24:66 Mk 6:30

66 And the servant told Isaac all things that he had done.

24:67 Gen 23:2; 25:20; 29:18

67 And Isaac brought her into his mother Sarah's tent, and took Rebekah, and she became his wife; and he loved her: and Isaac was comforted after his mother's *death.*

O. ABRAHAM'S LAST DAYS

1. Abraham's Children by Keturah

25:1 1 Chron 1:32

25 THEN again Abraham took a wife, and her name *was* Ke-tu′rah.
2 And she bare him Zim′ran, and Jok′shan, and Me′dan, and Mid′i-an, and Ish′-bak, and Shu′ah.

3 And Jok′shan begat She′ba, and De′dan. And the sons of De′dan were As-shu′rim, and Le-tu′shim, and Le-um′mim.

4 And the sons of Mid′i-an; E′phah, and E′pher, and Ha′noch, and A-bi′dah, and El′da-ah. All these *were* the children of Ke-tu′rah.

25:5☆ Gen 24:36

5 And Abraham gave all that he had unto Isaac.

25:6☆

6 But unto the sons of the concubines, which Abraham had, Abraham gave gifts, and sent them away from Isaac his son, while he yet lived, eastward, unto the east country.

2. Abraham's Death and Burial

25:7 Gen 12:4

7 And these *are* the days of the years of Abraham's life which he lived, an hundred threescore and fifteen years.

25:8 Gen 25:17; 35:29; 49:29, 33

8 Then Abraham gave up the ghost, and died in a good old age, an old man, and full *of years;* and was gathered to his people.

24:65 *she took a veil, and covered herself.* This was the custom in connection with marriages. Isaac had mourned the death of his mother and now is given a wife to fill the gap. We are not told whether the marriage took place immediately nor whether it was a public occasion with some formal ceremony and festivities.

25:5 Abraham married Keturah and she gave birth to six children. But since Isaac was the heir, he was given the bulk of Abraham's fortune. Gifts were given to Abraham's other children, who were sent away, so as to leave Isaac in full possession of what remained.

25:6 Hagar bore one son to Abraham; Keturah gave him six sons. Before his death Abraham distributed a portion of his wealth to these children and sent them "eastward, unto the east country." These descendants of Abraham were called *the children of the east.* They are mentioned in Judg. 6:3, 33, where they are said to be very numerous. They were enemies of the people of Israel. Today there may be multitudes of people in the Middle East who are lineal descendants of Abraham through these two concubines. When Abraham died and was buried, Isaac and Ishmael were in attendance. Especially interesting is the fact that 25:16 speaks of these children of Abraham through Ishmael, calling them "twelve princes according to their nations." Thus there were the twelve tribes of Israel through Isaac and Jacob, and twelve princes through Ishmael.

9 And his sons Isaac and Ish'ma-el buried him in the cave of Mach-pe'lah,
in the field of E'phron the son of Zo'har the Hittite, which *is* before
Mam're;
10 The field which Abraham purchased of the sons of Heth: there was
Abraham buried, and Sarah his wife.
11 And it came to pass after the death of Abraham, that God blessed his
son Isaac; and Isaac dwelt by the well La-hai'-roi.

☆25:9 Gen 23:17 49:29; 50:13

25:11 Gen 24:62; 26:3

3. The Descendants of Ishmael

12 ¶Now these *are* the generations of Ish'ma-el, Abraham's son, whom
Ha'gar the Egyptian, Sarah's handmaid, bare unto Abraham:
13 And these *are* the names of the sons of Ish'ma-el, by their names,
according to their generations: the firstborn of Ish'ma-el, Ne-ba'joth; and
Ke'dar, and Ad'be-el, and Mib'sam,
14 And Mish'ma, and Du'mah, and Mas'sa,
15 Ha'dar, and Te'ma, Je'tur, Na'phish, and Ked'e-mah:
16 These *are* the sons of Ish'ma-el, and these *are* their names, by their
towns, and by their castles; twelve princes according to their nations.
17 And these *are* the years of the life of Ish'ma-el, an hundred and thirty
and seven years: and he gave up the ghost and died; and was gathered unto
his people.
18 And they dwelt from Hav'i-lah unto Shur, that *is* before Egypt, as thou
goest toward Assyria: *and* he died in the presence of all his brethren.

25:12 Gen 16:15 1 Chron 1:28–31

25:13 Gen 17:20

25:17 Gen 25:8

25:18 a)Gen 20:1 b)Gen 16:12

VI. THE PATRIARCHS ISAAC AND JACOB (25:19—36:43)

A. THE WORD FROM GOD AT THE BIRTH OF JACOB AND ESAU

19 ¶And these *are* the generations of Isaac, Abraham's son: Abraham
begat Isaac:
20 And Isaac was forty years old when he took Rebekah to wife, the
daughter of Beth-u'el the Syrian of Pa'dan–a'ram, the sister to Laban the
Syrian.
21 And Isaac intreated the LORD for his wife, because she *was* barren: and
the LORD was intreated of him, and Rebekah his wife conceived.
22 And the children struggled together within her; and she said, If *it be* so,
why *am* I thus? And she went to inquire of the LORD.
23 And the LORD said unto her, Two nations *are* in thy womb, and two
manner of people shall be separated from thy bowels; and *the one* people
shall be stronger than *the other* people; and the elder shall serve the
younger.
24 ¶And when her days to be delivered were fulfilled, behold, *there were*
twins in her womb.

25:19 Gen 21:3 1 Chron 1:34

25:20 Gen 24:15, 29, 67; 35:28

☆25:21 Gen 21:2 1 Sam 1:19, 20

25:23 Gen 17:2–4 27:29; 48:19 Num 20:14 Deut 2:4, 8 Rom 9:12

25:9, 10 Isaac and Ishmael buried Abraham. Abraham lived 175 years. Isaac was born when Abraham was 100 years old. Thus Isaac was 75 years old when his father died. Ishmael was fourteen years older than Isaac. Whatever may have been the friction between Isaac and Ishmael, they must have lived close to each other and they did get together to bury their father. Abraham was interred next to Sarah in the cave of Machpelah. Nothing is said about the burial place of Hagar, Ishmael's mother. The descendants of Ishmael and Isaac have nothing in common today; they are inveterate enemies even though they came from a common father.

25:21 *she was barren*: Rebekah, like Sarah, was barren. Isaac, who married her when he was forty, prayed to God for a child. His prayer was answered when he was sixty years old. In the cases of both women, divine intervention was the answer to their dilemma.

25:25☆ Gen 27:11
25 And the first came out red, all over like an hairy garment; and they
called his name Esau.
25:26 Hos 12:3
26 And after that came his brother out, and his hand took hold on Esau's
heel; and his name was called Jacob: and Isaac *was* threescore years old
when she bare them.

B. ESAU TRADES AWAY THE BIRTHRIGHT

27 And the boys grew: and Esau was a cunning hunter, a man of the field;
and Jacob *was* a plain man, dwelling in tents.
25:28☆
28 And Isaac loved Esau, because he did eat of *his* venison: but Rebekah
loved Jacob.
29 ¶And Jacob sod pottage: and Esau came from the field, and he *was*
faint:
25:30 Gen 36:1, 9; Ex 15:15
30 And Esau said to Jacob, Feed me, I pray thee, with that same red
pottage; for I *am* faint: therefore was his name called Edom.
25:31☆ Deut 21:15–17
31 And Jacob said, Sell me this day thy birthright.
32 And Esau said, Behold, I *am* at the point to die: and what profit shall
this birthright do to me?
25:33 Gen 27:36; Heb 12:16
33 And Jacob said, Swear to me this day; and he sware unto him: and he
sold his birthright unto Jacob.
34 Then Jacob gave Esau bread and pottage of lentiles; and he did eat and
drink, and rose up, and went his way: thus Esau despised *his* birthright.

C. ISAAC AND ABIMELECH

1. Abraham's Covenant Confirmed to Isaac

26:1 Gen 12:10; 20:1, 2; 41:54
26 AND there was a famine in the land, beside the first famine that
was in the days of Abraham. And Isaac went unto A-bim'e-lech
king of the Philistines unto Ge'rar.
26:2 Gen 12:1, 7; 17:1; 18:1
2 And the LORD appeared unto him, and said, Go not down into Egypt;
dwell in the land which I shall tell thee of:
26:3 Gen 12:7; 15:8; 13:15; Gen 22:16–18; 26:24; 28:15
3 Sojourn in this land, and I will be with thee, and will bless thee; for unto
thee, and unto thy seed, I will give all these countries, and I will perform
the oath which I sware unto Abraham thy father;
26:4 Gen 15:15; 22:17; Ex 32:13; Gal 3:8
4 And I will make thy seed to multiply as the stars of heaven, and will give
unto thy seed all these countries; and in thy seed shall all the nations of the
earth be blessed;
26:5 Gen 18:19; 22:16
5 Because that Abraham obeyed my voice, and kept my charge, my
commandments, my statutes, and my laws.

25:25 Esau (whose name sounds a little like the Hebrew word for "hair") was Jacob's twin who emerged first from his mother's womb and thus was entitled to all of the rights of the firstborn, including the domestic priesthood, family headship and authority, and a double portion of the inheritance upon the death of his father. The Edomites were the descendants of Esau (*Edom* means "red"). The main points in Esau's life were: (1) the sale of the birthright for some of Jacob's stew (25:27–34), an act indicating his unconcern for the birthright; (2) the marriages Esau consummated with women unrelated to his father's family except for Mahalath, whom he married to placate Isaac and Rebekah; (3) his failure to obtain the patriarchal blessing before Isaac died; and (4) the resumption of brotherly relations with Jacob and his departure from Canaan for Seir. Esau was careless and indifferent to spiritual things.

25:28 For some reason Isaac and his wife had different loyalties. Rebekah loved Jacob more than Esau, while Isaac had a special affection for Esau. This difference led to marital problems. Rebekah practiced deceit on her husband, which led to a family separation when Jacob had to flee for his life.

25:31 The birthright was not especially important when there was only one son. It became important when Isaac had two sons. Esau, as the firstborn, should have been the one through whom the people of God would count their descent. But he sold his spiritual birthright for carnal needs and lost it to Jacob. Jacob got the birthright and from his loins came the Jewish patriarchs. Moreover, until the establishment of the Aaronic priesthood, the firstborn of the family exercised the priestly functions in the home after his father's death.

2. Isaac Misleads Abimelech about Rebekah

6 ¶And Isaac dwelt in Ge'rar:
7 And the men of the place asked *him* of his wife; and he said, She *is* my
sister: for he feared to say, *She is* my wife; lest, *said he,* the men of the place
should kill me for Rebekah; because she *was* fair to look upon.
8 And it came to pass, when he had been there a long time, that A-bim'e-
lech king of the Philistines looked out at a window, and saw, and, behold,
Isaac *was* sporting with Rebekah his wife.
9 And A-bim'e-lech called Isaac, and said, Behold, of a surety she *is* thy
wife: and how saidst thou, She *is* my sister? And Isaac said unto him,
Because I said, Lest I die for her.
10 And A-bim'e-lech said, What *is* this thou hast done unto us? one of the
people might lightly have lien with thy wife, and thou shouldest have
brought guiltiness upon us.
11 And A-bim'e-lech charged all *his* people, saying, He that toucheth this
man or his wife shall surely be put to death.

☆**26:7** Gen 12:11, 12; 20:12
☆**26:8** Prov 5:18, 19; Eccles 9:9
☆**26:9**
26:10 Gen 20:7–10
26:11 Prov 6:29

3. The LORD Blesses Isaac with Wealth

12 Then Isaac sowed in that land, and received in the same year an
hundredfold: and the LORD blessed him.
13 And the man waxed great, and went forward, and grew until he became
very great:
14 For he had possession of flocks, and possession of herds, and great
store of servants: and the Philistines envied him.
15 For all the wells which his father's servants had digged in the days of
Abraham his father, the Philistines had stopped them, and filled them with
earth.
16 And A-bim'e-lech said unto Isaac, Go from us; for thou art much
mightier than we.

☆**26:12** Gen 26:3
26:13 Gen 24:35; 25:5
26:15 Gen 21:15
26:16 Ex 1:9

4. Isaac and Abimelech Quarrel over Some Wells

17 ¶And Isaac departed thence, and pitched his tent in the valley of
Ge'rar, and dwelt there.
18 And Isaac digged again the wells of water, which they had digged in the
days of Abraham his father; for the Philistines had stopped them after the
death of Abraham: and he called their names after the names by which his
father had called them.
19 And Isaac's servants digged in the valley, and found there a well of
springing water.
20 And the herdmen of Ge'rar did strive with Isaac's herdmen, saying, The

☆**26:17**
26:19 Jn 4:10, 11
☆**26:20**

26:7 *She is my sister.* Isaac does what his father had done before him. He lies about his true relationship to Rebekah to protect himself against possible enemies. This evidenced his lack of faith in the protecting power of the God he professed to worship.

26:8 *Isaac was sporting with Rebekah.* "Sporting" has been translated "caressing" in the NASB. Whatever he was doing was not normal for a brother and sister to do. Either what he was doing was incestuous, or she was his wife and he was lying.

26:9 As in the case of Abraham, Abimelech knew that what Isaac was doing was something that belonged to a marriage relationship. Had any of his people had sexual relations with Rebekah, it would have been defiling.

26:12 *the LORD blessed him.* Abraham distributed his wealth among all of his children before his death. Isaac received a fair share. Now God blesses him and he "sowed in that land, and received in the same year a hundredfold . . . and waxed great." Wealth is the gift of God; there is nothing wrong in being wealthy. John Wesley said Christians should earn as much as they can, save as much as they can, and give as much as they can. Wesley himself died with very little wealth left. The major consideration about wealth for the believer is whether he uses it for the glory of God.

26:17 Gerar was located at the southern end of the territory belonging to the Canaanites, in the same region with Gaza.

26:20 *Esek,* or "Ezeb", meaning "The Well of Argument."†

water *is* ours: and he called the name of the well E′sek; because they strove
with him.

26:21☆ 21 And they digged another well, and strove for that also: and he called
the name of it Sit′nah.

26:22☆ 22 And he removed from thence, and digged another well; and for that
Ps 4:1; 18:19; 118:5 they strove not: and he called the name of it Re-ho′both; and he said, For
Isa 54:2 now the LORD hath made room for us, and we shall be fruitful in the land.

26:23 23 And he went up from thence to Be′er-she′ba.
Gen 21:31; 46:1

26:24☆ 24 And the LORD appeared unto him the same night, and said, I *am* the
Gen 12:1, 2 God of Abraham thy father: fear not, for I *am* with thee, and will bless
17:1–7 thee, and multiply thy seed for my servant Abraham's sake.

26:25 25 And he builded an altar there, and called upon the name of the LORD,
Gen 12:7 13:3, 4 and pitched his tent there: and there Isaac's servants digged a well.

26:26 26 ¶Then A-bim′e-lech went to him from Ge′rar, and A-huz′zath one of
Gen 21:22, 23 his friends, and Phi′chol the chief captain of his army.

26:27 27 And Isaac said unto them, Wherefore come ye to me, seeing ye hate me,
Gen 26:14, 16 and have sent me away from you?

26:28 28 And they said, We saw certainly that the LORD was with thee: and we
Gen 26:3, 12–16 said, Let there be now an oath betwixt us, *even* betwixt us and thee, and let
us make a covenant with thee;

26:29 29 That thou wilt do us no hurt, as we have not touched thee, and as we
Ps 115:15 have done unto thee nothing but good, and have sent thee away in peace:
thou *art* now the blessed of the LORD.

26:30 30 And he made them a feast, and they did eat and drink.
Gen 21:8; 31:54

26:31 31 And they rose up betimes in the morning, and sware one to another:
Gen 14:22 21:31; 31:55 and Isaac sent them away, and they departed from him in peace.

32 And it came to pass the same day, that Isaac's servants came, and told
him concerning the well which they had digged, and said unto him, We
have found water.

26:33☆ 33 And he called it She′bah: therefore the name of the city *is* Be′er-she′ba
Gen 21:31 unto this day.

5. Esau's Parents' Bitterness about His Marriages

26:34☆ 34 ¶And Esau was forty years old when he took to wife Judith the
Gen 28:6–8 36:2, 3 daughter of Be-e′ri the Hittite, and Bash′e-math the daughter of E′lon the
Hittite:

26:35☆ 35 Which were a grief of mind unto Isaac and to Rebekah.

D. JACOB STEALS HIS FATHER'S BLESSING

1. Esau Goes to Get Venison for His Father

Gen 27:46 **27:1**☆ Gen 25:25 48:10

27 AND it came to pass, that when Isaac was old, and his eyes were
dim, so that he could not see, he called Esau his eldest son, and said
unto him, My son: and he said unto him, Behold, *here am* I.

26:21 *Sitnah,* or, "The Well of Anger."†
26:22 *Rehoboth,* "The Well of Room Enough for Us at Last."†
26:24 The Lord appeared to Isaac and reconfirmed the covenant he had made with Abraham. In Isaac shall all the world be blessed and his descendants will be multiplied in number. Like his father Abraham, Isaac built an altar there to celebrate the holiness of the place associated with the appearance of his God.
26:33 *Shebah,* "The Well of the Oath." *Beer-sheba,* "Oath."†
26:34, 35 Esau foolishly married two Hittite women who were outside the family of faith. In doing this "he neither desired the blessing nor dreaded the curse of God."* This grieved his parents, particularly his father, Isaac, who had married in the family as a result of Abraham's sending his faithful servant who found Rebekah, the daughter of Bethuel and the sister of Laban, to be his wife. "It would seem, the wives Esau married were provoking in their conduct towards Isaac and Rebekah (with whom they lived); those children have little reason to expect the blessing of God who do that which is a grief of mind to their good parents."*
27:1 Isaac's eyes were dim. Apparently he suffered either from cataracts or glaucoma, both of which are common to that area of the world today.

[2]And he said, Behold now, I am old, I know not the day of my death:
[3]Now therefore take, I pray thee, thy weapons, thy quiver and thy bow,
and go out to the field, and take me *some* venison;
[4]And make me savoury meat, such as I love, and bring *it* to me, that I
may eat; that my soul may bless thee before I die.

27:2 Gen 47:29
27:3 Gen 25:28
☆**27:4** Gen 24:60; 27:19; 48:9

2. Rebekah Plots with Jacob to Steal the Blessing

[5]And Rebekah heard when Isaac spake to Esau his son. And Esau went
to the field to hunt *for* venison, *and* to bring *it*.
[6]¶And Rebekah spake unto Jacob her son, saying, Behold, I heard thy
father speak unto Esau thy brother, saying,
[7]Bring me venison, and make me savoury meat, that I may eat, and bless
thee before the LORD before my death.
[8]Now therefore, my son, obey my voice according to that which I
command thee.
[9]Go now to the flock, and fetch me from thence two good kids of the
goats; and I will make them savoury meat for thy father, such as he loveth:
[10]And thou shalt bring *it* to thy father, that he may eat, and that he may
bless thee before his death.
[11]And Jacob said to Rebekah his mother, Behold, Esau my brother *is* a
hairy man, and I *am* a smooth man:
[12]My father peradventure will feel me, and I shall seem to him as a
deceiver; and I shall bring a curse upon me, and not a blessing.
[13]And his mother said unto him, Upon me *be* thy curse, my son: only
obey my voice, and go fetch me *them*.
[14]And he went, and fetched, and brought *them* to his mother: and his
mother made savoury meat, such as his father loved.
[15]And Rebekah took goodly raiment of her eldest son Esau, which *were*
with her in the house, and put them upon Jacob her younger son:
[16]And she put the skins of the kids of the goats upon his hands, and upon
the smooth of his neck:
[17]And she gave the savoury meat and the bread, which she had prepared,
into the hand of her son Jacob.

27:6 Gen 25:28
27:8 Gen 27:13, 43
27:9 Judg 13:15
27:11 Gen 25:25
27:12 Gen 9:25; 27:21, 22
☆**27:13** Gen 27:8, 43
27:15 Gen 27:27

3. Jacob Claims to Be Esau and Gets the Blessing

[18]¶And he came unto his father, and said, My father: and he said, Here
am I; who *art* thou, my son?
[19]And Jacob said unto his father, I *am* Esau thy firstborn; I have done
according as thou badest me: arise, I pray thee, sit and eat of my venison,
that thy soul may bless me.

☆**27:19** Gen 27:21, 24, 31

27:4 *that my soul may bless thee.* It was Isaac's intention to give Esau the blessing which belonged to the firstborn. Whether he did not know of the stolen birthright or disregarded what had happened earlier we do not know. When Esau came for his blessing he knew that Jacob had received what he wanted even though he had despised it previously.

27:13 *Upon me be thy curse.* Rebekah was false to her marriage vows when she put her son Jacob before her husband Isaac. She could have honorably reasoned with Isaac and reminded him of God's promise that in Jacob should the seed be called. Rather, she planned the deceit and broke still another commandment: "Cursed be he that maketh the blind to wander out of the way" (Deut. 27:18). This applied to Isaac, whose sight was gone. Of this incident Matthew Henry says: "God left Rebekah to herself, to take this indirect course, that he might have the glory of bringing good out of evil, and of serving his own purposes by the sins and follies of men, and that we might have the satisfaction of knowing that, though there is much wickedness and deceit in the world, God governs it according to his will, to his own praise."

27:19 In order to obtain the blessing promised by God, Rebekah and Jacob deceived Isaac. Long before this happened, Esau had already sold the birthright (25:27–34) and God could and would have worked out the solution without any deception. One of the consequences of Jacob's deception was his exile and the fact that he never saw his mother again. Only God's will done God's way brings God's blessing.

20 And Isaac said unto his son, How *is it* that thou hast found *it* so quickly, my son? And he said, Because the LORD thy God brought *it* to me.

27:21 Gen 27:12

21 And Isaac said unto Jacob, Come near, I pray thee, that I may feel thee, my son, whether thou *be* my very son Esau or not.

22 And Jacob went near unto Isaac his father; and he felt him, and said, The voice *is* Jacob's voice, but the hands *are* the hands of Esau.

27:23 Gen 27:4, 16

23 And he discerned him not, because his hands were hairy, as his brother Esau's hands: so he blessed him.

27:24 Prov 12:19, 22
27:25 Gen 27:4

24 And he said, *Art* thou my very son Esau? And he said, I *am.*

25 And he said, Bring *it* near to me, and I will eat of my son's venison, that my soul may bless thee. And he brought *it* near to him, and he did eat: and he brought him wine, and he drank.

26 And his father Isaac said unto him, Come near now, and kiss me, my son.

27:27 Ps 65:9, 10 Heb 11:20

27 And he came near, and kissed him: and he smelled the smell of his raiment, and blessed him, and said, See, the smell of my son *is* as the smell of a field which the LORD hath blessed:

27:28 Gen 27:39 45:18 Deut 7:13; 33:13, 28 Zech 8:12
27:29 Gen 9:25; 12:3 22:17; 49:8 Num 24:9 Isa 45:14

28 Therefore God give thee of the dew of heaven, and the fatness of the earth, and plenty of corn and wine:

29 Let people serve thee, and nations bow down to thee: be lord over thy brethren, and let thy mother's sons bow down to thee: cursed *be* every one that curseth thee, and blessed *be* he that blesseth thee.

4. Esau Discovers Jacob's Deception

30 ¶And it came to pass, as soon as Isaac had made an end of blessing Jacob, and Jacob was yet scarce gone out from the presence of Isaac his father, that Esau his brother came in from his hunting.

27:31 Gen 27:4, 19

31 And he also had made savoury meat, and brought it unto his father, and said unto his father, Let my father arise, and eat of his son's venison, that thy soul may bless me.

27:32 Gen 27:18

32 And Isaac his father said unto him, Who *art* thou? And he said, I *am* thy son, thy firstborn Esau.

27:33 Gen 27:35 Ps 55:5

33 And Isaac trembled very exceedingly, and said, Who? where *is* he that hath taken venison, and brought *it* me, and I have eaten of all before thou camest, and have blessed him? yea, *and* he shall be blessed.

27:34 Heb 12:17

34 And when Esau heard the words of his father, he cried with a great and exceeding bitter cry, and said unto his father, Bless me, *even* me also, O my father.

27:35 Gen 27:12, 19–23

35 And he said, Thy brother came with subtilty, and hath taken away thy blessing.

27:36☆ Gen 25:26 32:28

36 And he said, Is not he rightly named Jacob? for he hath supplanted me these two times: he took away my birthright; and, behold, now he hath taken away my blessing. And he said, Hast thou not reserved a blessing for me?

27:37 Gen 27:27–29 2 Sam 8:14

37 And Isaac answered and said unto Esau, Behold, I have made him thy lord, and all his brethren have I given to him for servants; and with corn and wine have I sustained him: and what shall I do now unto thee, my son?

27:38☆ Gen 27:34 Heb 12:17

38 And Esau said unto his father, Hast thou but one blessing, my father? bless me, *even* me also, O my father. And Esau lifted up his voice, and wept.

27:39☆ Heb 11:20

39 And Isaac his father answered and said unto him, Behold, thy dwelling shall be the fatness of the earth, and of the dew of heaven from above;

27:36 *rightly named Jacob? Jacob* means "cheater."†
27:38 In some versions the following sentence is added at the end of the verse: "Isaac says nothing."

27:39, 40 God promised Esau, through the blessing of his father Isaac, a good living. He would have the fatness of the earth and the dew of heaven. But he

[40]And by thy sword shalt thou live, and shalt serve thy brother; and it shall come to pass when thou shalt have the dominion, that thou shalt break his yoke from off thy neck.

27:40 2 Kgs 8:20 2 Chron 21:8

5. Rebekah Plots to Send Jacob to Her Brother

[41]¶And Esau hated Jacob because of the blessing wherewith his father
blessed him: and Esau said in his heart, The days of mourning for my
father are at hand; then will I slay my brother Jacob.
[42]And these words of Esau her elder son were told to Rebekah: and she
sent and called Jacob her younger son, and said unto him, Behold, thy
brother Esau, as touching thee, doth comfort himself, *purposing* to kill thee.
[43]Now therefore, my son, obey my voice; and arise, flee thou to Laban
my brother to Ha'ran;
[44]And tarry with him a few days, until thy brother's fury turn away;
[45]Until thy brother's anger turn away from thee, and he forget *that* which
thou hast done to him: then I will send, and fetch thee from thence: why
should I be deprived also of you both in one day?
[46]And Rebekah said to Isaac, I am weary of my life because of the
daughters of Heth: if Jacob take a wife of the daughters of Heth, such as
these *which are* of the daughters of the land, what good shall my life do me?

☆**27:41** Gen 32:6 35:29; 37:4 Deut 34:8
27:43 Gen 11:31 12:4; 27:8, 13 28:10
27:44 Gen 31:41
27:45 Prov 20:21
☆**27:46** Gen 26:34, 35

6. Isaac Sends Jacob to Uncle Laban

28 AND Isaac called Jacob, and blessed him, and charged him, and
said unto him, Thou shalt not take a wife of the daughters of
Canaan.
[2]Arise, go to Pa'dan-a'ram, to the house of Beth-u'el thy mother's father;
and take thee a wife from thence of the daughters of Laban thy mother's
brother.
[3]And God Almighty bless thee, and make thee fruitful, and multiply
thee, that thou mayest be a multitude of people;
[4]And give thee the blessing of Abraham, to thee, and to thy seed with
thee; that thou mayest inherit the land wherein thou art a stranger, which
God gave unto Abraham.

☆**28:1** Gen 24:3, 4
28:2 Gen 25:20
28:3 Gen 17:1–4 27:4, 7 35:11
☆**28:4** Gen 12:1–3 15:7; 35:11 48:3

would not have the covenant blessing, which was the best of all. Jacob was given dominion over his brother. Isaac kissed Jacob but not Esau. We learn here that God gives good earth and good weather to many who reject his covenant of grace. This is due to common grace, but covenant grace is much better.

27:41 Wicked Esau hated his brother Jacob who had stolen his birthright; Esau was determined to kill him. He hated Jacob because Isaac had blessed him and God loved him. His hatred was so cruel that he went to great lengths to attain satisfaction. In his heart he committed a murder, even as Cain had slain his brother long before. He could call Jacob "brother" and vow his death. He intended to kill Jacob as soon as their father died and before Jacob was married and had a family. He would then have seized all of Isaac's goods.

27:46 Rebekah senses the danger to Jacob if he were to remain at home. She seizes on the pretext that Jacob might marry a Hittite girl. This works well with Isaac whose other son Esau had married outside the faith. Rebekah's plea to send him to her brother Laban is accepted and Jacob departs, to see his mother no more. In any event, the decision was a good one—for Jacob would indeed marry in the faith, despite evil treatment at the hands of his uncle Laban.

28:1 Isaac had learned enough from the marriages of Esau to two of the Canaanites; he wanted Jacob to return to Rebekah's kinsmen and there find a wife. At the same time, unknown to him, God would make Jacob suffer under Laban in punishment for his deceitful act against his father, Isaac. Jacob went from heir in his father's house to servant under Laban, who did to him what Jacob had done to his own father. Yet God included Jacob in the line of Abraham, looking toward the coming of the Messiah through Abraham's loins. Nonetheless, Jacob's harsh experiences under Laban only confirm the fact that God's providences often seem to contradict his promises.

28:4 Isaac was acutely aware that the blessing promised to his father Abraham had come to him. Now he wants to assure Jacob, the supplanter who stole the birthright from Esau, that the Abrahamic promise from God will be his too—and not only his, but it will pass on to Jacob's children. The two major promises to Abraham included an innumerable posterity through whom the nations of the earth would be blessed and the inheritance of the land of promise. In verse 3 Isaac refers to the first promise and in verse 4 to the second.

5 And Isaac sent away Jacob: and he went to Pa'dan–a'ram unto Laban,
son of Beth-u'el the Syrian, the brother of Rebekah, Jacob's and Esau's
mother.

7. Esau Marries to Please His Father

6 ¶When Esau saw that Isaac had blessed Jacob, and sent him away to
Pa'dan–a'ram, to take him a wife from thence; and that as he blessed him
he gave him a charge, saying, Thou shalt not take a wife of the daughters of
Canaan;
28:7 7 And that Jacob obeyed his father and his mother, and was gone to
Gen 27:8 Pa'dan–a'ram;
28:8☆ 8 And Esau seeing that the daughters of Canaan pleased not Isaac his
Gen 26:34 father;
28:9 9 Then went Esau unto Ish'ma-el, and took unto the wives which he had
Gen 36:3 Ma'ha-lath the daughter of Ish'ma-el Abraham's son, the sister of Ne-
ba'joth, to be his wife.

E. JACOB'S RELATIONS WITH HIS UNCLE LABAN

1. Jacob's Dream: The Ladder to Heaven

28:10 10 ¶And Jacob went out from Be'er–she'ba, and went toward Ha'ran.
Gen 12:4, 5; 26:23; 46:1 11 And he lighted upon a certain place, and tarried there all night, because
28:11 Gen 28:18, 19 the sun was set; and he took of the stones of that place, and put *them for* his
pillows, and lay down in that place to sleep.
28:12 12 And he dreamed, and behold a ladder set up on the earth, and the top
Gen 20:3; 32:1, 2; 37:5 of it reached to heaven: and behold the angels of God ascending and
Num 12:6; Jn 1:51 descending on it.
28:13☆ 13 And, behold, the LORD stood above it, and said, I *am* the LORD God of
Gen 15:18; 26:3; 31:53 Abraham thy father, and the God of Isaac: the land whereon thou liest, to
35:1 thee will I give it, and to thy seed;
28:14☆ 14 And thy seed shall be as the dust of the earth, and thou shalt spread
Gen 12:2; 13:14, 16; 22:18 abroad to the west, and to the east, and to the north, and to the south: and
in thee and in thy seed shall all the families of the earth be blessed.
28:15☆ 15 And, behold, I *am* with thee, and will keep thee in all *places* whither
Gen 26:3; 48:21; Deut 7:9; 31:6, 8 thou goest, and will bring thee again into this land; for I will not leave thee,
Ps 121:7, 8 until I have done *that* which I have spoken to thee of.
28:16 16 ¶And Jacob awaked out of his sleep, and he said, Surely the LORD is in
Ex 3:5; 1 Kgs 3:15; Ps 139:7–12 this place; and I knew *it* not.
28:17 17 And he was afraid, and said, How dreadful *is* this place! this *is* none
Gen 28:22; 2 Chron 5:14 other but the house of God, and this *is* the gate of heaven.
28:18 18 And Jacob rose up early in the morning, and took the stone that he had
Gen 35:14 put *for* his pillows, and set it up *for* a pillar, and poured oil upon the top of
it.

28:8 Esau, now that Jacob was gone, sought to appease his father Isaac. He saw that his father was displeased with Esau's unbelieving wives. So he took a wife, Mahalath, who was the daughter of Ishmael (Esau's half-uncle). He sought to satisfy his father, not God, and he wanted to strengthen his own position as heir to his father's goods, now that Jacob was far away. His acts in no way indicated that his inner self had changed for the better. It was purely an outward, calculating, and selfish decision.

28:13, 14 God certifies to Jacob what Isaac had told him in verses 3 and 4. He will get the land and he will have a posterity which will bless the nations of the earth.

28:15 At this point Jacob's future was obscure. He was fleeing from Esau but had not yet come to his uncle Laban's home. God now promises that he will protect him "in all places whither thou goest" and he will return him safely to the land of promise. Jacob would have plenty of time and opportunity to remember these promises—especially as he worked for Laban and when he returned to the land of promise, fearful that Esau would execute vengeance on him because of his transgression.

19And he called the name of that place Beth-el: but the name of that city
was called Luz at the first.
20And Jacob vowed a vow, saying, If God will be with me, and will keep
me in this way that I go, and will give me bread to eat, and raiment to put
on,
21So that I come again to my father's house in peace; then shall the LORD
be my God:
22And this stone, which I have set *for* a pillar, shall be God's house: and
of all that thou shalt give me I will surely give the tenth unto thee.

☆**28:19** Gen 12:8; 35:6 48:3
☆**28:20** Gen 28:15 31:13 Deut 7:9
☆**28:21** Gen 35:3 Ex 15:2
☆**28:22** Gen 14:20; 35:7 Deut 14:22

2. Jacob Meets Rachel

29 THEN Jacob went on his journey, and came into the land of the
people of the east.
2And he looked, and behold a well in the field, and, lo, there *were* three
flocks of sheep lying by it; for out of that well they watered the flocks: and
a great stone *was* upon the well's mouth.
3And thither were all the flocks gathered: and they rolled the stone from
the well's mouth, and watered the sheep, and put the stone again upon the
well's mouth in his place.
4And Jacob said unto them, My brethren, whence *be* ye? And they said,
Of Ha'ran *are* we.
5And he said unto them, Know ye Laban the son of Nahor? And they
said, We know *him.*
6And he said unto them, *Is* he well? And they said, *He is* well: and,
behold, Rachel his daughter cometh with the sheep.
7And he said, Lo, *it is* yet high day, neither *is it* time that the cattle
should be gathered together: water ye the sheep, and go *and* feed *them.*
8And they said, We cannot, until all the flocks be gathered together, and
till they roll the stone from the well's mouth; then we water the sheep.
9¶And while he yet spake with them, Rachel came with her father's
sheep: for she kept them.
10And it came to pass, when Jacob saw Rachel the daughter of Laban his
mother's brother, and the sheep of Laban his mother's brother, that Jacob
went near, and rolled the stone from the well's mouth, and watered the
flock of Laban his mother's brother.
11And Jacob kissed Rachel, and lifted up his voice, and wept.
12And Jacob told Rachel that he *was* her father's brother, and that he *was*
Rebekah's son: and she ran and told her father.
13And it came to pass, when Laban heard the tidings of Jacob his sister's
son, that he ran to meet him, and embraced him, and kissed him, and
brought him to his house. And he told Laban all these things.
14And Laban said to him, Surely thou *art* my bone and my flesh. And he
abode with him the space of a month.

29:1 Judg 6:3, 33
29:2 Gen 24:11
29:4 Gen 11:31 28:10
29:5 Gen 24:29
☆**29:6** Gen 37:14 43:27
29:10 Ex 2:16
29:11 Gen 27:26; 33:4
29:12 Gen 28:5
29:14 Judg 9:2 2 Sam 5:1

28:19 *of that city. Luz,* meaning "almond tree," was renamed *Bethel* ("House of God") by Jacob after God appeared to him in a dream. Bethel became a holy place for the Israelites and was located on land given to the tribe of Benjamin. The city was about twelve miles north of Jerusalem. Jeroboam defiled this sacred place when he caused a golden calf to be erected there (1 Kings 12:28–33). God ordered the destruction of the altar (1 Kings 13:1–5; 2 Kings 23:15–17; Amos 3:14, 15).

28:20–22 *If God will be with me.* Jacob was not promising to tithe in the event that God helped him. He was saying what Romans 8:31 says: "If God is on our side," which allows for no doubt. He was not making a bargain with God. He vowed simply to express his profound gratitude for what God had already done, for God's undeserved favor. This became the normal way for Israelites to thank God; the intention to tithe was accompanied by a votive offering.

29:6 Once again the mystery of God's providence is manifest. Jacob unwittingly comes upon Rachel, the daughter of Laban, who is keeping her father's sheep. Such coincidences are not accidental; they are acts of God.

29:15 Gen 30:28; 31:7, 41
29:16 Gen 29:25, 26
29:17☆ Gen 12:11; 26:7; 1 Sam 25:3
29:18 Gen 24:67; Hos 12:12
29:20 Song 8:6, 7; 1 Cor 13:7
29:21☆
29:22 Judg 14:10
29:23☆ Gen 24:65; 38:14
29:24 Gen 30:9
29:25☆ Gen 12:18; 27:35
29:27☆ Lev 18:18; Judg 14:10, 12
29:29☆ Gen 30:3–8
29:30 Gen 29:17
29:31 Gen 20:18; Deut 21:15; Mal 1:2, 3
29:32☆ Gen 35:23; 37:21; 42:22; 46:8, 9

3. Jacob Marries Leah and Rachel

15 ¶And Laban said unto Jacob, Because thou *art* my brother, shouldest
thou therefore serve me for nought? tell me, what *shall* thy wages *be?*
16 And Laban had two daughters: the name of the elder *was* Leah, and the
name of the younger *was* Rachel.
17 Leah *was* tender eyed; but Rachel was beautiful and well favoured.
18 And Jacob loved Rachel; and said, I will serve thee seven years for
Rachel thy younger daughter.
19 And Laban said, *It is* better that I give her to thee, than that I should
give her to another man: abide with me.
20 And Jacob served seven years for Rachel; and they seemed unto him
but a few days, for the love he had to her.
21 ¶And Jacob said unto Laban, Give *me* my wife, for my days are
fulfilled, that I may go in unto her.
22 And Laban gathered together all the men of the place, and made a
feast.
23 And it came to pass in the evening, that he took Leah his daughter, and
brought her to him; and he went in unto her.
24 And Laban gave unto his daughter Leah Zilpah his maid *for* an
handmaid.
25 And it came to pass, that in the morning, behold, it *was* Leah: and he
said to Laban, What *is* this thou hast done unto me? did not I serve with
thee for Rachel? wherefore then hast thou beguiled me?
26 And Laban said, It must not be so done in our country, to give the
younger before the firstborn.
27 Fulfil her week, and we will give thee this also for the service which
thou shalt serve with me yet seven other years.
28 And Jacob did so, and fulfilled her week: and he gave him Rachel his
daughter to wife also.
29 And Laban gave to Rachel his daughter Bil′hah his handmaid to be her
maid.
30 And he went in also unto Rachel, and he loved also Rachel more than
Leah, and served with him yet seven other years.

4. Jacob's Children

a. The Four Sons by Leah

31 ¶And when the LORD saw that Leah *was* hated, he opened her womb:
but Rachel *was* barren.
32 And Leah conceived, and bare a son, and she called his name Reuben:

29:17 *Leah was tender-eyed.* We are not told whether her eyesight was bad or that her eyes did not sparkle. Sparkling eyes were prized by the people of that day. Rachel had what Leah lacked.

29:21 *that I may go in unto her,* i.e., that we may be married and I can have sexual relations with her. Even today a marriage is not consummated until the bride and groom have had sexual relations.

29:23 Laban worked under the cover of darkness, for it was evening when he brought Leah to Jacob. The bride was also covered. Jacob went to bed with Leah under the impression that it was Rachel. If he had asked the girl whether she was Rachel, he might have gotten the same response that he used when he claimed to be Esau and stole the blessing under the pretext of being his brother. It served him right, even though what Laban did was wrong.

29:25 Jacob reaped as he had sown. He had cheated his brother Esau out of the birthright; now his uncle, Laban, practiced the same kind of deceit. Yet Jacob was under God's covenant watchcare and did not ultimately become a loser. Later Jacob's own sons deceived him about Joseph's abduction (37:32–36).

29:27 *fulfill her week, and we will give thee this also.* The week consisted in festivities connected with the marriage. Right after that, Jacob got his second bride. He had worked for Laban for seven years before his marriage to Leah. Now he agreed to work seven more years after being married to Rachel, the one he really loved.

29:29 Since Laban was wealthy, he gave each of his daughters a servant-girl as a wedding present. Leah got Zilpah and Rachel got Bilhah. From the four of these women Jacob begot his twelve sons, who founded the twelve tribes of Israel.

29:32 *Reuben* means "See, a son."

for she said, Surely the LORD hath looked upon my affliction; now therefore
my husband will love me.
33 And she conceived again, and bare a son; and said, Because the LORD ☆29:33
hath heard that I *was* hated, he hath therefore given me this *son* also: and Gen 30:6
she called his name Simeon.
34 And she conceived again, and bare a son; and said, Now this time will ☆29:34
my husband be joined unto me, because I have born him three sons: Gen 49:5
therefore was his name called Levi.
35 And she conceived again, and bare a son: and she said, Now will I ☆29:35
praise the LORD: therefore she called his name Judah; and left bearing. Gen 49:8

b. The Two Sons by Bilhah

30 AND when Rachel saw that she bare Jacob no children, Rachel ☆30:1
envied her sister; and said unto Jacob, Give me children, or else I 1 Sam 1:4–7 Eccles 4:4
die.
2 And Jacob's anger was kindled against Rachel: and he said, *Am* I in ☆30:2
God's stead, who hath withheld from thee the fruit of the womb? Gen 25:21 31:36
3 And she said, Behold my maid Bil'hah, go in unto her; and she shall 30:3
bear upon my knees, that I may also have children by her. Gen 16:2
4 And she gave him Bil'hah her handmaid to wife: and Jacob went in unto 30:4
her. Gen 22:24 35:22
5 And Bil'hah conceived, and bare Jacob a son.
6 And Rachel said, God hath judged me, and hath also heard my voice, ☆30:6
and hath given me a son: therefore called she his name Dan. Gen 29:32 35:25; 46:23
7 And Bil'hah Rachel's maid conceived again, and bare Jacob a second 49:16
son. Lam 3:59
8 And Rachel said, With great wrestlings have I wrestled with my sister, ☆30:8
and I have prevailed: and she called his name Naph'ta-li. Gen 32:24 Mt 4:13

c. The Two Sons by Zilpah

9 When Leah saw that she had left bearing, she took Zilpah her maid, and
gave her Jacob to wife.
10 And Zilpah Leah's maid bare Jacob a son.
11 And Leah said, A troop cometh: and she called his name Gad. ☆30:11
12 And Zilpah Leah's maid bare Jacob a second son. Gen 35:26 46:16; 49:19
13 And Leah said, Happy am I, for the daughters will call me blessed: and ☆30:13
she called his name Asher.

29:33 The name *Simeon* means "hearing" for God heard the prayer of Leah, who was hated.
29:34 *Levi* means "joined" or "attachment." Leah hoped that her victory over Rachel (who was barren) would seal her marriage with Jacob and bring her the love she so desperately wanted.
29:35 *Judah* means "praise." Jesus was of this tribe; thus Leah, the hated wife, was in his ancestral line, not Rachel, the adored wife.
30:1, 2 Jacob's household was characterized by feuds, the result of having children by two wives and two concubines. Here we see that Rachel, who had not yet borne any children, envied her sister and, in so doing, sinned against the God of providence. The hatred and feuding were not resolved until after the death of Rachel and the submission of Jacob's sons to Joseph in Egypt more than two decades after Joseph was sold into slavery. Rachel's child-bearing problem would have been solved had she applied the principle articulated years later in the Psalms: "Children are a heritage of the Lord" (Ps. 127:3).
30:6 *Dan* ("justice"). The meaning is not of the actual Hebrew name, but of a Hebrew word sounding like the name. The name is a Hebrew pun. An example in English might be, "Because of the large hospital bill the child was named 'Bill.' "†
30:8 *Naphtali* means "wrestling."
30:11 *Gad* means "fortune."
30:13 *Asher* means "happy."

d. Leah Has Two More Sons; Rachel Has Joseph

30:14☆ Song 7:13

14¶And Reuben went in the days of wheat harvest, and found mandrakes
in the field, and brought them unto his mother Leah. Then Rachel said to
Leah, Give me, I pray thee, of thy son's mandrakes.
15And she said unto her, *Is it* a small matter that thou hast taken my
husband? and wouldest thou take away my son's mandrakes also? And
Rachel said, Therefore he shall lie with thee to night for thy son's
mandrakes.
16And Jacob came out of the field in the evening, and Leah went out to
meet him, and said, Thou must come in unto me; for surely I have hired
thee with my son's mandrakes. And he lay with her that night.

30:17 Gen 29:31; 30:6 Ex 3:7

17And God hearkened unto Leah, and she conceived, and bare Jacob the
fifth son.

30:18☆ Gen 35:23 49:14, 15

18And Leah said, God hath given me my hire, because I have given my
maiden to my husband: and she called his name Is'sa-char.
19And Leah conceived again, and bare Jacob the sixth son.

30:20☆ Mt 4:13

20And Leah said, God hath endued me *with* a good dowry; now will my
husband dwell with me, because I have born him six sons: and she called
his name Zeb'u-lun.
21And afterwards she bare a daughter, and called her name Dinah.

30:22☆ 1 Sam 1:19

22¶And God remembered Rachel, and God hearkened to her, and opened
her womb.

30:23 Lk 1:25

23And she conceived, and bare a son; and said, God hath taken away my
reproach:

30:24☆ Gen 35:17

24And she called his name Joseph; and said, The LORD shall add to me
another son.

5. Jacob Bargains with Laban about His Wages

25¶And it came to pass, when Rachel had born Joseph, that Jacob said
unto Laban, Send me away, that I may go unto mine own place, and to my
country.

30:26 Gen 29:18, 27 Hos 12:12

26Give *me* my wives and my children, for whom I have served thee, and
let me go: for thou knowest my service which I have done thee.

30:27☆ Gen 18:3 39:2–5

27And Laban said unto him, I pray thee, if I have found favour in thine
eyes, *tarry: for* I have learned by experience that the LORD hath blessed me
for thy sake.

30:28☆ Gen 29:15; 31:7

28And he said, Appoint me thy wages, and I will give *it*.
29And he said unto him, Thou knowest how I have served thee, and how
thy cattle was with me.

30;14 Mandrakes were a leafy plant eaten by peasant women who supposed this would aid them in becoming pregnant. Rachel wanted to eat some in the hope she would have a child. She acquired some of the mandrakes from Leah by promising to allow her to go to bed with Jacob. Leah then had two more sons. Rachel, at last, did have a son, Joseph, then later died upon giving birth to Benjamin.

30:18 *Issachar* means "reward."

30:20 *Zebulun* means "dwelling."

30:22 *God remembered . . . God hearkened.* "God remembered Rachel, whom he seemed to have forgotten, and hearkened to her whose prayers had long been denied."*

30:24 *Joseph* means "he adds."

30:27 *by experience,* "by divination" (NIV, RSV). The same Hebrew word is used several other times and is variously translated: "divination," "soothsaying," "augury" (NIV, RSV). The KJV translates the same word in Lev. 19:26, and 2 Kings 21:6, and 2 Chron. 33:6 as "enchantment(s)." In any event, whether it was by personal experience or by enchantments, Laban did know that God had blessed him because of Jacob's presence and labors in their midst. Sometimes what we should know as a result of experience remains hidden and we must learn it directly from God in some other fashion.

30:28 *Appoint me thy wages,* i.e., he asks Jacob what wages he wished to receive, knowing he will ask less than Laban would have had to offer.

30 For *it was* little which thou hadst before I *came,* and it is *now* increased
unto a multitude; and the LORD hath blessed thee since my coming: and
now when shall I provide for mine own house also?
31 And he said, What shall I give thee? And Jacob said, Thou shalt not
give me any thing: if thou wilt do this thing for me, I will again feed *and*
keep thy flock:
32 I will pass through all thy flock to day, removing from thence all the
speckled and spotted cattle, and all the brown cattle among the sheep, and
the spotted and speckled among the goats: and *of such* shall be my hire.
33 So shall my righteousness answer for me in time to come, when it shall
come for my hire before thy face: every one that *is* not speckled and spotted
among the goats, and brown among the sheep, that shall be counted stolen
with me.
34 And Laban said, Behold, I would it might be according to thy word.
35 And he removed that day the he goats that were ringstraked and
spotted, and all the she goats that were speckled and spotted, *and* every one
that had *some* white in it, and all the brown among the sheep, and gave
them into the hand of his sons.
36 And he set three days' journey betwixt himself and Jacob: and Jacob
fed the rest of Laban's flocks.
37 ¶And Jacob took him rods of green poplar, and of the hazel and
chesnut tree; and pilled white strakes in them, and made the white appear
which *was* in the rods.
38 And he set the rods which he had pilled before the flocks in the gutters
in the watering troughs when the flocks came to drink, that they should
conceive when they came to drink.
39 And the flocks conceived before the rods, and brought forth cattle
ringstraked, speckled, and spotted.
40 And Jacob did separate the lambs, and set the faces of the flocks
toward the ringstraked, and all the brown in the flock of Laban; and he put
his own flocks by themselves, and put them not unto Laban's cattle.
41 And it came to pass, whensoever the stronger cattle did conceive, that
Jacob laid the rods before the eyes of the cattle in the gutters, that they
might conceive among the rods.
42 But when the cattle were feeble, he put *them* not in: so the feebler were
Laban's, and the stronger Jacob's.
43 And the man increased exceedingly, and had much cattle, and
maidservants, and menservants, and camels, and asses.

30:30 Gen 30:43
☆**30:31**
30:32 Gen 31:8, 10, 12
30:37 Gen 31:9–13
30:43 Gen 13:2; 24:35; 26:13; 33:11

6. Jacob Decides to Return to the Land of His Birth

31 AND he heard the words of Laban's sons, saying, Jacob hath taken
away all that *was* our father's; and of *that* which *was* our father's
hath he gotten all this glory.
2 And Jacob beheld the countenance of Laban, and, behold, it *was* not
toward him as before.
3 And the LORD said unto Jacob, Return unto the land of thy fathers, and
to thy kindred; and I will be with thee.
4 And Jacob sent and called Rachel and Leah to the field unto his flock,
5 And said unto them, I see your father's countenance, that it *is* not
toward me as before; but the God of my father hath been with me.
6 And ye know that with all my power I have served your father.

31:1 Prov 27:4
31:2 Gen 31:36; 1 Sam 18:9
31:3 Gen 28:15; 32:9
31:5 Gen 31:42, 53
31:6 Gen 30:29

30:31 Laban worked around the agreement with Jacob so he would benefit and Jacob would lose. In the long run it worked to Jacob's benefit, and he became a wealthy man. This only caused Laban and his sons to become envious of Jacob.

31:7 Gen 29:15; 30:28; 31:41
7 And your father hath deceived me, and changed my wages ten times; but God suffered him not to hurt me.

31:8 Gen 30:32
8 If he said thus, The speckled shall be thy wages; then all the cattle bare speckled: and if he said thus, The ringstraked shall be thy hire; then bare all the cattle ringstraked.

31:9 Gen 31:1, 16
9 Thus God hath taken away the cattle of your father, and given *them* to me.

31:10 Gen 31:24
10 And it came to pass at the time that the cattle conceived, that I lifted up mine eyes, and saw in a dream, and, behold, the rams which leaped upon the cattle *were* ringstraked, speckled, and grisled.

31:11☆ Gen 16:7–13; 18:1; 22:1, 11
11 And the angel of God spake unto me in a dream, *saying,* Jacob: and I said, Here *am* I.

31:12 Gen 30:37–43; Ex 3:7; Lev 19:13; Deut 24:14, 15
12 And he said, Lift up now thine eyes, and see, all the rams which leap upon the cattle *are* ringstraked, speckled, and grisled: for I have seen all that Laban doeth unto thee.

31:13 Gen 28:13–19; 35:7
13 I *am* the God of Beth–el, where thou anointedst the pillar, *and* where thou vowedst a vow unto me: now arise, get thee out from this land, and return unto the land of thy kindred.

14 And Rachel and Leah answered and said unto him, *Is there* yet any portion or inheritance for us in our father's house?

31:15 Gen 29:20, 27; 30:26–28
15 Are we not counted of him strangers? for he hath sold us, and hath quite devoured also our money.

16 For all the riches which God hath taken from our father, that *is* ours, and our children's: now then, whatsoever God hath said unto thee, do.

7. Jacob and His Family Flee from Laban

a. Jacob Heads toward Gilead

17 ¶Then Jacob rose up, and set his sons and his wives upon camels;

31:18 Gen 24:29; 25:20
18 And he carried away all his cattle, and all his goods which he had gotten, the cattle of his getting, which he had gotten in Pa'dan–a'ram, for to go to Isaac his father in the land of Canaan.

31:19☆
19 And Laban went to shear his sheep: and Rachel had stolen the images that *were* her father's.

31:20 Gen 31:27
20 And Jacob stole away unawares to Laban the Syrian, in that he told him not that he fled.

31:21 Gen 15:18; Num 32:1; Deut 3:12; Judg 17:4, 5; 18:20
21 So he fled with all that he had; and he rose up, and passed over the river, and set his face *toward* the mount Gilead.

b. Laban Catches Up with Jacob

31:22 Gen 30:36
22 And it was told Laban on the third day that Jacob was fled.

23 And he took his brethren with him, and pursued after him seven days' journey; and they overtook him in the mount Gilead.

31:24 Gen 25:20; 31:10
24 And God came to Laban the Syrian in a dream by night, and said unto him, Take heed that thou speak not to Jacob either good or bad.

31:25 Gen 33:18
25 ¶Then Laban overtook Jacob. Now Jacob had pitched his tent in the mount: and Laban with his brethren pitched in the mount of Gilead.

31:11 God's time for Jacob to return to the land of his father was at hand. This was revealed to him in a dream. When Rachel and Leah heard this they were in agreement and said, "Whatsoever God hath said unto thee, do" (31:16). This was at least one time when the two sisters saw eye to eye.

31:19 *Rachel had stolen the images.* Since the images belonged to Laban, Rachel was a thief. Yet the real problem was whether either Laban or Rachel was truly a child of God. They were idol-worshippers, and idolatry is forbidden in the Scriptures. Since Rachel had been married to Jacob for some time, apparently he had little influence on her spiritual state.

26And Laban said to Jacob, What hast thou done, that thou hast stolen
away unawares to me, and carried away my daughters, as captives *taken*
with the sword?
27Wherefore didst thou flee away secretly, and steal away from me; and
didst not tell me, that I might have sent thee away with mirth, and with
songs, with tabret, and with harp?
28And hast not suffered me to kiss my sons and my daughters? thou hast **31:28** Gen 29:13
now done foolishly in *so* doing. 31:55
29It is in the power of my hand to do you hurt: but the God of your Ex 4:27 **31:29**
father spake unto me yesternight, saying, Take thou heed that thou speak Gen 31:24, 42
not to Jacob either good or bad.
30And now, *though* thou wouldest needs be gone, because thou sore **31:30**
longedst after thy father's house, *yet* wherefore hast thou stolen my gods? Gen 31:21
31And Jacob answered and said to Laban, Because I was afraid: for I **31:31**
said, Peradventure thou wouldest take by force thy daughters from me. Gen 20:11
32With whomsoever thou findest thy gods, let him not live: before our **31:32**
brethren discern thou what *is* thine with me, and take *it* to thee. For Jacob Gen 44:9 1 Sam 12:3
knew not that Rachel had stolen them.

c. Rachel Hides the Stolen Idols

33And Laban went into Jacob's tent, and into Leah's tent, and into the
two maidservants' tents; but he found *them* not. Then went he out of Leah's
tent, and entered into Rachel's tent.
34Now Rachel had taken the images, and put them in the camel's
furniture, and sat upon them. And Laban searched all the tent, but found
them not.
35And she said to her father, Let it not displease my lord that I cannot ☆**31:35**
rise up before thee; for the custom of women *is* upon me. And he searched, Gen 18:11
but found not the images.
36¶And Jacob was wroth, and chode with Laban: and Jacob answered **31:36**
and said to Laban, What *is* my trespass? what *is* my sin, that thou hast so Gen 30:2 Num 16:15
hotly pursued after me?
37Whereas thou hast searched all my stuff, what hast thou found of all **31:37**
thy household stuff? set *it* here before my brethren and thy brethren, that Gen 31:32 Josh 7:23
they may judge betwixt us both.
38This twenty years *have* I *been* with thee; thy ewes and thy she goats **31:38**
have not cast their young, and the rams of thy flock have I not eaten. Gen 31:41
39That which was torn *of beasts* I brought not unto thee; I bare the loss of **31:39**
it; of my hand didst thou require it, *whether* stolen by day, or stolen by Ex 22:10–13
night.
40*Thus* I was; in the day the drought consumed me, and the frost by
night; and my sleep departed from mine eyes.
41Thus have I been twenty years in thy house; I served thee fourteen **31:41**
years for thy two daughters, and six years for thy cattle: and thou hast Gen 29:27 30:27–32
changed my wages ten times.
42Except the God of my father, the God of Abraham, and the fear of ☆**31:42**
Isaac, had been with me, surely thou hadst sent me away now empty. God Gen 28:13–15, 20; 31:29
hath seen mine affliction and the labour of my hands, and rebuked *thee*
yesternight.

31:35 *the custom of women* is *upon me,* i.e., "I'm having my monthly period." She was pregnant with Benjamin, but falsely claimed her menstrual period, which, under the later Mosaic law, caused ceremonial defilement of all that she sat upon. See Lev. 5.†

31:42 *the God of Abraham, and the fear of Isaac.* "Abraham was dead, and had gone to that world where perfect love casts out fear; but Isaac was yet alive, sanctifying the Lord in his heart, as his fear and his dread."*

d. Jacob and Laban Make the Watchtower (Mizpah) Covenant

43 ¶And Laban answered and said unto Jacob, *These* daughters *are* my daughters, and *these* children *are* my children, and *these* cattle *are* my cattle, and all that thou seest *is* mine: and what can I do this day unto these my daughters, or unto their children which they have born?

31:44 Gen 21:27; 26:28–31

44 Now therefore come thou, let us make a covenant, I and thou; and let it be for a witness between me and thee.

31:45 Gen 28:18; Josh 24:26, 27

45 And Jacob took a stone, and set it up *for* a pillar.

31:46 Gen 35:14; Josh 4:5

46 And Jacob said unto his brethren, Gather stones; and they took stones, and made an heap: and they did eat there upon the heap.

31:47☆

47 And Laban called it Je′gar-sa-ha-du′tha: but Jacob called it Gal′e-ed.

31:48 Gen 21:30; Deut 4:26

48 And Laban said, This heap *is* a witness between me and thee this day. Therefore was the name of it called Gal′e-ed;

31:49☆ Judg 10:17; 11:11, 29

49 And Mizpah; for he said, The LORD watch between me and thee, when we are absent one from another.

31:50 Judg 11:10; 1 Sam 12:5; Jer 29:23; 42:5

50 If thou shalt afflict my daughters, or if thou shalt take *other* wives beside my daughters, no man *is* with us; see, God *is* witness betwixt me and thee.

51 And Laban said to Jacob, Behold this heap, and behold *this* pillar, which I have cast betwixt me and thee;

31:52 Gen 31:29, 42

52 This heap *be* witness, and *this* pillar *be* witness, that I will not pass over this heap to thee, and that thou shalt not pass over this heap and this pillar unto me, for harm.

31:53 Gen 28:13; 31:29

53 The God of Abraham, and the God of Nahor, the God of their father, judge betwixt us. And Jacob sware by the fear of his father Isaac.

31:54 Gen 26:30; Ex 18:12

54 Then Jacob offered sacrifice upon the mount, and called his brethren to eat bread: and they did eat bread, and tarried all night in the mount.

31:55 Gen 31:28; 33:4

55 And early in the morning Laban rose up, and kissed his sons and his daughters, and blessed them: and Laban departed, and returned unto his place.

32:1☆ Gen 16:7; 18:1, 2; 19:1; 22:11; 31:11; 2 Kgs 6:16, 17; Ps 34:7

32 AND Jacob went on his way, and the angels of God met him.
2 And when Jacob saw them, he said, This *is* God's host: and he called the name of that place Ma-ha-na′im.

32:2 Josh 13:26; 21:38; 2 Sam 2:8

F. JACOB AND ESAU MEET

1. Jacob Prepares for the Meeting

32:3 Gen 14:5, 6; 25:30; 27:41; Mal 3:1

3 And Jacob sent messengers before him to Esau his brother unto the land of Se′ir, the country of Edom.

32:4 Gen 31:17, 18

4 And he commanded them, saying, Thus shall ye speak unto my lord Esau; Thy servant Jacob saith thus, I have sojourned with Laban, and stayed there until now:

32:5 Gen 30:43

5 And I have oxen, and asses, flocks, and menservants, and womenservants: and I have sent to tell my lord, that I may find grace in thy sight.

32:6 Gen 32:11; 33:1

6 ¶And the messengers returned to Jacob, saying, We came to thy brother Esau, and also he cometh to meet thee, and four hundred men with him.

31:47 *Jegar-sahadutha,* which in the Aramaic meant "the heap of witness." The Hebrew *Galeed* also meant "the heap of witness."

31:49 *Mizpah* means "Watchpost." Jacob and Laban made God their witness, the third party in their agreement. Each expected God to enforce the covenant if either man broke it.

32:1, 2 *Jacob went his way,* i.e., "Jacob and his household." *Mahanaim,* "God's territory," or, "two encampments." The angels constituted God's protecting hosts. Jacob saw them. Some commentators think there were two hosts, one in front of Jacob and the other behind him. Thus was he fully protected. In verse 2 Jacob calls the band of angels "God's host."

[7]Then Jacob was greatly afraid and distressed: and he divided the people
that *was* with him, and the flocks, and herds, and the camels, into two
bands;
[8]And said, If Esau come to the one company, and smite it, then the other
company which is left shall escape.
[9]¶And Jacob said, O God of my father Abraham, and God of my father
Isaac, the LORD which saidst unto me, Return unto thy country, and to thy
kindred, and I will deal well with thee:
[10]I am not worthy of the least of all the mercies, and of all the truth,
which thou hast shewed unto thy servant; for with my staff I passed over
this Jordan; and now I am become two bands.
[11]Deliver me, I pray thee, from the hand of my brother, from the hand of
Esau: for I fear him, lest he will come and smite me, *and* the mother with
the children.
[12]And thou saidst, I will surely do thee good, and make thy seed as the
sand of the sea, which cannot be numbered for multitude.
[13]¶And he lodged there that same night; and took of that which came to
his hand a present for Esau his brother;
[14]Two hundred she goats, and twenty he goats, two hundred ewes, and
twenty rams,
[15]Thirty milch camels with their colts, forty kine, and ten bulls, twenty
she asses, and ten foals.
[16]And he delivered *them* into the hand of his servants, every drove by
themselves; and said unto his servants, Pass over before me, and put a
space betwixt drove and drove.
[17]And he commanded the foremost, saying, When Esau my brother
meeteth thee, and asketh thee, saying, Whose *art* thou? and whither goest
thou? and whose *are* these before thee?
[18]Then thou shalt say, *They be* thy servant Jacob's; it *is* a present sent
unto my lord Esau: and, behold, also he *is* behind us.
[19]And so commanded he the second, and the third, and all that followed
the droves, saying, On this manner shall ye speak unto Esau, when ye find
him.
[20]And say ye moreover, Behold, thy servant Jacob *is* behind us. For he
said, I will appease him with the present that goeth before me, and
afterward I will see his face; peradventure he will accept of me.
[21]So went the present over before him: and himself lodged that night in
the company.

32:7 Ex 14:10
32:8 Gen 33:1–3
☆**32:9** Gen 28:13–15; 31:13
32:10 Gen 24:27
32:11 Gen 27:41; 33:4
32:12 Gen 28:14, 15
32:18 Gen 32:4, 5
☆**32:20** Gen 43:11, 12; 1 Sam 25:18; Prov 21:14

2. Jacob Wrestles with the Man and Becomes Israel

[22]And he rose up that night, and took his two wives, and his two
womenservants, and his eleven sons, and passed over the ford Jabbok.
[23]And he took them, and sent them over the brook, and sent over that he
had.
[24]¶And Jacob was left alone; and there wrestled a man with him until the
breaking of the day.

32:22 Deut 3:16; Josh 12:2
☆**32:24** Gen 18:3; Hos 12:3, 4

32:9 Here Jacob prays to God as an undeserving sinner who depended solely on the Lord's mercy. Jacob also worked as though everything depended upon his work, just as we should pray as though everything depended upon our praying.

32:20 *I will appease him.* Jacob had every reason to suppose that Esau might still hate him because of the stolen birthright and the blessing. He thought to buy him off by giving him a substantial bribe. Why did he not trust God to deliver him without resorting to such measures? "He longed to see his father, and yet he dreads to see his brother."*

32:24 *there wrestled a man with him.* Some think the man was the preincarnate Christ. Others hold that it was probably Michael, one of the highest of the angelic host. Whichever it was, we can be certain that God's name was in him. Jacob thought he had seen God face to face. Thus the notion that it was Jesus seems to have good support.

25 And when he saw that he prevailed not against him, he touched the
hollow of his thigh; and the hollow of Jacob's thigh was out of joint, as he
wrestled with him.

32:26 Ex 32:10 1 Chron 4:10 Ps 67:1, 6, 7
26 And he said, Let me go, for the day breaketh. And he said, I will not let
thee go, except thou bless me.
27 And he said unto him, What *is* thy name? And he said, Jacob.

32:28☆ Gen 35:10 1 Kgs 18:31
28 And he said, Thy name shall be called no more Jacob, but Israel: for as
a prince hast thou power with God and with men, and hast prevailed.

32:29 Ex 3:13 Judg 13:17
29 And Jacob asked *him,* and said, Tell *me,* I pray thee, thy name. And he
said, Wherefore *is* it *that* thou dost ask after my name? And he blessed him
there.

32:30☆ Gen 16:13 Ex 24:10; 33:20 Num 12:8 Deut 5:24; 34:10 Judg 6:22 Isa 6:5 Jn 1:18
30 And Jacob called the name of the place Pe-ni'el: for I have seen God
face to face, and my life is preserved.
31 And as he passed over Pe-nu'el the sun rose upon him, and he halted
upon his thigh.

32:31 Judg 8:8, 9, 17 1 Kgs 12:25 **32:32**☆
32 Therefore the children of Israel eat not *of* the sinew which shrank,
which *is* upon the hollow of the thigh, unto this day: because he touched
the hollow of Jacob's thigh in the sinew that shrank.

3. Jacob and Esau Meet

33:1 Gen 32:6, 16
33 AND Jacob lifted up his eyes, and looked, and, behold, Esau came,
and with him four hundred men. And he divided the children unto
Leah, and unto Rachel, and unto the two handmaids.

33:2☆
2 And he put the handmaids and their children foremost, and Leah and
her children after, and Rachel and Joseph hindermost.

33:3 Gen 18:2; 42:6 Prov 6:3
3 And he passed over before them, and bowed himself to the ground seven
times, until he came near to his brother.

33:4☆ Gen 45:14 46:29
4 And Esau ran to meet him, and embraced him, and fell on his neck, and
kissed him: and they wept.

33:5 Gen 48:8, 9
5 And he lifted up his eyes, and saw the women and the children; and
said, Who *are* those with thee? And he said, The children which God hath
graciously given thy servant.
6 Then the handmaidens came near, they and their children, and they
bowed themselves.
7 And Leah also with her children came near, and bowed themselves: and
after came Joseph near and Rachel, and they bowed themselves.

33:8☆ Gen 32:5, 13–16
8 And he said, What *meanest* thou by all this drove which I met? And he
said, *These are* to find grace in the sight of my lord.

33:9 Gen 27:39
9 And Esau said, I have enough, my brother; keep that thou hast unto
thyself.

33:10☆ Gen 19:19 47:29; 50:4
10 And Jacob said, Nay, I pray thee, if now I have found grace in thy
sight, then receive my present at my hand: for therefore I have seen thy
face, as though I had seen the face of God, and thou wast pleased with me.

32:28 *Israel* means "ruling with God." God had changed Abram's name to Abraham. He now changes Jacob's name to Israel, by which his descendants were to be known henceforth. It became the name for a nation, not simply for an individual. *Israel* normatively denotes the people as a whole, just as America denotes the citizens of the United States.
32:30 *Peniel* means "the face of God."
32:32 *eat not of the sinew which shrank.* This was a matter of custom, not of commandment. Nowhere is the eating of the sinew forbidden.
33:2 *Rachel and Joseph hindermost.* Jacob was not trusting Esau and what he might do by way of vengeance. He kept Rachel, whom he loved, and their one child, Joseph, as far away as possible. If Esau destroyed the others first, Rachel and Joseph might still be able to escape.
33:4 Only the working power of God in the heart of Esau can explain the friendly reception he gave the brother he had earlier intended to slay.
33:8 *this drove.* These were the animals Jacob had set apart as a gift for Esau.
33:10 *I have seen thy face, as though I had seen the face of God,* i.e., "I was as frightened of you as though approaching God!"†

[11]Take, I pray thee, my blessing that is brought to thee; because God
hath dealt graciously with me, and because I have enough. And he urged
him, and he took *it.*
[12]And he said, Let us take our journey, and let us go, and I will go before
thee.
[13]And he said unto him, My lord knoweth that the children *are* tender,
and the flocks and herds with young *are* with me: and if men should
overdrive them one day, all the flock will die.
[14]Let my lord, I pray thee, pass over before his servant: and I will lead on
softly, according as the cattle that goeth before me and the children be able
to endure, until I come unto my lord unto Se′ir.

33:11 Gen 32:13–15
33:14 Gen 32:3; Deut 2:1

4. Jacob Travels to Shechem in Canaan

[15]And Esau said, Let me now leave with thee *some* of the folk that *are*
with me. And he said, What needeth it? let me find grace in the sight of my
lord.
[16]¶So Esau returned that day on his way unto Se′ir.
[17]And Jacob journeyed to Suc′coth, and built him an house, and made
booths for his cattle: therefore the name of the place is called Suc′coth.
[18]¶And Jacob came to Sha′lem, a city of She′chem, which *is* in the land of
Canaan, when he came from Pa′dan–a′ram; and pitched his tent before the
city.
[19]And he bought a parcel of a field, where he had spread his tent, at the
hand of the children of Ha′mor, She′chem's father, for an hundred pieces of
money.
[20]And he erected there an altar, and called it El-e-lo′he-Israel.

☆**33:16**
☆**33:17** Josh 13:27; Judg 8:5; Ps 60:6
☆**33:18** Gen 12:6; 25:20; 28:6, 7
33:19 Gen 23:17
☆**33:20** Josh 24:32; Jn 4:5

G. JACOB'S LATER LIFE IN CANAAN

1. The Defilement of Dinah, Leah's Daughter

34 AND Dinah the daughter of Leah, which she bare unto Jacob, went
out to see the daughters of the land.
[2]And when She′chem the son of Ha′mor the Hi′vite, prince of the
country, saw her, he took her, and lay with her, and defiled her.
[3]And his soul clave unto Dinah the daughter of Jacob, and he loved the
damsel, and spake kindly unto the damsel.
[4]And She′chem spake unto his father Ha′mor, saying, Get me this damsel
to wife.
[5]And Jacob heard that he had defiled Dinah his daughter: now his sons
were with his cattle in the field: and Jacob held his peace until they were
come.
[6]¶And Ha′mor the father of She′chem went out unto Jacob to commune
with him.
[7]And the sons of Jacob came out of the field when they heard *it:* and the
men were grieved, and they were very wroth, because he had wrought folly
in Israel in lying with Jacob's daughter; which thing ought not to be done.
[8]And Ha′mor communed with them, saying, The soul of my son
She′chem longeth for your daughter: I pray you give her him to wife.

34:1 Gen 30:21
☆**34:2** Deut 21:14; 22:29; 2 Sam 11:2; Job 31:1
34:4 Judg 14:2, 6
34:7 2 Sam 13:12

33:16 *Seir,* i.e., *Edom.*
33:17 *Succoth,* i.e., "booths," a village which was East of the Jordan River. It was later called Sakut.
33:18 *Shechem,* which means "shoulder," was Jacob's residence some years after his stay at Succoth. Present-day Nablus is the site, or Shechem was near this town.
33:20 *El-el-ohe-Israel* means "God, the God of Israel."
34:2 Dinah had left the security of her home to go abroad among the Hivites. The passage does not say specifically whether she was raped or was guilty of fornication. Shechem sought to marry her because he loved her. The results were disastrous for all.

34:9 Gen 24:3; 28:1
9 And make ye marriages with us, *and* give your daughters unto us, and
take our daughters unto you.
10 And ye shall dwell with us: and the land shall be before you; dwell and
trade ye therein, and get you possessions therein.

34:11 Gen 33:10
11 And She′chem said unto her father and unto her brethren, Let me find
grace in your eyes, and what ye shall say unto me I will give.

34:12 Gen 24:53 29:18; 31:41 Ex 22:16
12 Ask me never so much dowry and gift, and I will give according as ye
shall say unto me: but give me the damsel to wife.

34:13 Gen 27:35 31:7; 34:31
13 And the sons of Jacob answered She′chem and Ha′mor his father
deceitfully, and said, because he had defiled Dinah their sister:

34:14☆ Gen 17:13, 14 Josh 5:2
14 And they said unto them, We cannot do this thing, to give our sister to
one that is uncircumcised; for that *were* a reproach unto us:
15 But in this will we consent unto you: If ye will be as we *be,* that every
male of you be circumcised;
16 Then will we give our daughters unto you, and we will take your
daughters to us, and we will dwell with you, and we will become one
people.
17 But if ye will not hearken unto us, to be circumcised; then will we take
our daughter, and we will be gone.

2. Dinah's Brothers Take Revenge

18 And their words pleased Ha′mor, and She′chem Ha′mor's son.

34:19 Gen 29:20
19 And the young man deferred not to do the thing, because he had
delight in Jacob's daughter: and he *was* more honourable than all the house
of his father.

34:20 Gen 23:10 Deut 17:5
20 ¶And Ha′mor and She′chem his son came unto the gate of their city,
and communed with the men of their city, saying,
21 These men *are* peaceable with us; therefore let them dwell in the land,
and trade therein; for the land, behold, *it is* large enough for them; let us
take their daughters to us for wives, and let us give them our daughters.

34:22 Gen 34:15
22 Only herein will the men consent unto us for to dwell with us, to be one
people, if every male among us be circumcised, as they *are* circumcised.
23 *Shall* not their cattle and their substance and every beast of theirs *be*
ours? only let us consent unto them, and they will dwell with us.

34:24 Gen 17:23 Josh 5:2
24 And unto Ha′mor and unto She′chem his son hearkened all that went
out of the gate of his city; and every male was circumcised, all that went out
of the gate of his city.

34:25☆ Gen 49:5, 6 Josh 5:8
25 ¶And it came to pass on the third day, when they were sore, that two of
the sons of Jacob, Simeon and Levi, Dinah's brethren, took each man his
sword, and came upon the city boldly, and slew all the males.
26 And they slew Ha′mor and She′chem his son with the edge of the
sword, and took Dinah out of She′chem's house, and went out.
27 The sons of Jacob came upon the slain, and spoiled the city, because
they had defiled their sister.

34:28 Josh 7:21
28 They took their sheep, and their oxen, and their asses, and that which
was in the city, and that which *was* in the field,
29 And all their wealth, and all their little ones, and their wives took they
captive, and spoiled even all that *was* in the house.

34:14 *to one that is uncircumcised.* Jacob's sons used this religious ceremony as a ploy to render the men of the town incapable of defending themselves. Then they slew them in revenge for the humbling of their sister. Whether all the sons of Jacob were involved in some episodes in connection with the story the Scripture does not say. In verse 25 only Simeon and Levi are mentioned, whereas in verse 13 the phrase "the sons of Jacob" is used.

34:25 *Simeon and Levi* were the second and third sons of Jacob by Leah. Dinah was also born of Leah. Reuben, Leah's first son by Jacob, is not mentioned by name in the account.

30 And Jacob said to Simeon and Levi, Ye have troubled me to make me
to stink among the inhabitants of the land, among the Canaanites and the
Per′iz-zites: and I *being* few in number, they shall gather themselves
together against me, and slay me; and I shall be destroyed, I and my house.
31 And they said, Should he deal with our sister as with an harlot?

3. Jacob Goes to Bethel; God Renews the Agreement

35 AND God said unto Jacob, Arise, go up to Beth-el, and dwell
there: and make there an altar unto God, that appeared unto thee
when thou fleddest from the face of Esau thy brother.
2 Then Jacob said unto his household, and to all that *were* with him, Put
away the strange gods that *are* among you, and be clean, and change your
garments:
3 And let us arise, and go up to Beth-el; and I will make there an altar
unto God, who answered me in the day of my distress, and was with me in
the way which I went.
4 And they gave unto Jacob all the strange gods which *were* in their hand,
and *all their* earrings which *were* in their ears; and Jacob hid them under the
oak which *was* by She′chem.
5 And they journeyed: and the terror of God was upon the cities that *were*
round about them, and they did not pursue after the sons of Jacob.
6 ¶So Jacob came to Luz, which *is* in the land of Canaan, that *is,* Beth-el,
he and all the people that *were* with him.
7 And he built there an altar, and called the place El-beth-el: because
there God appeared unto him, when he fled from the face of his brother.
8 But Deb′o-rah Rebekah's nurse died, and she was buried beneath Beth-
el under an oak: and the name of it was called Al′lon-bach′uth.
9 ¶And God appeared unto Jacob again, when he came out of Pa′dan-
a′ram, and blessed him.
10 And God said unto him, Thy name *is* Jacob: thy name shall not be
called any more Jacob, but Israel shall be thy name: and he called his name
Israel.
11 And God said unto him, I *am* God Almighty: be fruitful and multiply;
a nation and a company of nations shall be of thee, and kings shall come
out of thy loins;
12 And the land which I gave Abraham and Isaac, to thee I will give it,
and to thy seed after thee will I give the land.
13 And God went up from him in the place where he talked with him.
14 And Jacob set up a pillar in the place where he talked with him, *even* a
pillar of stone: and he poured a drink offering thereon, and he poured oil
thereon.

☆34:30 Gen 13:7; Gen 49:5-7; Ex 5:21; 1 Chron 16:19
35:1 Gen 12:1; 22:1; 28:19; 31:3
☆35:2 Gen 31:19; Ex 19:10
35:3 Gen 28:15-22
☆35:4 Ex 32:2; Josh 24:23-26; Judg 8:24; Hos 2:13
35:5 Gen 34:30; Ex 15:16; Deut 2:25; 2 Chron 14:14
35:6 Gen 12:8; 28:19; 48:3; Josh 16:2; Judg 1:23
☆35:7 Gen 28:19; 35:1, 3
☆35:8 Gen 24:59
35:9 Gen 26:2; 28:13; 48:3
35:10 Gen 17:5, 15; 32:28; 1 Kgs 18:31; 2 Kgs 17:34
35:11 Gen 12:1; 17:1, 5; 28:3
35:12 Gen 13:15; 28:13
☆35:13 Judg 6:21; 13:20
35:14 Gen 28:18, 19; 31:45; Ex 17:15

34:30 *make me to stink,* i.e., make me odious. Since the Canaanites and Perizzites were far more numerous than Jacob's small band, he feared they would revenge the death of their friends and exterminate Jacob and his family.
35:2 *put away the strange gods.* This was a sorry example of a family divided between those who worshipped the true God and those who had idols. However they had acquired these idols, Jacob commanded that they must be done away with. They were on their way to Bethel, where he was to build an altar and worship the true God with his family.
35:4 The strange gods and the earrings were not destroyed. They were only hidden under an oak tree where they could be recovered later.
35:7 *El-beth-el,* i.e., "the God of Bethel."
35:8 *Allon-bachuth,* i.e., "oak of weeping."
35:13, 14 This is the first recorded instance of the drink or wine offering. In Exod. 29:40 and Lev. 23:13 wine offerings are specified. In Num. 15:3–10 different quantities of wine are specified, depending on the kind of sacrifice offered. The Jews perverted the wine offering by using it along with sacrificial cakes offered to Ashtoreth, the Queen of Heaven (Jer. 44:17–19). God censured Israel for offering wine to idols (Jer. 19:13; Ezek. 20:28). The wine offering symbolizes the outpoured blood of Christ on Calvary (Isa. 53:12; Matt. 26:28; Heb. 9:11–14) and the outpouring of the Holy Spirit upon the church (Joel 2:28, Acts 2:13ff). Wine or grape juice is used at the Lord's Supper, but it is drunk, not poured out, and memorializes Christ's death till he comes again.

35:15 Gen 35:6

15 And Jacob called the name of the place where God spake with him,
Beth–el.

4. The Birth of Benjamin and the Death of Rachel

35:16 Ruth 4:11; Mic 5:2
35:17 Gen 30:23, 24; 1 Sam 4:19, 20
35:18☆ Gen 46:19; 49:27; 1 Chron 4:9
35:19 Gen 48:7
35:20 1 Sam 10:2

16 ¶And they journeyed from Beth–el; and there was but a little way to
come to Eph′rath: and Rachel travailed, and she had hard labour.
17 And it came to pass, when she was in hard labour, that the midwife said
unto her, Fear not; thou shalt have this son also.
18 And it came to pass, as her soul was in departing, (for she died) that she
called his name Ben–o′ni: but his father called him Benjamin.
19 And Rachel died, and was buried in the way to Eph′rath, which *is*
Beth–lehem.
20 And Jacob set a pillar upon her grave: that *is* the pillar of Rachel's
grave unto this day.

5. Reuben Sleeps with His Father's Concubine

35:22 Gen 49:4; Lev 18:8; 1 Chron 5:1

21 ¶And Israel journeyed, and spread his tent beyond the tower of E′dar.
22 And it came to pass, when Israel dwelt in that land, that Reuben went
and lay with Bil′hah his father's concubine: and Israel heard *it.* Now the
sons of Jacob were twelve:

6. Jacob's Twelve Sons: The Future Tribes of Israel

35:23 Gen 29:32–35; 30:18–20; 46:8–14
35:24 Gen 30:22–24; 35:18
35:25 Gen 30:4–8; 46:23–25
35:26 Gen 30:9–13; 46:16–18

23 The sons of Leah; Reuben, Jacob's firstborn, and Simeon, and Levi,
and Judah, and Is′sa-char, and Zeb′u-lun:
24 The sons of Rachel; Joseph, and Benjamin:
25 And the sons of Bil′hah, Rachel's handmaid; Dan, and Naph′ta-li:
26 And the sons of Zilpah, Leah's handmaid; Gad, and Asher: these *are*
the sons of Jacob, which were born to him in Pa′dan–a′ram.

7. Isaac's Death and Burial

35:27 Gen 13:18; 14:13; 18:1; 23:2; 37:14; Josh 14:13
35:28 Gen 23:1; 25:7; 25:20; 47:28; 50:26
35:29 Gen 25:8, 17; 49:33

27 ¶And Jacob came unto Isaac his father unto Mam′re, unto the city of
Ar′bah, which *is* Hebron, where Abraham and Isaac sojourned.
28 And the days of Isaac were an hundred and fourscore years.
29 And Isaac gave up the ghost, and died, and was gathered unto his
people, *being* old and full of days: and his sons Esau and Jacob buried him.

H. THE DESCENDANTS OF ESAU

36:1 Gen 25:25–34; 32:3–7; 1 Chron 1:35
36:2 Gen 26:34; 36:10, 14
36:3 Gen 25:13
36:4 Gen 36:10, 11, 13
36:5 Gen 36:18

36 NOW these *are* the generations of Esau, who *is* Edom.
2 Esau took his wives of the daughters of Canaan; Adah the
daughter of E′lon the Hittite, and A-hol-i-ba′mah the daughter of A′nah the
daughter of Zib′e-on the Hi′vite;
3 And Bash′e-math Ish′ma-el's daughter, sister of Ne-ba′joth.
4 And Adah bare to Esau El′i-phaz; and Bash′e-math bare Reu′el;
5 And A-hol-i-ba′mah bare Je′ush and Ja-a′lam, and Korah: these *are* the
sons of Esau, which were born unto him in the land of Canaan.
6 And Esau took his wives, and his sons, and his daughters, and all the
persons of his house, and his cattle, and all his beasts, and all his substance,

35:18 Benjamin was the twelfth son of Jacob and was born of Rachel, who died at his birth. He was the full brother of Joseph and half brother of the other ten sons of Jacob. He was born in Canaan and his mother's tomb may still be seen in Bethlehem. Jacob showed unusual affection for Joseph and Benjamin, who were the sons of the woman he really loved and for whom he spent seven years of hard labor with his uncle, Laban, who cheated him. Joseph's special concern for his full brother Benjamin may be understood in light of the hatred the ten other brothers had for them.

which he had got in the land of Canaan; and went into the country from the
face of his brother Jacob.
7For their riches were more than that they might dwell together; and the
land wherein they were strangers could not bear them because of their
cattle.
8Thus dwelt Esau in mount Se'ir: Esau *is* Edom.
9¶And these *are* the generations of Esau the father of the Edomites in
mount Se'ir:
10These *are* the names of Esau's sons; El'i-phaz the son of Adah the wife
of Esau, Reu'el the son of Bash'e-math the wife of Esau.
11And the sons of El'i-phaz were Te'man, Omar, Ze'pho, and Ga'tam,
and Ke'naz.
12And Tim'na was concubine to El'i-phaz Esau's son; and she bare to
El'i-phaz Am'a-lek: these *were* the sons of Adah Esau's wife.
13And these *are* the sons of Reu'el; Na'hath, and Ze'rah, Sham'mah, and
Miz'zah: these were the sons of Bash'e-math Esau's wife.
14¶And these were the sons of A-hol-i-ba'mah, the daughter of A'nah the
daughter of Zib'e-on, Esau's wife: and she bare to Esau Je'ush, and Ja-
a'lam, and Ko'rah.
15¶These *were* dukes of the sons of Esau: the sons of El'i-phaz the
firstborn *son* of Esau; duke Te'man, duke Omar, duke Ze'pho, duke Ke'naz,
16Duke Ko'rah, duke Ga'tam, *and* duke Am'a-lek: these *are* the dukes
that came of El'i-phaz in the land of Edom; these *were* the sons of Adah.
17¶And these *are* the sons of Reu'el Esau's son; duke Na'hath, duke
Ze'rah, duke Sham'mah, duke Miz'zah: these *are* the dukes *that came* of
Reu'el in the land of Edom; these *are* the sons of Bash'e-math Esau's wife.
18¶And these *are* the sons of A-hol-i-ba'mah Esau's wife; duke Je'ush,
duke Ja-a'lam, duke Ko'rah: these *were* the dukes *that came* of A-hol-i-
ba'mah the daughter of A'nah, Esau's wife.
19These *are* the sons of Esau, who *is* Edom, and these *are* their dukes.
20¶These *are* the sons of Se'ir the Ho'rite, who inhabited the land; Lo'tan,
and Sho'bal, and Zib'e-on, and A'nah,
21And Di'shon, and E'zer, and Di'shan: these *are* the dukes of the
Ho'rites, the children of Se'ir in the land of Edom.
22And the children of Lo'tan were Ho'ri and He'mam; and Lo'tan's sister
was Tim'na.
23And the children of Sho'bal *were* these; Al'van, and Man'a-hath, and
Ebal, She'pho, and O'nam.
24And these *are* the children of Zib'e-on; both A'jah, and A'nah: this *was*
that A'nah that found the mules in the wilderness, as he fed the asses of
Zib'e-on his father.
25And the children of A'nah *were* these; Di'shon, and A-hol-i-ba'mah the
daughter of A'nah.
26And these *are* the children of Di'shon; Hem'dan, and Esh'ban, and
Ith'ran, and Che'ran.
27The children of E'zer *are* these; Bil'han, and Za'a-van, and A'kan.
28The children of Di'shan *are* these; Uz, and A'ran.

36:7 Gen 13:6
36:8 Gen 14:6; 25:30; 32:3
☆**36:9** Gen 36:43; 1 Kgs 11:1
36:10 1 Chron 1:35
36:11 1 Chron 1:36
☆**36:14**
☆**36:15, 16**
36:18 1 Chron 1:35
36:19 Gen 36:1, 9
36:20 Gen 14:6; Deut 2:12, 22; 1 Chron 1:38–42
36:22 1 Chron 1:39
36:23 1 Chron 1:40
36:25 Gen 36:2, 5, 14, 18; 1 Chron 1:41
36:27 1 Chron 1:38, 42

36:9 Esau was the founding father of the Edomite peoples who lived in the hill country of Seir. They became Israel's deadly enemies (Ezek. 35:5). God told Israel not to hate or ravage them (Deut. 2:4–6; 23:7; 2 Chron. 20:10). The Edomites were unbelievers, and the prophets said they were to be the object of the wrath of God at the end of the age (Isa. 11:14; 34:5, 6; Obad. 1:1–4; Amos 9:12).

36:14 This verse repeats the names listed in 36:5.

36:15, 16 *dukes of the sons of Esau,* i.e., "Esau's grandchildren."

36:29, 30☆ Gen 36:20

29 These *are* the dukes *that came* of the Ho′rites; duke Lo′tan, duke Sho′bal, duke Zib′e-on, duke A′nah.

30 Duke Di′shon, duke E′zer, duke Di′shan: these *are* the dukes *that came* of Ho′ri, among their dukes in the land of Se′ir.

36:31 Gen 17:6, 16 20:14 1 Chron 1:43

31 ¶And these *are* the kings that reigned in the land of Edom, before there reigned any king over the children of Israel.

32 And Be′la the son of Be′or reigned in Edom: and the name of his city *was* Din′ha-bah.

33 And Be′la died, and Jo′bab the son of Ze′rah of Boz′rah reigned in his stead.

34 And Jo′bab died, and Hu′sham of the land of Tem′a-ni reigned in his stead.

36:35 1 Chron 1:46

35 And Hu′sham died, and Ha′dad the son of Be′dad, who smote Mid′i-an in the field of Moab, reigned in his stead: and the name of his city *was* A′vith.

36 And Ha′dad died, and Sam′lah of Mas′re-kah reigned in his stead.

36:37 1 Chron 1:48

37 And Sam′lah died, and Saul of Re-ho′both *by* the river reigned in his stead.

38 And Saul died, and Ba′al–ha′nan the son of Ach′bor reigned in his stead.

39 And Ba′al–ha′nan the son of Ach′bor died, and Ha′dar reigned in his stead: and the name of his city *was* Pa′u; and his wife's name *was* Me-het′a-bel, the daughter of Ma′tred, the daughter of Mez′a-hab.

36:40 1 Chron 1:51

40 ¶And these *are* the names of the dukes *that came* of Esau, according to their families, after their places, by their names; duke Tim′nah, duke Al′vah, duke Je′theth,

41 Duke A-hol-i-ba′mah, duke E′lah, duke Pi′non,

42 Duke Ke′naz, duke Te′man, duke Mib′zar,

43 Duke Mag′di-el, duke I′ram: these *be* the dukes of Edom, according to their habitations in the land of their possession: he *is* Esau the father of the Edomites.

VII. THE STORY OF JOSEPH'S LIFE (37:1—50:26)

A. JOSEPH IS SOLD AS A SLAVE

1. Joseph's Triumphal Dream

37:1 Gen 17:8; 28:4

37 AND Jacob dwelt in the land wherein his father was a stranger, in the land of Canaan.

37:2☆ Gen 6:9 35:22–26; 41:46

2 These *are* the generations of Jacob. Joseph, *being* seventeen years old, was feeding the flock with his brethren; and the lad *was* with the sons of Bil′hah, and with the sons of Zilpah, his father's wives: and Joseph brought unto his father their evil report.

37:3☆ Gen 37:23, 32 44:20 **37:4** Gen 27:41 37:5, 11, 18–24 **37:5☆** Gen 28:12 37:9; 40:5; 41:1 Num 12:6 Dan 2:1 **37:6** Gen 44:18

3 Now Israel loved Joseph more than all his children, because he *was* the son of his old age: and he made him a coat of *many* colours.

4 And when his brethren saw that their father loved him more than all his brethren, they hated him, and could not speak peaceably unto him.

5 ¶And Joseph dreamed a dream, and he told *it* his brethren: and they hated him yet the more.

6 And he said unto them, Hear, I pray you, this dream which I have dreamed:

36:29, 30 These verses repeat the names listed in 36:20, 21.

37:2 *Joseph brought unto his father their evil report* is better translated, "Joseph brought back a bad report about them to his father" (NASB).

37:3 *a coat of many colours,* literally, "an ornamented tunic," or, "long-sleeved tunic."

37:5 It was unwise for Joseph to tell his brothers about his dream. They understood the implications, and this was the cause for their hatred of him. No doubt he told of the dream in a fit of youthful enthusiasm—he was not yet tempered by age and discretion.

[7]For, behold, we *were* binding sheaves in the field, and, lo, my sheaf
arose, and also stood upright; and, behold, your sheaves stood round about,
and made obeisance to my sheaf.

37:7 Gen 42:6, 9 43:26

[8]And his brethren said to him, Shalt thou indeed reign over us? or shalt
thou indeed have dominion over us? And they hated him yet the more for
his dreams, and for his words.

37:8 Ex 2:14 Deut 33:16

[9]¶And he dreamed yet another dream, and told it his brethren, and said,
Behold, I have dreamed a dream more; and, behold, the sun and the moon
and the eleven stars made obeisance to me.

37:9 Gen 37:10 41:25, 32; 43:28

[10]And he told *it* to his father, and to his brethren: and his father rebuked
him, and said unto him, What *is* this dream that thou hast dreamed? Shall
I and thy mother and thy brethren indeed come to bow down ourselves to
thee to the earth?

37:10 Gen 27:29 Isa 60:14 Phil 2:10

[11]And his brethren envied him; but his father observed the saying.

37:11 Ps 106:16 Isa 11:13 Mt 27:18 Acts 7:9

2. Joseph's Brothers Plot to Kill Him

[12]¶And his brethren went to feed their father's flock in She'chem.

37:12 Gen 33:18; 37:1

[13]And Israel said unto Joseph, Do not thy brethren feed *the flock* in
She'chem? come, and I will send thee unto them. And he said to him, Here
am I.

[14]And he said to him, Go, I pray thee, see whether it be well with thy
brethren, and well with the flocks; and bring me word again. So he sent him
out of the vale of Hebron, and he came to She'chem.

37:14 Gen 29:6; 35:27

[15]¶And a certain man found him, and, behold, *he was* wandering in the
field: and the man asked him, saying, What seekest thou?

[16]And he said, I seek my brethren: tell me, I pray thee, where they feed
their flocks.

[17]And the man said, They are departed hence; for I heard them say, Let
us go to Do'than. And Joseph went after his brethren, and found them in
Do'than.

☆**37:17** 2 Kgs 6:13

[18]And when they saw him afar off, even before he came near unto them,
they conspired against him to slay him.

[19]And they said one to another, Behold, this dreamer cometh.

[20]Come now therefore, and let us slay him, and cast him into some pit,
and we will say, Some evil beast hath devoured him: and we shall see what
will become of his dreams.

37:20 Gen 37:33 Prov 1:11

[21]And Reuben heard *it,* and he delivered him out of their hands; and
said, Let us not kill him.

37:21 Gen 42:22

[22]And Reuben said unto them, Shed no blood, *but* cast him into this pit
that *is* in the wilderness, and lay no hand upon him; that he might rid him
out of their hands, to deliver him to his father again.

☆**37:22** Gen 37:29

[23]¶And it came to pass, when Joseph was come unto his brethren, that
they stript Joseph out of his coat, *his* coat of *many* colours that *was* on him;

37:23 Gen 37:3

[24]And they took him, and cast him into a pit: and the pit *was* empty,
there was no water in it.

37:24 Jer 38:6

[25]And they sat down to eat bread: and they lifted up their eyes and
looked, and, behold, a company of Ish'me-el-ites came from Gilead with

37:25 Gen 25:16–18 31:23; 37:28 Jer 8:22; 46:11

37:17 *Dothan,* which means "double feast," is mentioned only three times in the Old Testament. It has been excavated by Dr. Joseph Free and others. The results show that the site was occupied in Jacob's time. It was located near Mt. Gilboa and was occupied by the tribe of Mannaseh later.

37:22 As the eldest son, Reuben wanted to save Joseph from the fate that awaited him. He intended to return to the pit (probably a cistern without water but too deep for Joseph to escape from it) and free his brother. Joseph was sold into slavery when Reuben was absent. Later (Gen. 42:22) he reminded his brothers about his innocence and their guilt.

their camels bearing spicery and balm and myrrh, going to carry *it* down to Egypt.

3. Joseph Bought by the Ishmeelites; Reuben's Remorse

26 And Judah said unto his brethren, What profit *is it* if we slay our brother, and conceal his blood?

37:27 Ex 21:16 Neh 5:8

27 Come, and let us sell him to the Ish′me-el-ites, and let not our hand be upon him; for he *is* our brother *and* our flesh. And his brethren were content.

37:28☆ Gen 39:1; 45:4 Lev 27:5 Judg 8:22–24 Acts 7:9

28 Then there passed by Mid′i-an-ites merchantmen; and they drew and lifted up Joseph out of the pit, and sold Joseph to the Ish′me-el-ites for twenty *pieces* of silver: and they brought Joseph into Egypt.

37:29 Gen 37:34 44:13 Num 14:6

29 ¶And Reuben returned unto the pit; and, behold, Joseph *was* not in the pit; and he rent his clothes.

37:30 Gen 5:24 42:13, 32, 36

30 And he returned unto his brethren, and said, The child *is* not; and I, whither shall I go?

37:31 Gen 37:3, 23 Prov 28:13

31 ¶And they took Joseph's coat, and killed a kid of the goats, and dipped the coat in the blood;

37:32 Lk 15:30

32 And they sent the coat of *many* colours, and they brought *it* to their father; and said, This have we found: know now whether it *be* thy son's coat or no.

4. Jacob's Grief

37:33 Gen 37:20 44:28

33 And he knew it, and said, *It is* my son's coat; an evil beast hath devoured him; Joseph is without doubt rent in pieces.

37:34☆ Gen 37:29 44:13

34 And Jacob rent his clothes, and put sackcloth upon his loins, and mourned for his son many days.

37:35☆ Gen 31:43 44:29 2 Sam 12:17 Ps 77:2

35 And all his sons and all his daughters rose up to comfort him; but he refused to be comforted; and he said, For I will go down into the grave unto my son mourning. Thus his father wept for him.

37:36 Gen 39:1; 40:4

36 And the Mid′i-an-ites sold him into Egypt unto Pot′i-phar, an officer of Pharaoh's, *and* captain of the guard.

B. JUDAH AND TAMAR

1. Judah's Son Er Marries Tamar

38:1 Josh 12:15 15:35 1 Sam 22:1

38 AND it came to pass at that time, that Judah went down from his brethren, and turned in to a certain A-dul′lam-ite, whose name *was* Hi′rah.

38:2 Gen 24:3; 34:2 38:12

2 And Judah saw there a daughter of a certain Canaanite, whose name *was* Shu′ah; and he took her, and went in unto her.

38:3 Gen 46:12 Num 26:19

3 And she conceived, and bare a son; and he called his name Er.

4 And she conceived again, and bare a son; and she called his name O′nan.

5 And she yet again conceived, and bare a son; and called his name She′lah: and he was at Che′zib, when she bare him.

38:6 Mt 1:3

6 And Judah took a wife for Er his firstborn, whose name *was* Ta′mar.

37:28 The text is not clear on what the relationship was between the Midianite traders and the Ishmeelites. The Midianites were descendants of Abraham and Keturah; the Ishmeelites were descendants of Abraham and Hagar. 39:1 states that the Ishmeelites sold Joseph to Potiphar.

37:34 *Jacob . . . mourned.* Jacob's grief fully sustains the scriptural teaching that as a man sows, so shall he reap. He had cruelly deceived his own father; now his sons deceive him. Twenty years later, when retribution seemed likely, the sons were to experience their own anguish for their deception (see 42:21).

37:35 *grave,* i.e., *Sheol* for which see note to Deut. 32:22.

7 And Er, Judah's firstborn, was wicked in the sight of the LORD; and the
LORD slew him.
8 And Judah said unto O'nan, Go in unto thy brother's wife, and marry
her, and raise up seed to thy brother.
9 And O'nan knew that the seed should not be his; and it came to pass,
when he went in unto his brother's wife, that he spilled *it* on the ground,
lest that he should give seed to his brother.
10 And the thing which he did displeased the LORD: wherefore he slew
him also.
11 Then said Judah to Ta'mar his daughter in law, Remain a widow at thy
father's house, till She'lah my son be grown: for he said, Lest peradventure
he die also, as his brethren *did*. And Ta'mar went and dwelt in her father's
house.

38:7 Gen 6:5, 13:13; 19:13; 38:10; 2 Chron 33:6
☆**38:8** Lev 18:16; Num 36:8; Deut 25:5–10; Mt 22:24
☆**38:9**
38:10 2 Sam 11:27; 1 Chron 21:7
38:11 Ruth 1:13

2. Judah Commits Adultery with Er's Widow

12 ¶And in process of time the daughter of Shu'ah Judah's wife died; and
Judah was comforted, and went up unto his sheepshearers to Tim'nath, he
and his friend Hi'rah the A-dul'lam-ite.
13 And it was told Ta'mar, saying, Behold thy father in law goeth up to
Tim'nath to shear his sheep.
14 And she put her widow's garments off from her, and covered her with a
vail, and wrapped herself, and sat in an open place, which *is* by the way to
Tim'nath; for she saw that She'lah was grown, and she was not given unto
him to wife.
15 When Judah saw her, he thought her *to be* an harlot; because she had
covered her face.
16 And he turned unto her by the way, and said, Go to, I pray thee, let me
come in unto thee; (for he knew not that she *was* his daughter in law.) And
she said, What wilt thou give me, that thou mayest come in unto me?
17 And he said, I will send *thee* a kid from the flock. And she said, Wilt
thou give *me* a pledge, till thou send *it?*
18 And he said, What pledge shall I give thee? And she said, Thy signet,
and thy bracelets, and thy staff that *is* in thine hand. And he gave *it* her,
and came in unto her, and she conceived by him.
19 And she arose, and went away, and laid by her vail from her, and put
on the garments of her widowhood.
20 And Judah sent the kid by the hand of his friend the A-dul'lam-ite, to
receive *his* pledge from the woman's hand: but he found her not.
21 Then he asked the men of that place, saying, Where *is* the harlot, that
was openly by the way side? And they said, There was no harlot in this
place.
22 And he returned to Judah, and said, I cannot find her; and also the men
of the place said, *that* there was no harlot in this *place*.
23 And Judah said, Let her take *it* to her, lest we be shamed: behold, I sent
this kid, and thou hast not found her.

38:12 Gen 31:19; Josh 13:23–27; 1 Sam 25:4; 2 Sam 13:23–27
38:14 Gen 23:10; Josh 15:34
☆**38:15** Gen 24:65
38:16 2 Sam 13:11; Deut 23:18; Ezek 16:33
38:17 Gen 38:20, 25
38:18 Gen 41:42; Hos 4:11
38:23 Prov 6:32, 33

38:8 *raise up seed to thy brother.* This custom of levirate marriage, in which the nearest of kin was to continue the family line by marriage to the widow, is illustrated in the case of Ruth and Boaz. See note about this custom in Deut. 25:5–10.

38:9 Paraphrased, the verse reads: "But Onan was not willing to have a child who would not be counted as his own, and so, . . . whenever he went in to sleep with her, he spilled the sperm on the bed to prevent her from having a baby which would be his brother's."†

38:15 Tamar played the role of a prostitute in order to raise up seed for her dead husband. Judah refused to let Shelah his son raise up seed by Tamar. Judah himself was wrong not to give Shelah to Tamar for this purpose, and he was also guilty of committing adultery. He further aggravated his sins by accusing Tamar of being a prostitute and adulteress without inquiring into the circumstances surrounding her pregnancy.

3. Tamar's Virtue Vindicated: Pharez and Zarah Born

38:24 Gen 34:31; Lev 20:10; 21:9; Eccles 7:26

24 ¶And it came to pass about three months after, that it was told Judah,
saying, Ta'mar thy daughter in law hath played the harlot; and also,
behold, she *is* with child by whoredom. And Judah said, Bring her forth,
and let her be burnt.

38:25 Gen 37:32

25 When she *was* brought forth, she sent to her father in law, saying, By
the man, whose these *are, am* I with child: and she said, Discern, I pray
thee, whose *are* these, the signet, and bracelets, and staff.

38:26 1 Sam 24:17; Ezek 16:52

26 And Judah acknowledged *them*, and said, She hath been more righteous
than I; because that I gave her not to She'lah my son. And he knew her
again no more.

38:27 Gen 25:24

27 ¶And it came to pass in the time of her travail, that, behold, twins *were*
in her womb.

28 And it came to pass, when she travailed, that *the one* put out *his* hand:
and the midwife took and bound upon his hand a scarlet thread, saying,
This came out first.

38:29☆ Gen 46:12; Num 26:20; Ruth 4:12; 1 Chron 2:4; Mt 1:3; Lk 3:33

29 And it came to pass, as he drew back his hand, that, behold, his brother
came out: and she said, How hast thou broken forth? *this* breach *be* upon
thee: therefore his name was called Pha'rez.

30 And afterward came out his brother, that had the scarlet thread upon
his hand: and his name was called Za'rah.

C. GOD BLESSES JOSEPH THE SLAVE

1. Joseph's Prosperity

39:1 Gen 45:4; Ps 105:17; Acts 7:9

39 AND Joseph was brought down to Egypt; and Pot'i-phar, an officer
of Pharaoh, captain of the guard, an Egyptian, bought him of the
hands of the Ish'me-el-ites, which had brought him down thither.

39:2☆ Gen 21:22; 26:24, 28; 28:15; 1 Sam 3:19

2 And the LORD was with Joseph, and he was a prosperous man; and he
was in the house of his master the Egyptian.

39:3 Josh 1:8; 1 Sam 18:14; 1 Chron 22:13

3 And his master saw that the LORD *was* with him, and that the LORD
made all that he did to prosper in his hand.

39:4 Gen 32:5; 41:40; Prov 14:35; 17:2; 27:18

4 And Joseph found grace in his sight, and he served him: and he made
him overseer over his house, and all *that* he had he put into his hand.

39:5 Deut 28:3–6

5 And it came to pass from the time *that* he had made him overseer in his
house, and over all that he had, that the LORD blessed the Egyptian's house
for Joseph's sake; and the blessing of the LORD was upon all that he had in
the house, and in the field.

39:6 Gen 29:17; Ex 2:2; 1 Sam 16:12, 18; Lk 16:10; Acts 7:20

6 And he left all that he had in Joseph's hand; and he knew not ought he
had, save the bread which he did eat. And Joseph was *a* goodly *person*, and
well favoured.

2. Potiphar's Wife Tries to Seduce Joseph

39:7 Ps 119:37; Prov 2:16; 5:3; 7:13; Ezek 23:5

7 ¶And it came to pass after these things, that his master's wife cast her
eyes upon Joseph; and she said, Lie with me.

38:29, 30 *Pharez . . . and Zarah.* Pharez means "breach." Zarah means "sprout." Pharez is listed in the genealogy of Jesus in Matthew 1:3. Thus God brought forth good out of evil. The ancestors of Jesus included a number of wicked-acting people, yet the Son of God was born sinless and could be the Savior even of people like his own ancestors.

39:2 Joseph could hardly have known how God would use his brothers' evil to fulfill the divine purpose. Nor could he have known how and when his dreams were to be fulfilled. He did have faith in God, and here the Scriptures make plain that God was watching over this young man and caring for him. In 39:21, when Joseph had been thrown in jail for a crime he never committed and when his faith must have been hard-pressed, "the LORD was with Joseph." (See also 45:7; 50:20; Ps. 76:10.)

8 But he refused, and said unto his master's wife, Behold, my master
wotteth not what *is* with me in the house, and he hath committed all that he
hath to my hand;
9 *There is* none greater in this house than I; neither hath he kept back any
thing from me but thee, because thou *art* his wife: how then can I do this
great wickedness, and sin against God?
10 And it came to pass, as she spake to Joseph day by day, that he
hearkened not unto her, to lie by her, *or* to be with her.
11 And it came to pass about this time, that *Joseph* went into the house to
do his business; and *there was* none of the men of the house there within.
12 And she caught him by his garment, saying, Lie with me: and he left his
garment in her hand, and fled, and got him out.
13 And it came to pass, when she saw that he had left his garment in her
hand, and was fled forth,
14 That she called unto the men of her house, and spake unto them,
saying, See, he hath brought in an Hebrew unto us to mock us; he came in
unto me to lie with me, and I cried with a loud voice:
15 And it came to pass, when he heard that I lifted up my voice and cried,
that he left his garment with me, and fled, and got him out.
16 And she laid up his garment by her, until his lord came home.
17 And she spake unto him according to these words, saying, The Hebrew
servant, which thou hast brought unto us, came in unto me to mock me:
18 And it came to pass, as I lifted up my voice and cried, that he left his
garment with me, and fled out.

39:8 Gen 39:5 Prov 1:10 6:23, 24
☆**39:9** 2 Sam 12:13 Ps 51:4
39:10 1 Cor 6:18 15:33 1 Thess 5:22 2 Tim 2:22
☆**39:12** Prov 7:13 Eccles 7:26 Ezek 16:30
39:14 Isa 54:17
☆**39:17** Ex 20:16; 23:1 Ps 37:14; 55:3

3. Innocent Joseph Is Jailed

19 And it came to pass, when his master heard the words of his wife, which
she spake unto him, saying, After this manner did thy servant to me; that
his wrath was kindled.
20 And Joseph's master took him, and put him into the prison, a place
where the king's prisoners *were* bound: and he was there in the prison.
21 ¶But the LORD was with Joseph, and shewed him mercy, and gave him
favour in the sight of the keeper of the prison.
22 And the keeper of the prison committed to Joseph's hand all the
prisoners that *were* in the prison; and whatsoever they did there, he was the
doer *of it*.
23 The keeper of the prison looked not to any thing *that was* under his
hand; because the LORD was with him, and *that* which he did, the LORD
made *it* to prosper.

39:19 Prov 6:34; 18:17
39:20 Gen 40:1–3, 15 41:12, 14 Ps 105:18
☆**39:21** Gen 39:2, 3 49:25 Acts 7:9
39:22 Gen 39:4; 41:40
39:23 Gen 39:3 Ps 1:3

D. JOSEPH INTERPRETS TWO MEN'S DREAMS

1. The Chief Baker and the Butler (Wine Taster)

40 AND it came to pass after these things, *that* the butler of the king
of Egypt and *his* baker had offended their lord the king of Egypt.

40:1 Neh 1:11

39:9 Joseph's purity was tested here with his position at stake. He spurned Potiphar's wife, who sought to seduce him. She lied, and he was committed to prison for a crime he did not commit. What he could not know then was that this evil was part of the plan of God to make the fulfillment of his dreams possible. In prison he came in contact with the butler (wine taster), who later mentions Joseph to the Pharaoh.

39:12 *garment,* i.e., "sleeve." The word is not specific.†

39:17 This wicked woman, whose name is not given, wanted revenge against Joseph not because of vice but because of his virtue. She lied to her husband, implying that the fault lay with him for bringing Joseph into their household.

39:21 Joseph is isolated in prison from relatives and friends. But his God is the friend of the friendless. "The Lord was with Joseph, and shewed him mercy."* See also 39:2, where the Lord is said to be with Joseph.

40:2☆ Prov 16:14; 19:12
2 And Pharaoh was wroth against two *of* his officers, against the chief of
the butlers, and against the chief of the bakers.
40:3 Gen 39:20
3 And he put them in ward in the house of the captain of the guard, into
the prison, the place where Joseph *was* bound.
40:4 Gen 37:36; 39:1
4 And the captain of the guard charged Joseph with them, and he served
them: and they continued a season in ward.
40:5 Gen 20:3; 37:5–10; 40:8; 41:1–7, 11
5 ¶And they dreamed a dream both of them, each man his dream in one
night, each man according to the interpretation of his dream, the butler and
the baker of the king of Egypt, which *were* bound in the prison.
40:6 Gen 41:8
6 And Joseph came in unto them in the morning, and looked upon them,
and, behold, they *were* sad.
7 And he asked Pharaoh's officers that *were* with him in the ward of his
lord's house, saying, Wherefore look ye *so* sadly to day?
40:8☆ Gen 41:15, 16; Job 33:15, 16; Dan 2:28
8 And they said unto him, We have dreamed a dream, and *there is* no
interpreter of it. And Joseph said unto them, *Do* not interpretations *belong*
to God? tell me *them*, I pray you.

2. The Wine Taster's Dream and Joseph's Interpretation

40:9 Gen 37:5; Judg 7:13
9 And the chief butler told his dream to Joseph, and said to him, In my
dream, behold, a vine *was* before me;
10 And in the vine *were* three branches: and it *was* as though it budded,
and her blossoms shot forth; and the clusters thereof brought forth ripe
grapes:
11 And Pharaoh's cup *was* in my hand: and I took the grapes, and pressed
them into Pharaoh's cup, and I gave the cup into Pharaoh's hand.
40:12 Gen 41:12; Judg 7:14; Dan 2:36
12 And Joseph said unto him, This *is* the interpretation of it: The three
branches *are* three days:
40:13 Gen 40:19, 20
13 Yet within three days shall Pharaoh lift up thine head, and restore thee
unto thy place: and thou shalt deliver Pharaoh's cup into his hand, after the
former manner when thou wast his butler.
40:14 Josh 2:12; 1 Sam 20:13, 14
14 But think on me when it shall be well with thee, and shew kindness, I
pray thee, unto me, and make mention of me unto Pharaoh, and bring me
out of this house:
40:15 Gen 37:28; 39:1, 20
15 For indeed I was stolen away out of the land of the Hebrews: and here
also have I done nothing that they should put me into the dungeon.

3. The Chief Baker's Dream and Joseph's Interpretation

40:16 Gen 40:1, 2
16 When the chief baker saw that the interpretation was good, he said
unto Joseph, I also *was* in my dream, and, behold, *I had* three white baskets
on my head:
17 And in the uppermost basket *there was* of all manner of bakemeats for
Pharaoh; and the birds did eat them out of the basket upon my head.
40:18 Gen 40:12; 41:13
18 And Joseph answered and said, This *is* the interpretation thereof: The
three baskets *are* three days:
40:19 Gen 40:22; 41:13; Deut 21:22
19 Yet within three days shall Pharaoh lift up thy head from off thee, and
shall hang thee on a tree; and the birds shall eat thy flesh from off thee.

40:2 The butler and baker were important men to Pharaoh; their trustworthiness assured him he would not be poisoned either by food or by drink. Joseph interpreted their dreams accurately. The survivor, the butler, according to verse 23, forgot about Joseph as soon as he was freed from prison. He remembered him two years later.

40:8 Joseph gives glory to God as the interpreter of dreams. His gift of interpretation came from God.

4. Joseph's Interpretations Come True

[20]¶And it came to pass the third day, *which was* Pharaoh's birthday, that
he made a feast unto all his servants: and he lifted up the head of the chief
butler and of the chief baker among his servants.
[21]And he restored the chief butler unto his butlership again; and he gave
the cup into Pharaoh's hand:
[22]But he hanged the chief baker: as Joseph had interpreted to them.
[23]Yet did not the chief butler remember Joseph, but forgat him.

40:20 Gen 40:13, 18; 2 Kgs 25:27–30; Jer 52:31–34
40:22 Gen 40:19
40:23 Gen 40:14; 41:9

E. JOSEPH BECOMES SECOND TO PHARAOH

1. The Pharaoh Dreams a Dream

41 AND it came to pass at the end of two full years, that Pharaoh
dreamed: and, behold, he stood by the river.
[2]And, behold, there came up out of the river seven well favoured kine
and fatfleshed; and they fed in a meadow.
[3]And, behold, seven other kine came up after them out of the river, ill
favoured and leanfleshed; and stood by the *other* kine upon the brink of the
river.
[4]And the ill favoured and leanfleshed kine did eat up the seven well
favoured and fat kine. So Pharaoh awoke.
[5]And he slept and dreamed the second time: and, behold, seven ears of
corn came up upon one stalk, rank and good.
[6]And, behold, seven thin ears and blasted with the east wind sprung up
after them.
[7]And the seven thin ears devoured the seven rank and full ears. And
Pharaoh awoke, and, behold, *it was* a dream.
[8]And it came to pass in the morning that his spirit was troubled; and he
sent and called for all the magicians of Egypt, and all the wise men thereof:
and Pharaoh told them his dream; but *there was* none that could interpret
them unto Pharaoh.

41:2 Job 8:11; Isa 19:7
41:3 Gen 41:20, 21
41:4 1 Kgs 3:15
☆**41:6** Ezek 17:10; 19:12
41:8 Ex 7:11; Dan 2:1–3; 4:5; Mt 2:1

2. The Wine Taster Tells Pharaoh about Joseph

[9]¶Then spake the chief butler unto Pharaoh, saying, I do remember my
faults this day:
[10]Pharaoh was wroth with his servants, and put me in ward in the captain
of the guard's house, *both* me and the chief baker:
[11]And we dreamed a dream in one night, I and he; we dreamed each man
according to the interpretation of his dream.
[12]And *there was* there with us a young man, an Hebrew, servant to the
captain of the guard; and we told him, and he interpreted to us our dreams;
to each man according to his dream he did interpret.
[13]And it came to pass, as he interpreted to us, so it was; me he restored
unto mine office, and him he hanged.

41:9 Gen 40:14, 23
41:10 Gen 40:2
41:11 Gen 40:5–8
41:12 Gen 40:12–19
41:13 Gen 40:22

3. The Pharaoh Tells Joseph about His Dream

[14]¶Then Pharaoh sent and called Joseph, and they brought him hastily
out of the dungeon: and he shaved *himself*, and changed his raiment, and
came in unto Pharaoh.
[15]And Pharaoh said unto Joseph, I have dreamed a dream, and *there is*
none that can interpret it: and I have heard say of thee, *that* thou canst
understand a dream to interpret it.

41:14 Ex 10:16; Ps 105:16–22
41:15 Gen 41:8; Dan 2:25

41:6 *east wind,* i.e., a "sirocco," or, "a hot wind."

41:16☆ Gen 40:8 Num 12:6 Dan 2:28–30 Acts 3:12
41:17 Gen 41:1–7, 26–27
41:18 Gen 41:28, 32

16 And Joseph answered Pharaoh, saying, *It is* not in me: God shall give
Pharaoh an answer of peace.
17 And Pharaoh said unto Joseph, In my dream, behold, I stood upon the
bank of the river:
18 And, behold, there came up out of the river seven kine, fatfleshed and
well favoured; and they fed in a meadow:
19 And, behold, seven other kine came up after them, poor and very ill
favoured and leanfleshed, such as I never saw in all the land of Egypt for
badness:
20 And the lean and the ill favoured kine did eat up the first seven fat
kine:
21 And when they had eaten them up, it could not be known that they had
eaten them; but they *were* still ill favoured, as at the beginning. So I awoke.
22 And I saw in my dream, and, behold, seven ears came up in one stalk,
full and good:
23 And, behold, seven ears, withered, thin, *and* blasted with the east wind,
sprung up after them:
24 And the thin ears devoured the seven good ears: and I told *this* unto the
magicians; but *there was* none that could declare *it* to me.

4. Joseph Discloses the Meaning of the Dream and Makes a Proposal

41:26 Gen 40:12, 18
41:27 Gen 41:30, 54 2 Sam 24:13 2 Kgs 8:1
41:29 Gen 41:47
41:30 Gen 41:54 47:13

25 ¶And Joseph said unto Pharaoh, The dream of Pharaoh *is* one: God
hath shewed Pharaoh what he *is* about to do.
26 The seven good kine *are* seven years; and the seven good ears *are* seven
years: the dream *is* one.
27 And the seven thin and ill favoured kine that came up after them *are*
seven years; and the seven empty ears blasted with the east wind shall be
seven years of famine.
28 This *is* the thing which I have spoken unto Pharaoh: What God *is*
about to do he sheweth unto Pharaoh.
29 Behold, there come seven years of great plenty throughout all the land
of Egypt:
30 And there shall arise after them seven years of famine; and all the
plenty shall be forgotten in the land of Egypt; and the famine shall
consume the land;
31 And the plenty shall not be known in the land by reason of that famine
following; for it *shall be* very grievous.

41:32 Gen 37:9 Job 33:14 Isa 14:24; 46:10
41:33 Gen 41:39 Dan 4:27
41:34 Ex 18:19 Deut 1:13 2 Chron 34:12
41:35 Gen 41:48
41:36 Gen 47:13

32 And for that the dream was doubled unto Pharaoh twice; *it is* because
the thing *is* established by God, and God will shortly bring it to pass.
33 Now therefore let Pharaoh look out a man discreet and wise, and set
him over the land of Egypt.
34 Let Pharaoh do *this*, and let him appoint officers over the land, and take
up the fifth part of the land of Egypt in the seven plenteous years.
35 And let them gather all the food of those good years that come, and lay
up corn under the hand of Pharaoh, and let them keep food in the cities.
36 And that food shall be for store to the land against the seven years of
famine, which shall be in the land of Egypt; that the land perish not
through the famine.

5. The Pharaoh Appoints Joseph to a High Position

41:37 Prov 25:11 Acts 7:10

37 ¶And the thing was good in the eyes of Pharaoh, and in the eyes of all
his servants.

41:16 Joseph disclaimed any prophetic gifts and gave the glory to God. Thus he was a missionary to a pagan ruler, bearing testimony to his faith in the true God.

[38]And Pharaoh said unto his servants, Can we find *such a one* as this *is*, a
man in whom the Spirit of God *is?*
[39]And Pharaoh said unto Joseph, Forasmuch as God hath shewed thee
all this, *there is* none so discreet and wise as thou *art:*
[40]Thou shalt be over my house, and according unto thy word shall all my
people be ruled: only in the throne will I be greater than thou.
[41]And Pharaoh said unto Joseph, See, I have set thee over all the land of
Egypt.
[42]And Pharaoh took off his ring from his hand, and put it upon Joseph's
hand, and arrayed him in vestures of fine linen, and put a gold chain about
his neck;
[43]And he made him to ride in the second chariot which he had; and they
cried before him, Bow the knee: and he made him *ruler* over all the land of
Egypt.
[44]And Pharaoh said unto Joseph, I *am* Pharaoh, and without thee shall
no man lift up his hand or foot in all the land of Egypt.
[45]And Pharaoh called Joseph's name Zaph'nath-pa-a-ne'ah; and he gave
him to wife As'e-nath the daughter of Pot'i-phe'rah priest of On. And
Joseph went out over *all* the land of Egypt.

☆41:38 Job 32:8; Dan 4:8, 18; Dan 5:11, 14
41:39 Gen 41:28, 33
41:40 Gen 39:4, 22; 42:6; 45:8; Ps 105:21; Prov 22:29; Acts 7:10
41:41 Gen 42:6; Esth 10:3; Prov 17:2; Dan 6:3
41:42 Esth 3:10; Esth 6:8
41:43 Gen 42:6, 26, 30, 33; Esth 6:8
41:44 Gen 45:8; Ps 105:21, 22
☆**41:45** Gen 41:50; Ezek 30:17

6. Joseph's Interpretation Comes True

[46]¶And Joseph *was* thirty years old when he stood before Pharaoh king of
Egypt. And Joseph went out from the presence of Pharaoh, and went
throughout all the land of Egypt.
[47]And in the seven plenteous years the earth brought forth by handfuls.
[48]And he gathered up all the food of the seven years, which were in the
land of Egypt, and laid up the food in the cities: the food of the field, which
was round about every city, laid he up in the same.
[49]And Joseph gathered corn as the sand of the sea, very much, until he
left numbering; for *it was* without number.
[50]And unto Joseph were born two sons before the years of famine came,
which As'e-nath the daughter of Pot'i-phe'rah priest of On bare unto him.
[51]And Joseph called the name of the firstborn Ma-nas'seh: For God, *said*
he, hath made me forget all my toil, and all my father's house.
[52]And the name of the second called he E'phra-im: For God hath caused
me to be fruitful in the land of my affliction.
[53]¶And the seven years of plenteousness, that was in the land of Egypt,
were ended.
[54]And the seven years of dearth began to come, according as Joseph had
said: and the dearth was in all lands; but in all the land of Egypt there was
bread.

☆**41:46** Gen 37:2; 50:22
41:47 Gen 26:12
41:48 Gen 41:34–36; 47:21
41:49 Judg 6:5; 7:12; 1 Sam 13:5
41:50 Gen 41:45; 46:20
☆**41:51** Gen 48:5; Deut 33:17; Prov 31:7
☆**41:52** Gen 49:22
41:54 Gen 41:27; 45:11; Acts 7:11

41:38 The Pharaoh bears testimony to the fact that Joseph's God is with him and in him. He saw that Joseph had the gift of wisdom, which is one of the gifts of the Holy Spirit to some of the people of God, then and now.
41:45 *Zaphnath-paaneah.* The meaning of this is uncertain. Suggestions include: "the god speaks and he lives," or "the god said: he will live," or "He has the god-like power of life and death" (TLB). *he gave him to wife . . . the daughter of Poti-pherah priest of On* (Heliopolis). Heliopolis was a city in Northern Egypt noted for its chief temple of the sun dedicated to the sun god Re. References to it may be found in Isa. 19:18 and Jer. 43:13. Joseph married into a family of high nobility; his father-in-law was a major priest and politician of that time.
41:46 *Joseph was thirty years old.* Thirteen years had passed since Joseph dreamed his dreams. Now he has risen dramatically from being a slave of Potiphar to a position of prominence and eminence. But more years would have to pass before his most important dream could be fulfilled—the time when his brothers would bow before him. By this time Joseph spoke the Egyptian tongue and had learned Egyptian manners.
41:51, 52 *Manasseh,* Joseph's firstborn, means "making to forget." His second son was named *Ephraim.* This name comes from a Hebrew word meaning "to be fruitful."

41:55 Gen 41:40, 41, 49; Jer 14:1

55 And when all the land of Egypt was famished, the people cried to
Pharaoh for bread: and Pharaoh said unto all the Egyptians, Go unto
Joseph; what he saith to you, do.
56 And the famine was over all the face of the earth: and Joseph opened
all the storehouses, and sold unto the Egyptians; and the famine waxed sore
in the land of Egypt.

41:57 Gen 42:5; 50:20; Ps 105:16

57 And all countries came into Egypt to Joseph for to buy *corn;* because
that the famine was *so* sore in all lands.

F. JOSEPH'S BROTHERS COME TO EGYPT

1. Jacob Sends Ten Sons to Egypt for Food

42:1 Acts 7:12

42 NOW when Jacob saw that there was corn in Egypt, Jacob said
unto his sons, Why do ye look one upon another?

42:2 Gen 43:2; 45:9

2 And he said, Behold, I have heard that there is corn in Egypt: get you
down thither, and buy for us from thence; that we may live, and not die.

42:3 Gen 42:13 **42:4** Gen 43:8

3 ¶And Joseph's ten brethren went down to buy corn in Egypt.
4 But Benjamin, Joseph's brother, Jacob sent not with his brethren; for he
said, Lest peradventure mischief befall him.

42:5 Gen 41:57; Acts 7:11

5 And the sons of Israel came to buy *corn* among those that came: for the
famine was in the land of Canaan.

2. Joseph and His Brothers Meet

42:6 Ps 105:16–21

6 And Joseph *was* the governor over the land, *and* he *it was* that sold to all
the people of the land: and Joseph's brethren came, and bowed down
themselves before him *with* their faces to the earth.

42:7 Gen 42:14–17

7 And Joseph saw his brethren, and he knew them, but made himself
strange unto them, and spake roughly unto them; and he said unto them,
Whence come ye? And they said, From the land of Canaan to buy food.

42:8☆ Gen 37:2, 6–9 **42:9** Gen 42:16, 30–34 **42:10** Gen 27:29; 37:8; 42:2 **42:11** Gen 42:19, 31–34

8 And Joseph knew his brethren, but they knew not him.
9 And Joseph remembered the dreams which he dreamed of them, and
said unto them, Ye *are* spies; to see the nakedness of the land ye are come.
10 And they said unto him, Nay, my lord, but to buy food are thy servants
come.
11 We *are* all one man's sons; we *are* true *men,* thy servants are no spies.
12 And he said unto them, Nay, but to see the nakedness of the land ye are
come.

42:13 Gen 37:30; 42:4; 43:7; 44:20; 46:8–26

13 And they said, Thy servants *are* twelve brethren, the sons of one man in
the land of Canaan; and, behold, the youngest *is* this day with our father,
and one *is* not.

42:14 Gen 42:9

14 And Joseph said unto them, That *is it* that I spake unto you, saying, Ye
are spies:

42:15 Gen 42:34

15 Hereby ye shall be proved: By the life of Pharaoh ye shall not go forth
hence, except your youngest brother come hither.
16 Send one of you, and let him fetch your brother, and ye shall be kept in
prison, that your words may be proved, whether *there be any* truth in you:
or else by the life of Pharaoh surely ye *are* spies.

42:17 Gen 40:4

17 And he put them all together into ward three days.

3. Joseph Sends His Brothers Home with Free Food

42:18 Gen 20:11; Lev 25:43

18 And Joseph said unto them the third day, This do, and live: *for* I fear
God:

42:8 *they knew not him.* Little did the sons of Jacob know that the man they faced was their younger brother, Joseph. However, Joseph knew them. Verse 9 makes it clear that he had a long memory and had not forgotten his dreams or their wickedness.

19 If ye *be* true *men,* let one of your brethren be bound in the house of
your prison: go ye, carry corn for the famine of your houses:
20 But bring your youngest brother unto me; so shall your words be
verified, and ye shall not die. And they did so.

42:20 Gen 42:34 43:15

21 ¶And they said one to another, We *are* verily guilty concerning our
brother, in that we saw the anguish of his soul, when he besought us, and
we would not hear; therefore is this distress come upon us.

☆**42:21** Gen 37:23–28 41:9 Num 32:23

22 And Reuben answered them, saying, Spake I not unto you, saying, Do
not sin against the child; and ye would not hear? therefore, behold, also his
blood is required.

42:22 Gen 9:6 37:21, 22 Lk 23:41

23 And they knew not that Joseph understood *them;* for he spake unto
them by an interpreter.
24 And he turned himself about from them, and wept; and returned to
them again, and communed with them, and took from them Simeon, and
bound him before their eyes.

42:24 Gen 43:14, 23, 30; 45:14

25 ¶Then Joseph commanded to fill their sacks with corn, and to restore
every man's money into his sack, and to give them provision for the way:
and thus did he unto them.

42:25 Gen 44:1

26 And they laded their asses with the corn, and departed thence.
27 And as one of them opened his sack to give his ass provender in the inn,
he espied his money; for, behold, it *was* in his sack's mouth.

42:27 Gen 43:21 Ex 4:24

28 And he said unto his brethren, My money is restored; and, lo, *it is* even
in my sack: and their heart failed *them,* and they were afraid, saying one to
another, What *is* this *that* God hath done unto us?

42:28 Gen 27:33 Isa 45:7 Lam 3:37

29 ¶And they came unto Jacob their father unto the land of Canaan, and
told him all that befell unto them; saying,

4. Joseph's Brothers Tell Jacob Their Story

30 The man, *who is* the lord of the land, spake roughly to us, and took us
for spies of the country.

42:30 Gen 42:7

31 And we said unto him, We *are* true *men;* we are no spies:

42:31 Gen 42:11

32 We *be* twelve brethren, sons of our father; one *is* not, and the youngest
is this day with our father in the land of Canaan.

42:32 Gen 42:13

33 And the man, the lord of the country, said unto us, Hereby shall I know
that ye *are* true *men;* leave one of your brethren *here* with me, and take *food*
for the famine of your households, and be gone:

42:33 Gen 42:19

34 And bring your youngest brother unto me: then shall I know that ye *are*
no spies, but *that* ye *are* true *men: so* will I deliver you your brother, and ye
shall traffick in the land.

42:34 Gen 42:20

35 ¶And it came to pass as they emptied their sacks, that, behold, every
man's bundle of money *was* in his sack: and when *both* they and their father
saw the bundles of money, they were afraid.

42:35 Gen 42:27 43:12, 21

36 And Jacob their father said unto them, Me have ye bereaved *of my*
children: Joseph *is* not, and Simeon *is* not, and ye will take Benjamin *away:*
all these things are against me.

☆**42:36** Gen 43:14 44:20–22

42:21 *We are verily guilty concerning our brother.* The function of the conscience is to bring to mind sins committed long ago; in this instance it operated more than twenty years after the crime was committed. Time neither washes away the guilt of sin nor does it blot out the records of conscience. In 42:22 Reuben bespeaks his own innocence and the fact that he had been an advocate for Joseph. His brothers therefore sinned after they had been admonished to do right. This furthered their guilt.

42:36 *Simeon is no more.* Jacob bemoans the loss of both Joseph and Simeon. He is firm, at this point, that Benjamin will never be permitted to go to Egypt. Jacob did not yet know that God was working all things in his favor. "Through our ignorance and mistake, and the weakness of our faith, we often apprehend that to be against us which is really for us."* Joseph kept Simeon as a hostage. Simeon was Jacob's second son by Leah. Apparently Joseph let Reuben, the firstborn by Leah, go back because he exhibited concern for Joseph and would have freed him from the pit if he had been able to do so.

42:37 Gen 43:9; 44:32

37 And Reuben spake unto his father, saying, Slay my two sons, if I bring
him not to thee: deliver him into my hand, and I will bring him to thee
again.

42:38 Gen 37:35 44:20–22, 29 1 Kgs 2:6

38 And he said, My son shall not go down with you; for his brother is
dead, and he is left alone: if mischief befall him by the way in the which ye
go, then shall ye bring down my gray hairs with sorrow to the grave.

G. JOSEPH'S BROTHERS' SECOND TRIP TO EGYPT

1. Jacob Lets Benjamin Accompany His Brothers

43:1 Gen 41:5, 6, 7 42:5

43:2 Gen 43:15

43 AND the famine *was* sore in the land.
2 And it came to pass, when they had eaten up the corn which
they had brought out of Egypt, their father said unto them, Go again, buy
us a little food.

43:3 Gen 42:15 44:23

3 And Judah spake unto him, saying, The man did solemnly protest unto
us, saying, Ye shall not see my face, except your brother *be* with you.
4 If thou wilt send our brother with us, we will go down and buy thee
food:

43:5 Gen 44:26

5 But if thou wilt not send *him,* we will not go down: for the man said
unto us, Ye shall not see my face, except your brother *be* with you.
6 And Israel said, Wherefore dealt ye *so* ill with me, *as* to tell the man
whether ye had yet a brother?

43:7 Gen 42:13 43:27

7 And they said, The man asked us straitly of our state, and of our
kindred, saying, *Is* your father yet alive? have ye *another* brother? and we
told him according to the tenor of these words: could we certainly know
that he would say, Bring your brother down?

43:8 Gen 42:2 44:26; 45:18, 19

8 And Judah said unto Israel his father, Send the lad with me, and we will
arise and go; that we may live, and not die, both we, and thou, *and* also our
little ones.

43:9 Gen 42:37 44:32 Heb 7:22

9 I will be surety for him; of my hand shalt thou require him: if I bring
him not unto thee, and set him before thee, then let me bear the blame for
ever:
10 For except we had lingered, surely now we had returned this second
time.

43:11 Gen 32:13 37:25; 43:25

11 And their father Israel said unto them, If *it must be* so now, do this;
take of the best fruits in the land in your vessels, and carry down the man
a present, a little balm, and a little honey, spices, and myrrh, nuts, and
almonds:

43:12 Gen 42:35

12 And take double money in your hand; and the money that was brought
again in the mouth of your sacks, carry *it* again in your hand; peradventure
it *was* an oversight:

43:13 Gen 42:38; 43:4

43:14☆ Gen 39:21 42:36 Ps 106:46

13 Take also your brother, and arise, go again unto the man:
14 And God Almighty give you mercy before the man, that he may send
away your other brother, and Benjamin. If I be bereaved *of my children,* I
am bereaved.

2. Joseph Eats with His Half Brothers and Benjamin

15 ¶And the men took that present, and they took double money in their
hand, and Benjamin; and rose up, and went down to Egypt, and stood
before Joseph.

43:14 Jacob finally yielded to his sons and agreed to let Benjamin go with them to Egypt. But he prayed to God for mercy and for the deliverance of Simeon and Benjamin. This was Jacob at his best. He was pious and prayerful. "Those who would find mercy with men must seek it from God who has all hearts in his hands, and turns them as he pleases."* God not only delivered Simeon and Benjamin, he also brought Joseph back as it were from the dead. *God Almighty* is, in the Hebrew, *El Shaddai* (see note to Gen. 17:1).

[16]And when Joseph saw Benjamin with them, he said to the ruler of his
house, Bring *these* men home, and slay, and make ready; for *these* men shall
dine with me at noon.
[17]And the man did as Joseph bade; and the man brought the men into
Joseph's house.
[18]And the men were afraid, because they were brought into Joseph's
house; and they said, Because of the money that was returned in our sacks
at the first time are we brought in; that he may seek occasion against us,
and fall upon us, and take us for bondmen, and our asses.
[19]And they came near to the steward of Joseph's house, and they
communed with him at the door of the house,
[20]And said, O sir, we came indeed down at the first time to buy food:
[21]And it came to pass, when we came to the inn, that we opened our
sacks, and, behold, *every* man's money *was* in the mouth of his sack, our
money in full weight: and we have brought it again in our hand.
[22]And other money have we brought down in our hands to buy food: we
cannot tell who put our money in our sacks.
[23]And he said, Peace *be* to you, fear not: your God, and the God of your
father, hath given you treasure in your sacks: I had your money. And he
brought Simeon out unto them.
[24]And the man brought the men into Joseph's house, and gave *them*
water, and they washed their feet; and he gave their asses provender.
[25]And they made ready the present against Joseph came at noon: for they
heard that they should eat bread there.
[26]¶And when Joseph came home, they brought him the present which *was*
in their hand into the house, and bowed themselves to him to the earth.
[27]And he asked them of *their* welfare, and said, *Is* your father well, the
old man of whom ye spake? *Is* he yet alive?
[28]And they answered, Thy servant our father *is* in good health, he *is* yet
alive. And they bowed down their heads, and made obeisance.
[29]And he lifted up his eyes, and saw his brother Benjamin, his mother's
son, and said, *Is* this your younger brother, of whom ye spake unto me?
And he said, God be gracious unto thee, my son.
[30]And Joseph made haste; for his bowels did yearn upon his brother: and
he sought *where* to weep; and he entered into *his* chamber, and wept there.
[31]And he washed his face, and went out, and refrained himself, and said,
Set on bread.
[32]And they set on for him by himself, and for them by themselves, and
for the Egyptians, which did eat with him, by themselves: because the
Egyptians might not eat bread with the Hebrews; for that *is* an abomina-
tion unto the Egyptians.
[33]And they sat before him, the firstborn according to his birthright, and
the youngest according to his youth: and the men marvelled one at another.
[34]And he took *and sent* messes unto them from before him: but
Benjamin's mess was five times so much as any of theirs. And they drank,
and were merry with him.

43:16 Gen 31:54; 44:1
43:18 Gen 42:28, 35
43:21 Gen 42:27, 35 43:12
43:22 Gen 42:25
43:23 Gen 42:24
43:24 Gen 18:4; 24:32 Lk 7:44
43:26 Gen 42:6
43:27 Gen 43:7; 45:3 Ex 18:7
43:28 Ex 18:7
☆**43:29** Num 6:25 Ps 67:1
43:30 Gen 42:24 45:2, 14, 15 46:29
43:31 Gen 43:25; 45:1 Isa 42:14
43:32 Gen 46:34 Ex 8:26
43:33 Gen 44:12

43:29 *his mother's son.* Except for Benjamin, all Joseph's brothers were born of different mothers than he. He and Benjamin were the sons of Rachel, Jacob's beloved. He had not seen Benjamin for more than twenty years. Great changes in his appearance would have taken place. Joseph probably would not have recognized Benjamin in a crowd of people. This meeting was a touching reminder to him of their dead mother and of his love for his full brother.

3. Joseph's Soldiers Seize Benjamin

44:1 Gen 42:25; 43:16

44 AND he commanded the steward of his house, saying, Fill the men's sacks *with* food, as much as they can carry, and put every man's money in his sack's mouth.

2 And put my cup, the silver cup, in the sack's mouth of the youngest, and his corn money. And he did according to the word that Joseph had spoken.

3 As soon as the morning was light, the men were sent away, they and their asses.

44:4 Prov 17:13

4 *And* when they were gone out of the city, *and* not *yet* far off, Joseph said unto his steward, Up, follow after the men; and when thou dost overtake them, say unto them, Wherefore have ye rewarded evil for good?

44:5 Gen 30:27; Lev 19:26; Deut. 18:10–14

5 *Is* not this *it* in which my lord drinketh, and whereby indeed he divineth? ye have done evil in so doing.

6 ¶And he overtook them, and he spake unto them these same words.

7 And they said unto him, Wherefore saith my lord these words? God forbid that thy servants should do according to this thing:

44:8 Gen 43:21; Ex 20:15

8 Behold, the money, which we found in our sacks' mouths, we brought again unto thee out of the land of Canaan: how then should we steal out of thy lord's house silver or gold?

44:9 Gen 31:32; 44:16; Ps 7:3–5

9 With whomsoever of thy servants it be found, both let him die, and we also will be my lord's bondmen.

10 And he said, Now also *let* it *be* according unto your words: he with whom it is found shall be my servant; and ye shall be blameless.

11 Then they speedily took down every man his sack to the ground, and opened every man his sack.

44:12 Gen 44:2

12 And he searched, *and* began at the eldest, and left at the youngest: and the cup was found in Benjamin's sack.

44:13 Gen 37:29, 34; Num 14:6

13 Then they rent their clothes, and laded every man his ass, and returned to the city.

4. Joseph's Brothers Fall before Him and Beg

44:14☆ Gen 43:26

14 ¶And Judah and his brethren came to Joseph's house; for he *was* yet there: and they fell before him on the ground.

44:15 Gen 41:38; 44:5

15 And Joseph said unto them, What deed *is* this that ye have done? wot ye not that such a man as I can certainly divine?

44:16☆ Gen 42:21; 43:8, 9; Num 32:23; Ezra 9:10

16 And Judah said, What shall we say unto my lord? what shall we speak? or how shall we clear ourselves? God hath found out the iniquity of thy servants: behold, we *are* my lord's servants, both we, and *he* also with whom the cup is found.

17 And he said, God forbid that I should do so: *but* the man in whose hand the cup is found, he shall be my servant; and as for you, get you up in peace unto your father.

44:18 Gen 37:7, 8; 41:40

18 ¶Then Judah came near unto him, and said, Oh my lord, let thy servant, I pray thee, speak a word in my lord's ears, and let not thine anger burn against thy servant: for thou *art* even as Pharaoh.

44:19 Gen 42:13–16; 43:7

19 My lord asked his servants, saying, Have ye a father, or a brother?

44:14 When Joseph's brothers "fell before him on the ground," it was the first fulfillment of the dream Joseph had had when he was seventeen years old. Here his brothers acknowledged that they were his servants or vassals. After the death of their father they fell down before him again (50:18).

44:16 Judah becomes the spokesman for his brothers. Despite their sins Judah indicates that they believe in the God of their father, and he acknowledges their guilt. In verse 32 Judah indicates that he had become surety for the return of Benjamin. He pleads for mercy and offers himself as a substitute for Benjamin.

20 And we said unto my lord, We have a father, an old man, and a child of
his old age, a little one; and his brother is dead, and he alone is left of his
mother, and his father loveth him.
21 And thou saidst unto thy servants, Bring him down unto me, that I may
set mine eyes upon him.

44:21 Gen 42:20, 34 43:7

22 And we said unto my lord, The lad cannot leave his father: for *if* he
should leave his father, *his father* would die.

44:22 Gen 42:38

23 And thou saidst unto thy servants, Except your youngest brother come
down with you, ye shall see my face no more.

44:23 Gen 42:20

24 And it came to pass when we came up unto thy servant my father, we
told him the words of my lord.

44:24 Gen 42:29–34

25 And our father said, Go again, *and* buy us a little food.

44:25 Gen 43:2

26 And we said, We cannot go down: if our youngest brother be with us,
then will we go down: for we may not see the man's face, except our
youngest brother *be* with us.

44:26 Gen 43:4, 5

27 And thy servant my father said unto us, Ye know that my wife bare me
two *sons:*

44:27 Gen 46:19

28 And the one went out from me, and I said, Surely he is torn in pieces;
and I saw him not since:

44:28 Gen 37:33

29 And if ye take this also from me, and mischief befall him, ye shall bring
down my gray hairs with sorrow to the grave.

44:29 Gen 42:38

30 Now therefore when I come to thy servant my father, and the lad *be* not
with us; seeing that his life is bound up in the lad's life;

44:30 1 Sam 18:1

31 It shall come to pass, when he seeth that the lad *is* not *with us,* that he
will die: and thy servants shall bring down the gray hairs of thy servant our
father with sorrow to the grave.
32 For thy servant became surety for the lad unto my father, saying, If I
bring him not unto thee, then I shall bear the blame to my father for ever.

44:32 Gen 43:9

33 Now therefore, I pray thee, let thy servant abide instead of the lad a
bondman to my lord; and let the lad go up with his brethren.
34 For how shall I go up to my father, and the lad *be* not with me? lest
peradventure I see the evil that shall come on my father.

5. Joseph Tells Them Who He Is

45 THEN Joseph could not refrain himself before all them that stood
by him; and he cried, Cause every man to go out from me. And
there stood no man with him, while Joseph made himself known unto his
brethren.

45:1 Gen 42:24 43:30

2 And he wept aloud: and the Egyptians and the house of Pharaoh heard.
3 And Joseph said unto his brethren, I *am* Joseph; doth my father yet
live? And his brethren could not answer him; for they were troubled at his
presence.

45:3 Gen 50:17–19 Mt 14:27 Acts 7:13

4 And Joseph said unto his brethren, Come near to me, I pray you. And
they came near. And he said, I *am* Joseph your brother, whom ye sold into
Egypt.

45:4 Gen 37:28

5 Now therefore be not grieved, nor angry with yourselves, that ye sold me
hither: for God did send me before you to preserve life.

45:5 Gen 50:20

6 For these two years *hath* the famine *been* in the land: and yet *there are*
five years, in the which *there shall* neither *be* earing nor harvest.

45:6 Gen 41:29, 30 47:18, 23

7 And God sent me before you to preserve you a posterity in the earth,
and to save your lives by a great deliverance.

45:8☆ Gen 41:39; Judg 17:10; Ps 105:21; Jn 15:16; 19:11

8 So now *it was* not you *that* sent me hither, but God: and he hath made me a father to Pharaoh, and lord of all his house, and a ruler throughout all the land of Egypt.

45:9 Acts 7:14

9 Haste ye, and go up to my father, and say unto him, Thus saith thy son Joseph, God hath made me lord of all Egypt: come down unto me, tarry not:

45:10☆ Gen 46:28, 34; 47:6; Ex 8:22

10 And thou shalt dwell in the land of Goshen, and thou shalt be near unto me, thou, and thy children, and thy children's children, and thy flocks, and thy herds, and all that thou hast:

45:11 Gen 45:8; 47:12

11 And there will I nourish thee; for yet *there are* five years of famine; lest thou, and thy household, and all that thou hast, come to poverty.

12 And, behold, your eyes see, and the eyes of my brother Benjamin, that *it is* my mouth that speaketh unto you.

45:13 Acts 7:14

13 And ye shall tell my father of all my glory in Egypt, and of all that ye have seen; and ye shall haste and bring down my father hither.

45:14 Gen 43:30; 46:29

14 And he fell upon his brother Benjamin's neck, and wept; and Benjamin wept upon his neck.

15 Moreover he kissed all his brethren, and wept upon them: and after that his brethren talked with him.

6. The Pharaoh Encourages Joseph's Family to Come to Egypt

45:16 Acts 7:13

16 ¶And the fame thereof was heard in Pharaoh's house, saying, Joseph's brethren are come: and it pleased Pharaoh well, and his servants.

45:17 Gen 42:25; 44:1

17 And Pharaoh said unto Joseph, Say unto thy brethren, This do ye; lade your beasts, and go, get you unto the land of Canaan;

45:18 Gen 27:28; 47:6

18 And take your father and your households, and come unto me: and I will give you the good of the land of Egypt, and ye shall eat the fat of the land.

45:19 Gen 45:27; 46:5

19 Now thou art commanded, this do ye; take you wagons out of the land of Egypt for your little ones, and for your wives, and bring your father, and come.

45:20 Gen 20:15

20 Also regard not your stuff; for the good of all the land of Egypt *is* yours.

21 And the children of Israel did so: and Joseph gave them wagons, according to the commandment of Pharaoh, and gave them provision for the way.

45:22 Gen 43:34; Judg 14:12; 2 Kgs 5:5

22 To all of them he gave each man changes of raiment; but to Benjamin he gave three hundred *pieces* of silver, and five changes of raiment.

45:23 Gen 43:11

23 And to his father he sent after this *manner;* ten asses laden with the good things of Egypt, and ten she asses laden with corn and bread and meat for his father by the way.

45:24☆ Gen 37:22; 42:21; Ps 133:1–3

24 So he sent his brethren away, and they departed: and he said unto them, See that ye fall not out by the way.

25 ¶And they went up out of Egypt, and came into the land of Canaan unto Jacob their father,

45:26 Gen 37:31–35

26 And told him, saying, Joseph *is* yet alive, and he *is* governor over all the land of Egypt. And Jacob's heart fainted, for he believed them not.

45:8 Joseph states that it was God who has sent him to Egypt, even though his trip was brought about by the evil acts of his own brothers. He was a firm believer in the providence of God, who knows the end from the beginning and who accomplishes all things according to his divine will. Joseph's brothers wanted to defeat his dreams by selling him into slavery. But God turned their evil into good for Joseph and, ultimately, for them as well.

45:10 *Goshen,* (not the Goshen of Josh. 10:41, rather, that of Egypt, located in the eastern section of the Nile Delta, which was fertile grazing land). This verse confirms 47:6, where Pharaoh tells Joseph to settle his father and his kin in Goshen.

45:24 *See that ye fall not out by the way,* or "Don't quarrel along the way." Joseph knew that his brothers were not wholly sanctified, so his admonition was fitting.

27 And they told him all the words of Joseph, which he had said unto
them: and when he saw the wagons which Joseph had sent to carry him, the
spirit of Jacob their father revived:
28 And Israel said, *It is* enough; Joseph my son *is* yet alive: I will go and
see him before I die.

H. JACOB TRAVELS TO EGYPT TO JOSEPH

46 AND Israel took his journey with all that he had, and came to
Be′er-she′ba, and offered sacrifices unto the God of his father Isaac.
2 And God spake unto Israel in the visions of the night, and said, Jacob,
Jacob. And he said, Here *am* I.
3 And he said, I *am* God, the God of thy father: fear not to go down into
Egypt; for I will there make of thee a great nation:
4 I will go down with thee into Egypt; and I will also surely bring thee up
again: and Joseph shall put his hand upon thine eyes.
5 And Jacob rose up from Be′er-she′ba: and the sons of Israel carried
Jacob their father, and their little ones, and their wives, in the wagons
which Pharaoh had sent to carry him.
6 And they took their cattle, and their goods, which they had gotten in the
land of Canaan, and came into Egypt, Jacob, and all his seed with him:
7 His sons, and his sons' sons with him, his daughters, and his sons'
daughters, and all his seed brought he with him into Egypt.

I. THE DESCENDANTS OF ISRAEL (JACOB)

8 ¶And these *are* the names of the children of Israel, which came into
Egypt, Jacob and his sons: Reuben, Jacob's firstborn.
9 And the sons of Reuben; Ha′noch, and Phal′lu, and Hez′ron, and
Car′mi.
10 ¶And the sons of Simeon; Je-mu′el, and Ja′min, and O′had, and
Ja′chin, and Zo′har, and Sha′ul the son of a Canaanitish woman.
11 ¶And the sons of Levi; Ger′shon, Ko′hath, and Me-ra′ri.
12 ¶And the sons of Judah; Er, and O′nan, and She′lah, and Pha′rez, and
Ze′rah: but Er and O′nan died in the land of Canaan. And the sons of
Pha′rez were Hez′ron and Ha′mul.
13 ¶And the sons of Is′sa-char; To′la, and Phu′vah, and Job, and
Shim′ron.
14 ¶And the sons of Zeb′u-lun; Se′red, and E′lon, and Jah′le-el.
15 These *be* the sons of Leah, which she bare unto Jacob in Pa′dan-a′ram,
with his daughter Dinah: all the souls of his sons and his daughters *were*
thirty and three.
16 ¶And the sons of Gad; Ziph′i-on, and Hag′gi, Shu′ni, and Ez′bon, E′ri,
and Ar′o-di, and A-re′li.
17 ¶And the sons of Asher; Jim′nah, and Ish′u-ah, and Is′u-i, and Be-ri′ah,
and Se′rah their sister: and the sons of Be-ri′ah; He′ber, and Mal′chi-el.
18 These *are* the sons of Zilpah, whom Laban gave to Leah his daughter,
and these she bare unto Jacob, *even* sixteen souls.
19 The sons of Rachel Jacob's wife; Joseph, and Benjamin.

45:27 Gen 45:19, 21; Judg 15:19; 1 Sam 30:12
45:28 Gen 46:30; Lk 2:28–30
46:1 Gen 21:14; 26:22; 28:10, 13; 31:42; 33:20; 35:7
46:2 Gen 22:11; 31:11; Num 12:6
☆**46:3** Gen 15:1; 17:1; 26:2; Isa 41:10
☆**46:4** Gen 28–15; 48:21; 50:5; Ex 3:8
46:5 Gen 45:19
46:6 Num 20:15; Deut 10:22; 26:5; Acts 7:14, 15
46:8 Gen 29:32; 35:23; 49:3
46:9 Num 26:5; 1 Chron 5:3
46:10 Gen 29:33; 49:5; 1 Chron 4:24
46:11 Gen 29:34; 35:23; 1 Chron 6:1
☆**46:12** Gen 29:35; 38:3–11; 49:8; Deut 33:7; 1 Chron 2:3
46:13 Gen 30:18; 49:14; 1 Chron 7:1
46:14 Gen 30:20; 49:13
46:15 Gen 30:21; 49:31
46:16 Gen 30:11; 35:26; 49:19; Num 26:15; 1 Chron 5:11
46:17 Gen 30:13; 49:20; Num 26:44; 1 Chron 7:30
46:19 Gen 30:24; 35:18

46:3, 4 Some believe that Egypt always represents sin and compromise. Thus they suppose that Jacob's going to Egypt was against the directive will of God. This is not so, however, for God told Jacob to do this in order to develop a great nation which would be strong and numerous enough to conquer Canaan.

46:12 *Hezron and Hamul,* grandsons of Judah, were included to take the places of Er and Onan, who died in Canaan. They were probably born in Egypt. This is analogous to including Manasseh and Ephraim, who were born in Egypt, as among those who "came into Egypt."

46:20 Gen 41:45, 50–52
20¶And unto Joseph in the land of Egypt were born Ma-nas′seh and
E′phra-im, which As′e-nath the daughter of Pot′i-phe′rah priest of On bare
unto him.

46:21 Num 26:38; 1 Chron 7:6
21¶And the sons of Benjamin *were* Be′lah, and Be′cher, and Ash′bel,
Ge′ra, and Na′a-man, E′hi, and Rosh, Mup′pim, and Hup′pim, and Ard.

46:22 Gen 35:24
22These *are* the sons of Rachel, which were born to Jacob: all the souls
were fourteen.

46:23 Gen 30:6; 35:25; 49:16; Num 26:42
23¶And the sons of Dan; Hu′shim.

46:24 Gen 30:8; 49:21; Num 26:48; 1 Chron 7:13
24¶And the sons of Naph′ta-li; Jah′ze-el, and Gu′ni, and Je′zer, and
Shil′lem.
25These *are* the sons of Bil′hah, which Laban gave unto Rachel his
daughter, and she bare these unto Jacob: all the souls *were* seven.

46:25 Gen 35:25
26All the souls that came with Jacob into Egypt, which came out of his
loins, besides Jacob's sons' wives, all the souls *were* threescore and six;

46:27☆ Ex 1:5; 24:1; Deut 10:22; Acts 7:14
27And the sons of Joseph, which were born him in Egypt, *were* two souls:
all the souls of the house of Jacob, which came into Egypt, *were* threescore
and ten.

J. THE SETTLEMENT IN EGYPT

46:28 Gen 43:8; 45:10; 47:1
28¶And he sent Judah before him unto Joseph, to direct his face unto
Goshen; and they came into the land of Goshen.

46:29 Gen 33:4; 45:10, 14; Lk 15:20
29And Joseph made ready his chariot, and went up to meet Israel his
father, to Goshen, and presented himself unto him; and he fell on his neck,
and wept on his neck a good while.

46:30 Gen 45:28; Lk 2:29
30And Israel said unto Joseph, Now let me die, since I have seen thy face,
because thou *art* yet alive.

46:31 Gen 45:16; 47:1
31And Joseph said unto his brethren, and unto his father's house, I will go
up, and shew Pharaoh, and say unto him, My brethren, and my father's
house, which *were* in the land of Canaan, are come unto me;

46:32 Gen 37:2, 14; 47:3
32And the men *are* shepherds, for their trade hath been to feed cattle; and
they have brought their flocks, and their herds, and all that they have.

46:33 Gen 47:2
33And it shall come to pass, when Pharaoh shall call you, and shall say,
What *is* your occupation?

46:34 Gen 13:7; 43:32; 47:4
34That ye shall say, Thy servants' trade hath been about cattle from our
youth even until now, both we, *and* also our fathers: that ye may dwell in
the land of Goshen; for every shepherd *is* an abomination unto the
Egyptians.

47:1 Gen 46:31
47 THEN Joseph came and told Pharaoh, and said, My father and my
brethren, and their flocks, and their herds, and all that they have,
are come out of the land of Canaan; and, behold, they *are* in the land of
Goshen.

47:2 Acts 7:13
2And he took some of his brethren, *even* five men, and presented them
unto Pharaoh.

47:3 Gen 46:33; Amos 7:14
3And Pharaoh said unto his brethren, What *is* your occupation? And
they said unto Pharaoh, Thy servants *are* shepherds, both we, *and* also our
fathers.

47:4 Gen 15:13; 43:1; 46:34; Deut 26:5
4They said moreover unto Pharaoh, For to sojourn in the land are we
come; for thy servants have no pasture for their flocks; for the famine *is*
sore in the land of Canaan: now therefore, we pray thee, let thy servants
dwell in the land of Goshen.

46:27 Compare with Acts 7:14, where Joseph is said to have had seventy-five children. This number was probably taken from the Septuagint (LXX—Greek translation of the Old Testament Scriptures) which included five descendants of Manasseh and Ephraim, sons of Joseph. This meant there were five more people than the seventy of 46:27 of the Masoretic text (the standard Hebrew text of the Old Testament).

5And Pharaoh spake unto Joseph, saying, Thy father and thy brethren
are come unto thee:
6The land of Egypt *is* before thee; in the best of the land make thy father
and brethren to dwell; in the land of Goshen let them dwell: and if thou
knowest *any* men of activity among them, then make them rulers over my
cattle.
7And Joseph brought in Jacob his father, and set him before Pharaoh:
and Jacob blessed Pharaoh.
8And Pharaoh said unto Jacob, How old *art* thou?
9And Jacob said unto Pharaoh, The days of the years of my pilgrimage
are an hundred and thirty years: few and evil have the days of the years of
my life been, and have not attained unto the days of the years of the life of
my fathers in the days of their pilgrimage.
10And Jacob blessed Pharaoh, and went out from before Pharaoh.
11¶And Joseph placed his father and his brethren, and gave them a
possession in the land of Egypt, in the best of the land, in the land of
Ram′e-ses, as Pharaoh had commanded.
12And Joseph nourished his father, and his brethren, and all his father's
household, with bread, according to *their* families.

47:6 Gen 45:18; 46:34; 47:11; Ex 18:21
47:7 Gen 47:10; Ex 12:32; Num 6:23
☆**47:9** Gen 35:28; 1 Chron 29:15
☆**47:10** Gen 14:19
☆**47:11** Ex 1:11; 12:37
47:12 Gen 45:11; 47:24

K. JOSEPH BUYS THE LANDS FOR PHARAOH

13¶And *there was* no bread in all the land; for the famine *was* very sore, so
that the land of Egypt and *all* the land of Canaan fainted by reason of the
famine.
14And Joseph gathered up all the money that was found in the land of
Egypt, and in the land of Canaan, for the corn which they bought: and
Joseph brought the money into Pharaoh's house.
15And when money failed in the land of Egypt, and in the land of
Canaan, all the Egyptians came unto Joseph, and said, Give us bread: for
why should we die in thy presence? for the money faileth.
16And Joseph said, Give your cattle; and I will give you for your cattle, if
money fail.
17And they brought their cattle unto Joseph: and Joseph gave them bread
in exchange for horses, and for the flocks, and for the cattle of the herds,
and for the asses: and he fed them with bread for all their cattle for that
year.
18When that year was ended, they came unto him the second year, and
said unto him, We will not hide *it* from my lord, how that our money is
spent; my lord also hath our herds of cattle; there is not ought left in the
sight of my lord, but our bodies, and our lands:
19Wherefore shall we die before thine eyes, both we and our land? buy us
and our land for bread, and we and our land will be servants unto Pharaoh:
and give *us* seed, that we may live, and not die, that the land be not
desolate.

47:13 Gen 41:30; Jer 14:1–6; Acts 7:11
47:14 Gen 41:56; 1 Cor 4:2
47:15 Gen 47:18, 19, 24
47:17 Ex 9:3; 1 Kgs 10:28
47:19 Neh 5:2; Job 2:4; Lam 1:11; Mt 16:26

47:9 Jacob lived seventeen years in Egypt. He died at the age of 147, which was a shorter life-span than that of Abraham (175) and Isaac (180).

47:10 God's people are pilgrims, strangers, sojourners, and exiles, for their citizenship is in heaven. They are not of this world although they are in it (John 17:16). As pilgrims, they (1) look for the coming of the heavenly city whose maker is God (Heb. 11:6); (2) live in reverent fear of God during the days of this pilgrimage (1 Pet. 1:17); and (3) constitute a heavenly commonwealth (Phil. 3:20). The world will persecute God's people (John 17:14), but they are not to be anxious about worldly concerns (Matt. 6:25). They are commanded to lay up treasure in heaven (Matt. 6:19), to abstain from the passions of the flesh (1 Pet. 2:11), and to shine as lights in the world (Phil. 2:15).

47:11 *land of Rameses,* later known as *Goshen.*

47:20☆

20 And Joseph bought all the land of Egypt for Pharaoh; for the Egyptians sold every man his field, because the famine prevailed over them: so the land became Pharaoh's.

21 And as for the people, he removed them to cities from *one* end of the borders of Egypt even to the *other* end thereof.

47:22 Gen 41:45; Deut 12:19

22 Only the land of the priests bought he not; for the priests had a portion *assigned them* of Pharaoh, and did eat their portion which Pharaoh gave them: wherefore they sold not their lands.

47:23 Gen 45:6; Prov 11:26

23 Then Joseph said unto the people, Behold, I have bought you this day and your land for Pharaoh: lo, *here is* seed for you, and ye shall sow the land.

47:24 Gen 41:34; Lev 27:32

24 And it shall come to pass in the increase, that ye shall give the fifth *part* unto Pharaoh, and four parts shall be your own, for seed of the field, and for your food, and for them of your households, and for food for your little ones.

47:25 Gen 33:15; 45:7; 50:20; Ruth 2:13

25 And they said, Thou hast saved our lives: let us find grace in the sight of my lord, and we will be Pharaoh's servants.

47:26 Gen 47:22

26 And Joseph made it a law over the land of Egypt unto this day, *that* Pharaoh should have the fifth *part;* except the land of the priests only, *which* became not Pharaoh's.

L. JOSEPH MAKES A PROMISE TO HIS FATHER

47:27 Gen 13:16; 46:3; Ex 1:7

27 ¶And Israel dwelt in the land of Egypt, in the country of Goshen; and they had possessions therein, and grew, and multiplied exceedingly.

47:28 Gen 47:9

28 And Jacob lived in the land of Egypt seventeen years: so the whole age of Jacob was an hundred forty and seven years.

47:29 Gen 24:2, 49; 50:24, 25; Acts 7:15, 16; Heb 11:21

29 And the time drew nigh that Israel must die: and he called his son Joseph, and said unto him, If now I have found grace in thy sight, put, I pray thee, thy hand under my thigh, and deal kindly and truly with me; bury me not, I pray thee, in Egypt:

47:30 Gen 15:15; 23:19; 25:9; 49:29

30 But I will lie with my fathers, and thou shalt carry me out of Egypt, and bury me in their buryingplace. And he said, I will do as thou hast said.

47:31 Gen 21:23; 24:3; 1 Kgs 1:47

31 And he said, Swear unto me. And he sware unto him. And Israel bowed himself upon the bed's head.

M. JACOB GRANTS HIS BLESSINGS AND DIES

1. Jacob Blesses Ephraim and Manasseh, Joseph's Sons

48:1 Gen 41:50–52; 46:20; Heb 11:21

48 AND it came to pass after these things, that *one* told Joseph, Behold, thy father *is* sick: and he took with him his two sons, Manas′seh and E′phra-im.

2 And *one* told Jacob, and said, Behold, thy son Joseph cometh unto thee: and Israel strengthened himself, and sat upon the bed.

48:3 Gen 28:3, 12–19; 35:9–15

3 And Jacob said unto Joseph, God Almighty appeared unto me at Luz in the land of Canaan, and blessed me,

4 And said unto me, Behold, I will make thee fruitful, and multiply thee, and I will make of thee a multitude of people; and will give this land to thy seed after thee *for* an everlasting possession.

47:20 *bought all the land of Egypt for Pharaoh.* Before this the Egyptians owned their own land. The famine resulted in the consolidation of the land holdings in the name of Pharaoh. The landholders became tenant farmers who were allowed to keep 80 percent of their crops, while 20 percent went to the government. Verse 19 indicates their willingness to become slaves of Pharaoh in order to save their lives.

5 And now thy two sons, E′phra-im and Ma-nas′seh, which were born ☆48:5
unto thee in the land of Egypt before I came unto thee into Egypt, *are* Gen 46:20, 27
mine; as Reuben and Simeon, they shall be mine.
6 And thy issue, which thou begettest after them, shall be thine, *and* shall 48:6
be called after the name of their brethren in their inheritance. Josh 14:4
7 And as for me, when I came from Pa′dan, Rachel died by me in the land 48:7
of Canaan in the way, when yet *there was* but a little way to come unto Gen 35:19; 1 Sam 10:2
Eph′rath: and I buried her there in the way of Eph′rath; the same *is* Beth- Mt 2:18
lehem.
8 And Israel beheld Joseph's sons, and said, Who *are* these?
9 And Joseph said unto his father, They *are* my sons, whom God hath 48:9
given me in this *place.* And he said, Bring them, I pray thee, unto me, and Gen 27:4; 33:5; 49:28
I will bless them.
10 Now the eyes of Israel were dim for age, *so that* he could not see. And ☆48:10
he brought them near unto him; and he kissed them, and embraced them. Gen 27:1
11 And Israel said unto Joseph, I had not thought to see thy face: and, lo, 48:11
God hath shewed me also thy seed. Gen 37:33, 34; 42:36
12 And Joseph brought them out from between his knees, and he bowed 48:12
himself with his face to the earth. Gen 33:3; 42:6
13 And Joseph took them both, E′phra-im in his right hand toward Israel's ☆48:13
left hand, and Ma-nas′seh in his left hand toward Israel's right hand, and
brought *them* near unto him.
14 And Israel stretched out his right hand, and laid *it* upon E′phra-im's 48:14
head, who *was* the younger, and his left hand upon Ma-nas′seh's head, Gen 41:51, 52; Ex 15:6
guiding his hands wittingly; for Ma-nas′seh *was* the firstborn. Ps 110:1
15 ¶And he blessed Joseph, and said, God, before whom my fathers 48:15
Abraham and Isaac did walk, the God which fed me all my life long unto Gen 17:1; 27:4; 28:20, 21
this day, 49:24, 28
16 The Angel which redeemed me from all evil, bless the lads; and let my ☆48:16
name be named on them, and the name of my fathers Abraham and Isaac; Gen 22:11; 28:13; 31:11
and let them grow into a multitude in the midst of the earth. 32:28; Deut 28:11
17 And when Joseph saw that his father laid his right hand upon the head
of E′phra-im, it displeased him: and he held up his father's hand, to remove
it from E′phra-im's head unto Ma-nas′seh's head.
18 And Joseph said unto his father, Not so, my father: for this *is* the
firstborn; put thy right hand upon his head.
19 And his father refused, and said, I know *it,* my son, I know *it;* he also 48:19
shall become a people, and he also shall be great: but truly his younger Gen 28:14; 46:3; Deut 1:10
brother shall be greater than he, and his seed shall become a multitude of
nations.
20 And he blessed them that day, saying, In thee shall Israel bless, saying, 48:20
God make thee as E′phra-im and as Ma-nas′seh: and he set E′phra-im Gen 28:3; Ruth 4:11
before Ma-nas′seh.

48:5 Here Jacob adopts the two sons of Joseph and in doing so made them equal, for rights of inheritance, with all of his other sons. Joseph, through his sons, got a double portion of the inheritance, which may mean that he replaced Reuben who, technically, was the firstborn (see note to 49:4). Since the Levites did not share in the distribution of the land, there were still twelve tribes who got the land.

48:10 Undoubtedly Jacob's failing sight was due to cataracts, which in that day were impossible to correct. Modern medicine has reversed this, although there are still tens of thousands of cases of blindness in the Middle East due to untreated cataracts.

48:13 Jacob had deceived his father in order to obtain Esau's blessing. Now when Joseph wants his firstborn to receive the firstborn's blessing, Jacob deliberately crosses his hands and places his right hand on the head of Ephraim, who was the younger son. Manasseh was given second place by Jacob.

48:16 Christ is the Angel of the covenant who redeemed Jacob from all evil. As he bore this testimony, Jacob was "bidding an everlasting farewell to sin and sorrow."* As we approach death, it is good for us to witness to the graciousness of the God who has kept us through the long years of life. This is an encouragement to those we leave behind, and a pattern for them to follow through their daily walks.

21 And Israel said unto Joseph, Behold, I die: but God shall be with you, and bring you again unto the land of your fathers.

22 Moreover I have given to thee one portion above thy brethren, which I took out of the hand of the Am′or-ite with my sword and my bow.

2. Jacob Speaks His Last Words to His Sons

49 AND Jacob called unto his sons, and said, Gather yourselves together, that I may tell you *that* which shall befall you in the last days.

2 Gather yourselves together, and hear, ye sons of Jacob; and hearken unto Israel your father.

3 ¶Reuben, thou *art* my firstborn, my might, and the beginning of my strength, the excellency of dignity, and the excellency of power:

4 Unstable as water, thou shalt not excel; because thou wentest up to thy father's bed; then defiledst thou *it:* he went up to my couch.

5 ¶Simeon and Levi *are* brethren; instruments of cruelty *are in* their habitations.

6 O my soul, come not thou into their secret; unto their assembly, mine honour, be not thou united: for in their anger they slew a man, and in their selfwill they digged down a wall.

7 Cursed *be* their anger, for *it was* fierce; and their wrath, for it was cruel: I will divide them in Jacob, and scatter them in Israel.

8 ¶Judah, thou *art he* whom thy brethren shall praise: thy hand *shall be* in the neck of thine enemies; thy father's children shall bow down before thee.

9 Judah *is* a lion's whelp: from the prey, my son, thou art gone up: he stooped down, he couched as a lion, and as an old lion; who shall rouse him up?

10 The sceptre shall not depart from Judah, nor a lawgiver from between his feet, until Shi′loh come; and unto him *shall* the gathering of the people *be.*

11 Binding his foal unto the vine, and his ass's colt unto the choice vine; he washed his garments in wine, and his clothes in the blood of grapes:

12 His eyes *shall be* red with wine, and his teeth white with milk.

13 ¶Zeb′u-lun shall dwell at the haven of the sea; and he *shall be* for an haven of ships; and his border *shall be* unto Zi′don.

14 ¶Is′sa-char *is* a strong ass couching down between two burdens:

15 And he saw that rest *was* good, and the land that *it was* pleasant; and bowed his shoulder to bear, and became a servant unto tribute.

16 ¶Dan shall judge his people, as one of the tribes of Israel.

17 Dan shall be a serpent by the way, an adder in the path, that biteth the horse heels, so that his rider shall fall backward.

18 I have waited for thy salvation, O LORD.

48:21 Gen 28:15 46:4; 50:24
48:22 Gen 15:16 Josh 17:17, 18 24:32; Jn 4:5
49:1 Num 24:14 Deut 4:30; 31:12
49:2 Prov 1:8
49:3 Gen 46:8 Num 26:5 Deut 21:17 1 Chron 2:1; 5:1
49:4☆ Gen 35:22 Deut 27:20
49:5 Gen 29:33, 34 34:25
49:6 Gen 34:30 Ps 26:4; 64:2 Prov 1:15
49:7☆ Josh 1:9, 21:1–42
49:8 Gen 27:29 Deut 33:7 Judg 1:1, 2 20:18; Heb 7:14
49:9 Num 24:9 Ezek 19:5–7 Hos 5:14 Mic 5:8
49:10☆ Num 24:17 Ps 2:6–9; 60:7 Ps 108:8 Ezek 21:26, 27
49:11 Isa 63:2 Joel 3:18 Mic 4:4
49:13 Deut 33:19 Josh 19:10
49:14 Josh 19:17 Judg 5:16
49:16☆ Gen 30:6 Deut 33:22 Judg 13:2; 15:20 Judg 18:26
49:18 Ex 15:2; Ps 25:5 119:166, 174 Isa 25:9; Mic 7:7

49:4 *thou shalt not excel,* i.e., Reuben has lost his status, along with the rights, of the firstborn. Moreover, the Moabites seized the territory the Reubenites had occupied upon entering Canaan.

49:7 *I will . . . scatter them in Israel,* i.e., the tribes of Simeon and Levi were not given land holdings, as were their brother-tribes.

49:10 *until Shiloh come* means also "he to whom it belongs." The "he" here doubtless refers first to David and second to the reign of Messiah, who will come from the loins of David, even Jesus Christ. As one commentator wrote: "Dying Jacob, at a great distance, saw Christ's day, and it was his comfort and support on his death-bed."* There are other prophecies from the Old Testament related to the person of Jesus and his origin. Among them are (1) he would come from the stock of Israel, "a star from Jacob" (Num. 24:17; see note on that verse); (2) he would be of the family of David and of the tribe of Judah (49:10; Isa. 11:1; Luke 1:31–33); (3) he would be born in Bethlehem (Mic. 4:2; Luke 2:4, 6, 7); (4) he would be born of a virgin (Isa. 7:14; Matt. 1:18, 22); (5) he would come at the appointed time (Dan. 9:14–26); (6) his coming would be announced by John the Baptist (Isa. 40:3, Matt. 3:3); and (7) he would be God (Isa. 9:6; John 1:14).

49:16 *Dan shall judge his people.* Samson, one of the great judges of Israel, was a Danite.

19¶Gad, a troop shall overcome him: but he shall overcome at the last.
20¶Out of Asher his bread *shall be* fat, and he shall yield royal dainties.
21¶Naph'ta-li *is* a hind let loose: he giveth goodly words.
22¶Joseph *is* a fruitful bough, *even* a fruitful bough by a well; *whose*
branches run over the wall:
23The archers have sorely grieved him, and shot *at him,* and hated him:
24But his bow abode in strength, and the arms of his hands were made
strong by the hands of the mighty *God* of Jacob; (from thence *is* the
shepherd, the stone of Israel:)
25*Even* by the God of thy father, who shall help thee; and by the
Almighty, who shall bless thee with blessings of heaven above, blessings of
the deep that lieth under, blessings of the breasts, and of the womb:
26The blessings of thy father have prevailed above the blessings of my
progenitors unto the utmost bound of the everlasting hills: they shall be on
the head of Joseph, and on the crown of the head of him that was separate
from his brethren.
27¶Benjamin shall ravin *as* a wolf: in the morning he shall devour the
prey, and at night he shall divide the spoil.

49:19 Deut 33:20
49:20 Deut 33:24
49:21 Deut 33:23 Ps 18:33
49:22 Gen 41:52 Deut 33:13–17
49:23 Gen 37:4, 18, 24, 28 Ps 64:3, 4 105:18
49:24 Isa 1:24; 28:16 49:26 Ps 23:1; 80:1 132:2, 5 1 Pet 2:6–8
49:25 Gen 28:13 35:11; 43:23 Deut 33:13
49:26 Num 6:2 Deut 33:15, 16
☆**49:27** Num 23:24 Deut 33:12 Judg 3:15

3. The Death and Burial of Jacob

28¶All these *are* the twelve tribes of Israel: and this *is it* that their father
spake unto them, and blessed them; every one according to his blessing he
blessed them.
29And he charged them, and said unto them, I am to be gathered unto my
people: bury me with my fathers in the cave that *is* in the field of E'phron
the Hittite,
30In the cave that *is* in the field of Mach-pe'lah, which *is* before Mam're,
in the land of Canaan, which Abraham bought with the field of E'phron the
Hittite for a possession of a buryingplace.
31There they buried Abraham and Sarah his wife; there they buried Isaac
and Rebekah his wife; and there I buried Leah.
32The purchase of the field and of the cave that *is* therein *was* from the
children of Heth.
33And when Jacob had made an end of commanding his sons, he
gathered up his feet into the bed, and yielded up the ghost, and was
gathered unto his people.

49:29 Gen 23:16 25:8, 9; 35:29 47:29; 50:5
☆**49:31** Gen 23:19 25:9; 35:29
49:33 Gen 25:8, 17 35:29 Acts 7:15 Heb 11:21

50 AND Joseph fell upon his father's face, and wept upon him, and
kissed him.
2And Joseph commanded his servants the physicians to embalm his
father: and the physicians embalmed Israel.
3And forty days were fulfilled for him; for so are fulfilled the days of
those which are embalmed: and the Egyptians mourned for him threescore
and ten days.
4And when the days of his mourning were past, Joseph spake unto the
house of Pharaoh, saying, If now I have found grace in your eyes, speak, I
pray you, in the ears of Pharaoh, saying,

50:1 Gen 23:2 46:4, 29
☆**50:2** Gen 50:26
50:3 Num 20:29 Deut 34:8

49:27 King Saul was a Benjaminite; so was the Apostle Paul. Bad and good characters can come from the same family.

49:31 *there I buried Leah.* Rachel was buried in Bethlehem, where they happened to be when she died in childbirth. Ironically Jacob was to lie next to Leah in death, while Rachel, whom Jacob loved so dearly, was to lie alone. Leah had the first sons of Jacob and now, in death, she supplanted Rachel again.

50:2 *embalmed.* This was an Egyptian custom. It was used here for Jacob, whose body would have disintegrated had his children brought him back for burial beside Leah without having his body embalmed. Both the Egyptians and the Israelites believed in a life after death, but their viewpoints were quite different.

50:5
Gen 47:29
48:21

5 My father made me swear, saying, Lo, I die: in my grave which I have digged for me in the land of Canaan, there shalt thou bury me. Now therefore let me go up, I pray thee, and bury my father, and I will come again.

6 And Pharaoh said, Go up, and bury thy father, according as he made thee swear.

7 ¶And Joseph went up to bury his father: and with him went up all the servants of Pharaoh, the elders of his house, and all the elders of the land of Egypt,

50:8
Ex 10:9
Num 32:24

8 And all the house of Joseph, and his brethren, and his father's house: only their little ones, and their flocks, and their herds, they left in the land of Goshen.

50:9
Gen 41:43
46:29
Ex 14:7
50:10☆

9 And there went up with him both chariots and horsemen: and it was a very great company.

10 And they came to the threshingfloor of A'tad, which *is* beyond Jordan, and there they mourned with a great and very sore lamentation: and he made a mourning for his father seven days.

50:11☆

11 And when the inhabitants of the land, the Canaanites, saw the mourning in the floor of A'tad, they said, This *is* a grievous mourning to the Egyptians: wherefore the name of it was called A'bel-miz'ra-im, which *is* beyond Jordan.

50:12
Gen 47:29
49:29
Ex 20:12
Acts 7:16
50:13
Gen 23:16–18
25:9

12 And his sons did unto him according as he commanded them:

13 For his sons carried him into the land of Canaan, and buried him in the cave of the field of Mach-pe'lah, which Abraham bought with the field for a possession of a buryingplace of E'phron the Hittite, before Mam're.

N. JOSEPH'S KIND TREATMENT OF HIS BROTHERS

14 ¶And Joseph returned into Egypt, he, and his brethren, and all that went up with him to bury his father, after he had buried his father.

50:15
Gen 42:17, 22

15 ¶And when Joseph's brethren saw that their father was dead, they said, Joseph will peradventure hate us, and will certainly requite us all the evil which we did unto him.

50:16
Prov 29:25

16 And they sent a messenger unto Joseph, saying, Thy father did command before he died, saying,

50:17
Gen 45:5
Deut 32:35
Mt 6:12
Lk 6:27
Rom 12:19

17 So shall ye say unto Joseph, Forgive, I pray thee now, the trespass of thy brethren, and their sin; for they did unto thee evil: and now, we pray thee, forgive the trespass of the servants of the God of thy father. And Joseph wept when they spake unto him.

50:18☆
Gen 37:7–11
42:6; 44:14
50:19
Gen 30:2
50:20
Gen 37:26
Ps 76:10
105:17–19
50:21
Gen 45:11
47:12

18 And his brethren also went and fell down before his face; and they said, Behold, we *be* thy servants.

19 And Joseph said unto them, Fear not: for *am* I in the place of God?

20 But as for you, ye thought evil against me; *but* God meant it unto good, to bring to pass, as *it is* this day, to save much people alive.

21 Now therefore fear ye not: I will nourish you, and your little ones. And he comforted them, and spake kindly unto them.

50:10 *Atad.* Located just west of the Jordan River, near Jericho.†

50:11 *Abel-mizraim* means "meadow (or mourning) of Egypt."

50:18 The dreams of Joseph that were given him by God are now finally and completely fulfilled, as his brethren fall before him. The brothers somehow never did understand Joseph because they thought he was being kind to them only while their father Jacob was alive; after his death they expected Joseph would wreak vengeance on them. Instead he acted graciously and thus demonstrated his spiritual maturity and his understanding that what had happened was in the will of God and had worked together for good.

O. JOSEPH'S DEATH AND EMBALMING

22 ¶And Joseph dwelt in Egypt, he, and his father's house: and Joseph
lived an hundred and ten years.
23 And Joseph saw E'phra-im's children of the third *generation:* the
children also of Ma'chir the son of Ma-nas'seh were brought up upon
Joseph's knees.
24 And Joseph said unto his brethren, I die: and God will surely visit you,
and bring you out of this land unto the land which he sware to Abraham, to
Isaac, and to Jacob.
25 And Joseph took an oath of the children of Israel, saying, God will
surely visit you, and ye shall carry up my bones from hence.
26 So Joseph died, *being* an hundred and ten years old: and they
embalmed him, and he was put in a coffin in Egypt.

50:23 Gen 16:3; 30:3
☆**50:24** Gen 13:15 28:13; 35:12 48:21; 49:29
50:25 Gen 47:29 Ex 13:19 Josh 24:32 Heb 11:22
50:26 Gen 41:46 47:9; 50:2

50:24 Joseph understood and believed God's promise of a land for Abraham's descendants. Thus he knew that their stay in Egypt would end, although he probably did not foresee their slavery under later Pharaohs. He made his family promise that they would take his bones with them when the exodus came.

THE SECOND BOOK OF MOSES CALLED

EXODUS

Authorship, date, and background Exodus, like the other books of the Pentateuch, takes its name in the Hebrew Bible from the opening words of the text which mean "these are the names of." The Septuagint, or Greek translation, uses the title Exodos, meaning "departure" and this title has come into our English Bibles as *Exodus.* The book is the second of the five Books of Moses, to whom its authorship has been attributed (see the introduction to Genesis).

Exodus cannot be understood apart from Genesis. The book is simply a continuation of the story which commences in Genesis. The central character of Exodus is Moses, the great lawgiver, the leader of the people of Israel, the founding father of the nation of Israel, as well as the founding father of Israel's religion. Genesis ends with the family of Jacob in Egypt. Exodus opens with Jacob's descendants in slavery, a situation which developed after the death of Joseph. During the four and a half centuries in Egypt, the number of the Israelites increased very substantially. Now the time had come for God to free the slaves and deliver them from Egypt.

Scholars are divided about the date of Israel's flight from Egypt. Many conservatives place it around 1440 B.C., which fully fits the data of Scripture; others place it around 1290 B.C. Assuming that the exodus occurred around 1440 B.C., the composition of this book by Moses can be dated in the last two decades of the fifteenth century B.C.

The hard bondage to which the Israelites were subjected constituted a need for their liberation. God heard their prayers for help and chose Moses as their leader, through whom the liberation would take place. In preparation for that deliverance, Moses spent the first forty years of his life in the court of the Pharaoh, where he learned about politics and statecraft. He spent the second forty years on the backside of the desert, learning about God in preparation for the most important last forty years of his life. In the last part of his life Moses directed the destiny of the Israelites, during which time they became a nation under God, a theocracy governed by a covenant, which was spelled out in what might be called the constitution for the people of God.

Characteristics and content Probably the most notable event in Exodus is the crossing of the Red (Reed) Sea. This miraculous incident is referred to again and again in the Old and New Testaments. When the event takes place, Israel is a conglomerate mass of undisciplined slaves who need to be welded together into a nation. Moses describes how this comes to pass.

The exodus begins with the celebration of the Passover, at which time the firstborn of the Egyptians die. It is the story of redemption by blood which becomes the central motif of God's salvation for all men through animal sacrifices anticipating the death and resurrection of the Lord Jesus. It had been God's intention to bring the Israelites into the Promised Land shortly after their liberation from Egypt. When the people accept the adverse report of ten of the twelve spies, God condemns them to forty years of wandering before they are fit to enter the land; indeed, all Israelites thirty years or older are slated to perish. Only Joshua and Caleb of that generation will enter Canaan. Even Moses falls short when he sinfully strikes the rock in the wilderness instead of speaking to it.

During the long wilderness journey, God gives Israel the Law or the Ten Commandments by which they are to be governed. God establishes a covenant with Israel which binds the people to obey him. The Tabernacle in the wilderness is set up for the worship of God by the people and for the offering of the blood of bulls and goats for sin. Along with the Tabernacle God ordains the priesthood, choosing Aaron and his descendants to minister at the altar. When the Tabernacle is finished and dedicated, the glory of God enters the Holy Place, which is forbidden to all except the High Priest, who is to enter once a year to sprinkle blood on the mercy seat.

God marvelously provides for his people in the wilderness. He sends the cloud for day, and the pillar of fire by night. He gives them manna each day. Their clothes and their shoes never wear out. Yet they are a people who apostatize again and again. One divine punishment follows another as God seeks to teach them the truth that those who obey his voice prosper while those who disobey experience chastisement and sometimes even death.

Outline

I. Moses' background and preparation (1:1—4:31)
II. God delivers Israel from Egypt (5:1—15:21)
III. The journey to Mount Sinai (15:22—18:27)
IV. The book of the Covenant and the Law (19:1—24:18)
V. The Tabernacle and its ministry (25:1—40:38)

I. MOSES' BACKGROUND AND PREPARATION (1:1—4:31)

A. INTRODUCTION

1. Israel's Growth and Slavery in Egypt

1 NOW these *are* the names of the children of Israel, which came into
Egypt; every man and his household came with Jacob.
2 Reuben, Simeon, Levi, and Judah,
3 Is'sa-char, Zeb'u-lun, and Benjamin,
4 Dan, and Naph'ta-li, Gad, and Asher.
5 And all the souls that came out of the loins of Jacob were seventy souls:
for Joseph was in Egypt *already*.
6 And Joseph died, and all his brethren, and all that generation.
7 ¶And the children of Israel were fruitful, and increased abundantly, and
multiplied, and waxed exceeding mighty; and the land was filled with them.
8 Now there arose up a new king over Egypt, which knew not Joseph.
9 And he said unto his people, Behold, the people of the children of Israel
are more and mightier than we:
10 Come on, let us deal wisely with them; lest they multiply, and it come
to pass, that, when there falleth out any war, they join also unto our
enemies, and fight against us, and *so* get them up out of the land.
11 Therefore they did set over them taskmasters to afflict them with their
burdens. And they built for Pharaoh treasure cities, Pi'thom and Ra-am'ses.
12 But the more they afflicted them, the more they multiplied and grew.
And they were grieved because of the children of Israel.
13 And the Egyptians made the children of Israel to serve with rigour:
14 And they made their lives bitter with hard bondage, in morter, and in
brick, and in all manner of service in the field: all their service, wherein they
made them serve, *was* with rigour.

2. How the Midwives Saved the Babies

15 ¶And the king of Egypt spake to the Hebrew midwives, of which the
name of the one *was* Shiph'rah, and the name of the other Pu'ah:
16 And he said, When ye do the office of a midwife to the Hebrew women,
and see *them* upon the stools; if it *be* a son, then ye shall kill him: but if it
be a daughter, then she shall live.

1:1 Gen 46:8–26; 49:3–27; 1 Chron 2:1, 2; Rev 7:4–8
1:2 Ex 6:14–16
1:5 Gen 46:27; Ex 24:1; Deut 10:22; Judg 8:30; Acts 7:14
1:6 Gen 50:26; Acts 7:15, 16
1:7 Gen 1:27; 12:2; 35:11; 46:3; 47:27; 48:4; Ex 12:37; Acts 7:17
☆**1:8** Acts 7:18
☆**1:9** Ps 105:24
1:10 Num 22:6; Ps 105:25; Acts 7:19
1:11 Gen 47:11; Ex 2:11; 3:7; 5:10; Num 20:15; Deut 26:6
1:12 Prov 21:30
1:13 Gen 15:13
1:14 Ex 2:23; Deut 26:6, 7
☆**1:15**
☆**1:16** Acts 7:19

1:8 *there arose up a new king.* This incident occurred approximately 400 years after Joseph's death.
1:9 The Pharaoh feared the increasing number of Israelites, whose proliferation was part of God's plan before they entered the Promised Land. In Egypt the Israelites were able to build a mighty nation even though they were in bondage, for they presented a military threat to the military security of the Egyptian state.
1:15 There were many midwives. The two mentioned here were probably chief midwives.
1:16 *stools,* i.e., birthstools which were two stones that supported the females' thighs. The stones were separated so that the midwives could effect a delivery from beneath the mother. *Ye shall kill him.* The Egyptian Pharaoh did not hesitate to practice genocide—he ordered the killing of all Israelite male babies. In one form or another this practice has been the curse of many nations throughout history. The Pharaoh's evil mandate foreshadowed Hitler's slaughter of the Jews during World War II, the earlier genocide of the Kulaks in Russia under Stalin, and the ruthless murder of

1:17 Ps 31:19 Mt 10:28 Acts 4:19; 5:29

17 But the midwives feared God, and did not as the king of Egypt
commanded them, but saved the men children alive.
18 And the king of Egypt called for the midwives, and said unto them,
Why have ye done this thing, and have saved the men children alive?

1:19☆ Josh 2:4 2 Sam 17:20

19 And the midwives said unto Pharaoh, Because the Hebrew women *are*
not as the Egyptian women; for they *are* lively, and are delivered ere the
midwives come in unto them.

1:20 Ex 1:12

20 Therefore God dealt well with the midwives: and the people multiplied,
and waxed very mighty.
21 And it came to pass, because the midwives feared God, that he made
them houses.

1:22 Mt 2:16

22 And Pharaoh charged all his people, saying, Every son that is born ye
shall cast into the river, and every daughter ye shall save alive.

B. MOSES' BIRTH AND UPBRINGING

2:1☆ Ex 6:16, 20 Num 26:59

2 AND there went a man of the house of Levi, and took *to wife* a
daughter of Levi.

2:2 Acts 7:20 Heb 11:23

2 And the woman conceived, and bare a son: and when she saw him that
he *was a* goodly *child,* she hid him three months.

2:3☆ Gen 6:14 Ex 1:22 Isa 18:2; 19:6

3 And when she could not longer hide him, she took for him an ark of
bulrushes, and daubed it with slime and with pitch, and put the child
therein; and she laid *it* in the flags by the river's brink.

2:4 Ex 15:20 Num 26:59 Mic 6:4

4 And his sister stood afar off, to wit what would be done to him.

2:5 Ex 8:20 Acts 7:21

5 ¶And the daughter of Pharaoh came down to wash *herself* at the river;
and her maidens walked along by the river's side; and when she saw the ark
among the flags, she sent her maid to fetch it.

2:6 Ps 106:46

6 And when she had opened *it,* she saw the child: and, behold, the babe
wept. And she had compassion on him, and said, This *is one* of the
Hebrews' children.
7 Then said his sister to Pharaoh's daughter, Shall I go and call to thee a
nurse of the Hebrew women, that she may nurse the child for thee?
8 And Pharaoh's daughter said to her, Go. And the maid went and called
the child's mother.
9 And Pharaoh's daughter said unto her, Take this child away, and nurse
it for me, and I will give *thee* thy wages. And the woman took the child, and
nursed it.

2:10☆ 1 Sam 1:20 2 Sam 22:17

10 And the child grew, and she brought him unto Pharaoh's daughter, and
he became her son. And she called his name Moses: and she said, Because
I drew him out of the water.

---

several million Cambodians by their Communist masters following the Viet Nam War.

1:19 If this were true there would have been no need for midwives. Apparently the midwives lied. They are to be commended for preserving the lives of male babies, even though they lied.

2:1 We learn later that the father and mother of Moses are named Amram and Jochebed (6:20). Jochebed was the sister of Amram's father.

2:3 *bulrushes,* which came from the papyrus reeds. *slime and with pitch.* The ark basket was made waterproof by using asphalt or bitumen to cover the reeds.

2:10 Moses and Abraham were the two greatest Old Testament characters. Moses ranks among the greatest of all men who ever lived. He was well educated in Egypt; his training included literature, law, astronomy, geometry, writing, music, art, medicine, philosophy, and athletics. He could have been a politician, a writer, or a soldier. As Israel's leader he was deliverer, lawgiver, builder, military leader, judge, author, and intermediary between Israel and God. At 40 he fled from Egypt (according to Exod. 2:15; Acts 7:23–29). At 80 he delivered Israel from Egypt. At 120 he died in fullness of strength. He was from the tribe of Levi and consecrated his brother Aaron as high priest according to God's commandment. Moses was meek, faithful, and selfless, as well as courageous before men. The name *Moses* sounds like another Hebrew word meaning "to draw out."

C. MOSES SLAYS AN EGYPTIAN AND FLEES

11 ¶And it came to pass in those days, when Moses was grown, that he
went out unto his brethren, and looked on their burdens: and he spied an
Egyptian smiting an Hebrew, one of his brethren.
12 And he looked this way and that way, and when he saw that *there was*
no man, he slew the Egyptian, and hid him in the sand.
13 And when he went out the second day, behold, two men of the Hebrews
strove together: and he said to him that did the wrong, Wherefore smitest
thou thy fellow?
14 And he said, Who made thee a prince and a judge over us? intendest
thou to kill me, as thou killedst the Egyptian? And Moses feared, and said,
Surely this thing is known.
15 Now when Pharaoh heard this thing, he sought to slay Moses. But
Moses fled from the face of Pharaoh, and dwelt in the land of Mid'i-an: and
he sat down by a well.
16 Now the priest of Mid'i-an had seven daughters: and they came and
drew *water,* and filled the troughs to water their father's flock.
17 And the shepherds came and drove them away: but Moses stood up
and helped them, and watered their flock.
18 And when they came to Reu'el their father, he said, How *is it that* ye are
come so soon to day?
19 And they said, An Egyptian delivered us out of the hand of the
shepherds, and also drew *water* enough for us, and watered the flock.
20 And he said unto his daughters, And where *is* he? why *is* it *that* ye have
left the man? call him, that he may eat bread.
21 And Moses was content to dwell with the man: and he gave Moses Zip-
po'rah his daughter.
22 And she bare *him* a son, and he called his name Ger'shom: for he said,
I have been a stranger in a strange land.

D. GOD CALLS MOSES; THE SIGN OF THE BURNING BUSH

1. God's Conversation with Moses

23 ¶And it came to pass in process of time, that the king of Egypt died:
and the children of Israel sighed by reason of the bondage, and they cried,
and their cry came up unto God by reason of the bondage.
24 And God heard their groaning, and God remembered his covenant
with Abraham, with Isaac, and with Jacob.
25 And God looked upon the children of Israel, and God had respect unto
them.

3 NOW Moses kept the flock of Jeth'ro his father in law, the priest of
Mid'i-an: and he led the flock to the backside of the desert, and came
to the mountain of God, *even* to Ho'reb.
2 And the angel of the LORD appeared unto him in a flame of fire out of

2:11 Acts 7:23, 24; Heb 11:24
☆**2:12** Acts 7:24
2:13 Acts 7:26–28
2:14 Gen 19:9; 37:8; Num 16:3; Acts 7:28, 33
☆**2:15** Gen 24:11; 29:2; 1 Kgs 19:1–3; Acts 7:29
2:16 Gen 14:18; 24:11; Ex 3:1; 18:7, 12
2:17 Gen 29:10
☆**2:18** Num 10:29
2:20 Gen 18:5; 24:31; Job 31:32
2:21 Ex 4:25; 18:2; Acts 7:29
2:22 Gen 23:4; Ex 4:20; 18:3; Heb 11:13
2:23 Ex 6:5, 9; Deut 26:7; Acts 7:34; Jas 5:4
2:24 Gen 22:16–18; 26:2, 3; 28:13; 46:3, 4; Ps 105:8, 42
☆**2:25** Neh 9:9
☆**3:1** Ex 2:18; 4:18, 27; Ex 17:6; 18:5; 24:12
☆**3:2** Gen 22:11; Deut 33:16; Mk 12:26; Lk 20:37; Acts 7:30

2:12 Moses was guilty of murder even though his intention to help a fellow-Israelite was good. The end does not justify the means.
2:15 *land of Midian* was an area east and southeast of Canaan. It was peopled by descendants of Abraham born to Keturah, whom he married after the death of Sarah.
2:18 Reuel, Moses' father-in-law, was also called Jethro (3:1) and Hobab (Judg. 4:11). In Num. 10:29, Hobab is called the son of Reuel; this means that Reuel, who was also called Hobab, named his son Hobab.
2:25 *had respect unto them,* i.e., "knew their condition," or, "knew that the time had come for their rescue."†
3:1 *Jethro his father-in-law.* See note to 2:18.
3:2 The phrase *the angel of the LORD* may confirm what is elsewhere certain—that the preincarnate Christ made appearances in the Old Testament. In Judg. 2:1; 6:12–16; and 13:3–22, the texts indicate that the angel in these cases was God himself.

the midst of a bush: and he looked, and, behold, the bush burned with fire,
and the bush *was* not consumed.

3:3☆ Acts 7:31

3 And Moses said, I will now turn aside, and see this great sight, why the
bush is not burnt.

3:4 Gen 22:1, 46:2; Ex 4:5; 1 Sam 3:4

4 And when the LORD saw that he turned aside to see, God called unto
him out of the midst of the bush, and said, Moses, Moses. And he said,
Here *am* I.

3:5 Gen 28:16, 17; Ex 19:12; Josh 5:15; Acts 7:33

5 And he said, Draw not nigh hither: put off thy shoes from off thy feet,
for the place whereon thou standest *is* holy ground.

3:6 Gen 31:42; 32:9; Ex 4:5; 1 Kgs 18:36; Mt 22:32; Mk 12:26; Lk 20:37; Acts 7:32

6 Moreover he said, I *am* the God of thy father, the God of Abraham, the
God of Isaac, and the God of Jacob. And Moses hid his face; for he was
afraid to look upon God.

3:7☆ Isa 63:9; Acts 7:34

7 ¶And the LORD said, I have surely seen the affliction of my people which
are in Egypt, and have heard their cry by reason of their taskmasters; for I
know their sorrows;

3:8 a)Gen 15:16; 46:4; 50:24; b)Gen 15:19; Ex 3:17; Deut 6:3; 8:7–9; 11:9; 26:9; 27:3; Josh 5:6; 24:11

8 And I am come down to deliver them out of the hand of the Egyptians,
and to bring them up out of that land unto a good land and a large, unto a
land flowing with milk and honey; unto the place of the Canaanites, and
the Hittites, and the Am′or-ites, and the Per′iz-zites, and the Hi′vites, and
the Jeb′u-sites.

3:9 Ex 1:11; 2:23

9 Now therefore, behold, the cry of the children of Israel is come unto me:
and I have also seen the oppression wherewith the Egyptians oppress them.

3:10 Gen 15:13; Ex 12:40; Ps 105:26; Acts 7:34; 12:6

10 Come now therefore, and I will send thee unto Pharaoh, that thou
mayest bring forth my people the children of Israel out of Egypt.

3:11 Ex 4:10; 6:12; 1 Sam 18:18; Isa 6:5

11 ¶And Moses said unto God, Who *am* I, that I should go unto Pharaoh,
and that I should bring forth the children of Israel out of Egypt?

3:12 Gen 28:15; Ex 4:12; 19:2; Josh 1:5; Acts 7:7

12 And he said, Certainly I will be with thee; and this *shall be* a token unto
thee, that I have sent thee: When thou hast brought forth the people out of
Egypt, ye shall serve God upon this mountain.

3:13 Ex 15:3

13 And Moses said unto God, Behold, *when* I come unto the children of
Israel, and shall say unto them, The God of your fathers hath sent me unto
you; and they shall say to me, What *is* his name? what shall I say unto
them?

3:14☆ Ex 6:3; Jn 8:58; Rev 1:8; 4:8

14 And God said unto Moses, I AM THAT I AM: and he said, Thus
shalt thou say unto the children of Israel, I AM hath sent me unto you.

3:15☆ Ps 72:17; 102:12; 135:13; 145:1; Acts 7:32

15 And God said moreover unto Moses, Thus shalt thou say unto the
children of Israel, The LORD God of your fathers, the God of Abraham, the
God of Isaac, and the God of Jacob, hath sent me unto you: this *is* my
name for ever, and this *is* my memorial unto all generations.

3:16 Ex 4:29; 18:12

16 Go, and gather the elders of Israel together, and say unto them, The
LORD God of your fathers, the God of Abraham, of Isaac, and of Jacob,
appeared unto me, saying, I have surely visited you, and *seen* that which is
done to you in Egypt:

3:17 Ex 3:8; Josh 24:11

17 And I have said, I will bring you up out of the affliction of Egypt unto
the land of the Canaanites, and the Hittites, and the Am′or-ites, and the
Per′iz-zites, and the Hi′vites, and the Jeb′u-sites, unto a land flowing with
milk and honey.

3:3 The burning bush which was not consumed by the fire was evidence of the supernatural, and provided Moses with external, corroborating proof of the presence of God. In the history of redemption, God often gave such evidence in order that believers might know it was God who spoke.

3:7 *have heard their cry.* The Lord may delay in answering prayer but he never comes too late. The Israelites had been in bondage for four centuries. God was using Egypt to fashion a great people. The time had come for God to answer their prayers for deliverance.

3:14 *I AM THAT I AM,* or "I will be what I will be." God is "the Sovereign God," or "the Living God."†

3:15 *LORD God,* or, "Yahweh." Some translations use "Jehovah," others, "LORD."

18 And they shall hearken to thy voice: and thou shalt come, thou and the
elders of Israel, unto the king of Egypt, and ye shall say unto him, The
LORD God of the Hebrews hath met with us: and now let us go, we beseech
thee, three days' journey into the wilderness, that we may sacrifice to the
LORD our God.
19 ¶And I am sure that the king of Egypt will not let you go, no, not by a
mighty hand.
20 And I will stretch out my hand, and smite Egypt with all my wonders
which I will do in the midst thereof: and after that he will let you go.
21 And I will give this people favour in the sight of the Egyptians: and it
shall come to pass, that, when ye go, ye shall not go empty:
22 But every woman shall borrow of her neighbour, and of her that
sojourneth in her house, jewels of silver, and jewels of gold, and raiment:
and ye shall put *them* upon your sons, and upon your daughters; and ye
shall spoil the Egyptians.

3:18 Ex 4:31; 5:1, 3; Num 23:4, 16
☆**3:19** Ex 5:2; 6:1; 7:4; Deut 6:22
3:20 Ex 11:1; 12:31; 15:11; Neh 9:10; Acts 7:36
3:21 Ex 11:3; 12:36
3:22 Ex 11:2; 12:35

2. God Arms Moses with a Miraculous Rod

4 AND Moses answered and said, But, behold, they will not believe me,
nor hearken unto my voice: for they will say, The LORD hath not
appeared unto thee.
2 And the LORD said unto him, What *is* that in thine hand? And he said,
A rod.
3 And he said, Cast it on the ground. And he cast it on the ground, and it
became a serpent; and Moses fled from before it.
4 And the LORD said unto Moses, Put forth thine hand, and take it by the
tail. And he put forth his hand, and caught it, and it became a rod in his
hand:
5 That they may believe that the LORD God of their fathers, the God of
Abraham, the God of Isaac, and the God of Jacob, hath appeared unto
thee.
6 ¶And the LORD said furthermore unto him, Put now thine hand into thy
bosom. And he put his hand into his bosom: and when he took it out,
behold, his hand *was* leprous as snow.
7 And he said, Put thine hand into thy bosom again. And he put his hand
into his bosom again; and plucked it out of his bosom, and, behold, it was
turned again as his *other* flesh.
8 And it shall come to pass, if they will not believe thee, neither hearken
to the voice of the first sign, that they will believe the voice of the latter
sign.
9 And it shall come to pass, if they will not believe also these two signs,
neither hearken unto thy voice, that thou shalt take of the water of the river,
and pour *it* upon the dry *land:* and the water which thou takest out of the
river shall become blood upon the dry *land.*

4:1 Ex 3:11, 13–16
☆**4:2** Ex 4:17, 20
4:3 Ex 7:10–12
4:5 Ex 4:30, 31; 19:9
☆**4:6** Ex 12:10; Num 12:10; 2 Kgs 5:27
4:7 Num 12:13, 14; Deut 32:39; 2 Kgs 5:14; Mt 8:3; Lk 17:12–14
4:9 Ex 7:19

3:19 This verse is better translated: "But I know that the king of Egypt will not permit you to go, except under compulsion" (NASB).

4:2 Moses asked God to give him outward confirming evidence to present to Pharaoh which would show he was from God Almighty. He was given the rod-serpent, and the leprous hand (4:6). But Pharaoh's unbelief was not moved by signs and wonders. Indeed, the Pharaoh was not moved to free the Israelites by either sign. Scripture does show that small things in God's hands and under his control can bring about mighty results. Moses had the stick, David a sling and pebbles, and Samson the jawbone of an ass. In the case of Moses, even if the signs did not convince Pharaoh, they did convince the children of Israel that Moses was God's sure messenger of deliverance (4:29–31).

4:6 God enabled Moses to perform signs and wonders before the Pharaoh. Thus the king had no excuse. The corroborating evidences of God's power were externally visible, and the words of Moses were reinforced by these miraculous acts.

3. God Chooses Aaron to Be Moses' Voice

4:10 Ex 3:11; 6:12, 30; Jer 1:6; Acts 7:22
4:11 Ps 94:9; Isa 35:6; Mt 11:5
4:12 Deut 18:18; Isa 50:4; Jer 1:9; Mt 10:19
4:13 Ex 3:11
4:14 Ex 4:27; 6:7
4:15 Isa 51:16; Jer 1:9; Num 22:38
4:16 Ex 7:1; 18:19
4:17 Ex 14:16; 17:9

10 ¶And Moses said unto the LORD, O my Lord, I *am* not eloquent,
neither heretofore, nor since thou hast spoken unto thy servant: but I *am*
slow of speech, and of a slow tongue.
11 And the LORD said unto him, Who hath made man's mouth? or who
maketh the dumb, or deaf, or the seeing, or the blind? have not I the LORD?
12 Now therefore go, and I will be with thy mouth, and teach thee what
thou shalt say.
13 And he said, O my Lord, send, I pray thee, by the hand *of him whom*
thou wilt send.
14 And the anger of the LORD was kindled against Moses, and he said, *Is*
not Aaron the Levite thy brother? I know that he can speak well. And also,
behold, he cometh forth to meet thee: and when he seeth thee, he will be
glad in his heart.
15 And thou shalt speak unto him, and put words in his mouth: and I will
be with thy mouth, and with his mouth, and will teach you what ye shall do.
16 And he shall be thy spokesman unto the people: and he shall be, *even*
he shall be to thee instead of a mouth, and thou shalt be to him instead of
God.
17 And thou shalt take this rod in thine hand, wherewith thou shalt do
signs.

4. God Sends Moses to Egypt

4:18 Ex 3:1; 18:5
4:19 Ex 2:15, 23
4:20 Ex 4:17; 18:3; Mt 2:20
4:21☆ Ex 7:3, 13; 9:12; Deut 2:30; Jn 12:40
4:22 Isa 63:17; 64:8; Jer 31:9; Hos 11:1; Rom 9:4
4:23 Ex 5:1; 6:11; 7:16; 12:29
4:24 Num 22:22; 1 Chron 21:16
4:25☆ Gen 17:14; Josh 5:2

18 ¶And Moses went and returned to Jeth'ro his father in law, and said
unto him, Let me go, I pray thee, and return unto my brethren which *are* in
Egypt, and see whether they be yet alive. And Jeth'ro said to Moses, Go in
peace.
19 And the LORD said unto Moses in Mid'i-an, Go, return into Egypt: for
all the men are dead which sought thy life.
20 And Moses took his wife and his sons, and set them upon an ass, and
he returned to the land of Egypt: and Moses took the rod of God in his
hand.
21 And the LORD said unto Moses, When thou goest to return into Egypt,
see that thou do all those wonders before Pharaoh, which I have put in
thine hand: but I will harden his heart, that he shall not let the people go.
22 And thou shalt say unto Pharaoh, Thus saith the LORD, Israel *is* my
son, *even* my firstborn:
23 And I say unto thee, Let my son go, that he may serve me: and if thou
refuse to let him go, behold, I will slay thy son, *even* thy firstborn.
24 ¶And it came to pass by the way in the inn, that the LORD met him, and
sought to kill him.
25 Then Zip-po'rah took a sharp stone, and cut off the foreskin of her son,
and cast *it* at his feet, and said, Surely a bloody husband *art* thou to me.
26 So he let him go: then she said, A bloody husband *thou art,* because of
the circumcision.

4:21 The Scriptures say that God hardened Pharaoh's heart (9:12; 10:1) and that Pharaoh hardened his own heart (8:15, 32; 9:34). There is nothing to indicate that God violated Pharaoh's choice or will. Rather, he sent circumstances into Pharaoh's life which hardened his heart; Pharaoh rejected God's claims. Opposing God always results in a hardened heart.

4:25, 26 The Scriptures do not tell us why Moses had not circumcised his son. Perhaps it was to please his wife, who was not an Israelite. But this neglect of the covenant cut his son off from Israel, for circumcision was the seal of the covenant. Moses could not serve as God's deliverer unless and until he obeyed this ordinance. Zipporah, due to Moses' illness, performed the rite for her husband. In the New Testament, real circumcision is of the heart and not of the flesh (Rom. 2:29).

27¶And the LORD said to Aaron, Go into the wilderness to meet Moses.
And he went, and met him in the mount of God, and kissed him.

4:27 Ex 4:14

28And Moses told Aaron all the words of the LORD who had sent him,
and all the signs which he had commanded him.

4:28 Ex 4:15, 16

29¶And Moses and Aaron went and gathered together all the elders of the
children of Israel:

4:29 Ex 3:16

30And Aaron spake all the words which the LORD had spoken unto
Moses, and did the signs in the sight of the people.

☆**4:30** Ex 4:16, 17

31And the people believed: and when they heard that the LORD had
visited the children of Israel, and that he had looked upon their affliction,
then they bowed their heads and worshipped.

4:31 Ex 3:18; 12:27

II. GOD DELIVERS ISRAEL FROM EGYPT (5:1—15:21)

A. MOSES AND AARON APPEAR BEFORE PHARAOH

1. Pharaoh Will Not Let Israel Go

5 AND afterward Moses and Aaron went in, and told Pharaoh, Thus
saith the LORD God of Israel, Let my people go, that they may hold a
feast unto me in the wilderness.

5:1 Ex 3:18; 4:21 10:9

2And Pharaoh said, Who *is* the LORD, that I should obey his voice to let
Israel go? I know not the LORD, neither will I let Israel go.

☆**5:2** Ex 3:19 2 Kgs 18:35 Job 21:15

3And they said, The God of the Hebrews hath met with us: let us go, we
pray thee, three days' journey into the desert, and sacrifice unto the LORD
our God; lest he fall upon us with pestilence, or with the sword.

5:3 Ex 3:18 Deut 28:21

4And the king of Egypt said unto them, Wherefore do ye, Moses and
Aaron, let the people from their works? get you unto your burdens.
5And Pharaoh said, Behold, the people of the land now *are* many, and ye
make them rest from their burdens.

5:4, 5 Ex 1:11; 2:11 Jer 38:4 Amos 7:10

6And Pharaoh commanded the same day the taskmasters of the people,
and their officers, saying,

5:6 Ex 3:7; 5:10, 14

7Ye shall no more give the people straw to make brick, as heretofore: let
them go and gather straw for themselves.

☆**5:7** Gen 11:13

8And the tale of the bricks, which they did make heretofore, ye shall lay
upon them; ye shall not diminish *ought* thereof: for they *be* idle; therefore
they cry, saying, Let us go *and* sacrifice to our God.
9Let there more work be laid upon the men, that they may labour
therein; and let them not regard vain words.

2. Pharoah Increases Israel's Workload

10¶And the taskmasters of the people went out, and their officers, and
they spake to the people, saying, Thus saith Pharaoh, I will not give you
straw.
11Go ye, get you straw where ye can find it: yet not ought of your work
shall be diminished.

4:30 Aaron related to the elders of Israel the words Moses had spoken to him, and he performed the signs which testify to the divine origin of the words. The signs were done in the presence of the people, who were convinced and who "bowed their heads and worshipped" (4:31).

5:2 *I know not the LORD.* Those who refuse to listen will not hear, and those who do not want to know God will not know him.

5:7 *let them go and gather straw for themselves.* Bricks with straw were stronger than bricks without straw. Straw was provided the Israelites by their taskmasters. Now they must go some distance to the fields, gather straw for themselves, and still produce as many bricks as before. This was oppression with a vengeance (see 5:14).

12 So the people were scattered abroad throughout all the land of Egypt to
gather stubble instead of straw.
13 And the taskmasters hasted *them,* saying, Fulfil your works, *your* daily
tasks, as when there was straw.
5:14 14 And the officers of the children of Israel, which Pharaoh's taskmasters
Ex 5:6 had set over them, were beaten, *and* demanded, Wherefore have ye not
Isa 10:24 fulfilled your task in making brick both yesterday and to day, as heretofore?
15 ¶Then the officers of the children of Israel came and cried unto
Pharaoh, saying, Wherefore dealest thou thus with thy servants?
16 There is no straw given unto thy servants, and they say to us, Make
brick: and, behold, thy servants *are* beaten; but the fault *is* in thine own
people.
5:17 17 But he said, Ye *are* idle, *ye are* idle: therefore ye say, Let us go *and* do
Ex 5:8 sacrifice to the LORD.
18 Go therefore now, *and* work; for there shall no straw be given you, yet
shall ye deliver the tale of bricks.
19 And the officers of the children of Israel did see *that* they *were* in evil
case, after it was said, Ye shall not minish *ought* from your bricks of your
daily task.
20 ¶And they met Moses and Aaron, who stood in the way, as they came
forth from Pharaoh:
5:21☆ 21 And they said unto them, The LORD look upon you, and judge; because
Gen 16:5; 34:30 ye have made our savour to be abhorred in the eyes of Pharaoh, and in the
Ex 14:11; 15:24 eyes of his servants, to put a sword in their hand to slay us.

3. God Promises Moses That He Will Free Israel

5:22☆ 22 And Moses returned unto the LORD, and said, Lord, wherefore hast
Num 11:11 thou *so* evil entreated this people? why *is* it *that* thou hast sent me?
Jer 4:10; 20:7
5:23 23 For since I came to Pharaoh to speak in thy name, he hath done evil to
Ex 3:8, 19 this people; neither hast thou delivered thy people at all.

6:1 6 THEN the LORD said unto Moses, Now shalt thou see what I will do
Ex 3:19, 20 to Pharaoh: for with a strong hand shall he let them go, and with a
11:1; 12:31 strong hand shall he drive them out of his land.
Deut 4:34
6:2, 3☆ 2 And God spake unto Moses, and said unto him, I *am* the LORD:
Gen 15:7 3 And I appeared unto Abraham, unto Isaac, and unto Jacob, by *the name*
Ex 3:14; 14:18 *of* God Almighty, but by my name JEHOVAH was I not known to them.
Ps 83:18
Isa 42:8; 52:6 4 And I have also established my covenant with them, to give them the
Jer 16:21 land of Canaan, the land of their pilgrimage, wherein they were strangers.
Ezek 37:6, 13
Jn 8:58
6:4 5 And I have also heard the groaning of the children of Israel, whom the
Gen 15:18 Egyptians keep in bondage; and I have remembered my covenant.
6:5 6 Wherefore say unto the children of Israel, I *am* the LORD, and I will
Ex 2:24 bring you out from under the burdens of the Egyptians, and I will rid you
Deut 6:12 out of their bondage, and I will redeem you with a stretched out arm, and
Ps 105:8 with great judgments:
6:6
Ex 3:17; 7:4
Deut 26:8

5:21 Moses and Aaron were Israel's deliverers. Yet the people who had cried for deliverance unfairly reproached them for their efforts to answer those prayers.

5:22 Moses was perplexed when the situation worsened; God's guarantee to deliver Israel seemed farther away than ever. Moses did not understand that miraculous deliverances may be preceded by great difficulties and times when conditions appear most unfavorable. But we walk by faith and not by sight. Believers should not allow external circumstances to daunt them when they have express promises from God to deliver them. Before Joseph became the prime minister of Egypt he was first a slave, then imprisoned for a crime he never committed. Strong faith is challenged, not defeated, by adverse circumstances.

6:2, 3 Here we discover that God did not reveal his name *Jehovah* to the patriarchs. Yet Gen. 12:8 says that Abraham made an altar to the LORD (i.e., to Jehovah). The explanation is simple. While the patriarchs knew his name, they did not know him as to what the name meant, as now revealed in 6:3—as the God who performs what he has promised and who perfects what he has done and finishes his own work.

7 And I will take you to me for a people, and I will be to you a God: and
ye shall know that I *am* the LORD your God, which bringeth you out from
under the burdens of the Egyptians.
8 And I will bring you in unto the land, concerning the which I did swear
to give it to Abraham, to Isaac, and to Jacob; and I will give it you for an
heritage: I *am* the LORD.
9 ¶And Moses spake so unto the children of Israel: but they hearkened
not unto Moses for anguish of spirit, and for cruel bondage.
10 And the LORD spake unto Moses, saying,
11 Go in, speak unto Pharaoh king of Egypt, that he let the children of
Israel go out of his land.
12 And Moses spake before the LORD, saying, Behold, the children of
Israel have not hearkened unto me; how then shall Pharaoh hear me, who
am of uncircumcised lips?
13 And the LORD spake unto Moses and unto Aaron, and gave them a
charge unto the children of Israel, and unto Pharaoh king of Egypt, to bring
the children of Israel out of the land of Egypt.

6:7 Ex 16:12; Deut 4:20; Isa 60:16
6:8 Num 14:30; Josh 24:13; Ps 136:21; Ezek 20:5
☆6:9 Ex 5:21; 14:12; Num 21:4
6:11 Ex 5:1; 7:2
6:12 Ex 4:10; 6:30

4. The List of Israel's Chief Men

14 ¶These *be* the heads of their fathers' houses: The sons of Reuben the
firstborn of Israel; Ha'noch, and Pal'lu, Hez'ron, and Car'mi: these *be* the
families of Reuben.
15 And the sons of Simeon; Je-mu'el, and Ja'min, and O'had, and Ja'chin,
and Zo'har, and Sha'ul the son of a Canaanitish woman: these *are* the
families of Simeon.
16 ¶And these *are* the names of the sons of Levi according to their
generations; Ger'shon, and Ko'hath, and Me-ra'ri: and the years of the life
of Levi *were* an hundred thirty and seven years.
17 The sons of Ger'shon; Lib'ni, and Shi'mi, according to their families.
18 And the sons of Ko'hath; Amram, and Iz'har, and Hebron, and Uz'zi-
el: and the years of the life of Ko'hath *were* an hundred thirty and three
years.
19 And the sons of Me-ra'ri; Ma'ha-li and Mu'shi: these *are* the families of
Levi according to their generations.
20 And Amram took him Joch'e-bed his father's sister to wife; and she
bare him Aaron and Moses: and the years of the life of Amram *were* an
hundred and thirty and seven years.
21 ¶And the sons of Iz'har; Ko'rah, and Ne'pheg, and Zich'ri.
22 And the sons of Uz'zi-el; Mish'a-el, and El'za-phan, and Zith'ri.
23 And Aaron took him E-lish'e-ba, daughter of Am-min'a-dab, sister of
Na-ash'on, to wife; and she bare him Nadab, and A-bi'hu, E-le-a'zar, and
Ith'a-mar.
24 And the sons of Ko'rah; As'sir, and El-ka'nah, and A-bi'a-saph: these
are the families of the Kor'hites.
25 And E-le-a'zar Aaron's son took him *one* of the daughters of Pu'ti-el to
wife; and she bare him Phin'e-has: these *are* the heads of the fathers of the
Levites according to their families.

6:14 Gen 46:9; Num 26:5
6:15 Gen 46:10; Num 26:12
6:16 Gen 46:11; Num 3:18; 1 Chron 6:1, 16
6:17 Num 3:18–20
6:18 Num 3:25–30; 1 Chron 6:17
6:19 Num 3:33–35
☆6:20 Ex 2:1, 2; Lev 10:1; Num 1:7; 2:3; 3:2; Num 26:59
6:21 Num 16:1; 26:10
6:22 Lev 10:4
6:23 Ex 24:1; Ruth 4:19, 20; 1 Chron 2:10; Lk 1:5
6:24 Ex 6:21; Num 16:1; 1 Chron 6:22, 23, 37
6:25 Num 25:7, 11; Josh 22:13

6:9 *for anguish of spirit, and for cruel bondage,* i.e., "because they were too dispirited after the tragic consequences of what he had said before."† Moses' first contest with the Pharaoh only worsened the slave conditions of the Israelites; now they had to find their own straw to manufacture bricks. When Moses brought them a message of encouragement, promising that God would deliver them from their bondage, they did not listen. Their spirit had been broken and their bondage made more cruel. Matthew Henry has said: "By indulging ourselves in discontent and fretfulness, we deprive ourselves of the comfort we might have both from God's word and from his providence, and must thank ourselves if we go comfortless."

6:20 *Amram.* See 6:18.

6:26 Ex 6:13; Josh 24:5
[26] These *are* that Aaron and Moses, to whom the LORD said, Bring out the
children of Israel from the land of Egypt according to their armies.

6:27 Ex 5:1; 7:6
[27] These *are* they which spake to Pharaoh king of Egypt, to bring out the
children of Israel from Egypt: these *are* that Moses and Aaron.

6:28, 29 Ex 6:2; 7:16
[28] ¶And it came to pass on the day *when* the LORD spake unto Moses in
the land of Egypt,
[29] That the LORD spake unto Moses, saying, I *am* the LORD: speak thou
unto Pharaoh king of Egypt all that I say unto thee.

6:30 Ex 4:10; 6:12
[30] And Moses said before the LORD, Behold, I *am* of uncircumcised lips,
and how shall Pharaoh hearken unto me?

5. Moses Told to Speak to Pharoah Again

7:1☆ Ex 4:16; 18:19
7 AND the LORD said unto Moses, See, I have made thee a god to
Pharaoh: and Aaron thy brother shall be thy prophet.

7:2 Ex 4:15
[2] Thou shalt speak all that I command thee: and Aaron thy brother shall
speak unto Pharaoh, that he send the children of Israel out of his land.

7:3 Ex 4:21; 8:19; 9:16, 34
[3] And I will harden Pharaoh's heart, and multiply my signs and my
wonders in the land of Egypt.

7:4 Ex 11:9; 12:51
[4] But Pharaoh shall not hearken unto you, that I may lay my hand upon
Egypt, and bring forth mine armies, *and* my people the children of Israel,
out of the land of Egypt by great judgments.

7:5 Ex 8:10, 19; 14:4
[5] And the Egyptians shall know that I *am* the LORD, when I stretch forth
mine hand upon Egypt, and bring out the children of Israel from among
them.

7:6 Ex 12:28; 39:43; 40:16
7:7 Deut 31:2; 34:7; Acts 7:23, 30
[6] And Moses and Aaron did as the LORD commanded them, so did they.
[7] And Moses *was* fourscore years old, and Aaron fourscore and three
years old, when they spake unto Pharaoh.

B. MOSES PERFORMS WONDROUS MIRACLES

1. The Rod That Became a Serpent

[8] ¶And the LORD spake unto Moses and unto Aaron, saying,

7:9 Ex 4:3; Isa 7:11; Jn 2:18
[9] When Pharaoh shall speak unto you, saying, Shew a miracle for you:
then thou shalt say unto Aaron, Take thy rod, and cast *it* before Pharaoh,
and it shall become a serpent.
[10] ¶And Moses and Aaron went in unto Pharaoh, and they did so as the
LORD had commanded: and Aaron cast down his rod before Pharaoh, and
before his servants, and it became a serpent.

7:11 Gen 41:8; Ex 8:7, 18; Dan 2:4; 2 Tim 3:8, 9
[11] Then Pharaoh also called the wise men and the sorcerers: now the
magicians of Egypt, they also did in like manner with their enchantments.

7:12☆ Ex 8:19
[12] For they cast down every man his rod, and they became serpents: but
Aaron's rod swallowed up their rods.

7:13 Ex 4:21; Deut 2:30; Zech 7:11
[13] And he hardened Pharaoh's heart, that he hearkened not unto them; as
the LORD had said.

7:1 Aaron was eighty-three years old and Moses eighty. Some of God's servants wait a long time to be used and have been long in preparing for the service they render to God. On the other hand, John the Baptist served and died before he was thirty-two, and Jesus the Savior died at thirty-three.

7:12 At every important juncture God provided outward evidence which bore testimony to his divine work. Aaron's rod is a case in point. Two miracles took place here. The first was when the rod, in the hand of Aaron, was cast to the ground and became a serpent. (May it not have been a sign of what had happened in the Garden of Eden when Satan appeared as a serpent?) The Egyptian wise men and sorcerers were able to challenge Aaron by a counter-miracle. Then the second miracle occurred: the serpents of Pharaoh's

2. The River That Turned to Blood

14¶And the LORD said unto Moses, Pharaoh's heart *is* hardened, he refuseth to let the people go.

7:14 Ex 7:4; 8:15

15 Get thee unto Pharaoh in the morning; lo, he goeth out unto the water; and thou shalt stand by the river's brink against he come; and the rod which was turned to a serpent shalt thou take in thine hand.

7:15 Ex 2:5; 8:20

16 And thou shalt say unto him, The LORD God of the Hebrews hath sent me unto thee, saying, Let my people go, that they may serve me in the wilderness: and, behold, hitherto thou wouldest not hear.

7:16 Ex 4:23; 8:1

17 Thus saith the LORD, In this thou shalt know that I *am* the LORD: behold, I will smite with the rod that *is* in mine hand upon the waters which *are* in the river, and they shall be turned to blood.

7:17 Ex 7:20 Rev 11:6; 16:4–6

18 And the fish that *is* in the river shall die, and the river shall stink; and the Egyptians shall lothe to drink of the water of the river.

19¶And the LORD spake unto Moses, Say unto Aaron, Take thy rod, and stretch out thine hand upon the waters of Egypt, upon their streams, upon their rivers, and upon their ponds, and upon all their pools of water, that they may become blood; and *that* there may be blood throughout all the land of Egypt, both in *vessels of* wood, and in *vessels of* stone.

7:19 Ex 8:5, 16; 9:22

20 And Moses and Aaron did so, as the LORD commanded; and he lifted up the rod, and smote the waters that *were* in the river, in the sight of Pharaoh, and in the sight of his servants; and all the waters that *were* in the river were turned to blood.

7:20 Ps 78:44; 105:28, 29

21 And the fish that *was* in the river died; and the river stank, and the Egyptians could not drink of the water of the river; and there was blood throughout all the land of Egypt.

22 And the magicians of Egypt did so with their enchantments: and Pharaoh's heart was hardened, neither did he hearken unto them; as the LORD had said.

☆**7:22** Ex 8:7

23 And Pharaoh turned and went into his house, neither did he set his heart to this also.

7:23 Ex 9:21

24 And all the Egyptians digged round about the river for water to drink; for they could not drink of the water of the river.

25 And seven days were fulfilled, after that the LORD had smitten the river.

3. The Nile That Swarmed with Frogs

8 AND the LORD spake unto Moses, Go unto Pharaoh, and say unto him, Thus saith the LORD, Let my people go, that they may serve me.

8:1 Ex 5:1

2 And if thou refuse to let *them* go, behold, I will smite all thy borders with frogs:

☆**8:2** Rev 16:13

3 And the river shall bring forth frogs abundantly, which shall go up and come into thine house, and into thy bedchamber, and upon thy bed, and into the house of thy servants, and upon thy people, and into thine ovens, and into thy kneadingtroughs:

8:3 Ps 105:30

---

men were swallowed by Aaron's serpent, which then again became a rod.

7:22 Since the Nile was turned into blood by Moses, the magicians must have obtained water from newly dug wells—to turn it into blood by their arts. It was by God's permission that the magicians were able to "ape the miracle by their enchantments." Matthew Henry says, "Could they have turned the river of blood into water again, this would have been something to the purpose; then they would have proved their power, and Pharaoh would have been obliged to them as his benefactors."

8:2 *I will smite all thy borders with frogs.* This is the only time frogs are mentioned in the Scriptures. Moses told Aaron to use his rod, but it was the act of God who said, "I will smite." The irony of this judgment is that the magicians made the situation worse by adding more frogs to the ones God sent. Pharaoh should have asked his magicians to reverse the act of God and make the frogs disappear!

4And the frogs shall come up both on thee, and upon thy people, and
upon all thy servants.

8:5 Ex 7:19; 8:16

5¶And the LORD spake unto Moses, Say unto Aaron, Stretch forth thine
hand with thy rod over the streams, over the rivers, and over the ponds, and
cause frogs to come up upon the land of Egypt.

8:6 Ps 78:45; 105:30

6And Aaron stretched out his hand over the waters of Egypt; and the
frogs came up, and covered the land of Egypt.

8:7☆ Ex 7:11; 8:18

7And the magicians did so with their enchantments, and brought up frogs
upon the land of Egypt.

8:8☆ Ex 5:2; 9:28 10:10, 17

8¶Then Pharaoh called for Moses and Aaron, and said, Intreat the LORD,
that he may take away the frogs from me, and from my people; and I will
let the people go, that they may do sacrifice unto the LORD.
9And Moses said unto Pharaoh, Glory over me: when shall I intreat for
thee, and for thy servants, and for thy people, to destroy the frogs from thee
and thy houses, *that* they may remain in the river only?

8:10 Ex 9:14, 29 15:11 Deut 4:35 Ps 83:18 Isa 46:9

10And he said, To morrow. And he said, *Be it* according to thy word: that
thou mayest know that *there is* none like unto the LORD our God.
11And the frogs shall depart from thee, and from thy houses, and from
thy servants, and from thy people; they shall remain in the river only.

8:12☆ Ex 8:30; 9:33; 10:18

12And Moses and Aaron went out from Pharaoh: and Moses cried unto
the LORD because of the frogs which he had brought against Pharaoh.
13And the LORD did according to the word of Moses; and the frogs died
out of the houses, out of the villages, and out of the fields.
14And they gathered them together upon heaps: and the land stank.

8:15 Ex 7:22; 9:34 14:5 Prov 29:1 Eccles 8:11

15But when Pharaoh saw that there was respite, he hardened his heart,
and hearkened not unto them; as the LORD had said.

4. The Lice That Covered the Land

8:16 Ex 8:5; 9:22

16¶And the LORD said unto Moses, Say unto Aaron, Stretch out thy rod,
and smite the dust of the land, that it may become lice throughout all the
land of Egypt.

8:17 Ps 105:31

17And they did so; for Aaron stretched out his hand with his rod, and
smote the dust of the earth, and it became lice in man, and in beast; all the
dust of the land became lice throughout all the land of Egypt.

8:18 Ex 7:11; 9:11

18And the magicians did so with their enchantments to bring forth lice,
but they could not: so there were lice upon man, and upon beast.

8:19☆ Ex 7:5; 8:15 1 Sam 6:9

19Then the magicians said unto Pharaoh, This *is* the finger of God: and
Pharaoh's heart was hardened, and he hearkened not unto them; as the
LORD had said.

8:7 In 7:11, 22 and 8:7 the magicians of Egypt replicated the miracles of Moses and Aaron. But in 8:18 they failed to do so. Paul explains these kinds of phenomena when he speaks about "the working of Satan with all power and signs and lying wonders" in 2 Thess. 2:9. Miracles performed by Satan and his agents should not disturb us, and we should not attribute all miracles to God. Satan cannot harm the people of God, who are protected against the wiles of the evil one.

8:8 Pharaoh's servants could replicate what Moses and Aaron were doing. But that ability could not change the situation. Now the time comes when Pharaoh has a glimmer of understanding for he begs Moses and Aaron, "Entreat the LORD, that he may take away the frogs from me, and from my people."

8:12 Moses' prayer for God to remove the frogs was answered. But Moses had already told Pharaoh that the removal of the frogs would take place "that thou mayest know that there is none like unto the LORD our God" (8:10). The gods of the Egyptians were powerless; only Yahweh could deliver Egypt from this plague.

8:19 At last Pharaoh's magicians became convinced that Moses and Aaron had gifts from God that they could not match. No longer could they reproduce Moses' miracles. But the heart of Pharaoh remained adamant. He is a classic example of those who know the truth but still reject it in the face of all the evidences they need.

5. The Swarms of Flies

20¶And the LORD said unto Moses, Rise up early in the morning, and
stand before Pharaoh; lo, he cometh forth to the water; and say unto him,
Thus saith the LORD, Let my people go, that they may serve me.
21Else, if thou wilt not let my people go, behold, I will send swarms *of
flies* upon thee, and upon thy servants, and upon thy people, and into thy
houses: and the houses of the Egyptians shall be full of swarms *of flies,* and
also the ground whereon they *are.*
22And I will sever in that day the land of Goshen, in which my people
dwell, that no swarms *of flies* shall be there; to the end thou mayest know
that I *am* the LORD in the midst of the earth.
23And I will put a division between my people and thy people: to morrow
shall this sign be.
24And the LORD did so; and there came a grievous swarm *of flies* into the
house of Pharaoh, and *into* his servants' houses, and into all the land of
Egypt: the land was corrupted by reason of the swarm *of flies.*
25¶And Pharaoh called for Moses and for Aaron, and said, Go ye,
sacrifice to your God in the land.
26And Moses said, It is not meet so to do; for we shall sacrifice the
abomination of the Egyptians to the LORD our God: lo, shall we sacrifice
the abomination of the Egyptians before their eyes, and will they not stone
us?
27We will go three days' journey into the wilderness, and sacrifice to the
LORD our God, as he shall command us.
28And Pharaoh said, I will let you go, that ye may sacrifice to the LORD
your God in the wilderness; only ye shall not go very far away: intreat for
me.
29And Moses said, Behold, I go out from thee, and I will intreat the LORD
that the swarms *of flies* may depart from Pharaoh, from his servants, and
from his people, to morrow: but let not Pharaoh deal deceitfully any more
in not letting the people go to sacrifice to the LORD.
30And Moses went out from Pharaoh, and intreated the LORD.
31And the LORD did according to the word of Moses; and he removed the
swarms *of flies* from Pharaoh, from his servants, and from his people; there
remained not one.
32And Pharaoh hardened his heart at this time also, neither would he let
the people go.

8:20 Ex 7:15
8:22 Ex 8:10; 9:4; 10:23
8:24 Ps 78:45; 105:31
8:25 Gen 46:34; Ex 8:8; 10:8
☆**8:26** Ex 3:18; 9:3
8:27 Ex 10:26
8:28 Ex 8:8; 9:28; 1 Kgs 13:6
☆**8:30** Ex 8:12
8:31, 32 Ex 7:13; 9:12

6. The Egyptian Cattle That Died

9 THEN the LORD said unto Moses, Go in unto Pharaoh, and tell him,
Thus saith the LORD God of the Hebrews, Let my people go, that they
may serve me.
2For if thou refuse to let *them* go, and wilt hold them still,
3Behold, the hand of the LORD is upon thy cattle which *is* in the field,
upon the horses, upon the asses, upon the camels, upon the oxen, and upon
the sheep: *there shall be* a very grievous murrain.
4And the LORD shall sever between the cattle of Israel and the cattle of
Egypt: and there shall nothing die of all *that is* the children's of Israel.

9:1 Ex 8:1; 10:3
9:3 Ex 7:4; 9:18
☆**9:4** Ex 8:22; 9:26

8:26 "It would have been an abomination to God should they offer Egyptian sacrifices, and an abomination to the Egyptians should they offer to God their own sacrifices, as they ought; so that they could not sacrifice *in the land* without incurring the displeasure either of their God or of their taskmasters."* So Moses refused their offer.

8:30 Again Moses prays to God for the removal of a plague. By this time the Pharaoh should have been convinced that the God of Israel was greater than all the gods of Egypt.

9:4 God distinguished between the Israelites and the Egyptians. The judgments of God on Pharaoh did not touch Israel. God's people were supernaturally pre-

9:5☆ Ex 8:23; 10:4 [5]And the LORD appointed a set time, saying, To morrow the LORD shall
do this thing in the land.
[6]And the LORD did that thing on the morrow, and all the cattle of Egypt
died: but of the cattle of the children of Israel died not one.
9:7 Ex 7:14; 8:32 [7]And Pharaoh sent, and, behold, there was not one of the cattle of the
9:35 Israelites dead. And the heart of Pharaoh was hardened, and he did not let
the people go.

7. The Boils on Man and Beast

9:8 Ex 8:16 [8]¶And the LORD said unto Moses and unto Aaron, Take to you handfuls
of ashes of the furnace, and let Moses sprinkle it toward the heaven in the
sight of Pharaoh.
9:9 Lev 13:18 [9]And it shall become small dust in all the land of Egypt, and shall be a
Rev 16:2 boil breaking forth *with* blains upon man, and upon beast, throughout all
the land of Egypt.
[10]And they took ashes of the furnace, and stood before Pharaoh; and
Moses sprinkled it up toward heaven; and it became a boil breaking forth
with blains upon man, and upon beast.
9:11☆ Ex 8:18 [11]And the magicians could not stand before Moses because of the boils;
for the boil was upon the magicians, and upon all the Egyptians.
9:12 Ex 7:13; 10:1 [12]And the LORD hardened the heart of Pharaoh, and he hearkened not
unto them; as the LORD had spoken unto Moses.

8. The Hail and Lightning

9:13 Ex 8:20 [13]¶And the LORD said unto Moses, Rise up early in the morning, and
stand before Pharaoh, and say unto him, Thus saith the LORD God of the
Hebrews, Let my people go, that they may serve me.
9:14 Ex 8:10; 5:11 [14]For I will at this time send all my plagues upon thine heart, and upon
thy servants, and upon thy people; that thou mayest know that *there is*
none like me in all the earth.
9:15 Ex 11:6; 14:28 [15]For now I will stretch out my hand, that I may smite thee and thy
people with pestilence; and thou shalt be cut off from the earth.
9:16 Ex 14:4, 17 [16]And in very deed for this *cause* have I raised thee up, for to shew *in* thee
18:11 my power; and that my name may be declared throughout all the earth.
Rom 9:17 9:17 Job 9:4; 15:25 [17]As yet exaltest thou thyself against my people, that thou wilt not let
Isa 37:23 them go?
9:18☆ Ex 9:5; 10:4 [18]Behold, to morrow about this time I will cause it to rain a very grievous
hail, such as hath not been in Egypt since the foundation thereof even until
now.
[19]Send therefore now, *and* gather thy cattle, and all that thou hast in the
field; *for upon* every man and beast which shall be found in the field, and

served from the various plagues. Throughout the history of redemption, God has intervened on behalf of his people in many instances, delivering them, preserving them, and protecting them.

9:5 *Tomorrow the LORD will do this thing.* Before this, the plagues were brought on Egypt by the use of the rod in the hands of Moses and Aaron. Here, God performs the miracle without the use of the rod; no secondary agent is involved. If this would not move Pharaoh and change his heart, what would?

9:11 *the boil was upon the magicians.* God will not be mocked. The magicians now suffer from the boils. They had helped to harden the Pharaoh's heart by pretending to imitate the earlier plagues. Now all Egypt learns that the magicians cannot keep themselves from the plague. How then could they preserve the people from the plagues? God disarmed his adversary and made Satan look foolish.

9:18 Never had Egypt suffered a hailstorm as severe as that which God sent in this episode. Yet the storm stopped at the edge of the land of Goshen where the Israelites resided (9:26). In this catastrophe God was

shall not be brought home, the hail shall come down upon them, and they
shall die.
20 He that feared the word of the LORD among the servants of Pharaoh
made his servants and his cattle flee into the houses:
21 And he that regarded not the word of the LORD left his servants and his
cattle in the field.
22 ¶And the LORD said unto Moses, Stretch forth thine hand toward
heaven, that there may be hail in all the land of Egypt, upon man, and upon
beast, and upon every herb of the field, throughout the land of Egypt.
23 And Moses stretched forth his rod toward heaven: and the LORD sent
thunder and hail, and the fire ran along upon the ground; and the LORD
rained hail upon the land of Egypt.
24 So there was hail, and fire mingled with the hail, very grievous, such as
there was none like it in all the land of Egypt since it became a nation.
25 And the hail smote throughout all the land of Egypt all that *was* in the
field, both man and beast; and the hail smote every herb of the field, and
brake every tree of the field.
26 Only in the land of Goshen, where the children of Israel *were,* was there
no hail.
27 ¶And Pharaoh sent, and called for Moses and Aaron, and said unto
them, I have sinned this time: the LORD *is* righteous, and I and my people
are wicked.
28 Intreat the LORD (for *it is* enough) that there be no *more* mighty
thunderings and hail; and I will let you go, and ye shall stay no longer.
29 And Moses said unto him, As soon as I am gone out of the city, I will
spread abroad my hands unto the LORD; *and* the thunder shall cease,
neither shall there be any more hail; that thou mayest know how that the
earth *is* the LORD's.
30 But as for thee and thy servants, I know that ye will not yet fear the
LORD God.
31 And the flax and the barley was smitten: for the barley *was* in the ear,
and the flax *was* bolled.
32 But the wheat and the rie were not smitten: for they *were* not grown up.
33 And Moses went out of the city from Pharaoh, and spread abroad his
hands unto the LORD: and the thunders and hail ceased, and the rain was
not poured upon the earth.
34 And when Pharaoh saw that the rain and the hail and the thunders
were ceased, he sinned yet more, and hardened his heart, he and his
servants.
35 And the heart of Pharaoh was hardened, neither would he let the
children of Israel go; as the LORD had spoken by Moses.

☆**9:20** Prov 13:13; Heb 11:7
9:22 Ex 8:5
9:23 Ex 19:16; Josh 10:11; Ps 18:13; 78:47; 105:32; Rev 8:3; 16:21
9:24 Ex 10:6; Mt 24:21
9:25 Ps 105:33
9:26 Ex 8:22; 10:23
☆**9:27** 2 Chron 12:6; Ps 129:4
9:28 Ex 8:8; 10:17
9:29 Deut 10:14; Ps 24:1; 1 Cor 10:26, 28
☆**9:30** Ex 8:29; 11:9
☆**9:31**
9:34 Ex 8:15; 11:9

gracious enough to warn the Pharaoh to bring in the animals and the laborers from the fields so they would not perish (9:19).

9:20 Now God has gotten the attention of some of the Egyptians. Some now believe God and accept the warning. They bring their servants and animals into the houses. Others still refuse to believe; they and their animals are overtaken by a hail such as the Egyptians had never seen before.

9:27 The Pharaoh admitted that he was a sinner and beseeched Moses to pray to God for him. Convicted sinners may well repent at the moment judgment strikes them, but shortly thereafter they lapse into their old ways. This is not genuine repentance.

9:30 Moses exhibited spiritual insight into the true estate of the Pharaoh, for he said, in effect, "you will repent of your repentance." And he did, for his heart was hardened again.

9:31 It was January and the flax and barley crops were ready for harvesting. These crops were ruined. The wheat and the rie (rie was a variant form of wheat—*Triticum spelta*) were not ruined, for they would ripen a month or two later.

9. The Destroying Locusts

10:1 Ex 4:21; 7:13; 14:17

10 AND the LORD said unto Moses, Go in unto Pharaoh: for I have hardened his heart, and the heart of his servants, that I might shew these my signs before him:

10:2☆ Ex 13:8; Deut 4:9; Ps 44:1

2 And that thou mayest tell in the ears of thy son, and of thy son's son, what things I have wrought in Egypt, and my signs which I have done among them; that ye may know how that I *am* the LORD.

10:3 Ex 4:23; 16:28

3 And Moses and Aaron came in unto Pharaoh, and said unto him, Thus saith the LORD God of the Hebrews, How long wilt thou refuse to humble thyself before me? let my people go, that they may serve me.

10:4, 5 Ex 9:18; 11:4, 5; Joel 1:4; 2:25

4 Else, if thou refuse to let my people go, behold, to morrow will I bring the locusts into thy coast:

5 And they shall cover the face of the earth, that one cannot be able to see the earth: and they shall eat the residue of that which is escaped, which remaineth unto you from the hail, and shall eat every tree which groweth for you out of the field:

6 And they shall fill thy houses, and the houses of all thy servants, and the houses of all the Egyptians; which neither thy fathers, nor thy fathers' fathers have seen, since the day that they were upon the earth unto this day. And he turned himself, and went out from Pharaoh.

10:7 Ex 5:1; 12:33

7 And Pharaoh's servants said unto him, How long shall this man be a snare unto us? let the men go, that they may serve the LORD their God: knowest thou not yet that Egypt is destroyed?

10:8 Ex 5:1; 8:25

8 And Moses and Aaron were brought again unto Pharaoh: and he said unto them, Go, serve the LORD your God: *but* who *are* they that shall go?

10:9☆ Ex 12:37

9 And Moses said, We will go with our young and with our old, with our sons and with our daughters, with our flocks and with our herds will we go; for we *must hold* a feast unto the LORD.

10:10 Gen 50:8; Ex 12:31

10 And he said unto them, Let the LORD be so with you, as I will let you go, and your little ones: look *to it;* for evil *is* before you.

10:11☆ Ex 10:28; 11:8

11 Not so: go now ye *that are* men, and serve the LORD; for that ye did desire. And they were driven out from Pharaoh's presence.

10:12 Ex 7:19; 9:22

12 ¶And the LORD said unto Moses, Stretch out thine hand over the land of Egypt for the locusts, that they may come up upon the land of Egypt, and eat every herb of the land, *even* all that the hail hath left.

10:13 Ps 78:46; 105:34

13 And Moses stretched forth his rod over the land of Egypt, and the LORD brought an east wind upon the land all that day, and all *that* night; *and* when it was morning, the east wind brought the locusts.

10:14☆ Joel 1:4, 7; 2:1, 11

14 And the locusts went up over all the land of Egypt, and rested in all the coasts of Egypt: very grievous *were they;* before them there were no such locusts as they, neither after them shall be such.

10:15 Ex 10:5; Ps 78:46; 105:35

15 For they covered the face of the whole earth, so that the land was darkened; and they did eat every herb of the land, and all the fruit of the trees which the hail had left: and there remained not any green thing in the trees, or in the herbs of the field, through all the land of Egypt.

10:2 Seven plagues had overtaken Egypt. There were three more to come—locusts, darkness, and the death of the firstborn. God told Moses that the design of these plagues and the deliverance of the Israelites from Egypt will glorify his name and himself.

10:9 The Pharaoh's ministers of state saw the light before the king himself did. They recognized that Egypt was in danger of destruction. With the welfare of all the people in mind, they begged the Pharaoh to release the Israelites. Moses, they agreed, was a snare to Egypt and his people a burdensome stone to the Egyptians. It is unfortunate for a whole nation to be ruined by the obstinacy of its ruler or rulers. "To consult the welfare of the people is the first of laws."*

10:11 The Pharaoh made it plain that the men were permitted to depart from Egypt to offer their sacrifices, but not the women and children. Undoubtedly he supposed that the men would return because of their love for their families. Yet again, if they did not return, Egypt would still have the women and children as slaves. A half a loaf would be better than none.

10:14 *before them there were no such locusts as they,* i.e., "There never have been so many locusts" (NASB). The book of Joel later describes another invasion by

16 ¶Then Pharaoh called for Moses and Aaron in haste; and he said, I
have sinned against the LORD your God, and against you.
17 Now therefore forgive, I pray thee, my sin only this once, and intreat
the LORD your God, that he may take away from me this death only.
18 And he went out from Pharaoh, and intreated the LORD.
19 And the LORD turned a mighty strong west wind, which took away the
locusts, and cast them into the Red sea; there remained not one locust in all
the coasts of Egypt.
20 But the LORD hardened Pharaoh's heart, so that he would not let the
children of Israel go.

10:16 Ex 8:8; 9:27
10:17 Ex 8:28; Num 21:7; 1 Sam 15:25
10:18 Ex 8:30
10:20 Ex 4:21; 9:12; 11:10

10. Three Days of Thick Darkness

21 ¶And the LORD said unto Moses, Stretch out thine hand toward
heaven, that there may be darkness over the land of Egypt, even darkness
which may be felt.
22 And Moses stretched forth his hand toward heaven; and there was a
thick darkness in all the land of Egypt three days:
23 They saw not one another, neither rose any from his place for three
days: but all the children of Israel had light in their dwellings.
24 ¶And Pharaoh called unto Moses, and said, Go ye, serve the LORD;
only let your flocks and your herds be stayed: let your little ones also go
with you.
25 And Moses said, Thou must give us also sacrifices and burnt offerings,
that we may sacrifice unto the LORD our God.
26 Our cattle also shall go with us; there shall not an hoof be left behind;
for thereof must we take to serve the LORD our God; and we know not with
what we must serve the LORD, until we come thither.
27 ¶But the LORD hardened Pharaoh's heart, and he would not let them
go.
28 And Pharaoh said unto him, Get thee from me, take heed to thyself, see
my face no more; for in *that* day thou seest my face thou shalt die.
29 And Moses said, Thou hast spoken well, I will see thy face again no
more.

☆**10:21** Ex 9:22; Deut 28:29
10:22 Ex 20:21; Ps 105:28; Joel 2:2
☆**10:23** Ex 8:22; 9:4; 14:20
☆**10:24** Ex 8:28; 10:8
10:26 Ex 10:9; 12:32
10:27 Ex 4:21; 9:12; 11:10; 14:4
10:28 Ex 10:11
10:29 Heb 11:27

11. The Death of the Oldest Sons

a. The Announcement to Pharaoh

11 AND the LORD said unto Moses, Yet will I bring one plague *more*
upon Pharaoh, and upon Egypt; afterwards he will let you go
hence: when he shall let *you* go, he shall surely thrust you out hence
altogether.
2 Speak now in the ears of the people, and let every man borrow of his
neighbour, and every woman of her neighbour, jewels of silver, and jewels
of gold.

11:1 Ex 3:20, 21; 12:31
☆**11:2** Ex 12:35

---

locusts. The scene he pictures helps us understand how awful this plague was in Egypt.

10:21 God sent a total darkness over Egypt. The people could not see each other and they are said to have experienced a darkness "which may be felt." Neither the light of the sky nor of candles and fires was seen during those three days. So great was the pitch blackness that no one rose . . . from his place for three days" (10:23). The Egyptians had a foretaste of what hell is like—darkness, for God, who is light, is absent from there.

10:23 Again and again the Israelites were exempted from the plagues sent by God on the Egyptians. This affords us assurance that at the end of the age, when great evils occur, God will protect his people even as he then protected the Israelites.

10:24 The Pharaoh tried to bargain with God again. This time he offered to let the Israelites take their little ones with them so long as they left their flocks and herds behind. Moses refused to comply. He would not compromise the divine demands of his God.

11:2 The Israelites had been slaves who received no remuneration for their labors. Now God makes the Egyptians willing to give them silver and gold. The oppressors must pay for their oppression one way or another.

11:3 Deut 34:10–12

3 And the LORD gave the people favour in the sight of the Egyptians. Moreover the man Moses *was* very great in the land of Egypt, in the sight of Pharaoh's servants, and in the sight of the people.

11:4 Ex 12:29 Amos 4:10

4 And Moses said, Thus saith the LORD, About midnight will I go out into the midst of Egypt:

11:5 Ex 4:23; 12:12 13:15

5 And all the firstborn in the land of Egypt shall die, from the firstborn of Pharaoh that sitteth upon his throne, even unto the firstborn of the maidservant that *is* behind the mill; and all the firstborn of beasts.

11:6 Ex 12:30 Amos 5:17

6 And there shall be a great cry throughout all the land of Egypt, such as there was none like it, nor shall be like it any more.

11:7☆ Ex 8:22; 10:23

7 But against any of the children of Israel shall not a dog move his tongue, against man or beast: that ye may know how that the LORD doth put a difference between the Egyptians and Israel.

11:8 Ex 12:31 Heb 11:27

8 And all these thy servants shall come down unto me, and bow down themselves unto me, saying, Get thee out, and all the people that follow thee: and after that I will go out. And he went out from Pharaoh in a great anger.

11:9 Ex 7:4; 10:1

9 And the LORD said unto Moses, Pharaoh shall not hearken unto you; that my wonders may be multiplied in the land of Egypt.

11:10 Ex 4:21 10:20, 27 Rom 2:2; 9:17, 22

10 And Moses and Aaron did all these wonders before Pharaoh: and the LORD hardened Pharaoh's heart, so that he would not let the children of Israel go out of his land.

b. The Celebration of the First Passover

12 AND the LORD spake unto Moses and Aaron in the land of Egypt, saying,

12:2☆ Ex 12:14; 13:4 23:15; 34:18 Num 28:16

2 This month *shall be* unto you the beginning of months: it *shall be* the first month of the year to you.

12:3☆ Lev 1:5 Jn 12:1 1 Cor 5:7

3 ¶Speak ye unto all the congregation of Israel, saying, In the tenth *day* of this month they shall take to them every man a lamb, according to the house of *their* fathers, a lamb for an house:

4 And if the household be too little for the lamb, let him and his neighbour next unto his house take *it* according to the number of the souls; every man according to his eating shall make your count for the lamb.

12:5 Lev 22:18–20 23:12 Mal 1:8, 14 Heb 9:14

5 Your lamb shall be without blemish, a male of the first year: ye shall take *it* out from the sheep, or from the goats:

12:6 Lev 23:5 Num 9:3; 28:16 Deut 16:1 Mk 14:12

6 And ye shall keep it up until the fourteenth day of the same month: and the whole assembly of the congregation of Israel shall kill it in the evening.

12:7 Ex 12:22 Eph 1:7 Heb 9:13, 14 11:28

7 And they shall take of the blood, and strike *it* on the two side posts and on the upper door post of the houses, wherein they shall eat it.

12:8 Ex 13:3; 34:25 Num 9:11 Deut 16:7

8 And they shall eat the flesh in that night, roast with fire, and unleavened bread; *and* with bitter *herbs* they shall eat it.

12:9☆ Ex 29:17 Deut 16:7

9 Eat not of it raw, nor sodden at all with water, but roast *with* fire; his head with his legs, and with the purtenance thereof.

12:10 Ex 23:18; 29:34 Lev 7:15

10 And ye shall let nothing of it remain until the morning; and that which remaineth of it until the morning ye shall burn with fire.

12:11☆ Ex 12:27 Num 28:16

11 ¶And thus shall ye eat it; *with* your loins girded, your shoes on your

---

11:7 "While angels drew their swords against the Egyptians, there should not so much as a dog bark at any of the children of Israel."*

12:2 *the first month of the year to you.* God ordained that the calendar year should start with the month Nisan, which, in our calendar, is equivalent to the latter part of March and first part of April.

12:3, 4 The sacrificial lamb had to be perfect and its blood was offered as an atonement for sin. The lamb was a substitute for the offerer. So Christ, the perfect Lamb of God, offered his own blood as our substitute. He delivered us from the tyranny of sin as God delivered Israel from her Egyptian oppressor. The Hebrew word translated here as "lamb" can also mean "kid"—a baby goat.

12:9 *with the purtenance thereof,* i.e., "its inner parts."

12:11 On the Passover night the angel of death swept

feet, and your staff in your hand; and ye shall eat it in haste: it *is* the
LORD's passover.
12 For I will pass through the land of Egypt this night, and will smite all
the firstborn in the land of Egypt, both man and beast; and against all the
gods of Egypt I will execute judgment: I *am* the LORD.
13 And the blood shall be to you for a token upon the houses where ye
are: and when I see the blood, I will pass over you, and the plague shall not
be upon you to destroy *you,* when I smite the land of Egypt.
14 And this day shall be unto you for a memorial; and ye shall keep it a
feast to the LORD throughout your generations; ye shall keep it a feast by
an ordinance for ever.
15 Seven days shall ye eat unleavened bread; even the first day ye shall put
away leaven out of your houses: for whosoever eateth leavened bread from
the first day until the seventh day, that soul shall be cut off from Israel.
16 And in the first day *there shall be* an holy convocation, and in the
seventh day there shall be an holy convocation to you; no manner of work
shall be done in them, save *that* which every man must eat, that only may
be done of you.
17 And ye shall observe *the feast of* unleavened bread; for in this selfsame
day have I brought your armies out of the land of Egypt: therefore shall ye
observe this day in your generations by an ordinance for ever.
18 In the first *month,* on the fourteenth day of the month at even, ye shall
eat unleavened bread, until the one and twentieth day of the month at even.
19 Seven days shall there be no leaven found in your houses: for
whosoever eateth that which is leavened, even that soul shall be cut off from
the congregation of Israel, whether he be a stranger, or born in the land.
20 Ye shall eat nothing leavened; in all your habitations shall ye eat
unleavened bread.
21 ¶Then Moses called for all the elders of Israel, and said unto them,
Draw out and take you a lamb according to your families, and kill the
passover.
22 And ye shall take a bunch of hyssop, and dip *it* in the blood that *is* in
the bason, and strike the lintel and the two side posts with the blood that *is*
in the bason; and none of you shall go out at the door of his house until the
morning.
23 For the LORD will pass through to smite the Egyptians; and when he
seeth the blood upon the lintel, and on the two side posts, the LORD will
pass over the door, and will not suffer the destroyer to come in unto your
houses to smite *you.*
24 And ye shall observe this thing for an ordinance to thee and to thy sons
for ever.
25 And it shall come to pass, when ye be come to the land which the LORD
will give you, according as he hath promised, that ye shall keep this service.

12:12 Ex 11:4, 5 Num 33:4 Amos 5:17
12:13 Heb 11:28
☆**12:14** Ex 12:6 13:9, 10 Deut 16:11
☆**12:15** Ex 13:6; 34:18 Lev 23:5–8 Deut 16:3
12:16 Ex 20:10 Num 28:18
12:17 Ex 13:3 Num 9:4; 28:16 Josh 5:10 2 Kgs 23:21 Ezra 6:20 Mk 14:12–16
12:19 Ex 12:15
12:21 Ex 3:16; 17:5 Heb 11:28
☆**12:22** Lev 14:6 Num 19:18 Ps 51:7 Heb 9:13, 14 11:28
12:23 Ex 12:12 2 Sam 24:16 Isa 37:36
12:24 Gen 17:8 Ex 12:14
12:25 Gen 50:24 Ex 3:8 Deut 4:5; 12:9

---

through all of Egypt. It had respect only for those houses on whose lintels and over whose doors blood had been sprinkled (12:13). The characters and works of those inside had nothing to do with the saving efficacy of the sprinkled blood. It was the blood alone for which the angel of death had regard. Christ is our perfect sacrifice. His applied blood makes the unrighteous righteous and their sins are forgiven (Rom. 3:23; 1 Pet. 1:18, 19).

12:14 *ye shall keep it a feast to the LORD throughout your generations.* This the Jews still continue to do. In the evening at the beginning of Passover, Jewish families have a ceremonial meal and offer their worship to commemorate what happened in Egypt as their ancestors prepared for the exodus. For seven days no leaven is to be found in any home.

12:15 For the feast of unleavened bread see note to Lev. 23:6. The passover could not be celebrated the same way after the Holy of Holies was gone, for there would be no mercy-seat on which to sprinkle the blood of bulls and goats according to the prescribed ritual. The tradition, however, continues among many Israelites today who celebrate what is called the *seder* in their homes or communities to commemorate the exodus from Egypt.

12:22 *Hyssop.* See note to Ps. 51:7 for explanation.

12:26 Ex 13:8 Deut 6:7 Josh 4:6 Ps 78:5

26 And it shall come to pass, when your children shall say unto you, What
mean ye by this service?

12:27 a)Deut 16:2 1 Cor 5:7 b)Ex 4:31

27 That ye shall say, It *is* the sacrifice of the LORD's passover, who passed
over the houses of the children of Israel in Egypt, when he smote the
Egyptians, and delivered our houses. And the people bowed the head and
worshipped.
28 And the children of Israel went away, and did as the LORD had
commanded Moses and Aaron, so did they.

c. The Death of the Firstborn Sons

12:29 Ex 4:23 Ps 78:51 105:36

29 ¶And it came to pass, that at midnight the LORD smote all the firstborn
in the land of Egypt, from the firstborn of Pharaoh that sat on his throne
unto the firstborn of the captive that *was* in the dungeon; and all the
firstborn of cattle.

12:30 Ex 11:6

30 And Pharaoh rose up in the night, he, and all his servants, and all the
Egyptians; and there was a great cry in Egypt; for *there was* not a house
where *there was* not one dead.

12:31 Ex 3:19 10:9, 29; 11:8 Ps 105:38

31 ¶And he called for Moses and Aaron by night, and said, Rise up, *and*
get you forth from among my people, both ye and the children of Israel;
and go, serve the LORD, as ye have said.
32 Also take your flocks and your herds, as ye have said, and be gone; and
bless me also.

12:33 Gen 20:3 Ex 11:1 Num 17:12

33 And the Egyptians were urgent upon the people, that they might send
them out of the land in haste; for they said, We *be* all dead *men*.
34 And the people took their dough before it was leavened, their
kneadingtroughs being bound up in their clothes upon their shoulders.

12:35 Ex 3:22

35 And the children of Israel did according to the word of Moses; and
they borrowed of the Egyptians jewels of silver, and jewels of gold, and
raiment:

12:36 Gen 39:21 Ex 11:3 Ps 105:37

36 And the LORD gave the people favour in the sight of the Egyptians, so
that they lent unto them *such things as they required.* And they spoiled the
Egyptians.

C. THE EXODUS FROM EGYPT

1. The Unleavened Bread

12:37☆ Ex 1:11; 38:26 Num 1:46

37 ¶And the children of Israel journeyed from Ram′e-ses to Suc′coth,
about six hundred thousand on foot *that were* men, beside children.

12:38 Num 11:4 Deut 3:19 Zech 8:23

38 And a mixed multitude went up also with them; and flocks, and herds,
even very much cattle.

12:39 Ex 6:1; 11:1

39 And they baked unleavened cakes of the dough which they brought
forth out of Egypt, for it was not leavened; because they were thrust out of
Egypt, and could not tarry, neither had they prepared for themselves any
victual.

12:40, 41☆ Gen 15:13, 16 Acts 7:6 Gal 3:16, 17

40 ¶Now the sojourning of the children of Israel, who dwelt in Egypt, *was*
four hundred and thirty years.
41 And it came to pass at the end of the four hundred and thirty years,
even the selfsame day it came to pass, that all the hosts of the LORD went
out from the land of Egypt.

12:42 Ex 13:3 Deut 16:1

42 It *is* a night to be much observed unto the LORD for bringing them out
from the land of Egypt: this *is* that night of the LORD to be observed of all
the children of Israel in their generations.

12:37 The number of the Israelites probably totaled around two million.

12:40 Commentators offer various explanations for the 430 years spoken of here. It depends on which date is selected for the beginning of the period. Some state that it was the time span between God's promise to Abraham (when he first entered Caanan) and Israel's departure for Canaan.

2. The Rules Governing the Passover

43¶And the LORD said unto Moses and Aaron, This *is* the ordinance of
the passover: There shall no stranger eat thereof:
44But every man's servant that is bought for money, when thou hast
circumcised him, then shall he eat thereof.
45A foreigner and an hired servant shall not eat thereof.
46In one house shall it be eaten; thou shalt not carry forth ought of the
flesh abroad out of the house; neither shall ye break a bone thereof.
47All the congregation of Israel shall keep it.
48And when a stranger shall sojourn with thee, and will keep the passover
to the LORD, let all his males be circumcised, and then let him come near
and keep it; and he shall be as one that is born in the land: for no
uncircumcised person shall eat thereof.
49One law shall be to him that is homeborn, and unto the stranger that
sojourneth among you.
50Thus did all the children of Israel; as the LORD commanded Moses and
Aaron, so did they.
51And it came to pass the selfsame day, *that* the LORD did bring the
children of Israel out of the land of Egypt by their armies.

12:43 Num 9:14
12:44 Gen 17:12, 13; Lev 22:11
☆**12:46** a)1 Cor 12:12; Eph 2:19; b)Num 9:12; Jn 19:33, 36
12:48 Gen 17:12; Num 9:14; 15:15; Gal 3:28
12:49 Lev 24:22
12:50 Ex 12:28; Deut 4:1, 2; 12:32

13 AND the LORD spake unto Moses, saying,
2Sanctify unto me all the firstborn, whatsoever openeth the
womb among the children of Israel, *both* of man and of beast: it *is* mine.

13:1, 2 Ex 13:11; 22:29; 34:19; Lev 27:26; Num 3:13; Deut 15:19; Lk 2:23

3. Moses' Speech to His People

3¶And Moses said unto the people, Remember this day, in which ye came
out from Egypt, out of the house of bondage; for by strength of hand the
LORD brought you out from this *place:* there shall no leavened bread be
eaten.
4This day came ye out in the month Abib.
5¶And it shall be when the LORD shall bring thee into the land of the
Canaanites, and the Hittites, and the Am'or-ites, and the Hi'vites, and the
Jeb'u-sites, which he sware unto thy fathers to give thee, a land flowing with
milk and honey, that thou shalt keep this service in this month.
6Seven days thou shalt eat unleavened bread, and in the seventh day *shall
be* a feast to the LORD.
7Unleavened bread shall be eaten seven days; and there shall no leavened
bread be seen with thee, neither shall there be leaven seen with thee in all
thy quarters.
8¶And thou shalt shew thy son in that day, saying, *This is done* because of
that *which* the LORD did unto me when I came forth out of Egypt.
9And it shall be for a sign unto thee upon thine hand, and for a memorial
between thine eyes, that the LORD's law may be in thy mouth: for with a
strong hand hath the LORD brought thee out of Egypt.
10Thou shalt therefore keep this ordinance in his season from year to
year.
11¶And it shall be when the LORD shall bring thee into the land of the
Canaanites, as he sware unto thee and to thy fathers, and shall give it thee,

13:3 Ex 12:42; 23:15; Deut 5:15
☆**13:4, 5** Gen 17:7, 8; Ex 3:8, 17; 34:11; Deut 7:1
13:6 Ex 12:15, 19
13:8 Ex 12:26; 13:14; Deut 4:9
☆**13:9** Ex 12:14; Num 15:39; Deut 6:8
☆**13:10** Ex 12:14; 23:15; Lev 23:6–8; Deut 16:3, 4
13:11 Ex 13:5

12:46 No bone of the passover lamb was to be broken. According to John 19:36, this scripture was used to describe the condition of Jesus' body after the crucifixion—not one of whose bones was broken. Thus, Jesus fulfilled the type—he was the true passover Lamb.
13:4 *in the month Abib,* i.e., "at the end of March," or "at the appointed time each year."†
13:9 See note to Matt. 23:5 on phylacteries and fringes.
13:10 *in his season from year to year,* i.e., "in late March."†

13:12
Ex 13:2; 22:29
Num 8:17
Deut 15:19

12 That thou shalt set apart unto the LORD all that openeth the matrix,
and every firstling that cometh of a beast which thou hast; the males *shall*
be the LORD's.

13:13
Ex 34:20
Num 18:15
Rev 14:4

13 And every firstling of an ass thou shalt redeem with a lamb; and if thou
wilt not redeem it, then thou shalt break his neck: and all the firstborn of
man among thy children shalt thou redeem.

13:14
Ex 12:26; 13:8
Deut 6:20

14 ¶And it shall be when thy son asketh thee in time to come, saying,
What *is* this? that thou shalt say unto him, By strength of hand the LORD
brought us out from Egypt, from the house of bondage:

13:15
Ex 12:29; 13:12

15 And it came to pass, when Pharaoh would hardly let us go, that the
LORD slew all the firstborn in the land of Egypt, both the firstborn of man,
and the firstborn of beast: therefore I sacrifice to the LORD all that openeth
the matrix, being males; but all the firstborn of my children I redeem.

13:16
Ex 12:13; 13:9
Deut 6:7–9
11:18

16 And it shall be for a token upon thine hand, and for frontlets between
thine eyes: for by strength of hand the LORD brought us forth out of Egypt.

4. The Pillar of Cloud by Day and Fire by Night

13:17, 18☆
Ex 14:11; 16:12
Num 14:1–4
Deut 17:16
Josh 1:14; 4:12, 13

17 ¶And it came to pass, when Pharaoh had let the people go, that God led
them not *through* the way of the land of the Philistines, although that *was*
near; for God said, Lest peradventure the people repent when they see war,
and they return to Egypt:

18 But God led the people about, *through* the way of the wilderness of the
Red sea: and the children of Israel went up harnessed out of the land of
Egypt.

13:19
Gen 50:24, 25
Josh 24:32
Acts 7:15, 16

19 And Moses took the bones of Joseph with him: for he had straitly
sworn the children of Israel, saying, God will surely visit you; and ye shall
carry up my bones away hence with you.

13:20
Ex 12:37
Num 33:5, 6

20 ¶And they took their journey from Suc'coth, and encamped in E'tham,
in the edge of the wilderness.

13:21☆
Ex 14:19, 20
33:9, 10
Num 9:15; 10:34
Ps 105:39
1 Cor 10:1

21 And the LORD went before them by day in a pillar of a cloud, to lead
them the way; and by night in a pillar of fire, to give them light; to go by
day and night:

22 He took not away the pillar of the cloud by day, nor the pillar of fire by
night, *from* before the people.

5. Crossing the Red Sea Dryshod

14 AND the LORD spake unto Moses, saying,

14:2☆
Ex 13:17
Num 33:3, 7
Jer 44:1

2 Speak unto the children of Israel, that they turn and encamp
before Pi'-ha-hi'roth, between Mig'dol and the sea, over against Ba'al-
ze'phon: before it shall ye encamp by the sea.

3 For Pharaoh will say of the children of Israel, They *are* entangled in the
land, the wilderness hath shut them in.

13:18 Exactly where Israel crossed the Red Sea (which is literally "Sea of Reeds") is not known. Those who suppose that it was marshy land and less than knee-deep are incorrect. It was deep enough to allow for the drowning of the Egyptians who pursued them into that sea. The passage point was probably south of the present city of Suez.

13:21 *a pillar of a cloud,* later known as the *Shekinah* ("abiding," or "dwelling"), was called by various names in the Old Testament: (1) *my glory (kapod)* (29:43); (2) *cloud* and *pillar of cloud* (34:5, 33:9, 10; (3) *the cloud of the LORD* (Num. 10:34, RSV); and (4) *my presence* or *I will go with you* (33:14, 15). The *Shekinah:* (1) guided Israel (13:21; Neh. 9:19); (2) controlled Israel's movements in the wilderness (40:36, 37); and (3) defended Israel (14:19; Ps. 105:39). In the New Testament the cloud appeared at Jesus' transfiguration (Matt. 17:5) and at his ascension (Acts 1:9). When Christ comes again it will be "in a cloud with power and great glory" (Luke 21:27).

14:2 God directed the campaign against Egypt. He ordered Israel along a route that would keep them from having to face the armies of Egypt. The cloud by day and the pillar of fire by night would move as God determined, assuring Israel's safety. God hardened Pharaoh's heart, who tracked down Israel until he and his army fell into God's trap. God would be glorified in disposing of the Egyptians.

4 And I will harden Pharaoh's heart, that he shall follow after them; and
I will be honoured upon Pharaoh, and upon all his host; that the Egyptians
may know that I *am* the LORD. And they did so.
5 ¶And it was told the king of Egypt that the people fled: and the heart of
Pharaoh and of his servants was turned against the people, and they said,
Why have we done this, that we have let Israel go from serving us?
6 And he made ready his chariot, and took his people with him:
7 And he took six hundred chosen chariots, and all the chariots of Egypt,
and captains over every one of them.
8 And the LORD hardened the heart of Pharaoh king of Egypt, and he
pursued after the children of Israel: and the children of Israel went out with
an high hand.
9 But the Egyptians pursued after them, all the horses *and* chariots of
Pharaoh, and his horsemen, and his army, and overtook them encamping
by the sea, beside Pi'-ha-hi'roth, before Ba'al-ze'phon.
10 ¶And when Pharaoh drew nigh, the children of Israel lifted up their
eyes, and, behold, the Egyptians marched after them; and they were sore
afraid: and the children of Israel cried out unto the LORD.
11 And they said unto Moses, Because *there were* no graves in Egypt, hast
thou taken us away to die in the wilderness? wherefore hast thou dealt thus
with us, to carry us forth out of Egypt?
12 *Is* not this the word that we did tell thee in Egypt, saying, Let us alone,
that we may serve the Egyptians? For *it had been* better for us to serve the
Egyptians, than that we should die in the wilderness.
13 ¶And Moses said unto the people, Fear ye not, stand still, and see the
salvation of the LORD, which he will shew to you to day: for the Egyptians
whom ye have seen to day, ye shall see them again no more for ever.
14 The LORD shall fight for you, and ye shall hold your peace.
15 ¶And the LORD said unto Moses, Wherefore criest thou unto me? speak
unto the children of Israel, that they go forward:
16 But lift thou up thy rod, and stretch out thine hand over the sea, and
divide it: and the children of Israel shall go on dry *ground* through the
midst of the sea.
17 And I, behold, I will harden the hearts of the Egyptians, and they shall
follow them: and I will get me honour upon Pharaoh, and upon all his host,
upon his chariots, and upon his horsemen.
18 And the Egyptians shall know that I *am* the LORD, when I have gotten
me honour upon Pharaoh, upon his chariots, and upon his horsemen.
19 ¶And the angel of God, which went before the camp of Israel, removed
and went behind them; and the pillar of the cloud went from before their
face, and stood behind them:
20 And it came between the camp of the Egyptians and the camp of Israel;
and it was a cloud and darkness *to them,* but it gave light by night *to these:*
so that the one came not near the other all the night.

14:4 Ex 4:21; 7:3; 14:17; Rom 9:17, 22
14:5 Ex 12:33; Ps 105:25; Jer 34:10
14:7 Ex 14:23; 15:4
14:8 Ex 15:9
☆**14:9** Ex 14:2; Josh 24:6
14:10 Josh 24:7; Neh 9:9
14:11 Ex 5:21; 15:24; Ps 106:6, 7; Acts 7:39
☆**14:12**
☆**14:13** Gen 15:1; Ex 14:30; 20:20
14:14 Ex 15:3; Deut 1:30; 3:22; Isa 30:15; 31:4, 5
14:15 Josh 7:10
14:16 Ex 4:2; 7:9; 14:21; Num 20:8
14:17 Ex 14:4
14:18 Ex 7:5; 14:25
☆**14:19** Gen 24:7; Ex 13:21, 22; 23:20
14:20 Ps 18:11

14:9 The fortress towns named indicate that the Israelites crossed the waters to the north of the Red Sea proper (a more accurate translation is "Reed Sea"). The waters were deep enough for the forces of Pharaoh to drown in when they attempted to follow and recapture the Israelites.

14:12 Here we learn that the Israelites were constant complainers. Their complaints sprang from their lack of faith in God's delivering power. They preferred slavery to death. They lacked the eye of faith to see that there was a third alternative: life and freedom by God's strong hand.

14:13 Moses had strong faith. He told the people not to fear, knowing that fear comes from lack of faith. And he boldly promised them that God would deliver them from the Egyptians forever.

14:19 *the angel of God.* See note to Exod. 3:2. Sometimes this term designates Jesus Christ and sometimes an angel who helps the people of God (Heb. 1:14). The triune God—the Father, the Son, and the

21 And Moses stretched out his hand over the sea; and the LORD caused
the sea to go *back* by a strong east wind all that night, and made the sea dry
land, and the waters were divided.
22 And the children of Israel went into the midst of the sea upon the dry
ground: and the waters *were* a wall unto them on their right hand, and on
their left.
23 ¶And the Egyptians pursued, and went in after them to the midst of the
sea, *even* all Pharaoh's horses, his chariots, and his horsemen.
24 And it came to pass, that in the morning watch the LORD looked unto
the host of the Egyptians through the pillar of fire and of the cloud, and
troubled the host of the Egyptians,
25 And took off their chariot wheels, that they drave them heavily: so that
the Egyptians said, Let us flee from the face of Israel; for the LORD fighteth
for them against the Egyptians.
26 ¶And the LORD said unto Moses, Stretch out thine hand over the sea,
that the waters may come again upon the Egyptians, upon their chariots,
and upon their horsemen.
27 And Moses stretched forth his hand over the sea, and the sea returned
to his strength when the morning appeared; and the Egyptians fled against
it; and the LORD overthrew the Egyptians in the midst of the sea.
28 And the waters returned, and covered the chariots, and the horsemen,
and all the host of Pharaoh that came into the sea after them; there
remained not so much as one of them.
29 But the children of Israel walked upon dry *land* in the midst of the sea;
and the waters *were* a wall unto them on their right hand, and on their left.
30 Thus the LORD saved Israel that day out of the hand of the Egyptians;
and Israel saw the Egyptians dead upon the sea shore.
31 And Israel saw that great work which the LORD did upon the
Egyptians: and the people feared the LORD, and believed the LORD, and his
servant Moses.

6. The Song of Moses

15 THEN sang Moses and the children of Israel this song unto the
LORD, and spake, saying, I will sing unto the LORD, for he hath
triumphed gloriously: the horse and his rider hath he thrown into the sea.
2 The LORD *is* my strength and song, and he is become my salvation: he *is*
my God, and I will prepare him an habitation; my father's God, and I will
exalt him.
3 The LORD *is* a man of war: the LORD *is* his name.
4 Pharaoh's chariots and his host hath he cast into the sea: his chosen
captains also are drowned in the Red sea.
5 The depths have covered them: they sank into the bottom as a stone.
6 Thy right hand, O LORD, is become glorious in power: thy right hand, O
LORD, hath dashed in pieces the enemy.

14:21 Ex 7:19; Ps 106:9; 114:3, 5; 136:13; Isa 63:12, 13
14:22 Ex 14:29; Num 33:8; Ps 66:6; 78:13; Isa 11:15; Heb 11:29
14:23 Ex 14:4, 17; 15:9
14:24 Ex 13:21
14:25 Ex 14:4, 18
14:26 Ex 7:19; 14:21
14:27 Ex 15:1, 7; Deut 11:4; Josh 4:18
14:28 Ex 15:10; Neh 9:11; Ps 78:53; 106:11
14:29 Ex 14:21, 22; Ps 66:6; Isa 11:15
14:30 Ex 14:13; Ps 58:10; 106:10; Isa 63:11
14:31 Ex 4:31; 19:9; 2 Chron 20:20; Ps 106:12
15:1☆ Ps 106:12; Isa 12:5; 42:10–12; Jer 51:21; Rev 15:3
15:2 Ex 3:15, 16; Deut 10:21; 2 Sam 22:47, 51; Ps 18:1, 2; 140:7; Isa 12:2
15:3☆ Ex 6:2; 14:14; Ps 24:8
15:4 Ex 14:6, 7, 27, 28
15:5 Neh 9:11; Ezek 27:34; Jonah 2:2
15:6 Ex 3:20; Ps 17:7; 118:15

Holy Spirit—are found at work again and again in the Old Testament. In the Red Sea story the Father and the Son are active.

15:1 *Then sang Moses . . . this song.* This song of Moses and the people of Israel is part of the hymnody of the Christian faith. One of the most glorious contributions of the faith has been the hymnody composed by multitudes across the centuries. Words and music put together to be sung to God for his glory are inexpressably beautiful. According to Job 38:7, "the morning stars sang together." In Revelation 15:3 there is "the song of Moses . . . and the song of the Lamb" being sung by the angels. The Apostle Paul encourages the Ephesians to engage in "speaking to yourselves [one another] in psalms and hymns and spiritual songs, singing and making melody in your heart to the Lord" (Eph. 5:19).

15:3 *The LORD is a man of war.* This is like the depiction of Jesus Christ who comes with a sword in his mouth to wage the final war against Satan and to put away evil forever (Rev. 19:15).

7 And in the greatness of thine excellency thou hast overthrown them that rose up against thee: thou sentest forth thy wrath, *which* consumed them as stubble.

8 And with the blast of thy nostrils the waters were gathered together, the floods stood upright as an heap, *and* the depths were congealed in the heart of the sea.

9 The enemy said, I will pursue, I will overtake, I will divide the spoil; my lust shall be satisfied upon them; I will draw my sword, my hand shall destroy them.

10 Thou didst blow with thy wind, the sea covered them: they sank as lead in the mighty waters.

11 Who *is* like unto thee, O LORD, among the gods? who *is* like thee, glorious in holiness, fearful *in* praises, doing wonders?

12 Thou stretchedst out thy right hand, the earth swallowed them.

13 Thou in thy mercy hast led forth the people *which* thou hast redeemed: thou hast guided *them* in thy strength unto thy holy habitation.

14 The people shall hear, *and* be afraid: sorrow shall take hold on the inhabitants of Palestina.

15 Then the dukes of Edom shall be amazed; the mighty men of Moab, trembling shall take hold upon them; all the inhabitants of Canaan shall melt away.

16 Fear and dread shall fall upon them; by the greatness of thine arm they shall be *as* still as a stone; till thy people pass over, O LORD, till the people pass over, *which* thou hast purchased.

17 Thou shalt bring them in, and plant them in the mountain of thine inheritance, *in* the place, O LORD, *which* thou hast made for thee to dwell in, *in* the Sanctuary, O Lord, *which* thy hands have established.

18 The LORD shall reign for ever and ever.

19 For the horse of Pharaoh went in with his chariots and with his horsemen into the sea, and the LORD brought again the waters of the sea upon them; but the children of Israel went on dry *land* in the midst of the sea.

7. The Song of Miriam

20 ¶And Miriam the prophetess, the sister of Aaron, took a timbrel in her hand; and all the women went out after her with timbrels and with dances.

21 And Miriam answered them, Sing ye to the LORD, for he hath triumphed gloriously; the horse and his rider hath he thrown into the sea.

III. THE JOURNEY TO MOUNT SINAI (15:22—18:27)

A. HEALING THE BITTER WATER AT MARAH

22 So Moses brought Israel from the Red sea, and they went out into the wilderness of Shur; and they went three days in the wilderness, and found no water.

15:7
Ex 9:16; 14:24
Ps 78:49, 50
15:8
Ex 14:22, 29
2 Sam 22:16
Ps 78:13; 114:5; 118:15
Hab 3:8–10
15:9
Ex 14:5, 8, 9
15:10
Ex 14:27
Ps 74:13
147:18
☆**15:11**
Ex 8:10
Deut 3:24
1 Sam 2:2
2 Sam 7:22
Ps 22:3
Isa 6:3; 57:15
Jer 23:9
Mic 7:18
Rev 4:8
15:12
Ex 15:6
15:13
Neh 9:12
Ps 77:14, 15, 20
Jer 2:6
15:14
Num 14:14
Deut 2:25
Isa 14:29
15:15
Num 22:3
Deut 2:4
Josh 2:11
15:16
a)Ex 23:27
Deut 2:25
b)Ex 19:5, 6
Ps 74:2
Jer 31:11
15:17
Ex 23:20; 32:34
Ps 2:6
78:54, 68
Isa 5:1, 2
Jer 2:21
15:18
Ps 10:16; 29:10
Isa 57:15
Rev 11:15
15:19
Ex 14:22, 23, 29
15:5, 10
Heb 11:29
☆**15:20**
Ex 2:4
Num 26:59
1 Sam 18:6
Ps 150:4
15:21
Ex 15:1
Judg 5:3
Rev 5:9
15:22
Gen 16:7; 25:18
Ex 3:18

15:11 Among the chief attributes of God is his holiness. Whatever he does is right, true, and good. He cannot sin, nor is there any impurity in him. No one else's holiness can compare to that of God (1 Sam. 2:2). It is manifested in his name ("the high and lofty One that inhabiteth eternity," Isa. 57:15), in his words ("God has decreed holy words of judgment against them," Jer. 23:9, TLB), and in his character ("thou art holy," Ps. 22:3). His people are to imitate his holiness (Lev 11:44; 1 Pet 1:15, 16) and offer "thanks to his holy name" (Ps. 30:4, TLB).

15:20 Miriam (Mary) was a prophetess, that is, a female preacher. God was no respecter of sex. The Scriptures mention that Deborah, Huldah, Noadiah and Anna were all prophetesses. No one should underplay the role of women in God's scheme of redemption. Micah, in his prophecy, reports God as having said to him: "I sent before thee Moses, Aaron, and Miriam" (Mic. 6:4). If God identified Miriam along with Moses and Aaron as having been sent by him for the deliverance of Israel, she must have been an important figure in the divine plan.

15:23☆ Num 33:8; Ruth 1:20
15:24 Ex 14:11; 16:2; 17:3; Ps 106:13
15:25 Ex 14:10; 16:4; 17:4
15:26 Ex 19:5; 20:2-17; Deut 7:15; 12:28; Ps 103:3

23 ¶And when they came to Ma′rah, they could not drink of the waters of
Ma′rah, for they *were* bitter: therefore the name of it was called Ma′rah.
24 And the people murmured against Moses, saying, What shall we drink?
25 And he cried unto the LORD; and the LORD shewed him a tree, *which*
when he had cast into the waters, the waters were made sweet: there he
made for them a statute and an ordinance, and there he proved them,
26 And said, If thou wilt diligently hearken to the voice of the LORD thy
God, and wilt do that which is right in his sight, and wilt give ear to his
commandments, and keep all his statutes, I will put none of these diseases
upon thee, which I have brought upon the Egyptians: for I *am* the LORD
that healeth thee.

15:27 Num 33:9

27 ¶And they came to Elim, where *were* twelve wells of water, and
threescore and ten palm trees: and they encamped there by the waters.

B. GOD'S PROVISION FOR THE JOURNEY

1. The Complaining Israelites

16:1 Ex 17:1; 19:1; Num 33:10
16:2☆ Ex 14:11; Ps 106:7; Acts 7:39; 1 Cor 10:10
16:3☆ Ex 2:23; Num 11:4; 14:2-4; 20:3; Deut 28:67

16 AND they took their journey from Elim, and all the congregation
of the children of Israel came unto the wilderness of Sin, which *is*
between Elim and Si′nai, on the fifteenth day of the second month after
their departing out of the land of Egypt.
2 And the whole congregation of the children of Israel murmured against
Moses and Aaron in the wilderness:
3 And the children of Israel said unto them, Would to God we had died
by the hand of the LORD in the land of Egypt, when we sat by the flesh
pots, *and* when we did eat bread to the full; for ye have brought us forth
into this wilderness, to kill this whole assembly with hunger.

2. The Promise of Bread and Meat

16:4☆ Ex 15:25; Deut 8:2, 16; Ps 78:24; 105:40; Jn 6:31; 1 Cor 10:3
16:5 Ex 16:22; 35:2
16:6 Ex 12:51; 16:28
16:7-9 Ex 16:12; Num 14:27; 17:5; 21:7; 1 Sam 8:7; Mt 9:4

4 ¶Then said the LORD unto Moses, Behold, I will rain bread from heaven
for you; and the people shall go out and gather a certain rate every day,
that I may prove them, whether they will walk in my law, or no.
5 And it shall come to pass, that on the sixth day they shall prepare *that*
which they bring in; and it shall be twice as much as they gather daily.
6 And Moses and Aaron said unto all the children of Israel, At even, then
ye shall know that the LORD hath brought you out from the land of Egypt:
7 And in the morning, then ye shall see the glory of the LORD; for that he
heareth your murmurings against the LORD: and what *are* we, that ye
murmur against us?
8 And Moses said, *This shall be,* when the LORD shall give you in the
evening flesh to eat, and in the morning bread to the full; for that the LORD

15:23 *Marah* ("bitter") provides an illustration for believers. The Israelites, following God, came into difficulties not of their choosing, nor because of their transgressions. Without potable water they were in serious trouble. Their difficulty was God's opportunity. He made the bitter water sweet so they could drink of it. God does place his children in places of difficulty so that his deliverances will strengthen their faith.

16:2 The Israelites were already beginning to complain. They feared they would die from hunger. God told Moses to inform the people that they would be fed. They were to be given flesh for the evening meal and bread the following morning. After this first meal of flesh God did not design to give them any more flesh until they entered the land of promise, when the manna was no longer to be given. When they are told to look toward the wilderness (16:10) "the glory of the LORD appeared in the cloud." Once more God condescends to their incipient unbelief and manifests himself so unmistakably that they know that God is with them. Believers today do not have such manifestations. Rather, they have the full revelation of God in Jesus Christ and can walk by faith without sight.

16:3 *flesh pots . . . bread to the full.* The Israelites hark back to the food they had in Egypt and complain at what they now have. "Discontent magnifies what is past, and vilifies what is present without regard to truth or reason."*

16:4 Instead of raining fire and brimstone on Israel for their complaints, God graciously rains bread on them and does so for forty years.

heareth your murmurings which ye murmur against him: and what *are* we? your murmurings *are* not against us, but against the LORD.

9 ¶And Moses spake unto Aaron, Say unto all the congregation of the children of Israel, Come near before the LORD: for he hath heard your murmurings.

10 And it came to pass, as Aaron spake unto the whole congregation of the children of Israel, that they looked toward the wilderness, and, behold, the glory of the LORD appeared in the cloud.

☆16:10 Ex 13:21; 40:34 Num 14:10

11 ¶And the LORD spake unto Moses, saying,

12 I have heard the murmurings of the children of Israel: speak unto them, saying, At even ye shall eat flesh, and in the morning ye shall be filled with bread; and ye shall know that I *am* the LORD your God.

16:11, 12 Ex 4:5; 16:6

3. God Provides Quail and Manna

13 And it came to pass, that at even the quails came up, and covered the camp: and in the morning the dew lay round about the host.

16:13 Ex 16:31–33 Ps 78:27–29 105:40

14 And when the dew that lay was gone up, behold, upon the face of the wilderness *there lay a small round thing, as* small as the hoar frost on the ground.

16:14 Num 11:7–9 Deut 8:3

15 And when the children of Israel saw *it,* they said one to another, It *is* manna: for they wist not what it *was.* And Moses said unto them, This *is* the bread which the LORD hath given you to eat.

☆16:15 Ex 16:31 Josh 5:12 Neh 9:5 Jn 6:31

16 ¶This *is* the thing which the LORD hath commanded, Gather of it every man according to his eating, an omer for every man, *according to* the number of your persons; take ye every man for *them* which *are* in his tents.

☆16:16 Ex 16:18, 33, 36

17 And the children of Israel did so, and gathered, some more, some less.

18 And when they did mete *it* with an omer, he that gathered much had nothing over, and he that gathered little had no lack; they gathered every man according to his eating.

16:18 2 Cor 8:15

19 And Moses said, Let no man leave of it till the morning.

16:19 Ex 12:10; 23:18 Mt 6:34

20 Notwithstanding they hearkened not unto Moses; but some of them left of it until the morning, and it bred worms, and stank: and Moses was wroth with them.

16:20 Num 16:15

21 And they gathered it every morning, every man according to his eating: and when the sun waxed hot, it melted.

22 ¶And it came to pass, *that* on the sixth day they gathered twice as much bread, two omers for one *man:* and all the rulers of the congregation came and told Moses.

16:22 Ex 16:5; 34:31 Lev 25:11, 12, 22

4. The Sabbath Rest

23 And he said unto them, This *is that* which the LORD hath said, To morrow *is* the rest of the holy sabbath unto the LORD: bake *that* which ye

☆16:23 Gen 2:2 Ex 20:8; 23:12 31:14, 15 Neh 9:14 Mk 2:27

16:10 *the glory of the LORD.* Although Israel had the cloud of the Lord, they grew accustomed to it. And familiarity breeds contempt. Now God shows himself in even greater brilliance in the cloud, before he speaks to his people. Yet even great, divine manifestations become commonplace when looked upon for a period of time.

16:15 The manna (bread) supplied by God was a free gift and was sufficient for Israel's needs from day to day. It sustained life and was in plentiful supply. Christ is the Bread of life and is the fulfillment of this type, although in a far greater way. (See John 6:30–41.)

16:16 *an omer.* This word is used only in connection with the story about the manna in the wilderness. In Exodus an *omer* is said to be equal to one tenth of an *ephah.* Thus an *omer* would be equal to 2.087 dry quarts (2.299 liters). An *ephah* measured somewhere between three-eighths and two-thirds of a bushel. These measures were employed for such things as grain, flour, and meal. Liquids were measured by a unit called the *bath,* which has been estimated to be between five and six gallons.

16:23–26 Obviously the Sabbath existed before the commandment was given in Exod. 20:8–11, and it was kept before the Law was formally given.

will bake *to day,* and seethe that ye will seethe; and that which remaineth
over lay up for you to be kept until the morning.

16:24 Ex 16:20, 33

24 And they laid it up till the morning, as Moses bade: and it did not
stink, neither was there any worm therein.
25 And Moses said, Eat that to day; for to day *is* a sabbath unto the
LORD: to day ye shall not find it in the field.

16:26 Deut 5:13

26 Six days ye shall gather it; but on the seventh day, *which is* the sabbath,
in it there shall be none.
27 ¶And it came to pass, *that* there went out *some* of the people on the
seventh day for to gather, and they found none.

16:28, 29 Num 14:11; Ps 78:10, 18–24

28 And the LORD said unto Moses, How long refuse ye to keep my
commandments and my laws?
29 See, for that the LORD hath given you the sabbath, therefore he giveth
you on the sixth day the bread of two days; abide ye every man in his place,
let no man go out of his place on the seventh day.

16:30 Lev 23:3; Deut 5:12
16:31 Ex 16:15; Num 11:6; Deut 8:3, 16

30 So the people rested on the seventh day.
31 And the house of Israel called the name thereof Manna: and it *was* like
coriander seed, white; and the taste of it *was* like wafers *made* with honey.

5. Keeping the Omer of Manna as a Testimonial

16:32 Ps 111:4, 5

32 ¶And Moses said, This *is* the thing which the LORD commandeth, Fill
an omer of it to be kept for your generations; that they may see the bread
wherewith I have fed you in the wilderness, when I brought you forth from
the land of Egypt.

16:33 Heb 9:4; Rev 2:17

33 And Moses said unto Aaron, Take a pot, and put an omer full of
manna therein, and lay it up before the LORD, to be kept for your
generations.

16:34 Ex 25:16; 30:6; Num 1:50
16:35 Josh 5:12; Neh 9:15, 20, 21; Ps 78:24

34 As the LORD commanded Moses, so Aaron laid it up before the
Testimony, to be kept.
35 And the children of Israel did eat manna forty years, until they came to
a land inhabited; they did eat manna, until they came unto the borders of
the land of Canaan.
36 Now an omer *is* the tenth *part* of an ephah.

C. MOSES STRIKES THE ROCK; THE WATER FLOWS

17:1 Ex 16:1; 19:2; Num 33:14

17 AND all the congregation of the children of Israel journeyed from
the wilderness of Sin, after their journeys, according to the
commandment of the LORD, and pitched in Reph'i-dim: and *there was* no
water for the people to drink.

17:2 Ex 5:21; 14:11; 15:24; 16:2; Num 14:22; 20:2; Deut 6:16

2 Wherefore the people did chide with Moses, and said, Give us water that
we may drink. And Moses said unto them, Why chide ye with me?
wherefore do ye tempt the LORD?

17:3☆ Ex 16:3; Num 11:4, 5

3 And the people thirsted there for water; and the people murmured
against Moses, and said, Wherefore *is* this *that* thou hast brought us up out
of Egypt, to kill us and our children and our cattle with thirst?

17:4 Ex 15:25; Num 11:11; 14:10; 16:19

4 And Moses cried unto the LORD, saying, What shall I do unto this
people? they be almost ready to stone me.

17:3 The Israelites take every opportunity to complain and to find fault with Moses. Since God had given them manna, why should they suppose that he would not also provide water for them? Instead of exercising faith and praying to God for water, they once again contrast the lack of water with what they now think was a better situation when they were slaves in Egypt. Sometimes God allows his people to lack necessities in order for them to be tested, and to manifest whether their confidence is in him.

5 And the LORD said unto Moses, Go on before the people, and take with
thee of the elders of Israel; and thy rod, wherewith thou smotest the river,
take in thine hand, and go.
6 Behold, I will stand before thee there upon the rock in Ho'reb; and thou
shalt smite the rock, and there shall come water out of it, that the people
may drink. And Moses did so in the sight of the elders of Israel.
7 And he called the name of the place Mas'sah, and Mer'i-bah, because of
the chiding of the children of Israel, and because they tempted the LORD,
saying, Is the LORD among us, or not?

17:5, 6
Ex 3:1, 16; 7:20
Num 20:8–10
Neh 9:15
Ps 78:15
105:41
1 Cor 10:4
☆17:6
17:7
Deut 6:16; 9:22
33:8
Ps 81:7; 95:8
Heb 3:8

D. THE MILITARY VICTORY OVER THE AMALEKITES

8 ¶Then came Am'a-lek, and fought with Israel in Reph'i-dim.
9 And Moses said unto Joshua, Choose us out men, and go out, fight with
Am'a-lek: to morrow I will stand on the top of the hill with the rod of God
in mine hand.
10 So Joshua did as Moses had said to him, and fought with Am'a-lek: and
Moses, Aaron, and Hur went up to the top of the hill.
11 And it came to pass, when Moses held up his hand, that Israel
prevailed: and when he let down his hand, Am'a-lek prevailed.
12 But Moses' hands *were* heavy; and they took a stone, and put *it* under
him, and he sat thereon; and Aaron and Hur stayed up his hands, the one
on the one side, and the other on the other side; and his hands were steady
until the going down of the sun.
13 And Joshua discomfited Am'a-lek and his people with the edge of the
sword.
14 And the LORD said unto Moses, Write this *for* a memorial in a book,
and rehearse *it* in the ears of Joshua: for I will utterly put out the
remembrance of Am'a-lek from under heaven.
15 And Moses built an altar, and called the name of it Je-ho'vah–nis'si:
16 For he said, Because the LORD hath sworn *that* the LORD *will have* war
with Am'a-lek from generation to generation.

☆17:8
Gen 36:12, 16
Num 24:20
Deut 25:17
1 Sam 15:2
☆17:9
Ex 24:13
Num 11:28
☆17:10
Ex 24:14; 31:2
1 Chron 2:18, 19
17:11, 12
Heb 12:12
17:14
Ex 24:4; 34:27
Num 33:2
Deut 25:19
☆17:15, 16
Gen 22:14
Ps 60:4

E. JETHRO VISITS MOSES AND ISRAEL
1. Moses' Reunion with His Wife and Father-in-Law

18 WHEN Jeth'ro, the priest of Mid'i-an, Moses' father in law, heard
of all that God had done for Moses, and for Israel his people, *and*
that the LORD had brought Israel out of Egypt;
2 Then Jeth'ro, Moses' father in law, took Zip-po'rah, Moses' wife, after
he had sent her back,
3 And her two sons; of which the name of the one *was* Ger'shom; for he
said, I have been an alien in a strange land:
4 And the name of the other *was* E-li-e'zer; for the God of my father, *said*
he, was mine help, and delivered me from the sword of Pharaoh:

☆18:1
Ex 2:16, 18; 3:1
18:2
Ex 2:21; 4:25
☆18:3
Ex 2:22; 4:20
Acts 7:29
Heb 11:13
18:4
Gen 28:13
49:25
Ps 46:1
Isa 50:7

17:6 *thou shalt smite the rock,* "with your rod," implied. The rock which Moses struck and from which water flowed is a type of Christ (see 1 Cor. 10:4). He is our Rock; from him flow the waters of everlasting life. As water satisfies physical thirst, so Christ satisfies spiritual thirst. (See note on Num. 20:8.)
17:8 *Amalek,* a nomadic people who inhabited the Sinai Peninsula and the Negeb. Amalek considered the Israelites intruders.
17:9 *Joshua.* This is the first mention of the one who was a military leader, one of the twelve spies, and Moses' successor.
17:10 *Hur,* a man of Judah, of the family of Hezron, house of Caleb (1 Chron. 2:18, 19). He was the grandfather of Bezalel (31:1, 2).†
17:15 *Jehovah-nissi,* i.e., "the LORD (Jehovah) is my banner."
18:1 *Jethro, the priest of Midian.* Here is a priest who was a true believer, offering sacrifices to God as well as blessing him (verses 10 and 12). In verses 17ff he offers Moses excellent counsel on administrative matters.
18:3 Moses had two sons by Zipporah: Gershom (whose name means "a stranger there") and Eliezer

18:5, 6☆ Ex 3:1; 4:27

[5]And Jeth′ro, Moses' father in law, came with his sons and his wife unto
Moses into the wilderness, where he encamped at the mount of God:
[6]And he said unto Moses, I thy father in law Jeth′ro am come unto thee,
and thy wife, and her two sons with her.

18:7 Gen 43:26

[7]¶And Moses went out to meet his father in law, and did obeisance, and
kissed him; and they asked each other of *their* welfare; and they came into
the tent.

18:8 Ex 15:4, 8, 22 Num 20:14 Neh 9:9–15

[8]And Moses told his father in law all that the LORD had done unto
Pharaoh and to the Egyptians for Israel's sake, *and* all the travail that had
come upon them by the way, and *how* the LORD delivered them.

18:9 Isa 44:23; 63:7

[9]And Jeth′ro rejoiced for all the goodness which the LORD had done to
Israel, whom he had delivered out of the hand of the Egyptians.

18:10 1 Kgs 8:56 Ps 68:19 106:44–46

[10]And Jeth′ro said, Blessed *be* the LORD, who hath delivered you out of
the hand of the Egyptians, and out of the hand of Pharaoh, who hath
delivered the people from under the hand of the Egyptians.

18:11 Ex 10:2; 15:11

[11]Now I know that the LORD *is* greater than all gods: for in the thing
wherein they dealt proudly *he was* above them.

18:12 Gen 31:54 Ex 24:5 Job 1:5

[12]And Jeth′ro, Moses' father in law, took a burnt offering and sacrifices
for God: and Aaron came, and all the elders of Israel, to eat bread with
Moses' father in law before God.

2. Moses Appoints Judges on Jethro's Advice

[13]¶And it came to pass on the morrow, that Moses sat to judge the
people: and the people stood by Moses from the morning unto the evening.
[14]And when Moses' father in law saw all that he did to the people, he
said, What *is* this thing that thou doest to the people? why sittest thou
thyself alone, and all the people stand by thee from morning unto even?

18:15, 16 Lev 24:12–14 Num 9:6–8 15:34 Deut 17:8–13 2 Sam 15:3

[15]And Moses said unto his father in law, Because the people come unto
me to inquire of God:
[16]When they have a matter, they come unto me; and I judge between one
and another, and I do make *them* know the statutes of God, and his laws.
[17]And Moses' father in law said unto him, The thing that thou doest *is*
not good.

18:18 Num 11:14 Deut 1:9 Acts 6:1–4

[18]Thou wilt surely wear away, both thou, and this people that *is* with
thee: for this thing *is* too heavy for thee; thou art not able to perform it
thyself alone.

18:19, 20☆ Deut 1:17; 4:1

[19]Hearken now unto my voice, I will give thee counsel, and God shall be
with thee: Be thou for the people to God-ward, that thou mayest bring the
causes unto God:

18:21☆ Deut 1:12–15 16:18 1 Kgs 3:9 Ps 15:1–5

[20]And thou shalt teach them ordinances and laws, and shalt shew them
the way wherein they must walk, and the work that they must do.
[21]Moreover thou shalt provide out of all the people able men, such as fear

---

(whose name means "God is help"). Neither son became a leader in Israel after their father. Gershom had a son, Shebuel, who became "ruler of the treasures" under King David (1 Chron. 26:24).

18:5 *at the mount of God,* i.e., Mt. Sinai, or, Mt. Horeb.

18:19 The Scriptures consistently insist on the necessity for justice to prevail. Justice has to do with what is right or righteous. Thus God declares that a man's position in society, particularly if he is poor, shall not militate against him. Whatever is right must decide the judgment, whether one is rich or poor. Yet the rich do, on occasion, use their wealth to pervert justice, even as the poor can envy the rich and, by false claims, seek a share of that wealth. The term "social justice" is nowhere used in the Scriptures. That term comes from the Enlightenment; its guiding principle is egalitarianism, a concept contrary to biblical teaching. Social justice seeks the redistribution of wealth by taking from the rich and giving to the poor. This is stealing, which is contrary to the eighth commandment.

18:21ff Jethro, Moses' father-in-law, saw that Moses was overworked. He advised Moses to employ others to assist him in his labors. God called for a meeting with the seventy elders whom Moses had chosen, then had them take over some of Moses' duties. In the New Testament, in imitation of the seventy elders, the number of members of the Sanhedrin was set at seventy. In the early church, overworking, which burdened the apostles, led to the establishment of the office of deacon.

God, men of truth, hating covetousness; and place *such* over them, *to be*
rulers of thousands, *and* rulers of hundreds, rulers of fifties, and rulers of
tens:
22 And let them judge the people at all seasons: and it shall be, *that* every
great matter they shall bring unto thee, but every small matter they shall
judge: so shall it be easier for thyself, and they shall bear *the burden* with
thee.
23 If thou shalt do this thing, and God command thee *so,* then thou shalt
be able to endure, and all this people shall also go to their place in peace.
24 So Moses hearkened to the voice of his father in law, and did all that he
had said.
25 And Moses chose able men out of all Israel, and made them heads over
the people, rulers of thousands, rulers of hundreds, rulers of fifties, and
rulers of tens.
26 And they judged the people at all seasons: the hard causes they brought
unto Moses, but every small matter they judged themselves.
27 ¶And Moses let his father in law depart; and he went his way into his
own land.

18:22 Num 15:33; 27:2; 36:1; Deut 17:8
18:25 Deut 1:15; 16:18
18:26 Deut 17:8
18:27 Num 10:29, 30

IV. THE BOOK OF THE COVENANT AND THE LAW (19:1—24:18)

A. THE COVENANT PROMISE

1. God Offers His Promise

19 IN the third month, when the children of Israel were gone forth out
of the land of Egypt, the same day came they *into* the wilderness of
Si′nai.
2 For they were departed from Reph′i-dim, and were come *to* the desert of
Si′nai, and had pitched in the wilderness; and there Israel camped before
the mount.
3 And Moses went up unto God, and the LORD called unto him out of the
mountain, saying, Thus shalt thou say to the house of Jacob, and tell the
children of Israel;
4 Ye have seen what I did unto the Egyptians, and *how* I bare you on
eagles' wings, and brought you unto myself.
5 Now therefore, if ye will obey my voice indeed, and keep my covenant,
then ye shall be a peculiar treasure unto me above all people: for all the
earth *is* mine:
6 And ye shall be unto me a kingdom of priests, and an holy nation. These
are the words which thou shalt speak unto the children of Israel.
7 ¶And Moses came and called for the elders of the people, and laid
before their faces all these words which the LORD commanded him.
8 And all the people answered together, and said, All that the LORD hath
spoken we will do. And Moses returned the words of the people unto the
LORD.

19:1 Ex 12:51; 16:1; Deut 1:6; 4:10; 5:2
19:2, 3 Ex 17:1, 18:5; Num 33:15; Deut 5:5; Acts 7:38
☆**19:4** Deut 4:9; 32:11; Isa 40:31; 63:9; Rev 12:14
☆**19:5** Ex 15:26; 23:22; 24:7; Deut 4:20; 14:2; Isa 41:8
19:6 Lev 11:44, 45; Deut 33:2–4; Isa 61:6; 1 Pet 2:5, 9; Rev 1:6; 5:10
19:7 Ex 4:29, 30; 24:9
19:8 Ex 4:31; 24:3, 7; Deut 5:27; 26:17

19:4 Israel was a theocracy—it was governed directly by God. God told Israel when to move (40:36, 37); when to battle (Num. 31:1, 2); which leaders were to be appointed (Num. 27:18, 20); and how the land of Canaan was to be divided among the twelve tribes (Josh. 13:1–7). Moses, Joshua, and the prophets were used by God as intermediaries, through whom he governed. Saul was God's viceregent. When he proved unworthy, God chose David to serve as his theocratic king. This appointment was conditioned on David's obedience to the covenant; God promised him an everlasting successor in the person of God's Son, Jesus Christ.

19:5ff Israel accepted God's contract, an agreement in which he was recognized as their Lord. The contract was in fulfillment of God's promise to Abraham as well. It was a conditional arrangement based upon Israel's promise to believe God and to obey him. Only unbelief and disobedience could break the terms of the contract and lose the blessing God promised.

2. The Consecration of the People

19:9☆ Ex 14:31; 19:16 20:21 Deut 4:11 Ps 99:7 1 Kgs 8:12
19:10 Gen 35:2 Josh 3:5 Heb 10:22 Rev 7:14; 22:14
19:11 Ex 19:16; 34:5

9 And the LORD said unto Moses, Lo, I come unto thee in a thick cloud,
that the people may hear when I speak with thee, and believe thee for ever.
And Moses told the words of the people unto the LORD.
10 ¶And the LORD said unto Moses, Go unto the people, and sanctify
them to day and to morrow, and let them wash their clothes,
11 And be ready against the third day: for the third day the LORD will
come down in the sight of all the people upon mount Si′nai.
12 And thou shalt set bounds unto the people round about, saying, Take
heed to yourselves, *that ye* go *not* up into the mount, or touch the border of
it: whosoever toucheth the mount shall be surely put to death:

19:13 Ex 19:21 Heb 12:20

13 There shall not an hand touch it, but he shall surely be stoned, or shot
through; whether *it be* beast or man, it shall not live: when the trumpet
soundeth long, they shall come up to the mount.
14 ¶And Moses went down from the mount unto the people, and
sanctified the people; and they washed their clothes.

19:15 1 Sam 21:4 Mt 3:2 1 Cor 7:5

15 And he said unto the people, Be ready against the third day: come not
at *your* wives.

3. God and Moses Meet on Mount Sinai

19:16 Ex 9:23; 20:18 Heb 12:18, 19

16 ¶And it came to pass on the third day in the morning, that there were
thunders and lightnings, and a thick cloud upon the mount, and the voice
of the trumpet exceeding loud; so that all the people that *was* in the camp
trembled.

19:17 Deut 4:10; 5:5
19:18☆ Ex 24:17 Deut 5:4 Ps 68:7, 8; 104:32
19:19 Ps 81:7

17 And Moses brought forth the people out of the camp to meet with
God; and they stood at the nether part of the mount.
18 And mount Si′nai was altogether on a smoke, because the LORD
descended upon it in fire: and the smoke thereof ascended as the smoke of
a furnace, and the whole mount quaked greatly.
19 And when the voice of the trumpet sounded long, and waxed louder
and louder, Moses spake, and God answered him by a voice.

19:20 Ex 24:12 Neh 9:13
19:21 Ex 3:5; 33:20 1 Sam 6:19
19:22 Lev 10:2, 3 21:5–8

20 And the LORD came down upon mount Si′nai, on the top of the mount:
and the LORD called Moses *up* to the top of the mount; and Moses went up.
21 And the LORD said unto Moses, Go down, charge the people, lest they
break through unto the LORD to gaze, and many of them perish.
22 And let the priests also, which come near to the LORD, sanctify
themselves, lest the LORD break forth upon them.
23 And Moses said unto the LORD, The people cannot come up to mount
Si′nai: for thou chargedst us, saying, Set bounds about the mount, and
sanctify it.

19:24 Ex 24:1, 9, 12

24 And the LORD said unto him, Away, get thee down, and thou shalt
come up, thou, and Aaron with thee: but let not the priests and the people
break through to come up unto the LORD, lest he break forth upon them.
25 So Moses went down unto the people, and spake unto them.

20:1☆ Deut 4:33 5:4, 22 Acts 7:38
20:2 Ex 15:13 Deut 5:6; 7:8 15:15

B. THE GIVING OF THE TEN COMMANDMENTS

20 AND God spake all these words, saying,
2 I *am* the LORD thy God, which have brought thee out of the land
of Egypt, out of the house of bondage.

19:9 *the people . . . may believe thee for ever.* God had given Moses tokens so he could prove he was God's representative. Despite this, Israel doubted and disbelieved Moses time and again.

19:18 *the LORD* [Jehovah] *descended upon it in fire.* Fire symbolizes the holiness of God and is mentioned often in the Scriptures (3:2; 2 Kings 2:11; 2 Thess. 1:7, 8).

20:1 The Ten Commandments are an expression of the eternal moral law of God. They embody the basic

3 Thou shalt have no other gods before me.
4 Thou shalt not make unto thee any graven image, or any likeness *of any*
thing that *is* in heaven above, or that *is* in the earth beneath, or that *is* in the
water under the earth:
5 Thou shalt not bow down thyself to them, nor serve them: for I the
LORD thy God *am* a jealous God, visiting the iniquity of the fathers upon
the children unto the third and fourth *generation* of them that hate me;
6 And shewing mercy unto thousands of them that love me, and keep my
commandments.
7 Thou shalt not take the name of the LORD thy God in vain; for the
LORD will not hold him guiltless that taketh his name in vain.
8 Remember the sabbath day, to keep it holy.
9 Six days shalt thou labour, and do all thy work:
10 But the seventh day *is* the sabbath of the LORD thy God: *in it* thou shalt
not do any work, thou, nor thy son, nor thy daughter, thy manservant, nor
thy maidservant, nor thy cattle, nor thy stranger that *is* within thy gates:
11 For *in* six days the LORD made heaven and earth, the sea, and all that
in them *is,* and rested the seventh day: wherefore the LORD blessed the
sabbath day, and hallowed it.
12 ¶Honour thy father and thy mother: that thy days may be long upon
the land which the LORD thy God giveth thee.
13 Thou shalt not kill.
14 Thou shalt not commit adultery.
15 Thou shalt not steal.
16 Thou shalt not bear false witness against thy neighbour.
17 Thou shalt not covet thy neighbour's house, thou shalt not covet thy
neighbour's wife, nor his manservant, nor his maidservant, nor his ox, nor
his ass, nor any thing that *is* thy neighbour's.

C. ISRAEL IS GRIPPED BY FEAR

18 ¶And all the people saw the thunderings, and the lightnings, and the
noise of the trumpet, and the mountain smoking: and when the people saw
it, they removed, and stood afar off.
19 And they said unto Moses, Speak thou with us, and we will hear: but
let not God speak with us, lest we die.
20 And Moses said unto the people, Fear not: for God is come to prove
you, and that his fear may be before your faces, that ye sin not.

☆**20:3** Ex 15:11; 20:23 Deut 5:7; 6:14 1 Cor 8:4
20:4 Lev 26:1 Deut 4:15–20 27:15 Ps 97:7; 115:4-8 Rom 1:23
20:5 Ex 23:24; 34:14 Deut 4:24; 5:9, 10 Josh 23:16
20:6 Ex 34:6, 7 Deut 7:9
20:7 Lev 19:12 Deut 5:11; 6:13 Jer 4:2, Mt 5:33
20:8 Gen 2:3 Ex 16:23; 31:12–15 Deut 5:12
20:9 Ex 23:12; 34:21 Deut 5:13
20:11 Gen 2:2, 3 Mk 2:27
20:12 Deut 5:16, 33 Prov 1:8, 9 Mt 15:4; Eph 6:2
20:13 Gen 4:8–12; 9:5 Lev 24:21 Deut 5:17 Mt 5:21, 22
20:14 Prov 6:24–35 Mt 5:27, 28
☆**20:15** Lev 6:1–7 19:11, 13 Mt 15:19; 19:18
20:16 Deut 5:20; 19:15–21
20:18 Heb 12:18
20:19 Gen 32:30 Ex 33:20
20:20 Ex 14:13 Deut 4:10 6; 2, 24; 8:2

---

principles of life and state what would be true even if the commandments had never been given to Moses. They serve a twofold purpose: they are a schoolmaster to bring men to Christ (see Gal. 3:23–25) because they show men their guilt and make clear that no one ever keeps the law of God completely; they also help the Christian know what his duties are toward God and men, and to realize how he can please God and carry out his will. The commandments were summed up by Christ in two injunctions: men are to love God with their whole hearts, and their neighbors as themselves (Matt. 22:35–40). The Ten Commandments are said to have been spoken and written by God (32:16; Deut. 4:13; 5:4, 22; 10:4). The commandments condemn sinners, and drive those who wish to be right with God to Jesus Christ. The law is both external and internal in that some commandments pertain to overt acts while the last commandment ("Thou shalt not covet," 20:17) deals with the heart. Heart sin precedes overt acts of commission. Overt acts depict the condition of the heart.

20:3 Idolatry is expressly forbidden in the Scriptures. The objects of idol worship are denominated as "foreign gods," "gods of wood and stone," and "wooden idols." Idolatry takes a number of forms including: (1) bowing before or worshipping images, whether of God or of man (20:5; Isa. 44:17; Dan.3:5, 10, 15); (2) offering sacrifices to other gods or images (22:20; Ps. 106:38; Acts 7:41); (3) the worshipping of angels (Col. 2:18); (4) covetousness (Eph. 5:5); and (5) sensuality (Phil. 3:19). As a general rule, anything is idolatrous which takes first place away from God as the object of our love and obedience.

20:15 In the eighth commandment as well as by the word of Jesus (Matt. 19:18), stealing is always forbidden. This commandment presupposes the inalienability of private property—if what you take from me does not belong to me, then you have not stolen. Karl Marx claimed that this commandment was invented by Moses to support a *bourgeois* society. He condemned the right of individuals to own private property (such as land). God, though, gave the land to the Israelites and ordained that it should remain in the family forever. (See note to Lev. 25:16.)

D. THE LAWS GOVERNING ISRAEL

1. Rules for Making Altars

20:21 Deut 5:22 Ps 97:2
20:22 Deut 4:36 Neh 9:13 Heb 12:25
20:23 Ex 20:4; 32:4 Deut 29:17
20:24 Ex 10:25; 18:12 24:5; 27:1–8 Deut 12:4, 5

21 And the people stood afar off, and Moses drew near unto the thick
darkness where God *was*.
22 ¶And the LORD said unto Moses, Thus thou shalt say unto the children
of Israel, Ye have seen that I have talked with you from heaven.
23 Ye shall not make with me gods of silver, neither shall ye make unto
you gods of gold.
24 ¶An altar of earth thou shalt make unto me, and shalt sacrifice thereon
thy burnt offerings, and thy peace offerings, thy sheep, and thine oxen: in
all places where I record my name I will come unto thee, and I will bless
thee.

20:25 Deut 27:5 Josh 8:31
20:26 Ex 28:42

25 And if thou wilt make me an altar of stone, thou shalt not build it of
hewn stone: for if thou lift up thy tool upon it, thou hast polluted it.
26 Neither shalt thou go up by steps unto mine altar, that thy nakedness
be not discovered thereon.

2. Rules about Slavery

21:1☆ Lev 18:4, 5, 26 Deut 5:1, 31
21:2☆ Lev 25:39–43 Deut 15:12 Neh 5:1, 2 Jer 34:9–11

21 NOW these *are* the judgments which thou shalt set before them.
2 If thou buy an Hebrew servant, six years he shall serve: and in
the seventh he shall go out free for nothing.
3 If he came in by himself, he shall go out by himself: if he were married,
then his wife shall go out with him.
4 If his master have given him a wife, and she have born him sons or
daughters; the wife and her children shall be her master's, and he shall go
out by himself.

21:5 Deut 15:16
21:6 Ex 18:21

5 And if the servant shall plainly say, I love my master, my wife, and my
children; I will not go out free:
6 Then his master shall bring him unto the judges; he shall also bring him
to the door, or unto the door post; and his master shall bore his ear through
with an aul; and he shall serve him for ever.

21:7☆ Neh 5:5
21:8 Deut 21:11–14

7 ¶And if a man sell his daughter to be a maidservant, she shall not go out
as the menservants do.
8 If she please not her master, who hath betrothed her to himself, then
shall he let her be redeemed: to sell her unto a strange nation he shall have
no power, seeing he hath dealt deceitfully with her.
9 And if he have betrothed her unto his son, he shall deal with her after
the manner of daughters.

21:10 1 Cor 7:2–6
21:11 Ex 20:2, 3

10 If he take him another *wife;* her food, her raiment, and her duty of
marriage, shall he not diminish.
11 And if he do not these three unto her, then shall she go out free without
money.

21:1 God gave Israel its system of civil law under which society was to be governed. These laws were, in some instances, similar to those of Sumer and Babylonia, which are dated before Moses. Natural revelation presupposes that even pagan nations will know and use the laws of nature, for they apply to all people. The "thou shalt not" is peculiar to the laws of Israel. Some of the laws enacted in Moses' day are not applicable to our world today. Nevertheless, the underlying principles of justice, equality, and fairness are always foundational to any system of jurisprudence.

21:2 *If thou buy an Hebrew servant,* i.e., "if he owes you money and defaults in the payment, and thus becomes your slave."† Slavery was not forbidden in the Old Testament. Rather, its limits and governing principles were well regulated and legislated for the people of Israel.

21:7 *if a man sell his daughter.* Who would suppose that a father would sell a daughter? God, the author of these injunctions, knew what evils his own people were capable of and set up these regulations *before* they did these things.

3. Rules about Murder

12 ¶He that smiteth a man, so that he die, shall be surely put to death.

13 And if a man lie not in wait, but God deliver *him* into his hand; then I will appoint thee a place whither he shall flee.

14 But if a man come presumptuously upon his neighbour, to slay him with guile; thou shalt take him from mine altar, that he may die.

15 ¶And he that smiteth his father, or his mother, shall be surely put to death.

16 ¶And he that stealeth a man, and selleth him, or if he be found in his hand, he shall surely be put to death.

17 ¶And he that curseth his father, or his mother, shall surely be put to death.

4. Rules Governing Other Offenses

18 ¶And if men strive together, and one smite another with a stone, or with *his* fist, and he die not, but keepeth *his* bed:

19 If he rise again, and walk abroad upon his staff, then shall he that smote *him* be quit: only he shall pay *for* the loss of his time, and shall cause *him* to be thoroughly healed.

20 ¶And if a man smite his servant, or his maid, with a rod, and he die under his hand; he shall be surely punished.

21 Notwithstanding, if he continue a day or two, he shall not be punished: for he *is* his money.

22 If men strive, and hurt a woman with child, so that her fruit depart *from her*, and yet no mischief follow: he shall be surely punished, according as the woman's husband will lay upon him; and he shall pay as the judges *determine*.

23 And if *any* mischief follow, then thou shalt give life for life,

24 Eye for eye, tooth for tooth, hand for hand, foot for foot,

25 Burning for burning, wound for wound, stripe for stripe.

26 ¶And if a man smite the eye of his servant, or the eye of his maid, that it perish; he shall let him go free for his eye's sake.

27 And if he smite out his manservant's tooth, or his maidservant's tooth; he shall let him go free for his tooth's sake.

28 If an ox gore a man or a woman, that they die: then the ox shall be surely stoned, and his flesh shall not be eaten; but the owner of the ox *shall be* quit.

29 But if the ox were wont to push with his horn in time past, and it hath been testified to his owner, and he hath not kept him in, but that he hath killed a man or a woman; the ox shall be stoned, and his owner also shall be put to death.

30 If there be laid on him a sum of money, then he shall give for the ransom of his life whatsoever is laid upon him.

31 Whether he have gored a son, or have gored a daughter, according to this judgment shall it be done unto him.

32 If the ox shall push a manservant or a maidservant; he shall give unto their master thirty shekels of silver, and the ox shall be stoned.

☆**21:12** Gen 9:5; Ex 20:13; Lev 24:21
☆**21:13** Num 35:9–29, 32; Deut 19:1–10; Josh 20:1–10
☆**21:14** Ex 20:13; Num 35:30, 31; Deut 19:11–13; 1 Kgs 2:28–34
☆**21:15** Ex 20:12; Deut 21:18; Prov 30:11, 17
21:16 Deut 24:7; 1 Tim 1:10
21:17 Lev 20:9; Deut 27:16; Mt 15:4; Mk 7:10
21:18 Num 35:16, 17
☆**21:19**
21:21 Lev 25:44–46
21:23 Ex 20:13; 21:12
☆**21:24, 25** Lev 24:20–22; Deut 19:21; Mt 5:38
21:26 Job 31:13
21:28 Gen 9:5
21:30 Num 30:11, 12; 35:31
21:32 Gen 37:28; Zech 11:12; Mt 26:15; 27:3, 9

21:12–15 The law about murder distinguishes between that which is premeditated and springs from the heart and deaths caused by so-called accidents. The penalty for homicide is death. For the man who kills innocently, a place of refuge is provided to which he may flee. The phrase "God deliver him into his hand" indicates that nothing happens by chance, even accidental death. Today judges and juries guarantee the freedom of those who kill accidentally.

21:19 *if he . . . walk abroad upon his staff,* i.e., "if later he is able to walk again, even with a limp."†

21:24, 25 The idea that the punishment should be equal to the crime was a great advance over the law of revenge. The New Testament elevates both concepts with its principle of forgiveness. We must forgive those who hurt us even if they do it often, for thus we have been forgiven by God for our sins.

5. Rules about Property Rights

21:33ff☆
33 ¶And if a man shall open a pit, or if a man shall dig a pit, and not cover
it, and an ox or an ass fall therein;

21:34 Ex 22:5
34 The owner of the pit shall make *it* good, *and* give money unto the owner
of them; and the dead *beast* shall be his.
35 ¶And if one man's ox hurt another's, that he die; then they shall sell the
live ox, and divide the money of it; and the dead *ox* also they shall divide.
36 Or if it be known that the ox hath used to push in time past, and his
owner hath not kept him in; he shall surely pay ox for ox; and the dead
shall be his own.

22:1 Lev 6:1–7, 2 Sam 12:6, Prov 6:31, Lk 19:8

22

IF a man shall steal an ox, or a sheep, and kill it, or sell it; he shall
restore five oxen for an ox, and four sheep for a sheep.

22:2 Num 35:26, 27
2 If a thief be found breaking up, and be smitten that he die, *there shall* no
blood *be shed* for him.

22:3 Ex 20:13, 21:2, 14
3 If the sun be risen upon him, *there shall be* blood *shed* for him; *for* he
should make full restitution; if he have nothing, then he shall be sold for his
theft.

22:4 Prov 6:30, Jer 2:26, Jn 12:6
4 If the theft be certainly found in his hand alive, whether it be ox, or ass,
or sheep; he shall restore double.

22:5 Ex 21:34
5 If a man shall cause a field or vineyard to be eaten, and shall put in his
beast, and shall feed in another man's field; of the best of his own field, and
of the best of his own vineyard, shall he make restitution.
6 If fire break out, and catch in thorns, so that the stacks of corn, or the
standing corn, or the field, be consumed *therewith;* he that kindled the fire
shall surely make restitution.

22:7 Lev 6:1–7, Prov 6:30, 31
7 If a man shall deliver unto his neighbour money or stuff to keep, and it
be stolen out of the man's house; if the thief be found, let him pay double.

22:8 Ex 21:6, Deut 1:17
8 If the thief be not found, then the master of the house shall be brought
unto the judges, *to see* whether he have put his hand unto his neighbour's
goods.

22:9 Num 5:7, Deut 25:1, 2 Chron 19:10
9 For all manner of trespass, *whether it be* for ox, for ass, for sheep, for
raiment, *or* for any manner of lost thing, which *another* challengeth to be
his, the cause of both parties shall come before the judges; *and* whom the
judges shall condemn, he shall pay double unto his neighbour.
10 If a man deliver unto his neighbour an ass, or an ox, or a sheep, or any
beast, to keep; and it die, or be hurt, or driven away, no man seeing *it:*
11 *Then* shall an oath of the LORD be between them both, that he hath not
put his hand unto his neighbour's goods; and the owner of it shall accept
thereof, and he shall not make *it* good.

22:12 Lev 6:2
12 And if it be stolen from him, he shall make restitution unto the owner
thereof.

22:13☆ Gen 37:33
13 If it be torn in pieces, *then* let him bring it *for* witness, *and* he shall not
make good that which was torn.

22:14 Deut 23:19, Neh 5:4, Ps 37:21
14 ¶And if a man borrow *ought* of his neighbour, and it be hurt, or die, the
owner thereof *being* not with it, he shall surely make *it* good.
15 *But* if the owner thereof *be* with it, he shall not make *it* good: if it *be* an
hired *thing,* it came for his hire.

22:16☆ Gen 34:2–4, Deut 22:28, 29
16 ¶And if a man entice a maid that is not betrothed, and lie with her, he
shall surely endow her to be his wife.

21:33ff God guarantees property rights as well as human life. The right to property is inalienable, i.e., no one can take it from the owner; and if a loss is sustained through an accident, the one who caused the accident is liable for damages.

22:13 *torn in pieces,* i.e., torn by beasts. Acts of God do not require payment to those whose property has been lost or damaged. Earthquakes, fires, and volcanic eruptions are considered acts of God.

22:16 *a maid,* literally, "a virgin." *endow her,* literally, "give a customary marriage present to the bride's parents."†

17 If her father utterly refuse to give her unto him, he shall pay money
according to the dowry of virgins.

6. Other Regulations
a. Capital Crimes

18 ¶Thou shalt not suffer a witch to live.
19 ¶Whosoever lieth with a beast shall surely be put to death.
20 ¶He that sacrificeth unto *any* god, save unto the LORD only, he shall be
utterly destroyed.

b. Various Duties

21 ¶Thou shalt neither vex a stranger, nor oppress him: for ye were
strangers in the land of Egypt.
22 ¶Ye shall not afflict any widow, or fatherless child.
23 If thou afflict them in any wise, and they cry at all unto me, I will surely
hear their cry;
24 And my wrath shall wax hot, and I will kill you with the sword; and
your wives shall be widows, and your children fatherless.
25 If thou lend money to *any of* my people *that is* poor by thee, thou shalt
not be to him as an usurer, neither shalt thou lay upon him usury.
26 If thou at all take thy neighbour's raiment to pledge, thou shalt deliver
it unto him by that the sun goeth down:
27 For that *is* his covering only, it *is* his raiment for his skin: wherein shall
he sleep? and it shall come to pass, when he crieth unto me, that I will hear;
for I *am* gracious.
28 ¶Thou shalt not revile the gods, nor curse the ruler of thy people.
29 ¶Thou shalt not delay *to offer* the first of thy ripe fruits, and of thy
liquors: the firstborn of thy sons shalt thou give unto me.
30 Likewise shalt thou do with thine oxen, *and* with thy sheep: seven days
it shall be with his dam; on the eighth day thou shalt give it me.
31 ¶And ye shall be holy men unto me: neither shall ye eat *any* flesh *that*
is torn of beasts in the field; ye shall cast it to the dogs.

c. Ethical Matters

23 THOU shall not raise a false report: put not thine hand with the
wicked to be an unrighteous witness.
2 ¶Thou shalt not follow a multitude to *do* evil; neither shalt thou speak in
a cause to decline after many to wrest *judgment:*

22:17 Deut 7:3
22:18 Lev 19:26; 20:27 Deut 18:10 Jer 27:9
22:19 Lev 18:23; 20:15 Deut 27:21
22:20 Ex 32:8; 34:15 Num 25:2 Deut 13:1–16
22:21 Lev 19:33, 34 Deut 1:16 10:19; 27:19 Jer 7:6 Zech 7:10
22:22 Deut 24:17 Prov 23:10 Ps 94:5–10 Isa 1:17
22:23 Deut 10:18 Ps 10:14; 68:5 Lk 18:7 Jas 5:4
22:24 Ps 109:9
☆**22:25** Lev 25:36 Deut 23:19
22:26 Deut 24:6, 10–13 Job 22:6
☆**22:27** Ex 2:23 Ps 34:6; 72:12 Isa 19:20
22:28 Lev 24:15 Acts 23:5
22:29 Ex 13:2 23:16, 19 34:19, 20 Deut 26:2
22:30 Gen 17:12 Lev 12:3; 22:27
22:31 Ex 19:6 Lev 7:24; 17:15 22:8
☆**23:1** Deut 5:20; 19:16 Ps 35:11
23:2, 3 Deut 1:17; 16:19 Job 31:34 Prov 1:10 4:14, 15

22:25 Interest charges are forbidden when an Israelite lends money or goods to another Israelite. But a loan to a non-Israelite with interest charges is not forbidden. Usury is inordinate interest and runs counter to neighborly love.
22:27 *gracious,* i.e., "I am very compassionate." Grace, kindness, and compassion constitute one of God's attributes. God said he will be gracious and merciful to whom he wants (33:19). Grace may be defined as God's "unmerited favor" which he manifests to sinful man. It is everything for nothing to those who deserve the exact opposite. Concerning the grace or the kindness of God, the Scriptures teach that: (1) salvation is by God's grace or kindness (Eph. 1:7, 8); (2) justification (i.e., being declared "not guilty") is by God's grace or kindness (Rom. 3:24; Titus 3:7); (3) God's election (i.e., being chosen by God) is of God's kindness or grace (Rom. 11:5, 6); (4) faith itself is a gift of God's kindness or grace (Eph. 2:8, 9); (5) the call to Christian life and testimony is all of grace or kindness (Gal. 1:15, 16); (6) comfort, hope, and strength spring from grace (2 Thess. 2:16, 17).
23:1 Slander is a sin which is sternly forbidden in the Scriptures. It includes such sins as whispering, backbiting, tale-bearing, defaming, bearing false witness, and raising false reports (Prov. 6:16, 19; Eph. 4:31; James 4:11). The route to victory over slander is to walk in the Spirit so we can love our neighbors as we love ourselves.

Here and elsewhere the Scriptures deal with matters that fall under the rubric of *ethics.* Ethics is "a discipline dealing with what is good and bad and with moral duty and obligation" (Webster's *New Collegiate Dictionary*, Merriam, 1980). Christian ethics is based upon the biblical teachings of what is right and wrong and what the Bible asserts to be the believer's moral

23:4
Deut 22:1–4
Prov 24:17
25:21, 22
Rom 12:17–21
23:6
Ex 22:21–24
Deut 27:19
2 Chron 19:7
Ps 82:3
23:7
Ex 20:13, 16
Deut 27:15
Ps 119:29
23:8
Deut 16:19
1 Sam 8:3; 12:3
Prov 15:27
17:8, 23
23:9
Ex 22:21
Lev 19:33, 34
23:10
Lev 25:1
23:11☆
Lev 26:34, 35
23:12
Ex 20:8–11
Deut 5:13
23:13
Deut 4:9, 23
Josh 22:5
Ps 16:4
Jer 10:11
23:14☆
Ex 34:22
Lev 23:4
Deut 16:16
23:15
Ex 12:2; 13:4
34:18
Lev 23:5
Num 9:2
23:16☆
Ex 34:22
Lev 23:9, 34
Deut 16:9, 13
23:17
Deut 12:5; 16:16
23:18
Ex 12:10; 34:25
Lev 2:11; 7:15

3 ¶Neither shalt thou countenance a poor man in his cause.
4 If thou meet thine enemy's ox or his ass going astray, thou shalt surely
bring it back to him again.
5 If thou see the ass of him that hateth thee lying under his burden, and
wouldest forbear to help him, thou shalt surely help with him.
6 Thou shalt not wrest the judgment of thy poor in his cause.
7 Keep thee far from a false matter; and the innocent and righteous slay
thou not: for I will not justify the wicked.
8 ¶And thou shalt take no gift: for the gift blindeth the wise, and
perverteth the words of the righteous.
9 ¶Also thou shalt not oppress a stranger: for ye know the heart of a
stranger, seeing ye were strangers in the land of Egypt.

7. Rules about the Use of Land and Feasts

10 And six years thou shalt sow thy land, and shalt gather in the fruits
thereof:
11 But the seventh *year* thou shalt let it rest and lie still; that the poor of
thy people may eat: and what they leave the beasts of the field shall eat. In
like manner thou shalt deal with thy vineyard, *and* with thy oliveyard.
12 Six days thou shalt do thy work, and on the seventh day thou shalt rest:
that thine ox and thine ass may rest, and the son of thy handmaid, and the
stranger, may be refreshed.
13 And in all *things* that I have said unto you be circumspect: and make
no mention of the name of other gods, neither let it be heard out of thy
mouth.
14 ¶Three times thou shalt keep a feast unto me in the year.
15 Thou shalt keep the feast of unleavened bread: (thou shalt eat
unleavened bread seven days, as I commanded thee, in the time appointed
of the month Abib; for in it thou camest out from Egypt: and none shall
appear before me empty:)
16 And the feast of harvest, the firstfruits of thy labours, which thou hast
sown in the field: and the feast of ingathering, *which is* in the end of the
year, when thou hast gathered in thy labours out of the field.
17 Three times in the year all thy males shall appear before the Lord GOD.
18 Thou shalt not offer the blood of my sacrifice with leavened bread;
neither shall the fat of my sacrifice remain until the morning.

---

duty and obligation. Its basic presuppositions are twofold: Love God, and your neighbor as yourself. These basic commands are expanded on in the Scriptures and cover all aspects of the Christian life.

23:11 The feast of the sabbatical year was kept every seventh year. For six years the land was to be cultivated; the seventh year it was to lie fallow (Lev. 25:2). God promised there would be an adequate harvest on the sixth year (Lev. 25:21) so the people could live until the land was cultivated in the eighth year. Farming was to cease, the fruits of the earth became common property, debts were canceled, Hebrew servants were set free, and the law was read publicly (see Lev. 25:4ff; Deut. 15:1–3; Neh. 10:31; Deut. 15:12; 31:10–13). These arrangements did not necessarily apply to non-Israelites (Deut. 15:3). The later captivity by Babylonia was partially a consequence of Israel's failure to observe the sabbatical year (2 Chron. 36:20, 21).

23:14 All adult male Israelites were required to attend three yearly festivals at the tabernacle: the festival of unleavened bread (23:15), the festival of the harvest (23:16), and the festival (or pilgrimage) of ingathering (23:16). They are often known as the feasts of Passover, Pentecost, and tabernacles. (See notes on 12:11; Lev. 23:15, 16; Mark 14:1).

23:16 The pilgrimage of ingathering (34:22), also known as the feast of tabernacles, was one of three national festivals, (the other two were Passover and Pentecost). It started on the fifteenth day of *Tishri*, the seventh month (Lev. 23:34, 39). It lasted for eight days and came at the end of the harvest and vintage. All adult males were required to attend the three national festivals (23:17). The first and last days of the festival were celebrated by holy convocations (Lev. 23:35, 39; Num. 29:12, 35). The people camped out in booths for this festival, family by family (Lev. 23:42). The feast was to be celebrated annually and with thanksgiving (Lev. 23:41; Deut. 16:14, 15). It was also called the feast or festival of booths to recall Israel's redemption out of Egypt. Zechariah prophesied that it would become a memorial festival for all nations (Zech. 14:16–21).

[19]The first of the firstfruits of thy land thou shalt bring into the house of
the LORD thy God. Thou shalt not seethe a kid in his mother's milk.

23:19 Ex 22:29; 34:26 Lev 23:10

8. Instructions about the Land of Canaan

[20]¶Behold, I send an Angel before thee, to keep thee in the way, and to
bring thee into the place which I have prepared.
[21]Beware of him, and obey his voice, provoke him not; for he will not
pardon your transgressions: for my name *is* in him.
[22]But if thou shalt indeed obey his voice, and do all that I speak; then I
will be an enemy unto thine enemies, and an adversary unto thine
adversaries.
[23]For mine Angel shall go before thee, and bring thee in unto the Am'or-
ites, and the Hittites, and the Per'iz-zites, and the Canaanites, the Hi'vites,
and the Jeb'u-sites: and I will cut them off.
[24]Thou shalt not bow down to their gods, nor serve them; nor do after
their works: but thou shalt utterly overthrow them, and quite break down
their images.
[25]And ye shall serve the LORD your God, and he shall bless thy bread,
and thy water; and I will take sickness away from the midst of thee.
[26]¶There shall nothing cast their young, nor be barren, in thy land: the
number of thy days I will fulfil.
[27]I will send my fear before thee, and will destroy all the people to whom
thou shalt come, and I will make all thine enemies turn their backs unto
thee.
[28]And I will send hornets before thee, which shall drive out the Hi'vite,
the Canaanite, and the Hittite, from before thee.
[29]I will not drive them out from before thee in one year; lest the land
become desolate, and the beast of the field multiply against thee.
[30]By little and little I will drive them out from before thee, until thou be
increased, and inherit the land.
[31]And I will set thy bounds from the Red sea even unto the sea of the
Philistines, and from the desert unto the river: for I will deliver the
inhabitants of the land into your hand; and thou shalt drive them out
before thee.
[32]Thou shalt make no covenant with them, nor with their gods.
[33]They shall not dwell in thy land, lest they make thee sin against me: for
if thou serve their gods, it will surely be a snare unto thee.

23:20 Ex 3:2; 14:19 32:34
☆23:21 Ex 3:14; 34:5 Num 14:10, 11 Deut 9:7
23:22 Gen 12:3 Num 24:9 Deut 30:7
23:23 Gen 15:19–21 Deut 7:1 Josh 24:11
23:24 Ex 20:5; 34:13 Lev 26:1 Num 33:52 Deut 7:5 2 Kgs 18:4
23:25 Ex 15:26 Lev 26:3 Deut 7:15 28:1–14
23:26 Deut 7:14 Job 5:26 Ps 107:38
23:27 Gen 35:5 Ex 15:16 Deut 2:25
23:28 Ex 34:11 Deut 7:20 Josh 24:12
☆23:30 Deut 7:22 Josh 15:63 16:10; 17:12
23:31 Gen 15:18 Josh 21:44 24:12, 18
23:32 Ex 34:12 Deut 7:2 Josh 9:14, 15
23:33 Deut 7:16; 12:30

9. Israel Ratifies God's Covenant

a. The Blood of the Covenant

24 AND he said unto Moses, Come up unto the LORD, thou, and
Aaron, Na'dab, and A-bi'hu, and seventy of the elders of Israel;
and worship ye afar off.
[2]And Moses alone shall come near the LORD: but they shall not come
nigh; neither shall the people go up with him.

24:1 Ex 6:23; 19:24 28:1 Lev 10:1, 2 Num 11:16
24:2 Ex 20:21 Jer 30:21

23:21 *my name is in him,* i.e., "he is my representative—he bears my name."†
23:30 The expulsion of the inhabitants from the promised land and the granting of the land to Israel were the fixed purpose of God. But the execution of that purpose was conditioned by life's realities. Thus the inhabitants were not to be driven out immediately. In the interests of preserving the productivity of the land and of keeping it from being overrun by desolation, God told Israel that the divine strategy was to accomplish the intention over a period of time. This distinction between settled principle and the carrying out of that principle needs to be understood in the context of international situations today. Not every decision can be implemented immediately.

24:3☆ Ex 19:8; 24:7 Deut 5:27; 11:1
3 ¶And Moses came and told the people all the words of the LORD, and all
the judgments: and all the people answered with one voice, and said, All
the words which the LORD hath said will we do.

24:4 a)Ex 34:27 Deut 31:9 Josh 24:26 b)Gen 28:18
4 And Moses wrote all the words of the LORD, and rose up early in the
morning, and builded an altar under the hill, and twelve pillars, according
to the twelve tribes of Israel.

24:5 Ex 18:12 Lev 1:2; 7:11
5 And he sent young men of the children of Israel, which offered burnt
offerings, and sacrificed peace offerings of oxen unto the LORD.

24:6 Ex 12:7; 29:16
6 And Moses took half of the blood, and put *it* in basons; and half of the
blood he sprinkled on the altar.

24:7☆ Ex 19:8; 24:3 Deut 5:27
7 And he took the book of the covenant, and read in the audience of the
people: and they said, All that the LORD hath said will we do, and be
obedient.

24:8 Lev 8:30 Zech 9:11 Mt 26:28 1 Cor 11:25
8 And Moses took the blood, and sprinkled *it* on the people, and said,
Behold the blood of the covenant, which the LORD hath made with you
concerning all these words.

24:9 Ex 24:1
9 ¶Then went up Moses, and Aaron, Na'dab, and A-bi'hu, and seventy of
the elders of Israel:

24:10☆ Ex 33:20 Num 12:8 Isa 6:5 Ezek 1:26 Jn 1:18
10 And they saw the God of Israel: and *there was* under his feet as it were
a paved work of a sapphire stone, and as it were the body of heaven in *his*
clearness.

24:11 Ex 18:12
11 And upon the nobles of the children of Israel he laid not his hand: also
they saw God, and did eat and drink.

b. Moses Spends Forty Days with God on the Mount

24:12 Ex 31:18 Jer 31:33
12 ¶And the LORD said unto Moses, Come up to me into the mount, and
be there: and I will give thee tables of stone, and a law, and commandments
which I have written; that thou mayest teach them.

24:13☆ Ex 17:9; 32:17 33:11
13 And Moses rose up, and his minister Joshua: and Moses went up into
the mount of God.

24:14 Gen 22:5 Ex 17:10
14 And he said unto the elders, Tarry ye here for us, until we come again
unto you: and, behold, Aaron and Hur *are* with you: if any man have any
matters to do, let him come unto them.

24:15 Ex 19:9 2 Chron 6:1
15 ¶And Moses went up into the mount, and a cloud covered the mount.

24:16 Lev 9:23 Num 14:10
16 And the glory of the LORD abode upon mount Si'nai, and the cloud
covered it six days: and the seventh day he called unto Moses out of the
midst of the cloud.

24:3 The ordinances or commandments relating to community life are here said to have been given to Moses directly by God. Thus civil law derives from God himself, not from the whims and fancies of men. This means they are absolute in nature and not subject to any other authority.

24:7 *the book of the covenant* constituted all the words of the Lord, which God spoke to Moses (24:4). When the book of the covenant had been read to the people of Israel, they were called upon to accept and ratify what it contained. The people promised to do all God had said and they swore obedience. Then Moses sprinkled blood over the people (24:8) and said this symbolic act represented the blood of the covenant. It was the blood of bulls and goats which, in turn, were symbols of the blood of Christ shed on Calvary (Heb. 9:13, 14) which made up "the everlasting covenant" of Heb. 13:20.

24:10 A theophany is a visible appearance of God to men. Such appearances differed greatly. Among them were: (1) the appearance of God (in what may have been a vision) to Moses, Aaron, Nadab, Abihu, and the seventy elders in which his glory was manifested (24:10); (2) the time when God spoke to Moses face to face (33:11); (3) appearances to Isaiah (Isa. 6), Ezekiel (Ezek. 1), and Daniel (Dan. 7) when God was seen in a vision or a dream; (4) the appearance of the angel of the Lord to Hagar (Gen 16:7—although the angel of the Lord does not always mean the appearance of God or Christ); (5) the appearance of God in the pillar of cloud (14:19); (6) the time when God showed men of Israel his greatness and glory (Deut. 5:24); and (7) the appearance of God in the incarnation of Jesus Christ when the Son became a human being and "dwelt among us" (John 1:14).

24:13 *his minister Joshua.* Joshua served under Moses as a subordinate. Thus he had time to learn all he needed to know about the administration of justice and the supervision of Israel. After the death of Moses, he led the people of Israel into the land of promise. As God's choice, not man's, he was a well-trained replacement for Moses.

17 And the sight of the glory of the LORD *was* like devouring fire on the
top of the mount in the eyes of the children of Israel.
18 And Moses went into the midst of the cloud, and gat him up into the
mount: and Moses was in the mount forty days and forty nights.

24:17 Ex 3:2; 16:10; 19:18; Deut 4:24, 36; Ezek 1:27; Nah 1:6; Heb 12:29
24:18 Ex 19:20, 34:28; Deut 9:9; 10:10; 1 Kgs 19:8

V. THE TABERNACLE AND ITS MINISTRY (25:1—40:38)

A. GATHERING THE MATERIALS FOR THE TABERNACLE

25 AND the LORD spake unto Moses, saying,
2 Speak unto the children of Israel, that they bring me an offering:
of every man that giveth it willingly with his heart ye shall take my offering.
3 And this *is* the offering which ye shall take of them; gold, and silver, and
brass,
4 And blue, and purple, and scarlet, and fine linen, and goats' *hair*,
5 And rams' skins dyed red, and badgers' skins, and shittim wood,
6 Oil for the light, spices for anointing oil, and for sweet incense,
7 Onyx stones, and stones to be set in the ephod, and in the breastplate.
8 And let them make me a sanctuary; that I may dwell among them.
9 According to all that I shew thee, *after* the pattern of the tabernacle, and
the pattern of all the instruments thereof, even so shall ye make *it*.

25:1 Ex 35:5–9; Num 7:4, 5; 1 Chron 29:2–5; 2 Cor 8:10–12
25:8 Ex 29:45; 36:1; Deut 12:11; Rev 21:3
☆25:9 Acts 7:44; Heb 8:5

B. THE INSTRUCTIONS FOR MAKING THE ARK

10 ¶And they shall make an ark *of* shittim wood: two cubits and a half
shall be the length thereof, and a cubit and a half the breadth thereof, and
a cubit and a half the height thereof.
11 And thou shalt overlay it with pure gold, within and without shalt thou
overlay it, and shalt make upon it a crown of gold round about.
12 And thou shalt cast four rings of gold for it, and put *them* in the four
corners thereof; and two rings *shall be* in the one side of it, and two rings in
the other side of it.
13 And thou shalt make staves *of* shittim wood, and overlay them with
gold.
14 And thou shalt put the staves into the rings by the sides of the ark, that
the ark may be borne with them.
15 The staves shall be in the rings of the ark: they shall not be taken from
it.
16 And thou shalt put into the ark the testimony which I shall give thee.
17 And thou shalt make a mercy seat *of* pure gold: two cubits and a half
shall be the length thereof, and a cubit and a half the breadth thereof.
18 And thou shalt make two cherubims *of* gold, *of* beaten work shalt thou
make them, in the two ends of the mercy seat.

☆25:10 Ex 37:1–5; Deut 10:3
25:12 Ex 26:29; 27:7; 37:5; 38:7
25:13 Ex 30:5; 37:4; 40:20
25:15 1 Kgs 8:8; 2 Chron 5:9
25:16 Ex 16:34; 30:6; Deut 10:2; Heb 9:4
☆25:17 Ex 26:34; 37:6; 40:20; Lev 16:13; Rom 3:25; Heb 9:5
25:18 Ex 37:7

25:9 God commanded Moses to build the tabernacle. It was to be a removable tent because of the unsettled life of Israel (2 Sam. 7:6, 7). God appointed the Levites to have charge of it (Num. 1:50; 18:2–4) and assured Israel his presence would fill the holy place (25:22; Lev. 16:2; Num. 7:89). During the forty years in the wilderness, the glory of God rested over the tabernacle by day and by night. When the *shekinah* cloud moved, the people of Israel moved, too. God guided them this way for years (40:36–38; Num. 9:15, 16).

25:10 See notes on 25:17 and 26:33.

25:17 The mercy seat was made of pure gold. It was the lid of the ark, beaten out into the form of two cherubs (winged lions with human heads) facing each other. The wings of the cherubs were outspread and the cherubs looked down at the mercy seat. The tables of the law were inside the ark. Thus grace covers the law by mercy. Christ the perfect sacrifice met the full demands of the law, making divine mercy possible. The Hebrew term for "mercy seat" means "propitiatory" and derives from the verb *kippēr* ("to atone".) The high priest entered the Holy of Holies once a year with blood to make atonement. Christ entered the Holy of Holies in the heavenly sanctuary once for our sins, and his work is finished by that one act. Now all believers have immediate access to the mercy seat through Christ, our High Priest (Rom. 3:25; Heb. 4:14–16).

19 And make one cherub on the one end, and the other cherub on the other end: *even* of the mercy seat shall ye make the cherubims on the two ends thereof.

25:20 1 Kgs 8:7 1 Chron 28:18 Heb 9:5

20 And the cherubims shall stretch forth *their* wings on high, covering the mercy seat with their wings, and their faces *shall look* one to another; toward the mercy seat shall the faces of the cherubims be.

21 And thou shalt put the mercy seat above upon the ark; and in the ark thou shalt put the testimony that I shall give thee.

25:22 Ex 30:6, 36 Lev 1:1 Deut 5:26

22 And there I will meet with thee, and I will commune with thee from above the mercy seat, from between the two cherubims which *are* upon the ark of the testimony, of all *things* which I will give thee in commandment unto the children of Israel.

C. THE INSTRUCTIONS FOR MAKING THE TABLE

25:23 Ex 37:10; 40:22

23 ¶Thou shalt also make a table *of* shittim wood: two cubits *shall be* the length thereof, and a cubit the breadth thereof, and a cubit and a half the height thereof.

25:24 Ex 25:11

24 And thou shalt overlay it with pure gold, and make thereto a crown of gold round about.

25 And thou shalt make unto it a border of an hand breadth round about, and thou shalt make a golden crown to the border thereof round about.

26 And thou shalt make for it four rings of gold, and put the rings in the four corners that *are* on the four feet thereof.

27 Over against the border shall the rings be for places of the staves to bear the table.

28 And thou shalt make the staves *of* shittim wood, and overlay them with gold, that the table may be borne with them.

25:29 Ex 37:16 Num 4:7

29 And thou shalt make the dishes thereof, and spoons thereof, and covers thereof, and bowls thereof, to cover withal: *of* pure gold shalt thou make them.

25:30☆ Ex 35:13; 39:36 40:23 Lev 24:5 Num 4:7 2 Chron 13:11

30 And thou shalt set upon the table shewbread before me alway.

D. THE INSTRUCTIONS FOR MAKING THE LAMPSTAND

25:31☆ Ex 37:17; 40:24 1 Kgs 7:49 Heb 9:2

31 ¶And thou shalt make a candlestick *of* pure gold: *of* beaten work shall the candlestick be made: his shaft, and his branches, his bowls, his knops, and his flowers, shall be of the same.

32 And six branches shall come out of the sides of it; three branches of the candlestick out of the one side, and three branches of the candlestick out of the other side:

33 Three bowls made like unto almonds, *with* a knop and a flower in one branch; and three bowls made like almonds in the other branch, *with* a knop and a flower: so in the six branches that come out of the candlestick.

34 And in the candlestick *shall be* four bowls made like unto almonds, *with* their knops and their flowers.

25:30 The shewbread was set on the table. The twelve loaves represented the twelve tribes of Israel and were set in two rows of six loaves each. The tabernacle was God's house or palace. "In the royal palace it was fit that there should be a royal table."* The loaves were an acknowledgement of God's goodness to his people and a token of their uninterrupted communion with him. The shewbread is a type of the spiritual provision for the church in the gospel age. Best of all, God's people shall ever eat and drink with the Savior at his table in his kingdom (Luke 22:30).

25:31 The *candlestick,* or "lampstand," was of great significance in the tabernacle. It provided the only light in the tabernacle, for there were no windows in it. When Jesus, the sun of righteousness, came, the relative darkness of the old dispensation would be dissipated. For the Israelites, "the commandment was a lamp, and the law a light, and the prophets were branches from that lamp which gave light to their several ages."* We now have the entire Word of God, "a light that shineth in a dark place." The darkness of our minds and hearts can be regenerated by the Holy Spirit and given the light of the knowledge of God.

35 And *there shall be* a knop under two branches of the same, and a knop
under two branches of the same, and a knop under two branches of the
same, according to the six branches that proceed out of the candlestick.
36 Their knops and their branches shall be of the same: all it *shall be* one
beaten work *of* pure gold.
37 And thou shalt make the seven lamps thereof: and they shall light the
lamps thereof, that they may give light over against it.
38 And the tongs thereof, and the snuffdishes thereof, *shall be of* pure gold.
39 *Of* a talent of pure gold shall he make it, with all these vessels.
40 And look that thou make *them* after their pattern, which was shewed
thee in the mount.

25:37 Ex 37:23; Zech 4:2; Rev 1:4, 12, 20; 4:5
25:40 Ex 39:42; Num 8:4; Acts 7:44; Heb 8:5

E. THE INSTRUCTIONS FOR MAKING THE TABERNACLE

26 MOREOVER thou shalt make the tabernacle *with* ten curtains *of*
fine twined linen, and blue, and purple, and scarlet: *with* cherubims
of cunning work shalt thou make them.
2 The length of one curtain *shall be* eight and twenty cubits, and the
breadth of one curtain four cubits: and every one of the curtains shall have
one measure.
3 The five curtains shall be coupled together one to another; and *other* five
curtains *shall be* coupled one to another.
4 And thou shalt make loops of blue upon the edge of the one curtain
from the selvedge in the coupling; and likewise shalt thou make in the
uttermost edge of *another* curtain, in the coupling of the second.
5 Fifty loops shalt thou make in the one curtain, and fifty loops shalt thou
make in the edge of the curtain that *is* in the coupling of the second; that
the loops may take hold one of another.
6 And thou shalt make fifty taches of gold, and couple the curtains
together with the taches: and it shall be one tabernacle.
7 ¶And thou shalt make curtains *of* goats' *hair* to be a covering upon the
tabernacle: eleven curtains shalt thou make.
8 The length of one curtain *shall be* thirty cubits, and the breadth of one
curtain four cubits: and the eleven curtains *shall be all* of one measure.
9 And thou shalt couple five curtains by themselves, and six curtains by
themselves, and shalt double the sixth curtain in the forefront of the
tabernacle.
10 And thou shalt make fifty loops on the edge of the one curtain *that is*
outmost in the coupling, and fifty loops in the edge of the curtain which
coupleth the second.
11 And thou shalt make fifty taches of brass, and put the taches into the
loops, and couple the tent together, that it may be one.
12 And the remnant that remaineth of the curtains of the tent, the half
curtain that remaineth, shall hang over the backside of the tabernacle.
13 And a cubit on the one side, and a cubit on the other side of that which
remaineth in the length of the curtains of the tent, it shall hang over the
sides of the tabernacle on this side and on that side, to cover it.
14 And thou shalt make a covering for the tent *of* rams' skins dyed red,
and a covering above *of* badgers' skins.
15 ¶And thou shalt make boards for the tabernacle *of* shittim wood
standing up.

26:1 Ex 36:8–19
☆**26:2**
26:7 Ex 35:26; 36:14
26:14 Ex 36:19
26:15 Ex 36:20; 40:18, 19; Num 4:31

26:2 In antiquity, units of measure were determined by the use of the limbs of the human body. A cubit was the length of the forearm to the tip of the middle finger. Thus the people of that time had no absolute standard of measurement, for forearms differ in length. The cubit generally measured between seventeen and eighteen inches. Egypt and Babylon had longer or shorter cubits.

16 Ten cubits *shall be* the length of a board, and a cubit and a half *shall be* the breadth of one board.

17 Two tenons *shall there be* in one board, set in order one against another: thus shalt thou make for all the boards of the tabernacle.

18 And thou shalt make the boards for the tabernacle, twenty boards on the south side southward.

19 And thou shalt make forty sockets of silver under the twenty boards; two sockets under one board for his two tenons, and two sockets under another board for his two tenons.

20 And for the second side of the tabernacle on the north side *there shall be* twenty boards:

21 And their forty sockets *of* silver; two sockets under one board, and two sockets under another board.

22 And for the sides of the tabernacle westward thou shalt make six boards.

23 And two boards shalt thou make for the corners of the tabernacle in the two sides.

24 And they shall be coupled together beneath, and they shall be coupled together above the head of it unto one ring: thus shall it be for them both; they shall be for the two corners.

25 And they shall be eight boards, and their sockets *of* silver, sixteen sockets; two sockets under one board, and two sockets under another board.

26 ¶And thou shalt make bars *of* shittim wood; five for the boards of the one side of the tabernacle,

27 And five bars for the boards of the other side of the tabernacle, and five bars for the boards of the side of the tabernacle, for the two sides westward.

28 And the middle bar in the midst of the boards shall reach from end to end.

29 And thou shalt overlay the boards with gold, and make their rings *of* gold *for* places for the bars: and thou shalt overlay the bars with gold.

26:30 Ex 25:40; 39:42 Num 8:4 Acts 7:44 Heb 8:5

30 And thou shalt rear up the tabernacle according to the fashion thereof which was shewed thee in the mount.

F. THE INSTRUCTIONS FOR MAKING THE CURTAIN

26:31☆ Ex 36:35; 40:3 Lev 16:2 2 Chron 3:14 Mt 27:51 Heb 9:3; 10:20

31 ¶And thou shalt make a vail *of* blue, and purple, and scarlet, and fine twined linen of cunning work: with cherubims shall it be made:

32 And thou shalt hang it upon four pillars of shittim *wood* overlaid with gold: their hooks *shall be of* gold, upon the four sockets of silver.

26:33☆ Ex 25:16; 40:21

33 ¶And thou shalt hang up the vail under the taches, that thou mayest bring in thither within the vail the ark of the testimony: and the vail shall divide unto you between the holy *place* and the most holy.

26:31 *a vail of blue.* The curtain inside the tabernacle separated the Holy of Holies from all people except for the high priest, who entered the Holy of Holies once a year on the day of atonement. When the high priest entered the Holy of Holies he would always sprinkle blood on the mercy seat; sin separated men from God, and God would be satisfied only by the offering of blood through the priesthood.

26:33 The Holy of Holies was the innermost chamber of the tabernacle and temple. It was shielded by the veil through which no one but the high priest ever entered. The Holy of Holies was the place where the glory of God rested. The ark of the covenant was located in this sanctuary. The mercy seat was the ark's lid, made of pure gold. The cherubim sat atop the lid and were part of it. Inside the ark were (1) the golden urn holding manna from the wilderness journey (16:33); (2) Aaron's rod (Num. 17:10); and (3) the copy of the Law (Deut. 31:26; 2 Kings 22:8). The altar of incense was just outside the veil so that its smoke came through to cover the mercy seat. In Heb. 9:3, 4 it is spoken of as pertaining to the Holy of Holies, although outside of it. The Holy of Holies typifies the sanctuary in heaven which Christ entered once and for all to offer his own blood for the sins of men (Heb 9:23–26). When Christ hung on the cross, the veil of the temple was rent in two (Heb. 10:20), showing that the gateway to heaven is now open for all men through Christ's eternal priesthood.

34And thou shalt put the mercy seat upon the ark of the testimony in the
most holy *place*.

26:34
Ex 25:17; 37:6

35And thou shalt set the table without the vail, and the candlestick over
against the table on the side of the tabernacle toward the south: and thou
shalt put the table on the north side.
36And thou shalt make an hanging for the door of the tent, *of* blue, and
purple, and scarlet, and fine twined linen, wrought with needlework.

26:36
Ex 40:28

37And thou shalt make for the hanging five pillars *of* shittim *wood,* and
overlay them with gold, *and* their hooks *shall be of* gold: and thou shalt cast
five sockets of brass for them.

G. THE INSTRUCTIONS FOR MAKING THE ALTAR

27 AND thou shalt make an altar *of* shittim wood, five cubits long,
and five cubits broad; the altar shall be foursquare: and the height
thereof *shall be* three cubits.

☆**27:1**
Ex 20:24; 38:1
40:10, 29
Ezek 43:13
Heb 13:10

2And thou shalt make the horns of it upon the four corners thereof: his
horns shall be of the same: and thou shalt overlay it with brass.

27:2
Ex 29:12
Lev 4:7; 16:18
Num 16:38

3And thou shalt make his pans to receive his ashes, and his shovels, and
his basons, and his fleshhooks, and his firepans: all the vessels thereof thou
shalt make *of* brass.
4And thou shalt make for it a grate of network *of* brass; and upon the net
shalt thou make four brasen rings in the four corners thereof.
5And thou shalt put it under the compass of the altar beneath, that the
net may be even to the midst of the altar.
6And thou shalt make staves for the altar, staves *of* shittim wood, and
overlay them with brass.
7And the staves shall be put into the rings, and the staves shall be upon
the two sides of the altar, to bear it.
8Hollow with boards shalt thou make it: as it was shewed thee in the
mount, so shall they make *it*.

27:8
Ex 25:40; 26:30

H. THE INSTRUCTIONS ABOUT THE COURTYARD FOR THE TABERNACLE

9¶And thou shalt make the court of the tabernacle: for the south side
southward *there shall be* hangings for the court *of* fine twined linen of an
hundred cubits long for one side:

☆**27:9**
Ex 38:9–20; 40:8
1 Kgs 6:36; 8:64

10And the twenty pillars thereof and their twenty sockets *shall be of*
brass; the hooks of the pillars and their fillets *shall be of* silver.
11And likewise for the north side in length *there shall be* hangings of an
hundred *cubits* long, and his twenty pillars and their twenty sockets *of*
brass; the hooks of the pillars and their fillets *of* silver.
12¶And *for* the breadth of the court on the west side *shall be* hangings of
fifty cubits: their pillars ten, and their sockets ten.
13And the breadth of the court on the east side eastward *shall be* fifty
cubits.

27:1 The glory of God was manifested in the tabernacle itself. But only the priests were allowed to enter it. An altar was set up in the court before the tabernacle. The people came to it with their sacrifices and gifts. "The sacrifices were bound with cords to the horns of the altar, and to them malefactors fled for refuge" from the avenger of blood.* This brazen altar was a type of Christ; through his death on Calvary, atonement was made for our transgressions.

27:9 *the court of the tabernacle.* This court was one hundred by fifty cubits in size. Israelites could enter this court; only the priests were allowed to enter the tabernacle itself. Even kings could not enter the tabernacle. David wrote glowingly of his love for the courts of God: "A day in thy courts is better than a thousand" (Ps. 84:2, 10). Only a few people could enter this court at the same time. Since the coming of the gospel, men can pray everywhere and do not need to enter this sacred place. So the temporary, earthly court has given way to the eternal, heavenly court and is forever accessible to the people of God by prayer.

14The hangings of one side *of the gate shall be* fifteen cubits: their pillars three, and their sockets three.

15And on the other side *shall be* hangings fifteen *cubits:* their pillars three, and their sockets three.

16¶And for the gate of the court *shall be* an hanging of twenty cubits, *of* blue, and purple, and scarlet, and fine twined linen, wrought with needlework: *and* their pillars *shall be* four, and their sockets four.

17All the pillars round about the court *shall be* filleted with silver; their hooks *shall be of* silver, and their sockets *of* brass.

18¶The length of the court *shall be* an hundred cubits, and the breadth fifty every where, and the height five cubits *of* fine twined linen, and their sockets *of* brass.

19All the vessels of the tabernacle in all the service thereof, and all the pins thereof, and all the pins of the court, *shall be of* brass.

I. THE INSTRUCTIONS ABOUT THE SERVICES AND USE OF THE TABERNACLE

1. The Olive Oil for the Lamps

27:20☆ Ex 35:8 Lev 24:2 Zech 4:11, 12 **27:21** Lev 24:3 Ps 134:1

20¶And thou shalt command the children of Israel, that they bring thee pure oil olive beaten for the light, to cause the lamp to burn always.

21In the tabernacle of the congregation without the vail, which *is* before the testimony, Aaron and his sons shall order it from evening to morning before the LORD: *it shall be* a statute for ever unto their generations on the behalf of the children of Israel.

2. The Clothing for the Priests

28:1☆ Ex 24:1–9 Lev 8:2 Ps 99:6 Heb 5:4

28 AND take thou unto thee Aaron thy brother, and his sons with him, from among the children of Israel, that he may minister unto me in the priest's office, *even* Aaron, Na'dab and A-bi'hu, E-le-a'zar and Ith'a-mar, Aaron's sons.

28:2 Ex 29:5, 31:10 39:1 Lev 8:7, 30 Num 20:26 **28:3☆** Ex 31:6; 36:1

2And thou shalt make holy garments for Aaron thy brother for glory and for beauty.

3And thou shalt speak unto all *that are* wise hearted, whom I have filled with the spirit of wisdom, that they may make Aaron's garments to consecrate him, that he may minister unto me in the priest's office.

4And these *are* the garments which they shall make; a breastplate, and an ephod, and a robe, and a broidered coat, a mitre, and a girdle: and they shall make holy garments for Aaron thy brother, and his sons, that he may minister unto me in the priest's office.

28:5 Ex 39:2 Lev 8:7

5And they shall take gold, and blue, and purple, and scarlet, and fine linen.

28:6☆

6¶And they shall make the ephod *of* gold, *of* blue, and *of* purple, *of* scarlet, and fine twined linen, with cunning work.

27:20 A lamp without oil is like a well without water or clouds without rain. The lamp in the tabernacle was always to be kept lit and burning. This was the responsibility of the priests. So it is the responsibility of the Christian ministers, by the preaching and exposition of the Word of God, to bring light to believers, and the knowledge of salvation to unbelievers, and to do so without cessation until Christ returns.

28:1 Christ is our High Priest; Aaron, Israel's high priest, was a type of Christ. Heb. 5:6ff states that Christ had a better priesthood than Aaron, a priesthood similar to that of Melchizedek, to whom Abraham paid tithes. Thus Aaron paid tithes to Melchizedek as a descendant of Abraham, although he was not yet born.

28:3 *whom I have filled with the spirit of wisdom.* Wisdom is the gift of the Holy Spirit. Those filled with the Spirit of wisdom were chosen to make the garments for the priests, so that even the robes would bring glory to God.

28:6 The ephod, a priestly garment, was a close-fitting outer vest which generally extended down to the hips. The high priestly ephod was ornate with onyx stones and a lovely woven girdle.

7 It shall have the two shoulderpieces thereof joined at the two edges
thereof; and *so* it shall be joined together.
8 And the curious girdle of the ephod, which *is* upon it, shall be of the
same, according to the work thereof; *even of* gold, *of* blue, and purple, and
scarlet, and fine twined linen.
9 And thou shalt take two onyx stones, and grave on them the names of
the children of Israel:
10 Six of their names on one stone, and *the other* six names of the rest on
the other stone, according to their birth.
11 With the work of an engraver in stone, *like* the engravings of a signet,
shalt thou engrave the two stones with the names of the children of Israel:
thou shalt make them to be set in ouches of gold.
12 And thou shalt put the two stones upon the shoulders of the ephod *for* **28:12**
stones of memorial unto the children of Israel: and Aaron shall bear their Ex 39:7
names before the LORD upon his two shoulders for a memorial.
13 ¶And thou shalt make ouches *of* gold;
14 And two chains *of* pure gold at the ends; *of* wreathen work shalt thou
make them, and fasten the wreathen chains to the ouches.
15 ¶And thou shalt make the breastplate of judgment with cunning work; ☆**28:15**
after the work of the ephod thou shalt make it; *of* gold, *of* blue, and *of* Ex 39:8
purple, and *of* scarlet, and *of* fine twined linen, shalt thou make it.
16 Foursquare it shall be *being* doubled; a span *shall be* the length thereof,
and a span *shall be* the breadth thereof.
17 And thou shalt set in it settings of stones, *even* four rows of stones: *the* **28:17**
first row *shall be* a sardius, a topaz, and a carbuncle: *this shall be* the first Ex 39:10
row.
18 And the second row *shall be* an emerald, a sapphire, and a diamond.
19 And the third row a ligure, an agate, and an amethyst.
20 And the fourth row a beryl, and an onyx, and a jasper: they shall be set
in gold in their inclosings.
21 And the stones shall be with the names of the children of Israel, twelve,
according to their names, *like* the engravings of a signet; every one with his
name shall they be according to the twelve tribes.
22 ¶And thou shalt make upon the breastplate chains at the ends *of*
wreathen work *of* pure gold.
23 And thou shalt make upon the breastplate two rings of gold, and shalt
put the two rings on the two ends of the breastplate.
24 And thou shalt put the two wreathen *chains* of gold in the two rings
which are on the ends of the breastplate.
25 And *the other* two ends of the two wreathen *chains* thou shalt fasten in
the two ouches, and put *them* on the shoulderpieces of the ephod before it.
26 ¶And thou shalt make two rings of gold, and thou shalt put them upon
the two ends of the breastplate in the border thereof, which *is* in the side of
the ephod inward.
27 And two *other* rings of gold thou shalt make, and shalt put them on the
two sides of the ephod underneath, toward the forepart thereof, over
against the *other* coupling thereof, above the curious girdle of the ephod.
28 And they shall bind the breastplate by the rings thereof unto the rings
of the ephod with a lace of blue, that *it* may be above the curious girdle of
the ephod, and that the breastplate be not loosed from the ephod.
29 And Aaron shall bear the names of the children of Israel in the

28:15 *the breastplate of judgment,* a square piece of richly wrought cloth, was folded and attached to the ephod with wreathen chains of gold. Only the high priestly garment was so adorned.

breastplate of judgment upon his heart, when he goeth in unto the holy *place*, for a memorial before the LORD continually.

28:30☆ 30 ¶And thou shalt put in the breastplate of judgment the U'rim and the Thum'mim; and they shall be upon Aaron's heart, when he goeth in before the LORD: and Aaron shall bear the judgment of the children of Israel upon his heart before the LORD continually.

28:31 Ex 39:22 31 ¶And thou shalt make the robe of the ephod all *of* blue.

32 And there shall be an hole in the top of it, in the midst thereof: it shall have a binding of woven work round about the hole of it, as it were the hole of an habergeon, that it be not rent.

33 ¶And *beneath* upon the hem of it thou shalt make pomegranates *of* blue, and *of* purple, and *of* scarlet, round about the hem thereof; and bells of gold between them round about:

28:34☆ 34 A golden bell and a pomegranate, a golden bell and a pomegranate, upon the hem of the robe round about.

35 And it shall be upon Aaron to minister: and his sound shall be heard when he goeth in unto the holy *place* before the LORD, and when he cometh out, that he die not.

28:36☆ Ex 39:30 36 ¶And thou shalt make a plate *of* pure gold, and grave upon it, *like* the engravings of a signet, HOLINESS TO THE LORD.

28:37, 38 Lev 8:9 Lev 10:17; 22:16 Num 18:1 37 And thou shalt put it on a blue lace, that it may be upon the mitre; upon the forefront of the mitre it shall be.

38 And it shall be upon Aaron's forehead, that Aaron may bear the iniquity of the holy things, which the children of Israel shall hallow in all their holy gifts; and it shall be always upon his forehead, that they may be accepted before the LORD.

39 ¶And thou shalt embroider the coat of fine linen, and thou shalt make the mitre *of* fine linen, and thou shalt make the girdle *of* needlework.

28:40 Ex 39:27 Lev 8:13 40 ¶And for Aaron's sons thou shalt make coats, and thou shalt make for them girdles, and bonnets shalt thou make for them, for glory and for beauty.

41 And thou shalt put them upon Aaron thy brother, and his sons with him; and shalt anoint them, and consecrate them, and sanctify them, that they may minister unto me in the priest's office.

28:42 Ex 20:26 42 And thou shalt make them linen breeches to cover their nakedness; from the loins even unto the thighs they shall reach.

43 And they shall be upon Aaron, and upon his sons, when they come in unto the tabernacle of the congregation, or when they come near unto the altar to minister in the holy *place;* that they bear not iniquity, and die: *it shall be* a statute for ever unto him and his seed after him.

28:30 Urim and Thummim signify "lights" and "perfections." What they looked like is not known. They were perhaps two gemstones located in the breastplate of the high priest. They were specially marked, so that when they were cast to the ground, their markings and positions could be interpreted; by such decipherment, the high priest could know God's answers to questions involving national interest. In 1 Sam. 14 Urim and Thummim were used by Saul to uncover Jonathan's guilt. No mention is made of the use of the Urim and Thummim subsequent to the kingship of David. Ezra 2:63 and Neh. 7:65 indicate that, after the Babylonian exile, Israel had no priest with Urim and Thummim. The Bible does not refer to them after this.

28:34 *A golden bell.* The bells served notice to worshippers that Aaron was about the business of God in the tabernacle, where he could not be seen by men. They could then offer their prayers outside while their high priest was offering his inside. If Aaron attempted to minister without wearing the required garments, death would overtake him.

28:36 *HOLINESS TO THE LORD,* or, "The Holiness of Jehovah," by which sign Aaron is ever to remember that God is holy and his priests are to be holy in minds and hearts. Aaron, the high priest, is to "bear the iniquity of the holy things . . . that they may be accepted before the LORD" (28:38). Aaron is representative of Christ—our mediator between God and man. Through Christ the demands of the law are met; those who trust in him are accepted by God. Having such a High Priest, we can come "boldly unto the throne of grace, that we may obtain mercy, and find grace to help in time of need" (Heb. 4:16).

3. The Ceremony of Dedication of the Priests

a. The Dedication Ritual for Aaron and His Sons

29 AND this *is* the thing that thou shalt do unto them to hallow them, ☆29:1 Lev 8:1, 2; 9:2 16:3
to minister unto me in the priest's office: Take one young bullock,
and two rams without blemish,
2 And unleavened bread, and cakes unleavened tempered with oil, and 29:2 Lev 2:4; 6:19
wafers unleavened anointed with oil: *of* wheaten flour shalt thou make
them.
3 And thou shalt put them into one basket, and bring them in the basket,
with the bullock and the two rams.
4 And Aaron and his sons thou shalt bring unto the door of the tabernacle
of the congregation, and shalt wash them with water.
5 And thou shalt take the garments, and put upon Aaron the coat, and the 29:5 Ex 28:4, 8, 15, 31, 39
robe of the ephod, and the ephod, and the breastplate, and gird him with
the curious girdle of the ephod:
6 And thou shalt put the mitre upon his head, and put the holy crown 29:6 Ex 28:36
upon the mitre.
7 Then shalt thou take the anointing oil, and pour *it* upon his head, and 29:7 Ex 28:41 Lev 8:10; 10:7 Ps 133:2
anoint him.
8 And thou shalt bring his sons, and put coats upon them.
9 And thou shalt gird them with girdles, Aaron and his sons, and put the 29:9 Ex 40:15 Num 3:10; 18:7 25:13 Deut 18:5 Heb 5:4
bonnets on them: and the priest's office shall be theirs for a perpetual
statute: and thou shalt consecrate Aaron and his sons.

b. The Sin Offering

10 And thou shalt cause a bullock to be brought before the tabernacle of 29:10 Lev 1:4; 3:2 8:14
the congregation: and Aaron and his sons shall put their hands upon the
head of the bullock.
11 And thou shalt kill the bullock before the LORD, *by* the door of the
tabernacle of the congregation.
12 And thou shalt take of the blood of the bullock, and put *it* upon the 29:12 Ex 27:2 Lev 8:15, 16
horns of the altar with thy finger, and pour all the blood beside the bottom
of the altar.
13 And thou shalt take all the fat that covereth the inwards, and the caul 29:13 Lev 3:3–5
that is above the liver, and the two kidneys, and the fat that *is* upon them,
and burn *them* upon the altar.
14 But the flesh of the bullock, and his skin, and his dung, shalt thou burn ☆29:14 Lev 4:11, 12, 21 Heb 13:11, 12
with fire without the camp: it *is* a sin offering.

c. The Burnt Offering

15 ¶Thou shalt also take one ram; and Aaron and his sons shall put their 29:15 Ex 29:10 Lev 1:4
hands upon the head of the ram.
16 And thou shalt slay the ram, and thou shalt take his blood, and sprinkle
it round about upon the altar.
17 And thou shalt cut the ram in pieces, and wash the inwards of him, and
his legs, and put *them* unto his pieces, and unto his head.
18 And thou shalt burn the whole ram upon the altar: it *is* a burnt offering ☆29:18 Gen 8:21 Lev 2:2, 9; 6:15
unto the LORD: it *is* a sweet savour, an offering made by fire unto the LORD.

29:1ff This chapter contains the details about the ordination service for the priests, the sin and burnt offerings which were to be presented at the time of ordination, and sundry matters.

29:14 *it is a sin offering.* See note on Gen. 4:7.

29:18 *a burnt offering.* See note on Lev. 1:3.

d. Details of the Seven Days of Ordination

19¶And thou shalt take the other ram; and Aaron and his sons shall put their hands upon the head of the ram.

20Then shalt thou kill the ram, and take of his blood, and put *it* upon the tip of the right ear of Aaron, and upon the tip of the right ear of his sons, and upon the thumb of their right hand, and upon the great toe of their right foot, and sprinkle the blood upon the altar round about.

29:21 Ex 30:25, 31

21And thou shalt take of the blood that *is* upon the altar, and of the anointing oil, and sprinkle *it* upon Aaron, and upon his garments, and upon his sons, and upon the garments of his sons with him: and he shall be hallowed, and his garments, and his sons, and his sons' garments with him.

22Also thou shalt take of the ram the fat and the rump, and the fat that covereth the inwards, and the caul *above* the liver, and the two kidneys, and the fat that *is* upon them, and the right shoulder; for it *is* a ram of consecration:

29:23 Lev 8:26

23And one loaf of bread, and one cake of oiled bread, and one wafer out of the basket of the unleavened bread that *is* before the LORD:

29:24 Lev 7:30

24And thou shalt put all in the hands of Aaron, and in the hands of his sons; and shalt wave them *for* a wave offering before the LORD.

25And thou shalt receive them of their hands, and burn *them* upon the altar for a burnt offering, for a sweet savour before the LORD: it *is* an offering made by fire unto the LORD.

29:26 Lev 7:31; 8:29 9:21

26And thou shalt take the breast of the ram of Aaron's consecration, and wave it *for* a wave offering before the LORD: and it shall be thy part.

29:27 Lev 7:31–33 Num 18:11, 18 Deut 18:3

27And thou shalt sanctify the breast of the wave offering, and the shoulder of the heave offering, which is waved, and which is heaved up, of the ram of the consecration, *even* of *that* which *is* for Aaron, and of *that* which is for his sons:

28And it shall be Aaron's and his sons' by a statute for ever from the children of Israel: for it *is* an heave offering: and it shall be an heave offering from the children of Israel of the sacrifice of their peace offerings, *even* their heave offering unto the LORD.

29:29 Num 20:26, 28

29¶And the holy garments of Aaron shall be his sons' after him, to be anointed therein, and to be consecrated in them.

29:30 Lev 8:35

30*And* that son that is priest in his stead shall put them on seven days, when he cometh into the tabernacle of the congregation to minister in the holy *place*.

31¶And thou shalt take the ram of the consecration, and seethe his flesh in the holy place.

32And Aaron and his sons shall eat the flesh of the ram, and the bread that *is* in the basket, *by* the door of the tabernacle of the congregation.

29:33 Lev 22:10 Num 1:51 3:10, 38

33And they shall eat those things wherewith the atonement was made, to consecrate *and* to sanctify them: but a stranger shall not eat *thereof*, because they *are* holy.

34And if ought of the flesh of the consecrations, or of the bread, remain unto the morning, then thou shalt burn the remainder with fire: it shall not be eaten, because it *is* holy.

35And thus shalt thou do unto Aaron, and to his sons, according to all *things* which I have commanded thee: seven days shalt thou consecrate them.

36And thou shalt offer every day a bullock *for* a sin offering for atonement: and thou shalt cleanse the altar, when thou hast made an atonement for it, and thou shalt anoint it, to sanctify it.

37 Seven days thou shalt make an atonement for the altar, and sanctify it; and it shall be an altar most holy: whatsoever toucheth the altar shall be holy.

☆29:37 Mt 23:19

e. The Fragrant Burnt Offering

38 ¶Now this *is that* which thou shalt offer upon the altar; two lambs of the first year day by day continually.
39 The one lamb thou shalt offer in the morning; and the other lamb thou shalt offer at even:
40 And with the one lamb a tenth deal of flour mingled with the fourth part of an hin of beaten oil; and the fourth part of an hin of wine *for* a drink offering.
41 And the other lamb thou shalt offer at even, and shalt do thereto according to the meat offering of the morning, and according to the drink offering thereof, for a sweet savour, an offering made by fire unto the LORD.
42 *This shall be* a continual burnt offering throughout your generations *at* the door of the tabernacle of the congregation before the LORD: where I will meet you, to speak there unto thee.
43 And there I will meet with the children of Israel, and *the tabernacle shall be sanctified by my glory.*
44 And I will sanctify the tabernacle of the congregation, and the altar: I will sanctify also both Aaron and his sons, to minister to me in the priest's office.
45 ¶And I will dwell among the children of Israel, and will be their God.
46 And they shall know that I *am* the LORD their God, that brought them forth out of the land of Egypt, that I may dwell among them: I *am* the LORD their God.

29:38, 39 Num 28:3; 29:6 1 Chron 16:40 Ezra 3:3 Dan 12:11

29:41 1 Kgs 29:36 2 Kgs 16:15 Ezra 9:4 Ps 141:2

☆29:44

☆29:45 Ex 25:8 Lev 26:5 Num 5:3 Ps 68:18 Zech 2:10 Rev 21:3
29:46 Ex 20:2 Jer 31:33

4. The Small Altar for Burning of Incense

30 AND thou shalt make an altar to burn incense upon: *of* shittim wood shalt thou make it.
2 A cubit *shall be* the length thereof, and a cubit the breadth thereof; foursquare shall it be: and two cubits *shall be* the height thereof: the horns thereof *shall be* of the same.
3 And thou shalt overlay it with pure gold, the top thereof, and the sides thereof round about, and the horns thereof; and thou shalt make unto it a crown of gold round about.

☆30:1 Ex 27:1; 37:25 Lev 4:7 1 Kgs 6:22 Rev 8:3

29:37 *an atonement for the altar.* So holy is God that even the altar made by the hands of sinful men must first be cleansed from defilement by an atonement. The altar and men were unfit to be employed by God until this was done. The altar was also sanctified (i.e., set apart for holy use) and was made so holy that the gifts placed on the altar would also be sanctified (see Matt. 23:19). Jesus Christ is our altar. He sanctified himself for our sake so that we, in turn, might be sanctified by him, then recommended and made acceptable to God the Father.

29:44 God sanctified the altar, the tabernacle, and the priesthood; he took possession of those things which were sanctified to him. When this was accomplished, a holy God said: "I will dwell among the children of Israel, and will be their God" (29:45). Through all of this God gives to the Israelites the outward, corroborating evidences by which they will know that he is and will be their God.

29:45 *I will dwell among the children of Israel.* This promise was fulfilled when the shekinah glory of God filled the tabernacle. The temple had first been sanctified so as to make it occupiable by a holy God. So also should our bodies, which are indwelt by God the Spirit, be sanctified and kept in holiness.

30:1 The incense used on this altar was made of frankincense, salt, and equal parts of galbanum, stacte, and onycha. This comprised the holy incense, and was not to be used for non-religious purposes. The burning of the incense was to honor God, and represented prayer. In Rev. 5:8 and 8:3, 4 the burning incense or perfume is said to represent the prayers of the saints. In Luke 1:10 we read that it was at the hour of prayer and incense, that the angel appeared to Zacharias to tell him that his prayer had been heard and that John would be conceived in the womb of his elderly wife, Elizabeth.

4 And two golden rings shalt thou make to it under the crown of it, by the two corners thereof, upon the two sides of it shalt thou make *it;* and they shall be for places for the staves to bear it withal.

5 And thou shalt make the staves *of* shittim wood, and overlay them with gold.

6 And thou shalt put it before the vail that *is* by the ark of the testimony, before the mercy seat that *is* over the testimony, where I will meet with thee.

30:7 Ex 27:20; 30:34 1 Sam 2:28 Lk 1:9

7 And Aaron shall burn thereon sweet incense every morning: when he dresseth the lamps, he shall burn incense upon it.

8 And when Aaron lighteth the lamps at even, he shall burn incense upon it, a perpetual incense before the LORD throughout your generations.

9 Ye shall offer no strange incense thereon, nor burnt sacrifice, nor meat offering; neither shall ye pour drink offering thereon.

30:10☆ Lev 16:8

10 And Aaron shall make an atonement upon the horns of it once in a year with the blood of the sin offering of atonements: once in the year shall he make atonement upon it throughout your generations: it *is* most holy unto the LORD.

5. The Census and the Offering

30:11, 12☆ Ex 38:25 Num 1:2; 26:2 2 Sam 24:1 Mt 20:28 1 Pet 1:18, 19

11 ¶And the LORD spake unto Moses, saying,

12 When thou takest the sum of the children of Israel after their number, then shall they give every man a ransom for his soul unto the LORD, when thou numberest them; that there be no plague among them, when *thou* numberest them.

30:13 Mt 17:24

13 This they shall give, every one that passeth among them that are numbered, half a shekel after the shekel of the sanctuary: (a shekel *is* twenty gerahs:) an half shekel *shall be* the offering of the LORD.

14 Every one that passeth among them that are numbered, from twenty years old and above, shall give an offering unto the LORD.

30:15 Prov 22:2

15 The rich shall not give more, and the poor shall not give less than half a shekel, when *they* give an offering unto the LORD, to make an atonement for your souls.

16 And thou shalt take the atonement money of the children of Israel, and shalt appoint it for the service of the tabernacle of the congregation; that it may be a memorial unto the children of Israel before the LORD, to make an atonement for your souls.

6. The Bronze Basin for Washing

30:17 Ex 31:9; 38:8 Lev 8:11 **30:18☆**

17 ¶And the LORD spake unto Moses, saying,

18 Thou shalt also make a laver *of* brass, and his foot *also of* brass, to wash *withal:* and thou shalt put it between the tabernacle of the congregation and the altar, and thou shalt put water therein.

30:19 Ex 40:31

19 For Aaron and his sons shall wash their hands and their feet thereat:

20 When they go into the tabernacle of the congregation, they shall wash

---

30:10 *shall make an atonement upon the horns,* i.e., "must sanctify the altar."†

30:12 *a ransom for his soul.* See the note on 1 Pet. 1:18.

30:18 The priests washed their hands and feet in the laver of brass before they entered the tabernacle. Death by God was the penalty for failure to wash—this statute was imposed forever. When the Solomonic temple was built, a great molten sea replaced the laver of brass. The ceremonial washing typified the biblical truth that we need clean hands and a pure heart when we come before the Lord God. Since we are all priests unto God in the new age, care should be taken to cleanse ourselves from all impurity before coming into the presence of the living God.

with water, that they die not; or when they come near to the altar to
minister, to burn offering made by fire unto the LORD:
21 So they shall wash their hands and their feet, that they die not: and it
shall be a statute for ever to them, *even* to him and to his seed throughout
their generations.

30:21 Ex 28:43

7. The Recipe for the Anointing Oil

22 ¶Moreover the LORD spake unto Moses, saying,
23 Take thou also unto thee principal spices, of pure myrrh five hundred
shekels, and of sweet cinnamon half so much, *even* two hundred and fifty
shekels, and of sweet calamus two hundred and fifty *shekels*,
24 And of cassia five hundred *shekels*, after the shekel of the sanctuary,
and of oil olive an hin:
25 And thou shalt make it an oil of holy ointment, an ointment compound
after the art of the apothecary: it shall be an holy anointing oil.
26 And thou shalt anoint the tabernacle of the congregation therewith,
and the ark of the testimony,
27 And the table and all his vessels, and the candlestick and his vessels,
and the altar of incense,
28 And the altar of burnt offering with all his vessels, and the laver and his
foot.
29 And thou shalt sanctify them, that they may be most holy: whatsoever
toucheth them shall be holy.
30 And thou shalt anoint Aaron and his sons, and consecrate them, that
they may minister unto me in the priest's office.
31 And thou shalt speak unto the children of Israel, saying, This shall be
an holy anointing oil unto me throughout your generations.
32 Upon man's flesh shall it not be poured, neither shall ye make *any other*
like it, after the composition of it: it *is* holy, *and* it shall be holy unto you.
33 Whosoever compoundeth *any* like it, or whosoever putteth *any* of it
upon a stranger, shall even be cut off from his people.

30:22 Ps 45:8
30:25 Ex 37:29; 40:9 Lev 8:10
30:26 Num 7:1
☆30:32
30:33 Gen 17:4 Ex 12:15 Lev 7:20, 21

8. The Recipe for the Incense

34 ¶And the LORD said unto Moses, Take unto thee sweet spices, stacte,
and onycha, and galbanum; *these* sweet spices with pure frankincense: of
each shall there be a like *weight*:
35 And thou shalt make it a perfume, a confection after the art of the
apothecary, tempered together, pure *and* holy:
36 And thou shalt beat *some* of it very small, and put of it before the
testimony in the tabernacle of the congregation, where I will meet with
thee: it shall be unto you most holy.
37 And *as for* the perfume which thou shalt make, ye shall not make to
yourselves according to the composition thereof: it shall be unto thee holy
for the LORD.
38 Whosoever shall make like unto that, to smell thereto, shall even be cut
off from his people.

30:32 The holy oil was to be used only for the purposes ordained by God. No one else was ever to make it or use it in a common fashion, for its use was designed in perpetuity. However, in the second temple there was no holy oil and none is made today.

J. THE APPOINTMENT OF THE CHIEF WORKMEN

31:1☆ Ex 35:30, 36:1; 37:1; 1 Chron 2:20

31 AND the LORD spake unto Moses, saying,
2 See, I have called by name Be-zal'e-el the son of U'ri, the son of
Hur, of the tribe of Judah:

31:3 1 Kgs 7:14

3 And I have filled him with the spirit of God, in wisdom, and in
understanding, and in knowledge, and in all manner of workmanship,
4 To devise cunning works, to work in gold, and in silver, and in brass,
5 And in cutting of stones, to set *them*, and in carving of timber, to work
in all manner of workmanship.

31:6 Ex 35:34; 36:1

6 And I, behold, I have given with him A-ho'li-ab, the son of A-his'a-
mach, of the tribe of Dan: and in the hearts of all that are wise hearted I
have put wisdom, that they may make all that I have commanded thee;

31:7 Ex 25:9

7 The tabernacle of the congregation, and the ark of the testimony, and
the mercy seat that *is* thereupon, and all the furniture of the tabernacle,

31:8 Ex 25:31; Lev 24:4

8 And the table and his furniture, and the pure candlestick with all his
furniture, and the altar of incense,
9 And the altar of burnt offering with all his furniture, and the laver and
his foot,
10 And the cloths of service, and the holy garments for Aaron the priest,
and the garments of his sons, to minister in the priest's office,
11 And the anointing oil, and sweet incense for the holy *place:* according
to all that I have commanded thee shall they do.

K. THE SABBATH DAY REST

31:12 Ex 20:8, 12; Lev 19:30; 26:2; Deut 5:12; 31:13–17☆

12 ¶And the LORD spake unto Moses, saying,
13 Speak thou also unto the children of Israel, saying, Verily my sabbaths
ye shall keep: for it *is* a sign between me and you throughout your
generations; that *ye* may know that I *am* the LORD that doth sanctify you.

31:14 Ex 16:23; 35:2; Num 15:32; Jn 7:21

14 Ye shall keep the sabbath therefore; for it *is* holy unto you: every one
that defileth it shall surely be put to death: for whosoever doeth *any* work
therein, that soul shall be cut off from among his people.
15 Six days may work be done; but in the seventh *is* the sabbath of rest,
holy to the LORD: whosoever doeth *any* work in the sabbath day, he shall
surely be put to death.

31:16☆ Ex 20:9; Deut 5:13

16 Wherefore the children of Israel shall keep the sabbath, to observe the
sabbath throughout their generations, *for* a perpetual covenant.

31:17☆ Gen 2:2, 3; Ex 20:11; Heb 4:4

17 It *is* a sign between me and the children of Israel for ever: for *in* six
days the LORD made heaven and earth, and on the seventh day he rested,
and was refreshed.

31:18 Ex 24:12; 34:1, 28; 32:15; Deut 4:13

18 ¶And he gave unto Moses, when he had made an end of communing
with him upon mount Si'nai, two tables of testimony, tables of stone,
written with the finger of God.

31:1ff. Again and again in the Old Testament we see examples of saints of God who were filled with the Spirit of God. Here Bezaleel was filled with the Spirit of God (31:2, 3).

Moreover, the Spirit of God gave him the gift of craftsmanship so that he was endowed with the ability to construct the tabernacle. The power of the Holy Spirit gave him the enduement he needed to create what was to be the residence of God among his people. According to 31:6, Aholiab and others were given the gift of wisdom, so that they could make all that God had commanded made in connection with this task.

31:13–17 The sabbath was established by God as a sign between himself and the people of Israel. The seventh day was set apart as a holy day for the worship of God when no work was to be performed except works of necessity and mercy. Sabbath-breaking was a capital offense. The sign of the sabbath related to the six days of creation followed by the seventh day when God rested (31:17). It is this reference to seven literal twenty-four-hour days which gives added evidence for seven twenty-four-hour days of creation. A million years are as a day to God; looked at from man's perspective seven days of creation could be a long period of time.

L. ISRAEL'S ADULTEROUS IDOLATRY

1. Aaron Makes the Golden Calf and Builds an Altar

32 AND when the people saw that Moses delayed to come down out
of the mount, the people gathered themselves together unto Aaron,
and said unto him, Up, make us gods, which shall go before us; for *as for*
this Moses, the man that brought us up out of the land of Egypt, we wot not
what is become of him.
2 And Aaron said unto them, Break off the golden earrings, which *are* in
the ears of your wives, of your sons, and of your daughters, and bring *them*
unto me.
3 And all the people brake off the golden earrings which *were* in their ears,
and brought *them* unto Aaron.
4 And he received *them* at their hand, and fashioned it with a graving tool,
after he had made it a molten calf: and they said, These *be* thy gods, O
Israel, which brought thee up out of the land of Egypt.
5 And when Aaron saw *it*, he built an altar before it; and Aaron made
proclamation, and said, To morrow *is* a feast to the LORD.
6 And they rose up early on the morrow, and offered burnt offerings, and
brought peace offerings; and the people sat down to eat and to drink, and
rose up to play.

32:1 Ex 24:18; Deut 9:10; Acts 7:40
32:2 Ex 12:35; 35:22
☆**32:4** Ex 20:23; Deut 9:16; Ps 106:19; Acts 7:41
32:5 Hos 8:11
32:6 Num 25:2; Acts 7:41; 1 Cor 10:7

2. Moses Prays for Israel's Forgiveness

7 ¶And the LORD said unto Moses, Go, get thee down; for thy people,
which thou broughtest out of the land of Egypt, have corrupted *themselves:*
8 They have turned aside quickly out of the way which I commanded
them: they have made them a molten calf, and have worshipped it, and
have sacrificed thereunto, and said, These *be* thy gods, O Israel, which have
brought thee up out of the land of Egypt.
9 And the LORD said unto Moses, I have seen this people, and, behold, it
is a stiffnecked people:
10 Now therefore let me alone, that my wrath may wax hot against them,
and that I may consume them: and I will make of thee a great nation.
11 And Moses besought the LORD his God, and said, LORD, why doth thy
wrath wax hot against thy people, which thou hast brought forth out of the
land of Egypt with great power, and with a mighty hand?
12 Wherefore should the Egyptians speak, and say, For mischief did he
bring them out, to slay them in the mountains, and to consume them from
the face of the earth? Turn from thy fierce wrath, and repent of this evil
against thy people.

32:7 Ex 19:24; 33:1; Deut 9:12
32:8 Ex 22:20; 34:15; Deut 32:17
32:9 Ex 33:5; Num 14:11; Acts 7:42, 51
☆**32:10** Gen 18:32; Deut 9:13, 14
32:11 Num 14:17–19; Deut 9:18, 26; Ps 106:23
32:12 Deut 9:28; Josh 7:9

32:4 Aaron and the people of Israel were guilty of gross idolatry when they made the golden calf. God had worked many miracles on their behalf, yet at this moment they turned away from him. What they did was called: (1) terrible sin (32:21, 30, 31); (2) disobedience (Deut. 9:12, 16); and (3) a forgetting of their Savior (Ps. 106:21). The golden calf was supposed to be a representation of God (or of the pedestal upon which God invisibly stood). Then Aaron announced a feast to Jehovah which included gross immorality. God's anger resulted, for he had forbidden the use of any graven images. Surely any pictorial representation of God was and is included in the prohibition of the second commandment. This commandment also forbade bowing before any image of angel, man, bird, animal, or saint dwelling in heaven above. The Israelites knew this and were severely punished for their iniquity.

32:10 Israel's idolatry angered God. He threatened to destroy all of it, then rebuild a great nation through Moses, the only survivor. Surely there must have been some among the Israelites who did not engage in this idolatry. Babies and young children, for example, would have known nothing about the evil deed and would have had no part in the creation of the golden calf. Yet sin and its consequences often have a national character, and the judgment of God overtakes even those who appear to be innocent. Moses could easily have assented to what God said, for it would simply have lengthened the time span for God to raise a new nation and bring it into the land of promise. But Moses intervened in prayer for the guilty people and God repented of what he had intended to do. But there would come a time when the iniquity of Israel reached the point of no return, and the dispersion of the people to the ends of the earth would occur by way of divine judgment.

32:13 Gen 15:5; 22:16–18; Ex:13:5, 11; Lev 26:42; Deut 7:8; Lk 1:54, 55

13 Remember Abraham, Isaac, and Israel, thy servants, to whom thou swarest by thine own self, and saidst unto them, I will multiply your seed as the stars of heaven, and all this land that I have spoken of will I give unto your seed, and they shall inherit *it* for ever.

32:14 Gen 6:5, 6; 1 Sam 15:35; 2 Sam 24:16; Ps 106:45

14 And the LORD repented of the evil which he thought to do unto his people.

3. Moses Breaks the Stone Tablets and Burns the Golden Calf

32:15 Ex 24:18; Deut 9:15

15 ¶And Moses turned, and went down from the mount, and the two tables of the testimony *were* in his hand: the tables *were* written on both their sides; on the one side and on the other *were* they written.

32:16 Ex 31:18; 34:1; Deut 9:9

16 And the tables *were* the work of God, and the writing *was* the writing of God, graven upon the tables.

17 And when Joshua heard the noise of the people as they shouted, he said unto Moses, *There is* a noise of war in the camp.

18 And he said, *It is* not the voice of *them that* shout for mastery, neither *is it* the voice of *them that* cry for being overcome: *but* the noise of *them that* sing do I hear.

32:19 Ex 32:6; Deut 9:16, 17

19 ¶And it came to pass, as soon as he came nigh unto the camp, that he saw the calf, and the dancing: and Moses' anger waxed hot, and he cast the tables out of his hands, and brake them beneath the mount.

32:20 Deut 9:21

20 And he took the calf which they had made, and burnt *it* in the fire, and ground *it* to powder, and strawed *it* upon the water, and made the children of Israel drink *of it*.

21 And Moses said unto Aaron, What did this people unto thee, that thou hast brought so great a sin upon them?

32:22☆ Deut 9:6, 24; 31:27

22 And Aaron said, Let not the anger of my lord wax hot: thou knowest the people, that they *are set* on mischief.

32:23 Ex 32:1

23 For they said unto me, Make us gods, which shall go before us: for *as for* this Moses, the man that brought us up out of the land of Egypt, we wot not what is become of him.

24 And I said unto them, Whosoever hath any gold, let them break *it* off. So they gave *it* me: then I cast it into the fire, and there came out this calf.

4. The Levites Slay Three Thousand Sinners

32:25 1 Kgs 12:25

25 ¶And when Moses saw that the people *were* naked; (for Aaron had made them naked unto *their* shame among their enemies:)

32:26 2 Sam 20:11

26 Then Moses stood in the gate of the camp, and said, Who *is* on the LORD's side? *let him come* unto me. And all the sons of Levi gathered themselves together unto him.

32:27 Num 25:5

27 And he said unto them, Thus saith the LORD God of Israel, Put every man his sword by his side, *and* go in and out from gate to gate throughout the camp, and slay every man his brother, and every man his companion, and every man his neighbour.

32:28 Num 16:32; 25:9

28 And the children of Levi did according to the word of Moses: and there fell of the people that day about three thousand men.

32:29 Deut 13:6; 33:9

29 For Moses had said, Consecrate yourselves to day to the LORD, even every man upon his son, and upon his brother; that he may bestow upon you a blessing this day.

32:22 There is overwhelming evidence that Aaron was responsible for the creation of the golden calf. He was the high priest and had been Moses' closest ally in the deliverance from Egypt. Now he blames the people for what happened and speciously declares that when they threw the gold in the fire it spontaneously emerged as a golden calf. Aaron's high position did not keep him from compromise nor did he do anything significant to keep Israel from its idolatry.

5. Moses Prays Again; God Sends a Great Plague

30¶And it came to pass on the morrow, that Moses said unto the people,
Ye have sinned a great sin: and now I will go up unto the LORD;
peradventure I shall make an atonement for your sin.
31And Moses returned unto the LORD, and said, Oh, this people have
sinned a great sin, and have made them gods of gold.
32Yet now, if thou wilt forgive their sin—; and if not, blot me, I pray
thee, out of thy book which thou hast written.
33And the LORD said unto Moses, Whosoever hath sinned against me,
him will I blot out of my book.
34Therefore now go, lead the people unto *the place* of which I have
spoken unto thee: behold, mine Angel shall go before thee: nevertheless in
the day when I visit I will visit their sin upon them.
35And the LORD plagued the people, because they made the calf, which
Aaron made.

☆**32:31** Ex 20:23
32:32 Deut 9:14; Ps 139:16; Isa 4:3; Dan 12:1; Mal 3:16; Rev 3:5
32:33 Deut 29:20; Ps 9:5; 69:28; Ezek 18:4
32:34 Ex 3:17; 23:20; 33:2; Num 20:16

6. The Aftermath of Israel's Transgression

a. God's Judgment; Israel's Repentance

33 AND the LORD said unto Moses, Depart, *and* go up hence, thou
and the people which thou hast brought up out of the land of
Egypt, unto the land which I sware unto Abraham, to Isaac, and to Jacob,
saying, Unto thy seed will I give it:
2And I will send an angel before thee; and I will drive out the Canaanite,
the Am′or-ite, and the Hittite, and the Per′iz-zite, the Hi′vite, and the Jeb′u-site:
3Unto a land flowing with milk and honey: for I will not go up in the
midst of thee; for thou *art* a stiffnecked people: lest I consume thee in the
way.
4¶And when the people heard these evil tidings, they mourned: and no
man did put on him his ornaments.
5For the LORD had said unto Moses, Say unto the children of Israel, Ye
are a stiffnecked people: I will come up into the midst of thee in a moment,
and consume thee: therefore now put off thy ornaments from thee, that I
may know what to do unto thee.
6And the children of Israel stripped themselves of their ornaments by the
mount Ho′reb.

33:1 Gen 12:7; 22:16; Ex 32:13, 34
33:2 Ex 23:23, 27; 32:34
☆**33:3** Ex 3:8; 13:5; 32:9, 10, 14; 34:9
33:4 Num 14:1, 3, 9
33:5 Num 16:45

b. Moses Uses the Tent to Consult with God

7And Moses took the tabernacle, and pitched it without the camp, afar
off from the camp, and called it the Tabernacle of the congregation. And it

☆**33:7** Ex 18:26; 29:43

32:31 Moses interceded for the people in connection with the construction and worship of the golden calf. God forgave them on behalf of their intercessor, but sin often has consequences which cause sinners pain long after they have been forgiven. Guilt and penalty will be set aside upon repentance and confession, but the temporal consequences may remain, as evidenced in Moses' own life. He smote the rock the second time (Num. 20:11) when told to speak to it. He was purged from his sin, but, as a temporal consequence of that sinful act, he was forbidden to enter the Promised Land.

33:3 *a stiffnecked people,* i.e., a stubborn people who have resisted the commandments of their God. "Nothing in children is more offensive to their parents and teachers than stubbornness."* This hardness of heart against God is repeated by the Israelites in the New Testament age, especially at the time when Stephen was stoned to death. In his sermon before his death he said, "Ye stiffnecked and uncircumcised in heart and ears, ye do always resist the Holy Ghost [Spirit]: as your fathers did, so do ye" (Acts 7:51). Both in the Old and New Testaments Israel sinned against the Holy Spirit who had been wooing them and opening the door of salvation to them.

33:7 *tabernacle,* or, "the tent for meeting." When Moses entered the tent, a cloudy pillar appeared, indicating the presence of God in communion with Moses (and Joshua). Inside the tent, Moses got his instructions directly from God. This was direct revelation, no longer necessary since, in the Bible, we have the completed revelation of God. Israel operated under a theocracy at this time, with God as King.

came to pass, *that* every one which sought the LORD went out unto the
tabernacle of the congregation, which *was* without the camp.

33:8 Num 16:27

8 And it came to pass, when Moses went out unto the tabernacle, *that* all
the people rose up, and stood every man *at* his tent door, and looked after
Moses, until he was gone into the tabernacle.

33:9 Ex 13:21; 19:9; 25:22; Ps 99:7

9 And it came to pass, as Moses entered into the tabernacle, the cloudy
pillar descended, and stood *at* the door of the tabernacle, and *the LORD*
talked with Moses.
10 And all the people saw the cloudy pillar stand *at* the tabernacle door:
and all the people rose up and worshipped, every man *in* his tent door.

33:11☆ Gen 32:30; Num 12:8; Deut 34:10

11 And the LORD spake unto Moses face to face, as a man speaketh unto
his friend. And he turned again into the camp: but his servant Joshua, the
son of Nun, a young man, departed not out of the tabernacle.

c. Moses Prays to See God; God Reveals His Glory

33:12 Ex 3:10; 32:34; 33:1

12 ¶And Moses said unto the LORD, See, thou sayest unto me, Bring up
this people: and thou hast not let me know whom thou wilt send with me.
Yet thou hast said, I know thee by name, and thou hast also found grace in
my sight.

33:13 Ex 3:10; 5:1; Ps 25:4; 27:11

13 Now therefore, I pray thee, if I have found grace in thy sight, shew me
now thy way, that I may know thee, that I may find grace in thy sight: and
consider that this nation *is* thy people.

33:14 Ex 13:21; Josh 22:4; Isa 63:9 **33:15☆** Ps 80:3, 7, 19 **33:16** Ex 8:22; Lev 20:24, 26; Num 14:14

14 And he said, My presence shall go *with thee,* and I will give thee rest.
15 And he said unto him, If thy presence go not *with me,* carry us not up
hence.
16 For wherein shall it be known here that I and thy people have found
grace in thy sight? *is it* not in that thou goest with us? so shall we be
separated, I and thy people, from all the people that *are* upon the face of
the earth.

33:17 Gen 19:21; Ex 33:12 **33:18☆** Ps 4:6; Jn 1:18; 2 Cor 3:18 **33:19☆** Rom 9:15

17 And the LORD said unto Moses, I will do this thing also that thou hast
spoken: for thou hast found grace in my sight, and I know thee by name.
18 And he said, I beseech thee, shew me thy glory.
19 And he said, I will make all my goodness pass before thee, and I will
proclaim the name of the LORD before thee; and will be gracious to whom
I will be gracious, and will shew mercy on whom I will shew mercy.

33:11 God spoke to Moses *face to face, as a man speaketh unto his friend.* The implication is that God revealed himself to Moses more clearly than to others, manifesting a greater degree of his light to him. He talked, not as a king to a subject, but as a man to a friend whom he loves and with whom he has sweet counsel. Whenever Moses went into the tent of meeting, he took Joshua with him. Sometimes Moses allowed Joshua to remain in the tent while he came out to address Israel. Joshua was of the tribe of Ephraim, whereas Moses was a Levite. When Joshua succeeded Moses, it clearly meant that, to God, a man's gifts were more important than the tribe from which he came. *tabernacle. The* tabernacle had not yet been constructed (see Exod. 40). This was the tent set up by Moses to which he and Joshua came to meet with God and receive instructions. Thus there were two tents, one which was the tabernacle and the other a pre-tabernacle in which God met and talked with the key leaders of Israel, Moses and Joshua. Joshua, who came from the tribe of Ephraim, did not ever enter *the* tabernacle. Moses did, for he was commissioned by God to build it and to sanctify it.

33:15 Moses was a great and gifted man. Yet he knew that it was the presence of God in his life that made the difference between victory and defeat. Thus he did not wish to proceed unless he had the assurance of the presence of God. This is a lesson every believer needs to learn today. To move forward without the presence of God can only lead to disappointment, difficulty, and even disaster.

33:18ff This account is given in human terms. God is a spirit and is thus immaterial. Yet the language is anthropomorphic when it speaks about "face," "hand," and "back parts." No human being can look on God in his glory and live. Moses was a redeemed sinner who had not yet been glorified. He could not behold God in his full plenitude. But all of the redeemed will see God in all of his glory in eternity, when they will have been perfected.

33:19 *I will proclaim the name of the LORD before thee,* i.e., "I will announce to you the meaning of my name." His name, "LORD," or *"Jehovah"* means, "I will be what I will be." (See Exod. 3:14.)†

20 And he said, Thou canst not see my face: for there shall no man see me,
and live.
21 And the LORD said, Behold, *there is* a place by me, and thou shalt stand
upon a rock:
22 And it shall come to pass, while my glory passeth by, that I will put
thee in a clift of the rock, and will cover thee with my hand while I pass by:
23 And I will take away mine hand, and thou shalt see my back parts: but
my face shall not be seen.

7. The New Beginning; The Second Two Tablets of Stone
a. The Ten Commandments Engraved on Stone

34 AND the LORD said unto Moses, Hew thee two tables of stone like
unto the first: and I will write upon *these* tables the words that were
in the first tables, which thou brakest.
2 And be ready in the morning, and come up in the morning unto mount
Si′nai, and present thyself there to me in the top of the mount.
3 And no man shall come up with thee, neither let any man be seen
throughout all the mount; neither let the flocks nor herds feed before that
mount.
4 ¶And he hewed two tables of stone like unto the first; and Moses rose
up early in the morning, and went up unto mount Si′nai, as the LORD had
commanded him, and took in his hand the two tables of stone.
5 And the LORD descended in the cloud, and stood with him there, and
proclaimed the name of the LORD.
6 And the LORD passed by before him, and proclaimed, The LORD, The
LORD God, merciful and gracious, longsuffering, and abundant in goodness
and truth,
7 Keeping mercy for thousands, forgiving iniquity and transgression and
sin, and that will by no means clear *the guilty;* visiting the iniquity of the
fathers upon the children, and upon the children's children, unto the third
and to the fourth *generation.*
8 And Moses made haste, and bowed his head toward the earth, and
worshipped.
9 And he said, If now I have found grace in thy sight, O Lord, let my
Lord, I pray thee, go among us; for it *is* a stiffnecked people; and pardon
our iniquity and our sin, and take us for thine inheritance.
10 ¶And he said, Behold, I make a covenant: before all thy people I will do
marvels, such as have not been done in all the earth, nor in any nation: and
all the people among which thou *art* shall see the work of the LORD: for it
is a terrible thing that I will do with thee.

b. God's Prohibition against the Idolatry of Canaan

11 Observe thou that which I command thee this day: behold, I drive out
before thee the Am′or-ite, and the Canaanite, and the Hittite, and the
Per′iz-zite, and the Hi′vite, and the Jeb′u-site.
12 Take heed to thyself, lest thou make a covenant with the inhabitants of
the land whither thou goest, lest it be for a snare in the midst of thee:

33:20 Ex 24:10; Isa 6:5; Jn 1:18; 1 Tim 6:16
33:21 Ps 62:7
33:22 Ps 18:2; Isa 2:21; 49:2; 51:16
☆**34:1** Ex 24:12; 31:18; Deut 10:1
34:2 Ex 19:20
34:3 Ex 19:12; Lev 16:17
☆**34:5, 6** Ex 19:9; 33:9; Num 14:17, 18; Neh 9:17; Ps 86:15; 103:8
34:7 Ex 20:5, 6; 23:7; Deut 5:10; Neh 1:5
34:9 Num 14:19; Deut 4:20; 32:9; Ps 25:11
34:10 Ex 8:10; Deut 4:35; Ps 72:18; 136:4
34:11 Ex 33:2; Deut 4:1, 40; 6:3
34:12 Ex 23:32, 33; Deut 7:1–4

34:1 The Ten Commandments were engraved on the stone tablets by God himself. Exodus 32:16 says, "the writing was the writing of God"; here, when the second set of the Commandments were made, Moses quotes God as saying: "I will write upon these tables the words that were in the first tables." This constitutes a miracle from the human perspective but something hardly extraordinary from the divine vantage point.
34:5 *proclaimed the name of the LORD,* i.e., "announced the meaning of his name."†

34:13☆ Ex 23:24; Deut 7:5; 12:2; 16:21; 2 Chron 34:4

13 But ye shall destroy their altars, break their images, and cut down their
groves:

34:14☆ Ex 20:3, 4; Deut 4:24

14 For thou shalt worship no other god: for the LORD, whose name *is*
Jealous, *is* a jealous God:

34:15☆ Num 25:1, 2; Deut 31:16

15 Lest thou make a covenant with the inhabitants of the land, and they
go a whoring after their gods, and do sacrifice unto their gods, and *one* call
thee, and thou eat of his sacrifice;

34:16 Deut 7:3; Josh 23:12

16 And thou take of their daughters unto thy sons, and their daughters go
a whoring after their gods, and make thy sons go a whoring after their gods.

34:17 Lev 19:3, 4; Deut 29:17

17 Thou shalt make thee no molten gods.

c. Various Instructions

34:18 Ex 12:2, 15, 17; 23:15; Deut 16:1

18 ¶The feast of unleavened bread shalt thou keep. Seven days thou shalt
eat unleavened bread, as I commanded thee, in the time of the month Abib:
for in the month Abib thou camest out from Egypt.

34:19☆ Ex 13:2; 22:29, 30

19 All that openeth the matrix *is* mine; and every firstling among thy
cattle, *whether* ox or sheep, *that is male*.

34:20 Ex 13:13; Num 3:45; Lk 2:23

20 But the firstling of an ass thou shalt redeem with a lamb: and if thou
redeem *him* not, then shalt thou break his neck. All the firstborn of thy sons
thou shalt redeem. And none shall appear before me empty.

34:21 Ex 20:8; 31:15; 35:2

21 ¶Six days thou shalt work, but on the seventh day thou shalt rest: in
earing time and in harvest thou shalt rest.

34:22 Ex 23:16; Lev 23:4

22 ¶And thou shalt observe the feast of weeks, of the firstfruits of wheat
harvest, and the feast of ingathering at the year's end.

34:23 Ex 23:14–17; Deut 16:16

23 ¶Thrice in the year shall all your men children appear before the Lord
GOD, the God of Israel.

34:24 Ex 23:27; 33:2

24 For I will cast out the nations before thee, and enlarge thy borders:
neither shall any man desire thy land, when thou shalt go up to appear
before the LORD thy God thrice in the year.

34:25 Ex 12:10, 20; 23:18; Lev 2:11

25 Thou shalt not offer the blood of my sacrifice with leaven; neither shall
the sacrifice of the feast of the passover be left unto the morning.

34:26 Ex 23:19; Deut 26:2

26 The first of the firstfruits of thy land thou shalt bring unto the house of
the LORD thy God. Thou shalt not seethe a kid in his mother's milk.

34:27☆ Ex 17:14; 24:4; Deut 1:5; 31:9

27 And the LORD said unto Moses, Write thou these words: for after the
tenor of these words I have made a covenant with thee and with Israel.

34:28 Ex 24:18; Deut 4:13; 10:4

28 And he was there with the LORD forty days and forty nights; he did
neither eat bread, nor drink water. And he wrote upon the tables the words
of the covenant, the ten commandments.

d. Moses, the Man with the Glowing Face; the Veil

34:29 Ex 32:15; Mt 17:2; Acts 6:15; 2 Cor 3:7

29 ¶And it came to pass, when Moses came down from mount Si'nai with
the two tables of testimony in Moses' hand, when he came down from the
mount, that Moses wist not that the skin of his face shone while he talked
with him.

34:13 *Asherim* ("shameful idols") were symbols of *Asherah*, the Canaanite mother-goddess. The objects were carved from wood, which could be cut down, burned, or broken in pieces (Exod. 34:13; Deut. 16:21; Mic. 5:14; 2 Chron. 34:4). They were carved statues of male and female genital organs.

34:14 *a jealous God.* Here and in 20:5 God is called *jealous.* "Jealous" can be understood two ways: (1) Envious, resentful, suspicious, or distrustful; (2) solicitous in maintaining or guarding something, sleepless, scrupulous, or alert. It is in the second sense that God is jealous. He will maintain himself in his holiness, justice, and integrity and will not suffer anyone to malign or denigrate the divine person.

34:15 *go a whoring after their gods,* i.e., "committing adultery against me," or, "playing the harlot worshiping their gods."†

34:19 *All that openeth the matrix,* i.e., "Every firstborn male," or, "all that opens the womb."†

34:27 *Write thou these words,* i.e., the preceding laws in 34:12–26.†

30 And when Aaron and all the children of Israel saw Moses, behold, the
skin of his face shone; and they were afraid to come nigh him.
31 And Moses called unto them; and Aaron and all the rulers of the
congregation returned unto him: and Moses talked with them.
32 And afterward all the children of Israel came nigh: and he gave them in
commandment all that the LORD had spoken with him in mount Si'nai.
33 And *till* Moses had done speaking with them, he put a vail on his face.
34 But when Moses went in before the LORD to speak with him, he took
the vail off, until he came out. And he came out, and spake unto the
children of Israel *that* which he was commanded.
35 And the children of Israel saw the face of Moses, that the skin of
Moses' face shone: and Moses put the vail upon his face again, until he
went in to speak with him.

34:31 Ex 4:29; 24:1
☆34:33 2 Cor 3:13
34:34 2 Cor 3:16

M. THE CONSTRUCTION OF THE TABERNACLE
1. Assembling the Materials

35 AND Moses gathered all the congregation of the children of Israel
together, and said unto them, These *are* the words which the LORD
hath commanded, that *ye* should do them.
2 Six days shall work be done, but on the seventh day there shall be to you
an holy day, a sabbath of rest to the LORD: whosoever doeth work therein
shall be put to death.
3 Ye shall kindle no fire throughout your habitations upon the sabbath
day.
4 ¶And Moses spake unto all the congregation of the children of Israel,
saying, This *is* the thing which the LORD commanded, saying,
5 Take ye from among you an offering unto the LORD: whosoever *is* of a
willing heart, let him bring it, an offering of the LORD; gold, and silver, and
brass,
6 And blue, and purple, and scarlet, and fine linen, and goats' *hair*,
7 And rams' skins dyed red, and badgers' skins, and shittim wood,
8 And oil for the light, and spices for anointing oil, and for the sweet
incense,
9 And onyx stones, and stones to be set for the ephod, and for the
breastplate.
10 And every wise hearted among you shall come, and make all that the
LORD hath commanded;
11 The tabernacle, his tent, and his covering, his taches, and his boards,
his bars, his pillars, and his sockets,
12 The ark, and the staves thereof, *with* the mercy seat, and the vail of the
covering,
13 The table, and his staves, and all his vessels, and the shewbread,
14 The candlestick also for the light, and his furniture, and his lamps, with
the oil for the light,
15 And the incense altar, and his staves, and the anointing oil, and the
sweet incense, and the hanging for the door at the entering in of the
tabernacle,
16 The altar of burnt offering, with his brasen grate, his staves, and all his
vessels, the laver and his foot,

35:1 Ex 25:1; 34:32
35:2 Ex 16:23; 20:8; 23:12; 34:21; Num 15:32; Deut 5:13, 14
35:3 Ex 12:16; 16:23
35:5-9 Ex 25:1-7
35:10-19 Ex 39:32-41

34:33 The glory of God was reflected on the face of Moses whenever he left the tent of meeting. Israel then beheld Moses' face and knew he had been with God. But Moses, when he had finished speaking to the people under God's authority, would now put a veil over his face. He removed the veil when he re-entered the tent of meeting. The veil indicated his humility and modesty. In a real sense, the glory of God should be manifested in the faces of God's people. A shining face brings glory to God and moves people to emulate that person.

17 The hangings of the court, his pillars, and their sockets, and the
hanging for the door of the court,
18 The pins of the tabernacle, and the pins of the court, and their cords,
19 The cloths of service, to do service in the holy *place,* the holy garments
for Aaron the priest, and the garments of his sons, to minister in the priest's
office.
20 ¶And all the congregation of the children of Israel departed from the
presence of Moses.
35:21 Ex 25:2; 35:5
21 And they came, every one whose heart stirred him up, and every one
whom his spirit made willing, *and* they brought the LORD's offering to the
work of the tabernacle of the congregation, and for all his service, and for
the holy garments.
22 And they came, both men and women, as many as were willing hearted,
and brought bracelets, and earrings, and rings, and tablets, all jewels of
gold: and every man that offered *offered* an offering of gold unto the LORD.
23 And every man, with whom was found blue, and purple, and scarlet,
and fine linen, and goats' *hair,* and red skins of rams, and badgers' skins,
brought *them.*
24 Every one that did offer an offering of silver and brass brought the
LORD's offering: and every man, with whom was found shittim wood for
any work of the service, brought *it.*
35:25 Ex 28:3; 31:6; 36:1
25 And all the women that were wise hearted did spin with their hands,
and brought that which they had spun, *both* of blue, and of purple, *and* of
scarlet, and of fine linen.
26 And all the women whose heart stirred them up in wisdom spun goats'
hair.
35:27 1 Chron 29:6 Ezra 2:68
27 And the rulers brought onyx stones, and stones to be set, for the ephod,
and for the breastplate;
28 And spice, and oil for the light, and for the anointing oil, and for the
sweet incense.
35:29☆ 1 Chron 29:9
29 The children of Israel brought a willing offering unto the LORD, every
man and woman, whose heart made them willing to bring for all manner of
work, which the LORD had commanded to be made by the hand of Moses.

2. The Assembling of the Craftsmen

35:30 Ex 31:1; 38:22 1 Chron 2:20 1 Cor 3:10
30 ¶And Moses said unto the children of Israel, See, the LORD hath called
by name Be-zal'e-el the son of U'ri, the son of Hur, of the tribe of Judah;
35:31☆
31 And he hath filled him with the spirit of God, in wisdom, in under-
standing, and in knowledge, and in all manner of workmanship;
35:32 1 Kgs 7:13 2 Chron 2:14
32 And to devise curious works, to work in gold, and in silver, and in
brass,
33 And in the cutting of stones, to set *them,* and in carving of wood, to
make any manner of cunning work.

35:29 *a willing offering,* or, "a freewill offering." God wants our offerings to come from the heart and be given freely and generously. He could have laid a tax on the people for the cost of constructing the tabernacle. Instead, the Israelites were asked to give as they chose and out of glad hearts. The work of the church today should not depend on bazaars, stipends for services performed, or other carnal and material devices. The support of the churches should be voluntary, yet in accord with the principle of the tithe in a non-legalistic sense.
35:31 The Spirit of God filled Bezelel and gave him certain gifts which enabled him to construct the tabernacle for God's glory. Those gifts included wisdom, understanding, knowledge, and the ability to construct the tent. Bezelel's gifts were used in the religious work of making the tabernacle. Some of the Spirit's gifts are given to believers to be used, not directly in matters related to the church, but in non-religious callings such as medicine, law, business, or the like. Whoever is given the gift of making money has received that gift from the Spirit and should use his means to glorify God. The men and women who work in factories are likewise gifted by the Spirit and should labor as unto God.

34 And he hath put in his heart that he may teach, *both* he, and A-ho'li-ab, the son of A-his'a-mach, of the tribe of Dan.
35 Them hath he filled with wisdom of heart, to work all manner of work, of the engraver, and of the cunning workman, and of the embroiderer, in blue, and in purple, in scarlet, and in fine linen, and of the weaver, *even* of them that do any work, and of those that devise cunning work.

35:35 Ex 31:3; 1 Kgs 3:12; 7:13; 2 Chron 2:14; Isa 28:26

36 THEN wrought Be-zal'e-el and A-ho'li-ab, and every wise hearted man, in whom the LORD put wisdom and understanding to know how to work all manner of work for the service of the sanctuary, according to all that the LORD had commanded.
2 And Moses called Be-zal'e-el and A-ho'li-ab, and every wise hearted man, in whose heart the LORD had put wisdom, *even* every one whose heart stirred him up to come unto the work to do it:
3 And they received of Moses all the offering, which the children of Israel had brought for the work of the service of the sanctuary, to make it *withal.* And they brought yet unto him free offerings every morning.
4 And all the wise men, that wrought all the work of the sanctuary, came every man from his work which they made;
5 ¶And they spake unto Moses, saying, The people bring much more than enough for the service of the work, which the LORD commanded to make.
6 And Moses gave commandment, and they caused it to be proclaimed throughout the camp, saying, Let neither man nor woman make any more work for the offering of the sanctuary. So the people were restrained from bringing.
7 For the stuff they had was sufficient for all the work to make it, and too much.

36:2 1 Chron 29:5
36:5 2 Chron 31:10; 2 Cor 8:2, 3
☆36:6
36:7 1 Kgs 8:64

3. The Construction of the Sheets and Draperies

8 ¶And every wise hearted man among them that wrought the work of the tabernacle made ten curtains *of* fine twined linen, and blue, and purple, and scarlet: *with* cherubims of cunning work made he them.
9 The length of one curtain *was* twenty and eight cubits, and the breadth of one curtain four cubits: the curtains *were* all of one size.
10 And he coupled the five curtains one unto another: and *the other* five curtains he coupled one unto another.
11 And he made loops of blue on the edge of one curtain from the selvedge in the coupling: likewise he made in the uttermost side of *another* curtain, in the coupling of the second.
12 Fifty loops made he in one curtain, and fifty loops made he in the edge of the curtain which *was* in the coupling of the second: the loops held one *curtain* to another.
13 And he made fifty taches of gold, and coupled the curtains one unto another with the taches: so it became one tabernacle.
14 ¶And he made curtains *of* goats' *hair* for the tent over the tabernacle: eleven curtains he made them.
15 The length of one curtain *was* thirty cubits, and four cubits *was* the breadth of one curtain: the eleven curtains *were* of one size.
16 And he coupled five curtains by themselves, and six curtains by themselves.

36:8-38 Ex 26:1–37
36:14 Ex 26:7; 35:26

36:6 *the people were restrained from bringing.* When Moses had received all that was needed for the construction of the tabernacle, he stopped asking for or receiving additional monies. Had he been a materialist, he might have kept on taking the goods and monies, storing them for future needs. Today some churches are partially endowed, which means that the worshippers have less responsibility for the support of the work. The propriety of endowments is a question which needs further consideration.

17 And he made fifty loops upon the uttermost edge of the curtain in the coupling, and fifty loops made he upon the edge of the curtain which coupleth the second.

18 And he made fifty taches *of* brass to couple the tent together, that it might be one.

19 And he made a covering for the tent *of* rams' skins dyed red, and a covering *of* badgers' skins above *that*.

4. The Tabernacle Framework Constructed

36:20–34
Ex 26:15–29
40:18, 19
Num 4:31

20 ¶And he made boards for the tabernacle *of* shittim wood, standing up.

21 The length of a board *was* ten cubits, and the breadth of a board one cubit and a half.

22 One board had two tenons, equally distant one from another: thus did he make for all the boards of the tabernacle.

23 And he made boards for the tabernacle; twenty boards for the south side southward:

24 And forty sockets of silver he made under the twenty boards; two sockets under one board for his two tenons, and two sockets under another board for his two tenons.

25 And for the other side of the tabernacle, *which is* toward the north corner, he made twenty boards,

26 And their forty sockets of silver; two sockets under one board, and two sockets under another board.

27 And for the sides of the tabernacle westward he made six boards.

28 And two boards made he for the corners of the tabernacle in the two sides.

29 And they were coupled beneath, and coupled together at the head thereof, to one ring: thus he did to both of them in both the corners.

30 And there were eight boards; and their sockets *were* sixteen sockets of silver, under every board two sockets.

31 ¶And he made bars of shittim wood; five for the boards of the one side of the tabernacle,

32 And five bars for the boards of the other side of the tabernacle, and five bars for the boards of the tabernacle for the sides westward.

33 And he made the middle bar to shoot through the boards from the one end to the other.

34 And he overlaid the boards with gold, and made their rings *of* gold *to be* places for the bars, and overlaid the bars with gold.

5. The Construction of the Curtain

36:35–38☆
Ex 26:31–37;
40:3
Lev 16:2

35 ¶And he made a vail *of* blue, and purple, and scarlet, and fine twined linen: *with* cherubims made he it of cunning work.

36 And he made thereunto four pillars *of* shittim *wood*, and overlaid them with gold: their hooks *were of* gold; and he cast for them four sockets of silver.

37 ¶And he made an hanging for the tabernacle door *of* blue, and purple, and scarlet, and fine twined linen, of needlework;

38 And the five pillars of it with their hooks: and he overlaid their chapiters and their fillets with gold: but their five sockets *were of* brass.

36:35 *veil*, i.e., "the inner veil (or curtain)."

6. Bezaleel Constructs the Ark

37 AND Be-zal′e-el made the ark *of* shittim wood: two cubits and a half *was* the length of it, and a cubit and a half the breadth of it, and a cubit and a half the height of it:

☆**37:1-9** Ex 25:10-20; 26:33 Deut 10:3

2 And he overlaid it with pure gold within and without, and made a crown of gold to it round about.

3 And he cast for it four rings of gold, *to be set* by the four corners of it; even two rings upon the one side of it, and two rings upon the other side of it.

4 And he made staves *of* shittim wood, and overlaid them with gold.

5 And he put the staves into the rings by the sides of the ark, to bear the ark.

6 ¶And he made the mercy seat *of* pure gold: two cubits and a half *was* the length thereof, and one cubit and a half the breadth thereof.

7 And he made two cherubims *of* gold, beaten out of one piece made he them, on the two ends of the mercy seat;

8 One cherub on the end on this side, and another cherub on the *other* end on that side: out of the mercy seat made he the cherubims on the two ends thereof.

9 And the cherubims spread out *their* wings on high, *and* covered with their wings over the mercy seat, with their faces one to another; *even* to the mercy seatward were the faces of the cherubims.

7. Bezaleel Constructs the Table

10 ¶And he made the table *of* shittim wood: two cubits *was* the length thereof, and a cubit the breadth thereof, and a cubit and a half the height thereof:

37:10-16 Ex 25:23-29; 40:22

11 And he overlaid it with pure gold, and made thereunto a crown of gold round about.

12 Also he made thereunto a border of an handbreadth round about; and made a crown of gold for the border thereof round about.

13 And he cast for it four rings of gold, and put the rings upon the four corners that *were* in the four feet thereof.

14 Over against the border were the rings, the places for the staves to bear the table.

15 And he made the staves *of* shittim wood, and overlaid them with gold, to bear the table.

16 And he made the vessels which *were* upon the table, his dishes, and his spoons, and his bowls, and his covers to cover withal, *of* pure gold.

8. Bezaleel Constructs the Lampstand

17 ¶And he made the candlestick *of* pure gold: *of* beaten work made he the candlestick; his shaft, and his branch, his bowls, his knops, and his flowers, were of the same:

37:17-24 Ex 25:31-39; 40:24

18 And six branches going out of the sides thereof; three branches of the candlestick out of the one side thereof, and three branches of the candlestick out of the other side thereof:

19 Three bowls made after the fashion of almonds in one branch, a knop and a flower; and three bowls made like almonds in another branch, a knop and a flower: so throughout the six branches going out of the candlestick.

37:7 *cherubim.* See note to Ezek. 10:1 for this.

20 And in the candlestick *were* four bowls made like almonds, his knops, and his flowers:

21 And a knop under two branches of the same, and a knop under two branches of the same, and a knop under two branches of the same, according to the six branches going out of it.

22 Their knops and their branches were of the same: all of it *was* one beaten work *of* pure gold.

23 And he made his seven lamps, and his snuffers, and his snuffdishes, *of* pure gold.

24 *Of* a talent of pure gold made he it, and all the vessels thereof.

9. Bezaleel Constructs the Altar of Incense and Compounds the Oil

37:25–29
Ex 30:1-5
Lev 4:7
1 Kgs 6:22

25 ¶And he made the incense altar *of* shittim wood: the length of it *was* a cubit, and the breadth of it a cubit; *it was* foursquare; and two cubits *was* the height of it; the horns thereof were of the same.

26 And he overlaid it with pure gold, *both* the top of it, and the sides thereof round about, and the horns of it: also he made unto it a crown of gold round about.

27 And he made two rings of gold for it under the crown thereof, by the two corners of it, upon the two sides thereof, to be places for the staves to bear it withal.

28 And he made the staves *of* shittim wood, and overlaid them with gold.

37:29
Ex 30:22, 23
40:9
Lev 8:10

29 ¶And he made the holy anointing oil, and the pure incense of sweet spices, according to the work of the apothecary.

10. Bezaleel Constructs the Burnt-Offering Altar

38:1–7
Ex 20:24; 27:1-8
40:10, 29
Heb 13:10

38 AND he made the altar of burnt offering *of* shittim wood: five cubits *was* the length thereof, and five cubits the breadth thereof; *it was* foursquare; and three cubits the height thereof.

2 And he made the horns thereof on the four corners of it; the horns thereof were of the same: and he overlaid it with brass.

3 And he made all the vessels of the altar, the pots, and the shovels, and the basons, *and* the fleshhooks, and the firepans: all the vessels thereof made he *of* brass.

4 And he made for the altar a brasen grate of network under the compass thereof beneath unto the midst of it.

5 And he cast four rings for the four ends of the grate of brass, *to be* places for the staves.

6 And he made the staves *of* shittim wood, and overlaid them with brass.

7 And he put the staves into the rings on the sides of the altar, to bear it withal; he made the altar hollow with boards.

38:8
Ex 30:18; 31:9
Lev 8:11

8 ¶And he made the laver *of* brass, and the foot of it *of* brass, of the lookingglasses of *the women* assembling, which assembled *at* the door of the tabernacle of the congregation.

11. Bezaleel Constructs the Courtyard

38:9–20
Ex 27:9-19; 40:8
1 Kgs 6:36; 8:64

9 ¶And he made the court: on the south side southward the hangings of the court *were of* fine twined linen, an hundred cubits:

10 Their pillars *were* twenty, and their brasen sockets twenty; the hooks of the pillars and their fillets *were of* silver.

11 And for the north side *the hangings were* an hundred cubits, their pillars *were* twenty, and their sockets of brass twenty; the hooks of the pillars and their fillets *of* silver.

12 And for the west side *were* hangings of fifty cubits, their pillars ten, and their sockets ten; the hooks of the pillars and their fillets *of* silver.

13 And for the east side eastward fifty cubits.
14 The hangings of the one side *of the gate were* fifteen cubits; their pillars three, and their sockets three.
15 And for the other side of the court gate, on this hand and that hand, *were* hangings of fifteen cubits; their pillars three, and their sockets three.
16 All the hangings of the court round about *were* of fine twined linen.
17 And the sockets for the pillars *were of* brass; the hooks of the pillars and their fillets *of* silver; and the overlaying of their chapiters *of* silver; and all the pillars of the court *were* filleted with silver.
18 And the hanging for the gate of the court *was* needlework, *of* blue, and purple, and scarlet, and fine twined linen: and twenty cubits *was* the length, and the height in the breadth *was* five cubits, answerable to the hangings of the court.
19 And their pillars *were* four, and their sockets *of* brass four; their hooks *of* silver, and the overlaying of their chapiters and their fillets *of* silver.
20 And all the pins of the tabernacle, and of the court round about, *were of* brass.

12. A Summary of the Metals in the Tabernacle

21 ¶This is the sum of the tabernacle, *even* of the tabernacle of testimony, as it was counted, according to the commandment of Moses, *for* the service of the Levites, by the hand of Ith'a-mar, son to Aaron the priest.
22 And Be-zal'e-el the son of U'ri, the son of Hur, of the tribe of Judah, made all that the LORD commanded Moses.
23 And with him *was* A-ho'li-ab, son of A-his'a-mach, of the tribe of Dan, an engraver, and a cunning workman, and an embroiderer in blue, and in purple, and in scarlet, and fine linen.
24 All the gold that was occupied for the work in all the work of the holy *place*, even the gold of the offering, was twenty and nine talents, and seven hundred and thirty shekels, after the shekel of the sanctuary. ☆**38:24**
25 And the silver of them that were numbered of the congregation *was* an hundred talents, and a thousand seven hundred and threescore and fifteen shekels, after the shekel of the sanctuary: ☆**38:25, 26** Ex 12:37; 30:11–16 Num 1:2, 46 26:2, 51
26 A bekah for every man, *that is*, half a shekel, after the shekel of the sanctuary, for every one that went to be numbered, from twenty years old and upward, for six hundred thousand and three thousand and five hundred and fifty *men*.
27 And of the hundred talents of silver were cast the sockets of the sanctuary, and the sockets of the vail; an hundred sockets of the hundred talents, a talent for a socket.
28 And of the thousand seven hundred seventy and five *shekels* he made hooks for the pillars, and overlaid their chapiters, and filleted them.
29 And the brass of the offering *was* seventy talents, and two thousand and four hundred shekels.
30 And therewith he made the sockets to the door of the tabernacle of the congregation, and the brasen altar, and the brasen grate for it, and all the vessels of the altar,
31 And the sockets of the court round about, and the sockets of the court gate, and all the pins of the tabernacle, and all the pins of the court round about.

38:24 The value of the gold given by God's people was worth approximately ten million dollars according to today's currency market.

38:25 The value of the silver probably was worth in excess of one million dollars according to today's currency.

13. The Manufacture of the Priestly Garments
a. Bezalel Makes the Ephod

39 AND of the blue, and purple, and scarlet, they made cloths of service, to do service in the holy *place*, and made the holy garments for Aaron; as the LORD commanded Moses.

39:2 Ex 28:6 Lev 8:7

2 And he made the ephod *of* gold, blue, and purple, and scarlet, and fine twined linen.

3 And they did beat the gold into thin plates, and cut *it into* wires, to work *it* in the blue, and in the purple, and in the scarlet, and in the fine linen, *with* cunning work.

4 They made shoulderpieces for it, to couple *it* together: by the two edges was it coupled together.

5 And the curious girdle of his ephod, that *was* upon it, *was* of the same, according to the work thereof; *of* gold, blue, and purple, and scarlet, and fine twined linen; as the LORD commanded Moses.

6 ¶And they wrought onyx stones inclosed in ouches of gold, graven, as signets are graven, with the names of the children of Israel.

7 And he put them on the shoulders of the ephod, *that they should be* stones for a memorial to the children of Israel; as the LORD commanded Moses.

b. Bezalel Makes the Breastplate

39:8–21 Ex 28:15–28

8 ¶And he made the breastplate *of* cunning work, like the work of the ephod; *of* gold, blue, and purple, and scarlet, and fine twined linen.

9 It was foursquare; they made the breastplate double: a span *was* the length thereof, and a span the breadth thereof, *being* doubled.

10 And they set in it four rows of stones: *the first* row *was* a sardius, a topaz, and a carbuncle: this *was* the first row.

11 And the second row, an emerald, a sapphire, and a diamond.

12 And the third row, a ligure, an agate, and an amethyst.

13 And the fourth row, a beryl, an onyx, and a jasper: *they were* inclosed in ouches of gold in their inclosings.

39:14 Rev 21:12

14 And the stones *were* according to the names of the children of Israel, twelve, according to their names, *like* the engravings of a signet, every one with his name, according to the twelve tribes.

15 And they made upon the breastplate chains at the ends, *of* wreathen work *of* pure gold.

16 And they made two ouches *of* gold, and two gold rings; and put the two rings in the two ends of the breastplate.

17 And they put the two wreathen chains of gold in the two rings on the ends of the breastplate.

18 And the two ends of the two wreathen chains they fastened in the two ouches, and put them on the shoulderpieces of the ephod, before it.

19 And they made two rings of gold, and put *them* on the two ends of the breastplate, upon the border of it, which *was* on the side of the ephod inward.

20 And they made two *other* golden rings, and put them on the two sides of the ephod underneath, toward the forepart of it, over against the *other* coupling thereof, above the curious girdle of the ephod.

21 And they did bind the breastplate by his rings unto the rings of the ephod with a lace of blue, that it might be above the curious girdle of the ephod, and that the breastplate might not be loosed from the ephod; as the LORD commanded Moses.

c. Details Concerning Aaron's and His Sons' Robes

22¶And he made the robe of the ephod *of* woven work, all *of* blue. 39:22 Ex 28:31
23And *there was* an hole in the midst of the robe, as the hole of an
habergeon, *with* a band round about the hole, that it should not rend.
24And they made upon the hems of the robe pomegranates *of* blue, and
purple, and scarlet, *and* twined *linen.*
25And they made bells *of* pure gold, and put the bells between the
pomegranates upon the hem of the robe, round about between the
pomegranates;
26A bell and a pomegranate, a bell and a pomegranate, round about the
hem of the robe to minister *in;* as the LORD commanded Moses.
27¶And they made coats *of* fine linen *of* woven work for Aaron, and for 39:27 Ex 28:40 Lev 8:13
his sons,
28And a mitre *of* fine linen, and goodly bonnets *of* fine linen, and linen
breeches *of* fine twined linen,
29And a girdle *of* fine twined linen, and blue, and purple, and scarlet, *of*
needlework; as the LORD commanded Moses.
30¶And they made the plate of the holy crown *of* pure gold, and wrote 39:30 Ex 38:36 Lev 8:9
upon it a writing, *like to* the engravings of a signet, HOLINESS TO THE
LORD.
31And they tied unto it a lace of blue, to fasten *it* on high upon the mitre;
as the LORD commanded Moses.

14. Moses Accepts the Results and Blesses the Workmen

32¶Thus was all the work of the tabernacle of the tent of the congregation
finished: and the children of Israel did according to all that the LORD
commanded Moses, so did they.
33¶And they brought the tabernacle unto Moses, the tent, and all his
furniture, his taches, his boards, his bars, and his pillars, and his sockets,
34And the covering of rams' skins dyed red, and the covering of badgers'
skins, and the vail of the covering,
35The ark of the testimony, and the staves thereof, and the mercy seat,
36The table, *and* all the vessels thereof, and the shewbread,
37The pure candlestick, *with* the lamps thereof, *even with* the lamps to be
set in order, and all the vessels thereof, and the oil for light,
38And the golden altar, and the anointing oil, and the sweet incense, and
the hanging for the tabernacle door,
39The brasen altar, and his grate of brass, his staves, and all his vessels,
the laver and his foot,
40The hangings of the court, his pillars, and his sockets, and the hanging
for the court gate, his cords, and his pins, and all the vessels of the service
of the tabernacle, for the tent of the congregation,
41The cloths of service to do service in the holy *place*, and the holy
garments for Aaron the priest, and his sons' garments, to minister in the
priest's office. ☆39:43 Lev 9:22, 23 Num 6:23 Josh 22:6 1 Kgs 8:14 2 Chron 30:27
42According to all that the LORD commanded Moses, so the children of
Israel made all the work.
43And Moses did look upon all the work, and, behold, they had done it as

---

39:43 God had given Moses the pattern for the tabernacle. Although he did not construct it, it was done according to what had been revealed to him. Here he inspects the finished product and places his stamp of approval on it; it had met the specifications given to him by God. Moses blessed those who had done the work; he praised them and prayed for them. The blessing in the name of the Lord was adequate wages for the labors of those who constructed the tabernacle.

the LORD had commanded, even so had they done it: and Moses blessed
them.

15. The Tabernacle Put Together and Consecrated
a. God Orders the Tabernacle Put Together

40 AND the LORD spake unto Moses, saying,
2 On the first day of the first month shalt thou set up the
tabernacle of the tent of the congregation.
3 And thou shalt put therein the ark of the testimony, and cover the ark
with the vail.
4 And thou shalt bring in the table, and set in order the things that are to
be set in order upon it; and thou shalt bring in the candlestick, and light the
lamps thereof.
5 And thou shalt set the altar of gold for the incense before the ark of the
testimony, and put the hanging of the door to the tabernacle.
6 And thou shalt set the altar of the burnt offering before the door of the
tabernacle of the tent of the congregation.
7 And thou shalt set the laver between the tent of the congregation and
the altar, and shalt put water therein.
8 And thou shalt set up the court round about, and hang up the hanging
at the court gate.
9 And thou shalt take the anointing oil, and anoint the tabernacle, and all
that *is* therein, and shalt hallow it, and all the vessels thereof: and it shall be
holy.
10 And thou shalt anoint the altar of the burnt offering, and all his vessels,
and sanctify the altar: and it shall be an altar most holy.
11 And thou shalt anoint the laver and his foot, and sanctify it.
12 And thou shalt bring Aaron and his sons unto the door of the
tabernacle of the congregation, and wash them with water.
13 And thou shalt put upon Aaron the holy garments, and anoint him, and
sanctify him; that he may minister unto me in the priest's office.
14 And thou shalt bring his sons, and clothe them with coats:
15 And thou shalt anoint them, as thou didst anoint their father, that they
may minister unto me in the priest's office: for their anointing shall surely
be an everlasting priesthood throughout their generations.

40:2 Ex 12:1; 19:1
40:17 Num 1:1; 7:1
40:3 Ex 25:9, 10; Num 4:5
40:9☆
40:12 Ex 28:41; 29:1; Lev 8:1–13
40:15 Ex 29:9; Num 3:10; Deut 18:5; Heb 5:4

b. Moses Finishes the Project

16 Thus did Moses: according to all that the LORD commanded him, so
did he.
17 ¶And it came to pass in the first month in the second year, on the first
day of the month, *that* the tabernacle was reared up.
18 And Moses reared up the tabernacle, and fastened his sockets, and set
up the boards thereof, and put in the bars thereof, and reared up his pillars.
19 And he spread abroad the tent over the tabernacle, and put the
covering of the tent above upon it; as the LORD commanded Moses.
20 ¶And he took and put the testimony into the ark, and set the staves on
the ark, and put the mercy seat above upon the ark:
21 And he brought the ark into the tabernacle, and set up the vail of the
covering, and covered the ark of the testimony; as the LORD commanded
Moses.

40:17 Ex 40:2; Num 7:1
40:20 Deut 10:5; 1 Kgs 8:9; Heb 9:4

40:9 The completed tabernacle was not yet God's possession until it was first sanctified by the special anointing oil. The tent, and all the vessels and furniture therein were hallowed. When this was done, the tabernacle became holy; and once it was made holy, the glory of God filled that residence made for him.

[22]¶And he put the table in the tent of the congregation, upon the side of
the tabernacle northward, without the vail.
[23]And he set the bread in order upon it before the LORD; as the LORD
had commanded Moses.
[24]¶And he put the candlestick in the tent of the congregation, over
against the table, on the side of the tabernacle southward.
[25]And he lighted the lamps before the LORD; as the LORD commanded
Moses.
[26]¶And he put the golden altar in the tent of the congregation before the
vail:
[27]And he burnt sweet incense thereon; as the LORD commanded Moses.
[28]¶And he set up the hanging *at* the door of the tabernacle.
[29]And he put the altar of burnt offering *by* the door of the tabernacle of
the tent of the congregation, and offered upon it the burnt offering and the
meat offering; as the LORD commanded Moses.
[30]¶And he set the laver between the tent of the congregation and the
altar, and put water there, to wash *withal.*
[31]And Moses and Aaron and his sons washed their hands and their feet
thereat:
[32]When they went into the tent of the congregation, and when they came
near unto the altar, they washed; as the LORD commanded Moses.
[33]And he reared up the court round about the tabernacle and the altar,
and set up the hanging of the court gate. So Moses finished the work.

40:23 Ex 25:30; 35:13 Lev 24:5
40:31 Ex 30:19
☆**40:33**

c. The Glory of God Fills the Tabernacle

[34]¶Then a cloud covered the tent of the congregation, and the glory of the
LORD filled the tabernacle.
[35]And Moses was not able to enter into the tent of the congregation,
because the cloud abode thereon, and the glory of the LORD filled the
tabernacle.
[36]And when the cloud was taken up from over the tabernacle, the
children of Israel went onward in all their journeys:
[37]But if the cloud were not taken up, then they journeyed not till the day
that it was taken up.
[38]For the cloud of the LORD *was* upon the tabernacle by day, and fire was
on it by night, in the sight of all the house of Israel, throughout all their
journeys.

☆**40:34** Ex 13:21; 29:43 33:9 Num 9:15 1 Kgs 8:10, 11 2 Chron 5:13, 14; 7:2 Hag 2:7, 9 Jn 1:14 Eph 3:21 Rev 15:8
40:35 Lev 16:2 1 Kgs 8:1 2 Chron 5:14
40:36 Num 9:17; 10:11 Neh 9:19
40:37, 38 Num 9:15–23

40:33 Seven times in less than fourteen verses we learn that Moses was commanded to do certain things by God. Then comes the grand finale: "So Moses finished the work." His obedience in this task was ended, and the finished product given to God.

40:34 See note on 13:21. Here the cloud covered the tabernacle (the tent of the congregation) and the glory of the Lord filled it, as occurred later when the temple was dedicated (2 Chron. 5:13, 14). At the time of Zedekiah's apostasy the glory left the temple (cf. Ezek. 43:1–4) and never came back, even when the temple was rebuilt in 516 B.C. The Scriptures promised that the second temple would surpass the first one in glory. This occurred centuries later when Jesus came to cleanse the temple and to teach in it. Following his rejection and crucifixion, the spiritual glory departed from the temple forever and the building was destroyed in A.D. 70. God's temple today is the New Testament church.

THE THIRD BOOK OF MOSES CALLED

LEVITICUS

Authorship, date, and background Leviticus is the third Book of Moses and, like the other four books of the Pentateuch, was composed during the last two decades of the fifteenth century B.C. The Hebrew title for the book comes from the opening phrase of the text, meaning "and he called." The title used in the Septuagint, *Leviticus,* means "pertaining to the Levites." Since the Israeli priests were Levites, the title is appropriate, for the book discusses the ministry of the Levitical priesthood in some detail.

The key verse of Leviticus is 11:45, which says, "Ye shall therefore be holy, for I am holy." God chose Israel to be his holy people; they were a nation peculiarly set apart for God and his purposes. God, as this book constantly reiterates, gave his laws and regulations through Moses, who either wrote them down or had them written down under his aegis (4:1; 6:1; 8:1; 11:1; 12:1; 13:1, etc.). Israel was commanded to keep God's injunctions, not in order to become acceptable in his sight by their works, but rather because the keeping of God's laws would be an outward manifestation of hearts in tune with God and an expression of their love for him.

Leviticus lays down the rules for the proper presentation of sacrifices and clearly states what is clean and unclean.

Characteristics and content Law and grace kiss each other in this book. Superficially it appears to be the most legalistic book in the Old Testament. God demands that his people conform their conduct to his rules and regulations. Yet the gospel is truly to be found here, for the obedience God requires is a response to the grace and mercy of God which his people must first receive as a gift. This underlying truth is fully revealed and developed in the New Testament in the writings of Paul, who champions the doctrine of God's free grace in Jesus Christ, and through James, who emphasizes the necessity of the believer's response to God's grace through works.

The pages of Leviticus contain the laws of sacrifices, the rules for the consecration of the priesthood, and the regulations for the separation of God's people from defilement with respect to foods, childbirth, diseases like leprosy, and also bodily secretions. Great emphasis is laid on the Day of Atonement, the place of sacrifice, and the necessity to shed blood for the remission of sins. Then follow the laws for practical holiness, a summary of the duties of the priesthood, and a list of the holy convocations together with their meanings and requirements.

Economic regulations are laid down. The people of Israel are given title to their lands in perpetuity. Mortgaged properties are to be returned to their owners in the Year of Jubilee. Stipulations govern the cost of using the mortgaged lands, depending on how long they will be lost to the owners until the Jubilee. The sabbatical year for the land is set for every seventh year. The book comes to a close with the promise of God for blessings to be bestowed on the obedient and curses which accrue to the disobedient. The last chapter gives directions about vows and tithes.

Outline

I. The law of offerings (1:1—7:38)
II. Regulations concerning the priesthood (8:1—10:20)
III. Regulations about ceremonial defilement and purification (11:1—15:33)
IV. The Day of Atonement (16:1—35)
V. Maintaining a holy life before God (17:1—22:33)
VI. Regulations for festivals and seasons (23:1—25:55)
VII. How to secure God's blessing (26:1—27:34)

I. THE LAW OF OFFERINGS (1:1—7:38)

A. BURNT OFFERING

1 AND the LORD called unto Moses, and spake unto him out of the
tabernacle of the congregation, saying,
2 Speak unto the children of Israel, and say unto them, If any man of you
bring an offering unto the LORD, ye shall bring your offering of the cattle,
even of the herd, and of the flock.
3 If his offering *be* a burnt sacrifice of the herd, let him offer a male
without blemish: he shall offer it of his own voluntary will at the door of the
tabernacle of the congregation before the LORD.
4 And he shall put his hand upon the head of the burnt offering; and it
shall be accepted for him to make atonement for him.
5 And he shall kill the bullock before the LORD: and the priests, Aaron's
sons, shall bring the blood, and sprinkle the blood round about upon the
altar that *is by* the door of the tabernacle of the congregation.
6 And he shall flay the burnt offering, and cut it into his pieces.
7 And the sons of Aaron the priest shall put fire upon the altar, and lay
the wood in order upon the fire:
8 And the priests, Aaron's sons, shall lay the parts, the head, and the fat,
in order upon the wood that *is* on the fire which *is* upon the altar:
9 But his inwards and his legs shall he wash in water: and the priest shall
burn all on the altar, *to be* a burnt sacrifice, an offering made by fire, of a
sweet savour unto the LORD.
10 ¶And if his offering *be* of the flocks, *namely*, of the sheep, or of the
goats, for a burnt sacrifice; he shall bring it a male without blemish.
11 And he shall kill it on the side of the altar northward before the LORD:
and the priests, Aaron's sons, shall sprinkle his blood round about upon the
altar.
12 And he shall cut it into his pieces, with his head and his fat: and the
priest shall lay them in order on the wood that *is* on the fire which *is* upon
the altar:
13 But he shall wash the inwards and the legs with water: and the priest
shall bring *it* all, and burn *it* upon the altar: it *is* a burnt sacrifice, an
offering made by fire, of a sweet savour unto the LORD.
14 ¶And if the burnt sacrifice for his offering to the LORD *be* of fowls, then
he shall bring his offering of turtledoves, or of young pigeons.
15 And the priest shall bring it unto the altar, and wring off his head, and
burn *it* on the altar; and the blood thereof shall be wrung out at the side of
the altar:
16 And he shall pluck away his crop with his feathers, and cast it beside
the altar on the east part, by the place of the ashes:
17 And he shall cleave it with the wings thereof, *but* shall not divide *it*
asunder: and the priest shall burn it upon the altar, upon the wood that *is*
upon the fire: it *is* a burnt sacrifice, an offering made by fire, of a sweet
savour unto the LORD.

1:1 Ex 25:22 Num 7:89
1:2 Gen 4:3, 4 Ex 29:42 Lev 6:9–13; 17:1–8 22:19, 20–25 Num 29:8–11 Deut 12:4–6; 15:21 Deut 17:1 Mal 1:14 Heb 9:14 1 Pet 1:19
☆**1:3**
1:4 Ex 29:10, 15, 19 Lev 4:13–35 Num 8:10–12; 15:25 2 Chron 29:23, 24
1:5 Lev 1:11; 3:7, 8 16:15 Heb 12:24
1:6 Lev 7:8 Neh 13:31
1:8 Ex 29:17 Lev 3:3, 4, 5
1:9 Gen 8:21 Ex 29:17, 18 Num 15:8, 9 Eph 5:2 Phil 4:18
1:11 Lev 1:5
1:13 Lev 1:6-8
1:14 Gen 15:9 Lev 12:8
1:15 Lev 5:9

1:3 The burnt offering (sacrifice) is a type of Christ, who offered himself once for all for sin (Heb. 10:10). The animal was a substitute for the sinner even as Christ is our substitute. The offerer laid his hand on the animal (1:4) and thus identified himself with the offering. This was an act of faith. In the New Testament Christ stood in the sinner's place and made atonement for him as his representative and substitute (1 Pet. 1:18–20). The kind of animal offered depended on the financial condition of the offerer: it could be a healthy bull, sheep, goat, turtledove, or pigeon. The burnt offering was to be completely burned; no part of it was given to the priest or the offerer to be eaten. The Old Testament declares that the life is in the blood. No atonement is possible without the sacrifice of a life, for which the blood was the visible representation (17:11). When the blood was presented to God it was evidence that the life had been given. The blood that flowed from the Savior's wounds gave evidence of the offering of his life. And the presentation of his blood at the heavenly mercy seat meant that he had died for our salvation and had won the victory.

B. MEAT (GRAIN) OFFERING

2:1☆ Ex 29:2; Lev 6:14–18; 24:7; Num 15:4–21

2 AND when any will offer a meat offering unto the LORD, his offering shall be *of* fine flour; and he shall pour oil upon it, and put frankincense thereon:

2:2☆ Lev 2:9; 5:12, 13; 6:15–18

2 And he shall bring it to Aaron's sons the priests: and he shall take thereout his handful of the flour thereof, and of the oil thereof, with all the frankincense thereof; and the priest shall burn the memorial of it upon the altar, *to be* an offering made by fire, of a sweet savour unto the LORD:

2:3 Lev 10:12, 13; Num 8:8–11

3 And the remnant of the meat offering *shall be* Aaron's and his sons': *it is* a thing most holy of the offerings of the LORD made by fire.

2:4 Ex 29:2; Lev 7:12

4 ¶And if thou bring an oblation of a meat offering baken in the oven, *it shall be* unleavened cakes of fine flour mingled with oil, or unleavened wafers anointed with oil.

5 ¶And if thy oblation *be* a meat offering *baken* in a pan, it shall be *of* fine flour unleavened, mingled with oil.

6 Thou shalt part it in pieces, and pour oil thereon: it *is* a meat offering.

7 ¶And if thy oblation *be* a meat offering *baken* in the fryingpan, it shall be made *of* fine flour with oil.

8 And thou shalt bring the meat offering that is made of these things unto the LORD: and when it is presented unto the priest, he shall bring it unto the altar.

2:9 Gen 8:21; Ex 29:18; Lev 2:2; 6:15

9 And the priest shall take from the meat offering a memorial thereof, and shall burn *it* upon the altar: *it is* an offering made by fire, of a sweet savour unto the LORD.

2:10 Lev 2:3

10 And that which is left of the meat offering *shall be* Aaron's and his sons': *it is* a thing most holy of the offerings of the LORD made by fire.

2:11 Lev 6:16, 17

11 No meat offering, which ye shall bring unto the LORD, shall be made with leaven: for ye shall burn no leaven, nor any honey, in any offering of the LORD made by fire.

2:12 Lev 7:13; 23:9–14

12 ¶As for the oblation of the firstfruits, ye shall offer them unto the LORD: but they shall not be burnt on the altar for a sweet savour.

2:13☆ Num 18:19; 2 Chron 13:5; Ezek 43:24; Mk 9:49

13 And every oblation of thy meat offering shalt thou season with salt; neither shalt thou suffer the salt of the covenant of thy God to be lacking from thy meat offering: with all thine offerings thou shalt offer salt.

2:14 Lev 23:9–14; 2 Kgs 4:42

14 And if thou offer a meat offering of thy firstfruits unto the LORD, thou shalt offer for the meat offering of thy firstfruits green ears of corn dried by the fire, *even* corn beaten out of full ears.

15 And thou shalt put oil upon it, and lay frankincense thereon: it *is* a meat offering.

2:16 Lev 2:1, 2

16 And the priest shall burn the memorial of it, *part* of the beaten corn thereof, and *part* of the oil thereof, with all the frankincense thereof: *it is* an offering made by fire unto the LORD.

C. PEACE OFFERING

3:1☆ Lev 1:2; 7:11–21

3 AND if his oblation *be* a sacrifice of peace offering, if he offer *it* of the herd; whether *it be* a male or female, he shall offer it without blemish before the LORD.

2:1 *offering shall be made of fine flour.* The grain (or cereal or meal) offering was made of fine flour and was presented with oil and incense. It was unleavened. It was offered on the altar of burnt offering, not on the altar of incense (Exod. 30:9; 40:29). When offered by the priests it was to be totally burned up (6:23); when offered by the priests for others, a handful was put in the flames and the remainder eaten by the priests (6:15, 16).

2:2 *shall burn the memorial of it upon the altar, to be an offering made by fire,* i.e., "shall burn a small portion representing the entire amount."†

2:13 *season with salt.* In many of the languages of the ancient Near East, the word "salt" is a homonym of the word "good." It was used symbolically for "goodness" in making covenants.

3:1 The animal peace offering was to be eaten by the priests and the worshippers (except for the kidneys and

2 And he shall lay his hand upon the head of his offering, and kill it *at* the door of the tabernacle of the congregation: and Aaron's sons the priests shall sprinkle the blood upon the altar round about.

3:2 Ex 29:11 Lev 1:4; 7:14

3 And he shall offer of the sacrifice of the peace offering an offering made by fire unto the LORD; the fat that covereth the inwards, and all the fat that *is* upon the inwards,

3:3–5 Ex 29:13, 22 Lev 3:9–11, 14–16

4 And the two kidneys, and the fat that *is* on them, which *is* by the flanks, and the caul above the liver, with the kidneys, it shall he take away.

5 And Aaron's sons shall burn it on the altar upon the burnt sacrifice, which *is* upon the wood that *is* on the fire: *it is* an offering made by fire, of a sweet savour unto the LORD.

6 ¶And if his offering for a sacrifice of peace offering unto the LORD *be* of the flock; male or female, he shall offer it without blemish.

☆**3:6** Lev 1:2; 3:1

7 If he offer a lamb for his offering, then shall he offer it before the LORD.

8 And he shall lay his hand upon the head of his offering, and kill it before the tabernacle of the congregation: and Aaron's sons shall sprinkle the blood thereof round about upon the altar.

9 And he shall offer of the sacrifice of the peace offering an offering made by fire unto the LORD; the fat thereof, *and* the whole rump, it shall he take off hard by the backbone; and the fat that covereth the inwards, and all the fat that *is* upon the inwards,

10 And the two kidneys, and the fat that *is* upon them, which *is* by the flanks, and the caul above the liver, with the kidneys, it shall he take away.

11 And the priest shall burn it upon the altar: *it is* the food of the offering made by fire unto the LORD.

12 ¶And if his offering *be* a goat, then he shall offer it before the LORD.

3:12 Num 15:6, 11–16

13 And he shall lay his hand upon the head of it, and kill it before the tabernacle of the congregation: and the sons of Aaron shall sprinkle the blood thereof upon the altar round about.

3:13 Lev 1:2

14 And he shall offer thereof his offering, *even* an offering made by fire unto the LORD; the fat that covereth the inwards, and all the fat that *is* upon the inwards,

15 And the two kidneys, and the fat that *is* upon them, which *is* by the flanks, and the caul above the liver, with the kidneys, it shall he take away.

3:15, 16 Lev 4:26 7:23–25 Ezek 44:7

16 And the priest shall burn them upon the altar: *it is* the food of the offering made by fire for a sweet savour: all the fat *is* the LORD's.

17 *It shall be* a perpetual statute for your generations throughout all your dwellings, that ye eat neither fat nor blood.

3:17 Lev 7:26, 27 17:10 Deut 12:16 Acts 15:20, 27–29

D. OFFERINGS FOR UNINTENTIONAL SINS

1. Offering for Priestly Sin

4 AND the LORD spake unto Moses, saying,

2 Speak unto the children of Israel, saying, If a soul shall sin through ignorance against any of the commandments of the LORD *concerning things* which ought not to be done, and shall do against any of them:

☆**4:2** Lev 4:22, 22:14 Num 15:22–29

---

fat, which were to be burned). It was a fellowship meal, signifying that peace existed between God and the offerer as well as between man and man.

3:6 *peace offering . . . of the flock.* The offering was to come from the sheep or goats. Birds were excluded from this for two reasons: they did not have enough fat to warrant their use, and the meat was inconsiderable so as to make the offering of little worth for food. *without blemish.* This requirement was included because men would tend to offer a diseased or abnormal animal rather than a perfect one. God wanted no second-rate offerings from his people.

4:2 Sins which were intended to reject God's sovereignty were to be punished by executing the offender (Num. 15:30, 31). For unintentional sins or sins of ignorance, provision was made for repentance and atonement by an animal sacrifice. We all sin through ignorance and without any intention of renouncing God's sovereignty or control over our lives. Ignorance, then and now, was no excuse for failing to keep God's commandments. Believers are to study the Scriptures to learn and keep God's commandments. Paul says that even sins of ignorance are basically willful (Rom 1:20, 28).

4:3☆ Lev 4:14; 9:2 Ezek 43:19

3 If the priest that is anointed do sin according to the sin of the people; then let him bring for his sin, which he hath sinned, a young bullock without blemish unto the LORD for a sin offering.

4 And he shall bring the bullock unto the door of the tabernacle of the congregation before the LORD; and shall lay his hand upon the bullock's head, and kill the bullock before the LORD.

4:5, 6 Lev 4:17; 16:14 Num 19:4

5 And the priest that is anointed shall take of the bullock's blood, and bring it to the tabernacle of the congregation:

6 And the priest shall dip his finger in the blood, and sprinkle of the blood seven times before the LORD, before the vail of the sanctuary.

4:7 Ex 30:10 Lev 8:15

7 And the priest shall put *some* of the blood upon the horns of the altar of sweet incense before the LORD, which *is* in the tabernacle of the congregation; and shall pour all the blood of the bullock at the bottom of the altar of the burnt offering, which *is at* the door of the tabernacle of the congregation.

4:8 Lev 3:3

8 And he shall take off from it all the fat of the bullock for the sin offering; the fat that covereth the inwards, and all the fat that *is* upon the inwards,

9 And the two kidneys, and the fat that *is* upon them, which *is* by the flanks, and the caul above the liver, with the kidneys, it shall he take away,

10 As it was taken off from the bullock of the sacrifice of peace offerings: and the priest shall burn them upon the altar of the burnt offering.

4:11 Ex 29:14 Lev 6:11 Num 19:9 Heb 13:11

11 And the skin of the bullock, and all his flesh, with his head, and with his legs, and his inwards, and his dung,

12 Even the whole bullock shall he carry forth without the camp unto a clean place, where the ashes are poured out, and burn him on the wood with fire: where the ashes are poured out shall he be burnt.

2. Offering for National Sin

4:13☆ Num 15:23–26 1 Sam 14:32–34

13 ¶And if the whole congregation of Israel sin through ignorance, and the thing be hid from the eyes of the assembly, and they have done *somewhat against* any of the commandments of the LORD *concerning things* which should not be done, and are guilty;

4:14 Lev 4:3

14 When the sin, which they have sinned against it, is known, then the congregation shall offer a young bullock for the sin, and bring him before the tabernacle of the congregation.

4:15 Lev 8:14 Num 8:10–12

15 And the elders of the congregation shall lay their hands upon the head of the bullock before the LORD: and the bullock shall be killed before the LORD.

16 And the priest that is anointed shall bring of the bullock's blood to the tabernacle of the congregation:

4:3ff The Old Testament animal sacrifices prefigured Christ's sacrifice at Calvary. The sin offering spoken of here: (1) vindicated God's justice, i.e., it met the just demands of the Law (Heb. 10:10–12); (2) had to be a perfect animal (Christ was the sinless or perfect servant—Heb. 7:28); (3) was a substitute for the person offering the sin offering (Christ was our substitute who bore our sins—1 Pet. 2:24; 2 Cor. 5:21); and (4) took away the guilt and penalty of the sin. Sin offerings took care of specific sins. Once an animal was sacrificed, the sin or sins were forgiven. Burnt offerings, on the other hand, did not have to do with specific sins. Rather, they signified complete surrender to God and gave standing in God's sight. These two types of offerings were complementary.

4:13 Israel was a theocracy at this time. The point made here is that the nation's leaders, through lack of complete understanding of the law of God, might lead the nation astray. When the error was discovered, in order that wrath might not come upon the whole nation, a sin offering was to be presented before the Lord. Forgiveness would come and the wrath of God would not fall on the nation. Note that unwitting sin is talked of here; that is, sin which was not of a deliberate sort. If a nation, then or now, sins deliberately, the judgment of God can be executed for the sake of God's righteousness.

17 And the priest shall dip his finger *in some* of the blood, and sprinkle *it* **4:17** Lev 4:6
seven times before the LORD, *even* before the vail.
18 And he shall put *some* of the blood upon the horns of the altar which *is*
before the LORD, that *is* in the tabernacle of the congregation, and shall
pour out all the blood at the bottom of the altar of the burnt offering, which
is at the door of the tabernacle of the congregation.
19 And he shall take all his fat from him, and burn *it* upon the altar. **4:19** Lev 4:8
20 And he shall do with the bullock as he did with the bullock for a sin **4:20** Num 15:25
offering, so shall he do with this: and the priest shall make an atonement
for them, and it shall be forgiven them.
21 And he shall carry forth the bullock without the camp, and burn him as **4:21** Lev 4:11
he burned the first bullock: it *is* a sin offering for the congregation.

3. Offering for Ruler's Sins

22 ¶When a ruler hath sinned, and done *somewhat* through ignorance ☆**4:22** Lev 4:2, 13
against any of the commandments of the LORD his God *concerning things*
which should not be done, and is guilty;
23 Or if his sin, wherein he hath sinned, come to his knowledge; he shall
bring his offering, a kid of the goats, a male without blemish:
24 And he shall lay his hand upon the head of the goat, and kill it in the **4:24** Lev 6:25–30
place where they kill the burnt offering before the LORD: it *is* a sin offering. 9:2–11
25 And the priest shall take of the blood of the sin offering with his finger, **4:25** Lev 4:7
and put *it* upon the horns of the altar of burnt offering, and shall pour out
his blood at the bottom of the altar of burnt offering.
26 And he shall burn all his fat upon the altar, as the fat of the sacrifice of **4:26** Lev 4:8–12
peace offerings: and the priest shall make an atonement for him as
concerning his sin, and it shall be forgiven him.

4. Offering for Sins of Common People

27 ¶And if any one of the common people sin through ignorance, while he ☆**4:27** Lev 4:23
doeth *somewhat against* any of the commandments of the LORD *concerning*
things which ought not to be done, and be guilty;
28 Or if his sin, which he hath sinned, come to his knowledge: then he **4:28** Lev 1:2–4
shall bring his offering, a kid of the goats, a female without blemish, for his
sin which he hath sinned.
29 And he shall lay his hand upon the head of the sin offering, and slay the
sin offering in the place of the burnt offering.
30 And the priest shall take of the blood thereof with his finger, and put *it* **4:30** Lev 9:9–11
upon the horns of the altar of burnt offering, and shall pour out all the
blood thereof at the bottom of the altar.
31 And he shall take away all the fat thereof, as the fat is taken away from **4:31** Gen 8:21
off the sacrifice of peace offerings; and the priest shall burn *it* upon the altar Ex 29:18
for a sweet savour unto the LORD; and the priest shall make an atonement Lev 2:2; 4:8; 6:15
for him, and it shall be forgiven him.
32 And if he bring a lamb for a sin offering, he shall bring it a female **4:32** Lev 4:28
without blemish.
33 And he shall lay his hand upon the head of the sin offering, and slay it
for a sin offering in the place where they kill the burnt offering.

4:22 When a ruler sinned unwittingly, the sin was not to be covered over when discovered. It was to be atoned for by a sin offering; then the sin would be forgiven and God appeased.

4:27 God is no respecter of persons. Sin is sin whether committed by a nation, a ruler, a religious leader, or a common man. Here we read that God speaks of the atonement required on behalf of an individual who has unwittingly committed a trespass against the law of God. The individual cannot hide his transgression. It must be admitted, confessed by the sin offering, and thus remedied that judgment might be averted.

34 And the priest shall take of the blood of the sin offering with his finger, and put *it* upon the horns of the altar of burnt offering, and shall pour out all the blood thereof at the bottom of the altar:

4:35 Lev 3:3

35 And he shall take away all the fat thereof, as the fat of the lamb is taken away from the sacrifice of the peace offerings; and the priest shall burn them upon the altar, according to the offerings made by fire unto the LORD: and the priest shall make an atonement for his sin that he hath committed, and it shall be forgiven him.

5. Actions Calling for a Sin Offering

5:1☆ Prov 29:24

5 AND if a soul sin, and hear the voice of swearing, and *is* a witness, whether he hath seen or known *of it;* if he do not utter *it,* then he shall bear his iniquity.

5:2 Lev 11:4–11, 24–39 Num 19:11–16 Deut 14:3–21 Hag 2:13

2 Or if a soul touch any unclean thing, whether *it be* a carcase of an unclean beast, or a carcase of unclean cattle, or the carcase of unclean creeping things, and *if* it be hidden from him; he also shall be unclean, and guilty.

3 Or if he touch the uncleanness of man, whatsoever uncleanness *it be* that a man shall be defiled withal, and it be hid from him; when he knoweth *of it,* then he shall be guilty.

5:4 Judg 11:31 1 Sam 14:24, 25 Acts 23:12

4 Or if a soul swear, pronouncing with *his* lips to do evil, or to do good, whatsoever *it be* that a man shall pronounce with an oath, and it be hid from him; when he knoweth *of it,* then he shall be guilty in one of these.

5:5☆ Lev 16:21 Num 5:7 Josh 7:19 Ezra 10:11

5 And it shall be, when he shall be guilty in one of these *things,* that he shall confess that he hath sinned in that *thing:*

5:6 Lev 4:28, 32 7:1–10

6 And he shall bring his trespass offering unto the LORD for his sin which he hath sinned, a female from the flock, a lamb or a kid of the goats, for a sin offering; and the priest shall make an atonement for him concerning his sin.

6. Special Regulations for the Poor

5:7☆ Lev 12:8 14:21, 22 Lk 2:24

7 And if he be not able to bring a lamb, then he shall bring for his trespass, which he hath committed, two turtledoves, or two young pigeons, unto the LORD; one for a sin offering, and the other for a burnt offering.

5:8 Lev 1:15–17

8 And he shall bring them unto the priest, who shall offer *that* which *is* for the sin offering first, and wring off his head from his neck, but shall not divide *it* asunder:

5:9 Lev 4:7; 7:2

9 And he shall sprinkle of the blood of the sin offering upon the side of the altar; and the rest of the blood shall be wrung out at the bottom of the altar: it *is* a sin offering.

5:1 Jewish justice differed from English common law, in which a man is not obligated to testify against himself. In the Jewish judicial system, witnesses *and* the accused person were obligated to swear to tell the truth, the whole truth, and nothing but the truth. If a witness and/or the accused then lied, each "shall bear his iniquity." In Matt. 26:63, we read that when the high priest adjured Christ "by the living God, that thou tell us whether thou be the Christ, the Son of God," Jesus broke his silence, answering, "Yes, I am."† Thus Jesus, in this instance, subjected himself fully and without reservation to the law of God and so fully kept the law.

5:5 Confession of sin is essential in the Christian life. God requires it of those who have sinned (5:5; Hos. 5:15). Without repentance and confession, forgiveness is not possible. The New Testament calls believers to confession (James 5:16; 1 John 1:9). With it comes the assurance of forgiveness and cleansing. Biblical confession includes: (1) godly sorrow (Ps. 38:18); (2) self-abasement (Jer. 3:25); (3) prayer for forgiveness (Ps. 51:1); (4) restitution where necessary (Num. 5:6, 7); (5) acceptance of God's punishment (Ezra 9:13; Neh. 9:33); and (6) a turning away from sin (Prov. 28:13). The prodigal son and the tax collector are two examples of men who confessed and were forgiven.

5:7 God had respect for the poor. Thus he allowed for those who were poor to substitute a turtledove or pigeon for sin and burnt offerings, in place of a lamb. When presenting Jesus at the temple, Mary and Joseph brought no lamb, because they were poor. They substituted turtledoves or pigeons instead (Luke 2:24).

10And he shall offer the second *for* a burnt offering, according to the **5:10**
manner: and the priest shall make an atonement for him for his sin which Lev 1:14–17
he hath sinned, and it shall be forgiven him.
11¶But if he be not able to bring two turtledoves, or two young pigeons, **5:11**
then he that sinned shall bring for his offering the tenth part of an ephah of Lev 14:21 Num 15:3–9
fine flour for a sin offering; he shall put no oil upon it, neither shall he put 5:15
any frankincense thereon: for it *is* a sin offering.
12Then shall he bring it to the priest, and the priest shall take his handful **5:12**
of it, *even* a memorial thereof, and burn *it* on the altar, according to the Lev 6:25–30
offerings made by fire unto the LORD: it *is* a sin offering.
13And the priest shall make an atonement for him as touching his sin that
he hath sinned in one of these, and it shall be forgiven him: and *the remnant*
shall be the priest's, as a meat offering.

E. THE GUILT OFFERING

14¶And the LORD spake unto Moses, saying,
15If a soul commit a trespass, and sin through ignorance, in the holy **5:15**
things of the LORD; then he shall bring for his trespass unto the LORD a Ex 30:13
ram without blemish out of the flocks, with thy estimation by shekels of Lev 6:6; 7:1–10 22:14–16
silver, after the shekel of the sanctuary, for a trespass offering: 27:3, 25
16And he shall make amends for the harm that he hath done in the holy ☆**5:16**
thing, and shall add the fifth part thereto, and give it unto the priest: and Lev 6:4–6 22:15; 27:13
the priest shall make an atonement for him with the ram of the trespass
offering, and it shall be forgiven him.
17¶And if a soul sin, and commit any of these things which are forbidden ☆**5:17**
to be done by the commandments of the LORD; though he wist *it* not, yet is Lev 5:17, 19
he guilty, and shall bear his iniquity.
18And he shall bring a ram without blemish out of the flock, with thy
estimation, for a trespass offering, unto the priest: and the priest shall make
an atonement for him concerning his ignorance wherein he erred and wist *it*
not, and it shall be forgiven him.
19It *is* a trespass offering: he hath certainly trespassed against the LORD.

6 AND the LORD spake unto Moses, saying,
2If a soul sin, and commit a trespass against the LORD, and lie unto ☆**6:2**
his neighbour in that which was delivered him to keep, or in fellowship, or Ex 22:7–15 Num 5:6
in a thing taken away by violence, or hath deceived his neighbour; Col 3:9
3Or have found that which was lost, and lieth concerning it, and sweareth **6:3**
falsely; in any of all these that a man doeth, sinning therein: Lev 19:12 Deut 22:1–3
4Then it shall be, because he hath sinned, and is guilty, that he shall **6:4**
restore that which he took violently away, or the thing which he hath Ex 22:1, 4, 7, 9 Lev 5:16
deceitfully gotten, or that which was delivered him to keep, or the lost thing Prov 6:31 Jer 7:9
which he found, Zech 5:4 Lk 19:8
5Or all that about which he hath sworn falsely; he shall even restore it in
the principal, and shall add the fifth part more thereto, *and* give it unto him
to whom it appertaineth, in the day of his trespass offering.

5:16 The guilt offering (trespass offering) resembled the sin offering. It differed in that the guilt offering provided for sins in which the amount of the injury could be assessed and restitution made. The principle of atonement by blood was inherent in the offering (6:7). Restitution was made to the injured party on a six-fifths basis. Bringing the offering was evidence of repentance, confession of sin, faith in the blood of the slain sacrifice, and the certainty of forgiveness for the wrong act. In Isa. 53:10 the word translated as "an offering for sin" literally means "trespass (or guilt) offering" *(asham).*

5:17 See note to 4:2.

6:2 *hath deceived his neighbor.* Some read this as: "has deceitfully oppressed his neighbor." 6:4 speaks of what is violently taken or deceitfully obtained. Any and all forms of oppression of one's neighbor were forbidden by God, required a trespass offering for forgiveness, and were to be restored in the principal with a 20 percent addition.

6:6 Lev 5:15, 18

6 And he shall bring his trespass offering unto the LORD, a ram without blemish out of the flock, with thy estimation, for a trespass offering, unto the priest:

7 And the priest shall make an atonement for him before the LORD: and it shall be forgiven him for any thing of all that he hath done in trespassing therein.

F. PRIESTLY INSTRUCTIONS ABOUT VARIOUS OFFERINGS
1. The Burnt Offering

8 ¶And the LORD spake unto Moses, saying,

6:9 Ex 29:38–42 Lev 1:2–17 6:12, 13 Num 28:1–25

9 Command Aaron and his sons, saying, This *is* the law of the burnt offering: It *is* the burnt offering, because of the burning upon the altar all night unto the morning, and the fire of the altar shall be burning in it.

6:10 Ex 28:39–43 Lev 16:4

10 And the priest shall put on his linen garment, and his linen breeches shall he put upon his flesh, and take up the ashes which the fire hath consumed with the burnt offering on the altar, and he shall put them beside the altar.

6:11 Lev 16:23–25

11 And he shall put off his garments, and put on other garments, and carry forth the ashes without the camp unto a clean place.

6:12 Lev 3:3; 6:9

12 And the fire upon the altar shall be burning in it; it shall not be put out: and the priest shall burn wood on it every morning, and lay the burnt offering in order upon it; and he shall burn thereon the fat of the peace offerings.

6:13☆ Ex 27:20, 21 Lev 6:9, 12 24:1–4

13 The fire shall ever be burning upon the altar; it shall never go out.

2. The Meat (Grain) Offering

6:14 Lev 2:1–16

14 ¶And this *is* the law of the meat offering: the sons of Aaron shall offer it before the LORD, before the altar.

6:15 Lev 2:1, 2, 9

15 And he shall take of it his handful, of the flour of the meat offering, and of the oil thereof, and all the frankincense which *is* upon the meat offering, and shall burn *it* upon the altar *for* a sweet savour, *even* the memorial of it, unto the LORD.

6:16 Lev 10:12–15 Num 18:8–11

16 And the remainder thereof shall Aaron and his sons eat: with unleavened bread shall it be eaten in the holy place; in the court of the tabernacle of the congregation they shall eat it.

6:17 Ex 29:33, 34, 37 Lev 2:11 6:26, 29; 10:17

17 It shall not be baken with leaven. I have given it *unto them for* their portion of my offerings made by fire; it *is* most holy, as *is* the sin offering, and as the trespass offering.

6:18 Lev 6:29 Num 18:10 1 Cor 9:13

18 All the males among the children of Aaron shall eat of it. *It shall be* a statute for ever in your generations concerning the offerings of the LORD made by fire: every one that toucheth them shall be holy.

6:19 Ex 29:40 Lev 8:12

19 ¶And the LORD spake unto Moses, saying,

20 This *is* the offering of Aaron and of his sons, which they shall offer unto the LORD in the day when he is anointed; the tenth part of an ephah of fine flour for a meat offering perpetual, half of it in the morning, and half thereof at night.

6:21 Lev 2:5, 8; 7:9

21 In a pan it shall be made with oil; *and when it is* baken, thou shalt bring it in: *and* the baken pieces of the meat offering shalt thou offer *for* a sweet savour unto the LORD.

6:13 The fire for the burnt offering came down from God supernaturally and was never to go out. The supernatural origin of the altar fire meant, in effect, that only by the grace of God were sacrifices acceptable for atonement. Man-made fire was forbidden. The sin of bringing unholy (man-made) fire to the altar resulted in the deaths of Nadab and Abihu (10:1, 2).

22 And the priest of his sons that is anointed in his stead shall offer it: *it is*
a statute for ever unto the LORD; it shall be wholly burnt.
23 For every meat offering for the priest shall be wholly burnt: it shall not
be eaten.

3. The Sin Offering

24 ¶And the LORD spake unto Moses, saying,
25 Speak unto Aaron and to his sons, saying, This *is* the law of the sin
offering: In the place where the burnt offering is killed shall the sin offering
be killed before the LORD: it *is* most holy.
26 The priest that offereth it for sin shall eat it: in the holy place shall it be
eaten, in the court of the tabernacle of the congregation.
27 Whatsoever shall touch the flesh thereof shall be holy: and when there
is sprinkled of the blood thereof upon any garment, thou shalt wash that
whereon it was sprinkled in the holy place.
28 But the earthen vessel wherein it is sodden shall be broken: and if it be
sodden in a brasen pot, it shall be both scoured, and rinsed in water.
29 All the males among the priests shall eat thereof: it *is* most holy.
30 And no sin offering, whereof *any* of the blood is brought into the
tabernacle of the congregation to reconcile *withal* in the holy *place*, shall be
eaten: it shall be burnt in the fire.

4. The Trespass Offering

7 LIKEWISE this *is* the law of the trespass offering: it *is* most holy.
2 In the place where they kill the burnt offering shall they kill the
trespass offering: and the blood thereof shall he sprinkle round about upon
the altar.
3 And he shall offer of it all the fat thereof; the rump, and the fat that
covereth the inwards,
4 And the two kidneys, and the fat that *is* on them, which *is* by the flanks,
and the caul *that is* above the liver, with the kidneys, it shall he take away:
5 And the priest shall burn them upon the altar *for* an offering made by
fire unto the LORD: it *is* a trespass offering.
6 Every male among the priests shall eat thereof: it shall be eaten in the
holy place: it *is* most holy.
7 As the sin offering *is*, so *is* the trespass offering: *there is* one law for
them: the priest that maketh atonement therewith shall have *it*.
8 And the priest that offereth any man's burnt offering, *even* the priest
shall have to himself the skin of the burnt offering which he hath offered.
9 And all the meat offering that is baken in the oven, and all that is
dressed in the fryingpan, and in the pan, shall be the priest's that offereth it.
10 And every meat offering, mingled with oil, and dry, shall all the sons of
Aaron have, one *as much* as another.

6:22, 23 Ex 29:25
6:25 Lev 4:24, 29
☆6:27 Ex 29:37 30:29, 30 Lev 6:18
6:28 Lev 11:33; 15:12
6:29 Lev 6:18 Num 18:10
6:30 Lev 16:27 Heb 9:11; 13:11
7:1 Lev 5:14–19 6:1–7 Num 6:12
7:2 Lev 4:29
7:3 Lev 3:3, 9
☆7:6 Lev 6:18, 29 Num 18:10 1 Cor 9:13; 10:18
7:7 Lev 14:13
☆7:8
7:9 Lev 2:5, 8 Num 18:9 Ezek 44:29

6:27 The blood of the sin offering is representative of Christ. It is so precious that any garment which was stained by it had to be washed in a holy place to remove the stain. So Christ's blood shall not be counted common. It is to be sprinkled on our consciences. (Heb. 10:22) Thus we are cleansed and forgiven.
7:6 The meat of the trespass offering was to be eaten only by the priests and in the holy place. Whoever offered a peace offering could eat of the meat along with the priests. The peace offering symbolized thanksgiving for mercy and could be eaten by the offerer. But since the trespass offering signified sorrow for sin, fasting was more proper. It was a time for holy mourning and for a resolve to abstain from sin in the future.
7:8 *the priest shall have the skin.* Money could be earned from selling the skin. Some think this provision goes back to Adam who, as a priest, offered the animal-sacrifice and then received from God the skin to use for clothing for himself and for his wife.

5. Special Peace Offerings

7:11 Lev 3:1–17; 22:21–25; Ezek 45:15

11 And this *is* the law of the sacrifice of peace offerings, which he shall offer unto the LORD.

7:12 Lev 2:4; Num 6:15

12 If he offer it for a thanksgiving, then he shall offer with the sacrifice of thanksgiving unleavened cakes mingled with oil, and unleavened wafers anointed with oil, and cakes mingled with oil, of fine flour, fried.

7:13 Lev 2:12; 23:17

13 Besides the cakes, he shall offer *for* his offering leavened bread with the sacrifice of thanksgiving of his peace offerings.

7:14 Ex 29:27

14 And of it he shall offer one out of the whole oblation *for* an heave offering unto the LORD, *and* it shall be the priest's that sprinkleth the blood of the peace offerings.

7:15 Lev 22:29, 30

15 And the flesh of the sacrifice of his peace offerings for thanksgiving shall be eaten the same day that it is offered; he shall not leave any of it until the morning.

7:16 Lev 19:5–8; 22:18–21

16 But if the sacrifice of his offering *be* a vow, or a voluntary offering, it shall be eaten the same day that he offereth his sacrifice: and on the morrow also the remainder of it shall be eaten:

7:17 Ex 29:14

17 But the remainder of the flesh of the sacrifice on the third day shall be burnt with fire.

18 And if *any* of the flesh of the sacrifice of his peace offerings be eaten at all on the third day, it shall not be accepted, neither shall it be imputed unto him that offereth it: it shall be an abomination, and the soul that eateth of it shall bear his iniquity.

7:19 Lev 11:47

19 And the flesh that toucheth any unclean *thing* shall not be eaten; it shall be burnt with fire: and as for the flesh, all that be clean shall eat thereof.

7:20 Gen 17:14; Lev 22:3–7; Num 19:13; 1 Cor 11:27, 28

20 But the soul that eateth *of* the flesh of the sacrifice of peace offerings, that *pertain* unto the LORD, having his uncleanness upon him, even that soul shall be cut off from his people.

7:21 Lev 5:2, 3; Deut 14:8

21 Moreover the soul that shall touch any unclean *thing*, *as* the uncleanness of man, or *any* unclean beast, or any abominable unclean *thing*, and eat of the flesh of the sacrifice of peace offerings, which *pertain* unto the LORD, even that soul shall be cut off from his people.

6. Forbidden Food

22 ¶And the LORD spake unto Moses, saying,

7:23☆ Lev 3:17

23 Speak unto the children of Israel, saying, Ye shall eat no manner of fat, of ox, or of sheep, or of goat.

7:24 Ex 22:31; Lev 17:15; Deut 14:21

24 And the fat of the beast that dieth of itself, and the fat of that which is torn with beasts, may be used in any other use: but ye shall in no wise eat of it.

25 For whosoever eateth the fat of the beast, of which men offer an offering made by fire unto the LORD, even the soul that eateth *it* shall be cut off from his people.

7:26☆ Gen 9:4; Lev 3:17; 17:10–14; Ezek 33:25; John 6:53; Acts 15:20, 29

26 Moreover ye shall eat no manner of blood, *whether it be* of fowl or of beast, in any of your dwellings.

7:23 The eating of fat was forbidden. It appears, however, that this prohibition applied only to oxen, sheep, and goats—the animals which were offered as sacrifices. The fat of the roebuck, the hart, and of other clean beasts could be eaten. The fat of the inwards of those animals offered for sacrifice were to be burned, not eaten. The Jews had this rule of thumb: "If a man eat so much as an olive of forbidden fat—if he do it presumptuously, he is in danger of being cut off by the hand of God—if he do it ignorantly, he is to bring a sin-offering, and so to pay dearly for his carelessness."*

7:26 *eat no manner of blood.* This was God's express commandment, since blood represented the loss of life (Gen. 9:4) and was to be used as an atonement and for nothing else. It was never to be eaten or drunk. Some cultists believe that this commandment forbids blood transfusions. Transfusions, however, are not forbidden; rather, they serve as a wonderful illustration of the life-giving power of Christ's blood in atonement for us.

27 Whatsoever soul *it be* that eateth any manner of blood, even that soul
shall be cut off from his people.

7. Portions of Meat for the Priests

28 ¶And the LORD spake unto Moses, saying,
29 Speak unto the children of Israel, saying, He that offereth the sacrifice 7:29
of his peace offerings unto the LORD shall bring his oblation unto the LORD Ezek 45:15
of the sacrifice of his peace offerings.
30 His own hands shall bring the offerings of the LORD made by fire, the 7:30
fat with the breast, it shall he bring, that the breast may be waved *for* a Ex 29:24, 27 Lev 8:27; 9:21
wave offering before the LORD. Num 6:20
31 And the priest shall burn the fat upon the altar: but the breast shall be 7:31
Aaron's and his sons'. Lev 7:34 Num 18:18
32 And the right shoulder shall ye give unto the priest *for* an heave offering 7:32
of the sacrifices of your peace offerings. Num 18:18
33 He among the sons of Aaron, that offereth the blood of the peace
offerings, and the fat, shall have the right shoulder for *his* part.
34 For the wave breast and the heave shoulder have I taken of the children 7:34
of Israel from off the sacrifices of their peace offerings, and have given them Ex 29:28 Lev 7:31; 10:14,
unto Aaron the priest and unto his sons by a statute for ever from among 15
the children of Israel. Deut 18:3
35 ¶This *is the portion* of the anointing of Aaron, and of the anointing of ☆7:35
his sons, out of the offerings of the LORD made by fire, in the day *when* he
presented them to minister unto the LORD in the priest's office;
36 Which the LORD commanded to be given them of the children of Israel, 7:36
in the day that he anointed them, *by* a statute for ever throughout their Ex 29:22–34 40:13–15
generations.

8. Summary

37 This *is* the law of the burnt offering, of the meat offering, and of the sin
offering, and of the trespass offering, and of the consecrations, and of the
sacrifice of the peace offerings;
38 Which the LORD commanded Moses in mount Si'nai, in the day that he 7:38
commanded the children of Israel to offer their oblations unto the LORD, in Lev 26:46
the wilderness of Si'nai.

II. REGULATIONS CONCERNING THE PRIESTHOOD (8:1—10:20)

A. THE CONSECRATION OF PRIESTS

1. Anointing the Priests

8 AND the LORD spake unto Moses, saying, 8:1
2 Take Aaron and his sons with him, and the garments, and the Ex 29:1–4 8:2
anointing oil, and a bullock for the sin offering, and two rams, and a basket Ex 28:1
of unleavened bread;
3 And gather thou all the congregation together unto the door of the
tabernacle of the congregation.
4 And Moses did as the LORD commanded him; and the assembly was
gathered together unto the door of the tabernacle of the congregation.

7:35, 36 The Levites were given no land in Canaan. Thus they had no means by which they could support themselves and their families. So God made provision for them who serve at the altar by giving them the fruit of the altar. The priesthood was to be well-paid and well-provided for. Likewise the people of God today are under an indispensable obligation to provide for the support of those who give themselves to the service of God.

5 And Moses said unto the congregation, This *is* the thing which the LORD commanded to be done.

8:6 Ex 29:3, 4

6 And Moses brought Aaron and his sons, and washed them with water.

7 And he put upon him the coat, and girded him with the girdle, and clothed him with the robe, and put the ephod upon him, and he girded him with the curious girdle of the ephod, and bound *it* unto him therewith.

8:8☆ Ex 28:30, 31; Ezra 2:62, 63

8 And he put the breastplate upon him: also he put in the breastplate the U'rim and the Thum'mim.

8:9 Ex 28:4, 36–38; 29:6; 39:27–31; Zech 6:11–14

9 And he put the mitre upon his head; also upon the mitre, *even* upon his forefront, did he put the golden plate, the holy crown; as the LORD commanded Moses.

8:10 Ex 30:26–33; 40:9–11

10 And Moses took the anointing oil, and anointed the tabernacle and all that *was* therein, and sanctified them.

8:11 Ex 29:37; Lev 16:14

11 And he sprinkled thereof upon the altar seven times, and anointed the altar and all his vessels, both the laver and his foot, to sanctify them.

8:12 Ex 28:41; 30:30; Lev 21:10–12

12 And he poured of the anointing oil upon Aaron's head, and anointed him, to sanctify him.

8:13 Ex 28:36–38

13 And Moses brought Aaron's sons, and put coats upon them, and girded them with girdles, and put bonnets upon them; as the LORD commanded Moses.

2. The Bull for the Sin Offering

8:14 Ex 29:10–14; Lev 16:6

14 And he brought the bullock for the sin offering: and Aaron and his sons laid their hands upon the head of the bullock for the sin offering.

8:15☆ Ex 30:10; Lev 4:7

15 And he slew *it;* and Moses took the blood, and put *it* upon the horns of the altar round about with his finger, and purified the altar, and poured the blood at the bottom of the altar, and sanctified it, to make reconciliation upon it.

16 And he took all the fat that *was* upon the inwards, and the caul *above* the liver, and the two kidneys, and their fat, and Moses burned *it* upon the altar.

8:17 Lev 4:11; Num 19:9

17 But the bullock, and his hide, his flesh, and his dung, he burnt with fire without the camp; as the LORD commanded Moses.

3. The Ram for the Burnt Offering

8:18 Ex 29:15–19

18 ¶And he brought the ram for the burnt offering: and Aaron and his sons laid their hands upon the head of the ram.

19 And he killed *it;* and Moses sprinkled the blood upon the altar round about.

20 And he cut the ram into pieces; and Moses burnt the head, and the pieces, and the fat.

21 And he washed the inwards and the legs in water; and Moses burnt the whole ram upon the altar: it *was* a burnt sacrifice for a sweet savour, *and* an offering made by fire unto the LORD; as the LORD commanded Moses.

4. The Ram of Consecration

8:22 Ex 29:31; 8:23 Ex 29:19, 20

22 ¶And he brought the other ram, the ram of consecration: and Aaron and his sons laid their hands upon the head of the ram.

8:8 *the Urim and the Thummim.* These were apparently a kind of sacred lot used to determine the Lord's will by simple "yes" or "no" alternatives.† (See also note to Exo. 28:30).

8:15 Herein we see the formal institution of the Aaronic priesthood, with Moses acting as the priest. Moses inducted the priests into their office. Before they could function, blood atonement had to be made and the priests needed to be sanctified so that their service at the altar would be holy unto God.

23 And he slew *it;* and Moses took of the blood of it, and put *it* upon the tip of Aaron's right ear, and upon the thumb of his right hand, and upon the great toe of his right foot.

24 And he brought Aaron's sons, and Moses put of the blood upon the tip of their right ear, and upon the thumbs of their right hands, and upon the great toes of their right feet: and Moses sprinkled the blood upon the altar round about.

25 And he took the fat, and the rump, and all the fat that *was* upon the inwards, and the caul *above* the liver, and the two kidneys, and their fat, and the right shoulder:

8:25 Ex 29:22 Lev 3:9–11

26 And out of the basket of unleavened bread, that *was* before the LORD, he took one unleavened cake, and a cake of oiled bread, and one wafer, and put *them* on the fat, and upon the right shoulder:

8:26 Ex 29:23

27 And he put all upon Aaron's hands, and upon his sons' hands, and waved them *for* a wave offering before the LORD.

8:27 Ex 29:24

28 And Moses took them from off their hands, and burnt *them* on the altar upon the burnt offering: they *were* consecrations for a sweet savour: it *is* an offering made by fire unto the LORD.

8:28 Ex 29:25

29 And Moses took the breast, and waved it *for* a wave offering before the LORD: *for* of the ram of consecration it was Moses' part; as the LORD commanded Moses.

8:29 Ex 29:26 Lev 8:22

30 And Moses took of the anointing oil, and of the blood which *was* upon the altar, and sprinkled *it* upon Aaron, *and* upon his garments, and upon his sons, and upon his sons' garments with him; and sanctified Aaron, *and* his garments, and his sons, and his sons' garments with him.

8:30 Ex 29:21

5. The Seven-day Stay in the Tabernacle

31 ¶And Moses said unto Aaron and to his sons, Boil the flesh *at* the door of the tabernacle of the congregation: and there eat it with the bread that *is* in the basket of consecrations, as I commanded, saying, Aaron and his sons shall eat it.

8:31 Ex 29:31, 32 1 Sam 2:12–17

32 And that which remaineth of the flesh and of the bread shall ye burn with fire.

8:32 Lev 7:17, 18

33 And ye shall not go out of the door of the tabernacle of the congregation *in* seven days, until the days of your consecration be at an end: for seven days shall he consecrate you.

☆**8:33** Ex 29:35

34 As he hath done this day, *so* the LORD hath commanded to do, to make an atonement for you.

35 Therefore shall ye abide *at* the door of the tabernacle of the congregation day and night seven days, and keep the charge of the LORD, that ye die not: for so I am commanded.

8:35 Lev 8:33

36 So Aaron and his sons did all things which the LORD commanded by the hand of Moses.

B. THE SACRIFICES OF THE HIGH PRIEST AARON

1. Aaron Offers Sacrifices for the Priesthood

9 AND it came to pass on the eighth day, *that* Moses called Aaron and his sons, and the elders of Israel;

2 And he said unto Aaron, Take thee a young calf for a sin offering, and a ram for a burnt offering, without blemish, and offer *them* before the LORD.

9:2 Ex 29:24

8:33 *seven days.* The newly installed priests were not to go out of the door of the tabernacle for seven days. This symbolized the fact that they were giving themselves wholly to God. The seven days may well represent the creation days in Genesis, and they may indicate a new beginning. God was setting up an eternal priesthood which would find its ultimate fulfillment in his Son Jesus Christ.

9:3 Ezra 6:17
3 And unto the children of Israel thou shalt speak, saying, Take ye a kid
of the goats for a sin offering; and a calf and a lamb, *both* of the first year,
without blemish, for a burnt offering;
9:4☆ Ex 29:43; Lev 2:4
4 Also a bullock and a ram for peace offerings, to sacrifice before the
LORD; and a meat offering mingled with oil: for to day the LORD will
appear unto you.
5 ¶And they brought *that* which Moses commanded before the tabernacle
of the congregation: and all the congregation drew near and stood before
the LORD.
9:6 Ex 40:34; Lev 9:23
6 And Moses said, This *is* the thing which the LORD commanded that ye
should do: and the glory of the LORD shall appear unto you.
9:7 Heb 5:1–3; 7:27; 9:7
7 And Moses said unto Aaron, Go unto the altar, and offer thy sin
offering, and thy burnt offering, and make an atonement for thyself, and for
the people: and offer the offering of the people, and make an atonement for
them; as the LORD commanded.
8 ¶Aaron therefore went unto the altar, and slew the calf of the sin
offering, which *was* for himself.
9:9 Lev 4:6, 7; Heb 9:22
9 And the sons of Aaron brought the blood unto him: and he dipped his
finger in the blood, and put *it* upon the horns of the altar, and poured out
the blood at the bottom of the altar:
10 But the fat, and the kidneys, and the caul above the liver of the sin
offering, he burnt upon the altar; as the LORD commanded Moses.
11 And the flesh and the hide he burnt with fire without the camp.
12 And he slew the burnt offering; and Aaron's sons presented unto him
the blood, which he sprinkled round about upon the altar.
13 And they presented the burnt offering unto him, with the pieces
thereof, and the head: and he burnt *them* upon the altar.
14 And he did wash the inwards and the legs, and burnt *them* upon the
burnt offering on the altar.

2. Aaron Offers the People's Sacrifice and Blesses Them

9:15 Lev 4:27–31; 9:3; Heb 5:1–3; 7:27; 9:7
15 ¶And he brought the people's offering, and took the goat, which *was* the
sin offering for the people, and slew it, and offered it for sin, as the first.
9:16 Lev 1:3–10; 8:18–21
16 And he brought the burnt offering, and offered it according to the
manner.
9:17 Ex 29:38–42; Lev 2:1–16; 6:14–18
17 And he brought the meat offering, and took an handful thereof, and
burnt *it* upon the altar, beside the burnt sacrifice of the morning.
9:18 Lev 3:1–11; 7:11–18
18 He slew also the bullock and the ram *for* a sacrifice of peace offerings,
which *was* for the people: and Aaron's sons presented unto him the blood,
which he sprinkled upon the altar round about,
9:19 Lev 3:3; 9:10
19 And the fat of the bullock and of the ram, the rump, and that which
covereth *the inwards*, and the kidneys, and the caul *above* the liver:
20 And they put the fat upon the breasts, and he burnt the fat upon the
altar:
9:21 Lev 7:30, 32
21 And the breasts and the right shoulder Aaron waved *for* a wave offering
before the LORD; as Moses commanded.
9:22☆ Num 6:24–26
22 And Aaron lifted up his hand toward the people, and blessed them, and
came down from offering of the sin offering, and the burnt offering, and
peace offerings.

9:4 *for today the LORD will appear unto you.* Lest there be any doubt in the minds of the newly installed priests or in the minds of the people about the institution of the priesthood, Moses said the glory of God would appear to them. This promise was fulfilled in verse 23. At the same time, fire came from God to consume the sacrifice. Here, as always, when something new is given, there are corroborating signs and wonders from God. These acts of God established the priesthood of Aaron as coming from God, not from Moses. It was a divine institution through the human hands of Moses. **9:22** *lifted up his hand . . . and blessed them.* The

23 And Moses and Aaron went into the tabernacle of the congregation,
and came out, and blessed the people: and the glory of the LORD appeared
unto all the people.

9:23 Num 16:19, 42

24 And there came a fire out from before the LORD, and consumed upon
the altar the burnt offering and the fat: *which* when all the people saw, they
shouted, and fell on their faces.

☆**9:24** Gen 15:17 1 Kgs 18:38

3. Nadab and Abihu Offer Unholy Fire and Die

10 AND Na'dab and A-bi'hu, the sons of Aaron, took either of them
his censer, and put fire therein, and put incense thereon, and offered
strange fire before the LORD, which he commanded them not.

☆**10:1** Ex 6:23 Num 3:2

2 And there went out fire from the LORD, and devoured them, and they
died before the LORD.

10:2 Lev 16:1 Num 26:61

3 Then Moses said unto Aaron, This *is it* that the LORD spake, saying, I
will be sanctified in them that come nigh me, and before all the people I will
be glorified. And Aaron held his peace.

10:3 Ex 19:22 30:29, 30 Ezek 38:16 Rom 14:11

4 And Moses called Mish'a-el and El'za-phan, the sons of Uz'zi-el the
uncle of Aaron, and said unto them, Come near, carry your brethren from
before the sanctuary out of the camp.

10:4 Ex 6:18 Num 3:25–30

5 So they went near, and carried them in their coats out of the camp; as
Moses had said.

6 And Moses said unto Aaron, and unto E-le-a'zar and unto Ith'a-mar, his
sons, Uncover not your heads, neither rend your clothes; lest ye die, and
lest wrath come upon all the people: but let your brethren, the whole house
of Israel, bewail the burning which the LORD hath kindled.

10:6 Lev 21:1–15 Num 1:53 Deut 33:9 Josh 7:1

7 And ye shall not go out from the door of the tabernacle of the
congregation, lest ye die: for the anointing oil of the LORD *is* upon you.
And they did according to the word of Moses.

10:7 Lev 21:12

4. Alcohol Prohibited During Priestly Duties

8 ¶And the LORD spake unto Aaron, saying,

9 Do not drink wine nor strong drink, thou, nor thy sons with thee, when
ye go into the tabernacle of the congregation, lest ye die: *it shall be* a statute
for ever throughout your generations:

10 And that ye may put difference between holy and unholy, and between
unclean and clean;

11 And that ye may teach the children of Israel all the statutes which the
LORD hath spoken unto them by the hand of Moses.

☆**10:8, 9** Ezek 44:21
☆**10:10** Lev 11:47 Ezek 22:26
10:11 Deut 6:4–9 33:10

---

blessing of God is communicated to the people through the priest. His lifted hands indicated that the blessing came from God. Aaron here is a type of Christ who, at the time of his ascension, lifted up his hands and blessed them (Luke 24:50). Whoever lifts his hands to bless God's people has no power to do this on his own. He can only perform the function in the name of the Lord.

9:24 Fire has been regarded as a sacred symbol in many religions. It played a definite role in biblical faith. Fire came from the Lord (9:24). The altar had a perpetual flame (6:13). It was used by God as an instrument of vengeance (Ps. 97:3; Isa. 47:14; 66:16). Such was the case here. It appeared miraculously as in the case of the burning bush (Exod. 3:2), the plague God sent on the Egyptians (Exod. 9:23, 24), on Mount Sinai at the giving of the Law (Deut. 4:11, 36), and the destruction of the enemies of Elijah (2 Kings 1:10, 12). Christ is coming again in flaming fire (2 Thess. 1:7).

10:1 *offered strange fire before the LORD.* Their fatal error is not clearly identified. Some commentators have supposed that the prohibition against the consumption of wine by the priests who were about to enter the Tabernacle may imply that Nadab and Abihu were drunk when they committed their offense.

10:8, 9 *strong drink* must have been beer, since distilled liquors were unknown at that time.

10:10 *unclean and clean.* This is not a distinction between dirty things and clean things. It refers to that which is ceremonially unclean, i.e., not to be used in connection with the worship of God.

5. Regulations for Eating Meat (Grain) and Animal Offerings

10:12 Lev 2:1–3; 21:22 Num 3:2 12¶And Moses spake unto Aaron, and unto E-le-a'zar and unto Ith'a-
mar, his sons that were left, Take the meat offering that remaineth of the
offerings of the LORD made by fire, and eat it without leaven beside the
altar: for it *is* most holy:
10:13 Lev 16:14–18 13And ye shall eat it in the holy place, because it *is* thy due, and thy sons'
due, of the sacrifices of the LORD made by fire: for so I am commanded.
10:14 Lev 7:28–36 14And the wave breast and heave shoulder shall ye eat in a clean place;
thou, and thy sons, and thy daughters with thee: for *they be* thy due, and
thy sons' due, *which* are given out of the sacrifices of peace offerings of the
children of Israel.
10:15 Lev 7:30–34 15The heave shoulder and the wave breast shall they bring with the
offerings made by fire of the fat, to wave *it for* a wave offering before the
LORD; and it shall be thine, and thy sons' with thee, by a statute for ever;
as the LORD hath commanded.
10:16☆ 16¶And Moses diligently sought the goat of the sin offering, and, behold,
Lev 6:25–30; 9:3 10:17 it was burnt: and he was angry with E-le-a'zar and Ith'a-mar, the sons of
Lev 7:6 Aaron *which were* left *alive*, saying,
17Wherefore have ye not eaten the sin offering in the holy place, seeing it
is most holy, and *God* hath given it you to bear the iniquity of the
congregation, to make atonement for them before the LORD?
10:18 18Behold, the blood of it was not brought in within the holy *place:* ye
Lev 6:29, 30 should indeed have eaten it in the holy *place*, as I commanded.
19And Aaron said unto Moses, Behold, this day have they offered their
sin offering and their burnt offering before the LORD; and such things have
befallen me: and *if* I had eaten the sin offering to day, should it have been
accepted in the sight of the LORD?
20And when Moses heard *that*, he was content.

III. REGULATIONS ABOUT CEREMONIAL DEFILEMENT AND PURIFICATION (11:1—15:33)

A. CLEAN AND UNCLEAN FOODS

11 AND the LORD spake unto Moses and to Aaron, saying unto them,
11:2–19☆ 2Speak unto the children of Israel, saying, These *are* the beasts
Deut 14:3–21 which ye shall eat among all the beasts that *are* on the earth.
3Whatsoever parteth the hoof, and is clovenfooted, *and* cheweth the cud,
among the beasts, that shall ye eat.
11:4 4Nevertheless these shall ye not eat of them that chew the cud, or of them
Ezek 4:14 Dan 1:8 that divide the hoof: *as* the camel, because he cheweth the cud, but divideth
Mt 15:11 Acts 10:14 not the hoof; he *is* unclean unto you.
Rom 14:2, 3 5And the coney, because he cheweth the cud, but divideth not the hoof;
Heb 9:10; 13:9 he *is* unclean unto you.
6And the hare, because he cheweth the cud, but divideth not the hoof; he
is unclean unto you.
11:7 7And the swine, though he divide the hoof, and be clovenfooted, yet he
Isa 65:4; 66:3, 17 cheweth not the cud; he *is* unclean to you.

10:16 *which were left alive.* Nadab and Abihu, brothers of Eleazar and Ithamar, had lost their lives because they disobeyed God's instructions. Now Moses points out the sin of the two who are left alive and have become priests of God. They are warned not to repeat this error.

11:2, 3 The Old Testament dietary laws have been rendered obsolete by the work of Christ. Under the old covenant, the dietary regulations were based upon the following considerations: (1) some unclean birds and animals were forbidden because they fed on carrion or rotting foods; (2) pigs were associated with heathen worship and were offered to the gods of the nether world; and (3) these birds or animals were associated with objectionable connotations such as "creeping things," which were serpent-like in their movements, or bats, which lived in dark caves and hated the light. The dietary rules have changed under the new covenant.

8 Of their flesh shall ye not eat, and their carcase shall ye not touch; they
are unclean to you.

11:8 Mk 7:15, 18; Acts 10:14, 15; 1 Cor 8:8; Heb 9:10

9 ¶These shall ye eat of all that *are* in the waters: whatsoever hath fins and
scales in the waters, in the seas, and in the rivers, them shall ye eat.

☆11:9

10 And all that have not fins and scales in the seas, and in the rivers, of all
that move in the waters, and of any living thing which *is* in the waters, they
shall be an abomination unto you:
11 They shall be even an abomination unto you; ye shall not eat of their
flesh, but ye shall have their carcases in abomination.
12 Whatsoever hath no fins nor scales in the waters, that *shall be* an
abomination unto you.
13 ¶And these *are they which* ye shall have in abomination among the

☆11:13

fowls; they shall not be eaten, they *are* an abomination: the eagle, and the
ossifrage, and the ospray,
14 And the vulture, and the kite after his kind;
15 Every raven after his kind;
16 And the owl, and the night hawk, and the cuckow, and the hawk after
his kind,
17 And the little owl, and the cormorant, and the great owl,
18 And the swan, and the pelican, and the gier eagle,
19 And the stork, the heron after her kind, and the lapwing, and the bat.
20 All fowls that creep, going upon *all* four, *shall be* an abomination unto
you.
21 Yet these may ye eat of every flying creeping thing that goeth upon *all*
four, which have legs above their feet, to leap withal upon the earth;
22 *Even* these of them ye may eat; the locust after his kind, and the bald

11:22 Mt 3:4; Mk 1:6

locust after his kind, and the beetle after his kind, and the grasshopper after
his kind.
23 But all *other* flying creeping things, which have four feet, *shall be* an
abomination unto you.
24 And for these ye shall be unclean: whosoever toucheth the carcase of

☆11:24

them shall be unclean until the even.
25 And whosoever beareth *ought* of the carcase of them shall wash his

11:25 Lev 11:28, 40; Num 19:11–13

clothes, and be unclean until the even.
26 *The carcases* of every beast which divideth the hoof, and *is* not
clovenfooted, nor cheweth the cud, *are* unclean unto you: every one that
toucheth them shall be unclean.
27 And whatsoever goeth upon his paws, among all manner of beasts that
go on *all* four, those *are* unclean unto you: whoso toucheth their carcase
shall be unclean until the even.
28 And he that beareth the carcase of them shall wash his clothes, and be
unclean until the even: they *are* unclean unto you.
29 ¶These also *shall be* unclean unto you among the creeping things that
creep upon the earth; the weasel, and the mouse, and the tortoise after his
kind,
30 And the ferret, and the chameleon, and the lizard, and the snail, and
the mole.

11:9 From this we learn that under the old dispensation the Israelites were forbidden to eat shellfish, oysters, lobsters, crabs, and eels. Why they were considered unclean is not stated. The divine instructions were to be carried out, even though the reasons for them were not made plain.

11:13ff The regulations concerning the eating of fish, fowl, insects, and animal meat were not intended to remain in force forever. These ceremonial laws were superseded, according to Heb. 8:1—10:18 and in Acts 10:9ff, where God called "clean" what had been considered unclean under the old covenant. Peter needed this revelation in order to do what the Jewish law had forbidden.

11:24 *And for these ye shall be unclean,* i.e., ceremonially unclean, not dirty.

31 These *are* unclean to you among all that creep: whosoever doth touch them, when they be dead, shall be unclean until the even.

11:32 Lev 15:12

32 And upon whatsoever *any* of them, when they are dead, doth fall, it shall be unclean; whether *it be* any vessel of wood, or raiment, or skin, or sack, whatsoever vessel *it be*, wherein *any* work is done, it must be put into water, and it shall be unclean until the even; so it shall be cleansed.

11:33 Lev 6:28; 2 Tim 2:20, 21

33 And every earthen vessel, whereinto *any* of them falleth, whatsoever *is* in it shall be unclean; and ye shall break it.

34 Of all meat which may be eaten, *that* on which *such* water cometh shall be unclean: and all drink that may be drunk in every *such* vessel shall be unclean.

35 And every *thing* whereupon *any part* of their carcase falleth shall be unclean; *whether it be* oven, or ranges for pots, they shall be broken down: *for* they *are* unclean, and shall be unclean unto you.

36 Nevertheless a fountain or pit, *wherein there is* plenty of water, shall be clean: but that which toucheth their carcase shall be unclean.

37 And if *any part* of their carcase fall upon any sowing seed which is to be sown, it *shall be* clean.

38 But if *any* water be put upon the seed, and *any part* of their carcase fall thereon, it *shall be* unclean unto you.

39 And if any beast, of which ye may eat, die; he that toucheth the carcase thereof shall be unclean until the even.

11:40 Lev 11:25; 17:15; Deut 14:21; Ezek 4:14; 44:31

40 And he that eateth of the carcase of it shall wash his clothes, and be unclean until the even: he also that beareth the carcase of it shall wash his clothes, and be unclean until the even.

11:41 Lev 11:20, 23; Deut 14:19, 20

41 And every creeping thing that creepeth upon the earth *shall be* an abomination; it shall not be eaten.

42 Whatsoever goeth upon the belly, and whatsoever goeth upon *all* four, or whatsoever hath more feet among all creeping things that creep upon the earth, them ye shall not eat; for they *are* an abomination.

43 Ye shall not make yourselves abominable with any creeping thing that creepeth, neither shall ye make yourselves unclean with them, that ye should be defiled thereby.

11:44 Ex 19:6; 20:2; Lev 19:2; 20:7, 26; Isa 6:3, 4; Amos 3:3; Mt 5:48; 1 Thess 4:7; 1 Pet 1:16; Rev 4:8; 22:11

44 For I *am* the LORD your God: ye shall therefore sanctify yourselves, and ye shall be holy; for I *am* holy: neither shall ye defile yourselves with any manner of creeping thing that creepeth upon the earth.

11:45☆ Ex 20:2; Lev 22:32, 33

45 For I *am* the LORD that bringeth you up out of the land of Egypt, to be your God: ye shall therefore be holy, for I *am* holy.

46 This *is* the law of the beasts, and of the fowl, and of every living creature that moveth in the waters, and of every creature that creepeth upon the earth:

11:47 Lev 10:10; Ezek 22:26; 44:23

47 To make a difference between the unclean and the clean, and between the beast that may be eaten and the beast that may not be eaten.

B. PURIFICATION OF WOMEN FOLLOWING CHILDBIRTH

12:2☆ Lev 15:19; 18:19

12 AND the LORD spake unto Moses, saying,

2 Speak unto the children of Israel, saying, If a woman have conceived seed, and born a man child: then she shall be unclean seven days; according to the days of the separation for her infirmity shall she be unclean.

11:45 These restrictions lead us to the question whether God created creatures which he later disapproved of. It would appear that all things were perfect and good when created. But after the fall of Adam, even as a curse was placed on the serpent, so other animal life was ceremonially contaminated in the fall.

12:2 A woman who gave birth to a male child was strictly separated (isolated) for seven days. This meant that circumcision was performed on the eighth day, that is, after the mother was delivered from this

3 And in the eighth day the flesh of his foreskin shall be circumcised. **12:3**
4 And she shall then continue in the blood of her purifying three and Gen 17:12–14
thirty days; she shall touch no hallowed thing, nor come into the sanctuary, Josh 5:2–7 Lk 1:59; 2:21
until the days of her purifying be fulfilled. Phil 3:5
5 But if she bear a maid child, then she shall be unclean two weeks, as in
her separation: and she shall continue in the blood of her purifying
threescore and six days.
6 And when the days of her purifying are fulfilled, for a son, or for a **12:6**
daughter, she shall bring a lamb of the first year for a burnt offering, and a Lev 14:21, 22 Lk 2:22
young pigeon, or a turtledove, for a sin offering, unto the door of the
tabernacle of the congregation, unto the priest:
7 Who shall offer it before the LORD, and make an atonement for her; and
she shall be cleansed from the issue of her blood. This *is* the law for her that
hath born a male or a female.
8 And if she be not able to bring a lamb, then she shall bring two turtles, **12:8**
or two young pigeons; the one for the burnt offering, and the other for a sin Lev 5:7
offering: and the priest shall make an atonement for her, and she shall be 15:29–31 Lk 2:24
clean.

C. REGULATIONS CONCERNING LEPROSY

1. Priestly Diagnosis and Treatment of Leprosy among Men

13 AND the LORD spake unto Moses and Aaron, saying,
2 When a man shall have in the skin of his flesh a rising, a scab, or ☆**13:2, 3**
bright spot, and it be in the skin of his flesh *like* the plague of leprosy; then Lev 13:38; 14:56 Deut 24:8
he shall be brought unto Aaron the priest, or unto one of his sons the Lk 17:14
priests:
3 And the priest shall look on the plague in the skin of the flesh: and *when*
the hair in the plague is turned white, and the plague in sight *be* deeper than
the skin of his flesh, it *is* a plague of leprosy: and the priest shall look on
him, and pronounce him unclean.
4 If the bright spot *be* white in the skin of his flesh, and in sight *be* not
deeper than the skin, and the hair thereof be not turned white; then the
priest shall shut up *him that hath* the plague seven days:
5 And the priest shall look on him the seventh day: and, behold, *if* the
plague in his sight be at a stay, *and* the plague spread not in the skin; then
the priest shall shut him up seven days more:
6 And the priest shall look on him again the seventh day: and, behold, *if* **13:6**
the plague *be* somewhat dark, *and* the plague spread not in the skin, the Lev 11:25
priest shall pronounce him clean: it *is but* a scab: and he shall wash his
clothes, and be clean.
7 But if the scab spread much abroad in the skin, after that he hath been
seen of the priest for his cleansing, he shall be seen of the priest again:
8 And *if* the priest see that, behold, the scab spreadeth in the skin, then
the priest shall pronounce him unclean: it *is* a leprosy.

---

separation. If a female child were born, the separation was for fourteen days. It is not clear why the period was double for the female child. We must suppose that it was the will of the Lawmaker. A mother was required to be purified for thirty-three days after the birth of a male. She was to be purified for sixty-six days after the birth of a female child. During the time of purification, the mother could not come to the sanctuary, nor could she eat the Passover or peace offering. If the mother were the wife of a priest, she could not eat anything that was holy to the Lord. The child-bed situation and the need for purification emphasized the pollution of sin in which all of us are conceived and born.

13:2 *leprosy* was a term that covered a number of skin diseases. It also included molds and defects in garments (13:47–59) and in houses (14:35–53). Tetter (see 13:39), a cutaneous disease, was sometimes mistaken for leprosy.

13:9, 10☆ Num 12:10 2 Kgs 5:27

9¶When the plague of leprosy is in a man, then he shall be brought unto the priest;

10And the priest shall see *him:* and, behold, *if* the rising *be* white in the skin, and it have turned the hair white, and *there be* quick raw flesh in the rising;

11It *is* an old leprosy in the skin of his flesh, and the priest shall pronounce him unclean, and shall not shut him up: for he *is* unclean.

12And if a leprosy break out abroad in the skin, and the leprosy cover all the skin of *him that hath* the plague from his head even to his foot, wheresoever the priest looketh;

13Then the priest shall consider: and, behold, *if* the leprosy have covered all his flesh, he shall pronounce *him* clean *that hath* the plague: it is all turned white: he *is* clean.

14But when raw flesh appeareth in him, he shall be unclean.

15And the priest shall see the raw flesh, and pronounce him to be unclean: *for* the raw flesh *is* unclean: it *is* a leprosy.

16Or if the raw flesh turn again, and be changed unto white, he shall come unto the priest;

17And the priest shall see him: and, behold, *if* the plague be turned into white; then the priest shall pronounce *him* clean *that hath* the plague: he *is* clean.

13:18 Ex 9:9

18¶The flesh also, in which, *even* in the skin thereof, was a boil, and is healed,

19And in the place of the boil there be a white rising, or a bright spot, white, and somewhat reddish, and it be shewed to the priest;

20And if, when the priest seeth it, behold, it *be* in sight lower than the skin, and the hair thereof be turned white; the priest shall pronounce him unclean: it *is* a plague of leprosy broken out of the boil.

21But if the priest look on it, and, behold, *there be* no white hairs therein, and *if* it *be* not lower than the skin, but *be* somewhat dark; then the priest shall shut him up seven days:

22And if it spread much abroad in the skin, then the priest shall pronounce him unclean: it *is* a plague.

23But if the bright spot stay in his place, *and* spread not, it *is* a burning boil; and the priest shall pronounce him clean.

24¶Or if there be *any* flesh, in the skin whereof *there is* a hot burning, and the quick *flesh* that burneth have a white bright spot, somewhat reddish, or white;

25Then the priest shall look upon it: and, behold, *if* the hair in the bright spot be turned white, and it *be in* sight deeper than the skin; it *is* a leprosy broken out of the burning: wherefore the priest shall pronounce him unclean: it *is* the plague of leprosy.

26But if the priest look on it, and, behold, *there be* no white hair in the bright spot, and it *be* no lower than the *other* skin, but *be* somewhat dark; then the priest shall shut him up seven days:

13:27 Deut 24:8

27And the priest shall look upon him the seventh day: *and* if it be spread much abroad in the skin, then the priest shall pronounce him unclean: it *is* the plague of leprosy.

13:9 The diagnosis and treatment of certain diseases were responsibilities given to the priests. There is nothing in the Old Testament by which we can suppose that such responsibilities belong to the bishops or elders in the churches today. Luke was the beloved physician in the New Testament. The divine call to practice medicine is within the range of the gifts of the Holy Spirit, who endows and endues believers in all sorts of occupations for the common good of men.

28And if the bright spot stay in his place, *and* spread not in the skin, but
it *be* somewhat dark; it *is* a rising of the burning, and the priest shall
pronounce him clean: for it *is* an inflammation of the burning.
29If a man or woman have a plague upon the head or the beard;
30Then the priest shall see the plague: and, behold, if it *be* in sight deeper
than the skin; *and there be* in it a yellow thin hair; then the priest shall
pronounce him unclean: it *is* a dry scall, *even* a leprosy upon the head or
beard.
31And if the priest look on the plague of the scall, and, behold, it *be* not
in sight deeper than the skin, and *that there is* no black hair in it; then the
priest shall shut up *him that hath* the plague of the scall seven days:
32And in the seventh day the priest shall look on the plague: and, behold,
if the scall spread not, and there be in it no yellow hair, and the scall *be* not
in sight deeper than the skin;
33He shall be shaven, but the scall shall he not shave; and the priest shall **13:33** Lev 14:9
shut up *him that hath* the scall seven days more:
34And in the seventh day the priest shall look on the scall: and, behold, *if* **13:34** Lev 14:8
the scall be not spread in the skin, nor *be* in sight deeper than the skin; then
the priest shall pronounce him clean: and he shall wash his clothes, and be
clean.
35But if the scall spread much in the skin after his cleansing;
36Then the priest shall look on him: and, behold, if the scall be spread in
the skin, the priest shall not seek for yellow hair; he *is* unclean.
37But if the scall be in his sight at a stay, and *that* there is black hair
grown up therein; the scall is healed, he *is* clean: and the priest shall
pronounce him clean.
38If a man also or a woman have in the skin of their flesh bright spots,
even white bright spots;
39Then the priest shall look: and, behold, *if* the bright spots in the skin of
their flesh *be* darkish white; it *is* a freckled spot *that* groweth in the skin; he
is clean.
40And the man whose hair is fallen off his head, he *is* bald; *yet is* he clean.
41And he that hath his hair fallen off from the part of his head toward his
face, he *is* forehead bald: *yet is* he clean.
42And if there be in the bald head, or bald forehead, a white reddish sore;
it *is* a leprosy sprung up in his bald head, or his bald forehead.
43Then the priest shall look upon it: and, behold, *if* the rising of the sore
be white reddish in his bald head, or in his bald forehead, as the leprosy
appeareth in the skin of the flesh;
44He is a leprous man, he *is* unclean: the priest shall pronounce him
utterly unclean; his plague *is* in his head.
45And the leper in whom the plague *is*, his clothes shall be rent, and his ☆**13:45** Lam 4:15; Ezek 24:17, 22; Mic 3:7
head bare, and he shall put a covering upon his upper lip, and shall cry,
Unclean, unclean.
46All the days wherein the plague *shall be* in him he shall be defiled; he *is* **13:46** Num 5:1–4; 12:14; 2 Kgs 7:3; 15:5; 2 Chron 26:21; Lk 17:12
unclean: he shall dwell alone; without the camp *shall* his habitation *be*.

2. Priestly Diagnosis and Treatment of Leprosy in Garments

47¶The garment also that the plague of leprosy is in, *whether it be* a
woollen garment, or a linen garment;

13:45 Leprosy was a contagious disease and was known as such in the Old Testament. Provision was made for the separation of the contagious from general society, in order to prevent others from contracting the same disease.

48 Whether *it be* in the warp, or woof; of linen, or of woollen; whether in
a skin, or in any thing made of skin;
49 And if the plague be greenish or reddish in the garment, or in the skin,
either in the warp, or in the woof, or in any thing of skin; it *is* a plague of
leprosy, and shall be shewed unto the priest:
50 And the priest shall look upon the plague, and shut up *it that hath* the
plague seven days:
13:51 Lev 14:44 51 And he shall look on the plague on the seventh day: if the plague be
spread in the garment, either in the warp, or in the woof, or in a skin, *or* in
any work that is made of skin; the plague *is* a fretting leprosy; it *is* unclean.
52 He shall therefore burn that garment, whether warp or woof, in woollen
or in linen, or any thing of skin, wherein the plague is: for it *is* a fretting
leprosy; it shall be burnt in the fire.
53 And if the priest shall look, and, behold, the plague be not spread in the
garment, either in the warp, or in the woof, or in any thing of skin;
54 Then the priest shall command that they wash *the thing* wherein the
plague *is*, and he shall shut it up seven days more:
55 And the priest shall look on the plague, after that it is washed: and,
behold, *if* the plague have not changed his colour, and the plague be not
spread; it *is* unclean; thou shalt burn it in the fire; it *is* fret inward, *whether*
it *be* bare within or without.
56 And if the priest look, and, behold, the plague *be* somewhat dark after
the washing of it; then he shall rend it out of the garment, or out of the
skin, or out of the warp, or out of the woof:
57 And if it appear still in the garment, either in the warp, or in the woof,
or in any thing of skin; it *is* a spreading *plague:* thou shalt burn that
wherein the plague *is* with fire.
58 And the garment, either warp, or woof, or whatsoever thing of skin *it
be*, which thou shalt wash, if the plague be departed from them, then it shall
be washed the second time, and shall be clean.
13:59☆ 59 This *is* the law of the plague of leprosy in a garment of woollen or linen,
either in the warp, or woof, or any thing of skins, to pronounce it clean, or
to pronounce it unclean.

3. Regulations for Those Whose Leprosy Disappears

14 AND the LORD spake unto Moses, saying,
14:2 Mt 8:4 Mk 1:40–45 Lk 5:12–14 17:12–14 2 This shall be the law of the leper in the day of his cleansing: He
shall be brought unto the priest:
14:3 Lev 13:36 3 And the priest shall go forth out of the camp; and the priest shall look,
and, behold, *if* the plague of leprosy be healed in the leper;
14:4 Lev 14:6, 49–53 Num 19:6 4 Then shall the priest command to take for him that is to be cleansed two
birds alive *and* clean, and cedar wood, and scarlet, and hyssop:
5 And the priest shall command that one of the birds be killed in an
earthen vessel over running water:
14:6 Ps 51:7 Heb 9:19 6 As for the living bird, he shall take it, and the cedar wood, and the
scarlet, and the hyssop, and shall dip them and the living bird in the blood
of the bird *that was* killed over the running water:
14:7☆ 7 And he shall sprinkle upon him that is to be cleansed from the leprosy
seven times, and shall pronounce him clean, and shall let the living bird
loose into the open field.

13:59 The larger question in all of these instructions is why God allows sickness, disease, and such things as leprosy to afflict his own people, who have been redeemed. This happens because God has not ordained specific exceptions to his law. Even as the sun shines on the just and the unjust, so are all people, including believers, subjected to the ordinary hazards of life. They will be with us until we die.

14:7 The law of purification for deliverance from leprosy included the use of two birds. One was killed

8 And he that is to be cleansed shall wash his clothes, and shave off all his
hair, and wash himself in water, that he may be clean: and after that he
shall come into the camp, and shall tarry abroad out of his tent seven days.

14:8 Lev 14:9 Num 8:7

9 But it shall be on the seventh day, that he shall shave all his hair off his
head and his beard and his eyebrows, even all his hair he shall shave off:
and he shall wash his clothes, also he shall wash his flesh in water, and he
shall be clean.

14:9 Lev 13:33; 14:8 Num 6:9

10 And on the eighth day he shall take two he lambs without blemish, and
one ewe lamb of the first year without blemish, and three tenth deals of fine
flour *for* a meat offering, mingled with oil, and one log of oil.

14:10 Lev 23:12, 13 Num 6:14, 15

11 And the priest that maketh *him* clean shall present the man that is to be
made clean, and those things, before the LORD, *at* the door of the
tabernacle of the congregation:
12 And the priest shall take one he lamb, and offer him for a trespass
offering, and the log of oil, and wave them *for* a wave offering before the
LORD:

14:12 Ex 29:24

13 And he shall slay the lamb in the place where he shall kill the sin
offering and the burnt offering, in the holy place: for as the sin offering *is*
the priest's, *so is* the trespass offering: it *is* most holy:

14:13 Lev 1:11–13 4:4–12; 6:1—7:10

14 And the priest shall take *some* of the blood of the trespass offering, and
the priest shall put *it* upon the tip of the right ear of him that is to be
cleansed, and upon the thumb of his right hand, and upon the great toe of
his right foot:

14:14 Ex 29:19–21 Lev 8:23, 24

15 And the priest shall take *some* of the log of oil, and pour *it* into the
palm of his own left hand:
16 And the priest shall dip his right finger in the oil that *is* in his left hand,
and shall sprinkle of the oil with his finger seven times before the LORD:
17 And of the rest of the oil that *is* in his hand shall the priest put upon the
tip of the right ear of him that is to be cleansed, and upon the thumb of his
right hand, and upon the great toe of his right foot, upon the blood of the
trespass offering:
18 And the remnant of the oil that *is* in the priest's hand he shall pour
upon the head of him that is to be cleansed: and the priest shall make an
atonement for him before the LORD.

☆**14:18** Lev 8:30

19 And the priest shall offer the sin offering, and make an atonement for
him that is to be cleansed from his uncleanness; and afterward he shall kill
the burnt offering:

14:19 Lev 6:24–30

20 And the priest shall offer the burnt offering and the meat offering upon
the altar: and the priest shall make an atonement for him, and he shall be
clean.

14:20 Lev 23:12, 13

21 And if he *be* poor, and cannot get so much; then he shall take one lamb
for a trespass offering to be waved, to make an atonement for him, and one
tenth deal of fine flour mingled with oil for a meat offering, and a log of oil;

☆**14:21** Lev 5:7, 11 12:8

---

and the other dipped in the blood of the killed bird and then set free. What does this mean? "Some make the slain bird to typify Christ dying for our sins, and the living bird Christ rising again for our justification."* Believers have been sprinkled by the blood of Christ, and they have been set free from the law of sin and of death. They live to die no more, but in their living they glorify the one by whose blood they have been set free.

14:18 *make an atonement for him before the LORD.* If an atonement was required for one who had been delivered from leprosy, how much more is an atonement needed for those who have been separated from God because of their sins and need to be restored to God's fellowship.

14:21 God made provision both for the rich and for the poor. Those who were poor needed to bring one lamb, and one-tenth deal of fine flour. In place of the additional two lambs which well-to-do people brought, the poor needed only two turtledoves or two young pigeons. Under the gospel dispensation God again has respect for the poor: "My son, give me thy heart, and with that the calves of thy lips shall be accepted instead of the calves of the stall."* Mercy is deep and free. If you have nothing to bring, bring only yourself. That will be enough.

14:22 Lev 5:7 22 And two turtledoves, or two young pigeons, such as he is able to get; and the one shall be a sin offering, and the other a burnt offering.

14:23 Lev 14:11 23 And he shall bring them on the eighth day for his cleansing unto the priest, unto the door of the tabernacle of the congregation, before the LORD.

24 And the priest shall take the lamb of the trespass offering, and the log of oil, and the priest shall wave them *for* a wave offering before the LORD:

14:25 Lev 14:14 25 And he shall kill the lamb of the trespass offering, and the priest shall take *some* of the blood of the trespass offering, and put *it* upon the tip of the right ear of him that is to be cleansed, and upon the thumb of his right hand, and upon the great toe of his right foot:

26 And the priest shall pour of the oil into the palm of his own left hand:

27 And the priest shall sprinkle with his right finger *some* of the oil that *is* in his left hand seven times before the LORD:

28 And the priest shall put of the oil that *is* in his hand upon the tip of the right ear of him that is to be cleansed, and upon the thumb of his right hand, and upon the great toe of his right foot, upon the place of the blood of the trespass offering:

29 And the rest of the oil that *is* in the priest's hand he shall put upon the head of him that is to be cleansed, to make an atonement for him before the LORD.

30 And he shall offer the one of the turtledoves, or of the young pigeons, such as he can get;

31 *Even* such as he is able to get, the one *for* a sin offering, and the other *for* a burnt offering, with the meat offering: and the priest shall make an atonement for him that is to be cleansed before the LORD.

32 This *is* the law *of him* in whom *is* the plague of leprosy, whose hand is not able to get *that which pertaineth* to his cleansing.

4. Priestly Diagnosis and Treatment of Leprosy in Houses

33 ¶And the LORD spake unto Moses and unto Aaron, saying,

34 When ye be come into the land of Canaan, which I give to you for a possession, and I put the plague of leprosy in a house of the land of your possession;

14:35 Ps 91:10 Zech 5:4 35 And he that owneth the house shall come and tell the priest, saying, It seemeth to me *there is* as it were a plague in the house:

36 Then the priest shall command that they empty the house, before the priest go *into it* to see the plague, that all that *is* in the house be not made unclean: and afterward the priest shall go in to see the house:

37 And he shall look on the plague, and, behold, *if* the plague *be* in the walls of the house with hollow strakes, greenish or reddish, which in sight *are* lower than the wall;

38 Then the priest shall go out of the house to the door of the house, and shut up the house seven days:

14:39 Lev 13:6-8 39 And the priest shall come again the seventh day, and shall look: and, behold, *if* the plague be spread in the walls of the house;

40 Then the priest shall command that they take away the stones in which the plague *is*, and they shall cast them into an unclean place without the city:

41 And he shall cause the house to be scraped within round about, and they shall pour out the dust that they scrape off without the city into an unclean place:

42 And they shall take other stones, and put *them* in the place of those stones; and he shall take other morter, and shall plaister the house.

43 And if the plague come again, and break out in the house, after that he
hath taken away the stones, and after he hath scraped the house, and after
it is plaistered;
44 Then the priest shall come and look, and, behold, *if* the plague be
spread in the house, it *is* a fretting leprosy in the house: it *is* unclean.
45 And he shall break down the house, the stones of it, and the timber
thereof, and all the morter of the house; and he shall carry *them* forth out of
the city into an unclean place.
46 Moreover he that goeth into the house all the while that it is shut up
shall be unclean until the even.
47 And he that lieth in the house shall wash his clothes; and he that eateth
in the house shall wash his clothes.
48 And if the priest shall come in, and look *upon it*, and, behold, the
plague hath not spread in the house, after the house was plaistered: then
the priest shall pronounce the house clean, because the plague is healed.
49 And he shall take to cleanse the house two birds, and cedar wood, and
scarlet, and hyssop:
50 And he shall kill the one of the birds in an earthen vessel over running
water:
51 And he shall take the cedar wood, and the hyssop, and the scarlet, and
the living bird, and dip them in the blood of the slain bird, and in the
running water, and sprinkle the house seven times:
52 And he shall cleanse the house with the blood of the bird, and with the
running water, and with the living bird, and with the cedar wood, and with
the hyssop, and with the scarlet:
53 But he shall let go the living bird out of the city into the open fields, and
make an atonement for the house: and it shall be clean.
54 This *is* the law for all manner of plague of leprosy, and scall,
55 And for the leprosy of a garment, and of a house,
56 And for a rising, and for a scab, and for a bright spot:
57 To teach when *it is* unclean, and when *it is* clean: this *is* the law of
leprosy.

14:45 Lev 14:41–45

14:49 Lev 14:4–7; Num 19:6

☆**14:53**

14:57 Deut 24:8; Ezek 44:23

D. REGULATIONS CONCERNING BODILY SECRETIONS

1. Ceremonial Defilement in Man and Its Purification

15 AND the LORD spake unto Moses and to Aaron, saying,
2 Speak unto the children of Israel, and say unto them, When any
man hath a running issue out of his flesh, *because of* his issue he *is* unclean.
3 And this shall be his uncleanness in his issue: whether his flesh run with
his issue, or his flesh be stopped from his issue, it *is* his uncleanness.
4 Every bed, whereon he lieth that hath the issue, is unclean: and every
thing, whereon he sitteth, shall be unclean.
5 And whosoever toucheth his bed shall wash his clothes, and bathe
himself in water, and be unclean until the even.
6 And he that sitteth on *any* thing whereon he sat that hath the issue shall
wash his clothes, and bathe *himself* in water, and be unclean until the even.
7 And he that toucheth the flesh of him that hath the issue shall wash his
clothes, and bathe *himself* in water, and be unclean until the even.
8 And if he that hath the issue spit upon him that is clean; then he shall
wash his clothes, and bathe *himself* in water, and be unclean until the even.

15:1-3 Lev 22:4; Num 5:2

15:4 Lev 15:20–23

14:53 *an atonement for the house.* Deut. 20:5 indicates that the houses of the Israelites were dedicated. Their houses were to be kept free from ceremonial uncleanness; but when unclean, an atonement had to be made for the house. Our bodies are the houses of the Holy Spirit. Believers need to make their hearts fit for the service of the Lord by keeping them dedicated and clean.

9 And what saddle soever he rideth upon that hath the issue shall be
unclean.
10 And whosoever toucheth any thing that was under him shall be unclean
until the even: and he that beareth *any of* those things shall wash his
clothes, and bathe *himself* in water, and be unclean until the even.
11 And whomsoever he toucheth that hath the issue, and hath not rinsed
his hands in water, he shall wash his clothes, and bathe *himself* in water,
and be unclean until the even.
15:12 12 And the vessel of earth, that he toucheth which hath the issue, shall be
Lev 6:28; 11:33 broken: and every vessel of wood shall be rinsed in water.
15:13 13 And when he that hath an issue is cleansed of his issue; then he shall
Num 19:11, 12 number to himself seven days for his cleansing, and wash his clothes, and
bathe his flesh in running water, and shall be clean.
14 And on the eighth day he shall take to him two turtledoves, or two
young pigeons, and come before the LORD unto the door of the tabernacle
of the congregation, and give them unto the priest:
15:15 15 And the priest shall offer them, the one *for* a sin offering, and the other
Lev 14:22 *for* a burnt offering; and the priest shall make an atonement for him before
the LORD for his issue.
15:16 16 And if any man's seed of copulation go out from him, then he shall
Lev 15:5; 22:6 Deut 23:10, 11 wash all his flesh in water, and be unclean until the even.
17 And every garment, and every skin, whereon is the seed of copulation,
shall be washed with water, and be unclean until the even.
15:18☆ 18 The woman also with whom man shall lie *with* seed of copulation, they
Ex 19:15 1 Sam 21:4 shall *both* bathe *themselves* in water, and be unclean until the even.

2. Ceremonial Defilement in Woman and Its Purification

15:19 19 ¶And if a woman have an issue, *and* her issue in her flesh be blood, she
Lev 12:2–5 shall be put apart seven days: and whosoever toucheth her shall be unclean
until the even.
15:20 20 And every thing that she lieth upon in her separation shall be unclean:
Lev 15:4, 5 every thing also that she sitteth upon shall be unclean.
21 And whosoever toucheth her bed shall wash his clothes, and bathe
himself in water, and be unclean until the even.
22 And whosoever toucheth any thing that she sat upon shall wash his
clothes, and bathe *himself* in water, and be unclean until the even.
23 And if it *be* on *her* bed, or on any thing whereon she sitteth, when he
toucheth it, he shall be unclean until the even.
15:24 24 And if any man lie with her at all, and her flowers be upon him, he shall
Lev 15:33 18:19; 20:18 be unclean seven days; and all the bed whereon he lieth shall be unclean.
Ezek 18:6; 22:10 **15:25**☆ 25 And if a woman have an issue of her blood many days out of the time
Mt 9:20 Mk 5:25 of her separation, or if it run beyond the time of her separation; all the days
Lk 8:43, 44 of the issue of her uncleanness shall be as the days of her separation: she
shall be unclean.

15:18 Those who had sexual intercourse, or a woman who was menstruating, or a man who had a natural emission of semen became ceremonially unclean; but there was no need for them to bring an offering or make atonement. Sexual intercourse performed under the proper biblical conditions is beautiful, is the will of God, and has the divine blessing. It is the wrongful use of sex which is prohibited and which requires a sin offering.

15:25 A woman who had an issue of blood unrelated to her normal physical cycle was unclean. When she was healed of that condition, the usual sin and burnt offerings were required. While a woman had such a condition, she contaminated all that she touched. Jesus met such a woman, who was healed by touching his garment (see Luke 8:43–48). We are not told that the Savior became unclean or that an offering was required of him. The one who gave the law is above the law because he is the giver and cannot be contaminated by those who breach the law. God cannot lose his sanctity because of the sins of the people.

26 Every bed whereon she lieth all the days of her issue shall be unto her
as the bed of her separation: and whatsoever she sitteth upon shall be
unclean, as the uncleanness of her separation.
27 And whosoever toucheth those things shall be unclean, and shall wash
his clothes, and bathe *himself* in water, and be unclean until the even.
28 But if she be cleansed of her issue, then she shall number to herself
seven days, and after that she shall be clean.
29 And on the eighth day she shall take unto her two turtles, or two young
pigeons, and bring them unto the priest, to the door of the tabernacle of the
congregation.
30 And the priest shall offer the one *for* a sin offering, and the other *for* a
burnt offering; and the priest shall make an atonement for her before the
LORD for the issue of her uncleanness.
31 Thus shall ye separate the children of Israel from their uncleanness;
that they die not in their uncleanness, when they defile my tabernacle that
is among them.
32 This *is* the law of him that hath an issue, and *of him* whose seed goeth
from him, and is defiled therewith;
33 And of her that is sick of her flowers, and of him that hath an issue, of
the man, and of the woman, and of him that lieth with her that is unclean.

15:30 Lev 5:7; 14:22; 15:15
15:31 Num 5:3; 19:13, 20

IV. THE DAY OF ATONEMENT (16:1–35)

A. THE ONCE-A-YEAR OFFERING AT THE MERCY SEAT

16 AND the LORD spake unto Moses after the death of the two sons of
Aaron, when they offered before the LORD, and died;
2 And the LORD said unto Moses, Speak unto Aaron thy brother, that he
come not at all times into the holy *place* within the vail before the mercy
seat, which *is* upon the ark; that he die not: for I will appear in the cloud
upon the mercy seat.
3 Thus shall Aaron come into the holy *place:* with a young bullock for a
sin offering, and a ram for a burnt offering.
4 He shall put on the holy linen coat, and he shall have the linen breeches
upon his flesh, and shall be girded with a linen girdle, and with the linen
mitre shall he be attired: these *are* holy garments; therefore shall he wash
his flesh in water, and *so* put them on.
5 And he shall take of the congregation of the children of Israel two kids
of the goats for a sin offering, and one ram for a burnt offering.
6 And Aaron shall offer his bullock of the sin offering, which *is* for
himself, and make an atonement for himself, and for his house.
7 And he shall take the two goats, and present them before the LORD *at*
the door of the tabernacle of the congregation.

☆**16:1** Ex 25:17–22; 30:10; Lev 10:1, 2; Heb 9:7, 25
16:3 Lev 16:6, 7; Num 29:7–11
16:4 Ex 28:39–43; 39:27–29; Lev 6:10; Ezek 44:17–19
☆**16:6** Lev 9:7; Heb 5:1–3; 7:27, 28; 9:7

16:1, 2 Day of atonement. This event was celebrated once a year and was a high day for Israel. It was the only time the high priest entered the inner sanctuary, that is, when he went behind the curtain that separated the holy of holies with its mercy seat. The high priest had to enter the inner sanctuary with blood to make atonement, first for his own sins and then for the sins of the people. The sanctuary was representative of the heavenly sanctuary into which Christ entered with his own blood to make atonement for us. Whereas this event was celebrated over and over again under the old covenant, it was celebrated only once by Jesus and is a finished work which never needs to be repeated (see Heb. 9:12–28). Calvary, of course, is the place where Christ died and shed his blood.

16:6 The Hebrew word *kippūr* ("atonement") is derived from the verb kippĕr ("to atone") and means to cover over by an expiatory sacrifice. In the Old Testament animal sacrifices anticipated the great sacrifice at Calvary and provided a covering for the people of Israel. The animals were substituted for the offerers. Christ, in the New Testament, is the once-for-all substitute whose blood covers all our sins. The word used is "reconciliation" (*katallage* in Greek) and means "to effect legal and moral reparation for injury done"; this is man's offense against a holy God. The atonement makes forgiveness possible and restores to man what was lost by Adam's sin.

8 And Aaron shall cast lots upon the two goats; one lot for the LORD, and
the other lot for the scapegoat.
9 And Aaron shall bring the goat upon which the LORD's lot fell, and offer
him *for* a sin offering.
16:10☆ Isa 53:4–10 10 But the goat, on which the lot fell to be the scapegoat, shall be
presented alive before the LORD, to make an atonement with him, *and* to let
him go for a scapegoat into the wilderness.

B. THE SIN OFFERING FOR THE HIGH PRIEST AND HIS FAMILY

16:11 Lev 9:7; Heb 9:7 11 And Aaron shall bring the bullock of the sin offering, which *is* for
himself, and shall make an atonement for himself, and for his house, and
shall kill the bullock of the sin offering which *is* for himself:
16:12 Ex 30:34–38; Num 16:18, 46; Isa 6:6, 7; Rev 8:3–5 12 And he shall take a censer full of burning coals of fire from off the altar
before the LORD, and his hands full of sweet incense beaten small, and
bring *it* within the vail:
16:13 Ex 25:21; 30:1, 7, 8; Lev 22:9 13 And he shall put the incense upon the fire before the LORD, that the
cloud of the incense may cover the mercy seat that *is* upon the testimony,
that he die not:
16:14 Lev 4:17 14 And he shall take of the blood of the bullock, and sprinkle *it* with his
finger upon the mercy seat eastward; and before the mercy seat shall he
sprinkle of the blood with his finger seven times.

C. THE SIN OFFERING FOR THE PEOPLE

16:15 Heb 6:19; 9:3, 7, 12 15 ¶Then shall he kill the goat of the sin offering, that *is* for the people,
and bring his blood within the vail, and do with that blood as he did with
the blood of the bullock, and sprinkle it upon the mercy seat, and before
the mercy seat:
16:16 Ex 30:10; Ezek 45:18; Heb 9:22, 23 16 And he shall make an atonement for the holy *place,* because of the
uncleanness of the children of Israel, and because of their transgressions in
all their sins: and so shall he do for the tabernacle of the congregation, that
remaineth among them in the midst of their uncleanness.
16:17 Lk 1:10 17 And there shall be no man in the tabernacle of the congregation when
he goeth in to make an atonement in the holy *place,* until he come out, and
have made an atonement for himself, and for his household, and for all the
congregation of Israel.
16:18 Lev 4:7, 17, 25; Ezek 43:20 18 And he shall go out unto the altar that *is* before the LORD, and make an
atonement for it; and shall take of the blood of the bullock, and of the
blood of the goat, and put *it* upon the horns of the altar round about.
16:19 Lev 4:6; 16:14 19 And he shall sprinkle of the blood upon it with his finger seven times,
and cleanse it, and hallow it from the uncleanness of the children of Israel.

D. THE SENDING AWAY OF THE SCAPEGOAT

20 ¶And when he hath made an end of reconciling the holy *place,* and the
tabernacle of the congregation, and the altar, he shall bring the live goat:

16:10 *scapegoat,* literally, "for Azazel" or, "for removal." In the Scriptures two types of goats are mentioned: the first one was slain as a sin offering; the other one was placed before the Lord and then sent out into the wilderness. The Scriptures are unclear as to the meaning of this. In some manner, it is typical of Jesus Christ (Isa. 53:6, 11, 12). Some have suggested that the scapegoat is a name for Satan, but this theory has little to commend it. In the noncanonical Book of Enoch "scapegoat" is the name of a fallen angel who misled mankind. Some think the word is a reduplicated root from the Hebrew word *azal* which means "depart" or "remove." The silence of the Scriptures indicates that the whole matter must be quite incidental, for if it were not, the Holy Spirit would have given us more information.

21 And Aaron shall lay both his hands upon the head of the live goat, and
confess over him all the iniquities of the children of Israel, and all their
transgressions in all their sins, putting them upon the head of the goat, and
shall send *him* away by the hand of a fit man into the wilderness:

16:21 Lev 5:5 Num 5:7

22 And the goat shall bear upon him all their iniquities unto a land not
inhabited: and he shall let go the goat in the wilderness.

16:22 Isa 53:4–7

23 And Aaron shall come into the tabernacle of the congregation, and
shall put off the linen garments, which he put on when he went into the
holy *place,* and shall leave them there:

16:23 Ex 28:39–43 Lev 16:4

24 And he shall wash his flesh with water in the holy place, and put on his
garments, and come forth, and offer his burnt offering, and the burnt
offering of the people, and make an atonement for himself, and for the
people.

16:24 Ex 29:3–9

25 And the fat of the sin offering shall he burn upon the altar.
26 And he that let go the goat for the scapegoat shall wash his clothes, and
bathe his flesh in water, and afterward come into the camp.

16:26 Num 19:7

27 And the bullock *for* the sin offering, and the goat *for* the sin offering,
whose blood was brought in to make atonement in the holy *place,* shall *one*
carry forth without the camp; and they shall burn in the fire their skins, and
their flesh, and their dung.

16:27 Lev 4:11, 12 8:17

28 And he that burneth them shall wash his clothes, and bathe his flesh in
water, and afterward he shall come into the camp.

16:28 Lev 16:26

E. THE DAY OF ATONEMENT, A PERMANENT LAW

29 ¶And *this* shall be a statute for ever unto you: *that* in the seventh
month, on the tenth *day* of the month, ye shall afflict your souls, and do no
work at all, *whether it be* one of your own country, or a stranger that
sojourneth among you:

☆**16:29** Lev 23:26–32 Num 27:7 Ps 51:7

30 For on that day shall *the priest* make an atonement for you, to cleanse
you, *that* ye may be clean from all your sins before the LORD.
31 It *shall be* a sabbath of rest unto you, and ye shall afflict your souls, by
a statute for ever.

16:31 Ex 12:16; 20:10 Lev 23:32 Ezra 8:21

32 And the priest, whom he shall anoint, and whom he shall consecrate to
minister in the priest's office in his father's stead, shall make the atonement,
and shall put on the linen clothes, *even* the holy garments:

16:32 Ex 28:39–43

33 And he shall make an atonement for the holy sanctuary, and he shall
make an atonement for the tabernacle of the congregation, and for the
altar, and he shall make an atonement for the priests, and for all the people
of the congregation.
34 And this shall be an everlasting statute unto you, to make an atonement
for the children of Israel for all their sins once a year. And he did as the
LORD commanded Moses.

16:34 Ex 30:10 Lev 23:14, 21, 30, 31 Heb 9:7

16:29, 30 Fasting *(afflict your souls)* was a common practice in the Old and New Testaments. Mourning, self-abasement, and abstaining from food were normal practices (Deut. 9:18; Neh. 9:1; Joel 2:12). Sins were confessed (1 Sam. 7:6; Neh. 9:3), and supplicatory prayers were prayed (Ezra 8:23; Dan. 9:3). Fasting was an outward sign of an inward heart change. It was used in times of danger, affliction, calamities, and misfortune. It was practiced individually and nationally. Hypocrites used it to make men think they were pious. Examples of individuals who practiced fasting include David (2 Sam. 12:16), Daniel (Dan. 9:3), Cornelius (Acts 10:30), and Paul (2 Cor. 11:27). Fasting was required one day a year, *in the seventh month, on the tenth day of the month* (on our calendar, the twenty-fifth day of September).

V. MAINTAINING A HOLY LIFE BEFORE GOD (17:1—22:33)

A. FOLLOWING HEATHEN CUSTOMS FORBIDDEN

1. Sacrificing Animals Away from the Tabernacle Forbidden

17:1☆ 17 AND the LORD spake unto Moses, saying,
2Speak unto Aaron, and unto his sons, and unto all the children
of Israel, and say unto them; This *is* the thing which the LORD hath
commanded, saying,
17:3, 4☆ 3What man soever *there be* of the house of Israel, that killeth an ox, or
Lev 1:2, 3 Deut 12:5–7 lamb, or goat, in the camp, or that killeth *it* out of the camp,
4And bringeth it not unto the door of the tabernacle of the congregation,
to offer an offering unto the LORD before the tabernacle of the LORD; blood
shall be imputed unto that man; he hath shed blood; and that man shall be
cut off from among his people:
17:5 5To the end that the children of Israel may bring their sacrifices, which
Deut 12:4–7 they offer in the open field, even that they may bring them unto the LORD,
unto the door of the tabernacle of the congregation, unto the priest, and
offer them *for* peace offerings unto the LORD.
17:6 6And the priest shall sprinkle the blood upon the altar of the LORD *at* the
Ex 29:18 door of the tabernacle of the congregation, and burn the fat for a sweet
savour unto the LORD.
17:7 7And they shall no more offer their sacrifices unto devils, after whom
Ex 22:20; 32:8 Deut 32:17 they have gone a whoring. This shall be a statute for ever unto them
2 Chron 11:15 1 Cor 10:20 throughout their generations.
8¶And thou shalt say unto them, Whatsoever man *there be* of the house of
Israel, or of the strangers which sojourn among you, that offereth a burnt
offering or sacrifice,
17:9 9And bringeth it not unto the door of the tabernacle of the congregation,
Lev 17:3, 4 Deut 12:4–7 to offer it unto the LORD; even that man shall be cut off from among his
people.

2. The Eating of Blood Forbidden

17:10 10¶And whatsoever man *there be* of the house of Israel, or of the strangers
Lev 3:17; 19:26 Deut 12:23 that sojourn among you, that eateth any manner of blood; I will even set
my face against that soul that eateth blood, and will cut him off from
among his people.
17:11 11For the life of the flesh *is* in the blood: and I have given it to you upon
Gen 9:4 Lev 17:14 the altar to make an atonement for your souls: for it *is* the blood *that*
Matt 26:28 Rom 3:25 maketh an atonement for the soul.
Eph 1:7 Col 1:14, 20 12Therefore I said unto the children of Israel, No soul of you shall eat
Heb 9:22 blood, neither shall any stranger that sojourneth among you eat blood.
1 Pet 1:2 1 Jn 1:7 13And whatsoever man *there be* of the children of Israel, or of the
17:13 strangers that sojourn among you, which hunteth and catcheth any beast or
Deut 12:16, 24, 25; 15:23 fowl that may be eaten; he shall even pour out the blood thereof, and cover
Ezek 24:7 it with dust.
17:14 14For *it is* the life of all flesh; the blood of it *is* for the life thereof:
Lev 7:26, 27 17:11 therefore I said unto the children of Israel, Ye shall eat the blood of no
manner of flesh: for the life of all flesh *is* the blood thereof: whosoever
eateth it shall be cut off.

17:1, 2ff The laws recorded in 17:1—26:45 were given to Moses by God at Sinai. They are called "The Holiness Code" because they set forth how the Israelites were to act, think, and live if they were to be a holy people before the Lord.

17:3, 4 All animal sacrifices were to be made at the tabernacle, not at any shrine of man's own choosing. Disobeying God's command resulted in bloodguilt and banishment from the nation. The right sacrifice at the wrong place was useless.

15 And every soul that eateth that which died *of itself,* or that which was
torn *with beasts, whether it be* one of your own country, or a stranger, he
shall both wash his clothes, and bathe *himself* in water, and be unclean until
the even: then shall he be clean.
16 But if he wash *them* not, nor bathe his flesh; then he shall bear his
iniquity.

17:15 Lev 7:24; 11:24, 39; Num 19:8

B. REGULATIONS WITH REGARD TO SEXUAL RELATIONS

1. Incest Prohibited

18 AND the LORD spake unto Moses, saying,
2 Speak unto the children of Israel, and say unto them, I am the
LORD your God.
3 After the doings of the land of Egypt, wherein ye dwelt, shall ye not do:
and after the doings of the land of Canaan, whither I bring you, shall ye not
do: neither shall ye walk in their ordinances.
4 Ye shall do my judgments, and keep mine ordinances, to walk therein; I
am the LORD your God.
5 Ye shall therefore keep my statutes, and my judgments: which if a man
do, he shall live in them: I *am* the LORD.
6 ¶None of you shall approach to any that is near of kin to him, to
uncover *their* nakedness: I *am* the LORD.
7 The nakedness of thy father, or the nakedness of thy mother, shalt thou
not uncover: she *is* thy mother; thou shalt not uncover her nakedness.
8 The nakedness of thy father's wife shalt thou not uncover: it *is* thy
father's nakedness.
9 The nakedness of thy sister, the daughter of thy father, or daughter of
thy mother, *whether she be* born at home, or born abroad, *even* their
nakedness thou shalt not uncover.
10 The nakedness of thy son's daughter, or of thy daughter's daughter,
even their nakedness thou shalt not uncover: for theirs *is* thine own
nakedness.
11 The nakedness of thy father's wife's daughter, begotten of thy father,
she *is* thy sister, thou shalt not uncover her nakedness.
12 Thou shalt not uncover the nakedness of thy father's sister: she *is* thy
father's near kinswoman.
13 Thou shalt not uncover the nakedness of thy mother's sister: for she *is*
thy mother's near kinswoman.
14 Thou shalt not uncover the nakedness of thy father's brother, thou shalt
not approach to his wife: she *is* thine aunt.
15 Thou shalt not uncover the nakedness of thy daughter in law: she *is* thy
son's wife; thou shalt not uncover her nakedness.
16 Thou shalt not uncover the nakedness of thy brother's wife: it *is* thy
brother's nakedness.
17 Thou shalt not uncover the nakedness of a woman and her daughter,
neither shalt thou take her son's daughter, or her daughter's daughter, to
uncover her nakedness; *for* they *are* her near kinswomen: it *is* wickedness.

18:1 Ex 20:2
18:3 Ex 23:23, 24; Lev 18:29, 30; 20:23; Ezek 20:7, 8
18:4 Lev 19:37; 20:22; Deut 4:1; 6:1; Ezek 20:11; Rom 10:5; Gal 3:12
☆**18:6**
18:7 Lev 20:11
18:8 Gen 35:22; Lev 20:10; Deut 27:20
18:9 Lev 20:17
18:12 Lev 20:19
18:14 Lev 20:20
18:15 Lev 20:15; Ezek 22:11
☆**18:16** Lev 20:21; Deut 25:5; Mt 22:24
18:17 Lev 20:14

18:6 *uncover their nakedness,* i.e., "marry" or "have sexual intercourse with." God allowed sisters and brothers to marry in Adam's day. Later on, when the race was established, God laid down regulations forbidding intermarriage between close relatives. A man could not marry his sister, or his mother's sister, or his daughter-in-law. The same prohibitions are generally operative in the modern world even in non-Christian societies.

18:16 Sexual relations with a brother's wife was forbidden so long as the brother was alive. But if he died and left no heir, then the living brother was to raise up seed by the widow. This was the levirate custom.

18:18☆ Gen 4:19

18 Neither shalt thou take a wife to her sister, to vex *her,* to uncover her nakedness, beside the other in her life *time.*

2. Additional Forbidden Actions

18:19 Lev 15:24; 20:18 Ezek 18:6; 22:10
18:20 Ex 20:14 Lev 20:10 Deut 5:18 22:22–27
18:21 Lev 19:12 20:1–5; 21:6 22:2 Deut 12:31 18:10 2 Kgs 23:10 Mal 1:12
18:22☆ Gen 19:4–8 Lev 20:13 Judg 19:22–24 1 Kgs 14:24 Rom 1:26, 27 1 Cor 6:9, 10 1 Tim 1:10
18:23 Ex 22:19 Lev 20:15, 16 Deut 27:21

19 Also thou shalt not approach unto a woman to uncover her nakedness, as long as she is put apart for her uncleanness.

20 Moreover thou shalt not lie carnally with thy neighbour's wife, to defile thyself with her.

21 And thou shalt not let any of thy seed pass through *the fire* to Mo'lech, neither shalt thou profane the name of thy God: I *am* the LORD.

22 Thou shalt not lie with mankind, as with womankind: it *is* abomination.

23 Neither shalt thou lie with any beast to defile thyself therewith: neither shall any woman stand before a beast to lie down thereto: it *is* confusion.

3. Warnings of Judgment for Disobedience

18:24 Lev 18:2 Deut 12:31
18:25 Lev 20:22, 23 Deut 9:5 Isa 26:21
18:26 Lev 18:4
18:27 Lev 20:23

24 Defile not ye yourselves in any of these things: for in all these the nations are defiled which I cast out before you:

25 And the land is defiled: therefore I do visit the iniquity thereof upon it, and the land itself vomiteth out her inhabitants.

26 Ye shall therefore keep my statutes and my judgments, and shall not commit *any* of these abominations; *neither* any of your own nation, nor any stranger that sojourneth among you:

27 (For all these abominations have the men of the land done, which *were* before you, and the land is defiled;)

28 That the land spue not you out also, when ye defile it, as it spued out the nations that *were* before you.

29 For whosoever shall commit any of these abominations, even the souls that commit *them* shall be cut off from among their people.

30 Therefore shall ye keep mine ordinance, that *ye* commit not *any one* of these abominable customs, which were committed before you, and that ye defile not yourselves therein: I *am* the LORD your God.

C. THE LAWS OF HOLINESS

1. The Laws of Right Conduct

19:1 Ex 20:8–11 Lev 11:44, 45
19:3 Ex 20:3–5, 23 Lev 26:1 Deut 27:15
19:5 Lev 3:1–17 7:11–21, 28–38

19 AND the LORD spake unto Moses, saying,

2 Speak unto all the congregation of the children of Israel, and say unto them, Ye shall be holy: for I the LORD your God *am* holy.

3 ¶Ye shall fear every man his mother, and his father, and keep my sabbaths: I *am* the LORD your God.

4 ¶Turn ye not unto idols, nor make to yourselves molten gods: I *am* the LORD your God.

5 ¶And if ye offer a sacrifice of peace offerings unto the LORD, ye shall offer it at your own will.

18:18 Marrying two sisters is here forbidden. "If the sister of the wife be taken for the concubine, or secondary wife, nothing can be more vexing in her life, or as long as she lives."* Does this then mean that a man can have two wives so long as they are not sisters? (See Exod. 21:10.) Monogamy was God's rule from the beginning but concubinage, while not approved, was regulated if it took place.

18:22, 23 God here condemns sexual relations between two men, and with animals in verse 23. Sodomy and bestiality are sins against nature and the commandment has never been abrogated. These are sins "not to be named without the utmost abhorrence imaginable . . . That ever there should have been occasion for the making of these laws, and that since they are published they should ever have been broken, is the perpetual reproach and scandal of human nature."*

6 It shall be eaten the same day ye offer it, and on the morrow: and if
ought remain until the third day, it shall be burnt in the fire.
7 And if it be eaten at all on the third day, it *is* abominable; it shall not be
accepted.
8 Therefore *every one* that eateth it shall bear his iniquity, because he hath
profaned the hallowed thing of the LORD: and that soul shall be cut off
from among his people.
9 ¶And when ye reap the harvest of your land, thou shalt not wholly reap
the corners of thy field, neither shalt thou gather the gleanings of thy
harvest.
10 And thou shalt not glean thy vineyard, neither shalt thou gather *every*
grape of thy vineyard; thou shalt leave them for the poor and stranger: I *am*
the LORD your God.
11 ¶Ye shall not steal, neither deal falsely, neither lie one to another.
12 ¶And ye shall not swear by my name falsely, neither shalt thou profane
the name of thy God: I *am* the LORD.
13 ¶Thou shalt not defraud thy neighbour, neither rob *him:* the wages of
him that is hired shall not abide with thee all night until the morning.
14 ¶Thou shalt not curse the deaf, nor put a stumblingblock before the
blind, but shalt fear thy God: I *am* the LORD.
15 ¶Ye shall do no unrighteousness in judgment: thou shalt not respect the
person of the poor, nor honour the person of the mighty: *but* in righteous-
ness shalt thou judge thy neighbour.
16 ¶Thou shalt not go up and down *as* a talebearer among thy people:
neither shalt thou stand against the blood of thy neighbour: I *am* the LORD.
17 ¶Thou shalt not hate thy brother in thine heart: thou shalt in any wise
rebuke thy neighbour, and not suffer sin upon him.
18 ¶Thou shalt not avenge, nor bear any grudge against the children of thy
people, but thou shalt love thy neighbour as thyself: I *am* the LORD.
19 ¶Ye shall keep my statutes. Thou shalt not let thy cattle gender with a
diverse kind: thou shalt not sow thy field with mingled seed: neither shall a
garment mingled of linen and woollen come upon thee.
20 ¶And whosoever lieth carnally with a woman, that *is* a bondmaid,
betrothed to an husband, and not at all redeemed, nor freedom given her;
she shall be scourged; they shall not be put to death, because she was not
free.
21 And he shall bring his trespass offering unto the LORD, unto the door of
the tabernacle of the congregation, *even* a ram for a trespass offering.
22 And the priest shall make an atonement for him with the ram of the
trespass offering before the LORD for his sin which he hath done: and the
sin which he hath done shall be forgiven him.

19:8 Num 15:31
19:9 Lev 23:22 Deut 24:19–22
☆**19:10**
19:11 Ex 20:15, 16 Deut 5:19, 20
19:13 Ex 22:7–15, 21–27; 23:4–9 Deut 24:14, 15 Prov 22:22 Mal 3:5
19:14 Deut 27:18
☆**19:15** Ex 23:2, 3, 6 Deut 1:17 16:19, 20 Prov 24:23 Jas 2:1–7
19:16 Ex 23:1, 7 Prov 20:19 Ezek 22:9 Mt 26:60, 61 Acts 6:11–14
19:17 Prov 9:7, 8 27:5, 6 Mt 17:17, 18 Lk 17:2, 3 1 Jn 3:15
☆**19:18** Ex 23:4, 5 Deut 32:35 Ps 103:9 Mt 5:43; 19:19 Mk 12:31–33 Lk 10:27–37 Rom 12:17–21 13:9 Gal 5:14 Heb 10:30 Jas 2:8
19:19 Deut 22:9–11
19:20 Ex 21:20, 21
19:21 Lev 5:14–19 6:6; 7:1–10
☆**19:22**

19:10 It is clear from this and other scriptures that there never would be a time when there were no poor. Therefore works of piety must be accompanied by works of charity. Standing grain was to be left in a corner of the field for the poor and the sojourner. The Jewish doctors concluded that this meant a sixtieth part of the field. Successful farmers should be happy to see the poor helped from the fruit of their labors. Harvest time was particularly the right time for charity, amidst the rejoicing of the reaping of the harvest. As God had blessed the product of the fields, so the reaper should bless the poor by sharing. Thus the farmer rejoices when he shares and the poor rejoice with him for his charity.

19:15 Justice shall not favor a person because of his station in life. "Judges were obliged by this law to be so impartial as not to let one of the contending parties sit while the other stood, nor permit one to say what he pleased and bid the other be short."*

19:18 The two tables of the law could be reduced to two general commandments: love God and your neighbor as yourself (see Matt. 19:19 and Luke 10:27).

19:22 The atonement for guilt was followed by the forgiveness of the sin. Sacrifices which do not relieve the sinner of his guilt would be useless. God's grace includes forgiveness when atonement is made.

19:23 Deut 20:19
19:26☆ Ex 22:18 Lev 3:17 7:26, 27; 19:31 20:6, 27 Deut 18:10–12
19:27☆ Lev 21:5 Ezek 44:20
19:28☆ Deut 14:1 Jer 16:6; 48:37
19:29☆ Lev 21:9 Deut 23:17, 18 Hos 4:13
19:30 Ex 20:8–11 Lev 26:2
19:31 Lev 19:26
19:32 1 Tim 5:1, 2
19:34☆ Lev 19:18
19:35☆ Deut 25:13–16 Prov 11:1 16:11; 20:10 Amos 8:5 Mic 6:11

23 ¶And when ye shall come into the land, and shall have planted all manner of trees for food, then ye shall count the fruit thereof as uncircumcised: three years shall it be as uncircumcised unto you: it shall not be eaten of.

24 But in the fourth year all the fruit thereof shall be holy to praise the LORD *withal.*

25 And in the fifth year shall ye eat of the fruit thereof, that it may yield unto you the increase thereof: I *am* the LORD your God.

26 ¶Ye shall not eat *any thing* with the blood: neither shall ye use enchantment, nor observe times.

27 Ye shall not round the corners of your heads, neither shalt thou mar the corners of thy beard.

28 Ye shall not make any cuttings in your flesh for the dead, nor print any marks upon you: I *am* the LORD.

29 ¶Do not prostitute thy daughter, to cause her to be a whore; lest the land fall to whoredom, and the land become full of wickedness.

30 ¶Ye shall keep my sabbaths, and reverence my sanctuary: I *am* the LORD.

31 ¶Regard not them that have familiar spirits, neither seek after wizards, to be defiled by them: I *am* the LORD your God.

32 ¶Thou shalt rise up before the hoary head, and honour the face of the old man, and fear thy God: I *am* the LORD.

33 ¶And if a stranger sojourn with thee in your land, ye shall not vex him.

34 *But* the stranger that dwelleth with you shall be unto you as one born among you, and thou shalt love him as thyself; for ye were strangers in the land of Egypt: I *am* the LORD your God.

35 ¶Ye shall do no unrighteousness in judgment, in meteyard, in weight, or in measure.

36 Just balances, just weights, a just ephah, and a just hin, shall ye have: I *am* the LORD your God, which brought you out of the land of Egypt.

37 Therefore shall ye observe all my statutes, and all my judgments, and do them: I *am* the LORD.

2. The Consequences for Committing Certain Unholy Acts

a. Sacrificing Children to Molech

20:2 Lev 18:21 24:13, 14, 23 Deut 13:10 17:5–7
20:3 Lev 18:21 Num 19:20 Ezek 5:11; 23:38, 39

20 AND the LORD spake unto Moses, saying,

2 Again, thou shalt say to the children of Israel, Whosoever *he be* of the children of Israel, or of the strangers that sojourn in Israel, that giveth *any* of his seed unto Mo'lech; he shall surely be put to death: the people of the land shall stone him with stones.

3 And I will set my face against that man, and will cut him off from among his people; because he hath given of his seed unto Mo'lech, to defile my sanctuary, and to profane my holy name.

19:26–28 Eating blood as the heathen did, asking counsel of the devil through enchantment and divination, or cutting the edges of the beard and defacing oneself for the dead were heathen practices inconsonant with the worship of the true God. The Hebrew community was told again and again to refrain from incorporating pagan practices and ideas into its culture.

19:29 What is implied here and forbidden was the practice of temple prostitution, common to the pagans' idolatrous worship on the grounds that it pleased the spirits they worshipped. *lest . . . the land become full of wickedness.* Dishonoring God in the temple would lead to dishonoring God and themselves in their daily living.

19:34 Neighborly love was not limited to relationships between Israelites alone. It is here extended to strangers. The Good Samaritan story of Jesus demonstrates this.

19:35 Whoever shortchanged anyone was guilty of stealing. Honest weights and measures should be the rule of thumb.

[4]And if the people of the land do any ways hide their eyes from the man, when he giveth of his seed unto Mo'lech, and kill him not: ☆20:4
[5]Then I will set my face against that man, and against his family, and will cut him off, and all that go a whoring after him, to commit whoredom with Mo'lech, from among their people. 20:5 Lev 17:10

b. Consulting Mediums and Wizards

[6]¶And the soul that turneth after such as have familiar spirits, and after wizards, to go a whoring after them, I will even set my face against that soul, and will cut him off from among his people. 20:6 Lev 19:26, 31
[7]¶Sanctify yourselves therefore, and be ye holy: for I *am* the LORD your God. 20:7 Lev 11:44
[8]And ye shall keep my statutes, and do them: I *am* the LORD which sanctify you.
[9]¶For every one that curseth his father or his mother shall be surely put to death: he hath cursed his father or his mother; his blood *shall be* upon him. 20:9 Ex 21:17 Deut 27:16 Prov 20:20 Mt 15:4

c. Committing Adultery

[10]¶And the man that committeth adultery with *another* man's wife, *even he* that committeth adultery with his neighbour's wife, the adulterer and the adulteress shall surely be put to death. 20:10 Ex 20:14 Deut 22:22–24
[11]And the man that lieth with his father's wife hath uncovered his father's nakedness: both of them shall surely be put to death; their blood *shall be* upon them. 20:11 Lev 18:7, 8 Deut 27:20
[12]And if a man lie with his daughter in law, both of them shall surely be put to death: they have wrought confusion; their blood *shall be* upon them. 20:12 Lev 18:15
[13]If a man also lie with mankind, as he lieth with a woman, both of them have committed an abomination: they shall surely be put to death; their blood *shall be* upon them. ☆20:13 Gen 19:5 Lev 18:22 Deut 23:17 Judg 19:22
[14]And if a man take a wife and her mother, it *is* wickedness: they shall be burnt with fire, both he and they; that there be no wickedness among you. 20:14 Lev 18:17 Deut 27:23
[15]And if a man lie with a beast, he shall surely be put to death: and ye shall slay the beast. 20:15 Lev 18:23 Deut 27:21
[16]And if a woman approach unto any beast, and lie down thereto, thou shalt kill the woman, and the beast: they shall surely be put to death; their blood *shall be* upon them.

d. Other Sexual Sins

[17]And if a man shall take his sister, his father's daughter, or his mother's daughter, and see her nakedness, and she see his nakedness; it *is* a wicked thing; and they shall be cut off in the sight of their people: he hath uncovered his sister's nakedness; he shall bear his iniquity. 20:17 Lev 18:9
[18]And if a man shall lie with a woman having her sickness, and shall uncover her nakedness; he hath discovered her fountain, and she hath uncovered the fountain of her blood: and both of them shall be cut off from among their people. 20:18 Lev 15:24; 18:19

20:4 Whoever closed his eyes to the idolatrous practices of a neighbor was guilty—as an accessory after the fact—even though not a party to the transgression itself. So also "if magistrates will not do justice upon offenders, God will do justice upon them who sin by winking at the sin."*
20:13 The death penalty for adultery was the same penalty for homosexual offenders. See note to 20:19ff.

20:19☆ Lev 18:12, 13
20:20 Lev 18:14
20:21 Lev 18:16

19 And thou shalt not uncover the nakedness of thy mother's sister, nor of
thy father's sister: for he uncovereth his near kin: they shall bear their
iniquity.
20 And if a man shall lie with his uncle's wife, he hath uncovered his
uncle's nakedness: they shall bear their sin; they shall die childless.
21 And if a man shall take his brother's wife, it *is* an unclean thing: he
hath uncovered his brother's nakedness; they shall be childless.

e. The Command to Obey God's Laws

20:22 Lev 18:28
20:23 Lev 18:1–3, 24–30 Deut 9:5
20:24☆ Gen 15:16 Ex 3:17; 6:8, 9; Deut 6:3; 8:7–9 11:9; 26:9; 27:3 Josh 5:6; 24:11
20:25 Lev 11:1–47 Deut 14:3–5
20:26☆ Lev 11:44

22 ¶Ye shall therefore keep all my statutes, and all my judgments, and do
them: that the land, whither I bring you to dwell therein, spue you not out.
23 And ye shall not walk in the manners of the nation, which I cast out
before you: for they committed all these things, and therefore I abhorred
them.
24 But I have said unto you, Ye shall inherit their land, and I will give it
unto you to possess it, a land that floweth with milk and honey: I *am* the
LORD your God, which have separated you from *other* people.
25 Ye shall therefore put difference between clean beasts and unclean, and
between unclean fowls and clean: and ye shall not make your souls
abominable by beast, or by fowl, or by any manner of living thing that
creepeth on the ground, which I have separated from you as unclean.
26 And ye shall be holy unto me: for I the LORD *am* holy, and have
severed you from *other* people, that ye should be mine.

f. Stoning, the Penalty for Mediums and Wizards

20:27 Lev 19:26, 31 Deut 18:10–12

27 ¶A man also or woman that hath a familiar spirit, or that is a wizard,
shall surely be put to death: they shall stone them with stones: their blood
shall be upon them.

3. Regulations for the Priesthood

a. Proper Conduct for Priests Specified

21:1 Lev 21:11 Num 19:14, 16 Ezek 44:25
21:2 Lev 21:11
21:5 Lev 19:27, 28 Deut 14:1 Jer 16:6; 48:37
21:6 Ex 29:44 Lev 10:3

21 AND the LORD said unto Moses, Speak unto the priests the sons of
Aaron, and say unto them, There shall none be defiled for the dead
among his people:
2 But for his kin, that is near unto him, *that is,* for his mother, and for his
father, and for his son, and for his daughter, and for his brother,
3 And for his sister a virgin, that is nigh unto him, which hath had no
husband; for her may he be defiled.
4 *But* he shall not defile himself, *being* a chief man among his people, to
profane himself.
5 They shall not make baldness upon their head, neither shall they shave
off the corner of their beard, nor make any cuttings in their flesh.
6 They shall be holy unto their God, and not profane the name of their

---

20:19ff Despite present-day latitude, adultery, incest, homosexual and lesbian sexual relations, and coitus with animals are here and everywhere forbidden in the Scriptures. They were capital crimes punishable by death. These crimes against God and nature were prevalent among the heathen; they were also practiced among the Israelites, to some extent. There is nothing in the Scriptures to warrant the opinion that these illicit relationships are to be regarded as normal then, now, or ever. They are prohibited by the eternal moral law of God.

20:24 Whoever has the Lord for his God is thereby separated from the heathen round about him. Believers are advanced above unbelievers and should not devalue their estate by walking in the way of the heathen.

20:26 God is holy. Therefore, his people are to be like him. Holiness befits the people of God. It is a characteristic that pleases God, makes credible a witness to the heathen, encourages the hearts of believers who have not yet attained holiness, and is always open to further improvement.

God: for the offerings of the LORD made by fire, *and* the bread of their
God, they do offer: therefore they shall be holy.
7 They shall not take a wife *that is* a whore, or profane; neither shall they
take a woman put away from her husband: for he *is* holy unto his God.
8 Thou shalt sanctify him therefore; for he offereth the bread of thy God:
he shall be holy unto thee: for I the LORD, which sanctify you, *am* holy.
9 ¶And the daughter of any priest, if she profane herself by playing the
whore, she profaneth her father: she shall be burnt with fire.
10 And *he that is* the high priest among his brethren, upon whose head the
anointing oil was poured, and that is consecrated to put on the garments,
shall not uncover his head, nor rend his clothes;
11 Neither shall he go in to any dead body, nor defile himself for his
father, or for his mother;
12 Neither shall he go out of the sanctuary, nor profane the sanctuary of
his God; for the crown of the anointing oil of his God *is* upon him: I *am* the
LORD.
13 And he shall take a wife in her virginity.
14 A widow, or a divorced woman, or profane, *or* an harlot, these shall he
not take: but he shall take a virgin of his own people to wife.
15 Neither shall he profane his seed among his people: for I the LORD do
sanctify him.
16 ¶And the LORD spake unto Moses, saying,
17 Speak unto Aaron, saying, Whosoever *he be* of thy seed in their
generations that hath *any* blemish, let him not approach to offer the bread
of his God.
18 For whatsoever man *he be* that hath a blemish, he shall not approach:
a blind man, or a lame, or he that hath a flat nose, or any thing superfluous,
19 Or a man that is brokenfooted, or brokenhanded,
20 Or crookbackt, or a dwarf, or that hath a blemish in his eye, or be
scurvy, or scabbed, or hath his stones broken;
21 No man that hath a blemish of the seed of Aaron the priest shall come
nigh to offer the offerings of the LORD made by fire: he hath a blemish; he
shall not come nigh to offer the bread of his God.
22 He shall eat the bread of his God, *both* of the most holy, and of the
holy.
23 Only he shall not go in unto the vail, nor come nigh unto the altar,
because he hath a blemish; that he profane not my sanctuaries: for I the
LORD do sanctify them.
24 And Moses told *it* unto Aaron, and to his sons, and unto all the
children of Israel.

22 AND the LORD spake unto Moses, saying,
2 Speak unto Aaron and to his sons, that they separate themselves
from the holy things of the children of Israel, and that they profane not my
holy name *in those things* which they hallow unto me: I *am* the LORD.

21:7 Lev 21:14; Ezek 44:22
21:8 Lev 11:44
21:9 Lev 19:29; 20:14
21:10 Lev 10:6, 7
☆**21:11** Lev 21:1–4; Ezek 44:25
21:12 Ex 29:7; Lev 10:7; Num 19:11–13
21:13 Ezek 44:22
☆**21:14** Lev 21:7, 13; Ezra 2:62, 63; 9:2; Neh 13:29
☆**21:15**
☆**21:16, 17** Deut 23:1, 2
21:21 Lev 21:17–21
21:22 Lev 6:16, 29; 24:9; Num 18:8–11; 1 Cor 9:13
21:23 Lev 21:17
22:2 Lev 10:1–4

21:11 *for his father or for his mother.* Note that this rule applied to the high priest, while the contrary instructions in 21:1 applied to ordinary priests.†

21:14 The high priest could not marry a widow (as other priests could), much less one divorced, or a harlot. High priests were a type of Christ. As the church is to be presented as a chaste virgin to Christ (2 Cor. 11:2), so the high priest could marry only a virgin.

21:15 *Neither shall he profane his seed among his people,* i.e., "he must not be the father of children of mixed blood—half priestly and half ordinary."†

21:16, 17ff God laid down certain disqualifications which would prevent a Levite from being a priest. The physical disabilities and imperfections listed in 21:18–20 barred one from the office but not from receiving the proper share of the offerings for personal support (21:22). Thus the priest as well as the animal offered for sacrifice had to be without blemish to be satisfactory. Christ met both demands when he became our atonement. Today there are some things which disqualify a man from the office of elder or deacon, but which would not disqualify him from the worship and fellowship of the church.

22:3 Lev 7:20, 21; Num 19:13

3 Say unto them, Whosoever *he be* of all your seed among your genera-
tions, that goeth unto the holy things, which the children of Israel hallow
unto the LORD, having his uncleanness upon him, that soul shall be cut off
from my presence: I *am* the LORD.

22:4☆ Lev 11:24, 28, 31, 39, 40; 13:45, 46; 14:1–32; Num 5:1; 19:11

4 What man soever of the seed of Aaron *is* a leper, or hath a running
issue; he shall not eat of the holy things, until he be clean. And whoso
toucheth any thing *that is* unclean *by* the dead, or a man whose seed goeth
from him;

22:5 Lev 11:24, 25, 41–44

5 Or whosoever toucheth any creeping thing, whereby he may be made
unclean, or a man of whom he may take uncleanness, whatsoever unclean-
ness he hath;

22:6 Num 19:7–10

6 The soul which hath touched any such shall be unclean until even, and
shall not eat of the holy things, unless he wash his flesh with water.
7 And when the sun is down, he shall be clean, and shall afterward eat of
the holy things; because it *is* his food.

22:8 Ex 22:31; Lev 17:15; Deut 14:21; Ezek 44:31 **22:9** Ex 28:43; Lev 22:16; Num 18:1–7 **22:10** Ex 29:31–34; Lev 22:13 **22:11** Num 18:11

8 That which dieth of itself, or is torn *with beasts,* he shall not eat to defile
himself therewith: I *am* the LORD.
9 They shall therefore keep mine ordinance, lest they bear sin for it, and
die therefore, if they profane it: I the LORD do sanctify them.
10 There shall no stranger eat *of* the holy thing: a sojourner of the priest,
or an hired servant, shall not eat *of* the holy thing.
11 But if the priest buy *any* soul with his money, he shall eat of it, and he
that is born in his house: they shall eat of his meat.
12 If the priest's daughter also be *married* unto a stranger, she may not eat
of an offering of the holy things.

22:13 Lev 22:10

13 But if the priest's daughter be a widow, or divorced, and have no child,
and is returned unto her father's house, as in her youth, she shall eat of her
father's meat: but there shall no stranger eat thereof.

22:14 Lev 5:16; Num 15:22–26 **22:15** Lev 19:8 **22:16** Lev 22:9

14 ¶And if a man eat *of* the holy thing unwittingly, then he shall put the
fifth *part* thereof unto it, and shall give *it* unto the priest with the holy thing.
15 And they shall not profane the holy things of the children of Israel,
which they offer unto the LORD;
16 Or suffer them to bear the iniquity of trespass, when they eat their holy
things: for I the LORD do sanctify them.

b. Laws Governing Acceptable Sacrifices

17 ¶And the LORD spake unto Moses, saying,
18 Speak unto Aaron, and to his sons, and unto all the children of Israel,
and say unto them, Whatsoever *he be* of the house of Israel, or of the
strangers in Israel, that will offer his oblation for all his vows, and for all his
freewill offerings, which they will offer unto the LORD for a burnt offering;

22:19☆ Lev 1:2; 4:3

19 *Ye shall offer* at your own will a male without blemish, of the beeves, of
the sheep, or of the goats.

22:20 Lev 22:22–25; Deut 15:21

20 *But* whatsoever hath a blemish, *that* shall ye not offer: for it shall not be
acceptable for you.
21 And whosoever offereth a sacrifice of peace offerings unto the LORD to
accomplish *his* vow, or a freewill offering in beeves or sheep, it shall be
perfect to be accepted; there shall be no blemish therein.

22:4 Food from the offerings belonged to the priests. Yet those who were lepers or had a discharge could not eat the holy things. They had to find food which was common, i.e., food which was consumed by the ordinary people, who were not Levites.

22:19 One would assume that no consecrated believer would bring a deformed or defective sacrifice as an offering to the God of glory. Yet the prohibition stated here suggests either that the nature of man is such that this eventuality would occur or that it had already manifested itself among some of the people who professed to worship God, but not enough to keep them from offering the worst rather than the best of their beasts.

22 Blind, or broken, or maimed, or having a wen, or scurvy, or scabbed, ye
shall not offer these unto the LORD, nor make an offering by fire of them
upon the altar unto the LORD.
23 Either a bullock or a lamb that hath any thing superfluous or lacking in
his parts, that mayest thou offer *for* a freewill offering; but for a vow it shall
not be accepted.
24 Ye shall not offer unto the LORD that which is bruised, or crushed, or
broken, or cut; neither shall ye make *any offering thereof* in your land.
25 Neither from a stranger's hand shall ye offer the bread of your God of
any of these; because their corruption *is* in them, *and* blemishes *be* in them:
they shall not be accepted for you.
26 ¶And the LORD spake unto Moses, saying,
27 When a bullock, or a sheep, or a goat, is brought forth, then it shall be
seven days under the dam; and from the eighth day and thenceforth it shall
be accepted for an offering made by fire unto the LORD.
28 And *whether it be* cow or ewe, ye shall not kill it and her young both in
one day.
29 And when ye will offer a sacrifice of thanksgiving unto the LORD, offer
it at your own will.
30 On the same day it shall be eaten up; ye shall leave none of it until the
morrow: I *am* the LORD.
31 Therefore shall ye keep my commandments, and do them: I *am* the
LORD.
32 Neither shall ye profane my holy name; but I will be hallowed among
the children of Israel: I *am* the LORD which hallow you,
33 That brought you out of the land of Egypt, to be your God: I *am* the
LORD.

22:22 Lev 22:20; Mal 1:8
22:25 Num 15:15, 16; Mal 1:14
22:26 Ex 22:30
22:28 Deut 22:6
22:29 Ex 16:19; Lev 7:15
22:31 Ex 20:2; Lev 18:4
22:33 Lev 22:31

VI. REGULATIONS FOR FESTIVALS AND SEASONS (23:1—25:55)

A. THE SABBATH

23 AND the LORD spake unto Moses, saying,
2 Speak unto the children of Israel, and say unto them, *Concern-
ing* the feasts of the LORD, which ye shall proclaim *to be* holy convocations,
even these *are* my feasts.
3 Six days shall work be done: but the seventh day *is* the sabbath of rest,
an holy convocation; ye shall do no work *therein:* it *is* the sabbath of the
LORD in all your dwellings.

B. THE PASSOVER AND UNLEAVENED BREAD

4 ¶These *are* the feasts of the LORD, *even* holy convocations, which ye
shall proclaim in their seasons.
5 In the fourteenth *day* of the first month at even *is* the LORD's passover.
6 And on the fifteenth day of the same month *is* the feast of unleavened
bread unto the LORD: seven days ye must eat unleavened bread.

23:1 Ex 23:17; 34:22; Lev 23:4, 37, 44; Num 29:39
23:3 Ex 20:8–11; 23:12; 31:15; Deut 5:13, 14; Lk 13:14
23:4 Lev 23:1
☆**23:5** Ex 12:3–20; Num 9:2–7; Deut 16:1–8; Mt 26:17; Mk 14:12; Lk 22:7
☆**23:6** Mk 14:1–12; Lk 22:1

23:5 *In the fourteenth day of the first month* (of the Hebrew calendar), i.e., around the first day of April.
23:6 *the feast of unleavened bread.* This festival must be distinguished from the Passover, although they are closely connected. The Passover was celebrated on the fourteenth day of the first Jewish month; the feast of unleavened bread began the fifteenth day and lasted for seven days. Thus they constituted a double celebration, as did the day of atonement and the festival of tabernacles. In Mark 14:1–12 and Luke 22:1 the Passover and the feast of unleavened bread are mentioned as virtually one, doubtless because no period of time separated one from the other. The unleavened bread festival celebrated Israel's deliverance from Egypt. No unleavened bread was eaten during the festival. The regulations for the festival are found in 23:6–8 here.

23:7 Ex 12:6; Num 28:18

[7]In the first day ye shall have an holy convocation: ye shall do no servile work therein.

[8]But ye shall offer an offering made by fire unto the LORD seven days: in the seventh day *is* an holy convocation: ye shall do no servile work *therein.*

C. THE FESTIVAL OF FIRST FRUITS

23:9–11 Ex 23:16, 19; 34:22; Num 15:17–21; 28:26–31; Deut 16:9–12; Rom 11:16; Jas 1:18; Rev 14:4

[9]¶And the LORD spake unto Moses, saying,

[10]Speak unto the children of Israel, and say unto them, When ye be come into the land which I give unto you, and shall reap the harvest thereof, then ye shall bring a sheaf of the firstfruits of your harvest unto the priest:

[11]And he shall wave the sheaf before the LORD, to be accepted for you: on the morrow after the sabbath the priest shall wave it.

[12]And ye shall offer that day when ye wave the sheaf an he lamb without blemish of the first year for a burnt offering unto the LORD.

23:13 Lev 6:14–23; Num 15:3–10

[13]And the meat offering thereof *shall be* two tenth deals of fine flour mingled with oil, an offering made by fire unto the LORD *for* a sweet savour: and the drink offering thereof *shall be* of wine, the fourth *part* of an hin.

23:14 Lev 3:17

[14]And ye shall eat neither bread, nor parched corn, nor green ears, until the selfsame day that ye have brought an offering unto your God: *it shall be* a statute for ever throughout your generations in all your dwellings.

D. THE FESTIVAL OF PENTECOST

23:15☆ Lev 23:9–14; Num 28:26–31; Deut 16:9, 10; Acts 2:1

[15]¶And ye shall count unto you from the morrow after the sabbath, from the day that ye brought the sheaf of the wave offering; seven sabbaths shall be complete:

[16]Even unto the morrow after the seventh sabbath shall ye number fifty days; and ye shall offer a new meat offering unto the LORD.

23:17 Ex 23:16, 19; Lev 7:13; Num 15:17–21

[17]Ye shall bring out of your habitations two wave loaves of two tenth deals: they shall be of fine flour; they shall be baken with leaven; *they are* the firstfruits unto the LORD.

[18]And ye shall offer with the bread seven lambs without blemish of the first year, and one young bullock, and two rams: they shall be *for* a burnt offering unto the LORD, with their meat offering, and their drink offerings, *even* an offering made by fire, of sweet savour unto the LORD.

23:19 Lev 16:15

[19]Then ye shall sacrifice one kid of the goats for a sin offering, and two lambs of the first year for a sacrifice of peace offerings.

23:20 Num 18:12; Deut 18:4

[20]And the priest shall wave them with the bread of the firstfruits *for* a wave offering before the LORD, with the two lambs: they shall be holy to the LORD for the priest.

[21]And ye shall proclaim on the selfsame day, *that* it may be an holy convocation unto you: ye shall do no servile work *therein: it shall be* a statute for ever in all your dwellings throughout your generations.

23:22 Lev 19:9, 10; Deut 24:19–21; Prov 11:24, 25

[22]¶And when ye reap the harvest of your land, thou shalt not make clean riddance of the corners of thy field when thou reapest, neither shalt thou gather any gleaning of thy harvest: thou shalt leave them unto the poor, and to the stranger: I *am* the LORD your God.

23:15, 16 The festival of pentecost was also known as the feast of weeks, or feast of harvest. In the New Testament, the name derives from the Greek word for "fiftieth," which is used because the feast occurred fifty days after the feast of unleavened bread. (Using our reckoning, it would be forty-nine days.) The festival was prophetic, looking to the advent of the Holy Spirit, who came upon the apostolic believers on the fiftieth day after Christ rose from the dead (Acts 2:1ff). In the Old Testament the festival celebrated the harvest of fruits of the earth; in Acts, the 120 disciples represented the first-fruits of Christ's harvest. And the coming of the Holy Spirit represents the first-fruits of believers' heavenly inheritance. (See Rom. 8:23; 11:16; James 1:18.)

E. THE FESTIVAL OF TRUMPETS

23 ¶And the LORD spake unto Moses, saying,
24 Speak unto the children of Israel, saying, In the seventh month, in the
first *day* of the month, shall ye have a sabbath, a memorial of blowing of
trumpets, an holy convocation.
25 Ye shall do no servile work *therein:* but ye shall offer an offering made
by fire unto the LORD.

☆**23:23** Num 10:10 29:1–6
23:25 Lev 23:7

F. THE DAY OF ATONEMENT

26 ¶And the LORD spake unto Moses, saying,
27 Also on the tenth *day* of this seventh month *there shall be* a day of
atonement: it shall be an holy convocation unto you; and ye shall afflict
your souls, and offer an offering made by fire unto the LORD.
28 And ye shall do no work in that same day: for it *is* a day of atonement,
to make an atonement for you before the LORD your God.
29 For whatsoever soul *it be* that shall not be afflicted in that same day, he
shall be cut off from among his people.
30 And whatsoever soul *it be* that doeth any work in that same day, the
same soul will I destroy from among his people.
31 Ye shall do no manner of work: *it shall be* a statute for ever throughout
your generations in all your dwellings.
32 It *shall be* unto you a sabbath of rest, and ye shall afflict your souls: in
the ninth *day* of the month at even, from even unto even, shall ye celebrate
your sabbath.

23:26 Lev 16:3–34 Num 29:7–11
23:28 Lev 23-7
23:29 Lev 23:32
☆**23:32** Lev 16:29–31

G. THE FESTIVAL OF TABERNACLES

33 ¶And the LORD spake unto Moses, saying,
34 Speak unto the children of Israel, saying, The fifteenth day of this
seventh month *shall be* the feast of tabernacles *for* seven days unto the
LORD.
35 On the first day *shall be* an holy convocation: ye shall do no servile
work *therein.*
36 Seven days ye shall offer an offering made by fire unto the LORD: on the
eighth day shall be an holy convocation unto you; and ye shall offer an
offering made by fire unto the LORD: it *is* a solemn assembly; *and* ye shall
do no servile work *therein.*
37 These *are* the feasts of the LORD, which ye shall proclaim *to be* holy
convocations, to offer an offering made by fire unto the LORD, a burnt
offering, and a meat offering, a sacrifice, and drink offerings, every thing
upon his day:
38 Beside the sabbaths of the LORD, and beside your gifts, and beside all
your vows, and beside all your freewill offerings, which ye give unto the
LORD.
39 Also in the fifteenth day of the seventh month, when ye have gathered
in the fruit of the land, ye shall keep a feast unto the LORD seven days: on
the first day *shall be* a sabbath, and on the eighth day *shall be* a sabbath.

☆**23:33, 34** Ex 23:16 Lev 23:39–43 Num 29:12–39 Deut 16:13–16 Ezra 3:4 Neh 8:14 Zech 14:16 Jn 7:2
23:35 Lev 23:7
23:36 Lev 23:34 Neh 8:18 Jn 7:39
23:37 Ex 34:22 Deut 16:16
23:38 Num 29:39
23:39 Lev 23:34

23:23, 24 The festival of trumpets came the first day of the seventh month (mid-September) of the Hebrew calendar (*Tishri*). Trumpets were blown and sacrifices offered (Num. 29:1–6). The day was set apart for a holy convocation, celebration, and rest. It marked the first day of the Jewish new year and is celebrated today as *Rosh Hashanah.*

23:32 *ye shall afflict your souls.* This is better translated, "You shall begin your fast, and the expression of your humiliation. . . ." Except for children and sick people, the fast which began at sunset of the ninth day was continued until sundown of the tenth day. All worldly business was laid aside so that the people might better attend to spiritual matters on this day of atonement, spoken of as a sabbath.

23:33, 34 *The fifteenth day of this seventh month* (of the Hebrew calendar), i.e., "on the last day of September." *feast of tabernacles,* or "feast of shelters."†

40 And ye shall take you on the first day the boughs of goodly trees, branches of palm trees, and the boughs of thick trees, and willows of the brook; and ye shall rejoice before the LORD your God seven days.

41 And ye shall keep it a feast unto the LORD seven days in the year. *It shall be* a statute for ever in your generations: ye shall celebrate it in the seventh month.

23:42 Neh 8:14–18

42 Ye shall dwell in booths seven days; all that are Israelites born shall dwell in booths:

23:43 Ex 13:14–18 Deut 13:31 Ps 78:1–8

43 That your generations may know that I made the children of Israel to dwell in booths, when I brought them out of the land of Egypt: I *am* the LORD your God.

23:44 Lev 23:37

44 And Moses declared unto the children of Israel the feasts of the LORD.

H. INCIDENTAL INSTRUCTIONS

1. The Olive Oil and the Bread

24:1 Ex 27:20, 21

24 AND the LORD spake unto Moses, saying,

2 Command the children of Israel, that they bring unto thee pure oil olive beaten for the light, to cause the lamps to burn continually.

24:3 Ex 25:31–39 37:17–24

3 Without the vail of the testimony, in the tabernacle of the congregation, shall Aaron order it from the evening unto the morning before the LORD continually: *it shall be* a statute for ever in your generations.

4 He shall order the lamps upon the pure candlestick before the LORD continually.

24:5 Ex 25:30 37:10–13; 40:23 Lev 2:9, 16 5:12; 6:15 Heb 9:2

5 ¶And thou shalt take fine flour, and bake twelve cakes thereof: two tenth deals shall be in one cake.

6 And thou shalt set them in two rows, six on a row, upon the pure table before the LORD.

7 And thou shalt put pure frankincense upon *each* row, that it may be on the bread for a memorial, *even* an offering made by fire unto the LORD.

8 Every sabbath he shall set it in order before the LORD continually, *being taken* from the children of Israel by an everlasting covenant.

24:9 Lev 6:16–18 Mt 12:4

9 And it shall be Aaron's and his sons'; and they shall eat it in the holy place: for it *is* most holy unto him of the offerings of the LORD made by fire by a perpetual statute.

2. Capital Punishment for Blasphemy

10 ¶And the son of an Israelitish woman, whose father *was* an Egyptian, went out among the children of Israel: and this son of the Israelitish *woman* and a man of Israel strove together in the camp;

24:11 Ex 22:28 Job 1:5, 11, 22 Ps 74:18 Isa 8:21

11 And the Israelitish woman's son blasphemed the name *of the LORD*, and cursed. And they brought him unto Moses: (and his mother's name *was* Shel'o-mith, the daughter of Dib'ri, of the tribe of Dan:)

12 And they put him in ward, that the mind of the LORD might be shewed them.

24:13 Lev 4:15 Deut 13:9; 17:7 21:21

13 And the LORD spake unto Moses, saying,

14 Bring forth him that hath cursed without the camp; and let all that heard *him* lay their hands upon his head, and let all the congregation stone him.

24:15☆ Ex 22:28

15 And thou shalt speak unto the children of Israel, saying, Whosoever curseth his God shall bear his sin.

24:15, 16 To curse, scoff at, or revile God was blasphemous. The sentence for this sin was death. Idolatry was also regarded as blasphemy (Isa. 65:7) because it implied contempt for the divine name as the one true God. Unregenerate men are addicted to this sin (Ps. 74:18). Here we read that the profane Danite was a blasphemer (24:11). King Sennacherib was guilty of this crime (2 Kings 19:4, 10, 22). Hymenaeus

16 And he that blasphemeth the name of the LORD, he shall surely be put
to death, *and* all the congregation shall certainly stone him: as well the
stranger, as he that is born in the land, when he blasphemeth the name *of
the LORD*, shall be put to death.
17 ¶And he that killeth any man shall surely be put to death.
18 And he that killeth a beast shall make it good; beast for beast.
19 And if a man cause a blemish in his neighbour; as he hath done, so
shall it be done to him;
20 Breach for breach, eye for eye, tooth for tooth: as he hath caused a
blemish in a man, so shall it be done to him *again*.
21 And he that killeth a beast, he shall restore it: and he that killeth a man,
he shall be put to death.
22 Ye shall have one manner of law, as well for the stranger, as for one of
your own country: for I *am* the LORD your God.
23 ¶And Moses spake to the children of Israel, that they should bring forth
him that had cursed out of the camp, and stone him with stones. And the
children of Israel did as the LORD commanded Moses.

24:17 Gen 9:5 Ex 20:13 21:12, 14 Num 35:30, 31 Deut 19:11–13
24:18 Ex 21:33–36 Lev 24:21
24:20 Ex 21:24, 25 Deut 19:21 Mt 5:38
24:21 Lev 24:18
24:22 Ex 12:49 Num 15:15, 16, 29

I. THE CELEBRATION OF THE SABBATICAL YEAR AND THE YEAR OF JUBILEE

1. The Seventh Year of Rest for Land

25 AND the LORD spake unto Moses in mount Si'nai, saying,
2 Speak unto the children of Israel, and say unto them, When ye
come into the land which I give you, then shall the land keep a sabbath
unto the LORD.
3 Six years thou shalt sow thy field, and six years thou shalt prune thy
vineyard, and gather in the fruit thereof;
4 But in the seventh year shall be a sabbath of rest unto the land, a
sabbath for the LORD: thou shalt neither sow thy field, nor prune thy
vineyard.
5 That which groweth of its own accord of thy harvest thou shalt not reap,
neither gather the grapes of thy vine undressed: *for* it is a year of rest unto
the land.
6 And the sabbath of the land shall be meat for you; for thee, and for thy
servant, and for thy maid, and for thy hired servant, and for thy stranger
that sojourneth with thee,
7 And for thy cattle, and for the beast that *are* in thy land, shall all the
increase thereof be meat.

25:2 Ex 23:11 Lev 26:33–35, 43
25:3 Ex 23:10
25:4 Lev 25:1, 20–23
25:5 2 Kgs 19:29
25:6 Lev 25:20–22

2. The Year of Jubilee

8 ¶And thou shalt number seven sabbaths of years unto thee, seven times
seven years; and the space of the seven sabbaths of years shall be unto thee
forty and nine years.
9 Then shalt thou cause the trumpet of the jubile to sound on the tenth

☆25:9 Num 10:10

in the New Testament was also a blasphemer (1 Tim. 1:20). Unbelievers often accuse God's people of this sin of which they themselves are guilty. Jesus was called a blasphemer on the grounds that he made himself out to be God (Luke 22:66–71). Members of the early church were called blasphemers because they affirmed Jesus' diety (Acts 6:11–14).

25:9 *in the day of atonement*, literally, "the tenth day of the seventh month" (of the Hebrew calendar).† The year of jubilee occurred every fiftieth year. It commenced on the day of atonement. It was called by different names, such as the *year of release* (Ezek. 46:17), the *time of God's favor* (Isa. 61:2), and the *year of redemption* (Isa 63:4). It was introduced with the blowing of trumpets. All field labor ceased for that year. Nonurban property came back to the original owner, inheritances were restored, and slaves were freed. The year of jubilee is said to be fulfilled in the gospel (Luke 4:18, 19) when men are set free from their bondage and brought into the glorious liberty of the sons of God through Jesus Christ.

day of the seventh month, in the day of atonement shall ye make the trumpet sound throughout all your land.

25:10 Lev 25:8–16, 28–54; Isa 61:1, 2; Jer 34:8, 15, 17; Lk 4:17–20

10 And ye shall hallow the fiftieth year, and proclaim liberty throughout *all* the land unto all the inhabitants thereof: it shall be a jubile unto you; and ye shall return every man unto his possession, and ye shall return every man unto his family.

11 A jubile shall that fiftieth year be unto you: ye shall not sow, neither reap that which groweth of itself in it, nor gather *the grapes* in it of thy vine undressed.

25:12 Lev 25:5

12 For it *is* the jubile; it shall be holy unto you: ye shall eat the increase thereof out of the field.

25:13 Lev 25:10, 24–31

13 In the year of this jubile ye shall return every man unto his possession.

25:14 Lev 25:17, 51, 52

14 And if thou sell ought unto thy neighbour, or buyest *ought* of thy neighbour's hand, ye shall not oppress one another:

15 According to the number of years after the jubile thou shalt buy of thy neighbour, *and* according unto the number of years of the fruits he shall sell unto thee:

25:16☆

16 According to the multitude of years thou shalt increase the price thereof, and according to the fewness of years thou shalt diminish the price of it: for *according* to the number *of the years* of the fruits doth he sell unto thee.

25:17 Lev 25:14–16

17 Ye shall not therefore oppress one another; but thou shalt fear thy God: for I *am* the LORD your God.

18 ¶Wherefore ye shall do my statutes, and keep my judgments, and do them; and ye shall dwell in the land in safety.

19 And the land shall yield her fruit, and ye shall eat your fill, and dwell therein in safety.

20 And if ye shall say, What shall we eat the seventh year? behold, we shall not sow, nor gather in our increase:

25:21 Lev 25:3, 4

21 Then I will command my blessing upon you in the sixth year, and it shall bring forth fruit for three years.

22 And ye shall sow the eighth year, and eat *yet* of old fruit until the ninth year; until her fruits come in ye shall eat *of* the old *store*.

3. The Jubilee Redemption of Property

25:23 Ex 19:5; 2 Chron 7:20; Ezek 48:14

23 ¶The land shall not be sold for ever: for the land *is* mine; for ye *are* strangers and sojourners with me.

24 And in all the land of your possession ye shall grant a redemption for the land.

25:25☆ Lev 25:35; Ruth 2:20; 4:4, 6; Jer 32:6–8

25 If thy brother be waxen poor, and hath sold away *some* of his possession, and if any of his kin come to redeem it, then shall he redeem that which his brother sold.

26 And if the man have none to redeem it, and himself be able to redeem it;

25:16 In 25:23 God says the land belongs to him. But he gave it to the Israelites in perpetuity. They could not sell the land which belonged to them and to their posterity. But if economic hardship forced them to do so, they could, in effect, lease the land until the year of jubilee, when it would be returned to the rightful owner. 25:16 specifies that the price given to the owner of the land was to be computed on the basis of the number of crops (years) remaining until the jubilee. The owner was not to demand more nor the buyer fewer. Economic justice was to be the guiding principle.

25:25 *thy brother be waxen poor.* All Israelites had land which belonged to them in perpetuity. Thus all had equality of opportunity. Yet some were not successful and became poor. Some such ones would sell their land. Whoever sold part of his property could redeem it later, or it could be redeemed by the next kinsman. In any event, the land was to come back to the family in the year of jubilee.

27 Then let him count the years of the sale thereof, and restore the **25:27** Lev 25:50–53
overplus unto the man to whom he sold it; that he may return unto his
possession.
28 But if he be not able to restore *it* to him, then that which is sold shall **25:28** Lev 25:10, 13
remain in the hand of him that hath bought it until the year of jubile: and
in the jubile it shall go out, and he shall return unto his possession.
29 And if a man sell a dwelling house in a walled city, then he may redeem
it within a whole year after it is sold; *within* a full year may he redeem it.
30 And if it be not redeemed within the space of a full year, then the house
that *is* in the walled city shall be established for ever to him that bought it
throughout his generations: it shall not go out in the jubile.
31 But the houses of the villages which have no wall round about them
shall be counted as the fields of the country: they may be redeemed, and
they shall go out in the jubile.
32 Notwithstanding the cities of the Levites, *and* the houses of the cities of
their possession, may the Levites redeem at any time.
33 And if a man purchase of the Levites, then the house that was sold, and ☆**25:33**
the city of his possession, shall go out in *the year of* jubile: for the houses of
the cities of the Levites *are* their possession among the children of Israel.
34 But the field of the suburbs of their cities may not be sold; for it *is* their **25:34** Num 35:2–5
perpetual possession.

4. The Laws for Loans

35 ¶And if thy brother be waxen poor, and fallen in decay with thee; then ☆**25:35** Lev 25:25
thou shalt relieve him: *yea, though he be* a stranger, or a sojourner; that he Deut 15:7–11
may live with thee. Prov 14:21 19:17
36 Take thou no usury of him, or increase: but fear thy God; that thy **25:36** Ex 22:25
brother may live with thee. Deut 23:19, 20
37 Thou shalt not give him thy money upon usury, nor lend him thy Neh 5:10
victuals for increase.
38 I *am* the LORD your God, which brought you forth out of the land of **25:38** Ex 20:2
Egypt, to give you the land of Canaan, *and* to be your God. Lev 11:45

5. The Redemption of Slaves (Hired Servants)

39 ¶And if thy brother *that dwelleth* by thee be waxen poor, and be sold **25:39** Ex 21:2–11
unto thee; thou shalt not compel him to serve as a bondservant: Deut 15:12–18
40 *But* as an hired servant, *and* as a sojourner, he shall be with thee, *and* **25:40** Lev 25:53
shall serve thee unto the year of jubile:
41 And *then* shall he depart from thee, *both* he and his children with him,
and shall return unto his own family, and unto the possession of his fathers
shall he return.
42 For they *are* my servants, which I brought forth out of the land of **25:42** Rom 6:22
Egypt: they shall not be sold as bondmen. 1 Cor 7:23
43 Thou shalt not rule over him with rigour; but shalt fear thy God. **25:43** Eph 6:9
44 Both thy bondmen, and thy bondmaids, which thou shalt have, *shall be* ☆**25:44**
of the heathen that are round about you; of them shall ye buy bondmen
and bondmaids.

25:33 *the house . . . and the city of his possession,* i.e., "houses in their cities, and the surrounding fields."†
25:35 Neighbor love meant that when a fellow Israelite was poverty stricken, those able to help should lend him money but charge no interest. Matthew Henry observed: This law "could never be thought binding where money is borrowed for purchase of lands, trade, or other improvements; for there it is reasonable that the lender share with the borrower in the profit."
25:44 Among the Israelites, slavery was permitted when it involved non-Israelites. But no Israelite was to become a slave to another Israelite. The law permitted the slave owner to pass on his slaves to his sons by way of inheritance.

[45]Moreover of the children of the strangers that do sojourn among you,
of them shall ye buy, and of their families that *are* with you, which they
begat in your land: and they shall be your possession.

25:46 Lev 25:40, 53

[46]And ye shall take them as an inheritance for your children after you, to
inherit *them for* a possession; they shall be your bondmen for ever: but over
your brethren the children of Israel, ye shall not rule one over another with
rigour.

25:47 Lev 25:39

[47]¶And if a sojourner or stranger wax rich by thee, and thy brother *that*
dwelleth by him wax poor, and sell himself unto the stranger *or* sojourner by
thee, or to the stock of the stranger's family:

25:48 Neh 5:5

[48]After that he is sold he may be redeemed again; one of his brethren
may redeem him:

25:49 Lev 25:26

[49]Either his uncle, or his uncle's son, may redeem him, or *any* that is nigh
of kin unto him of his family may redeem him; or if he be able, he may
redeem himself.

25:50☆ Lev 25:27; Job 7:1

[50]And he shall reckon with him that bought him from the year that he
was sold to him unto the year of jubile: and the price of his sale shall be
according unto the number of years, according to the time of an hired
servant shall it be with him.
[51]If *there be* yet many years *behind,* according unto them he shall give
again the price of his redemption out of the money that he was bought for.
[52]And if there remain but few years unto the year of jubile, then he shall
count with him, *and* according unto his years shall he give him again the
price of his redemption.

25:53 Lev 25:40, 46

[53]*And* as a yearly hired servant shall he be with him: *and the other* shall
not rule with rigour over him in thy sight.

25:54 Ex 21:3–6; Lev 25:41

[54]And if he be not redeemed in these *years,* then he shall go out in the
year of jubile, *both* he, and his children with him.
[55]For unto me the children of Israel *are* servants; they *are* my servants
whom I brought forth out of the land of Egypt: I *am* the LORD your God.

VII. HOW TO SECURE GOD'S BLESSING (26:1—27:34)

A. THE BLESSINGS FOR KEEPING GOD'S LAWS

26:1 Ex 20:4; 34:17; Lev 19:3, 4; Num 33:52; Deut 16:21, 22

26 YE shall make you no idols nor graven image, neither rear you up
a standing image, neither shall ye set up *any* image of stone in your
land, to bow down unto it: for I *am* the LORD your God.

26:2 Ex 20:8–11

[2]¶Ye shall keep my sabbaths, and reverence my sanctuary: I *am* the
LORD.

26:3☆ Lev 18:4, 5

[3]If ye walk in my statutes, and keep my commandments, and do them;

26:4 Lev 25:19–22; Deut 11:14, 15; 28:12; Amos 9:13

[4]Then I will give you rain in due season, and the land shall yield her
increase, and the trees of the field shall yield their fruit.
[5]And your threshing shall reach unto the vintage, and the vintage shall
reach unto the sowing time: and ye shall eat your bread to the full, and
dwell in your land safely.

26:6 Ex 23:29, 30; Ps 29:11; 147:14

[6]And I will give peace in the land, and ye shall lie down, and none shall
make *you* afraid: and I will rid evil beasts out of the land, neither shall the
sword go through your land.

25:50 All God's people are his servants. Therefore all are subject to his sovereign rulership. They are to treat their brothers the way God treats them. Since God is merciful, they also must be merciful to those in need.
26:3ff God's invariable law is that those who obey him will be blessed by him. Paul repeats this truth: "Whatsoever a man soweth, that shall he also reap" (Gal. 6:7). If we sow righteousness and act in love toward our neighbor, we shall reap a rich reward in this life and in the one to come.

[7]And ye shall chase your enemies, and they shall fall before you by the
sword.
[8]And five of you shall chase an hundred, and an hundred of you shall put
ten thousand to flight: and your enemies shall fall before you by the sword.
[9]For I will have respect unto you, and make you fruitful, and multiply
you, and establish my covenant with you.
[10]And ye shall eat old store, and bring forth the old because of the new.
[11]And I will set my tabernacle among you: and my soul shall not abhor
you.
[12]And I will walk among you, and will be your God, and ye shall be my
people.
[13]I *am* the LORD your God, which brought you forth out of the land of
Egypt, that ye should not be their bondmen; and I have broken the bands
of your yoke, and made you go upright.

☆**26:8** Deut 28:7; 32:30
26:9 Ex 6:4, 5; Deut 28:2–6
26:10 Lev 26:5; 2 Kgs 19:29
26:11 Ex 29:45, 46; Ps 132:13, 14
26:12 Ex 6:7; Jer 32:38
26:13 Ex 20:2; Ps 116:6; Jer 2:20; Ezek 34:27

B. THE PUNISHMENTS FOR DISOBEDIENCE

[14]¶But if ye will not hearken unto me, and will not do all these
commandments;
[15]And if ye shall despise my statutes, or if your soul abhor my judgments,
so that ye will not do all my commandments, *but* that ye break my
covenant:
[16]I also will do this unto you; I will even appoint over you terror,
consumption, and the burning ague, that shall consume the eyes, and cause
sorrow of heart: and ye shall sow your seed in vain, for your enemies shall
eat it.
[17]And I will set my face against you, and ye shall be slain before your
enemies: they that hate you shall reign over you; and ye shall flee when
none pursueth you.
[18]And if ye will not yet for all this hearken unto me, then I will punish
you seven times more for your sins.
[19]And I will break the pride of your power; and I will make your heaven
as iron, and your earth as brass:
[20]And your strength shall be spent in vain: for your land shall not yield
her increase, neither shall the trees of the land yield their fruits.
[21]¶And if ye walk contrary unto me, and will not hearken unto me; I will
bring seven times more plagues upon you according to your sins.
[22]I will also send wild beasts among you, which shall rob you of your
children, and destroy your cattle, and make you few in number; and your
high ways shall be desolate.
[23]And if ye will not be reformed by me by these things, but will walk
contrary unto me;
[24]Then will I also walk contrary unto you, and will punish you yet seven
times for your sins.
[25]And I will bring a sword upon you, that shall avenge the quarrel of *my*
covenant: and when ye are gathered together within your cities, I will send
the pestilence among you; and ye shall be delivered into the hand of the
enemy.

26:15 Num 15:30, 31
26:16 Deut 28:22, 33, 65–67; 32:25; Jer 5:17; Ezek 33:10; Zech 14:12
26:17 Lev 26:36, 37; Deut 28:25; Neh 9:27–30; Ps 106:41, 42; Prov 28:1
26:18 Lev 26:21, 24, 28; Prov 6:31
26:19 Deut 28:23; Isa 25:11; 26:5
26:20 Ps 127:1; Hab 2:13
26:21 Lev 26:18
26:22 Lev 26:6; Deut 32:24
26:23 Isa 1:18–20
☆**26:24** Lev 26:18
26:25 Deut 28:21, 22, 27–29, 32:35

26:8 "Five of you will chase a hundred, and a hundred of you, ten thousand!" (TLB). In spiritual matters, arithmetic progression gives way to geometric progression. The greater the number of Christians praying, the greater the response; for five, the ratio is twenty-to-one, but when there are a hundred, the ratio of the response is one-hundred-to-one.

26:24 "Those that cast off God deserve that he should cast them off. As they continued obstinate, the judgments should increase yet more upon them."* God will punish them seven times more, for if "less judgments do not do their work, God will send greater judgments."*

26 *And* when I have broken the staff of your bread, ten women shall bake
your bread in one oven, and they shall deliver *you* your bread again by
weight: and ye shall eat, and not be satisfied.
27 And if ye will not for all this hearken unto me, but walk contrary unto
me;
28 Then I will walk contrary unto you also in fury; and I, even I, will
chastise you seven times for your sins.
29 And ye shall eat the flesh of your sons, and the flesh of your daughters
shall ye eat.
30 And I will destroy your high places, and cut down your images, and
cast your carcases upon the carcases of your idols, and my soul shall abhor
you.
31 And I will make your cities waste, and bring your sanctuaries unto
desolation, and I will not smell the savour of your sweet odours.
32 And I will bring the land into desolation: and your enemies which
dwell therein shall be astonished at it.
33 And I will scatter you among the heathen, and will draw out a sword
after you: and your land shall be desolate, and your cities waste.
34 Then shall the land enjoy her sabbaths, as long as it lieth desolate, and
ye *be* in your enemies' land; *even* then shall the land rest, and enjoy her
sabbaths.
35 As long as it lieth desolate it shall rest; because it did not rest in your
sabbaths, when ye dwelt upon it.
36 And upon them that are left *alive* of you I will send a faintness into
their hearts in the lands of their enemies; and the sound of a shaken leaf
shall chase them; and they shall flee, as fleeing from a sword; and they shall
fall when none pursueth.
37 And they shall fall one upon another, as it were before a sword, when
none pursueth: and ye shall have no power to stand before your enemies.
38 And ye shall perish among the heathen, and the land of your enemies
shall eat you up.
39 And they that are left of you shall pine away in their iniquity in your
enemies' lands; and also in the iniquities of their fathers shall they pine
away with them.
40 If they shall confess their iniquity, and the iniquity of their fathers, with
their trespass which they trespassed against me, and that also they have
walked contrary unto me;
41 And *that* I also have walked contrary unto them, and have brought
them into the land of their enemies; if then their uncircumcised hearts be
humbled, and they then accept of the punishment of their iniquity:
42 Then will I remember my covenant with Jacob, and also my covenant
with Isaac, and also my covenant with Abraham will I remember; and I will
remember the land.
43 The land also shall be left of them, and shall enjoy her sabbaths, while
she lieth desolate without them: and they shall accept of the punishment of
their iniquity: because, even because they despised my judgments, and
because their soul abhorred my statutes.
44 And yet for all that, when they be in the land of their enemies, I will not
cast them away, neither will I abhor them, to destroy them utterly, and to
break my covenant with them: for I *am* the LORD their God.

26:26 Isa 3:1; 9:19, 20; Ezek 4:16
26:28 Lev 26:18
26:29 Deut 28:53–57; 2 Kgs 6:26–30; Jer 19:9
26:30 1 Kgs 13:2–5; Isa 27:9; Ezek 6:13
26:31 2 Kgs 25:4–10; Ps 74:3; Isa 24:10–13; Jer 52:13
26:32☆ Deut 28:37; 29:23; Jer 12:11; 18:16; Ezek 33:28; Dan 9:2
26:33 Deut 28:64–68
26:34 Lev 26:43; 2 Chron 36:21; Jer 29:10
26:36 Deut 28:65, 67; Ezek 21:7
26:38 Deut 4:25–27; Jer 42:17, 18
26:39 Ezek 20:43; 33:10
26:40 Deut 30:1–3; 2 Chron 7:17; 12:7; Ezek 36:31; Mt 23:12; Lk 14:11; 1 Jn 1:9
26:42 Gen 12:1–3; 15:1–4, 13–16; 26:2–5; 28:13–15
26:43 Lev 26:34
26:44 Deut 4:29–31; Neh 9:31; Rom 11:2, 26

26:32 God reveals the punishment which would be exacted of his people if and when they disobeyed him and broke the covenant. This threat is repeated in Deut. 28:58–67. The first punishment was meted out in the Babylonian captivity of 587 B.C. The *diaspora*, or dispersion, of the Jews among the nations came later and has not been reversed to this day.

[45]But I will for their sakes remember the covenant of their ancestors,
whom I brought forth out of the land of Egypt in the sight of the heathen,
that I might be their God: I *am* the LORD.
[46]These *are* the statutes and judgments and laws, which the LORD made
between him and the children of Israel in mount Si'nai by the hand of
Moses.

26:45 Ex 2:24; 20:2 Lev 22:32, 33 25:38 Lk 1:72, 73
☆**26:46** Lev 27:34 Deut 6:1; 12:1

C. THE MAKING OF VOWS

1. The Price of Release from a Vow of Dedication

27 AND the LORD spake unto Moses, saying,
[2]Speak unto the children of Israel, and say unto them, When a
man shall make a singular vow, the persons *shall be* for the LORD by thy
estimation.
[3]And thy estimation shall be of the male from twenty years old even unto
sixty years old, even thy estimation shall be fifty shekels of silver, after the
shekel of the sanctuary.
[4]And if it *be* a female, then thy estimation shall be thirty shekels.
[5]And if *it be* from five years old even unto twenty years old, then thy
estimation shall be of the male twenty shekels, and for the female ten
shekels.
[6]And if *it be* from a month old even unto five years old, then thy
estimation shall be of the male five shekels of silver, and for the female thy
estimation *shall be* three shekels of silver.
[7]And if *it be* from sixty years old and above; if *it be* a male, then thy
estimation shall be fifteen shekels, and for the female ten shekels.
[8]But if he be poorer than thy estimation, then he shall present himself
before the priest, and the priest shall value him; according to his ability that
vowed shall the priest value him.

☆**27:2**
27:3 Ex 30:13 Lev 5:15; 27:25
27:6 Num 3:46–48 18:14–16
27:8 Lev 14:21, 22

2. Vows Involving Animals

[9]And if *it be* a beast, whereof men bring an offering unto the LORD, all
that *any man* giveth of such unto the LORD shall be holy.
[10]He shall not alter it, nor change it, a good for a bad, or a bad for a
good: and if he shall at all change beast for beast, then it and the exchange
thereof shall be holy.
[11]And if *it be* any unclean beast, of which they do not offer a sacrifice
unto the LORD, then he shall present the beast before the priest:

27:10 Lev 27:14–33

26:46 The Law of Moses takes in the total economy in which the people of Israel moved and lived. The Law can be divided into three segments: (1) the moral law of the Ten Commandments (Deut. 5:22; 10:4); (2) the ceremonial law which set forth the proper approach to God in worship (7:37, 38); (3) the civil law under which the people lived and were governed (Deut. 17:9–11). The ceremonial law, having been fulfilled by Jesus Christ, is no longer binding on people under the new covenant. The civil law was designed for the Old Testament theocracy, so other nations living under other conditions are not bound by it. The basic moral law, however, applies to all people of all eras and has for its purposes: (1) showing all men their need for a Savior (pedagogic use of the law); (2) laying down the rules which men of faith can follow in order to please him who has saved them (normative use); and (3) a restraining influence on all of mankind so that a government of law and not of men is made possible (political use).

27:2 *a singular vow.* While it was not required, some pious Israelites would consecrate themselves, their wives, or their children to serve in the tabernacle. This would involve inferior duties, such as sweeping the floor, carrying out the ashes, and running errands. But God had made full provision for all of the functions of the tabernacle through the Levites. Therefore, any singular vow or intention was redeemable by money, so non-Levites could accomplish the intentions of pious and devoted hearts. The priests had a money scale for the redemption of those who had such intentions. More was paid for a male than for a female. Why so? Apparently the value was related to the productivity of the sexes. In the Israelite community the male was the chief producer as a farmer. We know this because provision was made for widows and their children, but not for widowers. All were equal before God but there were (and still are) other differences which must be taken into account.

12 And the priest shall value it, whether it be good or bad: as thou valuest it, *who art* the priest, so shall it be.

13 But if he will at all redeem it, then he shall add a fifth *part* thereof unto thy estimation.

3. Vows Concerning a Dedicated House

14 ¶And when a man shall sanctify his house *to be* holy unto the LORD, then the priest shall estimate it, whether it be good or bad: as the priest shall estimate it, so shall it stand.

15 And if he that sanctified it will redeem his house, then he shall add the fifth *part* of the money of thy estimation unto it, and it shall be his.

4. Vows Concerning a Dedicated Field

16 And if a man shall sanctify unto the LORD *some part* of a field of his possession, then thy estimation shall be according to the seed thereof: an homer of barley seed *shall be valued* at fifty shekels of silver.

17 If he sanctify his field from the year of jubile, according to thy estimation it shall stand.

27:18 Lev 25:14–16

18 But if he sanctify his field after the jubile, then the priest shall reckon unto him the money according to the years that remain, even unto the year of the jubile, and it shall be abated from thy estimation.

19 And if he that sanctified the field will in any wise redeem it, then he shall add the fifth *part* of the money of thy estimation unto it, and it shall be assured to him.

27:20☆

20 And if he will not redeem the field, or if he have sold the field to another man, it shall not be redeemed any more.

27:21 Lev 25:8–54; Num 18:14; Ezek 44:29

21 But the field, when it goeth out in the jubile, shall be holy unto the LORD, as a field devoted; the possession thereof shall be the priest's.

22 And if *a man* sanctify unto the LORD a field which he hath bought, which *is* not of the fields of his possession;

23 Then the priest shall reckon unto him the worth of thy estimation, *even* unto the year of the jubile: and he shall give thine estimation in that day, *as* a holy thing unto the LORD.

27:24 Lev 27:21

24 In the year of the jubile the field shall return unto him of whom it was bought, *even* to him to whom the possession of the land *did belong*.

27:25☆ Ex 30:13; Lev 5:15; Num 3:47; 18:16; Ezek 45:12

25 And all thy estimations shall be according to the shekel of the sanctuary: twenty gerahs shall be the shekel.

5. Vows Concerning Dedicated Firstborn Animals and Other Dedicated Things

27:26 Ex 13:2, 12; 22:30

26 ¶Only the firstling of the beasts, which should be the LORD's firstling, no man shall sanctify it; whether *it be* ox, or sheep: it *is* the LORD's.

27 And if *it be* of an unclean beast, then he shall redeem *it* according to thine estimation, and shall add a fifth *part* of it thereto: or if it be not redeemed, then it shall be sold according to thy estimation.

27:28 Lev 27:21; Jos 6:17–19

28 Notwithstanding no devoted thing, that a man shall devote unto the LORD of all that he hath, *both* of man and beast, and of the field of his possession, shall be sold or redeemed: every devoted thing *is* most holy unto the LORD.

27:20 Paraphrased: "But if he decides not to redeem the field, or if he has sold the field to someone else (and has given the Lord his rights to it at the Year of Jubilee), it shall not be returned to him again."†

27:25 *And all your estimations shall be according to the shekel of the sanctuary: twenty gerahs shall be the shekel*, i.e., "all the valuations shall be stated in standard money."†

29 None devoted, which shall be devoted of men, shall be redeemed; *but* ☆27:29
shall surely be put to death.

6. Buying Back the Tithe

30 And all the tithe of the land, *whether* of the seed of the land, *or* of the ☆27:30
fruit of the tree, *is* the LORD'S: *it is* holy unto the LORD. Gen 28:22 Num 18:21, 24
31 And if a man will at all redeem *ought* of his tithes, he shall add thereto 2 Chron 31:5, 6 Neh 3:12
the fifth *part* thereof. Mal 3:8
32 And concerning the tithe of the herd, or of the flock, *even* of whatsoever
passeth under the rod, the tenth shall be holy unto the LORD.
33 He shall not search whether it be good or bad, neither shall he change 27:33
it: and if he change it at all, then both it and the change thereof shall be Lev 27:10
holy; it shall not be redeemed.
34 These *are* the commandments, which the LORD commanded Moses for 27:34
the children of Israel in mount Si'nai. Lev 26:46

27:29 Paraphrased: "No one sentenced by the courts to die may pay a fine instead; he shall surely be put to death." Or, "no one who is under the ban of God to be put to death may be ransomed."†
27:30 The Israelites were to tithe from the crops of their fields, from their trees, and from their cattle. If money were substituted as a ransom for any of these, a fifth was added to the value. The tithe acknowledged God's gracious material provision, for he fructified the labor of his people. It also was a token that they were mere tenants, for the true title to the land belonged to God himself.

THE FOURTH BOOK OF MOSES CALLED

NUMBERS

Authorship, date, and background Numbers is the fourth book of the Pentateuch. The English title for the book derives from the Septuagint, which selected this name because of the two numberings of the Israelites in the wilderness journey (chapters 1 and 26). The Hebrew title was "in the wilderness of," taken from the fifth word of the first line in the Hebrew text. It is the more appropriate title because the book describes the journey of the Israelites from Sinai to the plains of Moab. Moses is the chief figure in the book. It indicates that he wrote down their movements as the Lord instructed him (33:2). Thus he kept a record of the wanderings which was incorporated in the book of Numbers along with other source material which he used. The date for the book would be the last two decades of the fifteenth century, assuming the early date for the exodus.

Most of the events recorded in Numbers occurred in the second and the fortieth years of Israel's pilgrimage from Egypt to the Promised Land. The years in between were passed over in virtual silence. Genesis recorded the beginnings of the nation of Israel through the patriarchs; Exodus traced the deliverance of the Israelites from Egypt, the making of the covenant between them and God, the giving of the Law and the construction of the Tabernacle; Leviticus set forth the religious, political, social, and economic laws which were to govern Israel; Numbers recorded how God prepared his people for their entrance into, and the conquest of, the land he had promised to Abraham.

Characteristics and content Numbers describes how God leads, guides, disciplines, delivers, sustains, and protects his people. When they are disobedient he rewards them by judgment; when they repent he pardons and restores them. Their history is replete with backslidings and an account of all of the human passions common to man. Aaron and Miriam challenge the authority of their brother Moses. Miriam is chastened by God, who makes her leprous, after which Moses intervenes with God for her cleansing. The story of the quails, sent by God because of Israel's complaints against the manna, tells of the death of many at God's hands.

During this time Moses himself falls into sin. In an earlier event God instructed him to strike the rock to obtain water, which then flowed abundantly. On the second occasion God tells him to speak to the rock, undoubtedly because the rock is a type of Christ who can be smitten but once for the transgressions of men. Instead of speaking to the rock, Moses, in anger, smites the rock, and for this transgression God forbids him entrance into the Promised Land.

Numbers recounts rather fully the story of Israel's encounter with the Moabites and the hiring of Balaam by Balak to curse the people of God. Instead he pronounces a triple blessing and predicts Israel's ultimate triumph. In the latter section of the book, Moses records the preparations for entering Canaan, and apportions the Transjordan territory to Reuben, Gad, and Manasseh.

Outline

I. Preparing for the journey from Mount Sinai (1:1—10:10)
II. From Sinai to Kadesh-barnea (10:11—14:45)
III. From Kadesh-barnea to the plains of Moab (15:1—21:35)
IV. Israel encounters the Moabites and Balaam (22:1—25:18)
V. Preparations before entering the land of Canaan (26:1—36:13)

I. PREPARING FOR THE JOURNEY FROM MOUNT SINAI (1:1—10:10)

A. THE MILITARY CENSUS

1. The Census Takers Chosen

The Men of War Numbered

AND the LORD spake unto Moses in the wilderness of Si'nai, in the tabernacle of the congregation, on the first *day* of the second month, in the second year after they were come out of the land of Egypt, saying, ☆1:1

2 Take ye the sum of all the congregation of the children of Israel, after their families, by the house of their fathers, with the number of *their* names, every male by their polls; ☆1:2 Ex 25:22; 30:11, 12 38:26 Num 26:2–4, 63–65 2 Sam 24:1–3 1 Chron 21:2

3 From twenty years old and upward, all that are able to go forth to war in Israel: thou and Aaron shall number them by their armies.

4 And with you there shall be a man of every tribe; every one head of the house of his fathers.

5 ¶And these *are* the names of the men that shall stand with you: of *the tribe of* Reuben; E-li'zur the son of Shed'e-ur.

6 Of Simeon; She-lu'mi-el the son of Zu-ri-shad'da-i.

7 Of Judah; Nah'shon the son of Am-min'a-dab.

8 Of Is'sa-char; Ne-than'e-el the son of Zu'ar.

9 Of Zeb'u-lun; E-li'ab the son of He'lon.

10 Of the children of Joseph: of E'phra-im; E-lish'a-ma the son of Am-mi'hud: of Ma-nas'seh; Ga-ma'li-el the son of Pe-dah'zur.

11 Of Benjamin; Ab'i-dan the son of Gid-e-o'ni.

12 Of Dan; A-hi-e'zer the son of Am-mi-shad'da-i.

13 Of Asher; Pa'gi-el the son of Oc'ran.

14 Of Gad; E-li'a-saph the son of Deu'el.

15 Of Naph'ta-li; A-hi'ra the son of E'nan.

16 These *were* the renowned of the congregation, princes of the tribes of their fathers, heads of thousands in Israel. 1:16: Num 1:2–15 7:2; 26:3–51 1 Chron 27:16–22

2. The Counting of the Warriors

17 ¶And Moses and Aaron took these men which are expressed by *their* names: 1:17 Num 1:2 Ezra 2:59 Neh 7:61

18 And they assembled all the congregation together on the first *day* of the second month, and they declared their pedigrees after their families, by the house of their fathers, according to the number of the names, from twenty years old and upward, by their polls. ☆1:18

19 As the LORD commanded Moses, so he numbered them in the wilderness of Si'nai.

20 And the children of Reuben, Israel's eldest son, by their generations, after their families, by the house of their fathers, according to the number of the names, by their polls, every male from twenty years old and upward, all that were able to go forth to war; 1:20 Num 2:32, 33 26:5–51

21 Those that were numbered of them, *even* of the tribe of Reuben, *were* forty and six thousand and five hundred.

1:1 *on the first day of the second month* (of the Jewish calendar), i.e., around "the fifteenth day of April." (See also 1:18.)

1:2 Here God commands Moses to number the people. The census was to be limited, however, to males twenty years old or over. It was a military census in preparation for the wars to possess Caanan. Excluded from the census were the lame, the deaf, the blind, and others who had bodily infirmities or chronic diseases; only those who were "able to go forth to war" were numbered. Later, when David ordered a census, he paid dearly for so doing, since it was not commanded by God (2 Sam. 24:1ff). The Levites were not included in this census (see note on 1:49).

1:18 Anyone twenty years or older was eligible for military service. The tribe of Judah, from which Messiah came (1:27), supplied the largest number of warriors, 74,600.

22 ¶Of the children of Simeon, by their generations, after their families, by the house of their fathers, those that were numbered of them, according to the number of the names, by their polls, every male from twenty years old and upward, all that were able to go forth to war;
23 Those that were numbered of them, *even* of the tribe of Simeon, *were* fifty and nine thousand and three hundred.
24 ¶Of the children of Gad, by their generations, after their families, by the house of their fathers, according to the number of the names, from twenty years old and upward, all that were able to go forth to war;
25 Those that were numbered of them, *even* of the tribe of Gad, *were* forty and five thousand six hundred and fifty.
26 ¶Of the children of Judah, by their generations, after their families, by the house of their fathers, according to the number of the names, from twenty years old and upward, all that were able to go forth to war;
27 Those that were numbered of them, *even* of the tribe of Judah, *were* threescore and fourteen thousand and six hundred.
28 ¶Of the children of Is′sa-char, by their generations, after their families, by the house of their fathers, according to the number of the names, from twenty years old and upward, all that were able to go forth to war;
29 Those that were numbered of them, *even* of the tribe of Is′sa-char, *were* fifty and four thousand and four hundred.
30 ¶Of the children of Zeb′u-lun, by their generations, after their families, by the house of their fathers, according to the number of the names, from twenty years old and upward, all that were able to go forth to war;
31 Those that were numbered of them, *even* of the tribe of Zeb′u-lun, *were* fifty and seven thousand and four hundred.
1:32☆ 32 ¶Of the children of Joseph, *namely,* of the children of E′phra-im, by their generations, after their families, by the house of their fathers, according to the number of the names, from twenty years old and upward, all that were able to go forth to war;
33 Those that were numbered of them, *even* of the tribe of E′phra-im, *were* forty thousand and five hundred.
34 ¶Of the children of Ma-nas′seh, by their generations, after their families, by the house of their fathers, according to the number of the names, from twenty years old and upward, all that were able to go forth to war;
35 Those that were numbered of them, *even* of the tribe of Ma-nas′seh, *were* thirty and two thousand and two hundred.
36 ¶Of the children of Benjamin, by their generations, after their families, by the house of their fathers, according to the number of the names, from twenty years old and upward, all that were able to go forth to war;
37 Those that were numbered of them, *even* of the tribe of Benjamin, *were* thirty and five thousand and four hundred.
38 ¶Of the children of Dan, by their generations, after their families, by the house of their fathers, according to the number of the names, from twenty years old and upward, all that were able to go forth to war;
39 Those that were numbered of them, *even* of the tribe of Dan, *were* threescore and two thousand and seven hundred.
40 ¶Of the children of Asher, by their generations, after their families, by the house of their fathers, according to the number of the names, from twenty years old and upward, all that were able to go forth to war;

1:32 The Levites were exempted from going to war; yet there were twelve tribes participating in the military. Joseph's two sons, Ephraim and Manasseh, were counted as two tribes along with the other ten sons of Jacob.

41 Those that were numbered of them, *even* of the tribe of Asher, *were*
forty and one thousand and five hundred.
42 ¶Of the children of Naph'ta-li, throughout their generations, after their
families, by the house of their fathers, according to the number of the
names, from twenty years old and upward, all that were able to go forth to
war;
43 Those that were numbered of them, *even* of the tribe of Naph'ta-li, *were*
fifty and three thousand and four hundred.
44 ¶These *are* those that were numbered, which Moses and Aaron
numbered, and the princes of Israel, *being* twelve men: each one was for the
house of his fathers.
45 So were all those that were numbered of the children of Israel, by the
house of their fathers, from twenty years old and upward, all that were able
to go forth to war in Israel;
46 Even all they that were numbered were six hundred thousand and three
thousand and five hundred and fifty.
47 ¶But the Levites after the tribe of their fathers were not numbered
among them.

☆**1:47** Num 2:32, 33 26:62

48 For the LORD had spoken unto Moses, saying,
49 Only thou shalt not number the tribe of Levi, neither take the sum of
them among the children of Israel:
50 But thou shalt appoint the Levites over the tabernacle of testimony,
and over all the vessels thereof, and over all things that *belong* to it: they
shall bear the tabernacle, and all the vessels thereof; and they shall minister
unto it, and shall encamp round about the tabernacle.

1:50 Num 3:6–10, 25–37; 4:25–48

51 And when the tabernacle setteth forward, the Levites shall take it
down: and when the tabernacle is to be pitched, the Levites shall set it up:
and the stranger that cometh nigh shall be put to death.

1:51 Num 3:38; 18:22

52 And the children of Israel shall pitch their tents, every man by his own
camp, and every man by his own standard, throughout their hosts.

1:52 Num 2:1

53 But the Levites shall pitch round about the tabernacle of testimony,
that there be no wrath upon the congregation of the children of Israel: and
the Levites shall keep the charge of the tabernacle of testimony.

1:53 Num 1:50

54 And the children of Israel did according to all that the LORD com-
manded Moses, so did they.

1:54 Ex 39:43

B. THE CAMP ASSIGNMENTS

2 AND the LORD spake unto Moses and unto Aaron, saying,
2 Every man of the children of Israel shall pitch by his own standard,
with the ensign of their father's house: far off about the tabernacle of the
congregation shall they pitch.

2:1 Num 1:52

3 And on the east side toward the rising of the sun shall they of the
standard of the camp of Judah pitch throughout their armies: and
Nah'shon the son of Am-min'a-dab *shall be* captain of the children of
Judah.

☆**2:3**

4 And his host, and those that were numbered of them, *were* threescore
and fourteen thousand and six hundred.
5 And those that do pitch next unto him *shall be* the tribe of Is'sa-char:
and Ne-than'e-el the son of Zu'ar *shall be* captain of the children of Is'sa-
char.

1:47–49 The Levites were not to be included with the eleven other tribes. But later they were numbered separately (3:15).

2:3 Each of the tribes remained together. Apparently this was designed to maintain their separate identity. It also helped to keep them from extensive intermarriage among the tribes; thus when the land of Canaan was divided, each geographical area was sharply distinguished and easily identifiable.

6 And his host, and those that were numbered thereof, *were* fifty and four thousand and four hundred.

7 *Then* the tribe of Zeb′u-lun: and E-li′ab the son of He′lon *shall be* captain of the children of Zeb′u-lun.

8 And his host, and those that were numbered thereof, *were* fifty and seven thousand and four hundred.

9 All that were numbered in the camp of Judah *were* an hundred thousand and fourscore thousand and six thousand and four hundred, throughout their armies. These shall first set forth.

10 ¶On the south side *shall be* the standard of the camp of Reuben according to their armies: and the captain of the children of Reuben *shall be* E-li′zur the son of Shed′e-ur.

11 And his host, and those that were numbered thereof, *were* forty and six thousand and five hundred.

12 And those which pitch by him *shall be* the tribe of Simeon: and the captain of the children of Simeon *shall be* She-lu′mi-el the son of Zu-ri-shad′da-i.

13 And his host, and those that were numbered of them, *were* fifty and nine thousand and three hundred.

2:14☆ 14 Then the tribe of Gad: and the captain of the sons of Gad *shall be* E-li′a-saph the son of Reu′el.

15 And his host, and those that were numbered of them, *were* forty and five thousand and six hundred and fifty.

16 All that were numbered in the camp of Reuben *were* an hundred thousand and fifty and one thousand and four hundred and fifty, throughout their armies. And they shall set forth in the second rank.

17 ¶Then the tabernacle of the congregation shall set forward with the camp of the Levites in the midst of the camp: as they encamp, so shall they set forward, every man in his place by their standards.

18 ¶On the west side *shall be* the standard of the camp of E′phra-im according to their armies: and the captain of the sons of E′phra-im *shall be* E-lish′a-ma the son of Am-mi′hud.

19 And his host, and those that were numbered of them, *were* forty thousand and five hundred.

20 And by him *shall be* the tribe of Ma-nas′seh: and the captain of the children of Ma-nas′seh *shall be* Ga-ma′li-el the son of Pe-dah′zur.

21 And his host, and those that were numbered of them, *were* thirty and two thousand and two hundred.

22 Then the tribe of Benjamin: and the captain of the sons of Benjamin *shall be* Ab′i-dan the son of Gid-e-o′ni.

23 And his host, and those that were numbered of them, *were* thirty and five thousand and four hundred.

24 All that were numbered of the camp of E′phra-im *were* an hundred thousand and eight thousand and an hundred, throughout their armies. And they shall go forward in the third rank.

25 ¶The standard of the camp of Dan *shall be* on the north side by their armies: and the captain of the children of Dan *shall be* A-hi-e′zer the son of Am-mi-shad′da-i.

26 And his host, and those that were numbered of them, *were* threescore and two thousand and seven hundred.

27 And those that encamp by him *shall be* the tribe of Asher: and the captain of the children of Asher *shall be* Pa′gi-el the son of Oc′ran.

2:14 *Reuel.* Deuel in 1:14.

28 And his host, and those that were numbered of them, *were* forty and
one thousand and five hundred.
29 ¶Then the tribe of Naph'ta-li: and the captain of the children of
Naph'ta-li *shall be* A-hi'ra the son of E'nan.
30 And his host, and those that were numbered of them, *were* fifty and
three thousand and four hundred.
31 All they that were numbered in the camp of Dan *were* an hundred
thousand and fifty and seven thousand and six hundred. They shall go
hindmost with their standards.
32 ¶These *are* those which were numbered of the children of Israel by the **2:32** Ex 12:37; 38:26
house of their fathers: all those that were numbered of the camps Num 1:20
throughout their hosts *were* six hundred thousand and three thousand and 11:21; 26:51
five hundred and fifty.
33 But the Levites were not numbered among the children of Israel; as the
LORD commanded Moses.
34 And the children of Israel did according to all that the LORD com- **2:34** Num 1:54
manded Moses: so they pitched by their standards, and so they set forward,
every one after their families, according to the house of their fathers.

C. THE LEVITES AND THEIR DUTIES

1. The Sons of Aaron

3 THESE also *are* the generations of Aaron and Moses in the day *that*
the LORD spake with Moses in mount Si'nai.
2 And these *are* the names of the sons of Aaron; Na'dab the firstborn, and **3:2** Lev 10:1, 2, 6
A-bi'hu, E-le-a'zar, and Ith'a-mar. Num 26:60
3 These *are* the names of the sons of Aaron, the priests which were **3:3** Ex 29:1–37
anointed, whom he consecrated to minister in the priest's office.
4 And Na'dab and A-bi'hu died before the LORD, when they offered **3:4** Lev 10:1, 2
strange fire before the LORD, in the wilderness of Si'nai, and they had no Num 26:61
children: and E-le-a'zar and Ith'a-mar ministered in the priest's office in the
sight of Aaron their father.

2. The Duties of the Levites

5 ¶And the LORD spake unto Moses, saying,
6 Bring the tribe of Levi near, and present them before Aaron the priest, **3:6** Num 8:6–15,
that they may minister unto him. 22–26; 18:2–6
7 And they shall keep his charge, and the charge of the whole congrega- Deut 33:10
tion before the tabernacle of the congregation, to do the service of the **3:7** Num 3:11, 12,
tabernacle. 41; 8:16–18
8 And they shall keep all the instruments of the tabernacle of the
congregation, and the charge of the children of Israel, to do the service of
the tabernacle.
9 And thou shalt give the Levites unto Aaron and to his sons: they *are* ☆**3:9**
wholly given unto him out of the children of Israel.
10 And thou shalt appoint Aaron and his sons, and they shall wait on their **3:10** Num 1:51
priest's office: and the stranger that cometh nigh shall be put to death. 16:35, 40; 18:7
Ezek 44:8

3. The Levites in Substitution for the Oldest Sons of Israel

11 And the LORD spake unto Moses, saying, **3:11** Num 3:7, 41, 45
12 And I, behold, I have taken the Levites from among the children of

---

3:9 From among the tribe of Levi, only the descendants of Aaron participated in the priesthood; the remainder of the Levites were given to Aaron for service in connection with the tabernacle and its functions. No Levite, other than those of the priesthood, was ever to trespass into the areas or functions reserved especially for the priesthood.

Israel instead of all the firstborn that openeth the matrix among the
children of Israel: therefore the Levites shall be mine;
3:13 Ex 13:2, 12, 15 — 13 Because all the firstborn *are* mine; *for* on the day that I smote all the
Lev 27:26 — firstborn in the land of Egypt I hallowed unto me all the firstborn in Israel,
Num 8:16, 17 Lk 2:23 — both man and beast: mine shall they be: I *am* the LORD.

4. The Sons of Levi Numbered and Their Duties Assigned

3:14 Num 26:57–62 — 14 ¶And the LORD spake unto Moses in the wilderness of Si'nai, saying,
15 Number the children of Levi after the house of their fathers, by their
families: every male from a month old and upward shalt thou number
them.
3:16 Ex 16:16–22 — 16 And Moses numbered them according to the word of the LORD, as he
was commanded.
17 And these were the sons of Levi by their names; Ger'shon, and
Ko'hath, and Me-ra'ri.
18 And these *are* the names of the sons of Ger'shon by their families;
Lib'ni, and Shim'e-i.
19 And the sons of Ko'hath by their families; Amram, and Iz'e-har,
Hebron, and Uz'zi-el.
20 And the sons of Me-ra'ri by their families; Mah'li, and Mu'shi. These
are the families of the Levites according to the house of their fathers.
21 Of Ger'shon *was* the family of the Lib'nites, and the family of the
Shim'ites: these *are* the families of the Ger'shon-ites.
22 Those that were numbered of them, according to the number of all the
males, from a month old and upward, *even* those that were numbered of
them *were* seven thousand and five hundred.
23 The families of the Ger'shon-ites shall pitch behind the tabernacle
westward.
24 And the chief of the house of the father of the Ger'shon-ites *shall be*
E-li'a-saph the son of La'el.
3:25 Num 1:50 4:25–28 — 25 And the charge of the sons of Ger'shon in the tabernacle of the
congregation *shall be* the tabernacle, and the tent, the covering thereof, and
the hanging for the door of the tabernacle of the congregation,
26 And the hangings of the court, and the curtain for the door of the court,
which *is* by the tabernacle, and by the altar round about, and the cords of
it for all the service thereof.
27 ¶And of Ko'hath *was* the family of the Amra-mites, and the family of
the Iz'e-har-ites, and the family of the Hebronites, and the family of the
Uz'zi-el-ites: these *are* the families of the Ko'hath-ites.
28 In the number of all the males, from a month old and upward, *were*
eight thousand and six hundred, keeping the charge of the sanctuary.
29 The families of the sons of Ko'hath shall pitch on the side of the
tabernacle southward.
30 And the chief of the house of the father of the families of the Ko'hath-
ites *shall be* E-liz'a-phan the son of Uz'zi-el.
31 And their charge *shall be* the ark, and the table, and the candlestick,
and the altars, and the vessels of the sanctuary wherewith they minister,
and the hanging, and all the service thereof.
3:32☆ — 32 And E-le-a'zar the son of Aaron the priest *shall be* chief over the chief

3:32 Eleazar was the third of the four sons of Aaron. Nadab and Abihu were slain by God when they offered strange fire, probably when they were drunk. Apparently Eleazar had the primogeniture over Ithamar, the other brother. Eleazar became high priest upon his father's death. He supervised the Kohathites, who carried the ark and the holy furniture on their shoulders (see 3:30–32). He also had charge of the tabernacle and its furniture. For reasons we do not know, the sons of Ithamar supplanted Eleazar's descendants in the tabernacle at Shiloh. Eli was a descendant of Ithamar but God rejected his line.

of the Levites, *and have* the oversight of them that keep the charge of the
sanctuary.
33 ¶Of Me-ra'ri *was* the family of the Mah'lites, and the family of the
Mu'shites: these *are* the families of Me-ra'ri.
34 And those that were numbered of them, according to the number of all
the males, from a month old and upward, *were* six thousand and two
hundred.
35 And the chief of the house of the father of the families of Me-ra'ri *was*
Zu'ri-el the son of Ab-i-ha'il: *these* shall pitch on the side of the tabernacle
northward.
36 And *under* the custody and charge of the sons of Me-ra'ri *shall be* the
boards of the tabernacle, and the bars thereof, and the pillars thereof, and
the sockets thereof, and all the vessels thereof, and all that serveth thereto,
37 And the pillars of the court round about, and their sockets, and their
pins, and their cords.
38 ¶But those that encamp before the tabernacle toward the east, *even* ☆**3:38** Num 1:51; 3:10
before the tabernacle of the congregation eastward, *shall be* Moses, and
Aaron and his sons, keeping the charge of the sanctuary for the charge of
the children of Israel; and the stranger that cometh nigh shall be put to
death.
39 All that were numbered of the Levites, which Moses and Aaron ☆**3:39** Num 26:62
numbered at the commandment of the LORD, throughout their families, all
the males from a month old and upward, *were* twenty and two thousand.

5. The Census of All of Israel's Eldest Sons

40 ¶And the LORD said unto Moses, Number all the firstborn of the males **3:40** Num 1:2
of the children of Israel from a month old and upward, and take the
number of their names.
41 And thou shalt take the Levites for me (I *am* the LORD) instead of all **3:41** Num 3:11, 13, 45
the firstborn among the children of Israel; and the cattle of the Levites
instead of all the firstlings among the cattle of the children of Israel.
42 And Moses numbered, as the LORD commanded him, all the firstborn
among the children of Israel.
43 And all the firstborn males by the number of names, from a month old **3:43** Num 3:39
and upward, of those that were numbered of them, were twenty and two
thousand two hundred and threescore and thirteen.
44 ¶And the LORD spake unto Moses, saying,
45 Take the Levites instead of all the firstborn among the children of **3:45** Num 3:11, 13, 41
Israel, and the cattle of the Levites instead of their cattle; and the Levites
shall be mine: I *am* the LORD.
46 And for those that are to be redeemed of the two hundred and **3:46** Ex 13:13, 15 Num 18:14–16
threescore and thirteen of the firstborn of the children of Israel, which are
more than the Levites;
47 Thou shalt even take five shekels apiece by the poll, after the shekel of ☆**3:47** Lev 27:1–8 Num 18:16
the sanctuary shalt thou take *them:* (the shekel *is* twenty gerahs:)
48 And thou shalt give the money, wherewith the odd number of them is
to be redeemed, unto Aaron and to his sons.

3:38 Death was the sentence for any Levite not of the descendants of Aaron who sought to perform any of the religious rites.
3:39 The Levites were numbered from a month old and upward, not from twenty years old and upward as in the case of the other tribes. Still the number of Levites (which therefore included many more males) was the smallest of all the tribes—22,000. (Compare the 22,000 here with the 23,000 in 26:62. The difference may be accounted for by the increase in births between the first and the second mention. Round numbers were commonly used throughout history.)
3:47, 48 The 273 males of the other tribes were in excess of the 22,000 Levites and had to be redeemed. The price of redemption was five shekels, and the money went to Aaron and his sons.

49 And Moses took the redemption money of them that were over and
above them that were redeemed by the Levites:
3:50☆ Lev 25:25 Ezek 45:12
50 Of the firstborn of the children of Israel took he the money; a thousand
three hundred and threescore and five *shekels,* after the shekel of the
sanctuary:
51 And Moses gave the money of them that were redeemed unto Aaron
and to his sons, according to the word of the LORD, as the LORD
commanded Moses.

6. The Sons of Kohath and Their Duties

4:1 Num 3:25–30
4 AND the LORD spake unto Moses and unto Aaron, saying,
2 Take the sum of the sons of Ko'hath from among the sons of Levi,
after their families, by the house of their fathers,
4:3☆ Num 4:21–23 8:23, 24
3 From thirty years old and upward even until fifty years old, all that
enter into the host, to do the work in the tabernacle of the congregation.
4 This *shall be* the service of the sons of Ko'hath in the tabernacle of the
congregation, *about* the most holy things:
4:5 Num 4:15
5 ¶And when the camp setteth forward, Aaron shall come, and his sons,
and they shall take down the covering vail, and cover the ark of testimony
with it:
4:6 Ex 26:31 Num 4:25
6 And shall put thereon the covering of badgers' skins, and shall spread
over *it* a cloth wholly of blue, and shall put in the staves thereof.
4:7 Ex 37:10–16 Lev 24:5–8
7 And upon the table of shewbread they shall spread a cloth of blue, and
put thereon the dishes, and the spoons, and the bowls, and covers to cover
withal: and the continual bread shall be thereon:
4:8 Num 4:25
8 And they shall spread upon them a cloth of scarlet, and cover the same
with a covering of badgers' skins, and shall put in the staves thereof.
4:9 Ex 25:37, 38
9 And they shall take a cloth of blue, and cover the candlestick of the
light, and his lamps, and his tongs, and his snuffdishes, and all the oil
vessels thereof, wherewith they minister unto it:
10 And they shall put it and all the vessels thereof within a covering of
badgers' skins, and shall put *it* upon a bar.
11 And upon the golden altar they shall spread a cloth of blue, and cover
it with a covering of badgers' skins, and shall put to the staves thereof:
12 And they shall take all the instruments of ministry, wherewith they
minister in the sanctuary, and put *them* in a cloth of blue, and cover them
with a covering of badgers' skins, and shall put *them* on a bar:
13 And they shall take away the ashes from the altar, and spread a purple
cloth thereon:
14 And they shall put upon it all the vessels thereof, wherewith they
minister about it, *even* the censers, the fleshhooks, and the shovels, and the
basons, all the vessels of the altar; and they shall spread upon it a covering
of badgers' skins, and put to the staves of it.
4:15☆ Num 3:38 4:5, 17–19
15 And when Aaron and his sons have made an end of covering the
sanctuary, and all the vessels of the sanctuary, as the camp is to set
forward; after that, the sons of Ko'hath shall come to bear *it:* but they shall
not touch *any* holy thing, lest they die. These *things are* the burden of the
sons of Ko'hath in the tabernacle of the congregation.

3:50 *1365 shekels,* approximately $700.
4:3 *from thirty years old,* whereas in 8:24 the number twenty-five is used. "They were entered as probationers at twenty-five years old, and in David's time, when there was more work to be done, at twenty (1 Chron. 23:24, and so Ezra 3:8)."* They were taught their duties for five years and in David's time, ten years. Novices were not to be used in the temple duties.
4:15 The sons of Kohath were to carry, not cart, the furnishings of the sanctuary. Aaron and his sons first covered them and they were placed on carrying frames, at which time the Kohathites began their duties. They were never to touch the holy things lest they die.

16¶And to the office of E-le-a'zar the son of Aaron the priest *pertaineth*
the oil for the light, and the sweet incense, and the daily meat offering, and
the anointing oil, *and* the oversight of all the tabernacle, and of all that
therein *is*, in the sanctuary, and in the vessels thereof.

4:16 Ex 25:1–7 30:22–38

17¶And the LORD spake unto Moses and unto Aaron, saying,
18Cut ye not off the tribe of the families of the Ko'hath-ites from among
the Levites:

4:17 Num 4:15

19But thus do unto them, that they may live, and not die, when they
approach unto the most holy things: Aaron and his sons shall go in, and
appoint them every one to his service and to his burden:
20But they shall not go in to see when the holy things are covered, lest
they die.

7. The Sons of Gershon and Their Duties

21¶And the LORD spake unto Moses, saying,
22Take also the sum of the sons of Ger'shon, throughout the houses of
their fathers, by their families;

4:21 Num 3:3, 14–24, 35

23From thirty years old and upward until fifty years old shalt thou
number them; all that enter in to perform the service, to do the work in the
tabernacle of the congregation.
24This *is* the service of the families of the Ger'shon-ites, to serve, and for
burdens:
25And they shall bear the curtains of the tabernacle, and the tabernacle of
the congregation, his covering, and the covering of the badgers' skins that *is*
above upon it, and the hanging for the door of the tabernacle of the
congregation,

☆4:25 Num 3:25–30

26And the hangings of the court, and the hanging for the door of the gate
of the court, which *is* by the tabernacle and by the altar round about, and
their cords, and all the instruments of their service, and all that is made for
them: so shall they serve.
27At the appointment of Aaron and his sons shall be all the service of the
sons of the Ger'shon-ites, in all their burdens, and in all their service: and
ye shall appoint unto them in charge all their burdens.
28This *is* the service of the families of the sons of Ger'shon in the
tabernacle of the congregation: and their charge *shall be* under the hand of
Ith'a-mar the son of Aaron the priest.

8. The Sons of Merari and Their Duties

29¶As for the sons of Me-ra'ri, thou shalt number them after their
families, by the house of their fathers;

4:29 Num 3:31–35

30From thirty years old and upward even unto fifty years old shalt thou
number them, every one that entereth into the service, to do the work of the
tabernacle of the congregation.

4:30, 31 Ex 26:15, 16 Num 4:3

31And this *is* the charge of their burden, according to all their service in
the tabernacle of the congregation; the boards of the tabernacle, and the
bars thereof, and the pillars thereof, and sockets thereof,

☆4:31, 32

4:25 The Gershonites were responsible for transporting the curtains of the tabernacle and other items as specified in verses 25, 26. They were supervised by Ithamar, the son of Aaron (4:28).

4:31, 32 Herein the parts of the tabernacle to be carried by the sons of Merari are itemized. They also were supervised by Ithamar.

[32]And the pillars of the court round about, and their sockets, and their pins, and their cords, with all their instruments, and with all their service: and by name ye shall reckon the instruments of the charge of their burden.

[33]This *is* the service of the families of the sons of Me-ra'ri, according to all their service, in the tabernacle of the congregation, under the hand of Ith'a-mar the son of Aaron the priest.

9. The Results of Numbering the Sons of Kohath, Gershon, and Merari

[34]¶And Moses and Aaron and the chief of the congregation numbered the sons of the Ko'hath-ites after their families, and after the house of their fathers,

4:35 Num 3:3, 21, 35

[35]From thirty years old and upward even unto fifty years old, every one that entereth into the service, for the work in the tabernacle of the congregation:

[36]And those that were numbered of them by their families were two thousand seven hundred and fifty.

[37]These *were* they that were numbered of the families of the Ko'hath-ites, all that might do service in the tabernacle of the congregation, which Moses and Aaron did number according to the commandment of the LORD by the hand of Moses.

[38]¶And those that were numbered of the sons of Ger'shon, throughout their families, and by the house of their fathers,

[39]From thirty years old and upward even unto fifty years old, every one that entereth into the service, for the work in the tabernacle of the congregation,

[40]Even those that were numbered of them, throughout their families, by the house of their fathers, were two thousand and six hundred and thirty.

[41]These *are* they that were numbered of the families of the sons of Ger'shon, of all that might do service in the tabernacle of the congregation, whom Moses and Aaron did number according to the commandment of the LORD.

[42]¶And those that were numbered of the families of the sons of Me-ra'ri, throughout their families, by the house of their fathers,

[43]From thirty years old and upward even unto fifty years old, every one that entereth into the service, for the work in the tabernacle of the congregation,

[44]Even those that were numbered of them after their families, were three thousand and two hundred.

[45]These *be* those that were numbered of the families of the sons of Me-ra'ri, whom Moses and Aaron numbered according to the word of the LORD by the hand of Moses.

4:46 Num 3:39

[46]All those that were numbered of the Levites, whom Moses and Aaron and the chief of Israel numbered, after their families, and after the house of their fathers,

[47]From thirty years old and upward even unto fifty years old, every one that came to do the service of the ministry, and the service of the burden in the tabernacle of the congregation,

[48]Even those that were numbered of them, were eight thousand and five hundred and fourscore.

4:49 Num 1:47–49; 3:14, 15

[49]According to the commandment of the LORD they were numbered by the hand of Moses, every one according to his service, and according to his burden: thus were they numbered of him, as the LORD commanded Moses.

D. CAMP REGULATIONS
1. The Segregation of the Unclean

5 AND the LORD spake unto Moses, saying,
2 Command the children of Israel, that they put out of the camp
every leper, and every one that hath an issue, and whosoever is defiled by
the dead:
3 Both male and female shall ye put out, without the camp shall ye put
them; that they defile not their camps, in the midst whereof I dwell.
4 And the children of Israel did so, and put them out without the camp: as
the LORD spake unto Moses, so did the children of Israel.

5:1 Lev 13:45, 46; 15:1–5; Num 19:11
☆5:2
5:3 Lev 11:24, 25; 14:8; 26:11, 12; 2 Cor 6:16

2. Restitution for Damages

5 ¶And the LORD spake unto Moses, saying,
6 Speak unto the children of Israel, When a man or woman shall commit
any sin that men commit, to do a trespass against the LORD, and that
person be guilty;
7 Then they shall confess their sin which they have done: and he shall
recompense his trespass with the principal thereof, and add unto it the fifth
part thereof, and give *it* unto *him* against whom he hath trespassed.
8 But if the man have no kinsman to recompense the trespass unto, let the
trespass be recompensed unto the LORD, *even* to the priest; beside the ram
of the atonement, whereby an atonement shall be made for him.
9 And every offering of all the holy things of the children of Israel, which
they bring unto the priest, shall be his.
10 And every man's hallowed things shall be his: whatsoever any man
giveth the priest, it shall be his.

5:5 Lev 6:1–3
☆5:6
☆5:7 Lev 5:5, 16; 6:4, 5; 16:21
5:9 Ex 29:27, 28; Lev 6:17, 18; Num 18:8, 9

3. The Law of Jealousy*

11 ¶And the LORD spake unto Moses, saying,
12 Speak unto the children of Israel, and say unto them, If any man's wife
go aside, and commit a trespass against him,
13 And a man lie with her carnally, and it be hid from the eyes of her
husband, and be kept close, and she be defiled, and *there be* no witness
against her, neither she be taken *with the manner;*
14 And the spirit of jealousy come upon him, and he be jealous of his wife,
and she be defiled: or if the spirit of jealousy come upon him, and he be
jealous of his wife, and she be not defiled:
15 Then shall the man bring his wife unto the priest, and he shall bring her
offering for her, the tenth *part* of an ephah of barley meal; he shall pour no
oil upon it, nor put frankincense thereon; for it *is* an offering of jealousy, an
offering of memorial, bringing iniquity to remembrance.

☆5:11 Ex 20:14; Lev 18:20; 20:10; Num 5:4, 29
5:15 Num 15:1–10

5:2 One of the reasons for segregating lepers, those who had discharges, and those who had contact with the dead was to prevent contagion from spreading among other people. This principle of isolating people with contagious infections has a spiritual application (see note to 1 Cor. 5:11).

5:6 Restitution was required from those who have done wrong to a neighbor. The sin was to be confessed, an atonement made, and satisfaction rendered to the injured party. Verse 7 indicates that a fifth should be added to the wrong act. Thus the innocent person had a right to damages beyond the amount involved. This was a penalty the offender must pay. If a thousand dollars had been stolen, the offender would pay that back and two hundred dollars in addition.

5:7 *shall recompense his trespass,* i.e., "shall make full payment for what he has stolen," or "shall make full payment for his wrong."

5:11ff The law of jealousy was instituted so that God himself could determine the guilt or innocence of a wife whose conduct was suspect but for whose guilt there was no proof. It was to the advantage of an innocent party to go through the ordeal and have her name cleared and her husband reassured. The Scriptures afford no example of the use of this provision, nor was it used in postbiblical times, although church ordeals were employed which had some similarities to the law of jealousy.

16 And the priest shall bring her near, and set her before the LORD:

17 And the priest shall take holy water in an earthen vessel; and of the dust that is in the floor of the tabernacle the priest shall take, and put *it* into the water:

18 And the priest shall set the woman before the LORD, and uncover the woman's head, and put the offering of memorial in her hands, which *is* the jealousy offering: and the priest shall have in his hand the bitter water that causeth the curse:

19 And the priest shall charge her by an oath, and say unto the woman, If no man have lain with thee, and if thou hast not gone aside to uncleanness *with another* instead of thy husband, be thou free from this bitter water that causeth the curse:

20 But if thou hast gone aside *to another* instead of thy husband, and if thou be defiled, and some man have lain with thee beside thine husband:

5:21 2 Chron 21:15 Neh 10:29 Jer 29:22 Isa 65:16

21 Then the priest shall charge the woman with an oath of cursing, and the priest shall say unto the woman, The LORD make thee a curse and an oath among thy people, when the LORD doth make thy thigh to rot, and thy belly to swell;

22 And this water that causeth the curse shall go into thy bowels, to make *thy* belly to swell, and *thy* thigh to rot: And the woman shall say, Amen, amen.

23 And the priest shall write these curses in a book, and he shall blot *them* out with the bitter water:

24 And he shall cause the woman to drink the bitter water that causeth the curse: and the water that causeth the curse shall enter into her, *and become* bitter.

25 Then the priest shall take the jealousy offering out of the woman's hand, and shall wave the offering before the LORD, and offer it upon the altar:

5:26 Lev 5:12; 6:15

26 And the priest shall take an handful of the offering, *even* the memorial thereof, and burn *it* upon the altar, and afterward shall cause the woman to drink the water.

5:27☆ Num 5:11, 21 Jer 29:18; 42:18; 44:12

27 And when he hath made her to drink the water, then it shall come to pass, *that,* if she be defiled, and have done trespass against her husband, that the water that causeth the curse shall enter into her, *and become* bitter, and her belly shall swell, and her thigh shall rot: and the woman shall be a curse among her people.

28 And if the woman be not defiled, but be clean; then she shall be free, and shall conceive seed.

5:29☆ Num 5:11

29 This *is* the law of jealousies, when a wife goeth aside *to another* instead of her husband, and is defiled:

5:30 Num 5:15, 16

30 Or when the spirit of jealousy cometh upon him, and he be jealous over his wife, and shall set the woman before the LORD, and the priest shall execute upon her all this law.

31 Then shall the man be guiltless from iniquity, and this woman shall bear her iniquity.

5:27 The Jewish fathers held that a guilty woman would either die immediately or at a later time and that her companion in sin, the adulterer, would also die. "The Jewish doctors add that the waters had this effect upon the adulteress only in case the husband had never offended in the same kind; but that, if he had at any time defiled the marriage-bed, God did not thus right him against his injurious wife."*

5:29 The passage does not say what should be done if a wife suspected her husband of adultery but had no certainty that he had been unfaithful.

4. The Rules for Nazarites and the Aaronic Benediction

6 AND the LORD spake unto Moses, saying, ☆**6:1**
2 Speak unto the children of Israel, and say unto them, When either Lev 20:26 Num 6:3–8
man or woman shall separate *themselves* to vow a vow of a Nazarite, to Judg 13:4, 5 16:16, 17
separate *themselves* unto the LORD: Amos 2:11, 12
3 He shall separate *himself* from wine and strong drink, and shall drink no ☆**6:3**
vinegar of wine, or vinegar of strong drink, neither shall he drink any liquor Lev 10:8, 9 Jer 35:6–8
of grapes, nor eat moist grapes, or dried.
4 All the days of his separation shall he eat nothing that is made of the
vine tree, from the kernels even to the husk.
5 All the days of the vow of his separation there shall no razor come upon **6:5**
his head: until the days be fulfilled, in the which he separateth *himself* unto Num 1:1 1 Sam 1:11
the LORD, he shall be holy, *and* shall let the locks of the hair of his head
grow.
6 All the days that he separateth *himself* unto the LORD he shall come at **6:6**
no dead body. Lev 21:1–3 Num 19:11–22
7 He shall not make himself unclean for his father, or for his mother, for
his brother, or for his sister, when they die: because the consecration of his
God *is* upon his head.
8 All the days of his separation he *is* holy unto the LORD.
9 And if any man die very suddenly by him, and he hath defiled the head **6:9**
of his consecration; then he shall shave his head in the day of his cleansing, Num 6:18 Acts 18:18
on the seventh day shall he shave it. 21:23, 24
10 And on the eighth day he shall bring two turtles, or two young pigeons,
to the priest, to the door of the tabernacle of the congregation:
11 And the priest shall offer the one for a sin offering, and the other for a **6:11**
burnt offering, and make an atonement for him, for that he sinned by the Lev 5:7; 12:6–8
dead, and shall hallow his head that same day.
12 And he shall consecrate unto the LORD the days of his separation, and **6:12**
shall bring a lamb of the first year for a trespass offering: but the days that Lev 7:1–10 14:24, 25
were before shall be lost, because his separation was defiled.
13 ¶And this *is* the law of the Nazarite, when the days of his separation are ☆**6:13**
fulfilled: he shall be brought unto the door of the tabernacle of the
congregation:
14 And he shall offer his offering unto the LORD, one he lamb of the first **6:14**
year without blemish for a burnt offering, and one ewe lamb of the first year Lev 1:2–17 7:1–10
without blemish for a sin offering, and one ram without blemish for peace
offerings,
15 And a basket of unleavened bread, cakes of fine flour mingled with oil, **6:15**
and wafers of unleavened bread anointed with oil, and their meat offering, Num 15:1–7
and their drink offerings.
16 And the priest shall bring *them* before the LORD, and shall offer his sin
offering, and his burnt offering:

6:1, 2 Vows were made and kept in the Old and New Testaments. They were not to be made lightly (Prov. 20:25). Once made, they were to be kept (30:2). Vows were to be discharged promptly (Deut. 23:21–23). The Scriptures do not indicate that it is necessary to keep a vow which is made in good faith but which is later discovered to be wrong or sinful. Not to make vows was not sinful, but when made, certain restrictions were to be followed: (1) children needed parental consent for their vows (30:3–5); (2) wives needed the consent of their husbands (30:6–8, 10:13); (3) widows and divorced women were bound by their vows (30:9). Jephthah (Judg. 11:30, 31), Hannah (1 Sam. 1:11), David (Ps. 132:2–5), Paul (Acts 18:18), and certain Jews (Acts 21:23–26) all made vows.

6:3 See note on Judg. 13:5 for a description of a Nazarite.

6:13 This general rule concerning the ending of a Nazarite vow by going to the sanctuary and offering a sin and burnt offering was done by the Apostle Paul in Acts 21:24. In his case it worked to his harm, for he was taken prisoner and ultimately sent to Rome, where he was executed.

17 And he shall offer the ram *for* a sacrifice of peace offerings unto the
LORD, with the basket of unleavened bread: the priest shall offer also his
meat offering, and his drink offering.

6:18 Num 6:9

18 And the Nazarite shall shave the head of his separation *at* the door of
the tabernacle of the congregation, and shall take the hair of the head of his
separation, and put *it* in the fire which *is* under the sacrifice of the peace
offerings.
19 And the priest shall take the sodden shoulder of the ram, and one
unleavened cake out of the basket, and one unleavened wafer, and shall put
them upon the hands of the Nazarite, after *the hair of* his separation is
shaven:

6:20 Lev 7:28–34; Num 18:18

20 And the priest shall wave them *for* a wave offering before the LORD:
this *is* holy for the priest, with the wave breast and heave shoulder: and
after that the Nazarite may drink wine.

6:21 Num 6:1–5

21 This *is* the law of the Nazarite who hath vowed, *and of* his offering unto
the LORD for his separation, beside *that* that his hand shall get: according
to the vow which he vowed, so he must do after the law of his separation.

6:22☆ Deut 21:5; 33:1; Josh 8:33; 1 Chron 23:13

22 ¶And the LORD spake unto Moses, saying,
23 Speak unto Aaron and unto his sons, saying, On this wise ye shall bless
the children of Israel, saying unto them,

6:24–26 Deut 28:3–6; Ps 4:6, 17:8, 29:11; 44:3; 80:3, 7, 19; 2 Cor 13:14
6:27 2 Sam 7:23

24 The LORD bless thee, and keep thee:
25 The LORD make his face shine upon thee, and be gracious unto thee:
26 The LORD lift up his countenance upon thee, and give thee peace.
27 And they shall put my name upon the children of Israel; and I will
bless them.

E. THE TRIBAL OFFERINGS FOR THE TABERNACLE
1. The Dedication of the Altar

7:1 Ex 40:9–11; Lev 8:10

7 AND it came to pass on the day that Moses had fully set up the
tabernacle, and had anointed it, and sanctified it, and all the instru-
ments thereof, both the altar and all the vessels thereof, and had anointed
them, and sanctified them;

7:2 Num 1:2–16

2 That the princes of Israel, heads of the house of their fathers, who *were*
the princes of the tribes, and were over them that were numbered, offered:

7:3☆ Isa 66:20

3 And they brought their offering before the LORD, six covered wagons,
and twelve oxen; a wagon for two of the princes, and for each one an ox:
and they brought them before the tabernacle.
4 And the LORD spake unto Moses, saying,
5 Take *it* of them, that they may be to do the service of the tabernacle of
the congregation; and thou shalt give them unto the Levites, to every man
according to his service.
6 And Moses took the wagons and the oxen, and gave them unto the
Levites.

7:7☆ Num 4:26

7 Two wagons and four oxen he gave unto the sons of Ger'shon,
according to their service:

6:22ff God commanded Aaron and his sons to bless the people. Some say that the blessing was given at the close of the morning sacrifice, in order to show that when the Messiah came, in the evening of the world, the gospel would replace the law, and the blessing of Christ would be instituted. The value of the blessing was not due to the priest himself, but to God, through whom he gave the blessing. The priest was the conduit, God the source. Gospel ministers, like the priests of old, should dismiss their congregations with such a blessing. The New Testament contains a number of apostolic benedictions (e.g., Heb. 13:20, 21) which are often used today.

7:3–9 The covered wagons were used to carry certain parts of the tabernacle, but the furnishings were not to be placed on carts. They were to be borne on the shoulders of the Kohathites.

8And four wagons and eight oxen he gave unto the sons of Me-ra'ri, 7:8 Num 4:33
according unto their service, under the hand of Ith'a-mar the son of Aaron
the priest.
9But unto the sons of Ko'hath he gave none: because the service of the 7:9 Num 4:5–15
sanctuary belonging unto them *was that* they should bear upon their
shoulders.
10¶And the princes offered for dedicating of the altar in the day that it
was anointed, even the princes offered their offering before the altar.
11And the LORD said unto Moses, They shall offer their offering, each
prince on his day, for the dedicating of the altar.

2. Nahshon's Gift for Judah

12¶And he that offered his offering the first day was Nah'shon the son of
Am-min'a-dab, of the tribe of Judah:
13And his offering *was* one silver charger, the weight thereof *was* an
hundred and thirty *shekels,* one silver bowl of seventy shekels, after the
shekel of the sanctuary; both of them *were* full of fine flour mingled with oil
for a meat offering:
14One spoon of ten *shekels* of gold, full of incense:
15One young bullock, one ram, one lamb of the first year, for a burnt 7:15 Lev 6:9–13
offering:
16One kid of the goats for a sin offering: 7:16 Lev 6:25–30
17And for a sacrifice of peace offerings, two oxen, five rams, five he goats, 7:17 Lev 7:11–21
five lambs of the first year: this *was* the offering of Nah'shon the son of Am-
min'a-dab.

3. Nethaneel's Gift for Issachar

18¶On the second day Ne-than'e-el the son of Zu'ar, prince of Is'sa-char,
did offer:
19He offered *for* his offering one silver charger, the weight whereof *was* an
hundred and thirty *shekels,* one silver bowl of seventy shekels, after the
shekel of the sanctuary; both of them full of fine flour mingled with oil for
a meat offering:
20One spoon of gold of ten *shekels,* full of incense:
21One young bullock, one ram, one lamb of the first year, for a burnt
offering:
22One kid of the goats for a sin offering:
23And for a sacrifice of peace offerings, two oxen, five rams, five he goats,
five lambs of the first year: this *was* the offering of Ne-than'e-el the son of
Zu'ar.

4. Eliab's Gift for Zebulun

24¶On the third day E-li'ab the son of He'lon, prince of the children of
Zeb'u-lun, *did offer:*
25His offering *was* one silver charger, the weight whereof *was* an hundred
and thirty *shekels,* one silver bowl of seventy shekels, after the shekel of the
sanctuary; both of them full of fine flour mingled with oil for a meat
offering:
26One golden spoon of ten *shekels,* full of incense:
27One young bullock, one ram, one lamb of the first year, for a burnt
offering:
28One kid of the goats for a sin offering:
29And for a sacrifice of peace offerings, two oxen, five rams, five he goats,
five lambs of the first year: this *was* the offering of E-li'ab the son of He'lon.

5. Elizur's Gift for Reuben

30¶On the fourth day E-li'zur the son of Shed'e-ur, prince of the children of Reuben, *did offer:*

31His offering *was* one silver charger of the weight of an hundred and thirty *shekels,* one silver bowl of seventy shekels, after the shekel of the sanctuary; both of them full of fine flour mingled with oil for a meat offering:

32One golden spoon of ten *shekels,* full of incense:

33One young bullock, one ram, one lamb of the first year, for a burnt offering:

34One kid of the goats for a sin offering:

35And for a sacrifice of peace offerings, two oxen, five rams, five he goats, five lambs of the first year: this *was* the offering of E-li'zur the son of Shed'e-ur.

6. Shelumi-el's Gift for Simeon

36¶On the fifth day She-lu'mi-el the son of Zu-ri-shad'da-i, prince of the children of Simeon, *did offer:*

37His offering *was* one silver charger, the weight whereof *was* an hundred and thirty *shekels,* one silver bowl of seventy shekels, after the shekel of the sanctuary; both of them full of fine flour mingled with oil for a meat offering:

38One golden spoon of ten *shekels,* full of incense:

39One young bullock, one ram, one lamb of the first year, for a burnt offering:

40One kid of the goats for a sin offering:

41And for a sacrifice of peace offerings, two oxen, five rams, five he goats, five lambs of the first year: this *was* the offering of She-lu'mi-el the son of Zu-ri-shad'da-i.

7. Eliasaph's Gift for Gad

42¶On the sixth day E-li'a-saph the son of Deu'el, prince of the children of Gad, *offered:*

43His offering *was* one silver charger of the weight of an hundred and thirty *shekels,* a silver bowl of seventy shekels, after the shekel of the sanctuary; both of them full of fine flour mingled with oil for a meat offering:

44One golden spoon of ten *shekels,* full of incense:

45One young bullock, one ram, one lamb of the first year, for a burnt offering:

46One kid of the goats for a sin offering:

47And for a sacrifice of peace offerings, two oxen, five rams, five he goats, five lambs of the first year: this *was* the offering of E-li'a-saph the son of Deu'el.

8. Elishama's Gift for Ephraim

48¶On the seventh day E-lish'a-ma the son of Am-mi'hud, prince of the children of E'phra-im, *offered:*

49His offering *was* one silver charger, the weight whereof *was* an hundred and thirty *shekels,* one silver bowl of seventy shekels, after the shekel of the sanctuary; both of them full of fine flour mingled with oil for a meat offering:

50One golden spoon of ten *shekels,* full of incense:

[51]One young bullock, one ram, one lamb of the first year, for a burnt
offering:
[52]One kid of the goats for a sin offering:
[53]And for a sacrifice of peace offerings, two oxen, five rams, five he goats,
five lambs of the first year: this *was* the offering of E-lish'a-ma the son of
Am-mi'hud.

9. Gamaliel's Gift for Manasseh

[54]¶On the eighth day *offered* Ga-ma'li-el the son of Pe-dah'zur, prince of
the children of Ma-nas'seh:
[55]His offering *was* one silver charger of the weight of an hundred and
thirty *shekels,* one silver bowl of seventy shekels, after the shekel of the
sanctuary; both of them full of fine flour mingled with oil for a meat
offering:
[56]One golden spoon of ten *shekels,* full of incense:
[57]One young bullock, one ram, one lamb of the first year, for a burnt
offering:
[58]One kid of the goats for a sin offering:
[59]And for a sacrifice of peace offerings, two oxen, five rams, five he goats,
five lambs of the first year: this *was* the offering of Ga-ma'li-el the son of
Pe-dah'zur.

10. Abidan's Gift for Benjamin

[60]¶On the ninth day Ab'i-dan the son of Gid-e-o'ni, prince of the children
of Benjamin, *offered:*
[61]His offering *was* one silver charger, the weight whereof *was* an hundred
and thirty *shekels,* one silver bowl of seventy shekels, after the shekel of the
sanctuary; both of them full of fine flour mingled with oil for a meat
offering:
[62]One golden spoon of ten *shekels,* full of incense:
[63]One young bullock, one ram, one lamb of the first year, for a burnt
offering:
[64]One kid of the goats for a sin offering:
[65]And for a sacrifice of peace offerings, two oxen, five rams, five he goats,
five lambs of the first year: this *was* the offering of Ab'i-dan the son of Gid-
e-o'ni.

11. Ahiezer's Gift for Dan

[66]¶On the tenth day A-hi-e'zer the son of Am-mi-shad'da-i, prince of the
children of Dan, *offered:*
[67]His offering *was* one silver charger, the weight whereof *was* an hundred
and thirty *shekels,* one silver bowl of seventy shekels, after the shekel of the
sanctuary; both of them full of fine flour mingled with oil for a meat
offering:
[68]One golden spoon of ten *shekels,* full of incense:
[69]One young bullock, one ram, one lamb of the first year, for a burnt
offering:
[70]One kid of the goats for a sin offering:
[71]And for a sacrifice of peace offerings, two oxen, five rams, five he goats,
five lambs of the first year: this *was* the offering of A-hi-e'zer the son of
Am-mi-shad'da-i.

12. Pagiel's Gift for Asher

[72]¶On the eleventh day Pa'gi-el the son of Oc'ran, prince of the children
of Asher, *offered:*

73 His offering *was* one silver charger, the weight whereof *was* an hundred and thirty *shekels,* one silver bowl of seventy shekels, after the shekel of the sanctuary; both of them full of fine flour mingled with oil for a meat offering:
74 One golden spoon of ten *shekels,* full of incense:
75 One young bullock, one ram, one lamb of the first year, for a burnt offering:
76 One kid of the goats for a sin offering:
77 And for a sacrifice of peace offerings, two oxen, five rams, five he goats, five lambs of the first year: this *was* the offering of Pa′gi-el the son of Oc′ran.

13. Ahira's Gift for Naphtali

78 ¶On the twelfth day A-hi′ra the son of E′nan, prince of the children of Naph′ta-li, *offered:*
79 His offering *was* one silver charger, the weight whereof *was* an hundred and thirty *shekels,* one silver bowl of seventy shekels, after the shekel of the sanctuary; both of them full of fine flour mingled with oil for a meat offering:
80 One golden spoon of ten *shekels,* full of incense:
81 One young bullock, one ram, one lamb of the first year, for a burnt offering:
82 One kid of the goats for a sin offering:
83 And for a sacrifice of peace offerings, two oxen, five rams, five he goats, five lambs of the first year: this *was* the offering of A-hi′ra the son of E′nan.
7:84 Num 7:10
84 This *was* the dedication of the altar, in the day when it was anointed, by the princes of Israel: twelve chargers of silver, twelve silver bowls, twelve spoons of gold:
85 Each charger of silver *weighing* an hundred and thirty *shekels,* each bowl seventy: all the silver vessels *weighed* two thousand and four hundred *shekels,* after the shekel of the sanctuary:
86 The golden spoons *were* twelve, full of incense, *weighing* ten *shekels* apiece, after the shekel of the sanctuary: all the gold of the spoons *was* an hundred and twenty *shekels.*
7:87 Lev 1:2–17 6:9–13
87 All the oxen for the burnt offering *were* twelve bullocks, the rams twelve, the lambs of the first year twelve, with their meat offering: and the kids of the goats for sin offering twelve.
7:88 Num 7:17
88 And all the oxen for the sacrifice of the peace offerings *were* twenty and four bullocks, the rams sixty, the he goats sixty, the lambs of the first year sixty. This *was* the dedication of the altar, after that it was anointed.

14. Moses Hears the Voice Speak

7:89☆ Ex 25:22 33:9–11 Lev 1:1 Ps 80:1; 99:1
89 And when Moses was gone into the tabernacle of the congregation to speak with him, then he heard the voice of one speaking unto him from off the mercy seat that *was* upon the ark of testimony, from between the two cherubims: and he spake unto him.

7:89 Leaders from the various tribes had brought their offerings to God (7:12—88). Would God accept those offerings? "God signified his gracious acceptance of these presents that were brought to him, by speaking familiarly to Moses, as a man speaks to his friend, from off the mercy-seat; and in speaking to him he did in effect speak to all Israel, showing them this token for good."*

F. LAST EVENTS BEFORE THE MARCH BEGINS

1. The Candlestick (Lampstand)

8 AND the LORD spake unto Moses, saying,

2 Speak unto Aaron, and say unto him, When thou lightest the lamps, the seven lamps shall give light over against the candlestick. **8:2** Ex 25:37

3 And Aaron did so; he lighted the lamps thereof over against the candlestick, as the LORD commanded Moses.

4 And this work of the candlestick *was of* beaten gold, unto the shaft thereof, unto the flowers thereof, *was* beaten work: according unto the pattern which the LORD had shewed Moses, so he made the candlestick. **8:4** Ex 25:18, 31–36, 40; 37:17-22 Heb 8:5

2. The Purification and Installation of the Levites

5 ¶And the LORD spake unto Moses, saying,

6 Take the Levites from among the children of Israel, and cleanse them.

7 And thus shalt thou do unto them, to cleanse them: Sprinkle water of purifying upon them, and let them shave all their flesh, and let them wash their clothes, and *so* make themselves clean. **8:7** Ex 19:10 Lev 14:8, 9 15:6; 16:28

8 Then let them take a young bullock with his meat offering, *even* fine flour mingled with oil, and another young bullock shalt thou take for a sin offering. **8:8** Num 15:3–12

9 And thou shalt bring the Levites before the tabernacle of the congregation: and thou shalt gather the whole assembly of the children of Israel together:

10 And thou shalt bring the Levites before the LORD: and the children of Israel shall put their hands upon the Levites: **8:10** Lev 4:15

11 And Aaron shall offer the Levites before the LORD *for* an offering of the children of Israel, that they may execute the service of the LORD. ☆**8:11** Num 3:5–9

12 And the Levites shall lay their hands upon the heads of the bullocks: and thou shalt offer the one *for* a sin offering, and the other *for* a burnt offering, unto the LORD, to make an atonement for the Levites. **8:12** Ex 29:10–14 Lev 16:20–22 Num 8:10

13 And thou shalt set the Levites before Aaron, and before his sons, and offer them *for* an offering unto the LORD.

14 Thus shalt thou separate the Levites from among the children of Israel: and the Levites shall be mine. **8:14** Num 8:11

15 And after that shall the Levites go in to do the service of the tabernacle of the congregation: and thou shalt cleanse them, and offer them *for* an offering.

16 For they *are* wholly given unto me from among the children of Israel; instead of such as open every womb, *even instead of* the firstborn of all the children of Israel, have I taken them unto me. **8:16** Num 3:13

17 For all the firstborn of the children of Israel *are* mine, *both* man and beast: on the day that I smote every firstborn in the land of Egypt I sanctified them for myself. **8:17** Ex 13:12, 13

18 And I have taken the Levites for all the firstborn of the children of Israel.

19 And I have given the Levites *as* a gift to Aaron and to his sons from among the children of Israel, to do the service of the children of Israel in the tabernacle of the congregation, and to make an atonement for the **8:19** Num 1:53

8:11 Although the priesthood derived from the seed of Aaron, there were many Levites who were not of Aaron's line. Here we read that they were given over to God for other forms of religious service. In 8:19, we see that God gave them back to Aaron. Matthew Henry draws from that incident the following observation: "Whatever we give up to God, he will give back to us unspeakably to our advantage. Our hearts, our children, our estates, are never more ours, more truly, more comfortably ours, than when we have offered them up to God."

children of Israel: that there be no plague among the children of Israel, when the children of Israel come nigh unto the sanctuary.

20 And Moses, and Aaron, and all the congregation of the children of Israel, did to the Levites according unto all that the LORD commanded Moses concerning the Levites, so did the children of Israel unto them.

21 And the Levites were purified, and they washed their clothes; and Aaron offered them *as* an offering before the LORD; and Aaron made an atonement for them to cleanse them.

22 And after that went the Levites in to do their service in the tabernacle of the congregation before Aaron, and before his sons: as the LORD had commanded Moses concerning the Levites, so did they unto them.

3. The Retirement Provision for the Levites

8:23 Num 4:3 — 23 ¶And the LORD spake unto Moses, saying,

8:24☆ — 24 This *is it* that *belongeth* unto the Levites: from twenty and five years old and upward they shall go in to wait upon the service of the tabernacle of the congregation:

25 And from the age of fifty years they shall cease waiting upon the service *thereof,* and shall serve no more:

26 But shall minister with their brethren in the tabernacle of the congregation, to keep the charge, and shall do no service. Thus shalt thou do unto the Levites touching their charge.

4. The Keeping of the Passover Celebration

9:1 Ex 40:2, 17 — 9 AND the LORD spake unto Moses in the wilderness of Si′nai, in the first month of the second year after they were come out of the land of Egypt, saying,

9:2 Ex 12:1–6 — 2 Let the children of Israel also keep the passover at his appointed season.

3 In the fourteenth day of this month, at even, ye shall keep it in his appointed season: according to all the rites of it, and according to all the ceremonies thereof, shall ye keep it.

4 And Moses spake unto the children of Israel, that they should keep the passover.

5 And they kept the passover on the fourteenth day of the first month at even in the wilderness of Si′nai: according to all that the LORD commanded Moses, so did the children of Israel.

9:6 Lev 21:1–4 — 6 ¶And there were certain men, who were defiled by the dead body of a man, that they could not keep the passover on that day: and they came before Moses and before Aaron on that day:

7 And those men said unto him, We *are* defiled by the dead body of a man: wherefore are we kept back, that we may not offer an offering of the LORD in his appointed season among the children of Israel?

9:8☆ — 8 And Moses said unto them, Stand still, and I will hear what the LORD will command concerning you.

9 ¶And the LORD spake unto Moses, saying,

8:24 See note to Num. 4:3.

9:8 God commanded that all males were to keep the Passover. But the ceremonially unclean were not to appear before God until they first had met the requirements for cleansing. Here it seemed that one law contradicted another. Moses did not answer the question himself. He referred it to the Lawgiver, God. And God said that regardless of defilement for touching a dead body or from absence in another place, all were to keep the Passover. Today we have the Holy Spirit who leads us into all truth. When matters of such a nature arise we have the law, the testimony, and the Holy Spirit to aid us. We can rest in the assurance that we will be assisted in arriving at the right course of action. (See note to 9:10, 11 for the special provision.)

10 Speak unto the children of Israel, saying, If any man of you or of your
posterity shall be unclean by reason of a dead body, or *be* in a journey afar
off, yet he shall keep the passover unto the LORD.
11 The fourteenth day of the second month at even they shall keep it, *and*
eat it with unleavened bread and bitter *herbs.*
12 They shall leave none of it unto the morning, nor break any bone of it:
according to all the ordinances of the passover they shall keep it.
13 But the man that *is* clean, and is not in a journey, and forbeareth to
keep the passover, even the same soul shall be cut off from among his
people: because he brought not the offering of the LORD in his appointed
season, that man shall bear his sin.
14 And if a stranger shall sojourn among you, and will keep the passover
unto the LORD; according to the ordinance of the passover, and according
to the manner thereof, so shall he do: ye shall have one ordinance, both for
the stranger, and for him that was born in the land.

☆9:10, 11

9:12 Ex 12:1–50 Lev 23:5–14 Num 28:16–25 Jn 19:36

☆9:13 Ex 12:15 Num 15:30, 31

9:14 Ex 12:48, 49

5. God's Leading by the Cloud of Guidance

15 ¶And on the day that the tabernacle was reared up the cloud covered
the tabernacle, *namely,* the tent of the testimony: and at even there was
upon the tabernacle as it were the appearance of fire, until the morning.
16 So it was alway: the cloud covered it *by day,* and the appearance of fire
by night.
17 And when the cloud was taken up from the tabernacle, then after that
the children of Israel journeyed: and in the place where the cloud abode,
there the children of Israel pitched their tents.
18 At the commandment of the LORD the children of Israel journeyed, and
at the commandment of the LORD they pitched: as long as the cloud abode
upon the tabernacle they rested in their tents.
19 And when the cloud tarried long upon the tabernacle many days, then
the children of Israel kept the charge of the LORD, and journeyed not.
20 And *so* it was, when the cloud was a few days upon the tabernacle;
according to the commandment of the LORD they abode in their tents, and
according to the commandment of the LORD they journeyed.
21 And *so* it was, when the cloud abode from even unto the morning, and
that the cloud was taken up in the morning, then they journeyed: whether *it*
was by day or by night that the cloud was taken up, they journeyed.
22 Or *whether it were* two days, or a month, or a year, that the cloud
tarried upon the tabernacle, remaining thereon, the children of Israel abode
in their tents, and journeyed not: but when it was taken up, they journeyed.
23 At the commandment of the LORD they rested in the tents, and at the
commandment of the LORD they journeyed: they kept the charge of the
LORD, at the commandment of the LORD by the hand of Moses.

☆9:15 Ex 14:20, 24 40:2, 18 Num 14:14 Neh 9:12, 19 Ps 78:14

9:17 Ex 40:36–38 Num 10:11, 33, 34

9:23 Josh 22:2, 3

9:10, 11 So important was the keeping of the Passover that special provision was made for those who could not, for good reason, attend the celebration. Such people were permitted to observe it a month later.
9:13 Whoever is ceremonially clean, and is not on a journey, is to be cut off from the assembly of God if he fails to show up at the Passover celebration. Such failure is looked upon as an affront to God, an impious act against the divine majesty and the grace of God. Few Christians consider this sort of conduct unacceptable today, and indiscriminately absent themselves from the worship of God and participation in the ordinances or sacraments. Such people should not be surprised if the blessing of God no longer attends them, for God is not to be mocked.
9:15 Upon the dedication of the tabernacle, the cloud of the presence came upon the sanctuary. When it rose from the tabernacle, the people were to move with it. As long as it stayed still, they were to rest. God now had a house for himself.

6. The Two Trumpets of Beaten Silver

10 AND the LORD spake unto Moses, saying,

10:2☆ Lev 25:9; 2 Kgs 12:13

2 Make thee two trumpets of silver; of a whole piece shalt thou make them: that thou mayest use them for the calling of the assembly, and for the journeying of the camps.

3 And when they shall blow with them, all the assembly shall assemble themselves to thee at the door of the tabernacle of the congregation.

4 And if they blow *but* with one *trumpet,* then the princes, *which are* heads of the thousands of Israel, shall gather themselves unto thee.

10:5, 7☆ Ex 19:13; Judg 3:27; Joel 2:1

5 When ye blow an alarm, then the camps that lie on the east parts shall go forward.

6 When ye blow an alarm the second time, then the camps that lie on the south side shall take their journey: they shall blow an alarm for their journeys.

7 But when the congregation is to be gathered together, ye shall blow, but ye shall not sound an alarm.

10:8 Num 31:6; Josh 6:3–9; 2 Chron 5:11, 12

8 And the sons of Aaron, the priests, shall blow with the trumpets; and they shall be to you for an ordinance for ever throughout your generations.

10:9 Judg 3:27; Ezek 33:3; Joel 2:1; Zeph 2:5

9 And if ye go to war in your land against the enemy that oppresseth you, then ye shall blow an alarm with the trumpets; and ye shall be remembered before the LORD your God, and ye shall be saved from your enemies.

10:10☆ Lev 23:33, 34; Num 29:1; Ezra 3:10; Ps 81:3–5

10 Also in the day of your gladness, and in your solemn days, and in the beginnings of your months, ye shall blow with the trumpets over your burnt offerings, and over the sacrifices of your peace offerings; that they may be to you for a memorial before your God: I *am* the LORD your God.

II. FROM SINAI TO KADESH-BARNEA (10:11—14:45)

A. LEAVING SINAI

1. The Order of the March

10:11 Num 1:1; 9:11, 17–22; Ex 40:17

11 ¶And it came to pass on the twentieth *day* of the second month, in the second year, that the cloud was taken up from off the tabernacle of the testimony.

10:12 Gen 21:20, 21; Num 12:16; 13:3, 26

12 And the children of Israel took their journeys out of the wilderness of Si′nai; and the cloud rested in the wilderness of Paran.

10:13 Deut 1:6

13 And they first took their journey according to the commandment of the LORD by the hand of Moses.

10:14 Num 2:3–31

14 In the first *place* went the standard of the camp of the children of Judah according to their armies: and over his host *was* Nah′shon the son of Am-min′a-dab.

15 And over the host of the tribe of the children of Is′sa-char *was* Ne-than′e-el the son of Zu′ar.

16 And over the host of the tribe of the children of Zeb′u-lun *was* E-li′ab the son of He′lon.

10:2 The two silver trumpets were designed either to call the people to a public assembly in the presence of God or to signal that they should break camp and move. In Solomon's day 120 priests sounded the trumpets (2 Chron. 5:12). They needed only two trumpets at first because they were to be blown by Aaron's sons—and he had but two.

10:5–7 Paraphrased, this passage would begin: "Different trumpet blasts will be necessary to distinguish between the summons to assemble and the signal to break camp and move onward" (TLB).

10:10 The festival of the new moon was celebrated on the first day of each month. Sacrifices were to be offered (28:11–15) and the trumpets were to be blown (10:10; Ps. 81:3, 4). All labor stopped on that day (a practice detested by the ungodly—Amos 8:5). God condemned the formal observance of this and other religious festivals when insincerity marked the occasions (Isa. 1:13, 14). Under the new covenant these festivals have been abolished by the sacrifice of Jesus Christ (Col. 2:16; Gal. 4:10, 11).

17 And the tabernacle was taken down; and the sons of Ger′shon and the
sons of Me-ra′ri set forward, bearing the tabernacle.

10:17 Num 4:21–23

18 ¶And the standard of the camp of Reuben set forward according to
their armies: and over his host *was* E-li′zur the son of Shed′e-ur.

10:18 Num 2:3–31 26:5–18

19 And over the host of the tribe of the children of Simeon *was* She-lu′mi-
el the son of Zu-ri-shad′da-i.
20 And over the host of the tribe of the children of Gad *was* E-li′a-saph the
son of Deu′el.
21 And the Ko′hath-ites set forward, bearing the sanctuary: and *the other*
did set up the tabernacle against they came.

10:21 Num 4:1–20

22 ¶And the standard of the camp of the children of E′phra-im set forward
according to their armies: and over his host *was* E-lish′a-ma the son of Am-
mi′hud.

10:22 Num 2:3–31

23 And over the host of the tribe of the children of Ma-nas′seh *was* Ga-
ma′li-el the son of Pe-dah′zur.
24 And over the host of the tribe of the children of Benjamin *was* Ab′i-dan
the son of Gid-e-o′ni.
25 ¶And the standard of the camp of the children of Dan set forward,
which was the rereward of all the camps throughout their hosts: and over
his host *was* A-hi-e′zer the son of Am-mi-shad′da-i.
26 And over the host of the tribe of the children of Asher *was* Pa′gi-el the
son of Oc′ran.
27 And over the host of the tribe of the children of Naph′ta-li *was* A-hi′ra
the son of E′nan.
28 Thus *were* the journeyings of the children of Israel according to their
armies, when they set forward.

2. Moses Asks Hobab to Remain with Him

29 ¶And Moses said unto Ho′bab, the son of Ra-gu′el the Mid′i-an-ite,
Moses' father in law, We are journeying unto the place of which the LORD
said, I will give it you: come thou with us, and we will do thee good: for the
LORD hath spoken good concerning Israel.

10:29 Ex 2:18–21; 3:1 18:1, 5–27 Judg 1:16; 4:11

30 And he said unto him, I will not go; but I will depart to mine own land,
and to my kindred.
31 And he said, Leave us not, I pray thee; forasmuch as thou knowest how
we are to encamp in the wilderness, and thou mayest be to us instead of
eyes.
32 And it shall be, if thou go with us, yea, it shall be, that what goodness
the LORD shall do unto us, the same will we do unto thee.

10:32 Num 10:29 Ps 67:5–7

3. The Place of the Ark and the Cloud

33 ¶And they departed from the mount of the LORD three days' journey:
and the ark of the covenant of the LORD went before them in the three
days' journey, to search out a resting place for them.

☆**10:33** Josh 3:2–6, 11–17

34 And the cloud of the LORD *was* upon them by day, when they went out
of the camp.

10:34 Ex 14:20, 24 Num 9:15–22

35 And it came to pass, when the ark set forward, that Moses said, Rise
up, LORD, and let thine enemies be scattered; and let them that hate thee
flee before thee.

10:35 Ps 68:1, 2 132:8 1sa 51:9

36 And when it rested, he said, Return, O LORD, unto the many thousands
of Israel.

10:36 Gen 24:60 Deut 1:10, 11 Ps 90:13–17

10:33 *the mount of the LORD,* i.e., Mount Sinai.

B. ISRAEL'S SINS AGAINST GOD

1. Complaining at Taberah (The Place of Burning)

11:1☆ Ex 16:2–9; 17:2, 3; Lev 10:1, 2; Num 14:2; 16:35; 17:5; 20:2–5; Deut 32:22
11:2 Ex 32:9–14, 31, 32; Num 14:10–21; Deut 9:19, 20
11:3☆ Deut 9:22

11 AND *when* the people complained, it displeased the LORD: and the LORD heard *it;* and his anger was kindled; and the fire of the LORD burnt among them, and consumed *them that were* in the uttermost parts of the camp.

2 And the people cried unto Moses; and when Moses prayed unto the LORD, the fire was quenched.

3 And he called the name of the place Tab'e-rah: because the fire of the LORD burnt among them.

2. Israel's Demand for Meat

11:4☆ Ex 12:38; Lev 24:10, 11; Ps 78:18; 106:14; 1 Cor 10:6
11:6 Num 21:5
11:7 Ex 16:14, 31
11:9 Ex 16:13; Ps 78:23–25

4 ¶And the mixt multitude that *was* among them fell a lusting: and the children of Israel also wept again, and said, Who shall give us flesh to eat?

5 We remember the fish, which we did eat in Egypt freely; the cucumbers, and the melons, and the leeks, and the onions, and the garlick:

6 But now our soul *is* dried away: *there is* nothing at all, beside this manna, *before* our eyes.

7 And the manna *was* as coriander seed, and the colour thereof as the colour of bdellium.

8 *And* the people went about, and gathered *it,* and ground *it* in mills, or beat *it* in a mortar, and baked *it* in pans, and made cakes of it: and the taste of it was as the taste of fresh oil.

9 And when the dew fell upon the camp in the night, the manna fell upon it.

3. Moses Petitions God for Help

11:10 Num 11:1; 14:1, 2; 16:27; Deut 32:22; Isa 5:25
11:11☆ Ex 17:4; Num 11:15
11:12 Gen 13:14–17; 26:3; 50:24, 25; Ex 13:4, 5; Isa 49:15
11:14 Ex 18:18; Deut 1:9–13

10 ¶Then Moses heard the people weep throughout their families, every man in the door of his tent: and the anger of the LORD was kindled greatly; Moses also was displeased.

11 And Moses said unto the LORD, Wherefore hast thou afflicted thy servant? and wherefore have I not found favour in thy sight, that thou layest the burden of all this people upon me?

12 Have I conceived all this people? have I begotten them, that thou shouldest say unto me, Carry them in thy bosom, as a nursing father beareth the sucking child, unto the land which thou swarest unto their fathers?

13 Whence should I have flesh to give unto all this people? for they weep unto me, saying, Give us flesh, that we may eat.

14 I am not able to bear all this people alone, because *it is* too heavy for me.

11:1 How quickly the Israelites forgot God, whose glory they had seen and whose bread they ate day by day. They were discontented, mutinous, and complaining throughout the wilderness journey (which had been initially occasioned by their sin). In this age of grace this sort of attitude is not unknown among believers who are eager to manifest their lack of faith when God uses them differently from the way they think he should. Those who are Spirit-filled do not fall heir to such attitudes.

11:3 *Taberah,* i.e., "The Place of Burning."†

11:4 *the mixt multitude,* i.e., the rabble who came with the Israelites out of Egypt expecting almost instantaneous fulfillment of the promise of the land. When the fulfillment was delayed, they became pestilent discontents whose leaven worked its way through the whole community of God's children and wrought great evil. They infected the Israelites, who quickly copied their wretched ways.

11:11 Moses, the meekest of all men, was deeply affected by the grumbling of the Israelites. He felt he was being so badly treated by the God who called him that he began his own complaint, which rose to a crescendo when he passionately asked God to kill him out of hand. It is strange how life made difficult by others could turn Moses into a feeble and despairing servant, even though he had been appointed and strengthened by God and filled with his Holy Spirit. All believers on this earth have feet of clay.

[15]And if thou deal thus with me, kill me, I pray thee, out of hand, if I
have found favour in thy sight; and let me not see my wretchedness.

11:15
Ex 32:32

4. God Answers Moses' Petition
a. Seventy Leaders Appointed to Help Moses

[16]¶And the LORD said unto Moses, Gather unto me seventy men of the
elders of Israel, whom thou knowest to be the elders of the people, and
officers over them; and bring them unto the tabernacle of the congregation,
that they may stand there with thee.
[17]And I will come down and talk with thee there: and I will take of the
spirit which *is* upon thee, and will put *it* upon them; and they shall bear the
burden of the people with thee, that thou bear *it* not thyself alone.
[18]And say thou unto the people, Sanctify yourselves against to morrow,
and ye shall eat flesh: for ye have wept in the ears of the LORD, saying, Who
shall give us flesh to eat? for *it was* well with us in Egypt: therefore the
LORD will give you flesh, and ye shall eat.
[19]Ye shall not eat one day, nor two days, nor five days, neither ten days,
nor twenty days;
[20]*But* even a whole month, until it come out at your nostrils, and it be
loathsome unto you: because that ye have despised the LORD which *is*
among you, and have wept before him, saying, Why came we forth out of
Egypt?
[21]And Moses said, The people, among whom I *am, are* six hundred
thousand footmen; and thou hast said, I will give them flesh, that they may
eat a whole month.
[22]Shall the flocks and the herds be slain for them, to suffice them? or shall
all the fish of the sea be gathered together for them, to suffice them?
[23]And the LORD said unto Moses, Is the LORD's hand waxed short? thou
shalt see now whether my word shall come to pass unto thee or not.
[24]¶And Moses went out, and told the people the words of the LORD, and
gathered the seventy men of the elders of the people, and set them round
about the tabernacle.
[25]And the LORD came down in a cloud, and spake unto him, and took of
the spirit that *was* upon him, and gave *it* unto the seventy elders: and it
came to pass, *that,* when the spirit rested upon them, they prophesied, and
did not cease.
[26]But there remained two *of the* men in the camp, the name of the one
was El′dad, and the name of the other Me′dad: and the spirit rested upon
them; and they *were* of them that were written, but went not out unto the
tabernacle: and they prophesied in the camp.
[27]And there ran a young man, and told Moses, and said, El′dad and
Me′dad do prophesy in the camp.
[28]And Joshua the son of Nun, the servant of Moses, *one* of his young
men, answered and said, My lord Moses, forbid them.

11:16
Ex 4:29; 24:1, 9
Lk 10:1, 17

11:17
Ex 34:5, 6
Num 11:25; 12:5

11:18
Ex 19:10, 14, 15
Josh 7:13

11:21
Ex 12:37
Num 1:20–46
2:32, 33

11:23
Gen 18:14

☆11:25
Num 11:16, 17
Isa 50:2

☆11:26ff

11:28
Josh 1:1
Mk 9:38–40

11:25 *the LORD . . . took of the spirit that was upon him, and gave it unto the seventy elders: . . . when the spirit rested upon them, they prophesied, and did not cease.* This was the outward confirming evidence that the Spirit was in them and at work in their lives. In 11:26 we learn that two of the seventy were still in the camp. But the Spirit came upon them also and they prophesied. When what happened was questioned, Moses made it plain that he wished all of the people were prophets; he meant that he wished they too would have the Spirit laid upon them in power.

11:26ff A sectarian spirit prevailed here. Eldad and Medad prophesied by the Spirit. Someone informed Moses, and even Joshua wanted Moses to tell them to stop prophesying. Moses wisely declined and added that he wished all of the Israelites were prophets. The incident is similar to that recorded in Mark 9:38–41 when Jesus' disciples wanted him to stop those who were casting out demons in his name, since they did not belong to the apostolic band. Jesus condemned their attitude; this should be a warning for all believers today.

29 And Moses said unto him, Enviest thou for my sake? would God that all the LORD's people were prophets, *and* that the LORD would put his spirit upon them!

30 And Moses gat him into the camp, he and the elders of Israel.

b. God Sends Quail and a Plague

11:31☆ Ex 16:13; Ps 78:26–33; 105:40

31 ¶And there went forth a wind from the LORD, and brought quails from the sea, and let *them* fall by the camp, as it were a day's journey on this side, and as it were a day's journey on the other side, round about the camp, and as it were two cubits *high* upon the face of the earth.

32 And the people stood up all that day, and all *that* night, and all the next day, and they gathered the quails: he that gathered least gathered ten homers: and they spread *them* all abroad for themselves round about the camp.

11:33 Num 11:10

33 And while the flesh *was* yet between their teeth, ere it was chewed, the wrath of the LORD was kindled against the people, and the LORD smote the people with a very great plague.

11:34☆ Num 33:15–37; Deut 9:22

34 And he called the name of that place Kib'roth–hat-ta'a-vah: because there they buried the people that lusted.

11:35 Num 12:16

35 *And* the people journeyed from Kib'roth–hat-ta'a-vah unto Ha-ze'roth; and abode at Ha-ze'roth.

C. GOD'S JUDGMENT ON AARON AND MIRIAM FOR REBELLION

1. God Defends Moses

12:1☆ Ex 2:21; 15:20

12 AND Miriam and Aaron spake against Moses because of the E-thi-o'pi-an woman whom he had married: for he had married an E-thi-o'pi-an woman.

12:2 Num 16:3; Mic 6:4

2 And they said, Hath the LORD indeed spoken only by Moses? hath he not spoken also by us? And the LORD heard *it.*

12:3 Num 16:16–21

3 (Now the man Moses *was* very meek, above all the men which *were* upon the face of the earth.)

4 And the LORD spake suddenly unto Moses, and unto Aaron, and unto Miriam, Come out ye three unto the tabernacle of the congregation. And they three came out.

12:5 Num 11:25

12:6 Gen 15:1; 31:10; 46:2; 1 Kgs 3:5; Ezek 1:1; Dan 8:2; Mt 1:20; 2:12, 13, 19; Acts 22:17, 18

5 And the LORD came down in the pillar of the cloud, and stood *in* the door of the tabernacle, and called Aaron and Miriam: and they both came forth.

6 And he said, Hear now my words: If there be a prophet among you, *I* the LORD will make myself known unto him in a vision, *and* will speak unto him in a dream.

12:7☆ Ex 33:11; Num 14:14; Deut 18:15–19; 34:10; Acts 3:21–23; Heb 3:2, 5

7 My servant Moses *is* not so, who *is* faithful in all mine house.

8 With him will I speak mouth to mouth, even apparently, and not in dark speeches; and the similitude of the LORD shall he behold: wherefore then were ye not afraid to speak against my servant Moses?

11:31 This verse is paraphrased either: "There were quail flying there four feet above the ground," or, "The ground was covered with quail, three feet thick."†

11:34 *Kibroth-hattaavah,* i.e., "The Place of the Graves Caused by Lust."†

12:1 *because of the Ethiopian woman whom he had married.* The "Ethiopian woman" apparently was Moses' wife Zipporah, the Midianite daughter of Reuel (Exod. 2:21); for the land of Midian from which she came was sometimes called Cush. But areas of Ethiopia and Babylon were also known as Cush, so it is possible that the reference is to a second wife of Moses. It is indeterminate from the text whether she was criticized for being a Gentile, or (if she was a Cushite from Ethiopia) because of her color.†

12:7, 8 In many ways Moses is a type of Christ (see Heb. 3:1–6). As Moses was Israel's deliverer, so Jesus delivers his people from sin's bondage; Moses was a prophet and so was Jesus; Moses was a faithful servant, Jesus is God's Servant-Savior; Moses frequently interceded for Israel before God, and Jesus now intercedes for his people, the church.

2. Miriam Stricken with Leprosy; Moses Prays for Her Deliverance

9 And the anger of the LORD was kindled against them; and he departed.
10 And the cloud departed from off the tabernacle; and, behold, Miriam
became leprous, *white* as snow: and Aaron looked upon Miriam, and,
behold, *she was* leprous.
11 And Aaron said unto Moses, Alas, my lord, I beseech thee, lay not the
sin upon us, wherein we have done foolishly, and wherein we have sinned.
12 Let her not be as one dead, of whom the flesh is half consumed when he
cometh out of his mother's womb.
13 And Moses cried unto the LORD, saying, Heal her now, O God, I
beseech thee.
14 ¶And the LORD said unto Moses, If her father had but spit in her face,
should she not be ashamed seven days? let her be shut out from the camp
seven days, and after that let her be received in *again.*
15 And Miriam was shut out from the camp seven days: and the people
journeyed not till Miriam was brought in *again.*
16 And afterward the people removed from Ha-ze'roth, and pitched in the
wilderness of Paran.

12:9 Num 11:1
☆**12:10** Deut 24:9
12:11 2 Sam 19:19; Acts 8:24
12:13 Num 11:2
☆**12:14** Lev 14:8, 9; 15:8; Num 5:1–3; Deut 25:9
12:16 Num 11:35

D. ISRAEL'S GREAT REBELLION AFTER THE TWELVE SPIES' REPORT
1. The Choosing of the Spies

13 AND the LORD spake unto Moses, saying,
2 Send thou men, that they may search the land of Canaan, which
I give unto the children of Israel: of every tribe of their fathers shall ye send
a man, every one a ruler among them.
3 And Moses by the commandment of the LORD sent them from the
wilderness of Paran: all those men *were* heads of the children of Israel.
4 And these *were* their names: of the tribe of Reuben, Sham-mu'a the son
of Zac'cur.
5 Of the tribe of Simeon, Sha'phat the son of Ho'ri.
6 Of the tribe of Judah, Caleb the son of Je-phun'neh.
7 Of the tribe of Is'sa-char, I'gal the son of Joseph.
8 Of the tribe of E'phra-im, O-she'a the son of Nun.
9 Of the tribe of Benjamin, Pal'ti the son of Ra'phu.
10 Of the tribe of Zeb'u-lun, Gad'di-el the son of So'di.
11 Of the tribe of Joseph, *namely,* of the tribe of Ma-nas'seh, Gad'di the
son of Su'si.
12 Of the tribe of Dan, Am'mi-el the son of Ge-mal'li.
13 Of the tribe of Asher, Se'thur the son of Michael.
14 Of the tribe of Naph'ta-li, Nah'bi the son of Voph'si.
15 Of the tribe of Gad, Ge-u'el the son of Ma'chi.
16 These *are* the names of the men which Moses sent to spy out the land.
And Moses called O-she'a the son of Nun Je-hosh'u-a.

13:2 Ex 18:25; Num 11:16; 32:8; Deut 1:22–25; Josh 2:1
13:3 Num 1:2–15; 12:16; 13:26; 34:16–28
☆**13:8**
☆**13:16** Num 13:3–15; Acts 7:45

12:10 Miriam was the elder sister of Moses and Aaron. She had watched over Moses when he was placed in the basket in the Nile River. She was obviously a person of importance, since her two brothers were the titular heads of Israel. Yet she presumed to speak against Moses (as did Aaron, who married a Cushite woman). God judged Miriam by sending leprosy, a disease that covered her body and made her an outcast from the people of Israel. Aaron was repentant, and Moses prayed for God to heal his sister. His request was granted. Miriam died later (20:1) and is heard of no more.

12:14 Here we discover that mercy and justice kiss each other. Miriam is forgiven by Moses and by God for her transgression. That is mercy. But justice was fulfilled in that she was shut out from the camp for seven days. Mercy and justice kissed in our salvation. As sinners we are forgiven—that is mercy. And justice was met by the atoning death of Jesus Christ.

13:8 *Oshea,* or, "Joshua." (See 13:16.)

13:16 *Moses called Oshea . . . Jehoshuah. Oshea* means "salvation"; *Joshua* means "Jehovah is salvation". "Joshua" is the same name in Hebrew as the Greek name "Jesus."†

2. Moses Sends the Spies Out

13:17 Gen 12:9; 13:1 Num 13:22 Josh 15:1

17¶And Moses sent them to spy out the land of Canaan, and said unto
them, Get you up this *way* southward, and go up into the mountain:
18And see the land, what it *is;* and the people that dwelleth therein,
whether they *be* strong or weak, few or many;
19And what the land *is* that they dwell in, whether it *be* good or bad; and
what cities *they be* that they dwell in, whether in tents, or in strong holds;

13:20 Num 13:23, 24

20And what the land *is,* whether it *be* fat or lean, whether there be wood
therein, or not. And be ye of good courage, and bring of the fruit of the
land. Now the time *was* the time of the firstripe grapes.

13:21 Num 20:1, 27:14 Josh 19:28 Judg 1:31, 32 2 Sam 8:9 Amos 6:2
13:22☆ Num 13:33 Josh 11:21 15:14 Judg 1:10
13:23 Num 13:24; 32:9 Deut 1:24, 25
13:24☆

21¶So they went up, and searched the land from the wilderness of Zin
unto Re'hob, as men come to Ha'math.
22And they ascended by the south, and came unto Hebron; where
A-hi'man, She'shai, and Tal'mai, the children of Anak, *were.* (Now Hebron
was built seven years before Zo'an in Egypt.)
23And they came unto the brook of Esh'col, and cut down from thence a
branch with one cluster of grapes, and they bare it between two upon a
staff; and *they brought* of the pomegranates, and of the figs.
24The place was called the brook Esh'col, because of the cluster of grapes
which the children of Israel cut down from thence.

3. The Negative Reports of Ten of the Spies

25And they returned from searching of the land after forty days.

13:26☆ Num 12:16 13:3; 20:1; 32:8 Deut 1:19 Josh 14:6

26¶And they went and came to Moses, and to Aaron, and to all the
congregation of the children of Israel, unto the wilderness of Paran, to
Ka'desh; and brought back word unto them, and unto all the congregation,
and shewed them the fruit of the land.

13:27 Ex 13:5 Num 14:8 Deut 1:25

27And they told him, and said, We came unto the land whither thou
sentest us, and surely it floweth with milk and honey; and this *is* the fruit of
it.

13:28☆ Num 13:22, 23

28Nevertheless the people *be* strong that dwell in the land, and the cities
are walled, *and* very great: and moreover we saw the children of Anak
there.

13:29 Gen 15:19–21 Ex 3:8, 17 17:8–16 Num 14:43
13:30 Num 14:6–9 Josh 14:6–8 Isa 41:10–16

29The Am'a-lek-ites dwell in the land of the south: and the Hittites, and
the Jeb'u-sites, and the Am'or-ites, dwell in the mountains: and the
Canaanites dwell by the sea, and by the coast of Jordan.
30And Caleb stilled the people before Moses, and said, Let us go up at
once, and possess it; for we are well able to overcome it.

13:22 *Zoan,* or *Tanis,* also known as *Avaris,* was built ca. 1700 B.C. in the Nile delta by the Hyksos. Hebron (mentioned here) was built seven years earlier on a site known to Abraham as *Kiratha-arba* or *Mamre.* Ps. 78:43 refers to the plains of Zoan, which refers to Goshen, where the Israelites dwelt.
13:24 *Eshcol* meaning "cluster"—from the cluster of fruit the spies cut and bore back to the congregation of their people.
13:26 God had led Israel from Egypt toward the Promised Land. All the way the people exhibited signs of discontent, unbelief, and rebellion. God was patient. Despite God's many miracles, such as the opening of the Red Sea, the provision of manna, and protection against their foes, the Israelites murmured again and again. In 13:26, we see that they hear the report of the ten spies over against the testimony of Joshua and Caleb. The ten spies were negative in their description of the land; they were frightened by the giants there. The people accepted and endorsed the report of the ten spies despite God's promise that he would take care of them and would give them victory over the occupants of Canaan. They looked at outward circumstances rather than to the promises of God. Their unbelief was dealt with by the forty years of wandering through the wilderness, during which all adults who had voted to disobey would die off. The new generation, reared in freedom and aware of God's daily provision, would be prepared by God to enter Canaan along with Joshua and Caleb, who were men of faith.
13:28 *the cities are walled.* Some of their cities had walls thirty to fifty feet high and twelve to fifteen feet thick.

31 But the men that went up with him said, We be not able to go up
against the people; for they *are* stronger than we.
32 And they brought up an evil report of the land which they had searched
unto the children of Israel, saying, The land, through which we have gone
to search it, *is* a land that eateth up the inhabitants thereof; and all the
people that we saw in it *are* men of a great stature.
33 And there we saw the giants, the sons of Anak, *which come* of the
giants: and we were in our own sight as grasshoppers, and so we were in
their sight.

13:31 Num 32:9 Josh 14:8 Heb 3:19
13:32 Num 14:36, 37 Deut 1:28 Mt 23:13
13:33 1 Sam 17:4–7 2 Sam 21:20–22 1 Chron 11:23

4. The Great Rebellion of Israel

a. Israel's Chorus of Complaint

14 AND all the congregation lifted up their voice, and cried; and the
people wept that night.
2 And all the children of Israel murmured against Moses and against
Aaron: and the whole congregation said unto them, Would God that we
had died in the land of Egypt! or would God we had died in this
wilderness!
3 And wherefore hath the LORD brought us unto this land, to fall by the
sword, that our wives and our children should be a prey? were it not better
for us to return into Egypt?

☆**14:2** Ex 15:24; 16:3 Num 11:1, 5 16:41; 20:3, 4 21:5
☆**14:3** Ex 5:21; 16:3 Num 14:31 Deut 1:39

b. Joshua and Caleb Support Moses and Aaron

4 And they said one to another, Let us make a captain, and let us return
into Egypt.
5 Then Moses and Aaron fell on their faces before all the assembly of the
congregation of the children of Israel.
6 ¶And Joshua the son of Nun, and Caleb the son of Je-phun'neh, *which
were* of them that searched the land, rent their clothes:
7 And they spake unto all the company of the children of Israel, saying,
The land, which we passed through to search it, *is* an exceeding good land.
8 If the LORD delight in us, then he will bring us into this land, and give
it us; a land which floweth with milk and honey.
9 Only rebel not ye against the LORD, neither fear ye the people of the
land; for they *are* bread for us: their defence is departed from them, and the
LORD *is* with us: fear them not.

14:5 Gen 17:3 Lev 9:24 Num 16:22, 45 Josh 5:14
14:7 Num 13:27 Deut 1:25 6:10, 11; 8:7–9
14:8 Ex 3:8 Num 13:27
14:9 Deut 1:21, 29 7:18; 9:7, 23, 24

c. God's Anger against Israel

10 But all the congregation bade stone them with stones. And the glory of
the LORD appeared in the tabernacle of the congregation before all the
children of Israel.
11 ¶And the LORD said unto Moses, How long will this people provoke

☆**14:10** Ex 16:7, 10 17:4; 24:16, 17 32:9–13 Lev 9:23 Num 20:6 1 Sam 30:6
☆**14:11**

14:2, 3 The Israelites murmur again and repeat their pitiful refrain that they wished they were back in Egypt and in slavery. They complain against Moses and Aaron, and against the Lord also.

14:10 The Israelites wanted to choose another leader to replace Moses (14:4). Now they were ready to stone Moses, Aaron, Joshua and Caleb. At this point God intervened and manifested his glory in the tabernacle of the congregation before all the children of Israel. The people saw the glory of the living God. One would suppose that this would have been unnecessary, since they had seen the glory before this. God was ready to pronounce judgment upon them and destroy them. This would not have meant the end of God's plan of redemption. He would have raised up a new people. But Moses intervened and God pardoned them. Nevertheless, they were to smart for their transgression: they would never enter the Promised Land. Only their children and children's children would do this.

14:11 If the Israelites had a complaint against God, God had a greater complaint against them. God was provoked because his people still did not really believe, despite his sending them sign after sign and miracle after miracle. This same sort of attitude can be found today among certain believers who continue to doubt God despite his many blessings.

me? and how long will it be ere they believe me, for all the signs which I
have shewed among them?

14:12 Ex 32:10; Lev 26:25; Num 16:46–49; Deut 28:21

12 I will smite them with the pestilence, and disinherit them, and will
make of thee a greater nation and mightier than they.

d. Moses' Intercessory Prayer

14:13 Ex 9:28; 32:12

13 ¶And Moses said unto the LORD, Then the Egyptians shall hear *it,* (for
thou broughtest up this people in thy might from among them;)

14:14 Ex 13:21; 33:11; 40:38; Num 9:15–21; 12:8; Deut 5:4; 34:10

14 And they will tell *it* to the inhabitants of this land: *for* they have heard
that thou LORD *art* among this people, that thou LORD art seen face to face,
and *that* thy cloud standeth over them, and *that* thou goest before them, by
day time in a pillar of a cloud, and in a pillar of fire by night.

14:15 Ex 32:12; Num 14:13

15 ¶Now *if* thou shalt kill *all* this people as one man, then the nations
which have heard the fame of thee will speak, saying,
16 Because the LORD was not able to bring this people into the land which
he sware unto them, therefore he hath slain them in the wilderness.

14:17 Ex 20:5; 34:6, 7; Ps 103:8

17 And now, I beseech thee, let the power of my Lord be great, according
as thou hast spoken, saying,
18 The LORD *is* longsuffering, and of great mercy, forgiving iniquity and
transgression, and by no means clearing *the guilty,* visiting the iniquity of
the fathers upon the children unto the third and fourth *generation.*

14:19 Ex 32:32; 34:9

19 Pardon, I beseech thee, the iniquity of this people according unto the
greatness of thy mercy, and as thou hast forgiven this people, from Egypt
even until now.

e. God Condemns Israel to Forty Years of Wandering

14:20 Num 14:28; Deut 32:40; Mic 7:18–20

20 And the LORD said, I have pardoned according to thy word:
21 But *as* truly *as* I live, all the earth shall be filled with the glory of the
LORD.
22 Because all those men which have seen my glory, and my miracles,
which I did in Egypt and in the wilderness, and have tempted me now these
ten times, and have not hearkened to my voice;

14:23 Num 26:65; 32:11; Deut 1:35

23 Surely they shall not see the land which I sware unto their fathers,
neither shall any of them that provoked me see it:

14:24 Num 13:30; 14:6; 26:65; Josh 14:6–15

24 But my servant Caleb, because he had another spirit with him, and hath
followed me fully, him will I bring into the land whereinto he went; and his
seed shall possess it.

14:25 Num 13:29

25 (Now the Am'a-lek-ites and the Canaanites dwelt in the valley.) To
morrow turn you, and get you into the wilderness by the way of the Red
sea.

14:26 Num 11:1

26 ¶And the LORD spake unto Moses and unto Aaron, saying,
27 How long *shall I bear with* this evil congregation, which murmur against
me? I have heard the murmurings of the children of Israel, which they
murmur against me.

14:28 Num 14:21; Heb 3:17

28 Say unto them, *As truly as* I live, saith the LORD, as ye have spoken in
mine ears, so will I do to you:

14:29 Num 1:17–19; 26:2

14:30☆ Num 14:24, 38; 32:12

29 Your carcases shall fall in this wilderness; and all that were numbered
of you, according to your whole number, from twenty years old and
upward, which have murmured against me,
30 Doubtless ye shall not come into the land, *concerning* which I sware to

---

14:30 God passed sentence on all the Israelites twenty years of age or older. They would wander in the wilderness until the last one died. Only Caleb and Joshua would enter the land of promise. Since this was the tenth time the Israelites provoked God, it was about time that they smarted for their transgressions. The patience of God had worn thin and judgment was assessed. Pay day had come.

make you dwell therein, save Caleb the son of Je-phun'neh, and Joshua the son of Nun.
31But your little ones, which ye said should be a prey, them will I bring in, and they shall know the land which ye have despised.
32But *as for* you, your carcases, they shall fall in this wilderness.
33And your children shall wander in the wilderness forty years, and bear your whoredoms, until your carcases be wasted in the wilderness.
34After the number of the days in which ye searched the land, *even* forty days, each day for a year, shall ye bear your iniquities, *even* forty years, and ye shall know my breach of promise.
35I the LORD have said, I will surely do it unto all this evil congregation, that are gathered together against me: in this wilderness they shall be consumed, and there they shall die.
36And the men, which Moses sent to search the land, who returned, and made all the congregation to murmur against him, by bringing up a slander upon the land,
37Even those men that did bring up the evil report upon the land, died by the plague before the LORD.
38But Joshua the son of Nun, and Caleb the son of Je-phun'neh, *which were* of the men that went to search the land, lived *still.*
39And Moses told these sayings unto all the children of Israel: and the people mourned greatly.

14:31 Num 14:3
14:32 Num 14:29; 26:64; 32:13; 1 Cor 10:5
14:33 Num 33:38; Deut 2:7; 8:2
14:36 Num 13:26–29, 31–33; 16:49; 25:9
☆14:37
14:39 Ex 33:4

f. The Amalekites and Canaanites Defeat Israel

40¶And they rose up early in the morning, and gat them up into the top of the mountain, saying, Lo, we *be here,* and will go up unto the place which the LORD hath promised: for we have sinned.
41And Moses said, Wherefore now do ye transgress the commandment of the LORD? but it shall not prosper.
42Go not up, for the LORD *is* not among you; that ye be not smitten before your enemies.
43For the Am'a-lek-ites and the Canaanites *are* there before you, and ye shall fall by the sword: because ye are turned away from the LORD, therefore the LORD will not be with you.
44But they presumed to go up unto the hill top: nevertheless the ark of the covenant of the LORD, and Moses, departed not out of the camp.
45Then the Am'a-lek-ites came down, and the Canaanites which dwelt in that hill, and smote them, and discomfited them, *even* unto Hor'mah.

☆14:40 Deut 1:41–44
14:44 Num 10:33; 31:6
☆14:45 Num 21:3; Judg 1:17

III. FROM KADESH-BARNEA TO THE PLAINS OF MOAB (15:1—21:35)

A. GOD GIVES ISRAEL FURTHER RELIGIOUS REGULATIONS

1. Meat (Grain) Offerings

15 AND the LORD spake unto Moses, saying,
2Speak unto the children of Israel, and say unto them, When ye be come into the land of your habitations, which I give unto you,

☆15:2

14:37 God had intended for his people to enter into the land immediately. The ten spies, who brought in their evil report, hindered God's intention. For this they were punished. The sentence of death by plague was visited upon them. Surely it is always better to do the will of God and inherit his blessing than to disobey and suffer judgment and punishment.

14:40 The Israelites never seemed to learn their lessons. God had sentenced them to forty years of wandering. But now they thought they would return to the earlier promise and move forward to enter the land of promise. When they foolishly began their journey, leaving behind the ark of the covenant and Moses, they were defeated and chased away by the Amalekites and Canaanites. Nothing can end well that begins with sin.

14:45 As a result of this presumption, some of them died immediately, while the others would do so later.

15:2 The Israelites sinned twice: they refused to enter the promised land because of the report of the ten fearful spies, and then they presumptuously tried to

15:3 Lev 1:1; 2:1–16; 6:9–11; 6:14–21; 22:21; 23:37, 38; 27:2; Deut 12:6, 17; 16:16

15:5 Num 15:5–10; 28:7

15:8 Lev 3:1; 7:11–18

15:10 Num 15:5

15:15 Ex 12:49; Lev 24:22; Num 9:14; 15:29

15:19 Lev 23:10, 17; Num 18:12

15:23 Lev 4:2, 22, 27; 5:15, 18

3 And will make an offering by fire unto the LORD, a burnt offering, or a sacrifice in performing a vow, or in a freewill offering, or in your solemn feasts, to make a sweet savour unto the LORD, of the herd, or of the flock:
4 Then shall he that offereth his offering unto the LORD bring a meat offering of a tenth deal of flour mingled with the fourth *part* of an hin of oil.
5 And the fourth *part* of an hin of wine for a drink offering shalt thou prepare with the burnt offering or sacrifice, for one lamb.
6 Or for a ram, thou shalt prepare *for* a meat offering two tenth deals of flour mingled with the third *part* of an hin of oil.
7 And for a drink offering thou shalt offer the third *part* of an hin of wine, *for* a sweet savour unto the LORD.
8 And when thou preparest a bullock *for* a burnt offering, or *for* a sacrifice in performing a vow, or peace offerings unto the LORD:
9 Then shall he bring with a bullock a meat offering of three tenth deals of flour mingled with half an hin of oil.
10 And thou shalt bring for a drink offering half an hin of wine, *for* an offering made by fire, of a sweet savour unto the LORD.
11 Thus shall it be done for one bullock, or for one ram, or for a lamb, or a kid.
12 According to the number that ye shall prepare, so shall ye do to every one according to their number.
13 All that are born of the country shall do these things after this manner, in offering an offering made by fire, of a sweet savour unto the LORD.
14 And if a stranger sojourn with you, or whosoever *be* among you in your generations, and will offer an offering made by fire, of a sweet savour unto the LORD; as ye do, so he shall do.
15 One ordinance *shall be both* for you of the congregation, and also for the stranger that sojourneth *with you,* an ordinance for ever in your generations: as ye *are,* so shall the stranger be before the LORD.
16 One law and one manner shall be for you, and for the stranger that sojourneth with you.

2. Heave Offerings

17 ¶And the LORD spake unto Moses, saying,
18 Speak unto the children of Israel, and say unto them, When ye come into the land whither I bring you,
19 Then it shall be, that, when ye eat of the bread of the land, ye shall offer up an heave offering unto the LORD.
20 Ye shall offer up a cake of the first of your dough *for* an heave offering: as *ye do* the heave offering of the threshingfloor, so shall ye heave it.
21 Of the first of your dough ye shall give unto the LORD an heave offering in your generations.

3. Sacrifices for Sins Done Ignorantly

22 ¶And if ye have erred, and not observed all these commandments, which the LORD hath spoken unto Moses,
23 *Even* all that the LORD hath commanded you by the hand of Moses, from the day that the LORD commanded *Moses,* and henceforward among your generations;

enter. As a result, they were defeated by the Amalekites and Canaanites. Here God assures his people that they will enter the land despite their wickedness and the extension of their stay in the wilderness. God, then and now, stands willing to forgive his people (who through their sins break fellowship with him) if they repent and accept his chastening.

24Then it shall be, if *ought* be committed by ignorance without the ☆15:24
knowledge of the congregation, that all the congregation shall offer one
young bullock for a burnt offering, for a sweet savour unto the LORD, with
his meat offering, and his drink offering, according to the manner, and one
kid of the goats for a sin offering.
25And the priest shall make an atonement for all the congregation of the 15:25 Lev 4:20
children of Israel, and it shall be forgiven them; for it *is* ignorance: and
they shall bring their offering, a sacrifice made by fire unto the LORD, and
their sin offering before the LORD, for their ignorance:
26And it shall be forgiven all the congregation of the children of Israel,
and the stranger that sojourneth among them; seeing all the people *were* in
ignorance.
27¶And if any soul sin through ignorance, then he shall bring a she goat
of the first year for a sin offering.
28And the priest shall make an atonement for the soul that sinneth
ignorantly, when he sinneth by ignorance before the LORD, to make an
atonement for him; and it shall be forgiven him.
29Ye shall have one law for him that sinneth through ignorance, *both for* 15:29 Num 15:15
him that is born among the children of Israel, and for the stranger that
sojourneth among them.
30¶But the soul that doeth *ought* presumptuously, *whether he be* born in ☆15:30 Num 14:40–44 Deut 1:43 17:12, 13
the land, or a stranger, the same reproacheth the LORD; and that soul shall
be cut off from among his people.
31Because he hath despised the word of the LORD, and hath broken his
commandment, that soul shall utterly be cut off; his iniquity *shall be* upon
him.

4. God Ordains Death for Sabbath Breakers

32¶And while the children of Israel were in the wilderness, they found a ☆15:32 Ex 31:14, 15 35:2, 3
man that gathered sticks upon the sabbath day.
33And they that found him gathering sticks brought him unto Moses and
Aaron, and unto all the congregation.
34And they put him in ward, because it was not declared what should be
done to him.
35And the LORD said unto Moses, The man shall be surely put to death: 15:35 Lev 24:14, 23 Deut 21:21
all the congregation shall stone him with stones without the camp.
36And all the congregation brought him without the camp, and stoned ☆15:36
him with stones, and he died; as the LORD commanded Moses.

5. The Fringes to Remember God's Commandments

37¶And the LORD spake unto Moses, saying, ☆15:37, 38 Deut 22:12 Mt 9:20; 23:5 Lk 8:44
38Speak unto the children of Israel, and bid them that they make them

---

15:24 See note to Lev. 4:2 for sins of ignorance and the atonement prescribed.
15:30 *presumptuously,* literally, "with a high hand." The language of this sin is: "Eternal truth is not fit to be believed, the Lord is not fit to be obeyed, and almighty power is not fit to be feared or trusted."*
15:32 The gathering of sticks seems to be a small matter indeed. But it is presumptuous, a violation of the law, and tacit contempt of God, the author of that law.
15:36 The penalty for sabbath-breaking was death by stoning. This was Moses' injunction, given to him by God. It suggests the seriousness of the sin in which those who profess to love God defy the sabbath commandment, and insult their Creator. In abrogating God's commandments, sinners put themselves above their God. In 15:36, the man was punished not for the simple act of picking up sticks. He was put to death for what lay behind the action, an attitude of heart and mind in revolt against God.
15:38 *make fringes in the borders of their garments.* Verse 38 describes what the fringe was to be. Its purpose was to remind the Israelites of their duties and also to distinguish them in their dress from the heathen—even as their diet did. They were to be a separated people of God. Jesus wore those fringes, according to Matt. 9:20. Phylacteries were different things; they were inventions of the Israelites, unlike the fringes which came from a divine institution.

fringes in the borders of their garments throughout their generations, and
that they put upon the fringe of the borders a ribband of blue:

15:39 Ex 13:9 Deut 6:12; 8:11 Jude 16

39 And it shall be unto you for a fringe, that ye may look upon it, and
remember all the commandments of the LORD, and do them; and that ye
seek not after your own heart and your own eyes, after which ye use to go
a whoring:

15:40 1 Pet 1:15, 16

40 That ye may remember, and do all my commandments, and be holy
unto your God.

15:41 Ex 20:1

41 I *am* the LORD your God, which brought you out of the land of Egypt,
to be your God: I *am* the LORD your God.

B. THE GREAT REBELLIONS
1. Korah Incites a Revolt

16:1☆ Ex 6:21 Num 26:9, 10 Deut 11:6 Jude 11

16 NOW Ko'rah, the son of Iz'har, the son of Ko'hath, the son of Levi,
and Da'than and A-bi'ram, the sons of E-li'ab, and On, the son of
Pe'leth, sons of Reuben, took *men:*

16:2 Num 1:16

2 And they rose up before Moses, with certain of the children of Israel,
two hundred and fifty princes of the assembly, famous in the congregation,
men of renown:

16:3 Ex 19:6 Num 16:7; 35:34

3 And they gathered themselves together against Moses and against
Aaron, and said unto them, *Ye take* too much upon you, seeing all the
congregation *are* holy, every one of them, and the LORD *is* among them:
wherefore then lift ye up yourselves above the congregation of the LORD?

16:4 Num 14:5 16:45; 20:6

4 And when Moses heard *it,* he fell upon his face:

16:5 Lev 10:3 21:6–8, 12–15 Jn 15:16

5 And he spake unto Ko'rah and unto all his company, saying, Even to
morrow the LORD will shew who *are* his, and *who is* holy; and will cause
him to come near unto him: even *him* whom he hath chosen will he cause to
come near unto him.
6 This do; Take you censers, Ko'rah, and all his company;

16:7 Num 16:3

7 And put fire therein, and put incense in them before the LORD to
morrow: and it shall be *that* the man whom the LORD doth choose, he *shall
be* holy: *ye take* too much upon you, ye sons of Levi.
8 And Moses said unto Ko'rah, Hear, I pray you, ye sons of Levi:
9 *Seemeth it but* a small thing unto you, that the God of Israel hath
separated you from the congregation of Israel, to bring you near to himself
to do the service of the tabernacle of the LORD, and to stand before the
congregation to minister unto them?

16:10 Num 3:6–10

10 And he hath brought thee near *to him,* and all thy brethren the sons of
Levi with thee: and seek ye the priesthood also?

16:11 Num 16:3 1 Sam 8:7

11 For which cause *both* thou and all thy company *are* gathered together
against the LORD: and what *is* Aaron, that ye murmur against him?

16:12☆

12 ¶And Moses sent to call Da'than and A-bi'ram, the sons of E-li'ab:
which said, We will not come up:

16:13 Ex 16:3, 17 Num 11:5 14:2, 3; 20:3, 4

13 *Is it* a small thing that thou hast brought us up out of a land that
floweth with milk and honey, to kill us in the wilderness, except thou make
thyself altogether a prince over us?

16:1 Korah, who was of the tribe of Levi, challenged the authority of Moses and Aaron and was aided and abetted by Abiram and Dathan, who came from the tribe of Reuben. The revolt involved the assumption of priestly functions by non-Levites, which was forbidden by God. Korah himself was of the priestly tribe but his plot, which included Reubenites, was contrary to God's express commandment. God wiped out the entire families of Dathan and Abiram. He also killed Korah, but did not extend the punishment to his sons. The Israelites blamed Moses and Aaron for what happened (16:41); subsequently, God sent a plague that killed 14,700 Israelites (16:49).

16:12 With hot heads and hardened hearts Dathan and Abiram refused to obey the call of Moses, God's appointed leader. They were insolent, impudent, and treasonous.

14 Moreover thou hast not brought us into a land that floweth with milk
and honey, or given us inheritance of fields and vineyards: wilt thou put out
the eyes of these men? we will not come up.

16:14 Ex 22:5; Num 20:5

2. God's Judgment against the Rebels

15 And Moses was very wroth, and said unto the LORD, Respect not thou
their offering: I have not taken one ass from them, neither have I hurt one
of them.

16:15 Gen 4:4; 1 Sam 12:3

16 And Moses said unto Ko'rah, Be thou and all thy company before the
LORD, thou, and they, and Aaron, to morrow:
17 And take every man his censer, and put incense in them, and bring ye
before the LORD every man his censer, two hundred and fifty censers; thou
also, and Aaron, each *of you* his censer.
18 And they took every man his censer, and put fire in them, and laid
incense thereon, and stood in the door of the tabernacle of the congregation
with Moses and Aaron.
19 And Ko'rah gathered all the congregation against them unto the door
of the tabernacle of the congregation: and the glory of the LORD appeared
unto all the congregation.

☆**16:19** Lev 9:6; Num 12:5; 14:10; 16:42; 20:6

20 And the LORD spake unto Moses and unto Aaron, saying,
21 Separate yourselves from among this congregation, that I may consume
them in a moment.

16:21 Ex 32:10; Num 14:12

22 And they fell upon their faces, and said, O God, the God of the spirits
of all flesh, shall one man sin, and wilt thou be wroth with all the
congregation?

16:22 Gen 18:23-32

23 ¶And the LORD spake unto Moses, saying,
24 Speak unto the congregation, saying, Get you up from about the
tabernacle of Ko'rah, Da'than, and A-bi'ram.

16:24 Num 16:45

25 And Moses rose up and went unto Da'than and A-bi'ram; and the
elders of Israel followed him.
26 And he spake unto the congregation, saying, Depart, I pray you, from
the tents of these wicked men, and touch nothing of theirs, lest ye be
consumed in all their sins.

16:26 Gen 19:12-17; Deut 13:17

27 So they gat up from the tabernacle of Ko'rah, Da'than, and A-bi'ram,
on every side: and Da'than and A-bi'ram came out, and stood in the door
of their tents, and their wives, and their sons, and their little children.
28 And Moses said, Hereby ye shall know that the LORD hath sent me to
do all these works; for *I have* not *done them* of mine own mind.
29 If these men die the common death of all men, or if they be visited after
the visitation of all men; *then* the LORD hath not sent me.

16:28 Ex 3:12; 4:1-9; 7:9; Deut 18:22

30 But if the LORD make a new thing, and the earth open her mouth, and
swallow them up, with all that *appertain* unto them, and they go down
quick into the pit; then ye shall understand that these men have provoked
the LORD.
31 ¶And it came to pass, as he had made an end of speaking all these
words, that the ground clave asunder that *was* under them:
32 And the earth opened her mouth, and swallowed them up, and their
houses, and all the men that *appertained* unto Ko'rah, and all *their* goods.

16:32 Num 16:30; 26:10

33 They, and all that *appertained* to them, went down alive into the pit,
and the earth closed upon them: and they perished from among the
congregation.

16:19 Here the glory of God appears before Israel. This glory can be a sign of judgment (as in this case) or a sign of divine approval (as when the glory appeared to install Aaron in his office—Lev. 9:23).

[34]And all Israel that *were* round about them fled at the cry of them: for
they said, Lest the earth swallow us up *also*.
16:35☆ Lev 10:2 Num 11:1; 16:2 26:10 [35]And there came out a fire from the LORD, and consumed the two
hundred and fifty men that offered incense.
[36]¶And the LORD spake unto Moses, saying,
[37]Speak unto E-le-a'zar the son of Aaron the priest, that he take up the
censers out of the burning, and scatter thou the fire yonder; for they are
hallowed.
[38]The censers of these sinners against their own souls, let them make
them broad plates *for* a covering of the altar: for they offered them before
the LORD, therefore they are hallowed: and they shall be a sign unto the
children of Israel.
[39]And E-le-a'zar the priest took the brasen censers, wherewith they that
were burnt had offered; and they were made broad *plates for* a covering of
the altar:
16:40 Num 1:51 3:10, 38 [40]*To be* a memorial unto the children of Israel, that no stranger, which *is*
not of the seed of Aaron, come near to offer incense before the LORD; that
he be not as Ko'rah, and as his company: as the LORD said to him by the
hand of Moses.

3. The Murmurings against Moses and Aaron

16:41☆ Num 16:3 [41]¶But on the morrow all the congregation of the children of Israel
murmured against Moses and against Aaron, saying, Ye have killed the
people of the LORD.
16:42 Ex 24:16 40:34, 35 Num 14:10 16:19 [42]And it came to pass, when the congregation was gathered against
Moses and against Aaron, that they looked toward the tabernacle of the
congregation: and, behold, the cloud covered it, and the glory of the LORD
appeared.
[43]And Moses and Aaron came before the tabernacle of the congregation.
[44]¶And the LORD spake unto Moses, saying,
16:45 Num 16:21, 24 [45]Get you up from among this congregation, that I may consume them as
in a moment. And they fell upon their faces.
16:46 Ex 30:7–10 Lev 10:6 Num 8:19; 18:5 25:13 Deut 9:22 [46]¶And Moses said unto Aaron, Take a censer, and put fire therein from
off the altar, and put on incense, and go quickly unto the congregation, and
make an atonement for them: for there is wrath gone out from the LORD;
the plague is begun.
16:47 Num 16:36 25:7, 8, 13 Deut 33:10 [47]And Aaron took as Moses commanded, and ran into the midst of the
congregation; and, behold, the plague was begun among the people: and he
put on incense, and made an atonement for the people.
[48]And he stood between the dead and the living; and the plague was
stayed.
16:49 Num 16:32–35 25:9 1 Chron 21:14 [49]Now they that died in the plague were fourteen thousand and seven
hundred, beside them that died about the matter of Ko'rah.

16:35–38 The blaspheming malcontents were consumed by the fire of God for their transgression. They had offered incense and in so doing had taken fire from the altar, an act which was forbidden. As soon as they had kindled their fire, the fire of God consumed them. But the sacred fire which had been placed on their censer plates then became holy. God had no respect for the abominable sacrifice of the wicked. Yet he commanded that the censer plates containing the true fire be recovered and beaten into a cover for the altar. This was to remind the Israelites forever that rash actions provoke the wrath of God. Impressions that are deep are not always durable. So God provided this outward memorial to warn all future aspirants seeking to take over what belonged exclusively to the Levitical priesthood.

16:41 The Israelites blamed Moses for what God had done when the fire from heaven consumed two hundred and fifty Israelites and their leaders, Korah, Dathan, and Abiram. Blaming Moses was an insult to God, who stood behind his servant. Consequently, further judgment fell and 14,700 died from a plague. The malcontents obviously had no fear of God and suffered for their willfulness.

[50]And Aaron returned unto Moses unto the door of the tabernacle of the
congregation: and the plague was stayed.

4. Aaron's Budding Rod, a Sign of Authority from God

17 AND the LORD spake unto Moses, saying,
[2]Speak unto the children of Israel, and take of every one of them
a rod according to the house of *their* fathers, of all their princes according
to the house of their fathers twelve rods: write thou every man's name upon
his rod.
[3]And thou shalt write Aaron's name upon the rod of Levi: for one rod
shall be for the head of the house of their fathers.
[4]And thou shalt lay them up in the tabernacle of the congregation before
the testimony, where I will meet with you.

17:4 Ex 25:16–22 Num 17:10

[5]And it shall come to pass, *that* the man's rod, whom I shall choose, shall
blossom: and I will make to cease from me the murmurings of the children
of Israel, whereby they murmur against you.

☆**17:5** Num 16:5; 17:8 Heb 9:4

[6]¶And Moses spake unto the children of Israel, and every one of their
princes gave him a rod apiece, for each prince one, according to their
fathers' houses, *even* twelve rods: and the rod of Aaron *was* among
their rods.
[7]And Moses laid up the rods before the LORD in the tabernacle of
witness.

17:7 Num 18:2

[8]And it came to pass, that on the morrow Moses went into the tabernacle
of witness; and, behold, the rod of Aaron for the house of Levi was budded,
and brought forth buds, and bloomed blossoms, and yielded almonds.

☆**17:8** Num 17:5 Heb 9:4

[9]And Moses brought out all the rods from before the LORD unto all the
children of Israel: and they looked, and took every man his rod.
[10]¶And the LORD said unto Moses, Bring Aaron's rod again before the
testimony, to be kept for a token against the rebels; and thou shalt quite
take away their murmurings from me, that they die not.

☆**17:10** Num 17:4 Deut 9:7, 24

[11]And Moses did *so:* as the LORD commanded him, so did he.
[12]And the children of Israel spake unto Moses, saying, Behold, we die, we
perish, we all perish.

17:12 Num 1:51–53 18:4–7; 26:11 Isa 6:5

[13]Whosoever cometh any thing near unto the tabernacle of the LORD
shall die: shall we be consumed with dying?

C. RELATIONSHIPS BETWEEN THE PRIESTS AND THE LEVITES

1. The Functions of the Priests and Levites

18 AND the LORD said unto Aaron, Thou and thy sons and thy
father's house with thee shall bear the iniquity of the sanctuary: and
thou and thy sons with thee shall bear the iniquity of your priesthood.

18:1 Ex 28:38

[2]And thy brethren also of the tribe of Levi, the tribe of thy father, bring
thou with thee, that they may be joined unto thee, and minister unto thee:
but thou and thy sons with thee *shall minister* before the tabernacle of
witness.

18:2 Num 1:51 3:5–10 4:15–20 8:19, 22; 18:7

17:5 *the rod shall blossom.* "If anything shall convince them, they shall be convinced; and, if this will not convince them, nothing will."* Even this did not cause Israel to cease murmuring.

17:8 Both Moses and Aaron had rods. In this instance the rod of Aaron was placed in the inner room of the tabernacle along with rods for the other eleven tribes. His rod alone budded and blossomed—a sign from God that Aaron and his house were the sole priestly representatives before him. No longer were the Israelites to question Aaron's unique priestly authority. The rod was first kept in the sanctuary as a symbol and ultimately placed in the ark of the covenant (Heb. 9:4).

17:10 Implied in this verse is the idea that if there were further complaints about his authority, Aaron should bring out the rod and show it to the people.

3 And they shall keep thy charge, and the charge of all the tabernacle:
only they shall not come nigh the vessels of the sanctuary and the altar, that
neither they, nor ye also, die.
4 And they shall be joined unto thee, and keep the charge of the
tabernacle of the congregation, for all the service of the tabernacle: and a
stranger shall not come nigh unto you.
18:5 Num 8:19; 16:46
5 And ye shall keep the charge of the sanctuary, and the charge of the
altar: that there be no wrath any more upon the children of Israel.
18:6 Num 3:9 8:16–19
6 And I, behold, I have taken your brethren the Levites from among the
children of Israel: to you *they are* given *as* a gift for the LORD, to do the
service of the tabernacle of the congregation.
18:7 Ex 29:9 Num 1:51; 3:10
7 Therefore thou and thy sons with thee shall keep your priest's office for
every thing of the altar, and within the vail; and ye shall serve: I have given
your priest's office *unto you as* a service of gift: and the stranger that cometh
nigh shall be put to death.

2. The Offerings Designated for the Priests

18:8☆ Lev 7:28–34 Deut 12:6
8 ¶And the LORD spake unto Aaron, Behold, I also have given thee the
charge of mine heave offerings of all the hallowed things of the children of
Israel; unto thee have I given them by reason of the anointing, and to thy
sons, by an ordinance for ever.
18:9 Lev 2:2; 4:22 6:25–30 10:12, 13
9 This shall be thine of the most holy things, *reserved* from the fire: every
oblation of theirs, every meat offering of theirs, and every sin offering of
theirs, and every trespass offering of theirs, which they shall render unto
me, *shall be* most holy for thee and for thy sons.
10 In the most holy *place* shalt thou eat it; every male shall eat it: it shall
be holy unto thee.
18:11 Lev 22:2, 3, 11-13
11 And this *is* thine; the heave offering of their gift, with all the wave
offerings of the children of Israel: I have given them unto thee, and to thy
sons and to thy daughters with thee, by a statute for ever: every one that is
clean in thy house shall eat of it.
18:12 Ex 22:29 Num 15:19–21 Deut 18:4
12 All the best of the oil, and all the best of the wine, and of the wheat, the
firstfruits of them which they shall offer unto the LORD, them have I given
thee.
13 *And* whatsoever is first ripe in the land, which they shall bring unto the
LORD, shall be thine; every one that is clean in thine house shall eat *of* it.
18:14 Lev 27:28
14 Every thing devoted in Israel shall be thine.
18:15☆
15 Every thing that openeth the matrix in all flesh, which they bring unto
the LORD, *whether it be* of men or beasts, shall be thine: nevertheless the
firstborn of man shalt thou surely redeem, and the firstling of unclean
beasts shalt thou redeem.
16 And those that are to be redeemed from a month old shalt thou redeem,
according to thine estimation, for the money of five shekels, after the shekel
of the sanctuary, which *is* twenty gerahs.
17 But the firstling of a cow, or the firstling of a sheep, or the firstling of a
goat, thou shalt not redeem; they *are* holy: thou shalt sprinkle their blood
upon the altar, and shalt burn their fat *for* an offering made by fire, for a
sweet savour unto the LORD.
18 And the flesh of them shall be thine, as the wave breast and as the right
shoulder are thine.

18:8 God's provision for the material needs of the priesthood did not spring from their personal worthiness nor did it mean they were above their fellows. The material gifts came for the sake of the office to which they had been anointed.

18:15 Some beasts were ceremonially unclean but still necessary, such as asses. The firstborn of clean and unclean beasts had to be redeemed.

19 All the heave offerings of the holy things, which the children of Israel ☆**18:19**
offer unto the LORD, have I given thee, and thy sons and thy daughters with 2 Chron 13:5
thee, by a statute for ever: it *is* a covenant of salt for ever before the LORD
unto thee and to thy seed with thee.
20 ¶And the LORD spake unto Aaron, Thou shalt have no inheritance in **18:20** Num 18:23
their land, neither shalt thou have any part among them: I *am* thy part and Deut 10:9; 18:2 Josh 13:33
thine inheritance among the children of Israel. Ezek 44:28

3. The Tithe Designated for the Levites

21 And, behold, I have given the children of Levi all the tenth in Israel for ☆**18:21**
an inheritance, for their service which they serve, *even* the service of the Lev 27:30–33
tabernacle of the congregation.
22 Neither must the children of Israel henceforth come nigh the tabernacle
of the congregation, lest they bear sin, and die.
23 But the Levites shall do the service of the tabernacle of the congrega- **18:23**
tion, and they shall bear their iniquity: *it shall be* a statute for ever Num 18:1, 20
throughout your generations, that among the children of Israel they have
no inheritance.
24 But the tithes of the children of Israel, which they offer *as* an heave
offering unto the LORD, I have given to the Levites to inherit: therefore I
have said unto them, Among the children of Israel they shall have no
inheritance.

4. The Levites to Give a Tithe of the Tithe

25 ¶And the LORD spake unto Moses, saying, ☆**18:25, 26** Num 18:28
26 Thus speak unto the Levites, and say unto them, When ye take of the Neh 10:38
children of Israel the tithes which I have given you from them for your
inheritance, then ye shall offer up an heave offering of it for the LORD, *even*
a tenth *part* of the tithe.
27 And *this* your heave offering shall be reckoned unto you, as though *it*
were the corn of the threshingfloor, and as the fulness of the winepress.
28 Thus ye also shall offer an heave offering unto the LORD of all your **18:28**
tithes, which ye receive of the children of Israel; and ye shall give thereof Num 18:25
the LORD's heave offering to Aaron the priest.
29 Out of all your gifts ye shall offer every heave offering of the LORD, of
all the best thereof, *even* the hallowed part thereof out of it.
30 Therefore thou shalt say unto them, When ye have heaved the best
thereof from it, then it shall be counted unto the Levites as the increase of
the threshingfloor, and as the increase of the winepress.
31 And ye shall eat it in every place, ye and your households: for it *is* your **18:31** Mt 10:10
reward for your service in the tabernacle of the congregation. Lk 10:7
32 And ye shall bear no sin by reason of it, when ye have heaved from it 1 Cor 9:13 1 Tim 5:18
the best of it: neither shall ye pollute the holy things of the children of **18:32**
Israel, lest ye die. Lev 22:2, 15, 16

18:19 *a covenant of salt,* i.e., "a permanent contract."†
18:21 The tithe was assessed for the Levites. The priests had the first-fruits, said to be a fiftieth or sixtieth part, but the nonpriestly Levites did not share in this. The Levites were the fewest of the tribes in number. Since they received no land and therefore could not plow and sow, they needed support from the other tribes as a reward for their labors. In turn, the Levites who were not priests were to tithe their tithe to support the priests (18:26). Some have said the tithe of the tithe went to the high priest, for no specific provision was made for the one who occupied that office and he would have greater expenses.
18:26 See the note on Neh. 10:38 for information on the tithe of the tithes.

D. CLEANING OF THE UNCLEAN

1. The Red Heifer Sacrifice for Ceremonial Defilement

19 AND the LORD spake unto Moses and unto Aaron, saying,

19:2☆ Lev 10:6 22:20–25 Num 3:4 Deut 21:3

2 This *is* the ordinance of the law which the LORD hath commanded, saying, Speak unto the children of Israel, that they bring thee a red heifer without spot, wherein *is* no blemish, *and* upon which never came yoke:

3 And ye shall give her unto E-le-a'zar the priest, that he may bring her forth without the camp, and *one* shall slay her before his face:

19:4 Lev 4:6, 17 16:14

4 And E-le-a'zar the priest shall take of her blood with his finger, and sprinkle of her blood directly before the tabernacle of the congregation seven times:

5 And *one* shall burn the heifer in his sight; her skin, and her flesh, and her blood, with her dung, shall he burn:

19:6 Lev 14:4, 6, 49

6 And the priest shall take cedar wood, and hyssop, and scarlet, and cast *it* into the midst of the burning of the heifer.

19:7 Lev 11:25, 40 16:26–28

7 Then the priest shall wash his clothes, and he shall bathe his flesh in water, and afterward he shall come into the camp, and the priest shall be unclean until the even.

8 And he that burneth her shall wash his clothes in water, and bathe his flesh in water, and shall be unclean until the even.

19:9 Num 8:7 19:13, 20, 21

9 And a man *that is* clean shall gather up the ashes of the heifer, and lay *them* up without the camp in a clean place, and it shall be kept for the congregation of the children of Israel for a water of separation: it *is* a purification for sin.

19:10 Num 19:7, 8, 19

10 And he that gathereth the ashes of the heifer shall wash his clothes, and be unclean until the even: and it shall be unto the children of Israel, and unto the stranger that sojourneth among them, for a statute for ever.

2. The Water of Purification for Defilement

19:11 Lev 11:27, 31 21:1, 11

11 ¶He that toucheth the dead body of any man shall be unclean seven days.

19:12 Num 19:17–19

12 He shall purify himself with it on the third day, and on the seventh day he shall be clean: but if he purify not himself the third day, then the seventh day he shall not be clean.

19:13 Lev 7:20, 21 15:31; 20:3 22:3–7

13 Whosoever toucheth the dead body of any man that is dead, and purifieth not himself, defileth the tabernacle of the LORD; and that soul shall be cut off from Israel: because the water of separation was not sprinkled upon him, he shall be unclean; his uncleanness *is* yet upon him.

14 This *is* the law, when a man dieth in a tent: all that come into the tent, and all that *is* in the tent, shall be unclean seven days.

15 And every open vessel, which hath no covering bound upon it, *is* unclean.

19:16 Num 19:11 31:19

16 And whosoever toucheth one that is slain with a sword in the open fields, or a dead body, or a bone of a man, or a grave, shall be unclean seven days.

19:2 Whoever touched a corpse became unclean. The ritual of the *red heifer* provided cleansing for the uncleanness. The ashes of the burned animal were mixed with water (called "a water of separation," or a "water for impurity") which was sprinkled by someone who was clean on the tent of the dead person, the furnishings, and all those who had become unclean as a result of contact with the dead (see verse 18).

17And for an unclean *person* they shall take of the ashes of the burnt
heifer of purification for sin, and running water shall be put thereto in a
vessel:

19:17 Num 19:9

18And a clean person shall take hyssop, and dip *it* in the water, and
sprinkle *it* upon the tent, and upon all the vessels, and upon the persons
that were there, and upon him that touched a bone, or one slain, or one
dead, or a grave:

19And the clean *person* shall sprinkle upon the unclean on the third day,
and on the seventh day: and on the seventh day he shall purify himself, and
wash his clothes, and bathe himself in water, and shall be clean at even.

19:19 Num 19:9; Ps 51:7; Ezek 36:25-27

20But the man that shall be unclean, and shall not purify himself, that
soul shall be cut off from among the congregation, because he hath defiled
the sanctuary of the LORD: the water of separation hath not been sprinkled
upon him; he *is* unclean.

19:20 Num 15:30; 19:13

21And it shall be a perpetual statute unto them, that he that sprinkleth
the water of separation shall wash his clothes; and he that toucheth the
water of separation shall be unclean until even.

19:21 Lev 11:25, 40; 16:26-28; Num 19:7

22And whatsoever the unclean *person* toucheth shall be unclean; and the
soul that toucheth *it* shall be unclean until even.

19:22 Lev 5:2, 3; 7:21

E. EVENTS AT KADESH

1. The Death of Miriam

20 THEN came the children of Israel, *even* the whole congregation,
into the desert of Zin in the first month: and the people abode in
Ka'desh; and Miriam died there, and was buried there.

20:1 Num 13:21; 27:14

2. The Water from the Rock; Moses Disobeys God

2And there was no water for the congregation: and they gathered
themselves together against Moses and against Aaron.

20:2 Ex 15:23, 24; 17:1-4

3And the people chode with Moses, and spake, saying, Would God that
we had died when our brethren died before the LORD!

20:3 Ex 17:2; Num 11:1, 33, 34; 14:1, 2, 36, 37; 16:31-35

4And why have ye brought up the congregation of the LORD into this
wilderness, that we and our cattle should die there?

5And wherefore have ye made us to come up out of Egypt, to bring us in
unto this evil place? it *is* no place of seed, or of figs, or of vines, or of
pomegranates; neither *is* there any water to drink.

20:5 Num 16:14

6And Moses and Aaron went from the presence of the assembly unto the
door of the tabernacle of the congregation, and they fell upon their faces:
and the glory of the LORD appeared unto them.

7¶And the LORD spake unto Moses, saying,

8Take the rod, and gather thou the assembly together, thou, and Aaron
thy brother, and speak ye unto the rock before their eyes; and it shall give
forth his water, and thou shalt bring forth to them water out of the rock: so
thou shalt give the congregation and their beasts drink.

☆20:8 Ex 4:2, 17; Num 21:18

9And Moses took the rod from before the LORD, as he commanded him.

10And Moses and Aaron gathered the congregation together before the
rock, and he said unto them, Hear now, ye rebels; must we fetch you water
out of this rock?

20:8 In Exod. 17:6 God ordered Moses to smite the rock. Here we see that he was commanded to speak to the rock at *Kadesh* (later known as *Kadesh-barnea*). Due to his anger, he imprudently struck the rock twice. With an air of pride and self-importance he shouted: "Listen, you rebels! Must we bring you water from this rock?" (20:10, TLB). God punished Moses for his disobedience and unbelief by refusing to allow him to enter the Promised Land.

20:11 Ex 17:6 Ps 78:16 Isa 48:21 1 Cor 10:4

11 And Moses lifted up his hand, and with his rod he smote the rock
twice: and the water came out abundantly, and the congregation drank,
and their beasts *also.*

3. God Excludes Moses from Entering Canaan

20:12 Lev 10:3 Num 20:24 Ezek 36:23

12 ¶And the LORD spake unto Moses and Aaron, Because ye believed me
not, to sanctify me in the eyes of the children of Israel, therefore ye shall
not bring this congregation into the land which I have given them.

20:13 Ex 17:7 Deut 32:51

13 This *is* the water of Mer′i-bah; because the children of Israel strove
with the LORD, and he was sanctified in them.

4. The Edomites Refuse to Let Israel Pass over Their Land

20:14☆ Gen 36:31–39 Josh 2:10 9:9, 10

14 ¶And Moses sent messengers from Ka′desh unto the king of Edom,
Thus saith thy brother Israel, Thou knowest all the travail that hath
befallen us:
15 How our fathers went down into Egypt, and we have dwelt in Egypt a
long time; and the Egyptians vexed us, and our fathers:

20:16 Ex 3:2–6; 14:19 23:30

16 And when we cried unto the LORD, he heard our voice, and sent an
angel, and hath brought us forth out of Egypt: and, behold, we *are* in
Ka′desh, a city in the uttermost of thy border:

20:17☆

17 Let us pass, I pray thee, through thy country: we will not pass through
the fields, or through the vineyards, neither will we drink *of* the water of the
wells: we will go by the king's *high* way, we will not turn to the right hand
nor to the left, until we have passed thy borders.
18 And Edom said unto him, Thou shalt not pass by me, lest I come out
against thee with the sword.
19 And the children of Israel said unto him, We will go by the high way:
and if I and my cattle drink of thy water, then I will pay for it: I will only,
without *doing* any thing *else,* go through on my feet.
20 And he said, Thou shalt not go through. And Edom came out against
him with much people, and with a strong hand.

20:21 Num 20:1, 14 21:4 Deut 2:8, 29 Judg 11:17

21 Thus Edom refused to give Israel passage through his border: where-
fore Israel turned away from him.

F. INCIDENTS FROM KADESH TO MOAB

1. Aaron's Death on Mount Hor

22 ¶And the children of Israel, *even* the whole congregation, journeyed
from Ka′desh, and came unto mount Hor.
23 And the LORD spake unto Moses and Aaron in mount Hor, by the
coast of the land of Edom, saying,

20:24☆

24 Aaron shall be gathered unto his people: for he shall not enter into the
land which I have given unto the children of Israel, because ye rebelled
against my word at the water of Mer′i-bah.

20:25 Num 3:4; 19:3, 4 **20:26** Num 20:24

25 Take Aaron and E-le-a′zar his son, and bring them up unto mount Hor:
26 And strip Aaron of his garments, and put them upon E-le-a′zar his son:
and Aaron shall be gathered *unto his people,* and shall die there.
27 And Moses did as the LORD commanded: and they went up into mount
Hor in the sight of all the congregation.

20:14 *thy brother Israel.* The people of Edom were descended from Esau, while the people of Israel were descended from his brother Jacob, whose name was later changed to Israel.†

20:17 *the king's high way* was a well-traveled caravan route through that land. It is a paved road today.

20:24–28 We often forget that Aaron was also involved in the incident in which Moses smote the rock for water after God had commanded him to speak to the rock (20:10,11). For their transgression both of them were kept from entering the Promised Land. 20:28 tells us that Aaron died before entering Canaan; we are reminded that this was part of the judgment of God.

28 And Moses stripped Aaron of his garments, and put them upon E-le- **20:28**
a'zar his son; and Aaron died there in the top of the mount: and Moses and Num 33:38
E-le-a'zar came down from the mount.
29 And when all the congregation saw that Aaron was dead, they mourned
for Aaron thirty days, *even* all the house of Israel.

2. Israel's Military Victory over the King of Arad

21 AND *when* king A'rad the Canaanite, which dwelt in the south, **21:1**
heard tell that Israel came by the way of the spies; then he fought Num 33:40
against Israel, and took *some* of them prisoners. Josh 12:14 Judg 1:16
2 And Israel vowed a vow unto the LORD, and said, If thou wilt indeed
deliver this people into my hand, then I will utterly destroy their cities.
3 And the LORD hearkened to the voice of Israel, and delivered up the ☆**21:3**
Canaanites; and they utterly destroyed them and their cities: and he called Num 14:45
the name of the place Hor'mah. 1 Sam 30:30

3. Israel Murmurs Again; Poisonous Snakes Bite Them

4 ¶And they journeyed from mount Hor by the way of the Red sea, to **21:4**
compass the land of Edom: and the soul of the people was much Deut 2:8
discouraged because of the way.
5 And the people spake against God, and against Moses, Wherefore have ☆**21:5**
ye brought us up out of Egypt to die in the wilderness? for *there is* no bread, Ex 16:15 Num 11:1–9
neither *is there any* water; and our soul loatheth this light bread. 14:1–4; 16:13
6 And the LORD sent fiery serpents among the people, and they bit the **21:6**
people; and much people of Israel died. Deut 8:15 1 Cor 10:9
7 ¶Therefore the people came to Moses, and said, We have sinned, for we
have spoken against the LORD, and against thee; pray unto the LORD, that
he take away the serpents from us. And Moses prayed for the people.
8 And the LORD said unto Moses, Make thee a fiery serpent, and set it **21:8**
upon a pole: and it shall come to pass, that every one that is bitten, when he Isa 14:29
looketh upon it, shall live. Jn 3:14, 15
9 And Moses made a serpent of brass, and put it upon a pole, and it came ☆**21:9**
to pass, that if a serpent had bitten any man, when he beheld the serpent of 2 Kgs 18:4
brass, he lived. Jn 3:14; 12:32

4. Israel Marches toward Moab

10 ¶And the children of Israel set forward, and pitched in O'both.
11 And they journeyed from O'both, and pitched at I'je-ab'a-rim, in the
wilderness which *is* before Moab, toward the sunrising.
12 ¶From thence they removed, and pitched in the valley of Za'red.
13 From thence they removed, and pitched on the other side of Arnon,
which *is* in the wilderness that cometh out of the coasts of the Am'or-ites:
for Arnon *is* the border of Moab, between Moab and the Am'or-ites.
14 Wherefore it is said in the book of the wars of the LORD, What he did ☆**21:14**
in the Red sea, and in the brooks of Arnon,

21:3 *Hormah* means "destruction." It was in the Wilderness of Zin, east and slightly south of Beer-sheba.

21:5 Israel had bread enough and to spare. They now considered manna to be worthless compared to what they preferred. So they murmured again against God and Moses (not Aaron, who died and was buried before this event).

21:9 According to John 3:14, 15, the brass serpent is representative of Christ. Men bitten by the serpent suffered death; so also men bitten by the serpent of sin suffer spiritual death. As Moses lifted up the serpent in the wilderness, so Christ was lifted up to bear the sins of many (John 12:32). As men needed only to look at Moses' serpent and live, so sinners need only look to Jesus Christ to be healed from their transgressions. Christ saves sinners from the guilt, the penalty, and the power of sin.

21:14 *the book of the wars of the LORD.* This was probably a collection of songs used in war and/or a

21:15 Num 21:28 Deut 2:9
15 And at the stream of the brooks that goeth down to the dwelling of Ar,
and lieth upon the border of Moab.

21:16 Judg 9:21 Jn 4:14
16 And from thence *they went* to Beer: that *is* the well whereof the LORD
spake unto Moses, Gather the people together, and I will give them water.

21:17☆
17 ¶Then Israel sang this song, Spring up, O well; sing ye unto it:
18 The princes digged the well, the nobles of the people digged it, by *the
direction of* the lawgiver, with their staves. And from the wilderness *they
went* to Mat'ta-nah:
19 And from Mat'ta-nah to Na-ha'li-el: and from Na-ha'li-el to Ba'moth:
20 And from Ba'moth *in* the valley, that *is* in the country of Moab, to the
top of Pis'gah, which looketh toward Jesh'i-mon.

5. Israel's Victory over King Sihon, the Amorite

21:21 Deut 2:26–28 Judg 11:19–21
21:22 Num 20:17
21 ¶And Israel sent messengers unto Sihon king of the Am'or-ites, saying,
22 Let me pass through thy land: we will not turn into the fields, or into
the vineyards; we will not drink *of* the waters of the well: *but* we will go
along by the king's *high* way, until we be past thy borders.

21:23 Num 20:21 Deut 2:32 Judg 11:20
23 And Sihon would not suffer Israel to pass through his border: but
Sihon gathered all his people together, and went out against Israel into the
wilderness: and he came to Ja'haz, and fought against Israel.

21:24☆ Deut 2:19, 31–37 Josh 12:1–3 13:8–10
24 And Israel smote him with the edge of the sword, and possessed his
land from Arnon unto Jabbok, even unto the children of Ammon: for the
border of the children of Ammon *was* strong.

21:25, 26☆ Neh 9:22 Ps 135:9, 10; 136:19 Amos 2:9
25 And Israel took all these cities: and Israel dwelt in all the cities of the
Am'or-ites, in Hesh'bon, and in all the villages thereof.
26 For Hesh'bon *was* the city of Sihon the king of the Am'or-ites, who had
fought against the former king of Moab, and taken all his land out of his
hand, even unto Arnon.

21:27 Num 21:15 Deut 2:9, 18 Judg 11:24 1 Kgs 11:33 Jer 48:45, 46
27 Wherefore they that speak in proverbs say, Come into Hesh'bon, let the
city of Sihon be built and prepared:
28 For there is a fire gone out of Hesh'bon, a flame from the city of Sihon:
it hath consumed Ar of Moab, *and* the lords of the high places of Arnon.
29 Woe to thee, Moab! thou art undone, O people of Che'mosh: he hath
given his sons that escaped, and his daughters, into captivity unto Sihon
king of the Am'or-ites.
30 We have shot at them; Hesh'bon is perished even unto Di'bon, and we
have laid them waste even unto No'phah, which *reacheth* unto Med'e-ba.

6. Israel Defeats King Og of Bashan

21:31 Num 32:1, 35 Isa 16:8, 9 Jer 48:32
31 ¶Thus Israel dwelt in the land of the Am'or-ites.
32 And Moses sent to spy out Ja-a'zer, and they took the villages thereof,
and drove out the Am'or-ites that *were* there.

21:33 Deut 32:14
33 ¶And they turned and went up by the way of Ba'shan: and Og the king
of Ba'shan went out against them, he, and all his people, to the battle at
Ed're-i.

---

record of Israel's military victories. It is not noted as the "wars of Israel" but as the *wars of the LORD.* The operation of God in Israel's history was more important than what the people said and did.

21:17 *Israel sang this song.* Throughout the Bible singing is emphasized. Singing glorifies God and encourages those who sing. Music in the church meeting is one of the most significant parts of true worship.

21:24 *for the border of the children of Ammon was strong,* i.e., "but they were stopped by the rugged terrain." Deut. 2:19 indicates that God had promised the land of the Ammonites to the descendants of Lot.†

21:25 The Moabites had been given territory which Israel was forbidden by God to usurp. Here the land, which once had belonged to Moab, has been taken and settled by the Ammonites. Israel takes the land from the Ammonites and keeps it, for the title to it had long since passed from Moab to the Ammonites.

34 And the LORD said unto Moses, Fear him not: for I have delivered him
into thy hand, and all his people, and his land; and thou shalt do to him as
thou didst unto Sihon king of the Am'or-ites, which dwelt at Hesh'bon.
35 So they smote him, and his sons, and all his people, until there was
none left him alive: and they possessed his land.

IV. ISRAEL ENCOUNTERS THE MOABITES AND BALAAM (22:1—25:18)

A. BALAK, THE KING OF MOAB, AND BALAAM

1. Balak Summons Balaam to Curse Israel

22 AND the children of Israel set forward, and pitched in the plains of ☆22:1 Num 33:48, 49
Moab on this side Jordan *by* Jericho.
2 ¶And Balak the son of Zippor saw all that Israel had done to the Am'or- 22:2 Ex 15:15 Deut 2:25
ites.
3 And Moab was sore afraid of the people, because they *were* many: and
Moab was distressed because of the children of Israel.
4 And Moab said unto the elders of Mid'i-an, Now shall this company 22:4 Num 22:7 25:15–18
lick up all *that are* round about us, as the ox licketh up the grass of the field.
And Balak the son of Zippor *was* king of the Moabites at that time.
5 He sent messengers therefore unto Ba'laam the son of Be'or to Pe'thor, ☆22:5 Num 22:17 23:7, 8; 24:9 Deut 23:4
which *is* by the river of the land of the children of his people, to call him,
saying, Behold, there is a people come out from Egypt: behold, they cover
the face of the earth, and they abide over against me:
6 Come now therefore, I pray thee, curse me this people; for they *are* too
mighty for me: peradventure I shall prevail, *that* we may smite them, and
that I may drive them out of the land: for I wot that he whom thou blessest
is blessed, and he whom thou cursest is cursed.

2. God Tells Balaam Not to Go to King Balak

7 And the elders of Moab and the elders of Mid'i-an departed with the 22:7 1 Sam 9:7, 8 Isa 56:11
rewards of divination in their hand; and they came unto Ba'laam, and
spake unto him the words of Balak.
8 And he said unto them, Lodge here this night, and I will bring you word
again, as the LORD shall speak unto me: and the princes of Moab abode
with Ba'laam.
9 And God came unto Ba'laam, and said, What men *are* these with thee?
10 And Ba'laam said unto God, Balak the son of Zippor, king of Moab,
hath sent unto me, *saying,*
11 Behold, *there is* a people come out of Egypt, which covereth the face of
the earth: come now, curse me them; peradventure I shall be able to
overcome them, and drive them out.
12 And God said unto Ba'laam, Thou shalt not go with them; thou shalt 22:12 Num 23:13–15
not curse the people: for they *are* blessed.
13 And Ba'laam rose up in the morning, and said unto the princes of
Balak, Get you into your land: for the LORD refuseth to give me leave to go
with you.

22:1 Israel had now come close to the end of their wilderness journeys. They encamped in the plains of Moab, where they would remain until they passed over the Jordan under Joshua's leadership. Then they would begin to possess their inheritance.

22:5, 11 The land from which Balaam came was noted for its diviners. Balaam himself started as a good and true prophet of God. But he succumbed to the lure of money and became a hireling. In his sovereignty, however, God ordained that Balaam would not do what King Balak wanted him to do. Each time, Balaam failed to curse Israel; thus Balak was defeated. But Balaam did assist Balak, for he cunningly suggested to Balak that which led Israel to succumb to the sin of sexual license. This is what well may be called *the teaching of Balaam* as it is used here (23:1ff) and in Rev. 2:14 ("Balaam . . . taught Balak how to ruin the people of Israel by involving them in sexual sin . . . " TLB).

3. Balak Summons Balaam Again; God Lets Him Go

14 And the princes of Moab rose up, and they went unto Balak, and said,
Ba'laam refuseth to come with us.
15 ¶And Balak sent yet again princes, more, and more honourable than
they.
22:16 16 And they came to Ba'laam, and said to him, Thus saith Balak the son of
Num 22:6 Zippor, Let nothing, I pray thee, hinder thee from coming unto me:
17 For I will promote thee unto very great honour, and I will do
whatsoever thou sayest unto me: come therefore, I pray thee, curse me this
people.
22:18 18 And Ba'laam answered and said unto the servants of Balak, If Balak
Num 23:26 would give me his house full of silver and gold, I cannot go beyond the
24:13 word of the LORD my God, to do less or more.
22:19☆ 19 Now therefore, I pray you, tarry ye also here this night, that I may
know what the LORD will say unto me more.
22:20 20 And God came unto Ba'laam at night, and said unto him, If the men
Num 22:35 come to call thee, rise up, *and* go with them; but yet the word which I shall
23:12, 26 say unto thee, that shalt thou do.

4. The Angel of the Lord and Balaam's Speaking Ass

22:21 21 And Ba'laam rose up in the morning, and saddled his ass, and went
2 Pet 2:15 with the princes of Moab.
22:22, 23☆ 22 ¶And God's anger was kindled because he went: and the angel of the
LORD stood in the way for an adversary against him. Now he was riding
upon his ass, and his two servants *were* with him.
23 And the ass saw the angel of the LORD standing in the way, and his
sword drawn in his hand: and the ass turned aside out of the way, and went
into the field: and Ba'laam smote the ass, to turn her into the way.
24 But the angel of the LORD stood in a path of the vineyards, a wall *being*
on this side, and a wall on that side.
25 And when the ass saw the angel of the LORD, she thrust herself unto the
wall, and crushed Ba'laam's foot against the wall: and he smote her again.
26 And the angel of the LORD went further, and stood in a narrow place,
where *was* no way to turn either to the right hand or to the left.
27 And when the ass saw the angel of the LORD, she fell down under
Ba'laam: and Ba'laam's anger was kindled, and he smote the ass with a
staff.
22:28 28 And the LORD opened the mouth of the ass, and she said unto Ba'laam,
2 Pet 2:16 What have I done unto thee, that thou hast smitten me these three times?

22:19 God told Balaam that he was not to go to Balak (22:12). In 22:19 Balaam goes against God's directive will and says he needs further instruction about God's will. At this point God's directive will is put aside and his permissive will takes over. Balaam is allowed to do what he wanted to do but which God had forbidden. God still stipulates that Balaam shall do or say nothing which will harm the people of God. The donkey had better sense than his master (22:21–34). The story makes clear that he who disobeys God will smart for his transgression.
22:22, 23 *God's anger was kindled because he went,* i.e., "God was angry about Balaam's eager attitude."† Balaam said much more than God had told him to. See Num 25:1–3; 31:1. In the Hebrew text the angel is called "satan" or "the adversary." In the Book of Job "the satan" or "adversary" accuses Job of serving God for material benefit or gain. In the unfolding revelation of God, the word "satan" is applied to the archenemy of God. In Zech. 3:1 the Scriptures clearly distinguish between "the Angel of the Lord" and "Satan [who] was there too," (TLB). The work or mission of God's loyal angels includes the following: they (1) execute God's judgments and purposes (22:22; Matt. 13:41; Acts 12:23); (2) guide believers (Acts 8:26); (3) assist, protect, and strengthen God's people (1 Kings 19:5; Dan. 6:22); (4) will accompany the Lord Jesus at his second advent (Matt. 25:31; 2 Thess. 1:7, 8); (5) carry God's children to heaven (Luke 16:22). Men are superior to angels in at least one important regard: angels cannot preach the gospel whereas men can. Men are also superior in that believers will judge angels (1 Cor. 6:3).

29 And Ba'laam said unto the ass, Because thou hast mocked me: I would
there were a sword in mine hand, for now would I kill thee.
30 And the ass said unto Ba'laam, *Am* not I thine ass, upon which thou
hast ridden ever since *I was* thine unto this day? was I ever wont to do so
unto thee? And he said, Nay.
31 Then the LORD opened the eyes of Ba'laam, and he saw the angel of the
LORD standing in the way, and his sword drawn in his hand: and he bowed
down his head, and fell flat on his face.
32 And the angel of the LORD said unto him, Wherefore hast thou smitten
thine ass these three times? behold, I went out to withstand thee, because
thy way is perverse before me:
33 And the ass saw me, and turned from me these three times: unless she
had turned from me, surely now also I had slain thee, and saved her alive.
34 And Ba'laam said unto the angel of the LORD, I have sinned; for I knew
not that thou stoodest in the way against me: now therefore, if it displease
thee, I will get me back again.
35 And the angel of the LORD said unto Ba'laam, Go with the men: but
only the word that I shall speak unto thee, that thou shalt speak. So
Ba'laam went with the princes of Balak.

22:31 Num 24:4; Josh 5:13–15
22:34 Ex 9:27; 1 Sam 15:24
22:35 Num 22:20, 21

5. Balaam and Balak Meet

36 ¶And when Balak heard that Ba'laam was come, he went out to meet
him unto a city of Moab, which *is* in the border of Arnon, which *is* in the
utmost coast.
37 And Balak said unto Ba'laam, Did I not earnestly send unto thee to call
thee? wherefore camest thou not unto me? am I not able indeed to promote
thee to honour?
38 And Ba'laam said unto Balak, Lo, I am come unto thee: have I now any
power at all to say any thing? the word that God putteth in my mouth, that
shall I speak.
39 And Ba'laam went with Balak, and they came unto Kir'jath-hu'zoth.
40 And Balak offered oxen and sheep, and sent to Ba'laam, and to the
princes that *were* with him.
41 And it came to pass on the morrow, that Balak took Ba'laam, and
brought him up into the high places of Ba'al, that thence he might see the
utmost *part* of the people.

☆**22:37, 38** Num 22:18
22:41 Num 21:19, 20; 23:13

6. Balaam Blesses Israel

23 AND Ba'laam said unto Balak, Build me here seven altars, and
prepare me here seven oxen and seven rams.
2 And Balak did as Ba'laam had spoken; and Balak and Ba'laam offered
on *every* altar a bullock and a ram.
3 And Ba'laam said unto Balak, Stand by thy burnt offering, and I will go:
peradventure the LORD will come to meet me: and whatsoever he sheweth
me I will tell thee. And he went to an high place.
4 And God met Ba'laam: and he said unto him, I have prepared seven
altars, and I have offered upon *every* altar a bullock and a ram.
5 And the LORD put a word in Ba'laam's mouth, and said, Return unto
Balak, and thus thou shalt speak.
6 And he returned unto him, and, lo, he stood by his burnt sacrifice, he,
and all the princes of Moab.

23:5 Num 22:20, 35; 23:16

22:37, 38 Balak expected Balaam to curse Israel, for which he would be rewarded. But Balaam was rather noncommittal, for he wanted his fee yet he realized that God controls the prophecy.

23:7–10☆ Gen 10:22; 13:16; 22:17; 28:14; Ex 19:5, 6; 33:16; Num 22:5, 6, 11, 12, 17; Deut 33:28; Ps 37:37; Isa 57:1, 2

7 And he took up his parable, and said, Balak the king of Moab hath brought me from A'ram, out of the mountains of the east, *saying*, Come, curse me Jacob, and come, defy Israel.

8 How shall I curse, whom God hath not cursed? or how shall I defy, *whom* the LORD hath not defied?

9 For from the top of the rocks I see him, and from the hills I behold him: lo, the people shall dwell alone, and shall not be reckoned among the nations.

10 Who can count the dust of Jacob, and the number of the fourth *part* of Israel? Let me die the death of the righteous, and let my last end be like his!

11 And Balak said unto Ba'laam, What hast thou done unto me? I took thee to curse mine enemies, and, behold, thou hast blessed *them* altogether.

23:12 Num 22:38; 23:20, 26

12 And he answered and said, Must I not take heed to speak that which the LORD hath put in my mouth?

7. Balaam Blesses Israel a Second Time

13 And Balak said unto him, Come, I pray thee, with me unto another place, from whence thou mayest see them: thou shalt see but the utmost part of them, and shalt not see them all: and curse me them from thence.

23:14☆

14 ¶And he brought him into the field of Zo'phim, to the top of Pis'gah, and built seven altars, and offered a bullock and a ram on *every* altar.

15 And he said unto Balak, Stand here by thy burnt offering, while I meet *the LORD* yonder.

23:16 Num 22:35

16 And the LORD met Ba'laam, and put a word in his mouth, and said, Go again unto Balak, and say thus.

17 And when he came to him, behold, he stood by his burnt offering, and the princes of Moab with him. And Balak said unto him, What hath the LORD spoken?

23:18–24☆ Ex 3:12; 20:1, 2; Num 22:18, 38; Deut 31:23; 1 Sam 15:29; Isa 40:8; 43:13; 55:11

18 And he took up his parable, and said, Rise up, Balak, and hear; hearken unto me, thou son of Zippor:

19 God *is* not a man, that he should lie; neither the son of man, that he should repent: hath he said, and shall he not do *it?* or hath he spoken, and shall he not make it good?

20 Behold, I have received *commandment* to bless: and he hath blessed; and I cannot reverse it.

21 He hath not beheld iniquity in Jacob, neither hath he seen perverseness in Israel: the LORD his God *is* with him, and the shout of a king *is* among them.

22 God brought them out of Egypt; he hath as it were the strength of an unicorn.

23 Surely *there is* no enchantment against Jacob, neither *is there* any divination against Israel: according to this time it shall be said of Jacob and of Israel, What hath God wrought!

24 Behold, the people shall rise up as a great lion, and lift up himself as a young lion: he shall not lie down until he eat *of* the prey, and drink the blood of the slain.

23:7ff Balaam recited his first speech in poetic form. He asked the question: How can I curse what God has not cursed and denounce what God has not denounced? Yet he did not bless Israel positively. Balak, however, was keenly conscious that the words of Balaam constituted a blessing in disguise.

23:14 Balak took Balaam to a different place, where he built seven altars and offered sacrifices on all of them. These rites which were used by pagan Babylonian diviners did not have the acceptance or commendation of God. The genuine always gives rise to counterfeits, which outwardly resemble the real but inwardly are useless, vile, and constitute an affront to the true God.

23:18ff On this second effort Balaam helped Balak no more than he had helped him on the first effort. He predicted blessing for Israel, not the curse that Balak had hired him to express.

8. Balaam Blesses Israel the Third Time

25 ¶And Balak said unto Ba'laam, Neither curse them at all, nor bless
them at all.
26 But Ba'laam answered and said unto Balak, Told not I thee, saying, All
that the LORD speaketh, that I must do?
27 ¶And Balak said unto Ba'laam, Come, I pray thee, I will bring thee
unto another place; peradventure it will please God that thou mayest curse
me them from thence.
28 And Balak brought Ba'laam unto the top of Pe'or, that looketh toward
Jesh'i-mon.
29 And Ba'laam said unto Balak, Build me here seven altars, and prepare
me here seven bullocks and seven rams.
30 And Balak did as Ba'laam had said, and offered a bullock and a ram on
every altar.

☆23:25, 26 Num 22:18, 38
23:28 Num 31:16; Josh 22:17, 18

24 AND when Ba'laam saw that it pleased the LORD to bless Israel, he
went not, as at other times, to seek for enchantments, but he set his
face toward the wilderness.
2 And Ba'laam lifted up his eyes, and he saw Israel abiding *in his tents*
according to their tribes; and the spirit of God came upon him.
3 And he took up his parable, and said, Ba'laam the son of Be'or hath
said, and the man whose eyes are open hath said:
4 He hath said, which heard the words of God, which saw the vision of the
Almighty, falling *into a trance*, but having his eyes open:
5 How goodly are thy tents, O Jacob, *and* thy tabernacles, O Israel!
6 As the valleys are they spread forth, as gardens by the river's side, as the
trees of lign aloes which the LORD hath planted, *and* as cedar trees beside
the waters.
7 He shall pour the water out of his buckets, and his seed *shall be* in many
waters, and his king shall be higher than Agag, and his kingdom shall be
exalted.
8 God brought him forth out of Egypt; he hath as it were the strength of
an unicorn: he shall eat up the nations his enemies, and shall break their
bones, and pierce *them* through with his arrows.
9 He couched, he lay down as a lion, and as a great lion: who shall stir
him up? Blessed *is* he that blesseth thee, and cursed *is* he that curseth thee.

24:1 Num 23:3, 15
☆24:2 Num 11:25–29; 1 Sam 10:10; 2 Chron 15:1
☆24:3–9 Gen 12:3; 15:1, 2; 27:29; 49:9; Ex 20:1, 2; Num 12:6; 14:9; 22:20; 23:7–10, 18–24; 24:15-24; Deut 7:1; 1 Sam 15:8; Ps 45:8; 145:11–13; Dan 8:26, 27

9. Balaam Blesses Israel the Fourth Time and Prophesies about Jesus

10 ¶And Balak's anger was kindled against Ba'laam, and he smote his
hands together: and Balak said unto Ba'laam, I called thee to curse mine
enemies, and, behold, thou hast altogether blessed *them* these three times.
11 Therefore now flee thou to thy place: I thought to promote thee unto
great honour; but, lo, the LORD hath kept thee back from honour.
12 And Ba'laam said unto Balak, Spake I not also to thy messengers which
thou sentest unto me, saying,

23:25, 26 Balak now wanted to silence Balaam, who had not helped him. He wished for him to say nothing either way. If Balaam could not assist and encourage Balak's forces, then at least he did not want him to oppose or dishearten them. In verse 26 Balaam had to admit to Balak that he was not free to choose what to do; whatever God spoke, he must speak.

24:2 *the spirit of God came upon him.* When the Spirit of prophecy came upon Balaam he did not speak his own thoughts, but the language which came to him by the Spirit. In 24:4 he appears to be boasting that he has heard the Words of the Almighty and seen a vision of God. Balaam was one who became an agent of God's will even though he was filled with ambition and covetousness. God sometimes gets done what he wants done through strange agencies and even by those who have fallen far short of the glory of God.

24:3 *the man whose eyes are open.* Balaam's eyes had been shut. Now they are opened by the Spirit of God. He sees that his intention to curse Israel was a mistake, yet he is still blinded by covetousness and wrong ambition. His eyes were open but his heart is shut. He was enlightened but not sanctified. Balaam blessed Israel the third time, to the dismay of Balak.

24:13☆ Num 22:18, 20

13 If Balak would give me his house full of silver and gold, I cannot go beyond the commandment of the LORD, to do *either* good or bad of mine own mind; *but* what the LORD saith, that will I speak?

24:14☆

14 And now, behold, I go unto my people: come *therefore, and* I will advertise thee what this people shall do to thy people in the latter days.

24:15 Gen 49:10 Num 21:29 Isa 15:1—16:4 Amos 9:11, 12 Mt 2:2 Rev 22:16

15 ¶And he took up his parable, and said, Ba'laam the son of Be'or hath said, and the man whose eyes are open hath said:

16 He hath said, which heard the words of God, and knew the knowledge of the most High, *which* saw the vision of the Almighty, falling *into a trance,* but having his eyes open:

24:17☆

17 I shall see him, but not now: I shall behold him, but not nigh: there shall come a Star out of Jacob, and a Sceptre shall rise out of Israel, and shall smite the corners of Moab, and destroy all the children of Sheth.

18 And Edom shall be a possession, Se'ir also shall be a possession for his enemies; and Israel shall do valiantly.

19 Out of Jacob shall come he that shall have dominion, and shall destroy him that remaineth of the city.

24:20 Ex 17:14

20 ¶And when he looked on Am'a-lek, he took up his parable, and said, Am'a-lek *was* the first of the nations; but his latter end *shall be* that he perish for ever.

24:21 Gen 15:19 Judg 1:16 Ezra 4:2

21 And he looked on the Ken'ites, and took up his parable, and said, Strong is thy dwellingplace, and thou puttest thy nest in a rock.

24:22☆

22 Nevertheless the Ken'ite shall be wasted, until Asshur shall carry thee away captive.

24:23 Gen 10:4, 21–25 Dan 9:26, 27

23 And he took up his parable, and said, Alas, who shall live when God doeth this!

24 And ships *shall come* from the coast of Chit'tim, and shall afflict Asshur, and shall afflict E'ber, and he also shall perish for ever.

24:25☆

25 And Ba'laam rose up, and went and returned to his place: and Balak also went his way.

B. THE SIN OF IDOLATRY BY ISRAEL AT SHITTIM

1. Israelites Worship Baal

25:1☆ Num 33:49 Josh 2:1

25 AND Israel abode in Shit'tim, and the people began to commit whoredom with the daughters of Moab.

25:2 Ex 34:15, 16

2 And they called the people unto the sacrifices of their gods: and the people did eat, and bowed down to their gods.

25:3 Num 25:5 Deut 4:3, 4

3 And Israel joined himself unto Ba'al-pe'or: and the anger of the LORD was kindled against Israel.

4 And the LORD said unto Moses, Take all the heads of the people, and

---

24:13 In effect Balaam told Balak that what he had done was not his fault. His intention was to help Balak but God had interfered; he cannot help what he has done. It was all God's fault.

24:14 *what this people shall do to thy people.* Balak had dismissed Balaam; but before he left he blessed Israel for the fourth time, and he prophesied what Israel would do to the people of Balak.

24:17 *a Star out of Jacob.* Balaam prophesied that Israel would overcome Moab and Edom. This was fulfilled but there was a greater fulfillment to come, of which Balaam undoubtedly had no personal knowledge. He uttered what he himself did not understand. Jesus Christ is the star from Jacob. Christ holds the sceptre of his kingship with the promise that his dominion shall extend over the whole earth. In a spiritual sense, this is already true. Some believers in the millennial tradition look for the literal earthly manifestation of Christ's rule over the nations with a rod of iron, at the end of which period he will win the final victory over Satan and begin the eternal kingdom (Rev. 19:15). *Sheth,* an ancient name for Moab which has been found in nonbiblical texts.

24:22 *Kenite,* "smith" probably refers to the people who mined and smelted copper from Edomite mines.

24:25 *Balaam rose up, and went . . . and Balak also went his way.* They parted company, but not before Balaam gave insidious advice that brought about the situation described in 25:1–3. (See 13:16).†

25:1 The men of Israel committed whoredom, that is, harlotry, with the daughters of the Moabites. It was both spiritual and physical: they fornicated with them and worshipped their gods. It was not the sin of all the men but of enough of them to kindle the anger of God, who sent a plague that killed 24,000 Israelites.

hang them up before the LORD against the sun, that the fierce anger of the
LORD may be turned away from Israel.
[5]And Moses said unto the judges of Israel, Slay ye every one his men that
were joined unto Ba'al–pe'or.

2. God's Judgment: Phinehas Slays a Midianite Girl

[6]¶And, behold, one of the children of Israel came and brought unto his
brethren a Mid'i-an-it-ish woman in the sight of Moses, and in the sight of
all the congregation of the children of Israel, who *were* weeping *before* the
door of the tabernacle of the congregation.

25:6 Num 22:4; 31:2, 9–16

[7]And when Phin'e-has, the son of E-le-a'zar, the son of Aaron the priest,
saw *it*, he rose up from among the congregation, and took a javelin in his
hand;

25:7 Ex 6:25; Josh 22:30, 31

[8]And he went after the man of Israel into the tent, and thrust both of
them through, the man of Israel, and the woman through her belly. So the
plague was stayed from the children of Israel.
[9]And those that died in the plague were twenty and four thousand.
[10]¶And the LORD spake unto Moses, saying,
[11]Phin'e-has, the son of E-le-a'zar, the son of Aaron the priest, hath
turned my wrath away from the children of Israel, while he was zealous for
my sake among them, that I consumed not the children of Israel in my
jealousy.

☆**25:9** 1 Cor 10:8

[12]Wherefore say, Behold, I give unto him my covenant of peace:
[13]And he shall have it, and his seed after him, *even* the covenant of an
everlasting priesthood; because he was zealous for his God, and made an
atonement for the children of Israel.

25:12 Ex 29:9; 32:30; 40:15; Num 16:46; Isa 54:10; Ezek 37:26

[14]Now the name of the Israelite that was slain, *even* that was slain with
the Mid'i-an-it-ish woman, *was* Zimri, the son of Sa'lu, a prince of a chief
house among the Simeonites.
[15]And the name of the Mid'i-an-it-ish woman that was slain *was* Coz'bi,
the daughter of Zur; he *was* head over a people, *and* of a chief house in
Mid'i-an.

25:15 Num 25:18; 31:8; Josh 13:21

[16]¶And the LORD spake unto Moses, saying,
[17]Vex the Mid'i-an-ites, and smite them:
[18]For they vex you with their wiles, wherewith they have beguiled you in
the matter of Pe'or, and in the matter of Coz'bi, the daughter of a prince of
Mid'i-an, their sister, which was slain in the day of the plague for Pe'or's
sake.

25:16 Num 31:2
☆**25:17**
25:18 Num 25:15

V. PREPARATIONS BEFORE ENTERING THE LAND OF CANAAN (26:1—36:13)

A. THE SECOND CENSUS

1. God Orders the Census

26 AND it came to pass after the plague, that the LORD spake unto
Moses and unto E-le-a'zar the son of Aaron the priest, saying,
[2]Take the sum of all the congregation of the children of Israel, from

26:1 Num 25:6–9
☆**26:2** Num 1:2–15; 4:1–4

25:9 See the note on 1 Cor. 10:8 for the resolution of the apparent contradiction between the 24,000 mentioned here and the 23,000 referred to in 1 Cor. 10:8.
25:17 God has punished the Israelites with the plague; now he orders Moses to punish the Midianites with the sword, not with the rod of a father. While the Israelites who sinned were guilty, so also were the Midianites who caused them to sin. They must reap what they have sown. Evil men should not have the liberty to tempt the people of God, as though they have no responsibility for the crimes that follow.
26:2 The people were not to be numbered except by the command of God. A comparison of the statistics with the earlier census reveals minor differences from tribe to tribe. Later on King David numbered the people without receiving God's command to do so, and was severely punished.

twenty years old and upward, throughout their fathers' house, all that are able to go to war in Israel.

3 And Moses and E-le-a'zar the priest spake with them in the plains of Moab by Jordan *near* Jericho, saying,

4 *Take the sum of the people*, from twenty years old and upward; as the LORD commanded Moses and the children of Israel, which went forth out of the land of Egypt.

2. The Results of the Census

26:5 Gen 46:8–14; Num 1:20–46; 16:1; 1 Chron 5:1–5

5 ¶Reuben, the eldest son of Israel: the children of Reuben; Ha'noch, *of whom cometh* the family of the Ha'noch-ites: of Pal'lu, the family of the Pal'lu-ites:

6 Of Hez'ron, the family of the Hez'ron-ites: of Car'mi, the family of the Car'mites.

7 These *are* the families of the Reubenites: and they that were numbered of them were forty and three thousand and seven hundred and thirty.

8 And the sons of Pal'lu; E-li'ab.

9 And the sons of E-li'ab; Ne-mu'el, and Da'than, and A-bi'ram. This *is that* Da'than and A-bi'ram, *which were* famous in the congregation, who strove against Moses and against Aaron in the company of Ko'rah, when they strove against the LORD:

10 And the earth opened her mouth, and swallowed them up together with Ko'rah, when that company died, what time the fire devoured two hundred and fifty men: and they became a sign.

11 Notwithstanding the children of Ko'rah died not.

26:12 1 Chron 4:24–43

12 ¶The sons of Simeon after their families: of Ne-mu'el, the family of the Ne-mu'el-ites: of Ja'min, the family of the Ja'min-ites: of Ja'chin, the family of the Ja'chin-ites:

13 Of Ze'rah, the family of the Zar'hites: of Sha'ul, the family of the Sha'ul-ites.

14 These *are* the families of the Simeonites, twenty and two thousand and two hundred.

15 ¶The children of Gad after their families: of Ze'phon, the family of the Ze'phon-ites: of Hag'gi, the family of the Hag'gites: of Shu'ni, the family of the Shu'nites:

16 Of Oz'ni, the family of the Oz'nites: of E'ri, the family of the E'rites:

17 Of A'rod, the family of the A'rod-ites: of A-re'li, the family of the A-re'lites.

18 These *are* the families of the children of Gad according to those that were numbered of them, forty thousand and five hundred.

26:19 1 Chron 4:1–4

19 ¶The sons of Judah *were* Er and O'nan: and Er and O'nan died in the land of Canaan.

20 And the sons of Judah after their families were; of She'lah, the family of the She'lan-ites: of Pha'rez, the family of the Phar'zites: of Ze'rah, the family of the Zar'hites.

21 And the sons of Pha'rez were; of Hez'ron, the family of the Hez'ron-ites: of Ha'mul, the family of the Ha'mul-ites.

22 These *are* the families of Judah according to those that were numbered of them, threescore and sixteen thousand and five hundred.

26:23 1 Chron 7:1–5

23 ¶*Of* the sons of Is'sa-char after their families: *of* To'la, the family of the To'la-ites: of Pu'a, the family of the Pu'nites:

24 Of Jash'ub, the family of the Jash'ub-ites: of Shim'ron, the family of the Shim'ron-ites.

25 These *are* the families of Is'sa-char according to those that were numbered of them, threescore and four thousand and three hundred.

26 ¶*Of* the sons of Zeb′u-lun after their families: of Se′red, the family of
the Sar′dites: of E′lon, the family of the E′lon-ites: of Jah′le-el, the family of
the Jah′le-el-ites.
27 These *are* the families of the Zeb′u-lun-ites according to those that were
numbered of them, threescore thousand and five hundred.
28 ¶The sons of Joseph after their families *were* Ma-nas′seh and E′phra- **26:28** Gen 46:19–22
im. 1 Chron 7:14–40
29 Of the sons of Ma-nas′seh: of Ma′chir, the family of the Ma′chir-ites:
and Ma′chir begat Gilead: of Gilead *come* the family of the Gileadites.
30 These *are* the sons of Gilead: *of* Je-e′zer, the family of the Je-e′zer-ites:
of He′lek, the family of the He′lek-ites:
31 And *of* As′ri-el, the family of the As′ri-el-ites: and *of* She′chem, the
family of the She′chem-ites:
32 And *of* She-mi′da, the family of the She-mi′da-ites: and *of* He′pher, the
family of the He′pher-ites.
33 ¶And Ze-lo′phe-had the son of He′pher had no sons, but daughters:
and the names of the daughters of Ze-lo′phe-had *were* Mah′lah, and Noah,
Hog′lah, Mil′cah, and Tir′zah.
34 These *are* the families of Ma-nas′seh, and those that were numbered of
them, fifty and two thousand and seven hundred.
35 ¶These *are* the sons of E′phra-im after their families: of Shu′the-lah, the
family of the Shu′thal-hites: of Be′cher, the family of the Bach′rites: of
Ta′han, the family of the Ta′han-ites.
36 And these *are* the sons of Shu′the-lah: of E′ran, the family of the E′ran-
ites.
37 These *are* the families of the sons of E′phra-im according to those that
were numbered of them, thirty and two thousand and five hundred. These
are the sons of Joseph after their families.
38 ¶The sons of Benjamin after their families: of Be′la, the family of the **26:38** Gen 46:19–22
Be′la-ites: of Ash′bel, the family of the Ash′bel-ites; of A-hi′ram, the family 1 Chron 7:6–12
of the A-hi′ram-ites: 8:1–40
39 Of Shu′pham, the family of the Shu′pham-ites: of Hu′pham, the family
of the Hu′pham-ites.
40 And the sons of Be′la were Ard and Na′a-man: *of Ard*, the family of the
Ard′ites: *and* of Na′a-man, the family of the Na′a-mites.
41 These *are* the sons of Benjamin after their families: and they that were
numbered of them *were* forty and five thousand and six hundred.
42 ¶These *are* the sons of Dan after their families: of Shu′ham, the family **26:42** Gen 46:23–25
of the Shu′ham-ites. These *are* the families of Dan after their families.
43 All the families of the Shu′ham-ites, according to those that were
numbered of them, *were* threescore and four thousand and four hundred.
44 ¶*Of* the children of Asher after their families: of Jim′na, the family of **26:44** Gen 46:16, 17
the Jim′nites: of Jes′u-i, the family of the Jes′u-ites: of Be-ri′ah, the family
of the Be-ri′ites.
45 Of the sons of Be-ri′ah: of He′ber, the family of the He′ber-ites: of
Mal′chi-el, the family of the Mal′chi-el-ites.
46 And the name of the daughter of Asher *was* Sarah.
47 These *are* the families of the sons of Asher according to those that were
numbered of them; *who were* fifty and three thousand and four hundred.
48 ¶*Of* the sons of Naph′ta-li after their families: of Jah′ze-el, the family of **26:48** 1 Chron 7:13
the Jah′ze-el-ites: of Gu′ni, the family of the Gu′nites:
49 Of Je′zer, the family of the Je′zer-ites: of Shil′lem, the family of the
Shil′lem-ites.
50 These *are* the families of Naph′ta-li according to their families: and
they that were numbered of them *were* forty and five thousand and four
hundred.

26:51 Num 2:32, 33; 26:5
51 These *were* the numbered of the children of Israel, six hundred thousand and a thousand seven hundred and thirty.

3. The Land to Be Alloted According to the Size of Each Tribe

52 ¶And the LORD spake unto Moses, saying,
53 Unto these the land shall be divided for an inheritance according to the number of names.

26:54☆ Num 33:54
54 To many thou shalt give the more inheritance, and to few thou shalt give the less inheritance: to every one shall his inheritance be given according to those that were numbered of him.

26:55 Num 33:54; 34:13; Josh 14:2; 17:14
55 Notwithstanding the land shall be divided by lot: according to the names of the tribes of their fathers they shall inherit.
56 According to the lot shall the possession thereof be divided between many and few.

4. The Census among the Levites

26:57 Num 3:16–38; 1 Chron 6:1
57 ¶And these *are* they that were numbered of the Levites after their families: of Ger′shon, the family of the Ger′shon-ites: of Ko′hath, the family of the Ko′hath-ites: of Me-ra′ri, the family of the Me-ra′rites.

26:58 Num 3:16–35
58 These *are* the families of the Levites: the family of the Lib′nites, the family of the Hebronites, the family of the Mah′lites, the family of the Mu′shites, the family of the Ko′rath-ites. And Ko′hath begat Amram.
59 And the name of Amram's wife *was* Joch′e-bed, the daughter of Levi, whom *her mother* bare to Levi in Egypt: and she bare unto Amram Aaron and Moses, and Miriam their sister.

26:60 Num 3:2, 8
60 And unto Aaron was born Na′dab, and A-bi′hu, E-le-a′zar, and Ith′a-mar.

26:61 Lev 10:1, 2; Num 3:4
61 And Na′dab and A-bi′hu died, when they offered strange fire before the LORD.

26:62 Num 3:39; 4:46–48; Deut 10:9
62 And those that were numbered of them were twenty and three thousand, all males from a month old and upward: for they were not numbered among the children of Israel, because there was no inheritance given them among the children of Israel.

5. The Summary

63 ¶These *are* they that were numbered by Moses and E-le-a′zar the priest, who numbered the children of Israel in the plains of Moab by Jordan *near* Jericho.

26:64☆ Num 14:20–43; Deut 2:14, 15
64 But among these there was not a man of them whom Moses and Aaron the priest numbered, when they numbered the children of Israel in the wilderness of Si′nai.
65 For the LORD had said of them, They shall surely die in the wilderness. And there was not left a man of them, save Caleb the son of Je-phun′neh, and Joshua the son of Nun.

26:54 The division of the land was to be based on numbers, not on tribes. Tribes with more members received more land. It was the intention of God to set up an economic system by which each family received land and thus had a productive base for its support. The land was to be held forever by the families to which it was given. It was God's land, tenanted by God's people, with the external title in the name of the family. It belonged to the family by right and was to be passed down to the children and the children's children. See the note on Lev. 25:9 for information on the jubilee principle.

26:64 *there was not a man of them . . . numbered.* Forty years earlier, at the time of the first census, these men had been under twenty years of age, and so were not counted. All who at that time were older than twenty years of age were now dead.†

B. THE APPEAL OF ZELOPHEHAD'S DAUGHTERS

1. Zelophehad Dies without Male Issue

27 THEN came the daughters of Ze-lo'phe-had, the son of He'pher, ☆27:1 Num 26:28–37 36:1–4 Josh 17:3, 4
the son of Gilead, the son of Ma'chir, the son of Ma-nas'seh, of the
families of Ma-nas'seh the son of Joseph: and these *are* the names of his
daughters; Mah'lah, Noah, and Hog'lah, and Mil'cah, and Tir'zah.
2 And they stood before Moses, and before E-le-a'zar the priest, and
before the princes and all the congregation, *by* the door of the tabernacle of
the congregation, saying,
3 Our father died in the wilderness, and he was not in the company of
them that gathered themselves together against the LORD in the company of
Ko'rah; but died in his own sin, and had no sons.
4 Why should the name of our father be done away from among his
family, because he hath no son? Give unto us *therefore* a possession among
the brethren of our father.

2. God Allows the Daughters to Inherit Land

5 And Moses brought their cause before the LORD.
6 ¶And the LORD spake unto Moses, saying, **27:6, 7** Num 36:1–4 Josh 17:5, 6
7 The daughters of Ze-lo'phe-had speak right: thou shalt surely give them
a possession of an inheritance among their father's brethren; and thou shalt
cause the inheritance of their father to pass unto them.
8 And thou shalt speak unto the children of Israel, saying, If a man die,
and have no son, then ye shall cause his inheritance to pass unto his
daughter.
9 And if he have no daughter, then ye shall give his inheritance unto his
brethren.
10 And if he have no brethren, then ye shall give his inheritance unto his
father's brethren.
11 And if his father have no brethren, then ye shall give his inheritance **27:11** Lev 25:25, 49
unto his kinsman that is next to him of his family, and he shall possess it:
and it shall be unto the children of Israel a statute of judgment, as the LORD
commanded Moses.

C. MOSES LOOKS AT CANAAN; JOSHUA CHOSEN TO SUCCEED HIM

12 ¶And the LORD said unto Moses, Get thee up into this mount Ab'a-rim, ☆**27:12** Num 33:47 Deut 32:49
and see the land which I have given unto the children of Israel.
13 And when thou hast seen it, thou also shalt be gathered unto thy **27:13** Deut 32:50, 51 34–1-6
people, as Aaron thy brother was gathered.
14 For ye rebelled against my commandment in the desert of Zin, in the **27:14** Num 20:9–13 Deut 32:48–52 34:1–6
strife of the congregation, to sanctify me at the water before their eyes: that
is the water of Mer'i-bah in Ka'desh in the wilderness of Zin.
15 ¶And Moses spake unto the LORD, saying, ☆**27:15**
16 Let the LORD, the God of the spirits of all flesh, set a man over the
congregation,

27:1 The land was to be divided only among the males who had been numbered in the census. Women were not numbered. Zelophehad had no sons, only daughters. Zelophehad had died in the wilderness so there was no hope for a male heir. Thus the daughters would get no inheritance. The daughters ask for a exception to the general rule. God grants it and announces an amendment to the procedure (see 12:5–11).

27:12 *Mount Abarim,* i.e., "the regions beyond" in Hebrew. It here refers to the mountain ranges of Trans-Jordan, of which Mount Nebo was a part. Four thousand feet below these mountains is the Dead Sea.
27:15ff Moses asked God to appoint his successor. God's choice was Joshua (27:18), who had served under Moses and was well acquainted with the Israelites. Joshua was a Spirit-filled man of God.

27:17 1 Kgs 22:17 Ezek 34:1–24 Zech 10:2 Mt 9:36

[17]Which may go out before them, and which may go in before them, and which may lead them out, and which may bring them in; that the congregation of the LORD be not as sheep which have no shepherd.

27:18 Deut 3:28 31:7, 8; 34:9

[18]¶And the LORD said unto Moses, Take thee Joshua the son of Nun, a man in whom *is* the spirit, and lay thine hand upon him;

[19]And set him before E-le-a'zar the priest, and before all the congregation; and give him a charge in their sight.

27:20 Deut 31:3

[20]And thou shalt put *some* of thine honour upon him, that all the congregation of the children of Israel may be obedient.

27:21 Ex 28:30 Lev 8:8 Deut 33:8 1 Sam 28:6

[21]And he shall stand before E-le-a'zar the priest, who shall ask *counsel* for him after the judgment of U'rim before the LORD: at his word shall they go out, and at his word they shall come in, *both* he, and all the children of Israel with him, even all the congregation.

27:22–23☆

[22]And Moses did as the LORD commanded him: and he took Joshua, and set him before E-le-a'zar the priest, and before all the congregation:

[23]And he laid his hands upon him, and gave him a charge, as the LORD commanded by the hand of Moses.

D. RESTATEMENT OF THE LAWS OF SACRIFICES AND VOWS

1. The Morning and Evening Burnt Offering

28 AND the LORD spake unto Moses, saying,

28:2☆

[2]Command the children of Israel, and say unto them, My offering, *and* my bread for my sacrifices made by fire, *for* a sweet savour unto me, shall ye observe to offer unto me in their due season.

28:3 Ex 29:38–41 Ezek 46:13–15

[3]And thou shalt say unto them, This *is* the offering made by fire which ye shall offer unto the LORD; two lambs of the first year without spot day by day, *for* a continual burnt offering.

28:4 Lev 6:19, 20

[4]The one lamb shalt thou offer in the morning, and the other lamb shalt thou offer at even;

28:5 Num 15:3–12

[5]And a tenth *part* of an ephah of flour for a meat offering, mingled with the fourth *part* of an hin of beaten oil.

[6]*It is* a continual burnt offering, which was ordained in mount Si'nai for a sweet savour, a sacrifice made by fire unto the LORD.

28:7 Ex 29:41 Lev 23:12–14 Num 28:31

[7]And the drink offering thereof *shall be* the fourth *part* of an hin for the one lamb: in the holy *place* shalt thou cause the strong wine to be poured unto the LORD *for* a drink offering.

[8]And the other lamb shalt thou offer at even: as the meat offering of the morning, and as the drink offering thereof, thou shalt offer *it*, a sacrifice made by fire, of a sweet savour unto the LORD.

2. The Sabbath Offering

[9]¶And on the sabbath day two lambs of the first year without spot, and two tenth deals of flour *for* a meat offering, mingled with oil, and the drink offering thereof:

[10]*This is* the burnt offering of every sabbath, beside the continual burnt offering, and his drink offering.

27:22, 23 In a theocratic kingdom the religious and the secular aspects were conjoined. Joshua, Moses' successor, must be ordained for the position and this was done by his appearing before the high priest and the whole congregation of Israel. When Moses laid hands on Joshua, he passed the reins of his rule over to God's newly designated leader.

28:2ff Before entering the land, Moses repeats the divine instructions pertaining to the various offerings.

3. Offering on the First Day of Each Month

11¶And in the beginnings of your months ye shall offer a burnt offering
unto the LORD; two young bullocks, and one ram, seven lambs of the first
year without spot;
12And three tenth deals of flour *for* a meat offering, mingled with oil, for
one bullock; and two tenth deals of flour *for* a meat offering, mingled with
oil, for one ram;
13And a several tenth deal of flour mingled with oil *for* a meat offering
unto one lamb; *for* a burnt offering of a sweet savour, a sacrifice made by
fire unto the LORD.
14And their drink offerings shall be half an hin of wine unto a bullock,
and the third *part* of an hin unto a ram, and a fourth *part* of an hin unto a
lamb: this *is* the burnt offering of every month throughout the months of
the year.
15And one kid of the goats for a sin offering unto the LORD shall be
offered, beside the continual burnt offering, and his drink offering.

☆**28:11** Num 10:10; 28:19; 1 Chron 23:31; 2 Chron 2:4; Ezra 3:5; Neh 10:33; Isa 1:12, 13; Ezek 46:6, 7; Col 2:16
28:12 Num 15:4–12; 28:5
28:14 Num 28:7
28:15 Lev 6:8–13; Num 28:3

4. Offerings at the Feast of Unleavened Bread

16And in the fourteenth day of the first month *is* the passover of the
LORD.
17And in the fifteenth day of this month *is* the feast: seven days shall
unleavened bread be eaten.
18In the first day *shall be* an holy convocation; ye shall do no manner of
servile work *therein:*
19But ye shall offer a sacrifice made by fire *for* a burnt offering unto the
LORD; two young bullocks, and one ram, and seven lambs of the first year:
they shall be unto you without blemish:
20And their meat offering *shall be of* flour mingled with oil: three tenth
deals shall ye offer for a bullock, and two tenth deals for a ram;
21A several tenth deal shalt thou offer for every lamb, throughout the
seven lambs:
22And one goat *for* a sin offering, to make an atonement for you.
23Ye shall offer these beside the burnt offering in the morning, which *is*
for a continual burnt offering.
24After this manner ye shall offer daily, throughout the seven days, the
meat of the sacrifice made by fire, of a sweet savour unto the LORD: it shall
be offered beside the continual burnt offering, and his drink offering.
25And on the seventh day ye shall have an holy convocation; ye shall do
no servile work.

28:16 Ex 23:15; Lev 23:5–14; Num 9:3–5; Deut 16:1–8
☆**28:17**
28:19 Num 29:11

5. Offerings on the Day of Firstfruits (Pentecost)

26¶Also in the day of the firstfruits, when ye bring a new meat offering
unto the LORD, after your weeks *be out*, ye shall have an holy convocation;
ye shall do no servile work:
27But ye shall offer the burnt offering for a sweet savour unto the LORD;
two young bullocks, one ram, seven lambs of the first year;
28And their meat offering of flour mingled with oil, three tenth deals unto
one bullock, two tenth deals unto one ram,

☆**28:26** Ex 23:16; Lev 23:9–22; Deut 16:16; Acts 2:1

28:11 See note to Num. 10:10 for details on the new moon offering.
28:17 See note to Lev. 23:6 for details on the feast of unleavened bread.
28:26 *day of the firstfruits,* also called the harvest festival, Pentecost, and the feast of weeks. See note to Lev. 23:15 for details on this feast of firstfruits.

29 A several tenth deal unto one lamb, throughout the seven lambs;

30 *And* one kid of the goats, to make an atonement for you.

28:31 Num 28:3

31 Ye shall offer *them* beside the continual burnt offering, and his meat offering, (they shall be unto you without blemish) and their drink offerings.

6. Offerings at the Festival of Trumpets

29:1☆ Lev 23:23–25 Num 10:10

29 AND in the seventh month, on the first *day* of the month, ye shall have an holy convocation; ye shall do no servile work: it is a day of blowing the trumpets unto you.

2 And ye shall offer a burnt offering for a sweet savour unto the LORD; one young bullock, one ram, *and* seven lambs of the first year without blemish:

3 And their meat offering *shall be of* flour mingled with oil, three tenth deals for a bullock, *and* two tenth deals for a ram,

4 And one tenth deal for one lamb, throughout the seven lambs:

5 And one kid of the goats *for* a sin offering, to make an atonement for you:

29:6 Num 28:3

6 Beside the burnt offering of the month, and his meat offering, and the daily burnt offering, and his meat offering, and their drink offerings, according unto their manner, for a sweet savour, a sacrifice made by fire unto the LORD.

7. Offering on the Day of Atonement

29:7 Lev 16:29–31 23:23–27

7 ¶And ye shall have on the tenth *day* of this seventh month an holy convocation; and ye shall afflict your souls: ye shall not do any work *therein:*

29:8☆

8 But ye shall offer a burnt offering unto the LORD *for* a sweet savour; one young bullock, one ram, *and* seven lambs of the first year; they shall be unto you without blemish:

9 And their meat offering *shall be of* flour mingled with oil, three tenth deals to a bullock, *and* two tenth deals to one ram,

10 A several tenth deal for one lamb, throughout the seven lambs:

29:11 Lev 16:1–35 23:26–32

11 One kid of the goats *for* a sin offering; beside the sin offering of atonement, and the continual burnt offering, and the meat offering of it, and their drink offerings.

8. Offerings on the Seven-Day Feast of Tabernacles

29:12☆ Lev 23:33–43 Deut 16:13, 14 Ezek 45:25

12 ¶And on the fifteenth day of the seventh month ye shall have an holy convocation; ye shall do no servile work, and ye shall keep a feast unto the LORD seven days:

13 And ye shall offer a burnt offering, a sacrifice made by fire, of a sweet savour unto the LORD; thirteen young bullocks, two rams, *and* fourteen lambs of the first year; they shall be without blemish:

14 And their meat offering *shall be of* flour mingled with oil, three tenth deals unto every bullock of the thirteen bullocks, two tenth deals to each ram of the two rams,

15 And a several tenth deal to each lamb of the fourteen lambs:

16 And one kid of the goats *for* a sin offering; beside the continual burnt offering, his meat offering, and his drink offering.

29:1 *in the seventh month, on the first day of the month* (of the Hebrew calendar), i.e., "the fifteenth day of September." See note to Lev. 23:24 for details on the feast of trumpets.

29:8 See note to Lev. 16:6 for details on the day of atonement offering.

29:12 See note to Exod. 23:16 for details on the feast of tabernacles or booths.

17¶And on the second day *ye shall offer* twelve young bullocks, two rams,
fourteen lambs of the first year without spot:
18And their meat offering and their drink offerings for the bullocks, for
the rams, and for the lambs, *shall be* according to their number, after the
manner:
19And one kid of the goats *for* a sin offering; beside the continual burnt
offering, and the meat offering thereof, and their drink offerings.
20¶And on the third day eleven bullocks, two rams, fourteen lambs of the
first year without blemish;
21And their meat offering and their drink offerings for the bullocks, for
the rams, and for the lambs, *shall be* according to their number, after the
manner:
22And one goat *for* a sin offering; beside the continual burnt offering, and
his meat offering, and his drink offering.
23¶And on the fourth day ten bullocks, two rams, *and* fourteen lambs of
the first year without blemish:
24Their meat offering and their drink offerings for the bullocks, for the
rams, and for the lambs, *shall be* according to their number, after the
manner:
25And one kid of the goats *for* a sin offering; beside the continual burnt
offering, his meat offering, and his drink offering.
26¶And on the fifth day nine bullocks, two rams, *and* fourteen lambs of
the first year without spot:
27And their meat offering and their drink offerings for the bullocks, for
the rams, and for the lambs, *shall be* according to their number, after the
manner:
28And one goat *for* a sin offering; beside the continual burnt offering, and
his meat offering, and his drink offering.
29¶And on the sixth day eight bullocks, two rams, *and* fourteen lambs of
the first year without blemish:
30And their meat offering and their drink offerings for the bullocks, for
the rams, and for the lambs, *shall be* according to their number, after the
manner:
31And one goat *for* a sin offering; beside the continual burnt offering, his
meat offering, and his drink offering.
32¶And on the seventh day seven bullocks, two rams, *and* fourteen lambs
of the first year without blemish:
33And their meat offering and their drink offerings for the bullocks, for
the rams, and for the lambs, *shall be* according to their number, after the
manner:
34And one goat *for* a sin offering; beside the continual burnt offering, his
meat offering, and his drink offering.
35¶On the eighth day ye shall have a solemn assembly: ye shall do no
servile work *therein:*
36But ye shall offer a burnt offering, a sacrifice made by fire, of a sweet
savour unto the LORD: one bullock, one ram, seven lambs of the first year
without blemish:
37Their meat offering and their drink offerings for the bullock, for the
ram, and for the lambs, *shall be* according to their number, after the
manner:
38And one goat *for* a sin offering; beside the continual burnt offering, and
his meat offering, and his drink offering.
39These *things* ye shall do unto the LORD in your set feasts, beside your
vows, and your freewill offerings, for your burnt offerings, and for your
meat offerings, and for your drink offerings, and for your peace offerings.

29:19
Num 28:3, 11, 31

29:35
Lev 23:3, 7, 21, 36

29:39
Lev 22:20, 21
2 Chron 31:3
Ezra 3:5
Neh 10:33

[40]And Moses told the children of Israel according to all that the LORD commanded Moses.

9. Rules about Vows by Males and Females

30:1, 2 Lev 5:4; 27:2–13 Deut 23:21–25 Judg 11:30–35 Eccles 5:4 **30:2☆**

30 AND Moses spake unto the heads of the tribes concerning the children of Israel, saying, This *is* the thing which the LORD hath commanded.
[2]If a man vow a vow unto the LORD, or swear an oath to bind his soul with a bond; he shall not break his word, he shall do according to all that proceedeth out of his mouth.
[3]If a woman also vow a vow unto the LORD, and bind *herself* by a bond, *being* in her father's house in her youth;
[4]And her father hear her vow, and her bond wherewith she hath bound her soul, and her father shall hold his peace at her: then all her vows shall stand, and every bond wherewith she hath bound her soul shall stand.
[5]But if her father disallow her in the day that he heareth; not any of her vows, or of her bonds wherewith she hath bound her soul, shall stand: and the LORD shall forgive her, because her father disallowed her.

30:6 Judg 11:30, 31

[6]And if she had at all an husband, when she vowed, or uttered ought out of her lips, wherewith she bound her soul;
[7]And her husband heard *it*, and held his peace at her in the day that he heard *it:* then her vows shall stand, and her bonds wherewith she bound her soul shall stand.
[8]But if her husband disallowed her on the day that he heard *it;* then he shall make her vow which she vowed, and that which she uttered with her lips, wherewith she bound her soul, of none effect: and the LORD shall forgive her.
[9]But every vow of a widow, and of her that is divorced, wherewith they have bound their souls, shall stand against her.
[10]And if she vowed in her husband's house, or bound her soul by a bond with an oath;
[11]And her husband heard *it*, and held his peace at her, *and* disallowed her not: then all her vows shall stand, and every bond wherewith she bound her soul shall stand.
[12]But if her husband hath utterly made them void on the day he heard *them; then* whatsoever proceeded out of her lips concerning her vows, or concerning the bond of her soul, shall not stand: her husband hath made them void; and the LORD shall forgive her.
[13]Every vow, and every binding oath to afflict the soul, her husband may establish it, or her husband may make it void.
[14]But if her husband altogether hold his peace at her from day to day; then he establisheth all her vows, or all her bonds, which *are* upon her: he confirmeth them, because he held his peace at her in the day that he heard *them.*
[15]But if he shall any ways make them void after that he hath heard *them;* then he shall bear her iniquity.

30:16☆ Num 5:29

[16]These *are* the statutes, which the LORD commanded Moses, between a man and his wife, between the father and his daughter, *being yet* in her youth in her father's house.

30:2 See note to Num. 6:2 on the laws of vows.
30:16 No specific mention is made of male children making vows. Presumably they fall within the general prescription of men and do not need to have their vows approved by their fathers, as their sisters did. A woman was bound by her husband's decision but nothing is said to indicate that a married man is bound to the decision of his father-in-law. Since a married woman was bound by her husband's decision, there would be no reason for her husband to be bound to her father's.

E. THE SLAUGHTER OF THE MIDIANITES
1. The War against the Midianites

31 AND the LORD spake unto Moses, saying,
2 Avenge the children of Israel of the Mid'i-an-ites: afterward
shalt thou be gathered unto thy people.
3 And Moses spake unto the people, saying, Arm some of yourselves unto
the war, and let them go against the Mid'i-an-ites, and avenge the LORD of
Mid'i-an.
4 Of every tribe a thousand, throughout all the tribes of Israel, shall ye
send to the war.
5 So there were delivered out of the thousands of Israel, a thousand of
every tribe, twelve thousand armed for war.
6 And Moses sent them to the war, a thousand of *every* tribe, them and
Phin'e-has the son of E-le-a'zar the priest, to the war, with the holy
instruments, and the trumpets to blow in his hand.
7 And they warred against the Mid'i-an-ites, as the LORD commanded
Moses; and they slew all the males.
8 And they slew the kings of Mid'i-an, beside the rest of them that were
slain; *namely,* E'vi, and Re'kem, and Zur, and Hur, and Re'ba, five kings of
Mid'i-an: Ba'laam also the son of Be'or they slew with the sword.

☆31:1 Num 25:6–18 Deut 32:35

31:6 Num 10:10 Josh 6:4–6, 13–15 1 Sam 4:4, 5, 17 2 Chron 13:12–15

31:8 Josh 13:21, 22

2. Israel's Failure to Fully Obey God; The Rite of Purification

9 And the children of Israel took *all* the women of Mid'i-an captives, and
their little ones, and took the spoil of all their cattle, and all their flocks,
and all their goods.
10 And they burnt all their cities wherein they dwelt, and all their goodly
castles, with fire.
11 And they took all the spoil, and all the prey, *both* of men and of beasts.
12 And they brought the captives, and the prey, and the spoil, unto Moses,
and E-le-a'zar the priest, and unto the congregation of the children of
Israel, unto the camp at the plains of Moab, which *are* by Jordan *near*
Jericho.
13 ¶And Moses, and E-le-a'zar the priest, and all the princes of the
congregation, went forth to meet them without the camp.
14 And Moses was wroth with the officers of the host, *with* the captains
over thousands, and captains over hundreds, which came from the battle.
15 And Moses said unto them, Have ye saved all the women alive?
16 Behold, these caused the children of Israel, through the counsel of
Ba'laam, to commit trespass against the LORD in the matter of Pe'or, and
there was a plague among the congregation of the LORD.
17 Now therefore kill every male among the little ones, and kill every
woman that hath known man by lying with him.
18 But all the women children, that have not known a man by lying with
him, keep alive for yourselves.

31:16 Num 25:1–18 Deut 4:3 Josh 22:17, 18 2 Pet 2:15, 16

☆31:17 Judg 21:10–12 Deut 7:2; 20:16–18

31:1, 2 The Midianites were children of Abraham by Keturah (Gen. 25:2). Some of the Midianites settled east of Canaan. They had fallen into sin, and used some of their women to entice the Israelites to prostitution and idolatry. They were confederates of the Moabites. In 31:2ff we see that God commanded the Israelites to execute divine judgment on them by war in which all adults—male and female—were to be killed. Some modern liberals have said Moses was either mistaken, and carried out an order God could not have given, or that God was a "dirty bully." Such a judgment on God would then make any final judgment impossible. God is just; while we may not understand all he does, we must not attribute wrong conduct or evil intentions to the Creator.

31:17 All male children were to be killed, so that the Midianite race would become extinct. The women captives would intermarry with the Israelites and be absorbed into their society. However, the Midianites were not completely destroyed, for we read of them again in the Book of Judges (6:1, 2).

[19]And do ye abide without the camp seven days: whosoever hath killed
any person, and whosoever hath touched any slain, purify *both* yourselves
and your captives on the third day, and on the seventh day.
31:20 Lev 13:52 [20]And purify all *your* raiment, and all that is made of skins, and all work
of goats' *hair*, and all things made of wood.
[21]¶And E-le-a'zar the priest said unto the men of war which went to the
battle, This *is* the ordinance of the law which the LORD commanded Moses;
[22]Only the gold, and the silver, the brass, the iron, the tin, and the lead,
[23]Every thing that may abide the fire, ye shall make *it* go through the fire,
and it shall be clean: nevertheless it shall be purified with the water of
separation: and all that abideth not the fire ye shall make go through the
water.
31:24 Lev 11:25; 14:9 Num 19:19 [24]And ye shall wash your clothes on the seventh day, and ye shall be
clean, and afterward ye shall come into the camp.

3. The Distribution of the Booty

[25]¶And the LORD spake unto Moses, saying,
31:26☆ [26]Take the sum of the prey that was taken, *both* of man and of beast,
thou, and E-le-a'zar the priest, and the chief fathers of the congregation:
31:27 Josh 22:8 1 Sam 30:23, 24 [27]And divide the prey into two parts; between them that took the war
upon them, who went out to battle, and between all the congregation:
31:28 2 Sam 8:11, 12 [28]And levy a tribute unto the LORD of the men of war which went out to
battle: one soul of five hundred, *both* of the persons, and of the beeves, and
of the asses, and of the sheep:
31:29 Num 18:25, 26 [29]Take *it* of their half, and give *it* unto E-le-a'zar the priest, *for* an heave
offering of the LORD.
[30]And of the children of Israel's half, thou shalt take one portion of fifty,
of the persons, of the beeves, of the asses, and of the flocks, of all manner of
beasts, and give them unto the Levites, which keep the charge of the
tabernacle of the LORD.
[31]And Moses and E-le-a'zar the priest did as the LORD commanded
Moses.
[32]And the booty, *being* the rest of the prey which the men of war had
caught, was six hundred thousand and seventy thousand and five thousand
sheep,
[33]And threescore and twelve thousand beeves,
[34]And threescore and one thousand asses,
[35]And thirty and two thousand persons in all, of women that had not
known man by lying with him.
[36]And the half, *which was* the portion of them that went out to war, was
in number three hundred thousand and seven and thirty thousand and five
hundred sheep:
[37]And the LORD's tribute of the sheep was six hundred and threescore
and fifteen.
[38]And the beeves *were* thirty and six thousand; of which the LORD's
tribute *was* threescore and twelve.
[39]And the asses *were* thirty thousand and five hundred; of which the
LORD's tribute *was* threescore and one.
[40]And the persons *were* sixteen thousand; of which the LORD's tribute
was thirty and two persons.

31:26 The booty taken was to be divided among soldiers and civilians. One out of every five hundred men and animals were given to the high priest from the soldiers' booty. One in fifty of all men and animals were given to the Levites from the booty of the civilians.

41 And Moses gave the tribute, *which was* the LORD's heave offering, unto
E-le-a'zar the priest, as the LORD commanded Moses.
42 And of the children of Israel's half, which Moses divided from the men
that warred,
43 (Now the half *that pertained unto* the congregation was three hundred
thousand and thirty thousand *and* seven thousand and five hundred sheep,
44 And thirty and six thousand beeves,
45 And thirty thousand asses and five hundred,
46 And sixteen thousand persons;)
47 Even of the children of Israel's half, Moses took one portion of fifty,
both of man and of beast, and gave them unto the Levites, which kept the
charge of the tabernacle of the LORD; as the LORD commanded Moses.

4. The Metal Offerings by the Military Leaders

48 ¶And the officers which *were* over thousands of the host, the captains of
thousands, and captains of hundreds, came near unto Moses:
49 And they said unto Moses, Thy servants have taken the sum of the men
of war which *are* under our charge, and there lacketh not one man of us.
50 We have therefore brought an oblation for the LORD, what every man
hath gotten, of jewels of gold, chains, and bracelets, rings, earrings, and
tablets, to make an atonement for our souls before the LORD.
51 And Moses and E-le-a'zar the priest took the gold of them, *even* all
wrought jewels.
52 And all the gold of the offering that they offered up to the LORD, of the ☆31:52
captains of thousands, and of the captains of hundreds, was sixteen
thousand seven hundred and fifty shekels.
53 (*For* the men of war had taken spoil, every man for himself.) **31:53**
54 And Moses and E-le-a'zar the priest took the gold of the captains of Deut 20:14
thousands and of hundreds, and brought it into the tabernacle of the
congregation, *for* a memorial for the children of Israel before the LORD.

F. THE BEGINNING OF THE OCCUPATION; REUBEN, GAD AND THE HALF-TRIBE OF MANASSEH SETTLE IN THE TRANSJORDAN

1. Reuben and Gad Ask for Land East of the Jordan

32 NOW the children of Reuben and the children of Gad had a very **32:1**
great multitude of cattle: and when they saw the land of Ja'zer, and Num 21:32
the land of Gilead, that, behold, the place *was* a place for cattle; Josh 13:25 2 Sam 24:5
2 The children of Gad and the children of Reuben came and spake unto
Moses, and to E-le-a'zar the priest, and unto the princes of the congrega-
tion, saying,
3 At'a-roth, and Di'bon, and Ja'zer, and Nim'rah, and Hesh'bon, and **32:3**
E-le-a'leh, and She'bam, and Nebo, and Be'on, Num 32:33–42
4 *Even* the country which the LORD smote before the congregation of Josh 13:17–19 Isa 15:2–6; 16:8
Israel, *is* a land for cattle, and thy servants have cattle:
5 Wherefore, said they, if we have found grace in thy sight, let this land be
given unto thy servants for a possession, *and* bring us not over Jordan.

31:52 16,750 shekels of gold were offered to the Lord. It was an immense amount of money according to modern currency. There were no coins at this time, so that the gold and silver was bullion or comprised jewelry and ornaments. The shekel was obviously a measure of weight and this fluctuated at different times in the Scriptures. What was more important was what the silver or gold would buy. At this time a ram was priced at two shekels (Lev. 5:15). In Lev. 27:16 fifty shekels would buy a homer (estimated at four bushels or more) of barley seed. The value of silver and gold differed also. At any rate, the amount of the gold taken from the Midianites was in excess of two million dollars (in terms of 1984 American currency).

32:6☆
6 ¶And Moses said unto the children of Gad and to the children of
Reuben, Shall your brethren go to war, and shall ye sit here?
7 And wherefore discourage ye the heart of the children of Israel from
going over into the land which the LORD hath given them?

32:8 Num 13:2–26; 14:2; Deut 1:19–21
8 Thus did your fathers, when I sent them from Ka′desh-bar′ne-a to see
the land.

32:9 Num 13:23, 24, 27–33; 14:1–12
9 For when they went up unto the valley of Esh′col, and saw the land,
they discouraged the heart of the children of Israel, that they should not go
into the land which the LORD had given them.

32:10, 11 Num 14:28–30; Deut 1:34, 35
10 And the LORD's anger was kindled the same time, and he sware, saying,
11 Surely none of the men that came up out of Egypt, from twenty years
old and upward, shall see the land which I sware unto Abraham, unto
Isaac, and unto Jacob; because they have not wholly followed me:

32:12 Num 14:6, 24, 30; Deut 1:36; Josh 14:8, 9
12 Save Caleb the son of Je-phun′neh the Ken′ez-ite, and Joshua the son
of Nun: for they have wholly followed the LORD.

32:13 Num 14:31–39; Deut 2:14, 15
13 And the LORD's anger was kindled against Israel, and he made them
wander in the wilderness forty years, until all the generation, that had done
evil in the sight of the LORD, was consumed.
14 And, behold, ye are risen up in your fathers' stead, an increase of sinful
men, to augment yet the fierce anger of the LORD toward Israel.

32:15 Deut 30:17; Josh 22:16
15 For if ye turn away from after him, he will yet again leave them in the
wilderness; and ye shall destroy all this people.

2. Reuben and Gad Agree to Help in the Taking of Canaan

16 ¶And they came near unto him, and said, We will build sheepfolds here
for our cattle, and cities for our little ones:

32:17 Deut 3:18–20; Josh 4:12, 13
17 But we ourselves will go ready armed before the children of Israel, until
we have brought them unto their place: and our little ones shall dwell in the
fenced cities because of the inhabitants of the land.

32:18, 19 Josh 13:8; 22:4
18 We will not return unto our houses, until the children of Israel have
inherited every man his inheritance.
19 For we will not inherit with them on yonder side Jordan, or forward;
because our inheritance is fallen to us on this side Jordan eastward.
20 ¶And Moses said unto them, If ye will do this thing, if ye will go armed
before the LORD to war,

32:21 Deut 3:18; Josh 1:12–18
21 And will go all of you armed over Jordan before the LORD, until he
hath driven out his enemies from before him,

32:22 Deut 3:20; Josh 2:4–9
22 And the land be subdued before the LORD: then afterward ye shall
return, and be guiltless before the LORD, and before Israel; and this land
shall be your possession before the LORD.

32:23☆
23 But if ye will not do so, behold, ye have sinned against the LORD: and
be sure your sin will find you out.

32:24 Num 30:2
24 Build you cities for your little ones, and folds for your sheep; and do
that which hath proceeded out of your mouth.
25 And the children of Gad and the children of Reuben spake unto Moses,
saying, Thy servants will do as my lord commandeth.

32:6 Moses insisted that the tribes of Gad and Reuben who expected to settle on the east bank of the Jordan must help the other tribes who would face armed struggle as they sought to possess the land on the west bank of the Jordan. The Gadites and Reubenites agreed to war against the inhabitants who must be dispossessed.

32:23 Moses said that the men of Gad and Reuben would be sinning against God if they failed to keep their promise that they would help the other tribes take the land of Canaan. He said their sins would be found out by God from whom nothing—good or bad—can be concealed. God would reckon with those who broke their word, even though they may have made light of the breach of good ethics.

26 Our little ones, our wives, our flocks, and all our cattle, shall be there in the cities of Gilead:
27 But thy servants will pass over, every man armed for war, before the LORD to battle, as my lord saith.

3. Moses' Agreement with Reuben and Gad

28 So concerning them Moses commanded E-le-a'zar the priest, and Joshua the son of Nun, and the chief fathers of the tribes of the children of Israel:
29 And Moses said unto them, If the children of Gad and the children of Reuben will pass with you over Jordan, every man armed to battle, before the LORD, and the land shall be subdued before you; then ye shall give them the land of Gilead for a possession:
30 But if they will not pass over with you armed, they shall have possessions among you in the land of Canaan.
31 And the children of Gad and the children of Reuben answered, saying, As the LORD hath said unto thy servants, so will we do.
32 We will pass over armed before the LORD into the land of Canaan, that the possession of our inheritance on this side Jordan *may be* ours.

4. The Half-Tribe of Manasseh Settles in Gilead

33 And Moses gave unto them, *even* to the children of Gad, and to the children of Reuben, and unto half the tribe of Ma-nas'seh the son of Joseph, the kingdom of Sihon king of the Am'or-ites, and the kingdom of Og king of Ba'shan, the land, with the cities thereof in the coasts, *even* the cities of the country round about.

32:33 Num 21:23–26; 32:22; 34:14, 15; Deut 2:32–37; 3:8–17; Josh 12:1–6

34 ¶And the children of Gad built Di'bon, and At'a-roth, and Ar'o-er,
35 And At'roth, Sho'phan, and Ja-a'zer, and Jog'be-hah,
36 And Beth-nim'rah, and Beth-ha'ran, fenced cities: and folds for sheep.
37 And the children of Reuben built Hesh'bon, and E-le-a'leh, and Kir-jath-a'im,
38 And Nebo, and Ba'al-me'on, (their names being changed,) and Shib'mah: and gave other names unto the cities which they builded.
39 And the children of Ma'chir the son of Ma-nas'seh went to Gilead, and took it, and dispossessed the Am'or-ite which *was* in it.
40 And Moses gave Gilead unto Ma'chir the son of Ma-nas'seh; and he dwelt therein.
41 And Ja'ir the son of Ma-nas'seh went and took the small towns thereof, and called them Ha'voth-ja'ir.
42 And No'bah went and took Ke'nath, and the villages thereof, and called it No'bah, after his own name.

32:41 Deut 3:14; Josh 13:30; 1 Chron 2:22

G. A SUMMARY OF ISRAEL'S JOURNEY FROM EGYPT TO MOAB

33 THESE *are* the journeys of the children of Israel, which went forth out of the land of Egypt with their armies under the hand of Moses and Aaron.
2 And Moses wrote their goings out according to their journeys by the commandment of the LORD: and these *are* their journeys according to their goings out.

☆**33:1**

33:1, 2 Moses kept a record of the travels of the Israelites through the forty years of wandering. Chapter 33 contains that record.

33:3 3 And they departed from Ram′e-ses in the first month, on the fifteenth
Ex 12:11–51 day of the first month; on the morrow after the passover the children of
Israel went out with an high hand in the sight of all the Egyptians.
4 For the Egyptians buried all *their* firstborn, which the LORD had smitten
among them: upon their gods also the LORD executed judgments.
33:5 5 And the children of Israel removed from Ram′e-ses, and pitched in
Ex 13:20 Suc′coth.
6 And they departed from Suc′coth, and pitched in E′tham, which *is* in the
edge of the wilderness.
33:7 7 And they removed from E′tham, and turned again unto Pi′-ha-hi′roth,
Ex 14:2, 9 which *is* before Ba′al-ze′phon: and they pitched before Mig′dol.
33:8 8 And they departed from before Pi′-ha-hi′roth, and passed through the
Ex 14:21, 22 midst of the sea into the wilderness, and went three days' journey in the
wilderness of E′tham, and pitched in Ma′rah.
33:9 9 And they removed from Ma′rah, and came unto Elim: and in Elim *were*
Ex 15:27; 16:1 twelve fountains of water, and threescore and ten palm trees; and they
pitched there.
10 And they removed from Elim, and encamped by the Red sea.
33:11 11 And they removed from the Red sea, and encamped in the wilderness
Ex 16:1; 17:1 of Sin.
12 And they took their journey out of the wilderness of Sin, and encamped
in Doph′kah.
13 And they departed from Doph′kah, and encamped in A′lush.
33:14 14 And they removed from A′lush, and encamped at Reph′i-dim, where
Ex 17:1–8 was no water for the people to drink.
19:2, 3
33:15 15 And they departed from Reph′i-dim, and pitched in the wilderness of
Num 11:34, 35 Si′nai.
13:21; 20:1
Deut 2:2–8 16 And they removed from the desert of Si′nai, and pitched at Kib′roth–
10:6, 7; 32:51
1 Kgs 9:26 hat-ta′a-vah.
2 Chron 20:36
17 And they departed from Kib′roth–hat-ta′a-vah, and encamped at Ha-
ze′roth.
18 And they departed from Ha-ze′roth, and pitched in Rith′mah.
19 And they departed from Rith′mah, and pitched at Rim′mon–pa′rez.
20 And they departed from Rim′mon–pa′rez, and pitched in Lib′nah.
21 And they removed from Lib′nah, and pitched at Ris′sah.
22 And they journeyed from Ris′sah and pitched in Ke-hel′a-thah.
23 And they went from Ke-hel′a-thah, and pitched in mount Sha′pher.
24 And they removed from mount Sha′pher, and encamped in Har′a-dah.
25 And they removed from Har′a-dah, and pitched in Mak-he′loth.
26 And they removed from Mak-he′loth, and encamped at Ta′hath.
27 And they departed from Ta′hath, and pitched at Ta′rah.
28 And they removed from Ta′rah, and pitched in Mith′cah.
29 And they went from Mith′cah, and pitched in Hash-mo′nah.
30 And they departed from Hash-mo′nah, and encamped at Mo-se′roth.
31 And they departed from Mo-se′roth, and pitched in Ben′e–ja′a-kan.
32 And they removed from Ben′e–ja′a-kan, and encamped at Hor′–ha-
gid′gad.
33 And they went from Hor′–ha-gid′gad, and pitched in Jot′ba-thah.
34 And they removed from Jot′ba-thah, and encamped at E-bro′nah.
35 And they departed from E-bro′nah, and encamped at E′zi-on–ga′ber.
33:36☆ 36 And they removed from E′zi-on–ga′ber, and pitched in the wilderness
of Zin, which *is* Ka′desh.

33:36 *Ezion-geber,* see note to 1 Kings 9:26.

37 And they removed from Ka'desh, and pitched in mount Hor, in the
edge of the land of Edom.
38 And Aaron the priest went up into mount Hor at the commandment of
the LORD, and died there, in the fortieth year after the children of Israel
were come out of the land of Egypt, in the first *day* of the fifth month.
39 And Aaron *was* an hundred and twenty and three years old when he
died in mount Hor.
40 And king A'rad the Canaanite, which dwelt in the south in the land of
Canaan, heard of the coming of the children of Israel.
41 And they departed from mount Hor, and pitched in Zal-mo'nah.
42 And they departed from Zal-mo'nah, and pitched in Pu'non.
43 And they departed from Pu'non, and pitched in O'both.
44 And they departed from O'both, and pitched in I'je-ab'a-rim, in the
border of Moab.
45 And they departed from I'im, and pitched in Di'bon-gad.
46 And they removed from Di'bon-gad, and encamped in Al'mon-dib-la-
tha'im.
47 And they removed from Al'mon-dib-la-tha'im, and pitched in the
mountains of Ab'a-rim, before Nebo.
48 And they departed from the mountains of Ab'a-rim, and pitched in the
plains of Moab by Jordan *near* Jericho.
49 And they pitched by Jordan, from Beth-jes'i-moth *even* unto A'bel-
shit'tim in the plains of Moab.

33:38 Num 20:28
☆33:39
33:40 Num 21:1
☆33:41
33:42 Num 21:10, 11
33:47 Num 27:12
33:48 Num 22:1
33:49 Num 25:1; Josh 2:1; Joel 13:18; Mic 6:5

H. GOD'S ORDERS TO ISRAEL AS THEY POSSESS CANAAN

50 ¶And the LORD spake unto Moses in the plains of Moab by Jordan
near Jericho, saying,
51 Speak unto the children of Israel, and say unto them, When ye are
passed over Jordan into the land of Canaan;
52 Then ye shall drive out all the inhabitants of the land from before you,
and destroy all their pictures, and destroy all their molten images, and quite
pluck down all their high places:
53 And ye shall dispossess *the inhabitants of* the land, and dwell therein:
for I have given you the land to possess it.
54 And ye shall divide the land by lot for an inheritance among your
families: *and* to the more ye shall give the more inheritance, and to the
fewer ye shall give the less inheritance: every man's *inheritance* shall be in
the place where his lot falleth; according to the tribes of your fathers ye
shall inherit.
55 But if ye will not drive out the inhabitants of the land from before you;
then it shall come to pass, that those which ye let remain of them *shall be*
pricks in your eyes, and thorns in your sides, and shall vex you in the land
wherein ye dwell.
56 Moreover it shall come to pass, *that* I shall do unto you, as I thought to
do unto them.

33:52 Ex 23:24; 34:12–17; Deut 7:2–5, 25, 26; Josh 23:7; Judg 2:2
33:54 Num 26:53–56
☆33:55 Ex 23:33; Deut 7:4, 16–20; Ps 106:34–36
33:56 Lev 18:28; Deut 28:63; Ezek 33:27–29; Lk 21:22–24

33:39 Aaron died at the age of 123; Moses died at 120, according to Deut. 34:7. He was Aaron's younger brother. Miriam, their sister, preceded them in death (Num. 20:1). Her age is not stated.

33:41 *Zalmonah* means "dark" or "gloomy." In all probability it was located east of Jebel Harun, at Bir Madhkur.

33:55 Israel was commanded to drive out all of Canaan's inhabitants so she would not be defiled by their idolatry. This command was never completely fulfilled. As a consequence Israel was defiled and her people were contaminated; this ultimately resulted in apostasy and led to the Babylonian captivity.

I. PLANS FOR THE OCCUPATION OF CANAAN

1. The Boundaries of Canaan

34 AND the LORD spake unto Moses, saying,

34:2 Gen 17:8; Deut 1:7, 8; Ps 78:55; Ezek 47:14

2 Command the children of Israel, and say unto them, When ye come into the land of Canaan; (this *is* the land that shall fall unto you for an inheritance, *even* the land of Canaan with the coasts thereof:)

34:3 Ex 23:31; Josh 15:1–4

3 Then your south quarter shall be from the wilderness of Zin along by the coast of Edom, and your south border shall be the outmost coast of the salt sea eastward:

34:4 Num 34:4

4 And your border shall turn from the south to the ascent of Ak-rab′bim, and pass on to Zin: and the going forth thereof shall be from the south to Ka′desh–bar′ne-a, and shall go on to Ha′zar–ad′dar, and pass on to Az′mon:

5 And the border shall fetch a compass from Az′mon unto the river of Egypt, and the goings out of it shall be at the sea.

6 And *as for* the western border, ye shall even have the great sea for a border: this shall be your west border.

34:7 Josh 13:5; 15:5–11; 2 Sam 8:9; Jer 39:5; Ezek 47:15–17

7 And this shall be your north border: from the great sea ye shall point out for you mount Hor:

34:8☆

8 From mount Hor ye shall point out *your border* unto the entrance of Ha′math; and the goings forth of the border shall be to Ze′dad:

9 ¶And the border shall go on to Ziph′ron, and the goings out of it shall be at Ha′zar–e′nan: this shall be your north border.

34:10 Deut 3:17; Josh 15:5, 12; 2 Kgs 23:33; 25:6; Jer 52:9; Mt 14:34; Lk 5:1; Jn 6:1

10 And ye shall point out your east border from Ha′zar–e′nan to She′pham:

11 And the coast shall go down from She′pham to Rib′lah, on the east side of A′in; and the border shall descend, and shall reach unto the side of the sea of Chin′ne-reth eastward:

12 And the border shall go down to Jordan, and the goings out of it shall be at the salt sea: this shall be your land with the coasts thereof round about.

34:13 Josh 14:1, 2

13 And Moses commanded the children of Israel, saying, This *is* the land which ye shall inherit by lot, which the LORD commanded to give unto the nine tribes, and to the half tribe:

34:14 Num 32:33

14 For the tribe of the children of Reuben according to the house of their fathers, and the tribe of the children of Gad according to the house of their fathers, have received *their inheritance*; and half the tribe of Ma-nas′seh have received their inheritance:

15 The two tribes and the half tribe have received their inheritance on this side Jordan *near* Jericho eastward, toward the sunrising.

2. The Leaders Selected to Divide the Land

34:16 Num 1:2–15; 2:3–21

16 And the LORD spake unto Moses, saying,

17 These *are* the names of the men which shall divide the land unto you: E-le-a′zar the priest, and Joshua the son of Nun.

18 And ye shall take one prince of every tribe, to divide the land by inheritance.

19 And the names of the men *are* these: Of the tribe of Judah, Caleb the son of Je-phun′neh.

34:8 *unto the entrance of Hamath,* which was the ideal northern boundary of the land promised to Israel. It was not until the kingships of David, Solomon, and Jeroboam II that Israel's land extended to this point.

20 And of the tribe of the children of Simeon, She-mu'el the son of Am-
mi'hud.
21 Of the tribe of Benjamin, E-li'dad the son of Chis'lon.
22 And the prince of the tribe of the children of Dan, Buk'ki the son of
Jog'li.
23 The prince of the children of Joseph, for the tribe of the children of Ma-
nas'seh, Han'ni-el the son of E'phod.
24 And the prince of the tribe of the children of E'phra-im, Ke-mu'el the
son of Shiph'tan.
25 And the prince of the tribe of the children of Zeb'u-lun, E-liz'a-phan
the son of Par'nach.
26 And the prince of the tribe of the children of Is'sa-char, Pal'ti-el the son
of Az'zan.
27 And the prince of the tribe of the children of Asher, A-hi'hud the son of
Shel'o-mi.
28 And the prince of the tribe of the children of Naph'ta-li, Ped'a-hel the
son of Am-mi'hud.
29 These *are they* whom the LORD commanded to divide the inheritance
unto the children of Israel in the land of Canaan.

3. The Forty-Eight Levitical Cities

35 AND the LORD spake unto Moses in the plains of Moab by Jordan
near Jericho, saying,
2 Command the children of Israel, that they give unto the Levites of the
inheritance of their possession cities to dwell in; and ye shall give *also* unto
the Levites suburbs for the cities round about them.

35:2 Lev 25:32–34; Josh 14:3, 4; Ezek 45:1; 48:8

3 And the cities shall they have to dwell in; and the suburbs of them shall
be for their cattle, and for their goods, and for all their beasts.
4 And the suburbs of the cities, which ye shall give unto the Levites, *shall
reach* from the wall of the city and outward a thousand cubits round about.
5 And ye shall measure from without the city on the east side two
thousand cubits, and on the south side two thousand cubits, and on the
west side two thousand cubits, and on the north side two thousand cubits;
and the city *shall be* in the midst: this shall be to them the suburbs of the
cities.
6 And among the cities which ye shall give unto the Levites *there shall be*
six cities for refuge, which ye shall appoint for the manslayer, that he may
flee thither: and to them ye shall add forty and two cities.

35:6 Deut 4:41–43; Josh 20:2–9; 21:3, 13, 21–38

7 *So* all the cities which ye shall give to the Levites *shall be* forty and eight
cities: them *shall ye give* with their suburbs.

35:7 Josh 21:3–42; 1 Chron 6:54–81

8 And the cities which ye shall give *shall be* of the possession of the
children of Israel: from *them that have* many ye shall give many; but from
them that have few ye shall give few: every one shall give of his cities unto
the Levites according to his inheritance which he inheriteth.

35:8 Num 26:54

4. The Cities of Refuge

9 ¶And the LORD spake unto Moses, saying,
10 Speak unto the children of Israel, and say unto them, When ye be come
over Jordan into the land of Canaan;
11 Then ye shall appoint you cities to be cities of refuge for you; that the
slayer may flee thither, which killeth any person at unawares.

35:11 Num 35:6

35:12☆ Num 35:16–29

12 And they shall be unto you cities for refuge from the avenger; that the
manslayer die not, until he stand before the congregation in judgment.
13 And of these cities which ye shall give six cities shall ye have for refuge.
14 Ye shall give three cities on this side Jordan, and three cities shall ye
give in the land of Canaan, *which* shall be cities of refuge.
15 These six cities shall be a refuge, *both* for the children of Israel, and for
the stranger, and for the sojourner among them; that every one that killeth
any person unawares may flee thither.

35:16 Ex 21:12–14 Lev 24:17 Deut 19:11–13

16 And if he smite him with an instrument of iron, so that he die, he *is* a
murderer: the murderer shall surely be put to death.
17 And if he smite him with throwing a stone, wherewith he may die, and
he die, he *is* a murderer: the murderer shall surely be put to death.
18 Or *if* he smite him with an hand weapon of wood, wherewith he may
die, and he die, he *is* a murderer: the murderer shall surely be put to death.

35:19☆ Deut 19:6, 7, 12 Josh 20:3, 5

19 The revenger of blood himself shall slay the murderer: when he meeteth
him, he shall slay him.
20 But if he thrust him of hatred, or hurl at him by laying of wait, that he
die;
21 Or in enmity smite him with his hand, that he die: he that smote *him*
shall surely be put to death; *for* he *is* a murderer: the revenger of blood
shall slay the murderer, when he meeteth him.
22 But if he thrust him suddenly without enmity, or have cast upon him
any thing without laying of wait,
23 Or with any stone, wherewith a man may die, seeing *him* not, and cast
it upon him, that he die, and *was* not his enemy, neither sought his harm:
24 Then the congregation shall judge between the slayer and the revenger
of blood according to these judgments:
25 And the congregation shall deliver the slayer out of the hand of the
revenger of blood, and the congregation shall restore him to the city of his
refuge, whither he was fled: and he shall abide in it unto the death of the
high priest, which was anointed with the holy oil.
26 But if the slayer shall at any time come without the border of the city of
his refuge, whither he was fled;
27 And the revenger of blood find him without the borders of the city of
his refuge, and the revenger of blood kill the slayer; he shall not be guilty of
blood:
28 Because he should have remained in the city of his refuge until the
death of the high priest: but after the death of the high priest the slayer
shall return into the land of his possession.

35:30☆ Deut 17:6, 7 19:15 Mt 18:16 2 Cor 13:1 Heb 10:28

29 So these *things* shall be for a statute of judgment unto you throughout
your generations in all your dwellings.
30 Whoso killeth any person, the murderer shall be put to death by the

---

35:12 Here again we see that Moses repeated the law concerning killing, in which the avenger of blood was to slay the murderer. A clear distinction was made between accidental killing and unjustifiable homicide. The cities of refuge protected all killers, the innocent and the guilty. No one was to be killed until he stood before the congregation and was found guilty, after which the death penalty was enforced. Those who killed by accident and without malice stayed in the city of refuge until the death of the high priest, after which they were free to return home without being slain. Guilty murderers were to be slain by a near kinsman of the deceased, who was called "the avenger of blood."

35:19 *the avenger of blood* was the executor of the murderer. Obviously he was acting on behalf of the community which pronounced the murderer guilty. Whoever performed this function was not considered to be a murderer. So today, those who execute the guilty for the government are not guilty of a crime.

35:30, 31 Those accused of murder could not be convicted of the crime unless there were two or more witnesses. Today, circumstantial evidence is considered adequate to make a decision. The Mosaic provision was far stricter in that no murderer could be ransomed, that is, let off by payment. Most murderers today are sentenced to a longer or shorter term in jail, after which time they are freed.

mouth of witnesses: but one witness shall not testify against any person *to*
cause him to die.
31 Moreover ye shall take no satisfaction for the life of a murderer, which
is guilty of death: but he shall be surely put to death.
32 And ye shall take no satisfaction for him that is fled to the city of his
refuge, that he should come again to dwell in the land, until the death of the
priest.
33 So ye shall not pollute the land wherein ye *are:* for blood it defileth the
land: and the land cannot be cleansed of the blood that is shed therein, but
by the blood of him that shed it.
34 Defile not therefore the land which ye shall inhabit, wherein I dwell: for
I the LORD dwell among the children of Israel.

35:34 Lev 18:25 Deut 21:1-8 2 Kgs 24:4 Ezek 22:24-27

5. The Regulation about Marriages of Heiresses

36 AND the chief fathers of the families of the children of Gilead, the
son of Ma'chir, the son of Ma-nas'seh, of the families of the sons of
Joseph, came near, and spake before Moses, and before the princes, the
chief fathers of the children of Israel:
2 And they said, The LORD commanded my lord to give the land for an
inheritance by lot to the children of Israel: and my lord was commanded by
the LORD to give the inheritance of Ze-lo'phe-had our brother unto his
daughters.
3 And if they be married to any of the sons of the *other* tribes of the
children of Israel, then shall their inheritance be taken from the inheritance
of our fathers, and shall be put to the inheritance of the tribe whereunto
they are received: so shall it be taken from the lot of our inheritance.
4 And when the jubile of the children of Israel shall be, then shall their
inheritance be put unto the inheritance of the tribe whereunto they are
received: so shall their inheritance be taken away from the inheritance of
the tribe of our fathers.
5 And Moses commanded the children of Israel according to the word of
the LORD, saying, The tribe of the sons of Joseph hath said well.
6 This *is* the thing which the LORD doth command concerning the
daughters of Ze-lo'phe-had, saying, Let them marry to whom they think
best; only to the family of the tribe of their father shall they marry.
7 So shall not the inheritance of the children of Israel remove from tribe
to tribe: for every one of the children of Israel shall keep himself to the
inheritance of the tribe of his fathers.
8 And every daughter, that possesseth an inheritance in any tribe of the
children of Israel, shall be wife unto one of the family of the tribe of her
father, that the children of Israel may enjoy every man the inheritance of
his fathers.
9 Neither shall the inheritance remove from *one* tribe to another tribe; but
every one of the tribes of the children of Israel shall keep himself to his own
inheritance.
10 Even as the LORD commanded Moses, so did the daughters of Ze-
lo'phe-had:
11 For Mah'lah, Tir'zah, and Hog'lah, and Mil'cah, and Noah, the
daughters of Ze-lo'phe-had, were married unto their father's brothers' sons:

☆**36:1, 2** Num 27:1-11 Josh 17:3, 4

☆**36:6** Gen 24:3, 57, 58

36:8 1 Chron 23:22

36:11 Num 27:1-11 36:1

36:2 *Zelophehad.* See note to 27:1 for the rule of inheritance in connection with the daughters of this man.

36:6 Moses here commanded that the daughters of families who had no son should marry within their own tribes, so that no land would pass from one tribe to another. Thus tribal identity was to be preserved and the landed inheritance was to remain indefinitely within each tribe. 36:13 indicates that Moses' command came from God and was thus a divine fiat.

12 *And* they were married into the families of the sons of Ma-nas'seh the
son of Joseph, and their inheritance remained in the tribe of the family of
their father.

36:13☆ Lev 7:37, 38 27:34

13 These *are* the commandments and the judgments, which the LORD
commanded by the hand of Moses unto the children of Israel in the plains
of Moab by Jordan *near* Jericho.

36:13 These were Moses' last words to Israel before his death and prior to their entering the land of promise. The necessity of repeating the commands of God over and over again to his people and to successive generations is vital to a lively faith, a godly walk, and a useful testimony.

THE FIFTH BOOK OF MOSES CALLED
DEUTERONOMY

Authorship, date, and background The Hebrew title for this book is simply the opening words in the text: "these are the words," or just "words." The English title derives from the Greek word *deuteronomion,* which means "second law," or "repetition of the law." The Septuagint uses this word as the title for the last book of the Pentateuch. From the earliest days, Jewish and Samaritan traditions have attributed the authorship of the book to Moses. Thus the date for its composition would depend on whether one dates the Exodus around 1440 B.C. or 1220 B.C. The early date for the Exodus is preferable, however.

Deuteronomy itself supports Mosaic authorship by several statements such as: "On this side Jordan, in the land of Moab, began Moses to declare this law" (1:5); "And Moses wrote this law, and delivered it unto the priests the sons of Levi . . ." (31:9); "And it came to pass, when Moses had made an end of writing the words of this law in a book, until they were finished, that Moses commanded the Levites which bare the ark of the covenant of the LORD, saying, Take this book of the law, and put it in the side of the ark of the covenant of the LORD your God, that it may be there for a witness against thee" (31:24–26). Rationalist scholars have usually claimed that Deuteronomy was written in the seventh century B.C. The Graf-Wellhausen hypothesis is hardly in accord with the internal evidence of Deuteronomy as well as the external historical data common to the seventh and fifteenth centuries B.C. The testimony of Jesus, who endorses the Mosaic authorship of Deuteronomy in Matthew 19:8, forecloses the question for those who accept his Lordship.

The background against which Deuteronomy was written presupposes the existence of the material contained in Exodus and Leviticus. At the time Moses delivered the addresses in Deuteronomy, the children of Israel were encamped on the outskirts of the Promised Land, which they had not yet entered. Their forty years of probation and wandering, awaiting the death of the old generation, except Joshua and Caleb, were over. But God also told Moses not to enter the land because of his sin when he struck the rock rather than speaking to it at Meribah (Num 20:11ff.). God decreed that Joshua should lead Israel into the land, but Moses, prior to his own death, was to explain to the younger generation the terms and conditions of the covenant and the necessity for their obedience to it.

Characteristics and content Deuteronomy consists of a series of speeches which were delivered orally, no doubt, and which were written down for posterity. Moses first traces the background history of Israel in the wilderness journeys. The Ten Commandments are repeated and their implications expanded upon. Moses pays particular attention to the first commandment, which is basic to the covenant. From thence he goes on to discuss first the ceremonial laws having to do with such matters as places of worship, idolatry, clean and unclean foods, tithes, and holy seasons. In the second category he treats civil ordinances dealing with the appointment of judges, the election of a king, as well as regulations for priests, Levites, and prophets. This is followed by criminal laws relating to murder, cities of refuge, false testimony, waging war, and crimes punishable by hanging. Miscellaneous laws on marriage, disobedient sons, unchastity, wages, remarriage, parents, children, and even weights and measures are dealt with.

Moses' third discourse outlines the nature of God's covenant with Israel. He accents the need for repentance when the covenant is violated, and calls them to keep the covenant, with promises of blessing or of the severest punishment depending on Israel's faithfulness or unfaithfulness. Chapter 28 contains the prediction of future judgments on Israel. Moses closes the book with his final charge, a farewell and exhortation, the intimation of his death, and the pronouncement of blessing. The account of his death is apparently added to Moses' written record by Joshua, who takes over the leadership of Israel as the people prepare to enter the land.

Outline

I. Moses' first address (1:1—4:43)
II. Moses' second sermon (4:44—26:19)

III. The summary of various laws (27:1—28:68)
IV. Moses' last address and the naming of his successor (29:1—32:43)
V. Moses' final words and death (32:44—34:12)

I. MOSES' FIRST ADDRESS (1:1—4:43)

A. HOW GOD LED ISRAEL FROM HOREB TO MOAB

1. Introduction

1:1☆ Gen 32:3 1 THESE *be* the words which Moses spake unto all Israel on this side
Num 21:24, 33 Jordan in the wilderness, in the plain over against the Red *sea*,
Deut 2:8, 24 3:3; 4:1, 44–46 between Paran, and To'phel, and Laban, and Ha-ze'roth, and Diz'a-hab.
1:2☆ 2 (*There are* eleven days' *journey* from Ho'reb by the way of mount Se'ir
unto Ka'desh–bar'ne-a.)
3 And it came to pass in the fortieth year, in the eleventh month, on the
first *day* of the month, *that* Moses spake unto the children of Israel,
according unto all that the LORD had given him in commandment unto
them;
4 After he had slain Sihon the king of the Am'or-ites, which dwelt in
Hesh'bon, and Og the king of Ba'shan, which dwelt at As'ta-roth in Ed're-i:
1:5☆ 5 On this side Jordan, in the land of Moab, began Moses to declare this
law, saying,
1:6 6 The LORD our God spake unto us in Ho'reb, saying, Ye have dwelt long
Ex 19:1 Num 10:11–13 33:38 enough in this mount:

2. God's Command to Possess the Land

1:7 7 Turn you, and take your journey, and go to the mount of the Am'or-ites,
Gen 15:18–21 and unto all *the places* nigh thereunto, in the plain, in the hills, and in the
Deut 4:49 Josh 10:5, 40 vale, and in the south, and by the sea side, to the land of the Canaanites,
and unto Lebanon, unto the great river, the river Eu-phra'tes.
1:8 8 Behold, I have set the land before you: go in and possess the land which
Gen 12:7; 26:3 Ex 33:1 the LORD sware unto your fathers, Abraham, Isaac, and Jacob, to give unto
Num 32:10, 11 them and to their seed after them.

3. Tribal Leaders Appointed to Aid Moses

1:9 9 ¶And I spake unto you at that time, saying, I am not able to bear you
Ex 18:18, 24 myself alone:
1:10 Gen 15:5; 22:17 10 The LORD your God hath multiplied you, and, behold, ye *are* this day
Deut 10:22 26:5; 28:62 as the stars of heaven for multitude.
Heb 11:12 11 (The LORD God of your fathers make you a thousand times so many
1:11 Deut 8:1 more as ye *are*, and bless you, as he hath promised you!)
Ps 115:14 1:12 12 How can I myself alone bear your cumbrance, and your burden, and
Ex 18:13, 14 your strife?

1:1 *on this side Jordan.* Many say this should be thought of as the equivalent of "Trans-Jordan," as used today. However, in Deut. 3:20 and 3:25 the same expression clearly means Canaan; so does Deut. 11:30 which reads, "on the other side Jordan." Albeit, in the other verses quoted (e.g., Josh. 9:10; 13:8; 18:7) it is translated "beyond Jordan." Some have said that it means the writer of the introduction was in Canaan, but since Moses wrote the book it could not be so. It would be a proleptic word from God.

1:2 *eleven days' journey from Horeb by the way of mount Seir unto Kadesh-barnea.* This foot journey of eleven days makes vivid the fact that it was within this area that the Israelites wandered for thirty-eight lost years. They were always within just a few days of Canaan, yet they were prevented from entering the land because of their sin. *Horeb* is an alternate rendering of "Sinai." *Kadesh-barnea* was at the southern edge of the Promised Land.

1:5 *began Moses to declare this law* is better translated "undertook to explain this law" (RSV), or "undertook to expound this law" (NASB). Deuteronomy is an interpretation of the law, not just a repetition of it.

13Take you wise men, and understanding, and known among your tribes,
and I will make them rulers over you.
14And ye answered me, and said, The thing which thou hast spoken *is*
good *for us* to do.
15So I took the chief of your tribes, wise men, and known, and made
them heads over you, captains over thousands, and captains over hundreds,
and captains over fifties, and captains over tens, and officers among your
tribes.
16And I charged your judges at that time, saying, Hear *the causes* between
your brethren, and judge righteously between *every* man and his brother,
and the stranger *that is* with him.
17Ye shall not respect persons in judgment; *but* ye shall hear the small as
well as the great; ye shall not be afraid of the face of man; for the judgment
is God's: and the cause that is too hard for you, bring *it* unto me, and I will
hear it.
18And I commanded you at that time all the things which ye should do.

1:13 Ex 18:21, 22; Num 11:16, 17
☆1:15
1:16 Ex 22:21; 23:9; Deut 10:18; 24:14
1:17 Ex 18:25, 26; Deut 10:17; 16:19; 24:17; Prov 24:23; Jas 2:1, 9

4. Israel's Forty Years Wandering for Refusal to Enter the Land

19¶And when we departed from Ho'reb, we went through all that great
and terrible wilderness, which ye saw by the way of the mountain of the
Am'or-ites, as the LORD our God commanded us; and we came to Ka'desh-
bar'ne-a.
20And I said unto you, Ye are come unto the mountain of the Am'or-ites,
which the LORD our God doth give unto us.
21Behold, the LORD thy God hath set the land before thee: go up *and*
possess *it*, as the LORD God of thy fathers hath said unto thee; fear not,
neither be discouraged.
22¶And ye came near unto me every one of you, and said, We will send
men before us, and they shall search us out the land, and bring us word
again by what way we must go up, and into what cities we shall come.
23And the saying pleased me well: and I took twelve men of you, one of
a tribe:
24And they turned and went up into the mountain, and came unto the
valley of Esh'col, and searched it out.
25And they took of the fruit of the land in their hands, and brought *it*
down unto us, and brought us word again, and said, *It is* a good land which
the LORD our God doth give us.
26Notwithstanding ye would not go up, but rebelled against the com-
mandment of the LORD your God:
27And ye murmured in your tents, and said, Because the LORD hated us,
he hath brought us forth out of the land of Egypt, to deliver us into the
hand of the Am'or-ites, to destroy us.

☆1:19 Deut 1:2; 8:15; 32:10
☆1:22 Num 13:1, 2
1:23 Num 13:3–15
1:24 Num 13:21–25
☆1:26 Num 14:1–3
1:27 Ex 16:3; Num 14:3; Ps 106:25

1:15 See note to Exod. 18:25 where Moses appointed leaders from every tribe to help him in the governance of Israel—with the promise that the difficult cases could be referred to him.

1:19 *Kadesh-barnea* was on the southern border of the Promised Land.

1:22 *We will send men before us.* Moses here blames the Israelites for wanting to send the spies into Canaan. Before God allowed it to take place, the Israelites expressed a desire to have the survey made. "As if it were not enough that they were sure of a God before them, they must send men before them."* They should have entered the land by faith (without sight) and God would have given them the land forty years earlier.

1:26 *ye would not go up.* By this time most—if not all—of the men who had been condemned by God to die before entering the land of Cannan were gone from the scene. Yet Moses was addressing the present people of Israel as though they were in some way equally responsible for what happened. Thus we discover the unity of peoples and nations. The sins of the parents will be visited on the children to the third and fourth generation. So each generation needs to be reminded that the acts of their fathers have consequences in their lives. Those who were young when the judgment of the forty years began shared in the same penalty and are now warned by Moses not to repeat their fathers' sins.

1:28☆ Num 13:28, 33 Deut 9:1, 2

28 Whither shall we go up? our brethren have discouraged our heart,
saying, The people *is* greater and taller than we; the cities *are* great and
walled up to heaven; and moreover we have seen the sons of the Anakims
there.

1:29 Deut 3:22; 7:18 Josh 8:1

29 Then I said unto you, Dread not, neither be afraid of them.

1:30☆ Ex 14:14 Deut 20:4

30 The LORD your God which goeth before you, he shall fight for you,
according to all that he did for you in Egypt before your eyes;

1:31 Deut 32:11 Isa 40:11 Acts 13:18

31 And in the wilderness, where thou hast seen how that the LORD thy
God bare thee, as a man doth bear his son, in all the way that ye went, until
ye came into this place.
32 Yet in this thing ye did not believe the LORD your God,

1:33 Ex 13:21 Num 9:15–23 10:33–36

33 Who went in the way before you, to search you out a place to pitch
your tents *in*, in fire by night, to shew you by what way ye should go, and
in a cloud by day.

1:34 Num 14:28–30 32:8–12 Deut 2:14

34 And the LORD heard the voice of your words, and was wroth, and
sware, saying,
35 Surely there shall not one of these men of this evil generation see that
good land, which I sware to give unto your fathers,

1:36☆ Num 14:24 Josh 14:6

36 Save Caleb the son of Je-phun'neh; he shall see it, and to him will I give
the land that he hath trodden upon, and to his children, because he hath
wholly followed the LORD.

1:37 Num 20:12 27:18

37 Also the LORD was angry with me for your sakes, saying, Thou also
shalt not go in thither.

1:38 Num 34:16–28 Deut 3:28; 31:7

38 *But* Joshua the son of Nun, which standeth before thee, he shall go in
thither: encourage him: for he shall cause Israel to inherit it.

1:39 Num 14:3, 31

39 Moreover your little ones, which ye said should be a prey, and your
children, which in that day had no knowledge between good and evil, they
shall go in thither, and unto them will I give it, and they shall possess it.

1:40 Num 14:25

40 But *as for* you, turn you, and take your journey into the wilderness by
the way of the Red sea.

1:41 Num 14:40

41 Then ye answered and said unto me, We have sinned against the LORD,
we will go up and fight, according to all that the LORD our God com-
manded us. And when ye had girded on every man his weapons of war, ye
were ready to go up into the hill.

1:42 Num 14:41–43

42 And the LORD said unto me, Say unto them, Go not up, neither fight;
for I *am* not among you; lest ye be smitten before your enemies.

1:43☆ Num 14:44

43 So I spake unto you; and ye would not hear, but rebelled against the
commandment of the LORD, and went presumptuously up into the hill.

1:44 Num 14:45

44 And the Am'or-ites, which dwelt in that mountain, came out against
you, and chased you, as bees do, and destroyed you in Se'ir, *even* unto
Hor'mah.
45 And ye returned and wept before the LORD; but the LORD would not
hearken to your voice, nor give ear unto you.
46 So ye abode in Ka'desh many days, according unto the days that ye
abode *there*.

1:28 *the cities are . . . walled up to heaven.* The walls of the large Canaanite cities ranged from thirty to fifty feet in height.

1:30 Moses reassured Israel that God would go before them, leading them into Canaan. He would also deliver them from their enemies. Moses reminded them of what God had done for them in Egypt. What was true then is still true today. God forever promises to go before us to prepare the way; he assures us that we will be safe from all enemies and delivered from all opposition. But this protection is conditional; we must walk by faith and put our trust in God.

1:36 Caleb and Joshua were the only two of their generation who entered the Promised Land. They were commended as men who wholly followed the Lord. They were not perfect nor sinless, but they walked blamelessly before the Lord in obedience to his early command for Israel to enter Canaan.

1:43 Moses again and again reminds the people that they have failed because of their lack of faith and their refusal to obey the commands of God. Why have so few believers today learned their lessons from observing the tragic experiences of Israel? Must we repeat Israel's mistakes and suffer the same consequences?

5. The Forty Years of Wandering

2 THEN we turned, and took our journey into the wilderness by the way 2:1 Num 21:4
of the Red sea, as the LORD spake unto me: and we compassed mount
Se'ir many days.
2 And the LORD spake unto me, saying,
3 Ye have compassed this mountain long enough: turn you northward.
4 And command thou the people, saying, Ye *are* to pass through the coast ☆2:4 Ex 15:15 Num 20:14 Judg 11:17
of your brethren the children of Esau, which dwell in Se'ir; and they shall
be afraid of you: take ye good heed unto yourselves therefore:
5 Meddle not with them; for I will not give you of their land, no, not so 2:5 Deut 23:7
much as a foot breadth; because I have given mount Se'ir unto Esau *for* a
possession.
6 Ye shall buy meat of them for money, that ye may eat; and ye shall also 2:6 Num 20:19
buy water of them for money, that ye may drink.
7 For the LORD thy God hath blessed thee in all the works of thy hand: he 2:7 Deut 8:2; 29:5
knoweth thy walking through this great wilderness: these forty years the
LORD thy God *hath been* with thee; thou hast lacked nothing.
8 And when we passed by from our brethren the children of Esau, which 2:8 Num 20:20
dwelt in Se'ir, through the way of the plain from E'lath, and from E'zi-on-
ga'ber, we turned and passed by the way of the wilderness of Moab.

6. God Forbids an Attack on the Moabites

9 And the LORD said unto me, Distress not the Moabites, neither contend ☆2:9 Gen 19:37 Deut 1:1–5 2:18, 29
with them in battle: for I will not give thee of their land *for* a possession;
because I have given Ar unto the children of Lot *for* a possession.
10 The E'mims dwelt therein in times past, a people great, and many, and 2:10 Num 13:28 Josh 14:12
tall, as the Anakims;
11 Which also were accounted giants, as the Anakims; but the Moabites 2:11 Deut 2:20 3:11, 13 Josh 12:4
call them E'mims.
12 The Ho'rims also dwelt in Se'ir beforetime; but the children of Esau 2:12 Gen 14:5, 6 Num 21:25, 35 Deut 2:22
succeeded them, when they had destroyed them from before them, and
dwelt in their stead; as Israel did unto the land of his possession, which the
LORD gave unto them.
13 Now rise up, *said I*, and get you over the brook Ze'red. And we went
over the brook Ze'red.
14 And the space in which we came from Ka'desh-bar'ne-a, until we were 2:14, 15 Num 14:29–35 26:64, 65 Deut 2:7 Ps 106:26 1 Cor 10:5 Jude 5
come over the brook Ze'red, *was* thirty and eight years; until all the
generation of the men of war were wasted out from among the host, as the
LORD sware unto them.
15 For indeed the hand of the LORD was against them, to destroy them
from among the host, until they were consumed.

7. God's Command Not to Attack the Ammonites

16 ¶So it came to pass, when all the men of war were consumed and dead
from among the people,
17 That the LORD spake unto me, saying, 2:18 Num 21:15 Deut 2:9
18 Thou art to pass over through Ar, the coast of Moab, this day:

2:4 *the children of Esau . . . shall be afraid of you.* God was concerned for the children of Esau, who was the brother of Jacob. The Israelites were to pass through their land but leave them alone in safety. They were to trade with them honestly in their dealings. They were commanded to do this despite the fact that Edom earlier refused them permission to cross their territory (Num. 20:21).

2:9 See note to Gen. 19:36 on the Moabites, who descended from Lot. God granted protection to them and Israel was to leave them alone.

2:19☆

19 And *when* thou comest nigh over against the children of Ammon, distress them not, nor meddle with them: for I will not give thee of the land of the children of Ammon *any* possession; because I have given it unto the children of Lot *for* a possession.

2:20 Deut 2:11

20 (That also was accounted a land of giants: giants dwelt therein in old time; and the Ammonites call them Zam-zum′mims;

21 A people great, and many, and tall, as the Anakims; but the LORD destroyed them before them; and they succeeded them, and dwelt in their stead:

22 As he did to the children of Esau, which dwelt in Se′ir, when he destroyed the Ho′rims from before them; and they succeeded them, and dwelt in their stead even unto this day:

2:23☆ Gen 10:13, 14; 1 Chron 1:11, 12; Jer 47:4; Amos 9:7

23 And the A′vims which dwelt in Ha-ze′rim, *even* unto Az′zah, the Caph′to-rims, which came forth out of Caph′tor, destroyed them, and dwelt in their stead.)

2:24 Num 21:13; Judg 11:18

24 ¶Rise ye up, take your journey, and pass over the river Arnon: behold, I have given into thine hand Sihon the Am′or-ite, king of Hesh′bon, and his land: begin to possess *it*, and contend with him in battle.

2:25☆ Ex 15:14–16; 23:27; Deut 11:25; Josh 2:9

25 This day will I begin to put the dread of thee and the fear of thee upon the nations *that are* under the whole heaven, who shall hear report of thee, and shall tremble, and be in anguish because of thee.

8. The Military Defeats of the Ammonites

a. The successful war against King Sihon

2:26 Num 21:21; Deut 20:10–13; Judg 11:19

26 ¶And I sent messengers out of the wilderness of Ked′e-moth unto Sihon king of Hesh′bon with words of peace, saying,

27 Let me pass through thy land: I will go along by the high way, I will neither turn unto the right hand nor to the left.

28 Thou shalt sell me meat for money, that I may eat; and give me water for money, that I may drink: only I will pass through on my feet;

2:29 Deut 2:8, 9; 23:3

29 (As the children of Esau which dwell in Se′ir, and the Moabites which dwell in Ar, did unto me;) until I shall pass over Jordan into the land which the LORD our God giveth us.

2:30☆ Ex 11:10; Num 21:23; Josh 11:20

30 But Sihon king of Hesh′bon would not let us pass by him: for the LORD thy God hardened his spirit, and made his heart obstinate, that he might deliver him into thy hand, as *appeareth* this day.

31 And the LORD said unto me, Behold, I have begun to give Sihon and his land before thee: begin to possess, that thou mayest inherit his land.

32 Then Sihon came out against us, he and all his people, to fight at Ja′haz.

2:33 Num 21:24–30; Deut 3:6; 29:7

33 And the LORD our God delivered him before us; and we smote him, and his sons, and all his people.

2:34☆

34 And we took all his cities at that time, and utterly destroyed the men, and the women, and the little ones, of every city, we left none to remain:

2:35, 36 Num 31:9–11; Deut 3:7, 10; Ps 44:3

35 Only the cattle we took for a prey unto ourselves, and the spoil of the cities which we took.

2:19 The Ammonites, who descended from Lot by incest were given divine protection; Israel was required to leave them alone.

2:23 *Caphtor,* the island of Crete.

2:25 Israel was commanded to go into the land and begin to possess it. This was their work. But God also promised that, in his sovereignty, he would work among the enemies of Israel, terrifying and dispiriting them. Thus the divine power would work for Israel even though it was weaker than its enemies, and Israel would be victorious. In the battle against Satan we are to look to God, not at the strongest enemy. If we are clothed with God's power, no enemy can withstand us.

2:30 *the LORD thy God hardened his spirit.* See note on Exod. 4:21.

2:34 *we left none to remain.* This practice was called *herem* ("devoted to destruction"). Israel's enemies and their possessions were devoted to Yahweh ("Jehovah"). The males, and, in some cases, the females and children, were slain and the cities destroyed. The loot was divided among the victors.

36 From Ar′o-er, which *is* by the brink of the river of Arnon, and *from* the
city that *is* by the river, even unto Gilead, there was not one city too strong
for us: the LORD our God delivered all unto us:
37 Only unto the land of the children of Ammon thou camest not, *nor*
unto any place of the river Jabbok, nor unto the cities in the mountains, nor
unto whatsoever the LORD our God forbad us.

2:37 Deut 3:16

b. The Victory over King Og of Bashan

3 THEN we turned, and went up the way to Ba′shan: and Og the king of
Ba′shan came out against us, he and all his people, to battle at Ed′re-i.
2 And the LORD said unto me, Fear him not: for I will deliver him, and all
his people, and his land, into thy hand; and thou shalt do unto him as thou
didst unto Sihon king of the Am′or-ites, which dwelt at Hesh′bon.
3 So the LORD our God delivered into our hands Og also, the king of
Ba′shan, and all his people: and we smote him until none was left to him
remaining.
4 And we took all his cities at that time, there was not a city which we
took not from them, threescore cities, all the region of Ar′gob, the kingdom
of Og in Ba′shan.
5 All these cities *were* fenced with high walls, gates, and bars; beside
unwalled towns a great many.
6 And we utterly destroyed them, as we did unto Sihon king of Hesh′bon,
utterly destroying the men, women, and children, of every city.
7 But all the cattle, and the spoil of the cities, we took for a prey to
ourselves.
8 And we took at that time out of the hand of the two kings of the Am′or-
ites the land that *was* on this side Jordan, from the river of Arnon unto
mount Hermon;
9 (*Which* Hermon the Si-do′ni-ans call Sir′i-on; and the Am′or-ites call it
She′nir;)
10 All the cities of the plain, and all Gilead, and all Ba′shan, unto Sal′chah
and Ed′re-i, cities of the kingdom of Og in Ba′shan.
11 For only Og king of Ba′shan remained of the remnant of giants;
behold, his bedstead *was* a bedstead of iron; *is* it not in Rab′bath of the
children of Ammon? nine cubits *was* the length thereof, and four cubits the
breadth of it, after the cubit of a man.

☆3:1 Num 21:33–35 Deut 1:1–5
3:3 Josh 9:10
3:4 Num 32:33–42 Josh 12:4
3:6 Num 21:2 Deut 2:33, 34 20:16 Josh 11:11 Ps 135:10–12
3:7 2:35 Josh 8:27
3:8 Num 32:33–42 Josh 12:1–6 13:8–13 Amos 3:9, 10
3:9 Deut 4:48 Josh 11:17 Ps 29:5, 6
3:11 Deut 2:11, 20 2 Sam 11:1 12:26, 27 Jer 49:2 Ezek 21:19, 20

c. The Distribution of the Land to Reuben, Gad, and the Half-Tribe of Manasseh

12 And this land, *which* we possessed at that time, from Ar′o-er, which *is*
by the river Arnon, and half mount Gilead, and the cities thereof, gave I
unto the Reubenites and to the Gadites.
13 And the rest of Gilead, and all Ba′shan, *being* the kingdom of Og, gave
I unto the half tribe of Ma-nas′seh; all the region of Ar′gob, with all
Ba′shan, which was called the land of giants.
14 Ja′ir the son of Ma-nas′seh took all the country of Ar′gob unto the
coasts of Gesh′u-ri and Ma-ach′a-thi; and called them after his own name,
Ba′shan–ha′voth–ja′ir, unto this day.
15 And I gave Gilead unto Ma′chir.
16 And unto the Reubenites and unto the Gadites I gave from Gilead even
unto the river Arnon half the valley, and the border even unto the river
Jabbok, *which is* the border of the children of Ammon;

3:12 Num 32:33–42 Deut 2:35, 36 Josh 13:8–13
3:13 Num 32:41 Judg 10:4
3:15 Num 32:40

3:1 Og of Bashan was a giant who may have been nine or more feet tall. He was bold and daring, yet God gave the Israelites victory over him so that the Reubenites and Gadites could have that land (note verse 12).

3:17☆ Josh 13:27

17 The plain also, and Jordan, and the coast *thereof*, from Chin′ne-reth even unto the sea of the plain, *even* the salt sea, under Ash′doth-pis′gah eastward.

3:18 Num 32:20; Josh 1:12, 13; 4:12, 13

18 ¶And I commanded you at that time, saying, The LORD your God hath given you this land to possess it: ye shall pass over armed before your brethren the children of Israel, all *that are* meet for the war.

3:19 Num 32:26; Deut 20:5–8; Josh 1:14

19 But your wives, and your little ones, and your cattle, (*for* I know that ye have much cattle,) shall abide in your cities which I have given you;

20 Until the LORD have given rest unto your brethren, as well as unto you, and *until* they also possess the land which the LORD your God hath given them beyond Jordan: and *then* shall ye return every man unto his possession, which I have given you.

3:21☆ Num 27:18

21 ¶And I commanded Joshua at that time, saying, Thine eyes have seen all that the LORD your God hath done unto these two kings: so shall the LORD do unto all the kingdoms whither thou passest.

3:22 Deut 1:30; 20:4; Josh 10:25

22 Ye shall not fear them: for the LORD your God he shall fight for you.

d. Moses Looks over Canaan but Cannot Enter

3:23 Jer 15:1

23 And I besought the LORD at that time, saying,

24 O Lord GOD, thou hast begun to shew thy servant thy greatness, and thy mighty hand: for what God *is there* in heaven or in earth, that can do according to thy works, and according to thy might?

3:25☆

25 I pray thee, let me go over, and see the good land that *is* beyond Jordan, that goodly mountain, and Lebanon.

3:26 Num 20:12; 27:14; Deut 1:37; 32:51

26 But the LORD was wroth with me for your sakes, and would not hear me: and the LORD said unto me, Let it suffice thee; speak no more unto me of this matter.

3:27 Num 23:14; 27:12; Deut 1:37

27 Get thee up into the top of Pis′gah, and lift up thine eyes westward, and northward, and southward, and eastward, and behold *it* with thine eyes: for thou shalt not go over this Jordan.

3:28 Num 27:18; Deut 1:38; 31:3, 7, 23

28 But charge Joshua, and encourage him, and strengthen him: for he shall go over before this people, and he shall cause them to inherit the land which thou shalt see.

3:29☆ Deut 4:44, 45, 46; 34:6

29 So we abode in the valley over against Beth-pe′or.

9. Moses Pleads with Israel to Keep God's Law

4:1 Lev 19:37; Deut 5:32, 33; 8:1; 16:20; 30:16; Ezek 11:20; 20:11; Rom 10:5

4 NOW therefore hearken, O Israel, unto the statutes and unto the judgments, which I teach you, for to do *them*, that ye may live, and go in and possess the land which the LORD God of your fathers giveth you.

4:2☆ Deut 4:14, 40; 12:32; Prov 30:6; Eccles 12:13; Mt 5:18

2 Ye shall not add unto the word which I command you, neither shall ye diminish *ought* from it, that ye may keep the commandments of the LORD your God which I command you.

3:17 *Chinnereth,* Lake Genneserat, or Sea of Galilee.

3:21 What God allowed to happen to the two kings mentioned here should encourage the hearts of the Israelites because they are promised that God will do the same to their enemies in Canaan.

3:25 God had previously told Moses that he would not be permitted to enter the land of Canaan. Yet we see here that Moses prayed that God would allow him to do so. God's earlier judgment on Moses was not accompanied by an oath. In analogous situations Moses had prevailed with God and the circumstances had been reversed. Here, though, God told him to ask no more. But, although he was never allowed to walk on its earth, Moses was allowed to climb the mountain and look into Canaan (3:27). Thus God in judgment often remembers mercy.

3:29 *Beth-peor,* an above-sea-level area not far from the burial place of Moses.

4:2 Here and elsewhere we are warned against adding to or taking away from the Word of God. To commit such an act is a grievous breach against the Lawgiver and represents the ever-dangerous course of judging God.

3 Your eyes have seen what the LORD did because of Ba'al-pe'or: for all
the men that followed Ba'al-pe'or, the LORD thy God hath destroyed them
from among you.

4:3 Num 25; 1–9 Deut 3:29

4 But ye that did cleave unto the LORD your God *are* alive every one of
you this day.

5 Behold, I have taught you statutes and judgments, even as the LORD my
God commanded me, that ye should do so in the land whither ye go to
possess it.

4:5 Lev 26:46; 27:34 Deut 4:44–46 12:1

6 Keep therefore and do *them*; for this *is* your wisdom and your
understanding in the sight of the nations, which shall hear all these statutes,
and say, Surely this great nation *is* a wise and understanding people.

4:6 Deut 32:46, 47 Ps 19:7, 8 111:10 Prov 1:7–9

7 For what nation *is there so* great, who *hath* God *so* nigh unto them, as
the LORD our God *is* in all *things that* we call upon him *for?*

☆**4:7** Ps 148:14

8 And what nation *is there so* great, that hath statutes and judgments *so*
righteous as all this law, which I set before you this day?

4:8 Ps 89:14, 15

9 Only take heed to thyself, and keep thy soul diligently, lest thou forget
the things which thine eyes have seen, and lest they depart from thy heart
all the days of thy life: but teach them thy sons, and thy sons' sons;

4:9 Ex 13:8 Deut 6:2, 7 10-12a, 20-25 8:11; 11:19 32:46 Josh 4:6 Prov 3:1

10 *Specially* the day that thou stoodest before the LORD thy God in
Ho'reb, when the LORD said unto me, Gather me the people together, and
I will make them hear my words, that they may learn to fear me all the days
that they shall live upon the earth, and *that* they may teach their children.

4:10 Ex 19:7–9, 16 Deut 5:5, 22 17:19; 31:12

11 And ye came near and stood under the mountain; and the mountain
burned with fire unto the midst of heaven, with darkness, clouds, and thick
darkness.

4:11 Ex 19:18 Heb 12:18

12 And the LORD spake unto you out of the midst of the fire: ye heard the
voice of the words, but saw no similitude; only *ye heard* a voice.

13 And he declared unto you his covenant, which he commanded you to
perform, *even* ten commandments; and he wrote them upon two tables of
stone.

4:13 Ex 31:18 34:1, 28 Deut 10:4

14 ¶And the LORD commanded me at that time to teach you statutes and
judgments, that ye might do them in the land whither ye go over to possess
it.

10. The Warning against Idolatry

15 Take ye therefore good heed unto yourselves; for ye saw no manner of
similitude on the day *that* the LORD spake unto you in Ho'reb out of the
midst of the fire:

☆**4:15** Ex 19:9, 18, 21 24:10, 11

16 Lest ye corrupt *yourselves*, and make you a graven image, the similitude
of any figure, the likeness of male or female,

4:16 Ex 20:4, 5; 32:8 Deut 4:25; 5:8 9:12; 31:29

17 The likeness of any beast that *is* on the earth, the likeness of any winged
fowl that flieth in the air,

18 The likeness of any thing that creepeth on the ground, the likeness of
any fish that *is* in the waters beneath the earth:

19 And lest thou lift up thine eyes unto heaven, and when thou seest the
sun, and the moon, and the stars, *even* all the host of heaven, shouldest be
driven to worship them, and serve them, which the LORD thy God hath
divided unto all nations under the whole heaven.

4:19 Deut 17:2, 3 2 Kgs 17:16 Amos 5:25–27 Acts 7:43

4:7, 8 Moses extols the greatness of God and declares that none of the other nations have statutes or ordinances equal to those given to Israel by God through divine revelation. Those laws are still part of life today and the keeping or breaking of them will enable a nation to survive or go down in defeat.

4:15 *ye saw no manner of similitude,* i.e., "you didn't see the form of God."† God is spirit and is nonmaterial.

4:20☆ Deut 5:6; 7:6; 26:18; 1 Kgs 8:51; Jer 11:4
4:21 Num 27:14; Deut 1:37

20 But the LORD hath taken you, and brought you forth out of the iron
furnace, *even* out of Egypt, to be unto him a people of inheritance, as *ye are*
this day.
21 Furthermore the LORD was angry with me for your sakes, and sware
that I should not go over Jordan, and that I should not go in unto that good
land, which the LORD thy God giveth thee *for* an inheritance:
22 But I must die in this land, I must not go over Jordan: but ye shall go
over, and possess that good land.

4:23 Deut 4:9, 16; Josh 23:11; 1 Chron 16:15
4:24 Ex 24:17; 34:14; Deut 5:9, 10; 6:15; 9:3; Heb 12:29
4:25☆ Deut 4:16; 31:29

23 Take heed unto yourselves, lest ye forget the covenant of the LORD your
God, which he made with you, and make you a graven image, *or* the
likeness of any *thing*, which the LORD thy God hath forbidden thee.
24 For the LORD thy God *is* a consuming fire, *even* a jealous God.
25 ¶When thou shalt beget children, and children's children, and ye shall
have remained long in the land, and shall corrupt *yourselves*, and make a
graven image, *or* the likeness of any *thing*, and shall do evil in the sight of
the LORD thy God, to provoke him to anger:

4:26☆ Deut 7:4; 8:19; 31:29; Judg 2:10, 11
4:27☆ Deut 28:64; 29:28
4:28 Deut 28:36, 64; 29:17; Ps 115:4–8
4:29☆ Deut 6:5; 10:12; 30:1–3; 2 Chron 15:4; Neh 1:8, 9
4:30☆ Ps 18:6; 59:16; 107:13
4:31☆ Ex 34:6; Lev 26:45; Deut 31:6, 8; Josh 1:5; Jer 30:11; Heb 13:5

26 I call heaven and earth to witness against you this day, that ye shall
soon utterly perish from off the land whereunto ye go over Jordan to
possess it; ye shall not prolong *your* days upon it, but shall utterly be
destroyed.
27 And the LORD shall scatter you among the nations, and ye shall be left
few in number among the heathen, whither the LORD shall lead you.
28 And there ye shall serve gods, the work of men's hands, wood and
stone, which neither see, nor hear, nor eat, nor smell.
29 But if from thence thou shalt seek the LORD thy God, thou shalt find
him, if thou seek him with all thy heart and with all thy soul.
30 When thou art in tribulation, and all these things are come upon thee,
even in the latter days, if thou turn to the LORD thy God, and shalt be
obedient unto his voice;
31 (For the LORD thy God *is* a merciful God;) he will not forsake thee,
neither destroy thee, nor forget the covenant of thy fathers which he sware
unto them.

11. Israel Is God's Chosen Nation

4:32 Gen 1:27; Isa 45:12
4:33☆ Ex 20:22; Deut 5:24, 26
4:34☆ Ex 14:30; Deut 5:15; 6:21; 7:19; 33:29; Ps 136:12

32 For ask now of the days that are past, which were before thee, since the
day that God created man upon the earth, and *ask* from the one side of
heaven unto the other, whether there hath been *any such thing* as this great
thing *is*, or hath been heard like it?
33 Did *ever* people hear the voice of God speaking out of the midst of the
fire, as thou hast heard, and live?
34 Or hath God assayed to go *and* take him a nation from the midst of
another nation, by temptations, by signs, and by wonders, and by war, and
by a mighty hand, and by a stretched out arm, and by great terrors,
according to all that the LORD your God did for you in Egypt before your
eyes?

4:20 *brought you forth out of the iron furnace, i.e.,* "rescued you from prison." (See Jer. 11:4.)

4:25–31 Moses warns Israel about the consequences of disobedience. God will surely judge and chastise whoever disobeys him. But if and when they repent, God will be merciful. In 4:29 we learn that God will not seek the transgressor; the transgressor must seek God. When he does so with all his heart, he will find God. Disconsolate sinners from whom God has hidden his face must learn that the first step toward reconciliation must come from the offender, not the offended.

4:33, 34 God performed signs and wonders for Israel such as no other nation had experienced. By this extrinsic evidence their faith should have been strengthened; and with the knowledge of what God had done before, they could look to the future with expectation, knowing that he could and would show himself strong on behalf of his people in the future.

[35]Unto thee it was shewed, that thou mightest know that the LORD he *is*
God; *there is* none else beside him.
[36]Out of heaven he made thee to hear his voice, that he might instruct
thee: and upon earth he shewed thee his great fire; and thou heardest his
words out of the midst of the fire.
[37]And because he loved thy fathers, therefore he chose their seed after
them, and brought thee out in his sight with his mighty power out of Egypt;
[38]To drive out nations from before thee greater and mightier than thou
art, to bring thee in, to give thee their land *for* an inheritance, as *it is* this
day.
[39]Know therefore this day, and consider *it* in thine heart, that the LORD
he *is* God in heaven above, and upon the earth beneath: *there is* none else.
[40]Thou shalt keep therefore his statutes, and his commandments, which I
command thee this day, that it may go well with thee, and with thy children
after thee, and that thou mayest prolong *thy* days upon the earth, which the
LORD thy God giveth thee, for ever.

☆**4:35** Ex 8:10; 9:14 Deut 4:39 1 Sam 17:46 Mk 12:29
4:36 Ex 19:9, 19 20:18 Neh 9:13
4:37 Deut 7:7, 8 Ps 105:5–11 Isa 41:8
4:38 Ex 23:27–30 Num 32:3, 4 Deut 6:23 9:4, 28; 30:5
4:39 Deut 32:39
4:40 Ex 23:26 Deut 4:2 5:16, 29, 33 32:47

12. The Transjordan Cities of Refuge

[41]¶Then Moses severed three cities on this side Jordan toward the
sunrising;
[42]That the slayer might flee thither, which should kill his neighbour
unawares, and hated him not in times past; and that fleeing unto one of
these cities he might live:
[43]*Namely*, Be'zer in the wilderness, in the plain country, of the Reuben-
ites; and Ra'moth in Gilead, of the Gadites; and Go'lan in Ba'shan, of the
Ma-nas'sites.

4:41 Num 35:6 Deut 19:1–13 Josh 20:7

II. MOSES' SECOND SERMON (4:44—26:19)

A. INTRODUCTION

[44]¶And this *is* the law which Moses set before the children of Israel:
[45]These *are* the testimonies, and the statutes, and the judgments, which
Moses spake unto the children of Israel, after they came forth out of Egypt,
[46]On this side Jordan, in the valley over against Beth-pe'or, in the land of
Sihon king of the Am'or-ites, who dwelt at Hesh'bon, whom Moses and the
children of Israel smote, after they were come forth out of Egypt:
[47]And they possessed his land, and the land of Og king of Ba'shan, two
kings of the Am'or-ites, which *were* on this side Jordan toward the
sunrising;
[48]From Ar'o-er, which *is* by the bank of the river Arnon, even unto
mount Sion, which *is* Hermon,
[49]And all the plain on this side Jordan eastward, even unto the sea of the
plain, under the springs of Pis'gah.

4:48 Deut 2:35, 36

B. THE GIVING OF THE DECALOGUE: ISRAEL AND GOD'S COVENANT

1. The Statement of the Ten Commandments

[5] AND Moses called all Israel, and said unto them, Hear, O Israel, the
statutes and judgments which I speak in your ears this day, that ye
may learn them, and keep, and do them.

5:1 Deut 6:4; 9:1 20:3; 27:9

4:35 God is spirit (John 4:24), which means he has no body and is an invisible reality. There is only one God who has unchanging attributes. There is no one else like him. God is also a person who knows, feels, and wills (in Ps. 94:9, 10 we read that God sees, hears, punishes, and knows). His people pray to him as a person; they offer adoration and make known all their wishes.

5:2 Ex 19:5; Num 26:64, 65; Mal 4:4
5:4 Num 14:14; Deut 4:33
5:5 Ex 19:16, 25
5:6☆ Ex 20:2–17; Ps 81:5
5:7 Ex 20:3; Mt 4:10
5:8 Ex 20:4; Lev 26:1; Deut 4:16, 17
5:9, 10☆ Ex 20:4–6; 34:7, 14; Jer 32:18
5:11 Deut 6:13; 10:20; Jer 4:2; Mt 5:33
5:12☆ Ex 20:8–11; Lev 26:2
5:15☆ Ex 20:11; Deut 15:15; 16:12
5:16☆ Ex 20:12; 21:17; Deut 15:15; 16:12; Eph 6:2, 3; Col 3:20
5:17 Ex 20:13; Mt 5:21
5:18 Ex 20:14; Lk 18:20; Jas 2:11
5:19 Ex 20:15; Rom 13:9; Eph 4:28
5:20 Ex 20:16
5:21 Lk 12:5; Rom 7:7; 13:9

2 The LORD our God made a covenant with us in Ho'reb.
3 The LORD made not this covenant with our fathers, but with us, *even* us,
who *are* all of us here alive this day.
4 The LORD talked with you face to face in the mount out of the midst of
the fire,
5 (I stood between the LORD and you at that time, to shew you the word
of the LORD: for ye were afraid by reason of the fire, and went not up into
the mount;) saying,
6 I *am* the LORD thy God, which brought thee out of the land of Egypt,
from the house of bondage.
7 Thou shalt have none other gods before me.
8 Thou shalt not make thee *any* graven image, *or* any likeness *of any thing*
that *is* in heaven above, or that *is* in the earth beneath, or that *is* in the
waters beneath the earth:
9 Thou shalt not bow down thyself unto them, nor serve them: for I the
LORD thy God *am* a jealous God, visiting the iniquity of the fathers upon
the children unto the third and fourth *generation* of them that hate me,
10 And shewing mercy unto thousands of them that love me and keep my
commandments.
11 Thou shalt not take the name of the LORD thy God in vain: for the
LORD will not hold *him* guiltless that taketh his name in vain.
12 Keep the sabbath day to sanctify it, as the LORD thy God hath
commanded thee.
13 Six days thou shalt labour, and do all thy work:
14 But the seventh day *is* the sabbath of the LORD thy God: *in it* thou shalt
not do any work, thou, nor thy son, nor thy daughter, nor thy manservant,
nor thy maidservant, nor thine ox, nor thine ass, nor any of thy cattle, nor
thy stranger that *is* within thy gates; that thy manservant and thy
maidservant may rest as well as thou.
15 And remember that thou wast a servant in the land of Egypt, and *that*
the LORD thy God brought thee out thence through a mighty hand and by
a stretched out arm: therefore the LORD thy God commanded thee to keep
the sabbath day.
16 ¶Honour thy father and thy mother, as the LORD thy God hath
commanded thee; that thy days may be prolonged, and that it may go well
with thee, in the land which the LORD thy God giveth thee.
17 Thou shalt not kill.
18 Neither shalt thou commit adultery.
19 Neither shalt thou steal.
20 Neither shalt thou bear false witness against thy neighbour.
21 Neither shalt thou desire thy neighbour's wife, neither shalt thou covet
thy neighbour's house, his field, or his manservant, or his maidservant, his
ox, or his ass, or any *thing* that *is* thy neighbour's.

5:6 Moses here reminds Israel of the ten commandments, which had been given years ago to the fathers of the present generation. They need to recall them and to understand the implications. For example, Moses gives an added interpretation of the tenth commandment about coveting. He includes the fields they are to inherit, such as they had not had or owned for centuries. The poor who covet the wealth of the rich break this commandment, as do the rich when they are blind to the needs of the poor and do not love their neighbors as they love themselves.

5:9, 10 *a jealous God.* See note on Exod. 34:14.

5:12 *Keep,* whereas Exod. 20:8 says, "Remember."

5:15 In Exod. 20:11 the sabbath is said to be a creation ordinance. Here Moses has added another reason for keeping the sabbath—Israel's deliverance from slavery in Egypt.

5:16 *as the LORD thy God hath commanded thee.* In slightly different ways, this phrase is used throughout Deuteronomy.

2. The Details of Moses' Meeting with God at Sinai

22 ¶These words the LORD spake unto all your assembly in the mount out
of the midst of the fire, of the cloud, and of the thick darkness, with a great
voice: and he added no more. And he wrote them in two tables of stone,
and delivered them unto me.
23 And it came to pass, when ye heard the voice out of the midst of the
darkness, (for the mountain did burn with fire,) that ye came near unto me,
even all the heads of your tribes, and your elders;
24 And ye said, Behold, the LORD our God hath shewed us his glory and
his greatness, and we have heard his voice out of the midst of the fire: we
have seen this day that God doth talk with man, and he liveth.
25 Now therefore why should we die? for this great fire will consume us: if
we hear the voice of the LORD our God any more, then we shall die.
26 For who *is there of* all flesh, that hath heard the voice of the living God
speaking out of the midst of the fire, as we *have*, and lived?
27 Go thou near, and hear all that the LORD our God shall say: and speak
thou unto us all that the LORD our God shall speak unto thee; and we will
hear *it*, and do *it*.
28 And the LORD heard the voice of your words, when ye spake unto me;
and the LORD said unto me, I have heard the voice of the words of this
people, which they have spoken unto thee: they have well said all that they
have spoken.
29 O that there were such an heart in them, that they would fear me, and
keep all my commandments always, that it might be well with them, and
with their children for ever!
30 Go say to them, Get you into your tents again.
31 But as for thee, stand thou here by me, and I will speak unto thee all the
commandments, and the statutes, and the judgments, which thou shalt
teach them, that they may do *them* in the land which I give them to possess
it.
32 Ye shall observe to do therefore as the LORD your God hath com-
manded you: ye shall not turn aside to the right hand or to the left.
33 Ye shall walk in all the ways which the LORD your God hath
commanded you, that ye may live, and *that it may be* well with you, and *that*
ye may prolong *your* days in the land which ye shall possess.

5:22 Ex 19:16–19; 31:18; 32:15; Deut 4:13
☆**5:23**
5:25 Ex 20:18, 19; Deut 18:16; Heb 12:19
5:26 Ex 24:3
5:28 Deut 18:17
5:29 Deut 5:16, 33; Ps 81:13; Isa 48:18; Mt 23:37; Lk 19:42
5:31 Ex 24:12; Deut 5:1; 6:1, 2; 11:1, 2; Ezek 20:11
5:32 Deut 17:20; 28:14; Josh 1:7; 23:6
☆**5:33** Ex 20:12; Deut 4:1, 40; 5:16; 6:2; 25:13–15

3. The Command to Keep God's Commandments

6 NOW these *are* the commandments, the statutes, and the judgments,
which the LORD your God commanded to teach you, that ye might do
them in the land whither ye go to possess it:
2 That thou mightest fear the LORD thy God, to keep all his statutes and
his commandments, which I command thee, thou, and thy son, and thy
son's son, all the days of thy life; and that thy days may be prolonged.
3 ¶Hear therefore, O Israel, and observe to do *it*; that it may be well with
thee, and that ye may increase mightily, as the LORD God of thy fathers
hath promised thee, in the land that floweth with milk and honey.

6:1 Deut 5:1; 12:1
6:2 Deut 4:9; 10:12
6:3 Ex 3:8, 17; Deut 5:33

5:23 *the mountain did burn with fire,* cf. 4:24: "For the LORD thy God is a consuming fire," and 5:24: "we have heard his voice out of the midst of the fire." Everywhere in the Scriptures fire is connected with God. Here it is not clear whether there was a literal fire on the mountain or if the presence of God was an appearance of fire. In any case, the Israelites accepted the fact that "this great fire will consume us" (5:25) if God so chose. (See Deut. 4:33.)

5:33 Moses here says that it is highly to the advantage of Israel to walk in all the ways God had commanded. Blessing attends obedience.

4. God's Great Commandment: The Law of Love

6:4-9☆

6:4, 5☆ Deut 4:35, 39; 5:1; Mt 22:37; Mk 12:29, 30; Lk 10:27; 1 Cor 8:4, 6

6:6 Deut 10:12; 11:13; Josh 1:8

6:7☆ Ex 12:26; Deut 4:9; Ps 78:4–6

6:8 Ex 13:9; Deut 11:18

6:9 Deut 11:20

6:10 Deut 8:10; 9:1; 11:15; 19:1; Josh 24:13

4 Hear, O Israel: The LORD our God *is* one LORD:

5 And thou shalt love the LORD thy God with all thine heart, and with all thy soul, and with all thy might.

6 And these words, which I command thee this day, shall be in thine heart:

7 And thou shalt teach them diligently unto thy children, and shalt talk of them when thou sittest in thine house, and when thou walkest by the way, and when thou liest down, and when thou risest up.

8 And thou shalt bind them for a sign upon thine hand, and they shall be as frontlets between thine eyes.

9 And thou shalt write them upon the posts of thy house, and on thy gates.

10 And it shall be, when the LORD thy God shall have brought thee into the land which he sware unto thy fathers, to Abraham, to Isaac, and to Jacob, to give thee great and goodly cities, which thou buildedst not,

11 And houses full of all good *things*, which thou filledst not, and wells digged, which thou diggedst not, vineyards and olive trees, which thou plantedst not; when thou shalt have eaten and be full;

12 *Then* beware lest thou forget the LORD, which brought thee forth out of the land of Egypt, from the house of bondage.

6:13☆ Deut 5:11; 10:20; Mt 4:10; Lk 4:8

13 Thou shalt fear the LORD thy God, and serve him, and shalt swear by his name.

14 Ye shall not go after other gods, of the gods of the people which *are* round about you;

6:15 Deut 4:24; 5:9, 10; 11:16, 17

6:16☆ Ex 17:7; Mt 4:7; Lk 4:12; 1 Cor 10:9

6:17 Ex 15:26; Deut 11:22

6:18 Deut 4:40; 8:11; 12:24, 25; Ps 19:11

15 (For the LORD thy God *is* a jealous God among you) lest the anger of the LORD thy God be kindled against thee, and destroy thee from off the face of the earth.

16 ¶Ye shall not tempt the LORD your God, as ye tempted *him* in Mas'sah.

17 Ye shall diligently keep the commandments of the LORD your God, and his testimonies, and his statutes, which he hath commanded thee.

18 And thou shalt do *that which is* right and good in the sight of the LORD: that it may be well with thee, and that thou mayest go in and possess the good land which the LORD sware unto thy fathers,

19 To cast out all thine enemies from before thee, as the LORD hath spoken.

5. Teaching One's Children the Law

6:20 Ex 13:8, 14

20 *And* when thy son asketh thee in time to come, saying, What *mean* the testimonies, and the statutes, and the judgments, which the LORD our God hath commanded you?

21 Then thou shalt say unto thy son, We were Pharaoh's bondmen in Egypt; and the LORD brought us out of Egypt with a mighty hand:

6:4-9 The Jews still make a practice of repeating what they call the *Shema* ("hear") twice daily. These verses speak of the unity of the Godhead. Christians agree that God is one, but insist that the Godhead subsists in three persons—the Father, the Son, and the Holy Spirit, and that God is of one essence. This is a tri-unity, for God is one yet three. This is a great mystery. Peder Stiansen has said that "he who would try to understand the Trinity will lose his mind; but he who denies the Trinity will lose his soul." (See also note on 2 Cor. 13:14.)

6:5 The first table of the law is to love God with our whole hearts. Since "heart" in the Old Testament was considered the seat of the intellect, Jesus added the interpretation that we are to love God with our minds (see Mark 12:30 and Luke 10:27).

6:13 *shalt swear by his name,* i.e., "they must never appeal to any other, as the discerner of truth and avenger of wrong." In the courts today men take an oath on the Bible to tell the truth. Thus they swear by God's name. Woe betide those who swear by God's name and then speak falsehoods.

6:16 There should not be any circumstance or exigency which causes us to show distrust of the power, presence, or providence of God. Nor are we to quarrel with him. Simple, unquestioning faith is required of us.

[23]But the LORD thy God shall deliver them unto thee, and shall destroy
them with a mighty destruction, until they be destroyed.
[24]And he shall deliver their kings into thine hand, and thou shalt destroy
their name from under heaven: there shall no man be able to stand before
thee, until thou have destroyed them.
[25]The graven images of their gods shall ye burn with fire: thou shalt not
desire the silver or gold *that is* on them, nor take *it* unto thee, lest thou be
snared therein: for it *is* an abomination to the LORD thy God.
[26]Neither shalt thou bring an abomination into thine house, lest thou be
a cursed thing like it: *but* thou shalt utterly detest it, and thou shalt utterly
abhor it; for it *is* a cursed thing.

7:24 Deut 11:25 Josh 1:5; 6:2 10:8; 23:9
☆**7:25** Deut 7:2; 12:3 Josh 7:1, 21
7:26 Deut 13:17 Josh 6:18, 19

D. THE RECORD OF GOD'S MERCIES TOWARD ISRAEL

1. God's Mercies during Israel's Wandering

8 ALL the commandments which I command thee this day shall ye
observe to do, that ye may live, and multiply, and go in and possess the
land which the LORD sware unto your fathers.
[2]And thou shalt remember all the way which the LORD thy God led thee
these forty years in the wilderness, to humble thee, *and* to prove thee, to
know what *was* in thine heart, whether thou wouldest keep his command-
ments, or no.
[3]And he humbled thee, and suffered thee to hunger, and fed thee with
manna, which thou knewest not, neither did thy fathers know; that he
might make thee know that man doth not live by bread only, but by every
word that proceedeth out of the mouth of the LORD doth man live.
[4]Thy raiment waxed not old upon thee, neither did thy foot swell, these
forty years.
[5]Thou shalt also consider in thine heart, that, as a man chasteneth his
son, *so* the LORD thy God chasteneth thee.
[6]Therefore thou shalt keep the commandments of the LORD thy God, to
walk in his ways, and to fear him.
[7]For the LORD thy God bringeth thee into a good land, a land of brooks
of water, of fountains and depths that spring out of valleys and hills;
[8]A land of wheat, and barley, and vines, and fig trees, and pomegranates;
a land of oil olive, and honey;
[9]A land wherein thou shalt eat bread without scarceness, thou shalt not
lack any *thing* in it; a land whose stones *are* iron, and out of whose hills
thou mayest dig brass.
[10]When thou hast eaten and art full, then thou shalt bless the LORD thy
God for the good land which he hath given thee.

8:1 Lev 26:3 Deut 4:1; 7:11 11:13
8:2 Ex 15:25 Deut 13:3 2 Chron 32:31 Job 33:16–18 Ps 81:7
☆**8:3** Ps 78:24 Mt 4:4 Lk 4:4
8:4 Deut 29:5 Neh 9:21
8:5 Ps 89:30–32 Prov 3:11, 12 Heb 12:6
8:7 Deut 10:7 11:9–15 Jer 2:7
8:8 Deut 32:13
☆**8:9**
8:10 Ps 103:2

2. Moses' Warning against Pride

[11]Beware that thou forget not the LORD thy God, in not keeping his
commandments, and his judgments, and his statutes, which I command
thee this day:

8:11 Deut 4:9, 23 6:10–12

7:25 Images with silver and gold content are especially dangerous for their intrinsic value. Moses warned against them and ordered such images destroyed because they are abominable and detestable in the sight of God. Moses remembered that Israel had made a golden calf which they worshipped and around which they engaged in sexual immorality.

8:3 *man doth not live by bread only.* This immutable truth calls attention to the spiritual needs of men, as well as their physical needs. Jesus used this Scripture in his temptation and prefaced it by saying, "It is written." For him, that settled the matter. And it should settle matters for us. Whatever is written is true, good, and worthy of our attention and devotion.

8:9 *iron . . . brass* (copper). This has been confirmed by archeologists in the great rift of the Arabah south of the Dead Sea.

8:12☆ Prov 3:9 Hos 13:6

12 Lest *when* thou hast eaten and art full, and hast built goodly houses, and dwelt *therein*;

13 And *when* thy herds and thy flocks multiply, and thy silver and thy gold is multiplied, and all that thou hast is multiplied;

14 Then thine heart be lifted up, and thou forget the LORD thy God, which brought thee forth out of the land of Egypt, from the house of bondage;

8:15 Ex 17:6 Num 20:11; 21:6 Deut 1:19–21 32:13 Ps 78:15; 114:8

15 Who led thee through that great and terrible wilderness, *wherein were* fiery serpents, and scorpions, and drought, where *there was* no water; who brought thee forth water out of the rock of flint;

8:16 Ex 16:15 Deut 8:2 Jn 6:30, 31

16 Who fed thee in the wilderness with manna, which thy fathers knew not, that he might humble thee, and that he might prove thee, to do thee good at thy latter end;

8:17☆

17 And thou say in thine heart, My power and the might of *mine* hand hath gotten me this wealth.

8:18 Prov 10:22 Hos 2:8

18 But thou shalt remember the LORD thy God: for *it is* he that giveth thee power to get wealth, that he may establish his covenant which he sware unto thy fathers, as *it is* this day.

8:19 Deut 4:26; 30:18

19 And it shall be, if thou do at all forget the LORD thy God, and walk after other gods, and serve them, and worship them, I testify against you this day that ye shall surely perish.

8:20 Dan 9:11, 12

20 As the nations which the LORD destroyeth before your face, so shall ye perish; because ye would not be obedient unto the voice of the LORD your God.

3. God's Promise to Give Canaanland to Israel

9:1 Num 13:27–30 Deut 2:18; 12:10 Josh 1:10, 11:21

9 HEAR, O Israel: Thou *art* to pass over Jordan this day, to go in to possess nations greater and mightier than thyself, cities great and fenced up to heaven,

2 A people great and tall, the children of the Anakims, whom thou knowest, and *of whom* thou hast heard *say*, Who can stand before the children of Anak!

9:3 Deut 4:24 7:19, 20 Ps 78:52, 53 Heb 12:29

3 Understand therefore this day, that the LORD thy God *is* he which goeth over before thee; *as* a consuming fire he shall destroy them, and he shall bring them down before thy face: so shalt thou drive them out, and destroy them quickly, as the LORD hath said unto thee.

9:4☆ Lev 18:23–30 Deut 7:24 12:31; 18:9–14 31:27

4 Speak not thou in thine heart, after that the LORD thy God hath cast them out from before thee, saying, For my righteousness the LORD hath brought me in to possess this land: but for the wickedness of these nations the LORD doth drive them out from before thee.

5 Not for thy righteousness, or for the uprightness of thine heart, dost thou go to possess their land: but for the wickedness of these nations the LORD thy God doth drive them out from before thee, and that he may perform the word which the LORD sware unto thy fathers, Abraham, Isaac, and Jacob.

8:12ff Affluence is a powerful addiction which causes men to forget the God who gave them all they have. Poverty among believers is apt to cause them to concentrate on spiritual things and to look to God for the supply of material wants. Wealth, on the other hand, tends to lead to the opposite condition—producing pride and a sense of autonomy.

8:17 Moses warned Israel of the danger of supposing that they were self-sufficient. In 8:18 he enjoins the Israelites to remember that when they succeeded it was God "that giveth thee power to get wealth." The greatest danger of wealth arises when we begin to think we have made it on our own. This is the sin of the autonomous man. In 1 Kings 3:13, God tells Solomon that "I have also given thee . . . both riches, and honour: so that there shall not be any among the kings like unto thee all thy days."

9:4 Moses warned Israel against supposing that God would give them the land of Palestine because of their intrinsic righteousness. Moses feared they might think in their *hearts* that they were righteous. He knew that God would give the land to Israel out of his grace and because of "the wickedness of these nations the LORD doth drive them out before thee."

6Understand therefore, that the LORD thy God giveth thee not this good
land to possess it for thy righteousness; for thou *art* a stiffnecked people.

9:6 Deut 9:13, 14; 10:16; 31:27; Ps 78:17, 40

4. Israel's Idolatry: The Golden Calf

7¶Remember, *and* forget not, how thou provokedst the LORD thy God to
wrath in the wilderness: from the day that thou didst depart out of the land
of Egypt, until ye came unto this place, ye have been rebellious against the
LORD.

9:7 Ex 14:11; Num 11:4, 5; 14:20–22; Deut 8:2; 31:27; 32:5, 6

8Also in Ho'reb ye provoked the LORD to wrath, so that the LORD was
angry with you to have destroyed you.

9:8 Ex 32:7; Ps 106:19, 20

9When I was gone up into the mount to receive the tables of stone, *even*
the tables of the covenant which the LORD made with you, then I abode in
the mount forty days and forty nights, I neither did eat bread nor drink
water.

9:9 Ex 24:18; Deut 9:18

10And the LORD delivered unto me two tables of stone written with the
finger of God; and on them *was written* according to all the words, which
the LORD spake with you in the mount out of the midst of the fire in the day
of the assembly.
11And it came to pass at the end of forty days and forty nights, *that* the
LORD gave me the two tables of stone, *even* the tables of the covenant.
12And the LORD said unto me, Arise, get thee down quickly from hence;
for thy people which thou hast brought forth out of Egypt have corrupted
themselves; they are quickly turned aside out of the way which I com-
manded them; they have made them a molten image.

☆**9:12** Ex 32:7, 8

13Furthermore the LORD spake unto me, saying, I have seen this people,
and, behold, it *is* a stiffnecked people:

9:13 Ex 32:10

14Let me alone, that I may destroy them, and blot out their name from
under heaven: and I will make of thee a nation mightier and greater than
they.
15So I turned and came down from the mount, and the mount burned
with fire: and the two tables of the covenant *were* in my two hands.

9:15 Ex 32:15

16And I looked, and, behold, ye had sinned against the LORD your God,
and had made you a molten calf: ye had turned aside quickly out of the way
which the LORD had commanded you.

9:16 Ex 32:19; Acts 7:40, 41

17And I took the two tables, and cast them out of my two hands, and
brake them before your eyes.

9:17 Ex 32:19

18And I fell down before the LORD, as at the first, forty days and forty
nights: I did neither eat bread, nor drink water, because of all your sins
which ye sinned, in doing wickedly in the sight of the LORD, to provoke him
to anger.

☆**9:18** Ex 34:8, 9, 28; Deut 9:9; 10:10

19For I was afraid of the anger and hot displeasure, wherewith the LORD
was wroth against you to destroy you. But the LORD hearkened unto me at
that time also.

9:19 Ex 32:10, 11; Heb 12:21

20And the LORD was very angry with Aaron to have destroyed him: and
I prayed for Aaron also the same time.

9:20 Ex 32:2, 3, 21

9:12 See note to Exod. 32:4 on the golden calf incident.

9:18 God was angry with Israel and with Aaron for making and worshipping the golden calf, and for committing harlotry, like the heathen around them. Moses prayed for Israel and Aaron that the wrath of God might be stayed. He was in prayer for forty days and nights (see also 9:25). Moses was diligent and importunate. He refused to let go. Had he faltered and stopped praying before God relented, Israel would have been destroyed. This incident illustrates the fact that God's anger has waxed hot against sinful mankind and the judgment has been averted in that "no less a person than his Son, and no less a price than his own blood, would serve to turn it away."*

9:21 21 And I took your sin, the calf which ye had made, and burnt it with fire,
Ex 32:20 and stamped it, *and* ground *it* very small, *even* until it was as small as dust:
and I cast the dust thereof into the brook that descended out of the mount.

5. Israel's Other Transgressions

9:22 22 And at Tab'e-rah, and at Mas'sah, and at Kib'roth-hat-ta'a-vah, ye
Ex 17:7; Num 11:3, 34 provoked the LORD to wrath.
23 Likewise when the LORD sent you from Ka'desh-bar'ne-a, saying, Go
up and possess the land which I have given you; then ye rebelled against
the commandment of the LORD your God, and ye believed him not, nor
hearkened to his voice.
9:24 24 Ye have been rebellious against the LORD from the day that I knew
Ex 32:9; Deut 9:7; 31:27 you.
9:25☆ 25 Thus I fell down before the LORD forty days and forty nights, as I fell
Ex 34:8; Deut 9:18 down *at the first*; because the LORD had said he would destroy you.

6. Moses' Prayers for Israel's Forgiveness

9:26☆ 26 I prayed therefore unto the LORD, and said, O Lord GOD, destroy not
Ex 32:11–13; 34:9 thy people and thine inheritance, which thou hast redeemed through thy
Num 14:13 greatness, which thou hast brought forth out of Egypt with a mighty hand.
9:27 27 Remember thy servants, Abraham, Isaac, and Jacob; look not unto the
Ex 32:31; Ps 78:7, 8 stubbornness of this people, nor to their wickedness, nor to their sin:
28 Lest the land whence thou broughtest us out say, Because the LORD
was not able to bring them into the land which he promised them, and
because he hated them, he hath brought them out to slay them in the
wilderness.
9:29 29 Yet they *are* thy people and thine inheritance, which thou broughtest
Deut 4:34 out by thy mighty power and by thy stretched out arm.

7. The Second Set of the Two Tablets of the Law

10:1 10 AT that time the LORD said unto me, Hew thee two tables of stone
Ex 25:10; 34:1 like unto the first, and come up unto me into the mount, and make
thee an ark of wood.
10:2 2 And I will write on the tables the words that were in the first tables
Ex 25:16; Deut 4:13 which thou brakest, and thou shalt put them in the ark.
Heb 9:4 3 And I made an ark *of* shittim wood, and hewed two tables of stone like
10:3 Ex 34:4; 37:1 unto the first, and went up into the mount, having the two tables in mine
hand.
10:4 4 And he wrote on the tables, according to the first writing, the ten
Ex 34:28 commandments, which the LORD spake unto you in the mount out of the
Deut 4:13 midst of the fire in the day of the assembly: and the LORD gave them unto
me.
10:5 5 And I turned myself and came down from the mount, and put the tables
Ex 40:20 in the ark which I had made; and there they be, as the LORD commanded
me.

9:25, 26 In verse 18 and here again Moses reminds Israel that he spent forty days and forty nights alone with God after they had made the golden calf. In 12:25–26 he plainly states that God intended to destroy the people; but because of Moses' prayer, God refrained from slaying them. This teaches us the lesson of perseverance in prayer. (Suppose Moses had ceased praying the first day, before his prayer was answered?) He wrestled with God until God answered in the affirmative and Israel was saved from destruction.

10:4 Moses did not etch the ten commandments on the tables of stone; God wrote them. This supernatural act makes it clear that the commandments came directly from God and were not mediated through the writing of Moses.

6 ¶And the children of Israel took their journey from Be-e'roth of the
children of Ja'a-kan to Mo-se'ra: there Aaron died, and there he was
buried; and E-le-a'zar his son ministered in the priest's office in his stead.
7 From thence they journeyed unto Gud'go-dah; and from Gud'go-dah to
Jot'bath, a land of rivers of waters.
8 ¶At that time the LORD separated the tribe of Levi, to bear the ark of the
covenant of the LORD, to stand before the LORD to minister unto him, and
to bless in his name, unto this day.
9 Wherefore Levi hath no part nor inheritance with his brethren; the
LORD *is* his inheritance, according as the LORD thy God promised him.
10 And I stayed in the mount, according to the first time, forty days and
forty nights; and the LORD hearkened unto me at that time also, *and* the
LORD would not destroy thee.
11 And the LORD said unto me, Arise, take *thy* journey before the people,
that they may go in and possess the land, which I sware unto their fathers
to give unto them.

10:6 Num 20:25, 26; 33:15–38
10:8 Num 3:6; 18:1; Deut 18:5; 21:5; 31:9
10:9 Num 18:20, 24; 26:62; Deut 18:2; Josh 14:3, 4; Ezek 44:28
10:10 Deut 9:18
10:11 Ex 32:34; 33:1

8. God's Requirement: Obey the Commandments

12 ¶And now, Israel, what doth the LORD thy God require of thee, but to
fear the LORD thy God, to walk in all his ways, and to love him, and to
serve the LORD thy God with all thy heart and with all thy soul,
13 To keep the commandments of the LORD, and his statutes, which I
command thee this day for thy good?
14 Behold, the heaven and the heaven of heavens *is* the LORD'S thy God,
the earth *also*, with all that therein *is*.
15 Only the LORD had a delight in thy fathers to love them, and he chose
their seed after them, *even* you above all people, as *it is* this day.
16 Circumcise therefore the foreskin of your heart, and be no more
stiffnecked.
17 For the LORD your God *is* God of gods, and Lord of lords, a great God,
a mighty, and a terrible, which regardeth not persons, nor taketh reward:
18 He doth execute the judgment of the fatherless and widow, and loveth
the stranger, in giving him food and raiment.
19 Love ye therefore the stranger: for ye were strangers in the land of
Egypt.
20 Thou shalt fear the LORD thy God; him shalt thou serve, and to him
shalt thou cleave, and swear by his name.
21 He *is* thy praise, and he *is* thy God, that hath done for thee these great
and terrible things, which thine eyes have seen.
22 Thy fathers went down into Egypt with threescore and ten persons; and
now the LORD thy God hath made thee as the stars of heaven for multitude.

10:12 Deut 6:5; Jer 7:22, 23; Mic 6:8
10:14 1 Kgs 8:27; Neh 9:6; Ps 68:33; 115:16
10:15 Deut 4:37; 7:7; 9:6
☆**10:16** Lev 26:41, 42; Deut 30:6; Jer 4:4; Rom 2:29
☆**10:17** Deut 1:17, 16:19; Ps 136:2
10:18 Ex 22:22; Deut 27:19; Ps 68:5; 103:6; Isa 1:17
10:19 Ex 22:21; Lev 19:34; Ezek 47:22
10:20 Deut 5:11; 6:13; 11:22; 13:4
10:21 Ex 15:2; Ps 109:1; Isa 12:2, 6
☆**10:22** Gen 46:27; Deut 1:10; Acts 7:14

10:16 *Circumcise therefore the foreskin of your heart,* i.e., "cast away from you all corrupt affections and inclinations, which hinder you from fearing and loving God. . . . Rest not in the circumcision of the body, which was only the sign, but be circumcised in the heart, which is the thing signified."* (See Romans 2:29).

10:17 *God of gods, and Lord of lords.* The supremacy, greatness, and uniqueness of God are here pronounced. In Revelation 19:16 Jesus is called "KING OF KINGS AND LORD OF LORDS." Thus the divine titles used for God in the Old Testament are applied to Jesus in the New. Jesus is God, as well as man.

10:22 See the note on Gen. 46:27 concerning the so-called discrepancy between the number given in the Old Testament (10:22; Gen. 46:27) and the number quoted in Acts 7:14. A fuller explanation can be found in the *Encyclopedia of Bible Difficulties* by Gleason L. Archer (Zondervan, 1982).

9. Moses' Concluding Admonitions

a. Love the Lord God

11:1☆ Lev 18:29, 30; Deut 6:5, 6; 10:12, 13; 11:8, 31; 28:1
11:2 Deut 5:2, 3; 7:19; 8:3

11 THEREFORE thou shalt love the LORD thy God, and keep his
charge, and his statutes, and his judgments, and his command-
ments, alway.
2 And know ye this day: for *I speak* not with your children which have
not known, and which have not seen the chastisement of the LORD your
God, his greatness, his mighty hand, and his stretched out arm,
3 And his miracles, and his acts, which he did in the midst of Egypt unto
Pharaoh the king of Egypt, and unto all his land;

11:4 Ex 14:28; 15:4; Deut 1:40; Ps 106:6–11
11:5 Ps 77:19, 20; 78:11, 12
11:6 Num 16:31; 26:5–11; Ps 106:17

4 And what he did unto the army of Egypt, unto their horses, and to their
chariots; how he made the water of the Red sea to overflow them as they
pursued after you, and *how* the LORD hath destroyed them unto this day;
5 And what he did unto you in the wilderness, until ye came into this
place;
6 And what he did unto Da'than and A-bi'ram, the sons of E-li'ab, the son
of Reuben: how the earth opened her mouth, and swallowed them up, and
their households, and their tents, and all the substance that *was* in their
possession, in the midst of all Israel:
7 But your eyes have seen all the great acts of the LORD which he did.

b. Obey the Commandments

11:8 Deut 26:17; 31:6, 7, 23; Josh 1:6, 7
11:9 Deut 4:40; 5:33; 6:2; Ps 34:12; Prov 3:1, 2
11:10☆
11:11 Deut 8:7–9; Ps 104:10–13; Jer 2:7

8 Therefore shall ye keep all the commandments which I command you
this day, that ye may be strong, and go in and possess the land, whither ye
go to possess it;
9 And that ye may prolong *your* days in the land, which the LORD sware
unto your fathers to give unto them and to their seed, a land that floweth
with milk and honey.
10 ¶For the land, whither thou goest in to possess it, *is* not as the land of
Egypt, from whence ye came out, where thou sowedst thy seed, and
wateredst *it* with thy foot, as a garden of herbs:
11 But the land, whither ye go to possess it, *is* a land of hills and valleys,
and drinketh water of the rain of heaven:
12 A land which the LORD thy God careth for: the eyes of the LORD thy
God *are* always upon it, from the beginning of the year even unto the end
of the year.

c. Obedience Brings Blessing; Disobedience Brings Judgment

11:13 Deut 4:29; 6:5; 8:6
11:14 Lev 26:4, 5; Deut 28:12
11:15 Deut 6:10–12; 8:10; Joel 2:19

13 ¶And it shall come to pass, if ye shall hearken diligently unto my
commandments which I command you this day, to love the LORD your
God, and to serve him with all your heart and with all your soul,
14 That I will give *you* the rain of your land in his due season, the first rain
and the latter rain, that thou mayest gather in thy corn, and thy wine, and
thine oil.
15 And I will send grass in thy fields for thy cattle, that thou mayest eat
and be full.

11:1 *thou shalt love the LORD . . . and keep his charge.* The work of love is always obedience and obedience itself is acceptable to God only when it flows from a principle of love. (See 1 John 5:3.)

11:10 Here Canaan is compared with Egypt. Egypt lacked rain; its productive capacity depended on the overflow of the Nile River, which received its water from the lake region south of it. Canaan, on the other hand, "drinketh water of the rain of heaven" (11:11). It was ideally situated so that its fertility and productive capacity would be enhanced by rain. Then, as now, rain was under the sovereignty of God, who promised Israel an abundant supply of water from heaven. This was a conditional promise based on Israel's obedience. God attached the threat that disobedience would close the heavens and cut off the water (11:17).

16 Take heed to yourselves, that your heart be not deceived, and ye turn
aside, and serve other gods, and worship them;
17 And *then* the LORD's wrath be kindled against you, and he shut up the
heaven, that there be no rain, and that the land yield not her fruit; and *lest*
ye perish quickly from off the good land which the LORD giveth you.

11:16 Deut 8:19; 30:17
11:17 Deut 4:26; 28:24 Josh 23:13

d. Teach Your Children God's Laws; Lay Them Up in Your Heart

18 ¶Therefore shall ye lay up these my words in your heart and in your
soul, and bind them for a sign upon your hand, that they may be as
frontlets between your eyes.
19 And ye shall teach them your children, speaking of them when thou
sittest in thine house, and when thou walkest by the way, when thou liest
down, and when thou risest up.
20 And thou shalt write them upon the door posts of thine house, and
upon thy gates:
21 That your days may be multiplied, and the days of your children, in the
land which the LORD sware unto your fathers to give them, as the days of
heaven upon the earth.
22 ¶For if ye shall diligently keep all these commandments which I
command you, to do them, to love the LORD your God, to walk in all his
ways, and to cleave unto him;
23 Then will the LORD drive out all these nations from before you, and ye
shall possess greater nations and mightier than yourselves.
24 Every place whereon the soles of your feet shall tread shall be yours:
from the wilderness and Lebanon, from the river, the river Eu-phra′tes,
even unto the uttermost sea shall your coast be.
25 There shall no man be able to stand before you: *for* the LORD your God
shall lay the fear of you and the dread of you upon all the land that ye shall
tread upon, as he hath said unto you.

☆**11:18** Ex 13:16 Ps 119:11
11:19 Deut 4:9; 6:7 Ps 78:5, 6
11:22 Deut 6:17 10:20; 11:1
11:23 Deut 4:38; 7:1
☆**11:24** Gen 15:8 Ex 23:31 Deut 1:7, 8 Josh 1:3
11:25 Ex 23:27 Deut 7:24

e. Israel's Choice: Blessing or Cursing

26 ¶Behold, I set before you this day a blessing and a curse;
27 A blessing, if ye obey the commandments of the LORD your God, which
I command you this day:
28 And a curse, if ye will not obey the commandments of the LORD your
God, but turn aside out of the way which I command you this day, to go
after other gods, which ye have not known.
29 And it shall come to pass, when the LORD thy God hath brought thee in
unto the land whither thou goest to possess it, that thou shalt put the
blessing upon mount Ger′i-zim, and the curse upon mount Ebal.

☆**11:26** Deut 30:1, 15–20
11:29 Deut 27:12–26 Josh 8:30–35

11:18 *frontlets.* This word appears only three times in the Old Testament (here, 6:8, and Exod. 13:16). It is a metaphor which stresses the importance of the law in the lives of the Israelites. Jews later took the injunction quite literally. They wrote four passages of the law on small pieces of parchment, placed them in tiny boxes, then bound them on their arms and brows for use during morning prayers. Called *tephillin,* they were honored as highly as the Scriptures. Many believe the phylacteries of the Pharisees were the frontlets of which the Scriptures speak here.

11:24 Never in the history of Israel has this divine promise been literally fulfilled. We can expect this to take place before the consummation of history and the end of the age. None of the promises of God will fall short of literal fulfillment, however impossible they may appear to be.

11:26 Moses here presents two opposing options to Israel, which can be summed up in two words: blessing and cursing. Depending on which the Israelites chose, there would be rewards or punishments. Mount Gerizim would be the site of blessing and Mount Ebal of cursing. Doing the commandments of God would bring the blessing. Punishment would result from one of two sins: the sin of disobedience (by which the commandments are broken) and the sin of omission (by which the things Israel are supposed to do are simply not done).

11:30 Gen 12:6; Josh 4:19; 24:26
11:31 Deut 9:1; Josh 1:10, 11
11:32 Deut 11:1; 12:32

30 *Are* they not on the other side Jordan, by the way where the sun goeth
down, in the land of the Canaanites, which dwell in the champaign over
against Gilgal, beside the plains of Mo'reh?
31 For ye shall pass over Jordan to go in to possess the land which the
LORD your God giveth you, and ye shall possess it, and dwell therein.
32 And ye shall observe to do all the statutes and judgments which I set
before you this day.

E. MOSES' DISCUSSION OF GOD'S REGULATIONS AND COMMANDMENTS

1. The Canaan Altar; God Will Choose the Place

12:1 Deut 4:1; 6:1
12:2 Ex 34:13; Lev 26:30; Num 33:52; Deut 7:5; Judg 2:2
12:3☆
12:4, 5☆ Ex 20:24; Deut 26:2; Josh 9:27; 18:1; 2 Kgs 16:4; 17:10, 11; Jer 3:6; Jn 4:19, 20
12:6 Lev 17:3, 4; Deut 14:22; 26:2, 3
12:7 Deut 12:12, 18; 14:26; 15:20

12 THESE *are* the statutes and judgments, which ye shall observe to
do in the land, which the LORD God of thy fathers giveth thee to
possess it, all the days that ye live upon the earth.
2 Ye shall utterly destroy all the places, wherein the nations which ye shall
possess served their gods, upon the high mountains, and upon the hills, and
under every green tree:
3 And ye shall overthrow their altars, and break their pillars, and burn
their groves with fire; and ye shall hew down the graven images of their
gods, and destroy the names of them out of that place.
4 Ye shall not do so unto the LORD your God.
5 But unto the place which the LORD your God shall choose out of all
your tribes to put his name there, *even* unto his habitation shall ye seek, and
thither thou shalt come:
6 And thither ye shall bring your burnt offerings, and your sacrifices, and
your tithes, and heave offerings of your hand, and your vows, and your
freewill offerings, and the firstlings of your herds and of your flocks:
7 And there ye shall eat before the LORD your God, and ye shall rejoice in
all that ye put your hand unto, ye and your households, wherein the LORD
thy God hath blessed thee.

12:8 Judg 17:6
12:10 Josh 3:17; 11:23
12:11 Eph 2:21, 22; 1 Pet 2:5
12:12 Deut 10:9; 12:7, 18, 19; 26:11
12:13 Deut 12:4, 5

8 Ye shall not do after all *the things* that we do here this day, every man
whatsoever *is* right in his own eyes.
9 For ye are not as yet come to the rest and to the inheritance, which the
LORD your God giveth you.
10 But *when* ye go over Jordan, and dwell in the land which the LORD your
God giveth you to inherit, and *when* he giveth you rest from all your
enemies round about, so that ye dwell in safety;
11 Then there shall be a place which the LORD your God shall choose to
cause his name to dwell there; thither shall ye bring all that I command
you; your burnt offerings, and your sacrifices, your tithes, and the heave
offering of your hand, and all your choice vows which ye vow unto the
LORD:
12 And ye shall rejoice before the LORD your God, ye, and your sons, and
your daughters, and your menservants, and your maidservants, and the
Levite that *is* within your gates; forasmuch as he hath no part nor
inheritance with you.
13 Take heed to thyself that thou offer not thy burnt offerings in every
place that thou seest:

12:3 *pillars* (obelisks), large standing stones thought to have been symbols of Baal, the Canaanite's fertility god. *the graven images* "asherim". See note on Exod. 34:13.

12:5 *the place.* Paraphrased: "at a place (God) will select as his home."† Having one central sanctuary would help to avoid idolatry. David moved the sanctuary from Shiloh to Jerusalem, which subsequently became the center for the worship of God.

14 But in the place which the LORD shall choose in one of thy tribes, there
thou shalt offer thy burnt offerings, and there thou shalt do all that I
command thee.
15 Notwithstanding thou mayest kill and eat flesh in all thy gates,
whatsoever thy soul lusteth after, according to the blessing of the LORD thy
God which he hath given thee: the unclean and the clean may eat thereof,
as of the roebuck, and as of the hart.

12:15 Deut 12:20–23 14:3–5

16 Only ye shall not eat the blood; ye shall pour it upon the earth as water.

12:16 Lev 17:10–12 Deut 15:23

17 ¶Thou mayest not eat within thy gates the tithe of thy corn, or of thy
wine, or of thy oil, or the firstlings of thy herds or of thy flock, nor any of
thy vows which thou vowest, nor thy freewill offerings, or heave offering of
thine hand:

12:17 Deut 12:26 14:22; 26:12

18 But thou must eat them before the LORD thy God in the place which
the LORD thy God shall choose, thou, and thy son, and thy daughter, and
thy manservant, and thy maidservant, and the Levite that *is* within thy
gates: and thou shalt rejoice before the LORD thy God in all that thou
puttest thine hands unto.

12:18 Deut 12:4, 5, 26

19 Take heed to thyself that thou forsake not the Levite as long as thou
livest upon the earth.
20 ¶When the LORD thy God shall enlarge thy border, as he hath promised
thee, and thou shalt say, I will eat flesh, because thy soul longeth to eat
flesh; thou mayest eat flesh, whatsoever thy soul lusteth after.

☆**12:20** Lev 11:2, 3 Deut 12:16 15:23; 18:3–5

21 If the place which the LORD thy God hath chosen to put his name there
be too far from thee, then thou shalt kill of thy herd and of thy flock, which
the LORD hath given thee, as I have commanded thee, and thou shalt eat in
thy gates whatsoever thy soul lusteth after.
22 Even as the roebuck and the hart is eaten, so thou shalt eat them: the
unclean and the clean shall eat *of* them alike.
23 Only be sure that thou eat not the blood: for the blood *is* the life; and
thou mayest not eat the life with the flesh.
24 Thou shalt not eat it; thou shalt pour it upon the earth as water.
25 Thou shalt not eat it; that it may go well with thee, and with thy
children after thee, when thou shalt do *that which is* right in the sight of the
LORD.

12:24 Deut 4:40

26 Only thy holy things which thou hast, and thy vows, thou shalt take,
and go unto the place which the LORD shall choose:

12:26 Lev 3:1 Deut 12:20

27 And thou shalt offer thy burnt offerings, the flesh and the blood, upon
the altar of the LORD thy God: and the blood of thy sacrifices shall be
poured out upon the altar of the LORD thy God, and thou shalt eat the
flesh.
28 Observe and hear all these words which I command thee, that it may go
well with thee, and with thy children after thee for ever, when thou doest
that which is good and right in the sight of the LORD thy God.

12:28 Deut 4:40

29 ¶When the LORD thy God shall cut off the nations from before thee,
whither thou goest to possess them, and thou succeedest them, and dwellest
in their land;
30 Take heed to thyself that thou be not snared by following them, after
that they be destroyed from before thee; and that thou inquire not after
their gods, saying, How did these nations serve their gods? even so will I do
likewise.

12:30 Rom 16:19

12:20 In the wilderness Israel ate manna. In Canaan they would have all the meat to eat that they desired. The priests were commanded to eat meat. The people generally were free to eat meat or to abstain. Vegetarianism is a choice, not a commandment. Since God allowed for the use of meat, it is difficult to imagine that he would allow that which is dietetically wrong or inexpedient.

12:31☆ Lev 18:21; Deut 9:5; 18:10; Ps 106:37, 38

31 Thou shalt not do so unto the LORD thy God: for every abomination to the LORD, which he hateth, have they done unto their gods; for even their sons and their daughters they have burnt in the fire to their gods.

12:32 Deut 4:2

32 What thing soever I command you, observe to do it: thou shalt not add thereto, nor diminish from it.

2. No Other Gods

a. False Prophets Must Be Executed

13:1, 2☆ Num 12:6; Deut 18:20–22; Mt 24:24; Mk 13:22; 2 Thess 2:9

13 IF there arise among you a prophet, or a dreamer of dreams, and giveth thee a sign or a wonder,

2 And the sign or the wonder come to pass, whereof he spake unto thee, saying, Let us go after other gods, which thou hast not known, and let us serve them;

13:3 Deut 6:5; 8:2, 16; Ps 81:7

3 Thou shalt not hearken unto the words of that prophet, or that dreamer of dreams: for the LORD your God proveth you, to know whether ye love the LORD your God with all your heart and with all your soul.

13:4☆ Deut 10:20; Jer 7:23

4 Ye shall walk after the LORD your God, and fear him, and keep his commandments, and obey his voice, and ye shall serve him, and cleave unto him.

13:5 Deut 7:4; 13:9; 17:5; 22:21; Jer 14:15; Zech 13:3

5 And that prophet, or that dreamer of dreams, shall be put to death; because he hath spoken to turn *you* away from the LORD your God, which brought you out of the land of Egypt, and redeemed you out of the house of bondage, to thrust thee out of the way which the LORD thy God commanded thee to walk in. So shalt thou put the evil away from the midst of thee.

b. Idolaters Must Be Stoned

13:6☆ Deut 13:2; 17:2–7; 29:18; Mic 7:5

6 If thy brother, the son of thy mother, or thy son, or thy daughter, or the wife of thy bosom, or thy friend, which *is* as thine own soul, entice thee secretly, saying, Let us go and serve other gods, which thou hast not known, thou, nor thy fathers;

7 *Namely*, of the gods of the people which *are* round about you, nigh unto thee, or far off from thee, from the *one* end of the earth even unto the *other* end of the earth;

13:8☆ Deut 7:2; Ezek 9:5

8 Thou shalt not consent unto him, nor hearken unto him; neither shall thine eye pity him, neither shalt thou spare, neither shalt thou conceal him:

13:9☆ Lev 24:13, 14; Deut 13:5; 17:7

9 But thou shalt surely kill him; thine hand shall be first upon him to put him to death, and afterwards the hand of all the people.

12:31 The heathen had sunk so low and their views of the gods they worshipped were so depraved that they burned their children as sacrifices to their deities. The custom was barbarous and inhuman, violating the law of nature, and was a prostitution of every natural affection.

13:1 *giveth thee a sign or a wonder.* Whoever would cause a follower of God to go after strange gods is to be resisted and his counsel spurned. This is true even if that false prophet performs signs and wonders. The divine law against the worship of other gods is perpetual and unalterable. Paul expresses this same principle about the gospel: if even an angel from heaven were to give forth another gospel, it would be wrong and should be resisted (Gal. 1:8).

13:4 The acid test of one's faith lies in his obedience to God's commands. Obedience should come from the heart (Rom. 6:17); (2) it must be done willingly (Isa. 1:19; Josh. 22:2, 3); and (3) it must be done at all times (Phil 2:12). Believers are to be obedient to: (1) the law of God (11:27; Isa. 42:24); (2) the voice of God (Exod. 19:5; Jer. 7:23); (3) Christ (2 Cor. 10:5); (4) the gospel (Rom. 1:5; 6:17); and (5) governing authorities (Rom 13:1). The Bible contains many illustrations of faithful people who obeyed God immediately and without question. God promises blessings to those who obey and punishments for those who disobey.

13:6–9 Satan is quite likely to send us wrong signals by the mouths of those we love the most in this life. Satan tempted Adam by his wife, Eve. Christ was tempted by his dear friend Peter. No matter how much we love anyone, if that person tries to seduce us on behalf of anything or anyone other than the true God, he or she is to be resisted even if it means martyrdom for the resister.

[10]And thou shalt stone him with stones, that he die; because he hath
sought to thrust thee away from the LORD thy God, which brought thee out
of the land of Egypt, from the house of bondage.
[11]And all Israel shall hear, and fear, and shall do no more any such
wickedness as this is among you.

13:10 Lev 24:15 Num 15:35 Josh 7:25
13:11 Deut 17:13 19:20

c. Idolatrous Cities Must Be Destroyed

[12]If thou shalt hear *say* in one of thy cities, which the LORD thy God hath
given thee to dwell there, saying,
[13]*Certain* men, the children of Be'li-al, are gone out from among you, and
have withdrawn the inhabitants of their city, saying, Let us go and serve
other gods, which ye have not known;
[14]Then shalt thou inquire, and make search, and ask diligently, and,
behold, *if it be* truth, *and* the thing certain, *that* such abomination is
wrought among you;
[15]Thou shalt surely smite the inhabitants of that city with the edge of the
sword, destroying it utterly, and all that *is* therein, and the cattle thereof,
with the edge of the sword.
[16]And thou shalt gather all the spoil of it into the midst of the street
thereof, and shalt burn with fire the city, and all the spoil thereof every
whit, for the LORD thy God: and it shall be an heap for ever; it shall not be
built again.
[17]And there shall cleave nought of the cursed thing to thine hand: that
the LORD may turn from the fierceness of his anger, and shew thee mercy,
and have compassion upon thee, and multiply thee, as he hath sworn unto
thy fathers;
[18]When thou shalt hearken to the voice of the LORD thy God, to keep all
his commandments which I command thee this day, to do *that which is* right
in the eyes of the LORD thy God.

13:12 Deut 13:2 Josh 22:11
☆13:15
13:16 Num 21:2 Deut 7:25, 26 Josh 6:24
13:17 Ex 32:12 Num 25:4 Deut 7:13; 30:3
13:18 Deut 12:28 Mt 6:33, 34

3. Clean and Unclean Animals, Birds, and Fishlife

14 YE *are* the children of the LORD your God: ye shall not cut
yourselves, nor make any baldness between your eyes for the dead.
[2]For thou *art* an holy people unto the LORD thy God, and the LORD hath
chosen thee to be a peculiar people unto himself, above all the nations that
are upon the earth.
[3]¶Thou shalt not eat any abominable thing.
[4]These *are* the beasts which ye shall eat: the ox, the sheep, and the goat,
[5]The hart, and the roebuck, and the fallow deer, and the wild goat, and
the pygarg, and the wild ox, and the chamois.
[6]And every beast that parteth the hoof, and cleaveth the cleft into two
claws, *and* cheweth the cud among the beasts, that ye shall eat.
[7]Nevertheless these ye shall not eat of them that chew the cud, or of them
that divide the cloven hoof; *as* the camel, and the hare, and the coney: for
they chew the cud, but divide not the hoof; *therefore* they *are* unclean unto
you.

☆14:1 Lev 19:27, 28 21:5 Jer 16:6
14:2 Ex 19:5 Deut 7:6; 26:18
14:3 Lev 11:2–43 Ezek 4:14 Acts 10:12–14

13:15 Israel is ordered to slay not only the inhabitants of the idolatrous cities of Canaan, but also the animals which have been contaminated by the pagans. So holy is our God that what may not be unclean in itself may be considered by him to be unclean because of its association with his enemy.

14:1, 2 Three important truths are enunciated here. First, the Israelites are the sons of God. They belong to God by adoption, having been redeemed by blood. Thus they are God's children. Second, they have been chosen by God—they are the elect of God, known from eternity. Third, they have been sanctified by God, for they are a holy people. As a people set apart, the Israelites are devoted to the service of God, they are governed by the law of God, and they exist for the praise of his grace.

8 And the swine, because it divideth the hoof, yet cheweth not the cud, it
is unclean unto you: ye shall not eat of their flesh, nor touch their dead
carcase.
9 ¶These ye shall eat of all that *are* in the waters: all that have fins and
scales shall ye eat:
10 And whatsoever hath not fins and scales ye may not eat; it *is* unclean
unto you.
11 ¶*Of* all clean birds ye shall eat.
12 But these *are they* of which ye shall not eat: the eagle, and the ossifrage,
and the ospray,
13 And the glede, and the kite, and the vulture after his kind,
14 And every raven after his kind,
15 And the owl, and the night hawk, and the cuckow, and the hawk after
his kind,
16 The little owl, and the great owl, and the swan,
17 And the pelican, and the gier eagle, and the cormorant,
18 And the stork, and the heron after her kind, and the lapwing, and the
bat.
19 And every creeping thing that flieth *is* unclean unto you: they shall not
be eaten.
20 *But of* all clean fowls ye may eat.
14:21 21 ¶Ye shall not eat *of* any thing that dieth of itself: thou shalt give it unto
Ex 23:19; 34:26 Lev 17:15; 22:8 the stranger that *is* in thy gates, that he may eat it; or thou mayest sell it
Deut 14:2 Ezek 4:14 unto an alien: for thou *art* an holy people unto the LORD thy God. Thou
shalt not seethe a kid in his mother's milk.

4. Tithe of the Produce

14:22–27 **14:22** 22 Thou shalt truly tithe all the increase of thy seed, that the field bringeth
Deut 12:6, 17 forth year by year.
26:12 **14:23☆** 23 And thou shalt eat before the LORD thy God, in the place which he
Deut 4:10; 12:4 shall choose to place his name there, the tithe of thy corn, of thy wine, and
of thine oil, and the firstlings of thy herds and of thy flocks; that thou
mayest learn to fear the LORD thy God always.
14:24☆ 24 And if the way be too long for thee, so that thou art not able to carry it;
Deut 12:20 *or* if the place be too far from thee, which the LORD thy God shall choose
to set his name there, when the LORD thy God hath blessed thee:
25 Then shalt thou turn *it* into money, and bind up the money in thine
hand, and shalt go unto the place which the LORD thy God shall choose:
14:26☆ 26 And thou shalt bestow that money for whatsoever thy soul lusteth after,
Deut 12:18 for oxen, or for sheep, or for wine, or for strong drink, or for whatsoever thy
soul desireth: and thou shalt eat there before the LORD thy God, and thou
shalt rejoice, thou, and thine household,
14:27☆ 27 And the Levite that *is* within thy gates; thou shalt not forsake him; for
Num 18:20 he hath no part nor inheritance with thee.
Deut 10:9; 12:12 **14:28☆** 28 ¶At the end of three years thou shalt bring forth all the tithe of thine
Deut 26:12 increase the same year, and shalt lay *it* up within thy gates:

14:22–27 The law of the tithe here differs somewhat from that described in Num. 18:21–24. This law apparently superseded the earlier one.
14:26 *wine yayin* in Hebrew, fermented juice. *strong drink, shakar* in Hebrew, beer. There were no distilled liquors in Israel. *Shakar* comes from the verb meaning "to be drunk." Scriptural warnings against drunkenness indicate that whatever they drank contained enough alcohol to make men drunk.
14:28, 29 Every third year the tithe was allocated for the relief of the poor. God has a particular concern for widows and the fatherless. We must have a similar concern. We honor God when we help the helpless and we honor ourselves when we obey God's command. "It is an undoubted truth, though little believed, that to be charitable to the poor, and to be free and generous in the support of religion and any good work, is the surest way of thriving. What is lent to the Lord will be repaid with abundant interest."*

29 And the Levite, (because he hath no part nor inheritance with thee,)
and the stranger, and the fatherless, and the widow, which *are* within thy
gates, shall come, and shall eat and be satisfied; that the LORD thy God
may bless thee in all the work of thine hand which thou doest.

☆14:29 Deut 16:11, 14; 24:19

5. Slaves and the Poverty Stricken

a. The Seventh Year Release

15 AT the end of *every* seven years thou shalt make a release.
2 And this *is* the manner of the release: Every creditor that
lendeth *ought* unto his neighbour shall release *it;* he shall not exact *it* of his
neighbour, or of his brother; because it is called the LORD's release.
3 Of a foreigner thou mayest exact *it again:* but *that* which is thine with
thy brother thine hand shall release;
4 Save when there shall be no poor among you; for the LORD shall greatly
bless thee in the land which the LORD thy God giveth thee *for* an
inheritance to possess it:
5 Only if thou carefully hearken unto the voice of the LORD thy God, to
observe to do all these commandments which I command thee this day.
6 For the LORD thy God blesseth thee, as he promised thee: and thou
shalt lend unto many nations, but thou shalt not borrow; and thou shalt
reign over many nations, but they shall not reign over thee.
7 If there be among you a poor man of one of thy brethren within any of
thy gates in thy land which the LORD thy God giveth thee, thou shalt not
harden thine heart, nor shut thine hand from thy poor brother:
8 But thou shalt open thine hand wide unto him, and shalt surely lend him
sufficient for his need, *in that* which he wanteth.
9 Beware that there be not a thought in thy wicked heart, saying, The
seventh year, the year of release, is at hand; and thine eye be evil against
thy poor brother, and thou givest him nought; and he cry unto the LORD
against thee, and it be sin unto thee.
10 Thou shalt surely give him, and thine heart shall not be grieved when
thou givest unto him: because that for this thing the LORD thy God shall
bless thee in all thy works, and in all that thou puttest thine hand unto.
11 For the poor shall never cease out of the land: therefore I command
thee, saying, Thou shalt open thine hand wide unto thy brother, to thy
poor, and to thy needy, in thy land.

15:1 Deut 31:10, 11
15:2 Neh 5:7; Amos 8:4–8
☆15:3 Deut 23:20
15:4 Deut 14:29; 28:1–8
15:6 Deut 28:12, 13
15:7 Deut 15:11; Prov 19:11
☆15:9 Ex 22:22, 23; Deut 15:1; 24:14, 15; Job 34:28
15:10 2 Cor 9:7
☆15:11 Mt 26:11; Mk 14:7; Jn 12:8

15:3 The law which applied to the Israelites, that all debts owed each other were wiped out on the sabbatical year, did not apply to non-Israelites. God distinguished between his people Israel and those who were not. Is not such a distinction a breach of neighborly love? A similar question arose when Jesus gave the parable of the workers in the vineyard who all received the same wages though some worked shorter hours than others (Matt. 20:1ff). Was it fair? The reply is the same in both instances. God is free to do as he chooses. Since both Israelite and non-Israelite may be in debt, God is free to release one debtor and make the other pay. Favoring one debtor is a mark of grace and mercy, but it does not mean that God owes the other debtor anything.

15:9 God commanded those in Israel to relieve poverty by lending to the needy without taking into account the seven-year law for the release from debts. If there were only a short time until the sabbatical year came, a calculating mind might refuse to lend to the poor, for if not repaid by the sabbatical year, the loan would be wiped out. In its spiritual content the law restrains the thoughts of the "wicked heart." Our thoughts are monitored by God. All of us need to guard against thoughts of the heart which would divert us from doing our duty or which would discourage us from following God's law of charity. When we lend to the poor in obedience to God's command, we do not trust the one who borrows from us. We trust God without expecting recompense in this life, but with the assurance of repayment in the resurrection of the just.

15:11 *the poor shall never cease out of the land.* This prophetic word recognizes a truth that cannot be denied. In a sinful world, poverty should not be unexpected—whether due to lack of diligence on the part of the poor or circumstances beyond their control. The existence of poverty is a perennial challenge to the people of God to do what they can to alleviate the poverty-stricken.

b. The Freeing of Slaves

15:12 Ex 21:2; Lev 25:39; Jer 34:14

12 ¶*And* if thy brother, an Hebrew man, or an Hebrew woman, be sold unto thee, and serve thee six years; then in the seventh year thou shalt let him go free from thee.

13 And when thou sendest him out free from thee, thou shalt not let him go away empty:

14 Thou shalt furnish him liberally out of thy flock, and out of thy floor, and out of thy winepress: *of that* wherewith the LORD thy God hath blessed thee thou shalt give unto him.

15:15 Ex 20:2; Deut 5:15; 16:12

15 And thou shalt remember that thou wast a bondman in the land of Egypt, and the LORD thy God redeemed thee: therefore I command thee this thing to day.

15:16☆ Ex 21:5, 6

16 And it shall be, if he say unto thee, I will not go away from thee; because he loveth thee and thine house, because he is well with thee;

15:17☆ Lev 25:39

17 Then thou shalt take an aul, and thrust *it* through his ear unto the door, and he shall be thy servant for ever. And also unto thy maidservant thou shalt do likewise.

18 It shall not seem hard unto thee, when thou sendest him away free from thee; for he hath been worth a double hired servant *to thee,* in serving thee six years: and the LORD thy God shall bless thee in all that thou doest.

c. Consecration of the Firstborn Males

15:19 Ex 13:1; 34:19; Lev 27:26; Num 3:13

19 ¶All the firstling males that come of thy herd and of thy flock thou shalt sanctify unto the LORD thy God: thou shalt do no work with the firstling of thy bullock, nor shear the firstling of thy sheep.

15:20 Lev 7:15; Deut 12:7

20 Thou shalt eat *it* before the LORD thy God year by year in the place which the LORD shall choose, thou and thy household.

15:21 Lev 22:19; Mal 1:7, 8

21 And if there be *any* blemish therein, *as if it be* lame, or blind, *or have* any ill blemish, thou shalt not sacrifice it unto the LORD thy God.

15:22 Deut 12:15

22 Thou shalt eat it within thy gates: the unclean and the clean *person shall eat it* alike, as the roebuck, and as the hart.

15:23 Deut 12:16, 20–23

23 Only thou shalt not eat the blood thereof; thou shalt pour it upon the ground as water.

6. The Passover

16:1☆ Ex 12:2; Lev 23:5; Num 9:2, 3; 28:16

16 OBSERVE the month of Abib, and keep the passover unto the LORD thy God: for in the month of Abib the LORD thy God brought thee forth out of Egypt by night.

16:2 Ex 12:5

2 Thou shalt therefore sacrifice the passover unto the LORD thy God, of the flock and the herd, in the place which the LORD shall choose to place his name there.

16:3☆ Ex 12:8, 15; 34:18

3 Thou shalt eat no leavened bread with it; seven days shalt thou eat unleavened bread therewith, *even* the bread of affliction; for thou camest forth out of the land of Egypt in haste: that thou mayest remember the day when thou camest forth out of the land of Egypt all the days of thy life.

15:16, 17 Israel had no involuntary slavery. Manumission was provided for, unless the slave himself chose to continue as such.

16:1 See note on Exod. 12:11 and Mark. 14:1 for information on the passover. Here in chapter 16 Moses carefully reminds the men of Israel that they are to come to the holy place three times a year: for the passover (16:1–8), the feast of weeks (16:9–12, see note to Lev. 23:15, 16), and the feast of tabernacles or booths (16:13–17, see note to Exod. 23:16). They would come to perform their ceremonies "in the place which the LORD shall choose" (16:15). Later, this place would be the temple in Jerusalem.

16:3 *leavened bread.* See note on Matt. 13:33.

4And there shall be no leavened bread seen with thee in all thy coast
seven days; neither shall there *any thing* of the flesh, which thou sacrificedst
the first day at even, remain all night until the morning.
5Thou mayest not sacrifice the passover within any of thy gates, which
the LORD thy God giveth thee:
6But at the place which the LORD thy God shall choose to place his name
in, there thou shalt sacrifice the passover at even, at the going down of the
sun, at the season that thou camest forth out of Egypt.
7And thou shalt roast and eat *it* in the place which the LORD thy God
shall choose: and thou shalt turn in the morning, and go unto thy tents.
8Six days thou shalt eat unleavened bread: and on the seventh day *shall
be* a solemn assembly to the LORD thy God: thou shalt do no work *therein*.

16:4 Ex 13:6, 7; 34:25
16:6 Deut 12:4, 5; 2 Kgs 23:21–23; Jn 2:13; 11:55
16:7 2 Chron 35:13

7. The Feast of Weeks

9¶Seven weeks shalt thou number unto thee: begin to number the seven
weeks from *such time as* thou beginnest *to put* the sickle to the corn.
10And thou shalt keep the feast of weeks unto the LORD thy God with a
tribute of a freewill offering of thine hand, which thou shalt give *unto the
LORD thy God*, according as the LORD thy God hath blessed thee:
11And thou shalt rejoice before the LORD thy God, thou, and thy son,
and thy daughter, and thy manservant, and thy maidservant, and the Levite
that *is* within thy gates, and the stranger, and the fatherless, and the widow,
that *are* among you, in the place which the LORD thy God hath chosen to
place his name there.
12And thou shalt remember that thou wast a bondman in Egypt: and
thou shalt observe and do these statutes.

16:9 Ex 23:16; 34:22; Lev 23:15; Num 28:26
☆16:10 Lev 5:7; 12:8
16:11 Deut 12:7, 12; 14:29; 24:19
16:12 Ex 21:2; Deut 15:15

8. The Feast of Tabernacles

13¶Thou shalt observe the feast of tabernacles seven days, after that thou
hast gathered in thy corn and thy wine:
14And thou shalt rejoice in thy feast, thou, and thy son, and thy daughter,
and thy manservant, and thy maidservant, and the Levite, the stranger, and
the fatherless, and the widow, that *are* within thy gates.
15Seven days shalt thou keep a solemn feast unto the LORD thy God in
the place which the LORD shall choose: because the LORD thy God shall
bless thee in all thine increase, and in all the works of thine hands, therefore
thou shalt surely rejoice.
16¶Three times in a year shall all thy males appear before the LORD thy
God in the place which he shall choose; in the feast of unleavened bread,
and in the feast of weeks, and in the feast of tabernacles: and they shall not
appear before the LORD empty:
17Every man *shall give* as he is able, according to the blessing of the LORD
thy God which he hath given thee.

16:13 Lev 23:40; Ezek 45:25
16:16 Ex 22:29; 23:14; 34:20, 22–24
16:17 Deut 16:10

9. The Judicial System
a. The Appointment of Judges

18¶Judges and officers shalt thou make thee in all thy gates, which the
LORD thy God giveth thee, throughout thy tribes: and they shall judge the
people with just judgment.

16:18 Ex 18:25; Deut 1:17; 1 Chron 26:29

16:10 *feast of weeks.* See note on Lev. 23:15. This feast was also known as the feast of harvest.

16:19 Ex 23:2, 3; Lev 19:15; Deut 24:17; 27:19; 1 Sam 8:3; 12:3
16:20☆ Deut 25:13–15

19 Thou shalt not wrest judgment; thou shalt not respect persons, neither
take a gift: for a gift doth blind the eyes of the wise, and pervert the words
of the righteous.
20 That which is altogether just shalt thou follow, that thou mayest live,
and inherit the land which the LORD thy God giveth thee.

b. Breaches of the Law

16:21☆ Ex 34:13; Deut 7:5
16:22 Lev 26:1

21 ¶Thou shalt not plant thee a grove of any trees near unto the altar of
the LORD thy God, which thou shalt make thee.
22 Neither shalt thou set thee up *any* image; which the LORD thy God
hateth.

17:1☆ Lev 22:20; Deut 15:21
17:2 Deut 4:19, 23; 29:26; Josh 22:16; 2 Kgs 21:3–5; Acts 7:43
17:4 Deut 13:12–14; 19:18
17:5☆ Deut 13:10; 21:21
17:6 Num 35:30; Deut 19:15
17:7 Lev 24:13, 14; Deut 13:9

17 THOU shalt not sacrifice unto the LORD thy God *any* bullock, or
sheep, wherein is blemish, *or* any evilfavouredness: for that *is* an
abomination unto the LORD thy God.
2 If there be found among you, within any of thy gates which the LORD
thy God giveth thee, man or woman, that hath wrought wickedness in the
sight of the LORD thy God, in transgressing his covenant,
3 And hath gone and served other gods, and worshipped them, either the
sun, or moon, or any of the host of heaven, which I have not commanded;
4 And it be told thee, and thou hast heard *of it,* and inquired diligently,
and, behold, *it be* true, *and* the thing certain, *that* such abomination is
wrought in Israel:
5 Then shalt thou bring forth that man or that woman, which have
committed that wicked thing, unto thy gates, *even* that man or that woman,
and shalt stone them with stones, till they die.
6 At the mouth of two witnesses, or three witnesses, shall he that is worthy
of death be put to death; *but* at the mouth of one witness he shall not be put
to death.
7 The hands of the witnesses shall be first upon him to put him to death,
and afterward the hands of all the people. So thou shalt put the evil away
from among you.

c. Decisions of the Chief Judge Are Final

17:8☆ Deut 1:17; 19:17

8 If there arise a matter too hard for thee in judgment, between blood and
blood, between plea and plea, and between stroke and stroke, *being* matters

---

16:20 Israel was charged to do justice to all. We are to "adhere to the principles of justice, act by the rules of justice, imitate the patterns of justice, and pursue with resolution that which appears to be just."* The magistrate is to do right to all and wrong to none. The modern term "social justice" is a misnomer—it has an inherent injustice in its meaning. Thus it is wrong for government or magistrates to take what belongs to someone in order to give to a less fortunate person. Therefore the notion of the redistribution of wealth is an assault on the principle of justice.

16:21 Some things are wrong in themselves; others are inexpedient and may lead to sin. The pagan peoples had groves of trees where images were set up. Israel is forbidden to plant a grove or even a single tree near God's altar. It might cause the Israelites to sin. No image, no statue, and no pillar is to be erected with the pretense that it is for the worship of the true God. God is spirit and must be worshipped as such.

17:1 God knew that the "natural" inclination of his people would be to bring blemished animals for sacrifice while keeping the perfect ones for themselves. But to bring a blemished sacrifice is an insult to deity. He who performs such an evil deed shall eat the fruit of it.

17:5 Idolatry was a capital crime and punishable by stoning. The punishment mentioned by Moses looked toward the time when Israel would be settled in the land. The criminal was to be taken to the gates of the city, then hands were to be laid on him to transfer the guilt of the community to the offender. Two witnesses were required and they had to cast the first stones, after which the witnesses to the execution cast their stones until the victim was killed.

17:8ff Some legal cases were too difficult for local judges and courts to make a decision. They were referred to the priests and judges at the central sanctuary. Their verdicts were binding and could not be annulled. Whoever refused to conform to the sentence of the highest court was guilty of a capital crime.

of controversy within thy gates: then shalt thou arise, and get thee up into
the place which the LORD thy God shall choose;
9 And thou shalt come unto the priests the Levites, and unto the judge
that shall be in those days, and inquire; and they shall shew thee the
sentence of judgment:
10 And thou shalt do according to the sentence, which they of that place
which the LORD shall choose shall shew thee; and thou shalt observe to do
according to all that they inform thee:
11 According to the sentence of the law which they shall teach thee, and
according to the judgment which they shall tell thee, thou shalt do: thou
shalt not decline from the sentence which they shall shew thee, *to* the right
hand, nor *to* the left.
12 And the man that will do presumptuously, and will not hearken unto
the priest that standeth to minister there before the LORD thy God, or unto
the judge, even that man shall die: and thou shalt put away the evil from
Israel.
13 And all the people shall hear, and fear, and do no more presumptuously.

17:11 Deut 25:1
17:13 Deut 13:11 19:20

10. The Choosing of a King Belongs to God

14 ¶When thou art come unto the land which the LORD thy God giveth
thee, and shalt possess it, and shalt dwell therein, and shalt say, I will set a
king over me, like as all the nations that *are* about me;
15 Thou shalt in any wise set *him* king over thee, whom the LORD thy God
shall choose: *one* from among thy brethren shalt thou set king over thee:
thou mayest not set a stranger over thee, which *is* not thy brother.
16 But he shall not multiply horses to himself, nor cause the people to
return to Egypt, to the end that he should multiply horses: forasmuch as
the LORD hath said unto you, Ye shall henceforth return no more that way.
17 Neither shall he multiply wives to himself, that his heart turn not away:
neither shall he greatly multiply to himself silver and gold.
18 And it shall be, when he sitteth upon the throne of his kingdom, that he
shall write him a copy of this law in a book out of *that which is* before the
priests the Levites:
19 And it shall be with him, and he shall read therein all the days of his
life: that he may learn to fear the LORD his God, to keep all the words of
this law and these statutes, to do them:
20 That his heart be not lifted up above his brethren, and that he turn not
aside from the commandment, *to* the right hand, or *to* the left: to the end
that he may prolong *his* days in his kingdom, he, and his children, in the
midst of Israel.

☆**17:14** Deut 11:31 Josh 21:43 1 Sam 8:5, 19, 20
17:16 1 Kgs 4:26 10:26 Isa 31:1 Ezek 17:15
17:17 2 Sam 5:13 1 Kgs 11:3, 4
☆**17:18** Deut 31:9, 24 2 Kgs 11:12; 22:8
17:19 Deut 6:6; 11:18 Ps 119

11. The Remuneration for the Priests and Levites

18 THE priests the Levites, *and* all the tribe of Levi, shall have no part
nor inheritance with Israel: they shall eat the offerings of the LORD
made by fire, and his inheritance.

18:1 Deut 10:9 1 Cor 9:13

17:14 Moses said that Israel would opt for a king. This was in the plan of God. The king, according to 17:19, was to keep a copy of the law before him and read it every day of his life.

17:18 God ordained that every king of Israel was to write down for himself a copy of the law. We do not know whether he was referring to the five books of the Pentateuch or only to Deuteronomy. The Levitical priests kept the word of God; it was regarded as sacred and was to be kept inviolate from profane hands. Yet God insisted that the king make a copy of the law for himself. He was to study the law and keep it close to him at all times (17:19). He was also to obey the law and practice its precepts. The king was not the law nor was he above the law. He and all the people were *under* the law of God.

18:2 Deut 12:12; 14:27; Ps 16:5

2 Therefore shall they have no inheritance among their brethren: the LORD *is* their inheritance, as he hath said unto them.

18:3 Lev 7:32; Num 18:11

3 ¶And this shall be the priest's due from the people, from them that offer a sacrifice, whether *it be* ox or sheep; and they shall give unto the priest the shoulder, and the two cheeks, and the maw.

18:4 Ex 22:29; 23:19

4 The firstfruit *also* of thy corn, of thy wine, and of thine oil, and the first of the fleece of thy sheep, shalt thou give him.

18:5 Ex 28:1; Num 3:10; Deut 10:8

5 For the LORD thy God hath chosen him out of all thy tribes, to stand to minister in the name of the LORD, him and his sons for ever.

18:6 Num 35:2, 3

6 ¶And if a Levite come from any of thy gates out of all Israel, where he sojourned, and come with all the desire of his mind unto the place which the LORD shall choose;

7 Then he shall minister in the name of the LORD his God, as all his brethren the Levites *do*, which stand there before the LORD.

18:8 Lev 27:30; Num 18:21

8 They shall have like portions to eat, beside that which cometh of the sale of his patrimony.

12. Prophets—False and True

a. Heathen Practices Forbidden

18:9 Lev 18:26; Deut 9:5; 12:29, 30

9 ¶When thou art come into the land which the LORD thy God giveth thee, thou shalt not learn to do after the abominations of those nations.

18:10☆ Ex 22:18; Lev 19:26, 31; 20:6; Deut 12:31; Jer 27:9, 10

10 There shall not be found among you *any one* that maketh his son or his daughter to pass through the fire, *or* that useth divination, *or* an observer of times, or an enchanter, or a witch,

11 Or a charmer, or a consulter with familiar spirits, or a wizard, or a necromancer.

12 For all that do these things *are* an abomination unto the LORD: and because of these abominations the LORD thy God doth drive them out from before thee.

18:13 Gen 6:7–10; 17:1; Job 1:1; Mt 5:48

13 Thou shalt be perfect with the LORD thy God.

14 For these nations, which thou shalt possess, hearkened unto observers of times, and unto diviners: but as for thee, the LORD thy God hath not suffered thee so *to do*.

b. The Test for a Prophet; the Promise of the Prophet Messiah

18:15 Lk 24:19; Jn 1:21, 24, 25; 6:14; 7:52; Acts 3:20–22; 7:37; Heb 3:2; **18:15–22**☆

15 ¶The LORD thy God will raise up unto thee a Prophet from the midst of thee, of thy brethren, like unto me; unto him ye shall hearken;

18:16 Deut 5:23–27

16 According to all that thou desiredst of the LORD thy God in Ho'reb in the day of the assembly, saying, Let me not hear again the voice of the LORD my God, neither let me see this great fire any more, that I die not.

17 And the LORD said unto me, They have well *spoken that* which they have spoken.

18:18 Acts 3:21–23

18 I will raise them up a Prophet from among their brethren, like unto thee, and will put my words in his mouth; and he shall speak unto them all that I shall command him.

18:10 The Scriptures forbid divination, divining, sorcery, augury, fortune telling, mediums, wizardry, and other heathen practices. Ancient army leaders had diviners who were quite influential in major decisions. Israel was led by the true God; thus heathen practices were inconsistent with genuine faith. In the Old Testament we read that those who engaged in these practices were sentenced to death (Exod. 22:18; Lev. 20:27). The New Testament says that spiritists and sorcerers shall not inherit the kingdom of God (Gal. 5:20; Rev. 22:15).

18:15–22 God would raise up a prophet like Moses. The ultimate fulfilling of that prophecy was Jesus Christ. Other good prophets who spoke the true word of God were raised up after Moses. False prophets were to be shown to be wrong and would die for their presumption.

19And it shall come to pass, *that* whosoever will not hearken unto my
words which he shall speak in my name, I will require *it* of him.
20But the prophet, which shall presume to speak a word in my name,
which I have not commanded him to speak, or that shall speak in the name
of other gods, even that prophet shall die.
21And if thou say in thine heart, How shall we know the word which the
LORD hath not spoken?
22When a prophet speaketh in the name of the LORD, if the thing follow
not, nor come to pass, that *is* the thing which the LORD hath not spoken,
but the prophet hath spoken it presumptuously: thou shalt not be afraid of
him.

18:19 Deut 17:12; Heb 12:25
18:20 Deut 13:1–4; Jer 28:15, 16
☆18:22 Isa 41:22; Jer 28:9

13. Crime and Punishment

a. Unpremeditated Killing

19 WHEN the LORD thy God hath cut off the nations, whose land the
LORD thy God giveth thee, and thou succeedest them, and dwellest
in their cities, and in their houses;
2Thou shalt separate three cities for thee in the midst of thy land, which
the LORD thy God giveth thee to possess it.
3Thou shalt prepare thee a way, and divide the coasts of thy land, which
the LORD thy God giveth thee to inherit, into three parts, that every slayer
may flee thither.
4¶And this *is* the case of the slayer, which shall flee thither, that he may
live: Whoso killeth his neighbour ignorantly, whom he hated not in time
past;
5As when a man goeth into the wood with his neighbour to hew wood,
and his hand fetcheth a stroke with the axe to cut down the tree, and the
head slippeth from the helve, and lighteth upon his neighbour, that he die;
he shall flee unto one of those cities, and live:
6Lest the avenger of the blood pursue the slayer, while his heart is hot,
and overtake him, because the way is long, and slay him; whereas he *was*
not worthy of death, inasmuch as he hated him not in time past.
7Wherefore I command thee, saying, Thou shalt separate three cities for
thee.
8And if the LORD thy God enlarge thy coast, as he hath sworn unto thy
fathers, and give thee all the land which he promised to give unto thy
fathers;
9If thou shalt keep all these commandments to do them, which I
command thee this day, to love the LORD thy God, and to walk ever in his
ways; then shalt thou add three cities more for thee, beside these three:
10That innocent blood be not shed in thy land, which the LORD thy God
giveth thee *for* an inheritance, and *so* blood be upon thee.

19:1 Deut 6:10–12; 17:14
☆19:2 Num 35:6; Deut 4:41, 42; Josh 20:7
☆19:4 Num 35:9–34
☆19:8 Deut 11:24; 12:20–24
☆19:9 Deut 6:15; 11:22
☆19:10 Num 35:33; Deut 21:1–9

18:22 The test of a false prophet is simple: what he prophesies does not come to pass. Israel need not fear such people. Scripture says that, in Samuel's case, God "let none of his words fall to the ground" (1 Sam. 3:19). None of Jesus' prophecies remain unfulfilled except those that have a future reference, such as his second advent. False prophets were subject to capital punishment. This provision would make intelligent people careful about assuming the prophetic role.

19:2–13 Six cities of refuge were to be erected for the protection of those who accidentally were responsible for the death of another. The first three were to be set up on the east side of the Jordan. Here Moses speaks specifically about the additional three cities to be set up on the west side of the Jordan River. The emphasis on innocent blood indicates the need for such refuges against avengers of blood who might kill someone who was not guilty of murder according to the precepts set up by God through Moses.

b. The Avenger of Blood for Murder

19:11 Deut 27:24

11¶But if any man hate his neighbour, and lie in wait for him, and rise up
against him, and smite him mortally that he die, and fleeth into one of these
cities:

19:12 Num 35:21, 24

12Then the elders of his city shall send and fetch him thence, and deliver
him into the hand of the avenger of blood, that he may die.

19:13 Deut 7:16; 13:8

13Thine eye shall not pity him, but thou shalt put away *the guilt of*
innocent blood from Israel, that it may go well with thee.

c. Prohibition against Moving Landmarks

19:14☆ Deut 27:17; Prov 23:10, 11

14¶Thou shalt not remove thy neighbour's landmark, which they of old
time have set in thine inheritance, which thou shalt inherit in the land that
the LORD thy God giveth thee to possess it.

d. The Rule about the Number of Witnesses to a Crime

19:15☆ Num 35:30; Deut 17:16; Mt 18:16; 2 Cor 13:1

15¶One witness shall not rise up against a man for any iniquity, or for any
sin, in any sin that he sinneth: at the mouth of two witnesses, or at the
mouth of three witnesses, shall the matter be established.

19:16 Ex 23:1; Prov 14:5, 25

16If a false witness rise up against any man to testify against him *that
which is* wrong;

19:17 Deut 17:9; 21:5

17Then both the men, between whom the controversy *is*, shall stand
before the LORD, before the priests and the judges, which shall be in those
days;
18And the judges shall make diligent inquisition: and, behold, *if* the
witness *be* a false witness, *and* hath testified falsely against his brother;

19:19 Deut 13:5; 17:7; Prov 19:5, 9; Jer 14:15

19Then shall ye do unto him, as he had thought to have done unto his
brother: so shalt thou put the evil away from among you.

19:20 Deut 21:21

20And those which remain shall hear, and fear, and shall henceforth
commit no more any such evil among you.

19:21☆ Ex 21:23; Lev 24:17, 20; Mt 5:38

21And thine eye shall not pity; *but* life *shall go* for life, eye for eye, tooth
for tooth, hand for hand, foot for foot.

14. The Laws of War

a. Exemption from Military Service

20:1 Deut 1:29, 30; 3:22; 7:18; 31:6, 7; Josh 11:6

20 WHEN thou goest out to battle against thine enemies, and seest
horses, and chariots, *and* a people more than thou, be not afraid of
them: for the LORD thy God *is* with thee, which brought thee up out of the
land of Egypt.

20:2 Num 10:8; 31:6

2And it shall be, when ye are come nigh unto the battle, that the priest
shall approach and speak unto the people,

20:3 Ps 27:1–3; Isa 35:4; 41:10

3And shall say unto them, Hear, O Israel, ye approach this day unto
battle against your enemies: let not your hearts faint, fear not, and do not
tremble, neither be ye terrified because of them;

19:14 *landmark*, i.e., "boundary marker." Some Israelites apparently moved property markers so as to steal land from their neighbors. This was prohibited.
19:15 Here and elsewhere God required that no one be declared guilty of an offense on the basis of one person's testimony. This guaranteed better justice. Whoever witnessed falsely to another's guilt would pay the same penalty which would have been exacted against the accused. The very existence of this provision was based on the presumption that some people would witness falsely. The provision would, according to 19:20, keep other people from doing the same thing.
19:21 *an eye for an eye.* No law could be any more just than that retributive justice must equal the crime. Here a false witness must receive the penalty that would have ensued if judgment had been executed on the basis of his testimony. The false witness must die, even as the indicted would have been executed if the testimony of the false witness had been accepted. So also with civil affairs. Whoever is harmed must be repaid in equal amount for the damage.

4For the LORD your God *is* he that goeth with you, to fight for you
against your enemies, to save you.
5¶And the officers shall speak unto the people, saying, What man *is there* **20:5** Neh 12:27
that hath built a new house, and hath not dedicated it? let him go and
return to his house, lest he die in the battle, and another man dedicate it.
6And what man *is he* that hath planted a vineyard, and hath not *yet* eaten **20:6** Lev 19:23
of it? let him *also* go and return unto his house, lest he die in the battle, and
another man eat of it.
7And what man *is there* that hath betrothed a wife, and hath not taken ☆**20:7** Deut 24:5
her? let him go and return unto his house, lest he die in the battle, and
another man take her.
8And the officers shall speak further unto the people, and they shall say, **20:8** Judg 7:3
What man *is there that is* fearful and fainthearted? let him go and return
unto his house, lest his brethren's heart faint as well as his heart.
9And it shall be, when the officers have made an end of speaking unto the
people, that they shall make captains of the armies to lead the people.

b. Truces and Sieges

10¶When thou comest nigh unto a city to fight against it, then proclaim ☆**20:10** 2 Sam 20:17–21
peace unto it.
11And it shall be, if it make thee answer of peace, and open unto thee,
then it shall be, *that* all the people *that is* found therein shall be tributaries
unto thee, and they shall serve thee.
12And if it will make no peace with thee, but will make war against thee,
then thou shalt besiege it:
13And when the LORD thy God hath delivered it into thine hands, thou ☆**20:13** Num 31:7–11
shalt smite every male thereof with the edge of the sword: 1 Kgs 11:15
14But the women, and the little ones, and the cattle, and all that is in the ☆**20:14** Josh 8:2
city, *even* all the spoil thereof, shalt thou take unto thyself; and thou shalt 11:14
eat the spoil of thine enemies, which the LORD thy God hath given thee. 2 Chron 14:13–15
15Thus shalt thou do unto all the cities *which are* very far off from thee,
which *are* not of the cities of these nations.
16But of the cities of these people, which the LORD thy God doth give ☆**20:16** Ex 23:31
thee *for* an inheritance, thou shalt save alive nothing that breatheth: Deut 7:1, 2
17But thou shalt utterly destroy them; *namely*, the Hittites, and the
Am′or-ites, the Canaanites, and the Per′iz-zites, the Hi′vites, and the Jeb′u-
sites; as the LORD thy God hath commanded thee:
18That they teach you not to do after all their abominations, which they ☆**20:18** Deut 7:4; 9:5
have done unto their gods; so should ye sin against the LORD your God. 12:31
19¶When thou shalt besiege a city a long time, in making war against it to ☆**20:19, 20** 2 Chron 26:15
take it, thou shalt not destroy the trees thereof by forcing an axe against
them: for thou mayest eat of them, and thou shalt not cut them down (for
the tree of the field *is* man's *life*) to employ *them* in the siege:
20Only the trees which thou knowest that they *be* not trees for meat, thou
shalt destroy and cut them down; and thou shalt build bulwarks against the
city that maketh war with thee, until it be subdued.

20:7 The law of military service exempted a man who was engaged to marry but the marriage had not yet been consummated. He was free to remain at home for a year after the marriage—presumably so that he could raise up seed before going to war and thus preserve the family inheritance.

20:10–18 See note on 2:34.

20:19, 20 War, by its very nature, is destructive. So God protected man's best interests by forbidding the destruction of fruit trees (except for those which bore no fruit). Jewish theologians took this to be a prohibition against willful waste on any account. Thus they said that "whoso willfully breaks vessels, tears clothes, stops wells, pulls down buildings, or destroys meat, transgresses this law: *Thou shalt not destroy.*"* Modern warfare, accompanied by mass bombings and the threat of nuclear destruction, suggests how far mankind has departed from such injunctions.

15. Incidental Laws

a. Sacrifice for an Unsolved Murder

21 IF *one* be found slain in the land which the LORD thy God giveth
thee to possess it, lying in the field, *and* it be not known who hath
slain him:
2 Then thy elders and thy judges shall come forth, and they shall measure
unto the cities which *are* round about him that is slain:
3 And it shall be, *that* the city *which is* next unto the slain man, even the
elders of that city shall take an heifer, which hath not been wrought with,
and which hath not drawn in the yoke;
4 And the elders of that city shall bring down the heifer unto a rough
valley, which is neither eared nor sown, and shall strike off the heifer's neck
there in the valley:
21:5 Deut 10:8; 17:9; 19:17
5 And the priests the sons of Levi shall come near; for them the LORD thy
God hath chosen to minister unto him, and to bless in the name of the
LORD; and by their word shall every controversy and every stroke be *tried:*
21:6, 7☆ Ps 26:6; Mt 27:24
6 And all the elders of that city, *that are* next unto the slain *man*, shall
wash their hands over the heifer that is beheaded in the valley:
7 And they shall answer and say, Our hands have not shed this blood,
neither have our eyes seen *it.*
21:8 Num 35:33, 34; Jonah 1:14
8 Be merciful, O LORD, unto thy people Israel, whom thou hast redeemed,
and lay not innocent blood unto thy people of Israel's charge. And the
blood shall be forgiven them.
21:9 Deut 19:13
9 So shalt thou put away the *guilt of* innocent blood from among you,
when thou shalt do *that which is* right in the sight of the LORD.

b. Marriage to a Captive Woman

21:10 Deut 20:1
10 ¶When thou goest forth to war against thine enemies, and the LORD thy
God hath delivered them into thine hands, and thou hast taken them
captive,
21:11☆ Deut 20:14
11 And seest among the captives a beautiful woman, and hast a desire
unto her, that thou wouldest have her to thy wife;
21:12 Lev 14:8, 9; Num 6:9
12 Then thou shalt bring her home to thine house; and she shall shave her
head, and pare her nails;
21:13 Ps 45:10
13 And she shall put the raiment of her captivity from off her, and shall
remain in thine house, and bewail her father and her mother a full month:
and after that thou shalt go in unto her, and be her husband, and she shall
be thy wife.
21:14 Ex 21:8, 11; Deut 22:19
14 And it shall be, if thou have no delight in her, then thou shalt let her go
whither she will; but thou shalt not sell her at all for money, thou shalt not
make merchandise of her, because thou hast humbled her.

c. Inheritance Law for the Firstborn

15 If a man have two wives, one beloved, and another hated, and they
have born him children, *both* the beloved and the hated; and *if* the firstborn
son be hers that was hated:

21:7 Many crimes are committed for which the guilty cannot be identified. The community as a whole bears the responsibility and must offer the proper sacrifice, asking for divine forgiveness and professing innocence with respect to the crime.

21:11 Provision is made here for a soldier to marry a woman taken captive. She is provided protection against misuse. If she came from a pagan nation it was wrong for an Israelite to marry her in the first place, but provision is made in advance in case such a marriage were to take place.

16Then it shall be, when he maketh his sons to inherit *that* which he hath,
that he may not make the son of the beloved firstborn before the son of the
hated, *which is indeed* the firstborn:
17But he shall acknowledge the son of the hated *for* the firstborn, by
giving him a double portion of all that he hath: for he *is* the beginning of
his strength; the right of the firstborn *is* his.

☆**21:17** Gen 49:3

d. Executing Rebellious Sons

18If a man have a stubborn and rebellious son, which will not obey the
voice of his father, or the voice of his mother, and *that,* when they have
chastened him, will not hearken unto them:

21:18 Deut 27:16 Prov 28:24 30:11, 12

19Then shall his father and his mother lay hold on him, and bring him out
unto the elders of his city, and unto the gate of his place;
20And they shall say unto the elders of his city, This our son *is* stubborn
and rebellious, he will not obey our voice; *he is* a glutton, and a drunkard.

☆**21:20**

21And all the men of his city shall stone him with stones, that he die: so
shalt thou put evil away from among you; and all Israel shall hear, and fear.

21:21 Lev 20:2, 27 24:13, 14 Num 15:35

e. Burying Hanged Criminals the Same Day

22¶And if a man have committed a sin worthy of death, and he be to be
put to death, and thou hang him on a tree:
23His body shall not remain all night upon the tree, but thou shalt in any
wise bury him that day; (for he that is hanged *is* accursed of God;) that thy
land be not defiled, which the LORD thy God giveth thee *for* an inheritance.

☆**21:22** 2 Sam 21:5, 6, 9 Mt 26:65, 66 Mk 14:63, 64
21:23 Josh 8:29 10:26, 27 Jn 19:31 Gal 3:13

f. Helping One's Neighbor

22 THOU shalt not see thy brother's ox or his sheep go astray, and
hide thyself from them: thou shalt in any case bring them again
unto thy brother.

22:1 Ex 23:4 Lev 20:4

2And if thy brother *be* not nigh unto thee, or if thou know him not, then
thou shalt bring it unto thine own house, and it shall be with thee until thy
brother seek after it, and thou shalt restore it to him again.
3In like manner shalt thou do with his ass; and so shalt thou do with his
raiment; and with all lost thing of thy brother's, which he hath lost, and
thou hast found, shalt thou do likewise: thou mayest not hide thyself.
4¶Thou shalt not see thy brother's ass or his ox fall down by the way, and
hide thyself from them: thou shalt surely help him to lift *them* up again.

g. Various Regulations

5¶The woman shall not wear that which pertaineth unto a man, neither
shall a man put on a woman's garment: for all that do so *are* abomination
unto the LORD thy God.

☆**22:5**

21:17 The Scriptures nowhere endorse polygamy or concubinage. But they recognize the unhappy fact that polygamy may exist. Thus, if a man had two wives and loved one more than the other, he could not transfer the rights of the firstborn son of the woman he loved less to a younger son of the woman he loved more. The double portion of the inheritance belonged to the firstborn, regardless of whether he was mothered by the loved or the unloved wife.

21:20 A stubborn and rebellious son who is a glutton and a drunkard is here subjected to capital punishment. Presumably such a man was warned not to commit such sins. Anarchy in the home would not be permitted. The judgment was pronounced by the community according to its laws, not by the father as an individual.

21:22 Capital punishment normally was executed by stoning. But the corpse might then be hung on a tree to warn others against committing similar crimes. However, the body was not to be left hanging overnight; it was to be buried the same day.

22:5 Since normal dress for male and female was similar, provision was made to distinguish male from female and to keep either sex from using the distinctive signs of the opposite sex.

22:6 Lev 22:28 6 If a bird's nest chance to be before thee in the way in any tree, or on the
ground, *whether they be* young ones, or eggs, and the dam sitting upon the
young, or upon the eggs, thou shalt not take the dam with the young:
7 *But* thou shalt in any wise let the dam go, and take the young to thee;
that it may be well with thee, and *that* thou mayest prolong *thy* days.
8 ¶When thou buildest a new house, then thou shalt make a battlement
for thy roof, that thou bring not blood upon thine house, if any man fall
from thence.
22:9 Lev 19:19 9 ¶Thou shalt not sow thy vineyard with divers seeds: lest the fruit of thy
seed which thou hast sown, and the fruit of thy vineyard, be defiled.
22:10 2 Cor 6:14 10 ¶Thou shalt not plow with an ox and an ass together.
11 ¶Thou shalt not wear a garment of divers sorts, *as* of woollen and linen
together.
22:12☆ Num 15:37–39 Mt 23:5 12 ¶Thou shalt make thee fringes upon the four quarters of thy vesture,
wherewith thou coverest *thyself*.

h. Laws Regarding the Use of Sex

22:13☆ Deut 24:1 13 If any man take a wife, and go in unto her, and hate her,
14 And give occasions of speech against her, and bring up an evil name
upon her, and say, I took this woman, and when I came to her, I found her
not a maid:
15 Then shall the father of the damsel, and her mother, take and bring
forth *the tokens of* the damsel's virginity unto the elders of the city in the
gate:
16 And the damsel's father shall say unto the elders, I gave my daughter
unto this man to wife, and he hateth her;
17 And, lo, he hath given occasions of speech *against her,* saying, I found
not thy daughter a maid; and yet these *are the tokens of* my daughter's
virginity. And they shall spread the cloth before the elders of the city.
18 And the elders of that city shall take that man and chastise him;
19 And they shall amerce him in an hundred *shekels* of silver, and give
them unto the father of the damsel, because he hath brought up an evil
name upon a virgin of Israel: and she shall be his wife; he may not put her
away all his days.
20 But if this thing be true, *and the tokens of* virginity be not found for the
damsel:
22:21 Lev 19:29; 21:9 Deut 23:17, 18 21 Then they shall bring out the damsel to the door of her father's house,
and the men of her city shall stone her with stones that she die: because she
hath wrought folly in Israel, to play the whore in her father's house: so shalt
thou put evil away from among you.
22:22 Lev 20:10 Ezek 16:38 Jn 8:5 22 If a man be found lying with a woman married to an husband, then
they shall both of them die, *both* the man that lay with the woman, and the
woman: so shalt thou put away evil from Israel.
22:23 Lev 19:20 Deut 20:7 23 If a damsel *that is* a virgin be betrothed unto an husband, and a man
find her in the city, and lie with her;

22:12 Here as well as in Num. 15:37, 38 the Israelites were told to make fringes or tassels on the four corners of their garments. This was to distinguish them from other people by showing they were not ashamed of their country or of their religion. It would also remind them of their own origins and faith. Later the Jews ceased to wear these externally in order to avoid both heathen and Christian persecution. They often substituted a kind of undergarment which covered the chest and back which had four corners to which they attached the fringes or tassels. In Jesus' day the scribes and Pharisees made the tassels long, so that men might think more highly of their persons.

22:13ff A woman was presumed to be a virgin at the time of her marriage. If her husband had reason to suspect that she was not a virgin, an inquiry must take place. If she was not a virgin she had to be stoned. If she was, her husband must be beaten, fined and not allowed to put his wife away.

24 Then ye shall bring them both out unto the gate of that city, and ye
shall stone them with stones that they die; the damsel, because she cried
not, *being* in the city; and the man, because he hath humbled his
neighbour's wife: so thou shalt put away evil from among you.
25 ¶But if a man find a betrothed damsel in the field, and the man force ☆**22:25**
her, and lie with her: then the man only that lay with her shall die:
26 But unto the damsel thou shalt do nothing; *there is* in the damsel no sin
worthy of death: for as when a man riseth against his neighbour, and slayeth
him, even so *is* this matter:
27 For he found her in the field, *and* the betrothed damsel cried, and *there*
was none to save her.
28 If a man find a damsel *that is* a virgin, which is not betrothed, and lay **22:28** Ex 22:16
hold on her, and lie with her, and they be found;
29 Then the man that lay with her shall give unto the damsel's father fifty
shekels of silver, and she shall be his wife; because he hath humbled her, he
may not put her away all his days.
30 ¶A man shall not take his father's wife, nor discover his father's skirt. ☆**22:30** Lev 18:8; 20:11 Deut 27:20

i. Those Who May and May Not Enter the Sanctuary

23 HE that is wounded in the stones, or hath his privy member cut off, **23:1** Lev 21:20; 22:24
shall not enter into the congregation of the LORD.
2 A bastard shall not enter into the congregation of the LORD; even to his
tenth generation shall he not enter into the congregation of the LORD.
3 An Ammonite or Moabite shall not enter into the congregation of the ☆**23:3** Deut 7:1
LORD; even to their tenth generation shall they not enter into the
congregation of the LORD for ever:
4 Because they met you not with bread and with water in the way, when **23:4** Num 23:4, 7–10 Neh 13:1 2 Pet 2:15 Jude 11
ye came forth out of Egypt; and because they hired against thee Ba'laam
the son of Be'or of Pe'thor of Mes-o-po-ta'mi-a, to curse thee.
5 Nevertheless the LORD thy God would not hearken unto Ba'laam; but **23:5** Num 22:35 24:3–9
the LORD thy God turned the curse into a blessing unto thee, because the
LORD thy God loved thee.
6 Thou shalt not seek their peace nor their prosperity all thy days for ever.
7 ¶Thou shalt not abhor an Edomite; for he *is* thy brother: thou shalt not ☆**23:7** Lev 19:34 Num 20:14 Deut 10:19
abhor an Egyptian; because thou wast a stranger in his land.
8 The children that are begotten of them shall enter into the congregation **23:8** Num 11:4
of the LORD in their third generation.

j. Sanitary Rules of War

9 ¶When the host goeth forth against thine enemies, then keep thee from
every wicked thing.
10 If there be among you any man, that is not clean by reason of
uncleanness that chanceth him by night, then shall he go abroad out of the
camp, he shall not come within the camp:
11 But it shall be, when evening cometh on, he shall wash *himself* with **23:11** Lev 15:5, 16
water: and when the sun is down, he shall come into the camp *again*.

22:25 If a betrothed woman were raped, the rapist would be put to death. If the rape victim were not betrothed, the rapist had to either pay a fine to her father or marry her (in the latter case, he would be forbidden to put her away).
22:30 *his father's wife,* i.e., "his father's widow." The general law against adultery protected her and other wives while their husbands were living.†
23:3 See notes on Ezek. 25:2, 9 for information on the Ammonites and Moabites.
23:7 The Edomites were descendants of Esau and thus were in the Abrahamic family. (See note on Gen. 36:9.) No reason is given why Israel should not abhor an Egyptian. God orders them to forget, in effect, their bondage in Egypt and remember instead the delivering power of their God. Thus the grandchildren of Edomites or Egyptians who turned to God were to be looked upon as members of the congregation of Israel.

12¶Thou shalt have a place also without the camp, whither thou shalt go
forth abroad:
13And thou shalt have a paddle upon thy weapon; and it shall be, when
thou wilt ease thyself abroad, thou shalt dig therewith, and shalt turn back
and cover that which cometh from thee:
23:14 Lev 26:12 14For the LORD thy God walketh in the midst of thy camp, to deliver
thee, and to give up thine enemies before thee; therefore shall thy camp be
holy: that he see no unclean thing in thee, and turn away from thee.

k. Various Regulations

23:15☆ 1 Sam 22:2 15¶Thou shalt not deliver unto his master the servant which is escaped
25:10 from his master unto thee:
16He shall dwell with thee, *even* among you, in that place which he shall
choose in one of thy gates, where it liketh him best: thou shalt not oppress
him.
23:17☆ 17¶There shall be no whore of the daughters of Israel, nor a sodomite of
Lev 18:22; 20:13 Deut 22:21 the sons of Israel.
23:18☆ 18Thou shalt not bring the hire of a whore, or the price of a dog, into the
house of the LORD thy God for any vow: for even both these *are*
abomination unto the LORD thy God.
23:19 19¶Thou shalt not lend upon usury to thy brother; usury of money, usury
Ex 22:25 Lev 25:36 of victuals, usury of any thing that is lent upon usury:
23:20 20Unto a stranger thou mayest lend upon usury; but unto thy brother
Deut 28:12 thou shalt not lend upon usury: that the LORD thy God may bless thee in
all that thou settest thine hand to in the land whither thou goest to possess
it.
23:21 21¶When thou shalt vow a vow unto the LORD thy God, thou shalt not
Lev 5:4 Num 15:4 slack to pay it: for the LORD thy God will surely require it of thee; and it
30:1, 2 Eccles 5:4 would be sin in thee.
Mt 5:33 22But if thou shalt forbear to vow, it shall be no sin in thee.
23That which is gone out of thy lips thou shalt keep and perform; *even* a
freewill offering, according as thou hast vowed unto the LORD thy God,
which thou hast promised with thy mouth.
23:24☆ 24¶When thou comest into thy neighbour's vineyard, then thou mayest
eat grapes thy fill at thine own pleasure; but thou shalt not put *any* in thy
vessel.
23:25☆ 25When thou comest into the standing corn of thy neighbour, then thou
Mt 12:1, 2 Mk 2:23 mayest pluck the ears with thine hand; but thou shalt not move a sickle
Lk 6:1 unto thy neighbour's standing corn.

1. Variety of Incidental Rules

24:1☆ Num 5:12–28 Deut 22:13–21 24 WHEN a man hath taken a wife, and married her, and it come to
Jer 3:1 Mal 2:16 pass that she find no favour in his eyes, because he hath found some
Mt 5:31; 19:7 uncleanness in her: then let him write her a bill of divorcement, and give *it*
Mk 10:4 in her hand, and send her out of his house.

23:15 God provided sanctuary in Israel for a slave from any neighboring nation who escaped and who, apparently, had been abused in his servitude. So today, international law provides sanctuary for a citizen of another nation who flees from that nation if the cause for flight is legitimate.

23:17 Canaanite worship included the use of male and female cult prostitutes. God forbade this practice for Israel.

23:18 *the price of a dog,* i.e., of a sodomite.

23:24, 25 Anyone was permitted to eat grapes or grain while in another's field, but no one was permitted to carry anything away with him.

24:1 Divorce was never in the will of God, but it was permitted with certain restrictions as a concession to man's waywardness. In this instance the provision was designed to protect the property rights of a woman whose husband sent her away. He was required to surrender his claim to her dowry. Jesus said divorce sprang from the hardness of men's hearts (Matt. 19:8)

2 And when she is departed out of his house, she may go and be another
man's *wife*.
3 And *if* the latter husband hate her, and write her a bill of divorcement,
and giveth *it* in her hand, and sendeth her out of his house; or if the latter
husband die, which took her *to be* his wife;
4 Her former husband, which sent her away, may not take her again to be
his wife, after that she is defiled; for that *is* abomination before the LORD:
and thou shalt not cause the land to sin, which the LORD thy God giveth
thee *for* an inheritance.
5 ¶When a man hath taken a new wife, he shall not go out to war, neither **24:5** Deut 20:7
shall he be charged with any business: *but* he shall be free at home one year,
and shall cheer up his wife which he hath taken.
6 ¶No man shall take the nether or the upper millstone to pledge: for he ☆**24:6**
taketh *a man's* life to pledge.
7 If a man be found stealing any of his brethren of the children of Israel,
and maketh merchandise of him, or selleth him; then that thief shall die;
and thou shalt put evil away from among you.
8 ¶Take heed in the plague of leprosy, that thou observe diligently, and do **24:8** Lev 13:1, 59
according to all that the priests the Levites shall teach you: as I com-
manded them, *so* ye shall observe to do.
9 Remember what the LORD thy God did unto Miriam by the way, after **24:9** Num 12:10
that ye were come forth out of Egypt.
10 ¶When thou dost lend thy brother any thing, thou shalt not go into his **24:10** Deut 15:8
house to fetch his pledge.
11 Thou shalt stand abroad, and the man to whom thou dost lend shall
bring out the pledge abroad unto thee.
12 And if the man *be* poor, thou shalt not sleep with his pledge: **24:12** Ex 22:26
13 In any case thou shalt deliver him the pledge again when the sun goeth
down, that he may sleep in his own raiment, and bless thee: and it shall be
righteousness unto thee before the LORD thy God.
14 ¶Thou shalt not oppress an hired servant *that is* poor and needy, ☆**24:14** Lev 19:13
whether he be of thy brethren, or of thy strangers that *are* in thy land within Mt 20:8
thy gates: 1 Tim 5:18 Jas 5:4
15 At his day thou shalt give *him* his hire, neither shall the sun go down
upon it; for he *is* poor, and setteth his heart upon it: lest he cry against thee
unto the LORD: and it be sin unto thee.
16 The fathers shall not be put to death for the children, neither shall the **24:16** 2 Kgs 14:6
children be put to death for the fathers: every man shall be put to death for 2 Chron 25:4
his own sin. Ezek 18:4, 20
17 ¶Thou shalt not pervert the judgment of the stranger, *nor* of the **24:17** Ex 22:21, 22
fatherless; nor take a widow's raiment to pledge: 23:2, 3 Deut 1:17; 10:17
18 But thou shalt remember that thou wast a bondman in Egypt, and the **24:18**
LORD thy God redeemed thee thence: therefore I command thee to do this Deut 5:15, 24:22
thing.

---

and forbade it among Christians except on the ground of adultery (Matt. 5:32 and 19:9). Adultery breaks the marriage bond; in the Old Testament those guilty of adultery were stoned to death. Thus the innocent parties were free to remarry. We do not stone people to death for adultery today. But remarriage appears to be quite appropriate for a truly innocent party whose mate has committed adultery. Some say that willful desertion is also ground for remarriage, but the Scriptures do not explicitly say this. The Christian who marries the divorced innocent party does not sin. But, in the eyes of heaven, any Christian who marries someone divorced for other than a biblical reason commits adultery. Some argue that there is no biblical basis for any divorce. They say marriage can be broken only by the death of a spouse.

24:6 The mill for grinding grain was essential to life. Neither the mill nor one of the stones was to be taken as security for a loan.

24:14 God was and is interested in those who earn their keep by working for others. Hired servants were not to be overloaded with work, unreasonably rebuked, or improperly cared for. This rule of thumb applied to Israelite servants and to foreign sojourners.

24:19 Lev 19:9, 10 Deut 14:28, 29

19 ¶When thou cuttest down thine harvest in thy field, and hast forgot a
sheaf in the field, thou shalt not go again to fetch it: it shall be for the
stranger, for the fatherless, and for the widow: that the LORD thy God may
bless thee in all the work of thine hands.

24:20 Lev 19:10

20 When thou beatest thine olive tree, thou shalt not go over the boughs
again: it shall be for the stranger, for the fatherless, and for the widow.
21 When thou gatherest the grapes of thy vineyard, thou shalt not glean *it*
afterward: it shall be for the stranger, for the fatherless, and for the widow.

24:22 Deut 15:15 16:12

22 And thou shalt remember that thou wast a bondman in the land of
Egypt: therefore I command thee to do this thing.

25:1–3☆ Deut 17:11 Acts 16:33 2 Cor 11:24

25 IF there be a controversy between men, and they come unto
judgment, that *the judges* may judge them; then they shall justify
the righteous, and condemn the wicked.
2 And it shall be, if the wicked man *be* worthy to be beaten, that the judge
shall cause him to lie down, and to be beaten before his face, according to
his fault, by a certain number.
3 Forty stripes he may give him, *and* not exceed: lest, *if* he should exceed,
and beat him above these with many stripes, then thy brother should seem
vile unto thee.

25:4 1 Cor 9:9 1 Tim 5:18

25:5–10☆

25:5☆ Gen 38:8 Ruth 1:11, 12 Mt 22:24 Mk 12:19 Lk 20:28

25:6☆ Ruth 4:5

4 ¶Thou shalt not muzzle the ox when he treadeth out *the corn.*
5 If brethren dwell together, and one of them die, and have no child, the
wife of the dead shall not marry without unto a stranger: her husband's
brother shall go in unto her, and take her to him to wife, and perform the
duty of an husband's brother unto her.
6 And it shall be, *that* the firstborn which she beareth shall succeed in the
name of his brother *which is* dead, that his name be not put out of Israel.
7 And if the man like not to take his brother's wife, then let his brother's
wife go up to the gate unto the elders, and say, My husband's brother
refuseth to raise up unto his brother a name in Israel, he will not perform
the duty of my husband's brother.
8 Then the elders of his city shall call him, and speak unto him: and *if* he
stand *to it*, and say, I like not to take her;

25:9, 10☆ Ruth 4:7, 8

9 Then shall his brother's wife come unto him in the presence of the
elders, and loose his shoe from off his foot, and spit in his face, and shall
answer and say, So shall it be done unto that man that will not build up his
brother's house.
10 And his name shall be called in Israel, The house of him that hath his
shoe loosed.
11 ¶When men strive together one with another, and the wife of the one
draweth near for to deliver her husband out of the hand of him that smiteth
him, and putteth forth her hand, and taketh him by the secrets:

25:12 Deut 7:2

12 Then thou shalt cut off her hand, thine eye shall not pity *her*.

25:1ff The law provided that a guilty man not be beaten with more than forty strokes of the lash. The apostle Paul said he had been beaten in this manner five times by the Jews. Thus we have an apt illustration of the fact that there can be miscarriages of justice. Such miscarriages in no way invalidate the law or require that punishments be eliminated. In an imperfect world justice can only be approximated. But the judgments of God are always perfect and no miscarriage of justice ever occurs when divine decisions are handed down.

25:5–10 Levirate marriage was established under the Deuteronomic code. If a man died childless, his unmarried brother was supposed to produce children by the widow. This was probably intended to protect the property rights of the deceased. The first son of the levirate marriage had the same rights he would have had if he had been fathered by his mother's dead husband. All additional children were regarded as legal heirs of the father and not of his dead brother. The custom is pre-Mosaic, and was mentioned in the Nuzi Tablets. Tamar, in Gen. 38, insisted upon this right against her father-in-law, Judah, and contrived his compliance before it was written into the Mosaic law. Later this regulation was the basis of the Sadducean argument against bodily resurrection (Matt. 22:23–33).

25:9, 10 Compare this with the custom described in Ruth 4:7, 8.

13¶Thou shalt not have in thy bag divers weights, a great and a small.
14Thou shalt not have in thine house divers measures, a great and a small.
15*But* thou shalt have a perfect and just weight, a perfect and just measure
shalt thou have: that thy days may be lengthened in the land which the
LORD thy God giveth thee.
16For all that do such things, *and* all that do unrighteously, *are* an
abomination unto the LORD thy God.
17¶Remember what Am'a-lek did unto thee by the way, when ye were
come forth out of Egypt;
18How he met thee by the way, and smote the hindmost of thee, *even* all
that were feeble behind thee, when thou *wast* faint and weary; and he feared
not God.
19Therefore it shall be, when the LORD thy God hath given thee rest from
all thine enemies round about, in the land which the LORD thy God giveth
thee *for* an inheritance to possess it, *that* thou shalt blot out the remem-
brance of Am'a-lek from under heaven; thou shalt not forget *it*.

☆**25:13** Lev 19:35; Prov 11:1; 16:11; Ezek 45:10, 11
25:16 Deut 18:12; 22:5
☆**25:17** Ex 17:8–16
25:19 Deut 12:9

m. Offerings and Prayers to God

26 AND it shall be, when thou *art* come in unto the land which the
LORD thy God giveth thee *for* an inheritance, and possessest it, and
dwellest therein;
2That thou shalt take of the first of all the fruit of the earth, which thou
shalt bring of thy land that the LORD thy God giveth thee, and shalt put *it*
in a basket, and shalt go unto the place which the LORD thy God shall
choose to place his name there.
3And thou shalt go unto the priest that shall be in those days, and say
unto him, I profess this day unto the LORD thy God, that I am come unto
the country which the LORD sware unto our fathers for to give us.
4And the priest shall take the basket out of thine hand, and set it down
before the altar of the LORD thy God.
5And thou shalt speak and say before the LORD thy God, A Syrian ready
to perish *was* my father, and he went down into Egypt, and sojourned there
with a few, and became there a nation, great, mighty, and populous:
6And the Egyptians evil entreated us, and afflicted us, and laid upon us
hard bondage:
7And when we cried unto the LORD God of our fathers, the LORD heard
our voice, and looked on our affliction, and our labour, and our oppression:
8And the LORD brought us forth out of Egypt with a mighty hand, and
with an outstretched arm, and with great terribleness, and with signs, and
with wonders:
9And he hath brought us into this place, and hath given us this land, *even*
a land that floweth with milk and honey.
10And now, behold, I have brought the firstfruits of the land, which thou,
O LORD, hast given me. And thou shalt set it before the LORD thy God, and
worship before the LORD thy God:
11And thou shalt rejoice in every good *thing* which the LORD thy God
hath given unto thee, and unto thine house, thou, and the Levite, and the
stranger that *is* among you.

26:1 Deut 6:1
26:2 Ex 22:29; 23:16, 19
☆**26:5** Gen 43:1; 46:27; Deut 1:10; 10:22
26:6 Ex 1:11, 12; Deut 4:20
26:8 Deut 4:34
26:9 Ex 3:8, 17; Deut 27:2–4; Josh 5:6
26:11 Deut 12:7, 12

25:13 Quite obviously there was a common system of weights and measures in use among the Israelites. Equally obvious was the fact that some were cheats who shortchanged those who did business with them. This form of stealing was prohibited, even as it is today.
25:17 Israel is reminded that the Amalekites were their enemy and that God had sworn to blot out the remembrance of them (see Exod. 17:14). This judgment was deferred until Saul's time (see 1 Samuel 15).
26:5 *A Syrian*, i.e., "migrant Aramean." This refers to Jacob; he had close ties to Paddan-aram.

26:12☆ Deut 14:28, 29; Heb 7:5, 9, 10

12 ¶When thou hast made an end of tithing all the tithes of thine increase the third year, *which is* the year of tithing, and hast given *it* unto the Levite, the stranger, the fatherless, and the widow, that they may eat within thy gates, and be filled;

13 Then thou shalt say before the LORD thy God, I have brought away the hallowed things out of *mine* house, and also have given them unto the Levite, and unto the stranger, to the fatherless, and to the widow, according to all thy commandments which thou hast commanded me: I have not transgressed thy commandments, neither have I forgotten *them:*

26:14☆

14 I have not eaten thereof in my mourning, neither have I taken away *ought* thereof for *any* unclean *use,* nor given *ought* thereof for the dead: *but* I have hearkened to the voice of the LORD my God, *and* have done according to all that thou hast commanded me.

26:15 1 Kgs 8:30; 2 Chron 30:27; Zech 2:13

15 Look down from thy holy habitation, from heaven, and bless thy people Israel, and the land which thou hast given us, as thou swarest unto our fathers, a land that floweth with milk and honey.

16. Moses' Injunction for Israel's Obedience to God

26:16 Deut 6:5, 17

16 ¶This day the LORD thy God hath commanded thee to do these statutes and judgments: thou shalt therefore keep and do them with all thine heart, and with all thy soul.

26:17 Ex 24:3; Lev 18:4, 5; Deut 5:1

17 Thou hast avouched the LORD this day to be thy God, and to walk in his ways, and to keep his statutes, and his commandments, and his judgments, and to hearken unto his voice:

26:18 Deut 7:6

18 And the LORD hath avouched thee this day to be his peculiar people, as he hath promised thee, and that *thou* shouldest keep all his commandments;

26:19☆ Deut 28:1, 13

19 And to make thee high above all nations which he hath made, in praise, and in name, and in honour; and that thou mayest be an holy people unto the LORD thy God, as he hath spoken.

III. THE SUMMARY OF VARIOUS LAWS (27:1—28:68)

A. THE COMMAND TO ERECT AN ALTAR AT MOUNT EBAL

27 AND Moses with the elders of Israel commanded the people, saying, Keep all the commandments which I command you this day.

27:2 Deut 26:9; Josh 8:30–32

2 And it shall be on the day when ye shall pass over Jordan unto the land which the LORD thy God giveth thee, that thou shalt set thee up great stones, and plaister them with plaister:

3 And thou shalt write upon them all the words of this law, when thou art passed over, that thou mayest go in unto the land which the LORD thy God

---

26:12 See note to Deut. 14:28, 29 about the third-year tithe for the poor, etc. This commandment to use the fruit of the land for the poor, the widow, and the Levites was entrusted to the individual. At the end of that third year everyone was required to take an oath before God that he had used the tithe of the land for the purpose for which it was taken and that there had been no holding back or misuse of it. This oath was based on the knowledge of the potential sinfulness of men and was designed to curb coveteousness.

26:14 *nor given aught thereof for the dead.* Heathens sacrificed to the spirits of the dead. This practice was forbidden in Israel; there is no indication that Israelites did this.

26:19 If Israel obeyed God and kept his commandments God would make it high above all nations, and the Israelites would be a holy people to him. "High above all nations" implies that God would accept the Israelites, their friends would admire them, and their enemies would envy them. As holy unto God, they would be separated unto him, devoted to him, and rightly employed in the divine service. The same things may be said of the Church and its people since Pentecost. God raises it above the unregenerate and it is a holy people whose service glorifies the Redeemer.

giveth thee, a land that floweth with milk and honey; as the LORD God of
thy fathers hath promised thee.
4 Therefore it shall be when ye be gone over Jordan, *that* ye shall set up
these stones, which I command you this day, in mount Ebal, and thou shalt
plaister them with plaister.
5 And there shalt thou build an altar unto the LORD thy God, an altar of
stones: thou shalt not lift up *any* iron *tool* upon them.
6 Thou shalt build the altar of the LORD thy God of whole stones: and
thou shalt offer burnt offerings thereon unto the LORD thy God:
7 And thou shalt offer peace offerings, and shalt eat there, and rejoice
before the LORD thy God.
8 And thou shalt write upon the stones all the words of this law very
plainly.
9 ¶And Moses and the priests the Levites spake unto all Israel, saying,
Take heed, and hearken, O Israel; this day thou art become the people of
the LORD thy God.
10 Thou shalt therefore obey the voice of the LORD thy God, and do his
commandments and his statutes, which I command thee this day.
11 ¶And Moses charged the people the same day, saying,
12 These shall stand upon mount Ger'i-zim to bless the people, when ye
are come over Jordan; Simeon, and Levi, and Judah, and Is'sa-char, and
Joseph, and Benjamin:
13 And these shall stand upon mount Ebal to curse; Reuben, Gad, and
Asher, and Zeb'u-lun, Dan, and Naph'ta-li.
14 ¶And the Levites shall speak, and say unto all the men of Israel with a
loud voice,

27:7 Lev 7:11; Num 6:14; 7:88
27:9 Deut 26:17
☆**27:11**
27:12 Deut 11:26; Josh 8:33–35

B. THE TWELVE CURSES PROCLAIMED BY THE LEVITES

15 Cursed *be* the man that maketh *any* graven or molten image, an
abomination unto the LORD, the work of the hands of the craftsman, and
putteth *it* in *a* secret *place.* And all the people shall answer and say, Amen.
16 Cursed *be* he that setteth light by his father or his mother. And all the
people shall say, Amen.
17 Cursed *be* he that removeth his neighbour's landmark. And all the
people shall say, Amen.
18 Cursed *be* he that maketh the blind to wander out of the way. And all
the people shall say, Amen.
19 Cursed *be* he that perverteth the judgment of the stranger, fatherless,
and widow. And all the people shall say, Amen.
20 Cursed *be* he that lieth with his father's wife; because he uncovereth his
father's skirt. And all the people shall say, Amen.
21 Cursed *be* he that lieth with any manner of beast. And all the people
shall say, Amen.
22 Cursed *be* he that lieth with his sister, the daughter of his father, or the
daughter of his mother. And all the people shall say, Amen.
23 Cursed *be* he that lieth with his mother in law. And all the people shall
say, Amen.

27:15 Ex 20:4, 23; 34:17; Lev 19:3, 4; 26:1; Deut 4:16; 5:8
27:16 Ex 21:15; Lev 20:9; Deut 21:18; Ezek 22:7
27:17 Deut 19:14
27:18 Lev 19:14
27:19 Ex 22:21; Lev 19:33; Deut 10:18; 24:17; Ezek 22:7
27:20 Lev 18:8; 20:11; Deut 22:30
27:21 Ex 22:19; Lev 18:23; 20:15
27:22 Lev 18:9; 20:17
27:23 Lev 18:17; 20:14

27:11ff Once Israel has entered the land, the covenant must be publicly renewed and accepted by oral testimony. Six of the tribes were to be stationed on Mount Ebal and the other six on Mount Gerazim. The six on Mount Gerazim were children of Leah and Rachel; the other six were children of the bondwomen. Curses were to be declared as judgments against those things that were prohibited and the Israelites were to shout Amen. By this, Israel acknowledged the equity of the curses and promised they would not do what was prohibited. Their assent would make any disobedience their own fault and any judgment that followed would be what they deserved.

27:24 Ex 21:12; Lev 24:17; Num 35:30; Deut 19:13; Ps 64:4
27:25 Ex 23:8; Deut 10:17; 16:19; Prov 15:27; 17:23
27:26 Deut 5:1; 28:15; Gal 3:10

24 Cursed *be* he that smiteth his neighbour secretly. And all the people
shall say, Amen.
25 Cursed *be* he that taketh reward to slay an innocent person. And all the
people shall say, Amen.
26 Cursed *be* he that confirmeth not *all* the words of this law to do them.
And all the people shall say, Amen.

C. GOD'S SPECIFIC BLESSING FOR OBEDIENCE

28:1 Ex 15:26; 23:22; Lev 26:3; Deut 7:12; 11:13

28 AND it shall come to pass, if thou shalt hearken diligently unto the
voice of the LORD thy God, to observe *and* to do all his command-
ments which I command thee this day, that the LORD thy God will set thee
on high above all nations of the earth:

28:2☆ Lev 26:9; Deut 28:8; Ps 107:36–38; Amos 9:13

2 And all these blessings shall come on thee, and overtake thee, if thou
shalt hearken unto the voice of the LORD thy God.
3 Blessed *shalt* thou *be* in the city, and blessed *shalt* thou *be* in the field.
4 Blessed *shall be* the fruit of thy body, and the fruit of thy ground, and
the fruit of thy cattle, the increase of thy kine, and the flocks of thy sheep.
5 Blessed *shall be* thy basket and thy store.
6 Blessed *shalt* thou *be* when thou comest in, and blessed *shalt* thou *be*
when thou goest out.

28:7 Lev 26:7; Deut 32:30; Josh 10:10; Ps 89:23
28:8 Lev 25:21, 22; 26:4, 5

7 The LORD shall cause thine enemies that rise up against thee to be
smitten before thy face: they shall come out against thee one way, and flee
before thee seven ways.
8 The LORD shall command the blessing upon thee in thy storehouses, and
in all that thou settest thine hand unto; and he shall bless thee in the land
which the LORD thy God giveth thee.

28:9 Ex 19:5; Deut 7:6; 26:18

9 The LORD shall establish thee an holy people unto himself, as he hath
sworn unto thee, if thou shalt keep the commandments of the LORD thy
God, and walk in his ways.
10 And all people of the earth shall see that thou art called by the name of
the LORD; and they shall be afraid of thee.

28:11☆ Lev 26:9; Deut 28:2–6, 8; 30:9

11 And the LORD shall make thee plenteous in goods, in the fruit of thy
body, and in the fruit of thy cattle, and in the fruit of thy ground, in the
land which the LORD sware unto thy fathers to give thee.

28:12 Lev 26:4; Deut 11:14; 23:20

12 The LORD shall open unto thee his good treasure, the heaven to give the
rain unto thy land in his season, and to bless all the work of thine hand:
and thou shalt lend unto many nations, and thou shalt not borrow.

28:13 Deut 28:1, 44

13 And the LORD shall make thee the head, and not the tail; and thou
shalt be above only, and thou shalt not be beneath; if that thou hearken
unto the commandments of the LORD thy God, which I command thee this
day, to observe and to do *them:*

28:14 Deut 5:32, 33; 19:9

14 And thou shalt not go aside from any of the words which I command
thee this day, *to* the right hand, or *to* the left, to go after other gods to serve
them.

28:2 If there are cursings for disobedience, there are also blessings for obedience. Here God made promises to his people—for better or for worse; unfortunately, they were for the worst and even resulted in the captivity and the diminution of the nation before the first coming of Jesus Christ. At some later time, a repentant Israel will have the blessings restored.

28:11 *And the LORD shall make thee plenteous in goods,* i.e., the Lord will grant his people material prosperity. A number of evangelicals have succumbed to the faddish notion that there is something intrinsically wrong in having much of this world's goods. Yet God has promised to bless his people materially. But the more God gives them, the greater their stewardship responsibilities. Riches can be either a snare or an instrument for the glory of God and the advancement of world evangelization.

D. GOD'S SPECIFIC PUNISHMENTS FOR DISOBEDIENCE

15 ¶But it shall come to pass, if thou wilt not hearken unto the voice of the LORD thy God, to observe to do all his commandments and his statutes which I command thee this day; that all these curses shall come upon thee, and overtake thee:

28:15 Lev 26:14 Deut 27:15 28:1–6 Josh 23:15, 16

16 Cursed *shalt* thou *be* in the city, and cursed *shalt* thou *be* in the field.
17 Cursed *shall be* thy basket and thy store.
18 Cursed *shall be* the fruit of thy body, and the fruit of thy land, the increase of thy kine, and the flocks of thy sheep.
19 Cursed *shalt* thou *be* when thou comest in, and cursed *shalt* thou *be* when thou goest out.
20 The LORD shall send upon thee cursing, vexation, and rebuke, in all that thou settest thine hand unto for to do, until thou be destroyed, and until thou perish quickly; because of the wickedness of thy doings, whereby thou hast forsaken me.

28:20 Deut 8:11; 28:25

21 The LORD shall make the pestilence cleave unto thee, until he have consumed thee from off the land, whither thou goest to possess it.
22 The LORD shall smite thee with a consumption, and with a fever, and with an inflammation, and with an extreme burning, and with the sword, and with blasting, and with mildew; and they shall pursue thee until thou perish.

28:21 Lev 26:25 Num 14:12 1 Kgs 8:37 Amos 4:10

23 And thy heaven that *is* over thy head shall be brass, and the earth that *is* under thee *shall be* iron.

28:23 Lev 26:19

24 The LORD shall make the rain of thy land powder and dust: from heaven shall it come down upon thee, until thou be destroyed.
25 The LORD shall cause thee to be smitten before thine enemies: thou shalt go out one way against them, and flee seven ways before them: and shalt be removed into all the kingdoms of the earth.
26 And thy carcase shall be meat unto all fowls of the air, and unto the beasts of the earth, and no man shall fray *them* away.
27 The LORD will smite thee with the botch of Egypt, and with the emerods, and with the scab, and with the itch, whereof thou canst not be healed.
28 The LORD shall smite thee with madness, and blindness, and astonishment of heart:

28:24 Deut 11:17 1 Kgs 17:1 Jer 14:1
28:25 Lev 26:17, 36 2 Chron 29:8 Isa 30:17 Jer 15:4
28:26 Ps 79:2 Jer 7:33; 16:4 19:7; 34:20
28:27 Ex 9:9; 15:26 Lev 13:1, 2 Deut 7:15 1 Sam 5:6, 9, 12
28:28 Isa 19:14

29 And thou shalt grope at noonday, as the blind gropeth in darkness, and thou shalt not prosper in thy ways: and thou shalt be only oppressed and spoiled evermore, and no man shall save *thee*.

28:29 Ex 10:21 Job 5:14 Ps 69:23 Isa 59:10

30 Thou shalt betroth a wife, and another man shall lie with her: thou shalt build an house, and thou shalt not dwell therein: thou shalt plant a vineyard, and shalt not gather the grapes thereof.
31 Thine ox *shall be* slain before thine eyes, and thou shalt not eat thereof: thine ass *shall be* violently taken away from before thy face, and shall not be restored to thee: thy sheep *shall be* given unto thine enemies, and thou shalt have none to rescue *them*.

28:30 Deut 20:6, 7 Job 31:10 Isa 65:21 Jer 8:10 Amos 5:11

32 Thy sons and thy daughters *shall be* given unto another people, and thine eyes shall look, and fail *with longing* for them all the day long: and *there shall be* no might in thine hand.

28:32 2 Chron 29:9 Neh 5:2, 5

33 The fruit of thy land, and all thy labours, shall a nation which thou knowest not eat up; and thou shalt be only oppressed and crushed alway:
34 So that thou shalt be mad for the sight of thine eyes which thou shalt see.

28:34 Deut 28:28

35 The LORD shall smite thee in the knees, and in the legs, with a sore botch that cannot be healed, from the sole of thy foot unto the top of thy head.

28:35 Job 2:7 Isa 3:17

28:36☆ Deut 4:28; 2 Kgs 17:4, 6; 24:12, 14; 25:7, 11

36 The LORD shall bring thee, and thy king which thou shalt set over thee,
unto a nation which neither thou nor thy fathers have known; and there
shalt thou serve other gods, wood and stone.

28:37 Deut 29:22

37 And thou shalt become an astonishment, a proverb, and a byword,
among all nations whither the LORD shall lead thee.

28:38 Lev 26:20; Isa 5:10; Joel 1:4; Mic 6:15
28:39 Amos 5:11; Mic 6:15

38 Thou shalt carry much seed out into the field, and shalt gather *but* little
in; for the locust shall consume it.
39 Thou shalt plant vineyards, and dress *them*, but shalt neither drink *of*
the wine, nor gather *the grapes;* for the worms shall eat them.
40 Thou shalt have olive trees throughout all thy coasts, but thou shalt not
anoint *thyself* with the oil; for thine olive shall cast *his fruit*.

28:41 Deut 28:32

41 Thou shall beget sons and daughters, but thou shalt not enjoy them; for
they shall go into captivity.

28:42 Deut 28:38; Amos 7:11

42 All thy trees and fruit of thy land shall the locust consume.
43 The stranger that *is* within thee shall get up above thee very high; and
thou shalt come down very low.

28:44 Deut 28:12, 13

44 He shall lend to thee, and thou shalt not lend to him: he shall be the
head, and thou shalt be the tail.

28:45 Lev 26:28; Deut 4:25, 26; 29:20

45 Moreover all these curses shall come upon thee, and shall pursue thee,
and overtake thee, till thou be destroyed; because thou hearkenedst not
unto the voice of the LORD thy God, to keep his commandments and his
statutes which he commanded thee:
46 And they shall be upon thee for a sign and for a wonder, and upon thy
seed for ever.

28:47 Lev 26:13; Deut 28:36; Jer 28:14; Lam 1:3

47 Because thou servedst not the LORD thy God with joyfulness, and with
gladness of heart, for the abundance of all *things;*
48 Therefore shalt thou serve thine enemies which the LORD shall send
against thee, in hunger, and in thirst, and in nakedness, and in want of all
things: and he shall put a yoke of iron upon thy neck, until he have
destroyed thee.

28:49☆ Deut 28:36; Isa 5:26; 7:18; Jer 5:15

49 The LORD shall bring a nation against thee from far, from the end of
the earth, *as swift* as the eagle flieth; a nation whose tongue thou shalt not
understand;
50 A nation of fierce countenance, which shall not regard the person of the
old, nor shew favour to the young:
51 And he shall eat the fruit of thy cattle, and the fruit of thy land, until
thou be destroyed: which *also* shall not leave thee *either* corn, wine, or oil,
or the increase of thy kine, or flocks of thy sheep, until he have destroyed
thee.

28:52 2 Kgs 19:30; 25:1; 2 Chron 32:1; Jer 10:17, 18; Zeph 1:14, 15

52 And he shall besiege thee in all thy gates, until thy high and fenced
walls come down, wherein thou trustedst, throughout all thy land: and he
shall besiege thee in all thy gates throughout all thy land, which the LORD
thy God hath given thee.

28:53 Lev 26:29; Jer 19:9; Lam 2:20; 4:10; Ezek 5:10

53 And thou shalt eat the fruit of thine own body, the flesh of thy sons and
of thy daughters, which the LORD thy God hath given thee, in the siege, and
in the straitness, wherewith thine enemies shall distress thee:
54 *So that* the man *that is* tender among you, and very delicate, his eye
shall be evil toward his brother, and toward the wife of his bosom, and
toward the remnant of his children which he shall leave:

28:36 This prophetic word was literally fulfilled when the ten tribes were carried captive into Assyria (2 Kings 17:6) and later when the other two tribes were taken to Babylon in the captivity of seventy years (2 Kings 24:14, 15; 25:7, 21).

28:49 Some think this judgment refers to the Babylonian captivity; others think it is the destruction of Jerusalem by the Romans in A.D. 70, as later prophesied by Jesus; still others think it refers to both judgments.

55 So that he will not give to any of them of the flesh of his children whom
he shall eat: because he hath nothing left him in the siege, and in the
straitness, wherewith thine enemies shall distress thee in all thy gates.
56 The tender and delicate woman among you, which would not adventure
to set the sole of her foot upon the ground for delicateness and tenderness,
her eye shall be evil toward the husband of her bosom, and toward her son,
and toward her daughter,
57 And toward her young one that cometh out from between her feet, and
toward her children which she shall bear: for she shall eat them for want of
all *things* secretly in the siege and straitness, wherewith thine enemy shall
distress thee in thy gates.
58 If thou wilt not observe to do all the words of this law that are written **28:58**
in this book, that thou mayest fear this glorious and fearful name, THE Lev 26:14 Deut 28:15
LORD THY GOD;
59 Then the LORD will make thy plagues wonderful, and the plagues of thy
seed, *even* great plagues, and of long continuance, and sore sicknesses, and
of long continuance.
60 Moreover he will bring upon thee all the diseases of Egypt, which thou **28:60**
wast afraid of; and they shall cleave unto thee. Deut 28:21, 27
61 Also every sickness, and every plague, which *is* not written in the book
of this law, them will the LORD bring upon thee, until thou be destroyed.
62 And ye shall be left few in number, whereas ye were as the stars of ☆**28:62**
heaven for multitude; because thou wouldest not obey the voice of the Deut 1:10
LORD thy God.
63 And it shall come to pass, *that* as the LORD rejoiced over you to do you **28:63**
good, and to multiply you; so the LORD will rejoice over you to destroy Deut 30:9 Jer 45:4
you, and to bring you to nought; and ye shall be plucked from off the land
whither thou goest to possess it.
64 And the LORD shall scatter thee among all people, from the one end of **28:64**
the earth even unto the other; and there thou shalt serve other gods, which Lev 26:33 Deut 4:27; 32:17
neither thou nor thy fathers have known, *even* wood and stone. Neh 1:8 Jer 16:13
65 And among these nations shalt thou find no ease, neither shall the sole Lk 21:24 **28:65**
of thy foot have rest: but the LORD shall give thee there a trembling heart, Lam 1:3
and failing of eyes, and sorrow of mind:
66 And thy life shall hang in doubt before thee; and thou shalt fear day **28:66**
and night, and shalt have none assurance of thy life: Heb 10:27
67 In the morning thou shalt say, Would God it were even! and at even **28:67**
thou shalt say, Would God it were morning! for the fear of thine heart Deut 28:34
wherewith thou shalt fear, and for the sight of thine eyes which thou shalt
see.
68 And the LORD shall bring thee into Egypt again with ships, by the way **28:68**
whereof I spake unto thee, Thou shalt see it no more again: and there ye Deut 17:16
shall be sold unto your enemies for bondmen and bondwomen, and no man
shall buy *you*.

28:62 This prophecy concerning the Jews was fulfilled in the *diaspora* ("dispersion") when the Northern Kingdom came under attack by the Assyrians in 722 B.C., when Nebuchadnezzar overcame Jerusalem in 586 B.C., and finally when Titus and Vespasian finished this work in A.D. 70, when Jerusalem was destroyed. The Bible is filled with prophecies concerning future events which either have been fulfilled or await fulfillment. Fulfilled prophecy attests to the inspiration and inerrancy of the Word of God. (See also Jesus' Olivet Discourse—Matt. 24:1—25:46; Mark 13; Luke 21—for the course of this present age.)

IV. MOSES' LAST ADDRESS AND THE NAMING OF HIS SUCCESSOR (29:1—32:43)

A. ISRAEL EXHORTED TO KEEP GOD'S CONTRACT

29:1☆ Lev 27:34; Deut 1:1–5; 5:1

29 THESE *are* the words of the covenant, which the LORD com-
manded Moses to make with the children of Israel in the land of
Moab, beside the covenant which he made with them in Ho′reb.

29:2 Lev 8:1; Num 1:17–19; 30:1

2¶And Moses called unto all Israel, and said unto them, Ye have seen all
that the LORD did before your eyes in the land of Egypt unto Pharaoh, and
unto all his servants, and unto all his land;
3The great temptations which thine eyes have seen, the signs, and those
great miracles:

29:4 Isa 6:9, 10; Acts 28:26; Rom 11:8

4Yet the LORD hath not given you an heart to perceive, and eyes to see,
and ears to hear, unto this day.

29:5 Deut 8:2, 4

5And I have led you forty years in the wilderness: your clothes are not
waxen old upon you, and thy shoe is not waxen old upon thy foot.
6Ye have not eaten bread, neither have ye drunk wine or strong drink:
that ye might know that I *am* the LORD your God.

29:7 Num 21:21; Deut 1:2–5; 2:26

7And when ye came unto this place, Sihon the king of Hesh′bon, and Og
the king of Ba′shan, came out against us unto battle, and we smote them:

29:8 Num 32:31; Deut 3:12

8And we took their land, and gave it for an inheritance unto the
Reubenites, and to the Gadites, and to the half tribe of Ma-nas′seh.

29:9 Ex 19:5; Deut 4:6; Josh 1:7

9Keep therefore the words of this covenant, and do them, that ye may
prosper in all that ye do.

29:10☆ Deut 4:10; 31:12

10¶Ye stand this day all of you before the LORD your God; your captains
of your tribes, your elders, and your officers, *with* all the men of Israel,

29:11 Josh 9:21, 23, 27

11Your little ones, your wives, and thy stranger that *is* in thy camp, from
the hewer of thy wood unto the drawer of thy water:

29:12 Deut 5:2

12That thou shouldest enter into covenant with the LORD thy God, and
into his oath, which the LORD thy God maketh with thee this day:

29:13 Gen 17:7; Ex 6:7; Deut 7:6; 26:18

13That he may establish thee to day for a people unto himself, and *that* he
may be unto thee a God, as he hath said unto thee, and as he hath sworn
unto thy fathers, to Abraham, to Isaac, and to Jacob.

B. GOD WILL NOT PARDON CONTRACT BREAKERS

29:14 Jer 31:31; Heb 8:7

14Neither with you only do I make this covenant and this oath;
15But with *him* that standeth here with us this day before the LORD our
God, and also with *him* that *is* not here with us this day:

29:16 Deut 2:4

16(For ye know how we have dwelt in the land of Egypt; and how we
came through the nations which ye passed by;

29:17 Ex 20:23; Deut 4:28; 28:36

17And ye have seen their abominations, and their idols, wood and stone,
silver and gold, which *were* among them:)

29:18 Deut 13:6; 32:32; Jer 9:15; Hos 10:4; Heb 12:15

18Lest there should be among you man, or woman, or family, or tribe,
whose heart turneth away this day from the LORD our God, to go *and* serve
the gods of these nations; lest there should be among you a root that
beareth gall and wormwood;

29:1 This agreement between God and Israel was made in Moab and is an extension of the Abrahamic covenant. The conditions: (1) God's blessings are conditioned upon Israel's obedience (28:1ff); (2) God will punish Israel for disobedience (28:15ff); (3) God will disperse his people if they become apostate (28:63ff); (4) God will regather Israel after dispersion if and when they repent (30:1ff); (5) God promises that Israel will some day repossess the land (30:5); (6) God promises judgment on Israel's enemies (30:7); and (7) God assures them of future prosperity (30:9).

29:10ff This was an all-embracing covenant which included the children, the wives, and the sojourners, as well as the elders, officers, and obviously the priests too. The inclusion of the sojourners or foreigners was an indication of God's concern for all men, as was demonstrated when Peter and Paul preached the gospel to the Gentiles.

[19]And it come to pass, when he heareth the words of this curse, that he
bless himself in his heart, saying, I shall have peace, though I walk in the
imagination of mine heart, to add drunkenness to thirst:
[20]The LORD will not spare him, but then the anger of the LORD and his
jealousy shall smoke against that man, and all the curses that are written in
this book shall lie upon him, and the LORD shall blot out his name from
under heaven.
[21]And the LORD shall separate him unto evil out of all the tribes of Israel,
according to all the curses of the covenant that are written in this book of
the law:
[22]So that the generation to come of your children that shall rise up after
you, and the stranger that shall come from a far land, shall say, when they
see the plagues of that land, and the sicknesses which the LORD hath laid
upon it;
[23]*And that* the whole land thereof *is* brimstone, and salt, *and* burning, *that*
it is not sown, nor beareth, nor any grass groweth therein, like the
overthrow of Sodom, and Go-mor'rah, Ad'mah, and Ze-bo'im, which the
LORD overthrew in his anger, and in his wrath:
[24]Even all nations shall say, Wherefore hath the LORD done thus unto
this land? what *meaneth* the heat of this great anger?
[25]Then men shall say, Because they have forsaken the covenant of the
LORD God of their fathers, which he made with them when he brought
them forth out of the land of Egypt:
[26]For they went and served other gods, and worshipped them, gods
whom they knew not, and *whom* he had not given unto them:
[27]And the anger of the LORD was kindled against this land, to bring upon
it all the curses that are written in this book:
[28]And the LORD rooted them out of their land in anger, and in wrath, and
in great indignation, and cast them into another land, as *it is* this day.
[29]The secret *things belong* unto the LORD our God: but those *things which*
are revealed *belong* unto us and to our children for ever, that *we* may do all
the words of this law.

29:19 Num 15:30, 39; Ps 10:4–6; 49:18, 19; Prov 29:1; Jer 5:12
29:20 Deut 9:14; 2 Kgs 14:27; Ps 74:1; 80:4
29:22 Jer 19:8
☆**29:23** Gen 19:24; Isa 1:7; 34:9; 64:11
29:24 1 Kgs 9:8; 2 Chron 7:21; Jer 22:8; Lam 2:15
29:25 2 Kgs 17:9; 2 Chron 36:13; Jer 40:2, 3; 50:7
29:27 Deut 29:20
29:28 1 Kgs 14:15; Ezek 19:12
☆**29:29** Job 11:6, 7; Ps 25:14; 78:2–7

C. THE MERCY OF GOD FOR THE REPENTANT SINNERS

30 AND it shall come to pass, when all these things are come upon
thee, the blessing and the curse, which I have set before thee, and
thou shalt call *them* to mind among all the nations, whither the LORD thy
God hath driven thee,
[2]And shalt return unto the LORD thy God, and shalt obey his voice
according to all that I command thee this day, thou and thy children, with
all thine heart, and with all thy soul;
[3]That then the LORD thy God will turn thy captivity, and have
compassion upon thee, and will return and gather thee from all the nations,
whither the LORD thy God hath scattered thee.

30:1 Lev 26:40, 41; Deut 4:30; 11:26
☆**30:2** Lev 26:3; Deut 26:16; Neh 1:8, 9
30:3 Gen 28:15; 48:21; Ps 106:45–47; Isa 56:8; Mt 23:37; Jn 12:51, 52

29:23 Even as Canaan would be a garden of the Lord, so it could become a barren waste like Sodom if Israel turned from God. The judgment would begin with plagues and sicknesses (verse 22), followed by judgment on the land itself. This was true in a later age, when Rome left Canaan desolate and barren.

29:29 This verse makes plain that God has not told us everything, but he has told us all we need to know. Disobedience indicates a lack of motivation or will, not a lack of knowledge.

30:2 God promised Israel that if the nation repented after having been judged and dispersed by God, he would regather his people "from the outmost parts of heaven" (30:4). This promise has never been fulfilled; the fulfillment will come in the future. There are different opinions as to when and how this will take place, but take place it will.

30:4 Isa 43:5, 6; 48:20; 62:11

[4]If *any* of thine be driven out unto the outmost *parts* of heaven, from thence will the LORD thy God gather thee, and from thence will he fetch thee:

30:5 Deut 13:17; Jer 29:14; 30:3

[5]And the LORD thy God will bring thee into the land which thy fathers possessed, and thou shalt possess it; and he will do thee good, and multiply thee above thy fathers.

[6]And the LORD thy God will circumcise thine heart, and the heart of thy seed, to love the LORD thy God with all thine heart, and with all thy soul, that thou mayest live.

30:7 Ex 23:22; Deut 25:19; 28:7; 30:2

[7]And the LORD thy God will put all these curses upon thine enemies, and on them that hate thee, which persecuted thee.

[8]And thou shalt return and obey the voice of the LORD, and do all his commandments which I command thee this day.

30:9 Deut 15:10; 29:9

[9]And the LORD thy God will make thee plenteous in every work of thine hand, in the fruit of thy body, and in the fruit of thy cattle, and in the fruit of thy land, for good: for the LORD will again rejoice over thee for good, as he rejoiced over thy fathers:

30:10 Deut 4:29; Ezek 18:21

[10]If thou shalt hearken unto the voice of the LORD thy God, to keep his commandments and his statutes which are written in this book of the law, *and* if thou turn unto the LORD thy God with all thine heart, and with all thy soul.

D. THE CLOSING EXHORTATION

1. The Nearness of the Word of God in Hearts and on Lips

30:11–14☆ Isa 45:19; Rom 16:25–27

[11]¶For this commandment which I command thee this day, it *is* not hidden from thee, neither *is* it far off.

30:12–14 Rom 10:6–8

[12]It *is* not in heaven, that thou shouldest say, Who shall go up for us to heaven, and bring it unto us, that we may hear it, and do it?

[13]Neither *is* it beyond the sea, that thou shouldest say, Who shall go over the sea for us, and bring it unto us, that we may hear it, and do it?

[14]But the word *is* very nigh unto thee, in thy mouth, and in thy heart, that thou mayest do it.

2. The Choice of Life or Death, Blessing or Curse

30:15 Deut 11:26; Jer 21:8; Mt 7:13, 14

30:16 Deut 4:1; 6:5; 30:6

[15]¶See, I have set before thee this day life and good, and death and evil;

[16]In that I command thee this day to love the LORD thy God, to walk in his ways, and to keep his commandments and his statutes and his judgments, that thou mayest live and multiply: and the LORD thy God shall bless thee in the land whither thou goest to possess it.

30:17 Deut 28:15, 36, 64; 29:18

[17]But if thine heart turn away, so that thou wilt not hear, but shalt be drawn away, and worship other gods, and serve them;

30:18 Deut 25:13–15; 31:29

[18]I denounce unto you this day, that ye shall surely perish, *and that* ye shall not prolong *your* days upon the land, whither thou passest over Jordan to go to possess it.

30:19 Deut 4:26; 31:28; 32:1; Isa 1:2

[19]I call heaven and earth to record this day against you, *that* I have set before you life and death, blessing and cursing: therefore choose life, that both thou and thy seed may live:

30:20 Deut 10:20; 13:4; Josh 22:5

[20]That thou mayest love the LORD thy God, *and* that thou mayest obey his voice, and that thou mayest cleave unto him: for he *is* thy life, and the

---

30:11–14 What God revealed to Israel, and to us through Israel, does not require more revelation or the need to seek it by sending messengers to heaven. His word is forever written in the Scriptures and is available to all. The translation of the Bible into thousands of languages brings to virtually all the peoples of the world the knowledge of God and the commandments they are called upon to obey with thankful hearts.

length of thy days: that thou mayest dwell in the land which the LORD sware unto thy fathers, to Abraham, to Isaac, and to Jacob, to give them.

E. MOSES' LAST ACTIONS
1. The Appointment of Joshua as Leader

31 AND Moses went and spake these words unto all Israel.
2 And he said unto them, I *am* an hundred and twenty years old this day; I can no more go out and come in: also the LORD hath said unto me, Thou shalt not go over this Jordan.
3 The LORD thy God, he will go over before thee, *and* he will destroy these nations from before thee, and thou shalt possess them: *and* Joshua, he shall go over before thee, as the LORD hath said.
4 And the LORD shall do unto them as he did to Sihon and to Og, kings of the Am'or-ites, and unto the land of them, whom he destroyed.
5 And the LORD shall give them up before your face, that ye may do unto them according unto all the commandments which I have commanded you.
6 Be strong and of a good courage, fear not, nor be afraid of them: for the LORD thy God, he *it is* that doth go with thee; he will not fail thee, nor forsake thee.
7 ¶And Moses called unto Joshua, and said unto him in the sight of all Israel, Be strong and of a good courage: for thou must go with this people unto the land which the LORD hath sworn unto their fathers to give them; and thou shalt cause them to inherit it.
8 And the LORD, he *it is* that doth go before thee; he will be with thee, he will not fail thee, neither forsake thee: fear not, neither be dismayed.

☆31:2 Deut 1:37; 34:7 Acts 7:23, 30
31:3 Num 27:18 Deut 3:28; 34:9 Josh 1:2; 3:7
31:4 Deut 2:32–34 3:3
31:6 Deut 20:1 Heb 13:5
☆31:7 Deut 1:38; 3:28

2. The Command to Read the Laws to Israel at Stated Times

9 ¶And Moses wrote this law, and delivered it unto the priests the sons of Levi, which bare the ark of the covenant of the LORD, and unto all the elders of Israel.
10 And Moses commanded them, saying, At the end of *every* seven years, in the solemnity of the year of release, in the feast of tabernacles,
11 When all Israel is come to appear before the LORD thy God in the place which he shall choose, thou shalt read this law before all Israel in their hearing.
12 Gather the people together, men, and women, and children, and thy stranger that *is* within thy gates, that they may hear, and that they may learn, and fear the LORD your God, and observe to do all the words of this law:
13 And *that* their children, which have not known *any thing*, may hear, and learn to fear the LORD your God, as long as ye live in the land whither ye go over Jordan to possess it.

31:9 Num 4:5, 6 Deut 10:8
☆31:10–13
31:10 Deut 12:4, 5 15:1
31:12 Deut 4:10; 29:11

31:2 *I can no more go out and come in,* i.e., "I am no longer able to lead you."† Moses was not disabled by physical disability or senility of mind, for "his natural force [was not] abated" (34:7). Rather he was under the divine sentence that he could not go over the Jordan because of his sin. Israel was ready to enter the land. Moses was, therefore, relieved of his responsibility.

31:7 The appointment of Joshua was by God's command. He had been under training for a long time. God never removes a leader without raising up someone else to take his place and to carry on the work of God.

31:10–13 There were not many copies of the Pentateuch available. But we do know that Moses' writings were read in the synagogues every sabbath (Acts 15:21). Even pious Israelites could not read Moses' writings to their families every day unless they had copies of the law, which most of them did not have. Thus Moses appointed a time for the public reading of the law: every seventh year. Today most people have copies of the Bible they can read at home. Home reading of the Bible, though, is often neglected. In all likelihood, the Israelites memorized the law and could probably repeat much of it from memory. Private reading, public reading, and memorization of the Word of God are important.

3. Moses and Joshua Meet with God

31:14☆ Num 27:13; Deut 34:5

14 ¶And the LORD said unto Moses, Behold, thy days approach that thou must die: call Joshua, and present yourselves in the tabernacle of the congregation, that I may give him a charge. And Moses and Joshua went, and presented themselves in the tabernacle of the congregation.

31:15☆ Ex 16:10

15 And the LORD appeared in the tabernacle in a pillar of a cloud: and the pillar of the cloud stood over the door of the tabernacle.

31:16 Deut 4:25; 32:50; Judg 2:11; 10:6

16 ¶And the LORD said unto Moses, Behold, thou shalt sleep with thy fathers; and this people will rise up, and go a whoring after the gods of the strangers of the land, whither they go *to be* among them, and will forsake me, and break my covenant which I have made with them.

31:17 Judg 2:12–14

17 Then my anger shall be kindled against them in that day, and I will forsake them, and I will hide my face from them, and they shall be devoured, and many evils and troubles shall befall them; so that they will say in that day, Are not these evils come upon us, because our God *is* not among us?

18 And I will surely hide my face in that day for all the evils which they shall have wrought, in that they are turned unto other gods.

19 Now therefore write ye this song for you, and teach it the children of Israel: put it in their mouths, that this song may be a witness for me against the children of Israel.

31:20 Deut 6:10–12; 8:10, 19; 11:16, 17

20 For when I shall have brought them into the land which I sware unto their fathers, that floweth with milk and honey; and they shall have eaten and filled themselves, and waxen fat; then will they turn unto other gods, and serve them, and provoke me, and break my covenant.

31:21 Lev 26:40, 41

21 And it shall come to pass, when many evils and troubles are befallen them, that this song shall testify against them as a witness; for it shall not be forgotten out of the mouths of their seed: for I know their imagination which they go about, even now, before I have brought them into the land which I sware.

22 ¶Moses therefore wrote this song the same day, and taught it the children of Israel.

23 And he gave Joshua the son of Nun a charge, and said, Be strong and of a good courage: for thou shalt bring the children of Israel into the land which I sware unto them: and I will be with thee.

4. Moses' Last Words to the Levites

31:24–26☆

24 ¶And it came to pass, when Moses had made an end of writing the words of this law in a book, until they were finished,

31:25 Deut 31:9

25 That Moses commanded the Levites, which bare the ark of the covenant of the LORD, saying,

26 Take this book of the law, and put it in the side of the ark of the covenant of the LORD your God, that it may be there for a witness against thee.

31:27 Deut 9:6, 7, 13, 14

27 For I know thy rebellion, and thy stiff neck: behold, while I am yet alive with you this day, ye have been rebellious against the LORD; and how much more after my death?

31:14, 15 God now charges Moses to bring Joshua with him to the tabernacle. He is then presented to God as the new leader of Israel. This is the only time in Deuteronomy we hear of the glory of the Lord appearing. In these later times, we should not expect to see the appearance of the glory of the Lord since we have the sure word of prophecy; and if we will not hear that, we will not heed a supernatural appearance of God.

31:24–26 Moses completed the written word of the law of God and gave it to the priests to be deposited beside the ark of God. The two tables of the law were kept in the ark. For the writing of Moses to be placed beside the ark indicates how wonderfully sacred that Word was and ever will be.

28 ¶Gather unto me all the elders of your tribes, and your officers, that I
may speak these words in their ears, and call heaven and earth to record
against them.
29 For I know that after my death ye will utterly corrupt *yourselves*, and
turn aside from the way which I have commanded you; and evil will befall
you in the latter days; because ye will do evil in the sight of the LORD, to
provoke him to anger through the work of your hands.

31:28 Deut 30:19; 32:1
31:29 Deut 32:5

5. The Song Moses Sang

a. The Prelude

30 And Moses spake in the ears of all the congregation of Israel the words
of this song, until they were ended.

32 GIVE ear, O ye heavens, and I will speak; and hear, O earth, the
words of my mouth.
2 My doctrine shall drop as the rain, my speech shall distil as the dew, as
the small rain upon the tender herb, and as the showers upon the grass:
3 Because I will publish the name of the LORD: ascribe ye greatness unto
our God.

32:1 Deut 4:26 Isa 1:2
32:2 Ps 72:6 Isa 55:10
32:3 Gen 18:25 Ex 34:5, 6 Deut 3:23–25 5:24

b. God Is Faithful; Israel Is Faithless

4 *He is* the Rock, his work *is* perfect: for all his ways *are* judgment: a God
of truth and without iniquity, just and right *is* he.
5 They have corrupted themselves, their spot *is* not *the spot* of his
children: *they are* a perverse and crooked generation.
6 Do ye thus requite the LORD, O foolish people and unwise? *is* not he thy
father *that* hath bought thee? hath he not made thee, and established thee?
7 ¶Remember the days of old, consider the years of many generations: ask
thy father, and he will shew thee; thy elders, and they will tell thee.
8 When the Most High divided to the nations their inheritance, when he
separated the sons of Adam, he set the bounds of the people according to
the number of the children of Israel.
9 For the LORD's portion *is* his people; Jacob *is* the lot of his inheritance.
10 He found him in a desert land, and in the waste howling wilderness; he
led him about, he instructed him, he kept him as the apple of his eye.
11 As an eagle stirreth up her nest, fluttereth over her young, spreadeth
abroad her wings, taketh them, beareth them on her wings:
12 *So* the LORD alone did lead him, and *there was* no strange god with him.
13 He made him ride on the high places of the earth, that he might eat the
increase of the fields; and he made him to suck honey out of the rock, and
oil out of the flinty rock;
14 Butter of kine, and milk of sheep, with fat of lambs, and rams of the
breed of Ba'shan, and goats, with the fat of kidneys of wheat; and thou
didst drink the pure blood of the grape.
15 ¶But Jesh'u-run waxed fat, and kicked: thou art waxen fat, thou art
grown thick, thou art covered *with fatness;* then he forsook God *which* made
him, and lightly esteemed the Rock of his salvation.
16 They provoked him to jealousy with strange *gods*, with abominations
provoked they him to anger.

☆**32:4** Gen 49:24 Deut 32:18 2 Sam 22:2
32:5 Deut 4:25; 31:27 Mt 17:17
32:6 Deut 1:31; 32:28
32:7 Deut 7:18, 19 8:2
32:9 Deut 1:19–21 1 Kgs 8:51 Jer 10:16
32:10 Ps 17:8
32:11 Ex 19:4 Ps 17:8; 91:4
32:12 Deut 4:36 Isa 43:12
32:13 Job 29:6 Ps 81:16
32:14 Ps 147:14
☆**32:15** Judg 10:6
32:16 Ps 78:58 106:29

32:4 *He is the Rock.* Outside of Deuteronomy, a reference to God as the Rock appears eighteen times in the Old Testament. "He is in himself immutable, immovable, and he is to all that seek him and fly to him an impenetrable shelter, and to all that trust in him an everlasting foundation."*

32:15 *Jeshurun,* i.e., "Israel."

32:17 Lev 17:7; 1 Cor 10:20
32:18 Ps 106:21; Deut 8:11; 32:4

17 They sacrificed unto devils, not to God; to gods whom they knew not,
to new *gods that* came newly up, whom your fathers feared not.
18 Of the Rock *that* begat thee thou art unmindful, and hast forgotten
God that formed thee.

c. Why God Was Angry with Israel

32:19 Lev 26:30; Ps 106:40
32:20 Deut 32:5; Mt 17:17

19 And when the LORD saw *it*, he abhorred *them*, because of the provoking
of his sons, and of his daughters.
20 And he said, I will hide my face from them, I will see what their end
shall be: for they *are* a very froward generation, children in whom *is* no
faith.

32:21 1 Kgs 16:13, 26; Rom 10:19

21 They have moved me to jealousy with *that which is* not God; they have
provoked me to anger with their vanities: and I will move them to jealousy
with *those which are* not a people; I will provoke them to anger with a
foolish nation.

32:22☆ Lev 26:20; Ps 18:7, 8
32:23 Lev 26:18; Deut 28:15–19; 2 Sam 22:15; Ps 85:5
32:24 Deut 28:53; Ps 91:6
32:25 2 Chron 36:17; Lam 1:20; 2:21; Ezek 7:15
32:26 Deut 4:27; 28:64

22 For a fire is kindled in mine anger, and shall burn unto the lowest hell,
and shall consume the earth with her increase, and set on fire the
foundations of the mountains.
23 I will heap mischiefs upon them; I will spend mine arrows upon them.
24 *They shall be* burnt with hunger, and devoured with burning heat, and
with bitter destruction: I will also send the teeth of beasts upon them, with
the poison of serpents of the dust.
25 The sword without, and terror within, shall destroy both the young man
and the virgin, the suckling *also* with the man of gray hairs.
26 I said, I would scatter them into corners, I would make the remem-
brance of them to cease from among men:
27 Were it not that I feared the wrath of the enemy, lest their adversaries
should behave themselves strangely, *and* lest they should say, Our hand *is*
high, and the LORD hath not done all this.
28 For they *are* a nation void of counsel, neither *is there any* understanding
in them.

32:29 Deut 5:29

29 O that they were wise, *that* they understood this, *that* they would
consider their latter end!

32:30 Lev 26:7, 8; Josh 23:10; Judg 7:22; Deut 32:4, 18

30 How should one chase a thousand, and two put ten thousand to flight,
except their Rock had sold them, and the LORD had shut them up?
31 For their rock *is* not as our Rock, even our enemies themselves *being*
judges.

32:32☆ Gen 19:4, 5; Deut 29:18

32 For their vine *is* of the vine of Sodom, and of the fields of Go-mor'rah:
their grapes *are* grapes of gall, their clusters *are* bitter:
33 Their wine *is* the poison of dragons, and the cruel venom of asps.

d. God Will Have Mercy on Israel and Take Vengeance on Her Enemies

32:35 Jer 23:12; Ezek 7:5; Rom 12:19

34 *Is* not this laid up in store with me, *and* sealed up among my treasures?
35 To me *belongeth* vengeance, and recompence; their foot shall slide in

---

32:22 *lowest hell* (the underworld). The Hebrew word *sheol* (translated "hell" in the KJV) was the abode of the departed spirits of the dead, both righteous and wicked. God's Spirit was there (Ps. 139:8), the anger of God was felt there (32:22), and it was a gloomy place with worms (Job 17:13–15), a place where God could not be praised (Ps 6:5; Isa. 38:18). The Old Testament view of sheol was quite complex. We read in Ps. 9:17 that "the wicked shall be turned into hell (sheol)." *Sheol* was carried over into the New Testament as *hades*, the place where only the wicked dead dwelt. It was also associated with *gehenna* (see note on Matt. 18:9 for information on *gehenna*). But the idea that sheol was the abode of the wicked dead was understood more clearly during the intertestamental period.

32:32 *their vine is of the vine of Sodom.* The enemies of Israel fell before them because they were ripe for ruin; the measure of their iniquity was full. These heathen had come from wicked forbears and their sins were offensive and malignant. *their grapes are grapes of gall*, i.e., their "deeds" are poison.

due time: for the day of their calamity *is* at hand, and the things that shall
come upon them make haste.
36 For the LORD shall judge his people, and repent himself for his
servants, when he seeth that *their* power is gone, and *there is* none shut up,
or left.
37 And he shall say, Where *are* their gods, *their* rock in whom they trusted,
38 Which did eat the fat of their sacrifices, *and* drank the wine of their
drink offerings? let them rise up and help you, *and* be your protection.
39 See now that I, *even* I, *am* he, and *there is* no god with me: I kill, and I
make alive; I wound, and I heal: neither *is there any* that can deliver out of
my hand.
40 For I lift up my hand to heaven, and say, I live for ever.
41 If I whet my glittering sword, and mine hand take hold on judgment; I
will render vengeance to mine enemies, and will reward them that hate me.
42 I will make mine arrows drunk with blood, and my sword shall devour
flesh; *and that* with the blood of the slain and of the captives, from the
beginning of revenges upon the enemy.
43 Rejoice, O ye nations, *with* his people: for he will avenge the blood of
his servants, and will render vengeance to his adversaries, and will be
merciful unto his land, *and* to his people.

32:36 Lev 26:44, 45; Deut 30:2, 3; Heb 10:30
32:37 Jer 2:28
32:38 Num 25:1, 2; Jer 11:12
☆**32:39** 1 Sam 2:6; Ps 50:22; Isa 41:4; 43:10
32:40 Num 8:21; Ps 65:5; Isa 1:24; 34:6; Jer 12:12; 46:10; 50:28–32
☆**32:41, 42**
☆**32:43**

V. MOSES' FINAL WORDS AND DEATH (32:44—34:12)

A. MOSES' CONCLUDING INJUNCTION

44 ¶And Moses came and spake all the words of this song in the ears of
the people, he, and Ho-she'a the son of Nun.
45 And Moses made an end of speaking all these words to all Israel:
46 And he said unto them, Set your hearts unto all the words which I
testify among you this day, which ye shall command your children to
observe to do, all the words of this law.
47 For it *is* not a vain thing for you; because it *is* your life: and through
this thing ye shall prolong *your* days in the land, whither ye go over Jordan
to possess it.

32:46 Deut 4:9; Ezek 40:4; 44:5
32:47 Deut 4:40; 8:3; 30:20

B. GOD ORDERS MOSES TO GO TO MOUNT NEBO TO DIE

48 And the LORD spake unto Moses that selfsame day, saying,
49 Get thee up into this mountain Ab'a-rim, *unto* mount Nebo, which *is* in
the land of Moab, that *is* over against Jericho; and behold the land of
Canaan, which I give unto the children of Israel for a possession:
50 And die in the mount whither thou goest up, and be gathered unto thy
people; as Aaron thy brother died in mount Hor, and was gathered unto his
people:

32:49 Num 27:12; Deut 3:27
☆**32:50** Gen 25:17; Num 27:13, 14; Deut 31:16

32:39 Israel's God is the self-existent One. He is supreme, for there is no other god with him or greater than he. He is absolute Sovereign who does as he pleases. No one can deliver out of his hand those who have been marked for destruction. And elsewhere it is stated that those who are marked for everlasting life cannot be taken from his hands either (see John 10:28–29).

32:41, 42 The God of love and grace is also the God of wrath, whose sentence cannot be escaped. He makes his "arrows drunk with blood." When the sword of God's wrath is drawn, it will make bloody work, blood to the horse-bridles (Rev. 14:20).

32:43 Moses now ends the song with a triumphant refrain. There is a remnant who will experience God's ultimate peace. God avenges his servants and punishes his adversaries. And atonement is made for the people of God and the land. "The people of God will rejoice and they will rejoice everlastingly."*

32:50 *die in the mount.* Unlike Elijah, who was taken into heaven without experiencing death, Moses was to die. Thus at the transfiguration of Jesus, Elijah, who never died, appeared in his earthly body and Moses, who did die, appeared in a body. The place of Moses' burial was undoubtedly to remain unknown so that his grave would not become a focal point of worship and lead to a depreciation of the true worship of God.

32:51 Num 20:12; 27:14
32:52 Deut 1:37; 3:27

51 Because ye trespassed against me among the children of Israel at the
waters of Mer'i-bah–Ka'desh, in the wilderness of Zin; because ye
sanctified me not in the midst of the children of Israel.
52 Yet thou shalt see the land before *thee;* but thou shalt not go thither
unto the land which I give the children of Israel.

C. MOSES' BLESSING ON EACH TRIBE

33:1 1 Sam 2:27
33:2☆ Ex 19:18, 20; Judg 5:4; Ps 68:8, 17; Dan 7:10; Hab 3:3; Gal 3:19
33:3 Deut 4:37; 6:1–9; 7:6; 14:2
33:4 Deut 4:2; Ps 119:111
33:5☆ Num 23:18–24; Ps 10:16; 22:28
33:6☆ Gen 49:3
33:7☆ Gen 49:8–12

33 AND this *is* the blessing, wherewith Moses the man of God blessed
the children of Israel before his death.
2 And he said, The LORD came from Si'-nai, and rose up from Se'ir unto
them; he shined forth from mount Paran, and he came with ten thousands
of saints: from his right hand *went* a fiery law for them.
3 Yea, he loved the people; all his saints *are* in thy hand: and they sat
down at thy feet; *every one* shall receive of thy words.
4 Moses commanded us a law, *even* the inheritance of the congregation of
Jacob.
5 And he was king in Jesh'u-run, when the heads of the people *and* the
tribes of Israel were gathered together.
6 ¶Let Reuben live, and not die; and let *not* his men be few.
7 ¶And this *is the blessing* of Judah: and he said, Hear, LORD, the voice of
Judah, and bring him unto his people: let his hands be sufficient for him;
and be thou an help *to him* from his enemies.

33:8–11☆
33:8 Ex 17:7; Lev 8:8; Num 20:13, 24; Deut 6:16
33:9 Ex 32:27; Lev 10:6; 21:11; Mt 10:37
33:10 Lev 10:11; 16:12, 13; Deut 17:9; 31:9

8 ¶And of Levi he said, *Let* thy Thum'mim and thy U'rim *be* with thy holy
one, whom thou didst prove at Mas'sah, *and with* whom thou didst strive at
the waters of Mer'i-bah;
9 Who said unto his father and to his mother, I have not seen him; neither
did he acknowledge his brethren, nor knew his own children: for they have
observed thy word, and kept thy covenant.
10 They shall teach Jacob thy judgments, and Israel thy law: they shall put
incense before thee, and whole burnt sacrifice upon thine altar.
11 Bless, LORD, his substance, and accept the work of his hands: smite
through the loins of them that rise against him, and of them that hate him,
that they rise not again.

33:12☆ Gen 49:27; Deut 12:10; 32:11
33:13☆ Gen 27:27–29; 49:22
33:14 Deut 28:8

12 ¶*And* of Benjamin he said, The beloved of the LORD shall dwell in
safety by him; *and the LORD* shall cover him all the day long, and he shall
dwell between his shoulders.
13 ¶And of Joseph he said, Blessed of the LORD *be* his land, for the
precious things of heaven, for the dew, and for the deep that coucheth
beneath,
14 And for the precious fruits *brought forth* by the sun, and for the
precious things put forth by the moon,

33:2 *saints,* i.e., "holy ones," or "holy angels."
33:5 *Jeshurun,* ("the upright one") was a poetic name for Israel. It suggests the kind of people who live ideally or righteously. The word appears three times in Deuteronomy and once in Isaiah.
33:6 Moses, the military strategist, knew that the Reubenites on the east bank of the Jordan would face the people of Moab. They especially needed prayer for their survival and increase.
33:7 Simeon's name and blessing are missing. Perhaps the reason was that the tribe of Simeon lived within the borders of Judah and so was implicitly included in that tribe's blessing. Moses prayed for the leadership to come from *Judah,* which prayer would be fulfilled in the Messiah.
33:8–11 Moses prayed that God would prosper the tribe of Levi and supply their material needs, that God would accept the work of their hands in their service for him, and that God would take the side of the Levites against all of their enemies.
33:12 Moses blessed *Benjamin,* the second son of Jacob's beloved Rachel, who died giving birth to him. He will have divine protection. And since Mount Moriah and Jerusalem are in Benjamin's territory, that tribe is close to the heart of God because he takes up his residence in those sacred places.
33:13 Moses' blessing for *Joseph* included both Manasseh and Ephraim. These two tribes have the choicest lands, with rich blessings and thousands of descendants.

15 And for the chief things of the ancient mountains, and for the precious
things of the lasting hills,
16 And for the precious things of the earth and fulness thereof, and *for* the
good will of him that dwelt in the bush: let *the blessing* come upon the head
of Joseph, and upon the top of the head of him *that was* separated from his
brethren.
17 His glory *is like* the firstling of his bullock, and his horns *are like* the
horns of unicorns: with them he shall push the people together to the ends
of the earth: and they *are* the ten thousands of E′phra-im, and they *are* the
thousands of Ma-nas′seh.
18 ¶And of Zeb′u-lun he said, Rejoice, Zeb′u-lun, in thy going out; and,
Is′sa-char, in thy tents.
19 They shall call the people unto the mountain; there they shall offer
sacrifices of righteousness: for they shall suck *of* the abundance of the seas,
and *of* treasures hid in the sand.
20 ¶And of Gad he said, Blessed *be* he that enlargeth Gad: he dwelleth as
a lion, and teareth the arm with the crown of the head.
21 And he provided the first part for himself, because there, *in* a portion of
the lawgiver, *was he* seated; and he came with the heads of the people, he
executed the justice of the LORD, and his judgments with Israel.
22 ¶And of Dan he said, Dan *is* a lion's whelp: he shall leap from Ba′shan.
23 ¶And of Naph′ta-li he said, O Naph′ta-li, satisfied with favour, and full
with the blessing of the LORD: possess thou the west and the south.
24 ¶And of Asher he said, *Let* Asher *be* blessed with children; let him be
acceptable to his brethren, and let him dip his foot in oil.
25 Thy shoes *shall be* iron and brass; and as thy days, *so shall* thy strength
be.
26 ¶*There is* none like unto the God of Jesh′u-run, *who* rideth upon the
heaven in thy help, and in his excellency on the sky.
27 The eternal God *is thy* refuge, and underneath *are* the everlasting arms:
and he shall thrust out the enemy from before thee; and shall say, Destroy
them.
28 Israel then shall dwell in safety alone: the fountain of Jacob *shall be*
upon a land of corn and wine; also his heavens shall drop down dew.
29 Happy *art* thou, O Israel: who *is* like unto thee, O people saved by the
LORD, the shield of thy help, and who *is* the sword of thy excellency! and
thine enemies shall be found liars unto thee; and thou shalt tread upon
their high places.

33:16 Ps 24:1; 50:12 89:11
33:17 Num 23:22; 24:8 1 Kgs 22:11
☆**33:18** Gen 49:13
☆**33:19** Deut 32:13 Ps 4:5; 51:19
☆**33:20** Gen 49:19
☆**33:21** Num 32:1 34:14, 15 Josh 4:12; 22:1
☆**33:22** Gen 49:16 Josh 19:47, 48 Ezek 19:2
☆**33:23** Gen 49:21 Isa 9:1, 2
☆**33:24** Gen 49:20 Job 29:6
☆**33:25** Ps 147:13
33:26 Ex 15:11 Deut 4:35 Ps 68:33
☆**33:27** Gen 49:24 Deut 7:2 Josh 24:18 Ps 90:1
33:28 Gen 27:27–29, 37 Deut 33:12, 13
33:29 Gen 15:1 Deut 4:32 2 Sam 22:3 Ps 66:3; 115:11

33:18, 19 The tribe of *Zebulun* were to be successful businessmen and sea-traders, whereas the tribe of *Issachar* would be blessed as farmers and cattle raisers.
33:20, 21 *Gad* would be enlarged, and be a valiant, victorious tribe with great military strength against the enemy. They were commended for what they had done, especially for fulfilling their responsibilities to those of other tribes of Israel.
33:22 *Dan* was blessed with courage and resolution to overcome the enemy. From Dan there was to come Samson, a lion's whelp.
33:23 *Naphtali* was to be a happy people, loved by other tribes and favored by God. Wealthy Bethsaida and Capernaum lay within Naphtali's borders. Of Naphtali later Jews said: "The portion of the tribe of Naphtali was so fruitful, and the productions so forward, though it lay north, that those of that tribe were generally the first that brought their first-fruits to the temple; and so they had first the blessing from the priest, which was the blessing of the Lord."
33:24, 25 *Asher* would be prolific. Their land would be productive because beneath the surface of the land is vast mineral wealth. The strength of this tribe in old age will equal that of their youth.
33:27 The *eternal God* is the mansion-house of all who believe. In that house they will be safe and at ease. As they settle in Canaan, Israel must remember they have God for their dwelling-place and that Canaan without him would be a wilderness and a place of darkness. God's everlasting arms would be beneath them for protection and consolation. Whoever is right with God is at home with God, and his soul will return to God and there repose in him as its resting-place.

D. MOSES' DEATH AND BURIAL

34 AND Moses went up from the plains of Moab unto the mountain
of Nebo, to the top of Pis'gah, that *is* over against Jericho. And the
LORD shewed him all the land of Gilead, unto Dan,
2 And all Naph'ta-li, and the land of E'phra-im, and Ma-nas'seh, and all
the land of Judah, unto the utmost sea,
3 And the south, and the plain of the valley of Jericho, the city of palm
trees, unto Zo'ar.
4 And the LORD said unto him, This *is* the land which I sware unto
Abraham, unto Isaac, and unto Jacob, saying, I will give it unto thy seed: I
have caused thee to see *it* with thine eyes, but thou shalt not go over thither.
5 ¶So Moses the servant of the LORD died there in the land of Moab,
according to the word of the LORD.
6 And he buried him in a valley in the land of Moab, over against Beth-
pe'or: but no man knoweth of his sepulchre unto this day.
7 ¶And Moses *was* an hundred and twenty years old when he died: his eye
was not dim, nor his natural force abated.
8 ¶And the children of Israel wept for Moses in the plains of Moab thirty
days: so the days of weeping *and* mourning for Moses were ended.
9 ¶And Joshua the son of Nun was full of the spirit of wisdom; for Moses
had laid his hands upon him: and the children of Israel hearkened unto
him, and did as the LORD commanded Moses.
10 ¶And there arose not a prophet since in Israel like unto Moses, whom
the LORD knew face to face,
11 In all the signs and the wonders, which the LORD sent him to do in the
land of Egypt to Pharaoh, and to all his servants, and to all his land,
12 And in all that mighty hand, and in all the great terror which Moses
shewed in the sight of all Israel.

34:1☆ Num 21:20; 27:12; Deut 32:49, 52
34:2 Ex 23:31; Deut 11:24; Josh 19:32
34:4☆ Gen 12:7; 26:3; 28:13; Ps 105:10, 11
34:5 Num 12:7, 8; Deut 32:50
34:6 Deut 3:29; 4:44–46; Jude 9
34:7 Deut 31:2; Acts 7:23, 30
34:8 Gen 50:3; Num 20:29
34:9 Ex 31:3; Num 27:18; Isa 11:2
34:10 Num 12:7, 8; Acts 3:22, 23
34:11 Deut 4:34; 7:19

34:1 Some hold that this story of Moses' death was added by a different writer at a later time. Others accept it as a form of predictive prophecy penned by Moses himself, who had been informed of the details of his approaching death and who told the story in advance of its actual occurrence.

34:4 *I have caused thee to see it with thine eyes.* God granted Moses a last look at the land promised to Israel, a land which was his by faith and by sight but not by physical presence. His sin had cut him off from what had been his goal from the beginning—to inherit the land promised to his forefathers years ago. God took his spirit and buried his body in an unmarked grave—to await the resurrection, when he would see the Messiah he had talked about in prophecy.

THE BOOK OF
JOSHUA

Authorship, date, and background This book was named for Joshua, the chief personage involved in the events which are described in it. Undoubtedly large sections of the book were written by Joshua himself. Many items in the work could have been known only by Joshua, who included them in the book or passed them on to others who included them. Some of the material, however, such as the decease of Joshua and a few events which took place subsequent to Joshua's death, have led scholars to conclude that the book was written after Joshua's death. Eleazar and Phinehas, his son, have been suggested as possible inspired writers under the Holy Spirit who brought the full work to fruition.

Liberal critics formulated the theory that the first six books of the Old Testament, that is, the five Books of Moses and Joshua, formed the Hexateuch (or six books) comprising materials from Moses and Joshua which were reworked or redacted. The final editing took place in the seventh century B.C. At that time the anonymous compiler of Deuteronomy incorporated Joshua into the five Books of Moses, forming the Hexateuch. Conservative scholars, however, are in agreement that the five Books of Moses were written by Moses and that Joshua was written shortly after the death of Joshua (fourteenth century B.C.) but not later than the twelfth century B.C. in any event.

The children of Israel had spent forty years in the wilderness because of their refusal to enter the Promised Land when ten of the twelve spies reported unfavorably on the possibility of subduing its occupants. Now Moses had died and Joshua, their new leader, was ready to bring the people into the land which God had promised them. Thus, the book of Joshua is a continuation of the history of Israel, covering the period from the entrance into Canaan, the distribution of the land to the twelve tribes, and the pacification of the land, up to the period of the Judges.

Characteristics and content The book of Joshua tells the story of Israel's triumphant occupation of the land of promise. In it the mighty power of God is manifested over the enemies who inhabit the land. The Canaanites living in the land are pictured in all of their degeneracy, which consists of polytheism, religious prostitution, and other abominations which anger God and occasion his command for the Israelites to exterminate the seven heathen nations. Some scholars say that venereal disease was rampant among the heathen due to sexual license. Surely the Israelites need to be kept from contact with the Canaanites which will result in spiritual degeneration as well as the possibility of contracting their loathsome diseases. God wants the Canaanites destroyed.

The first part of Joshua tells of the conquest of the land and includes Joshua's commission by God, the miraculous crossing of the Jordan River, the capture of Jericho, the failure at Ai, and the erection of an altar at Mount Ebal where the law is solemnly read to the people. The crafty Gibeonites manage to preserve themselves in the land by deception due to the failure of Joshua to seek God's guidance before making a treaty with them. A most unusual event occurs during the conquest of southern Canaan in the battle of Gibeon when the "sun stood still in the midst of heaven, and hasted not to go down about a whole day" (10:13). The text leaves no other alternative than that the earth stopped rotating on its axis. Thus God performs a stupendous miracle. But it takes no greater power for God to do this than for him to perform any other miracle, since he is the almighty God.

The latter half of Joshua describes the division of the land among the tribes. The book concludes with Joshua's final charge to Israel wherein he points out that the Israelis are a covenant people who are to trust God and who are not to permit sins of disobedience to mar their relationship to him, lest they incur God's anger and feel the lash of his judgment upon them.

Outline

I. The entrance into and the conquest of the land (1:1—12:24)
II. The division of the land of Canaan (13:1—21:45)
III. Joshua's farewell and charge to Israel (22:1—24:33)

I. THE ENTRANCE INTO AND THE CONQUEST OF THE LAND (1:1—12:24)

A. GOD COMMISSIONS JOSHUA

1:1☆ 1 NOW after the death of Moses the servant of the LORD it came to
Num 13:16 Deut 34:7, 8 pass, that the LORD spake unto Joshua the son of Nun, Moses'
minister, saying,
1:2 2 Moses my servant is dead; now therefore arise, go over this Jordan,
Num 12:7, 8 Deut 34:9 thou, and all this people, unto the land which I do give to them, *even* to the
1 Kgs 8:56 children of Israel.
1:3 3 Every place that the sole of your foot shall tread upon, that have I given
Deut 11:24 unto you, as I said unto Moses.
4 From the wilderness and this Lebanon even unto the great river, the
river Eu-phra'tes, all the land of the Hittites, and unto the great sea toward
the going down of the sun, shall be your coast.
1:5☆ 5 There shall not any man be able to stand before thee all the days of thy
Deut 7:24 31:6–8 life: as I was with Moses, *so* I will be with thee: I will not fail thee, nor
Heb 13:5 forsake thee.
6 Be strong and of a good courage: for unto this people shalt thou divide
for an inheritance the land, which I sware unto their fathers to give them.
1:7 7 Only be thou strong and very courageous, that thou mayest observe to
Deut 5:29, 32 28:14; 29:9 do according to all the law, which Moses my servant commanded thee: turn
not from it *to* the right hand or *to* the left, that thou mayest prosper
whithersoever thou goest.
1:8☆ 8 This book of the law shall not depart out of thy mouth; but thou shalt
Deut 6:6, 7 11:18; 17:19 meditate therein day and night, that thou mayest observe to do according
Josh 8:35 Ps 1:1–3 to all that is written therein: for then thou shalt make thy way prosperous,
and then thou shalt have good success.
1:9 9 Have not I commanded thee? Be strong and of a good courage; be not
Deut 31:6, 8 afraid, neither be thou dismayed: for the LORD thy God *is* with thee
whithersoever thou goest.

B. THE PREPARATIONS TO CROSS THE JORDAN

1. Joshua's Instructions

1:10 10 ¶Then Joshua commanded the officers of the people, saying,
Deut 3:2–4, 15–17 11 Pass through the host, and command the people, saying, Prepare you
victuals; for within three days ye shall pass over this Jordan, to go in to
possess the land, which the LORD your God giveth you to possess it.

2. Joshua Reminds the Tribes of Reuben, Gad, and the Half-Tribe of Manasseh of Their Agreement

1:12 Num 32:20 Deut 3:18 12 ¶And to the Reubenites, and to the Gadites, and to half the tribe of
Josh 22:1 Ma-nas'seh, spake Joshua, saying,

1:1 *Joshua,* a shortened version of *Jehoshua* ("Yahweh is salvation"). Joshua was Moses' assistant and, along with Caleb, had urged Israel to enter Canaan forty years earlier. Moses had trained Joshua to become his successor. God chose him for this role. Joshua led Israel successfully into Canaan and was a victorious military commander. He is a type of Christ, who is his people's captain, who saves them, brings them to the place of rest, intercedes for them, and makes the conquest of sin possible (7:5–9; Acts 20:32; Rom. 8:37; 2 Cor. 1:10; 2:14; Heb. 2:10; 4:8, 9).

1:5 God gave Joshua the same promise he made to Moses—that he would be with him all the days of his life. Joshua had seen this fulfilled in the life of Moses and by faith believed it would be fulfilled in his life and ministry. Similar promises are made to the people of God today.

1:8 God enjoined Joshua to study the book of the law day and night. Joshua was admonished to do all that was commanded in it. The promise of success and prosperity was attached to obedience. Churches and believers are seriously weakened today by their failure to do what is here commanded. Moreover, even when the Bible is read, discipline is often lacking and malefactors go unpunished. The situation is worsened by the current drift away from the commandments brought about by the charge that the Bible is outdated and no longer normative for society and culture.

13 Remember the word which Moses the servant of the LORD commanded
you, saying, The LORD your God hath given you rest, and hath given you
this land.
14 Your wives, your little ones, and your cattle, shall remain in the land
which Moses gave you on this side Jordan; but ye shall pass before your
brethren armed, all the mighty men of valour, and help them;
15 Until the LORD have given your brethren rest, as *he hath given* you, and **1:15** Josh 22:4
they also have possessed the land which the LORD your God giveth them:
then ye shall return unto the land of your possession, and enjoy it, which
Moses the LORD's servant gave you on this side Jordan toward the
sunrising.
16 ¶And they answered Joshua, saying, All that thou commandest us we ☆**1:16** Num 32:25
will do, and whithersoever thou sendest us, we will go.
17 According as we hearkened unto Moses in all things, so will we hearken ☆**1:17** Ex 19:8; 24:3
unto thee: only the LORD thy God be with thee, as he was with Moses. Deut 5:27
18 Whosoever *he be* that doth rebel against thy commandment, and will
not hearken unto thy words in all that thou commandest him, he shall be
put to death: only be strong and of a good courage.

3. Two Spies Sent to Jericho
a. Rahab the Harlot Hides the Spies

2 AND Joshua the son of Nun sent out of Shit'tim two men to spy ☆**2:1** Num 13:2
secretly, saying, Go view the land, even Jericho. And they went, and Mt 1:5
came into an harlot's house, named Rahab, and lodged there.
2 And it was told the king of Jericho, saying, Behold, there came men in
hither to night of the children of Israel to search out the country.
3 And the king of Jericho sent unto Rahab, saying, Bring forth the men
that are come to thee, which are entered into thine house: for they be come
to search out all the country.
4 And the woman took the two men, and hid them, and said thus, There ☆**2:4** Ex 1:19
came men unto me, but I wist not whence they *were:* 2 Sam 17:20
5 And it came to pass *about the time* of shutting of the gate, when it was
dark, that the men went out: whither the men went I wot not: pursue after
them quickly; for ye shall overtake them.
6 But she had brought them up to the roof of the house, and hid them **2:6** Jas 2:25
with the stalks of flax, which she had laid in order upon the roof.
7 And the men pursued after them the way to Jordan unto the fords: and
as soon as they which pursued after them were gone out, they shut the gate.

b. Rahab Exacts a Promise from the Spies

8 ¶And before they were laid down, she came up unto them upon the
roof;
9 And she said unto the men, I know that the LORD hath given you the **2:9** Ex 23:27
land, and that your terror is fallen upon us, and that all the inhabitants of Deut 2:25
the land faint because of you. Josh 9:24; Heb 11:31

1:16, 17 In response to Joshua's speech the Israelites promised to obey him and prayed that God would be with him as he was with Moses. Unfortunately, the Israelites frequently disobeyed Moses and complained against him many times. Joshua was well aware of this proclivity; but his faith and confidence were not in the Israelites, but in God.

2:1 Joshua was taking no chances. He sent two, not twelve men, and he sent them secretly so that if they brought back a bad report it would not be known to Israel. He did not want to wait another forty years before entering the promised land.

2:4 Rahab lied in order to save the lives of the spies. This has subsequently occasioned the conclusion that lying is sometimes permissible. But this inference is erroneous. John Calvin says of this incident: "As to the falsehood, we must admit that though it was done for a good purpose, it was not free from fault." In the New Testament Rahab is commended, but never for having lied (Heb. 11:31; James 2:25). The spies would somehow have been delivered by God even if Rahab had told the truth. The Scriptures do not say lying is ever justifiable (Exod. 20:16; Deut. 5:20; Matt. 19:19).

2:10 Ex 14:21–31 Num 21:21 Deut 2:30; 3:1

10 For we have heard how the LORD dried up the water of the Red sea for you, when ye came out of Egypt; and what ye did unto the two kings of the Am′or-ites, that *were* on the other side Jordan, Sihon and Og, whom ye utterly destroyed.

2:11 Deut 4:39 1 Kgs 8:60 Ps 83:18

11 And as soon as we had heard *these things*, our hearts did melt, neither did there remain any more courage in any man, because of you: for the LORD your God, he *is* God in heaven above, and in earth beneath.

2:12☆ Josh 6:22, 23 9:14, 15, 18

12 Now therefore, I pray you, swear unto me by the LORD, since I have shewed you kindness, that ye will also shew kindness unto my father's house, and give me a true token:

13 And *that* ye will save alive my father, and my mother, and my brethren, and my sisters, and all that they have, and deliver our lives from death.

14 And the men answered her, Our life for yours, if ye utter not this our business. And it shall be, when the LORD hath given us the land, that we will deal kindly and truly with thee.

2:15☆ Josh 2:17, 18, 21

15 Then she let them down by a cord through the window: for her house *was* upon the town wall, and she dwelt upon the wall.

2:16 Jas 2:25

16 And she said unto them, Get you to the mountain, lest the pursuers meet you; and hide yourselves there three days, until the pursuers be returned: and afterward may ye go your way.

c. The Sign of the Scarlet Rope

17 And the men said unto her, We *will be* blameless of this thine oath which thou hast made us swear.

2:18☆

18 Behold, *when* we come into the land, thou shalt bind this line of scarlet thread in the window which thou didst let us down by: and thou shalt bring thy father, and thy mother, and thy brethren, and all thy father's household, home unto thee.

19 And it shall be, *that* whosoever shall go out of the doors of thy house into the street, his blood *shall be* upon his head, and we *will be* guiltless: and whosoever shall be with thee in the house, his blood *shall be* on our head, if *any* hand be upon him.

20 And if thou utter this our business, then we will be quit of thine oath which thou hast made us to swear.

21 And she said, According unto your words, so *be* it. And she sent them away, and they departed: and she bound the scarlet line in the window.

d. The Report of the Two Spies

22 And they went, and came unto the mountain, and abode there three days, until the pursuers were returned: and the pursuers sought *them* throughout all the way, but found *them* not.

23 ¶So the two men returned, and descended from the mountain, and passed over, and came to Joshua the son of Nun, and told him all *things* that befell them:

2:12 Rahab exacted a pledge or oath from the two spies—that they will save her and her family when the invasion takes place. She demanded that they do it in the name of their God.

2:15 Rahab's house was on the top of the city wall. This Canaanite city was enclosed by two walls approximately twelve to fifteen feet apart. Houses were built on timbers stretched from one wall to the other. It was easy to escape from within the city by means of windows on houses built on the outer wall.

2:18 *scarlet thread,* or, "cord." Years before this episode, Israelite families living in Egypt had sprinkled blood on their lintels to avert the angel of death. The angel, upon seeing the blood, passed over their homes. Similarly, the scarlet cord was a sign to all Israel that it should leave that house and its inhabitants unscathed. The presence of the scarlet cord, not the righteousness of the people in the dwelling place, made the difference.

24 And they said unto Joshua, Truly the LORD hath delivered into our ☆2:24 Josh 5:1; 9:24
hands all the land; for even all the inhabitants of the country do faint
because of us.

C. ISRAEL PASSES OVER THE JORDAN
1. Last Minute Preparations

3 AND Joshua rose early in the morning; and they removed from 3:1 Josh 2:1
Shit'tim, and came to Jordan, he and all the children of Israel, and
lodged there before they passed over.
2 And it came to pass after three days, that the officers went through the 3:2 Deut 31:9 Josh 1:10, 11
host;
3 And they commanded the people, saying, When ye see the ark of the ☆3:3
covenant of the LORD your God, and the priests the Levites bearing it, then
ye shall remove from your place, and go after it.
4 Yet there shall be a space between you and it, about two thousand
cubits by measure: come not near unto it, that ye may know the way by
which ye must go: for ye have not passed *this* way heretofore.
5 And Joshua said unto the people, Sanctify yourselves: for to morrow the 3:5 Ex 19:10 Josh 7:13
LORD will do wonders among you.
6 And Joshua spake unto the priests, saying, Take up the ark of the
covenant, and pass over before the people. And they took up the ark of the
covenant, and went before the people.

2. God's Promise to Joshua

7 ¶And the LORD said unto Joshua, This day will I begin to magnify thee ☆3:7 Josh 4:14
in the sight of all Israel, that they may know that, as I was with Moses, *so*
I will be with thee.
8 And thou shalt command the priests that bear the ark of the covenant, 3:8 Josh 3:13, 14
saying, When ye are come to the brink of the water of Jordan, ye shall stand
still in Jordan.
9 ¶And Joshua said unto the children of Israel, Come hither, and hear the
words of the LORD your God.
10 And Joshua said, Hereby ye shall know that the living God *is* among 3:10 Gen 15:19, 20, 21 Deut 7:1
you, and *that* he will without fail drive out from before you the Canaanites,
and the Hittites, and the Hi'vites, and the Per'iz-zites, and the Gir'ga-shites,
and the Am'or-ites, and the Jeb'u-sites.
11 Behold, the ark of the covenant of the Lord of all the earth passeth over
before you into Jordan.

3. The Jordan Parts; Israel Crosses Dryshod

12 Now therefore take you twelve men out of the tribes of Israel, out of 3:12 Josh 4:2, 3
every tribe a man.
13 And it shall come to pass, as soon as the soles of the feet of the priests 3:13 Ex 15:8
that bear the ark of the LORD, the Lord of all the earth, shall rest in the
waters of Jordan, *that* the waters of Jordan shall be cut off *from* the waters
that come down from above; and they shall stand upon an heap.
14 ¶And it came to pass, when the people removed from their tents, to

2:24 The spies brought back an encouraging report based on their faith that God had given them the land and on the knowledge that the inhabitants were fearful of the approaching Israelites. Their faith was corroborated by external evidence.
3:3 Here the Levites rather than the Kohathites carry the ark. The Levites and the ark preceded the people, a guarantee that God was going before them in victory.
3:7 God is now going to demonstrate that he is with Joshua as he was with Moses by showing signs and wonders which will provide the Israelites with external evidences that would justify their faith.

pass over Jordan, and the priests bearing the ark of the covenant before the people;

3:15☆ 1 Chron 12:15 Ps 66:6; 74:15 114:3, 5
15 And as they that bare the ark were come unto Jordan, and the feet of the priests that bare the ark were dipped in the brim of the water, (for Jordan overfloweth all his banks all the time of harvest,)

3:16☆
16 That the waters which came down from above stood *and* rose up upon an heap very far from the city Adam, that *is* beside Zar'e-tan: and those that came down toward the sea of the plain, *even* the salt sea, failed, *and* were cut off: and the people passed over right against Jericho.

3:17 Ex 14:21, 22, 29 Josh 3:6–8 2 Kgs 2:8
17 And the priests that bare the ark of the covenant of the LORD stood firm on dry ground in the midst of Jordan, and all the Israelites passed over on dry ground, until all the people were passed clean over Jordan.

4. The Monument to the Crossing Set Up

4 AND it came to pass, when all the people were clean passed over Jordan, that the LORD spake unto Joshua, saying,

2 Take you twelve men out of the people, out of every tribe a man,

3 And command ye them, saying, Take you hence out of the midst of Jordan, out of the place where the priests' feet stood firm, twelve stones, and ye shall carry them over with you, and leave them in the lodging place, where ye shall lodge this night.

4 Then Joshua called the twelve men, whom he had prepared of the children of Israel, out of every tribe a man:

5 And Joshua said unto them, Pass over before the ark of the LORD your God into the midst of Jordan, and take you up every man of you a stone upon his shoulder, according unto the number of the tribes of the children of Israel:

4:6 Ex 12:26; 13:14 Deut 6:20 Josh 4:20, 21
6 That this may be a sign among you, *that* when your children ask *their fathers* in time to come, saying, What *mean* ye by these stones?

4:7☆
7 Then ye shall answer them, That the waters of Jordan were cut off before the ark of the covenant of the LORD; when it passed over Jordan, the waters of Jordan were cut off: and these stones shall be for a memorial unto the children of Israel for ever.

4:8 Josh 1:16
8 And the children of Israel did so as Joshua commanded, and took up twelve stones out of the midst of Jordan, as the LORD spake unto Joshua, according to the number of the tribes of the children of Israel, and carried them over with them unto the place where they lodged, and laid them down there.

4:9☆ Josh 5:8, 9
9 And Joshua set up twelve stones in the midst of Jordan, in the place where the feet of the priests which bare the ark of the covenant stood: and they are there unto this day.

10 ¶For the priests which bare the ark stood in the midst of Jordan, until everything was finished that the LORD commanded Joshua to speak unto the people, according to all that Moses commanded Joshua: and the people hasted and passed over.

3:15, 16 The Jordan River has been blocked on occasion by a "dam" of earth caused by an earthquake which dislodges portions of cliffs overlooking the river. We do not know whether God sent such an earthquake to dam the Jordan or whether he opened the waters such as he had done when the Israelites crossed the Red Sea. Either way, the remarkable act of providence was a special miracle.

4:7 *these stones shall be for a memorial.* The memorial stones were set up for more than a commemoration. They were to be a testimony to future generations of what God had done. From then on, whenever Israel faced trouble, this memorial would cause the people to look to the same God who would deliver them again. Every believer should set up in his heart stones of remembrance of what God has done in the past; then when trouble overtakes him he can have the same confidence he once had.

4:9 The author of this book apparently knew that, at the time of the writing, the stones in the middle of the river could be seen when the water level was low.

[11]And it came to pass, when all the people were clean passed over, that
the ark of the LORD passed over, and the priests, in the presence of the
people.
[12]And the children of Reuben, and the children of Gad, and half the tribe
of Ma-nas′seh, passed over armed before the children of Israel, as Moses
spake unto them:
[13]About forty thousand prepared for war passed over before the LORD
unto battle, to the plains of Jericho.

4:12 Num 32:1, 17, 25; Josh 1:12, 13

5. The Jordan Flows Again

[14]¶On that day the LORD magnified Joshua in the sight of all Israel; and
they feared him, as they feared Moses, all the days of his life.
[15]And the LORD spake unto Joshua, saying,
[16]Command the priests that bear the ark of the testimony, that they come
up out of Jordan.
[17]Joshua therefore commanded the priests, saying, Come ye up out of
Jordan.
[18]And it came to pass, when the priests that bare the ark of the covenant
of the LORD were come up out of the midst of Jordan, *and* the soles of the
priests' feet were lifted up unto the dry land, that the waters of Jordan
returned unto their place, and flowed over all his banks, as *they did* before.
[19]¶And the people came up out of Jordan on the tenth *day* of the first
month, and encamped in Gilgal, in the east border of Jericho.
[20]And those twelve stones, which they took out of Jordan, did Joshua
pitch in Gilgal.

4:14 Josh 24:31; 1 Chron 29:25
4:15 Josh 3:8
4:19 Ex 12:3

6. The Meaning of the Monument

[21]And he spake unto the children of Israel, saying, When your children
shall ask their fathers in time to come, saying, What *mean* these stones?
[22]Then ye shall let your children know, saying, Israel came over this
Jordan on dry land.
[23]For the LORD your God dried up the waters of Jordan from before you,
until ye were passed over, as the LORD your God did to the Red sea, which
he dried up from before us, until we were gone over:
[24]That all the people of the earth might know the hand of the LORD, that
it *is* mighty: that ye might fear the LORD your God for ever.

☆**4:21**
4:22 Josh 3:17
4:24 Ex 7:3

D. ISRAEL AT GILGAL

1. The Circumcision of the Males

5 AND it came to pass, when all the kings of the Am′or-ites, which *were*
on the side of Jordan westward, and all the kings of the Canaanites,
which *were* by the sea, heard that the LORD had dried up the waters of
Jordan from before the children of Israel, until we were passed over, that
their heart melted, neither was there spirit in them any more, because of the
children of Israel.
[2]¶At that time the LORD said unto Joshua, Make thee sharp knives, and
circumcise again the children of Israel the second time.

5:1 Num 13:29; Josh 2:9–11
☆**5:2, 3** Gen 17:9, 10, 23

4:21 Later generations of children in Israel would see the stones that had been set up by God's commandment and would want to know what they meant. Parents would have the opportunity to teach their children about the true faith, about God's signs and wonders, and about trusting in God, who would do for them great or greater things than he did when their forebearers crossed the Jordan dryshod.

5:2, 3 Circumcision was the seal of the covenant with Abraham (see Gen. 17:9, 10). It had no value unless faith were present. The rite was neglected during the wilderness wandering. When Israel was about to enter Canaan, God ordered Joshua to command all males to be circumcised, "rolling away the shame of Egypt" by so doing. In the early church, water baptism replaced circumcision as the seal of the new covenant and as a prerequisite for church membership.

[3]And Joshua made him sharp knives, and circumcised the children of
Israel at the hill of the foreskins.
5:4 Deut 2:14 [4]And this *is* the cause why Joshua did circumcise: All the people that
came out of Egypt, *that were* males, *even* all the men of war, died in the
wilderness by the way, after they came out of Egypt.
[5]Now all the people that came out were circumcised: but all the people
that were born in the wilderness by the way as they came forth out of Egypt,
them they had not circumcised.
5:6 Num 14:29–35 26:64, 65 Deut 2:7 [6]For the children of Israel walked forty years in the wilderness, till all the
people *that were* men of war, which came out of Egypt, were consumed,
because they obeyed not the voice of the LORD: unto whom the LORD sware
that he would not shew them the land, which the LORD sware unto their
fathers that he would give us, a land that floweth with milk and honey.
5:7 Deut 1:39 [7]And their children, *whom* he raised up in their stead, them Joshua
circumcised: for they were uncircumcised, because they had not circum-
cised them by the way.
[8]And it came to pass, when they had done circumcising all the people,
that they abode in their places in the camp, till they were whole.
[9]And the LORD said unto Joshua, This day have I rolled away the
reproach of Egypt from off you. Wherefore the name of the place is called
Gilgal unto this day.

2. The Celebration of the Passover

5:10 Ex 12:18 Josh 4:19 [10]¶And the children of Israel encamped in Gilgal, and kept the passover
on the fourteenth day of the month at even in the plains of Jericho.
5:11 Ex 16:35 Neh 9:20 [11]And they did eat of the old corn of the land on the morrow after the
passover, unleavened cakes, and parched *corn* in the selfsame day.
5:12☆ [12]¶And the manna ceased on the morrow after they had eaten of the old
corn of the land; neither had the children of Israel manna any more; but
they did eat of the fruit of the land of Canaan that year.

3. Joshua Encounters God's Commander-In-Chief

5:13 Gen 18:2 32:22, 23, 24 Ex 23:23 Num 22:31 Judg 13:9 [13]¶And it came to pass, when Joshua was by Jericho, that he lifted up his
eyes and looked, and, behold, there stood a man over against him with his
sword drawn in his hand: and Joshua went unto him, and said unto him,
Art thou for us, or for our adversaries?
5:14☆ Ex 3:5 [14]And he said, Nay; but *as* captain of the host of the LORD am I now
come. And Joshua fell on his face to the earth, and did worship, and said
unto him, What saith my lord unto his servant?
5:15☆ [15]And the captain of the LORD's host said unto Joshua, Loose thy shoe
from off thy foot; for the place whereon thou standest *is* holy. And Joshua
did so.

5:12 *the manna ceased.* Following the Passover in Egypt, the people of Israel fled and were fed manna by God for forty years. Here we see that as they began their entrance into Canaan they celebrated another Passover. Following that celebration, when they entered the land, *the manna ceased.* It was no longer necessary for God to use supernatural means to care for his people. They were now back to the normal situation where they could provide for themselves under the eye of their God.

5:14, 15 This *captain of the host* was no mere angel. His presence was a theophany, an appearance of Christ in person. Joshua worshipped the captain; his worship was accepted and he was neither rebuked nor instructed otherwise. The captain said the place was holy and Joshua removed his shoes. Just as God used the burning bush to give Moses outward, confirming evidence of the divine presence in his life, so God now gave similar assurance to Joshua as he began a new phase of his life following the assault on Canaan. Joshua did not need to fear, for God was on his side and victory was assured. In the same manner, Christ, as the captain of our salvation, brings us every assurance (see Heb. 2:10). He guarantees his continuing presence among his people with the promise of available power for every contingency.

E. THE CAPTURE OF JERICHO
1. Marching around Jericho for Six Days

6 NOW Jericho was straitly shut up because of the children of Israel: ☆6:1 Josh 5:1
none went out, and none came in.
2And the LORD said unto Joshua, See, I have given into thine hand 6:2 Deut 7:24 Josh 10:8
Jericho, and the king thereof, *and* the mighty men of valour.
3And ye shall compass the city, all *ye* men of war, *and* go round about the 6:3 Lev 25:9
city once. Thus shalt thou do six days.
4And seven priests shall bear before the ark seven trumpets of rams'
horns: and the seventh day ye shall compass the city seven times, and the
priests shall blow with the trumpets.
5And it shall come to pass, that when they make a long *blast* with the
ram's horn, *and* when ye hear the sound of the trumpet, all the people shall
shout with a great shout; and the wall of the city shall fall down flat, and
the people shall ascend up every man straight before him.
6¶And Joshua the son of Nun called the priests, and said unto them, 6:6 Josh 1:10; 3:2
Take up the ark of the covenant, and let seven priests bear seven trumpets
of rams' horns before the ark of the LORD.
7And he said unto the people, Pass on, and compass the city, and let him
that is armed pass on before the ark of the LORD.
8¶And it came to pass, when Joshua had spoken unto the people, that the
seven priests bearing the seven trumpets of rams' horns passed on before
the LORD, and blew with the trumpets: and the ark of the covenant of the
LORD followed them.
9¶And the armed men went before the priests that blew with the ☆6:9
trumpets, and the rereward came after the ark, *the priests* going on, and
blowing with the trumpets.
10And Joshua had commanded the people, saying, Ye shall not shout, nor
make any noise with your voice, neither shall *any* word proceed out of your
mouth, until the day I bid you shout; then shall ye shout.
11So the ark of the LORD compassed the city, going about *it* once: and
they came into the camp, and lodged in the camp.
12¶And Joshua rose early in the morning, and the priests took up the ark 6:12 Josh 6:3, 4
of the LORD.
13And seven priests bearing seven trumpets of rams' horns before the ark
of the LORD went on continually, and blew with the trumpets: and the
armed men went before them; but the rereward came after the ark of the
LORD, *the priests* going on, and blowing with the trumpets.
14And the second day they compassed the city once, and returned into
the camp: so they did six days.

2. The Capture of the City

15And it came to pass on the seventh day, that they rose early about the
dawning of the day, and compassed the city after the same manner seven
times: only on that day they compassed the city seven times.
16And it came to pass at the seventh time, when the priests blew with the

---

6:1 Jericho was not taken by carnal means, but by spiritual, supernatural means. God used apparently foolish things to confound the wise and the mighty: e.g., the wooden stick of Moses, the slingshot of David, and the ram's-horn trumpets of Joshua. It is not important whether the walls of Jericho collapsed because of an earthquake or because of a special miracle. God always chooses his own means to accomplish his purposes. Jericho's walls fell at the right moment so that the means, natural or supernatural, were secondary.

6:9 The inhabitants of Jericho must have observed with incredulity the Israelites marching around the city day after day. No war had ever been fought like that and none has been like it since then. The Israelites themselves probably thought what they were doing was strange and they must have waited breathlessly to see what the result would be.

trumpets, Joshua said unto the people, Shout; for the LORD hath given you
the city.

6:17☆ Josh 2:15; 6:22

17¶And the city shall be accursed, *even* it, and all that *are* therein, to the
LORD: only Rahab the harlot shall live, she and all that *are* with her in the
house, because she hid the messengers that we sent.

6:18 Deut 20:17 Josh 7:1

18And ye, in any wise keep *yourselves* from the accursed thing, lest ye
make *yourselves* accursed, when ye take of the accursed thing, and make the
camp of Israel a curse, and trouble it.

6:19 Num 31:22, 23

19But all the silver, and gold, and vessels of brass and iron, *are*
consecrated unto the LORD: they shall come into the treasury of the LORD.

6:20☆ Heb 11:30

20So the people shouted when *the priests* blew with the trumpets: and it
came to pass, when the people heard the sound of the trumpet, and the
people shouted with a great shout, that the wall fell down flat, so that the
people went up into the city, every man straight before him, and they took
the city.

6:21 Deut 20:16

21And they utterly destroyed all that *was* in the city, both man and
woman, young and old, and ox, and sheep, and ass, with the edge of the
sword.

3. The Rescue of Rahab and Her Family

6:22 Josh 2:15 Judg 1:25

22But Joshua had said unto the two men that had spied out the country,
Go into the harlot's house, and bring out thence the woman, and all that
she hath, as ye sware unto her.

6:23☆ Heb 11:31

23And the young men that were spies went in, and brought out Rahab,
and her father, and her mother, and her brethren, and all that she had; and
they brought out all her kindred, and left them without the camp of Israel.
24And they burnt the city with fire, and all that *was* therein: only the
silver, and the gold, and the vessels of brass and of iron, they put into the
treasury of the house of the LORD.

6:25 Josh 2:6 Heb 11:31

25And Joshua saved Rahab the harlot alive, and her father's household,
and all that she had; and she dwelleth in Israel *even* unto this day; because
she hid the messengers, which Joshua sent to spy out Jericho.

4. Joshua Lays a Curse on Jericho

6:26☆ 2 Sam 10:5 1 Kgs 16:34

26¶And Joshua adjured *them* at that time, saying, Cursed *be* the man
before the LORD, that riseth up and buildeth this city Jericho: he shall lay
the foundation thereof in his firstborn, and in his youngest *son* shall he set
up the gates of it.

6:27☆ Deut 31:7

27So the LORD was with Joshua; and his fame was *noised* throughout all
the country.

6:17 The first part of this verse is better translated: "And the city shall be under the ban, it and all that is in it belongs to the Lord." The Hebrew word *herem* is used. See note to Deut. 2:34 for explanation.

6:20 The soldiers marched around the city once a day for six days. On the seventh day they circled the city seven times then blew their trumpets. It is absurd to think that this sound caused the walls to fall down. It was God who miraculously caused the walls to collapse. The text gives no specific explanation for the happening. It only records the facts.

6:23 Although Rahab was a harlot, the mercy of God wrought wonders in that depraved life. Her works demonstrated her faith. In Matt. 1:15 we read that she married Salmon, then gave birth to Boaz. Rahab was an Israelite by redemption, not by birth. Although an alien and a sinful woman, she came to stand in the promised line of the Messiah. Such is the wonderful grace of God.

6:26 See 1 Kings 16:34 for the fulfillment of this curse.†

6:27 The events magnified Joshua before Israel but they also made him appear as a formidable enemy to the Canaanites, who could see that his God was with him.

F. THE TRAGEDY AND VICTORY AT AI

1. Israel's Defeat and Joshua's Grief

7 BUT the children of Israel committed a trespass in the accursed thing:
for A'chan, the son of Car'mi, the son of Zab'di, the son of Ze'rah, of
the tribe of Judah, took of the accursed thing: and the anger of the LORD
was kindled against the children of Israel.

☆7:1 Josh 6:17–19; 1 Chron 2:7

2And Joshua sent men from Jericho to A'i, which *is* beside Beth–a'ven,
on the east side of Beth–el, and spake unto them, saying, Go up and view
the country. And the men went up and viewed A'i.

7:2 Gen 28:19; Josh 16:2

3And they returned to Joshua, and said unto him, Let not all the people
go up; but let about two or three thousand men go up and smite A'i; *and*
make not all the people to labour thither; for they *are but* few.
4So there went up thither of the people about three thousand men: and
they fled before the men of A'i.
5And the men of A'i smote of them about thirty and six men: for they
chased them *from* before the gate *even* unto Sheb'a-rim, and smote them in
the going down: wherefore the hearts of the people melted, and became as
water.

7:5 Josh 8:1

6¶And Joshua rent his clothes, and fell to the earth upon his face before
the ark of the LORD until the eventide, he and the elders of Israel, and put
dust upon their heads.

☆7:6 Job 2:12; 42:6; Lam 2:10

7And Joshua said, Alas, O Lord GOD, wherefore hast thou at all brought
this people over Jordan, to deliver us into the hand of the Am'or-ites, to
destroy us? would to God we had been content, and dwelt on the other side
Jordan!

7:7 Ex 14:11; 17:3

8O Lord, what shall I say, when Israel turneth their backs before their
enemies!
9For the Canaanites and all the inhabitants of the land shall hear *of it*,
and shall environ us round, and cut off our name from the earth: and what
wilt thou do unto thy great name?

7:9 Ex 32:12; Deut 9:28

2. God Uncovers Israel's Sin

10¶And the LORD said unto Joshua, Get thee up; wherefore liest thou
thus upon thy face?

7:10 Ex 14:15; 1 Sam 15:22; 16:1

11Israel hath sinned, and they have also transgressed my covenant which
I commanded them: for they have even taken of the accursed thing, and
have also stolen, and dissembled also, and they have put *it* even among
their own stuff.

☆7:11

12Therefore the children of Israel could not stand before their enemies,
but turned *their* backs before their enemies, because they were accursed:

7:1 The sin for which Achan was punished was not the seizure of the enemy's valuable goods. Nor was it the fact that he coveted these things. His chief sin lay in his refusal to unconditionally obey God's express command. Moreover, his sin involved corporate Israel, for no man lives or dies to himself. Consequently, God's displeasure included Israel as a whole; the nation was not released from responsibility until Achan and his family had been dealt with. Had Achan not sinned, Israel's first attack on Ai would have been successful and lives would have been saved.

7:6 Joshua had been promised success in his warfare, but now he suffered a significant defeat at Ai. He was led to ask God why he had allowed his people to be defeated (7:7). Joshua learned quickly that the defeat had been caused by the sin of Achan. One bad apple in a barrel can contaminate all the good apples. This apparently small transgression brought incalculable harm to all Israel. When the situation had been rectified, Israel continued its successful takeover of Canaan.

7:11 *the accursed thing.* (See also 7:1, 12, 13, 15.) This is better translated "the devoted thing," in reference to persons or things irrevocably given over to God, sometimes by their total destruction, as in these verses.

neither will I be with you any more, except ye destroy the accursed from among you.

7:13 Ex 19:10 Joel 2:16, 17 Zeph 2:1–3

13 Up, sanctify the people, and say, Sanctify yourselves against to morrow: for thus saith the LORD God of Israel, *There is* an accursed thing in the midst of thee, O Israel: thou canst not stand before thine enemies, until ye take away the accursed thing from among you.

14 In the morning therefore ye shall be brought according to your tribes: and it shall be, *that* the tribe which the LORD taketh shall come according to the families *thereof;* and the family which the LORD shall take shall come by households; and the household which the LORD shall take shall come man by man.

15 And it shall be, *that* he that is taken with the accursed thing shall be burnt with fire, he and all that he hath: because he hath transgressed the covenant of the LORD, and because he hath wrought folly in Israel.

3. The Guilt of Achan

16 ¶So Joshua rose up early in the morning, and brought Israel by their tribes; and the tribe of Judah was taken:

17 And he brought the family of Judah; and he took the family of the Zar′hites: and he brought the family of the Zar′hites man by man; and Zab′di was taken:

18 And he brought his household man by man; and A′chan, the son of Car′mi, the son of Zab′di, the son of Ze′rah, of the tribe of Judah, was taken.

7:19☆ Jer 13:16 Jn 9:24

19 And Joshua said unto A′chan, My son, give, I pray thee, glory to the LORD God of Israel, and make confession unto him; and tell me now what thou hast done; hide *it* not from me.

7:20 Ex 10:16

20 And A′chan answered Joshua, and said, Indeed I have sinned against the LORD God of Israel, and thus and thus have I done:

21 When I saw among the spoils a goodly Babylonish garment, and two hundred shekels of silver, and a wedge of gold of fifty shekels weight, then I coveted them, and took them; and, behold, they *are* hid in the earth in the midst of my tent, and the silver under it.

4. The Execution of Achan and His Family

22 ¶So Joshua sent messengers, and they ran unto the tent; and, behold, *it was* hid in his tent, and the silver under it.

23 And they took them out of the midst of the tent, and brought them unto Joshua, and unto all the children of Israel, and laid them out before the LORD.

7:24 Josh 15:7

24 And Joshua, and all Israel with him, took A′chan the son of Ze′rah, and the silver, and the garment, and the wedge of gold, and his sons, and his daughters, and his oxen, and his asses, and his sheep, and his tent, and all that he had: and they brought them unto the valley of A′chor.

7:25 Deut 13:17 24:16 Josh 6:18

25 And Joshua said, Why hast thou troubled us? the LORD shall trouble thee this day. And all Israel stoned him with stones, and burned them with fire, after they had stoned them with stones.

7:26☆ Gen 31:46, 51, 52 Josh 8:28, 29 Isa 65:10 Hos 2:15

26 And they raised over him a great heap of stones unto this day. So the LORD turned from the fierceness of his anger. Wherefore the name of that place was called, The valley of A′chor, unto this day.

7:19 *Tell me now what thou hast done.* It is the same old story. Just before crossing the Jordan all Israel promised solemnly to obey Joshua and God. This pledge was broken by Achan who (with his family) suffered the penalty of death.

7:26 *Achor,* i.e., "trouble," "calamity," or "disaster."

5. The Victory at Ai

a. The Military Plan

8 AND the LORD said unto Joshua, Fear not, neither be thou dismayed: take all the people of war with thee, and arise, go up to A'i: see, I have given into thy hand the king of A'i, and his people, and his city, and his land:

8:1 Deut 1:19, 20, 21; 31:8 Josh 1:9; 6:2 10:8

2 And thou shalt do to A'i and her king as thou didst unto Jericho and her king: only the spoil thereof, and the cattle thereof, shall ye take for a prey unto yourselves: lay thee an ambush for the city behind it.

☆**8:2** Josh 6:18; 8:27

3 ¶So Joshua arose, and all the people of war, to go up against A'i: and Joshua chose out thirty thousand mighty men of valour, and sent them away by night.

4 And he commanded them, saying, Behold, ye shall lie in wait against the city, *even* behind the city: go not very far from the city, but be ye all ready:

5 And I, and all the people that *are* with me, will approach unto the city: and it shall come to pass, when they come out against us, as at the first, that we will flee before them,

6 (For they will come out after us) till we have drawn them from the city; for they will say, They flee before us, as at the first: therefore we will flee before them.

8:6 Josh 7:5

7 Then ye shall rise up from the ambush, and seize upon the city: for the LORD your God will deliver it into your hand.

8 And it shall be, when ye have taken the city, *that* ye shall set the city on fire: according to the commandment of the LORD shall ye do. See, I have commanded you.

8:8 Josh 6:24 8:20, 21

9 ¶Joshua therefore sent them forth: and they went to lie in ambush, and abode between Beth–el and A'i, on the west side of A'i: but Joshua lodged that night among the people.

b. The Capture of the City

10 And Joshua rose up early in the morning, and numbered the people, and went up, he and the elders of Israel, before the people to A'i.

11 And all the people, *even the people* of war that *were* with him, went up, and drew nigh, and came before the city, and pitched on the north side of A'i: now *there was* a valley between them and A'i.

12 And he took about five thousand men, and set them to lie in ambush between Beth–el and A'i, on the west side of the city.

☆**8:12**

13 And when they had set the people, *even* all the host that *was* on the north of the city, and their liers in wait on the west of the city, Joshua went that night into the midst of the valley.

☆**8:13**

14 ¶And it came to pass, when the king of A'i saw *it*, that they hasted and rose up early, and the men of the city went out against Israel to battle, he and all his people, at a time appointed, before the plain; but he wist not that *there were* liers in ambush against him behind the city.

8:14 Deut 1:1; 4:49 Josh 11:1

15 And Joshua and all Israel made as if they were beaten before them, and fled by the way of the wilderness.

16 And all the people that *were* in A'i were called together to pursue after them: and they pursued after Joshua, and were drawn away from the city.

8:2 Whereas the spoil from Jericho was dedicated in its entirety to God, the Israelites were free to keep all they took at Ai.

8:12 *five thousand men.* These were evidently additional to the thirty thousand men already hiding there. Perhaps the additional five thousand were to intercept the forces expected from Beth-el (8:17).†

8:13 *went that night into the midst of the valley* is better translated that he "spent that night in the midst of the valley." Some have suggested that he spent the night in prayer, seeking the blessing of God before the battle started the next day.

8:17 Josh 12:8–24
17 And there was not a man left in A'i or Beth–el, that went not out after Israel: and they left the city open, and pursued after Israel.

8:18 Ex 14:16; 17:9 Josh 8:26
18 And the LORD said unto Joshua, Stretch out the spear that *is* in thy hand toward A'i; for I will give it into thine hand. And Joshua stretched out the spear that *he had* in his hand toward the city.

19 And the ambush arose quickly out of their place, and they ran as soon as he had stretched out his hand: and they entered into the city, and took it, and hasted and set the city on fire.

20 And when the men of A'i looked behind them, they saw, and, behold, the smoke of the city ascended up to heaven, and they had no power to flee this way or that way: and the people that fled to the wilderness turned back upon the pursuers.

21 And when Joshua and all Israel saw that the ambush had taken the city, and that the smoke of the city ascended, then they turned again, and slew the men of A'i.

8:22 Num 21:35 Deut 3:6
22 And the other issued out of the city against them; so they were in the midst of Israel, some on this side, and some on that side: and they smote them, so that they let none of them remain or escape.

23 And the king of A'i they took alive, and brought him to Joshua.

c. The Slaughter of the People of Ai

24 And it came to pass, when Israel had made an end of slaying all the inhabitants of A'i in the field, in the wilderness wherein they chased them, and when they were all fallen on the edge of the sword, until they were consumed, that all the Israelites returned unto A'i, and smote it with the edge of the sword.

8:25 Deut 20:16
25 And *so* it was, *that* all that fell that day, both of men and women, *were* twelve thousand, *even* all the men of A'i.

8:26 Ex 17:11 Josh 8:18
26 For Joshua drew not his hand back, wherewith he stretched out the spear, until he had utterly destroyed all the inhabitants of A'i.

8:27 Josh 8:2
27 Only the cattle and the spoil of that city Israel took for a prey unto themselves, according unto the word of the LORD which he commanded Joshua.

8:28☆ Josh 7:26
28 And Joshua burnt A'i, and made it an heap for ever, *even* a desolation unto this day.

8:29☆ Deut 21:22, 23
29 And the king of A'i he hanged on a tree until eventide: and as soon as the sun was down, Joshua commanded that they should take his carcase down from the tree, and cast it at the entering of the gate of the city, and raise thereon a great heap of stones, *that remaineth* unto this day.

8:30☆ Gen 8:20 12:7, 8 Josh 22:10 Judg 6:24
d. An Altar Built on Mount Ebal

30 ¶Then Joshua built an altar unto the LORD God of Israel in mount Ebal,

---

8:28 *Ai* ("the heap" or "the ruin") was destroyed by Israel. It appears to have been located in the area near Jericho, Jerusalem, and Beth-el. Its exact site is still undetermined. Ai may have been a military outpost of Beth-el which Joshua seized.

8:29 "The king of Ai was taken prisoner and cut off, not by the sword of war as a soldier, but by the sword of justice as a malefactor."* This king was apparently notoriously wicked, a blasphemer of the God of Israel, justly deserving the judgment that fell on him.

8:30 Joshua built an altar on Mount Ebal according to the instruction of Moses in Deut. 27:2–8. Building the altar was more than a simple act of obedience to Moses' command. The Israelites were giving glory to God for the victory at Ai which had first been denied them by Achan's sin. When they erected the altar, they acknowledged that they were the people of God. In 8:32 we read that Joshua engraved the Ten Commandments on the stones of the altar, demonstrating that they accepted God's law. This dedication was a renewal of God's covenant arrangements with Israel, a covenant which promised the blessing of God on an obedient people.

31 As Moses the servant of the LORD commanded the children of Israel, as
it is written in the book of the law of Moses, an altar of whole stones, over
which no man hath lift up *any* iron: and they offered thereon burnt
offerings unto the LORD, and sacrificed peace offerings.
32 ¶And he wrote there upon the stones a copy of the law of Moses, which
he wrote in the presence of the children of Israel.
33 And all Israel, and their elders, and officers, and their judges, stood on
this side the ark and on that side before the priests the Levites, which bare
the ark of the covenant of the LORD, as well the stranger, as he that was
born among them; half of them over against mount Ger'i-zim, and half of
them over against mount Ebal; as Moses the servant of the LORD had
commanded before, that they should bless the people of Israel.
34 And afterward he read all the words of the law, the blessings and
cursings, according to all that is written in the book of the law.
35 There was not a word of all that Moses commanded, which Joshua read
not before all the congregation of Israel, with the women, and the little
ones, and the strangers that were conversant among them.

8:31 Ex 20:25 Deut 27:5, 6
8:33 Deut 27:12, 13
8:34 Deut 11:26 28:2–6, 15-19

G. THE TRICKERY OF THE GIBEONITES
1. The Alliance Formed against Israel

9 AND it came to pass, when all the kings which *were* on this side
Jordan, in the hills, and in the valleys, and in all the coasts of the great
sea over against Lebanon, the Hittite, and the Am'or-ite, the Canaanite, the
Per'iz-zite, the Hi'vite, and the Jeb'u-site, heard *thereof;*
2 That they gathered themselves together, to fight with Joshua and with
Israel, with one accord.

9:1 Num 13:17, 29 Deut 1:7 Josh 3:10 10:40; 11:16
☆9:2

2. The Gibeonite Peace Treaty

3 ¶And when the inhabitants of Gibeon heard what Joshua had done unto
Jericho and to A'i,
4 They did work wilily, and went and made as if they had been
ambassadors, and took old sacks upon their asses, and wine bottles, old,
and rent, and bound up;
5 And old shoes and clouted upon their feet, and old garments upon
them; and all the bread of their provision was dry *and* mouldy.
6 And they went to Joshua unto the camp at Gilgal, and said unto him,
and to the men of Israel, We be come from a far country: now therefore
make ye a league with us.
7 And the men of Israel said unto the Hi'vites, Peradventure ye dwell
among us; and how shall we make a league with you?
8 And they said unto Joshua, We *are* thy servants. And Joshua said unto
them, Who *are* ye? and from whence come ye?
9 And they said unto him, From a very far country thy servants are come
because of the name of the LORD thy God: for we have heard the fame of
him, and all that he did in Egypt,
10 And all that he did to the two kings of the Am'or-ites, that *were* beyond
Jordan, to Sihon king of Hesh'bon, and to Og king of Ba'shan, which *was* at
Ash'ta-roth.
11 Wherefore our elders and all the inhabitants of our country spake to us,
saying, Take victuals with you for the journey, and go to meet them, and

9:3 Josh 10:2, 7 11:19 Prov 13:17
9:7 Ex 23:32 Josh 11:19
9:9 Josh 2:9 9:16, 17

9:2 When the inhabitants of Canaan learned about the fate of Ai, they formed a military alliance to fight against Israel. The number of Israelites in itself presented a grave threat to these peoples who were far fewer in numbers.

say unto them, We *are* your servants: therefore now make ye a league with us.

12 This our bread we took hot *for* our provision out of our houses on the day we came forth to go unto you; but now, behold, it is dry, and it is mouldy:

13 And these bottles of wine, which we filled, *were* new; and, behold, they be rent: and these our garments and our shoes are become old by reason of the very long journey.

9:14☆ Ex 23:32 Num 27:21

14 And the men took of their victuals, and asked not *counsel* at the mouth of the LORD.

9:15☆

15 And Joshua made peace with them, and made a league with them, to let them live: and the princes of the congregation sware unto them.

3. Joshua's Punishment of the Gibeonites

16 ¶And it came to pass at the end of three days after they had made a league with them, that they heard that they *were* their neighbours, and *that* they dwelt among them.

9:17 Josh 18:15, 25, 26; 15:9, 60 1 Sam 7:1, 2 1 Chron 13:5, 6

17 And the children of Israel journeyed, and came unto their cities on the third day. Now their cities *were* Gibeon, and Che-phi'rah, and Be-e'roth, and Kir'jath-je'a-rim.

18 And the children of Israel smote them not, because the princes of the congregation had sworn unto them by the LORD God of Israel. And all the congregation murmured against the princes.

9:19☆

19 But all the princes said unto all the congregation, We have sworn unto them by the LORD God of Israel: now therefore we may not touch them.

9:20 2 Sam 21:1

20 This we will do to them; we will even let them live, lest wrath be upon us, because of the oath which we sware unto them.

9:21 Gen 9:25

21 And the princes said unto them, Let them live; but let them be hewers of wood and drawers of water unto all the congregation; as the princes had promised them.

22 ¶And Joshua called for them, and he spake unto them, saying, Wherefore have ye beguiled us, saying, We *are* very far from you; when ye dwell among us?

9:23☆

23 Now therefore ye *are* cursed, and there shall none of you be freed from being bondmen, and hewers of wood and drawers of water for the house of my God.

9:24 Deut 7:1 20:16, 17 Josh 2:24; 5:1

24 And they answered Joshua, and said, Because it was certainly told thy servants, how that the LORD thy God commanded his servant Moses to give you all the land, and to destroy all the inhabitants of the land from before you, therefore we were sore afraid of our lives because of you, and have done this thing.

25 And now, behold, we *are* in thine hand: as it seemeth good and right unto thee to do unto us, do.

26 And so did he unto them, and delivered them out of the hand of the children of Israel, that they slew them not.

9:14, 15 The Gibeonites deceived Israel when working out their treaty. Israel, however, was not without responsibility; it was not necessary for them to be deceived. *The men . . . asked not counsel at the mouth of the LORD* makes clear that the error would have been avoided if they sought God's advice. No matter how favorable or unfavorable external circumstances may be, believers should not rely on their own judgment when they have divine resources at hand to help them.

9:19 The leaders of Israel were constrained to keep the oath they made with the Gibeonites, for it was taken in the name of God. Even though the oath was taken as a result of the false pretensions of the Gibeonites, it was to be kept. The Psalmist says, "he that sweareth to his own hurt, and changeth not" (15:4).

9:23 The Gibeonites preferred to live as slaves than as dead heroes. Some things are worth fighting for, even though it may mean death. Life is not the supreme goal for the believer. It may be better to be dead than a slave.

27 And Joshua made them that day hewers of wood and drawers of water for the congregation, and for the altar of the LORD, even unto this day, in the place which he should choose.

9:27 Deut 12:4, 5, 6

H. THE VICTORY OVER SOUTHERN CANAAN

1. The Amorite Confederation

10 NOW it came to pass, when A-do'ni-ze'dec king of Jerusalem had heard how Joshua had taken A'i, and had utterly destroyed it; as he had done to Jericho and her king, so he had done to A'i and her king; and how the inhabitants of Gibeon had made peace with Israel, and were among them;

☆10:1 Josh 8:25; 9:14, 15

2 That they feared greatly, because Gibeon *was* a great city, as one of the royal cities, and because it *was* greater than A'i, and all the men thereof *were* mighty.

10:2 1 Kgs 3:4, 5; 9:2, 3; 1 Chron 21:29; 2 Chron 1:2, 3

3 Wherefore A-do'ni-ze'dec king of Jerusalem sent unto Ho'ham king of Hebron, and unto Pi'ram king of Jar'muth, and unto Ja-phi'a king of La'chish, and unto De'bir king of Eg'lon, saying,

4 Come up unto me, and help me, that we may smite Gibeon: for it hath made peace with Joshua and with the children of Israel.

5 Therefore the five kings of the Am'or-ites, the king of Jerusalem, the king of Hebron, the king of Jar'muth, the king of La'chish, the king of Eg'lon, gathered themselves together, and went up, they and all their hosts, and encamped before Gibeon, and made war against it.

10:5 Num 13:29; Josh 9:1

2. The Hailstorm and the Victory

6 ¶And the men of Gibeon sent unto Joshua to the camp to Gilgal, saying, Slack not thy hand from thy servants; come up to us quickly, and save us, and help us: for all the kings of the Am'or-ites that dwell in the mountains are gathered together against us.

7 So Joshua ascended from Gilgal, he, and all the people of war with him, and all the mighty men of valour.

8 ¶And the LORD said unto Joshua, Fear them not: for I have delivered them into thine hand; there shall not a man of them stand before thee.

10:8 Josh 1:5, 9; 6:2; 8:1

9 Joshua therefore came unto them suddenly, *and* went up from Gilgal all night.

10 And the LORD discomfited them before Israel, and slew them with a great slaughter at Gibeon, and chased them along the way that goeth up to Beth-ho'ron, and smote them to A-ze'kah, and unto Mak-ke'dah.

10:10 Judg 4:15

11 And it came to pass, as they fled from before Israel, *and* were in the going down to Beth-ho'ron, that the LORD cast down great stones from heaven upon them unto A-ze'kah, and they died: *they were* more which died with hailstones than *they* whom the children of Israel slew with the sword.

☆10:11

10:1 The Gibeonites go from the frying pan into the fire. They have made a treaty with Israel, but now five kings set up an alliance to attack Gibeon and retake it from the Israelites who are its masters. Gibeon appeals to Joshua for help. (Those who pay allegiance can rightly expect the protection of their masters.) Moreover, they had a binding treaty with Israel. Joshua had been waiting for the right time to attack the Amorites, who stood in the way of Israel's occupation of the land. Now that time had come, and Joshua was prepared. Again God intervened and manifested himself through signs and wonders.

10:11 God providentially sent a storm in which hailstones killed more enemies than the troops of Israel had killed. Job mentions the weapons of nature that God sometimes uses to defend and help his people. "Hast thou entered into the treasures of the snow? or hast thou seen the treasures of the hail which I have reserved against the time of trouble, against the day of battle and war?" (Job 38:22, 23). No secular historian can understand how a sovereign God can intervene in warfare and in other affairs of men through the forces of nature that appear to be accidental or based on luck.

3. God Makes the Sun Stand Still

12 ¶Then spake Joshua to the LORD in the day when the LORD delivered
up the Am'or-ites before the children of Israel, and he said in the sight of
Israel, Sun, stand thou still upon Gibeon; and thou, Moon, in the valley of
Aj'a-lon.

10:13☆ Isa 38:8

13 And the sun stood still, and the moon stayed, until the people had
avenged themselves upon their enemies. *Is* not this written in the book of
Ja'sher? So the sun stood still in the midst of heaven, and hasted not to go
down about a whole day.

10:14 Ex 14:14; Deut 1:30

14 And there was no day like that before it or after it, that the LORD
hearkened unto the voice of a man: for the LORD fought for Israel.

10:15 Josh 10:6, 43

15 ¶And Joshua returned, and all Israel with him, unto the camp to Gilgal.

4. The Execution of the Five Kings

10:16 Josh 10:28

16 But these five kings fled, and hid themselves in a cave at Mak-ke'dah.
17 And it was told Joshua, saying, The five kings are found hid in a cave at
Mak-ke'dah.
18 And Joshua said, Roll great stones upon the mouth of the cave, and set
men by it for to keep them:
19 And stay ye not, *but* pursue after your enemies, and smite the hindmost
of them; suffer them not to enter into their cities: for the LORD your God
hath delivered them into your hand.

10:20 Deut 20:16

20 And it came to pass, when Joshua and the children of Israel had made
an end of slaying them with a very great slaughter, till they were consumed,
that the rest *which* remained of them entered into fenced cities.

10:21 Josh 10:16

21 And all the people returned to the camp to Joshua at Mak-ke'dah in
peace: none moved his tongue against any of the children of Israel.

10:22 Deut 7:24; 1 Sam 15:32, 33

22 Then said Joshua, Open the mouth of the cave, and bring out those five
kings unto me out of the cave.
23 And they did so, and brought forth those five kings unto him out of the
cave, the king of Jerusalem, the king of Hebron, the king of Jar'muth, the
king of La'chish, *and* the king of Eg'lon.

10:24☆

24 And it came to pass, when they brought out those kings unto Joshua,
that Joshua called for all the men of Israel, and said unto the captains of
the men of war which went with him, Come near, put your feet upon the
necks of these kings. And they came near, and put their feet upon the necks
of them.

10:25 Josh 10:8

25 And Joshua said unto them, Fear not, nor be dismayed, be strong and
of good courage: for thus shall the LORD do to all your enemies against
whom ye fight.

10:26 Josh 8:29

26 And afterward Joshua smote them, and slew them, and hanged them on
five trees: and they were hanging upon the trees until the evening.

10:27 Deut 21:22, 23

27 And it came to pass at the time of the going down of the sun, *that*
Joshua commanded, and they took them down off the trees, and cast them
into the cave wherein they had been hid, and laid great stones in the cave's
mouth, *which remain* until this very day.

10:13 *the sun stood still, and the moon stayed.* The historicity of this event has been questioned even by people in the conservative tradition. They have leaned toward the notion that this is a figure of speech; the sun only *seemed* to stand still, or the day *seemed* longer than it actually was. Nevertheless, for an all-powerful God to stop the rotation of the earth for a day without the universe collapsing is no harder than to raise the dead or create the universe. This was a miracle—a great one, to be sure.

10:24 *put your feet upon the necks of these kings.* This was customary as a symbol of victory. Egyptian and Assyrian sculptures frequently portray this custom.

5. The Completion of the Military Conquest

28¶And that day Joshua took Mak-ke′dah, and smote it with the edge of ☆10:28 Deut 20:16 Josh 10:20
the sword, and the king thereof he utterly destroyed, them, and all the souls
that *were* therein; he let none remain: and he did to the king of Mak-
ke′dah, as he did unto the king of Jericho.
29Then Joshua passed from Mak-ke′dah, and all Israel with him, unto 10:29 Num 33:15–37 Josh 12:8–24
Lib′nah, and fought against Lib′nah:
30And the LORD delivered it also, and the king thereof, into the hand of
Israel; and he smote it with the edge of the sword, and all the souls that
were therein; he let none remain in it; but did unto the king thereof as he
did unto the king of Jericho.
31¶And Joshua passed from Lib′nah, and all Israel with him, unto
La′chish, and encamped against it, and fought against it:
32And the LORD delivered La′chish into the hand of Israel, which took it
on the second day, and smote it with the edge of the sword, and all the
souls that *were* therein, according to all that he had done to Lib′nah.
33¶Then Ho′ram king of Ge′zer came up to help La′chish; and Joshua
smote him and his people, until he had left him none remaining.
34¶And from La′chish Joshua passed unto Eg′lon, and all Israel with him;
and they encamped against it, and fought against it:
35And they took it on that day, and smote it with the edge of the sword,
and all the souls that *were* therein he utterly destroyed that day, according
to all that he had done to La′chish.
36And Joshua went up from Eg′lon, and all Israel with him, unto Hebron; 10:36 Josh 10:3
and they fought against it:
37And they took it, and smote it with the edge of the sword, and the king ☆10:37
thereof, and all the cities thereof, and all the souls that *were* therein; he left
none remaining, according to all that he had done to Eg′lon; but destroyed
it utterly, and all the souls that *were* therein.
38¶And Joshua returned, and all Israel with him, to De′bir; and fought
against it:
39And he took it, and the king thereof, and all the cities thereof; and they
smote them with the edge of the sword, and utterly destroyed all the souls
that *were* therein; he left none remaining: as he had done to Hebron, so he
did to De′bir, and to the king thereof; as he had done also to Lib′nah, and
to her king.
40¶So Joshua smote all the country of the hills, and of the south, and of ☆10:40 Deut 1:7; 7:24 20:16
the vale, and of the springs, and all their kings: he left none remaining, but
utterly destroyed all that breathed, as the LORD God of Israel commanded.
41And Joshua smote them from Ka′desh-bar′ne-a even unto Ga′za, and ☆10:41 Josh 11:16 15:48–62
all the country of Goshen, even unto Gibeon.
42And all these kings and their land did Joshua take at one time, because
the LORD God of Israel fought for Israel.
43And Joshua returned, and all Israel with him, unto the camp to Gilgal. 10:43 Josh 10:6

10:28 Following the slaughter of the five kings Joshua extends his military campaign and razes city after city—Makkedah, Libnah, Lachish, Eglon, Hebron, and Debar. Also the Negeb and the hill country. It was a massive assault and a complete victory, with no evidence of a contrary spirit on the part of the Israelites.

10:37 *the king thereof.* Joshua slew the king of Hebron (10:26). This must have been a new king, i.e., a successor to the old king or a claimant to the throne. Whenever a monarch dies there is always someone to take his place.

10:40 *smote all the country.* This statement pertains to certain areas of Canaan, for in Judg. 1:27–33 a number of Canaanite cities are said to have remained uncaptured. The full conquest of the land did not come until the days of David and Solomon. But Joshua did win nominal control of the whole land, although pockets of resistance were left.

10:41 *Goshen,* not the Goshen of Egypt.

I. THE VICTORY OVER NORTHERN CANAAN

11:1☆ Josh 10:3, 4; 11:10; 12:8–24; 19:35–39; Judg 4:2, 17

11 AND it came to pass, when Ja'bin king of Ha'zor had heard *those things*, that he sent to Jo'bab king of Ma'don, and to the king of Shim'ron, and to the king of Ach'shaph,

2 And to the kings that *were* on the north of the mountains, and of the plains south of Chin'ne-roth, and in the valley, and in the borders of Dor on the west,

3 *And to* the Canaanite on the east and on the west, and *to* the Am'or-ite, and the Hittite, and the Per'iz-zite, and the Jeb'u-site in the mountains, and *to* the Hi'vite under Hermon in the land of Miz'peh.

11:4 Josh 11:20

4 And they went out, they and all their hosts with them, much people, even as the sand that *is* upon the sea shore in multitude, with horses and chariots very many.

5 And when all these kings were met together, they came and pitched together at the waters of Me'rom, to fight against Israel.

11:6☆ Josh 8:1; 10:8; 2 Sam 8:4

6 ¶And the LORD said unto Joshua, Be not afraid because of them: for to morrow about this time will I deliver them up all slain before Israel: thou shalt hough their horses, and burn their chariots with fire.

7 So Joshua came, and all the people of war with him, against them by the waters of Me'rom suddenly; and they fell upon them.

11:8☆

8 And the LORD delivered them into the hand of Israel, who smote them, and chased them unto great Zi'don, and unto Mis're-photh–ma'im, and unto the valley of Miz'peh eastward; and they smote them, until they left them none remaining.

9 And Joshua did unto them as the LORD bade him: he houghed their horses, and burnt their chariots with fire.

11:10 Judg 4:2, 3; 1 Sam 12:9; 1 Kgs 9:15; 2 Kgs 15:29

10 ¶And Joshua at that time turned back, and took Ha'zor, and smote the king thereof with the sword: for Ha'zor beforetime was the head of all those kingdoms.

11:11 Deut 20:16; Josh 8:8, 20, 21; 10:28, 30

11 And they smote all the souls that *were* therein with the edge of the sword, utterly destroying *them;* there was not any left to breathe: and he burnt Ha'zor with fire.

12 And all the cities of those kings, and all the kings of them, did Joshua take, and smote them with the edge of the sword, *and* he utterly destroyed them, as Moses the servant of the LORD commanded.

13 But *as for* the cities that stood still in their strength, Israel burned none of them, save Ha'zor only; *that* did Joshua burn.

11:14 Josh 8:27

14 And all the spoil of these cities, and the cattle, the children of Israel took for a prey unto themselves; but every man they smote with the edge of the sword, until they had destroyed them, neither left they any to breathe.

11:15☆ Ex 34:11; Deut 31:7

15 ¶As the LORD commanded Moses his servant, so did Moses command Joshua, and so did Joshua; he left nothing undone of all that the LORD commanded Moses.

11:1 The rulers of Northern Canaan formed a coalition against Joshua. They came against Israel in large numbers but Joshua defeated the coalition. There were no supernatural signs or wonders in this campaign; God granted strength to his people to win the war without them. We should not expect God to perform miracles on every occasion, for miracles by their very nature are extraordinary. What appears to be ordinary is no less of God than the extraordinary.

11:6 *hough their horses and burn their chariots.* Israel did not need the armaments of the enemy. They had God on their side. They were not to put their trust in horses or in chariots.

11:8 *the LORD delivered them into the hand of Israel.* God is the Lord of history. Victory is not always in the hands of those who have superior military force. God determines the outcome of the events in history and stands behind it to accomplish the divine purpose. Unbelieving men heedlessly suppose they can make their own history apart from God.

11:15 Joshua was obedient to the commands of Moses which had been given to his predecessor by God. "Those that rule others at their will must themselves be ruled by the divine will."* Joshua neither spared the idols nor the idolaters according to the commission given him. He was faithful to God.

J. THE SUMMARY OF JOSHUA'S CONQUESTS

1. A General Review of the Conquest

16So Joshua took all that land, the hills, and all the south country, and all
the land of Goshen, and the valley, and the plain, and the mountain of
Israel, and the valley of the same;
17*Even* from the mount Ha'lak, that goeth up to Se'ir, even unto Ba'al-
gad in the valley of Lebanon under mount Hermon: and all their kings he
took, and smote them, and slew them.
18Joshua made war a long time with all those kings.
19There was not a city that made peace with the children of Israel, save
the Hi'vites the inhabitants of Gibeon: all *other* they took in battle.
20For it was of the LORD to harden their hearts, that they should come
against Israel in battle, that he might destroy them utterly, *and* that they
might have no favour, but that he might destroy them, as the LORD
commanded Moses.
21¶And at that time came Joshua, and cut off the Anakims from the
mountains, from Hebron, from De'bir, from Anab, and from all the
mountains of Judah, and from all the mountains of Israel: Joshua
destroyed them utterly with their cities.
22There was none of the Anakims left in the land of the children of Israel:
only in Ga'za, in Gath, and in Ash'dod, there remained.
23So Joshua took the whole land, according to all that the LORD said unto
Moses; and Joshua gave it for an inheritance unto Israel according to their
divisions by their tribes. And the land rested from war.

11:16 Josh 10:40, 41
11:17 Deut 7:24; Josh 12:7
11:19 Josh 9:3–15
☆**11:20** Ex 14:17; Deut 20:16; Josh 11:4
11:21 Num 13:33; Deut 9:1, 2; Josh 14:12; 15:13
11:23 Deut 1:38; 12:9, 10; 25:19; Heb 4:8

2. The Conquest of the Kings of East Canaan

12 NOW these *are* the kings of the land, which the children of Israel
smote, and possessed their land on the other side Jordan toward the
rising of the sun, from the river Arnon unto mount Hermon, and all the
plain on the east:
2Sihon king of the Am'or-ites, who dwelt in Hesh'bon, *and* ruled from
Ar'o-er, which *is* upon the bank of the river Arnon, and from the middle of
the river, and from half Gilead, even unto the river Jabbok, *which is* the
border of the children of Ammon;
3And from the plain to the sea of Chin'ne-roth on the east, and unto the
sea of the plain, *even* the salt sea on the east, the way to Beth-jesh'i-moth;
and from the south, under Ash'doth-pis'gah:
4¶And the coast of Og king of Ba'shan, *which was* of the remnant of the
giants, that dwelt at Ash'ta-roth and at Ed're-i,
5And reigned in mount Hermon, and in Sal'cah, and in all Ba'shan, unto
the border of the Gesh'u-rites, and the Ma-ach'a-thites, and half Gilead, the
border of Sihon king of Hesh'bon.
6Them did Moses the servant of the LORD and the children of Israel
smite: and Moses the servant of the LORD gave it *for* a possession unto the
Reubenites, and the Gadites, and the half tribe of Ma-nas'seh.

☆**12:1** Num 32:33; Deut 3:8; Josh 11:1–3
12:2 Num 21:23; Deut 2:35
12:4 Num 21:33; Josh 13:12

11:20 The hearts of the enemy were hardened by God so that his immutable will against them for their idolatry and other crimes might be executed through the people of Israel. These peoples were ripe for judgment, even as sinners in the end will be ripe for the great assize of God.

12:1 The account of the conquest of the land of Canaan is reported quickly and not in great detail. In chapter 12 a summary of the conquest is given. It starts with the victories on the east side of the Jordan and goes on from there to the west side. The abridgement reports the defeat of thirty-one kings. It marks the end of the conquest for the time being, and is a preface to the dividing of the land to the various tribes. However, there were still islands of resistance and enemies which still must be dealt with. The successors to Joshua would have to do this.

3. The Conquest of the Kings of West Canaan

12:7 Josh 11:17

7¶And these *are* the kings of the country which Joshua and the children of Israel smote on this side Jordan on the west, from Ba′al-gad in the valley of Lebanon even unto the mount Ha′lak, that goeth up to Se′ir; which Joshua gave unto the tribes of Israel *for* a possession according to their divisions;

12:8 Num 21:1–3 Deut 7:24 Josh 11:16

8In the mountains, and in the valleys, and in the plains, and in the springs, and in the wilderness, and in the south country; the Hittites, the Am′or-ites, and the Canaanites, the Per′iz-zites, the Hi′vites, and the Jeb′u-sites:

9¶The king of Jericho, one; the king of A′i, which *is* beside Beth–el, one;
10The king of Jerusalem, one; the king of Hebron, one;
11The king of Jar′muth, one; the king of La′chish, one;
12The king of Eg′lon, one; the king of Ge′zer, one;
13The king of De′bir, one; the king of Ge′der, one;
14The king of Hor′mah, one; the king of A′rad, one;
15The king of Lib′nah, one; the king of A-dul′lam, one;
16The king of Mak-ke′dah, one; the king of Beth–el, one;
17The king of Tap′pu-ah, one; the king of He′pher, one;
18The king of A′phek, one; the king of La-shar′on, one;
19The king of Ma′don, one; the king of Ha′zor, one;
20The king of Shim′ron–me′ron, one; the king of Ach′shaph, one;
21The king of Ta′a-nach, one; the king of Me-gid′do, one;
22The king of Ke′desh, one; the king of Jok′ne-am of Carmel, one;
23The king of Dor in the coast of Dor, one; the king of the nations of Gilgal, one;
24The king of Tir′zah, one: all the kings thirty and one.

II. THE DIVISION OF THE LAND OF CANAAN (13:1—21:45)

A. GOD COMMANDS JOSHUA TO DIVIDE THE LAND

13:1☆ Josh 14:10

13 NOW Joshua was old *and* stricken in years; and the LORD said unto him, Thou art old *and* stricken in years, and there remaineth yet very much land to be possessed.

13:2 Josh 12:3 Judg 3:1–3

2This *is* the land that yet remaineth: all the borders of the Philistines, and all Gesh′u-ri,

3From Si′hor, which *is* before Egypt, even unto the borders of Ekron northward, *which* is counted to the Canaanite: five lords of the Philistines; the Ga′zath-ites, and the Ash′doth-ites, the Esh′ka-lon-ites, the Git′tites, and the Ekronites; also the A′vites:

4From the south, all the land of the Canaanites, and Me-a′rah that *is* beside the Si-do′ni-ans, unto A′phek, to the borders of the Am′or-ites:

5And the land of the Gib′lites, and all Lebanon, toward the sunrising, from Ba′al-gad under mount Hermon unto the entering into Ha′math.

6All the inhabitants of the hill country from Lebanon unto Mis′re-photh-ma′im, *and* all the Si-do′ni-ans, them will I drive out from before the

---

13:1 Joshua was getting old and his death was near at hand. God commanded him to divide the land according to the numbers of the families in each tribe. The division was made by lot (Josh. 14:2). The Scriptures do not tell us precisely how lots were cast, nor do they say whether the practice was approved or disapproved by God. Lots were used in the New Testament as well as the Old Testament and were employed when important decisions were required. Prov. 16:33 says: "The lot is cast into the lap; but the whole disposing thereof is of the LORD." It was supposed that God, who is sovereign, was behind the way the lot fell. In some instances the people of God followed Gideon's example (Judg. 6:36ff), and put out fleeces.

children of Israel: only divide thou it by lot unto the Israelites for an
inheritance, as I have commanded thee.
7 Now therefore divide this land for an inheritance unto the nine tribes, ☆13:7
and the half tribe of Ma-nas'seh,

B. THE INHERITANCE ASSIGNED TO THE EASTERN TRIBES

1. The Boundaries

8 With whom the Reubenites and the Gadites have received their ☆13:8
inheritance, which Moses gave them, beyond Jordan eastward, *even* as Num 32:33
Moses the servant of the LORD gave them; Deut 3:12
9 From Ar'o-er, that *is* upon the bank of the river Arnon, and the city that
is in the midst of the river, and all the plain of Med'e-ba unto Di'bon;
10 And all the cities of Sihon king of the Am'or-ites, which reigned in
Hesh'bon, unto the border of the children of Ammon;
11 And Gilead, and the border of the Gesh'u-rites and Ma-ach'a-thites,
and all mount Hermon, and all Ba'shan unto Sal'cah;
12 All the kingdom of Og in Ba'shan, which reigned in Ash'ta-roth and in 13:12
Ed're-i, who remained of the remnant of the giants: for these did Moses Josh 12:4
smite, and cast them out.
13 Nevertheless the children of Israel expelled not the Gesh'u-rites, nor the 13:13
Ma-ach'a-thites: but the Gesh'u-rites and the Ma-ach'a-thites dwell among Josh 6:25; 13:13
the Israelites until this day.
14 Only unto the tribe of Levi he gave none inheritance; the sacrifices of 13:14
the LORD God of Israel made by fire *are* their inheritance, as he said unto Deut 18:1
them.

2. The Assignment to the Reubenites

15 ¶And Moses gave unto the tribe of the children of Reuben *inheritance* 13:15
according to their families. Josh 18:7
16 And their coast was from Ar'o-er, that *is* on the bank of the river
Arnon, and the city that *is* in the midst of the river, and all the plain by
Med'e-ba;
17 Hesh'bon, and all her cities that *are* in the plain; Di'bon, and Ba'moth–
ba'al, and Beth–ba'al–me'on,
18 And Ja-ha'zah, and Ked'e-moth, and Meph'a-ath,
19 And Kir-jath-a'im, and Sib'mah, and Za'reth–sha'har in the mount of
the valley,
20 And Beth–pe'or, and Ash'doth–pis'gah, and Beth–jesh'i-moth,
21 And all the cities of the plain, and all the kingdom of Sihon king of the 13:21
Am'or-ites, which reigned in Hesh'bon, whom Moses smote with the Num 31:8
princes of Mid'i-an, E'vi, and Re'kem, and Zur, and Hur, and Re'ba, *which*
were dukes of Sihon, dwelling in the country.
22 ¶Ba'laam also the son of Be'or, the soothsayer, did the children of Israel 13:22
slay with the sword among them that were slain by them. Num 22:5
23 And the border of the children of Reuben was Jordan, and the border 32:34–36
thereof. This *was* the inheritance of the children of Reuben after their
families, the cities and the villages thereof.

13:7 The division of the land to the nine and a half tribes was to be done by lot in accordance with God's instructions to Moses (Num. 34:13). This procedure avoided friction and exempted Joshua from making decisions that might be unpopular and for which he could be blamed. Providence is better than the counsels of men.

13:8 The Gadites, Reubenites, and half the tribe of Manasseh had already come into their possession on the east side of the Jordan. Moses gave them that land before his death. The other half of the tribe of Manasseh settled on the west side of Jordan.

3. The Assignment to the Gadites

[24]And Moses gave *inheritance* unto the tribe of Gad, *even* unto the
children of Gad according to their families.
[25]And their coast was Ja'zer, and all the cities of Gilead, and half the land
of the children of Ammon, unto Ar'o-er that *is* before Rab'bah;
[26]And from Hesh'bon unto Ra-math–miz'peh, and Bet'o-nim; and from
Ma-ha-na'im unto the border of De'bir;
13:27 Deut 3:17 [27]And in the valley, Beth–a'ram, and Beth–nim'rah, and Suc'coth, and
Za'phon, the rest of the kingdom of Sihon king of Hesh'bon, Jordan and *his*
border, *even* unto the edge of the sea of Chin'ne-reth on the other side
Jordan eastward.
[28]This *is* the inheritance of the children of Gad after their families, the
cities, and their villages.

4. The Assignment to the Half-Tribe of Manasseh

[29]¶And Moses gave *inheritance* unto the half tribe of Ma-nas'seh: and *this*
was *the possession* of the half tribe of the children of Ma-nas'seh by their
families.
[30]And their coast was from Ma-ha-na'im, all Ba'shan, all the kingdom of
Og king of Ba'shan, and all the towns of Ja'ir, which *are* in Ba'shan,
threescore cities:
[31]And half Gilead, and Ash'ta-roth, and Ed're-i, cities of the kingdom of
Og in Ba'shan, *were pertaining* unto the children of Ma'chir the son of Ma-
nas'seh, *even* to the one half of the children of Ma'chir by their families.
[32]These *are the countries* which Moses did distribute for inheritance in the
plains of Moab, on the other side Jordan, by Jericho, eastward.
13:33☆ Josh 13:14 [33]But unto the tribe of Levi Moses gave not *any* inheritance: the LORD
God of Israel *was* their inheritance, as he said unto them.

C. THE INHERITANCE ASSIGNED TO THE WESTERN TRIBES
1. The Introduction

14:1 Num 34:10–29 Josh 18:5, 6 14 AND these *are the countries* which the children of Israel inherited in
the land of Canaan, which E-le-a'zar the priest, and Joshua the son
of Nun, and the heads of the fathers of the tribes of the children of Israel,
distributed for inheritance to them.
[2]By lot *was* their inheritance, as the LORD commanded by the hand of
Moses, for the nine tribes, and *for* the half tribe.
14:3 Num 32:33 Josh 13:14 [3]For Moses had given the inheritance of two tribes and an half tribe on
the other side Jordan: but unto the Levites he gave none inheritance among
them.
[4]For the children of Joseph were two tribes, Ma-nas'seh and E'phra-im:
therefore they gave no part unto the Levites in the land, save cities to dwell
in, with their suburbs for their cattle and for their substance.
[5]As the LORD commanded Moses, so the children of Israel did, and they
divided the land.

2. The Land Given to Caleb of Judah

14:6 Num 13:30 14:6, 24, 30 Josh 15:13 [6]¶Then the children of Judah came unto Joshua in Gilgal: and Caleb the
son of Je-phun'neh the Ken'ez-ite said unto him, Thou knowest the thing

13:33 In verses 14 and 33 the tribe of Levi is stated to have no inheritance in Canaan. God provided for them in another manner. They were distributed among all of the tribes to maintain the true religion and to instruct the people of God. This provision also made visible to the various tribes the tribe they were to support inasmuch as the tribe of Levi would not be far removed from their borders. There must always be settled ministers in the communities they serve.

that the LORD said unto Moses the man of God concerning me and thee in Ka′desh-bar′ne-a.

7 Forty years old *was* I when Moses the servant of the LORD sent me from Ka′desh-bar′ne-a to espy out the land; and I brought him word again as *it was* in mine heart.

8 Nevertheless my brethren that went up with me made the heart of the people melt: but I wholly followed the LORD my God.

9 And Moses sware on that day, saying, Surely the land whereon thy feet have trodden shall be thine inheritance, and thy children's for ever, because thou hast wholly followed the LORD my God. **14:9** Deut 1:36

10 And now, behold, the LORD hath kept me alive, as he said, these forty and five years, even since the LORD spake this word unto Moses, while *the children of* Israel wandered in the wilderness: and now, lo, I *am* this day fourscore and five years old. ☆**14:10, 11**

11 As yet I *am as* strong this day as *I was* in the day that Moses sent me: as my strength *was* then, even so *is* my strength now, for war, both to go out, and to come in.

12 Now therefore give me this mountain, whereof the LORD spake in that day; for thou heardest in that day how the Anakims *were* there, and *that* the cities *were* great *and* fenced: if so be the LORD *will be* with me, then I shall be able to drive them out, as the LORD said. **14:12** Num 13:33

13 And Joshua blessed him, and gave unto Caleb the son of Je-phun′neh Hebron for an inheritance.

14 Hebron therefore became the inheritance of Caleb the son of Je-phun′neh the Ken′ez-ite unto this day, because that he wholly followed the LORD God of Israel. ☆**14:14**

15 And the name of Hebron before *was* Kir′jath-ar′ba; *which Arba was* a great man among the Anakims. And the land had rest from war. **14:15** Gen 35:27 Josh 15:48–62 20:7 Judg 1:10

3. The Inheritance of Judah's Descendants

a. Judah's Boundaries

15 *THIS* then was the lot of the tribe of the children of Judah by their families; *even* to the border of Edom the wilderness of Zin southward *was* the uttermost part of the south coast. **15:1** Num 34:3, 4 Deut 32:51 Josh 15:13 19:1, 36

2 And their south border was from the shore of the salt sea, from the bay that looketh southward:

3 And it went out to the south side to Ma-al′eh-ac-rab′bim, and passed along to Zin, and ascended up on the south side unto Ka′desh-bar′ne-a, and passed along to Hez′ron, and went up to A′dar, and fetched a compass to Kar′ka-a:

4 *From thence* it passed toward Az′mon, and went out unto the river of Egypt; and the goings out of that coast were at the sea: this shall be your south coast.

5 And the east border *was* the salt sea, *even* unto the end of Jordan. And *their* border in the north quarter *was* from the bay of the sea at the uttermost part of Jordan: **15:5** Josh 18:15

6 And the border went up to Beth-hog′la, and passed along by the north of Beth-ar′a-bah; and the border went up to the stone of Bo′han the son of Reuben:

14:10, 11 Caleb was eighty-five years old and stated that he was as strong and physically able as he had been when he spied out the land at forty years of age. On the other hand, Joshua apparently was feeling the infirmities of age and could not say this (13:1).

14:14 Of those who left Egypt, Caleb and Joshua were the only two male Israelites to enter the land of Canaan. All the others, including Moses, died before the Jordan was crossed. The most fitting memorial for the life of Caleb is: "He wholly followed the LORD God of Israel." This epitaph is one any believer should like to have engraved on his tombstone.

7 And the border went up toward De′bir from the valley of A′chor, and so northward, looking toward Gilgal, that *is* before the going up to A-dum′mim, which *is* on the south side of the river: and the border passed toward the waters of En–she′mesh, and the goings out thereof were at En–ro′gel:

15:8 Josh 15:63

8 And the border went up by the valley of the son of Hin′nom unto the south side of the Jeb′u-site; the same *is* Jerusalem: and the border went up to the top of the mountain that *lieth* before the valley of Hin′nom westward, which *is* at the end of the valley of the giants northward:

9 And the border was drawn from the top of the hill unto the fountain of the water of Neph′to-ah, and went out to the cities of mount E′phron; and the border was drawn to Ba′al-ah, which *is* Kir′jath–je′a-rim:

10 And the border compassed from Ba′al-ah westward unto mount Se′ir, and passed along unto the side of mount Je′a-rim, which *is* Ches′a-lon, on the north side, and went down to Beth–she′mesh, and passed on to Tim′nah:

11 And the border went out unto the side of Ekron northward: and the border was drawn to Shi′cron, and passed along to mount Ba′al-ah, and went out unto Jab′ne-el; and the goings out of the border were at the sea.

12 And the west border *was* to the great sea, and the coast *thereof.* This *is* the coast of the children of Judah round about according to their families.

b. The Land Assigned to Caleb's Descendants

15:13 Josh 14:13–15; Judg 1:12–15

13 ¶And unto Caleb the son of Je-phun′neh he gave a part among the children of Judah, according to the commandment of the LORD to Joshua, *even* the city of Arba the father of Anak, which *city is* Hebron.

15:14 Num 13:33; Deut 9:2; Josh 11:21, 22

14 And Caleb drove thence the three sons of Anak, She′shai, and A-hi′man, and Tal′mai, the children of Anak.

15 And he went up thence to the inhabitants of De′bir: and the name of De′bir before *was* Kir′jath–se′pher.

16 ¶And Caleb said, He that smiteth Kir′jath–se′pher, and taketh it, to him will I give Ach′sah my daughter to wife.

15:17☆ Judg 1:13; 3:9

17 And Oth′ni-el the son of Ke′naz, the brother of Caleb, took it: and he gave him Ach′sah his daughter to wife.

18 And it came to pass, as she came *unto him,* that she moved him to ask of her father a field: and she lighted off *her* ass; and Caleb said unto her, What wouldest thou?

19 Who answered, Give me a blessing; for thou hast given me a south land; give me also springs of water. And he gave her the upper springs, and the nether springs.

c. The Cities Assigned to the Sons of Judah

20 This *is* the inheritance of the tribe of the children of Judah according to their families.

15:21 Gen 21:31; 35:21; 1 Sam 27:6; 30:1; 2 Kgs 14:19

21 And the uttermost cities of the tribe of the children of Judah toward the coast of Edom southward were Kab′ze-el, and E′der, and Ja′gur,

22 And Ki′nah, and Di-mo′nah, and Ad′a-dah,

23 And Ke′desh, and Ha′zor, and Ith′nan,

24 Ziph, and Te′lem, and Be′a-loth,

25 And Ha′zor, Ha-dat′tah, and Ke′ri-oth, *and* Hez′ron, which *is* Ha′zor,

26 A′mam, and She′ma, and Mol′a-dah,

15:17 Othniel, Caleb's younger brother, was to become one of the judges of Israel after Joshua's death.

27 And Ha'zar-gad'dah, and Hesh'mon, and Beth-pa'let,
28 And Ha'zar-shu'al, and Be'er-she'ba, and Biz-joth'jah,
29 Ba'al-ah, and I'im, and A'zem,
30 And El'to-lad, and Che'sil, and Hor'mah,
31 And Ziklag, and Mad-man'nah, and San-san'nah.
32 And Leb'a-oth, and Shil'him, and A'in, and Rimmon: all the cities *are* ☆15:32
twenty and nine, with their villages:
33 *And* in the valley, Esh'ta-ol, and Zo're-ah, and Ash'nah,
34 And Za-no'ah, and En-gan'nim, Tap'pu-ah, and E'nam,
35 Jar'muth, and A-dul'lam, So'coh, and A-ze'kah,
36 And Sha-ra'im, and Ad-i-tha'im, and Ge-de'rah, and Ged-e-roth-a'im;
fourteen cities with their villages:
37 Ze'nan, and Had'a-shah, and Mig'dal-gad,
38 And Dil'e-an, and Miz'peh, and Jok'the-el,
39 La'chish, and Boz'kath, and Eg'lon,
40 And Cab'bon, and Lah'mam, and Kith'lish,
41 And Ge-de'roth, Beth-da'gon, and Na'a-mah, and Mak-ke'dah; sixteen
cities with their villages:
42 Lib'nah, and E'ther, and A'shan,
43 And Jiph'tah, and Ash'nah, and Ne'zib,
44 And Kei'lah, and Ach'zib, and Ma-re'shah; nine cities with their
villages:
45 Ekron, with her towns and her villages:
46 From Ekron even unto the sea, all that *lay* near Ash'dod, with their
villages:
47 Ash'dod with her towns and her villages, Ga'za with her towns and her
villages, unto the river of Egypt, and the great sea, and the border *thereof*:
48 ¶And in the mountains, Sha'mir, and Jat'tir, and So'coh,
49 And Dan'nah, and Kir'jath-san'nah, which *is* De'bir,
50 And Anab, and Esh'te-moh, and A'nim,
51 And Goshen, and Ho'lon, and Gi'loh; eleven cities with their villages:
52 A'rab, and Du'mah, and E'she-an,
53 And Ja'num, and Beth-tap'pu-ah, and A-phe'kah,
54 And Hum'tah, and Kir'jath-ar'ba, which *is* Hebron, and Zi'or; nine
cities with their villages:
55 Ma'on, Carmel, and Ziph, and Jut'tah,
56 And Jez're-el, and Jok'de-am, and Za-no'ah,
57 Cain, Gib'e-ah, and Tim'nah; ten cities with their villages:
58 Hal'hul, Beth'-zur, and Ge'dor,
59 And Ma'a-rath, and Beth-a'noth, and El'te-kon; six cities with their
villages:
60 Kir'jath-ba'al, which *is* Kir'jath-je'a-rim, and Rab'bah; two cities with
their villages:
61 In the wilderness, Beth-ar'a-bah, Mid'din, and Sec'a-cah,
62 And Nib'shan, and the city of Salt, and En-ge'di; six cities with their ☆15:62
villages.
63 ¶As for the Jeb'u-sites the inhabitants of Jerusalem, the children of
Judah could not drive them out: but the Jeb'u-sites dwell with the children
of Judah at Jerusalem unto this day.

15:33 Judg 13:25; 16:31; 1 Sam 22:1
15:37 Josh 10:3; 2 Kgs 14:19
15:47 Josh 13:2–7
15:63 Judg 1:21; 2 Sam 5:6

15:32 "Here are thirty-eight named, and yet said to be twenty-nine, because nine of these were afterwards transferred to the lot of Simeon, and are reckoned as belonging to that, as appears by comparing Ch. 19:2ff; therefore those only are counted (though the rest are named) which remained to Judah."*
15:62 *the city of Salt* may well be the ancient name for Qumran, the site where the Dead Sea Scrolls were found.

4. The Land Assigned to the Tribes of Joseph
a. The General Boundaries

16:1 Josh 8:15; 10:33; 18:13; 1 Kgs 9:17

16 AND the lot of the children of Joseph fell from Jordan by Jericho, unto the water of Jericho on the east, to the wilderness that goeth up from Jericho throughout mount Beth–el,

2 And goeth out from Beth–el to Luz, and passeth along unto the borders of Ar′chi to At′a-roth,

3 And goeth down westward to the coast of Japh-le′ti, unto the coast of Beth–ho′ron the nether, and to Ge′zer; and the goings out thereof are at the sea.

4 So the children of Joseph, Ma-nas′seh and E′phra-im, took their inheritance.

b. The Land Assigned to Ephraim

16:5 Josh 17:7; 18:13

5 ¶And the border of the children of E′phra-im according to their families was *thus:* even the border of their inheritance on the east side was At′a-roth–ad′dar, unto Beth–ho′ron the upper;

6 And the border went out toward the sea to Mich′me-thah on the north side; and the border went about eastward unto Ta′a-nath–shi′loh, and passed by it on the east to Ja-no′hah;

7 And it went down from Ja-no′hah to At′a-roth, and to Na′a-rath, and came to Jericho, and went out at Jordan.

16:8 Josh 17:8

8 The border went out from Tap′pu-ah westward unto the river Ka′nah; and the goings out thereof were at the sea. This *is* the inheritance of the tribe of the children of E′phra-im by their families.

9 And the separate cities for the children of E′phra-im *were* among the inheritance of the children of Ma-nas′seh, all the cities with their villages.

16:10☆ Josh 13:13; 15:63; 17:12, 13; Judg 1:29; 1 Kgs 9:16

10 And they drave not out the Canaanites that dwelt in Ge′zer: but the Canaanites dwell among the E′phra-im-ites unto this day, and serve under tribute.

c. The Land Assigned to the Half-Tribe of Manasseh

17:1 Josh 13:8

17 THERE was also a lot for the tribe of Ma-nas′seh; for he *was* the firstborn of Joseph; *to wit,* for Ma′chir the firstborn of Ma-nas′seh, the father of Gilead: because he was a man of war, therefore he had Gilead and Ba′shan.

2 There was also *a lot* for the rest of the children of Ma-nas′seh by their families; for the children of A-bi-e′zer, and for the children of He′lek, and for the children of As′ri-el, and for the children of She′chem, and for the children of He′pher, and for the children of She-mi′da: these *were* the male children of Ma-nas′seh the son of Joseph by their families.

17:3 Num 26:28–37; 27:1–7; 36:1–12

3 ¶But Ze-lo′phe-had, the son of He′pher, the son of Gilead, the son of Ma′chir, the son of Ma-nas′seh, had no sons, but daughters: and these *are* the names of his daughters, Mah′lah, and Noah, Hog′lah, Mil′cah, and Tir′zah.

4 And they came near before E-le-a′zar the priest, and before Joshua the son of Nun, and before the princes, saying, The LORD commanded Moses to give us an inheritance among our brethren. Therefore according to the commandment of the LORD he gave them an inheritance among the brethren of their father.

16:10 *unto this day,* i.e., to the time of the writing of this book.

[5]And there fell ten portions to Ma-nas'seh, beside the land of Gilead and 17:5 Josh 13:30
Ba'shan, which *were* on the other side Jordan;
[6]Because the daughters of Ma-nas'seh had an inheritance among his
sons: and the rest of Ma-nas'seh's sons had the land of Gilead.
[7]¶And the coast of Ma-nas'seh was from Asher to Mich'me-thah, that
lieth before She'chem; and the border went along on the right hand unto
the inhabitants of En-tap'pu-ah.
[8]*Now* Ma-nas'seh had the land of Tap'pu-ah: but Tap'pu-ah on the
border of Ma-nas'seh *belonged* to the children of E'phra-im:
[9]And the coast descended unto the river Ka'nah, southward of the river:
these cities of E'phra-im *are* among the cities of Ma-nas'seh: the coast of
Ma-nas'seh also *was* on the north side of the river, and the outgoings of it
were at the sea:
[10]Southward *it was* E'phra-im's, and northward *it was* Ma-nas'seh's, and
the sea is his border; and they met together in Asher on the north, and in
Is'sa-char on the east.
[11]And Ma-nas'seh had in Is'sa-char and in Asher Beth-she'an and her 17:11 1 Chron 7:29
towns, and Ib'le-am and her towns, and the inhabitants of Dor and her
towns, and the inhabitants of En-dor and her towns, and the inhabitants of
Ta'a-nach and her towns, and the inhabitants of Me-gid'do and her towns,
even three countries.
[12]Yet the children of Ma-nas'seh could not drive out *the inhabitants of* 17:12 Josh 16:10 Judg 1:27
those cities; but the Canaanites would dwell in that land.
[13]Yet it came to pass, when the children of Israel were waxen strong, that ☆17:13
they put the Canaanites to tribute, but did not utterly drive them out.

d. The Complaint of Joseph's Descendants

[14]And the children of Joseph spake unto Joshua, saying, Why hast thou 17:14 Num 26:28–37
given me *but* one lot and one portion to inherit, seeing I *am* a great people,
forasmuch as the LORD hath blessed me hitherto?
[15]And Joshua answered them, If thou *be* a great people, *then* get thee up
to the wood *country,* and cut down for thyself there in the land of the Per'iz-
zites and of the giants, if mount E'phra-im be too narrow for thee.
[16]And the children of Joseph said, The hill is not enough for us: and all 17:16 Judg 1:19 4:3, 13
the Canaanites that dwell in the land of the valley have chariots of iron,
both they who *are* of Beth-she'an and her towns, and *they* who *are* of the
valley of Jez're-el.
[17]And Joshua spake unto the house of Joseph, *even* to E'phra-im and to ☆17:17
Ma-nas'seh, saying, Thou *art* a great people, and hast great power: thou
shalt not have one lot *only:*
[18]But the mountain shall be thine; for it *is* a wood, and thou shalt cut it
down: and the outgoings of it shall be thine: for thou shalt drive out the
Canaanites, though they have iron chariots, *and* though they *be* strong.

5. The Assignment of the Remaining Land

a. The Mapping Out of the Territory

18 AND the whole congregation of the children of Israel assembled 18:1 Gen 49:10 Deut 12:10, 11 Judg 21:19 1 Sam 4:3 Jer 7:12; 26:6, 9
together at Shi'loh, and set up the tabernacle of the congregation
there. And the land was subdued before them.

17:13 *the Canaanites serve under tribute.* The children of Joseph did not destroy some of the Canaanites but subdued them and made them pay tribute. This caused problems later.

17:17 In response to the complaints of Joseph's progeny that they did not have as much land as they needed, Joshua told them to clear the trees and settle the forested areas and put away the Canaanites. The failure to exterminate the Canaanites was contrary to God's original command—that all the former inhabitants of the land were to be destroyed lest they contaminate Israel. The fact the Canaanites had iron chariots was no problem, so long as God's people trusted in him to deliver them.

2 And there remained among the children of Israel seven tribes, which had not yet received their inheritance.

18:3 Josh 14:1 — 3 And Joshua said unto the children of Israel, How long *are* ye slack to go to possess the land, which the LORD God of your fathers hath given you?

4 Give out from among you three men for *each* tribe: and I will send them, and they shall rise, and go through the land, and describe it according to the inheritance of them; and they shall come *again* to me.

5 And they shall divide it into seven parts: Judah shall abide in their coast on the south, and the house of Joseph shall abide in their coasts on the north.

18:6☆ — 6 Ye shall therefore describe the land *into* seven parts, and bring *the description* hither to me, that I may cast lots for you here before the LORD our God.

18:7 Num 18:7, 20 Josh 13:32, 33 — 7 But the Levites have no part among you; for the priesthood of the LORD *is* their inheritance: and Gad, and Reuben, and half the tribe of Manas'seh, have received their inheritance beyond Jordan on the east, which Moses the servant of the LORD gave them.

18:8 Judg 1:22 — 8 ¶And the men arose, and went away: and Joshua charged them that went to describe the land, saying, Go and walk through the land, and describe it, and come again to me, that I may here cast lots for you before the LORD in Shi'loh.

9 And the men went and passed through the land, and described it by cities into seven parts in a book, and came *again* to Joshua to the host at Shi'loh.

18:10☆ Num 34:16–29 Josh 19:51 — 10 ¶And Joshua cast lots for them in Shi'loh before the LORD: and there Joshua divided the land unto the children of Israel according to their divisions.

b. The Land Assigned to the Benjaminites

11 ¶And the lot of the tribe of the children of Benjamin came up according to their families: and the coast of their lot came forth between the children of Judah and the children of Joseph.

12 And their border on the north side was from Jordan; and the border went up to the side of Jericho on the north side, and went up through the mountains westward; and the goings out thereof were at the wilderness of Beth–a'ven.

13 And the border went over from thence toward Luz, to the side of Luz, which *is* Beth–el, southward; and the border descended to At'a-roth–a'dar, near the hill that *lieth* on the south side of the nether Beth–ho'ron.

18:14 Josh 15:9, 48–62 — 14 And the border was drawn *thence,* and compassed the corner of the sea southward, from the hill that *lieth* before Beth–ho'ron southward; and the goings out thereof were at Kir'jath–ba'al, which *is* Kir'jath–je'a-rim, a city of the children of Judah: this *was* the west quarter.

15 And the south quarter *was* from the end of Kir'jath–je'a-rim, and the border went out on the west, and went out to the well of waters of Neph'to-ah:

16 And the border came down to the end of the mountain that *lieth* before the valley of the son of Hin'nom, *and* which *is* in the valley of the giants on the north, and descended to the valley of Hin'nom, to the side of Je-bu'si on the south, and descended to En–ro'gel,

---

18:6 *that I may cast lots for you here before the LORD our God.* This was to be done before God in solemn assembly so that all the mouths would be shut and the decision accepted without murmuring.

18:10 The land was apportioned to all families except for the Levites, for whom other arrangements were made. The title to the land could not be prescribed; it was to remain in the same family for all generations.

[17]And was drawn from the north, and went forth to En-she'mesh, and
went forth toward Gel'i-loth, which *is* over against the going up of
A-dum'mim, and descended to the stone of Bo'han the son of Reuben,
[18]And passed along toward the side over against Ar'a-bah northward,
and went down unto Ar'a-bah:
[19]And the border passed along to the side of Beth-hog'lah northward:
and the outgoings of the border were at the north bay of the salt sea at the
south end of Jordan: this *was* the south coast.
[20]And Jordan was the border of it on the east side. This *was* the
inheritance of the children of Benjamin, by the coasts thereof round about,
according to their families.
[21]Now the cities of the tribe of the children of Benjamin according to
their families were Jericho, and Beth-hog'lah, and the valley of Ke'ziz,
[22]And Beth-ar'a-bah, and Zem-a-ra'im, and Beth-el,
[23]And A'vim, and Pa'rah, and Oph'rah,
[24]And Che'phar-ha-am'mo-nai, and Oph'ni, and Ga'ba; twelve cities
with their villages:
[25]Gibeon, and Ra'mah, and Be-e'roth,
[26]And Miz'peh, and Che-phi'rah, and Mo'zah,
[27]And Re'kem, and Ir'pe-el, and Tar'a-lah,
[28]And Ze'lah, E'leph, and Je-bu'si, which *is* Jerusalem, Gib'e-ath, *and*
Kir'jath; fourteen cities with their villages. This *is* the inheritance of the
children of Benjamin according to their families.

c. The Land Assigned to the Simeonites

19 AND the second lot came forth to Simeon, *even* for the tribe of the ☆19:1
children of Simeon according to their families: and their inheri-
tance was within the inheritance of the children of Judah.
[2]And they had in their inheritance Be'er-she'ba, and She'ba, and Mol'a-
dah,
[3]And Ha'zar-shu'al, and Ba'lah, and A'zem,
[4]And El'to-lad, and Be'thul, and Hor'mah,
[5]And Ziklag, and Beth-mar'ca-both, and Ha'zar-su'sah,
[6]And Beth-leb'a-oth, and Sha-ru'hen; thirteen cities and their villages:
[7]A'in, Rem'mon, and E'ther, and A'shan; four cities and their villages:
[8]And all the villages that *were* round about these cities to Ba'al-ath-be'er,
Ra'math of the south. This *is* the inheritance of the tribe of the children of
Simeon according to their families.
[9]Out of the portion of the children of Judah *was* the inheritance of the
children of Simeon: for the part of the children of Judah was too much for
them: therefore the children of Simeon had their inheritance within the
inheritance of them.

d. The Land Assigned to the Zebulunites

[10]¶And the third lot came up for the children of Zeb'u-lun according to ☆19:10
their families: and the border of their inheritance was unto Sa'rid:
[11]And their border went up toward the sea, and Mar'a-lah, and reached
to Dab'ba-sheth, and reached to the river that *is* before Jok'ne-am;
[12]And turned from Sa'rid eastward toward the sunrising unto the border

19:1 The territory assigned to Simeon was in the southern section of Judah's land grant. Eventually the tribe of Simeon was absorbed into the tribe of Judah and lost its tribal identity.
19:10 The land assigned to Zebulun included the town of Nazareth, which was to be the home of Jesus.

of Chis'loth-ta'bor, and then goeth out to Dab'e-rath, and goeth up to Ja-
phi'a,
13 And from thence passeth on along on the east to Git'tah-he'pher, to
It'tah-ka'zin, and goeth out to Rem'mon-meth'o-ar to Ne'ah;
14 And the border compasseth it on the north side to Han'na-thon: and
the outgoings thereof are in the valley of Jiph'thah-el:
15 And Kat'tath, and Na-hal'lal, and Shim'ron, and Id'a-lah, and Beth-
lehem: twelve cities with their villages.
16 This *is* the inheritance of the children of Zeb'u-lun according to their
families, these cities with their villages.

e. The Land Assigned to the Tribe of Issachar

17 ¶*And* the fourth lot came out to Is'sa-char, for the children of Is'sa-char
according to their families.
18 And their border was toward Jez're-el, and Che-sul'loth, and Shu'nem,
19 And Haph-a-ra'im, and Shi'hon, and An-a-ha'rath,
20 And Rab'bith, and Kish'i-on, and A'bez,
21 And Re'meth, and En-gan'nim, and En-had'dah, and Beth-paz'zez;
22 And the coast reacheth to Ta'bor, and Sha-haz'i-mah, and Beth-
she'mesh; and the outgoings of their border were at Jordan: sixteen cities
with their villages.
23 This *is* the inheritance of the tribe of the children of Is'sa-char
according to their families, the cities and their villages.

f. The Land Assigned to the Tribe of Asher

19:24☆ 24 ¶And the fifth lot came out for the tribe of the children of Asher
according to their families.
25 And their border was Hel'kath, and Ha'li, and Be'ten, and Ach'shaph,
26 And A-lam'me-lech, and A'mad, and Mi'she-al; and reacheth to
Carmel westward, and to Shi'hor-lib'nath;
27 And turneth toward the sunrising to Beth-da'gon, and reacheth to
Zeb'u-lun, and to the valley of Jiph'thah-el toward the north side of Beth-
e'mek, and Ne-i'el, and goeth out to Ca'bul on the left hand,
28 And Hebron, and Re'hob, and Ham'mon, and Ka'nah, *even* unto great
Zi'don;
29 And *then* the coast turneth to Ra'mah, and to the strong city Tyre; and
the coast turneth to Ho'sah; and the outgoings thereof are at the sea from
the coast to Ach'zib:
30 Um'mah also, and A'phek, and Re'hob: twenty and two cities with
their villages.
31 This *is* the inheritance of the tribe of the children of Asher according to
their families, these cities with their villages.

g. The Land Assigned to the Tribe of Naphtali

19:32☆ 32 ¶The sixth lot came out to the children of Naph'ta-li, *even* for the
children of Naph'ta-li according to their families.
33 And their coast was from He'leph, from Al'lon to Za-a-nan'nim, and
Ad'a-mi, Ne'keb, and Jab'ne-el, unto La'kum; and the outgoings thereof
were at Jordan:

19:24 Asher's territory gave them land on the Mediterranean. Other tribes were landlocked. The boundary-line went as far north as Tyre, where the Phoenicians pursued their sea-trade with vigor.

19:32 Naphtali was assigned land just east of Asher and shared a common border with that tribe.

34 And *then* the coast turneth westward to Az'noth–ta'bor, and goeth out
from thence to Huk'kok, and reacheth to Zeb'u-lun on the south side, and
reacheth to Asher on the west side, and to Judah upon Jordan toward the
sunrising.
35 And the fenced cities *are* Zid'dim, Zer, and Ham'math, Rak'kath, and
Chin'ne-reth,
36 And Ad'a-mah, and Ra'mah, and Ha'zor,
37 And Ke'desh, and Ed're-i, and En–ha'zor,
38 And I'ron, and Mig'dal-el, Ho'rem, and Beth–a'nath, and Beth-
she'mesh; nineteen cities with their villages.
39 This *is* the inheritance of the tribe of the children of Naph'ta-li
according to their families, the cities and their villages.

h. The Land Assigned to the Tribe of Dan

40 ¶*And* the seventh lot came out for the tribe of the children of Dan
according to their families.
41 And the coast of their inheritance was Zo'rah, and Esh'ta-ol, and Ir-
she'mesh,
42 And Sha-al-ab'bin, and Aj'a-lon, and Jeth'lah,
43 And E'lon, and Thim'na-thah, and Ekron,
44 And El'te-keh, and Gib'be-thon, and Ba'al-ath,
45 And Je'hud, and Ben'e–be'rak, and Gath–rim'mon,
46 And Me-jar'kon, and Rak'kon, with the border before Ja'pho.
47 And the coast of the children of Dan went out *too little* for them:
therefore the children of Dan went up to fight against Le'shem, and took it,
and smote it with the edge of the sword, and possessed it, and dwelt therein,
and called Le'shem, Dan, after the name of Dan their father.
48 This *is* the inheritance of the tribe of the children of Dan according to
their families, these cities with their villages.

i. The Summary

49 ¶When they had made an end of dividing the land for inheritance by ☆**19:49**
their coasts, the children of Israel gave an inheritance to Joshua the son of
Nun among them:
50 According to the word of the LORD they gave him the city which he **19:50** Josh 24:30 Judg 2:7–9
asked, *even* Tim'nath–se'rah in mount E'phra-im: and he built the city, and
dwelt therein.
51 These *are* the inheritances, which E-le-a'zar the priest, and Joshua the ☆**19:51** Josh 14:1; 18:10
son of Nun, and the heads of the fathers of the tribes of the children of
Israel, divided for an inheritance by lot in Shi'loh before the LORD, at the
door of the tabernacle of the congregation. So they made an end of dividing
the country.

6. The Cities of Refuge

20 THE LORD also spake unto Joshua, saying, ☆**20:2** Num 35:6 Deut 4:41 19:2, 3 1 Chron 6:58, 59
2 Speak to the children of Israel, saying, Appoint out for you
cities of refuge, whereof I spake unto you by the hand of Moses:

19:49 When the land had been assigned, Joshua was given Timnath-serah by the people of Israel. This city was in the hill country of Ephraim. He rebuilt it and occupied it until his death.
19:51 This marks the end of the division of the land to the twelve tribes of Israel. The assignment of cities and pasture lands for the Levites had yet to be accomplished.
20:2 In line with earlier instruction, the six cities of refuge were designated, three on the east bank and three on the west bank of the Jordan. They constituted a refuge for those who accidentally killed someone with

3 That the slayer that killeth *any* person unawares *and* unwittingly may flee thither: and they shall be your refuge from the avenger of blood.

4 And when he that doth flee unto one of those cities shall stand at the entering of the gate of the city, and shall declare his cause in the ears of the elders of that city, they shall take him into the city unto them, and give him a place, that he may dwell among them.

20:5☆
5 And if the avenger of blood pursue after him, then they shall not deliver the slayer up into his hand; because he smote his neighbour unwittingly, and hated him not beforetime.

6 And he shall dwell in that city, until he stand before the congregation for judgment, *and* until the death of the high priest that shall be in those days: then shall the slayer return, and come unto his own city, and unto his own house, unto the city from whence he fled.

20:7
Josh 21:9–16, 32
1 Chron 6:76
Lk 1:39
7 ¶And they appointed Ke′desh in Galilee in mount Naph′ta-li, and She′chem in mount E′phra-im, and Kir′jath-ar′ba, which *is* Hebron, in the mountain of Judah.

8 And on the other side Jordan by Jericho eastward, they assigned Be′zer in the wilderness upon the plain out of the tribe of Reuben, and Ra′moth in Gilead out of the tribe of Gad, and Go′lan in Ba′shan out of the tribe of Ma-nas′seh.

9 These were the cities appointed for all the children of Israel, and for the stranger that sojourneth among them, that whosoever killeth *any* person at unawares might flee thither, and not die by the hand of the avenger of blood, until he stood before the congregation.

7. The Levite Cities and Pastureland

a. The Distribution by Sacred Lot

21:1
Josh 14:1; 17:4
21 THEN came near the heads of the fathers of the Levites unto E-le-a′zar the priest, and unto Joshua the son of Nun, and unto the heads of the fathers of the tribes of the children of Israel;

21:2☆
Num 35:1, 2
1 Chron 6:54
2 And they spake unto them at Shi′loh in the land of Canaan, saying, The LORD commanded by the hand of Moses to give us cities to dwell in, with the suburbs thereof for our cattle.

3 And the children of Israel gave unto the Levites out of their inheritance, at the commandment of the LORD, these cities and their suburbs.

4 And the lot came out for the families of the Ko′hath-ites: and the children of Aaron the priest, *which were* of the Levites, had by lot out of the tribe of Judah, and out of the tribe of Simeon, and out of the tribe of Benjamin, thirteen cities.

5 And the rest of the children of Ko′hath *had* by lot out of the families of the tribe of E′phra-im, and out of the tribe of Dan, and out of the half tribe of Ma-nas′seh, ten cities.

---

no malicious forethought. Whoever fled to any one of these cities stood trial in the community nearest the scene of the killing. When the accused was found to be innocent, he went back to the city of refuge and remained there until the death of the high priest. Then he could return to his own home.

20:5 *the avenger of blood.* In the ancient world, the nearest of kin was supposed to avenge the murder of a relative. God authorized retributive justice for murder, but distinguished between accidental and deliberate homicide. Cities of refuge were established, to which a murderer could flee until his guilt or innocence was established by the elders of Israel. These elders represented the community in such matters (see Num. 35:9–15, Deut. 19:11, 12). No one could be executed unless there were two or more witnesses to the crime. If the elders determined that the slayer was guilty of homicide, he was denied further asylum in the city of refuge and the avenger of blood was free to find him and execute him. Many Christians today endorse the principle of retributive justice and allow for capital punishment. Individuals no longer take the law into their own hands. This has become a formal function of the state (see Rom. 13).

21:2 The Levites were given forty-eight cities and their pasturelands. This meant that the Levites could exercise pastoral oversight of all Israel, since none of the other Israelites lived more than ten miles away from a Levitical city.

6And the children of Ger'shon *had* by lot out of the families of the tribe
of Is'sa-char, and out of the tribe of Asher, and out of the tribe of Naph'ta-
li, and out of the half tribe of Ma-nas'seh in Ba'shan, thirteen cities.
7The children of Me-ra'ri by their families *had* out of the tribe of Reuben,
and out of the tribe of Gad, and out of the tribe of Zeb'u-lun, twelve cities.
8And the children of Israel gave by lot unto the Levites these cities with
their suburbs, as the LORD commanded by the hand of Moses.

b. The Actual Distribution Itself

9¶And they gave out of the tribe of the children of Judah, and out of the
tribe of the children of Simeon, these cities which are *here* mentioned by
name,
10Which the children of Aaron, *being* of the families of the Ko'hath-ites,
who were of the children of Levi, had: for theirs was the first lot.
11And they gave them the city of Arba the father of Anak, which *city is*
Hebron, in the hill *country* of Judah, with the suburbs thereof round about
it.
12But the fields of the city, and the villages thereof, gave they to Caleb the
son of Je-phun'neh for his possession.
13¶Thus they gave to the children of Aaron the priest Hebron with her
suburbs, *to be* a city of refuge for the slayer; and Lib'nah with her suburbs,
14And Jat'tir with her suburbs, and Esh-te-mo'a with her suburbs,
15And Ho'lon with her suburbs, and De'bir with her suburbs,
16And A'in with her suburbs, and Jut'tah with her suburbs, *and* Beth-
she'mesh with her suburbs; nine cities out of those two tribes.
17And out of the tribe of Benjamin, Gibeon with her suburbs, Ge'ba with
her suburbs,
18An'a-thoth with her suburbs, and Al'mon with her suburbs; four cities.
19All the cities of the children of Aaron, the priests, *were* thirteen cities
with their suburbs.
20¶And the families of the children of Ko'hath, the Levites which
remained of the children of Ko'hath, even they had the cities of their lot out
of the tribe of E'phra-im.
21For they gave them She'chem with her suburbs in mount E'phra-im, *to
be* a city of refuge for the slayer; and Ge'zer with her suburbs,
22And Kib'za-im with her suburbs, and Beth-ho'ron with her suburbs;
four cities.
23And out of the tribe of Dan, El'te-keh with her suburbs, Gib'be-thon
with her suburbs,
24Ai'ja-lon with her suburbs, Gath-rim'mon with her suburbs; four cities.
25And out of the half tribe of Ma-nas'seh, Ta'nach with her suburbs, and
Gath-rim'mon with her suburbs; two cities.
26All the cities *were* ten with their suburbs for the families of the children
of Ko'hath that remained.
27¶And unto the children of Ger'shon, of the families of the Levites, out
of the *other* half tribe of Ma-nas'seh *they gave* Go'lan in Ba'shan with her
suburbs, *to be* a city of refuge for the slayer; and Be-esh'-te-rah with her
suburbs; two cities.
28And out of the tribe of Is'sa-char, Ki'shon with her suburbs, Dab'a-reh
with her suburbs,
29Jar'muth with her suburbs, En-gan'nim with her suburbs; four cities.
30And out of the tribe of Asher, Mi'shal with her suburbs, Abdon with
her suburbs,
31Hel'kath with her suburbs, and Re'hob with her suburbs; four cities.
32And out of the tribe of Naph'ta-li, Ke'desh in Galilee with her suburbs,

to be a city of refuge for the slayer; and Ham'moth-dor with her suburbs,
and Kar'tan with her suburbs; three cities.
33 All the cities of the Ger'shon-ites according to their families *were*
thirteen cities with their suburbs.
34 ¶And unto the families of the children of Me-ra'ri, the rest of the
Levites, out of the tribe of Zeb'u-lun, Jok'ne-am with her suburbs, and
Kar'tah with her suburbs,
35 Dim'nah with her suburbs, Na'ha-lal with her suburbs; four cities.
36 And out of the tribe of Reuben, Be'zer with her suburbs, and Ja-ha'zah
with her suburbs,
37 Ked'e-moth with her suburbs, and Meph'a-ath with her suburbs; four
cities.
38 And out of the tribe of Gad, Ra'moth in Gilead with her suburbs, *to be*
a city of refuge for the slayer; and Ma-ha-na'im with her suburbs,
21:39☆ 39 Hesh'bon with her suburbs, Ja'zer with her suburbs; four cities in all.
40 So all the cities for the children of Me-ra'ri by their families, which were
remaining of the families of the Levites, were *by* their lot twelve cities.
21:41 Num 35:7 41 All the cities of the Levites within the possession of the children of
Israel *were* forty and eight cities with their suburbs.
42 These cities were every one with their suburbs round about them: thus
were all these cities.

8. The Blessing of God on Israel

21:43☆ Num 33:53; Deut 11:31; 17:14; 34:4 43 ¶And the LORD gave unto Israel all the land which he sware to give
unto their fathers; and they possessed it, and dwelt therein.
21:44 Ex 23:31; Deut 7:24; Josh 1:14, 15; 23:1 44 And the LORD gave them rest round about, according to all that he
sware unto their fathers: and there stood not a man of all their enemies
before them; the LORD delivered all their enemies into their hand.
21:45 Josh 23:14; 1 Kgs 8:56; 1 Cor 1:9; 1 Thess 5:24 45 There failed not ought of any good thing which the LORD had spoken
unto the house of Israel; all came to pass.

III. JOSHUA'S FAREWELL AND CHARGE TO ISRAEL (22:1—24:33)

A. THE ADDRESS TO THE TWO-AND-A-HALF TRIBES

1. Joshua Blesses Them before Their Departure

22:1 Num 32:29–41 22 THEN Joshua called the Reubenites, and the Gadites, and the half
tribe of Ma-nas'seh,
22:2 Josh 1:12–18 2 And said unto them, Ye have kept all that Moses the servant of the
LORD commanded you, and have obeyed my voice in all that I commanded
you:
3 Ye have not left your brethren these many days unto this day, but have
kept the charge of the commandment of the LORD your God.
22:4 Num 32:18; Deut 3:20 4 And now the LORD your God hath given rest unto your brethren, as he
promised them: therefore now return ye, and get you unto your tents, *and*
unto the land of your possession, which Moses the servant of the LORD
gave you on the other side Jordan.
22:5 Deut 5:1 5 But take diligent heed to do the commandment and the law, which
Moses the servant of the LORD charged you, to love the LORD your God,

---

21:39 *Heshbon,* originally assigned to Reuben (13:17) and is mentioned here under Gad. Both the Reubenites and the Simeonites were absorbed; as a result, they lost their special identity. The allocation of territory had been made; the land itself, though, remained to be taken and possessed by the individual tribes.

21:43 God's promise of the land to Israel had been fulfilled in its major part. God had indicated that the takeover would require time and the unpossessed areas would be brought under the jurisdiction of Israel bit by bit, in due season, if the people obeyed the orders of God.

and to walk in all his ways, and to keep his commandments, and to cleave
unto him, and to serve him with all your heart and with all your soul.
6So Joshua blessed them, and sent them away: and they went unto their
tents.
7¶Now to the *one* half of the tribe of Ma-nas'seh Moses had given 22:7 Num 32:33 Josh 17:1
possession in Ba'shan: but unto the *other* half thereof gave Joshua among
their brethren on this side Jordan westward. And when Joshua sent them
away also unto their tents, then he blessed them,
8And he spake unto them, saying, Return with much riches unto your
tents, and with very much cattle, with silver, and with gold, and with brass,
and with iron, and with very much raiment: divide the spoil of your
enemies with your brethren.

2. The Altar of Witness by the Jordan

9¶And the children of Reuben and the children of Gad and the half tribe
of Ma-nas'seh returned, and departed from the children of Israel out of
Shi'loh, which *is* in the land of Canaan, to go unto the country of Gilead, to
the land of their possession, whereof they were possessed, according to the
word of the LORD by the hand of Moses.
10¶And when they came unto the borders of Jordan, that *are* in the land ☆22:10 Deut 12:5
of Canaan, the children of Reuben and the children of Gad and the half
tribe of Ma-nas'seh built there an altar by Jordan, a great altar to see to.
11¶And the children of Israel heard say, Behold, the children of Reuben 22:11 Deut 13:12–14
and the children of Gad and the half tribe of Ma-nas'seh have built an altar
over against the land of Canaan, in the borders of Jordan, at the passage of
the children of Israel.
12And when the children of Israel heard *of it,* the whole congregation of
the children of Israel gathered themselves together at Shi'loh, to go up to
war against them.
13And the children of Israel sent unto the children of Reuben, and to the 22:13 Num 25:7, 10, 11; 31:6
children of Gad, and to the half tribe of Ma-nas'seh, into the land of
Gilead, Phin'e-has the son of E-le-a'zar the priest,
14And with him ten princes, of each chief house a prince throughout all
the tribes of Israel; and each one *was* an head of the house of their fathers
among the thousands of Israel.
15¶And they came unto the children of Reuben, and to the children of
Gad, and to the half tribe of Ma-nas'seh, unto the land of Gilead, and they
spake with them, saying,
16Thus saith the whole congregation of the LORD, What trespass *is* this
that ye have committed against the God of Israel, to turn away this day
from following the LORD, in that ye have builded you an altar, that ye
might rebel this day against the LORD?
17*Is* the iniquity of Pe'or too little for us, from which we are not cleansed 22:17 Num 25:1–9
until this day, although there was a plague in the congregation of the LORD,
18But that ye must turn away this day from following the LORD? and it
will be, *seeing* ye rebel to day against the LORD, that to morrow he will be
wroth with the whole congregation of Israel.
19Notwithstanding, if the land of your possession *be* unclean, *then* pass ye
over unto the land of the possession of the LORD, wherein the LORD's

22:10 God had specifically commanded that there be only one central place for offering sacrifices. When the Reubenites, Gadites, and half the tribe of Manasseh built a huge altar by the Jordan River, it appeared to run counter to the altar set up on Mount Ebal. The other tribes protested until they discovered that it had been intended to be a memorial which would keep the eyes of the people on the Lord God. There was no intention of offering any sacrifices there. The erection of the altar was a tribute to the spiritual sensitivities of those who wanted to perpetuate the name and the worship of the true God.

tabernacle dwelleth, and take possession among us: but rebel not against
the LORD, nor rebel against us, in building you an altar beside the altar of
the LORD our God.

22:20 Josh 7:1

20 Did not A'chan the son of Ze'rah commit a trespass in the accursed
thing, and wrath fell on all the congregation of Israel? and that man
perished not alone in his iniquity.
21 ¶Then the children of Reuben and the children of Gad and the half
tribe of Ma-nas'seh answered, and said unto the heads of the thousands of
Israel,

22:22☆ Deut 12:1, 2

22 The LORD God of gods, the LORD God of gods, he knoweth, and Israel
he shall know; if *it be* in rebellion, or if in transgression against the LORD,
(save us not this day,)
23 That we have built us an altar to turn from following the LORD, or if to
offer thereon burnt offering or meat offering, or if to offer peace offerings
thereon, let the LORD himself require *it;*
24 And if we have not *rather* done it for fear of *this* thing, saying, In time
to come your children might speak unto our children, saying, What have ye
to do with the LORD God of Israel?
25 For the LORD hath made Jordan a border between us and you, ye
children of Reuben and children of Gad; ye have no part in the LORD: so
shall your children make our children cease from fearing the LORD.
26 Therefore we said, Let us now prepare to build us an altar, not for
burnt offering, nor for sacrifice:
27 But *that* it *may be* a witness between us, and you, and our generations
after us, that we might do the service of the LORD before him with our
burnt offerings, and with our sacrifices, and with our peace offerings; that
your children may not say to our children in time to come, Ye have no part
in the LORD.
28 Therefore said we, that it shall be, when they should *so* say to us or to
our generations in time to come, that we may say *again,* Behold the pattern
of the altar of the LORD, which our fathers made, not for burnt offerings,
nor for sacrifices; but it *is* a witness between us and you.
29 God forbid that we should rebel against the LORD, and turn this day
from following the LORD, to build an altar for burnt offerings, for meat
offerings, or for sacrifices, beside the altar of the LORD our God that *is*
before his tabernacle.
30 ¶And when Phin'e-has the priest, and the princes of the congregation
and heads of the thousands of Israel which *were* with him, heard the words
that the children of Reuben and the children of Gad and the children of
Ma-nas'seh spake, it pleased them.
31 And Phin'e-has the son of E-le-a'zar the priest said unto the children of
Reuben, and to the children of Gad, and to the children of Ma-nas'seh,
This day we perceive that the LORD *is* among us, because ye have not
committed this trespass against the LORD: now ye have delivered the
children of Israel out of the hand of the LORD.
32 ¶And Phin'e-has the son of E-le-a'zar the priest, and the princes,
returned from the children of Reuben, and from the children of Gad, out of
the land of Gilead, unto the land of Canaan, to the children of Israel, and
brought them word again.
33 And the thing pleased the children of Israel; and the children of Israel

---

22:22 When the tribes on the west bank of Jordan heard of the altar erected by the two and a half tribes in the east bank, they were upset for they thought it might represent idolatry. The east bank settlers swore before God that their intentions were pure and expressed a willingness for the judgment of God to overtake them if they were really guilty of a crime. Verses 33 and 34 indicate the satisfactory conclusion of what could have been a serious breach of the law. Everybody was happy with the outcome of the inquiry.

blessed God, and did not intend to go up against them in battle, to destroy
the land wherein the children of Reuben and Gad dwelt.
34 And the children of Reuben and the children of Gad called the altar
Ed: for it *shall be* a witness between us that the LORD *is* God.

22:34 Gen 31:47–49

B. THE ADDRESS TO THE NINE-AND-A-HALF TRIBES

23 AND it came to pass a long time after that the LORD had given rest
unto Israel from all their enemies round about, that Joshua waxed
old *and* stricken in age.
2 And Joshua called for all Israel, *and* for their elders, and for their heads,
and for their judges, and for their officers, and said unto them, I am old *and*
stricken in age:
3 And ye have seen all that the LORD your God hath done unto all these
nations because of you; for the LORD your God *is* he that hath fought for
you.
4 Behold, I have divided unto you by lot these nations that remain, to be
an inheritance for your tribes, from Jordan, with all the nations that I have
cut off, even unto the great sea westward.
5 And the LORD your God, he shall expel them from before you, and drive
them from out of your sight; and ye shall possess their land, as the LORD
your God hath promised unto you.
6 Be ye therefore very courageous to keep and to do all that is written in
the book of the law of Moses, that ye turn not aside therefrom *to* the right
hand or *to* the left;
7 That ye come not among these nations, these that remain among you;
neither make mention of the name of their gods, nor cause to swear *by*
them, neither serve them, nor bow yourselves unto them:
8 But cleave unto the LORD your God, as ye have done unto this day.
9 For the LORD hath driven out from before you great nations and strong:
but *as for* you, no man hath been able to stand before you unto this day.
10 One man of you shall chase a thousand: for the LORD your God, he *it*
is that fighteth for you, as he hath promised you.
11 Take good heed therefore unto yourselves, that ye love the LORD your
God.
12 Else if ye do in any wise go back, and cleave unto the remnant of these
nations, *even* these that remain among you, and shall make marriages with
them, and go in unto them, and they to you:
13 Know for a certainty that the LORD your God will no more drive out
any of these nations from before you; but they shall be snares and traps
unto you, and scourges in your sides, and thorns in your eyes, until ye
perish from off this good land which the LORD your God hath given you.
14 And, behold, this day I *am* going the way of all the earth: and ye know
in all your hearts and in all your souls, that not one thing hath failed of all

23:1 Josh 21:44
23:2 Deut 31:28; Josh 24:1
23:3 Deut 1:30
23:4 Ex 23:30; Num 33:53
23:6 Deut 5:32; Josh 1:7; 22:5
23:7 Ex 20:5; 23:13; Deut 6:13; 10:20; Ps 16:4
23:9 Ex 23:23, 30; Deut 7:24
☆23:10 Lev 26:8; Deut 28:7; Judg 15:15
☆23:12 Deut 7:3; Ezra 9:2
☆23:13 Ex 23:33; 34:12; Deut 7:16
☆23:14

23:10 The hyperbole that one can chase a thousand is representative of the difference that God makes in any situation. It has been said that one man and God constitute a majority. The Scriptures teach that having God on one's side does make the difference between victory or defeat, regardless of the size of the opposition.

23:12, 13 Joshua warned Israel against intermarriage with the heathen. Theoretically, there would have been none of this if the original mandate to slay all of the heathen peoples had been obeyed. Intermarriage between believers and unbelievers always works to the disadvantage of the true religion. The New Testament says: "Be ye not unequally yoked . . . with unbelievers" (2 Cor. 6:14).

23:14 Joshua bears testimony to the faithfulness of God in fulfilling all of the promises made to Israel. Every believer should exhibit thanksgiving to God for his blessings and express it in such a way that God will know that that person is indeed grateful. This is especially true for one on the edge of death, which is an opportune time to deposit something positive to the bereft, something which will help them face death later on.

the good things which the LORD your God spake concerning you; all are
come to pass unto you, *and* not one thing hath failed thereof.
23:15 Lev 26:14 Deut 4:25 28:15–19; 32:30
15 Therefore it shall come to pass, *that* as all good things are come upon
you, which the LORD your God promised you; so shall the LORD bring
upon you all evil things, until he have destroyed you from off this good land
which the LORD your God hath given you.
16 When ye have transgressed the covenant of the LORD your God, which
he commanded you, and have gone and served other gods, and bowed
yourselves to them; then shall the anger of the LORD be kindled against
you, and ye shall perish quickly from off the good land which he hath given
unto you.

C. JOSHUA'S FINAL SPEECH
1. Joshua Recounts God's Dealing with Israel

24:1 Josh 23:1
24 AND Joshua gathered all the tribes of Israel to She'chem, and
called for the elders of Israel, and for their heads, and for their
judges, and for their officers; and they presented themselves before God.
24:2 Gen 11:27–32
2 And Joshua said unto all the people, Thus saith the LORD God of Israel,
Your fathers dwelt on the other side of the flood in old time, *even* Te'rah,
the father of Abraham, and the father of Na'chor: and they served other
gods.
24:3☆ Gen 12:1; 15:5 21:1–3; 24:7
3 And I took your father Abraham from the other side of the flood, and
led him throughout all the land of Canaan, and multiplied his seed, and
gave him Isaac.
24:4 Gen 25:25, 26 36:9; 46:6 Deut 2:5
4 And I gave unto Isaac Jacob and Esau: and I gave unto Esau mount
Se'ir, to possess it; but Jacob and his children went down into Egypt.
24:5 Ex 4:14–17 Ps 105:26
5 I sent Moses also and Aaron, and I plagued Egypt, according to that
which
I did among them: and afterward I brought you out.
24:6 Ex 14:2–8 Neh 9:11 Ps 77:15
6 And I brought your fathers out of Egypt: and ye came unto the sea; and
the Egyptians pursued after your fathers with chariots and horsemen unto
the Red sea.
24:7 Ex 14:19–31 Num 14:33 Deut 1:46; 2:14
7 And when they cried unto the LORD, he put darkness between you and
the Egyptians, and brought the sea upon them, and covered them; and your
eyes have seen what I have done in Egypt: and ye dwelt in the wilderness a
long season.
24:8 Num 21:21–35
8 And I brought you into the land of the Am'or-ites, which dwelt on the
other side Jordan; and they fought with you: and I gave them into your
hand, that ye might possess their land; and I destroyed them from before
you.
24:9 Num 22:2–6
9 Then Balak the son of Zippor, king of Moab, arose and warred against
Israel, and sent and called Ba'laam the son of Be'or to curse you:
10 But I would not hearken unto Ba'laam; therefore he blessed you still:
so I delivered you out of his hand.
24:11 Ex 23:23, 31 Deut 7:1 Josh 3:15–17
11 And ye went over Jordan, and came unto Jericho: and the men of
Jericho fought against you, the Am'or-ites, and the Per'iz-zites, and the
Canaanites, and the Hittites, and the Gir'ga-shites, the Hi'vites, and the
Jeb'u-sites; and I delivered them into your hand.
24:12 Ex 23:28 Deut 7:20 Ps 44:3
12 And I sent the hornet before you, which drave them out from before
you, *even* the two kings of the Am'or-ites; *but* not with thy sword, nor with
thy bow.

24:3 Beginning with this verse Joshua quotes God as saying that he sovereignly gave the Israelites all they had, and that he worked his will among their enemies to bring the divine purposes to pass. The God of Abraham, Isaac, and Jacob works among the people of God today to do the same thing for them.

13 And I have given you a land for which ye did not labour, and cities
which ye built not, and ye dwell in them; of the vineyards and oliveyards
which ye planted not do ye eat.

24:13 Deut 6:10–12

2. The Challenge to Love and Serve God

14 ¶Now therefore fear the LORD, and serve him in sincerity and in truth:
and put away the gods which your fathers served on the other side of the
flood, and in Egypt; and serve ye the LORD.
15 And if it seem evil unto you to serve the LORD, choose you this day
whom ye will serve; whether the gods which your fathers served that *were*
on the other side of the flood, or the gods of the Am′or-ites, in whose land
ye dwell: but as for me and my house, we will serve the LORD.

☆**24:14** Deut 10:12, 13; 18:13; 1 Sam 12:24; Ps 111:10
24:15 Ruth 1:15, 16; 1 Kgs 18:21

3. Israel's Commitment to Worship and Serve God

16 And the people answered and said, God forbid that we should forsake
the LORD, to serve other gods;
17 For the LORD our God, he *it is* that brought us up and our fathers out
of the land of Egypt, from the house of bondage, and which did those great
signs in our sight, and preserved us in all the way wherein we went, and
among all the people through whom we passed:
18 And the LORD drave out from before us all the people, even the Am′or-
ites which dwelt in the land: *therefore* will we also serve the LORD; for he *is*
our God.
19 And Joshua said unto the people, Ye cannot serve the LORD: for he *is*
an holy God; he *is* a jealous God; he will not forgive your transgressions
nor your sins.
20 If ye forsake the LORD, and serve strange gods, then he will turn and do
you hurt, and consume you, after that he hath done you good.
21 And the people said unto Joshua, Nay; but we will serve the LORD.
22 And Joshua said unto the people, Ye *are* witnesses against yourselves
that ye have chosen you the LORD, to serve him. And they said, *We are*
witnesses.
23 Now therefore put away, *said he,* the strange gods which *are* among
you, and incline your heart unto the LORD God of Israel.
24 And the people said unto Joshua, The LORD our God will we serve, and
his voice will we obey.
25 So Joshua made a covenant with the people that day, and set them a
statute and an ordinance in She′chem.
26 ¶And Joshua wrote these words in the book of the law of God, and
took a great stone, and set it up there under an oak, that *was* by the
sanctuary of the LORD.
27 And Joshua said unto all the people, Behold, this stone shall be a
witness unto us; for it hath heard all the words of the LORD which he spake
unto us: it shall be therefore a witness unto you, lest ye deny your God.
28 So Joshua let the people depart, every man unto his inheritance.

24:19 Ex 20:5; 23:21; 34:14; Lev 19:1, 2; 20:7, 26
24:20 Deut 4:25; Josh 23:12; Acts 7:42
☆**24:23**
24:24 Ex 19:8; 24:3, 7; Deut 5:26, 27
24:25 Ex 24:8
24:27 Ex 22:26, 27

24:14 *Now therefore.* Having spoken of God's mercies toward Israel, Joshua says here that Israel must continue to fear God, defer to his authority, and live in accord with the principles they have professed.

24:23 In 24:16 the Israelites told Joshua: "God forbid that we should forsake the LORD, to serve other gods." Joshua followed up on this affirmation by ordering them to put away their strange or foreign gods and to serve the Lord. The command to put away the strange gods suggests that some of the people of Israel had already fallen into the trap of keeping images and relics secured from the heathen or similar to those worshipped by those whose land they had entered. This constituted idolatry, however innocent it may have appeared, and was a serious offense against the majesty and holiness of the true God. Every appearance of idolatry must be put away by those who truly love God and wish to maintain a proper relationship to him.

D. THE DEATH AND BURIAL OF JOSHUA

24:29 Judg 2:7–9

29 ¶And it came to pass after these things, that Joshua the son of Nun, the servant of the LORD, died, *being* an hundred and ten years old.

24:30 Josh 19:50

30 And they buried him in the border of his inheritance in Tim′nath-se′rah, which *is* in mount E′phra-im, on the north side of the hill of Ga′ash.

31 And Israel served the LORD all the days of Joshua, and all the days of the elders that overlived Joshua, and which had known all the works of the LORD, that he had done for Israel.

E. THE BURIAL OF JOSEPH'S BONES

24:32☆ Gen 50:25 Ex 13:19 Acts 7:16 Heb 11:22

32 ¶And the bones of Joseph, which the children of Israel brought up out of Egypt, buried they in She′chem, in a parcel of ground which Jacob bought of the sons of Ha′mor the father of She′chem for an hundred pieces of silver: and it became the inheritance of the children of Joseph.

F. THE DEATH AND BURIAL OF ELEAZAR

24:33☆ Judg 19:12, 13 1 Sam 10:26

33 And E-le-a′zar the son of Aaron died; and they buried him in a hill *that pertained to* Phin′e-has his son, which was given him in mount E′phra-im.

24:32 Joseph died in Egypt approximately two hundred years before he was buried at last in Canaan. He had carefully left instructions with the Israelites that he was not to be buried in that land but was to be taken away when Israel left Egypt. The coffin containing his mummy was cared for by the Israelites through the long wilderness journey and was now interred in Shechem in the plot of ground purchased by Jacob from the sons of Hamor. His coffin must have been a constant reminder to the Israelites and their offspring of their great ancestor, who believed the promise made to Abraham about Canaan and of his desire to be buried in its sacred soil.

24:33 *Eleazar* was the third son of Aaron. He succeeded his father in the high-priestly office. He supervised the Kohathites who carried the ark and the holy furniture on their shoulders in the wilderness. He played a major role in assuaging God's wrath in connection with the rebellion of Korah, Dathan, and Abiram. He was the first one to prepare holy water from the ashes of the red heifer. He was also Joshua's high priest. Along with Joshua he had part in the division of the land of Canaan among the various tribes. He married an unnamed girl, a daughter of Putiel.

THE BOOK OF

JUDGES

Authorship, date, and background The title for Judges in the Hebrew is the word *Shophetim,* which means *executive leaders* or *judges.* It expresses what was the type of government or leadership of the people of Israel between the time of Joshua's death and the beginning of the monarchy under King Saul. The author's identity is unknown. Whoever he was, his use of original sources included materials from northern Israel with its dialect which differed from that of the southern section of the nation.

Dating the book of Judges depends upon a number of factors. One has to do with the length of the period under discussion. Undoubtedly some of the judges overlapped each other or were contemporaneous. Adding the years of each judge consecutively yields a period of approximately 410 years. A statement in 1 Kings 6:1 (this was 480 years after the people of Israel left their slavery in Egypt) leaves a time span of slightly less than three hundred years for the period between Eli and Othniel. Overlapping reigns account for the difference. What is more important is the date for the Exodus from Egypt. Some evangelical scholars date the Israelite conquest of Canaan at ca. 1290 B.C. Other scholars date the beginning of the Exodus from Egypt at ca. 1440 B.C. The latter date appears to be the better choice as a result of the Tell el-Amarna letters concerning the dating of the conquest of Canaan. The best date for the composition of Judges is the eleventh century B.C.

Judges must be understood against the background of a recurring cycle of apostasy, repentance, and renewal. The theocracy had been set up by God through Moses, but the people backslid again and again. The period was a disordered one filled with times of violence. The book of Ruth shows how the common people lived, loved, and died amidst these great difficulties. Life simply went on despite the turmoil. The Judges were part of the total history of Israel, providing the indispensable connecting link between the beginning of the conquest of Canaan and the emergence of the kingship.

Characteristics and content Judges contains many statements such as "the children of Israel did evil in the sight of the Lord"; and statements like "the land had rest" for *x* number of years (see here 3:7, 12; 4:1; 6:1; 10:6; 13:1; and 3:11, 30; 5:31; 8:28). It has been noted that Othniel and Samson "stand alone at the beginning and at the end of the series" of the fourteen judges, and that "those who come in between are usually connected in pairs." Shamgar and Ehud are linked together. Barak and Deborah are paired up. And Gideon and his natural son, Abimelech, are connected.

Judges clearly teaches that the people of Israel are covenant-breakers who fail to maintain the demands of God's theocracy. They are delivered from their oppressors again and again, only to fall into sin again and repeat the mistakes of their predecessors. The key phrase of the book is found in 21:25, the last verse in Judges: "There was no king in Israel in those days, and every man did that which was right in his own eyes."

Judges depicts the strengths and the weaknesses of those who lead Israel in times of turmoil. Deborah, Gideon, and Samson are sharply etched. The story of Gideon's fleece, by which he determines the will of God for his life, stands out boldly. The Song of Deborah and Barak is a paean of praise to the wonderful victory God gives his people in their moment of distress. The tragic life of Samson is filled with pathos. His miserable departure from the faith of his fathers and his period of blindness when the Philistines take away his sight remind every Christian of the need for perseverance through all the days of this life. The closing section of Judges speaks about the strange case of the priest of Micah and the men of Dan who come to Micah's home. They take away his priest and his idols, which become a source of evil among them thereafter. The closing chapters picture the death of the unfortunate concubine and the war against the Benjaminites, whose tribal members are guilty of the atrocity. The other tribes slay so many Benjaminites that the tribe faces extinction. But the survivors are allowed to take brides from among the maidens of Shiloh whom they kidnap and take home as their wives.

Outline

I. The background for the book (1:1—3:7)
II. The cycle of apostasy and deliverances (3:8—16:31)
III. The cultural situation during the time of the judges (17:1—21:25)

I. THE BACKGROUND FOR THE BOOK (1:1—3:7)
A. ISRAEL'S INCOMPLETE CONQUEST OF CANAAN
1. The Victories of the Tribes of Judah and Simeon

1:1☆ 1 NOW after the death of Joshua it came to pass, that the children of
Num 27:21 Israel asked the LORD, saying, Who shall go up for us against the
Canaanites first, to fight against them?
1:2 2 And the LORD said, Judah shall go up: behold, I have delivered the land
Gen 49:8 into his hand.
1:3 3 And Judah said unto Simeon his brother, Come up with me into my lot,
Josh 19:1 that we may fight against the Canaanites; and I likewise will go with thee
into thy lot. So Simeon went with him.
1:4☆ 4 And Judah went up; and the LORD delivered the Canaanites and the
Gen 13:7; 34:30 Per′iz-zites into their hand: and they slew of them in Be′zek ten thousand
1 Sam 11:8 men.
5 And they found A-do′ni–be′zek in Be′zek: and they fought against him,
and they slew the Canaanites and the Per′iz-zites.
1:6☆ 6 But A-do′ni–be′zek fled; and they pursued after him, and caught him,
and cut off his thumbs and his great toes.
7 And A-do′ni–be′zek said, Threescore and ten kings, having their thumbs
and their great toes cut off, gathered *their meat* under my table: as I have
done, so God hath requited me. And they brought him to Jerusalem, and
there he died.
1:8 8 Now the children of Judah had fought against Jerusalem, and had taken
Josh 15:63 it, and smitten it with the edge of the sword, and set the city on fire.
9 ¶And afterward the children of Judah went down to fight against the
Canaanites, that dwelt in the mountain, and in the south, and in the valley.
1:10 10 And Judah went against the Canaanites that dwelt in Hebron: (now the
Josh 15:14 20:7, 21:9–16 name of Hebron before *was* Kir′jath–ar′ba:) and they slew She′shai, and
A-hi′man, and Tal′mai.
1:11 11 And from thence he went against the inhabitants of De′bir: and the
Josh 15:15 name of De′bir before *was* Kir′jath–se′pher:
1:12 12 And Caleb said, He that smiteth Kir′jath–se′pher, and taketh it, to him
Josh 15:16 will I give Ach′sah my daughter to wife.
1:13 13 And Oth′ni-el the son of Ke′naz, Caleb's younger brother, took it: and
Judg 3:9 he gave him Ach′sah his daughter to wife.
14 And it came to pass, when she came *to him,* that she moved him to ask
of her father a field: and she lighted from off *her* ass; and Caleb said unto
her, What wilt thou?

1:1 Joshua and Judges are complementary, not contradictory. Some have the impression that by the time of Joshua's death the land had been fully occupied by Israel. But the book of Judges describes the conquest as gradual and lengthy. Joshua did fight and overcome many enemies. Many Canaanites were defeated, but not all of Canaan was occupied by Israel. Judges continues the story of the conquest, but when the book ends, the story is still incomplete. It was left to each tribe, until the time of the monarchy, to take full possession of the territory allocated to it.

1:4 *Perizzites.* There are no references to this name outside of the Bible except the mention of *Pirati* in Egyptian vocabulary and possibly in a fragment from Amarna. Sometimes the Bible speaks of the Canaanites and then all of the other peoples as the Perizzites.

1:6 In Josh. 10:1 Adoni-bezek is identified as the king of Jerusalem (which was then called Jebus and was an Amorite city.) Judah captured the city and then it reverted to the Amorites. It was King David who took the city permanently from the Amorites and named it after himself, "The City of David" (2 Sam. 5:9). The word *Jerusalem* means "foundation of peace."

15 And she said unto him, Give me a blessing: for thou hast given me a
south land; give me also springs of water. And Caleb gave her the upper
springs and the nether springs.
16 ¶And the children of the Ken'ite, Moses' father in law, went up out of
the city of palm trees with the children of Judah into the wilderness of
Judah, which *lieth* in the south of A'rad; and they went and dwelt among
the people.

1:16 Deut 34:3 Judg 3:13; 4:11

17 And Judah went with Simeon his brother, and they slew the Canaanites
that inhabited Ze'phath, and utterly destroyed it. And the name of the city
was called Hor'mah.

1:17 Num 21:3

18 Also Judah took Ga'za with the coast thereof, and As'ke-lon with the
coast thereof, and Ekron with the coast thereof.
19 And the LORD was with Judah; and he drave out *the inhabitants of* the
mountain; but could not drive out the inhabitants of the valley, because
they had chariots of iron.

☆**1:19** Josh 17:16 Judg 4:2, 3

20 And they gave Hebron unto Caleb, as Moses said: and he expelled
thence the three sons of Anak.

1:20 Josh 14:6–9 15:14

21 And the children of Benjamin did not drive out the Jeb'u-sites that
inhabited Jerusalem; but the Jeb'u-sites dwell with the children of
Benjamin in Jerusalem unto this day.

1:21 Josh 15:63 2 Sam 5:6

2. Israel's Failure to Complete the Conquest

22 ¶And the house of Joseph, they also went up against Beth-el: and the
LORD *was* with them.

☆**1:22** Gen 28:19 Josh 14:3, 4

23 And the house of Joseph sent to descry Beth-el. (Now the name of the
city before *was* Luz.)

☆**1:23**

24 And the spies saw a man come forth out of the city, and they said unto
him, Shew us, we pray thee, the entrance into the city, and we will shew
thee mercy.

☆**1:24** Josh 6:22

25 And when he shewed them the entrance into the city, they smote the
city with the edge of the sword; but they let go the man and all his family.

1:25 Josh 6:25

26 And the man went into the land of the Hittites, and built a city, and
called the name thereof Luz: which *is* the name thereof unto this day.
27 ¶Neither did Ma-nas'seh drive out *the inhabitants of* Beth-she'an and
her towns, nor Ta'a-nach and her towns, nor the inhabitants of Dor and her
towns, nor the inhabitants of Ib'le-am and her towns, nor the inhabitants of
Me-gid'do and her towns: but the Canaanites would dwell in that land.

☆**1:27** Josh 17:11, 12

28 And it came to pass, when Israel was strong, that they put the
Canaanites to tribute, and did not utterly drive them out.

☆**1:28**

29 ¶Neither did E'phra-im drive out the Canaanites that dwelt in Ge'zer;
but the Canaanites dwelt in Ge'zer among them.

1:29 Josh 16:10

30 Neither did Zeb'u-lun drive out the inhabitants of Kit'ron, nor the
inhabitants of Na'ha-lol; but the Canaanites dwelt among them, and
became tributaries.
31 Neither did Asher drive out the inhabitants of Ac'cho, nor the

---

1:19 In the hill country, where hand-to-hand battle was important, the Israelites prevailed. In the plains Israel was at a disadvantage, for the enemy had chariots of iron. From the human perspective it looked as if Israel were at a loss. But God is always behind history and he is not always on the side of the most powerful armies. God is the ultimate source of power; man is the proximate, secondary source. In this instance, though, the superior armed might of the enemy prevailed.

1:22 *the house of Joseph,* i.e., the two tribes of Ephraim and Manasseh.

1:23 *descry,* i.e. to "spy out."

1:24 *the entrance into the city,* i.e., "the passage through the wall."† This obviously refers to a small, obscure entrance, not the entrance via the city gates.

1:27 See notes on Josh. 10:40; 12:9–24.

1:28 *to tribute,* i.e. "to forced labor."

inhabitants of Zi′don, nor of Ah′lab, nor of Ach′zib, nor of Hel′bah, nor of
A′phik, nor of Re′hob:
32 But the Asherites dwelt among the Canaanites, the inhabitants of the
land: for they did not drive them out.
33 Neither did Naph′ta-li drive out the inhabitants of Beth–she′mesh, nor
the inhabitants of Beth–a′nath; but he dwelt among the Canaanites, the
inhabitants of the land: nevertheless the inhabitants of Beth–she′mesh and
of Beth–a′nath became tributaries unto them.

1:34 Josh 19:47; Judg 18:1

34 And the Am′or-ites forced the children of Dan into the mountain: for
they would not suffer them to come down to the valley:
35 But the Am′or-ites would dwell in mount He′res in Ai′ja-lon, and in
Sha-al′bim: yet the hand of the house of Joseph prevailed, so that they
became tributaries.
36 And the coast of the Am′or-ites *was* from the going up to Ak-rab′bim,
from the rock, and upward.

B. ISRAEL, BREAKER OF GOD'S COVENANT

2:1☆ Ex 20:2; Josh 3:10; Judg 6:11; 13:2, 3

2 AND an angel of the LORD came up from Gilgal to Bo′chim, and said,
I made you to go up out of Egypt, and have brought you unto the land
which I sware unto your fathers; and I said, I will never break my covenant
with you.

2:2 Gen 17:7, 8; Ex 23:32; 34:12, 13; Lev 26:1, 14, 42, 44; Deut 7:12
2:3 Num 33:55, 56; Deut 29:25; Josh 23:12, 13; Ps 81:9

2 And ye shall make no league with the inhabitants of this land; ye shall
throw down their altars: but ye have not obeyed my voice: why have ye
done this?
3 Wherefore I also said, I will not drive them out from before you; but
they shall be *as thorns* in your sides, and their gods shall be a snare unto
you.
4 And it came to pass, when the angel of the LORD spake these words unto
all the children of Israel, that the people lifted up their voice, and wept.

2:5☆ Josh 7:26

5 And they called the name of that place Bo′chim: and they sacrificed
there unto the LORD.

C. JOSHUA'S DEATH AND BURIAL

2:6 Josh 24:28
2:7 Josh 24:29

6 ¶And when Joshua had let the people go, the children of Israel went
every man unto his inheritance to possess the land.
7 And the people served the LORD all the days of Joshua, and all the days
of the elders that outlived Joshua, who had seen all the great works of the
LORD, that he did for Israel.
8 And Joshua the son of Nun, the servant of the LORD, died, *being* an
hundred and ten years old.
9 And they buried him in the border of his inheritance in Tim′nath–he′res,
in the mount of E′phra-im, on the north side of the hill Ga′ash.

D. ISRAEL ABANDONS JEHOVAH

2:10☆ Ps 81:11

10 And also all that generation were gathered unto their fathers: and there
arose another generation after them, which knew not the LORD, nor yet the
works which he had done for Israel.

2:1 This verse reiterates the Abrahamic covenant as renewed in Exodus 34. Its seal was obedience to the voice of God. Israel failed to drive out of Canaan all of the inhabitants, thus breaking the covenant. This transgression led to disaster (see 2:2, 3). *angel of the LORD,* the Lord himself.

2:5 *Bochim,* i.e. "weepers."

2:10 A new generation arose which was somehow detached from its spiritual inheritance. These Israelites neither knew the Lord nor were they aware of his great works on their behalf among their forebears. It is possible, although quite difficult, for generation after generation to be brought up in the true faith. The first and principal business of parents is to raise their children in the nurture and admonition of the Lord. As we see in this verse, some of the Israelites failed to do this. But there remained a remnant which would carry on the ancient traditions.

[11]¶And the children of Israel did evil in the sight of the LORD, and served
Ba'al-im:
[12]And they forsook the LORD God of their fathers, which brought them
out of the land of Egypt, and followed other gods, of the gods of the people
that *were* round about them, and bowed themselves unto them, and
provoked the LORD to anger.
[13]And they forsook the LORD, and served Ba'al and Ash'ta-roth.
[14]¶And the anger of the LORD was hot against Israel, and he delivered
them into the hands of spoilers that spoiled them, and he sold them into the
hands of their enemies round about, so that they could not any longer stand
before their enemies.

2:11 Judg 4:1; 6:1 8:33; 10:6
☆**2:12** Deut 28:25 31:16, 17; 32:30 Judg 10:6 Ps 106-40
☆**2:13**
☆**2:14**

E. GOD DELIVERS ISRAEL BUT ISRAEL BREAKS GOD'S TREATY

[15]Whithersoever they went out, the hand of the LORD was against them
for evil, as the LORD had said, and as the LORD had sworn unto them: and
they were greatly distressed.
[16]¶Nevertheless the LORD raised up judges, which delivered them out of
the hand of those that spoiled them.
[17]And yet they would not hearken unto their judges, but they went a
whoring after other gods, and bowed themselves unto them: they turned
quickly out of the way which their fathers walked in, obeying the
commandments of the LORD; *but* they did not so.
[18]And when the LORD raised them up judges, then the LORD was with the
judge, and delivered them out of the hand of their enemies all the days of
the judge: for it repented the LORD because of their groanings by reason of
them that oppressed them and vexed them.
[19]And it came to pass, when the judge was dead, *that* they returned, and
corrupted *themselves* more than their fathers, in following other gods to
serve them, and to bow down unto them; they ceased not from their own
doings, nor from their stubborn way.
[20]¶And the anger of the LORD was hot against Israel; and he said,
Because that this people hath transgressed my covenant which I com-
manded their fathers, and have not hearkened unto my voice;
[21]I also will not henceforth drive out any from before them of the nations
which Joshua left when he died:
[22]That through them I may prove Israel, whether they will keep the way
of the LORD to walk therein, as their fathers did keep *it,* or not.
[23]Therefore the LORD left those nations, without driving them out
hastily; neither delivered he them into the hand of Joshua.

☆**2:16** Judg 6:6 Ps 106:43–45
2:17 Ps 81:11, 12
☆**2:19** Judg 3:11, 12 4:1; 8:33 2 Chron 24:17, 18 Ps 78:8
2:21 Josh 23:13
2:22 2 Chron 32:31
☆**2:23**

2:12–14 *gods,* local representations of Baal, the lord of the Canaanite pantheon and a male consort of Ashtaroth, a Canaanite goddess of fertility and war. *Ashtaroth,* the plural of Astarte. Those who will not have God as their father often look to something else to take his place. Even those who profess atheism are seen as having their own gods of various sorts. Few people, if any, are totally bereft of any commitment to something higher than themselves.

2:16 Subsequent to the death of Joshua there was a decline of Israel, occasioned by religious apostasy. The nation experienced a recurring pattern of subjugation by neighboring peoples, followed by repentance and deliverance by God. During this period, before the appointment of prophets, God raised up deliverers such as Othniel, Ehud, Deborah, and Samson. These heroes were called *judges* (a title which, in Hebrew, meant leadership in war, government, politics, and law). Israel was still a theocratic nation; God was still the ruler. None of the judges reached the stature of Moses and Joshua before them, or of David and Samuel after them. The period of the judges was marked by confusion and disorder: "everyone did whatever he wanted to—whatever seemed right in his own eyes" (17:6, TLB; see also 21:25).

2:19 While living, the judges were generally able to restrain their countrymen from apostasy. This verse indicates that when the judges died, the people easily departed from the true faith and *corrupted themselves more than their fathers.* The judges did not restrain the people through legalistic legislation, but through force of character, quality of leadership, and their own example of fidelity to God.

2:23 *into the hand of Joshua.* Joshua here is a euphemism for Israel.

F. THE NATIONS GOD LEAVES IN THE LAND

3:1☆ Ps 78:7; Josh 11:19

3 NOW these *are* the nations which the LORD left, to prove Israel by
them, *even* as many *of Israel* as had not known all the wars of Canaan;
2 Only that the generations of the children of Israel might know, to teach
them war, at the least such as before knew nothing thereof;
3 *Namely,* five lords of the Philistines, and all the Canaanites, and the Si-
do′ni-ans, and the Hi′vites that dwelt in mount Lebanon, from mount
Ba′al–her′mon unto the entering in of Ha′math.

3:4 Deut 8:2; Judg 2:22

4 And they were to prove Israel by them, to know whether they would
hearken unto the commandments of the LORD, which he commanded their
fathers by the hand of Moses.

3:5 Judg 1:29–32

5 ¶And the children of Israel dwelt among the Canaanites, Hittites, and
Am′or-ites, and Per′iz-zites, and Hi′vites, and Jeb′u-sites:

3:6 Ex 34:15, 16; Deut 7:3, 4; Josh 23:12

6 And they took their daughters to be their wives, and gave their
daughters to their sons, and served their gods.

3:7☆ Judg 2:11–13

7 And the children of Israel did evil in the sight of the LORD, and forgat
the LORD their God, and served Ba′al-im and the groves.

II. THE CYCLE OF APOSTASY AND DELIVERANCES (3:8—16:31)

A. OTHNI-EL, ISRAEL'S DELIVERER FROM MESOPOTAMIA

3:8☆ Ex 22:24; Deut 29:20; Judg 2:12–14, 20

8 ¶Therefore the anger of the LORD was hot against Israel, and he sold
them into the hand of Chu′shan–rish-a-tha′im king of Mes-o-po-ta′mi-a:
and the children of Israel served Chu′shan–rish-a-tha′im eight years.

3:9 Judg 1:13

9 And when the children of Israel cried unto the LORD, the LORD raised
up a deliverer to the children of Israel, who delivered them, *even* Oth′ni-el
the son of Ke′naz, Caleb's younger brother.

3:10☆ Num 11:17; 27:18; Judg 6:34; 11:29; 1 Sam 10:6

10 And the Spirit of the LORD came upon him, and he judged Israel, and
went out to war: and the LORD delivered Chu′shan–rish-a-tha′im king of
Mes-o-po-ta′mi-a into his hand; and his hand prevailed against Chu′shan–
rish-a-tha′im.

3:11 Judg 5:31; 8:28

11 And the land had rest forty years. And Oth′ni-el the son of Ke′naz died.

B. EHUD DELIVERS ISRAEL FROM MOAB

1. God Puts Israel under Moabite Control

3:12☆ Judg 2:19; Hos 6:4

12 ¶And the children of Israel did evil again in the sight of the LORD: and
the LORD strengthened Eg′lon the king of Moab against Israel, because
they had done evil in the sight of the LORD.

3:1 Several nations remained in Canaan after its occupation by Israel. God allowed them to exist in order to keep the Israelites on their guard. Knowing that enemies surrounded them, the Israelites had to be militarily prepared at all times. This kept them from falling into a life of ease, luxury, and effeminacy.

3:7 *the groves,* i.e., "Asheroth" (the plural of "Asherah"), the Canaanite mother-goddess who, like Ashtaroth in 2:3, was prominent in Canaanite fertility rites.

3:8 *Mesopotamia* (eastern Syria), in Hebrew, *Aram-naha-raim.* Mesopotamia was located near Haran. (See note on Gen. 24:10, which speaks of Iraq.) *Chushan-rishathaim,* an Aramean prince.

3:10 *the Spirit of the LORD came upon him.* In the Old Testament we often read of the Spirit of the Lord coming upon someone. When this happened, the person on whom the Spirit came received useful gifts and experienced the power of God in his life so that he could perform great exploits for God, Israel, and the advancement of the true faith. Here we read that Othniel enjoyed a forty-year judgeship and that the Israelites under his leadership prospered spiritually and materially.

The Pentecost marked the beginning of the age of the Holy Spirit. Before Pentecost, however, the Spirit came upon men and women as he pleased to accomplish the will of God the Father. He came upon some of the judges (6:34; 11:29), upon David (1 Sam. 16:13), and upon Zechariah (2 Chron. 24:20), among others. The life of Jesus also manifests the work of the Holy Spirit. Jesus was "full of the Holy Ghost" (Luke 4:1); he was "led up of the Spirit into the wilderness to be tempted of the devil" (Matt. 4:1); and "through the eternal Spirit [Christ] offered himself without spot to God" (Heb. 9:14). The Spirit of God was also active in creation (Gen. 1:2).

3:12–15 Subsequent to Othniel's death, Israel became apostate. After eighteen years of oppression under Eglon, Israel sought the help of God, who heard and delivered them.

[13]And he gathered unto him the children of Ammon and Am'a-lek, and **3:13**
went and smote Israel, and possessed the city of palm trees. Judg 1:16
[14]So the children of Israel served Eg'lon the king of Moab eighteen years.

2. Ehud Slays King Eglon

[15]But when the children of Israel cried unto the LORD, the LORD raised **3:15**
them up a deliverer, E'hud the son of Ge'ra, a Benjamite, a man lefthanded: Judg 3:9, 20:16
and by him the children of Israel sent a present unto Eg'lon the king of 1 Chron 12:2
Moab.
[16]But E'hud made him a dagger which had two edges, of a cubit length;
and he did gird it under his raiment upon his right thigh.
[17]And he brought the present unto Eg'lon king of Moab: and Eg'lon *was*
a very fat man.
[18]And when he had made an end to offer the present, he sent away the
people that bare the present.
[19]But he himself turned again from the quarries that *were* by Gilgal, and
said, I have a secret errand unto thee, O king: who said, Keep silence. And
all that stood by him went out from him.
[20]And E'hud came unto him; and he was sitting in a summer parlour, ☆**3:20**
which he had for himself alone. And E'hud said, I have a message from
God unto thee. And he arose out of *his* seat.
[21]And E'hud put forth his left hand, and took the dagger from his right
thigh, and thrust it into his belly:
[22]And the haft also went in after the blade; and the fat closed upon the
blade, so that he could not draw the dagger out of his belly; and the dirt
came out.
[23]Then E'hud went forth through the porch, and shut the doors of the
parlour upon him, and locked them.
[24]When he was gone out, his servants came; and when they saw that, ☆**3:24**
behold, the doors of the parlour *were* locked, they said, Surely he covereth 1 Sam 24:3
his feet in his summer chamber.
[25]And they tarried till they were ashamed: and, behold, he opened not
the doors of the parlour; therefore they took a key, and opened *them:* and,
behold, their lord *was* fallen down dead on the earth.

3. Israel Delivered from Moab

[26]And E'hud escaped while they tarried, and passed beyond the quarries,
and escaped unto Se'i-rath.
[27]And it came to pass, when he was come, that he blew a trumpet in the
mountain of E'phra-im, and the children of Israel went down with him
from the mount, and he before them.
[28]And he said unto them, Follow after me: for the LORD hath delivered **3:28**
your enemies the Moabites into your hand. And they went down after him, Judg 7:24; 12:5
and took the fords of Jordan toward Moab, and suffered not a man to pass
over.
[29]And they slew of Moab at that time about ten thousand men, all lusty,
and all men of valour; and there escaped not a man.
[30]So Moab was subdued that day under the hand of Israel. And the land ☆**3:30**
had rest fourscore years.

3:20 *summer parlor,* "cool roof chamber" (RSV).
3:24 *covereth his feet,* i.e., relieving himself or "going to the toilet."

3:30 The power of the Moabites was so broken that the land had rest for eighty years, quite an extended period of time.

C. JUDGE SHAMGAR DELIVERS ISRAEL FROM PHILISTIA

3:31☆ [31]¶And after him was Sham'gar the son of A'nath, which slew of the
Judg 5:6 Philistines six hundred men with an ox goad: and he also delivered Israel.

D. DEBORAH AND BARAK DELIVER ISRAEL FROM CANAAN (HAZOR)

1. Canaan Oppresses Israel

4:1☆ 4 AND the children of Israel again did evil in the sight of the LORD,
Judg 2:19 when E'hud was dead.
4:2 [2]And the LORD sold them into the hand of Ja'bin king of Canaan, that
Josh 11:1
Ps 83:9 reigned in Ha'zor; the captain of whose host *was* Sis'e-ra, which dwelt in
Ha-ro'sheth of the Gentiles.
[3]And the children of Israel cried unto the LORD: for he had nine hundred
chariots of iron; and twenty years he mightily oppressed the children of
Israel.

2. Deborah Enlists Barak

4:4☆ [4]¶And Deb'o-rah, a prophetess, the wife of Lap'i-doth, she judged Israel
at that time.
4:5☆ [5]And she dwelt under the palm tree of Deb'o-rah between Ra'mah and
Beth-el in mount E'phra-im: and the children of Israel came up to her for
judgment.
4:6 [6]And she sent and called Ba'rak the son of A-bin'o-am out of Ke'desh-
1 Sam 12:11
Heb 11:32 naph'ta-li, and said unto him, Hath not the LORD God of Israel com-
manded, *saying,* Go and draw toward mount Ta'bor, and take with thee ten
thousand men of the children of Naph'ta-li and of the children of Zeb'u-
lun?
4:7 [7]And I will draw unto thee to the river Ki'shon Sis'e-ra, the captain of
Ps 83:9 Ja'bin's army, with his chariots and his multitude; and I will deliver him
into thine hand.
[8]And Ba'rak said unto her, If thou wilt go with me, then I will go: but if
thou wilt not go with me, *then* I will not go.
[9]And she said, I will surely go with thee: notwithstanding the journey
that thou takest shall not be for thine honour; for the LORD shall sell Sis'e-
ra into the hand of a woman. And Deb'o-rah arose, and went with Ba'rak
to Ke'desh.

3. Barak Defeats Sisera's Army

4:10 [10]¶And Ba'rak called Zeb'u-lun and Naph'ta-li to Ke'desh; and he went
Judg 5:18 up with ten thousand men at his feet: and Deb'o-rah went up with him.
4:11☆ [11]Now He'ber the Ken'ite, *which was* of the children of Ho'bab the father
Josh 19:33
Judg 1:16 in law of Moses, had severed himself from the Ken'ites, and pitched his tent
unto the plain of Za-a-na'im, which *is* by Ke'desh.

3:31 *ox goad.* The Israelites lacked real armaments. An ox goad was a sharp stick used to prod cattle, and also to clean plows. It probably had a blade on the other end. Shamgar used it as a spear.

4:1 For eighty years Ehud kept a sharp eye on the people, and they did not turn away from God. But after his death they became apostate. They feared Ehud more than God.

4:4 *Deborah, a prophetess,* is the only judge so described. As a prophetess, she conveyed to the people the word she received from the Holy Spirit. In this role she was able to foretell the future with the help of the Spirit. God is not partial to men over women in principle, for the Scriptures are full of incidents in which God chose to employ women in his service. There were prophetesses, deaconesses, and other women who played an important part in the unfolding scheme of redemption. Miriam, Rahab, Lydia, Elizabeth, Mary, and others stand out as illustrations of God's choice of godly women who served him well.

4:5 *the children of Israel came up to her for judgment,* i.e., "came to her to decide their disputes."†

4:11 *Hobab.* See note on Exod. 2:18.

[12]And they shewed Sis′e-ra that Ba′rak the son of A-bin′o-am was gone
up to mount Ta′bor.
[13]And Sis′e-ra gathered together all his chariots, *even* nine hundred
chariots of iron, and all the people that *were* with him, from Ha-ro′sheth of
the Gentiles unto the river of Ki′shon.
[14]And Deb′o-rah said unto Ba′rak, Up; for this *is* the day in which the
LORD hath delivered Sis′e-ra into thine hand: is not the LORD gone out
before thee? So Ba′rak went down from mount Ta′bor, and ten thousand
men after him.
[15]And the LORD discomfited Sis′e-ra, and all *his* chariots, and all *his* host, ☆4:15 Josh 10:10 Judg 7:21
with the edge of the sword before Ba′rak; so that Sis′e-ra lighted down off
his chariot, and fled away on his feet.
[16]But Ba′rak pursued after the chariots, and after the host, unto Ha- 4:16 Judg 4:2, 3 Ps 83:9
ro′sheth of the Gentiles: and all the host of Sis′e-ra fell upon the edge of the
sword; *and* there was not a man left.
[17]Howbeit Sis′e-ra fled away on his feet to the tent of Ja′el the wife of
He′ber the Ken′ite: for *there was* peace between Ja′bin the king of Ha′zor
and the house of He′ber the Ken′ite.

4. Jael Kills Sisera

[18]¶And Ja′el went out to meet Sis′e-ra, and said unto him, Turn in, my
lord, turn in to me; fear not. And when he had turned in unto her into the
tent, she covered him with a mantle.
[19]And he said unto her, Give me, I pray thee, a little water to drink; for 4:19 Judg 5:25
I am thirsty. And she opened a bottle of milk, and gave him drink, and
covered him.
[20]Again he said unto her, Stand in the door of the tent, and it shall be,
when any man doth come and inquire of thee, and say, Is there any man
here? that thou shalt say, No.
[21]Then Ja′el He′ber's wife took a nail of the tent, and took an hammer in ☆4:21
her hand, and went softly unto him, and smote the nail into his temples,
and fastened it into the ground: for he was fast asleep and weary. So he
died.

5. King Jabin of Canaan Destroyed

[22]And, behold, as Ba′rak pursued Sis′e-ra, Ja′el came out to meet him,
and said unto him, Come, and I will shew thee the man whom thou seekest.
And when he came into her *tent,* behold, Sis′e-ra lay dead, and the nail *was*
in his temples.
[23]So God subdued on that day Ja′bin the king of Canaan before the
children of Israel.
[24]And the hand of the children of Israel prospered, and prevailed against
Ja′bin the king of Canaan, until they had destroyed Ja′bin king of Canaan.

6. The Song of Triumph of Deborah and Barak

5 THEN sang Deb′o-rah and Ba′rak the son of A-bin′o-am on that day, ☆5:1 Ex 15:1, 21 Num 21:17, 18 1 Sam 2:1
saying,

4:15 *the LORD discomfited Sisera,* i.e., "The Lord routed Sisera," and he did this by some sort of flood or great rainstorm, according to 5:21. In any event it was God, not the people of God, who made the difference in this encounter.

4:21 What Jael did "was a divine warrant that justified her in the doing of it; and, therefore, since no such extraordinary commissions can now be pretended, it ought not in any case to be imitated. The laws of friendship and hospitality must be religiously observed, and we must abhor the thought of betraying any whom we have invited and encouraged to put a confidence in us."*

5:1 It is good to praise God by song. Deborah "used her gifts as a prophetess in composing the song, and the strain throughout is very fine and lofty, the images

5:2 [2]Praise ye the LORD for the avenging of Israel, when the people willingly
Ps 110:3 offered themselves.
[3]Hear, O ye kings; give ear, O ye princes; I, *even* I, will sing unto the
LORD; I will sing *praise* to the LORD God of Israel.
5:4☆ [4]LORD, when thou wentest out of Se'ir, when thou marchedst out of the
Deut 33:2 Hab 3:3 field of Edom, the earth trembled, and the heavens dropped, the clouds also
dropped water.
5:5☆ [5]The mountains melted from before the LORD, *even* that Si'nai from
Ex 19:18; 20:18 Ps 97:5; 114:6 before the LORD God of Israel.
Isa 64:3 5:6 [6]In the days of Sham'gar the son of A'nath, in the days of Ja'el, the
Judg 3:31; 4:17 highways were unoccupied, and the travellers walked through byways.
[7]*The inhabitants of* the villages ceased, they ceased in Israel, until that I
Deb'o-rah arose, that I arose a mother in Israel.
5:8 [8]They chose new gods; then *was* war in the gates: was there a shield or
Deut 32:17 1 Sam 13:22 spear seen among forty thousand in Israel?
[9]My heart *is* toward the governors of Israel, that offered themselves
willingly among the people. Bless ye the LORD.
5:10☆ [10]Speak, ye that ride on white asses, ye that sit in judgment, and walk by
Judg 10:4; 12:14 the way.
5:11☆ [11]*They that are delivered* from the noise of archers in the places of
Gen 24:11 1 Sam 12:7 drawing water, there shall they rehearse the righteous acts of the LORD,
even the righteous acts *toward the inhabitants* of his villages in Israel: then
shall the people of the LORD go down to the gates.
[12]Awake, awake, Deb'o-rah: awake, awake, utter a song: arise, Ba'rak,
and lead thy captivity captive, thou son of A-bin'o-am.
5:13☆ [13]Then he made him that remaineth have dominion over the nobles
among the people: the LORD made me have dominion over the mighty.
[14]Out of E'phra-im *was there* a root of them against Am'a-lek; after thee,
Benjamin, among thy people; out of Ma'chir came down governors, and
out of Zeb'u-lun they that handle the pen of the writer.
5:15☆ [15]And the princes of Is'sa-char *were* with Deb'o-rah; even Is'sa-char, and
also Ba'rak: he was sent on foot into the valley. For the divisions of Reuben
there were great thoughts of heart.
5:16☆ [16]Why abodest thou among the sheepfolds, to hear the bleatings of the
Num 32:24 flocks? For the divisions of Reuben *there were* great searchings of heart.
5:17☆ [17]Gilead abode beyond Jordan: and why did Dan remain in ships? Asher
Josh 13:25; 22:9 continued on the sea shore, and abode in his breaches.
[18]Zeb'u-lun and Naph'ta-li *were* a people *that* jeoparded their lives unto
the death in the high places of the field.
5:19 [19]The kings came *and* fought, then fought the kings of Canaan in Ta'a-
Josh 11:1, 2 Judg 1:27 nach by the waters of Me-gid'do; they took no gain of money.
5:20☆ [20]They fought from heaven; the stars in their courses fought against
Sis'e-ra.

---

are lively, the expressions elegant, and an admirable mixture there is in it of sweetness and majesty. No poetry is comparable to the sacred poetry."* When God gives the victory his people should offer their thanksgiving, and singing is one of the beautiful ways to do this.

5:4, 5 Recalling to mind what God had done for Israel in the exodus and wanderings, Deborah likens what God has just done for Israel as comparable to what he had done for that nation in the past. Past mercies give God's people the hope and expectation that he will repeat them in the days to come.

5:10, 11 Deborah calls for people of all classes to speak forth their praise to God for his great deliverance: those who ride on the rare white asses, those who walk because they have nothing to ride on, those whose wells have not been stopped up by the enemy so they can still get water, and those who dispense justice—let all praise the Lord.

5:13 The glorious victory over the enemy made Israel and Deborah and Barak look great. However, they owed that victory entirely to God who delivered them.

5:15–17 Some of Israel gave no support to those who battled Sisera. Reuben, Gilead, Asher, and Dan sat on the sidelines and contributed nothing to the victory. This was a word of reproof.

5:20 It may be said that "from heaven, from the place where the stars go forth, war was waged against Sisera."* The God of heaven waged war against the enemy.

[21]The river of Ki′shon swept them away, that ancient river, the river Ki′shon. O my soul, thou hast trodden down strength.
[22]Then were the horsehoofs broken by the means of the pransings, the pransings of their mighty ones.
[23]Curse ye Me′roz, said the angel of the LORD, curse ye bitterly the inhabitants thereof; because they came not to the help of the LORD, to the help of the LORD against the mighty.
[24]Blessed above women shall Ja′el the wife of He′ber the Ken′ite be, blessed shall she be above women in the tent.
[25]He asked water, *and* she gave *him* milk; she brought forth butter in a lordly dish.
[26]She put her hand to the nail, and her right hand to the workmen's hammer; and with the hammer she smote Sis′e-ra, she smote off his head, when she had pierced and stricken through his temples.
[27]At her feet he bowed, he fell, he lay down: at her feet he bowed, he fell: where he bowed, there he fell down dead.
[28]The mother of Sis′e-ra looked out at a window, and cried through the lattice, Why is his chariot *so* long in coming? why tarry the wheels of his chariots?
[29]Her wise ladies answered her, yea, she returned answer to herself,
[30]Have they not sped? have they *not* divided the prey; to every man a damsel *or* two; to Sis′e-ra a prey of divers colours, a prey of divers colours of needlework, of divers colours of needlework on both sides, *meet* for the necks of *them that take* the spoil?
[31]So let all thine enemies perish, O LORD: but *let* them that love him *be* as the sun when he goeth forth in his might. And the land had rest forty years.

☆**5:21** Judg 4:7
☆**5:22** Job 39:19–25
☆**5:23**
☆**5:24**
5:30 Ex 15:9
5:31 Ps 68:1, 2; 92:8, 9

E. DELIVERANCE FROM MIDIAN BY JUDGE GIDEON
1. Israel's Slavery under the Midianites

6 AND the children of Israel did evil in the sight of the LORD: and the LORD delivered them into the hand of Mid′i-an seven years.
[2]And the hand of Mid′i-an prevailed against Israel: *and* because of the Mid′i-an-ites the children of Israel made them the dens which *are* in the mountains, and caves, and strong holds.
[3]And *so* it was, when Israel had sown, that the Mid′i-an-ites came up, and the Am′a-lek-ites, and the children of the east, even they came up against them;
[4]And they encamped against them, and destroyed the increase of the earth, till thou come unto Ga′za, and left no sustenance for Israel, neither sheep, nor ox, nor ass.
[5]For they came up with their cattle and their tents, and they came as grasshoppers for multitude; *for* both they and their camels were without number: and they entered into the land to destroy it.
[6]And Israel was greatly impoverished because of the Mid′i-an-ites; and the children of Israel cried unto the LORD.

☆**6:1** Num 22:4; 25:15; 31:1; Judg 2:11–14
☆**6:3** Isa 21:2
☆**6:5** 1 Sam 30:17
6:6 Deut 28:43

5:21, 22 Kishon was ordinarily a shallow river. But a rainstorm so swelled the torrents that those who sought to cross it were drowned and their chariots mired in the mud. Even the horses' hooves were broken.
5:23 All Meroz was cursed because the inhabitants did not come to the help of the Lord. They were condemned, not because they were unwilling to help their friends, but because they failed to come to help the Lord.
5:24 Deborah rises to poetic heights as she pictures heroic Jael, the one who smote Sisera. Sisera's mother will have to wait long for her son to come home, for this enemy of God has perished. She ends with the prayer that all the enemies of God may also perish. The upshot of the victory was that the land had rest for forty years, until the advent of Gideon.
6:1 *Midian.* See note to Exod. 2:15.
6:3 *Amalekites.* See note to Exod. 17:8.
6:5 This is the first instance recorded in the Scriptures of the use of camels in warfare.

2. God Speaks through His Prophet

7 ¶And it came to pass, when the children of Israel cried unto the LORD
because of the Mid'i-an-ites,
6:8☆ 8 That the LORD sent a prophet unto the children of Israel, which said
Ex 18:9 Judg 2:1, 2, 18 unto them, Thus saith the LORD God of Israel, I brought you up from
10:12 Egypt, and brought you forth out of the house of bondage;
9 And I delivered you out of the hand of the Egyptians, and out of the
hand of all that oppressed you, and drave them out from before you, and
gave you their land;
6:10 10 And I said unto you, I *am* the LORD your God; fear not the gods of the
Josh 24:15 Am'or-ites, in whose land ye dwell: but ye have not obeyed my voice.

3. God Calls Gideon

6:11☆ 11 ¶And there came an angel of the LORD, and sat under an oak which *was*
Judg 13:2, 3 Heb 11:32 in Oph'rah, that *pertained* unto Jo'ash the A'bi-ez'rite: and his son Gideon
threshed wheat by the winepress, to hide *it* from the Mid'i-an-ites.
12 And the angel of the LORD appeared unto him, and said unto him, The
LORD *is* with thee, thou mighty man of valour.
6:13 13 And Gideon said unto him, Oh my Lord, if the LORD be with us, why
Deut 31:17 2 Chron 15:2 then is all this befallen us? and where *be* all his miracles which our fathers
Ps 44:9 told us of, saying, Did not the LORD bring us up from Egypt? but now the
LORD hath forsaken us, and delivered us into the hands of the Mid'i-an-ites.
14 And the LORD looked upon him, and said, Go in this thy might, and
thou shalt save Israel from the hand of the Mid'i-an-ites: have not I sent
thee?
6:15 15 And he said unto him, Oh my Lord, wherewith shall I save Israel?
Ex 3:11 behold, my family *is* poor in Ma-nas'seh, and I *am* the least in my father's
house.
6:16☆ 16 And the LORD said unto him, Surely I will be with thee, and thou shalt
smite the Mid'i-an-ites as one man.
6:17☆ 17 And he said unto him, If now I have found grace in thy sight, then shew
Isa 38:7 me a sign that thou talkest with me.
6:18☆ 18 Depart not hence, I pray thee, until I come unto thee, and bring forth
my present, and set *it* before thee. And he said, I will tarry until thou come
again.
6:19 19 ¶And Gideon went in, and made ready a kid, and unleavened cakes of
Gen 18:8 an ephah of flour: the flesh he put in a basket, and he put the broth in a pot,
and brought *it* out unto him under the oak, and presented *it*.
6:20☆ 20 And the angel of God said unto him, Take the flesh and the unleavened
cakes, and lay *them* upon this rock, and pour out the broth. And he did so.

6:8 God sent a prophet to speak to Israel on his behalf; the prophet is not named. His sole duty was to call Israel back to faithfulness to the God they had deserted in favor of the gods of the Amorites. Eternity alone will reveal the numberless people of God who served him faithfully without being identified in the Scriptures.

6:11 *an angel of the LORD.* This was evidently an appearance of Christ. In 6:14 we read that "the LORD looked upon him." The Hebrew word for this use of LORD is *Jehovah* or *Yahweh.* The angel called Gideon to the office of judge; he promised that he would be with Gideon. When Gideon asked for some outward sign that he was indeed called of God, the angel destroyed the meat and unleavened cakes with supernatural fire. Gideon later put out the fleece, and on the strength of that providential sign, he led the people of Israel to victory over the oppressive Midianites.

6:16 *I will be with thee,* i.e., "I Am will be with you." The name "I Am" is also used in Exod. 3:14. God was telling Gideon that the same One who appeared to Moses and rescued Israel from Egypt (see 6:13) would now rescue Israel from Midian.†

6:17–21 *show me a sign.* How was Gideon to know that this personage was God speaking to him? He begged for a sign. Since the commission came to him in extraordinary fashion, he thought the confirmation of that command might also be extraordinary. It was. In verse 21 fire sprung from the rock and consumed the flesh and the unleavened bread. Then Gideon knew that the call was from God.

21 ¶Then the angel of the LORD put forth the end of the staff that *was* in 6:21 Lev 9:24
his hand, and touched the flesh and the unleavened cakes; and there rose up
fire out of the rock, and consumed the flesh and the unleavened cakes. Then
the angel of the LORD departed out of his sight.
22 And when Gideon perceived that he *was* an angel of the LORD, Gideon 6:22 Gen 16:13
said, Alas, O Lord GOD! for because I have seen an angel of the LORD face 32:30
to face. Ex 33:20 Judg 13:22
23 And the LORD said unto him, Peace *be* unto thee; fear not: thou shalt
not die.
24 Then Gideon built an altar there unto the LORD, and called it Je- ☆6:24
ho'vah-sha'lom: unto this day it *is* yet in Oph'rah of the A'bi-ez'rites.

4. Gideon Pulls Down Baal's Altar

25 ¶And it came to pass the same night, that the LORD said unto him, 6:25 Ex 34:13
Take thy father's young bullock, even the second bullock of seven years old, Deut 7:5
and throw down the altar of Ba'al that thy father hath, and cut down the
grove that *is* by it:
26 And build an altar unto the LORD thy God upon the top of this rock, in
the ordered place, and take the second bullock, and offer a burnt sacrifice
with the wood of the grove which thou shalt cut down.
27 Then Gideon took ten men of his servants, and did as the LORD had
said unto him: and *so* it was, because he feared his father's household, and
the men of the city, that he could not do *it* by day, that he did *it* by night.
28 ¶And when the men of the city arose early in the morning, behold, the
altar of Ba'al was cast down, and the grove was cut down that *was* by it,
and the second bullock was offered upon the altar *that was* built.
29 And they said one to another, Who hath done this thing? And when
they inquired and asked, they said, Gideon the son of Jo'ash hath done this
thing.
30 Then the men of the city said unto Jo'ash, Bring out thy son, that he
may die: because he hath cast down the altar of Ba'al, and because he hath
cut down the grove that *was* by it.
31 And Jo'ash said unto all that stood against him, Will ye plead for Ba'al? ☆6:31
will ye save him? he that will plead for him, let him be put to death whilst
it is yet morning: if he *be* a god, let him plead for himself, because *one* hath
cast down his altar.
32 Therefore on that day he called him Je-rub'ba-al, saying, Let Ba'al
plead against him, because he hath thrown down his altar.
33 ¶Then all the Mid'i-an-ites and the Am'a-lek-ites and the children of 6:33 Josh 17:16–18
the east were gathered together, and went over, and pitched in the valley of Judg 7:1, 12, 13
Jez're-el.
34 But the Spirit of the LORD came upon Gideon, and he blew a trumpet; ☆6:34 Judg 3:10
and A'bi-e'zer was gathered after him. 1 Chron 12:18
35 And he sent messengers throughout all Ma-nas'seh; who also was 2 Chron 24:20 6:35
gathered after him: and he sent messengers unto Asher, and unto Zeb'u- Judg 7:24; 9:31
lun, and unto Naph'ta-li; and they came up to meet them.

6:24 *Jehovah-shalom,* "the LORD is peace." In Jer. 33:16 the Lord is said to be our righteousness; here we learn that he is also our peace (see Eph. 2:14).

6:31 Joash, Gideon's father, asked the right question: Is it not folly to pray to Baal and to solicit his help when he cannot avenge himself on the person who has pulled his statue down? And we might well ask: If our God cannot help himself why should we expect that he would be able to help us? The fact that he is almighty means he can defend himself and protect us.

6:34 The Spirit came upon Gideon. He was then empowered and could not fail. But he wanted to be sure that what he was about to do was from God and not from self, so he put out the fleece (see 6:37).

5. Gideon Puts Out the Fleece

6:36 Judg 6:14 36¶And Gideon said unto God, If thou wilt save Israel by mine hand, as
thou hast said,
6:37☆ 37Behold, I will put a fleece of wool in the floor; *and* if the dew be on the
fleece only, and *it be* dry upon all the earth *beside,* then shall I know that
thou wilt save Israel by mine hand, as thou hast said.
38And it was so: for he rose up early on the morrow, and thrust the fleece
together, and wringed the dew out of the fleece, a bowl full of water.
6:39 Gen 18:32 39And Gideon said unto God, Let not thine anger be hot against me, and
I will speak but this once: let me prove, I pray thee, but this once with the
fleece; let it now be dry only upon the fleece, and upon all the ground let
there be dew.
40And God did so that night: for it was dry upon the fleece only, and
there was dew on all the ground.

6. Gideon Defeats the Midianites
a. The Choice of the Three Hundred Soldiers

7:1 Gen 12:6 Deut 11:30 Judg 6:32 7 THEN Je-rub′ba-al, who *is* Gideon, and all the people that *were* with
him, rose up early, and pitched beside the well of Ha′rod: so that the
host of the Mid′i-an-ites were on the north side of them, by the hill of
Mo′reh, in the valley.
7:2☆ Deut 8:18 Isa 10:13 Ezek 28:2, 17 2And the LORD said unto Gideon, The people that *are* with thee *are* too
many for me to give the Mid′i-an-ites into their hands, lest Israel vaunt
themselves against me, saying, Mine own hand hath saved me.
7:3☆ Deut 20:8 3Now therefore go to, proclaim in the ears of the people, saying,
Whosoever *is* fearful and afraid, let him return and depart early from
mount Gilead. And there returned of the people twenty and two thousand;
and there remained ten thousand.
7:4 1 Sam 14:6 4And the LORD said unto Gideon, The people *are* yet *too* many; bring
them down unto the water, and I will try them for thee there: and it shall
be, *that* of whom I say unto thee, This shall go with thee, the same shall go
with thee; and of whomsoever I say unto thee, This shall not go with thee,
the same shall not go.
5So he brought down the people unto the water: and the LORD said unto
Gideon, Every one that lappeth of the water with his tongue, as a dog
lappeth, him shalt thou set by himself; likewise every one that boweth down
upon his knees to drink.
6And the number of them that lapped, *putting* their hand to their mouth,
were three hundred men: but all the rest of the people bowed down upon
their knees to drink water.
7:7☆ 7And the LORD said unto Gideon, By the three hundred men that lapped
will I save you, and deliver the Mid′i-an-ites into thine hand: and let all the
other people go every man unto his place.

6:37 Gideon used the fleece to obtain an outward token from God; he wanted to be sure that he knew the will of God. Once he was certain, he led the campaign against the Midianites and won a spectacular victory. At many important junction points in the Scriptures, God provided external, corroborating evidence by which men could know he was at work. The Pharaoh saw what the rods of Aaron and Moses could do. At Carmel, God sent fire from heaven. At Pentecost, he sent the wind, the fire, and the gift of tongues.

7:2, 3 The army consisted of 32,000 men. Gideon thought the number too few. God told him he had more than he needed. Ten thousand went home almost immediately. They were fearful ones who would be of no use to Gideon anyhow.

7:7 When the number God wanted was reduced to three hundred, all the others went home and God promised to deliver Israel with this tiny number. God chose to glorify himself by making certain that Gideon and all the people could not, by themselves, win the victory. When the fight was over they would have to give God the glory. And this would diminish the stature of Baal, in whom they had sinfully placed their trust.

[8]So the people took victuals in their hand, and their trumpets: and he
sent all *the rest of* Israel every man unto his tent, and retained those three
hundred men: and the host of Mid′i-an was beneath him in the valley.
[9]¶And it came to pass the same night, that the LORD said unto him,
Arise, get thee down unto the host; for I have delivered it into thine hand.

7:8 Josh 2:24; 10:8; 11:6; Judg 3:28; 4:14

☆**7:9**

b. God's Prophecy of Victory

[10]But if thou fear to go down, go thou with Phu′rah thy servant down to
the host:
[11]And thou shalt hear what they say; and afterward shall thine hands be
strengthened to go down unto the host. Then went he down with Phu′rah
his servant unto the outside of the armed men that *were* in the host.
[12]And the Mid′i-an-ites and the Am′a-lek-ites and all the children of the
east lay along in the valley like grasshoppers for multitude; and their
camels *were* without number, as the sand by the sea side for multitude.
[13]And when Gideon was come, behold, *there was* a man that told a dream
unto his fellow, and said, Behold, I dreamed a dream, and, lo, a cake of
barley bread tumbled into the host of Mid′i-an, and came unto a tent, and
smote it that it fell, and overturned it, that the tent lay along.
[14]And his fellow answered and said, This *is* nothing else save the sword of
Gideon the son of Jo′ash, a man of Israel: *for* into his hand hath God
delivered Mid′i-an, and all the host.

☆**7:12** Josh 11:4; Judg 6:5; 8:10

c. The Battle and Defeat of the Midianites

[15]¶And it was *so,* when Gideon heard the telling of the dream, and the
interpretation thereof, that he worshipped, and returned into the host of
Israel, and said, Arise; for the LORD hath delivered into your hand the host
of Mid′i-an.
[16]And he divided the three hundred men *into* three companies, and he
put a trumpet in every man's hand, with empty pitchers, and lamps within
the pitchers.
[17]And he said unto them, Look on me, and do likewise: and, behold,
when I come to the outside of the camp, it shall be *that,* as I do, so shall ye
do.
[18]When I blow with a trumpet, I and all that *are* with me, then blow ye
the trumpets also on every side of all the camp, and say, *The sword* of the
LORD, and of Gideon.
[19]¶So Gideon, and the hundred men that *were* with him, came unto the
outside of the camp in the beginning of the middle watch; and they had but
newly set the watch: and they blew the trumpets, and brake the pitchers
that *were* in their hands.
[20]And the three companies blew the trumpets, and brake the pitchers,
and held the lamps in their left hands, and the trumpets in their right hands
to blow *withal:* and they cried, The sword of the LORD, and of Gideon.

7:9 The circumstances would cause any intelligent commander to suppose that it would be indiscreet and militarily rash to attack the enemy with three hundred soldiers. Yet when Gideon was told to go ahead he had no choice but to do so. God gave him further evidence to strengthen his faith (7:13, 14); consequently, Gideon raised an altar and worshipped God. He told his troops that God had *already* given them the victory. All they needed to do was obey orders.

7:12 Here we see the vast numbers of the enemy against whom Gideon is to fight with a mere three hundred followers armed with trumpets, jars, and torches. From the human perspective, who would have supposed that Gideon would emerge victorious? As we have seen before, though, God could deliver his people at any time, regardless of the size of the enemy. The grossest error any believer can make is to leave God out of the picture when faced with small or large difficulties.

7:21 Ex 14:25 2 Kgs 7:7
21 And they stood every man in his place round about the camp: and all
the host ran, and cried, and fled.
7:22☆
22 And the three hundred blew the trumpets, and the LORD set every
man's sword against his fellow, even throughout all the host: and the host
fled to Beth–shit'tah in Zer'e-rath, *and* to the border of A'bel-me-ho'lah,
unto Tab'bath.
23 And the men of Israel gathered themselves together out of Naph'ta-li,
and out of Asher, and out of all Ma-nas'seh, and pursued after the Mid'i-
an-ites.
7:24 Judg 3:28; 12:5
24 ¶And Gideon sent messengers throughout all mount E'phra-im, saying,
Come down against the Mid'i-an-ites, and take before them the waters unto
Beth–ba'rah and Jordan. Then all the men of E'phra-im gathered them-
selves together, and took the waters unto Beth–ba'rah and Jordan.
7:25 Judg 8:2, 3 Ps 83:11 Isa 10:26
25 And they took two princes of the Mid'i-an-ites, O'reb and Ze'eb; and
they slew O'reb upon the rock O'reb, and Ze'eb they slew at the winepress
of Ze'eb, and pursued Mid'i-an, and brought the heads of O'reb and Ze'eb
to Gideon on the other side Jordan.

d. Ephraim's Quarrel with Gideon

8:1☆ Judg 12:1
8 AND the men of E'phra-im said unto him, Why hast thou served us
thus, that thou calledst us not, when thou wentest to fight with the
Mid'i-an-ites? And they did chide with him sharply.
2 And he said unto them, What have I done now in comparison of you? *Is*
not the gleaning of the grapes of E'phra-im better than the vintage of A'bi-
e'zer?
3 God hath delivered into your hands the princes of Mid'i-an, O'reb and
Ze'eb: and what was I able to do in comparison of you? Then their anger
was abated toward him, when he had said that.

e. Succoth and Penuel Refuse to Give Gideon Food

4 ¶And Gideon came to Jordan, *and* passed over, he, and the three
hundred men that *were* with him, faint, yet pursuing *them.*
8:5☆ Gen 33:17 Judg 8:15
5 And he said unto the men of Suc'coth, Give, I pray you, loaves of bread
unto the people that follow me; for they *be* faint, and I am pursuing after
Ze'bah and Zal-mun'na, kings of Mid'i-an.
6 ¶And the princes of Suc'coth said, *Are* the hands of Ze'bah and Zal-
mun'na now in thine hand, that we should give bread unto thine army?
8:7 Judg 4:14; 7:15
7 And Gideon said, Therefore when the LORD hath delivered Ze'bah and
Zal-mun'na into mine hand, then I will tear your flesh with the thorns of
the wilderness and with briers.
8:8 Gen 32:30 1 Kgs 12:25
8 ¶And he went up thence to Pe-nu'el, and spake unto them likewise: and
the men of Pe-nu'el answered him as the men of Suc'coth had answered
him.

7:22 In the darkness of the night the trumpets and lights frightened the enemy out of their wits. Then God confused them so that they fought against each other and killed each other. So it is today; God can make the enemies of the church instruments to destroy one another.

8:1 Gideon was from the tribe of Manasseh. The Ephraimites, who also sprang from Joseph's loins, peevishly and unreasonably picked a quarrel with Gideon as to why he had not called them when he went after the Midianites. Gideon realized that a soft answer turns away wrath. He suggests that they have done far more than he, for the fleeing princes of Midian have fallen into their hands. Compared to what you have done, he suggests, I have not done as much. The Ephraimites were satisfied.

8:5 When Gideon crossed the Jordan, he sought bread from the people of Succoth who refused to give it to him. They feared that the Midian princes he was pursuing might escape, come back, and hurt them for helping Gideon. So they refused Gideon bread; so do the men of Penuel. Gideon was chasing the two kings of Midian, Zebah and Zalmunna. He promised Succoth and Penuel that he would repay them for their enmity when he had finished his job.

9 And he spake also unto the men of Pe-nu'el, saying, When I come again
in peace, I will break down this tower.

f. Gideon Defeats Zebah and Zalmunna at Karkor

10 ¶Now Ze'bah and Zal-mun'na *were* in Kar'kor, and their hosts with **8:10**
them, about fifteen thousand *men,* all that were left of all the hosts of the Ps 83:9
children of the east: for there fell an hundred and twenty thousand men Isa 9:4
that drew sword.
11 ¶And Gideon went up by the way of them that dwelt in tents on the
east of No'bah and Jog'be-hah, and smote the host: for the host was secure.
12 And when Ze'bah and Zal-mun'na fled, he pursued after them, and
took the two kings of Mid'i-an, Ze'bah and Zal-mun'na, and discomfited all
the host.

g. Gideon's Revenge on Succoth and Penuel

13 ¶And Gideon the son of Jo'ash returned from battle before the sun *was*
up,
14 And caught a young man of the men of Suc'coth, and inquired of him:
and he described unto him the princes of Suc'coth, and the elders thereof,
even threescore and seventeen men.
15 And he came unto the men of Suc'coth, and said, Behold Ze'bah and **8:15**
Zal-mun'na, with whom ye did upbraid me, saying, *Are* the hands of Ze'bah Judg 8:7
and Zal-mun'na now in thine hand, that we should give bread unto thy men
that are weary?
16 And he took the elders of the city, and thorns of the wilderness and ☆**8:16**
briers, and with them he taught the men of Suc'coth.
17 And he beat down the tower of Pe-nu'el, and slew the men of the city. ☆**8:17** Judg 8:8

h. The Slaying of Zebah and Zalmunna

18 ¶Then said he unto Ze'bah and Zal-mun'na, What manner of men *were*
they whom ye slew at Ta'bor? And they answered, As thou *art,* so *were*
they; each one resembled the children of a king.
19 And he said, They *were* my brethren, *even* the sons of my mother: *as* the
LORD liveth, if ye had saved them alive, I would not slay you.
20 And he said unto Je'ther his firstborn, Up, *and* slay them. But the youth ☆**8:20**
drew not his sword: for he feared, because he *was* yet a youth.
21 Then Ze'bah and Zal-mun'na said, Rise thou, and fall upon us: for as
the man *is, so is* his strength. And Gideon arose, and slew Ze'bah and Zal-
mun'na, and took away the ornaments that *were* on their camels' necks.

7. Gideon Spurns the Offer of the Kingship

22 ¶Then the men of Israel said unto Gideon, Rule thou over us, both ☆**8:22**
thou, and thy son, and thy son's son also: for thou hast delivered us from
the hand of Mid'i-an.
23 And Gideon said unto them, I will not rule over you, neither shall my
son rule over you: the LORD shall rule over you.

8:16, 17 Gideon returned to pay off his debt to Succoth and Penuel for refusing him help when he was pursuing the kings of Midian. He had captured Zebah and Zalmunna, so the men of Succoth and Penuel had no excuse left. He disciplined the men of Succoth with thorns and briars and tore down the tower of Penuel.

8:20 Jether, Gideon's firstborn, was told by his father to slay the two kings, but his youth and a sense of fear caused him to decline what was obviously a honor and what was also an indignity to the kings—i.e. to be slain by a youth. So Gideon slew them himself.

8:22 Since Israel still lived under a theocracy, they should never have proposed to make Gideon ruler over them. We do not know whether it was modesty or a spiritual sense of discernment which kept him from doing so. Either way his decision was wise.

24¶And Gideon said unto them, I would desire a request of you, that ye would give me every man the earrings of his prey. (For they had golden earrings, because they *were* Ish'ma-el-ites.)

25And they answered, We will willingly give *them.* And they spread a garment, and did cast therein every man the earrings of his prey.

26And the weight of the golden earrings that he requested was a thousand and seven hundred *shekels* of gold; beside ornaments, and collars, and purple raiment that *was* on the kings of Mid'i-an, and beside the chains that *were* about their camels' necks.

8:27☆ Ex 28:5, 6 Judg 17:4, 5

27And Gideon made an ephod thereof, and put it in his city, *even* in Oph'rah: and all Israel went thither a whoring after it: which thing became a snare unto Gideon, and to his house.

28¶Thus was Mid'i-an subdued before the children of Israel, so that they lifted up their heads no more. And the country was in quietness forty years in the days of Gideon.

8. Gideon's Death and Israel's Idolatry

29¶And Je-rub'ba-al the son of Jo'ash went and dwelt in his own house.

8:30 Judg 9:2, 5

30And Gideon had threescore and ten sons of his body begotten: for he had many wives.

8:31 Judg 9:1, 2

31And his concubine that *was* in She'chem, she also bare him a son, whose name he called A-bim'e-lech.

32¶And Gideon the son of Jo'ash died in a good old age, and was buried in the sepulchre of Jo'ash his father, in Oph'rah of the A'bi-ez'rites.

8:33☆ Judg 2:11

33And it came to pass, as soon as Gideon was dead, that the children of Israel turned again, and went a whoring after Ba'al-im, and made Ba'al-be'rith their god.

8:34 Deut 4:9 Judg 3:7

34And the children of Israel remembered not the LORD their God, who had delivered them out of the hands of all their enemies on every side:

35Neither shewed they kindness to the house of Je-rub'ba-al, *namely,* Gideon, according to all the goodness which he had shewed unto Israel.

F. ABIMELECH'S (SON OF GIDEON) JUDGESHIP

1. Abimelech Becomes King and Slays Seventy of His Brothers

9:1☆

9 AND A-bim'e-lech the son of Je-rub'ba-al went to She'chem unto his mother's brethren, and communed with them, and with all the family of the house of his mother's father, saying,

2Speak, I pray you, in the ears of all the men of She'chem, Whether *is* better for you, either that all the sons of Je-rub'ba-al, *which* are threescore and ten persons, reign over you, or that one reign over you? remember also that I *am* your bone and your flesh.

3And his mother's brethren spake of him in the ears of all the men of She'chem all these words: and their hearts inclined to follow A-bim'e-lech; for they said, He *is* our brother.

9:4 Judg 8:33; 9:46

4And they gave him threescore and ten *pieces* of silver out of the house of Ba'al-be'rith, wherewith A-bim'e-lech hired vain and light persons, which followed him.

8:27 *ephod* usually referred to the priestly garment of white linen worn upon the chest. Here, though, it seems to refer to some kind of image or idol set up in the city. It became an object of idolatrous worship.
8:33 *Baal-berith,* or, "Baal (Lord) of the Covenant." Baal-berith was the god worshipped by the Canaanites at Shechem and elsewhere. In 9:46 he is called Berith, "God of the Covenant." Archeologists have found the ruins of a temple to this god.
9:1 Abimelech was Gideon's son by a concubine. Whereas his father refused to start a monarchy, his son had no qualms about seeking kingly status. He slew his seventy brothers, except for Jotham, who escaped. Then he was made king (9:6).

[5]And he went unto his father's house at Oph'rah, and slew his brethren
the sons of Je-rub'ba-al, *being* threescore and ten persons, upon one stone:
notwithstanding yet Jo'tham the youngest son of Je-rub'ba-al was left; for
he hid himself.

9:5 Judg 6:11; 8:32

[6]And all the men of She'chem gathered together, and all the house of
Mil'lo, and went, and made A-bim'e-lech king, by the plain of the pillar
that *was* in She'chem.

☆**9:6** Josh 24:26

2. Jotham's Illustration of the Thorn Bush

[7]¶And when they told *it* to Jo'tham, he went and stood in the top of
mount Ger'i-zim, and lifted up his voice, and cried, and said unto them,
Hearken unto me, ye men of She'chem, that God may hearken unto you.
[8]The trees went forth *on a time* to anoint a king over them; and they said
unto the olive tree, Reign thou over us.
[9]But the olive tree said unto them, Should I leave my fatness, wherewith
by me they honour God and man, and go to be promoted over the trees?
[10]And the trees said to the fig tree, Come thou, *and* reign over us.
[11]But the fig tree said unto them, Should I forsake my sweetness, and my
good fruit, and go to be promoted over the trees?
[12]Then said the trees unto the vine, Come thou, *and* reign over us.
[13]And the vine said unto them, Should I leave my wine, which cheereth
God and man, and go to be promoted over the trees?
[14]Then said all the trees unto the bramble, Come thou, *and* reign over us.
[15]And the bramble said unto the trees, If in truth ye anoint me king over
you, *then* come *and* put your trust in my shadow: and if not, let fire come
out of the bramble, and devour the cedars of Lebanon.

9:7 Deut 11:29 27:12 Jn 4:20

9:8 2 Kgs 14:9 Ezek 17:3 Dan 4:10

3. The Application of the Illustration

[16]Now therefore, if ye have done truly and sincerely, in that ye have made
A-bim'e-lech king, and if ye have dealt well with Je-rub'ba-al and his house,
and have done unto him according to the deserving of his hands;
[17](For my father fought for you, and adventured his life far, and
delivered you out of the hand of Mid'i-an:
[18]And ye are risen up against my father's house this day, and have slain
his sons, threescore and ten persons, upon one stone, and have made
A-bim'e-lech, the son of his maidservant, king over the men of She'chem,
because he *is* your brother;)
[19]If ye then have dealt truly and sincerely with Je-rub'ba-al and with his
house this day, *then rejoice ye in A*-bim'e-lech, and let him also rejoice in
you:
[20]But if not, let fire come out from A-bim'e-lech, and devour the men of
She'chem, and the house of Mil'lo; and let fire come out from the men of
She'chem, and from the house of Mil'lo, and devour A-bim'e-lech.
[21]And Jo'tham ran away, and fled, and went to Beer, and dwelt there, for
fear of A-bim'e-lech his brother.

9:18 Judg 9:5

4. The Revolt of the Shechemites

[22]¶When A-bim'e-lech had reigned three years over Israel,
[23]Then God sent an evil spirit between A-bim'e-lech and the men of
She'chem; and the men of She'chem dealt treacherously with A-bim'e-lech:

9:22 1 Sam 16:14

9:6 Gideon's son Abimelech was made king after he had mercilessly murdered all his half-brothers except for Jotham, who had escaped. In naming Abimelech king, the Israelites did not consult God or any of his representatives. Thus the action was doomed to failure and tragedy. In 9:53, 54 we read that a woman dropped a millstone on Abimelech's head, fracturing his skull. Then, upon Abimelech's insistence, his armor-bearer finished the job.

9:24 Num 35:33 Deut 27:25

24That the cruelty *done* to the threescore and ten sons of Je-rub′ba-al might come, and their blood be laid upon A-bim′e-lech their brother, which slew them; and upon the men of She′chem, which aided him in the killing of his brethren.

25And the men of She′chem set liers in wait for him in the top of the mountains, and they robbed all that came along that way by them: and it was told A-bim′e-lech.

5. The Revolt of Gaal

26And Ga′al the son of E′bed came with his brethren, and went over to She′chem: and the men of She′chem put their confidence in him.

9:27 Judg 8:33

27And they went out into the fields, and gathered their vineyards, and trode *the grapes,* and made merry, and went into the house of their god, and did eat and drink, and cursed A-bim′e-lech.

28And Ga′al the son of E′bed said, Who *is* A-bim′e-lech, and who *is* She′chem, that we should serve him? *is* not *he* the son of Je-rub′ba-al? and Ze′bul his officer? serve the men of Ha′mor the father of She′chem: for why should we serve him?

29And would to God this people were under my hand! then would I remove A-bim′e-lech. And he said to A-bim′e-lech, Increase thine army, and come out.

6. Abimelech Drives Gaal Out of Shechem and Destroys It

30¶And when Ze′bul the ruler of the city heard the words of Ga′al the son of E′bed, his anger was kindled.

31And he sent messengers unto A-bim′e-lech privily, saying, Behold, Ga′al the son of E′bed and his brethren be come to She′chem; and, behold, they fortify the city against thee.

32Now therefore up by night, thou and the people that *is* with thee, and lie in wait in the field:

9:33 1 Sam 10:7

33And it shall be, *that* in the morning, as soon as the sun is up, thou shalt rise early, and set upon the city: and, behold, *when* he and the people that *is* with him come out against thee, then mayest thou do to them as thou shalt find occasion.

9:34☆

34¶And A-bim′e-lech rose up, and all the people that *were* with him, by night, and they laid wait against She′chem in four companies.

35And Ga′al the son of E′bed went out, and stood in the entering of the gate of the city: and A-bim′e-lech rose up, and the people that *were* with him, from lying in wait.

36And when Ga′al saw the people, he said to Ze′bul, Behold, there come people down from the top of the mountains. And Ze′bul said unto him, Thou seest the shadow of the mountains as *if they were* men.

37And Ga′al spake again and said, See there come people down by the middle of the land, and another company come along by the plain of Me-on′e-nim.

38Then said Ze′bul unto him, Where *is* now thy mouth, wherewith thou saidst, Who *is* A-bim′e-lech, that we should serve him? *is* not this the people that thou hast despised? go out, I pray now, and fight with them.

39And Ga′al went out before the men of She′chem, and fought with A-bim′e-lech.

9:34 Abimelech came down on Shechem to do battle with Gaal. Zebul taunted him and challenged him to go out and fight with Abimelech. He did so and was defeated; therefore, he and his kinsmen could no longer live in Shechem.

40And A-bim'e-lech chased him, and he fled before him, and many were
overthrown *and* wounded, *even* unto the entering of the gate.
41And A-bim'e-lech dwelt at A-ru'mah: and Ze'bul thrust out Ga'al and
his brethren, that they should not dwell in She'chem.
42And it came to pass on the morrow, that the people went out into the ☆9:42
field; and they told A-bim'e-lech.
43And he took the people, and divided them into three companies, and
laid wait in the field, and looked, and, behold, the people *were* come forth
out of the city; and he rose up against them, and smote them.
44And A-bim'e-lech, and the company that *was* with him, rushed
forward, and stood in the entering of the gate of the city: and the two *other*
companies ran upon all *the people* that *were* in the fields, and slew them.
45And A-bim'e-lech fought against the city all that day; and he took the
city, and slew the people that *was* therein, and beat down the city, and
sowed it with salt.
46¶And when all the men of the tower of She'chem heard *that,* they 9:46 Judg 8:33
entered into an hold of the house of the god Be'rith.
47And it was told A-bim'e-lech, that all the men of the tower of She'chem 9:47 Ps 68:14
were gathered together.
48And A-bim'e-lech gat him up to mount Zal'mon, he and all the people
that *were* with him; and A-bim'e-lech took an axe in his hand, and cut
down a bough from the trees, and took it, and laid *it* on his shoulder, and
said unto the people that *were* with him, What ye have seen me do, make
haste, *and* do as I *have done.*
49And all the people likewise cut down every man his bough, and
followed A-bim'e-lech, and put *them* to the hold, and set the hold on fire
upon them; so that all the men of the tower of She'chem died also, about a
thousand men and women.

7. The Death of Abimelech

50¶Then went A-bim'e-lech to The'bez, and encamped against The'bez, ☆9:50
and took it.
51But there was a strong tower within the city, and thither fled all the men
and women, and all they of the city, and shut *it* to them, and gat them up
to the top of the tower.
52And A-bim'e-lech came unto the tower, and fought against it, and went
hard unto the door of the tower to burn it with fire.
53And a certain woman cast a piece of a millstone upon A-bim'e-lech's 9:53 2 Sam 11:19–21
head, and all to brake his skull.
54Then he called hastily unto the young man his armourbearer, and said
unto him, Draw thy sword, and slay me, that men say not of me, A woman
slew him. And his young man thrust him through, and he died.
55And when the men of Israel saw that A-bim'e-lech was dead, they
departed every man unto his place.
56¶Thus God rendered the wickedness of A-bim'e-lech, which he did unto
his father, in slaying his seventy brethren:

9:42 Little did Zebul know that what he had done would lead to the razing of Shechem. Abimelech, following the defeat of Gaal, came to Shechem, slew the inhabitants, razed the city and sowed it with salt. Then he burned the Tower of Shechem and slew all the people, a thousand or so in number. The people of Shechem, who had made Abimelech ruler over the territory, had now paid their transgressions.

9:50ff Abimelech had gone to Thebez to take it by force. Unknown to him, his date with destiny had come. A woman threw an upper millstone over the wall of the city and it struck Abimelech, who then was finished off by his armor-bearer. Abimelech did not want it said that he was slain by a woman. Verse 56 sums up the matter: "Thus God repaid the wickedness of Abimelech, which he had done to his father, in killing his seventy brothers" (NASB). "The Lord is known by the judgments which he executes, when the wicked is snared in the work of his own hands. Though wickedness may prosper awhile, it will not prosper always."*

57 And all the evil of the men of She'chem did God render upon their
heads: and upon them came the curse of Jo'tham the son of Je-rub'ba-al.

G. THE JUDGESHIPS OF TOLA AND JAIR

10:1–3☆ 10 AND after A-bim'e-lech there arose to defend Israel To'la the son
of Pu'ah, the son of Dodo, a man of Is'sa-char; and he dwelt in
Sha'mir in mount E'phra-im.
2 And he judged Israel twenty and three years, and died, and was buried
in Sha'mir.
3 ¶And after him arose Ja'ir, a Gileadite, and judged Israel twenty and
two years.
10:4 Num 32:41 4 And he had thirty sons that rode on thirty ass colts, and they had thirty
cities, which are called Ha'voth–ja'ir unto this day, which *are* in the land of
Gilead.
5 And Ja'ir died, and was buried in Ca'mon.

H. JUDGE JEPHTHAH; DELIVERANCE FROM AMMON

1. Israel Apostatizes Again

10:6☆ Judg 4:1; 6:1 10:16; 13:1 2 Kgs 17:7 2 Chron 7:21, 22 6 ¶And the children of Israel did evil again in the sight of the LORD, and
served Ba'al-im, and Ash'ta-roth, and the gods of Syria, and the gods of
Zi'don, and the gods of Moab, and the gods of the children of Ammon, and
the gods of the Philistines, and forsook the LORD, and served not him.
10:7 Judg 4:2 1 Sam 12:9 7 And the anger of the LORD was hot against Israel, and he sold them into
the hands of the Philistines, and into the hands of the children of Ammon.
8 And that year they vexed and oppressed the children of Israel: eighteen
years, all the children of Israel that *were* on the other side Jordan in the
land of the Am'or-ites, which *is* in Gilead.
9 Moreover the children of Ammon passed over Jordan to fight also
against Judah, and against Benjamin, and against the house of E'phra-im;
so that Israel was sore distressed.

2. Israel Pleads to God for Help

10:10 Judg 3:9 Ps 106:43 10 ¶And the children of Israel cried unto the LORD, saying, We have
sinned against thee, both because we have forsaken our God, and also
served Ba'al-im.
10:11 Judg 2:1–3 1 Kgs 9:9 11 And the LORD said unto the children of Israel, *Did* not *I deliver you*
from the Egyptians, and from the Am'or-ites, from the children of Ammon,
and from the Philistines?
12 The Zi-do'ni-ans also, and the Am'a-lek-ites, and the Ma'on-ites, did
oppress you; and ye cried to me, and I delivered you out of their hand.
13 Yet ye have forsaken me, and served other gods: wherefore I will
deliver you no more.
10:14☆ Deut 32:37 14 Go and cry unto the gods which ye have chosen; let them deliver you in
the time of your tribulation.

10:1–3 "Quiet and peaceable reigns, though the best to live in, are the worst to write of, as yielding least variety of matter for the historian to entertain his reader with; such were the reigns of these two judges, Tola and Jair, who make but a small figure and take up but small room in this history."*

10:6 Once again Israel apostasizes. This time they serve a number of gods from Syria, Sidon, Moab, the Ammonites, and the Philistines. It appears that they did not even give the true God any attention. Those Israelites on the east bank of Jordan were especially oppressed. Then the oppression spread, as the tribes on the west bank began to feel the weight of their enemies. Ironically, Israel found that worshipping other gods did not improve their condition; it only made it worse.

10:14 The Israelites had turned from God to other gods. Now they found themselves in great distress, so they turned toward the true God. But God rebuked them by suggesting that if the gods they were serving

15 ¶And the children of Israel said unto the LORD, We have sinned: do
thou unto us whatsoever seemeth good unto thee; deliver us only, we pray
thee, this day.

10:15
2 Sam 12:13

16 And they put away the strange gods from among them, and served the
LORD: and his soul was grieved for the misery of Israel.

☆**10:16**
Deut 32:43
Josh 24:23
2 Chron 7:14
15:8, 33:15
Jer 18:7, 8

17 Then the children of Ammon were gathered together, and encamped in
Gilead. And the children of Israel assembled themselves together, and
encamped in Miz'peh.
18 And the people *and* princes of Gilead said one to another, What man *is*
he that will begin to fight against the children of Ammon? he shall be head
over all the inhabitants of Gilead.

3. Jephthah, a Son of a Harlot

11 NOW Jeph'thah the Gileadite was a mighty man of valour, and he
was the son of an harlot: and Gilead begat Jeph'thah.

☆**11:1**
1 Sam 12:11
20:30
Heb 11:32

2 And Gilead's wife bare him sons; and his wife's sons grew up, and they
thrust out Jeph'thah, and said unto him, Thou shalt not inherit in our
father's house; for thou *art* the son of a strange woman.

4. Israel Asks Jephthah for His Help

3 Then Jeph'thah fled from his brethren, and dwelt in the land of Tob:
and there were gathered vain men to Jeph'thah, and went out with him.

11:3
Judg 9:4; 12:4
1 Sam 22:2
30:22
2 Sam 10:6, 8

4 ¶And it came to pass in process of time, that the children of Ammon
made war against Israel.

11:4
Judg 10:9

5 And it was so, that when the children of Ammon made war against
Israel, the elders of Gilead went to fetch Jeph'thah out of the land of Tob:
6 And they said unto Jeph'thah, Come, and be our captain, that we may
fight with the children of Ammon.
7 And Jeph'thah said unto the elders of Gilead, Did not ye hate me, and
expel me out of my father's house? and why are ye come unto me now when
ye are in distress?
8 And the elders of Gilead said unto Jeph'thah, Therefore we turn again
to thee now, that thou mayest go with us, and fight against the children of
Ammon, and be our head over all the inhabitants of Gilead.
9 And Jeph'thah said unto the elders of Gilead, If ye bring me home again
to fight against the children of Ammon, and the LORD deliver them before
me, shall I be your head?

☆**11:9**

10 And the elders of Gilead said unto Jeph'thah, The LORD be witness
between us, if we do not so according to thy words.

11:10
Gen 21:23
31:51–53

---

were as great as they thought them to be, then those gods should deliver them from their distress. God would have men learn by experience that other gods are limited and incapable of delivering their anguished worshippers. Genuine repentance always means that "there be a full conviction of the utter insufficiency of those things to help us and do us any kindness which we have idolized and set upon the throne of our hearts in competition with God."*

10:16 Israel now begins to repent and turn to the true God. God responds to their repentance and "his soul was grieved for the misery of Israel." Once again deliverance begins to take place.

11:1 God used strange instruments to accomplish his purposes. Jephthah was a son of a harlot, not of a wife or even a concubine. He was thrust out of his father's house, suffering indignity for something he had no control over. He became a mighty warrior and led a band of rabble in raids. When the Gileadites were attacked by the Ammonites, they appealed to Jephthah for help.

11:9 Jephthah, despite his background, is a worshipper of God. He speaks about victory over the Ammonites and demands that if "the LORD deliver them before me" are you willing for me to be your head? In verse 11 Jephthah "uttered all his words before the LORD in Mizpeh." By this we learn that he wanted the presence and power of God exercised on his behalf when he led the armies of the Israelites against their enemies.

5. The Ammonites Demand East Canaan

11:11 Judg 9:14, 15
[11]Then Jeph'thah went with the elders of Gilead, and the people made
him head and captain over them: and Jeph'thah uttered all his words before
the LORD in Miz'peh.
[12]¶And Jeph'thah sent messengers unto the king of the children of
Ammon, saying, What hast thou to do with me, that thou art come against
me to fight in my land?
11:13 Josh 13:10
[13]And the king of the children of Ammon answered unto the messengers
of Jeph'thah, Because Israel took away my land, when they came up out of
Egypt, from Arnon even unto Jabbok, and unto Jordan: now therefore
restore those *lands* again peaceably.
11:14☆
[14]And Jeph'thah sent messengers again unto the king of the children of
Ammon:
[15]And said unto him, Thus saith Jeph'thah, Israel took not away the land
of Moab, nor the land of the children of Ammon:
11:16 Num 20:1–22
[16]But when Israel came up from Egypt, and walked through the
wilderness unto the Red sea, and came to Ka'desh;
11:17 Josh 24:9
[17]Then Israel sent messengers unto the king of Edom, saying, Let me, I
pray thee, pass through thy land: but the king of Edom would not hearken
thereto. And in like manner they sent unto the king of Moab: but he would
not *consent:* and Israel abode in Ka'desh.
11:18 Num 21:4 Deut 2:8, 9, 18, 19
[18]Then they went along through the wilderness, and compassed the land
of Edom, and the land of Moab, and came by the east side of the land of
Moab, and pitched on the other side of Arnon, but came not within the
border of Moab: for Arnon *was* the border of Moab.
11:19 Num 21:21–32
[19]And Israel sent messengers unto Sihon king of the Am'or-ites, the king
of Hesh'bon; and Israel said unto him, Let us pass, we pray thee, through
thy land into my place.
[20]But Sihon trusted not Israel to pass through his coast: but Sihon
gathered all his people together, and pitched in Ja'haz, and fought against
Israel.
11:21 Deut 2:19, 37 3:3
[21]And the LORD God of Israel delivered Sihon and all his people into the
hand of Israel, and they smote them: so Israel possessed all the land of the
Am'or-ites, the inhabitants of that country.
[22]And they possessed all the coasts of the Am'or-ites, from Arnon even
unto Jabbok, and from the wilderness even unto Jordan.
[23]So now the LORD God of Israel hath dispossessed the Am'or-ites from
before his people Israel, and shouldest thou possess it?
11:24 Num 21:27–30 1 Kgs 11:7
[24]Wilt not thou possess that which Che'mosh thy god giveth thee to
possess? So whomsoever the LORD our God shall drive out from before us,
them will we possess.
[25]And now *art* thou any thing better than Balak the son of Zippor, king
of Moab? did he ever strive against Israel, or did he ever fight against them,
11:26☆
[26]While Israel dwelt in Hesh'bon and her towns, and in Ar'o-er and her
towns, and in all the cities that *be* along by the coasts of Arnon, three
hundred years? why therefore did ye not recover *them* within that time?

11:14ff Jephthah first tried to settle the matter peacefully. He indicated that the Ammonite claims to some of Israel's territory was based on a false premise. Israel took the land from the Amorites, not the Ammonites, and therefore the Ammonites had no cause for complaint. He attributed the success of Israel in taking the land from the Amorites to God (11:23). His conclusion (in 11:24) is that "whatever our God has driven out before us, we will possess it" (NASB).

11:26 *three hundred years.* This is probably a round figure; it may be that some of the judges ruled concurrently. If regarded seriously, this figure establishes that the Exodus took place during the fifteenth century B.C. (this fact is accepted by many evangelicals). This runs contrary to the belief of rationalist scholars that it occured during the thirteenth century B.C.

27 Wherefore I have not sinned against thee, but thou doest me wrong to
war against me: the LORD the Judge be judge this day between the children
of Israel and the children of Ammon.
28 Howbeit the king of the children of Ammon hearkened not unto the
words of Jeph'thah which he sent him.

6. Jephthah Defeats the Ammonites and Fulfills His Vow

29 ¶Then the Spirit of the LORD came upon Jeph'thah, and he passed over ☆**11:29**
Gilead, and Ma-nas'seh, and passed over Miz'peh of Gilead, and from Judg 3:10; 6:34
Miz'peh of Gilead he passed over *unto* the children of Ammon. 13:25
30 And Jeph'thah vowed a vow unto the LORD, and said, If thou shalt ☆**11:30, 31**
without fail deliver the children of Ammon into mine hands,
31 Then it shall be, that whatsoever cometh forth of the doors of my house
to meet me, when I return in peace from the children of Ammon, shall
surely be the LORD'S, and I will offer it up for a burnt offering.
32 ¶So Jeph'thah passed over unto the children of Ammon to fight against ☆**11:32**
them; and the LORD delivered them into his hands.
33 And he smote them from Ar'o-er, even till thou come to Min'nith, *even*
twenty cities, and unto the plain of the vineyards, with a very great
slaughter. Thus the children of Ammon were subdued before the children
of Israel.
34 ¶And Jeph'thah came to Miz'peh unto his house, and, behold, his **11:34**
daughter came out to meet him with timbrels and with dances: and she *was* Ex 15:20; 1 Sam 18:6
his only child; beside her he had neither son nor daughter. Jer 31:4
35 And it came to pass, when he saw her, that he rent his clothes, and said, **11:35**
Alas, my daughter! thou hast brought me very low, and thou art one of Num 30:1, 2; Eccles 5:4, 5
them that trouble me: for I have opened my mouth unto the LORD, and I
cannot go back.
36 And she said unto him, My father, *if* thou hast opened thy mouth unto
the LORD, do to me according to that which hath proceeded out of thy
mouth; forasmuch as the LORD hath taken vengeance for thee of thine
enemies, *even* of the children of Ammon.
37 And she said unto her father, Let this thing be done for me: let me
alone two months, that I may go up and down upon the mountains, and
bewail my virginity, I and my fellows.
38 And he said, Go. And he sent her away *for* two months: and she went
with her companions, and bewailed her virginity upon the mountains.
39 And it came to pass at the end of two months, that she returned unto
her father, who did with her *according* to his vow which he had vowed: and
she knew no man. And it was a custom in Israel,
40 *That* the daughters of Israel went yearly to lament the daughter of ☆**11:40**
Jeph'thah the Gileadite four days in a year.

11:29 *Jephthah* was the son of a harlot (11:1), yet God was pleased to deliver Israel through him. Jephthah was one of the many men upon whom the Spirit of God descended, endowing him with the gifts and power needed to deliver Israel. The Spirit who sovereignly came upon certain people in the Old Testament is the same Spirit who presently fills all believers who seek his infilling.

11:30, 31 Jephthah vowed to offer up a sacrifice if God gave him victory over the Ammonites. Scholars differ as to whether Jephthah offered a human sacrifice. The Hebrew term used here, *'olah,* means "whole burnt offering," which required the death of the object offered. He may well have killed his daughter, but the Scriptures do not imply that he was right in making such a vow or in executing it. His background may account for his lack of understanding (cf 11:1–3).

11:32 *the LORD delivered them into his hands.* The Ammonites seek by war what was not theirs, and lost. God makes "those feel the force of war that would not yield to the force of reason."*

11:40 The annual four-day period of lamentation became a custom in Israel (11:39), but it is never mentioned again in the Scriptures. Evidently, it was observed only in Gilead and never became part of the whole community's customs.

7. Jephthah's Dispute with Ephraim: Shibboleth or Sibboleth

12:1☆ Judg 8:1 12 AND the men of E′phra-im gathered themselves together, and went northward, and said unto Jeph′thah, Wherefore passedst thou over to fight against the children of Ammon, and didst not call us to go with thee? we will burn thine house upon thee with fire.

2 And Jeph′thah said unto them, I and my people were at great strife with the children of Ammon; and when I called you, ye delivered me not out of their hands.

12:3 1 Sam 19:5 Job 13:14 3 And when I saw that ye delivered *me* not, I put my life in my hands, and passed over against the children of Ammon, and the LORD delivered them into my hand: wherefore then are ye come up unto me this day, to fight against me?

12:4 Judg 11:3 1 Sam 22:2 4 Then Jeph′thah gathered together all the men of Gilead, and fought with E′phra-im: and the men of Gilead smote E′phra-im, because they said, Ye Gileadites *are* fugitives of E′phra-im among the E′phra-im-ites, *and* among the Ma-nas′sites.

12:5–7☆ Josh 2:7 Judg 3:28; 7:24 5 And the Gileadites took the passages of Jordan before the E′phra-im-ites: and it was *so,* that when those E′phra-im-ites which were escaped said, Let me go over; that the men of Gilead said unto him, *Art* thou an E′phra-im-ite? If he said, Nay;

6 Then said they unto him, Say now Shib′bo-leth: and he said Sib′bo-leth: for he could not frame to pronounce *it* right. Then they took him, and slew him at the passages of Jordan: and there fell at that time of the E′phra-im-ites forty and two thousand.

7 And Jeph′thah judged Israel six years. Then died Jeph′thah the Gileadite, and was buried in *one of* the cities of Gilead.

I. THE JUDGESHIPS OF IBZAN, ELON, AND ABDON

12:8–15☆ 8 ¶And after him Ib′zan of Beth–lehem judged Israel.

9 And he had thirty sons, and thirty daughters, *whom* he sent abroad, and took in thirty daughters from abroad for his sons. And he judged Israel seven years.

10 Then died Ib′zan, and was buried at Beth–lehem.

11 ¶And after him E′lon, a Zeb′u-lon-ite, judged Israel; and he judged Israel ten years.

12 And E′lon the Zeb′u-lon-ite died, and was buried in Ai′ja-lon in the country of Zeb′u-lun.

13 ¶And after him Abdon the son of Hil′lel, a Pir′a-thon-ite, judged Israel.

14 And he had forty sons and thirty nephews, that rode on threescore and ten ass colts: and he judged Israel eight years.

15 And Abdon the son of Hil′lel the Pir′a-thon-ite died, and was buried in Pir′a-thon in the land of E′phra-im, in the mount of the Am′a-lek-ites.

12:1 The Ephraimites complained that they should have been told of the upcoming war, for they would have joined forces with Jephthah. They threatened to use force against him because of this.

12:5–7 Jephthah controlled the fords over Jordan River and when the Ephramites sought to cross over, a linguistic test was employed. Although they all spoke the same language, there were regional differences. The Ephraimites said Sibboleth instead of Shibboleth and those who failed the test were slain, a total of 42,000. Jephthah's judgeship lasted only six years, to his death.

12:8–15 The judgeships of Ibzan, Elon, and Abdon are passed over swiftly. They ruled for twenty-five years, a period in which there was peace. The strange fact is that during all of these judgeships no mention is made of Israel's High Priest, or any other priest, or even the Levites. No explanation is given for this absence of Israel's spiritual leaders who were so prominent in the wilderness and in the taking of the land when the Israelites first entered it.

J. JUDGE SAMSON DELIVERS ISRAEL FROM THE PHILISTINES

1. Samson's Early Years

a. The Angel's Promise to Manoah's Wife

13 AND the children of Israel did evil again in the sight of the LORD; ☆13:1 Judg 2:11; 3:8
and the LORD delivered them into the hand of the Philistines forty 4:2, 3; 10:6–8
years.
2 ¶And there was a certain man of Zo'rah, of the family of the Danites, 13:2 Gen 16:7; 17:17
whose name *was* Ma-no'ah; and his wife *was* barren, and bare not. Judg 2:1
3 And the angel of the LORD appeared unto the woman, and said unto 6:11, 12
her, Behold now, thou *art* barren, and bearest not: but thou shalt conceive,
and bear a son.
4 Now therefore beware, I pray thee, and drink not wine nor strong drink, 13:4 Num 6:1–4
and eat not any unclean *thing:* Judg 13:13, 14
5 For, lo, thou shalt conceive, and bear a son; and no razor shall come on ☆13:5 Judg 16:16, 17
his head: for the child shall be a Nazarite unto God from the womb: and he
shall begin to deliver Israel out of the hand of the Philistines.
6 ¶Then the woman came and told her husband, saying, A man of God
came unto me, and his countenance *was* like the countenance of an angel of
God, very terrible: but I asked him not whence he *was,* neither told he me
his name:
7 But he said unto me, Behold, thou shalt conceive, and bear a son; and
now drink no wine nor strong drink, neither eat any unclean *thing:* for the
child shall be a Nazarite to God from the womb to the day of his death.

b. The Appearance of the Angel to Manoah and His Wife

8 ¶Then Ma-no'ah intreated the LORD, and said, O my Lord, let the man ☆13:8
of God which thou didst send come again unto us, and teach us what we
shall do unto the child that shall be born.
9 And God hearkened to the voice of Ma-no'ah; and the angel of God
came again unto the woman as she sat in the field: but Ma-no'ah her
husband *was* not with her.
10 And the woman made haste, and ran, and shewed her husband, and
said unto him, Behold, the man hath appeared unto me, that came unto me
the *other* day.
11 And Ma-no'ah arose, and went after his wife, and came to the man, and
said unto him, *Art* thou the man that spakest unto the woman? And he said,
I *am.*
12 And Ma-no'ah said, Now let thy words come to pass. How shall we
order the child, and *how* shall we do unto him?
13 And the angel of the LORD said unto Ma-no'ah, Of all that I said unto 13:13 Judg 13:4
the woman let her beware.
14 She may not eat of any *thing* that cometh of the vine, neither let her

---

13:1 According to Deut. 2:23, Amos 9:7, and Jer. 47:4, the Philistines came from Caphtor, the island of Crete. They settled along the coast of Canaan and lodged in the foothills of the territory assigned to Dan and Judah. Samson's deliverance of Israel from the Philistines was not permanent, for the Philistines plagued Israel until David's time. (See note on 14:4 for Israel's deliverance under Samson.)

13:5 A Nazarite was a man or a woman consecrated to God by a special vow. Samson and John the Baptist were Nazarites from their mothers' wombs, i.e., committed to God before they were born (13:5; Luke 1:15). Nazarites (1) used neither wine nor strong drink (Num. 6:3; Luke 1:15); (2) avoided contact with the dead (Num. 6:6, 7); (3) did not shave their heads (Num. 6:5; Judg. 13:5; 16:17); and (4) had no contact with grapes or any product of the vine (Num 6:3, 4; Judg. 13:14). The prohibitions continued as long as the vow was in effect. When the vow was ended, the Nazarite was brought to the door of the tabernacle, his head was shaved, sacrifices were offered, and the left shoulder of a ram was presented by the priest as a wave-offering (Num. 6:13–20; Acts 18:18; Lev. 7:32).

13:8 Manoah believed what his wife told him. Having confidence that they would have a son, he prayed and humbly asked that the angel might appear to him also, to instruct him as to what they should do with the boy. God heard and answered that prayer (13:9–14).

drink wine or strong drink, nor eat any unclean *thing:* all that I commanded her let her observe.

13:15 Gen 18:3, 4 Judg 6:18

15 ¶And Ma-no'ah said unto the angel of the LORD, I pray thee, let us detain thee, until we shall have made ready a kid for thee.

16 And the angel of the LORD said unto Ma-no'ah, Though thou detain me, I will not eat of thy bread: and if thou wilt offer a burnt offering, thou must offer it unto the LORD. For Ma-no'ah knew not that he *was* an angel of the LORD.

13:17 Gen 32:29

17 And Ma-no'ah said unto the angel of the LORD, What *is* thy name, that when thy sayings come to pass we may do thee honour?

13:18☆

18 And the angel of the LORD said unto him, Why askest thou thus after my name, seeing it *is* secret?

13:19 Judg 6:19

19 So Ma-no'ah took a kid with a meat offering, and offered *it* upon a rock unto the LORD: and *the angel* did wondrously; and Ma-no'ah and his wife looked on.

13:20☆

20 For it came to pass, when the flame went up toward heaven from off the altar, that the angel of the LORD ascended in the flame of the altar. And Ma-no'ah and his wife looked on *it,* and fell on their faces to the ground.

21 But the angel of the LORD did no more appear to Ma-no'ah and to his wife. Then Ma-no'ah knew that he *was* an angel of the LORD.

13:22 Gen 32:30 Ex 33:20 Judg 6:22

22 And Ma-no'ah said unto his wife, We shall surely die, because we have seen God.

23 But his wife said unto him, If the LORD were pleased to kill us, he would not have received a burnt offering and a meat offering at our hands, neither would he have shewed us all these *things,* nor would as at this time have told us *such things* as these.

c. The Birth of Samson

13:24☆ Heb 11:32

24 ¶And the woman bare a son, and called his name Samson: and the child grew, and the LORD blessed him.

13:25☆ Judg 3:10; 6:34 14:6 1 Sam 10:6, 10

25 And the Spirit of the LORD began to move him at times in the camp of Dan between Zo'rah and Esh'ta-ol.

2. Samson's Courtship and Marriage

a. Samson Courts the Woman of Timnah

14 AND Samson went down to Tim'nath, and saw a woman in Tim'nath of the daughters of the Philistines.

2 And he came up, and told his father and his mother, and said, I have seen a woman in Tim'nath of the daughters of the Philistines: now therefore get her for me to wife.

14:3 Deut 7:3 Josh 23:12

3 Then his father and his mother said unto him, *Is there* never a woman among the daughters of thy brethren, or among all my people, that thou

---

13:18 *secret,* i.e., "wonderful" or, "beyond knowledge." (See Ps. 139:6.)

13:20 Here God does what he had done many times before. Supernatural acts are performed to confirm to Manoah and his wife (who is not named) the words the angel spoke. From what happened Manoah (13:21) knew that it was an angel. "It was plain it was not the body of a man they saw, since it was not chained to the earth, nor prejudiced by fire; but ascended in flame and therefore with good reason they conclude it was an angel."*

13:24 As a Nazarite, Samson was separated unto God from his mother's womb. But he started off better than he finished. He was a backslider whose carnal nature overtook him. One small sin led to larger and more grievous ones.

13:25 The Spirit of the Lord came on Samson in mighty power. He did exploits for God by that power. "Strong men think themselves greatly animated by wine, but Samson drank no wine, and yet excelled in strength and courage, and every thing that was bold and brave, for he had the Spirit of God moving him; 'therefore, be not drunk with wine, but be filled with the Spirit,' who will come to those that are sober and temperate."*

goest to take a wife of the uncircumcised Philistines? And Samson said unto his father, Get her for me; for she pleaseth me well.
4But his father and his mother knew not that it *was* of the LORD, that he sought an occasion against the Philistines: for at that time the Philistines had dominion over Israel.

☆**14:4** Josh 11:20; 1 Kgs 12:15

b. Samson's Conquest of the Lion

5¶Then went Samson down, and his father and his mother, to Tim'nath, and came to the vineyards of Tim'nath: and, behold, a young lion roared against him.
6And the Spirit of the LORD came mightily upon him, and he rent him as he would have rent a kid, and *he had* nothing in his hand: but he told not his father or his mother what he had done.
7And he went down, and talked with the woman; and she pleased Samson well.
8¶And after a time he returned to take her, and he turned aside to see the carcase of the lion: and, behold, *there was* a swarm of bees and honey in the carcase of the lion.
9And he took thereof in his hands, and went on eating, and came to his father and mother, and he gave them, and they did eat: but he told not them that he had taken the honey out of the carcase of the lion.

☆**14:6** Judg 11:29; 13:25; 15:14; 1 Sam 17:34–36

c. Samson's Riddle at His Premarital Party

10¶So his father went down unto the woman: and Samson made there a feast; for so used the young men to do.
11And it came to pass, when they saw him, that they brought thirty companions to be with him.
12¶And Samson said unto them, I will now put forth a riddle unto you: if ye can certainly declare it me within the seven days of the feast, and find *it* out, then I will give you thirty sheets and thirty change of garments:
13But if ye cannot declare *it* me, then shall ye give me thirty sheets and thirty change of garments. And they said unto him, Put forth thy riddle, that we may hear it.
14And he said unto them, Out of the eater came forth meat, and out of the strong came forth sweetness. And they could not in three days expound the riddle.

14:12 Gen 29:27; Dan 5:12; Ezek 17:2

d. Samson's Wife Betrays His Secret of the Riddle

15And it came to pass on the seventh day, that they said unto Samson's wife, Entice thy husband, that he may declare unto us the riddle, lest we burn thee and thy father's house with fire: have ye called us to take that we have? *is it* not *so?*
16And Samson's wife wept before him, and said, Thou dost but hate me, and lovest me not: thou hast put forth a riddle unto the children of my people, and hast not told *it* me. And he said unto her, Behold, I have not told *it* my father nor my mother, and shall I tell *it* thee?

☆**14:15** Judg 15:6

14:4 Samson married a heathen woman. This was against the will of God. Yet God used his transgression to accomplish the divine purpose of delivering Israel from its bondage to the Philistines. Nevertheless, God's higher purpose in no way excused Samson for his sinful decision to marry the heathen woman, visit the prostitute, or ally himself to Delilah.

14:6 "God let Samson know what he could do in the strength of the Spirit of the Lord, that he might never be afraid to look the greatest difficulties in the face."*

14:15 When the Philistines could not solve Samson's riddle, they forced his wife to secure the answer for them by threatening to burn her and her father's house. It was a brutish thing to say. But it was even worse for them to ask her to betray her husband. She pretended that she was not sure of Samson's love and wept profusely. Samson told her the answer and lost the contest to the Philistines.

[17]And she wept before him the seven days, while their feast lasted: and it
came to pass on the seventh day, that he told her, because she lay sore upon
him: and she told the riddle to the children of her people.
14:18☆ [18]And the men of the city said unto him on the seventh day before the
sun went down, What *is* sweeter than honey? and what *is* stronger than a
lion? And he said unto them, If ye had not plowed with my heifer, ye had
not found out my riddle.
14:19 Judg 14:6; 15:14 [19]¶And the Spirit of the LORD came upon him, and he went down to
Ash'ke-lon, and slew thirty men of them, and took their spoil, and gave
change of garments unto them which expounded the riddle. And his anger
was kindled, and he went up to his father's house.
14:20 Jn 3:29 [20]But Samson's wife was *given* to his companion, whom he had used as
his friend.

3. Samson Loses His Wife, Takes Revenge; the Philistines Kill His Wife and Father-In-Law

15 BUT it came to pass within a while after, in the time of wheat
harvest, that Samson visited his wife with a kid; and he said, I will
go in to my wife into the chamber. But her father would not suffer him to
go in.
[2]And her father said, I verily thought that thou hadst utterly hated her;
therefore I gave her to thy companion: *is* not her younger sister fairer than
she? take her, I pray thee, instead of her.
[3]¶And Samson said concerning them, Now shall I be more blameless
than the Philistines, though I do them a displeasure.
[4]And Samson went and caught three hundred foxes, and took firebrands,
and turned tail to tail, and put a firebrand in the midst between two tails.
15:5☆ [5]And when he had set the brands on fire, he let *them* go into the standing
corn of the Philistines, and burnt up both the shocks, and also the standing
corn, with the vineyards *and* olives.
15:6 Judg 14:15 [6]¶Then the Philistines said, Who hath done this? And they answered,
Samson, the son in law of the Tim'nite, because he had taken his wife, and
given her to his companion. And the Philistines came up, and burnt her and
her father with fire.
[7]¶And Samson said unto them, Though ye have done this, yet will I be
avenged of you, and after that I will cease.
[8]And he smote them hip and thigh with a great slaughter: and he went
down and dwelt in the top of the rock E'tam.

4. Judah Delivers Samson to the Philistines; Samson Slays a Thousand of Them in Revenge

[9]¶Then the Philistines went up, and pitched in Judah, and spread
themselves in Le'hi.
[10]And the men of Judah said, Why are ye come up against us? And they
answered, To bind Samson are we come up, to do to him as he hath done to
us.

14:18 Samson disrespectfully said, "If you had not ploughed with my heifer," and in so doing exhibited his distaste for the infidelity of his bride to whom he had been married for only a few days. What a way to begin a honeymoon!

15:5 Samson avenged himself on the Philistines for their trick and also for the loss of his wife who had been given by her father to another man. Ironically, the Philistines burned Samson's wife and her father. Her people threatened her with this revenge if she did not discover Samson's secret. Now they burn her despite her having complied with their demand. How could she be held responsible for Samson's act? The life of Samson was unique. He was the only judge who operated by himself, without having recourse to servants or soldiers to assist him. He was a loner.

11 Then three thousand men of Judah went to the top of the rock E'tam, **15:11** Judg 13:1; 15:20
and said to Samson, Knowest thou not that the Philistines *are* rulers over
us? what *is* this *that* thou hast done unto us? And he said unto them, As
they did unto me, so have I done unto them.
12 And they said unto him, We are come down to bind thee, that we may ☆**15:12, 13**
deliver thee into the hand of the Philistines. And Samson said unto them,
Swear unto me, that ye will not fall upon me yourselves.
13 And they spake unto him, saying, No; but we will bind thee fast, and
deliver thee into their hand: but surely we will not kill thee. And they
bound him with two new cords, and brought him up from the rock.
14 ¶*And* when he came unto Le'hi, the Philistines shouted against him: **15:14** Judg 14:6, 19
and the Spirit of the LORD came mightily upon him, and the cords that *were*
upon his arms became as flax that was burnt with fire, and his bands loosed
from off his hands.
15 And he found a new jawbone of an ass, and put forth his hand, and ☆**15:15**
took it, and slew a thousand men therewith.
16 And Samson said, With the jawbone of an ass, heaps upon heaps, with
the jaw of an ass have I slain a thousand men.
17 And it came to pass, when he had made an end of speaking, that he cast
away the jawbone out of his hand, and called that place Ra'math–le'hi.
18 ¶And he was sore athirst, and called on the LORD, and said, Thou hast
given this great deliverance into the hand of thy servant: and now shall I
die for thirst, and fall into the hand of the uncircumcised?
19 But God clave an hollow place that *was* in the jaw, and there came **15:19** Gen 45:27
water thereout; and when he had drunk, his spirit came again, and he 1 Sam 30:11
revived: wherefore he called the name thereof En–hak'ko-re, which *is* in
Le'hi unto this day.
20 And he judged Israel in the days of the Philistines twenty years. **15:20** Judg 13:1, 5; 16:31; Heb 11:32

5. Samson and the Harlot at Gaza

16 THEN went Samson to Ga'za, and saw there an harlot, and went in ☆**16:1** Josh 15:47
unto her.
2 *And it was told* the Ga'zites, saying, Samson is come hither. And they
compassed *him* in, and laid wait for him all night in the gate of the city, and
were quiet all the night, saying, In the morning, when it is day, we shall kill
him.
3 And Samson lay till midnight, and arose at midnight, and took the
doors of the gate of the city, and the two posts, and went away with them,
bar and all, and put *them* upon his shoulders, and carried them up to the
top of an hill that *is* before Hebron.

6. Samson and Delilah

a. The Philistines Bribe Delilah to Find the Source of Samson's Strength

4 ¶And it came to pass afterward, that he loved a woman in the valley of ☆**16:4**
So'rek, whose name *was* De-li'lah,

15:12, 13 Samson, instead of resisting the Judeans, tamely allowed them to bind him with ropes, securing from them the promise that they would not hurt him. By being delivered over to the Philistines, he would have an opportunity to slay many of them and thus begin the delivery of Israel from their servitude.

15:15 Samson's strength did not come from his Nazarite vow, his spurning of strong drink or from his hair. It lay in his relationship to God, of which these other things were only symbols. Samson himself acknowledged that God was the author of his power (15:18).

16:1 Here Samson is on the downward path. If it was wrong to marry a pagan, it was worse to fornicate with a prostitute. The sin began with the eyegate, and when lust had its way, he went in to her and broke one of the ten commandments.

16:4 Samson continues his evil pattern of life: now he lives in sin with a woman he has not married. For money, she uncovered the true source of Samson's power and sold her paramour into the hands of the enemy.

5 And the lords of the Philistines came up unto her, and said unto her, Entice him, and see wherein his great strength *lieth,* and by what *means* we may prevail against him, that we may bind him to afflict him: and we will give thee every one of us eleven hundred *pieces* of silver.

6 ¶And De-li'lah said to Samson, Tell me, I pray thee, wherein thy great strength *lieth,* and wherewith thou mightest be bound to afflict thee.

7 And Samson said unto her, If they bind me with seven green withs that were never dried, then shall I be weak, and be as another man.

8 Then the lords of the Philistines brought up to her seven green withs which had not been dried, and she bound him with them.

9 Now *there were* men lying in wait, abiding with her in the chamber. And she said unto him, The Philistines *be* upon thee, Samson. And he brake the withs, as a thread of tow is broken when it toucheth the fire. So his strength was not known.

b. Delilah Tries the Second Time

10 And De-li'lah said unto Samson, Behold, thou hast mocked me, and told me lies: now tell me, I pray thee, wherewith thou mightest be bound.

11 And he said unto her, If they bind me fast with new ropes that never were occupied, then shall I be weak, and be as another man.

12 De-li'lah therefore took new ropes, and bound him therewith, and said unto him, The Philistines *be* upon thee, Samson. And *there were* liers in wait abiding in the chamber. And he brake them from off his arms like a thread.

c. Delilah Tries the Third Time

13 And De-li'lah said unto Samson, Hitherto thou hast mocked me, and told me lies: tell me wherewith thou mightest be bound. And he said unto her, If thou weavest the seven locks of my head with the web.

14 And she fastened *it* with the pin, and said unto him, The Philistines *be* upon thee, Samson. And he awaked out of his sleep, and went away with the pin of the beam, and with the web.

d. Samson Tells Delilah His Secret

16:15 Judg 14:16

15 ¶And she said unto him, How canst thou say, I love thee, when thine heart *is* not with me? thou hast mocked me these three times, and hast not told me wherein thy great strength *lieth.*

16:16 Num 6:5 Judg 13:5

16 And it came to pass, when she pressed him daily with her words, and urged him, *so* that his soul was vexed unto death;

17 That he told her all his heart, and said unto her, There hath not come a razor upon mine head; for I *have been* a Nazarite unto God from my mother's womb: if I be shaven, then my strength will go from me, and I shall become weak, and be like any *other* man.

e. The Philistines Seize Samson and Blind Him

18 And when De-li'lah saw that he had told her all his heart, she sent and called for the lords of the Philistines, saying, Come up this once, for he hath shewed me all his heart. Then the lords of the Philistines came up unto her, and brought money in their hand.

19 And she made him sleep upon her knees; and she called for a man, and she caused him to shave off the seven locks of his head; and she began to afflict him, and his strength went from him.

20And she said, The Philistines *be* upon thee, Samson. And he awoke out ☆16:20 1 Sam 16:14 18:11, 12
of his sleep, and said, I will go out as at other times before, and shake
myself. And he wist not that the LORD was departed from him.
21¶But the Philistines took him, and put out his eyes, and brought him
down to Ga'za, and bound him with fetters of brass; and he did grind in the
prison house.
22Howbeit the hair of his head began to grow again after he was shaven.

f. Samson's Recovery, Revenge, and Death

23Then the lords of the Philistines gathered them together for to offer a 16:23 1 Sam 5:1, 2
great sacrifice unto Da'gon their god, and to rejoice: for they said, Our god
hath delivered Samson our enemy into our hand.
24And when the people saw him, they praised their god: for they said,
Our god hath delivered into our hands our enemy, and the destroyer of our
country, which slew many of us.
25And it came to pass, when their hearts were merry, that they said, Call
for Samson, that he may make us sport. And they called for Samson out of
the prison house; and he made them sport: and they set him between the
pillars.
26And Samson said unto the lad that held him by the hand, Suffer me
that I may feel the pillars whereupon the house standeth, that I may lean
upon them.
27Now the house was full of men and women; and all the lords of the
Philistines *were* there; and *there were* upon the roof about three thousand
men and women, that beheld while Samson made sport.
28And Samson called unto the LORD, and said, O Lord GOD, remember ☆16:28 Judg 15:18
me, I pray thee, and strengthen me, I pray thee, only this once, O God, that
I may be at once avenged of the Philistines for my two eyes.
29And Samson took hold of the two middle pillars upon which the house
stood, and on which it was borne up, of the one with his right hand, and of
the other with his left.
30And Samson said, Let me die with the Philistines. And he bowed
himself with *all his* might; and the house fell upon the lords, and upon all
the people that *were* therein. So the dead which he slew at his death were
more than *they* which he slew in his life.
31Then his brethren and all the house of his father came down, and took
him, and brought *him* up, and buried him between Zo'rah and Esh'ta-ol in
the buryingplace of Ma-no'ah his father. And he judged Israel twenty years.

16:20 Samson was a Spirit-filled Nazarite who performed great deeds of valor. According to 14:6 and 19, "the Spirit of the LORD came upon him." Again in 15:14 the Spirit of God came upon him in mighty power. But the saddest words come from the experience of Samson in this verse. He has disclosed the source of his strength to Delilah. When she wakens him as the Philistines come after him, once more he thinks he still has the power of the Spirit in his life. When he rises to use that power it is gone, and the Scripture says, "he wist not that the LORD was departed from him." The Spirit was gone from him and he did not even know it. He had slept in the lap of his lust and awoke a prisoner of his enemies who blind him. He *did* repent before death, however, and was subsequently numbered among the heroes of the faith (Heb. 11:32) as one who vindicated God before the ungodly heathen. He was justified by his faith, not by any of his carnal acts.

16:28 *remember me . . . strengthen me.* Samson had repented; his hair had grown and his blinded eyes turn again to the God he had sinned against. Now he sought the help of God. He searched for the power he once had, and God graciously heard him. He slew more Philistines in death than he had slain in life. He died in this incident, leaving behind for all ages a reminder of what it means to be without the presence of God in one's life.

III. THE CULTURAL SITUATION DURING THE TIME OF THE JUDGES (17:1—21:25)

A. MICAH: HIS IDOLATRY AND HIS PRIEST

1. Micah and His Idol Shrine

17:1☆ 17 AND there was a man of mount E′phra-im, whose name *was*
Mi′cah.
2 And he said unto his mother, The eleven hundred *shekels* of silver that
were taken from thee, about which thou cursedst, and spakest of also in
mine ears, behold, the silver *is* with me; I took it. And his mother said,
Blessed *be thou* of the LORD, my son.
17:3☆ 3 And when he had restored the eleven hundred *shekels* of silver to his
Ex 20:4, 23; 34:17 mother, his mother said, I had wholly dedicated the silver unto the LORD
Deut 12:3; Judg 10:10 from my hand for my son, to make a graven image and a molten image:
18:31 now therefore I will restore it unto thee.
17:4 4 Yet he restored the money unto his mother; and his mother took two
Judg 8:27; 1 Sam 19:13 hundred *shekels* of silver, and gave them to the founder, who made thereof
a graven image and a molten image: and they were in the house of Mi′cah.
5 And the man Mi′cah had an house of gods, and made an ephod, and
teraphim, and consecrated one of his sons, who became his priest.
17:6☆ 6 In those days *there was* no king in Israel, *but* every man did *that which*
Deut 12:8; Judg 18:1; 19:1; 21:25 *was* right in his own eyes.

2. Micah Employs a Levite to Be His Priest

17:7 7 ¶And there was a young man out of Beth–lehem–judah of the family of
Judg 19:1; Ruth 1:1, 2 Judah, who *was* a Levite, and he sojourned there.
Mic 5:2; Mt 2:1 8 And the man departed out of the city from Beth–lehem–judah to
sojourn where he could find *a place:* and he came to mount E′phra-im to
the house of Mi′cah, as he journeyed.
9 And Mi′cah said unto him, Whence comest thou? And he said unto him,
I *am* a Levite of Beth–lehem–judah, and I go to sojourn where I may find *a*
place.
10 And Mi′cah said unto him, Dwell with me, and be unto me a father and
a priest, and I will give thee ten *shekels* of silver by the year, and a suit of
apparel, and thy victuals. So the Levite went in.
11 And the Levite was content to dwell with the man; and the young man
was unto him as one of his sons.
17:12 12 And Mi′cah consecrated the Levite; and the young man became his
Num 16:10; Judg 18:30 priest, and was in the house of Mi′cah.
1 Kgs 12:31 17:13☆ 13 Then said Mi′cah, Now know I that the LORD will do me good, seeing
I have a Levite to *my* priest.

17:1 Chapter 16 brings an end to the story of the judges; the remainder of the book constitutes an appendix. The priesthood, which is absent in the stories connected with the judges, appears again.

17:3 This is the sad story of Micah and his mother. Micah stole eleven hundred shekels of silver. When he returned the money after she had cursed the thief, she dedicated the silver to the Lord. But she used only two hundred shekels to make the graven image. Like Ananias and Sapphira, she kept some for herself. In using the balance, she broke the second commandment. Her son was left with an idolatrous shrine and hired a Levite to be his priest. The judgment of God overtook him and the Danites took his gods away from him. His evil deeds then led to idolatry among those who stole his gods. The lesson is clear: whoever has a god or gods which can be taken away, has no real god. No one can take God from his people.

17:6 *there was no king in Israel.* This statement, the substance of which is repeated in 18:1, 19:1, and 21:25, indicates that Judges was written sometime during the days of the monarchy. (See the introduction to Judges.)

17:13 Sin against God always results in muddled thinking. Micah thought God would bless his idolatrous lifestyle because he had a Levite as his priest. But no priest or minister can shield a guilty sinner from the judgment and anger of God. Micah's priest was a counterfeit, for he allowed himself to be used in a way forbidden by God. He should never have attached himself to Micah, who had made his own gods and in so doing had departed from the true faith, even though he outwardly professed it.

3. The Danites and the Plan to Seize Laish

18 IN those days *there was* no king in Israel: and in those days the tribe of the Danites sought them an inheritance to dwell in; for unto that day *all their* inheritance had not fallen unto them among the tribes of Israel. ☆18:1 Josh 19:40 Judg 17:6; 21:25

2 And the children of Dan sent of their family five men from their coasts, men of valour, from Zo'rah, and from Esh'ta-ol, to spy out the land, and to search it; and they said unto them, Go, search the land: who when they came to mount E'phra-im, to the house of Mi'cah, they lodged there. 18:2 Judg 13:2, 3, 25

3 When they *were* by the house of Mi'cah, they knew the voice of the young man the Levite: and they turned in thither, and said unto him, Who brought thee hither? and what makest thou in this *place?* and what hast thou here?

4 And he said unto them, Thus and thus dealeth Mi'cah with me, and hath hired me, and I am his priest. 18:4 Judg 17:10, 11

5 And they said unto him, Ask counsel, we pray thee, of God, that we may know whether our way which we go shall be prosperous. ☆18:5

6 And the priest said unto them, Go in peace: before the LORD *is* your way wherein ye go.

7 ¶Then the five men departed, and came to La'ish, and saw the people that *were* therein, how they dwelt careless, after the manner of the Zi-do'ni-ans, quiet and secure; and *there was* no magistrate in the land, that might put *them* to shame in *any* thing; and they *were* far from the Zi-do'ni-ans, and had no business with *any* man. 18:7 Josh 19:47, 48

8 And they came unto their brethren to Zo'rah and Esh'ta-ol: and their brethren said unto them, What *say* ye?

9 And they said, Arise, that we may go up against them: for we have seen the land, and, behold, it *is* very good: and *are* ye still? be not slothful to go, *and* to enter to possess the land.

10 When ye go, ye shall come unto a people secure, and to a large land: for God hath given it into your hands; a place where *there is* no want of any thing that *is* in the earth.

11 ¶And there went from thence of the family of the Danites, out of Zo'rah and out of Esh'ta-ol, six hundred men appointed with weapons of war.

12 And they went up, and pitched in Kir'jath–je'a-rim, in Judah: wherefore they called that place Ma'ha-neh–dan unto this day: behold, *it is* behind Kir'jath–je'a-rim. ☆18:12

13 And they passed thence unto mount E'phra-im, and came unto the house of Mi'cah.

4. The Danites Take Micah's Priest and Steal His Idols

14 ¶Then answered the five men that went to spy out the country of La'ish, and said unto their brethren, Do ye know that there is in these houses an ephod, and teraphim, and a graven image, and a molten image? now therefore consider what ye have to do. 18:14 Judg 17:4, 5

15 And they turned thitherward, and came to the house of the young man the Levite, *even* unto the house of Mi'cah, and saluted him.

18:1 *all their inheritance had not fallen unto them.* The Danites still had much land to be taken from the enemy. They had occupied the highlands. Now they wanted the lowlands, which were fertile, but the Amorites occupied the plains and had iron chariots. The Danites lacked the faith they needed to secure the land they were given.

18:5 The five spies came to Micah's home and inquired of his priest whether their effort would succeed. The priest told them to go ahead. At that time they obviously saw the idols which the priest consulted. Upon their return home, they reported the existence of these idols in Micah's house.

18:12 *Mahaneh-dan,* i.e., "Camp of Dan."

16 And the six hundred men appointed with their weapons of war, which
were of the children of Dan, stood by the entering of the gate.

18:17☆ 17 And the five men that went to spy out the land went up, *and* came in
thither, *and* took the graven image, and the ephod, and the teraphim, and
the molten image: and the priest stood in the entering of the gate with the
six hundred men *that were* appointed with weapons of war.

18 And these went into Mi'cah's house, and fetched the carved image, the
ephod, and the teraphim, and the molten image. Then said the priest unto
them, What do ye?

18:19 Judg 17:10, 11 19 And they said unto him, Hold thy peace, lay thine hand upon thy
mouth, and go with us, and be to us a father and a priest: *is it* better for
thee to be a priest unto the house of one man, or that thou be a priest unto
a tribe and a family in Israel?

20 And the priest's heart was glad, and he took the ephod, and the
teraphim, and the graven image, and went in the midst of the people.

5. Micah Fails to Recover His Priest or His Property

18:21 Gen 33:2 Ex 12:37 21 So they turned and departed, and put the little ones and the cattle and
the carriage before them.

22 ¶*And* when they were a good way from the house of Mi'cah, the men
that *were* in the houses near to Mi'cah's house were gathered together, and
overtook the children of Dan.

23 And they cried unto the children of Dan. And they turned their faces,
and said unto Mi'cah, What aileth thee, that thou comest with such a
company?

18:24☆ 24 And he said, Ye have taken away my gods which I made, and the priest,
and ye are gone away: and what have I more? and what *is* this *that* ye say
unto me, What aileth thee?

25 And the children of Dan said unto him, Let not thy voice be heard
among us, lest angry fellows run upon thee, and thou lose thy life, with the
lives of thy household.

26 And the children of Dan went their way: and when Mi'cah saw that
they *were* too strong for him, he turned and went back unto his house.

6. The Danites Destroy and Rebuild Laish; They Use Micah's Idols

27 And they took *the things* which Mi'cah had made, and the priest which
he had, and came unto La'ish, unto a people *that were* at quiet and secure:
and they smote them with the edge of the sword, and burnt the city with
fire.

18:28 2 Sam 10:6 28 And *there was* no deliverer, because it *was* far from Zi'don, and they
had no business with *any* man; and it was in the valley that *lieth* by Beth-
re'hob. And they built a city, and dwelt therein.

18:29☆ 29 And they called the name of the city Dan, after the name of Dan their
father, who was born unto Israel: howbeit the name of the city *was* La'ish
at the first.

18:17 Six hundred armed Danites stood by as the five spies returned to seize the carved image, the ephod, the teraphim, and the molten image of Micah. The priest took the idols and went with the men from Dan. Instead of serving a single household he would have an enlarged ministry and profit more from it. Coveteousness is not limited to the laity; even the priesthood can defect.

18:24 The irony of Micah's situation is revealed here. He had lost his gods and his priest, and he had nothing left. While he had them, he thought he had everything. He had not realized he was poor, wretched, and blind. When he had lost his gods and his priest, he at least knew that he was bereft of all he had depended on. This now put him in a situation where he might have turned to the living God. Nothing in the Scriptures say he did, however.

18:29 *Laish,* called "Leshem" in Josh. 19:47.

30¶And the children of Dan set up the graven image: and Jonathan, the son of Ger′shom, the son of Ma-nas′seh, he and his sons were priests to the tribe of Dan until the day of the captivity of the land.
31And they set them up Mi′cah's graven image, which he made, all the time that the house of God was in Shi′loh.

☆18:30 Ex 2:22; 18:3

B. THE CRIME AT GIBEAH AND THE WAR AGAINST BENJAMIN
1. The Levite and the Concubine Who Left Him

19 AND it came to pass in those days, when *there was* no king in
Israel, that there was a certain Levite sojourning on the side of
mount E′phra-im, who took to him a concubine out of Beth–lehem–judah,
2And his concubine played the whore against him, and went away from
him unto her father's house to Beth–lehem–judah, and was there four whole months.
3And her husband arose, and went after her, to speak friendly unto her, *and* to bring her again, having his servant with him, and a couple of asses: and she brought him into her father's house: and when the father of the damsel saw him, he rejoiced to meet him.
4And his father in law, the damsel's father, retained him; and he abode with him three days: so they did eat and drink, and lodged there.
5¶And it came to pass on the fourth day, when they arose early in the morning, that he rose up to depart: and the damsel's father said unto his son in law, Comfort thine heart with a morsel of bread, and afterward go your way.
6And they sat down, and did eat and drink both of them together: for the damsel's father had said unto the man, Be content, I pray thee, and tarry all night, and let thine heart be merry.
7And when the man rose up to depart, his father in law urged him: therefore he lodged there again.
8And he arose early in the morning on the fifth day to depart: and the damsel's father said, Comfort thine heart, I pray thee. And they tarried until afternoon, and they did eat both of them.
9And when the man rose up to depart, he, and his concubine, and his servant, his father in law, the damsel's father, said unto him, Behold, now the day draweth toward evening, I pray you tarry all night: behold, the day groweth to an end, lodge here, that thine heart may be merry; and to morrow get you early on your way, that thou mayest go home.

19:1 Judg 17:6; 21:25

☆19:2

19:3 Gen 34:3

19:5 Gen 18:5

2. En Route Home They Stop at Gibeah

10But the man would not tarry that night, but he rose up and departed, and came over against Je′bus, which *is* Jerusalem; and *there were* with him two asses saddled, his concubine also *was* with him.
11*And* when they *were* by Je′bus, the day was far spent; and the servant said unto his master, Come, I pray thee, and let us turn in into this city of the Jeb′u-sites, and lodge in it.

19:10 Josh 15:8 18:21–28 1 Chron 11:4

18:30 *captivity of the land.* Some scholars believe this refers to the time of the captivity of the Ark under Eli. Others believe this refers to the captivity of the Northern Kingdom by the Assyrians under Tiglath-pileser in the eighth century. If the latter is correct, the date for the composition of Judges would obviously be at or after that time. 18:31 must have been written around 1050 B.C. when the Philistines took the Ark. This further confirms the theory that the writing of Judges was done in the early days of the monarchy.

19:2 Here is the story of a Levite whose wife plays the harlot and leaves her husband for the other man. Why he did not press his case against her and have her stoned is not stated. Instead, he seeks to get her back from his father-in-law's home to which she has come. He starts back with her, arriving in Gibeah with no place to stay.

19:12 Josh 24:33 Judg 20:4 12 And his master said unto him, We will not turn aside hither into the
city of a stranger, that *is* not of the children of Israel; we will pass over to
Gib'e-ah.
13 And he said unto his servant, Come, and let us draw near to one of
these places to lodge all night, in Gib'e-ah, or in Ra'mah.
14 And they passed on and went their way; and the sun went down upon
them *when they were* by Gib'e-ah, which *belongeth* to Benjamin.
19:15☆ 15 And they turned aside thither, to go in *and* to lodge in Gib'e-ah: and
when he went in, he sat him down in a street of the city: for *there was* no
man that took them into his house to lodging.

3. An Ephraimite Takes Them In

16 ¶And, behold, there came an old man from his work out of the field at
even, which *was* also of mount E'phra-im; and he sojourned in Gib'e-ah:
but the men of the place *were* Benjamites.
19:17 Esth 4:6 17 And when he had lifted up his eyes, he saw a wayfaring man in the
street of the city: and the old man said, Whither goest thou? and whence
comest thou?
18 And he said unto him, We *are* passing from Beth-lehem-judah toward
the side of mount E'phra-im; from thence *am* I: and I went to Beth-lehem-
judah, but I *am now* going to the house of the LORD; and there *is* no man
that receiveth me to house.
19 Yet there is both straw and provender for our asses; and there is bread
and wine also for me, and for thy handmaid, and for the young man *which*
is with thy servants: *there is* no want of any thing.
20 And the old man said, Peace *be* with thee; howsoever *let* all thy wants
lie upon me; only lodge not in the street.
19:21 Gen 18:4; 19:2 24:32 21 So he brought him into his house, and gave provender unto the asses:
and they washed their feet, and did eat and drink.

4. The Rape and Death of the Levite's Concubine

19:22 Gen 19:4, 5 22 ¶*Now* as they were making their hearts merry, behold, the men of the
city, certain sons of Be'li-al, beset the house round about, *and* beat at the
door, and spake to the master of the house, the old man, saying, Bring forth
the man that came into thine house, that we may know him.
19:23 2 Sam 13:12 23 And the man, the master of the house, went out unto them, and said
unto them, Nay, my brethren, *nay,* I pray you, do not *so* wickedly; seeing
that this man is come into mine house, do not this folly.
19:24 Gen 19:8 24 Behold, *here is* my daughter a maiden, and his concubine; them I will
bring out now, and humble ye them, and do with them what seemeth good
unto you: but unto this man do not so vile a thing.
25 But the men would not hearken to him: so the man took his concubine,
and brought her forth unto them; and they knew her, and abused her all the
night until the morning: and when the day began to spring, they let her go.
26 Then came the woman in the dawning of the day, and fell down at the
door of the man's house where her lord *was,* till it was light.
19:27☆ 27 And her lord rose up in the morning, and opened the doors of the
house, and went out to go his way: and, behold, the woman his concubine

19:15 In those days there were no inns or hotels. Unless the inhabitants of a town opened their homes to travelers and strangers, there was no place to which they could go. Partly for this reason Jesus said, "I was a stranger, and ye took me not in" (Matt. 25:43). When we fail to care for those who follow Jesus, it is as though we have failed to care for Jesus himself.

19:27 The moral of this episode is ambiguous. Why did the Levite fail to protect the concubine with his own life? Why did he wait until morning to open the door was fallen down *at* the door of the house, and her hands *were* upon the threshold.

5. The Levite Seeks Vengeance against the Benjaminites

28 And he said unto her, Up, and let us be going. But none answered.
Then the man took her *up* upon an ass, and the man rose up, and gat him
unto his place.
29 ¶And when he was come into his house, he took a knife, and laid hold
on his concubine, and divided her, *together* with her bones, into twelve
pieces, and sent her into all the coasts of Israel.
30 And it was so, that all that saw it said, There was no such deed done
nor seen from the day that the children of Israel came up out of the land of
Egypt unto this day: consider of it, take advice, and speak *your minds.*

6. Israel's Civil War with Benjamin

a. The Levite Tells Israel His Story at Mizpah

20 THEN all the children of Israel went out, and the congregation was
gathered together as one man, from Dan even to Be'er-she'ba, with
the land of Gilead, unto the LORD in Miz'peh.
2 And the chief of all the people, *even* of all the tribes of Israel, presented
themselves in the assembly of the people of God, four hundred thousand
footmen that drew sword.
3 (Now the children of Benjamin heard that the children of Israel were
gone up to Miz'peh.) Then said the children of Israel, Tell *us,* how was this
wickedness?
4 And the Levite, the husband of the woman that was slain, answered and
said, I came into Gib'e-ah that *belongeth* to Benjamin, I and my concubine,
to lodge.
5 And the men of Gib'e-ah rose against me, and beset the house round
about upon me by night, *and* thought to have slain me: and my concubine
have they forced, that she is dead.
6 And I took my concubine, and cut her in pieces, and sent her
throughout all the country of the inheritance of Israel: for they have
committed lewdness and folly in Israel.
7 Behold, ye *are* all children of Israel: give here your advice and counsel.
8 ¶And all the people arose as one man, saying, We will not any *of us* go
to his tent, neither will we any *of us* turn into his house.
9 But now this *shall be* the thing which we will do to Gib'e-ah; *we will go
up* by lot against it;
10 And we will take ten men of an hundred throughout all the tribes of
Israel, and an hundred of a thousand, and a thousand out of ten thousand,
to fetch victual for the people, that they may do, when they come to Gib'e-
ah of Benjamin, according to all the folly that they have wrought in Israel.
11 So all the men of Israel were gathered against the city, knit together as
one man.

20:1 1 Sam 7:5; 2 Sam 19:14

☆**20:10**

and see her dead? Would not the second table of the law have required him to act differently, even if it meant the loss of his own life? Would a believer today not have a moral obligation to preserve the integrity of his wife, even if it meant resorting to violence in order to protect her in such a contingency? Does not a woman—a member of the weaker sex—have entitlement to the strength of the male for her physical well-being?

20:10 The Benjamites must pay for *the folly they have wrought* ("wanton crime" in the RSV; "disgraceful acts" in the NASV) in Israel. The armed forces gather for battle.

b. God Approves the War against Unrepentant Benjamin

12¶And the tribes of Israel sent men through all the tribe of Benjamin,
saying, What wickedness *is* this that is done among you?
20:13☆ 13Now therefore deliver *us* the men, the children of Be'li-al, which *are* in
Gib'e-ah, that we may put them to death, and put away evil from Israel.
But the children of Benjamin would not hearken to the voice of their
brethren the children of Israel:
20:14 Num 2:23 14But the children of Benjamin gathered themselves together out of the
cities unto Gib'e-ah, to go out to battle against the children of Israel.
15And the children of Benjamin were numbered at that time out of the
cities twenty and six thousand men that drew sword, beside the inhabitants
of Gib'e-ah, which were numbered seven hundred chosen men.
20:16 Judg 3:15 16Among all this people *there were* seven hundred chosen men left-
handed; every one could sling stones at an hair *breadth,* and not miss.
17And the men of Israel, beside Benjamin, were numbered four hundred
thousand men that drew sword: all these *were* men of war.
20:18☆ Num 27:21 Judg 1:1 18¶And the children of Israel arose, and went up to the house of God,
and asked counsel of God, and said, Which of us shall go up first to the
battle against the children of Benjamin? And the LORD said, Judah *shall go
up* first.

c. Benjamin's First and Second Military Victories

19And the children of Israel rose up in the morning, and encamped
against Gib'e-ah.
20And the men of Israel went out to battle against Benjamin; and the
men of Israel put themselves in array to fight against them at Gib'e-ah.
21And the children of Benjamin came forth out of Gib'e-ah, and
destroyed down to the ground of the Israelites that day twenty and two
thousand men.
20:22 Josh 7:6, 7 22And the people the men of Israel encouraged themselves, and set their
battle again in array in the place where they put themselves in array the first
day.
23(And the children of Israel went up and wept before the LORD until
even, and asked counsel of the LORD, saying, Shall I go up again to battle
against the children of Benjamin my brother? And the LORD said, Go up
against him.)
24And the children of Israel came near against the children of Benjamin
the second day.
25And Benjamin went forth against them out of Gib'e-ah the second day,
and destroyed down to the ground of the children of Israel again eighteen
thousand men; all these drew the sword.
20:26 Judg 21:4 1 Sam 13:9 2 Sam 24:25 26¶Then all the children of Israel, and all the people, went up, and came
unto the house of God, and wept, and sat there before the LORD, and fasted
that day until even, and offered burnt offerings and peace offerings before
the LORD.
20:27☆ Judg 7:9 27And the children of Israel inquired of the LORD, (for the ark of the
covenant of God *was* there in those days,

20:13 Before the battle took place, Israel presented a solution which would have made war unnecessary: they wanted the guilty men surrendered to them, judged, and executed for their crime.
20:18 Before the first and the second battles, Israel asked counsel from God as to what they should do and how they should do it. Benjamin won the first two battles and Israel went back to God, to fast and to offer burnt and peace offerings (20:26). They are told to start the third battle, the results of which are reported in versus 35 and 36. Israel won the day.
20:27 *the ark of the covenant.* Throughout the wilderness journeys the ark rested in the tent of meeting. During the period of the judges a house or "temple" was built for the ark at Shiloh (see Judg. 18:31). When Samuel was a lad he slept in this temple (1 Sam. 3:3).

28 And Phin'e-has, the son of E-le-a'zar, the son of Aaron, stood before it ☆20:28
in those days,) saying, Shall I yet again go out to battle against the children
of Benjamin my brother, or shall I cease? And the LORD said, Go up; for to
morrow I will deliver them into thine hand.

d. The Israeli Defeat of Benjamin

29 And Israel set liers in wait round about Gib'e-ah.
30 And the children of Israel went up against the children of Benjamin on
the third day, and put themselves in array against Gib'e-ah, as at other
times.
31 And the children of Benjamin went out against the people, *and* were **20:31** Josh 8:16
drawn away from the city; and they began to smite of the people, *and* kill,
as at other times, in the highways, of which one goeth up to the house of
God, and the other to Gib'e-ah in the field, about thirty men of Israel.
32 And the children of Benjamin said, They *are* smitten down before us, as
at the first. But the children of Israel said, Let us flee, and draw them from
the city unto the highways.
33 And all the men of Israel rose up out of their place, and put themselves **20:33** Josh 8:19
in array at Ba'al-ta'mar: and the liers in wait of Israel came forth out of
their places, *even* out of the meadows of Gib'e-ah.
34 And there came against Gib'e-ah ten thousand chosen men out of all
Israel, and the battle was sore: but they knew not that evil *was* near them.
35 And the LORD smote Benjamin before Israel: and the children of Israel ☆20:35–39
destroyed of the Benjamites that day twenty and five thousand and an
hundred men: all these drew the sword.
36 So the children of Benjamin saw that they were smitten: for the men of
Israel gave place to the Benjamites, because they trusted unto the liers in
wait which they had set beside Gib'e-ah.
37 And the liers in wait hasted, and rushed upon Gib'e-ah; and the liers in
wait drew *themselves* along, and smote all the city with the edge of the
sword.
38 Now there was an appointed sign between the men of Israel and the
liers in wait, that they should make a great flame with smoke rise up out of
the city.
39 And when the men of Israel retired in the battle, Benjamin began to
smite *and* kill of the men of Israel about thirty persons: for they said, Surely
they are smitten down before us, as *in* the first battle.
40 But when the flame began to arise up out of the city with a pillar of
smoke, the Benjamites looked behind them, and, behold, the flame of the
city ascended up to heaven.
41 And when the men of Israel turned again, the men of Benjamin were
amazed: for they saw that evil was come upon them.
42 Therefore they turned *their backs* before the men of Israel unto the way **20:42** Josh 8:15, 24
of the wilderness; but the battle overtook them; and them which *came* out
of the cities they destroyed in the midst of them.
43 *Thus* they inclosed the Benjamites round about, *and* chased them, *and*
trode them down with ease over against Gib'e-ah toward the sunrising.
44 And there fell of Benjamin eighteen thousand men; all these *were* men
of valour.

We do not know what happened to the tent of meeting. The ark, however, was preserved for centuries until the time of Nebuchadnezzar. It has been presumed that the ark was destroyed when Nebuchadnezzar burned the temple in 586 B.C. It is, of course, possible that God may have miraculously preserved the ark, but this appears unlikely.

20:28 The first defeats did not signal final defeat. Victory followed these first defeats.

20:35–39 Archeologists have uncovered evidences of the destruction of Gibeah.

20:45 Judg 21:13 45And they turned and fled toward the wilderness unto the rock of
Rimmon: and they gleaned of them in the highways five thousand men;
and pursued hard after them unto Gi′dom, and slew two thousand men of
them.
46So that all which fell that day of Benjamin were twenty and five
thousand men that drew the sword; all these *were* men of valour.
47But six hundred men turned and fled to the wilderness unto the rock
Rimmon, and abode in the rock Rimmon four months.
48And the men of Israel turned again upon the children of Benjamin, and
smote them with the edge of the sword, as well the men of *every* city, as the
beast, and all that came to hand: also they set on fire all the cities that they
came to.

7. The Tribe of Benjamin Restored
a. Israel's Sorrow over Benjamin

21:1☆ Judg 20:1 21 NOW the men of Israel had sworn in Miz′peh, saying, There shall
not any of us give his daughter unto Benjamin to wife.
21:2 Judg 20:31; 21:19 2And the people came to the house of God, and abode there till even
before God, and lifted up their voices, and wept sore;
3And said, O LORD God of Israel, why is this come to pass in Israel, that
there should be to day one tribe lacking in Israel?
21:4 Deut 12:4, 5; 2 Sam 24:25 4And it came to pass on the morrow, that the people rose early, and built
there an altar, and offered burnt offerings and peace offerings.
5And the children of Israel said, Who *is there* among all the tribes of
Israel that came not up with the congregation unto the LORD? For they had
made a great oath concerning him that came not up to the LORD to
Miz′peh, saying, He shall surely be put to death.
6And the children of Israel repented them for Benjamin their brother,
and said, There is one tribe cut off from Israel this day.
7How shall we do for wives for them that remain, seeing we have sworn
by the LORD that we will not give them of our daughters to wives?

b. Seeking Wives for the Benjaminites
(1) The Virgins from Jabesh-gilead

8¶And they said, What one *is there* of the tribes of Israel that came not
up to Miz′peh to the LORD? And, behold, there came none to the camp
from Ja′besh-gil′e-ad to the assembly.
21:8, 9☆ 9For the people were numbered, and, behold, *there were* none of the
inhabitants of Ja′besh-gil′e-ad there.
21:10 Num 31:18 10And the congregation sent thither twelve thousand men of the
valiantest, and commanded them, saying, Go and smite the inhabitants of
Ja′besh-gil′e-ad with the edge of the sword, with the women and the
children.
11And this *is* the thing that ye shall do, Ye shall utterly destroy every
male, and every woman that hath lain by man.
21:12☆ 12And they found among the inhabitants of Ja′besh-gil′e-ad four

21:1ff The destruction of the men of Benjamin left only a few alive. And the women had also been slain. It appeared that the tribe of Benjamin was faced with extinction because the other tribes of Israel made a solemn pact that none of their daughters would be given in marriage to a Benjamite. Israel sought for a resolution to the problem without breaking their own vow.

21:8, 9 Evidently the earlier marriage ties between the Gileadites (Machir) and the people of Benjamin (see 1 Chron. 7:12, 15) explain why no one from Jabesh-gilead came to fight against the Benjamites.

21:12 When the people of Jabesh-Gilead were slain, four hundred virgins were saved from the slaughter. They were sent to the camp at Shiloh—there to await their disposition, as a solution to the lack of wives available for the few men of Benjamin who were left alive.

hundred young virgins, that had known no man by lying with any male:
and they brought them unto the camp to Shi'loh, which *is* in the land of
Canaan.
13 And the whole congregation sent *some* to speak to the children of **21:13**
Benjamin that *were* in the rock Rimmon, and to call peaceably unto them. Deut 20:10
14 And Benjamin came again at that time; and they gave them wives
which they had saved alive of the women of Ja'besh-gil'e-ad: and yet so
they sufficed them not.
15 And the people repented them for Benjamin, because that the LORD
had made a breach in the tribes of Israel.

(2) The Kidnapping of the Girls from Shiloh

16 ¶Then the elders of the congregation said, How shall we do for wives
for them that remain, seeing the women are destroyed out of Benjamin?
17 And they said, *There must be* an inheritance for them that be escaped of
Benjamin, that a tribe be not destroyed out of Israel.
18 Howbeit we may not give them wives of our daughters: for the children
of Israel have sworn, saying, Cursed *be* he that giveth a wife to Benjamin.
19 Then they said, Behold, *there is* a feast of the LORD in Shi'loh yearly *in* **21:19**
a place which *is* on the north side of Beth-el, on the east side of the highway Josh 18:1 Judg 18:31
that goeth up from Beth-el to She'chem, and on the south of Le-bo'nah. 1 Sam 1:3
20 Therefore they commanded the children of Benjamin, saying, Go and
lie in wait in the vineyards;
21 And see, and, behold, if the daughters of Shi'loh come out to dance in **21:21**
dances, then come ye out of the vineyards, and catch you every man his Ex 15:20 Judg 11:34
wife of the daughters of Shi'loh, and go to the land of Benjamin.
22 And it shall be, when their fathers or their brethren come unto us to
complain, that we will say unto them, Be favourable unto them for our
sakes: because we reserved not to each man his wife in the war: for ye did
not give unto them at this time, *that* ye should be guilty.
23 And the children of Benjamin did so, and took *them* wives, according to ☆**21:23**
their number, of them that danced, whom they caught: and they went and Judg 20:48
returned unto their inheritance, and repaired the cities, and dwelt in them.
24 And the children of Israel departed thence at that time, every man to
his tribe and to his family, and they went out from thence every man to his
inheritance.

8. The Anarchy during the Age of the Judges

25 In those days *there was* no king in Israel: every man did *that which was* ☆**21:25**
right in his own eyes.

21:23 Amidst the festivities, the men of Benjamin took for themselves virgins and went home to repopulate the tribe decimated from the battles with Israel. Thus, the tribe of Benjamin was not wiped out completely.

21:25 As the book of Judges closes, anarchy was the order of the day. "Though God was their king, every man would be his own master, as if there were no king."*

THE BOOK OF RUTH

Authorship, date, and background Jewish tradition has it that Samuel wrote the books of Samuel, Judges, and Ruth. The statement about David in 4:17, 21 suggests that it was not written earlier than David's time. This means it was written either during his time or later. Thus Samuel could have been the author if the book was written in David's lifetime. The book itself mentions no author. Therefore, no one can be dogmatic as to the authorship.

The events recorded in Ruth occurred during the time of the Judges. The chronology depends on when the Exodus from Egypt is dated. If the early date of the Exodus is taken (ca. 1440 B.C.), then Ruth and Boaz lived during the latter times of the Judges. In any event, they were the great-grandparents of David, who was the third generation after Boaz. Thus the events occurred around 1100 B.C., even though the book may have been put into written form later.

The period of the Judges was marked by anarchy in which men did what was right in their own eyes. A recurring pattern of apostasy followed by repentance and restoration marked this period. Dislocations were common, intermarriage with non-Israelite peoples took place, and yet everyday life went on amidst the turbulent times. Ruth is a refreshing story, not fiction or fable, of how common people lived through disasters and managed to love, marry, raise children, and worship the true God.

The book of Ruth is one of the five Megilloth or scrolls, shorter Old Testament books which could be read publicly at certain religious festivals. The Song of Songs was read at Passover, Lamentations the ninth of Aba, Ecclesiastes at Tabernacles, Esther at Purim, and Ruth at Pentecost (Feast of Weeks). In the Hebrew Bible, Ruth was in the last section known as the Hagiographa (Holy Writings). The book of Ruth follows the book of Judges in our English Bibles, after the pattern of the Septuagint. It appears after Psalms, Job, and Proverbs in the Hebrew Bible.

Characteristics and content The book of Ruth is one of the loveliest books in the Bible. It deals with the pilgrimage of ordinary families exemplified by the lives of Elimelech and Naomi of Bethlehem, who go with their two sons to Moab because of famine conditions in their own land. Their sons marry and die without leaving any children. One widow, Orpah, does not return to Bethlehem with Naomi after the death of her husband. Faithful Ruth clings to Naomi. Strong emphasis is placed on levirate marriage (the nearest male must preserve the name of the deceased by producing offspring with the widow). Boaz is a near kinsman. After Naomi has set the stage for Boaz to play the kinsman's role, he first arranges for a nearer kinsman to decline so that he can marry Ruth and continue the line of Elimelech, Ruth's father-in-law, and her first husband, Mahlon. After a period of suspense, the happy ending is marked not only by Ruth's marriage to Boaz, but by the birth of a son whose grandson is King David. Thus a Gentile, Ruth, becomes part of the kingly line of David. She is a convert to Judaism, and thoroughly identifies herself with the chosen people of God.

Outline

I. The migration of Naomi and Elimelech (1:1–22)
II. Boaz, a kindly friend (2:1–23)
III. Naomi's plan (3:1–18)
IV. Boaz carries out his pledge (4:1–22)

I. THE MIGRATION OF NAOMI AND ELIMELECH (1:1–22)

A. NAOMI'S WIDOWHOOD AND SORROW

1 NOW it came to pass in the days when the judges ruled, that there was ☆1:1
a famine in the land. And a certain man of Beth–lehem–judah went to Judg 2:16–18
sojourn in the country of Moab, he, and his wife, and his two sons.
2 And the name of the man *was* E-lim'e-lech, and the name of his wife
Naomi, and the name of his two sons Mah'lon and Chil'i-on, Eph'rath-ites
of Beth–lehem–judah. And they came into the country of Moab, and
continued there.
3 And E-lim'e-lech Naomi's husband died; and she was left, and her two ☆1:3
sons.
4 And they took them wives of the women of Moab; the name of the one ☆1:4
was Or'pah, and the name of the other Ruth: and they dwelled there about
ten years.
5 And Mah'lon and Chil'i-on died also both of them; and the woman was
left of her two sons and her husband.
6 ¶Then she arose with her daughters in law, that she might return from 1:6
the country of Moab: for she had heard in the country of Moab how that Ex 4:31
the LORD had visited his people in giving them bread.
7 Wherefore she went forth out of the place where she was, and her two
daughters in law with her; and they went on the way to return unto the land
of Judah.

B. NAOMI'S RETURN TO JUDAH

8 And Naomi said unto her two daughters in law, Go, return each to her
mother's house: the LORD deal kindly with you, as ye have dealt with the
dead, and with me.
9 The LORD grant you that ye may find rest, each *of you* in the house of
her husband. Then she kissed them; and they lifted up their voice, and
wept.
10 And they said unto her, Surely we will return with thee unto thy people.
11 And Naomi said, Turn again, my daughters: why will ye go with me? ☆1:11
are there yet *any more* sons in my womb, that they may be your husbands? Deut 25:5
12 Turn again, my daughters, go *your way;* for I am too old to have an
husband. If I should say, I have hope, *if* I should have an husband also to
night, and should also bear sons;
13 Would ye tarry for them till they were grown? would ye stay for them ☆1:13
from having husbands? nay, my daughters; for it grieveth me much for your
sakes that the hand of the LORD is gone out against me.

1:1 *when the judges ruled.* The earlier account of the days of the judges is noticeably different from the story of the times in which Ruth lived. There was no king in Israel—every man did what was right in his own eyes. The days were dark and gloomy, for Israel went through a series of highs and lows marked by apostasy, captivity, repentance, and restoration. *Man of Beth-lehem-judah,* literally, "Ephrathite from Bethlehem in Judah."

1:3 The death of Elimelech was only the beginning of Naomi's sorrow. In addition to having fled from Canaan because of the famine and the loss of her husband, she would lose both sons and neither one of them would leave any grandchildren for her. Her afflictions were many but her consolation in the end would be greater than all the afflictions. It was her attitude that was negative: her laments were woeful, her complaints restated again and again. She wore the black garb of mourning in her speech and apparently had not forgiven God for what happened to her.

1:4 The people of Moab were descendants of Lot through incest with his daughter (Gen. 19:36, 37). Ruth was a Moabite. She became an ancestress of Jesus (Matt. 1:3–6).

1:11 *Are there yet any more sons in my womb that they may be your husbands?* This refers to the custom of the day—levirate marriage (Deut. 25:5–10) was a common practice. The brother of a deceased husband was to marry the widow. (See note on 3:1.)†

1:13 *the hand of the LORD has gone out against me.* As she seeks to send her daughters-in-law back to their homes she says, in effect, that God's quarrel is with

14 And they lifted up their voice, and wept again: and Or'pah kissed her
mother in law; but Ruth clave unto her.

C. RUTH DECIDES TO GO WITH NAOMI TO BETHLEHEM

15 And she said, Behold, thy sister in law is gone back unto her people,
and unto her gods: return thou after thy sister in law.
1:16☆ 16 And Ruth said, Intreat me not to leave thee, *or* to return from following
after thee: for whither thou goest, I will go; and where thou lodgest, I will
lodge: thy people *shall be* my people, and thy God my God:
17 Where thou diest, will I die, and there will I be buried: the LORD do so
to me, and more also, *if ought* but death part thee and me.
18 When she saw that she was stedfastly minded to go with her, then she
left speaking unto her.
19 ¶So they two went until they came to Beth-lehem. And it came to pass,
when they were come to Beth-lehem, that all the city was moved about
them, and they said, *Is* this Naomi?
1:20☆ Job 6:4 20 And she said unto them, Call me not Naomi, call me Ma'ra: for the
Almighty hath dealt very bitterly with me.
21 I went out full, and the LORD hath brought me home again empty: why
then call ye me Naomi, seeing the LORD hath testified against me, and the
Almighty hath afflicted me?
22 So Naomi returned, and Ruth the Moabitess, her daughter in law, with
her, which returned out of the country of Moab: and they came to Beth-
lehem in the beginning of barley harvest.

II. BOAZ, A KINDLY FRIEND (2:1–23)

A. RUTH GLEANS FREE GRAIN IN BOAZ'S FIELD

2:1☆ 2 AND Naomi had a kinsman of her husband's, a mighty man of wealth,
of the family of E-lim'e-lech; and his name *was* Bo'az.
2:2☆ Lev 19:9, 10; 23:22 2 And Ruth the Moabitess said unto Naomi, Let me now go to the field,
and glean ears of corn after *him* in whose sight I shall find grace. And she
said unto her, Go, my daughter.
2:3☆ 3 And she went, and came, and gleaned in the field after the reapers: and
her hap was to light on a part of the field *belonging* unto Bo'az, who *was* of
the kindred of E-lim'e-lech.

---

her. Affliction is not a sign that God is against the one afflicted. If it comes because of disobedience, it is deserved and should be accepted gladly; if it comes and there is no apparent reason for it, it should be welcomed and God should be praised for sending it, even before the deliverance appears.

1:16 Many brides use this passage as part of their wedding ceremonies. But no bride should make her husband's God her God unless her husband's God is the true God; her decision should be rooted in her own faith and commitment to Jesus Christ.

1:20 Now in Bethlehem, Naomi continues her sorry complaint. Call me Mara, that is, "bitter." "The Lord hath afflicted me." "The Almighty hath dealt very bitterly with me." "What a poor figure does Naomi make now, compared to what it was when it was blooming."*

2:1 *Boaz.* In Matt. 1:5 we are told that Boaz was the son of Salmon by Rahab (Rachab). For Rahab to be in the lineage of the Messiah sounds strange. She had three strikes against her. She was a Canaanitess, a prostitute and a liar. Divine grace covers a multitude of sins. Apparently she was converted and her life transformed. From her womb came Boaz, a distinguished, moral, and God-believing man. God works in mysterious ways. The Rahab story manifests one of those ways. This Gentile in the lineage of the Redeemer expresses again the truth that Jesus is the cosmic Christ (for Jew and Gentile) and the Man for all seasons.

2:2 *glean ears of corn.* See note on Lev. 19:10.

2:3 *her hap was to light on a part of the field belonging to Boaz.* Ruth was humble enough to glean, industrious enough to work, concerned enough about Naomi to help feed them, and utterly dependent on the God of grace whom she had embraced as her Redeemer. It was no accident that she gleaned in the field belonging to Boaz. God in his providence directed her steps to this particular field.

4¶And, behold, Bo'az came from Beth–lehem, and said unto the reapers,
The LORD *be* with you. And they answered him, The LORD bless thee.
5Then said Bo'az unto his servant that was set over the reapers, Whose
damsel *is* this?
6And the servant that was set over the reapers answered and said, It *is*
the Moabitish damsel that came back with Naomi out of the country of
Moab:
7And she said, I pray you, let me glean and gather after the reapers ☆2:7
among the sheaves: so she came, and hath continued even from the
morning until now, that she tarried a little in the house.

B. BOAZ'S CONCERN FOR RUTH

8Then said Bo'az unto Ruth, Hearest thou not, my daughter? Go not to
glean in another field, neither go from hence, but abide here fast by my
maidens:
9*Let* thine eyes *be* on the field that they do reap, and go thou after them:
have I not charged the young men that they shall not touch thee? and when
thou art athirst, go unto the vessels, and drink of *that* which the young men
have drawn.
10Then she fell on her face, and bowed herself to the ground, and said ☆2:10
unto him, Why have I found grace in thine eyes, that thou shouldest take
knowledge of me, seeing I *am* a stranger?
11And Bo'az answered and said unto her, It hath fully been shewed me, ☆2:11
all that thou hast done unto thy mother in law since the death of thine
husband: and *how* thou hast left thy father and thy mother, and the land of
thy nativity, and art come unto a people which thou knewest not
heretofore.
12The LORD recompense thy work, and a full reward be given thee of the ☆2:12
LORD God of Israel, under whose wings thou art come to trust. Ruth 1:16
13Then she said, Let me find favour in thy sight, my lord; for that thou
hast comforted me, and for that thou hast spoken friendly unto thine
handmaid, though I be not like unto one of thine handmaidens.
14And Bo'az said unto her, At mealtime come thou hither, and eat of the
bread, and dip thy morsel in the vinegar. And she sat beside the reapers:
and he reached her parched *corn*, and she did eat, and was sufficed, and left.
15And when she was risen up to glean, Bo'az commanded his young men,
saying, Let her glean even among the sheaves, and reproach her not:
16And let fall also *some* of the handfuls of purpose for her, and leave ☆2:16
them, that she may glean *them*, and rebuke her not.
17So she gleaned in the field until even, and beat out that she had
gleaned: and it was about an ephah of barley.
18¶And she took *it* up, and went into the city: and her mother in law saw
what she had gleaned: and she brought forth, and gave to her that she had
reserved after she was sufficed.

C. RUTH TELLS HER STORY TO NAOMI

19And her mother in law said unto her, Where hast thou gleaned to day?
and where wroughtest thou? blessed be he that did take knowledge of thee.

2:7 Some of the grain or grapes were left for gleaning by the poor. Anyone could glean in the fields, but Ruth did not intrude. She asked permission to glean, and so demonstrated her humility and concern to do only the right thing.
2:10 *I am a stranger*, i.e., "I am a foreigner," not of your people by birth.
2:11 Boaz evidently knew all about Ruth even though he had not personally met her (2:5).
2:12 *under whose wings thou art come to trust.* Boaz knew that she was a convert to the true faith. Her confidence was in his God, who had become her God. He was impressed by her.
2:16 Boaz was so moved that he saw to it that Ruth would get more than normally would be the case for a gleaner. His heart went out to this widow in distress.

And she shewed her mother in law with whom she had wrought, and said,
The man's name with whom I wrought to day *is* Bo'az.
2:20☆ [20]And Naomi said unto her daughter in law, Blessed *be* he of the LORD,
who hath not left off his kindness to the living and to the dead. And Naomi
said unto her, The man *is* near of kin unto us, one of our next kinsmen.
[21]And Ruth the Moabitess said, He said unto me also, Thou shalt keep
fast by my young men, until they have ended all my harvest.
2:22☆ [22]And Naomi said unto Ruth her daughter in law, *It is* good, my
daughter, that thou go out with his maidens, that they meet thee not in any
other field.
2:23☆ [23]So she kept fast by the maidens of Bo'az to glean unto the end of barley
harvest and of wheat harvest; and dwelt with her mother in law.

III. NAOMI'S PLAN (3:1–18)

A. NAOMI TELLS RUTH WHAT TO DO

3:1☆ 3 THEN Naomi her mother in law said unto her, My daughter, shall I
not seek rest for thee, that it may be well with thee?
3:2☆ [2]And now *is* not Bo'az of our kindred, with whose maidens thou wast?
Deut 25:5–10 Behold, he winnoweth barley to night in the threshingfloor.
[3]Wash thyself therefore, and anoint thee, and put thy raiment upon thee,
and get thee down to the floor: *but* make not thyself known unto the man,
until he shall have done eating and drinking.
[4]And it shall be, when he lieth down, that thou shalt mark the place
where he shall lie, and thou shalt go in, and uncover his feet, and lay thee
down; and he will tell thee what thou shalt do.
[5]And she said unto her, All that thou sayest unto me I will do.

B. RUTH OBEYS NAOMI'S INSTRUCTIONS; BOAZ MAKES HIS DECISION

[6]¶And she went down unto the floor, and did according to all that her
mother in law bade her.
[7]And when Bo'az had eaten and drunk, and his heart was merry, he went
to lie down at the end of the heap of corn: and she came softly, and
uncovered his feet, and laid her down.
[8]¶And it came to pass at midnight, that the man was afraid, and turned
himself: and, behold, a woman lay at his feet.
3:9☆ [9]And he said, Who *art* thou? And she answered, I *am* Ruth thine
handmaid: spread therefore thy skirt over thine handmaid; for thou *art* a
near kinsman.
3:10☆ [10]And he said, Blessed *be* thou of the LORD, my daughter: *for* thou hast

---

2:20 *The man is near of kin*, i.e., "he is a near relative, one of our redeemers."†

2:22 *that they meet thee not in any other field* is translated "lest in another field you be molested" (RSV), or "lest others fall upon you in another field" (NASB). Apparently it was not uncommon for a female gleaner to be taken advantage of, particularly if she was a stranger.

2:23 Ruth's submissive obedience and sterling qualities attracted Boaz to her.

3:1 Here we see that Naomi referred to the Israeli custom of levirate marriage (see note on 1:11). The first child of such a marriage was recognized as the son of the widow's deceased husband and was entitled to the land ownership of his dead father. Additional children begotten by the dead man's brother were regarded as his own, not those of the deceased.

3:2 The grain was winnowed and then guarded overnight. Boaz remained there to oversee the harvesting activities. Again we note that grain might have been stolen if not watched over.

3:9 Ruth's invitation to Boaz to perform the role of kinsman was devoid of any immorality. It was part of the societal customs of the day. Today, though, there is no biblical sanction which validates its use.

3:10 Boaz was impressed by the fact that Ruth had not sought out a younger and perhaps more vigorous man to play the role of kinsman. He happened to be rich, but a younger woman might be more interested in having children than in wealth.

shewed more kindness in the latter end than at the beginning, inasmuch as thou followedst not young men, whether poor or rich.

11 And now, my daughter, fear not; I will do to thee all that thou requirest: for all the city of my people doth know that thou *art* a virtuous woman.

3:11 Prov 31:10

12 And now it is true that I *am thy* near kinsman: howbeit there is a kinsman nearer than I.

13 Tarry this night, and it shall be in the morning, *that* if he will perform unto thee the part of a kinsman, well; let him do the kinsman's part: but if he will not do the part of a kinsman to thee, then will I do the part of a kinsman to thee, *as* the LORD liveth: lie down until the morning.

C. RUTH TELLS NAOMI WHAT HAPPENED

14 ¶And she lay at his feet until the morning: and she rose up before one could know another. And he said, Let it not be known that a woman came into the floor.

15 Also he said, Bring the vail that *thou hast* upon thee, and hold it. And when she held it, he measured six *measures* of barley, and laid *it* on her: and she went into the city.

16 And when she came to her mother in law, she said, Who *art* thou, my daughter? And she told her all that the man had done to her.

17 And she said, These six *measures* of barley gave he me; for he said to me, Go not empty unto thy mother in law.

18 Then said she, Sit still, my daughter, until thou know how the matter will fall: for the man will not be in rest, until he have finished the thing this day.

☆3:18

IV. BOAZ CARRIES OUT HIS PLEDGE (4:1–22)

A. BOAZ SPEAKS TO THE NEAREST RELATIVE (KINSMAN), WHO REFUSES TO MARRY RUTH

4 THEN went Bo'az up to the gate, and sat him down there: and, behold, the kinsman of whom Bo'az spake came by; unto whom he said, Ho, such a one! turn aside, sit down here. And he turned aside, and sat down.

☆4:1

2 And he took ten men of the elders of the city, and said, Sit ye down here. And they sat down.

3 And he said unto the kinsman, Naomi, that is come again out of the country of Moab, selleth a parcel of land, which *was* our brother E-lim'e-lech's:

4:3 Lev 25:25

4 And I thought to advertise thee, saying, Buy *it* before the inhabitants, and before the elders of my people. If thou wilt redeem *it*, redeem *it:* but if thou wilt not redeem *it*, *then* tell me, that I may know: for *there is* none to redeem *it* beside thee; and I *am* after thee. And he said, I will redeem *it*.

5 Then said Bo'az, What day thou buyest the field of the hand of Naomi, thou must buy *it* also of Ruth the Moabitess, the wife of the dead, to raise up the name of the dead upon his inheritance.

☆4:5

3:18 When Naomi heard Ruth's report of what had happened, she was wise enough in the affairs of life to know that Boaz meant business and would not rest until he had taken care of the problem.
4:1 *Then Boaz went up to the gate* (of the city), where legal affairs were usually transacted.†
4:5 Boaz made certain that the purchaser of the land was also ready to marry Ruth. He probably knew that the nearer kinsman would decline to purchase the land if he had to marry Ruth as well. (See Deut. 25:5, 6.) When Boaz redeemed the property and married Ruth, the details were not all in accord with what the regulations demanded, for while Boaz was a near kinsman he was not the brother of Mahlon.

4:6☆ Lev 25:25 [6]¶And the kinsman said, I cannot redeem *it* for myself, lest I mar mine own inheritance: redeem thou my right to thyself; for I cannot redeem *it*.

B. BOAZ CARRIES OUT THE ISRAELITE CUSTOM

4:7☆ Deut 25:8–10 [7]Now this *was the manner* in former time in Israel concerning redeeming and concerning changing, for to confirm all things; a man plucked off his shoe, and gave *it* to his neighbour: and this *was* a testimony in Israel.
[8]Therefore the kinsman said unto Bo′az, Buy *it* for thee. So he drew off his shoe.
[9]¶And Bo′az said unto the elders, and *unto* all the people, Ye *are* witnesses this day, that I have bought all that *was* E-lim′e-lech's, and all that *was* Chil′i-on's and Mah′lon's, of the hand of Naomi.
[10]Moreover Ruth the Moabitess, the wife of Mah′lon, have I purchased to be my wife, to raise up the name of the dead upon his inheritance, that the name of the dead be not cut off from among his brethren, and from the gate of his place: ye *are* witnesses this day.
4:11 Gen 29:25–30 [11]And all the people that *were* in the gate, and the elders, said, *We are* witnesses. The LORD make the woman that is come into thine house like Rachel and like Leah, which two did build the house of Israel: and do thou worthily in Eph′ra-tah, and be famous in Beth-lehem:
4:12☆ Gen 38:29 46:12 [12]And let thy house be like the house of Pha′rez, whom Ta′mar bare unto Judah, of the seed which the LORD shall give thee of this young woman.

C. BOAZ MARRIES RUTH; OBED IS BORN

4:13☆ [13]¶So Bo′az took Ruth, and she was his wife: and when he went in unto her, the LORD gave her conception, and she bare a son.
[14]And the women said unto Naomi, Blessed *be* the LORD, which hath not left thee this day without a kinsman, that his name may be famous in Israel.
[15]And he shall be unto thee a restorer of *thy* life, and a nourisher of thine old age: for thy daughter in law, which loveth thee, which is better to thee than seven sons, hath born him.
[16]And Naomi took the child, and laid it in her bosom, and became nurse unto it.
[17]And the women her neighbours gave it a name, saying, There is a son born to Naomi; and they called his name O′bed: he *is* the father of Jesse, the father of David.

D. RUTH AND BOAZ BECOME THE GREAT-GRANDPARENTS OF KING DAVID

4:18–22☆ [18]¶Now these *are* the generations of Pha′rez: Pha′rez begat Hez′ron,
[19]And Hez′ron begat Ram, and Ram begat Am-min′a-dab,
[20]And Am-min′a-dab begat Nah′shon, and Nah′shon begat Sal′mon,
[21]And Sal′mon begat Bo′az, and Bo′az begat O′bed,
[22]And O′bed begat Jesse, and Jesse begat David.

4:6 *lest I mar mine own inheritance,* i.e., complicate his estate for the children he already had.†
4:7 The handing over of the sandal was a token that the right of redemption was transmitted to another. Boaz now had the right to raise up seed for the dead son of Naomi, so that the family property would remain in the same hands to which it had been originally given.
4:12 Tamar played the role of a prostitute in order to make Judah perform his function as a near kinsman when he refused to allow his living son to marry Tamar. Tamar protected her purity—the fault lay with Judah, not with her.
4:13 When Ruth became the wife of Boaz, the purpose for which she had returned to the land was fulfilled. She gave birth to a son. It was the Lord who "gave her conception." She became the joyful mother of one who would be in the lineage of the Messiah. And Naomi, who had complained so much, was blessed far beyond her wildest dreams by becoming the grandmother and nurse of the lovely little boy.
4:18–22 The genealogy of David and thus of Jesus is traced from Perez, the son of Tamar by Judah, in a situation marked by duplicity, in contrast to the lovely and moving account of the birth of Obed by levirate marriage consummated without any moral taint.

THE FIRST BOOK OF
SAMUEL
OTHERWISE CALLED THE FIRST BOOK OF THE KINGS

Authorship, date, and background 1 and 2 Samuel, as also 1 and 2 Kings (and 1 and 2 Chronicles), were originally single books. In the Greek Septuagint the two larger books of Samuel and Kings were divided into four books which were called "Books of the Kingdoms" since they dealt with the history of the kingdoms of Israel and Judah. In the Latin Vulgate Bible, Jerome followed the Septuagint translators except that he called the four books the "Books of Kings." Thus, what is called today 1 and 2 Samuel and 1 and 2 Kings were known as "The First, Second, Third, and Fourth Books of the Kings."

The date and authorship of the books of Samuel cannot be determined with certainty. From the evidence contained in them, it appears that the writer lived after the events occurred. He made use of extant material such as the Chronicles of Samuel, Nathan, and Gad. A late Jewish tradition which attributed the authorship of these two books to Samuel indicates the degree of respect with which he was held by the Jews. He was certainly important as a prophet, priest, and judge. He started the schools of the prophets. He was the nexus between the period of the Judges and the beginning of the monarchy. And he trained David, who was to become Israel's shepherd-king. Conservative scholars have usually set the date for the composition of the books of Samuel somewhere from the death of Solomon in 930 B.C. to 722 B.C., which marked the end of the Northern Kingdom.

Characteristics and content 1 Samuel recounts the history of Israel from the end of the Judges to the death of Saul by special reference to the leading characters—Eli, Samuel, Saul, David, and Jonathan. The book begins with the birth of Samuel, the son of Elkanah who lived in Ramathaim-zophim. Elkanah may well have been a Levite, since they were distributed among the various tribes including the tribe of Ephraim, among whose people he resides. Little Samuel lives with Eli, whose sons are reprobates. Upon the death of Eli, Samuel, now grown up, succeeds him and serves Israel as judge, prophet, and priest.

When Israel insists upon having a king like the surrounding nations, God discloses to Samuel that Saul is his choice. At the same time he foretells what the king will be like. Saul gets off to a good start. He wins military victories. But he becomes heady and disobeys the commands of Samuel. Samuel pronounces judgment upon him for God, who says that he delights more in obedience than in burnt offerings. Young David enters the picture when he slays Goliath, makes friends with Jonathan, and eventually serves King Saul at the royal court. Saul persecutes David, who is forced to flee. He maintains his friendship with Jonathan despite Saul's objections to his son's love for David. God reveals to Samuel that David is his choice to replace Saul in the kingship. David has a number of opportunities to slay Saul but refuses to do so lest he smite the Lord's anointed.

Saul becomes demented. His conduct indicates his state of mind. At last he consults the witch at Endor because the Spirit of God has left him. Meanwhile, David flees to the Philistines. Finally Saul dies in a battle against the Philistines as do his sons Jonathan, Abinadab, and Malchishua. A new day is about to dawn for Israel with David coming into prominence as king.

Outline

I. Eli, the priest and judge (1:1—4:22)
II. The ministry of Samuel as prophet, priest, and judge (5:1—7:17)
III. The reign of King Saul (8:1—31:13)

I. ELI, THE PRIEST AND JUDGE (1:1—4:22)
A. THE BIRTH AND GROWTH OF SAMUEL
1. Hannah's Prayer for a Son

1:1☆ 1 Chron 6:22–28 6:33–38

1 NOW there was a certain man of Ra-math-a'im-zo'phim, of mount
E'phra-im, and his name *was* El-ka'-nah, the son of Jer'o-ham, the son
of E-li'hu, the son of To'hu, the son of Zuph, an Eph'rath-ite:

1:2☆ Gen 29:30; 30:1 Deut 21:15–17

2 And he had two wives; the name of the one *was* Hannah, and the name
of the other Pe-nin'nah: and Pe-nin'nah had children, but Hannah had no
children.

1:3☆ Ex 34:22, 23 Deut 12:4–7 Josh 18:1, 2 1 Sam 2:12 4:4, 11 Lk 2:41, 42

3 And this man went up out of his city yearly to worship and to sacrifice
unto the LORD of hosts in Shi'loh. And the two sons of Eli, Hoph'ni and
Phin'e-has, the priests of the LORD, *were* there.
4 And when the time was that El-ka'nah offered, he gave to Pe-nin'nah his
wife, and to all her sons and her daughters, portions:

1:5 Gen 20:18; 30:2

5 But unto Hannah he gave a worthy portion; for he loved Hannah: but
the LORD had shut up her womb.

1:6☆

6 And her adversary also provoked her sore, for to make her fret, because
the LORD had shut up her womb.
7 And *as* he did so year by year, when she went up to the house of the
LORD, so she provoked her; therefore she wept, and did not eat.

1:8 Ruth 4:15

8 Then said El-ka'nah her husband to her, Hannah, why weepest thou?
and why eatest thou not? and why is thy heart grieved? *am* not I better to
thee than ten sons?
9 ¶So Hannah rose up after they had eaten in Shi'loh, and after they had
drunk. Now Eli the priest sat upon a seat by a post of the temple of the
LORD.

1:10☆

10 And she *was* in bitterness of soul, and prayed unto the LORD, and wept
sore.

1:11☆ Gen 29:32 Num 6:1–6 30:6–11 Judg 13:5 Lk 1:15

11 And she vowed a vow, and said, O LORD of hosts, if thou wilt indeed
look on the affliction of thine handmaid, and remember me, and not forget
thine handmaid, but wilt give unto thine handmaid a man child, then I will
give him unto the LORD all the days of his life, and there shall no razor
come upon his head.
12 And it came to pass, as she continued praying before the LORD, that Eli
marked her mouth.
13 Now Hannah, she spake in her heart; only her lips moved, but her voice
was not heard: therefore Eli thought she had been drunken.

1:14 Acts 2:13

14 And Eli said unto her, How long wilt thou be drunken? put away thy
wine from thee.

1:1 Samuel's father was *Elkanah.* He was a Levite of the family of the Kohathites. *Zuph* was from Bethlehem-Judah. The family moved to Mount Ephraim. Elkanah lived in Ramathaim-zophim; the name signifies *the double Ramah.* Ramah and Ramathaim-zophim are the same towns.

1:2 In the case of a childless marriage, a man was permitted to take a second wife. A second wife with children would protect the land rights of the family. But in the case of the Levites the land problem was not important, for they were dispersed among all of the tribes.

1:3 *LORD of hosts,* i.e., *Jehovah* (or Yahweh) *Sabaoth.* This is the first appearance of this appellation (at a time when Israel's hosts were few and feeble). It is a military term, for God has his hosts of angels who do his will and serve him at his pleasure.

1:6 Elkanah had two wives, Hannah and Peninnah. He loved Hannah, but Peninnah was the one who bore his children. As in Jacob's household—where, as a result of Laban's treachery, Jacob was married to Leah as well as Rachel—Elkanah's family was in a state of turmoil. Peninnah, the unloved wife, made fun of Hannah and bragged about her children when Hannah had none. Polygamy has never enjoyed the approval of God.

1:10 Hannah's prayer was effective because (1) she was a true believer; (2) she fervently desired what she prayed for; (3) she asked God for what she wanted; (4) she had faith to believe God was able and willing to answer her prayer; and (5) she received the promise by faith even before the answer actually came. When her son was born, Hannah acknowledged what God had done by naming the child Samuel, which means either "His name is God," or "Asked of God."

1:11 *no razor (shall) come upon his head.* This was an approved custom for those who were wholly dedicated to God.†

15 And Hannah answered and said, No, my lord, I *am* a woman of a
sorrowful spirit: I have drunk neither wine nor strong drink, but have
poured out my soul before the LORD.
16 Count not thine handmaid for a daughter of Be'li-al: for out of the
abundance of my complaint and grief have I spoken hitherto.
17 Then Eli answered and said, Go in peace: and the God of Israel grant
thee thy petition that thou hast asked of him.
18 And she said, Let thine handmaid find grace in thy sight. So the woman
went her way, and did eat, and her countenance was no more *sad*.
19 ¶And they rose up in the morning early, and worshipped before the
LORD, and returned, and came to their house to Ra'mah: and El-ka'-nah
knew Hannah his wife; and the LORD remembered her.
20 Wherefore it came to pass, when the time was come about after
Hannah had conceived, that she bare a son, and called his name Samuel,
saying, Because I have asked him of the LORD.

1:15 Ps 42:4; 142:1, 2; Lam 2:19
1:17 Ps 20:3
☆**1:19** Gen 21:1, 2; 30:22; Ex 2:24; Ps 106:45
☆**1:20**

2. The Dedication of Samuel

21 And the man El-ka'nah, and all his house, went up to offer unto the
LORD the yearly sacrifice, and his vow.
22 But Hannah went not up; for she said unto her husband, *I will not go up*
until the child be weaned, and *then* I will bring him, that he may appear
before the LORD, and there abide for ever.
23 And El-ka'nah her husband said unto her, Do what seemeth thee good;
tarry until thou have weaned him; only the LORD establish his word. So the
woman abode, and gave her son suck until she weaned him.
24 ¶And when she had weaned him, she took him up with her, with three
bullocks, and one ephah of flour, and a bottle of wine, and brought him
unto the house of the LORD in Shi'loh: and the child *was* young.
25 And they slew a bullock, and brought the child to Eli.
26 And she said, Oh my lord, *as* thy soul liveth, my lord, I *am* the woman
that stood by thee here, praying unto the LORD.
27 For this child I prayed; and the LORD hath given me my petition which
I asked of him:
28 Therefore also I have lent him to the LORD; as long as he liveth he shall
be lent to the LORD. And he worshipped the LORD there.

1:21 Lk 2:22
1:24 Num 15:8, 9, 10
☆**1:25**

3. Hannah's Prayer of Praise

2 AND Hannah prayed, and said, My heart rejoiceth in the LORD, mine
horn is exalted in the LORD: my mouth is enlarged over mine enemies;
because I rejoice in thy salvation.
2 *There is* none holy as the LORD: for *there is* none beside thee: neither *is*
there any rock like our God.

☆**2:1** Ex 15:1, 2; Deut 32:3, 4; Isa 12:2, 3; Lk 1:47, 68
☆**2:2** Ex 15:11; Deut 4:35; 32:30, 31; 1 Sam 2:2; 2 Sam 22:32; Ps 18:2

1:19 Elkanah and Hannah maintained a righteous relationship with God. Before returning home, they rose early to worship God. It is good to begin every day worshipping God by reading his Word and praying. When we practice the faith that we profess, God blesses us in a special way. In this instance Hannah conceived the baby for which she had longed; the family tensions were somewhat abated. The phrase "The LORD remembered her" clearly indicates that the baby was conceived as a direct result of God's intervention. He ever remains the author of life.

1:20 *Samuel*, i.e., "asked of God." This was a play on words. The word *Samuel* in Hebrew sounds like the word which means "to ask."†

1:25 *they*, i.e., "Elkanah and Hannah." Elkanah went home from Shiloh after Hannah's prayer (2:11).

2:1 After Hannah conceived, a prayer of thanksgiving to God rose in her heart by the spirit of prayer and of prophecy. She acknowledged that God was the author of life in the womb. Thanksgiving for the mercies of God constitutes our rent, or tribute. If we do not pay it, we are unjust to the God who gave us the gift. Hannah's prayer is a foretaste of that prayer which would later be offered by the virgin Mary upon conceiving in an even more miraculous fashion.

2:2 *there is none beside thee.* There may be other Samuels but there is no other God. His perfection is unparalleled and his being peerless.

2:3☆ 1 Sam 16:7; 1 Kgs 8:39; Prov 8:13; 16:2; 29:11, 12
2:4☆ Ps 37:15; 46: 7–9
2:5 Ruth 4:15; Ps 113:9; Jer 15:9; Lk 1:53
2:6☆ Deut 32:39; 2 Kgs 5:7; Rev 1:17, 18
2:7☆ Deut 8:17, 18; Job 1:21; 5:10, 11; Eccl 2:24–26; Jas 4:10
2:8☆ Job 36:7; 38:4–7; 42:10; Ps 75:6, 7; Jas 2:5
2:9☆ Ps 33:16, 17; Jer 9:23, 24; Zech 4:6; Mt 8:12
2:10☆ Ex 15:6; 19:18; 1 Sam 7:10; Ps 18:13; 21:1, 7; 96:13

3 Talk no more so exceeding proudly; let *not* arrogancy come out of your mouth: for the LORD *is* a God of knowledge, and by him actions are weighed.

4 The bows of the mighty men *are* broken, and they that stumbled are girded with strength.

5 *They that were* full have hired out themselves for bread; and *they that were* hungry ceased: so that the barren hath born seven; and she that hath many children is waxed feeble.

6 The LORD killeth, and maketh alive: he bringeth down to the grave, and bringeth up.

7 The LORD maketh poor, and maketh rich: he bringeth low, and lifteth up.

8 He raiseth up the poor out of the dust, *and* lifteth up the beggar from the dunghill, to set *them* among princes, and to make them inherit the throne of glory: for the pillars of the earth *are* the LORD's, and he hath set the world upon them.

9 He will keep the feet of his saints, and the wicked shall be silent in darkness; for by strength shall no man prevail.

10 The adversaries of the LORD shall be broken to pieces; out of heaven shall he thunder upon them: the LORD shall judge the ends of the earth; and he shall give strength unto his king, and exalt the horn of his anointed.

4. Young Samuel, the Lord's Helper

2:11☆
2:12☆ 1 Sam 1:3; 4:4, 11; Jer 2:8; 9:3, 6
2:13 Lev 7:20, 28–36

11 And El-ka'nah went to Ra'mah to his house. And the child did minister unto the LORD before Eli the priest.

12 Now the sons of Eli *were* sons of Be'li-al; they knew not the LORD.

13 And the priest's custom with the people *was, that,* when any man offered sacrifice, the priest's servant came, while the flesh was in seething, with a fleshhook of three teeth in his hand;

14 And he struck *it* into the pan, or kettle, or caldron, or pot; all that the fleshhook brought up the priest took for himself. So they did in Shi'loh unto all the Israelites that came thither.

2:15 Lev 3:2–5; 7:30

15 Also before they burnt the fat, the priest's servant came, and said to the man that sacrificed, Give flesh to roast for the priest; for he will not have sodden flesh of thee, but raw.

16 And *if* any man said unto him, Let them not fail to burn the fat presently, and *then* take *as much* as thy soul desireth; then he would answer him, *Nay;* but thou shalt give *it me* now: and if not, I will take *it* by force.

2:17 Mal 2:7–9

17 Wherefore the sin of the young men was very great before the LORD: for men abhorred the offering of the LORD.

18 ¶But Samuel ministered before the LORD, *being* a child, girded with a linen ephod.

2:3 *a God of knowledge.* His wisdom is unsearchable. He gives knowledge and understanding to whoever seeks him in faith.
2:4 *the bows of the mighty men are broken.* However mighty men may be, all God needs to do is speak and they are disarmed, disabled, and beaten in battle.
2:6 *killeth and maketh alive.* God is the sovereign Lord of both death and life. He is the one who holds in his hand the keys of death and the grave.
2:7, 8 Promotion does not come by chance. God lifts up and pulls down whom he pleases. Unlikely people are advanced and advantaged "from a prison to a palace, from a sheep-hook to a sceptre."*
2:9, 10 This prophetic word announces that God will care for and keep safely those whom he has chosen. Those who oppose him are adversaries, who will be cut off and judged. *he shall give strength to his king* has messianic implications, for "the power and honor of Messiah the prince shall grow and increase more and more"* until the end of the age, when every knee shall bow before him.
2:11ff In these verses the contrast is drawn between the good character of Elkanah's family and the bad character of Eli's family. Later, the children of Samuel will be no better than the children of Eli. Grace does not run through the bloodline.
2:12 See note on 1 Sam. 3:13, concerning the sons of Eli who were judged by God for their sinfulness.

[19]Moreover his mother made him a little coat, and brought *it* to him from
year to year, when she came up with her husband to offer the yearly
sacrifice.
[20]¶And Eli blessed El-ka'nah and his wife, and said, The LORD give thee
seed of this woman for the loan which is lent to the LORD. And they went
unto their own home.
[21]And the LORD visited Hannah, so that she conceived, and bare three
sons and two daughters. And the child Samuel grew before the LORD.
[22]¶Now Eli was very old, and heard all that his sons did unto all Israel;
and how they lay with the women that assembled *at* the door of the
tabernacle of the congregation.
[23]And he said unto them, Why do ye such things? for I hear of your evil
dealings by all this people.
[24]Nay, my sons; for *it is* no good report that I hear: ye make the LORD's
people to transgress.
[25]If one man sin against another, the judge shall judge him: but if a man
sin against the LORD, who shall intreat for him? Notwithstanding they
hearkened not unto the voice of their father, because the LORD would slay
them.
[26]And the child Samuel grew on, and was in favour both with the LORD,
and also with men.

2:19 1 Sam 1:3
☆2:21 Gen 21:1; 1 Sam 3:19–21; Lk 2:40
2:23 Num 15:30; Deut 1:17
2:26 Lk 1:80; 2:40, 52

5. A Prophet's Word of God's Judgment on Eli's House

[27]¶And there came a man of God unto Eli, and said unto him, Thus saith
the LORD, Did I plainly appear unto the house of thy father, when they
were in Egypt in Pharaoh's house?
[28]And did I choose him out of all the tribes of Israel *to be* my priest, to
offer upon mine altar, to burn incense, to wear an ephod before me? and
did I give unto the house of thy father all the offerings made by fire of the
children of Israel?
[29]Wherefore kick ye at my sacrifice and at mine offering, which I have
commanded *in my* habitation; and honourest thy sons above me, to make
yourselves fat with the chiefest of all the offerings of Israel my people?
[30]Wherefore the LORD God of Israel saith, I said indeed *that* thy house,
and the house of thy father, should walk before me for ever: but now the
LORD saith, Be it far from me; for them that honour me I will honour, and
they that despise me shall be lightly esteemed.
[31]Behold, the days come, that I will cut off thine arm, and the arm of thy
father's house, that there shall not be an old man in thine house.
[32]And thou shalt see an enemy *in my* habitation, in all *the wealth* which
God shall give Israel: and there shall not be an old man in thine house for
ever.
[33]And the man of thine, *whom* I shall not cut off from mine altar, *shall be*
to consume thine eyes, and to grieve thine heart: and all the increase of
thine house shall die in the flower of their age.
[34]And this *shall be* a sign unto thee, that shall come upon thy two sons,
on Hoph'ni and Phin'e-has; in one day they shall die both of them.

☆2:27 Ex 13:16; Deut 6:21; Jos 2:10; Judg 6:8
☆2:28 Ex 28: 1–4; 30:7, 8; Deut 10:9
2:29 Mt 10:37
2:30 Num 25: 12, 13; Ps 50:23; Mal 2:7–9
2:31 1 Sam 4:11; 22:17–20
2:34 1 Sam 4:11, 17

2:21ff The descendants of Eli shall "be stripped of their authority, should be deposed, and have no influence upon the people as once they had."* One writer commented that a family lived in Jerusalem long after this, whose life spans generally did not exceed eighteen years. It was found that they were descendants of Eli's house.
2:27 *a man of God,* i.e., "a prophet." The Scriptures do not identify this man of God. God has always had unidentified servants who carry out the divine will and who serve as preachers of the prophetic word, even when it is unwelcome. God sharply rebuked Eli for failing to discipline his sons. By his failure to take action against them, "he strengthened their hands in their wickedness."*
2:28 *wear an ephod,* i.e., "wear a priestly robe."†

2:35☆ 35 And I will raise me up a faithful priest, *that* shall do according to *that*
which *is* in mine heart and in my mind: and I will build him a sure house;
and he shall walk before mine anointed for ever.
36 And it shall come to pass, *that* every one that is left in thine house shall
come *and* crouch to him for a piece of silver and a morsel of bread, and
shall say, Put me, I pray thee, into one of the priests' offices, that I may eat
a piece of bread.

6. Samuel's Message to Eli from God
a. The Lord's Call to Samuel

3:1☆ 3 AND the child Samuel ministered unto the LORD before Eli. And the
1 Sam 3:21 Isa 1:1 Jer 1:1 Ezek 13:17 word of the LORD was precious in those days; *there was* no open
vision.
2 And it came to pass at that time, when Eli *was* laid down in his place,
and his eyes began to wax dim, *that* he could not see;
3:3☆ 3 And ere the lamp of God went out in the temple of the LORD, where the
ark of God *was*, and Samuel was laid down *to sleep;*
3:4 Isa 6:8 4 That the LORD called Samuel: and he answered, Here *am* I.
5 And he ran unto Eli, and said, Here *am* I; for thou calledst me. And he
said, I called not; lie down again. And he went and lay down.
6 And the LORD called yet again, Samuel. And Samuel arose and went to
Eli, and said, Here *am* I; for thou didst call me. And he answered, I called
not, my son; lie down again.
7 Now Samuel did not yet know the LORD, neither was the word of the
LORD yet revealed unto him.
8 And the LORD called Samuel again the third time. And he arose and
went to Eli, and said, Here *am* I; for thou didst call me. And Eli perceived
that the LORD had called the child.
9 Therefore Eli said unto Samuel, Go, lie down: and it shall be, if he call
thee, that thou shalt say, Speak, LORD; for thy servant heareth. So Samuel
went and lay down in his place.

b. God Tells Samuel about Eli's Fate

10 And the LORD came, and stood, and called as at other times, Samuel,
Samuel. Then Samuel answered, Speak; for thy servant heareth.
3:11☆ 11 ¶And the LORD said to Samuel, Behold, I will do a thing in Israel, at
Deut 31:21 2 Kgs 21:12 Isa 29:14 Jer 19:3 which both the ears of every one that heareth it shall tingle.
12 In that day I will perform against Eli all *things* which I have spoken
concerning his house: when I begin, I will also make an end.
3:13☆ 13 For I have told him that I will judge his house for ever for the iniquity
which he knoweth; because his sons made themselves vile, and he
restrained them not.

2:35 *I will raise me up a faithful priest.* This promise and prediction was fulfilled when Solomon appointed Zadok to replace Abiathar, Eli's great-grandson (1 Kings 2.27, 35).

3:1 *there was no open vision.* The silence of God prevailed. No one was known (publicly) to have visions from God in those days.

3:3 This verse marks the beginning of God's open dealing with Samuel, who is shortly to be called to replace Eli.

3:11 God's first message to Samuel is one of judgment on the sons of Eli for blasphemy (3:13) and Eli's failure to restrain them in their evil. Samuel has to reveal this sentence to Eli.

3:13 Eli the priest favored his sons above his God. In 2:12 we are told that the "sons of Eli were sons of Belial; they knew not the LORD." These sons were adulterers and they abused their privilege as priests by breaking ceremonial arrangements (2:12–17). They treated the offering of the Lord with contempt (see 2:17, RSV). Even after Eli discovered their transgressions, he did nothing to correct the situation. He failed to restrain his sons and thus was guilty of being an accessory to their crimes against God. God pronounced his judgment, ending the priestly succession through Eli. When Eli died, he was replaced by Samuel.

14 And therefore I have sworn unto the house of Eli, that the iniquity of
Eli's house shall not be purged with sacrifice nor offering for ever.

3:14 Lev 15:31; 1 Sam 2:25; Ps 51:16, 17; Isa 22:14; Jer 7:16

c. Samuel Informs Eli about His Fate

15 ¶And Samuel lay until the morning, and opened the doors of the house
of the LORD. And Samuel feared to shew Eli the vision.
16 Then Eli called Samuel, and said, Samuel, my son. And he answered,
Here *am* I.
17 And he said, What *is* the thing that *the LORD* hath said unto thee? I
pray thee hide *it* not from me: God do so to thee, and more also, if thou
hide *any* thing from me of all the things that he said unto thee.
18 And Samuel told him every whit, and hid nothing from him. And he
said, It *is* the LORD: let him do what seemeth him good.

3:15 Jer 1:8
3:18 2 Sam 16:10; Job 2:10; Ps 39:9; Isa 39:8

d. Samuel Becomes God's Prophet

19 ¶And Samuel grew, and the LORD was with him, and did let none of his
words fall to the ground.
20 And all Israel from Dan even to Be'er–she'ba knew that Samuel *was*
established *to be* a prophet of the LORD.
21 And the LORD appeared again in Shi'loh: for the LORD revealed himself
to Samuel in Shi'loh by the word of the LORD.

☆**3:19** Gen 21:22; Judg 13:24; Lk 1:80; 2:40, 52
3:20 Judg 20:1; 2 Sam 3:9, 10; 17:11

B. GOD'S JUDGMENT ON ELI
1. Israel Defeated; the Ark Captured

4 AND the word of Samuel came to all Israel. Now Israel went out
against the Philistines to battle, and pitched beside Eb'en–e'zer: and
the Philistines pitched in A'phek.
2 And the Philistines put themselves in array against Israel: and when
they joined battle, Israel was smitten before the Philistines: and they slew
of the army in the field about four thousand men.
3 ¶And when the people were come into the camp, the elders of Israel
said, Wherefore hath the LORD smitten us to day before the Philistines? Let
us fetch the ark of the covenant of the LORD out of Shi'loh unto us, that,
when it cometh among us, it may save us out of the hand of our enemies.
4 So the people sent to Shi'loh, that they might bring from thence the ark
of the covenant of the LORD of hosts, which dwelleth *between* the
cherubims: and the two sons of Eli, Hoph'ni and Phin'e-has, *were* there
with the ark of the covenant of God.
5 And when the ark of the covenant of the LORD came into the camp, all
Israel shouted with a great shout, so that the earth rang again.
6 And when the Philistines heard the noise of the shout, they said, What
meaneth the noise of this great shout in the camp of the Hebrews? And they
understood that the ark of the LORD was come into the camp.
7 And the Philistines were afraid, for they said, God is come into the
camp. And they said, Woe unto us! for there hath not been such a thing
heretofore.

☆**4:1** Josh 13:2–7; Judg 13:1; 1 Sam 29:1
☆**4:2** Josh 7:5, 12; Ps 44:9, 10
☆**4:3** Num 10:35; 31:6; Josh 7:7; 1 Sam 14:18
☆**4:4** 1 Sam 1:3; 4:11; 2 Sam 6:2; 2 Kgs 19:15; Ps 80:1
4:5 Josh 6:5
4:7 Ex 14:25; 15:14

3:19 *let none of his words fall to the ground.* Every word that Samuel spoke as a prophet proved true and all was accomplished in its season.
4:1 *Philistines.* See note on Judg. 13:1 for background information on these people.
4:2 *Israel was smitten,* i.e., they lost the battle against a well armed and aggressive foe. They think the absence of the ark is the reason for the defeat (4:3).
4:3 Israel superstitiously believed that bringing the ark to the battle will enable them to defeat the Philistines. But since the ark had become an idol for the absence of God's presence, it was useless.
4:4 *cherubims.* See note on Exod. 25:22.

4:8☆ 8 Woe unto us! who shall deliver us out of the hand of these mighty Gods?
these *are* the Gods that smote the Egyptians with all the plagues in the
wilderness.
4:9 9 Be strong, and quit yourselves like men, O ye Philistines, that ye be not
Judg 13:1 2 Sam 10:12 servants unto the Hebrews, as they have been to you: quit yourselves like
men, and fight.
4:10 10 ¶And the Philistines fought, and Israel was smitten, and they fled every
Deut 28:15, 25 Ps 78:9 man into his tent: and there was a very great slaughter; for there fell of
Israel thirty thousand footmen.
4:11☆ 11 And the ark of God was taken; and the two sons of Eli, Hoph′ni and
1 Sam 2:34 Ps 78:60–61 Phin′e-has, were slain.

2. The Death of Eli

4:12☆ 12 ¶And there ran a man of Benjamin out of the army, and came to
Josh 7:6 2 Sam 1:1, 2 Shi′loh the same day with his clothes rent, and with earth upon his head.
13:19 Neh 9:1 13 And when he came, lo, Eli sat upon a seat by the wayside watching: for
his heart trembled for the ark of God. And when the man came into the
city, and told *it*, all the city cried out.
4:14 14 And when Eli heard the noise of the crying, he said, What *meaneth* the
2 Sam 1:4 noise of this tumult? And the man came in hastily, and told Eli.
4:15 15 Now Eli was ninety and eight years old; and his eyes were dim, that he
Gen 27:1 1 Sam 3:2 could not see.
16 And the man said unto Eli, I *am* he that came out of the army, and I
fled to day out of the army. And he said, What is there done, my son?
4:17 17 And the messenger answered and said, Israel is fled before the
1 Sam 2:34 4:11 Philistines, and there hath been also a great slaughter among the people,
and thy two sons also, Hoph′ni and Phin′e-has, are dead, and the ark of
God is taken.
4:18☆ 18 And it came to pass, when he made mention of the ark of God, that he
fell from off the seat backward by the side of the gate, and his neck brake,
and he died: for he was an old man, and heavy. And he had judged Israel
forty years.

3. The Birth of Ichabod

4:19☆ 19 ¶And his daughter in law, Phin′e-has′ wife, was with child, *near* to be
delivered: and when she heard the tidings that the ark of God was taken,
and that her father in law and her husband were dead, she bowed herself
and travailed; for her pains came upon her.
4:20 20 And about the time of her death the women that stood by her said unto
Gen 35:17, 18 her, Fear not; for thou hast born a son. But she answered not, neither did
she regard *it*.
4:21 21 And she named the child I′-cha-bod, saying, The glory is departed
1 Sam 14:3 Ps 78:61 from Israel: because the ark of God was taken, and because of her father in
106:19, 20 law and her husband.

4:8 The Philistines regarded the ark as deity. But their attitude is understandable because they had no knowledge of the true God, whereas Israel did.

4:11 The presence of Hophni and Phinehas with the ark was a sure guarantee of defeat. These sons of Eli were apostates, who denied the true faith and sinned against God. They died for their transgressions.

4:12 *Shiloh*. This verse does not mention the destruction of Shiloh, but archeological findings confirm the fact reported in Jer. 7:12; 26:6.

4:18 To the credit of Eli, it may be said that it was the loss of the ark, not the death of his sons, that was the immediate cause of his death. Here we also learn that Eli served as judge, as well as priest.

4:19 Phinehas' wife appears to have been a devout believer who was concerned about the ark and the glory of her God. She dies giving birth to the child she named Ichabod, whose name means "without glory." This gracious woman was married to a wicked husband—which happens more frequently than we suppose.

22 And she said, The glory is departed from Israel: for the ark of God is taken.

II. THE MINISTRY OF SAMUEL AS PROPHET, PRIEST, AND JUDGE (5:1—7:17)

A. THE SEIZURE AND RELEASE OF THE ARK

1. The Ark in Ashdod in Dagon's Temple

5 AND the Philistines took the ark of God, and brought it from Eb'en-
e'zer unto Ash'dod.
2 When the Philistines took the ark of God, they brought it into the house
of Da'gon, and set it by Da'gon.
3 ¶And when they of Ash'dod arose early on the morrow, behold, Da'gon
was fallen upon his face to the earth before the ark of the LORD. And they
took Da'gon, and set him in his place again.
4 And when they arose early on the morrow morning, behold, Da'gon *was*
fallen upon his face to the ground before the ark of the LORD; and the head
of Da'gon and both the palms of his hands *were* cut off upon the threshold;
only *the stump of* Da'gon was left to him.
5 Therefore neither the priests of Da'gon, nor any that come into Da'gon's
house, tread on the threshold of Da'gon in Ash'dod unto this day.

5:1 Josh 13:3; Judg 16:23–30; 1 Sam 4:11, 17; 1 Chron 10:8–10; Ps 78:61
☆5:2
☆5:3 Isa 19:1; 46:1, 2, 7

2. The Ark at Gath and Ekron

6 But the hand of the LORD was heavy upon them of Ash'dod, and he
destroyed them, and smote them with emerods, *even* Ash'dod and the
coasts thereof.
7 And when the men of Ash'dod saw that *it was* so, they said, The ark of
the God of Israel shall not abide with us: for his hand is sore upon us, and
upon Da'gon our god.
8 They sent therefore and gathered all the lords of the Philistines unto
them, and said, What shall we do with the ark of the God of Israel? And
they answered, Let the ark of the God of Israel be carried about unto Gath.
And they carried the ark of the God of Israel about *thither*.
9 And it was *so*, that, after they had carried it about, the hand of the LORD
was against the city with a very great destruction: and he smote the men of
the city, both small and great, and they had emerods in their secret parts.
10 ¶Therefore they sent the ark of God to Ekron. And it came to pass, as
the ark of God came to Ekron, that the Ekronites cried out, saying, They
have brought about the ark of the God of Israel to us, to slay us and our
people.
11 So they sent and gathered together all the lords of the Philistines, and
said, Send away the ark of the God of Israel, and let it go again to his own
place, that it slay us not, and our people: for there was a deadly destruction
throughout all the city; the hand of God was very heavy there.
12 And the men that died not were smitten with the emerods: and the cry
of the city went up to heaven.

5:6 Ex 9:3; Deut 28:27; 1 Sam 6:4, 5
5:7 Ex 8:8; 12:33; 1 Sam 6:20
☆5:8
5:9 1 Sam 7:13; 12:15
5:10 Josh 15:45; Judg 1:18; 2 Kgs 1:2
☆5:11

5:2 *Dagon* was the chief god of the Philistines. Temples were erected in his honor in Ashdod, Gaza, Bethshan, and Ugarit. He was a fertility god (or grain god) in Philistia, a land which produced much grain.
5:3 This marks the story of a god against the true God. Dagon falls on his face before the ark of God. God is not mocked. Nothing, living or dead, stone or human can stand before the majesty of the most high God unless they stand in the righteousness of Jesus Christ.
5:8 The Philistines, whose hands are unclean, carry the sacred ark of God to another resting place. They pay a high price for their error. God sends sickness so grievous that they begin to panic and want to rid themselves of the ark.
5:11 *let it go again to his own place.* It took dire sickness for the Philistines to decide to return the ark to the place from whence it came. At least they still had enough sense to know when they were defeated and what they needed to do about it. Some of God's people do not always evince this common sense.

3. The Return of the Ark
a. The Philistine Guilt Offering

6:1 1 Sam 5:1

6 AND the ark of the LORD was in the country of the Philistines seven
months.

6:2 Gen 41:8; Ex 7:11; Isa 47:12, 13; Dan 2:1; 5:7

2 And the Philistines called for the priests and the diviners, saying, What
shall we do to the ark of the LORD? tell us wherewith we shall send it to his
place.

6:3 Lev 5:15, 16; 7:1–7; 1 Sam 6:9

3 And they said, If ye send away the ark of the God of Israel, send it not
empty; but in any wise return him a trespass offering: then ye shall be
healed, and it shall be known to you why his hand is not removed from you.

6:4☆

4 Then said they, What *shall be* the trespass offering which we shall return
to him? They answered, Five golden emerods, and five golden mice,
according to the number of the lords of the Philistines: for one plague *was*
on you all, and on your lords.
5 Wherefore ye shall make images of your emerods, and images of your
mice that mar the land; and ye shall give glory unto the God of Israel:
peradventure he will lighten his hand from off you, and from off your gods,
and from off your land.

6:6 Ex 8:15, 31, 32; 12:31

6 Wherefore then do ye harden your hearts, as the Egyptians and Pharaoh
hardened their hearts? when he had wrought wonderfully among them, did
they not let the people go, and they departed?

6:7 Deut 21:3; 2 Sam 6:3

7 Now therefore make a new cart, and take two milch kine, on which there
hath come no yoke, and tie the kine to the cart, and bring their calves home
from them:
8 And take the ark of the LORD, and lay it upon the cart; and put the
jewels of gold, which ye return him *for* a trespass offering, in a coffer by the
side thereof; and send it away, that it may go.

6:9 Josh 15:10, 11; Judg 1:33; 1 Sam 6:3

9 And see, if it goeth up by the way of his own coast to Beth–she′mesh,
then he hath done us this great evil: but if not, then we shall know that *it is*
not his hand *that* smote us; it *was* a chance *that* happened to us.
10 ¶And the men did so; and took two milch kine, and tied them to the
cart, and shut up their calves at home:

6:11 2 Sam 6:3; 1 Chron 13:7

11 And they laid the ark of the LORD upon the cart, and the coffer with the
mice of gold and the images of their emerods.

6:12☆

12 And the kine took the straight way to the way of Beth–she′mesh, *and*
went along the highway, lowing as they went, and turned not aside *to* the
right hand or *to* the left; and the lords of the Philistines went after them
unto the border of Beth–she′mesh.
13 And *they of* Beth–she′mesh *were* reaping their wheat harvest in the
valley: and they lifted up their eyes, and saw the ark, and rejoiced to see *it*.

6:14 Judg 6:26; 1 Kgs 18:30; 2 Sam 24:22

14 And the cart came into the field of Joshua, a Beth–she′mite, and stood
there, where *there was* a great stone: and they clave the wood of the cart,
and offered the kine a burnt offering unto the LORD.

6:15 Josh 3:2–4

15 And the Levites took down the ark of the LORD, and the coffer that *was*
with it, wherein the jewels of gold *were*, and put *them* on the great stone:
and the men of Beth–she′mesh offered burnt offerings and sacrificed
sacrifices the same day unto the LORD.
16 And when the five lords of the Philistines had seen *it*, they returned to
Ekron the same day.

6:4 The Philistines knew that they had violated the God of Israel and they decided to make a sacrifice, even in unbelief, to arrest the sickness which has spread through their ranks.

6:12 God uses dumb animals to do his will. And sometimes animals evidence more good sense than the humans who own them. The cows headed straight for Beth-shemesh without missing a turn. They shamed the stupidity of the Israelites, who had made no effort to bring the ark to its home.

b. The Ark Sent from Beth-shemesh to Kirjath-jearim

17 And these *are* the golden emerods which the Philistines returned *for* a **6:17** 1 Sam 6:4, 5
trespass offering unto the LORD; for Ash'dod one, for Ga'za one, for As'ke-
lon one, for Gath one, for Ekron one;
18 And the golden mice, *according to* the number of all the cities of the **6:18** Num 4:1, 15, 20; Deut 3:5; 2 Sam 6:7
Philistines *belonging* to the five lords, *both* of fenced cities, and of country
villages, even unto the great *stone of* Abel, whereon they set down the ark of
the LORD: *which stone remaineth* unto this day in the field of Joshua, the
Beth-she'mite.
19 ¶And he smote the men of Beth-she'mesh, because they had looked ☆**6:19**
into the ark of the LORD, even he smote of the people fifty thousand and
threescore and ten men: and the people lamented, because the LORD had
smitten *many* of the people with a great slaughter.
20 And the men of Beth-she'mesh said, Who is able to stand before this **6:20** Lev 11:44, 45; 2 Sam 6:9
holy LORD God? and to whom shall he go up from us?
21 ¶And they sent messengers to the inhabitants of Kir'jath-je'a-rim, **6:21** Josh 15:9, 60
saying, The Philistines have brought again the ark of the LORD; come ye
down, *and* fetch it up to you.

7 AND the men of Kir'jath-je'a-rim came, and fetched up the ark of the **7:1** 2 Sam 6:3, 4
LORD, and brought it into the house of A-bin'a-dab in the hill, and
sanctified E-le-a'zar his son to keep the ark of the LORD.
2 And it came to pass, while the ark abode in Kir'jath-je'a-rim, that the **7:2** Judg 2:3
time was long; for it was twenty years: and all the house of Israel lamented
after the LORD.

B. SAMUEL'S VICTORY OVER THE PHILISTINES
1. Samuel's Call for Repentance

3 ¶And Samuel spake unto all the house of Israel, saying, If ye do return ☆**7:3** Deut 6:13; 13:4; Josh 24:14, 23; Judg 2:12–14; 10:16; 2 Chron 19:13; Joel 2:12–14
unto the LORD with all your hearts, *then* put away the strange gods and
Ash'ta-roth from among you, and prepare your hearts unto the LORD, and
serve him only: and he will deliver you out of the hand of the Philistines.
4 Then the children of Israel did put away Ba'al-im and Ash'ta-roth, and
served the LORD only.

2. The Philistines Defeated; the Stone of Help (Ebenezer)

5 And Samuel said, Gather all Israel to Miz'peh, and I will pray for you **7:5** 1 Sam 12:17–19; 1 Kgs 18:24
unto the LORD.
6 And they gathered together to Miz'peh, and drew water, and poured *it* ☆**7:6** Judg 10:10; Neh 9:1; Lam 2:19
out before the LORD, and fasted on that day, and said there, We have
sinned against the LORD. And Samuel judged the children of Israel in
Miz'peh.
7 And when the Philistines heard that the children of Israel were gathered **7:7** 1 Sam 13:6

6:19 The ark of the Lord was originally placed within the Holy of Holies, into which only the high priest could enter. Here we see that the ark was returned to Israel from the hands of the Philistines, who had previously seized it. But the tent of meeting was no longer set up. Thus the ark was exposed to all. When it was returned to Israel, some of the people, in the same manner as Adam, were "ruined by an ambition of forbidden knowledge."* They wanted to look into the ark, perhaps to see the two tables of the law. When they invaded God's privacy, judgment fell upon them and 50,070 men died at the hands of an angry God. (Evangelicals think this figure is too large. Archer says, "The received Hebrew text of this passage gives rise to a very justified suspicion that the text was inadvertently garbled in the course of transmission," *Encyclopedia of Bible Difficulties,* G. L. Archer, Zondervan, 1982.)

7:3 Israel may have had a high regard for the ark, but they also had been worshipping other gods. Samuel calls them to repent and return to the worship of the one true God. Revival takes place (according to 7:4) and Israel serves only the Lord.

7:6 Prayer, fasting, repentance, and pouring out of water before the Lord were evidences of revival.

together to Miz'peh, the lords of the Philistines went up against Israel. And
when the children of Israel heard *it*, they were afraid of the Philistines.
[8]And the children of Israel said to Samuel, Cease not to cry unto the
LORD our God for us, that he will save us out of the hand of the Philistines.
[9]¶And Samuel took a sucking lamb, and offered *it for* a burnt offering
wholly unto the LORD: and Samuel cried unto the LORD for Israel; and the
LORD heard him.
[10]And as Samuel was offering up the burnt offering, the Philistines drew
near to battle against Israel: but the LORD thundered with a great thunder
on that day upon the Philistines, and discomfited them; and they were
smitten before Israel.
[11]And the men of Israel went out of Miz'peh, and pursued the Philistines,
and smote them, until *they came* under Beth-car.
[12]Then Samuel took a stone, and set *it* between Miz'peh and Shen, and
called the name of it Eb'en-e'zer, saying, Hitherto hath the LORD helped us.
[13]¶So the Philistines were subdued, and they came no more into the coast
of Israel: and the hand of the LORD was against the Philistines all the days
of Samuel.
[14]And the cities which the Philistines had taken from Israel were restored
to Israel, from Ekron even unto Gath; and the coasts thereof did Israel
deliver out of the hands of the Philistines. And there was peace between
Israel and the Am'or-ites.

7:8 1 Sam 12:19; Isa 37:4
7:9☆ Lev 22:26, 27; Jer 15:1
7:10 1 Sam 2:10; 2 Sam 22:14; Ps 18:14
7:12☆ Gen 28:18; 35:13–15; Josh 4:9; 24:26
7:13☆ Judg 13:1; 1 Sam 13:5

3. A Summary of Samuel's Ministry

[15]¶And Samuel judged Israel all the days of his life.
[16]And he went from year to year in circuit to Beth-el, and Gilgal, and
Miz'peh, and judged Israel in all those places.
[17]And his return *was* to Ra'mah; for there *was* his house; and there he
judged Israel; and there he built an altar unto the LORD.

7:15 1 Sam 7:6; 12:11
7:16 Gen 28:19; Josh 5:8; 11:1; 1 Sam 7:5
7:17☆ 1 Sam 1:1, 19; 2:11; 15:34; 16:13

III. THE REIGN OF KING SAUL (8:1—31:13)

A. SAUL APPOINTED TO THE KINGSHIP

1. The Israelis Ask for a King

8 AND it came to pass, when Samuel was old, that he made his sons
judges over Israel.

8:1☆ Deut 16:18, 19

7:9 Samuel is a praying prophet and priest. His prayers are heard and answered by God almost instantaneously. Thunder and lightning overtook the Philistines, who retreat. Once again God answers by a providential act.

7:12 *called the name of it Eben-ezer. Eben-ezer* means "stone of help," and represented the great victory God had given the Israelites over the Philistines. It was intended to be a memorial for future generations to see, so that their faith in God might be strengthened and that they might experience the same delivering power of their fathers' God. Believers today should also raise "Eben-ezers" in their souls, in order to remember the mighty deliverances of which God was, and is, capable.

7:13 Samuel, by means of prayer and the work of reformation among the Israelites, brought peace from the threat of the Philistines all the days of his ministry. God now fought for Israel and raised his hand against the Philistines. If God is on our side, who can be against us?

7:17 *his return was to Ramah.* Ramah was Samuel's home town. It was also known as Ramathaim-zuphim. Since Shiloh was in ruins, Samuel found it convenient to make his headquarters in Ramah.

8:1ff Samuel should have learned something from the experience of Eli, his predecessor. But he did not. Like Eli, he appointed his sons as judges over Israel, even though his sons did not follow in their father's footsteps. His sons were guilty of taking bribes and of perverting judgment. It was this situation which prompted the elders of Israel to ask for a king; they were tired of being ruled by scoundrels. Samuel was displeased, but God ordered him to anoint the man God had chosen to be king over Israel.

2 Now the name of his firstborn was Jo'el; and the name of his second, A-
bi'ah: *they were* judges in Be'er–she'ba.
3 And his sons walked not in his ways, but turned aside after lucre, and
took bribes, and perverted judgment.
4 Then all the elders of Israel gathered themselves together, and came to
Samuel unto Ra'mah,
5 And said unto him, Behold, thou art old, and thy sons walk not in thy
ways: now make us a king to judge us like all the nations.
6 ¶But the thing displeased Samuel, when they said, Give us a king to
judge us. And Samuel prayed unto the LORD.
7 And the LORD said unto Samuel, Hearken unto the voice of the people
in all that they say unto thee: for they have not rejected thee, but they have
rejected me, that I should not reign over them.
8 According to all the works which they have done since the day that I
brought them up out of Egypt even unto this day, wherewith they have
forsaken me, and served other gods, so do they also unto thee.
9 Now therefore hearken unto their voice: howbeit yet protest solemnly
unto them, and shew them the manner of the king that shall reign over
them.
10 ¶And Samuel told all the words of the LORD unto the people that asked
of him a king.
11 And he said, This will be the manner of the king that shall reign over
you: He will take your sons, and appoint *them* for himself, for his chariots,
and *to be* his horsemen; and *some* shall run before his chariots.
12 And he will appoint him captains over thousands, and captains over
fifties; and *will set them* to ear his ground, and to reap his harvest, and to
make his instruments of war, and instruments of his chariots.
13 And he will take your daughters *to be* confectionaries, and *to be* cooks,
and *to be* bakers.
14 And he will take your fields, and your vineyards, and your oliveyards,
even the best *of them*, and give *them* to his servants.
15 And he will take the tenth of your seed, and of your vineyards, and give
to his officers, and to his servants.
16 And he will take your menservants, and your maidservants, and your
goodliest young men, and your asses, and put *them* to his work.
17 He will take the tenth of your sheep: and ye shall be his servants.
18 And ye shall cry out in that day because of your king which ye shall
have chosen you; and the LORD will not hear you in that day.
19 ¶Nevertheless the people refused to obey the voice of Samuel; and they
said, Nay; but we will have a king over us;

☆**8:2** 1 Kgs 19:3; 1 Chron 6:28; Amos 5:5
8:3 Ex 23:6, 8; Deut 16:19; 1 Sam 2:12
8:4 1 Sam 7:17
☆**8:5** Deut 17:14, 15; 1 Sam 12:19
8:6 1 Sam 12:17; 15:11
8:7 Ex 16:8
8:8 Ex 14:11; 16:3; Deut 9:24; Judg 2:1, 2; 1 Sam 10:18, 19
☆**8:9**
8:11 Deut 17:14–20; 1 Sam 10:24; 14:52; 2 Sam 15:1; 1 Kgs 1:5
8:12 1 Sam 22:7; 1 Kgs 4:7
8:14 1 Sam 22:7; 1 Kgs 21:7; Ezek 46:18
8:18 Job 27:9; Prov 1:25–28; Isa 8:21; Mic 3:4
☆**8:19** 1 Sam 8:5

8:2 It is surely ironic that the sons of Samuel were no better than Eli's sons, whom God slew. Since Samuel witnessed the experience of Eli and noted the conduct of Eli's sons, one would have expected something better of Samuel's own sons. This demonstrates that good men can have bad children, and that good children sometimes come from bad homes. Grace does not run through the blood of the family; it comes from God.

8:5ff After the Exodus God ruled Israel through his servant Moses. This rule continued through the days of Joshua and the judges. Samuel was God's representative. When his sons sinned, the people asked for a king. Samuel was unhappy but consented to the request because God commanded him to do so. He told the people what was in store for them, but they failed to heed the warning. They probably thought that serving *any* king would be better than serving the wicked sons of Samuel. God predicted that the kingship would prove to be disastrous, and this prophecy was fulfilled with the rule of the ungodly kings of Judah and those of Israel. At the consummation of the present age, the theocracy will be restored. God will reign over his people through his Son Jesus Christ, whose kingdom shall endure forever (Luke 1:32; 1 Tim. 1:17; 6:14–16).

8:9 Israel, like all nations, wanted a king to judge them. Little did they dream that they would get this kind of king in Saul. He turned out to be a king just like the ones the nations around about Israel had, and the result was disaster. God said that Israel's desire for a king was tantamount to a rejection of his theocratic reign, and any rejection of God leads to trouble and difficulty sooner or later.

8:19–22 Again, the stubborness of Israel manifested

20 That we also may be like all the nations; and that our king may judge
us, and go out before us, and fight our battles.
21 And Samuel heard all the words of the people, and he rehearsed them
in the ears of the LORD.
22 And the LORD said to Samuel, Hearken unto their voice, and make
them a king. And Samuel said unto the men of Israel, Go ye every man
unto his city.

2. God Chooses Saul

a. The Genealogy of Saul

9:1 1 Sam 10:21; 14:51; 1 Chron 8:33; 9:36–39
9:2☆ 1 Sam 10:24; 2 Sam 14:25

9 NOW there was a man of Benjamin, whose name *was* Kish, the son of
A-bi′el, the son of Ze′ror, the son of Be-cho′rath, the son of A-phi′ah,
a Benjamite, a mighty man of power.
2 And he had a son, whose name *was* Saul, a choice young man, and a
goodly: and *there was* not among the children of Israel a goodlier person
than he: from his shoulders and upward *he was* higher than any of the
people.

b. Saul Searches for His Father's Donkeys

9:3 1 Sam 10:2, 14

3 And the asses of Kish Saul's father were lost. And Kish said to Saul his
son, Take now one of the servants with thee, and arise, go seek the asses.
4 And he passed through mount E′phra-im, and passed through the land
of Shal′i-sha, but they found *them* not: then they passed through the land of
Sha′lim, and *there they were* not: and he passed through the land of the
Benjamites, but they found *them* not.

9:5☆ 1 Sam 1:1

5 *And* when they were come to the land of Zuph, Saul said to his servant
that *was* with him, Come, and let us return; lest my father leave *caring* for
the asses, and take thought for us.

9:6☆ Deut 18:20, 21; 1 Sam 3:19, 20; 2 Kgs 5:8

6 And he said unto him, Behold now, *there is* in this city a man of God,
and *he is* an honourable man; all that he saith cometh surely to pass: now
let us go thither; peradventure he can shew us our way that we should go.

9:7 1 Kgs 14:3; 2 Kgs 5:15; 8:8, 9; Ezek 13:19

7 Then said Saul to his servant, But, behold, *if* we go, what shall we bring
the man? for the bread is spent in our vessels, and *there is* not a present to
bring to the man of God: what have we?
8 And the servant answered Saul again, and said, Behold, I have here at
hand the fourth part of a shekel of silver: *that* will I give to the man of God,
to tell us our way.

9:9☆ Ex 2:16; 1 Chron 26:28

9 (Beforetime in Israel, when a man went to inquire of God, thus he
spake, Come, and let us go to the seer: for *he that is* now *called* a Prophet
was beforetime called a Seer.)
10 Then said Saul to his servant, Well said; come, let us go. So they went
unto the city where the man of God *was*.
11 ¶*And* as they went up the hill to the city, they found young maidens
going out to draw water, and said unto them, Is the seer here?

---

itself. They refused to heed the counsel of Samuel and insisted on having a king. God ordered Samuel to give them what they craved.

9:2 From the human vantage point Saul was everything Israel could want in a king, that is, in outward appearance. He was handsome, wealthy, and came from the tribe of Benjamin.

9:5 Providence in the search for the lost asses brings Saul to Zuph, where Samuel awaits God's choice for the kingship. God has not told Samuel who it will be.

9:6 *this city,* apparently Ramah, where Samuel now had his headquarters. *all that he saith cometh surely to pass.* This is the supreme test of a true prophet, as set forth in Deut. 18:21, 22.

9:9 Saul's servant suggests that they visit Samuel, who is here called a *seer* (which meant that he could see things others did not see). They give him a piece of silver out of respect for his office and with the expectation that Samuel will tell them what they need to know.

12And they answered them, and said, He is; behold, *he is* before you: ☆9:12 Lk 9:16 Jn 6:11
make haste now, for he came to day to the city; for *there is* a sacrifice of the
people to day in the high place:
13As soon as ye be come into the city, ye shall straightway find him,
before he go up to the high place to eat: for the people will not eat until he
come, because he doth bless the sacrifice; *and* afterwards they eat that be
bidden. Now therefore get you up; for about this time ye shall find him.

c. God Tells Samuel to Anoint Saul as King

14And they went up into the city: *and* when they were come into the city,
behold, Samuel came out against them, for to go up to the high place.
15¶Now the LORD had told Samuel in his ear a day before Saul came, ☆9:15 1 Sam 15:1 Acts 13:21
saying,
16To morrow about this time I will send thee a man out of the land of ☆9:16 Ex 3:7, 9 Ps 106:44
Benjamin, and thou shalt anoint him *to be* captain over my people Israel,
that he may save my people out of the hand of the Philistines: for I have
looked upon my people, because their cry is come unto me.
17And when Samuel saw Saul, the LORD said unto him, Behold the man 9:17 1 Sam 10:1 12:13; 16:12
whom I spake to thee of! this same shall reign over my people.
18Then Saul drew near to Samuel in the gate, and said, Tell me, I pray 9:18
thee, where the seer's house *is*.
19And Samuel answered Saul, and said, I *am* the seer: go up before me ☆9:19
unto the high place; for ye shall eat with me to day, and to morrow I will let
thee go, and will tell thee all that *is* in thine heart.
20And as for thine asses that were lost three days ago, set not thy mind on ☆9:20 1 Sam 9:6 1 Sam 10:16
them; for they are found. And on whom *is* all the desire of Israel? *Is it* not
on thee, and on all thy father's house?
21And Saul answered and said, *Am* not I a Benjamite, of the smallest of ☆9:21 Judg 20:46–48 1 Sam 15:17
the tribes of Israel? and my family the least of all the families of the tribe of
Benjamin? wherefore then speakest thou so to me?
22And Samuel took Saul and his servant, and brought them into the
parlour, and made them sit in the chiefest place among them that were
bidden, which *were* about thirty persons.
23And Samuel said unto the cook, Bring the portion which I gave thee, of 9:23 Gen 43:34
which I said unto thee, Set it by thee.
24And the cook took up the shoulder, and *that* which *was* upon it, and set ☆9:24
it before Saul. And *Samuel* said, Behold that which is left! set *it* before thee,
and eat: for unto this time hath it been kept for thee since I said, I have
invited the people. So Saul did eat with Samuel that day.

9:12 *in the high place.* Now that Shiloh was in ruins, Samuel had built an altar on a hill in Ramah. This became the central place for worship (see 7:17).

9:15, 16 the *LORD had told Samuel in his ear,* i.e., "he uncovered the ear of Samuel." He spoke to Samuel in a familiar and secret way so that his will was made known to the prophet. Amos says, ". . . the LORD God . . . revealeth his secret unto his servants the prophets" (3:7). Whether this was done through prayer or through the Holy Spirit or directly by God the Father is of no account. It was a private revelation from the triune God to the listening ear of the prophet. Samuel was in a right relationship to God and his ear was open to the voice of God. Today we have the revelation of God who speaks to us by the Spirit through the Word. But wherever and whenever it is necessary, God can and still does speak to us what he wants us to hear—however he chooses to do it. This is the God who works by design and not by accident. Saul was sent by God to arrive the next day. He had a date with destiny. God was going to give Israel a king. (See note to 1 Sam. 8:5.)

9:18–21 Evidently Samuel wore no distinctive clothing and presented no special appearance. Saul asked for directions from him as to where Samuel could be found. He got more than he expected. Samuel told him about his asses before Saul even mentioned them, and he ordered Saul to eat with him. When he uttered the prophetic statement, "And on whom is all the desire of Israel? Is it not thee . . .?" Saul showed a spirit of humility and deference (9:21).

9:24 Giving Saul the shoulder of the meat was a symbol of honor, which placed him above all the other guests.

9:25 Deut 22:8 2 Kgs 4:10 Neh 8:16 Acts 10:9, 10
9:26☆

25 ¶And when they were come down from the high place into the city,
Samuel communed with Saul upon the top of the house.
26 And they arose early: and it came to pass about the spring of the day,
that Samuel called Saul to the top of the house, saying, Up, that I may send
thee away. And Saul arose, and they went out both of them, he and Samuel,
abroad.

9:27☆

27 *And* as they were going down to the end of the city, Samuel said to Saul,
Bid the servant pass on before us, (and he passed on,) but stand thou still a
while, that I may shew thee the word of God.

3. Saul's Coronation

a. Samuel Anoints Saul; the Donkeys Are Found

10:1 Ex 30:22–25 Lev 8:12 1 Sam 9:16 16:13; 26:9 2 Sam 1:14
10:2 Gen 35:19; 48:7

10 THEN Samuel took a vial of oil, and poured *it* upon his head, and
kissed him, and said, *Is it* not because the LORD hath anointed thee
to be captain over his inheritance?
2 When thou art departed from me to day, then thou shalt find two men
by Rachel's sepulchre in the border of Benjamin at Zel′zah; and they will
say unto thee, The asses which thou wentest to seek are found: and, lo, thy
father hath left the care of the asses, and sorroweth for you, saying, What
shall I do for my son?

10:3 Gen 28:16, 22 35:1, 3, 7

3 Then shalt thou go on forward from thence, and thou shalt come to the
plain of Ta′bor, and there shall meet thee three men going up to God to
Beth–el, one carrying three kids, and another carrying three loaves of bread,
and another carrying a bottle of wine:
4 And they will salute thee, and give thee two *loaves* of bread; which thou
shalt receive of their hands.

10:5 1 Sam 19:20 2 Kgs 2:3, 5, 15 1 Chron 25:1

5 After that thou shalt come to the hill of God, where *is* the garrison of
the Philistines: and it shall come to pass, when thou art come thither to
the city, that thou shalt meet a company of prophets coming down from the
high place with a psaltery, and a tabret, and a pipe, and a harp, before
them; and they shall prophesy:

10:6☆ Num 11:25, 29 Judg 3:10; 14:6 1 Sam 16:13 19:23, 24

6 And the Spirit of the LORD will come upon thee, and thou shalt
prophesy with them, and shalt be turned into another man.
7 And let it be, when these signs are come unto thee, *that* thou do as
occasion serve thee; for God *is* with thee.

10:8 1 Sam 7:16 11:14, 15; 13:7 15:33

8 And thou shalt go down before me to Gilgal; and, behold, I will come
down unto thee, to offer burnt offerings, *and* to sacrifice sacrifices of peace
offerings: seven days shalt thou tarry, till I come to thee, and shew thee
what thou shalt do.

10:9 1 Sam 10:6

9 ¶And it was *so,* that when he had turned his back to go from Samuel,
God gave him another heart: and all those signs came to pass that day.
10 And when they came thither to the hill, behold, a company of prophets
met him; and the Spirit of God came upon him, and he prophesied among
them.

10:11 1 Sam 19:24 Amos 7:14, 15 Mt 13:54–57

11 And it came to pass, when all that knew him beforetime saw that,
behold, he prophesied among the prophets, then the people said one to

---

9:26 *spring of the day,* i.e., *"the dawn of the day."*
9:27 We may suppose here that Samuel informed Saul what God had told him about the kingship and his appointment by God to that office. It must have been a great surprise to Saul, who had no idea that he was God's choice to lead Israel.
10:1 *the LORD hath anointed thee.* God assured Saul that he was God's choice by two external signs: he would receive two loaves of bread, and he would prophesy.
10:6 Samuel prophesied that the Spirit of the Lord would come mightily upon Saul and that he would prophesy. The Spirit empowered Saul and enabled him to put down Israel's enemies. (See note on 1 Sam. 16:13—because of sin the Spirit of God left Saul and rendered him incapable of doing God's will and of performing great feats.)

another, What *is* this *that* is come unto the son of Kish? *Is* Saul also among
the prophets?
12And one of the same place answered and said, But who *is* their father? ☆10:12
Therefore it became a proverb, *Is* Saul also among the prophets?
13And when he had made an end of prophesying, he came to the high
place.
14¶And Saul's uncle said unto him and to his servant, Whither went ye? ☆10:14 1 Sam 9:3
And he said, To seek the asses: and when we saw that *they were* no where,
we came to Samuel.
15And Saul's uncle said, Tell me, I pray thee, what Samuel said unto you.
16And Saul said unto his uncle, He told us plainly that the asses were 10:16 1 Sam 9:20
found. But of the matter of the kingdom, whereof Samuel spake, he told
him not.

b. Saul Accepted by the Israelis as King

17¶And Samuel called the people together unto the LORD to Miz'peh; 10:17 Judg 20:1 1 Sam 7:5, 6
18And said unto the children of Israel, Thus saith the LORD God of
Israel. I brought up Israel out of Egypt, and delivered you out of the hand 10:18 Josh 24:5 Judg 6:8 1 Sam 8:6, 7
of the Egyptians, and out of the hand of all kingdoms, *and* of them that
oppressed you:
19And ye have this day rejected your God, who himself saved you out of
all your adversities and your tribulations; and ye have said unto him, *Nay,*
but set a king over us. Now therefore present yourselves before the LORD
by your tribes, and by your thousands.
20And when Samuel had caused all the tribes of Israel to come near, the ☆10:20 Josh 7:16 1 Sam 14:41 Acts 1:24, 25
tribe of Benjamin was taken.
21When he had caused the tribe of Benjamin to come near by their
families, the family of Ma'tri was taken, and Saul the son of Kish was
taken: and when they sought him, he could not be found.
22Therefore they inquired of the LORD further, if the man should yet 10:22 Num 27:21
come thither. And the LORD answered, Behold, he hath hid himself among
the stuff.
23And they ran and fetched him thence: and when he stood among the 10:23 1 Sam 9:2; 16:7
people, he was higher than any of the people from his shoulders and
upward.
24And Samuel said to all the people, See ye him whom the LORD hath ☆10:24 1 Kgs 1:25, 34, 39 2 Kgs 11:12
chosen, that *there is* none like him among all the people? And all the people
shouted, and said, God save the king.
25Then Samuel told the people the manner of the kingdom, and wrote *it* ☆10:25 Deut 17:15 1 Sam 8:11–18
in a book, and laid *it* up before the LORD. And Samuel sent all the people
away, every man to his house.

10:12 *Is Saul also among the prophets?* This was an expression of surprise. Saul's friends were incredulous that Saul had become religious. A modern paraphrase of this question might be: "He got religion?"†
10:14 *Saul's uncle.* This could have been Ner.
10:20ff God's will that Saul become king was manifested by the use of the lot. This outward sign was for Israel's benefit. Samuel presented him fittingly by saying there was none like him in all Israel. And for the first time in Israel's history they shout: "God save the king." (This saying is still in use in Britain.)
10:24 The choice of Saul for the kingship is somewhat of an enigma; Saul came from the tribe of Benjamin, whereas Jacob's blessing gave the kingship to Judah (Gen. 49:10). Why did God choose Saul to be king? Some have surmised that he did so for the following reasons: (1) just as God used Samson and the other judges to lead until a king could be chosen, so also he used Saul until David was full-grown and ready for the kingship; (2) Saul prepared the way for David's later conquests of the entire territory promised by God to Abraham (Gen. 15:18), and made it possible for David to consolidate the kingdom on a permanent basis.
10:25 No king serving under God was autonomous. God, after all, had appointed him to the kingship. Thus Samuel wrote down the "regulations of the kingship" (NIV) or "the rights and duties of the kingship" (RSV). This document was "laid . . . up before the LORD," signifying that it was a binding authority which came from God and stood over the king.

26¶And Saul also went home to Gib′e-ah; and there went with him a
band of men, whose hearts God had touched.

10:27 1 Kgs 10:24 Ps 72:10

27But the children of Be′li-al said, How shall this man save us? And they
despised him, and brought him no presents. But he held his peace.

B. SAUL'S EARLY REIGN

1. Saul Defeats the Ammonites

11:1☆ Judg 11:4–6 21:8 1 Sam 31:11

11 THEN Na′hash the Ammonite came up, and encamped against
Ja′besh-gil′e-ad: and all the men of Ja′besh said unto Na′hash,
Make a covenant with us, and we will serve thee.
2And Na′hash the Ammonite answered them, On this *condition* will I
make *a covenant* with you, that I may thrust out all your right eyes, and lay
it *for* a reproach upon all Israel.
3And the elders of Ja′besh said unto him, Give us seven days' respite,
that we may send messengers unto all the coasts of Israel: and then, if *there*
be no man to save us, we will come out to thee.

11:4 1 Sam 10:26 14:2; 30:4 **11:5** 1 Kgs 19:19

4¶Then came the messengers to Gib′e-ah of Saul, and told the tidings in
the ears of the people: and all the people lifted up their voices, and wept.
5And, behold, Saul came after the herd out of the field; and Saul said,
What *aileth* the people that they weep? And they told him the tidings of the
men of Ja′besh.

11:6☆ Judg 3:10; 6:34 1 Sam 10:6, 7, 10 **11:7** Judg 19:29; 20:1

6And the Spirit of God came upon Saul when he heard those tidings, and
his anger was kindled greatly.
7And he took a yoke of oxen, and hewed them in pieces, and sent *them*
throughout all the coasts of Israel by the hands of messengers, saying,
Whosoever cometh not forth after Saul and after Samuel, so shall it be done
unto his oxen. And the fear of the LORD fell on the people, and they came
out with one consent.

11:8 Judg 1:4–6

8And when he numbered them in Be′zek, the children of Israel were three
hundred thousand, and the men of Judah thirty thousand.
9And they said unto the messengers that came, Thus shall ye say unto the
men of Ja′besh-gil′e-ad, To morrow, by *that time* the sun be hot, ye shall
have help. And the messengers came and shewed *it* to the men of Ja′besh;
and they were glad.
10Therefore the men of Ja′besh said, To morrow we will come out unto
you, and ye shall do with us all that seemeth good unto you.

11:11 Judg 7:16; 9:43

11And it was *so* on the morrow, that Saul put the people in three
companies; and they came into the midst of the host in the morning watch,
and slew the Ammonites until the heat of the day: and it came to pass, that
they which remained were scattered, so that two of them were not left
together.

11:12 1 Sam 10:27 Lk 19:27 **11:13** Ex 14:13 1 Sam 14:45 19:5 2 Sam 19:22 **11:14** 1 Sam 10:1, 8 **11:15☆**

12¶And the people said unto Samuel, Who *is* he that said, Shall Saul reign
over us? bring the men, that we may put them to death.
13And Saul said, There shall not a man be put to death this day: for to
day the LORD hath wrought salvation in Israel.
14Then said Samuel to the people, Come, and let us go to Gilgal, and
renew the kingdom there.
15And all the people went to Gilgal; and there they made Saul king

---

11:1 Despite the lot which showed Israel what God's choice was for the kingship, some in Israel did not like or want to accept that verdict. The opposition must be overcome and Saul must show himself to be the leader who has strength, wisdom, and confidence.

11:6 Note that the Spirit of God came on Saul in mighty power. In the New Testament we learn that all of God's people are indwelt by the Spirit and that all should be filled with the Spirit (Eph. 5:18).

11:15 *they made Saul king.* Samuel had announced God's choice of Saul in 10:24. Saul became king in the fullest sense only after his victory over the Ammonites and the summoning of the people to Gilgal.

before the LORD in Gilgal; and there they sacrificed sacrifices of peace
offerings before the LORD; and there Saul and all the men of Israel rejoiced
greatly.

2. Samuel Retires as Judge

12 AND Samuel said unto all Israel, Behold, I have hearkened unto
your voice in all that ye said unto me, and have made a king over
you.
2 And now, behold, the king walketh before you: and I am old and
grayheaded; and, behold, my sons *are* with you: and I have walked before
you from my childhood unto this day.
3 Behold, here I *am:* witness against me before the LORD, and before his
anointed: whose ox have I taken? or whose ass have I taken? or whom have
I defrauded? whom have I oppressed? or of whose hand have I received *any*
bribe to blind mine eyes therewith? and I will restore it you.
4 And they said, Thou hast not defrauded us, nor oppressed us, neither
hast thou taken ought of any man's hand.
5 And he said unto them, The LORD *is* witness against you, and his
anointed *is* witness this day, that ye have not found ought in my hand. And
they answered, *He is* witness.
6 ¶And Samuel said unto the people, *It is* the LORD that advanced Moses
and Aaron, and that brought your fathers up out of the land of Egypt.
7 Now therefore stand still, that I may reason with you before the LORD
of all the righteous acts of the LORD, which he did to you and to your
fathers.
8 When Jacob was come into Egypt, and your fathers cried unto the
LORD, then the LORD sent Moses and Aaron, which brought forth your
fathers out of Egypt, and made them dwell in this place.
9 And when they forgat the LORD their God, he sold them into the hand
of Sis′e-ra, captain of the host of Ha′zor, and into the hand of the
Philistines, and into the hand of the king of Moab, and they fought against
them.
10 And they cried unto the LORD, and said, We have sinned, because we
have forsaken the LORD, and have served Ba′al-im and Ash′ta-roth: but
now deliver us out of the hand of our enemies, and we will serve thee.
11 And the LORD sent Je-rub′ba-al, and Be′dan, and Jeph′thah, and
Samuel, and delivered you out of the hand of your enemies on every side,
and ye dwelled safe.
12 And when ye saw that Na′hash the king of the children of Ammon
came against you, ye said unto me, Nay; but a king shall reign over us:
when the LORD your God *was* your king.
13 Now therefore behold the king whom ye have chosen, *and* whom ye
have desired! and, behold, the LORD hath set a king over you.

☆**12:1** 1 Sam 8:7, 9, 22
12:2 1 Sam 3:10, 19, 20; 8:1, 5
☆**12:3** Ex 23:8; Num 16:15; Deut 16:19
12:4 1 Sam 8:3
12:5 Ex 22:4; Ps 17:3
☆**12:6** Ex 6:26
12:7 Deut 4:9; Judg 5:11; Ps 78:4; Mic 6:4
12:8 Ex 2:23–25; 3:10; 4:14–16
12:9 Deut 32:18; Judg 3:7; 10:7; 13:1; Ps 106:21
12:10 Judg 3:15; 10:10, 15, 16
12:11 Judg 4:6; 6:32; 11:1; 1 Sam 1:19, 20; Heb 11:32
12:12 Judg 8:23, 24; 1 Sam 11:1
12:13 1 Sam 10:24; 11:15; Hos 13:11

12:1 Now that Saul had been elevated to the kingship, he would be Israel's judge and thus there was no longer any need for Samuel to act as judge. His ministry as judge was over and he continued as priest and had the privilege of anointing David as king over Israel following Saul's downfall for disobedience. The death of Samuel is mentioned in 25:1.

12:3 Samuel himself may have rendered fair and just judgment, but his hands were not wholly clean. He favored his sons over the God he served, for he knew and approved (at least by his failure to put them out of office) of what they did. Yet God was gracious enough to allow him to serve out his judgeship over Israel until Saul was in place as king.

12:6ff Samuel reminded Israel of its history and God's saving deeds among them. He traced events from Jacob's trip to Egypt through the exodus, the entry into the land and the period of the judges. He spoke of Israel's ups and downs and God's continuing grace.

12:14☆ Josh 24:14, 20 Ps 81:12–15 Isa 3:10
12:15 Deut 28:15 Josh 24:20 Isa 1:2, 20
12:16☆ Ex 14:13, 21
12:17 Josh 10:12 1 Sam 7:10 Ps 99:6 Jer 15:1
12:19 Gen 20:7 Ex 9:28; 10:17 1 Sam 7:5; 8
12:20 Ex 20:20 Deut 11:16 Josh 23:6
12:21 Isa 41:29 Hab 2:18 1 Cor 8:4
12:22 Ex 32:12 Num 14:13 Deut 7:6; 31:6 1 Pet 2:9
12:23 Prov 4:11 Rom 1:9 Col 1:9 1 Thess 3:10
12:24☆ Deut 10:21 1 Sam 12:16 Eccles 12:13 Rom 12:1
12:25☆ Josh 24:20 1 Sam 12:15 31:1–5 Isa 1:20 Hos 10:3
13:1☆
13:2 1 Sam 10:26 13:23 14:2, 5, 52

14If ye will fear the LORD, and serve him, and obey his voice, and not
rebel against the commandment of the LORD, then shall both ye and also
the king that reigneth over you continue following the LORD your God:
15But if ye will not obey the voice of the LORD, but rebel against the
commandment of the LORD, then shall the hand of the LORD be against
you, as *it was* against your fathers.
16¶Now therefore stand and see this great thing, which the LORD will do
before your eyes.
17*Is it* not wheat harvest to day? I will call unto the LORD, and he shall
send thunder and rain; that ye may perceive and see that your wickedness
is great, which ye have done in the sight of the LORD, in asking you a king.
18So Samuel called unto the LORD; and the LORD sent thunder and rain
that day: and all the people greatly feared the LORD and Samuel.
19And all the people said unto Samuel, Pray for thy servants unto the
LORD thy God, that we die not: for we have added unto all our sins *this*
evil, to ask us a king.
20¶And Samuel said unto the people, Fear not: ye have done all this
wickedness: yet turn not aside from following the LORD, but serve the
LORD with all your heart;
21And turn ye not aside: for *then should ye go* after vain *things*, which
cannot profit nor deliver; for they *are* vain.
22For the LORD will not forsake his people for his great name's sake:
because it hath pleased the LORD to make you his people.
23Moreover as for me, God forbid that I should sin against the LORD in
ceasing to pray for you: but I will teach you the good and the right way:
24Only fear the LORD, and serve him in truth with all your heart: for
consider how great *things* he hath done for you.
25But if ye shall still do wickedly, ye shall be consumed, both ye and your
king.

3. The War against the Philistines
a. The Opening Battle of the War

13 SAUL reigned one year; and when he had reigned two years over
Israel,
2Saul chose him three thousand *men* of Israel; *whereof* two thousand were
with Saul in Mich'mash and in mount Beth-el, and a thousand were with
Jonathan in Gib'e-ah of Benjamin: and the rest of the people he sent every
man to his tent.

12:14 God accepted the kingship on condition that the king and the people alike followed the commandments of God, the real king. The kingship was an expression of the *secret* will of God in contrast to the *declared* will of God. It was God's declared will to be king in a theocratic kingdom, but his secret will was to appoint a Davidic king, because he foreknew that Israel would be unfaithful to him.

12:16 *this great thing, which the LORD will do before your eyes.* Once again God deigned to give his people outward, corroborating evidence of his presence and power. In 12:17 we see that Samuel asked God to send thunder and rain as a token of his power and approval (this request was made on wheat-harvest day, when rain and thunder were unexpected). God responded to Samuel's prayer, and the rain and thunder came. The people *"greatly feared the LORD and Samuel"* (12:18).

12:24, 25 Samuel concluded his admonitions to Israel with "an earnest exhortation to practical religion and serious godliness."* He told them to fear God—this is the first principle of a righteous life. Then they were to serve him with all their hearts. Profession and practice belong together; one without the other is hypocrisy. Samuel appealed to them on the basis of the wonderful manner in which God had provided for them. The speech ended with a prophetic word: If Israel and the king ever failed to heed the warning, God would consume them. Both king and people finally did *do wickedly,* and at last God dispersed them to the four corners of the earth; he awaits for them to turn back to him for restoration.

13:1 *Saul reigned one year.* The Hebrew text, from which specific numbers evidently were omitted by ancient scribes, reads: "Saul was . . . years old when he began to reign, and he reigned . . . and two years over Israel."†

3And Jonathan smote the garrison of the Philistines that *was* in Ge'ba, and the Philistines heard *of it.* And Saul blew the trumpet throughout all the land, saying, Let the Hebrews hear.

☆13:3 Judg 3:27; 6:34 2 Sam 2:28 20:1

4And all Israel heard say *that* Saul had smitten a garrison of the Philistines, and *that* Israel also was had in abomination with the Philistines. And the people were called together after Saul to Gilgal.

☆13:4

5¶And the Philistines gathered themselves together to fight with Israel, thirty thousand chariots, and six thousand horsemen, and people as the sand which *is* on the sea shore in multitude: and they came up, and pitched in Mich'mash, eastward from Beth–a'ven,

13:5 Josh 11:4

b. Saul Wrongly Performs a Priestly Duty

6When the men of Israel saw that they were in a strait, (for the people were distressed,) then the people did hide themselves in caves, and in thickets, and in rocks, and in high places, and in pits.

13:6 Judg 6:2 1 Sam 14:11 23:19

7And *some of* the Hebrews went over Jordan to the land of Gad and Gilead. As for Saul, he *was* yet in Gilgal, and all the people followed him trembling.

8¶And he tarried seven days, according to the set time that Samuel *had appointed:* but Samuel came not to Gilgal; and the people were scattered from him.

13:8 1 Sam 10:8

9And Saul said, Bring hither a burnt offering to me, and peace offerings. And he offered the burnt offering.

☆13:9 2 Sam 24:25 1 Kgs 3:4

10And it came to pass, that as soon as he had made an end of offering the burnt offering, behold, Samuel came; and Saul went out to meet him, that he might salute him.

13:10 1 Sam 15:13

11¶And Samuel said, What hast thou done? And Saul said, Because I saw that the people were scattered from me, and *that* thou camest not within the days appointed, and *that* the Philistines gathered themselves together at Mich'mash;

13:11 2 Sam 3:23, 24

12Therefore said I, The Philistines will come down now upon me to Gilgal, and I have not made supplication unto the LORD: I forced myself therefore, and offered a burnt offering.

13And Samuel said to Saul, Thou hast done foolishly: thou hast not kept the commandment of the LORD thy God, which he commanded thee: for now would the LORD have established thy kingdom upon Israel for ever.

☆13:13 1 Sam 15:22, 28 2 Chron 16:9

14But now thy kingdom shall not continue: the LORD hath sought him a man after his own heart, and the LORD hath commanded him *to be* captain over his people, because thou hast not kept *that* which the LORD commanded thee.

13:14 Acts 13:22

c. Saul's Ragtag Army

15And Samuel arose, and gat him up from Gilgal unto Gib'e-ah of Benjamin. And Saul numbered the people *that were* present with him, about six hundred men.

13:3, 4 After subjugating Israel, the Philistines had set up military posts throughout the land.

13:9 Saul intruded into the office reserved for the Levitical priesthood. As a Benjamite, he was ineligible for the priesthood. This intrusion brought condemnation upon him. In 13:13 and 14 we read that Samuel announced that Saul's kingship would be terminated and another man would be appointed in his place.

13:13 *Thou hast done foolishly.* Saul was forbidden to act as religious leader or to assume any functions of the priesthood. Despite the apparent need for a burnt offering, Saul should never have disobeyed God, who would have provided for the nation's needs some other way.

13:16 1 Sam 14:2

16 And Saul, and Jonathan his son, and the people *that were* present with
them, abode in Gib'e-ah of Benjamin: but the Philistines encamped in
Mich'mash.

13:17 1 Sam 11:11

17 ¶And the spoilers came out of the camp of the Philistines in three
companies: one company turned unto the way *that leadeth to* Oph'rah, unto
the land of Shu'al:

13:18 1 Kgs 9:17 Neh 11:31–35

18 And another company turned the way *to* Beth–ho'ron: and another
company turned *to* the way of the border that looketh to the valley of Ze-
bo'im toward the wilderness.

13:19☆ Judg 5:8 1 Sam 17:47 2 Kgs 24:14 Jer 24:1

19 ¶Now there was no smith found throughout all the land of Israel: for
the Philistines said, Lest the Hebrews make *them* swords or spears:
20 But all the Israelites went down to the Philistines, to sharpen every man
his share, and his coulter, and his axe, and his mattock.
21 Yet they had a file for the mattocks, and for the coulters, and for the
forks, and for the axes, and to sharpen the goads.
22 So it came to pass in the day of battle, that there was neither sword nor
spear found in the hand of any of the people that *were* with Saul and
Jonathan: but with Saul and with Jonathan his son was there found.

13:23 1 Sam 14:5, 31 Isa 10:28

23 And the garrison of the Philistines went out to the passage of
Mich'mash.

d. Prince Jonathan's Exploit
(1) Jonathan's Military Victory

14:1☆ 1 Sam 13:2, 22 14:39–45; 18:1

14 NOW it came to pass upon a day, that Jonathan the son of Saul
said unto the young man that bare his armour, Come, and let us go
over to the Philistines' garrison, that *is* on the other side. But he told not his
father.

14:2 1 Sam 13:16

2 And Saul tarried in the uttermost part of Gib'e-ah under a pomegranate
tree which *is* in Mig'ron: and the people that *were* with him *were* about six
hundred men;

14:3☆ 1 Sam 1:3 4:21, 22 22:11, 12

3 And A-hi'ah, the son of A-hi'tub, I'-cha-bod's brother, the son of
Phin'e-has, the son of Eli, the LORD's priest in Shi'loh, wearing an ephod.
And the people knew not that Jonathan was gone.

14:4

4 ¶And between the passages, by which Jonathan sought to go over unto
the Philistines' garrison, *there was* a sharp rock on the one side, and a sharp
rock on the other side: and the name of the one *was* Bo'zez, and the name
of the other Se'neh.

14:5 1 Sam 13:23

5 The forefront of the one *was* situate northward over against Mich'mash,
and the other southward over against Gib'e-ah.

14:6 Judg 7:4 2 Chron 14:11

6 And Jonathan said to the young man that bare his armour, Come, and
let us go over unto the garrison of these uncircumcised: it may be that the
LORD will work for us: for *there is* no restraint to the LORD to save by many
or by few.

13:19 *smith,* i.e., "blacksmiths." The Philistines overpowered Israel with their superior weaponry. Without blacksmiths Israel had no armaments.

14:1 Jonathan was Saul's firstborn and his heir apparent. He was a man of sterling character who loved God with his whole heart. The friendship of Jonathan and David has never been surpassed by any friendship. Jonathan had nothing to gain and everything to lose in this friendship. Three covenants between David and Jonathan are recorded in the Old Testament. Yet Jonathan remained faithful to his father even as he tried to bridge the gap which separated his father Saul from David, God's anointed choice to succeed Saul. Jonathan never breached his friendship with David. He died heroically in his last act of devotion to his father. David wrote Jonathan's finest epitaph when he said of him and Saul: "in their death they were not divided" (2 Sam. 1:23).

14:3 *wearing an ephod.* Saul sent for a priest from Shiloh, and Ahiah (Ahijah) came wearing an ephod. This was used to ask God's advice in times of trouble. Apparently the Urim and Thummim were in the ephod and the stones meant either a yes or a no to the question asked.

7 And his armourbearer said unto him, Do all that *is* in thine heart: turn
thee; behold, I *am* with thee according to thy heart.
8 Then said Jonathan, Behold, we will pass over unto *these* men, and we ☆**14:8**
will discover ourselves unto them.
9 If they say thus unto us, Tarry until we come to you; then we will stand
still in our place, and will not go up unto them.
10 But if they say thus, Come up unto us; then we will go up: for the LORD **14:10** Gen 24:14
hath delivered them into our hand: and this *shall be* a sign unto us. Judg 6:36
11 And both of them discovered themselves unto the garrison of the **14:11**
Philistines: and the Philistines said, Behold, the Hebrews come forth out of 1 Sam 13:6
the holes where they had hid themselves.
12 And the men of the garrison answered Jonathan and his armourbearer, **14:12**
and said, Come up to us, and we will shew you a thing. And Jonathan said Judg 5:14; 7:15 2 Sam 5:24
unto his armourbearer, Come up after me: for the LORD hath delivered
them into the hand of Israel.
13 And Jonathan climbed up upon his hands and upon his feet, and his
armourbearer after him: and they fell before Jonathan; and his armour-
bearer slew after him.
14 And that first slaughter, which Jonathan and his armourbearer made,
was about twenty men, within as it were an half acre of land, *which* a yoke
of oxen might plow.
15 And there was trembling in the host, in the field, and among all the ☆**14:15**
people: the garrison, and the spoilers, they also trembled, and the earth Josh 2:9 1 Sam 7:10
quaked: so it was a very great trembling. 2 Kgs 7:6

(2) The Flight of the Philistines

16 And the watchmen of Saul in Gib′e-ah of Benjamin looked; and,
behold, the multitude melted away, and they went on beating down *one*
another.
17 Then said Saul unto the people that *were* with him, Number now, and
see who is gone from us. And when they had numbered, behold, Jonathan
and his armourbearer *were* not *there.*
18 And Saul said unto A-hi′ah, Bring hither the ark of God. For the ark of ☆**14:18**
God was at that time with the children of Israel. 1 Sam 4:3 23:9; 30:7
19 ¶And it came to pass, while Saul talked unto the priest, that the noise **14:19**
that *was* in the host of the Philistines went on and increased: and Saul said Num 27:21
unto the priest, Withdraw thine hand.
20 And Saul and all the people that *were* with him assembled themselves, **14:20**
and they came to the battle: and, behold, every man's sword was against his Judg 7:21
fellow, *and there was* a very great discomfiture. 2 Chron 20:23
21 Moreover the Hebrews *that* were with the Philistines before that time, **14:21**
which went up with them into the camp *from the country* round about, even 1 Sam 29:4
they also *turned* to be with the Israelites that *were* with Saul and Jonathan.
22 Likewise all the men of Israel which had hid themselves in mount **14:22**
E′phra-im, *when* they heard that the Philistines fled, even they also followed 1 Sam 13:6 31:7
hard after them in the battle.
23 So the LORD saved Israel that day: and the battle passed over unto **14:23** Ex 14:30
Beth–a′ven. 2 Chron 32:22

14:8 Jonathan determines to follow providence, believing that God would guide him with his eye. He laid out a fleece before God; and when God gave him the sign he expected, he answered the signal.

14:15 At the opportune moment in the battle, God sent an earthquake, causing the Philistines to tremble and become panic-stricken. The Philistines were soundly defeated, despite their superior military strength.

14:18 The ark was stationed at Kirjath-jearim at this time. Probably it was borrowed for a short time and brought to the battlefield as a symbol of their faith in God.

(3) Jonathan Unknowingly Breaks His Father's Order

14:24☆ Josh 6:26

24¶And the men of Israel were distressed that day: for Saul had adjured the people, saying, Cursed *be* the man that eateth *any* food until evening, that I may be avenged on mine enemies. So none of the people tasted *any* food.

25And all *they of* the land came to a wood; and there was honey upon the ground.

26And when the people were come into the wood, behold, the honey dropped; but no man put his hand to his mouth: for the people feared the oath.

27But Jonathan heard not when his father charged the people with the oath: wherefore he put forth the end of the rod that *was* in his hand, and dipped it in an honeycomb, and put his hand to his mouth; and his eyes were enlightened.

28Then answered one of the people, and said, Thy father straitly charged the people with an oath, saying, Cursed *be* the man that eateth *any* food this day. And the people were faint.

29Then said Jonathan, My father hath troubled the land: see, I pray you, how mine eyes have been enlightened, because I tasted a little of this honey.

30How much more, if haply the people had eaten freely to day of the spoil of their enemies which they found? for had there not been now a much greater slaughter among the Philistines?

14:31 Josh 10:12

31And they smote the Philistines that day from Mich'mash to Ai'ja-lon: and the people were very faint.

14:32☆ Gen 9:4; Lev 17:10; 1 Sam 15:19; Acts 15:20

32And the people flew upon the spoil, and took sheep, and oxen, and calves, and slew *them* on the ground: and the people did eat *them* with the blood.

33¶Then they told Saul, saying, Behold, the people sin against the LORD, in that they eat with the blood. And he said, Ye have transgressed: roll a great stone unto me this day.

34And Saul said, Disperse yourselves among the people, and say unto them, Bring me hither every man his ox, and every man his sheep, and slay *them* here, and eat; and sin not against the LORD in eating with the blood. And all the people brought every man his ox with him that night, and slew *them* there.

14:35☆ 1 Sam 7:12, 17

35And Saul built an altar unto the LORD: the same was the first altar that he built unto the LORD.

(4) Jonathan's Error Uncovered

14:36 Josh 10:14

36¶And Saul said, Let us go down after the Philistines by night, and spoil them until the morning light, and let us not leave a man of them. And they said, Do whatsoever seemeth good unto thee. Then said the priest, Let us draw near hither unto God.

14:37 1 Sam 23:4; 28:5, 6; 30:7, 8

37And Saul asked counsel of God, Shall I go down after the Philistines?

14:24 Saul foolishly forbade his troops to touch any food until the evening. He enforced the command by cursing any who would disobey. But Saul's curse fell upon his own son, who, in ignorance of the command, had eaten some honey. Saul decided to execute Jonathan. The people, however, protested the action against Jonathan, whom they loved; they subsequently ransomed him from his guilt (14:45). In Ps. 109:17, 18, David writes of the foolishness of cursing; he may have been referring to this incident.

14:32 Although it was forbidden to eat blood, due to the extreme conditions, the soldiers do what is forbidden. Saul had enough good sense to reprove them for that act and ordered it to be stopped.

14:35 Saul built an altar to keep the people from eating blood (see Lev. 7:26, 27; 17:12). He supervised the sacrifices.

wilt thou deliver them into the hand of Israel? But he answered him not
that day.
38 And Saul said, Draw ye near hither, all the chief of the people: and
know and see wherein this sin hath been this day.

14:38 Josh 7:10–12

39 For, *as* the LORD liveth, which saveth Israel, though it be in Jonathan
my son, he shall surely die. But *there was* not a man among all the people
that answered him.

14:39 1 Sam 14:24–44 19:6

40 Then said he unto all Israel, Be ye on one side, and I and Jonathan my
son will be on the other side. And the people said unto Saul, Do what
seemeth good unto thee.
41 Therefore Saul said unto the LORD God of Israel, Give a perfect *lot.*
And Saul and Jonathan were taken: but the people escaped.
42 And Saul said, Cast *lots* between me and Jonathan my son. And
Jonathan was taken.

☆**14:41** Prov 16:33 Acts 1:24

(5) The People Save Jonathan from Death

43 Then Saul said to Jonathan, Tell me what thou hast done. And
Jonathan told him, and said, I did but taste a little honey with the end of
the rod that *was* in mine hand, *and,* lo, I must die.

14:43 Josh 7:19 1 Sam 14:27

44 And Saul answered, God do so and more also: for thou shalt surely die,
Jonathan.
45 And the people said unto Saul, Shall Jonathan die, who hath wrought
this great salvation in Israel? God forbid: *as* the LORD liveth, there shall not
one hair of his head fall to the ground; for he hath wrought with God this
day. So the people rescued Jonathan, that he died not.
46 Then Saul went up from following the Philistines: and the Philistines
went to their own place.

☆**14:44** Gen 38:24 1 Sam 3:17 14:39; 25:22 2 Sam 12:5
☆**14:45** 2 Sam 14:11 Lk 21:18 Acts 27:34

e. Saul's Victories over the Surrounding Nations

47 ¶So Saul took the kingdom over Israel, and fought against all his
enemies on every side, against Moab, and against the children of Ammon,
and against Edom, and against the kings of Zo'bah, and against the
Philistines: and whithersoever he turned himself, he vexed *them.*

☆**14:47**

48 And he gathered an host, and smote the Am'a-lek-ites, and delivered
Israel out of the hands of them that spoiled them.

14:48 1 Sam 15:3, 7

f. Saul's Children and His Army Leaders

49 ¶Now the sons of Saul were Jonathan, and Ish'u-i, and Mel'chi-shu'a:
and the names of his two daughters *were these;* the name of the firstborn
Me'rab, and the name of the younger Mi'chal:
50 And the name of Saul's wife *was* A-hin'o-am, the daughter of A-him'a-
az: and the names of the captain of his host *was* Abner, the son of Ner,
Saul's uncle.
51 And Kish *was* the father of Saul; and Ner the father of Abner *was* the
son of A-bi'el.

14:49 1 Sam 18:17, 20, 27; 19:11, 12 31:2 2 Sam 6:20 1 Chron 10:2
14:50 1 Sam 17:55 2 Sam 2:8

14:41 *perfect lot,* i.e., "Urim and Thummin." (See note on Exod. 28:30.)

14:44, 45 Jonathan was guilty of disobeying his father's order, and Saul was willing for him to be slain. The soldiers thought the judgment was unfair and therefore rescued Jonathan. They did it not by violence but by reason and resolution.

14:47ff In a few words the writer tells how Saul extended his control over Edom, Moab, Ammon, Zobah, and Philistia by successful warfare. In verses 49–52 a short account of the kingly family and its members is mentioned. It ends with the statement that Saul attached all the strong men to himself, as Samuel had prophesied the king would do when he began to reign.

14:52 1 Sam 8:11 / 1 Kgs 9:22

52 And there was sore war against the Philistines all the days of Saul: and
when Saul saw any strong man, or any valiant man, he took him unto him.

C. SAUL DISOBEYS GOD AND IS REJECTED

1. The Command to Destroy the Amalekites

15:1☆ 1 Sam 9:16 / 10:1

15 SAMUEL also said unto Saul, The LORD sent me to anoint thee *to*
be king over his people, over Israel: now therefore hearken thou
unto the voice of the words of the LORD.

15:2 Ex 17:8–16 / Num 24:20 / Deut 25:17
15:3☆ Deut 20:16–18 / Josh 6:17, 18

2 Thus saith the LORD of hosts, I remember *that* which Am'a-lek did to
Israel, how he laid *wait* for him in the way, when he came up from Egypt.
3 Now go and smite Am'a-lek, and utterly destroy all that they have, and
spare them not; but slay both man and woman, infant and suckling, ox and
sheep, camel and ass.

2. Saul's Disobedience

4 And Saul gathered the people together, and numbered them in Tel'a-im,
two hundred thousand footmen, and ten thousand men of Judah.
5 And Saul came to a city of Am'a-lek, and laid wait in the valley.

15:6 Num 24:21, 22 / Judg 1:16; 4:11

6 ¶And Saul said unto the Ken'ites, Go, depart, get you down from
among the Am'a-lek-ites, lest I destroy you with them: for ye shewed
kindness to all the children of Israel, when they came up out of Egypt. So
the Ken'ites departed from among the Am'a-lek-ites.

15:7 Gen 16:7; 25:18 / Ex 15:22 / 1 Sam 27:8
15:8☆ Num 24:7
15:9☆ 1 Sam 15:15, 21

7 And Saul smote the Am'a-lek-ites from Hav'i-lah *until* thou comest to
Shur, that *is* over against Egypt.
8 And he took Agag the king of the Am'a-lek-ites alive, and utterly
destroyed all the people with the edge of the sword.
9 But Saul and the people spared Agag, and the best of the sheep, and of
the oxen, and of the fatlings, and the lambs, and all *that was* good, and
would not utterly destroy them: but every thing *that was* vile and refuse,
that they destroyed utterly.

3. God's Judgment on Saul's Disobedience

15:10
15:11☆ Gen 6:6, 7 / Ex 32:9, 11, 14 / 2 Sam 24:16 / Luke 6:12

10 ¶Then came the word of the LORD unto Samuel, saying,
11 It repenteth me that I have set up Saul *to be* king: for he is turned back
from following me, and hath not performed my commandments. And it
grieved Samuel; and he cried unto the LORD all night.
12 And when Samuel rose early to meet Saul in the morning, it was told
Samuel, saying, Saul came to Carmel, and, behold, he set him up a place,
and is gone about, and passed on, and gone down to Gilgal.

15:13☆

13 And Samuel came to Saul: and Saul said unto him, Blessed *be* thou of
the LORD: I have performed the commandment of the LORD.

15:1 God through Samuel ordered Saul to smite Amalek for its opposition to Israel on the wilderness journey.

15:3 *utterly destroy,* i.e., *"devote to God or destruction"* (*charam* or *herem*). The condition of the Amalekites was irremediable; God had given them sufficient time to repent. The hour of judgment had arrived for them. (See note on Deut. 2:34.)

15:8 Evidently not all the Amalekites were slain, for a strong enclave existed in David's day (27:8; 30:1, 18; 2 Sam. 1:1). Apparently some of the Amalekites were elsewhere at the time. (See note on Est. 3:1 for information on the Amalekites.)

15:9 Saul saved Agag and some of the sheep, oxen, and lambs. He destroyed only the useless and worthless, despite God's command to slay all human and animal life.

15:11 *It repenteth me* is translated "I regret" in the NASB and "I am grieved" in the NIV. The word *repent* has a deeper theological connotation than is called for in this instance.

15:13 Saul piously told Samuel he had followed the commandment of God, but the bleating of the sheep and the lowing of the oxen told a different tale. Samuel already knew of Saul's disobedience and had to proclaim the judgment of God to this impenitent sinner.

14 And Samuel said, What *meaneth* then this bleating of the sheep in mine
ears, and the lowing of the oxen which I hear?
15 And Saul said, They have brought them from the Am′a-lek-ites: for the
people spared the best of the sheep and of the oxen, to sacrifice unto the
LORD thy God; and the rest we have utterly destroyed.
16 Then Samuel said unto Saul, Stay, and I will tell thee what the LORD
hath said to me this night. And he said unto him, Say on.
17 And Samuel said, When thou *wast* little in thine own sight, *wast* thou
not *made* the head of the tribes of Israel, and the LORD anointed thee king
over Israel?
18 And the LORD sent thee on a journey, and said, Go and utterly destroy
the sinners the Am′a-lek-ites, and fight against them until they be
consumed.
19 Wherefore then didst thou not obey the voice of the LORD, but didst fly
upon the spoil, and didst evil in the sight of the LORD?
20 And Saul said unto Samuel, Yea, I have obeyed the voice of the LORD,
and have gone the way which the LORD sent me, and have brought Agag
the king of Am′a-lek, and have utterly destroyed the Am′a-lek-ites.
21 But the people took of the spoil, sheep and oxen, the chief of the things
which should have been utterly destroyed, to sacrifice unto the LORD thy
God in Gilgal.
22 And Samuel said, Hath the LORD *as great* delight in burnt offerings and
sacrifices, as in obeying the voice of the LORD? Behold, to obey *is* better
than sacrifice, *and* to hearken than the fat of rams.
23 For rebellion *is as* the sin of witchcraft, and stubbornness *is as* iniquity
and idolatry. Because thou hast rejected the word of the LORD, he hath also
rejected thee from *being* king.

4. Saul's Repentance of No Avail

24 ¶And Saul said unto Samuel, I have sinned: for I have transgressed the
commandment of the LORD, and thy words: because I feared the people,
and obeyed their voice.
25 Now therefore, I pray thee, pardon my sin, and turn again with me, that
I may worship the LORD.
26 And Samuel said unto Saul, I will not return with thee: for thou hast
rejected the word of the LORD, and the LORD hath rejected thee from being
king over Israel.
27 And as Samuel turned about to go away, he laid hold upon the skirt of
his mantle, and it rent.
28 And Samuel said unto him, The LORD hath rent the kingdom of Israel
from thee this day, and hath given it to a neighbour of thine, *that is* better
than thou.
29 And also the Strength of Israel will not lie nor repent: for he *is* not a
man, that he should repent.

15:15 Gen 3:12, 13; 1 Sam 15:9, 21
15:17 Judg 6:15; 1 Sam 9:21; 10:22
15:19 1 Sam 14:32
☆**15:21** 1 Sam 15:9, 15
☆**15:22** Ps 40:6–8; 51:16–17; Isa 1:11; Jer 7:22; Hos 6:6; Mic 6:7, 8; Mk 12:33
15:23 Deut 18:10; 1 Sam 13:14
15:24 Num 22:34; 2 Sam 12:13; Ps 51:4
15:25 Ex 10:17
15:27 1 Kgs 11:30, 31
15:28 1 Sam 28:17, 18
☆**15:29** Num 23:19; Ezek 24:14; 2 Tim 2:13

15:21 *the people took of the spoil.* This was Saul's excuse for his disobedience. But he too was guilty of covetousness. In an earlier episode, Aaron was guilty of blaming "the people" for a sin of which he too was guilty (Exod. 32:22–24).

15:22 Saul foolishly failed to fulfill God's orders completely. When Samuel faced him with his disobedience, Saul argued that he had saved some of the sheep and oxen in order to sacrifice them to God. This incident was the final step in Saul's downfall. Divine judgment was pronounced and Saul was rejected by God, for he had rejected the word of the Lord. Samuel enunciated a vital truth: obedience is better than sacrifice. It is always possible for a disobedient person to offer sacrifice. But when obedience rules the heart, sacrifices will also be made.

Samuel likens disobedience and stubbornness to idolatry and divination. Nothing so offends and provokes God more than setting up our wills in competition with his.

15:29 *Strength of Israel,* translated "Glory of Israel" in the NASB, RSV, and NIV. The term emphasizes the eternal nature and immutability of God.

15:30 30 Then he said, I have sinned: *yet* honour me now, I pray thee, before the
Isa 29:13 elders of my people, and before Israel, and turn again with me, that I may
worship the LORD thy God.
31 So Samuel turned again after Saul; and Saul worshipped the LORD.

5. Samuel Slays Agag and Mourns for Saul

32 ¶Then said Samuel, Bring ye hither to me Agag the king of the Am'a-
lek-ites. And Agag came unto him delicately. And Agag said, Surely the
bitterness of death is past.
15:33☆ 33 And Samuel said, As thy sword hath made women childless, so shall
Gen 9:5, 6 Judg 1:7 thy mother be childless among women. And Samuel hewed Agag in pieces
before the LORD in Gilgal.
15:34☆ 34 ¶Then Samuel went to Ra'mah; and Saul went up to his house to Gib'e-
1 Sam 7:17 11:4; 15:35 ah of Saul.
1 Sam 15:11 35 And Samuel came no more to see Saul until the day of his death:
15:35☆ nevertheless Samuel mourned for Saul: and the LORD repented that he had
made Saul king over Israel.

D. THE DECLINE OF SAUL; THE RISE OF DAVID
1. David to Be Saul's Successor
a. Samuel Visits David's Father

16:1☆ 16 AND the LORD said unto Samuel, How long wilt thou mourn for
Ruth 4:18–22 1 Sam 9:16 Saul, seeing I have rejected him from reigning over Israel? fill thine
13:13; 14 horn with oil, and go, I will send thee to Jesse the Beth-lehemite: for I have
2 Kgs 9:1, 2 provided me a king among his sons.
16:2☆ 2 And Samuel said, How can I go? if Saul hear *it,* he will kill me. And the
1 Sam 20:28, 29 LORD said, Take an heifer with thee, and say, I am come to sacrifice to the
LORD.
16:3☆ 3 And call Jesse to the sacrifice, and I will shew thee what thou shalt do:
Deut 17:14, 15 and thou shalt anoint unto me *him* whom I name unto thee.
16:4☆ 4 And Samuel did that which the LORD spake, and came to Beth-lehem.
1 Sam 16:18 Lk 2:4 And the elders of the town trembled at his coming, and said, Comest thou
peaceably?
16:5☆ 5 And he said, Peaceably: I am come to sacrifice unto the LORD: sanctify
Gen 35:2 Ex 19:10 yourselves, and come with me to the sacrifice. And he sanctified Jesse and
Josh 3:5 his sons, and called them to the sacrifice.

b. David Chosen and Anointed King

16:6☆ 6 ¶And it came to pass, when they were come, that he looked on E-li'ab,
and said, Surely the LORD'S anointed *is* before him.

15:33 Why did Saul not slay Agag immediately? Samuel performed this deed, for it appears that Saul still shirked his duty.

15:34, 35 Samuel went to Ramah, never to see Saul again while he was living. Both Samuel and God grieved over what happened to Saul. He got off to a promising start but fell into sin.

16:1 God announced to Samuel that he had selected Saul's successor from the sons of Jesse, but he did not tell Samuel which one. The remainder of 1 Samuel depicts the struggle between Saul and David and ends with the death of Saul.

16:2, 3 Samuel feared that Saul might kill him. God told him to go to Bethlehem and offer an animal sacrifice. During that stay he was to anoint David as the new king. There was no deception on the part of God.

16:4 When Samuel came to Bethlehem, the elders of the town thought he might be coming to pronounce some adverse judgment of God against them. Samuel reassured them. Little did they know that the tribe of Judah, their tribe, would produce the next king and that he would start a line that would last eternally.

16:5 In order to appear at the sacrifice it was first necessary to go through the ritual of ceremonial washings and purification. Jesse and the family did this.

16:6 Starting with the eldest, Samuel looked at each son and was told by God that none of them was the divine choice. Finally David, the youngest, who had been tending the sheep, was sent for; and when he appeared, God said, "Arise, anoint him: for this is he" (16:12).

7 But the LORD said unto Samuel, Look not on his countenance, or on the
height of his stature; because I have refused him: for *the LORD seeth* not as
man seeth; for man looketh on the outward appearance, but the LORD
looketh on the heart.

16:7 1 Sam 9:2; 1 Kgs 8:39; 1 Chron 28:9; Lk 16:15

8 Then Jesse called A-bin′a-dab, and made him pass before Samuel. And
he said, Neither hath the LORD chosen this.

16:8 1 Sam 17:13

9 Then Jesse made Sham′mah to pass by. And he said, Neither hath the
LORD chosen this.

10 Again, Jesse made seven of his sons to pass before Samuel. And Samuel
said unto Jesse, The LORD hath not chosen these.

16:10 2 Sam 7:8; 1 Chron 17:7

11 And Samuel said unto Jesse, Are here all *thy* children? And he said,
There remaineth yet the youngest, and, behold, he keepeth the sheep. And
Samuel said unto Jesse, Send and fetch him: for we will not sit down till he
come hither.

12 And he sent, and brought him in. Now he *was ruddy, and* withal of a
beautiful countenance, and goodly to look to. And the LORD said, Arise,
anoint him: for this *is* he.

☆16:12 Gen 39:6; Ex 2:1, 2; 1 Sam 9:17; Acts 7:20

13 Then Samuel took the horn of oil, and anointed him in the midst of his
brethren: and the Spirit of the LORD came upon David from that day
forward. So Samuel rose up, and went to Ra′mah.

16:13 1 Sam 10:6, 9, 10

2. The Spirit of the Lord Leaves Saul

14 ¶But the Spirit of the LORD departed from Saul, and an evil spirit from
the LORD troubled him.

☆16:14 1 Sam 11:6; 18:10–12; 19:9; 1 Kgs 22:22

15 And Saul's servants said unto him, Behold now, an evil spirit from God
troubleth thee.

16:15 2 Kgs 3:15

16 Let our lord now command thy servants, *which are* before thee, to seek
out a man, *who is* a cunning player on an harp: and it shall come to pass,
when the evil spirit from God is upon thee, that he shall play with his hand,
and thou shalt be well.

17 And Saul said unto his servants, Provide me now a man that can play
well, and bring *him* to me.

18 Then answered one of the servants, and said, Behold, I have seen a son
of Jesse the Beth–lehemite, *that is* cunning in playing, and a mighty valiant
man, and a man of war, and prudent in matters, and a comely person, and
the LORD *is* with him.

16:18 1 Sam 3:19; 18:11, 12

19 ¶Wherefore Saul sent messengers unto Jesse, and said, Send me David
thy son, which *is* with the sheep.

20 And Jesse took an ass *laden* with bread, and a bottle of wine, and a kid,
and sent *them* by David his son unto Saul.

21 And David came to Saul, and stood before him: and he loved him
greatly; and he became his armourbearer.

16:21 1 Sam 22:14

22 And Saul sent to Jesse, saying, Let David, I pray thee, stand before me;
for he hath found favour in my sight.

16:12 David, the shepherd-king, is a type of Christ. David left the sheep to become king of Israel. Christ came as the good shepherd to give his life for the sheep (John 10:11). Christ the shepherd rose from the dead, ascended into glory, and is now king of kings, sitting upon the heavenly throne of his father David, for he is David's greater son (Luke 1:32; Acts 2:30).

16:13 *the Spirit of the LORD came upon David from that day forward.* The Spirit came upon believers in the Old Testament as he pleased. When David was anointed to be king, the Spirit of God filled him. 16:14 is a pathetic illustration of how the Spirit departed from disobedient servants of God: "The Spirit of the LORD departed from Saul." Note how the Spirit of the Lord came upon Samson (Judg. 14:19), then how Samson's sins caused the loss of the Spirit's presence and power: "And he wist not that the LORD was departed from him" (Judg. 16:20).

16:14 Saul's punishment was from God, who sent *an evil spirit* "that filled him with depression and fear."†

16:23☆ 23 And it came to pass, when the *evil* spirit from God was upon Saul, that
David took an harp, and played with his hand: so Saul was refreshed, and
was well, and the evil spirit departed from him.

E. DAVID'S RISE TO FAME AND SAUL'S PERSECUTIONS

1. Goliath, the Philistine Champion

17:1 1 Sam 13:5 1 Chron 11:13

17 NOW the Philistines gathered together their armies to battle, and
were gathered together at Sho'choh, which *belongeth* to Judah, and
pitched between Sho'choh and A-ze'kah, in E'phes–dam'mim,

17:2 1 Sam 21:9

2 And Saul and the men of Israel were gathered together, and pitched by
the valley of E'lah, and set the battle in array against the Philistines.
3 And the Philistines stood on a mountain on the one side, and Israel
stood on a mountain on the other side: and *there was* a valley between
them.

17:4☆ Josh 11:21, 22 2 Sam 21:19

4 ¶And there went out a champion out of the camp of the Philistines,
named Goliath, of Gath, whose height *was* six cubits and a span.
5 And *he had* an helmet of brass upon his head, and he *was* armed with a
coat of mail; and the weight of the coat *was* five thousand shekels of brass.
6 And *he had* greaves of brass upon his legs, and a target of brass between
his shoulders.
7 And the staff of his spear *was* like a weaver's beam; and his spear's head
weighed six hundred shekels of iron: and one bearing a shield went before
him.
8 And he stood and cried unto the armies of Israel, and said unto them,
Why are ye come out to set *your* battle in array? *am* not I a Philistine, and
ye servants to Saul? choose you a man for you, and let him come down to
me.

17:9☆ 2 Sam 2:12–16

9 If he be able to fight with me, and to kill me, then will we be your
servants: but if I prevail against him, and kill him, then shall ye be our
servants, and serve us.
10 And the Philistine said, I defy the armies of Israel this day; give me a
man, that we may fight together.

17:11☆

11 When Saul and all Israel heard those words of the Philistine, they were
dismayed, and greatly afraid.

2. David's Victory over Goliath

17:12 Gen 35:19 Ruth 4:18–22 1 Chron 2:13

12 ¶Now David *was* the son of that Eph'rath-ite of Beth–lehem–judah,
whose name *was* Jesse; and he had eight sons: and the man went among
men *for* an old man in the days of Saul.
13 And the three eldest sons of Jesse went *and* followed Saul to the battle:
and the names of his three sons that went to the battle *were* E-li'ab the
firstborn, and next unto him A-bin'a-dab, and the third Sham'mah.
14 And David *was* the youngest: and the three eldest followed Saul.
15 But David went and returned from Saul to feed his father's sheep at
Beth–lehem.
16 And the Philistine drew near morning and evening, and presented
himself forty days.

16:23 "David is made a physician to Saul, and by this means brought to court, a physician that helped him against the worst of diseases, when none else could."* Here David refreshed the king, and the evil spirit left him for a moment.

17:4 Goliath was approximately ten feet tall and his armor weighed more than a hundred pounds.

17:9 Goliath challenged Israel to a two-man fight, winner take all. Israel had no one who wished to take up the challenge, until David showed up.

17:11 *When Saul.* Saul was probably especially worried, for he was the tallest of the Israelites, and was obviously the best match!†

[17]And Jesse said unto David his son, Take now for thy brethren an ephah of this parched *corn,* and these ten loaves, and run to the camp to thy brethren;
[18]And carry these ten cheeses unto the captain of *their* thousand, and look how thy brethren fare, and take their pledge.
[19]Now Saul, and they, and all the men of Israel, *were* in the valley of E'lah, fighting with the Philistines.
[20]¶And David rose up early in the morning, and left the sheep with a keeper, and took, and went, as Jesse had commanded him; and he came to the trench, as the host was going forth to the fight, and shouted for the battle.
[21]For Israel and the Philistines had put the battle in array, army against army.
[22]And David left his carriage in the hand of the keeper of the carriage, and ran into the army, and came and saluted his brethren.
[23]And as he talked with them, behold, there came up the champion, the Philistine of Gath, Goliath by name, out of the armies of the Philistines, and spake according to the same words: and David heard *them.*
[24]And all the men of Israel, when they saw the man, fled from him, and were sore afraid.
[25]And the men of Israel said, Have ye seen this man that is come up? surely to defy Israel is he come up: and it shall be, *that* the man who killeth him, the king will enrich him with great riches, and will give him his daughter, and make his father's house free in Israel.
[26]And David spake to the men that stood by him, saying, What shall be done to the man that killeth this Philistine, and taketh away the reproach from Israel? for who *is* this uncircumcised Philistine, that he should defy the armies of the living God?
[27]And the people answered him after this manner, saying, So shall it be done to the man that killeth him.
[28]¶And E-li'ab his eldest brother heard when he spake unto the men; and E-li'ab's anger was kindled against David, and he said, Why camest thou down hither? and with whom hast thou left those few sheep in the wilderness? I know thy pride, and the naughtiness of thine heart; for thou art come down that thou mightest see the battle.
[29]And David said, What have I now done? *Is there* not a cause?
[30]¶And he turned from him toward another, and spake after the same manner: and the people answered him again after the former manner.
[31]And when the words were heard which David spake, they rehearsed *them* before Saul: and he sent for him.
[32]¶And David said to Saul, Let no man's heart fail because of him; thy servant will go and fight with this Philistine.
[33]And Saul said to David, Thou art not able to go against this Philistine

☆**17:17** 1 Sam 25:18
17:18 Gen 37:13, 14
17:20 1 Sam 26:5, 7
17:25 Josh 15:16; 1 Sam 18:17
☆**17:26** 1 Sam 14:6; 2 Kgs 19:4
☆**17:28** Gen 37:4, 8
17:32 Deut 20:1; Ps 27:3
☆**17:33**

17:17 Saul's enmity against David caused him to plan for David's death. He promised to give David his eldest daughter in marriage. He urged him to fight against the Philistines, hoping he would be slain. Then he broke his word and gave Merab to another man. When Saul learned that another of his daughters, Michal, was in love with David, he planned to use her to entrap David. His servants told David that the king wanted a hundred foreskins of the Philistines from the man who would marry Michal. To secure these, David endangered his life. David produced the foreskins, won Michal, and frustrated Saul.

17:26 David spoke the language of faith when he asked, *Who is this uncircumcised Philistine, that he should defy the armies of the living God?* His confidence was not in himself but in the living God. The Spirit of the Lord had come upon him in mighty power, and it was from that day onward that he was filled (1 Sam. 16:13).

17:28 Eliab, David's oldest brother, suspected that David wanted to take on Goliath. He browbeat the young man by using abusive language. He would not take the challenge himself; for this youngster to do so, would make him lose face. He was envious of David's daring.

17:33 Saul sought to dissuade David from tackling Goliath. David argued that if he could slay a lion and a bear, he could slay Goliath.

to fight with him: for thou *art but* a youth, and he a man of war from his
youth.
34 And David said unto Saul, Thy servant kept his father's sheep, and
there came a lion, and a bear, and took a lamb out of the flock:

17:35 Amos 3:12

35 And I went out after him, and smote him, and delivered *it* out of his
mouth: and when he arose against me, I caught *him* by his beard, and
smote him, and slew him.

17:36 1 Sam 17:26

36 Thy servant slew both the lion and the bear: and this uncircumcised
Philistine shall be as one of them, seeing he hath defied the armies of the
living God.

17:37 1 Sam 20:13; Ps 18:16, 17; 2 Tim 4:17

37 David said moreover, The LORD that delivered me out of the paw of the
lion, and out of the paw of the bear, he will deliver me out of the hand of
this Philistine. And Saul said unto David, Go, and the LORD be with thee.
38 ¶And Saul armed David with his armour, and he put an helmet of brass
upon his head; also he armed him with a coat of mail.
39 And David girded his sword upon his armour, and he assayed to go; for
he had not proved *it.* And David said unto Saul, I cannot go with these; for
I have not proved *them.* And David put them off him.
40 And he took his staff in his hand, and chose him five smooth stones out
of the brook, and put them in a shepherd's bag which he had, even in a
scrip; and his sling *was* in his hand: and he drew near to the Philistine.
41 And the Philistine came on and drew near unto David; and the man
that bare the shield *went* before him.

17:42 1 Sam 16:12

42 And when the Philistine looked about, and saw David, he disdained
him: for he was *but* a youth, and ruddy, and of a fair countenance.

17:43☆ 2 Sam 3:8; 9:8; 16:9; 1 Kgs 20:10

43 And the Philistine said unto David, *Am* I a dog, that thou comest to me
with staves? And the Philistine cursed David by his gods.
44 And the Philistine said to David, Come to me, and I will give thy flesh
unto the fowls of the air, and to the beasts of the field.

17:45☆ 2 Chron 32:8; Ps 124:8; Prov 18:10; Heb 11:34

45 Then said David to the Philistine, Thou comest to me with a sword, and
with a spear, and with a shield: but I come to thee in the name of the LORD
of hosts, the God of the armies of Israel, whom thou hast defied.

17:46 Ex 7:5; Josh 4:24; 2 Kgs 19:19; Isa 37:20; Dan 2:47

46 This day will the LORD deliver thee into mine hand; and I will smite
thee, and take thine head from thee; and I will give the carcases of the host
of the Philistines this day unto the fowls of the air, and to the wild beasts of
the earth; that all the earth may know that there is a God in Israel.

17:47 1 Sam 14:6; 2 Chron 14:11; 20:15; Ps 44:6

47 And all this assembly shall know that the LORD saveth not with sword
and spear: for the battle *is* the LORD's, and he will give you into our hands.
48 And it came to pass, when the Philistine arose, and came and drew nigh
to meet David, that David hasted, and ran toward the army to meet the
Philistine.
49 And David put his hand in his bag, and took thence a stone, and slang
it, and smote the Philistine in his forehead, that the stone sunk into his
forehead; and he fell upon his face to the earth.

17:50 1 Sam 21:9; 2 Sam 23:21

50 So David prevailed over the Philistine with a sling and with a stone,
and smote the Philistine, and slew him; but *there was* no sword in the hand
of David.

17:43 When Goliath saw this shorter, younger, and ill-armed contender stand before him, he was disdainful and contemptuous. In effect he said, "Do you think you can beat me as easily as you would a shepherd dog?" He cursed David by his gods and thus cursed the God of David.

17:45 From the perspective of the unbeliever, David's eagerness to confront Goliath appears to be based on adolescent naiveté. Yet we know the outcome of this confrontation. David declared that God had called, anointed, and authorized him to fulfill this task. David knew that his God was the God of the armies of the Israelites; he was certain that God would deliver Goliath into his hand before the end of the battle (17:46). Who can withstand even the weakest, most unprepared of God's servants when he comes as the chosen of God for a particular task?

51 Therefore David ran, and stood upon the Philistine, and took his
sword, and drew it out of the sheath thereof, and slew him, and cut off his
head therewith. And when the Philistines saw their champion was dead,
they fled.
52 And the men of Israel and of Judah arose, and shouted, and pursued
the Philistines, until thou come to the valley, and to the gates of Ekron.
And the wounded of the Philistines fell down by the way to Sha-a-ra'im,
even unto Gath, and unto Ekron.
53 And the children of Israel returned from chasing after the Philistines,
and they spoiled their tents.
54 And David took the head of the Philistine, and brought it to Jerusalem;
but he put his armour in his tent.
55 ¶And when Saul saw David go forth against the Philistine, he said unto
Abner, the captain of the host, Abner, whose son *is* this youth? And Abner
said, *As* thy soul liveth, O king, I cannot tell.
56 And the king said, Inquire thou whose son the stripling *is.*
57 And as David returned from the slaughter of the Philistine, Abner took
him, and brought him before Saul with the head of the Philistine in his
hand.
58 And Saul said to him, Whose son *art* thou, *thou* young man? And David
answered, I *am* the son of thy servant Jesse the Beth-lehemite.

17:52 Josh 15:10, 11, 33–36

☆**17:55** 1 Sam 14:50, 51

17:58 1 Sam 16:18

3. David and Jonathan Become Close Friends

18 AND it came to pass, when he had made an end of speaking unto
Saul, that the soul of Jonathan was knit with the soul of David, and
Jonathan loved him as his own soul.
2 And Saul took him that day, and would let him go no more home to his
father's house.
3 Then Jonathan and David made a covenant, because he loved him as his
own soul.
4 And Jonathan stripped himself of the robe that *was* upon him, and gave
it to David, and his garments, even to his sword, and to his bow, and to his
girdle.
5 ¶And David went out whithersoever Saul sent him, *and* behaved himself
wisely: and Saul set him over the men of war, and he was accepted in the
sight of all the people, and also in the sight of Saul's servants.

☆**18:1** 1 Sam 20:8; 23:18; 2 Sam 1:26; 9:1

18:4 Gen 41:42; Esther 6:8

☆**18:5**

4. Saul's Hatred of David

6 And it came to pass as they came, when David was returned from the
slaughter of the Philistine, that the women came out of all cities of Israel,
singing and dancing, to meet king Saul, with tabrets, with joy, and with
instruments of musick.
7 And the women answered *one another* as they played, and said, Saul
hath slain his thousands, and David his ten thousands.

18:6 Judg 11:34; Ps 68:24; 149:3

18:7 1 Sam 21:11; 29:5

17:55 Neither Saul nor Abner could remember the name of David's father. Saul was indebted to the family for what David had done and in order to reward them he needed to know who headed up the family. David himself answered the question in verse 58.

18:1 Jonathan and David became fast friends and cleaved to each other through thick and thin. Later Saul cursed his son for what he considered to be his infidelity toward himself.

18:5 David rose rapidly to a place of standing and honor and was well-thought-of by the people. Even the servants of Saul were partial toward him. "Those that climb so fast have need of good heads and good hearts. It is more difficult to know how to abound than how to be abased."*

18:8 8And Saul was very wroth, and the saying displeased him; and he said,
1 Sam 15:28 16:13 They have ascribed unto David ten thousands, and to me they have
ascribed *but* thousands: and *what* can he have more but the kingdom?
9And Saul eyed David from that day and forward.
18:10☆ 10¶And it came to pass on the morrow, that the evil spirit from God came
1 Sam 16:14, 23 upon Saul, and he prophesied in the midst of the house: and David played
with his hand, as at other times: and *there was* a javelin in Saul's hand.
11And Saul cast the javelin; for he said, I will smite David even to the
wall *with it.* And David avoided out of his presence twice.
18:12☆ 12¶And Saul was afraid of David, because the LORD was with him, and
was departed from Saul.
18:13 13Therefore Saul removed him from him, and made him his captain over
2 Sam 5:2 a thousand; and he went out and came in before the people.
18:14 14And David behaved himself wisely in all his ways; and the LORD *was*
1 Sam 14:47 with him.
16:18; 18:30
2 Sam 5:10 15Wherefore when Saul saw that he behaved himself very wisely, he was
afraid of him.
16But all Israel and Judah loved David, because he went out and came in
before them.

5. David Loses Merab but Marries Michal, Saul's Daughter

18:17 17¶And Saul said to David, Behold my elder daughter Me'rab, her will I
1 Sam 17:25 25:28 give thee to wife: only be thou valiant for me, and fight the LORD's battles.
For Saul said, Let not mine hand be upon him, but let the hand of the
Philistines be upon him.
18:18 18And David said unto Saul, Who *am* I? and what *is* my life, *or* my
Ex 3:11 1 Sam 9:21 father's family in Israel, that I should be son in law to the king?
2 Sam 7:18 **18:19** 19But it came to pass at the time when Me'rab Saul's daughter should
2 Sam 21:8 have been given to David, that she was given unto A'dri-el the Me-hol'ath-
ite to wife.
20And Mi'chal Saul's daughter loved David: and they told Saul, and the
thing pleased him.
21And Saul said, I will give him her, that she may be a snare to him, and
that the hand of the Philistines may be against him. Wherefore Saul said to
David, Thou shalt this day be my son in law in *the one of* the twain.
22¶And Saul commanded his servants, *saying,* Commune with David
secretly, and say, Behold, the king hath delight in thee, and all his servants
love thee: now therefore be the king's son in law.
18:23 23And Saul's servants spake those words in the ears of David. And David
Gen 29:20 34:12 said, Seemeth it to you *a* light *thing* to be a king's son in law, seeing that I
am a poor man, and lightly esteemed?
24And the servants of Saul told him, saying, On this manner spake David.
18:25☆ 25And Saul said, Thus shall ye say to David, The king desireth not any
dowry, but an hundred foreskins of the Philistines, to be avenged of the

---

18:10 Saul, jealous and malicious, gave place to the devil who came upon him. He pretended to be in a religious ecstasy and simulated the gestures and motions of a prophet; these were in no sense genuine. This counterfeit play-acting was designed to entice David so that Saul could slay him. David, who was filled with the Holy Spirit (see Ps. 51:10), was given the wisdom and grace to avoid a premature death on two occasions as Saul sought to pin him to the wall with his javelin. The basis for Saul's hatred for David rose from the fact expressed in 18:12: "Saul was afraid of David, because the LORD was with him, and was departed from Saul."

18:12 Saul now feared David for the best of reasons. He knew that God the Holy Spirit was with him and that the Holy Spirit had departed from his own soul. Since he once had the power of the Spirit, he knew that whoever had the same power was greater than he. Instead of making peace with the situation and manifesting a willingness to accept the one whom God had promoted, Saul demoted David to a lower position and with less public visibility. Thus Saul was really engaged in a fight against God.

18:25 *an hundred foreskins of the Philistines.* 18:27 says David brought two hundred foreskins to the king. In 2 Sam. 3:14 the number is said to be one hundred.

king's enemies. But Saul thought to make David fall by the hand of the
Philistines.
26And when his servants told David these words, it pleased David well to
be the king's son in law: and the days were not expired.
27Wherefore David arose and went, he and his men, and slew of the **18:27** 2 Sam 3:14
Philistines two hundred men; and David brought their foreskins, and they
gave them in full tale to the king, that he might be the king's son in law.
And Saul gave him Mi'chal his daughter to wife.
28¶And Saul saw and knew that the LORD *was* with David, and *that*
Mi'chal Saul's daughter loved him.
29And Saul was yet the more afraid of David; and Saul became David's
enemy continually.
30Then the princes of the Philistines went forth: and it came to pass, after **18:30** 1 Sam 18:14
they went forth, *that* David behaved himself more wisely than all the
servants of Saul; so that his name was much set by.

6. Saul Tries to Murder David

a. Jonathan Pleads for David to His Father

19 AND Saul spake to Jonathan his son, and to all his servants, that ☆**19:1** 1 Sam 18:1–3
they should kill David.
2But Jonathan Saul's son delighted much in David: and Jonathan told ☆**19:2**
David, saying, Saul my father seeketh to kill thee: now therefore, I pray
thee, take heed to thyself until the morning, and abide in a secret *place,* and
hide thyself:
3And I will go out and stand beside my father in the field where thou *art,* **19:3** 1 Sam 20:9
and I will commune with my father of thee; and what I see, that I will tell
thee.
4¶And Jonathan spake good of David unto Saul his father, and said unto
him, Let not the king sin against his servant, against David; because he
hath not sinned against thee, and because his works *have been* to thee-ward
very good:
5For he did put his life in his hand, and slew the Philistine, and the LORD **19:5** Deut 19:10–13; 1 Sam 17:49, 50; Ps 94:21
wrought a great salvation for all Israel: thou sawest *it,* and didst rejoice:
wherefore then wilt thou sin against innocent blood, to slay David without
a cause?
6And Saul hearkened unto the voice of Jonathan: and Saul sware, *As* the
LORD liveth, he shall not be slain.
7And Jonathan called David, and Jonathan shewed him all those things. **19:7** 1 Sam 16:21
And Jonathan brought David to Saul, and he was in his presence, as in
times past.
8¶And there was war again: and David went out, and fought with the
Philistines, and slew them with a great slaughter; and they fled from him.

Two possibilities may explain this apparent discrepancy. Either some sleepy scribe miscopied the original text at 18:27, or David brought back twice as many as was required of him. However, when David said what he had done, in 2 Sam. 3:14, he states the original price demanded by Saul.

19:1 Saul then went one step further. He told Jonathan and all his servants to murder David. Saul knew of Jonathan's friendship with David but supposed that since he was heir to the throne, he would be happy to dispose of a contender. Saul gauged his son's intentions by his own. But Jonathan was made of different stuff and was a man of honor.

19:2 Jonathan warned David against his father and proved that blood is not always thicker than water. He spoke to Saul and secured a pledge from him (19:6) that David would not be murdered.

b. Saul Tries to Spear David

19:9☆ 1 Sam 16:14; 18:10–12

9 And the evil spirit from the LORD was upon Saul, as he sat in his house
with his javelin in his hand: and David played with *his* hand.
10 And Saul sought to smite David even to the wall with the javelin; but
he slipped away out of Saul's presence, and he smote the javelin into the
wall: and David fled, and escaped that night.

c. Michal Aids David to Escape

19:11 Judg 16:2; Ps 59 (title), vss 3, 4, 6

11 Saul also sent messengers unto David's house, to watch him, and to slay
him in the morning: and Mi′chal David's wife told him, saying, If thou save
not thy life to night, to morrow thou shalt be slain.
12 ¶So Mi′chal let David down through a window: and he went, and fled,
and escaped.

19:13 Judg 17:4, 5; 18:14, 17

13 And Mi′chal took an image, and laid *it* in the bed, and put a pillow of
goats' *hair* for his bolster, and covered *it* with a cloth.
14 And when Saul sent messengers to take David, she said, He *is* sick.
15 And Saul sent the messengers *again* to see David, saying, Bring him up
to me in the bed, that I may slay him.
16 And when the messengers were come in, behold, *there was* an image in
the bed, with a pillow of goats' *hair* for his bolster.
17 And Saul said unto Mi′chal, Why hast thou deceived me so, and sent
away mine enemy, that he is escaped? And Mi′chal answered Saul, He said
unto me, Let me go; why should I kill thee?

d. Saul Chases David to Naioth and Prophesies

19:18 1 Sam 7:17; 15:34; 19:22

18 ¶So David fled, and escaped, and came to Samuel to Ra′mah, and told
him all that Saul had done to him. And he and Samuel went and dwelt in
Nai′oth.

19:19☆

19 And it was told Saul, saying, Behold, David *is* at Nai′oth in Ra′mah.

19:20 Num 11:24, 25; 1 Sam 10:5, 6, 10; Joel 2:28

20 And Saul sent messengers to take David: and when they saw the
company of the prophets prophesying, and Samuel standing *as* appointed
over them, the Spirit of God was upon the messengers of Saul, and they
also prophesied.
21 And when it was told Saul, he sent other messengers, and they
prophesied likewise. And Saul sent messengers again the third time, and
they prophesied also.

19:22 1 Sam 19:18

22 Then went he also to Ra′mah, and came to a great well that *is* in
Se′chu: and he asked and said, Where *are* Samuel and David? And *one* said,
Behold, *they be* at Nai′oth in Ra′mah.

19:23 1 Sam 19:20

23 And he went thither to Nai′oth in Ra′mah: and the Spirit of God was

---

19:9 Saul had sworn to Jonathan that he would not seek the murder of David, but when the evil spirit overtook him he forgot that pledge and personally sought to kill David. Then he sent men to take David at home, but Michal his daughter was faithful to her husband and arranged for his escape from this ploy (19:11ff). One would have supposed that the actions of Michal and Jonathan would have shown their father that he was in error and he would have turned from his schemes to kill David.

19:19 Naioth in Ramah was the site of the school of the prophets. Samuel and David went there. Saul heard of it and sent messengers to take David. The men who intended to seize David were themselves seized by the Spirit of God and joined the prophets in worshiping God and prophesying. This happened three times. Then Saul went there himself. He too was seized by the Spirit (19:23) and prophesied. He stripped off his clothes and went naked all night. The question was asked: "Is Saul also among the prophets?" (19:24). This is a good question. The Spirit can and does overtake evil men and uses them to accomplish the divine will. Thus Jesus said there were those who in his name prophesied, cast out devils, and did mighty works (Matt. 7:21, 22). But even though they did these things, Jesus disowned them and said they worked iniquity. They used good things for wrong purposes. So Saul also did a good thing by the Spirit; his heart was unchanged, however, and he stood condemned.

upon him also, and he went on, and prophesied, until he came to Nai'oth in Ra'mah.

24 And he stripped off his clothes also, and prophesied before Samuel in like manner, and lay down naked all that day and all that night. Wherefore they say, *Is* Saul also among the prophets?

19:24 1 Sam 10:10–12; 2 Sam 6:20; Mic 1:8

7. Jonathan Saves David's Life

a. Jonathan and David Discuss Saul's Hatred

20 AND David fled from Nai'oth in Ra'mah, and came and said
before Jonathan, What have I done? what *is* mine iniquity? and
what *is* my sin before thy father, that he seeketh my life?
2 And he said unto him, God forbid; thou shalt not die: behold, my father
will do nothing either great or small, but that he will shew it me: and why
should my father hide this thing from me? it *is* not *so*.
3 And David sware moreover, and said, Thy father certainly knoweth that
I have found grace in thine eyes; and he saith, Let not Jonathan know this,
lest he be grieved: but truly *as* the LORD liveth, and *as* thy soul liveth, *there*
is but a step between me and death.
4 Then said Jonathan unto David, Whatsoever thy soul desireth, I will
even do *it* for thee.
5 And David said unto Jonathan, Behold, to morrow *is* the new moon,
and I should not fail to sit with the king at meat: but let me go, that I may
hide myself in the field unto the third *day* at even.
6 If thy father at all miss me, then say, David earnestly asked *leave* of me
that he might run to Beth–lehem his city: for *there is* a yearly sacrifice there
for all the family.
7 If he say thus, *It is* well; thy servant shall have peace: but if he be very
wroth, *then* be sure that evil is determined by him.
8 Therefore thou shalt deal kindly with thy servant; for thou hast brought
thy servant into a covenant of the LORD with thee: notwithstanding, if there
be in me iniquity, slay me thyself; for why shouldest thou bring me to thy
father?
9 And Jonathan said, Far be it from thee: for if I knew certainly that evil
were determined by my father to come upon thee, then would not I tell it
thee?
10 Then said David to Jonathan, Who shall tell me? or what *if* thy father
answer thee roughly?
11 ¶And Jonathan said unto David, Come, and let us go out into the field.
And they went out both of them into the field.

☆**20:1** 1 Sam 24:9, 11, 17
☆**20:3** Deut 6:13; 2 Kgs 2:6, 7; Jer 4:2
20:5 Num 10:10; 28:11–17
20:6 1 Sam 16:2; 17:58; 20:28
20:8 1 Sam 18:1–3; 23:18; 2 Sam 1:26
☆**20:9** 1 Sam 19:2

b. Jonathan Makes a Covenant with David

12 And Jonathan said unto David, O LORD God of Israel, when I have
sounded my father about to morrow any time, *or* the third *day*, and, behold,
if there be good toward David, and I then send not unto thee, and shew it
thee;
13 The LORD do so and much more to Jonathan: but if it please my father

20:13 Ruth 1:17; 1 Sam 3:17; 14:44; 18:11, 12; 1 Chron 28:20

20:1 "It was happy for David that he had such a friend at court, when he had such an enemy on the throne. If there be those that hate and despise us, let us not be disturbed at that, for there are those also that love and respect us."* Jonathan was a "brother that was born for adversity" (Prov. 17:17).

20:3ff David shared his inner thoughts with his friend Jonathan and presented the facts to show that he was innocent of any crimes and that he was no enemy of Saul.

20:9 Jonathan assured David of his own integrity in David's moment of distress. He swore allegiance to David, whatever the cost and whatever the outcome.

to do thee evil, then I will shew it thee, and send thee away, that thou
mayest go in peace: and the LORD be with thee, as he hath been with my
father.

14 And thou shalt not only while yet I live shew me the kindness of the
LORD, that I die not:

20:15☆ 1 Sam 24:21 15 But *also* thou shalt not cut off thy kindness from my house for ever: no,
2 Sam 9:1; 21:7 not when the LORD hath cut off the enemies of David every one from the
face of the earth.

20:16 Deut 23:21 16 So Jonathan made *a covenant* with the house of David, *saying*, Let the
1 Sam 25:22 LORD even require *it* at the hand of David's enemies.

17 And Jonathan caused David to swear again, because he loved him: for
he loved him as he loved his own soul.

18 Then Jonathan said to David, To morrow *is* the new moon: and thou
shalt be missed, because thy seat will be empty.

c. Jonathan's Secret Sign

19 And *when* thou hast stayed three days, *then* thou shalt go down quickly,
and come to the place where thou didst hide thyself when the business was
in hand, and shalt remain by the stone E′zel.

20:20☆ 20 And I will shoot three arrows on the side *thereof*, as though I shot at a
mark.

21 And, behold, I will send a lad, *saying*, Go, find out the arrows. If I
expressly say unto the lad, Behold, the arrows *are* on this side of thee, take
them; then come thou: for *there is* peace to thee, and no hurt; *as* the LORD
liveth.

22 But if I say thus unto the young man, Behold, the arrows *are* beyond
thee; go thy way: for the LORD hath sent thee away.

20:23☆ Gen 31:49, 53 23 And *as touching* the matter which thou and I have spoken of, behold,
the LORD *be* between thee and me for ever.

d. Jonathan Talks to Saul About David

24 ¶So David hid himself in the field: and when the new moon was come,
the king sat him down to eat meat.

25 And the king sat upon his seat, as at other times, *even* upon a seat by
the wall: and Jonathan arose, and Abner sat by Saul's side, and David's
place was empty.

20:26 Lev 7:21 26 Nevertheless Saul spake not any thing that day: for he thought,
Num 19:16 Something hath befallen him, he *is* not clean; surely he *is* not clean.
1 Sam 16:5 27 And it came to pass on the morrow, *which was* the second *day* of the
month, that David's place was empty: and Saul said unto Jonathan his son,
Wherefore cometh not the son of Jesse to meat, neither yesterday, nor to
day?

20:28 1 Sam 20:6 28 And Jonathan answered Saul, David earnestly asked *leave* of me *to go*
to Beth–lehem:

29 And he said, Let me go, I pray thee; for our family hath a sacrifice in
the city; and my brother, he hath commanded me *to be there*: and now, if I
have found favour in thine eyes, let me get away, I pray thee, and see my
brethren. Therefore he cometh not unto the king's table.

20:15 David did what Jonathan requested when he spared Jonathan's son, Mephibosheth.

20:20 Jonathan arranged the signal by which he would tell David of his father's intentions. If he should shoot his arrow beyond the lad who was assigned to recover the arrows, David would know that his life was in danger and would flee.

20:23 *the LORD be between thee and me for ever,* literally, "The Lord is our mediator forever."†

e. Saul's Rage against Jonathan

30 Then Saul's anger was kindled against Jonathan, and he said unto him, ☆20:30 Judg 11:1
Thou son of the perverse rebellious *woman*, do not I know that thou hast
chosen the son of Jesse to thine own confusion, and unto the confusion of
thy mother's nakedness?
31 For as long as the son of Jesse liveth upon the ground, thou shalt not be 20:31 1 Sam 26:16 2 Sam 12:5
established, nor thy kingdom. Wherefore now send and fetch him unto me,
for he shall surely die.
32 And Jonathan answered Saul his father, and said unto him, Wherefore
shall he be slain? what hath he done?
33 And Saul cast a javelin at him to smite him: whereby Jonathan knew 20:33 1 Sam 18:11 19:10, 11
that it was determined of his father to slay David.
34 So Jonathan arose from the table in fierce anger, and did eat no meat
the second day of the month: for he was grieved for David, because his
father had done him shame.

f. Jonathan Warns David of the Danger

35 ¶And it came to pass in the morning, that Jonathan went out into the
field at the time appointed with David, and a little lad with him.
36 And he said unto his lad, Run, find out now the arrows which I shoot. 20:36 1 Sam 20:20, 21
And as the lad ran, he shot an arrow beyond him.
37 And when the lad was come to the place of the arrow which Jonathan ☆20:37
had shot, Jonathan cried after the lad, and said, *Is* not the arrow beyond
thee?
38 And Jonathan cried after the lad, Make speed, haste, stay not. And
Jonathan's lad gathered up the arrows, and came to his master.
39 But the lad knew not any thing: only Jonathan and David knew the
matter.
40 And Jonathan gave his artillery unto his lad, and said unto him, Go,
carry *them* to the city.
41 ¶*And* as soon as the lad was gone, David arose out of *a place* toward the
south, and fell on his face to the ground, and bowed himself three times:
and they kissed one another, and wept one with another, until David
exceeded.
42 And Jonathan said to David, Go in peace, forasmuch as we have sworn 20:42 1 Sam 20:14, 15; 23:18
both of us in the name of the LORD, saying, The LORD be between me and
thee, and between my seed and thy seed for ever. And he arose and
departed: and Jonathan went into the city.

8. David Flees from Saul
a. Ahimelech the Priest Gives David Some Holy Bread

21 THEN came David to Nob to A-him'e-lech the priest: and ☆21:1 1 Sam 22:19 Neh 11:32 Mk 2:25, 26
A-him'e-lech was afraid at the meeting of David, and said unto
him, Why *art* thou alone, and no man with thee?

20:30 *son of the perverse rebellious woman.* The modern equivalent is "son of a bitch." *son of Jesse,* i.e., "son of a nobody."†

At this point, Saul appears to have reached a point of no return. He accused his son Jonathan of being a traitor by his support of David. When Jonathan withstood his father, asking what David had done that made him worthy of death, Saul attempted to kill Jonathan (20:32, 33). This was the last straw. Jonathan knew then that his father was irrevocably commited to slaying David.

20:37ff Jonathan shot the arrow beyond the lad and thus warned David that Saul meant to kill him. The lad went off with the arrows, and David and Jonathan had a farewell meeting. In verse 41 David fell to the ground and bowed three times to Jonathan, thus acknowledging the good services done him by his friend. In a touching scene they took leave of each other with tears and sorrow, as Jonathan said words to this effect: "We have sworn both of us in the name of the Lord, for ourselves and our heirs, that we and they will be faithful and kind to each other from generation to generation." So spoke a man whose integrity and love overshadowed the deceitfulness and hatred of his own father.

21:1 David came to Ahimelech the priest and asked for two things: bread and a weapon. David wanted five

21:2☆ 1 Sam 19:17

2 And David said unto A-him′e-lech the priest, The king hath commanded me a business, and hath said unto me, Let no man know any thing of the business whereabout I send thee, and what I have commanded thee: and I have appointed *my* servants to such and such a place.

3 Now therefore what is under thine hand? give *me* five *loaves of* bread in mine hand, or what there is present.

21:4 Ex 19:14, 15 Lev 24:5–8 Mt 12:4

4 And the priest answered David, and said, *There is* no common bread under mine hand, but there is hallowed bread; if the young men have kept themselves at least from women.

5 And David answered the priest, and said unto him, Of a truth women *have been* kept from us about these three days, since I came out, and the vessels of the young men are holy, and *the bread is* in a manner common, yea, though it were sanctified this day in the vessel.

21:6☆ Mt 12:3, 4 Mk 2:25, 26 Lk 6:4

6 So the priest gave him hallowed *bread:* for there was no bread there but the shewbread, that was taken from before the LORD, to put hot bread in the day when it was taken away.

21:7 1 Sam 22:9 Ps 52:1

7 Now a certain man of the servants of Saul *was* there that day, detained before the LORD; and his name *was* Do′eg, an Edomite, the chiefest of the herdmen that *belonged* to Saul.

b. David Takes Goliath's Sword

8 ¶And David said unto A-him′e-lech, And is there not here under thine hand spear or sword? for I have neither brought my sword nor my weapons with me, because the king's business required haste.

21:9 1 Sam 17:2, 50, 51

9 And the priest said, The sword of Goliath the Philistine, whom thou slewest in the valley of E′lah, behold, it *is here* wrapped in a cloth behind the ephod: if thou wilt take that, take *it:* for *there is* no other save that here. And David said, *There is* none like that; give it me.

c. David Flees to Gath

21:10☆ 1 Sam 27:1–3 28:1

10 ¶And David arose, and fled that day for fear of Saul, and went to A′chish the king of Gath.

21:11 1 Sam 18:7 29:5

11 And the servants of A′chish said unto him, *Is* not this David the king of the land? did they not sing one to another of him in dances, saying, Saul hath slain his thousands, and David his ten thousands?

12 And David laid up these words in his heart, and was sore afraid of A′chish the king of Gath.

13 And he changed his behaviour before them, and feigned himself mad in their hands, and scrabbled on the doors of the gate, and let his spittle fall down upon his beard.

---

loaves of bread. But Ahimelech had no common bread, only hallowed bread (shewbread) which normally stood for a week on the golden table and, when replaced by fresh bread, was to be eaten by the priest and his family. David argued that after the holy use of the bread was finished, the bread could be considered common. Later Jesus supported this argument, saying that ritual observances must give way to moral duties and that, in emergencies, what normally was forbidden could be done (see Matt. 12:3–8 for an illustration of this). Ahimelech consented to give him the bread; he also gave David the sword of Goliath.

21:2 Here David lied to Ahimelech, for he had no charge from Saul. This lie brought about the death of many people (22:9ff).

21:6 *So the priest gave him hallowed bread.* See the note on Mark 2:26 for the explanation of a supposed error in which Jesus is misunderstood as saying that Abiathar, not Ahimelech, gave out the holy bread. At any rate, the priest broke the cermonial law by giving David the bread. Perhaps he was aware of the fact that the saving of a life was morally superior to keeping a secondary law which endangered another's life.

21:10 On two occasions David took refuge in Gath, which was ruled over by a Philistine king. He saved his life on this occasion by feigning madness (21:10–15; Ps. 56:1). The second time he sought refuge with his wives and six hundred followers (1 Sam. 27:1—28:2).

[14]Then said A′chish unto his servants, Lo, ye see the man is mad: wherefore *then* have ye brought him to me?
[15]Have I need of mad men, that ye have brought this *fellow* to play the mad man in my presence? shall this *fellow* come into my house?

d. David Flees to Adullam's Cave

22 DAVID therefore departed thence, and escaped to the cave A-dul′lam: and when his brethren and all his father's house heard *it*, they went down thither to him.
[2]And every one *that was* in distress, and every one that *was* in debt, and every one *that was* discontented, gathered themselves unto him; and he became a captain over them: and there were with him about four hundred men.

22:1 Josh 15:33–36; 2 Sam 23:13
22:2 Judg 9:4; 11:3; 1 Sam 23:13; 25:13; 30:22

e. David Seeks the Protection of the King of Moab

[3]¶And David went thence to Miz′peh of Moab: and he said unto the king of Moab, Let my father and my mother, I pray thee, come forth, *and be* with you, till I know what God will do for me.
[4]And he brought them before the king of Moab: and they dwelt with him all the while that David was in the hold.
[5]¶And the prophet Gad said unto David, Abide not in the hold; depart, and get thee into the land of Judah. Then David departed, and came into the forest of Ha′reth.

☆22:3 Judg 11:29
22:5 2 Sam 24:11; 1 Chron 21:9; 29:29; 2 Chron 29:25, 26

f. Doeg of Edom Tells Saul How Ahimelech Helped David

[6]¶When Saul heard that David was discovered, and the men that *were* with him, (now Saul abode in Gib′e-ah under a tree in Ra′mah, having his spear in his hand, and all his servants *were* standing about him;)
[7]Then Saul said unto his servants that stood about him, Hear now, ye Benjamites; will the son of Jesse give every one of you fields and vineyards, *and* make you all captains of thousands, and captains of hundreds;
[8]That all of you have conspired against me, and *there is* none that sheweth me that my son hath made a league with the son of Jesse, and *there is* none of you that is sorry for me, or sheweth unto me that my son hath stirred up my servant against me, to lie in wait, as at this day?
[9]¶Then answered Do′eg the Edomite, which was set over the servants of Saul, and said, I saw the son of Jesse coming to Nob, to A-him′e-lech the son of A-hi′tub.
[10]And he inquired of the LORD for him, and gave him victuals, and gave him the sword of Goliath the Philistine.

22:6 Judg 4:5; 1 Sam 11:4; 14:2
☆22:7 1 Sam 8:14; 1 Chron 12:16
☆22:8 1 Sam 23:21
22:9 1 Sam 21:1, 7; Ps 52:1

g. Saul Murders Ahimelech and the Priests

[11]Then the king sent to call A-him′e-lech the priest, the son of A-hi′tub, and all his father's house, the priests that *were* in Nob: and they came all of them to the king.
[12]And Saul said, Here now, thou son of A-hi′tub. And he answered, Here I *am*, my lord.
[13]And Saul said unto him, Why have ye conspired against me, thou and the son of Jesse, in that thou hast given him bread, and a sword, and hast

22:11 1 Sam 14:3

22:3 David so feared—not only for himself but also for his family—that he took his aged parents beyond the Dead Sea to the country of Moab for safety.
22:7, 8 Saul spread the fictitious story that David and his son Jonathan waited for him and sought to kill him. David and Jonathan were friends, but not enemies of the king. Saul was so beside himself that his chief business in life was to find David and slay him.

inquired of God for him, that he should rise against me, to lie in wait, as at this day?

22:14 1 Sam 19:4; 5 20:32; 24:11

14 Then A-him'e-lech answered the king, and said, And who *is so* faithful among all thy servants as David, which is the king's son in law, and goeth at thy bidding, and is honourable in thine house?

22:15 2 Sam 5:19, 23

15 Did I then begin to inquire of God for him? be it far from me: let not the king impute *any* thing unto his servant, *nor* to all the house of my father: for thy servant knew nothing of all this, less or more.

22:16☆

16 And the king said, Thou shalt surely die, A-him'e-lech, thou, and all thy father's house.

22:17 1 Sam 14:45 2 Kgs 10:25

17 ¶And the king said unto the footmen that stood about him, Turn, and slay the priests of the LORD; because their hand also *is* with David, and because they knew when he fled, and did not shew it to me. But the servants of the king would not put forth their hand to fall upon the priests of the LORD.

22:18 1 Sam 2:30–33

18 And the king said to Do'eg, Turn thou, and fall upon the priests. And Do'eg the Edomite turned, and he fell upon the priests, and slew on that day fourscore and five persons that did wear a linen ephod.

19 And Nob, the city of the priests, smote he with the edge of the sword, both men and women, children and sucklings, and oxen, and asses, and sheep, with the edge of the sword.

h. Abiathar Escapes; David Vows to Protect Him

22:20 1 Sam 2:30–33 23:9, 30:7 1 Kgs 2:26, 27

20 ¶And one of the sons of A-him'e-lech the son of A-hi'tub, named A-bi'a-thar, escaped, and fled after David.

21 And A-bi'a-thar shewed David that Saul had slain the LORD's priests.

22:22☆

22 And David said unto A-bi'a-thar, I knew *it* that day, when Do'eg the Edomite *was* there, that he would surely tell Saul: I have occasioned *the death* of all the persons of thy father's house.

23 Abide thou with me, fear not: for he that seeketh my life seeketh thy life: but with me thou *shalt be* in safeguard.

i. David Saves Keilah from the Philistines

23:1☆ Josh 15:44 Neh 3:17

23 THEN they told David, saying, Behold, the Philistines fight against Kei'lah, and they rob the threshingfloors.

23:2 1 Sam 22:15 23:9; 30:8 2 Sam 5:19, 23

2 Therefore David inquired of the LORD, saying, Shall I go and smite these Philistines? And the LORD said unto David, Go, and smite the Philistines, and save Kei'lah.

3 And David's men said unto him, Behold, we be afraid here in Judah: how much more then if we come to Kei'lah against the armies of the Philistines?

22:16 Saul decided to slay Ahimelech for helping David. Then he went even further, condemning Ahimelech's whole house. Saul had reached a point where he assumed to himself an authority above the office of king. He did not appeal to any judge or prophet; he did not seek advice from a privy council or a council of war. It was the act of a dictator, wicked in design and capricious in execution. His own soldiers refused to execute the priest and his famiy. Saul finally ordered Doeg, an unbelieving Edomite, to proceed with the slaughter; when he was finished, eighty-five people lay dead (22:18).

22:22 David here assumed full responsibility for the death of the priests and their loved ones. His lie produced dreadful consequences, especially since he intuitively knew that Doeg the Edomite (who was not an Israelite but a convert to Judaism) would report his presence to Saul. Later David wrote Psalm 52 in which "he represents Doeg not only as malicious and spiteful, but as false and deceitful, because though what he said was, for the substance of it, true, yet he put false colors upon it, with a design to do mischief."*

23:1 Keilah was in Judah but bordered on land occupied by the Philistines, who would seize the grain after it had been reaped and threshed. David was told by God to go up against the Philistines in order to stop the pillaging.

4Then David inquired of the LORD yet again. And the LORD answered him and said, Arise, go down to Kei'lah; for I will deliver the Philistines into thine hand.

23:4 Josh 8:7 Judg 7:7 2 Sam 5:19 2 Kgs 3:18

5So David and his men went to Kei'lah, and fought with the Philistines, and brought away their cattle, and smote them with a great slaughter. So David saved the inhabitants of Kei'lah.

6And it came to pass, when A-bi'a-thar the son of A-him'e-lech fled to David to Kei'lah, *that* he came down *with* an ephod in his hand.

7¶And it was told Saul that David was come to Kei'lah. And Saul said, God hath delivered him into mine hand; for he is shut in, by entering into a town that hath gates and bars.

☆23:7

8And Saul called all the people together to war, to go down to Kei'lah, to besiege David and his men.

9¶And David knew that Saul secretly practised mischief against him; and he said to A-bi'a-thar the priest, Bring hither the ephod.

☆23:9 1 Sam 22:15 23:2; 30:7

10Then said David, O LORD God of Israel, thy servant hath certainly heard that Saul seeketh to come to Kei'lah, to destroy the city for my sake.

11Will the men of Kei'lah deliver me up into his hand? will Saul come down, as thy servant hath heard? O LORD God of Israel, I beseech thee, tell thy servant. And the LORD said, He will come down.

12Then said David, Will the men of Kei'lah deliver me and my men into the hand of Saul? And the LORD said, They will deliver *thee* up.

13¶Then David and his men, *which were* about six hundred, arose and departed out of Kei'lah, and went whithersoever they could go. And it was told Saul that David was escaped from Kei'lah; and he forbare to go forth.

23:13 1 Sam 22:2 25:13 2 Sam 15:20

14And David abode in the wilderness in strong holds, and remained in a mountain in the wilderness of Ziph. And Saul sought him every day, but God delivered him not into his hand.

23:14 Josh 15:55 1 Sam 26:1 2 Chron 11:8

15And David saw that Saul was come out to seek his life: and David *was* in the wilderness of Ziph in a wood.

☆23:15

j. The Men of Ziph Betray David to Saul

16¶And Jonathan Saul's son arose, and went to David into the wood, and strengthened his hand in God.

17And he said unto him, Fear not: for the hand of Saul my father shall not find thee; and thou shalt be king over Israel, and I shall be next unto thee; and that also Saul my father knoweth.

23:17 1 Sam 20:31 24:20

18And they two made a covenant before the LORD: and David abode in the wood, and Jonathan went to his house.

23:18 1 Sam 20:16

19¶Then came up the Ziph'ites to Saul to Gib'e-ah, saying, Doth not David hide himself with us in strong holds in the wood, in the hill of Hach'i-lah, which *is* on the south of Jesh'i-mon?

23:19 1 Sam 22:6 26:1

23:7 Saul erroneously assumed that God had providentially delivered David into his hands. Since David was in the center of God's will, God brought to naught the counsel of Saul and delivered David. The designs of men cannot annul God's sovereign purposes, as illustrated in Neh.4:15; 2 Sam.17:14; and Job 5:12.

23:9 David asked directions from God through Abiathar, who apparently had taken the ephod with him when he escaped the massacre of the priests at Nob. When God informed him that the people of Keilah (whom David had come to help) would turn him over to Saul, he fled.

23:15 Saul was now in hot pursuit of David. He had many more troops than David and the situation looked grim. The Ziphites reported his movements to Saul (23:19). In this particular episode David was on one side of the mountain in the wilderness of Maon, and Saul was on the other. Saul's troops were closing in on David (23:26) when God intervened to rescue him; the Philistines started raids, and Saul stopped the search for David and went back to fend off the Philistines. David was saved for the moment.

20 Now therefore, O king, come down according to all the desire of thy soul to come down; and our part *shall be* to deliver him into the king's hand.

23:21 1 Sam 22:8
21 And Saul said, Blessed *be* ye of the LORD; for ye have compassion on me.

22 Go, I pray you, prepare yet, and know and see his place where his haunt is, *and* who hath seen him there: for it is told me *that* he dealeth very subtilly.

23 See therefore, and take knowledge of all the lurking places where he hideth himself, and come ye again to me with the certainty, and I will go with you: and it shall come to pass, if he be in the land, that I will search him out throughout all the thousands of Judah.

23:24 Josh 15:55
24 And they arose, and went to Ziph before Saul: but David and his men *were* in the wilderness of Ma′on, in the plain on the south of Jesh′i-mon.

25 Saul also and his men went to seek *him*. And they told David: wherefore he came down into a rock, and abode in the wilderness of Ma′on. And when Saul heard *that*, he pursued after David in the wilderness of Ma′on.

23:26 Ps 17:9; 22:12
26 And Saul went on this side of the mountain, and David and his men on that side of the mountain: and David made haste to get away for fear of Saul; for Saul and his men compassed David and his men round about to take them.

27 ¶But there came a messenger unto Saul, saying, Haste thee, and come; for the Philistines have invaded the land.

28 Wherefore Saul returned from pursuing after David, and went against the Philistines: therefore they called that place Se′la-ham′mah-le′koth.

23:29 Josh 15:62 2 Chron 20:2
29 ¶And David went up from thence, and dwelt in strong holds at En-ge′di.

k. David Cuts Off the Bottom of Saul's Robe at En-gedi and Rebukes Him

24 AND it came to pass, when Saul was returned from following the Philistines, that it was told him, saying, Behold, David *is* in the wilderness of En-ge′di.

24:2 1 Sam 13:2 26:2
2 Then Saul took three thousand chosen men out of all Israel, and went to seek David and his men upon the rocks of the wild goats.

3 And he came to the sheepcotes by the way, where *was* a cave; and Saul went in to cover his feet: and David and his men remained in the sides of the cave.

24:4☆ 1 Sam 26:8
4 And the men of David said unto him, Behold the day of which the LORD said unto thee, Behold, I will deliver thine enemy into thine hand, that thou mayest do to him as it shall seem good unto thee. Then David arose, and cut off the skirt of Saul's robe privily.

24:5 2 Sam 24:10
5 And it came to pass afterward, that David's heart smote him, because he had cut off Saul's skirt.

24:6 1 Sam 26:11 2 Sam 1:14
6 And he said unto his men, The LORD forbid that I should do this thing unto my master, the LORD's anointed, to stretch forth mine hand against him, seeing he *is* the anointed of the LORD.

24:4 David, on several occasions, could have killed Saul. But he refused to do so on the ground that Saul was God's anointed king. He was willing to let God work out his will. The end would not justify the means, for good ends must be secured through good means. David would not seize the crown by murder. Believers should learn that God's will done God's way results in God's blessing.

[7]So David stayed his servants with these words, and suffered them not to rise against Saul. But Saul rose up out of the cave, and went on *his* way. **24:7** 1 Kgs 1:31
[8]David also arose afterward, and went out of the cave, and cried after Saul, saying, My lord the king. And when Saul looked behind him, David stooped with his face to the earth, and bowed himself. ☆**24:8**
[9]¶And David said to Saul, Wherefore hearest thou men's words, saying, Behold, David seeketh thy hurt? **24:9** 1 Sam 26:19 Ps 7:3, 4
[10]Behold, this day thine eyes have seen how that the LORD had delivered thee to day into mine hand in the cave: and *some* bade *me* kill thee: but *mine eye* spared thee; and I said, I will not put forth mine hand against my lord; for he *is* the LORD's anointed.
[11]Moreover, my father, see, yea, see the skirt of thy robe in my hand: for in that I cut off the skirt of thy robe, and killed thee not, know thou and see that *there is* neither evil nor transgression in mine hand, and I have not sinned against thee; yet thou huntest my soul to take it. **24:11** 1 Sam 23:14, 23; 26:20
[12]The LORD judge between me and thee, and the LORD avenge me of thee: but mine hand shall not be upon thee. **24:12** Gen 31:53 Judg 11:27
[13]As saith the proverb of the ancients, Wickedness proceedeth from the wicked: but mine hand shall not be upon thee. **24:13** Mt 7:16–20 12:33; 15:19
[14]After whom is the king of Israel come out? after whom dost thou pursue? after a dead dog, after a flea. **24:14** 1 Sam 26:20
[15]The LORD therefore be judge, and judge between me and thee, and see, and plead my cause, and deliver me out of thine hand. **24:15** 1 Sam 26:17 Ps 35:1; 84:9

I. Saul Acknowledges His Sin

[16]¶And it came to pass, when David had made an end of speaking these words unto Saul, that Saul said, *Is* this thy voice, my son David? And Saul lifted up his voice, and wept. ☆**24:16**
[17]And he said to David, Thou *art* more righteous than I: for thou hast rewarded me good, whereas I have rewarded thee evil. **24:17** 1 Sam 26:21 Mt 5:44
[18]And thou hast shewed this day how that thou hast dealt well with me: forasmuch as when the LORD had delivered me into thine hand, thou killedst me not.
[19]For if a man find his enemy, will he let him go well away? wherefore the LORD reward thee good for that thou hast done unto me this day. **24:19** 1 Sam 26:23
[20]And now, behold, I know well that thou shalt surely be king, and that the kingdom of Israel shall be established in thine hand. **24:20** 1 Sam 13:14 20:31; 23:17
[21]Swear now therefore unto me by the LORD, that thou wilt not cut off my seed after me, and that thou wilt not destroy my name out of my father's house. **24:21** Gen 21:23 1 Sam 20:14–17 2 Sam 21:7
[22]And David sware unto Saul. And Saul went home; but David and his men gat them up unto the hold. ☆**24:22**

24:8 After David had taken the skirt of Saul's robe, he addressed the king from a distance and pleaded his case. He could have murdered Saul but refused to do so. Why then should Saul wish to kill him? He quoted an old proverb that wickedness proceeds from the wicked. If his heart had been wicked his deeds would have been wicked, and he would have slain Saul (24:13). Contrariwise, Saul could see by this statement his own wicked condition.

24:16 Saul was moved to tears by David's words. Superficially, he appeared to be penitent. David responded to Saul's petition by swearing that he would not cut down Saul's descendants—an obvious indication on the part of Saul that he knew his days were numbered and that David would succeed him in the kingship.

24:22 *Saul went home* "convinced but not converted; ashamed of his envy of David, yet retaining in his breast that root of bitterness; vexed that, when at last he had found David, he could not at that time find in his heart to destroy him, as he had designed."*

m. David, Nabal, and Abigail
(1) Nabal Refuses to Help David

25:1☆ Num 10:12; 13:3; 1 Sam 2:11; 7:17; 15:35; 28:3
25:2☆ Josh 15:55; 1 Sam 27:2; 3; 1 Kgs 18:19
25:3☆ Gen 24:15, 16; 29:17; Josh 15:13; 1 Sam 30:14

25 AND Samuel died; and all the Israelites were gathered together,
and lamented him, and buried him in his house at Ra′mah. And
David arose, and went down to the wilderness of Paran.
2 And *there was* a man in Ma′on, whose possessions *were* in Carmel; and
the man *was* very great, and he had three thousand sheep, and a thousand
goats: and he was shearing his sheep in Carmel.
3 Now the name of the man *was* Na′bal; and the name of his wife Ab′i-
gail: and *she was* a woman of good understanding, and of a beautiful
countenance: but the man *was* churlish and evil in his doings; and he *was* of
the house of Caleb.
4 ¶And David heard in the wilderness that Na′bal did shear his sheep.
5 And David sent out ten young men, and David said unto the young
men, Get you up to Carmel, and go to Na′bal, and greet him in my name:
6 And thus shall ye say to him that liveth *in prosperity,* Peace *be* both to
thee, and peace *be* to thine house, and peace *be* unto all that thou hast.

25:7 1 Sam 15:21

7 And now I have heard that thou hast shearers: now thy shepherds which
were with us, we hurt them not, neither was there ought missing unto them,
all the while they were in Carmel.
8 Ask thy young men, and they will shew thee. Wherefore let the young
men find favour in thine eyes: for we come in a good day: give, I pray thee,
whatsoever cometh to thine hand unto thy servants, and to thy son David.
9 And when David's young men came, they spake to Na′bal according to
all those words in the name of David, and ceased.

25:10 Ex 5:2; Judg 9:28

10 ¶And Na′bal answered David's servants, and said, Who *is* David? and
who *is* the son of Jesse? there be many servants now a days that break away
every man from his master.

25:11☆

11 Shall I then take my bread, and my water, and my flesh that I have
killed for my shearers, and give *it* unto men, whom I know not whence they
be?
12 So David's young men turned their way, and went again, and came and
told him all those sayings.

25:13 1 Sam 23:13; 25:13

13 And David said unto his men, Gird ye on every man his sword. And
they girded on every man his sword; and David also girded on his sword:
and there went up after David about four hundred men; and two hundred
abode by the stuff.

(2) Abigail Intercedes for Nabal

14 ¶But one of the young men told Ab′i-gail, Na′bal's wife, saying, Behold,
David sent messengers out of the wilderness to salute our master; and he
railed on them.
15 But the men *were* very good unto us, and we were not hurt, neither

---

25:1 Samuel the prophet died and was buried. He had been a good friend of David and had had the pleasure of anointing him to the kingship on the command of God. He was a man of prayer and we can be sure that many prayers were offered on behalf of David with the expectation that God would place him on the throne at the proper time.

25:2 Perchance David went to the wilderness of Paran after Samuel's death to mourn the prophet's death—but surely to stay away from Saul, whose intentions had not really changed toward David. The incident with Nabal resulted from this journey.

25:3 Nabal, which means "a fool," was a fitting name. His wife Abigail, whose name means "the joy of her father," was a good woman married to a bad man. They lived in Maon but they had sheep and pasture in Carmel (not to be confused with Mount Carmel). David and his men protected Nabal's workers and animals from predators. So David asked for Nabal's help, which he so churlishly refused that David decided to seize by force what he had asked for.

25:11 Nabal's men had solicited David's help and now their master refused to recognize what good David and his men had done. He pretended that he was unaware of the agreement made on his behalf and turned David's messengers away in scorn.

missed we any thing, as long as we were conversant with them, when we
were in the fields:
16They were a wall unto us both by night and day, all the while we were
with them keeping the sheep.
17Now therefore know and consider what thou wilt do; for evil is
determined against our master, and against all his household: for he *is such*
a son of Be'li-al, that *a man* cannot speak to him.
18¶Then Ab'i-gail made haste, and took two hundred loaves, and two
bottles of wine, and five sheep ready dressed, and five measures of parched
corn, and an hundred clusters of raisins, and two hundred cakes of figs, and
laid *them* on asses.
19And she said unto her servants, Go on before me; behold, I come after
you. But she told not her husband Na'bal.
20And it was *so, as* she rode on the ass, that she came down by the covert
of the hill, and, behold, David and his men came down against her; and she
met them.
21Now David had said, Surely in vain have I kept all that this *fellow* hath
in the wilderness, so that nothing was missed of all that *pertained* unto him:
and he hath requited me evil for good.
22So and more also do God unto the enemies of David, if I leave of all
that *pertain* to him by the morning light any that pisseth against the wall.
23And when Ab'i-gail saw David, she hasted, and lighted off the ass, and
fell before David on her face, and bowed herself to the ground,
24And fell at his feet, and said, Upon me, my lord, *upon* me *let this*
iniquity *be:* and let thine handmaid, I pray thee, speak in thine audience,
and hear the words of thine handmaid.
25Let not my lord, I pray thee, regard this man of Be'li-al, *even* Na'bal:
for as his name *is,* so *is* he; Na'bal *is* his name, and folly *is* with him: but I
thine handmaid saw not the young men of my lord, whom thou didst send.
26Now therefore, my lord, *as* the LORD liveth, and *as* thy soul liveth,
seeing the LORD hath withholden thee from coming to *shed* blood, and from
avenging thyself with thine own hand, now let thine enemies, and they that
seek evil to my lord, be as Na'bal.
27And now this blessing which thine handmaid hath brought unto my
lord, let it even be given unto the young men that follow my lord.
28I pray thee, forgive the trespass of thine handmaid: for the LORD will
certainly make my lord a sure house; because my lord fighteth the battles of
the LORD, and evil hath not been found in thee *all* thy days.
29Yet a man is risen to pursue thee, and to seek thy soul: but the soul of
my lord shall be bound in the bundle of life with the LORD thy God; and
the souls of thine enemies, them shall he sling out, *as out* of the middle of a
sling.
30And it shall come to pass, when the LORD shall have done to my lord
according to all the good that he hath spoken concerning thee, and shall
have appointed thee ruler over Israel;
31That this shall be no grief unto thee, nor offence of heart unto my lord,
either that thou hast shed blood causeless, or that my lord hath avenged
himself: but when the LORD shall have dealt well with my lord, then
remember thine handmaid.

☆**25:18** 2 Sam 16:1; 1 Chron 12:40
25:19 Gen 32:16, 20
25:22 1 Sam 3:17; 14:44
☆**25:25**
25:26 2 Sam 18:32
25:27 Gen 33:11; 1 Sam 30:26; 2 Kgs 5:15
25:28 2 Sam 7:16
25:29 1 Sam 2:9; Ps 66:9
25:30 Gen 40:14; 1 Sam 13:14

25:18 Nabal's wife Abigail had more good sense than her husband. She gathered food and personally visited David to seek deliverance from the impending attack. She was a true believer whose faith in God came to her assistance. David complied with her request and granted her petition; she could go home in peace, with the assurance that all was well.

25:25 *Nabal.* The name *Nabal* is also a Hebrew word translated "fool" nine times in the Old Testament, "foolish" five times, "vile person" twice, "foolish man" once, and "foolish woman" once. Nabal was well named indeed!

25:32 Ex 18:10 1 Sam 24:19 26:9, 10

32 ¶And David said to Ab′i-gail, Blessed *be* the LORD God of Israel, which sent thee this day to meet me:

33 And blessed *be* thy advice, and blessed *be* thou, which hast kept me this day from coming to *shed* blood, and from avenging myself with mine own hand.

34 For in very deed, *as* the LORD God of Israel liveth, which hath kept me back from hurting thee, except thou hadst hasted and come to meet me, surely there had not been left unto Na′bal by the morning light any that pisseth against the wall.

25:35 Gen 19:21

35 So David received of her hand *that* which she had brought him, and said unto her, Go up in peace to thine house; see, I have hearkened to thy voice, and have accepted thy person.

(3) Nabal's Sudden Death

36 ¶And Ab′i-gail came to Na′bal; and, behold, he held a feast in his house, like the feast of a king; and Na′bal's heart *was* merry within him, for he *was* very drunken: wherefore she told him nothing, less or more, until the morning light.

37 But it came to pass in the morning, when the wine was gone out of Na′bal, and his wife had told him these things, that his heart died within him, and he became *as* a stone.

25:38☆

38 And it came to pass about ten days *after,* that the LORD smote Na′bal, that he died.

25:39☆ 2 Sam 3:28, 29

39 ¶And when David heard that Na′bal was dead, he said, Blessed *be* the LORD, that hath pleaded the cause of my reproach from the hand of Na′bal, and hath kept his servant from evil: for the LORD hath returned the wickedness of Na′bal upon his own head. And David sent and communed with Ab′i-gail, to take her to him to wife.

25:40☆

40 And when the servants of David were come to Ab′i-gail to Carmel, they spake unto her, saying, David sent us unto thee, to take thee to him to wife.

41 And she arose, and bowed herself on *her* face to the earth, and said, Behold, *let* thine handmaid *be* a servant to wash the feet of the servants of my lord.

25:42 Gen 24:61

42 And Ab′i-gail hasted, and arose, and rode upon an ass, with five damsels of hers that went after her; and she went after the messengers of David, and became his wife.

25:43 1 Sam 27:2, 3 30:5 2 Sam 2:2; 3:2

43 David also took A-hin′o-am of Jez′re-el; and they were also both of them his wives.

25:44 1 Sam 18:27 2 Sam 3:14, 15

44 ¶But Saul had given Mi′chal his daughter, David's wife, to Phal′ti the son of La′ish, which *was* of Gal′lim.

n. David Again Refuses to Kill Saul

26:1 1 Sam 23:19

26 AND the Ziph′ites came unto Saul to Gib′e-ah, saying, Doth not David hide himself in the hill of Hach′i-lah, *which is* before Jesh′i-mon?

26:2☆ 1 Sam 13:2 24:2

2 Then Saul arose, and went down to the wilderness of Ziph, having three

---

25:38 Whatever may have been the human causes which lay behind the death of Nabal, it is here said that it was God who smote him. Bishop Hall said, "It is just that those who live without grace, should die without comfort, nor can we expect better while we go on in our sins."

25:39, 40 David rejoiced that God had kept him from killing Nabal and that his death had come by the hand of God in a natural way. In due season he courted the widow of Nabal, whom he had found wise as well as gracious. The courtship was by proxy, in that his servants put David's proposal of marriage before Abigail. Without hesitation she accepted, followed after the messengers, and became David's spouse.

26:2 When the Ziphites reported the presence of David among them to Saul, the king hastened with troops to track David down and kill him. This was to be the last time David and Saul saw each other. And again David refused to take advantage of what some might have considered a God-given opportunity for revenge.

thousand chosen men of Israel with him, to seek David in the wilderness of
Ziph.
3 And Saul pitched in the hill of Hach'i-lah, which *is* before Jesh'i-mon,
by the way. But David abode in the wilderness, and he saw that Saul came
after him into the wilderness.
4 David therefore sent out spies, and understood that Saul was come in
very deed.
5 ¶And David arose, and came to the place where Saul had pitched: and
David beheld the place where Saul lay, and Abner the son of Ner, the
captain of his host: and Saul lay in the trench, and the people pitched
round about him.
6 Then answered David and said to A-him'e-lech the Hittite, and to
A-bish'a-i the son of Zer-u-i'ah, brother to Jo'ab, saying, Who will go down
with me to Saul to the camp? And A-bish'a-i said, I will go down with thee.
7 So David and A-bish'a-i came to the people by night: and, behold, Saul
lay sleeping within the trench, and his spear stuck in the ground at his
bolster: but Abner and the people lay round about him.
8 Then said A-bish'a-i to David, God hath delivered thine enemy into
thine hand this day: now therefore let me smite him, I pray thee, with the
spear even to the earth at once, and I will not *smite* him the second time.
9 And David said to A-bish'a-i, Destroy him not: for who can stretch
forth his hand against the LORD's anointed, and be guiltless?
10 David said furthermore, *As* the LORD liveth, the LORD shall smite him;
or his day shall come to die; or he shall descend into battle, and perish.
11 The LORD forbid that I should stretch forth mine hand against the
LORD's anointed: but, I pray thee, take thou now the spear that *is* at his
bolster, and the cruse of water, and let us go.
12 So David took the spear and the cruse of water from Saul's bolster; and
they gat them away, and no man saw *it,* nor knew *it,* neither awaked: for
they *were* all asleep; because a deep sleep from the LORD was fallen upon
them.
13 ¶Then David went over to the other side, and stood on the top of an hill
afar off; a great space *being* between them:
14 And David cried to the people, and to Abner the son of Ner, saying,
Answerest thou not, Abner? Then Abner answered and said, Who *art* thou
that criest to the king?
15 And David said to Abner, *Art* not thou a *valiant* man? and who *is* like
to thee in Israel? wherefore then hast thou not kept thy lord the king? for
there came one of the people in to destroy the king thy lord.
16 This thing *is* not good that thou hast done. *As* the LORD liveth, ye *are*
worthy to die, because ye have not kept your master, the LORD's anointed.
And now see where the king's spear *is,* and the cruse of water that *was* at his
bolster.
17 And Saul knew David's voice, and said, *Is* this thy voice, my son
David? And David said, *It is* my voice, my lord, O king.

26:3 1 Sam 23:19
26:5 Judg 7:10, 11; 1 Sam 14:50, 51; 2 Sam 3:29; 1 Chron 2:15, 16
☆**26:8** 1 Sam 24:4
26:9 1 Sam 24:6; 2 Sam 1:14, 16
☆**26:12** Gen 2:21; 15:12; Isa 29:10
26:14 1 Sam 14:50; 17:55
26:16 2 Sam 12:5
☆**26:17** 1 Sam 24:16

26:8 David once again had an opportunity to kill Saul, who was prepared to kill David and had tried to do so on several occasions. Abishai was quite willing to commit the murder but was restrained by David. David continued to trust God to deliver him and to make him king when the right time came. David, however, took advantage of this opportunity to remove the spear and the jar of water from Saul's side as he slept. Then he announced what he had done and proved again that he had not chosen to be Saul's enemy. Both Saul and he knew that if the situation were reversed, Saul would have slain him without hesitation.

26:12 God's providence was at work again. So sound was the sleep of Saul and his troops that David could do his work unheard and unseen. David was successful; he removed Saul's spear and water container to show he had been there and could have slain him.

26:17 David bantered with Saul's military leader, Abner, accusing him of leaving his king open to assault (26:15). Then he talked again (and for the last time) to Saul in order to plead his innocence (26:18–20). Once again Saul was touched, although this time he did not weep. He admitted, "I have played the fool." Thus he bore testimony against himself and his unceasing

18 And he said, Wherefore doth my lord thus pursue after his servant? for
what have I done? or what evil *is* in mine hand?

26:19 1 Sam 24:9 2 Sam 16:11

19 Now therefore, I pray thee, let my lord the king hear the words of his
servant. If the LORD have stirred thee up against me, let him accept an
offering: but if *they be* the children of men, cursed *be* they before the LORD;
for they have driven me out this day from abiding in the inheritance of the
LORD, saying, Go, serve other gods.
20 Now therefore, let not my blood fall to the earth before the face of the
LORD: for the king of Israel is come out to seek a flea, as when one doth
hunt a partridge in the mountains.

26:21 1 Sam 15:24 24:17

21 ¶Then said Saul, I have sinned: return, my son David: for I will no
more do thee harm, because my soul was precious in thine eyes this day:
behold, I have played the fool, and have erred exceedingly.
22 And David answered and said, Behold the king's spear! and let one of
the young men come over and fetch it.

26:23 1 Sam 24:19 2 Sam 22:21

23 The LORD render to every man his righteousness and his faithfulness:
for the LORD delivered thee into *my* hand to day, but I would not stretch
forth mine hand against the LORD's anointed.

26:24 Ps 54:7

24 And, behold, as thy life was much set by this day in mine eyes, so let
my life be much set by in the eyes of the LORD, and let him deliver me out
of all tribulation.

26:25☆

25 Then Saul said to David, Blessed *be* thou, my son David: thou shalt
both do great *things*, and also shalt still prevail. So David went on his way,
and Saul returned to his place.

F. THE DEATH OF KING SAUL
1. David Flees to Philistia
a. David Joins Achish

27:1☆ 1 Sam 17:52 28:1

27 AND David said in his heart, I shall now perish one day by the
hand of Saul: *there is* nothing better for me than that I should
speedily escape into the land of the Philistines; and Saul shall despair of
me, to seek me any more in any coast of Israel: so shall I escape out of his
hand.

27:2 1 Sam 21:10 25:42, 43 2 Sam 2:2, 3 1 Kgs 2:39

2 And David arose, and he passed over with the six hundred men that
were with him unto A'chish, the son of Ma'och, king of Gath.
3 And David dwelt with A'chish at Gath, he and his men, every man with
his household, *even* David with his two wives, A-hin'o-am the Jez're-el-it-
ess, and Ab'i-gail the Carmelitess, Na'bal's wife.

b. David Receives Ziklag from Achish and Ravages the Surrounding Villages

4 And it was told Saul that David was fled to Gath: and he sought no
more again for him.

---

sinfulness. He wanted David to return to him, but David resisted his plea.

26:25 David had heard the pious words of Saul on other occasions, yet he saw that his heart had not changed. Thus he did not join himself to Saul, and never saw him alive again. The journey toward the kingship had been long and hard, the dangers had been many; but David still trusted that God would fulfill his promise and the kingship would be his at last.

27:1 David was around fifteen years of age when he was anointed to become king of Israel. He was not made king until he was thirty. This means that he waited for approximately fifteen years before the promise of God to him was fulfilled. These fifteen years were filled with difficulties. They teach us a lesson. It takes time for God to do his work; while we wait for his will to be fulfilled, we are exposed to difficulties and testings in which we come to know what God can do. If David had found that God could not meet his needs in the years before he became king, he would have had no reason to believe that God would help after he became king. If God could not sustain him when he occupied a lesser place, why should David think God would help him when he was in a position of great prominence and more in need of God's help than ever before.

5¶And David said unto A'chish, If I have now found grace in thine eyes, let them give me a place in some town in the country, that I may dwell there: for why should thy servant dwell in the royal city with thee? ☆27:5
6Then A'chish gave him Ziklag that day: wherefore Ziklag pertaineth unto the kings of Judah unto this day. **27:6** Josh 15:31 2 Sam 1:1 Neh 11:28
7And the time that David dwelt in the country of the Philistines was a full year and four months. **27:7** 1 Sam 29:3
8¶And David and his men went up, and invaded the Gesh'u-rites, and the Gez'rites, and the Am'a-lek-ites: for those *nations were* of old the inhabitants of the land, as thou goest to Shur, even unto the land of Egypt. ☆**27:8** Ex 17:8 Josh 13:2–7, 13 1 Sam 15:7, 8
9And David smote the land, and left neither man nor woman alive, and took away the sheep, and the oxen, and the asses, and the camels, and the apparel, and returned, and came to A'chish. **27:9** 1 Sam 15:3
10And A'chish said, Whither have ye made a road to day? And David said, Against the south of Judah, and against the south of the Je-rah'me-el-ites, and against the south of the Ken'ites. **27:10** Judg 1:16; 4:11 1 Sam 30:27–31 1 Chron 2:9, 25
11And David saved neither man nor woman alive, to bring *tidings* to Gath, saying, Lest they should tell on us, saying, So did David, and so *will be* his manner all the while he dwelleth in the country of the Philistines.
12And A'chish believed David, saying, He hath made his people Israel utterly to abhor him; therefore he shall be my servant for ever.

2. The Philistine War against Israel

a. The Philistines Plan to Fight

28 AND it came to pass in those days, that the Philistines gathered their armies together for warfare, to fight with Israel. And A'chish said unto David, Know thou assuredly, that thou shalt go out with me to battle, thou and thy men. ☆**28:1** 1 Sam 21:10 27:1–3
2And David said to A'chish, Surely thou shalt know what thy servant can do. And A'chish said to David, Therefore will I make thee keeper of mine head for ever. ☆**28:2**

b. Saul Visits the Medium at Endor

(1) God No Longer Answers Saul

3¶Now Samuel was dead, and all Israel had lamented him, and buried him in Ra'mah, even in his own city. And Saul had put away those that had familiar spirits, and the wizards, out of the land. **28:3** Lev 19:31 Deut 18:10 1 Sam 15:23 25:1
4And the Philistines gathered themselves together, and came and pitched in Shu'nem: and Saul gathered all Israel together, and they pitched in Gil-bo'a. **28:4** 1 Sam 31:1 2 Sam 1:6
5And when Saul saw the host of the Philistines, he was afraid, and his heart greatly trembled. **28:5** Ex 28:30, 31 Num 12:6
6And when Saul inquired of the LORD, the LORD answered him not, neither by dreams, nor by U'rim, nor by prophets. ☆**28:6**

27:5 David was a well-known soldier who had been successful in his military ventures. Achish the Philistine knew this and was willing to give David the town of Ziklag. He wanted to use him against Israel and especially against Saul. Saul's enmity for David made him a good prospect for cultivation by Achish.

27:8ff Next, David conducted raids against the Geshurites, the Gezrites, and the Amalekites. He slew them all and reported back to Achish that he had conducted raids but led him to think they were against his own people. This was a falsehood on David's part and heinous because of Achish's fidelity to him and confidence in him. Given this report, Achish thought David would be hated by Israel and would cling to him.

28:1, 2 When David first went to Achish, he concluded that the circumstances were unfavorable, so he feigned madness. Achish learned to trust David, finally inviting him to join his forces in the upcoming battle. David agreed to this. But the lords of the Philistines objected, and Achish was forced to withdraw his offer. David then, did not fight against Saul and his army.

28:6 *nor by Urim.* The Urim and Thummim were holy instruments used as lots in determining the will of God. See Exod. 28:30.†

(2) Saul Visits the Medium

28:7☆ 2 Chron 18:29; 35:22; Ps 83:10; Isa 8:19; Acts 16:16

28:8☆

7 ¶Then said Saul unto his servants, Seek me a woman that hath a familiar spirit, that I may go to her, and inquire of her. And his servants said to him, Behold, *there is* a woman that hath a familiar spirit at En-dor.

8 And Saul disguised himself, and put on other raiment, and he went, and two men with him, and they came to the woman by night: and he said, I pray thee, divine unto me by the familiar spirit, and bring me *him* up, whom I shall name unto thee.

9 And the woman said unto him, Behold, thou knowest what Saul hath done, how he hath cut off those that have familiar spirits, and the wizards, out of the land: wherefore then layest thou a snare for my life, to cause me to die?

10 And Saul sware to her by the LORD, saying, *As* the LORD liveth, there shall no punishment happen to thee for this thing.

11 Then said the woman, Whom shall I bring up unto thee? And he said, Bring me up Samuel.

12 And when the woman saw Samuel, she cried with a loud voice: and the woman spake to Saul, saying, Why hast thou deceived me? for thou *art* Saul.

13 And the king said unto her, Be not afraid: for what sawest thou? And the woman said unto Saul, I saw gods ascending out of the earth.

14 And he said unto her, What form *is* he of? And she said, An old man cometh up; and he *is* covered with a mantle. And Saul perceived that it *was* Samuel, and he stooped with *his* face to the ground, and bowed himself.

(3) The Medium Brings Up Samuel

28:15☆ 1 Sam 16:13, 14; 28:4-6

15 ¶And Samuel said to Saul, Why hast thou disquieted me, to bring me up? And Saul answered, I am sore distressed; for the Philistines make war against me, and God is departed from me, and answereth me no more, neither by prophets, nor by dreams: therefore I have called thee, that thou mayest make known unto me what I shall do.

16 Then said Samuel, Wherefore then dost thou ask of me, seeing the LORD is departed from thee, and is become thine enemy?

28:17 1 Sam 15:28; 16:13

17 And the LORD hath done to him, as he spake by me: for the LORD hath rent the kingdom out of thine hand, and given it to thy neighbour, *even* to David:

18 Because thou obeyedst not the voice of the LORD, nor executedst his fierce wrath upon Am'a-lek, therefore hath the LORD done this thing unto thee this day.

28:19 1 Sam 31:2, 6

19 Moreover the LORD will also deliver Israel with thee into the hand of the Philistines: and to morrow *shalt* thou and thy sons *be* with me: the LORD also shall deliver the host of Israel into the hand of the Philistines.

28:7, 8 God prohibited divination. He alone could guide his people; there was no need to use witches, mediums, diviners, or soothsayers. Saul, after God's Spirit left him, sought help from the medium at En-dor, in order to find the will of God. Saul hoped Samuel might help him if only he could speak with him. Some commentators doubt that the medium brought up Samuel, since the Scriptures are opposed to divination, but Saul evidently thought it was Samuel he saw. In any event, this incident provides no justification for efforts to make contact with the spirits of the dead.

28:15 Saul believed that he was talking to Samuel and received from him the unwelcome message that God would now take the kingdom from him because of his disobedience. He would give David the throne, and Saul and his sons would be with Samuel the next day. From this we could conclude that although Saul was a disobedient servant, yet he was apparently a saved man, as were his sons—especially Jonathan, whose heart was surely right with God. They would join Samuel in paradise.

(4) The Medium Gives Saul Food

20Then Saul fell straightway all along on the earth, and was sore afraid, ☆28:20 1 Sam 25:37, 38
because of the words of Samuel: and there was no strength in him; for he
had eaten no bread all the day, nor all the night.
21¶And the woman came unto Saul, and saw that he was sore troubled, ☆28:21
and said unto him, Behold, thine handmaid hath obeyed thy voice, and I
have put my life in my hand, and have hearkened unto thy words which
thou spakest unto me.
22Now therefore, I pray thee, hearken thou also unto the voice of thine
handmaid, and let me set a morsel of bread before thee; and eat, that thou
mayest have strength, when thou goest on thy way.
23But he refused, and said, I will not eat. But his servants, together with 28:23 2 Kgs 5:13
the woman, compelled him; and he hearkened unto their voice. So he arose
from the earth, and sat upon the bed.
24And the woman had a fat calf in the house; and she hasted, and killed 28:24 Gen 18:6, 7
it, and took flour, and kneaded *it*, and did bake unleavened bread thereof:
25And she brought *it* before Saul, and before his servants; and they did
eat. Then they rose up, and went away that night.

c The Philistines Refuse David's Help

29 NOW the Philistines gathered together all their armies to A'phek: 29:1 Josh 12:18 1 Sam 4:1 2 Kgs 9:30
and the Israelites pitched by a fountain which *is* in Jez're-el.
2And the lords of the Philistines passed on by hundreds, and by
thousands: but David and his men passed on in the rereward with A'chish.
3Then said the princes of the Philistines, What *do* these Hebrews *here?* ☆29:3 1 Sam 27:1–6 1 Chron 12:19, 20
And A'chish said unto the princes of the Philistines, *Is* not this David, the
servant of Saul the king of Israel, which hath been with me these days, or
these years, and I have found no fault in him since he fell *unto me* unto this
day?
4And the princes of the Philistines were wroth with him; and the princes ☆29:4
of the Philistines said unto him, Make this fellow return, that he may go
again to his place which thou hast appointed him, and let him not go down
with us to battle, lest in the battle he be an adversary to us: for wherewith
should he reconcile himself unto his master? *should it* not *be* with the heads
of these men?
5*Is* not this David, of whom they sang one to another in dances, saying, ☆29:5 1 Sam 18:7 21:11
Saul slew his thousands, and David his ten thousands?
6¶Then A'chish called David, and said unto him, Surely, *as* the LORD 29:6 1 Sam 27:12
liveth, thou hast been upright, and thy going out and thy coming in with me
in the host *is* good in my sight: for I have not found evil in thee since the
day of thy coming unto me unto this day: nevertheless the lords favour thee
not.
7Wherefore now return, and go in peace, that thou displease not the lords
of the Philistines.

28:20 Saul was filled with fright. He had asked in verse 15, "What shall I do?" He was "only told what he had not done and what should be done to him."* He was wretchedly disappointed, but he got what he deserved. He could not expect good counsel or compassion from God at this point.
28:21 Apparently the medium was afraid that Saul might die on her premises and she would be held responsible. She urged Saul to take food so that he could be strengthened and leave her house. Saul and his soldiers departed that night, the last of all nights for Saul. One wonders why, in this extremity, he did not become penitent, confess his sins, and ask for divine pardon and help.
29:3–5 Achish wanted David to be part of his army when the battle with the Israelites started. David's forces were placed behind those of Achish. David would be fighting against his own people and this would be a reproach against him. God providentially delivered him by using other Philistines to counter the order of Achish. Some thought that in the thick of battle David might prove to be a turncoat and fight against the Philistines. Achish offered support by speaking of David's military exploits and how he would help the Philistines.

8 ¶And David said unto A'chish, But what have I done? and what hast
thou found in thy servant so long as I have been with thee unto this day,
that I may not go fight against the enemies of my lord the king?

29:9☆ 2 Sam 14:17, 20; 19:27

9 And A'chish answered and said to David, I know that thou *art* good in
my sight, as an angel of God: notwithstanding the princes of the Philistines
have said, He shall not go up with us to the battle.
10 Wherefore now rise up early in the morning with thy master's servants
that are come with thee: and as soon as ye be up early in the morning, and
have light, depart.
11 So David and his men rose up early to depart in the morning, to return
into the land of the Philistines. And the Philistines went up to Jez're-el.

d. David's War against the Amalekites
(1) The Raid on Ziklag

30:1☆ 1 Sam 15:7; 27:6, 8; 30:26

30 AND it came to pass, when David and his men were come to Ziklag
on the third day, that the Am'a-lek-ites had invaded the south, and
Ziklag, and smitten Ziklag, and burned it with fire;
2 And had taken the women captives, that *were* therein: they slew not any,
either great or small, but carried *them* away, and went on their way.
3 ¶So David and his men came to the city, and, behold, *it was* burned with
fire; and their wives, and their sons, and their daughters, were taken
captives.
4 Then David and the people that *were* with him lifted up their voice and
wept, until they had no more power to weep.

30:5 1 Sam 25:39, 43; 30:18, 19; 2 Sam 2:2; 3:2
30:6 Ex 17:4; 1 Sam 23:16; Ps 18:2

5 And David's two wives were taken captives, A-hin'o-am the Jez're-el-it-
ess, and Ab'i-gail the wife of Na'bal the Carmelite.
6 And David was greatly distressed; for the people spake of stoning him,
because the soul of all the people was grieved, every man for his sons and
for his daughters: but David encouraged himself in the LORD his God.

(2) God Tells David to Chase the Amalekites

30:7☆ 1 Sam 23:9

7 And David said to A-bi'a-thar the priest, A-him'e-lech's son, I pray thee,
bring me hither the ephod. And A-bi'a-thar brought thither the ephod to
David.

30:8 Judg 20:18; 1 Sam 23:2, 4; 2 Sam 5:19

8 And David inquired at the LORD, saying, Shall I pursue after this troop?
shall I overtake them? And he answered him, Pursue: for thou shalt surely
overtake *them,* and without fail recover *all.*

30:9 1 Sam 27:2

9 So David went, he and the six hundred men that *were* with him, and
came to the brook Be'sor, where those that were left behind stayed.
10 But David pursued, he and four hundred men: for two hundred abode
behind, which were so faint that they could not go over the brook Be'sor.

30:11☆ Judg 15:19

11 ¶And they found an Egyptian in the field, and brought him to David,
and gave him bread, and he did eat; and they made him drink water;

29:9 Achish was forced to accede to the request of his allies. He spoke to David about his continued confidence in him but gently eased him out of the picture. David responded with some dissimulation, for which he could not be excused inasmuch as he appeared to be sincere in wanting to fight against Saul. David did not know at this juncture that he was needed at Ziklag. So God was doubly gracious by keeping him from fighting against his own people and by sending him home to rescue his loved ones.

30:1 Strangely but providentially the Amalekites captured all of David's people without killing any of them. They burned the town and kept its treasures. Apparently they would make the captured people their slaves.

30:7 David called for Abiathar and requested that he bring the ephod so that he could consult God. Clearly Abiathar must have been with David and his troops. This leaves us with the puzzle as to why David had not consulted God while he was still with Achish. At least here he did the right thing. The extremity of the hour caused him to put his trust in his God, especially when his own men talked of stoning him on account of the tragedy.

30:11 Again providence intervened on behalf of David: the Egyptian slave agreed to lead David and his men to the place where they would find the Amalekites, their prisoners, and the booty. David promised to protect the Egyptian (30:15).

12And they gave him a piece of a cake of figs, and two clusters of raisins: and when he had eaten, his spirit came again to him: for he had eaten no bread, nor drunk *any* water, three days and three nights.

13And David said unto him, To whom *belongest* thou? and whence *art* thou? And he said, I *am* a young man of Egypt, servant to an Am'a-lek-ite; and my master left me, because three days agone I fell sick.

14We made an invasion *upon* the south of the Cher'e-thites, and upon *the coast* which *belongeth* to Judah, and upon the south of Caleb; and we burned Ziklag with fire.

15And David said to him, Canst thou bring me down to this company? And he said, Swear unto me by God, that thou wilt neither kill me, nor deliver me into the hands of my master, and I will bring thee down to this company.

☆**30:14** 1 Sam 30:1; 2 Sam 1:1; 15:17, 18; 1 Chron 18:17
30:15 Josh 2:12; 9:19

(3) David Defeats the Amalekites

16¶And when he had brought him down, behold, *they were* spread abroad upon all the earth, eating and drinking, and dancing, because of all the great spoil that they had taken out of the land of the Philistines, and out of the land of Judah.

17And David smote them from the twilight even unto the evening of the next day: and there escaped not a man of them, save four hundred young men, which rode upon camels, and fled.

18And David recovered all that the Am'a-lek-ites had carried away: and David rescued his two wives.

19And there was nothing lacking to them, neither small nor great, neither sons nor daughters, neither spoil, nor any *thing* that they had taken to them: David recovered all.

20And David took all the flocks and the herds, *which* they drave before those *other* cattle, and said, This *is* David's spoil.

30:17 1 Sam 15:3

(4) The Division of the Spoils

21¶And David came to the two hundred men, which were so faint that they could not follow David, whom they had made also to abide at the brook Be'sor: and they went forth to meet David, and to meet the people that *were* with him: and when David came near to the people, he saluted them.

22Then answered all the wicked men and *men of Be'li-*al, of those that went with David, and said, Because they went not with us, we will not give them *ought* of the spoil that we have recovered, save to every man his wife and his children, that they may lead *them* away, and depart.

23Then said David, Ye shall not do so, my brethren, with that which the LORD hath given us, who hath preserved us, and delivered the company that came against us into our hand.

24For who will hearken unto you in this matter? but as his part *is* that goeth down to the battle, so *shall* his part *be* that tarrieth by the stuff: they shall part alike.

30:21 1 Sam 30:10, 11
☆**30:22**
30:24 Num 31:27; Josh 22:7, 8

30:14 *Cherethites,* i.e., Cherethites in the Negeb. The Negeb, now a desertlike land in southern Canaan, was divided into five segments, all of which belonged to the Cherethites, who were related to the Philistines and possibly some of the sea peoples who started settlements along the sea coast of Canaan.

30:22 Not all those who fought with David were honest and compassionate men. When the battle was won and the spoils were being distributed, those who had fought argued that those who merely stood by the stuff without fighting were unworthy of receiving any of the spoils of war. The warriors would let them go with their wives and children; they were permitted to have the mouths to be fed, but not the meat to feed them. David rightly ruled that *all* who were involved, including those who stood by the stuff while the others fought, were entitled to a fair share of the booty. This became a standing arrangement for Israel.

25 And it was *so* from that day forward, that he made it a statute and an ordinance for Israel unto this day.

30:26☆ Gen 33:11 1 Sam 25:27 2 Kgs 5:15

26 ¶And when David came to Ziklag, he sent of the spoil unto the elders of Judah, *even* to his friends, saying, Behold a present for you of the spoil of the enemies of the LORD;

27 To *them* which *were* in Beth–el, and to *them* which *were* in south Ra'moth, and to *them* which *were* in Jat'tir,

28 And to *them* which *were* in Ar'o-er, and to *them* which *were* in Siph'moth, and to *them* which *were* in Esh-te-mo'a,

29 And to *them* which *were* in Ra'chal, and to *them* which *were* in the cities of the Je-rah'me-el-ites, and to *them* which *were* in the cities of the Ken'ites,

30 And to *them* which *were* in Hor'mah, and to *them* which *were* in Chor-a'shan, and to *them* which *were* in A'thach,

31 And to *them* which *were* in Hebron, and to all the places where David himself and his men were wont to haunt.

e. The Death of Saul

31:1 1 Sam 28:4 1 Chr 10:1–12

31 NOW the Philistines fought against Israel: and the men of Israel fled from before the Philistines, and fell down slain in mount Gil-bo'a.

31:2☆

2 And the Philistines followed hard upon Saul and upon his sons; and the Philistines slew Jonathan, and A-bin'a-dab, and Mel'chi-shu'a, Saul's sons.

31:3 Judg 9:54 2 Sam 1:6, 10

3 And the battle went sore against Saul, and the archers hit him; and he was sore wounded of the archers.

31:4☆

4 Then said Saul unto his armourbearer, Draw thy sword, and thrust me through therewith; lest these uncircumcised come and thrust me through, and abuse me. But his armourbearer would not; for he was sore afraid. Therefore Saul took a sword, and fell upon it.

5 And when his armourbearer saw that Saul was dead, he fell likewise upon his sword, and died with him.

31:6☆

6 So Saul died, and his three sons, and his armourbearer, and all his men, that same day together.

7 ¶And when the men of Israel that *were* on the other side of the valley, and *they* that *were* on the other side Jordan, saw that the men of Israel fled, and that Saul and his sons were dead, they forsook the cities, and fled; and the Philistines came and dwelt in them.

f. The Beheading of Saul and His Three Sons

8 And it came to pass on the morrow, when the Philistines came to strip the slain, that they found Saul and his three sons fallen in mount Gil-bo'a.

31:9☆ Judg 16:23, 24 2 Sam 1:20

9 And they cut off his head, and stripped off his armour, and sent into the land of the Philistines round about, to publish *it in* the house of their idols, and among the people.

30:26 David generously sent some of the booty to the elders of Judah. It was an expression of gratitude toward those who had helped him on other occasions. He said the gifts were spoils from the enemies of God. And his gifts served the further purpose of gaining their affection and support, for he knew that Saul's reign would terminate shortly and his own begin.

31:2 Saul and three of his four sons were gathered in the battle against the Philistines. The sons, including David's firmest friend Jonathan, were slain; Saul fell wounded to the ground and then killed himself with his sword.

31:4 *Saul took a sword, and fell upon it.* Compare this account with 2 Sam. 1:9, 10, where an Amalekite lied to David.

31:6 *and his three sons.* Jonathan left a son named Mephibosheth.

31:9 God used the Philistines to accomplish the divine purpose, thus freeing David from any necessity to dispose of Saul. The Philistines understood their victory to mean that their gods were on their side. We learn from 1 Chron. 10:10 that Saul's head was fastened in the temple of Dagon. What the Philistines did not know was that their victory was of no consequence, for David would conquer the Philistines and put them to flight.

10 And they put his armour in the house of Ash'ta-roth: and they fastened
his body to the wall of Beth'-shan.
11 ¶And when the inhabitants of Ja'besh-gil'e-ad heard of that which the
Philistines had done to Saul;
12 All the valiant men arose, and went all night, and took the body of Saul
and the bodies of his sons from the wall of Beth'-shan, and came to
Ja'besh, and burnt them there.
13 And they took their bones, and buried *them* under a tree at Ja'besh, and
fasted seven days.

31:10 Josh 17:11; Judg 2:12–14; 1 Sam 7:3; 2 Sam 21:12–14
31:11 1 Sam 11:1–13
31:12 2 Sam 2:4–7
☆**31:13**

31:13 1 Samuel begins with the birth of Samuel and ends with the burial of Saul. It marks the transition from the period of the judges to the beginning of the monarchy. The house of Saul the Benjamite had now given way to the Davidic throne. From David's loins would come that one who is the true Messiah and the Savior of the world. God's program of redemption was being forwarded, despite the attacks of Satan to hinder that plan and to thwart the divine will.

THE SECOND BOOK OF
SAMUEL
OTHERWISE CALLED THE SECOND BOOK OF THE KINGS

Authorship, date, and background See 1 Samuel.

Characteristics and content 1 Samuel ends with the death of King Saul. 2 Samuel records the story of David's kingship and ends before his death, which is recounted in 1 Kings. David expresses his anguish over the deaths of Saul and Jonathan. He is anointed king over Judah and civil war begins with Israel. Abner makes Ish-bosheth, a son of Saul, king of Israel. Joab, David's nephew and commander of his army, slays Abner. David grieves over this act. Ish-bosheth is slain by Rechab and Baanah, who report their deed to David. He executes them for their transgression. David becomes king over all Israel.

David consolidates his kingship, takes the city of Jerusalem, which becomes the national capital, and brings back the ark to the city. He wishes to build the Temple but is forbidden by God, who leaves that task for his son. David wins many victories over the surrounding nations. In the midst of these successes he falls into sin with Bathsheba, the wife of Uriah whom he then has killed to cover his adultery. Nathan arrives to pronounce God's judgment on David, and although he is forgiven when he repents, God ordains that he shall smart for his sins. This is fulfilled at a later time when his own son leads a revolt against him. He faces many trials, but the worst of them involves Absalom, who tries to overthrow his father. David flees from Jerusalem and a civil war commences. It ends in the death of Absalom and David's poignant cry, "O my son Absalom, my son, my son Absalom! Would God I had died for thee, O Absalom, my son, my son" (18:33).

Following restoration to his kingship after the death of Absalom, David has to face one emergency after another. A famine comes, due to the bloodguilt on Saul, who put the Gibeonites to death. Seven of Saul's kin are hanged to stop the famine. The later years of David's kingship are described, including his sin of numbering the people. David chooses the punishment of pestilence in the land. The angel of the Lord is about to destroy Jerusalem, when God orders the angel to stay his hand. David builds an altar on the threshing floor of Araunah to stay the pestilence and his burnt offering is accepted by God. The story of David's death is related in 1 Kings, which follows 2 Samuel.

Outline

I. The beginning of David's kingship (1:1—4:12)
II. David becomes king over all Israel and Judah (5:1—10:19)
III. David's great sin (11:1—12:31)
IV. David's difficulties (13:1—18:33)
V. The kingdom becomes David's again (19:1—20:26)
VI. David's latter years (21:1—24:25)

I. THE BEGINNING OF DAVID'S KINGSHIP (1:1—4:12)

A. DAVID LEARNS OF SAUL'S DEATH

1:1☆ 1 Sam 30:1, 17, 26; 31:6; 2 Sam 4:9, 10

1 NOW it came to pass after the death of Saul, when David was returned
from the slaughter of the Am'a-lek-ites, and David had abode two days
in Ziklag;
2It came even to pass on the third day, that, behold, a man came out of

---

1:1 Saul is now dead and David is back in Ziklag with his family. 2 Samuel covers the life of David from the beginning of his kingship until almost the end of it. He was to reign for forty years, during which time some of the lands occupied by non-Israelites would be conquered and added to David's kingdom.

the camp from Saul with his clothes rent, and earth upon his head: and *so*
it was, when he came to David, that he fell to the earth, and did obeisance.
3 And David said unto him, From whence comest thou? And he said unto
him, Out of the camp of Israel am I escaped.
4 And David said unto him, How went the matter? I pray thee, tell me.
And he answered, That the people are fled from the battle, and many of the
people also are fallen and dead; and Saul and Jonathan his son are dead
also.
5 And David said unto the young man that told him, How knowest thou
that Saul and Jonathan his son be dead?
6 And the young man that told him said, As I happened by chance upon
mount Gil-bo'a, behold, Saul leaned upon his spear; and, lo, the chariots
and horsemen followed hard after him.
7 And when he looked behind him, he saw me, and called unto me. And I
answered, Here *am* I.
8 And he said unto me, Who *art* thou? And I answered him, I *am* an
Am'a-lek-ite.
9 He said unto me again, Stand, I pray thee, upon me, and slay me: for
anguish is come upon me, because my life *is* yet whole in me.
10 So I stood upon him, and slew him, because I was sure that he could
not live after that he was fallen: and I took the crown that *was* upon his
head, and the bracelet that *was* on his arm, and have brought them hither
unto my lord.
11 Then David took hold on his clothes, and rent them; and likewise all
the men that *were* with him:
12 And they mourned, and wept, and fasted until even, for Saul, and for
Jonathan his son, and for the people of the LORD, and for the house of
Israel; because they were fallen by the sword.
13 ¶And David said unto the young man that told him, Whence *art* thou?
And he answered, I *am* the son of a stranger, an Am'a-lek-ite.
14 And David said unto him, How wast thou not afraid to stretch forth
thine hand to destroy the LORD's anointed?
15 And David called one of the young men, and said, Go near, *and* fall
upon him. And he smote him that he died.
16 And David said unto him, Thy blood *be* upon thy head; for thy mouth
hath testified against thee, saying, I have slain the LORD's anointed.

1:4 1 Sam 4:16; 31:2–4; 1 Chron 10:1
1:6 1 Sam 28:4; 31:1
1:8 1 Sam 15:3; 30:1, 13
1:9
☆**1:10** 1 Sam 31:3, 4
1:11 Gen 37:29, 34
1:14 1 Sam 24:6; 26:9, 11
1:15 2 Sam 4:10, 12
1:16 1 Sam 26:9; 2 Sam 1:10

B. DAVID'S DIRGE FOR SAUL AND JONATHAN

17 ¶And David lamented with this lamentation over Saul and over
Jonathan his son:
18 (Also he bade them teach the children of Judah *the use of* the bow:
behold, *it is* written in the book of Ja'sher.)
19 The beauty of Israel is slain upon thy high places: how are the mighty
fallen!

☆**1:17** Josh 10:13; 2 Chron 35:27
☆**1:18**
☆**1:19** 2 Sam 3:38

1:10 The Amalekite was evidently lying. See 1 Sam. 31:3 for the true account. He had probably found Saul dead upon the field and thought David would reward him for killing his great rival.†

1:17 David had refused to kill Saul. Now, on the event of Saul's death, he rent his clothes, mourned, wept and fasted (as the ethos of the times called for). It is significant that no mention is made of any of the sons of Saul except for Jonathan, with whom David had the closest fellowship. Perhaps David's mourning was more a sign of his love for Jonathan than his sorrow over the death of Saul. It is hard to suppose that David was not relieved that the long battle with Saul for the kingship was over.

1:18 *the Book of Jasher*, an extrabiblical collection of poems and other literary matter. Parts of it are also quoted in Josh. 10:12 and Judg. 5.

1:19 In this elegy David is generous in his praise of Saul, recalling some of the good things he had done for Israel. In all lives there are good as well as bad things to be considered. Three times he speaks of "the mighty" who have fallen (1:19, 25, 27), and he does so in sorrow not in judgment.

1:20☆ 1 Sam 6:17; 31:8
[20]Tell *it* not in Gath, publish *it* not in the streets of As′ke-lon; lest the
daughters of the Philistines rejoice, lest the daughters of the uncircumcised
triumph.

1:21 1 Sam 31:1; Ezek 31:15
[21]Ye mountains of Gil-bo′a, *let there be* no dew, neither *let there be* rain,
upon you, nor fields of offerings: for there the shield of the mighty is vilely
cast away, the shield of Saul, *as though he had* not *been* anointed with oil.

1:22☆
[22]From the blood of the slain, from the fat of the mighty, the bow of
Jonathan turned not back, and the sword of Saul returned not empty.

1:23 Judg 14:18; Prov 31:29–31
[23]Saul and Jonathan *were* lovely and pleasant in their lives, and in their
death they were not divided: they were swifter than eagles, they were
stronger than lions.
[24]Ye daughters of Israel, weep over Saul, who clothed you in scarlet, with
other delights, who put on ornaments of gold upon your apparel.

1:25 2 Sam 1:19
[25]How are the mighty fallen in the midst of the battle! O Jonathan, *thou*
wast slain in thine high places.

1:26 1 Sam 18:1; 19:1; 20:17
[26]I am distressed for thee, my brother Jonathan: very pleasant hast thou
been unto me: thy love to me was wonderful, passing the love of women.
[27]How are the mighty fallen, and the weapons of war perished!

C. DAVID CROWNED KING OF JUDAH

2:1☆ Josh 14:13, 14; 1 Sam 23:2, 4, 9; 2 Sam 5:19
2 AND it came to pass after this, that David inquired of the LORD,
saying, Shall I go up into any of the cities of Judah? And the LORD
said unto him, Go up. And David said, Whither shall I go up? And he said,
Unto Hebron.

2:2 1 Sam 25:39, 43; 30:5
[2]So David went up thither, and his two wives also, A-hin′o-am the Jez′re-
el-it-ess, and Ab′i-gail Na′bal's wife the Carmelite.

2:3 1 Sam 22:2; 2 Sam 3:19; 4:8; 1 Chron 12:1
[3]And his men that *were* with him did David bring up, every man with his
household: and they dwelt in the cities of Hebron.

2:4☆ 1 Sam 16:13; 31:11; 2 Sam 5:3; 21:12–14
[4]And the men of Judah came, and there they anointed David king over
the house of Judah. And they told David, saying, *That* the men of Ja′besh-
gil′e-ad *were they* that buried Saul.

2:5☆ 1 Sam 24:19; 25:32
[5]¶And David sent messengers unto the men of Ja′besh-gil′e-ad, and said
unto them, Blessed *be* ye of the LORD, that ye have shewed this kindness
unto your lord, *even* unto Saul, and have buried him.

2:6 Ex 34:5, 6
[6]And now the LORD shew kindness and truth unto you: and I also will
requite you this kindness, because ye have done this thing.
[7]Therefore now let your hands be strengthened, and be ye valiant: for
your master Saul is dead, and also the house of Judah have anointed me
king over them.

1:20 He did not wish the uncircumcised and their daughters to rejoice over what was a temporary defeat of Israel, a defeat that would be reversed as soon as possible by David himself.

1:22 In verses 22 and 26 David pays special tribute to Jonathan. Nothing is so welcome as friendship with one who is wise, good, and faithful to all of our interests. And nothing is so distressing as the loss of such a friend, for the more we love the more we grieve.

2:1 *Shall I go up into any of the cities of Judah?* David sought guidance from God as to how he should proceed, having earlier been secretly anointed king (16:1–13).

2:4 The people of Judah anointed David as their king. They were not speaking for the rest of Israel. David was at this time king only of Judah. His kingdom would be set up piece by piece until all Israel would acknowledge him as God's choice for them.

2:5 David here began a policy of conciliation by sending a word of appreciation to the people of Jabesh-gilead for their kindness to Saul after his death. He wished to honor the memory of Saul against whom he would not speak an evil word. His action was also designed to indicate that he was not seeking the kingship from pride or ambition but only because it had been pressed on him by the command of God, as the kingship had been pressed on Saul too. He carefully revealed that only Judah had anointed him king.

D. ISH-BOSHETH CROWNED KING OF ISRAEL BY ABNER

8¶But Abner the son of Ner, captain of Saul's host, took Ish–bo'sheth the
son of Saul, and brought him over to Ma-ha-na'im;
9And made him king over Gilead, and over the Ash'ur-ites, and over
Jez're-el, and over E'phra-im, and over Benjamin, and over all Israel.
10Ish–bo'sheth Saul's son *was* forty years old when he began to reign over
Israel, and reigned two years. But the house of Judah followed David.
11And the time that David was king in Hebron over the house of Judah
was seven years and six months.

☆2:8 1 Sam 14:50; 17:55; 26:14; 2 Sam 2:29; 17:24
2:10 2 Sam 5:4, 5

E. JOAB DEFEATS ABNER

12¶And Abner the son of Ner, and the servants of Ish–bo'sheth the son of
Saul, went out from Ma-ha-na'im to Gibeon.
13And Jo'ab the son of Zer-u-i'ah, and the servants of David, went out,
and met together by the pool of Gibeon: and they sat down, the one on the
one side of the pool, and the other on the other side of the pool.
14And Abner said to Jo'ab, Let the young men now arise, and play before
us. And Jo'ab said, Let them arise.
15Then there arose and went over by number twelve of Benjamin, which
pertained to Ish–bo'sheth the son of Saul, and twelve of the servants of
David.
16And they caught every one his fellow by the head, and *thrust* his sword
in his fellow's side; so they fell down together: wherefore that place was
called Hel'kath-haz'zu-rim, which *is* in Gibeon.
17And there was a very sore battle that day; and Abner was beaten, and
the men of Israel, before the servants of David.

☆2:12 Josh 10:12; 2 Sam 19:5; 21:5, 6
☆2:13 2 Sam 8:16; 1 Chron 2:16; 11:5, 6
☆2:16
2:17 2 Sam 3:1

F. ABNER KILLS ASAHEL

18¶And there were three sons of Zer-u-i'ah there, Jo'ab, and A-bish'a-i,
and As'a-hel: and As'a-hel *was as* light of foot as a wild roe.
19And As'a-hel pursued after Abner; and in going he turned not to the
right hand nor to the left from following Abner.
20Then Abner looked behind him, and said, *Art* thou As'a-hel? And he
answered, I *am*.
21And Abner said to him, Turn thee aside to thy right hand or to thy left,
and lay thee hold on one of the young men, and take thee his armour. But
As'a-hel would not turn aside from following of him.
22And Abner said again to As'a-hel, Turn thee aside from following me:

☆2:18 1 Chron 2:16; 11:26; 12:8

2:8 *Ish-bosheth,* i.e., "Man of Shame." According to 1 Chron. 8:33 his name was *Esh-baal* (*Ishbaal*), "Man of Baal." Since the Israelites detested the use of Baal in a proper name, someone may have substituted *bosheth* ("shame") in place of *baal*. *Ish-bosheth* was the youngest son of Saul and had not fought with his father in his last battle and thus was not killed as his three brothers had been. Abner, a skilled military leader, was responsible for installing Ish-bosheth as king over the remainder of Israel. He appeared to be more important in this phase of David's rise to power than the king himself.

2:12 This event was not in its beginning a major battle between two opposing dynasties. It was simply a skirmish involving two small groups of men. It was Abner who engineered the scenario and David who quietly played it. Twelve men from both sides engaged in the conflict and all of the contestants were killed. Then the full forces of both sides engaged in battle and Abner's forces were turned back.

2:13 *pool of Gibeon.* This pool was located in 1956 by excavators at El-jib, the site of ancient Gibeon.

2:16 *Helkath-hazzurim,* i.e., "the field of sword-edges."

2:18ff Asahel was the son of Zeruiah, who was either David's sister or half-sister. Asahel was one of David's thirty mighty men. In the battle of Gibeon he foolishly pursued Abner, a stronger warrior than he, and was brutally slain by him. Later Joab, the brother of Asahel, slew Abner in an act of vengeance. In 1 Chron. 27:7 Asahel is named as the fourth of King David's monthly captains. Some suppose that this is an error, for Asahel was dead before David was established as king. It appears that the post actually had been given to Zebediah, Asahel's son, as a posthumous honor to Asahel.

wherefore should I smite thee to the ground? how then should I hold up my
face to Jo'ab thy brother?
23 Howbeit he refused to turn aside: wherefore Abner with the hinder end
of the spear smote him under the fifth *rib,* that the spear came out behind
him; and he fell down there, and died in the same place: and it came to
pass, *that* as many as came to the place where As'a-hel fell down and died
stood still.

G. JOAB AND ABNER AGREE TO A CEASE-FIRE

2:24☆ 24 Jo'ab also and A-bish'a-i pursued after Abner: and the sun went down
1 Sam 26:5–7 2 Sam 10:10 when they were come to the hill of Am'mah, that *lieth* before Gi'ah by the
way of the wilderness of Gibeon.
2:25 2 Sam 2:9 25 ¶And the children of Benjamin gathered themselves together after
Abner, and became one troop, and stood on the top of an hill.
26 Then Abner called to Jo'ab, and said, Shall the sword devour for ever?
knowest thou not that it will be bitterness in the latter end? how long shall
it be then, ere thou bid the people return from following their brethren?
27 And Jo'ab said, *As* God liveth, unless thou hadst spoken, surely then in
the morning the people had gone up every one from following his brother.
28 So Jo'ab blew a trumpet, and all the people stood still, and pursued
after Israel no more, neither fought they any more.
2:29 2 Sam 2:8 29 And Abner and his men walked all that night through the plain, and
passed over Jordan, and went through all Bith'ron, and they came to Ma-
ha-na'im.
30 And Jo'ab returned from following Abner: and when he had gathered
all the people together, there lacked of David's servants nineteen men and
As'a-hel.
31 But the servants of David had smitten of Benjamin, and of Abner's
men, *so that* three hundred and threescore men died.
2:32 1 Sam 17:58 32 ¶And they took up As'a-hel, and buried him in the sepulchre of his
father, which *was in* Beth–lehem. And Jo'ab and his men went all night, and
they came to Hebron at break of day.

H. ISH-BOSHETH'S TROUBLES WITH ABNER

3:1☆ 1 Kgs 14:30 15:16, 32, 33 3 NOW there was long war between the house of Saul and the house of
3:2☆ 2 Sam 13:1 1 Chron 3:1 David: but David waxed stronger and stronger, and the house of Saul
waxed weaker and weaker.
3:3☆ 2 ¶And unto David were sons born in Hebron: and his firstborn was
1 Sam 25:39 2 Sam 13:20 Am'non, of A-hin'o-am the Jez're-el-it-ess;
1 Chron 3:2 3 And his second, Chil'e-ab, of Ab'i-gail the wife of Na'bal the Carmelite;

2:24 Joab and his forces had defeated Abner and now were in hot pursuit of those who remained. Abner came to his senses, realizing that he was in danger of extermination. Had he been victorious in the war that he started, things would have looked different. Now he was in a desperate plight and used all possible strategems to extricate himself. He spoke of the evil of a civil war among brethren and begged Joab to sound the retreat and leave things as they are. Joab placed the blame squarely where it belonged. If Abner had not started the fracas by unsheathing the sword, there would have been no need for him to plead for mercy after the defeat.

3:1 God's earlier actions in the life of David had prepared him for further delays in the fulfillment of God's promise of the kingship. The war between the two dynasties was prolonged; David's faith and patience were tested still further. But there was something good in the delay, for during this period of time David grew stronger, while the forces of Abner and Ish-bosheth grew weaker. Meanwhile God was silently at work, arranging for a debacle between Abner and Ish-bosheth.

3:2ff All of David's first six sons were born of different mothers. Not one of them inherited the throne. Rather, Solomon, who was born of Bath-sheba, succeeded his father. Adonijah, David's fourth son, opposed this action. Secretly seeking to prevent Solomon's succession, Adonijah asked Bath-sheba to convince Solomon to permit Adonijah to marry Abishag, King David's nurse in his last days. Solomon rightly suspected the true intentions of Adonijah, and had him put to death.

and the third, Ab′sa-lom the son of Ma′a-cah the daughter of Tal′mai king
of Ge′shur;
4And the fourth, Ad-o-ni′jah the son of Hag′gith; and the fifth, Sheph-a- **3:4** 1 Kgs 1:5
ti′ah the son of Ab′i-tal; 1 Chron 3:2, 3
5And the sixth, Ith′re-am, by Eg′lah David's wife. These were born to **3:5** 1 Chron 3:3
David in Hebron.
6¶And it came to pass, while there was war between the house of Saul ☆**3:6**
and the house of David, that Abner made himself strong for the house of
Saul.
7And Saul had a concubine, whose name *was* Riz′pah, the daughter of ☆**3:7** 2 Sam 21:8
A-i′ah: and *Ish–bo′sheth* said to Abner, Wherefore hast thou gone in unto
my father's concubine?
8Then was Abner very wroth for the words of Ish–bo′sheth, and said, *Am* ☆**3:8** 1 Sam 24:14
I a dog's head, which against Judah do shew kindness this day unto the 2 Sam 9:8; 16:9
house of Saul thy father, to his brethren, and to his friends, and have not
delivered thee into the hand of David, that thou chargest me to day with a
fault concerning this woman?
9So do God to Abner, and more also, except, as the LORD hath sworn to **3:9** 1 Sam 3:16, 17
David, even so I do to him; 14:44
10To translate the kingdom from the house of Saul, and to set up the
throne of David over Israel and over Judah, from Dan even to Be′er–she′ba.
11And he could not answer Abner a word again, because he feared him.
12¶And Abner sent messengers to David on his behalf, saying, Whose *is*
the land? saying *also,* Make thy league with me, and, behold, my hand *shall*
be with thee, to bring about all Israel unto thee.
13¶And he said, Well; I will make a league with thee: but one thing I **3:13** 1 Sam 18:20
require of thee, that is, Thou shalt not see my face, except thou first bring 1 Chron 15:29
Mi′chal Saul's daughter, when thou comest to see my face.
14And David sent messengers to Ish–bo′sheth Saul's son, saying, Deliver **3:14** 1 Sam 18:26, 27
me my wife Mi′chal, which I espoused to me for an hundred foreskins of the
Philistines.
15And Ish–bo′sheth sent, and took her from *her* husband, *even* from **3:15** 1 Sam 25:44
Phal′ti-el the son of La′ish.
16And her husband went with her along weeping behind her to Ba- **3:16** 2 Sam 16:5
hu′rim. Then said Abner unto him, Go, return. And he returned.

I. ABNER VISITS DAVID AND IS SLAIN BY JOAB

17¶And Abner had communication with the elders of Israel, saying, Ye ☆**3:17**
sought for David in times past *to be* king over you:
18Now then do *it:* for the LORD hath spoken of David, saying, By the ☆**3:18** 1 Sam 9:16
hand of my servant David I will save my people Israel out of the hand of 15:28
the Philistines, and out of the hand of all their enemies.

3:6, 7 Abner proved to be a self-seeking aspirant for the throne occupied by Ish-bosheth. He went to bed with Saul's concubine, Rizpah. This was the clearest sign of a claim to succeed Saul. Apparently only kings had concubines. For Abner to sleep with Rizpah was an act of treason, which led to a dispute between Abner and Ish-bosheth.

3:8 We do not know whether Ish-bosheth's charge was in fact true, but the failure of Abner to deny the charge makes it appear to be true. Abner arrogantly and insolently told Ish-bosheth that he raised him to the kingship and he could now take it away from him and he would do so. Ish-bosheth (3:11) was weak-kneed and lacked a martial spirit. In fear of Abner who indeed had the power to destroy him, he remained silent.

3:12–14 Abner sent a message to David in which he acknowledged David's right to the throne. He would bring about a reunion of the twelve tribes under David. He wanted David to make a covenant with him, one which was designed to benefit him as well as David. David agreed with one condition: Michal must be returned to him. Abner consented.

3:17–21 Abner worked out the details for the ten tribes of Israel to reunite with Judah. There was no indication that he talked with Ish-bosheth or that the king had any part in the decision. David received Abner and made a feast to celebrate the agreement between them that would unite the nation.

3:19 1 Sam 10:20

19 And Abner also spake in the ears of Benjamin: and Abner went also to
speak in the ears of David in Hebron all that seemed good to Israel, and
that seemed good to the whole house of Benjamin.
20 So Abner came to David to Hebron, and twenty men with him. And
David made Abner and the men that *were* with him a feast.
21 And Abner said unto David, I will arise and go, and will gather all
Israel unto my lord the king, that they may make a league with thee, and
that thou mayest reign over all that thine heart desireth. And David sent
Abner away; and he went in peace.

3:22☆ 1 Sam 27:8

22 ¶And, behold, the servants of David and Jo'ab came from *pursuing* a
troop, and brought in a great spoil with them: but Abner *was* not with
David in Hebron; for he had sent him away, and he was gone in peace.
23 When Jo'ab and all the host that *was* with him were come, they told
Jo'ab, saying, Abner the son of Ner came to the king, and he hath sent him
away, and he is gone in peace.

3:24 1 Sam 29:3

24 Then Jo'ab came to the king, and said, What hast thou done? behold,
Abner came unto thee; why *is* it *that* thou hast sent him away, and he is
quite gone?
25 Thou knowest Abner the son of Ner, that he came to deceive thee, and
to know thy going out and thy coming in, and to know all that thou doest.

3:26☆

26 And when Jo'ab was come out from David, he sent messengers after
Abner, which brought him again from the well of Si'rah: but David knew *it*
not.

3:27 2 Sam 2:23; 20:8–10; 1 Kgs 2:5

27 And when Abner was returned to Hebron, Jo'ab took him aside in the
gate to speak with him quietly, and smote him there under the fifth *rib,* that
he died, for the blood of As'a-hel his brother.
28 ¶And afterward when David heard *it,* he said, I and my kingdom *are*
guiltless before the LORD for ever from the blood of Abner the son of Ner:

3:29 Lev 13:45, 46; Deut 21:7, 8; 1 Kgs 2:31

29 Let it rest on the head of Jo'ab, and on all his father's house; and let
there not fail from the house of Jo'ab one that hath an issue, or that is a
leper, or that leaneth on a staff, or that falleth on the sword, or that lacketh
bread.

3:30☆ 2 Sam 2:23

30 So Jo'ab and A-bish'a-i his brother slew Abner, because he had slain
their brother As'a-hel at Gibeon in the battle.

J. DAVID WEEPS OVER THE MURDER OF ABNER

3:31 Gen 37:34; Judg 11:35; 2 Sam 1:11

31 ¶And David said to Jo'ab, and to all the people that *were* with him,
Rend your clothes, and gird you with sackcloth, and mourn before Abner.
And king David *himself* followed the bier.
32 And they buried Abner in Hebron: and the king lifted up his voice, and
wept at the grave of Abner; and all the people wept.

3:22 Joab had little use for Abner because he had slain his brother Asahel. When he learned that David had made a covenant and sent Abner away happy, he was angry. He accused the king of being deceived by Abner and implied that David was a fool for having trusted him. David exhibited patience when insulted and did so because he despised Joab and did not fear him as Ish-bosheth feared Abner.

3:26 Joab acted with presumption and without authority from David, when he secretly planned the murder of Abner. He accomplished his purpose, to the dismay of David, who expressed his unbounded anger and placed an imprecation on the head of Joab and his posterity.

3:30 Abner served as military commander under Saul and David. He was the most important military man of the day. When Saul and Jonathan were killed, Abner installed Ish-bosheth as king in their place. When Abner had sexual relations with Rizpah, one of Saul's royal concubines, Ish-bosheth's anger and suspicions caused Abner to turn from him and to work for the acceptance of David as king. Abner had earlier alienated all of the tribes except Judah against David. Joab, the brother of Asahel whom Abner had killed, plotted against Abner and finally murdered him. King David disclaimed all knowledge of the treacherous act, gave Abner a great funeral, placed a curse on the house of Joab, and penned the immortal line: "Know ye not that there is a prince and a great man fallen this day in Israel?" (2 Sam. 3:38).

33 And the king lamented over Abner, and said, Died Abner as a fool
dieth?
34 Thy hands *were* not bound, nor thy feet put into fetters: as a man
falleth before wicked men, *so* fellest thou. And all the people wept again
over him.
35 And when all the people came to cause David to eat meat while it was
yet day, David sware, saying, So do God to me, and more also, if I taste
bread, or ought else, till the sun be down.
36 And all the people took notice *of it,* and it pleased them: as whatsoever
the king did pleased all the people.
37 For all the people and all Israel understood that day that it was not of
the king to slay Abner the son of Ner.
38 And the king said unto his servants, Know ye not that there is a prince
and a great man fallen this day in Israel?
39 And I *am* this day weak, though anointed king; and these men the sons
of Zer-u-i′ah *be* too hard for me: the LORD shall reward the doer of evil
according to his wickedness.

☆3:33ff

3:35 2 Sam 1:12; 12:17

3:39 1 Sam 26:5–7; 2 Sam 8:16; 19:5; 1 Chron 11:5, 6

K. THE SLAYING OF ISH-BOSHETH

4 AND when Saul's son heard that Abner was dead in Hebron, his
hands were feeble, and all the Israelites were troubled.
2 And Saul's son had two men *that were* captains of bands: the name of
the one *was* Ba′a-nah, and the name of the other Re′chab, the sons of
Rimmon a Be-e′roth-ite, of the children of Benjamin: (for Be-e′roth also
was reckoned to Benjamin:
3 And the Be-e′roth-ites fled to Git′ta-im, and were sojourners there until
this day.)
4 And Jonathan, Saul's son, had a son *that was* lame of *his* feet. He was
five years old when the tidings came of Saul and Jonathan out of Jez′re-el,
and his nurse took him up, and fled: and it came to pass, as she made haste
to flee, that he fell, and became lame. And his name *was* Me-phib′o-sheth.
5 And the sons of Rimmon the Be-e′roth-ite, Re′chab and Ba′a-nah, went,
and came about the heat of the day to the house of Ish-bo′sheth, who lay
on a bed at noon.
6 And they came thither into the midst of the house, *as though* they would
have fetched wheat; and they smote him under the fifth *rib:* and Re′chab
and Ba′a-nah his brother escaped.
7 For when they came into the house, he lay on his bed in his bed-
chamber, and they smote him, and slew him, and beheaded him, and took
his head, and gat them away through the plain all night.
8 And they brought the head of Ish-bo′sheth unto David to Hebron, and
said to the king, Behold the head of Ish-bo′sheth the son of Saul thine
enemy, which sought thy life; and the LORD hath avenged my lord the king
this day of Saul, and of his seed.

☆4:1 2 Sam 3:27

4:2 Josh 9:17; 18:25; Neh 11:33

☆4:3

☆4:4 1 Sam 31:1–4; 2 Sam 9:3, 5, 6; 1 Chron 8:34

4:5 2 Sam 2:8

4:6 1 Sam 17:54; 31:9; 2 Kgs 10:6; Mt 14:11

3:33ff David showed admirable sorrow at the untimely death of Abner, who was the victim of treachery. The people of Israel exempted David from any guilt, for they saw he was not privy to the counsel of Joab. The people wept and yet were pleased with the way David conducted himself.

4:1 Baanah and Rechab, captains of raiding bands under Ish-bosheth's sovereignty, formed a plot against their master. The incidents connected with the crime are recorded in verses 5–7. Having beheaded their king, they took the head to David, expecting to be accorded high honors for having disposed of his chief competitor for the affection of Israel.

4:3 *to Gittaim,* which is not in Benjamin. The Beerothites in Gittaim continued to be considered as part of the tribe of Benjamin, even though they lived outside its boundaries.

4:4 *Mephibosheth* was also called *Merib-baal* in 1 Chron. 8:34. The name *Merib-baal* ("my Lord is Baal") was offensive to Israelites because of its idolatrous connections. This son of Jonathan was, technically speaking, heir to the throne, for his father was older than Ish-bosheth. But he was so crippled that he had little chance of inheriting the throne, especially when his uncle was vigorous and had the support of Abner.

4:9 2 Sam 22:20; 1 Kgs 1:29

9¶And David answered Re'chab and Ba'a-nah his brother, the sons of
Rimmon the Be-e'roth-ite, and said unto them, *As* the LORD liveth, who
hath redeemed my soul out of all adversity,

4:10 2 Sam 1:1, 2, 4, 15

10When one told me, saying, Behold, Saul is dead, thinking to have
brought good tidings, I took hold of him, and slew him in Ziklag, who
thought that I would have given him a reward for his tidings:

4:11☆ Gen 9:5; 1 Kgs 2:32; Ps 9:12

11How much more, when wicked men have slain a righteous person in his
own house upon his bed? shall I not therefore now require his blood of your
hand, and take you away from the earth?

4:12 2 Sam 1:15; 3:32

12And David commanded his young men, and they slew them, and cut off
their hands and their feet, and hanged *them* up over the pool in Hebron.
But they took the head of Ish-bo'sheth, and buried *it* in the sepulchre of
Abner in Hebron.

II. DAVID BECOMES KING OVER ALL ISRAEL AND JUDAH (5:1—10:19)

A. ISRAEL ACCEPTS DAVID AS KING

5:1☆ 2 Sam 2:3, 10; 1 Chron 11:1

5 THEN came all the tribes of Israel to David unto Hebron, and spake,
saying, Behold, we *are* thy bone and thy flesh.

5:2 1 Sam 18:5, 14; 25:30, 31; 2 Sam 7:8

2Also in time past, when Saul was king over us, thou wast he that leddest
out and broughtest in Israel: and the LORD said to thee, Thou shalt feed my
people Israel, and thou shalt be a captain over Israel.

5:3☆ 1 Sam 16:1, 13; 2 Sam 2:4; 3:21

3So all the elders of Israel came to the king to Hebron; and king David
made a league with them in Hebron before the LORD: and they anointed
David king over Israel.

5:4 Gen 41:46; 2 Sam 2:10, 11; 1 Kgs 2:11; 1 Chron 26:31, 32; Lk 3:23

4¶David *was* thirty years old when he began to reign, *and* he reigned forty
years.
5In Hebron he reigned over Judah seven years and six months: and in
Jerusalem he reigned thirty and three years over all Israel and Judah.

B. DAVID CAPTURES JERUSALEM

5:6☆ Josh 15:63; Judg 1:21; 1 Chron 11:4

6¶And the king and his men went to Jerusalem unto the Jeb'u-sites, the
inhabitants of the land: which spake unto David, saying, Except thou take
away the blind and the lame, thou shalt not come in hither: thinking, David
cannot come in hither.

5:7 1 Kgs 2:10

7Nevertheless David took the strong hold of Zion: the same *is* the city of
David.
8And David said on that day, Whosoever getteth up to the gutter, and
smiteth the Jeb'u-sites, and the lame and the blind, *that are* hated of
David's soul, *he shall be chief and captain.* Wherefore they said, The blind
and the lame shall not come into the house.

4:11 David executed vengeance on Baanah and Rechab for murdering Ish-bosheth, whom he considered to be innocent of any crime warranting such action. They cut off their hands and feet and hung (the whole bodies were not hung for that was contrary to the law) them in public as a symbol of justice and to frighten others from committing such heinous crimes. The body of Ish-bosheth was laid in the tomb of Abner so that in death he lay beside the man who betrayed him and with whom he had a great quarrel (4:12).

5:1 The event for which David had been waiting for many years now comes to pass. The ten tribes beseech him to become their king, for he is one of them and has a great record of splendid service. They want him to be both shepherd and prince.

5:3 At Hebron a covenant is made between David and the ten tribes, and he is anointed as their king. At thirty years of age he has reached the pinnacle; that which God had promised years ago has become a reality at last.

5:6 The very first exploit of David (after he became king of all Israel) was to seize Jerusalem, which lay in the territory assigned to Benjamin. The Jebusites were haughty and insolent when they learned of David's intention. They thought they were safe within the walls of the great city. In spite of this, David took the city and dwelt in it. It was to become, under him and his son Solomon, the center of the nation and the site of the magnificent temple. *Jebusites.* See Judg. 1:21.

9 So David dwelt in the fort, and called it the city of David. And David
built round about from Mil'lo and inward.
10 And David went on, and grew great, and the LORD God of hosts *was*
with him.
11 ¶And Hiram king of Tyre sent messengers to David, and cedar trees,
and carpenters, and masons: and they built David an house.
12 And David perceived that the LORD had established him king over
Israel, and that he had exalted his kingdom for his people Israel's sake.
13 ¶And David took *him* more concubines and wives out of Jerusalem,
after he was come from Hebron: and there were yet sons and daughters
born to David.
14 And these *be* the names of those that were born unto him in Jerusalem;
Sham-mu'a, and Sho'bab, and Nathan, and Solomon,
15 Ib'har also and El-i-shu'a, and Ne'pheg, and Ja-phi'a,
16 And E-lish'a-ma, and E-li'a-da, and E-liph'a-let.

☆**5:9** 1 Kgs 9:15, 24
☆**5:10** 1 Sam 18:14; 2 Sam 3:1
5:11 1 Kgs 5:10, 18; 1 Chron 14:1
5:12 Deut 7:14; 2 Sam 7:15; 1 Kgs 10:9
☆**5:13** Deut 17:17; 1 Chron 3:9; 14:3
5:14 1 Chron 3:5–8; 14:4–7

C. DAVID'S VICTORY OVER THE PHILISTINES

17 ¶But when the Philistines heard that they had anointed David king over
Israel, all the Philistines came up to seek David; and David heard *of it*, and
went down to the hold.
18 The Philistines also came and spread themselves in the valley of
Reph'a-im.
19 And David inquired of the LORD, saying, Shall I go up to the
Philistines? wilt thou deliver them into mine hand? And the LORD said unto
David, Go up: for I will doubtless deliver the Philistines into thine hand.
20 And David came to Ba'al-per'a-zim, and David smote them there, and
said, The LORD hath broken forth upon mine enemies before me, as the
breach of waters. Therefore he called the name of that place Ba'al-per'a-
zim.
21 And there they left their images, and David and his men burned them.
22 ¶And the Philistines came up yet again, and spread themselves in the
valley of Reph'a-im.
23 And when David inquired of the LORD, he said, Thou shalt not go up;
but fetch a compass behind them, and come upon them over against the
mulberry trees.
24 And let it be, when thou hearest the sound of a going in the tops of the
mulberry trees, that then thou shalt bestir thyself: for then shall the LORD
go out before thee, to smite the host of the Philistines.

☆**5:17** 2 Sam 23:14; 1 Chron 11:16
5:18 Josh 15:8; 18:16; 2 Sam 23:13
5:19 1 Sam 23:2; 30:8
5:20 Num 33:3, 4; 1 Chron 14:11
☆**5:22**
☆**5:24** Judg 4:14; 7:15; 2 Kgs 7:6

5:9 *Millo,* or, "the Filling." While we cannot be certain, Millo was apparently a fortification or citadel near Jerusalem. Solomon added to the Millo's existing defense works. (See 1 Kings 9:15; 11:27; 1 Chron. 11:8; 2 Chron. 32:5.)

5:10 The reason for the increasing greatness of David is stated in these terms: "The LORD God of hosts was with him." This is always true for all of God's people who rise to heights which they could not have attained without God's gifts and help.

5:13 It was the prerogative of kings to have many concubines. But nowhere did God place his stamp of approval on this. It was to David's shame that he did not seek the counsel of God about this. We cannot praise, justify, or excuse David. "David had many wives, and yet that did not keep him from coveting his neighbor's wife and defiling her; for men that have once broken the fence will wander endlessly."*

5:17 The Philistines, as soon as they knew David was king, sought to undo him and crush him before he had time to establish himself firmly in Israel. David sought the counsel of God when the Philistines came toward him. He asked God three questions: Shall I go up against them? Shall I go at this time? Shall I be victorious over them? God responded in the affirmative, and when the victory was won David gave God the glory: "The LORD hath broken forth upon mine enemies before me."

5:22 The Philistines tried the second time to defeat David and again God intervened saying that he would go before David to smite the army of the Philistines.

5:24 God reveals his will to the believer in three ways: (1) directly and indirectly through the Word of God—for example, God does not wish believers to marry unbelievers (2 Cor. 6:17; Judg. 14:1–3); (2) through circumstances (5:24); and (3) through the inward persuasion of the Holy Spirit, which is subsequently confirmed by circumstances (Jer. 32:6–8).

5:25 Josh 12:12; 21:20-22

25And David did so, as the LORD had commanded him; and smote the
Philistines from Ge'ba until thou come to Ga'zer.

D. DAVID BRINGS THE ARK TO JERUSALEM

1. The Beginning of the Journey

6:1 Ex 25:22; 1 Sam 7:1; 2 Kgs 19:15; 1 Chron 13:5, 6

6 AGAIN, David gathered together all *the* chosen *men* of Israel, thirty
thousand.

6:2☆

2And David arose, and went with all the people that *were* with him from
Ba'al-e of Judah, to bring up from thence the ark of God, whose name is
called by the name of the LORD of hosts that dwelleth *between* the
cherubims.

6:3☆ Num 7:9; 1 Sam 6:7; 7:1

3And they set the ark of God upon a new cart, and brought it out of the
house of A-bin'a-dab that *was* in Gib'e-ah: and Uz'zah and A-hi'o, the sons
of A-bin'a-dab, drave the new cart.
4And they brought it out of the house of A-bin'a-dab which *was* at Gib'e-
ah, accompanying the ark of God: and A-hi'o went before the ark.

6:5 1 Sam 10:5; 16:16; 1 Chron 13:7, 8; 16:5

5And David and all the house of Israel played before the LORD on all
manner of *instruments made of* fir wood, even on harps, and on psalteries,
and on timbrels, and on cornets, and on cymbals.

2. Uzzah's Sin

6:6☆ Num 4:15; 1 Chron 13:9

6¶And when they came to Na'chon's threshingfloor, Uz'zah put forth *his
hand* to the ark of God, and took hold of it; for the oxen shook *it*.

6:7 Lev 10:1, 2; 1 Sam 6:19

7And the anger of the LORD was kindled against Uz'zah; and God smote
him there for *his* error; and there he died by the ark of God.

6:8☆

8And David was displeased, because the LORD had made a breach upon
Uz'zah: and he called the name of the place Pe'rez-uz'zah to this day.
9And David was afraid of the LORD that day, and said, How shall the ark
of the LORD come to me?

6:10 1 Chron 13:13; 26:4, 5

10So David would not remove the ark of the LORD unto him into the city
of David: but David carried it aside into the house of O'bed-e'dom the
Git'tite.
11And the ark of the LORD continued in the house O'bed-e'dom the
Git'tite three months: and the LORD blessed O'bed-e'dom, and all his
household.

3. The Ark Arrives at the City of David

6:12☆ 1 Kgs 8:1; 1 Chron 15:1-3, 25

12¶And it was told king David, saying, The LORD hath blessed the house
of O'bed-e'dom, and all that *pertaineth* unto him, because of the ark of

---

6:2 *Baale of Judah*, i.e., *Kiriath-jearim* (1 Chron.13:6). *cherubims*, or, *"Guardian Angels"* (TLB). See note on Exod. 25:22.

6:3 The instructions by God for transporting the ark were simple. It was to be carried by four priests, with the ark resting on two carrying poles suspended on the shoulders of the priests. David disregarded God's specific instructions, and however pious his intention, disaster followed his disobedience.

6:6 If the ark had been carried as it was supposed to be, this incident would never have occurred. The oxen stumbled, or got mired, or jumped under the goad and shook the ark, which might have been dislodged and fallen from the cart. Uzzah, a Levite, knew that he should not touch the ark. Only those who were priests could do that. The punishment for doing this was death. But the Philistines had handled the ark and nothing had happened to them. Possibly Uzzah took this to mean that he was equally free to touch the ark. He was mistaken and God judged him immediately, so that he died there and then. David refers to this error and acknowledges guilt in 1 Chron. 15:13.

6:8 David was angry with God for slaying Uzzah and so the ark was not brought to Jerusalem but left in the house of Obed-edom. "The ark is a guest which none shall lose by that bid it welcome. Josephus says that, whereas before Obed-edom was poor, on a sudden, in these three months, his estate increased, to the envy of his neighbors. Piety is the best friend to prosperity."*

6:12 When David learned what happened to Obed-edom and how he prospered, he decided to bring the ark in the proper fashion to Jerusalem. He did it and danced all the way to show his joy. He laid aside his purple robe as a sign of his humility.

God. So David went and brought up the ark of God from the house of
O'bed–e'dom into the city of David with gladness.
13 And it was *so,* that when they that bare the ark of the LORD had gone
six paces, he sacrificed oxen and fatlings.
14 And David danced before the LORD with all *his* might; and David *was*
girded with a linen ephod.

6:14 Ex 15:20; 1 Sam 2:18, 28

15 So David and all the house of Israel brought up the ark of the LORD
with shouting, and with the sound of the trumpet.
16 And as the ark of the LORD came into the city of David, Mi'chal Saul's
daughter looked through a window, and saw king David leaping and
dancing before the LORD; and she despised him in her heart.

☆**6:16** 1 Sam 18:27; 2 Sam 3:14

17 ¶And they brought in the ark of the LORD, and set it in his place, in the
midst of the tabernacle that David had pitched for it: and David offered
burnt offerings and peace offerings before the LORD.

6:17 1 Kgs 8:62; 1 Chron 15:1; 2 Chron 1:4

18 And as soon as David had made an end of offering burnt offerings and
peace offerings, he blessed the people in the name of the LORD of hosts.
19 And he dealt among all the people, *even* among the whole multitude of
Israel, as well to the women as men, to every one a cake of bread, and a
good piece *of flesh,* and a flagon *of wine.* So all the people departed every
one to his house.

4. Michal Scolds David

☆**6:20**

20 ¶Then David returned to bless his household. And Mi'chal
the daughter of Saul came out to meet David, and said, How glorious was
the king of Israel to day, who uncovered himself to day in the eyes of the
handmaids of his servants, as one of the vain fellows shamelessly uncover-
eth himself!
21 And David said unto Mi'chal, *It was* before the LORD, which chose me
before thy father, and before all his house, to appoint me ruler over the
people of the LORD, over Israel: therefore will I play before the LORD.
22 And I will yet be more vile than thus, and will be base in mine own
sight: and of the maidservants which thou hast spoken of, of them shall I be
had in honour.
23 Therefore Mi'chal the daughter of Saul had no child unto the day of her
death.

E. THE PLAN TO BUILD THE TEMPLE

1. Nathan Approves the Plan

7 AND it came to pass, when the king sat in his house, and the LORD
had given him rest round about from all his enemies;
2 That the king said unto Nathan the prophet, See now, I dwell in an
house of cedar, but the ark of God dwelleth within curtains.

☆**7:1** Josh 21:44; 23:1; 1 Kgs 5:4; 2 Chron 14:7
7:2 2 Sam 5:11; 6:17; 1 Kgs 1:22; 8:17, 18; 1 Chron 17:1; 29:29; Acts 7:46

6:16 Unknown to David, his wife Michal watched him dance before the Lord as the ark was being carried to Jerusalem. She despised her husband and soon told him so. Possibly she was looking for something like this to find fault for David's having recovered her from her husband, who apparently loved her greatly. Or she thought it unbecoming for a great soldier, statesman, and monarch so to act. Either way she missed the true intention of David, which was to glorify God. However that is carried out, it can never be thought unbecoming or mean.

6:20ff Michal greeted David in a critical and condemnatory manner. In her judgment what he did was vulgar and shameless, and she said so with delight. Verse 23 indicates her sentence for her own error: she had no child unto the day of her death.

7:1 David was now at peace and had time to think. His mind turned toward a permanent house for the ark of God. It was, of course, impossible to have a building for the ark during the wilderness journeys. But now Israel was in the land, while the ark was still housed in a tent. David surmised that a building to house the ark was now a necessity for permanence and he spoke to Nathan the prophet. Nathan endorsed the idea, even though at this time there was no word from God on the matter (7:3).

3And Nathan said to the king, Go, do all that *is* in thine heart; for the
LORD *is* with thee.

2. God's Disapproval of the Plan

4¶And it came to pass that night, that the word of the LORD came unto
Nathan, saying,
5Go and tell my servant David, Thus saith the LORD, Shalt thou build me
an house for me to dwell in?
6Whereas I have not dwelt in *any* house since the time that I brought up
the children of Israel out of Egypt, even to this day, but have walked in a
tent and in a tabernacle.
7:7 1 Chron 17:6
7In all *the places* wherein I have walked with all the children of Israel
spake I a word with any of the tribes of Israel, whom I commanded to feed
my people Israel, saying, Why build ye not me an house of cedar?
7:8☆ 1 Sam 16:10 2 Sam 5:2 Ps 78:70
8Now therefore so shalt thou say unto my servant David, Thus saith the
LORD of hosts, I took thee from the sheepcote, from following the sheep, to
be ruler over my people, over Israel:
9And I was with thee whithersoever thou wentest, and have cut off all
thine enemies out of thy sight, and have made thee a great name, like unto
the name of the great *men* that *are* in the earth.
7:10 1 Sam 12:9–11 Ps 89:22 Isa 60:18
10Moreover I will appoint a place for my people Israel, and will plant
them, that they may dwell in a place of their own, and move no more;
neither shall the children of wickedness afflict them any more, as before-
time,
7:11☆
11And as since the time that I commanded judges *to be* over my people
Israel, and have caused thee to rest from all thine enemies. Also the LORD
telleth thee that he will make thee an house.
7:12☆ 1 Kgs 2:1; 5:4
12¶And when thy days be fulfilled, and thou shalt sleep with thy fathers,
I will set up thy seed after thee, which shall proceed out of thy bowels, and
I will establish his kingdom.
7:13☆ 1 Kgs 6:11, 12 8:19 Isa 9:7 Acts 7:46, 47
13He shall build an house for my name, and I will stablish the throne of
his kingdom for ever.
7:14 Ps 89:26 Heb 1:5, 6
14I will be his father, and he shall be my son. If he commit iniquity, I will
chasten him with the rod of men, and with the stripes of the children of
men:
7:15 1 Sam 15:23 16:14 Ps 89:35, 36
15But my mercy shall not depart away from him, as I took *it* from Saul,
whom I put away before thee.
7:16 1 Sam 25:28
16And thine house and thy kingdom shall be established for ever before
thee: thy throne shall be established for ever.
7:17☆
17According to all these words, and according to all this vision, so did
Nathan speak unto David.

7:8ff God's covenant with David was built upon the Abrahamic covenant; it was strengthened by the kingship and prophecies of the Davidic Messiah. The agreement anticipated the kingly rule of Jesus Christ. The covenant was both conditional and unconditional. God promised punishment for the breaking of the covenant, and he also promised that even if there were disobedience, the covenant itself would not be abrogated. The covenant had four promises connected with it: (1) the promise of a dynasty; (2) the promise of a kingdom to rule over; (3) the promise of a land and people; and (4) the promise that the house of David would endure forever. The fulfillment of this covenant was announced to Jesus' mother Mary in Luke 1:31ff. The spiritual fulfillment of the covenant is referred to in Acts 2:25ff, which states that Christ, since his resurrection, has been exalted to supreme and eternal rule over the kingdom of God.

7:11–13 David wanted to build a house for God, but he was forbidden to do so. Yet God was pleased with David's intention. He told David that he would build a house for him, i.e., a posterity to sit upon the throne of David. And from that posterity God would raise up one who would build the temple David had in mind.

7:17 When Nathan first encouraged David to build the temple, he did not at that time have a word from God. Now Nathan speaks after having received a vision from God. The temple project had divine approval.

3. David's Prayer of Acceptance

18 ¶Then went king David in, and sat before the LORD, and he said, Who
am I, O Lord GOD? and what *is* my house, that thou hast brought me
hitherto?
19 And this was yet a small thing in thy sight, O Lord GOD; but thou hast
spoken also of thy servant's house for a great while to come. And *is* this the
manner of man, O Lord GOD?
20 And what can David say more unto thee? for thou, Lord GOD, knowest
thy servant.
21 For thy word's sake, and according to thine own heart, hast thou done
all these great things, to make thy servant know *them*.
22 Wherefore thou art great, O LORD God: for *there is* none like thee,
neither *is there any* God beside thee, according to all that we have heard
with our ears.
23 And what one nation in the earth *is* like thy people, *even* like Israel,
whom God went to redeem for a people to himself, and to make him a
name, and to do for you great things and terrible, for thy land, before thy
people, which thou redeemedst to thee from Egypt, *from* the nations and
their gods?
24 For thou hast confirmed to thyself thy people Israel *to be* a people unto
thee for ever: and thou, LORD, art become their God.
25 And now, O LORD God, the word that thou hast spoken concerning thy
servant, and concerning his house, establish *it* for ever, and do as thou hast
said.
26 And let thy name be magnified for ever, saying, The LORD of hosts *is*
the God over Israel: and let the house of thy servant David be established
before thee.
27 For thou, O LORD of hosts, God of Israel, hast revealed to thy servant,
saying, I will build thee an house: therefore hath thy servant found in his
heart to pray this prayer unto thee.
28 And now, O Lord GOD, thou *art* that God, and thy words be true, and
thou hast promised this goodness unto thy servant:
29 Therefore now let it please thee to bless the house of thy servant, that it
may continue for ever before thee: for thou, O Lord GOD, hast spoken *it*:
and with thy blessing let the house of thy servant be blessed for ever.

☆7:18 Ex 3:11; 1 Sam 18:18; Judg 6:15; Ps 8:4
7:19 1 Chron 17:17; Isa 55:8, 9
7:20 1 Sam 16:7; Ps 139:1; Jn 21:17
7:21 1 Chron 17:19; Isa 37:35
7:22 Ex 10:2; 15:11; 1 Sam 2:2; Ps 48:1
7:23 Deut 4:32; 10:21; 15:15; Ps 40:5; 65:5
7:24 Gen 17:7, 8; Ex 6:7; Deut 32:6; 1 Chron 17:22; Ps 48:14
7:26 1 Chron 17:23; Ps 89:35, 36
7:28 Ex 34:5, 6; Jn 17:17
7:29 Num 6:24–26

F. DAVID'S CONQUEST OF THE SURROUNDING NATIONS

8 AND after this it came to pass, that David smote the Philistines, and
subdued them: and David took Me'theg-am'mah out of the hand of
the Philistines.
2 And he smote Moab, and measured them with a line, casting them down
to the ground; even with two lines measured he to put to death, and with
one full line to keep alive. And *so* the Moabites became David's servants,
and brought gifts.
3 ¶David smote also Had-ad-e'zer, the son of Re'hob, king of Zo'bah, as
he went to recover his border at the river Eu-phra'tes.

8:1 1 Chron 18:1
8:2 Num 24:15–19; 1 Kgs 4:21; 2 Kgs 3:4; 17:3
☆8:3 1 Sam 14:47; 2 Sam 10:19; 1 Kgs 11:23; Ps 60 Title

7:18ff Nathan had brought God's message to David. Now David went to God himself without any intermediary. He offered a prayer in humility and solemnity to his great God. He began by acknowledging his own nothingness in comparison to God. He expressed gratitude for the undeserved favors God had given him. All that God had done had come from his free grace (7:21), and David adored the greatness and glory of his God (7:22). He praised God that he had brought Israel into being and had blessed this people. He closed with petitions for God to bless him and his posterity, and he magnified the fact that God's words are true (7:28).

8:3 Ironically, David's defeat of Hadadezer helped make possible the rise of Assyria, which would be the enemy of Israel and Judah.

8:4☆ Josh 11:6

4 And David took from him a thousand *chariots,* and seven hundred
horsemen, and twenty thousand footmen: and David houghed all the
chariot *horses,* but reserved of them *for* an hundred chariots.
5 And when the Syrians of Damascus came to succour Had-ad-e'zer king
of Zo'bah, David slew of the Syrians two and twenty thousand men.

8:6☆ 2 Sam 3:18; 2 Chron 17:2; 26:8

6 Then David put garrisons in Syria of Damascus: and the Syrians
became servants to David, *and* brought gifts. And the LORD preserved
David whithersoever he went.

8:7 1 Kgs 10:16; 14:26; 1 Chron 18:7

7 And David took the shields of gold that were on the servants of Had-ad-
e'zer, and brought them to Jerusalem.

8:8 Ezek 47:16

8 And from Be'tah, and from Ber'o-thai, cities of Had-ad-e'zer, king
David took exceeding much brass.
9 ¶When To'i king of Ha'math heard that David had smitten all the host
of Had-ad-e'zer,
10 Then To'i sent Joram his son unto king David, to salute him, and to
bless him, because he had fought against Had-ad-e'zer, and smitten him:
for Had-ad-e'zer had wars with To'i. And *Joram* brought with him vessels
of silver, and vessels of gold, and vessels of brass:

8:11 1 Sam 27:8; 2 Sam 7:9; 1 Kgs 7:51; 1 Chron 18:11

11 Which also king David did dedicate unto the LORD, with the silver and
gold that he had dedicated of all nations which he subdued;
12 Of Syria, and of Moab, and of the children of Ammon, and of the
Philistines, and of Am'a-lek, and of the spoil of Had-ad-e'zer, son of
Re'hob, king of Zo'bah.

8:13☆ 2 Kgs 14:7; 1 Chron 18:12

13 And David gat *him* a name when he returned from smiting of the
Syrians in the valley of salt, *being* eighteen thousand *men.*

8:14 Gen 27:30, 37

14 ¶And he put garrisons in Edom; throughout all Edom put he garrisons,
and all they of Edom became David's servants. And the LORD preserved
David whithersoever he went.
15 And David reigned over all Israel; and David executed judgment and
justice unto all his people.

8:16 2 Sam 3:39; 19:5; 1 Kgs 4:1

16 And Jo'ab the son of Zer-u-i'ah *was* over the host; and Je-hosh'a-phat
the son of A-hi'lud *was* recorder;

8:17☆

17 And Za'dok the son of A-hi'tub, and A-him'e-lech the son of A-bi'a-
thar, *were* the priests; and Ser-a-i'ah *was* the scribe;

8:18☆ 2 Sam 20:7, 23; 1 Kgs 1:38; 1 Chron 18:17

18 And Be-nai'ah the son of Je-hoi'a-da *was over* both the Cher'e-thites
and the Pel'e-thites; and David's sons were chief rulers.

8:4 Compare with 1 Chron. 18:4, where the numbers are somewhat different. The Hebrew text is unclear at this point; some words have been dropped out. Because of the way numbers were written, it was easy for copyists to misread the text, particularly when it was well worn.

8:6 Here, as well as in 8:14 and in 1 Chron. 18:6, 13, the Scriptures say that the Lord "preserved David whithersoever he went." Under God's divine protection, David was kept from harm. It was part of the covenant God made with David, and the same promise belongs to God's people who are under the Lordship of Christ, their preserver, by his Holy Spirit.

8:13 *Syrians,* i.e., "Edomites." The difference in the Hebrew spellings of Edom and Syria consists of but one letter—a letter *d* which resembles the Hebrew *r.* The RSV reads *Edomites,* the KJV *Syrians,* and TLB accepts *Syrians* as literal. 1 Chron. 18:12 is a parallel account. Some scholars believe *Edomites* to be the right word, since the location of the military engagement was the Valley of Salt, on the south end of the Dead Sea. The Syrians dwelt to the north of Israel.

8:17 *scribe.* A scribe was one who numbered or who wrote. He was a learned person who could perform a variety of duties at a time when many Hebrews could not write. In the Old Testament many of these people apparently came from the tribe of Levi. They usually were (1) men of great wisdom (1 Chron. 27:32); (2) competent and able writers (Ps. 45:1); (3) well versed in the law (Ezra 7:6); (4) secretaries to kings (20:25; 2 Kings 12:10); (5) notaries (Jer. 32:11, 12); (6) keepers of state records (1 Chron. 24:6); (7) secretaries to prophets (Jer. 36:4, 26); and (8) secretaries who kept the rolls of the armies for the military leaders (2 Chron. 26:11; Jer. 52:25). *Zadok* is mentioned here for the first time. After this time the recognized priesthood descended from him (1 Kings 2:35). According to 1 Chron. 6:8 he was in the priestly line of Aaron, Eleazar, and Phinehas. Aside from this genealogical data, the Bible says nothing about where his father, Ahitub, and his other ancestors served as priests.

8:18 *Benaiah . . . was over both the Cherethites and the Pelethites,* i.e., "Benaial was Captain of his bodyguard." *were chief rulers,* literally, "were priests."

G. DAVID'S GENEROSITY TO MEPHIBOSHETH, SAUL'S GRANDSON

9 AND David said, Is there yet any that is left of the house of Saul, that ☆9:1 1 Sam 20:14, 42; 23:18
I may shew him kindness for Jonathan's sake?
2 And *there was* of the house of Saul a servant whose name *was* Zi'ba. And 9:2 2 Sam 16:1 19:17
when they had called him unto David, the king said unto him, *Art* thou
Zi'ba? And he said, Thy servant *is he.*
3 And the king said, *Is* there not yet any of the house of Saul, that I may 9:3 2 Sam 4:4
shew the kindness of God unto him? And Zi'ba said unto the king,
Jonathan hath yet a son, *which is* lame on *his* feet.
4 And the king said unto him, Where *is* he? And Zi'ba said unto the king, 9:4 2 Sam 17:27
Behold, he *is* in the house of Ma'chir, the son of Am'mi-el, in Lo–de'bar.
5 ¶Then king David sent, and fetched him out of the house of Ma'chir, the 9:5 2 Sam 19:24 21:7 1 Chron 8:34
son of Am'mi-el, from Lo–de'bar.
6 Now when Me-phib'o-sheth, the son of Jonathan, the son of Saul, was
come unto David, he fell on his face, and did reverence. And David said,
Me-phib'o-sheth. And he answered, Behold thy servant!
7 ¶And David said unto him, Fear not: for I will surely shew thee ☆9:7 2 Sam 19:28 2 Kgs 25:29
kindness for Jonathan thy father's sake, and will restore thee all the land of
Saul thy father; and thou shalt eat bread at my table continually.
8 And he bowed himself, and said, What *is* thy servant, that thou
shouldest look upon such a dead dog as I *am?*
9 ¶Then the king called to Zi'ba, Saul's servant, and said unto him, I have 9:9 2 Sam 16:4 19:29
given unto thy master's son all that pertained to Saul and to all his house.
10 Thou therefore, and thy sons, and thy servants, shall till the land for 9:10 2 Sam 19:28
him, and thou shalt bring in *the fruits,* that thy master's son may have food
to eat: but Me-phib'o-sheth thy master's son shall eat bread alway at my
table. Now Zi'ba had fifteen sons and twenty servants.
11 Then said Zi'ba unto the king, According to all that my lord the king
hath commanded his servant, so shall thy servant do. As for Me-phib'o-
sheth, *said the king,* he shall eat at my table, as one of the king's sons.
12 And Me-phib'o-sheth had a young son, whose name *was* Mi'cha. And
all that dwelt in the house of Zi'ba *were* servants unto Me-phib'o-sheth.
13 So Me-phib'o-sheth dwelt in Jerusalem: for he did eat continually at
the king's table; and was lame on both his feet.

H. DAVID'S DEFEAT OF THE AMMONITES

1. Hanun Embarrasses David's Ambassadors

10 AND it came to pass after this, that the king of the children of ☆10:1 1 Chron 19:1–19
Ammon died, and Ha'nun his son reigned in his stead.
2 Then said David, I will shew kindness unto Ha'nun the son of Na'hash, ☆10:2
as his father shewed kindness unto me. And David sent to comfort him by
the hand of his servants for his father. And David's servants came into the
land of the children of Ammon.

Since David and his offspring were not in the Levitical line, they were not supposed to serve as priests.

9:1 David had not forgotten his agreement with Jonathan. (See 1 Sam. 20:14-17.)

9:7 Mephibosheth (which means "he scatters shame") was the son of Jonathan, to whom David had pledged that he would look with favor upon his offspring. Technically Mephibosheth should have succeeded Saul; but his uncle, who was younger than his father Jonathan, seized the throne. Since Mephibosheth was lame he could not do very much. Here David welcomes this only son of Jonathan and provides for him to eat at his table. He restores Saul's lands to him. Ziba, Saul's servant, is part of this scene. Later, he will besmirch the memory of Mephibosheth by accusing him of treachery and of having a desire to take the throne from David.

10:1 *the king of . . . Ammon,* i.e., "Nahash."

10:2 Nahash, an enemy of Israel, had nonetheless shown kindness to David. Upon his death David sent messengers to console the new king and to express David's kind intentions towards them. The king, Hanun, listened to his princes and therefore degraded the messengers by shaving off half of each beard and cutting their garments to the waist. This, of course, was meant as an insult to David.

3 And the princes of the children of Ammon said unto Ha′nun their lord, Thinkest thou that David doth honour thy father, that he hath sent comforters unto thee? hath not David *rather* sent his servants unto thee to search the city, and to spy it out, and to overthrow it?

10:4 Isa 15:2; 20:4; 47:2, 3; Jer 41:5

4 Wherefore Ha′nun took David's servants, and shaved off the one half of their beards, and cut off their garments in the middle, *even* to their buttocks, and sent them away.

5 When they told *it* unto David, he sent to meet them, because the men were greatly ashamed: and the king said, Tarry at Jericho until your beards be grown, and *then* return.

2. The Ammonites and the Syrians Flee from Joab

10:6☆ 2 Kgs 7:6

6 ¶And when the children of Ammon saw that they stank before David, the children of Ammon sent and hired the Syrians of Beth–re′hob, and the Syrians of Zo′ba, twenty thousand footmen, and of king Ma′a-cah a thousand men, and of Ish′–tob twelve thousand men.

10:7 Judg 11:3

7 And when David heard of *it,* he sent Jo′ab, and all the host of the mighty men.

8 And the children of Ammon came out, and put the battle in array at the entering in of the gate: and the Syrians of Zo′ba, and of Re′hob, and Ish′–tob, and Ma′a-cah, *were* by themselves in the field.

9 When Jo′ab saw that the front of the battle was against him before and behind, he chose of all the choice *men* of Israel, and put *them* in array against the Syrians:

10:10 2 Sam 2:18; 16:9

10 And the rest of the people he delivered into the hand of A-bish′a-i his brother, that he might put *them* in array against the children of Ammon.

11 And he said, If the Syrians be too strong for me, then thou shalt help me: but if the children of Ammon be too strong for thee, then I will come and help thee.

10:12 Deut 31:6; 1 Sam 3:18; 1 Cor 16:13
10:13 1 Kgs 20:20; 1 Chron 19:14

12 Be of good courage, and let us play the men for our people, and for the cities of our God: and the LORD do that which seemeth him good.

13 And Jo′ab drew nigh, and the people that *were* with him, unto the battle against the Syrians: and they fled before him.

14 And when the children of Ammon saw that the Syrians were fled, then fled they also before A-bish′a-i, and entered into the city. So Jo′ab returned from the children of Ammon, and came to Jerusalem.

10:15☆ 2 Sam 8:3; 1 Chron 19:16

15 ¶And when the Syrians saw that they were smitten before Israel, they gathered themselves together.

16 And Had-ar-e′zer sent, and brought out the Syrians that *were* beyond the river: and they came to He′lam; and Sho′bach the captain of the host of Had-ar-e′zer *went* before them.

3. David Defeats the Coalition at Helam

17 And when it was told David, he gathered all Israel together, and passed over Jordan, and came to He′lam. And the Syrians set themselves in array against David, and fought with him.

10:6 The Ammonites hired the Syrians and looked for a military engagement with Israel. Joab led David's army and skillfully managed the campaign which resulted in a defeat for the enemy—when first the Syrians fled and then the soldiers of the Ammonites did the same. Joab came home to Jerusalem the victor.
10:15 The Ammonites and Syrians gathered still larger forces and looked for a battle against David. The enemy soldiers came from as far away as the region beyond the Euphrates. They congregated on the east bank of Jordan, at Helem, where the battle took place. In this instance David himself headed up his forces and won a great victory.

[18]And the Syrians fled before Israel; and David slew *the men of* seven
hundred chariots of the Syrians, and forty thousand horsemen, and smote
Sho'bach the captain of their host, who died there.
[19]And when all the kings *that were* servants to Had-ar-e'zer saw that they
were smitten before Israel, they made peace with Israel, and served them.
So the Syrians feared to help the children of Ammon any more.

☆**10:18** 1 Chron 19:17, 18

10:19 2 Sam 8:6

III. DAVID'S GREAT SIN (11:1—12:31)

A. DAVID AND BATH-SHEBA COMMIT ADULTERY

11 AND it came to pass, after the year was expired, at the time when
kings go forth *to battle,* that David sent Jo'ab, and his servants with
him, and all Israel; and they destroyed the children of Ammon, and
besieged Rab'bah. But David tarried still at Jerusalem.
[2]¶And it came to pass in an eveningtide, that David arose from off his
bed, and walked upon the roof of the king's house: and from the roof he
saw a woman washing herself; and the woman *was* very beautiful to look
upon.
[3]And David sent and inquired after the woman. And *one* said, *Is* not this
Bath'-she-ba, the daughter of E-li'am, the wife of U-ri'ah the Hittite?
[4]And David sent messengers, and took her; and she came in unto him,
and he lay with her; for she was purified from her uncleanness: and she
returned unto her house.
[5]And the woman conceived, and sent and told David, and said, I *am* with
child.

☆**11:1** 2 Sam 12:26; 1 Chron 20:1; Jer 49:2; Amos 1:14

11:2 Deut 22:8; 1 Sam 9:25; Acts 10:9, 10

11:3 1 Chron 3:5; 2 Sam 23:39

☆**11:4** Lev 15:19; 18:19; Ps 51 Title

11:5 Lev 20:10; Deut 22:22; 2 Sam 12:13

B. DAVID'S PLAN TO COVER HIS SIN

[6]¶And David sent to Jo'ab, *saying,* Send me U-ri'ah the Hittite. And
Jo'ab sent U-ri'ah to David.
[7]And when U-ri'ah was come unto him, David demanded *of him* how
Jo'ab did, and how the people did, and how the war prospered.
[8]And David said to U-ri'ah, Go down to thy house, and wash thy feet.
And U-ri'ah departed out of the king's house, and there followed him a
mess *of meat* from the king.
[9]But U-ri'ah slept at the door of the king's house with all the servants of
his lord, and went not down to his house.
[10]And when they had told David, saying, U-ri'ah went not down unto his
house, David said unto U-ri'ah, Camest thou not from *thy* journey? why
then didst thou not go down unto thine house?

11:8, 9 Job 5:12

10:18 *seven hundred chariots.* This number is recorded as seven thousand in 1 Chron. 19:18, but the smaller figure seems more accurate. The scribal error probably derived from confusion over one of the digits of the decimal system used for computation. Another discrepancy appears between these verses: 10:18 mentions *forty thousand horsemen* whereas 1 Chron. 19:18 reads "forty thousand footmen." Most copyists' errors occurred either because the manuscripts from which they worked were worn or torn, or because of human carelessness and weariness.

11:1 David should have been with his soldiers battling for the Lord. Instead he remained at ease at home and promptly fell into sin. Is it not strange that a man who had many wives and concubines found that he did not have as many as he would like and defiled a neighbor's wife? The nature of sin is that no matter how much a man has in life, he always wants more.

11:4 The anatomy of sin may be seen plainly in David's act of adultery with Bath-sheba. When he saw her from a distance, all he needed to do was to go down from the roof and forget about it. Instead, he sent for Bath-sheba. She then made her decision. She knew that the king was not asking her to come for mere innocent conversation. She was a married woman; all she needed to do was decline the invitation, even though it had been made by the king. What happened when they met was a foregone conclusion. The adultery was not committed in a moment of passion brought on by accidental circumstances. It was a deliberate act which wrought changes in the life of David. He paid a price for his transgression all the days of his life, even though he was forgiven when he repented and confessed.

11:11 2 Sam 7:2; 20:6
[11]And U-ri'ah said unto David, The ark, and Israel, and Judah, abide in tents; and my lord Jo'ab, and the servants of my lord, are encamped in the open fields; shall I then go into mine house, to eat and to drink, and to lie with my wife? *as* thou livest, and *as* thy soul liveth, I will not do this thing.
[12]And David said to U-ri'ah, Tarry here to day also, and to morrow I will let thee depart. So U-ri'ah abode in Jerusalem that day, and the morrow.
[13]And when David had called him, he did eat and drink before him; and he made him drunk: and at even he went out to lie on his bed with the servants of his lord, but went not down to his house.

C. DAVID ARRANGES THE MURDER OF URIAH

[14]¶And it came to pass in the morning, that David wrote a letter to Jo'ab, and sent *it* by the hand of U-ri'ah.
11:15☆ 2 Sam 12:9
[15]And he wrote in the letter, saying, Set ye U-ri'ah in the forefront of the hottest battle, and retire ye from him, that he may be smitten, and die.
[16]And it came to pass, when Jo'ab observed the city, that he assigned U-ri'ah unto a place where he knew that valiant men *were*.
[17]And the men of the city went out, and fought with Jo'ab: and there fell *some* of the people of the servants of David; and U-ri'ah the Hittite died also.
[18]¶Then Jo'ab sent and told David all the things concerning the war;
11:19 Judg 9:53
[19]And charged the messenger, saying, When thou hast made an end of telling the matters of the war unto the king,
[20] And if so be that the king's wrath arise, and he say unto thee, Wherefore approached ye so nigh unto the city when ye did fight? knew ye not that they would shoot from the wall?
[21]Who smote A-bim'e-lech the son of Je-rub'be-sheth? did not a woman cast a piece of a millstone upon him from the wall, that he died in The'bez? why went ye nigh the wall? then say thou, Thy servant U-ri'ah the Hittite is dead also.
[22]¶So the messenger went, and came and shewed David all that Jo'ab had sent him for.
[23]And the messenger said unto David, Surely the men prevailed against us, and came out unto us into the field, and we were upon them even unto the entering of the gate.
[24]And the shooters shot from off the wall upon thy servants; and *some* of the king's servants be dead, and thy servant U-ri'ah the Hittite is dead also.
[25]Then David said unto the messenger, Thus shalt thou say unto Jo'ab, Let not this thing displease thee, for the sword devoureth one as well as another: make thy battle more strong against the city, and overthrow it: and encourage thou him.

11:26 Gen 50:10 Deut 34:8 1 Sam 31:13

D. DAVID AND BATH-SHEBA MARRY

[26]¶And when the wife of U-ri'ah heard that U-ri'ah her husband was dead, she mourned for her husband.
11:27☆ 1 Sam 3:2–5 Ps 51:4, 5
[27]And when the mourning was past, David sent and fetched her to his

11:15 David sought to deliver himself from the dilemma created by the pregnancy of Bath-sheba. He planned to have Uriah the Hittite come home and lie with his wife. Then the baby would be thought to be his. When David's plan failed he had Uriah slain. One sin often leads to another; one transgression requires a second and a third to cover it. David had become both an adulterer and a murderer, and the second crime was worse than the first. It was committed in cold blood and with malicious forethought against an innocent military man who was more righteous than the king.

11:27 "The birth of the child so soon after the marriage published the crime."* Sin will be found out; and even if it had been covered and glossed over, it was known to God, who searches the heart and whose anger would not be satisfied until the matter was settled.

house, and she became his wife, and bare him a son. But the thing that
David had done displeased the LORD.

E. NATHAN THE PROPHET CONDEMNS DAVID

1. Nathan Tells David a Story

12 AND the LORD sent Nathan unto David. And he came unto him, ☆12:1 2 Sam 7:2, 17
and said unto him, There were two men in one city; the one rich, 1 Kgs 20:35
and the other poor. Ps 51 Title
2The rich *man* had exceeding many flocks and herds:
3But the poor *man* had nothing, save one little ewe lamb, which he had
bought and nourished up: and it grew up together with him, and with his
children; it did eat of his own meat, and drank of his own cup, and lay in
his bosom, and was unto him as a daughter.
4And there came a traveller unto the rich man, and he spared to take of
his own flock and of his own herd, to dress for the wayfaring man that was
come unto him; but took the poor man's lamb, and dressed it for the man
that was come to him.
5And David's anger was greatly kindled against the man; and he said to ☆12:5 1 Sam 26:16
Nathan, *As* the LORD liveth, the man that hath done this *thing* shall surely 1 Kgs 20:39
die:
6And he shall restore the lamb fourfold, because he did this thing, and ☆12:6 Ex 22:1
because he had no pity.

2. Nathan Tells David He Is the Sinner

7¶And Nathan said to David, Thou *art* the man. Thus saith the LORD ☆12:7 1 Sam 16:13
God of Israel, I anointed thee king over Israel, and I delivered thee out of
the hand of Saul;
8And I gave thee thy master's house, and thy master's wives into thy 12:8 2 Sam 7:2; 9:7
bosom, and gave thee the house of Israel and of Judah; and if *that had been*
too little, I would moreover have given unto thee such and such things.
9Wherefore hast thou despised the commandment of the LORD, to do evil 12:9 1 Sam 15:23
in his sight? thou hast killed U-ri'ah the Hittite with the sword, and hast 2 Sam 11:14, 27
taken his wife *to be* thy wife, and hast slain him with the sword of the
children of Ammon.
10Now therefore the sword shall never depart from thine house; because 12:10 2 Sam 13:29
thou hast despised me, and hast taken the wife of U-ri'ah the Hittite to be 18:14
thy wife. 1 Kgs 2:23
11Thus saith the LORD, Behold, I will raise up evil against thee out of 12:11 2 Sam 16:21
thine own house, and I will take thy wives before thine eyes, and give *them* 15:6, 10
unto thy neighbour, and he shall lie with thy wives in the sight of this sun.

12:1 God was angry with David. He sent Nathan the prophet to David. The prophet spoke a parable about injustice; it was designed to trap David into making a condemning statement about someone else. Nathan finally pointed the finger at David and said: "Thou art the man." Great was the courage of the prophet. Apart from the preserving power of God, he could have expected the same kind of treatment accorded to Uriah. Fortunately, David came under deep conviction of sin, repented, and asked for divine forgiveness. Ps. 51 was subsequently written to warn all men of all ages about the awfulness of sinning against God. Even though he was forgiven, the temporal consequences of David's transgression remained to cloud his days.

12:5, 6 Little did David know at this point that the judgment he would mete out to the man who had committed a far lesser crime would be used against him. He would be charged with guilt by his own words. He who judges must himself be free from the same or worse sins.

12:7 Since David had not repented on his own, Nathan pointed the finger at him directly and accused him of the two crimes he had committed. From verse 14 it appears that David had gone for at least nine months with guilt hanging over him, for the child had already been born. God gave him plenty of time to repent on his own; but when he did not, then God sent Nathan to do two things: to tell David that God was angry and to pronounce the penalty which God would exact for his transgression. Since he had killed Uriah with the sword, the sword would not depart from his own house all the days of his life. And as he had sinned publicly, so would men have sexual relations with David's own wives in broad daylight.

12 For thou didst *it* secretly: but I will do this thing before all Israel, and
before the sun.

12:13☆ Lev 20:10; 24:17 2 Sam 11:5 24:10 Prov 28:13 Mic 7:18 Lk 18:13
12:14 Isa 52:5 Rom 2:23

13 And David said unto Nathan, I have sinned against the LORD. And
Nathan said unto David, The LORD also hath put away thy sin; thou shalt
not die.
14 Howbeit, because by this deed thou hast given great occasion to the
enemies of the LORD to blaspheme, the child also *that is* born unto thee
shall surely die.

3. Bath-sheba's Baby Dies

12:15☆
12:16☆ 2 Sam 1:12 13:31 Ps 69:10
12:17 2 Sam 3:35

15 ¶And Nathan departed unto his house. And the LORD struck the child
that U-ri'ah's wife bare unto David, and it was very sick.
16 David therefore besought God for the child; and David fasted, and
went in, and lay all night upon the earth.
17 And the elders of his house arose, *and went* to him, to raise him up from
the earth: but he would not, neither did he eat bread with them.
18 And it came to pass on the seventh day, that the child died. And the
servants of David feared to tell him that the child was dead: for they said,
Behold, while the child was yet alive, we spake unto him, and he would not
hearken unto our voice: how will he then vex himself, if we tell him that the
child is dead?
19 But when David saw that his servants whispered, David perceived that
the child was dead: therefore David said unto his servants, Is the child
dead? And they said, He is dead.
20 Then David arose from the earth, and washed, and anointed *himself*,
and changed his apparel, and came into the house of the LORD, and
worshipped: then he came to his own house; and when he required, they set
bread before him, and he did eat.
21 Then said his servants unto him, What thing *is* this that thou hast done?
thou didst fast and weep for the child, *while it was* alive; but when the child
was dead, thou didst rise and eat bread.

12:22 Isa 38:1–5 Jonah 3:9
12:23 Job 7:9–10

22 And he said, While the child was yet alive, I fasted and wept: for I said,
Who can tell *whether* GOD will be gracious to me, that the child may live?
23 But now he is dead, wherefore should I fast? can I bring him back
again? I shall go to him, but he shall not return to me.

4. Bath-sheba Gives Birth to Solomon

12:24☆ 1 Chron 22:9
12:25☆

24 ¶And David comforted Bath'-she-ba his wife, and went in unto her,
and lay with her: and she bare a son, and he called his name Solomon: and
the LORD loved him.
25 And he sent by the hand of Nathan the prophet; and he called his name
Jed-i-di'ah, because of the LORD.

12:13 *I have sinned.* Ps. 51 records the lament of David as he repented of his sins of adultery and murder.
12:15 The child conceived in sin was struck by God with a grave illness that would lead to its death. The sins of the parents are sometimes visited upon their children, so that the innocent suffer along with the guilty.
12:16 God sent a sickness on the child born of David and Bath-sheba's adultery. David fasted and prayed for seven days and nights before the child died. He had hoped that God would have mercy and permit the baby to live. God said no to his prayer. When David learned of the death, he stopped praying, began to eat, and was solaced by the knowledge that he had done all he could to repair the damage. In 12:23 we see that he expressed the great truth of life after death when he proclaimed: "I shall go to him, but he shall not return to me."
12:24, 25 David and Bath-sheba were blessed by the gift of Solomon. Nathan was sent by God to tell David that this child would succeed David to the throne. *Jedidiah,* "beloved of the Lord."
12:25 *sent by the hand of Nathan,* i.e., "sent congratulations through Nathan." *because of the LORD,* i.e., "because of the Lord's interest."†

F. DAVID'S VICTORY OVER THE AMMONITES

26 ¶And Jo'ab fought against Rab'bah of the children of Ammon, and took the royal city.

27 And Jo'ab sent messengers to David, and said, I have fought against Rab'bah, and have taken the city of waters.

28 Now therefore gather the rest of the people together, and encamp against the city, and take it: lest I take the city, and it be called after my name.

29 And David gathered all the people together, and went to Rab'bah, and fought against it, and took it.

30 And he took their king's crown from off his head, the weight whereof *was* a talent of gold with the precious stones: and it was *set* on David's head. And he brought forth the spoil of the city in great abundance.

31 And he brought forth the people that *were* therein, and put *them* under saws, and under harrows of iron, and under axes of iron, and made them pass through the brickkiln: and thus did he unto all the cities of the children of Ammon. So David and all the people returned unto Jerusalem.

☆**12:26** Deut 3:11; 2 Sam 11:1; 1 Chron 20:1

12:29 1 Chron 20:2, 3

IV. DAVID'S DIFFICULTIES (13:1—18:33)

A. TAMAR'S RAPE BY AMNON

1. Amnon Falls in with Jonadab's Scheme

13 AND it came to pass after this, that Ab'sa-lom the son of David had a fair sister, whose name *was* Ta'mar; and Am'non the son of David loved her.

2 And Am'non was so vexed, that he fell sick for his sister Ta'mar; for she *was* a virgin; and Am'non thought it hard for him to do anything to her.

3 But Am'non had a friend, whose name *was* Jon'a-dab, the son of Shim'e-ah David's brother: and Jon'a-dab *was* a very subtil man.

4 And he said unto him, Why *art* thou, *being* the king's son, lean from day to day? wilt thou not tell me? And Am'non said unto him, I love Ta'mar, my brother Ab'sa-lom's sister.

5 And Jon'a-dab said unto him, Lay thee down on thy bed, and make thyself sick: and when thy father cometh to see thee, say unto him, I pray thee, let my sister Ta'mar come, and give me meat, and dress the meat in my sight, that I may see *it,* and eat *it* at her hand.

6 ¶So Am'non lay down, and made himself sick: and when the king was come to see him, Am'non said unto the king, I pray thee, let Ta'mar my sister come, and make me a couple of cakes in my sight, that I may eat at her hand.

7 Then David sent home to Ta'mar, saying, Go now to thy brother Am'non's house, and dress him meat.

8 So Ta'mar went to her brother Am'non's house; and he was laid down. And she took flour, and kneaded *it,* and made cakes in his sight, and did bake the cakes.

9 And she took a pan, and poured *them* out before him; but he refused to

☆**13:1** 2 Sam 3:2, 3; 1 Chron 3:2, 9

☆**13:2**

12:26 This scripture does not say when this struggle with the Ammonites took place. It may well have occurred between the time of Uriah's death and the birth of the baby to Bath-sheba and David. The Ammonites were defeated and their capital city seized.

13:1ff Subsequent to the birth of Solomon the troubles of David from within his own household began to mount. They were part of the judgment of God on David for his sin. Absalom's beautiful sister, Tamar, was coveted by Amnon, her half-brother, who raped her. From that moment on he expressed hatred for the girl he had abused. She told her story to Absalom, who worked out a plan to kill Amnon in revenge. Two years went by before Absalom's plan bore its evil fruit. As a result of the murder, Absalom fled from Jerusalem, to the sorrow of his father who loved him. (See note on 2 Sam. 13:25 for the remainder of this grim story.)

13:2 *for she was a virgin: and Amnon thought it hard for him to do anything to her,* i.e., "for the girls and young men were kept strictly apart."†

eat. And Am′non said, Have out all men from me. And they went out every
man from him.
10 And Am′non said unto Ta′mar, Bring the meat into the chamber, that
I may eat of thine hand. And Ta′mar took the cakes which she had made,
and brought *them* into the chamber to Am′non her brother.
11 And when she had brought *them* unto him to eat, he took hold of her,
and said unto her, Come lie with me, my sister.
13:12☆ Lev 18:9, 11 20:17
12 And she answered him, Nay, my brother, do not force me; for no such
thing ought to be done in Israel: do not thou this folly.
13 And I, whither shall I cause my shame to go? and as for thee, thou shalt
be as one of the fools in Israel. Now therefore, I pray thee, speak unto the
king; for he will not withhold me from thee.
14 Howbeit he would not hearken unto her voice: but, being stronger than
she, forced her, and lay with her.
15 ¶Then Am′non hated her exceedingly; so that the hatred wherewith he
hated her *was* greater than the love wherewith he had loved her. And
Am′non said unto her, Arise, be gone.
16 And she said unto him, *There is* no cause: this evil in sending me away
is greater than the other that thou didst unto me. But he would not hearken
unto her.
13:17 Gen 37:3, 32
17 Then he called his servant that ministered unto him, and said, Put now
this *woman* out from me, and bolt the door after her.
18 And *she had* a garment of divers colours upon her: for with such robes
were the king's daughters *that were* virgins apparelled. Then his servant
brought her out, and bolted the door after her.
13:19☆ Gen 37:29 2 Sam 1:11 Esth 4:1
19 ¶And Ta′mar put ashes on her head, and rent her garment of divers
colours that *was* on her, and laid her hand on her head, and went on crying.

2. Absalom, Tamar's Brother, Murders Amnon

20 And Ab′sa-lom her brother said unto her, Hath Am′non thy brother
been with thee? but hold now thy peace, my sister: he *is* thy brother; regard
not this thing. So Ta′mar remained desolate in her brother Ab′sa-lom's
house.
13:21☆
21 ¶But when king David heard of all these things, he was very wroth.
22 And Ab′sa-lom spake unto his brother Am′non neither good nor bad:
for Ab′sa-lom hated Am′non, because he had forced his sister Ta′mar.
13:23☆
23 ¶And it came to pass after two full years, that Ab′sa-lom had
sheepshearers in Ba′al–ha′zor, which *is* beside E′phra-im: and Ab′sa-lom
invited all the king's sons.
24 And Ab′sa-lom came to the king, and said, Behold now, thy servant
hath sheepshearers; let the king, I beseech thee, and his servants go with thy
servant.
13:25☆
25 And the king said to Ab′sa-lom, Nay, my son, let us not all now go, lest

13:12 *no such thing ought to be done in Israel; do not thou this folly,* i.e., "You know what a serious crime it is in Israel."†

13:19 Tamar "bitterly lamented the injury she had received, as it was a stain to her honor, though no real blemish to her virtue."* She returned to her brother's house. Absalom learned that Amnon was the seducer and so he planned revenge.

13:21 David was angry with Amnon for his sin and he had every reason to be. He should have punished Amnon, for as father and king he had the right and the power to do so. But his anger served instead of justice. Eventually Amnon was slain by Absalom who acted as judge when his father failed to do so.

13:23 Two years elapsed before Absalom's plan to slay Amnon matured. It may be that Absalom had more in mind than to avenge the rape of his sister. Amnon was David's firstborn and technically was likely to inherit the throne. Absalom later indicated his own desire to become king.

13:25 The story of Absalom provides its own lesson. King David could see in his son the very defects he had exhibited in his own life, defects that God had mastered but which ran wild in his son. What Absalom did was

we be chargeable unto thee. And he pressed him: howbeit he would not go,
but blessed him.
26 Then said Ab'sa-lom, If not, I pray thee, let my brother Am'non go
with us. And the king said unto him, Why should he go with thee?
27 But Ab'sa-lom pressed him, that he let Am'non and all the king's sons
go with him.
28 ¶Now Ab'sa-lom had commanded his servants, saying, Mark ye now **13:28** 2 Sam 3:27
when Am'non's heart is merry with wine, and when I say unto you, Smite 11:13
Am'non; then kill him, fear not: have not I commanded you? be coura-
geous, and be valiant.
29 And the servants of Ab'sa-lom did unto Am'non as Ab'sa-lom had **13:29** 2 Sam 18:9
commanded. Then all the king's sons arose, and every man gat him up
upon his mule, and fled.
30 ¶And it came to pass, while they were in the way, that tidings came to
David, saying, Ab'sa-lom hath slain all the king's sons, and there is not one
of them left.
31 Then the king arose, and tare his garments, and lay on the earth; and ☆**13:31** 2 Sam 1:11
all his servants stood by with their clothes rent. 12:16
32 And Jon'a-dab, the son of Shim'e-ah David's brother, answered and **13:32** 2 Sam 13:4, 14
said, Let not my lord suppose *that* they have slain all the young men the
king's sons; for Am'non only is dead: for by the appointment of Ab'sa-lom
this hath been determined from the day that he forced his sister Ta'mar.
33 Now therefore let not my lord the king take the thing to his heart, to
think that all the king's sons are dead: for Am'non only is dead.

3. Absalom Flees to Geshur

34 But Ab'sa-lom fled. And the young man that kept the watch lifted up ☆**13:34** 2 Sam 18:24
his eyes, and looked, and, behold, there came much people by the way of
the hill side behind him.
35 And Jon'a-dab said unto the king, Behold, the king's sons come: as thy
servant said, so it is.
36 And it came to pass, as soon as he had made an end of speaking, that,
behold, the king's sons came, and lifted up their voice and wept: and the
king also and all his servants wept very sore.
37 ¶But Ab'sa-lom fled, and went to Tal'mai, the son of Am-mi'hud, king **13:37** 2 Sam 3:3
of Ge'shur, And *David* mourned for his son every day. 12:21; 14:23, 32
38 So Ab'sa-lom fled, and went to Ge'shur, and was there three years.
39 And *the soul of* king David longed to go forth unto Ab'sa-lom: for he
was comforted concerning Am'non, seeing he was dead.

---

simply the fulfillment of what God had promised because of David's adultery with Bath-sheba. God had remanded the eternal punishment, but he did not take away the temporal consequences. When David wept over Absalom's death (18:33), he knew he was in some sense responsible for what happened as one consequence of his own adultery. God used wicked Absalom as an instrument for the chastisement of David, his father.

13:31 When David received tidings that all his sons had been slain, he tore his garments and lay on the ground, grief-stricken. Jonadab brought the good news that only Amnon was slain. This nephew of David's was a despicable character. He acknowledged that he knew of Absalom's plan to kill Amnon, for it was planned two years before it took place. Yet he never warned the king, who then could have prevented it from happening. By failing to prevent this mischief, Jonadab became an accessory to the crime and should have been punished.

13:34 Absalom fled and went to Geshur for three years. He did not flee to an Israelite city of refuge, for they offered no refuge to a willful murderer. David came short of proper conduct, for instead of loathing Absalom for his murder and executing justice on behalf of the dead Amnon, he yearned for Absalom. Eventually David would bring him home and restore his fortunes, little knowing that Absalom would turn against him and force him to flee from Jerusalem.

B. JOAB GETS DAVID TO REINSTATE ABSALOM
1. The Woman of Tekoa Tells David a Story

14:1☆ 14 NOW Jo'ab the son of Zer-u-i'ah perceived that the king's heart *was* toward Ab'sa-lom.

14:2☆ 2 Chron 11:5–10 Amos 1:1 [2]And Jo'ab sent to Te-ko'ah, and fetched thence a wise woman, and said unto her, I pray thee, feign thyself to be a mourner, and put on now mourning apparel, and anoint not thyself with oil, but be as a woman that had a long time mourned for the dead:

[3]And come to the king, and speak on this manner unto him. So Jo'ab put the words in her mouth.

14:4 2 Sam 12:1, 2 [4]¶And when the woman of Te-ko'ah spake to the king, she fell on her face to the ground, and did obeisance, and said, Help, O king.

[5]And the king said unto her, What aileth thee? And she answered, I *am* indeed a widow woman, and mine husband is dead.

[6]And thy handmaid had two sons, and they two strove together in the field, and *there was* none to part them, but the one smote the other, and slew him.

14:7 Num 35:19 Deut 19:12, 13 [7]And, behold, the whole family is risen against thine handmaid, and they said, Deliver him that smote his brother, that we may kill him, for the life of his brother whom he slew; and we will destroy the heir also: and so they shall quench my coal which is left, and shall not leave to my husband *neither* name nor remainder upon the earth.

[8]And the king said unto the woman, Go to thine house, and I will give charge concerning thee.

14:9 Gen 43:9 1 Sam 25:24 [9]And the woman of Te-ko'ah said unto the king, My lord, O king, the iniquity *be* on me, and on my father's house: and the king and his throne *be* guiltless.

[10]And the king said, Whosoever saith *ought* unto thee, bring him to me, and he shall not touch thee any more.

14:11 Num 35:19, 21 Deut 19:4–10 1 Sam 14:45 [11]Then said she, I pray thee, let the king remember the LORD thy God, that thou wouldest not suffer the revengers of blood to destroy any more, lest they destroy my son. And he said, *As* the LORD liveth, there shall not one hair of thy son fall to the earth.

2. The Woman Pleads Absalom's Case

14:12☆ [12]Then the woman said, Let thine handmaid, I pray thee, speak *one* word unto my lord the king. And he said, Say on.

14:13 2 Sam 12:7 13:37–39 1 Kgs 20:40–42 [13]And the woman said, Wherefore then hast thou thought such a thing against the people of God? for the king doth speak this thing as one which is faulty, in that the king doth not fetch home again his banished.

14:1 Crafty Joab (who had murdered Abner) perceived that David really wanted to pardon Absalom, bring him home, and reverse his standing. He was aware that the Israelites accepted Absalom as their darling; and he may have feared that if David died while Absalom was far away, a civil war might erupt for the succession. He wanted to have Absalom in Jerusalem as a provision against such a contingency. So he planned a strategem which would commend him both to David and to Absalom if it succeeded.

14:2–11 Joab solicited the services of an unnamed woman from Tekoa, who came to David with her sad story. She posed as a widow whose one son had been killed by his brother. If sentence were to be executed on the only remaining son she has, the family would become extinct and she would have lost both sons. She pleaded on his behalf. In verse 11 David rendered a verdict. No avenger of blood should touch the son. She was free to go home and rejoice.

14:12 The woman from Tekoa now used her supposititious case and applied it to David and Absalom. She asked whether the king who had just rendered a verdict ought not apply the same principle and the same grace to his son Absalom. David "smelled a rat" and deftly got from her the admission that she was acting as an agent for Joab.

[14]For we must needs die, and *are* as water spilt on the ground, which ☆14:14 Job 34:14, 15 Heb 9:27
cannot be gathered up again; neither doth God respect *any* person: yet
doth he devise means, that his banished be not expelled from him.
[15]Now therefore that I am come to speak of this thing unto my lord the
king, *it is* because the people have made me afraid: and thy handmaid said,
I will now speak unto the king; it may be that the king will perform the
request of his handmaid.
[16]For the king will hear, to deliver his handmaid out of the hand of the
man *that would* destroy me and my son together out of the inheritance of
God.
[17]Then thine handmaid said, The word of my lord the king shall now be 14:17 1 Sam 29:9 2 Sam 19:27
comfortable: for as an angel of God, so *is* my lord the king to discern good
and bad: therefore the LORD thy God will be with thee.

3. David Asks about Joab's Role

[18]Then the king answered and said unto the woman, Hide not from me,
I pray thee, the thing that I shall ask thee. And the woman said, Let my
lord the king now speak.
[19]And the king said, *Is not* the hand of Jo'ab with thee in all this? And the
woman answered and said, *As* thy soul liveth, my lord the king, none can
turn to the right hand or to the left from ought that my lord the king hath
spoken: for thy servant Jo'ab, he bade me, and he put all these words in the
mouth of thine handmaid:
[20]To fetch about this form of speech hath thy servant Jo'ab done this
thing: and my lord *is* wise, according to the wisdom of an angel of God, to
know all *things* that *are* in the earth.

4. David Has Joab Bring Absalom Back

[21]¶And the king said unto Jo'ab, Behold now, I have done this thing: go ☆14:21
therefore, bring the young man Ab'sa-lom again.
[22]And Jo'ab fell to the ground on his face, and bowed himself, and
thanked the king: and Jo'ab said, To day thy servant knoweth that I have
found grace in thy sight, my lord, O king, in that the king hath fulfilled the
request of his servant.
[23]So Jo'ab arose and went to Ge'shur, and brought Ab'sa-lom to 14:23 2 Sam 13:37–39
Jerusalem.
[24]And the king said, Let him turn to his own house, and let him not see
my face. So Ab'sa-lom returned to his own house, and saw not the king's
face.

C. ABSALOM'S PLOT TO UNSEAT DAVID

1. Absalom's Demand to See King David

[25]¶But in all Israel there was none to be so much praised as Ab'sa-lom for
his beauty: from the sole of his foot even to the crown of his head there was
no blemish in him.
[26]And when he polled his head, (for it was at every year's end that he
polled *it:* because *the hair* was heavy on him, therefore he polled it:) he
weighed the hair of his head at two hundred shekels after the king's weight.

14:14 *yet doth he devise means, that his banished be not expelled from him,* or, "God does not sweep life away, but has made provision to bring back those he banishes, so that they will not be forever exiles."†

14:21 David ordered Joab to bring Absalom back to Jerusalem, with the understanding that he would not lay eyes on Absalom and that his son would live in his own house. This interdict against coming to the king's court was a punishment—showing that David could not countenance so great a criminal nor forgive him too easily.

14:27☆ 2 Sam 13:1

27 And unto Ab'sa-lom there were born three sons, and one daughter, whose name *was* Ta'mar: she was a woman of a fair countenance.

14:28 2 Sam 14:24

28 ¶So Ab'sa-lom dwelt two full years in Jerusalem, and saw not the king's face.

29 Therefore Ab'sa-lom sent for Jo'ab, to have sent him to the king; but he would not come to him: and when he sent again the second time, he would not come.

30 Therefore he said unto his servants, See, Jo'ab's field is near mine, and he hath barley there; go and set it on fire. And Ab'sa-lom's servants set the field on fire.

31 Then Jo'ab arose, and came to Ab'sa-lom unto *his* house, and said unto him, Wherefore have thy servants set my field on fire?

14:32☆ 1 Sam 20:8

32 And Ab'sa-lom answered Jo'ab, Behold, I sent unto thee, saying, Come hither, that I may send thee to the king, to say, Wherefore am I come from Ge'shur? *it had been* good for me *to have been* there still: now therefore let me see the king's face; and if there be *any* iniquity in me, let him kill me.

14:33 Gen 27:26; 33:4 Lk 15:20

33 So Jo'ab came to the king, and told him: and when he had called for Ab'sa-lom, he came to the king, and bowed himself on his face to the ground before the king: and the king kissed Ab'sa-lom.

2. Absalom's Treason

15:1☆ 1 Kgs 1:5

15 AND it came to pass after this, that Ab'sa-lom prepared him chariots and horses, and fifty men to run before him.

15:2 2 Sam 19:8

2 And Ab'sa-lom rose up early, and stood beside the way of the gate: and it was *so,* that when any man that had a controversy came to the king for judgment, then Ab'sa-lom called unto him, and said, Of what city *art* thou? And he said, Thy servant *is* of one of the tribes of Israel.

3 And Ab'sa-lom said unto him, See, thy matters *are* good and right; but *there is* no man *deputed* of the king to hear thee.

15:4 Judg 9:1–3

4 Ab'sa-lom said moreover, Oh that I were made judge in the land, that every man which hath any suit or cause might come unto me, and I would do him justice!

15:5 2 Sam 14:33

5 And it was *so,* that when any man came nigh *to him* to do him obeisance, he put forth his hand, and took him, and kissed him.

6 And on this manner did Ab'sa-lom to all Israel that came to the king for judgment: so Ab'sa-lom stole the hearts of the men of Israel.

15:7☆ Gen 28:20, 21 2 Sam 13:37–39

7 ¶And it came to pass after forty years, that Ab'sa-lom said unto the king, I pray thee, let me go and pay my vow, which I have vowed unto the LORD, in Hebron.

15:8☆

8 For thy servant vowed a vow while I abode at Ge'shur in Syria, saying, If the LORD shall bring me again indeed to Jerusalem, then I will serve the LORD.

15:9☆

9 And the king said unto him, Go in peace. So he arose, and went to Hebron.

14:27 *three sons.* Compare this to 18:18, where Absalom says, "I have no son . . ." One of two possibilities supplies the answer to this apparent discrepancy. Either the monument in 18:18 was set up before any of Absalom's sons were born, or the event occurred after the death of all three sons. In any case, Absalom was left without any male heirs, and none is mentioned in any of the genealogies.

14:32 Insolent and imperious Absalom demanded to stand before his father and challenged him to kill him if he wished to do so. He well knew that David loved him too much to do this. His conduct was unbecoming of either a son or a subject. He already had great plans in mind to unseat his father and become king of Israel in his stead.

15:1 Absalom was now fully engaged in his plot to unseat David and seize the throne for himself. A civil war was in the making, with unexpected results for all parties involved.

15:7, 8 David continued to love Absalom even though he had used deceit and treachery in winning the hearts of the people, who turned against David their king.

15:9 *So he arose, and went to Hebron.* Hebron was King David's first capital. It was also Absalom's

10¶But Ab′sa-lom sent spies throughout all the tribes of Israel, saying, As soon as ye hear the sound of the trumpet, then ye shall say, Ab′sa-lom reigneth in Hebron.
11And with Ab′sa-lom went two hundred men out of Jerusalem, *that were* called; and they went in their simplicity, and they knew not any thing.
12And Ab′sa-lom sent for A-hith′o-phel the Gi′lo-nite, David's counsellor, from his city, *even* from Gi′loh, while he offered sacrifices. And the conspiracy was strong; for the people increased continually with Ab′-sa-lom.

15:10 1 Kgs 1:34 2 Kgs 9:13
15:12 2 Sam 16:20 17:14

3. David's Hasty Flight

13¶And there came a messenger to David, saying, The hearts of the men of Israel are after Ab′sa-lom.
14And David said unto all his servants that *were* with him at Jerusalem, Arise, and let us flee; for we shall not *else* escape from Ab′sa-lom: make speed to depart, lest he overtake us suddenly, and bring evil upon us, and smite the city with the edge of the sword.
15And the king's servants said unto the king, Behold, thy servants *are ready to do* whatsoever my lord the king shall appoint.
16And the king went forth, and all his household after him. And the king left ten women, *which were* concubines, to keep the house.
17And the king went forth, and all the people after him, and tarried in a place that was far off.
18And all his servants passed on beside him; and all the Cher′e-thites, and all the Pel′e-thites, and all the Git′tites, six hundred men which came after him from Gath, passed on before the king.

☆15:13 Judg 9:3
15:14 2 Sam 12:11 Ps 3 Title
15:16 2 Sam 16:21
15:17 1 Sam 23:13 25:13; 30:9 2 Sam 8:18 18:1, 2

4. Ittai, the Gittite, Refuses to Leave David

19¶Then said the king to It′ta-i the Git′tite, Wherefore goest thou also with us? return to thy place, and abide with the king: for thou *art* a stranger, and also an exile.
20Whereas thou camest *but* yesterday, should I this day make thee go up and down with us? seeing I go whither I may, return thou, and take back thy brethren: mercy and truth *be* with thee.
21And It′ta-i answered the king, and said, *As* the LORD liveth, and *as* my lord the king liveth, surely in what place my lord the king shall be, whether in death or life, even there also will thy servant be.
22And David said to It′ta-i, Go and pass over. And It′ta-i the Git′tite passed over, and all his men, and all the little ones that *were* with him.
23And all the country wept with a loud voice, and all the people passed over: the king also himself passed over the brook Kidron, and all the people passed over, toward the way of the wilderness.

☆15:19 1 Sam 23:13 Ruth 1:16
15:23 1 Kgs 15:13 2 Chron 15:16 29:16

---

hometown; its people doubtless were very proud of him.†

15:13 David learned that Absalom had rebelled against him and, even worse, that the people of Israel were in league with his son. David had loved his son and been indulgent with him, not repaying him for the killing of Amnon. How unnaturally and ungratefully does Absalom seek the kingdom from his father. David flees from Absalom.

15:19 Ittai the Gittite fled with David, who urged him to return to Jerusalem. Ittai was a stranger, an exile, a proselyte, and a new convert. Ittai was made of sterner stuff, and he refused the suggestion of David. His resolution and faithfulness led him to say that whether it be for life or for death he would stay with the king he served and loved. He is a good model for believers who belong to Jesus, who should also cling to the Savior whether it means life or death. Jesus has given us his promise that nothing will cause him to leave us. Why then should we ever leave him?

5. The Return of the Ark to Jerusalem

15:24 Num 4:15; 1 Sam 4:4; 2 Sam 8:17; 20:25

24¶And lo Za'dok also, and all the Levites *were* with him, bearing the ark of the covenant of God: and they set down the ark of God; and A-bi'a-thar went up, until all the people had done passing out of the city.

15:25 1 Sam 3:18

25And the king said unto Za'dok, Carry back the ark of God into the city: if I shall find favour in the eyes of the LORD, he will bring me again, and shew me *both* it, and his habitation:

15:26☆

26But if he thus say, I have no delight in thee; behold, *here am* I, let him do to me as seemeth good unto him.

15:27 2 Sam 17:17; 18:19

27The king said also unto Za'dok the priest, *Art not* thou a seer? return into the city in peace, and your two sons with you, A-him'a-az thy son, and Jonathan the son of A-bi'a-thar.

15:28 Judg 3:28; 7:4; 12:5; 2 Sam 17:16

28See, I will tarry in the plain of the wilderness, until there come word from you to certify me.

29Za'dok therefore and A-bi'a-thar carried the ark of God again to Jerusalem: and they tarried there.

6. Ahithophel the Deserter; Hushai the Faithful

15:30☆ Ezek 24:23

30¶And David went up by the ascent of *mount* Olivet, and wept as he went up, and had his head covered, and he went barefoot: and all the people that *was* with him covered every man his head, and they went up, weeping as they went up.

15:31☆ 2 Sam 15:12; 16:23; 17:14, 23

31¶And *one* told David, saying, A-hith'o-phel *is* among the conspirators with Ab'sa-lom. And David said, O LORD, I pray thee, turn the counsel of A-hith'o-phel into foolishness.

15:32 2 Sam 16:16; 17:5

32¶And it came to pass, that *when* David was come to the top *of the mount,* where he worshipped God, behold, Hu'shai the Ar'chite came to meet him with his coat rent, and earth upon his head:

15:33 2 Sam 16:19

33Unto whom David said, If thou passest on with me, then thou shalt be a burden unto me:

34But if thou return to the city, and say unto Ab'sa-lom, I will be thy servant, O king; *as* I *have been* thy father's servant hitherto, so *will* I now also *be* thy servant: then mayest thou for me defeat the counsel of A-hith'o-phel.

15:35 2 Sam 16:15; 17:15; 1 Chron 27:33

35And *hast thou* not there with thee Za'dok and A-bi'a-thar the priests? therefore it shall be, *that* what thing soever thou shalt hear out of the king's house, thou shalt tell *it* to Za'dok and A-bi'a-thar the priests.

36Behold, *they have* there with them their two sons, A-him'a-az Za'dok's *son,* and Jonathan A-bi'a-thar's *son;* and by them ye shall send unto me every thing that ye can hear.

37So Hu'shai David's friend came into the city, and Ab'sa-lom came into Jerusalem.

15:26 Here we see David at his spiritual best. He prayed that God would deliver him from his present plight, in which his own son had seized the throne and precipitated civil war. He accepted the fact that whatever God does is good. He waited patiently for either deliverance or the end of his kingship, according to the good pleasure of God. As a servant expecting orders he cried out: "Behold, here am I."

15:30 David wept, went barefoot, and had his head covered. These were expressions of humiliation, sadness over the revolt of a beloved son, and a tasting of the wormwood and the gall. Even for the righteous there are moments in life when the face of God seems hidden and his will seems obscure.

15:31ff Tense moments in life bring out the good in some and the bad in others. Ahithophel was a traitor who gave allegiance to Absalom. In 16:1–4 we see that Ziba bore false witness against Mephibosheth (a son of Jonathan, who had been David's closest friend and associate). Ziba was given all of his master's possessions by David. As David fled, he was met by Shimei, of the house of Saul. Shimei cursed the king, predicting his ruin with malicious pleasure. David accepted this, and attributed it to the Lord (16:11). He prayed that God would bless him because of the curses he had received that day. In the strains and stresses of life, one finds out who are his friends and his enemies.

7. Ziba's Conspiracy against Mephibosheth

16 AND when David was a little past the top *of the hill,* behold, Zi'ba
the servant of Me-phib'o-sheth met him, with a couple of asses
saddled, and upon them two hundred *loaves* of bread, and an hundred
bunches of raisins, and an hundred of summer fruits, and a bottle of wine.
2 And the king said unto Zi'ba, What meanest thou by these? And Zi'ba
said, The asses *be* for the king's household to ride on; and the bread and
summer fruit for the young men to eat; and the wine, that such as be faint
in the wilderness may drink.
3 And the king said, And where *is* thy master's son? And Zi'ba said unto
the king, Behold, he abideth at Jerusalem: for he said, To day shall the
house of Israel restore me the kingdom of my father.
4 Then said the king to Zi'ba, Behold, thine *are* all that *pertained* unto Me-
phib'o-sheth. And Zi'ba said, I humbly beseech thee *that* I may find grace
in thy sight, my lord, O king.

☆**16:1** 2 Sam 9:2
16:2 Judg 5:10; 10:4; 2 Sam 17:28
☆**16:3** 2 Sam 9:9; 19:26, 27

8. Shimei Curses David

5 ¶And when king David came to Ba-hu'rim, behold, thence came out a
man of the family of the house of Saul, whose name *was* Shim'e-i, the son of
Ge'ra: he came forth, and cursed still as he came.
6 And he cast stones at David, and at all the servants of king David: and
all the people and all the mighty men *were* on his right hand and on his left.
7 And thus said Shim'e-i when he cursed, Come out, come out, thou
bloody man, and thou man of Be'li-al:
8 The LORD hath returned upon thee all the blood of the house of Saul, in
whose stead thou hast reigned; and the LORD hath delivered the kingdom
into the hand of Ab'sa-lom thy son: and, behold, thou *art taken* in thy
mischief, because thou *art* a bloody man.
9 ¶Then said A-bish'a-i the son of Zer-u-i'ah unto the king, Why should
this dead dog curse my lord the king? let me go over, I pray thee, and take
off his head.
10 And the king said, What have I to do with you, ye sons of Zer-u-i'ah? so
let him curse, because the LORD hath said unto him, Curse David. Who
shall then say, Wherefore hast thou done so?
11 And David said to A-bish'a-i, and to all his servants, Behold, my son,
which came forth of my bowels, seeketh my life: how much more now *may*
this Benjamite *do it?* let him alone, and let him curse; for the LORD hath
bidden him.
12 It may be that the LORD will look on mine affliction, and that the LORD
will requite me good for his cursing this day.

☆**16:5** Ex 22:28; 1 Sam 17:43; 2 Sam 3:16; 17:18; 19:16; 1 Kgs 2:8
16:7 2 Sam 12:9; 21:1
16:9 Ex 22:28; 1 Sam 26:8; 2 Sam 19:21
16:10 2 Sam 3:39; 19:22; Jn 18:11; Rom 9:20
16:11 Gen 45:5; 1 Sam 26:19; 2 Sam 12:11
☆**16:12** Deut 23:5; Rom 8:28

16:1 Ziba had been the manager of the estate of Mephibosheth who had been David's table-guest for years. Ziba was a mean and calculating person who wanted to own, not manage, his master's estate. So he craftily bore false witness by saying that his master had designs on David's throne. David accepted his statement at face value and gave him the possessions of his master (16:4). "Great men ought always be jealous of flattery, and remember that nature has given them two ears, that they may hear both sides."*

16:3 *my father,* i.e., "Saul." Saul was Mephibosheth's grandfather. The word "father" can extend to mean grandfather, great-grandfather, etc. For example, Jesus was called the son of David even though David was a distant ancestor.

16:5 "We here find that David bore Shimei's curses much better than he had borne Ziba's flattery. By the latter he was brought to a wrong judgment on another, by the former to pass a right judgment on himself."* This descendant of Saul cursed David, pelted him with stones, and pronounced maledictions on him. David refused to let his men kill Shimei, supposing the possibility that God was using him for his divine purposes, which David was willing to accept with humility.

16:12 David piously hoped that God would have mercy on him and use this evil to repay him with good things. Faith and hope must ever be the Christian's strength in the hour of adversity.

[13]And as David and his men went by the way, Shim′e-i went along on the hill's side over against him, and cursed as he went, and threw stones at him, and cast dust.

[14]And the king, and all the people that *were* with him, came weary, and refreshed themselves there.

9. Absalom Usurps His Father's Throne
a. Hushai Pretends to Be for Absalom

16:15 2 Sam 15:12, 37
[15]¶And Ab′sa-lom, and all the people the men of Israel, came to Jerusalem, and A-hith′o-phel with him.

16:16☆ 1 Sam 10:24; 2 Sam 15:33; 17:5; 2 Kgs 11:12
[16]And it came to pass, when Hu′shai the Ar′chite, David's friend, was come unto Ab′sa-lom, that Hu′shai said unto Ab′sa-lom, God save the king, God save the king.

[17]And Ab′sa-lom said to Hu′shai, *Is* this thy kindness to thy friend? why wentest thou not with thy friend?

[18]And Hu′shai said unto Ab′sa-lom, Nay; but whom the LORD, and this people, and all the men of Israel, choose, his will I be, and with him will I abide.

16:19 2 Sam 15:33, 34
[19]And again, whom should I serve? *should I* not *serve* in the presence of his son? as I have served in thy father's presence, so will I be in thy presence.

b. Ahithophel Gets Absalom to Lie with His Father's Concubines

[20]¶Then said Ab′sa-lom to A-hith′o-phel, Give counsel among you what we shall do.

16:21☆ 2 Sam 15:16
[21]And A-hith′o-phel said unto Ab′sa-lom, Go in unto thy father's concubines, which he hath left to keep the house; and all Israel shall hear that thou art abhorred of thy father: then shall the hands of all that *are* with thee be strong.

16:22☆ 2 Sam 12:11; 20:3
[22]So they spread Ab′sa-lom a tent upon the top of the house; and Ab′sa-lom went in unto his father's concubines in the sight of all Israel.

16:23 2 Sam 15:12; 17:14
[23]And the counsel of A-hith′o-phel, which he counselled in those days, *was* as if a man had inquired at the oracle of God: so *was* all the counsel of A-hith′o-phel both with David and with Ab′sa-lom.

c. Ahithophel's Plan to Chase after David

17:1☆
17 MOREOVER A-hith′o-phel said unto Ab′sa-lom, Let me now choose out twelve thousand men, and I will arise and pursue after David this night:

17:2 2 Sam 16:14; 1 Kgs 22:31
[2]And I will come upon him while he *is* weary and weak handed, and will

---

16:16 Hushai, an Archite, is called King David's companion in 1 Chron. 27:33. The same verse reports that Ahithophel was the king's "counsellor." Even in this role, however, Ahithophel was not the king's friend. He defected to Absalom. But when David was fleeing, his friend Hushai came out to be with him and support him. David sent him back to Jerusalem in order to offset the advice of Ahithophel. Hushai was successful in his mission; his counsel was accepted by Absalom and that of Ahithophel rejected. Ahithophel then committed suicide. Meanwhile, Hushai advised David to escape across the Jordan River (2 Sam. 17:15–22).

16:21 *then shall the hands of all that art with thee be strong,* i.e., "they will all close ranks behind you."†

16:22 Thus was the word of the Lord fulfilled in accord with God's promise to David that someone would have sexual relations with his wives as he had had sexual relations with Bath-sheba, the wife of his servant Uriah (2 Sam. 12:11). Ahithophel suggested that Absalom defile his father's concubines for all Israel to hear about it. But wicked Absalom went farther than that; he wanted all Israel to see, as well as hear of his defilement.

17:1 Ahithophel counselled Absalom to pursue David. Since David had no time to gather his own army, it would be simple for Ahithophel and his men to capture and kill David without causing numerous deaths in a larger conflict. Kill one man and all the people would be at peace. For some unexplained reason, undoubtedly the providence of God, Absalom wanted to hear what Hushai had to say.

for the people that *were* with him, to eat: for they said, The people *is*
hungry, and weary, and thirsty, in the wilderness.

2. The Decisive Battle in the Forest of Ephraim

18 AND David numbered the people that *were* with him, and set
captains of thousands and captains of hundreds over them.
2 And David sent forth a third part of the people under the hand of Jo'ab,
and a third part under the hand of A-bish'a-i the son of Zer-u-i'ah, Jo'ab's
brother, and a third part under the hand of It'ta-i the Git'tite. And the king
said unto the people, I will surely go forth with you myself also.
3 But the people answered, Thou shalt not go forth: for if we flee away,
they will not care for us; neither if half of us die, will they care for us: but
now *thou art* worth ten thousand of us: therefore now *it is* better that thou
succour us out of the city.
4 And the king said unto them, What seemeth you best I will do. And the
king stood by the gate side, and all the people came out by hundreds and by
thousands.
5 And the king commanded Jo'ab and A-bish'a-i and It'ta-i, saying, *Deal*
gently for my sake with the young man, *even* with Ab'sa-lom. And all the
people heard when the king gave all the captains charge concerning Ab'sa-
lom.
6 ¶So the people went out into the field against Israel: and the battle was
in the wood of E'phra-im;
7 Where the people of Israel were slain before the servants of David, and
there was there a great slaughter that day of twenty thousand *men*.
8 For the battle was there scattered over the face of all the country: and
the wood devoured more people that day than the sword devoured.
9 ¶And Ab'sa-lom met the servants of David. And Ab'sa-lom rode upon a
mule, and the mule went under the thick boughs of a great oak, and his
head caught hold of the oak, and he was taken up between the heaven and
the earth; and the mule that *was* under him went away.
10 And a certain man saw *it*, and told Jo'ab, and said, Behold, I saw
Ab'sa-lom hanged in an oak.

3. The Death of Absalom

11 And Jo'ab said unto the man that told him, And, behold, thou sawest
him, and why didst thou not smite him there to the ground? and I would
have given thee ten *shekels* of silver, and a girdle.
12 And the man said unto Jo'ab, Though I should receive a thousand
shekels of silver in mine hand, *yet* would I not put forth mine hand against
the king's son: for in our hearing the king charged thee and A-bish'a-i and
It'ta-i, saying, Beware that none *touch* the young man Ab'sa-lom.
13 Otherwise I should have wrought falsehood against mine own life: for

☆**18:1** Ex 18:25; 1 Sam 8:12; 22:7
18:2 1 Sam 11:11; 2 Sam 15:19
18:3 2 Sam 17:2, 3; 21:17; 1 Kgs 22:31
18:4 2 Sam 18:24
☆**18:5**
☆**18:6** Josh 17:15
18:7 2 Sam 2:17
18:9 2 Sam 14:26
☆**18:11** 2 Sam 3:27; 11:15; 14:20

18:1 David now assembled his own army under the leadership of three skilled warriors—Joab, Zeruiah, and Ittai the Gittite. He wished to go with them to battle but they urged him to remain on the sideline, which he did. He gave them one warning: "Deal gently for my sake with the young man."

18:5 The climactic battle in the forest of Ephraim was shaping up—the battle that would end the civil war. David appealed to his commanders to deal gently with Absalom, his beloved son. In the ensuing battle, Absalom accidentally got caught in the limb of an oak tree and was left hanging, helpless. Joab learned of it and slew Absalom after one of the bystanders refused to do so (18:14, 15).

18:6 The battlefield was the forest of Ephraim. It was in the territory of Gad in the Transjordan but was named from some memorable action of the Ephraimites there. It was a treacherous place.

18:11 *given thee ten shekels of silver, and a girdle,* i.e., "made you a commissioned officer." There is no way of knowing the value of the silver. The girdle was probably worn by a commissioned officer.†

there is no matter hid from the king, and thou thyself wouldest have set
thyself against *me.*
18:14☆ 14 Then said Jo′ab, I may not tarry thus with thee. And he took three darts
in his hand, and thrust them through the heart of Ab′sa-lom, while he *was*
yet alive in the midst of the oak.
15 And ten young men that bare Jo′ab's armour compassed about and
smote Ab′sa-lom, and slew him.
18:16☆ 16 And Jo′ab blew the trumpet, and the people returned from pursuing
2 Sam 2:28; 20:22 after Israel: for Jo′ab held back the people.
17 And they took Ab′sa-lom, and cast him into a great pit in the wood,
and laid a very great heap of stones upon him: and all Israel fled every one
to his tent.
18:18 18 ¶Now Ab′sa-lom in his lifetime had taken and reared up for himself a
1 Sam 15:12; 2 Sam 14:27 pillar, which *is* in the king's dale: for he said, I have no son to keep my
name in remembrance: and he called the pillar after his own name: and it
is called unto this day, Ab′sa-lom's place.

4. Ahimaaz Races to Tell King David the News

18:19☆ 19 ¶Then said A-him′a-az the son of Za′dok, Let me now run, and bear the
2 Sam 15:35, 36; 17:17 king tidings, how that the LORD hath avenged him of his enemies.
20 And Jo′ab said unto him, Thou shalt not bear tidings this day, but thou
shalt bear tidings another day: but this day thou shalt bear no tidings,
because the king's son is dead.
21 Then said Jo′ab to Cu′shi, Go tell the king what thou hast seen. And
Cu′shi bowed himself unto Jo′ab, and ran.
22 Then said A-him′a-az the son of Za′dok yet again to Jo′ab, But
howsoever, let me, I pray thee, also run after Cu′shi. And Jo′ab said,
Wherefore wilt thou run, my son, seeing that thou hast no tidings ready?
18:23☆ 23 But howsoever, *said he,* let me run. And he said unto him, Run. Then
A-him′a-az ran by the way of the plain, and overran Cu′shi.
18:24 24 And David sat between the two gates: and the watchman went up to
2 Sam 13:34; 18:4; 19:8–10; 2 Kgs 9:17 the roof over the gate unto the wall, and lifted up his eyes, and looked, and
behold a man running alone.
25 And the watchman cried, and told the king. And the king said, If he *be*
alone, *there is* tidings in his mouth. And he came apace, and drew near.
26 And the watchman saw another man running: and the watchman called
unto the porter, and said, Behold *another* man running alone. And the king
said, He also bringeth tidings.
18:27 27 And the watchman said, Me thinketh the running of the foremost is like
1 Kgs 1:42 the running of A-him′a-az the son of Za′dok, And the king said, He *is* a
good man, and cometh with good tidings.
18:28 28 And A-him′a-az called, and said unto the king, All is well. And he fell
1 Sam 17:46; 25:23 down to the earth upon his face before the king, and said, Blessed *be* the

---

18:14 Joab wasted no time in disposing of Absalom, even though it was an act of disobedience against his commander's orders. Doubtless, David would not have permitted this to happen had he been in the battle himself. Joab performed a good service for the nation, for king and country would still have been endangered had he let him live.

18:16 Once Absalom was dead, there was no longer any reason for the war to continue. Joab blew the trumpet and the fighting ceased. David needed only return to Jerusalem and regain the enthusiastic support of those who had favored Absalom.

18:19 Ahimaaz, the young priest who had brought David the news of Absalom's intentions, wanted to run to tell David the good news. Joab knew what David's reaction would be and did not want this man to suffer any untoward consequences. So he sent an Ethiopian, who may have been black (called "Cushi" in the KJV but "a Cushite" in NASB, RSV, and NIV) to carry the tidings to David.

18:23 Ahimaaz outran the Cushite and arrived first to tell David the results of the civil war. David was expecting good news.

LORD thy God, which hath delivered up the men that lifted up their hand
against my lord the king.
29And the king said, Is the young man Ab'sa-lom safe? And A-him'a-az ☆18:29
answered, When Jo'ab sent the king's servant, and *me* thy servant, I saw a
great tumult, but I knew not what *it was*.
30And the king said *unto him*, Turn aside, *and* stand here. And he turned
aside, and stood still.
31And, behold, Cu'shi came; and Cu'shi said, Tidings, my lord the king: 18:31 Judg 5:31
for the LORD hath avenged thee this day of all them that rose up against
thee.
32And the king said unto Cu'shi, *Is* the young man Ab'sa-lom safe? And ☆18:32
Cu'shi answered, The enemies of my lord the king, and all that rise against
thee to do *thee* hurt, be as *that* young man *is*.
33¶And the king was much moved, and went up to the chamber over the ☆18:33 2 Sam 19:4 Rom 9:1–3
gate, and wept: and as he went, thus he said, O my son Ab'sa-lom, my son,
my son Ab'sa-lom! would God I had died for thee, O Ab'sa-lom, my son,
my son!

V. THE KINGDOM BECOMES DAVID'S AGAIN (19:1—20:26)

A. JOAB REPROVES THE KING

19 AND it was told Jo'ab, Behold, the king weepeth and mourneth for ☆19:1 2 Sam 18:5, 14
Ab'sa-lom.
2And the victory that day was *turned* into mourning unto all the people: ☆19:2
for the people heard say that day how the king was grieved for his son.
3And the people gat them by stealth that day into the city, as people
being ashamed steal away when they flee in battle.
4But the king covered his face, and the king cried with a loud voice, O my 19:4 2 Sam 15:30 18:33
son Ab'sa-lom, O Ab'sa-lom, my son, my son!
5And Jo'ab came into the house to the king, and said, Thou hast shamed ☆19:5 2 Sam 3:39 20:8–10
this day the faces of all thy servants, which this day have saved thy life, and
the lives of thy sons and of thy daughters, and the lives of thy wives, and
the lives of thy concubines;
6In that thou lovest thine enemies, and hatest thy friends. For thou hast ☆19:6
declared this day, that thou regardest neither princes nor servants: for this
day I perceive, that if Ab'sa-lom had lived, and all we had died this day,
then it had pleased thee well.

18:29 *I knew not what it was*, i.e., "I didn't know what was happening." Ahimaaz apparently was afraid to tell the king what actually had happened.†

18:32 Ahimaaz realized that David was not prepared for news of the death of Absalom, so he wisely deferred making any definitive statement, knowing that the Cushite was about to arrive and would be sure to tell David the unhappy fact that Absalom was dead. Since the Cushite had been charged by Joab to do this, David could not take offense at a messenger who was not even an Israelite.

18:33 The death of Absalom brought David to the depths of despair. The king here displays his humanness and his weaknesses. David showed a preference for a graceless son who, although he was witty and handsome, had been abandoned by God and man. Instead of weeping, he should have been rejoicing that the divine providence of God had worked the will of God. Moreover, as king he should have preferred the nation over his son and realized that the public interest had been served by the death of Absalom and the end of the civil war. He should have rejoiced in God's divine deliverance, rather than suggesting—by his weeping—that God's mercy was not worth giving thanks for. Because he overloved, he overgrieved when he should have kept a strict guard on his emotions.

19:1, 2 David was more concerned about the death of Absalom than he was about the nation, the army that won the battle, or the deaths of those who perished to save David and his kingship. This news spread through the army and great dissatisfaction arose. By his actions David threatened himself and Israel more than Absalom had done by his revolution.

19:5, 6 Joab courageously faced King David, pointing out to him the implications of his conduct with regard to the death of Absalom. David's soldiers had saved the kingdom from Absalom. They were worthy of commen-

7 Now therefore arise, go forth, and speak comfortably unto thy servants:
for I swear by the LORD, if thou go not forth, there will not tarry one with
thee this night: and that will be worse unto thee than all the evil that befell
thee from thy youth until now.

B. DAVID GOES HOME TO JERUSALEM

1. The Elders Ask David to Come Back

19:8 8 Then the king arose, and sat in the gate. And they told unto all the
2 Sam 8:1 15:2; 18:24 people, saying, Behold, the king doth sit in the gate. And all the people
came before the king: for Israel had fled every man to his tent.
19:9☆ 9 ¶And all the people were at strife throughout all the tribes of Israel,
saying, The king saved us out of the hand of our enemies, and he delivered
us out of the hand of the Philistines; and now he is fled out of the land for
Ab′sa-lom.
10 And Ab′sa-lom, whom we anointed over us, is dead in battle. Now
therefore why speak ye not a word of bringing the king back?
19:11☆ 11 ¶And king David sent to Za′dok and to A-bi′a-thar the priests, saying,
2 Sam 5:1 Speak unto the elders of Judah, saying, Why are ye the last to bring the
king back to his house? seeing the speech of all Israel is come to the king,
even to his house.
12 Ye *are* my brethren, ye *are* my bones and my flesh: wherefore then are
ye the last to bring back the king?
19:13☆ 13 And say ye to Am′a-sa, *Art* thou not of my bone, and of my flesh? God
2 Sam 8:16 17:25 do so to me, and more also, if thou be not captain of the host before me
20:23 1 Chron 2:16, 17 continually in the room of Jo′ab.
14 And he bowed the heart of all the men of Judah, even as *the heart of* one
man; so that they sent *this word* unto the king, Return thou, and all thy
servants.
19:15 15 So the king returned, and came to Jordan. And Judah came to Gilgal,
Josh 5:8, 9 1 Sam 11:14 to go to meet the king, to conduct the king over Jordan.

2. Shimei Repents and Is Forgiven

19:16 16 ¶And Shim′e-i the son of Ge′ra, a Benjamite, which *was* of Ba-hu′rim,
2 Sam 16:5 1 Kgs 2:8 hasted and came down with the men of Judah to meet king David.
19:17 17 And *there were* a thousand men of Benjamin with him, and Zi′ba the
2 Sam 9:2; 16:1 servant of the house of Saul, and his fifteen sons and his twenty servants
with him; and they went over Jordan before the king.
19:18☆ 18 And there went over a ferry boat to carry over the king's household,

---

dation and rightly were offended at being slighted. Joab warned David that unless his attitude changed, he would lose the affection of his people and bring about the very state of affairs which would have come had the revolt of Absalom succeeded. David heeded Joab's rebuke and changed his attitude.

19:9 The ten tribes of Israel were disenchanted and angry that David had not promptly returned to Jerusalem to resume his kingship. David had apparently been waiting for the people of Judah and Israel to call for his return. The ten tribes, who had anointed Absalom to be king over them, now asked why nothing was being done to promote the return of David.

19:11 David sent word to Abiathar and Zadok, asking why the people of Judah had not sent for him to come home to Jerusalem, whereas the ten tribes desired that he do so. He wanted a vote of confidence from his own tribe of Judah.

19:13 Joab faithfully served King David. He did not carry out David's request to protect Absalom, for he knew the whole kingdom was at stake. David, angry at Joab for this single act of disobedience, rashly promised to make Amasa, the leader of Absalom's army, the commander of his army, instead of Joab.

19:18 Crafty Shimei, who had cursed David when he was fleeing from Absalom now falls at the feet of the king and begs for pardon. Abishai wants to know why Shimei should not be executed for his treason and his gall. David forgives him and assures him he will not die. We who have cursed God and his Son are also forgiven when we fall at the feet of the Savior and ask for forgiveness. This is what grace is all about, and David displayed that on this occasion.

and to do what he thought good. And Shim'e-i the son of Ge'ra fell down
before the king, as he was come over Jordan;
19 And said unto the king, Let not my lord impute iniquity unto me, **19:19** 1 Sam 26:21 2 Sam 16:6–9 1 Kgs 1:31
neither do thou remember that which they servant did perversely the day
that my lord the king went out of Jerusalem, that the king should take it to
his heart.
20 For thy servant doth know that I have sinned: therefore, behold, I am
come the first this day of all the house of Joseph to go down to meet my
lord the king.
21 But A-bish'a-i the son of Zer-u-i'ah answered and said, Shall not **19:21** Ex 22:28 1 Sam 24:6 1 Kgs 21:10
Shim'e-i be put to death for this, because he cursed the LORD's anointed?
22 And David said, What have I to do with you, ye sons of Zer-u-i'ah, that **19:22** 1 Sam 11:13 2 Sam 3:39
ye should this day be adversaries unto me? shall there any man be put to
death this day in Israel? for do not I know that I *am* this day king over
Israel?
23 Therefore the king said unto Shim'e-i, Thou shalt not die. And the king **19:23** 1 Kgs 2:8
sware unto him.

3. Mephibosheth Explains Ziba's Treachery

24 ¶And Me-phib'o-sheth the son of Saul came down to meet the king, ☆**19:24** 2 Sam 9:5, 6 21:7
and had neither dressed his feet, nor trimmed his beard, nor washed his
clothes, from the day the king departed until the day he came *again* in
peace.
25 And it came to pass, when he was come to Jerusalem to meet the king,
that the king said unto him, Wherefore wentest not thou with me, Me-
phib'o-sheth?
26 And he answered, My lord, O king, my servant deceived me: for thy ☆**19:26** 2 Sam 9:3, 13
servant said, I will saddle me an ass, that I may ride thereon, and go to the
king; because thy servant *is* lame.
27 And he hath slandered thy servant unto my lord the king; but my lord ☆**19:27** 2 Sam 14:17, 20; 16:3, 4
the king *is* as an angel of God: do therefore *what is* good in thine eyes.
28 For all *of* my father's house were but dead men before my lord the king: ☆**19:28** 2 Sam 9:7, 10, 13
yet didst thou set thy servant among them that did eat at thine own table.
What right therefore have I yet to cry any more unto the king?
29 And the king said unto him, Why speakest thou any more of thy
matters? I have said, Thou and Zi'ba divide the land.
30 And Me-phib'o-sheth said unto the king, Yea, let him take all,
forasmuch as my lord the king is come again in peace unto his own house.

4. Barzillai Blesses King David

31 ¶And Bar-zil'la-i the Gileadite came down from Ro-ge'lim, and went ☆**19:31** 2 Sam 17:27 1 Kgs 2:7
over Jordan with the king, to conduct him over Jordan.
32 Now Bar-zil'la-i was a very aged man, *even* fourscore years old: and he

---

19:24–30 Being lame, Mephibosheth was unable to join David's army and fight for his king. He did the next best thing. He was melancholy over David's plight and forsook the amenities of life, spending his time in mourning as he waited for the return of David. He explained his innocence of the crime attributed to him by Ziba and received back his estate, which he promptly refused in his delight that the king had come back safely. David apparently forgave Ziba either because he feared him or he loved him so much that the penalty was not laid on him according to the law (see Deut. 19:18, 19).

19:31 Faithful Barzillai had rendered great service to David when he was in great need. He supplied David with provisions and thus supported him against Absalom and the revolution. He came with David on his return to Jerusalem when he crossed the Jordan. David wanted to reward him by inviting him to be his guest in royal splendor at the court. Barzillai, who was eighty years old, quietly and tactfully declined the honor so that he could return to his own home in quietness and peace.

had provided the king of sustenance while he lay at Ma-ha-na'im; for he
was a very great man.
33 And the king said unto Bar-zil'la-i, Come thou over with me, and I will
feed thee with me in Jerusalem.
34 And Bar-zil'la-i said unto the king, How long have I to live, that I
should go up with the king unto Jerusalem?
19:35 Ps 90:10, 13 — 35 I *am* this day fourscore years old: *and* can I discern between good and
evil? can thy servant taste what I eat or what I drink? can I hear any more
the voice of singing men and singing women? wherefore then should thy
servant be yet a burden unto my lord the king?
36 Thy servant will go a little way over Jordan with the king: and why
should the king recompense it me with such a reward?
19:37☆ 1 Kgs 2:7 — 37 Let thy servant, I pray thee, turn back again, that I may die in mine
own city, *and be buried* by the grave of my father and of my mother. But
behold thy servant Chim'ham; let him go over with my lord the king; and
do to him what shall seem good unto thee.
38 And the king answered, Chim'ham shall go over with me, and I will do
to him that which shall seem good unto thee: and whatsoever thou shalt
require of me, *that* will I do for thee.
19:39 Gen 31:55; Ruth 1:14; 2 Sam 14:33 — 39 And all the people went over Jordan. And when the king was come
over, the king kissed Bar-zil'la-i, and blessed him; and he returned unto his
own place.
40 Then the king went on to Gilgal, and Chim'ham went on with him: and
all the people of Judah conducted the king, and also half the people of
Israel.

5. Israel's Jealousy of Judah

19:41☆ — 41 ¶And, behold, all the men of Israel came to the king, and said unto the
king, Why have our brethren the men of Judah stolen thee away, and have
brought the king, and his household, and all David's men with him, over
Jordan?
42 And all the men of Judah answered the men of Israel, Because the king
is near of kin to us: wherefore then be ye angry for this matter? have we
eaten at all of the king's *cost?* or hath he given us any gift?
19:43 2 Sam 5:1 — 43 And the men of Israel answered the men of Judah, and said, We have
ten parts in the king, and we have also more *right* in David than ye: why
then did ye despise us, that our advice should not be first had in bringing
back our king? And the words of the men of Judah were fiercer than the
words of the men of Israel.

C. SHEBA'S REBELLION

1. The Call to Insurrection

20:1☆ 1 Sam 16:7, 8; 1 Kgs 12:16; 2 Chron 10:16

20 AND there happened to be there a man of Be'li-al, whose name *was*
She'ba, the son of Bich'ri, a Benjamite: and he blew a trumpet, and

---

19:37 *Chimham.* According to Josephus, Chimham was Barzillai's son.†

19:41ff Here David is returning home to a divided people. The ten tribes had been overlooked, as the people of Judah brought David home. They were angry for not having been invited to participate and said so with some vehemence. Explanations were offered to the effect that David came from the tribe of Judah and is their own kin. The last line is clear enough: "The words of the men of Judah were fiercer than the words of the men of Israel." The Judeans lacked humility and trusted in force.

20:1 Sheba used the disaffection between the north and the south to gain the support of the northerners against David and Judah.

said, We have no part in David, neither have we inheritance in the son of
Jesse: every man to his tents, O Israel.
2So every man of Israel went up from after David, *and* followed She'ba
the son of Bich'ri: but the men of Judah clave unto their king, from Jordan
even to Jerusalem.

20:2 2 Sam 19:15, 41

3¶And David came to his house at Jerusalem; and the king took the ten
women *his* concubines, whom he had left to keep the house, and put them
in ward, and fed them, but went not in unto them. So they were shut up
unto the day of their death, living in widowhood.

☆**20:3** 2 Sam 15:16 16:21, 22

2. Joab Slays Amasa

4¶Then said the king to Am'a-sa, Assemble me the men of Judah within
three days, and be thou here present.

☆**20:4** 2 Sam 17:25 19:13

5So Am'a-sa went to assemble *the men of* Judah: but he tarried longer
than the set time which he had appointed him.

☆**20:5**

6And David said to A-bish'a-i, Now shall She'ba the son of Bich'ri do us
more harm than *did* Ab'sa-lom: take thou thy lord's servants, and pursue
after him, lest he get him fenced cities, and escape us.

20:6 2 Sam 18:2, 12 21:7

7And there went out after him Jo'ab's men, and the Cher'e-thites, and the
Pel'e-thites, and all the mighty men: and they went out of Jerusalem, to
pursue after She'ba the son of Bich'ri,

20:7 2 Sam 8:18 15:17, 18 1 Kgs 1:38

8When they *were* at the great stone which *is* in Gibeon, Am'a-sa went
before them. And Jo'ab's garment that he had put on was girded unto him,
and upon it a girdle *with* a sword fastened upon his loins in the sheath
thereof; and as he went forth it fell out.

20:8 2 Sam 2:13 3:27 1 Kgs 2:5 Mt 26:49

9And Jo'ab said to Am'a-sa, *Art* thou in health, my brother? And Jo'ab
took Am'a-sa by the beard with the right hand to kiss him.
10But Am'a-sa took no heed to the sword that *was* in Jo'ab's hand: so he
smote him therewith in the fifth *rib*, and shed out his bowels to the ground,
and struck him not again; and he died. So Jo'ab and A-bish'a-i his brother
pursued after She'ba the son of Bich'ri,

3. Joab's Pursuit of Sheba

11And one of Jo'ab's men stood by him, and said, He that favoureth
Jo'ab, and he that *is* for David, *let him go* after Jo'ab.
12And Am'a-sa wallowed in blood in the midst of the highway. And when
the man saw that all the people stood still, he removed Am'a-sa out of the
highway into the field, and cast a cloth upon him, when he saw that every
one that came by him stood still.
13When he was removed out of the highway, all the people went on after
Jo'ab, to pursue after She'ba the son of Bich'ri.

20:3 David's ten concubines, who had been left behind when he fled, were rendered unclean by their defilement by Absalom. Those Absalom had sinfully taken for pleasure must now be put away for life. In order that Absalom's "villany might be buried in oblivion, they must be buried in obscurity."*

20:4 Amasa's mother was a sister of David. He was Joab's cousin. Amasa led Absalom's army. Following the defeat of Absalom, King David pardoned Amasa, then appointed him as captain of his army instead of Joab. Some have suggested that Joab had lost favor with the king when he deliberately disobeyed David's instructions to deal gently with Absalom. When Sheba revolted, David commanded Amasa to call up the army in three days. When he failed to fulfill the deadline, Abishai was called upon to suppress the revolt. At Gibeon, Amasa's army joined that of Abishai. Joab slew Amasa (20:10) and then led the combined forces to victory over Sheba.

20:5 *Amasa* was hardly the equal of Joab, whom he replaced.

4. The Death of Sheba

20:14☆ 14¶And he went through all the tribes of Israel unto Abel, and to Beth-
ma′a-chah, and all the Be′rites: and they were gathered together, and went
also after him.
20:15 15And they came and besieged him in Abel of Beth-ma′a-chah, and they
2 Kgs 19:32 Ezek 4:2 cast up a bank against the city, and it stood in the trench: and all the people
that *were* with Jo′ab battered the wall, to throw it down.
20:16☆ 16¶Then cried a wise woman out of the city, Hear, hear; say, I pray you,
unto Jo′ab, Come near hither, that I may speak with thee.
17And when he was come near unto her, the woman said, *Art* thou Jo′ab?
And he answered, I *am he.* Then she said unto him, Hear the words of thine
handmaid. And he answered, I do hear.
18Then she spake, saying, They were wont to speak in old time, saying,
They shall surely ask *counsel* at Abel: and so they ended *the matter.*
20:19 19I *am one of them that are* peaceable *and* faithful in Israel: thou seekest
Deut 20:10 2 Sam 14:15, 16 to destroy a city and a mother in Israel: why wilt thou swallow up the
inheritance of the LORD?
20And Jo′ab answered and said, Far be it, far be it from me, that I should
swallow up or destroy.
20:21 21The matter *is* not so: but a man of mount E′phra-im, She′ba the son of
Josh 24:33 2 Sam 20:2 Bich′ri by name, hath lifted up his hand against the king, *even* against
David: deliver him only, and I will depart from the city. And the woman
said unto Jo′ab, Behold, his head shall be thrown to thee over the wall.
20:22 22Then the woman went unto all the people in her wisdom. And they cut
2 Sam 2:28 8:16 off the head of She′ba the son of Bich′ri, and cast *it* out to Jo′ab. And he
blew a trumpet, and they retired from the city, every man to his tent. And
Jo′ab returned to Jerusalem unto the king.
20:23☆ 23¶Now Jo′ab *was* over all the host of Israel: and Be-nai′ah the son of Je-
hoi′a-da *was* over the Cher′e-thites and over the Pel′e-thites:
20:24 24And A-do′ram *was* over the tribute: and Je-hosh′a-phat the son of
1 Kgs 12:18 A-hi′lud *was* recorder:
25And She′va *was* scribe: and Za′dok and A-bi′a-thar *were* the priests:
20:26 26And Ira also the Ja′ir-ite was a chief ruler about David.
2 Sam 23:34

VI. DAVID'S LATTER YEARS (21:1—24:25)

A. THE THREE-YEAR FAMINE

1. The Cause of the Famine: Saul's Slaughter of the Gibeonites

21:1☆ 21 THEN there was a famine in the days of David three years, year
Gen 12:10 26:1; 42:5 after year; and David inquired of the LORD. And the LORD
Num 27:21 answered, *It is* for Saul, and for *his* bloody house, because he slew the
Gib′e-o-nites.

20:14 *Abel, . . . Beth-maachah* ("Beth-maacah" in TLB, RSV). Abel was located in the most northern part of what is now Palestine, an area populated by the sons of Naphtali.

20:16 Apparently the men of Beth-maachah either feared Sheba or were unconcerned for the safety of their community, for they did nothing. An unnamed, discreet, and wise woman played the role of mediator by going to Joab and pleading for the city. Joab wisely declared that his only interest was to capture Sheba, the leader of the revolt. She agreed to throw the head of the rebel over the wall of the city, if Joab would leave the city and its inhabitants free from war. He consented. And after counsel in the city, Sheba was slain and his head dropped over the wall. The revolt ended and Joab, who had slain Amasa, was once again in full control of the military.

20:23 *the Cherithites and over the Pelethites,* i.e., "the king's bodyguard."†

21:1 God had promised Israel plentiful harvests and adequate rain. Yet here drought, or famine, occurred for three years. Apparently, it was expected that the situation would be reversed at the end of the first year. But it did not change. We wonder why David did not ask God about the reason for the famine until the end of the third year. He appears to have been remiss. This much we do know: Saul had violated the agreement

[2]And the king called the Gib'e-o-nites, and said unto them; (now the
Gib'e-o-nites *were* not of the children of Israel, but of the remnant of the
Am'or-ites; and the children of Israel had sworn unto them: and Saul
sought to slay them in his zeal to the children of Israel and Judah.)
[3]Wherefore David said unto the Gib'e-o-nites, What shall I do for you?
and wherewith shall I make the atonement, that ye may bless the
inheritance of the LORD?
[4]And the Gib'e-o-nites said unto him, We will have no silver nor gold of
Saul, nor of his house; neither for us shalt thou kill any man in Israel. And
he said, What ye shall say, *that* will I do for you.
[5]And they answered the king, The man that consumed us, and that
devised against us *that* we should be destroyed from remaining in any of the
coasts of Israel,
[6]Let seven men of his sons be delivered unto us, and we will hang them
up unto the LORD in Gib'e-ah of Saul, *whom* the LORD did choose. And the
king said, I will give *them*.

21:2 Ex 34:11; Josh 9:15–20; 1 Sam 7:14
21:4 Num 35:31
21:5 Num 25:4; 2 Sam 21:1

2. The Gibeonites Hang Seven of Saul's Relatives

[7]But the king spared Me-phib'o-sheth, the son of Jonathan the son of
Saul, because of the LORD's oath that *was* between them, between David
and Jonathan the son of Saul.
[8]But the king took the two sons of Riz'pah the daughter of A-i'ah, whom
she bare unto Saul, Ar-mo'ni and Me-phib'o-sheth; and the five sons of
Mi'chal the daughter of Saul, whom she brought up for A'dri-el the son of
Bar-zil'la-i the Me-hol'ath-ite:
[9]And he delivered them into the hands of the Gib'e-o-nites and they
hanged them in the hill before the LORD: and they fell *all* seven together,
and were put to death in the days of harvest, in the first *days,* in the
beginning of barley harvest.

21:7 1 Sam 18:1–3; 20:14, 15; 23:18; 2 Sam 4:4
☆**21:8** 1 Sam 18:19; 2 Sam 3:7

3. Saul, Jonathan, and the Seven Buried in the Grave of Kish

[10]¶And Riz'pah the daughter of A-i'ah took sackcloth, and spread it for
her upon the rock, from the beginning of harvest until water dropped upon
them out of heaven, and suffered neither the birds of the air to rest on them
by day, nor the beasts of the field by night.
[11]And it was told David what Riz'pah the daughter of A-i'ah, the
concubine of Saul, had done.
[12]¶And David went and took the bones of Saul and the bones of
Jonathan his son from the men of Ja'besh-gil'e-ad, which had stolen them
from the street of Beth'-shan, where the Philistines had hanged them, when
the Philistines had slain Saul in Gil-bo'a:

21:10 Deut 21:23; 1 Sam 17:44
21:12 2 Sam 2:4, 5; 24:25

---

with the Gibeonites, and even though the consequences were delayed, they arrived at last. When David asked God about the famine, he was told that it was caused by Saul's failure. When the proper steps were taken, the famine ceased. Thus we learn that famines are sometimes sent by God because of transgressions. Therefore, we should never presume that famines are accidental until we have sought God to discover the reason for them, and with the intention of correcting the problem if there is any.

21:8 David saved the life of Mephibosheth so that while he avenged the breaking of the oath to the Gibeonites, he would not break his oath to Jonathan and his son. He turned over seven sons of Saul, who were hung by the Gibeonites who did so as unto the Lord God. Hanging was the symbol of being accursed. So Christ was to be accursed for our transgressions as he hung upon the tree. In this instance the guilt of the house of Saul was expiated for the blood of the priests and their families, as well as for the breach of the oath with the Gibeonites. "These executions must not be complained of as cruel which have become necessary to the public welfare. Better that seven of Saul's bloody house be hanged than that all Israel be famished."*

13 And he brought up from thence the bones of Saul and the bones of
Jonathan his son; and they gathered the bones of them that were hanged.
14 And the bones of Saul and Jonathan his son buried they in the country
of Benjamin in Ze′lah, in the sepulchre of Kish his father: and they
performed all that the king commanded. And after that God was intreated
for the land.

B. DAVID DEFEATS THE PHILISTINES AGAIN

21:15 2 Sam 5:17
15 ¶Moreover the Philistines had yet war again with Israel; and David
went down, and his servants with him, and fought against the Philistines:
and David waxed faint.

21:16 Num 13:28; Deut 1:28
16 And Ish′bi–be′nob, which *was* of the sons of the giant, the weight of
whose spear *weighed* three hundred *shekels* of brass in weight, he being
girded with a new *sword,* thought to have slain David.

21:17 2 Sam 18:2; 20:6
17 But A-bish′a-i the son of Zer-u-i′ah succoured him, and smote the
Philistine, and killed him. Then the men of David sware unto him, saying,
Thou shalt go no more out with us to battle, that thou quench not the light
of Israel.

21:18 1 Chron 11:29; 20:4–8; 27:11
18 And it came to pass after this, that there was again a battle with the
Philistines at Gob: then Sib′be-chai the Hu′shath-ite slew Saph, which *was*
of the sons of the giant.

21:19☆ 1 Sam 17:4–7
19 And there was again a battle in Gob with the Philistines, where El-
ha′nan the son of Ja-ar′e–or′e-gim, a Beth–lehemite, slew *the brother of*
Goliath the Git′tite, the staff of whose spear *was* like a weaver's beam.
20 And there was yet a battle in Gath, where was a man of *great* stature,
that had on every hand six fingers, and on every foot six toes, four and
twenty in number; and he also was born to the giant.
21 And when he defied Israel, Jonathan the son of Shim′e-a the brother of
David slew him.

21:22 1 Chron 20:8
22 These four were born to the giant in Gath, and fell by the hand of
David, and by the hand of his servants.

C. DAVID'S SONG OF PRAISE TO THE LORD

22:1☆ Ex 15:1; Deut 31:30; Judg 5:1; Ps 18 Title
22:2 Deut 32:4; 1 Sam 2:2; Ps 31:3; 71:3
22:3 Gen 15:1; Deut 33:29; Ps 3:3; 9:9; Lk 1:69
22:4 Ps 66:2, 3; 96:4
22:5 Ps 69:14; 93:4; Jonah 2:3

22 AND David spake unto the LORD the words of this song in the day
that the LORD had delivered him out of the hand of all his enemies,
and out of the hand of Saul:
2 And he said, The LORD *is* my rock, and my fortress, and my deliverer;
3 The God of my rock; in him will I trust: *he is* my shield, and the horn of
my salvation, my high tower, and my refuge, my saviour; thou savest me
from violence.
4 I will call on the LORD, *who is* worthy to be praised: so shall I be saved
from mine enemies.
5 When the waves of death compassed me, the floods of ungodly men
made me afraid;

21:19 *slew the brother of Goliath the Gittite.* The words *the brother of* do not appear in the Masoretic Text; they were added on the basis of 1 Chron. 20:5, the parallel record. David slew Goliath; Elhanan slew Goliath's brother.

22:1 David sang this glorious song *in the day that the LORD had delivered him.* He did not wait until long after the deliverance to praise God. He expressed his gratitude quickly. He expressed what he declared in Psalm 34:19: "Many are the afflictions of the righteous: but the LORD delivereth him out of them all." The believer will experience affliction and will not be delivered from all of his enemies until he gets to heaven. But God will preserve him so that he does get there. The song of David was no doubt inspired by the Holy Spirit. It is replete with delightful phrases such as "my fortress," "my rock," "my salvation," "my shield," and "the tower of salvation."

6 The sorrows of hell compassed me about; the snares of death prevented
me;
7 In my distress I called upon the LORD, and cried to my God: and he did
hear my voice out of his temple, and my cry *did enter* into his ears.
8 Then the earth shook and trembled; the foundations of heaven moved
and shook, because he was wroth.
9 There went up a smoke out of his nostrils, and fire out of his mouth
devoured: coals were kindled by it.
10 He bowed the heavens also, and came down; and darkness *was* under
his feet.
11 And he rode upon a cherub, and did fly: and he was seen upon the
wings of the wind.
12 And he made darkness pavilions round about him, dark waters, *and*
thick clouds of the skies.
13 Through the brightness before him were coals of fire kindled.
14 The LORD thundered from heaven, and the most High uttered his voice.
15 And he sent out arrows, and scattered them; lightning, and discomfited
them.
16 And the channels of the sea appeared, the foundations of the world
were discovered, at the rebuking of the LORD, at the blast of the breath of
his nostrils.
17 He sent from above, he took me; he drew me out of many waters;
18 He delivered me from my strong enemy, *and* from them that hated me:
for they were too strong for me.
19 They prevented me in the day of my calamity: but the LORD was my
stay.
20 He brought me forth also into a large place: he delivered me, because
he delighted in me.
21 The LORD rewarded me according to my righteousness: according to
the cleanness of my hands hath he recompensed me.
22 For I have kept the ways of the LORD, and have not wickedly departed
from my God.
23 For all his judgments *were* before me: and *as for* his statutes, I did not
depart from them.
24 I was also upright before him, and have kept myself from mine iniquity.
25 Therefore the LORD hath recompensed me according to my righteous-
ness; according to my cleanness in his eye sight.
26 With the merciful thou wilt shew thyself merciful, *and* with the upright
man thou wilt shew thyself upright.
27 With the pure thou wilt shew thyself pure; and with the froward thou
wilt shew thyself unsavoury.
28 And the afflicted people thou wilt save: but thine eyes *are* upon the
haughty, *that* thou mayest bring *them* down.
29 For thou *art* my lamp, O LORD; and the LORD will lighten my darkness.

22:6 Ps 116:3, 4
☆**22:7**
☆**22:8** Judg 5:4; Job 26:11; Ps 97:4
22:9 Ex 15:7; 19:18; Deut 32:22; Heb 12:29
22:10 Ex 20:21; 1 Kgs 8:12, 13; Ps 97:2; Nah 1:3
22:11 Ps 68:17, 18
22:12 Ps 18:11, 12; 97:2
22:14 Ex 19:19; Job 37:2; Ps 29:3
22:15 Deut 32:23; Josh 10:10; 1 Sam 7:10
22:16 Ex 15:8; Nah 1:4
22:17 Ps 144:7
22:18 Ps 23:4
☆**22:20** 2 Sam 4:9; 1 Kgs 1:29; Ps 31:8; 118:5
22:21 1 Sam 26:23; Ps 24:5; 128:1
☆**22:22**
☆**22:23** Deut 6:6; Ps 119:6
☆**22:24** Gen 6:9, 10; 7:1; Job 1:8; 9:20
☆**22:25** Isa 3:10
22:26 Mt 5:7; Jas 2:13
22:27 Lev 26:23, 24; Deut 28:58, 59; Ps 125:4, 5; Mt 5:8
22:28 Ex 3:7, 8; Ps 72:12, 13; Isa 2:11, 12, 17; 5:15
22:29 Ps 27:1; 84:11

22:7 David's deliverance was an answer to prayer. Distress is always an occasion for us to seek the face of God and plead for help.

22:8ff In response to David's prayers God manifested himself and his power in great and unusual ways. God is ready to help and to protect those who know him and love him. No one can stand up against God when he is angry on behalf of his people.

22:20 God's favor and deliverance did not come from common providence. Rather it sprang from his covenant-love, which guarantees the promise of God to deliver those who trust in him.

22:22–25 David here claims he has followed the commandments of God and thus stands righteous in his sight. He did not, in fact, always keep the commandments of God. But he did repent, confess, and was cleansed from his iniquity. We, like David, do sin and like him we can repent, confess, and be cleansed so that our relationship may remain unimpaired.

22:30☆ Ps 18:29
22:31 Deut 32:4; 2 Sam 22:3; Ps 12:6; 119:140; Prov 30:5; Mt 5:48
22:32☆ 1 Sam 2:2; Isa 44:6, 8
22:33☆
22:34 Ps 18:33
22:35 Ps 144:1
22:36 2 Sam 22:3; Eph 6:16
22:37 Ps 18:36; 31:8; 66:9
22:38 2 Sam 8:1, 2; Ps 18:37; 21:8–10; 110:1
22:39 Mal 4:3
22:40 Ps 18:32; Isa 45:5
22:41 Ex 23:27; Ps 18:40, 41
22:42 1 Sam 28:5, 6; Job 27:9; Isa 1:15
22:43 Ps 18:42; Isa 10:6; Mic 7:10
22:44 2 Sam 3:1; 5:1; 8:1; 19:8–10
22:45☆ Ps 66:3; 72:8–10; Isa 55:5; 60:12
22:46☆ Isa 2:19; Mic 7:17
22:47 2 Sam 22:2, 32; Ps 89:26
22:48 1 Sam 24:12; 25:39; 2 Sam 18:19; Ps 94:1; 144:2
22:49 Ps 44:5; 140:1, 4, 11
22:50 Ps 18:49; Rom 15:9
22:51☆ 2 Sam 7:12; Ps 18:50; 89:20; 144:10

30 For by thee I have run through a troop: by my God have I leaped over a wall.

31 *As for* God, his way *is* perfect; the word of the LORD *is* tried: he *is* a buckler to all them that trust in him.

32 For who *is* God, save the LORD? and who *is* a rock, save our God?

33 God *is* my strength *and* power: and he maketh my way perfect.

34 He maketh my feet like hinds' *feet:* and setteth me upon my high places.

35 He teacheth my hands to war; so that a bow of steel is broken by mine arms.

36 Thou hast also given me the shield of thy salvation: and thy gentleness hath made me great.

37 Thou hast enlarged my steps under me; so that my feet did not slip.

38 I have pursued mine enemies, and destroyed them; and turned not again until I had consumed them.

39 And I have consumed them, and wounded them, that they could not arise: yea, they are fallen under my feet.

40 For thou hast girded me with strength to battle: them that rose up against me hast thou subdued under me.

41 Thou hast also given me the necks of mine enemies, that I might destroy them that hate me.

42 They looked, but *there was* none to save; *even* unto the LORD, but he answered them not.

43 Then did I beat them as small as the dust of the earth, I did stamp them as the mire of the street, *and* did spread them abroad.

44 Thou also hast delivered me from the strivings of my people, thou hast kept me *to be* head of the heathen: a people *which* I knew not shall serve me.

45 Strangers shall submit themselves unto me: as soon as they hear, they shall be obedient unto me.

46 Strangers shall fade away, and they shall be afraid out of their close places.

47 The LORD liveth; and blessed *be* my rock; and exalted be the God of the rock of my salvation.

48 It *is* God that avengeth me, and that bringeth down the people under me,

49 And that bringeth me forth from mine enemies: thou also hast lifted me up on high above them that rose up against me: thou hast delivered me from the violent man.

50 Therefore I will give thanks unto thee, O LORD, among the heathen, and I will sing praises unto thy name.

51 *He is* the tower of salvation for his king: and sheweth mercy to his anointed, unto David, and to his seed for evermore.

22:30 With God's help David can do anything that he needs to do. So can we, according to Phil. 4:13.

22:32 There is no God beside our God and he is a rock or foundation which cannot be shaken. Those who find their rest on that foundation may quake on the rock but the rock will never quake under them.

22:33 *God is my strength and power,* i.e., "God is my strong fortress" (NASB).

22:45, 46 "Even *the sons of the stranger,* that would hear the report of his victories and the tokens of God's presence with him, would be possessed with a fear of him, would be forced to submit to him . . . and would be obedient to him."*

22:51 This verse has messianic implications. The promise of God is to David and to his offspring forever. The Christ of God has a throne and kingdom which shall continue to the end. By the eye of faith, David sees this. Thus, "all his joys and all his hopes terminate, as ours should, in the great Redeemer."*

D. DAVID'S LAST WORDS

23 NOW these *be* the last words of David. David the son of Jesse said,
and the man *who was* raised up on high, the anointed of the God of
Jacob, and the sweet psalmist of Israel, said,
2 The Spirit of the LORD spake by me, and his word *was* in my tongue.
3 The God of Israel said, the Rock of Israel spake to me, He that ruleth
over men *must be* just, ruling in the fear of God.
4 And *he shall be* as the light of the morning, *when* the sun riseth, *even* a
morning without clouds; *as* the tender grass *springing* out of the earth by
clear shining after rain.
5 Although my house *be* not so with God; yet he hath made with me an
everlasting covenant, ordered in all *things,* and sure: for *this is* all my
salvation, and all *my* desire, although he make *it* not to grow.
6 ¶But *the sons* of Be'li-al *shall be* all of them as thorns thrust away,
because they cannot be taken with hands:
7 But the man *that* shall touch them must be fenced with iron and the staff
of a spear; and they shall be utterly burned with fire in the *same* place.

☆**23:1** Gen 49:1; Deut 33:1; Josh 23:2; 1 Sam 16:12, 13; 2 Sam 7:8, 9; Ps 78:70–72; 89:20
☆**23:2** 2 Pet 1:20, 21
☆**23:3** 2 Sam 22:2, 32; 2 Chron 19:7, 9; Ps 72:1; Isa 11:3, 4
23:4 Deut 32:2; Judg 5:31; Ps 72:6; 110:3
☆**23:5** 2 Sam 7:12; Ps 89:29; Isa 55:3
23:6 Mt 13:41, 42
23:7 Mt 3:10; 13:30; Heb 6:8

E. THE DEEDS OF DAVID'S HEROIC MEN

8 ¶These *be* the names of the mighty men whom David had: The
Tach'mo-nite that sat in the seat, chief among the captains; the same *was*
Ad'i-no the Ez'nite: *he lift up his spear* against eight hundred, whom he slew
at one time.
9 And after him *was* E-le-a'zar the son of Dodo the A-ho'hite, *one* of the
three mighty men with David, when they defied the Philistines *that* were
there gathered together to battle, and the men of Israel were gone away:
10 He arose, and smote the Philistines until his hand was weary, and his
hand clave unto the sword: and the LORD wrought a great victory that day;
and the people returned after him only to spoil.
11 And after him *was* Sham'mah the son of Ag'ee the Ha'ra-rite. And the
Philistines were gathered together into a troop, where was a piece of ground
full of lentiles: and the people fled from the Philistines.
12 But he stood in the midst of the ground, and defended it, and slew the
Philistines: and the LORD wrought a great victory.
13 And three of the thirty chief went down, and came to David in the
harvest time unto the cave of A-dul'lam: and the troop of the Philistines
pitched in the valley of Reph'a-im.
14 And David *was* then in an hold, and the garrison of the Philistines *was*
then *in* Beth-lehem.

☆**23:8** 1 Chron 11:11; 27:2
☆**23:9** 1 Chron 11:12; 27:4
☆**23:13** 1 Sam 22:1; 2 Sam 5:18

23:1–3 *The God of Israel said.* The phrase "thus saith the LORD" or its equivalent occurs more than two thousand times in the Old Testament. Thus the prophets attest that what they say is the Word of God. Here David identified the Spirit as speaking through him and says, *his word was in my tongue.* He also claimed that *the Rock of Israel spake* (said) *to me,* and he then stated what God did say. (See also Isa. 8:1, 11; Jer. 1:14; 7:27; 13:12; Ezek. 3:4; Micah 3:8; Hab. 2:2; Heb. 1:1; Matt. 1:22; 2:15; Acts 1:16; 28:25.)

23:5 *all my desire, although he make it not to grow,* or, "He will cause my help and my desire to sprout."†

23:8 *Adino* (also known as *Josheb-basshebeth*) is said to have slain eight hundred enemies at one time. In 1 Chron. 11:11 Jashobeam (the same person with a different name) is said to have slain three hundred. In Hebrew, the first letter of the words for three and eight is the same. This, then, is a copyist's error.

23:9–12 Eleazar and Shammah along with Adino are said to have been the three mightiest of David's soldiers. Except here and in 1 Chron. 11, there is no mention of these men who are singled out as great warriors. God has not chosen by his Spirit to give us a detailed account of all the glories of David's reign nor does he tell us a great deal about some of its greatest heroes. In eternity we will discover that multitudes of unnamed saints through the ages have done exploits which, unknown now, will be remembered and celebrated in due season.

23:13–17 Of the three mentioned for their devotion to David when he was in flight and who risked their lives

15 And David longed, and said, Oh that one would give me drink of the
water of the well of Beth–lehem, which *is* by the gate!
23:16☆ Gen 35:13 1 Sam 7:6
16 And the three mighty men brake through the host of the Philistines,
and drew water out of the well of Beth–lehem, that *was* by the gate, and
took *it,* and brought *it* to David: nevertheless he would not drink thereof,
but poured it out unto the LORD.
17 And he said, Be it far from me, O LORD, that I should do this: *is not this*
the blood of the men that went in jeopardy of their lives? therefore he
would not drink it. These things did these three mighty men.
23:18☆ 2 Sam 10:10 18:2 1 Chron 11:20
18 And A-bish′a-i, the brother of Jo′ab, the son of Zer-u-i′ah, was chief
among three. And he lifted up his spear against three hundred, *and* slew
them, and had the name among three.
19 Was he not most honourable of three? therefore he was their captain:
howbeit he attained not unto the *first* three.
23:20☆ Josh 15:21 2 Sam 8:18 20:23 1 Kgs 4:1–6
20 And Be-nai′ah the son of Je-hoi′a-da, the son of a valiant man, of
Kab′ze-el, who had done many acts, he slew two lionlike men of Moab: he
went down also and slew a lion in the midst of a pit in time of snow:
21 And he slew an Egyptian, a goodly man: and the Egyptian had a spear
in his hand; but he went down to him with a staff, and plucked the spear
out of the Egyptian's hand, and slew him with his own spear.
22 These *things* did Be-nai′ah the son of Je-hoi′a-da, and had the name
among three mighty men.
23 He was more honourable than the thirty, but he attained not to the *first*
three. And David set him over his guard.
23:24–39☆
24 As′a-hel the brother of Jo′ab *was* one of the thirty; El-ha′nan the son of
Dodo of Beth–lehem.
25 Sham′mah the Ha′rod-ite, E-li′ka the Ha′rod-ite,
26 He′lez the Pal′tite, Ira the son of Ik′kesh the Te-ko′ite,
27 A-bi-e′zer the An′e-thoth-ite, Me-bun′nai the Hu′shath-ite,
28 Zal′mon the A-ho′hite, Ma-har′a-i the Ne-toph′a-thite,
29 He′leb the son of Ba′a-nah, a Ne-toph′a-thite, It′ta-i the son of Ri′bai
out of Gib′e-ah of the children of Benjamin,
30 Be-nai′ah the Pir′a-thon-ite, Hid′da-i of the brooks of Ga′ash,
31 A′bi-al′bon the Ar′bath-ite, Az′ma-veth the Bar-hu′mite,
32 E-li′ah-ba the Sha-al′bo-nite, of the sons of Ja′shen, Jonathan,
33 Sham′mah the Ha′ra-rite, A-hi′am the son of Sha′rar the Ha′ra-rite,
34 E-liph′e-let the son of A-has′ba-i, the son of the Ma-ach′a-thite, E-li′am
the son of A-hith′o-phel the Gi′lo-nite,
35 Hez′ra-i the Carmelite, Pa′a-rai the Ar′bite,
36 I′gal the son of Nathan of Zo′bah, Ba′ni the Gadite,
37 Ze′lek the Ammonite, Na′ha-ri the Be-e′roth-ite, armourbearer to Jo′ab
the son of Zer-u-i′ah,
38 Ira an Ith′rite, Ga′reb an Ith′rite,
39 U-ri′ah the Hittite: thirty and seven in all.

---

to bring him water, only two are named in the Scriptures: Abishai and Benaiah. Their exceptional bravery for labor beyond the call of duty is recorded for us who may follow their example by works above what we are commanded to do.

23:18–23 Abishai and Benaiah, who were two of the three who brought water to David, are here mentioned for other acts of bravery by which they distinguished themselves. There are degrees of greatness and while they did not match the first three mighty men, they are worthy of acclaim. We cannot all be Luthers, Calvins, or Grahams, but we can do notable works for God on a lesser level.

23:24–39 The remainder of the thirty great soldiers are here recorded. Perhaps the one of special interest is Uriah the Hittite, who was basely treated by David. The number thirty-seven indicates that the "thirty" comprised an elite group to which was added successors for those who died in battle or from some disease. While thirty composed the group, there were different people in that group for the reason just mentioned.

F. DAVID TAKES A NATIONAL CENSUS
1. The Headcount of the People

24 AND again the anger of the LORD was kindled against Israel, and
he moved David against them to say, Go, number Israel and Judah.
2 For the king said to Jo'ab the captain of the host, which *was* with him,
Go now through all the tribes of Israel, from Dan even to Be'er-she'ba, and
number ye the people, that I may know the number of the people.
3 And Jo'ab said unto the king, Now the LORD thy God add unto the
people, how many soever they be, an hundredfold, and that the eyes of my
lord the king may see *it:* but why doth my lord the king delight in this
thing?
4 Notwithstanding the king's word prevailed against Jo'ab, and against
the captains of the host. And Jo'ab and the captains of the host went out
from the presence of the king, to number the people of Israel.
5 ¶And they passed over Jordan, and pitched in Ar'o-er, on the right side
of the city that *lieth* in the midst of the river of Gad, and toward Ja'zer:
6 Then they came to Gilead, and to the land of Tah'tim-hod'shi; and they
came to Dan-ja'an, and about to Zi'don,
7 And came to the strong hold of Tyre, and to all the cities of the Hi'vites,
and of the Canaanites: and they went out to the south of Judah, *even* to
Be'er-she'ba.
8 So when they had gone through all the land, they came to Jerusalem at
the end of nine months and twenty days.
9 And Jo'ab gave up the sum of the number of the people unto the king:
and there were in Israel eight hundred thousand valiant men that drew the
sword; and the men of Judah *were* five hundred thousand men.

☆**24:1** 2 Sam 6:7; 1 Kgs 16:33
24:2 Judg 20:1; 2 Sam 3:9, 10
☆**24:3** Deut 1:11
24:5 Num 21:32; 32:34–36; Josh 13:9, 16
24:6 Gen 31:21, 47; Josh 19:28; 2 Sam 17:26
☆**24:9** Num 1:20–46; 1 Chron 21:5

2. David Chooses His Punishment

10 ¶And David's heart smote him after that he had numbered the people.
And David said unto the LORD, I have sinned greatly in that I have done:
and now, I beseech thee, O LORD, take away the iniquity of thy servant; for
I have done very foolishly.
11 For when David was up in the morning, the word of the LORD came
unto the prophet Gad, David's seer, saying,
12 Go and say unto David, Thus saith the LORD, I offer thee three *things;*
choose thee one of them, that I may *do it* unto thee.
13 So Gad came to David, and told him, and said unto him, Shall seven
years of famine come unto thee in thy land? or wilt thou flee three months
before thine enemies, while they pursue thee? or that there be three days'

☆**24:10** 1 Sam 24:5; 2 Sam 12:13; 1 Chron 21:8
24:11 1 Sam 22:5; 1 Chron 29:29; 2 Chron 29:25, 26
24:13 1 Chron 21:12

24:1 Here the text says that *God* incited David against Israel. 1 Chron. 21:1 says that *Satan* made David do it. Both are true. God was the ultimate cause, Satan the proximate one. We do not know why God was angry with David and allowed Satan as the secondary agent to cause David to number the people. David did not consult with God before he gave the order nor was there any pressing need to count heads. Yet good was to come out of this evil, for the land David bought from Araunah was later to become the site on which the temple was built.

24:3 At this point Joab seems to have had more wisdom than David. He pointed out to the king that there was no good reason for taking a census. This raises the question whether the taking of a census was forbidden by God. There is nothing in the Scriptures which forbade the taking of a census. But since the previous ones were mandated by God, it appears that David would have been well advised to consult God before he ordered this census. This he failed to do. When believers move forward on their own, without consulting God, they often make mistakes that could have been averted.

24:9 The numbers here differ from those in 1 Chron. 21:5. The difference may be accounted for by the inclusion or exclusion of the men in the standing army.

24:10 The census was nine months in the taking, and it was not until the job was finished that David came under conviction of sin. His penitent reflection came before the prophet Gad arrived by God's order to pronounce judgment on his act. He was given a choice from three options, any one of which would serve as a proper penalty for his transgression. David did not wish to fall under the hand of any man and so he chose pestilence from the hand of God.

pestilence in thy land? now advise, and see what answer I shall return to him that sent me.

24:14 Ps 51:1; 130:3, 4

14 And David said unto Gad, I am in a great strait: let us fall now into the hand of the LORD; for his mercies *are* great: and let me not fall into the hand of man.

3. The Plague

24:15☆ Num 16:46; 24:9; 1 Sam 6:19; 1 Chron 21:14; 27:24

15 ¶So the LORD sent a pestilence upon Israel from the morning even to the time appointed: and there died of the people from Dan even to Be′er-she′ba seventy thousand men.

24:16☆ Ex 12:23; 32:14; 2 Kgs 19:35; 2 Chron 32:21

16 And when the angel stretched out his hand upon Jerusalem to destroy it, the LORD repented him of the evil, and said to the angel that destroyed the people, It is enough: stay now thine hand. And the angel of the LORD was by the threshingplace of A-rau′nah the Jeb′u-site.

24:17 2 Sam 7:8; 1 Kgs 22:17; Ps 74:1

17 And David spake unto the LORD when he saw the angel that smote the people, and said, Lo, I have sinned, and I have done wickedly: but these sheep, what have they done? let thine hand, I pray thee, be against me, and against my father's house.

4. David's Offering Stops the Plague

24:18 1 Chron 21:15; 2 Chron 3:1

18 ¶And Gad came that day to David, and said unto him, Go up, rear an altar unto the LORD in the threshingfloor of A-rau′nah the Jeb′u-site.

19 And David, according to the saying of Gad, went up as the LORD commanded.

20 And A-rau′nah looked, and saw the king and his servants coming on toward him: and A-rau′nah went out, and bowed himself before the king on his face upon the ground.

21 And A-rau′nah said, Wherefore is my lord the king come to his servant? And David said, To buy the threshingfloor of thee, to build an altar unto the LORD, that the plague may be stayed from the people.

24:22☆ 1 Sam 6:14; 1 Kgs 19:21

22 And A-rau′nah said unto David, Let my lord the king take and offer up what *seemeth* good unto him: behold, *here be* oxen for burnt sacrifice, and threshing instruments and *other* instruments of the oxen for wood.

23 All these *things* did A-rau′nah, *as* a king, give unto the king. And A-rau′nah said unto the king, The LORD thy God accept thee.

24:24 Gen 23:16; 1 Chron 21:24

24 And the king said unto A-rau′nah, Nay; but I will surely buy *it* of thee at a price: neither will I offer burnt offerings unto the LORD my God of that which doth cost me nothing. So David bought the threshingfloor and the oxen for fifty shekels of silver.

24:25☆

25 And David built there an altar unto the LORD, and offered burnt offerings and peace offerings. So the LORD was intreated for the land, and the plague was stayed from Israel.

24:15 The angel of God's vengeance slew seventy thousand men, from Dan to Beersheba. He was about to destroy Jerusalem when God ordered the angel to stay his hand. Nothing is said to indicate that the plague struck children or women. If it did, the total number who died would have been much greater. Why it should be limited only to the men is not stated.

24:16 When the angel was about to destroy Jerusalem, God stayed his hand. It says *the Lord repented of the evil.* The NASB translates it better: "The LORD relented from the calamity." The NIV says, "The LORD was grieved because of the calamity."

24:22 Araunah was willing to donate the ground on which the offering was to be made, while David was determined to buy it from him. The king had already sinned; he was not about to offer a sacrifice to God on land which cost him nothing. Sometimes believers are cheapskates who profess to love and obey God but wish to do so at the least cost and with a minimum of effort. If God is all he claims to be, then the best is none too good to offer him. After all, he gave the best he had when his Son died on Calvary's cross.

24:25 God was entreated by the sacrifice and in mercy removed the plague. "Christ is our altar, our sacrifice; in him alone we may expect to find favor with God, to escape his wrath, and the sword, the flaming sword of the cherubim who *keep the way of the tree of life.*"*

THE FIRST AND SECOND BOOK OF THE
KINGS
OTHERWISE CALLED THE THIRD AND FOURTH BOOK OF THE KINGS

Authorship, date, and background In the Hebrew canon 1 and 2 Kings were accounted as one book. (See also the introduction to 1 Samuel.) In the Hebrew consonantal text one scroll was sufficient for the present two books. When the vowels were added in the Greek and Latin Bibles, twice as much space was required, and the one book was divided arbitrarily into two.

The title *The Kings* is appropriate since the two books comprised a history of the Jewish people from the death of David and the accession of Solomon to the defeat of Judah before the armies of Nebuchadnezzar in 586 B.C. In the Septuagint, which divided the books of Samuel and Kings into the Books of Kingdoms, 1 and 2 Kings were the third and fourth Books of Kingdoms.

The period of the Kings ranged from the accession of Solomon in 971 B.C. to Jehoiachin in 562 B.C., or more than four centuries. A composite authorship of the book is obvious, for nothing in the text attributes the composition to a single person. It was a compilation of writings which undoubtedly were composed by different prophets across the years who were intent on preserving the religious history of the Jewish people. Prior written documents were used when Kings was finally put together. The book itself mentions the use of the book of The Acts of Solomon (1 Kings 11:41), The Chronicles of the Kings of Judah (passim), and The Chronicles of the Kings of Israel (passim). In addition, large sections of Isaiah 36—39 are found in 2 Kings 18–20. These segments were copied from Isaiah and not vice versa.

Talmudic tradition associated Jeremiah the prophet with the book of Kings except for the final chapter. Since the book was written from a prophetic standpoint, either he or a number of prophets like him wrote the accounts from which the compiler produced the final product and the last chapter. A sixth century B.C. date for the final composition is likely, although much of the material used by the writer existed earlier.

Characteristics and content Kings is characterized by its consistent methodology of handling the reigns of the various monarchs. In general, the accounts report the length of each reign for Judah and Israel. In the case of Judah, the reader is told the name of the monarch's mother and the age of the king at the time of his accession. For the kings who were assassinated, the formula is not used. Each king is appraised (something a court historian would not do), especially in his relationship to God and the covenant. The kings of Israel beginning with Jeroboam are all idolaters who break the first commandment and are unfaithful to God's covenant with his people. Persistent apostasy marks the Northern Kingdom once the division takes place after Solomon's reign. The story of the judgment of God against Israel and its dissolution in 722 B.C. with the fall of Samaria into the hands of Sennacherib is recounted in all of its tragic dimensions.

Prior to the division of the kingdom, the golden age of Solomon is depicted. He erects his own palace and builds the Solomonic Temple. His ventures in commerce and his international relations mark the highest tide in the fortunes of the Israelis. Despite the gift of wisdom, Solomon in his later years is unfaithful to God largely through the influence of his many foreign wives and concubines who lead him into idolatry. Solomon gives recognition to Ashtoreth of the Sidonians; Molech, the god of the Ammonites; and Chemosh, the god of the Moabites for whom he builds shrines east of Jerusalem and within sight of the Temple. This remains a source of spiritual temptation for more than three and a half centuries before it is done away with during the reign of Josiah (2 Kings 23:13).

Kings constantly reinforces the notion that Jerusalem is the only true place for worship. Whoever constructs other shrines or engages in idolatrous worship is looked upon with a critical eye. Kings endorses every reform movement in which idolatry is stamped out and when the covenant between God and his people is renewed or takes on new force. The kingdom of Judah differs from that of Israel (Samaria) in that it experiences periodic revival under good kings such as Jehosphaphat, Hezekiah, and Josiah. Asa and Uzziah too are mentioned as kings who are concerned about the spiritual welfare of their citizens. Hezekiah and Josiah are the only kings of Judah the book of 1 Kings approves wholeheartedly. Jehoram, Ahaz, and Manasseh come in for the harshest denunciations for their iniquitous conduct.

Kings also tells the story of the two greatest prophets of Jewish history after the death of David: Elijah and Elisha, who succeeded him. 1 Kings recounts the miracles and ministry of Elijah; 2 Kings picks up the story of his successor. Four clusters of miracles mark the progress of God's scheme of redemption. The first series comes during Moses' day; the second cluster of miracles occurs under the ministries of Elijah and Elisha; the third cluster comes in the life of Jesus; and the fourth cluster appears in the ministry of the early church at the hands of the apostles. Other miraculous events are scattered through the Bible, of course, but they do not come in marked numbers.

The red thread which runs through 1 and 2 Kings consistently is the spiritual decline of God's people and their loss of affection for God's covenants and his commandments. During the period of the Jewish kingdom(s), as during the forty years in the wilderness, the people of God turn away from him and at last end up in captivity.

Outline

1 Kings:
I. The accession of King Solomon (1:1—2:46)
II. Solomon's kingship (3:1—11:43)
III. The two kingdoms (12:1—22:53)
2 Kings:
IV. The continued history of the divided kingdom (1:1—9:37)
V. The decline and fall of Israel (10:1—17:41)
VI. The kingdom of Judah to the fall of Jerusalem (18:1—25:30)

1 KINGS

I. THE ACCESSION OF KING SOLOMON (1:1—2:46)
A. THE BATTLE FOR THE SUCCESSION
1. David's Last Days

1:1☆ 1 NOW king David was old *and* stricken in years; and they covered him
with clothes, but he gat no heat.
2 Wherefore his servants said unto him, Let there be sought for my lord
the king a young virgin: and let her stand before the king, and let her
cherish him, and let her lie in thy bosom, that my lord the king may get
heat.
1:3 3 So they sought for a fair damsel throughout all the coasts of Israel, and
1 Sam 28:4 found Ab'i-shag a Shu'nam-mite, and brought her to the king.
1 Kgs 2:17
4 And the damsel *was* very fair, and cherished the king, and ministered to
him: but the king knew her not.

2. Adonijah Seeks the Kingship

1:5☆ 5 ¶Then Ad-o-ni'jah the son of Hag'gith exalted himself, saying, I will be
2 Sam 3:4 king: and he prepared him chariots and horsemen, and fifty men to run
1 Chron 3:2 before him.

1:1 David was now seventy years old. His virility and vigor had waned. He who had wives and concubines needed them no more. At the close of his life God was perhaps chastising him because of his escapade with Bath-sheba and the murder of her husband. "Let not the strong man glory in his strength"* for sooner or later it is gone. His youthful lusts had given way to old age and infirmity. Verse 4 is significant: "the king knew her not," i.e., they had no sexual relations.

1:5 *Adonijah* was King David's eldest son after the death of Absalom. He normally would have expected to become king upon his father's death. David did not, however, inform Adonijah that the custom was to be bypassed and that Solomon was the preferred heir. Thus Adonijah was not totally at fault when he made preparations for assuming the throne (see 2:15).

[6]And his father had not displeased him at any time in saying, Why hast
thou done so? and he also *was a* very goodly *man;* and *his mother* bare him
after Ab'sa-lom.
[7]And he conferred with Jo'ab the son of Zer-u-i'ah, and with A-bi'a-thar
the priest: and they following Ad-o-ni'jah helped *him.*
[8]But Za'dok the priest, and Be-nai'ah the son of Je-hoi'a-da, and Nathan
the prophet, and Shim'e-i, and Re'i, and the mighty men which *belonged* to
David, were not with Ad-o-ni'jah.
[9]And Ad-o-ni'jah slew sheep and oxen and fat cattle by the stone of
Zo'he-leth, which *is* by En-ro'gel, and called all his brethren the king's
sons, and all the men of Judah the king's servants:
[10]But Nathan the prophet, and Be-nai'ah, and the mighty men, and
Solomon his brother, he called not.

1:7 1 Sam 22:20; 2 Sam 20:25; 1 Kgs 2:28
1:8 2 Sam 8:18; 12:1; 20:25; 23:20
1:10 2 Sam 12:24

3. Nathan Warns Bath-sheba about Adonijah

[11]¶Wherefore Nathan spake unto Bath'-she-ba the mother of Solomon,
saying, Hast thou not heard that Ad-o-ni'jah the son of Hag'gith doth reign,
and David our lord knoweth *it* not?
[12]Now therefore come, let me, I pray thee, give thee counsel, that thou
mayest save thine own life, and the life of thy son Solomon.
[13]Go and get thee in unto king David, and say unto him, Didst not thou,
my lord, O king, swear unto thine handmaid, saying, Assuredly Solomon
thy son shall reign after me, and he shall sit upon my throne? why then
doth Ad-o-ni'jah reign?
[14]Behold, while thou yet talkest there with the king, I also will come in
after thee, and confirm thy words.

☆1:13 1 Chron 22:9

4. Bath-sheba Asks David to Crown Solomon

[15]¶And Bath'-she-ba went in unto the king into the chamber: and the
king was very old; and Ab'i-shag the Shu'nam-mite ministered unto the
king.
[16]And Bath'-she-ba bowed, and did obeisance unto the king. And the
king said, What wouldest thou?
[17]And she said unto him, My lord, thou swarest by the LORD thy God
unto thine handmaid, *saying,* Assuredly Solomon thy son shall reign after
me, and he shall sit upon my throne.
[18]And now, behold, Ad-o-ni'jah reigneth; and now, my lord the king,
thou knowest *it* not:
[19]And he hath slain oxen and fat cattle and sheep in abundance, and hath
called all the sons of the king, and A-bi'a-thar the priest, and Jo'ab the
captain of the host: but Solomon thy servant hath he not called.
[20]And thou, my lord, O king, the eyes of all Israel *are* upon thee, that
thou shouldest tell them who shall sit on the throne of my lord the king
after him.
[21]Otherwise it shall come to pass, when my lord the king shall sleep with
his fathers, that I and my son Solomon shall be counted offenders.

☆1:16–18
1:20 2 Sam 7:12

1:13 David apparently had sworn to Bath-sheba that Solomon would be his successor. But he certainly had not made that fact public, otherwise Adonijah would have acted differently. Verse 6 leaves the impression that David's relationship to Adonijah in no way disabused him (as heir apparent) that the throne would be his. But Nathan knew what the will of God was in this matter, and he planned to bring it to pass.

1:16–18 Bath-sheba informed David that Adonijah was acting as though he was to inherit the throne. She was asking him to keep his vow and make clear to the nation that Solomon would be king. Why David had not made Solomon co-regent with him at an earlier date and worked him into the high position is not explained.

5. Nathan Supports Bath-sheba's Plea

22¶And, lo, while she yet talked with the king, Nathan the prophet also
came in.
23And they told the king, saying, Behold Nathan the prophet. And when
he was come in before the king, he bowed himself before the king with his
face to the ground.
1:24☆ 24And Nathan said, My lord, O king, hast thou said, Ad-o-ni'jah shall
reign after me, and he shall sit upon my throne?
1:25☆ 25For he is gone down this day, and hath slain oxen and fat cattle and
1 Sam 10:24 sheep in abundance, and hath called all the king's sons, and the captains of
2 Sam 24:24 the host, and A-bi'a-thar the priest; and, behold, they eat and drink before
1 Kgs 1:9 him, and say, God save king Ad-o-ni'jah.
26But me, *even* me thy servant, and Za'dok the priest, and Be-nai'ah the
son of Je-hoi'a-da, and thy servant Solomon, hath he not called.
27Is this thing done by my lord the king, and thou hast not shewed *it* unto
thy servant, who should sit on the throne of my lord the king after him?

6. David Chooses Solomon to Be King

a. David Tells Bath-sheba of His Decision

28¶Then king David answered and said, Call me Bath'-she-ba. And she
came into the king's presence, and stood before the king.
1:29 2 Sam 4:9 29And the king sware, and said, *As* the LORD liveth, that hath redeemed
22:20 my soul out of all distress,
30Even as I sware unto thee by the LORD God of Israel, saying, Assuredly
Solomon thy son shall reign after me, and he shall sit upon my throne in my
stead; even so will I certainly do this day.
1:31 31Then Bath'-she-ba bowed with *her* face to the earth, and did reverence
to the king, and said, Let my lord king David live for ever.

b. David Instructs Zadock and Nathan

1:32ff☆ 32¶And king David said, Call me Za'dok the priest, and Nathan the
2 Sam 19:19 prophet, and Be-nai'ah the son of Je-hoi'a-da. And they came before the
king.
33The king also said unto them, Take with you the servants of your lord,
and cause Solomon my son to ride upon mine own mule, and bring him
down to Gi'hon:
1:34 34And let Za'dok the priest and Nathan the prophet anoint him there
1 Sam 10:1 16:3, 12 king over Israel: and blow ye with the trumpet, and say, God save king
2 Sam 15:10 2 Kgs 9:13 Solomon.
11:13, 14 35Then ye shall come up after him, that he may come and sit upon my

---

1:24 Nathan skillfully reinforced the words of Bath-sheba by asking a question, not stating a conclusion: is Adonijah to be your successor? And he added that people were already shouting, "God save King Adonijah." That was the prompting David needed. (Probably David's memory was failing, as was his strength.)

1:25 Plots and counterplots for kingships were quite common in those days and Israel was no exception. Adonijah employed all the devices he could to obtain the kingship when his father David died. In this verse, we learn that Joab and Abiathar supported Adonijah. This meant he had the backing of the chief priest and the commander of the armed forces. Nathan the prophet was not a supporter of Adonijah, and Zadok, an influential priest, stood with Nathan. Adonijah carefully excluded Nathan, Zadok, Benaiah, and Solomon from the festivities.

1:32ff Once the issue of the succession had been raised, David promptly took steps to ensure that Solomon would succeed him. The details of the decision made clear to all that only another civil war could alter the king's arrangements. His actions were carried out while Adonijah was still feasting with his friends. When it became known that Solomon had ridden on his father's mule, that he had been anointed, and that the people had shouted, "God save King Solomon," Adonijah and his friends feared for their lives. Adonijah promptly "caught hold of the horns of the altar" (1:50).

throne; for he shall be king in my stead: and I have appointed him to be
ruler over Israel and over Judah.
36 And Be-nai′ah the son of Je-hoi′a-da answered the king, and said,
Amen: the LORD God of my lord the king say so *too.*
37 As the LORD hath been with my lord the king, even so be he with
Solomon, and make his throne greater than the throne of my lord king
David.

1:37 Josh 1:5, 17; 1 Sam 20:13; 1 Chron 28:20

c. Solomon Anointed as King

38 So Za′dok the priest, and Nathan the prophet, and Be-nai′ah the son of
Je-hoi′a-da, and the Cher′e-thites, and the Pel′e-thites, went down, and
caused Solomon to ride upon king David's mule, and brought him to
Gi′hon.
39 And Za′dok the priest took an horn of oil out of the tabernacle, and
anointed Solomon. And they blew the trumpet; and all the people said,
God save king Solomon.
40 And all the people came up after him, and the people piped with pipes,
and rejoiced with great joy, so that the earth rent with the sound of them.

1:39 1 Sam 16:3, 13; 1 Kgs 1:34; 1 Chron 16:39; 29:22
1:40 1 Sam 11:15; 2 Kgs 11:13, 14

7. Adonijah Bows before Solomon

41 ¶And Ad-o-ni′jah and all the guests that *were* with him heard *it* as they
had made an end of eating. And when Jo′ab heard the sound of the
trumpet, he said, Wherefore *is this* noise of the city being in an uproar?
42 And while he yet spake, behold, Jonathan the son of A-bi′a-thar the
priest came; and Ad-o-ni′jah said unto him, Come in; for thou *art* a valiant
man, and bringest good tidings.
43 And Jonathan answered and said to Ad-o-ni′jah, Verily our lord king
David hath made Solomon king.
44 And the king hath sent with him Za′dok the priest, and Nathan the
prophet, and Be-nai′ah the son of Je-hoi′a-da, and the Cher′e-thites, and
the Pel′e-thites, and they have caused him to ride upon the king's mule:
45 And Za′dok the priest and Nathan the prophet have anointed him king
in Gi′hon: and they are come up from thence rejoicing, so that the city rang
again. This *is* the noise that ye have heard.
46 And also Solomon sitteth on the throne of the kingdom.
47 And moreover the king's servants came to bless our lord king David,
saying, God make the name of Solomon better than thy name, and make
his throne greater than thy throne. And the king bowed himself upon the
bed.
48 And also thus said the king, Blessed *be* the LORD God of Israel, which
hath given *one* to sit on my throne this day, mine eyes even seeing *it.*
49 And all the guests that *were* with Ad-o-ni′jah were afraid, and rose up,
and went every man his way.
50 ¶And Ad-o-ni′jah feared because of Solomon, and arose, and went, and
caught hold on the horns of the altar.
51 And it was told Solomon, saying, Behold, Ad-o-ni′jah feareth king
Solomon: for, lo, he hath caught hold on the horns of the altar, saying, Let
king Solomon swear unto me to day that he will not slay his servant with
the sword.
52 And Solomon said, If he will shew himself a worthy man, there shall

1:42 2 Sam 18:27
1:48 2 Sam 7:12; 1 Kgs 3:6
1:49 1 Kgs 2:28
☆**1:50**

1:50 *caught hold on the horns of the altar.* This constituted an appeal for sanctuary until his case could be heard in court.

not an hair of him fall to the earth: but if wickedness shall be found in him,
he shall die.

1:53☆

53 So king Solomon sent, and they brought him down from the altar. And
he came and bowed himself to king Solomon: and Solomon said unto him,
Go to thine house.

B. DAVID'S WORDS TO SOLOMON AND HIS DEATH

1. David's Charge to Solomon

2:1 Josh 23:14; Job 16:22; 30:23; Ps 89:48

2 NOW the days of David drew nigh that he should die; and he charged
Solomon his son, saying,
2 I go the way of all the earth: be thou strong therefore, and shew thyself
a man;

2:3☆ Deut 18:18, 19; Josh 1:7; 1 Chron 22:12

3 And keep the charge of the LORD thy God, to walk in his ways, to keep
his statutes, and his commandments, and his judgments, and his testimo-
nies, as it is written in the law of Moses, that thou mayest prosper in all that
thou doest, and whithersoever thou turnest thyself:

2:4 2 Sam 7:12; 1 Kgs 8:25; 9:5; 1 Chron 17:11

4 That the LORD may continue his word which he spake concerning me,
saying, If thy children take heed to their way, to walk before me in truth
with all their heart and with all their soul, there shall not fail thee (said he)
a man on the throne of Israel.

2. David's Last Commands

2:5☆ 2 Sam 3:27; 20:10

5 Moreover thou knowest also what Jo'ab the son of Zer-u-i'ah did to me,
and what he did to the two captains of the hosts of Israel, unto Abner the
son of Ner, and unto Am'a-sa the son of Je'ther, whom he slew, and shed
the blood of war in peace, and put the blood of war upon his girdle that *was*
about his loins, and in his shoes that *were* on his feet.

2:6☆ 1 Kgs 2:31

6 Do therefore according to thy wisdom, and let not his hoar head go
down to the grave in peace.

2:7☆ 2 Sam 17:27; 19:31, 39

7 But shew kindness unto the sons of Bar-zil'la-i the Gileadite, and let
them be of those that eat at thy table: for so they came to me when I fled
because of Ab'sa-lom thy brother.

2:8☆ 2 Sam 16:5–8; 19:16

8 And, behold, *thou hast* with thee Shim'e-i the son of Ge'ra, a Benjamite
of Ba-hu'rim, which cursed me with a grievous curse in the day when I went
to Ma-ha-na'im: but he came down to meet me at Jordan, and I sware to
him by the LORD, saying, I will not put thee to death with the sword.

2:9☆ 1 Kgs 2:46

9 Now therefore hold him not guiltless: for thou *art* a wise man, and
knowest what thou oughtest to do unto him; but his hoar head bring thou
down to the grave with blood.

3. David's Death

2:10 2 Sam 5:7; 1 Chron 29:28; Acts 2:29; 13:36
2:11 2 Sam 5:4, 5; 1 Chron 29:26, 27

10 So David slept with his fathers, and was buried in the city of David.
11 And the days that David reigned over Israel *were* forty years: seven

---

1:53 Solomon told Adonijah to go to his house and retire there. All he had lost was the kingship. Since Adonijah bowed before Solomon, the issue was closed—unless and until Adonijah reopened the matter later, which is exactly what he did.

2:3 David charged Solomon to keep the law of God. He tied that conviction to the belief that this is the way to prosper in all things. He bore witness to the fact that the law of Moses was written and available to the future king. Solomon could not, however, keep the precepts he knew nothing about. Thus David was implicitly ordering Solomon to study the law diligently and do what it commanded.

2:5–9 David entrusted to Solomon the duty of executing judgment against Joab, who was responsible for the deaths of Abner and Amasa. The bloodguilt would be removed only after Joab himself was executed.

2:8 Shimei had cursed David when he fled from Absalom. When the civil war was over, David swore that he would not put him to death. But David's successor was not bound to his oath. On his deathbed, David instructs Solomon to execute Shimei who cursed David *with a grievous curse.* The Jews said that Shimei upbraided David with his descent from Ruth the Moabitess, intimating that with his mixed blood he was not a real Jew.

years reigned he in Hebron, and thirty and three years reigned he in
Jerusalem.
12¶Then sat Solomon upon the throne of David his father; and his
kingdom was established greatly.

2:12 1 Chron 29:23 2 Chron 1:1

C. SOLOMON OBEYS DAVID'S COMMANDS
1. The Slaying of Adonijah

13¶And Ad-o-ni'jah the son of Hag'gith came to Bath'-she-ba the mother
of Solomon. And she said, Comest thou peaceably? And he said, Peaceably.
14He said moreover, I have somewhat to say unto thee. And she said, Say
on.
15And he said, Thou knowest that the kingdom was mine, and *that* all
Israel set their faces on me, that I should reign: howbeit the kingdom is
turned about, and is become my brother's: for it was his from the LORD.
16And now I ask one petition of thee, deny me not. And she said unto
him, Say on.
17And he said, Speak, I pray thee, unto Solomon the king, (for he will not
say thee nay,) that he give me Ab'i-shag the Shu'nam-mite to wife.
18And Bath'-she-ba said, Well; I will speak for thee unto the king.
19¶Bath'-she-ba therefore went unto king Solomon, to speak unto him for
Ad-o-ni'jah. And the king rose up to meet her, and bowed himself unto her,
and sat down on his throne, and caused a seat to be set for the king's
mother; and she sat on his right hand.
20Then she said, I desire one small petition of thee; *I pray thee,* say me
not nay. And the king said unto her, Ask on, my mother: for I will not say
thee nay.
21And she said, Let Ab'i-shag the Shu'nam-mite be given to Ad-o-ni'jah ☆2:21
thy brother to wife.
22And king Solomon answered and said unto his mother, And why dost
thou ask Ab'i-shag the Shu'nam-mite for Ad-o-ni'jah? ask for him the
kingdom also; for he *is* mine elder brother; even for him, and for A-bi'a-
thar the priest, and for Jo'ab the son of Zer-u-i'ah.
23Then king Solomon sware by the LORD, saying, God do so to me, and
more also, if Ad-o-ni'jah have not spoken this word against his own life.
24Now therefore, *as* the LORD liveth, which hath established me, and set
me on the throne of David my father, and who hath made me an house, as
he promised, Ad-o-ni'jah shall be put to death this day.
25And king Solomon sent by the hand of Be-nai'ah the son of Je-hoi'a-da;
and he fell upon him that he died.

2:23 Ruth 1:17 1 Sam 14:44 1 Kgs 20:10

2:25 2 Sam 8:18

2. Abiathar Banished to Anathoth

26¶And unto A-bi'a-thar the priest said the king, Get thee to An'a-thoth,
unto thine own fields; for thou *art* worthy of death: but I will not at this
time put thee to death, because thou barest the ark of the Lord GOD before
David my father, and because thou hast been afflicted in all wherein my
father was afflicted.
27So Solomon thrust out A-bi'a-thar from being priest unto the LORD;

2:26 Josh 21:17, 18 1 Sam 22:20 26:16 2 Sam 15:24 Jer 1:1

☆2:27 1 Sam 2:30, 31

2:21 Adonijah used Bath-sheba to get her son Solomon to give him Abishag as his wife. Since Abishag was the last wife of David, Adonijah might claim the throne for himself. Realizing the threat and knowing of Adonijah's treasonous intentions, Solomon refused the request.

2:27 God foretold the end of the line of Eli the priest. Abiathar was Eli's great-grandson. Following King David's death and Solomon's accession, Adonijah revolted and was supported by Abiathar. When King Solomon put down the revolt, he expelled Abiathar to Anathoth, which was accepted as the fulfillment of 1 Sam. 2:31–36. It marked the end of Eli's line. Jeremiah the prophet was a descendant of the priests from Anathoth (Jer. 1:1).

that he might fulfil the word of the LORD, which he spake concerning the
house of Eli in Shi'loh.

3. The Slaying of Joab

2:28 2 Sam 17:25 1 Kgs 1:49

28¶Then tidings came to Jo'ab: for Jo'ab had turned after Ad-o-ni'jah,
though he turned not after Ab'sa-lom, And Jo'ab fled unto the tabernacle of
the LORD, and caught hold on the horns of the altar.
29And it was told king Solomon that Jo'ab was fled unto the tabernacle of
the LORD; and, behold, *he is* by the altar. Then Solomon sent Be-nai'ah the
son of Je-hoi'a-da, saying, Go, fall upon him.
30And Be-nai'ah came to the tabernacle of the LORD, and said unto him,
Thus saith the king, Come forth. And he said, Nay; but I will die here. And
Be-nai'ah brought the king word again, saying, Thus said Jo'ab, and thus he
answered me.

2:31 Ex 21:14 Num 35:33 Deut 19:13

31And the king said unto him, Do as he hath said, and fall upon him, and
bury him; that thou mayest take away the innocent blood, which Jo'ab
shed, from me, and from the house of my father.

2:32 Gen 9:5, 6 Judg 9:24, 56, 57 2 Sam 3:27 20:8–10

32And the LORD shall return his blood upon his own head, who fell upon
two men more righteous and better than he, and slew them with the sword,
my father David not knowing *thereof, to wit,* Abner the son of Ner, captain
of the host of Israel, and Am'a-sa the son of Je'ther, captain of the host of
Judah.

2:33 2 Sam 3:29 Prov 25:5

33Their blood shall therefore return upon the head of Jo'ab, and upon the
head of his seed for ever: but upon David, and upon his seed, and upon his
house, and upon his throne, shall there be peace for ever from the LORD.
34So Be-nai'ah the son of Je-hoi'a-da went up, and fell upon him, and
slew him: and he was buried in his own house in the wilderness.

2:35☆ 1 Chron 29:22

35¶And the king put Be-nai'ah the son of Je-hoi'a-da in his room over the
host: and Za'dok the priest did the king put in the room of A-bi'a-thar.

4. Shimei Breaks His Word and Loses His Life

2:36☆ 2 Sam 16:5 1 Kgs 2:8

36¶And the king sent and called for Shim'e-i, and said unto him, Build
thee an house in Jerusalem, and dwell there, and go not forth thence any
whither.
37For it shall be, *that* on the day thou goest out, and passest over the
brook Kidron, thou shalt know for certain that thou shalt surely die: thy
blood shall be upon thine own head.
38And Shim'e-i said unto the king, The saying *is* good: as my lord the
king hath said, so will thy servant do. And Shim'e-i dwelt in Jerusalem
many days.
39And it came to pass at the end of three years, that two of the servants
of Shim'e-i ran away unto A'chish son of Ma'a-chah king of Gath. And
they told Shim'e-i, saying, Behold, thy servants *be* in Gath.
40And Shim'e-i arose, and saddled his ass, and went to Gath to A'chish to
seek his servants: and Shim'e-i went, and brought his servants from Gath.
41And it was told Solomon that Shim'e-i had gone from Jerusalem to
Gath, and was come again.
42And the king sent and called for Shim'e-i, and said unto him, Did I not

---

2:35 Zadok replaced Abiathar so that his descendants constituted the priestly line.
2:36, 37 Solomon did not execute Shimei immediately. Instead, he ordered Shimei to remain forever in Jerusalem, apparently to keep him well within his purview. In what might have appeared to be excusable circumstances, Shimei crossed the brook Kidron in a search for two of his slaves who had run away. But it was a breach of his agreement with Solomon, who then had him executed.

make thee to swear by the LORD, and protested unto thee, saying, Know for
a certain, on the day thou goest out, and walkest abroad any whither, that
thou shalt surely die? and thou saidst unto me, The word *that* I have heard
is good.
43 Why then hast thou not kept the oath of the LORD, and the command-
ment that I have charged thee with?
44 The king said moreover to Shim'e-i, Thou knowest all the wickedness
which thine heart is privy to, that thou didst to David my father: therefore
the LORD shall return thy wickedness upon thine own head;
45 And king Solomon *shall be* blessed, and the throne of David shall be
established before the LORD for ever.
46 So the king commanded Be-nai'ah the son of Je-hoi'a-da; which went
out, and fell upon him, that he died. And the kingdom was established in
the hand of Solomon.

II. SOLOMON'S KINGSHIP (3:1—11:43)

A. THE EARLY YEARS; MARRIAGE TO PHARAOH'S DAUGHTER

3 AND Solomon made affinity with Pharaoh king of Egypt, and took
Pharaoh's daughter, and brought her into the city of David, until he
had made an end of building his own house, and the house of the LORD,
and the wall of Jerusalem round about.
2 Only the people sacrificed in high places, because there was no house
built unto the name of the LORD, until those days.

B. SOLOMON'S PRAYER FOR WISDOM

3 And Solomon loved the LORD, walking in the statutes of David his
father: only he sacrificed and burnt incense in high places.
4 And the king went to Gibeon to sacrifice there; for that *was* the great
high place: a thousand burnt offerings did Solomon offer upon that altar.
5 In Gibeon the LORD appeared to Solomon in a dream by night: and
God said, Ask what I shall give thee.
6 And Solomon said, Thou hast shewed unto thy servant David my father
great mercy, according as he walked before thee in truth, and in righteous-
ness, and in uprightness of heart with thee; and thou hast kept for him this
great kindness, that thou hast given him a son to sit on his throne, as *it is*
this day.
7 And now, O LORD my God, thou hast made thy servant king instead of
David my father: and I *am but* a little child: I know not *how* to go out or
come in.
8 And thy servant *is* in the midst of thy people which thou hast chosen, a
great people, that cannot be numbered nor counted for multitude.
9 Give therefore thy servant an understanding heart to judge thy people,

2:44 1 Sam 25:39; 2 Sam 16:5
2:45 2 Sam 7:13; Isa 9:7
2:46 2 Chron 1:1
☆**3:1** 1 Kgs 7:8; 9:24; 11:1
3:2 Lev 17:3–5; Deut 12:13, 14; 1 Kgs 5:2, 3
☆**3:3** 1 Kgs 9:4; 11:4, 6, 38; Ps 31:23
☆**3:4** 1 Chron 16:39; 21:29; 2 Chron 1:2, 3
☆**3:5** Gen 28:12; Num 12:6; 1 Kgs 9:2, 3; 2 Chron 1:7; Mt 1:20
3:6 2 Sam 7:8; 12:7; 1 Kgs 9:4; 2 Chron 1:8
3:7 1 Chron 22:9; 29:1; Jer 1:6; Dan 2:21
3:8 Gen 13:16; 15:5; 22:17; Ex 19:6; Deut 7:6; 1 Sam 12:22
3:9 2 Sam 14:17; 1 Kgs 3:12, 13; 2 Chron 1:10; Ps 72:1; Prov 2:3–5, 9; Jas 1:5

3:1 Some of Solomon's many marriages were political, designed to protect his kingdom. Peace with Egypt by marriage to the princess of that realm was one of those instances.

3:3, 4 Contrary to Deut. 12:13, 14, Solomon maintained *high places* outside of Jerusalem. Evidently he did not think of Jerusalem as the unique, central shrine. (See note on 12:31 for more information on "high places.")

3:5 Here God visits Solomon in a dream and offers to give him whatever he asks for. Solomon knew that the task before him was great and that to replace David was no easy job. So he asked for wisdom or discernment. He did not ask for a long life, great riches, or even a great reputation. God was pleased to give him what he asked for. We need to be reminded that whatever gifts we have come from God, who is the giver through the Holy Spirit. There is no reason why we cannot ask God for some gift or gifts we think we need for his service. The mystery is why Solomon lacked wisdom about marriage and took so many wives and concubines.

that I may discern between good and bad: for who is able to judge this thy so great a people?

10 And the speech pleased the LORD, that Solomon had asked this thing.

11 And God said unto him, Because thou hast asked this thing, and hast not asked for thyself long life; neither hast asked riches for thyself, nor hast asked the life of thine enemies; but hast asked for thyself understanding to discern judgment;

3:12 1 Kgs 4:29; 5:12

12 Behold, I have done according to thy words: lo, I have given thee a wise and an understanding heart; so that there was none like thee before thee, neither after thee shall any arise like unto thee.

3:13 1 Kgs 3:28 4:20; 10:23

13 And I have also given thee that which thou hast not asked, both riches, and honour: so that there shall not be any among the kings like unto thee all thy days.

3:14 Deut 5:16 25:13–15 Ps 21:4; 91:16 Prov 3:1, 2, 16

14 And if thou wilt walk in my ways, to keep my statutes and my commandments, as thy father David did walk, then I will lengthen thy days.

3:15☆ 2 Sam 6:17, 18 1 Kgs 8:63 2 Chron 7:4, 5

15 And Solomon awoke; and, behold, *it was* a dream. And he came to Jerusalem, and stood before the ark of the covenant of the LORD, and offered up burnt offerings, and offered peace offerings, and made a feast to all his servants.

C. SOLOMON'S WISDOM ILLUSTRATED

3:16☆

16 ¶Then came there two women, *that were* harlots, unto the king, and stood before him.

17 And the one woman said, O my lord, I and this woman dwell in one house; and I was delivered of a child with her in the house.

18 And it came to pass the third day after that I was delivered, that this woman was delivered also: and we *were* together; *there was* no stranger with us in the house, save we two in the house.

19 And this woman's child died in the night; because she overlaid it.

20 And she arose at midnight, and took my son from beside me, while thine handmaid slept, and laid it in her bosom, and laid her dead child in my bosom.

21 And when I rose in the morning to give my child suck, behold, it was dead: but when I had considered it in the morning, behold, it was not my son, which I did bear.

22 And the other woman said, Nay; but the living *is* my son, and the dead *is* thy son. And this said, No; but the dead *is* thy son, and the living *is* my son. Thus they spake before the king.

23 Then said the king, The one saith, This *is* my son that liveth, and thy son *is* the dead: and the other saith, Nay; but thy son *is* the dead, and my son *is* the living.

24 And the king said, Bring me a sword. And they brought a sword before the king.

25 And the king said, Divide the living child in two, and give half to the one, and half to the other.

3:26 Isa 49:15

26 Then spake the woman whose the living child *was* unto the king, for her bowels yearned upon her son, and she said, O my lord, give her the living

---

3:15 The first application of wisdom may be seen here. Before this, Solomon had offered sacrifices at Gibeon. Now he comes to Jerusalem where the ark is and offers the proper sacrifices before the ark.

3:16 In the case of the two harlots fighting over the possession of the live baby, Solomon must decide which of the two is telling the truth. His decision to give each one half of the living baby caused the true mother to relinquish her claim. When the other harlot indicated a willingness to let the baby be sliced in two, Solomon discerned that she was a fraud. The news of this incident served to satisfy the people everywhere that their king indeed had the gift of wisdom.

child, and in no wise slay it. But the other said, Let it be neither mine nor
thine, *but* divide *it.*
27Then the king answered and said, Give her the living child, and in no
wise slay it: she *is* the mother thereof.
28And all Israel heard of the judgment which the king had judged; and
they feared the king: for they saw that the wisdom of God *was* in him, to do
judgment.

3:28 1 Kgs 3:9; 4:29

D. SOLOMON'S OFFICIAL APPOINTMENTS

4 SO king Solomon was king over all Israel.
2And these *were* the princes which he had; Az-a-ri'ah the son of Za'dok
the priest,
3El-i-ho'reph and A-hi'ah, the sons of Shi'sha, scribes; Je-hosh'a-phat the
son of A-hi'lud, the recorder.
4And Be-nai'ah the son of Je-hoi'a-da *was* over the host: and Za'dok and
A-bi'a-thar *were* the priests:
5And Az-a-ri'ah the son of Nathan *was* over the officers: and Za'bud the
son of Nathan *was* principal officer, *and* the king's friend:
6And A-hi'shar *was* over the household: and Ad-o-ni'ram the son of
Abda *was* over the tribute.
7¶And Solomon had twelve officers over all Israel, which provided
victuals for the king and his household: each man his month in a year made
provision.
8And these *are* their names: The son of Hur, in mount E'phra-im:
9The son of De'kar, in Ma'kaz, and in Sha-al'bim, and Beth-she'mesh,
and E'lon-beth-ha'nan:
10The son of He'sed, in Ar'u-both; to him *pertained* So'choh, and all the
land of He'pher:
11The son of A-bin'a-dab, in all the region of Dor; which had Ta'phath
the daughter of Solomon to wife:
12Ba'a-na the son of A-hi'lud; *to him pertained* Ta'a-nach and Me-gid'do,
and all Beth-she'an, which *is* by Zar'ta-nah beneath Jez're-el, from Beth-
she'an to A'bel-me-ho'lah, *even* unto *the place that is* beyond Jok'ne-am:
13The son of Ge'ber, in Ra'moth-gil'e-ad; to him *pertained* the towns of
Ja'ir the son of Ma-nas'seh, which *are* in Gilead; to him *also pertained* the
region of Ar'gob, which *is* in Ba'shan, threescore great cities with walls and
brasen bars:
14A-hin'a-dab the son of Id'do *had* Ma-ha-na'im:
15A-him'a-az *was* in Naph'ta-li; he also took Bas'math the daughter of
Solomon to wife:
16Ba'a-nah the son of Hu'shai *was* in Asher and in A'loth:
17Je-hosh'a-phat the son of Par'u-ah, in Is'sa-char:
18Shim'e-i the son of E'lah, in Benjamin:
19Ge'ber the son of U'ri *was* in the country of Gilead, *in* the country of
Sihon king of the Am'or-ites, and of Og king of Ba'shan; and *he was* the
only officer which *was* in the land.

☆4:7

E. SOLOMON'S DAILY PROVISIONS

20¶Judah and Israel *were* many, as the sand which *is* by the sea in
multitude, eating and drinking, and making merry.

☆4:20 Gen 32:12 Prov 14:28

4:7 Apparently Solomon divided the kingdom into twelve segments and appointed twelve officials over them in order to provide the means to support his extensive building and military ventures.

4:20 The contentment here expressed turned to discontent when Solomon laid a heavy yoke on the people, as may be inferred from 12:10.

4:21 2 Sam 8:2, 6 2 Chron 9:26 Ps 68:29 72:10, 11

21 And Solomon reigned over all kingdoms from the river unto the land of
the Philistines, and unto the border of Egypt: they brought presents, and
served Solomon all the days of his life.
22 ¶And Solomon's provision for one day was thirty measures of fine flour,
and threescore measures of meal,
23 Ten fat oxen, and twenty oxen out of the pastures, and an hundred
sheep, beside harts, and roebucks, and fallowdeer, and fatted fowl.

4:24 1 Kgs 5:4 1 Chron 22:9

24 For he had dominion over all *the region* on this side the river, from
Tiph'sah even to Az'zah, over all the kings on this side the river: and he had
peace on all sides round about him.

4:25☆ Isa 60:18 Jer 23:5, 6 Mic 4:4 Zech 3:10 4:26☆ 1 Kgs 10:26 2 Chron 1:14

25 And Judah and Israel dwelt safely, every man under his vine and under
his fig tree, from Dan even to Be'er–she'ba, all the days of Solomon.
26 ¶And Solomon had forty thousand stalls of horses for his chariots, and
twelve thousand horsemen.
27 And those officers provided victual for king Solomon, and for all that
came unto king Solomon's table, every man in his month: they lacked
nothing.
28 Barley also and straw for the horses and dromedaries brought they unto
the place where *the officers* were, every man according to his charge.

F. SOLOMON'S GREAT WISDOM

4:29☆ 1 Kgs 3:9, 28 10:23 4:30 Isa 19:11 Acts 7:22

29 ¶And God gave Solomon wisdom and understanding exceeding much,
and largeness of heart, even as the sand that *is* on the sea shore.
30 And Solomon's wisdom excelled the wisdom of all the children of the
east country, and all the wisdom of Egypt.
31 For he was wiser than all men; than Ethan the Ez'ra-hite, and He'man,
and Chal'col, and Dar'da, the sons of Ma'hol: and his fame was in all
nations round about.

4:32 Prov 1:1 Eccles: 12:9 Song 1:1

32 And he spake three thousand proverbs: and his songs were a thousand
and five.
33 And he spake of trees, from the cedar tree that *is* in Lebanon even unto
the hyssop that springeth out of the wall: he spake also of beasts, and of
fowl, and of creeping things, and of fishes.

4:34 1 Kgs 10:1 2 Chron 9:23

34 And there came of all people to hear the wisdom of Solomon, from all
kings of the earth, which had heard of his wisdom.

G. THE CONSTRUCTION OF THE TEMPLE

1. The Arrangements with Hiram

5:1☆ 2 Sam 5:11 1 Chron 14:1 2 Chron 14:1

5 AND Hiram king of Tyre sent his servants unto Solomon; for he had
heard that they had anointed him king in the room of his father: for
Hiram was ever a lover of David.

4:25 Solomon had reached the height of his splendor. The twelve tribes lived in peace and were provided for by God. Nothing was lacking. God had fulfilled his promises and his people could expect him to help them maintain that state of affairs. No longer did the people hark back to Egypt and its fare. However, contentment would continue only if the people and the king remained faithful to God.

4:26 Compare the forty thousand in this verse with the four thousand mentioned in 2 Chron. 9:25. The copyist misread the Hebrew cipher for *four* as the Hebrew cipher for *forty*. The lower number is probably the correct one, especially since the number of chariots is stated to be 1,400 in 10:26. Archaeologists have found some of the stalls in Megiddo.

4:29 The gift of wisdom was God's gift to Solomon. Prov. 2:6 says that wisdom comes from God. Chaldea and Egypt were famed for their knowledge. Some of it rubbed off on the Greeks. But Solomon is said to have possessed far greater wisdom than the finest scholars of all the nations (4:30). Yet wisdom, when it is not accompanied by right actions, loses much of its value. Wisdom did not keep him from loving and marrying heathen women from the surrounding nations; these women helped to turn his heart away from God.

5:1 Hiram had been David's friend. His people built David a house (2 Sam. 5:11), and we can be sure it was magnificent.

2 And Solomon sent to Hiram, saying, **5:2**
3 Thou knowest how that David my father could not build an house unto 2 Sam 7:5, 13; 1 Chron 22:8
the name of the LORD his God for the wars which were about him on every 28:2, 3
side, until the LORD put them under the soles of his feet.
4 But now the LORD my God hath given me rest on every side, *so that* **5:4** 1 Kgs 4:24
there is neither adversary nor evil occurrent. 1 Chron 22:9
5 And, behold, I purpose to build an house unto the name of the LORD my ☆**5:5**
God, as the LORD spake unto David my father, saying, Thy son, whom I 2 Sam 7:12, 13; 1 Chron 17:12
will set upon thy throne in thy room, he shall build an house unto my name.
6 Now therefore command thou that they hew me cedar trees out of
Lebanon; and my servants shall be with thy servants: and unto thee will I
give hire for thy servants according to all that thou shalt appoint: for thou
knowest that *there is* not among us any that can skill to hew timber like
unto the Si-do′ni-ans.
7 ¶And it came to pass, when Hiram heard the words of Solomon, that he
rejoiced greatly, and said, Blessed *be* the LORD this day, which hath given
unto David a wise son over this great people.
8 And Hiram sent to Solomon, saying, I have considered the things which
thou sentest to me for: *and* I will do all thy desire concerning timber of
cedar, and concerning timber of fir.
9 My servants shall bring *them* down from Lebanon unto the sea: and I ☆**5:9**
will convey them by sea in floats unto the place that thou shalt appoint me, 2 Chron 2:16; Ezra 3:7
and will cause them to be discharged there, and thou shalt receive *them:*
and thou shalt accomplish my desire, in giving food for my household.
10 So Hiram gave Solomon cedar trees and fir trees *according to* all his
desire.
11 And Solomon gave Hiram twenty thousand measures of wheat *for* food
to his household, and twenty measures of pure oil: thus gave Solomon to
Hiram year by year.
12 And the LORD gave Solomon wisdom, as he promised him: and there ☆**5:12**
was peace between Hiram and Solomon; and they two made a league 1 Kgs 3:12; 4:29
together.
13 ¶And king Solomon raised a levy out of all Israel; and the levy was ☆**5:13**
thirty thousand men.
14 And he sent them to Lebanon, ten thousand a month by courses: a
month they were in Lebanon, *and* two months at home: and Ad-o-ni′ram
was over the levy.
15 And Solomon had threescore and ten thousand that bare burdens, and
fourscore thousand hewers in the mountains;
16 Beside the chief of Solomon's officers which *were* over the work, three
thousand and three hundred, which ruled over the people that wrought in
the work.
17 And the king commanded, and they brought great stones, costly stones, ☆**5:17**
and hewed stones, to lay the foundation of the house.
18 And Solomon's builders and Hiram's builders did hew *them,* and the
stonesquarers: so they prepared timber and stones to build the house.

5:5–12 Solomon asked Hiram for help in the construction of the temple, which God had forbidden David to erect. It was to be a joint effort of Israelites and the people of Hiram. Solomon indicated his willingness to reimburse Hiram for his troubles. They signed a treaty to seal the bargain (5:12).

5:13 Solomon employed thirty thousand Israelites in the work of building the temple. Ten thousand worked for a month and then had two months off to tend their own affairs. The additional workers came from tributary peoples who did not share the same time-off advantages. The labor engaged in the enterprise was enormous.

5:17 When the foundation for the temple was laid, Solomon was apparently present. No doubt it was a splendid occasion accompanied by festivities. In the New Testament we learn that Christ is our sure foundation.

2. The Specifications of the Temple

6:1☆ Judg 11:26 2 Chron 3:1 Acts 7:47

6 AND it came to pass in the four hundred and eightieth year after the
children of Israel were come out of the land of Egypt, in the fourth
year of Solomon's reign over Israel, in the month Zif, which *is* the second
month, that he began to build the house of the LORD.

6:2 1 Chron 28:11 Ezek 40:5

2 And the house which king Solomon built for the LORD, the length
thereof *was* threescore cubits, and the breadth thereof twenty *cubits,* and the
height thereof thirty cubits.

6:3☆

3 And the porch before the temple of the house, twenty cubits *was* the
length thereof, according to the breadth of the house; *and* ten cubits *was* the
breadth thereof before the house.
4 And for the house he made windows of narrow lights.
5 ¶And against the wall of the house he built chambers round about,
against the walls of the house round about, *both* of the temple and of the
oracle: and he made chambers round about:
6 The nethermost chamber *was* five cubits broad, and the middle *was* six
cubits broad, and the third *was* seven cubits broad: for without *in the wall*
of the house he made narrowed rests round about, that *the beams* should
not be fastened in the walls of the house.

6:7 Ex 20:25 Deut 27:5, 6

7 And the house, when it was in building, was built of stone made ready
before it was brought thither: so that there was neither hammer nor axe *nor*
any tool of iron heard in the house, while it was in building.
8 The door for the middle chamber *was* in the right side of the house: and
they went up with winding stairs into the middle *chamber,* and out of the
middle into the third.

6:9 2 Sam 7:7 1 Kgs 6:14, 38

9 So he built the house, and finished it; and covered the house with beams
and boards of cedar.
10 And *then* he built chambers against all the house, five cubits high: and
they rested on the house with timber of cedar.

6:11 1 Kgs 3:14

11 ¶And the word of the LORD came to Solomon, saying,
12 *Concerning* this house which thou art in building, if thou wilt walk in
my statutes, and execute my judgments, and keep all my commandments to
walk in them; then will I perform my word with thee, which I spake unto
David thy father:

6:13☆ Ex 25:8 Deut 31:6 Josh 1:5

13 And I will dwell among the children of Israel, and will not forsake my
people Israel.
14 So Solomon built the house, and finished it.
15 And he built the walls of the house within with boards of cedar, both
the floor of the house, and the walls of the ceiling: *and* he covered *them* on
the inside with wood, and covered the floor of the house with planks of fir.

6:16☆ Ex 26:33 Lev 16:1, 2 2 Chron 3:8

16 And he built twenty cubits on the sides of the house, both the floor and
the walls with boards of cedar: he even built *them* for it within, *even* for the
oracle, *even* for the most holy *place.*

6:1 *four hundred and eightieth year after . . . Egypt.* This means that the Exodus occurred around 1440 B.C. Scholars have argued at length for this date or for the later date in the middle of the thirteenth century B.C.

6:3 Solomon's temple was erected some four centuries after the tabernacle (tent) was constructed. For seven years some 30,000 Israelites and 150,000 Canaanites labored to finish building the temple. The materials were secured and prepared elsewhere and simply assembled on the site of the building.

6:13 God promised Solomon that he would dwell among the people of Israel in the temple and would not forsake them. But this was a conditional promise—they must keep God's commandments. When the temple was finally dedicated, the glory of God entered the sanctuary and remained there until Ezekiel's day.

6:16, 17 One-third of the temple comprised the holy of holies area, the other two-thirds the remaining interior of the temple. In the New Testament the veil between the holy of holies and the other part of the temple was torn asunder at the death of Christ, signifying his entrance into the holy of holies to obtain eternal redemption. Only the high priest could enter the holy of holies and that on special occasions, and always with blood to sprinkle on the altar.

17 And the house, that *is,* the temple before it, was forty cubits *long.*
18 And the cedar of the house within *was* carved with knops and open
flowers: all *was* cedar; there was no stone seen.
19 And the oracle he prepared in the house within, to set there the ark of
the covenant of the LORD.
20 And the oracle in the forepart *was* twenty cubits in length, and twenty
cubits in breadth, and twenty cubits in the height thereof: and he overlaid
it with pure gold; and *so* covered the altar *which was of* cedar.
21 So Solomon overlaid the house within with pure gold: and he made a **6:21**
partition by the chains of gold before the oracle; and he overlaid it with Ex 30:1
gold.
22 And the whole house he overlaid with gold, until he had finished all the ☆**6:22**
house: also the whole altar that *was* by the oracle he overlaid with gold.
23 ¶And within the oracle he made two cherubims *of* olive tree, *each* ten ☆**6:23**
cubits high. Ex 25:20; 37:7 2 Chron 3:10
24 And five cubits *was* the one wing of the cherub, and five cubits the other
wing of the cherub: from the uttermost part of the one wing unto the
uttermost part of the other *were* ten cubits.
25 And the other cherub *was* ten cubits: both the cherubims *were* of one
measure and one size.
26 The height of the one cherub *was* ten cubits, and so *was it* of the other
cherub.
27 And he set the cherubims within the inner house: and they stretched
forth the wings of the cherubims, so that the wing of the one touched the
one wall, and the wing of the other cherub touched the other wall; and their
wings touched one another in the midst of the house.
28 And he overlaid the cherubims with gold.
29 And he carved all the walls of the house round about with carved ☆**6:29**
figures of cherubims and palm trees and open flowers, within and without.
30 And the floor of the house he overlaid with gold, within and without.
31 ¶And for the entering of the oracle he made doors *of* olive tree: the
lintel *and* side posts *were* a fifth part *of the wall.*
32 The two doors also *were of* olive tree; and he carved upon them
carvings of cherubims and palm trees and open flowers, and overlaid *them*
with gold, and spread gold upon the cherubims, and upon the palm trees.
33 So also made he for the door of the temple posts *of* olive tree, a fourth
part *of the wall.*
34 And the two doors *were of* fir tree: the two leaves of the one door *were* **6:34**
folding, and the two leaves of the other door *were* folding. Ezek 41:23
35 And he carved *thereon* cherubims and palm trees and open flowers: and
covered *them* with gold fitted upon the carved work.
36 ¶And he built the inner court with three rows of hewed stone, and a
row of cedar beams.
37 In the fourth year was the foundation of the house of the LORD laid, in **6:37**
the month Zif: 2 Chron 3:3

6:22 The immense amount of gold used in the construction of the temple would make it a special attraction to foreign powers when they converged on Jerusalem.

6:23 *made two cherubims,* i.e., "two statues of Guardian Angels."† Some think these resembled winged lions with human heads. God was thought of as invisibly enthroned on the cherubim (see Exod. 25:22). This led people to incorrectly suppose that God would never allow the temple to be destroyed since he dwelt there (see Jer. 7:4).

6:29 The Israelites had been cured of their desire for idols. Despite their later departures from the true faith, the people of Israel rarely stooped to erect figures to represent their God. The art of Israel compared to that of pagan nations (like Egypt, Greece, and Rome) was remarkably lacking in statues.

6:38☆ 38 And in the eleventh year, in the month Bul, which *is* the eighth month,
was the house finished throughout all the parts thereof, and according to all
the fashion of it. So was he seven years in building it.

3. Solomon's Palace

7:1☆ 1 Kgs 3:1; 9:10 2 Chron 8:1 7 BUT Solomon was building his own house thirteen years, and he
finished all his house.
7:2☆ 1 Kgs 10:17 2 Chron 9:16 2 ¶He built also the house of the forest of Lebanon; the length thereof *was*
an hundred cubits, and the breadth thereof fifty cubits, and the height
thereof thirty cubits, upon four rows of cedar pillars, with cedar beams
upon the pillars.
3 And *it was* covered with cedar above upon the beams, that *lay* on forty
five pillars, fifteen *in* a row.
4 And *there were* windows *in* three rows, and light *was* against light *in*
three ranks.
5 And all the doors and posts *were* square, with the windows: and light
was against light *in* three ranks.
6 ¶And he made a porch of pillars; the length thereof *was* fifty cubits, and
the breadth thereof thirty cubits: and the porch *was* before them: and the
other pillars and the thick beam *were* before them.
7:7 1 Kgs 6:9 7 ¶Then he made a porch for the throne where he might judge, *even* the
porch of judgment: and *it was* covered with cedar from one side of the floor
to the other.
7:8☆ 1 Kgs 3:1; 7:8 2 Chron 8:11 8 ¶And his house where he dwelt *had* another court within the porch,
which was of the like work. Solomon made also an house for Pharaoh's
daughter, whom he had taken *to wife,* like unto this porch.
9 All these *were of* costly stones, according to the measures of hewed
stones, sawed with saws, within and without, even from the foundation
unto the coping, and *so* on the outside toward the great court.
10 And the foundation *was of* costly stones, even great stones, stones of
ten cubits, and stones of eight cubits.
11 And above *were* costly stones, after the measures of hewed stones, and
cedars.
12 And the great court round about *was* with three rows of hewed stones,
and a row of cedar beams, both for the inner court of the house of the
LORD, and for the porch of the house.

4. Hiram of Tyre, the Skilled Workman
a. The Casting of the Hollow Bronze Pillars

7:13☆ 1 Kgs 7:40 2 Chron 2:13 13 ¶And king Solomon sent and fetched Hiram out of Tyre.
14 He *was* a widow's son of the tribe of Naph'ta-li, and his father *was* a
man of Tyre, a worker in brass: and he was filled with wisdom, and

---

6:38 In less than eight years the temple was finished. No noise of axes and hammers was heard. It was quiet and serene, just as heaven will be for us.

7:1 We give Solomon the benefit of the doubt and do not suppose his own dwelling was more ornate than the temple because it took six years longer than the temple to build. Rather, he was less anxious to build his house than the temple; and so greater effort and therefore less time was spent on God's house than on his own. The splendor of Solomon's own buildings was not to be compared with the temple.

7:2 *The house of the forest of Lebanon* was a country dwelling near Jerusalem. Some think it was a retreat in the forest of Lebanon itself. Apparently Solomon's throne was not there but in Jerusalem and was called "the hall of the throne" and "the hall of judgment" (NASB).

7:8 Pharaoh's daughter had her own home built by Solomon. This was a political marriage. Since Solomon had 700 wives and 300 concubines, it is hardly to be expected that their names would appear in holy writ. Solomon's successor, Rehoboam, was born of Naamah, an Ammonitess.

7:13 The Hiram mentioned here is not the king spoken of in 5:1. He was the chief craftsman and architect for King Solomon.

understanding, and cunning to work all works in brass. And he came to
king Solomon, and wrought all his work.
15 For he cast two pillars of brass, of eighteen cubits high apiece: and a 7:15 2 Kgs 25:13
line of twelve cubits did compass either of them about. 2 Chron 3:15
16 And he made two chapiters *of* molten brass, to set upon the tops of the 4:12
pillars: the height of the one chapiter *was* five cubits, and the height of the Jer 52:17
other chapiter *was* five cubits:
17 *And* nets of checker work, and wreaths of chain work, for the chapiters
which *were* upon the top of the pillars; seven for the one chapiter, and
seven for the other chapiter.
18 And he made the pillars, and two rows round about upon the one
network, to cover the chapiters that *were* upon the top, with pomegranates:
and so did he for the other chapiter.
19 And the chapiters that *were* upon the top of the pillars *were* of lily work
in the porch, four cubits.
20 And the chapiters upon the two pillars *had pomegranates* also above,
over against the belly which *was* by the network: and the pomegranates
were two hundred in rows round about upon the other chapiter.
21 And he set up the pillars in the porch of the temple: and he set up the ☆7:21
right pillar, and called the name thereof Ja′chin: and he set up the left
pillar, and called the name thereof Bo′az.
22 And upon the top of the pillars *was* lily work: so was the work of the
pillars finished.

b. The Round Bronze Tank

23 ¶And he made a molten sea, ten cubits from the one brim to the other: ☆7:23
it was round all about, and his height *was* five cubits: and a line of thirty
cubits did compass it round about.
24 And under the brim of it round about *there were* knops compassing it,
ten in a cubit, compassing the sea round about: the knops *were* cast in two
rows, when it was cast.
25 It stood upon twelve oxen, three looking toward the north, and three
looking toward the west, and three looking toward the south, and three
looking toward the east: and the sea *was set* above upon them, and all their
hinder parts *were* inward.
26 And it *was* an hand breadth thick, and the brim thereof was wrought ☆7:26
like the brim of a cup, with flowers of lilies: it contained two thousand
baths.

c. The Ten Four-Wheeled Movable Stands

27 ¶And he made ten bases of brass; four cubits *was* the length of one ☆7:27
base, and four cubits the breadth thereof, and three cubits the height of it. 2 Kgs 16:17
28 And the work of the bases *was* on this *manner:* they had borders, and
the borders *were* between the ledges:
29 And on the borders that *were* between the ledges *were* lions, oxen, and
cherubims: and upon the ledges *there was* a base above: and beneath the
lions and oxen *were* certain additions made of thin work.

7:21 *Jachin,* i.e. "to establish." *Boaz,* i.e., "strength."
7:23 *a molten sea* ("bronze tank," TLB) was filled with water by the Gibeonites or Nethinim, who supplied all of the water for the house of God.
7:26 *two thousand baths,* i.e., approximately twelve thousand gallons. In 2 Chron. 4:5 the stated capacity is three thousand baths. Different Hebrew verbs were used; the bronze tank probably normally contained two thousand baths, but when filled to the brim would contain three thousand. Some think there is an error in transmission, due to a copyist's mistake. Based on the dimensions of the tank, it normally may have had in it some ten thousand gallons of water.
7:27 The ten brass lavers for washing were set on wheels (7:32) so they could be moved when desired. The molten sea was stationary.

30And every base had four brasen wheels, and plates of brass: and the four corners thereof had undersetters: under the laver *were* undersetters molten, at the side of every addition.

31And the mouth of it within the chapiter and above *was* a cubit: but the mouth thereof *was* round *after* the work of the base, a cubit and an half: and also upon the mouth of it *were* gravings with their borders, foursquare, not round.

32And under the borders *were* four wheels; and the axletrees of the wheels *were joined* to the base: and the height of a wheel *was* a cubit and half a cubit.

33And the work of the wheels *was* like the work of a chariot wheel: their axletrees, and their naves, and their felloes, and their spokes, *were* all molten.

34And *there were* four undersetters to the four corners of one base: *and* the undersetters *were* of the very base itself.

35And in the top of the base *was there* a round compass of half a cubit high: and on the top of the base the ledges thereof and the borders thereof *were* of the same.

36For on the plates of the ledges thereof, and on the borders thereof, he graved cherubims, lions, and palm trees, according to the proportion of every one, and additions round about.

37After this *manner* he made the ten bases: all of them had one casting, one measure, *and* one size.

7:38 2 Kgs 25:14 2 Chron 4:6

38¶Then made he ten lavers of brass: one laver contained forty baths: *and* every laver was four cubits: *and* upon every one of the ten bases one laver.

39And he put five bases on the right side of the house, and five on the left side of the house: and he set the sea on the right side of the house eastward over against the south.

d. Hiram's Other Vessels

40¶And Hiram made the lavers, and the shovels, and the basons. So Hiram made an end of doing all the work that he made king Solomon for the house of the LORD:

7:41 2 Chron 4:12

41The two pillars, and the *two* bowls of the chapiters that *were* on the top of the two pillars; and the two networks, to cover the two bowls of the chapiters which *were* upon the top of the pillars;

42And four hundred pomegranates for the two networks, *even* two rows of pomegranates for one network, to cover the two bowls of the chapiters that *were* upon the pillars;

43And the ten bases, and ten lavers on the bases;

44And one sea, and twelve oxen under the sea;

45And the pots, and the shovels, and the basons: and all these vessels, which Hiram made to king Solomon for the house of the LORD, *were of* bright brass.

46In the plain of Jordan did the king cast them, in the clay ground between Suc'coth and Zar'than.

7:47 1 Chron 22:3, 14

47And Solomon left all the vessels *unweighed*, because they were exceeding many: neither was the weight of the brass found out.

e. The Vessels of Gold

7:48 Ex 37:10, 15, 16

48And Solomon made all the vessels that *pertained* unto the house of the LORD: the altar of gold, and the table of gold, whereupon the shewbread *was*,

[49]And the candlesticks of pure gold, five on the right *side*, and five on the
left, before the oracle, with the flowers, and the lamps, and the tongs *of*
gold,
[50]And the bowls, and the snuffers, and the basons, and the spoons, and
the censers *of* pure gold; and the hinges *of* gold, *both* for the doors of the
inner house, the most holy *place, and* for the doors of the house, *to wit,* of
the temple.
[51]So was ended all the work that king Solomon made for the house of the
LORD. And Solomon brought in the things which David his father had
dedicated; *even* the silver, and the gold, and the vessels, did he put among
the treasures of the house of the LORD.

7:49 Ex 25:31; 37:14
7:50 2 Kgs 25:14, 15
7:51 2 Sam 8:11; 2 Chron 5:1

H. THE CONSECRATION OF THE TEMPLE
1. Bringing the Ark into the Temple

8 THEN Solomon assembled the elders of Israel, and all the heads of the
tribes, the chief of the fathers of the children of Israel, unto king
Solomon in Jerusalem, that they might bring up the ark of the covenant of
the LORD out of the city of David, which *is* Zion.
[2]And all the men of Israel assembled themselves unto king Solomon at
the feast in the month Eth'a-nim, which *is* the seventh month.
[3]And all the elders of Israel came, and the priests took up the ark.
[4]And they brought up the ark of the LORD, and the tabernacle of the
congregation, and all the holy vessels that *were* in the tabernacle, even those
did the priests and the Levites bring up.
[5]And king Solomon, and all the congregation of Israel, that were
assembled unto him, *were* with him before the ark, sacrificing sheep and
oxen, that could not be told nor numbered for multitude.
[6]And the priests brought in the ark of the covenant of the LORD unto his
place, into the oracle of the house, to the most holy *place, even* under the
wings of the cherubims.
[7]For the cherubims spread forth *their* two wings over the place of the ark,
and the cherubims covered the ark and the staves thereof above.
[8]And they drew out the staves, that the ends of the staves were seen out
in the holy *place* before the oracle, and they were not seen without: and
there they are unto this day.
[9]*There was* nothing in the ark save the two tables of stone, which Moses
put there at Ho'reb, when the LORD made *a covenant* with the children of
Israel, when they came out of the land of Egypt.
[10]And it came to pass, when the priests were come out of the holy *place*,
that the cloud filled the house of the LORD,
[11]So that the priests could not stand to minister because of the cloud: for
the glory of the LORD had filled the house of the LORD.

☆**8:1** Num 7:2; Josh 23:2; 24:1; 2 Sam 5:7; 6:17; 2 Chron 5:2
8:2 Lev 23:33, 34; 2 Chron 5:3; 7:8; Ezra 3:4; Neh 8:14
8:3 Num 7:9; 1 Chron 15:2, 12
8:5 1 Kgs 8:62, 63; 2 Chron 1:5, 6
8:8 Ex 25:13, 14; 37:4, 5
8:9 Ex 24:7; 25:16; Deut 4:13, 14; 10:2; Heb 9:4
☆**8:10** Ex 40:34; 2 Chron 7:1
☆**8:11**

8:1 When the ark was brought into the newly constructed temple, the need for the tent no longer existed. Though nothing is said about its disposition, it must have been destroyed.

8:10 *the cloud filled the house of the LORD.* The cloud signified both the presence and the blessing of God in the temple. The *shekinah* departed from Jerusalem and the first temple, and did not return after that. Ezekiel prophesied the return of the *shekinah* glory to the new temple, which has not yet been erected (Ezek. 43:1ff).

8:11 The glory of the Solomonic temple was not its size, beauty, or cost. Its glory came from the divine presence which came after the ark was carried into the holy place by the priests. Once the ark was in place and the priests were departing from the temple, the *shekinah* filled the edifice. It was the dark cloud of the presence. From that time forward, only the high priest would enter the holy of holies once a year to make atonement for the sins of the people. The dark cloud signified the darkness of the old dispensation when compared with the light of the gospel, which would come with the advent of the Messiah, the Lord Jesus. In heaven, the divine glory will be unveiled and the darkness of that which is hidden will be replaced by the light.

8:12☆ 2 Sam 7:13; 22:10; 2 Chron 6:1; Ps 97:2; 132:14

12 ¶Then spake Solomon, The LORD said that he would dwell in the thick
darkness.
13 I have surely built thee an house to dwell in, a settled place for thee to
abide in for ever.

2. Solomon's Consecration Speech

8:15 2 Sam 7:12; 1 Kgs 8:24; 1 Chron 22:10; 29:10
8:16 Deut 12:4, 5, 11; 1 Sam 16:1
8:17 2 Sam 7:2, 3; 1 Chron 17:1
8:19 2 Sam 7:12, 13; 1 Chron 17:11, 12; 22:8; 28:6
8:20 Neh 9:8; Jer 29:10

14 And the king turned his face about, and blessed all the congregation of
Israel: (and all the congregation of Israel stood;)
15 And he said, Blessed *be* the LORD God of Israel, which spake with his
mouth unto David my father, and hath with his hand fulfilled *it*, saying,
16 Since the day that I brought forth my people Israel out of Egypt, I
chose no city out of all the tribes of Israel to build an house, that my name
might be therein; but I chose David to be over my people Israel.
17 And it was in the heart of David my father to build an house for the
name of the LORD God of Israel.
18 And the LORD said unto David my father, Whereas it was in thine heart
to build an house unto my name, thou didst well that it was in thine heart.
19 Nevertheless thou shalt not build the house; but thy son that shall come
forth out of thy loins, he shall build the house unto my name.
20 And the LORD hath performed his word that he spake, and I am risen
up in the room of David my father, and sit on the throne of Israel, as the
LORD promised, and have built an house for the name of the LORD God of
Israel.
21 And I have set there a place for the ark, wherein *is* the covenant of the
LORD, which he made with our fathers, when he brought them out of the
land of Egypt.

3. Solomon's Prayer

8:22☆ Deut 7:9; 1 Sam 2:2; 2 Sam 7:22; 2 Chron 6:12; Neh 1:5; 9:32
8:24 1 Kgs 8:15
8:25 2 Sam 7:12, 16; 1 Kgs 2:4; 1 Chron 17:23
8:27 2 Chron 6:18; Ps 139:7; Isa 66:1; Jer 23:24; Acts 7:48, 49

22 ¶And Solomon stood before the altar of the LORD in the presence of all
the congregation of Israel, and spread forth his hands toward heaven:
23 And he said, LORD God of Israel, *there is* no God like thee, in heaven
above, or on earth beneath, who keepest covenant and mercy with thy
servants that walk before thee with all their heart:
24 Who hast kept with thy servant David my father that thou promisedst
him: thou spakest also with thy mouth, and hast fulfilled *it* with thine hand,
as *it is* this day.
25 Therefore now, LORD God of Israel, keep with thy servant David my
father that thou promisedst him, saying, There shall not fail thee a man in
my sight to sit on the throne of Israel; so that thy children take heed to
their way, that they walk before me as thou hast walked before me.
26 And now, O God of Israel, let thy word, I pray thee, be verified, which
thou spakest unto thy servant David my father.
27 But will God indeed dwell on the earth? behold, the heaven and heaven

---

8:12 Solomon spoke to the priests and encouraged their hearts about the mystery they had experienced and the darkness they had encountered. He told them that the Lord had said *that he would dwell in the thick darkness.* He is the God who hides himself so that the holy faith may be exercised and holy fear increased. "Where God dwells in light, faith is swallowed up in vision and fear in love."* The dark cloud of the presence certified God's acceptance of the temple Solomon had built, and endorsed the kingship of this son of David to whom wisdom was imparted.

8:22 It is good for the ruler of a nation to so love God that he can offer public prayer before the people and for them. When God is so honored in prayer, the nation will be blessed and honored in turn by God. Not only was this prayer offered in connection with the dedication and acceptance of the temple by God; it had a larger frame of reference—Isaiah proclaimed that this place of worship should be a "house of prayer for all people" (Isa. 56:7). This refers to the fact that the God of the temple is the God of all nations and ruler over all people and things.

of heavens cannot contain thee; how much less this house that I have
builded?
28 Yet have thou respect unto the prayer of thy servant, and to his
supplication, O LORD my God, to hearken unto the cry and to the prayer,
which thy servant prayeth before thee to day:
29 That thine eyes may be open toward this house night and day, *even*
toward the place of which thou hast said, My name shall be there: that thou
mayest hearken unto the prayer which thy servant shall make toward this
place.

8:29
2 Chron 7:12, 15, 16

30 And hearken thou to the supplication of thy servant, and of thy people
Israel, when they shall pray toward this place: and hear thou in heaven thy
dwelling place: and when thou hearest, forgive.

8:30
Neh 1:5–7

31 If any man trespass against his neighbour, and an oath be laid upon
him to cause him to swear, and the oath come before thine altar in this
house:

8:31
Ex 22:8
Lev 5:1

32 Then hear thou in heaven, and do, and judge thy servants, condemning
the wicked, to bring his way upon his head; and justifying the righteous, to
give him according to his righteousness.
33 ¶When thy people Israel be smitten down before the enemy, because
they have sinned against thee, and shall turn again to thee, and confess thy
name, and pray, and make supplication unto thee in this house:

8:33
Lev 26:14–17, 40, 41
Deut 28:25, 47, 48

34 Then hear thou in heaven, and forgive the sin of thy people Israel, and
bring them again unto the land which thou gavest unto their fathers.
35 ¶When heaven is shut up, and there is no rain, because they have
sinned against thee; if they pray toward this place, and confess thy name,
and turn from their sin, when thou afflictest them:
36 Then hear thou in heaven, and forgive the sin of thy servants, and of
thy people Israel, that thou teach them the good way wherein they should
walk, and give rain upon thy land, which thou hast given to thy people for
an inheritance.

8:35
Lev 26:19
Deut 11:16, 17
28:23
1 Sam 12:23
2 Sam 21:1
1 Kgs 18:41

37 If there be in the land famine, if there be pestilence, blasting, mildew,
locust, *or* if there be caterpiller; if their enemy besiege them in the land of
their cities; whatsoever plague, whatsoever sickness *there be;*

8:37
Lev 26:16, 25
Deut 28:21, 31
2 Kgs 6:25

38 What prayer and supplication soever be *made* by any man, *or* by all thy
people Israel, which shall know every man the plague of his own heart, and
spread forth his hands toward this house:
39 Then hear thou in heaven thy dwelling place, and forgive, and do, and
give to every man according to his ways, whose heart thou knowest; (for
thou, *even* thou only, knowest the hearts of all the children of men;)

8:39
1 Sam 2:3
1 Chron 28:9
Jer 17:10
Jn 2:24

40 That they may fear thee all the days that they live in the land which
thou gavest unto our fathers.
41 Moreover concerning a stranger, that *is* not of thy people Israel, but
cometh out of a far country for thy name's sake;

8:41
1 Kgs 10:1
2 Chron 6:32

42 (For they shall hear of thy great name, and of thy strong hand, and of
thy stretched out arm;) when he shall come and pray toward this house;
43 Hear thou in heaven thy dwelling place, and do according to all that the
stranger calleth to thee for: that all people of the earth may know thy name,
to fear thee, as *do* thy people Israel; and that they may know that this
house, which I have builded, is called by thy name.

8:43
1 Sam 17:46
2 Kgs 19:19
Ps 22:27
102:15

44 If thy people go out to battle against their enemy, whithersoever thou
shalt send them, and shall pray unto the LORD toward the city which thou
hast chosen, and *toward* the house that I have built for thy name:

8:44
2 Chron 14:11

45 Then hear thou in heaven their prayer and their supplication, and
maintain their cause.
46 If they sin against thee, (for *there is* no man that sinneth not,) and thou

8:46
2 Kgs 17:6, 18
25:21
2 Chron 6:36
Ps 130:3, 4
Prov 20:9
1 Jn 1:8

be angry with them, and deliver them to the enemy, so that they carry them away captives unto the land of the enemy, far or near;

8:47 Lev 26:40 Ezra 9:5, 6 Neh 1:6, 7 Ps 106:6, 7 Dan 9:5

47 *Yet* if they shall bethink themselves in the land whither they were carried captives, and repent, and make supplication unto thee in the land of them that carried them captives, saying, We have sinned, and have done perversely, we have committed wickedness;

8:48 Deut 4:29 1 Sam 7:3 Jer 29:12

48 And *so return unto thee with all their heart, and with all their soul, in the land of their enemies, which led them away captive, and pray* unto thee toward their land, which thou gavest unto their fathers, the city which thou hast chosen, and the house which I have built for thy name:

49 Then hear thou their prayer and their supplication in heaven thy dwelling place, and maintain their cause,

8:50 2 Chron 30:9 Ezra 7:6 Neh 1:11 Ps 106:46

50 And forgive thy people that have sinned against thee, and all their transgressions wherein they have transgressed against thee, and give them compassion before them who carried them captive, that they may have compassion on them:

8:51 Ex 32:11 Deut 4:20; 9:26 1 Sam 8:8 Jer 11:4

51 For they *be* thy people, and thine inheritance, which thou broughtest forth out of Egypt, from the midst of the furnace of iron:

52 That thine eyes may be open unto the supplication of thy servant, and unto the supplication of thy people Israel, to hearken unto them in all that they call for unto thee.

8:53 Ex 19:5, 6 33:16 Deut 4:34

53 For thou didst separate them from among all the people of the earth, *to be* thine inheritance, as thou spakest by the hand of Moses thy servant, when thou broughtest our fathers out of Egypt, O Lord GOD.

4. Solomon Blesses His People

8:54 1 Kgs 8:22

54 And it was *so*, that when Solomon had made an end of praying all this prayer and supplication unto the LORD, he arose from before the altar of the LORD, from kneeling on his knees with his hands spread up to heaven.

55 And he stood, and blessed all the congregation of Israel with a loud voice, saying,

8:56 Josh 21:45 23:14 2 Kgs 10:9, 10 Lk 1:54

56 Blessed *be* the LORD, that hath given rest unto his people Israel, according to all that he promised: there hath not failed one word of all his good promise, which he promised by the hand of Moses his servant.

8:57 Josh 1:5 1 Sam 12:22 Isa 41:17 Heb 13:5

57 The LORD our God be with us, as he was with our fathers: let him not leave us, nor forsake us:

8:58 Ps 119:36 Jer 31:33

58 That he may incline our hearts unto him, to walk in all his ways, and to keep his commandments, and his statutes, and his judgments, which he commanded our fathers.

8:59 2 Chron 6:40

59 And let these my words, wherewith I have made supplication before the LORD, be nigh unto the LORD our God day and night, that he maintain the cause of his servant, and the cause of his people Israel at all times, as the matter shall require:

8:60☆ Deut 4:35 1 Sam 17:46 1 Kgs 18:39 Jer 10:10

60 That all the people of the earth may know that the LORD *is* God, *and that there is* none else.

8:61☆ Deut 18:13 1 Kgs 20:3

61 Let your heart therefore be perfect with the LORD our God, to walk in his statutes, and to keep his commandments, as at this day.

8:60 Solomon's benediction had in it a missionary perspective. He did not want all nations to be subject to his rulership. Rather, he expressed the wish that the people of all nations might know the true God and acknowledge that there is nothing above him.

8:61 The ideal standard for the believer's daily walk is characterized by obedience that is universal, not divided; that is upright, with no dissembling; that is constant, so that it continues all the days of life.

5. The Great Festal Celebration

62¶And the king, and all Israel with him, offered sacrifice before the
LORD.

8:62 2 Sam 6:17; 2 Chron 7:4

63And Solomon offered a sacrifice of peace offerings, which he offered
unto the LORD, two and twenty thousand oxen, and an hundred and twenty
thousand sheep. So the king and all the children of Israel dedicated the
house of the LORD.

☆**8:63**

64The same day did the king hallow the middle of the court that *was*
before the house of the LORD: for there he offered burnt offerings, and meat
offerings, and the fat of the peace offerings: because the brasen altar that
was before the LORD *was* too little to receive the burnt offerings, and meat
offerings, and the fat of the peace offerings.

8:64 2 Chron 7:7

65And at that time Solomon held a feast, and all Israel with him, a great
congregation, from the entering in of Ha'math unto the river of Egypt,
before the LORD our God, seven days and seven days, *even* fourteen days.

8:65 2 Chron 7:9, 10

66On the eighth day he sent the people away: and they blessed the king,
and went unto their tents joyful and glad of heart for all the goodness that
the LORD had done for David his servant, and for Israel his people.

I. GOD'S COVENANTAL PROMISE TO SOLOMON

9 AND it came to pass, when Solomon had finished the building of the
house of the LORD, and the king's house, and all Solomon's desire
which he was pleased to do,

9:1 1 Kgs 7:1; 2 Chron 8:6

2That the LORD appeared to Solomon the second time, as he had
appeared unto him at Gibeon.

☆**9:2** 1 Kgs 3:5; 11:9

3And the LORD said unto him, I have heard thy prayer and thy
supplication, that thou hast made before me: I have hallowed this house,
which thou hast built, to put my name there for ever; and mine eyes and
mine heart shall be there perpetually.

4And if thou wilt walk before me, as David thy father walked, in integrity
of heart, and in uprightness, to do according to all that I have commanded
thee, *and* wilt keep my statutes and my judgments:

9:4 1 Kgs 3:14; 11:4

5Then I will establish the throne of thy kingdom upon Israel for ever, as
I promised to David thy father, saying, There shall not fail thee a man upon
the throne of Israel.

9:5 2 Sam 7:12; 1 Kgs 8:25

6*But* if ye shall at all turn from following me, ye or your children, and will
not keep my commandments *and* my statutes which I have set before you,
but go and serve other gods, and worship them:

☆**9:6** 2 Sam 7:14; 1 Chron 28:9; 2 Chron 7:19

7Then will I cut off Israel out of the land which I have given them; and
this house, which I have hallowed for my name, will I cast out of my sight;
and Israel shall be a proverb and a byword among all people:

9:7 Lev 18:24; Deut 4:26, 27; 2 Kgs 17:23; Jer 7:4

8:63 Some have questioned whether this number of animals could have been sacrificed in such a short period. 8:64 explains that some animals were offered a short distance away from the middle court of the temple.

9:2 Since God appeared the second time to Solomon in the same manner as he had at Gibeon, it can only mean that it was a vision or dream. Solomon had dedicated the temple to God, but only God could hallow or consecrate it. It would be sanctified by the presence of the glory of God in the midst of the temple.

9:6 The word "if" consistently appears in God's conversations with the leaders and the people of Israel. The promised blessings of God were conditional, that is, they would come only if God's people obeyed his commandments and walked before him with a whole heart. But if they did not do so, evil consequences would flow from their disobedience and the blessings would turn to curses and disaster. The promises to Solomon are of special note, since his latter days would be marked by a turning away from the deep-seated convictions expressed at the time of the dedication of the house of God.

9:8☆ Deut 29:24; 2 Chron 7:21; Jer 22:8

8 And at this house, *which* is high, every one that passeth by it shall be astonished, and shall hiss; and they shall say, Why hath the LORD done thus unto this land, and to this house?

9:9 Deut 29:25; 2 Chron 7:22

9 And they shall answer, Because they forsook the LORD their God, who brought forth their fathers out of the land of Egypt, and have taken hold upon other gods, and have worshipped them, and served them: therefore hath the LORD brought upon them all this evil.

J. INCIDENTAL DETAILS ABOUT SOLOMON'S DAYS

9:10 1 Kgs 6:37

10 ¶And it came to pass at the end of twenty years, when Solomon had built the two houses, the house of the LORD, and the king's house,

9:11 1 Kgs 5:4; 2 Chron 2:4

11 (*Now* Hiram the king of Tyre had furnished Solomon with cedar trees and fir trees, and with gold, according to all his desire,) that then king Solomon gave Hiram twenty cities in the land of Galilee.

12 And Hiram came out from Tyre to see the cities which Solomon had given him; and they pleased him not.

13 And he said, What cities *are* these which thou hast given me, my brother? And he called them the land of Ca'bul unto this day.

14 And Hiram sent to the king sixscore talents of gold.

9:15☆ 2 Sam 5:9; 1 Kgs 6:38; 7:1; 2 Chron 8:1, 2

15 ¶And this *is* the reason of the levy which king Solomon raised; for to build the house of the LORD, and his own house, and Mil'lo, and the wall of Jerusalem, and Ha'zor, and Me-gid'do, and Ge'zer.

16 *For* Pharaoh king of Egypt had gone up, and taken Ge'zer, and burnt it with fire, and slain the Canaanites that dwelt in the city, and given it *for* a present unto his daughter, Solomon's wife.

17 And Solomon built Ge'zer, and Beth–ho'ron the nether,

18 And Ba'al-ath, and Tad'mor in the wilderness, in the land,

19 And all the cities of store that Solomon had, and cities for his chariots, and cities for his horsemen, and that which Solomon desired to build in Jerusalem, and in Lebanon, and in all the land of his dominion.

9:20 Gen 9:24, 25; Josh 15:63; Judg 1:28, 35

20 *And* all the people *that were* left of the Am'or-ites, Hittites, Per'iz-zites, Hi'vites, and Jeb'u-sites, which *were* not of the children of Israel,

21 Their children that were left after them in the land, whom the children of Israel also were not able utterly to destroy, upon those did Solomon levy a tribute of bondservice unto this day.

22 But of the children of Israel did Solomon make no bondmen: but they *were* men of war, and his servants, and his princes, and his captains, and rulers of his chariots, and his horsemen.

23 These *were* the chief of the officers that *were* over Solomon's work, five hundred and fifty, which bare rule over the people that wrought in the work.

9:24 1 Kgs 3:1; 7:8; 11:1, 27; 2 Chron 32:5

24 ¶But Pharaoh's daughter came up out of the city of David unto her house which *Solomon* had built for her: then did he build Mil'lo.

9:25 Ex 23:14; Deut 16:16; 2 Chron 8:13

25 ¶And three times in a year did Solomon offer burnt offerings and peace offerings upon the altar which he built unto the LORD, and he burnt incense upon the altar that *was* before the LORD. So he finished the house.

9:26☆

26 ¶And king Solomon made a navy of ships in E'zi-on-ge'ber, which *is* beside E'loth, on the shore of the Red sea, in the land of Edom.

9:8 If the temple of God is ever destroyed and people ask why God permitted it to happen, the answer is plain: God was first abandoned by his people before he abandoned them.

9:15 *Millo* ("The Filling," possible translation). *Hazor, and Megiddo, and Gezer.* Remains from Solomon's time have been found by archaeologists in these Canaanite cities.

9:26 *Eziongeber,* a seaport for which evidences have not yet been found, although a copper-smelting refinery has been unearthed in that area.

27 And Hiram sent in the navy his servants, shipmen that had knowledge of the sea, with the servants of Solomon. 9:27 1 Kgs 10:11 1 Chron 29:4

28 And they came to O'phir, and fetched from thence gold, four hundred and twenty talents, and brought *it* to king Solomon. ☆9:28

K. THE QUEEN OF SHEBA VISITS SOLOMON

10 AND when the queen of She'ba heard of the fame of Solomon concerning the name of the LORD, she came to prove him with hard questions. ☆10:1 2 Chron 9:1 Ps 72:10, 15 Isa 60:6 Mt 12:42

2 And she came to Jerusalem with a very great train, with camels that bare spices, and very much gold, and precious stones: and when she was come to Solomon, she communed with him of all that was in her heart.

3 And Solomon told her all her questions: there was not *any* thing hid from the king, which he told her not.

4 And when the queen of She'ba had seen all Solomon's wisdom, and the house that he had built,

5 And the meat of his table, and the sitting of his servants, and the attendance of his ministers, and their apparel, and his cupbearers, and his ascent by which he went up unto the house of the LORD; there was no more spirit in her.

6 And she said to the king, It was a true report that I heard in mine own land of thy acts and of thy wisdom.

7 Howbeit I believed not the words, until I came, and mine eyes had seen *it:* and, behold, the half was not told me: thy wisdom and prosperity exceedeth the fame which I heard.

8 Happy *are* thy men, happy *are* these thy servants, which stand continually before thee, *and* that hear thy wisdom.

9 Blessed be the LORD thy God, which delighted in thee, to set thee on the throne of Israel: because the LORD loved Israel for ever, therefore made he thee king, to do judgment and justice. 10:9 2 Sam 8:15 23:3 1 Kgs 5:7 2 Chron 2:11

10 And she gave the king an hundred and twenty talents of gold, and of spices very great store, and precious stones: there came no more such abundance of spices as these which the queen of She'ba gave to king Solomon.

11 And the navy also of Hiram, that brought gold from O'phir, brought in from O'phir great plenty of almug trees, and precious stones. 10:11 1 Kgs 9:27

12 And the king made of the almug trees pillars for the house of the LORD, and for the king's house, harps also and psalteries for singers: there came no such almug trees, nor were seen unto this day.

13 And king Solomon gave unto the queen of She'ba all her desire, whatsoever she asked, beside *that* which Solomon gave her of his royal bounty. So she turned and went to her own country, she and her servants.

L. SOLOMON'S GREAT WEALTH

14 ¶Now the weight of gold that came to Solomon in one year was six hundred threescore and six talents of gold, ☆10:14 2 Chron 9:13

9:28 *Ophir,* thought by some to be located in southern Arabia. More likely, it was located along the African coast in the area of what is now Somaliland.

10:1 *Sheba,* the land of the Sabeans in southwestern Arabia, now part of modern Yemen. It controlled the caravan routes through which incense and spice were brought from Arabia to Palestine.

10:14 The 666 talents would make approximately eight hundred thousand ounces of gold. According to American currency in 1984, it would amount to more than three hundred million dollars a year.

15 Beside *that he had* of the merchantmen, and of the traffick of the spice merchants, and of all the kings of Arabia, and of the governors of the country.

10:16 1 Kgs 14:26 2 Chron 9:15 12:9

16 ¶And king Solomon made two hundred targets *of* beaten gold: six hundred *shekels* of gold went to one target.

17 And *he made* three hundred shields *of* beaten gold; three pound of gold went to one shield: and the king put them in the house of the forest of Lebanon.

18 ¶Moreover the king made a great throne of ivory, and overlaid it with the best gold.

19 The throne had six steps, and the top of the throne *was* round behind: and *there were* stays on either side on the place of the seat, and two lions stood beside the stays.

20 And twelve lions stood there on the one side and on the other upon the six steps: there was not the like made in any kingdom.

10:21☆ 1 Kgs 7:2

21 ¶And all king Solomon's drinking vessels *were of* gold, and all the vessels of the house of the forest of Lebanon *were of* pure gold; none *were of* silver: it was nothing accounted of in the days of Solomon.

22 For the king had at sea a navy of Thar′shish with the navy of Hiram: once in three years came the navy of Thar′shish, bringing gold, and silver, ivory, and apes, and peacocks.

10:23 1 Kgs 3:12, 13 4:30 2 Chron 9:22

23 So king Solomon exceeded all the kings of the earth for riches and for wisdom.

24 ¶And all the earth sought to Solomon, to hear his wisdom, which God had put in his heart.

25 And they brought every man his present, vessels of silver, and vessels of gold, and garments, and armour, and spices, horses, and mules, a rate year by year.

26 ¶And Solomon gathered together chariots and horsemen: and he had a thousand and four hundred chariots, and twelve thousand horsemen, whom he bestowed in the cities for chariots, and with the king at Jerusalem.

10:27 2 Chron 1:15 9:27

27 And the king made silver *to be* in Jerusalem as stones, and cedars made he *to be* as the sycomore trees that *are* in the vale, for abundance.

10:28 2 Chron 1:16 9:28

28 ¶And Solomon had horses brought out of Egypt, and linen yarn: the king's merchants received the linen yarn at a price.

10:29 2 Kgs 7:7

29 And a chariot came up and went out of Egypt for six hundred *shekels* of silver, and an horse for an hundred and fifty: and so for all the kings of the Hittites, and for the kings of Syria, did they bring *them* out by their means.

M. SOLOMON'S BACKSLIDING; BREAKING THE COVENANT

1. Building His Harem

11:1 1 Kgs 3:1; 7:8 9:24 Neh 13:26

11 BUT king Solomon loved many strange women, together with the daughter of Pharaoh, women of the Moabites, Ammonites, Edomites, Zi-do′ni-ans, *and* Hittites;

10:21 So plentiful was gold that silver "was nothing accounted of in the days of Solomon." Even the cups were made of gold.

10:22 *navy of Tharshish* (Tarshish), i.e., "ships of Tarshish" (RSV). These were probably large vessels trading with Tarshish, which was in Sardinia or southern Spain. W. F. Albright thinks *Tarshish* may mean "refinery." If so, ships of Tarshish would mean that the port of origin was the refinery at Eziongeber.

10:23 Solomon had asked God for wisdom. He got both wisdom and riches. None was greater than he. Yet Solomon "wrote a whole book to show the vanity of all worldly things and the vexation of spirit that attends them, their insufficiency to make us happy and the folly of setting our hearts upon them."*

[2]Of the nations *concerning* which the LORD said unto the children of
Israel, Ye shall not go in to them, neither shall they come in unto you: *for*
surely they will turn away your heart after their gods: Solomon clave unto
these in love.
[3]And he had seven hundred wives, princesses, and three hundred
concubines: and his wives turned away his heart.
[4]For it came to pass, when Solomon was old, *that* his wives turned away
his heart after other gods: and his heart was not perfect with the LORD his
God, as *was* the heart of David his father.
[5]For Solomon went after Ash'to-reth the goddess of the Zi-do'ni-ans, and
after Mil'com the abomination of the Ammonites.
[6]And Solomon did evil in the sight of the LORD, and went not fully after
the LORD, as *did* David his father.
[7]Then did Solomon build an high place for Che'mosh, the abomination
of Moab, in the hill that *is* before Jerusalem, and for Mo'lech, the
abomination of the children of Ammon.
[8]And likewise did he for all his strange wives, which burnt incense and
sacrificed unto their gods.

11:2 Ex 23:32, 33; 34:12–14; Deut 7:3, 4; 17:17
☆**11:3** 2 Sam 5:13
☆**11:4**
☆**11:5** Judg 2:12–14; 10:6; 1 Sam 7:3, 4; 12:10; 1 Kgs 11:33; 2 Kgs 23:13
11:7 Lev 20:2; Num 21:27–30; Judg 11:24; 2 Kgs 23:10, 13

2. God's Judgment on Solomon

[9]¶And the LORD was angry with Solomon, because his heart was turned
from the LORD God of Israel, which had appeared unto him twice,
[10]And had commanded him concerning this thing, that he should not go
after other gods: but he kept not that which the LORD commanded.
[11]Wherefore the LORD said unto Solomon, Forasmuch as this is done of
thee, and thou hast not kept my covenant and my statutes, which I have
commanded thee, I will surely rend the kingdom from thee, and will give it
to thy servant.
[12]Notwithstanding in thy days I will not do it for David thy father's sake:
but I will rend it out of the hand of thy son.
[13]Howbeit I will not rend away all the kingdom; *but* will give one tribe to
thy son for David my servant's sake, and for Jerusalem's sake which I have
chosen.

☆**11:9** 1 Kgs 3:5; 9:2, 3
☆**11:10**
☆**11:11** 1 Sam 2:30; 1 Kgs 6:11, 12; 11:31
☆**11:12** 1 Kgs 21:29
☆**11:13**

11:3 Solomon's acquisition of wives, horses, silver, and gold constituted a violation of Deut. 17:16, 17.
11:4 Solomon's many wives turned his heart away from God, which eventually led to his downfall. David was bad in this regard and Solomon was worse. His wisdom failed him at this point. Curiously, there is no record that Israel ever witnessed to God in such a way that other nations decided to follow Israel's God. Rather it worked the other way. Israel again and again came into contact with pagan peoples who influenced them for evil. In the modern world the same thing has happened. Nations that once were generally Christian have now been lost to the faith and only small numbers of their people ever enter a church on the Lord's Day.
11:5 *Ashtoreth,* also known as Astarte, a Canaanite goddess of fertility. *Milcom* was another name for Molech, the god to whom children were sacrificed (Lev. 20:1–5). (See note on Zeph. 1:5.)
11:9, 10 To backslide is to turn away from God, to leave one's first love. When this happens, fellowship is broken. Backsliding occurs in a variety of ways. In David's case, it was a breach of the moral law when he committed adultery and murder (2 Sam. 11). It may be a verbal denial of Jesus, as by Peter (Matt. 26:70–74). It may be disobedience to an express command of God, as in the case of Saul (1 Sam. 15:11). Backsliding is not incurable. Repentance, confession, and restitution change matters. Samson changed (Judg. 16:28); David repented and was restored (2 Sam. 12:13); Peter repented and was changed after Pentecost (Acts 2:14ff).
11:11–13 God now informs Solomon that he is angry with the king because of his backsliding. How he did this we are not told. No prophet is mentioned here who speaks for God. God gave Solomon all a king could desire and still he chose not to remain faithful. The judgment would result in the division of Solomon's kingdom, with the loss of the ten tribes to another monarch. For the sake of David's memory, this would be delayed until after the death of Solomon.

3. Tribulation in Solomon's Time
a. Hadad the Edomite

11:14☆ 14 ¶And the LORD stirred up an adversary unto Solomon, Ha'dad the
Edomite: he *was* of the king's seed in Edom.
11:15 15 For it came to pass, when David was in Edom, and Jo'ab the captain of
2 Sam 8:13, 14 1 Chron 18:12 the host was gone up to bury the slain, after he had smitten every male in
Edom;
11:16 16 (For six months did Jo'ab remain there with all Israel, until he had cut
Num 10:12 off every male in Edom:)
17 That Ha'dad fled, he and certain Edomites of his father's servants with
him, to go into Egypt; Ha'dad *being* yet a little child.
18 And they arose out of Mid'i-an, and came to Paran: and they took men
with them out of Paran, and they came to Egypt, unto Pharaoh king of
Egypt; which gave him an house, and appointed him victuals, and gave him
land.
19 And Ha'dad found great favour in the sight of Pharaoh, so that he gave
him to wife the sister of his own wife, the sister of Tah'pen-es the queen.
20 And the sister of Tah'pen-es bare him Ge-nu'bath his son, whom
Tah'pen-es weaned in Pharaoh's house: and Ge-nu'bath was in Pharaoh's
household among the sons of Pharaoh.
11:21 21 And when Ha'dad heard in Egypt that David slept with his fathers, and
1 Kgs 2:10, 34 that Jo'ab the captain of the host was dead, Ha'dad said to Pharaoh, Let me
depart, that I may go to mine own country.
22 Then Pharaoh said unto him, But what hast thou lacked with me, that,
behold, thou seekest to go to thine own country? And he answered,
Nothing: howbeit let me go in any wise.

b. Rezon

11:23 23 ¶And God stirred him up *another* adversary, Re'zon the son of E-li'a-
2 Sam 8:3 10:15, 16 dah, which fled from his lord Had-ad-e'zer king of Zo'bah:
11:24 24 And he gathered men unto him, and became captain over a band, when
2 Sam 10:7, 8 David slew them *of Zo'bah:* and they went to Damascus, and dwelt therein,
and reigned in Damascus.
25 And he was an adversary to Israel all the days of Solomon, beside the
mischief that Ha'dad *did:* and he abhorred Israel, and reigned over Syria.

c. Jeroboam

11:26 26 ¶And Jer-o-bo'am the son of Ne'bat, an Eph'rath-ite of Zer'e-da,
1 Kgs 13:1 2 Chron 13:6 Solomon's servant, whose mother's name *was* Ze-ru'ah, a widow woman,
even he lifted up *his* hand against the king.
11:27 27 And this *was* the cause that he lifted up *his* hand against the king:
Prov 22:29 Solomon built Mil'lo, *and* repaired the breaches of the city of David his
father.
28 And the man Jer-o-bo'am *was* a mighty man of valour: and Solomon
seeing the young man that he was industrious, he made him ruler over all
the charge of the house of Joseph.
11:29 29 And it came to pass at that time when Jer-o-bo'am went out of
1 Kgs 12:15 14:2 2 Chron 10:15 Jerusalem, that the prophet A-hi'jah the Shi'lo-nite found him in the way;

11:14 Beginning with this verse we learn that God raised up three enemies to act as his agents in judgment upon Solomon. The first was Hadad the Edomite, whose pilgrimage is traced in 11:14–22. Then in 11:23–25 we learn of Rezon, who reigned over Syria and who hated Israel fervently. He played the adversary role for God. The third was Jeroboam, who came from the tribe of Ephraim. He became king of Israel.

and he had clad himself with a new garment; and they two *were* alone in the field:

30And A-hi'jah caught the new garment that *was* on him, and rent it *in* 11:30 1 Sam 15:27
twelve pieces:

31And he said to Jer-o-bo'am, Take thee ten pieces: for thus saith the 11:31 1 Kgs 11:11
LORD, the God of Israel, Behold, I will rend the kingdom out of the hand of
Solomon, and will give ten tribes to thee:

32(But he shall have one tribe for my servant David's sake, and for ☆11:32
Jerusalem's sake, the city which I have chosen out of all the tribes of Israel:)

33Because that they have forsaken me, and have worshipped Ash'to-reth 11:33 1 Kgs 11:5, 7
the goddess of the Zi-do'ni-ans, Che'mosh the god of the Moabites, and
Mil'com the god of the children of Ammon, and have not walked in my
ways, to do *that which is* right in mine eyes, and *to keep* my statutes and my
judgments, as *did* David his father.

34Howbeit I will not take the whole kingdom out of his hand: but I will
make him prince all the days of his life for David my servant's sake, whom
I chose, because he kept my commandments and my statutes:

35But I will take the kingdom out of his son's hand, and will give it unto 11:35 1 Kgs 12:16
thee, *even* ten tribes.

36And unto his son will I give one tribe, that David my servant may have 11:36 1 Kgs 15:4 2 Kgs 8:19 2 Chron 21:7
a light alway before me in Jerusalem, the city which I have chosen me to
put my name there.

37And I will take thee, and thou shalt reign according to all that thy soul
desireth, and shalt be king over Israel.

38And it shall be, if thou wilt hearken unto all that I command thee, and 11:38 2 Sam 7:11, 27 1 Kgs 14:7-9
wilt walk in my ways, and do *that is* right in my sight, to keep my statutes
and my commandments, as David my servant did; that I will be with thee,
and build thee a sure house, as I built for David, and will give Israel unto
thee.

39And I will for this afflict the seed of David, but not for ever.

40Solomon sought therefore to kill Jer-o-bo'am. And Jer-o-bo'am arose, ☆11:40 1 Kgs 12:2-4 14:25 2 Chron 12:2
and fled into Egypt, unto Shi'shak king of Egypt, and was in Egypt until the
death of Solomon.

N. THE DEATH OF SOLOMON

41¶And the rest of the acts of Solomon, and all that he did, and his 11:41 2 Chron 9:29
wisdom, *are* they not written in the book of the acts of Solomon?

42And the time that Solomon reigned in Jerusalem over all Israel *was*
forty years.

43And Solomon slept with his fathers, and was buried in the city of David ☆11:43 1 Kgs 14:21 2 Chron 9:31
his father: and Re-ho-bo'am his son reigned in his stead.

11:32 *he shall have one tribe.* Of the twelve tribes, Judah and Benjamin were left to Solomon's son. Benjamin had already been assimilated by Judah, the more numerous and powerful neighbor, and both were often called "Judah."

11:40 Jeroboam was an industrious worker, "a man of valour" (11:28). Ahijah the prophet told him that God would give him ten tribes, for Solomon's kingdom was to be divided into two parts because of his sins. Solomon obviously knew of this coming judgment from God, and his spiritual state was such that he refused to accept the consequences for his transgressions. In full rebellion against the word from God, he tried to slay Jeroboam. Jeroboam was forced to flee to Egypt for his life, until the death of Solomon.

11:43 Solomon may have been wise and wealthy, and he may have written many words that are helpful. But when the writer of the Hebrews spoke of the great saints of the Old Testament he mentioned David and Samuel but not a word about Solomon. Perhaps it was due to the fact that when God spoke the word of judgment, Solomon is not said to have repented as his father did.

III. THE TWO KINGDOMS (12:1—22:53)

A. THE BREAKING UP OF SOLOMON'S KINGDOM

1. The Rebellion of the Ten Tribes of Israel

12:1☆ Josh 20:7; 24:1 Judg 9:1, 6 2 Chron 10:1 12:2 1 Sam 8:18

12 AND Re-ho-bo'am went to She'chem: for all Israel were come to
She'chem to make him king.
[2]And it came to pass, when Jer-o-bo'am the son of Ne'bat, who was yet
in Egypt, heard *of it*, (for he was fled from the presence of king Solomon,
and Jer-o-bo'am dwelt in Egypt;)
[3]That they sent and called him. And Jer-o-bo'am and all the congrega-
tion of Israel came, and spake unto Re-ho-bo'am, saying,
[4]Thy father made our yoke grievous: now therefore make thou the
grievous service of thy father, and his heavy yoke which he put upon us,
lighter, and we will serve thee.

12:5 1 Kgs 12:12

[5]And he said unto them, Depart yet *for* three days, then come again to
me. And the people departed.
[6]¶And king Re-ho-bo'am consulted with the old men, that stood before
Solomon his father while he yet lived, and said, How do ye advise that I
may answer this people?
[7]And they spake unto him, saying, If thou wilt be a servant unto this
people this day, and wilt serve them, and answer them, and speak good
words to them, then they will be thy servants for ever.
[8]But he forsook the counsel of the old men, which they had given him,
and consulted with the young men that were grown up with him, *and* which
stood before him:

12:9 2 Chron 10:8 18:3–5

[9]And he said unto them, What counsel give ye that we may answer this
people, who have spoken to me, saying, Make the yoke which thy father did
put upon us lighter?
[10]And the young men that were grown up with him spake unto him,
saying, Thus shalt thou speak unto this people that spake unto thee, saying,
Thy father made our yoke heavy, but make thou *it* lighter unto us; thus
shalt thou say unto them, My little *finger* shall be thicker than my father's
loins.
[11]And now whereas my father did lade you with a heavy yoke, I will add
to your yoke: my father hath chastised you with whips, but I will chastise
you with scorpions.

12:12 1 Kgs 12:5

[12]¶So Jer-o-bo'am and all the people came to Re-ho-bo'am the third day,
as the king had appointed, saying, Come to me again the third day.

12:13☆

[13]And the king answered the people roughly, and forsook the old men's
counsel that they gave him;
[14]And spake to them after the counsel of the young men, saying, My
father made your yoke heavy, and I will add to your yoke: my father *also*
chastised you with whips, but I will chastise you with scorpions.

12:1ff Rehoboam was Solomon's successor to the throne. Solomon had already introduced foreign elements and practices into Israel. Moreover, Solomon's heavy taxation policies and use of forced labor alienated the Israelites from the North. Israel had assembled at Shechem to formally make Rehoboam king. Before his investiture, though, he was asked to lighten the heavy yoke placed on the people by Solomon. He inadvisedly responded with great rigor, "I will add to your yoke: my father also chastised you with whips, but I will chastise you with scorpions" (12:14). Jeroboam, who had come back from Egypt, was the leader of the northern Israelis who had asked for relief. When it was not granted, the northern tribes defected from the Davidic monarchy and set up Jeroboam as their king. Thus began the history of the two kingdoms of Israel and Judah.

12:13 Unlike his grandfather, Rehoboam sought the advice of old and young men instead of seeking God for his will. He was "the son of the wisest of men, yet he did not inherit his father's wisdom."* Neither wisdom nor grace runs in the blood. If at forty (as Rehoboam was when he became king) he did not have wisdom, he was not likely to gain it thereafter.

15 Wherefore the king hearkened not unto the people; for the cause was
from the LORD, that he might perform his saying, which the LORD spake by
A-hi′jah the Shi′lo-nite unto Jer-o-bo′am the son of Ne′bat.
16 ¶So when all Israel saw that the king hearkened not unto them, the
people answered the king, saying, What portion have we in David? neither
have we inheritance in the son of Jesse: to your tents, O Israel: now see to
thine own house, David. So Israel departed unto their tents.
17 But *as for* the children of Israel which dwelt in the cities of Judah, Re-
ho-bo′am reigned over them.
18 Then king Re-ho-bo′am sent A-do′ram, who *was* over the tribute; and
all Israel stoned him with stones, that he died. Therefore king Re-ho-bo′am
made speed to get him up to his chariot, to flee to Jerusalem.
19 So Israel rebelled against the house of David unto this day.
20 And it came to pass, when all Israel heard that Jer-o-bo′am was come
again, that they sent and called him unto the congregation, and made him
king over all Israel: there was none that followed the house of David, but
the tribe of Judah only.

☆12:15 Deut 2:30; Judg 14:4; 2 Chron 10:15; 22:7; Amos 3:6
12:16 2 Sam 20:1
12:18 2 Sam 20:24
12:19 2 Kgs 17:21; 2 Chron 10:19; Isa 7:17
☆12:20 1 Kgs 12:2–4

2. Rehoboam Forbidden to Fight Jeroboam

21 ¶And when Re-ho-bo′am was come to Jerusalem, he assembled all the
house of Judah, with the tribe of Benjamin, an hundred and fourscore
thousand chosen men, which were warriors, to fight against the house of
Israel, to bring the kingdom again to Re-ho-bo′am the son of Solomon.
22 But the word of God came unto Shem-a-i′ah the man of God, saying,
23 Speak unto Re-ho-bo′am, the son of Solomon, king of Judah, and unto
all the house of Judah and Benjamin, and to the remnant of the people,
saying,
24 Thus saith the LORD, Ye shall not go up, nor fight against your brethren
the children of Israel: return every man to his house; for this thing is from
me. They hearkened therefore to the word of the LORD, and returned to
depart, according to the word of the LORD.

☆12:21 2 Chron 11:1
12:22 2 Chron 11:2; 12:5

3. Jeroboam Makes Two Calf-Idols

25 ¶Then Jer-o-bo′am built She′chem in mount E′phra-im, and dwelt
therein; and went out from thence, and built Pe-nu′el.
26 And Jer-o-bo′am said in his heart, Now shall the kingdom return to the
house of David:
27 If this people go up to do sacrifice in the house of the LORD at
Jerusalem, then shall the heart of this people turn again unto their lord,
even unto Re-ho-bo′am king of Judah, and they shall kill me, and go again
to Re-ho-bo′am king of Judah.
28 Whereupon the king took counsel, and made two calves *of* gold, and

☆12:25 Judg 8:8, 17
12:27 Deut 12:4, 5
☆12:28 Ex 32:4; 2 Kgs 10:29; 17:16; 2 Chron 11:15; Hos 8:5

12:15 The God of providence brought about the decision of Rehoboam, which would lead to the fulfillment of the divine prophecy uttered by Ahijah the Shilonite, who said the kingdom would be divided and Solomon's heir left with only Judah for his lot.

12:20 *the tribe of Judah only.* Judah and Benjamin were sometimes (as in this instance) counted together as one tribe.†

12:21 Rehoboam's desire to conquer Israel by force and re-establish his father's undivided kingdom was forbidden him by God, who sent Shemaiah the prophet to tell him so. God had visited Solomon by direct communication but made no such visitation to Rehoboam.

12:25 *Jeroboam built Shechem,* i.e., "Jeroboam fortified and rebuilt the city."

12:28 When the kingdom of Solomon was divided, Jeroboam, king of the Northern Kingdom, did not wish his people to go to Jerusalem for their religious services. So he set up two calves for their worship, one in Beth-el, not far from Jerusalem, and the other in Dan in the far north. Jeroboam's statement *behold thy gods* was taken from Exod. 32:4, implying that his images were similar to the golden calf of Aaron. Some think Jeroboam only intended the calves to be pedestals, much like the cherubim, over which the invisible God was enthroned. Later, the people worshipped the visible objects (bringing about the most awful apostasy which permeated the kingdom), incurred the wrath of God, and brought about the end of the ten tribes in 722 B.C.

said unto them, It is too much for you to go up to Jerusalem: behold thy gods, O Israel, which brought thee up out of the land of Egypt.

12:29 Gen 28:19; 35:1 Judg 20:1

29 And he set the one in Beth–el, and the other put he in Dan.

12:30 1 Kgs 13:34 2 Kgs 10:31 17:21

30 And this thing became a sin: for the people went *to worship* before the one, *even* unto Dan.

12:31☆ Num 3:10 2 Kgs 17:32 2 Chron 11:13, 14; 13:9

31 And he made an house of high places, and made priests of the lowest of the people, which were not of the sons of Levi.

12:32 Lev 23:33, 34

32 And Jer-o-bo'am ordained a feast in the eighth month, on the fifteenth day of the month, like unto the feast that *is* in Judah, and he offered upon the altar. So did he in Beth–el, sacrificing unto the calves that he had made: and he placed in Beth–el the priests of the high places which he had made.

33 So he offered upon the altar which he had made in Beth–el the fifteenth day of the eighth month, *even* in the month which he had devised of his own heart; and ordained a feast unto the children of Israel: and he offered upon the altar, and burnt incense.

B. GOD SENDS A JUDEAN PROPHET TO JEROBOAM

1. The Birth of Josiah Prophesied

13:1☆ 2 Kgs 23:17

13 AND, behold, there came a man of God out of Judah by the word of the LORD unto Beth–el: and Jer-o-bo'am stood by the altar to burn incense.

13:2 2 Kgs 23:15, 16

2 And he cried against the altar in the word of the LORD, and said, O altar, altar, thus saith the LORD; Behold, a child shall be born unto the house of David, Jo-si'ah by name; and upon thee shall he offer the priests of the high places that burn incense upon thee, and men's bones shall be burnt upon thee.

13:3 2 Kgs 20:8

3 And he gave a sign the same day, saying, This *is* the sign which the LORD hath spoken; Behold, the altar shall be rent, and the ashes that *are* upon it shall be poured out.

13:4☆

4 And it came to pass, when king Jer-o-bo'am heard the saying of the man of God, which had cried against the altar in Beth–el, that he put forth his hand from the altar, saying, Lay hold on him. And his hand, which he put forth against him, dried up, so that he could not pull it in again to him.

5 The altar also was rent, and the ashes poured out from the altar, according to the sign which the man of God had given by the word of the LORD.

13:6 Ex 8:8, 28; 9:28 Jer 37:3 Acts 8:24

6 And the king answered and said unto the man of God, Intreat now the face of the LORD thy God, and pray for me, that my hand may be restored me again. And the man of God besought the LORD, and the king's hand was restored him again, and became as *it was* before.

13:7 1 Sam 9:7 2 Kgs 5:15

7 And the king said unto the man of God, Come home with me, and refresh thyself, and I will give thee a reward.

12:31 Generally, *high places* were places of worship located on a hill or mountain and associated with false religions. Before the end of the Northern Kingdom and the destruction of Jerusalem by Nebuchadnezzar, the Israelites built many such shrines and engaged in pagan worship ceremonies.

12:32 *the eighth month, on the fifteenth day* (of the Hebrew calendar) i.e., "the first of November." This was a month later than the annual celebration in Jerusalem, which God had ordained.†

13:1ff Jeroboam turned out to be an idolatrous king. He revived the bull worship of Mesopotamian origin, established high places for worship, and appointed non-Levites as priests. He even changed the date of the feast of tabernacles. He reigned for twenty-two years and was succeeded by his son Nadab, who was assassinated by Baasha less than two years after his kingship began.

13:4 Jeroboam was about to offer sacrifices to God on a strange altar. "How could the gift be acceptable when the altar that should sanctify it was an abomination?"* God's anger and the prophetic word of the man of God were confirmed by signs and wonders. Jeroboam's arm was dried up and he could not move it. The altar was rent and the ashes poured out from the altar. But none of this moved Jeroboam to repentance. He invited the man of God to go home with him.

8 And the man of God said unto the king, If thou wilt give me half thine
house, I will not go in with thee, neither will I eat bread nor drink water in
this place:
9 For so was it charged me by the word of the LORD, saying, Eat no bread, **13:9** Num 22:18 24:13
nor drink water, nor turn again by the same way that thou camest.
10 So he went another way, and returned not by the way that he came to
Beth–el.

2. The Prophet from Judah Deceived

11 ¶Now there dwelt an old prophet in Beth–el; and his sons came and ☆**13:11**
told him all the works that the man of God had done that day in Beth–el:
the words which he had spoken unto the king, them they told also to their
father.
12 And their father said unto them, What way went he? For his sons had
seen what way the man of God went, which came from Judah.
13 And he said unto his sons, Saddle me the ass. So they saddled him the
ass: and he rode thereon,
14 And went after the man of God, and found him sitting under an oak:
and he said unto him, *Art* thou the man of God that camest from Judah?
And he said, I *am*.
15 Then he said unto him, Come home with me, and eat bread.
16 And he said, I may not return with thee, nor go in with thee: neither
will I eat bread nor drink water with thee in this place:
17 For it was said to me by the word of the LORD, Thou shalt eat no bread
nor drink water there, nor turn again to go by the way that thou camest.
18 He said unto him, I *am* a prophet also as thou *art;* and an angel spake
unto me by the word of the LORD, saying, Bring him back with thee into
thine house, that he may eat bread and drink water. *But* he lied unto him.
19 So he went back with him, and did eat bread in his house, and drank
water.

3. God Kills the Judean Prophet for Disobedience

20 ¶And it came to pass, as they sat at the table, that the word of the LORD ☆**13:20**
came unto the prophet that brought him back:
21 And he cried unto the man of God that came from Judah, saying, Thus **13:21** 1 Sam 15:26
saith the LORD, Forasmuch as thou hast disobeyed the mouth of the LORD,
and hast not kept the commandment which the LORD thy God commanded
thee,
22 But camest back, and hast eaten bread and drunk water in the place, of
the which *the LORD* did say to thee, Eat no bread, and drink no water; thy
carcase shall not come unto the sepulchre of thy fathers.

13:11 God's unnamed prophet received an invitation to visit and eat with an unnamed old prophet. God had told him not to eat and drink. He had already refused to be honored by Jeroboam, but now he falls into sin through the words of a false prophet, who pretends to have received a word from God through an angel countermanding what God had told the true prophet in the first place. God's good prophet believes the lie and eats and drinks with the bad one. It reminds us of the Pauline injunction that if an angel claiming to be from heaven preached any other gospel than the one Paul had received, he was to be disbelieved—for the gospel does not change. Neither does the word from God. The prophet here should have believed God, not the false prophet. Whatever countermands what God has said is to be regarded as false.

13:20 Now God gives a true word to the lying prophet and through him pronounces judgment on the one who ate and drank contrary to God's specific command. Herein we learn that "no man shall be protected in disobedience by the sanctity of his profession, the dignity of his office, his nearness to God, or any good services he has done for him . . . by this God intended to warn all those whom he employs strictly to observe their orders at their peril."*

[23]¶And it came to pass, after he had eaten bread, and after he had drunk, that he saddled for him the ass, *to wit*, for the prophet whom he had brought back.

13:24 1 Kgs 20:36
[24]And when he was gone, a lion met him by the way, and slew him: and his carcase was cast in the way, and the ass stood by it, the lion also stood by the carcase.

[25]And, behold, men passed by, and saw the carcase cast in the way, and the lion standing by the carcase: and they came and told *it* in the city where the old prophet dwelt.

13:26☆
[26]And when the prophet that brought him back from the way heard *thereof*, he said, It *is* the man of God, who was disobedient unto the word of the LORD: therefore the LORD hath delivered him unto the lion, which hath torn him, and slain him, according to the word of the LORD, which he spake unto him.

[27]And he spake to his sons, saying, Saddle me the ass. And they saddled *him*.

[28]And he went and found his carcase cast in the way, and the ass and the lion standing by the carcase: the lion had not eaten the carcase, nor torn the ass.

[29]And the prophet took up the carcase of the man of God, and laid it upon the ass, and brought it back: and the old prophet came to the city, to mourn and to bury him.

[30]And he laid his carcase in his own grave; and they mourned over him, *saying*, Alas, my brother!

13:31 2 Kgs 23:17
[31]And it came to pass, after he had buried him, that he spake to his sons, saying, When I am dead, then bury me in the sepulchre wherein the man of God *is* buried; lay my bones beside his bones:

[32]For the saying which he cried by the word of the LORD against the altar in Beth-el, and against all the houses of the high places which *are* in the cities of Sa-ma′ri-a, shall surely come to pass.

4. Jeroboam Persists in His Apostasy

13:33☆ 2 Chron 13:9
[33]¶After this thing Jer-o-bo′am returned not from his evil way, but made again of the lowest of the people priests of the high places: whosoever would, he consecrated him, and he became *one* of the priests of the high places.

13:34 1 Kgs 14:10 15:29 2 Kgs 17:21
[34]And this thing became sin unto the house of Jer-o-bo′am, even to cut *it* off, and to destroy *it* from off the face of the earth.

14:1☆
5. Ahijah Foretells the Death of Abijah, Jeroboam's Son

14:2 1 Sam 28:7, 8 2 Sam 14:2, 3 2 Chron 18:29
14 AT that time A-bi′jah the son of Jer-o-bo′am fell sick.
[2]And Jer-o-bo′am said to his wife, Arise, I pray thee, and disguise

---

13:26 The lying prophet concluded that the death of the true prophet was the result of disobeying the command of God. He wished to be buried in the same grave with the dead prophet. If God's judgment was fair, the lying prophet should have asked himself why God did not send the lion to consume *him* for his transgression because, after all, he was an accessory before the fact. See 2 Kings 23:15ff for the sequel.

13:33 Jeroboam spurned the evidences God sent to convince him of his own iniquity. The pagan altar had been rent, the ashes poured out, his arm withered, and the true prophet was lying in his grave. What more could God do to make a case against this wicked king?

14:1 This sickness of Jeroboam's son causes him to seek the counsel of Ahijah the prophet. He sends his wife, who is disguised as another woman. Perhaps he thought that since Ahijah foretold his kingship over Israel, he would get good news a second time from the prophet. God told Ahijah that Jeroboam's wife was on the way. Before she could enter into his presence he identifies her and gives forth a prophetic word: the child will die, and all the descendants of Jeroboam shall perish and their bodies be disposed of in an ignominious way. The child who died was the only one who had a normal burial. Again the reason for the adverse prophecy is this: God who had given Israel to him was angry because he disobeyed the commands of God to him and was guilty of dreadful sin.

thyself, that thou be not known to be the wife of Jer-o-bo'am; and get thee
to Shi'loh: behold, there *is* A-hi'jah the prophet, which told me that *I should*
be king over this people.
3 And take with thee ten loaves, and cracknels, and a cruse of honey, and
go to him: he shall tell thee what shall become of the child.
4 And Jer-o-bo'am's wife did so, and arose, and went to Shi'loh, and came
to the house of A-hi'jah. But A-hi'jah could not see; for his eyes were set by
reason of his age.
5 ¶And the LORD said unto A-hi'jah, Behold, the wife of Jer-o-bo'am
cometh to ask a thing of thee for her son; for he *is* sick: thus and thus shalt
thou say unto her: for it shall be, when she cometh in, that she shall feign
herself *to be* another *woman.*
6 And it was *so,* when A-hi'jah heard the sound of her feet, as she came in
at the door, that he said, Come in, thou wife of Jer-o-bo'am; why feignest
thou thyself *to be* another? for I *am* sent to thee *with* heavy *tidings.*
7 Go, tell Jer-o-bo'am, Thus saith the LORD God of Israel, Forasmuch as
I exalted thee from among the people, and made thee prince over my
people Israel,
8 And rent the kingdom away from the house of David, and gave it thee:
and *yet* thou hast not been as my servant David, who kept my command-
ments, and who followed me with all his heart, to do *that* only *which was*
right in mine eyes;
9 But hast done evil above all that were before thee: for thou hast gone
and made thee other gods, and molten images, to provoke me to anger, and
hast cast me behind thy back:
10 Therefore, behold, I will bring evil upon the house of Jer-o-bo'am, and
will cut off from Jer-o-bo'am him that pisseth against the wall, *and* him that
is shut up and left in Israel, and will take away the remnant of the house of
Jer-o-bo'am, as a man taketh away dung, till it be all gone.
11 Him that dieth of Jer-o-bo'am in the city shall the dogs eat; and him
that dieth in the field shall the fowls of the air eat: for the LORD hath
spoken *it.*
12 Arise thou therefore, get thee to thine own house: *and* when thy feet
enter into the city, the child shall die.
13 And all Israel shall mourn for him, and bury him: for he only of Jer-o-
bo'am shall come to the grave, because in him there is found *some* good
thing toward the LORD God of Israel in the house of Jer-o-bo'am.
14 Moreover the LORD shall raise him up a king over Israel, who shall cut
off the house of Jer-o-bo'am that day: but what? even now.
15 For the LORD shall smite Israel, as a reed is shaken in the water, and he
shall root up Israel out of this good land, which he gave to their fathers, and
shall scatter them beyond the river, because they have made their groves,
provoking the LORD to anger.
16 And he shall give Israel up because of the sins of Jer-o-bo'am, who did
sin, and who made Israel to sin.

14:3 1 Sam 9:7, 8; 2 Kgs 4:42
14:4 1 Sam 3:2, 3; 4:15
14:7 1 Kgs 11:28, 31; 12:20
14:8 1 Kgs 11:30, 33; 15:5
14:9 Ex 34:17; 1 Kgs 13:33; 2 Chron 11:15; Ps 50:17; Ezek 23:35
☆**14:10** 1 Kgs 21:22; 2 Kgs 9:8
14:11 1 Kgs 16:4–7; 21:24
14:12 1 Kgs 14:17
14:14 1 Kgs 15:27, 29
14:15 Ex 34:17; Deut 12:3; 1 Sam 12:25; Ps 52:5

6. The Death of Jeroboam; Nadab Becomes King

17 ¶And Jer-o-bo'am's wife arose, and departed, and came to Tir'zah: *and*
when she came to the threshold of the door, the child died;
18 And they buried him; and all Israel mourned for him, according to the

☆**14:17** 1 Kgs 15:21; 16:9

14:10 *him that pisseth against the wall, and him that is shut up and left in Israel,* i.e., "this boy who is sick and all those who are well."†

14:17 *Tirzah* (meaning "a delight"), the first capital of Northern Israel, formerly a Canaanite city.

word of the LORD, which he spake by the hand of his servant A-hi′jah the
prophet.

14:19☆ 1 Kgs 14:29; 15:7, 23, 31; 16:4–7, 14, 20; 1 Chron 9:1

19 And the rest of the acts of Jer-o-bo′am, how he warred, and how he
reigned, behold, they *are* written in the book of the chronicles of the kings
of Israel.
20 And the days which Jer-o-bo′am reigned *were* two and twenty years:
and he slept with his fathers, and Na′dab his son reigned in his stead.

C. THE KINGDOM OF JUDAH
1. Rehoboam's Reign
a. The Depravity of Judah

14:21 1 Kgs 11:32, 36; 2 Kgs 21:7; 2 Chron 12:13; 13:7

21 ¶And Re-ho-bo′am the son of Solomon reigned in Judah. Re-ho-bo′am
was forty and one years old when he began to reign, and he reigned
seventeen years in Jerusalem, the city which the LORD did choose out of all
the tribes of Israel, to put his name there. And his mother's name *was* Na′a-
mah an Ammonitess.

14:22☆ 1 Kgs 14:9; 2 Chron 12:1, 14

22 And Judah did evil in the sight of the LORD, and they provoked him to
jealousy with their sins which they had committed, above all that their
fathers had done.

14:23 Deut 16:22; 2 Kgs 17:10; Isa 57:5; Jer 2:20; Ezek 16:24

23 For they also built them high places, and images, and groves, on every
high hill, and under every green tree.

14:24 Deut 23:17, 18; 1 Kgs 15:12; 22:46; 2 Kgs 23:7

24 And there were also sodomites in the land: *and* they did according to
all the abominations of the nations which the LORD cast out before the
children of Israel.

b. Shishak of Egypt Conquers Jerusalem

14:25☆ 2 Chron 12:2, 9

25 ¶And it came to pass in the fifth year of king Re-ho-bo′am, *that*
Shi′shak king of Egypt came up against Jerusalem:

14:26☆ 1 Kgs 7:51; 10:16, 17; 15:18

26 And he took away the treasures of the house of the LORD, and the
treasures of the king's house; he even took away all: and he took away all
the shields of gold which Solomon had made.
27 And king Re-ho-bo′am made in their stead brasen shields, and
committed *them* unto the hands of the chief of the guard, which kept the
door of the king's house.
28 And it was *so*, when the king went into the house of the LORD, that the
guard bare them, and brought them back into the guard chamber.

c. Rehoboam Dies; Abijam Reigns

29 ¶Now the rest of the acts of Re-ho-bo′am, and all that he did, *are* they
not written in the book of the chronicles of the kings of Judah?

14:30☆ 1 Kgs 15:6; 2 Chron 12:15

30 And there was war between Re-ho-bo′am and Jer-o-bo′am all *their*
days.
31 And Re-ho-bo′am slept with his fathers, and was buried with his fathers

---

14:19 *The book of the chronicles.* These and the chronicles (annals) of Judah (14:29) were the official court records from which the books of Kings and Chronicles are derived in part.

14:22 Both Jeroboam and Rehoboam were wicked kings. It is possible to have a bad ruler who lives among good people. Here the scripture says that Judah was no better than the king. The people did evil in the sight of God so that like the husband whose wife was adulterous, God was offended by the breaking of the covenant relationship.

14:25, 26 God sent Shishak, the king of Egypt, to afflict Judah and to remove the treasures of both the house of God and the house of the king. This was only the beginning of the diminishing of the Davidic throne—until the day of Christ, who would spring from dry ground.

14:30 Rehoboam died and the sorry note of continual warfare between him and Jeroboam (who outlived him) is left for us to ponder. He went into the house of the Lord (14:28), but those visits seem to have had no good effect on him or on his kingdom. Outward performances of devotion cannot hide a heart that is not right with God.

in the city of David. And his mother's name *was* Na'a-mah an Ammonitess.
And A-bi'jam his son reigned in his stead.

2. Abijam's Short Reign; Asa Becomes King

15 NOW in the eighteenth year of king Jer-o-bo'am the son of Ne'bat
reigned A-bi'jam over Judah.
☆15:1 2 Chron 13:1

2 Three years reigned he in Jerusalem. And his mother's name *was* Ma'a-
chah, the daughter of A-bish'a-lom,
3 And he walked in all the sins of his father, which he had done before
him: and his heart was not perfect with the LORD his God, as the heart of
David his father.
15:3 1 Kgs 11:4

4 Nevertheless for David's sake did the LORD his God give him a lamp in
Jerusalem, to set up his son after him, and to establish Jerusalem.
15:4 2 Chron 21:7

5 Because David did *that which was* right in the eyes of the LORD, and
turned not aside from any *thing* that he commanded him all the days of his
life, save only in the matter of U-ri'ah the Hittite.
15:5 2 Sam 11:4, 15; 12:9; 1 Kgs 9:4; 14:8

6 And there was war between Re-ho-bo'am and Jer-o-bo'am all the days
of his life.
☆15:6 1 Kgs 14:30

7 Now the rest of the acts of A-bi'jam, and all that he did, *are* they not
written in the book of the chronicles of the kings of Judah? And there was
war between A-bi'jam and Jer-o-bo'am.
15:7 1 Kgs 14:29; 2 Chron 13:1, 2

8 And A-bi'jam slept with his fathers; and they buried him in the city of
David: and Asa his son reigned in his stead.
15:8 1 Chron 3:10–14; 2 Chron 14:1

3. Asa's Long Reign

a. Asa's Reformation; He Pleased the Lord

9 ¶And in the twentieth year of Jer-o-bo'am king of Israel reigned Asa
over Judah.
☆15:9

10 And forty and one years reigned he in Jerusalem. And his mother's
name *was* Ma'a-chah, the daughter of A-bish'a-lom,
11 And Asa did *that which was* right in the eyes of the LORD, as *did* David
his father.
15:11 2 Chron 14:2; 15:17

12 And he took away the sodomites out of the land, and removed all the
idols that his fathers had made.
15:12 Deut 23:17, 18; 1 Kgs 22:46; 2 Chron 15:3

13 And also Ma'a-chah his mother, even her he removed from *being* queen,
because she had made an idol in a grove; and Asa destroyed her idol, and
burnt *it* by the brook Kidron.
15:13 2 Chron 15:16

14 But the high places were not removed: nevertheless Asa's heart was
perfect with the LORD all his days.
☆15:14 1 Kgs 22:43; 2 Kgs 12:3; 14:4

15 And he brought in the things which his father had dedicated, and the
things which himself had dedicated, into the house of the LORD, silver, and
gold, and vessels.
15:15 1 Kgs 14:27

15:1 *Abijam* here but "Abijah" in 2 Chron. 13:1. Abijah means "My father is the Lord." He is called by the name Abijah in 2 Chron. for there he called upon God for help, was heard, and was given a great victory against Jeroboam. The Chronicler lays no wickedness to his charge. The writer of Kings, however, charges him with his faults. "Jah," the name of God, is removed from his name as a disgrace to him; instead, he is called "Abijam" which means "father of light."

15:6 *between Rehoboam and Jeroboam,* i.e., "between Israel and Judah."

15:9 Asa's reign is compressed in this account. 2 Chron. 14–16 enlarges on it considerably. Asa's reign was considerably better than those of Rehoboam and Abijam. He began a reform movement and is said to have had a heart that followed God (15:14), yet he did not do as much as was needed to offset the reigns of his two predecessors.

15:14 *nevertheless Asa's heart was perfect with the LORD all his days,* i.e., "Asa did not realize that the high places were wrong."†

b. The War between Asa and Baasha; Asa's Death and Jehoshaphat His Successor

16¶And there was war between Asa and Ba'a-sha king of Israel all their
days.

15:17 2 Chron 16:1

17And Ba'a-sha king of Israel went up against Judah, and built Ra'mah,
that he might not suffer any to go out or come in to Asa king of Judah.

15:18☆ 1 Kgs 14:26; 20:1-5; 2 Kgs 12:18

18Then Asa took all the silver and the gold *that were* left in the treasures
of the house of the LORD, and the treasures of the king's house, and
delivered them into the hand of his servants: and king Asa sent them to
Ben-ha'dad, the son of Tab'ri-mon, the son of He'zi-on, king of Syria, that
dwelt at Damascus, saying,

15:19 2 Chron 16:7

19*There is* a league between me and thee, *and* between my father and thy
father: behold, I have sent unto thee a present of silver and gold; come and
break thy league with Ba'a-sha king of Israel, that he may depart from me.
20So Ben-ha'dad hearkened unto king Asa, and sent the captains of the
hosts which he had against the cities of Israel, and smote I'jon, and Dan,
and A'bel-beth-ma'a-chah, and all Cin'ne-roth, with all the land of
Naph'ta-li.

15:21 2 Chron 16:5

21And it came to pass, when Ba'a-sha heard *thereof*, that he left off
building of Ra'mah, and dwelt in Tir'zah.

15:22 2 Chron 16:6

22Then king Asa made a proclamation throughout all Judah; none *was*
exempted: and they took away the stones of Ra'mah, and the timber
thereof, wherewith Ba'a-sha had builded; and king Asa built with them
Ge'ba of Benjamin, and Mizpah.

15:23 1 Kgs 15:7, 31; 2 Chron 16:11

23The rest of all the acts of Asa, and all his might, and all that he did, and
the cities which he built, *are* they not written in the book of the chronicles
of the kings of Judah? Nevertheless in the time of his old age he was
diseased in his feet.

15:24☆ 1 Kgs 22:41; 2 Chron 16:13, 14; 17:1

24And Asa slept with his fathers, and was buried with his fathers in the
city of David his father: and Je-hosh'a-phat his son reigned in his stead.

D. JEROBOAM'S SUCCESSORS IN ISRAEL (NORTHERN KINGDOM)

1. Nadab, an Evil King

15:25☆ 1 Kgs 14:20

25¶And Na'dab the son of Jer-o-bo'am began to reign over Israel in the
second year of Asa king of Judah, and reigned over Israel two years.

15:26 1 Kgs 12:28; 13:33; 14:16

26And he did evil in the sight of the LORD, and walked in the way of his
father, and in his sin wherewith he made Israel to sin.

15:27 Josh 21:23, 24

27¶And Ba'a-sha the son of A-hi'jah, of the house of Is'sa-char, conspired
against him; and Ba'a-sha smote him at Gib'be-thon, which *belonged* to the
Philistines; for Na'dab and all Israel laid siege to Gib'be-thon.
28Even in the third year of Asa king of Judah did Ba'a-sha slay him, and
reigned in his stead.

15:18 The Old Testament mentions three Ben-hadads of Damascus. The first one is mentioned in this verse. His son, Ben-hadad II, was the one who warred against Ahab and besieged Samaria unsuccessfully. Ahab defeated him at Aphek and he was smothered by Hazael, who seized the crown (see 1 Kings 20; 2 Kings 7, 8). The third king named Ben-hadad was the son of Hazael, mentioned in 2 Kings 13:24. He lost the territories his father had taken from the Israelites.

15:24 Asa, for the most part, prospered. Yet there were wars fought between Judah and Israel that vexed and weakened each of them. This civil war syndrome aided the external enemies of God's people. Toward the end of his life Asa suffered from what probably was gout; moreover, his temperament suffered—making him peevish and difficult.

15:25 In the second year of Asa's reign, Jeroboam died. From that time until the reign of Ahab (who came to the throne at the end of Asa's reign), Israel was in turmoil. From the end of Jeroboam's reign to the beginning of Ahab's kingship there were six monarchs: Nadab, Baasha, Elah, Zimri, Tibni, and Omri. Nadab lasted two years. He was slain by Baasha, who promptly killed off all of the house of Jeroboam, thus fulfilling the prophecy of Ahijah the Shilonite, a prophet of God.

29 And it came to pass, when he reigned, *that* he smote all the house of ☆15:29 1 Kgs 14:14
Jer-o-bo′am; he left not to Jer-o-bo′am any that breathed, until he had
destroyed him, according unto the saying of the LORD, which he spake by
his servant A-hi′jah the Shi′lo-nite:
30 Because of the sins of Jer-o-bo′am which he sinned, and which he made
Israel sin, by his provocation wherewith he provoked the LORD God of
Israel to anger.
31 ¶Now the rest of the acts of Na′dab, and all that he did, *are* they not 15:31 1 Kgs 14:19
written in the book of the chronicles of the kings of Israel? 16:4–7, 14

2. Baasha, a Wicked Monarch

32 And there was war between Asa and Ba′a-sha king of Israel all their 15:32 1 Kgs 15:16
days. 2 Chron 15:19
33 In the third year of Asa king of Judah began Ba′a-sha the son of ☆15:33
A-hi′jah to reign over all Israel in Tir′zah, twenty and four years.
34 And he did evil in the sight of the LORD, and walked in the way of Jer-
o-bo′am, and in his sin wherewith he made Israel to sin.

16 THEN the word of the LORD came to Jehu the son of Ha-na′ni 16:1 1 Kgs 16:12
against Ba′a-sha, saying, 2 Chron 19:2 20:34
2 Forasmuch as I exalted thee out of the dust, and made thee prince over 16:2 1 Sam 2:8
my people Israel; and thou hast walked in the way of Jer-o-bo′am, and hast 1 Kgs 14:7
made my people Israel to sin, to provoke me to anger with their sins;
3 Behold, I will take away the posterity of Ba′a-sha, and the posterity of 16:3 1 Kgs 14:10
his house; and will make thy house like the house of Jer-o-bo′am the son of 15:29; 21:21
Ne′bat.
4 Him that dieth of Ba′a-sha in the city shall the dogs eat; and him that 16:4 1 Kgs 14:11
dieth of his in the fields shall the fowls of the air eat. 15:31; 16:14
5 Now the rest of the acts of Ba′a-sha, and what he did, and his might, *are* 21:19 Isa 66:24
they not written in the book of the chronicles of the kings of Israel?
6 So Ba′a-sha slept with his fathers, and was buried in Tir′zah: and E′lah
his son reigned in his stead.
7 And also by the hand of the prophet Jehu the son of Ha-na′ni came
the word of the LORD against Ba′a-sha, and against his house, even for
all the evil that he did in the sight of the LORD, in provoking him to anger
with the work of his hands, in being like the house of Jer-o-bo′am; and
because he killed him.

3. Elah's Short Reign

8 In the twenty and sixth year of Asa king of Judah began E′lah the son of ☆16:8
Ba′a-sha to reign over Israel in Tir′zah, two years.
9 And his servant Zimri, captain of half *his* chariots, conspired against ☆16:9 2 Kgs 9:31
him, as he was in Tir′zah, drinking himself drunk in the house of Ar′za
steward of *his* house in Tir′zah.

15:29 Baasha murdered all the possible aspirants to the throne from the house of Jeroboam. The history of the Northern Kingdom is replete with the rise and fall of one dynasty after another. The descendants of David, however, sat on the throne of Judah without interruption until the kingship of Zedekiah, at which time the kingdom practically ceased. The Northern Kingdom of Israel did not have a single good king. Judah, on the other hand, had some good kings and some bad ones.

15:33 *Baasha* lasted twenty-four years. He was a wicked king who led his people into sin. God gave a word to Jehu (the son of Hanani) against Baasha, in which the divine judgment was mandated that the whole house of Baasha should be wiped out, as was the house of Jeroboam (16:3). On the death of Baasha, his son Elah became king (16:6).

16:8–11 Elah's kingship lasted two years. He was murdered by one of his own soldiers, Zimri, who replaced him. Whereas Nadab died more honorably (on the field of battle), Elah was a drunken sot who died in his servant's house. Zimri proceeded to wipe out the entire family of Elah, as Baasha had wiped out that of Jeroboam. Zimri's vengeance went so far that he slew his friends also, so that no one was left to act as avenger for the death of Elah.

10 And Zimri went in and smote him, and killed him, in the twenty and
seventh year of Asa king of Judah, and reigned in his stead.

4. Zimri's Seven Day Reign

16:11 1 Kgs 14:10 15:29

11 ¶And it came to pass, when he began to reign, as soon as he sat on his
throne, *that* he slew all the house of Ba'a-sha: he left him not one that
pisseth against a wall, neither of his kinsfolks, nor of his friends.

16:12 1 Kgs 16:1

12 Thus did Zimri destroy all the house of Ba'a-sha, according to the word
of the LORD, which he spake against Ba'a-sha by Jehu the prophet,

16:13 Deut 32:21 1 Kgs 15:30

13 For all the sins of Ba'a-sha, and the sins of E'lah his son, by which they
sinned, and by which they made Israel to sin, in provoking the LORD God
of Israel to anger with their vanities.

16:14 1 Kgs 16:4–7, 20, 28, 30

14 Now the rest of the acts of E'lah, and all that he did, *are* they not
written in the book of the chronicles of the kings of Israel?

16:15☆

15 In the twenty and seventh year of Asa king of Judah did Zimri reign
seven days in Tir'zah. And the people *were* encamped against Gib'be-thon,
which *belonged* to the Philistines.

16:16☆

16 And the people *that were* encamped heard say, Zimri hath conspired,
and hath also slain the king: wherefore all Israel made Omri, the captain of
the host, king over Israel that day in the camp.

16:17☆

17 And Omri went up from Gib'be-thon, and all Israel with him, and they
besieged Tir'zah.

16:18☆ 1 Sam 31:4, 5 2 Sam 17:23

18 And it came to pass, when Zimri saw that the city was taken, that he
went into the palace of the king's house, and burnt the king's house over
him with fire, and died.

16:19☆ 1 Kgs 12:28 14:6

19 For his sins which he sinned in doing evil in the sight of the LORD, in
walking in the way of Jer-o-bo'am, and in his sin which he did, to make
Israel to sin.

16:20 1 Kgs 16:14, 27

20 Now the rest of the acts of Zimri, and his treason that he wrought, *are*
they not written in the book of the chronicles of the kings of Israel?

5. Omri a Wicked King; Ahab His Successor

16:21, 22☆

21 ¶Then were the people of Israel divided into two parts: half of the
people followed Tib'ni the son of Gi'nath, to make him king; and half
followed Omri.

22 But the people that followed Omri prevailed against the people that
followed Tib'ni the son of Gi'nath: so Tib'ni died, and Omri reigned.

16:24☆ 1 Kgs 13:32 18:2 Jn 4:4

23 In the thirty and first year of Asa king of Judah began Omri to reign
over Israel, twelve years: six years reigned he in Tir'zah.

24 And he bought the hill Sa-ma'ri-a of She'mer for two talents of silver,

---

16:15–19 Zimri had a very short reign. While he was killing off the relatives and friends of Elah, the army of Israel was busy at Gibbethon. When it was learned that Zimri had slain Elah, Omri was made king of Israel in the field—as was done by the Romans on occasion. Thus there were two kings at the same time. Omri and the army went to Tirzah where Zimri was. They took the city and went to the king's house where Zimri was hiding. Rather than being killed by Omri and his body being given to the birds and beasts of the field, Zimri burned the house and perished in the flames.

16:21, 22 Omri became king only to find that Tibni was a rival claimant to the throne. Half of the people of Israel followed Tibni. The contest lasted for some years before Tibni died (in what fashion the account does not say) and Omri reigned alone. Omri was a wicked king known for his idolatry. He left for posterity one who would do greater works of wickedness and leave his name stained in the pages of sacred writ. Ahab, his son, succeeded to the throne on Omri's death.

16:24 *Samaria.* Omri was the originator of the scheme to build Samaria, which became the capital of the Northern Kingdom of the ten tribes of Israel. Omri did more evil than all the kings who preceded him. But he was an important secular figure. For almost one hundred years the Assyrians called Israel the House of Omri. (See Mic. 6:16 for Omri's importance relative to official Baal worship.)

and built on the hill, and called the name of the city which he built, after
the name of She'mer, owner of the hill, Sa-ma'ri-a.
25¶But Omri wrought evil in the eyes of the LORD, and did worse than all
that *were* before him.
26For he walked in all the way of Jer-o-bo'am the son of Ne'bat, and in
his sin wherewith he made Israel to sin, to provoke the LORD God of Israel
to anger with their vanities.
27Now the rest of the acts of Omri which he did, and his might that he
shewed, *are* they not written in the book of the chronicles of the kings of
Israel?
28So Omri slept with his fathers, and was buried in Sa-ma'ri-a: and Ahab
his son reigned in his stead.

16:25 1 Kgs 14:9; Mic 6:16
16:26 1 Kgs 13:33, 34
16:27 1 Kgs 16:20; 22:39
16:28 2 Chron 18:1

E. KING AHAB OF ISRAEL VERSUS ELIJAH, GOD'S PROPHET
1. Ahab and Jezebel, an Evil Combination

29¶And in the thirty and eighth year of Asa king of Judah began Ahab
the son of Omri to reign over Israel: and Ahab the son of Omri reigned over
Israel in Sa-ma'ri-a twenty and two years.
30And Ahab the son of Omri did evil in the sight of the LORD above all
that *were* before him.
31And it came to pass, as if it had been a light thing for him to walk in the
sins of Jer-o-bo'am the son of Ne'bat, that he took to wife Jez'e-bel the
daughter of Eth-ba'al king of the Zi-do'ni-ans, and went and served Ba'al,
and worshipped him.
32And he reared up an altar for Ba'al in the house of Ba'al, which he had
built in Sa-ma'ri-a.
33And Ahab made a grove; and Ahab did more to provoke the LORD
God of Israel to anger than all the kings of Israel that were before him.
34In his days did Hi'el the Beth-elite build Jericho: he laid the foundation
thereof in A-bi'ram his firstborn, and set up the gates thereof in his
youngest *son* Se'gub, according to the word of the LORD, which he spake by
Joshua the son of Nun.

☆**16:29**
16:31 Deut 7:3, 4; 1 Kgs 11:5; 2 Kgs 10:18; 17:16
16:32 2 Kgs 10:21, 26
16:33 1 Kgs 21:19, 25; 2 Kgs 13:6
☆**16:34** Josh 6:26

2. Elijah, the Prophet, and the Drought
a. The Ravens Feed Elijah

17 AND E-li'jah the Tish'bite, *who was* of the inhabitants of Gilead,
said unto Ahab, *As* the LORD God of Israel liveth, before whom I
stand, there shall not be dew nor rain these years, but according to my
word.
2And the word of the LORD came unto him, saying,
3Get thee hence, and turn thee eastward, and hide thyself by the brook
Che'rith, that *is* before Jordan.

☆**17:1** Judg 12:4; 1 Kgs 22:14; Lk 4:25; Jas 5:17
☆**17:3**

16:29 Ahab had the distinction of being the worst of all the kings of Israel. Jezebel, his wife, was equally wicked and brought in the vilest notions and practices of the Baal cult. Their daughter, Athaliah, married Jehoram, the king of Judah, and brought with her all the evils she had learned from her mother.
16:34 *the word of the LORD, which he spake by Joshua,* i.e., "the Lord's curse on whoever would seek to rebuild Jericho" (see Josh. 6:26).
17:1 Elijah springs to our attention out of nowhere. We are told nothing about his family background. The names of his mother and father are never mentioned. Thus God called a rough man for a rough work against a determined and scoundrelly king, Ahab. Similarly, God would later call a rough man like Martin Luther to spearhead the Reformation. Elijah stood before Ahab and prophesied the great famine, which would last until Elijah announced its end. He said to Ahab, in effect, "Expect no dew or rain until you hear from me again." Then he disappeared to an obscure, unfrequented place until the time God had set for the end of the famine. As the famine began and continued, we can imagine the thoughts which crossed the mind of Ahab as he searched desperately to locate the prophet of the bad news so he could twist his arm and force him to announce the end to the famine.
17:3 Elijah, by the express direction of God, fled from Ahab to the brook Cherith. There he was fed by ravens and drank from the brook. When the brook dried up, he could have gone to the Jordan, where there was water. But God directed him elsewhere.

17:4 1 Kgs 19:5

4 And it shall be, *that* thou shalt drink of the brook; and I have
commanded the ravens to feed thee there.
5 So he went and did according unto the word of the LORD: for he went
and dwelt by the brook Che'rith, that *is* before Jordan.
6 And the ravens brought him bread and flesh in the morning, and bread
and flesh in the evening; and he drank of the brook.
7 And it came to pass after a while, that the brook dried up, because there
had been no rain in the land.

b. The Widow and the Miraculous Supply of Food

17:8☆ Obad 20 Lk 4:25; 26

8 ¶And the word of the LORD came unto him, saying,
9 Arise, get thee to Zar'e-phath, which *belongeth* to Zi'don, and dwell
there: behold, I have commanded a widow woman there to sustain thee.

17:10 Gen 24:17 Jn 4:7

10 So he arose and went to Zar'e-phath. And when he came to the gate of
the city, behold, the widow woman *was* there gathering of sticks: and he
called to her, and said, Fetch me, I pray thee, a little water in a vessel, that
I may drink.
11 And as she was going to fetch *it*, he called to her, and said, Bring me, I
pray thee, a morsel of bread in thine hand.

17:12 2 Kgs 4:2 Mt 15:33

12 And she said, *As* the LORD thy God liveth, I have not a cake, but an
handful of meal in a barrel, and a little oil in a cruse: and, behold, I *am*
gathering two sticks, that I may go in and dress it for me and my son, that
we may eat it, and die.
13 And E-li'jah said unto her, Fear not; go *and* do as thou hast said: but
make me thereof a little cake first, and bring *it* unto me, and after make for
thee and for thy son.
14 For thus saith the LORD God of Israel, The barrel of meal shall not
waste, neither shall the cruse of oil fail, until the day *that* the LORD sendeth
rain upon the earth.
15 And she went and did according to the saying of E-li'jah: and she, and
he, and her house, did eat *many* days.

17:16☆

16 *And* the barrel of meal wasted not, neither did the cruse of oil fail,
according to the word of the LORD, which he spake by E-li'jah.

c. Elijah Revives the Widow's Dead Son

17:17☆

17 ¶And it came to pass after these things, *that* the son of the woman, the
mistress of the house, fell sick; and his sickness was so sore, that there was
no breath left in him.

17:8 Jezebel, the wife of wicked Ahab, was a Sidonian. God sent Elijah to the very place from which she came and protected him from Ahab among Gentiles. Zarephath was on the Mediterranean seacoast between Sidon and Tyre. The home to which he was sent was impoverished. The widow and her son expected to die, but a miracle was performed so that the cruse of oil and the jar of meal remained fillled. Elijah, the widow, and her son were fed despite the famine.

17:16 Elijah and Elisha together performed more miracles than any other two men since Israel had entered the land of Canaan. Elijah performed five miracles; Elisha no fewer than twelve miracles, according to the record. Of course, they may have performed more miracles than were recorded. Given the span of time from creation to the opening of the New Testament, the number of miracles was few, and those which were performed came in clusters and were available at times of national crisis. Most of the Old Testament miracles came during the time of Elisha and Elijah, and during these eras: (1) the time of Israel's deliverance from Egypt and before the entrance into the Promised Land; (2) the middle of the ninth century before the kingdom of Israel was finally obliterated; and (3) during the Babylonian exile, when the question of Judah's return to the land and its viability was in doubt.

17:17 The widow's son died suddenly, to the surprise of the mother, who was living well and entertaining a prophet who performed miracles. Why then should she expect difficulties? When this sharp affliction comes (in the midst of helping the prophet), she speaks as though Elijah were the cause of all her trouble. She thinks God may have sent Elijah to remind her of her past sins. (In the moment of trial and affliction we do well to remember our transgressions.) Elijah takes the boy and stretches over him and prays; and lo, the dead one comes to life and is received back into the arms of his loving mother.

18And she said unto E-li'jah, What have I to do with thee, O thou man of
God? art thou come unto me to call my sin to remembrance, and to slay my
son?
19And he said unto her, Give me thy son. And he took him out of her
bosom, and carried him up into a loft, where he abode, and laid him upon
his own bed.
20And he cried unto the LORD, and said, O LORD my God, hast thou also
brought evil upon the widow with whom I sojourn, by slaying her son?
21And he stretched himself upon the child three times, and cried unto the **17:21**
LORD, and said, O LORD my God, I pray thee, let this child's soul come into 2 Kgs 4:34 Acts 20:10–12
him again.
22And the LORD heard the voice of E-li'jah; and the soul of the child
came into him again, and he revived.
23And E-li'jah took the child, and brought him down out of the chamber **17:23**
into the house, and delivered him unto his mother: and E-li'jah said, See, 2 Kgs 4:36 Lk 7:15
thy son liveth. Acts 9:41 Heb 11:35
24¶And the woman said to E-li'jah, Now by this I know that thou *art* a ☆**17:24**
man of God, *and* that the word of the LORD in thy mouth *is* truth. Jn 2:11; 3:1, 2 11:15

3. Elijah's Triumph over Baal on Mount Carmel

a. Elijah and Obadiah Hold a Conversation

18 AND it came to pass *after* many days, that the word of the LORD ☆**18:1**
came to E-li'jah in the third year, saying, Go, shew thyself unto Jas 5:18
Ahab; and I will send rain upon the earth.
2And E-li'jah went to shew himself unto Ahab. And *there was* a sore **18:2**
famine in Sa-ma'ri-a. 1 Kgs 16:24
3And Ahab called O-ba-di'ah, which *was* the governor of *his* house. (Now ☆**18:3**
O-ba-di'ah feared the LORD greatly: 1 Kgs 18:16
4For it was *so*, when Jez'e-bel cut off the prophets of the LORD, that ☆**18:4**
O-ba-di'ah took an hundred prophets, and hid them by fifty in a cave, and
fed them with bread and water.)
5And Ahab said unto O-ba-di'ah, Go into the land, unto all fountains of
water, and unto all brooks: peradventure we may find grass to save the
horses and mules alive, that we lose not all the beasts.
6So they divided the land between them to pass throughout it: Ahab
went one way by himself, and O-ba-di'ah went another way by himself.
7¶And as O-ba-di'ah was in the way, behold, E-li'jah met him: and he
knew him, and fell on his face, and said, *Art* thou that my lord E-li'jah?
8And he answered him, I *am:* go, tell thy lord, Behold, E-li'jah *is here.* ☆**18:8**
9And he said, What have I sinned, that thou wouldest deliver thy servant ☆**18:9**
into the hand of Ahab, to slay me?

17:24 This woman knew that Elijah was a man of God when the cruse and the jar remained filled. At the death of her son she began to doubt. When her son came back to life "she was abundantly satisfied that Elijah had both the power and goodness of a man of God, and will never doubt of it again, but give herself to the direction of his word and the worship of the God of Israel."*

18:1 God's time to end the drought and to show Ahab the error of his ways has come. He dispatches Elijah to stand before Ahab. Since the priests and Levites had long since left Israel and gone to Judah, God raised up prophets to speak to Israel.

18:3, 4 Obadiah was a true believer who feared God, and was honest, industrious, and ingenious. Thus he was useful to a wicked king. But why he remained to serve such a man is not explained. Obadiah was not corrupted by the king, and the king evidently was not influenced spiritually by his servant. Perhaps God allowed him to remain with Ahab so that he could protect the prophets, who otherwise might have been murdered (18:4). Sometimes some of God's people are forced to live in a land from which there is no escape, and yet they do not succumb to evil nor do they transfer their allegiance from their God to other gods.

18:8–12 Elijah told Obadiah to inform Ahab that Elijah was on his way to meet the king face to face. Obadiah was frightened, for he thought Ahab would blame him for not seizing Elijah and bringing him back captive. He thought the Spirit of God might carry him away (18:12). In order to quell Obadiah's fears, Elijah promised to confront Ahab that very day.

10 *As* the LORD thy God liveth, there is no nation or kingdom, whither my
lord hath not sent to seek thee: and when they said, *He is* not *there;* he took
an oath of the kingdom and nation, that they found thee not.
11 And now thou sayest, Go, tell thy lord, Behold, E-li'jah *is here.*
18:12 2 Kgs 2:16; Ezek 3:12; Acts 8:39
12 And it shall come to pass, *as soon as* I am gone from thee, that the
Spirit of the LORD shall carry thee whither I know not; and *so* when I come
and tell Ahab, and he cannot find thee, he shall slay me: but I thy servant
fear the LORD from my youth.
18:13 1 Kgs 18:3; 4
13 Was it not told my lord what I did when Jez'e-bel slew the prophets of
the LORD, how I hid an hundred men of the LORD's prophets by fifty in a
cave, and fed them with bread and water?
14 And now thou sayest, Go, tell thy lord, Behold, E-li'jah *is here:* and he
shall slay me.
15 And E-li'jah said, *As* the LORD of hosts liveth, before whom I stand, I
will surely shew myself unto him to day.
16 So O-ba-di'ah went to meet Ahab, and told him: and Ahab went to
meet E-li'jah.

b. Elijah Appears before Ahab

18:17☆ Josh 7:25
17 ¶And it came to pass, when Ahab saw E-li'jah, that Ahab said unto
him, *Art* thou he that troubleth Israel?
18:18 1 Kgs 9:9; 21:25; 2 Chron 15:5
18 And he answered, I have not troubled Israel; but thou, and thy father's
house, in that ye have forsaken the commandments of the LORD, and thou
hast followed Ba'al-im.
19 Now therefore send, *and* gather to me all Israel unto mount Carmel,
and the prophets of Ba'al four hundred and fifty, and the prophets of the
groves four hundred, which eat at Jez'e-bel's table.

c. Baal's Priests Produce No Fire

18:20☆
20 So Ahab sent unto all the children of Israel, and gathered the prophets
together unto mount Carmel.
18:21 Josh 24:15; 2 Kgs 17:41; Zeph 1:5
21 And E-li'jah came unto all the people, and said, How long halt ye
between two opinions? if the LORD *be* God, follow him: but if Ba'al, *then*
follow him. And the people answered him not a word.
18:22 1 Kgs 19:10, 14
22 Then said E-li'jah unto the people, I, *even* I only, remain a prophet of
the LORD; but Ba'al's prophets *are* four hundred and fifty men.
23 Let them therefore give us two bullocks; and let them choose one
bullock for themselves, and cut it in pieces, and lay *it* on wood, and put no
fire *under:* and I will dress the other bullock, and lay *it* on wood, and put no
fire *under:*
18:24☆ 1 Sam 7:5; 1 Chron 21:26
24 And call ye on the name of your gods, and I will call on the name of the

---

18:17 Here we read of the meeting of "as bad a king as ever the world was plagued with and as good a prophet as ever the church was blessed with."* Ahab rudely and roughly accused Elijah of being the source of all his troubles. Elijah fearlessly pointed his finger right back at the wicked king and announced that it was Ahab who had followed Baalim and who had forsaken the commandments of God. Elijah majestically commanded Ahab to meet him at Mount Carmel and to bring with him the four hundred and fifty prophets of Baal and the four hundred prophets of Asherah, who were indentified with Jezebel. This would become the climactic moment of the prophet's life.
18:20 Presumably Ahab and Israel expected that Elijah, who had pronounced the coming of the famine, would now lift the judgment and bless the people. But Elijah had more important work to do first. Israel must be reproved for its idolatry and the name of the true God must, by word and miracle, be lifted above Baal.
18:24 Elijah knew that the people would not heed his words. They needed external corroborating evidence that God is the true God. He made them a proposition based on the coming of supernatural fire from heaven. The God who can give fire can also give rain. And if Baal can do this, Elijah told them, they ought to worship him. But if Baal cannot do this and the God of Israel can, then they should worship him. The people agreed and the pageant began.

LORD: and the God that answereth by fire, let him be God. And all the
people answered and said, It is well spoken.
25 And E-li'jah said unto the prophets of Ba'al, Choose you one bullock
for yourselves, and dress *it* first; for ye *are* many; and call on the name of
your gods, but put no fire *under.*
26 And they took the bullock which was given them, and they dressed *it,* 18:26
and called on the name of Ba'al from morning even until noon, saying, O Ps 115:5 Jer 10:5
Ba'al, hear us. But *there was* no voice, nor any that answered. And they 1 Cor 12:2
leaped upon the altar which was made.
27 And it came to pass at noon, that E-li'jah mocked them, and said, Cry
aloud: for he *is* a god; either he is talking, or he is pursuing, or he is in a
journey, *or* peradventure he sleepeth, and must be awaked.
28 And they cried aloud, and cut themselves after their manner with 18:28 Lev 19:28
knives and lancets, till the blood gushed out upon them. Deut 14:1
29 And it came to pass, when midday was past, and they prophesied until ☆18:29
the *time* of the offering of the *evening* sacrifice, that *there was* neither voice,
nor any to answer, nor any that regarded.

d. God's Fire Consumes Elijah's Sacrifice

30 And E-li'jah said unto all the people, Come near unto me. And all the 18:30 1 Kgs 19:10, 14
people came near unto him. And he repaired the altar of the LORD *that was*
broken down.
31 And E-li'jah took twelve stones, according to the number of the tribes 18:31
of the sons of Jacob, unto whom the word of the LORD came, saying, Israel Josh 4:2, 3
shall be thy name:
32 And with the stones he built an altar in the name of the LORD: and he ☆18:32
made a trench about the altar, as great as would contain two measures of
seed.
33 And he put the wood in order, and cut the bullock in pieces, and laid 18:33
him on the wood, and said, Fill four barrels with water, and pour *it* on the Gen 22:9
burnt sacrifice, and on the wood.
34 And he said, Do *it* the second time. And they did *it* the second time.
And he said, Do *it* the third time. And they did *it* the third time.
35 And the water ran round about the altar; and he filled the trench also
with water.
36 And it came to pass at *the time of* the offering of the *evening* sacrifice, 18:36
that E-li'jah the prophet came near, and said, LORD God of Abraham, Ex 3:6; 4:5 Num 16:28
Isaac, and of Israel, let it be known this day that thou *art* God in Israel, and 1 Sam 17:46 2 Kgs 19:19
that I *am* thy servant, and *that* I have done all these things at thy word. 1 Chron 29:18
37 Hear me, O LORD, hear me, that this people may know that thou *art* the
LORD God, and *that* thou hast turned their heart back again.
38 Then the fire of the LORD fell, and consumed the burnt sacrifice, and ☆18:38 Gen 15:17
the wood, and the stones, and the dust, and licked up the water that *was* in Lev 9:24; 10:1 2 Kgs 1:12
the trench. Job 1:16

18:29 Elijah did not interrupt the priests of Baal from cavorting around their sacrifice while they invoked Baal to send the fire. Their idols could do neither good nor evil. "The prince of the power of the air, if God had permitted him, could have caused *fire to come down from heaven* on this occasion, and gladly would have done it for the support of his Baal. We find that the beast which deceives the world does it. *He maketh fire come down from heaven in the sight of men and so deceiveth them* (Rev. 13:13, 14). But God would not suffer the devil to do it now, because the trial of his title was on that issue by consent of parties."*

18:32 *a trench about the altar, as great as would contain two measures of seed,* i.e., "three feet wide."†

18:38 *the fire of the LORD fell.* Unlike the gods of Ahab and Jezebel, God was not sleeping nor did he need to be persuaded by the cutting of the flesh of the body. Before Elijah finished speaking, God was already answering. The holy fire consumed the sacrifice, sucked up the water, and burned up the stones of the altar and even the dust itself. It was so mighty a miracle that terror overtook guilty Ahab and all the worshippers of Baal. They fled in fear, lest they too be consumed by the holy fire from heaven.

18:39 1 Kgs 8:60
39 And when all the people saw *it*, they fell on their faces: and they said, The LORD, he *is* the God; the LORD, he *is* the God.

18:40☆ Deut 13:5; 18:20 2 Kgs 10:24
40 And E-li'jah said unto them, Take the prophets of Ba'al; let not one of them escape. And they took them: and E-li'jah brought them down to the brook Ki'shon, and slew them there.

e. The Rain Falls

41 ¶And E-li'jah said unto Ahab, Get thee up, eat and drink; for *there is* a sound of abundance of rain.

42 So Ahab went up to eat and to drink. And E-li'jah went up to the top of Carmel; and he cast himself down upon the earth, and put his face between his knees,

43 And said to his servant, Go up now, look toward the sea. And he went up, and looked, and said, *There is* nothing. And he said, Go again seven times.

18:44☆
44 And it came to pass at the seventh time, that he said, Behold, there ariseth a little cloud out of the sea, like a man's hand. And he said, Go up, say unto Ahab, Prepare *thy chariot*, and get thee down, that the rain stop thee not.

45 And it came to pass in the mean while, that the heaven was black with clouds and wind, and there was a great rain. And Ahab rode, and went to Jez're-el.

18:46☆
46 And the hand of the LORD was on E-li'jah; and he girded up his loins, and ran before Ahab to the entrance of Jez're-el.

4. Elijah's Stay at Mount Horeb

a. Jezebel Threatens Elijah

19:1☆
19 AND Ahab told Jez'e-bel all that E-li'jah had done, and withal how he had slain all the prophets with the sword.

19:2☆ 2 Kgs 6:31
2 Then Jez'e-bel sent a messenger unto E-li'jah, saying, So let the gods do *to me*, and more also, if I make not thy life as the life of one of them by to morrow about this time.

19:3☆ Gen 21:31 Amos 7:12
3 And when he saw *that*, he arose, and went for his life, and came to Be'er–she'ba, which *belongeth* to Judah, and left his servant there.

b. Elijah Flees for His Life

19:4 Num 11:5 Job 3:20, 21 Jer 20:14 Jonah 4:3, 8
4 ¶But he himself went a day's journey into the wilderness, and came and sat down under a juniper tree: and he requested for himself that he might die; and said, It is enough; now, O LORD, take away my life; for I *am* not better than my fathers.

5 And as he lay and slept under a juniper tree, behold, then an angel touched him, and said unto him, Arise *and* eat.

18:40 Baal's prophets were seized. As criminals they were condemned and executed according to the law of God (see Deut. 13:1–11).

18:44 The prayer of Elijah, which was according to the will of God, was not answered when it was first offered. Seven times the servant rose to look for the cloud in the sky. Petitions delayed are not petitions denied. Perseverance in prayer is called for until the answer comes. We are to remain instant in prayer and neither faint nor cease praying.

18:46 *ran before Ahab* is translated *outran Ahab* in the NASB. Ahab rode in his chariot in ease and comfort. God gave Elijah the ability to outrun the chariot and arrive before Ahab did.

19:1–3 Ahab now recounted to Jezebel what Elijah had done. He gave credit to Elijah for what happened, thereby insulting the God of Elijah who was directly responsible for the fire. His heart remained unchanged. He excited the hatred of his wife, who was angry that Ahab had not killed Elijah. This she intended to accomplish, so Elijah fled for his life.

6 And he looked, and, behold, *there was* a cake baken on the coals, and a
cruse of water at his head. And he did eat and drink, and laid him down
again.
7 And the angel of the LORD came again the second time, and touched
him, and said, Arise *and* eat; because the journey *is* too great for thee.
8 And he arose, and did eat and drink, and went in the strength of that
meat forty days and forty nights unto Ho′reb the mount of God.

☆**19:8** Ex 3:1; 4:27; 24:18; 34:28; Deut 9:9; Mt 4:2

c. Elijah's Encounter with God

9 ¶And he came thither unto a cave, and lodged there; and, behold, the
word of the LORD *came* to him, and he said unto him, What doest thou
here, E-li′jah?
10 And he said, I have been very jealous for the LORD God of hosts: for
the children of Israel have forsaken thy covenant, thrown down thine altars,
and slain thy prophets with the sword; and I, *even* I only, am left; and they
seek my life, to take it away.
11 And he said, Go forth, and stand upon the mount before the LORD.
And, behold, the LORD passed by, and a great and strong wind rent the
mountains, and brake in pieces the rocks before the LORD; *but* the LORD
was not in the wind: and after the wind an earthquake; *but* the LORD *was*
not in the earthquake:
12 And after the earthquake a fire; *but* the LORD *was* not in the fire: and
after the fire a still small voice.
13 And it was *so*, when E-li′jah heard *it*, that he wrapped his face in his
mantle, and went out, and stood in the entering in of the cave. And, behold,
there came a voice unto him, and said, What doest thou here, E-li′jah?
14 And he said, I have been very jealous for the LORD God of hosts:
because the children of Israel have forsaken thy covenant, thrown down
thine altars, and slain thy prophets with the sword; and I, *even* I only, am
left; and they seek my life, to take it away.
15 And the LORD said unto him, Go, return on thy way to the wilderness
of Damascus: and when thou comest, anoint Haz′a-el *to be* king over Syria:
16 And Jehu the son of Nim′shi shalt thou anoint *to be* king over Israel:
and E-li′sha the son of Sha′phat of A′bel-me-ho′lah shalt thou anoint *to be*
prophet in thy room.
17 And it shall come to pass, *that* him that escapeth the sword of Haz′a-el
shall Jehu slay: and him that escapeth from the sword of Jehu shall E-li′sha
slay.
18 Yet I have left *me* seven thousand in Israel, all the knees which have not
bowed unto Ba′al, and every mouth which hath not kissed him.

☆**19:9**
19:10 Rom 11:2, 3
19:11 Ex 19:16, 19, 20; 24:12; Ezek 1:4
19:12 Ex 3:2, 6; Deut 4:11; Job 4:16
19:15 2 Kgs 8:8
☆**19:16** 2 Kgs 2:9; 9:1
19:17 2 Kgs 8:12, 13; 9:14; 13:3
☆**19:18** Hos 13:2; Rom 11:4

19:8 *Horeb,* i.e., "Mount Sinai," where Moses had gone. He hoped in his despondency to be renewed by God.
19:9 Elijah here displayed his humanity and thus disclosed his own weakness in the flesh. Great faith may be less great on some occasions. Elijah feared Jezebel would kill him, so he ran from that death to seek another death at the hand of God. He pleaded that he has had enough and asked God to kill him. Is this the Elijah who stood tall on Mount Carmel? "Can that great and gallant spirit shrink thus? God has left him to himself to show that when he was bold and strong it was *in the Lord and the power of his might,* but of himself he was *no better than his fathers* or brethren."* God still had something for him to do. He sent him to anoint Jehu to be king of Israel and to anoint Elisha to be Elijah's successor. Elijah was not allowed to die then so that he might never die but be translated for God's glory.
19:16 God announced to Elijah that the dynasty of Ahab was to end. Jehu was to be the successor. Elijah's ministry also was fast coming to its close. Therefore, he was to anoint Elisha to be prophet in his place. Before Ahab died, Elijah was to see him face to face, but God also employed an unnamed prophet to speak the divine word to this wicked king. In 20:13, 22 we see that this anonymous prophet spoke God's word to Ahab. In 20:35 "a certain man of the sons of the prophets" is used by God to prophesy the death of Ahab.
19:18 Despite Elijah's pessimism, 7,000 people were still faithful. God always has his remnant.

d. Elijah Puts His Coat over Elisha

19:19☆ 2 Kgs 2:8, 13, 14

19¶So he departed thence, and found E-li'sha the son of Sha'phat, who *was* plowing *with* twelve yoke *of oxen* before him, and he with the twelfth: and E-li'jah passed by him, and cast his mantle upon him.

20And he left the oxen, and ran after E-li'jah, and said, Let me, I pray thee, kiss my father and my mother, and *then* I will follow thee. And he said unto him, Go back again: for what have I done to thee?

21And he returned back from him, and took a yoke of oxen, and slew them, and boiled their flesh with the instruments of the oxen, and gave unto the people, and they did eat. Then he arose, and went after E-li'jah, and ministered unto him.

5. Ahab's War with Ben-hadad of Syria

a. Ben-hadad's Ultimatum

20:1☆ 2 Kgs 6:24

20 AND Ben-ha'dad the king of Syria gathered all his host together: and *there were* thirty and two kings with him, and horses, and chariots: and he went up and besieged Sa-ma'ri-a, and warred against it.

20:2 1 Kgs 15:18; 2 Chron 16:2

2And he sent messengers to Ahab king of Israel into the city, and said unto him, Thus saith Ben-ha'dad,

3Thy silver and thy gold *is* mine; thy wives also and thy children, *even* the goodliest, *are* mine.

4And the king of Israel answered and said, My lord, O king, according to thy saying, I *am* thine, and all that I have.

5And the messengers came again, and said, Thus speaketh Ben-ha'dad, saying, Although I have sent unto thee, saying, Thou shalt deliver me thy silver, and thy gold, and thy wives, and thy children;

6Yet I will send my servants unto thee to morrow about this time, and they shall search thine house, and the houses of thy servants; and it shall be, *that* whatsoever is pleasant in thine eyes, they shall put *it* in their hand, and take *it* away.

b. Ahab's Insulting Reply

7Then the king of Israel called all the elders of the land, and said, Mark, I pray you, and see how this *man* seeketh mischief: for he sent unto me for my wives, and for my children, and for my silver, and for my gold; and I denied him not.

8And all the elders and all the people said unto him, Hearken not *unto him*, nor consent.

9Wherefore he said unto the messengers of Ben-ha'dad, Tell my lord the king, All that thou didst send for to thy servant at the first I will do: but this thing I may not do. And the messengers departed, and brought him word again.

20:10 1 Kgs 19:2; 2 Kgs 6:31

10And Ben-ha'dad sent unto him, and said, The gods do so unto me, and more also, if the dust of Sa-ma'ri-a shall suffice for handfuls for all the people that follow me.

19:19 Elisha was plowing when the call of God came to him to take over Elijah's mantle and become God's prophet. That call of God was effectual, for God is sovereign. He was chosen; he did not choose his office himself. He merely accepted the divine will.

20:1ff Ahab was confronted by Ben-hadad, the king of Syria, who imperiously made demands on him. Ahab meekly accepted. Having lost confidence in God, he was without a defender, since Baal had been of no help (20:4). Then Ben-hadad sent a more ominous note. He wished to search every house and take anything he wanted. Ahab talked with his elders and they got him to refuse to submit. Ben-hadad intended to destroy Samaria. God intervened. He sent a prophet to tell Ahab that he would win the battle (20:13). Ahab was successful and the Syrians went home defeated but would return to battle against Ahab the next spring, as it was prophesied by the prophet God sent (20:22).

[11]And the king of Israel answered and said, Tell *him*, Let not him that girdeth on *his harness* boast himself as he that putteth it off. 20:11 Prov 27:1

[12]And it came to pass, when *Ben-ha'dad* heard this message, as he *was* drinking, he and the kings in the pavilions, that he said unto his servants, Set *yourselves in array*. And they set *themselves in array* against the city.

c. God's Prophet Promises Ahab Victory

[13]¶And, behold, there came a prophet unto Ahab king of Israel, saying, Thus saith the LORD, Hast thou seen all this great multitude? behold, I will deliver it into thine hand this day; and thou shalt know that I *am* the LORD. 20:13 2 Kgs 6:8–10

[14]And Ahab said, By whom? And he said, Thus saith the LORD, *Even* by the young men of the princes of the provinces. Then he said, Who shall order the battle? And he answered, Thou.

[15]Then he numbered the young men of the princes of the provinces, and they were two hundred and thirty two: and after them he numbered all the people, *even* all the children of Israel, *being* seven thousand.

d. Ahab's Military Success

[16]And they went out at noon. But Ben-ha'dad *was* drinking himself drunk in the pavilions, he and the kings, the thirty and two kings that helped him.

[17]And the young men of the princes of the provinces went out first; and Ben-ha'dad sent out, and they told him, saying, There are men come out of Sa-ma'ri-a.

[18]And he said, Whether they be come out for peace, take them alive; or whether they be come out for war, take them alive.

[19]So these young men of the princes of the provinces came out of the city, and the army which followed them.

[20]And they slew every one his man: and the Syrians fled; and Israel pursued them: and Ben-ha'dad the king of Syria escaped on an horse with the horsemen.

[21]And the king of Israel went out, and smote the horses and chariots, and slew the Syrians with a great slaughter.

e. The Prophet Foretells a Second Campaign

[22]¶And the prophet came to the king of Israel, and said unto him, Go, strengthen thyself, and mark, and see what thou doest: for at the return of the year the king of Syria will come up against thee.

6. The Second Campaign of Ahab against Ben-hadad

a. The Second Defeat of Ben-hadad

[23]And the servants of the king of Syria said unto him, Their gods *are* gods of the hills; therefore they were stronger than we; but let us fight against them in the plain, and surely we shall be stronger than they. ☆20:23

[24]And do this thing, Take the kings away, every man out of his place, and put captains in their rooms:

[25]And number thee an army, like the army that thou hast lost, horse for

20:23 The Syrians prepared for the second phase of the war against Israel. With little knowledge of the God of Israel they supposed that they lost the first battle because of Israel's "gods of the hills." They were polytheists and thought that Israel was too. (They may have known about Israel's commitment to Baal and in that event they would have been correct.) This time they plan to fight on the plains where the "gods of the hills" may have no power.

horse, and chariot for chariot: and we will fight against them in the plain,
and surely we shall be stronger than they. And he hearkened unto their
voice, and did so.
20:26 26 And it came to pass at the return of the year, that Ben-ha'dad
1 Sam 4:1; 29:1 2 Kgs 13:17 numbered the Syrians, and went up to A'phek, to fight against Israel.
20:27 27 And the children of Israel were numbered, and were all present, and
Judg 6:5 1 Sam 13:5 went against them: and the children of Israel pitched before them like two
little flocks of kids; but the Syrians filled the country.
20:28, 29☆ 28 ¶And there came a man of God, and spake unto the king of Israel, and
said, Thus saith the LORD, Because the Syrians have said, The LORD *is* God
of the hills, but he *is* not God of the valleys, therefore will I deliver all this
great multitude into thine hand, and ye shall know that I *am* the LORD.
29 And they pitched one over against the other seven days. And *so* it was,
that in the seventh day the battle was joined: and the children of Israel slew
of the Syrians an hundred thousand footmen in one day.
20:30 30 But the rest fled to A'phek, into the city; and *there* a wall fell upon
1 Kgs 22:25 2 Chron 18:24 twenty and seven thousand of the men *that were* left. And Ben-ha'dad fled,
and came into the city, into an inner chamber.

b. Ahab Makes a Covenant with Ben-hadad

20:31 31 ¶And his servants said unto him, Behold now, we have heard that the
Gen 37:34 1 Kgs 21:27 kings of the house of Israel *are* merciful kings: let us, I pray thee, put
Esth 4:3 sackcloth on our loins, and ropes upon our heads, and go out to the king of
Israel: peradventure he will save thy life.
20:32☆ 32 So they girded sackcloth on their loins, and *put* ropes on their heads,
and came to the king of Israel, and said, Thy servant Ben-ha'dad saith, I
pray thee, let me live. And he said, *Is* he yet alive? he *is* my brother.
20:33☆ 33 Now the men did diligently observe whether *any thing would come* from
him, and did hastily catch *it:* and they said, Thy brother Ben-ha'dad. Then
he said, Go ye, bring him. Then Ben-ha'dad came forth to him; and he
caused him to come up into the chariot.
20:34☆ 34 And *Ben-ha'dad* said unto him, The cities, which my father took from
1 Kgs 15:20 thy father, I will restore; and thou shalt make streets for thee in Damascus,
as my father made in Sa-ma'ri-a. Then *said Ahab,* I will send thee away with
this covenant. So he made a covenant with him, and sent him away.

c. God Pronounces the Coming Judgment on Ahab for Disobedience

20:35☆ 35 ¶And a certain man of the sons of the prophets said unto his neighbour
1 Kgs 13:16, 17 in the word of the LORD, Smite me, I pray thee. And the man refused to
smite him.
20:36 36 Then said he unto him, Because thou hast not obeyed the voice of the
1 Kgs 13:24 LORD, behold, as soon as thou art departed from me, a lion shall slay thee.
And as soon as he was departed from him, a lion found him, and slew him.

20:28 Ahab did not consult with the prophet of God. Instead, God sent the prophet to speak to Ahab. He said that God would enable Ahab to defeat the Syrians and would do this solely because the Syrians had insulted deity (by thinking it to be polytheistic). In this war both parties were defective: Ahab had neither praised God nor prayed to him; the Syrians had blasphemed God. God would preserve the honor of his name by giving Ahab the victory.
20:29 Syria's army was far greater in size than that of Israel, yet God allowed the lesser to destroy the greater.

20:32–34 Ben-hadad lost the battle and tamely pleaded for his life by ingratiating himself with Ahab. A covenant was made between the two leaders and Ben-hadad was set free, contrary to the instructions of God.
20:35 God commanded a certain prophet to let himself be smitten by another man. When this man refused to smite the prophet, he was slain by a lion for his refusal. Still another man smote the prophet, who now waits for Ahab along the highway. God would have no direct dealings with Ahab, who had ignored him; he dealt with him through an intermediary.

37 Then he found another man, and said, Smite me, I pray thee. And the
man smote him, so that in smiting he wounded *him.*
38 So the prophet departed, and waited for the king by the way, and
disguised himself with ashes upon his face.

20:38 2 Sam 14:2, 3 1 Kgs 14:2 22:30

39 And as the king passed by, he cried unto the king: and he said, Thy
servant went out into the midst of the battle; and, behold, a man turned
aside, and brought a man unto me, and said, Keep this man: if by any
means he be missing, then shall thy life be for his life, or else thou shalt pay
a talent of silver.

20:39 2 Kgs 10:24

40 And as thy servant was busy here and there, he was gone. And the king
of Israel said unto him, So *shall* thy judgment *be;* thyself hast decided *it.*
41 And he hasted, and took the ashes away from his face; and the king of
Israel discerned him that he *was* of the prophets.
42 And he said unto him, Thus saith the LORD, Because thou hast let go
out of *thy* hand a man whom I appointed to utter destruction, therefore thy
life shall go for his life, and thy people for his people.

☆**20:42**

43 And the king of Israel went to his house heavy and displeased, and
came to Sa-ma'ri-a.

7. Ahab Covets Naboth's Vineyard

a. Naboth Refuses to Sell the Vineyard

21 AND it came to pass after these things, *that* Na'both the Jez're-el-
ite had a vineyard, which *was* in Jez're-el, hard by the palace of
Ahab king of Sa-ma'ri-a.

☆**21:1** 2 Kgs 9:21

2 And Ahab spake unto Na'both, saying, Give me thy vineyard, that I
may have it for a garden of herbs, because it *is* near unto my house: and
I will give thee for it a better vineyard than it; *or,* if it seem good to thee,
I will give thee the worth of it in money.
3 And Na'both said to Ahab, The LORD forbid it me, that I should give
the inheritance of my fathers unto thee.

21:3 Lev 25:23 Num 36:6 Ezek 46:18

4 And Ahab came into his house heavy and displeased because of the
word which Na'both the Jez're-el-ite had spoken to him: for he had said, I
will not give thee the inheritance of my fathers. And he laid him down upon
his bed, and turned away his face, and would eat no bread.

b. Jezebel Has Naboth Killed

5 ¶But Jez'e-bel his wife came to him, and said unto him, Why is thy spirit
so sad, that thou eatest no bread?
6 And he said unto her, Because I spake unto Na'both the Jez're-el-ite,
and said unto him, Give me thy vineyard for money; or else, if it please
thee, I will give thee *another* vineyard for it: and he answered, I will not give
thee my vineyard.

20:42 King Ahab disobeyed God when he spared Ben-hadad. Ahab's excuse was that he had been busy. Busyness is neither an excuse nor a virtue when it interferes with the plan and will of God. Sometimes it merely means choosing the good instead of the best. True believers put God and his will first and busyness second (James 4:15; Matt. 6:10; Rom. 1:10; 15:32; Acts 21:14; Deut. 28:1ff).

21:1ff Ahab coveted the field which belonged to Naboth. Yet he offered to buy the field, for who would deny the king such a small request? Naboth had sufficient knowledge of the Word of God that he refused to sell what was his by tenancy, since it belonged to God. God forbade the sale of one's patrimony, which represented a stake in the economic order of the day. Ahab was angry and sullen. But Jezebel would not let her husband be denied that which he coveted. So, by her evil actions, she brought about the death of Naboth and the seizure of his land. This led to Elijah's final confrontation with the king, the announcement of the end of his dynasty, and the promise that "The dogs shall eat Jezebel by the wall of Jezreel" (21:23).

21:7 1 Sam 8:14 7 And Jez′e-bel his wife said unto him, Dost thou now govern the
kingdom of Israel? arise, *and* eat bread, and let thine heart be merry: I will
give thee the vineyard of Na′both the Jez′re-el-ite.
21:8 2 Sam 11:14 8 So she wrote letters in Ahab's name, and sealed *them* with his seal, and
2 Chron 32:17 sent the letters unto the elders and to the nobles that *were* in his city,
Esth 3:12; 8:8 dwelling with Na′both.
21:9☆ 9 And she wrote in the letters, saying, Proclaim a fast, and set Na′both on
high among the people:
21:10 10 And set two men, sons of Be′li-al, before him, to bear witness against
Ex 22:28 Lev 24:15, 16 him, saying, Thou didst blaspheme God and the king. And *then* carry him
Mt 26:59 Acts 6:11 out, and stone him, that he may die.
11 And the men of his city, *even* the elders and the nobles who were the
inhabitants in his city, did as Jez′e-bel had sent unto them, *and* as it *was*
written in the letters which she had sent unto them.
12 They proclaimed a fast, and set Na′both on high among the people.
13 And there came in two men, children of Be′li-al, and sat before him:
and the men of Be′li-al witnessed against him, *even* against Na′both, in the
presence of the people, saying, Na′both did blaspheme God and the king.
Then they carried him forth out of the city, and stoned him with stones,
that he died.
14 Then they sent to Jez′e-bel, saying, Na′both is stoned, and is dead.
15 ¶And it came to pass, when Jez′e-bel heard that Na′both was stoned,
and was dead, that Jez′e-bel said to Ahab, Arise, take possession of the
vineyard of Na′both the Jez′re-el-ite, which he refused to give thee for
money: for Na′both is not alive, but dead.
21:16☆ 16 And it came to pass, when Ahab heard that Na′both was dead, that
Ahab rose up to go down to the vineyard of Na′both the Jez′re-el-ite, to
take possession of it.

C. Elijah Pronounces Judgment on Ahab and Jezebel

17 ¶And the word of the LORD came to E-li′jah the Tish′bite, saying,
18 Arise, go down to meet Ahab king of Israel, which *is* in Sa-ma′ri-a:
behold, *he is* in the vineyard of Na′both, whither he is gone down to possess
it.
21:19 1 Kgs 22:38 19 And thou shalt speak unto him, saying, Thus saith the LORD, Hast thou
2 Kgs 9:26 killed, and also taken possession? And thou shalt speak unto him, saying,
Thus saith the LORD, In the place where dogs licked the blood of Na′both
shall dogs lick thy blood, even thine.
20 And Ahab said to E-li′jah, Hast thou found me, O mine enemy? And he
answered, I have found *thee:* because thou hast sold thyself to work evil in
the sight of the LORD.
21:21☆ 1 Kgs 14:10 21 Behold, I will bring evil upon thee, and will take away thy posterity,
2 Kgs 9:8 and will cut off from Ahab him that pisseth against the wall, and him that
is shut up and left in Israel,
21:22 1 Kgs 14:16 22 And will make thine house like the house of Jer-o-bo′am the son of
15:29; 16:3 Ne′bat, and like the house of Ba′a-sha the son of A-hi′jah, for the

---

21:9 *Proclaim a fast, and set Naboth on high among the people,* i.e., "Call the citizens together for fasting and prayer." Perhaps this inquiry was conducted ostensibly to discover whose sins had caused the famine.†

21:16 Ahab went in person, and probably with great fanfare, to take possession of the land that had been acquired as a result of murdering Naboth. Can God let such actions go unrequited?

21:21 God sent Elijah to confront Ahab and deliver the bad news of the approaching judgment on him and his house. Elijah had never brought him good news, so he expected the worst from his enemy. And he got it. What had happened to the house of Jeroboam and to Baasha's house would happen to him.

provocation wherewith thou hast provoked *me* to anger, and made Israel to
sin.
23 And of Jez'e-bel also spake the LORD, saying, The dogs shall eat Jez'e-
bel by the wall of Jez're-el.
24 Him that dieth of Ahab in the city the dogs shall eat; and him that
dieth in the field shall the fowls of the air eat.
25 ¶But there was none like unto Ahab, which did sell himself to work
wickedness in the sight of the LORD, whom Jez'e-bel his wife stirred up.
26 And he did very abominably in following idols, according to all *things*
as did the Am'or-ites, whom the LORD cast out before the children of Israel.

21:23 2 Kgs 9:10 33, 34
21:24 1 Kgs 14:11 16:4–7
21:26 Gen 15:16 Lev 18:25 Judg 6:10 2 Kgs 21:11

d. Ahab Humbles Himself

27 And it came to pass, when Ahab heard those words, that he rent his
clothes, and put sackcloth upon his flesh, and fasted, and lay in sackcloth,
and went softly.
28 And the word of the LORD came to E-li'jah the Tish'bite, saying,
29 Seest thou how Ahab humbleth himself before me? because he
humbleth himself before me, I will not bring the evil in his days: *but* in his
son's days will I bring the evil upon his house.

☆21:27 Gen 37:34 2 Kgs 6:26–30 18:37
21:29 1 Kgs 22:38 2 Kgs 9:25, 26 2 Chron 12:7 34:27

8. Ahab's Last Syrian Campaign

a. Jehoshaphat Agrees to Help Ahab

22 AND they continued three years without war between Syria and
Israel.
2 And it came to pass in the third year, that Je-hosh'a-phat the king of
Judah came down to the king of Israel.
3 And the king of Israel said unto his servants, Know ye that Ra'moth in
Gilead *is* ours, and we *be* still, *and* take it not out of the hand of the king of
Syria?
4 And he said unto Je-hosh'a-phat, Wilt thou go with me to battle to
Ra'moth–gil'e-ad? And Je-hosh'a-phat said to the king of Israel, I *am* as
thou *art*, my people as thy people, my horses as thy horses.

22:2 1 Kgs 15:24
22:3 Deut 4:43 Josh 20:8 2 Kgs 8:28
☆22:4 2 Kgs 3:6–8

b. Ahab Listens to the Lying Prophets

5 And Je-hosh'a-phat said unto the king of Israel, Inquire, I pray thee, at
the word of the LORD to day.
6 Then the king of Israel gathered the prophets together, about four
hundred men, and said unto them, Shall I go against Ra'moth–gil'e-ad to
battle, or shall I forbear? And they said, Go up; for the Lord shall deliver
it into the hand of the king.
7 And Je-hosh'a-phat said, *Is there* not here a prophet of the LORD
besides, that we might inquire of him?
8 And the king of Israel said unto Je-hosh'a-phat, *There is* yet one man,

22:5 Num 27:21 Josh 9:14, 15 1 Sam 23:2
☆22:6
22:7 2 Kgs 3:11 2 Chron 18:6, 7
22:8 1 Kgs 18:17

21:27 Now at last Ahab "gets religion"; he dons the sackcloth and fasts. Even at this late stage, God is merciful and suspends the judgment against Ahab; it will fall on his house after his death.

22:4 Little did Ahab know that he would be the cause of his own death. He wanted to take Ramoth-gilead away from the Syrians. Jehoshaphat, the king of Judah, visited him and they arranged to fight together against the Syrians. Jehoshaphat had enough good sense to seek the counsel of God about this. Ahab gathered a band of four hundred false prophets, and they gave him the message he wanted. They said Syria would be defeated; that God would give the enemy into their hands. Jehoshaphat had spiritual insight; he wanted a word from a true prophet of God. He consulted Micaiah.

22:6 *the king of Israel gathered the prophets together, about four hundred men.* These were evidently the four hundred Asherah priests left alive by Elijah at Carmel, though the four hundred fifty prophets of Baal were slain. See 18:19, 40.†

Mi-cai'ah the son of Im'lah, by whom we may inquire of the LORD: but I
hate him; for he doth not prophesy good concerning me, but evil. And Je-
hosh'a-phat said, Let not the king say so.
9 Then the king of Israel called an officer, and said, Hasten *hither* Mi-
cai'ah the son of Im'lah.
10 And the king of Israel and Je-hosh'a-phat the king of Judah sat each on
his throne, having put on their robes, in a void place in the entrance of the
gate of Sa-ma'ri-a; and all the prophets prophesied before them.

22:11 2 Chron 18:10

11 And Zed-e-ki'ah the son of Che-na'a-nah made him horns of iron: and
he said, Thus saith the LORD, With these shalt thou push the Syrians, until
thou have consumed them.
12 And all the prophets prophesied so, saying, Go up to Ra'moth-gil'e-ad,
and prosper: for the LORD shall deliver *it* into the king's hand.

c. Micaiah Prophesies Ahab's Doom

22:13☆

13 And the messenger that was gone to call Mi-cai'ah spake unto him,
saying, Behold now, the words of the prophets *declare* good unto the king
with one mouth: let thy word, I pray thee, be like the word of one of them,
and speak *that which is* good.

22:14 Num 22:18; 24:13; 2 Chron 18:13; Jer 23:28; Ezek 2:4
22:15, 16☆

14 And Mi-cai'ah said, *As* the LORD liveth, what the LORD saith unto me,
that will I speak.
15 ¶So he came to the king. And the king said unto him, Mi-cai'ah, shall
we go against Ra'moth-gil'e-ad to battle, or shall we forbear? And he
answered him, Go, and prosper: for the LORD shall deliver *it* into the hand
of the king.
16 And the king said unto him, How many times shall I adjure thee that
thou tell me nothing but *that which is* true in the name of the LORD?

22:17☆ Num 27:17; 1 Kgs 22:36; 37; Jer 23:1

17 And he said, I saw all Israel scattered upon the hills, as sheep that have
not a shepherd: and the LORD said, These have no master: let them return
every man to his house in peace.
18 And the king of Israel said unto Je-hosh'a-phat, Did I not tell thee that
he would prophesy no good concerning me, but evil?

22:19 Isa 6:1; Dan 7:9

19 And he said, Hear thou therefore the word of the LORD: I saw the
LORD sitting on his throne, and all the host of heaven standing by him on
his right hand and on his left.
20 And the LORD said, Who shall persuade Ahab, that he may go up and
fall at Ra'moth-gil'e-ad? And one said on this manner, and another said on
that manner.
21 And there came forth a spirit, and stood before the LORD, and said, I
will persuade him.

22:22 2 Thess 2:11

22 And the LORD said unto him, Wherewith? And he said, I will go forth,
and I will be a lying spirit in the mouth of all his prophets. And he said,
Thou shalt persuade *him,* and prevail also: go forth, and do so.

22:13 Ahab's messenger found Micaiah and warned him that the false prophets had promised victory for Ahab. He expected Micaiah to join the chorus and do the same. Being a true prophet, his reply was, "what the LORD saith to me, that will I speak." He could do no other.

22:15, 16 Ahab asked Micaiah whether they should go or forbear. Ironically and with derision he said, "Go, and prosper." Ahab perceived that Micaiah was mocking him, and he adjured him to tell the truth. Let all jesting stop. What do you really believe?

22:17 Micaiah then prophesied that Syria would win the battle. One would suppose that Ahab would heed the word of a prophet he knew to be from God and spoke the word of truth. Instead he made light of Micaiah and said to Jehoshaphat that this was to be expected from one like him. Micaiah went so far as to assert that God had put a lying spirit in the mouth of all of Ahab's false prophets. What is hard to understand is why Jehoshaphat, who had some spiritual insight, did not then and there divorce himself from Ahab and go home without joining the fray.

23 Now therefore, behold, the LORD hath put a lying spirit in the mouth of
all these thy prophets, and the LORD hath spoken evil concerning thee.
24 But Zed-e-ki'ah the son of Che-na'a-nah went near, and smote Mi-
cai'ah on the cheek, and said, Which way went the Spirit of the LORD from
me to speak unto thee?
25 And Mi-cai'ah said, Behold, thou shalt see in that day, when thou shalt
go into an inner chamber to hide thyself.
26 And the king of Israel said, Take Mi-cai'ah, and carry him back unto
A'mon the governor of the city, and to Jo'ash the king's son;
27 And say, Thus saith the king, Put this *fellow* in the prison, and feed him
with bread of affliction and with water of affliction, until I come in peace.
28 And Mi-cai'ah said, If thou return at all in peace, the LORD hath not
spoken by me. And he said, Hearken, O people, every one of you.

22:23 Isa 9:14, 15; Ezek 14:9
22:24 2 Chron 18:23
☆**22:27** 2 Chron 16:10; 18:25; Jer 20:2
22:28 Deut 18:22; Isa 44:26

d. The Defeat of Ahab and His Death

29 So the king of Israel and Je-hosh'a-phat the king of Judah went up to
Ra'moth–gil'e-ad.
30 And the king of Israel said unto Je-hosh'a-phat, I will disguise myself,
and enter into the battle; but put thou on thy robes. And the king of Israel
disguised himself, and went into the battle.
31 But the king of Syria commanded his thirty and two captains that had
rule over his chariots, saying, Fight neither with small nor great, save only
with the king of Israel.
32 And it came to pass, when the captains of the chariots saw Je-hosh'a-
phat, that they said, Surely it *is* the king of Israel. And they turned aside to
fight against him: and Je-hosh'a-phat cried out.
33 And it came to pass, when the captains of the chariots perceived that it
was not the king of Israel, that they turned back from pursuing him.
34 And a *certain* man drew a bow at a venture, and smote the king of
Israel between the joints of the harness: wherefore he said unto the driver
of his chariot, Turn thine hand, and carry me out of the host; for I am
wounded.
35 And the battle increased that day: and the king was stayed up in his
chariot against the Syrians, and died at even: and the blood ran out of the
wound into the midst of the chariot.
36 And there went a proclamation throughout the host about the going
down of the sun, saying, Every man to his city, and every man to his own
country.
37 ¶So the king died, and was brought to Sa-ma'ri-a; and they buried the
king in Sa-ma'ri-a.
38 And *one* washed the chariot in the pool of Sa-ma'ri-a; and the dogs
licked up his blood; and they washed his armour; according unto the word
of the LORD which he spake.

22:30 1 Kgs 14:2; 2 Chron 35:22
22:31 2 Chron 18:30
☆**22:34**
☆**22:38**

22:27 The role of prophet sometimes led to imprisonment and suffering. This happened in the case of Micaiah, who faithfully proclaimed the true Word of God. On the other hand, Zedekiah, the false prophet, assured Ahab that he would be victorious. Ahab imprisoned Micaiah, saying that he was to be fed coarse bread and puddle-water. Ahab did not doubt that he would return from the battle as victor, at which time he would slay Micaiah as a false prophet.

22:34 *a bow at a venture,* i.e., "an arrow at random."† Ahab was wearing the uniform of a common soldier. He was shot by a Syrian soldier who simply shot an arrow into the air at no particular target. God directed the arrow to its proper target. Ahab was struck in the abdomen where his armor was of no avail. Man cannot finally hide himself from the judgment of God. What appears to be accidental often comes directly from the hand of God.

22:38 God's prophetic word must always be fulfilled. The bloody chariot and bloody armor of Ahab were washed in the pool of Samaria and the dogs licked up his blood.

22:39 1 Kgs 16:27; 22:44; 2 Kgs 1:18 — 39 Now the rest of the acts of Ahab, and all that he did, and the ivory
house which he made, and all the cities that he built, *are* they not written in
the book of the chronicles of the kings of Israel?
40 So Ahab slept with his fathers; and A-ha-zi'ah his son reigned in his
stead.

9. The Reign of Jehoshaphat over Judah; Jehoram Succeeds Him

22:41☆ 1 Chron 3:10; 2 Chron 20:31 — 41 ¶And Je-hosh'a-phat the son of Asa began to reign over Judah in the
fourth year of Ahab king of Israel.
42 Je-hosh'a-phat *was* thirty and five years old when he began to reign;
and he reigned twenty and five years in Jerusalem. And his mother's name
was A-zu'bah the daughter of Shil'hi.
22:43 1 Kgs 14:23; 15:14; 2 Kgs 12:3 — 43 And he walked in all the ways of Asa his father; he turned not aside
from it, doing *that which was* right in the eyes of the LORD: nevertheless the
high places were not taken away; *for* the people offered and burnt incense
yet in the high places.
44 And Je-hosh'a-phat made peace with the king of Israel.
22:45 1 Kgs 22:39; 2 Kgs 1:18 — 45 Now the rest of the acts of Je-hosh'a-phat, and his might that he
shewed, and how he warred, *are* they not written in the book of the
chronicles of the kings of Judah?
22:46 Deut 23:17; 1 Kgs 15:12; 2 Kgs 23:7 — 46 And the remnant of the sodomites, which remained in the days of his
father Asa, he took out of the land.
22:47 2 Sam 8:14; 2 Kgs 3:9 — 47 *There was* then no king in Edom: a deputy *was* king.
48 Je-hosh'a-phat made ships of Thar'shish to go to O'phir for gold: but
22:48 1 Kgs 9:26–28; 2 Chron 8:17, 18 — they went not; for the ships were broken at E'zi-on–ge'ber.
49 Then said A-ha-zi'ah the son of Ahab unto Je-hosh'a-phat, Let my
servants go with thy servants in the ships. But Je-hosh'a-phat would not.
22:50 2 Kgs 8:16; 2 Chron 21:1 — 50 ¶And Je-hosh'a-phat slept with his fathers, and was buried with his
fathers in the city of David his father: and Je-ho'ram his son reigned in his
stead.

10. Wicked Ahaziah Reigns in Israel for Two Years

22:51☆ — 51 ¶A-ha-zi'ah the son of Ahab began to reign over Israel in Sa-ma'ri-a the
seventeenth year of Je-hosh'a-phat king of Judah, and reigned two years
over Israel.
22:52 15:26; 16:30 — 52 And he did evil in the sight of the LORD, and walked in the way of his
father, and in the way of his mother, and in the way of Jer-o-bo'am the son
of Ne'bat, who made Israel to sin:
53 For he served Ba'al, and worshipped him, and provoked to anger the
LORD God of Israel, according to all that his father had done.

22:41ff A short account of Jehoshaphat's reign is given here. The longer account is found in 2 Chron. 17–20. Jehoshaphat may have learned a lesson, for verse 49 indicates he was unwilling to assist Ahaziah, the son of Ahab, in one of his ventures.

22:51 Ahaziah succeeded his father Ahab. All nineteen kings of Israel served either the calf or Baal. Baal worship was halted through the efforts of Elijah, Elisha, and Jehu. Jezebel had introduced Baalism in Israel. Athaliah, her daughter, married Jehoram, the king of Judah, and she promptly propagated Baalism in Judah. The influence of these two wicked women was tremendous and deleterious.

2 KINGS

IV. THE CONTINUED HISTORY OF THE DIVIDED KINGDOM (1:1—9:37)

A. AHAZIAH OF ISRAEL

1. Ahaziah Inquires of Baal-zebub; Elijah Pronounces Judgment

1 THEN Moab rebelled against Israel after the death of Ahab. **1:1**
2 And A-ha-zi'ah fell down through a lattice in his upper chamber 2 Sam 8:2 2 Kgs 3:5
that *was* in Sa-ma'ri-a, and was sick: and he sent messengers, and said unto 1 Chron 18:2
them, Go, inquire of Ba'al-ze'bub the god of Ekron whether I shall recover ☆**1:2** 1 Kgs 14:3
of this disease. 2 Kgs 8:7

3 But the angel of the LORD said to E-li'jah the Tish'bite, Arise, go up to ☆**1:3**
meet the messengers of the king of Sa-ma'ri-a, and say unto them, *Is it* not 1 Kgs 17:1
because *there is* not a God in Israel, *that* ye go to inquire of Ba'al-ze'bub
the god of Ekron?

4 Now therefore thus saith the LORD, Thou shalt not come down from **1:4**
that bed on which thou art gone up, but shalt surely die. And E-li'jah 2 Kgs 1:16, 17
departed.

5 ¶And when the messengers turned back unto him, he said unto them,
Why are ye now turned back?

6 And they said unto him, There came a man up to meet us, and said unto
us, Go, turn again unto the king that sent you, and say unto him, Thus saith
the LORD, *Is it* not because *there is* not a God in Israel, *that* thou sendest to
inquire of Ba'al-ze'bub the god of Ekron? therefore thou shalt not come
down from that bed on which thou art gone up, but shalt surely die.

7 And he said unto them, What manner of man *was he* which came up to
meet you, and told you these words?

8 And they answered him, *He was* an hairy man, and girt with a girdle of **1:8**
leather about his loins. And he said, It *is* E-li'jah the Tish'bite. Mt 3:4 Mk 1:6

2. Ahaziah's Failures to Seize Elijah

9 Then the king sent unto him a captain of fifty with his fifty. And he went
up to him: and, behold, he sat on the top of an hill. And he spake unto him,
Thou man of God, the king hath said, Come down.

10 And E-li'jah answered and said to the captain of fifty, If I *be* a man of ☆**1:10**
God, then let fire come down from heaven, and consume thee and thy fifty. 1 Kgs 18:36 22:28
And there came down fire from heaven, and consumed him and his fifty. 2 Chron 36:16 Job 1:16

11 Again also he sent unto him another captain of fifty with his fifty. And Lk 9:54
he answered and said unto him, O man of God, thus hath the king said,
Come down quickly.

1:2 *Baal-zebub*, the "Lord of flies," was the Philistine god Ahaziah spoke to after he had fallen from his upper room in Samaria. There has been much speculation over this god's strange name. Some think the god protected his devotees from flies, or that the god sent messages as swiftly as the fly's flight, or that the seeming omnipresence of flies represents an all-seeing god. The name appears in the New Testament as Beelzebub (Matt. 12:24), "the king of the devils." This is in line with one of the Canaanite titles for Baal, which was "Prince (Zabul), Lord of the Earth."

1:3 Ahaziah had learned nothing from the life of his father. Instead of consulting God, he turned to idols. God sent Elijah to inquire why he had not sought the true God. The prophet pronounced judgment: Ahaziah will die.

1:10 The public ministry of Elijah came to its close with two amazing miracles. When wicked Ahaziah sent soldiers to capture the prophet, they and their captain were consumed by fire. The second military company suffered the same fate. But this did not deter Ahaziah from persisting in an effort which had already shown itself to be imprudent. The third group of soldiers were led by a captain who begged for their lives. God's angel then told Elijah to go with the fifty servants of Ahaziah. When Elijah faced Ahaziah, he brought the bad news to the king that he would not rise from his bed of sickness. After reigning for less than two years, Ahaziah died.

12 And E-li'jah answered and said unto them, If I *be* a man of God, let fire come down from heaven, and consume thee and thy fifty. And the fire of God came down from heaven, and consumed him and his fifty.

13 ¶And he sent again a captain of the third fifty with his fifty. And the third captain of fifty went up, and came and fell on his knees before E-li'jah, and besought him, and said unto him, O man of God, I pray thee, let my life, and the life of these fifty thy servants, be precious in thy sight.

14 Behold, there came fire down from heaven, and burnt up the two captains of the former fifties with their fifties: therefore let my life now be precious in thy sight.

1:15 2 Kgs 1:3

15 And the angel of the LORD said unto E-li'jah, Go down with him: be not afraid of him. And he arose, and went down with him unto the king.

16 And he said unto him, Thus saith the LORD, Forasmuch as thou hast sent messengers to inquire of Ba'al-ze'bub the god of Ekron, *is it* not because *there is* no God in Israel to inquire of his word? therefore thou shalt not come down off that bed on which thou art gone up, but shalt surely die.

3. Jehoram Succeeds Ahaziah

1:17☆ 2 Kgs 3:1; 8:16

17 ¶So he died according to the word of the LORD which E-li'jah had spoken. And Je-ho'ram reigned in his stead in the second year of Je-ho'ram the son of Je-hosh'a-phat king of Judah; because he had no son.

1:18 2 Kgs 10:34; 13:8, 12; 14:15

18 Now the rest of the acts of A-ha-zi'ah which he did, *are* they not written in the book of the chronicles of the kings of Israel?

B. KING JEHORAM OF ISRAEL

1. Elijah Goes to Heaven in a Whirlwind

2:1☆ Gen 5:23, 24; 1 Kgs 19:16; 2 Kgs 2:11; Heb 11:5

2 AND it came to pass, when the LORD would take up E-li'jah into heaven by a whirlwind, that E-li'jah went with E-li'sha from Gilgal.

2 And E-li'jah said unto E-li'sha, Tarry here, I pray thee; for the LORD hath sent me to Beth-el. And E-li'sha said *unto him, As* the LORD liveth, and *as* thy soul liveth, I will not leave thee. So they went down to Beth-el.

2:3 2 Kgs 2:5, 7, 15

3 And the sons of the prophets that *were* at Beth-el came forth to E-li'sha, and said unto him, Knowest thou that the LORD will take away thy master from thy head to day? And he said, Yea, I know *it;* hold ye your peace.

2:4 1 Kgs 16:34; 2 Kgs 2:15

4 And E-li'jah said unto him, E-li'sha, tarry here, I pray thee; for the LORD hath sent me to Jericho. And he said, *As* the LORD liveth, and *as* thy soul liveth, I will not leave thee. So they came to Jericho.

5 And the sons of the prophets that *were* at Jericho came to E-li'sha, and said unto him, Knowest thou that the LORD will take away thy master from thy head to day? And he answered, Yea, I know *it:* hold ye your peace.

2:6 Ruth 1:15–17; 2 Sam 15:19–21; 2 Kgs 2:1, 2

6 And E-li'jah said unto him, Tarry, I pray thee, here; for the LORD hath sent me to Jordan. And he said, *As* the LORD liveth, and *as* thy soul liveth, I will not leave thee. And they two went on.

7 And fifty men of the sons of the prophets went, and stood to view afar off: and they two stood by Jordan.

2:8 Ex 14:21; 1 Kgs 19:19; Ps 114:5

8 And E-li'jah took his mantle, and wrapped *it* together, and smote the waters, and they were divided hither and thither, so that they two went over on dry ground.

1:17 Since Ahaziah left no children, his brother Jehoram ascended the throne. Ahab had reigned twenty-two years; Ahaziah less than two.

2:1 *Gilgal.* Perhaps this refers to the city located in southwest Samaria.

9¶And it came to pass, when they were gone over, that E-li'jah said unto
E-li'sha, Ask what I shall do for thee, before I be taken away from thee.
And E-li'sha said, I pray thee, let a double portion of thy spirit be upon me.
10And he said, Thou hast asked a hard thing: *nevertheless,* if thou see me
when I am taken from thee, it shall be so unto thee; but if not, it shall not
be *so.*
11And it came to pass, as they still went on, and talked, that, behold,
there appeared a chariot of fire, and horses of fire, and parted them both
asunder; and E-li'jah went up by a whirlwind into heaven.
12¶And E-li'sha saw *it,* and he cried, My father, my father, the chariot of
Israel, and the horsemen thereof. And he saw him no more: and he took
hold of his own clothes, and rent them in two pieces.

☆2:9 1 Kgs 3:5; 2 Chron 1:7

☆2:11 2 Kgs 2:1; 6:17

2:12 2 Kgs 13:14

2. Elisha Replaces Elijah

13He took up also the mantle of E-li'jah that fell from him, and went
back, and stood by the bank of Jordan;
14And he took the mantle of E-li'jah that fell from him, and smote the
waters, and said, Where *is* the LORD God of E-li'jah? and when he also had
smitten the waters, they parted hither and thither: and E-li'sha went over.
15And when the sons of the prophets which *were* to view at Jericho saw
him, they said, The spirit of E-li'jah doth rest on E-li'sha. And they came to
meet him, and bowed themselves to the ground before him.
16¶And they said unto him, Behold now, there be with thy servants fifty
strong men; let them go, we pray thee, and seek thy master: lest peradven-
ture the Spirit of the LORD hath taken him up, and cast him upon some
mountain, or into some valley. And he said, Ye shall not send.
17And when they urged him till he was ashamed, he said, Send. They sent
therefore fifty men; and they sought three days, but found him not.
18And when they came again to him, (for he tarried at Jericho,) he said
unto them, Did I not say unto you, Go not?
19¶And the men of the city said unto E-li'sha, Behold, I pray thee, the
situation of this city *is* pleasant, as my lord seeth: but the water *is* naught,
and the ground barren.
20And he said, Bring me a new cruse, and put salt therein. And they
brought *it* to him.
21And he went forth unto the spring of the waters, and cast the salt in
there, and said, Thus saith the LORD, I have healed these waters; there shall
not be from thence any more death or barren *land.*
22So the waters were healed unto this day, according to the saying of
E-li'sha which he spake.
23¶And he went up from thence unto Beth-el: and as he was going up by
the way, there came forth little children out of the city, and mocked him,
and said unto him, Go up, thou bald head; go up, thou bald head.

☆2:14

2:16 1 Kgs 18:12; Ezek 3:14, 15; 8:3; 11:24; Acts 8:39

2:21 Ex 15:25; 2 Kgs 4:41

2:9 *a double portion.* Elisha was not asking to be greater than Elijah. A double share was always given to the heir apparent or firstborn son. Elisha was asking if he could be Elijah's spiritual heir.
2:11 *a chariot of fire, and horses of fire.* "The chariot and horses appeared like fire, not for burning, but for brightness, not to torture or consume him, but to render his ascension conspicuous and illustrious in the eyes of those that stood afar off to view it. Elijah had burned with holy zeal for God and his honour, and now with the heavenly fire he was refined and translated."*

2:14 Elisha began his ministry as the waters of the Jordan divided to let him through. Some members of the school of the prophets at Jericho had come near the Jordan; when they saw that river was divided, they welcomed Elisha as one on whom "the spirit of Elijah doth rest." They bowed down to him in acknowledgement of his office under God. Elisha's ministry consisted of aiding the needy, acting as a spokesman for God, advising the king, and performing miracles. It was a distinguished ministry, unequaled until the days of John the Baptist.

2:24☆ Judg 9:20, 57; 1 Kgs 21:19; 2 Kgs 1:10; Jer 28:16

24 And he turned back, and looked on them, and cursed them in the name
of the LORD. And there came forth two she bears out of the wood, and tare
forty and two children of them.
25 And he went from thence to mount Carmel, and from thence he
returned to Sa-ma'ri-a.

3. Jehoram Wars against Moab

3:1☆ 1 Kgs 22:51; 2 Kgs 1:17; 8:16

3 NOW Je-ho'ram the son of Ahab began to reign over Israel in Sa-
ma'ri-a the eighteenth year of Je-hosh'a-phat king of Judah, and
reigned twelve years.

3:2 1 Kgs 16:31, 32; 2 Kgs 10:26

2 And he wrought evil in the sight of the LORD; but not like his father,
and like his mother: for he put away the image of Ba'al that his father had
made.

3:3 1 Kgs 12:28; 14:16

3 Nevertheless he cleaved unto the sins of Jer-o-bo'am the son of Ne'bat,
which made Israel to sin; he departed not therefrom.

3:4 2 Sam 8:2; 1 Chron 18:2; Ps 60:8; Isa 16:1

4 ¶And Me'sha king of Moab was a sheepmaster, and rendered unto the
king of Israel an hundred thousand lambs, and an hundred thousand rams,
with the wool.

3:5☆ 2 Kgs 1:1

5 But it came to pass, when Ahab was dead, that the king of Moab
rebelled against the king of Israel.
6 ¶And king Je-ho'ram went out of Sa-ma'ri-a the same time, and
numbered all Israel.
7 And he went and sent to Je-hosh'a-phat the king of Judah, saying, The
king of Moab hath rebelled against me: wilt thou go with me against Moab
to battle? And he said, I will go up: I *am* as thou *art,* my people as thy
people, *and* my horses as thy horses.
8 And he said, Which way shall we go up? And he answered, The way
through the wilderness of Edom.

3:9, 10☆

9 So the king of Israel went, and the king of Judah, and the king of Edom:
and they fetched a compass of seven days' journey: and there was no water
for the host, and for the cattle that followed them.
10 And the king of Israel said, Alas! that the LORD hath called these three
kings together, to deliver them into the hand of Moab!

3:11☆ 1 Kgs 19:21; 22:7

11 But Je-hosh'a-phat said, *Is there* not here a prophet of the LORD, that
we may inquire of the LORD by him? And one of the king of Israel's
servants answered and said, Here *is* E-li'sha the son of Sha'phat, which
poured water on the hands of E-li'jah.

3:12☆

12 And Je-hosh'a-phat said, The word of the LORD is with him. So the
king of Israel and Je-hosh'a-phat and the king of Edom went down to him.

2:24 Many have wondered about the rightness of what Elisha did here. Matthew Henry wrote, "Elisha knew, by the Spirit, the bad character of these children. He knew what a generation of vipers they were, and what mischievous enemies they would be to God's prophets if they should live to be men, who began so early to be abusive to them." Even the curse of a prophet would have no effect if the cause were not right. Thus in Prov. 26:2 it says: "the curse causeless shall not come." No believer need ever fear the curse of anyone, so long as he is not guilty of that which occasioned the curse.
3:1 *the eighteenth year of Jehoshaphat.* 1:17 says King Jehoram was the king of Judah at this time. Possibly there was a co-regency.†
3:2 *his mother.* Ahab, the father of Jehoram, was dead, but his mother, Jezebel, lived through his entire kingship.
3:5 Approximately one hundred years ago a missionary discovered a stone inscription (called the Moabite Stone) describing Mesha's revolt against Israel.
3:9, 10 Jehoram boldly blamed God for his predicament and expected that God would let himself, Jehoshaphat, and the king of Edom fall at the hands of the Moabites. At this time, Jehoram and his friends lacked water and were in desperate straits.
3:11–15 Even as Jehoshaphat joined Ahab against Syria, so now he joined himself to Jehoram against Moab. Jehoshaphat asked for a consultation with a prophet of God. Elisha was close by, so both kings went to see him. Elisha wanted nothing to do with Jehoram and declared, in insulting fashion (3:14), that if it were not for the presence of Jehoshaphat he would neither look at nor see Jehoram, who should consult his pagan deities for his heart was not right with God.

13 And E-li'sha said unto the king of Israel, What have I to do with thee? 3:13 1 Kgs 22:6, 22
get thee to the prophets of thy father, and to the prophets of thy mother.
And the king of Israel said unto him, Nay: for the LORD hath called these
three kings together, to deliver them into the hand of Moab.
14 And E-li'sha said, *As* the LORD of hosts liveth, before whom I stand,
surely, were it not that I regard the presence of Je-hosh'a-phat the king of
Judah, I would not look toward thee, nor see thee.
15 But now bring me a minstrel. And it came to pass, when the minstrel 3:15 1 Sam 10:5 16:23
played, that the hand of the LORD came upon him.
16 And he said, Thus saith the LORD, Make this valley full of ditches.
17 For thus saith the LORD, Ye shall not see wind, neither shall ye see rain; ☆3:17
yet that valley shall be filled with water, that ye may drink, both ye, and
your cattle, and your beasts.
18 And this is *but* a light thing in the sight of the LORD: he will deliver the
Moabites also into your hand.
19 And ye shall smite every fenced city, and every choice city, and shall
fell every good tree, and stop all wells of water, and mar every good piece of
land with stones.
20 And it came to pass in the morning, when the meat offering was 3:20 Ex 29:39
offered, that, behold, there came water by the way of Edom, and the
country was filled with water.
21 ¶And when all the Moabites heard that the kings were come up to fight
against them, they gathered all that were able to put on armour, and
upward, and stood in the border.
22 And they rose up early in the morning, and the sun shone upon the
water, and the Moabites saw the water on the other side *as* red as blood:
23 And they said, This *is* blood: the kings are surely slain, and they have 3:23 2 Kgs 6:18; 7:6
smitten one another: now therefore, Moab, to the spoil.
24 And when they came to the camp of Israel, the Israelites rose up and
smote the Moabites, so that they fled before them: but they went forward
smiting the Moabites, even in *their* country.
25 And they beat down the cities, and on every good piece of land cast 3:25 Isa 16:7 Jer 48:31, 36
every man his stone, and filled it; and they stopped all the wells of water,
and felled all the good trees: only in Kir-har'a-seth left they the stones
thereof; howbeit the slingers went about *it,* and smote it.
26 ¶And when the king of Moab saw that the battle was too sore for him,
he took with him seven hundred men that drew swords, to break through
even unto the king of Edom: but they could not.
27 Then he took his eldest son that should have reigned in his stead, and ☆3:27 2 Kgs 16:3 17:17; 21:6 Mic 6:7
offered him *for* a burnt offering upon the wall. And there was great
indignation against Israel: and they departed from him, and returned to
their own land.

4. Miracles Performed by Elisha
a. The Miracle of the Widow's Jar of Oil

4 NOW there cried a certain woman of the wives of the sons of the 4:1 Lev 25:39, 48 Neh 5:2–4 Jer 34:14
prophets unto E-li'sha, saying, Thy servant my husband is dead; and
thou knowest that thy servant did fear the LORD: and the creditor is come
to take unto him my two sons to be bondmen.

3:17ff Elisha prophesied that Jehoram and his allies would get the water they needed and they would also win the war. Verse 20 indicates the miraculous fulfillment of the promise of water. Verse 24 records the defeat and flight of the Moabites.

3:27 King Mesha sacrificed his son to Molech; the Israelis turned back in disgust.

4:2 1 Kgs 17:12 2And E-li'sha said unto her, What shall I do for thee? tell me, what hast
thou in the house? And she said, Thine handmaid hath not any thing in the
house, save a pot of oil.
4:3ff☆ 3Then he said, Go, borrow thee vessels abroad of all thy neighbours, *even*
empty vessels; borrow not a few.
4And when thou art come in, thou shalt shut the door upon thee and
upon thy sons, and shalt pour out into all those vessels, and thou shalt set
aside that which is full.
5So she went from him, and shut the door upon her and upon her sons,
who brought *the vessels* to her; and she poured out.
6And it came to pass, when the vessels were full, that she said unto her
son, Bring me yet a vessel. And he said unto her, *There is* not a vessel more.
And the oil stayed.
4:7☆ 7Then she came and told the man of God. And he said, Go, sell the oil,
and pay thy debt, and live thou and thy children of the rest.

b. The Woman of Shunem Promised a Son

4:8 1 Sam 28:4 1 Kgs 1:3, 4 8¶And it fell on a day, that E-li'sha passed to Shu'nem, where *was* a great
woman; and she constrained him to eat bread. And *so* it was, *that* as oft as
he passed by, he turned in thither to eat bread.
4:9 Deut 33:1 1 Kgs 13:1 17:18 9And she said unto her husband, Behold now, I perceive that this *is* an
holy man of God, which passeth by us continually.
10Let us make a little chamber, I pray thee, on the wall; and let us set for
him there a bed, and a table, and a stool, and a candlestick: and it shall be,
when he cometh to us, that he shall turn in thither.
4:11 2 Kgs 4:29 5:20; 8:4 11And it fell on a day, that he came thither, and he turned into the
chamber, and lay there.
4:12☆ 12And he said to Ge-ha'zi his servant, Call this Shu'nam-mite. And when
he had called her, she stood before him.
13And he said unto him, Say now unto her, Behold, thou hast been
careful for us with all this care; what *is* to be done for thee? wouldest thou
be spoken for to the king, or to the captain of the host? And she answered,
I dwell among mine own people.
14And he said, What then *is* to be done for her? and Ge-ha'zi answered,
Verily she hath no child, and her husband is old.
4:15 Gen 18:14 15And he said, Call her. And when he had called her, she stood in the
door.
16And he said, About this season, according to the time of life, thou shalt
embrace a son. And she said, Nay, my lord, *thou* man of God, do not lie
unto thine handmaid.
17And the woman conceived, and bare a son at that season that E-li'sha
had said unto her, according to the time of life.

c. Raising the Widow's Son from the Dead

18¶And when the child was grown, it fell on a day, that he went out to his
father to the reapers.

4:3ff Elisha performed a miracle by increasing the oil supply for a poor widow in need. He provided enough oil for her to pay her debt and to maintain her family. He put her in business selling oil. Thus his charity enabled her to improve what she had by her own industry and ingenuity. It was not simply a handout.
4:7 *the man of God,* i.e., "Shemaiah" (see 1 Kgs 12:22).
4:12ff Elisha appreciated what the Shunammite woman had done for him and for his servant. He wanted to do something for her. Gehazi noted that she had no heir and her husband was aged. Her case was like that of Sarah, and Hannah. Elisha summoned her and said that in a year's time she would have a child. She found it hard to believe (4:16) and suggested that the prophet must be teasing her. She had received Elisha in the name of a prophet and she had a

19 And he said unto his father, My head, my head. And he said to a lad,
Carry him to his mother.
20 And when he had taken him, and brought him to his mother, he sat on
her knees till noon, and *then* died.
21 And she went up, and laid him on the bed of the man of God, and shut
the door upon him, and went out.
22 And she called unto her husband, and said, Send me, I pray thee, one of
the young men, and one of the asses, that I may run to the man of God, and
come again.
23 And he said, Wherefore wilt thou go to him to day? *it is* neither new
moon, nor sabbath. And she said, *It shall be* well.
24 Then she saddled an ass, and said to her servant, Drive, and go
forward; slack not *thy* riding for me, except I bid thee.
25 So she went and came unto the man of God to mount Carmel. And it ☆4:25
came to pass, when the man of God saw her afar off, that he said to Ge-
ha'zi his servant, Behold, *yonder is* that Shu'nam-mite:
26 Run now, I pray thee, to meet her, and say unto her, *Is it* well with
thee? *is it* well with thy husband? *is it* well with the child? And she
answered, *It is* well.
27 And when she came to the man of God to the hill, she caught him by 4:27 Mt 28:9
the feet: but Ge-ha'zi came near to thrust her away. And the man of God
said, Let her alone; for her soul *is* vexed within her: and the LORD hath hid
it from me, and hath not told me.
28 Then she said, Did I desire a son of my lord? did I not say, Do not
deceive me?
29 Then he said to Ge-ha'zi, Gird up thy loins, and take my staff in thine ☆4:29 Ex 4:17; 7:19 14:16
hand, and go thy way: if thou meet any man, salute him not; and if any
salute thee, answer him not again: and lay my staff upon the face of the
child.
30 And the mother of the child said, *As* the LORD liveth, and *as* thy soul
liveth, I will not leave thee. And he arose, and followed her.
31 And Ge-ha'zi passed on before them, and laid the staff upon the face of
the child; but *there was* neither voice, nor hearing. Wherefore he went again
to meet him, and told him, saying, The child is not awaked.
32 And when E-li'sha was come into the house, behold, the child was dead,
and laid upon his bed.
33 He went in therefore, and shut the door upon them twain, and prayed
unto the LORD.
34 And he went up, and lay upon the child, and put his mouth upon his 4:34 1 Kgs 17:21
mouth, and his eyes upon his eyes, and his hands upon his hands: and he
stretched himself upon the child; and the flesh of the child waxed warm.
35 Then he returned, and walked in the house to and fro; and went up,
and stretched himself upon him: and the child sneezed seven times, and the
child opened his eyes.

---

prophet's reward. A son was born to her, so the family wealth could be passed on to the next generation.

4:25ff The son of the Shunammite woman was dead. She was perplexed, for she thought that the birth of the child meant that he would survive her and her husband and then take over the family wealth. In her agony she sought out the prophet who was at Mt. Carmel. Elisha sent Gehazi ahead of him with the prophet's staff in his hand. He laid it on the body of the dead boy and nothing happened. The power lay not in the staff but in the prophet. Elisha and the lad's mother arrived and Elisha took over. He laid his mouth on the child's mouth and his hands on the child's hands and fastened his eyes on the eyes of dead. The flesh of the corpse became warm. Elisha rose from the body, walked to and fro, and lo, the dead corpse breathed—life was restored. It was a great miracle!

4:29 Why did Elisha send Gehazi to raise the dead child instead of going himself? Did he suppose that his staff without his presence would resolve the problem? A Puritan writer suggested that Elisha's act was done out of conceit, not by divine direction, and thereby failed. When Elisha came, he did what Elijah had done before him when he revivified the son of the widow of Zarephath—he stretched himself on the child, and the miracle took place.

36 And he called Ge-ha'zi, and said, Call this Shu'nam-mite. So he called
her. And when she was come in unto him, he said, Take up thy son.
4:37 Heb 11:35 37 Then she went in, and fell at his feet, and bowed herself to the ground,
and took up her son, and went out.

d. The Poisonous Stew Made Edible

4:38☆ 2 Sam 21:1 2 Kgs 8:1 38 ¶And E-li'sha came again to Gilgal: and *there was* a dearth in the land;
and the sons of the prophets *were* sitting before him: and he said unto his
servant, Set on the great pot, and seethe pottage for the sons of the
prophets.
39 And one went out into the field to gather herbs, and found a wild vine,
and gathered thereof wild gourds his lap full, and came and shred *them* into
the pot of pottage: for they knew *them* not.
40 So they poured out for the men to eat. And it came to pass, as they were
eating of the pottage, that they cried out, and said, O *thou* man of God,
there is death in the pot. And they could not eat *thereof*.
4:41 Ex 15:25 2 Kgs 2:22 41 But he said, Then bring meal. And he cast *it* into the pot; and he said,
Pour out for the people, that they may eat. And there was no harm in the
pot.

e. A Hundred Men Fed Miraculously

42 ¶And there came a man from Ba'al–shal'i-sha, and brought the man of
God bread of the firstfruits, twenty loaves of barley, and full ears of corn in
the husk thereof. And he said, Give unto the people, that they may eat.
43 And his servitor said, What, should I set this before an hundred men?
He said again, Give the people, that they may eat: for thus saith the LORD,
They shall eat, and shall leave *thereof*.
4:44☆ Mt 14:16, 20 44 So he set *it* before them, and they did eat, and left *thereof*, according to
the word of the LORD.

5. The Healing of Naaman the Leper

a. The Servant Girl Tells Her Mistress about Elisha

5:1 Lk 4:27 5 NOW Na'a-man, captain of the host of the king of Syria, was a great
man with his master, and honourable, because by him the LORD had
given deliverance unto Syria: he was also a mighty man in valour, *but he
was* a leper.
5:2☆ 2 Kgs 6:23 2 And the Syrians had gone out by companies, and had brought away
captive out of the land of Israel a little maid; and she waited on Na'a-man's
wife.

4:38 A famine had come. Elisha had been spending his time teaching in the school of the prophets. Word comes about death in the pot. The stew Elisha ordered to be made for the students was discovered to be lethal. The prophet casts meal into the pot and the danger ceases. The students ate and were not made ill. What God did then, God can do today. "Those who wait upon God in the way of duty may hope to be both protected and supplied by a particular care of divine Providence."*

4:44 Elisha fed a hundred men who had only a small food supply. This miracle was small when compared with Jesus' miracles of the feeding of the five thousand and then of the four thousand. But whether large or small, a miracle is no less a miracle and should not be discounted because of its size.

5:2ff The little maid from Israel was not old enough to have become cynical. Thus she could earnestly and faithfully extol the virtue of God's prophet; she was sure he could cure her master's illness. When Naaman finally came face to face with the prophet Elisha, he expected something big to take place. He was disappointed when Elisha suggested that he bathe seven times in the Jordan, a muddy river not to be compared with the mighty rivers of Damascus. He presently learned that big things can come out of small things. It was not the river, the water, or the prophet himself who made the difference. It was God working through the prophet who performed the miracle. We should never despise the day of small things.

[3]And she said unto her mistress, Would God my lord *were* with the
prophet that *is* in Sa-ma'ri-a! for he would recover him of his leprosy.
[4]And *one* went in, and told his lord, saying, Thus and thus said the maid
that *is* of the land of Israel.
[5]And the king of Syria said, Go to, go, and I will send a letter unto the **5:5** 1 Sam 9:8
king of Israel. And he departed, and took with him ten talents of silver, and 1 Kgs 13:7
six thousand *pieces* of gold, and ten changes of raiment. 2 Kgs 8:8, 9

b. Jehoram's Letter from the Syrian King

[6]And he brought the letter to the king of Israel, saying, Now when this ☆**5:6**
letter is come unto thee, behold, I have *therewith* sent Na'a-man my servant
to thee, that thou mayest recover him of his leprosy.
[7]And it came to pass, when the king of Israel had read the letter, that he **5:7** Gen 30:2; 37:29
rent his clothes, and said, *Am* I God, to kill and to make alive, that this man 1 Sam 2:6
doth send unto me to recover a man of his leprosy? wherefore consider, I
pray you, and see how he seeketh a quarrel against me.

c. Elisha Heals Naaman's Leprosy

[8]¶And it was *so,* when E-li'sha the man of God had heard that the king of ☆**5:8**
Israel had rent his clothes, that he sent to the king, saying, Wherefore hast
thou rent thy clothes? let him come now to me, and he shall know that there
is a prophet in Israel.
[9]So Na'a-man came with his horses and with his chariot, and stood at the
door of the house of E-li'sha.
[10]And E-li'sha sent a messenger unto him, saying, Go and wash in Jordan **5:10** Jn 9:7
seven times, and thy flesh shall come again to thee, and thou shalt be clean.
[11]But Na'a-man was wroth, and went away, and said, Behold, I thought, ☆**5:11**
He will surely come out to me, and stand, and call on the name of the LORD
his God, and strike his hand over the place, and recover the leper.
[12]*Are* not Ab'a-na and Phar'par, rivers of Damascus, better than all the
waters of Israel? may I not wash in them, and be clean? So he turned and
went away in a rage.
[13]And his servants came near, and spake unto him, and said, My father, ☆**5:13**
if the prophet had bid thee *do some* great thing, wouldest thou not have
done *it?* how much rather then, when he saith to thee, Wash, and be clean?
[14]Then went he down, and dipped himself seven times in Jordan, **5:14** Job 33:23–25
according to the saying of the man of God: and his flesh came again like Lk 4:27; 5:13
unto the flesh of a little child, and he was clean.

d. Elisha Refuses Naaman's Gifts

5:15 Josh 2:9; 9:9 1 Sam 17:46 1 Kgs 18:36 Isa 43:10
[15]¶And he returned to the man of God, he and all his company, and
came, and stood before him: and he said, Behold, now I know that *there is*

5:6 When Jehoram received the letter from the king of Syria asking him to cure Naaman of his leprosy, he rent his clothes inasmuch as the Syrian king was guilty of blasphemy for supposing that Jehoram had a power which belonged to God alone. He was frightened and dismayed, and yet he failed to send for God's prophet.
5:8 Elisha offered his service to the king to show that God was able to heal and that his prophet had power because he belonged to God. Elisha could do what Jehoram could not do and what the gods and prophets of Syria had been unable to do.
5:11 Naaman had a tantrum because Elisha failed to speak to him face to face. Only a servant was sent. And instead of the prophet standing tall, calling on his God, and performing an immediate cure, he was sent to bathe in the Jordan river. Bathing, of course, would not cure his leprosy. But if he did it on the orders of the prophet, it would be an evidence of faith and humility; and God would honor that and cure him.
5:13 Masters who have sense should be willing to hear reason from their servants. One of them argued that if Elisha had asked Naaman to do something great, he would have done it. Why not do the small order since what was important was the cure, not how the cure would come about. Naaman followed this counsel and was healed.

no God in all the earth, but in Israel: now therefore, I pray thee, take a
blessing of thy servant.

5:16 Gen 14:22 2 Kgs 3:14
16 But he said, *As* the LORD liveth, before whom I stand, I will receive
none. And he urged him to take *it;* but he refused.

5:17☆ Ex 20:24
17 And Na'a-man said, Shall there not then, I pray thee, be given to thy
servant two mules' burden of earth? for thy servant will henceforth offer
neither burnt offering nor sacrifice unto other gods, but unto the LORD.
18 In this thing the LORD pardon thy servant, *that* when my master goeth
into the house of Rimmon to worship there, and he leaneth on my hand,
and I bow myself in the house of Rimmon: when I bow down myself in the
house of Rimmon, the LORD pardon thy servant in this thing.
19 And he said unto him, Go in peace. So he departed from him a little
way.

e. Gehazi's Avarice and Condemnation

5:20☆ 2 Kgs 4:11, 12, 31, 36
20 ¶But Ge-ha'zi, the servant of E-li'sha the man of God, said, Behold, my
master hath spared Na'a-man this Syrian, in not receiving at his hands that
which he brought: but, *as* the LORD liveth, I will run after him, and take
somewhat of him.
21 So Ge-ha'zi followed after Na'a-man. And when Na'a-man saw *him*
running after him, he lighted down from the chariot to meet him, and said,
Is all well?
22 And he said, All *is* well. My master hath sent me, saying, Behold, even
now there be come to me from mount E'phra-im two young men of the sons
of the prophets: give them, I pray thee, a talent of silver, and two changes
of garments.
23 And Na'a-man said, Be content, take two talents. And he urged him,
and bound two talents of silver in two bags, with two changes of garments,
and laid *them* upon two of his servants; and they bare *them* before him.
24 And when he came to the tower, he took *them* from their hand, and
bestowed *them* in the house: and he let the men go, and they departed.
25 But he went in, and stood before his master. And E-li'sha said unto
him, Whence *comest thou,* Ge-ha'zi? And he said, Thy servant went no
whither.

5:26☆
26 And he said unto him, Went not mine heart *with thee,* when the man
turned again from his chariot to meet thee? *Is it* a time to receive money,
and to receive garments, and oliveyards, and vineyards, and sheep, and
oxen, and menservants, and maidservants?

5:27 Ex 4:6 Num 12:10
27 The leprosy therefore of Na'a-man shall cleave unto thee, and unto thy
seed for ever. And he went out from his presence a leper *as white* as snow.

6. Elisha's Expanded Ministry

a. Recovering the Sunken Axhead

6:1 2 Kgs 2:3, 5, 7
6 AND the sons of the prophets said unto E-li'sha, Behold now, the
place where we dwell with thee is too strait for us.

5:17 *two mules' burden of earth,* i.e., "two muleloads of earth." Thus even in a foreign land Naaman could worship God on Israel's soil.†

5:20 Many a servant of God has come to grief by expecting rewards from those he has helped through the power of God. Elisha had no thought of taking anything from Naaman for his services. But Gehazi was covetous, wily, and deceitful. He got what he wanted from Naaman, but he also got something he did not want from the prophet—the sentence of leprosy upon him and his descendants.

5:26 Elisha affirmed the fact that God had given him a preternatural gift. Elisha knew what Gehazi was doing at the exact moment he sought a gift from Naaman for the services of his master. Gehazi did not dream that the leprosy which went from Naaman by the act of Elisha would come to him by another of the prophet's acts.

2 Let us go, we pray thee, unto Jordan, and take thence every man a
beam, and let us make us a place there, where we may dwell. And he
answered, Go ye.
3 And one said, Be content, I pray thee, and go with thy servants. And he
answered, I will go.
4 So he went with them. And when they came to Jordan, they cut down
wood.
5 But as one was felling a beam, the axe head fell into the water: and he
cried, and said, Alas, master! for it was borrowed.
6 And the man of God said, Where fell it? And he shewed him the place.
And he cut down a stick, and cast *it* in thither; and the iron did swim.
7 Therefore said he, Take *it* up to thee. And he put out his hand, and took
it.

☆**6:6**
Ex 15:25
2 Kgs 2:21, 4:41

b. Elisha Warns Jehoram of Ben-hadad's Plans

8 ¶Then the king of Syria warred against Israel, and took counsel with his
servants, saying, In such and such a place *shall be* my camp.
9 And the man of God sent unto the king of Israel, saying, Beware that
thou pass not such a place; for thither the Syrians are come down.
10 And the king of Israel sent to the place which the man of God told him
and warned him of, and saved himself there, not once nor twice.

6:9
1 Kgs 20:13, 28

☆**6:10**

c. Elisha Blinds the Syrians by Prayer

11 Therefore the heart of the king of Syria was sore troubled for this thing;
and he called his servants, and said unto them, Will ye not shew me which
of us *is* for the king of Israel?
12 And one of his servants said, None, my lord, O king: but E-li′sha, the
prophet that *is* in Israel, telleth the king of Israel the words that thou
speakest in thy bedchamber.
13 ¶And he said, Go and spy where he *is,* that I may send and fetch him.
And it was told him, saying, Behold, *he is* in Do′than.
14 Therefore sent he thither horses, and chariots, and a great host: and
they came by night, and compassed the city about.
15 And when the servant of the man of God was risen early, and gone
forth, behold, an host compassed the city both with horses and chariots.
And his servant said unto him, Alas, my master! how shall we do?
16 And he answered, Fear not: for they that *be* with us *are* more than they
that *be* with them.

☆**6:12**

☆**6:13**
Gen 37:17

6:14
2 Kgs 1:9

6:16
Ex 14:13
2 Chron 32:7
Ps 3:6; 11:1
Rom 8:31

6:6 Elisha was a man of great power. "He could make the iron to swim, contrary to its nature, for the God of nature is not tied to its laws."* If God by his grace can soften stony hearts which rest in the mud of life, can he not also make iron float?
6:10 God gave Elisha a word of knowledge on several occasions, so that he could warn the king of Israel concerning the plans and activities of Ben-hadad. The king had regard for these warnings about danger from the Syrians, but he paid no attention to Elisha's warning about his sins. Thus he would be saved from physical death but not from hell itself.
6:12 The king of Syria suspected that his thoughts and statements were being communicated to the king of Israel by some treacherous servant. But a more observant servant told the king that Elisha knew every word the king spoke, even when the king was in his own bedroom. "Nothing done, said, or thought by any person, in any place, at any time, is out of reach of God's cognizance."* By divine power this cognizance was passed on to God's prophets at his good pleasure.
6:13 Ben-hadad sent a large complement of soldiers to seize Elisha. If Elisha knew what the plans of Ben-hadad were, would he not also know the plans afoot to take him prisoner?

6:17☆ 2 Kgs 2:11; Ps 34:7; Isa 42:7; Acts 26:18

17 And E-li′sha prayed, and said, LORD, I pray thee, open his eyes, that he may see. And the LORD opened the eyes of the young man; and he saw: and, behold, the mountain *was* full of horses and chariots of fire round about E-li′sha.

6:18☆ Gen 19:11

18 And when they came down to him, E-li′sha prayed unto the LORD, and said, Smite this people, I pray thee, with blindness. And he smote them with blindness according to the word of E-li′sha.

6:19 1 Kgs 20:1; 2 Kgs 3:1

19 ¶And E-li′sha said unto them, This *is* not the way, neither *is* this the city: follow me, and I will bring you to the man whom ye seek. But he led them to Sa-ma′ri-a.

d. The Blind Syrians Are Led to Samaria

20 And it came to pass, when they were come into Sa-ma′ri-a, that E-li′sha said, LORD, open the eyes of these *men,* that they may see. And the LORD opened their eyes, and they saw; and, behold, *they were* in the midst of Sa-ma′ri-a.

6:21 1 Sam 24:4, 19; 26:8

21 And the king of Israel said unto E-li′sha, when he saw them, My father, shall I smite *them?* shall I smite *them?*

6:22 2 Chron 28:8; Rom 12:20

22 And he answered, Thou shalt not smite *them:* wouldest thou smite those whom thou hast taken captive with thy sword and with thy bow? set bread and water before them, that they may eat and drink, and go to their master.

6:23 2 Kgs 5:2

23 And he prepared great provision for them: and when they had eaten and drunk, he sent them away, and they went to their master. So the bands of Syria came no more into the land of Israel.

e. Ben-hadad Besieges Samaria: Elisha Prophesies Deliverance

6:24 1 Kgs 20:1

24 ¶And it came to pass after this, that Ben–ha′dad king of Syria gathered all his host, and went up, and besieged Sa-ma′ri-a.

6:25☆ 2 Kgs 7:12

25 And there was a great famine in Sa-ma′ri-a: and, behold, they besieged it, until an ass's head was *sold* for fourscore *pieces* of silver, and the fourth part of a cab of dove's dung for five *pieces* of silver.

6:26 Lev 26:29; Deut 28:53; 1 Kgs 21:27; Lam 4:10

26 And as the king of Israel was passing by upon the wall, there cried a woman unto him, saying, Help, my lord, O king.

27 And he said, If the LORD do not help thee, whence shall I help thee? out of the barnfloor, or out of the winepress?

28 And the king said unto her, What aileth thee? And she answered, This woman said unto me, Give thy son, that we may eat him to day, and we will eat my son to morrow.

29 So we boiled my son, and did eat him: and I said unto her on the next day, Give thy son, that we may eat him: and she hath hid her son.

6:17 Elisha's servant was striken with fear at the sight of the enemy. But Elisha had a cure for his malady. He prayed that God would *open his eyes, that he may see.* That was an odd prayer because the servant was not blind. With the eyes of his body he saw the danger. But Elisha's prayer brought him the eyes of faith. He then saw the protection they were under. The veil which separates the seen from the unseen world was parted, and he saw chariots of fire and horses of fire more numerous than the enemy. When our spiritual eyes are opened, our fears are silenced. God's angels are messengers; they are also his soldiers, his legions, and his armies; they are powerful enough to defeat any and all enemies.

6:18 In response to Elisha's prayers, God struck the Syrians blind and then the prophet led them to Samaria where their eyes were opened—face to face with the king of Israel. Instead of their being slain, a feast was prepared for them. They never tried to seize Elisha again.

6:25 Ben-hadad still wished to destroy Israel. So he besieged Samaria which shortly was left without food. So great was the famine that an unclean animal's head sold for an exorbitant price. The king was distraught, but he neither removed Israel's idols, nor sought the face of God in repentance.

30¶And it came to pass, when the king heard the words of the woman,
that he rent his clothes; and he passed by upon the wall, and the people
looked, and, behold, *he had* sackcloth within upon his flesh.
31Then he said, God do so and more also to me, if the head of E-li'sha the
son of Sha'phat shall stand on him this day.
32But E-li'sha sat in his house, and the elders sat with him; and *the king*
sent a man from before him: but ere the messenger came to him, he said to
the elders, See ye how this son of a murderer hath sent to take away mine
head? look, when the messenger cometh, shut the door, and hold him fast at
the door: *is* not the sound of his master's feet behind him?
33And while he yet talked with them, behold, the messenger came down
unto him: and he said, Behold, this evil *is* of the LORD; what should I wait
for the LORD any longer?

☆**6:31** 2 Sam 3:9, 10; 1 Kgs 2:23, 24; 19:2
6:32 1 Kgs 18:14; Ezek 8:1; 14:1; 20:1
6:33 Isa 8:21

7 THEN E-li'sha said, Hear ye the word of the LORD; Thus saith the
LORD, To morrow about this time *shall* a measure of fine flour *be sold*
for a shekel, and two measures of barley for a shekel, in the gate of Sa-
ma'ri-a.
2Then a lord on whose hand the king leaned answered the man of God,
and said, Behold, *if* the LORD would make windows in heaven, might this
thing be? And he said, Behold, thou shalt see *it* with thine eyes, but shalt
not eat thereof.
3¶And there were four leprous men at the entering in of the gate: and
they said one to another, Why sit we here until we die?
4If we say, We will enter into the city, then the famine *is* in the city, and
we shall die there: and if we sit still here, we die also. Now therefore come,
and let us fall unto the host of the Syrians: if they save us alive, we shall
live; and if they kill us, we shall but die.
5And they rose up in the twilight, to go unto the camp of the Syrians: and
when they were come to the uttermost part of the camp of Syria, behold,
there was no man there.
6For the Lord had made the host of the Syrians to hear a noise of
chariots, and a noise of horses, *even* the noise of a great host: and they said
one to another, Lo, the king of Israel hath hired against us the kings of the
Hittites, and the kings of the Egyptians, to come upon us.
7Wherefore they arose and fled in the twilight, and left their tents, and
their horses, and their asses, even the camp as it *was,* and fled for their life.
8And when these lepers came to the uttermost part of the camp, they
went into one tent, and did eat and drink, and carried thence silver, and
gold, and raiment, and went and hid *it;* and came again, and entered into
another tent, and carried thence *also,* and went and hid *it.*

☆**7:1**
7:2 Mal 3:10
7:3 Lev 13:45; Num 5:1, 2; 2 Kgs 5:1; Mt 8:4
7:4 2 Kgs 6:24
☆**7:6** 2 Sam 5:24; 2 Chron 12:3

6:31 A woman told the king that his people were now eating human flesh. Her son had been eaten, and when the other woman who had agreed to give her son for food refused to do so, she complained to the king. He was struck by the horror of the situation and placed the blame upon Elisha, the prophet. This appeared to be reasonable, for God had intervened previously without the king's having to repent. He thought that God did this because of Elisha and supposed that Elisha was responsible for the famine because he had done nothing to gain the assistance of God for the king.

7:1 Elisha called the king a murderer (6:32). While the king and his royal officer and prophet stand face to face, Elisha has a good word from God: the famine will be over. Man's extremity is God's opportunity and he will do the impossible. When the king's royal officer heard the word of prophecy, he exhibited disbelief. God through Elisha passed immediate judgment on the royal officer. He was told that indeed he would see the food and know the crisis was past, but he would not eat of the food.

7:6ff The Syrians unexpectedly fled from the scene of the siege. Terror came upon them by a divine visitation from God. They heard the noise of chariots and horses and thought relief had come to Israel from Egypt and the Hittites. The deliverance was not by power or by might but by the Spirit of God. Four lepers who lived outside the camp observed what happened and found food and wealth left behind by the Syrians due to their flight. They brought the good news to the city and told the king and his court what had happened. But the king thought it was only a military device and disbelieved that the enemy had gone.

9 Then they said one to another, We do not well: this day *is* a day of good
tidings, and we hold our peace: if we tarry till the morning light, some
mischief will come upon us: now therefore come, that we may go and tell
the king's household.
10 So they came and called unto the porter of the city: and they told them,
saying, We came to the camp of the Syrians, and, behold, *there was* no man
there, neither voice of man, but horses tied, and asses tied, and the tents as
they *were.*
11 And he called the porters; and they told *it* to the king's house within.
7:12 Josh 8:6, 7 2 Kgs 6:25 — 12 ¶And the king arose in the night, and said unto his servants, I will now
shew you what the Syrians have done to us. They know that we *be* hungry;
therefore are they gone out of the camp to hide themselves in the field,
saying, When they come out of the city, we shall catch them alive, and get
into the city.
13 And one of his servants answered and said, Let *some* take, I pray thee,
five of the horses that remain, which are left in the city, (behold, they *are* as
all the multitude of Israel that are left in it: behold, *I say,* they *are* even as
all the multitude of the Israelites that are consumed:) and let us send and
see.
14 They took therefore two chariot horses; and the king sent after the host
of the Syrians, saying, Go and see.
15 And they went after them unto Jordan: and, lo, all the way *was* full of
garments and vessels, which the Syrians had cast away in their haste. And
the messengers returned, and told the king.
16 And the people went out, and spoiled the tents of the Syrians. So a
measure of fine flour was *sold* for a shekel, and two measures of barley for
a shekel, according to the word of the LORD.
7:17☆ 2 Kgs 7:2 — 17 ¶And the king appointed the lord on whose hand he leaned to have the
charge of the gate: and the people trode upon him in the gate, and he died,
as the man of God had said, who spake when the king came down to him.
18 And it came to pass as the man of God had spoken to the king, saying,
Two measures of barley for a shekel, and a measure of fine flour for a
shekel, shall be to morrow about this time in the gate of Sa-ma'ri-a:
19 And that lord answered the man of God, and said, Now, behold, *if* the
LORD should make windows in heaven, might such a thing be? And he said,
Behold, thou shalt see it with thine eyes, but shalt not eat thereof.
20 And so it fell out unto him: for the people trode upon him in the gate,
and he died.

7. The Woman of Shunem Comes Home

8:1☆ Gen 41:27 Deut 28:22 Ps 105:16 Hag 1:11 — 8 THEN spake E-li'sha unto the woman, whose son he had restored to
life, saying, Arise, and go thou and thine household, and sojourn
wheresoever thou canst sojourn: for the LORD hath called for a famine; and
it shall also come upon the land seven years.
8:2☆ — 2 And the woman arose, and did after the saying of the man of God: and

---

7:17 The starving people rushed out to find food and booty. The king appointed his royal officer to guard the gate. The mob trampled on him and he died. He saw the food but did not eat of it. His disbelief was repaid by his own death, and the prophetic word of Elisha was fulfilled.

8:1 God often sent famines to accomplish the divine purpose. In this instance it was to last seven years.

8:2 The Shunammite woman to whom God had given a son was warned by Elisha to leave Israel and go to the land of the Philistines until the seven-year famine sent by God is over. She did so. On her return she asked the king for her land to be returned to her. When the king heard the story of her life and how God visited her with a son he was moved by this testimony from the lips of Gehazi.

she went with her household, and sojourned in the land of the Philistines
seven years.
3 And it came to pass at the seven years' end, that the woman returned
out of the land of the Philistines: and she went forth to cry unto the king
for her house and for her land.
4 And the king talked with Ge-ha'zi the servant of the man of God, ☆8:4
saying, Tell me, I pray thee, all the great things that E-li'sha hath done. 2 Kgs 4:11, 12 5:20
5 And it came to pass, as he was telling the king how he had restored a 8:5
dead body to life, that, behold, the woman, whose son he had restored to 2 Kgs 4:34
life, cried to the king for her house and for her land. And Ge-ha'zi said, My
lord, O king, this *is* the woman, and this *is* her son, whom E-li'sha restored
to life.
6 And when the king asked the woman, she told him. So the king
appointed unto her a certain officer, saying, Restore all that *was* hers, and
all the fruits of the field since the day that she left the land, even until now.

8. Elisha Informs Hazael He Will Succeed Ben-hadad

7 ¶And E-li'sha came to Damascus; and Ben–ha'dad the king of Syria was 8:7
sick; and it was told him, saying, The man of God is come hither. 2 Kgs 6:24; 13:3
8 And the king said unto Haz'a-el, Take a present in thine hand, and go, ☆8:8
meet the man of God, and inquire of the LORD by him, saying, Shall I 1 Kgs 14:3 19:15
recover of this disease?
9 So Haz'a-el went to meet him, and took a present with him, even of
every good thing of Damascus, forty camels' burden, and came and stood
before him, and said, Thy son Ben–ha'dad king of Syria hath sent me to
thee, saying, Shall I recover of this disease?
10 And E-li'sha said unto him, Go, say unto him, Thou mayest certainly ☆8:10
recover: howbeit the LORD hath shewed me that he shall surely die.
11 And he settled his countenance stedfastly, until he was ashamed: and ☆8:11
the man of God wept. 2 Kgs 2:17
12 And Haz'a-el said, Why weepeth my lord? And he answered, Because I ☆8:12
know the evil that thou wilt do unto the children of Israel: their strong 2 Kgs 10:32, 33 12:17; 13:3
holds wilt thou set on fire, and their young men wilt thou slay with the 15:16
sword, and wilt dash their children, and rip up their women with child.
13 And Haz'a-el said, But what, *is* thy servant a dog, that he should do this ☆8:13
great thing? And E-li'sha answered, The LORD hath shewed me that thou 1 Sam 17:43 2 Sam 9:8
shalt be king over Syria.
14 So he departed from E-li'sha, and came to his master; who said to him,
What said E-li'sha to thee? And he answered, He told me *that* thou
shouldest surely recover.
15 And it came to pass on the morrow, that he took a thick cloth, and ☆8:15

8:4 Even though Gehazi became a leper Elisha did not dismiss him from his service. Here we find him engaged in the service of his master, speaking with the king about the great things Elisha had done. Lepers were separated from society according to the law, but they were not forbidden to talk with nonlepers.

8:8 Elisha, the prophet whom God sent to Israel, is now in Damascus. Why he came is not stated here, but 1 Kings 19:15 says Elijah was to go to Damascus to anoint Hazael. Some think it was done to fulfill the command given to Elijah which he had not been able to complete because of his translation to heaven. The king of Syria was ill and called for Elisha. Is it not strange that a pagan king would do what the house of Ahab had often refused to do—consult God through his prophet? Ben-hadad wanted to know whether he would get well. He sent Hazael to secure an answer from Elisha.

8:10–13 Elisha responded to the inquiry of Hazael in a curious manner. "Indeed," he said, "tell the king he will recover, but he will die." By that he meant that the illness would not kill him but Hazael would. Elisha then wept because he knew that Hazael would do terrible things to Israel when he became king. Hazael was unhappy with what the prophet said and assured him he was a decent man who would never be unfaithful. Then Elisha replied, "The LORD hath showed me that thou shalt be king over Syria." How God showed him this we do not know.

8:15 The *thick cloth* was a heavy bedcover which when wet made an effective implement with which to smother someone.

dipped *it* in water, and spread *it* on his face, so that he died: and Haz'a-el
reigned in his stead.

C. JEHORAM'S SHORT REIGN IN JUDAH

8:16☆ 16 ¶And in the fifth year of Joram the son of Ahab king of Israel, Je-
2 Kgs 1:17; 3:1 hosh'a-phat *being* then king of Judah, Je-ho'ram the son of Je-hosh'a-phat
king of Judah began to reign.
8:17 17 Thirty and two years old was he when he began to reign; and he reigned
2 Chron 21:5 eight years in Jerusalem.
8:18☆ 18 And he walked in the way of the kings of Israel, as did the house of
Ahab: for the daughter of Ahab was his wife: and he did evil in the sight of
the LORD.
8:19 19 Yet the LORD would not destroy Judah for David his servant's sake, as
2 Sam 7:12, 13 1 Kgs 11:36 he promised him to give him alway a light, *and* to his children.
8:20 20 In his days Edom revolted from under the hand of Judah, and made a
2 Kgs 3:9, 26 2 Chron 21:8 king over themselves.
8:21☆ 21 So Joram went over to Za'ir, and all the chariots with him: and he rose
by night, and smote the Edomites which compassed him about, and the
captains of the chariots: and the people fled into their tents.
8:22 22 Yet Edom revolted from under the hand of Judah unto this day. Then
Gen 27:39, 40 Lib'nah revolted at the same time.
8:23 23 And the rest of the acts of Joram, and all that he did, *are* they not
1 Kgs 15:23 22:45 written in the book of the chronicles of the kings of Judah?
2 Kgs 12:19 14:18; 15:6 24 And Joram slept with his fathers, and was buried with his fathers in the
8:24☆ city of David: and A-ha-zi'ah his son reigned in his stead.
1 Kgs 2:10 11:43 2 Chron 21:20 22:1

D. AHAZIAH'S ONE YEAR REIGN IN JUDAH

8:25☆ 25 In the twelfth year of Joram the son of Ahab king of Israel did A-ha-
zi'ah the son of Je-ho'ram king of Judah begin to reign.
8:26☆ 26 Two and twenty years old *was* A-ha-zi'ah when he began to reign; and
2 Kgs 11:1 he reigned one year in Jerusalem. And his mother's name *was* Ath-a-li'ah,
the daughter of Omri king of Israel.
8:27 27 And he walked in the way of the house of Ahab, and did evil in the
1 Kgs 16:30 sight of the LORD, as *did* the house of Ahab: for he *was* the son in law of the
house of Ahab.

8:16 *Joram,* also called *Jehoram,* was the brother of Ahaziah who died childless. The name Joram here distinguishes him from Jehoram (also called Joram), the son of Jehoshaphat, who began a co-regency with his father. Joram was the king of Israel and Jehoram the king of Judah.

8:18 Jehoram of Judah succeeded Jehoshaphat, who was a good king. Jehoram was a very bad king. "He did as the house of Ahab, and worse he could not do."* He married the daughter of Jezebel, Athaliah, who was as wicked as her mother, who had raised her in her pagan tradition. Why Jehoshaphat ever permitted this to happen is a mystery, since he was fully acquainted with the house of Ahab.

8:21 The Edomites revolted against Judah and king Joram (Jehoram). They had been overcome in David's day and had spent a hundred and fifty years under the yoke of Judah. They were descendants of Esau. In Gen. 27:40 it was predicted that the older, who would serve the younger, would have offspring who would someday "break that yoke from off his neck." The Edomites became independent and remained as inveterate enemies of the Jews. The king of Judah, Joram, was unable to keep them in bondage. Judah was weak enough to have been overcome, but God would not destroy Judah.

8:24 Joram (Jehoram) died and was buried at the age of forty, having served as king for only eight years. His "bowels fell out . . . so he died of sore diseases" and "without being desired," according to 2 Chron. 21:19, 20.

8:25ff Ahaziah (an alternate form of the name Jehoahaz) aged twenty-two, became king when Joram (Jehoram) his father died. He was the son of Athaliah, who taught him the way her mother had taught her. Ahaziah was a wicked king. He helped Joram the son of Ahab against the king of Syria at Ramoth-gilead. Joram was wounded in the battle. He went to Jezreel to recover. It was located in the hill country of Judah. Ahab, Joram's father, had a royal residence in that city. Ahaziah made a visit to his relative while he still was ill.

8:26 *Athaliah,* the daughter of Jezebel and Ahab, and the granddaughter of Omri, carried her idolatrous religious practices to Judah when she married Jehoram. As queen, she was a powerful force in religious matters.

28¶And he went with Joram the son of Ahab to the war against Haz'a-el
king of Syria in Ra'moth-gil'e-ad; and the Syrians wounded Joram.
29And king Joram went back to be healed in Jez're-el of the wounds
which the Syrians had given him at Ra'mah, when he fought against Haz'a-
el king of Syria. And A-ha-zi'ah the son of Je-ho'ram king of Judah went
down to see Joram the son of Ahab in Jez're-el, because he was sick.

8:29 2 Kgs 9:14; 2 Chron 22:6

E. JEHU'S REIGN IN ISRAEL

1. Jehu Is Anointed to Replace Jehoram (Joram) of Israel

9 AND E-li'sha the prophet called one of the children of the prophets,
and said unto him, Gird up thy loins, and take this box of oil in thine
hand, and go to Ra'moth-gil'e-ad:
2And when thou comest thither, look out there Jehu the son of Je-hosh'a-
phat the son of Nim'shi, and go in, and make him arise up from among his
brethren, and carry him to an inner chamber;
3Then take the box of oil, and pour *it* on his head, and say, Thus saith the
LORD, I have anointed thee king over Israel. Then open the door, and flee,
and tarry not.
4¶So the young man, *even* the young man the prophet, went to Ra'moth-
gil'e-ad.
5And when he came, behold, the captains of the host *were* sitting; and he
said, I have an errand to thee, O captain. And Jehu said, Unto which of all
us? And he said, To thee, O captain.
6And he arose, and went into the house; and he poured the oil on his
head, and said unto him, Thus saith the LORD God of Israel, I have
anointed thee king over the people of the LORD, *even* over Israel.
7And thou shalt smite the house of Ahab thy master, that I may avenge
the blood of my servants the prophets, and the blood of all the servants of
the LORD, at the hand of Jez'e-bel.
8For the whole house of Ahab shall perish: and I will cut off from Ahab
him that pisseth against the wall, and him that is shut up and left in Israel:
9And I will make the house of Ahab like the house of Jer-o-bo'am the son
of Ne'bat, and like the house of Ba'a-sha the son of A-hi'jah:
10And the dogs shall eat Jez'e-bel in the portion of Jez're-el, and *there
shall be* none to bury *her*. And he opened the door, and fled.
11¶Then Jehu came forth to the servants of his lord: and *one* said unto
him, *Is* all well? wherefore came this mad *fellow* to thee? And he said unto
them, Ye know the man, and his communication.
12And they said, *It is* false; tell us now. And he said, Thus and thus spake
he to me, saying, Thus saith the LORD, I have anointed thee king over
Israel.
13Then they hasted, and took every man his garment, and put *it* under
him on the top of the stairs, and blew with trumpets, saying, Jehu is king.

9:1 1 Sam 10:1; 16:1; 1 Kgs 1:39; 2 Kgs 8:28
☆**9:2** 1 Kgs 19:16
9:3 1 Sam 9:16; 16:12; 2 Chron 22:7
☆**9:4**
9:7 Deut 32:35; 1 Kgs 18:3, 4; 21:15, 21; 2 Kgs 10:17
9:9 1 Kgs 14:10; 15:29; 16:3, 11
9:10 1 Kgs 21:23; 2 Kgs 9:35, 36
9:12 2 Kgs 9:6
☆**9:13** 2 Sam 15:10; 1 Kgs 1:34, 39

9:2 Jehu was appointed to be king of Israel by divine fiat; this brought an end to the dynasty of Ahab.

9:4ff Elisha ordered a young prophet to anoint Jehu to become king of Israel. And he told him to flee as soon as his job was done. The prophet not only anointed Jehu, he also prophesied that Jezebel (the wife of Ahab, the mother of Athaliah, and a wicked schemer who was responsible for the death of Naboth) should die ignominiously. Dogs would eat her body and no one would bury her. What a calamitous end to any life!

9:13 Jehu's fellow warriors thought little of the young prophet who anointed him to be king. But when Jehu explained it to them, they put their garments on the ground for him to walk over them. The trumpets were blown and Jehu was accepted as their new monarch. He made haste to go to Jezreel, where the kings of Israel and Judah were holding their own gathering. Jehoram (Joram) of Israel sensed what had happened and prepared himself, along with Ahaziah of Judah, for battle against Jehu. Jehu slew Jehoram and his body was cast into the field of Naboth the Jezreelite, from whom Ahab had taken his property. Jehoram died a criminal under the sentence of God's law, and the execution was performed by Jehu, God's surrogate.

2. Jehoram's (Joram's) Defeat and Death

9:14 2 Kgs 8:28

14 So Jehu the son of Je-hosh'a-phat the son of Nim'shi conspired against Joram. (Now Joram had kept Ra'moth-gil'e-ad, he and all Israel, because of Haz'a-el king of Syria.

15 But king Joram was returned to be healed in Jez're-el of the wounds which the Syrians had given him, when he fought with Haz'a-el king of Syria.) And Jehu said, If it be your minds, *then* let none go forth *nor* escape out of the city to go to tell *it* in Jez're-el.

16 So Jehu rode in a chariot, and went to Jez're-el; for Joram lay there. And A-ha-zi'ah king of Judah was come down to see Joram.

9:17 2 Sam 13:34; 18:24; Isa 21:6, 7

17 And there stood a watchman on the tower in Jez're-el, and he spied the company of Jehu as he came, and said, I see a company. And Joram said, Take an horseman, and send to meet them, and let him say, *Is it* peace?

18 So there went one on horseback to meet him, and said, Thus saith the king, *Is it* peace? And Jehu said, What hast thou to do with peace? turn thee behind me. And the watchman told, saying, The messenger came to them, but he cometh not again.

19 Then he sent out a second on horseback, which came to them, and said, Thus saith the king, *Is it* peace? And Jehu answered, What hast thou to do with peace? turn thee behind me.

20 And the watchman told, saying, He came even unto them, and cometh not again: and the driving *is* like the driving of Jehu the son of Nim'shi; for he driveth furiously.

9:21 1 Kgs 21:1

21 And Joram said, Make ready. And his chariot was made ready. And Joram king of Israel and A-ha-zi'ah king of Judah went out, each in his chariot, and they went out against Jehu, and met him in the portion of Na'both the Jez're-el-ite.

9:22 1 Kgs 16:31; 18:19

22 And it came to pass, when Joram saw Jehu, that he said, *Is it* peace, Jehu? And he answered, What peace, so long as the whoredoms of thy mother Jez'e-bel and her witchcrafts *are so* many?

9:23 2 Kgs 11:14

23 And Joram turned his hands, and fled, and said to A-ha-zi'ah, *There is* treachery, O A-ha-zi'ah.

9:24 1 Kgs 22:34

24 And Jehu drew a bow with his full strength, and smote Je-ho'ram between his arms, and the arrow went out at his heart, and he sunk down in his chariot.

9:25 1 Kgs 21:1, 19

25 Then said *Jehu* to Bid'kar his captain, Take up, *and* cast him in the portion of the field of Na'both the Jez're-el-ite: for remember how that, when I and thou rode together after Ahab his father, the LORD laid this burden upon him;

26 Surely I have seen yesterday the blood of Na'both, and the blood of his sons, saith the LORD; and I will requite thee in this plat, saith the LORD. Now therefore take *and* cast him into the plat *of ground,* according to the word of the LORD.

3. The Death of Ahaziah of Judah

9:27☆ Josh 17:11; Judg 1:27; 2 Chron 22:7

27 ¶But when A-ha-zi'ah the king of Judah saw *this,* he fled by the way of the garden house. And Jehu followed after him, and said, Smite him also in the chariot. *And they did so* at the going up to Gur, which *is* by Ib'le-am. And he fled to Me-gid'do, and died there.

9:27 Ahaziah of Judah also was slain by Jehu's men. He went to Megiddo, where he died. Had Ahaziah not associated with evil company and had he remained at home he would not have died at this time. Jehu rightly presumed that those who were associated with the man he was to slay were worthy of the same treatment.

28 And his servants carried him in a chariot to Jerusalem, and buried him **9:28** 2 Kgs 8:25
in his sepulchre with his fathers in the city of David. 23:30
29 And in the eleventh year of Joram the son of Ahab began A-ha-zi′ah to **9:29** 2 Kgs 8:28
reign over Judah.

4. The Slaying of Jezebel

30 ¶And when Jehu was come to Jez′re-el, Jez′e-bel heard *of it;* and she ☆**9:30** Jer 4:30
painted her face, and tired her head, and looked out at a window. Ezek 23:40
31 And as Jehu entered in at the gate, she said, *Had* Zimri peace, who slew **9:31** 1 Kgs 16:9, 10
his master?
32 And he lifted up his face to the window, and said, Who *is* on my side?
who? And there looked out to him two *or* three eunuchs.
33 And he said, Throw her down. So they threw her down: and *some* of her
blood was sprinkled on the wall, and on the horses: and he trode her under
foot.
34 And when he was come in, he did eat and drink, and said, Go, see now **9:34** 1 Kgs 16:30
this cursed *woman,* and bury her: for she *is* a king's daughter. 21:20
35 And they went to bury her: but they found no more of her than the ☆**9:35**
skull, and the feet, and the palms of *her* hands.
36 Wherefore they came again, and told him. And he said, This *is* the word **9:36** 1 Kgs 21:23
of the LORD, which he spake by his servant E-li′jah the Tish′bite, saying, In
the portion of Jez′re-el shall dogs eat the flesh of Jez′e-bel:
37 And the carcase of Jez′e-bel shall be as dung upon the face of the field
in the portion of Jez′re-el; *so* that they shall not say, This *is* Jez′e-bel.

V. THE DECLINE AND FALL OF ISRAEL (10:1—17:41)

A. JEHU EXTERMINATES THE HOUSE OF OMRI AND THE WORSHIPPERS OF BAAL

1. Ahab's Seventy Sons Killed

10 AND Ahab had seventy sons in Sa-ma′ri-a. And Jehu wrote letters, ☆**10:1** Judg 8:30; 12:14
and sent to Sa-ma′ri-a, unto the rulers of Jez′re-el, to the elders, and 1 Kgs 16:24
to them that brought up Ahab's *children,* saying,
2 Now as soon as this letter cometh to you, seeing your master's sons *are*
with you, and *there are* with you chariots and horses, a fenced city also, and
armour;
3 Look even out the best and meetest of your master's sons, and set *him*
on his father's throne, and fight for your master's house.
4 But they were exceedingly afraid, and said, Behold, two kings stood not
before him: how then shall we stand?
5 And he that *was* over the house, and he that *was* over the city, the elders **10:5** Josh 9:8
also, and the bringers up *of the children,* sent to Jehu, saying, We *are* thy
servants, and will do all that thou shalt bid us; we will not make any king:
do thou *that which is* good in thine eyes.

9:30 Here Jezebel, unafraid and painted for the occasion, stands in the sight of Jehu and tries to put him on the defensive. Some of her attendants throw her over the railing. She plunges to her death and is trodden over by Jehu. She died as she lived, outside the circle of grace, and ever an opponent of the God of all Israel.

9:35 The dogs ate the body of Jezebel till there was nothing left to bury except a skull, feet, and hands. To this day the name of Jezebel is a title of opprobrium and no one would dare to stigmatize a daughter by naming her after that wretched and wicked woman.

10:1ff Jehu was relentless, intrepid, and without pity. He not only killed two kings; he also killed Ahab's seventy sons, the friends and supporters of the house of Ahab, the priests of Baal, and the worshippers of that god. He destroyed the temple and the pillars of Baal, as well. God used a bad man to exterminate even more wicked people, who had been among the worst enemies God ever had in the ancient world.

10:6 2 Kgs 9:32

6 Then he wrote a letter the second time to them, saying, If ye *be* mine, and *if* ye will hearken unto my voice, take ye the heads of the men your master's sons, and come to me to Jez're-el by to morrow this time. Now the king's sons, *being* seventy persons, *were* with the great men of the city, which brought them up.

10:7 Judg 9:5; 2 Kgs 11:1

7 And it came to pass, when the letter came to them, that they took the king's sons, and slew seventy persons, and put their heads in baskets, and sent him *them* to Jez're-el.

8 ¶And there came a messenger, and told him, saying, They have brought the heads of the king's sons. And he said, Lay ye them in two heaps at the entering in of the gate until the morning.

10:9 1 Kgs 8:56; 21:19; 2 Kgs 9:7

9 And it came to pass in the morning, that he went out, and stood, and said to all the people, Ye *be* righteous: behold, I conspired against my master, and slew him: but who slew all these?

10 Know now that there shall fall unto the earth nothing of the word of the LORD, which the LORD spake concerning the house of Ahab: for the LORD hath done *that* which he spake by his servant E-li'jah.

10:11☆ 1 Kgs 21:22; 2 Kgs 9:8; 10:17

11 So Jehu slew all that remained of the house of Ahab in Jez're-el, and all his great men, and his kinsfolks, and his priests, until he left him none remaining.

2. The Kinsmen of Ahaziah Slain

12 ¶And he arose and departed, and came to Sa-ma'ri-a. *And* as he *was* at the shearing house in the way,

10:13☆ 2 Chron 22:8

13 Jehu met with the brethren of A-ha-zi'ah king of Judah, and said, Who *are* ye? And they answered, We *are* the brethren of A-ha-zi'ah; and we go down to salute the children of the king and the children of the queen.

10:14☆

14 And he said, Take them alive. And they took them alive, and slew them at the pit of the shearing house, *even* two and forty men; neither left he any of them.

10:15☆ 2 Kgs 10:23; 1 Chron 2:55; Jer 35:6

15 ¶And when he was departed thence, he lighted on Je-hon'a-dab the son of Re'chab *coming* to meet him: and he saluted him, and said to him, Is thine heart right, as my heart *is* with thy heart? And Je-hon'a-dab answered, It is. If it be, give *me* thine hand. And he gave *him* his hand; and he took him up to him into the chariot.

16 And he said, Come with me, and see my zeal for the LORD. So they made him ride in his chariot.

10:17 2 Kgs 9:8

17 And when he came to Sa-ma'ri-a, he slew all that remained unto Ahab in Sa-ma'ri-a, till he had destroyed him, according to the saying of the LORD, which he spake to E-li'jah.

3. The Massacre of the Baal Worshippers

10:18☆ 1 Kgs 16:31; 18:19; 22:6

18 ¶And Jehu gathered all the people together, and said unto them, Ahab served Ba'al a little; *but* Jehu shall serve him much.

10:11 *he left him none remaining,* i.e., "no one was left who had been close to him in any way" (TLB). Apparently Jehu in his zeal exceeded the Lord's command in this bloodbath, for he was blamed for it by the prophet Hosea (Hos. 1:4).†

10:13 *brethen,* literally, "kinsmen."†

10:14 These people were from branches of the house of Ahab who descended from Athaliah. They were tainted with the wickedness of Ahab and his house. These people, forty-two of them of high positions, were slain by Jehu.

10:15 *Jehonadab,* an ascetic, is mentioned (as "Jonadab," another of his names) in Jer. 35:6, where his descendants are tested by Jeremiah. Jehu accepted Jehonadab at face value as honest.

10:18 The worship of Baal was so extensive that it had penetrated most of the Northern Kingdom. Jehu wanted to stamp out Baal worship. So he pretended to be a worshipper of Baal and called all the Baal worshippers to a convocation. There they were slain and the pillar of Baal was demolished. The house of Baal was made into a latrine. 10:28 says: "Thus Jehu destroyed Baal out of Israel."

19 Now therefore call unto me all the prophets of Ba'al, all his servants,
and all his priests; let none be wanting: for I have a great sacrifice *to do* to
Ba'al; whosoever shall be wanting, he shall not live. But Jehu did *it* in
subtilty, to the intent that he might destroy the worshippers of Ba'al.
20 And Jehu said, Proclaim a solemn assembly for Ba'al. And they **10:20**
proclaimed *it.* 1 Kgs 16:32; 2 Kgs 11:18
21 And Jehu sent through all Israel: and all the worshippers of Ba'al came,
so that there was not a man left that came not. And they came into the
house of Ba'al; and the house of Ba'al was full from one end to another.
22 And he said unto him that *was* over the vestry, Bring forth vestments
for all the worshippers of Ba'al. And he brought them forth vestments.
23 And Jehu went, and Je-hon'a-dab the son of Re'chab, into the house of ☆**10:23**
Ba'al, and said unto the worshippers of Ba'al, Search, and look that there
be here with you none of the servants of the LORD, but the worshippers of
Ba'al only.
24 And when they went in to offer sacrifices and burnt offerings, Jehu **10:24**
appointed fourscore men without, and said, *If* any of the men whom I have 1 Kgs 20:40
brought into your hands escape, *he that letteth him go,* his life *shall be* for
the life of him.
25 And it came to pass, as soon as he had made an end of offering the **10:25**
burnt offering, that Jehu said to the guard and to the captains, Go in, *and* 1 Sam 22:17; 1 Kgs 18:40
slay them; let none come forth. And they smote them with the edge of the
sword; and the guard and the captains cast *them* out, and went to the city
of the house of Ba'al.
26 And they brought forth the images out of the house of Ba'al, and **10:26**
burned them. 1 Kgs 14:23; 2 Kgs 3:2
27 And they brake down the image of Ba'al, and brake down the house of ☆**10:27**
Ba'al, and made it a draught house unto this day.
28 Thus Jehu destroyed Ba'al out of Israel. ☆**10:28**
29 ¶Howbeit *from* the sins of Jer-o-bo'am the son of Ne'bat, who made **10:29**
Israel to sin, Jehu departed not from after them, *to wit,* the golden calves 1 Kgs 12:28; 13:33, 34
that *were* in Beth-el, and that *were* in Dan.

4. A Summary of Jehu's Kingship

30 And the LORD said unto Jehu, Because thou hast done well in executing **10:30**
that which is right in mine eyes, *and* hast done unto the house of Ahab 2 Kgs 13:1; 15:12
according to all that *was* in mine heart, thy children of the fourth *generation*
shall sit on the throne of Israel.
31 But Jehu took no heed to walk in the law of the LORD God of Israel **10:31**
with all his heart: for he departed not from the sins of Jer-o-bo'am, which 1 Kgs 12:28, 29
made Israel to sin.
32 In those days the LORD began to cut Israel short: and Haz'a-el smote **10:32**
them in all the coasts of Israel; Deut 2:36; 2 Kgs 8:12; 13:22; 14:25
33 From Jordan eastward, all the land of Gilead, the Gadites, and the
Reubenites, and the Ma-nas'sites, from Ar'o-er, which *is* by the river
Arnon, even Gilead and Ba'shan.
34 Now the rest of the acts of Jehu, and all that he did, and all his might, **10:34**
are they not written in the book of the chronicles of the kings of Israel? 2 Kgs 1:18; 13:8; 2 Chron 20:34

10:23 Jehu was careful to distinguish between those who worshipped Baal and those who did not. Only Baal-worshippers were to be killed.

10:27 *a draught house,* i.e., a toilet which according to Hebrew law and tradition was unclean.

10:28 Jehu was by no means devoted to God in a meaningful way. He did not walk according to God's commandments, but he did do what God wanted done: he removed the house of Ahab and destroyed Baal worship. For this God said his line would continue for four generations. He died after a reign of twenty-eight years and was succeeded by his son Jehoahaz.

10:35 2 Kgs 13:1 35 And Jehu slept with his fathers: and they buried him in Sa-ma'ri-a. And
Je-ho'a-haz his son reigned in his stead.
36 And the time that Jehu reigned over Israel in Sa-ma'ri-a *was* twenty and
eight years.

B. QUEEN ATHALIAH OF JUDAH, DAUGHTER OF AHAB

1. Athaliah Takes over the Kingdom

11:1☆ 2 Kgs 8:26 2 Chron 22:10 11 AND when Ath-a-li'ah the mother of A-ha-zi'ah saw that her son
was dead, she arose and destroyed all the seed royal.
11:2☆ 2 But Je-hosh'e-ba, the daughter of king Joram, sister of A-ha-zi'ah, took
Jo'ash the son of A-ha-zi'ah, and stole him from among the king's sons
which were slain; and they hid him, *even* him and his nurse, in the
bedchamber from Ath-a-li'ah, so that he was not slain.
11:3☆ 3 And he was with her hid in the house of the LORD six years. And Ath-
a-li'ah did reign over the land.

2. Jehoiada the Priest Overthrows Athaliah; Joash Reigns

11:4☆ 2 Chron 23:1 4 ¶And the seventh year Je-hoi'a-da sent and fetched the rulers over
hundreds, with the captains and the guard, and brought them to him into
the house of the LORD, and made a covenant with them, and took an oath
of them in the house of the LORD, and shewed them the king's son.
5 And he commanded them, saying, This *is* the thing that ye shall do; A
third part of you that enter in on the sabbath shall even be keepers of the
watch of the king's house;
6 And a third part *shall be* at the gate of Sur; and a third part at the gate
behind the guard: so shall ye keep the watch of the house, that it be not
broken down.
7 And two parts of all you that go forth on the sabbath, even they shall
keep the watch of the house of the LORD about the king.
8 And ye shall compass the king round about, every man with his
weapons in his hand: and he that cometh within the ranges, let him be
slain: and be ye with the king as he goeth out and as he cometh in.
9 And the captains over the hundreds did according to all *things* that Je-
hoi'a-da the priest commanded: and they took every man his men that were

---

11:1 God had promised to have a man on the throne of David forever. Here that promise is almost ended and the Davidic line extinguished by Athaliah. She was Jezebel's daughter and Jehoram's wife. Following the death of her son, Ahaziah, this angry woman destroyed all of the royal seed (so far as she knew). Her malice knew no bounds and revenge was the order of the day for her. She was not alone in this endeavor. Her husband, Jehoram, had killed all of the sons of Jehoshaphat to prevent anyone from usurping his kingship. Thus he was the only heir left, unless he had children. The Arabians, according to 2 Chron. 22:1, had killed all of Jehoram's sons except Ahaziah. Because she was the grandmother of all of Ahaziah's children, one would have supposed that she would have loved them, not destroyed them. Ahaziah's sons were the only ones left to inherit the throne when he was slain after a two-year reign.

11:2, 3 Jehosheba, the wife of the priest Jehoiada and the aunt of Joash preserved Joash's life by hiding him in a place where bedroom equipment was stored. She did this for six years while Athaliah reigned over Judah. Here was God at work to frustrate the evil purposes of one who sought to undo the divine arrangements. The tyrannous Athaliah would surely have destroyed Joash, too, had she known of his existence. *in the house of the LORD,* i.e., "in a storeroom in the temple." This arrangement was practical, for Jehosheba was the wife of Jehoiada the high priest.

11:4 State and church or state and Israel were not explicitly divided in the Old Testament. There was a state church, if we use today's parlance. Here the religious leaders involve themselves in political affairs. They do it with the connivance of the military leaders. The plot was simple: they wished to elevate young Joash to the kingship and rid themselves of Athaliah, who had no right to the throne and who had slain every contender known to her. She reintroduced Baalism to Judah, was wholly out of tune with Judah's God, and introduced for the first time the notion that a woman could succeed to the kingship. God had promised that a man would occupy the throne and made no provision for a female to occupy the post. Had there been such a provision, then Jehosheba could have become the monarch instead of Athaliah, for she was of royal blood.

to come in on the sabbath, with them that should go out on the sabbath,
and came to Je-hoi′a-da the priest.
10 And to the captains over hundreds did the priest give king David's
spears and shields, that *were* in the temple of the LORD.

11:10 2 Sam 8:7; 1 Chron 18:7, 8; 2 Chron 23:9

11 And the guard stood, every man with his weapons in his hand, round
about the king, from the right corner of the temple to the left corner of the
temple, *along* by the altar and the temple.
12 And he brought forth the king's son, and put the crown upon him, and
gave him the testimony; and they made him king, and anointed him; and
they clapped their hands, and said, God save the king.

☆**11:12** Ex 31:18; 1 Sam 10:24; 2 Kgs 12:1

13 ¶And when Ath-a-li′ah heard the noise of the guard *and* of the people,
she came to the people into the temple of the LORD.

☆**11:13** Gen 37:29; 44:13; 1 Kgs 1:39, 40; 2 Chron 23:12

14 And when she looked, behold, the king stood by a pillar, as the manner
was, and the princes and the trumpeters by the king, and all the people of
the land rejoiced, and blew with trumpets: and Ath-a-li′ah rent her clothes,
and cried, Treason, Treason.
15 But Je-hoi′a-da the priest commanded the captains of the hundreds, the
officers of the host, and said unto them, Have her forth without the ranges:
and him that followeth her kill with the sword. For the priest had said, Let
her not be slain in the house of the LORD.
16 And they laid hands on her; and she went by the way by the which the
horses came into the king's house: and there was she slain.

☆**11:16**

17 ¶And Je-hoi′a-da made a covenant between the LORD and the king and
the people, that they should be the LORD's people; between the king also
and the people.

☆**11:17** Josh 24:25; 2 Sam 5:3; 2 Chron 15:12

18 And all the people of the land went into the house of Ba′al, and brake
it down; his altars and his images brake they in pieces thoroughly, and slew
Mat′tan the priest of Ba′al before the altars. And the priest appointed
officers over the house of the LORD.

11:18 Deut 12:2; 1 Kgs 18:40; 2 Kgs 10:24

19 And he took the rulers over hundreds, and the captains, and the guard,
and all the people of the land; and they brought down the king from the
house of the LORD, and came by the way of the gate of the guard to the
king's house. And he sat on the throne of the kings.
20 And all the people of the land rejoiced, and the city was in quiet: and
they slew Ath-a-li′ah with the sword *beside* the king's house.
21 Seven years old *was* Je-ho′ash when he began to reign.

11:21 2 Chron 24:1

C. JOASH (JEHOASH), THE KING OF JUDAH

1. Joash (Jehoash) a Good King

12 IN the seventh year of Jehu Je-ho′ash began to reign; and forty
years reigned he in Jerusalem. And his mother's name *was* Zib′i-ah
of Be′er–she′ba.

☆**12:1** 1 Kgs 19:16; 2 Chron 24:1

11:12 Joash was crowned king at the temple. Jehoiada had laid his plans well. Joash was given the testimony, that is, the Word of God, to read and to obey. He was anointed, and a crown was placed on his young head. The soldiers and those assembled recognized him as the legitimate heir to his father's throne and cried out, "God save the king."

11:13 When Athaliah heard what had happened, she came to the temple and was amazed to see this young man of whom she had no knowledge standing there as the king of Judah. To her it was treason, and she shouted that aloud for all to hear. They removed her from the house of the Lord and killed her.

11:16 Athaliah's death was the result of her upbringing. Her father, Ahab, was a nominal Yahweh worshipper married to Jezebel, a Baal worshipper, who raised and trained her daughter in all the evil she knew. Even as Jezebel evilly influenced Ahab, so Athaliah influenced her unresisting husband, the king of Judah. She brought naught but evil into the kingdom of Judah and, no doubt, hastened its spiritual decline.

11:17 Jehoiada now made a covenant with God, the people, and the king that they would be the Lord's people. The house of Baal was destroyed and all the paraphernalia connected with that worship was wiped out. Mattan the priest of Baal was also killed. Renewal had come to Judah and the prospects were bright.

12:1, 2 Joash (Jehoash) came to the throne at seven years of age and reigned for forty years. He was instructed by Jehoiada, who was his mentor and his faithful steward until he reached a proper age.

12:2 2 Kgs 14:3

2 And Je-ho'ash did *that which was* right in the sight of the LORD all his days wherein Je-hoi'a-da the priest instructed him.

12:3☆ 1 Kgs 14:23; 15:14; 2 Kgs 14:4; 15:34, 35

3 But the high places were not taken away: the people still sacrificed and burnt incense in the high places.

2. The Repair of the Temple

12:4 Ex 35:5–9, 22, 29; 2 Kgs 22:3–6; 1 Chron 29:3

4 ¶And Je-ho'ash said to the priests, All the money of the dedicated things that is brought into the house of the LORD, *even* the money of every one that passeth *the account,* the money that every man is set at, *and* all the money that cometh into any man's heart to bring into the house of the LORD,

5 Let the priests take *it* to them, every man of his acquaintance: and let them repair the breaches of the house, wheresoever any breach shall be found.

6 But it was *so, that* in the three and twentieth year of king Je-ho'ash the priests had not repaired the breaches of the house.

7 Then king Je-ho'ash called for Je-hoi'a-da the priest, and the *other* priests, and said unto them, Why repair ye not the breaches of the house? now therefore receive no *more* money of your acquaintance, but deliver it for the breaches of the house.

8 And the priests consented to receive no *more* money of the people, neither to repair the breaches of the house.

12:9☆ Mk 12:41; Lk 21:1

9 But Je-hoi'a-da the priest took a chest, and bored a hole in the lid of it, and set it beside the altar, on the right side as one cometh into the house of the LORD: and the priests that kept the door put therein all the money *that was* brought into the house of the LORD.

10 And it was *so,* when they saw that *there was* much money in the chest, that the king's scribe and the high priest came up, and they put up in bags, and told the money that was found in the house of the LORD.

12:11 2 Kgs 22:5, 6; 2 Chron 24:11

11 And they gave the money, being told, into the hands of them that did the work, that had the oversight of the house of the LORD: and they laid it out to the carpenters and builders, that wrought upon the house of the LORD,

12 And to masons, and hewers of stone, and to buy timber and hewed stone to repair the breaches of the house of the LORD, and for all that was laid out for the house to repair *it.*

12:13 1 Kgs 7:48, 50

13 Howbeit there were not made for the house of the LORD bowls of silver, snuffers, basons, trumpets, any vessels of gold, or vessels of silver, of the money *that was* brought into the house of the LORD:

14 But they gave that to the workmen, and repaired therewith the house of the LORD.

12:15 2 Kgs 22:7

15 Moreover they reckoned not with the men, into whose hand they delivered the money to be bestowed on workmen: for they dealt faithfully.

16 The trespass money and sin money was not brought into the house of the LORD: it was the priests'.

12:3 In Judah, high places for worship had been set up and altars for incense and sacrifice were in vogue. While they were not removed in Jehoash's day, efforts were made to bring the people to the temple for their religious observances. Private altars for worship were in tacit competition with the temple and its observances and were an offense to God, however well intended.

12:9 The temple was in need of repairs. The efforts of the priests to repair the temple were ineffective, for in the twenty-third year of Jehoash's reign no repairs had been made. Now money is gathered in a public chest and used for the purpose for which it was given. The repair of the house of God begins in earnest.

3. Joash (Jehoash) Pays Tribute to Hazael of Syria

17 ¶Then Haz'a-el king of Syria went up, and fought against Gath, and took it: and Haz'a-el set his face to go up to Jerusalem.
18 And Je-ho'ash king of Judah took all the hallowed things that Je-hosh'a-phat, and Je-ho'ram, and A-ha-zi'ah, his fathers, kings of Judah, had dedicated, and his own hallowed things, and all the gold *that was* found in the treasures of the house of the LORD, and in the king's house, and sent *it* to Haz'a-el king of Syria: and he went away from Jerusalem.

☆12:17 2 Kgs 8:12; 10:32, 33
12:18 1 Kgs 15:18; 2 Kgs 16:8; 18:15, 16

4. Joash's Death; Amaziah His Successor

19 ¶And the rest of the acts of Jo'ash, and all that he did, *are* they not written in the book of the chronicles of the kings of Judah?
20 And his servants arose, and made a conspiracy, and slew Jo'ash in the house of Mil'lo, which goeth down to Sil'la.
21 For Joz'a-char the son of Shim'e-ath, and Je-hoz'a-bad the son of Sho'mer, his servants, smote him, and he died; and they buried him with his fathers in the city of David: and Am-a-zi'ah his son reigned in his stead.

12:19 2 Kgs 8:23; 2 Chron 24:27
☆12:20 2 Sam 5:9; 2 Chron 24:25
12:21 2 Kgs 13:12; 2 Chron 25:1

D. JEHOAHAZ THE KING OF ISRAEL; JOASH HIS SUCCESSOR

13 IN the three and twentieth year of Jo'ash the son of A-ha-zi'ah king of Judah Je-ho'a-haz the son of Jehu began to reign over Israel in Sa-ma'ri-a, *and reigned* seventeen years.
2 And he did *that which was* evil in the sight of the LORD, and followed the sins of Jer-o-bo'am the son of Ne'bat, which made Israel to sin; he departed not therefrom.
3 ¶And the anger of the LORD was kindled against Israel, and he delivered them into the hand of Haz'a-el king of Syria, and into the hand of Ben-ha'dad the son of Haz'a-el, all *their* days.
4 And Je-ho'a-haz besought the LORD, and the LORD hearkened unto him: for he saw the oppression of Israel, because the king of Syria oppressed them.
5 (And the LORD gave Israel a saviour, so that they went out from under the hand of the Syrians: and the children of Israel dwelt in their tents, as beforetime.
6 Nevertheless they departed not from the sins of the house of Jer-o-bo'am, who made Israel sin, *but* walked therein: and there remained the grove also in Sa-ma'ri-a.)
7 Neither did he leave of the people to Je-ho'a-haz but fifty horsemen, and

☆13:1 2 Kgs 10:35; 2 Chron 25:17
13:2 1 Kgs 12:28; 2 Kgs 10:29
13:3 Judg 2:12–14; 2 Kgs 8:8, 9; 10:32, 33; 12:17; 13:22
13:4 Ex 3:7, 9; Num 21:7; Judg 10:15; 2 Kgs 14:26; 2 Chron 33:12
13:5 Judg 2:18, 19; Neh 9:27
13:6 2 Kgs 10:29; 17:21
13:7 Ps 18:42; Isa 41:2

12:17 Joash (Jehoash) of Judah revolted against God and became a fierce persecutor as well as an idolater. He had begun in the Spirit and ended up in the flesh. When he forsook God, he forfeited the divine protection which was his, and Hazael of Syria extracted great wealth from him by threats. By paying a ransom, Joash got Hazael to leave him alone.
12:20 Jehoash's own servants plotted against the king and finally slew him. The king had slain the son of Jehoiada, who had been his counselor as well as his friend. This may have been the provocation that resulted in his death. Those who slew him were not averse to the kingship, for Amaziah was permitted to succeed his father without any revolution. (See 2 Chron. 24:17–19 for an account of his wickedness.)
13:1 Jehoahaz was the first of the four descendants of Jehu to occupy the throne in Israel. He started out very badly and only after many setbacks did he begin to seek the face and the aid of God. "It becomes kings to be beggars at God's door, and the greatest of men to be humble petitioners at the footstool of this throne. Need will drive them to it."* God heard the cry of Jehoahaz and sent him a savior, Jehoahaz's own son, who won battles against the Syrians and recovered the cities they had taken from his father. On his death (after a seventeen-year reign) his son, Joash, ascended to the throne.

ten chariots, and ten thousand footmen; for the king of Syria had destroyed
them, and had made them like the dust by threshing.

13:8 2 Kgs 10:34 13:12; 14:15
8 ¶Now the rest of the acts of Je-ho'a-haz, and all that he did, and his
might, *are* they not written in the book of the chronicles of the kings of
Israel?

E. JOASH'S WICKED REIGN OVER ISRAEL
1. Joash's Sin

13:9 2 Kgs 13:1
9 And Je-ho'a-haz slept with his fathers; and they buried him in Sa-ma'-
ri-a: and Jo'ash his son reigned in his stead.

13:10☆
10 In the thirty and seventh year of Jo'ash king of Judah began Je-ho'ash
the son of Je-ho'a-haz to reign over Israel in Sa-ma'ri-a, *and reigned* sixteen
years.

13:11 1 Kgs 12:28 2 Kgs 10:29 13:2
11 And he did *that which was* evil in the sight of the LORD; he departed not
from all the sins of Jer-o-bo'am the son of Ne'bat, who made Israel sin: *but*
he walked therein.

13:12 2 Kgs 10:34 14:8, 15, 28 2 Chron 25:17
12 And the rest of the acts of Jo'ash, and all that he did, and his might
wherewith he fought against Am-a-zi'ah king of Judah, *are* they not written
in the book of the chronicles of the kings of Israel?

13:13 2 Kgs 14:24, 27 Amos 7:10
13 And Jo'ash slept with his fathers; and Jer-o-bo'am sat upon his throne:
and Jo'ash was buried in Sa-ma'ri-a with the kings of Israel.

2. Elisha and the Arrow of the Lord

13:14☆ 2 Kgs 2:12
14 ¶Now E-li'sha was fallen sick of his sickness whereof he died. And
Jo'ash the king of Israel came down unto him, and wept over his face, and
said, O my father, my father, the chariot of Israel, and the horsemen
thereof.

13:15☆
15 And E-li'sha said unto him, Take bow and arrows. And he took unto
him bow and arrows.
16 And he said to the king of Israel, Put thine hand upon the bow. And he
put his hand *upon it:* and E-li'sha put his hands upon the king's hands.
17 And he said, Open the window eastward. And he opened *it.* Then
E-li'sha said, Shoot. And he shot. And he said, The arrow of the LORD's
deliverance, and the arrow of deliverance from Syria: for thou shalt smite
the Syrians in A'phek, till thou have consumed *them.*
18 And he said, Take the arrows. And he took *them.* And he said unto the
king of Israel, Smite upon the ground. And he smote thrice, and stayed.
19 And the man of God was wroth with him, and said, Thou shouldest
have smitten five or six times; then hadst thou smitten Syria till thou hadst
consumed *it:* whereas now thou shalt smite Syria *but* thrice.

13:10 Joash, or Jehoash, was the second descendant of Jehu to rule over Israel. His reign was one of wickedness. Idolatry continued. He was also in conflict with Amaziah, king of Judah. When he died, the third descendant of Jehu, his son Jeroboam, occupied the throne (14:15,16). Jehoash, the grandson of Jehu, was named after Joash (Jehoash), the king of Judah. This occurred several times and makes for difficulty in distinguishing some of the kings of Israel from the kings of Judah. Usually the text calls one Joash and the other Jehoash when this happens.

13:14 Elisha had served God for about sixty years after he was called to the prophetic office. He was sick unto death. The Scriptures tell us nothing about his later life, a period of forty-five years subsequent to the anointing of Jehu. Life is usually like that: we rise, we level off, we decline, and then we die. *the chariot of Israel, and the horsemen thereof,* i.e., "you are the strength of Israel."†

13:15 Elisha still had one more thing to do before he died. He ordered Joash of Israel to shoot an arrow into the air and then to take arrows and smite the ground. He interpreted the meaning of the prophetic word. The flight of the arrow meant that God would assist Israel against Syria and deliver them. The striking of the arrow on the ground meant that there would be three victories over the Syrians. Elisha upbraided Joash that he had not struck the ground five or six times. He had limited the number of victories by his failure to strike repeatedly—until Syria was completely overthrown.

3. Elisha's Death; the Miracle at His Tomb

20 ¶And E-li'sha died, and they buried him. And the bands of the
Moabites invaded the land at the coming in of the year.
21 And it came to pass, as they were burying a man, that, behold, they
spied a band *of men;* and they cast the man into the sepulchre of E-li'sha:
and when the man was let down, and touched the bones of E-li'sha, he
revived, and stood up on his feet.

☆**13:20** 2 Kgs 3:7; 5:2 24:2
☆**13:21**

4. Israel's Victories over Syria

22 ¶But Haz'a-el king of Syria oppressed Israel all the days of Je-ho'a-haz.
23 And the LORD was gracious unto them, and had compassion on them,
and had respect unto them, because of his covenant with Abraham, Isaac,
and Jacob, and would not destroy them, neither cast he them from his
presence as yet.
24 So Haz'a-el king of Syria died; and Ben–ha'dad his son reigned in his
stead.
25 And Je-ho'ash the son of Je-ho'a-haz took again out of the hand of
Ben–ha'dad the son of Haz'a-el the cities, which he had taken out of the
hand of Je-ho'a-haz his father by war. Three times did Jo'ash beat him, and
recovered the cities of Israel.

13:22 2 Kgs 8:12; 13:3
13:23 Gen 13:16 17:2–4 2 Kgs 14:27
13:24 2 Kgs 8:8, 9 13:3
☆**13:25** 2 Kgs 10:32 14:25

F. KING AMAZIAH OF JUDAH

1. His Activities

14 IN the second year of Jo'ash son of Je-ho'a-haz king of Israel
reigned Am-a-zi'ah the son of Jo'ash king of Judah.
2 He was twenty and five years old when he began to reign, and reigned
twenty and nine years in Jerusalem. And his mother's name *was* Je-ho-
ad'dan of Jerusalem.
3 And he did *that which was* right in the sight of the LORD, yet not like
David his father: he did according to all things as Jo'ash his father did.
4 Howbeit the high places were not taken away: as yet the people did
sacrifice and burnt incense on the high places.
5 ¶And it came to pass, as soon as the kingdom was confirmed in his
hand, that he slew his servants which had slain the king his father.
6 But the children of the murderers he slew not: according unto that
which is written in the book of the law of Moses, wherein the LORD
commanded, saying, The fathers shall not be put to death for the children,
nor the children be put to death for the fathers; but every man shall be put
to death for his own sin.
7 He slew of Edom in the valley of salt ten thousand, and took Se'lah by
war, and called the name of it Jok'the-el unto this day.

☆**14:1** 2 Kgs 13:9, 10 14:17 2 Chron 25:1
☆**14:2**
☆**14:3** 1 Kgs 11:4; 15:3 2 Kgs 15:3
☆**14:4** 1 Kgs 14:23 15:14 2 Kgs 12:3 15:4, 34, 35 16:4
☆**14:5** 2 Kgs 12:20
☆**14:6** Deut 24:16 2 Chron 25:4 Jer 31:30 Ezek 18:4, 20
☆**14:7** 2 Sam 8:13 1 Chron 18:12 2 Chron 25:11 Isa 16:1

13:20, 21 Nothing is said about Elisha on his deathbed. We are told simply that he died. But this was not the end of Elisha or of his ministry. He was the only prophet of God of whom it was said that when a dead man was cast into Elisha's grave, the man revived and stood on his feet. Elisha in life and in death raised the dead.

13:25 Elisha's prediction came to pass. Joash defeated the Syrians three times and recovered the cities they had taken from Israel.

14:1–7 Amaziah of Judah was a relatively good king, at least in his beginnings. Yet he did not remove the high places. He killed those who had murdered his father, but he spared their children. He was successful in his warfare against the Edomites (see 2 Chron. 25:5ff).

14:7 *Selah,* "rock," the capital of Edom.

2. His Wars against Israel

14:8 2 Chron 25:17

8 ¶Then Am-a-zi'ah sent messengers to Je-ho'ash, the son of Je-ho'a-haz son of Jehu, king of Israel, saying, Come, let us look one another in the face.

14:9 Judg 9:14, 15

9 And Je-ho'ash the king of Israel sent to Am-a-zi'ah king of Judah, saying, The thistle that *was* in Lebanon, sent to the cedar that *was* in Lebanon, saying, Give thy daughter to my son to wife: and there passed by a wild beast that *was* in Lebanon, and trode down the thistle.

14:10 Prov 16:18

10 Thou hast indeed smitten Edom, and thine heart hath lifted thee up: glory *of this,* and tarry at home: for why shouldest thou meddle to *thy* hurt, that thou shouldest fall, *even* thou, and Judah with thee?

14:11 Josh 19:35–39; 1 Sam 6:9

11 But Am-a-zi'ah would not hear. Therefore Je-ho'ash king of Israel went up; and he and Am-a-zi'ah king of Judah looked one another in the face at Beth–she'mesh, which *belongeth* to Judah.

12 And Judah was put to the worse before Israel; and they fled every man to their tents.

14:13 2 Chron 25:23; Neh 8:16; 12:39

13 And Je-ho'ash king of Israel took Am-a-zi'ah king of Judah, the son of Je-ho'ash the son of A-ha-zi'ah, at Beth–she'mesh, and came to Jerusalem, and brake down the wall of Jerusalem from the gate of E'phra-im unto the corner gate, four hundred cubits.

14:14 2 Kgs 12:18

14 And he took all the gold and silver, and all the vessels that were found in the house of the LORD, and in the treasures of the king's house, and hostages, and returned to Sa-ma'ri-a.

3. The Death of Joash of Israel

14:15☆ 2 Kgs 13:12, 13; 14:28; 2 Chron 25:26

15 ¶Now the rest of the acts of Je-ho'ash which he did, and his might, and how he fought with Am-a-zi'ah king of Judah, *are* they not written in the book of the chronicles of the kings of Israel?

14:16☆ 2 Kgs 10:35; 13:13

16 And Je-ho'ash slept with his fathers, and was buried in Sa-ma'ri-a with the kings of Israel; and Jer-o-bo'am his son reigned in his stead.

4. Amaziah's Death; Azariah (Uzziah) His Successor

14:17☆ 2 Chron 25:25

17 ¶And Am-a-zi'ah the son of Jo'ash king of Judah lived after the death of Je-ho'ash son of Je-ho'a-haz king of Israel fifteen years.

14:18 2 Kgs 12:19; 15:15

18 And the rest of the acts of Am-a-zi'ah, *are* they not written in the book of the chronicles of the kings of Judah?

14:19 2 Kgs 12:20; 15:10

19 Now they made a conspiracy against him in Jerusalem: and he fled to La'chish; but they sent after him to La'chish, and slew him there.

14:20 2 Kgs 8:24, 25; 9:28; 12:21

20 And they brought him on horses: and he was buried at Jerusalem with his fathers in the city of David.

14:21 1 Chron 3:10–14; 2 Chron 26:1; Mt 1:9

21 ¶And all the people of Judah took Az-a-ri'ah, which *was* sixteen years old, and made him king instead of his father Am-a-zi'ah.

14:8 Amaziah had shortcomings that annihilated him: he was proud and presumptuous, and challenged Jehoash of Israel to battle. Jehoash sent back a letter in which he compared Amaziah to a thistle that was trodden down by a wild beast and he compared himself to a cedar of Lebanon. He conquered Amaziah and took him prisoner. He entered Jerusalem and removed all that was valuable. He broke down part of the city's walls; and according to Josephus, he rode his chariot in triumph through the breach.

14:15, 16 Jehoash's death is reported in 13:12, 13 and again here. His son Jeroboam, who succeeded him, was the third king of the four promised to Jehu by Elisha years before.

14:17 Amaziah got off to a good start but had a bad ending. His insolence, the defeat at the hands of Jehoash, and the virtual sack of Jerusalem led the people of Judah to detest him. He fled to Lachish where he was concealed for some time before he was slain by his own people. He was succeeded by Azariah (Uzziah), who was four years old at the time of his father's death. He was under his protectors until he was sixteen, at which time he became king on his own. We meet him later in Scripture, in Isaiah 6:1.

[22]He built E'lath, and restored it to Judah, after that the king slept with
his fathers.

14:22 2 Kgs 16:6

G. JEROBOAM II AND HIS LONG AND EVIL REIGN OVER ISRAEL

[23]In the fifteenth year of Am-a-zi'ah the son of Jo'ash king of Judah Jer-
o-bo'am the son of Jo'ash king of Israel began to reign in Sa-ma'ri-a, *and*
reigned forty and one years.
[24]And he did *that which was* evil in the sight of the LORD: he departed not
from all the sins of Jer-o-bo'am the son of Ne'bat, who made Israel to sin.
[25]He restored the coast of Israel from the entering of Ha'math unto the
sea of the plain, according to the word of the LORD God of Israel, which he
spake by the hand of his servant Jonah, the son of A-mit'ta-i, the prophet,
which *was* of Gath–he'pher.
[26]For the LORD saw the affliction of Israel, *that it was* very bitter: for
there was not any shut up, nor any left, nor any helper for Israel.
[27]And the LORD said not that he would blot out the name of Israel from
under heaven: but he saved them by the hand of Jer-o-bo'am the son of
Jo'ash.
[28]¶Now the rest of the acts of Jer-o-bo'am, and all that he did, and his
might, how he warred, and how he recovered Damascus, and Ha'math,
which belonged to Judah, for Israel, *are* they not written in the book of the
chronicles of the kings of Israel?
[29]And Jer-o-bo'am slept with his fathers, *even* with the kings of Israel;
and Zach-a-ri'ah his son reigned in his stead.

☆**14:23** 2 Kgs 13:13; Hos 1:1; Amos 1:2
14:24 1 Kgs 12:28; 2 Kgs 13:2, 6
14:25 2 Kgs 13:25; Jonah 1:1
14:26 Ex 3:7, 9; Deut 32:36; 2 Kgs 13:4
14:27 2 Kgs 13:5, 23
14:28 2 Kgs 14:15; 15:11

H. AZARIAH (UZZIAH) AND HIS LONG AND GOOD REIGN OVER JUDAH

15 IN the twenty and seventh year of Jer-o-bo'am king of Israel began
Az-a-ri'ah son of Am-a-zi'ah king of Judah to reign.
[2]Sixteen years old was he when he began to reign, and he reigned two
and fifty years in Jerusalem. And his mother's name *was* Jech-o-li'ah of
Jerusalem.
[3]And he did *that which was* right in the sight of the LORD, according to all
that his father Am-a-zi'ah had done;
[4]Save that the high places were not removed: the people sacrificed and
burnt incense still on the high places.
[5]¶And the LORD smote the king, so that he was a leper unto the day of
his death, and dwelt in a several house. And Jo'tham the king's son *was*
over the house, judging the people of the land.
[6]And the rest of the acts of Az-a-ri'ah, and all that he did, *are* they not
written in the book of the chronicles of the kings of Judah?
[7]So Az-a-ri'ah slept with his fathers; and they buried him with his fathers
in the city of David: and Jo'tham his son reigned in his stead.

☆**15:1** 2 Kgs 14:21; 15:13, 17
15:3 2 Kgs 14:3
15:4 Lev 13:46; 2 Kgs 12:3; 14:3; 2 Chron 26:21
☆**15:5**
15:6 2 Kgs 14:18; 15:36
15:7 2 Kgs 14:20; 15:32, 33

14:23 Jeroboam of Israel was named after Jeroboam of Nebat, the first king of Israel. Thus he is called Jeroboam II. He represented the third generation of the Jehu line. He reigned longer than any other king of Israel—forty-one years. He was a wicked king who did not depart from the sins of Jeroboam I. God was long-suffering with Israel, and despite the wickedness of the king God helped him. He gained back some of the territory that had been taken from Israel, for God had compassion on the people of those regions. He was succeeded by Zechariah, who was the fourth generation of Jehu and the last of that line to sit on Israel's throne.

15:1 This is a short account of Ahaziah's reign over Judah. 2 Chron. 16 has a fuller report of his life and acts. Like Amaziah, he began well and finished poorly. His fifty-two year reign was the longest of all the kings of either Israel or Judah. Jotham succeeded him and his reign is reported in 15:32ff.

15:5 Azariah (Uzziah) is spoken of as a leper here, but the cause of his leprosy is not stated. In 2 Chron. 26:16–21, however, we learn that he sought to burn incense on the altar of incense, a job reserved for the Levitical priesthood. God punished his transgression by sending leprosy. Because of his disease, he was forever banned from entering the house of worship.

I. ZECHARIAH'S (SON OF JEROBOAM II) HALF-YEAR REIGN OVER ISRAEL

15:8☆ 2 Kgs 14:29 8In the thirty and eighth year of Az-a-ri'ah king of Judah did Zach-a-
ri'ah the son of Jer-o-bo'am reign over Israel in Sa-ma'ri-a six months.
15:9 2 Kgs 10:29 13:2; 14:24 9And he did *that which was* evil in the sight of the LORD, as his fathers
had done: he departed not from the sins of Jer-o-bo'am the son of Ne'bat,
who made Israel to sin.
15:10 Amos 7:9 10And Shal'lum the son of Ja'besh conspired against him, and smote him
before the people, and slew him, and reigned in his stead.
15:11 2 Kgs 14:28 15:15, 21 11And the rest of the acts of Zach-a-ri'ah, behold, they *are* written in the
book of the chronicles of the kings of Israel.
15:12 2 Kgs 10:30 12This *was* the word of the LORD which he spake unto Jehu, saying, Thy
sons shall sit on the throne of Israel unto the fourth *generation*. And so it
came to pass.

J. SHALLUM'S ONE-MONTH REIGN (ISRAEL)

15:13☆ 2 Kgs 15:1 13¶Shal'lum the son of Ja'besh began to reign in the nine and thirtieth
year of Uz-zi'ah king of Judah; and he reigned a full month in Sa-ma'ri-a.
14For Men'a-hem the son of Ga'di went up from Tir'zah, and came to Sa-
ma'ri-a, and smote Shal'lum the son of Ja'besh in Sa-ma'ri-a, and slew him,
and reigned in his stead.
15:15 2 Kgs 15:11, 21 15And the rest of the acts of Shal'lum, and his conspiracy which he made,
behold, they *are* written in the book of the chronicles of the kings of Israel.
15:16 2 Kgs 8:12 16¶Then Men'a-hem smote Tiph'sah, and all that *were* therein, and the
coasts thereof from Tir'zah: because they opened not *to him,* therefore he
smote *it; and* all the women therein that were with child he ripped up.

K. MENAHEM'S TEN-YEAR REIGN OVER ISRAEL

15:17☆ 17In the nine and thirtieth year of Az-a-ri'ah king of Judah began Men'a-
hem the son of Ga'di to reign over Israel, *and reigned* ten years in Sa-ma'-
ri-a.
15:18 2 Kgs 14:24 18And he did *that which was* evil in the sight of the LORD: he departed not
all his days from the sins of Jer-o-bo'am the son of Ne'bat, who made Israel
to sin.
15:19☆ 19*And* Pul the king of Assyria came against the land: and Men'a-hem
gave Pul a thousand talents of silver, that his hand might be with him to
confirm the kingdom in his hand.
20And Men'a-hem exacted the money of Israel, *even* of all the mighty
men of wealth, of each man fifty shekels of silver, to give to the king of
Assyria. So the king of Assyria turned back, and stayed not there in the
land.

15:8 Zechariah was the fourth and last descendant of Jehu on the throne of Israel. His reign lasted six months. The best days of the kingdom of Israel were while the kingship was in the hands of Jehu and his family. Verse 12 states that God's promise to Jehu of four generations of kings had been fulfilled. A conspiracy started by Shallum the son of Jabesh led to Zechariah's death and the ascension of the revolter, Shallum, to the throne.

15:13 The four kings who followed Zechariah were "a disaster." Confusion abounded for approximately thirty-three years. Shallum lasted one month before he was killed by Menahem, the son of Gadi. He was a very bad king.

15:17 Menahem reigned for ten years. He had sacked Tappuah and ripped open the pregnant women. Pul of Asssyria came down on Israel, and Menahem exacted money from the richer people to pay tribute. He paid a thousand talents of silver to Pul to help keep him on the throne. On his death he was succeeded by his son, Pekahiah.

15:19 *Pul,* another name for Tiglath-pileser III (744–727 B.C.). His inscriptions record payment of tribute by Menahem.

21¶And the rest of the acts of Men'a-hem, and all that he did, *are* they not
written in the book of the chronicles of the kings of Israel?
22And Men'a-hem slept with his fathers; and Pek-a-hi'ah his son reigned
in his stead.

L. PEKAHIAH'S TWO-YEAR REIGN OVER ISRAEL

23In the fiftieth year of Az-a-ri'ah king of Judah Pek-a-hi'ah the son of
Men'a-hem began to reign over Israel in Sa-ma'ri-a, *and reigned* two years.
24And he did *that which was* evil in the sight of the LORD: he departed not
from the sins of Jer-o-bo'am the son of Ne'bat, who made Israel to sin.
25But Pe'kah the son of Rem-a-li'ah, a captain of his, conspired against
him, and smote him in Sa-ma'ri-a, in the palace of the king's house, with
Ar'gob and A-ri'eh, and with him fifty men of the Gileadites: and he killed
him, and reigned in his room.
26And the rest of the acts of Pek-a-hi'ah, and all that he did, behold, they
are written in the book of the chronicles of the kings of Israel.

☆**15:23**

M. PEKAH'S TWENTY-YEAR REIGN OVER ISRAEL

27In the two and fiftieth year of Az-a-ri'ah king of Judah Pe'kah the son
of Rem-a-li'ah began to reign over Israel in Sa-ma'ri-a, *and reigned* twenty
years.
28And he did *that which was* evil in the sight of the LORD: he departed not
from the sins of Jer-o-bo'am the son of Ne'bat, who made Israel to sin.
29In the days of Pe'kah king of Israel came Tig'lath-pi-le'ser king of
Assyria, and took I'jon, and A'bel-beth-ma'a-chah, and Ja-no'ah, and
Ke'desh, and Ha'zor, and Gilead, and Galilee, all the land of Naph'ta-li,
and carried them captive to Assyria.
30And Ho-she'a the son of E'lah made a conspiracy against Pe'kah the
son of Rem-a-li'ah, and smote him, and slew him, and reigned in his stead,
in the twentieth year of Jo'tham the son of Uz-zi'ah.
31And the rest of the acts of Pe'kah, and all that he did, behold, they *are*
written in the book of the chronicles of the kings of Israel.

☆**15:27** 2 Kgs 15:32 16:5

15:29 2 Kgs 17:6

☆**15:30** 2 Kgs 17:4; 18:1

N. JOTHAM'S REIGN OVER JUDAH

32In the second year of Pe'kah the son of Rem-a-li'ah king of Israel began
Jo'tham the son of Uz-zi'ah king of Judah to reign.
33Five and twenty years old was he when he began to reign, and he
reigned sixteen years in Jerusalem. And his mother's name *was* Je-ru'sha,
the daughter of Za'dok.
34And he did *that which was* right in the sight of the LORD: he did
according to all that his father Uz-zi'ah had done.

☆**15:32** 2 Kgs 15:7, 27 2 Chron 27:1 Mt 1:9

15:34 2 Kgs 12:2, 3 14:4; 15:4 2 Chron 26:4 27:1, 2

15:23 Pekahiah lasted two years. He followed in the footsteps of the first king, Jeroboam, and did evil in the sight of God. Pekah, a captain in his army, conspired against him and slew him, then became the new king of Israel.

15:27 The *twenty years* assigned to Pekah have been thought by some to be an error. He reigned alone for eight of the twenty years. During the twelve years before that, he was co-ruler with the two previous kings, Pekahiah and Menahem.

15:30 Again a king of Israel is slain. Hoshea, the son of Elah, was the murderer and successor to Pekah. He acted as he did because Pekah had failed to keep Tiglath-pileser (also known as Pul) from taking over parts of Israel. Hoshea was the nineteenth and the last king of Israel. His reign began in 732 B.C. Tiglath-pileser died in 727 B.C. Hoshea sought relief from Assyria by calling on Egypt for help. Shalmaneser led a campaign against Israel in 724 B.C. Hoshea capitulated and paid tribute. He was later imprisoned by Shalmaneser. See further details in 17:1ff.

15:32 Jotham's sixteen-year reign over Judah is covered quickly. Generally he was a good king, but the high places remained, where sacrifices and incense were offered instead of at the temple in Jerusalem. Ahaz succeeded him.

35 ¶Howbeit the high places were not removed: the people sacrificed and burned incense still in the high places. He built the higher gate of the house of the LORD.

15:36 2 Kgs 15:6 16:19; 20:20

36 ¶Now the rest of the acts of Jo'tham, and all that he did, *are* they not written in the book of the chronicles of the kings of Judah?

15:37 2 Kgs 16:5 Isa 7:1

37 In those days the LORD began to send against Judah Re'zin the king of Syria, and Pe'kah the son of Rem-a-li'ah.

15:38 2 Kgs 14:20 15:7; 16:20

38 And Jo'tham slept with his fathers, and was buried with his fathers in the city of David his father: and Ahaz his son reigned in his stead.

O. AHAZ'S (JOTHAM'S SON) REIGN OVER JUDAH

1. Resumé of Ahaz's Reign

16:1☆ 2 Chron 28:1 Mt 1:9

16 IN the seventeenth year of Pe'kah the son of Rem-a-li'ah Ahaz the son of Jo'tham king of Judah began to reign.

16:2 2 Kgs 14:3

2 Twenty years old *was* Ahaz when he began to reign, and reigned sixteen years in Jerusalem, and did not *that which was* right in the sight of the LORD his God, like David his father.

16:3 Lev 18:21 Deut 12:31 2 Kgs 3:27 17:17; 21:6

3 But he walked in the way of the kings of Israel, yea, and made his son to pass through the fire, according to the abominations of the heathen, whom the LORD cast out from before the children of Israel.

16:4 Deut 12:2; 14:4

4 And he sacrificed and burnt incense in the high places, and on the hills, and under every green tree.

2. Tiglath-pileser of Assyria Rescues Ahaz from War with Israel and Syria

16:5☆ 2 Kgs 15:37 2 Chron 28:5 Isa 7:1

5 ¶Then Re'zin king of Syria and Pe'kah son of Rem-a-li'ah king of Israel came up to Jerusalem to war: and they besieged Ahaz, but could not overcome *him.*

16:6 2 Kgs 14:22 2 Chron 26:2

6 At that time Re'zin king of Syria recovered E'lath to Syria, and drave the Jews from E'lath: and the Syrians came to E'lath, and dwelt there unto this day.

16:7 2 Kgs 15:29 2 Chron 28:20

7 So Ahaz sent messengers to Tig'lath–pi-le'ser king of Assyria, saying, I *am* thy servant and thy son: come up, and save me out of the hand of the king of Syria, and out of the hand of the king of Israel, which rise up against me.

16:8 2 Kgs 12:18 18:15

8 And Ahaz took the silver and gold that was found in the house of the LORD, and in the treasures of the king's house, and sent *it for* a present to the king of Assyria.

16:9 Isa 7:15, 16 Amos 1:3–5

9 And the king of Assyria hearkened unto him: for the king of Assyria went up against Damascus, and took it, and carried *the people of* it captive to Kir, and slew Re'zin.

3. Ahaz Builds a Heathen Altar

16:10 2 Chron 28:23 Isa 8:2

10 ¶And king Ahaz went to Damascus to meet Tig'lath–pi-le'ser king of Assyria, and saw an altar that *was* at Damascus: and king Ahaz sent to U-ri'jah the priest the fashion of the altar, and the pattern of it, according to all the workmanship thereof.

16:1 Ahaz, who followed two good kings, was a bad one. He walked according to the sins of Israel. He was only twenty when he began to reign and died at thirty-six. He burned some of his sons to dunghill-deities. Others he passed through fire, as a token of their commitment to idols. Instead of worshipping only at the temple, he sacrificed and burned incense at the high places.

16:5 Syria and Israel conspired against Ahaz. Eventually Ahaz sent tribute money to Tiglath-pileser and asked for help. The Assyrians descended on Damascus and so kept Syria from attacking Ahaz and his country.

11 And U-ri'jah the priest built an altar according to all that king Ahaz ☆16:11
had sent from Damascus: so U-ri'jah the priest made *it* against king Ahaz
came from Damascus.
12 And when the king was come from Damascus, the king saw the altar:
and the king approached to the altar, and offered thereon.
13 And he burnt his burnt offering and his meat offering, and poured his
drink offering, and sprinkled the blood of his peace offerings, upon the
altar.
14 And he brought also the brasen altar, which *was* before the LORD, from **16:14** Ex 40:6
the forefront of the house, from between the altar and the house of the 1 Kgs 8:22, 23
LORD, and put it on the north side of the altar.
15 And king Ahaz commanded U-ri'jah the priest, saying, Upon the great **16:15** Lev 4:14
altar burn the morning burnt offering, and the evening meat offering, and Num 28:1, 2
the king's burnt sacrifice, and his meat offering, with the burnt offering of
all the people of the land, and their meat offering, and their drink offerings;
and sprinkle upon it all the blood of the burnt offering, and all the blood of
the sacrifice: and the brasen altar shall be for me to inquire *by*.
16 Thus did U-ri'jah the priest, according to all that king Ahaz com-
manded.
17 ¶And king Ahaz cut off the borders of the bases, and removed the laver **16:17**
from off them; and took down the sea from off the brasen oxen that *were* 1 Kgs 7:23
under it, and put it upon a pavement of stones.
18 And the covert for the sabbath that they had built in the house, and the
king's entry without, turned he from the house of the LORD for the king of
Assyria.

4. Ahaz's Death; Hezekiah His Successor

19 ¶Now the rest of the acts of Ahaz which he did, *are* they not written in **16:19**
the book of the chronicles of the kings of Judah? 2 Kgs 15:36 20:20
20 And Ahaz slept with his fathers, and was buried with his fathers in the ☆**16:20**
city of David: and Hez-e-ki'ah his son reigned in his stead. 2 Kgs 18:1 2 Chron 28:27 29:1

P. THE FALL OF THE KINGDOM OF ISRAEL
1. Shalmaneser of Assyria Captures Samaria

17 IN the twelfth year of Ahaz king of Judah began Ho-she'a the son ☆**17:1**
of E'lah to reign in Sa-ma'ri-a over Israel nine years. 2 Kgs 15:30
2 And he did *that which was* evil in the sight of the LORD, but not as the
kings of Israel that were before him.
3 ¶Against him came up Shal-man-e'ser king of Assyria; and Ho-she'a **17:3**
became his servant, and gave him presents. 2 Kgs 18:9
4 And the king of Assyria found conspiracy in Ho-she'a: for he had sent **17:4**
messengers to So king of Egypt, and brought no present to the king of 2 Kgs 18:20, 21

16:11 The altar in God's temple was not good enough for Ahaz. He had Urijah the priest, who should have known better, make a copy of an altar he had seen in Damascus. Urijah "prostituted his authority and profaned the crown of his priesthood, making himself a servant to the lusts of men."* In short, he betrayed his trust as the leader of Judea. Ahaz offered sacrifices on the new altar which had been placed near the brazen altar. Then Ahaz removed God's altar to an obscure corner of the sanctuary and replaced it with his pagan altar; he made his sacrifices not to the God of Israel but to the gods of pagans.

16:20 Ahaz died and was succeeded by Hezekiah, who was to be as much a friend to the temple as his father had been an enemy of it. Hezekiah is one instance of a bad father who had a good son.

17:1 Hoshea was the last king of Israel. The captivity was to begin under his kingship. He was in his ninth year as king, when the Assyrians captured Samaria and sent the ten tribes into captivity in Assyria. One would have supposed that the end of the Northern Kingdom would have warned Judah about its own disobedience and caused king and people to repent in order to avoid their own catastrophe.

Assyria, as *he had done* year by year: therefore the king of Assyria shut him up, and bound him in prison.

5 ¶Then the king of Assyria came up throughout all the land, and went up to Sa-ma′ri-a, and besieged it three years.

17:6☆ Deut 28:64 29:28 2 Kgs 18:11 1 Chron 5:26 Hos 13:16

6 In the ninth year of Ho-she′a the king of Assyria took Sa-ma′ri-a, and carried Israel away into Assyria, and placed them in Ha′lah and in Ha′bor *by* the river of Go′zan, and in the cities of the Medes.

2. The Reasons for Israel's Downfall

17:7☆ Josh 23:15, 16

7 For *so* it was, that the children of Israel had sinned against the LORD their God, which had brought them up out of the land of Egypt, from under the hand of Pharaoh king of Egypt, and had feared other gods,

17:8 Lev 18:3 Deut 18:9 Judg 6:10

8 And walked in the statutes of the heathen, whom the LORD cast out from before the children of Israel, and of the kings of Israel, which they had made.

17:9 Ex 34:12 1 Kgs 14:23

9 And the children of Israel did secretly *those* things that *were* not right against the LORD their God, and they built them high places in all their cities, from the tower of the watchmen to the fenced city.

10 And they set them up images and groves in every high hill, and under every green tree:

11 And there they burnt incense in all the high places, as *did* the heathen whom the LORD carried away before them; and wrought wicked things to provoke the LORD to anger:

12 For they served idols, whereof the LORD had said unto them, Ye shall not do this thing.

17:13☆ Neh 9:29, 30 Jer 7:5, 6; 18:11 Acts 7:51, 52

13 Yet the LORD testified against Israel, and against Judah, by all the prophets, *and by* all the seers, saying, Turn ye from your evil ways, and keep my commandments *and* my statutes, according to all the law which I commanded your fathers, and which I sent to you by my servants the prophets.

17:14 Ex 32:9; 33:3 2 Chron 36:15

14 Notwithstanding they would not hear, but hardened their necks, like to the neck of their fathers, that did not believe in the LORD their God.

17:15 Ex 24:7, 8 Deut 12:30, 31 29:25

15 And they rejected his statutes, and his covenant that he made with their fathers, and his testimonies which he testified against them; and they followed vanity, and became vain, and went after the heathen that *were* round about them, *concerning* whom the LORD had charged them, that they should not do like them.

17:16 Deut 4:16, 17 1 Kgs 12:28 16:31

16 And they left all the commandments of the LORD their God, and made them molten images, *even* two calves, and made a grove, and worshipped all the host of heaven, and served Ba′al.

17:17☆ Lev 19:26 Deut 18:10 2 Kgs 3:27 16:3; 21:6

17 And they caused their sons and their daughters to pass through the fire, and used divination and enchantments, and sold themselves to do evil in the sight of the LORD, to provoke him to anger.

17:6 Shalmaneser, the Assyrian king (727–722 B.C.), began the siege of Samaria, but he died before the city surrendered. Sargon II (722–705 B.C.), his successor, captured Samaria and took the people captive. The Northern Kingdom came to an end late in 722 B.C. or early in 721 B.C.

17:7 The captivity of the ten tribes (Israel or the Northern Kingdom) resulted from national wickedness. That captivity has never ended. The returnees from the seventy years' captivity in Babylon were largely the offspring of the people of Judah, although a small number of the returnees were from Israel. Hosea predicted that the Northern Kingdom would never be set up again (Hos. 1:6, 9). From Paul's statement in Rom. 9:22–26, perhaps their ranks were to be filled by Gentile converts in the church of Jesus Christ.

17:13 Although this account explains why the ten tribes went into captivity, it also points out that all the prophets and all the seers warned Judah even as they warned Israel.

17:17 *caused their sons and their daughters to pass through the fire,* i.e., "They even burned their own sons and daughters to death on the altars of Molech."†

[18]Therefore the LORD was very angry with Israel, and removed them out of his sight: there was none left but the tribe of Judah only.

[19]Also Judah kept not the commandments of the LORD their God, but walked in the statutes of Israel which they made. 17:19 1 Kgs 14:24

[20]And the LORD rejected all the seed of Israel, and afflicted them, and delivered them into the hand of spoilers, until he had cast them out of his sight. 17:20 Jer 6:30 Rom 11:1–3

[21]For he rent Israel from the house of David; and they made Jer-o-bo'am the son of Ne'bat king: and Jer-o-bo'am drave Israel from following the LORD, and made them sin a great sin. 17:21 1 Kgs 11:11, 31 12:20 2 Chron 10:16–19 Isa 7:17

[22]For the children of Israel walked in all the sins of Jer-o-bo'am which he did; they departed not from them;

[23]Until the LORD removed Israel out of his sight, as he had said by all his servants the prophets. So was Israel carried away out of their own land to Assyria unto this day. 17:23 2 Kgs 18:11, 12

3. Samaria Repeopled; the Beginning of the Samaritans

[24]¶And the king of Assyria brought *men* from Babylon, and from Cu'thah, and from A'va, and from Ha'math, and from Seph-ar-va'im, and placed *them* in the cities of Sa-ma'ri-a instead of the children of Israel: and they possessed Sa-ma'ri-a, and dwelt in the cities thereof. ☆17:24 2 Kgs 18:34

[25]And *so* it was at the beginning of their dwelling there, *that* they feared not the LORD: therefore the LORD sent lions among them, which slew *some* of them. 17:25 1 Kgs 13:24, 25 20:36

[26]Wherefore they spake to the king of Assyria, saying, The nations which thou hast removed, and placed in the cities of Sa-ma'ri-a, know not the manner of the God of the land: therefore he hath sent lions among them, and, behold, they slay them, because they know not the manner of the God of the land.

[27]Then the king of Assyria commanded, saying, Carry thither one of the priests whom ye brought from thence; and let them go and dwell there, and let him teach them the manner of the God of the land.

[28]Then one of the priests whom they had carried away from Sa-ma'ri-a came and dwelt in Beth–el, and taught them how they should fear the LORD.

[29]Howbeit every nation made gods of their own, and put *them* in the houses of the high places which the Sa-mar'i-tans had made, every nation in their cities wherein they dwelt. ☆17:29 1 Kgs 12:31 13:32

[30]And the men of Babylon made Suc'coth–be'noth, and the men of Cuth made Ner'gal, and the men of Ha'math made Ash'i-ma,

[31]And the A'vites made Nib'haz and Tartak, and the Seph'ar-vites burnt their children in fire to A-dram'me-lech and A-nam'me-lech, the gods of Seph-ar-va'im. 17:31 2 Kgs 19:37

[32]So they feared the LORD, and made unto themselves of the lowest of them priests of the high places, which sacrificed for them in the houses of the high places. 17:32 1 Kgs 12:31 13:33

[33]They feared the LORD, and served their own gods, after the manner of the nations whom they carried away from thence.

17:24 The relocation of peoples was a policy carried on by Esar-haddon (681–669 B.C.). He was the grandson of Sargon. Sargon's great-grandson, Ashurbanipal (669–633 B.C.), who was called Osnapper, did the same thing (Ezra 4:10).

17:29 *Samaritans.* This is the first time this word appears in the Old Testament (Hebrew text—RSV and KJV). This name was given by the people of Judah to the mixed-breed people of Samaria. The Samaritans worshipped their own gods while saying they served the Lord. (See note on John 4:5.)

17:34 Gen 32:28 35:10

34 Unto this day they do after the former manners: they fear not the
LORD, neither do they after their statutes, or after their ordinances, or after
the law and commandment which the LORD commanded the children of
Jacob, whom he named Israel;

17:35 Ex 19:5; 24:7 Judg 6:10

35 With whom the LORD had made a covenant, and charged them, saying,
Ye shall not fear other gods, nor bow yourselves to them, nor serve them,
nor sacrifice to them:
36 But the LORD, who brought you up out of the land of Egypt with great
power and a stretched out arm, him shall ye fear, and him shall ye worship,
and to him shall ye do sacrifice.

17:37 Deut 5:32

37 And the statutes, and the ordinances, and the law, and the command-
ment, which he wrote for you, ye shall observe to do for evermore; and ye
shall not fear other gods.

17:38 Deut 4:23 6:10–12

38 And the covenant that I have made with you ye shall not forget; neither
shall ye fear other gods.

17:39 1 Sam 12:24

39 But the LORD your God ye shall fear; and he shall deliver you out of
the hand of all your enemies.
40 Howbeit they did not hearken, but they did after their former manner.

17:41 Zeph 1:5 Mt 6:24 Acts 7:42

41 So these nations feared the LORD, and served their graven images, both
their children, and their children's children: as did their fathers, so do they
unto this day.

VI. THE KINGDOM OF JUDAH TO THE FALL OF JERUSALEM (18:1—25:30)

A. HEZEKIAH AND SENNACHERIB

1. Resumé of Hezekiah's Kingship

18:1☆ 2 Kgs 15:30 16:20; 20:3 2 Chron 28:27 31:20
18:2☆

18 NOW it came to pass in the third year of Ho-she'a son of E'lah king
of Israel, *that* Hez-e-ki'ah the son of Ahaz king of Judah began to
reign.
2 Twenty and five years old was he when he began to reign; and he
reigned twenty and nine years in Jerusalem. His mother's name also *was*
A'bi, the daughter of Zach-a-ri'ah.
3 And he did *that which was* right in the sight of the LORD, according to all
that David his father did.

18:4☆ Num 21:8, 9 2 Kgs 12:3 2 Chron 31:1

4 ¶He removed the high places, and brake the images, and cut down the
groves, and brake in pieces the brasen serpent that Moses had made: for
unto those days the children of Israel did burn incense to it: and he called
it Ne-hush'tan.

18:5 2 Kgs 23:25

5 He trusted in the LORD God of Israel; so that after him was none like
him among all the kings of Judah, nor *any* that were before him.
6 For he clave to the LORD, *and* departed not from following him, but
kept his commandments, which the LORD commanded Moses.

18:7 Gen 39:2 1 Sam 18:14 2 Chron 15:2 Job 1:10 Dan 6:28

7 And the LORD was with him; *and* he prospered whithersoever he went
forth: and he rebelled against the king of Assyria, and served him not.

18:1 Here and in 18:9, 10 the reigns of Hezekiah and Hoshea (who succeeded Pekah) are synchronized. From 18:13 we know that Sennacherib invaded Judah in the fourteenth year of Hezekiah's reign. Thus the invasion occurred in 701 B.C. Hoshea, though, had ceased to reign in 722 B.C. The probable solution is that Hezekiah was co-regent with his father for twelve years, beginning in Hoshea's third year.

18:2 *Abi.* Her other name was Abijah (2 Chron. 29:1).

18:4 *the brasen serpent.* This refers to the bronze serpent which Moses had made in the wilderness and which, when looked upon, enabled any serpent-bit Israelite to be saved from an untimely death. It had now become an idolatrous object. Hezekiah broke it into pieces and disposed of it. It is easy to take something which has religious significance and turn it into an idol, so that something which at one time served a good purpose now becomes a stumblingblock and an offense to God.

8 He smote the Philistines, *even* unto Ga′za, and the borders thereof, from
the tower of the watchmen to the fenced city.

18:8 2 Chron 28:18

2. The Fall of Israel (the Northern Kingdom)

9 ¶And it came to pass in the fourth year of king Hez-e-ki′ah, which *was*
the seventh year of Ho-she′a son of E′lah king of Israel, *that* Shal-man-e′ser
king of Assyria came up against Sa-ma′ri-a, and besieged it.
10 And at the end of three years they took it: *even* in the sixth year of Hez-
e-ki′ah, that *is* the ninth year of Ho-she′a king of Israel, Sa-ma′ri-a was
taken.
11 And the king of Assyria did carry away Israel unto Assyria, and put
them in Ha′lah and in Ha′bor *by* the river of Go′zan, and in the cities of the
Medes:
12 Because they obeyed not the voice of the LORD their God, but
transgressed his covenant, *and* all that Moses the servant of the LORD
commanded, and would not hear *them,* nor do *them.*

18:9 2 Kgs 17:3
18:11 2 Kgs 17:6; 19:11
18:12 Num 12:7, 8; 1 Kgs 8:56; 2 Kgs 17:7, 13; Neh 9:17; Isa 1:20

3. Sennacherib's Invasion of Judah
a. Hezekiah Forced to Pay Tribute

13 ¶Now in the fourteenth year of king Hez-e-ki′ah did Sen-nach′e-rib
king of Assyria come up against all the fenced cities of Judah, and took
them.
14 And Hez-e-ki′ah king of Judah sent to the king of Assyria to La′chish,
saying, I have offended; return from me: that which thou puttest on me will
I bear. And the king of Assyria appointed unto Hez-e-ki′ah king of Judah
three hundred talents of silver and thirty talents of gold.
15 And Hez-e-ki′ah gave *him* all the silver that was found in the house of
the LORD, and in the treasures of the king's house.
16 At that time did Hez-e-ki′ah cut off *the gold from* the doors of the
temple of the LORD, and *from* the pillars which Hez-e-ki′ah king of Judah
had overlaid, and gave it to the king of Assyria.
17 ¶And the king of Assyria sent Tartan and Rab′-sa-ris and Rab′-sha-
keh from La′chish to king Hez-e-ki′ah with a great host against Jerusalem.
And they went up and came to Jerusalem. And when they were come up,
they came and stood by the conduit of the upper pool, which *is* in the
highway of the fuller's field.
18 And when they had called to the king, there came out to them E-li′a-
kim the son of Hil-ki′ah, which *was* over the household, and Sheb′na the
scribe, and Jo′ah the son of A′saph the recorder.

18:13 2 Chron 32:1; Isa 36:1
☆**18:14**
18:15 1 Kgs 15:18; 2 Kgs 12:18
☆**18:17** 2 Kgs 20:20; Isa 20:1
18:18 2 Kgs 19:2; Isa 22:15, 16, 20; 36:3

b. Assyria Threatens to Conquer Judah

19 And Rab′-sha-keh said unto them, Speak ye now to Hez-e-ki′ah, Thus
saith the great king, the king of Assyria, What confidence *is* this wherein
thou trustest?

☆**18:19**

18:14 Hezekiah meekly accepted the dictates of Sennacherib of Assyria and agreed to pay him tribute. Nowhere does the account suggest that Hezekiah in the midst of his difficulty did either of these two things: he neither sought God directly nor did he ask help from Isaiah, who was available to him. Up to this point, God had said nothing to Isaiah about this situation.
18:17 *Tartan and Rab-saris and Rab-shakeh,* i.e., "his field marshall, his chief treasurer, and his chief of staff" (TLB).
18:19–26 Here Hezekiah has to put up with the taunts of Sennacherib's leaders. Jerusalem was besieged and the enemy was telling Hezekiah that he had better capitulate, for he could not escape the might of the Assyrian army. The Judean negotiators pleaded with the enemy to speak Aramaic rather than the language of Judah, so that the people would not understand what was being said.

18:20 Isa 30:2, 7 Ezek 29:2, 6

20 Thou sayest, (but *they are but* vain words,) *I have* counsel and strength
for the war. Now on whom dost thou trust, that thou rebellest against me?
21 Now, behold, thou trustest upon the staff of this bruised reed, *even*
upon Egypt, on which if a man lean, it will go into his hand, and pierce it:
so *is* Pharaoh king of Egypt unto all that trust on him.
22 But if ye say unto me, We trust in the LORD our God: *is* not that he,
whose high places and whose altars Hez-e-ki'ah hath taken away, and hath
said to Judah and Jerusalem, Ye shall worship before this altar in
Jerusalem?
23 Now therefore, I pray thee, give pledges to my lord the king of Assyria,
and I will deliver thee two thousand horses, if thou be able on thy part to
set riders upon them.
24 How then wilt thou turn away the face of one captain of the least of my
master's servants, and put thy trust on Egypt for chariots and for
horsemen?
25 Am I now come up without the LORD against this place to destroy it?
The LORD said to me, Go up against this land, and destroy it.

18:26 Ezra 4:7 Isa 36:11, 12 Dan 2:4

26 Then said E-li'a-kim the son of Hil-ki'ah, and Sheb'na, and Jo'ah, unto
Rab'-sha-keh, Speak, I pray thee, to thy servants in the Syrian language;
for we understand *it:* and talk not with us in the Jews' language in the ears
of the people that *are* on the wall.
27 But Rab'-sha-keh said unto them, Hath my master sent me to thy
master, and to thee, to speak these words? *hath he* not *sent me* to the men
which sit on the wall, that they may eat their own dung, and drink their
own piss with you?

18:28☆

28 ¶Then Rab'-sha-keh stood and cried with a loud voice in the Jews'
language, and spake, saying, Hear the word of the great king, the king of
Assyria:
29 Thus saith the king, Let not Hez-e-ki'ah deceive you: for he shall not be
able to deliver you out of his hand:
30 Neither let Hez-e-ki'ah make you trust in the LORD, saying, The LORD
will surely deliver us, and this city shall not be delivered into the hand of
the king of Assyria.

18:31 Deut 8:7–9

31 Hearken not to Hez-e-ki'ah: for thus saith the king of Assyria, Make *an
agreement* with me by a present, and come out to me, and *then* eat ye every
man of his own vine, and every one of his fig tree, and drink ye every one
the waters of his cistern:
32 Until I come and take you away to a land like your own land, a land of
corn and wine, a land of bread and vineyards, a land of oil olive and of
honey, that ye may live, and not die: and hearken not unto Hez-e-ki'ah,
when he persuadeth you, saying, The LORD will deliver us.

18:33 2 Kgs 19:12 Isa 10:7, 9

33 Hath any of the gods of the nations delivered at all his land out of the
hand of the king of Assyria?

18:34 2 Kgs 17:24 19:13

34 Where *are* the gods of Ha'math, and of Ar'pad? where *are* the gods of
Seph-ar-va'im, He'na, and I'vah? have they delivered Sa-ma'ri-a out of
mine hand?
35 Who *are* they among all the gods of the countries, that have delivered
their country out of mine hand, that the LORD should deliver Jerusalem out
of mine hand?

18:28 Here the Rab-shakeh now made his biggest mistake. He appealed to the people of Judah over the head of the king and suggested they should capitulate, for then they would be at peace and enjoy many good things under the Assyrians. His most potent argument was that their God could not deliver them even if Hezekiah called on him. This affront to God, as well as to Hezekiah, led to the divine intervention that changed the picture quickly.

36 But the people held their peace, and answered him not a word: for the
king's commandment was, saying, Answer him not.
37 Then came E-li'a-kim the son of Hil-ki'ah, which *was* over the
household, and Sheb'na the scribe, and Jo'ah the son of A'saph the
recorder, to Hez-e-ki'ah with *their* clothes rent, and told him the words of
Rab'-sha-keh.

c. Isaiah's Good Word from God to Hezekiah

19 AND it came to pass, when king Hez-e-ki'ah heard *it*, that he rent
his clothes, and covered himself with sackcloth, and went into the
house of the LORD.
2 And he sent E-li'a-kim, which *was* over the household, and Sheb'na the
scribe, and the elders of the priests, covered with sackcloth, to Isaiah the
prophet the son of Amoz.
3 And they said unto him, Thus saith Hez-e-ki'ah, This day *is* a day of
trouble, and of rebuke, and blasphemy: for the children are come to the
birth, and *there is* not strength to bring forth.
4 It may be the LORD thy God will hear all the words of Rab'-sha-keh,
whom the king of Assyria his master hath sent to reproach the living God;
and will reprove the words which the LORD thy God hath heard: wherefore
lift up *thy* prayer for the remnant that are left.
5 So the servants of king Hez-e-ki'ah came to Isaiah.
6 ¶And Isaiah said unto them, Thus shall ye say to your master, Thus
saith the LORD, Be not afraid of the words which thou hast heard, with
which the servants of the king of Assyria have blasphemed me.
7 Behold, I will send a blast upon him, and he shall hear a rumour, and
shall return to his own land; and I will cause him to fall by the sword in his
own land.
8 ¶So Rab'-sha-keh returned, and found the king of Assyria warring
against Lib'nah: for he had heard that he was departed from La'chish.
9 And when he heard say of Tir'ha-kah king of E-thi-o'pi-a, Behold, he is
come out to fight against thee: he sent messengers again unto Hez-e-ki'ah,
saying,
10 Thus shall ye speak to Hez-e-ki'ah king of Judah, saying, Let not thy
God in whom thou trustest deceive thee, saying, Jerusalem shall not be
delivered into the hand of the king of Assyria.
11 Behold, thou hast heard what the kings of Assyria have done to all
lands, by destroying them utterly: and shalt thou be delivered?
12 Have the gods of the nations delivered them which my fathers have
destroyed; *as* Go'zan, and Ha'ran, and Re'zeph, and the children of Eden
which *were* in The-la'sar?
13 Where *is* the king of Ha'math, and the king of Ar'pad, and the king of
the city of Seph-ar-va'im, of He'na, and I'vah?

☆**19:1** 2 Chron 32:20; Isa 37:1
☆**19:2** Isa 1:1
☆**19:3**
☆**19:4** 2 Kgs 18:35; Isa 1:9
19:5 2 Kgs 18:22
☆**19:6**
19:7 2 Kgs 19:37
19:10 2 Kgs 18:5, 30
19:12 2 Kgs 17:6; 18:33; Isa 37:12
19:13 2 Kgs 17:24; 18:34

19:1 Chapter 19 is the same as Isaiah 37. From the dating of the book of 2 Kings, it appears that the unknown writer was familiar with the book of Isaiah and, under the aegis of the Holy Spirit, used material from Isaiah here.

19:2–4 Hezekiah has donned the sackcloth and gone before God in the house of the Lord. Now he sends Eliakim to Isaiah the prophet to beseech his help in the emergency. Hezekiah's message is interesting, for in verse 4 we read, "It may be the LORD *thy* God (that is, the God of Isaiah) will hear all the words of Rab-shakeh." Then he asks Isaiah to pray to God for Judah. Hezekiah's view of God was small indeed. Should he not have known that no word goes out of the mouth of any man that God does know even before he says it? And why did he not say to Isaiah "our God," not "thy God?" Is not the God of the prophets the God of all believers? And can not the believers offer their own prayers? Had not Solomon prayed to God and been answered? Had not David often sought the face of God in prayer?

19:6 Isaiah then sent back a message for Hezekiah not to fear: God will take care of him. The word is explicit, "the servants of the king of Assyria have blasphemed me." God had heard the words of the Assyrians and he would defend his own honor.

d. Hezekiah's Humble Prayer for Help

19:14☆ Isa 37:14

14 ¶And Hez-e-ki'ah received the letter of the hand of the messengers, and
read it: and Hez-e-ki'ah went up into the house of the LORD, and spread it
before the LORD.

19:15 1 Sam 4:4; 2 Sam 6:2; Ps 80:1; Isa 37:16, 17

15 And Hez-e-ki'ah prayed before the LORD, and said, O LORD God of
Israel, which dwellest *between* the cherubims, thou art the God, *even* thou
alone, of all the kingdoms of the earth; thou hast made heaven and earth.

19:16 1 Kgs 8:29, 30; 2 Chron 6:40; Ps 31:2

16 LORD, bow down thine ear, and hear: open, LORD, thine eyes, and see:
and hear the words of Sen-nach'e-rib, which hath sent him to reproach the
living God.
17 Of a truth, LORD, the kings of Assyria have destroyed the nations and
their lands,

19:18 Isa 44:9; Acts 17:29

18 And have cast their gods into the fire: for they *were* no gods, but the
work of men's hands, wood and stone: therefore they have destroyed them.

19:19 Ex 9:14; 1 Sam 17:46; 1 Kgs 8:42, 43

19 Now therefore, O LORD our God, I beseech thee, save thou us out of his
hand, that all the kingdoms of the earth may know that thou *art* the LORD
God, *even* thou only.

e. Isaiah's Prophecy of Deliverance

19:20☆ 2 Kgs 20:5; Ps 65:1, 2; Isa 65:24

20 ¶Then Isaiah the son of Amoz sent to Hez-e-ki'ah, saying, Thus saith
the LORD God of Israel, *That* which thou hast prayed to me against Sen-
nach'e-rib king of Assyria I have heard.
21 This *is* the word that the LORD hath spoken concerning him; The virgin
the daughter of Zion hath despised thee, *and* laughed thee to scorn; the
daughter of Jerusalem hath shaken her head at thee.

19:22 Ex 5:2; Isa 5:24; 30:10, 11; Jer 51:5

22 Whom hast thou reproached and blasphemed? and against whom hast
thou exalted *thy* voice, and lifted up thine eyes on high? *even* against the
Holy *One* of Israel.
23 By thy messengers thou hast reproached the Lord, and hast said, With
the multitude of my chariots I am come up to the height of the mountains,
to the sides of Lebanon, and will cut down the tall cedar trees thereof, *and*
the choice fir trees thereof: and I will enter into the lodgings of his borders,
and into the forest of his Carmel.
24 I have digged and drunk strange waters, and with the sole of my feet
have I dried up all the rivers of besieged places.

19:25 Isa 10:5–7; 37:26; 45:5–7; Hab 1:6

25 Hast thou not heard long ago *how* I have done it, *and* of ancient times
that I have formed it? now have I brought it to pass, that thou shouldest be
to lay waste fenced cities *into* ruinous heaps.

19:26 Ps 129:6, 7

26 Therefore their inhabitants were of small power, they were dismayed
and confounded; they were *as* the grass of the field, and *as* the green herb,
as the grass on the housetops, and *as corn* blasted before it be grown up.

19:27 Ps 139:1; Jer 23:23, 24

27 But I know thy abode, and thy going out, and thy coming in, and thy
rage against me.

19:28 Ps 32:9; Ezek 29:4; Amos 4:2

28 Because thy rage against me and thy tumult is come up into mine ears,
therefore I will put my hook in thy nose, and my bridle in thy lips, and I
will turn thee back by the way by which thou camest.

19:14 See note on 1 Sam. 1:10. Here is another illustration of prayer principles properly used and productive of a great response. Hezekiah battled against an impossible situation from which there was no deliverance, humanly speaking. But he sought God's face, asked for divine help, and was sent a word from God by the prophet Isaiah. He believed God for the answer and waited expectantly until it came, having accepted the answer by faith before its fulfillment.

19:20 The word that Isaiah spoke to Hezekiah was the word he had received from God. It is there for us, as it was for him. God is no different today. This great God who was scorned by the Assyrians will execute judgment on them. This was determined by God from days of old (19:25), even before the event came to pass. God will put a hook in the king's nose and a bit in his mouth (19:28).

[29]And this *shall be* a sign unto thee, Ye shall eat this year such things as grow of themselves, and in the second year that which springeth of the same; and in the third year sow ye, and reap, and plant vineyards, and eat the fruits thereof.
[30]And the remnant that is escaped of the house of Judah shall yet again take root downward, and bear fruit upward.
[31]For out of Jerusalem shall go forth a remnant, and they that escape out of mount Zion: the zeal of the LORD *of hosts* shall do this.
[32]Therefore thus saith the LORD concerning the king of Assyria, He shall not come into this city, nor shoot an arrow there, nor come before it with shield, nor cast a bank against it.
[33]By the way that he came, by the same shall he return, and shall not come into this city, saith the LORD.
[34]For I will defend this city, to save it, for mine own sake, and for my servant David's sake.

19:29 Ex 3:12; 2 Kgs 20:8; Isa 7:11
19:30 2 Chron 32:22, 23; Isa 1:9
☆**19:32**
19:34 1 Kgs 11:12, 13; 2 Kgs 20:6; Isa 43:25; 48:9, 11

f. God's Vengeance on Assyria

[35]¶And it came to pass that night, that the angel of the LORD went out, and smote in the camp of the Assyrians an hundred fourscore and five thousand: and when they arose early in the morning, behold, they *were* all dead corpses.
[36]So Sen-nach'e-rib king of Assyria departed, and went and returned, and dwelt at Nin'e-veh.
[37]And it came to pass, as he was worshipping in the house of Nis'roch his god, that A-dram'me-lech and Sha-re'zer his sons smote him with the sword: and they escaped into the land of Ar-me'ni-a, And E'sar-had'don his son reigned in his stead.

☆**19:35** 2 Chron 32:21; Isa 10:16
19:36 Jonah 1:2; Nah 1:1
☆**19:37** Gen 8:4; Ezra 4:2

B. HEZEKIAH'S SICKNESS AND FOOLISHNESS
1. God Answers Hezekiah's Prayer Not to Die

20 IN those days was Hez-e-ki'ah sick unto death. And the prophet Isaiah the son of Amoz came to him, and said unto him, Thus saith the LORD, Set thine house in order; for thou shalt die, and not live.
[2]Then he turned his face to the wall, and prayed unto the LORD, saying,
[3]I beseech thee, O LORD, remember now how I have walked before thee in truth and with a perfect heart, and have done *that which is* good in thy sight. And Hez-e-ki'ah wept sore.
[4]And it came to pass, afore Isaiah was gone out into the middle court, that the word of the LORD came to him, saying,
[5]Turn again, and tell Hez-e-ki'ah the captain of my people, Thus saith

☆**20:1** 2 Chron 32:24; Isa 38:1
20:3 2 Kgs 18:6; 2 Chron 17:3
20:5 2 Kgs 19:20; Ps 39:12

19:32 God promised Hezekiah that (1) the enemy would not enter the city; (2) nor would he shoot an arrow over the city walls; (3) nor would the soldiers stand before the city with their shields; (4) nor would they build an embankment against the walls so that the troops could clamber up and over the walls into the city. The most gracious part of the promise was the assurance that this would all take place without Hezekiah and his small army having to do anything except trust in God.

19:35 We do not know how God defeated Sennacherib; the death of the soldiers may have come from a sudden plague, or the angel of the Lord may have slain these troops in an exercise of the divine wrath. In any event, it was a miraculous deliverance.

19:37 *Esar-haddon*, Sennacherib's successor, was not his eldest son. Like David, Sennacherib chose a *favored* son to replace him, not the eldest.

20:1ff Hezekiah was taken ill and Isaiah the prophet brought him word from the Lord that he was about to die. He was approximately forty years old at the time. And there was no heir to the throne. He pled with God for an extension of his life, and was granted fifteen years. Manasseh was born several years later and was twelve years old when he succeeded his father. Manasseh enjoyed the longest reign of all the kings of Judah (fifty-five years). God had promised an unbroken succession for the house of David; therefore, we can conclude that Hezekiah's prayer was in accord with the will of God.

the LORD, the God of David thy father, I have heard thy prayer, I have seen thy tears: behold, I will heal thee: on the third day thou shalt go up unto the house of the LORD.

20:6 2 Kgs 19:34

6 And I will add unto thy days fifteen years; and I will deliver thee and this city out of the hand of the king of Assyria; and I will defend this city for mine own sake, and for my servant David's sake.

20:7 2 Kgs 2:20; 4:41 Isa 38:21

7 And Isaiah said, Take a lump of figs. And they took and laid *it* on the boil, and he recovered.

2. The Sign of God's Mercy: the Sundial Goes Backward

8 ¶And Hez-e-ki'ah said unto Isaiah, What *shall be* the sign that the LORD will heal me, and that I shall go up into the house of the LORD the third day?

20:9 Isa 38:7, 8 Mt 16:1

9 And Isaiah said, This sign shalt thou have of the LORD, that the LORD will do the thing that he hath spoken: shall the shadow go forward ten degrees, or go back ten degrees?

10 And Hez-e-ki'ah answered, It is a light thing for the shadow to go down ten degrees: nay, but let the shadow return backward ten degrees.

20:11☆ Josh 10:12 2 Chron 32:24, 31

11 And Isaiah the prophet cried unto the LORD: and he brought the shadow ten degrees backward, by which it had gone down in the dial of Ahaz.

3. Hezekiah Wrongly Shows His Wealth to Berodach-Baladan

12 ¶At that time Be-ro'dach-bal'a-dan, the son of Bal'a-dan, king of Babylon, sent letters and a present unto Hez-e-ki'ah: for he had heard that Hez-e-ki'ah had been sick.

20:13 2 Chron 32:27

13 And Hez-e-ki'ah hearkened unto them, and shewed them all the house of his precious things, the silver, and the gold, and the spices, and the precious ointment, and *all* the house of his armour, and all that was found in his treasures: there was nothing in his house, nor in all his dominion, that Hez-e-ki'ah shewed them not.

14 ¶Then came Isaiah the prophet unto king Hez-e-ki'ah, and said unto him, What said these men? and from whence came they unto thee? And Hez-e-ki'ah said, They are come from a far country, *even* from Babylon.

15 And he said, What have they seen in thine house? And Hez-e-ki'ah answered, All *the things* that *are* in mine house have they seen: there is nothing among my treasures that I have not shewed them.

16 And Isaiah said unto Hez-e-ki'ah, Hear the word of the LORD.

20:17 2 Kgs 24:13 25:13 Jer 52:17

17 Behold, the days come, that all that *is* in thine house, and that which thy fathers have laid up in store unto this day, shall be carried into Babylon: nothing shall be left, saith the LORD.

20:18 2 Kgs 24:12 2 Chron 33:11

18 And of thy sons that shall issue from thee, which thou shalt beget, shall they take away; and they shall be eunuchs in the palace of the king of Babylon.

19 Then said Hez-e-ki'ah unto Isaiah, Good *is* the word of the LORD which

---

20:11 *in the dial of Ahaz,* or, "on the steps of Ahaz." Egyptian sundials were made in the form of miniature staircases so that the shadow moved up and down the steps.† Hezekiah's long day has been the subject of much discussion. The account simply states that the sun dial of Ahaz went ten degrees backward. If it had been merely an optical illusion rather than an actual lengthening of the day, Hezekiah would hardly have been impressed that it was a real sign. He expected something more than an illusion. We must conclude that a miracle was performed here, that it occurred without disorder or harm to the celestial system. An infinite, all-powerful God who called the world into being can also stop, start, or rearrange the universe as he pleases.

thou hast spoken. And he said, *Is it* not *good,* if peace and truth be in my days?

4. Hezekiah's Death; Manasseh His Successor

20 ¶And the rest of the acts of Hez-e-ki'ah, and all his might, and how he made a pool, and a conduit, and brought water into the city, *are* they not written in the book of the chronicles of the kings of Judah?
21 And Hez-e-ki'ah slept with his fathers: and Ma-nas'seh his son reigned in his stead.

C. THE REIGN OF WICKED MANASSEH

1. Manasseh's Evil Deeds

21 MA-NAS'SEH *was* twelve years old when he began to reign, and reigned fifty and five years in Jerusalem. And his mother's name *was* Heph'zi-bah.
2 And he did *that which was* evil in the sight of the LORD, after the abominations of the heathen, whom the LORD cast out before the children of Israel.
3 For he built up again the high places which Hez-e-ki'ah his father had destroyed; and he reared up altars for Ba'al, and made a grove, as did Ahab king of Israel; and worshipped all the host of heaven, and served them.
4 And he built altars in the house of the LORD, of which the LORD said, In Jerusalem will I put my name.
5 And he built altars for all the host of heaven in the two courts of the house of the LORD.
6 And he made his son pass through the fire, and observed times, and used enchantments, and dealt with familiar spirits and wizards: he wrought much wickedness in the sight of the LORD, to provoke *him* to anger.
7 And he set a graven image of the grove that he had made in the house, of which the LORD said to David, and to Solomon his son, In this house, and in Jerusalem, which I have chosen out of all tribes of Israel, will I put my name for ever:
8 Neither will I make the feet of Israel move any more out of the land which I gave their fathers; only if they will observe to do according to all that I have commanded them, and according to all the law that my servant Moses commanded them.
9 But they hearkened not: and Ma-nas'seh seduced them to do more evil than did the nations whom the LORD destroyed before the children of Israel.

2. Jerusalem's Fall Foretold

10 ¶And the LORD spake by his servants the prophets, saying,
11 Because Ma-nas'seh king of Judah hath done these abominations, *and* hath done wickedly above all that the Am'or-ites did, which *were* before him, and hath made Judah also to sin with his idols:

☆**20:20** 2 Kgs 16:19 21:17 2 Chron 32:32
20:21 2 Chron 32:33
☆**21:1** 1 Chron 3:10–14 2 Chron 33:1
☆**21:2**
21:3 Lev 18:25 Deut 12:31 17:2, 3 1 Kgs 16:29–31
21:6 Lev 18:21 19:26, 31 Deut 18:10 2 Kgs 3:27 16:3; 17:17
21:7 Deut 16:21 1 Kgs 9:3 2 Kgs 23:6
21:8 2 Kgs 18:12 2 Chron 15:2
21:9 2 Chron 36:16 Ezra 9:10 Neh 9:26 Ps 81:11
☆**21:10**
☆**21:11** Gen 15:16 1 Kgs 21:26 2 Kgs 21:16 24:3, 4

20:20 This tunnel of Hezekiah was dug through solid rock by two crews starting at either end of the tunnel and meeting in the middle. An ancient inscription tells of the exciting moment when the two crews met.
21:1 Manasseh was co-regent with Hezekiah for ten years. This practice, when the years of a co-regency are included in a king's total time of reign, has sometimes complicated the regal chronologies.
21:2 Good fathers can have bad sons. Grace does not run through blood but through regeneration. Manasseh undid much, if not all, of the good things wrought by his father. He went so far as to burn his son as an offering to a pagan god. The judgment of God was pronounced against Judah by God's prophets in 21:10–15.
21:10–15 Judah has reached the point of no return. God's judgment is pronounced: Jerusalem will be sacked; the people will be given into the hand of the conqueror. It was not going to happen immediately, for the time was not ripe; but it was coming and nothing could prevent it.

21:12 2 Kgs 22:15, 16; Jer 19:3; Mic 3:12

12 Therefore thus saith the LORD God of Israel, Behold, I *am* bringing
such evil upon Jerusalem and Judah, that whosoever heareth of it, both his
ears shall tingle.
13 And I will stretch over Jerusalem the line of Sa-ma′ri-a, and the
plummet of the house of Ahab: and I will wipe Jerusalem as *a man* wipeth
a dish, wiping *it,* and turning *it* upside down.
14 And I will forsake the remnant of mine inheritance, and deliver them
into the hand of their enemies; and they shall become a prey and a spoil to
all their enemies;
15 Because they have done *that which was* evil in my sight, and have
provoked me to anger, since the day their fathers came forth out of Egypt,
even unto this day.

3. Resumé of Manasseh's Kingship; Amon His Successor

21:16 2 Kgs 24:3, 4

16 Moreover Ma-nas′seh shed innocent blood very much, till he had filled
Jerusalem from one end to another; beside his sin wherewith he made
Judah to sin, in doing *that which was* evil in the sight of the LORD.

21:17☆ 2 Kgs 20:20; 21:25; 2 Chron 33:18

17 ¶Now the rest of the acts of Ma-nas′seh, and all that he did, and his sin
that he sinned, *are* they not written in the book of the chronicles of the
kings of Judah?

21:18 2 Kgs 21:26; 2 Chron 33:20

18 And Ma-nas′seh slept with his fathers, and was buried in the garden of
his own house, in the garden of Uz′za: and A′mon his son reigned in his
stead.

D. WICKED AMON'S TWO-YEAR REIGN

21:19☆

19 ¶A′mon *was* twenty and two years old when he began to reign, and he
reigned two years in Jerusalem. And his mother's name *was* Me-shul′le-
meth, the daughter of Ha′ruz of Jot′bah.
20 And he did *that which was* evil in the sight of the LORD, as his father
Ma-nas′seh did.

21:21 2 Kgs 21:3–5

21 And he walked in all the way that his father walked in, and served the
idols that his father served, and worshipped them:

21:22 Deut 32:15; 2 Kgs 22:17

22 And he forsook the LORD God of his fathers, and walked not in the way
of the LORD.

21:23 2 Kgs 12:20; 14:19; 15:25

23 ¶And the servants of A′mon conspired against him, and slew the king
in his own house.
24 And the people of the land slew all them that had conspired against
king A′mon; and the people of the land made Jo-si′ah his son king in his
stead.

21:25 2 Kgs 21:17; 23:28

25 Now the rest of the acts of A′mon which he did, *are* they not written in
the book of the chronicles of the kings of Judah?

21:26 2 Kgs 21:18

26 And he was buried in his sepulchre in the garden of Uz′za: and Jo-si′ah
his son reigned in his stead.

E. THE GOOD REIGN OF JOSIAH, AMON'S SON

1. Faithful Josiah Repairs the Temple

22:1☆ Deut 5:32; Josh 1:7; 2 Chron 34:1; Jer 1:2; Zeph 1:1

22 JO-SI′AH *was* eight years old when he began to reign, and he
reigned thirty and one years in Jerusalem. And his mother's name
was Je-di′dah, the daughter of Ad-a-i′ah of Bos′cath.

21:17 Manasseh was a bad ruler, but (according to 2 Chron. 33:11–19) he had a change of heart near the end of his days. That is not recorded here.

21:19 The reign of Amon was inglorious and his wickedness great. He was given to idolatry in every form. He lasted for two years, at which time his servants killed him and his son Josiah became king.

22:1 Josiah was a good king. He did right in the eyes of God. When he grew up, he began the repair of the house of God. It had been allowed to deteriorate while his father had put time and effort into idolatry.

2And he did *that which was* right in the sight of the LORD, and walked in
all the way of David his father, and turned not aside to the right hand or to
the left.
3¶And it came to pass in the eighteenth year of king Jo-si'ah, *that* the
king sent Sha'phan the son of Az-a-li'ah, the son of Me-shul'lam, the scribe,
to the house of the LORD, saying,
4Go up to Hil-ki'ah the high priest, that he may sum the silver which is
brought into the house of the LORD, which the keepers of the door have
gathered of the people:
5And let them deliver it into the hand of the doers of the work, that have
the oversight of the house of the LORD: and let them give it to the doers of
the work which *is* in the house of the LORD, to repair the breaches of the
house,
6Unto carpenters, and builders, and masons, and to buy timber and
hewn stone to repair the house.
7Howbeit there was no reckoning made with them of the money that was
delivered into their hand, because they dealt faithfully.

22:3 2 Kgs 12:4, 5; 2 Chron 34:9
22:5 2 Kgs 12:11, 12; Ezra 3:7
22:7 2 Kgs 12:15; 2 Chron 34:13

2. The Discovery of the Scroll in the Temple

8¶And Hil-ki'ah the high priest said unto Sha'phan the scribe, I have
found the book of the law in the house of the LORD. And Hil-ki'ah gave the
book to Sha'phan, and he read it.
9And Sha'phan the scribe came to the king, and brought the king word
again, and said, Thy servants have gathered the money that was found in
the house, and have delivered it into the hand of them that do the work,
that have the oversight of the house of the LORD.

☆**22:8** Deut 31:24-26; 2 Chron 34:14-16

3. Josiah Hears the Word of God

10And Sha'phan the scribe shewed the king, saying, Hil-ki'ah the priest
hath delivered me a book. And Sha'phan read it before the king.
11And it came to pass, when the king had heard the words of the book of
the law, that he rent his clothes.
12And the king commanded Hil-ki'ah the priest, and A-hi'kam the son of
Sha'phan, and Ach'bor the son of Mi-chai'ah, and Sha'phan the scribe, and
A-sa-hi'ah a servant of the king's, saying,
13Go ye, inquire of the LORD for me, and for the people, and for all
Judah, concerning the words of this book that is found: for great *is* the
wrath of the LORD that is kindled against us, because our fathers have not
hearkened unto the words of this book, to do according unto all that which
is written concerning us.

☆**22:11** Josh 7:6
22:12 Deut 29:24, 25; 31:17; 2 Kgs 25:22; 2 Chron 34:20; Jer 26:24

4. Huldah the Prophetess Speaks to Josiah for God

14So Hil-ki'ah the priest, and A-hi'kam, and Ach'bor, and Sha'phan, and
A-sa-hi'ah, went unto Hul'dah the prophetess, the wife of Shal'lum the son

☆**22:14** 2 Chron 34:22

22:8 The scroll that Hilkiah discovered contained material from Deuteronomy (Josiah's reforms indicate this to be so), as well as some material in Jeremiah. This undermines the view that Deuteronomy was a late production that did not come from the pen of Moses.

22:11 The book of the law was not known to Josiah. When it was discovered and read to him, he was moved by it. He acknowledged that the fathers of Judah had not obeyed the commandments of the book, and for that reason judgment had come upon the nation.

22:14 Hilkiah the priest and others consulted with Huldah, who was a prophetess. She confirmed the word that had been spoken by the prophets who preceded her—that the judgment of God would fall on Jerusalem and all Judah. They were sent by the king and her reply was to the king through them. She had a good word. God had seen the good heart of Josiah and had deferred the time of the fall of Jerusalem until after his death. He would die in peace, and his eyes would not behold the evil that was coming.

of Tik′vah, the son of Har′has, keeper of the wardrobe; (now she dwelt in
Jerusalem in the college;) and they communed with her.
15¶And she said unto them, Thus saith the LORD God of Israel, Tell the
man that sent you to me,
16Thus saith the LORD, Behold, I will bring evil upon this place, and upon
the inhabitants thereof, *even* all the words of the book which the king of
Judah hath read:
22:17 Deut 29:27 17Because they have forsaken me, and have burned incense unto other
gods, that they might provoke me to anger with all the works of their
hands; therefore my wrath shall be kindled against this place, and shall not
be quenched.
22:18 Lev 26:31 Ps 51:17 Isa 51:17 18But to the king of Judah which sent you to inquire of the LORD, thus
shall ye say to him, Thus saith the LORD God of Israel, *As touching* the
words which thou hast heard;
19Because thine heart was tender, and thou hast humbled thyself before
the LORD, when thou heardest what I spake against this place, and against
the inhabitants thereof, that they should become a desolation and a curse,
and hast rent thy clothes, and wept before me; I also have heard *thee,* saith
the LORD.
22:20 1 Kgs 21:29 20Behold therefore, I will gather thee unto thy fathers, and thou shalt be
gathered into thy grave in peace; and thine eyes shall not see all the evil
which I will bring upon this place. And they brought the king word again.

5. Josiah Covenants to Obey God

23:1☆ 2 Kgs 22:8 2 Chron 34:29 23 AND the king sent, and they gathered unto him all the elders of
Judah and of Jerusalem.
2And the king went up into the house of the LORD, and all the men of
Judah and all the inhabitants of Jerusalem with him, and the priests, and
the prophets, and all the people, both small and great: and he read in their
ears all the words of the book of the covenant which was found in the house
of the LORD.
23:3 Ex 24:7 2 Kgs 11:17 3¶And the king stood by a pillar, and made a covenant before the LORD,
to walk after the LORD, and to keep his commandments and his testimonies
and his statutes with all *their* heart and all *their* soul, to perform the words
of this covenant that were written in this book. And all the people stood to
the covenant.

6. Josiah Institutes Important Reforms

23:4☆ 2 Kgs 22:3, 4 4And the king commanded Hil-ki′ah the high priest, and the priests of
the second order, and the keepers of the door, to bring forth out of the
temple of the LORD all the vessels that were made for Ba′al, and for
the grove, and for all the host of heaven: and he burned them with-
out Jerusalem in the fields of Kidron, and carried the ashes of them unto
Beth-el.

23:1 The bad news given to Josiah did not leave him in a state of shock nor did he cultivate a spirit of lethargy. He called the elders, went to the house of God, and read the Word of God to the assembled crowd. He made a public covenant with God to walk according to the law of God, and the people joined him in that covenant.

23:4 So great was the extent of idolatry that objects belonging to the worship of Baal, Asherah, and the host of heaven had been found lodging in the house of God itself. Josiah had these things taken out and burned. He got rid of the priests who had been ordained by former kings to burn incense to Baal, the sun, the moon, and the constellations. He stopped the activities of the male cult prostitutes. The long list of what he did makes it clear that Judah had sunk into the pit of degradation, after having enjoyed a brilliant and powerful kingdom established by their father David.

5 And he put down the idolatrous priests, whom the kings of Judah had
ordained to burn incense in the high places in the cities of Judah, and in the
places round about Jerusalem; them also that burned incense unto Ba'al, to
the sun, and to the moon, and to the planets, and to all the host of heaven.
6 And he brought out the grove from the house of the LORD, without
Jerusalem, unto the brook Kidron, and burned it at the brook Kidron, and
stamped *it* small to powder, and cast the powder thereof upon the graves of
the children of the people.

23:6 2 Kgs 21:7; 2 Chron 34:4

7 And he brake down the houses of the sodomites, that *were* by the house
of the LORD, where the women wove hangings for the grove.

23:7 1 Kgs 14:24; 15:12; 22:46

8 And he brought all the priests out of the cities of Judah, and defiled the
high places where the priests had burned incense, from Ge'ba to Be'er-
she'ba, and brake down the high places of the gates that *were* in the
entering in of the gate of Joshua the governor of the city, which *were* on a
man's left hand at the gate of the city.

23:8 1 Kgs 15:22

9 Nevertheless the priests of the high places came not up to the altar of
the LORD in Jerusalem, but they did eat of the unleavened bread among
their brethren.

23:9 Ezek 44:9–11

10 And he defiled To'pheth, which *is* in the valley of the children of
Hin'nom, that no man might make his son or his daughter to pass through
the fire to Mo'lech.

23:10 Lev 18:21; 1 Kgs 11:7; Jer 7:31, 32

11 And he took away the horses that the kings of Judah had given to the
sun, at the entering in of the house of the LORD, by the chamber of
Na'than–me'lech the chamberlain, which *was* in the suburbs, and burned
the chariots of the sun with fire.
12 And the altars that *were on the top of the upper chamber of Ahaz, which*
*the kings of Judah had made, and the altars which Ma-*nas'seh had made in
the two courts of the house of the LORD, did the king beat down, and brake
them down from thence, and cast the dust of them into the brook Kidron.

23:12 2 Kgs 21:3–5; 2 Chron 33:4, 5; Jer 19:13; Zeph 1:5

13 And the high places that *were* before Jerusalem, which *were* on the right
hand of the mount of corruption, which Solomon the king of Israel had
builded for Ash'to-reth the abomination of the Zi-do'ni-ans, and for
Che'mosh the abomination of the Moabites, and for Mil'com the abomina-
tion of the children of Ammon, did the king defile.

23:13 1 Kgs 11:5; Jer 48:7

14 And he brake in pieces the images, and cut down the groves, and filled
their places with the bones of men.

23:14 Deut 7:5, 25; 2 Chron 34:3, 4

15 ¶Moreover the altar that *was* at Beth–el, *and* the high place which Jer-
o-bo'am the son of Ne'bat, who made Israel to sin, had made, both that
altar and the high place he brake down, and burned the high place, *and*
stamped *it* small to powder, and burned the grove.

23:15 1 Kgs 12:28; 14:16

7. Josiah Leaves the Bones of the Man of God Untouched

16 And as Jo-si'ah turned himself, he spied the sepulchres that *were* there
in the mount, and sent, and took the bones out of the sepulchres, and
burned *them* upon the altar, and polluted it, according to the word of the
LORD which the man of God proclaimed, who proclaimed these words.

☆23:16 1 Kgs 13:2, 32

17 Then he said, What title *is* that that I see? And the men of the city told
him, *It is* the sepulchre of the man of God, which came from Judah, and
proclaimed these things that thou hast done against the altar of Beth–el.

23:17 1 Kgs 13:1, 2, 30

18 And he said, Let him alone; let no man move his bones. So they let his
bones alone, with the bones of the prophet that came out of Sa-ma'ri-a.

23:18 1 Kgs 13:11, 31

23:16 This was the altar constructed by Jeroboam. (See 1 Kings 13:2.)

23:19 2 Kgs 17:19; 2 Chron 34:6, 7

19 And all the houses also of the high places that *were* in the cities of Sa-
ma'ri-a, which the kings of Israel had made to provoke *the LORD* to anger,
Jo-si'ah took away, and did to them according to all the acts that he had
done in Beth–el.

23:20 2 Kgs 10:26; 11:18; 2 Chron 34:5

20 And he slew all the priests of the high places that *were* there upon the
altars, and burned men's bones upon them, and returned to Jerusalem.

8. Josiah Observes the Passover Ceremonies

23:21☆ Num 9:2, 3; Deut 16:2; 2 Chron 35:1
23:22 2 Chron 35:18

21 ¶And the king commanded all the people, saying, Keep the passover
unto the LORD your God, as *it is* written in the book of this covenant.
22 Surely there was not holden such a passover from the days of the judges
that judged Israel, nor in all the days of the kings of Israel, nor of the kings
of Judah;
23 But in the eighteenth year of king Jo-si'ah, *wherein* this passover was
holden to the LORD in Jerusalem.

9. Josiah's Faithful Obedience

23:24 Lev 19:31; Deut 18:10; 2 Kgs 21:6; 22:8

24 ¶Moreover the *workers with* familiar spirits, and the wizards, and the
images, and the idols, and all the abominations that were spied in the land
of Judah and in Jerusalem, did Jo-si'ah put away, that he might perform the
words of the law which were written in the book that Hil-ki'ah the priest
found in the house of the LORD.

23:25☆ 2 Kgs 18:5

25 And like unto him was there no king before him, that turned to the
LORD with all his heart, and with all his soul, and with all his might,
according to all the law of Moses; neither after him arose there *any* like
him.

10. God's Unabated Anger against Judah

23:26 2 Kgs 21:11; 22:15, 16

26 ¶Notwithstanding the LORD turned not from the fierceness of his great
wrath, wherewith his anger was kindled against Judah, because of all the
provocations that Ma-nas'seh had provoked him withal.

23:27 2 Kgs 17:18; 21:13; Ezek 23:32

27 And the LORD said, I will remove Judah also out of my sight, as I have
removed Israel, and will cast off this city Jerusalem which I have chosen,
and the house of which I said, My name shall be there.

11. Josiah's Death; Jehoahaz His Successor

23:28 2 Kgs 20:20; 24:5
23:29☆ 2 Chron 35:20

28 Now the rest of the acts of Jo-si'ah, and all that he did, *are* they not
written in the book of the chronicles of the kings of Judah?
29 In his days Pharaoh–nechoh king of Egypt went up against the king of
Assyria to the river Eu-phra'tes: and king Jo-si'ah went against him; and he
slew him at Me-gid'do, when he had seen him.

23:21 Josiah, the grandson of Manasseh, was a good king. He reigned for thirty-one years and was the best of all Judah's kings since the days of Rehoboam. Here we learn that he kept the Passover in a manner far better than any of his predecessors as far back as the days of the judges. He rooted out the abominable customs taken over by Judah from the pagan world; the religion of Jehovah flourished and the feasts were kept. He not only caused Judah to cease to do evil; he also taught them to do good.

23:25 After Josiah, Judah went lower and lower until the captivity came and Judah was ruined—never to rise again to the heights of splendor enjoyed during the days of David and Solomon.

23:29 *Pharaoh-nechoh* was rushing to assist the Assyrians whose capital, Nineveh, fell under the onslaughts of the Babylonians in 612 B.C. He had no quarrel with Josiah, who foolishly insisted on this encounter. Josiah's death in 609–608 B.C. hastened the subsequent downfall of Judah.

30 And his servants carried him in a chariot dead from Me-gid'do, and
brought him to Jerusalem, and buried him in his own sepulchre. And the
people of the land took Je-ho'a-haz the son of Jo-si'ah, and anointed him,
and made him king in his father's stead.

☆**23:30** 2 Chron 36:1

F. JUDAH'S LAST KINGS AND THE FALL OF JERUSALEM
1. Jehoahaz's Three-Months' Reign

31 ¶Je-ho'a-haz *was* twenty and three years old when he began to reign;
and he reigned three months in Jerusalem. And his mother's name *was* Ha-
mu'tal, the daughter of Jer-e-mi'ah of Lib'nah.
32 And he did *that which was* evil in the sight of the LORD, according to all
that his fathers had done.
33 And Pharaoh-nechoh put him in bands at Rib'lah in the land of
Ha'math, that he might not reign in Jerusalem; and put the land to a tribute
of an hundred talents of silver, and a talent of gold.
34 And Pharaoh-nechoh made E-li'a-kim the son of Jo-si'ah king in the
room of Jo-si'ah his father, and turned his name to Je-hoi'a-kim, and took
Je-ho'a-haz away: and he came to Egypt, and died there.
35 And Je-hoi'a-kim gave the silver and the gold to Pharaoh; but he taxed
the land to give the money according to the commandment of Pharaoh: he
exacted the silver and the gold of the people of the land, of every one
according to his taxation, to give *it* unto Pharaoh-nechoh.

☆**23:31** 2 Kgs 21:2; 24:18; Jer 22:11
☆**23:32**
☆**23:33** 2 Kgs 23:29; 2 Chron 35:20; 36:3
23:34 1 Chron 3:15; 2 Chron 36:4; Ezek 19:3

2. Jehoiakim's Kingship; the First Seizure of Jerusalem

36 ¶Je-hoi'a-kim *was* twenty and five years old when he began to reign;
and he reigned eleven years in Jerusalem. And his mother's name *was* Ze-
bu'dah, the daughter of Pe-dai'ah of Ru'mah.
37 And he did *that which was* evil in the sight of the LORD, according to all
that his fathers had done.

23:36 2 Chron 36:5; Jer 1:3; 26:21

24 IN his days Neb-u-chad-nez'zar king of Babylon came up, and Je-
hoi'a-kim became his servant three years: then he turned and
rebelled against him.
2 And the LORD sent against him bands of the Chal'dees, and bands of
the Syrians, and bands of the Moabites, and bands of the children of
Ammon, and sent them against Judah to destroy it, according to the word
of the LORD, which he spake by his servants the prophets.
3 Surely at the commandment of the LORD came *this* upon Judah, to
remove *them* out of his sight, for the sins of Ma-nas'seh, according to all
that he did;
4 And also for the innocent blood that he shed: for he filled Jerusalem
with innocent blood; which the LORD would not pardon.
5 ¶Now the rest of the acts of Je-hoi'a-kim, and all that he did, *are* they
not written in the book of the chronicles of the kings of Judah?

☆**24:1** 2 Chron 36:6; Jer 25:1; 46:1, 2
☆**24:2** 2 Kgs 13:20, 21; 23:27
24:3 2 Kgs 18:25; 21:16; 23:26
24:5 2 Kgs 23:28

23:30 The people chose Jehoahaz to be king, bypassing his older brother Eliakim (Jehoiakim).

23:31–33 Jehoahaz reigned for three months as a prince before becoming a prisoner. Pharaoh-nechoh seized him, made him his prisoner, and carried him to Egypt where he died shortly thereafter. He was a bad king.

23:34 Eliakim means "God is setting up." When the Pharaoh made this son of Josiah king in place of his brother Jehoahaz, he named him Jehoiakim which name means "Jah sets up."

24:1 This is the first mention in the Scriptures of Nebuchadnezzar, about whom we learn a great deal in the book of Daniel. Jehoiakim's eleven-year reign (608–597 B.C.) was marked by bondage to Nebuchadnezzar of Babylon. In 606/605 B.C. Nebuchadnezzar conquered Jehoiakim. He took the temple treasures and the royal seed to Babylon. Along with him went Daniel the prophet (see 2 Chron. 36:6, 7; Dan. 1:1–3). Jehoiakim "slept with his fathers," but he was not buried with them. His son Jehoiachin succeeded him.

24:2 *the Chaldees*, i.e., the Babylonians.

24:6 Jer 22:24, 25 6 So Je-hoi′a-kim slept with his fathers: and Je-hoi′a-chin his son reigned
in his stead.
24:7 Jer 37:5, 7; 46:2 7 And the king of Egypt came not again any more out of his land: for the
king of Babylon had taken from the river of Egypt unto the river Eu-
phra′tes all that pertained to the king of Egypt.

3. Jehoiachin's Reign; the Second Seizure of Jerusalem

24:8 1 Chron 3:16 8 ¶Je-hoi′a-chin *was* eighteen years old when he began to reign, and he
2 Chron 36:9 reigned in Jerusalem three months. And his mother's name *was* Ne-hush′ta,
the daughter of El-na′than of Jerusalem.
9 And he did *that which was* evil in the sight of the LORD, according to all
that his father had done.
24:10☆ 2 Kgs 25:2 10 ¶At that time the servants of Neb-u-chad-nez′zar king of Babylon came
up against Jerusalem, and the city was besieged.
11 And Neb-u-chad-nez′zar king of Babylon came against the city, and his
servants did besiege it.
24:12 2 Chron 36:10 12 And Je-hoi′a-chin the king of Judah went out to the king of Babylon,
Jer 24:1; 29:1 he, and his mother, and his servants, and his princes, and his officers: and
Ezek 17:12, 13 the king of Babylon took him in the eighth year of his reign.
24:13 1 Kgs 7:48 13 And he carried out thence all the treasures of the house of the LORD,
2 Kgs 20:17; 25:13 and the treasures of the king's house, and cut in pieces all the vessels of gold
Isa 39:6 which Solomon king of Israel had made in the temple of the LORD, as the
Jer 20:5 LORD had said.
24:14☆ 2 Kgs 25:12 14 And he carried away all Jerusalem, and all the princes, and all the
Jer 24:1; 52:28 mighty men of valour, *even* ten thousand captives, and all the craftsmen
and smiths: none remained, save the poorest sort of the people of the land.
15 And he carried away Je-hoi′a-chin to Babylon, and the king's mother,
and the king's wives, and his officers, and the mighty of the land, *those*
carried he into captivity from Jerusalem to Babylon.
16 And all the men of might, *even* seven thousand, and craftsmen and
smiths a thousand, all *that were* strong *and* apt for war, even them the king
of Babylon brought captive to Babylon.
24:17☆ 2 Chron 36:10 17 ¶And the king of Babylon made Mat-ta-ni′ah his father's brother king
Jer 37:1; 52:1 in his stead, and changed his name to Zed-e-ki′ah.

4. Zedekiah's Kingship

a. The Revolt of Judah against Babylon

24:18 2 Kgs 23:31 18 Zed-e-ki′ah *was* twenty and one years old when he began to reign, and
he reigned eleven years in Jerusalem. And his mother's name *was* Ha-
mu′tal, the daughter of Jer-e-mi′ah of Lib′nah.
19 And he did *that which was* evil in the sight of the LORD, according to all
that Je-hoi′a-kim had done.

24:10 At this point, the Babylonian captivity was about to start. It was predicted to last seventy years, according to Jer. 25:11. Some compute the seventy years from the first deportation mentioned here. This event took place in 605 B.C., Others start with 586 B.C., when the last deportation took place. In any case, the end of the kingdom of Judah was at hand. The kingdom would languish until the birth of Jesus as a root out of a dry ground. (See note on Jer. 25:11.)

24:14 Jehoiachin had a short reign of three months in Jerusalem. He was removed and taken to Babylon along with the rest of Judah's treasures and ten thousand of the princes, officers, and chief men. This took place in 597 B.C.

24:17 Jehoiachin was a prisoner in Babylon. Nebuchadnezzar made his uncle, Mattaniah (whose name means "Gift of Yahweh"), king of Jerusalem and renamed him Zedekiah. The books of Jeremiah and Ezekiel provide the most information about Zedekiah and the events that transpired during his reign. Zedekiah rebelled against Nebuchadnezzar, even though he had taken a solemn oath of loyalty to Nebuchadnezzar in the name of Yahweh. He was warned by Jeremiah not to revolt.

20 For through the anger of the LORD it came to pass in Jerusalem and
Judah, until he had cast them out from his presence, that Zed-e-ki′ah
rebelled against the king of Babylon.

24:20 2 Chron 36:13; Jer 27:12; 38:17, 21, 22; 39:1

25

AND it came to pass in the ninth year of his reign, in the tenth
month, in the tenth *day* of the month, *that* Neb-u-chad-nez′zar king
of Babylon came, he, and all his host, against Jerusalem, and pitched
against it; and they built forts against it round about.
2 And the city was besieged unto the eleventh year of king Zed-e-ki′ah.
3 And on the ninth *day* of the *fourth* month the famine prevailed in the
city, and there was no bread for the people of the land.
4 ¶And the city was broken up, and all the men of war *fled* by night by the
way of the gate between two walls, which *is* by the king's garden: (now the
Chal′dees *were* against the city round about:) and *the king* went the way
toward the plain.
5 And the army of the Chal′dees pursued after the king, and overtook him
in the plains of Jericho: and all his army were scattered from him.
6 So they took the king, and brought him up to the king of Babylon to
Rib′lah; and they gave judgment upon him.
7 And they slew the sons of Zed-e-ki′ah before his eyes, and put out the
eyes of Zed-e-ki′ah, and bound him with fetters of brass, and carried him to
Babylon.

25:1 2 Chron 36:17; Jer 39:1; Ezek 24:2
25:3 2 Kgs 6:24, 25; Lam 4:9
☆**25:6** Jer 32:4
25:7 Jer 39:6; Ezek 12:13

b. Jerusalem Captured; the Temple Destroyed

8 ¶And in the fifth month, on the seventh *day* of the month, which *is* the
nineteenth year of king Neb-u-chad-nez′zar king of Babylon, came Neb′u-
zar-a′dan, captain of the guard, a servant of the king of Babylon, unto
Jerusalem:
9 And he burnt the house of the LORD, and the king's house, and all the
houses of Jerusalem, and every great *man's* house burnt he with fire.
10 And all the army of the Chal′dees, that *were with* the captain of the
guard, brake down the walls of Jerusalem round about.
11 Now the rest of the people *that were* left in the city, and the fugitives
that fell away to the king of Babylon, with the remnant of the multitude,
did Neb′u-zar-a′dan the captain of the guard carry away.
12 But the captain of the guard left of the poor of the land *to be*
vinedressers and husbandmen.
13 And the pillars of brass that *were* in the house of the LORD, and the
bases, and the brasen sea that *was* in the house of the LORD, did the
Chal′dees break in pieces, and carried the brass of them to Babylon.
14 And the pots, and the shovels, and the snuffers, and the spoons, and all
the vessels of brass wherewith they ministered, took they away.
15 And the firepans, and the bowls, *and* such things as *were* of gold, *in*
gold, and of silver, *in* silver, the captain of the guard took away.
16 The two pillars, one sea, and the bases which Solomon had made for
the house of the LORD; the brass of all these vessels was without weight.
17 The height of the one pillar *was* eighteen cubits, and the chapiter upon

☆**25:8** Jer 52:12
25:9 2 Chron 36:19; Ps 74:3; Isa 64:10, 11; Jer 7:13, 14; Amos 2:5
25:10 Neh 1:3; Jer 52:14
25:11 2 Chron 36:20
25:12 2 Chron 24:14; Jer 40:7; 52:16
25:13 1 Kgs 7:15; 2 Kgs 20:17; 2 Chron 36:18
25:14 1 Kgs 7:48–50; Jer 39:10; 42:18
25:17 1 Kgs 7:15; Jer 52:20; Ezek 26:11

25:6 This event marks the end of the Judean kingship over Jerusalem. Both Zedekiah and Jehoiachin are in Babylon. How did this affect the promise of God about the house of David? Jesus was to come from a root out of a dry ground (see Isa. 53:2). David's house becomes a dry root. Six hundred years will pass before the son of David, Jesus, will emerge.

25:8 The destruction of the temple and of Jerusalem occurred in 586 B.C. Before the destruction of the temple, the glory of God had already left the sanctuary, signifying that God had left his people to a just judgment for their transgressions. However, the door is always left open to a renewal of the covenant, when Israel repents and turns to the Messiah.

it *was* brass: and the height of the chapiter three cubits; and the wreathen work, and pomegranates upon the chapiter round about, all of brass: and like unto these had the second pillar with wreathen work.

c. The Leaders of Judah Slain

25:18 Ezra 7:1; Jer 29:25, 26, 29

18 ¶And the captain of the guard took Ser-a-i'ah the chief priest, and Zeph-a-ni'ah the second priest, and the three keepers of the door:

19 And out of the city he took an officer that was set over the men of war, and five men of them that were in the king's presence, which were found in the city, and the principal scribe of the host, which mustered the people of the land, and threescore men of the people of the land *that were* found in the city:

25:20 2 Kgs 23:33; Jer 52:9

20 And Neb'u-zar-a'dan captain of the guard took these, and brought them to the king of Babylon to Rib'lah:

25:21 Deut 28:64; 1 Kgs 9:7; 2 Kgs 23:27; Jer 24:9, 10; Ezek 12:25

21 And the king of Babylon smote them, and slew them at Rib'lah in the land of Ha'math. So Judah was carried away out of their land.

G. THE AFTERMATH

1. Gedaliah Made Governor; His Assassination

25:22☆ Jer 39:14

22 ¶And *as for* the people that remained in the land of Judah, whom Neb-u-chad-nez'zar king of Babylon had left, even over them he made Ged-a-li'ah the son of A-hi'kam, the son of Sha'phan, ruler.

25:23 Jer 40:7

23 And when all the captains of the armies, they and their men, heard that the king of Babylon had made Ged-a-li'ah governor, there came to Ged-a-li'ah to Mizpah, even Ish'ma-el the son of Neth-a-ni'ah, and Jo-ha'nan the son of Ca-re'ah, and Ser-a-i'ah the son of Tan'hu-meth the Ne-toph'a-thite, and Ja-az-a-ni'ah the son of a Ma-ach'a-thite, they and their men.

24 And Ged-a-li'ah sware to them, and to their men, and said unto them, Fear not to be the servants of the Chal'dees: dwell in the land, and serve the king of Babylon; and it shall be well with you.

25:25 Jer 41:1

25 But it came to pass in the seventh month, that Ish'ma-el the son of Neth-a-ni'ah, the son of E-lish'a-ma, of the seed royal, came, and ten men with him, and smote Ged-a-li'ah, that he died, and the Jews and the Chal'dees that were with him at Mizpah.

25:26 Jer 43:5

26 And all the people, both small and great, and the captains of the armies, arose, and came to Egypt: for they were afraid of the Chal'dees.

2. Evil-merodach Shows Favor to Jehoiachin

25:27☆ Jer 52:31

27 ¶And it came to pass in the seven and thirtieth year of the captivity of Je-hoi'a-chin king of Judah, in the twelfth month, on the seven and twentieth *day* of the month, *that* E'vil–me-ro'dach king of Babylon in the year that he began to reign did lift up the head of Je-hoi'a-chin king of Judah out of prison;

25:22ff *Gedaliah* was a political moderate. He avoided political intrigue, seeking to promote the interests of the Israelites who remained in Palestine. Ishmael assassinated him and his court—both the Jews and the Babylonians. The Jewish community virtually ceased to exist after this. Gedaliah's followers fled to Egypt and forced Jeremiah to go with them. In Jewish tradition the anniversary of Gedaliah's death is celebrated by a fast.

25:27 *Evil-merodach,* Nebuchadnezzar's son, reigned from 561 to 560 B.C. His Babylonian name was Amel-Marduk ("Man of Marduk") which was a variant form of Awel-merodach (the source of his Hebrew name, Evil-Merodach). "Evil" in the name has nothing whatever to do with the English word *evil.* This king released Jehoiachin from prison and took good care of him, for he represented to the Babylonians the legitimate king of Judah. Clay tablets found in the ruins of Babylon mention that food was supplied by their conquerors to Jehoiachin and five of his sons.

28 And he spake kindly to him, and set his throne above the throne of the
kings that *were* with him in Babylon;
29 And changed his prison garments: and he did eat bread continually
before him all the days of his life.
30 And his allowance *was* a continual allowance given him of the king, a
daily rate for every day, all the days of his life.

THE FIRST AND SECOND BOOK OF THE

CHRONICLES

Authorship, date, and background 1 and 2 Chronicles in modern translations were one book in the Hebrew Bible. The name given to Chronicles in the Greek and Latin versions was *Paraleipomena,* which simply means the record of the things left out of Samuel and Kings. Chronicles was placed at the end of the Writings (Kethubim) in the Hebrew Bible.

The authorship and dating of Chronicles stand together. Ezra, according to Jewish tradition, was the author. This view is held by many conservative scholars today. They have placed the composition of the book (or books) somewhere between 450 and 425 B.C. Chronicles was put together by Ezra after considerable research had been done. Nehemiah, with whom he was associated, was said to have had a large library (2 Maccabees 2:13–15). No doubt Ezra had access to it. In Chronicles there is a list of the various sources used; these included various books of the kings of Judah and Israel. Writings of Samuel the seer, Nathan the prophet, Gad the seer, Ahijah the Shilonite, Iddo the seer, Shemaiah the prophet, Jehu the son of Hanani, Isaiah the prophet, and "The Chronicles of the Seers" were all consulted. Some passages of Chronicles parallel the books of Samuel and Kings.

The Israelis who had come back from Babylon were apparently unaware of their national heritage. A new generation had grown up who were unfamiliar with the land. Jerusalem was in shambles, the Temple had been destroyed, and the religious ceremonies centering around it had not been celebrated for more than half a century. A need existed to unify the people by teaching them something about their former glory and about the work of God in their midst. The purpose was to give the Israelis in the new commonwealth an understanding of their covenant relationship to God, what the theocracy and the monarchy were all about, and to trace for them the beginning of the Davidic line and what followed thereafter.

Characteristics and content Ezra traces the rise of the Hebrew peoples from Adam and carries it through the exile under Nebuchadnezzar to the return to the land under Cyrus' edict. No doubt he does this to encourage the returnees to appreciate their heritage and to develop a national spirit. This history will give them a sense of belonging, and also show that the God of mighty miracles had been with their ancestors despite the trials and tribulations brought upon them because of disobedience.

The first nine chapters of 1 Chronicles are genealogical tables showing that the Israelis are direct descendants of the first human pair, who are the creation of God. The writer does not describe the reign of Saul. He only records the fact that his reign ended ingloriously because he was unfaithful to God. He did not keep God's commandments and he consulted a medium instead of the Lord. Beginning with chapter 11, Ezra recounts the life of King David. He leaves out the bad items in David's pilgrimage, such as his adultery with Bath-sheba, the rebellion of his own household, and family affairs, all of which are extensively covered in 2 Samuel 11–20.

The Chronicler speaks of David's major interests as king of the nation, his religious acts such as bringing the ark to Jerusalem, the organization of the priests and Levites, David's covenantal relation with God who promises him an eternal throne, and his gathering of the materials for the construction of the temple, which is to be the responsibility of Solomon.

As the author sets down the incidents of Solomon's reign, he omits his apostasy and idolatry while stressing the good things he did, such as erecting the temple. Following the division of the Solomonic kingdom into the Northern and Southern Kingdoms, nothing is said about the kings of Samaria (Israel) except for those who have a direct connection with affairs involving the kingdom of Judah. He follows the kings of Judah, one by one, devoting the greatest attention to the ones who fear God, keep his law, and promote and teach the law to their people. He stresses over and over again those kings and their acts which contribute to the upbuilding and the preservation of the Jewish theocracy over which God is the Head.

The central theme which pervades the story of the Chronicler is the proposition that those who fear God and follow his commandments can expect the blessing and favor of God over all their works. Disobedience brings disaster; obedience brings blessing. This theme is also to be found in the New Testament for the people of God, the church, and the promise of future blessing for an obedient Israel, so many of whom will seek God and his face in the closing days of the present age.

Outline

1 Chronicles
I. The genealogies from Adam to King David (1:1—9:44)
II. The history of David's reign (10:1—29:30)

2 Chronicles
III. The reign of Solomon (1:1—9:31)
IV. The kings of Judah from Rehoboam to the captivity (10:1—36:23)

---

1 CHRONICLES

I. THE GENEALOGIES FROM ADAM TO KING DAVID (1:1—9:44)

A. THE GENEALOGICAL LIST FROM ADAM TO ISRAEL (JACOB)

1 ADAM, Sheth, E'nosh,
2 Ke'nan, Ma-ha'la-le-el, Je'red,
3 He'noch, Me-thu'se-lah, La'mech,
4 Noah, Shem, Ham, and Ja'pheth.
5 ¶The sons of Ja'pheth; Go'mer, and Ma'gog, and Mad'a-i, and Ja'van,
and Tu'bal, and Me'shech, and Ti'ras.
6 And the sons of Go'mer; Ash'che-naz, and Ri'phath, and To-gar'mah.
7 And the sons of Ja'van; E-li'shah, and Tarshish, Kit'tim, and Do'da-
nim.
8 ¶The sons of Ham; Cush, and Miz'ra-im, Put, and Canaan.
9 And the sons of Cush; Se'ba, and Hav'i-lah, and Sab'ta, and Ra'a-mah,
and Sab'te-cha. And the sons of Ra'a-mah; She'ba, and De'dan.
10 And Cush begat Nimrod: he began to be mighty upon the earth.
11 And Miz'ra-im begat Lu'dim, and An'a-mim, and Le'ha-bim, and
Naph'tu-him,
12 And Path-ru'sim, and Cas'lu-him, (of whom came the Philistines,) and
Caph'tho-rim.
13 And Canaan begat Zi'don his firstborn, and Heth,
14 The Jeb'u-site also, and the Am'or-ite, and the Gir'ga-shite,
15 And the Hi'vite, and the Ark'ite, and the Sin'ite,
16 And the Ar'vad-ite, and the Zem'a-rite, and the Ha'math-ite.
17 ¶The sons of Shem; E'lam, and Asshur, and Ar-phax'ad, and Lud, and
A'ram, and Uz, and Hul, and Ge'ther, and Me'shech.

☆**1:1** Gen 4:25; 5:3–32; 10:1; Isa 54:9, 10; Ezek 14:14; Mt 24:37; Lk 3:38; Heb 11:7
☆**1:3**
☆**1:4**
1:5 Gen 10:2–4, 6–8; 1 Chron 4:40, 42; Ezek 27:13
1:10 Gen 10:8
1:11 Gen 9:22; 10:13–18
1:13 Gen 15:19–21
1:17 Gen 10:21, 22; 11:10; Lk 3:36

1:1 The first twenty-seven verses start with *Adam* and end with *Abraham.* Despite modern denials of the historicity of Adam, the biblical writers all state that Adam was the first man in a literal sense. He was the common father of the entire human race. By his breach of God's covenant with him, we were all made miserable. By God's grace Abraham was the common father of the faithful, and by the covenant of grace made between Abraham and God we are all made happy. By nature we are of the seed of Adam. By faith we are of the seed of Abraham and have been grafted into the good olive tree.

1:3 *Henoch,* i.e., Enoch, "was translated that he should not see death" (Heb. 11:5). The line of Cain is not included in this list.

1:4 *Shem* is mentioned here and again in verse 24. The line of Shem was the line of Abraham and thus the line of Jesus Christ. When Jesus came he was challenged to show from whence he had come. Matthew carefully traced his genealogy back to Abraham, the father of Israel. Luke traced Jesus' genealogy back to Adam through Abraham. No one would have been the Messiah who could not trace his lineage very specifically to Adam through Abraham.

18 And Ar-phax'ad begat She'lah, and She'lah begat E'ber.
1:19 Gen 11:16 19 And unto E'ber were born two sons: the name of the one *was* Pe'leg;
because in his days the earth was divided: and his brother's name *was*
Jok'tan.
20 And Jok'tan begat Al-mo'dad, and She'leph, and Ha'zar-ma'veth, and
Je'rah,
21 Ha-do'ram also, and U'zal, and Dik'lah,
22 And Ebal, and A-bim'a-el, and She'ba,
23 And O'phir, and Hav'i-lah, and Jo'bab. All these *were* the sons of
Jok'tan.
1:24 Gen 11:10–26 Lk 3:34 24 ¶Shem, Ar-phax'ad, She'lah,
25 E'ber, Pe'leg, Re'u,
26 Se'rug, Nahor, Te'rah,
27 Abram; the same *is* Abraham.
1:28☆ 28 The sons of Abraham; Isaac, and Ish'ma-el.
Gen 16:9–12 17:19; 21:3, 9 25:9, 10 29 ¶These *are* their generations: The firstborn of Ish'ma-el, Ne-bai'oth;
1:29☆ then Ke'dar, and Ad'be-el, and Mib'sam,
1:30☆ 30 Mish'ma, and Du'mah, Mas'sa, Ha'dad, and Te'ma,
1:31☆ 31 Je'tur, Na'phish, and Ked'e-mah. These are the sons of Ish'ma-el.
1:32 Gen 25:1, 2 32 ¶Now the sons of Ke-tu'rah, Abraham's concubine: she bare Zim'ran,
and Jok'shan, and Me'dan, and Mid'i-an, and Ish'bak, and Shu'ah. And the
sons of Jok'shan; She'ba, and De'dan.
33 And the sons of Mid'i-an; E'phah, and E'pher, and He'noch, and
A-bi'da, and El'da-ah. All these *are* the sons of Ke-tu'rah.
1:34☆ 34 And Abraham begat Isaac. The sons of Isaac; Esau and Israel.
Gen 25:25, 26 32:28 35 ¶The sons of Esau; El'i-phaz, Reu'el, and Je'ush, and Ja-a'lam, and
Mal 1:2, 3 Mt 1:2 Ko'rah.
1:35☆ Gen 36:4–12 36 The sons of El'i-phaz; Te'man, and Omar, Ze'phi, and Ga'tam, Ke'naz,
and Tim'na, and Am'a-lek.
37 The sons of Reu'el; Na'hath, Ze'rah, Sham'mah, and Miz'zah.
1:38☆ 38 And the sons of Se'ir; Lo'tan, and Sho'bal, and Zib'e-on, and A'nah,
Gen 36:18–21 and Di'shon, and E'zer, and Di'shan.
39 And the sons of Lo'tan; Ho'ri, and Ho'mam: and Tim'na *was* Lo'tan's
sister.
40 The sons of Sho'bal; A-li'an, and Man'a-hath, and Ebal, She'phi, and
O'nam. And the sons of Zib'e-on; A-i'ah, and A'nah.
41 The sons of A'nah; Di'shon. And the sons of Di'shon; Amram, and
Esh'ban, and Ith'ran, and Che'ran.
42 The sons of E'zer; Bil'han, and Za'van, *and* Ja'kan. The sons of
1:43 Di'shan; Uz, and A'ran.
Gen 36:31–39 43 ¶Now these *are* the kings that reigned in the land of Edom before *any*

1:28 Abraham had many sons through Sarah, Hagar, and Keturah. But Sarah had only one son, and through that one son the seed of the Messiah was to be traced. Isaac and only Isaac was the successor to God's covenant promise to Abraham.

1:29–31 The twelve tribes of Ishmael are here named. Jacob had twelve sons and his uncle Ishmael had twelve, and thus the two are juxtaposed.

1:34 As it was in the case of Abraham, so it was also in the case of Isaac. The latter had two sons, but it was only through Jacob and not through Esau that Messiah was to come. Yet the Scriptures trace the non-Messianic line so as to guarantee who could *not* be the Messiah, even though one might spring from the loins of Abraham and Isaac. It is apparent that multiplied millions of people have come from the line of Abraham, but they are not from the line of promise. In this verse Jacob is called Israel and the text thereby suggests a larger context in that it designates the people of Israel as a nation.

1:35 Esau was not in the line of promise. From him and from other sons of Abraham, his grandfather, many nations came into being. This does not mean that those who were not in the line of promise were not and could not be sons and daughters of God. God has called out multitudes from all nations and we may well be astonished to discover how many of those had their names in the book of life. Not all of those attached to Israel will be saved and not all of those unattached to Israel by birth will be lost.

1:38 *Seir,* i.e., "Esau."

king reigned over the children of Israel; Be'la the son of Be'or: and the
name of his city *was* Din'ha-bah.
44 And when Be'la was dead, Jo'bab the son of Ze'rah of Boz'rah reigned
in his stead.
45 And when Jo'bab was dead, Hu'sham of the land of the Te'man-ites
reigned in his stead.
46 And when Hu'sham was dead, Ha'dad the son of Be'dad, which smote
Mid'i-an in the field of Moab, reigned in his stead: and the name of his city
was A'vith.
47 And when Ha'dad was dead, Sam'lah of Mas're-kah reigned in his
stead.
48 And when Sam'lah was dead, Sha'ul of Re-ho'both by the river reigned
in his stead.
49 And when Sha'ul was dead, Ba'al-ha'nan the son of Ach'bor reigned in
his stead.
50 And when Ba'al-ha'nan was dead, Ha'dad reigned in his stead: and the
name of his city *was* Pa'i; and his wife's name *was* Me-het'a-bel, the
daughter of Ma'tred, the daughter of Mez'a-hab.
51 ¶Ha'dad died also. And the dukes of Edom were; duke Tim'nah, duke
A-li'ah, duke Je'theth,
52 Duke A-hol-i-ba'mah, duke E'lah, duke Pi'non,
53 Duke Ke'naz, duke Te'man, duke Mib'zar,
54 Duke Mag'di-el, duke I'ram. These *are* the dukes of Edom.

1:45 Job 2:11

B. ISRAEL'S (JACOB'S) DESCENDANTS

1. From Israel (Jacob) to David

2 THESE *are* the sons of Israel; Reuben, Simeon, Levi, and Judah, Is'sa-
char, and Zeb'u-lun,
2 Dan, Joseph, and Benjamin, Naph'ta-li, Gad, and Asher.
3 ¶The sons of Judah; Er, and O'nan, and She'lah: *which* three were born
unto him of the daughter of Shu'a the Canaanitess. And Er, the firstborn of
Judah, was evil in the sight of the LORD; and he slew him.
4 And Ta'mar his daughter in law bare him Pha'rez and Ze'rah. All the
sons of Judah *were* five.
5 The sons of Pha'rez; Hez'ron, and Ha'mul.
6 And the sons of Ze'rah; Zimri, and E'than, and He'man, and Cal'col,
and Da'ra: five of them in all.
7 And the sons of Car'mi; A'char, the troubler of Israel, who transgressed
in the thing accursed.
8 And the sons of E'than; Az-a-ri'ah.
9 The sons also of Hez'ron, that were born unto him; Je-rah'me-el, and
Ram, and Che-lu'bai.
10 And Ram begat Am-min'a-dab; and Am-min'a-dab begat Nah'shon,
prince of the children of Judah;
11 And Nah'shon begat Sal'ma, and Sal'ma begat Bo'az,
12 And Bo'az begat O'bed, and O'bed begat Jesse,
13 ¶And Jesse begat his firstborn E-li'ab, and A-bin'a-dab the second, and
Shim'ma the third,

☆2:1 Gen 35:22–26 46:8–25 Ex 1:1–4 Num 1:2–15 Rev 7:4–8
2:3 Gen 38:2–10
2:4 Gen 38:13–30 46:8–14
☆2:7 Josh 7:17; 22:20
2:10 Num 7:12; 10:14 Mt 1:4 Lk 3:32
2:12 Ruth 4:16, 17 Mt 1:5
2:13 1 Sam 16:8

2:1 Jacob preferred Rachel over Leah, yet it was from Leah that the two most important tribes of Israel came: Judah and Levi. Thus the Messiah came from Jacob but not from Rachel.

2:7 *Achar*, i.e., Achan, here called "the troubler of Israel." Every family tree has in it those who are illustrious and those who are a disgrace. Scripture is no respecter of persons; it mentions the blemishes as well as the perfections.

14 Ne-than'e-el the fourth, Rad'da-i the fifth,

2:15☆ 15 O'zem the sixth, David the seventh:

2:16☆ 1 Sam 26:5–7 16 Whose sisters *were* Zer-u-i'ah, and Ab'i-gail. And the sons of Zer-u-
2 Sam 2:13 1 Chron 11:5, 6 i'ah; A-bish'a-i, and Jo'ab, and As'a-hel, three.

2:17 2 Sam 17:25 17 And Ab'i-gail bare Am'a-sa: and the father of Am'a-sa *was* Je'ther the
19:13 1 Kgs 2:5 Ish'me-el-ite.

2:18☆ 18 ¶And Caleb the son of Hez'ron begat *children* of A-zu'bah *his* wife, and of Je'ri-oth: her sons *are* these; Je'sher, and Sho'bab, and Ardon.

19 And when A-zu'bah was dead, Caleb took unto him Eph'rath, which bare him Hur.

2:20☆ 20 And Hur begat U'ri, and U'ri begat Be-zal'e-el.

21 ¶And afterward Hez'ron went in to the daughter of Ma'chir the father of Gilead, whom he married when he *was* threescore years old; and she bare him Se'gub.

22 And Se'gub begat Ja'ir, who had three and twenty cities in the land of Gilead.

23 And he took Ge'shur, and A'ram, with the towns of Ja'ir, from them, with Ke'nath, and the towns thereof, *even* threescore cities. All these *belonged to* the sons of Ma'chir the father of Gilead.

24 And after that Hez'ron was dead in Ca'leb–eph'ra-tah, then A-bi'ah Hez'ron's wife bare him Ashur the father of Te-ko'a.

2:25☆ 25 ¶And the sons of Je-rah'me-el the firstborn of Hez'ron were, Ram the firstborn, and Bu'nah, and O'ren, and O'zem, *and* A-hi'jah.

26 Je-rah'me-el had also another wife, whose name *was* At'a-rah; she *was* the mother of O'nam.

27 And the sons of Ram the firstborn of Je-rah'me-el were, Ma'az, and Ja'min, and E'ker.

28 And the sons of O'nam were, Sham'ma-i, and Ja'da. And the sons of Sham'ma-i; Na'dab, and Ab'i-shur.

29 And the name of the wife of Ab'i-shur *was* Ab-i-ha'il, and she bare him Ah'ban, and Mo'lid.

30 And the sons of Na'dab; Se'led, and Ap'pa-im: but Se'led died without children.

31 And the sons of Ap'pa-im; I'shi. And the sons of I'shi; She'shan. And the children of She'shan; Ah'lai.

32 And the sons of Ja'da the brother of Sham'ma-i; Je'ther, and Jonathan: and Je'ther died without children.

33 And the sons of Jonathan; Pe'leth, and Za'za, These were the sons of Je-rah'me-el.

34 ¶Now She'shan had no sons, but daughters. And She'shan had a servant, an Egyptian, whose name *was* Jar'ha.

2:15 *David the seventh.* According to 1 Sam. 16:10, 11 Jesse had eight sons, of whom David was the youngest. Seven of Jesse's sons appeared before Samuel: none of them was God's choice for the kingship and all were older than David. Since the situation mentioned in 1 Chronicles occurred later than what had been reported in 1 Samuel, one of Jesse's sons must have died without issue—so that when the 1 Chronicles genealogy was drawn up there were only seven sons of Jesse left.

2:16 David's three great commanders, Joab, Abisha, and Asahel, were the sons of one of his own sisters. The fourth great leader, Amasa, was the son of his other sister. Evidently they were selected, not because of their family relationship to David, but for their excellence in military matters. Otherwise, we have a classic instance of nepotism.

2:18 This *Caleb* is not to be confused with the famous Caleb who was one of the twelve spies mentioned in 4:15. Of the Caleb in this verse we have no other information apart from who were his ancestors and descendants.

2:20 Bezaleel was the overseer of the construction of the tabernacle. He was given the gift of craftsmanship by the Holy Spirit.

2:25 The name *Jerahmeel* means "may God have compassion." Some non-Israelis, subjects of David, called themselves Jerahmeelites. See 1 Sam. 27:10 for mention of them.

35 And She'shan gave his daughter to Jar'ha his servant to wife; and she bare him At'tai.
36 And At'tai begat Nathan, and Nathan begat Za'bad, ☆2:36 1 Chron 11:41
37 And Za'bad begat Eph'lal, and Eph'lal begat O'bed,
38 And O'bed begat Jehu, and Jehu begat Az-a-ri'ah,
39 And Az-a-ri'ah begat He'lez, and He'lez begat E-le'a-sah,
40 And E-le'a-sah begat Si-sam'a-i, and Si-sam'a-i begat Shal'lum,
41 And Shal'lum begat Jek-a-mi'ah, and Jek-a-mi'ah begat E-lish'a-ma.
42 ¶Now the sons of Caleb the brother of Je-rah'me-el *were,* Me'sha his firstborn, which *was* the father of Ziph; and the sons of Ma-re'shah the father of Hebron.
43 And the sons of Hebron; Ko'rah, and Tap'pu-ah, and Re'kem, and She'ma.
44 And She'ma begat Raham, the father of Jor'ko-am: and Re'kem begat Sham'ma-i.
45 And the son of Sham'ma-i *was* Ma'on: and Ma'on *was* the father of Beth'–zur.
46 And E'phah, Caleb's concubine, bare Ha'ran, and Mo'za, and Ga'zez: and Ha'ran begat Ga'zez.
47 And the sons of Jah'da-i; Re'gem, and Jo'tham, and Ge'sham, and Pe'let, and E'phah, and Sha'aph.
48 Ma'a-chah, Caleb's concubine, bare She'ber, and Tir'ha-nah. 2:48 Josh 15:17 Judg 1:2
49 She bare also Sha'aph the father of Mad-man'nah, She'va the father of Mach'be-nah, and the father of Gib'e-a: and the daughter of Caleb *was* Ach'sa.
50 ¶These were the sons of Caleb the son of Hur, the firstborn of Eph'ra-tah; Sho'bal the father of Kir'jath–je'a-rim, ☆2:50, 51
51 Sal'ma the father of Beth–lehem, Ha'reph the father of Beth–ga'der.
52 And Sho'bal the father of Kir'jath–je'a-rim had sons; Har'o-eh, *and* half of the Ma-na'heth-ites.
53 And the families of Kir'jath–je'a-rim; the Ith'rites, and the Pu'hites, and the Shu'math-ites, and the Mish'ra-ites; of them came the Za're-ath-ites, and the Esh'ta-ul-ites. 2:53 1 Chron 4:2
54 The sons of Sal'ma; Beth–lehem, and the Ne-toph'a-thites, At'a-roth, the house of Jo'ab, and half of the Ma-na'heth-ites, the Zo'rites.
55 And the families of the scribes which dwelt at Ja'bez; the Ti'rath-ites, the Shim'e-ath-ites, *and* Su'chath-ites. These *are* the Ken'ites that came of He'math, the father of the house of Re'chab. ☆2:55 2 Kgs 10:15

2. David's Descendants

3 NOW these were the sons of David, which were born unto him in Hebron; the firstborn Am'non, of A-hin'o-am the Jez're-el-it-ess; the second Daniel, of Ab'i-gail the Carmelitess: 3:1 1 Sam 25:42 2 Sam 3:2–5 13:1 1 Chron 2:3
2 The third, Ab'sa-lom the son of Ma'a-chah the daughter of Tal'mai king of Ge'shur: the fourth, Ad-o-ni'jah the son of Hag'gith: 3:2 2 Sam 3:4 13:20; 14:23
3 The fifth, Sheph-a-ti'ah of Ab'i-tal: the sixth, Ith're-am by Eg'lah his wife.
4 *These* six were born unto him in Hebron; and there he reigned seven years and six months: and in Jerusalem he reigned thirty and three years. 3:4 2 Sam 5:4, 5

2:36 *Attai,* not to be confused with the Gadite warrior mentioned in 12:11.
2:50, 51 The pedigree of several men terminated not in a person but in a place or country. Shobal is called the father of Kirjath-jearim and Salma the father of Jerusalem. These places fell to their lot in the distribution of the land.
2:55 *the scribes,* or, "the writers," were non-Levitical writers, even though some of the Levites also were called writers.

3:5☆ 2 Sam 5:14–16; 11:3; 12:24; 1 Chron 14:4–7

5 And these were born unto him in Jerusalem; Shim'e-a, and Sho'bab, and
Nathan, and Solomon, four, of Bath'–shu-a the daughter of Am'mi-el:
6 Ib'har also, and E-lish'a-ma, and E-liph'e-let,
7 And No'gah, and Ne'pheg, and Ja-phi'a,
8 And E-lish'a-ma, and E-li'a-da, and E-liph'e-let, nine.

3:9☆

9 *These were* all the sons of David, beside the sons of the concubines, and
Ta'mar their sister.

3:10 1 Kgs 11:43; 15:1, 8, 24; 22:50; 2 Kgs 8:24, 25; 11:21; 14:1, 21; 15:30, 32, 33; 16:1; 18:1; 21:1, 2, 19, 20; 22:1; 2 Chron 9:30; 13:1; 14:1; 17:1; 21:1, 17; 24:1; 25:1; 26:1; 27:1; 28:1; 29:1; 33:1, 20, 21; 34:1; Mt 1:7–10
3:11, 12☆
3:15☆ 2 Kgs 23:30, 34; 2 Chron 36:1, 4
3:16☆
3:17☆
3:19☆

10 ¶And Solomon's son *was* Re-ho-bo'am, A-bi'a his son, Asa his son, Je-
hosh'a-phat his son,
11 Joram his son, A-ha-zi'ah his son, Jo'ash his son,
12 Am-a-zi'ah his son, Az-a-ri'ah his son, Jo'tham his son,
13 Ahaz his son, Hez-e-ki'ah his son, Ma-nas'seh his son,
14 A'mon his son, Jo-si'ah his son.
15 And the sons of Jo-si'ah *were,* the firstborn Jo-ha'nan, the second Je-
hoi'a-kim, the third Zed-e-ki'ah, the fourth Shal'lum.
16 And the sons of Je-hoi'a-kim: Jec-o-ni'ah his son, Zed-e-ki'ah his son.
17 ¶And the sons of Jec-o-ni'ah; As'sir, Sa-la'thi-el his son,
18 Mal-chi'ram also, and Pe-dai'ah, and She-na'zar, Jec-a-mi'ah, Hosh'a-
ma, and Ned-a-bi'ah.
19 And the sons of Pe-dai'ah *were,* Ze-rub'ba-bel, and Shim'e-i: and the
sons of Ze-rub'ba-bel; Me-shul'lam, and Han-a-ni'ah, and Shel'o-mith their
sister:
20 And Ha-shu'bah, and O'hel, and Ber-e-chi'ah, and Has-a-di'ah,
Ju'shab–he'sed, five.

3:21 Ezra 8:2–14

21 And the sons of Han-a-ni'ah; Pel-a-ti'ah, and Je-sai'ah: the sons of
Reph-a-i'ah, the sons of Arnan, the sons of O-ba-di'ah, the sons of Shech-
a-ni'ah.
22 And the sons of Shech-a-ni'ah; Shem-a-i'ah: and the sons of Shem-a-
i'ah; Hat'tush, and Ig'e-al, and Ba-ri'ah, and Ne-a-ri'ah, and Sha'phat, six.
23 And the sons of Ne-a-ri'ah; E-li-o-e'na-i, and Hez-e-ki'ah, and Az'ri-
kam, three.
24 And the sons of E-li-o-e'na-i *were,* Hod-a-i'ah, and E-li'a-shib, and Pel-
a-i'ah, and Ak'kub, and Jo-ha'nan, and Dal-a-i'ah, and An-a'ni, seven.

3. Judah's Descendants

4:1 Gen 38:29; 46:12; Num 26:19–22; Ruth 4:18; 1 Chron 2:3; Mt 1:3; Lk 3:33
4:2 1 Chron 2:53
4:3 1 Chron 2:19

4 THE sons of Judah; Pha'rez, Hez'ron, and Car'mi, and Hur, and
Sho'bal.
2 And Re-a-i'ah the son of Sho'bal begat Ja'hath; and Ja'hath begat
A-hu'ma-i, and La'had. These *are* the families of the Zo'rath-ites.
3 And these *were of* the father of E'tam; Jez're-el, and Ish'ma, and
Id'bash: and the name of their sister *was* Haz-e-lel-po'ni:
4 And Pe-nu'el the father of Ge'dor, and E'zer the father of Hu'shah.

3:5 *Bath-shua,* i.e., "Bath-sheba."†
3:9 This is the Tamar who was sexually assaulted by her half brother Amnon, who was later slain by Absalom, the full brother of Tamar. The sons of David by his concubines are mentioned in general, but none of them has his name recorded in particular.
3:11, 12 *Joram,* or, "Jehoram." *Azariah,* or, "Uzziah."
3:15 *Johanan.* He died young, never reigned, and is never mentioned in the historical accounts. *Shallum,* i.e., "Jehoahaz" (see Jer. 22:11).
3:16 *Jehoiakim,* i.e., "Jehoiachin," or, "Coniah."
3:17 *Assir.* The NASB, RSV, and NIV do not regard Assir as a name but as an adjective modifying Jeconiah (who is also known as Jehoiachin, king of Judah). In these newer translations the wording generally is: "the sons of Jeconiah, the captive", since he was a captive under Nebuchadnezzar.
3:19 *Zerubbabel.* The man by this name who led the returnees from Babylon to Palestine was said to be "the son of Shealtiel" (Ezra 3:2; Neh. 12:1). Apparently Shealtiel and Pedaiah both had sons with the same name (Zerubbabel). The descendants listed here are most likely from the line of Shealtiel, not Pedaiah.

These *are* the sons of Hur, the firstborn of Eph'ra-tah, the father of Beth-
lehem.
5 ¶And Ashur the father of Te-ko'a had two wives, He'lah and Na'a-rah.
6 And Na'a-rah bare him A-hu'zam, and He'pher, and Tem'e-ni, and Ha-
a-hash'ta-ri. These *were* the sons of Na'a-rah.
7 And the sons of He'lah *were*, Ze'reth, and Je-zo'ar, and Eth'nan.
8 And Coz begat A'nub, and Zo-be'bah, and the families of A-har'hel the
son of Ha'rum.
9 ¶And Ja'bez was more honourable than his brethren: and his mother ☆4:9
called his name Ja'bez, saying, Because I bare him with sorrow.
10 And Ja'bez called on the God of Israel, saying, Oh that thou wouldest ☆4:10 Gen 32:26
bless me indeed, and enlarge my coast, and that thine hand might be with Ps 72:17
me, and that thou wouldest keep *me* from evil, that it may not grieve me! Eph 1:3
And God granted him that which he requested.
11 ¶And Che'lub the brother of Shu'ah begat Me'hir, which *was* the father
of Esh'ton.
12 And Esh'ton begat Beth-ra'pha, and Pa-se'ah, and Te-hin'nah the
father of Ir-na'hash. These *are* the men of Re'chah.
13 And the sons of Ke'naz; Oth'ni-el, and Ser-a-i'ah: and the sons of 4:13 Josh 15:17
Oth'ni-el; Ha'thath.
14 And Me-on'o-thai begat Oph'rah: and Ser-a-i'ah begat Jo'ab, the father ☆4:14
of the valley of Char'a-shim; for they were craftsmen.
15 And the sons of Caleb the son of Je-phun'neh; I'ru, E'lah, and Na'am:
and the sons of E'lah, even Ke'naz.
16 And the sons of Je-hal'e-le-el; Ziph, and Zi'phah, Tir'i-a, and A-sa're-
el.
17 And the sons of Ezra *were*, Je'ther, and Me'red, and E'pher, and Jal'on:
and she bare Miriam, and Sham'ma-i, and Ish'bah the father of Esh-te-
mo'a.
18 And his wife Je-hu-di'jah bare Je'red the father of Ge'dor, and He'ber
the father of So'cho, and Je-ku'thi-el the father of Za-no'ah. And these *are*
the sons of Bith'i-ah the daughter of Pharaoh, which Me'red took.
19 And the sons of *his* wife Ho-di'ah the sister of Naham, the father of
Kei'lah the Gar'mite, and Esh-te-mo'a the Ma-ach'a-thite.
20 And the sons of Shi'mon *were*, Amnon, and Rin'nah, Ben-ha'nan, and
Ti'lon. And the sons of I'shi *were*, Zo'heth, and Ben-zo'heth.
21 ¶The sons of She'lah the son of Judah *were*, Er the father of Le'cah, and ☆4:21
La'a-dah the father of Ma-re'shah, and the families of the house of them
that wrought fine linen, of the house of Ash-be'a,
22 And Jo'kim, and the men of Cho-ze'ba, and Jo'ash, and Sa'raph, who 4:22
had the dominion in Moab, and Jash'u-bi-le'hem. And *these are* ancient
things.
23 These *were* the potters, and those that dwelt among plants and hedges: ☆4:23 Gen 38:5
there they dwelt with the king for his work.

4:9 *Jabez.* His name is a play on words. Jabez sounds like *ozeb,* the Hebrew word meaning "distress."†

4:10 *Jabez* must have been an unusual character whose quality of life stood out above many others. Tradition has it that he was a doctor of the law. He was a man of excellent character, whose prayer life could be emulated by Christians today. He sought the blessing of God and received what he asked for. His petition included a request for God's blessing, an enlargement of his coast, that the hand of God would be with him, and that he would be kept from evil. God gave him success in his conflicts with the Canaanites, in his secular pursuits, in his studies, and in his undertakings. What God did for him he can do for us today.

4:14, 21 In the midst of the genealogical tables the writer takes time to express appreciation for the craftsmen who were ingenious, industrious, and stood far above others of the same trade. In verse 21 those who excelled in the production of fine linens are mentioned. For potters see note to 4:23.

4:23 *potters . . . dwelt with the king for his work.* Stamped jar handles discovered in excavations by archeologists have verified that the king did indeed have royal potters who worked for him.

4. Simeon's Descendants

24 ¶The sons of Simeon *were*, Ne-mu'el, and Ja'min, Ja'rib, Ze'rah, *and*
Sha'ul:
25 Shal'lum his son, Mib'sam his son, Mish'ma his son.
26 And the sons of Mish'ma; Ha-mu'el his son, Zac'chur his son, Shim'-
e-i his son.
27 And Shim'e-i had sixteen sons and six daughters; but his brethren had
not many children, neither did all their family multiply, like to the children
of Judah.
28 And they dwelt at Be'er–she'ba, and Mol'a-dah, and Ha'zar–shu'al,
29 And at Bil'hah, and at E'zem, and at To'lad,
30 And at Beth-u'el, and at Hor'mah, and at Ziklag,
31 And at Beth–mar'ca-both, and Ha'zar–su'sim, and at Beth-bir'e-i, and
at Sha-a-ra'im. These *were* their cities unto the reign of David.
32 And their villages *were*, E'tam, and A'in, Rimmon, and To'chen, and
A'shan, five cities:
33 And all their villages that *were* round about the same cities, unto Ba'al.
These *were* their habitations, and their genealogy.
34 And Me-sho'bab, and Jam'lech, and Jo'shah the son of Am-a-zi'ah,
35 And Jo'el, and Jehu the son of Jos-i-bi'ah, the son of Ser-a-i'ah, the son
of A'si-el,
36 And E-li-o-e'na-i, and Ja-ak'o-bah, and Jesh-o-hai'ah, and A-sa-i'ah,
and A'di-el, and Je-sim'i-el, and Be-nai'ah,
37 And Zi'za the son of Shi'phi, the son of Al'lon, the son of Je-dai'ah, the
son of Shim'ri, the son of Shem-a-i'ah;
38 These mentioned by *their* names *were* princes in their families: and the
house of their fathers increased greatly.
39 ¶And they went to the entrance of Ge'dor, *even* unto the east side of the
valley, to seek pasture for their flocks.
4:40☆ 40 And they found fat pasture and good, and the land *was* wide, and quiet,
Judg 18:7–10 and peaceable; for *they* of Ham had dwelt there of old.
4:41☆ 41 And these written by name came in the days of Hez-e-ki'ah king of
Judah, and smote their tents, and the habitations that were found there,
and destroyed them utterly unto this day, and dwelt in their rooms: because
there was pasture there for their flocks.
4:42 42 And *some* of them, *even* of the sons of Simeon, five hundred men, went
Gen 36:8 to mount Se'ir, having for their captains Pel-a-ti'ah, and Ne-a-ri'ah, and
Reph-a-i'ah, and Uz'zi-el, the sons of I'shi.
4:43 43 And they smote the rest of the Am'a-lek-ites that were escaped, and
1 Sam 15:7, 8 30:16, 17 dwelt there unto this day.

5. Reuben's Descendants

5:1☆ 5 NOW the sons of Reuben the firstborn of Israel, (for he *was* the
Gen 29:32 35:22 firstborn; but, forasmuch as he defiled his father's bed, his birthright
48:15–22; 49:4 1 Chron 2:1 was given unto the sons of Joseph the son of Israel: and the genealogy is
not to be reckoned after the birthright.
5:2☆ Gen 49:8–10 2 For Judah prevailed above his brethren, and of him *came* the chief ruler;
Mic 5:2 Mt 2:6 but the birthright *was* Joseph's:)
5:3 Ex 6:14 3 The sons, *I say*, of Reuben the firstborn of Israel *were*, Ha'noch, and
Num 26:5 Pal'lu, Hez'ron, and Car'mi.

4:40, 41 *they of Ham had dwelt there of old*, i.e., "the land belonged to the descendants of Ham,"† the Canaanites who are listed under Ham's progeny (Gen. 10:6).

5:1, 2 Although the birthright was lost to Reuben and given to the sons of Joseph, Ephraim and Manasseh, it was the tribe of Judah that became the most powerful tribe.

4The sons of Jo'el; Shem-a-i'ah his son, Gog his son, Shim'e-i his son,
5Mi'cah his son, Re-ai'a his son, Ba'al his son,
6Be-e'rah his son, whom Til'gath-pil-ne'ser king of Assyria carried away
captive: he *was* prince of the Reubenites.
7And his brethren by their families, when the genealogy of their
generations was reckoned, *were* the chief, Je-i'el, and Zech-a-ri'ah,
8And Be'la the son of A'zaz, the son of She'ma, the son of Jo'el, who
dwelt in Ar'o-er, even unto Nebo and Ba'al-me'on:
9And eastward he inhabited unto the entering in of the wilderness from
the river Eu-phra'tes: because their cattle were multiplied in the land of
Gilead.
10And in the days of Saul they made war with the Ha'gar-ites, who fell by
their hand: and they dwelt in their tents throughout all the east *land* of
Gilead.

6. Gad's Descendants

11¶And the children of Gad dwelt over against them, in the land of
Ba'shan unto Sal'cah:
12Jo'el the chief, and Sha'pham the next, and Ja-a'nai, and Sha'phat in
Ba'shan.
13And their brethren of the house of their fathers *were,* Michael, and Me-
shul'lam, and She'ba, and Jo'rai, and Ja'chan, and Zi'a, and He'ber, seven.
14These *are* the children of Ab-i-ha'il the son of Hu'ri, the son of Ja-ro'ah,
the son of Gilead, the son of Michael, the son of Je-shish'a-i, the son of
Jah'do, the son of Buz;
15A'hi the son of Ab'di-el, the son of Gu'ni, chief of the house of their
fathers.
16And they dwelt in Gilead in Ba'shan, and in her towns, and in all the
suburbs of Shar'on, upon their borders.
17All these were reckoned by genealogies in the days of Jo'tham king of
Judah, and in the days of Jer-o-bo'am king of Israel.
18¶The sons of Reuben, and the Gadites, and half the tribe of Ma-
nas'seh, of valiant men, men able to bear buckler and sword, and to shoot
with bow, and skilful in war, *were* four and forty thousand seven hundred
and threescore, that went out to the war.
19And they made war with the Ha'gar-ites, with Je'tur, and Ne'phish, and
No'dab.
20And they were helped against them, and the Ha'gar-ites were delivered
into their hand, and all that *were* with them: for they cried to God in the
battle, and he was intreated of them; because they put their trust in him.
21And they took away their cattle; of their camels fifty thousand, and of
sheep two hundred and fifty thousand, and of asses two thousand, and of
men an hundred thousand.
22For there fell down many slain, because the war *was* of God. And they
dwelt in their steads until the captivity.

5:6 2 Kgs 15:29; 16:7; 1 Chron 5:26
☆**5:7** Num 32:34; Josh 12:2
5:9 Josh 22:8, 9
☆**5:10** 1 Chron 5:18–21
5:11 Num 32:34–36; Josh 13:11, 24
5:16 1 Chron 27:29
5:17 2 Kgs 14:16, 28; 15:5, 32, 33
5:18 Num 1:3
5:19 Chron 1:31; 5:10
☆**5:20** Josh 10:42; 2 Chron 14:11–13; Ps 9:10
5:22 Josh 23:10; 2 Kgs 17:6; 2 Chron 32:8

5:7, 8 *Jeiel, . . . Zechariah, And Bela* were Reubenites who dwelt in Aroer.

5:10 *Hagarites.* Whether these people descended from Hagar is uncertain. They and other Arab tribes are mentioned in an inscription of Tiglath-pileser III (745–727 B.C.).

5:20 The author attributes the victory of the Israelites on the east bank of the Jordan to their petition to God for help. However, in verse 25 they are said to have gone "a whoring after the gods of the people of the land," and this resulted in God's judgment on them and their captivity by Pul and Tiglath-pileser.

7. Manasseh's (a Half-Tribe) Descendants

5:23☆ [23]¶And the children of the half tribe of Ma-nas′seh dwelt in the land:
Deut 3:9; 4:48 they increased from Ba′shan unto Ba′al–her′mon and Se′nir, and unto
mount Hermon.
[24]And these *were* the heads of the house of their fathers, even E′pher, and
I′shi, and E-li′el, and Az′ri-el, and Jer-e-mi′ah, and Hod-a-vi′ah, and Jah′di-
el, mighty men of valour, famous men, *and* heads of the house of their
fathers.
5:25 [25]¶And they transgressed against the God of their fathers, and went a
Ex 34:15 2 Kgs 17:7 whoring after the gods of the people of the land, whom God destroyed
before them.
5:26 [26]And the God of Israel stirred up the spirit of Pul king of Assyria, and
2 Kgs 15:19, 29 the spirit of Til′gath–pil-ne′ser king of Assyria, and he carried them away,
even the Reubenites, and the Gadites, and the half tribe of Ma-nas′seh, and
brought them unto Ha′lah, and Ha′bor, and Ha′ra, and to the river Go′zan,
unto this day.

8. Levi's Descendants

6:1☆ 6 THE sons of Levi; Ger′shon, Ko′hath, and Me-ra′ri.
Gen 46:11 [2]And the sons of Ko′hath; Amram, Iz′har, and Hebron, and Uz′zi-el.
Ex 6:16 Num 3:17 [3]And the children of Amram; Aaron, and Moses, and Miriam. The sons
6:3 1 Chron 23:13 also of Aaron; Na′dab, and A-bi′hu, E-le-a′zar, and Ith′a-mar.
6:4 [4]¶E-le-a′zar begat Phin′e-has, Phin′e-has begat A-bish′u-a,
1 Chron 9:20 [5]And A-bish′u-a begat Buk′ki, and Buk′ki begat Uz′zi,
[6]And Uz′zi begat Zer-a-hi′ah, and Zer-a-hi′ah begat Me-rai′oth,
[7]Me-rai′oth begat Am-a-ri′ah, and Am-a-ri′ah begat A-hi′tub,
6:8☆ [8]And A-hi′tub begat Za′dok, and Za′dok begat A-him′a-az,
[9]And A-him′a-az begat Az-a-ri′ah, and Az-a-ri′ah begat Jo-ha′nan,
[10]And Jo-ha′nan begat Az-a-ri′ah, (he *it is* that executed the priest's office
in the temple that Solomon built in Jerusalem:)
[11]And Az-a-ri′ah begat Am-a-ri′ah, and Am-a-ri′ah begat A-hi′tub,
[12]And A-hi′tub begat Za′dok, and Za′dok begat Shal′lum,
6:13☆ [13]And Shal′lum begat Hil-ki′ah, and Hil-ki′ah begat Az-a-ri′ah,
[14]And Az-a-ri′ah begat Ser-a-i′ah, and Ser-a-i′ah begat Je-hoz′a-dak,
6:15☆ [15]And Je-hoz′a-dak went *into captivity*, when the LORD carried away
Judah and Jerusalem by the hand of Neb-u-chad-nez′zar.
[16]¶The sons of Levi; Ger′shom, Ko′hath, and Me-ra′ri.
[17]And these *be* the names of the sons of Ger′shom; Lib′ni, and Shim′e-i.
[18]And the sons of Ko′hath *were*, Amram, and Iz′har, and Hebron, and
Uz′zi-el.

5:23 *Mount Hermon* is probably a scribal explanation for *Senir*, the Amorite name for Mount Hermon. (See Deut. 3:9.)

6:1 The Levites were especially careful to keep their genealogical tables in order. From this tribe came the priesthood and no one, not even a Levite, who was not in the priestly line could offer sacrifices. For one not of the priesthood to offer sacrifices was an abomination punishable by death.

6:8 Zadok was the high priest during the reigns of David and Solomon.

6:13 Some priests were more useful to God than others. Hilkiah discovered the book of the law—whether by accident or by search we do not know. But it can only mean that the book of the law was not in general use before his discovery; therefore, Hilkiah could not use what he did not have. There is a difference today between those who do not have the Bible and therefore cannot use it and those who possess copies of the sacred Book and choose not to be informed by it. The latter is far worse than the former.

6:15 Jehozadak is also called Josedech in Haggai and Zechariah in the KJV. It is shortened to Jozadak in Ezra and Nehemiah. He was the father of Joshua, who was the high priest at the time of the rebuilding of the temple after the captivity.

19The sons of Me-ra'ri; Mah'li, and Mu'shi. And these *are* the families of
the Levites according to their fathers.
20Of Ger'shom; Lib'ni his son, Ja'hath his son, Zimmah his son,
21Jo'ah his son, Id'do his son, Ze'rah his son, Je-at'e-rai his son.
22The sons of Ko'hath; Am-min'a-dab his son, Ko'rah his son, As'sir his
son,
23El-ka'nah his son, and E-bi'a-saph his son, and As'sir his son,
24Ta'hath his son, U'ri-el his son, Uz-zi'ah his son, and Sha'ul his son.
25And the sons of El-ka'nah; A-mas'a-i, and A-hi'moth.
26*As for* El-ka'nah: the sons of El-ka'nah; Zo'phai his son, and Na'hath
his son,
27E-li'ab his son, Jer'o-ham his son, El-ka'nah his son.
28And the sons of Samuel; the firstborn Vash'ni, and A-bi'ah.
29The sons of Me-ra'ri; Mah'li, Lib'ni his son, Shim'e-i his son, Uz'za his
son,
30Shim'e-a his son, Hag-gi'ah his son, A-sa-i'ah his son.
31And these *are they* whom David set over the service of song in the
house of the LORD, after that the ark had rest.
32And they ministered before the dwelling place of the tabernacle of the
congregation with singing, until Solomon had built the house of the LORD
in Jerusalem: and *then* they waited on their office according to their order.
33And these *are* they that waited with their children. Of the sons of the
Ko'hath-ites: He'man a singer, the son of Jo'el, the son of She-mu'el,
34The son of El-ka'nah, the son of Jer'o-ham, the son of E-li'el, the son of
To'ah,
35The son of Zuph, the son of El-ka'nah, the son of Ma'hath, the son of
A-mas'a-i,
36The son of El-ka'nah, the son of Jo'el, the son of Az-a-ri'ah, the son of
Zeph-a-ni'ah,
37The son of Ta'hath, the son of As'sir, the son of E-bi'a-saph, the son of
Ko'rah,
38The son of Iz'har, the son of Ko'hath, the son of Levi, the son of Israel.
39And his brother A'saph, who stood on his right hand, *even* A'saph the
son of Ber-a-chi'ah, the son of Shim'e-a,
40The son of Michael, the son of Ba'a-sei'ah, the son of Mal-chi'ah,
41The son of Eth'ni, the son of Ze'rah, the son of Ad-a-i'ah,
42The son of E'than, the son of Zimmah, the son of Shim'e-i,
43The son of Ja'hath, the son of Ger'shom, the son of Levi.
44And their brethren the sons of Me-ra'ri *stood* on the left hand: E'than
the son of Kish'i, the son of Ab'di, the son of Mal'luch,
45The son of Hash-a-bi'ah, the son of Am-a-zi'ah, the son of Hil-ki'ah,
46The son of Am'zi, the son of Ba'ni, the son of Sha'mer,
47The son of Mah'li, the son of Mu'shi, the son of Me-ra'ri, the son of
Levi.
48Their brethren also the Levites *were* appointed unto all manner of
service of the tabernacle of the house of God.
49¶But Aaron and his sons offered upon the altar of the burnt offering,
and on the altar of incense, *and were appointed* for all the work of the *place*
most holy, and to make an atonement for Israel, according to all that Moses
the servant of God had commanded.
50And these *are* the sons of Aaron; E-le-a'zar his son, Phin'e-has his son,
A-bish'u-a his son,

6:19 1 Chron 23:21
6:25 1 Sam 1:1
6:28 1 Sam 8:2
☆6:31 2 Sam 6:17; 1 Chron 15:16, 27; 16:4–6; 25:1
6:49 Ex 29:33, 34
6:50 1 Chron 6:4–8

6:31 The authority of King David in matters of temple ritual and song was equal to that of Moses in the area of law. David actively exercised his authority in these matters.

[51]Buk'ki his son, Uz'zi his son, Zer-a-hi'ah his son,
[52]Me-rai'oth his son, Am-a-ri'ah his son, A-hi'tub his son,
[53]Za'dok his son, A-him'a-az his son.

6:54☆ Josh 21:4, 10
[54]¶Now these *are* their dwelling places throughout their castles in their coasts, of the sons of Aaron, of the families of the Ko'hath-ites: for theirs was the lot.

6:55 Josh 14:13; 15:13; 21:13, 19
[55]And they gave them Hebron in the land of Judah, and the suburbs thereof round about it.
[56]But the fields of the city, and the villages thereof, they gave to Caleb the son of Je-phun'neh.

6:57☆
[57]And to the sons of Aaron they gave the cities of Judah, *namely*, Hebron, *the city* of refuge, and Lib'nah with her suburbs, and Jat'tir, and Esh-te-mo'a, with their suburbs,

6:58 Num 35:6; Deut 4:41; 19:2; Josh 20:2
[58]And Hi'len with her suburbs, De'bir with her suburbs,
[59]And A'shan with her suburbs, and Beth-she'mesh with her suburbs:
[60]And out of the tribe of Benjamin; Ge'ba with her suburbs, and Al'e-meth with her suburbs, and An'a-thoth with her suburbs. All their cities throughout their families *were* thirteen cities.

6:61 Josh 21:5; 1 Chron 6:66–70
[61]And unto the sons of Ko'hath, *which were* left of the family of that tribe, *were cities given* out of the half tribe, *namely, out of* the half *tribe* of Ma-nas'seh, by lot, ten cities.
[62]And to the sons of Ger'shom throughout their families out of the tribe of Is'sa-char, and out of the tribe of Asher, and out of the tribe of Naph'ta-li, and out of the tribe of Ma-nas'seh in Ba'shan, thirteen cities.

6:63 Josh 21:7, 34–40; 1 Chron 6:77
[63]Unto the sons of Me-ra'ri *were given* by lot, throughout their families, out of the tribe of Reuben, and out of the tribe of Gad, and out of the tribe of Zeb'u-lun, twelve cities.

6:64 Josh 21:3, 41, 42; 1 Chron 6:57–60
[64]And the children of Israel gave to the Levites *these* cities with their suburbs.
[65]And they gave by lot out of the tribe of the children of Judah, and out of the tribe of the children of Simeon, and out of the tribe of the children of Benjamin, these cities, which are called by *their* names.

6:66 Josh 21:20–26; 1 Chron 6:61
[66]And *the residue* of the families of the sons of Ko'hath had cities of their coasts out of the tribe of E'phra-im.
[67]And they gave unto them, *of* the cities of refuge, She'chem in mount E'phra-im with her suburbs; *they gave* also Ge'zer with her suburbs,
[68]And Jok'me-am with her suburbs, and Beth-ho'ron with her suburbs,
[69]And Ai'ja-lon with her suburbs, and Gath-rim'mon with her suburbs:
[70]And out of the half tribe of Ma-nas'seh; Aner with her suburbs, and Bil'e-am with her suburbs, for the family of the remnant of the sons of Ko'hath.
[71]Unto the sons of Ger'shom *were given* out of the family of the half tribe of Ma-nas'seh, Go'lan in Ba'shan with her suburbs, and Ash'ta-roth with her suburbs:
[72]And out of the tribe of Is'sa-char; Ke'desh with her suburbs, Dab'e-rath with her suburbs,
[73]And Ra'moth with her suburbs, and A'nem with her suburbs:
[74]And out of the tribe of Asher; Ma'shal with her suburbs, and Abdon with her suburbs,

---

6:54 *castles,* a word from the Hebrew, "tirah" which means dwelling places, not castles as we understand the term popularly.
6:57 The text here makes it appear that all of the cities named were cities of refuge. Only Hebron was such a city. The NIV has correctly translated the verse: "So the descendants of Aaron were given Hebron (a city of Refuge), and Libnah . . . ." Two letters of the Hebrew text were interchanged and need to be inverted.

75 And Hu'kok with her suburbs, and Re'hob with her suburbs:

76 And out of the tribe of Naph'ta-li; Ke'desh in Galilee with her suburbs, and Ham'mon with her suburbs, and Kir-jath-a'im with her suburbs.

77 Unto the rest of the children of Me-ra'ri *were given* out of the tribe of Zeb'u-lun, Rimmon with her suburbs, Ta'bor with her suburbs: **6:77** 1 Chron 6:63

78 And on the other side Jordan by Jericho, on the east side of Jordan, *were given them* out of the tribe of Reuben, Be'zer in the wilderness with her suburbs, and Jah'zah with her suburbs,

79 Ked'e-moth also with her suburbs, and Meph'a-ath with her suburbs:

80 And out of the tribe of Gad; Ra'moth in Gilead with her suburbs, and Ma-ha-na'im with her suburbs,

81 And Hesh'bon with her suburbs, and Ja'zer with her suburbs.

9. Issachar's Descendants

7 NOW the sons of Is'sa-char *were*, To'la, and Pu'ah, Jash'ub, and Shim'rom, four. **7:1** Gen 46:13 Num 26:23

2 And the sons of To'la; Uz'zi, and Reph-a-i'ah, and Je'ri-el, and Jah'-ma-i, and Jib'sam, and She-mu'el, heads of their father's house, *to wit*, of To'la: *they were* valiant men of might in their generations; whose number *was* in the days of David two and twenty thousand and six hundred. **7:2** 2 Sam 24:1–9 1 Chron 21:1

3 And the sons of Uz'zi; Iz-ra-hi'ah: and the sons of Iz-ra-hi'ah; Michael, and O-ba-di'ah, and Jo'el, I-shi'ah, five: all of them chief men.

4 And with them, by their generations, after the house of their fathers, *were* bands of soldiers for war, six and thirty thousand *men:* for they had many wives and sons.

5 And their brethren among all the families of Is'sa-char *were* valiant men of might, reckoned in all by their genealogies fourscore and seven thousand.

10. Benjamin's Descendants

6 ¶*The sons* of Benjamin; Be'la, and Be'cher, and Je-di'a-el, three. **☆7:6** 1 Chron 8:1

7 And the sons of Be'la; Ez'bon, and Uz'zi, and Uz'zi-el, and Jer'i-moth, and I'ri, five; heads of the house of *their* fathers, mighty men of valour; and were reckoned by their genealogies twenty and two thousand and thirty and four.

8 And the sons of Be'cher; Ze-mi'ra, and Jo'ash, and E-li-e'zer, and E-li-o-e'na-i, and Omri, and Jer'i-moth, and A-bi'ah, and An'a-thoth, and Al'a-meth. All these *are* the sons of Be'cher.

9 And the number of them, after their genealogy by their generations, heads of the house of their fathers, mighty men of valour, *was* twenty thousand and two hundred.

10 The sons also of Je-di'a-el; Bil'han: and the sons of Bil'han; Je'ush, and Benjamin, and E'hud, and Che-na'a-nah, and Ze'than, and Thar'shish, and A-hish'a-har.

11 All these the sons of Je-di'a-el, by the heads of their fathers, mighty men of valour, *were* seventeen thousand and two hundred *soldiers*, fit to go out for war *and* battle.

12 Shup'pim also, and Hup'pim, the children of Ir, *and* Hu'shim, the sons of A'her. **☆7:12**

7:6 *sons of Benjamin.* A second genealogy for Benjamin appears in 8:1–40. There is a textual question as to whether Zebulun, whose genealogy is otherwise missing, appeared in the autograph in place of Benjamin. The names *Zebulun* and *Benjamin* are much closer in the Hebrew than in the English.

7:12 Since the genealogy of Dan is missing, some scholars think that the text here originally read, "the sons of Dan, Hushim his one son," which is in accord with Gen. 46:23 ("the sons of Dan; Hushim"). Chronicles presents a number of textual problems.

11. Naphtali's Descendants

7:13 Gen 46:23–25 Num 26:49

13¶The sons of Naph'ta-li; Jah'zi-el, and Gu'ni, and Je'zer, and Shal'lum, the sons of Bil'hah.

7:14 Gen 50:23 Num 26:29 Josh 13:31

14¶The sons of Ma-nas'seh; Ash'ri-el, whom she bare: (*but* his concubine the A'ram-it-ess bare Ma'chir the father of Gilead:

7:15☆

15And Ma'chir took to wife *the sister* of Hup'pim and Shup'pim, whose sister's name *was* Ma'a-chah;) and the name of the second *was* Ze-lo'phe-had: and Ze-lo'phe-had had daughters.

16And Ma'a-chah the wife of Ma'chir bare a son, and she called his name Pe'resh; and the name of his brother *was* She'resh; and his sons *were* U'lam and Ra'kem.

17And the sons of U'lam; Be'dan. These *were* the sons of Gilead, the son of Ma'chir, the son of Ma-nas'seh.

18And his sister Ham-mol'e-keth bare I'shod, and A-bi-e'zer, and Ma-ha'lah.

19And the sons of She-mi'dah were, A-hi'an, and She'chem, and Lik'hi, and A'ni-am.

12. Ephraim's Descendants

7:20 Num 26:35, 36

20¶And the sons of E'phra-im; Shu'the-lah, and Be'red his son, and Ta'hath his son, and El'a-dah his son, and Ta'hath his son,

21¶And Za'bad his son, and Shu'the-lah his son, and E'zer, and E'le-ad, whom the men of Gath *that were* born in *that* land slew, because they came down to take away their cattle.

22And E'phra-im their father mourned many days, and his brethren came to comfort him.

23¶And when he went in to his wife, she conceived, and bare a son, and he called his name Be-ri'ah, because it went evil with his house.

7:24 Josh 16:3, 5

24(And his daughter *was* She'rah, who built Beth–ho'ron the nether, and the upper, and Uz'zen–she'rah.)

7:25–27 Ex 17:9–14 24:13

25And Re'phah *was* his son, also Re'sheph, and Te'lah his son, and Ta'han his son,

26La'a-dan his son, Am-mi'hud his son, E-lish'a-ma his son,

27Non his son, Je-hosh'u-a his son.

28¶And their possessions and habitations *were*, Beth–el and the towns thereof, and eastward Na'a-ran, and westward Ge'zer, with the towns thereof; She'chem also and the towns thereof, unto Ga'za and the towns thereof:

7:29 Josh 17:7–11

29And by the borders of the children of Ma-nas'seh, Beth–she'an and her towns, Ta'a-nach and her towns, Me-gid'do and her towns, Dor and her towns. In these dwelt the children of Joseph the son of Israel.

13. Asher's Descendants

7:30 Gen 46:17 Num 26:44–46

30¶The sons of Asher; Im'nah, and Is'u-ah, and Ish'u-ai, and Be-ri'ah, and Se'rah their sister.

31And the sons of Be-ri'ah; He'ber, and Mal'chi-el, who *is* the father of Bir'za-vith.

7:15 *Zelophehad* had five daughters and no sons. In Num. 27:1ff the daughters asked Moses if the female descendants could inherit the property of their father when there were no sons. This became standard practice; and this rule was later changed (Num. 36:2ff) to require female descendants to marry within their own tribe so that their offspring would be of the same tribe, thus preventing land from going to other tribes or to strangers.

32And He'ber begat Japh'let, and Sho'mer, and Ho'tham, and Shu'a their
sister.
33And the sons of Japh'let; Pa'sach, and Bim'hal, and Ash'vath. These
are the children of Japh'let.
34And the sons of Sha'mer; A'hi, and Roh'gah, Je-hub'bah, and A'ram,
35And the sons of his brother He'lem; Zo'phah, and Im'na, and She'lesh,
and A'mal.
36The sons of Zo'phah; Su'ah, and Har'ne-pher, and Shu'al, and Be'ri,
and Im'rah,
37Be'zer, and Hod, and Sham'ma, and Shil'shah, and Ith'ran, and Be-e'ra.
38And the sons of Je'ther; Je-phun'neh, and Pis'pah, and A'ra.
39And the sons of Ul'la; A'rah, and Han'i-el, and Re-zi'a.
40All these *were* the children of Asher, heads of *their* father's house,
choice *and* mighty men of valour, chief of the princes. And the number
throughout the genealogy of them that were apt to the war *and* to battle *was*
twenty and six thousand men.

14. Benjamin's Descendants

8 NOW Benjamin begat Be'la his firstborn, Ash'bel the second, and
A-har'ah the third,
2No'hah the fourth, and Ra'pha the fifth.
3And the sons of Be'la were, Ad'dar, and Ge'ra, and A-bi'hud,
4And A-bish'u-a, and Na'a-man, and A-ho'ah,
5And Ge'ra, and She-phu'phan, and Hu'ram.
6And these *are* the sons of E'hud: these are the heads of the fathers of the
inhabitants of Ge'ba, and they removed them to Man'a-hath:
7And Na'a-man, and A-hi'ah, and Ge'ra, he removed them, and begat
Uz'za, and A-hi'hud.
8And Sha-ha-ra'im begat *children* in the country of Moab, after he had
sent them away; Hu'shim and Ba'a-ra *were* his wives.
9And he begat of Ho'desh his wife, Jo'bab, and Zib'i-a, and Me'sha, and
Mal'cham,
10And Je'uz, and Sha-chi'a, and Mir'ma. These *were* his sons, heads of the
fathers.
11And of Hu'shim he begat Ab'i-tub, and El'pa-al.
12The sons of El'pa-al; E'ber, and Mi'sham, and Sha'med, who built
O'no, and Lod, with the towns thereof:
13Be-ri'ah also, and She'ma, who *were* heads of the fathers of the
inhabitants of Ai'ja-lon, who drove away the inhabitants of Gath:
14And A-hi'o, Sha'shak, and Jer'e-moth,
15And Zeb-a-di'ah, and A'rad and A'der,
16And Michael, and Is'pah, and Jo'ha, the sons of Be-ri'ah;
17And Zeb-a-di'ah, and Me-shul'lam, and Hez'e-ki, and He'ber,
18Ish'me-rai also, and Jez-li'ah, and Jo'bab, the sons of El'pa-al;
19And Ja'kim, and Zich'ri, and Zab'di,
20And E-li-e'na-i, and Zil'thai, and E-li'el,
21And A-da-i'ah, and Ber-a-i'ah, and Shim'rath, the sons of Shim'hi;
22And Ish'pan, and He'ber, and E-li'el,

☆**8:1** Gen 46:21; 1 Chron 7:6–12

8:1 The lineage of Benjamin which began in 7:6–12 is taken up again in this chapter. Its importance springs from the fact that the first king of Israel came from this tribe. Moreover, the people of Benjamin supported the Davidic monarchy, occupied parts of Jerusalem, were taken into the captivity with Judah, and returned from the captivity to repopulate the land. Apart from the genealogy, there is little or nothing of history about Benjamin and its people.

23 And Abdon, and Zich'ri, and Ha'nan,
24 And Han-a-ni'ah, and E'lam, and An-to-thi'jah,
25 And Iph-e-de-i'ah, and Pe-nu'el, the sons of Sha'shak;
26 And Sham-she-ra'i, and She-ha-ri'ah, and Ath-a-li'ah,
27 And Jar-e-si'ah, and E-li'ah, and Zich'ri, the sons of Jer'o-ham.
28 These *were* heads of the fathers, by their generations, chief *men*. These
dwelt in Jerusalem.
8:29 1 Chron 9:35–38 29 And at Gibeon dwelt the father of Gibeon; whose wife's name *was*
Ma'a-chah:
30 And his firstborn son Abdon, and Zur, and Kish, and Ba'al, and
Na'dab,
31 And Ge'dor, and A-hi'o, and Za'cher.
32 And Mik'loth begat Shim'e-ah. And these also dwelt with their
brethren in Jerusalem, over against them.
8:33☆ 1 Sam 9:1 14:50 1 Chron 9:39–44 33 ¶And Ner begat Kish, and Kish begat Saul, and Saul begat Jonathan,
and Mal'chi-shu'a, and A-bin'a-dab, and Esh-ba'al.
8:34☆ 2 Sam 4:4 34 And the son of Jonathan *was* Mer'ib-ba'al; and Mer'ib-ba'al begat
Mi'cah.
35 And the sons of Mi'cah *were*, Pi'thon, and Me'lech, and Ta're-a, and
Ahaz.
36 And Ahaz begat Je-ho'a-dah; and Je-ho'a-dah begat Al'e-meth, and
Az'ma-veth, and Zimri; and Zimri begat Mo'za,
37 And Mo'za begat Bin'e-a: Ra'pha *was* his son, E-le'a-sah his son, A'zel
his son:
38 And A'zel had six sons, whose names *are* these, Az'ri-kam, Boch'e-ru,
and Ish'ma-el, and She-a-ri'ah, and O-ba-di'ah, and Ha'nan. All these *were*
the sons of A'zel.
39 And the sons of E'shek his brother *were*, U'lam his firstborn, Je'hush
the second, and E-liph'e-let the third.
40 And the sons of U'lam were mighty men of valour, archers, and had
many sons, and sons' sons, an hundred and fifty. All these *are* of the sons of
Benjamin.

15. The List of Returnees from Babylon

9:1☆ 1 Kgs 14:19 22:39 2 Kgs 1:18 2 Chron 16:11 20:34 9 SO all Israel were reckoned by genealogies; and, behold, they *were*
written in the book of the kings of Israel and Judah, *who* were carried
away to Babylon for their transgression.
9:2 Ezra 2:43, 58 8:20 Neh 11:3–22 2 ¶Now the first inhabitants that *dwelt* in their possessions in their cities
were, the Israelites, the priests, Levites, and the Neth'i-nims.
3 And in Jerusalem dwelt of the children of Judah, and of the children of
9:3☆ Benjamin, and of the children of E'phra-im, and Ma-nas'seh;
4 U'tha-i the son of Am-mi'hud, the son of Omri, the son of Im'ri, the son
of Ba'ni, of the children of Pha'rez the son of Judah.
5 And of the Shi'lo-nites; A-sa-i'ah the firstborn, and his sons.

8:33 *Esh-baal.* See note on 2 Sam. 2:8.
8:34 *Merib-baal,* or, *Mephibosheth."* See note on 2 Sam 4:4. The writer traces the descendants of Jonathan for about ten generations. While the other sons of Saul are named, their offspring are omitted. This may be due to David's commitment to Jonathan and his desire to honor his friend.
9:1 The writer reminds us that Judah was taken captive by Babylon as a warning to future generations. Should anyone suppose that God had been unable to prevent the Babylonian calamity, the text specifies that the captivity had been caused by Judah's transgressions. Let no one ever accuse God of injustice or suppose that his mercies have failed to protect his people. When God chastises any believer, he should always be ready to say, "It was for my transgression." *the book of the kings of Israel and Judah.* This refers to court records, not to the books of First and Second Kings.
9:3 When the Northern Kingdom was overthrown, some people from those tribes escaped to Judah and Jerusalem. They were then taken in the Babylonian

6And of the sons of Ze'rah; Je-u'el, and their brethren, six hundred and ninety.
7And of the sons of Benjamin; Sal'lu the son of Me-shul'lam, the son of Hod-a-vi'ah, the son of Has-e-nu'ah,
8And Ib-nei'ah the son of Jer'o-ham, and E'lah the son of Uz'zi, the son of Mich'ri, and Me-shul'lam the son of Sheph-a-thi'ah, the son of Reu'el, the son of Ib-ni'jah;
9And their brethren, according to their generations, nine hundred and fifty and six. All these men *were* chief of the fathers in the house of their fathers.
10¶And of the priests; Je-dai'ah, and Je-hoi'a-rib, and Ja'chin,
11And Az-a-ri'ah the son of Hil-ki'ah, the son of Me-shul'lam, the son of Za'dok, the son of Me-rai'oth, the son of A-hi'tub, the ruler of the house of God;
12And Ad-a-i'ah the son of Jer'o-ham, the son of Pash'ur, the son of Mal-chi'jah, and Ma-as'i-ai the son of A'di-el, the son of Jah'ze-rah, the son of Me-shul'lam, the son of Me-shil'le-mith, the son of Im'mer;
13And their brethren, heads of the house of their fathers, a thousand and seven hundred and threescore; very able men for the work of the service of the house of God.
14And of the Levites; Shem-a-i'ah the son of Has'shub, the son of Az'ri-kam, the son of Hash-a-bi'ah, of the sons of Me-ra'ri;
15And Bak-bak'kar, He'resh, and Ga'lal, and Mat-ta-ni'ah the son of Mi'cah, the son of Zich'ri, the son of A'saph;
16And O-ba-di'ah the son of Shem-a-i'ah, the son of Ga'lal, the son of Jed'u-thun, and Ber-e-chi'ah the son of Asa, the son of El-ka'nah, that dwelt in the villages of the Ne-toph'a-thites.
17And the porters *were*, Shal'lum, and Ak'kub, and Tal'mon, and A-hi'man, and their brethren: Shal'lum *was* the chief;
18Who hitherto *waited* in the king's gate eastward: they *were* porters in the companies of the children of Levi.
19And Shal'lum the son of Ko're, the son of E-bi'a-saph, the son of Ko'rah, and his brethren, of the house of his father, the Ko'rah-ites, *were* over the work of the service, keepers of the gates of the tabernacle: and their fathers, *being* over the host of the LORD, *were* keepers of the entry.
20And Phin'e-has the son of E-le-a'zar was the ruler over them in time past, *and* the LORD *was* with him.
21*And* Zech-a-ri'ah the son of Me-shel-e-mi'ah *was* porter of the door of the tabernacle of the congregation.
22All these *which were* chosen to be porters in the gates *were* two hundred and twelve. These were reckoned by their genealogy in their villages, whom David and Samuel the seer did ordain in their set office.
23So they and their children *had* the oversight of the gates of the house of the LORD, *namely*, the house of the tabernacle, by wards.
24In four quarters were the porters, toward the east, west, north, and south.
25And their brethren, *which were* in their villages, *were* to come after seven days from time to time with them.

9:9 Neh 11:8
9:10 Neh 11:10–14; Jer 20:1
☆**9:14** Neh 11:15–19
9:17 Ezek 46:1, 2
9:20 Num 25:7–13
9:21 1 Chron 26:2, 14
9:22 1 Chron 26:1; 2 Chron 31:15, 18
9:25 2 Kgs 11:5, 7; 2 Chron 23:8

captivity, and some of their descendants returned to the land in the days of Ezra and Nehemiah.
9:14ff The Israelites in Babylon had learned the lesson that infidelity leads to punishment. As they returned to the land, they were more careful to restore the true worship of God. There was no temple, however, since verse 19 speaks of a tabernacle. Verse 27 indicates that the priests lodged around the house of God to be near their religious duties. Verse 33 indicates that singers were employed night and day. Thus God was continually praised.

26For these Levites, the four chief porters, were in *their* set office, and
were over the chambers and treasuries of the house of God.
9:27 1 Chron 23:30–32 27¶And they lodged round about the house of God, because the charge
was upon them, and the opening thereof every morning *pertained* to them.
28And *certain* of them had the charge of the ministering vessels, that they
should bring them in and out by tale.
9:29 1 Chron 23:29 29*Some* of them also *were* appointed to oversee the vessels, and all the
instruments of the sanctuary, and the fine flour, and the wine, and the oil,
and the frankincense, and the spices.
9:30 Ex 30:23–25 30And *some* of the sons of the priests made the ointment of the spices.
31And Mat-ti-thi′ah, *one* of the Levites, who *was* the firstborn of Shal′lum
the Ko′rah-ite, had the set office over the things that were made in the pans.
9:32 Lev 24:5–8 32And *other* of their brethren, of the sons of the Ko′hath-ites, *were* over
the shewbread, to prepare *it* every sabbath.
9:33 1 Chron 6:31–47; 25:1 33And these *are* the singers, chief of the fathers of the Levites, *who*
remaining in the chambers *were* free: for they were employed in *that* work
day and night.
34These chief fathers of the Levites *were* chief throughout their genera-
tions; these dwelt at Jerusalem.

16. Saul's Descendants

9:35☆ 1 Chron 8:29–32 35¶And in Gibeon dwelt the father of Gibeon, Je-hi′el, whose wife's name
was Ma′a-chah:
36And his firstborn son Abdon, then Zur, and Kish, and Ba′al, and Ner,
and Na′dab,
37And Ge′dor, and A-hi′o, and Zech-a-ri′ah, and Mik′loth.
38And Mik′loth begat Shim′e-am. And they also dwelt with their brethren
at Jerusalem, over against their brethren.
9:39 1 Chron 8:33–38 39And Ner begat Kish; and Kish begat Saul; and Saul begat Jonathan,
and Mal′chi-shu′a, and A-bin′a-dab, and Esh–ba′al.
9:40☆ 40And the son of Jonathan *was* Mer′ib–ba′al: and Mer′ib–ba′al begat
Mi′cah.
9:41 1 Chron 8:35–37 41And the sons of Mi′cah *were*, Pi′thon, and Me′lech, and Tah′re-a, *and*
Ahaz.
42And Ahaz begat Ja′rah; and Ja′rah begat Al′e-meth, and Az′ma-veth,
and Zimri; and Zimri begat Mo′za;
43And Mo′za begat Bin′e-a; and Reph-a-i′ah his son, E-le′a-sah his son,
A′zel his son.
44And A′zel had six sons, whose names *are* these, Az′ri-kam, Boch′e-ru,
and Ish′ma-el, and She′a-ri-ah, and O-ba-di′ah, and Ha′nan: these *were* the
sons of A′zel.

II. THE HISTORY OF DAVID'S REIGN (10:1—29:30)

A. SAUL'S LAST DAYS

10:1☆ 1 Sam 31:1 10 NOW the Philistines fought against Israel; and the men of Israel
fled from before the Philistines, and fell down slain in mount Gil-
bo′a.

9:35ff These verses are the same as 8:29–38. Was this a scribal blunder? Or was it a redundancy for the sake of repetition that would, of course, do no harm? There are other places in the Scriptures where the same words are repeated in other books (e.g., see 2 Kings 19 and Isaiah 37).

9:40 *Merib-baal,* or, "Mephibosheth." See note on 2 Sam. 4:4.

10:1 The remainder of 1 Chronicles deals with events preceding the data about the returnees from the Babylonian captivity as given in chapter 9.

2 And the Philistines followed hard after Saul, and after his sons; and the 10:2
Philistines slew Jonathan, and A-bin'a-dab, and Mal'chi-shu'a, the sons of 1 Sam 31:2
Saul.
3 And the battle went sore against Saul, and the archers hit him, and he
was wounded of the archers.
4 Then said Saul to his armourbearer, Draw thy sword, and thrust me ☆10:4
through therewith; lest these uncircumcised come and abuse me. But his
armourbearer would not; for he was sore afraid. So Saul took a sword, and
fell upon it.
5 And when his armourbearer saw that Saul was dead, he fell likewise on
the sword, and died.
6 So Saul died, and his three sons, and all his house died together.
7 And when all the men of Israel that *were* in the valley saw that they fled,
and that Saul and his sons were dead, then they forsook their cities, and
fled: and the Philistines came and dwelt in them.
8 ¶And it came to pass on the morrow, when the Philistines came to strip
the slain, that they found Saul and his sons fallen in mount Gil-bo'a.
9 And when they had stripped him, they took his head, and his armour, 10:9
and sent into the land of the Philistines round about, to carry tidings unto 1 Sam 31:9
their idols, and to the people.
10 And they put his armour in the house of their gods, and fastened his ☆10:10
head in the temple of Da'gon.
11 ¶And when all Ja'besh-gil'e-ad heard all that the Philistines had done
to Saul,
12 They arose, all the valiant men, and took away the body of Saul, and
the bodies of his sons, and brought them to Ja'besh, and buried their bones
under the oak in Ja'besh, and fasted seven days.
13 ¶So Saul died for his transgression which he committed against the ☆10:13
LORD, *even* against the word of the LORD, which he kept not, and also for 1 Sam 13:13, 14
asking *counsel* of *one that had* a familiar spirit, to inquire *of it*; 15:23; 28:7
14 And inquired not of the LORD: therefore he slew him, and turned the ☆10:14
kingdom unto David the son of Jesse. 1 Sam 15:28
1 Chron 12:23

B. DAVID BECOMES KING

1. David Captures Jerusalem (Jebus)

11 THEN all Israel gathered themselves to David unto Hebron, 11:1
saying, Behold, we *are* thy bone and thy flesh. 2 Sam 5:1, 3, 6
2 And moreover in time past, even when Saul was king, thou *wast* he that 11:2
leddest out and broughtest in Israel: and the LORD thy God said unto thee, 2 Sam 5:2; 7:7
Thou shalt feed my people Israel, and thou shalt be ruler over my people
Israel.
3 Therefore came all the elders of Israel to the king to Hebron; and David 11:3
made a covenant with them in Hebron before the LORD; and they anointed 1 Sam 16:1, 3,
David king over Israel, according to the word of the LORD by Samuel. 12, 13

10:4 The story of Saul's death here makes clear the fact that the story of the Amalekite who claimed that he had killed Saul (and expected David to be grateful) was a fabrication. David had the Amalekite slain for claiming to have done away with Saul. If David would not touch the Lord's anointed, why would he be grateful to a man who had done what he himself thought was wrong?

10:10 First Samuel 31:10 says the body of Saul was fastened to the wall of Beth-shan and his armor was placed in the temple of Ashtaroth. Here we see added details: Saul's head was put in Dagon's temple. Since there were four Canaanite temples, all of this is possible.

10:13 *one that had a familiar spirit,* i.e., "medium." (See 1 Sam. 28). The writer explains the reasons for Saul's tragic end. It was not that God had deserted him; rather, Saul had deserted God. When that happened, the justice of God overtook him. All the ways of the Lord are right.

10:14 God did not slay Saul. That was done by the enemy and by Saul himself. Yet it was done "by the determinate counsel and foreknowledge of God" (Acts 2:23). Disobedience can have fatal consequences; however great and powerful a man may be, he is not exempted from the judgment of God. The ruin of Saul was a triumph of divine justice.

11:4 Josh 15:8, 63 Judg 1:21

[4]¶And David and all Israel went to Jerusalem, which *is* Je'bus; where the
Jeb'u-sites *were*, the inhabitants of the land.
[5]And the inhabitants of Je'bus said to David, Thou shalt not come hither.
Nevertheless David took the castle of Zion, which *is* the city of David.

11:6 2 Sam 8:16

[6]And David said, Whosoever smiteth the Jeb'u-sites first shall be chief
and captain. So Jo'ab the son of Zer-u-i'ah went first up, and was chief.
[7]And David dwelt in the castle; therefore they called it the city of David.
[8]And he built the city round about, even from Mil'lo round about: and
Jo'ab repaired the rest of the city.

11:9☆ 2 Sam 3:1

[9]So David waxed greater and greater: for the LORD of hosts *was* with
him.

2. David's Brave Warriors Listed

11:10 2 Sam 23:8–39 1 Chron 11:3

[10]¶These also *are* the chief of the mighty men whom David had, who
strengthened themselves with him in his kingdom, *and* with all Israel, to
make him king, according to the word of the LORD concerning Israel.

11:11 2 Sam 23:8 2 Chron 27:2

[11]And this *is* the number of the mighty men whom David had; Ja-sho'be-
am, an Hach'mo-nite, the chief of the captains: he lifted up his spear
against three hundred slain *by him* at one time.

11:12 1 Chron 27:4

[12]And after him *was* E-le-a'zar the son of Dodo, the A-ho'hite, who *was*
one of the three mighties.

11:13 2 Sam 23:11, 12

[13]He was with David at Pas–dam'mim, and there the Philistines where
gathered together to battle, where was a parcel of ground full of barley; and
the people fled from before the Philistines.
[14]And they set themselves in the midst of *that* parcel, and delivered it,
and slew the Philistines; and the LORD saved *them* by a great deliverance.

11:15 1 Chron 14:9

[15]¶Now three of the thirty captains went down to the rock to David, into
the cave of A-dul'lam; and the host of the Philistines encamped in the
valley of Reph'a-im.

11:16 1 Sam 10:5

[16]And David *was* then in the hold, and the Philistines' garrison *was* then
at Beth–lehem.
[17]And David longed, and said, Oh that one would give me drink of the
water of the well of Beth–lehem, that *is* at the gate!
[18]And the three brake through the host of the Philistines, and drew water
out of the well of Beth–lehem, that *was* by the gate, and took *it*, and
brought *it* to David: but David would not drink *of* it, but poured it out to
the LORD,
[19]And said, My God forbid it me, that I should do this thing: shall I
drink the blood of these men that have put their lives in jeopardy? for with
the jeopardy of their lives they brought it. Therefore he would not drink it.
These things did these three mightiest.
[20]¶And A-bish'a-i the brother of Jo'ab, he was chief of the three: for
lifting up his spear against three hundred, he slew *them*, and had a name
among the three.
[21]Of the three, he was more honourable than the two; for he was their
captain: howbeit he attained not to the *first* three.

11:22☆ 2 Sam 8:18

[22]Be-nai'ah the son of Je-hoi'a-da, the son of a valiant man of Kab'ze-el,
who had done many acts; he slew two lionlike men of Moab: also he went
down and slew a lion in a pit in a snowy day.

11:9 The reason David *waxed greater and greater* was that God was with him. Promotion comes neither from the east nor the west. God sets up and pulls down as he pleases. Let every man know that whatever success he attains in life is from God. And the one who gives it is also the one who can take it away when pride, disobedience, or carelessness overtakes the one God has blessed.

11:22 *lionlike men* ("giants"), literally, "ariels." The meaning of the term is uncertain.†

22 For at *that* time day by day there came to David to help him, until *it*
was a great host, like the host of God.

12:22
Josh 5:13–15

23 ¶And these *are* the numbers of the bands *that were* ready armed to the
war, *and* came to David to Hebron, to turn the kingdom of Saul to him,
according to the word of the LORD.

☆**12:23**
2 Sam 2:3, 4
1 Chron 10:14
11:10

24 The children of Judah that bare shield and spear *were* six thousand and
eight hundred, ready armed to the war.

12:24
2 Sam 2:8, 9
8:17
1 Chron 6:8, 53
12:2
Esth 1:13
Ps 12:2

25 Of the children of Simeon, mighty men of valour for the war, seven
thousand and one hundred.
26 Of the children of Levi four thousand and six hundred.
27 And Je-hoi′a-da *was* the leader of the Aaronites, and with him *were*
three thousand and seven hundred;
28 And Za′dok, a young man mighty of valour, and of his father's house
twenty and two captains.
29 And of the children of Benjamin, the kindred of Saul, three thousand:
for hitherto the greatest part of them had kept the ward of the house of
Saul.
30 And of the children of E′phra-im twenty thousand and eight hundred,
mighty men of valour, famous throughout the house of their fathers.
31 And of the half tribe of Ma-nas′seh eighteen thousand, which were
expressed by name, to come and make David king.
32 And of the children of Is′sa-char, *which were men* that had understand-
ing of the times, to know what Israel ought to do; the heads of them *were*
two hundred; and all their brethren *were* at their commandment.
33 Of Zeb′u-lun, such as went forth to battle, expert in war, with all
instruments of war, fifty thousand, which could keep rank: *they were* not of
double heart.
34 And of Naph′ta-li a thousand captains, and with them with shield and
spear thirty and seven thousand.
35 And of the Danites expert in war twenty and eight thousand and six
hundred.
36 And of Asher, such as went forth to battle, expert in war, forty
thousand.
37 And on the other side of Jordan, of the Reubenites, and the Gadites,
and of the half tribe of Ma-nas′seh, with all manner of instruments of war
for the battle, an hundred and twenty thousand.
38 All these men of war, that could keep rank, came with a perfect heart to
Hebron, to make David king over all Israel: and all the rest also of Israel
were of one heart to make David king.

☆**12:38**
2 Sam 5:1–3
1 Chron 12:33

39 And there they were with David three days, eating and drinking: for
their brethren had prepared for them.
40 Moreover they that were nigh them, *even* unto Is′sa-char and Zeb′u-lun
and Naph′ta-li, brought bread on asses, and on camels, and on mules, and
on oxen, *and* meat, meal, cakes of figs, and bunches of raisins, and wine,
and oil, and oxen, and sheep abundantly: for *there was* joy in Israel.

12:40
1 Sam 25:18

12:23 David's army increased substantially, as men from the various tribes joined him in the overthrow of Saul. The author of Chronicles was careful to say that the turning over of the kingdom was "according to the word of the LORD." The will of God against Saul and for David must have been known to Israel. They now are moved by God to join David to end the reign of Saul.

12:38 Israel was now of a single mind to make David king. Their unity for David shows their opposition to Saul, who has lost their affection. No man can rule over a people for long, when he has lost their confidence and they spurn his dominion.

C. DAVID BRINGS THE ARK OF GOD TO JERUSALEM
1. The Ark in the House of Obed-edom

13:1☆ **13** AND David consulted with the captains of thousands and hun-
dreds, *and* with every leader.
2 And David said unto all the congregation of Israel, If *it seem* good unto
you, and *that it be* of the LORD our God, let us send abroad unto our
brethren every where, *that are* left in all the land of Israel, and with them
also to the priests and Levites *which are* in their cities *and* suburbs, that they
may gather themselves unto us:
13:3 3 And let us bring again the ark of our God to us: for we inquired not at
1 Sam 7:l, 2 it in the days of Saul.
4 And all the congregation said that they would do so: for the thing was
right in the eyes of all the people.
13:5 5 So David gathered all Israel together, from Shi'hor of Egypt even unto
1 Sam 6:21; 7:1 / 2 Sam 6:1 the entering of He'math, to bring the ark of God from Kir'jath–je'a-rim.
1 Kgs 8:65 / 1 Chron 15:3 6 And David went up, and all Israel, to Ba'al-ah, *that is*, to Kir'jath–je'a-
13:6 / Josh 15:9 rim, which *belonged* to Judah, to bring up thence the ark of God the LORD,
2 Kgs 19:15 that dwelleth *between* the cherubims, whose name is called *on it*.
13:7 7 And they carried the ark of God in a new cart out of the house of
1 Sam 7:1 A-bin'a-dab: and Uz'za and A-hi'o drave the cart.
13:8 8 And David and all Israel played before God with all *their* might, and
1 Chron 15:16 with singing, and with harps, and with psalteries, and with timbrels, and
with cymbals, and with trumpets.
13:9☆ 9 ¶And when they came unto the threshingfloor of Chi'don, Uz'za put
2 Sam 6:6 forth his hand to hold the ark; for the oxen stumbled.
13:10 10 And the anger of the LORD was kindled against Uz'za, and he smote
Lev 10:2 / 1 Chron 15:13, him, because he put his hand to the ark: and there he died before God.
15 11 And David was displeased, because the LORD had made a breach upon
Uz'za: wherefore that place is called Pe'rez–uz'za to this day.
12 And David was afraid of God that day, saying, How shall I bring the
ark of God *home* to me?
13:13☆ 13 So David brought not the ark *home* to himself to the city of David, but
2 Chron 25:24 carried it aside into the house of O'bed–e'dom the Git'tite.
13:14 14 And the ark of God remained with the family of O'bed–e'dom in his
1 Chron 26:4, 5 house three months. And the LORD blessed the house of O'bed–e'dom, and
all that he had.

2. David's Good Fortune
a. The Greatness of David's Kingship

14:1☆ **14** NOW Hiram king of Tyre sent messengers to David, and timber of
2 Sam 5:11 cedars, with masons and carpenters, to build him an house.

13:1 This part of David's story is not to be found in the book of Samuel. David proposes to bring the ark to Jerusalem so that the royal city might be the holy city. Saul had neglected the ark and thereby showed his neglect of God. Here David manifests respect for the ark, and shows that in his government he will use his power to advance the cause of true religion—something that any Christian ruler ought to do. Those who honor God are blessed by him; those who begin with the fear of God experience the favor of God.

13:9 The story of Uzza's error is told in 2 Sam. 6:66ff. Familiarity may breed contempt, and those who handle spiritual things may come to regard them in a secular spirit. Since God is a jealous God, those who claim his name must approach him in adoration and subjection.

13:13 Despite the breach made by Uzza's act, David should have gone ahead with his plan to bring the ark to Jerusalem. God's reproof to David for this failure was shown by the blessing that attended the house of Obed-edom, into whose care the ark was committed. The ark was a savor of life unto life, even as the cross is a savor of Christ's death unto endless life for those who abide in its shadow.

14:1 The chronicler may have taken what is recorded here from 2 Samuel 5:11ff. It would appear that Hiram was moved by God to offer what David needed for the construction of the temple. Hiram had a little kingdom; David had a large one. But David needed both the materials and the manual help Hiram could give. We are never so great that we do not need the help afforded by those who may seem to be insignificant.

2 And David perceived that the LORD had confirmed him king over Israel, ☆14:2
for his kingdom was lifted up on high, because of his people Israel.
3 ¶And David took more wives at Jerusalem: and David begat more sons
and daughters.
4 Now these *are* the names of *his* children which he had in Jerusalem; 14:4 2 Sam 5:14 1 Chron 3:5–8
Sham-mu'a, and Sho'bab, Nathan, and Solomon,
5 And Ib'har, and El-i-shu'a, and El'pa-let.
6 And No'gah, and Ne'pheg, and Ja-phi'a,
7 And E-lish'a-ma, and Be-el-i'a-da, and E-liph'a-let.

b. David's Victories over the Philistines

8 ¶And when the Philistines heard that David was anointed king over all
Israel, all the Philistines went up to seek David. And David heard *of it*, and
went out against them.
9 And the Philistines came and spread themselves in the valley of Reph'a- 14:9 1 Chron 11:15 14:13
im.
10 And David inquired of God, saying, Shall I go up against the ☆14:10
Philistines? And wilt thou deliver them into mine hand? And the LORD said
unto him, Go up; for I will deliver them into thine hand.
11 So they came up to Ba'al-per'a-zim; and David smote them there. Then
David said, God hath broken in upon mine enemies by mine hand like the
breaking forth of waters: therefore they called the name of that place Ba'al-
per'a-zim.
12 And when they had left their gods there, David gave a commandment,
and they were burned with fire.
13 And the Philistines yet again spread themselves abroad in the valley. 14:13 1 Chron 14:9
14 Therefore David inquired again of God; and God said unto him, Go
not up after them; turn away from them, and come upon them over against
the mulberry trees.
15 And it shall be, when thou shalt hear a sound of going in the tops of the
mulberry trees, *that* then thou shalt go out to battle: for God is gone forth
before thee to smite the host of the Philistines.
16 David therefore did as God commanded him: and they smote the host
of the Philistines from Gibeon even to Ga'zer.
17 And the fame of David went out into all lands; and the LORD brought ☆14:17 Ex 15:14 Deut 2:25
the fear of him upon all nations.

3. Bringing the Ark to Jerusalem

a. Arrangements for the Ark's Transport

15 AND *David* made him houses in the city of David, and prepared a ☆15:1 1 Chron 16:1 17:1 Ps 132:2–5
place for the ark of God, and pitched for it a tent.
2 Then David said, None ought to carry the ark of God but the Levites: 15:2 Num 4:15 Deut 10:8
for them hath the LORD chosen to carry the ark of God, and to minister
unto him for ever.

14:2 David had waited for a long time before the promise of Samuel the prophet—that David would be king—was fulfilled. Here we learn that David now knows beyond a shadow of doubt that God has confirmed him in the kingship for the sake of Israel. This confirmation spurred him on to serve God with his whole heart.

14:10 David is king but he gets his instructions from the one who gave him his throne. Here he inquires from God as to what course of action he should take against the Philistines, who have challenged him to a war. God assures him of victory over the enemy and gives him a sign. When he hears "a sound of going in the tops of the mulberry trees" ("the sound of marching in the tops of the balsam trees," NASB) he is to engage in battle "for God is gone forth *before* you to smite the host of the Philistines" (14:15). If God be for us who can be against us?

14:17 The fame of David and the fear of his enemies has in it the providential movement of God. It was the Lord who "brought the fear of him upon all nations."

15:1 David pitched a tent to house the ark, for as yet there was no temple which had been constructed. The tent was probably built according to the pattern given by Moses, who obtained it from God.

15:3 2 Sam 6:12, 17; 1 Kgs 8:1; 1 Chron 13:5; 15:1, 12
15:4 1 Chron 6:16; 12:26

3 And David gathered all Israel together to Jerusalem, to bring up the ark
of the LORD unto his place, which he had prepared for it.
4 And David assembled the children of Aaron, and the Levites:
5 Of the sons of Ko'hath; U'ri-el the chief, and his brethren an hundred
and twenty:
6 Of the sons of Me-ra'ri; A-sa-i'ah the chief, and his brethren two
hundred and twenty:
7 Of the sons of Ger'shom; Jo'el the chief, and his brethren an hundred
and thirty:
8 Of the sons of E-liz'a-phan; Shem-a-i'ah the chief, and his brethren two
hundred:
9 Of the sons of Hebron; E-li'el the chief, and his brethren fourscore:
10 Of the sons of Uz'zi-el; Am-min'a-dab the chief, and his brethren an
hundred and twelve.

15:11 1 Sam 22:20; 1 Kgs 2:26, 35; 1 Chron 12:28

11 And David called for Za'dok and A-bi'a-thar the priests, and for the
Levites, for U'ri-el, A-sa-i'ah, and Jo'el, Shem-a-i'ah, and E-li'el, and Am-
min'a-dab,

15:12 Ex 19:14, 15; 2 Chron 35:6

12 And said unto them, Ye *are* the chief of the fathers of the Levites:
sanctify yourselves, *both* ye and your brethren, that ye may bring up the ark
of the LORD God of Israel unto *the place that* I have prepared for it.
13 For because ye *did it* not at the first, the LORD our God made a breach
upon us, for that we sought him not after the due order.
14 So the priests and the Levites sanctified themselves to bring up the ark
of the LORD God of Israel.

15:15☆ Ex 25:14; Num 4:5

15 And the children of the Levites bare the ark of God upon their
shoulders with the staves thereon, as Moses commanded according to the
word of the LORD.

b. The Selection of the Singers and Orchestra

15:16 1 Chron 13:8; 25:1

16 And David spake to the chief of the Levites to appoint their brethren *to
be* the singers with instruments of musick, psalteries and harps and
cymbals, sounding, by lifting up the voice with joy.

15:17 1 Chron 25:1

17 So the Levites appointed He'man the son of Jo'el; and of his brethren,
A'saph the son of Ber-e-chi'ah; and of the sons of Me-ra'ri their brethren,
E'than the son of Ku-shai'ah;
18 And with them their brethren of the second *degree*, Zech-a-ri'ah, Ben,
and Ja-a'zi-el, and She-mir'a-moth, and Je-hi'el, and Un'ni, E-li'ab, and Be-
nai'ah, and Ma-a-sei'ah, and Mat-ti-thi'ah, and E-liph'e-leh, and Mik-
nei'ah, and O'bed-e'dom, and Je-i'el, the porters.
19 So the singers, He'man, A'saph, and E'than, *were appointed* to sound
with cymbals of brass;

15:20☆

20 And Zech-a-ri'ah, and A'zi-el, and She-mir'a-moth, and Je-hi'el, and
Un'ni, and E-li'ab, and Ma-a-sei'ah, and Be-nai'ah, with psalteries on Al'a-
moth;

15:21☆

21 And Mat-ti-thi'ah, and E-liph'e-leh, and Mik-nei'ah, and O'bed-e'dom,
and Je-i'el, and Az-a-zi'ah, with harps on the Shem'i-nith to excel.

15:15 In the first effort to bring the ark of God to Jerusalem, it was placed on a cart pulled by oxen. Uzzah touched the ark when the oxen stumbled, and was immediately killed by God. So the ark was placed in the home of Obed-edom, whom God chose to bless. This time the ark was carried on the shoulders of the Levites using the proper poles according to the commandment of God. In 16:1 we see that the ark was placed inside the tent David had pitched for it. (See the note on 1 Chron. 16:39.)

15:20 *with psalteries on Alamoth,* i.e., "accompanied by harps."†

15:21 *Mattithiah, . . . Azaziah* "were the harpists." Their music was set to Shiminith (the meaning of this word is uncertain).†

22 And Chen-a-ni'ah, chief of the Levites, *was* for song: he instructed
about the song, because he *was* skilful.
23 And Ber-e-chi'ah and El-ka'nah *were* doorkeepers for the ark.
24 And Sheb-a-ni'ah, and Je-hosh'a-phat, and Ne-than'e-el, and A-mas'- **15:21**
a-i, and Zech-a-ri'ah, and Be-nai'ah, and E-li-e'zer, the priests, did blow **15:24** 1 Chron 16:6
with the trumpets before the ark of God: and O'bed–e'dom and Je-hi'ah
were doorkeepers for the ark.

c. David's Dance before the Ark

25 ¶So David, and the elders of Israel, and the captains over thousands, **15:25** 2 Sam 6:12, 15
went to bring up the ark of the covenant of the LORD out of the house of 1 Chron 13:13
O'bed–e'dom with joy.
26 And it came to pass, when God helped the Levites that bare the ark of ☆**15:26**
the covenant of the LORD, that they offered seven bullocks and seven rams. Num 23:1, 29
27 And David *was* clothed with a robe of fine linen, and all the Levites
that bare the ark, and the singers, and Chen-a-ni'ah the master of the song
with the singers: David also *had* upon him an ephod of linen.
28 Thus all Israel brought up the ark of the covenant of the LORD with
shouting, and with sound of the cornet, and with trumpets, and with
cymbals, making a noise with psalteries and harps.
29 ¶And it came to pass, *as* the ark of the covenant of the LORD came to ☆**15:29**
the city of David, that Mi'chal the daughter of Saul looking out at a
window saw king David dancing and playing: and she despised him in her
heart.

d. The Sacrifices and Music

16 SO they brought the ark of God, and set it in the midst of the tent **16:1**
that David had pitched for it: and they offered burnt sacrifices and 2 Sam 6:17 1 Kgs 8:5
peace offerings before God. 1 Chron 15:1
2 And when David had made an end of offering the burnt offerings and
the peace offerings, he blessed the people in the name of the LORD.
3 And he dealt to every one of Israel, both man and woman, to every one
a loaf of bread, and a good piece of flesh, and a flagon *of wine*.
4 ¶And he appointed *certain* of the Levites to minister before the ark of ☆**16:4**
the LORD, and to record, and to thank and praise the LORD God of Israel: 1 Chron 15:16
5 A'saph the chief, and next to him Zech-a-ri'ah, Je-i'el, and She-mir'a-
moth, and Je-hi'el, and Mat-ti-thi'ah, and E-li'ab, and Be-nai'ah, and
O'bed–e'dom: and Je-i'el with psalteries and with harps; but A'saph made
a sound with cymbals;
6 Be-nai'ah also and Ja-ha'zi-el the priests with trumpets continually
before the ark of the covenant of God.

e. The Choral Psalm of Praise

7 ¶Then on that day David delivered first *this psalm* to thank the LORD **16:7**
into the hand of A'saph and his brethren. 2 Sam 22:1

15:26 No doubt the Levites who carried the ark remembered what had happened to Uzza and they were frightened. Had they stumbled and someone touched the ark, there might be another tragic incident. Since they were doing the right thing, we are told that "God helped the Levites." If God is in anything it will go well. We need not fear.

15:29 See note to 2 Sam. 6:16 on Michal's reaction to David's dancing before the Lord.

16:4 Prayer consists of more than petitions and intercessions. They are to be preceded by adoration and thanksgiving. Our rejoicing should lead to thanksgiving to God for his provision and goodness. In the New Jerusalem there will be no need to confess our sins or to ask God to meet our needs. Prayer will consist of praise and thanksgiving to him from whom our salvation and all our comforts are received.

16:8☆ 1 Kgs 8:43 2 Kgs 19:19 Ps 105:1–15

8 Give thanks unto the LORD, call upon his name, make known his deeds
among the people.
9 Sing unto him, sing psalms unto him, talk ye of all his wondrous works.
10 Glory ye in his holy name: let the heart of them rejoice that seek the
LORD.
11 Seek the LORD and his strength, seek his face continually.

16:12 Ps 78:43; 103:2

12 Remember his marvellous works that he hath done, his wonders, and
the judgments of his mouth;
13 O ye seed of Israel his servant, ye children of Jacob, his chosen ones.

16:14 Ps 48:10

14 He *is* the LORD our God; his judgments *are* in all the earth.

16:15☆

15 Be ye mindful always of his covenant; the word *which* he commanded
to a thousand generations;

16:16 Gen 17:2 22:16–18; 26:3

16 *Even of the covenant* which he made with Abraham, and of his oath
unto Isaac;

16:17 Gen 35:11, 12

17 And hath confirmed the same to Jacob for a law, *and* to Israel *for* an
everlasting covenant,

16:18 Gen 13:15

18 Saying, Unto thee will I give the land of Canaan, the lot of your
inheritance;

16:19 Gen 34:30 Deut 7:7

19 When ye were but few, even a few, and strangers in it.
20 And *when* they went from nation to nation, and from *one* kingdom to
another people;

16:21 Gen 12:17; 20:3 Ex 7:15

21 He suffered no man to do them wrong: yea, he reproved kings for their
sakes,

16:22 Gen 20:7

22 *Saying*, Touch not mine anointed, and do my prophets no harm.

16:23 Ps 96:1–13

23 Sing unto the LORD, all the earth; shew forth from day to day his
salvation.
24 Declare his glory among the heathen: his marvellous works among all
nations.

16:25☆ Ps 89:7 144:3, 4

25 For great *is* the LORD, and greatly to be praised: he also *is* to be feared
above all gods.

16:26☆ Lev 19:4 Ps 102:25

26 For all the gods of the people *are* idols: but the LORD made the
heavens.
27 Glory and honour *are* in his presence; strength and gladness *are* in his
place.
28 Give unto the LORD, ye kindreds of the people, give unto the LORD
glory and strength.

16:29 Ps 29:2

29 Give unto the LORD the glory *due* unto his name: bring an offering, and
come before him: worship the LORD in the beauty of holiness.
30 Fear before him, all the earth: the world also shall be stable, that it be
not moved.

16:31 Ps 93:1; 96:10 Isa 44:23; 49:13

31 Let the heavens be glad, and let the earth rejoice: and let *men* say
among the nations, The LORD reigneth.

16:32 Ps 98:7

32 Let the sea roar, and the fulness thereof: let the fields rejoice, and all
that *is* therein.
33 Then shall the trees of the wood sing out at the presence of the LORD,
because he cometh to judge the earth.

16:8 This psalm of gratitude is found in Psalm 105:1–15. Its preservation here and in the Psalms assures us that repetition does no harm; and when we meet the same theme in each place, our spirits are fortified and our pilgrimage helped.

16:15 David's refrain about God's covenant is based on the assurance that he will keep his promise and do what he has said he will do. A covenant that is not intended to be kept is no covenant at all. Since God keeps his covenant promises, how great is the transgression when the recipients of the covenant promises break their commitment to him.

16:25, 26 *he also is to be feared above all gods.* David did not endorse the notion that there are other gods. In verse 26 he says that the gods of men are idols. They have no existence. But whatever it is that men worship becomes a substitute for the true God, and David wants all men to worship the one and only God, who is creator of all things.

34 O give thanks unto the LORD; for *he is* good; for his mercy *endureth* for
ever.

16:34 Ps 106:1; 136:1

35 And say ye, Save us, O God of our salvation, and gather us together,
and deliver us from the heathen, that we may give thanks to thy holy name,
and glory in thy praise.

16:35 Ps 106:47, 48

36 Blessed *be* the LORD God of Israel for ever and ever. And all the people
said, Amen, and praised the LORD.

☆16:36 Deut 27:15; 1 Kgs 8:15, 56; Neh 8:6; Ps 72:18

37 ¶So he left there before the ark of the covenant of the LORD A'saph and
his brethren, to minister before the ark continually, as every day's work
required:

16:37 2 Chron 8:14; Ezra 3:4

38 And O'bed-e'dom with their brethren, threescore and eight; O'bed-
e'dom also the son of Jed'u-thun and Ho'sah *to be* porters:

16:38 1 Chron 13:14; 26:10

39 And Za'dok the priest, and his brethren the priests, before the
tabernacle of the LORD in the high place that *was* at Gibeon,

☆16:39 1 Kgs 3:4; 1 Chron 15:11

40 To offer burnt offerings unto the LORD upon the altar of the burnt
offering continually morning and evening, and *to do* according to all that is
written in the law of the LORD, which he commanded Israel;

16:40 Ex 29:38; Num 28:3, 4

41 And with them He'man and Jed'u-thun, and the rest that were chosen,
who were expressed by name, to give thanks to the LORD, because his
mercy *endureth* for ever;

16:41 1 Chron 6:33; 25:1; 2 Chron 5:13

42 And with them He'man and Jed'u-thun with trumpets and cymbals for
those that should make a sound, and with musical instruments of God. And
the sons of Jed'u-thun *were* porters.

16:42 1 Chron 25:7; 2 Chron 7:6; 29:27

43 And all the people departed every man to his house: and David
returned to bless his house.

☆16:43

D. THE CONSTRUCTION OF THE TEMPLE

1. David's Desire to Build the Temple

17 NOW it came to pass, as David sat in his house, that David said to
Nathan the prophet, Lo, I dwell in an house of cedars, but the ark
of the covenant of the LORD *remaineth* under curtains.

17:1 2 Sam 7:1, 2

2 Then Nathan said unto David, Do all that *is* in thine heart; for God *is*
with thee.

2. God's Order for David's Son to Erect the Temple

3 ¶And it came to pass the same night, that the word of God came to
Nathan, saying,

4 Go and tell David my servant, Thus saith the LORD, Thou shalt not
build me an house to dwell in:

☆17:4 1 Chron 28:3; Acts 7:42

5 For I have not dwelt in an house since the day that I brought up Israel
unto this day; but have gone from tent to tent, and from *one* tabernacle *to*
another.

17:5 Ex 40:2, 3; 2 Sam 7:6

16:36 Asaph and the singers had sung this song before the people in public. The people responded by saying "Amen" and by praising the Lord. The amen represented their consent and concurrence. Unfortunately later events would demonstrate the transiency of their religious affections, for apostasy overtook the nation. A good start is no guarantee of perseverance.

16:39 *tabernacle . . . at Gibeon.* According to this verse and 21:29, Israel had two sanctuaries in David's day: one was at Jerusalem with the ark; the other was at Gibeon with the tabernacle and its furniture.

16:43 David was careful to see that public worship was provided for Israel; and when this was accomplished, he went home to maintain his own family worship. The mystery is why he did not bring the tabernacle and the altar which were at Gibeon to Jerusalem at the same time he brought the ark there. Or he could have brought the ark to Gibeon. This state of affairs continued until the temple was built.

17:4 David's intention to build the temple was good and God approved of the desire of his servant to do this. But God did not wish David to be the builder nor was it to be done during David's reign. When God's will was made plain to David through Nathan, he accepted the decision without complaint and began to gather the materials with zeal.

17:6 [6]Wheresoever I have walked with all Israel, spake I a word to any of the
2 Sam 7:7 judges of Israel, whom I commanded to feed my people, saying, Why have
ye not built me an house of cedars?
17:7☆ [7]Now therefore thus shalt thou say unto my servant David, Thus saith
the LORD of hosts, I took thee from the sheepcote, *even* from following the
sheep, that thou shouldest be ruler over my people Israel:
[8]And I have been with thee whithersoever thou hast walked, and have cut
off all thine enemies from before thee, and have made thee a name like the
name of the great men that *are* in the earth.
[9]Also I will ordain a place for my people Israel, and will plant them, and
they shall dwell in their place, and shall be moved no more; neither shall
the children of wickedness waste them any more, as at the beginning,
[10]And since the time that I commanded judges *to be* over my people
Israel. Moreover I will subdue all thine enemies. Furthermore I tell thee
that the LORD will build thee an house.
17:11 [11]¶And it shall come to pass, when thy days be expired that thou must go
2 Sam 7:12 *to be* with thy fathers, that I will raise up thy seed after thee, which shall be
1 Kgs 2:4; 5:5 8:25 of thy sons; and I will establish his kingdom.
[12]He shall build me an house, and I will stablish his throne for ever.
17:13 [13]I will be his father, and he shall be my son: and I will not take my
1 Chron 10:14 mercy away from him, as I took *it* from *him* that was before thee:
Heb 1:5 [14]But I will settle him in mine house and in my kingdom for ever: and his
throne shall be established for evermore.
[15]According to all these words, and according to all this vision, so did
Nathan speak unto David.

3. David's Humble Prayer

17:16☆ [16]¶And David the king came and sat before the LORD, and said, Who *am*
I, O LORD God, and what *is* mine house, that thou hast brought me
hitherto?
17:17 [17]And *yet* this was a small thing in thine eyes, O God; for thou hast *also*
2 Sam 7:19 spoken of thy servant's house for a great while to come, and hast regarded
me according to the estate of a man of high degree, O LORD God.
[18]What can David *speak* more to thee for the honour of thy servant? for
thou knowest thy servant.
17:19 [19]O LORD, for thy servant's sake, and according to thine own heart, hast
2 Sam 7:21 Isa 37:35 thou done all this greatness, in making known all *these* great things.
[20]O LORD, *there is* none like thee, neither *is there any* God beside thee,
according to all that we have heard with our ears.
[21]And what one nation in the earth *is* like thy people Israel, whom God
went to redeem *to be* his own people, to make thee a name of greatness and
terribleness, by driving out nations from before thy people, whom thou hast
redeemed out of Egypt?
17:22 [22]For thy people Israel didst thou make thine own people for ever; and
Ex 19:5, 6 thou, LORD, becamest their God.

17:7 Beginning with this verse, God reminds David that he was a mere shepherd boy who was raised to power by God. God has overcome David's enemies and raised him to a high place. He guarantees him posterity, that from his loins will come kings who will sit on a throne which is established forever. And best of all, David's seed will build God a dwelling place, where the ark may rest and sacrifices may be made in the divine name.

17:16 When David received God's message from the mouth of his servant Nathan, he responded. He received the promises by faith, he was persuaded they were true, and he cordially embraced them. He abased himself before God and acknowledged his unworthiness. He rejoiced that God is the God of Israel; and so long as that was so, Israel had nothing to fear. But if Israel broke faith with God, nothing could keep them from judgment.

23 Therefore now, LORD, let the thing that thou hast spoken concerning
thy servant and concerning his house be established for ever, and do as
thou hast said.
24 Let it even be established, that thy name may be magnified for ever, **17:24**
saying, The LORD of hosts *is* the God of Israel, *even* a God to Israel: and *let* 2 Sam 7:12, 16 1 Kgs 2:4; 8:25
the house of David thy servant *be* established before thee.
25 For thou, O my God, hast told thy servant that thou wilt build him an
house: therefore thy servant hath found *in his heart* to pray before thee.
26 And now, LORD, thou art God, and hast promised this goodness unto
thy servant:
27 Now therefore let it please thee to bless the house of thy servant, that it
may be before thee for ever: for thou blessest, O LORD, and *it shall be*
blessed for ever.

E. DAVID'S MANY EXPLOITS AND VICTORIES

18 NOW after this it came to pass, that David smote the Philistines, **☆18:1** 2 Sam 8:1
and subdued them, and took Gath and her towns out of the hand of
the Philistines.
2 And he smote Moab; and the Moabites became David's servants, *and*
brought gifts.
3 ¶And David smote Had-ar-e'zer king of Zo'bah unto Ha'math, as he
went to stablish his dominion by the river Eu-phra'tes.
4 And David took from him a thousand chariots, and seven thousand
horsemen, and twenty thousand footmen: David also houghed all the
chariot *horses*, but reserved of them an hundred chariots.
5 And when the Syrians of Damascus came to help Had-ar-e'zer king of
Zo'bah, David slew of the Syrians two and twenty thousand men.
6 Then David put *garrisons* in Syria–damascus; and the Syrians became
David's servants, *and* brought gifts. Thus the LORD preserved David
whithersoever he went.
7 And David took the shields of gold that were on the servants of Had-ar-
e'zer, and brought them to Jerusalem.
8 Likewise from Tib'hath, and from Chun, cities of Had-ar-e'zer, brought
David very much brass, wherewith Solomon made the brasen sea, and the
pillars, and the vessels of brass.
9 ¶Now when To'u king of Ha'math heard how David had smitten all the
host of Had-ar-e'zer king of Zo'bah;
10 He sent Ha-do'ram his son to king David, to inquire of his welfare, and
to congratulate him, because he had fought against Had-ar-e'zer, and
smitten him; (for Had-ar-e'zer had war with To'u;) and *with him* all manner
of vessels of gold and silver and brass.
11 ¶Them also king David dedicated unto the LORD, with the silver and **☆18:11**
the gold that he brought from all *these* nations; from Edom, and from
Moab, and from the children of Ammon, and from the Philistines, and
from Am'a-lek.
12 Moreover A-bish'a-i the son of Zer-u-i'ah slew of the Edomites in the
valley of salt eighteen thousand.

18:1 Following David's sweet fellowship with God, he rose to subdue the enemies of Israel. He succeeded against the Philistines, the Moabites, and Hadarezer. When the Syrians of Damascus intervened, they were defeated too.

18:11 The strength of David's commitment to God was demonstrated when the king of Hamath, named Tou, sent him great wealth, for David set these treasures apart for God. "That is most truly and most comfortably our own which we have consecrated unto the Lord, and which we use for his glory."*

[13]And he put garrisons in Edom; and all the Edomites became David's
servants. Thus the LORD preserved David whithersoever he went.
18:14☆ [14]¶So David reigned over all Israel, and executed judgment and justice
among all his people.
18:15 1 Chron 11:6 [15]And Jo'ab the son of Zer-u-i'ah *was* over the host; and Je-hosh'a-phat
the son of A-hi'lud, recorder.
[16]And Za'dok the son of A-hi'tub, and A-bim'e-lech the son of A-bi'a-
thar, *were* the priests; and Shav'sha was scribe;
[17]And Be-nai'ah the son of Je-hoi'a-da *was* over the Cher'e-thites and the
Pel'e-thites; and the sons of David *were* chief about the king.

19:1 2 Sam 10:1 19 NOW it came to pass after this, that Na'hash the king of the
children of Ammon died, and his son reigned in his stead.
[2]And David said, I will shew kindness unto Ha'nun the son of Na'hash,
because his father shewed kindness to me. And David sent messengers to
comfort him concerning his father. So the servants of David came into the
land of the children of Ammon to Ha'nun, to comfort him.
[3]But the princes of the children of Ammon said to Ha'nun, Thinkest thou
that David doth honour thy father, that he hath sent comforters unto thee?
are not his servants come unto thee for to search, and to overthrow, and to
spy out the land?
19:4☆ [4]Wherefore Ha'nun took David's servants, and shaved them, and cut off
their garments in the midst hard by their buttocks, and sent them away.
[5]Then there went *certain*, and told David how the men were served. And
he sent to meet them: for the men were greatly ashamed. And the king said,
Tarry at Jericho until your beards be grown, and *then* return.
19:6☆ [6]¶And when the children of Ammon saw that they had made themselves
odious to David, Ha'nun and the children of Ammon sent a thousand
talents of silver to hire them chariots and horsemen out of Mes-o-po-ta'-
mi-a and out of Syr'i-a-ma'a-chah, and out of Zo'bah.
19:7 Num 21:30 Josh 13:9, 16 [7]So they hired thirty and two thousand chariots, and the king of Ma'a-
chah and his people; who came and pitched before Med'e-ba, And the
children of Ammon gathered themselves together from their cities, and
came to battle.
[8]And when David heard *of it*, he sent Jo'ab, and all the host of the mighty
men.
[9]And the children of Ammon came out, and put the battle in array before
the gate of the city: and the kings that were come *were* by themselves in the
field.
[10]Now when Jo'ab saw that the battle was set against him before and
behind, he chose out of all the choice of Israel, and put *them* in array
against the Syrians.
[11]And the rest of the people he delivered unto the hand of A-bish'a-i his
brother, and they set *themselves* in array against the children of Ammon.
[12]And he said, If the Syrians be too strong for me, then thou shalt help
me: but if the children of Ammon be too strong for thee, then I will help
thee.

18:14 David was not so committed to the expansion of his kingdom that he forgot the home base. He did not neglect the administration of justice for his people. The leader who deals well with his people can sleep comfortably at night.

19:4 David's kindness in sending messengers of comfort was interpreted as an act of aggression, with a view to seizing of Hanun's territory. Good acts can be misunderstood and the hand of friendship can be rebuffed. This should in no way deter the believer from doing right things.

19:6 "The hearts of sinners that are marked for ruin are hardened to their destruction." The children of Ammon attributed to David the kind of evil thoughts they had themselves. They prepared to war against him, "and so brought upon themselves, by David's hand, those desolations which he never intended them."*

13 Be of good courage, and let us behave ourselves valiantly for our
people, and for the cities of our God: and let the LORD do *that which is*
good in his sight.
14 So Jo'ab and the people that *were* with him drew nigh before the **19:14** 2 Sam 10:14
Syrians unto the battle; and they fled before him.
15 And when the children of Ammon saw that the Syrians were fled, they
likewise fled before A-bish'a-i his brother, and entered into the city. Then
Jo'ab came to Jerusalem.
16 ¶And when the Syrians saw that they were put to the worse before **19:16** 2 Sam 10:15, 16
Israel, they sent messengers, and drew forth the Syrians that *were* beyond
the river: and Sho'phach the captain of the host of Had-ar-e'zer *went* before
them.
17 And it was told David; and he gathered all Israel, and passed over
Jordan, and came upon them, and set *the battle* in array against them. So
when David had put the battle in array against the Syrians, they fought
with him.
18 But the Syrians fled before Israel; and David slew of the Syrians seven
thousand *men which fought in* chariots, and forty thousand footmen, and
killed Sho'phach the captain of the host.
19 And when the servants of Had-ar-e'zer saw that they were put to the ☆**19:19**
worse before Israel, they made peace with David, and became his servants:
neither would the Syrians help the children of Ammon any more.

20 AND it came to pass, that after the year was expired, at the time ☆**20:1** 2 Sam 11:1; 12:26
that kings go out *to battle,* Jo'ab led forth the power of the army,
and wasted the country of the children of Ammon, and came and besieged
Rab'bah. But David tarried at Jerusalem. And Jo'ab smote Rab'bah, and
destroyed it.
2 And David took the crown of their king from off his head, and found it ☆**20:2** 2 Sam 12:29, 30
to weigh a talent of gold, and *there were* precious stones in it; and it was set
upon David's head: and he brought also exceeding much spoil out of the
city.
3 And he brought out the people that *were* in it, and cut *them* with saws, ☆**20:3** 2 Sam 12:31
and with harrows of iron, and with axes. Even so dealt David with all the
cities of the children of Ammon. And David and all the people returned to
Jerusalem.
4 ¶And it came to pass after this, that there arose war at Ge'zer with the **20:4** 2 Sam 21:18
Philistines; at which time Sib'be-chai the Hu'shath-ite slew Sip'pai, *that was*
of the children of the giant: and they were subdued.
5 And there was war again with the Philistines; and El-ha'nan the son of **20:5** 1 Sam 17:4–7; 2 Sam 21:19; 1 Chron 11:23
Ja'ir slew Lah'mi the brother of Goliath the Git'tite, whose spear staff *was*
like a weaver's beam.
6 And yet again there was war at Gath, where was a man of *great* stature,
whose fingers and toes *were* four and twenty, six *on each hand,* and six *on
each foot:* and he also was the son of the giant.

19:19 The Ammonites had hired the Syrians to help them against Israel. When David defeated the Syrians, they sought peace and paid tribute. "Those who have meddled with strife that belongs not to them, and have found that they meddled to their own hurt, do well to learn wit at length and meddle no further."*

20:1–3 This segment of the chronicler's history covers the same time span as 2 Sam. 11:1—12:31. The chronicler features the good kings of Judah and says little about the Northern Kingdom except when it impinges on Judah. He also leaves out some material given in 2 Samuel, such as David's adultery with Bathsheba, David's struggle with Saul and his seven-year stay at Hebron, and Solomon's idolatry and punishment. David's disobedience in taking the census and God's chastisement of him are mentioned here. Chronicles pays close attention to the temple, its importance, its personnel, and the rituals. The picture painted is on the positive side rather than the negative.

20:2 *their king,* i.e., "Milcom." See 1 Kings 11:5.

20:3 *with axes,* literally, "he conducted them to the saw." It is uncertain whether this means that he made them labor with saws or that he sawed them to pieces.†

7But when he defied Israel, Jonathan the son of Shim′e-a David's brother
slew him.
8These were born unto the giant in Gath; and they fell by the hand of
David, and by the hand of his servants.

F. DAVID'S SIN OF TAKING A CENSUS
1. The Census

21:1☆ 2 Sam 24:1 **21** AND Satan stood up against Israel, and provoked David to
number Israel.
21:2 1 Chron 27:23, 24 2And David said to Jo′ab and to the rulers of the people, Go, number
Israel from Be′er–she′ba even to Dan; and bring the number of them to me,
that I may know *it.*
21:3 Deut 1:11 3And Jo′ab answered, The LORD make his people an hundred times so
many more as they *be:* but, my lord the king, *are* they not all my lord's
servants? why then doth my lord require this thing? why will he be a cause
of trespass to Israel?
4Nevertheless the king's word prevailed against Jo′ab. Wherefore Jo′ab
departed, and went throughout all Israel, and came to Jerusalem.
21:5 Num 1:17–19 2 Sam 24:9 5¶And Jo′ab gave the sum of the number of the people unto David. And
all *they of* Israel were a thousand thousand and an hundred thousand men
that drew sword: and Judah *was* four hundred threescore and ten thousand
men that drew sword.
21:6 1 Chron 27:24 6But Levi and Benjamin counted he not among them: for the king's word
was abominable to Jo′ab.

2. God Sends the Plague as Punishment

7And God was displeased with this thing; therefore he smote Israel.
21:8 2 Sam 12:13 8And David said unto God, I have sinned greatly, because I have done
this thing: but now, I beseech thee, do away the iniquity of thy servant; for
I have done very foolishly.
21:9 1 Sam 9:9 2 Sam 24:11 1 Chron 29:29 9¶And the LORD spake unto Gad, David's seer, saying,
10Go and tell David, saying, Thus saith the LORD, I offer thee three
things: choose thee one of them, that I may do *it* unto thee.
11So Gad came to David, and said unto him, Thus saith the LORD,
Choose thee
21:12 2 Sam 24:13 12Either three years' famine; or three months to be destroyed before thy
foes, while that the sword of thine enemies overtaketh *thee;* or else three
days the sword of the LORD, even the pestilence, in the land, and the angel
of the LORD destroying throughout all the coasts of Israel. Now therefore
advise thyself what word I shall bring again to him that sent me.
21:13☆ Ps 51:1 130:4, 7 13And David said unto Gad, I am in a great strait: let me fall now into
the hand of the LORD; for very great *are* his mercies: but let me not fall into
the hand of man.
21:14☆ 14¶So the LORD sent pestilence upon Israel: and there fell of Israel
seventy thousand men.

21:1 *Satan* (the Adversary) is mentioned in the Bible by the use of more than thirty different names and titles. Each one speaks about some aspect about him or his work. Among the many names are: (1) the serpent (Gen. 3:4); (2) prince of this world (John 14:30); (3) prince of the devils (Matt. 12:24); (4) the god of this world (2 Cor. 4:4); (5) the tempter (1 Thess. 3:5). See note to 2 Sam. 24:1 where it says God moved David to number the people.

21:13 David confessed his sin, accepted the punishment gracefully, cast himself on the mercy of God, and was greatly concerned that the people had to suffer for his transgression. He knew that the mercy of God is better than the mercilessness of man, should he have chosen devastation by his foes.

21:14 Punishment sometimes affects the innocent as well as the guilty. It also shows something about the unity of a nation. David disobediently numbered the people of Israel. Seventy thousand people perished as a result of one man's act. Perhaps the people of Israel embraced the same spirit of pride exhibited by David, but this is not stated. God's ways are inscrutable, for in war, people who have wanted no war are killed along with its initiators.

15 And God sent an angel unto Jerusalem to destroy it: and as he was
destroying, the LORD beheld, and he repented him of the evil, and said to
the angel that destroyed, It is enough, stay now thine hand. And the angel
of the LORD stood by the threshingfloor of Or′nan the Jeb′u-site.

21:15 Ex 32:14; 1 Sam 15:11; Jonah 3:10

16 And David lifted up his eyes, and saw the angel of the LORD stand
between the earth and the heaven, having a drawn sword in his hand
stretched out over Jerusalem. Then David and the elders *of Israel, who were*
clothed in sackcloth, fell upon their faces.

21:16 1 Kgs 21:27

17 And David said unto God, *Is it* not I *that* commanded the people to be
numbered? even I it is that have sinned and done evil indeed; but *as for*
these sheep, what have they done? let thine hand, I pray thee, O LORD my
God, be on me, and on my father's house; but not on thy people, that they
should be plagued.

21:17 2 Sam 7:8; Ps 74:1

18 ¶Then the angel of the LORD commanded Gad to say to David, that
David should go up, and set up an altar unto the LORD in the threshingfloor
of Or′nan the Jeb′u-site.

21:18 2 Chron 3:1

19 And David went up at the saying of Gad, which he spake in the name
of the LORD.

20 And Or′nan turned back, and saw the angel; and his four sons with him
hid themselves. Now Or′nan was threshing wheat.

21 And as David came to Or′nan, Or′nan looked and saw David, and went
out of the threshingfloor, and bowed himself to David with *his* face to the
ground.

22 Then David said to Or′nan, Grant me the place of *this* threshingfloor,
that I may build an altar therein unto the LORD: thou shalt grant it me for
the full price: that the plague may be stayed from the people.

23 And Or′nan said unto David, Take *it* to thee, and let my lord the king
do *that which is* good in his eyes: lo, I give *thee* the oxen *also* for burnt
offerings, and the threshing instruments for wood, and the wheat for the
meat offering; I give it all.

24 And king David said to Or′nan, Nay; but I will verily buy it for the full
price: for I will not take *that* which *is* thine for the LORD, nor offer burnt
offerings without cost.

21:24 2 Sam 24:24

25 So David gave to Or′nan for the place six hundred shekels of gold by
weight.

☆**21:25**

26 And David built there an altar unto the LORD, and offered burnt
offerings and peace offerings, and called upon the LORD; and he answered
him from heaven by fire upon the altar of burnt offering.

21:26 Lev 9:24; Judg 6:21

27 And the LORD commanded the angel; and he put up his sword again
into the sheath thereof.

28 ¶At that time when David saw that the LORD had answered him in the
threshingfloor of Or′nan the Jeb′u-site, then he sacrificed there.

29 For the tabernacle of the LORD, which Moses made in the wilderness,
and the altar of the burnt offering, *were* at that season in the high place at
Gibeon.

21:29 1 Kgs 3:4; 1 Chron 16:39

30 But David could not go before it to inquire of God: for he was afraid
because of the sword of the angel of the LORD.

21:25 *six hundred shekels of gold by weight,* i.e., "$4,300 in gold."† Compare this with 2 Sam. 24:24, where it is said David paid fifty silver shekels for a threshing floor and oxen. The difference is explained by the fact that six hundred shekels of gold were paid for the entire property (Hebrew *māqōm* or "place"), although the *goren* ("threshing floor") cost only fifty silver shekels. David obviously bought more than the threshing floor, for the temple and other buildings were erected on the site later. All of Mount Moriah must have included considerable land, and with rising real estate values, it must have been well worth six hundred shekels of gold. Ornan's name in 2 Sam. 24 is given as *Araunah,* a name which differs from Ornan by only one or two secondary letters in the Hebrew consonants, probably representing the earlier form.

G. DAVID'S ARRANGEMENTS FOR BUILDING THE TEMPLE
1. Collecting the Construction Materials

22:1☆ 2 Sam 24:18; 1 Chron 21:18; 2 Chron 3:1; 6:5, 6

22 THEN David said, This *is* the house of the LORD God, and this *is* the altar of the burnt offering for Israel.

22:2 1 Kgs 5:17, 18; 9:20, 21; 2 Chron 2:17

[2]And David commanded to gather together the strangers that *were* in the land of Israel; and he set masons to hew wrought stones to build the house of God.

22:3 1 Chron 22:14

[3]And David prepared iron in abundance for the nails for the doors of the gates, and for the joinings; and brass in abundance without weight;

22:4 1 Kgs 5:6

[4]Also cedar trees in abundance: for the Zi-do′ni-ans and they of Tyre brought much cedar wood to David.

22:5 1 Kgs 3:7; 1 Chron 29:1

[5]And David said, Solomon my son *is* young and tender, and the house *that is* to be builded for the LORD *must be* exceeding magnifical, of fame and of glory throughout all countries: I will *therefore* now make preparation for it. So David prepared abundantly before his death.

2. David's Instructions to Solomon

22:6☆

[6]¶Then he called for Solomon his son, and charged him to build an house for the LORD God of Israel.

22:7 2 Sam 7:2, 3; 1 Chron 17:1

[7]And David said to Solomon, My son, as for me, it was in my mind to build an house unto the name of the LORD my God:

22:8 1 Chron 28:3; Acts 7:46

[8]But the word of the LORD came to me, saying, Thou hast shed blood abundantly, and hast made great wars: thou shalt not build an house unto my name, because thou hast shed much blood upon the earth in my sight.

22:9 2 Sam 12:24, 25; 1 Kgs 4:20, 25

[9]Behold, a son shall be born to thee, who shall be a man of rest; and I will give him rest from all his enemies round about: for his name shall be Solomon, and I will give peace and quietness unto Israel in his days.

22:10 2 Sam 12:24, 25; 1 Chron 17:12

[10]He shall build an house for my name; and he shall be my son, and I *will be* his father; and I will establish the throne of his kingdom over Israel for ever.

22:11 1 Chron 22:16

[11]Now, my son, the LORD be with thee; and prosper thou, and build the house of the LORD thy God, as he hath said of thee.

22:12 1 Kgs 3:9; 2 Chron 1:10

[12]Only the LORD give thee wisdom and understanding, and give thee charge concerning Israel, that thou mayest keep the law of the LORD thy God.

22:13☆ 1 Chron 28:7; Josh 1:6

[13]Then shalt thou prosper, if thou takest heed to fulfil the statutes and judgments which the LORD charged Moses with concerning Israel: be strong, and of good courage; dread not, nor be dismayed.

22:14☆ 1 Chron 22:3; 29:4

[14]Now, behold, in my trouble I have prepared for the house of the LORD an hundred thousand talents of gold, and a thousand thousand talents of silver; and of brass and iron without weight; for it is in abundance: timber also and stone have I prepared; and thou mayest add thereto.

22:1 David knew that the altar of burnt offering which was then in Gibeon belonged with the ark of the covenant which was then in Jerusalem. He had enough sense to realize that they belonged together and should not be separated.

22:6 David charged Solomon to build the temple after his decease and began gathering the building materials. This action should have made it obvious to David's other sons that Solomon would succeed him. Apparently this did not deter Adonijah from making an effort to supplant his brother Solomon when David appeared to be getting senile. Adonijah, of course, may have rested his case on the fact that he was the eldest son of [illegible]id at the time of his father's death.

[illegible]avid charged Solomon to keep God's commandments and assured him that he would prosper if he did. This meant failure to do so would result in disaster. Even though Solomon would be king of Israel, he was still the subject of God Almighty. He and any monarch or national leader should always be number 2.

22:14 *an hundred thousand talents of gold, and a thousand thousand (million) talents of silver,* i.e., "several billion dollars worth of gold bullion and millions in silver."† The huge amount of gold has been questioned by some. They suppose that there is a copyist's mistake here so that the figure has been enlarged. We do know, however, that when Jerusalem was sacked in A.D. 70, so much gold was taken that the market price for that metal declined by 50 percent. And

15 Moreover *there are* workmen with thee in abundance, hewers and
workers of stone and timber, and all manner of cunning men for every
manner of work.
16 Of the gold, the silver, and the brass, and the iron, *there is* no number.
Arise *therefore,* and be doing, and the LORD be with thee.

22:16
1 Chron 22:11

3. David Orders the Leaders to Help Solomon

17 ¶David also commanded all the princes of Israel to help Solomon his
son, *saying,*
18 *Is* not the LORD your God with you? and hath he *not* given you rest on
every side? for he hath given the inhabitants of the land into mine hand;
and the land is subdued before the LORD, and before his people.

☆**22:18**
1 Chron 22:9
23:25

19 Now set your heart and your soul to seek the LORD your God; arise
therefore, and build ye the sanctuary of the LORD God, to bring the ark of
the covenant of the LORD, and the holy vessels of God, into the house that
is to be built to the name of the LORD.

22:19
1 Kgs 8:6, 21
1 Chron 28:9
2 Chron 5:7

H. DAVID'S ARRANGEMENTS FOR THE TEMPLE RITES

1. The Grouping of the Levites

23 SO when David was old and full of days, he made Solomon his son
king over Israel.

☆**23:1**
1 Chron 28:5
29:22, 28

2 ¶And he gathered together all the princes of Israel, with the priests and
the Levites.
3 Now the Levites were numbered from the age of thirty years and
upward: and their number by their polls, man by man, was thirty and eight
thousand.

23:3
Num 4:3, 48
1 Chron 23:24

4 Of which, twenty and four thousand *were* to set forward the work of the
house of the LORD; and six thousand *were* officers and judges:
5 Moreover four thousand *were* porters; and four thousand praised the
LORD with the instruments which I made, *said David,* to praise *therewith.*

23:4
1 Chron 15:16
26:29
Ezra 3:8, 9

6 And David divided them into courses among the sons of Levi, *namely,*
Ger'shon, Ko'hath, and Me-ra'ri.

23:6
1 Chron 6:1

7 ¶Of the Ger'shon-ites *were,* La'a-dan, and Shim'e-i.
8 The sons of La'a-dan; the chief *was* Je-hi'el, and Ze'tham, and Jo'el,
three.
9 The sons of Shim'e-i; Shel'o-mith, and Ha'zi-el, and Ha'ran, three.
These *were* the chief of the fathers of La'a-dan.
10 And the sons of Shim'e-i *were,* Ja'hath, Zi'na, and Je'ush, and Be-ri'ah.
These four *were* the sons of Shim'e-i.
11 And Ja'hath was the chief, and Zi'zah the second: but Je'ush and Be-
ri'ah had not many sons; therefore they were in one reckoning, according to
their father's house.
12 ¶The sons of Ko'hath; Amram, Iz'har, Hebron, and Uz'zi-el, four.
13 The sons of Amram; Aaron and Moses: and Aaron was separated, that

23:13
Ex 6:20; 28:1
30:6
Num 3:25–30
26:58, 59

---

when we remember that the amount of gold seized by the Babylonians and carried off to Babylon was great, we cannot simply dismiss the value stated here as though it were impossible for Israel to have accumulated this much of the metal.

22:18 Israel as a kingdom reached its greatest heights under David and Solomon. God fulfilled his word by giving Israel a land, a stable government, and a people. But the favor of God would disappear in a few short centuries because of unbelief and apostasy, and the kingdom would shrivel into nothingness.

23:1 David "made Solomon king, not to reign with him, or reign under him, but only to reign after him."* Was this not a blunder? Had he made Solomon co-regent with him he might have avoided the difficulty which arose with Adonijah, who was the eldest son and who had some right (humanly speaking) to succeed his father. David may have been unfair in not settling the matter before his death. Long before this, he knew that Solomon was to succeed him.

he should sanctify the most holy things, he and his sons for ever, to burn
incense before the LORD, to minister unto him, and to bless in his name for
ever.
23:14 14 Now *concerning* Moses the man of God, his sons were named of the
Deut 32:30 tribe of Levi.
15 The sons of Moses *were,* Ger′shom, and E-li-e′zer.
16 Of the sons of Ger′shom, Sheb′u-el *was* the chief.
17 And the sons of E-li-e′zer *were,* Re-ha-bi′ah the chief. And E-li-e′zer
had none other sons; but the sons of Re-ha-bi′ah were very many.
18 Of the sons of Iz′har; Shel′o-mith the chief.
19 Of the sons of Hebron; Je-ri′ah the first, Am-a-ri′ah the second, Ja-
ha′zi-el the third, and Jek-a-me′am the fourth.
20 Of the sons of Uz′zi-el; Mi′chah the first, and Je-si′ah the second.
23:21 21 ¶The sons of Me-ra′ri; Mah′li, and Mu′shi. The sons of Mah′li; E-le-
1 Chron 6:19–21 a′zar, and Kish.
22 And E-le-a′zar died, and had no sons, but daughters: and their brethren
the sons of Kish took them.
23 The sons of Mu′shi; Mah′li, and E′der, and Jer′e-moth, three.

2. The Ministry of the Levites

23:24☆ 24 ¶These *were* the sons of Levi after the house of their fathers; *even* the
Num 10:17, 21 chief of the fathers, as they were counted by number of names by their
1 Chron 23:3 polls, that did the work for the service of the house of the LORD, from the
age of twenty years and upward.
23:25 25 For David said, The LORD God of Israel hath given rest unto his
1 Chron 22:18 people, that they may dwell in Jerusalem for ever:
23:26☆ 26 And also unto the Levites; they shall no *more* carry the tabernacle, nor
Num 4:5, 15; 7:9 any vessels of it for the service thereof.
27 For by the last words of David the Levites *were* numbered from twenty
years old and above:
28 Because their office *was* to wait on the sons of Aaron for the service of
the house of the LORD, in the courts, and in the chambers, and in the
purifying of all holy things, and the work of the service of the house of
God;
23:29 29 Both for the shewbread, and for the fine flour for meat offering, and for
Lev 6:20, 21; 19:35, 36; 24:5 the unleavened cakes, and for *that which is baked in* the pan, and for that
1 Kgs 7:48 which is fried, and for all manner of measure and size;
1 Chron 9:31 30 And to stand every morning to thank and praise the LORD, and likewise
at even;
23:31 31 And to offer all burnt sacrifices unto the LORD in the sabbaths, in the
Lev 23:2–4; Isa 1:13, 14 new moons, and on the set feasts, by number, according to the order
commanded unto them, continually before the LORD:
23:32 32 And that they should keep the charge of the tabernacle of the
Num 1:53; 3:6, 38 congregation, and the charge of the holy *place,* and the charge of the sons of
1 Chron 9:27 Aaron their brethren, in the service of the house of the LORD.

23:24 In Num. 4:30 we read that the Levites who served and assisted the priests began at age thirty and retired at age fifty. The number of the Israelites had increased and the services of the priests also increased. Here we see that the age of service has been changed to start at twenty years; the retirement age remained the same.

23:26 When the temple was constructed and dedicated, there was no need for anyone to carry the ark, the furniture, etc. These were permanently attached to the temple. David, therefore, made a reassignment for those who had earlier performed these duties. It is interesting to speculate why this was done by David and not by the high priest. It adds to the mystery of the relationship between state and church, then and now.

3. The Grouping of the Priests

24 NOW *these are* the divisions of the sons of Aaron. The sons of **24:1**
Aaron; Na'dab, and A-bi'hu, E-le-a'zar, and Ith'a-mar. Ex 6:23
2 But Na'dab and A-bi'hu died before their father, and had no children: ☆**24:2**
therefore E-le-a'zar and Ith'a-mar executed the priest's office. Lev 10:2
3 And David distributed them, both Za'dok of the sons of E-le-a'zar, and **24:3**
A-him'e-lech of the sons of Ith'a-mar, according to their offices in their 1 Chron 6:8
service.
4 And there were more chief men found of the sons of E-le-a'zar than of
the sons of Ith'a-mar; and *thus* were they divided. Among the sons of E-le-
a'zar *there were* sixteen chief men of the house of *their* fathers, and eight
among the sons of Ith'a-mar according to the house of their fathers.
5 Thus were they divided by lot, one sort with another; for the governors ☆**24:5**
of the sanctuary, and governors *of the house* of God, were of the sons of
E-le-a'zar, and of the sons of Ith'a-mar.
6 And Shem-a-i'ah the son of Ne-than'e-el the scribe, *one* of the Levites, **24:6**
wrote them before the king, and the princes, and Za'dok the priest, and 1 Chron 18:16 24:31
A-him'e-lech the son of A-bi'a-thar, and *before* the chief of the fathers of
the priests and Levites: one principal household being taken for E-le-a'zar,
and *one* taken for Ith'a-mar.
7 Now the first lot came forth to Je-hoi'a-rib, the second to Je-dai'ah, **24:7**
8 The third to Ha'rim, the fourth to Se-o'rim, Neh 12:4 Lk 1:5
9 The fifth to Mal-chi'jah, the sixth to Mij'a-min,
10 The seventh to Hak'koz, the eighth to A-bi'jah,
11 The ninth to Jesh'u-a, the tenth to Shec-a-ni'ah,
12 The eleventh to E-li'a-shib, the twelfth to Ja'kim,
13 The thirteenth to Hup'pah, the fourteenth to Je-sheb'e-ab,
14 The fifteenth to Bil'gah, the sixteenth to Im'mer,
15 The seventeenth to He'zir, the eighteenth to Aph'ses,
16 The nineteenth to Peth-a-hi'ah, the twentieth to Je-hez'e-kel,
17 The one and twentieth to Ja'chin, the two and twentieth to Ga'mul,
18 The three and twentieth to Del-a-i'ah, the four and twentieth to Ma-a-
zi'ah.
19 These *were* the orderings of them in their service to come into the house ☆**24:19**
of the LORD, according to their manner, under Aaron their father, as the 1 Chron 9:25
LORD God of Israel had commanded him.
20 ¶And the rest of the sons of Levi *were these:* Of the sons of Amram;
Shu'ba-el: of the sons of Shu'ba-el; Jeh-dei'ah.
21 Concerning Re-ha-bi'ah: of the sons of Re-ha-bi'ah, the first *was* Is-
shi'ah.
22 Of the Iz'har-ites; Shel'o-moth: of the sons of Shel'o-moth; Ja'hath.
23 And the sons *of Hebron;* Je-ri'ah *the first,* Am-a-ri'ah the second, Ja- **24:23**
ha'zi-el the third, Jek-a-me'am the fourth. 1 Chron 23:19
24 *Of* the sons of Uz'zi-el; Mi'chah: of the sons of Mi'chah; Sha'mir.
25 The brother of Mi'chah *was* Is-shi'ah: of the sons of Is-shi'ah; Zech-a-
ri'ah.

24:2 See notes on Lev. 10:1 and 10:16 for the sin of Nadab and Abihu and God's warning to his brothers.
24:5 The lot was cast publicly and with great solemnity in the presence of the king, the priests, and the princes. This was to guarantee against fraud. The lot was an appeal to God for his will. Matthias, for example, was chosen by lot (Acts 1:24, 26). There may be times today when the lot is necessary, remembering that "The lot is cast into the lap; but the whole disposing thereof is of the LORD" (Prov. 16:33).
24:19 The casting of the lot had nothing to do with procedure or duty. These things had been decided by Aaron on the command from God long before this event took place. The only question here was who was to perform the duties.

26 The sons of Me-ra′ri *were* Mah′li and Mu′shi: the sons of Ja-a-zi′ah;
Be′no.
27 ¶The sons of Me-ra′ri by Ja-a-zi′ah; Be′no, and Sho′ham, and Zac′cur,
and Ib′ri.
28 Of Mah′li *came* E-le-a′zar, who had no sons.
29 Concerning Kish: the son of Kish *was* Je-rah′me-el.
30 The sons also of Mu′shi; Mah′li, and E′der, and Jer′i-moth. These *were*
the sons of the Levites after the house of their fathers.
24:31☆ 31 These likewise cast lots over against their brethren the sons of Aaron in
1 Chron 24:5, 6 the presence of David the king, and Za′dok, and A-him′e-lech, and the chief
of the fathers of the priests and Levites, even the principal fathers over
against their younger brethren.

4. The Arrangements for the Music

25:1☆ 25 MOREOVER David and the captains of the host separated to the
2 Kgs 3:15 service of the sons of A′saph, and of He′man, and of Jed′u-thun,
1 Chron 6:33, 39; 15:16 who should prophesy with harps, with psalteries, and with cymbals: and the
number of the workmen according to their service was:
25:2☆ 2 Of the sons of A′saph; Zac′cur, and Joseph, and Neth-a-ni′ah, and As-
a-re′lah, the sons of A′saph under the hands of A′saph, which prophesied
according to the order of the king.
25:3☆ 3 Of Jed′u-thun: the sons of Jed′u-thun; Ged-a-li′ah, and Ze′ri, and Je-
1 Chron 16:41, 42 shai′ah, Hash-a-bi′ah, and Mat-ti-thi′ah, six, under the hands of their father
Jed′u-thun, who prophesied with a harp, to give thanks and to praise the
LORD.
25:4 4 Of He′man: the sons of He′man; Buk-ki′ah, Mat-ta-ni′ah, Uz′zi-el,
2 Sam 24:11 Sheb′u-el, and Jer′i-moth, Han-a-ni′ah, Ha-na′ni, E-li′a-thah, Gid-dal′ti,
1 Chron 21:9 and Ro-mam′ti-e′zer, Josh-bek′a-shah, Mal′lo-thi, Ho′thir, *and* Ma-ha′zi-
oth:
5 All these *were* the sons of He′man the king's seer in the words of God, to
lift up the horn. And God gave to He′man fourteen sons and three
daughters.
25:6☆ 6 All these *were* under the hands of their father for song *in* the house of
1 Chron 15:16, 19; 23:5 the LORD, with cymbals, psalteries, and harps, for the service of the house
of God, according to the king's order to A′saph, Jed′u-thun, and He′man.
7 So the number of them, with their brethren that were instructed in the
songs of the LORD, *even* all that were cunning, was two hundred fourscore
and eight.
25:8☆ 8 ¶And they cast lots, ward against *ward,* as well the small as the great, the
1 Chron 26:13 teacher as the scholar.

24:31 The procedure for the casting of the lot is again stated. The public nature of the act and who was present guaranteed objectivity. There could be no collusion.

25:1–3 Singing praises to God is here called *prophesying.* This does not mean that all who performed this function could fortell the future or had special visions from God. Perhaps this is what Paul intended in 1 Cor. 11:4 and 14:24.

25:3 The purpose of singing was to praise God. The use of instruments such as harps and cymbals was for a similar purpose. Here, at least, music was for sacred purposes. This does not mean that music for entertainment is wrong; but it should be free from immorality and profanity—i.e., anything that would violate the law of God.

25:6 Singing and instrumental music were under the oversight of the fathers whose children were gifted by the Spirit and had a function to fulfill. This suggests the children were skilled in these arts and that such skill was due in part to constant practice with a view to perfection. If God is worthy of being praised by instrument and song, the best is none too good for him. But God is pleased with the intention when the gift is not given. Those who cannot sing well are loved by God for their effort, not for their talent.

25:8 This verse is better translated: "And they cast lots for their duties, all alike, the small as well as the great, the teacher as well as the pupil." There were 228 teachers (25:7). The students numbered four thousand according to 23:5. The twenty-four groups matched the twenty-four courses of priests.

[9]Now the first lot came forth for A'saph to Joseph: the second to Ged-a-
li'ah, who with his brethren and sons *were* twelve:
[10]The third to Zac'cur, *he,* his sons, and his brethren, *were* twelve:
[11]The fourth to Iz'ri, *he,* his sons, and his brethren, *were* twelve:
[12]The fifth to Neth-a-ni'ah, *he,* his sons, and his brethren, *were* twelve:
[13]The sixth to Buk-ki'ah, *he,* his sons, and his brethren, *were* twelve:
[14]The seventh to Je-shar'e-lah, *he,* his sons, and his brethren, *were* twelve:
[15]The eighth to Je-shai'ah, *he,* his sons, and his brethren, *were* twelve:
[16]The ninth to Mat-ta-ni'ah, *he,* his sons, and his brethren, *were* twelve:
[17]The tenth to Shim'e-i, *he,* his sons, and his brethren, *were* twelve:
[18]The eleventh to A-zar'e-el, *he,* his sons, and his brethren, *were* twelve:
[19]The twelfth to Hash-a-bi'ah, *he,* his sons, and his brethren, *were* twelve:
[20]The thirteenth to Shu'ba-el, *he,* his sons, and his brethren, *were* twelve:
[21]The fourteenth to Mat-ti-thi'ah, *he,* his sons, and his brethren, *were*
twelve:
[22]The fifteenth to Jer'e-moth, *he,* his sons, and his brethren, *were* twelve:
[23]The sixteenth to Han-a-ni'ah, *he,* his sons, and his brethren, *were*
twelve:
[24]The seventeenth to Josh-bek'a-shah, *he,* his sons, and his brethren, *were*
twelve:
[25]The eighteenth to Ha-na'ni, *he,* his sons, and his brethren, *were* twelve:
[26]The nineteenth to Mal'lo-thi, *he,* his sons, and his brethren, *were*
twelve:
[27]The twentieth to E-li'a-thah, *he,* his sons, and his brethren, *were* twelve:
[28]The one and twentieth to Ho'thir, *he,* his sons, and his brethren, *were*
twelve:
[29]The two and twentieth to Gid-dal'ti, *he,* his sons, and his brethren, *were*
twelve:
[30]The three and twentieth to Ma-ha'zi-oth, *he,* his sons, and his brethren,
were twelve:
[31]The four and twentieth to Ro-mam'ti–e'zer, *he,* his sons, and his
brethren, *were* twelve.

5. The Divisions of the Temple Guards

26 CONCERNING the divisions of the porters: Of the Kor'hites *was* ☆26:1
Me-shel-e-mi'ah the son of Ko're, of the sons of A'saph.
[2]And the sons of Me-shel-e-mi'ah *were,* Zech-a-ri'ah the firstborn, Je-
di'a-el the second, Zeb-a-di'ah the third, Jath'ni-el the fourth,
[3]E'lam the fifth, Je-ho-ha'nan the sixth, E-li-o-e'na-i the seventh.
[4]Moreover the sons of O'bed–e'dom *were,* Shem-a-i'ah the firstborn, Je-
hoz'a-bad the second, Jo'ah the third, and Sa'car the fourth, and Ne-than'e-
el the fifth,
[5]Am'mi-el the sixth, Is'sa-char the seventh, Pe-ul'thai the eighth: for God
blessed him.
[6]Also unto Shem-a-i'ah his son were sons born, that ruled throughout the ☆26:6ff
house of their father: for they *were* mighty men of valour.
[7]The sons of Shem-a-i'ah; Oth'ni, and Re'pha-el and O'bed, El'za-bad,
whose brethren *were* strong men, E-li'hu, and Sem-a-chi'ah.

26:1 The porters attended to certain duties pertaining to the temple. They guarded the avenues that led to it; they opened and shut the outer gates; they were charged to keep decorum among the worshippers; they turned back those who were unclean; and they guarded against thieves and any enemies.

26:6ff Some of the people named here are marked out as having special gifts and attributes. There are mighty men of valor, strong men, able men and even a wise counsellor. When God calls men, he either chooses them because they are fit or he makes them so.

8 All these of the sons of O'bed–e'dom: they and their sons and their
brethren, able men for strength for the service, *were* threescore and two of
O'bed–e'dom.
9 And Me-shel-e-mi'ah had sons and brethren, strong men, eighteen.
26:10☆ 1 Chron 16:38 10 Also Ho'sah, of the children of Me-ra'ri, had sons; Sim'ri the chief, (for
though he was not the firstborn, yet his father made him the chief;)
11 Hil-ki'ah the second, Teb-a-li'ah the third, Zech-a-ri'ah the fourth: all
the sons and brethren of Ho'sah *were* thirteen.
12 Among these *were* the divisions of the porters, *even* among the chief
men, *having* wards one against another, to minister in the house of the
LORD.
26:13 1 Chron 24:5, 31; 25:8 13 ¶And they cast lots, as well the small as the great, according to the
house of their fathers, for every gate.
14 And the lot eastward fell to Shel-e-mi'ah. Then for Zech-a-ri'ah his son,
a wise counsellor, they cast lots; and his lot came out northward.
15 To O'bed–e'dom southward; and to his sons the house of A-sup'pim.
16 To Shup'pim and Ho'sah *the lot came forth* westward, with the gate
Shal'le-cheth, by the causeway of the going up, ward against ward.
17 Eastward *were* six Levites, northward four a day, southward four a day,
and toward A-sup'pim two *and* two.
18 At Par'bar westward, four at the causeway, *and* two at Par'bar.
19 These *are* the divisions of the porters among the sons of Ko're, and
among the sons of Me-ra'ri.

6. The Oversight of the Treasury

26:20☆ 1 Chron 26:22, 24 20 ¶And of the Le'vites, A-hi'jah *was* over the treasures of the house of
God, and over the treasures of the dedicated things.
21 *As concerning* the sons of La'a-dan; the sons of the Ger'shon-ite La'a-
dan, chief fathers, *even* of La'a-dan the Ger'shon-ite, *were* Je-hi'e-li.
22 The sons of Je-hi'e-li; Ze'tham, and Jo'el his brother, *which were* over
the treasures of the house of the LORD.
23 Of the Amramites, *and* the Iz'har-ites, the Hebronites, *and* the Uz'zi-el-
ites:
24 And Sheb'u-el the son of Ger'shom, the son of Moses, *was* ruler of the
treasures.
25 And his brethren by E-li-e'zer; Re-ha-bi'ah his son, and Je-shai'ah his
son, and Joram his son, and Zich'ri his son, and Shel'o-mith his son.
26 Which Shel'o-mith and his brethren *were* over all the treasures of the
dedicated things, which David the king, and the chief fathers, the captains
over thousands and hundreds, and the captains of the host, had dedicated.
27 Out of the spoils won in battles did they dedicate to maintain the house
of the LORD.
28 And all that Samuel the seer, and Saul the son of Kish, and Abner the
son of Ner, and Jo'ab the son of Zer-u-i'ah, had dedicated; *and* whosoever
had dedicated *any thing, it was* under the hand of Shel'o-mith, and of his
brethren.

26:10 Simri was elevated above the firstborn (i.e., he was made chief) either because he enjoyed special excellence or the firstborn was very weak. This decision did not pertain to the inheritance rights of the firstborn but only to his service for God, which called for special personal qualifications.

26:20 The treasures of the house of God included such things as flour, wine, oil, salt, fuel, lamps, sacred vestments, and utensils. Money, that is, silver and gold, would have been among the treasures that called for a keeper. The spoils from David's wars were given by him to the temple. What they were is not mentioned specifically.

7. The Public Administrators and Judges

29 ¶Of the Iz'har-ites, Chen-a-ni'ah and his sons *were* for the outward
business over Israel, for officers and judges.

☆26:29 1 Chron 23:4

30 *And* of the Hebronites, Hash-a-bi'ah and his brethren, men of valour, a
thousand and seven hundred, *were* officers among them of Israel on this
side Jordan westward in all the business of the LORD, and in the service of
the king.

26:30 1 Chron 27:17

31 Among the Hebronites *was* Je-ri'jah the chief, *even* among the Hebron-
ites, according to the generations of his fathers. In the fortieth year of the
reign of David they were sought for, and there were found among them
mighty men of valour at Ja'zer of Gilead.

26:31 1 Chron 19:11 23:19

32 And his brethren, men of valour, *were* two thousand and seven hundred
chief fathers, whom king David made rulers over the Reubenites, the
Gadites, and the half tribe of Ma-nas'seh, for every matter pertaining to
God, and affairs of the king.

I. THE ARRANGEMENTS FOR THE ISRAELI ARMY

27 NOW the children of Israel after their number, *to wit,* the chief
fathers and captains of thousands and hundreds, and their officers
that served the king in any matter of the courses, which came in and went
out month by month throughout all the months of the year, of every course
were twenty and four thousand.

☆27:1

2 Over the first course for the first month *was* Ja-sho'be-am the son of
Zab'di-el: and in his course *were* twenty and four thousand.

27:2 2 Sam 23:8 1 Chron 11:11

3 Of the children of Pe'rez *was* the chief of all the captains of the host for
the first month.
4 And over the course of the second month *was* Do'da-i an A-ho'hite, and
of his course *was* Mik'loth also the ruler: in his course likewise *were* twenty
and four thousand.
5 The third captain of the host for the third month *was* Be-nai'ah the son
of Je-hoi'a-da, a chief priest: and in his course *were* twenty and four
thousand.
6 This *is that* Be-nai'ah, *who was* mighty *among* the thirty, and above the
thirty: and in his course *was* Am-miz'a-bad his son.
7 The fourth *captain* for the fourth month *was* As'a-hel the brother of
Jo'ab, and Zeb-a-di'ah his son after him: and in his course *were* twenty and
four thousand.
8 The fifth captain for the fifth month *was* Sham'huth the Iz'ra-hite: and
in his course *were* twenty and four thousand.
9 The sixth *captain* for the sixth month *was* I'ra the son of Ik'kesh the Te-
ko'ite: and in his course *were* twenty and four thousand.
10 The seventh *captain* for the seventh month *was* He'lez the Pel'o-nite, of
the children of E'phra-im: and in his course *were* twenty and four thousand.
11 The eighth *captain* for the eighth month *was* Sib'be-cai the Hu'shath-ite,
of the Zar'hites: and in his course *were* twenty and four thousand.

26:29 Some of the Levites were employed in the affairs of government, with no responsibilities at the temple. They were ministers of justice in the civil realm, caring for God's tithes, the king's tax money, and the affairs of the nation. They served the nation in secular matters and also in religious matters having to do with such things as idolatry and the like.

27:1 King David maintained a standing army and had control over the military operations of the nation. The military was divided into courses, as were the priests. This made their support less burdensome. The whole number of those under arms totaled 288,000. There were various divisions among the soldiers similar to those of armies in our day. The captains might be considered as being equivalent to the generals in our armies today.

12 The ninth *captain* for the ninth month *was* A-bi-e'zer the An'e-toth-ite,
of the Benjamites: and in his course *were* twenty and four thousand.
13 The tenth *captain* for the tenth month *was* Ma-har'a-i the Ne-toph'a-
thite, of the Zar'hites: and in his course *were* twenty and four thousand.
14 The eleventh *captain* for the eleventh month *was* Be-nai'ah the Pir'a-
thon-ite, of the children of E'phra-im: and in his course *were* twenty and
four thousand.
15 The twelfth *captain* for the twelfth month *was* Hel'da-i the Ne-toph'a-
thite, of Oth'ni-el: and in his course *were* twenty and four thousand.

27:16☆ 1 Chron 28:1

16 ¶Furthermore over the tribes of Israel: the ruler of the Reubenites *was*
E-li-e'zer the son of Zich'ri: of the Simeonites, Sheph-a-ti'ah the son of
Ma'a-chah:
17 Of the Levites, Hash-a-bi'ah the son of Ke-mu'el: of the Aaronites,
Za'dok:
18 Of Judah, E-li'hu, *one* of the brethren of David: of Is'sa-char, Omri the
son of Michael:
19 Of Zeb'u-lun, Ish-ma-i'ah the son of O-ba-di'ah: of Naph'ta-li, Jer'i-
moth the son of Az'ri-el:
20 Of the children of E'phra-im, Ho-she'a the son of Az-a-zi'ah: of the half
tribe of Ma-nas'seh, Jo'el the son of Pe-dai'ah:
21 Of the half *tribe* of Ma-nas'seh in Gilead, Id'do the son of Zech-a-ri'ah:
of Benjamin, Ja-a'si-el the son of Abner:
22 Of Dan, A-zar'e-el the son of Jer'o-ham. These were the princes of the
tribes of Israel.

27:23 Gen 15:5; Num 1:17–19; 2 Sam 24:1

23 ¶But David took not the number of them from twenty years old and
under: because the LORD had said he would increase Israel like to the stars
of the heavens.

27:24 2 Sam 24:12; 1 Chron 21:1

24 Jo'ab the son of Zer-u-i'ah began to number, but he finished not,
because there fell wrath for it against Israel; neither was the number put in
the account of the chronicles of king David.

27:25☆

25 ¶And over the king's treasures *was* Az'ma-veth the son of A'di-el: and
over the storehouses in the fields, in the cities, and in the villages, and in the
castles, *was* Je-hon'a-than the son of Uz-zi'ah:
26 And over them that did the work of the field for tillage of the ground
was Ez'ri the son of Che'lub:
27 And over the vineyards *was* Shim'e-i the Ra'math-ite: over the increase
of the vineyards for the wine cellars *was* Zab'di the Shiph'mite:

27:28 1 Kgs 10:27; 2 Chron 1:15

28 And over the olive trees and the sycomore trees that *were* in the low
plains *was* Ba'al-ha'nan the Ged'e-rite: and over the cellars of oil *was*
Jo'ash:

27:29 1 Chron 5:16

29 And over the herds that fed in Shar'on *was* Shit'ra-i the Shar'on-ite:
and over the herds *that were* in the valleys *was* Sha'phat the son of Ad'la-i:
30 Over the camels also *was* O'bil the Ish'ma-el-ite: and over the asses *was*
Jeh-dei'ah the Me-ron'o-thite:

27:31 1 Chron 5:10

31 And over the flocks *was* Ja'ziz the Ha'ger-ite. All these *were* the rulers of
the substance which *was* king David's.
32 Also Jonathan David's uncle was a counsellor, a wise man, and a
scribe: and Je-hi'el the son of Hach'mo-ni *was* with the king's sons:

27:16 There were rulers over the tribes of Israel. Once the monarchy was established, their role was a lesser one than when there was no king. These leaders might be considered as governors under the supreme head, the king.

27:25 Beginning here we learn that King David's large possessions were managed by subordinates who oversaw those possessions. These served the king himself rather than the nation.

33 And A-hith'o-phel *was* the king's counsellor: and Hu'shai the Ar'chite
was the king's companion:

27:33 2 Sam 15:12, 32, 37

34 And after A-hith'o-phel *was* Je-hoi'a-da the son of Be-nai'ah,
and A-bi'a-thar: and the general of the king's army *was* Jo'ab.

27:34 Kgs 1:7; 1 Chron 11:6; 27:5

J. DAVID'S FINAL INSTRUCTIONS AND DEATH
1. The Leaders Commanded to Aid Solomon

28 AND David assembled all the princes of Israel, the princes of the
tribes, and the captains of the companies that ministered to the
king by course, and the captains over the thousands, and captains over
the hundreds, and the stewards over all the substance and possession of the
king, and of his sons, with the officers, and with the mighty men, and with
all the valiant men, unto Jerusalem.

☆28:1 1 Chron 11:10; 23:2; 27:1

2 Then David the king stood up upon his feet, and said, Hear me, my
brethren, and my people: *As for me,* I *had* in mine heart to build an house
of rest for the ark of the covenant of the LORD, and for the footstool of our
God, and had made ready for the building:

28:2 1 Chron 17:1, 2; Ps 132:7; Isa 66:1

3 But God said unto me, Thou shalt not build an house for my name,
because thou *hast been* a man of war, and hast shed blood.

28:3 1 Chron 17:4; 22:8; Acts 7:46, 47

4 Howbeit the LORD God of Israel chose me before all the house of my
father to be king over Israel for ever: for he hath chosen Judah *to be* the
ruler; and of the house of Judah, the house of my father; and among the
sons of my father he liked me to make *me* king over all Israel:

28:4 Gen 49:8; 1 Sam 16:1, 6; 1 Chron 5:2; 17:23, 27

5 And of all my sons, (for the LORD hath given me many sons,) he hath
chosen Solomon my son to sit upon the throne of the kingdom of the LORD
over Israel.

28:5 1 Chron 3:1; 14:3; 22:9, 10

6 And he said unto me, Solomon thy son, he shall build my house and my
courts: for I have chosen him *to be* my son, and I will be his father.

☆28:6 2 Sam 7:13, 14

7 Moreover I will establish his kingdom for ever, if he be constant to do
my commandments and my judgments, as at this day.

28:7 1 Chron 22:13

2. David's Last Words to Solomon

8 Now therefore in the sight of all Israel the congregation of the LORD,
and in the audience of our God, keep and seek for all the commandments
of the LORD your God: that ye may possess this good land, and leave *it* for
an inheritance for your children after you for ever.

9 ¶And thou, Solomon my son, know thou the God of thy father, and
serve him with a perfect heart and with a willing mind: for the LORD
searcheth all hearts, and understandeth all the imaginations of the
thoughts: if thou seek him, he will be found of thee; but if thou forsake
him, he will cast thee off for ever.

☆28:9 1 Sam 17:7; 1 Kgs 8:61; 1 Chron 29:17; 2 Chron 15:2; Jer 29:13

10 Take heed now; for the LORD hath chosen thee to build an house for
the sanctuary: be strong, and do *it.*

☆28:10 1 Chron 22:13

28:1 Whatever may have been the indisposition of David when his body gave no heat and the young virgin was brought to him, he is very much in charge of matters as the time of death approaches. He gathers a large crowd of the leaders of the nation to spell out for them what the future would be upon his decease.

28:6 David had many sons. But it was God himself who determined who would succeed him. Solomon was David's choice because he was God's choice. The choice was not based on primogeniture. It was worth, not age, that brought Solomon to the throne.

28:9, 10 David publicly presented his successor to the leadership of the nation and did so by committing him to God and charging him to know God and obey him in all things. "We cannot serve God aright if we do not know him; and in vain do we know him if we do not serve him, serve him with heart and mind."* Since God knows the hearts, he cannot be fooled by pretense. Moreover, David commanded Solomon to build the house for God that he wanted to erect but was forbidden to do so.

28:11 Ex 25:17, 40 11¶Then David gave to Solomon his son the pattern of the porch, and of
the houses thereof, and of the treasuries thereof, and of the upper chambers
thereof, and of the inner parlours thereof, and of the place of the mercy
seat,
28:12 1 Chron 26:20, 28 12And the pattern of all that he had by the spirit, of the courts of the
house of the LORD, and of all the chambers round about, of the treasuries
of the house of God, and of the treasuries of the dedicated things:
28:13 1 Chron 23:6 24:1 13Also for the courses of the priests and the Levites, and for all the work
of the service of the house of the LORD, and for all the vessels of service in
the house of the LORD.
14*He gave* of gold by weight for *things* of gold, for all instruments of all
manner of service; *silver also* for all instruments of silver by weight, for all
instruments of every kind of service:
28:15 Ex 25:31 15Even the weight for the candlesticks of gold, and for their lamps of
gold, by weight for every candlestick, and for the lamps thereof: and for the
candlesticks of silver by weight, *both* for the candlestick, and *also* for the
lamps thereof, according to the use of every candlestick.
16And by weight *he gave* gold for the tables of shewbread, for every table;
and *likewise* silver for the tables of silver:
17Also pure gold for the fleshhooks, and the bowls, and the cups: and for
the golden basons *he gave gold* by weight for every bason; and *likewise silver*
by weight for every bason of silver:
28:18 Ex 25:18; 30:1 18And for the altar of incense refined gold by weight; and gold for the
pattern of the chariot of the cherubims, that spread out *their wings,* and
covered the ark of the covenant of the LORD.
28:19☆ 1 Chron 28:11, 12 19All *this, said David,* the LORD made me understand in writing by *his*
hand upon me, *even* all the works of this pattern.
28:20☆ Josh 1:5 1 Sam 20:13 1 Kgs 1:37 1 Chron 22:13 Heb 13:5 20And David said to Solomon his son, Be strong and of good courage,
and do *it:* fear not, nor be dismayed: for the LORD God, *even* my God, *will
be* with thee; he will not fail thee, nor forsake thee, until thou hast finished
all the work for the service of the house of the LORD.
28:21 Ex 35:25 36:1, 2 21And, behold, the courses of the priests and the Levites, *even they shall
be with thee* for all the service of the house of God: and *there shall be* with
thee for all manner of workmanship every willing skilful man, for any
manner of service: also the princes and all the people *will be* wholly at thy
commandment.

3. David's Plea for Funds for the Temple

29:1☆ 1 Chron 22:5 29 FURTHERMORE David the king said unto all the congregation,
Solomon my son, whom alone God hath chosen, *is yet* young and
tender, and the work *is* great: for the palace *is* not for man, but for the
LORD God.
29:2 1 Chron 22:3 2Now I have prepared with all my might for the house of my God the
gold for *things to be made* of gold, and the silver for *things* of silver, and the

28:19 David here claims that the plan for the temple had come directly from God to him. As he wrote down the instructions for Solomon to follow, they were written under the aegis of God in much the same way God supervised the giving of his own words to Moses and the prophets.

28:20 The "fear not, be not dismayed, God is with you, he will not fail you" promise can be found everywhere in Scripture, Old and New Testament alike. The God of David is our God today, and the conditional promise remains forever true. It is based on the requirement that if we obey his commandments, the blessings will follow.

29:1 David here calls the temple of God the *palace* of God. The Hebrew word for palace is *birah* and usually refers to the house of a king, as in Esther and Daniel. The word for temple is *hekal.* As for David, the building would be the temple of God and also the palace of God, for God has a kingdom over which he rules and the ruler of a kingdom has a royal residence.

brass for *things* of brass, the iron for *things* of iron, and wood for *things* of
wood; onyx stones, and *stones* to be set, glistering stones, and of divers
colours, and all manner of precious stones, and marble stones in abun-
dance.
3 Moreover, because I have set my affection to the house of my God, I
have of mine own proper good, of gold and silver, *which* I have given to the
house of my God, over and above all that I have prepared for the holy
house,
4 *Even* three thousand talents of gold, of the gold of O'phir, and seven
thousand talents of refined silver, to overlay the walls of the houses *withal:*

29:4 1 Kgs 9:28; 1 Chron 22:14

5 The gold for *things* of gold, and the silver for *things* of silver, and for all
manner of work *to be made* by the hands of artificers. And who *then* is
willing to consecrate his service this day unto the LORD?
6 ¶Then the chief of the fathers and princes of the tribes of Israel, and the
captains of thousands and of hundreds, with the rulers of the king's work,
offered willingly,

☆**29:6** 1 Chron 27:1, 25; 28:1

7 And gave for the service of the house of God of gold five thousand
talents and ten thousand drams, and of silver ten thousand talents, and of
brass eighteen thousand talents, and one hundred thousand talents of iron.

☆**29:7**

8 And they with whom *precious* stones were found gave *them* to the
treasure of the house of the LORD, by the hand of Je-hi'el the Ger'shon-ite.

29:8 1 Chron 23:8

9 Then the people rejoiced, for that they offered willingly, because with
perfect heart they offered willingly to the LORD: and David the king also
rejoiced with great joy.

29:9 1 Kgs 8:61; 2 Cor 9:7

4. David's Prayer of Praise to God

10 ¶Wherefore David blessed the LORD before all the congregation: and
David said, Blessed *be* thou, LORD God of Israel our father, for ever and
ever.
11 Thine, O LORD, *is* the greatness, and the power, and the glory, and the
victory, and the majesty: for all *that is* in the heaven and in the earth *is*
thine; thine *is* the kingdom, O LORD, and thou art exalted as head above all.

29:11 Rev 5:13

12 Both riches and honour *come* of thee, and thou reignest over all; and in
thine hand *is* power and might; and in thine hand *it is* to make great, and
to give strength unto all.

29:12 2 Chron 1:12; 20:6

13 Now therefore, our God, we thank thee, and praise thy glorious name.
14 But who *am* I, and what *is* my people, that we should be able to offer so
willingly after this sort? for all things *come* of thee, and of thine own have
we given thee.

☆**29:14**

15 For we *are* strangers before thee, and sojourners, as *were* all our fathers:
our days on the earth *are* as a shadow, and *there is* none abiding.

29:15 Lev 25:23; Job 14:2, 10

16 O LORD our God, all this store that we have prepared to build thee an
house for thine holy name *cometh* of thine hand, and *is* all thine own.
17 I know also, my God, that thou triest the heart, and hast pleasure in
uprightness. As for me, in the uprightness of mine heart I have willingly

29:17 1 Chron 28:9

29:6 The temple of God must not be built by tax money. It must come from the hearts of God's people—thus the free-will offerings. The free-will gifts were occasion for rejoicing by both king and people. In present-day giving, there rarely is a lack of money, only a lack of desire.

29:7 *drams,* i.e., "ten thousand darics of gold." A daric was a Persian coin of that day.

29:14 David knew that God was the source of all things, including his wealth and his kingship. What he gave back to God by way of gifts was God's to begin with. Thus David and all of God's people are only stewards of God's possessions, which are loaned to us and for which we will be held responsible before the judgment seat of Christ at the end of the age. We came into the world with nothing and we go out the way we came in—with nothing, save the treasure we have laid up in heaven.

offered all these things: and now have I seen with joy thy people, which are
present here, to offer willingly unto thee.
29:18 1 Kgs 18:36
18 O LORD God of Abraham, Isaac, and of Israel, our fathers, keep this
for ever in the imagination of the thoughts of the heart of thy people, and
prepare their heart unto thee:
29:19 1 Chron 28:9 Ps 72:1
19 And give unto Solomon my son a perfect heart, to keep thy command-
ments, thy testimonies, and thy statutes, and to do all *these things,* and to
build the palace, *for* the which I have made provision.
29:20 Josh 22:33
20 ¶And David said to all the congregation, Now bless the LORD your
God. And all the congregation blessed the LORD God of their fathers, and
bowed down their heads, and worshipped the LORD, and the king.
29:21 1 Kgs 8:62, 63
21 And they sacrificed sacrifices unto the LORD, and offered burnt
offerings unto the LORD, on the morrow after that day, *even* a thousand
bullocks, a thousand rams, *and* a thousand lambs, with their drink
offerings, and sacrifices in abundance for all Israel:

5. The Second Crowning of Solomon

29:22☆ 1 Kgs 1:33 1 Chron 29:1
22 And did eat and drink before the LORD on that day with great gladness.
And they made Solomon the son of David king the second time, and
anointed *him* unto the LORD *to be* the chief governor, and Za'dok *to be*
priest.
23 Then Solomon sat on the throne of the LORD as king instead of David
his father, and prospered; and all Israel obeyed him.
29:24☆
24 And all the princes, and the mighty men, and all the sons likewise of
king David, submitted themselves unto Solomon the king.
29:25 1 Kgs 3:13 2 Chron 1:1, 12
25 And the LORD magnified Solomon exceedingly in the sight of all Israel,
and bestowed upon him *such* royal majesty as had not been on any king
before him in Israel.

6. The Death of King David

29:26 2 Sam 5:4, 5 1 Kgs 2:11 1 Chron 18:14
26 ¶Thus David the son of Jesse reigned over all Israel.
27 And the time that he reigned over Israel *was* forty years; seven years
reigned he in Hebron, and thirty and three *years* reigned he in Jerusalem.
29:28 Gen 15:15 1 Chron 23:1 Acts 13:36
28 And he died in a good old age, full of days, riches, and honour: and
Solomon his son reigned in his stead.
29:29☆ 1 Sam 9:9; 22:5 2 Sam 7:2 12:1
29 Now the acts of David the king, first and last, behold, they *are* written
in the book of Samuel the seer, and in the book of Nathan the prophet, and
in the book of Gad the seer,
30 With all his reign and his might, and the times that went over him, and
over Israel, and over all the kingdoms of the countries.

29:22 *Solomon . . . the second time,* i.e., "and they installed him as co-regent" (with the elderly and soon-to-die King David).†

29:24 God moved the hearts of David's other sons to accept Solomon as king. They gave their oaths of allegiance by the traditional manner of putting the hand under the thigh when taking an oath. The chronicler did not mention the incident involving Adonijah and Abishag (See 1 Kings 1 and 2). Adonijah must have taken the oath with mental reservations, as is betrayed by his later actions.

29:29 *the book of Samuel the seer* evidently refers to the two books of Samuel. The chronicler was selective in what he reported and did not include some of the materials contained in the book of Samuel. In Chronicles there is no treatment of the plots and counterplots for the kingship at the time of David's death. The writer assumed that the reader would be familiar with the book of Samuel.

2 CHRONICLES

III. THE REIGN OF SOLOMON (1:1—9:31)

A. THE WEALTH AND WISDOM OF KING SOLOMON

1 AND Solomon the son of David was strengthened in his kingdom, and ☆1:1 1 Kgs 2:12, 46
the LORD his God *was* with him, and magnified him exceedingly. 1 Chron 29:25
2 Then Solomon spake unto all Israel, to the captains of thousands and of 1:2 Ex 36:8
hundreds, and to the judges, and to every governor in all Israel, the chief of 1 Kgs 3:4
the fathers. 1 Chron 28:1
3 So Solomon, and all the congregation with him, went to the high place ☆1:3
that *was* at Gibeon; for there was the tabernacle of the congregation of
God, which Moses the servant of the LORD had made in the wilderness.
4 But the ark of God had David brought up from Kir'jath-je'a-rim to *the* 1:4 1 Chron
place which David had prepared for it: for he had pitched a tent for it at 15:25–28
Jerusalem.
5 Moreover the brasen altar, that Be-zal'e-el the son of U'ri, the son of 1:5
Hur, had made, he put before the tabernacle of the LORD: and Solomon Ex 31:9; 38:1–7 1 Kgs 3:4
and the congregation sought unto it.
6 And Solomon went up thither to the brasen altar before the LORD, ☆1:6
which *was* at the tabernacle of the congregation, and offered a thousand
burnt offerings upon it.
7 In that night did God appear unto Solomon, and said unto him, Ask 1:7
what I shall give thee. 1 Kgs 3:5–14
8 And Solomon said unto God, Thou hast shewed great mercy unto David 1:8
my father, and hast made me to reign in his stead. 1 Chron 28:5
9 Now, O LORD God, let thy promise unto David my father be estab- 1:9
lished: for thou hast made me king over a people like the dust of the earth Gen 13:16 22:17
in multitude. 2 Sam 7:12–16
10 Give me now wisdom and knowledge, that I may go out and come in ☆1:10
before this people: for who can judge this thy people, *that is so* great? 2 Sam 5:2
11 And God said to Solomon, Because this was in thine heart, and thou ☆1:11
hast not asked riches, wealth, or honour, nor the life of thine enemies,
neither yet hast asked long life; but hast asked wisdom and knowledge for
thyself, that thou mayest judge my people, over whom I have made thee
king:
12 Wisdom and knowledge *is* granted unto thee; and I will give thee 1:12
riches, and wealth, and honour, such as none of the kings have had that 1 Chron 29:25 2 Chron 9:22
have been before thee, neither shall there any after thee have the like.
13 ¶Then Solomon came *from his journey* to the high place that *was* at 1:13
Gibeon to Jerusalem, from before the tabernacle of the congregation, and 2 Chron 1:3
reigned over Israel.
14 And Solomon gathered chariots and horsemen: and he had a thousand ☆1:14
and four hundred chariots, and twelve thousand horsemen, which he placed 1 Kgs 4:26 9:19; 10:26–29
in the chariot cities, and with the king at Jerusalem.
15 And the king made silver and gold at Jerusalem *as plenteous* as stones, ☆1:15

1:1 *was strengthened,* i.e., *he established himself in his kingdom.* The reason for this was that "the LORD his God was with him."

1:3 *there was the tabernacle.* Moses had built the tabernacle five hundred years before the reign of King Solomon.†

1:6 According to Deut. 12:13, 14, burnt offerings were prohibited except in Jerusalem. The chronicler explained the reason for Solomon's thousand burnt offerings at Gibeon: the tent of meeting (tabernacle) and the bronze altar were there.

1:10 Solomon's request for wisdom was granted. Wisdom is a unique gift, a gift for using knowledge correctly.

1:11 Here it is said that Solomon became king because God loved his people. This was a humbling fact that all rulers should take to heart.

1:14–17 See note on 1 Kings 11:3 regarding Solomon's propensity for horses, silver, and gold.

and cedar trees made he as the sycomore trees that *are* in the vale for
abundance.
16 And Solomon had horses brought out of Egypt, and linen yarn: the
king's merchants received the linen yarn at a price.
17 And they fetched up, and brought forth out of Egypt a chariot for six
hundred *shekels* of silver, and an horse for an hundred and fifty: and so
brought they out *horses* for all the kings of the Hittites, and for the kings of
Syria, by their means.

B. THE CONSTRUCTION AND DEDICATION OF THE TEMPLE

1. The Arrangements for the Construction

2:1☆ 2 AND Solomon determined to build an house for the name of the
1 Kgs 5:5 LORD, and an house for his kingdom.
2:2 2 And Solomon told out threescore and ten thousand men to bear
1 Kgs 5:15, 16 2 Chron 2:18 burdens, and fourscore thousand to hew in the mountain, and three
thousand and six hundred to oversee them.
2:3 3 ¶And Solomon sent to Hu'ram the king of Tyre, saying, As thou didst
1 Kgs 5:2–11 1 Chron 14:1 deal with David my father, and didst send him cedars to build him an
house to dwell therein, *even so deal with me.*
2:4☆ 4 Behold, I build an house to the name of the LORD my God, to dedicate
Ex 25:30 29:38–42; 30:7 *it* to him, *and* to burn before him sweet incense, and for the continual
Num 28:9, 10 shewbread, and for the burnt offerings morning and evening, on the
sabbaths, and on the new moons, and on the solemn feasts of the LORD our
God. This *is an ordinance* for ever to Israel.
2:5 5 And the house which I build *is* great: for great *is* our God above all
Ex 15:11 1 Chron 16:25 gods.
2:6 6 But who is able to build him an house, seeing the heaven and heaven of
1 Kgs 8:27 2 Chron 6:18 heavens cannot contain him? who *am* I then, that I should build him an
house, save only to burn sacrifice before him?
2:7 7 Send me now therefore a man cunning to work in gold, and in silver,
Ex 31:3–5 1 Chron 22:15 and in brass, and in iron, and in purple, and crimson, and blue, and that
2 Chron 2:13, 14 can skill to grave with the cunning men that *are* with me in Judah and in
Jerusalem, whom David my father did provide.
2:8 8 Send me also cedar trees, fir trees, and algum trees, out of Lebanon: for
2 Chron 9:10, 11 I know that thy servants can skill to cut timber in Lebanon; and, behold,
my servants *shall be* with thy servants,
9 Even to prepare me timber in abundance: for the house which I am
about to build *shall be* wonderful great.
10 And, behold, I will give to thy servants, the hewers that cut timber,
twenty thousand measures of beaten wheat, and twenty thousand measures
of barley, and twenty thousand baths of wine, and twenty thousand baths
of oil.
2:11 11 ¶Then Hu'ram the king of Tyre answered in writing, which he sent to
1 Kgs 10:9 2 Chron 9:8 Solomon, Because the LORD hath loved his people, he hath made thee king
2:12 over them.
2 Chron 2:1 Ps 33:6; 102:25 12 Hu'ram said moreover, Blessed *be* the LORD God of Israel, that made

2:1 Three sanctuaries have existed during Israel's long history. The first was the tabernacle in the wilderness. The second was Solomon's temple. The third was the temple erected after the captivity. This third temple was virtually rebuilt or renovated by Herod the Great over a period of nearly fifty years (John 2:20). The great temple, of course, was Solomon's. His father, David, when forbidden by God to erect the structure, collected the material for Solomon to do so (1 Chron. 22:2–5, 8, 14–16; 29:2–5). Solomon spent seven years building the temple. It was called "the house of the God of Zion (Isa. 2:3), and "Mount Zion" (Ps. 74:2). At the dedication of the temple, fire came down from heaven upon the altar and the glory cloud of God filled it (7:2, 3; 1 Kings 8:10, 11; 2 Chron. 5:13). The Scriptures prophesied the destruction of the first temple (Mic. 3:12; Jer. 26:18), and this was fulfilled by the Chaldeans (Babylonians) under Nebuchadnezzar (2 Kings 25:9, 13–17; 2 Chron. 36:18, 19).

2:4 *shewbread,* literally, "the Bread of the Presence."

heaven and earth, who hath given to David the king a wise son, endued
with prudence and understanding, that might build an house for the LORD,
and an house for his kingdom.
13 And now I have sent a cunning man, endued with understanding, of ☆2:13
Hu'ram my father's,
14 The son of a woman of the daughters of Dan, and his father *was* a man 2:14
of Tyre, skilful to work in gold, and in silver, in brass, in iron, in stone, and 1 Kgs 7:14
in timber, in purple, in blue, and in fine linen, and in crimson; also to grave
any manner of graving, and to find out every device which shall be put to
him, with thy cunning men, and with the cunning men of my lord David
thy father.
15 Now therefore the wheat, and the barley, the oil, and the wine, which 2:15
my lord hath spoken of, let him send unto his servants: 2 Chron 2:10
16 And we will cut wood out of Lebanon, as much as thou shalt need: and ☆2:16
we will bring it to thee in floats by sea to Joppa; and thou shalt carry it up 1 Kgs 5:8, 9
to Jerusalem.
17 ¶And Solomon numbered all the strangers that *were* in the land of
Israel, after the numbering wherewith David his father had numbered
them; and they were found an hundred and fifty thousand and three
thousand and six hundred.
18 And he set threescore and ten thousand of them *to be* bearers of 2:18
burdens, and fourscore thousand *to be* hewers in the mountain, and three 1 Chron 22:2
thousand and six hundred overseers to set the people a work. 2 Chron 2:2

2. The Actual Construction of the Temple
a. The Description of the Construction

3 THEN Solomon began to build the house of the LORD at Jerusalem in ☆3:1
mount Mo-ri'ah, where *the LORD* appeared unto David his father, in 1 Kgs 6:1
the place that David had prepared in the threshingfloor of Or'nan the 1 Chron 21:18
Jeb'u-site.
2 And he began to build in the second *day* of the second month, in the ☆3:2
fourth year of his reign.
3 ¶Now these *are the things wherein* Solomon was instructed for the ☆3:3
building of the house of God. The length by cubits after the first measure
was threescore cubits, and the breadth twenty cubits.
4 And the porch that *was* in the front *of the house,* the length *of it was* 3:4
according to the breadth of the house, twenty cubits, and the height *was* an 1 Kgs 6:3
hundred and twenty: and he overlaid it within with pure gold.
5 And the greater house he cieled with fir tree, which he overlaid with fine 3:5
gold, and set thereon palm trees and chains. 1 Kgs 6:17
6 And he garnished the house with precious stones for beauty: and the ☆3:6
gold *was* gold of Par-va'im.
7 He overlaid also the house, the beams, the posts, and the walls thereof, 3:7
and the doors thereof, with gold; and graved cherubims on the walls. 1 Kgs 6:20–22, 29–35
8 And he made the most holy house, the length whereof *was* according to 3:8
the breadth of the house, twenty cubits, and the breadth thereof twenty Ex 26:33
cubits: and he overlaid it with fine gold, *amounting* to six hundred talents. 1 Kgs 6:16

2:13 Huram (or *Hiram,* or *Huramabi*) is said to have been the son of a widow of the tribe of Naphtali (1 Kings 7:14). He was an architect and artist.
2:16 *flotes,* i.e., rafts.
3:1 The site for the temple was decided by David (1 Chron. 22:1). It is the place thought by many to be where Abraham offered Isaac many years before.
3:2 Solomon began the construction of the temple almost four years after he became king. Time was needed to gather the materials for the construction.
3:3 *after the first measure,* i.e., "cubits of the old standard" (NIV, RSV); "by cubits according to the former measure" (NKJV). The length of the cubit differed at various times. There were longer and shorter cubits. The cubit was the distance from the beginning of the forearm to the tip of the middle finger. Generally it was approximately 17.5 inches long.
3:6 *Parvaim.* We do not know where this was located.

3:9 1 Chron 28:11 9 And the weight of the nails *was* fifty shekels of gold. And he overlaid the
upper chambers with gold.
3:10 1 Kgs 6:23–28 10 And in the most holy house he made two cherubims of image work, and
overlaid them with gold.
11 ¶And the wings of the cherubims *were* twenty cubits long: one wing *of*
the one cherub was five cubits, reaching to the wall of the house: and the
other wing *was likewise* five cubits, reaching to the wing of the other cherub.
12 And *one* wing of the other cherub *was* five cubits, reaching to the wall
of the house: and the other wing *was* five cubits *also,* joining to the wing of
the other cherub.
13 The wings of these cherubims spread themselves forth twenty cubits:
and they stood on their feet, and their faces *were* inward.
3:14 Ex 26:31 14 ¶And he made the vail *of* blue, and purple, and crimson, and fine linen,
and wrought cherubims thereon.
3:15 1 Kgs 7:15–20 15 Also he made before the house two pillars of thirty and five cubits high,
and the chapiter that *was* on the top of each of them *was* five cubits.
16 And he made chains, *as* in the oracle, and put *them* on the heads of the
pillars; and made an hundred pomegranates, and put *them* on the chains.
3:17☆ 1 Kgs 7:21 17 And he reared up the pillars before the temple, one on the right hand,
and the other on the left; and called the name of that on the right hand
Ja'chin, and the name of that on the left Bo'az.

b. The Furniture of the Temple

4:1☆ Ex 27:1, 2 2 Kgs 16:14 4 MOREOVER he made an altar of brass, twenty cubits the length
thereof, and twenty cubits the breadth thereof, and ten cubits the
height thereof.
4:2☆ 1 Kgs 7:23–26 2 ¶Also he made a molten sea of ten cubits from brim to brim, round in
compass, and five cubits the height thereof; and a line of thirty cubits did
compass it round about.
3 And under it *was* the similitude of oxen, which did compass it round
about: ten in a cubit, compassing the sea round about. Two rows of oxen
were cast, when it was cast.
4 It stood upon twelve oxen, three looking toward the north, and three
looking toward the west, and three looking toward the south, and three
looking toward the east: and the sea *was set* above upon them, and all their
hinder parts *were* inward.
4:5 1 Kgs 7:26 5 And the thickness of it *was* an handbreadth, and the brim of it like the
work of the brim of a cup, with flowers of lilies; *and* it received and held
three thousand baths.
4:6 1 Kgs 7:38, 40 6 ¶He made also ten lavers, and put five on the right hand, and five on the
left, to wash in them: such things as they offered for the burnt offering they
washed in them; but the sea *was* for the priests to wash in.
4:7 1 Kgs 7:49 7 And he made ten candlesticks of gold according to their form, and set
them in the temple, five on the right hand, and five on the left.
8 He made also ten tables, and placed *them* in the temple, five on the right
side, and five on the left. And he made an hundred basons of gold.
4:9 1 Kgs 6:36 9 ¶Furthermore he made the court of the priests, and the great court, and
doors for the court, and overlaid the doors of them with brass.

3:17 Why Solomon named the pillars Jachin and Boaz is not known. Jachin was the fourth son of Simeon. Boaz was the husband of Ruth, who gave birth to Obed, the grandfather of David.

4:1 *altar of bronze.* This was the burnt offering altar. See note to Lev. 1:2, 3.

4:2 The molten sea could hold 3,000 baths of water. Normally only 2,000 baths were in it. The New Testament speaks about the washing of regeneration (Titus 3:5). Thus the molten sea may be a type of this washing.

[10]And he set the sea on the right side of the east end, over against the south.
4:10 1 Kgs 7:39

[11]¶And Hu'ram made the pots, and the shovels, and the basons. And Hu'ram finished the work that he was to make for king Solomon for the house of God;

[12]*To wit,* the two pillars, and the pommels, and the chapiters *which were* on top of the two pillars, and the two wreaths to cover the two pommels of the chapiters which *were* on the top of the pillars;
☆4:12 1 Kgs 7:14; 20, 27–43 2 Chron 2:13

[13]And four hundred pomegranates on the two wreaths; two rows of pomegranates on each wreath, to cover the two pommels of the chapiters which *were* upon the pillars.

[14]He made also bases, and lavers made he upon the bases;

[15]One sea, and twelve oxen under it.

[16]The pots also, and the shovels, and the fleshhooks, and all their instruments, did Hu'ram his father make to king Solomon for the house of the LORD of bright brass.

[17]In the plain of Jordan did the king cast them, in the clay ground between Suc'coth and Ze-red'a-thah.
4:17 1 Kgs 7:47

[18]Thus Solomon made all these vessels in great abundance: for the weight of the brass could not be found out.

[19]¶And Solomon made all the vessels that *were for* the house of God, the golden altar also, and the tables whereon the shewbread *was set;*
☆4:19

[20]Moreover the candlesticks with their lamps, that they should burn after the manner before the oracle, of pure gold;
☆4:20 Ex 25:31–37

[21]And the flowers, and the lamps, and the tongs, *made he of* gold, *and* that perfect gold;

[22]And the snuffers, and the basons, and the spoons, and the censers, *of* pure gold: and the entry of the house, the inner doors thereof for the most holy *place,* and the doors of the house of the temple, *were of* gold.

5 THUS all the work that Solomon made for the house of the LORD was finished: and Solomon brought in *all* the things that David his father had dedicated; and the silver, and the gold, and all the instruments, put he among the treasures of the house of God.
☆5:1

3. The Dedication of the Temple

a. The Ark Brought to the Temple

[2]¶Then Solomon assembled the elders of Israel, and all the heads of the tribes, the chief of the fathers of the children of Israel, unto Jerusalem, to bring up the ark of the covenant of the LORD out of the city of David, which *is* Zion.
☆5:2 1 Kgs 8:1–9 2 Chron 1:4

[3]Wherefore all the men of Israel assembled themselves unto the king in the feast which *was* in the seventh month.
☆5:3

[4]And all the elders of Israel came; and the Levites took up the ark.
5:4 2 Chron 5:7

[5]And they brought up the ark, and the tabernacle of the congregation, and all the holy vessels that *were* in the tabernacle, these did the priests *and* the Levites bring up.

[6]Also king Solomon, and all the congregation of Israel that were

---

4:12 *pommels,* i.e., bowls.
4:19 *shewbread.* See note to Mark 2:25.
4:20 *before the oracle,* i.e., "in front of the inner sanctuary" or "before the holy of holies."
5:1 See 1 Chron. 29:2–5 for the things David had dedicated to the temple.
5:2 *Zion,* another name for Jerusalem. The word is used extensively in the Psalms and in Isaiah.
5:3 *in the feast,* i.e., the feast of tabernacles, for which see note to Exod. 23:16.

assembled unto him before the ark, sacrificed sheep and oxen, which could not be told nor numbered for multitude.

7 And the priests brought in the ark of the covenant of the LORD unto his place, to the oracle of the house, into the most holy *place*, *even* under the wings of the cherubims:

5:8☆
8 For the cherubims spread forth *their* wings over the place of the ark, and the cherubims covered the ark and the staves thereof above.

5:9 1 Kgs 8:8, 9
9 And they drew out the staves *of the ark*, that the ends of the staves were seen from the ark before the oracle; but they were not seen without. And there it is unto this day.

5:10☆ Deut 10:2–5 Heb 9:4
10 *There was* nothing in the ark save the two tables which Moses put *therein* at Ho′reb, when the LORD made *a covenant* with the children of Israel, when they came out of Egypt.

5:11 1 Chron 13:8 15:16, 24 24:1–5; 25:1–4 2 Chron 7:6
11 ¶And it came to pass, when the priests were come out of the holy *place*: (for all the priests *that were* present were sanctified, *and* did not *then* wait by course:

12 Also the Levites *which were* the singers, all of them of A′saph, of He′man, of Jed′u-thun, with their sons and their brethren, *being* arrayed in white linen, having cymbals and psalteries and harps, stood at the east end of the altar, and with them an hundred and twenty priests sounding with trumpets:)

5:13 1 Kgs 8:11 1 Chron 16:34, 42 2 Chron 7:3
13 It came even to pass, as the trumpeters and singers *were* as one, to make one sound to be heard in praising and thanking the LORD; and when they lifted up *their* voice with the trumpets and cymbals and instruments of musick, and praised the LORD, *saying*, For *he is* good; for his mercy *endureth* for ever: that *then* the house was filled with a cloud, *even* the house of the LORD;

5:14☆
14 So that the priests could not stand to minister by reason of the cloud: for the glory of the LORD had filled the house of God.

b. Solomon Blesses God and the People

6:1☆ 1 Kgs 8:12–50
6 THEN said Solomon, The LORD hath said that he would dwell in the thick darkness.

2 But I have built an house of habitation for thee, and a place for thy dwelling for ever.

3 And the king turned his face, and blessed the whole congregation of Israel: and all the congregation of Israel stood.

4 And he said, Blessed *be* the LORD God of Israel, who hath with his hands fulfilled *that* which he spake with his mouth to my father David, saying,

6:5 1 Chron 28:4 2 Chron 12:13
5 Since the day that I brought forth my people out of the land of Egypt I chose no city among all the tribes of Israel to build an house in, that my name might be there; neither chose I any man to be a ruler over my people Israel:

5:8 *cherubims.* See note to Ezek. 10:1.

5:10 *nothing in the ark save the two tables.* The golden jar of manna (Exod. 16:33, 34) was placed in the ark and so was Aaron's rod that budded (Num. 17:10). Aside from these two items the ark had in it ony the two tables of the law. However, by the time of Solomon only the two tables of the law remained in the ark. We do not know when the other items were removed or what happened to them. Hebrews 9:4 specifically states that the golden jar and Aaron's rod were in the ark.

5:14 The temple became the house of God when the glory of God filled it. It was the divine presence that made it holy. The glory of God indwelling the temple also indicated that God was pleased with the temple. His presence remained in the temple until Ezekiel's day, when it was seen to leave the temple because God abandoned it due to the sins of Israel.

6:1 Because there were no windows to give light, the temple lay in darkness. The light of the temple came from the candles, but most of all from the presence of God who is light. God was the light of the world before he created the sun, and he will be the unique source of light for the New Jerusalem.

6 But I have chosen Jerusalem, that my name might be there; and have
chosen David to be over my people Israel.
7 Now it was in the heart of David my father to build an house for the
name of the LORD God of Israel.
8 But the LORD said to David my father, Forasmuch as it was in thine **6:8**
heart to build an house for my name, thou didst well in that it was in thine 1 Kgs 5:3
heart:
9 Notwithstanding thou shalt not build the house; but thy son which shall
come forth out of thy loins, he shall build the house for my name.
10 The LORD therefore hath performed his word that he hath spoken: for
I am risen up in the room of David my father, and am set on the throne of
Israel, as the LORD promised, and have built the house for the name of the
LORD God of Israel.
11 And in it have I put the ark, wherein *is* the covenant of the LORD, that **6:11**
he made with the children of Israel. 2 Chron 5:7, 10

c. Solomon Consecrates the Temple in Prayer

12 ¶And he stood before the altar of the LORD in the presence of all the ☆**6:12**
congregation of Israel, and spread forth his hands: 1 Kgs 8:54 Neh 8:4
13 For Solomon had made a brasen scaffold, of five cubits long, and five
cubits broad, and three cubits high, and had set it in the midst of the court:
and upon it he stood, and kneeled down upon his knees before all the
congregation of Israel, and spread forth his hands toward heaven,
14 And said, O LORD God of Israel, *there is* no God like thee in the **6:14**
heaven, nor in the earth; which keepest covenant, and *shewest* mercy unto Ex 15:11 Deut 3:24; 7:9
thy servants, that walk before thee with all their hearts:
15 Thou which hast kept with thy servant David my father that which thou **6:15**
hast promised him; and spakest with thy mouth, and hast fulfilled *it* with 1 Chron 22:9, 10
thine hand, as *it is* this day.
16 Now therefore, O LORD God of Israel, keep with thy servant David my **6:16**
father that which thou hast promised him, saying, There shall not fail thee 1 Kgs 2:4 2 Chron 7:18
a man in my sight to sit upon the throne of Israel; yet so that thy children
take heed to their way to walk in my law, as thou hast walked before me.
17 Now then, O LORD God of Israel, let thy word be verified, which thou
hast spoken unto thy servant David.
18 But will God in very deed dwell with men on the earth? behold, heaven ☆**6:18**
and the heaven of heavens cannot contain thee; how much less this house 2 Chron 2:6
which I have built!
19 Have respect therefore to the prayer of thy servant, and to his
supplication, O LORD my God, to hearken unto the cry and the prayer
which thy servant prayeth before thee:
20 That thine eyes may be open upon this house day and night, upon the **6:20**
place whereof thou hast said that thou wouldest put thy name there; to Mic 7:18
hearken unto the prayer which thy servant prayeth toward this place.
21 Hearken therefore unto the supplications of thy servant, and of thy ☆**6:21**

6:12 Verses 12ff describe what Solomon did and reiterate the prayer he offered. He stood on a bronze platform but then prayed on his knees. The day will come when every knee shall bow to Jesus Christ (Phil. 2:10). Solomon's act was symbolic of this future certainty and expresses the greatness and glory of God before whom all hearts must bow, as well as every knee.

6:18 The universe itself, however large and commodious, cannot contain God. "He is infinitely beyond the bounds of his creation and infinitely above the praises of all intelligent creatures."*

6:21 Solomon prays that God would hear the prayers of his people and help them. Those prayers were directed to the temple, not because the temple had worth but because it housed the glory of God. Without that presence, prayer toward the temple would lose all significance.

people Israel, which they shall make toward this place: hear thou from thy
dwelling place, *even* from heaven; and when thou hearest, forgive.
22 If a man sin against his neighbour, and an oath be laid upon him to
make him swear, and the oath come before thine altar in this house;
23 Then hear thou from heaven, and do, and judge thy servants, by
requiting the wicked, by recompensing his way upon his own head; and by
justifying the righteous, by giving him according to his righteousness.
24 ¶And if thy people Israel be put to the worse before the enemy, because
they have sinned against thee; and shall return and confess thy name, and
pray and make supplication before thee in this house;
25 Then hear thou from the heavens, and forgive the sin of thy people
Israel, and bring them again unto the land which thou gavest to them and
to their fathers.
6:26☆ 26 ¶When the heaven is shut up, and there is no rain, because they have
sinned against thee; *yet* if they pray toward this place, and confess thy
name, and turn from their sin, when thou dost afflict them;
27 Then hear thou from heaven, and forgive the sin of thy servants, and of
thy people Israel, when thou hast taught them the good way, wherein they
should walk; and send rain upon thy land, which thou hast given unto thy
people for an inheritance.
28 If there be dearth in the land, if there be pestilence, if there be blasting,
or mildew, locusts, or caterpillers; if their enemies besiege them in the cities
of their land; whatsoever sore or whatsoever sickness *there be:*
29 *Then* what prayer *or* what supplication soever shall be made of any
man, or of all thy people Israel, when every one shall know his own sore
and his own grief, and shall spread forth his hands in this house:
6:30 30 Then hear thou from heaven thy dwelling place, and forgive, and render
1 Sam 16:7 unto every man according unto all his ways, whose heart thou knowest; (for
1 Chron 28:9 thou only knowest the hearts of the children of men:)
31 That they may fear thee, to walk in thy ways, so long as they live in the
land which thou gavest unto our fathers.
32 ¶Moreover concerning the stranger, which is not of thy people Israel,
but is come from a far country for thy great name's sake, and thy mighty
hand, and thy stretched out arm; if they come and pray in this house;
33 Then hear thou from the heavens, *even* from thy dwelling place, and do
according to all that the stranger calleth to thee for; that all people of the
earth may know thy name, and fear thee, as *doth* thy people Israel, and may
know that this house which I have built is called by thy name.
6:34☆ 34 If thy people go out to war against their enemies by the way that thou
shalt send them, and they pray unto thee toward this city which thou hast
chosen, and the house which I have built for thy name;
35 Then hear thou from the heavens their prayer and their supplication,
and maintain their cause.
6:36 36 If they sin against thee, (for *there is* no man which sinneth not,) and
Job 15:14–16 thou be angry with them, and deliver them over before *their* enemies, and
Jas 3:2 they carry them away captives unto a land far off or near;
1 Jn 1:8–10 37 Yet *if* they bethink themselves in the land whither they are carried
captive, and turn and pray unto thee in the land of their captivity, saying,
We have sinned, we have done amiss, and have dealt wickedly;

6:26ff All nature is subject to God's will. When natural phenomena occur and people suffer, it may well be a sign of God's wrath for sins committed. Implicit in this segment of Solomon's prayer about natural catastrophe is that when people repent, God is gracious and circumstances right themselves.

6:34 While the petition here concerns Israel at war against its enemies, it is also true for the believer today when he fights against the forces of darkness. Prayer will result in maintaining the cause of God's servants.

38 If they return to thee with all their heart and with all their soul in the
land of their captivity, whither they have carried them captives, and pray
toward their land, which thou gavest unto their fathers, and *toward* the city
which thou hast chosen, and toward the house which I have built for thy
name:
39 Then hear thou from the heavens, *even* from thy dwelling place, their
prayer and their supplications, and maintain their cause, and forgive thy
people which have sinned against thee.
40 Now, my God, let, I beseech thee, thine eyes be open, and *let* thine ears
be attent unto the prayer *that is made* in this place.
41 Now therefore arise, O LORD God, into thy resting place, thou, and the
ark of thy strength: let thy priests, O LORD God, be clothed with salvation,
and let thy saints rejoice in goodness.
42 O LORD God, turn not away the face of thine anointed: remember the
mercies of David thy servant.

6:40 2 Chron 7:15; Neh 1:6, 11; Ps 17:1
☆6:41 Ps 132:8, 9

d. God's Response to Solomon's Prayer

(1) The Fire and the Glory of the Lord

7 NOW when Solomon had made an end of praying, the fire came down
from heaven, and consumed the burnt offering and the sacrifices; and
the glory of the LORD filled the house.
2 And the priests could not enter into the house of the LORD, because the
glory of the LORD had filled the LORD's house.
3 And when all the children of Israel saw how the fire came down, and the
glory of the LORD upon the house, they bowed themselves with their faces
to the ground upon the pavement, and worshipped, and praised the LORD,
saying, For *he is* good; for his mercy *endureth* for ever.
4 ¶Then the king and all the people offered sacrifices before the LORD.
5 And king Solomon offered a sacrifice of twenty and two thousand oxen,
and an hundred and twenty thousand sheep: so the king and all the people
dedicated the house of God.
6 And the priests waited on their offices: the Levites also with instruments
of musick of the LORD, which David the king had made to praise the LORD,
because his mercy *endureth* for ever, when David praised by their ministry;
and the priests sounded trumpets before them, and all Israel stood.
7 Moreover Solomon hallowed the middle of the court that *was* before the
house of the LORD: for there he offered burnt offerings, and the fat of the
peace offerings, because the brasen altar which Solomon had made was not
able to receive the burnt offerings, and the meat offerings, and the fat.
8 ¶Also at the same time Solomon kept the feast seven days, and all Israel
with him, a very great congregation, from the entering in of Ha'math unto
the river of Egypt.

☆7:1 1 Kgs 8:54; 18:24, 38
☆7:3 2 Chron 5:13; 20:21
7:4 1 Kgs 8:62, 63
7:6 1 Chron 15:16–21; 2 Chron 5:12
☆7:7 1 Kgs 8:64–66
7:8 1 Kgs 8:65

6:41 Here Solomon asks God to take possession of the house that has been built for him and to keep possession of it as his resting place. Believers should ask God to take possession of their hearts and to remain on the thrones of all hearts for time and in eternity.

7:1 Even as fire came down from heaven to consume the sacrifice of Elijah on Mount Carmel, so now at the dedication of the Solomonic temple, God sent down supernatural fire to consume the burnt offerings and the sacrifices. The glory of the Lord also filled the house. The priests had to leave the temple, for they were blinded by the cloud of darkness. The glory did not fill Ezra's temple, which was erected after the end of the Babylonian captivity.

7:3 When the fire came down, the worshippers bowed their faces to the ground. This indicated their dread of the divine majesty, the sense of their utter unworthiness, and their willingness to submit themselves to the authority of God.

7:7 So many were the sacrifices that the altar could not contain them. The more God blesses, the more offerings should we bring and the greater should be our commitment to the giver of all good things. Solomon's own example stirred the people to great heights of giving.

7:9 Lev 23:26 9 And in the eighth day they made a solemn assembly: for they kept the
dedication of the altar seven days, and the feast seven days.
10 And on the three and twentieth day of the seventh month he sent the
people away into their tents, glad and merry in heart for the goodness that
the LORD had shewed unto David, and to Solomon, and to Israel his
people.

(2) God's Appearance to Solomon and His Covenant

11 Thus Solomon finished the house of the LORD, and the king's house:
and all that came into Solomon's heart to make in the house of the LORD,
and in his own house, he prosperously effected.
7:12☆ 12 ¶And the LORD appeared to Solomon by night, and said unto him, I
have heard thy prayer, and have chosen this place to myself for an house of
sacrifice.
7:13 13 If I shut up heaven that there be no rain, or if I command the locusts to
2 Chron 6:26–28 devour the land, or if I send pestilence among my people;
7:14☆ 14 If my people, which are called by my name, shall humble themselves,
2 Chron 6:37–39 and pray, and seek my face, and turn from their wicked ways; then will I
hear from heaven, and will forgive their sin, and will heal their land.
7:15 15 Now mine eyes shall be open, and mine ears attent unto the prayer *that*
2 Chron 6:20, 40 *is made* in this place.
7:16 16 For now have I chosen and sanctified this house, that my name may be
2 Chron 7:12 there for ever: and mine eyes and mine heart shall be there perpetually.

(3) God's Sure Judgment against Apostasy

7:17☆ 17 And as for thee, if thou wilt walk before me, as David thy father
walked, and do according to all that I have commanded thee, and shalt
observe my statutes and my judgments;
7:18 18 Then will I stablish the throne of thy kingdom, according as I have
2 Chron 6:16 covenanted with David thy father, saying, There shall not fail thee a man *to
be* ruler in Israel.
7:19 19 But if ye turn away, and forsake my statutes and my commandments,
Lev 26:14, 33 Deut 28:15 which I have set before you, and shall go and serve other gods, and worship
them;
7:20 20 Then will I pluck them up by the roots out of my land which I have
Deut 28:37 29:28 given them; and this house, which I have sanctified for my name, will I cast
1 Kgs 14:15 out of my sight, and will make it *to be* a proverb and a byword among all
nations.
7:21 21 And this house, which is high, shall be an astonishment to every one
Deut 29:24, 25 that passeth by it; so that he shall say, Why hath the LORD done thus unto
this land, and unto this house?
22 And it shall be answered, Because they forsook the LORD God of their
fathers, which brought them forth out of the land of Egypt, and laid hold
on other gods, and worshipped them, and served them: therefore hath he
brought all this evil upon them.

7:12 How God appeared to Solomon we do not know, but the message God gave him was quite clear.

7:14 This famous passage has been used in connection with revival and renewal. The conditions that result in the blessing of God are national repentance, national prayer, and national reformation. Any nation that humbles itself and does these things in a true spirit will be helped and blessed by God.

7:17 Solomon had asked for God's blessing. God promised that blessing but it was a contingent promise—Solomon must walk in the ways of God and keep his commandments. God knows how prone his people are to backslide. If they turn from him, a temple, an ark, and all the sacrifices in the world will not help them unless and until they meet the conditions stated in verse 14.

4. Solomon's Activities and Death
a. Solomon's Building Activities

8 AND it came to pass at the end of twenty years, wherein Solomon had — **8:1** 1 Kgs 9:1–28
built the house of the LORD, and his own house,
2 That the cities which Hu'ram had restored to Solomon, Solomon built — ☆**8:2**
them, and caused the children of Israel to dwell there.
3 And Solomon went to Ha'math–zo'bah, and prevailed against it.
4 And he built Tad'mor in the wilderness, and all the store cities, which he — ☆**8:4**
built in Ha'math.
5 Also he built Beth–ho'ron the upper, and Beth–ho'ron the nether, fenced — **8:5** 1 Chron 7:24
cities, with walls, gates, and bars; — 2 Chron 14:7
6 And Ba'al-ath, and all the store cities that Solomon had, and all the
chariot cities, and the cities of the horsemen, and all that Solomon desired
to build in Jerusalem, and in Lebanon, and throughout all the land of his
dominion.
7 ¶*As for* all the people *that were* left of the Hittites, and the Am'or-ites, — **8:7** Gen 15:18–21
and the Per'iz-zites, and the Hi'vites, and the Jeb'u-sites, which *were* not of — 1 Kgs 3:1; 7:8
Israel,
8 *But* of their children, who were left after them in the land, whom the
children of Israel consumed not, them did Solomon make to pay tribute
until this day.
9 But of the children of Israel did Solomon make no servants for his work;
but they *were* men of war, and chief of his captains, and captains of his
chariots and horsemen.
10 And these *were* the chief of king Solomon's officers, *even* two hundred
and fifty, that bare rule over the people.

b. The New Palace for Pharaoh's Daughter

11 ¶And Solomon brought up the daughter of Pharaoh out of the city of — ☆**8:11** 1 Kgs 3:1; 7:8
David unto the house that he had built for her: for he said, My wife shall
not dwell in the house of David king of Israel, because *the places are* holy,
whereunto the ark of the LORD hath come.

c. The Solomonic Sacrifices

12 ¶Then Solomon offered burnt offerings unto the LORD on the altar of — **8:12** 2 Chron 4:1
the LORD, which he had built before the porch,
13 Even after a certain rate every day, offering according to the command- — **8:13** Ex 23:14–17
ment of Moses, on the sabbaths, and on the new moons, and on the solemn — 29:38–42
feasts, three times in the year, *even* in the feast of unleavened bread, and in — Num 28:3
the feast of weeks, and in the feast of tabernacles.
14 And he appointed, according to the order of David his father, the — **8:14** 1 Chron 24:1
courses of the priests to their service, and the Levites to their charges, to — 25:1; 26:1
praise and minister before the priests, as the duty of every day required: the — Neh 12:24, 36
porters also by their courses at every gate: for so had David the man of
God commanded.

8:2 The same account may be found in 1 Kings 9:10–24.
8:4 *Tadmor*, also named Palmyra, located in the Syrian desert. It appears that some copyist confused this with Tamar (1 Kings 9:18), a caravan station in the wilderness southwest of the Dead Sea.
8:11 Solomon married the Egyptian Pharaoh's daughter for political reasons. Had he trusted wholly in God, this would never have happened. But he still had sufficient spiritual insight at this stage in his life to build a separate palace for this wife. He had respect for the house in which his father David had lived and in which the ark of God rested for a considerable length of time. The presence of his wife would have defiled the house and the ark unless she became a true believer. But there is no evidence that she did.

[15]And they departed not from the commandment of the king unto the
priests and Levites concerning any matter, or concerning the treasures.
[16]Now all the work of Solomon was prepared unto the day of the
foundation of the house of the LORD, and until it was finished. *So* the house
of the LORD was perfected.

d. Solomon's Great Wealth

8:17☆ 1 Kgs 9:26 [17]¶Then went Solomon to E′zi-on-ge′ber, and to E′loth, at the sea side in
2 Kgs 14:22 the land of Edom.
2 Chron 9:10, 13 [18]And Hu′ram sent him by the hands of his servants ships, and servants
that had knowledge of the sea; and they went with the servants of Solomon
to O′phir, and took thence four hundred and fifty talents of gold, and
brought *them* to king Solomon.

e. The Queen of Sheba Comes to Visit

9:1☆ 1 Kgs 10:1–13 9 AND when the queen of She′ba heard of the fame of Solomon, she
Mt 12:42 came to prove Solomon with hard questions at Jerusalem, with a very
Lk 11:31 great company, and camels that bare spices, and gold in abundance, and
precious stones: and when she was come to Solomon, she communed with
him of all that was in her heart.
9:2☆ [2]And Solomon told her all her questions: and there was nothing hid from
Solomon which he told her not.
[3]And when the queen of She′ba had seen the wisdom of Solomon, and
the house that he had built,
[4]And the meat of his table, and the sitting of his servants, and the
attendance of his ministers, and their apparel; his cupbearers also, and their
apparel; and his ascent by which he went up into the house of the LORD;
there was no more spirit in her.
[5]And she said to the king, *It was* a true report which I heard in mine own
land of thine acts, and of thy wisdom:
[6]Howbeit I believed not their words, until I came, and mine eyes had
seen *it:* and, behold, the one half of the greatness of thy wisdom was not
told me: *for* thou exceedest the fame that I heard.
[7]Happy *are* thy men, and happy *are* these thy servants, which stand
continually before thee, and hear thy wisdom.
9:8☆ [8]Blessed be the LORD thy God, which delighted in thee to set thee on his
Deut 7:8 1 Chron 28:5 throne, *to be* king for the LORD thy God: because thy God loved Israel, to
29:23 2 Chron 2:11 establish them for ever, therefore made he thee king over them, to do
judgment and justice.
[9]And she gave the king an hundred and twenty talents of gold, and of
spices great abundance, and precious stones: neither was there any such
spice as the queen of She′ba gave king Solomon.
9:10 [10]And the servants also of Hu′ram, and the servants of Solomon, which
2 Chron 8:18 brought gold from O′phir, brought algum trees and precious stones.
[11]And the king made *of* the algum trees terraces to the house of the LORD,
and to the king's palace, and harps and psalteries for singers: and there
were none such seen before in the land of Judah.

8:17 *Ezion-geber.* See note on 1 Kings 9:26.
8:18 1 Kings 9:28 speaks about 420 talents of gold; here the figure is 450 talents. This is obviously a copyist's error in reading worn manuscripts, which were often illegible.
9:1 *Sheba,* the land of the Sabeans. (See note on 1 Kings 10:1).
9:2 Solomon had greatly honored God and God honored him. The Queen of Sheba was amazed at his knowledge and understanding. However great Solomon was, we learn that a greater than Solomon came in the person of Jesus (Luke 11:31).
9:8 The Queen of Sheba exhibited some wisdom herself. She knew that Solomon was "to be king for the LORD thy God." So also should every ruler understand that he is under the rule of God. Furthermore, the purpose of every ruler should be to execute judgment against wickedness and to establish justice.

12 And king Solomon gave to the queen of She'ba all her desire,
whatsoever she asked, beside *that* which she had brought unto the king. So
she turned, and went away to her own land, she and her servants.

f. The Riches and Wisdom of Solomon Retold

13 ¶Now the weight of gold that came to Solomon in one year was six
hundred and threescore and six talents of gold;

☆**9:13**
1 Kgs 10:14–28

14 Beside *that which* chapmen and merchants brought. And all the kings of
Arabia and governors of the country brought gold and silver to Solomon.
15 ¶And king Solomon made two hundred targets *of* beaten gold: six
hundred *shekels* of beaten gold went to one target.
16 And three hundred shields *made he of* beaten gold: three hundred
shekels of gold went to one shield. And the king put them in the house of
the forest of Lebanon.
17 Moreover the king made a great throne of ivory, and overlaid it with
pure gold.
18 And *there were* six steps to the throne, with a footstool of gold, *which*
were fastened to the throne, and stays on each side of the sitting place, and
two lions standing by the stays:
19 And twelve lions stood there on the one side and on the other upon the
six steps. There was not the like made in any kingdom.
20 ¶And all the drinking vessels of king Solomon *were of* gold, and all the
vessels of the house of the forest of Lebanon *were of* pure gold: none *were*
of silver; it was *not* any thing accounted of in the days of Solomon.
21 For the king's ships went to Tarshish with the servants of Hu'ram:
every three years once came the ships of Tarshish bringing gold, and silver,
ivory, and apes, and peacocks.

9:21
2 Chron 20:36, 37

22 And king Solomon passed all the kings of the earth in riches and
wisdom.

9:22
1 Kgs 3:13
2 Chron 1:12

23 ¶And all the kings of the earth sought the presence of Solomon, to hear
his wisdom, that God had put in his heart.
24 And they brought every man his present, vessels of silver, and vessels of
gold, and raiment, harness, and spices, horses, and mules, a rate year by
year.
25 ¶And Solomon had four thousand stalls for horses and chariots, and
twelve thousand horsemen; whom he bestowed in the chariot cities, and
with the king at Jerusalem.

☆**9:25**
Deut 17:16
1 Kgs 4:26
10:26
2 Chron 1:14

26 ¶And he reigned over all the kings from the river even unto the land of
the Philistines, and to the border of Egypt.

9:26
1 Kgs 4:21, 24

27 And the king made silver in Jerusalem as stones, and cedar trees made
he as the sycomore trees that *are* in the low plains in abundance.

9:27
2 Chron 1:15–17

28 And they brought unto Solomon horses out of Egypt, and out of all
lands.

9:28
2 Chron 1:16

g. The Death and Burial of Solomon; Rehoboam Succeeds Him

29 ¶Now the rest of the acts of Solomon, first and last, *are* they not written
in the book of Nathan the prophet, and in the prophecy of A-hi'jah the

☆**9:29**
1 Kgs 11:41–43
1 Chron 29:29

9:13ff Solomon was known for his wisdom and his wealth. Both were the gift of God. Therefore he had nothing about which to boast.
9:25 *four thousand stalls.* See 1 Kings 4:26 where it says forty thousand stalls. This is a copyist's error in either that reference or this.
9:29 The chronicler said nothing about Solomon's one thousand wives and concubines. He glossed over the sins of Solomon, generally limiting himself to the good points connected with Solomon's reign. Yet it was intermarriage with these foreign women that brought about Solomon's spiritual decline, according to 1 Kings 11:1ff.

Shi′lo-nite, and in the visions of Id′do the seer against Jer-o-bo′am the son
of Ne′bat?
30 And Solomon reigned in Jerusalem over all Israel forty years.
9:31 1 Kgs 2:10 31 And Solomon slept with his fathers, and he was buried in the city of
David his father: and Re-ho-bo′am his son reigned in his stead.

IV. THE KINGS OF JUDAH FROM REHOBOAM TO THE CAPTIVITY (10:1—36:23)

A. THE DIVISION OF THE SOLOMONIC KINGDOM

1. Rehoboam's Ill-Chosen Words at His Coronation

10:1 1 Kgs 12:1–20 10 AND Re-ho-bo′am went to She′chem: for to She′chem were all
Israel come to make him king.
10:2 1 Kgs 11:40 2 And it came to pass, when Jer-o-bo′am the son of Ne′bat, who *was* in
Egypt, whither he had fled from the presence of Solomon the king, heard *it,*
that Jer-o-bo′am returned out of Egypt.
3 And they sent and called him. So Jer-o-bo′am and all Israel came and
spake to Re-ho-bo′am, saying,
10:4☆ 4 Thy father made our yoke grievous: now therefore ease thou somewhat
the grievous servitude of thy father, and his heavy yoke that he put upon us,
and we will serve thee.
5 And he said unto them, Come again unto me after three days. And the
people departed.
6 ¶And king Re-ho-bo′am took counsel with the old men that had stood
before Solomon his father while he yet lived, saying, What counsel give ye
me to return answer to this people?
7 And they spake unto him, saying, If thou be kind to this people, and
please them, and speak good words to them, they will be thy servants for
ever.
10:8☆ 8 But he forsook the counsel which the old men gave him, and took
counsel with the young men that were brought up with him, that stood
before him.
9 And he said unto them, What advice give ye that we may return answer
to this people, which have spoken to me, saying, Ease somewhat the yoke
that thy father did put upon us?
10 And the young men that were brought up with him spake unto him,
saying, Thus shalt thou answer the people that spake unto thee, saying, Thy
father made our yoke heavy, but make thou *it* somewhat lighter for us; thus
shalt thou say unto them, My little *finger* shall be thicker than my father's
loins.
10:11☆ 11 For whereas my father put a heavy yoke upon you, I will put more to
your yoke: my father chastised you with whips, but I *will chastise you* with
scorpions.

10:4 Now that Solomon was dead, the people expressed their unhappiness with the yoke he had laid upon them. His many marriages and his splendor required large expenditures. Solomon's latter days were much worse than the former ones. He had given the people reason to complain. We who are under the yoke of Christ can never say that he gives us any reason for complaint.

10:8 Solomon knew God and consulted him. Here there is no indication that Rehoboam sought God for help in stilling the complaints of the people. He had learned nothing in this regard either from his father's life style or his prayers.

10:11 Rough answers are likely to stir up anger and worsen any situation. Rehoboam's obstinacy and lack of charity brought its own reward. The kingdom was torn in two.

2. The Rebellion of the Ten Tribes

12So Jer-o-bo'am and all the people came to Re-ho-bo'am on the third ☆10:12
day, as the king bade, saying, Come again to me on the third day.
13And the king answered them roughly; and king Re-ho-bo'am forsook
the counsel of the old men,
14And answered them after the advice of the young men, saying, My
father made your yoke heavy, but I will add thereto: my father chastised
you with whips, but I *will chastise you* with scorpions.
15So the king hearkened not unto the people: for the cause was of God, 10:15 1 Kgs 11:29–39 2 Chron 25:16–20
that the LORD might perform his word, which he spake by the hand of
A-hi'jah the Shi'lo-nite to Jer-o-bo'am the son of Ne'bat.
16¶And when all Israel *saw* that the king would not hearken unto them, ☆10:16 2 Sam 20:1 2 Chron 10:19
the people answered the king, saying, What portion have we in David? and
we have none inheritance in the son of Jesse: every man to your tents, O
Israel: *and* now, David, see to thine own house. So all Israel went to their
tents.
17But *as for* the children of Israel that dwelt in the cities of Judah, Re-ho-
bo'am reigned over them.
18Then king Re-ho-bo'am sent Ha-do'ram that *was* over the tribute; and ☆10:18 1 Kgs 4:6; 5:14
the children of Israel stoned him with stones, that he died. But king Re-ho-
bo'am made speed to get him up to *his* chariot, to flee to Jerusalem.
19And Israel rebelled against the house of David unto this day.

3. Judah Forbidden to Fight Israel

11 AND when Re-ho-bo'am was come to Jerusalem, he gathered of 11:1 1 Kgs 12:21–24
the house of Judah and Benjamin an hundred and fourscore
thousand chosen *men,* which were warriors, to fight against Israel, that he
might bring the kingdom again to Re-ho-bo'am.
2But the word of the LORD came to Shem-a-i'ah the man of God, saying, ☆11:2 2 Chron 12:5–7, 15
3Speak unto Re-ho-bo'am the son of Solomon, king of Judah, and to all
Israel in Judah and Benjamin, saying,
4Thus saith the LORD, Ye shall not go up, nor fight against your 11:4 2 Chron 10:15 28:8–11
brethren: return every man to his house: for this thing is done of me. And
they obeyed the words of the LORD, and returned from going against Jer-o-
bo'am.

4. Rehoboam Fortifies the Cities

5¶And Re-ho-bo'am dwelt in Jerusalem, and built cities for defence in ☆11:5 2 Chron 8:2–6 11:23
Judah.
6He built even Beth-lehem, and E'tam, and Te-ko'a,
7And Beth'-zur, and Sho'co, and A-dul'lam,

10:12 After Solomon's death the kingdom was divided into two parts: Israel, the Northern Kingdom led by Jeroboam, who engaged in Baal- and calf-worship; and Judah, the Southern Kingdom, which was led by Rehoboam. Assyria destroyed the Northern Kingdom after it had been misruled by evil kings for two centuries. Judah was blessed by having several good rulers.

10:16 *went to their tents,* a fitting demonstration that the ten tribes wanted no more of Rehoboam. They went home to set up their own kingdom and face a civil war if necessary.

10:18 Apparently Rehoboam went along with Hadoram and when he was stoned, the king had enough sense to flee to Jerusalem. But this incident did not bring him to his senses. The kingdom was divided forever—or until God at some future date brings Israel together again.

11:2 God had spoken directly to David and to Solomon. Rehoboam was beyond this sort of relationship. So God sent his prophet Shemaiah to tell Rehoboam not to fight against the revolting tribes. He obeyed the order given him by the prophet.

11:5 Rehoboam was prudent enough to defend his smaller kingdom against possible incursions by the ten revolting tribes. He fortified Jerusalem and built fortress cities surrounding Jerusalem for its protection.

8 And Gath, and Ma-re'shah, and Ziph,
9 And Ad-o-ra'im, and La'chish, and A-ze'kah,
10 And Zo'rah, and Ai'ja-lon, and Hebron, which *are* in Judah and in
Benjamin fenced cities.
11 And he fortified the strong holds, and put captains in them, and store
of victual, and of oil and wine.
12 And in every several city *he put* shields and spears, and made them
exceeding strong, having Judah and Benjamin on his side.

5. The Northern Priests and Levites Move to Judah

11:13☆ Num 35:2–5; 1 Kgs 12:28–33; 2 Chron 13:9

13 ¶And the priests and the Levites that *were* in all Israel resorted to him
out of all their coasts.
14 For the Levites left their suburbs and their possession, and came to
Judah and Jerusalem: for Jer-o-bo'am and his sons had cast them off from
executing the priest's office unto the LORD:

11:15 1 Kgs 12:31; 13:33

15 And he ordained him priests for the high places, and for the devils, and
for the calves which he had made.

11:16 2 Chron 15:9

16 And after them out of all the tribes of Israel such as set their hearts to
seek the LORD God of Israel came to Jerusalem, to sacrifice unto the LORD
God of their fathers.

11:17 2 Chron 12:1

17 So they strengthened the kingdom of Judah, and made Re-ho-bo'am
the son of Solomon strong, three years: for three years they walked in the
way of David and Solomon.

6. Rehoboam's Plural Marriages

11:18 1 Sam 16:6

18 ¶And Re-ho-bo'am took him Ma'ha-lath the daughter of Jer'i-moth the
son of David to wife, *and* Ab-i-ha'il the daughter of E-li'ab the son of Jesse;
19 Which bare him children; Je'ush, and Shem-a-ri'ah, and Za'ham.
20 And after her he took Ma'a-chah the daughter of Ab'sa-lom; which
bare him A-bi'jah, and At'tai, and Zi'za, and Shel'o-mith.

11:21☆ Deut 17:17

21 And Re-ho-bo'am loved Ma'a-chah the daughter of Ab'sa-lom above
all his wives and his concubines: (for he took eighteen wives, and threescore
concubines; and begat twenty and eight sons, and threescore daughters.)

11:22 Deut 21:15–17

22 And Re-ho-bo'am made A-bi'jah the son of Ma'a-chah the chief, *to be*
ruler among his brethren: for *he thought* to make him king.
23 And he dealt wisely, and dispersed of all his children throughout all the
countries of Judah and Benjamin, unto every fenced city: and he gave them
victual in abundance. And he desired many wives.

7. Shishak of Egypt's Military Victory over Rehoboam

12:1☆ 2 Chron 11:17; 12:13; 26:13–16

12 AND it came to pass, when Re-ho-bo'am had established the
kingdom, and had strengthened himself, he forsook the law of the
LORD, and all Israel with him.

11:13 Jeroboam had turned from God and cast off the priests and Levites. They now swarm into Jerusalem, leaving their possessions behind them. Their influence on Rehoboam was for good, for a short time. Verse 16 indicates that pious believers from the ten tribes followed the priests and Levites. Thus when the Northern Kingdom was destroyed, there were still people from those tribes who were not involved in the captivity and destruction. Jerusalem became their haven.

11:21 Rehoboam indulged himself in pleasure, as did his father Solomon. It did neither of them any good. Rehoboam had eighteen wives and sixty concubines. This was a violation of God's commandments and a lack of common sense, even apart from the commandments.

12:1 *Rehoboam,* Solomon's son and successor, was responsible for the breakup of the Solomonic kingdom because of his stupidity. He turned against God and suffered for his folly (2 Chron. 12:2). Nineteen kings followed after him. Some were good and others were evil. Judah, the Southern Kingdom, survived for more than three hundred years before it was destroyed by the Babylonian (Chaldean) conquest.

2 And it came to pass, *that* in the fifth year of king Re-ho-bo'am Shi'shak
king of Egypt came up against Jerusalem, because they had transgressed
against the LORD,

12:2 1 Kgs 11:40; 14:25

3 With twelve hundred chariots, and threescore thousand horsemen: and
the people *were* without number that came with him out of Egypt; the
Lu'bims, the Suk'ki-ims, and the E-thi-o'pi-ans.

12:3 2 Chron 16:8; Nah 3:9

4 And he took the fenced cities which *pertained* to Judah, and came to
Jerusalem.

12:4 2 Chron 11:5–12

5 ¶Then came Shem-a-i'ah the prophet to Re-ho-bo'am, and *to* the princes
of Judah, that were gathered together to Jerusalem because of Shi'shak, and
said unto them, Thus saith the LORD, Ye have forsaken me, and therefore
have I also left you in the hand of Shi'shak.

☆**12:5** Deut 28:15; 2 Chron 11:2; 15:2

6 Whereupon the princes of Israel and the king humbled themselves; and
they said, The LORD *is* righteous.

☆**12:6** Ex 9:27; Dan 9:14

7 And when the LORD saw that they humbled themselves, the word of the
LORD came to Shem-a-i'ah, saying, They have humbled themselves;
therefore I will not destroy them, but I will grant them some deliverance;
and my wrath shall not be poured out upon Jerusalem by the hand of
Shi'shak.

☆**12:7** 1 Kgs 21:29; 2 Chron 34:25–27; Ps 78:38

8 Nevertheless they shall be his servants; that they may know my service,
and the service of the kingdoms of the countries.

☆**12:8** Deut 28:47, 48

9 So Shi'shak king of Egypt came up against Jerusalem, and took away
the treasures of the house of the LORD, and the treasures of the king's
house; he took all: he carried away also the shields of gold which Solomon
had made.

☆**12:9** 1 Kgs 14:26–28; 2 Chron 9:15, 16

10 Instead of which king Re-ho-bo'am made shields of brass, and
committed *them* to the hands of the chief of the guard, that kept the
entrance of the king's house.
11 And when the king entered into the house of the LORD, the guard came
and fetched them, and brought them again into the guard chamber.
12 And when he humbled himself, the wrath of the LORD turned from him,
that he would not destroy *him* altogether: and also in Judah things went
well.

12:12 2 Chron 12:6, 7

8. The Death of Rehoboam; Abijah Succeeds Him

13 ¶So king Re-ho-bo'am strengthened himself in Jerusalem, and reigned:
for Re-ho-bo'am *was* one and forty years old when he began to reign, and
he reigned seventeen years in Jerusalem, the city which the LORD had
chosen out of all the tribes of Israel, to put his name there. And his
mother's name *was* Na'a-mah an Ammonitess.

12:13 1 Kgs 14:21

14 And he did evil, because he prepared not his heart to seek the LORD.

12:14 2 Chron 19:3

15 Now the acts of Re-ho-bo'am, first and last, *are* they not written in the
book of Shem-a-i'ah the prophet, and of Id'do the seer concerning
genealogies? And *there were* wars between Re-ho-bo'am and Jer-o-bo'am
continually.

☆**12:15** 1 Kgs 14:29; 2 Chron 9:29; 12:5

16 And Re-ho-bo'am slept with his fathers, and was buried in the city of
David: and A-bi'jah his son reigned in his stead.

12:16 2 Chron 11:20

12:5–8 Shishak came down on Judah at the instigation of God (12:2). It was a divine punishment for departing from the faith. In verse 6 there was a turning back to God and a seeking for his help. Thus the counsel of 2 Chron. 7:14 was followed, and help from God stayed the hand of Shishak so that the kingdom was not destroyed. It became a tributary to Shishak.

12:9 Shishak helped himself generously to the treasures of Judah and the temple. He raided the palace and the temple. Verse 12 indicates that once again Rehoboam learned his lesson the hard way and God helped him so that "in Judah things went well."

12:15 Shishak was a problem for Rehoboam; so also were the ten tribes that had revolted, and "there were wars continually between Rehoboam and Jeroboam."* The splendor of Solomon had already departed from Israel, and the promise of blessing lost because of transgression.

B. KING ABIJAH

1. Abijah and Jeroboam at War

13:1 1 Kgs 15:1, 2, 7; 2 Chron 11:20

13 NOW in the eighteenth year of king Jer-o-bo'am began A-bi'jah to reign over Judah.

13:2☆

2 He reigned three years in Jerusalem. His mother's name also *was* Mi-chai'ah the daughter of U'ri-el of Gib'e-ah. And there was war between A-bi'jah and Jer-o-bo'am.

3 And A-bi'jah set the battle in array with an army of valiant men of war, *even* four hundred thousand chosen men: Jer-o-bo'am also set the battle in array against him with eight hundred thousand chosen men, *being* mighty men of valour.

13:4 Josh 18:22

4 ¶And A-bi'jah stood up upon mount Zem-a-ra'im, which *is* in mount E'phra-im, and said, Hear me, thou Jer-o-bo'am, and all Israel;

13:5☆ Num 18:19; 2 Sam 7:12–16

5 Ought ye not to know that the LORD God of Israel gave the kingdom over Israel to David for ever, *even* to him and to his sons by a covenant of salt?

13:6 1 Kgs 11:26

6 Yet Jer-o-bo'am the son of Ne'bat, the servant of Solomon the son of David, is risen up, and hath rebelled against his lord.

13:7 2 Chron 12:13

7 And there are gathered unto him vain men, the children of Be'li-al, and have strengthened themselves against Re-ho-bo'am the son of Solomon, when Re-ho-bo'am was young and tenderhearted, and could not withstand them.

13:8☆ 1 Kgs 12:28; 2 Chron 11:15

8 And now ye think to withstand the kingdom of the LORD in the hand of the sons of David; and ye *be* a great multitude, and *there are* with you golden calves, which Jer-o-bo'am made you for gods.

13:9 Ex 29:29–33; 2 Chron 11:14; Jer 2:11; 5:7

9 Have ye not cast out the priests of the LORD, the sons of Aaron, and the Levites, and have made you priests after the manner of the nations of *other* lands? so that whosoever cometh to consecrate himself with a young bullock and seven rams, *the same* may be a priest of *them that are* no gods.

10 But as for us, the LORD *is* our God, and we have not forsaken him; and the priests, which minister unto the LORD, *are* the sons of Aaron, and the Levites *wait* upon *their* business:

13:11 Ex 25:30–39; 29:38; Lev 24:5–9; 2 Chron 2:4

11 And they burn unto the LORD every morning and every evening burnt sacrifices and sweet incense: the shewbread also *set they in order* upon the pure table; and the candlestick of gold with the lamps thereof, to burn every evening: for we keep the charge of the LORD our God; but ye have forsaken him.

13:12 Num 10:8, 9

12 And, behold, God himself *is* with us for *our* captain, and his priests with sounding trumpets to cry alarm against you. O children of Israel, fight ye not against the LORD God of your fathers; for ye shall not prosper.

2. Abijah Defeats Jeroboam

13:13☆ Josh 8:4–9; 2 Chron 14:11

13 ¶But Jer-o-bo'am caused an ambushment to come about behind them: so they were before Judah, and the ambushment *was* behind them.

13:2 God had forbidden Rehoboam to war against Jeroboam (11:4). He allowed his son Abijah to do so and gave him the victory over Jeroboam.

13:5 Abijah speaks to Jeroboam and apprises him of an undeniable fact. God had given the kingship to David and to his posterity in a covenant of salt. Therefore Jeroboam was a rebel who had done the wrong thing. Moreover he had taken advantage of the youthfulness of Rehoboam and his lack of tact.

13:8 Abijah's case against Jeroboam centered around the godlessness of the ruler who made golden calves and turned Israel away from the true God. While Abijah was by no means fully obedient and under the rule of God, yet he did call on God and seek divine help against this awful apostate. He was the lesser of two evils.

13:13 Apparently Jeroboam was talking peace to Abijah at the same time he was preparing an ambush to take him and the soldiers of Judah by surprise. His ploy did not work.

14 And when Judah looked back, behold, the battle *was* before and
behind: and they cried unto the LORD, and the priests sounded with the
trumpets.
☆13:14
15 Then the men of Judah gave a shout: and as the men of Judah shouted,
it came to pass, that God smote Jer-o-bo'am and all Israel before A-bi'jah
and Judah.
13:15 2 Chron 16:8
16 And the children of Israel fled before Judah: and God delivered them
into their hand.
17 And A-bi'jah and his people slew them with a great slaughter: so there
fell down slain of Israel five hundred thousand chosen men.
18 Thus the children of Israel were brought under at that time, and the
children of Judah prevailed, because they relied upon the LORD God of
their fathers.
13:18 2 Chron 14:11
19 And A-bi'jah pursued after Jer-o-bo'am, and took cities from him,
Beth-el with the towns thereof, and Jesh'a-nah with the towns thereof, and
E'phra-in with the towns thereof.
20 Neither did Jer-o-bo'am recover strength again in the days of A-bi'jah:
and the LORD struck him, and he died.
13:20 1 Sam 25:38; 1 Kgs 14:20
21 ¶But A-bi'jah waxed mighty, and married fourteen wives, and begat
twenty and two sons, and sixteen daughters.
☆13:21
22 And the rest of the acts of A-bi'jah, and his ways, and his sayings, *are*
written in the story of the prophet Id'do.
13:22 2 Chron 9:20; 24:27

C. KING ASA

1. God Blesses Faithful Asa

14 SO A-bi'jah slept with his fathers, and they buried him in the city of
David: and Asa his son reigned in his stead. In his days the land
was quiet ten years.
14:1 1 Kgs 15:8
2 And Asa did *that which was* good and right in the eyes of the LORD his
God:
☆14:2
3 For he took away the altars of the strange *gods,* and the high places, and
brake down the images, and cut down the groves:
14:3 Ex 34:13; Deut 7:5; 1 Kgs 15:12–14
4 And commanded Judah to seek the LORD God of their fathers, and to
do the law and the commandment.
5 Also he took away out of all the cities of Judah the high places and the
images: and the kingdom was quiet before him.
14:5 2 Chron 15:15; 34:4, 7
6 ¶And he built fenced cities in Judah: for the land had rest, and he had
no war in those years; because the LORD had given him rest.
☆14:6 2 Chron 11:5
7 Therefore he said unto Judah, Let us build these cities, and make about
them walls, and towers, gates, and bars, *while* the land *is* yet before us;
because we have sought the LORD our God, we have sought *him,* and he
hath given us rest on every side. So they built and prospered.
☆14:7 2 Chron 8:5
8 And Asa had an army *of men* that bare targets and spears, out of Judah
three hundred thousand; and out of Benjamin, that bare shields and drew
bows, two hundred and fourscore thousand: all these *were* mighty men of
valour.
14:8 2 Chron 13:3

13:14 The priests accompanied the troops of Abijah in battle. They blew their trumpets, thus calling on the name of God. Judah prevailed, and Jeroboam never recovered from the defeat he suffered.

13:21 Abijah followed in the steps of his father and grandfather. He multiplied wives to himself and begat twenty-two sons and sixteen daughters. He prospered and, fortunately for Judah, he had a good son, Asa, to succeed him.

14:2 Asa was a good king who enjoyed peace in his time. He aimed to please God and in so doing he abolished idolatry among his people. The strange altars, images, and groves were destroyed.

14:6, 7 The clue to the peace Asa and Judah enjoyed was based on God's graciousness. "The LORD had given him (Asa) rest." All who trust in God will find peace and rest, which are the reward of faithfulness.

2. Asa's Military Victory over Zerah of Egypt

14:9☆ 2 Chron 11:8; 12:2, 3; 16:8
9¶And there came out against them Ze'rah the E-thi-o'pi-an with an host
of a thousand thousand, and three hundred chariots; and came unto Ma-
re'shah.
14:10☆
10Then Asa went out against him, and they set the battle in array in the
valley of Zeph'a-thah at Ma-re'shah.
14:11 2 Chron 13:14, 18
11And Asa cried unto the LORD his God, and said, LORD, *it is* nothing
with thee to help, whether with many, or with them that have no power:
help us, O LORD our God; for we rest on thee, and in thy name we go
against this multitude. O LORD, thou *art* our God; let not man prevail
against thee.
14:12☆ 2 Chron 13:15
12So the LORD smote the E-thi-o'pi-ans before Asa, and before Judah;
and the E-thi-o'pi-ans fled.
14:13 Gen 10:19
13And Asa and the people that *were* with him pursued them unto Ge'rar:
and the E-thi-o'pi-ans were overthrown, that they could not recover
themselves; for they were destroyed before the LORD, and before his host;
and they carried away very much spoil.
14:14 2 Chron 17:10
14And they smote all the cities round about Ge'rar; for the fear of the
LORD came upon them: and they spoiled all the cities; for there was
exceeding much spoil in them.
15They smote also the tents of cattle, and carried away sheep and camels
in abundance, and returned to Jerusalem.

3. Asa's Reforms

15:1☆ 2 Chron 20:14; 24:20
15 AND the Spirit of God came upon Az-a-ri'ah the son of O'ded:
2And he went out to meet Asa, and said unto him, Hear ye me,
15:2 2 Chron 15:4, 15; 20:17
Asa, and all Judah and Benjamin; The LORD *is* with you, while ye be with
him; and if ye seek him, he will be found of you; but if ye forsake him, he
will forsake you.
15:3 Lev 10:8–11; 1 Kgs 12:28–33; 2 Chron 17:9
3Now for a long season Israel *hath been* without the true God, and
without a teaching priest, and without law.
15:4 Deut 4:29
4But when they in their trouble did turn unto the LORD God of Israel,
and sought him, he was found of them.
5And in those times *there was* no peace to him that went out, nor to him
that came in, but great vexations *were* upon all the inhabitants of the
countries.
6And nation was destroyed of nation, and city of city: for God did vex
them with all adversity.
15:7 Josh 1:7, 9
7Be ye strong therefore, and let not your hands be weak: for your work
shall be rewarded.
15:8☆ 2 Chron 4:1; 8:12; 13:19
8And when Asa heard these words, and the prophecy of O'ded the
prophet, he took courage, and put away the abominable idols out of all the
land of Judah and Benjamin, and out of the cities which he had taken from

---

14:9 *thousand thousand,* i.e., "one million." In view of the three-hundred chariots, the million soldiers is probably a hyperbole or the result of misreading an illegible or worn manuscript when it was copied.

14:10 Asa enjoyed internal peace until Zerah the Ethiopian came down with a mighty army against him. Asa put his trust in God and prayed for divine help. God heard and helped.

14:12 The victory over Zerah is stated to be God's victory. "The LORD smote the Ethiopians." How and under what circumstances God did this is not stated here. But at least Judah knew that they had not won the victory by their own strength.

15:1 The Spirit of God came on God's people in the Old Testament according to his good pleasure. He came upon Azariah to instruct him as to what he should say to the king and to enable him to say it with boldness and clarity. He did not come to compliment the king, for the victory was God's not the king's. He came rather to tell Asa what he should do as a servant of God.

15:8 Revival came to Judah after Azariah spoke to the

mount E'phra-im, and renewed the altar of the LORD, that *was* before the
porch of the LORD.
9 And he gathered all Judah and Benjamin, and the strangers with them **15:9**
out of E'phra-im and Ma-nas'seh, and out of Simeon: for they fell to him 2 Chron 11:16
out of Israel in abundance, when they saw that the LORD his God *was* with
him.
10 So they gathered themselves together at Jerusalem in the third month,
in the fifteenth year of the reign of Asa.
11 And they offered unto the LORD the same time, of the spoil *which* they **15:11** 2 Chron
had brought, seven hundred oxen and seven thousand sheep. 14:13–15
12 And they entered into a covenant to seek the LORD God of their fathers **15:12**
with all their heart and with all their soul; 2 Chron 23:16
13 That whosoever would not seek the LORD God of Israel should be put **15:13** Ex 22:20
to death, whether small or great, whether man or woman. Deut 13:6–9
14 And they sware unto the LORD with a loud voice, and with shouting,
and with trumpets, and with cornets.
15 And all Judah rejoiced at the oath: for they had sworn with all their ☆**15:15**
heart, and sought him with their whole desire; and he was found of them: 2 Chron 14:7
and the LORD gave them rest round about.
16 ¶And also *concerning* Ma'a-chah the mother of Asa the king, he ☆**15:16**
removed her from *being* queen, because she had made an idol in a grove: Ex 34:13 1 Kgs 15:13–15
and Asa cut down her idol, and stamped *it*, and burnt *it* at the brook 2 Chron 14:2–5
Kidron.
17 But the high places were not taken away out of Israel: nevertheless the
heart of Asa was perfect all his days.
18 ¶And he brought into the house of God the things that his father had
dedicated, and that he himself had dedicated, silver, and gold, and vessels.
19 And there was no *more* war unto the five and thirtieth year of the reign
of Asa.

4. Asa's Unholy Alliance with Ben-hadad

16 IN the six and thirtieth year of the reign of Asa Ba'a-sha king of ☆**16:1**
Israel came up against Judah, and built Ra'mah, to the intent that 1 Kgs 15:17–22
he might let none go out or come in to Asa king of Judah.
2 Then Asa brought out silver and gold out of the treasures of the house ☆**16:2**
of the LORD and of the king's house, and sent to Ben-ha'dad king of Syria,
that dwelt at Damascus, saying,
3 *There is* a league between me and thee, as *there was* between my father ☆**16:3**
and thy father: behold, I have sent thee silver and gold; go, break thy
league with Ba'a-sha king of Israel, that he may depart from me.
4 And Ben-ha'dad hearkened unto king Asa, and sent the captains of his **16:4**
armies against the cities of Israel; and they smote I'jon, and Dan, and Ex 1:11
A'bel-ma'im, and all the store cities of Naph'ta-li.

---

king. Azariah encouraged Asa to be strong. He followed that advice—by repairing the altar of God, by destroying all the idols he could find in his kingdom, and by calling the people to the true worship of God.
15:15 The revival led Judah, Benjamin, and the people from the Northern Kingdom (who had come to live in Judea) to take an oath before God that they would serve him faithfully. When they did this, God gave them rest.
15:16 *an idol*, "an abominable image" (RSV); an "Asherah-idol" (TLB). (See note on Deut. 12:3.)
16:1 Reconciling the date here with the history of the kings presents a problem. There are two good explanations for the supposed error, both found in G. L. Archer's *Encyclopedia of Bible Difficulties*, Zondervan, 1982, pp. 225–226.
16:2 Ben-hadad. See note on 1 Kings 15:18.
16:3 Instead of trusting in God, Asa bribed Ben-hadad and worked out a military alliance with him. He was successful in repulsing Baasha, the king of Israel.

5 And it came to pass, when Ba'a-sha heard *it,* that he left off building of
Ra'mah, and let his work cease.
6 Then Asa the king took all Judah; and they carried away the stones of
Ra'mah, and the timber thereof, wherewith Ba'a-sha was building; and he
built therewith Ge'ba and Mizpah.

5. Hanani, God's Prophet, Condemns the Alliance

16:7☆ 7 ¶And at that time Ha-na'ni the seer came to Asa king of Judah, and said
1 Kgs 16:1 2 Chron 14:11 unto him, Because thou hast relied on the king of Syria, and not relied on
19:2; 32:7, 8 the LORD thy God, therefore is the host of the king of Syria escaped out of
thine hand.
16:8☆ 8 Were not the E-thi-o'pi-ans and the Lu'bims a huge host, with very
2 Chron 12:3 13:16, 18; 14:9 many chariots and horsemen? yet, because thou didst rely on the LORD, he
delivered them into thine hand.
16:9☆ 9 For the eyes of the LORD run to and fro throughout the whole earth, to
2 Chron 15:17 Prov 15:3 shew himself strong in the behalf of *them* whose heart *is* perfect toward him.
Zech 4:10 Herein thou hast done foolishly: therefore from henceforth thou shalt have
wars.
16:10☆ 10 Then Asa was wroth with the seer, and put him in a prison house; for
he was in a rage with him because of this *thing.* And Asa oppressed *some* of
the people the same time.

6. Asa's Disease and Death

16:11 11 ¶And, behold, the acts of Asa, first and last, lo, they *are* written in the
1 Kgs 15:23, 24 book of the kings of Judah and Israel.
12 And Asa in the thirty and ninth year of his reign was diseased in his
feet, until his disease *was* exceeding *great:* yet in his disease he sought not to
the LORD, but to the physicians.
16:13 13 ¶And Asa slept with his fathers, and died in the one and fortieth year of
Gen 50:2 2 Chron 21:19 his reign.
Jn 12:1–7 19:39, 40 14 And they buried him in his own sepulchres, which he had made for
himself in the city of David, and laid him in the bed which was filled with
sweet odours and divers kinds *of spices* prepared by the apothecaries' art:
and they made a very great burning for him.

D. KING JEHOSHAPHAT

1. Jehoshaphat the Faithful: Teaching *The Book of the Law* of the Lord

17:1 17 AND Je-hosh'a-phat his son reigned in his stead, and strengthened
1 Kgs 15:24 himself against Israel.
17:2 2 And he placed forces in all the fenced cities of Judah, and set garrisons
2 Chron 11:5 15:8 in the land of Judah, and in the cities of E'phra-im, which Asa his father
had taken.

16:7–9 The prophet Hanani rebuked Asa for substituting Ben-hadad for God and for forming an alliance with him instead of trusting God alone. He reminded him that God gave Judah a great victory over the Ethiopians and this should have taught him to rely on God alone. Then follows verse 9: here God is pictured as searching the farthest corners of the earth to find those who trust in him. And when he finds them he shows his might on their behalf. Those whose hearts are not upright can expect no help from God. Thus the condition for blessing and help always derives from the rightness of one's relation to God.

16:10 Blessed is the man who meekly accepts criticism when he is found wanting. Asa angrily threw Hanani into prison and thus insulted God who sent him. After spurning the rebuke, he was afflicted with a disease; and in that sorry condition he still refused to seek the face of God. The implication is plain. Had he sought God, he would have been helped. The physicians did him no good, and he died for his stubborn attitude toward his God.

3 And the LORD was with Je-hosh'a-phat, because he walked in the first ☆17:3
ways of his father David, and sought not unto Ba'al-im;
4 But sought to the *LORD* God of his father, and walked in his command- 17:4 1 Kgs 12:28
ments, and not after the doings of Israel.
5 Therefore the LORD stablished the kingdom in his hand; and all Judah 17:5 2 Chron 18:1
brought to Je-hosh'a-phat presents; and he had riches and honour in
abundance.
6 And his heart was lifted up in the ways of the LORD: moreover he took ☆17:6 2 Chron 15:17
away the high places and groves out of Judah.
7 ¶Also in the third year of his reign he sent to his princes, *even* to Ben- 17:7 Deut 6:4–9
ha'il, and to O-ba-di'ah, and to Zech-a-ri'ah, and to Ne-than'e-el, and to 2 Chron 15:3
Mi-chai'ah, to teach in the cities of Judah. 19:8; 35:3
8 And with them *he sent* Levites, *even* Shem-a-i'ah, and Neth-a-ni'ah, and
Zeb-a-di'ah, and As'a-hel, and She-mir'a-moth, and Je-hon'a-than, and Ad-
o-ni'jah, and To-bi'jah, and Tob'-ad-o-ni'jah, Levites; and with them
E-lish'a-ma and Je-ho'ram, priests.
9 And they taught in Judah, and *had* the book of the law of the LORD with ☆17:9
them, and went about throughout all the cities of Judah, and taught the
people.

2. God's Blessing on Jehoshaphat

10 ¶And the fear of the LORD fell upon all the kingdoms of the lands that ☆17:10 2 Chron 14:14
were round about Judah, so that they made no war against Je-hosh'a-phat.
11 Also *some* of the Philistines brought Je-hosh'a-phat presents, and ☆17:11 2 Chron 9:14
tribute silver; and the Arabians brought him flocks, seven thousand and 26:8
seven hundred rams, and seven thousand and seven hundred he goats.
12 ¶And Je-hosh'a-phat waxed great exceedingly; and he built in Judah
castles, and cities of store.
13 And he had much business in the cities of Judah: and the men of war,
mighty men of valour, *were* in Jerusalem.
14 And these *are* the numbers of them according to the house of their
fathers: Of Judah, the captains of thousands; Ad'nah the chief, and with
him mighty men of valour three hundred thousand.
15 And next to him *was* Je-ho-ha'nan the captain, and with him two
hundred and fourscore thousand.
16 And next him *was* Am-a-si'ah the son of Zich'ri, who willingly offered 17:16 Judg 5:2; 9
himself unto the LORD; and with him two hundred thousand mighty men of 1 Chron 29:9
valour.
17 And of Benjamin; E-li'a-da a mighty man of valour, and with him
armed men with bow and shield two hundred thousand.
18 And next him *was* Je-hoz'a-bad, and with him an hundred and
fourscore thousand ready prepared for the war.
19 These waited on the king, beside *those* whom the king put in the fenced 17:19 2 Chron 17:2
cities throughout all Judah.

17:3 This verse presents some problems for the translators. The RSV has it, "because he walked in the earlier ways of his father." The NASB says, "because he followed the example of his father David's earlier days." In either event, he was one of the better kings of Judah.

17:6 Evidently idol worship had not been completely extirpated in Judah. Jehoshaphat destroyed high places and groves, which were forbidden by God.

17:9–11 The Word of God was known to the spiritual leaders of Judah. They taught its doctrines to the people and diffused a blessed light among them. The devotion of the king and people to the Word of God brought happiness, prosperity, and peace. Great revivals and great reforms are founded in the rediscovery of God's Word.

3. Jehoshaphat's Military Pact with Ahab
a. Ahab's Proposal

18:1☆ 2 Chron: 17:5 **18** NOW Je-hosh'a-phat had riches and honour in abundance, and
joined affinity with Ahab.
18:2 1 Kgs 22:2–35 [2]And after *certain* years he went down to Ahab to Sa-ma'ri-a. And Ahab
killed sheep and oxen for him in abundance, and for the people that *he had*
with him, and persuaded him to go up *with him* to Ra'moth-gil'e-ad.
[3]And Ahab king of Israel said unto Je-hosh'a-phat king of Judah, Wilt
thou go with me to Ra'moth-gil'e-ad? And he answered him, I *am* as thou
art, and my people as thy people; and *we will be* with thee in the war.

b. The Counsel of the False Prophets

[4]¶And Je-hosh'a-phat said unto the king of Israel, Inquire, I pray thee, at
the word of the LORD to day.
18:4ff☆ [5]Therefore the king of Israel gathered together of prophets four hundred
men, and said unto them, Shall we go to Ra'moth-gil'e-ad to battle, or shall
I forbear? And they said, Go up; for God will deliver *it* into the king's
hand.
[6]But Je-hosh'a-phat said, *Is there* not here a prophet of the LORD besides,
that we might inquire of him?
[7]And the king of Israel said unto Je-hosh'a-phat, *There is* yet one man,
by whom we may inquire of the LORD: but I hate him; for he never
prophesied good unto me, but always evil: the same *is* Mi-cai'ah the son of
Im'la. And Je-hosh'a-phat said, Let not the king say so.
[8]And the king of Israel called for one *of his* officers, and said, Fetch
quickly Mi-cai'ah the son of Im'la.
[9]And the king of Israel and Je-hosh'a-phat king of Judah sat either of
them on his throne, clothed in *their* robes, and they sat in a void place at the
entering in of the gate of Sa-ma'ri-a; and all the prophets prophesied before
them.
[10]And Zed-e-ki'ah the son of Che-na'a-nah had made him horns of iron,
and said, Thus saith the LORD, With these thou shalt push Syria until they
be consumed.
[11]And all the prophets prophesied so, saying, Go up to Ra'moth-gil'e-ad,
and prosper: for the LORD shall deliver *it* into the hand of the king.

c. Micaiah's God-given Prophecy

[12]And the messenger that went to call Mi-cai'ah spake to him, saying,
Behold, the words of the prophets *declare* good to the king with one assent;
let thy word therefore, I pray thee, be like one of theirs, and speak thou
good.
18:13 Num 22:18–20, 35 [13]And Mi-cai'ah said, *As* the LORD liveth, even what my God saith, that
will I speak.
[14]And when he was come to the king, the king said unto him, Mi-cai'ah,
shall we go to Ra'moth-gil'e-ad to battle, or shall I forbear? And he said,
Go ye up, and prosper, and they shall be delivered into your hand.
[15]And the king said to him, How many times shall I adjure thee that thou
say nothing but the truth to me in the name of the LORD?

18:1 Jehoshaphat grew greater but he did not grow wiser. He made an alliance by marriage with Ahab, whose daughter Athaliah became the wife of Jehoram, the son of Jehoshaphat. "What good could Jehoshaphat get from a man (Ahab) that was so bad? What good could he do to a man that was so obstinately wicked—an idolator, a persecutor?"*

18:4ff The passage from verse 4 through verse 34 is similar to that found in 1 Kings 22. See the notes in that chapter for further information on the text here.

16Then he said, I did see all Israel scattered upon the mountains, as sheep
that have no shepherd: and the LORD said, These have no master; let them
return *therefore* every man to his house in peace.

18:16 Num 27:17 Ezek 34:5–8 Mt 9:36

17And the king of Israel said to Je-hosh′a-phat, Did I not tell thee *that* he
would not prophesy good unto me, but evil?
18Again he said, Therefore hear the word of the LORD; I saw the LORD
sitting upon his throne, and all the host of heaven standing on his right
hand and *on* his left.

18:18 Isa 6:1–5 Dan 7:9, 10

19And the LORD said, Who shall entice Ahab king of Israel, that he may
go up and fall at Ra′moth-gil′e-ad? And one spake saying after this
manner, and another saying after that manner.
20Then there came out a spirit, and stood before the LORD, and said, I
will entice him. And the LORD said unto him, Wherewith?
21And he said, I will go out, and be a lying spirit in the mouth of all his
prophets. And *the LORD* said, Thou shalt entice *him,* and thou shalt also
prevail: go out, and do *even* so.
22Now therefore, behold, the LORD hath put a lying spirit in the mouth of
these thy prophets, and the LORD hath spoken evil against thee.
23Then Zed-e-ki′ah the son of Che-na′a-nah came near, and smote Mi-
cai′ah upon the cheek, and said, Which way went the Spirit of the LORD
from me to speak unto thee?
24And Mi-cai′ah said, Behold, thou shalt see on that day when thou shalt
go into an inner chamber to hide thyself.
25Then the king of Israel said, Take ye Mi-cai′ah, and carry him back to
A′mon the governor of the city, and to Jo′ash the king's son;

18:25 2 Chron 18:8 34:8

26And say, Thus saith the king, Put this *fellow* in the prison, and feed him
with bread of affliction and with water of affliction, until I return in peace.

18:26 2 Chron 16:10

27And Mi-cai′ah said, If thou certainly return in peace, *then* hath not the
LORD spoken by me. And he said, Hearken, all ye people.

18:27 Mic 1:2

d. The Death of Ahab in Battle

28So the king of Israel and Je-hosh′a-phat the king of Judah went up to
Ra′moth-gil′e-ad.
29And the king of Israel said unto Je-hosh′a-phat, I will disguise myself,
and will go to the battle; but put thou on thy robes. So the king of Israel
disguised himself; and they went to the battle.
30Now the king of Syria had commanded the captains of the chariots that
were with him, saying, Fight ye not with small or great, save only with the
king of Israel.
31And it came to pass, when the captains of the chariots saw Je-hosh′a-
phat, that they said, It *is* the king of Israel. Therefore they compassed about
him to fight: but Je-hosh′a-phat cried out, and the LORD helped him; and
God moved them *to depart* from him.

18:31 2 Chron 13:14, 15

32For it came to pass, that, when the captains of the chariots perceived
that it was not the king of Israel, they turned back again from pursuing
him.
33And a *certain* man drew a bow at a venture, and smote the king of
Israel between the joints of the harness: therefore he said to his chariot
man, Turn thine hand, that thou mayest carry me out of the host; for I am
wounded.

☆18:33

34And the battle increased that day: howbeit the king of Israel stayed

18:33 "No art, no arms, can save those whom God has appointed to ruin. What can hurt those whom God will protect? And what can shelter those whom God will destroy? . . . The race is not to the swift nor the battle to the strong."*

himself up in *his* chariot against the Syrians until the even: and about the time of the sun going down he died.

4. The Prophet Jehu Rebukes Jehoshaphat

19 AND Je-hosh'a-phat the king of Judah returned to his house in peace to Jerusalem.

19:2☆ 1 Kgs 16:1; 2 Chron 18:1, 3; 20:34; 24:18

[2]And Jehu the son of Ha-na'ni the seer went out to meet him, and said to king Je-hosh'a-phat, Shouldest thou help the ungodly, and love them that hate the LORD? therefore *is* wrath upon thee from before the LORD.

19:3 2 Chron 12:12, 14; 17:6

[3]Nevertheless there are good things found in thee, in that thou hast taken away the groves out of the land, and hast prepared thine heart to seek God.

5. Jehoshaphat's Reforms

19:4☆ Deut 16:18–20

[4]And Je-hosh'a-phat dwelt at Jerusalem: and he went out again through the people from Be'er-she'ba to mount E'phra-im, and brought them back unto the LORD God of their fathers.

[5]And he set judges in the land throughout all the fenced cities of Judah, city by city,

19:6 Lev 19:15; Deut 1:17

[6]And said to the judges, Take heed what ye do: for ye judge not for man, but for the LORD, who *is* with you in the judgment.

19:7 Gen 18:25; Deut 10:17, 18; 32:4

[7]Wherefore now let the fear of the LORD be upon you; take heed and do *it:* for *there is* no iniquity with the LORD our God, nor respect of persons, nor taking of gifts.

19:8 2 Chron 17:8, 9

[8]¶Moreover in Jerusalem did Je-hosh'a-phat set of the Levites, and *of* the priests, and of the chief of the fathers of Israel, for the judgment of the LORD, and for controversies, when they returned to Jerusalem.

19:9☆

[9]And he charged them, saying, Thus shall ye do in the fear of the LORD, faithfully, and with a perfect heart.

19:10 Deut 17:8; 2 Chron 19:2

[10]And what cause soever shall come to you of your brethren that dwell in their cities, between blood and blood, between law and commandment, statutes and judgments, ye shall even warn them that they trespass not against the LORD, and *so* wrath come upon you, and upon your brethren: this do, and ye shall not trespass.

19:11☆ 1 Chron 28:20; 2 Chron 19:8

[11]And, behold, Am-a-ri'ah the chief priest *is* over you in all matters of the LORD; and Zeb-a-di'ah the son of Ish'ma-el, the ruler of the house of Judah, for all the king's matters: also the Levites *shall be* officers before you. Deal courageously, and the LORD shall be with the good.

6. Jehoshaphat's Delivery from the Moabites, Ammonites, and Syrians

a. Jehoshaphat Seeks God and Prays for Help

20:1☆

20 IT came to pass after this also, *that* the children of Moab, and the children of Ammon, and with them *other* beside the Ammonites, came against Je-hosh'a-phat to battle.

19:2 It is of God's mercy that he reproves us of our errors. Jehu the son of Hanani was sent by God to tell Jehoshaphat he had erred in allying himself with Ahab. He asked the question: Should a godly man help an ungodly one? God was angry but Jehoshaphat repented, so God did not cast him off.

19:4 Jehoshaphat revived and continued his efforts to reform the nation. He brought the people back to the God of their fathers. God approved of this.

19:9 The king wanted justice to be done by the nation's judges, who were to render judgment in the fear of the Lord. They were to judge not for man but for God. This meant impartiality, with no respect for persons.

19:11 There was a separation of church and state. Jehoshaphat stated that Amariah would deal with ecclesiastical matters and that Ishmael would handle civil matters. Neither could say that one had no need of the other. "Some best understand the matters of the Lord, others the king's matters."* God uses both kinds for his glory.

20:1 The enemies of Jehoshaphat organized an alliance and conspired to ruin him and Judah. They were Ammonites, Moabites, and Meunites. The king sensed his danger and called the nation to fast and pray.

2 Then there came some that told Je-hosh'a-phat, saying, There cometh a
great multitude against thee from beyond the sea on this side Syria; and,
behold, they *be* in Haz'a-zon–ta'mar, which *is* En–ge'di.

20:2 Gen 14:7

3 And Je-hosh'a-phat feared, and set himself to seek the LORD, and
proclaimed a fast throughout all Judah.

20:3 1 Sam 7:6; 2 Chron 19:3; Ezra 8:21

4 And Judah gathered themselves together, to ask *help* of the LORD: even
out of all the cities of Judah they came to seek the LORD.
5 ¶And Je-hosh'a-phat stood in the congregation of Judah and Jerusalem,
in the house of the LORD, before the new court,
6 And said, O LORD God of our fathers, *art* not thou God in heaven? and
rulest *not* thou over all the kingdoms of the heathen? and in thine hand *is*
there not power and might, so that none is able to withstand thee?

☆**20:6** Deut 4:39; 1 Chron 29:11

7 *Art* not thou our God, *who* didst drive out the inhabitants of this land
before thy people Israel, and gavest it to the seed of Abraham thy friend for
ever?

20:7 Isa 41:8

8 And they dwelt therein, and have built thee a sanctuary therein for thy
name, saying,
9 If, *when* evil cometh upon us, *as* the sword, judgment, or pestilence, or
famine, we stand before this house, and in thy presence, (for thy name *is* in
this house,) and cry unto thee in our affliction, then thou wilt hear and help.

20:9 2 Chron 6:20, 28–30

10 And now, behold, the children of Ammon and Moab and mount Se'ir,
whom thou wouldest not let Israel invade, when they came out of the land
of Egypt, but they turned from them, and destroyed them not;

20:10 Num 20:17–21; 2 Chron 20:1, 22

11 Behold, *I say, how* they reward us, to come to cast us out of thy
possession, which thou hast given us to inherit.
12 O our God, wilt thou not judge them? for we have no might against this
great company that cometh against us; neither know we what to do: but
our eyes *are* upon thee.

20:12 Judg 11:27; Ps 25:15; 121:1, 2

b. Jahaziel Promises God's Deliverance

13 And all Judah stood before the LORD, with their little ones, their wives,
and their children.
14 ¶Then upon Ja-ha'zi-el the son of Zech-a-ri'ah, the son of Be-nai'ah, the
son of Je-i'el, the son of Mat-ta-ni'ah, a Levite of the sons of A'saph, came
the Spirit of the LORD in the midst of the congregation;

☆**20:14** 2 Chron 15:1; 24:20

15 And he said, Hearken ye, all Judah, and ye inhabitants of Jerusalem,
and thou king Je-hosh'a-phat, Thus saith the LORD unto you, Be not afraid
nor dismayed by reason of this great multitude; for the battle *is* not yours,
but God's.

20:15 Ex 14:13; 1 Sam 17:47; 2 Chron 32:7, 8

16 To morrow go ye down against them: behold, they come up by the cliff
of Ziz; and ye shall find them at the end of the brook, before the wilderness
of Jer'u-el.
17 Ye shall not *need* to fight in this *battle:* set yourselves, stand ye *still,* and
see the salvation of the LORD with you, O Judah and Jerusalem: fear not,
nor be dismayed; to morrow go out against them: for the LORD *will be* with
you.

20:17 Ex 14:13; 2 Chron 15:2

18 And Je-hosh'a-phat bowed his head with *his* face to the ground: and all

20:6ff Jehoshaphat's prayer includes certain elements which most of our prayers should follow. First, he adored God and acknowledged his mighty power (20:6). Second, he reminded God of his divine promises to Israel. Third, he set forth the problem even though God knew it before he said it. Then he asked God specifically for help. He was confident that God heard his prayer and would do something about the problem (20:20). Jehoshaphat and his people thanked God for the answer before it came (20:21ff). (See note on Luke 11:1 regarding the conditions of effectual prayer.)

20:14 The Spirit of the LORD came on Jahaziel, who brought God's message to Jehoshaphat the king. The king was to do nothing except stand still and watch God work. Judah need not fear nor be dismayed.

Judah and the inhabitants of Jerusalem fell before the LORD, worshipping
the LORD.
20:19 2 Chron 7:3 19 And the Levites, of the children of the Ko'hath-ites, and of the children
of the Kor'hites, stood up to praise the LORD God of Israel with a loud
voice on high.

c. God Fulfills His Promise

20:20 Isa 7:9 20 ¶And they rose early in the morning, and went forth into the wilderness
of Te-ko'a: and as they went forth, Je-hosh'a-phat stood and said, Hear me,
O Judah, and ye inhabitants of Jerusalem; Believe in the LORD your God,
so shall ye be established; believe his prophets, so shall ye prosper.
20:21☆ 1 Chron 16:29, 34 21 And when he had consulted with the people, he appointed singers unto
the LORD, and that should praise the beauty of holiness, as they went out
Ps 29:2 before the army, and to say, Praise the LORD; for his mercy *endureth* for
ever.
20:22 2 Chron 13:13 22 ¶And when they began to sing and to praise, the LORD set ambush-
20:10 ments against the children of Ammon, Moab, and mount Se'ir, which were
come against Judah; and they were smitten.
20:23 Judg 7:22 23 For the children of Ammon and Moab stood up against the inhabitants
1 Sam 14:20 of mount Se'ir, utterly to slay and destroy *them:* and when they had made
an end of the inhabitants of Se'ir, every one helped to destroy another.
24 And when Judah came toward the watch tower in the wilderness, they
looked unto the multitude, and, behold, they *were* dead bodies fallen to the
earth, and none escaped.
20:25☆ 25 And when Je-hosh'a-phat and his people came to take away the spoil of
them, they found among them in abundance both riches with the dead
bodies, and precious jewels, which they stripped off for themselves, more
than they could carry away: and they were three days in gathering of the
spoil, it was so much.
26 ¶And on the fourth day they assembled themselves in the valley of
Ber'a-chah; for there they blessed the LORD: therefore the name of the
same place was called, The valley of Ber'a-chah, unto this day.
27 Then they returned, every man of Judah and Jerusalem, and Je-hosh'a-
phat in the forefront of them, to go again to Jerusalem with joy; for the
LORD had made them to rejoice over their enemies.
28 And they came to Jerusalem with psalteries and harps and trumpets
unto the house of the LORD.
20:29 2 Chron 14:6, 7 29 And the fear of God was on all the kingdoms of *those* countries, when
15:15 they had heard that the LORD fought against the enemies of Israel.
20:30 1 Kgs 22:41–43 30 So the realm of Je-hosh'a-phat was quiet: for his God gave him rest
round about.

d. A Summary of Jehoshaphat's Kingship

20:31 2 Chron 17:6 31 ¶And Je-hosh'a-phat reigned over Judah: *he was* thirty and five years
old when he began to reign, and he reigned twenty and five years in
Jerusalem. And his mother's name *was* A-zu'bah the daughter of Shil'hi.
32 And he walked in the way of Asa his father, and departed not from it,
doing *that which was* right in the sight of the LORD.

20:21 As the army went out to war, nothing is said of their swords, spears, shields, or bows. Their faith was their armor in this situation because God told them not to fight. They believed him and that settled the matter. The battle was won without Judah's having to fight.

20:25 This incident consists in four parts: the problem, the prayer, the promise, and the provision. Now the troops get busy removing the spoils of the battle they never fought.

33 Howbeit the high places were not taken away: for as yet the people had
not prepared their hearts unto the God of their fathers.

☆20:33 2 Chron 17:6 19:3

34 Now the rest of the acts of Je-hosh′a-phat, first and last, behold, they
are written in the book of Jehu the son of Ha-na′ni, who *is* mentioned in the
book of the kings of Israel.

20:34 1 Kgs 16:1, 7 2 Chron 19:2

35 ¶And after this did Je-hosh′a-phat king of Judah join himself with
A-ha-zi′ah king of Israel, who did very wickedly:

☆20:35 1 Kgs 22:48, 49

36 And he joined himself with him to make ships to go to Tarshish: and
they made the ships in E′zi-on–ga′ber.

20:36 2 Chron 9:21

37 Then E-li-e′zer the son of Do′da-vah of Ma-re′shah prophesied against
Je-hosh′a-phat, saying, Because thou hast joined thyself with A-ha-zi′ah,
the LORD hath broken thy works. And the ships were broken, that they
were not able to go to Tarshish.

E. KING JEHORAM (JORAM)

1. Wicked Jehoram

21 NOW Je-hosh′a-phat slept with his fathers, and was buried with his
fathers in the city of David. And Je-ho′ram his son reigned in his
stead.

☆21:1 1 Kgs 22:50

2 And he had brethren the sons of Je-hosh′a-phat, Az-a-ri′ah, and Je-hi′el,
and Zech-a-ri′ah, and Az-a-ri′ah, and Michael, and Sheph-a-ti′ah: all these
were the sons of Je-hosh′a-phat king of Israel.
3 And their father gave them great gifts of silver, and of gold, and of
precious things, with fenced cities in Judah: but the kingdom gave he to Je-
ho′ram; because he *was* the firstborn.

21:3 2 Kgs 8:17–22 2 Chron 11:5

4 Now when Je-ho′ram was risen up to the kingdom of his father, he
strengthened himself, and slew all his brethren with the sword, and *divers*
also of the princes of Israel.
5 ¶Je-ho′ram *was* thirty and two years old when he began to reign, and he
reigned eight years in Jerusalem.
6 And he walked in the way of the kings of Israel, like as did the house of
Ahab: for he had the daughter of Ahab to wife: and he wrought *that which*
was evil in the eyes of the LORD.

☆21:6 1 Kgs 12:28–30 2 Chron 18:1

7 Howbeit the LORD would not destroy the house of David, because of the
covenant that he had made with David, and as he promised to give a light
to him and to his sons for ever.

21:7 2 Sam 7:12–17 1 Kgs 11:13

2. Edom and Libnah Revolt

8 In his days the Edomites revolted from under the dominion of Judah,
and made themselves a king.

☆21:8 2 Chron 20:22, 23; 21:10

9 Then Je-ho′ram went forth with his princes, and all his chariots with
him: and he rose up by night, and smote the Edomites which compassed
him in, and the captains of the chariots.

20:33 The chronicler explains why Jehoshaphat, a godly king, did not remove the high places. The people were not yet spiritually ready for that. (See 1 Kings 22:43.)

20:35 Jehoshaphat had a short memory. He should have learned from his experience with Ahab that righteousness and wickedness should not bind themselves together. He joined with wicked Ahaziah, the king of Israel, in a commercial venture, building ships to go to Tarshish. God was displeased and the ships were wrecked. God's displeasure was spoken for him by the prophet Eliezer. Had Jehoshaphat sought God for guidance before the venture was started, he would have avoided trouble.

21:1 Good fathers do not always have good sons to succeed them. Jehoram turned out to be a wicked king. One of his first acts was to kill all of the possible aspirants to the throne. His reign was to be very short—eight years, to be exact.

21:6 *the daughter of Ahab,* i.e., Athaliah, who patterned herself after her wicked mother, Jezebel.

21:8 Jehoram's subjects, the Edomites, revolted against him; and although he chastised them, he did not reduce them. This should have warned him that God was not favorable to him, as he had been to his father.

10 So the Edomites revolted from under the hand of Judah unto this day.
The same time *also* did Lib'nah revolt from under his hand; because he had
forsaken the LORD God of his fathers.

21:11 Lev 20:5; 1 Kgs 11:7

11 Moreover he made high places in the mountains of Judah, and caused
the inhabitants of Jerusalem to commit fornication, and compelled Judah
thereto.

3. Elijah Pronounces God's Judgment on Jehoram

21:12 2 Chron 14:2–5; 17:3, 4

12 ¶And there came a writing to him from E-li'jah the prophet, saying,
Thus saith the LORD God of David thy father, Because thou hast not
walked in the ways of Je-hosh'a-phat thy father, nor in the ways of Asa king
of Judah,

21:13 1 Kgs 16:31–33; 2 Chron 21:4, 6

13 But hast walked in the way of the kings of Israel, and hast made Judah
and the inhabitants of Jerusalem to go a whoring, like to the whoredoms of
the house of Ahab, and also hast slain thy brethren of thy father's house,
which were better than thyself:
14 Behold, with a great plague will the LORD smite thy people, and thy
children, and thy wives, and all thy goods:

21:15 2 Chron 21:18, 19

15 And thou *shalt have* great sickness by disease of thy bowels, until thy
bowels fall out by reason of the sickness day by day.

4. Jehoram's Terrible Suffering and Death

21:16 2 Chron 17:11; 22:1; 33:11

16 ¶Moreover the LORD stirred up against Je-ho'ram the spirit of the
Philistines, and of the Arabians, that *were* near the E-thi-o'pi-ans:

21:17☆ 2 Chron 25:23

17 And they came up into Judah, and brake into it, and carried away all
the substance that was found in the king's house, and his sons also, and his
wives; so that there was never a son left him, save Je-ho'a-haz, the youngest
of his sons.

21:18☆ 2 Chron 21:15

18 And after all this the LORD smote him in his bowels with an incurable
disease.

21:19☆ 2 Chron 16:14

19 And it came to pass, that in process of time, after the end of two years,
his bowels fell out by reason of his sickness: so he died of sore diseases.
And his people made no burning for him, like the burning of his fathers.

21:20☆ 2 Chron 24:25; 28:27; Jer 22:18, 28

20 Thirty and two years old was he when he began to reign, and he reigned
in Jerusalem eight years, and departed without being desired. Howbeit they
buried him in the city of David, but not in the sepulchres of the kings.

F. KING AHAZIAH AND QUEEN ATHALIAH

1. Wicked Ahaziah

22:1☆ 2 Kgs 8:24–29; 2 Chron 21:16

22 AND the inhabitants of Jerusalem made A-ha-zi'ah his youngest
son king in his stead: for the band of men that came with the
Arabians to the camp had slain all the eldest. So A-ha-zi'ah the son of Je-
ho'ram king of Judah reigned.

22:2☆ 2 Chron 21:6

2 Forty and two years old *was* A-ha-zi'ah when he began to reign, and he
reigned one year in Jerusalem. His mother's name also *was* Ath-a-li'ah the
daughter of Omri.

21:17 This incident appears only here. The books of Kings do not mention it. Apparently some of the wives were recovered or not all of the wives were taken, for Athaliah took charge of the realm after the death of her husband.

21:18–20 Jehoram, whose wickedness may have been helped by his pagan wife Athaliah (who was the daughter of Jezebel), suffered for his transgression. He was diseased and died a painful death at age forty. Verse 20 reveals that no one mourned his passing. He was an unsung king whom God and Judah lightly esteemed.

22:1 *Ahaziah,* also called "Jehoahaz."

22:2 *Forty and two years old.* Compare to 2 Kings 8:26. This is a copyist's error. The correct age is twenty-two years old.

3 He also walked in the ways of the house of Ahab: for his mother was his
counsellor to do wickedly.
4 Wherefore he did evil in the sight of the LORD like the house of Ahab:
for they were his counsellors after the death of his father to his destruction.
5 ¶He walked also after their counsel, and went with Je-ho'ram the son of
Ahab king of Israel to war against Haz'a-el king of Syria at Ra'moth-gil'e-
ad: and the Syrians smote Joram.
6 And he returned to be healed in Jez're-el because of the wounds which
were given him at Ra'mah, when he fought with Haz'a-el king of Syria. And
Az-a-ri'ah the son of Je-ho'ram king of Judah went down to see Je-ho'ram
the son of Ahab at Jez're-el, because he was sick.
7 And the destruction of A-ha-zi'ah was of God by coming to Joram: for ☆22:7 2 Kgs 9:6, 7, 21 2 Chron 10:15
when he was come, he went out with Je-ho'ram against Jehu the son of
Nim'shi, whom the LORD had anointed to cut off the house of Ahab.

2. Jehu Slays Ahaziah

8 And it came to pass, that, when Jehu was executing judgment upon the 22:8 2 Kgs 10:11-14
house of Ahab, and found the princes of Ju'dah, and the sons of the
brethren of A-ha-zi'ah, that ministered to A-ha-zi'ah, he slew them.
9 And he sought A-ha-zi'ah: and they caught him, (for he was hid in Sa- ☆22:9 2 Kgs 9:27, 28 2 Chron 17:4
ma'ri-a,) and brought him to Jehu: and when they had slain him, they
buried him: Because, said they, he *is* the son of Je-hosh'a-phat, who sought
the LORD with all his heart. So the house of A-ha-zi'ah had no power to
keep still the kingdom.

3. Athaliah Takes Over the Kingship

a. Athaliah Slays the Royal Heirs except Joash

10 ¶But when Ath-a-li'ah the mother of A-ha-zi'ah saw that her son was ☆22:10 2 Kgs 11:1-3
dead, she arose and destroyed all the seed royal of the house of Judah.
11 But Je-ho-shab'e-ath, the daughter of the king, took Jo'ash the son of ☆22:11
A-ha-zi'ah, and stole him from among the king's sons that were slain, and
put him and his nurse in a bedchamber. So Je-ho-shab'e-ath, the daughter
of king Je-ho'ram, the wife of Je-hoi'a-da the priest, (for she was the sister
of A-ha-zi'ah,) hid him from Ath-a-li'ah, so that she slew him not.
12 And he was with them hid in the house of God six years: and Ath-a-
li'ah reigned over the land.

b. Jehoiada Secures the Crown for Joash; Athaliah is Slain

23 AND in the seventh year Je-hoi'a-da strengthened himself, and ☆23:1 2 Kgs 11:4-20
took the captains of hundreds, Az-a-ri'ah the son of Jer'o-ham,
and Ish'ma-el the son of Je-ho-ha'nan, and Az-a-ri'ah the son of O'bed, and

---

22:7 *the destruction of Ahaziah was of God* is translated in the RSV, "It was ordained of God that the downfall of Ahaziah should come about. . . ." This emphasizes the biblical truth that God sets up on the throne and pulls down from the throne whom he pleases.

22:9 At Ahaziah's death he was given a decent burial only because he was "the grandson of Jehoshaphat, who sought the LORD with all his heart." "The memory of the just is blessed, but the name of the wicked shall rot."*

22:10 *Athaliah,* the daughter of Ahab and Jezebel is said to have been a wicked woman (2 Chron. 24:7). She married Jehoram of Judah, who later inherited his father's throne. He died after a reign of eight years, leaving Athaliah as queen. She gained the distinction of being the only woman in history to usurp the Davidic throne. After reigning six years, Athaliah was slain and Joash became king at seven years of age.

22:11 *the daughter of the king.* Her father was King Jehoram and her brother was King Ahaziah.

23:1 Six years of Athaliah was enough for the people of Judah. An ecclesiastical-political plot was formed which resulted in the death of Athaliah and the accession of Joash to the throne at the tender age of seven.

Ma-a-sei′ah the son of Ad-a-i′ah, and E-lish′a-phat the son of Zich′ri, into
covenant with him.
23:2 2 And they went about in Judah, and gathered the Levites out of all the
2 Chron 21:7 cities of Judah, and the chief of the fathers of Israel, and they came to
Jerusalem.
3 And all the congregation made a covenant with the king in the house of
God. And he said unto them, Behold, the king's son shall reign, as the
LORD hath said of the sons of David.
23:4 4 This *is* the thing that ye shall do; A third part of you entering on the
1 Chron 9:25 sabbath, of the priests and of the Levites, *shall be* porters of the doors;
5 And a third part *shall be* at the king's house; and a third part at the gate
of the foundation: and all the people *shall be* in the courts of the house of
the LORD.
23:6 6 But let none come into the house of the LORD, save the priests, and they
1 Chron 23:28–32 that minister of the Levites; they shall go in, for they *are* holy: but all the
people shall keep the watch of the LORD.
7 And the Levites shall compass the king round about, every man with his
weapons in his hand; and whosoever *else* cometh into the house, he shall be
put to death: but be ye with the king when he cometh in, and when he goeth
out.
8 So the Levites and all Judah did according to all things that Je-hoi′a-da
the priest had commanded, and took every man his men that were to come
in on the sabbath, with them that were to go *out* on the sabbath: for Je-
hoi′a-da the priest dismissed not the courses.
9 Moreover Je-hoi′a-da the priest delivered to the captains of hundreds
spears, and bucklers, and shields, that *had been* king David's, which *were* in
the house of God.
10 And he set all the people, every man having his weapon in his hand,
from the right side of the temple to the left side of the temple, along by the
altar and the temple, by the king round about.
23:11 11 Then they brought out the king's son, and put upon him the crown, and
Ex 25:16, 21 *gave him* the testimony, and made him king. And Je-hoi′a-da and his sons
1 Sam 10:24 anointed him, and said, God save the king.
12 ¶Now when Ath-a-li′ah heard the noise of the people running and
praising the king, she came to the people into the house of the LORD:
13 And she looked, and, behold, the king stood at his pillar at the entering
in, and the princes and the trumpets by the king: and all the people of the
land rejoiced, and sounded with trumpets, also the singers with instruments
of musick, and such as taught to sing praise. Then Ath-a-li′ah rent her
clothes, and said, Treason, Treason.
23:14☆ 14 Then Je-hoi′a-da the priest brought out the captains of hundreds that
were set over the host, and said unto them, Have her forth of the ranges:
and whoso followeth her, let him be slain with the sword. For the priest
said, Slay her not in the house of the LORD.
23:15 15 So they laid hands on her; and when she was come to the entering of
Deut 13:6–9 the horse gate by the king's house, they slew her there.
1 Kgs 18:40
2 Chron 22:10 16 ¶And Je-hoi′a-da made a covenant between him, and between all the
23:16☆ people, and between the king, that they should be the LORD's people.
17 Then all the people went to the house of Ba′al, and brake it down, and

23:14 Like mother like daughter. Athaliah's ambitions and wickedness brought about her own death by the sword. Jehoiada insisted that she not be killed in the house of the Lord, so she was removed to the entrance of the horse gate of the king's house for her execution.

23:16 Following the death of Athaliah the people of Judah returned to the Lord. Jehoiada sparked this renewal and advised the young king. He cleaned up the wickedness connected with the use of the temple. The people rejoiced and peace descended for a season.

brake his altars and his images in pieces, and slew Mat′tan the priest of
Ba′al before the altars.
18 Also Je-hoi′a-da appointed the offices of the house of the LORD by the
hand of the priests the Levites, whom David had distributed in the house of
the LORD, to offer the burnt offerings of the LORD, as *it is* written in the law
of Moses, with rejoicing and with singing, *as it was ordained* by David.

23:18 1 Chron 9:22; 23:6, 25–31; 2 Chron 5:5

19 And he set the porters at the gates of the house of the LORD, that none
which was unclean in any thing should enter in.
20 And he took the captains of hundreds, and the nobles, and the
governors of the people, and all the people of the land, and brought down
the king from the house of the LORD: and they came through the high gate
into the king's house, and set the king upon the throne of the kingdom.
21 And all the people of the land rejoiced: and the city was quiet, after
that they had slain Ath-a-li′ah with the sword.

G. KING JOASH

1. Joash Pleases God

24 JO′ASH *was* seven years old when he began to reign, and he
reigned forty years in Jerusalem. His mother's name also *was* Zib′i-
ah of Be′er–she′ba.

24:1 2 Kgs 11:21; 12:1–15

2 And Jo′ash did *that which was* right in the sight of the LORD all the days
of Je-hoi′a-da the priest.

☆**24:2** 2 Chron 26:4, 5

3 And Je-hoi′a-da took for him two wives; and he begat sons and
daughters.

2. Joash Repairs the Temple

4 ¶And it came to pass after this, *that* Jo′ash was minded to repair the
house of the LORD.

24:4 2 Chron 24:7

5 And he gathered together the priests and the Levites, and said to them,
Go out unto the cities of Judah, and gather of all Israel money to repair the
house of your God from year to year, and see that ye hasten the matter.
Howbeit the Levites hastened *it* not.
6 And the king called for Je-hoi′a-da the chief, and said unto him, Why
hast thou not required of the Levites to bring in out of Judah and out of
Jerusalem the collection, *according to the commandment* of Moses the
servant of the LORD, and of the congregation of Israel, for the tabernacle of
witness?

24:6 Ex 30:12–16

7 For the sons of Ath-a-li′ah, that wicked woman, had broken up the
house of God; and also all the dedicated things of the house of the LORD
did they bestow upon Ba′al-im.

☆**24:7**

8 And at the king's commandment they made a chest, and set it without at
the gate of the house of the LORD.
9 And they made a proclamation through Judah and Jerusalem, to bring
in to the LORD the collection *that* Moses the servant of God *laid* upon Israel
in the wilderness.

24:9 2 Chron 24:6; 36:22

10 And all the princes and all the people rejoiced, and brought in, and cast
into the chest, until they had made an end.

24:2 Joash got off to a good start. Under the benign influence of Jehoiada, he followed God, but this lasted only while he was young enough to be under the influence of his godly tutor. His end was worse than his beginning. Whoever refuses to be counseled cannot be helped.

24:7 The house of God had been entered by Athaliah, and its treasures were used for the worship of Baal. This was an awful prostitution of things dedicated to the glory of God. Sacred things that are used for wicked purposes become unclean and ultimately worthless to the user, and they are an offense to God.

[11]Now it came to pass, that at what time the chest was brought unto the
king's office by the hand of the Levites, and when they saw that *there was*
much money, the king's scribe and the high priest's officer came and
emptied the chest, and took it, and carried it to his place again. Thus they
did day by day, and gathered money in abundance.
[12]And the king and Je-hoi'a-da gave it to such as did the work of the
service of the house of the LORD, and hired masons and carpenters to repair
the house of the LORD, and also such as wrought iron and brass to mend
the house of the LORD.
[13]So the workmen wrought, and the work was perfected by them, and
they set the house of God in his state, and strengthened it.
[14]And when they had finished *it,* they brought the rest of the money
before the king and Je-hoi'a-da, whereof were made vessels for the house of
the LORD, *even* vessels to minister, and to offer *withal,* and spoons, and
vessels of gold and silver. And they offered burnt offerings in the house of
the LORD continually all the days of Je-hoi'a-da.

3. Jehoiada, the Priest, Dies

[15]¶But Je-hoi'a-da waxed old, and was full of days when he died; an
hundred and thirty years old *was he* when he died.
24:16 2 Chron 21:20
[16]And they buried him in the city of David among the kings, because he
had done good in Israel, both toward God, and toward his house.

4. King Joash and Judah Apostatize

24:17☆ Ex 34:12–14; Josh 22:20; 2 Chron 24:4
[17]Now after the death of Je-hoi'a-da came the princes of Judah, and
made obeisance to the king. Then the king hearkened unto them.
[18]And they left the house of the LORD God of their fathers, and served
groves and idols: and wrath came upon Judah and Jerusalem for this their
trespass.
24:19☆ Jer 7:25
[19]Yet he sent prophets to them, to bring them again unto the LORD; and
they testified against them: but they would not give ear.

5. Joash Executes Zechariah the Priest

24:20☆ Num 14:41; 2 Chron 20:14
[20]And the Spirit of God came upon Zech-a-ri'ah the son of Je-hoi'a-da
the priest, which stood above the people, and said unto them, Thus saith
God, Why transgress ye the commandments of the LORD, that ye cannot
prosper? because ye have forsaken the LORD, he hath also forsaken you.
[21]And they conspired against him, and stoned him with stones at the
commandment of the king in the court of the house of the LORD.
24:22 Mt 23:34, 35
[22]Thus Jo'ash the king remembered not the kindness which Je-hoi'a-da
his father had done to him, but slew his son. And when he died, he said,
The LORD look upon *it,* and require *it.*

24:17 The king and the princes had done well, but did so under compulsion while Jehoiada lived. After his death they showed their true colors. They left the house of God and worshipped idols in the groves. Apostasy was the order of the day.

24:19 God was gracious and sent not one but many prophets to warn Judah concerning its apostasy. But the leaders and people were so wedded to their idols that neither warning, reproofs, nor threatenings moved them. They were ripe for judgment.

24:20 The Spirit of God took possession of Zechariah the priest. Zechariah was given the prophetic power and used it to pronounce the verdict of God against disobedience. He lost his life as a result of his faithful preaching. God executed judgment on Joash, whose spiritual life declined after a good beginning, and the Syrians slew him. Many a believer has commended himself to God in the early years after conversion only to backslide in later years, finding himself cut off from the God he once professed to love and serve.

6. Joash's Military Defeat and Death

23 ¶And it came to pass at the end of the year, *that* the host of Syria came up against him: and they came to Judah and Jerusalem, and destroyed all the princes of the people from among the people, and sent all the spoil of them unto the king of Damascus.

☆**24:23** Gen 9:5

24 For the army of the Syrians came with a small company of men, and the LORD delivered a very great host into their hand, because they had forsaken the LORD God of their fathers. So they executed judgment against Jo'ash.

24:24 2 Kgs 12:17; 2 Chron 16:7, 8

25 And when they were departed from him, (for they left him in great diseases,) his own servants conspired against him for the blood of the sons of Je-hoi'a-da the priest, and slew him on his bed, and he died: and they buried him in the city of David, but they buried him not in the sepulchres of the kings.

☆**24:25** 2 Kgs 12:20, 21

26 And these are they that conspired against him; Za'bad the son of Shim'e-ath an Ammonitess, and Je-hoz'a-bad the son of Shim'rith a Moabitess.

27 ¶Now *concerning* his sons, and the greatness of the burdens *laid* upon him, and the repairing of the house of God, behold, they *are* written in the story of the book of the kings. And Am-a-zi'ah his son reigned in his stead.

24:27 2 Chron 13:22; 24:12

H. KING AMAZIAH

1. His Early Acts

25 AM-A-ZI'AH *was* twenty and five years old *when* he began to reign, and he reigned twenty and nine years in Jerusalem. And his mother's name *was* Je-ho-ad'dan of Jerusalem.

25:1 2 Kgs 14:1–6

2 And he did *that which was* right in the sight of the LORD, but not with a perfect heart.

☆**25:2**

3 ¶Now it came to pass, when the kingdom was established to him, that he slew his servants that had killed the king his father.

4 But he slew not their children, but *did* as *it is* written in the law in the book of Moses, where the LORD commanded, saying, The fathers shall not die for the children, neither shall the children die for the fathers, but every man shall die for his own sin.

25:4 Deut 24:16

2. The Victory over the Edomites (in the Valley of Salt)

5 ¶Moreover Am-a-zi'ah gathered Judah together, and made them captains over thousands, and captains over hundreds, according to the houses of *their* fathers, throughout all Judah and Benjamin: and he numbered them from twenty years old and above, and found them three hundred thousand choice *men, able* to go forth to war, that could handle spear and shield.

25:5 Num 1:3; 2 Chron 26:13

24:23 Zechariah prayed for God to avenge his death, and God did. A small band of Syrians were God's instrument for judgment. They made themselves masters of Jerusalem. They plundered the city, slew the princes, and sent the spoil to the king of Damascus. God can save or destory through a few instruments as well as through many.

24:25 Ironically, those who slew Joash were sons of Israelites who had married pagans. Intermarriage was forbidden to prevent idolatry and here the sons of mixed marriages cause the death of a king who had embraced idolatrous practices.

25:2 Amaziah had a long reign (twenty-nine years) and he did what was right in the sight of God. He kept the temple services going and supported true religion. But he was not a serious and devout follower. He was an indifferent and cool friend. He was like those of the Laodicean age mentioned in the book of the Revelation; the good they did was not done with a perfect heart.

25:6☆ 6 He hired also an hundred thousand mighty men of valour out of Israel
for an hundred talents of silver.
25:7 7 But there came a man of God to him, saying, O king, let not the army of
2 Kgs 4:9 Israel go with thee; for the LORD *is* not with Israel, *to wit, with* all the
children of E′phra-im.
25:8 8 But if thou wilt go, do *it,* be strong for the battle: God shall make thee
2 Chron 14:11; 20:6 fall before the enemy: for God hath power to help, and to cast down.
9 And Am-a-zi′ah said to the man of God, But what shall we do for the
hundred talents which I have given to the army of Israel? And the man of
God answered, The LORD is able to give thee much more than this.
10 Then Am-a-zi′ah separated them, *to wit,* the army that was come to him
out of E′phra-im, to go home again: wherefore their anger was greatly
kindled against Judah, and they returned home in great anger.
25:11 11 And Am-a-zi′ah strengthened himself, and led forth his people, and
2 Kgs 14:7 went to the valley of salt, and smote of the children of Se′ir ten thousand.
12 And *other* ten thousand *left* alive did the children of Judah carry away
captive, and brought them unto the top of the rock, and cast them down
from the top of the rock, that they all were broken in pieces.
13 ¶But the soldiers of the army which Am-a-zi′ah sent back, that they
should not go with him to battle, fell upon the cities of Judah, from Sa-
ma′ri-a even unto Beth–ho′ron, and smote three thousand of them, and
took much spoil.

3. Amaziah and His Idols

25:14☆ 14 ¶Now it came to pass, after that Am-a-zi′ah was come from the
2 Chron 28:23 slaughter of the Edomites, that he brought the gods of the children of Se′ir,
and set them up *to be* his gods, and bowed down himself before them, and
burned incense unto them.
25:15 15 Wherefore the anger of the LORD was kindled against Am-a-zi′ah, and
2 Chron 25:11, 12 he sent unto him a prophet, which said unto him, Why hast thou sought
after the gods of the people, which could not deliver their own people out of
thine hand?
16 And it came to pass, as he talked with him, that *the king* said unto him,
Art thou made of the king's counsel? forbear; why shouldest thou be
smitten? Then the prophet forbare, and said, I know that God hath
determined to destroy thee, because thou hast done this, and hast not
hearkened unto my counsel.

4. Joash of Israel's Victory over Amaziah

25:17☆ 17 ¶Then Am-a-zi′ah king of Judah took advice, and sent to Jo′ash, the
2 Kgs 14:8–14 son of Je-ho′a-haz, the son of Jehu, king of Israel, saying, Come, let us see
one another in the face.
25:18 Judg 9:8–15 18 And Jo′ash king of Israel sent to Am-a-zi′ah king of Judah, saying, The

---

25:6 Amaziah finds that his forces are too small to wage war against the Edomites, so he hires mercenaries from Israel to assist him. He had no qualms about allying himself with those who had become idolatrous. When he was confronted by God's prophet, he dismissed the mercenaries at God's command. But his heart was not changed.

25:14 The gods of the Edomites had not protected them against the battle with Amaziah. Yet Amaziah stupidly takes these gods, makes them his own, and bows before them in idolatrous worship. When God's prophet remonstrated with him, the king angrily dismissed him and even threatened him with death. Amaziah's doom was set and certain.

25:17ff Amaziah foolishly invited Israel to war with him. He sought the counsel of others rather than God, and paid a price for so doing. Joash of Israel won the war and stripped the house of God of silver, gold, and sacred vessels. He also took whatever was valuable from the king's house. Amaziah lived for fifteen years after the death of Joash (25:25) but finally had to flee to Lachish where he was slain as a result of a conspiracy against him (25:27).

thistle that *was* in Lebanon sent to the cedar that *was* in Lebanon, saying,
Give thy daughter to my son to wife: and there passed by a wild beast that
was in Lebanon, and trode down the thistle.
19 Thou sayest, Lo, thou hast smitten the Edomites; and thine heart lifteth
thee up to boast: abide now at home; why shouldest thou meddle to *thine*
hurt, that thou shouldest fall, *even* thou, and Judah with thee?
20 But Am-a-zi'ah would not hear; for it *came* of God, that he might
deliver them into the hand *of their enemies,* because they sought after the
gods of Edom.
21 So Jo'ash the king of Israel went up; and they saw one another in the
face, *both* he and Am-a-zi'ah king of Judah, at Beth-she'mesh, which
belongeth to Judah.
22 And Judah was put to the worse before Israel, and they fled every man
to his tent.
23 And Jo'ash the king of Israel took Am-a-zi'ah king of Judah, the son of
Jo'ash, the son of Je-ho'a-haz, at Beth-she'mesh, and brought him to
Jerusalem, and brake down the wall of Jerusalem from the gate of E'phra-
im to the corner gate, four hundred cubits.
24 And *he took* all the gold and the silver, and all the vessels that were
found in the house of God with O'bed-e'dom, and the treasures of the
king's house, the hostages also, and returned to Sa-ma'ri-a.

25:19 2 Chron 26:16 32:25

25:24 1 Chron 26:15

5. The Assassination of Amaziah

25 ¶And Am-a-zi'ah the son of Jo'ash king of Judah lived after the death
of Jo'ash son of Je-ho'a-haz king of Israel fifteen years.
26 Now the rest of the acts of Am-a-zi'ah, first and last, behold, *are* they
not written in the book of the kings of Judah and Israel?
27 ¶Now after the time that Am-a-zi'ah did turn away from following the
LORD they made a conspiracy against him in Jerusalem; and he fled to
La'chish: but they sent to La'chish after him, and slew him there.
28 And they brought him upon horses, and buried him with his fathers in
the city of Judah.

25:25 2 Kgs 14:17–22

I. KING UZZIAH (AZARIAH)

1. Uzziah's Desire to Please God

26 THEN all the people of Judah took Uz-zi'ah, who *was* sixteen years
old, and made him king in the room of his father Am-a-zi'ah.
2 He built E'loth, and restored it to Judah, after that the king slept with
his fathers.
3 Sixteen years old *was* Uz-zi'ah when he began to reign, and he reigned
fifty and two years in Jerusalem. His mother's name also *was* Jec-o-li'ah of
Jerusalem.
4 And he did *that which was* right in the sight of the LORD, according to all
that his father Am-a-zi'ah did.
5 And he sought God in the days of Zech-a-ri'ah, who had understanding
in the visions of God: and as long as he sought the LORD, God made him
to prosper.

☆26:1 2 Kgs 15:2, 3

☆26:5 2 Chron 15:2

26:1 *Uzziah,* i.e., the Azariah mentioned in 2 Kings 15:1.
26:5 Uzziah prospered as long as he kept close to God and obeyed his voice. His pride led him to disregard the will of God; he subsequently suffered failure and loss (26:19–21).

2. Uzziah's Military Successes

26:6 Isa 14:29

6 And he went forth and warred against the Philistines, and brake down the wall of Gath, and the wall of Jab'neh, and the wall of Ash'dod, and built cities about Ash'dod, and among the Philistines.

26:7☆ 2 Chron 21:16

7 And God helped him against the Philistines, and against the Arabians that dwelt in Gur–ba'al, and the Me-hu'nims.

26:8 2 Chron 17:11

8 And the Ammonites gave gifts to Uz-zi'ah: and his name spread abroad *even* to the entering in of Egypt; for he strengthened *himself* exceedingly.

26:9 2 Chron 25:23 Neh 3:13 21:13, 15

9 Moreover Uz-zi'ah built towers in Jerusalem at the corner gate, and at the valley gate, and at the turning *of the wall,* and fortified them.

26:10 Gen 26:18–21

10 Also he built towers in the desert, and digged many wells: for he had much cattle, both in the low country, and in the plains: husbandmen *also,* and vine dressers in the mountains, and in Carmel: for he loved husbandry.

11 ¶Moreover Uz-zi'ah had an host of fighting men, that went out to war by bands, according to the number of their account by the hand of Je-i'el the scribe and Ma-a-sei'ah the ruler, under the hand of Han-a-ni'ah, *one* of the king's captains.

12 The whole number of the chief of the fathers of the mighty men of valour *were* two thousand and six hundred.

26:13 2 Chron 25:5

13 And under their hand *was* an army, three hundred thousand and seven thousand and five hundred, that made war with mighty power, to help the king against the enemy.

14 And Uz-zi'ah prepared for them throughout all the host shields, and spears, and helmets, and habergeons, and bows, and slings *to cast* stones.

15 And he made in Jerusalem engines, invented by cunning men, to be on the towers and upon the bulwarks, to shoot arrows and great stones withal. And his name spread far abroad; for he was marvellously helped, till he was strong.

3. Uzziah's Transgression and Leprosy

26:16☆ Deut 32:15 1 Kgs 13:1–4 2 Chron 25:19

16 ¶But when he was strong, his heart was lifted up to *his* destruction: for he transgressed against the LORD his God, and went into the temple of the LORD to burn incense upon the altar of incense.

26:17☆ Ex 30:7, 8 Num 16:39, 40 1 Chron 6:10 2 Chron 19:2

17 And Az-a-ri'ah the priest went in after him, and with him fourscore priests of the LORD, *that were* valiant men:

26:18☆

18 And they withstood Uz-zi'ah the king and said unto him, *It appertaineth* not unto thee, Uz-zi'ah, to burn incense unto the LORD, but to the priests the sons of Aaron, that are consecrated to burn incense: go out of the sanctuary; for thou hast trespassed; neither *shall it be* for thine honour from the LORD God.

26:19 2 Kgs 5:25–27

19 Then Uz-zi'ah was wroth, and *had* a censer in his hand to burn incense: and while he was wroth with the priests, the leprosy even rose up in his forehead before the priests in the house of the LORD, from beside the incense altar.

26:20☆

20 And Az-a-ri'ah the chief priest, and all the priests, looked upon him, and, behold, he *was* leprous in his forehead, and they thrust him out from

---

26:7 *God helped him.* This tells the same old story: those who trust God are helped, whereas those who turn to idols are judged and forsaken by God. Uzziah raised a large army to defend his kingdom. His fame spread, his kingdom prospered, and he became very strong.

26:16–20 Some people, including kings, find prosperity more dangerous than poverty. Uzziah's folly consisted in intruding into the house of God to burn incense on the sacred altar. This was most presumptuous, for only the Levitical priests could do this. God had honored him, yet he turned to dishonor God by performing a rite that was expressly forbidden him. He was angry when he was reproved by the priests. With censer in hand, he was about to do the forbidden act when leprosy broke out on his forehead. This was an act of divine judgment which took Uzziah and the priests by surprise. He died a leper.

thence; yea, himself hasted also to go out, because the LORD had smitten
him.
21 And Uz-zi'ah the king was a leper unto the day of his death, and dwelt
in a several house, *being* a leper; for he was cut off from the house of the
LORD: and Jo'tham his son *was* over the king's house, judging the people of
the land.

26:21 Lev 13:46; 2 Kgs 15:5–7

4. Uzziah's Death

22 ¶Now the rest of the acts of Uz-zi'ah, first and last, did Isaiah the
prophet, the son of Amoz, write.
23 So Uz-zi'ah slept with his fathers, and they buried him with his fathers
in the field of the burial which *belonged* to the kings; for they said, He *is* a
leper: and Jo'tham his son reigned in his stead.

☆26:22 Isa 1:1
26:23 2 Chron 21:20; 28:27

J. KING JOTHAM

27 JO'THAM *was* twenty and five years old when he began to reign,
and he reigned sixteen years in Jerusalem. His mother's name also
was Je-ru'shah, the daughter of Za'dok.
2 And he did *that which was* right in the sight of the LORD, according to all
that his father Uz-zi'ah did: howbeit he entered not into the temple of the
LORD. And the people did yet corruptly.
3 He built the high gate of the house of the LORD, and on the wall of
O'phel he built much.
4 Moreover he built cities in the mountains of Judah, and in the forests he
built castles and towers.
5 ¶He fought also with the king of the Ammonites, and prevailed against
them. And the children of Ammon gave him the same year an hundred
talents of silver, and ten thousand measures of wheat, and ten thousand of
barley. So much did the children of Ammon pay unto him, both the second
year, and the third.
6 So Jo'tham became mighty, because he prepared his ways before the
LORD his God.
7 ¶Now the rest of the acts of Jo'tham, and all his wars, and his ways, lo,
they *are* written in the book of the kings of Israel and Judah.
8 He was five and twenty years old when he began to reign, and reigned
sixteen years in Jerusalem.
9 ¶And Jo'tham slept with his fathers, and they buried him in the city of
David: and Ahaz his son reigned in his stead.

☆27:1 2 Kgs 15:33–35
27:2 2 Chron 26:16
27:3 2 Chron 33:14; Neh 3:26
27:4 2 Chron 11:5
27:6 2 Chron 26:5
27:7 2 Kgs 15:36
27:8 2 Chron 27:1

K. KING AHAZ

1. Ahaz's Wickedness

28 AHAZ *was* twenty years old when he began to reign, and he reigned
sixteen years in Jerusalem: but he did not *that which was* right in the
sight of the LORD, like David his father:

☆28:1 2 Kgs 16:2–4

26:22 Isaiah the prophet is mentioned here. It was in the year that Uzziah died that Isaiah saw the Lord.

27:1 Jotham succeeded Uzziah, and for sixteen years Judah prospered and was at peace. He followed his father in his devotion to God but was careful not to follow him in his folly of trying to burn incense in the place of the priests. The people, however, did not follow their king. Their practices in religion were corrupt. They were laying up wrath against the day of wrath when God would judge them. He died young (forty-one) but he finished his course with honor. Unfortunately, he did not have a son who would walk in his father's ways.

28:1 Ahaz had everything going for him. The kingdom was at peace and prospered. But he chose evil instead of good. He followed the example of the wicked kings of Israel rather than his forefather David. He was wretched, corrupted, and debauched. He offered sacrifices and burned incense literally everywhere except at the house of God. He also made idols to Baal.

28:2 Ex 34:17; 2 Chron 22:3

2 For he walked in the ways of the kings of Israel, and made also molten
images for Ba'al-im.

28:3 Lev 18:21; Josh 15:8; 2 Chron 33:2, 6

3 Moreover he burnt incense in the valley of the son of Hin'nom, and
burnt his children in the fire, after the abominations of the heathen whom
the LORD had cast out before the children of Israel.
4 He sacrificed also and burnt incense in the high places, and on the hills,
and under every green tree.

2. God Allows Syria and Israel to Defeat Him

28:5☆ 2 Chron 24:24

5 Wherefore the LORD his God delivered him into the hand of the king of
Syria; and they smote him, and carried away a great multitude of them
captives, and brought *them* to Damascus. And he was also delivered into
the hand of the king of Israel, who smote him with a great slaughter.

28:6 2 Kgs 16:5

6 For Pe'kah the son of Rem-a-li'ah slew in Judah an hundred and twenty
thousand in one day, *which were* all valiant men; because they had forsaken
the LORD God of their fathers.
7 And Zich'ri, a mighty man of E-phra'im, slew Ma-a-sei'ah the king's
son, and Az'ri-kam the governor of the house, and El-ka'nah *that was* next
to the king.

28:8 Deut 28:25, 41

8 And the children of Israel carried away captive of their brethren two
hundred thousand, women, sons, and daughters, and took also away much
spoil from them, and brought the spoil to Sa-ma'ri-a.

28:9☆ 2 Chron 25:15; Ezra 9:6; Isa 47:6; Rev 18:5

9 But a prophet of the LORD was there, whose name *was* O'ded: and he
went out before the host that came to Sa-ma'ri-a, and said unto them,
Behold, because the LORD God of your fathers was wroth with Judah, he
hath delivered them into your hand, and ye have slain them in a rage *that*
reacheth up unto heaven.

28:10 2 Chron 28:8

10 And now ye purpose to keep under the children of Judah and Jerusalem
for bondmen and bondwomen unto you: *but are there* not with you, even
with you, sins against the LORD your God?
11 Now hear me therefore, and deliver the captives again, which ye have
taken captive of your brethren: for the fierce wrath of the LORD *is* upon
you.
12 Then certain of the heads of the children of E'phra-im, Az-a-ri'ah the
son of Jo-ha'nan, Ber-e-chi'ah the son of Me-shil'le-moth, and Je-hiz-ki'ah
the son of Shal'lum, and Am'a-sa the son of Had'la-i, stood up against them
that came from the war,
13 And said unto them, Ye shall not bring in the captives hither: for
whereas we have offended against the LORD *already*, ye intend to add *more*
to our sins and to our trespass: for our trespass is great, and *there is* fierce
wrath against Israel.
14 So the armed men left the captives and the spoil before the princes and
all the congregation.

28:15 Deut 34:3; 2 Kgs 6:22; 2 Chron 28:12; Prov 25:21, 22

15 And the men which were expressed by name rose up, and took the
captives, and with the spoil clothed all that were naked among them, and
arrayed them, and shod them, and gave them to eat and to drink, and

---

28:5 *Wherefore,* i.e., because of his wickedness God delivered him and his people over to the hands of Syria and Israel. The blood of his people "was shed, their country wasted, their familes ruined."* Their good king Jotham caused God to delay his judgment; but now that they have a bad king and are a bad people, justice catches up with them.

28:9 Oded the prophet had a word for Pekah the king of Samaria. He was about to make slaves of his blood relatives, contrary to the law. Oded informed him that Israel's victory over Judah was no sign that God thought Israel was good. Rather, God was punishing one wicked nation by using another wicked nation to execute divine justice. He must not take the people of Judah for slavery. He accepted the word of the prophet and the people returned home.

anointed them, and carried all the feeble of them upon asses, and brought
them to Jericho, the city of palm trees, to their brethren: then they returned
to Sa-ma′ri-a.

3. Ahaz's Further Defeats, Apostasy, and Death

16 ¶At that time did king Ahaz send unto the kings of Assyria to help him. ☆**28:16** 2 Kgs 16:7
17 For again the Edomites had come and smitten Judah, and carried away **28:17**
captives. Ezek 16:57
18 The Philistines also had invaded the cities of the low country, and of
the south of Judah, and had taken Beth-she′mesh, and Aj′a-lon, and Ge-
de′roth, and Sho′cho with the villages thereof, and Tim′nah with the
villages thereof, Gim′zo also and the villages thereof: and they dwelt there.
19 For the LORD brought Judah low because of Ahaz king of Israel; for he ☆**28:19**
made Judah naked, and transgressed sore against the LORD.
20 And Til′gath-pil-ne′ser king of Assyria came unto him, and distressed **28:20**
him, but strengthened him not. 1 Chron 5:26
21 For Ahaz took away a portion *out* of the house of the LORD, and *out* of **28:21**
the house of the king, and of the princes, and gave *it* unto the king of 2 Kgs 16:8, 9
Assyria: but he helped him not.
22 ¶And in the time of his distress did he trespass yet more against the ☆**28:22**
LORD: this *is that* king Ahaz.
23 For he sacrificed unto the gods of Damascus, which smote him: and he ☆**28:23**
said, Because the gods of the kings of Syria help them, *therefore* will I 2 Chron 25:14 Jer 44:17, 18
sacrifice to them, that they may help me. But they were the ruin of him, and
of all Israel.
24 And Ahaz gathered together the vessels of the house of God, and cut in ☆**28:24**
pieces the vessels of the house of God, and shut up the doors of the house 2 Kgs 16:17 2 Chron 29:7
of the LORD, and he made him altars in every corner of Jerusalem. 30:14; 33:3–5
25 And in every several city of Judah he made high places to burn incense
unto other gods, and provoked to anger the LORD God of his fathers.
26 ¶Now the rest of his acts and of all his ways, first and last, behold, they **28:26**
are written in the book of the kings of Judah and Israel. 2 Kgs 16:19, 20
27 And Ahaz slept with his fathers, and they buried him in the city, *even* in **28:27**
Jerusalem: but they brought him not into the sepulchres of the kings of 2 Chron 24:25
Israel: and Hez-e-ki′ah his son reigned in his stead.

L. KING HEZEKIAH

1. The Restoration of the Temple and Its Services

a. Hezekiah's Good Intentions

29 HEZ-E-KI′AH began to reign *when he was* five and twenty years ☆**29:1**
old, and he reigned nine and twenty years in Jerusalem. And his 2 Kgs 18:1–3
mother's name *was* A-bi′jah, the daughter of Zech-a-ri′ah.

28:16 Judah was brought so low that the Edomites and the Philistines were able to do them extensive harm. Instead of repenting and turning to God, Ahaz made an appeal to the Assyrians for military help. Ironically, Tilgath-pilneser the king of Assyria saw Judah's weakness and, as the RSV has it, "afflicted him instead of strengthening him" (28:20).

28:19 King Ahaz ruled two tribes of Israel—Judah and Benjamin—and so is referred to here in this unusual way as a king of Israel. "For the Lord brought Judah very low on account of the evil deeds of King Ahaz of Israel, . . ."†

28:22, 23 One would have supposed that Ahaz had learned his lesson. Instead his spiritual condition worsened and he "trespasses yet more against the LORD." What an indictment! He adds the gods of the Assyrians to his collection of false gods, expecting them to help him. Tersely, the Scripture says, "they were the ruin of him."

28:24 So rash and angry had Ahaz become that he closed the temple doors to all true worship and set up altars in every corner of Jerusalem. Who could stoop lower than this wicked king?

29:1 Hezekiah was a devout follower of God. His soul must have been vexed as he watched the antics of his father, having no power to change the situation for good. He came to the kingship at a low time. The challenge was great and the need for reformation and a return to God a pressing necessity. He rose to his opportunity and performed magnificently for God.

29:2 2 Chron 28:1; 34:2
2 And he did *that which was* right in the sight of the LORD, according to all
that David his father had done.

29:3☆ 2 Chron 28:24; 29:7
3 ¶He in the first year of his reign, in the first month, opened the doors of
the house of the LORD, and repaired them.
4 And he brought in the priests and the Levites, and gathered them
together into the east street,

29:5☆ 2 Chron 29:15, 34; 35:6
5 And said unto them, Hear me, ye Levites, sanctify now yourselves, and
sanctify the house of the LORD God of your fathers, and carry forth the
filthiness out of the holy *place*.

29:6 Ezek 8:16
6 For our fathers have trespassed, and done *that which was* evil in the eyes
of the LORD our God, and have forsaken him, and have turned away their
faces from the habitation of the LORD, and turned *their* backs.
7 Also they have shut up the doors of the porch, and put out the lamps,
and have not burned incense nor offered burnt offerings in the holy *place*
unto the God of Israel.

29:8 Deut 28:25; 2 Chron 24:18; 28:5; Jer 25:9, 18
8 Wherefore the wrath of the LORD was upon Judah and Jerusalem, and
he hath delivered them to trouble, to astonishment, and to hissing, as ye see
with your eyes.

29:9 2 Chron 28:5–8, 17
9 For, lo, our fathers have fallen by the sword, and our sons and our
daughters and our wives *are* in captivity for this.

29:10 2 Chron 23:16
10 Now *it is* in mine heart to make a covenant with the LORD God of
Israel, that his fierce wrath may turn away from us.

29:11 Num 3:6; 8:6
11 My sons, be not now negligent: for the LORD hath chosen you to stand
before him, to serve him, and that ye should minister unto him, and burn
incense.

b. The Levites Clean Up the Temple

29:12 Num 3:19, 20; 2 Chron 31:13
12 ¶Then the Levites arose, Ma'hath the son of A-mas'a-i, and Jo'el the
son of Az-a-ri'ah, of the sons of the Ko'hath-ites: and of the sons of Me-
ra'ri, Kish the son of Ab'di, and Az-a-ri'ah the son of Je-hal'e-lel: and of the
Ger'shon-ites; Jo'ah the son of Zimmah, and Eden the son of Jo'ah:
13 And of the sons of E-liz'a-phan; Shim'ri, and Je-i'el: and of the sons of
A'saph; Zech-a-ri'ah, and Mat-ta-ni'ah:
14 And of the sons of He'man; Je-hi'el, and Shim'e-i: and of the sons of
Jed'u-thun; Shem-a-i'ah, and Uz'zi-el.

29:15☆ 1 Chron 23:28; 2 Chron 29:5; 30:12
15 And they gathered their brethren, and sanctified themselves, and came,
according to the commandment of the king, by the words of the LORD, to
cleanse the house of the LORD.

29:16 2 Chron 15:16
16 And the priests went into the inner part of the house of the LORD, to
cleanse *it*, and brought out all the uncleanness that they found in the temple
of the LORD into the court of the house of the LORD. And the Levites took
it, to carry *it* out abroad into the brook Kidron.
17 Now they began on the first *day* of the first month to sanctify, and on
the eighth day of the month came they to the porch of the LORD: so they
sanctified the house of the LORD in eight days; and in the sixteenth day of
the first month they made an end.

29:3 Hezekiah began his reforms immediately. He opened the house of God and began to repair the damage done by his father.

29:5 The house of God had been defiled. Refuse had accumulated in it, the lamps had not been lit, incense had not been burned (29:6, 7), and the priests had not been carrying out their responsibilities. This meant that the state of religion in the whole of the kingdom was one of benign neglect, disinterest, and decay. Hezekiah intended to revive the true religion.

29:15 We may well ask where the priests were and what were they doing to have let the house of God become ill-kept and filled with filth. We also may ask why God did not remove his glory from such a house. He was long-suffering, providing his people with every opportunity to mend their ways and follow his precepts. When the captivity came, it was not from want of divine patience and repeated efforts to get the people to repent.

18 Then they went in to Hez-e-ki'ah the king, and said, We have cleansed all the house of the LORD, and the altar of burnt offering, with all the vessels thereof, and the shewbread table, with all the vessels thereof.

19 Moreover all the vessels, which king Ahaz in his reign did cast away in his transgression, have we prepared and sanctified, and, behold, they *are* before the altar of the LORD.

29:19 2 Chron 28:24

c. Hezekiah Reconsecrates the Temple

20 ¶Then Hez-e-ki'ah the king rose early, and gathered the rulers of the city, and went up to the house of the LORD.

21 And they brought seven bullocks, and seven rams, and seven lambs, and seven he goats, for a sin offering for the kingdom, and for the sanctuary, and for Judah. And he commanded the priests the sons of Aaron to offer *them* on the altar of the LORD.

☆29:21 Lev 4:3–14

22 So they killed the bullocks, and the priests received the blood, and sprinkled *it* on the altar: likewise, when they had killed the rams, they sprinkled the blood upon the altar: they killed also the lambs, and they sprinkled the blood upon the altar.

29:22 Lev 4:18

23 And they brought forth the he goats *for* the sin offering before the king and the congregation; and they laid their hands upon them:

☆29:23 Lev 4:15

24 And the priests killed them, and they made reconciliation with their blood upon the altar, to make an atonement for all Israel: for the king commanded *that* the burnt offering and the sin offering *should be made* for all Israel.

29:24 Lev 4:26

25 And he set the Levites in the house of the LORD with cymbals, with psalteries, and with harps, according to the commandment of David, and of Gad the king's seer, and Nathan the prophet: for *so was* the commandment of the LORD by his prophets.

29:25 2 Sam 7:2 24:11 1 Chron 25:6 2 Chron 5:12 8:14

26 And the Levites stood with the instruments of David, and the priests with the trumpets.

27 And Hez-e-ki'ah commanded to offer the burnt offering upon the altar. And when the burnt offering began, the song of the LORD began *also* with the trumpets, and with the instruments *ordained* by David king of Israel.

29:27 2 Chron 23:18

28 And all the congregation worshipped, and the singers sang, and the trumpeters sounded: *and* all *this continued* until the burnt offering was finished.

29 And when they had made an end of offering, the king and all that were present with him bowed themselves, and worshipped.

29:29 2 Chron 20:18

30 Moreover Hez-e-ki'ah the king and the princes commanded the Levites to sing praise unto the LORD with the words of David, and of A'saph the seer. And they sang praises with gladness, and they bowed their heads and worshipped.

d. The Sacrificial Offerings

31 Then Hez-e-ki'ah answered and said, Now ye have consecrated yourselves unto the LORD, come near and bring sacrifices and thank offerings into the house of the LORD. And the congregation brought in sacrifices and thank offerings; and as many as were of a free heart burnt offerings.

29:31 Ex 35:5, 22

32 And the number of the burnt offerings, which the congregation

29:21, 23 Blood atonement must be made for the sins of the people. Seven of each kind of animal were brought for sacrifice. The king and others laid their hands on these animals to confess their guilt before God. The revival of true religion was on the way.

brought, was threescore and ten bullocks, an hundred rams, *and* two
hundred lambs: all these *were* for a burnt offering to the LORD.
33 And the consecrated things *were* six hundred oxen and three thousand
sheep.
29:34☆ 2 Chron 35:11 — 34 But the priests were too few, so that they could not flay all the burnt
offerings: wherefore their brethren the Levites did help them, till the work
was ended, and until the *other* priests had sanctified themselves: for the
Levites *were* more upright in heart to sanctify themselves than the priests.
29:35 Num 15:5–10; 2 Chron 29:32 — 35 And also the burnt offerings *were* in abundance, with the fat of the
peace offerings, and the drink offerings for *every* burnt offering. So the
service of the house of the LORD was set in order.
36 And Hez-e-ki'ah rejoiced, and all the people, that God had prepared
the people: for the thing was *done* suddenly.

2. The Reinstitution of the Passover

a. Hezekiah's Invitation to All Israelis to Come

30:1ff☆ — 30 AND Hez-e-ki'ah sent to all Israel and Judah, and wrote letters
also to E'phra-im and Ma-nas'seh, that they should come to the
house of the LORD at Jerusalem, to keep the passover unto the LORD God
of Israel.
30:2 Num 9:10; 11; 2 Chron 30:13, 15 — 2 For the king had taken counsel, and his princes, and all the congrega-
tion in Jerusalem, to keep the passover in the second month.
3 For they could not keep it at that time, because the priests had not
sanctified themselves sufficiently, neither had the people gathered them-
selves together to Jerusalem.
4 And the thing pleased the king and all the congregation.
30:5☆ Judg 20:1 — 5 So they established a decree to make proclamation throughout all Israel,
from Be'er–she'ba even to Dan, that they should come to keep the passover
unto the LORD God of Israel at Jerusalem: for they had not done *it* of a
long *time in such sort* as it was written.
30:6 2 Chron 28:20 — 6 So the posts went with the letters from the king and his princes
throughout all Israel and Judah, and according to the commandment of the
king, saying, Ye children of Israel, turn again unto the LORD God of
Abraham, Isaac, and Israel, and he will return to the remnant of you, that
are escaped out of the hand of the kings of Assyria.
30:7 2 Chron 29:8; Ezek 20:13 — 7 And be not ye like your fathers, and like your brethren, which
trespassed against the LORD God of their fathers, *who* therefore gave them
up to desolation, as ye see.
30:8 Ex 3:29; 2 Chron 29:10 — 8 Now be ye not stiffnecked, as your fathers *were*, *but* yield yourselves
unto the LORD, and enter into his sanctuary, which he hath sanctified for
30:9 Ex 34:6, 7; Deut 30:2; Mic 7:18 — ever: and serve the LORD your God, that the fierceness of his wrath may
turn away from you.
9 For if ye turn again unto the LORD, your brethren and your children

---

29:34 Not all the Levites were priests; only those who descended from Aaron. Here there were not enough priests, so other Levites, contrary to the law, were called upon to help. The legality was dispensed with in cases of necessity, even as the Sabbath was violated in cases of necessity.

30:1ff Hezekiah sent messengers all over Israel as well as Judah, inviting all to assemble for the celebration of the Passover. The citizens of the north laughed, scorned and mocked the messengers, refusing to come to Jerusalem to celebrate. The people of Judah, on the other hand, accepted the invitation and came to Jerusalem. The people were revived and true religion prospered.

30:5 *they had not done it of a long time in such sort as it was written,* or, "The Passover had not been celebrated by the northern tribes of Israel for a long time; only a faithful few had been doing it in the proper way."† Clearly the Northern Kingdom was finished; otherwise, Hezekiah would not have extended an invitation for people from the Northern Kingdom to come to Jerusalem to celebrate the Passover.

shall find compassion before them that lead them captive, so that they shall
come again into this land: for the LORD your God *is* gracious and merciful,
and will not turn away *his* face from you, if ye return unto him.
10So the posts passed from city to city through the country of E′phra-im
and Ma-nas′seh even unto Zeb′u-lun: but they laughed them to scorn, and
mocked them.

30:10 2 Chron 36:16

11Nevertheless divers of Asher and Ma-nas′seh and of Zeb′u-lun humbled
themselves, and came to Jerusalem.

30:11 2 Chron 30, 18, 21, 35

12Also in Judah the hand of God was to give them one heart to do the
commandment of the king and of the princes, by the word of the LORD.
13¶And there assembled at Jerusalem much people to keep the feast of
unleavened bread in the second month, a very great congregation.

30:13 2 Chron 30:2

14And they arose and took away the altars that *were* in Jerusalem, and all
the altars for incense took they away, and cast *them* into the brook Kidron.

30:14 2 Chron 28:24 29:16

b. The Celebration of the Passover

15Then they killed the passover on the fourteenth *day* of the second
month: and the priests and the Levites were ashamed, and sanctified
themselves, and brought in the burnt offerings into the house of the LORD.

30:15 2 Chron 29:34 30:2, 3

16And they stood in their place after their manner, according to the law
of Moses the man of God: the priests sprinkled the blood, *which they
received* of the hand of the Levites.

30:16 2 Chron 35:10, 15

17For *there were* many in the congregation that were not sanctified:
therefore the Levites had the charge of the killing of the passovers for every
one *that was* not clean, to sanctify *them* unto the LORD.

30:17 Ex 12:43-49 Num 9:10 2 Chron 19:3 29:34; 30:11, 25

18For a multitude of the people, *even* many of E′phra-im, and Ma-
nas′seh, Is′sa-char, and Zeb′u-lun, had not cleansed themselves, yet did
they eat the passover otherwise than it was written. But Hez-e-ki′ah prayed
for them, saying, The good LORD pardon every one
19*That* prepareth his heart to seek God, the LORD God of his fathers,
though *he be* not *cleansed* according to the purification of the sanctuary.
20And the LORD hearkened to Hez-e-ki′ah, and healed the people.

☆30:20

21And the children of Israel that were present at Jerusalem kept the feast
of unleavened bread seven days with great gladness: and the Levites and
the priests praised the LORD day by day, *singing* with loud instruments unto
the LORD.

30:21 Ex 12:15; 13:6

22And Hez-e-ki′ah spake comfortably unto all the Levites that taught the
good knowledge of the LORD: and they did eat throughout the feast seven
days, offering peace offerings, and making confession to the LORD God of
their fathers.

30:22 Ezra 10:11

c. The Feast Continued for Seven More Days

23And the whole assembly took counsel to keep other seven days: and
they kept *other* seven days with gladness.

30:23 1 Kgs 8:65

24For Hez-e-ki′ah king of Judah did give to the congregation a thousand
bullocks and seven thousand sheep; and the princes gave to the congrega-
tion a thousand bullocks and ten thousand sheep: and a great number of
priests sanctified themselves.

30:24 2 Chron 29:34 30:3; 35:7, 8

25And all the congregation of Judah, with the priests and the Levites, and

30:25 2 Chron 30:11, 18

30:20 *healed the people.* Hezekiah prayed that God would accept those who came to worship but who had not cleansed themselves properly. Their heart-intention was right but their performance fell short of the requirements. Thus the healing here is not physical healing from disease or sickness but forgiveness, comfort, and peace. The word for healing (*rapha*) is used in the Old Testament in several different ways.

all the congregation that came out of Israel, and the strangers that came out of the land of Israel, and that dwelt in Ju'dah, rejoiced.

30:26 2 Chron 7:8–10

[26]So there was great joy in Jerusalem: for since the time of Solomon the son of David king of Israel *there was* not the like in Jerusalem.

30:27☆ Num 6:23 Deut 26:15 2 Chron 23:18 Ps 68:5

[27]¶Then the priests the Levites arose and blessed the people: and their voice was heard, and their prayer came *up* to his holy dwelling place, *even* unto heaven.

3. Hezekiah's Reforms Continued

a. The Idol Centers Torn Down

31:1☆ 2 Kgs 18:4

31 NOW when all this was finished, all Israel that were present went out to the cities of Judah, and brake the images in pieces, and cut down the groves, and threw down the high places and the altars out of all Judah and Benjamin, in E'phra-im also and Ma-nas'seh, until they had utterly destroyed them all. Then all the children of Israel returned, every man to his possession, into their own cities.

b. The Reform of the Levitical Service

31:2 1 Chron 23:28–31; 24:1

[2]¶And Hez-e-ki'ah appointed the courses of the priests and the Levites after their courses, every man according to his service, the priests and Levites for burnt offerings and for peace offerings, to minister, and to give thanks, and to praise in the gates of the tents of the LORD.

31:3 Num 28:1–29, 40 2 Chron 35:7

[3]*He appointed* also the king's portion of his substance for the burnt offerings, *to wit,* for the morning and evening burnt offerings, and the burnt offerings for the sabbaths, and for the new moons, and for the set feasts, as *it is* written in the law of the LORD.

31:4☆ Num 18:8

[4]Moreover he commanded the people that dwelt in Jerusalem to give the portion of the priests and the Levites, that they might be encouraged in the law of the LORD.

31:5 Lev 27:30 Deut 14:28 Neh 13:12

[5]¶And as soon as the commandment came abroad, the children of Israel brought in abundance the firstfruits of corn, wine, and oil, and honey, and of all the increase of the field; and the tithe of all *things* brought they in abundantly.

[6]And *concerning* the children of Israel and Judah, that dwelt in the cities of Judah, they also brought in the tithe of oxen and sheep, and the tithe of holy things which were consecrated unto the LORD their God, and laid *them* by heaps.

[7]In the third month they began to lay the foundation of the heaps, and finished *them* in the seventh month.

[8]And when Hez-e-ki'ah and the princes came and saw the heaps, they blessed the LORD, and his people Israel.

[9]Then Hez-e-ki'ah questioned with the priests and the Levites concerning the heaps.

31:10 1 Chron 6:8, 9 Mal 3:10

[10]And Az-a-ri'ah the chief priest of the house of Za'dok answered him,

---

30:27 God in heaven was pleased with what happened and said his own Amen to the blessing of the priests. "The prayer that comes up to heaven in a cloud of incense will come down again to this earth in showers of blessing."*

31:1 Hezekiah and his officers undoubtedly could not know of or find all of the places where monuments of idolatry existed. Here the people finish the work by destroying all those places that had escaped the king's notice. Isaiah may have had this in mind when he wrote, "In that day a man shall cast his idols of silver, and his idols of gold, which they made each for himself to worship, to the moles and to the bats" (Isa. 2:20).

31:4 Apparently the people had not supported the Levites, and those who were priests had to find means in other ways. This resulted in the neglect of their duties which included the study of the Word of God. Ministers should be paid well and encouraged to pursue their study, use, and exposition of the Word of God for their own sake and for the sake of the people. Seeing the need, Hezekiah contributed to this end and urged others to do the same.

and said, Since *the people* began to bring the offerings into the house of the
LORD, we have had enough to eat, and have left plenty: for the LORD hath
blessed his people; and that which is left *is* this great store.
11 ¶Then Hez-e-ki'ah commanded to prepare chambers in the house of the
LORD; and they prepared *them*,

31:11 1 Kgs 6:5, 8

12 And brought in the offerings and the tithes and the dedicated *things*
faithfully: over which Con-o-ni'ah the Levite *was* ruler, and Shim'e-i his
brother *was* the next.

31:12 2 Chron 31:10

13 And Je-hi'el, and Az-a-zi'ah, and Na'hath, and As'a-hel, and Jer'i-
moth, and Joz'a-bad, and E-li'el, and Is-ma-chi'ah, and Ma'hath, and Be-
nai'ah, *were* overseers under the hand of Con-o-ni'ah and Shim'e-i his
brother, at the commandment of Hez-e-ki'ah the king, and Az-a-ri'ah the
ruler of the house of God.
14 And Ko're the son of Im'nah the Levite, the porter toward the east, *was*
over the freewill offerings of God, to distribute the oblations of the LORD,
and the most holy things.

31:14 Josh 21:9–19 2 Chron 29:12

15 And next him *were* Eden, and Min'i-a-min, and Jesh'u-a, and Shem-a-
i'ah, Am-a-ri'ah, and Shec-a-ni'ah, in the cities of the priests, in *their* set
office, to give to their brethren by courses, as well to the great as to the
small:
16 Beside their genealogy of males, from three years old and upward, *even*
unto every one that entereth into the house of the LORD, his daily portion
for their service in their charges according to their courses;
17 Both to the genealogy of the priests by the house of their fathers, and
the Levites from twenty years old and upward, in their charges by their
courses;

☆31:17 1 Chron 23:24

18 And to the genealogy of all their little ones, their wives, and their sons,
and their daughters, through all the congregation: for in their set office they
sanctified themselves in holiness:
19 Also of the sons of Aaron the priests, *which were* in the fields of the
suburbs of their cities, in every several city, the men that were expressed by
name, to give portions to all the males among the priests, and to all that
were reckoned by genealogies among the Levites.

31:19 2 Chron 31:12–15

c. Summary of Hezekiah's Reforms

20 ¶And thus did Hez-e-ki'ah throughout all Judah, and wrought *that*
which was good and right and truth before the LORD his God.

31:20 2 Kgs 20:3; 22:2

21 And in every work that he began in the service of the house of God, and
in the law, and in the commandments, to seek his God, he did *it* with all his
heart, and prospered.

4. Sennacherib's Invasion of Judah
a. The Invasion of Judah by Sennacherib

32 AFTER these things, and the establishment thereof, Sen-nach'e-rib
king of Assyria came, and entered into Judah, and encamped
against the fenced cities, and thought to win them for himself.

☆32:1 2 Kgs 18:13–19, 37 Isa 36:1—37:38

31:17 It was essential for records to be kept of those who were Levites. This included those of the priesthood and those who were not. All Levites were supported by those who were not Levites and apportionment was made according to the numbers of the Levites. Evidently Levites with wives and children received more than those who were single or married and without children.

32:1 Sennacherib took it upon himself to assault Judah. Hezekiah prepared for this eventuality by gathering an army and manufacturing armaments. He reinforced the city of Jerusalem. His most important contribution was his faith in God, which he communicated to the people: "with us is the LORD our God to help us and to fight our battles" (32:8, NASB). Judah was soon to learn the meaning of Hezekiah's confidence when they saw the power of God displayed on their behalf.

32:2☆ 2 And when Hez-e-ki'ah saw that Sen-nach'e-rib was come, and that he
was purposed to fight against Jerusalem,
32:3 3 He took counsel with his princes and his mighty men to stop the waters
2 Kgs 20:20 of the fountains which *were* without the city: and they did help him.
32:4 4 So there was gathered much people together, who stopped all the
2 Chron 32:30 fountains, and the brook that ran through the midst of the land, saying,
Why should the kings of Assyria come, and find much water?
32:5 5 Also he strengthened himself, and built up all the wall that was broken,
1 Kgs 9:24 2 Kgs 25:4 and raised *it* up to the towers, and another wall without, and repaired
2 Chron 25:23 Mil'lo *in* the city of David, and made darts and shields in abundance.
32:6 6 And he set captains of war over the people, and gathered them together
2 Chron 30:22 to him in the street of the gate of the city, and spake comfortably to them,
saying,
32:7 7 Be strong and courageous, be not afraid nor dismayed for the king of
2 Kgs 6:16 1 Chron 22:13 Assyria, nor for all the multitude that *is* with him: for *there be* more with us
than with him:
32:8 8 With him *is* an arm of flesh; but with us *is* the LORD our God to help us,
2 Chron 20:17 Jer 17:5 and to fight our battles. And the people rested themselves upon the words
of Hez-e-ki'ah king of Judah.

b. Sennacherib's Arrogant Message

9 ¶After this did Sen-nach'e-rib king of Assyria send his servants to
Jerusalem, (but he *himself laid siege* against La'chish, and all his power with
him,) unto Hez-e-ki'ah king of Judah, and unto all Judah that *were* at
Jerusalem, saying,
10 Thus saith Sen-nach'e-rib king of Assyria, Whereon do ye trust, that ye
abide in the siege in Jerusalem?
11 Doth not Hez-e-ki'ah persuade you to give over yourselves to die by
famine and by thirst, saying, The LORD our God shall deliver us out of the
hand of the king of Assyria?
32:12 12 Hath not the same Hez-e-ki'ah taken away his high places and his
2 Chron 31:1 altars, and commanded Judah and Jerusalem, saying, Ye shall worship
before one altar, and burn incense upon it?
13 Know ye not what I and my fathers have done unto all the people of
other lands? were the gods of the nations of those lands any ways able to
deliver their lands out of mine hand?
32:14 14 Who *was there* among all the gods of those nations that my fathers
Isa 10:9–11 utterly destroyed, that could deliver his people out of mine hand, that your
God should be able to deliver you out of mine hand?
15 Now therefore let not Hez-e-ki'ah deceive you, nor persuade you on
this manner, neither yet believe him: for no god of any nation or kingdom
was able to deliver his people out of mine hand, and out of the hand of my
fathers: how much less shall your God deliver you out of mine hand?

c. Sennacherib Blasphemes God

16 And his servants spake yet *more* against the LORD God, and against his
servant Hez-e-ki'ah.
32:17 17 He wrote also letters to rail on the LORD God of Israel, and to speak
2 Chron 32:14 against him, saying, As the gods of the nations of *other* lands have not
delivered their people out of mine hand, so shall not the God of Hez-e-ki'ah
deliver his people out of mine hand.

32:2 The chronicler leaves out the fact that before this, Hezekiah meekly paid tribute to Sennacherib and at that time neither consulted God or the prophet Isaiah (see note to 2 Kings 18:14).

18 Then they cried with a loud voice in the Jews' speech unto the people of
Jerusalem that *were* on the wall, to affright them, and to trouble them; that
they might take the city.
19 And they spake against the God of Jerusalem, as against the gods of the
people of the earth, *which were* the work of the hands of man.

d. God's Angel Destroys Sennacherib's Army

20 And for this *cause* Hez-e-ki'ah the king, and the prophet Isaiah the son
of Amoz, prayed and cried to heaven.
21 ¶And the LORD sent an angel, which cut off all the mighty men of
valour, and the leaders and captains in the camp of the king of Assyria. So
he returned with shame of face to his own land. And when he was come
into the house of his god, they that came forth of his own bowels slew him
there with the sword.
22 Thus the LORD saved Hez-e-ki'ah and the inhabitants of Jerusalem
from the hand of Sen-nach'e-rib the king of Assyria, and from the hand of
all *other*, and guided them on every side.
23 And many brought gifts unto the LORD to Jerusalem, and presents to
Hez-e-ki'ah king of Judah: so that he was magnified in the sight of all
nations from thenceforth.

☆32:20
☆32:21
32:23 2 Sam 8:10

e. God Extends Hezekiah's Life

24 In those days Hez-e-ki'ah was sick to the death, and prayed unto the
LORD: and he spake unto him, and he gave him a sign.
25 But Hez-e-ki'ah rendered not again according to the benefit *done* unto
him; for his heart was lifted up: therefore there was wrath upon him, and
upon Judah and Jerusalem.
26 Notwithstanding Hez-e-ki'ah humbled himself for the pride of his
heart, *both* he and the inhabitants of Jerusalem, so that the wrath of the
LORD came not upon them in the days of Hez-e-ki'ah.

☆32:24 2 Kgs 20:1–11 Isa 38:1–8
32:25 2 Chron 24:18 26:16
32:26 Jer 26:18, 19

f. Hezekiah's Accomplishments

27 ¶And Hez-e-ki'ah had exceeding much riches and honour: and he made
himself treasuries for silver, and for gold, and for precious stones, and for
spices, and for shields, and for all manner of pleasant jewels;
28 Storehouses also for the increase of corn, and wine, and oil; and stalls
for all manner of beasts, and cotes for flocks.
29 Moreover he provided him cities, and possessions of flocks and herds in
abundance: for God had given him substance very much.
30 This same Hez-e-ki'ah also stopped the upper watercourse of Gi'hon,
and brought it straight down to the west side of the city of David. And Hez-
e-ki'ah prospered in all his works.
31 ¶Howbeit in *the business of* the ambassadors of the princes of Babylon,
who sent unto him to inquire of the wonder that was *done* in the land, God
left him, to try him, that he might know all *that was* in his heart.

32:30 1 Kgs 1:33 2 Kgs 20:20
32:31 2 Kgs 20:12 2 Chron 32:24 Isa 38:7; 8; 39:1

32:20 When Jerusalem was threatened, both King Hezekiah and the prophet Isaiah laid hold of God in prayer. The account here is further compressed, for nothing is said about how the angel of God slew 185,000 Assyrians in one night. The victory over Sennacherib was so great that Hezekiah "was magnified in the sight of all nations from thenceforth" (32:23).

32:21 See note on 2 Kings 19:35. God sent an avenging angel to execute judgment against Sennacherib, who fled from the scene of the disaster, never to return to Israel.

32:24 A more extended account of Hezekiah's healing is found in 2 Kings 20:1–11. The turning back of the sundial is not recorded here. But Hezekiah's pride after his healing is said to be the cause of transgression after which Isaiah prophesied the destruction of Judah. This was held off until after Hezekiah's day so that it could be said that there was peace and truth in his days (2 Kings 20:19).

g. Hezekiah's Death; Manasseh His Successor

32 ¶Now the rest of the acts of Hez-e-ki'ah, and his goodness, behold, they *are* written in the vision of Isaiah the prophet, the son of Amoz, *and* in the book of the kings of Judah and Israel.

33 And Hez-e-ki'ah slept with his fathers, and they buried him in the chiefest of the sepulchres of the sons of David: and all Judah and the inhabitants of Jerusalem did him honour at his death. And Ma-nas'seh his son reigned in his stead.

M. KINGS MANASSEH AND AMON

1. Manasseh's Evil Reign

33:1☆ 2 Kgs 21:1–9

33 MA-NAS'SEH *was* twelve years old when he began to reign, and he reigned fifty and five years in Jerusalem:

33:2 2 Chron 28:3

2 But did *that which was* evil in the sight of the LORD, like unto the abominations of the heathen, whom the LORD had cast out before the children of Israel.

33:3☆ Deut 16:21; 2 Kgs 23:5, 6; 2 Chron 31:1

3 ¶For he built again the high places which Hez-e-ki'ah his father had broken down, and he reared up altars for Ba'al-im, and made groves, and worshipped all the host of heaven, and served them.

33:4 2 Chron 4:9; 7:16; 28:24

4 Also he built altars in the house of the LORD, whereof the LORD had said, In Jerusalem shall my name be for ever.

5 And he built altars for all the host of heaven in the two courts of the house of the LORD.

33:6 Lev 19:31; 20:27; 2 Chron 28:3

6 And he caused his children to pass through the fire in the valley of the son of Hin'nom: also he observed times, and used enchantments, and used witchcraft, and dealt with a familiar spirit, and with wizards: he wrought much evil in the sight of the LORD, to provoke him to anger.

33:7 2 Chron 3:4, 15

7 And he set a carved image, the idol which he had made, in the house of God, of which God had said to David and to Solomon his son, In this house, and in Jerusalem, which I have chosen before all the tribes of Israel, will I put my name for ever:

33:8 2 Sam 7:10

8 Neither will I any more remove the foot of Israel from out of the land which I have appointed for your fathers; so that they will take heed to do all that I have commanded them, according to the whole law and the statutes and the ordinances by the hand of Moses.

9 So Ma-nas'seh made Judah and the inhabitants of Jerusalem to err, *and* to do worse than the heathen, whom the LORD had destroyed before the children of Israel.

2. Manasseh's Babylonian Imprisonment and Release

33:10☆

10 And the LORD spake to Ma-nas'seh, and to his people: but they would not hearken.

33:11 Deut 28:36; 2 Chron 36:6

11 Wherefore the LORD brought upon them the captains of the host of the king of Assyria, which took Ma-nas'seh among the thorns, and bound him with fetters, and carried him to Babylon.

33:12 2 Chron 32:26

12 And when he was in affliction, he besought the LORD his God, and humbled himself greatly before the God of his fathers,

---

33:1 The first ten years of Manasseh's reign was a co-regency with his father Hezekiah.

33:3 Manasseh reversed the pattern established by his father. Judah resorted to idolatry again. The high places were rebuilt and altars to the Baals were set up. He burned his sons (33:6). He also committed the vilest of sins: he set up an idol in the house of God (33:7). All of his numerous transgressions were as nothing compared to this. It was the supreme insult to Almighty God.

33:10 God had warned Manasseh; when the divine injunctions were ignored, God's judgment fell and the king was humbled.

[13]And prayed unto him: and he was intreated of him, and heard his ☆33:13
supplication, and brought him again to Jerusalem into his kingdom. Then Ezra 8:23 Dan 4:32
Ma-nas'seh knew that the LORD he *was* God.

3. Manasseh Tears Down the Heathen Altars

[14]Now after this he built a wall without the city of David, on the west 33:14
side of Gi'hon, in the valley, even to the entering in at the fish gate, and 1 Kgs 1:33 Neh 3:3
compassed about O'phel, and raised it up a very great height, and put
captains of war in all the fenced cities of Judah.
[15]And he took away the strange gods, and the idol out of the house of the 33:15
LORD, and all the altars that he had built in the mount of the house of the 2 Chron 33:3–7
LORD, and in Jerusalem, and cast *them* out of the city.
[16]And he repaired the altar of the LORD, and sacrificed thereon peace
offerings and thank offerings, and commanded Judah to serve the LORD
God of Israel.
[17]Nevertheless the people did sacrifice still in the high places, *yet* unto the 33:17
LORD their God only. 2 Chron 32:12

4. Summary of Manasseh's Kingship; His Death

[18]¶Now the rest of the acts of Ma-nas'seh, and his prayer unto his God, ☆33:18
and the words of the seers that spake to him in the name of the LORD God 2 Chron 33:10, 12, 13
of Israel, behold, they *are written* in the book of the kings of Israel.
[19]His prayer also, and *how God* was intreated of him, and all his sins, and ☆33:19
his trespass, and the places wherein he built high places, and set up groves 2 Chron 33:3, 13
and graven images, before he was humbled: behold, they *are* written among
the sayings of the seers.
[20]¶So Ma-nas'seh slept with his fathers, and they buried him in his own 33:20
house: and A'mon his son reigned in his stead. 2 Kgs 21:19–24
[21]¶A'mon *was* two and twenty years old when he began to reign, and
reigned two years in Jerusalem.

5. King Amon's Two-Year Evil Regin

[22]But he did *that which was* evil in the sight of the LORD, as did Ma- 33:22
nas'seh his father: for A'mon sacrificed unto all the carved images which 2 Chron 33:2–7
Ma-nas'seh his father had made, and served them;
[23]And humbled not himself before the LORD, as Ma-nas'seh his father ☆33:23
had humbled himself; but A'mon trespassed more and more. 2 Chron 33:12, 19
[24]And his servants conspired against him, and slew him in his own house. 33:24
[25]¶But the people of the land slew all them that had conspired against 2 Chron 25:27
king A'mon; and the people of the land made Jo-si'ah his son king in his
stead.

N. KING JOSIAH
1. Josiah Destroys the Pagan Altars and the Idols

[34] JO-SI'AH *was* eight years old when he began to reign, and he 34:1
reigned in Jerusalem one and thirty years. 2 Kgs 22:1, 2
[2]And he did *that which was* right in the sight of the LORD, and walked in 34:2 2 Chron 29:2

33:13 It was only after Manasseh had been taken captive and brought to Babylon in chains that he came to his senses. He pleaded with God for help and was returned to Jerusalem. By then he knew the power of God and changed somewhat for the better.
33:18, 19 So remarkable was the turning around of Manasseh and so unexpected that the chronicler twice says "and his prayer." He began praying to the true God late in life. Better late than never.
33:23 Amon, who had a very short reign, distinguished himself by his wickedness. He "trespassed more and more" or "incurred guilt more and more" as the RSV has it. He was cut off when he was young, and nothing is said about any repentance on his part.

the ways of David his father, and declined *neither* to the right hand, nor to
the left.

34:3☆ 2 Chron 33:22
3 ¶For in the eighth year of his reign, while he was yet young, he began to
seek after the God of David his father: and in the twelfth year he began to
purge Judah and Jerusalem from the high places, and the groves, and the
carved images, and the molten images.

34:4☆ Ex 32:20; 2 Kgs 23:4, 5
4 And they brake down the altars of Ba'al-im in his presence; and the
images, that *were* on high above them, he cut down; and the groves, and the
carved images, and the molten images, he brake in pieces, and made dust *of*
them, and strowed *it* upon the graves of them that had sacrificed unto them.

34:5 2 Kgs 23:20
5 And he burnt the bones of the priests upon their altars, and cleansed
Judah and Jerusalem.

34:6 2 Kgs 23:15, 19
6 And *so did he* in the cities of Ma-nas'seh, and E'phra-im, and Simeon,
even unto Naph'ta-li, with their mattocks round about.

34:7 Chron 31:1
7 And when he had broken down the altars and the groves, and had
beaten the graven images into powder, and cut down all the idols
throughout all the land of Israel, he returned to Jerusalem.

2. The Repair of the Temple

34:8☆ 2 Kgs 22:3–20; 2 Chron 18:25
8 ¶Now in the eighteenth year of his reign, when he had purged the land,
and the house, he sent Sha'phan the son of Az-a-li'ah, and Ma-a-sei'ah the
governor of the city, and Jo'ah the son of Jo'a-haz the recorder, to repair
the house of the LORD his God.

34:9 2 Chron 30:10, 18; 35:8
9 And when they came to Hil-ki'ah the high priest, they delivered the
money that was brought into the house of God, which the Levites that kept
the doors had gathered of the hand of Ma-nas'seh and E'phra-im, and of all
the remnant of Israel, and of all Judah and Benjamin; and they returned to
Jerusalem.
10 And they put *it* in the hand of the workmen that had the oversight of
the house of the LORD, and they gave it to the workmen that wrought in the
house of the LORD, to repair and amend the house:
11 Even to the artificers and builders gave they *it*, to buy hewn stone, and
timber for couplings, and to floor the houses which the kings of Judah had
destroyed.

34:12 1 Chron 25:1
12 And the men did the work faithfully: and the overseers of them *were*
Ja'hath and O-ba-di'ah, the Levites, of the sons of Me-ra'ri; and Zech-a-
ri'ah and Me-shul'lam, of the sons of the Ko'hath-ites, to set *it* forward; and
other of the Levites, all that could skill of instruments of musick.

34:13 2 Chron 8:10; Neh 4:10
13 Also *they were* over the bearers of burdens, and *were* overseers of all
that wrought the work in any manner of service: and of the Levites *there*
were scribes, and officers, and porters.

3. The Discovery of the Scroll (The Laws of God)

34:14☆ 2 Chron 34:9
14 ¶And when they brought out the money that was brought into the
house of the LORD, Hil-ki'ah the priest found a book of the law of the LORD
given by Moses.

34:3 While Josiah was yet a boy (sixteen years of age) he set his heart to seek God; he found him and was found of him.

34:4 When Josiah was twenty years old and firmly settled in his kingship, he destroyed the places of idolatry. He moved through the country, making a clean sweep of everything contrary to the law and will of God.

34:8 When Josiah was twenty-six, he rehabilitated the house of the Lord. Repairs were made and the proper services of worship carried on.

34:14 Hilkiah the priest discovered a copy of the Pentateuch. One must ask why it had been misplaced. Evidently the priests had strayed from the book of the law or it was not sufficiently important for them to keep track of it. But even if they had, it would be of no value unless they used it. When Josiah heard the words of the book, he was profoundly moved by them and rent his clothes (34:19).

15 And Hil-ki'ah answered and said to Sha'phan the scribe, I have found
the book of the law in the house of the LORD. And Hil-ki'ah delivered the
book to Sha'phan.
16 And Sha'phan carried the book to the king, and brought the king word
back again, saying, All that was committed to thy servants, they do *it*.
17 And they have gathered together the money that was found in the
house of the LORD, and have delivered it into the hand of the overseers, and
to the hand of the workmen.
18 Then Sha'phan the scribe told the king, saying, Hil-ki'ah the priest hath
given me a book. And Sha'phan read it before the king.
19 And it came to pass, when the king had heard the words of the law, that **34:19**
he rent his clothes. Josh 7:6
20 And the king commanded Hil-ki'ah, and A-hi'kam the son of Sha'phan,
and Abdon the son of Mi'cah, and Sha'phan the scribe, and A-sa-i'ah a
servant of the king's, saying,
21 Go, inquire of the LORD for me, and for them that are left in Israel and **34:21**
in Judah, concerning the words of the book that is found: for great *is* the 2 Chron 29:8
wrath of the LORD that is poured out upon us, because our fathers have not
kept the word of the LORD, to do after all that is written in this book.
22 And Hil-ki'ah, and *they* that the king *had appointed*, went to Hul'dah ☆**34:22**
the prophetess, the wife of Shal'lum the son of Tik'vath, the son of Has'rah,
keeper of the wardrobe; (now she dwelt in Jerusalem in the college:) and
they spake to her to that *effect*.
23 And she answered them, Thus saith the LORD God of Israel, Tell ye the
man that sent you to me,
24 Thus saith the LORD, Behold, I will bring evil upon this place, and upon **34:24**
the inhabitants thereof, *even* all the curses that are written in the book Deut 28:15–68 2 Chron
which they have read before the king of Judah: 36:14–20
25 Because they have forsaken me, and have burned incense unto other **34:25**
gods, that they might provoke me to anger with all the works of their 2 Chron 33:3
hands; therefore my wrath shall be poured out upon this place, and shall
not be quenched.

4. The Law Read and the Covenant Renewed

26 And as for the king of Judah, who sent you to inquire of the LORD, so
shall ye say unto him, Thus saith the LORD God of Israel *concerning* the
words which thou hast heard;
27 Because thine heart was tender, and thou didst humble thyself before **34:27**
God, when thou heardest his words against this place, and against the 2 Chron 12:7 32:26
inhabitants thereof, and humbledst thyself before me, and didst rend thy
clothes, and weep before me; I have even heard *thee* also, saith the LORD.
28 Behold, I will gather thee to thy fathers, and thou shalt be gathered to ☆**34:28**
thy grave in peace, neither shall thine eyes see all the evil that I will bring
upon this place, and upon the inhabitants of the same. So they brought the
king word again.
29 ¶Then the king sent and gathered together all the elders of Judah and **34:29**
Jerusalem. 2 Kgs 23:1–3
30 And the king went up into the house of the LORD, and all the men of **34:30**
Judah, and the inhabitants of Jerusalem, and the priests, and the Levites, Neh 8:1–3

34:22 See note on 2 Kings 22:14 about Huldah the prophetess.
34:28 Josiah was so moved by the Word of God that he placed himself under that Word and promised to obey it and the God who gave it. God promised that judgment against Judah would be deferred and that Josiah would be gathered to his grave in peace.

and all the people, great and small: and he read in their ears all the words
of the book of the covenant that was found in the house of the LORD.
34:31 2 Chron 23:16 29:10
31 And the king stood in his place, and made a covenant before the LORD,
to walk after the LORD, and to keep his commandments, and his testimo-
nies, and his statutes, with all his heart, and with all his soul, to perform the
words of the covenant which are written in this book.
32 And he caused all that were present in Jerusalem and Benjamin to
stand *to it.* And the inhabitants of Jerusalem did according to the covenant
of God, the God of their fathers.
34:33 2 Chron 34:3–7
33 And Jo-si'ah took away all the abominations out of all the countries
that *pertained* to the children of Israel, and made all that were present in
Israel to serve, *even* to serve the LORD their God. *And* all his days they
departed not from following the LORD, the God of their fathers.

5. The Celebration of the Passover

35:1☆ Ex 12:6 Num 9:3 2 Kgs 23:21
35 MOREOVER Jo-si'ah kept a passover unto the LORD in Jerusalem:
and they killed the passover on the fourteenth *day* of the first
month.
35:2 2 Chron 29:11
2 And he set the priests in their charges, and encouraged them to the
service of the house of the LORD,
35:3 1 Chron 23:26 2 Chron 17:8, 9 Neh 8:7
3 And said unto the Levites that taught all Israel, which were holy unto
the LORD, Put the holy ark in the house which Solomon the son of David
king of Israel did build; *it shall* not *be* a burden upon *your* shoulders: serve
now the LORD your God, and his people Israel,
35:4 1 Chron 9:10–13 2 Chron 8:14
4 And prepare *yourselves* by the houses of your fathers, after your courses,
according to the writing of David king of Israel, and according to the
writing of Solomon his son.
5 And stand in the holy *place* according to the divisions of the families of
the fathers of your brethren the people, and *after* the division of the families
of the Levites.
35:6 2 Chron 29:5 35:1
6 So kill the passover, and sanctify yourselves, and prepare your brethren,
that *they* may do according to the word of the LORD by the hand of Moses.
7 And Jo-si'ah gave to the people, of the flock, lambs and kids, all for the
passover offerings, for all that were present, to the number of thirty
thousand, and three thousand bullocks: these *were* of the king's substance.
35:8 2 Chron 31:13
8 And his princes gave willingly unto the people, to the priests, and to the
Levites: Hil-ki'ah and Zech-a-ri'ah and Je-hi'el, rulers of the house of God,
gave unto the priests for the passover offerings two thousand and six
hundred *small cattle,* and three hundred oxen.
35:9 2 Chron 31:12
9 Con-a-ni'ah also, and Shem-a-i'ah and Ne-than'e-el, his brethren, and
Hash-a-bi'ah and Je-i'el and Joz'a-bad, chief of the Levites, gave unto the
Levites for passover offerings five thousand *small cattle,* and five hundred
oxen.
35:10 2 Chron 35:5
10 So the service was prepared, and the priests stood in their place, and
the Levites in their courses, according to the king's commandment.
35:11 2 Chron 29:22 35:1, 6
11 And they killed the passover, and the priests sprinkled *the blood* from
their hands, and the Levites flayed *them.*
12 And they removed the burnt offerings, that they might give according

---

35:1 The celebration of the Passover is mentioned very briefly in 2 Kings 23:21–23. Here it is enlarged upon and many details added for our knowledge. The king provided many animals from his own flocks for the people to offer. The king, priests, singers, porters and people alike participated in what was to be an epic event in Judah's recent history. The failure to keep the Passover celebration regularly and in large numbers suggests how deeply idolatry had robbed the people of their tradition and their faith.

to the divisions of the families of the people, to offer unto the LORD, as *it is*
written in the book of Moses. And so *did they* with the oxen.
13And they roasted the passover with fire according to the ordinance: but
the *other* holy *offerings* sod they in pots, and in caldrons, and in pans, and
divided *them* speedily among all the people.
14And afterward they made ready for themselves, and for the priests:
because the priests the sons of Aaron *were busied* in offering of burnt
offerings and the fat until night; therefore the Levites prepared for
themselves, and for the priests the sons of Aaron.
15And the singers the sons of A'saph *were* in their place, according to the
commandment of David, and A'saph, and He'man, and Jed'u-thun the
king's seer; and the porters *waited* at every gate; they might not depart from
their service; for their brethren the Levites prepared for them.
16So all the service of the LORD was prepared the same day, to keep the
passover, and to offer burnt offerings upon the altar of the LORD, according
to the commandment of king Jo-si'ah.
17And the children of Israel that were present kept the passover at that
time, and the feast of unleavened bread seven days.
18And there was no passover like to that kept in Israel from the days of
Samuel the prophet; neither did all the kings of Israel keep such a passover
as Jo-si'ah kept, and the priests, and the Levites, and all Judah and Israel
that were present, and the inhabitants of Jerusalem.
19In the eighteenth year of the reign of Jo-si'ah was this passover kept.

35:13 Ex 12:8, 9; Lev 6:25
35:15 1 Chron 25:1; 26:12–19
35:17 2 Chron 30:21
☆**35:18** 2 Kgs 23:21, 22; 2 Chron 30:5

6. Josiah's Death in the Battle with King Neco of Egypt

20¶After all this, when Jo-si'ah had prepared the temple, Ne'cho king of
Egypt came up to fight against Car'che-mish by Eu-phra'tes: and Jo-si'ah
went out against him.
21But he sent ambassadors to him, saying, What have I to do with thee,
thou king of Judah? *I come* not against thee this day, but against the house
wherewith I have war: for God commanded me to make haste: forbear thee
from *meddling with* God, who *is* with me, that he destroy thee not.
22Nevertheless Jo-si'ah would not turn his face from him, but disguised
himself, that he might fight with him, and hearkened not unto the words of
Ne'cho from the mouth of God, and came to fight in the valley of Me-
gid'do.
23And the archers shot at king Jo-si'ah; and the king said to his servants,
Have me away; for I am sore wounded.
24His servants therefore took him out of that chariot, and put him in the
second chariot that he had; and they brought him to Jerusalem, and he
died, and was buried in *one of* the sepulchres of his fathers. And all Judah
and Jerusalem mourned for Jo-si'ah.
25¶And Jer-e-mi'ah lamented for Jo-si'ah: and all the singing men and the
singing women spake of Jo-si'ah in their lamentations to this day, and made

☆**35:20** 2 Kgs 23:29, 30; Isa 10:9; Jer 46:2
☆**35:21**
☆**35:22** Judg 5:19; 2 Chron 18:29; 35:21
☆**35:24**
35:25 Jer 22:10–13; Lam 4:20; Zech 12:11

35:18 Hezekiah's celebration of the Passover exceeded any such celebration as far back as Solomon's day (30:26). But Josiah's celebration was to exceed that of Hezekiah, Solomon, and David, for none like it was seen since the days of the judges (2 Kings 23:22).
35:20 *against Carchemish,* i.e., "against the Assyrians." (See 2 Kings 23:29).
35:21 *the house wherewith I have war,* i.e., "the king of Assyria."
35:22 *valley of Megiddo.* The fortress of Megiddo was named *Har-megiddo* ("the hill of Megiddo"). It rose above the plain in the southern part of the Jezreel (Esdraelon) Valley. It guarded the pass of the best north-south trade route in Canaan. It was here that many great battles were fought in ancient times. And according to Rev. 16:16, it is here that the great climactic battle of the age will be fought, with Christ the victor.
35:24 Josiah was still in his early thirties when he died. Had he lived, the history of Judah might have been different. The next four kings reigned a total of less than twenty-three years. Two of the four reigned less than four months each.

them an ordinance in Israel: and, behold, they *are* written in the lamenta-
tions.
26 Now the rest of the acts of Jo-si'ah, and his goodness, according to *that*
which was written in the law of the LORD,
27 And his deeds, first and last, behold, they *are* written in the book of the
kings of Israel and Judah.

O. FROM JOSIAH'S DEATH TO THE BABYLONIAN CAPTIVITY

1. Jehoahaz, Neco's Prisoner in Egypt

36:1☆ Jer 22:11 — 36 THEN the people of the land took Je-ho'a-haz the son of Jo-si'ah,
and made him king in his father's stead in Jerusalem.
36:2 2 Kgs 23:30–34 — 2 Je-ho'a-haz *was* twenty and three years old when he began to reign, and
he reigned three months in Jerusalem.
3 And the king of Egypt put him down at Jerusalem, and condemned the
land in an hundred talents of silver and a talent of gold.
36:4 Jer 22:10, 12 — 4 And the king of Egypt made E-li'a-kim his brother king over Judah and
Jerusalem, and turned his name to Je-hoi'a-kim. And Ne'cho took Je-ho'a-
haz his brother, and carried him to Egypt.

2. Jehoiakim, Nebuchadnezzar's Prisoner in Babylon

36:5☆ 2 Kgs 22:36, 37 Jer 22:13–19 — 5 ¶Je-hoi'a-kim *was* twenty and five years old when he began to reign, and
he reigned eleven years in Jerusalem: and he did *that which was* evil in the
sight of the LORD his God.
36:6 2 Kgs 24:1 2 Chron 33:11 Jer 22:19, 20 — 6 Against him came up Neb-u-chad-nez'zar king of Babylon, and bound
him in fetters, to carry him to Babylon.
36:7 2 Kgs 24:13 — 7 Neb-u-chad-nez'zar also carried of the vessels of the house of the LORD
to Babylon, and put them in his temple at Babylon.
36:8☆ 2 Kgs 24:5 — 8 Now the rest of the acts of Je-hoi'a-kim, and his abominations which he
did, and that which was found in him, behold, they *are* written in the book
of the kings of Israel and Judah: and Je-hoi'a-chin his son reigned in his
stead.

3. Jehoiachin Brought to Babylon

36:9☆ 2 Kgs 24:8–17 — 9 ¶Je-hoi'a-chin *was* eight years old when he began to reign, and he
reigned three months and ten days in Jerusalem: and he did *that which was*
evil in the sight of the LORD.
36:10 2 Sam 11:1 Jer 37:1 — 10 And when the year was expired, king Neb-u-chad-nez'zar sent, and
brought him to Babylon, with the goodly vessels of the house of the LORD,
and made Zed-e-ki'ah his brother king over Judah and Jerusalem.

4. Zedekiah: the End of the Kingdom

a. The Rebellion of Zedekiah

36:11☆ 2 Kgs 24:18–20 Jer 52:1 — 11 ¶Zed-e-ki'ah *was* one and twenty years old when he began to reign, and
reigned eleven years in Jerusalem.

36:1 In 2 Kings we are told what the chronicler does not speak about Jehoahaz—"he did evil in the sight of the LORD" and reigned for three months before being taken captive to Egypt.

36:5 Jehoiakim, whose throne name was Eliakim, was chosen to become king by Pharaoh-Necho. He reigned in Jerusalem for eleven years. Nebuchadnezzar took him to Babylon in chains.

36:8 See note to 2 Kings 24:14 on Jehoiachin.

36:9 *eight years old.* Although some manuscripts read "eight years old," the correct age is eighteen, as in 2 Kings 24:8, unless Jehoiachin had been co-regent for ten years before the death of his father.

36:11 See note to 2 Kings 24:17 for information on Zedekiah.

[12]And he did *that which was* evil in the sight of the LORD his God, *and*
humbled not himself before Jer-e-mi'ah the prophet *speaking* from the
mouth of the LORD.

36:12 Jer 21:3–7

[13]And he also rebelled against king Neb-u-chad-nez'zar, who had made
him swear by God: but he stiffened his neck, and hardened his heart from
turning unto the LORD God of Israel.

36:13 2 Chron 30:8 Jer 52:3 Ezek 17:15

[14]¶Moreover all the chief of the priests, and the people, transgressed very
much after all the abominations of the heathen; and polluted the house of
the LORD which he had hallowed in Jerusalem.

[15]And the LORD God of their fathers sent to them by his messengers,
rising up betimes, and sending; because he had compassion on his people,
and on his dwelling place:

36:15 Jer 7:13; 25:3

[16]But they mocked the messengers of God, and despised his words, and
misused his prophets, until the wrath of the LORD arose against his people,
till *there was* no remedy.

36:16 2 Chron 30:10 Ezra 5:12 Prov 1:24–32 Jer 5:12, 13

b. The Captivity; the Temple and Jerusalem Destroyed

[17]Therefore he brought upon them the king of the Chal'dees, who slew
their young men with the sword in the house of their sanctuary, and had no
compassion upon young man or maiden, old man, or him that stooped for
age: he gave *them* all into his hand.

36:17 2 Kgs 25:1–7

[18]And all the vessels of the house of God, great and small, and the
treasures of the house of the LORD, and the treasures of the king, and of his
princes; all *these* he brought to Babylon.

36:18 2 Chron 36:7, 10

[19]And they burnt the house of God, and brake down the wall of
Jerusalem, and burnt all the palaces thereof with fire, and destroyed all the
goodly vessels thereof.

☆36:19 2 Kgs 25:9 Jer 52:13

[20]And them that had escaped from the sword carried he away to
Babylon; where they were servants to him and his sons until the reign of the
kingdom of Persia:

36:20 2 Kgs 25:11 Jer 27:7

[21]To fulfil the word of the LORD by the mouth of Jer-e-mi'ah, until the
land had enjoyed her sabbaths: *for* as long as she lay desolate she kept
sabbath, to fulfil threescore and ten years.

☆36:21 Lev 25:4; 26:33 Jer 29:10

c. Cyrus's Prophecy of the Return from the Captivity

[22]¶Now in the first year of Cyrus king of Persia, that the word of the
LORD *spoken* by the mouth of Jer-e-mi'ah might be accomplished, the LORD
stirred up the spirit of Cyrus king of Persia, that he made a proclamation
throughout all his kingdom, and *put it* also in writing, saying,

☆36:22 Ezra 1:1–3 Isa 44:28 Jer 25:12 29:10

[23]Thus saith Cyrus king of Persia, All the kingdoms of the earth hath the
LORD God of heaven given me; and he hath charged me to build him an
house in Jerusalem, which *is* in Judah. Who *is there* among you of all his
people? The LORD his God *be* with him, and let him go up.

☆36:23

36:19 *they burnt the house of God.* The Jews thought God would never let his house be destroyed. How wrong they were! If they had no use for God, neither should they have had any concern for the house of the God they no longer worshipped. Scripture does not tell us what happened to the ark. We can suppose it was destroyed in the fire and was irreplaceable.

36:21 *threescore and ten years.* Jeremiah spoke of the seventy years' captivity in Jer. 25:11, 12; 29:10.

36:22, 23 *Cyrus,* who founded the Persian Empire, presided over what was the largest empire the world had ever seen up to that time.

EZRA

Authorship, date, and background The books of Ezra and Nehemiah were at one time considered a single book under the title The Book of Ezra in the Hebrew Bible. Both must be related to the books of Chronicles as well as to the book of Esther. The authorship of Ezra and Nehemiah has never been finally resolved. Gleason L. Archer says that "Ezra himself undoubtedly wrote most of the book named after him . . . But he evidently incorporated into the final edition the personal memoirs of Nehemiah (i.e., the book of Nehemiah) including even his form of the list of the returnees."

Ezra returned to the land in 458 or 457 B.C. during the reign of Artaxerxes I (465–424 B.C.). Nehemiah returned twelve years later, in 445 B.C. Nehemiah's first governorship started in 445 B.C.; his second one in 433 B.C. Ezra was the son of Jozadak, whose genealogy went back to Aaron. He was a ready scribe of the Law of Moses. He led the return of the second group of immigrants, totaling approximately 5000 people. The temple had been finished years ago (516 B.C.) but the walls of the city had not been rebuilt. It was to be the labors of Ezra and Nehemiah which brought this to fruition. Ezra, upon his return to the land, was given a blank check by the king. As a priest of the line of Zadock he was expected to teach the Law. There is no record of his acting in the political office of governor as was true of Nehemiah.

Characteristics and content Ezra traces the return of the Jews to the land following the edict of Cyrus, who reversed the policy of the Chaldeans. He describes the preparations for the return, lists the various family groups, and notes that upon their return they went to the site of the former temple and contributed offerings of approximately five hundred thousand dollars for its rebuilding. Then follows the story of the rebuilding of the temple and the restoration of worship there. It is hampered by the malicious attacks of the Samaritans but, after a careful investigation, Darius gives order to continue the work of rebuilding. When it is completed, the feasts of the Passover and Unleavened Bread are celebrated.

Ezra, a patriotic Jew, secures permission to return to the land himself and does so. He describes the details of his return and poignantly notes that he refused to ask for armed protection, since his trust was in the Lord God. Ezra's anger knows no bounds when he discovers that the first group of returnees have intermarried with the heathen. He says, "I rent my garment and my mantle and plucked off the hair of my head and my beard and sat down astonied" (9:3). He prays, lies on the ground weeping, and forcefully insists that this evil must be remedied. As a result, many marriages contracted by priests, Levites, singers, gatekeepers, and ordinary citizens are annulled.

Outline

I. The return of the Jews from Babylon to Jerusalem (1:1—2:70)
II. Rebuilding the city and the temple (3:1—6:22)
III. The return of Ezra: the reforms begun (7:1—10:44)

I. THE RETURN OF THE JEWS FROM BABYLON TO JERUSALEM (1:1—2:70)

A. THE PROCLAMATION OF CYRUS

1:1-3☆
1:1 2 Chron 36:22, 23; Ezra 5:13-17; 6:3-5; Jer 25:12-14; 29:10

1 NOW in the first year of Cyrus king of Persia, that the word of the
LORD by the mouth of Jer-e-mi'-ah might be fulfilled, the LORD stirred
up the spirit of Cyrus king of Persia, that he made a proclamation
throughout all his kingdom, and *put it* also in writing, saying,

---

1:1 *the first year,* i.e., "539 B.C." Cyrus reigned 559–530 B.C., but his control of Babylonia began in 539 B.C. *the word of the LORD by the mouth of Jeremiah,* i.e., "the prediction that the Jews would remain in captivity in Babylon for seventy years." (See Jer. 25:12; 29:10.)†

1:1-3 These verses are also found in 2 Chron. 36:22, 23. This suggests that Ezra may well have written Chronicles as well as the book of Ezra.

[2]Thus saith Cyrus king of Persia, The LORD God of heaven hath given
me all the kingdoms of the earth; and he hath charged me to build him an
house at Jerusalem, which *is* in Judah.

☆1:2 Ezra 3:1, 2 Isa 44:28 45:1–13

[3]Who *is there* among you of all his people? his God be with him, and let
him go up to Jerusalem, which *is* in Judah, and build the house of the LORD
God of Israel, (he *is* the God,) which *is* in Jerusalem.

☆1:3

[4]And whosoever remaineth in any place where he sojourneth, let the men
of his place help him with silver, and with gold, and with goods, and with
beasts, beside the freewill offering for the house of God that *is* in Jerusalem.

☆1:4

B. THE PLANS FOR THE RETURN

[5]¶Then rose up the chief of the fathers of Judah and Benjamin, and the
priests, and the Levites, with all *them* whose spirit God had raised, to go up
to build the house of the LORD which *is* in Jerusalem.

☆1:5 2 Chron 36:22

[6]And all they that *were* about them strengthened their hands with vessels
of silver, with gold, with goods, and with beasts, and with precious things,
beside all *that* was willingly offered.
[7]¶Also Cyrus the king brought forth the vessels of the house of the LORD,
which Neb-u-chad-nez′zar had brought forth out of Jerusalem, and had put
them in the house of his gods;

1:7 2 Kgs 24:13 25:13–16 2 Chron 36:7–18 Ezra 1:9–11; 6:5

[8]Even those did Cyrus king of Persia bring forth by the hand of Mith′re-
dath the treasurer, and numbered them unto Shesh-baz′zar, the prince of
Judah.

☆1:8 Ezra 1:11 5:14–16

[9]And this *is* the number of them: thirty chargers of gold, a thousand
chargers of silver, nine and twenty knives,

1:9 Ezra 1:7

[10]Thirty basons of gold, silver basons of a second *sort* four hundred and
ten, *and* other vessels a thousand.
[11]All the vessels of gold and of silver *were* five thousand and four
hundred. All *these* did Shesh-baz′zar bring up with *them of* the captivity
that were brought up from Babylon unto Jerusalem.

1:11 Ezra 1:8

C. THE LIST OF THE JEWISH EMIGRANTS

2 NOW these *are* the children of the province that went up out of the
captivity, of those which had been carried away, whom Neb-u-chad-
nez′zar the king of Babylon had carried away unto Babylon, and came
again unto Jerusalem and Judah, every one unto his city;

2:1 2 Kgs 24:14–16 25:11 2 Chron 36:20

[2]Which came with Ze-rub′ba-bel: Jesh′u-a, Ne-he-mi′ah, Ser-a-i′ah, Re-
el-ai′ah, Mor′de-cai, Bil′shan, Miz′par, Big′va-i, Re′hum, Ba′a-nah. The
number of the men of the people of Israel:

☆2:2 Neh 7:7

1:2-4 The hearts of all rulers are in the hands of God, who turns them as he wills. Isa. 45:4 says Cyrus did not know God nor did he "serve" him, as we popularly think of that term. But God knew him and used him to accomplish the divine purpose. Yet in these verses Cyrus says that what he possesses was given to him by God, and that he was ordered by God to build him a house in Jerusalem. If God can use unbelievers to do his will, how much more should believers expect God to use them who know him and who are in tune with his purposes. In the case of Cyrus we do not know whether his statement that "he is the God" in 1:3 means only that he wanted to acknowledge the existence of another god and conciliate the people, or that he believed in that God too. God alone knows the heart.

1:5 It was the Spirit of God who moved, not only Cyrus but also "the chief of the fathers" to return to the land. During the seventy years' captivity, the Israelites had found a safe refuge in Babylon. There was nothing to come back to in Jerusalem and the task of rebuilding was seemingly impossible. God gave the vision, the daring, and the power to the remnant who finally went back. And they succeeded.

1:8 Perhaps *Sheshbazzar* is the Shenazar named in 1 Chron. 3:18, although some have thought the name Sheshbazzar was the pseudonym for Zerubbabel. As a son of Jehoiachin he would have been the one entrusted with the priceless jewels of the temple. This "prince of Judah" was so highly regarded that Cyrus later appointed him to be governor over the people (see 5:14).

2:2 Only two Mordecais are named in the Old Testament. This one is not the Mordecai in the book of Esther.

2:3☆ 1 Chron 9:1–44 Neh 7:8–38 3 The children of Pa'rosh, two thousand an hundred seventy and two.
4 The children of Sheph-a-ti'ah, three hundred seventy and two.
2:5☆ 5 The children of A'rah, seven hundred seventy and five.
6 The children of Pa'hath-mo'ab, of the children of Jesh'u-a *and* Jo'ab,
two thousand eight hundred and twelve.
7 The children of E'lam, a thousand two hundred fifty and four.
8 The children of Zat'tu, nine hundred forty and five.
9 The children of Zac'ca-i, seven hundred and threescore.
10 The children of Ba'ni, six hundred forty and two.
11 The children of Beb'a-i, six hundred twenty and three.
12 The children of Az'gad, a thousand two hundred twenty and two.
13 The children of A-don'i-kam, six hundred sixty and six.
14 The children of Big'va-i, two thousand fifty and six.
15 The children of A'din, four hundred fifty and four.
16 The children of A'ter of Hez-e-ki'ah, ninety and eight.
17 The children of Be'zai, three hundred twenty and three.
18 The children of Jo'rah, an hundred and twelve.
19 The children of Ha'shum, two hundred twenty and three.
20 The children of Gib'bar, ninety and five.
21 The children of Beth–lehem, an hundred twenty and three.
22 The men of Ne-to'phah, fifty and six.
23 The men of An'a-thoth, an hundred twenty and eight.
24 The children of Az'ma-veth, forty and two.
25 The children of Kir'jath–a'rim, Che-phi'rah, and Be-e'roth, seven
hundred and forty and three.
26 The children of Ra'mah and Ge'ba, six hundred twenty and one.
27 The men of Mich'mas, an hundred twenty and two.
28 The men of Beth–el and A'i, two hundred twenty and three.
29 The children of Nebo, fifty and two.
30 The children of Mag'bish, an hundred fifty and six.
31 The children of the other E'lam, a thousand two hundred fifty and four.
32 The children of Ha'rim, three hundred and twenty.
33 The children of Lod, Ha'did, and O'no, seven hundred twenty and five.
34 The children of Jericho, three hundred forty and five.
35 The children of Se-na'ah, three thousand and six hundred and thirty.
2:36 1 Chron 9:10, 11; 24:7–18 Neh 7:39–42 36 ¶The priests: the children of Je-dai'ah, of the house of Jesh'u-a, nine
hundred seventy and three.
37 The children of Im'mer, a thousand fifty and two.
38 The children of Pash'ur, a thousand two hundred forty and seven.
39 The children of Ha'rim, a thousand and seventeen.
2:40☆ Neh 7:43–45 40 ¶The Levites: the children of Jesh'u-a and Kad'mi-el, of the children of
Hod-a-vi'ah, seventy and four.
2:41☆ 41 ¶The singers: the children of A'saph, an hundred twenty and eight.

2:3ff Apparently the genealogical tables of the deportees to Babylon were carefully maintained. This was for the benefit of succeeding generations, that they might know their "roots" and understand their family relationships. The names of those who returned are listed in a family sequence.

2:5 *children of Arah, seven hundred seventy and five.* Compare this figure with that given in Neh. 7:10—six hundred fifty-two. It could be a copyist's error; Jewish letters were used to represent numbers, and this often created confusion. See Gleason L. Archer's explanation in *The Encyclopedia of Biblical Difficulties* (Zondervan, 1982).

2:40 Generally, there were fewer priests than there were Levites. Yet only seventy-four Levites (350 if the singers and porters are included) returned to the land, while there were 4,289 priests. No reason is given for this disparity. It may well be that the priests were spiritually discerning and wanted to reestablish proper worship according to the Mosaic pattern, whereas the other Levites were comfortable and possibly better off financially than they had been in Jerusalem. Since they were not of the priestly line, their spiritual perceptions may have been faulty.

2:41 This is the Asaph who composed Psalms 50, 73–83. He was appointed by David as musician for the house of God, and these listed here were his descendants.

[42]¶The children of the porters: the children of Shal'lum, the children of
A'ter, the children of Tal'mon, the children of Ak'kub, the children of
Hat'i-ta, the children of Sho'ba-i, *in* all an hundred thirty and nine.
[43]¶The Neth'i-nims: the children of Zi'ha, the children of Ha-su'pha, the
children of Tab'ba-oth,
[44]The children of Ke'ros, the children of Si'a-ha, the children of Pa'don,
[45]The children of Leb'a-nah, the children of Hag'a-bah, the children of
Ak'kub,
[46]The children of Ha'gab, the children of Shal'ma-i, the children of
Ha'nan,
[47]The children of Gid'del, the children of Ga'har, the children of Re-a-
i'ah,
[48]The children of Re'zin, the children of Ne-ko'da, the children of
Gaz'zam,
[49]The children of Uz'za, the children of Pa-se'ah, the children of Be'sai,
[50]The children of As'nah, the children of Me-hu'nim, the children of Ne-
phu'sim,
[51]The children of Bak'buk, the children of Ha-ku'pha, the children of
Har'hur,
[52]The children of Baz'luth, the children of Me-hi'da, the children of
Har'sha,
[53]The children of Bar'kos, the children of Sis'e-ra, the children of
Tha'mah,
[54]The children of Ne-zi'ah, the children of Hat'i-pha.
[55]¶The children of Solomon's servants: the children of So'ta-i, the
children of Soph'e-reth, the children of Pe-ru'da,
[56]The children of Ja-a'lah, the children of Dar'kon, the children of
Gid'del,
[57]The children of Sheph-a-ti'ah, the children of Hat'til, the children of
Poch'e-reth of Ze-ba'im, the children of A'mi.
[58]All the Neth'i-nims, and the children of Solomon's servants, *were* three
hundred ninety and two.
[59]And these *were* they which went up from Tel-me'lah, Tel-har'sa,
Cherub, Ad'dan, *and* Im'mer: but they could not shew their father's house,
and their seed, whether they *were* of Israel.
[60]The children of Del-a-i'ah, the children of To-bi'ah, the children of Ne-
ko'da, six hundred fifty and two.
[61]¶And of the children of the priests: the children of Ha-bai'ah, the
children of Koz, the children of Bar-zil'la-i; which took a wife of the
daughters of Bar-zil'la-i the Gileadite, and was called after their name:
[62]These sought their register *among* those that were reckoned by
genealogy, but they were not found: therefore were they, as polluted, put
from the priesthood.
[63]And the Tir'sha-tha said unto them, that they should not eat of the
most holy things, till there stood up a priest with U'rim and with
Thum'mim.
[64]¶The whole congregation together *was* forty and two thousand three
hundred *and* threescore,

☆**2:42**
☆**2:43** Neh 7:46–56
2:55 Neh 7:57–59
2:59 Neh 7:61, 63–65
2:60 Neh 7:62
2:61 2 Sam 17:27
2:62 Ex 28:30 Lev 21:21–23 Num 3:10 16:39, 40 Ezra 2:59
☆**2:63**
2:64 Neh 7:66, 67

2:42 *porters,* i.e., the gatekeepers who guarded the doors to keep intruders and the unclean from entering the sacred precincts of the house of God.
2:43 The *Nethinim* were assigned by David to help the Levites. They are spoken of mostly in Ezra and Nehemiah. Ezra 8:20 provides the most specific clues concerning their identity and origin. Ezra lists the heads of the families who came back to Jerusalem.
2:63 *Urim . . . Thummim.* See note on Exod. 28:30. The last mention of these in the Bible occurs in Neh. 7:65.

65 Beside their servants and their maids, of whom *there were* seven thousand three hundred thirty and seven: and *there were* among them two hundred singing men and singing women.

66 Their horses *were* seven hundred thirty and six; their mules, two hundred forty and five;

67 Their camels, four hundred thirty and five; *their* asses, six thousand seven hundred and twenty.

2:68 Neh 7:70–72

68 ¶And *some* of the chief of the fathers, when they came to the house of the LORD which *is* at Jerusalem, offered freely for the house of God to set it up in his place:

2:69☆

69 They gave after their ability unto the treasure of the work threescore and one thousand drams of gold, and five thousand pound of silver, and one hundred priests' garments.

2:70 Neh 7:73

70 So the priests, and the Levites, and *some* of the people, and the singers, and the porters, and the Neth'i-nims, dwelt in their cities, and all Israel in their cities.

II. REBUILDING THE CITY AND THE TEMPLE (3:1—6:22)

A. REBUILDING THE ALTAR; THE SACRIFICES COMMENCED

3:1 Lev 1:1–17; 6:8–13; Deut 12:4–7; 1 Chron 3:17–20; Ezra 2:2; Neh 12:1, 8; Hag 1:1; Zech 3:1; 4:6–10; 6:10, 11

3 AND when the seventh month was come, and the children of Israel *were* in the cities, the people gathered themselves together as one man to Jerusalem.

3:2☆

2 Then stood up Jesh'u-a the son of Joz'a-dak, and his brethren the priests, and Ze-rub'ba-bel the son of She-al'ti-el, and his brethren, and builded the altar of the God of Israel, to offer burnt offerings thereon, as *it is* written in the law of Moses the man of God.

3:3 Ex 29:38–42; Num 28:1–8

3 And they set the altar upon his bases; for fear *was* upon them because of the people of those countries: and they offered burnt offerings thereon unto the Lord, *even* burnt offerings morning and evening.

3:4–6☆
3:4 Lev 23:34–36; Num 8:14–17

4 They kept also the feast of tabernacles, as *it is* written, and *offered* the daily burnt offerings by number, according to the custom, as the duty of every day required;

3:5 Ex 29:42; Lev 1:3; Num 28:11–14; 29:39; Deut 12:6, 17

5 And afterward *offered* the continual burnt offering, both of the new moons, and of all the set feasts of the LORD that were consecrated, and of every one that willingly offered a freewill offering unto the LORD.

6 From the first day of the seventh month began they to offer burnt offerings unto the LORD. But the foundation of the temple of the LORD was not *yet* laid.

3:7 1 Kgs 5:9–11; 2 Chron 2:10–16

7 They gave money also unto the masons, and to the carpenters; and

---

2:69 *drams* and *pounds,* literally "darics" and "minas." The amount of gold was approximately 300,000 ounces and the silver 6,000 pounds.

3:2 *son of Shealtiel.* Zerubbabel was the legitimate heir, since his father was the eldest son of Jehoiachin. (See 1 Chron. 3:17; and note on 1 Chron. 3:19.) *builded the altar.* The old altar had been destroyed when the Solomonic Temple was demolished by the forces of Nebuchadnezzar. Ezra and the people were now in no position to build another temple, but they had to have an altar on which to offer sacrifices of animals and for prayer and praise. Abraham had built an altar on occasion. So Ezra rightly began with what was possible to do and awaited the time when the new temple could be started.

There is nothing to suppose that there was such an altar and such sacrifices while they were in Babylon. Today there is no priesthood, no altar, and no animal sacrifice. Whatever genealogical tables were kept of the priestly families, there are none extant from which the priestly line could be established.

3:4 See note to Exod. 23:16 for the feast of booths or tabernacles. It was one of three national festivals (Passover, pentecost, and tabernacles). All males were expected to attend.

3:5 *the new moons.* See note to Num. 10:10 for the festival of the new moon.

3:6 Fire came from heaven in the times of Moses and Solomon when the burnt offerings were commenced in the tabernacle and in the temple. There is no indication that fire came down from heaven on this occasion.

meat, and drink, and oil, unto them of Zi'don, and to them of Tyre, to bring
cedar trees from Lebanon to the sea of Joppa, according to the grant that
they had of Cyrus king of Persia.

B. THE CONSTRUCTION OF THE TEMPLE BEGUN

8¶Now in the second year of their coming unto the house of God at
Jerusalem, in the second month, began Ze-rub'ba-bel the son of She-al'ti-el,
and Jesh'u-a the son of Joz'a-dak, and the remnant of their brethren the
priests and the Levites, and all they that were come out of the captivity
unto Jerusalem; and appointed the Levites, from twenty years old and
upward, to set forward the work of the house of the LORD.

☆3:8 Num 4:3; 1 Chron 23:24-32

9Then stood Jesh'u-a *with* his sons and his brethren, Kad'mi-el and his
sons, the sons of Judah, together, to set forward the workmen in the house
of God: the sons of Hen'a-dad, *with* their sons and their brethren the
Levites.

10And when the builders laid the foundation of the temple of the LORD,
they set the priests in their apparel with trumpets, and the Levites the sons
of A'saph with cymbals, to praise the LORD, after the ordinance of David
king of Israel.

3:10 1 Chron 28:11-13, 19

11And they sang together by course in praising and giving thanks unto
the LORD; because *he is* good, for his mercy *endureth* for ever toward Israel.
And all the people shouted with a great shout, when they praised the LORD,
because the foundation of the house of the LORD was laid.

3:11 1 Chron 16:34, 41; 29:20; Neh 12:24; Ps 24:7-10; 103:17; 106:1; Isa 12:6

12But many of the priests and Levites and chief of the fathers, *who were*
ancient men, that had seen the first house, when the foundation of this
house was laid before their eyes, wept with a loud voice; and many shouted
aloud for joy:

☆3:12 Hag 2:3

13So that the people could not discern the noise of the shout of joy from
the noise of the weeping of the people: for the people shouted with a loud
shout, and the noise was heard afar off.

C. OPPOSITION FROM THE ENEMY

1. Zerubbabel Refuses Help

4 NOW when the adversaries of Judah and Benjamin heard that the
children of the captivity builded the temple unto the LORD God of
Israel;

☆4:1

2Then they came to Ze-rub'ba-bel, and to the chief of the fathers, and
said unto them, Let us build with you: for we seek your God, as ye *do*; and
we do sacrifice unto him since the days of E'sar–had'don king of Assur,
which brought us up hither.

☆4:2 2 Kgs 19:37; Ezra 4:7-10; Neh 4:1-13

3But Ze-rub'ba-bel, and Jesh'u-a, and the rest of the chief of the fathers
of Israel, said unto them, Ye have nothing to do with us to build an house
unto our God; but we ourselves together will build unto the LORD God of
Israel, as king Cyrus the king of Persia hath commanded us.

4:3 Ezra 1:1-4; 6:3-5; Neh 2:20

4Then the people of the land weakened the hands of the people of Judah,
and troubled them in building,

4:4 Ezra 4:24; 5:5-7; Neh 12:22; Hag 1:1, 14, 15

3:8 There was never any doubt that a new temple would be constructed. It was begun in the second year after the celebration of the Passover. The leaders, the priests, and the people were enthused for the work, and when the foundation was laid, there was a time of praise and rejoicing (3:10, 11).

3:12 The weeping of those who had seen Solomon's temple was occasioned by the fact that the new temple was to be smaller and far less ornate and beautiful. It was decidedly inferior.

4:1 *the adversaries* were those who had mixed blood, partly Jewish and partly foreign. The offer of help by a people of mixed religious sympathies was designed to hinder, not help the project. Zerubbabel and Joshua refused this help.

4:2 *Esar-haddon.* See note on 2 Kings 17:24.

4:5☆ 5 And hired counsellors against them, to frustrate their purpose, all the
days of Cyrus king of Persia, even until the reign of Darius king of Persia.

2. The Stoppage of Work on the Temple by King Artaxerxes

4:6☆ 6 And in the reign of A-has-u-e′rus, in the beginning of his reign, wrote
Esth 1:1; 2:1, 12–14 they *unto him* an accusation against the inhabitants of Judah and Jerusa-
Dan 9:1 lem.
4:7☆ 7 ¶And in the days of Ar-ta-xer′xes wrote Bish′lam, Mith′re-dath, Ta′be-
2 Kgs 18:26; Ezra 4:11, 23 el, and the rest of their companions, unto Ar-ta-xer′xes king of Persia; and
7:1–21; Neh 1:1; 5:14 the writing of the letter *was* written in the Syrian tongue, and interpreted in
Isa 36:11; Dan 2:4 the Syrian tongue.
4:8 8 Re′hum the chancellor and Shim′shai the scribe wrote a letter against
Ezra 5:6; 6:13 Jerusalem to Ar-ta-xer′xes the king in this sort:
9 Then *wrote* Re′hum the chancellor, and Shim′shai the scribe, and the
rest of their companions; the Di′na-ites, the A-phar′sath-chites, the Tar′pel-
ites, the A-phar′sites, the Ar′che-vites, the Babylonians, the Su′san-chites,
the De-ha′vites, *and* the E′lam-ites,
4:10☆ 10 And the rest of the nations whom the great and noble As-nap′per
brought over, and set in the cities of Sa-ma′ri-a, and the rest *that are* on this
side the river, and at such a time.
11 ¶This *is* the copy of the letter that they sent unto him, *even* unto Ar-ta-
xer′xes the king; Thy servants the men on this side the river, and at such a
time.
4:12 12 Be it known unto the king, that the Jews which came up from thee to us
Ezra 5:3; Neh 1:3 are come unto Jerusalem, building the rebellious and the bad city, and have
Dan 9:25 set up the walls *thereof*, and joined the foundations.
4:13☆ 13 Be it known now unto the king, that, if this city be builded, and the
Ezra 4:20; 7:24; Neh 5:4 walls set up *again, then* will they not pay toll, tribute, and custom, and *so*
thou shalt endamage the revenue of the kings.
14 Now because we have maintenance from *the king's* palace, and it was
not meet for us to see the king's dishonour, therefore have we sent and
certified the king;
15 That search may be made in the book of the records of thy fathers: so
shalt thou find in the book of the records, and know that this city *is* a
rebellious city, and hurtful unto kings and provinces, and that they have
moved sedition within the same of old time: for which cause was this city
destroyed.
16 We certify the king that, if this city be builded *again*, and the walls
thereof set up, by this means thou shalt have no portion on this side the
river.
17 ¶*Then* sent the king an answer unto Re′hum the chancellor, and *to*
Shim′shai the scribe, and *to* the rest of their companions that dwell in Sa-
ma′ri-a, and *unto* the rest beyond the river, Peace, and at such a time.
18 The letter which ye sent unto us hath been plainly read before me.
19 And I commanded, and search hath been made, and it is found that
this city of old time hath made insurrection against kings, and *that* rebellion
and sedition have been made therein.

4:5 *Darius* reigned 522–486 B.C.
4:6 *Ahasuerus,* i.e., "Xerxes" (468–465 B.C.).
4:7 *Artaxerxes* reigned 465–423 B.C.
4:10 *Asnappar,* i.e., "Ashurbanipal." (See note on 2 Kings 17:24.)
4:13ff The Samaritans wrote to Artaxerxes to stop the rebuilding of temple and city. They argued that (1) the Samaritans were loyal to the king and concerned for his interests; (2) the Jews were disloyal and dangerous to the kingdom; (3) their past history proved they were seditious. Their accusations were inaccurate, their fears absurd and without reason. And the claims that the Jews would not pay tribute and would lead a revolt of all the territories west of the Euphrates lacked any foundation.

[20]There have been mighty kings also over Jerusalem, which have ruled
over all *countries* beyond the river; and toll, tribute, and custom, was paid
unto them.
[21]Give ye now commandment to cause these men to cease, and that this
city be not builded, until *another* commandment shall be given from me.
[22]Take heed now that ye fail not to do this: why should damage grow to
the hurt of the kings?
[23]¶Now when the copy of king Ar-ta-xer'xes' letter *was* read before
Re'hum, and Shim'shai the scribe, and their companions, they went up in
haste to Jerusalem unto the Jews, and made them to cease by force and
power.
[24]Then ceased the work of the house of God which *is* at Jerusalem. So it
ceased unto the second year of the reign of Darius king of Persia.

4:20 1 Kgs 4:21, 24; 1 Chron 18:3, 4, 6, 13; 19:19; 2 Chron 17:11; Ezra 4:13

☆**4:24** Neh 6:3, 9; Hag 1:14, 15

3. Haggai and Zechariah Start Building Again

a. The Rebuilding Started

5 THEN the prophets, Hag'ga-i the prophet, and Zech-a-ri'ah the son of
Id'do, prophesied unto the Jews that *were* in Judah and Jerusalem in
the name of the God of Israel, *even* unto them.
[2]Then rose up Ze-rub'ba-bel the son of She-al'ti-el, and Jesh'u-a the son
of Joz'a-dak, and began to build the house of God which *is* at Jerusalem:
and with them *were* the prophets of God helping them.

☆**5:1** Ezra 3:2; 6:14; Hag 1:1; Zech 1:1

☆**5:2**

b. Tatnai's Objections

[3]¶At the same time came to them Tat'na-i, governor on this side the river,
and She'thar-boz'na-i and their companions, and said thus unto them, Who
hath commanded you to build this house, and to make up this wall?
[4]Then said we unto them after this manner, What are the names of the
men that make this building?
[5]But the eye of their God was upon the elders of the Jews, that they could
not cause them to cease, till the matter came to Darius: and they they
returned answer by letter concerning this *matter*.

☆**5:3** Ezra 5:6, 9, 17; 6:6, 13

5:4 Ezra 5:10

☆**5:5** Ezra 4:4; 6:1; 7:6, 12; 8:22; Ps 33:18; 1 Pet 3:12

c. Tatnai's Letter to King Darius

[6]¶The copy of the letter that Tat'na-i, governor on this side the river, and
She'thar-boz'na-i, and his companions the A-phar'sach-ites, which *were* on
this side the river, sent unto Darius the king:
[7]They sent a letter unto him, wherein was written thus; Unto Darius the
king, all peace.

☆**5:6** Ezra 4:11, 23

4:24 The work on the temple was halted for a time. Verses 6–23 are a parenthesis here and can be understood better as continuing the narrative between chapters 6 and 7.

5:1 The Books of Haggai and Zechariah should be read here in connection with the return to the land, the construction of the temple, and the fact that God still provided prophets to speak for him to the remnant.

5:2 The altar had been built (Ezra 3:2—see note) and now the time had come to commence the construction of the house of God. Note that the prophets of God were providing leadership in rebuilding the house of God. "It is the business of God's prophets to stir up God's people to do that which is good, and to help them in it, to strengthen their hands, and . . . to quicken them to their duty and encourage them in it."*

5:3 *Tatnai,* i.e., Tattenai, was governor of the region west of the Euphrates during the reign of Darius Hystaspis. In the book of Esdras he is called Sisinnes. He made a report to the king of Persia about the complaints of the Samaritans concerning the rebuilding of the temple.

5:5 God's eye was on the elders of the Jews, to keep them from yielding to their enemies. Whoever is employed in God's work is under God's eye and protection. This knowledge "will keep us in our duty and encourage us in it when the difficulties are ever so discouraging."*

5:6 *the Apharsachites* were from the Samaritans who signed the letter of complaint to the Persian officials against those who sought to rebuild the temple.

5:8☆ 8 Be it known unto the king, that we went into the province of Judea, to
the house of the great God, which is builded with great stones, and timber
is laid in the walls, and this work goeth fast on, and prospereth in their
hands.
5:9☆ 9 Then asked we those elders, *and* said unto them thus, Who commanded
you to build this house, and to make up these walls?
5:10 Ezra 5:4 10 We asked their names also, to certify thee, that we might write the
names of the men that *were* the chief of them.
5:11 1 Kgs 6:1–38 11 And thus they returned us answer, saying, We are the servants of the
2 Chron 3:1—5:14 God of heaven and earth, and build the house that was builded these many
years ago, which a great king of Israel builded and set up.
5:12 2 Kgs 24:2, 10 12 But after that our fathers had provoked the God of heaven unto wrath,
25:1, 8–11 he gave them into the hand of Neb-u-chad-nez'zar the king of Babylon, the
2 Chron 36:6–20 Chal-de'an, who destroyed this house, and carried the people away into
Babylon.
5:13 2 Chron 36:22 13 But in the first year of Cyrus the king of Babylon *the same* king Cyrus
23 made a decree to build this house of God.
Ezra 1:1–8 14 And the vessels also of gold and silver of the house of God, which Neb-
6:3–5 u-chad-nez'zar took out of the temple that *was* in Jerusalem, and brought
5:14 Ezra 1:7, 8, 11 them into the temple of Babylon, those did Cyrus the king take out of the
5:16; 6:3–5 temple of Babylon, and they were delivered unto *one*, whose name *was*
Shesh-baz'zar, whom he had made governor;
15 And said unto him, Take these vessels, go, carry them into the temple
that *is* in Jerusalem, and let the house of God be builded in his place.
16 Then came the same Shesh-baz'zar, *and* laid the foundation of the
house of God which *is* in Jerusalem: and since that time even until now
hath it been in building, and *yet it is not finished.*
5:17 Ezra 6:1, 2 17 Now therefore, if *it seem* good to the king, let there be search made in
the king's treasure house, which *is* there at Babylon, whether it be *so*, that a
decree was made of Cyrus the king to build this house of God at Jerusalem,
and let the king send his pleasure to us concerning this matter.

d. King Darius Supports the Rebuilding

6:1 Ezra 5:17 6 THEN Darius the king made a decree, and search was made in the
house of the rolls, where the treasures were laid up in Babylon.
6:2☆ Esth 1:1, 13–15 2 And there was found at Ach'me-tha, in the palace that *is* in the province
10:2 of the Medes, a roll, and therein *was* a record thus written:
Jer 25:25 3 In the first year of Cyrus the king *the same* Cyrus the king made a decree
6:3☆ Ezra 1:2–4 *concerning* the house of God at Jerusalem, Let the house be builded, the
place where they offered sacrifices, and let the foundations thereof be
strongly laid; the height thereof threescore cubits, *and* the breadth thereof
threescore cubits;
6:4☆ 1 Kgs 6:36 4 *With* three rows of great stones, and a row of new timber: and let the
expences be given out of the king's house:

5:8 *great stones,* "huge stones" (in the RSV) were those which had to be moved on rollers because of their size and weight.
5:9 In response to the question, "Who authorized you to rebuild the temple and the walls of the city?" the Jews provided the historical background for their labors (5:11–15). Their claim that they had the right to rebuild by a royal decree from King Cyrus shut the Samaritans' mouths—unless and until it could be shown that this claim was fraudulent. The enemies asked for the records to be searched and a decision rendered.

6:2 *Achmetha,* a form of *Ecbatana.* This city was located more than a mile above sea level and was a summer capital of the Parthian kings. The modern city of Hamadan has taken its place. The records kept on papyrus or leather were better preserved at a higher altitude and it was here that the decree of Cyrus was found by Darius. Later (330 B.C.), Alexander the Great looted the palaces and pulled down the city walls.
6:3–5 The researchers discovered information in the record left by Cyrus which had added details not contained in the earlier proclamation mentioned in Ezra 1:2–4.

5 And also let the golden and silver vessels of the house of God, which Neb-u-chad-nez'zar took forth out of the temple which *is* at Jerusalem, and brought unto Babylon, be restored, and brought again unto the temple which *is* at Jerusalem, *every one* to his place, and place *them* in the house of God.

6 Now *therefore,* Tat'na-i, governor beyond the river, She'thar-boz'na-i, and your companions the A-phar'sach-ites, which *are* beyond the river, be ye far from thence:

7 Let the work of this house of God alone; let the governor of the Jews and the elders of the Jews build this house of God in his place.

8 Moreover I make a decree what ye shall do to the elders of these Jews for the building of this house of God: that of the king's goods, *even* of the tribute beyond the river, forthwith expences be given unto these men, that they be not hindered. ☆**6:8, 9**

9 And that which they have need of, both young bullocks, and rams, and lambs, for the burnt offerings of the God of heaven, wheat, salt, wine, and oil, according to the appointment of the priests which *are* at Jerusalem, let it be given them day by day without fail:

10 That they may offer sacrifices of sweet savours unto the God of heaven, and pray for the life of the king, and of his sons.

11 Also I have made a decree, that whosoever shall alter this word, let timber be pulled down from his house, and being set up, let him be hanged thereon; and let his house be made a dunghill for this. **6:11** Ezra 7:26 Dan 2:5; 3:29

12 And the God that hath caused his name to dwell there destroy all kings and people, that shall put to their hand to alter *and* to destroy this house of God which *is* at Jerusalem. I Darius have made a decree; let it be done with speed. ☆**6:12** Deut 12:4, 5, 11 1 Kgs 9:2, 3

e. The Temple Completed

13 ¶Then Tat'na-i, governor on this side the river, She'thar-boz'na-i, and their companions, according to that which Darius the king had sent, so they did speedily.

14 And the elders of the Jews builded, and they prospered through the prophesying of Hag'ga-i the prophet and Zech-a-ri'ah the son of Id'do. And they builded, and finished *it*, according to the commandment of the God of Israel, and according to the commandment of Cyrus, and Darius, and Ar-ta-xer'xes king of Persia. ☆**6:14** Ezra 1:1; 5:1 6:12; 7:1 7–9, 11 Zech 4:9

15 And this house was finished on the third day of the month A'dar, which was in the sixth year of the reign of Darius the king.

f. The Temple Dedicated and the Feasts Begun

16 ¶And the children of Israel, the priests, and the Levites, and the rest of the children of the captivity, kept the dedication of this house of God with joy, ☆**6:16** Ezra 3:11, 12 6:21, 22

6:8, 9 God not only ruled in the uncovering of Cyrus' decree but he also opened the heart of Darius to provide additional monies to the Jews from the tribute they paid. Thus Tatnai became a partial loser as a consequence of this action, for his share of the tribute was cut down.

6:12 Darius pronounced a curse on kings or people who should seek to destroy the house of God. If he could not prevent this himself, he left it in the hand of the Jews' God to execute his own vengeance on any destroyers.

6:14 This Artaxerxes was Artaxerxes I Longimanus, the son and heir of Xerxes. He reigned from 464–424 B.C. Ezra came to Jerusalem in the seventh year of this king and Nehemiah in the twentieth year of the same king.

6:16 Ezra contains the last mention of the temple in the Old Testament. In the account nothing is said about a high priest nor is there any mention of an ark of the covenant. The two tables of the law, which were apparently destroyed when Solomon's temple was burned, were not in the new temple.

6:17☆ 17 And offered at the dedication of this house of God an hundred
bullocks, two hundred rams, four hundred lambs; and for a sin offering for
all Israel, twelve he goats, according to the number of the tribes of Israel.
6:18 2 Chron 35:4, 5 18 And they set the priests in their divisions, and the Levites in their
courses, for the service of God, which *is* at Jerusalem; as it is written in the
book of Moses.
6:19 Ex 12:6 19 And the children of the captivity kept the passover upon the fourteenth
day of the first month.
6:20 2 Chron 29:34 30:15–17 20 For the priests and the Levites were purified together, all of them *were*
pure, and killed the passover for all the children of the captivity, and for
their brethren the priests, and for themselves.
6:21☆ Ex 19:10, 14 Num 9:6, 7, 10–14 Ezra 9:1–15 21 And the children of Israel, which were come again out of captivity, and
all such as had separated themselves unto them from the filthiness of the
heathen of the land, to seek the LORD God of Israel, did eat,
6:22☆ 22 And kept the feast of unleavened bread seven days with joy: for the
LORD had made them joyful, and turned the heart of the king of Assyria
unto them, to strengthen their hands in the work of the house of God, the
God of Israel.

III. THE RETURN OF EZRA; THE REFORMS BEGUN (7:1—10:44)

A. EZRA'S GENEALOGY AND BACKGROUND

7:1☆ Ezra 7:12, 21 8:1—10:44 Neh 2:1; 8:1–18 7 NOW after these things, in the reign of Ar-ta-xer′xes king of Persia,
Ezra the son of Ser-a-i′ah, the son of Az-a-ri′ah, the son of Hil-ki′ah,
2 The son of Shal′lum, the son of Za′dok, the son of A-hi′tub,
3 The son of Am-a-ri′ah, the son of Az-a-ri′ah, the son of Me-rai′oth,
4 The son of Zer-a-hi′ah, the son of Uz′zi, the son of Buk′ki,
5 The son of A-bish′u-a, the son of Phin′e-has, the son of E-le-a′zar, the
son of Aaron the chief priest:
7:6☆ Ezra 7:10, 21, 25 Neh 8:9, 13 6 This Ezra went up from Babylon; and he *was* a ready scribe in the law
of Moses, which the LORD God of Israel had given: and the king granted
him all his request, according to the hand of the LORD his God upon him.
7:7☆ 1 Chron 6:31, 48, 49 Ezra 2:40–58 Neh 7:39–60 7 And there went up *some* of the children of Israel, and of the priests, and
the Levites, and the singers, and the porters, and the Neth′i-nims, unto
Jerusalem, in the seventh year of Ar-ta-xer′xes the king.
8 And he came to Jerusalem in the fifth month, which *was* in the seventh
year of the king.
9 For upon the first *day* of the first month began he to go up from
Babylon, and on the first *day* of the fifth month came he to Jerusalem,
according to the good hand of his God upon him.

6:17 Following the return of the remnant from Babylon, the second temple was constructed. It never attained the glory of the Solomonic structure nor was the kingship restored after the captivity. Nowhere do the Scriptures state specifically that the glory of God filled the second temple as he did the first. The second temple was enlarged and spruced up by Herod the Great and his successors. It was destroyed in A.D. 70 when the Roman armies sacked Jerusalem.

6:21 Judaism has always been a missionary faith, having provisions for non-Jews to participate in the worship of God. Here the Jews who had returned from the exile and all those who had sought God, separated from their false religions, and stopped their idolatries and immoralities were received as fellow-citizens with the saints and of the household of God. God will also receive such people today.

6:22 The reason for the Assyrian designation here is not clear.

7:1 Ezra's pedigree takes him back to Aaron, from whom he had descended. Thus he was of the priestly line. His grandfather or great grandfather, Seraiah, was high priest at the time of the deportation (586 B.C.).

7:6 Matthew 23:34, in the words of Jesus, speaks of prophets, wise men, and scribes as being ones sent from God. Ezra was a scribe held in great repute by the Jews who said he had collected and collated all the copies of the law he could find and then published an accurate edition. He also, according to this tradition, may have put together the books which make up the canon of the Old Testament. In any event he was a gifted scholar and fervent student of the Word of God.

7:7 *the Nethinims,* i.e., the gatekeepers.

10For Ezra had prepared his heart to seek the law of the LORD, and to do
it, and to teach in Israel statutes and judgments.

☆7:10 Ezra 7:6

B. KING ARTAXERXES' SUPPORT OF EZRA

11¶Now this *is* the copy of the letter that the king Ar-ta-xer'xes gave unto
Ezra the priest, the scribe, *even* a scribe of the words of the commandments
of the LORD, and of his statutes to Israel.
12Ar-ta-xer'xes, king of kings, unto Ezra the priest, a scribe of the law of
the God of heaven, perfect *peace*, and at such a time.
13I make a decree, that all they of the people of Israel, and *of* his priests
and Levites, in my realm, which are minded of their own freewill to go up
to Jerusalem, go with thee.
14Forasmuch as thou art sent of the king, and of his seven counsellors, to
inquire concerning Judah and Jerusalem, according to the law of thy God
which *is* in thine hand;
15And to carry the silver and gold, which the king and his counsellors
have freely offered unto the God of Israel, whose habitation *is* in Jerusalem,
16And all the silver and gold that thou canst find in all the province of
Babylon, with the freewill offering of the people, and of the priests, offering
willingly for the house of their God which *is* in Jerusalem:
17That thou mayest buy speedily with this money bullocks, rams, lambs,
with their meat offerings and their drink offerings, and offer them upon the
altar of the house of your God which *is* in Jerusalem.
18And whatsoever shall seem good to thee, and to thy brethren, to do
with the rest of the silver and the gold, that do after the will of your God.
19The vessels also that are given thee for the service of the house of thy
God, *those* deliver thou before the God of Jerusalem.
20And whatsoever more shall be needful for the house of thy God, which
thou shalt have occasion to bestow, bestow *it* out of the king's treasure
house.
21And I, *even* I Ar-ta-xer'xes the king, do make a decree to all the
treasurers which *are* beyond the river, that whatsoever Ezra the priest, the
scribe of the law of the God of heaven, shall require of you, it be done
speedily,
22Unto an hundred talents of silver, and to an hundred measures of
wheat, and to an hundred baths of wine, and to an hundred baths of oil,
and salt without prescribing *how much*.
23Whatsoever is commanded by the God of heaven, let it be diligently
done for the house of the God of heaven: for why should there be wrath
against the realm of the king and his sons?
24Also we certify you, that touching any of the priests and Levites,
singers, porters, Neth'i-nims, or ministers of this house of God, it shall not
be lawful to impose toll, tribute, or custom, upon them.
25And thou, Ezra, after the wisdom of thy God, that *is* in thine hand, set
magistrates and judges, which may judge all the people that *are* beyond the

☆7:11 Ezra 4:11; 5:6
7:12 Ezek 26:7; Dan 2:37, 47; 1 Tim 6:15; Rev 17:14; 19:16
7:14 Ezra 7:28; Esth 1:14
7:16 Deut 16:10; Ezra 1:4, 6; 8:28
7:17 Ex 30:9; Lev 23:13; Num 6:15; Deut 12:4–11
7:24 Gen 47:26
7:25 Ex 18:21–25; Deut 16:18; Ezra 7:6, 10

7:10 Here we learn that Ezra was a student of the Word, a man who obeyed the commands of the Word, and one who taught others the Word of God. "Moses in Egypt, Ezra in Babylon, and both in captivity, were wonderfully fitted for eminent services to the church."*
7:11-26 This segment comprises the letter from Artaxerxes to Ezra granting him permission to settle in Jerusalem and take with him as many of his people as he wished. He gave Ezra money (silver and gold) and provided him with a warrant to secure further funds from the king's treasury east of the Euphrates. Ezra and all those connected with the temple were to pay tribute (i.e., taxes). Furthermore, he could appoint judges and magistrates for the realm.

river, all such as know the laws of thy God; and teach ye them that know
them not.
7:26 26 And whosoever will not do the law of thy God, and the law of the king,
Ezra 6:11 let judgment be executed speedily upon him, whether *it be* unto death, or to
Ps 52:5 banishment, or to confiscation of goods, or to imprisonment.

C. EZRA'S PRAISE TO GOD

7:27☆ 27 ¶Blessed *be* the LORD God of our fathers, which hath put *such a thing* as
this in the king's heart, to beautify the house of the LORD which *is* in
Jerusalem:
7:28☆ 28 And hath extended mercy unto me before the king, and his counsellors,
Ezra 7:14 and before all the king's mighty princes. And I was strengthened as the
hand of the LORD my God *was* upon me, and I gathered together out of
Israel chief men to go up with me.

D. THE LIST OF THOSE WHO RETURNED

8:1☆ 8 THESE *are* now the chief of their fathers, and *this is* the genealogy of
Ezra 2:2–35; 62, 63; 7:1–5 them that went up with me from Babylon, in the reign of Ar-ta-xer'xes
the king.
2 Of the sons of Phin'e-has; Ger'shom: of the sons of Ith'a-mar; Daniel:
of the sons of David; Hat'tush.
3 Of the sons of Shech-a-ni'ah, of the sons of Pha'rosh; Zech-a-ri'ah: and
with him were reckoned by genealogy of the males an hundred and fifty.
4 Of the sons of Pa'hath–mo'ab; E-li-ho-e'na-i the son of Zer-a-hi'ah, and
with him two hundred males.
5 Of the sons of Shech-a-ni'ah; the son of Ja-ha'zi-el, and with him three
hundred males.
6 Of the sons also of A'din; E'bed the son of Jonathan, and with him fifty
males.
7 And of the sons of E'lam; Je-shai'ah the son of Ath-a-li'ah, and with
him seventy males.
8 And of the sons of Sheph-a-ti'ah; Zeb-a-di'ah the son of Michael, and
with him fourscore males.
9 Of the sons of Jo'ab; O-ba-di'ah the son of Je-hi'el, and with him two
hundred and eighteen males.
10 And of the sons of Shel'o-mith; the son of Jos-i-phi'ah, and with him an
hundred and threescore males.
11 And of the sons of Beb'a-i; Zech-a-ri'ah the son of Beb'a-i, and with
him twenty and eight males.
12 And of the sons of Az'gad; Jo-ha'nan the son of Hak'ka-tan, and with
him an hundred and ten males.
13 And of the last sons of A-don'i-kam, whose names *are* these, E-liph'e-
let, Je-i'el, and Shem-a-i'ah, and with them threescore males.
14 Of the sons also of Big'va-i; U'tha-i, and Zab'bud, and with them
seventy males.

7:27 Ezra knew that what the king had done was the work of God in the king's heart. He took courage from this, since he knew that God was with him also (7:28) and was thus persuaded to move forward in the work to which he had been called.

7:28 *unto me,* i.e., "Ezra," who is the speaker in the remainder of the book.†

8:1 This list of the returning remnant (8:1–14) constitutes the second group of returning exiles. The first group had returned under Zerubbabel, and this period is covered in chapters 1–6 of the book. Beginning with chapter 7 the story turns to the second group of returnees under Ezra. The total number was 1,496, listed not individually, but by families.

E. STAFFING THE TEMPLE

15¶And I gathered them together to the river that runneth to A-ha'va; ☆8:15 Ezra 8:21, 31
and there abode we in tents three days: and I viewed the people, and the
priests, and found there none of the sons of Levi.
16Then sent I for E-li-e'zer, for A'ri-el, for Shem-a-i'ah, and for El- ☆8:16
na'than, and for Ja'rib, and for El-na'than, and for Na-than, and for Zech-
a-ri'ah, and for Me-shul'lam, chief men; also for Joi'a-rib, and for El-
na'than, men of understanding.
17And I sent them with commandment unto Id'do the chief at the place 8:17
Ca-siph'i-a, and I told them what they should say unto Id'do, *and* to his Ezra 2:43–54 8:20
brethren the Neth'i-nims, at the place Ca-siph'i-a, that they should bring Neh 7:46–56
unto us ministers for the house of our God.
18And by the good hand of our God upon us they brought us a man of
understanding, of the sons of Mah'li, the son of Levi, the son of Israel; and
Sher-e-bi'ah, with his sons and his brethren, eighteen;
19And Hash-a-bi'ah, and with him Je-shai'ah of the sons of Me-ra'ri, his
brethren and their sons, twenty;
20Also of the Neth'i-nims, whom David and the princes had appointed 8:20
for the service of the Levites, two hundred and twenty Neth'i-nims: all of Ezra 8:17
them were expressed by name.

F. THE RETURN TO JERUSALEM

1. Fasting and Prayer

21¶Then I proclaimed a fast there, at the river of A-ha'va, that we might ☆8:21
afflict ourselves before our God, to seek of him a right way for us, and for Lev 23:32 2 Chron 7:14 20:3
our little ones, and for all our substance. Ezra 8:15, 31
22For I was ashamed to require of the king a band of soldiers and Ps 37:11 Jonah 3:5
horsemen to help us against the enemy in the way: because we had spoken ☆8:22
unto the king, saying, The hand of our God *is* upon all them for good that 2 Chron 15:2 Ezra 7:6
seek him; but his power and his wrath *is* against all them that forsake him.
23So we fasted and besought our God for this: and he was intreated of us. ☆8:23

2. Transporting the Silver and Gold

24¶Then I separated twelve of the chief of the priests, Sher-e-bi'ah, Hash- ☆8:24
a-bi'ah, and ten of their brethren with them,
25And weighed unto them the silver, and the gold, and the vessels, *even*
the offering of the house of our God, which the king, and his counsellors,
and his lords, and all Israel *there* present, had offered:

8:15 In the first return of the remnant to Jerusalem under Zebubbabel, there were a few Levites and many priests. In the second group led by Ezra, there were no Levites, only priests. These non-priestly Levites preferred to remain in Babylon. (The location of *Ahava* in this text remains a mystery.)

8:16 Noting the absence of Levites, Ezra began a campaign to enlist some of them. He succeeded in drafting about forty of them to come with him. Among them was Sherebiah, a man of distinction and discretion. Also two hundred of the Nethinim who were temple servants under David's appointment were enlisted to go back with him.

8:21, 22 Ezra had boldly stated that God was his confidence. He was therefore loath to ask the king for a military escort, lest it be said he did not trust God. He called for a fast and implored divine protection against all enemies on the trek. Verse 23 makes it plain that God was entreated and protection was promised. The small band went forward with confidence. This incident does not establish a principle. At times God is pleased to deliver through human help. Fasting in verse 21 was designed to do two things: (1) to express their humiliation corporately before God by denying themselves food; (2) to engage in concerted and corporate prayer *to seek of him a right way for us.*

8:23 Here we see the consequences of the fast. *he was intreated of us.* They were confident that God had heard and was answering their petitions.

8:24 Ezra not only prayed; he also acted with discretion. He committed the treasures into the hands of faithful men. In this instance it was the priests and Levites who could be trusted to care for the wealth (perhaps as much as 20 million dollars). And when they arrived in Jerusalem, it was to be checked carefully to see there was no loss.

26 I even weighed unto their hand six hundred and fifty talents of silver, and silver vessels an hundred talents, *and* of gold an hundred talents;

27 Also twenty basons of gold, of a thousand drams; and two vessels of fine copper, precious as gold.

8:28 Lev 21:6–8 Ezra 7:16 Isa 52:11

28 And I said unto them, Ye *are* holy unto the LORD; the vessels *are* holy also; and the silver and the gold *are* a freewill offering unto the LORD God of your fathers.

29 Watch ye, and keep *them,* until ye weigh *them* before the chief of the priests and the Levites, and chief of the fathers of Israel, at Jerusalem, in the chambers of the house of the LORD.

3. The Arrival at Jerusalem

30 So took the priests and the Levites the weight of the silver, and the gold, and the vessels, to bring *them* to Jerusalem unto the house of our God.

8:31 Ezra 7:15, 21

31 ¶Then we departed from the river of A-ha'va on the twelfth *day* of the first month, to go unto Jerusalem: and the hand of our God was upon us, and he delivered us from the hand of the enemy, and of such as lay in wait by the way.

32 And we came to Jerusalem, and abode there three days.

33 ¶Now on the fourth day was the silver and the gold and the vessels weighed in the house of our God by the hand of Mer'e-moth the son of U-ri'ah the priest; and with him *was* E-le-a'zar the son of Phin'e-has; and with them *was* Joz'a-bad the son of Jesh'u-a, and No-a-di'ah the son of Bin'nu-i, Levites;

8:34☆

34 By number *and* by weight of every one: and all the weight was written at that time.

35 *Also* the children of those that had been carried away, which were come out of the captivity, offered burnt offerings unto the God of Israel, twelve bullocks for all Israel, ninety and six rams, seventy and seven lambs, twelve he goats *for* a sin offering: all *this was* a burnt offering unto the LORD.

8:36 Ezra 5:3, 6

36 ¶And they delivered the king's commissions unto the king's lieutenants, and to the governors on this side the river: and they furthered the people, and the house of God.

G. THE REFORMATION IN JERUSALEM

1. The Evil of Mixed Marriages

9:1 Ex 23:23 Lev 18:3, 24–30 Deut 12:30, 31 18:9; 20:17, 18

9 NOW when these things were done, the princes came to me, saying, The people of Israel, and the priests, and the Levites, have not separated themselves from the people of the lands, *doing* according to their abominations, *even* of the Canaanites, the Hittites, the Per'iz-zites, the Jeb'u-sites, the Ammonites, the Moabites, the Egyptians, and the Am'or-ites.

9:2☆ Ex 34:16 Deut 7:3–6 Ezra 10:16–44 Neh 13:23, 24

2 For they have taken of their daughters for themselves, and for their sons: so that the holy seed have mingled themselves with the people of *those* lands: yea, the hand of the princes and rulers hath been chief in this trespass.

8:34 Ezra and his company arrived safely. The money was counted and found to be correct. In the church today accountability is most important, and believers do well to follow the pattern set up by Ezra so as to guarantee that none of the Lord's resources be lost.

9:2 Time and again in the history of Israel intermarriage with the heathen had led to grave problems—such intermarriage was forbidden by God. The returning Jews still had not learned their lesson. Ezra discovered that intermarriage with the heathen was widespread. His subsequent prayer included an admission of this grave sin: "We have forsaken thy commandments" (9:10). Repentance and correction were called for.

3 And when I heard this thing, I rent my garment and my mantle, and
plucked off the hair of my head and of my beard, and sat down astonied.
4 Then were assembled unto me every one that trembled at the words of
the God of Israel, because of the transgression of those that had been
carried away; and I sat astonied until the evening sacrifice..

☆**9:3**
Josh 7:6
2 Kgs 18:37
19:1
Neh 1:4
Job 2:12, 13
☆**9:4**
Ex 29:38, 39

2. Ezra's Prayer to God

5 ¶And at the evening sacrifice I arose up from my heaviness; and having
rent my garment and my mantle, I fell upon my knees, and spread out my
hands unto the LORD my God,
6 And said, O my God, I am ashamed and blush to lift up my face to thee,
my God: for our iniquities are increased over *our* head, and our trespass is
grown up unto the heavens.
7 Since the days of our fathers *have* we *been* in a great trespass unto this
day; and for our iniquities have we, our kings, *and* our priests, been
delivered into the hand of the kings of the lands, to the sword, to captivity,
and to a spoil, and to confusion of face, as *it is* this day.
8 And now for a little space grace hath been *shewed* from the LORD our
God, to leave us a remnant to escape, and to give us a nail in his holy place,
that our God may lighten our eyes, and give us a little reviving in our
bondage.
9 For we *were* bondmen; yet our God hath not forsaken us in our
bondage, but hath extended mercy unto us in the sight of the kings of
Persia, to give us a reviving, to set up the house of our God, and to repair
the desolations thereof, and to give us a wall in Judah and in Jerusalem.
10 And now, O our God, what shall we say after this? for we have forsaken
thy commandments,
11 Which thou hast commanded by thy servants the prophets, saying, The
land, unto which ye go to possess it, is an unclean land with the filthiness of
the people of the lands, with their abominations, which have filled it from
one end to another with their uncleanness.
12 Now therefore give not your daughters unto their sons, neither take
their daughters unto your sons, nor seek their peace or their wealth for ever:
that ye may be strong, and eat the good of the land, and leave *it* for an
inheritance to your children for ever.
13 And after all that is come upon us for our evil deeds, and for our great
trespass, seeing that thou our God hast punished us less than our iniquities
deserve, and hast given us *such* deliverance as this;
14 Should we again break thy commandments, and join in affinity with the
people of these abominations? wouldest not thou be angry with us till thou
hadst consumed *us*, so that *there should be* no remnant nor escaping?

☆**9:5**
Ex 9:29
2 Chron 6:12, 13
1 Tim 2:8
☆**9:6**
2 Chron 28:9
Lk 15:21
Rev 18:5
9:7
2 Kgs 24:1–4
2 Chron
36:16–20
9:8
2 Kgs 19:4, 30,
31
Isa 1:9
Jer 44:14
9:9
Ex 1:11–14
Neh 9:36, 37
Ps 106:45, 46
Ezek 11:16
9:12
Deut 7:3
Josh 1:6–9
23:12, 13
Ezra 9:2
9:14
Num 16:21, 22,
45, 46
Deut 9:7, 8, 13,
14
Ezra 9:2

9:3 Ezra's reaction to the mixed marriages indicates the seriousness with which he regarded this transgression. It was made worse by reason of the fact that priests and Levites were among the offenders. When religious leaders defect from the faith, what can be expected of their church members? Ezra rent his clothes, plucked out his hair, and sat down astonished. Long before the captivity the Israelites had broken the command of God in this regard again and again.

9:4 So great was the influence of Ezra that the upright believers, who took the Word of God seriously, voluntarily joined Ezra for fasting and prayer to keep the judgment of God from falling upon them all.

9:5 The prayer Ezra was about to offer came at the time of the evening sacrifice and it was a public act before all who gathered before him. He rose from his heaviness, knelt, and spread out his hands before the Lord God. He was an innocent suppliant under deep conviction about the sins of the people.

9:6ff Ezra now offers a prayer of confession of sin. He identifies himself with the sinners by the use of the words "I," "my," and "our." He acknowledges the greatness of the transgression, the length of time it has been practiced, the judgments that have come as a result of sin. He asks for the great mercies of God and the need for a reviving. He bespeaks the justice and anger of a righteous God, even as he boldly proclaims the guilt of the people who cannot stand before God because of their sins. This prayer, along with those of Daniel 9 and Nehemiah 9, is among the most moving of all the prayers in the Scriptures.

9:15 Neh 9:33, 34; Job 9:2, 3; Ps 130:3; Dan 9:7–11; Rom 3:19; 10:3

15 O LORD God of Israel, thou *art* righteous: for we remain yet escaped, as
it is this day: behold, we *are* before thee in our trespasses: for we cannot
stand before thee because of this.

3. The Confession and Repentance of the Guilty

10 NOW when Ezra had prayed, and when he had confessed, weeping
and casting himself down before the house of God, there assembled
unto him out of Israel a very great congregation of men and women and
children: for the people wept very sore.

10:2☆ Ezra 10:11

2 And Shech-a-ni′ah the son of Je-hi′el, *one* of the sons of E′lam, answered
and said unto Ezra, We have trespassed against our God, and have taken
strange wives of the people of the land: yet now there is hope in Israel
concerning this thing.

10:3☆ Deut 7:2, 3; 24:1, 29:12; Josh 1:17, 18; Mt 5:32

3 Now therefore let us make a covenant with our God to put away all the
wives, and such as are born of them, according to the counsel of my lord,
and of those that tremble at the commandment of our God; and let it be
done according to the law.

10:4 Josh 1:6–9; 1 Chron 28:10

4 Arise; for *this* matter *belongeth* unto thee: we also *will be* with thee: be of
good courage, and do *it*.

10:5☆ Ezra 10:3; Neh 5:12; 13:25

5 Then arose Ezra, and made the chief priests, the Levites, and all Israel,
to swear that they should do according to this word. And they sware.

10:6 Deut 9:18

6 ¶Then Ezra rose up from before the house of God, and went into the
chamber of Jo-ha′nan the son of E-li′a-shib: and *when* he came thither, he
did eat no bread, nor drink water: for he mourned because of the
transgression of them that had been carried away.

7 And they made proclamation throughout Judah and Jerusalem unto all
the children of the captivity, that they should gather themselves together
unto Jerusalem;

8 And that whosoever would not come within three days, according to the
counsel of the princes and the elders, all his substance should be forfeited,
and himself separated from the congregation of those that had been carried
away.

10:9 1 Sam 12:17, 18; Jer 10:10, 13

9 ¶Then all the men of Judah and Benjamin gathered themselves together
unto Jerusalem within three days. It *was* the ninth month, on the twentieth
day of the month; and all the people sat in the street of the house of God,
trembling because of *this* matter, and for the great rain.

10:11☆ Ezra 10:2; Neh 13:3; 2 Cor 6:17

10 And Ezra the priest stood up, and said unto them, Ye have trans-
gressed, and have taken strange wives, to increase the trespass of Israel.
11 Now therefore make confession unto the LORD God of your fathers,

---

10:2 *Shechaniah*, under conviction of sin, was truly repentant.

10:3 Conviction of sin came upon the congregation regarding the marriage of some Jews to pagan women. Nothing is said as to whether any Jewish women married pagan men. The larger question was what remedy was to be applied to erase the wrong. In this instance, the foreign wives were to be divorced by the Jewish men who had married them. While the marriages were sinful, they were not null. Divorce was the only answer. Yet in the New Testament it is stated that "if any brother hath a wife that believeth not, and she be pleased to dwell with him, let him not put her away" (1 Cor. 7:12). The Corinthian passage, however, seems to apply to a marriage of two unbelievers, one of whom gets converted. Thus this teaching would not apply to the situation under Ezra. What had been sinfully gotten could not be justly kept. There had to be a separation to cure the sin.

10:5 A revival of true religion took place on this occasion. There was deep conviction of sin followed by confession and a determination to correct the difficulty—they would put away their pagan spouses. The priests, the Levites, and all Israel solemnly swore they would do this. The forsaking of sin often involves a strong remedy. The harder the decision the greater the evidence that true repentance exists.

10:6 *Johanan,* called Jehohanan in the RSV and TLB. He is said to be the grandson of Eliashib. (See Neh. 12:22.)

10:11 Here we learn that the marriages with pagan women had brought about concourse with a mass of unbelieving persons. The covenant agreement included a separation not only from the pagan wives but also "from the people of the land." Undoubtedly many of the Jews (who had not married pagan women) nonetheless had close relationships with pagan communities.

and do his pleasure: and separate yourselves from the people of the land,
and from the strange wives.
12 Then all the congregation answered and said with a loud voice, As thou
hast said, so must we do.
13 But the people *are* many, and *it is* a time of much rain, and we are not
able to stand without, neither *is this* a work of one day or two: for we are
many that have transgressed in this thing.
14 Let now our rulers of all the congregation stand, and let all them which
have taken strange wives in our cities come at appointed times, and with
them the elders of every city, and the judges thereof, until the fierce wrath
of our God for this matter be turned from us.
15 ¶Only Jonathan the son of As'a-hel and Ja-ha-zi'ah the son of Tik'vah
were employed about this *matter:* and Me-shul'lam and Shab'be-thai the
Levite helped them.

10:14 Num 25:4 Deut 13:17 2 Chron 29:10 Ezra 9:14

☆**10:15**

4. The Names of the Offenders

16 And the children of the captivity did so. And Ezra the priest, *with*
certain chief of the fathers, after the house of their fathers, and all of them
by *their* names, were separated, and sat down in the first day of the tenth
month to examine the matter.
17 And they made an end with all the men that had taken strange wives by
the first day of the first month.
18 ¶And among the sons of the priests there were found that had taken
strange wives: *namely,* of the sons of Jesh'u-a the son of Joz'a-dak, and his
brethren; Ma-a-sei'ah, and E-li-e'zer, and Ja'rib, and Ged-a-li'ah.
19 And they gave their hands that they would put away their wives; and
being guilty, *they offered* a ram of the flock for their trespass.
20 And of the sons of Im'mer; Ha-na'ni, and Zeb-a-di'ah.
21 And of the sons of Ha'rim; Ma-a-sei'ah, and E-li'jah, and Shem-a-i'ah,
and Je-hi'el, and Uz-zi'ah.
22 And of the sons of Pash'ur; E-li-o-e'na-i, Ma-a-sei'ah, Ish'ma-el, Ne-
than'e-el, Joz'a-bad, and El'a-sah.
23 Also of the Levites; Joz'a-bad, and Shim'e-i, and Ke-lai'ah, (the same *is*
Kel'i-ta,) Peth-a-hi'ah, Judah, and E-li-e'zer.
24 Of the singers also; E-li'a-shib: and of the porters; Shal'lum, and
Te'lem, and U'ri.
25 Moreover of Israel: of the sons of Pa'rosh; Ra-mi'ah, and Je-zi'ah, and
Mal-chi'ah, and Mi'a-min, and E-le-a'zar, and Mal-chi'jah, and Be-nai'ah.
26 And of the sons of E'lam; Mat-ta-ni'ah, Zech-a-ri'ah, and Je-hi'el, and
Ab'di, and Jer'e-moth, and E-li'ah.
27 And of the sons of Zat'tu; E-li-o-e'na-i, E-li'a-shib, Mat-ta-ni'ah, and
Jer'e-moth, and Za'bad, and A-zi'za.
28 Of the sons also of Beb'a-i; Je-ho-ha'nan, Han-a-ni'ah, Zab'bai, *and*
Ath'lai.
29 And of the sons of Ba'ni; Me-shul'lam, Mal'luch, and Ad-a-i'ah,
Jash'ub, and She'al, and Ra'moth.

☆**10:18**

10:15 Since four men opposed the plan, there was not complete unanimity. What is not clear is whether they opposed the procedure which was to be followed or the agreement to put away strange wives. Meshullam was one who opposed the agreement and yet gave up his foreign wife. Nothing is said of the others, so we cannot render any verdict in the absence of all the facts.

10:18ff One hundred thirteen men are listed as having obeyed the agreement to put away their strange wives. Among them were seventeen priests and ten Levites. The remainder were from other tribes. Greater was the guilt of those from the tribe of Levi, who had been given special functions by God and who were expected to serve as an example for the other tribes.

30And of the sons of Pa'hath-mo'ab; Ad'na, and Che'lal, Be-nai'ah, Ma-
a-sei'ah, Mat-ta-ni'ah, Be-zal'e-el, and Bin'nu-i, and Ma-nas'seh.
31And *of* the sons of Ha'rim; E-li-e'zer, I-shi'jah, Mal-chi'ah, Shem-a-i'ah,
Shim'e-on,
32Benjamin, Mal'luch, *and* Shem-a-ri'ah.
33Of the sons of Ha'shum; Mat-te-na'i, Mat'ta-thah, Za'bad, E-liph'e-let,
Jer'e-mai, Ma-nas'seh, *and* Shim'e-i.
34Of the sons of Ba'ni; Ma-ad'ai, Amram, and U'el,
35Be-nai'ah, Be-dei'ah, Chel'luh,
36Va-ni'ah, Mer'e-moth, E-li'a-shib,
37Mat-ta-ni'ah, Mat-te-na'i, and Ja'a-sau,
38And Ba'ni, and Bin'nu-i, Shim'e-i,
39And Shel-e-mi'ah, and Nathan, and Ad-a-i'ah,
40Mach-na-de'bai, Shash'a-i, Shar'a-i,
41A-zar'e-el, and Shel-e-mi'ah, Shem-a-ri'ah,
42Shal'lum, Am-a-ri'ah, *and* Joseph.
43Of the sons of Nebo; Je-i'el, Mat-ti-thi'ah, Za'bad, Ze-bi'na, Ja-da'u,
and Jo'el, Be-nai'ah.
44All these had taken strange wives: and *some* of them had wives by
whom they had children.

THE BOOK OF
NEHEMIAH

Authorship, date, and background See the introduction to Ezra. Ezra and Nehemiah were one book in the Hebrew Bible. Both books are part of the Hagiographa, which include the Poetical Books and the Scrolls (the Megilloth). The book of Nehemiah consists of the personal memoirs of Nehemiah, who can logically be considered the author despite objections raised by liberal scholars. This book picks up the story where the book of Ezra leaves off. Ezra had returned to the land in 458 or 457 B.C.; Nehemiah followed him twelve years later. The Elephantine letter #30, an external source, clearly shows that the book of Nehemiah cannot be dated after 400 B.C.

Nehemiah did not return to the land with the first contingent. He was very successful in the land of his captivity, becoming cupbearer for Artaxerxes. It was nearly a hundred years after the first return that he became exercised about conditions and was moved by God to go back. Discouraging reports had come via Hanani, a kinsman. Providentially, Artaxerxes granted him permission to return. He was an astute politician who became governor. Energetic and self-sacrificial, Nehemiah was able to cope with the plots against the Jews by the enemies who surrounded them. His account indicates the success of his efforts in the rebuilding of the walls of Jerusalem and the reassignment of Jews to strategic sections of the city to ward off possible attacks by enemy invaders.

Characteristics and content Nehemiah records his own memoirs. He recounts his sorrow over the plight of his people, the willingness of the king to allow him to return, and the supplies which were provided to ensure the rebuilding of the city walls. Upon his return, Nehemiah surveys the situation and calls for the completion of the reconstruction. Sanballat and Tobiah try to stop him. Tobiah, an Ammonite who had married a Jewish woman, has been given a guest room in the temple compound by Eliashib, the High Priest. This complicates the problem. Despite the opposition, Nehemiah persists in his efforts to rebuild the walls. He defends the poor and stops usury so that the work will not be interrupted. The Herculean task of finishing the rebuilding is completed in a fifty-two-day frenzy of activity. The names of the returnees and their families are listed.

The people assemble to hear the Law read to them. Ezra does the reading and expounds the meaning. The Feast of Booths is held and the covenant is renewed and signed. In the covenant are prohibitions against mixed marriages, something Ezra dealt with earlier, the observance of the sabbath, a tax to support the temple, along with pledges about tithing and food offering and first fruits.

The second reform movement of Nehemiah begins with chapter 11. Israelis living outside the city of Jerusalem are relocated inside the city, the genealogies of the priests and Levites are written down, the walls of the city dedicated, and collectors, singers and gatekeepers appointed. Following this, Nehemiah, who has temporarily returned to Babylon, comes home and casts Tobiah out of the temple chamber provided for him by Eliashib. He concludes his memoirs by mentioning the sabbath reforms which forbade work on the holy day. He institutes marriage reforms, for the men had intermarried with women from Ashdod, Ammon, and Moab. He summarizes his labors by saying, "Thus cleansed I them from all strangers, and appointed the wards of the priests and the Levites. . . . Remember me, O my God, for good" (13:30, 31).

Outline

I. Nehemiah goes to Jerusalem and rebuilds the walls (1:1—6:19)
II. Nehemiah's first reform (7:1—10:39)
III. Nehemiah's second reform (11:1—13:31)

I. NEHEMIAH GOES TO JERUSALEM AND REBUILDS THE WALLS (1:1—6:19)

A. NEHEMIAH'S RETURN TO JERUSALEM

1. The Bad News from Jerusalem

1:1☆ Neh 2:1; 10:1 Esth 1:2 Zech 7:1

1 THE words of Ne-he-mi'ah the son of Hach-a-li'ah. And it came to pass in the month Chis'leu, in the twentieth year, as I was in Shu'shan the palace,

1:2 Neh 7:2

2 That Ha-na'ni, one of my brethren, came, he and *certain* men of Judah; and I asked them concerning the Jews that had escaped, which were left of the captivity, and concerning Jerusalem.

1:3 Neh 2:3, 17

3 And they said unto me, The remnant that are left of the captivity there in the province *are* in great affliction and reproach: the wall of Jerusalem also *is* broken down, and the gates thereof are burned with fire.

2. Nehemiah's Prayer to God

1:4☆ Ezra 9:3; 10:1 Dan 9:3

4 ¶And it came to pass, when I heard these words, that I sat down and wept, and mourned *certain* days, and fasted, and prayed before the God of heaven,

5 And said, I beseech thee, O LORD God of heaven, the great and terrible God, that keepeth covenant and mercy for them that love him and observe his commandments:

1:6 Deut 28:14, 15 Ezra 10:1 Ps 32:5 Dan 9:8, 17–20

6 Let thine ear now be attentive, and thine eyes open, that thou mayest hear the prayer of thy servant, which I pray before thee now, day and night, for the children of Israel thy servants, and confess the sins of the children of Israel, which we have sinned against thee: both I and my father's house have sinned.

7 We have dealt very corruptly against thee, and have not kept the commandments, nor the statutes, nor the judgments, which thou commandedst thy servant Moses.

1:8 Lev 26:33

8 Remember, I beseech thee, the word that thou commandedst thy servant Moses, saying, *If* ye transgress, I will scatter you abroad among the nations:

1:9 Deut 12:5 30:2–4 Jer 29:11–14

9 But *if* ye turn unto me, and keep my commandments, and do them; though there were of you cast out unto the uttermost part of the heaven, *yet* will I gather them from thence, and will bring them unto the place that I have chosen to set my name there.

1:10 Ex 32:11 Deut 9:29

10 Now these *are* thy servants and thy people, whom thou hast redeemed by thy great power, and by thy strong hand.

1:11☆ Gen 40:21 Neh 2:1

11 O Lord, I beseech thee, let now thine ear be attentive to the prayer of

1:1 *Nehemiah.* We know little about this man in relation to his forebears. Since he offered sacrifices, it is supposed he may have been from the tribe of Levi and was a priest. This book he wrote is the last of the historical books in the Old Testament, just as Malachi is the last of the prophetical books. He lived at a time when the bright ornaments of Greece lived and wrote: Xenophon, Plato, and Demosthenes. Nowhere do their names appear in the Bible. Great as these Greeks were, from the biblical perspective and from revelation, Nehemiah was greater. *Chisleu,* i.e., "early December." *in the twentieth year,* i.e., "the twentieth year of the reign of King Artaxerxes (445 B.C.)."

1:4 Nehemiah was a devout believer. When he heard of the sad situation in Jerusalem, he turned to prayer and fasting on behalf of the people of God. He fasted and prayed for an unspecified period of time. God does not always respond to our prayers as soon as they are spoken. In this instance God moved the heart of Nehemiah to do more than pray for the peace of Jerusalem. He commissioned him to give up his cozy job with the king and to identify himself with the suffering saints where they were. The king responded to Nehemiah's request for a leave of absence and this called forth his statement, "the good hand of my God [was] upon me" (2:8). God had heard; God had blessed. Providence was at work in his life.

1:11 *cupbearer.* Ancient monarchs were fearful of being poisoned. The cupbearer had to be a faithful and trustworthy servant of the king. Most frequently he was a eunuch, and such may have been the case with Nehemiah, especially since he was allowed in the presence of the queen (2:6). Deut. 23:1 excluded emasculated persons from the Jewish community. So either Nehemiah was not a eunuch or an exception was made in his case.

thy servant, and to the prayer of thy servants, who desire to fear thy name:
and prosper, I pray thee, thy servant this day, and grant him mercy in the
sight of this man. For I was the king's cupbearer.

3. Nehemiah's Request of King Artaxerxes

2 AND it came to pass in the month Ni'san, in the twentieth year of Ar- ☆2:1 Neh 1:11
ta-xer'xes the king, *that* wine *was* before him: and I took up the wine,
and gave *it* unto the king. Now I had not been *beforetime* sad in his
presence.
2Wherefore the king said unto me, Why *is* thy countenance sad, seeing
thou *art* not sick? this *is* nothing *else* but sorrow of heart. Then I was very
sore afraid,
3And said unto the king, Let the king live for ever: why should not my 2:3 Neh 1:3
countenance be sad, when the city, the place of my fathers' sepulchres, *lieth*
waste, and the gates thereof are consumed with fire?
4Then the king said unto me, For what dost thou make request? So I ☆2:4
prayed to the God of heaven.
5And I said unto the king, If it please the king, and if thy servant have
found favour in thy sight, that thou wouldest send me unto Judah, unto the
city of my fathers' sepulchres, that I may build it.
6And the king said unto me, (the queen also sitting by him,) For how ☆2:6
long shall thy journey be? and when wilt thou return? So it pleased the king
to send me; and I set him a time.
7Moreover I said unto the king, If it please the king, let letters be given 2:7 Ezra 6:6; 7:21; 8:36; Neh 2:9
me to the governors beyond the river, that they may convey me over till I
come into Judah;
8And a letter unto A'saph the keeper of the king's forest, that he may give ☆2:8 Neh 7:2; Eccles 2:5, 6
me timber to make beams for the gates of the palace which *appertained* to
the house, and for the wall of the city, and for the house that I shall enter
into. And the king granted me, according to the good hand of my God
upon me.

4. Nehemiah Goes to Jerusalem and Inspects the Walls

9¶Then I came to the governors beyond the river, and gave them the 2:9 Ezra 8:22; Neh 2:7
king's letters. Now the king had sent captains of the army and horsemen
with me.
10When San-bal'lat the Hor'o-nite, and To-bi'ah the servant, the 2:10 Neh 2:19; 4:1–3; 6:1
Ammonite, heard *of it*, it grieved them exceedingly that there was come a
man to seek the welfare of the children of Israel.
11So I came to Jerusalem, and was there three days. ☆2:11

2:1 *Nisan,* the first month of the Jewish calendar (March/April). No one who served the king would have been sad or melancholy in the presence of the monarch. The fact that the king noticed his condition and remarked about it caused Nehemiah to be "very sore afraid" (2:2). Unknown to him, God was at work and used the king to make his return to Jerusalem possible.
2:4 *So I prayed to the God of heaven.* This must have been a very short prayer asking God for help as to what he should say. Compare the promise of Jesus that when we stand before men and know not what to say, it "will be given to you . . . for it is not you who speak, but the Spirit of your Father speaking through you" (Matt. 10:19, 20, RSV). Nehemiah received divine assistance and his prayer was answered.
2:6 *I set him a time,* i.e., when he expected to return to the king's service. What the set time was we do not know. It must have been extended, for he spent at least twelve years in Jerusalem, according to 5:14.
2:8 *the good hand of my God* [was] *upon me.* God supplied his material needs, and letters were given him to the governors of the king who could help him. Moreover (2:9) "captains of the army and horsemen" accompanied him and protected him. Ezra had refused military help and was safe. Nehemiah accepted the help and was also safe. God works differently on some occasions.
2:11 Nehemiah wisely kept his intentions to himself. When those intentions were discovered, the persecution began. He clearly stated that what he intended to do had been put into his heart by God himself. Every believer should find the will of God for his life and then pursue it with vigor, perseverance, and faith.

[12]¶And I arose in the night, I and some few men with me; neither told I
any man what my God had put in my heart to do at Jerusalem: neither *was*
there any beast with me, save the beast that I rode upon.
2:13 Neh 1:3; 2:15 3:13; 12:31 [13]And I went out by night by the gate of the valley, even before the
dragon well, and to the dung port, and viewed the walls of Jerusalem, which
were broken down, and the gates thereof were consumed with fire.
2:14 2 Kgs 20:20 2 Chron 32:30 Neh 2:13; 3:15 [14]Then I went on to the gate of the fountain, and to the king's pool: but
there was no place for the beast *that was* under me to pass.
[15]Then went I up in the night by the brook, and viewed the wall, and
turned back, and entered by the gate of the valley, and *so* returned.
2:16☆ [16]And the rulers knew not whither I went, or what I did; neither had I as
yet told *it* to the Jews, nor to the priests, nor to the nobles, nor to the rulers,
nor to the rest that did the work.

5. Nehemiah Decides to Rebuild the Wall; Sanballat and Tobiah Resist Him

2:17 Neh 1:3; 2:14 [17]¶Then said I unto them, Ye see the distress that we *are* in, how
Jerusalem *lieth* waste, and the gates thereof are burned with fire: come, and
let us build up the wall of Jerusalem, that we be no more a reproach.
2:18☆ [18]Then I told them of the hand of my God which was good upon me; as
also the king's words that he had spoken unto me. And they said, Let us
rise up and build. So they strengthened their hands for *this* good *work.*
2:19☆ Neh 2:10; 6:6 [19]But when San-bal'lat the Hor'o-nite, and To-bi'ah the servant, the
Ammonite, and Ge'shem the Arabian, heard *it,* they laughed us to scorn,
and despised us, and said, What *is* this thing that ye do? will ye rebel
against the king?
2:20 Ezra 4:3 [20]Then answered I them, and said unto them, the God of heaven, he will
prosper us; therefore we his servants will arise and build: but ye have no
portion, nor right, nor memorial, in Jerusalem.

B. REBUILDING THE WALLS AND GATES

1. The Workmen and Their Labors

3:1☆ Neh 3:20, 32 12:39; 13:28 Jer 31:38 3 THEN E-li'a-shib the high priest rose up with his brethren the priests,
and they builded the sheep gate; they sanctified it, and set up the doors
of it; even unto the tower of Me'ah they sanctified it, unto the tower of Ha-
nan'e-el.
3:2 Neh 7:36 [2]And next unto him builded the men of Jericho. And next to them
builded Zac'cur the son of Im'ri.

2:16 Nehemiah's first job was to view the situation discreetly in order to determine what needed to be done and how he would accomplish it. He carefully refrained from letting anyone know about his reconnaisance.

2:18 *Let us rise up and build.* Once Nehemiah disclosed what the king had promised him, how he had surveyed the situation, and how he decided the walls of the city should be rebuilt, the people rallied behind him. He gave them the divine assurance that the hand of God was upon him and therefore upon those who would assist him. What God wants done can and will be accomplished by his servants through his power.

2:19 Whoever does the will of God will encounter opposition. Nehemiah was scorned, despised, and accused of rebelling against the king. This would have deterred a lesser mortal. But Nehemiah was a man of resolve; he was certain of his call and insistent on fulfilling it. He simply refused to quit or be stopped by enemies of his cause. His watchword was this: "The God of heaven, he will prosper us" (2:20). With that assurance he was unbeatable.

3:1 *the sheep gate.* This was the gate through which the animals came that were to be sacrificed in the temple. Since the sacrifices benefited the priests, it was to their advantage to see that this gate was reconstructed. Moreover this route led to the temple itself. The energy of the high priest, Eliashib, who himself worked on the project, was impressive. His example was worth a dozen sermons, and his willingness to engage in common labor unusual. Jesus did precisely this in the *kenosis*—when he emptied himself for us and our salvation. (Phil. 2:7).

3 But the fish gate did the sons of Has-se-na'ah build, who *also* laid the ☆**3:3**
beams thereof, and set up the doors thereof, the locks thereof, and the bars Neh 12:39
thereof.
4 And next unto them repaired Mer'e-moth the son of U-ri'jah, the son of
Koz. And next unto them repaired Me-shul'lam the son of Ber-e-chi'ah, the
son of Me-shez'a-be-el. And next unto them repaired Za'dok the son of
Ba'a-na.
5 And next unto them the Te-ko'ites repaired; but their nobles put not ☆**3:5**
their necks to the work of their Lord. Neh 3:27
6 Moreover the old gate repaired Je-hoi'a-da the son of Pa-se'ah, and Me- ☆**3:6**
shul'lam the son of Bes-o-dei'ah; they laid the beams thereof, and set up the Neh 12:39
doors thereof, and the locks thereof, and the bars thereof.
7 And next unto them repaired Mel-a-ti'ah the Gib'e-o-nite, and Ja'don
the Me-ron'o-thite, the men of Gibeon, and of Mizpah, unto the throne of
the governor on this side the river.
8 Next unto him repaired Uz'zi-el the son of Har-ha-i'ah, of the gold- ☆**3:8**
smiths. Next unto him also repaired Han-a-ni'ah the son of *one of* the Neh 3:31
apothecaries, and they fortified Jerusalem unto the broad wall.
9 And next unto them repaired Reph-a-i'ah the son of Hur, the ruler of **3:9**
the half part of Jerusalem. Neh 3:12, 17
10 And next unto them repaired Je-dai'ah the son of Ha-ru'maph, even
over against his house. And next unto him repaired Hat'tush the son of
Hash-ab-ni'ah.
11 Mal-chi'jah the son of Ha'rim, and Ha'shub the son of Pa'hath-mo'ab, ☆**3:11**
repaired the other piece, and the tower of the furnaces. Neh 12:38
12 And next unto him repaired Shal'lum the son of Ha-lo'hesh, the ruler of **3:12**
the half part of Jerusalem, he and his daughters. Neh 3:9
13 The valley gate repaired Ha'nun, and the inhabitants of Za-no'ah; they ☆**3:13**
built it, and set up the doors thereof, the locks thereof, and the bars thereof, Neh 2:13
and a thousand cubits on the wall unto the dung gate.
14 But the dung gate repaired Mal-chi'ah the son of Re'chab, the ruler of ☆**3:14**
part of Beth-hac'ce-rem; he built it, and set up the doors thereof, the locks Neh 2:13; 3:13
thereof, and the bars thereof.
15 But the gate of the fountain repaired Shal'lun the son of Col-ho'zeh, ☆**3:15**
the ruler of part of Mizpah; he built it, and covered it, and set up the doors 2 Kgs 25:4, 5
thereof, the locks thereof, and the bars thereof, and the wall of the pool of Neh 2:14; 12:37
Si-lo'ah by the king's garden, and unto the stairs that go down from the city **3:16**
of David. 1 Kgs 14:28 2 Kgs 20:20 2 Chron 12:10, 11; 16:14
16 After him repaired Ne-he-mi'ah the son of Az'buk, the ruler of the half Neh 2:14

3:3 *the fish gate* was apparently so named because of the fish market nearby. Evidently those who sold fish would bring their wares through this gate. All commerce brought into the city would of necessity have to come through some gate.

3:5 *put not their necks to the work of their LORD.* The nobles of Tekoa thought their high status exempted them from doing the work of God. Nothing is below us that will advance the interests of our nation and its people.

3:6 *the old gate* was located on the north side of post-exilic Jerusalem. Some think the gate of Ephraim was on its west and the fish gate on its east side.

3:8 *the broad wall,* i.e., the western wall.

3:11 *tower of the furnaces,* i.e., "tower of the ovens," which was close to the Corner Gate in the northwest angle of the Jerusalem wall. There were baking ovens in the area, thus it probably got its name from these.

3:13 *gate of the valley,* i.e., "The Valley Gate," which had had towers built by Uzziah. It was the point from which Nehemiah started his tour of Jerusalem before the work of reconstruction began. The gate was five hundred yards from the dung gate. Since Jerusalem's size differed from time to time, there are exegetical problems connected with some such items.

3:14 *the dung gate* was on the south end of the city not far from the pool of Siloam. Refuse from the city was carried out this gate to the Valley of Hinnom where it was burned. *Hinnom,* which comes from the Hebrew *Ge-ben-Hinnom,* became corrupted into *Gehenna* (Greek), which is used in the New Testament to designate the place of eternal punishment.

3:15 *the gate of the fountain,* i.e., the "Fountain Gate," was located in the southeast section of the wall below the Pool of Siloam and along the Kidron Valley.

part of Beth′-zur, unto *the place* over against the sepulchres of David, and
to the pool that was made, and unto the house of the mighty.
17 After him repaired the Levites, Re′hum the son of Ba′ni. Next unto him
repaired Hash-a-bi′ah, the ruler of the half part of Kei′lah, in his part.
18 After him repaired their brethren, Bav′a-i the son of Hen′a-dad, the
ruler of the half part of Kei′lah.
3:19 19 And next to him repaired E′zer the son of Jesh′u-a, the ruler of Mizpah,
Neh 3:16 another piece over against the going up to the armoury at the turning *of the*
2 Chron 26:9 *wall.*
3:20 20 After him Ba′ruch the son of Zab′bai earnestly repaired the other piece,
Neh 3:1 from the turning *of the wall* unto the door of the house of E-li′a-shib the
high priest.
21 After him repaired Mer′e-moth the son of U-ri′jah the son of Koz
another piece, from the door of the house of E-li′a-shib even to the end of
the house of E-li′a-shib.
3:22 22 And after him repaired the priests, the men of the plain.
Neh 12:28 23 After him repaired Benjamin and Ha′shub over against their house.
After him repaired Az-a-ri′ah the son of Ma-a-sei′ah the son of An-a-ni′ah
by his house.
24 After him repaired Bin′nu-i the son of Hen′a-dad another piece, from
the house of Az-a-ri′ah unto the turning *of the wall*, even unto the corner.
3:25 25 Pa′lal the son of U′za-i, over against the turning *of the wall*, and the
Jer 32:2 tower which lieth out from the king's high house, that *was* by the court of
the prison. After him Pe-dai′ah the son of Pa′rosh.
3:26☆ 26 Moreover the Neth′i-nims dwelt in O′phel, unto *the place* over against
Neh 3:27; 7:46 8:1, 3; 11:21 the water gate toward the east, and the tower that lieth out.
12:37 3:27 27 After them the Te-ko′ites repaired another piece, over against the great
Neh 3:5, 26 tower that lieth out, even unto the wall of O′phel.
3:28☆ 28 From above the horse gate repaired the priests, every one over against
2 Kgs 11:16 2 Chron 23:15 the house.
Jer 31:40 3:29☆ 29 After them repaired Za′dok the son of Im′mer over against his house.
Jer 19:2 After him repaired also Shem-a-i′ah the son of Shech-a-ni′ah, the keeper of
the east gate.
30 After him repaired Han-a-ni′ah the son of Shel-e-mi′ah, and Ha′nun
the sixth son of Za′laph, another piece. After him repaired Me-shul′lam the
son of Ber-e-chi′ah over against his chamber.
3:31 31 After him repaired Mal-chi′ah the goldsmith's son unto the place of the
Neh 3:1, 8 Neth′i-nims, and of the merchants, over against the gate Miph′kad, and to
the going up of the corner.
3:32 32 And between the going up of the corner unto the sheep gate repaired
Neh 3:1; 12:39 the goldsmiths and the merchants.

2. The Resistance to the Rebuilding
a. The Evil Plans of Sanballat and Tobiah

4:1☆ 4 BUT it came to pass, that when San-bal′lat heard that we builded the
Ezra 4:9, 10 Neh 2:10 wall, he was wroth, and took great indignation, and mocked the Jews.
2 And he spake before his brethren and the army of Sa-ma′ri-a, and said,

---

3:26 *the water gate* was close by the Gihon spring. There was an open square where the people assembled to hear the reading of the law by Ezra. There was space for erecting booths for the festival of Tabernacles.

3:28 *the horse gate* was at the southeast corner of the temple area. Athaliah was killed there. Nehemiah restored it.

3:29 *the east gate* is not specifically stated to have been repaired by Nehemiah. It was a temple gate. It may have been the gate through which Jesus entered Jerusalem on "Palm Sunday."

4:1 The work of God will always be opposed by the forces of evil. Sanballat and Tobiah, who were Samaritans, indignantly protested what Nehemiah was doing. They were derogatory, scornful, and malicious.

house, and from his labour, that performeth not this promise, even thus be
he shaken out, and emptied. And all the congregation said, Amen, and
praised the LORD. And the people did according to this promise.
14¶Moreover from the time that I was appointed to be their governor in
the land of Judah, from the twentieth year even unto the two and thirtieth
year of Ar-ta-xer'xes the king, *that is,* twelve years, I and my brethren have
not eaten the bread of the governor.
15But the former governors that *had been* before me were chargeable unto
the people, and had taken of them bread and wine, beside forty shekels of
silver; yea, even their servants bare rule over the people: but so did not I,
because of the fear of God.
16Yea, also I continued in the work of this wall, neither bought we any
land: and all my servants *were* gathered thither unto the work.
17Moreover *there were* at my table an hundred and fifty of the Jews and
rulers, beside those that came unto us from among the heathen that *are*
about us.
18Now *that* which was prepared *for me* daily *was* one ox *and* six choice
sheep; also fowls were prepared for me, and once in ten days store of all
sorts of wine: yet for all this required not I the bread of the governor,
because the bondage was heavy upon this people.
19Think upon me, my God, for good, *according* to all that I have done for
this people.

☆5:14 Neh 1:1; 13:6
5:15 Neh 5:9
5:17 1 Kgs 18:19
5:18 1 Kgs 4:22, 23; 2 Thess 3:8
☆5:19 Neh 13:14, 22, 31

c. The Continuing Opposition of Sanballat and Tobiah

6 NOW it came to pass, when San-bal'lat, and To-bi'ah, and Ge'shem
the Arabian, and the rest of our enemies, heard that I had builded the
wall, and *that* there was no breach left therein; (though at that time I had
not set up the doors upon the gates;)
2That San-bal'lat and Ge'shem sent unto me, saying, Come, let us meet
together in *some one of* the villages in the plain of O'no. But they thought to
do me mischief.
3And I sent messengers unto them, saying, I *am* doing a great work, so
that I cannot come down: why should the work cease, whilst I leave it, and
come down to you?
4Yet they sent unto me four times after this sort; and I answered them
after the same manner.
5Then sent San-bal'lat his servant unto me in like manner the fifth time
with an open letter in his hand;
6Wherein *was* written, It is reported among the heathen, and Gash'mu
saith *it, that* thou and the Jews think to rebel: for which cause thou buildest
the wall, that thou mayest be their king, according to these words.

☆6:1
6:2 1 Chron 8:12
☆6:5 Neh 2:19
☆6:6

5:14 Nehemiah did the work of the governor but he did not eat the bread of the governor, that is, he did not demand the perquisites of the office. Rather, he served sacrificially. He practiced self-denial, identifying himself with the sufferings of the common people. He preferred to do good, not to enrich himself at the expense of others.

5:19 Nehemiah here is not boasting of what he had done. He was shaming those who had broken God's law. He wanted them to follow his example and forsake greed. He had given up everything for God and his people, and he wanted others to do likewise. He knew that the approbation of God is worth more than the approval of men. He wanted nothing more than for God to think on him.

6:1 The enemies now hatch two plots to undo the work of Nehemiah. They are frustrated by God's providence and Nehemiah's prudence, and they do not succeed. The first plot is to get him away from Jerusalem for a conference, some twenty miles from there in the plain of Ono (6:1, 2). In his absence they might be able to assault the city or they might kill Nehemiah at Ono, when he is not accompanied by his armed helpers. He declines their invitation and remains in Jerusalem. Four times they sought to have him meet with them, and four times he rejects their plea.

6:5, 6 Now the foes of Nehemiah employ their second strategem. In an open letter they accuse him of wanting to be king, which would mean rebellion against Artaxerxes. They hoped this would frighten Nehemiah and stop the work.

7 And thou hast also appointed prophets to preach of thee at Jerusalem,
saying, *There is* a king in Judah: and now shall it be reported to the king
according to these words. Come now therefore, and let us take counsel
together.
8 Then I sent unto him, saying, There are no such things done as thou
sayest, but thou feignest them out of thine own heart.
9 For they all made us afraid, saying, Their hands shall be weakened from
the work, that it be not done. Now therefore, *O God,* strengthen my hands.
10 Afterward I came unto the house of Shem-a-i′ah the son of Del-a-i′ah
the son of Me-het′a-be-el, who *was* shut up; and he said, Let us meet
together in the house of God, within the temple, and let us shut the doors of
the temple: for they will come to slay thee; yea, in the night will they come
to slay thee.
6:11☆ 11 And I said, Should such a man as I flee? and who *is there,* that, *being* as
I *am,* would go into the temple to save his life? I will not go in.
6:12 12 And, lo, I perceived that God had not sent him; but that he pro-
Neh 6:6 nounced this prophecy against me: for To-bi′ah and San-bal′lat had hired
him.
13 Therefore *was* he hired, that I should be afraid, and do so, and sin, and
that they might have *matter* for an evil report, that they might reproach me.
6:14 14 My God, think thou upon To-bi′ah and San-bal′lat according to these
Ezek 13:17 Joel 2:28 their works, and on the prophetess No-a-di′ah, and the rest of the prophets,
that would have put me in fear.
6:15☆ 15 ¶So the wall was finished in the twenty and fifth *day* of *the month* E′lul,
Neh 4:1, 2 in fifty and two days.
6:16 16 And it came to pass, that when all our enemies heard *thereof,* and all
Neh 2:10; 4:1, 7 the heathen that *were* about us saw *these things,* they were much cast down
in their own eyes: for they perceived that this work was wrought of our
God.
6:17☆ 17 ¶Moreover in those days the nobles of Ju′dah sent many letters unto
To-bi′ah, and *the letters* of To-bi′ah came unto them.
18 For *there were* many in Judah sworn unto him, because he *was* the son
in law of Shech-a-ni′ah the son of A′rah; and his son Jo-ha′nan had taken
the daughter of Me-shul′lam the son of Ber-e-chi′ah.
19 Also they reported his good deeds before me, and uttered my words to
him. *And* To-bi′ah sent letters to put me in fear.

II. NEHEMIAH'S FIRST REFORM (7:1—10:39)

A. NEHEMIAH'S APPOINTMENT OF HANANI AND HANANIAH

7:1☆ 7 NOW it came to pass, when the wall was built, and I had set up the
doors, and the porters and the singers and the Levites were appointed,

---

6:11 Nehemiah got word that he might be assassinated. It was suggested that he leave his work and flee to the house of God for refuge. But he was made of sterner stuff. He refused to desert God's work or, by leaving, to discourage the workmen he had engaged in the task of rebuilding Jerusalem. He would not be anxious about his own safety. He would rather have died while doing his duty than have lived retreating from that duty. The goal of his life was never to decline a good work, nor ever to do a bad one.

6:15 *fifty and two days* refers to the last phase of the construction. Josephus said it took two years and four months to rebuild the walls.

6:17 Nehemiah had to face the secret treason of some nobles who exchanged communications with Tobiah, to the hurt of his cause. This secret confederacy, based partially on blood ties, became known to Nehemiah and did not succeed, even though spies reported his very words to the enemy.

7:1 Nehemiah's task was not finished when the walls were built and the gates to the doors set up. "Dead walls, without living watchmen, are but a poor defence to a city."* The porters, singers, and Levites were chosen for the temple. He still needed to appoint someone to administer Jerusalem.

[2]That I gave my brother Ha-na'ni, and Han-a-ni'ah the ruler of the ☆7:2 Neh 1:2; 10:23
palace, charge over Jerusalem: for he *was* a faithful man, and feared God
above many.
[3]And I said unto them, Let not the gates of Jerusalem be opened until the ☆7:3
sun be hot; and while they stand by, let them shut the doors, and bar *them:*
and appoint watches of the inhabitants of Jerusalem, every one in his
watch, and every one *to be* over against his house.
[4]Now the city *was* large and great: but the people *were* few therein, and
the houses *were* not builded.

B. THE GENEALOGIES OF THE RETURNEES

[5]¶And my God put into mine heart to gather together the nobles, and the ☆7:5
rulers, and the people, that they might be reckoned by genealogy. And I
found a register of the genealogy of them which came up at the first and
found written therein,
[6]These *are* the children of the province, that went up out of the captivity, 7:6 Ezra 2:1–70
of those that had been carried away, whom Neb-u-chad-nez'zar the king of
Babylon had carried away, and came again to Jerusalem and to Judah,
every one unto his city;
[7]Who came with Ze-rub'ba-bel, Jesh'u-a, Ne-he-mi'ah, Az-a-ri'ah, Ra-a- 7:7 Ezra 2:2
mi'ah, Na-ham'a-ni, Mor'de-cai, Bil'shan, Mis'pe-reth, Big'va-i, Ne'hum,
Ba'a-nah. The number, *I say*, of the men of the people of Israel *was this;*
[8]The children of Pa'rosh, two thousand an hundred seventy and two. 7:8 Ezra 2:3–35
[9]The children of Sheph-a-ti'ah, three hundred seventy and two.
[10]The children of A'rah, six hundred fifty and two.
[11]The children of Pa'hath–mo'ab, of the children of Jesh'u-a and Jo'ab,
two thousand and eight hundred *and* eighteen.
[12]The children of E'lam, a thousand two hundred fifty and four.
[13]The children of Zat'tu, eight hundred forty and five.
[14]The children of Zac'ca-i, seven hundred and threescore.
[15]The children of Bin'nu-i, six hundred forty and eight.
[16]The children of Beb'a-i, six hundred twenty and eight.
[17]The children of Az'gad, two thousand three hundred twenty and two.
[18]The children of A-don'i-kam, six hundred threescore and seven.
[19]The children of Big'va-i, two thousand threescore and seven.
[20]The children of A'din, six hundred fifty and five.
[21]The children of A'ter of Hez-e-ki'ah, ninety and eight.
[22]The children of Ha'shum, three hundred twenty and eight.
[23]The children of Be'zai, three hundred twenty and four.
[24]The children of Ha'riph, an hundred and twelve.
[25]The children of Gibeon, ninety and five.
[26]The men of Beth–lehem and Ne-to'phah, an hundred fourscore and
eight.

7:2 Nehemiah chose Hanani his brother and Hananiah to oversee the city of Jerusalem. These two were governors or consuls, who were charged to provide for the public peace and safety for the people, from enemies within and without. Hananiah was marked out by Nehemiah for being a faithful man who feared God above many others that were less committed and trustworthy. He had already demonstrated his ability, for he had been ruler of the palace. Some think Nehemiah was about to return to the Persian court and have his commission renewed; thus, he wanted to leave good men in charge in his absence.

7:3 Nehemiah wanted to be sure that the city gates were opened and shut at proper times to guarantee the safety of the city. Sentinels were to be posted to give the alarm should any contingency arise. Inside the gates there was great need for the building of homes and businesses.

7:5 Nehemiah carefully preserved the genealogical records of the people. They probably were stored carefully in the temple rooms. The records of the first returnees were examined, and, along with those of the second wave of immigrants, were updated and kept current. There follows the listing by families, although the temple records probably included the names of all the children in every family.

27The men of An′a-thoth, an hundred twenty and eight.
28The men of Beth–az′ma-veth, forty and two.
29The men of Kir′jath–je′a-rim, Che-phi′rah, and Be-e′roth, seven hundred forty and three.
30The men of Ra′mah and Ge′ba, six hundred twenty and one.
31The men of Mich′mas, an hundred and twenty and two.
32The men of Beth–el and A′i, an hundred twenty and three.
33The men of the other Nebo, fifty and two.
34The children of the other E′lam, a thousand two hundred fifty and four.
35The children of Ha′rim, three hundred and twenty.
36The children of Jericho, three hundred forty and five.
37The children of Lod, Ha′did, and O′no, seven hundred twenty and one.
38The children of Se-na′ah, three thousand nine hundred and thirty.
7:39 Ezra 2:36–39 39¶The priests: the children of Je-dai′ah, of the house of Jesh′u-a, nine hundred seventy and three.
40The children of Im′mer, a thousand fifty and two.
41The children of Pash′ur, a thousand two hundred forty and seven.
42The children of Ha′rim, a thousand and seventeen.
7:43 Ezra 2:40–42 43¶The Levites: the children of Jesh′u-a, of Kad′mi-el, *and* of the children of Ho-de′vah, seventy and four.
44¶The singers: the children of A′saph, an hundred forty and eight.
45¶The porters: the children of Shal′lum, the children of A′ter, the children of Tal′mon, the children of Ak′kub, the children of Hat′i-ta, the children of Sho′ba-i, an hundred thirty and eight.
7:46 Ezra 2:43–54 46¶The Neth′i-nims: the children of Zi′ha, the children of Ha-shu′pha, the children of Tab′ba-oth,
47The children of Ke′ros, the children of Si′a, the children of Pa′don,
48The children of Leb′a-na, the children of Hag′a-ba, the children of Shal′ma-i,
49The children of Ha′nan, the children of Gid′del, the children of Ga′har,
50The children of Re-a-i′ah, the children of Re′zin, the children of Ne-ko′da,
51The children of Gaz′zam, the children of Uz′za, the children of Pha-se′ah,
52The children of Be′sai, the children of Me-u′nim, the children of Ne-phish′e-sim,
53The children of Bak′buk, the children of Ha-ku′pha, the children of Har′hur,
54The children of Baz′lith, the children of Me-hi′da, the children of Har′sha,
55The children of Bar′kos, the children of Sis′e-ra, the children of Ta′mah,
56The children of Ne-zi′ah, the children of Hat′i-pha.
7:57 Ezra 2:55–57 57¶The children of Solomon's servants: the children of So′ta-i, the children of Soph′e-reth, the children of Pe-ri′da,
58The children of Ja-a′la, the children of Dar′kon, the children of Gid′del,
59The children of Sheph-a-ti′ah, the children of Hat′til, the children of Poch′e-reth of Ze-ba′im, the children of A′mon.
7:60 Ezra 2:58 60All the Neth′i-nims, and the children of Solomon's servants, *were* three hundred ninety and two.
7:61 Ezra 2:59, 60 61And these *were* they which went up *also* from Tel–me′lah, Tel-ha-re′sha, Cherub, Ad′don, and Im′mer: but they could not shew their father's house, nor their seed, whether they *were* of Israel.
62The children of Del-a-i′ah, the children of To-bi′ah, the children of Ne-ko′da, six hundred forty and two.
7:63 Ezra 2:61 63¶And of the priests: the children of Ha-bai′ah, the children of Koz, the

children of Bar-zil'la-i, which took *one* of the daughters of Bar-zil'la-i the
Gileadite to wife, and was called after their name.
64 These sought their register *among* those that were reckoned by **7:64** Ezra 2:62, 63
genealogy, but it was not found: therefore were they, as polluted, put from
the priesthood.
65 And the Tir'sha-tha said unto them, that they should not eat of the
most holy things, till there stood *up* a priest with U'rim and Thum'mim.
66 ¶The whole congregation together *was* forty and two thousand three **7:66** Ezra 2:64–67
hundred and threescore,
67 Beside their manservants and their maidservants, of whom *there were*
seven thousand three hundred thirty and seven: and they had two hundred
forty and five singing men and singing women.
68 Their horses, seven hundred thirty and six: their mules, two hundred
forty and five:
69 *Their* camels, four hundred thirty and five: six thousand seven hundred
and twenty asses.
70 ¶And some of the chief of the fathers gave unto the work. The Tir'sha- **7:70** Ezra 2:68, 69
tha gave to the treasure a thousand drams of gold, fifty basons, five
hundred and thirty priests' garments.
71 And *some* of the chief of the fathers gave to the treasure of the work
twenty thousand drams of gold, and two thousand and two hundred pound
of silver.
72 And *that* which the rest of the people gave *was* twenty thousand drams
of gold, and two thousand pound of silver, and threescore and seven priests'
garments.
73 So the priests, and the Levites, and the porters, and the singers, and **7:73** Ezra 2:70
some of the people, and the Neth'i-nims, and all Israel, dwelt in their cities;
and when the seventh month came, the children of Israel *were* in their cities.

C. THE LAW READ AND THE COVENANT RENEWED

1. The Word of God Read and Explained

8 AND all the people gathered themselves together as one man into the **☆8:1** 2 Chron 34:15 Ezra 7:6 Neh 3:26
street that *was* before the water gate; and they spake unto Ezra the
scribe to bring the book of the law of Moses, which the LORD had
commanded to Israel.
2 And Ezra the priest brought the law before the congregation both of
men and women, and all that could hear with understanding, upon the first
day of the seventh month.
3 And he read therein before the street that *was* before the water gate **☆8:3**
from the morning until midday, before the men and the women, and those
that could understand; and the ears of all the people *were attentive* unto the
book of the law.
4 And Ezra the scribe stood upon a pulpit of wood, which they had made **☆8:4**
for the purpose; and beside him stood Mat-ti-thi'ah, and She'ma, and An-

---

8:1 This was a solemn religious assembly of people gathered to honor God and to receive edification for the advancement of their spiritual state.

8:3 This event took place on the first day of the seventh month. This was the feast of trumpets and as such was a sabbath or holy day. It was a day of holy convocation when the people gathered together. Since copies of the law were few, the public reading of the Word of God was of great importance. Ezra stood on a wooden pulpit to read. As he opened the scroll, the people stood, a tribute to their reverence for the Word of God. This was a high moment in the lives of the returnees from Babylon.

8:4 *pulpit of wood.* This is the first and only time this Hebrew word *(migdal)* is translated "pulpit" in the KJV. Forty-seven times it is translated "tower." Obviously Ezra the scribe needed a platform from which to address the multitude so that all could see and hear him. Ezra had come to Jerusalem thirteen years before Nehemiah came. It was Nehemiah's zeal that set Ezra to work instructing the people in the Word of God.

a-i'ah, and U-ri'jah, and Hil-ki'ah, and Ma-a-sei'ah, on his right hand; and
on his left hand, Pe-dai'ah, and Mish'a-el, and Mal-chi'ah, and Ha'shum,
and Hash-bad'a-na, Zech-a-ri'ah, *and* Me-shul'lam.
[5]And Ezra opened the book in the sight of all the people; (for he was
above all the people;) and when he opened it, all the people stood up:
8:6 [6]And Ezra blessed the LORD, the great God. And all the people
Gen 14:22 Ex 4:31 answered, Amen, Amen, with lifting up their hands: and they bowed their
2 Chron 20:18 Neh 5:13 heads, and worshipped the LORD with *their* faces to the ground.
1 Tim 2:8 8:7 [7]Also Jesh'u-a, and Ba'ni, and Sher-e-bi'ah, Ja'min, Ak'kub, Shab'be-
Lev 10:11 thai, Ho-di'jah, Ma-a-sei'ah, Kel'i-ta, Az-a-ri'ah, Joz'a-bad, Ha'nan, Pel-a-
Deut 33:10 i'ah, and the Levites, caused the people to understand the law: and the
people *stood* in their place.
8:8☆ [8]So they read in the book in the law of God distinctly, and gave the
sense, and caused *them* to understand the reading.
8:9☆ [9]¶And Ne-he-mi'ah, which *is* the Tir'sha-tha, and Ezra the priest the
Deut 12:7, 12 Neh 8:2 scribe, and the Levites that taught the people, said unto all the people, This
day *is* holy unto the LORD your God; mourn not, nor weep. For all the
people wept, when they heard the words of the law.
8:10 [10]Then he said unto them, Go your way, eat the fat, and drink the sweet,
Deut 26:11–13 Esth 9:19, 22 and send portions unto them for whom nothing is prepared: for *this* day *is*
Ps 28:6–8 holy unto our Lord: neither be ye sorry; for the joy of the LORD is your
strength.
[11]So the Levites stilled all the people, saying, Hold your peace, for the
day *is* holy; neither be ye grieved.
8:12 [12]And all the people went their way to eat, and to drink, and to send
Neh 8:7, 8, 10 Rom 7:7 portions, and to make great mirth, because they had understood the words
that were declared unto them.

2. The Festival of Tabernacles Kept

[13]¶And on the second day were gathered together the chief of the fathers
of all the people, the priests, and the Levites, unto Ezra the scribe, even to
understand the words of the law.
8:14☆ [14]And they found written in the law which the LORD had commanded by
Lev 23:34, 40, 42 Moses, that the children of Israel should dwell in booths in the feast of the
seventh month:
[15]And that they should publish and proclaim in all their cities, and in
Jerusalem, saying, Go forth unto the mount, and fetch olive branches, and
pine branches, and myrtle branches, and palm branches, and branches of
thick trees, to make booths, as *it is* written.
8:16 [16]¶So the people went forth, and brought *them,* and made themselves
2 Kgs 14:13 Neh 8:1; 12:39 booths, every one upon the roof of his house, and in their courts, and in the
Jer 32:29 courts of the house of God, and in the street of the water gate, and in the
street of the gate of E'phra-im.
8:17 [17]And all the congregation of them that were come again out of the
2 Chron 7:8 8:13; 30:21 captivity made booths, and sat under the booths: for since the days of

8:8 *gave the sense.* The Hebrew language was being rapidly replaced by Aramaic; therefore, some scholars think these verses mean that Ezra's helpers gave the people a *Targum,* a translation of the Hebrew text in Aramaic, which they could understand.
8:9 *Tirshatha,* i.e., "governor." The people wept when they heard the Word of God. But since it was the festival of tabernacles or trumpets, Ezra and Nehemiah enjoined them not to weep. It was a holy day of rejoicing and the time to celebrate the completion of the task of rebuilding the walls of their sacred city.

8:14 From the reading and interpretation of the Word of God, they learned about the tradition of dwelling in booths for the festival they now celebrated. They proceeded to use tree branches to build booths on the rooftops of their houses, in the courts of the house of God, and in the streets. This celebration was comparable to that inaugurated in Joshua's day, when Israel first entered the land. Now they have re-entered the land and this is the first time they celebrated the festival of tabernacles as returnees.

thy law behind their backs, and slew thy prophets which testified against
them to turn them to thee, and they wrought great provocations.
27 Therefore thou deliveredst them into the hand of their enemies, who
vexed them: and in the time of their trouble, when they cried unto thee,
thou heardest *them* from heaven; and according to thy manifold mercies
thou gavest them saviours, who saved them out of the hand of their
enemies.

9:27 Judg 2:16; 1 Sam 12:10, 11; 2 Kgs 13:5

28 But after they had rest, they did evil again before thee: therefore leftest
thou them in the hand of their enemies, so that they had the dominion over
them: yet when they returned, and cried unto thee, thou heardest *them* from
heaven; and many times didst thou deliver them according to thy mercies;
29 And testifiedst against them, that thou mightest bring them again unto
thy law: yet they dealt proudly, and hearkened not unto thy commandments,
but sinned against thy judgments, (which if a man do, he shall live in
them;) and withdrew the shoulder, and hardened their neck, and would not
hear.

9:29 Lev 18:5; Neh 9:26–30; Zech 7:11

30 Yet many years didst thou forbear them, and testifiedst against them by
thy spirit in thy prophets: yet would they not give ear: therefore gavest thou
them into the hand of the people of the lands.

☆**9:30** Neh 9:20

31 Nevertheless for thy great mercies' sake thou didst not utterly consume
them, nor forsake them; for thou *art* a gracious and merciful God.

9:31 Neh 9:17; Jer 4:27

32 Now therefore, our God, the great, the mighty, and the terrible God,
who keepest covenant and mercy, let not all the trouble seem little before
thee, that hath come upon us, on our kings, on our princes, and on our
priests, and on our prophets, and on our fathers, and on all thy people,
since the time of the kings of Assyria unto this day.

9:32 2 Kgs 15:19, 29; 17:3; Isa 7:17, 18

33 Howbeit thou *art* just in all that is brought upon us; for thou hast done
right, but we have done wickedly:

☆**9:33** Gen 18:25; Jer 12:1

34 Neither have our kings, our princes, our priests, nor our fathers, kept
thy law, nor hearkened unto thy commandments and thy testimonies,
wherewith thou didst testify against them.
35 For they have not served thee in their kingdom, and in thy great
goodness that thou gavest them, and in the large and fat land which thou
gavest before them, neither turned they from their wicked works.

9:35 Deut 8:7–10; 32:12–15

36 Behold, we *are* servants this day, and *for* the land that thou gavest unto
our fathers to eat the fruit thereof and the good thereof, behold, we *are*
servants in it:

9:36 Deut 28:48

37 And it yieldeth much increase unto the kings whom thou hast set over
us because of our sins: also they have dominion over our bodies, and over
our cattle, at their pleasure, and we *are* in great distress.
38 And because of all this we make a sure *covenant,* and write *it;* and our
princes, Levites, *and* priests, seal *unto it.*

9:38 1 Kgs 21:8; Neh 10:1, 29

c. *The Signers of the Covenant*

10 NOW those that sealed *were,* Ne-he-mi'ah, the Tir'sha-tha, the son
of Hach-a-li'ah, and Zid-ki'jah,
2 Ser-a-i'ah, Az-a-ri'ah, Jer-e-mi'ah,

10:1 Neh 1:1; 9:38; 12:26

9:30 "Admonished them by thy Spirit through thy prophets" (NASB). The Holy Spirit, then and now, brings conviction of sin. He did his work through the prophets, who spoke what the Holy Spirit wanted said at a time when the full revelation of God had not yet been given. Today the same Spirit speaks through the Word of God and the preaching of that Word by faithful servants. The Spirit and the Word function together to accomplish the divine will and bring us renewal.

9:33 *thou hast done right, but we have done wickedly.* The coming of the New Testament and the complete revelation of God does not mean that what was prayed in Ezra's day is no longer necessary. Believers today also do wickedly and must acknowledge that God has done right. Revival tarries unless and until God's people confess their wickedness, receive forgiveness, and enjoy the fullness of the Holy Spirit.

3 Pash'ur, Am-a-ri'ah, Mal-chi'jah,
4 Hat'tush, Sheb-a-ni'ah, Mal'luch,
5 Ha'rim, Mer'e-moth, O-ba-di'ah,
6 Daniel, Gin'ne-thon, Ba'ruch,
7 Me-shul'lam, A-bi'jah, Mij'a-min,
8 Ma-a-zi'ah, Bil'ga-i, Shem-a-i'ah: these *were* the priests.

10:9 Neh 3:19; 7:43 8:7; 9:4

9 And the Levites: both Jesh'u-a the son of Az-a-ni'ah, Bin'nu-i of the sons of Hen'a-dad, Kad'mi-el;
10 And their brethren, Sheb-a-ni'ah, Ho-di'jah, Kel'i-ta, Pel-a-i'ah, Ha'nan,
11 Mi'cha, Re'hob, Hash-a-bi'ah,
12 Zac'cur, Sher-e-bi'ah, Sheb-a-ni'ah,
13 Ho-di'jah, Ba'ni, Ben'i-nu.
14 The chief of the people; Pa'rosh, Pa'hath–mo'ab, E'lam, Zat'thu, Ba'ni,
15 Bun'ni, Az'gad, Beb'a-i,
16 Ad-o-ni'jah, Big'va-i, A'din,
17 A'ter, Hiz-ki'jah, Az'zur,
18 Ho-di'jah, Ha'shum, Be'zai,
19 Ha'riph, An'a-thoth, Neb'a-i,
20 Mag'pi-ash, Me-shul'lam, He'zir,
21 Me-shez'a-be-el, Za'dok, Jad-du'a,
22 Pel-a-ti'ah, Ha'nan, An-a-i'ah,
23 Ho-she'a, Han-a-ni'ah, Ha'shub,
24 Hal-lo'hesh, Pil'e-ha, Sho'bek,
25 Re'hum, Ha-shab'nah, Ma-a-sei'ah,
26 And A-hi'jah, Ha'nan, A'nan,
27 Mal'luch, Ha'rim, Ba'a-nah.

10:28☆ Neh 9:2

28 ¶And the rest of the people, the priests, the Levites, the porters, the singers, the Neth'i-nims, and all they that had separated themselves from the people of the lands unto the law of God, their wives, their sons, and their daughters, every one having knowledge, and having understanding;

10:29 Neh 5:12

29 They clave to their brethren, their nobles, and entered into a curse, and into an oath, to walk in God's law, which was given by Moses the servant of God, and to observe and do all the commandments of the LORD our Lord, and his judgments and his statutes;

10:30☆ Ex 34:16 Deut 7:3 Ezra 9:1–3, 12–14; 10:10–12

30 And that we would not give our daughters unto the people of the land, nor take their daughters for our sons:

10:31☆ Ex 23:10 Lev 25:1–7 Deut 15:1, 2 Neh 13:15–22

31 And *if* the people of the land bring ware or any victuals on the sabbath day to sell, *that* we would not buy it of them on the sabbath, or on the holy day: and *that* we would leave the seventh year, and the exaction of every debt.

10:32☆ Ex 30:11–16 Mt 17:24

32 Also we made ordinances for us, to charge ourselves yearly with the third part of a shekel for the service of the house of our God;

10:33 Ex 20:8–11 Lev 1:1–17 2:1–16; 6:8–23 23:1–44; 24:5 Num 10:10 28:11–15 Deut 16:1–17 Ezra 3:5

33 For the shewbread, and for the continual meat offering, and for the continual burnt offering, of the sabbaths, of the new moons, for the set feasts, and for the holy *things,* and for the sin offerings to make an atonement for Israel, and *for* all the work of the house of our God.

10:28 *Nethinims,* i.e., "temple servants" for which see note to Ezra 2:43.

10:30 In Ezra the chief sin was intermarriage with heathen women. Here the promise is that the Israelites would neither take heathen women to wife or let Jewish women marry heathen men.

10:31, 32 The Sabbath had no meaning for non-Jews. Here the Jews promise to refrain from commercial activities on the Sabbath and holy days. Why they did not prevent the movement of goods into the city by shutting the gates on the Sabbath is not stated here. In verse 32 they promise also to support the temple by paying a per capita tax of one-third of a shekel. Exod. 30:13 speaks of the tax as a half shekel. Perhaps the people in Nehemiah's day were much poorer.

[34]And we cast the lots among the priests, the Levites, and the people, for
the wood offering, to bring *it* into the house of our God, after the houses of
our fathers, at times appointed year by year, to burn upon the altar of the
LORD our God, as *it is* written in the law:
[35]And to bring the firstfruits of our ground, and the firstfruits of all fruit
of all trees, year by year, unto the house of the LORD:
[36]Also the firstborn of our sons, and of our cattle, as *it is* written in the
law, and the firstlings of our herds and of our flocks, to bring to the house
of our God, unto the priests that minister in the house of our God:
[37]And *that* we should bring the firstfruits of our dough, and our offerings,
and the fruit of all manner of trees, of wine and of oil, unto the priests, to
the chambers of the house of our God; and the tithes of our ground unto
the Levites, that the same Levites might have the tithes in all the cities of
our tillage.
[38]And the priest the son of Aaron shall be with the Levites, when the
Levites take tithes: and the Levites shall bring up the tithe of the tithes unto
the house of our God, to the chambers, into the treasure house.
[39]For the children of Israel and the children of Levi shall bring the
offering of the corn, of the new wine, and the oil, unto the chambers, where
are the vessels of the sanctuary, and the priests that minister, and the
porters, and the singers: and we will not forsake the house of our God.

☆**10:34** Neh 11:1; 13:31
10:35 Ex 23:19; Lev 23:17
10:37 Lev 27:30
☆**10:38** Neh 13:12, 13; 1 Chron 9:26; 2 Chron 31:11, 12

III. NEHEMIAH'S SECOND REFORM (11:1—13:31)

A. REPEOPLING JERUSALEM

11 AND the rulers of the people dwelt at Jerusalem: the rest of the
people also cast lots, to bring one of ten to dwell in Jerusalem the
holy city, and nine parts *to dwell* in *other* cities.
[2]And the people blessed all the men, that willingly offered themselves to
dwell at Jerusalem.

☆**11:1** Neh 7:4; 11:18

B. THE LIST OF THE OFFICIALS WHO SETTLED IN JERUSALEM

[3]¶Now these *are* the chief of the province that dwelt in Jerusalem: but in
the cities of Judah dwelt every one in his possession in their cities, *to wit,*
Israel, the priests, and the Levites, and the Neth'i-nims, and the children of
Solomon's servants.
[4]And at Jerusalem dwelt *certain* of the children of Judah, and of the
children of Benjamin. Of the children of Judah; Ath-a-i'ah the son of Uz-
zi'ah, the son of Zech-a-ri'ah, the son of Am-a-ri'ah, the son of Sheph-a-
ti'ah, the son of Ma-ha'la-le-el, of the children of Pe'rez;
[5]And Ma-a-sei'ah the son of Ba'ruch, the son of Col-ho'zeh, the son of
Ha-zai'ah, the son of Ad-a-i'ah, the son of Joi'a-rib, the son of Zech-a-ri'ah,
the son of Shi-lo'ni.

☆**11:3** 1 Chron 9:2–34; Ezra 2:43–57; 8:2–14; Neh 7:57–59; 11:20

10:34 The wood offering was designed to keep the altar fires burning for the sacrifices.
10:38 *the tithe of the tithes.* In Num. 18:26 God commanded that the Levites, who constituted the priesthood and who were supported by the tithe of the other eleven tribes of Israel, were themselves required to tithe. It was one-tenth of the tenth they received. Thus no one was exempted from returning the tenth to God, the giver of all we have. God plays no favorites; even the ministers of the gospel who live by the gospel have a financial obligation to God. (See note on Mal. 3:8 on tithing and consult Lev. 27:3–33.)
11:1 Jerusalem is here called "the holy city." Due to lack of numbers in the city one-tenth of the people outside its walls were chosen by lot to dwell within the walls of the city. There was nothing to keep people from moving into the city on their own volition. It was to become a much larger city as the years rolled by.
11:3 Beginning with this verse, the names of the families and their numbers who resided in Jerusalem are enumerated.

6 All the sons of Pe'rez that dwelt at Jerusalem *were* four hundred
threescore and eight valiant men.
7 And these *are* the sons of Benjamin; Sal'lu the son of Me-shul'lam, the
son of Jo'ed, the son of Pe-dai'ah, the son of Kol-a-i'ah, the son of Ma-a-
sei'ah, the son of Ith'i-el, the son of Je-sai'ah.
8 And after him Gab'ba-i, Sal'la-i, nine hundred twenty and eight.
9 And Jo'el the son of Zich'ri *was* their overseer: and Judah the son of Se-
nu'ah *was* second over the city.
10 Of the priests: Je-dai'ah the son of Joi'a-rib, Ja'chin.
11 Ser-a-i'ah the son of Hil-ki'ah, the son of Me-shul'lam, the son of
Za'dok, the son of Me-rai'oth, the son of A-hi'tub, *was* the ruler of the
house of God.
12 And their brethren that did the work of the house *were* eight hundred
twenty and two: and Ad-a-i'ah the son of Jer'o-ham, the son of Pel-a-li'ah,
the son of Am'zi, the son of Zech-a-ri'ah, the son of Pash'ur, the son of
Mal-chi'ah,
13 And his brethren, chief of the fathers, two hundred forty and two: and
A-mash'a-i the son of A-zar'e-el, the son of A-has'a-i, the son of Me-shil'le-
moth, the son of Im'mer,
14 And their brethren, mighty men of valour, an hundred twenty and
eight: and their overseer *was* Zab'di-el, the son of *one of* the great men.
11:15 15 Also of the Levites: Shem-a-i'ah the son of Ha'shub, the son of Az'ri-
1 Chron 26:29–32 kam, the son of Hash-a-bi'ah, the son of Bun'ni;
16 And Shab'be-thai and Joz'a-bad, of the chief of the Levites, *had* the
oversight of the outward business of the house of God.
17 And Mat-ta-ni'ah the son of Mi'cha, the son of Zab'di, the son of
A'saph, *was* the principal to begin the thanksgiving in prayer: and Bak-buk-
i'ah the second among his brethren, and Ab'da the son of Sham-mu'a, the
son of Ga'lal, the son of Jed'u-thun.
11:18 Neh 11:3 18 All the Levites in the holy city *were* two hundred fourscore and four.
11:19 2 Chron 27:3 33:14 19 Moreover the porters, Ak'kub, Tal'mon, and their brethren that kept
the gates, *were* an hundred seventy and two.
Neh 3:26, 27 20 ¶And the residue of Israel, of the priests, *and* the Levites, *were* in all the
cities of Judah, every one in his inheritance.
21 But the Neth'i-nims dwelt in O'phel: and Zi'ha and Gis'pa *were* over
the Neth'i-nims.
11:22 22 The overseer also of the Levites at Jerusalem *was* Uz'zi the son of Ba'ni,
1 Chron 9:33 25:1–6 the son of Hash-a-bi'ah, the son of Mat-ta-ni'ah, the son of Mi'cha. Of the
Ezra 3:10; 6:8 7:20 sons of A'saph, the singers *were* over the business of the house of God.
Neh 11:17 12:46 23 For *it was* the king's commandment concerning them, that a certain
portion should be for the singers, due for every day.
24 And Peth-a-hi'ah the son of Me-shez'a-be-el, of the children of Ze'rah
the son of Judah, *was* at the king's hand in all matters concerning the
people.

C. SETTLING THE VILLAGES SURROUNDING JERUSALEM

11:25☆ 25 And for the villages, with their fields, *some* of the children of Judah
Josh 13:9, 17 14:15; 15:31 dwelt at Kir'jath–ar'ba, and *in* the villages thereof, and at Di'bon, and *in*
1 Sam 27:6 the villages thereof, and at Je-kab'ze-el, and *in* the villages thereof,
26 And at Jesh'u-a, and at Mol'a-dah, and at Beth–phe'let,

11:25 Beginning here, the towns outside Jerusalem inhabited by Judeans and Benjaminites are enumerated. *with their fields* probably refers to the lands outside the towns which were used for a variety of agricultural and pastoral purposes.

[27]And at Ha'zar–shu'al, and at Be'er–she'ba, and *in* the villages thereof,
[28]And at Ziklag, and at Mek'o-nah, and in the villages thereof,
[29]And at En–rim'mon, and at Za're-ah, and at Jar'muth,
[30]Za-no'ah, A-dul'lam, and *in* their villages, at La'chish, and the fields
thereof, at A-ze'kah, and *in* the villages thereof. And they dwelt from Be'er–
she'ba unto the valley of Hin'nom.
[31]The children also of Benjamin from Ge'ba *dwelt* at Mich'mash, and
A-i'ja, and Beth–el, and *in* their villages,
[32]*And* at An'a-thoth, Nob, An-a-ni'ah,
[33]Ha'zor, Ra'mah, Git'ta-im.
[34]Ha'did, Ze-bo'im, Ne-bal'lat,
[35]Lod, and O'no, the valley of craftsmen.
[36]And of the Levites *were* divisions *in* Judah, *and* in Benjamin.

11:31 Gen 28:19 Josh 18:13 1 Chron 4:14 8:12 Neh 6:2

D. THE GENEALOGIES OF THE PRIESTS AND LEVITES

12 NOW these *are* the priests and the Levites that went up with Ze-
rub'ba-bel the son of She-al'ti-el, and Jesh'u-a: Ser-a-i'ah, Jer-e-
mi'ah, Ezra,
[2]Am-a-ri'ah, Mal'luch, Hat'tush,
[3]Shech-a-ni'ah, Re'hum, Mer'e-moth,
[4]Id'do, Gin'ne-tho, A-bi'jah,
[5]Mi'a-min, Ma-a-di'ah, Bil'gah,
[6]Shem-a-i'ah, and Joi'a-rib, Je-dai'ah,
[7]Sal'lu, A'mok, Hil-ki'ah, Je-dai'ah. These *were* the chief of the priests
and of their brethren in the days of Jesh'u-a.
[8]Moreover the Levites: Jesh'u-a, Bin'nu-i, Kad'mi-el, Sher-e-bi'ah,
Judah, *and* Mat-ta-ni'ah, *which was* over the thanksgiving, he and his
brethren.
[9]Also Bak-buk-i'ah and Un'ni, their brethren, *were* over against them in
the watches.
[10]¶And Jesh'u-a begat Joi'a-kim, Joi'a-kim also begat E-li'a-shib, and
E-li'a-shib begat Joi'a-da,
[11]And Joi'a-da begat Jonathan, and Jonathan begat Jad-du'a.
[12]And in the days of Joi'a-kim were priests, the chief of the fathers: of
Ser-a-i'ah, Mer-a-i'ah; of Jer-e-mi'ah, Han-a-ni'ah;
[13]Of Ezra, Me-shul'lam; of Am-a-ri'ah, Je-ho-ha'nan;
[14]Of Mel'i-cu, Jonathan; of Sheb-a-ni'ah, Joseph;
[15]Of Ha'rim, Ad'na; of Me-rai'oth, Hel'ka-i;
[16]Of Id'do, Zech-a-ri'ah; of Gin'ne-thon, Me-shul'lam;
[17]Of A-bi'jah, Zich'ri; of Min'i-a-min, of Mo-a-di'ah, Pil'tai;
[18]Of Bil'gah, Sham-mu'a; of Shem-a-i'ah, Je-hon'a-than;
[19]And of Joi'a-rib, Mat-te-na'i; of Je-dai'ah, Uz'zi;
[20]Of Sal'la-i, Kal'la-i; of A'mok, E'ber;
[21]Of Hil-ki'ah, Hash-a-bi'ah; of Je-dai'ah, Ne-than'e-el.

☆**12:1** Ezra 2:36–39 Neh 7:39–42

☆**12:10** Ezra 2:2; 7:1–5 Neh 7:7

☆**12:11**

☆**12:16**

12:1 Beginning here, names of priests and Levites are listed. For what purpose they were inscribed is not stated here.

12:10, 11 Herein is listed the succession of high priests during the Persian monarchy from Jeshua (or, Jesus) to Jaddua (or, Jaddus), who was the high priest at the time Alexander the Great came to Jerusalem after his conquest of Tyre. Alexander is said to have paid him his respects, and he also showed Jaddua the prophecy of Daniel in which his conquests were foretold. *Jonathan* is probably a scribal error for *Johanan* (12:22, 23).

12:16 *Zechariah.* Iddo, his grandfather, (12:4) came back from the captivity with Zerubbabel and Joshua. Zechariah the priest was the author of the book of Zechariah, which contains more prophecies about the Messiah than any other Old Testament book except Psalms and Isaiah. Berechiah, the father of Zechariah, probably died young so that his son became the immediate successor to Iddo the grandfather.

12:22☆ 1 Chron 9:1–44; Ezra 4:5, 24; 5:5; 6:1–15; 8:2–14
12:23 Josh 10:13; 1 Sam 10:25; 1 Chron 29:29; Esth 6:1; 9:32; Jer 32:12
12:24 Neh 11:15

22¶The Levites in the days of E-li'a-shib, Joi'a-da, and Jo-ha'nan, and
Jad-du'a, *were* recorded chief of the fathers: also the priests, to the reign of
Darius the Persian.
23The sons of Levi, the chief of the fathers, *were* written in the book of the
chronicles, even until the days of Jo-ha'nan the son of E-li'a-shib.
24And the chief of the Levites: Hash-a-bi'ah, Sher-e-bi'ah, and Jesh'u-a
the son of Kad'mi-el, with their brethren over against them, to praise *and* to
give thanks, according to the commandment of David the man of God,
ward over against ward.

12:25 1 Chron 26:15
12:26 Neh 1:1; 10:1

25Mat-ta-ni'ah, and Bak-buk-i'ah, O-ba-di'ah, Me-shul'lam, Tal'mon,
Ak'kub, *were* porters keeping the ward at the thresholds of the gates.
26These *were* in the days of Joi'a-kim the son of Jesh'u-a, the son of Joz'a-
dak, and in the days of Ne-he-mi'ah the governor, and of Ezra the priest,
the scribe.

E. THE DEDICATION OF THE NEW JERUSALEM WALL

12:27☆ 1 Chron 15:16, 28; Ezra 3:10, 11
12:28 1 Chron 2:54; 9:16

27¶And at the dedication of the wall of Jerusalem they sought the Levites
out of all their places, to bring them to Jerusalem, to keep the dedication
with gladness, both with thanksgivings, and with singing, *with* cymbals,
psalteries, and with harps.
28And the sons of the singers gathered themselves together, both out of
the plain country round about Jerusalem, and from the villages of Ne-
toph'a-thi;
29Also from the house of Gilgal, and out of the fields of Ge'ba and
Az'ma-veth: for the singers had builded them villages round about
Jerusalem.

12:30 Ezra 10:11; Neh 10:28; 13:22, 30
12:31☆ Neh 2:13; 3:13, 14

30And the priests and the Levites purified themselves, and purified the
people, and the gates, and the wall.
31Then I brought up the princes of Judah upon the wall, and appointed
two great *companies of them that gave* thanks, *whereof one* went on the right
hand upon the wall toward the dung gate:
32And after them went Hosh-a-i'ah, and half of the princes of Judah,
33And Az-a-ri'ah, Ezra, and Me-shul'lam,
34Judah, and Benjamin, and Shem-a-i'ah, and Jer-e-mi'ah.

12:35☆ Neh 12:28
12:36☆

35And *certain* of the priests' sons with trumpets; *namely,* Zech-a-ri'ah the
son of Jonathan, the son of Shem-a-i'ah, the son of Mat-ta-ni'ah, the son of
Mi-chai'ah, the son of Zac'cur, the son A'saph:
36And his brethren, Shem-a-i'ah, and A-zar'a-el, Mil-a-la'i, Gil'a-lai, Ma-

---

12:22 *Eliashib* was the grandson of Joshua, the high priest. He allied himself with Tobiah, who joined company with Sanballat and others who opposed the work of Nehemiah. Tobiah and his son both married Jewish women. Basically Eliashib was unfaithful to his calling, for he supplied Tobiah with a guest room in the temple compound (see note to 13:4). *Jaddua* was a high priest during the reign of Darius the Persian. He probably was the one to whom Josephus made reference in the account of Alexander the Great's entry into Jerusalem. He is not to be confused with the Jaddua of 10:21, who was one of the Jewish princes who signed Nehemiah's covenant.

12:27 *the dedication of the wall.* The construction was accomplished with fear and trembling; now it is dedicated with a sense of joy and triumph. Probably the dedication included the entire city, which was now safely enclosed. It was God's city, possessed by him, and holy unto the Lord. By this act the city was placed under divine protection. Every person and thing was purified (12:30) so that all was presented without spot or blemish.

12:31 Two companies walked on the top of the walls of the city, one group led by Ezra and the other by Nehemiah. They went in opposite directions and met at the place where the temple stood. The people walked on the ground inside and outside the city walls. All joined together at the temple to rejoice and to voice their thanksgiving to God. Songs of praise, the music from instruments, and the shouts of the crowd filled the air. "The wives also and the children rejoiced" (12:43). Sacrifices were offered as a climax to the celebration.

12:35, 36 Ezra and Nehemiah were co-workers for a time, with Nehemiah as governor and Ezra as priest.

a'i, Ne-than'e-el, and Judah, Ha-na'ni, with the musical instruments of
David the man of God, and Ezra the scribe before them.
37 And at the fountain gate, which was over against them, they went up by
the stairs of the city of David, at the going up of the wall, above the house
of David, even unto the water gate eastward.
38 And the other *company of them that gave* thanks went over against *them,*
and I after them, and the half of the people upon the wall, from beyond the
tower of the furnaces even unto the broad wall;
39 And from above the gate of E'phra-im, and above the old gate, and
above the fish gate, and the tower of Ha-nan'e-el, and the tower of Me'ah,
even unto the sheep gate: and they stood still in the prison gate.
40 So stood the two *companies of them that gave* thanks in the house of
God, and I, and the half of the rulers with me:
41 And the priests; E-li'a-kim, Ma-a-sei'ah, Min'i-a-min, Mi-chai'ah, E-li-
o-e'na-i, Zech-a-ri'ah, *and* Han-a-ni'ah, with trumpets;
42 And Ma-a-sei'ah, and Shem-a-i'ah, and E-le-a'zar, and Uz'zi, and Je-
ho-ha'nan, and Mal-chi'jah, and E'lam, and E'zer. And the singers sang
loud, with Jez-ra-hi'ah *their* overseer.
43 Also that day they offered great sacrifices, and rejoiced: for God had
made them rejoice with great joy: the wives also and the children rejoiced:
so that the joy of Jerusalem was heard even afar off.

12:37 2 Sam 5:7–9; Neh 2:14; 3:15, 26; 8:1, 3, 16
12:38 Neh 3:8, 11
12:39 2 Kgs 14:13; Neh 3:1, 3, 6, 25, 31, 32; 8:16; Jer 31:38

F. APPOINTING THE COLLECTORS, SINGERS, AND GATEKEEPERS

44 ¶And at that time were some appointed over the chambers for the
treasures, for the offerings, for the firstfruits, and for the tithes, to gather
into them out of the fields of the cities the portions of the law for the priests
and Levites: for Judah rejoiced for the priests and for the Levites that
waited.
45 And both the singers and the porters kept the ward of their God, and
the ward of the purification, according to the commandment of David, *and*
of Solomon his son.
46 For in the days of David and A'saph of old *there were* chief of the
singers, and songs of praise and thanksgiving unto God.
47 And all Israel in the days of Ze-rub'ba-bel, and in the days of Ne-he-
mi'ah, gave the portions of the singers and the porters, every day his
portion: and they sanctified *holy things* unto the Levites; and the Levites
sanctified *them* unto the children of Aaron.

12:44 Ex 29:26–28; Lev 7:29–34; 23:20; 27:30–33; Deut 26:3–10; Neh 10:35–39; Neh 13:5, 12, 13
12:45 1 Chron 25:1–8; 26:1–32
12:46 1 Chron 25:1, 7; 26:1; 2 Chron 29:30; Neh 11:23
12:47 Num 18:21–29

G. THE LAST OF NEHEMIAH'S REFORMS
1. The Expulsion of the Foreigners

13 ON that day they read in the book of Moses in the audience of the
people; and therein was found written, that the Ammonite and the
Moabite should not come into the congregation of God for ever;
2 Because they met not the children of Israel with bread and with water,
but hired Ba'laam against them, that he should curse them: howbeit our
God turned the curse into a blessing.
3 Now it came to pass, when they had heard the law, that they separated
from Israel all the mixed multitude.

☆**13:1** Deut 23:3–5; Neh 13:23
☆**13:2** Num 22:3–11
☆**13:3** Ezra 10:11; Neh 9:2; 10:28

13:1 According to Deut. 23:3–5, no Ammonite or Moabite could enter the Temple.
13:2 *hired Balaam* [to] . . . *curse them.* See Num. 22:6.
13:3 The "mixed multitude" comprised those of Samaritan blood, who were not counted as Jews. A separation of the non-Jews from the Jews was effected in obedience to the command of God in the Torah. This action by no means solved the problem permanently (13:23).

2. The Removal of Tobiah's Furnishings from the Temple

13:4☆ Neh 6:17–19 12:44 4¶And before this, E-li'a-shib the priest, having the oversight of the
chamber of the house of our God, *was* allied unto To-bi'ah:
13:5☆ Neh 2:10 6:1, 17, 18; 13:7 5And he had prepared for him a great chamber, where aforetime they laid
the meat offerings, the frankincense, and the vessels, and the tithes of the
corn, the new wine, and the oil, which was commanded *to be given* to the
Levites, and the singers, and the porters; and the offerings of the priests.
13:6☆ Ezra 4:11 7:1, 11, 12, 21 Neh 1:1; 5:14 6But in all this *time* was not I at Jerusalem: for in the two and thirtieth
year of Ar-ta-xer'xes king of Babylon came I unto the king, and after
certain days obtained I leave of the king:
13:7☆ Neh 13:5 7And I came to Jerusalem, and understood of the evil that E-li'a-shib did
for To-bi'ah, in preparing him a chamber in the courts of the house of God.
13:8☆ 8And it grieved me sore: therefore I cast forth all the household stuff of
To-bi'ah out of the chamber.
13:9☆ 2 Chron 29:5, 15–19 9Then I commanded, and they cleansed the chambers: and thither
brought I again the vessels of the house of God, with the meat offering and
the frankincense.

3. The Support of the Levites Begun Again

13:10☆ Neh 12:28, 29 10¶And I perceived that the portions of the Levites had not been given
them: for the Levites and the singers, that did the work, were fled every one
to his field.
11Then contended I with the rulers, and said, Why is the house of God
forsaken? And I gathered them together, and set them in their place.
13:12 Neh 10:37 12:44 12Then brought all Judah the tithe of the corn and the new wine and the
oil unto the treasuries.
13:13 Neh 7:2 13And I made treasurers over the treasuries, Shel-e-mi'ah the priest, and
Za'dok the scribe, and of the Levites, Pe-dai'ah: and next to them *was*
Ha'nan the son of Zac'cur, the son of Mat-ta-ni'ah: for they were counted
faithful, and their office *was* to distribute unto their brethren.
13:14☆ 14Remember me, O my God, concerning this, and wipe not out my good
deeds that I have done for the house of my God, and for the offices thereof.

4. Sabbath Reforms Begun

13:15☆ Ex 20:8–11 34:21 Neh 13:21 15In those days saw I in Judah *some* treading wine presses on the sabbath,
and bringing in sheaves, and lading asses; as also wine, grapes, and figs,
and all *manner of* burdens, which they brought into Jerusalem on the
sabbath day: and I testified *against them* in the day wherein they sold
victuals.

13:4–9 Eliashib provided Tobiah (an Ammonite) a room in the temple compound, in the absence of Nehemiah, who had returned to the court of King Artaxerxes for a short time. Had he been there he might have prevented this incursion. Upon his return Nehemiah saw what had been done; he acted promptly and vigorously. He ejected Tobiah and his effects. Eliashib was a base and faithless high priest who defiled the sacred site by his wrongful acts. Nehemiah had the room Tobiah occupied sprinkled with the water of purification and so reclaimed its sanctity.

13:10 Nehemiah also discovered that the Levites had been wronged, for their portions ("salaries") had not been paid them. Apparently their portions had been collected but not given to the Levites. Nehemiah corrected this evil. Four reliable treasurers were appointed to oversee the payments. How quickly subordinates are likely to fail in their duties when the voice of the master is absent!

13:14 As is typical of his devotion to God and his commandments, Nehemiah calls on his God to remember what he had done, but not for the purpose of reward; he was pure of heart and faithful to duty when others failed.

13:15 Three of the major and recurring sins of Israel were (1) breaking of the sabbath (Num. 15:32–36; Neh. 13:17, 18; Isa. 58:13, 14; Ezek. 20:13; 22:8), (2) contracting marriage with the heathen (13:23–25; 1 Kings 11:1, 2; Deut. 7:3, 4), (3) worshipping of idols (1 Kings 21:26; 2 Kings 17:12; Ezek. 6:1–5; Zech. 13:2). These national sins could not be overlooked. They had to be dealt with if Israel was to carry out its mission.

16There dwelt men of Tyre also therein, which brought fish, and all
manner of ware, and sold on the sabbath unto the children of Judah, and in
Jerusalem.
17Then I contended with the nobles of Judah, and said unto them, What
evil thing *is* this that ye do, and profane the sabbath day?
18Did not your fathers thus, and did not our God bring all this evil upon
us, and upon this city? yet ye bring more wrath upon Israel by profaning
the sabbath.
19And it came to pass, that when the gates of Jerusalem began to be dark
before the sabbath, I commanded that the gates should be shut, and
charged that they should not be opened till after the sabbath: and *some* of
my servants set I at the gates, *that* there should no burden be brought in on
the sabbath day.
20So the merchants and sellers of all kind of ware lodged without
Jerusalem once or twice.
21Then I testified against them, and said unto them, Why lodge ye about
the wall? if ye do *so* again, I will lay hands on you. From that time forth
came they no *more* on the sabbath.
22And I commanded the Levites that they should cleanse themselves, and
that they should come *and* keep the gates, to sanctify the sabbath day.
Remember me, O my God, *concerning* this also, and spare me according to
the greatness of thy mercy.

☆**13:19** Lev 23:32

13:22 1 Chron 15:12; Neh 12:30

5. Mixed Marriages Dealt With

23In those days also saw I Jews *that* had married wives of Ash'dod, of
Ammon, *and* of Moab:
24And their children spake half in the speech of Ash'dod, and could not
speak in the Jews' language, but according to the language of each people.
25And I contended with them, and cursed them, and smote certain of
them, and plucked off their hair, and made them swear by God, *saying,* Ye
shall not give your daughters unto their sons, nor take their daughters unto
your sons, or for yourselves.
26Did not Solomon king of Israel sin by these things? yet among many
nations was there no king like him, who was beloved of his God, and God
made him king over all Israel: nevertheless even him did outlandish women
cause to sin.
27Shall we then hearken unto you to do all this great evil, to transgress
against our God in marrying strange wives?

13:23 Neh 10:30

☆**13:24** 2 Kgs 18:26, 28; Ezra 4:7; 9:2; Isa 19:18; 36:11; Dan 2:4; Zeph 3:9

☆**13:25** Deut 25:2; Neh 10:29, 30; 13:11, 17,

13:26 1 Kgs 11:1–8

13:19 Until this point, the gates of the city had been open on the Sabbath. Now that the sabbath has been desecrated, more severe action is required: the gates are to be shut from sundown Friday to sundown Saturday. But this did not keep faithless Jews and non-Jews from hawking their wares outside the walls of the city on the sabbath. Nehemiah threatened to lay hands on any who acted this way on the sabbath. This again illustrates the principle that laws exist for the sake of the wicked and are enacted to prevent improper acts. Today, the profanation of the Christian sabbath (Sunday) is so widespread that little attention is paid to something God may regard as contrary to his will.

13:24 Language is a unifying force among people. When God confused the tongues of men at Babel, his purpose was to disunify men. Here we see that some Jews had married women who taught their offspring their own languages instead of Hebrew. This prevented the offspring from hearing and understanding the Word of God, which was spoken and read in the Hebrew tongue. At this time there were no translations of the Word of God into other languages. The real solution to this problem was simply not to marry heathen women; marrying them, then teaching them the Hebrew tongue, provided no guarantee that they would turn to God in true faith.

13:25 Nehemiah did not hesitate to use police force to curb wrongful intermarriage with the heathen. He cursed them, pulled out their hair, beat them, and made them swear not to allow sons or daughters to engage in mixed marriages. Strong medicine is required to stop contagious disease.

13:28☆ Num 25:13 Neh 2:10, 19
[28] And *one* of the sons of Joi'a-da, the son of E-li'a-shib the high priest,
was son in law to San-bal'lat the Hor'o-nite: therefore I chased him from
me.
[29] Remember them, O my God, because they have defiled the priesthood,
and the covenant of the priesthood, and of the Levites.

6. The Summary

13:30 Neh 10:30
[30] Thus cleansed I them from all strangers, and appointed the wards of
the priests and the Levites, every one in his business;
13:31 Neh 10:34 13:14, 22
[31] And for the wood offering, at times appointed, and for the firstfruits.
Remember me, O my God, for good.

13:28 A grandson of the high priest had married a daughter of Sanballat, who was a well-known enemy of the Jews. When this young priest would not put away his wife, Nehemiah expelled him from the priesthood. According to Josephus, the man in question was Manasseh, whose father-in-law, Sanballat, then built a temple on Mount Gerazim and made him its high priest. This laid the foundation for Samaritan pretensions of having true religion, even in Jesus' day (see John 4).

THE BOOK OF
ESTHER

Authorship, date, and background Who authored the book of Esther is unknown. Tradition has accorded this role to Mordecai or Ezra or Nehemiah. The latter two are hardly credible possibilities when any survey of the books attributed to them is compared with Esther. The name Esther is derived from a Persian word meaning "star"; her Hebrew name, Hadassah, means "Myrtle." The book itself is the last of the five books of the Megilloth (Five Scrolls) which include Ruth, Song of Solomon, Ecclesiastes, and Lamentations. Esther is thought to be the greatest of them all.

The writer of this book knew a great deal about Persian life and customs. The setting was the king's palace in Shushan (Susa), which was the Persian capital. The incident occurred during the reign of Xerxes (the Greek rendering of his name) or Ahasuerus as recorded in Esther. Ahasuerus or Xerxes died in 465 B.C., so scholars have dated the composition of the book somewhere in the latter half of the fifth century. This means that the Jews involved in the incident were the ones who had not returned to Jerusalem with the first remnant. They had either lost their attachment to the faith of their fathers, or had been so successful that they preferred remaining in their new environment.

Mordecai (whose name had a Babylonian equivalent of *Mardukaia*) was Esther's guardian. She was his Uncle Abihail's daughter whom Mordecai adopted. He occupied a position of importance in the Persian court. Nothing is known about his own spiritual commitment. He was a strong nationalist, a brave man, and one who kept his Jewish identity hidden for what may have been opportunistic reasons.

Characteristics and content Nowhere in the book of Esther does the author mention the name of God. Fasting, which always includes prayer, is part of the story. In any event, the hand of a sovereign God at work in the lives of his people is everywhere evident. The book speaks of the Feast of Purim (the word Purim comes from the term *puru,* meaning *lot,* found in Assyrian inscriptions), which marks the deliverance of the Jews from extinction. Ahasuerus' wife, Vashti, refuses to make a public appearance before the males of the kingdom at a drunken revelry. She is demoted from her queenship and a successor is sought for her. Esther is chosen. Later Haman, in anger over the refusal of Mordecai to bow before him, plans the massacre of all the Jews. The king assents.

When Mordecai learns of the plot, he seeks the help of Esther, asking her to intercede with the king. She willingly risks her life by entering the king's presence without being summoned. She arranges a first and second banquet with the king, herself, and Haman. Between the first and second banquet, Haman prepares the gallows on which to hang Mordecai. Before this comes about, Mordecai discovers a plot against the king's life which he reports and the assassins are apprehended and executed. Mordecai goes unrewarded.

As the story reaches its climax, Haman has gained the king's unchanging commitment to execute all Jews. When Haman hears his plot disclosed to Ahasuerus by Esther, he pleads with her after the king has left the room. The king upon his return finds Haman on the couch of his queen and interprets it as an assault upon his wife. He orders Haman to be hanged on the gallows prepared for Mordecai. Mordecai takes over the vacant position of Haman. Orders are given for the Jews to defend themselves when the day of reckoning comes, since the king's edict cannot be annulled. The Jews successfully defend themselves. Mordecai ends up as Prime Minister next to King Ahasuerus, "great among the Jews, and accepted of the multitude of his brethren, seeking the wealth of his people, and speaking peace to all his seed" (10:3). The Feast of Purim is instituted as a reminder of God's great deliverance of his people.

Outline

I. Intrigues in Ahasuerus' court at Shushan (1:1—2:23)
II. Haman's plot against the Jews (3:1—5:14)
III. The victory of the Jews (6:1—10:3)

I. INTRIGUES IN AHASUERUS' COURT AT SHUSHAN (1:1—2:23)

A. AHASUERUS' GREAT BANQUET

1:1☆ Ezra 1:2; 4:6 Neh 1:2 Esth 2:1, 3, 12–14; 3:5–12, 15; 8:9, 10; 9:12–15, 29–31 Isa 37:8, 9 Dan 5:28; 8:2; 9:1
1:2☆
1:4☆

1 NOW it came to pass in the days of A-has-u-e'rus, (this *is* A-has-u-
e'rus which reigned, from India even unto E-thi-o'pi-a, *over* an
hundred and seven and twenty provinces:)
2 *That* in those days, when the king A-has-u-e'rus sat on the throne of his
kingdom, which *was* in Shu'shan the palace,
3 In the third year of his reign, he made a feast unto all his princes and his
servants; the power of Persia and Me'di-a, the nobles and princes of the
provinces, *being* before him:
4 When he shewed the riches of his glorious kingdom and the honour of
his excellent majesty many days, *even* an hundred and fourscore days.

1:5 Esth 7:7, 8

5 And when these days were expired, the king made a feast unto all the
people that were present in Shu'shan the palace, both unto great and small,
seven days, in the court of the garden of the king's palace;
6 *Where were* white, green, and blue, *hangings,* fastened with cords of fine
linen and purple to silver rings and pillars of marble: the beds *were of* gold
and silver, upon a pavement of red, and blue, and white, and black, marble.

1:7 Esth 2:18

7 And they gave *them* drink in vessels of gold, (the vessels being diverse
one from another,) and royal wine in abundance, according to the state of
the king.
8 And the drinking *was* according to the law; none did compel: for so the
king had appointed to all the officers of his house, that they should do
according to every man's pleasure.

1:9 Esth 1:11, 12, 16–19; 2:1, 4

9 Also Vash'ti the queen made a feast for the women *in* the royal house
which *belonged* to king A-has-u-e'rus.

B. THE DEMOTION OF QUEEN VASHTI

1. Queen Vashti's Refusal

1:10☆ Judg 16:25 Esth 2:21; 6:2 Dan 1:3–5, 18, 19

10 ¶On the seventh day, when the heart of the king was merry with wine,
he commanded Me-hu'man, Biz'tha, Har-bo'na, Big'tha, and A-bag'tha,
Ze'thar, and Car'cas, the seven chamberlains that served in the presence of
A-has-u-e'rus the king,
11 To bring Vash'ti the queen before the king with the crown royal, to
shew the people and the princes her beauty: for she *was* fair to look on.
12 But the queen Vash'ti refused to come at the king's commandment by

---

1:1 *Ahasuerus,* identified as Xerxes (486–465 B.C.).
1:2 *Shushan* (Susa) was the capital of Xerxes' empire. It was located in Iran near the Persian Gulf. The palace was opulently appointed, as we learn from the account in Esther. In later history it became one of Alexander's prized acquisitions. It was here that a mass marriage of royal Persian women and Greek army officers was performed. The site has been excavated by French archeologists since the middle of the nineteenth century.
1:4 Ahasuerus (Xerxes) had but one purpose in arranging the feast. He wanted to show the wealth of his holdings and the honor of his majesty. There were two feasts, one for the nobility and the other for the common people. The feast for the nobility lasted for six months; the one for the people "great and small" lasted a week. It was at this feast that the incident occurred that ultimately brought Esther to the royal throne, as wife of the monarch.
1:10ff At the end of the seventh day of the second feast, the king was drunk. So were the guests. He summoned his queen to appear before this multitude of men whose wives were not present—for women were sequestered from appearing in public. The honor of Vashti was at stake. She either had to lose her honor or disobey her husband, who was king. Ahasuerus wanted to parade the beauty of his wife before the multitude, and this could not be done unless she was unveiled. Had the king been sober he would never have done this, nor would he have endorsed such conduct by anyone else. Vashti's refusal to debase herself may have been stated unwisely. Josephus alleges that the messengers were sent again and again. Repeated refusals by Vashti angered the king, whose authority was at stake. Ahasuerus asked the question, What should be done to the queen who refused to obey the command of the king?

his chamberlains: therefore was the king very wroth, and his anger burned
in him.
13¶Then the king said to the wise men, which knew the times, (for so *was*
the king's manner toward all that knew law and judgment:
14And the next unto him *was* Car-she'na, She'thar, Ad'ma-tha, Tarshish,
Me'res, Mar'se-na, *and* Me-mu'can, the seven princes of Persia and Me'-
di-a, which saw the king's face, *and* which sat the first in the kingdom;)
15What shall we do unto the queen Vash'ti according to law because she
hath not performed the commandment of the king A-has-u-e'rus by the
chamberlains?

1:13 Ezra 7:14; Esth 1:16

2. Queen Vashti Dethroned

16And Me-mu'can answered before the king and princes, Vash'ti the
queen hath not done wrong to the king only, but also to all the princes, and
to all the people that *are* in all the provinces of the king A-has-u-e'rus.
17For *this* deed of the queen shall come abroad unto all women, so that
they shall despise their husbands in their eyes, when it shall be reported,
The king A-has-u-e'rus commanded Vash'ti the queen to be brought in
before him, but she came not.
18*Likewise* shall the ladies of Persia and Me'di-a say this day unto all the
king's princes, which have heard of the deed of the queen. Thus *shall there
arise* too much contempt and wrath.
19If it please the king, let there go a royal commandment from him, and
let it be written among the laws of the Persians and the Medes, that it be
not altered, That Vash'ti come no more before king A-has-u-e'rus; and let
the king give her royal estate unto another that is better than she.
20And when the king's decree which he shall make shall be published
throughout all his empire, (for it is great,) all the wives shall give to their
husbands honour, both to great and small.
21And the saying pleased the king and the princes; and the king did
according to the word of Me-mu'can:
22For he sent letters into all the king's provinces, into every province
according to the writing thereof, and to every people after their language,
that every man should bear rule in his own house, and that *it* should be
published according to the language of every people.

☆**1:16** Esth 1:9; 13

☆**1:19** Esth 8:8; Dan 6:8–15, 17

1:20 Eph 5:33; Col 3:18; 1 Pet 3:1–7

1:21 Esth 1:13, 16

1:22 Esth 3:12; 8:9, 10

C. ESTHER CHOSEN AS QUEEN

1. The Hunt for a Queen

2 AFTER these things, when the wrath of king A-has-u-e'rus was
appeased, he remembered Vash'ti, and what she had done, and what
was decreed against her.
2Then said the king's servants that ministered unto him, Let there be fair
young virgins sought for the king:
3And let the king appoint officers in all the provinces of his kingdom,
that they may gather together all the fair young virgins unto Shu'shan the
palace, to the house of the women, unto the custody of He'ge the king's
chamberlain, keeper of the women; and let their things for purification be
given *them:*

2:1 Esth 1:9

☆**2:2**

2:3 Esth 1:1–3; 2:9, 15

1:16 In a segregated society where the females were decidedly unequal, one could expect what happened. Her act was turned into a national crisis involving male supremacy. Vashti was removed from her queenship. Nothing is said as to what ultimately was done to her except that she was never to appear before the king again.

1:19 *that it be not altered,* a notion of immutability expressed in 8:8 and in Dan. 6:8.

2:2 The removal of Vashti required the appointment of a new queen. The servants of the king initiated a search for the most beautiful women from among whom the king would choose another queen. Esther was to be one of those chosen for consideration.

4 And let the maiden which pleaseth the king be queen instead of Vash'ti. And the thing pleased the king; and he did so.

2. Esther's Ancestry

2:5☆ Esth 3:2–6; 10:3
5 ¶*Now* in Shu'shan the palace there was a certain Jew, whose name *was* Mor'de-cai, the son of Ja'ir, the son of Shim'e-i, the son of Kish, a Benjamite;

2:6 2 Kgs 24:14, 15 2 Chron 36:17–20
6 Who had been carried away from Jerusalem with the captivity which had been carried away with Jec-o-ni'ah king of Judah, whom Neb-u-chad-nez'zar the king of Babylon had carried away.

2:7☆ Dan 1:6, 7
7 And he brought up Ha-das'sah, that *is,* Esther, his uncle's daughter: for she had neither father nor mother, and the maid *was* fair and beautiful; whom Mor'de-cai, when her father and mother were dead, took for his own daughter.

2:8☆
8 ¶So it came to pass, when the king's commandment and his decree was heard, and when many maidens were gathered together unto Shu'shan the palace, to the custody of Heg'a-i, that Esther was brought also unto the king's house, to the custody of Heg'a-i, keeper of the women.

9 And the maiden pleased him, and she obtained kindness of him; and he speedily gave her her things for purification, with such things as belonged to her, and seven maidens, *which were* meet to be given her, out of the king's house: and he preferred her and her maids unto the best *place* of the house of the women.

2:10 Esth 2:20
10 Esther had not shewed her people nor her kindred: for Mor'de-cai had charged her that she should not shew *it.*

11 And Mor'de-cai walked every day before the court of the women's house, to know how Esther did, and what should become of her.

3. Esther Chosen to Be Queen

12 ¶Now when every maid's turn was come to go in to king A-has-u-e'rus, after that she had been twelve months, according to the manner of the women, (for so were the days of their purifications accomplished, *to wit,* six months with oil of myrrh, and six months with sweet odours, and with *other* things for the purifying of the women;)

13 Then thus came *every* maiden unto the king; whatsoever she desired was given her to go with her out of the house of the women unto the king's house.

14 In the evening she went, and on the morrow she returned into the second house of the women, to the custody of Sha-ash'gaz, the king's chamberlain, which kept the concubines: she came in unto the king no more, except the king delighted in her, and that she were called by name.

2:5 The Mordecai of Ezra 2:2 is not to be confused with this Mordecai. Both had been involved in the captivity. The Mordecai of Ezra returned with Zerubbabel to Jerusalem. The Mordecai of Esther did not leave his adopted land.

2:7 *Hadassah,* i.e., "Myrtle." *Esther,* meaning "star" in Persian or "Ishtar" (the Babylonian goddess). *for his own daughter.* Apparently Mordecai had adopted his cousin as his daughter.

2:8 Esther was selected along with many other young women and secluded in the seraglio of the king until such time as he called for her. She won the favor of Hegai, who oversaw the women and who was a eunuch, and thus no threat to the king. Mordecai told Esther not to indicate that she was a Jewess, by which one can conclude that Jews were not among the people favored by the monarch. Since she was an orphan, it was easier to conceal her nationality than if her parents had been alive and were known to those who chose her as a candidate for the queenship.

15 ¶Now when the turn of Esther, the daughter of Ab-i-ha'il the uncle of
Mor'de-cai, who had taken her for his daughter, was come to go in unto the
king, she required nothing but what Heg'a-i the king's chamberlain, the
keeper of the women, appointed. And Esther obtained favour in the sight of
all them that looked upon her.
16 So Esther was taken unto king A-has-u-e'rus into his house royal in the
tenth month, which *is* the month Te'beth, in the seventh year of his reign.
17 And the king loved Esther above all the women, and she obtained grace
and favour in his sight more than all the virgins; so that he set the royal
crown upon her head, and made her queen instead of Vash'ti.
18 Then the king made a great feast unto all his princes and his servants,
even Esther's feast; and he made a release to the provinces, and gave gifts,
according to the state of the king.

☆**2:15**

2:17 Esth 1:11 Zech 6:10, 11

2:18 Esth 1:5–8

4. The Plan to Assassinate Ahasuerus

19 And when the virgins were gathered together the second time, then
Mor'de-cai sat in the king's gate.
20 Esther had not *yet* shewed her kindred nor her people; as Mor'de-cai
had charged her: for Esther did the commandment of Mor'de-cai, like as
when she was brought up with him.
21 In those days, while Mor'de-cai sat in the king's gate, two of the king's
chamberlains, Big'than and Te'resh, of those which kept the door, were
wroth, and sought to lay hand on the king A-has-u-e'rus.
22 And the thing was known to Mor'de-cai, who told *it* unto Esther the
queen; and Esther certified the king *thereof* in Mor'de-cai's name.
23 And when inquisition was made of the matter, it was found out;
therefore they were both hanged on a tree: and it was written in the book of
the chronicles before the king.

2:20 Esth 2:10

2:21 Esth 1:10; 6:2

2:22 Esth 6:1, 2

☆**2:23** Ezra 6:11 Esth 5:14 6:1, 2; 7:10

II. HAMAN'S PLOT AGAINST THE JEWS (3:1—5:14)

A. MORDECAI GAINS THE HATRED OF HAMAN

3 AFTER these things did king A-has-u-e'rus promote Ha'man the son
of Ham-med'a-tha the A'gag-ite, and advanced him, and set his seat
above all the princes that *were* with him.
2 And all the king's servants, that *were* in the king's gate, bowed, and

☆**3:1** Num 24:3–9 1 Sam 15:8, 31–33 Esth 3:10; 5:11 7:6; 8:2 9:24, 25; 10:3 Dan 6:2

☆**3:2** Esth 5:9

2:15 After Esther had been purified and thus prepared for the bed of the king, she was called upon to attend him. The king married every woman he took to his bed; each one became a wife of a lower rank than the queen. It was a custom also practiced by the kings of Israel and even by the patriarchs, as in the case of Jacob who was married to four women. Had the king never called for Esther again, she would have remained secluded for the remainder of her life. But Ahasuerus loved her above all the other of his wives and chose her to become his queen. Her accession to the queenship was celebrated by a great banquet. In addition, the king "granted a remission of taxes to the provinces" (RSV) which added to their happiness and no doubt made Esther a favorite with them.

2:23 *hanged on a tree,* i.e., "impaled alive." Possibly the meaning is that they were crucified.† *written in the book of the chronicles,* i.e., court records of daily happenings. It was providential that Mordecai's action went into the book, for later it would prove to be most important to the story.

3:1 Haman is said to be a descendant of the line of Agag. An Agag of Amalekite extraction is mentioned in 1 Sam. 15 as the last of a tribe destroyed by King Saul, who was following God's command. An ancient rabbinic tradition traces Haman to this Agag. If this is so, we can see the continuing conflict between the descendants of Esau and Jacob, since Esau was an ancestor of Amalek. A more likely explanation for the use of the word Agagite is that a region of the Persian Empire was called Agag. Haman's father and all of Haman's sons had Persian names, which would probably not have been the case if the family had not been related to Amalek.

3:2 Haman was the prime minister of Persia. He must have been an able man to have been promoted to such a high post. But he was also an ambitious and vainglorious man. When Mordecai refused to bow down to him, the enmity of Haman against him was aroused. He was so incensed that he determined to exterminate Mordecai along with all the other Jews in the kingdom. Apparently anti-Semitism is not simply a modern expression of hatred against the chosen people of God.

reverenced Ha'man: for the king had so commanded concerning him. But
Mor'de-cai bowed not, nor did *him* reverence.
[3]Then the king's servants, which *were* in the king's gate, said unto
Mor'de-cai, Why transgressest thou the king's commandment?
3:4☆ [4]Now it came to pass, when they spake daily unto him, and he hearkened
not unto them, that they told Ha'man, to see whether Mor'de-cai's matters
would stand: for he had told them that he *was* a Jew.
[5]And when Ha'man saw that Mor'de-cai bowed not, nor did him
reverence, then was Ha'man full of wrath.
[6]And he thought scorn to lay hands on Mor'de-cai alone; for they had
shewed him the people of Mor'de-cai: wherefore Ha'man sought to destroy
all the Jews that *were* throughout the whole kingdom of A-has-u-e'rus, *even*
the people of Mor'de-cai.

B. HAMAN'S PLAN TO KILL THE JEWS

3:7☆ [7]In the first month, that *is,* the month Ni'san, in the twelfth year of king
Esth 9:24–26 Prov 16:33 A-has-u-e'rus, they cast Pur, that *is,* the lot, before Ha'man from day to
Ezek 21:21, 22 day, and from month to month, *to* the twelfth *month,* that *is,* the month
Mt 27:35 A'dar.
3:8☆ [8]¶And Ha'man said unto king A-has-u-e'rus, There is a certain people
Acts 16:20, 21 scattered abroad and dispersed among the people in all the provinces of thy
kingdom; and their laws *are* diverse from all people; neither keep they the
king's laws: therefore it *is* not for the king's profit to suffer them.
3:9 [9]If it please the king, let it be written that they may be destroyed: and I
Esth 4:7 will pay ten thousand talents of silver to the hands of those that have the
charge of the business, to bring *it* into the king's treasuries.
3:10☆ [10]And the king took his ring from his hand, and gave it unto Ha'man the
Esth 8:2, 9, 10 son of Ham-med'a-tha the A'gag-ite, the Jews' enemy.
[11]And the king said unto Ha'man, The silver *is* given to thee, the people
also, to do with them as it seemeth good to thee.
3:12☆ [12]Then were the king's scribes called on the thirteenth day of the first
1 Kgs 21:8 Esth 1:22 month, and there was written according to all that Ha'man had com-
8:8–10 manded unto the king's lieutenants, and to the governors that *were* over
every province, and to the rulers of every people of every province
according to the writing thereof, and *to* every people after their language; in
the name of king A-has-u-e'rus was it written, and sealed with the king's
ring.
3:13 [13]And the letters were sent by posts into all the king's provinces, to
Esth 1:1, 2 8:9–11, 14 destroy, to kill, and to cause to perish, all Jews, both young and old, little
9:2, 7–10, 17 Isa 10:5, 6 children and women, in one day, *even* upon the thirteenth *day* of the twelfth
month, which *is* the month A'dar, and *to take* the spoil of them for a prey.

3:4 Mordecai refused to bow before Haman. When he was asked the reason for his refusal to do so, he told those associated with him that he was a Jew. He acted much as Daniel and the three Hebrew children did. To bow was against his religious convictions and he would not violate his conscience. His Jewishness was reported to Haman. Haman's anger did not stop with Mordecai. If one Jew would not bow before him, neither would any other Jew. Therefore, he determined to exterminate all Jews for this affront.

3:7 *they cast Pur.* Having determined to do away with the Jews, Haman now casts lots to discover what is the best time to do this evil deed. The lot fell on the twelfth month, which was February/March. This gave him plenty of time to work out the details of the pogrom.

3:8 The plot was simple. Haman accused the Jews of breaking the laws of the land. He offered the king a huge bribe for his royal consent, expecting to recover what it cost him by taking over the property of the dead Jews. He did not say who the people were, and the king did not inquire.

3:10 So great was the king's confidence in this prince of the realm that he readily assented to the scheme, and even gave his signet ring to Haman to have the decree sealed.

3:12 The plot now develops; the orders go out to the farthest reaches of the empire: "Annihilate the Jews." By this time the king must have known that the edict was directed against the Jews, although he did not yet know that Esther was a Jewess.

[14]The copy of the writing for a commandment to be given in every province was published unto all people, that they should be ready against that day.

☆3:14 Esth 4:8 8:13, 14

[15]The posts went out, being hastened by the king's commandment, and the decree was given in Shu'shan the palace. And the king and Ha'man sat down to drink; but the city Shu'shan was perplexed.

☆3:15 Esth 1:1–3

C. MORDECAI SEEKS THE HELP OF ESTHER

4 WHEN Mor'de-cai perceived all that was done, Mor'de-cai rent his clothes, and put on sackcloth with ashes, and went out into the midst of the city, and cried with a loud and a bitter cry;

☆4:1 Gen 27:34 2 Sam 1:11 13:19 Isa 15:4 Ezek 27:30 Jonah 3:4–9 Mic 1:8

[2]And came even before the king's gate: for none *might* enter into the king's gate clothed with sackcloth.

[3]And in every province, whithersoever the king's commandment and his decree came, *there was* great mourning among the Jews, and fasting, and weeping, and wailing; and many lay in sackcloth and ashes.

☆4:3

[4]¶So Esther's maids and her chamberlains came and told *it* her. Then was the queen exceedingly grieved; and she sent raiment to clothe Mor'de-cai, and to take away his sackcloth from him: but he received *it* not.

[5]Then called Esther for Ha'tach, *one* of the king's chamberlains, whom he had appointed to attend upon her, and gave him a commandment to Mor'de-cai, to know what it *was,* and why it *was.*

[6]So Ha'tach went forth to Mor'de-cai unto the street of the city, which *was* before the king's gate.

[7]And Mor'de-cai told him of all that had happened unto him, and of the sum of the money that Ha'man had promised to pay to the king's treasuries for the Jews, to destroy them.

4:7 Esth 3:9

[8]Also he gave him the copy of the writing of the decree that was given at Shu'shan to destroy them, to shew *it* unto Esther, and to declare *it* unto her, and to charge her that she should go in unto the king, to make supplication unto him, and to make request before him for her people.

☆4:8 Esth 3:14 8:13, 14

[9]And Ha'tach came and told Esther the words of Mor'de-cai.

[10]¶Again Esther spake unto Ha'tach, and gave him commandment unto Mor'de-cai;

[11]All the king's servants, and the people of the king's provinces, do know, that whosoever, whether man or woman, shall come unto the king into the

4:11 Esth 5:1, 2; 8:4

3:14 Mordecai clearly ordered Esther to appeal to the king against the plot of Haman to slaughter the Jews. But his strong faith impelled him to tell her that if she failed to do his bidding, deliverance would come some other way. Obviously salvation could only come from the God of the Israelites. Mordecai assured her that if she failed to do her duty and the Jews were delivered some other way, she could be sure that she and her father's house would perish. Mordecai believed that God had brought Esther into the kingdom for just such a time that the Jews now faced.

3:15 The king and Haman sat down to drink and congratulate themselves on the upcoming massacre. It is difficult to understand how the king could have rejoiced in what he had agreed to do, since the Jews really had done nothing to deserve what was coming. Mordecai had done nothing to offend the king, and what one person did could hardly constitute sufficient reason to kill off all the others—unless it could be shown that they were in agreement with Mordecai.

4:1 *rent his clothes.* This was an external sign of mourning. Some Jews now have substituted the wearing of a black ribbon. *sackcloth* was a garment made from goat and camel hair. It was coarse and dark-colored. Jews wore this garment when in mourning as they waited for deliverance from a national catastrophe.

4:3 The name of God is not mentioned in the book of Esther nor is anything said about prayers to God; yet the sackcloth, fasting, and ashes must have told their own story. All of these things without God would have meant nothing and accomplished nothing. Indeed the refusal of Mordecai to bow before Haman cannot be understood apart from divine providence. If he had not been faithful to the God of Judaism, his conduct would have made no sense at all.

4:8 Esther placed her confidence in Hatach by telling him that Mordecai and the Jews were her people. If he had spoken of this to the king, it would have become immediately apparent to him that Esther would have to die with the rest of the Jews, according to the law of the Medes and Persians. Mordecai sent Esther a message that she must go to the king and make supplication for her people.

inner court, who is not called, *there is* one law of his to put *him* to death,
except such to whom the king shall hold out the golden sceptre, that he may
live: but I have not been called to come in unto the king these thirty days.
12 And they told to Mor'de-cai Esther's words.
4:13☆ 13 Then Mor'de-cai commanded to answer Esther, Think not with thyself
that thou shalt escape in the king's house, more than all the Jews.
14 For if thou altogether holdest thy peace at this time, *then* shall there
enlargement and deliverance arise to the Jews from another place; but thou
and thy father's house shall be destroyed: and who knoweth whether thou
art come to the kingdom for *such* a time as this?
4:15☆ 15 ¶Then Esther bade *them* return Mor'de-cai *this answer,*
4:16☆ 16 Go, gather together all the Jews that are present in Shu'shan, and fast
2 Chron 20:3 ye for me, and neither eat nor drink three days, night or day: I also and my
Joel 2:2–17 maidens will fast likewise; and so will I go in unto the king, which *is* not
Jonah 3:4–9 according to the law: and if I perish, I perish.
4:17☆ 17 So Mor'de-cai went his way, and did according to all that Esther had
commanded him.

D. ESTHER'S INTERCESSION

1. Esther's Request of King Ahasuerus

5:1☆ 5 NOW it came to pass on the third day, that Esther put on *her* royal
Esth 4:11 *apparel,* and stood in the inner court of the king's house, over against
the king's house: and the king sat upon his royal throne in the royal house,
over against the gate of the house.
5:2☆ 2 And it was so, when the king saw Esther the queen standing in the court,
Esth 4:11; 8:4 *that* she obtained favour in his sight: and the king held out to Esther the
golden sceptre that *was* in his hand. So Esther drew near, and touched the
top of the sceptre.
5:3☆ 3 Then said the king unto her, What wilt thou, queen Esther? and what *is*
1 Kgs 2:20 Esth 5:6; 7:2 9:12 thy request? it shall be even given thee to the half of the kingdom.
Mt 20:20–22 4 And Esther answered, If *it seem* good unto the king, let the king and
Lk 18:41 Ha'man come this day unto the banquet that I have prepared for him.
5:5 5 Then the king said, Cause Ha'man to make haste, that he may do as
Esth 6:14 Esther hath said. So the king and Ha'man came to the banquet that Esther
had prepared.

4:13 Mordecai sent an explicit word to Esther. If she did nothing she would die because she was a Jewess. If she made an appeal to the king or her entrance to his presence was denied and she suffered death, she would be no worse off than having done nothing. Her only hope was to make an appearance before the king, come what may.

4:15 Many a believer needs to see that he or she has come into the kingdom for such a time as that experienced by Esther and Mordecai. Every missionary, minister, and lay person lives in that kind of situation and has a calling of God to be faithful, whatever the price.

4:16 Fasting in and of itself is a sign of confidence in the delivering power of God. It connotes a sense of need, a desire for a right relationship to God, and constitutes an unspoken but nevertheless genuine prayer for help. Without those elements, fasting has no spiritual value.

4:17 Here there is a reversal of roles. Mordecai has given orders to Esther. Now she gives orders to him, and he obeys them. She will approach the king with holy resolution to do her duty and trust God for the outcome. Should not all believers do the same?

5:1 *on the third day.* A day began at sundown, and a part of a day was considered to be a whole day. The first day began the night before and the three-day period ended before the fourth sundown. Thus 4:16 and this verse coincide.

5:2 No one came into the king's presence without permission. Esther dared to violate a perceived tradition. The king held out the royal sceptre to show that she might come before him. She touched the tip of the sceptre; this signified that she was coming before him as a humble petitioner who sought his favor. God granted her favor with the king and preserved her in her daring. But her actions were preceded by prayer and fasting; she had the assurance that she was in the will of God.

5:3 Josephus and the apocryphal author paint an interesting picture in which Esther is accompanied by two maids who support her. She faints in the presence of the king, who leaps from his throne to her aid and lovingly embraces her. Whatever the details, the king granted her request, and the dinner with Haman, the king, and Esther took place.

6¶And the king said unto Esther at the banquet of wine, What *is* thy ☆5:6
petition? and it shall be granted thee: and what *is* thy request? even to the
half of the kingdom it shall be performed.
7Then answered Esther, and said, My petition and my request *is;*
8If I have found favour in the sight of the king, and if it please the king ☆5:8
to grant my petition, and to perform my request, let the king and Ha'man
come to the banquet that I shall prepare for them, and I will do to morrow
as the king hath said.

2. Haman's Plan to Hang Mordecai

9¶Then went Ha'man forth that day joyful and with a glad heart: but ☆5:9 Esth 3:2
when Ha'man saw Mor'de-cai in the king's gate, that he stood not up, nor
moved for him, he was full of indignation against Mor'de-cai.
10Nevertheless Ha'man refrained himself: and when he came home, he 5:10 Esth 5:14; 6:13
sent and called for his friends, and Ze'resh his wife.
11And Ha'man told them of the glory of his riches, and the multitude of
his children, and all *the things* wherein the king had promoted him, and how
he had advanced him above the princes and servants of the king.
12Ha'man said moreover, Yea, Esther the queen did let no man come in
with the king unto the banquet that she had prepared but myself; and to
morrow am I invited unto her also with the king.
13Yet all this availeth me nothing, so long as I see Mor'de-cai the Jew
sitting at the king's gate.
14¶Then said Ze'resh his wife and all his friends unto him, Let a gallows ☆5:14 Esth 5:10; 7:9
be made of fifty cubits high, and to morrow speak thou unto the king that
Mor'de-cai may be hanged thereon: then go thou in merrily with the king
unto the banquet. And the thing pleased Ha'man; and he caused the
gallows to be made.

III. THE VICTORY OF THE JEWS (6:1—10:3)

A. THE FAILURE OF HAMAN'S PLOT

6 ON that night could not the king sleep, and he commanded to bring ☆6:1 Esth 2:21–23
the book of records of the chronicles; and they were read before the
king.
2And it was found written, that Mor'de-cai had told of Big'tha-na and
Te'resh, two of the king's chamberlains, the keepers of the door, who sought
to lay hand on the king A-has-u-e'rus.
3And the king said, What honour and dignity hath been done to Mor'de-
cai for this? Then said the king's servants that ministered unto him, There
is nothing done for him.

5:6 The heart of the king was in the hands of God. Vashti had refused to come when sent for and lost her queenship; Esther comes when she was not sent for, and God moves the king's heart to grant her request.
5:8 We can assume that Esther sensed that a second banquet would be more advantageous for her cause, and that the delay would increase the chance for success. Since Haman was the king's favorite, she wanted to present her case under the best circumstances.
5:9 Haman, puffed up, rejoices in his good fortune, boasts of his greatness, and is more angered than ever that stubborn Mordecai refuses to bow before him once more. He assumes that the private banquet will be the summit of his career.
5:14 On the advice of family and friends, Haman moves to construct the gallows on which he will hang Mordecai before going to the banquet with the king and Esther. Here the providence of God can be seen, for the hanging is delayed by "chance."
6:1 God works his providences in mysterious and unfathomable ways. There is no explanation as to why the king should spend a sleepless night and ask for the very document that would call to his mind the fact that Mordecai had saved him from assassination. The unspiritual mind would call this luck or accident, but there are no accidents in God's economy. It was part of the will of God, whether perceived by the eye of faith or denied and derided by the skeptic.

6:4☆ [4]¶And the king said, Who *is* in the court? Now Ha'man was come into
the outward court of the king's house, to speak unto the king to hang
Mor'de-cai on the gallows that he had prepared for him.
[5]And the king's servants said unto him, Behold, Ha'man standeth in the
court. And the king said, Let him come in.
[6]So Ha'man came in. And the king said unto him, What shall be done
unto the man whom the king delighteth to honour? Now Ha'man thought
in his heart, To whom would the king delight to do honour more than to
myself?
6:7 1 Kgs 1:33 [7]And Ha'man answered the king, For the man whom the king delighteth
Zech 9:9 to honour,
[8]Let the royal apparel be brought which the king *useth* to wear, and the
horse that the king rideth upon, and the crown royal which is set upon his
head:
6:9 [9]And let this apparel and horse be delivered to the hand of one of the
Gen 41:43 1 Kgs 1:34 king's most noble princes, that they may array the man *withal* whom the
king delighteth to honour, and bring him on horseback through the street of
the city, and proclaim before him, Thus shall it be done to the man whom
the king delighteth to honour.
6:10☆ [10]Then the king said to Ha'man, Make haste, *and* take the apparel and
the horse, as thou hast said, and do even so to Mor'de-cai the Jew, that
sitteth at the king's gate: let nothing fail of all that thou hast spoken.
[11]Then took Ha'man the apparel and the horse, and arrayed Mor'de-cai,
and brought him on horseback through the street of the city, and
proclaimed before him, Thus shall it be done unto the man whom the king
delighteth to honour.
6:12 2 Sam 15:30 [12]¶And Mor'de-cai came again to the king's gate. But Ha'man hasted to
Esth 7:8 his house mourning, and having his head covered.
Jer 14:3 [13]And Ha'man told Ze'resh his wife and all his friends every *thing* that
6:13☆ Esth 5:10, 14 had befallen him. Then said his wise men and Ze'resh his wife unto him, If
Mor'de-cai *be* of the seed of the Jews, before whom thou hast begun to fall,
thou shalt not prevail against him, but shalt surely fall before him.
6:14 [14]And while they *were* yet talking with him, came the king's chamber-
Esth 5:5–8 lains, and hasted to bring Ha'man unto the banquet that Esther had
prepared.

B. THE DEFEAT OF HAMAN

7 SO the king and Ha'man came to banquet with Esther the queen.
7:2 [2]And the king said again unto Esther on the second day at the
Esth 5:3, 6 7:3–6 banquet of wine, What *is* thy petition, queen Esther? and it shall be granted
thee: and what *is* thy request? and it shall be performed, *even* to the half of
the kingdom.
7:3☆ Esth 5:7, 8; 8:5 [3]Then Esther the queen answered and said, If I have found favour in thy

---

6:4 God, the Great Disposer, caused Haman to visit the king's court at the moment the monarch wanted advice on how to honor Haman's worst enemy, Mordecai. Ironically Haman supposed the king wished to honor him and so he selected the highest award he could think of.

6:10 Who can imagine the consternation and surprise of Haman who selected the honor to be conferred on his hated foe and was charged by the king to oversee the conferring of that honor on him? The Lord is in the heavens but he does what he pleases on earth.

6:13 Friends and relatives alike now predict the fall of Haman and the failure of his plot to hang Mordecai. Somehow they know that because Mordecai is a Jew, Haman cannot defeat him. Why they did not recommend that he repent, ask Mordecai for his forgiveness, and rejoice in the exaltation of his foe is not explained. Let those who worship Christ always be ready to repent of their sins and make things right.

7:3 Here Esther pleads for her own life and thus tells her husband that she is a Jewess. She also asks for the lives of all Jews who are under the edict by which they will be slaughtered. Knowing that her husband loves her, she rightly expects that he will be angry at anyone who would touch the life of his wife and the lives of her friends.

H. MORDECAI'S GREATNESS UNDER KING AHASUERUS

10 AND the king A-has-u-e'rus laid a tribute upon the land, and *upon*
the isles of the sea.
2 And all the acts of his power and of his might, and the declaration of the
greatness of Mor'de-cai, whereunto the king advanced him, *are* they not
written in the book of the chronicles of the kings of Me'di-a and Persia?
3 For Mor'de-cai the Jew *was* next unto king A-has-u-e'rus, and great
among the Jews, and accepted of the multitude of his brethren, seeking the
wealth of his people, and speaking peace to all his seed.

10:2 Esth 2:23; 6:1

☆**10:3** Gen 41:43, 44; Esth 5:11; 8:2; Dan 6:2

10:3 Mordecai, a good man, became a great man by the providence of God. "Men of merit may for a time seem buried alive; but often, by some means or other, they are discovered and preferred at last."*

THE BOOK OF
JOB

Authorship, date, and background The book of Job is listed among the five poetical books, which include Psalms, Proverbs, Ecclesiastes, and the Song of Songs (Solomon). The poetical books are not historical or prophetical works. The book of Job nowhere indicates who the author might have been. Jewish tradition has suggested writers from the time of Moses to the time of Ahasuerus. The events recorded in the book suggest a time frame early in the second millennium B.C. But this does not mean the book was authored at that time or even shortly later. Scholars have placed the date anywhere from the time of Moses to the return of the Jews from the Babylonian exile. In all probability a date around the age of Solomon is preferable.

Job does not make reference to historical events, although Job himself is said to have come from the land of Uz, which may have been located in southeastern Edom. Job's three friends are spoken of as having come from the Temanites, the Shuhites, and Naamathites. Elihu is called a Buzite. The main character, Job, was a wealthy man who lived a seminomadic existence. He was a real person, and the story tells how he was suddenly caught up in a series of disasters such as many people have faced in all ages. Thus the background for the book is applicable to all ages and all circumstances. The heart of the problem for Job was to find an answer to the dilemma why there is human suffering and how a loving God can allow it. It is further complicated by the inescapable fact that Job had really done nothing, humanly speaking, to deserve the disasters as a punishment for transgressions.

Characteristics and content S. J. Schultz has said that the book of Job exhibits "vast resources of knowledge, a superb style of forceful expression, profundity of thought, excellent command of language, noble ideals, a high standard of ethics and a genuine love for nature." The literary style is poetry with a prose introduction and epilogue. It is regarded by many as one of the truly great literary works of all times. The writer skillfully describes the contest between Job and his friends as they labor over the question of the cause of Job's plight. He faces the inquisition after losing his children, his possessions, and his great wealth. His own body is wracked with sores and he himself reaches the place where he wishes he had never been born.

Neither Job nor anyone else has ever been able to solve the problem that is posed in this book. But answers to the question emerge in a somewhat different pattern. Clearly it is shown that the thoughts and ways of God are beyond man's ability to understand them. He can only accept what God allows, believing that in the end all is for the glory of God and for the good of the sufferer. This does not answer the question, "Why me?" but it does provide a framework for acceptance of what may not always be understood. Moreover, Job teaches that God sometimes uses suffering to purify and strengthen the suffering soul. The third lesson Job teaches is that a believer must love God wholly apart from whether God sends blessings or disasters into his life.

What Job does not know is that in his case it is Satan who seeks permission from God to afflict him with the expectation that he will lose his faith, curse his God, and allow Satan to win a victory over the Almighty. Job's friends never do see the rightness of Job's defense until they are rebuked by God, who allows Job to pray for his friends. The final answer the life of Job brings to every believer is that God will deliver his suffering people either in this life or in that which is to come.

Outline

I. The historical setting (1:1—2:13)
II. Job's dialogue with his three friends (3:1—31:40)
III. The speeches of Elihu (32:1—37:24)
IV. God intervenes to speak (38:1—41:34)
V. The conclusion of the matter (42:1–17)

I. THE HISTORICAL SETTING (1:1—2:13)

A. JOB'S BACKGROUND

1 THERE was a man in the land of Uz, whose name *was* Job; and that man was perfect and upright, and one that feared God, and eschewed evil.

2 And there were born unto him seven sons and three daughters.

3 His substance also was seven thousand sheep, and three thousand camels, and five hundred yoke of oxen, and five hundred she asses, and a very great household; so that this man was the greatest of all the men of the east.

4 And his sons went and feasted *in their* houses, every one his day; and sent and called for their three sisters to eat and to drink with them.

5 And it was so, when the days of *their* feasting were gone about, that Job sent and sanctified them, and rose up early in the morning, and offered burnt offerings *according* to the number of them all: for Job said, It may be that my sons have sinned, and cursed God in their hearts. Thus did Job continually.

☆**1:1** Gen 6:9; 17:1 22:12 Ex 18:21 Job 28:28 29:25; 42:12 Jer 25:20 Ezek 14:14 Lam 4:21 Jas 5:11
1:2 Job 42:13
1:5 Job 8:4; 42:8

B. SATAN CHALLENGES GOD TO TRY JOB

1. God Allows Satan to Test Job

6 ¶Now there was a day when the sons of God came to present themselves before the LORD, and Satan came also among them.

7 And the LORD said unto Satan, Whence comest thou? Then Satan answered the LORD, and said, From going to and fro in the earth, and from walking up and down in it.

8 And the LORD said unto Satan, Hast thou considered my servant Job, that *there is* none like him in the earth, a perfect and an upright man, one that feareth God, and escheweth evil?

9 Then Satan answered the LORD, and said, Doth Job fear God for nought?

10 Hast not thou made an hedge about him, and about his house, and about all that he hath on every side? thou hast blessed the work of his hands, and his substance is increased in the land.

11 But put forth thine hand now, and touch all that he hath, and he will curse thee to thy face.

12 And the LORD said unto Satan, Behold, all that he hath *is* in thy power; only upon himself put not forth thine hand. So Satan went forth from the presence of the LORD.

☆**1:6**
1:7 1 Pet 5:8
1:8 Num 12:7 Josh 1:2, 7 Job 7:8
☆**1:9**
1:10 Job 29:2–6 31:25 Prov 10:22
☆**1:11** Job 2:5; 19:21
☆**1:12**

1:1 *the land of Uz* was probably in Edom, east of the region occupied by Israel. *Job* lived during the age of the patriarchs. Nothing in the book refers to any of the fathers such as Abraham, Isaac, or Jacob. God has his own people from every tribe and nation (Rev. 7:9) and Job was among that multitude. Job was a religious man who feared or had a reverential trust in God. He was a true worshipper who lived according to the will of God. He was governed by God's divine law in all things. He was not sinless but he was righteous, which means he was looking to God for salvation through the blood of the Lamb. He dreaded the thought of doing evil and was constant in his desire to please God. He was both pious and prosperous.
1:6 *the sons of God,* i.e., "the angels."
1:9 *Does Job fear God for nought?* Satan suggests that Job feared God because he gained something from so doing. It is true that godliness is great gain, but it was not true that Job would not have continued to fear God if he had not gained from doing so. Satan accused Job of being a hypocrite because he gained something from pretending to be what he was not; later Job's friends said the opposite, that his afflictions proved he was a hypocrite—otherwise he would not have suffered.
1:11 Satan had no power to afflict Job without first securing God's permission. Job lost his wealth (1:14–17), his children (1:18, 19), and his health (2:1–8). Deprived of his most important blessings, his life hardly seemed worth preserving; he had good reason to turn away from God, who allowed him to suffer so much.
1:12 *all that he hath is in thy power.* Satan now has God's permission to touch Job who, until this permission was given, was protected. The permission was limited to Job's possessions and did not include any attack upon his person.

2. Job Loses His Wealth and Children

13 ¶And there was a day when his sons and his daughters *were* eating and
drinking wine in their eldest brother's house:

1:14☆ Gen 25:3; Job 1:16–19; 6:19

14 And there came a messenger unto Job, and said, The oxen were
plowing, and the asses feeding beside them:
15 And the Sa-be'ans fell *upon them,* and took them away; yea, they have
slain the servants with the edge of the sword; and I only am escaped alone
to tell thee.

1:16 Gen 19:24; Lev 10:2; Num 11:1–3

16 While he *was* yet speaking, there came also another, and said, The fire
of God is fallen from heaven, and hath burned up the sheep, and the
servants, and consumed them; and I only am escaped alone to tell thee.

1:17 Gen 11:28, 31

17 While he *was* yet speaking, there came also another, and said, The
Chal-de'ans made out three bands, and fell upon the camels, and have
carried them away, yea, and slain the servants with the edge of the sword;
and I only am escaped alone to tell thee.
18 While he *was* yet speaking, there came also another, and said, Thy sons
and thy daughters *were* eating and drinking wine in their eldest brother's
house:
19 And, behold, there came a great wind from the wilderness, and smote
the four corners of the house, and it fell upon the young men, and they are
dead; and I only am escaped alone to tell thee.

3. Job Accepts the Test

1:20 Gen 37:29, 34; Josh 7:6; Ezra 9:3
1:21 1 Sam 2:7, 8; Job 2:10; Eccles 5:15; 1 Tim 6:7
1:22☆ Job 2:10

20 Then Job arose, and rent his mantle, and shaved his head, and fell
down upon the ground, and worshipped,
21 And said, Naked came I out of my mother's womb, and naked shall I
return thither: the LORD gave, and the LORD hath taken away; blessed be
the name of the LORD.
22 In all this Job sinned not, nor charged God foolishly.

C. SATAN'S SECOND ATTACK ON JOB

1. God Grants Satan His Desire

2:1☆ Job 1:6–8; Isa 6:1, 2

2 AGAIN there was a day when the sons of God came to present
themselves before the LORD, and Satan came also among them to
present himself before the LORD.
2 And the LORD said unto Satan, From whence comest thou? And Satan
answered the LORD, and said, From going to and fro in the earth, and from
walking up and down in it.

2:3☆

3 And the LORD said unto Satan, Hast thou considered my servant Job,
that *there is* none like him in the earth, a perfect and an upright man, one
that feareth God, and escheweth evil? and still he holdeth fast his integrity,
although thou movedst me against him, to destroy him without cause.

2:4☆ Job 1:11; 19:20, 21

4 And Satan answered the LORD, and said, Skin for skin, yea, all that a
man hath will he give for his life.

1:14 First Job lost his wealth (1:14–17), then he lost his children (1:18–19), then he lost his health (2:1–8). What more could a man lose? These three possessions are among the things most prized by all men. Satan thought that the loss of them would cause Job to defect from God and curse the divine name. Moreover, the loss of these possessions would make life itself worthless. Might not a man so afflicted commit suicide?

1:22 Paraphrased: "In all of this, Job did not sin or revile God."† Job did not understand why God permitted him to suffer. But, great as his complaint was, he did not question God's sovereignty over him.

2:1 *the sons of God,* i.e., "the angels."

2:3 *he holdeth fast his integrity,* i.e., "he is the same in adversity that he was in prosperity." His confidence in God is firmer and more deeply rooted than ever.

2:4 *Skin for skin* was probably a common expression used by tradesmen. When Job does not sin against God through his response to the loss of possessions and loved ones, Satan thinks Job will turn away if God allows physical affliction to come to him.

5 But put forth thine hand now, and touch his bone and his flesh, and he
will curse thee to thy face.
6 And the LORD said unto Satan, Behold, he *is* in thine hand; but save his
life.

2. Satan Ruins Job's Health

7 ¶So went Satan forth from the presence of the LORD, and smote Job
with sore boils from the sole of his foot unto his crown.
8 And he took him a potsherd to scrape himself withal; and he sat down
among the ashes.

☆2:7 Deut 28:35; Job 7:5; 13:28
2:8 Job 42:6; Jer 6:26; Jonah 3:6; Mt 11:21

3. Job Continues to Trust God

9 ¶Then said his wife unto him, Dost thou still retain thine integrity? curse
God, and die.
10 But he said unto her, Thou speakest as one of the foolish women
speaketh. What? shall we receive good at the hand of God, and shall we not
receive evil? In all this did not Job sin with his lips.

2:10 Job 1:21, 22; Mt 12:34–37; Jas 3:2

4. Job's Friends Come to Visit

11 ¶Now when Job's three friends heard of all this evil that was come upon
him, they came every one from his own place: El'i-phaz the Te'man-ite, and
Bildad the Shu'hite, and Zo'phar the Na'a-math-ite; for they had made an
appointment together to come to mourn with him and to comfort him.
12 And when they lifted up their eyes afar off, and knew him not, they
lifted up their voice, and wept; and they rent every one his mantle, and
sprinkled dust upon their heads toward heaven.
13 So they sat down with him upon the ground seven days and seven
nights, and none spake a word unto him: for they saw that *his* grief was
very great.

☆2:11
2:12 Josh 7:6; Job 1:20; Lam 2:10; Rev 18:19
2:13 Ezek 3:15

II. JOB'S DIALOGUE WITH HIS THREE FRIENDS (3:1—31:40)

A. JOB'S GREAT DISTRESS

1. "Let the Day of My Birth Be Cursed"

3 AFTER this opened Job his mouth, and cursed his day.
2 And Job spake, and said,
3 Let the day perish wherein I was born, and the night *in which* it was said,
There is a man child conceived.
4 Let that day be darkness; let not God regard it from above, neither let
the light shine upon it.
5 Let darkness and the shadow of death stain it; let a cloud dwell upon it;
let the blackness of the day terrify it.

☆3:2 Jer 20:14–18
☆3:3

2:7 God indeed had protected Job from physical suffering. Now he permits Satan to touch Job's body. We do not know how much Satan may have the capacity, under God's permissive hand, of striking the sons of men (and particularly the sons of God) with grievous diseases. Jesus said that one daughter of Abraham had been bound by Satan with illness for eighteen years before she was delivered (Luke 13:16).

2:11 *when Job's three friends heard.* When Job's friends, who came to console him and to help him, had finished their work, one might have asked the question, With friends like that who needs enemies? They were sincere, yet wrong; thus their intentions were good. These friends came from northern Arabia. *Teman* is the name of a clan from Edom (Gen. 36:4, 11). The Shuhites were probably a brother tribe to Midian (cf. Gen. 25:2; 1 Chron. 1:32). Nowhere else in the Scriptures are the Naamathites mentioned.

3:2, 3 Job will not curse God. But he does curse the day of his birth. He wishes he had not been born or that he had been born dead (3:3–19).

6 *As for* that night, let darkness seize upon it; let it not be joined unto the days of the year, let it not come into the number of the months.

7 Lo, let that night be solitary, let no joyful voice come therein.

3:8☆ Job 41:25

8 Let them curse it that curse the day, who are ready to raise up their mourning.

3:9 Job 41:18

9 Let the stars of the twilight thereof be dark; let it look for light, but *have* none; neither let it see the dawning of the day:

10 Because it shut not up the doors of my *mother's* womb, nor hid sorrow from mine eyes.

2. "Why Didn't I Die at Birth?"

3:11☆ Job 10:18, 19 Ps 139:13–16

11 Why died I not from the womb? *why* did I *not* give up the ghost when I came out of the belly?

12 Why did the knees prevent me? or why the breasts that I should suck?

3:13 Job 3:13–19 6:8, 9 14:10–15 19:25–27 Eccles 6:3–5 **3:14** Job 15:28

13 For now should I have lain still and been quiet, I should have slept: then had I been at rest,

14 With kings and counsellors of the earth, which built desolate places for themselves;

15 Or with princes that had gold, who filled their houses with silver:

16 Or as an hidden untimely birth I had not been; as infants *which* never saw light.

3:17 Job 17:16

17 There the wicked cease *from* troubling; and there the weary be at rest.

18 *There* the prisoners rest together; they hear not the voice of the oppressor.

19 The small and great are there; and the servant *is* free from his master.

3. His Great Groanings

3:20☆

20 Wherefore is light given to him that is in misery, and life unto the bitter *in* soul;

21 Which long for death, but it *cometh* not; and dig for it more than for hid treasures;

22 Which rejoice exceedingly, *and* are glad, when they can find the grave?

3:23 Job 19:6, 8, 12 Ps 88:8 Hos 2:6 **3:24** Job 6:7; 30:16 33:20 Ps 42:4 Isa 59:11 **3:25** Job 9:28; 30:15 **3:26** Job 7:13, 14

23 *Why is light given* to a man whose way is hid, and whom God hath hedged in?

24 For my sighing cometh before I eat, and my roarings are poured out like the waters.

25 For the thing which I greatly feared is come upon me, and that which I was afraid of is come unto me.

26 I was not in safety, neither had I rest, neither was I quiet; yet trouble came.

3:8 *Let them curse it that curse the day,* literally, "Let them who can curse the sea, knowing how to rouse the sea monster (leviathan), curse it."† NASB translates it: "Let those curse it who curse the day, who are prepared to rouse Leviathan." *to raise up their mourning* is better translated "who are skilled to raise up Leviathan." Leviathan or "sea monster" was thought to swallow up the sun in times of an eclipse. Job thinks that if Leviathan had been aroused and the sun eclipsed, he might never have been born!

3:11 Job wished that he had died at birth or that he had never been born in the first place. Jesus made some reference to this idea when he said, "Blessed are the barren, and the wombs that never bare, and the paps which never gave suck" (Luke 23:29). However, in blessing the barren womb, Jesus did not curse the fruitful one. Job welcomes death and curses life, regarding the grave as the best of all things. In this he was mistaken, and he was unwilling to make the most of his affliction.

3:20 Job "tacitly reflects on the divine Providence as unjust and unkind in continuing life when the comforts of life are removed."* He goes on to argue that life is like the light of a candle. The longer it burns, the shorter it is, and the nearer it is to the socket. It must be renewed each day and this renewal is a task men would be better without if it only serves them to see their misery by it.

B. THE FIRST SET OF SPEECHES WITH JOB'S FRIENDS
1. Eliphaz Speaks
a. Innocent People Are Not Punished

4 THEN El'i-phaz the Te'man-ite answered and said, ☆4:1
2 *If* we assay to commune with thee, wilt thou be grieved? but who ☆4:2
can withhold himself from speaking?
3 Behold, thou hast instructed many, and thou hast strengthened the weak ☆4:3
hands. Job 29:21, 25
4 Thy words have upholden him that was falling, and thou hast
strengthened the feeble knees.
5 But now it is come upon thee, and thou faintest; it toucheth thee, and
thou art troubled.
6 *Is* not *this* thy fear, thy confidence, thy hope, and the uprightness of thy ☆4:6
ways? Prov 3:26; 14:26
7 Remember, I pray thee, who *ever* perished, being innocent? or where ☆4:7
were the righteous cut off? Job 8:20
8 Even as I have seen, they that plow iniquity, and sow wickedness, reap Ps 37:25; Prov 22:8; Gal 6:7
the same. 2 Pet 2:9
9 By the blast of God they perish, and by the breath of his nostrils are 4:9
they consumed. Job 15:30; 2 Thess 2:8
10 The roaring of the lion, and the voice of the fierce lion, and the teeth of Rev 2:16
the young lions, are broken. 4:10 Ps 58:6
11 The old lion perisheth for lack of prey, and the stout lion's whelps are 4:11
scattered abroad. Job 5:4; 29:17; Jer 4:7; Hos 11:10

b. Man Is Not More Just Than God

12 Now a thing was secretly brought to me, and mine ear received a little 4:12
thereof. Job 33:15–18
13 In thoughts from the visions of the night, when deep sleep falleth on
men,
14 Fear came upon me, and trembling, which made all my bones to shake.
15 Then a spirit passed before my face; the hair of my flesh stood up: ☆4:15
16 It stood still, but I could not discern the form thereof: an image *was*
before mine eyes, *there was* silence, and I heard a voice, *saying,* 4:17 Gen 18:25
17 Shall mortal man be more just than God? shall a man be more pure Job 9:2; 25:4
than his maker? 35:10; 36:3 ☆4:18
18 Behold, he put no trust in his servants; and his angels he charged with Gen 2:7; 3:19
folly: Job 15:15; 22:16; Isa 6:2, 3

4:1 The speeches of Eliphaz, Bildad, and Zophar are written in poetic form. The Scriptures record what they said, but this does not mean that all they said is necessarily true. God judged them defective. Nonetheless, some of their statements are true and are quoted as such in the New Testament (e.g., the statements of Eliphaz in 5:11–13 are echoed in Luke 1:52 and quoted as true in 1 Cor. 3:19).
4:2ff Eliphaz claimed that (1) if Job were righteous he would trust God and not wish to die; (2) his suffering follows the rule that as a man sows so shall he reap (4:8, 9); (3) Job should accept God's chastening by humbly repenting, at which time he would be restored. Eliphaz's theories were inaccurate, and did not apply to Job because he was not being punished for having committed secret sins, as his friends intimated.
4:3 *thou hast instructed many,* i.e., "you have told many a troubled soul to trust in God."†
4:6 Eliphaz's question is: "Shouldn't you believe that God will care for those who are good?"†
4:7 *who ever perished, being innocent?* Job's friends tell him that only the wicked suffer. Thus if he is suffering he must be wicked. Job must confess his sin, get right with God, trust in his mercy, and all will be well. Unfortunately their premise was wrong. All who suffer are not necessarily wicked, as they learn later.
4:15 Eliphaz here relates the incident in which an apparition passed before him, causing his hair to stand on end. We know little about spirits, but we do know there are both good and bad ones. Whether good or bad, apparitions make a deep impression on the souls of men. Yet God sends us his messages, not through apparitions, but through men who have given us the Word of God under the guidance of the Holy Spirit. Spirits are to be tried by testing what they say against what the Scriptures teach.
4:18 This verse has been understood by some to read as follows: "He will put no trust in his saints; nor will he glory in his angels or make boast of them"* (as if their praises or services added anything to him). God is infinitely happy with the angels and, for that matter, with men.

19How much less *in* them that dwell in houses of clay, whose foundation
is in the dust, *which* are crushed before the moth?

4:20 Job 14:2, 20
20They are destroyed from morning to evening: they perish for ever
without any regarding *it*.

4:21 Job 8:22; 36:12
21Doth not their excellency *which is* in them go away? they die, even
without wisdom.

c. Punishment Comes Only to the Wicked

5:1☆ Job 15:15
5 CALL now, if there be any that will answer thee; and to which of the
saints wilt thou turn?

5:2 Prov 12:16; 27:3
2For wrath killeth the foolish man, and envy slayeth the silly one.

5:3 Job 24:18; 31:30 Jer 12:2
3I have seen the foolish taking root: but suddenly I cursed his habitation.
4His children are far from safety, and they are crushed in the gate,
neither *is there* any to deliver *them*.

5:5 Job 18:8–10 22:10
5Whose harvest the hungry eateth up, and taketh it even out of the
thorns, and the robber swalloweth up their substance.

5:6 Job 15:35
6Although affliction cometh not forth of the dust, neither doth trouble
spring out of the ground;

5:7 Job 14:1 Eccl 5:15–17 1 Cor 10:13
7Yet man is born unto trouble, as the sparks fly upward.

d. He Advises Job to Confess His Sins

5:8☆ Job 13:2, 3
8I would seek unto God, and unto God would I commit my cause:

5:9 Job 9:10 37:14, 16; 42:3
9Which doeth great things and unsearchable; marvellous things without
number:

5:10 Job 36:27–29 37:6 Ps 65:9–11 Amos 4:7
10Who giveth rain upon the earth, and sendeth waters upon the fields:

5:11 Job 22:29; 36:7
11To set up on high those that be low; that those which mourn may be
exalted to safety.

5:12 Ps 33:10
12He disappointeth the devices of the crafty, so that their hands cannot
perform *their* enterprise.

5:13 Job 37:24 1 Cor 3:19
13He taketh the wise in their own craftiness: and the counsel of the
froward is carried headlong.

5:14 Deut 28:29 Prov 4:19
14They meet with darkness in the daytime, and grope in the noonday as
in the night.

5:15 Job 4:10, 11 29:17; 36:6, 15 Ps 35:10
15But he saveth the poor from the sword, from their mouth, and from the
hand of the mighty.

5:16 Ps 107:42
16So the poor hath hope, and iniquity stoppeth her mouth.

5:17☆ Ps 94:12 Prov 3:1 Heb 12:5–11
17Behold, happy *is* the man whom God correcteth: therefore despise not
thou the chastening of the Almighty:

5:18 Deut 32:39 Isa 30:26 Hos 6:1
18For he maketh sore, and bindeth up: he woundeth, and his hands make
whole.
19He shall deliver thee in six troubles: yea, in seven there shall no evil
touch thee.

5:20 Ps 33:19 144:10 Prov 10:3
20In famine he shall redeem thee from death: and in war from the power
of the sword.

5:1 Eliphaz charges Job to show him a single case of any saint who was reduced to the same circumstances in which Job now found himself. If God never dealt in this manner with any saint who loved his name, then it must be clear that Job is not one of them.

5:8 *I would seek unto God, and unto God would I commit my cause,* i.e., "Go to God and confess your sins to him."† Eliphaz is certain that Job is suffering for his sins. But even though he is wrong, he is right in speaking of the solution to such a problem. He affirms that if he were in Job's shoes, he would seek God. God is, of course, the sinner's only refuge, and from him comes his great salvation.

5:17ff Eliphaz says that Job should glory in affliction; he correctly states that God is the great deliverer, whether the problem be famine, war, reproach, or false accusation. From six, even seven troubles God will deliver the righteous, says 5:19. Yet this does not resolve Job's problems; they have sprung from a different situation than that envisioned by Eliphaz.

21 Thou shalt be hid from the scourge of the tongue: neither shalt thou be
afraid of destruction when it cometh.
22 At destruction and famine thou shalt laugh: neither shalt thou be afraid
of the beasts of the earth.
23 For thou shalt be in league with the stones of the field: and the beasts
of the field shall be at peace with thee.
24 And thou shalt know that thy tabernacle *shall be* in peace; and thou
shalt visit thy habitation, and shalt not sin.
25 Thou shalt know also that thy seed *shall be* great, and thine offspring as
the grass of the earth.
26 Thou shalt come to *thy* grave in a full age, like as a shock of corn
cometh in in his season.
27 Lo this, we have searched it, so it *is;* hear it, and know thou *it* for thy
good.

5:21 Ps 31:20; 91:5, 6; Prov 12:18; Jas 3:5–8
5:22 Ps 91:13; Ezek 34:25; Hos 2:18
5:23 Isa 11:6–9; 65:25
5:25 Ps 112:2; Isa 44:3, 4; 48:19
5:26 Gen 15:15; Job 42:17; Prov 9:11; 10:27
☆**5:27**

2. Job Responds to Eliphaz

a. He Wishes God Would Let Him Die

6 BUT Job answered and said,
2 Oh that my grief were throughly weighed, and my calamity laid in
the balances together!
3 For now it would be heavier than the sand of the sea: therefore my
words are swallowed up.
4 For the arrows of the Almighty *are* within me, the poison whereof
drinketh up my spirit: the terrors of God do set themselves in array against
me.
5 Doth the wild ass bray when he hath grass? or loweth the ox over his
fodder?
6 Can that which is unsavoury be eaten without salt? or is there *any* taste
in the white of an egg?
7 The things *that* my soul refused to touch *are* as my sorrowful meat.
8 Oh that I might have my request; and that God would grant *me* the
thing that I long for!
9 Even that it would please God to destroy me; that he would let loose his
hand, and cut me off!
10 Then should I yet have comfort; yea, I would harden myself in sorrow:
let him not spare; for I have not concealed the words of the Holy One.
11 What *is* my strength, that I should hope? and what *is* mine end, that I
should prolong my life?
12 *Is* my strength the strength of stones? or *is* my flesh of brass?
13 *Is* not my help in me? and is wisdom driven quite from me?

☆**6:1ff**
6:2 Job 31:6
6:3 Job 23:2
6:4 Job 16:13; 21:20; 30:15; Ps 38:2
6:5 Job 3:24; 33:20; 39:5–8; Jer 14:6
☆**6:8** Num 11:15; 1 Kgs 19:4; Job 7:16; 9:21; 10:1
6:11 Job 21:4
6:13 Job 26:2, 3

b. He Charges His Friends with Unfaithfulness

14 To him that is afflicted pity *should be shewed* from his friend; but he
forsaketh the fear of the Almighty.

☆**6:14** Job 1:5; 4:5; 15:4

5:27 The words spoken by Eliphaz are true. We must hear and know the truth. But that is not enough; we must be improved and made wiser by what we know. We must submit to the commanding power of truth.

6:1ff Job replies to Eliphaz that his troubles are far worse than his friends'; he is suffering deeply. But he insists that his sufferings are not a result of transgressions. He justifies himself and feels that his friends have been unfaithful to him. He demands evidence to show that he has sinned, even as he explains the depths of his suffering while addressing his Maker, the only source of his deliverance.

6:8 Job passionately desires to die. Apparently he expects never to see any better days (and in this he would be proved wrong). He thinks only death would solve his problem. Why then did he not commit suicide? Behind his words lie his knowledge that life and death come only from God. He gives and takes life; man shall not die by his own hand.

6:14 Job argues that compassion is a debt owed to those who are afflicted. Eliphaz has not shown compassion. Thus inhumanity is a sign of the lack of piety. Job is deeply disappointed in his friends.

6:15 Job 24:19; Jer 15:18

15 My brethren have dealt deceitfully as a brook, *and* as the stream of
brooks they pass away;
16 Which are blackish by reason of the ice, *and* wherein the snow is hid:
17 What time they wax warm, they vanish: when it is hot, they are
consumed out of their place.
18 The paths of their way are turned aside; they go to nothing, and perish.

6:19 Gen 25:15; Job 1:15; Isa 21:14; Jer 14:3

19 The troops of Te′ma looked, the companies of She′ba waited for them.
20 They were confounded because they had hoped; they came thither, and
were ashamed.
21 For now ye are nothing; ye see *my* casting down, and are afraid.

c. Job Asks: "What Have I Done Wrong?"

22 Did I say, Bring unto me? or, Give a reward for me of your substance?
23 Or, Deliver me from the enemy's hand? or, Redeem me from the hand
of the mighty?

6:24☆

24 Teach me, and I will hold my tongue: and cause me to understand
wherein I have erred.

6:25 Job 8:2; 15:2; 16:3; Mt 12:37

25 How forcible are right words! but what doth your arguing reprove?
26 Do ye imagine to reprove words, and the speeches of one that is
desperate, *which are* as wind?

6:27 Job 22:9; 24:9; Joel 3:3; Nah 3:10; 2 Pet 2:3
6:28 Job 27:4; 33:3; 36:4
6:29 Job 13:18; 27:5, 6; 42:1–6
6:30 Job 12:11; Heb 5:14

27 Yea, ye overwhelm the fatherless, and ye dig *a pit* for your friend.
28 Now therefore be content, look upon me; for *it is* evident unto you if I
lie.
29 Return, I pray you, let it not be iniquity; yea, return again, my
righteousness *is* in it.
30 Is there iniquity in my tongue? cannot my taste discern perverse things?

d. Life Is Hopeless

7:1☆ Lev 25:50; Deut 15:18; Mt 20:1–15
7:2☆

7 *IS there* not an appointed time to man upon earth? *are not* his days
also like the days of an hireling?
2 As a servant earnestly desireth the shadow, and as an hireling looketh
for *the reward of* his work:
3 So am I made to possess months of vanity, and wearisome nights are
appointed to me.

7:4 Deut 28:67; Job 7:13, 14; Isa 54:11
7:5 Ps 38:5–7
7:6 Job 9:25; 13:15; 17:15, 16; 19:10; Prov 14:32

4 When I lie down, I say, When shall I arise, and the night be gone? and
I am full of tossings to and fro unto the dawning of the day.
5 My flesh is clothed with worms and clods of dust; my skin is broken,
and become loathsome.
6 My days are swifter than a weaver's shuttle, and are spent without hope.

e. Job Prays to God in Despair

7:7☆ Job 7:16; 9:25

7 O remember that my life *is* wind: mine eye shall no more see good.
8 The eye of him that hath seen me shall see me no *more:* thine eyes *are*
upon me, and I *am* not.

6:24 Job acknowledges that he and his friends do have a difference of opinion. He insists that he is not obstinate and is ready to change his mind if he can be shown that what he holds to is, in fact, wrong and untrue. If they can teach him, he will hold his tongue.

7:1, 2 Job thinks he has as much reason to wish for death as a hired servant who is tired of his work and looks for the setting of the sun.

7:7 Job reflects that we all must take our leave of temporal things that are seen. We pass this way only once; there is no repassing. We pass from this life to return no more. The spiritual lesson is plain: glorified saints return no more to the cares, concerns, burdens, and sorrows of this life; nor do damned sinners return to the gaieties and worldly pleasures they once enjoyed.

9*As* the cloud is consumed and vanisheth away: so he that goeth down to
the grave shall come up no *more.*
10He shall return no more to his house, neither shall his place know him
any more.
11Therefore I will not refrain my mouth; I will speak in the anguish of my
spirit; I will complain in the bitterness of my soul.
12*Am* I a sea, or a whale, that thou settest a watch over me?
13When I say, My bed shall comfort me, my couch shall ease my
complaint;
14Then thou scarest me with dreams, and terrifiest me through visions:
15So that my soul chooseth strangling, *and* death rather than my life.
16I loathe *it;* I would not live alway: let me alone; for my days *are* vanity.
17What *is* man, that thou shouldest magnify him? and that thou shouldest
set thine heart upon him?
18And *that* thou shouldest visit him every morning, *and* try him every
moment?
19How long wilt thou not depart from me, nor let me alone till I swallow
down my spittle?
20I have sinned; what shall I do unto thee, O thou preserver of men? why
hast thou set me as a mark against thee, so that I am a burden to myself?
21And why dost thou not pardon my transgression, and take away mine
iniquity? for now shall I sleep in the dust; and thou shalt seek me in the
morning, but I *shall* not *be.*

7:9 Ps 39:13; Isa 38:11
7:10 Ps 103:16
7:11 Job 10:1; 21:4; 23:2
☆**7:12** Ezek 32:2, 3; Lam 3:7
7:13 Job 7:4; Ps 6:6; 77:4
7:16 Job 6:9; 7:7; 9:21; 10:1
7:17 1 Sam 24:14; Job 22:2; Ps 8:4; 144:3; Heb 2:6
7:19 Ps 6:3
7:20 Job 35:3, 6; Ps 80:4
☆**7:21** Job 10:9, 14; Tit 2:14; 1 Jn 1:9; 3:5

3. Bildad Charges Job with Hypocrisy and Urges Repentance

8 THEN answered Bildad the Shu'hite, and said,
2How long wilt thou speak these *things?* and *how long shall* the words
of thy mouth *be like* a strong wind?
3Doth God pervert judgment? or doth the Almighty pervert justice?
4If thy children have sinned against him, and he have cast them away for
their transgression;
5If thou wouldest seek unto God betimes, and make thy supplication to
the Almighty;
6If thou *wert* pure and upright; surely now he would awake for thee, and
make the habitation of thy righteousness prosperous.
7Though thy beginning was small, yet thy latter end should greatly
increase.
8For inquire, I pray thee, of the former age, and prepare thyself to the
search of their fathers:

☆**8:1ff**
☆**8:2**
8:3 Gen 18:25; Deut 32:4; 2 Chron 19:7; Job 34:10, 12; 36:23; Rom 3:5
8:4 Job 1:15–19
8:5 Job 5:17–27; Isa 55:6, 7; Mt 7:7, 8; Heb 3:7, 8
8:6 Job 22:27; Ps 7:6; Prov 15:8
☆**8:7** Job 42:12
☆**8:8** Deut 4:32; 32:7; Ps 44:1; Rom 15:4

7:12 That Job is suffering allows for no doubt. But he peevishly declares that the restraints laid upon him are more than the circumstances require. He is neither so strong nor so distempered that he needs to be restrained by force to keep him from devouring all the fishes of the sea!

7:21 *why dost thou not pardon my transgression?* Job knows of no sin he has committed that has harmed God. Let God forgive him, for he does not merit the awful scourging he has experienced. Job is not irreverent here. He is only seeking to reason with God as he tries to understand what, at that moment, is not understandable and what can at last only be known to him by revelation from God.

8:1ff Bildad's argument hardly differs from that of Eliphaz: If only Job would stop rebelling against his afflictions and accept the rightness of God's dealing with him, he would shortly be restored.

8:2 Bildad hits Job hard by saying that he is a bag of wind. He accuses Job of being blustering, threatening, boisterous, and dangerous. Bildad felt he had to take God's side against his friend Job.

8:7 Bildad expresses confidence that God can restore good things to Job. But it all is based on the notion that Job is a sinner who needs to repent, turn to God, and be forgiven. All that Bildad said was true for most of us who indeed have sinned. In Job's case, however, Bildad's primary assumption was false. Job was not guilty of the sins his friends thought he had committed.

8:8 Eliphaz had appealed to mystical experience, that is, to the apparition he had seen. Bildad appeals to past history and tradition, to scholarship rather than to mystical events. His philosophy, however, is the same as that of Eliphaz: Job is in error and needs correction.

9(For we *are but of* yesterday, and know nothing, because our days upon
earth *are* a shadow:)
10Shall not they teach thee, *and* tell thee, and utter words out of their
heart?
11Can the rush grow up without mire? can the flag grow without water?
12Whilst it *is* yet in his greenness, *and* not cut down, it withereth before
any *other* herb.
13So *are* the paths of all that forget God; and the hypocrite's hope shall
perish:
14Whose hope shall be cut off, and whose trust *shall be* a spider's web.
15He shall lean upon his house, but it shall not stand: he shall hold it fast,
but it shall not endure.
16He *is* green before the sun, and his branch shooteth forth in his garden.
17His roots are wrapped about the heap, *and* seeth the place of stones.
18If he destroy him from his place, then *it* shall deny him, *saying,* I have
not seen thee.
19Behold, this *is* the joy of his way, and out of the earth shall others grow.
20Behold, God will not cast away a perfect *man,* neither will he help the
evil doers:
21Till he fill thy mouth with laughing and thy lips with rejoicing.
22They that hate thee shall be clothed with shame; and the dwelling place
of the wicked shall come to nought.

4. Job Responds to Bildad

a. Job Says God Is Just

9 THEN Job answered and said,
2I know *it is* so of a truth: but how should man be just with God?
3If he will contend with him, he cannot answer him one of a thousand.
4*He is* wise in heart, and mighty in strength: who hath hardened *himself*
against him, and hath prospered?
5Which removeth the mountains, and they know not: which overturneth
them in his anger.
6Which shaketh the earth out of her place, and the pillars thereof
tremble.
7Which commandeth the sun, and it riseth not; and sealeth up the stars.
8Which alone spreadeth out the heavens, and treadeth upon the waves of
the sea.
9Which maketh Arc-tu′rus, O-ri′on, and Plei′a-des, and the chambers of
the south.
10Which doeth great things past finding out; yea, and wonders without
number.
11Lo, he goeth by me, and I see *him* not: he passeth on also, but I
perceive him not.
12Behold, he taketh away, who can hinder him? who will say unto him,
What doest thou?

8:11 Ex 2:3; Ps 9:17; Isa 19:5–7
8:14 Isa 59:5, 6
8:15 Job 27, 18; Ps 49:11
8:16 Ps 37:35; 80:11
8:20☆ Isa 45:1
8:21 Ps 126:1, 2; 132:16; Lk 6:21
8:22 Ps 132:18
9:1☆
9:2 Job 4:17; 25:4
9:3☆ Job 10:2; 40:2; Rom 9:20
9:4 2 Chron 13:12
9:5 Job 26:6–14; Zech 4:7; Rev 6:14
9:6 Isa 2:19; 13:13; Hag 2:6; Heb 12:26
9:7 Job 38:12–15; Isa 13:10; Lk 21:25, 26
9:8 Gen 1:1; Ps 77:19; 104:2; Isa 40:22; Jn 6:19
9:9 Job 38:31, 32; Amos 5:8
9:10☆
9:11 Job 23:8, 9; 1 Tim 6:16
9:12 Job 10:7; Isa 45:9

8:20 Bildad sums up his case that as Job was, so he should fare, and that as he fared, so he was. Since Job had fared so badly, it simply proved he was a sinner. Let him repent and his mouth would be filled with laughing and his lips with shouting.

9:1 Whoever argues with his opponent should be willing to accept anything that he says that is true. It is true that God brings wicked men to ruin. It is also true that the godly are under the wings and the protection of the Almighty.

9:3 Job asserts that no man is an equal match against his Maker. Man cannot win in an argument nor can he overcome his Maker in combat.

9:10 God acts invisibly and undiscerned. Men who are finite cannot understand God's counsels nor can they apprehend his motions or comprehend the measures he takes. They are not competent to judge his proceedings because they do not know what he does or what he designs.

b. Job Says He Is a Sinner

13 *If* God will not withdraw his anger, the proud helpers do stoop under
him.
14 How much less shall I answer him, *and* choose out my words *to reason*
with him?
15 Whom, though I were righteous, *yet* would I not answer, *but* I would
make supplication to my judge.
16 If I had called, and he had answered me; *yet* would I not believe that he
had hearkened unto my voice.
17 For he breaketh me with a tempest, and multiplieth my wounds
without cause.
18 He will not suffer me to take my breath, but filleth me with bitterness.
19 If *I speak* of strength, lo, *he is* strong: and if of judgment, who shall set
me a time *to plead?*
20 If I justify myself, mine own mouth shall condemn me: *if I say,* I *am*
perfect, it shall also prove me perverse.
21 *Though* I *were* perfect, *yet* would I not know my soul: I would despise
my life.
22 This *is* one *thing,* therefore I said *it,* He destroyeth the perfect and the
wicked.
23 If the scourge slay suddenly, he will laugh at the trial of the innocent.
24 The earth is given into the hand of the wicked: he covereth the faces of
the judges thereof; if not, where, *and* who *is* he?

c. Job's Complaint against God

25 Now my days are swifter than a post: they flee away, they see no good.
26 They are passed away as the swift ships: as the eagle *that* hasteth to the
prey.
27 If I say, I will forget my complaint, I will leave off my heaviness, and
comfort *myself:*
28 I am afraid of all my sorrows, I know that thou wilt not hold me
innocent.
29 *If* I be wicked, why then labour I in vain?
30 If I wash myself with snow water, and make my hands never so clean;
31 Yet shalt thou plunge me in the ditch, and mine own clothes shall
abhor me.
32 For *he is* not a man, as I *am, that* I should answer him, *and* we should
come together in judgment.
33 Neither is there any daysman betwixt us, *that* might lay his hand upon
us both.
34 Let him take his rod away from me, and let not his fear terrify me:
35 *Then* would I speak, and not fear him; but *it is* not so with me.

d. Job Persists in Complaining

10 MY soul is weary of my life; I will leave my complaint upon
myself; I will speak in the bitterness of my soul.

☆**9:13** Ps 89:10
9:15 Job 8:5; 10:15 Dan 9:3, 18
9:17 Job 16:12, 14
9:18 Job 27:2 Ps 39:13
9:20 Prov 10:19 Jas 3:2
9:21 Prov 28:26
☆**9:22** Eccles 9:2
☆**9:23**
☆**9:24** Job 12:6, 17 16:11 Dan 4:17 5:18–21
9:26 2 Sam 1:23 Job 39:29 Isa 18:2 Hab 1:8
9:28 Job 3:25; 7:21 10:14
9:29 Ps 37:33 Jer 2:35
9:30 Job 31:7 Jer 2:22 Rom 10:3 1 Jn 1:8
9:32 1 Sam 2:25 Isa 1:18 Rom 9:20
9:34 Ps 39:10; 90:11
10:1 Num 11:15 1 Kgs 19:4 Job 7:11, 16 Isa 38:15, 17

9:13 *the proud helpers do stoop under him,* i.e., "the pride of man collapses before him."† The Hebrew has it "helpers of Rahab," which suggests God's triumph over evil in primordial times.

9:22–24 Job repeats the main point of difference between him and his friends. It is common for the wicked to prosper and for the righteous to be greatly afflicted. Let God's children reconcile their troubles with the fact that they are designed for their honor and benefit. What we see happen in this life is not the end of the matter. Some who suffer much will be saved at last; the wicked who have flourished will at last end up in hell.

9:25 In this passage we see that Job becomes more complaining, more peevish. In chapter 10 he gives vent to resentment. He refuses to impeach God but he uses violent words, making clear the bitterness of his soul. Somehow he finds it difficult to perceive that "in acceptance lieth peace."

10:2☆ Job 9:29 Ps 139:23, 24 **10:3** Job 9:22–24 10:8; 19:6 21:16; 22:18 Ps 138:8 **10:4** 1 Sam 16:7 Job 9:12; 36:26 Lk 16:15 **10:7**☆

2 I will say unto God, Do not condemn me; shew me wherefore thou
contendest with me.
3 *Is it* good unto thee that thou shouldest oppress, that thou shouldest
despise the work of thine hands, and shine upon the counsel of the wicked?
4 Hast thou eyes of flesh? or seest thou as man seeth?
5 *Are* thy days as the days of man? *are* thy years as man's days,
6 That thou inquirest after mine iniquity, and searchest after my sin?
7 Thou knowest that I am not wicked; and *there is* none that can deliver
out of thine hand.

e. Job Says God Is Creator and Preserver

10:8☆ Job 9:22 Ps 119:73 Isa 43:7 **10:9** Job 4:19; 7:21 33:6 Eccles 12:7 Rom 9:21

8 Thine hands have made me and fashioned me together round about; yet
thou dost destroy me.
9 Remember, I beseech thee, that thou hast made me as the clay; and wilt
thou bring me into dust again?
10 Hast thou not poured me out as milk, and curdled me like cheese?
11 Thou hast clothed me with skin and flesh, and hast fenced me with
bones and sinews.

10:12 Job 33:4 Mt 6:25 **10:13** Job 7:20, 21 9:28; 23:13 **10:14**☆

12 Thou hast granted me life and favour, and thy visitation hath preserved
my spirit.
13 And these *things* hast thou hid in thine heart: I know that this *is* with
thee.
14 If I sin, then thou markest me, and thou wilt not acquit me from mine
iniquity.

f. Job Continues to Complain

10:15 Job 6:29 Rom 2:8, 9 **10:16** Job 5:9 Isa 38:13 Lam 3:10 Hos 13:7, 8 **10:17** Job 7:1; 16:8 **10:18**☆ Job 3:11–13 Jer 20:14–18 Mt 26:24 **10:20** 2 Sam 12:23 Job 7:19; 14:1 16:22 Ps 39:13

15 If I be wicked, woe unto me; and *if* I be righteous, *yet* will I not lift up
my head. *I am* full of confusion; therefore see thou mine affliction;
16 For it increaseth. Thou huntest me as a fierce lion: and again thou
shewest thyself marvellous upon me.
17 Thou renewest thy witnesses against me, and increasest thine indigna-
tion upon me; changes and war *are* against me.
18 Wherefore then hast thou brought me forth out of the womb? Oh that
I had given up the ghost, and no eye had seen me!
19 I should have been as though I had not been; I should have been
carried from the womb to the grave.
20 *Are* not my days few? cease *then, and* let me alone, that I may take
comfort a little,
21 Before I go *whence* I shall not return, *even* to the land of darkness and
the shadow of death;

10:2 Job wants to be delivered from his afflictions. Though he lies under the cross, he does not wish to lie under the curse. He smarts under the rod of the Father, but he prays not to be cut off by the sword of the Judge. It is the comfort of all believers who are in affliction that there is no condemnation to them. They are chastened that they may not be condemned with the world (1 Cor. 11:32).

10:7 Job knows that under the grace of God he can say, "I am not guilty." He appeals to God, who knows that he is a man of integrity.

10:8 It is God who has made us, not we ourselves. Who then can ask, "Why hast thou made me thus?" God who lights the lamp of life in us does not let it burn of itself. He supplies it with fresh oil every day. Job calls upon God to remember that he made him. Because God has made him, he submits to God and will serve him. This is his argument for mercy.

10:14 Job has a complaint and he says so. He cannot be justified but he can be excused, for he had a reason to complain. Let this be a warning to us that we keep our tempers better when under the severe lash of God.

10:18 Job now asserts that life is a burden. He challenges God to tell him why he gave him life if it was to become such a burden. One commentator favors Job at this point by saying, "We may charitably suppose that that which troubled Job was that he was in a condition of life which (as he conceived) hindered the main end of his life, which was the glorifying of God. His harp was hung on the willow trees, and he was quite out of tune for praising God."*

22 A land of darkness, as darkness *itself; and* of the shadow of death,
without any order, and *where* the light *is* as darkness.

5. Zophar Speaks
a. Job Is a Lying Hypocrite

11 THEN answered Zo'phar the Na'a-math-ite, and said,
2 Should not the multitude of words be answered? and should a
man full of talk be justified?
3 Should thy lies make men hold their peace? and when thou mockest,
shall no man make thee ashamed?
4 For thou hast said, My doctrine *is* pure, and I am clean in thine eyes.
5 But oh that God would speak, and open his lips against thee;
6 And that he would shew thee the secrets of wisdom, that *they are* double
to that which is! Know therefore that God exacteth of thee *less* than thine
iniquity *deserveth*.

b. God Is Sovereign and Cannot Be Judged

7 Canst thou by searching find out God? canst thou find out the Almighty
unto perfection?
8 *It is* as high as heaven; what canst thou do? deeper than hell; what canst
thou know?
9 The measure thereof *is* longer than the earth, and broader than the sea.
10 If he cut off, and shut up, or gather together, then who can hinder him?
11 For he knoweth vain men: he seeth wickedness also; will he not then
consider *it*?
12 For vain man would be wise, though man be born *like* a wild ass's colt.

c. He Urges Job to Repent and Be Delivered

13 If thou prepare thine heart, and stretch out thine hands toward him;
14 If iniquity *be* in thine hand, put it far away, and let not wickedness
dwell in thy tabernacles.
15 For then shalt thou lift up thy face without spot; yea, thou shalt be
stedfast, and shalt not fear:
16 Because thou shalt forget *thy* misery, *and* remember *it* as waters *that*
pass away:
17 And *thine* age shall be clearer than the noonday; thou shalt shine forth,
thou shalt be as the morning.
18 And thou shalt be secure, because there is hope; yea, thou shalt dig
about thee, and thou shalt take thy rest in safety.
19 Also thou shalt lie down, and none shall make *thee* afraid; yea, many
shall make suit unto thee.
20 But the eyes of the wicked shall fail, and they shall not escape, and their
hope *shall be as* the giving up of the ghost.

☆**11:1ff**
11:2 Job 8:2; 15:2 Prov 10:19 Jas 1:19
11:3 Job 17:2; 21:3
11:4 Job 6:10 1 Pet 3:15
☆**11:6** Job 22:5
11:7 Job 33:12, 13 36:26; 37:5 Isa 40:28 Eph 3:8
11:8 2 Chron 6:18 Job 22:12; 38:17 Prov 25:2, 3
11:10 Dan 4:35
11:11 Job 24:23 34:21–23 Heb 4:13 Rev 2:23
11:12 Ps 62:9
☆**11:13** Ps 78:8; 88:9 143:6 Lk 12:47
11:15 Ps 27:3; 46:2
11:16 Isa 65:16
11:17 Ps 37:6
11:19 Lev 26:6 Isa 45:14 Zeph 3:13
☆**11:20** Job 6:9; 34:22

11:1ff *Zophar* simply repeats the arguments advanced by Bildad and Eliphaz. According to him, Job is a liar and a hypocrite, and his plight is the just recompense for his sins.

11:6 *God exacteth of thee less than thine iniquity deserveth.* Zophar arrogantly insists that Job is a hypocrite who deserves more, not less, punishment. His conclusion is based upon his own notion of right and wrong, not on the mysticism of Eliphaz or the scholarship of Bildad.

11:13ff Zophar is certain that Job is at fault. But even in error, the remedy he suggests is excellent for those who are at fault. He tells Job to (1) prepare his heart for a change, (2) turn his hands toward God, (3) put away his transgressions, and (4) "let not wickedness dwell in thy tabernacles" (11:14), that is, implying that Job had sheltered wicked people and permitted wicked practices and that, for this, God had taken away his offspring as punishment. Zophar believed Job's home life had to be changed.

11:20 Zophar concludes his statement by saying that the eyes of the wicked shall fail. Apparently, he suspects that Job will not take his counsel. He warns him that those who persist in their wickedness and will not reform are doomed. Thus he passed adverse judgment against this poor suffering saint.

6. Job Responds to Zophar
a. Job Claims He Is Innocent

12 AND Job answered and said,
2No doubt but ye *are* the people, and wisdom shall die with you.
3But I have understanding as well as you; I *am* not inferior to you: yea,
who knoweth not such things as these?
4I am *as* one mocked of his neighbour, who calleth upon God, and he
answereth him: the just upright *man is* laughed to scorn.
5He that is ready to slip with *his* feet *is as* a lamp despised in the thought
of him that is at ease.
6The tabernacles of robbers prosper, and they that provoke God are
secure; into whose hand God bringeth *abundantly*.

b. God Knows What We Should Do

7But ask now the beasts, and they shall teach thee; and the fowls of the
air, and they shall tell thee:
8Or speak to the earth, and it shall teach thee: and the fishes of the sea
shall declare unto thee.
9Who knoweth not in all these that the hand of the LORD hath wrought
this?
10In whose hand *is* the soul of every living thing, and the breath of all
mankind.
11Doth not the ear try words? and the mouth taste his meat?
12With the ancient *is* wisdom; and in length of days understanding.
13With him *is* wisdom and strength, he hath counsel and understanding.

c. God Is Sovereign

14Behold, he breaketh down, and it cannot be built again: he shutteth up
a man, and there can be no opening.
15Behold, he withholdeth the waters, and they dry up: also he sendeth
them out, and they overturn the earth.
16With him *is* strength and wisdom: the deceived and the deceiver *are* his.
17He leadeth counsellors away spoiled, and maketh the judges fools.
18He looseth the bond of kings, and girdeth their loins with a girdle.
19He leadeth princes away spoiled, and overthroweth the mighty.
20He removeth away the speech of the trusty, and taketh away the
understanding of the aged.
21He poureth contempt upon princes, and weakeneth the strength of the
mighty.
22He discovereth deep things out of darkness, and bringeth out to light
the shadow of death.
23He increaseth the nations, and destroyeth them: he enlargeth the
nations, and straiteneth them *again*.

12:2☆ Job 16:1, 2; 17:10; Prov 28:11; 1 Cor 4:10
12:3 2 Cor 11:5, 21–23
12:4 Job 6:29; 17:6; 30:1, 9, 10
12:6 Job 9:24; 21:9; Jer 5:27
12:7☆ Isa 41:20; Prov 6:6
12:9☆
12:10 Acts 17:28
12:11☆ Job 34:3; 1 Cor 10:15
12:12 Job 32:7
12:13☆ Prov 2:6, 7; Col 2:3
12:14 Job 19:10; 37:7; Isa 25:2; Mal 1:4
12:15 Gen 7:11–24; Deut 11:17; 1 Kgs 8:35
12:16 Job 13:7, 9
12:17 Isa 19:12–14; 1 Cor 1:19, 20
12:18 Ps 116:16; Dan 2:21
12:19 Job 34:24–28; Rev 17:14; 19:19–21
12:20 Job 32:9; Prov 10:21
12:21 2 Kgs 9:26; Job 12:18; 34:19; Ps 107:40; Eph 6:10, 14
12:22 Dan 2:22; 1 Cor 4:5
12:23☆ Isa 9:3; Zech 10:8

12:2 *wisdom shall die with you.* Job ironically concedes that his friends are the human embodiment of wisdom. They "know it all," so that when they perish from the earth wisdom will be gone also!
12:7 *ask now the beasts.* Job puts down his friends. They think they have all the wisdom in the world. He suggests that the beasts and the birds of the earth can teach *them* things they do not know. So also they can learn from the fishes in the seas (12:8).
12:9 All creatures and men derive their being from God. They depend on him for their continuance and are used by him for his purposes. He does with them as he pleases (Ps. 115:3).
12:11 The mind of man has as good a faculty for discerning between truth and error as the palate has of discerning between the sweet and the sour. The wicked indeed will learn that their minds, although reprobate, will not excuse them from their responsibility to discern the good from the evil.
12:13 This discourse of Job's deals with the wisdom, power, and sovereignty of God, who orders and disposes man's affairs according to his own will. No one can contradict or resist God.
12:23 Job has a right understanding of the providence of God who causes droughts (12:15), who controls kings and priests (12:18, 19), and who makes nations rise and fall at his good pleasure. No nation is so strong that it can keep itself from falling and none is so weak that God cannot make it strong.

24 He taketh away the heart of the chief of the people of the earth, and
causeth them to wander in a wilderness *where there is* no way.
25 They grope in the dark without light, and he maketh them to stagger
like *a* drunken *man*.

12:24 Dan 4:16, 33; Hos 7:11; Acts 13:11; 1 Jn 2:11

d. Job Is Angry with His Friends

13 LO, mine eye hath seen all *this*, mine ear hath heard and understood it.
2 What ye know, *the same* do I know also: I *am* not inferior unto you.
3 Surely I would speak to the Almighty, and I desire to reason with God.
4 But ye *are* forgers of lies, ye *are* all physicians of no value.
5 O that ye would altogether hold your peace! and it should be your
wisdom.
6 Hear now my reasoning, and hearken to the pleadings of my lips.
7 Will ye speak wickedly for God? and talk deceitfully for him?
8 Will ye accept his person? will ye contend for God?
9 Is it good that he should search you out? or as one man mocketh
another, do ye *so* mock him?
10 He will surely reprove you, if ye do secretly accept persons.
11 Shall not his excellency make you afraid? and his dread fall upon you?
12 Your remembrances *are* like unto ashes, your bodies to bodies of clay.

13:1 Job 12:9
☆**13:2** Job 12:3
13:3 Job 13:22; 23:4; Jer 12:1, 2
☆**13:4** Ps 119:69; Jer 23:32; Hos 5:13; Mk 2:17
13:5 Job 21:5; Prov 17:28
13:7 Job 27:4
☆**13:9** Ps 44:21; Jer 17:10
☆**13:10** Job 32:21
☆**13:11** Job 31:23
13:12 Job 15:3

e. Job Says, "I Know That I Am Righteous"

13 Hold your peace, let me alone, that I may speak, and let come on me
what *will*.
14 Wherefore do I take my flesh in my teeth, and put my life in mine
hand?
15 Though he slay me, yet will I trust in him: but I will maintain mine own
ways before him.
16 He also *shall be* my salvation: for an hypocrite shall not come before
him.
17 Hear diligently my speech, and my declaration with your ears.
18 Behold now, I have ordered *my* cause; I know that I shall be justified.
19 Who *is* he *that* will plead with me? for now, if I hold my tongue, I shall
give up the ghost.

☆**13:15** Job 7:6; 27:5
13:16 Job 34:21–23
13:18 Job 9:21; 23:4
☆**13:19** Job 7:21

13:2 Job declares that he does not need his friends to teach him. He is not inferior to them in understanding. He vehemently says his friends "are forgers of lies" (13:4). These are strong words in his own defense. In 13:8, 9 Job turns the tables on his friends. He suggests that God does not need them to conduct the divine business and that those who pass judgment on others should ask themselves whether they are righteous. If they are not, they have no reason to examine and damn others.

13:4 Job's temper has shortened; he chastises his friends. He compares himself to them, then condemns them for their falsehoods, their willingness to act as his judge, and their deceitfulness under cover of taking God's side against him.

13:9–11 Job threatens his friends with the judgment of God against them for what they have done to him. The fulfillment of this prophetic admonition was to take place later when Job is called upon by God to pray for these benighted people who sinned against God when they judged Job unfairly.

13:12 One commentator suggests that this verse might be interpreted as saying that their protestations on behalf of God against Job "are not better than dust" and their arguments are "like so many heaps of dirt."*

13:15 Or, "Though he slay me, yet will I trust in him. I will argue my case before him."† Despite his low estate, Job continues to depend on God. Even if God slays him he will still trust him. This is a high expression of faith. "We must be well pleased with God as a friend even when he seems to come forth against us as an enemy" (33:8–10).* All things will work together for good, even when everything appears to be against this (Rom. 8:28).

13:19 Job knows of no sins he has committed. He does not know why he is suffering. He can only think God is dealing with him capriciously or arbitrarily; this he cannot comprehend.

f. Job Prays to God

20 Only do not two *things* unto me: then will I not hide myself from thee.
13:21 21 Withdraw thine hand far from me: and let not thy dread make me
Job 9:34 Ps 39:10 afraid.
13:22 22 Then call thou, and I will answer: or let me speak, and answer thou me.
Job 14:15 13:23☆ 23 How many *are* mine iniquities and sins? make me to know my
1 Sam 26:18 13:24 transgression and my sin.
Job 19:11; 33:10 24 Wherefore hidest thou thy face, and holdest me for thine enemy?
Ps 13:1 13:25 25 Wilt thou break a leaf driven to and fro? and wilt thou pursue the dry
Lev 26:36 Job 11:18 stubble?
13:26 26 For thou writest bitter things against me, and makest me to possess the
Job 9:18 iniquities of my youth.
13:27 27 Thou puttest my feet also in the stocks, and lookest narrowly unto all
Job 2:7 my paths; thou settest a print upon the heels of my feet.
28 And he, as a rotten thing, consumeth, as a garment that is moth eaten.

14:1☆ **14** MAN *that is* born of a woman *is* of few days, and full of trouble.
Job 5:7 14:2 2 He cometh forth like a flower, and is cut down: he fleeth also as
Job 8:9 Ps 90:5, 6 a shadow, and continueth not.
Isa 40:6, 7 3 And dost thou open thine eyes upon such an one, and bringest me into
judgment with thee?
14:4 4 Who can bring a clean *thing* out of an unclean? not one.
Job 15:14; 25:4 14:5☆ 5 Seeing his days *are* determined, the number of his months *are* with thee,
Job 21:21 thou hast appointed his bounds that he cannot pass;
14:6 6 Turn from him, that he may rest, till he shall accomplish, as an hireling,
Job 7:19 his day.
14:7☆ 7 For there is hope of a tree, if it be cut down, that it will sprout again,
and that the tender branch thereof will not cease.
8 Though the root thereof wax old in the earth, and the stock thereof die
in the ground;
9 *Yet* through the scent of water it will bud, and bring forth boughs like a
plant.
14:10 10 But man dieth, and wasteth away: yea, man giveth up the ghost, and
Job 13:19 where *is* he?
14:11 11 *As* the waters fail from the sea, and the flood decayeth and drieth up:
Job 3:13 Isa 19:5 12 So man lieth down, and riseth not: till the heavens *be* no more, they
shall not awake, nor be raised out of their sleep.
14:13 13 O that thou wouldest hide me in the grave, that thou wouldest keep me
Isa 26:20 secret, until thy wrath be past, that thou wouldest appoint me a set time,
and remember me!
14:14☆ 14 If a man die, shall he live *again?* all the days of my appointed time will
I wait, till my change come.
15 Thou shalt call, and I will answer thee: thou wilt have a desire to the
14:16 work of thine hands.
Job 10:6; 31:4 34:21 16 For now thou numberest my steps: dost thou not watch over my sin?

13:23ff Job complains that he is at a loss to understand what God has against him and why his Maker has treated him so rigorously.

14:1 Job reminds himself of his own frailties and mortality. Men's lives are short, sorrowful, and sinful. He pleads for God to mitigate his miseries and deliver him from his agonies.

14:5 Men's days are numbered, not numberless, determined in advance by God who sets their dates, and cannot be extended or shortened by anyone.

14:7 Cut down a tree and it will sprout again. Thus the fate of the tree is better than that of a man, since he cannot sprout again.

14:14 *If a man die shall he live again?* Job knows that all men must die. The greater question is whether they will have life beyond the grave. His answer is in the affirmative. For believers we must expect death to come; we must even desire that it come, as those who long to be with Christ. Yet we must be willing to wait for death to come, believing that God's will in this regard is best; we must prepare for death with diligence so that the change will be a blessed one.

34 For the congregation of hypocrites *shall be* desolate, and fire shall
consume the tabernacles of bribery.
35 They conceive mischief, and bring forth vanity, and their belly
prepareth deceit.

15:34 Job 8:13, 22
15:35 Ps 7:14; Isa 59:4

2. Job Responds to Eliphaz

a. Job Calls His Friends Miserable Comforters

16 THEN Job answered and said,
2 I have heard many such things: miserable comforters *are* ye all.
3 Shall vain words have an end? or what emboldeneth thee that thou
answerest?
4 I also could speak as ye *do:* if your soul were in my soul's stead, I could
heap up words against you, and shake mine head at you.
5 *But* I would strengthen you with my mouth, and the moving of my lips
should asswage *your grief.*

☆**16:1**
16:2 Job 13:4; 21:34
16:3 Job 6:26
16:4 Ps 22:7; 109:25; Lam 2:15; Mt 27:39

b. "God Has Made Me Weary"

6 Though I speak, my grief is not asswaged: and *though* I forbear, what
am I eased?
7 But now he hath made me weary: thou hast made desolate all my
company.
8 And thou hast filled me with wrinkles, *which* is a witness *against me:* and
my leanness rising up in me beareth witness to my face.
9 He teareth *me* in his wrath, who hateth me: he gnasheth upon me with
his teeth; mine enemy sharpeneth his eyes upon me.
10 They have gaped upon me with their mouth; they have smitten me
upon the cheek reproachfully; they have gathered themselves together
against me.
11 God hath delivered me to the ungodly, and turned me over into the
hands of the wicked.
12 I was at ease, but he hath broken me asunder: he hath also taken *me* by
my neck, and shaken me to pieces, and set me up for his mark.
13 His archers compass me round about, he cleaveth my reins asunder,
and doth not spare; he poureth out my gall upon the ground.
14 He breaketh me with breach upon breach, he runneth upon me like a
giant.
15 I have sewed sackcloth upon my skin, and defiled my horn in the dust.

☆**16:6** Job 9:27, 28
16:7 Job 7:3; 19:13–15
16:8 Job 10:17; 19:20
16:9 Job 13:24; 33:10; Ps 35:16; Hos 6:1
16:10 Job 30:12; Ps 22:13; 35:15; Lam 3:30
16:12 Job 7:20; 9:17; Lam 3:12
16:13 Job 6:4; 19:12; 20:25
16:14 Job 9:17; Joel 2:7
16:15 Gen 37:34; Job 30:19; Ps 69:11; Lam 2:3

c. Job Affirms His Innocence

16 My face is foul with weeping, and on my eyelids *is* the shadow of death;
17 Not for *any* injustice in mine hands: also my prayer *is* pure.
18 O earth, cover not thou my blood, and let my cry have no place.
19 Also now, behold, my witness *is* in heaven, and my record *is* on high.
20 My friends scorn me: *but* mine eye poureth out *tears* unto God.
21 O that one might plead for a man with God, as a man *pleadeth* for his
neighbour!

16:16 Job 16:20; 24:17
16:17 Job 27:4; Jonah 3:8
16:19 Job 19:25–27; 31:2; Phil 1:18
16:20 Lam 2:19

16:1 Job replies to Eliphaz. He accuses him of endless repetition, wrong conclusions, continuing impertinence, and causeless obstinacy. He also says he has broken all the laws of friendship by doing to his brother what his brother would not have done to him.

16:6ff In this passage Job argues that (1) his family has been scattered; (2) he is a skeleton from his disease and pains; (3) his adversaries are a terror to him; (4) he is being insolently abused; (5) instead of delivering him God has turned him over to the hands of the wicked (his so-called friends); (6) God has also afflicted him furiously; and (7) Job has stripped himself of all his honor and comfort, using sackcloth rather than silks.

16:22 Job 3:13
22 When a few years are come, then I shall go the way *whence* I shall not
return.

d. Job Wants God to Vindicate Him

17:1☆ Ps 88:3, 4
17 MY breath is corrupt, my days are extinct, the graves *are ready* for
me.
17:2☆ Job 12:4
2 *Are there* not mockers with me? and doth not mine eye continue in their
provocation?
17:3☆ Job 12:20
3 Lay down now, put me in a surety with thee; who *is* he *that* will strike
hands with me?
17:4☆
4 For thou hast hid their heart from understanding: therefore shalt thou
not exalt *them.*
17:5☆ Lev 19:13, 16 Job 11:20
5 He that speaketh flattery to *his* friends, even the eyes of his children
shall fail.
17:6☆ Job 30:10
6 He hath made me also a byword of the people; and aforetime I was as a
tabret.
17:7☆ Job 16:8, 16
7 Mine eye also is dim by reason of sorrow, and all my members *are* as a
shadow.
17:8 Job 22:19
8 Upright *men* shall be astonied at this, and the innocent shall stir up
himself against the hypocrite.
17:9 Job 22:30 Prov 4:18
9 The righteous also shall hold on his way, and he that hath clean hands
shall be stronger and stronger.
17:10 Job 12:2
10 But as for you all, do ye return, and come now: for I cannot find *one*
wise *man* among you.
17:11 Job 7:6
11 My days are past, my purposes are broken off, *even* the thoughts of my
heart.
12 They change the night into day: the light *is* short because of darkness.
17:13 Job 3:13; 21:26 25:6
13 If I wait, the grave *is* mine house: I have made my bed in the darkness.
14 I have said to corruption, Thou *art* my father: to the worm, *Thou art* my
mother, and my sister.
17:15 Job 7:6
15 And where *is* now my hope? as for my hope, who shall see it?
17:16–17ff☆ 17:16 Job 3:17; 21:33
16 They shall go down to the bars of the pit, when *our* rest together *is* in
the dust.

3. Bildad's Second Speech

a. Job Cannot Fool His Friends

18:1☆
18 THEN answered Bildad the Shu'hite, and said,
2 How long *will it be ere* ye make an end of words? mark, and
afterwards we will speak.
18:3 Ps 73:22
3 Wherefore are we counted as beasts, *and* reputed vile in your sight?
4 He teareth himself in his anger: shall the earth be forsaken for thee? and
shall the rock be removed out of his place?

17:1ff Job has reached a point of no return. He says (1) he is a dying man (17:1); (2) he is a despised man (17:6); and (3) he is a man of sorrows (17:7).

17:2–7 Job makes his appeal to God and begs for him to appear on his behalf. He asks God to right him against these friends who have wronged him. He needs God to do this, for he does not know how to do it himself.

17:16 "Job and his friends could not agree now, but they will both be quiet in the grave; the dust of that will shortly stop their mouths and put an end to the controversy."*

17:17ff Job professes that his conscience is clear. His walk is upright and he has committed no gross sins. His conscience is void of offense against man and God. If he is guilty, he wants that fact shown him. He does not want the earth to cover the blood of his transgression. He has integrity and looks to the end of his days with good conscience.

18:1 Bildad now strikes at Job with bitter words and adds to his affliction. He says Job is an obstinate, haughty sinner who refuses to repent. He goes on to describe the misery and the end of the wicked. Obviously he believes sincerely, albeit wrongly, that Job is a wretched sinner.

b. The Consequence of Being Wicked

5 Yea, the light of the wicked shall be put out, and the spark of his fire
shall not shine.
6 The light shall be dark in his tabernacle, and his candle shall be put out
with him.
7 The steps of his strength shall be straitened, and his own counsel shall
cast him down.
8 For he is cast into a net by his own feet, and he walketh upon a snare.
9 The gin shall take *him* by the heel, *and* the robber shall prevail against
him.
10 The snare *is* laid for him in the ground, and a trap for him in the way.
11 Terrors shall make him afraid on every side, and shall drive him to his
feet.
12 His strength shall be hungerbitten, and destruction *shall be* ready at his
side.
13 It shall devour the strength of his skin: *even* the firstborn of death shall
devour his strength.
14 His confidence shall be rooted out of his tabernacle, and it shall bring
him to the king of terrors.
15 It shall dwell in his tabernacle, because *it is* none of his: brimstone shall
be scattered upon his habitation.
16 His roots shall be dried up beneath, and above shall his branch be cut
off.
17 His remembrance shall perish from the earth, and he shall have no
name in the street.
18 He shall be driven from light into darkness, and chased out of the
world.
19 He shall neither have son nor nephew among his people, nor any
remaining in his dwellings.
20 They that come after *him* shall be astonied at his day, as they that went
before were affrighted.
21 Surely such *are* the dwellings of the wicked, and this *is* the place *of him*
that knoweth not God.

☆**18:5** Job 21:17; Prov 13:9; 20:20; 24:20
18:6 Job 12:25
18:8 Job 22:10; Ps 9:15; 35:8
18:11 Job 15:21; 18:18
18:12 Isa 8:21
18:13 Zech 14:12
18:14 Job 8:22; 15:21; 27:18
18:15 Ps 11:6
18:16 Job 15:30, 32; Hos 9:16; Amos 2:9
18:17 Job 24:20; Ps 34:16; Prov 2:22; 10:7
18:18 Job 5:14; 27:21–23; Prov 14:32; Dan 4:33; 5:21
18:19 Job 27:14, 15; Isa 14:22; Jer 22:30
18:20 Jer 50:27; Obad 12; Lk 19:42, 44

4. Job Responds to Bildad

a. Job Asks for Proof of His Guilt

19 THEN Job answered and said,
2 How long will ye vex my soul, and break me in pieces with
words?
3 These ten times have ye reproached me: ye are not ashamed *that* ye
make yourselves strange to me.
4 And be it indeed *that* I have erred, mine error remaineth with myself.
5 If indeed ye will magnify *yourselves* against me, and plead against me
my reproach:

☆**19:1ff**
19:5 Ps 35:26; 38:16; 55:12

b. God Has Sent My Troubles

6 Know now that God hath overthrown me, and hath compassed me with
his net.

19:6 Job 16:11; 18:8–10; 27:2; Ps 66:11

18:5ff Bildad takes into account the miserable estate in which Job finds himself. He cites Job's own words that he sits in the dark, is bewildered, frightened, ensnared, and on his way out of this present evil world. Since he assumes that this is the condition of wicked men, he concludes that Job must be one of them.

19:1ff Job arraigns his friends for vexing his soul, breaking him in pieces, giving him a bad character, estranging themselves from him, and magnifying themselves against him. In an unkind and unjust fashion, they have impugned his integrity.

19:7 Job 30:20, 24 Hab 1:2 **19:8**☆ Job 3:23; 30:26 Lam 3:7, 9 **19:9** Job 12:17, 19 Ps 89:39, 44 Lam 5:16 **19:10** Job 7:6; 12:14 **19:11** Job 13:24; 16:9 33:10 **19:12** Job 16:13

7 Behold, I cry out of wrong, but I am not heard: I cry aloud, but *there is*
no judgment.
8 He hath fenced up my way that I cannot pass, and he hath set darkness
in my paths.
9 He hath stripped me of my glory, and taken the crown *from* my head.
10 He hath destroyed me on every side, and I am gone: and mine hope
hath he removed like a tree.
11 He hath also kindled his wrath against me, and he counteth me unto
him as *one of* his enemies.
12 His troops come together, and raise up their way against me, and
encamp round about my tabernacle.

c. Men Have Abandoned Me

19:13 Job 16:7, 20 Ps 69:8 88:8, 18

13 He hath put my brethren far from me, and mine acquaintance are verily
estranged from me.
14 My kinsfolk have failed, and my familiar friends have forgotten me.
15 They that dwell in mine house, and my maids, count me for a stranger:
I am an alien in their sight.
16 I called my servant, and he gave *me* no answer; I intreated him with my
mouth.
17 My breath is strange to my wife, though I intreated for the children's
sake of mine own body.

19:18 2 Kgs 2:23 Isa 3:5 **19:19** Ps 38:11; 55:13 **19:20** Job 33:21 Ps 102:5 Lam 4:8

18 Yea, young children despised me; I arose, and they spake against me.
19 All my inward friends abhorred me: and they whom I loved are turned
against me.
20 My bone cleaveth to my skin and to my flesh, and I am escaped with
the skin of my teeth.

d. Have Pity on Me

19:21 Job 1:11 Ps 38:2 **19:22** Ps 16:11; 69:26 **19:23** Isa 30:8 Jer 36:2

21 Have pity upon me, have pity upon me, O ye my friends; for the hand
of God hath touched me.
22 Why do ye persecute me as God, and are not satisfied with my flesh?
23 Oh that my words were now written! oh that they were printed in a
book!
24 That they were graven with an iron pen and lead in the rock for ever!

19:25☆ Job 16:19 Isa 43:14 Jer 50:34 **19:26**☆ Ps 17:15 Mt 5:8 1 Cor 13:12 1 Jn 3:2

e. My Confidence Is in My Redeemer

25 For I know *that* my redeemer liveth, and *that* he shall stand at the latter
day upon the earth:
26 And *though* after my skin *worms* destroy this *body*, yet in my flesh shall
I see God:

19:8 Job himself errs in thinking that what has happened to him comes from God. He does not yet see that it springs from God's conflict with Satan and from God's own confidence that Job will not wilt under the attacks.

19:25 Job cannot convince his friends of his innocence. His last and only confidence is that God will vindicate him—be his Redeemer!

19:26 The doctrine of the resurrection appears in undeveloped form in the Old Testament. It awaits fuller explication in the New Testament. Among the Old Testament references to the resurrection are Ps. 16:10; 49:15; Isa. 26:19; Dan. 12:2; and Hos. 13:14. In Jesus' day the Jews looked for the resurrection of the body (John 11:24; Heb. 6:1, 2). It was denied by the Sadducees, the theological liberals of the day, whereas it was basic to Pharisee teaching (Acts 23:6–8). Jesus believed and taught the resurrection of the body (Matt. 22:29–32; Luke 14:14; John 5:28, 29). The early apostles preached it constantly and consistently (Acts 4:2; 17:18; 24:15). The central theme of the Christian hope is the resurrection of the dead. This doctrine has its foundation in the resurrection of Jesus, a historical event. The second part of 19:26 has been interpreted as meaning: "then even without my flesh I shall see God." This is not linguistically legitimate; the correct meaning is that we shall see him in our bodies. 19:27 makes it even clearer, for it says "I shall see for myself." To interpret this as other than physical or bodily has no warrant.

27 Whom I shall see for myself, and mine eyes shall behold, and not
another; *though* my reins be consumed within me.
28 But ye should say, Why persecute we him, seeing the root of the matter **19:28** Job 19:22
is found in me?
29 Be ye afraid of the sword: for wrath *bringeth* the punishments of the **19:29** Job 15:22; 22:4
sword, that ye may know *there is* a judgment. Ps 9:7 Eccles 12:14

5. Zophar's Second Speech: the Wrath of God Awaits the Wicked

20 THEN answered Zo′phar the Na′a-math-ite, and said, **☆20:1ff**
2 Therefore do my thoughts cause me to answer, and for *this* I
make haste.
3 I have heard the check of my reproach, and the spirit of my understand- **20:3** Job 19:3
ing causeth me to answer.
4 Knowest thou *not* this of old, since man was placed upon earth, **☆20:4** Deut 4:32
5 That the triumphing of the wicked *is* short, and the joy of the hypocrite **☆20:5** Job 8:12, 13
but for a moment? Ps 37:35, 36
6 Though his excellency mount up to the heavens, and his head reach unto **☆20:6** Isa 14:13, 14
the clouds; Obad 3, 4
7 *Yet* he shall perish for ever like his own dung: they which have seen him **☆20:7** Job 4:20; 7:10
shall say, Where *is* he? 8:18; 14:20
8 He shall fly away as a dream, and shall not be found: yea, he shall be **☆20:8** Ps 73:20; 90:5
chased away as a vision of the night.
9 The eye also *which* saw him shall *see him* no more; neither shall his place **☆20:9** Job 7:8, 10
any more behold him. 8:18
10 His children shall seek to please the poor, and his hands shall restore **20:10** Job 5:4
their goods. 27:16, 17
11 His bones are full *of the sin* of his youth, which shall lie down with him **☆20:11** Job 13:26
in the dust.
12 Though wickedness be sweet in his mouth, *though* he hide it under his **20:12** Job 15:16
tongue;
13 *Though* he spare it, and forsake it not; but keep it still within his
mouth:
14 *Yet* his meat in his bowels is turned, *it is* the gall of asps within him.
15 He hath swallowed down riches, and he shall vomit them up again:
God shall cast them out of his belly.
16 He shall suck the poison of asps: the viper's tongue shall slay him. **20:16** Deut 32:24, 33
17 He shall not see the rivers, the floods, the brooks of honey and butter. **☆20:17**
18 That which he laboured for shall he restore, and shall not swallow *it* **☆20:18**
down: according to *his* substance *shall* the restitution *be*, and he shall not
rejoice *therein.*
19 Because he hath oppressed *and* hath forsaken the poor; *because* he hath **☆20:19**
violently taken away an house which he builded not; Job 24:2-4; 35:9
20 Surely he shall not feel quietness in his belly, he shall not save of that **☆20:20**
which he desired. Eccles 5:13-15
21 There shall none of his meat be left; therefore shall no man look for his **20:21** Job 15:29
goods.

20:1ff Zophar is now angry with Job, whom he charges with provocation for his failure to accept the judgment of his condemning friends. Zophar speaks about "the triumphing of the wicked," "the joy of the hypocrite," "wickedness . . . in [Job's] mouth," and charges that "he hath oppressed and hath forsaken the poor." According to him, Job was indeed a great sinner.

20:4-9 The prosperity of the wicked man does not last for long; his ruin is certain and will come upon him shortly.

20:11ff Zophar insists that Job is guilty of the lusts of the flesh (20:11), the love of the world and its wealth (20:15), and has been mistreating his neighbors by injustice, oppression, and violence (20:19).

20:17-20 Zophar says Job will be disappointed in his expectation of worldly wealth, that he will lose his estate, and that his mind will have no rest.

20:22☆ Job 5:5; 15:21
22 In the fulness of his sufficiency he shall be in straits: every hand of the
wicked shall come upon him.

20:23 Num 11:33 Ps 78:30, 31
23 *When* he is about to fill his belly, *God* shall cast the fury of his wrath
upon him, and shall rain *it* upon him while he is eating.
24 He shall flee from the iron weapon, *and* the bow of steel shall strike him
through.

20:25 Job 16:13 18:11, 14
25 It is drawn, and cometh out of the body; yea, the glittering sword
cometh out of his gall: terrors *are* upon him.

20:26 Job 15:30; 18:18
26 All darkness *shall be* hid in his secret places: a fire not blown shall
consume him; it shall go ill with him that is left in his tabernacle.

20:27 Deut 31:28
27 The heaven shall reveal his iniquity; and the earth shall rise up against
him.

20:28 Deut 28:31 Job 21:30
28 The increase of his house shall depart, *and his goods* shall flow away in
the day of his wrath.

20:29 Job 27:13 31:2, 3
29 This *is* the portion of a wicked man from God, and the heritage
appointed unto him by God.

6. Job Responds to Zophar

a. He Asks Not to Be Interrupted

21:2 Job 11:3; 17:2 **21:4**☆ Job 6:11; 7:11 **21:5** Judg 18:19 Job 29:9; 40:4 Prov 30:32 **21:6** Ps 55:5 Hab 3:16

21 BUT Job answered and said,
2 Hear diligently my speech, and let this be your consolations.
3 Suffer me that I may speak; and after that I have spoken, mock on.
4 As for me, *is* my complaint to man? and if *it were so*, why should not my
spirit be troubled?
5 Mark me, and be astonished, and lay *your* hand upon *your* mouth.
6 Even when I remember I am afraid, and trembling taketh hold on my
flesh.

b. The Wicked Seem to Prosper at Times

21:7☆ Ps 73:3 Jer 12:1 Hab 1:13 Rev 17:2–4 **21:8** Ps 17:14 **21:9** Job 12:6 Ps 73:5

7 Wherefore do the wicked live, become old, yea, are mighty in power?
8 Their seed is established in their sight with them, and their offspring
before their eyes.
9 Their houses *are* safe from fear, neither *is* the rod of God upon them.
10 Their bull gendereth, and faileth not; their cow calveth, and casteth not
her calf.
11 They send forth their little ones like a flock, and their children dance.

21:12 Job 36:11
12 They take the timbrel and harp, and rejoice at the sound of the organ.
13 They spend their days in wealth, and in a moment go down to the
grave.

21:14 Job 22:17
14 Therefore they say unto God, Depart from us; for we desire not the
knowledge of thy ways.

21:15 Job 22:17; 34:9
15 What *is* the Almighty, that we should serve him? and what profit should
we have, if we pray unto him?

21:16 Job 22:18
16 Lo, their good *is* not in their hand: the counsel of the wicked is far from
me.

20:22ff Job can expect wrath and vengeance against him from God. His ruin is inevitable and inescapable. It will be a terrible ruin that will make his family suffer and it will be a righteous and just judgment. "Never was any doctrine better explained, or worse applied, than this by Zophar, who intended by all this to prove Job a hypocrite."*

21:4 *Is my complaint to man?* Rather, "I am complaining about God, not man."†

21:7 Job argues that, contrary to what his friends have said, the wicked sometimes prosper like the green bay tree. They do not reap their just deserts. Indirectly he is saying that those who appear to be reaping bad rewards for their wickedness may not be wicked, even as the prosperous may not be just.

17 How oft is the candle of the wicked put out! and *how oft* cometh their
destruction upon them! *God* distributeth sorrows in his anger.
18 They are as stubble before the wind, and as chaff that the storm carrieth
away.

☆21:17 Job 18:5, 6
21:18 Job 13:25; Ps 1:4; 35:5; 83:13; Isa 17:13

c. God, the Supreme Judge, Does as He Chooses

19 God layeth up his iniquity for his children: he rewardeth him, and he
shall know *it*.
20 His eyes shall see his destruction, and he shall drink of the wrath of the
Almighty.
21 For what pleasure *hath* he in his house after him, when the number of
his months is cut off in the midst?
22 Shall *any* teach God knowledge? seeing he judgeth those that are high.
23 One dieth in his full strength, being wholly at ease and quiet.
24 His breasts are full of milk, and his bones are moistened with marrow.
25 And another dieth in the bitterness of his soul, and never eateth with
pleasure.
26 They shall lie down alike in the dust, and the worms shall cover them.

21:19 Ex 20:5; Ps 109:9; Mt 23:31–35
21:20 Isa 51:17; Jer 25:15; Ezek 18:4; Rev 14:10
21:22 Job 36:22; Ps 82:1; Isa 40:14; Rom 11:34
21:23 Job 20:11
21:26 Job 3:13; 24:20; Eccles 9:2; Isa 14:11

d. Job Knows His Friends Will Disagree with Him

27 Behold, I know your thoughts, and the devices *which* ye wrongfully
imagine against me.
28 For ye say, Where *is* the house of the prince? and where *are* the
dwelling places of the wicked?
29 Have ye not asked them that go by the way? and do ye not know their
tokens,
30 That the wicked is reserved to the day of destruction? they shall be
brought forth to the day of wrath.
31 Who shall declare his way to his face? and who shall repay him *what* he
hath done?
32 Yet shall he be brought to the grave, and shall remain in the tomb.
33 The clods of the valley shall be sweet unto him, and every man shall
draw after him, as *there are* innumerable before him.
34 How then comfort ye me in vain, seeing in your answers there
remaineth falsehood?

21:28 Num 16:26–34; Job 1:3; Ps 37:36; 52:5, 6
21:30 Job 20:29; Prov 16:4; Rom 2:5; 2 Pet 2:9
21:33 Job 3:19, 22; 17:16; 24:24
☆21:34 Job 16:2; 42:7

D. THE THIRD SET OF SPEECHES WITH JOB'S FRIENDS

1. Eliphaz's Third Speech

a. God Is Just; Job Is Being Punished for His Sins

22 THEN El'i-phaz the Te'man-ite answered and said,
2 Can a man be profitable unto God, as he that is wise may be
profitable unto himself?
3 *Is it* any pleasure to the Almighty, that thou art righteous? or *is it* gain
to him, that thou makest thy ways perfect?

☆22:1ff
22:2 Job 35:7; Lk 17:10

21:17ff Job argues that the wicked often end their days in pomp and prosperity. They do not always reap as they have sown in this present life. Thus he shows that "no certain judgment can be made of men's characters by their outward condition."* The righteous may suffer and the wicked may prosper. But we need not think God will let the wicked go forever unpunished or the righteous left forever in their misery. There is a payday some day.

21:34 Job says that his friends will disagree with him. But he concludes that because they begin with the wrong premise, they come out with the wrong conclusion. They cannot comfort him as they think they are doing when they argue that piety will be crowned by prosperity. This, he says, is an erroneous conclusion, so they cannot deliver him from his misery.

22:1ff Eliphaz makes a true statement but draws a false conclusion. He argues that Job has complained so much about his afflictions that he is accusing God of being unjust by sending them. This is true enough in itself, but inappropriate, for Job was not a wretched sinner, and he was not accusing God of injustice.

22:4 Job 14:3
4 Will he reprove thee for fear of thee? will he enter with thee into judgment?

22:5 Job 11:6; 15:5
5 *Is* not thy wickedness great? and thine iniquities infinite?

b. He Lists Job's Transgressions

22:6☆ Ex 22:26; Deut 24:6, 17; Job 24:3, 9; 31:19, 20; Ezek 18:16
6 For thou hast taken a pledge from thy brother for nought, and stripped the naked of their clothing.

22:7 Job 31:31; Mt 10:42
7 Thou hast not given water to the weary to drink, and thou hast withholden bread from the hungry.

22:8 Job 9:24; 12:19
8 But *as for* the mighty man, he had the earth; and the honourable man dwelt in it.

22:9☆ Job 6:27; 24:3, 21
9 Thou hast sent widows away empty, and the arms of the fatherless have been broken.

22:10 Job 15:21; 18:8
10 Therefore snares *are* round about thee, and sudden fear troubleth thee;
11 Or darkness, *that* thou canst not see; and abundance of waters cover thee.

22:12 Job 11:7–9
12 *Is* not God in the height of heaven? and behold the height of the stars, how high they are!

22:13 Ps 10:11; 64:5; 94:7; Isa 29:15
13 And thou sayest, How doth God know? can he judge through the dark cloud?

22:14 Job 26:9
14 Thick clouds *are* a covering to him, that he seeth not; and he walketh in the circuit of heaven.

c. Job Should Admit His Sins, Repent, and Be Restored

22:15☆ Job 14:19; 15:32; 34:36; Isa 28:2; Mt 7:26, 27
15 Hast thou marked the old way which wicked men have trodden?
16 Which were cut down out of time, whose foundation was overflown with a flood:

22:17 Job 21:14, 15
17 Which said unto God, Depart from us: and what can the Almighty do for them?

22:18 Job 12:6; 21:16
18 Yet he filled their houses with good *things:* but the counsel of the wicked is far from me.

22:19 Ps 58:10; 107:42
19 The righteous see *it,* and are glad: and the innocent laugh them to scorn.

22:20 Job 15:30
20 Whereas our substance is not cut down, but the remnant of them the fire consumeth.

22:21☆ Ps 34:10
21 Acquaint now thyself with him, and be at peace: thereby good shall come unto thee.

22:22 Job 6:10; 23:12; Prov 2:6
22 Receive, I pray thee, the law from his mouth, and lay up his words in thine heart.

22:23 Job 8:5; 11:14; Isa 19:22; Zech 1:3
23 If thou return to the Almighty, thou shalt be built up, thou shalt put away iniquity far from thy tabernacles.

22:6 Eliphaz says in effect that they have been very lenient with Job. Now he takes off his gloves and catalogues the numerous sins he thinks Job has committed. He says all of Job's present troubles are the result of having committed these supposed sins. Never was a friend more ill-used than was Job by this searing indictment.

22:9 Eliphaz's indictment against Job contradicted God's own appraisal of his servant. Job's friends were guilty of false accusations and they were committing sin when they so accused him. In retrospect, their own sin seems to be far greater than all of their accusations against Job.

22:15 Wrong as Eliphaz was, he must be given credit for seeking to get Job to repent and thus to recover his lost estate. He assures him of restoration if only he will follow what Eliphaz has laid before him. But if Job were to do this, he would then have lost his own integrity, for he was innocent of the charge they pressed against him.

22:21 It is strange that from the same fountain both sweet and bitter water may come. Eliphaz's excellent counsel was built on the mistaken notion that Job was a wicked man and an enemy and stranger to God. But for those who are wicked, Eliphaz's counsel, if followed, will bring about restitution and assurance to sinners that God's grace will cover their transgressions and discharge them from their indebtedness.

24 Then shalt thou lay up gold as dust, and the *gold* of O'phir as the stones
of the brooks.
25 Yea, the Almighty shall be thy defence, and thou shalt have plenty of
silver.
26 For then shalt thou have thy delight in the Almighty, and shalt lift up
thy face unto God.
27 Thou shalt make thy prayer unto him, and he shall hear thee, and thou
shalt pay thy vows.
28 Thou shalt also decree a thing, and it shall be established unto thee:
and the light shall shine upon thy ways.
29 When *men* are cast down, then thou shalt say, *There is* lifting up; and
he shall save the humble person.
30 He shall deliver the island of the innocent: and it is delivered by the
pureness of thine hands.

2. Job Responds to Eliphaz

a. Job Wants to Find God and Be Judged by Him

23 THEN Job answered and said,
2 Even to day *is* my complaint bitter: my stroke is heavier than
my groaning.
3 Oh that I knew where I might find him! *that* I might come *even* to his
seat!
4 I would order *my* cause before him, and fill my mouth with arguments.
5 I would know the words *which* he would answer me, and understand
what he would say unto me.
6 Will he plead against me with *his* great power? No; but he would put
strength in me.
7 There the righteous might dispute with him; so should I be delivered for
ever from my judge.
8 Behold, I go forward, but he *is* not *there;* and backward, but I cannot
perceive him:
9 On the left hand, where he doth work, but I cannot behold *him;* he
hideth himself on the right hand, that I cannot see *him;*
10 But he knoweth the way that I take: *when* he hath tried me, I shall come
forth as gold.
11 My foot hath held his steps, his way have I kept, and not declined.
12 Neither have I gone back from the commandment of his lips; I have
esteemed the words of his mouth more than my necessary *food.*
13 But he *is* in one *mind,* and who can turn him? and *what* his soul
desireth, even *that* he doeth.
14 For he performeth *the thing that is* appointed for me: and many such
things are with him.
15 Therefore am I troubled at his presence: when I consider, I am afraid of
him.
16 For God maketh my heart soft, and the Almighty troubleth me:

22:24 Job 31:24, 25
22:26 Job 27:10; Ps 37:4; Isa 58:14
22:27 Job 33:26; 34:28; Isa 58:9
22:28 Job 11:17; Ps 112:4
22:29 Job 5:11; Mt 23:12; Jas 4:6; 1 Pet 5:5
☆**22:30** Ps 42:7; Ps 18:20; 24:3, 4
23:2 Job 6:2, 3; 7:11
☆**23:3**
23:4 Job 13:18; Isa 43:26
23:6 Job 9:4; 2 Cor 12:9, 10
23:7 Job 13:3, 16
23:8 Job 9:11
☆**23:10** Job 7:18; Ps 7:9; 11:5
23:11 Job 31:7; Ps 17:5; 44:18; 1 Thess 2:10
23:12 Job 6:10
☆**23:13**
23:16 Deut 20:3; Job 10:18, 19; 19:8; Jer 51:46

22:30 "A good man is a public good. Sinners fare the better for the saints, whether they are aware of it or not."*

23:3 Job realizes that his only refuge is God himself. His friends will not believe him, but he is confident that God will sustain his innocence. But the face of God is hidden from him. The inscrutibility of the Almighty is now his problem. Why does God not intervene on his behalf and succor him?

23:10 Job knows that these friends have judged him about what they knew not and thus charged him with that of which he was never guilty. But his God, who knew every step he had taken, would not do so. God understands honest intentions though some men do not, cannot, or will not.

23:13 God's counsels are immutable and his power is irresistible. Men desire things they may not do, or cannot do, or dare not do. But the sovereign God, whose ways are true and pure, will do all he chooses, for all that he does is in accord with the counsel of his will.

17 Because I was not cut off before the darkness, *neither* hath he covered
the darkness from my face.

b. God's Punishment of the Wicked Is Sometimes Deferred

24 WHY, seeing times are not hidden from the Almighty, do they that
know him not see his days?
2 *Some* remove the landmarks; they violently take away flocks, and feed
thereof.
3 They drive away the ass of the fatherless, they take the widow's ox for a
pledge.
4 They turn the needy out of the way: the poor of the earth hide
themselves together.
5 Behold, *as* wild asses in the desert, go they forth to their work; rising
betimes for a prey: the wilderness *yieldeth* food for them *and* for *their*
children.
6 They reap *every one* his corn in the field: and they gather the vintage of
the wicked.
7 They cause the naked to lodge without clothing, that *they have* no
covering in the cold.
8 They are wet with the showers of the mountains, and embrace the rock
for want of a shelter.
9 They pluck the fatherless from the breast, and take a pledge of the poor.
10 They cause *him* to go naked without clothing, and they take away the
sheaf *from* the hungry;
11 *Which* make oil within their walls, *and* tread *their* winepresses, and
suffer thirst.
12 Men groan from out of the city, and the soul of the wounded crieth out:
yet God layeth not folly *to them.*
13 They are of those that rebel against the light; they know not the ways
thereof, nor abide in the paths thereof.
14 The murderer rising with the light killeth the poor and needy, and in
the night is as a thief.
15 The eye also of the adulterer waiteth for the twilight, saying, No eye
shall see me: and disguiseth *his* face.
16 In the dark they dig through houses, *which* they had marked for
themselves in the daytime: they know not the light.
17 For the morning *is* to them even as the shadow of death: if *one* know
them, they are in the terrors of the shadow of death.
18 He *is* swift as the waters; their portion is cursed in the earth: he
beholdeth not the way of the vineyards.
19 Drought and heat consume the snow waters: *so doth* the grave *those*
which have sinned.
20 The womb shall forget him; the worm shall feed sweetly on him; he
shall be no more remembered; and wickedness shall be broken as a tree.
21 He evil entreateth the barren *that* beareth not: and doeth not good to
the widow.

24:1☆ Isa 2:12; Jer 46:10
24:2 Deut 19:14; 27:17
24:3 Ex 22:26
24:4 Job 29:16; 30:25; Prov 14:31; Amos 8:4
24:5 Job 39:5–8; Ps 104:23
24:8 Lam 4:5; Heb 11:38
24:9 Job 6:27
24:12 Job 9:23, 24; Mal 2:17; Rom 2:4, 5
24:13☆
24:14☆ Ps 10:8; Prov 7:9; Mic 2:1
24:15☆
24:16☆ Ex 22:2; Mt 6:19
24:17☆ Ps 91:5
24:18 Job 5:3; 22:11, 16; 27:20
24:19 Job 6:16, 17; 21:13
24:20 Job 18:17; 19:10; 21:26; Prov 10:7; Isa 49:15; Dan 4:14
24:21☆ Job 22:9

24:1 Job once again speaks concerning the prosperity of wicked people. He argues that many who act corruptly and live in open defiance of the rules of justice and common honesty, thrive and succeed in their wrongful practices. We do not see them get their just deserts in this life.

24:13–17 Job says here that those who secretly practice villainy may go undiscovered and therefore unpunished. But their time is coming.

24:21 Again Job insists that experience proves that daring sinners prosper and often end their days in apparent peace. Such sinners seem to have the protection of deity (24:23). Job insists that they are exalted for a time, perhaps even till they die. But a day comes when they are cut off forever. Their death, even if they die in ease, will prove to be their ruin. The grave at last will consume those who have sinned. The land of darkness will be their habitation because they loved darkness rather than light. In 24:25 Job challenges the opposition to show him that he is wrong. Those who speak the truth need never fear being brought to the test, for a fair examination will sustain them.

22 He draweth also the mighty with his power: he riseth up, and no *man* is
sure of life.
23 *Though* it be given him *to be* in safety, whereon he resteth; yet his eyes
are upon their ways.
24 They are exalted for a little while, but are gone and brought low; they
are taken out of the way as all *other,* and cut off as the tops of the ears of
corn.
25 And if *it be* not *so* now, who will make me a liar, and make my speech
nothing worth?

24:22 Job 9:4, 10:4; 11:11; 12:6
☆**24:24** Job 14:21; Ps 37:10
24:25 Job 6:28; 27:4

3. Bildad's Third Speech: No Man Is Righteous

25 THEN answered Bildad the Shu'hite, and said,
2 Dominion and fear *are* with him, he maketh peace in his high
places.
3 Is there any number of his armies? and upon whom doth not his light
arise?
4 How then can man be justified with God? or how can he be clean *that is*
born of a woman?
5 Behold even to the moon, and it shineth not; yea, the stars are not pure
in his sight.
6 How much less man, *that is* a worm? and the son of man, *which is* a
worm?

☆**25:1ff**
25:2 Job 9:4; 16:19; 31:2; 36:5; 37:23
25:3 Jas 1:17
25:4 Job 4:17; 9:2; 14:4
25:5 Job 15:15; 31:26
25:6 Job 7:17

4. Job's Response to Bildad: God Is Great and Good

26 BUT Job answered and said,
2 How hast thou helped *him that is* without power? *how* savest
thou the arm *that hath* no strength?
3 How hast thou counselled *him that hath* no wisdom? and *how* hast thou
plentifully declared the thing as it is?
4 To whom hast thou uttered words? and whose spirit came from thee?
5 Dead *things* are formed from under the waters, and the inhabitants
thereof.
6 Hell *is* naked before him, and destruction hath no covering.
7 He stretcheth out the north over the empty place, *and* hangeth the earth
upon nothing.
8 He bindeth up the waters in his thick clouds; and the cloud is not rent
under them.
9 He holdeth back the face of his throne, *and* spreadeth his cloud upon it.
10 He hath compassed the waters with bounds, until the day and night
come to an end.
11 The pillars of heaven tremble and are astonished at his reproof.
12 He divideth the sea with his power, and by his understanding he
smiteth through the proud.

☆**26:1ff**
26:2 Ps 71:9; Isa 35:3, 4; 41:5–7
26:5 Job 3:13; Ps 88:10
☆**26:7** Job 9:8
26:8 Job 37:11; Prov 30:4
26:9 Job 22:14; Ps 97:2; 105:39
26:10 Job 38:1–11, 19, 20, 24; Prov 8:29
26:12 Isa 51:15; Jer 31:35

24:24 Job concludes that no one can say or prove that all who are in trouble are wicked, for it is certain that not all who are rich are righteous.

25:1ff Bildad either knows he cannot best Job in the argument or he feels that the pursuit of the issue is no longer profitable. He contents himself in saying that God is glorious and man is guilty and impure before God. At this point he might have profitably applied this theology to himself and joined Job in common prayer for both of them. But he was not yet ready for that.

26:1ff Here Job employs irony in making light of Bildad's discourse. He goes on to praise the majesty and greatness of God, who performs deeds no one can match. Job then begins an extensive discourse that will end his argument at 31:40. Then follows the extended statement of Elihu, which leads to the intervention of God into the disputation. God puts an end to the matter; Job is delivered and his friends are dealt with in judgment.

26:7 Job gives many illustrations of the wisdom and power of God in the creation and the preservation of this planet earth. God hung the earth on nothing; he set the bounds of the waters; he created giant amphibians under the waters; he shook and even now shakes the mountains by mighty storms and tempests.

26:13 Job 9:8; Isa 27:1
26:14 Job 36:29; 37:4, 5

13 By his spirit he hath garnished the heavens; his hand hath formed the
crooked serpent.
14 Lo, these *are* parts of his ways: but how little a portion is heard of him?
but the thunder of his power who can understand?

5. Job Sums Up His Situation
a. He Is Righteous

27:1☆ Job 13:12; 29:1
27:2 Job 9:18; 16:11; 34:5
27:3 Job 32:8; 33:4
27:4 Job 6:28; 33:3; Jn 8:55; 2 Cor 11:10
27:5 Job 6:29
27:6 Job 2:3; 13:18

27 MOREOVER Job continued his parable, and said,
2 *As* God liveth, *who* hath taken away my judgment; and the
Almighty, *who* hath vexed my soul;
3 All the while my breath *is* in me, and the spirit of God *is* in my nostrils;
4 My lips shall not speak wickedness, nor my tongue utter deceit.
5 God forbid that I should justify you: till I die I will not remove mine
integrity from me.
6 My righteousness I hold fast, and will not let it go: my heart shall not
reproach *me* so long as I live.

b. The Wicked Will Be Condemned at Last

27:7☆
27:8 Job 8:13; 11:20; 12:10
27:9 Job 35:12, 13; Prov 1:27, 28; Isa 1:15
27:10 Job 22:26, 27; Hab 3:18
27:13ff☆
27:13 Job 20:29; Prov 22:23
27:14 Job 18:19; 20:10
27:15 Ps 78:64
27:17 Job 20:18–21
27:18 Job 8:15
27:19 Job 7:8, 21
27:20 Job 15:21; 20:8; 34:20
27:21 Job 7:10; 21:18

7 Let mine enemy be as the wicked, and he that riseth up against me as
the unrighteous.
8 For what *is* the hope of the hypocrite, though he hath gained, when God
taketh away his soul?
9 Will God hear his cry when trouble cometh upon him?
10 Will he delight himself in the Almighty? will he always call upon God?
11 I will teach you by the hand of God: *that* which *is* with the Almighty
will I not conceal.
12 Behold, all ye yourselves have seen *it;* why then are ye thus altogether
vain?
13 This *is* the portion of a wicked man with God, and the heritage of
oppressors, *which* they shall receive of the Almighty.
14 If his children be multiplied, *it is* for the sword: and his offspring shall
not be satisfied with bread.
15 Those that remain of him shall be buried in death: and his widows shall
not weep.
16 Though he heap up silver as the dust, and prepare raiment as the clay;
17 He may prepare *it,* but the just shall put *it* on, and the innocent shall
divide the silver.
18 He buildeth his house as a moth, and as a booth *that* the keeper
maketh.
19 The rich man shall lie down, but he shall not be gathered: he openeth
his eyes, and he *is* not.
20 Terrors take hold on him as waters, a tempest stealeth him away in the
night.
21 The east wind carrieth him away, and he departeth: and as a storm
hurleth him out of his place.

27:1 The purpose of Job from this point on is to back up all he has said with a solemn oath, to silence his critics, and to assume all blame if it can be shown that he is a liar.

27:7ff In this passage Job expresses his own hatred of the wicked. He makes clear the fact that whatever prosperity, power, and adulation they attain will come to an unhappy end. Their wealth will disappear, terror will overtake them, and the wrath of God will be their portion. The gates of hell are locked and barred. A great gulf is fixed between the good and the bad so that whoever has not fled to the arms of divine grace will not be able to flee from the arm of divine wrath. The wicked will be cut off.

27:13ff The wicked who have long enjoyed prosperity come to a miserable end. They are cursed by God, and their wives and offspring participate in the calamity. Thus no man lives or dies to himself. What he does has effects in the lives of his loved ones and neighbors.

[22]For *God* shall cast upon him, and not spare: he would fain flee out of
his hand.
[23]*Men* shall clap their hands at him, and shall hiss him out of his place.

27:22 Job 11:20; Jer 13:14; Ezek 5:11; 24:14
27:23 Job 18:18; 20:8

c. The Fear of the Lord Is Wisdom

28 SURELY there is a vein for the silver, and a place for gold *where*
they fine *it.*
[2]Iron is taken out of the earth, and brass *is* molten *out of* the stone.
[3]He setteth an end to darkness, and searcheth out all perfection: the
stones of darkness, and the shadow of death.
[4]The flood breaketh out from the inhabitant: *even the waters* forgotten of
the foot: they are dried up, they are gone away from men.
[5]*As for* the earth, out of it cometh bread: and under it is turned up as it
were fire.
[6]The stones of it *are* the place of sapphires: and it hath dust of gold.
[7]*There is* a path which no fowl knoweth, and which the vulture's eye hath
not seen:
[8]The lion's whelps have not trodden it, nor the fierce lion passed by it.
[9]He putteth forth his hand upon the rock; he overturneth the mountains
by the roots.
[10]He cutteth out rivers among the rocks; and his eye seeth every precious
thing.
[11]He bindeth the floods from overflowing; and *the thing that is* hid
bringeth he forth to light.
[12]But where shall wisdom be found? and where *is* the place of under-
standing?
[13]Man knoweth not the price thereof; neither is it found in the land of the
living.
[14]The depth saith, It *is* not in me: and the sea saith, *It is* not with me.
[15]It cannot be gotten for gold, neither shall silver be weighed *for* the price
thereof.
[16]It cannot be valued with the gold of O′phir, with the precious onyx, or
the sapphire.
[17]The gold and the crystal cannot equal it: and the exchange of it *shall
not be for* jewels of fine gold.
[18]No mention shall be made of coral, or of pearls: for the price of wisdom
is above rubies.
[19]The topaz of E-thi-o′pi-a shall not equal it, neither shall it be valued
with pure gold.
[20]Whence then cometh wisdom? and where *is* the place of understanding?
[21]Seeing it is hid from the eyes of all living, and kept close from the fowls
of the air.
[22]Destruction and death say, We have heard the fame thereof with our
ears.
[23]God understandeth the way thereof, and he knoweth the place thereof.
[24]For he looketh to the ends of the earth, *and* seeth under the whole
heaven;
[25]To make the weight for the winds; and he weigheth the waters by
measure.

☆28:1ff
☆28:12 Job 28:23, 28
28:17 Prov 8:10; 16:16
28:18 Prov 8:11
28:19 Prov 8:19
28:22 Job 26:6
28:23 Ps 11:4; 33:13, 14; Prov 8:22–36; 15:3
28:25 Job 12:15; 38:8–11; Ps 135:7

28:1ff Job now declares that wisdom, not wealth and power, is man's greatest need. Its value is unequaled. All other things shrink into insignificance if there is no wisdom. He concludes with a sparkling statement: "The fear of the LORD, that is wisdom; and to depart from evil is understanding" (28:28).

28:12ff Job says that the price of wisdom is inestimable. Whoever has it is richer and happier than those who only have silver and gold. Wisdom, he says, can be found only in true religion. Men must utterly despair of finding it anywhere but in God.

28:26 Job 37:3, 6, 11, 12; 38:25

26 When he made a decree for the rain, and a way for the lightning of the
thunder:
27 Then did he see it, and declare it; he prepared it, yea, and searched it
out.

28:28☆ Ps 111:10 Prov 1:7; 9:10

28 And unto man he said, Behold, the fear of the Lord, that *is* wisdom;
and to depart from evil *is* understanding.

d. Job Describes His Pilgrim Journey
(1) His Earlier Prosperity

29:1☆ Job 13:12; 27:1
29:2☆ Jer 31:28 Ps 37:28
29:3 Job 11:17

29 MOREOVER Job continued his parable, and said,
2 Oh that I were as *in* months past, as *in* the days *when* God
preserved me;
3 When his candle shined upon my head, *and when* by his light I walked
through darkness;

29:4 Job 15:8 Ps 25:14

4 As I was in the days of my youth, when the secret of God *was* upon my
tabernacle;
5 When the Almighty *was* yet with me, *when* my children *were* about me;

29:6 Deut 32:13 Ps 81:16

6 When I washed my steps with butter, and the rock poured me out rivers
of oil;
7 When I went out to the gate through the city, *when* I prepared my seat
in the street!
8 The young men saw me, and hid themselves: and the aged arose, *and*
stood up.

29:9 Job 21:5

9 The princes refrained talking, and laid *their* hand on their mouth.
10 The nobles held their peace, and their tongue cleaved to the roof of
their mouth.

29:11 Job 4:3, 4

11 When the ear heard *me,* then it blessed me; and when the eye saw *me,*
it gave witness to me:

29:12 Job 24:4, 9 31:17, 21; 34:28
29:13 Job 31:19 Isa 27:13
29:14 Job 27:5, 6 Ps 132:9

12 Because I delivered the poor that cried, and the fatherless, and *him that*
had none to help him.
13 The blessing of him that was ready to perish came upon me: and I
caused the widow's heart to sing for joy.
14 I put on righteousness, and it clothed me: my judgment *was* as a robe
and a diadem.

29:16 Prov 29:7 Eph 5:1 Jas 1:27
29:17 Ps 3:7 Prov 30:14
29:19 Jer 17:8 Hos 14:5
29:20 Gen 49:24 Ps 18:34
29:21 Job 4:3 32:11, 12
29:22 Deut 32:2 Ezek 20:46 Amos 7:11

15 I was eyes to the blind, and feet *was* I to the lame.
16 I *was* a father to the poor: and the cause *which* I knew not I searched
out.
17 And I brake the jaws of the wicked, and plucked the spoil out of his
teeth.
18 Then I said, I shall die in my nest, and I shall multiply *my* days as the
sand.
19 My root *was* spread out by the waters, and the dew lay all night upon
my branch.
20 My glory *was* fresh in me, and my bow was renewed in my hand.
21 Unto me *men* gave ear, and waited, and kept silence at my counsel.
22 After my words they spake not again; and my speech dropped upon
them.

28:28 The thought of Job may be summed up this way: to be truly religious is to be truly wise. God is the author of wisdom. It is attained by those who fear God, who then gives them wisdom. No one can learn to do well who has not first ceased to do evil.

29:1ff Job rehearses the details of his life before his present catastrophe. In it he defends himself by a presentation of how he lived and acted; he has the sure conviction that he had followed the law of love in his treatment of neighbors and was himself accepted among men as a man of honor, integrity, and wisdom.

29:2 Job describes the heights to which he had attained and the depths to which he had fallen. He had enjoyed family, wealth, and peace; he had honor and power among men; he had done good to all he could. His prospects for the future were bright. All of this made his present situation more calamitous and difficult to bear. Like Naomi he had gone out full only to return home again empty.

23 And they waited for me as for the rain; and they opened their mouth
wide *as* for the latter rain.
24 *If* I laughed on them, they believed *it* not; and the light of my
countenance they cast not down.
25 I chose out their way, and sat chief, and dwelt as a king in the army, as
one *that* comforteth the mourners.

(2) His Present Calamities

30 BUT now *they that are* younger than I have me in derision, whose
fathers I would have disdained to have set with the dogs of my
flock.
2 Yea, whereto *might* the strength of their hands *profit* me, in whom old
age was perished?
3 For want and famine *they were* solitary; fleeing into the wilderness in
former time desolate and waste.
4 Who cut up mallows by the bushes, and juniper roots *for* their meat.
5 They were driven forth from among *men,* (they cried after them as *after*
a thief;)
6 To dwell in the cliffs of the valleys, *in* caves of the earth, and *in* the
rocks.
7 Among the bushes they brayed; under the nettles they were gathered
together.
8 *They were* children of fools, yea, children of base men: they were viler
than the earth.
9 And now am I their song, yea, I am their byword.
10 They abhor me, they flee far from me, and spare not to spit in my face.
11 Because he hath loosed my cord, and afflicted me, they have also let
loose the bridle before me.
12 Upon *my* right *hand* rise the youth; they push away my feet, and they
raise up against me the ways of their destruction.
13 They mar my path, they set forward my calamity, they have no helper.
14 They came *upon me* as a wide breaking in *of waters:* in the desolation
they rolled themselves *upon me.*
15 Terrors are turned upon me: they pursue my soul as the wind: and my
welfare passeth away as a cloud.
16 And now my soul is poured out upon me; the days of affliction have
taken hold upon me.
17 My bones are pierced in me in the night season: and my sinews take no
rest.
18 By the great force *of my disease* is my garment changed: it bindeth me
about as the collar of my coat.
19 He hath cast me into the mire, and I am become like dust and ashes.
20 I cry unto thee, and thou dost not hear me: I stand up, and thou
regardest me *not.*
21 Thou art become cruel to me: with thy strong hand thou opposest
thyself against me.
22 Thou liftest me up to the wind; thou causest me to ride *upon it,* and
dissolvest my substance.
23 For I know *that* thou wilt bring me *to* death, and *to* the house appointed
for all living.

29:25 Job 1:3; 4:4; 16:5; 31:37; Isa 61:1–3
☆30:1 Job 12:4; Isa 3:5; Mk 14:65
☆30:2
30:9 Job 12:4; 17:6; Ps 35:15, 16; 69:12
30:10 Isa 50:6; Mt 26:67
30:11 Ruth 1:21; Ps 32:9; 88:7
30:12 Ps 140:4, 5; Isa 3:5
30:15 Job 3:25; 7:9; Ps 55:3–5
30:16 Ps 22:14
30:19 Ps 69:2, 14; Jer 38:6
30:20 Job 19:7; Ps 80:4, 5; Lam 38:8, 44; Mt 15:23
30:21 Job 16:9, 14; 19:6, 22
30:22 Job 9:17; 27:21
30:23 Job 9:22; 10:8

30:1ff Job speaks of his great fall from prosperity, status, and acceptability to a place of suffering in which even people of low estate make light of him. They compose songs to affront him, shun him, maliciously attack him, and do all the mischief they can to him. He ends with a vivid description of his present plight and bemoans the fact that his harp has turned to mourning.

30:2ff Job's ignominy includes the fact that those whom he had befriended and helped now have turned against him and are insulting him. They compose songs and sing them to rejoice in his downfall. He is a byword to them and they abhor him.

30:24☆ Job 19:7
30:25☆ Job 24:4; Ps 35:13, 14; Rom 12:15
30:26 Job 19:8; Jer 8:15; Mic 1:12
30:27 Lam 2:11
30:28 Job 19:7; Ps 44:19; Mic 1:8
30:30 Job 2:7; Ps 102:3; 119:83

24 Howbeit he will not stretch out *his* hand to the grave, though they cry in his destruction.

25 Did not I weep for him that was in trouble? was *not* my soul grieved for the poor?

26 When I looked for good, then evil came *unto me:* and when I waited for light, there came darkness.

27 My bowels boiled, and rested not: the days of affliction prevented me.

28 I went mourning without the sun: I stood up, *and* I cried in the congregation.

29 I am a brother to dragons, and a companion to owls.

30 My skin is black upon me, and my bones are burned with heat.

31 My harp also is *turned* to mourning, and my organ into the voice of them that weep.

(3) His Final Defense of Himself

31:1 Gen 6:2; 2 Sam 11:2–4; Mt 5:28
31:2 Job 18:12

31 I MADE a covenant with mine eyes: why then should I think upon a maid?

2 For what portion of God *is there* from above? and *what* inheritance of the Almighty from on high?

3 *Is* not destruction to the wicked? and a strange *punishment* to the workers of iniquity?

31:4 Job 14:16; 28:24; 34:21; Prov 5:21
31:5 Mic 2:11
31:6 Prov 16:11; Isa 26:7
31:7 Lev 26:16; Job 9:30; 23:11; Mic 6:15

4 Doth not he see my ways, and count all my steps?

5 If I have walked with vanity, or if my foot hath hasted to deceit;

6 Let me be weighed in an even balance that God may know mine integrity.

7 If my step hath turned out of the way, and mine heart walked after mine eyes, and if any blot hath cleaved to mine hands;

8 *Then* let me sow, and let another eat; yea, let my offspring be rooted out.

9 If mine heart have been deceived by a woman, or *if* I have laid wait at my neighbour's door;

31:10 Deut 28:30; Jer 8:10; Hos 4:13, 14
31:11 Lev 20:10; Deut 22:24; Ezek 16:38
31:12 Job 15:30
31:13 Deut 24:14, 15

10 *Then* let my wife grind unto another, and let others bow down upon her.

11 For this *is* an heinous crime; yea, it *is* an iniquity *to be punished by* the judges.

12 For it *is* a fire *that* consumeth to destruction, and would root out all mine increase.

13 If I did despise the cause of my manservant or of my maidservant, when they contended with me;

14 What then shall I do when God riseth up? and when he visiteth, what shall I answer him?

31:15 Job 10:3
31:16 Ex 22:22–24; Job 20:19
31:17 Job 22:7, 9; 29:12
31:19 Job 22:6; 24:4; 29:13

15 Did not he that made me in the womb make him? and did not one fashion us in the womb?

16 If I have withheld the poor from *their* desire, or have caused the eyes of the widow to fail;

17 Or have eaten my morsel myself alone, and the fatherless hath not eaten thereof;

18 (For from my youth he was brought up with me, as *with* a father, and I have guided her from my mother's womb;)

19 If I have seen any perish for want of clothing, or any poor without covering;

20 If his loins have not blessed me, and *if* he were *not* warmed with the fleece of my sheep;

30:24, 25 Job consoled himself by the thought that his troubles would not follow him to the grave and that in his own prosperity he identified with and had sympathy for those who lived in misery. "Those who mourn with them that mourn will bear their own sorrows the better when it comes their turn to drink the bitter cup."*

21 If I have lifted up my hand against the fatherless, when I saw my help
in the gate:
22 *Then* let mine arm fall from my shoulder blade, and mine arm be
broken from the bone.
23 For destruction *from* God *was* a terror to me, and by reason of his
highness I could not endure.
24 If I have made gold my hope, or have said to the fine gold, *Thou art* my
confidence;
25 If I rejoiced because my wealth *was* great, and because mine hand had
gotten much;
26 If I beheld the sun when it shined, or the moon walking *in* brightness;
27 And my heart hath been secretly enticed, or my mouth hath kissed my
hand:
28 This also *were* an iniquity *to be punished by* the judge: for I should have
denied the God *that is* above.
29 If I rejoiced at the destruction of him that hated me, or lifted up myself
when evil found him:
30 Neither have I suffered my mouth to sin by wishing a curse to his soul.
31 If the men of my tabernacle said not, Oh that we had of his flesh! we
cannot be satisfied.
32 The stranger did not lodge in the street: *but* I opened my doors to the
traveller.
33 If I covered my transgressions as Adam, by hiding mine iniquity in my
bosom:
34 Did I fear a great multitude, or did the contempt of families terrify me,
that I kept silence, *and* went not out of the door?
35 Oh that one would hear me! behold, my desire *is*, *that* the Almighty
would answer me, and *that* mine adversary had written a book.
36 Surely I would take it upon my shoulder, *and* bind it *as* a crown to me.
37 I would declare unto him the number of my steps; as a prince would I
go near unto him.
38 If my land cry against me, or that the furrows likewise thereof
complain;
39 If I have eaten the fruits thereof without money, or have caused the
owners thereof to lose their life:
40 Let thistles grow instead of wheat, and cockle instead of barley. The
words of Job are ended.

31:23 Job 13:11
31:24 Job 22:24; Mk 10:24
31:25 Ps 62:10
31:26 Deut 4:19; 17:3; Ezek 8:16
31:28 Deut 17:2–7; Josh 24:27; Isa 59:13; Prov 30:9; 2 Pet 2:1
31:29 Prov 17:5; 24:17; Obad 12
31:30 Job 5:3; Ps 7:4
31:33 Gen 3:10; Josh 7:11; Prov 28:13; 1 Jn 1:8–10
31:34 Ex 23:2; Prov 29:25
31:35 Job 19:7; 27:7; 30:20, 24, 28; 35:14; Ps 26:1
31:38 1 Kgs 21:19; Job 24:2, 6, 10–12; Hab 2:11; Jas 5:4
31:40 Isa 5:6; Zeph 2:9

III. THE SPEECHES OF ELIHU (32:1—37:24)

A. ELIHU'S ANGER BECAUSE JOB JUSTIFIES HIMSELF

32 SO these three men ceased to answer Job, because he *was* righteous
in his own eyes.
2 Then was kindled the wrath of E-li'hu the son of Bar'a-chel the Bu'zite,
of the kindred of Ram: against Job was his wrath kindled, because he
justified himself rather than God.
3 Also against his three friends was his wrath kindled, because they had
found no answer, and *yet* had condemned Job.
4 Now E-li'hu had waited till Job had spoken, because they *were* elder
than he.

32:1 Job 10:7; 13:18; 31:6; 33:9
☆**32:2**

32:2 Elihu is unhappy with Job's statement that God deals capriciously with men in this life. He sees that Job's three friends have lost the argument because they entertained too narrow a viewpoint. Elihu's main thesis is that God allowed Job to suffer in order to improve him. 36:6–15 contains Elihu's clearest statement on his theory of suffering. (See note on 37:24.)

5 When E-li'hu saw that *there was* no answer in the mouth of *these* three
men, then his wrath was kindled.

32:6 Job 15:10; Rom 13:7; 1 Tim 5:1; Tit 2:6

6 And E-li'hu the son of Bar'a-chel the Bu'zite answered and said, I *am*
young, and ye *are* very old; wherefore I was afraid, and durst not shew you
mine opinion.
7 I said, Days should speak, and multitude of years should teach wisdom.

32:8 Job 33:4; 38:36; Prov 2:6; Dan 2:21; Jas 1:5

8 But *there is* a spirit in man: and the inspiration of the Almighty giveth
them understanding.
9 Great men are not *always* wise: neither do the aged understand
judgment.

32:10☆

10 Therefore I said, Hearken to me; I also will shew mine opinion.

32:11 Prov 18:17

11 Behold, I waited for your words; I gave ear to your reasons, whilst ye
searched out what to say.
12 Yea, I attended unto you, and, behold, *there was* none of you that
convinced Job, *or* that answered his words:
13 Lest ye should say, We have found out wisdom: God thrusteth him
down, not man.
14 Now he hath not directed *his* words against me: neither will I answer
him with your speeches.
15 They were amazed, they answered no more: they left off speaking.

32:16 Prov 17:28; Amos 5:13

16 When I had waited, (for they spake not, but stood still, *and* answered
no more;)
17 *I said,* I will answer also my part, I also will shew mine opinion.

32:18☆

18 For I am full of matter, the spirit within me constraineth me.
19 Behold, my belly *is* as wine *which* hath no vent; it is ready to burst like
new bottles.
20 I will speak, that I may be refreshed: I will open my lips and answer.

32:21 Lev 19:15; Job 13:8, 10; 34:19; Prov 24:23

21 Let me not, I pray you, accept any man's person, neither let me give
flattering titles unto man.
22 For I know not to give flattering titles; *in so doing* my maker would
soon take me away.

B. GOD USES CALAMITIES TO CHASTEN MEN

33:1☆

33 WHEREFORE, Job, I pray thee, hear my speeches, and hearken to
all my words.
2 Behold, now I have opened my mouth, my tongue hath spoken in my
mouth.

33:3 Job 6:28; 27:4; 36:4

3 My words *shall be of* the uprightness of my heart: and my lips shall utter
knowledge clearly.

33:4☆ Job 10:3; 27:3; 32:8

4 The Spirit of God hath made me, and the breath of the Almighty hath
given me life.

32:10 *Hearken to me.* Elihu knew how to keep silent and listen to older and wiser friends. He also knew when and how to speak. He would betray his friends if he continued his silence. Even though his friends were superior to him in every way, they should not be offended by being contradicted and instructed by their inferiors for "Better is a poor and wise child than an old and foolish king" (Eccles. 4:13).

32:18 The God of providence can raise up younger people to speak, when aged men have gone dry and said all they can. God can give younger people things to say that will edify the church. The subject of their dispute can never be exhausted even though those who address the matter may be. Elihu will speak his piece with freedom and sincerity. He will say what is true, not what he thinks will please the listener.

33:1 Elihu did not agree with what his three companions had said earlier. He wanted to be deliberate and solemn in his speech. He would speak as he thought and not otherwise. He would speak so he could be understood, and he was willing to listen to Job for his comments when he had finished (33:5).

33:4 The Holy Spirit is the third person of the Trinity. He is God and has existed eternally with the Father and the Son. He is called by more than thirty different names or titles in the Scriptures. Here he is called *the spirit of God . . . and breath of the Almighty.* Elsewhere he is called (1) "the Spirit of life" (Rom. 8:2); (2) "the spirit of wisdom and understanding, the spirit of counsel and might, the spirit of knowledge" (Isa. 11:2); (3) "the Spirit of truth" (John 14:17); and (4) the "Spirit of God" (1 Cor. 12:3). As God, the Holy Spirit is a person who knows, feels, and wills. He has all the attributes of deity. (See note on Gen 17:1.)

5If thou canst answer me, set *thy words* in order before me, stand up.
6Behold, I *am* according to thy wish in God's stead: I also am formed out
of the clay.
7Behold, my terror shall not make thee afraid, neither shall my hand be
heavy upon thee.
8Surely thou hast spoken in mine hearing, and I have heard the voice of
thy words, *saying,*
9I am clean without transgression, I *am* innocent; neither *is there* iniquity
in me.
10Behold, he findeth occasions against me, he counteth me for his enemy,
11He putteth my feet in the stocks, he marketh all my paths.
12Behold, *in* this thou art not just: I will answer thee, that God is greater
than man.
13Why dost thou strive against him? for he giveth not account of any of
his matters.
14For God speaketh once, yea twice, *yet man* perceiveth it not.
15In a dream, in a vision of the night, when deep sleep falleth upon men,
in slumberings upon the bed;
16Then he openeth the ears of men, and sealeth their instruction,
17That he may withdraw man *from his* purpose, and hide pride from man.
18He keepeth back his soul from the pit, and his life from perishing by the
sword.
19He is chastened also with pain upon his bed, and the multitude of his
bones with strong *pain:*
20So that his life abhorreth bread, and his soul dainty meat.
21His flesh is consumed away, that it cannot be seen; and his bones *that*
were not seen stick out.
22Yea, his soul draweth near unto the grave, and his life to the destroyers.
23If there be a messenger with him, an interpreter, one among a
thousand, to shew unto man his uprightness:
24Then he is gracious unto him, and saith, Deliver him from going down
to the pit: I have found a ransom.
25His flesh shall be fresher than a child's: he shall return to the days of his
youth:
26He shall pray unto God, and he will be favourable unto him: and he
shall see his face with joy: for he will render unto man his righteousness.
27He looketh upon men, and *if any* say, I have sinned, and perverted *that*
which was right, and it profited me not;
28He will deliver his soul from going into the pit, and his life shall see the
light.
29Lo, all these *things* worketh God oftentimes with man,

☆**33:8ff**

☆**33:9** Job 7:21; 9:21; 10:7, 14
33:10 Job 13:23, 24; 16:17
33:11 Job 13:27
33:13 Job 40:2; Isa 45:9
33:14 Job 40:5; Ps 62:11
33:15 Job 4:12–17
33:16 Job 36:10, 15
33:17 Job 15:22
☆**33:19** Job 30:17
33:20 Job 3:24; 6:7; Ps 107:18
33:21 Job 16:8; 19:20; Ps 22:17
33:23 Job 36:18; Ps 49:7; Isa 38:17
33:26 Job 22:26, 27; 34:28
33:27 2 Sam 12:13; Lk 15:21; Rom 6:21
33:28 Job 22:28
33:29 Eph 1:11; Phil 2:13

33:8ff Elihu charges Job with saying things that reflect upon the justice and goodness of God. He carefully says that he is not speaking secondhand, but that he had heard Job say these things publicly. Had it been in private conversation, Elihu would not have repeated them. But since it was done in public, he would reprove Job in public.
33:9 Elihu strikes at Job from a somewhat different perspective. He knows that Job thinks himself to be innocent. But in thinking himself to be innocent, he then is guilty of charging God with injustice and with doing wrong in afflicting Job. According to Elihu, this is Job's sin.
33:19ff Elihu says that God has spoken to men through conscience; when nothing happens, he speaks through providence, which includes sensible instructions from God's ministers. Elihu argues that all of them were mistaken, for God often afflicts the body in love and has gracious designs for improving the soul. Sickness and suffering have their benefits.

30 To bring back his soul from the pit, to be enlightened with the light of
the living.
31 Mark well, O Job, hearken unto me: hold thy peace, and I will speak.
33:32☆ 32 If thou hast any thing to say, answer me: speak, for I desire to justify
thee.
33 If not, hearken unto me: hold thy peace, and I shall teach thee wisdom.

C. GOD DOESN'T SIN; HE IS NOT UNJUST

34:1☆ 34 FURTHERMORE E-li'hu answered and said,
2 Hear my words, O ye wise *men;* and give ear unto me, ye that
have knowledge.
34:3 1 Cor 2:15 Heb 5:14 3 For the ear trieth words, as the mouth tasteth meat.
4 Let us choose to us judgment: let us know among ourselves what *is*
good.
34:5☆ 5 For Job hath said, I am righteous: and God hath taken away my
judgment.
6 Should I lie against my right? my wound *is* incurable without transgres-
sion.
34:7 Ps 50:18 7 What man *is* like Job, *who* drinketh up scorning like water?
8 Which goeth in company with the workers of iniquity, and walketh with
wicked men.
34:9 Job 21:15; 35:3 Mal 3:14 9 For he hath said, It profiteth a man nothing that he should delight
himself with God.
34:10☆ Ps 92:15 10 Therefore hearken unto me, ye men of understanding: far be it from
God, *that he should do* wickedness; and *from* the Almighty, *that he should*
commit iniquity.
34:11 Ps 62:12 Prov 24:12 Mt 16:27 Rom 2:6 2 Cor 5:10 Rev 22:12 11 For the work of a man shall he render unto him, and cause every man
to find according to *his* ways.
12 Yea, surely God will not do wickedly, neither will the Almighty pervert
judgment.
34:13 Prov 8:23–30 Dan 4:35 13 Who hath given him a charge over the earth? or who hath disposed the
whole world?
34:14 Ps 104:29 14 If he set his heart upon man *if* he gather unto himself his spirit and his
breath;
34:15 Gen 3:19; 7:21 Job 9:22; 10:9 Ps 90:3–10 15 All flesh shall perish together, and man shall turn again unto dust.
16 If now *thou hast* understanding, hear this: hearken to the voice of my
34:16☆ words.
34:17 2 Sam 23:3 Job 40:8 17 Shall even he that hateth right govern? and wilt thou condemn him that
is most just?
18 *Is it fit* to say to a king, *Thou art* wicked? *and* to princes, *Ye are*
ungodly?

33:32 Elihu is so confident of his analysis of the case that he challenges Job to answer his charge. He says he really wants to justify Job, and not simply win a debating victory over him, as his three friends sought to do. If Job has nothing to say to the charge, then Elihu wants him to know that he has further words for Job. He says: "I shall teach thee wisdom" (33:33).

34:1 Elihu humbly seeks to gain the good will of his brethren and get favorable attention to his arguments. He calls them wise men who can judge what he says.

34:5ff Elihu warmly accuses Job of having spoken peevish words against God's divine government. Job was wrong in charging God with injustice because he thought himself to be righteous. He paints Job as one sitting in the seat of the scornful.

34:10 Elihu asserts that, as all good men know, God is not unjust. Therefore, God cannot do wickedness, and whatever he has done to Job cannot be wicked. Moreover, man should not quarrel with God for what he does. What God does must be acknowledged and submitted to.

34:16 Elihu now speaks directly to Job and says he has no business quarreling with God for anything he chooses to do. It is presumptuous to make God stand in the dock and to condemn his proceedings—as demonstrated by Job's repeated discontents. The almighty, omniscient, righteous God proceeds with equity and has an invincible dominion over all the affairs of men; he does as he pleases because he is wise in all his doings.

19 *How much less to him* that accepteth not the persons of princes, nor
regardeth the rich more than the poor? for they all *are* the work of his
hands.
20 In a moment shall they die, and the people shall be troubled at
midnight, and pass away: and the mighty shall be taken away without
hand.
21 For his eyes *are* upon the ways of man, and he seeth all his goings.
22 *There is* no darkness, nor shadow of death, where the workers of
iniquity may hide themselves.
23 For he will not lay upon man more *than right;* that he should enter into
judgment with God.
24 He shall break in pieces mighty men without number, and set others in
their stead.
25 Therefore he knoweth their works, and he overturneth *them* in the
night, so that they are destroyed.
26 He striketh them as wicked men in the open sight of others;
27 Because they turned back from him, and would not consider any of his
ways:
28 So that they cause the cry of the poor to come unto him, and he heareth
the cry of the afflicted.
29 When he giveth quietness, who then can make trouble? and when he
hideth *his* face, who then can behold him? whether *it be done* against a
nation, or against a man only:
30 That the hypocrite reign not, lest the people be ensnared.
31 Surely it is meet to be said unto God, I have borne *chastisement,* I will
not offend *any more:*
32 *That which* I see not teach thou me: if I have done iniquity, I will do no
more.
33 *Should it be* according to thy mind? he will recompense it, whether thou
refuse, or whether thou choose; and not I: therefore speak what thou
knowest.
34 Let men of understanding tell me, and let a wise man hearken unto me.
35 Job hath spoken without knowledge, and his words *were* without
wisdom.
36 My desire *is that* Job may be tried unto the end because of *his* answers
for wicked men.
37 For he addeth rebellion unto his sin, he clappeth *his hands* among us,
and multiplieth his words against God.

35 E-LI'HU spake moreover, and said,
2 Thinkest thou this to be right, *that* thou saidst, My righteousness
is more than God's?
3 For thou saidst, What advantage will it be unto thee? *and,* What profit
shall I have, *if I be cleansed* from my sin?
4 I will answer thee, and thy companions with thee.
5 Look unto the heavens, and see; and behold the clouds *which* are higher
than thou.
6 If thou sinnest, what doest thou against him? or *if* thy transgressions be
multiplied, what doest thou unto him?
7 If thou be righteous, what givest thou him? or what receiveth he of thine
hand?

34:19 Deut 10:17 Acts 10:34 Rom 2:11 Eph 6:9 1 Pet 1:17
34:20 Ex 12:29 Job 12:19; 36:20
34:21 Prov 5:21; 15:3 Amos 9:8
34:22 Ps 139:11, 12 Amos 9:2, 3 Heb 4:13
34:24 Job 12:19
34:26 Ps 9:5; 11:5 Isa 66:24
34:27 1 Sam 15:11 Zeph 1:6 Lk 17:31, 32
34:28 Ex 22:23 Job 22:27; 35:9
34:29 Job 5:15; 20:5 Jer 27:8 Jn 14:27 Rom 8:31–34
☆**34:31** Dan 9:7–14
34:32 Prov 28:13
34:34 Job 35:16
34:36 Ps 17:3; 26:2 Jas 5:11
☆**35:1ff**
35:2 Job 27:2 Mt 12:36, 37
35:4 Prov 13:20
35:5 Gen 15:5 1 Kgs 8:27 Ps 8:3, 4 Isa 55:9
35:6 Job 7:20 Prov 8:36 Jer 7:19
35:7 Job 22:2, 3 Prov 9:12 Lk 17:10 Rom 11:35

34:31 Elihu wants Job only to admit that he had spoken inadvisedly. Therefore, he should humble himself before God and ask him to make his sins known to him. Job should also promise reformation, says Elihu.

35:1ff Elihu reproves Job for justifying himself more than justifying God. He also condemns Job for seeming to say that because he has suffered all of these things, there are no advantages or benefits to having faith in God.

8 Thy wickedness *may hurt* a man as thou *art;* and thy righteousness *may profit* the son of man.

35:9 Job 27:10; 36:13 Ps 42:8; 77:6 Acts 16:25
35:10☆
35:11 Job 36:33 Ps 94:12 Jer 32:33

9 By reason of the multitude of oppressions they make *the oppressed* to cry: they cry out by reason of the arm of the mighty.
10 But none saith, Where *is* God my maker, who giveth songs in the night;
11 Who teacheth us more than the beasts of the earth, and maketh us wiser than the fowls of heaven?
12 There they cry, but none giveth answer, because of the pride of evil men.

35:13 Job 27:9 Isa 1:15 Jer 11:11 Jas 4:3
35:14 Job 31:35 Ps 37:5, 6
35:16☆ Job 34:35; 38:2

13 Surely God will not hear vanity, neither will the Almighty regard it.
14 Although thou sayest thou shalt not see him, *yet* judgment *is* before him; therefore trust thou in him.
15 But now, because *it is* not *so,* he hath visited in his anger; yet he knoweth *it* not in great extremity:
16 Therefore doth Job open his mouth in vain; he multiplieth words without knowledge.

D. THE WAYS OF A JUST GOD ARE PAST FINDING OUT

36:1ff☆
36:3 Job 8:3; 37:23 Dan 9:7, 14
36:4 Job 33:3; 37:16 Lk 1:3 1 Cor 14:20
36:5 Ps 22:24; 69:33 102:17 Jer 10:12 1 Cor 1:24–28
36:6 Job 5:15; 8:22 34:26
36:7 Job 5:11 Ps 33:18; 34:15 113:8 1 Pet 3:12
36:9 Job 15:25
36:10 2 Kgs 17:13 Job 33:16; 36:21 Jonah 3:8 Acts 16:14
36:12 Job 4:21; 15:22 Jn 18:21–24

36 E-LI'HU also proceeded, and said,
2 Suffer me a little, and I will shew thee that *I have* yet to speak on God's behalf.
3 I will fetch my knowledge from afar, and will ascribe righteousness to my Maker.
4 For truly my words *shall* not *be* false: he that is perfect in knowledge *is* with thee.
5 Behold, God *is* mighty, and despiseth not *any: he is* mighty in strength *and* wisdom.
6 He preserveth not the life of the wicked: but giveth right to the poor.
7 He withdraweth not his eyes from the righteous: but with kings *are they* on the throne; yea, he doth establish them for ever, and they are exalted.
8 And if *they be* bound in fetters, *and* be holden in cords of affliction;
9 Then he sheweth them their work, and their transgressions that they have exceeded.
10 He openeth also their ear to discipline, and commandeth that they return from iniquity.
11 If they obey and serve *him,* they shall spend their days in prosperity, and their years in pleasures.
12 But if they obey not, they shall perish by the sword, and they shall die without knowledge.
13 But the hypocrites in heart heap up wrath: they cry not when he bindeth them.
14 They die in youth, and their life *is* among the unclean.
15 He delivereth the poor in his affliction, and openeth their ears in oppression.

35:10 Many who groan under their distresses never mind God. Afflictions work to gain the attention of the sufferer. When such people turn to God, they will learn a great deal from their afflictions and bear them more patiently. God gives those who call on him songs in the night, such as was experienced by Paul and Silas at Philippi (Acts 16:25).

35:16 When we do not behave rightly and when afflictions overtake us, "we quarrel with God, are fretful and impatient, and distrustful of the divine Providence."* Job opens his mouth in vain because he does not rest his case with God, wait for him, and turn to him for help and sustaining grace.

36:1ff Elihu continues to build up his case as an advocate who favors God and who remains convinced that Job is wrong. He argues that God is a God of equity who takes care of the least of his subjects, who does not sustain the greatest if they are bad, who avenges the poor, who protects his own people, and who withstands the hypocrites. He supposes that God would have delivered Job had he humbled himself under his affliction; Job must cease his argument against God and obtain right knowledge. He wants Job to entertain the highest thoughts about God and cheerfully submit to God's providence. Much of what he says is true, of course, but he still has failed to understand God's actions in the life of Job. And only God could make that known to man.

[16]Even so would he have removed thee out of the strait *into* a broad
place, where *there is* no straitness: and that which should be set on thy table
should be full of fatness.
[17]But thou hast fulfilled the judgment of the wicked: judgment and
justice take hold *on thee.*
[18]Because *there is* wrath, *beware* lest he take thee away with *his* stroke:
then a great ransom cannot deliver thee.
[19]Will he esteem thy riches? *no,* not gold, nor all the forces of strength.
[20]Desire not the night, when people are cut off in their place.
[21]Take heed, regard not iniquity: for this hast thou chosen rather than
affliction.
[22]Behold, God exalteth by his power: who teacheth like him?
[23]Who hath enjoined him his way? or who can say, Thou hast wrought
iniquity?
[24]Remember that thou magnify his work, which men behold.
[25]Every man may see it; man may behold *it* afar off.
[26]Behold, God *is* great, and we know *him* not, neither can the number of
his years be searched out.
[27]For he maketh small the drops of water: they pour down rain according
to the vapour thereof:
[28]Which the clouds do drop *and* distil upon man abundantly.
[29]Also can *any* understand the spreadings of the clouds, *or* the noise of
his tabernacle?
[30]Behold, he spreadeth his light upon it, and covereth the bottom of the
sea.
[31]For by them judgeth he the people; he giveth meat in abundance.
[32]With clouds he covereth the light; and commandeth it *not to shine* by
the cloud that cometh betwixt.
[33]The noise thereof sheweth concerning it, the cattle also concerning the
vapour.

36:16 Hos 2:14
36:17 Job 22:5, 10, 11
36:18 Job 33:24; 34:33 Jonah 4:4, 9 Heb 2:3
36:20 Job 34:20, 25
36:21 Ps 31:6; 66:18 Mt 5:29, 30
36:22 Job 35:11 Jer 31:33
36:23 Job 8:3 Rom 2:5; 3:5 9:14
☆**36:24**
☆**36:26** Job 11:7–9 37:23 Ps 90:2 102:24, 27
36:27 Job 5:10 37:6, 11 Ps 147:8 Jer 14:22
36:29 Job 26:14 Ps 136:25
36:31 Job 37:11, 13, 16 Ps 65:9–13 Acts 14:17
36:32 Job 37:11, 12, 15
36:33 Job 37:2

37

AT this also my heart trembleth, and is moved out of his place.
[2]Hear attentively the noise of his voice, and the sound *that* goeth
out of his mouth.
[3]He directeth it under the whole heaven, and his lightning unto the ends
of the earth.
[4]After it a voice roareth: he thundereth with the voice of his excellency;
and he will not stay them when his voice is heard.
[5]God thundereth marvellously with his voice; great things doeth he,
which we cannot comprehend.
[6]For he saith to the snow, Be thou *on* the earth; likewise to the small rain,
and to the great rain of his strength.
[7]He sealeth up the hand of every man; that all men may know his work.
[8]Then the beasts go into dens, and remain in their places.
[9]Out of the south cometh the whirlwind: and cold out of the north.
[10]By the breath of God frost is given: and the breadth of the waters is
straitened.
[11]Also by watering he wearieth the thick cloud: he scattereth his bright
cloud:

☆**37:2** Job 36:33 37:4, 5 Ps 29:3–9
37:3 Job 37:12
37:5 Job 5:9; 26:14 Rom 11:33
☆**37:6** Job 36:27; 38:22 Prov 28:3
☆**37:7** Job 12:14
37:8 Job 38:40 Ps 104:22
37:9 Job 9:9 Isa 21:1 Zech 9:14
37:10 Job 38:29 Ps 147:17
37:11 Job 36:27, 29

36:24 God does nothing mean. We should behold his works and magnify his name. He is infinite and unsearchable. "We know that he is, but not what he is. We know what he is not, but not what he is. We know in part, but not in perfection."* Therefore we must not arraign Deity or find fault with what he does.

36:26 Finite man cannot comprehend an infinite God. And man can only know what God chooses to reveal.

37:2 God controls the thunder and the lightning. All nature is under his sway.

37:6, 7 God sends the snow, the rain, and storms. Through his dominion over the elements God controls the actions of men. In winter, the farmer cannot plow, and in blizzards, airplanes can't fly and salesmen cannot go to work.

37:12 Job 36:32; Ps 148:8; Isa 14:21; 27:6
37:13 Ex 9:18, 19; 1 Kgs 18:45; Ezra 10:9; Joel 2:23

12 And it is turned round about by his counsels: that they may do whatsoever he commandeth them upon the face of the world in the earth.

13 He causeth it to come, whether for correction, or for his land, or for mercy.

14 Hearken unto this, O Job: stand still, and consider the wondrous works of God.

15 Dost thou know when God disposed them, and caused the light of his cloud to shine?

37:16 Job 36:4

16 Dost thou know the balancings of the clouds, the wondrous works of him which is perfect in knowledge?

17 How thy garments *are* warm, when he quieteth the earth by the south *wind?*

37:18 Gen 1:6–8; Job 9:8, 9; Ps 104:2; Isa 45:12; Jer 10:12

18 Hast thou with him spread out the sky, *which is* strong, *and* as a molten looking glass?

19 Teach us what we shall say unto him; *for* we cannot order *our speech* by reason of darkness.

20 Shall it be told him that I speak? if a man speak, surely he shall be swallowed up.

21 And now *men* see not the bright light which *is* in the clouds: but the wind passeth, and cleanseth them.

22 Fair weather cometh out of the north: with God *is* terrible majesty.

37:23 Isa 63:9; Nah 1:12; Rom 11:13
37:24☆ Job 5:13; 1 Cor 1:26

23 *Touching* the Almighty, we cannot find him out: *he is* excellent in power, and in judgment, and in plenty of justice: he will not afflict.

24 Men do therefore fear him: he respecteth not any *that are* wise of heart.

IV. GOD INTERVENES TO SPEAK (38:1—41:34)

A. GOD CHALLENGES JOB

38:1☆ Job 40:6
38:2☆ Job 35:16; 42:3

38 THEN the LORD answered Job out of the whirlwind, and said,

2 Who *is* this that darkeneth counsel by words without knowledge?

38:3 Job 40:7; 42:4

3 Gird up now thy loins like a man: for I will demand of thee, and answer thou me.

B. GOD THE CREATOR SPEAKS OF HIS INFINITY VERSUS JOB'S FINITUDE

38:4 Job 15:7; Ps 104:5; Prov 30:4
38:5 Prov 8:29; Isa 40:12; Zech 2:1, 2
38:6 Job 1:6; 26:7
38:7☆

4 Where wast thou when I laid the foundations of the earth? declare, if thou hast understanding.

5 Who hath laid the measures thereof, if thou knowest? or who hath stretched the line upon it?

6 Whereupon are the foundations thereof fastened? or who laid the corner stone thereof;

7 When the morning stars sang together, and all the sons of God shouted for joy?

37:24 Elihu argued that God cannot be charged with injustice. Job's sufferings were designed to uphold the glory of God against the allegations of Satan. His sufferings also were the instrument by which God was perfecting his sanctification. Surely God was not unjust to allow Job to keep on suffering in order that he might be conformed to the image of God.

38:1 This is the climax of the book: God makes his appearance. God shows Job the greatness of creation compared to man's ignorance and finitude. Job will learn that, while he had committed no sin for which the affliction was laid on him, he erred in thinking too highly of his own ability to rationalize the actions of his Creator. Soon he will kneel before his Maker in abject humiliation and surrender.

38:2 *words without knowledge.* They spoke in ignorance instead of teaching what needed to be taught.

38:7 *the sons of God* [who] *shouted for joy* were the angels, the first creation of God before men. They rejoiced when the foundations of the earth were laid and when the morning stars sang together. This latter reference is probably a figure of speech indicating that even inanimate nature sings the praises of the One who made it.

8 Or *who* shut up the sea with doors, when it brake forth, *as if* it had
issued out of the womb?
9 When I made the cloud the garment thereof, and thick darkness a
swaddlingband for it,
10 And brake up for it my decreed *place*, and set bars and doors,
11 And said, Hitherto shalt thou come, but no further: and here shall thy
proud waves be stayed?
12 Hast thou commanded the morning since thy days; *and* caused the
dayspring to know his place;
13 That it might take hold of the ends of the earth, that the wicked might
be shaken out of it?
14 It is turned as clay *to* the seal; and they stand as a garment.
15 And from the wicked their light is withholden, and the high arm shall
be broken.

C. MAN CANNOT KNOW THE MYSTERY OF GOD'S CREATION

16 Hast thou entered into the springs of the sea? or hast thou walked in
the search of the depth?
17 Have the gates of death been opened unto thee? or hast thou seen the
doors of the shadow of death?
18 Hast thou perceived the breadth of the earth? declare if thou knowest it
all.
19 Where *is* the way *where* light dwelleth? and *as for* darkness, where *is* the
place thereof,
20 That thou shouldest take it to the bound thereof, and that thou
shouldest know the paths *to* the house thereof?
21 Knowest thou *it*, because thou wast then born? or *because* the number
of thy days *is* great?
22 Hast thou entered into the treasures of the snow? or hast thou seen the
treasures of the hail,
23 Which I have reserved against the time of trouble, against the day of
battle and war?
24 By what way is the light parted, *which* scattereth the east wind upon the
earth?
25 Who hath divided a watercourse for the overflowing of waters, or a way
for the lightning of thunder;
26 To cause it to rain on the earth, *where* no man *is;* *on* the wilderness,
wherein *there is* no man;
27 To satisfy the desolate and waste *ground;* and to cause the bud of the
tender herb to spring forth?
28 Hath the rain a father? or who hath begotten the drops of dew?
29 Out of whose womb came the ice? and the hoary frost of heaven, who
hath gendered it?
30 The waters are hid as *with* a stone, and the face of the deep is frozen.
31 Canst thou bind the sweet influences of Plei'a-des, or loose the bands of
O-ri'on?
32 Canst thou bring forth Maz'za-roth in his season? or canst thou guide
Arc-tu'rus with his sons?
33 Knowest thou the ordinances of heaven? canst thou set the dominion
thereof in the earth?

38:10 Gen 1:9; Ps 33:7; Prov 8:29; Jer 5:22
38:13 Job 37:3; 34:25, 26
38:15 Num 15:30; Job 5:14; Ps 10:15; 37:17
☆**38:16** Gen 7:11; 8:2; Prov 8:24, 28; Jer 51:36
38:17 Job 28:24; 34:22; Ps 9:13
38:20 Job 26:10
38:21 Job 15:7
38:22 Ex 9:18; Josh 10:11; Job 37:6; Isa 30:30; Ezek 13:11, 13; Rev 16:21
38:24 Job 26:10
38:25 Job 36:27; Ps 104:13, 14
☆**38:28** 1 Sam 12:17, 18; Job 36:27, 28; Ps 147:8; Jer 14:22
38:29 Job 37:10; Ps 147:17
38:31 Job 9:9; Amos 5:8
38:33 Ps 148:6; Jer 31:35, 36

38:16 God asks Job puzzling questions about nature so as to convince him of his ignorance. Job will shortly come to the place where he realizes that, compared to God, he knows next to nothing.

38:28ff As God continues to deal with Job, he makes the point that if Job cannot understand the things of nature (which are ever a mystery to men) how is it then possible for him to understand the God of nature. The answer is plain: no one can understand unless God chooses to reveal it himself.

38:34 Job 22:11; 36:27, 28
38:35 Job 36:32; 37:3

34 Canst thou lift up thy voice to the clouds, that abundance of waters
may cover thee?
35 Canst thou send lightnings, that they may go, and say unto thee, Here
we *are?*

38:36 Job 32:8; Ps 51:6; Eccles 2:26

36 Who hath put wisdom in the inward parts? or who hath given
understanding to the heart?
37 Who can number the clouds in wisdom? or who can stay the bottles of
heaven,
38 When the dust groweth into hardness, and the clods cleave fast
together?

D. MAN CANNOT KNOW THE MYSTERIES OF ANIMAL AND BIRD LIFE

38:39☆ Job 37:8; Ps 104:21
38:41 Ps 147:9; Mt 6:26; Lk 12:24

39 Wilt thou hunt the prey for the lion? or fill the appetite of the young
lions,
40 When they couch in *their* dens, *and* abide in the covert to lie in wait?
41 Who provideth for the raven his food? when his young ones cry unto
God, they wander for lack of meat.

39:1☆ Deut 14:5; Ps 29:9

39 KNOWEST thou the time when the wild goats of the rock bring
forth? *or* canst thou mark when the hinds do calve?
2 Canst thou number the months *that* they fulfil? or knowest thou the time
when they bring forth?
3 They bow themselves, they bring forth their young ones, they cast out
their sorrows.
4 Their young ones are in good liking, they grow up with corn; they go
forth, and return not unto them.

39:5☆ Job 6:5; 11:12; 24:5; Dan 5:21; Hos 8:9
39:6 Job 24:5; Jer 2:24

5 Who hath sent out the wild ass free? or who hath loosed the bands of the
wild ass?
6 Whose house I have made the wilderness, and the barren land his
dwellings.
7 He scorneth the multitude of the city, neither regardeth he the crying of
the driver.
8 The range of the mountains *is* his pasture, and he searcheth after every
green thing.

39:9 Num 23:22; Deut 33:17; Ps 92:10; Isa 1:3

9 Will the unicorn be willing to serve thee, or abide by thy crib?
10 Canst thou bind the unicorn with his band in the furrow? or will he
harrow the valleys after thee?
11 Wilt thou trust him, because his strength *is* great? or wilt thou leave thy
labour to him?
12 Wilt thou believe him, that he will bring home thy seed, and gather *it*
into thy barn?

39:13☆

13 *Gavest thou* the goodly wings unto the peacocks? or wings and feathers
unto the ostrich?
14 Which leaveth her eggs in the earth, and warmeth them in dust,
15 And forgetteth that the foot may crush them, or that the wild beast may
break them.

38:39 If Job knows little or nothing about nature, God now turns to the mysteries hidden from the ken of man about animals and birds. He asks about lions, goats, asses, unicorns, peacocks, ostriches, horses, and hawks. The closer God gets to things Job can see and know about, the more it is apparent that what he knows is insignificant when compared to what he does not know.

39:1ff God here informs Job about divine compassion toward the inferior creatures on the planet. He takes tender care of them. Therefore Job has no reason for charging God with unkindness toward him. He who cares for the lesser will be equally or more concerned for the higher.

39:5 The wild ass is bound by no fetters. He can range as he pleases and need not labor under any yoke. Men should not covet this freedom, for it is better to labor and be good for something than to ramble aimlessly and be good for nothing.

39:13ff The ostrich drops her eggs anywhere on the ground and leaves them to fend for themselves. God hatches the abandoned eggs by sun and sand, even as he feeds the neglected young ones of the raven. Most animals are orchestrated to care for their offspring, for

5 Wilt thou play with him as *with* a bird? or wilt thou bind him for thy
maidens?
6 Shall the companions make a banquet of him? shall they part him
among the merchants?
7 Canst thou fill his skin with barbed irons? or his head with fish spears?
8 Lay thine hand upon him, remember the battle, do no more.
9 Behold, the hope of him is in vain: shall not *one* be cast down even at
the sight of him?
10 None *is so* fierce that dare stir him up: who then is able to stand before
me?
11 Who hath prevented me, that I should repay *him? whatsoever is* under
the whole heaven is mine.
12 I will not conceal his parts, nor his power, nor his comely proportion.
13 Who can discover the face of his garment? *or* who can come *to him* with
his double bridle?
14 Who can open the doors of his face? his teeth *are* terrible round about.
15 *His* scales *are his* pride, shut up together *as with* a close seal.
16 One is so near to another, that no air can come between them.
17 They are joined one to another, they stick together, that they cannot be
sundered.
18 By his neesings a light doth shine, and his eyes *are* like the eyelids of the
morning.
19 Out of his mouth go burning lamps, *and* sparks of fire leap out.
20 Out of his nostrils goeth smoke, as *out* of a seething pot or caldron.
21 His breath kindleth coals, and a flame goeth out of his mouth.
22 In his neck remaineth strength, and sorrow is turned into joy before
him.
23 The flakes of his flesh are joined together: they are firm in themselves;
they cannot be moved.
24 His heart is as firm as a stone; yea, as hard as a piece of the nether
millstone.
25 When he raiseth up himself, the mighty are afraid: by reason of
breakings they purify themselves.
26 The sword of him that layeth at him cannot hold: the spear, the dart,
nor the habergeon.
27 He esteemeth iron as straw, *and* brass as rotten wood.
28 The arrow cannot make him flee: slingstones are turned with him into
stubble.
29 Darts are counted as stubble: he laugheth at the shaking of a spear.
30 Sharp stones *are* under him: he spreadeth sharp pointed things upon
the mire.
31 He maketh the deep to boil like a pot: he maketh the sea like a pot of
ointment.
32 He maketh a path to shine after him; *one* would think the deep *to be*
hoary.
33 Upon earth there is not his like, who is made without fear.
34 He beholdeth all high *things:* he *is* a king over all the children of pride.

41:8 1 Kgs 20:11; 2 Kgs 10:4; Lk 14:31, 33
41:10 Job 3:8
41:11 Ex 19:5; Deut 10:14; Ps 24:1; 50:12; 1 Cor 10:26
41:18 Job 3:9
41:33 Job 40:19
☆**41:34** Job 28:8; Ezek 29:3

41:34 God stresses the strength and power of the crocodile, who cannot be conquered nor tamed. This fearless monster is indomitable. But God limited him to the waters—not to roam the earth where he might damage other created things. However strong men may be, the crocodile is stronger. So also God is stronger than any man or all men together. He is king over all the children of pride. And God, who controls elephant and crocodile, cannot be displaced or put down by men. The lofty looks of all men shall be humbled. The haughty shall bow down. The Lord God alone shall be exalted now and forevermore.

V. THE CONCLUSION OF THE MATTER (42:1–17)

A. JOB ACKNOWLEDGES HIS TRANSGRESSION

42 THEN Job answered the LORD, and said,
2 I know that thou canst do every *thing*, and *that* no thought can
be withholden from thee.

42:3☆ Job 38:2 Ps 40:5; 131:1 139:6

3 Who *is* he that hideth counsel without knowledge? therefore have I
uttered that I understood not; things too wonderful for me, which I knew
not.

42:4 Gen 18:27, 30–32 Job 38:3; 40:7

4 Hear, I beseech thee, and I will speak: I will demand of thee, and
declare thou unto me.

42:5 Job 26:14 Isa 6:5 Jn 1:18; 12:41

5 I have heard of thee by the hearing of the ear: but now mine eye seeth
thee.
6 Wherefore I abhor *myself*, and repent in dust and ashes.

B. JOB PRAYS FOR HIS FRIENDS

42:7☆ Job 40:3–5

7 ¶And it was *so*, that after the LORD had spoken these words unto Job,
the LORD said to El′i-phaz the Te′man-ite, My wrath is kindled against
thee, and against thy two friends: for ye have not spoken of me *the thing*
that is right, as my servant Job *hath*.

42:8 Job 1:5; 22:30

8 Therefore take unto you now seven bullocks and seven rams, and go to
my servant Job, and offer up for yourselves a burnt offering; and my
servant Job shall pray for you: for him will I accept: lest I deal with you
after your folly, in that ye have not spoken of me *the thing which is* right, like
my servant Job.
9 So El′i-phaz the Te′man-ite and Bildad the Shu′hite *and* Zo′phar the
Na′a-math-ite went, and did according as the LORD commanded them: the
LORD also accepted Job.

C. SATAN IS DEFEATED; JOB'S END IS GREATER THAN HIS BEGINNING

42:10☆ Ps 14:7; 85:1–3 126:1–6

10 And the LORD turned the captivity of Job, when he prayed for his
friends: also the LORD gave Job twice as much as he had before.

42:11 Job 2:11; 19:13

11 Then came there unto him all his brethren, and all his sisters, and all
they that had been of his acquaintance before, and did eat bread with him
in his house: and they bemoaned him, and comforted him over all the evil
that the LORD had brought upon him: every man also gave him a piece of
money, and every one an earring of gold.

42:12 Job 1:3, 10 Prov 10:22 1 Tim 6:17

12 So the LORD blessed the latter end of Job more than his beginning: for
he had fourteen thousand sheep, and six thousand camels, and a thousand
yoke of oxen, and a thousand she asses.

42:13 Job 1:2 Ps 107:41

13 He had also seven sons and three daughters.
14 And he called the name of the first, Je-mi′ma; and the name of the
second, Ke-zi′a; and the name of the third, Ker′en–hap′puch.
15 And in all the land were no women found *so* fair as the daughters of
Job: and their father gave them inheritance among their brethren.

42:17 Gen 15:15; 25:8 Job 5:26 Prov 3:16

16 After this lived Job an hundred and forty years, and saw his sons, and
his sons' sons, *even* four generations.
17 So Job died, *being* old and full of days.

***42:3** Job has learned from his experience*, even though full understanding has not come to him in time as it will in eternity.

42:7 Job's repentance did not mean that his friends were correct in their assessment. God says they were wrong. They must offer sacrifices; God tells them that Job will pray for them. Thus Job forgave them their words of condemnation and God answers his prayer for his friends (42:9). Job's restoration followed (42:10).

42:10 God restored to Job twice the wealth he had when Satan began to afflict him.

THE BOOK OF
PSALMS

Authorship, date, and background The book of Psalms has followed the tradition of the Septuagint for its name. The Greek rendering *Psalmoi* means, literally, "song to the accompaniment of a stringed instrument." The Hebrew title for the book is *Tehillim*, which means *Praise Songs.* Psalms contains 150 chapters or psalms and has been divided into five segments, each division ending with a doxology. The division is as follows: Book I: Psalms 1—41; Book II: Psalms 42—72; Book III: Psalms 73—89; Book IV: Psalms 90—106; Book V: Psalms 107—150.

The date and authorship of this book is unique in that some of the authors are known and others are not, and the dates for the composition of the various psalms go back to Moses and forward to the period of the Exile and shortly thereafter. The Psalms have been dated from ca. 1400 to 500 B.C. Seventy-three of the psalms are ascribed to David, two to Solomon, one each to Ethan and Heman, one to Moses, and twenty-three to Levitical clans of Asaph, leaving forty-nine psalms whose authors cannot be ascertained. Rationalist critics have vigorously denied the Davidic authorship of a number of the psalms attributed to him. They have also opted for a late dating of virtually all of the psalms. Interestingly, this seems to be quite inconsistent, because some of the instructions for the singing of the psalms were written in language which had already become untranslatable in the sixth century B.C.

Characteristics and content The psalms vary widely in their purposes. Scholars have noted eight different categories of psalms: (1) personal psalms; (2) prayer psalms; (3) liturgical psalms; (4) historical psalms; (5) praise psalms; (6) penitential psalms; (7) Messianic psalms; (8) psalms which bespeak the majesty and might of God. Some psalms fit neatly into a particular category; others might fit into several categories. The book of Psalms has always occupied a unique place in the hearts of all believers. The range of human emotions includes heavenly praises as well as imprecatory petitions for God to smite the enemy. Some of the sayings spoken by Christ on Calvary are found in psalms, the greatest of which is the cry: "My God, my God, why hast thou forsaken me?" (22:1). Nowhere in Scripture does any sinner more eloquently confess his transgressions and seek the mercy of God in forgiveness than does David in Psalm 51. It was written after Nathan the prophet pointed an accusing finger at him and pronounced the judgment of God upon him for his adultery with Bath-sheba and the murder of Uriah the Hittite, her husband.

The psalms not only praise the Creator; they also explore nature with respect to the universe and to its occupants. The heavens, the earth, the seas, the abyss, reptiles sheep, pastures, deer, sparrows, and the night seasons are mentioned. In historical matters the Exodus from Egypt, the travels of Israel during the years of wandering, the covenants of God with his people, and the redeeming and delivering hand of God are referred to. Other psalms speak about man in all of his social relationships. The Messianic psalms tell of the humiliation and glory of David's Son, Jesus Christ, of his eternity, his priesthood and ascension, his incorruption, his passion, his incarnation; and in Acts 1:20, two psalms are quoted with regard to Judas who betrayed him (69:25; 109:8). The Shepherd's Psalm (23) will remain fixed forever in the affections of God's people everywhere.

Outline

Book I (1—41)
Book II (42—72)
Book III (73—89)
Book IV (90—106)
Book V (107—150)

Book I (Psalms 1—41)

I. THE TREE OF LIFE

A. THE BLESSEDNESS OF THE RIGHTEOUS

1:1☆ Ps 17:4; 26:5 Prov 4:14

1 BLESSED *is* the man that walketh not in the counsel of the ungodly,
nor standeth in the way of sinners, nor sitteth in the seat of the
scornful.

1:2 Ps 25:5 63:5, 6 119:1, 13–16, 35

2 But his delight *is* in the law of the LORD; and in his law doth he
meditate day and night.

1:3 Ps 92:12–14 128:2 Jer 17:7, 8 Ezek 47:12

3 And he shall be like a tree planted by the rivers of water, that bringeth
forth his fruit in his season; his leaf also shall not wither; and whatsoever
he doeth shall prosper.

B. THE MISERY OF THE UNRIGHTEOUS

1:4 Job 21:18 Ps 35:5 Isa 17:13

4 The ungodly *are* not so: but *are* like the chaff which the wind driveth
away.

1:5 Ps 5:5; 9:7, 8 89:5

5 Therefore the ungodly shall not stand in the judgment, nor sinners in
the congregation of the righteous.

1:6 Neh 1:7 Ps 9:5, 6; 11:6 Jn 10:14 2 Tim 2:19

6 For the LORD knoweth the way of the righteous: but the way of the
ungodly shall perish.

I. THE PSALM OF THE MESSIAH KING

A. THE PLOT AGAINST THE MESSIAH

2:1☆ Ps 21:11; 46:6 83:2–5 Acts 4:25, 26

2 WHY do the heathen rage, and the people imagine a vain thing?

2:2☆ Ps 48:4–6 74:18, 23

2 The kings of the earth set themselves, and the rulers take counsel
together, against the LORD, and against his anointed, *saying,*

2:3☆ Jer 5:5

3 Let us break their bands asunder, and cast away their cords from us.

B. MESSIAH'S VICTORY; THE CONFUSION OF HIS OPPONENTS

2:4☆ Ps 37:12, 13 59:8

4 He that sitteth in the heavens shall laugh: the Lord shall have them in
derision.

2:5☆ Ps 21:8–10 76:7; 78:49, 50

5 Then shall he speak unto them in his wrath, and vex them in his sore
displeasure.

2:6☆ Ps 3:4; 45:6 48:1, 2

6 Yet have I set my king upon my holy hill of Zion.

1:1ff This Psalm instructs us concerning good and evil. The children of men are divided into saints and sinners, the seed of the woman and the seed of the serpent. This distinction is lasting and will survive all other classifications such as rich and poor, young and old. By this distinction will the everlasting state of all men be determined.

2:1–12 A number of the Psalms were composed a millennium before the first coming of Jesus. Many Psalms are thus predictive in substance since they refer to Jesus. Mention is made of David in many Psalms, but these references often have messianic implications. David is a type of the Messiah. Among the *Psalms that are clearly messianic are 2, 8, 16, 22, 72,* 89, 110, and 132.

Psalm 2 is messianic. 2:2 speaks about *the LORD, and . . . his anointed. King upon my holy hill of Zion,* 2:6, pictures Christ, the ascended one. Christ will indeed reign over a reconstituted Zion in the future. In 2:7, *Thou art my Son,* while it includes human kings, also refers to the incarnation of Jesus Christ, confirmed by the words from heaven. (Matt. 3:17 says: "This is my beloved Son.") Psalm 2 was written, no doubt, against a background of a rebellion against David or some other ruler of that line. The revolt is futile, however, for God has willed that the Davidic king shall reign over all nations. Jesus, as the Messiah and the anointed one, the Son of David, ultimately fulfills this cosmic claim. More than sixty prophecies concerning Christ were fulfilled by his earthly ministry, death, and resurrection. There are other prophecies that either have been partially fulfilled or are yet to be fulfilled. Among them are (1) the conversion of the Gentiles (Isa. 11:10; 42:1; John 10:16; Acts 10:45, 47), (2) Christ's universal dominion (72:8; Dan. 7:14), (3) Christ enthroned in Jerusalem (2:6), and (4) the establishment of his righteous and eternal government (45:6, 7).

C. THE MESSIAH KING SPEAKS

7 I will declare the decree: the LORD hath said unto me, Thou *art* my Son;
this day have I begotten thee.
8 Ask of me, and I shall give *thee* the heathen *for* thine inheritance, and
the uttermost parts of the earth *for* thy possession.

D. CALLING THE KINGS OF THE EARTH TO SERVE THE LORD

9 Thou shalt break them with a rod of iron; thou shalt dash them in pieces
like a potter's vessel.
10 Be wise now therefore, O ye kings: be instructed, ye judges of the earth.
11 Serve the LORD with fear, and rejoice with trembling.
12 Kiss the Son, lest he be angry, and ye perish *from* the way, when his
wrath is kindled but a little. Blessed *are* all they that put their trust in him.

I. GOD IS DAVID'S HELP

A. DAVID'S COMPLAINT AND HIS FAITH IN GOD

A Psalm of David, when he fled from Absalom his son

3 LORD, how are they increased that trouble me! many *are* they that
rise up against me.
2 Many *there be* which say of my soul, *There is* no help for him in God.
Se'lah.
3 But thou, O LORD, *art* a shield for me; my glory, and the lifter up of
mine head.

B. DAVID'S PRAYER; GOD'S DELIVERANCE

4 I cried unto the LORD with my voice, and he heard me out of his holy
hill. Se'lah.
5 I laid me down and slept; I awaked; for the LORD sustained me.
6 I will not be afraid of ten thousands of people, that have set *themselves*
against me round about.
7 Arise, O LORD; save me, O my God: for thou hast smitten all mine
enemies *upon* the cheek bone; thou hast broken the teeth of the ungodly.
8 Salvation *belongeth* unto the LORD: thy blessing *is* upon thy people.
Se'lah.

I. A PSALM FOR THE NIGHT

A. THE PETITION FOR HELP

To the chief Musician on Neginoth, A Psalm of David

4 HEAR me when I call, O God of my righteousness: thou hast enlarged
me *when I was* in distress; have mercy upon me, and hear my prayer.
2 O ye sons of men, how long *will ye turn* my glory into shame? *how long*
will ye love vanity, *and* seek after leasing? Se'lah.

B. THE ASSURANCE THAT GOD ANSWERS PRAYER

3 But know that the LORD hath set apart him that is godly for himself: the
LORD will hear when I call unto him.

☆**2:7** Acts 13:32, 33 Heb 1:5, 6; 5:5
☆**2:8** Ps 21:1, 2 22:27
☆**2:9** Ps 28:5; 72:4 110:5, 6 Rev 2:27; 12:5 19:15
☆**2:10** Prov 8:14, 15
☆**2:11** Ps 5:7; 32:8 119:119, 120 Heb 12:28
☆**2:12** Ps 5:11 34:8, 22 Jn 5:23 Rom 9:33
3:1 2 Sam 15:12 Ps 69:4
3:2 Ps 22:7, 8 71:11
3:3 Ps 5:12 27:5, 6; 28:7 62:7
3:4 Ps 4:3; 34:4 99:9
3:5 Lev 26:6 Ps 4:8 139:17, 18 Prov 3:24–26
3:6 Ps 23:4; 27:3 118:10–13
3:7 Job 16:10 Ps 7:6; 22:21 57:4; 58:6
☆**3:8** Ps 28:8; 29:11 Isa 43:11 Jer 3:23
☆**4:1** Ps 3:4; 17:6 18:6, 18, 19 27:7
4:2 Ps 3:3 31:6, 18 69:7–10, 19
4:3 Ps 6:8, 9; 17:6 31:23; 50:5 135:4

3:8 *Salvation belongeth to the LORD.* Those who speak experientially, that is, as a result of what has happened to them, speak best about how God delivers and saves his people.

4:1 Some Psalms are devotional; others are doctrinal and practical. This one is of the latter category. It is a prayer that preaches; herein we learn many things about the nature of God in relation to his people.

4:4 Ps 33:8; 77:6; 119:11; Eph 4:26
4:5 Ps 37:3, 5; 50:14; 51:19; 62:8

4 Stand in awe, and sin not: commune with your own heart upon your
bed, and be still. Se'lah.
5 Offer the sacrifices of righteousness, and put your trust in the LORD.

C. THE PSALMIST'S CONFIDENCE IN GOD

4:6 Num 6:26; Job 7:7; 9:25; Ps 80:3, 7, 19
4:7 Ps 97:11, 12; 119:14; Acts 14:17
4:8 Deut 12:10; Job 11:19; Ps 3:5; 16:9

6 *There be* many that say, Who will shew us *any* good? LORD, lift thou up
the light of thy countenance upon us.
7 Thou hast put gladness in my heart, more than in the time *that* their
corn and their wine increased.
8 I will both lay me down in peace, and sleep: for thou, LORD, only
makest me dwell in safety.

I. A MORNING PRAYER

A. INSTANT IN PRAYER

To the chief Musician upon Nehiloth, A Psalm of David

5:1☆ Ps 54:2; 84:3; 140:6–8
5:3 Ps 88:13; 130:5

5 GIVE ear to my words, O LORD, consider my meditation.
2 Hearken unto the voice of my cry, my King, and my God: for unto
thee will I pray.
3 My voice shalt thou hear in the morning, O LORD; in the morning will
I direct *my prayer* unto thee, and will look up.

B. GOD'S HATRED OF SIN

5:4 Ps 11:5; 34:16; 92:15
5:5 Ps 1:5; 11:5; 45:7; 75:4
5:6 Ps 52:4, 5; 55:23

4 For thou *art* not a God that hath pleasure in wickedness: neither shall
evil dwell with thee.
5 The foolish shall not stand in thy sight: thou hatest all workers of
iniquity.
6 Thou shalt destroy them that speak leasing: the LORD will abhor the
bloody and deceitful man.

C. THE ASSURANCE THAT GOD BLESSES THE GODLY

5:7☆ Ps 69:13; 115:11, 13; 138:2
5:8 Ps 27:11; 31:1, 3
5:9 Ps 7:14; 52:3; Rom 3:13; Lk 11:44
5:10 Ps 9:16; 36:12; 107:10, 11
5:11☆ Ps 2:12; 12:7; 33:1; 64:10; Isa 65:13
5:12 Ps 29:11; 32:7, 10

7 But as for me, I will come *into* thy house in the multitude of thy mercy:
and in thy fear will I worship toward thy holy temple.
8 Lead me, O LORD, in thy righteousness because of mine enemies; make
thy way straight before my face.
9 For *there is* no faithfulness in their mouth; their inward part *is* very
wickedness; their throat *is* an open sepulchre; they flatter with their tongue.
10 Destroy thou them, O God; let them fall by their own counsels; cast
them out in the multitude of their transgressions; for they have rebelled
against thee.
11 But let all those that put their trust in thee rejoice: let them ever shout
for joy, because thou defendest them: let them also that love thy name be
joyful in thee.
12 For thou, LORD, wilt bless the righteous; with favour wilt thou compass
him as *with* a shield.

5:1ff This is a prayer of David when faced with enemies who would destroy him. David assures us that God hears his people's prayers, delivers them, and acts righteously on their behalf.

5:7 David is resolved to engage in the public worship of God by attending God's house. Secret worship and prayer are necessary and good. But the gathering of God's people for worship is also very important.

5:11 *let those that put their trust in thee rejoice* is better translated "let all who take refuge in you be glad" (NIV). All men need this refuge, for without it they are lost. All have wandered from the way and are lost and undone. Without this refuge they remain alienated and forever wander in the darkness of night.

I. A PENITENT'S PRAYER FOR PARDON AND HEALING

A. A PLEA FOR MERCY AND HEALING

To the chief Musician on Neginoth upon Sheminith, A Psalm of David

6 O LORD, rebuke me not in thine anger, neither chasten me in thy hot
displeasure.
2 Have mercy upon me, O LORD; for I *am* weak: O LORD, heal me; for my
bones are vexed.
3 My soul is also sore vexed: but thou, O LORD, how long?
4 Return, O LORD, deliver my soul: oh save me for thy mercies' sake.
5 For in death *there is* no remembrance of thee: in the grave who shall
give thee thanks?
6 I am weary with my groaning; all the night make I my bed to swim; I
water my couch with my tears.
7 Mine eye is consumed because of grief; it waxeth old because of all mine
enemies.

☆**6:1** Ps 2:5; 38:1
6:2 Ps 22:14; 31:9, 10; 41:4; 51:1; 102:3, 4, 11
6:3 Ps 88:3; 90:13; Jn 12:27
☆**6:5** Ps 30:9; 88:10–12; 115:17; Eccles 9:10; Isa 38:18
6:6 Ps 42:3; 69:3
6:7 Ps 31:9

B. THE ASSURANCE OF GOD'S ANSWER

8 Depart from me, all ye workers of iniquity; for the LORD hath heard the
voice of my weeping.
9 The LORD hath heard my supplication; the LORD will receive my prayer.
10 Let all mine enemies be ashamed and sore vexed: let them return *and*
be ashamed suddenly.

6:8 Ps 119:115; 28:6
6:9 Ps 66:19, 20; 116:1
☆**6:10** Ps 71:24; 73:19

I. THE SONG OF THE SLANDERED SAINT

A. THE PSALMIST TRUSTS GOD

Shiggaion of David, which he sang unto the LORD, concerning the words of Cush the Benjamite

7 O LORD my God, in thee do I put my trust: save me from all them
that persecute me, and deliver me:
2 Lest he tear my soul like a lion, rending *it* in pieces, while *there is* none
to deliver.

☆**7:1** Ps 11:1; 31:1, 14, 15; 71:1
7:2 Ps 17:12; 57:4

B. THE PSALMIST PLEADS HIS INNOCENCE

3 O LORD my God, if I have done this; if there be iniquity in my hands;
4 If I have rewarded evil unto him that was at peace with me; (yea, I have
delivered him that without cause is mine enemy:)
5 Let the enemy persecute my soul, and take *it;* yea, let him tread down
my life upon the earth, and lay mine honour in the dust. Se'lah.

7:3 1 Sam 24:11
7:4 1 Sam 26:9; Ps 109:4, 5

C. THE PSALMIST ASKS FOR JUSTICE

6 Arise, O LORD, in thine anger, lift up thyself because of the rage of mine
enemies: and awake for me *to* the judgment *that* thou hast commanded.

7:6 Ps 3:7; 35:23; 138:7

6:1ff This is a Psalm for all who are afflicted and who express their complaints to a listening, caring God. It ends with the cheerful assurance that God hears and helps, and that those who afflict the servants of God will be turned back.

6:5 Paraphrased: "For if I die I cannot give you glory by praising you before my friends." Isa. 57:1, 2 may indicate that Old Testament saints believed in a conscious, pleasant hereafter for those who love God.†

6:10 This verse is either a prayer for the conversion of David's enemies or a prediction of their destruction.

7:1ff This Psalm will encourage the hearts of those who have been unjustly and maliciously attacked by those who hate and despise them. David proclaims his innocence, is convinced that God will deal with the unrighteous, and ends by thanking and praising the Lord most high.

7:7 Ps 18:20; 35:24; 43:1; 96:13; 98:8, 9
7:9 1 Chron 28:9; Ps 11:4, 5; 40:2; 94:23; Jer 11:20; Rev 2:23

7So shall the congregation of the people compass thee about: for their
sakes therefore return thou on high.
8The LORD shall judge the people: judge me, O LORD, according to my
righteousness, and according to mine integrity *that is* in me.
9Oh let the wickedness of the wicked come to an end; but establish the
just: for the righteous God trieth the hearts and reins.

D. GOD WILL DEFEND THE RIGHTEOUS AND REWARD THE WICKED

7:10 Ps 18:2, 30; 97:10, 11
7:11 Deut 32:41; Ps 50:6; 90:9
7:12☆ Ps 64:7; Ezek 33:9
7:13 Ps 18:14; 45:5; 64:7
7:14 Job 15:35; Isa 59:4; Jas 1:15
7:15☆ Job 4:7, 8; Ps 57:6
7:16 Esth 9:24, 25; Ps 140:9, 11
7:17 Ps 9:2; 66:1, 2, 4; 71:15, 16

10My defence *is* of God, which saveth the upright in heart.
11God judgeth the righteous, and God is angry *with the wicked* every day.
12If he turn not, he will whet his sword; he hath bent his bow, and made
it ready.
13He hath also prepared for him the instruments of death; he ordaineth
his arrows against the persecutors.
14Behold, he travaileth with iniquity, and hath conceived mischief, and
brought forth falsehood.
15He made a pit, and digged it, and is fallen into the ditch *which* he made.
16His mischief shall return upon his own head, and his violent dealing
shall come down upon his own pate.
17I will praise the LORD according to his righteousness: and will sing
praise to the name of the LORD most high.

I. GOD'S GLORY AND HIS CREATURES' GREATNESS

A. THE CREATOR'S MAJESTY AND GLORY

To the chief Musician upon Gittith, A Psalm of David

8:1☆ Ps 57:5, 11; 66:2; 113:4; 148:13
8:2 Mt 21:16
8:3 Ps 89:11; 136:9
8:4 Job 7:17; Ps 144:3; Heb 2:6–8

8 O LORD our Lord, how excellent *is* thy name in all the earth! who
hast set thy glory above the heavens.
2Out of the mouth of babes and sucklings hast thou ordained strength
because of thine enemies, that thou mightest still the enemy and the
avenger.
3When I consider thy heavens, the work of thy fingers, the moon and the
stars, which thou hast ordained;
4What is man, that thou art mindful of him? and the son of man, that
thou visitest him?

B. MAN: GOD'S STEWARD OVER CREATION

8:5☆ Ps 21:5; 82:6; 103:4
8:6 Gen 1:26, 28; 1 Cor 15:27

5For thou hast made him a little lower than the angels, and hast crowned
him with glory and honour.
6Thou madest him to have dominion over the works of thy hands: thou
hast put all *things* under his feet:
7All sheep and oxen, yea, and the beasts of the field;

7:12 Sword and bow are ready when God executes vengeance on his enemies. However, while he is preparing his instruments of destruction, he warns men of their danger and gives them time to repent.

7:15 There is a sense in which sinners prepare to *destroy themselves. They are like Haman,* who constructed the gallows on which he was hung, although the gallows was intended for Mordecai. So sinners dig a pit for others, only to fall into it themselves.

8:1ff This hymn of praise exalts the glory of the Creator and speaks of the relationship of man—a lower form—to the One who has made him. Even though man is finite, God has crowned him with glory and honor. The Psalm ends on a note of the excellency or majesty of God our Lord.

8:5 *a little lower than the angels.* Man, when compared with the size of the cosmos, is insignificant. Yet God has "put him in charge of everything" (8:6, TLB) he has made. Jesus, the Son of God, as true man, is sovereign over all the universe and is in charge of everything. This is a messianic Psalm (see Heb. 2:5–9).

8 The fowl of the air, and the fish of the sea, *and whatsoever* passeth
through the paths of the seas.
9 O LORD our Lord, how excellent *is* thy name in all the earth!

I. GOD, THE GREAT DELIVERER

A. HYMN OF PRAISE FOR GOD'S PERSON AND WORKS

To the chief Musician upon Muth-labben, A Psalm of David

9 I WILL praise *thee*, O LORD, with my whole heart; I will shew forth all
thy marvellous works.
☆**9:1** Ps 26:7; 86:12

2 I will be glad and rejoice in thee: I will sing praise to thy name, O thou
most High.
9:2 Ps 66:2, 4 92:1; 104:34

3 When mine enemies are turned back, they shall fall and perish at thy
presence.
9:3 Ps 27:2; 56:9

4 For thou hast maintained my right and my cause; thou satest in the
throne judging right.
9:4 Ps 47:8; 140:12 1 Pet 2:23

5 Thou hast rebuked the heathen, thou hast destroyed the wicked, thou
hast put out their name for ever and ever.
9:5 Ps 69:28 119:21

6 O thou enemy, destructions are come to a perpetual end: and thou hast
destroyed cities; their memorial is perished with them.
9:6 Ps 34:16; 40:15

7 But the LORD shall endure for ever: he hath prepared his throne for
judgment.
8 And he shall judge the world in righteousness, he shall minister
judgment to the people in uprightness.
9:7 Ps 10:16 89:14, 15 96:13; 98:8, 9

9 The LORD also will be a refuge for the oppressed, a refuge in times of
trouble.
9:9 Ps 18:2; 37:39 59:9, 16, 17

10 And they that know thy name will put their trust in thee: for thou,
LORD, hast not forsaken them that seek thee.
9:10 Ps 37:28; 91:14 94:14

11 Sing praises to the LORD, which dwelleth in Zion: declare among the
people his doings.
9:11 Ps 76:2; 105:1

12 When he maketh inquisition for blood, he remembereth them: he
forgetteth not the cry of the humble.
9:12 Gen 9:5, 6 Ps 72:14

B. THE PSALMIST'S PETITION FOR DELIVERANCE

13 Have mercy upon me, O LORD; consider my trouble *which I suffer* of
them that hate me, thou that liftest me up from the gates of death:
9:13 Ps 30:3; 38:19 86:13

14 That I may shew forth all thy praise in the gates of the daughter of
Zion: I will rejoice in thy salvation.
9:14 Ps 13:5; 20:5 35:9; 51:12 106:2

15 The heathen are sunk down in the pit *that* they made: in the net which
they hid is their own foot taken.
9:15 Ps 7:15; 35:8 57:6

16 The LORD is known *by* the judgment *which* he executeth: the wicked is
snared in the work of his own hands. Hig-gai′-on. Se′lah.
☆**9:16**

17 The wicked shall be turned into hell, *and* all the nations that forget
God.
9:17 Job 8:13 Ps 49:14; 50:22

18 For the needy shall not alway be forgotten: the expectation of the poor
shall *not* perish for ever.
9:18 Ps 62:5; 71:5

19 Arise, O LORD; let not man prevail: let the heathen be judged in thy
sight.
9:19 Num 10:35 2 Chron 14:11

20 Put them in fear, O LORD: *that* the nations may know themselves *to be*
but men. Se′lah.
9:20 Ps 62:9 83:17, 18

9:1ff This hymn of deliverance goes far beyond David as an individual and speaks about the nations. Implicit in this Psalm is the truth that nations do sin and are judged by God. They rise and fall according to God's righteous judgments. God knows that nations are composed of men, whose views and actions determine their destiny.

I. THE LORD WHO JUDGES THE WICKED
A. THE CHARACTER AND DEEDS OF THE WICKED

10 WHY standest thou afar off, O LORD? *why* hidest thou *thyself* in
times of trouble?
2 The wicked in *his* pride doth persecute the poor: let them be taken in the
devices that they have imagined.
3 For the wicked boasteth of his heart's desire, and blesseth the covetous,
whom the LORD abhorreth.
4 The wicked, through the pride of his countenance, will not seek *after*
God: God *is* not in all his thoughts.
5 His ways are always grievous; thy judgments *are* far above out of his
sight: *as for* all his enemies, he puffeth at them.
6 He hath said in his heart, I shall not be moved: for *I shall* never *be* in
adversity.
7 His mouth is full of cursing and deceit and fraud: under his tongue *is*
mischief and vanity.
8 He sitteth in the lurking places of the villages: in the secret places doth
he murder the innocent: his eyes are privily set against the poor.
9 He lieth in wait secretly as a lion in his den: he lieth in wait to catch the
poor: he doth catch the poor, when he draweth him into his net.
10 He croucheth, *and* humbleth himself, that the poor may fall by his
strong ones.
11 He hath said in his heart, God hath forgotten: he hideth his face; he
will never see *it*.

B. THE PETITION FOR HELP AND ASSURANCE OF THE ANSWER

12 Arise, O LORD; O God, lift up thine hand: forget not the humble.
13 Wherefore doth the wicked contemn God? he hath said in his heart,
Thou wilt not require *it*.
14 Thou hast seen *it;* for thou beholdest mischief and spite, to requite *it*
with thy hand: the poor committeth himself unto thee; thou art the helper
of the fatherless.
15 Break thou the arm of the wicked and the evil *man:* seek out his
wickedness *till* thou find none.
16 The LORD *is* King for ever and ever: the heathen are perished out of his
land.
17 LORD, thou hast heard the desire of the humble: thou wilt prepare their
heart, thou wilt cause thine ear to hear:
18 To judge the fatherless and the oppressed, that the man of the earth
may no more oppress.

I. THE LORD, OUR FAITHFUL DEFENDER
A. THE TEMPTATION NOT TO TRUST THE LORD

To the chief Musician, A Psalm of David

11 IN the LORD put I my trust: how say ye to my soul, Flee *as* a bird
to your mountain?

10:1☆ Ps 13:1; 22:1; 55:1
10:2 Ps 7:15; 9:16; 73:6, 8
10:3 Ps 49:6; 94:3, 4
10:4 Ps 14:1; 36:1, 2
10:5 Ps 28:5; 52:7
10:6 Ps 30:6, 7; 49:11
10:7 Job 20:12; Ps 59:12; 73:8; 140:3; Rom 3:14
10:8 Ps 11:2; 94:6, 7; Prov 1:11
10:9☆ Ps 17:12; 59:3; 140:5
10:11 Ps 10:4
10:12 Ps 9:12; 17:7; Mic 5:9
10:14 Job 11:11; Ps 9:12; 22:9–11; 37:5; 68:5
10:15 Ps 37:17; 140:11
10:16 Deut 8:20; Ps 29:10
10:17 Ps 9:18; 34:15; 145:19
10:18 Ps 9:9; 74:21; 146:9; Isa 29:20
11:1☆ Ps 56:10, 11; 121:1, 2

10:1ff God is long-suffering. The wicked are not *always punished immediately;* they continue in their evil ways with apparent impunity. A prayer is offered to God to take action against the wicked and ends with the assurance that justice will prevail at last and the wicked will be punished.
10:9 *to catch the poor.* The wicked treat the poor unkindly but it is not to be supposed that only wealthy sinners do this. Poor sinners may not have the same opportunity as do the rich, but they are no less sinners. God looks on the heart, not on the pocketbook. Rich and poor sinners alike are condemned.
11:1 When in trouble we are tempted to distrust God or to quit. There is one thing the righteous can and

2 For, lo, the wicked bend *their* bow, they make ready their arrow upon
the string, that they may privily shoot at the upright in heart.
3 If the foundations be destroyed, what can the righteous do?

11:2 Ps 7:12; 64:3, 4
11:3 Ps 82:5

B. THE PSALMIST AFFIRMS HIS FAITH IN THE LORD

4 The LORD *is* in his holy temple, the LORD's throne *is* in heaven: his eyes
behold, his eyelids try, the children of men.
5 The LORD trieth the righteous: but the wicked and him that loveth
violence his soul hateth.
6 Upon the wicked he shall rain snares, fire and brimstone, and an
horrible tempest: *this shall be* the portion of their cup.
7 For the righteous LORD loveth righteousness; his countenance doth
behold the upright.

11:4 Mic 1:2; Ps 34:15, 16; 103:19; Isa 66:1; Mt 5:34; Rev 4:2
11:5 Gen 22:1; Ps 5:5; 34:19; Jas 1:12
11:6 Gen 19:24; Ezek 38:22; Jer 4:11, 12
☆**11.7** Ps 7:9–11; 16:11; 17:15; 33:5

I. DELIVERING THE RIGHTEOUS AMONG THE UNGODLY

A. THE RIGHTEOUS MAN'S PRAYER FOR HELP

To the chief Musician upon Sheminith, A Psalm of David

12 HELP, LORD; for the godly man ceaseth; for the faithful fail from
among the children of men.
2 They speak vanity every one with his neighbour: *with* flattering lips *and*
with a double heart do they speak.
3 The LORD shall cut off all flattering lips, *and* the tongue that speaketh
proud things:
4 Who have said, With our tongue will we prevail; our lips *are* our own:
who *is* lord over us?

☆**12:1** Mic 7:1, 2
12:2 Ps 28:3; 41:6; Jer 9:8; Rom 16:18
12:3 Ps 73:8, 9; Dan 7:8; Rev 13:5

B. THE LORD'S PROMISE OF DELIVERANCE IS SURE

5 For the oppression of the poor, for the sighing of the needy, now will I
arise, saith the LORD; I will set *him* in safety *from him that* puffeth at him.
6 The words of the LORD *are* pure words: *as* silver tried in a furnace of
earth, purified seven times.
7 Thou shalt keep them, O LORD, thou shalt preserve them from this
generation for ever.
8 The wicked walk on every side, when the vilest men are exalted.

☆**12:5** Ps 3:7; 9:9; 34:6; 35:10
12:6 Ps 19:8–10; 119:140; Prov 30:5
12:7 Ps 37:28; 97:10
12:8 Ps 55:10, 11

I. THE FRIENDLESS SOUL

A. THE PSALMIST FEELS DESERTED

To the chief Musician, A Psalm of David

13 HOW long wilt thou forget me, O LORD? for ever? how long wilt
thou hide thy face from me?

☆**13:1** Job 13:24; Ps 44:24; 89:46

---

ought to do—trust God and be assured that he will deal with the wicked, for God loves the righteous and approves of their deeds.

11:7 Paraphrased: "For God is good, and he loves goodness; the godly shall see his face" or, "His face shines down in mercy and joy upon the good."†

12:1 There are times when people generally lack piety and when honesty and integrity are in short supply. Men on every side prowl about to destroy, but the righteous shall be refined and purified in the midst of all this evil.

12:5 There are good thoughts for bad times in this psalm. God will come to the aid of his saints. Though men are false, God is faithful. His word is precious and his promises pure and sure.

13:1ff This Psalm is for the soul who experiences the silence of God and feels the absence of the divine in his life. When God is veiled and we cannot see him, this is the time when we should continually call on him, for he is speaking when we do not hear him and present when he seems to be absent.

13:2 Ps 42:4, 5, 9

2 How long shall I take counsel in my soul, *having* sorrow in my heart
daily? how long shall mine enemy be exalted over me?

B. THE PSALMIST PRAYS FOR HELP

13:3 Ezra 9:8 Job 33:29, 30 Ps 5:1; 18:28 **13:4** Ps 25:2; 38:16 Jer 20:10

3 Consider *and* hear me, O LORD my God: lighten mine eyes, lest I sleep
the *sleep of* death;
4 Lest mine enemy say, I have prevailed against him; *and* those that
trouble me rejoice when I am moved.

C. THE PSALMIST'S SONG OF FAITH

13:5 Ps 52:8 **13:6☆** Ps 59:16 96:1, 2; 116:7

5 But I have trusted in thy mercy; my heart shall rejoice in thy salvation.
6 I will sing unto the LORD, because he hath dealt bountifully with me.

I. THE CORRUPTION OF THE WORLD
A. THE WICKEDNESS OF MEN

To the chief Musician, A Psalm of David

14:1☆ Ps 10:4; 53:1 Rom 3:10–12 **14:2** Ezra 6:21, 22 Ps 33:13–15 102:19 **14:3** Ps 58:3; 143:2 2 Pet 2:7, 8 **14:4** Isa 64:7 Jer 10:25 Amos 8:4 Mic 3:2, 3

14 THE fool hath said in his heart, *There is* no God. They are corrupt,
they have done abominable works, *there is* none that doeth good.
2 The LORD looked down from heaven upon the children of men, to see if
there were any that did understand, *and* seek God.
3 They are all gone aside, they are *all* together become filthy: *there is* none
that doeth good, no, not one.
4 Have all the workers of iniquity no knowledge? who eat up my people *as*
they eat bread, and call not upon the LORD.

B. GOD'S DELIGHT IN THOSE WHO LOVE HIM

14:5 Ps 112:2 **14:6** Ps 9:9; 40:17 46:1 **14:7☆** Ps 53:6; 85:1, 2 Job 42:10

5 There were they in great fear: for God *is* in the generation of the
righteous.
6 Ye have shamed the counsel of the poor, because the LORD *is* his refuge.
7 Oh that the salvation of Israel *were come* out of Zion! when the LORD
bringeth back the captivity of his people, Jacob shall rejoice, *and* Israel
shall be glad.

I. THE CHARACTER OF THOSE WHO LOVE THE LORD

A Psalm of David

15:1☆ Ps 24:3; 27:5, 6 **15:2** Ps 24:4 Isa 33:15 Zech 8:16 Eph 4:25

15 LORD, who shall abide in thy tabernacle? who shall dwell in thy
holy hill?
2 He that walketh uprightly, and worketh righteousness, and speaketh the
truth in his heart.

13:6 *he hath dealt bountifully with me.* David speaks of this in the past tense, for by faith he has received the pledge of God for something which has not yet come.

14:1 *fool.* Here the atheist is called a fool. The reason is simple: no one can deny the existence of God without being omniscient, which would make that person God. Since the doubter is not omniscient, God *can exist outside the limits of his knowledge.* One *can* be an agnostic and say, "I don't know whether there is a God." But to be an atheist is to be anti-intellectual, irrational, or simply a fool.

14:7 The wicked practice what is in accord with their principles. They act corruptly, but there is a God who will come out of Zion and deliver his people. Israel shall rejoice. And so shall all believers and nations whose God is the Lord.

15:1ff The way to heaven and to happiness is to be holy and honest. Christ is the way, and we are to walk in his way as described in this lovely Psalm. *thy tabernacle.* God's presence by way of the cloud of glory was manifested to his people in the tabernacle and also in the temple. Those who find refuge in God do so not only because they trust in God but also because that trust is exhibited in a new life marked by the characteristics stated in 15:2–5.

3 *He that* backbiteth not with his tongue, nor doeth evil to his neighbour,
nor taketh up a reproach against his neighbour.
4 In whose eyes a vile person is contemned; but he honoureth them that
fear the LORD. *He that* sweareth to *his own* hurt, and changeth not.
5 *He that* putteth not out his money to usury, nor taketh reward against
the innocent. He that doeth these *things* shall never be moved.

15:3 Ex 23:1 Lev 19:16 Ps 28:3
15:4 Acts 28:10 Judg 11:35
15:5 Ex 22:25; 23:8 23:20

I. THE RESURRECTION; A MESSIANIC PSALM

A. TRUST IN GOD, OUR REFUGE

Michtam of David

16 PRESERVE me, O God: for in thee do I put my trust.
2 *O my soul,* thou hast said unto the LORD, Thou *art* my Lord: my
goodness *extendeth* not to thee;
3 *But* to the saints that *are* in the earth, and *to* the excellent, in whom *is* all
my delight.
4 Their sorrows shall be multiplied *that* hasten *after* another *god:* their
drink offerings of blood will I not offer, nor take up their names into my
lips.
5 The LORD *is* the portion of mine inheritance and of my cup: thou
maintainest my lot.

☆**16:1** Ps 7:1; 17:8
16:2 Ps 73:25
16:3 Deut 33:3 Ps 101:6 119:63
16:4 Ex 23:13 Josh 23:7 Ps 32:10 106:37, 38
16:5 Ps 23:5; 73:26 125:3 Lam 3:24

B. DOING THE WILL OF GOD

6 The lines are fallen unto me in pleasant *places;* yea, I have a goodly
heritage.
7 I will bless the LORD, who hath given me counsel: my reins also instruct
me in the night seasons.
8 I have set the LORD always before me: because *he is* at my right hand, I
shall not be moved.

16:6 Ps 78:55 Jer 3:19
16:7 Ps 73:24; 77:6
16:8 Ps 27:8; 73:23 110:5; 123:1, 2 131:5

C. THE PROMISE OF THE RESURRECTION

9 Therefore my heart is glad, and my glory rejoiceth: my flesh also shall
rest in hope.
10 For thou wilt not leave my soul in hell; neither wilt thou suffer thine
Holy One to see corruption.
11 Thou wilt shew me the path of life: in thy presence *is* fulness of joy; at
thy right hand *there are* pleasures for evermore.

16:9 Ps 4:7; 13:5 57:8, 9; 108:1
☆**16:10** Ps 49:15; 86:13 Acts 2:27; 13:35
16:11 Ps 21:6 36:7, 8; 43:4 46:4

I. DAVID IN THE SHADOW OF GOD'S WINGS

A. HIS CLAIM OF FAITHFULNESS

A Prayer of David

17 HEAR the right, O LORD, attend unto my cry, give ear unto my
prayer, *that goeth* not out of feigned lips.

☆**17:1** Ps 61:1; 88:2 142:6

16:1 This Psalm has much of David in it but much more about Christ. It is messianic, and it will close with a confidence in the resurrection. David did not fully understand what was implied in this Psalm, but we rest in the assurance that the Holy Spirit inspired David to write it.

16:10 This messianic Psalm predicts the resurrection of Jesus Christ from the grave. The Apostle Peter quotes from 16:8–11 in Acts 2:25–28 to show this to be true. The Hebrew word *nephesh* here refers to the whole person, not merely to the soul as distinct from the body. Thus the verse "You will not leave my soul in hell or let the body of your Holy Son decay" (Acts 2:27, TLB) is an apt paraphrase. The KJV and the RSV are not as clear.

17:1 Here David claims the correctness of his life. He prays for God to conserve and protect him from his enemies, whose character he describes here. As a result of his confidence in God, David experienced God's comfort.

17:2 Ps 98:8, 9; 99:4; 103:6
2 Let my sentence come forth from thy presence; let thine eyes behold the
things that are equal.

17:3 Job 23:10; Ps 26:1, 2; 66:10; Jer 50:20
3 Thou hast proved mine heart; thou hast visited *me* in the night; thou
hast tried me, *and* shalt find nothing; I am purposed *that* my mouth shall
not transgress.

17:4 Ps 10:5–11; 119:9, 101; Prov 1:15
4 Concerning the works of men, by the word of thy lips I have kept *me*
from the paths of the destroyer.

17:5 Ps 18:36; 37:30, 31; 44:18
5 Hold up my goings in thy paths, *that* my footsteps slip not.

B. HIS PRAYER FOR HELP

17:6☆ Ps 86:7; 88:2
6 I have called upon thee, for thou wilt hear me, O God: incline thine ear
unto me, *and hear* my speech.

17:7 Ps 20:6; 31:21
7 Shew thy marvellous lovingkindness, O thou that savest by thy right
hand them which put their trust *in thee* from those that rise up *against them.*

17:8☆ Deut 32:10; Ruth 2:12; Ps 36:7; 91:1, 4; Zech 2:8
8 Keep me as the apple of the eye, hide me under the shadow of thy wings,

17:9 Ps 27:12; 38:12
9 From the wicked that oppress me, *from* my deadly enemies, *who*
compass me about.

C. HE DESCRIBES HIS ENEMIES

17:10 1 Sam 2:3; Ps 31:18; 73:7, 8
10 They are inclosed in their own fat: with their mouth they speak
proudly.

17:11 Ps 37:14; 88:17
11 They have now compassed us in our steps: they have set their eyes
bowing down to the earth;

17:12 Ps 7:2; 10:9
12 Like as a lion *that* is greedy of his prey, and as it were a young lion
lurking in secret places.

D. HE CLAIMS GOD'S DELIVERANCE

17:13 Ps 22:20; 49:6; 73:3–7; Lk 16:25
13 Arise, O LORD, disappoint him, cast him down: deliver my soul from
the wicked, *which is* thy sword:
14 From men *which are* thy hand, O LORD, from men of the world, *which*
have their portion in *this* life, and whose belly thou fillest with thy hid
treasure: they are full of children, and leave the rest of their *substance* to
their babes.

17:15 Ps 4:6, 7; 16:11; 140:13; 1 Jn 3:2
15 As for me, I will behold thy face in righteousness: I shall be satisfied,
when I awake, with thy likeness.

I. DAVID'S SONG OF DELIVERANCE

A. PRAISE TO THE LORD

To the chief Musician, A Psalm of David, the servant of the LORD, who spake unto the LORD the words of this song in the day that the LORD delivered him from the hand of all his enemies, and from the hand of Saul: And he said,

18:1☆ Ps 59:17
18 I WILL love thee, O LORD, my strength.

18:2 1 Sam 2:2; Ps 28:1; 19:14; 59:9, 11; 71:3; 75:10; 144:2
2 The LORD *is* my rock, and my fortress, and my deliverer; my
God, my strength, in whom I will trust; my buckler, and the horn of my
salvation, *and* my high tower.

18:3 Num 10:9; Ps 34:6; 96:4; 145:3
3 I will call upon the LORD, *who is worthy* to be praised: so shall I be saved
from mine enemies.

17:6 Persecution and suffering have a way of concentrating our attention on God and his mercies. People pray more when they are in trouble than when all is *going well.*

17:8 "If we keep God's law as the *apple of our eye* (Prov. 7:2), we may expect that God will so keep us."* Whoever touches any believer touches the apple of God's eye (Zech. 2:8).

18:1ff This Psalm is found in 2 Sam. 22. While it has been altered here, its substance is the same. David expresses thanksgiving to God for having often delivered him. As a result of God's faithfulness, David has the courage and assurance that this same God will deliver him in the days which lie ahead. Such should be the attitude of all believers in this age; because of the incarnation, we have the full and final revelation of God in Jesus Christ, our preserver and helper through life's journey.

B. THE PSALMIST'S DIFFICULTIES AND THE LORD'S DELIVERANCE

4 The sorrows of death compassed me, and the floods of ungodly men
made me afraid.
5 The sorrows of hell compassed me about: the snares of death prevented
me.
6 In my distress I called upon the LORD, and cried unto my God: he heard
my voice out of his temple, and my cry came before him, *even* into his ears.
7 Then the earth shook and trembled; the foundations also of the hills
moved and were shaken, because he was wroth.
8 There went up a smoke out of his nostrils, and fire out of his mouth
devoured: coals were kindled by it.
9 He bowed the heavens also, and came down: and darkness *was* under
his feet.
10 And he rode upon a cherub, and did fly: yea, he did fly upon the wings
of the wind.
11 He made darkness his secret place; his pavilion round about him *were*
dark waters *and* thick clouds of the skies.
12 At the brightness *that was* before him his thick clouds passed, hail
stones and coals of fire.
13 The LORD also thundered in the heavens, and the Highest gave his
voice; hail *stones* and coals of fire.
14 Yea, he sent out his arrows, and scattered them; and he shot out
lightnings, and discomfited them.
15 Then the channels of waters were seen, and the foundations of the
world were discovered at thy rebuke, O LORD, at the blast of the breath of
thy nostrils.
16 He sent from above, he took me, he drew me out of many waters.
17 He delivered me from my strong enemy, and from them which hated
me: for they were too strong for me.
18 They prevented me in the day of my calamity: but the LORD was my
stay.
19 He brought me forth also into a large place; he delivered me, because
he delighted in me.

C. THE PSALMIST'S DEFENSE OF HIS INTEGRITY

20 The LORD rewarded me according to my righteousness; according to
the cleanness of my hands hath he recompensed me.
21 For I have kept the ways of the LORD, and have not wickedly departed
from my God.
22 For all his judgments *were* before me, and I did not put away his
statutes from me.
23 I was also upright before him, and I kept myself from mine iniquity.
24 Therefore hath the LORD recompensed me according to my righteous-
ness, according to the cleanness of my hands in his eyesight.
25 With the merciful thou wilt shew thyself merciful; with an upright man
thou wilt shew thyself upright;
26 With the pure thou wilt shew thyself pure; and with the froward thou
wilt shew thyself froward.
27 For thou wilt save the afflicted people; but wilt bring down high looks.
28 For thou wilt light my candle: the LORD my God will enlighten my
darkness.
29 For by thee I have run through a troop; and by my God have I leaped
over a wall.

18:4 Ps 69:1, 2; 116:3; 124:2–5
18:6 Ps 3:4; 34:15; 120:1
18:7 Judg 5:4; Ps 114:4, 6, 7; Isa 13:13; Hag 2:6
18:8 Ps 50:3
18:9 Ex 20:21; Ps 97:2; 144:5
18:10 Ps 80:1; 99:1; 104:3
18:11 Deut 4:11
18:12 Ps 104:1, 2; Isa 30:30
18:13 Ps 29:3; 104:7, 8
18:14 Judg 4:15; Ps 144:6
18:15 Ex 15:8; Ps 106:9
18:16 Ps 144:7
18:17 Ps 35:10; 142:6
18:18 Ps 16:8; 59:16
18:19 Ps 31:8; 37:23; 41:1, 11; 118:5
18:20 Job 33:26; Ps 7:8; 24:4
18:21 2 Chron 34:33; Ps 37:34; 119:33, 102, 103
18:22 Ps 119:30, 83
18:24 Prov 8:32
18:25 Ps 62:12; Mt 5:7
18:26 Lev 26:23, 24; Prov 3:34; Hab 1:13
18:27 Ps 72:12; 101:5; Prov 6:16–19
18:28 Job 18:6; Ps 27:1
18:29 Ps 118:10–12; 2 Cor 12:9

D. THE PSALMIST ASCRIBES HIS DELIVERANCE TO THE LORD

18:30 Ps 12:6; 19:7
18:31☆ Deut 32:31, 39 Ps 62:2; 86:8–10
18:32 Isa 45:5 1 Pet 5:10
18:33 Hab 3:19
18:34 Ps 144:1
18:35 Ps 33:20, 63:8 119:117
18:36 Ps 31:8; 66:9
18:37 Ps 44:5
18:38 Ps 36:12; 47:3
18:40 Ps 94:23; 21:12
18:41 Job 27:8, 9 Ps 50:22 Prov 1:28
18:42 Ps 83:13
18:43 2 Sam 3:1 Ps 89:27 Isa 55:5 Mic 7:17

30 *As for* God, his way *is* perfect: the word of the LORD is tried: he *is* a
buckler to all those that trust in him.
31 For who *is* God save the LORD? or who *is* a rock save our God?
32 *It is* God that girdeth me with strength, and maketh my way perfect.
33 He maketh my feet like hinds' *feet,* and setteth me upon my high places.
34 He teacheth my hands to war, so that a bow of steel is broken by mine
arms.
35 Thou hast also given me the shield of thy salvation: and thy right hand
hath holden me up, and thy gentleness hath made me great.
36 Thou hast enlarged my steps under me, that my feet did not slip.
37 I have pursued mine enemies, and overtaken them: neither did I turn
again till they were consumed.
38 I have wounded them that they were not able to rise: they are fallen
under my feet.
39 For thou hast girded me with strength unto the battle: thou hast
subdued under me those that rose up against me.
40 Thou hast also given me the necks of mine enemies; that I might
destroy them that hate me.
41 They cried, but *there was* none to save *them: even* unto the LORD, but he
answered them not.
42 Then did I beat them small as the dust before the wind: I did cast them
out as the dirt in the streets.
43 Thou hast delivered me from the strivings of the people; *and* thou hast
made me the head of the heathen: a people *whom* I have not known shall
serve me.
44 As soon as they hear of me, they shall obey me: the strangers shall
submit themselves unto me.
45 The strangers shall fade away, and be afraid out of their close places.

E. HIS CONFIDENCE FOR THE FUTURE IS IN THE LORD

18:46 Job 19:25
18:47 Ps 47:3 94:1, 2; 144:2
18:48 Ps 3:7; 27:5, 6
18:49 Ps 108:1 Rom 15:9
18:50 Ps 21:1; 28:8 89:4

46 The LORD liveth; and blessed *be* my rock; and let the God of my
salvation be exalted.
47 *It is* God that avengeth me, and subdueth the people under me.
48 He delivereth me from mine enemies: yea, thou liftest me up above
those that rise up against me: thou hast delivered me from the violent man.
49 Therefore will I give thanks unto thee, O LORD, among the heathen,
and sing praises unto thy name.
50 Great deliverance giveth he to his king; and sheweth mercy to his
anointed, to David, and to his seed for evermore.

I. THE GOD OF NATURE AND THE WORD

A. THE HEAVENS REVEAL GOD'S GLORY

19:1☆ 1 Gen 1:6–8 Ps 8:1 Rom 1:20

To the chief Musician, A Psalm of David

19 THE heavens declare the glory of God; and the firmament sheweth
his handywork.

18:31 *who is a rock save our God?* God indeed is the rock or foundation on which his people rest their confidence. His Word is also a rock which stands forever. Christ, too, is our Rock and sure defense. No one else and nothing else can be compared to this Rock.

19:1 Here we discover that God has revealed himself in two ways: (1) in nature, for the heavens show forth the divine glory and the firmament testifies to his creative power, and (2) in the written Word of God, without which no man can find God. Even nature does no more than manifest the fact that God exists. Unlike the Word, nature does not disclose who he is or what he has done for our salvation.

2 Day unto day uttereth speech, and night unto night sheweth knowledge.
3 *There is* no speech nor language, *where* their voice is not heard.
4 Their line is gone out through all the earth, and their words to the end of
the world. In them hath he set a tabernacle for the sun,
5 Which *is* as a bridegroom coming out of his chamber, *and* rejoiceth as a
strong man to run a race.
6 His going forth *is* from the end of the heaven, and his circuit unto the
ends of it: and there is nothing hid from the heat thereof.

19:2 Ps 74:16
19:3 Rom 10:18
☆**19:5**
☆**19:6** Ps 113:3

B. THE WORD OF GOD REVEALS THE LAWS OF GOD

7 The law of the LORD *is* perfect, converting the soul: the testimony of the
LORD *is* sure, making wise the simple.
8 The statutes of the LORD *are* right, rejoicing the heart: the command-
ment of the LORD *is* pure, enlightening the eyes.
9 The fear of the LORD *is* clean, enduring for ever: the judgments of the
LORD *are* true *and* righteous altogether.
10 More to be desired *are they* than gold, yea, than much fine gold: sweeter
also than honey and the honeycomb.
11 Moreover by them is thy servant warned: *and* in keeping of them *there*
is great reward.
12 Who can understand *his* errors? cleanse thou me from secret *faults.*
13 Keep back thy servant also from presumptuous *sins;* let them not have
dominion over me: then shall I be upright, and I shall be innocent from the
great transgression.
14 Let the words of my mouth, and the meditation of my heart, be
acceptable in thy sight, O LORD, my strength, and my redeemer.

19:7 Ps 36:9; 119:14, 98–100, 160
19:9 Ps 119:138, 142
19:10 Ps 119:127; Prov 8:10; 16:24
19:11 Ps 17:4; Prov 29:18, 19
19:12 Ps 51:1, 2; 90:8; 139:23, 24
19:13 Ps 25:11; 32:2; 119:133
☆**19:14** Ps 18:2; 104:34; Isa 41:14

I. THE PRAYER FOR THE MESSIAH KING

A. THE PRAYER OF THE CONGREGATION FOR THE KING

To the chief Musician, A Psalm of David

20 THE LORD hear thee in the day of trouble; the name of the God of
Jacob defend thee;
2 Send thee help from the sanctuary, and strengthen thee out of Zion;
3 Remember all thy offerings, and accept thy burnt sacrifice; Se'lah.
4 Grant thee according to thine own heart, and fulfil all thy counsel.
5 We will rejoice in thy salvation, and in the name of our God we will set
up *our* banners: the LORD fulfil all thy petitions.

☆**20:1** Ps 46:7, 11; 59:1
20:2 Ps 3:4; 110:2; 119:28
20:3 Ps 51:19; Acts 10:4
20:4 1 Sam 1:17; Ps 21:2; 145:19
20:5 Ps 9:14; 60:4

B. THE FAITH OF THE MESSIAH KING

6 Now know I that the LORD saveth his anointed; he will hear him from
his holy heaven with the saving strength of his right hand.

20:6 Ps 28:8

19:5 *is as a bridegroom,* i.e., "as radiant as a bridegroom." *coming out of his chamber,* i.e., "going to his wedding."†

19:6 This is the language of the apparent. Even though we know better, we still speak of the sun rising and setting. Neither what is written here nor what we say today can or should be construed as teaching that the sun revolves around the earth.

19:14 Redemption, of which the Psalmist speaks, begins and ends with God and is all of grace and not of works. (Isa. 49:26; Job 19:25). Redemption is by Christ (1 Cor. 1:30; Gal. 3:13; Eph. 1:7). The cost of this salvation is the precious lifeblood of Christ (1 Pet. 1:18, 19), who gave his life for all mankind (1 Tim. 2:6).

20:1ff God commands believers to pray for kings and those in authority—Ps. 20 does this precisely. It supposes, of course, that the cause for which the nation prays is just. Beyond this, though, there is the larger reference to the kingdom of God headed by Jesus Christ. We are to pray for this kingdom to come and for the enthroning of Christ in connection with the second advent.

20:7 2 Chron 32:8 Ps 33:16, 17 Isa 31:1 **20:8** Isa 2:11, 17 Mic 7:8

7 Some *trust* in chariots, and some in horses: but we will remember the name of the LORD our God.

8 They are brought down and fallen: but we are risen, and stand upright.

C. THE CONGREGATION'S PETITION

20:9☆ Ps 17:6

9 Save, LORD: let the king hear us when we call.

I. THE ASCENSION DAY SONG
A. THE REDEEMER'S VICTORY AND GLORY

To the chief Musician, A Psalm of David

21:1☆ Ps 59:16, 17

21 THE king shall joy in thy strength, O LORD; and in thy salvation how greatly shall he rejoice!

21:2 Ps 37:4

2 Thou hast given him his heart's desire, and hast not withholden the request of his lips. Se'lah.

21:3 Ps 59:10

3 For thou preventest him with the blessings of goodness: thou settest a crown of pure gold on his head.

21:4 Ps 61:6; 91:16 133:3

4 He asked life of thee, *and* thou gavest *it* him, *even* length of days for ever and ever.

21:5 Ps 8:5; 96:6

5 His glory *is* great in thy salvation: honour and majesty hast thou laid upon him.

21:6 1 Chron 17:27 Ps 16:11

6 For thou hast made him most blessed for ever: thou hast made him exceeding glad with thy countenance.

21:7☆ Ps 112:6; 125:1

7 For the king trusteth in the LORD, and through the mercy of the most High he shall not be moved.

B. THE REDEEMER'S FUTURE VICTORY

21:8 Isa 10:10

8 Thine hand shall find out all thine enemies: thy right hand shall find out those that hate thee.

21:9 Ps 37:28 Mal 4:1

9 Thou shalt make them as a fiery oven in the time of thine anger: the LORD shall swallow them up in his wrath, and the fire shall devour them.

10 Their fruit shalt thou destroy from the earth, and their seed from among the children of men.

21:11 Ps 2:1–3

11 For they intended evil against thee: they imagined a mischievous device, *which* they are not able *to perform*.

21:12 Ps 7:12, 13 18:40

12 Therefore shalt thou make them turn their back, *when* thou shalt make ready *thine arrows* upon thy strings against the face of them.

21:13 Ps 59:16; 81:1

13 Be thou exalted, LORD, in thine own strength: *so* will we sing and praise thy power.

I. THE CRUCIFIXION PSALM
A. THE SAVIOR FORSAKEN

22:1☆ Job 3:24 Ps 10:1; 38:8 Mt 27:46 Mk 15:34

To the chief Musician upon Aijeleth Shahar, A Psalm of David

22 MY God, my God, why hast thou forsaken me? *why art thou so* far from helping me, *and from* the words of my roaring?

20:9 ". . . many interpreters give another reading of this verse [as do the RSV and NIV] by altering the pause, *LORD, save the king, and hear us when we call.*" *Thus the Anglican liturgy says:* "O Lord! save the king, and mercifully hear us when we call upon thee."*

21:1 When we pray for kings and those in authority and God answers those prayers, we are to return thanks to God. This should then encourage us to ask God for divine help as other emergencies arise and difficulties confront the nation. He who helped us yesterday will help us again today and tomorrow.

21:7 *the king trusteth in the LORD.* David did trust in the Lord, but many rulers in our day do not trust in the Lord. We believers are to pray for those in authority that we may live a quiet and peaceable-life (1 Tim. 2:2).

22:1 This verse sets forth one of the seven last sayings of Jesus on the cross. The whole Psalm graphically portrays the suffering of the Messiah and adds a

2 O my God, I cry in the daytime, but thou hearest not; and in the night
season, and am not silent.
3 But thou *art* holy, *O thou* that inhabitest the praises of Israel.
4 Our fathers trusted in thee: they trusted, and thou didst deliver them.
5 They cried unto thee, and were delivered: they trusted in thee, and were
not confounded.

22:2 Ps 42:3; 88:1
22:3 Ps 99:9; 78:53 107:6; 148:14

B. THE SAVIOR SCORNED

6 But I *am* a worm, and no man; a reproach of men, and despised of the
people.
7 All they that see me laugh me to scorn: they shoot out the lip, they
shake the head, *saying,*
8 He trusted on the LORD *that* he would deliver him: let him deliver him,
seeing he delighted in him.
9 But thou *art* he that took me out of the womb: thou didst make me hope
when I was upon my mother's breasts.
10 I was cast upon thee from the womb: thou *art* my God from my
mother's belly.
11 Be not far from me; for trouble *is* near; for *there is* none to help.
12 Many bulls have compassed me: strong *bulls* of Ba'shan have beset me
round.

☆**22:6** Job 25:6 Ps 31:11 Isa 41:14
22:7 Isa 53:3 Mt 27:39 Mk 15:29, 30
22:9 2 Kgs 14:26 Ps 71:5, 6, 12 72:12 Isa 46:3; 49:1
22:12 Ps 22:21 Amos 4:1

C. THE SAVIOR SURROUNDED AND PIERCED

13 They gaped upon me *with* their mouths, *as* a ravening and a roaring
lion.
14 I am poured out like water, and all my bones are out of joint; my heart
is like wax; it is melted in the midst of my bowels.
15 My strength is dried up like a potsherd; and my tongue cleaveth to my
jaws; and thou hast brought me into the dust of death.
16 For dogs have compassed me: the assembly of the wicked have inclosed
me: they pierced my hands and my feet.
17 I may tell all my bones: they look *and* stare upon me.
18 They part my garments among them, and cast lots upon my vesture.

22:13 Job 16:10 Ps 17:12 Lam 2:16
22:14 Job 30:16 Ps 31:9, 10 73:26
22:15 Ps 38:10 104:29
22:16 Ps 59:6, 7 Mt 27:35 Jn 20:25
☆**22:18** Mt 27:35 Lk 23:34 Jn 19:23, 24

D. THE SAVIOR'S PRAYER

19 But be not thou far from me, O LORD: O my strength, haste thee to
help me.
20 Deliver my soul from the sword; my darling from the power of the dog.
21 Save me from the lion's mouth: for thou hast heard me from the horns
of the unicorns.

22:19 Ps 70:5
☆**22:20** Ps 35:17; 37:14
22:21 Ps 34:4; 118:5 120:1

E. THE SAVIOR'S PRAISE

22 I will declare thy name unto my brethren: in the midst of the
congregation will I praise thee.
23 Ye that fear the LORD, praise him; all ye the seed of Jacob, glorify him;
and fear him, all ye the seed of Israel.

22:22 Ps 40:10 Heb 2:12
22:23 Ps 33:8; 86:12 135:19, 20

---

second prophecy fulfilled at the crucifixion, namely, that the soldiers would gamble over the seamless robe of the Savior (Matt. 27:35; Luke 23:34; John 19:23, 24).

22:6 *I am a worm.* A worm is a lowly thing, stepped on by men, and regarded with contempt. So was the Son of God treated by men at his crucifixion.

22:18 According to John 19:23, 24, this prophetic word was fulfilled exactly. Those who performed the deed knew nothing of the prophecy. Unknown to them, they were doing what the omniscient and omnipotent God had determined long before the event.

22:20 *Deliver my soul from the sword, my darling from the power of the dog,* i.e., "Rescue me from death, spare my precious life from all these evil men."†

22:24 Ps 27:9; 31:22 69:33; 102:2 Heb 5:7
22:25 Ps 35:18 40:9, 10

24 For he hath not despised nor abhorred the affliction of the afflicted;
neither hath he hid his face from him; but when he cried unto him, he
heard.
25 My praise *shall be* of thee in the great congregation: I will pay my vows
before them that fear him.

F. THE SAVIOR'S OFFER OF SALVATION

22:26 Ps 40:16; 69:32 107:9
22:27 Ps 2:8; 86:9
22:28 Ps 47:6, 7, 8 Obad 21 Zech 14:9
22:29 Ps 89:48
22:30 Ps 102:18, 28
22:31 Ps 71:18; 78:6

26 The meek shall eat and be satisfied: they shall praise the LORD that seek
him: your heart shall live for ever.
27 All the ends of the world shall remember and turn unto the LORD: and
all the kindreds of the nations shall worship before thee.
28 For the kingdom *is* the LORD'S: and he *is* the governor among the
nations.
29 All *they that be* fat upon earth shall eat and worship: all they that go
down to the dust shall bow before him: and none can keep alive his own
soul.
30 A seed shall serve him; it shall be accounted to the Lord for a
generation.
31 They shall come, and shall declare his righteousness unto a people that
shall be born, that he hath done *this.*

I. THE SHEPHERD PSALM

A. THE PRESENCE OF THE SHEPHERD

A Psalm of David

23:1☆ Ps 78:52 Isa 40:11 Ezek 34:11–13 Jn 10:11 1 Pet 2:25
23:2 Ps 5:8; 46:4 65:11–13 Ezek 34:14 Rev 7:17
23:4 Ps 27:1; 107:14 Isa 43:2

23 THE LORD *is* my shepherd; I shall not want.
2 He maketh me to lie down in green pastures: he leadeth me
beside the still waters.
3 He restoreth my soul: he leadeth me in the paths of righteousness for his
name's sake.
4 Yea, though I walk through the valley of the shadow of death, I will fear
no evil: for thou *art* with me; thy rod and thy staff they comfort me.

B. THE PROVISION OF THE SHEPHERD

23:5 Ps 16:5; 92:10
23:6 Ps 25:6, 7, 10 27:4–6

5 Thou preparest a table before me in the presence of mine enemies: thou
anointest my head with oil; my cup runneth over.
6 Surely goodness and mercy shall follow me all the days of my life: and
I will dwell in the house of the LORD for ever.

I. THE KING OF GLORY PSALM

A. THE SOVEREIGN LORD

A Psalm of David

24:1☆ Ps 89:11 1 Cor 10:26

24 THE earth *is* the LORD'S, and the fulness thereof; the world, and
they that dwell therein.
2 For he hath founded it upon the seas, and established it upon the floods.

23:1ff Of all the messianic Psalms, this is the best known and the greatest. It pictures Jesus as the shepherd, an identification which is picked up in the New Testament, where Jesus is called the good shepherd (John 10:11), the great shepherd (Heb. 13:20), and the chief shepherd (1 Pet. 5:4).

24:1ff This Psalm has to do with the kingdom of Jesus Christ, a kingdom which has come and is coming in its fullness when he returns in glory. It describes the subjects of the kingdom and their character. 24:7–10 beautifully describes the "King of glory," the Lord Christ.

B. THE CHARACTER OF THE LORD'S PEOPLE

3 Who shall ascend into the hill of the LORD? or who shall stand in his
holy place?
4 He that hath clean hands, and a pure heart; who hath not lifted up his
soul unto vanity, nor sworn deceitfully.
5 He shall receive the blessing from the LORD, and righteousness from the
God of his salvation.
6 This *is* the generation of them that seek him, that seek thy face, O Jacob.
Se′lah.

24:3 Ps 15:1; 65:4
24:4 Job 17:9 Ps 51:10; 73:1 Mt 5:8
24:5 Deut 11:26, 27 Ps 36:10

C. THE OPEN GATES FOR THE KING OF GLORY

7 Lift up your heads, O ye gates; and be ye lift up, ye everlasting doors;
and the King of glory shall come in.
8 Who *is* this King of glory? The LORD strong and mighty, the LORD
mighty in battle.
9 Lift up your heads, O ye gates; even lift *them* up, ye everlasting doors;
and the King of glory shall come in.
10 Who is this King of glory? The LORD of hosts, he *is* the King of glory.
Se′lah.

24:7 Ps 29:2, 9 118:20 Isa 26:2 1 Cor 2:8
24:8 Ex 15:3, 6 Deut 4:3, 4 Ps 76:3–6
24:9 Ps 26:8 Zech 9:9 Mt 21:5
☆**24:10** Josh 5:14

I. THE PRAYER OF THE HUMBLE
A. THE PRAYER TO FIND THE RIGHT ROAD

A Psalm of David

25 UNTO thee, O LORD, do I lift up my soul.
2 O my God, I trust in thee: let me not be ashamed, let not mine
enemies triumph over me.
3 Yea, let none that wait on thee be ashamed: let them be ashamed which
transgress without cause.
4 Shew me thy ways, O LORD; teach me thy paths.
5 Lead me in thy truth, and teach me: for thou *art* the God of my
salvation; on thee do I wait all the day.
6 Remember, O LORD, thy tender mercies and thy lovingkindnesses; for
they *have been* ever of old.
7 Remember not the sins of my youth, nor my transgressions: according
to thy mercy remember thou me for thy goodness' sake, O LORD.

☆**25:1** Ps 86:4
25:2 Ps 31:1, 6
25:3 Ps 37:9; 40:1 Isa 49:23
☆**25:4** Ps 5:8; 86:11
25:5 Ps 24:5; 40:1 Jn 16:13
25:6 Job 13:26 Ps 51:1 Jer 3:25

B. GOD WILL HELP THE HUMBLE

8 Good and upright *is* the LORD: therefore will he teach sinners in the
way.
9 The meek will he guide in judgment: and the meek will he teach his way.
10 All the paths of the LORD *are* mercy and truth unto such as keep his
covenant and his testimonies.
11 *For thy name's* sake, O LORD, pardon mine iniquity; for it *is* great.

25:8 Ps 86:5
25:9 Ps 23:3; 32:8
25:10 Ps 40:11 103:17, 18
25:11 Ex 34:9 Ps 79:9

24:10 The King of glory is Jehovah (Yahweh). He is our righteousness, imputed to us by faith through Christ's shed blood. He is omnipotent and desires to come into our souls, but only if we welcome him.
25:1 This psalmist (David) is full of zealous attachment to God and holy desires. He looks for God's favor and seeks his grace. We are to pray for pardon, seek his direction concerning our duty, and by faith claim his deliverance from our troubles and his protection from all our enemies of whom, of course, Satan is the worst.
25:4 God has a perfect will for each of his children. David asks God to reveal that perfect will to him. He exultantly declares that God will guide him in the way he should go (25:9, 10). The same truth is taught in Col. 1:9 and Isa. 30:20, 21. The way to know and do the perfect will of God is to surrender one's life to God (Rom. 12:2).

25:12 Ps 31:19 12 What man *is* he that feareth the LORD? him shall he teach in the way
that he shall choose.
25:13 Ps 37:11; 69:36 Prov 19:23 13 His soul shall dwell at ease; and his seed shall inherit the earth.
25:14 Prov 3:32 14 The secret of the LORD *is* with them that fear him; and he will shew
them his covenant.

C. THE PRAYER OF THE HELPLESS FOR DELIVERANCE

25:15 Ps 31:4; 123:2 15 Mine eyes *are* ever toward the LORD; for he shall pluck my feet out of
the net.
25:16 Ps 69:16 16 Turn thee unto me, and have mercy upon me; for I *am* desolate and
afflicted.
25:17 Ps 40:12; 107:6 17 The troubles of my heart are enlarged: *O* bring thou me out of my
distresses.
25:18 Ps 31:7; 103:3 18 Look upon mine affliction and my pain; and forgive all my sins.
25:19 Ps 3:1; 9:13 19 Consider mine enemies; for they are many; and they hate me with cruel
hatred.
25:20 Ps 25:2; 86:2 20 O keep my soul, and deliver me: let me not be ashamed; for I put my
25:21☆ Ps 25:3 trust in thee.
21 Let integrity and uprightness preserve me; for I wait on thee.
25:22 Ps 130:8 22 Redeem Israel, O God, out of all his troubles.

I. A PETITION FOR EXONERATION

A. THE PLEA FOR JUSTICE

A Psalm of David

26:1☆ Ps 7:8; 13:5 Heb 10:23 **26** JUDGE me, O LORD; for I have walked in mine integrity: I have
trusted also in the LORD; *therefore* I shall not slide.
26:2 Ps 7:9; 139:23 2 Examine me, O LORD, and prove me; try my reins and my heart.
26:3 Ps 1:2; 48:9 3 For thy lovingkindness *is* before mine eyes: and I have walked in thy
truth.

B. THE PSALMIST'S DEFENSE OF HIMSELF

26:4 Ps 1:1 4 I have not sat with vain persons, neither will I go in with dissemblers.
26:5 Ps 1:1; 31:6 139:21 5 I have hated the congregation of evil doers; and will not sit with the
wicked.
26:6 Ps 43:3, 4 6 I will wash mine hands in innocency: so will I compass thine altar, O
LORD:
26:7 Ps 9:1 7 That I may publish with the voice of thanksgiving, and tell of all thy
wondrous works.

C. THE PRAYER FOR THE LORD'S HELP

26:8 Ps 27:4 8 LORD, I have loved the habitation of thy house, and the place where
thine honour dwelleth.
26:9 Ps 28:3; 139:19 9 Gather not my soul with sinners, nor my life with bloody men;
10 In whose hands *is* mischief, and their right hand is full of bribes.
26:11☆ Ps 26:1; 44:26 69:18 11 But as for me, I will walk in mine integrity: redeem me, and be merciful
unto me.

25:21 David pleads his own integrity—not that he was sinless, but that he had the witness of his conscience that he had done his enemies no wrong. Thus he would *be preserved against those* who hated him. Clearly he was intimating that should he abuse and hate his enemies, he would not be preserved.

26:1ff David apparently has suffered from slander, defamation, and utterly false accusations. Such has been and always will be the lot of God's people (see, for example, Matt. 5:11 and John 15:20). David places his case in God's hands and looks to him for justification from the wrong judgments of men.

26:11 Herein David purposes in his heart that no matter what anyone else may do, he will walk according to God's precepts (i.e., in integrity). Divine grace will enable him to do this and comfort him in the doing of it.

12 My foot standeth in an even place: in the congregations will I bless the
LORD.

26:12 Ps 22:22; 40:2

I. THE PSALMIST'S TRUST AND ASSURANCE OF VICTORY (27:1–6)

A Psalm of David

27 THE LORD *is* my light and my salvation; whom shall I fear? the
LORD *is* the strength of my life; of whom shall I be afraid?
2 When the wicked, *even* mine enemies and my foes, came upon me to eat
up my flesh, they stumbled and fell.
3 Though an host should encamp against me, my heart shall not fear:
though war should rise against me, in this *will* I *be* confident.
4 One *thing* have I desired of the LORD, that will I seek after; that I may
dwell in the house of the LORD all the days of my life, to behold the beauty
of the LORD, and to inquire in his temple.
5 For in the time of trouble he shall hide me in his pavilion: in the secret
of his tabernacle shall he hide me; he shall set me up upon a rock.
6 And now shall mine head be lifted up above mine enemies round about
me: therefore will I offer in his tabernacle sacrifices of joy; I will sing, yea,
I will sing praises unto the LORD.

☆**27:1** Ex 15:2; Ps 18:28; 118:6, 14; Isa 60:20; Jonah 2:9; Mic 7:8
27:2 Ps 9:3
27:3 Ps 3:6, 7
☆**27:4** Ps 23:6; 26:8
27:5 Ps 17:8; 31:20; 40:2
27:6 Ps 13:6; 107:22

II. THE EARNEST PRAYER FOR PROTECTION AND SUPPORT (27:7–14)

7 Hear, O LORD, *when* I cry with my voice: have mercy also upon me, and
answer me.
8 *When thou saidst,* Seek ye my face; my heart said unto thee, Thy face,
LORD, will I seek.
9 Hide not thy face *far* from me; put not thy servant away in anger: thou
hast been my help; leave me not, neither forsake me, O God of my
salvation.
10 When my father and my mother forsake me, then the LORD will take
me up.
11 Teach me thy way, O LORD, and lead me in a plain path, because of
mine enemies.
12 Deliver me not over unto the will of mine enemies: for false witnesses
are risen up against me, and such as breathe out cruelty.
13 *I had fainted,* unless I had believed to see the goodness of the LORD in
the land of the living.
14 Wait on the LORD: be of good courage, and he shall strengthen thine
heart: wait, I say, on the LORD.

27:7 Ps 13:3; 37:12; 61:1
27:8 Ps 105:4; Amos 5:4
27:9 Ps 6:1; 40:17; 69:17; 94:14
27:10 Isa 40:11; 49:15
27:11 Ps 5:8; 25:4; 86:11
27:12 Ps 35:11; Jer 11:19; Mt 26:60; Acts 9:1
27:13 Ps 116:9; 142:5; Isa 38:11
27:14 Ps 31:24; 37:34; 130:5; Prov 20:22; Isa 25:9

I. DAVID'S PRAYER FOR DELIVERANCE (28:1–5)

A Psalm of David

28 UNTO thee will I cry, O LORD my rock; be not silent to me: lest, *if*
thou be silent to me, I become like them that go down into the pit.

☆**28:1** Ps 18:2; 35:22; 143:7

27:1ff This Psalm could have been written either before David became king or at the end of his life. The Psalm manifests the courage and bravery of David, his happiness in communion with God, how he seeks the face of the Lord, and what his expectations are of what God can and will do. It ends on a high note.

27:4 The ardent desire of David's heart was to *dwell in the house of the LORD.* Here he would engage in meditation as he worshipped his God, and be instructed as to his duty. Worship and teaching go hand in hand and are to be followed up by obedience to God's commandments.

28:1ff Here we find David as a saint militant, battling along in life, beseeching God for help. In the latter half of the Psalm David reflects the saint triumphant, thanking God for deliverance in the knowledge that God is the strength of his people—how then can they fail?

28:2☆ Ps 141:2; Lam 2:19; 1 Tim 2:8
28:3 Ps 26:9, 10; 55:21; 62:4; Jer 9:8
28:4 Ps 62:12; 2 Tim 4:14; Rev 18:6
28:5 Isa 5:12

2 Hear the voice of my supplications, when I cry unto thee, when I lift up
my hands toward thy holy oracle.
3 Draw me not away with the wicked, and with the workers of iniquity,
which speak peace to their neighbours, but mischief *is* in their hearts.
4 Give them according to their deeds, and according to the wickedness of
their endeavours: give them after the work of their hands; render to them
their desert.
5 Because they regard not the works of the LORD, nor the operation of his
hands, he shall destroy them, and not build them up.

II. DAVID'S SONG OF TRIUMPH FOR THE LORD'S HELP (28:6–9)

28:6 Ps 116:1
28:7 Ps 13:5, 6; 16:9; 40:3; 59:17
28:8☆ Ps 20:6
28:9 Deut 9:29; 32:9; Ps 33:12; 80:1; Isa 40:11

6 Blessed *be* the LORD, because he hath heard the voice of my supplica-
tions.
7 The LORD *is* my strength and my shield; my heart trusted in him, and I
am helped: therefore my heart greatly rejoiceth; and with my song will I
praise him.
8 The LORD *is* their strength, and he *is* the saving strength of his anointed.
9 Save thy people, and bless thine inheritance: feed them also, and lift
them up for ever.

I. THE VOICE OF THE LORD

A. THE CALL TO GLORIFY THE LORD

A Psalm of David

29:1☆ 1 Chron 16:28, 29; Ps 96:7–9
29:2 2 Chron 20:21; Ps 110:3

29 GIVE unto the LORD, O ye mighty, give unto the LORD glory and
strength.
2 Give unto the LORD the glory due unto his name; worship the LORD in
the beauty of holiness.

B. THE POWER OF THE VOICE OF THE LORD

29:3 Job 37:1–5
29:4 Ps 104:3
29:5 Judg 9:15; Ps 104:16; 114:4, 6; Isa 2:13
29:8 Num 13:26
29:9☆ Ps 26:8

3 The voice of the LORD *is* upon the waters: the God of glory thundereth:
the LORD *is* upon many waters.
4 The voice of the LORD *is* powerful; the voice of the LORD *is* full of
majesty.
5 The voice of the LORD breaketh the cedars; yea, the LORD breaketh the
cedars of Lebanon.
6 He maketh them also to skip like a calf; Lebanon and Sir′i-on like a
young unicorn.
7 The voice of the LORD divideth the flames of fire.
8 The voice of the LORD shaketh the wilderness; the LORD shaketh the
wilderness of Ka′desh.
9 The voice of the LORD maketh the hinds to calve, and discovereth the
forests: and in his temple doth every one speak of *his* glory.

C. PRAYER FOR THE LORD TO STRENGTHEN HIS PEOPLE

29:10☆ Gen 6:17; Ps 10:16

10 The LORD sitteth upon the flood; yea, the LORD sitteth King for ever.

28:2 *thy holy oracle,* or, "your innermost shrine," i.e., the Holy of Holies within the tabernacle.†
28:8 The sooner the saints learn that God is their strength and not themselves, the better their lives will be and the more they will put their trust in him.
29:1 It has been supposed that David wrote this at a time when there was great thunder, lightning, and rain. Despite the inclemency of nature, his heart is at rest, for God sits enthroned in the heavens and is not disturbed by the threats of nature. This is the great God of his people Israel, and, of course, of us today.
29:9 *maketh the hinds to calve,* or, "spins and topples the mighty oaks."†
29:10 *The LORD sitteth upon the flood.* The Hebrew

11 The LORD will give strength unto his people; the LORD will bless his
people with peace.

29:11 Ps 37:11; 68:35 Isa 40:29

I. DELIVERANCE FROM SICKNESS
A. PRAISE FOR DELIVERANCE FROM SICKNESS

A Psalm and Song at the dedication of the house of David

30 I WILL extol thee, O LORD; for thou hast lifted me up, and hast
not made my foes to rejoice over me.
2 O LORD my God, I cried unto thee, and thou hast healed me.
3 O LORD, thou hast brought up my soul from the grave: thou hast kept
me alive, that I should not go down to the pit.

☆30:1 Ps 25:2 35:19, 24 118:28; 145:1
30:2 Ps 6:2; 88:13
30:3 PS 86:13; 103:3

B. EXHORTATION FOR THE SAINTS TO PRAISE THE LORD

4 Sing unto the LORD, O ye saints of his, and give thanks at the
remembrance of his holiness.
5 For his anger *endureth but* a moment; in his favour *is* life: weeping may
endure for a night, but joy *cometh* in the morning.
6 And in my prosperity I said, I shall never be moved.
7 LORD, by thy favour thou hast made my mountain to stand strong: thou
didst hide thy face, *and* I was troubled.
8 I cried to thee, O LORD; and unto the LORD I made supplication.
9 What profit *is there* in my blood, when I go down to the pit? Shall the
dust praise thee? shall it declare thy truth?
10 Hear, O LORD, and have mercy upon me: LORD, be thou my helper.
11 Thou hast turned for me my mourning into dancing: thou hast put off
my sackcloth, and girded me with gladness;
12 To the end that *my* glory may sing praise to thee, and not be silent. O
LORD my God, I will give thanks unto thee for ever.

30:4 Ex 3:15 Ps 97:12; 149:1
30:5 Ps 54:7, 8 103:9; 118:1 2 Cor 4:17
☆30:6 Ps 10:6; 104:29 143:7
30:9 Ps 6:5
30:10 Ps 4:1; 27:7, 9
30:11 Ps 6:8 Jer 31:4, 13
30:12 Ps 44:8; 57:8 108:1

I. A PSALM OF MISERY AND MERCY
A. THE PSALMIST TURNS TO THE LORD FOR DELIVERANCE

To the chief Musician, A Psalm of David

31 IN thee, O LORD, do I put my trust; let me never be ashamed:
deliver me in thy righteousness.
2 Bow down thine ear to me; deliver me speedily: be thou my strong rock,
for an house of defence to save me.
3 For thou *art* my rock and my fortress; therefore for thy name's sake lead
me, and guide me.
4 Pull me out of the net that they have laid privily for me: for thou *art* my
strength.

☆31:1 Ps 25:2; 71:1–3 143:1
31:2 Ps 71:3; 86:1 102:2
31:3 Ps 18:2; 23:2, 3
31:4 Ps 25:15

---

word for flood (*mabbul*) is used only for the Noahic flood and in this verse here. God did sit on the flood in the sense that he was the Judge pronouncing justice on a wicked world. This Judge is enthroned as king forever. He will judge the world in righteousness at the end of the age.

30:1ff David offers praise for God's deliverance and exhorts the saints to praise God too. During a time of prosperity he was brought low. As a result of his prayers, his mourning was turned to gladness and he promises to give thanks to God forever. Indeed, past mercies are to be recalled and thanks offered even after a long passage of time. Suffering saints will read this Psalm with gratitude.

30:6 David became complacent in the midst of prosperity. He was secure and overconfident that it would continue. Suddenly he fell into great trouble and distress, and then realized what he had forgotten—the help of God.

31:1ff This is a Psalm of prayer, praise, and an expression of confidence in God. This triad of graces encourages our hearts to be strong and to wait for the Lord, the great Deliverer. Difficulties and setbacks should afford us no occasion to lose these precious characteristics. Rather, they should be more visibly present during times of trouble.

5 Into thine hand I commit my spirit: thou hast redeemed me, O LORD
God of truth.
6 I have hated them that regard lying vanities: but I trust in the LORD.
7 I will be glad and rejoice in thy mercy: for thou hast considered my
trouble; thou hast known my soul in adversities;
8 And hast not shut me up into the hand of the enemy: thou hast set my
feet in a large room.

31:5 Deut 32:4; Ps 55:18; 71:22, 23; Jonah 2:8, 9; Lk 23:46; Acts 7:59
31:7 Ps 10:14; 90:14
31:8 Ps 37:33

B. A CATALOG OF THE PSALMIST'S MISERIES

9 Have mercy upon me, O LORD, for I am in trouble: mine eye is
consumed with grief, *yea,* my soul and my belly.
10 For my life is spent with grief, and my years with sighing: my strength
faileth because of mine iniquity, and my bones are consumed.
11 I was a reproach among all mine enemies, but especially among my
neighbours, and a fear to mine acquaintance: they that did see me without
fled from me.
12 I am forgotten as a dead man out of mind: I am like a broken vessel.
13 For I have heard the slander of many: fear *was* on every side: while
they took counsel together against me, they devised to take away my life.
14 But I trusted in thee, O LORD: I said, Thou *art* my God.
15 My times *are* in thy hand: deliver me from the hand of mine enemies,
and from them that persecute me.
16 Make thy face to shine upon thy servant: save me for thy mercies' sake.
17 Let me not be ashamed, O LORD; for I have called upon thee: let the
wicked be ashamed, *and* let them be silent in the grave.
18 Let the lying lips be put to silence; which speak grievous things proudly
and contemptuously against the righteous.

31:9 Ps 6:7; 32:3; 38:3, 4; 39:11; 63:1; 69:17; 102:1, 3, 4
31:11 Ps 38:11; 88:8, 18; Isa 53:4
31:12 Ps 88:5
31:13 Ps 41:7; Jer 20:10; Mt 27:1
31:14 Job 14:5; Ps 140:6; 143:9
31:15☆
31:16 Num 6:24–26; Ps 6:4; 80:3
31:17 1 Sam 2:9; Ps 25:2, 3, 20
31:18 1 Sam 2:3; Ps 94:4; 120:2; Jude 15

C. PRAISE TO THE LORD WHO RESCUES AND DELIVERS

19 *Oh* how great *is* thy goodness, which thou hast laid up for them that
fear thee; *which* thou hast wrought for them that trust in thee before the
sons of men!
20 Thou shalt hide them in the secret of thy presence from the pride of
man: thou shalt keep them secretly in a pavilion from the strife of tongues.
21 Blessed *be* the LORD: for he hath shewed me his marvellous kindness in
a strong city.
22 For I said in my haste, I am cut off from before thine eyes: nevertheless
thou heardest the voice of my supplications when I cried unto thee.
23 O love the LORD, all ye his saints: *for* the LORD preserveth the faithful,
and plentifully rewardeth the proud doer.
24 Be of good courage, and he shall strengthen your heart, all ye that hope
in the LORD.

31:19 Ps 5:11; Isa 64:14; Rom 11:22
31:20 Job 5:21; Ps 27:5; 31:13
31:21 Ps 17:7; 28:7
31:22 Ps 66:19; 116:11, 12; 145:19; Lam 3:54–56
31:23 Deut 32:40, 41; Ps 37:28; 145:20; Rev 2:10
31:24 Ps 27:14

I. THE HAPPINESS OF THE FORGIVEN

A. THE JOY OF FORGIVENESS

A Psalm of David, Maschil

32 BLESSED *is he whose* transgression *is* forgiven, *whose* sin *is*
covered.

32:1☆ Ps 85:2; Rom 4:7, 8

31:15 *My times are in thy hand.* If God has our times in his hand he can help us. If he is our God he will help us. He can "lengthen or shorten, embitter or sweeten, as he pleases, according to the counsel of his will."*
32:1ff This Psalm speaks of the blessedness of imputed righteousness, which excludes good works. Believers are protected and guided by grace. Confession of sin, living rightly, and rejoicing in God are the attributes of the redeemed. One commentator says that this Psalm was sung on the day of atonement.

2 Blessed *is* the man unto whom the LORD imputeth not iniquity, and in whose spirit *there is* no guile.

B. FORGIVENESS FOLLOWS CONFESSION

3 When I kept silence, my bones waxed old through my roaring all the day long.

32:3 Ps 31:10; 39:2

4 For day and night thy hand was heavy upon me: my moisture is turned into the drought of summer. Se′lah.

32:4 Ps 22:15; 39:10

5 I acknowledged my sin unto thee, and mine iniquity have I not hid. I said, I will confess my transgressions unto the LORD; and thou forgavest the iniquity of my sin. Se′lah.

32:5 Lev 26:40 Job 31:33 Ps 38:18 1 Jn 1:9

6 For this shall every one that is godly pray unto thee in a time when thou mayest be found: surely in the floods of great waters they shall not come nigh unto him.

32:6 Ps 69:13 Isa 43:2

7 Thou *art* my hiding place; thou shalt preserve me from trouble; thou shalt compass me about with songs of deliverance. Se′lah.

32:7 Ex 15:1 Ps 31:20; 40:3 121:7

C. A GENERAL EXHORTATION FOR ALL SINNERS TO REPENT

8 I will instruct thee and teach thee in the way which thou shalt go: I will guide thee with mine eye.

32:8 Ps 25:8 33:18, 19

9 Be ye not as the horse, *or* as the mule, *which* have no understanding: whose mouth must be held in with bit and bridle, lest they come near unto thee.

32:9 Prov 26:3 Jas 3:3

10 Many sorrows *shall be* to the wicked: but he that trusteth in the LORD, mercy shall compass him about.

32:10 Ps 16:4 Prov 13:21 Rom 2:9, 10

11 Be glad in the LORD, and rejoice, ye righteous: and shout for joy, all *ye that are* upright in heart.

32:11 Ps 64:10; 97:12

I. A PSALM FOR THE NATION

A. THE JOY OF PRAISING THE LORD

33 REJOICE in the LORD, O ye righteous: *for* praise is comely for the upright.

☆**33:1** Ps 32:11; 147:1 Phil 4:4

2 Praise the LORD with harp: sing unto him with the psaltery *and* an instrument of ten strings.

33:2 Ps 92:3

3 Sing unto him a new song; play skilfully with a loud noise.

33:3 Ps 98:1 Isa 42:10 Rev 5:9

B. THE LORD'S RULE OVER THE WORLD

4 For the word of the LORD *is* right; and all his works *are done* in truth.

☆**33:4** Ps 19:8

5 He loveth righteousness and judgment: the earth is full of the goodness of the LORD.

☆**33:5** Ps 11:7; 119:64

6 By the word of the LORD were the heavens made; and all the host of them by the breath of his mouth.

33:6 Gen 1:6, 7 Ps 148:5 Heb 11:3

7 He gathereth the waters of the sea together as an heap: he layeth up the depth in storehouses.

33:7 Ex 15:8

33:1 This is a psalm of praise that may have been written by David. In any event it takes us beyond the realm of man to the blessed Holy Spirit who moved the writer and guided him to say what the Spirit wanted said. We are to praise the Lord God, who is Creator, Preserver, and Deliverer.

33:4, 5 God makes himself known to man through his Word and his works. His Word is right and any deviation from it is wrong. We are in the right when we agree with it. Nothing is amiss in his Word. It is backed up by his works, which are according to truth. According to verse 5 the works of God are based on his inflexible justice. He never has done or will do wrong to any creature. He is ready to relieve those who are wronged, and delights to do so. The earth is full of his goodness, for his bounty is inexhaustible. The tragedy of life is that a world so full of goodness is so empty of his praises. When will men learn to praise him?

33:8 Ps 67:7; 96:9
8 Let all the earth fear the LORD: let all the inhabitants of the world stand
in awe of him.
33:9 Gen 1:3; Ps 148:5
9 For he spake, and it was *done;* he commanded, and it stood fast.
33:10 Gen 11:8; Isa 8:9, 10
10 The LORD bringeth the counsel of the heathen to nought: he maketh
the devices of the people of none effect.
33:11 Job 23:13; Prov 19:21
11 The counsel of the LORD standeth for ever, the thoughts of his heart to
all generations.

C. THE LORD'S PROVIDENCES OVER ISRAEL

33:12 Ex 19:5; Ps 144:15
12 Blessed *is* the nation whose God *is* the LORD: *and* the people *whom* he
hath chosen for his own inheritance.
33:13 1 Kgs 8:39; Job 34:21; Ps 11:4; 14:2; Jer 32:19
13 The LORD looketh from heaven; he beholdeth all the sons of men.
14 From the place of his habitation he looketh upon all the inhabitants of
the earth.
15 He fashioneth their hearts alike; he considereth all their works.
33:16 Ps 44:6; 147:10
16 There is no king saved by the multitude of an host: a mighty man is not
delivered by much strength.
17 An horse *is* a vain thing for safety: neither shall he deliver *any* by his
great strength.
33:18 Job 5:20; Ps 34:15; 37:19; Acts 12:11; 1 Pet 3:12
18 Behold, the eye of the LORD *is* upon them that fear him, upon them that
hope in his mercy;
19 To deliver their soul from death, and to keep them alive in famine.
33:20☆ Ps 115:9; Isa 8:17
20 Our soul waiteth for the LORD: he *is* our help and our shield.
33:21 Ps 28:7; Jn 16:22
21 For our heart shall rejoice in him, because we have trusted in his holy
name.
22 Let thy mercy, O LORD, be upon us, according as we hope in thee.

I. A PSALM OF PRAISE FOR DELIVERANCE

A. MAGNIFYING THE LORD FOR PROTECTION FROM DANGER

A Psalm of David, when he changed his behaviour before Abimelech; who drove him away, and he departed

34:1 Ps 71:6; Eph 5:20; 1 Thess 5:18
34 I WILL bless the LORD at all times: his praise *shall* continually *be*
in my mouth.
34:2 Jer 9:24; 1 Cor 1:31
2 My soul shall make her boast in the LORD: the humble shall hear
thereof, and be glad.
34:3 Lk 1:46; Ps 69:32
3 O magnify the LORD with me, and let us exalt his name together.
34:4☆ Ps 35:27; Mt 7:7
4 I sought the LORD, and he heard me, and delivered me from all my
fears.
5 They looked unto him, and were lightened: and their faces were not
34:5 Ps 25:3; 36:9
ashamed.
6 This poor man cried, and the LORD heard *him,* and saved him out of all
his troubles.
34:7☆ Ps 91:14; Dan 6:22
7 The angel of the LORD encampeth round about them that fear him, and
delivereth them.

33:20 *Our soul waits for the LORD.* God does not always deliver his waiting servant as soon as he hopes for. The believer must accommodate himself to God's providences in the dark night of the soul. Waiting *implies* that God has not yet answered. While he may delay in coming he never comes too late. Therefore the believing servant waits in faith and with assurance that deliverance will come.

34:4 David had feigned madness before Ahimelech. He sought the Lord who delivered him from all his fears—especially the death that he feared and the disquiet that the thought of death brought to him. If he really loved God, why then did he fear? Since none is totally sanctified in this life, anyone can be subject to fear and held in its bondage. But God can and does deliver the faithful one from his fears.

34:7 Angels are ministering servants sent forth to minister to those who are the heirs of salvation (Heb. 1:14). God's holy angels guard and protect believers and do them more good than they are aware of. Thanksgiving should be raised to God for these angels who minister to the saints.

B. EXHORTATION TO PROVE THE LORD'S GOODNESS

8 O taste and see that the LORD *is* good: blessed *is* the man *that* trusteth
in him.
9 O fear the LORD, ye his saints: for *there is* no want to them that fear
him.
10 The young lions do lack, and suffer hunger: but they that seek the
LORD shall not want any good *thing*.

34:8 Ps 23:1; 1 Pet 2:3
34:9 Ps 23:1; 31:23
34:10 Ps 84:11

C. HOW TO INSURE LENGTH OF DAYS

11 Come, ye children, hearken unto me: I will teach you the fear of the
LORD.
12 What man *is he that* desireth life, *and* loveth *many* days, that he may see
good?
13 Keep thy tongue from evil, and thy lips from speaking guile.
14 Depart from evil, and do good; seek peace, and pursue it.

☆**34:11** Ps 111:10
34:12 1 Pet 3:10–12
34:13 Prov 13:3; Jas 1:26; 1 Pet 2:22
34:14 Ps 37:27; Isa 1:16, 17; Rom 14:18, 19; Heb 12:14

D. THE CERTAINTY OF DELIVERANCE FOR THE RIGHTEOUS

15 The eyes of the LORD *are* upon the righteous, and his ears *are open* unto
their cry.
16 The face of the LORD *is* against them that do evil, to cut off the
remembrance of them from the earth.
17 *The righteous* cry, and the LORD heareth, and delivereth them out of all
their troubles.
18 The LORD *is* nigh unto them that are of a broken heart; and saveth such
as be of a contrite spirit.
19 Many *are* the afflictions of the righteous: but the LORD delivereth him
out of them all.
20 He keepeth all his bones: not one of them is broken.
21 Evil shall slay the wicked: and they that hate the righteous shall be
desolate.
22 The LORD redeemeth the soul of his servants: and none of them that
trust in him shall be desolate.

34:15 Ps 33:18, 19
☆**34:16** Ps 9:6; 109:15; Jer 44:11
34:17 Ps 34:6; 145:19
34:18 Ps 51:17; 145:18; Isa 57:15
34:19 Ps 71:20; 2 Tim 3:11, 12
34:21 Ps 94:23
34:22 1 Kgs 1:29; Ps 71:23

I. A HUMBLE PETITION FOR DELIVERANCE

A. FROM THOSE WHO ATTACK US

A Psalm of David

35 PLEAD *my cause,* O LORD, with them that strive with me: fight
against them that fight against me.
2 Take hold of shield and buckler, and stand up for mine help.
3 Draw out also the spear, and stop *the way* against them that persecute
me: say unto my soul, I *am* thy salvation.

☆**35:1** Ps 56:1, 2; Isa 49:25
35:2 Ps 91:4
35:3 Ps 62:2

34:11 David would teach children how they should live and what sins they should avoid. He would teach them the fear of the Lord. Unfortunately he did not succeed with some of his own sons, for they turned out to be disobedient to God and broke his commandments. Let those who would teach other people's sons be sure that their own sons have learned that lesson.

34:16 *The face of the LORD is against them that do evil.* Though the wicked may bless themselves, God is against them, and at last they will be miserable. Sad should that man be who has caused God to be his destroyer. Here we learn that God has set his face *against* them. He is their opponent; therefore they will be ruined. He will cut off the remembrance of them. On the other hand, all is well for the righteous.

35:1ff Probably every believer can identify with this Psalm; it speaks of prayers offered for indignities suffered through persecution, slander, and ill-will. Vindication is desired and there is the certainty that it will come—God's servant will speak of God's righteousness and sing his praises all day long.

35:4☆ Ps 40:14; 70:2, 3

4 Let them be confounded and put to shame that seek after my soul: let them be turned back and brought to confusion that devise my hurt.

35:5 Ps 1:4; 83:13; Isa 29:5

5 Let them be as chaff before the wind: and let the angel of the LORD chase *them.*

35:6 Ps 73:18; Jer 23:12

6 Let their way be dark and slippery: and let the angel of the LORD persecute them.

35:7 Ps 69:4; 109:3

7 For without cause have they hid for me their net *in* a pit, *which* without cause they have digged for my soul.

35:8 Ps 9:15; Isa 47:11; 1 Thess 5:3

8 Let destruction come upon him at unawares; and let his net that he hath hid catch himself: into that very destruction let him fall.

35:9 Isa 61:10; Lk 1:47

9 And my soul shall be joyful in the LORD: it shall rejoice in his salvation.

35:10 Ex 15:11, 12; Ps 18:17; 37:14; Mic 7:18

10 All my bones shall say, LORD, who *is* like unto thee, which deliverest the poor from him that is too strong for him, yea, the poor and the needy from him that spoileth him?

B. FROM THOSE WHO SLANDER US

35:11 Ps 27:12

11 False witnesses did rise up; they laid to my charge *things* that I knew not.

35:12 Ps 38:20; Jn 10:32

12 They rewarded me evil for good *to* the spoiling of my soul.

35:13☆ Job 30:25; Jer 18:20

13 But as for me, when they were sick, my clothing *was* sackcloth: I humbled my soul with fasting; and my prayer returned into mine own bosom.

14 I behaved myself as though *he had been* my friend *or* brother: I bowed down heavily, as one that mourneth *for his* mother.

35:15 Job 16:10; Obad 12

15 But in mine adversity they rejoiced, and gathered themselves together: *yea,* the abjects gathered themselves together against me, and I knew *it* not; they did tear *me,* and ceased not:

35:16 Job 30:1, 8, 14; Lam 2:16

16 With hypocritical mockers in feasts, they gnashed upon me with their teeth.

35:17 Ps 13:1; 22:20, 21; Hab 1:13

17 Lord, how long wilt thou look on? rescue my soul from their destructions, my darling from the lions.

35:18 Ps 22:23, 25

18 I will give thee thanks in the great congregation: I will praise thee among much people.

C. FROM THOSE WHO HATE US AND LIE ABOUT US

35:19☆ Ps 13:4; 38:16, 19; 69:4; 70:3; Jn 15:25

19 Let not them that are mine enemies wrongfully rejoice over me: *neither* let them wink with the eye that hate me without a cause.

35:20 Prov 6:12–14; Mic 6:12

20 For they speak not peace: but they devise deceitful matters against *them that are* quiet in the land.

35:21 Ps 22:13; 40:15; Job 16:10

21 Yea, they opened their mouth wide against me, *and* said, Aha, aha, our eye hath seen *it.*

35:22 Ex 3:7; 22:9–11; 28:1; Ps 10:14

22 *This* thou hast seen, O LORD: keep not silence: O Lord, be not far from me.

35:4 Here David fervently prays not simply for deliverance from his enemies but for God to bring them to shame and dishonor. Some think it was a prophetic statement rather than an imprecatory prayer. In that event it was a foretelling of what would happen to those who hated and abused David, not a prayer asking God to do this to them.

35:13 David resorted to sackcloth, fasting, and prayer. He serves us as a striking example of practices that few use today but would be better off if they did.

35:19 *neither let them wink with the eye,* i.e., "Don't let them rejoice."† To be hated for one's evil is one thing; to be hated for no cause is difficult to understand. But Jesus was hated thus, and so will his people be. For the wicked to hate someone simply because he is a Christian shows how deep the rebellion of man against his Maker is.

23 Stir up thyself, and awake to my judgment, *even* unto my cause, my
God and my Lord.

35:23 Ps 7:6; 44:23

24 Judge me, O LORD my God, according to thy righteousness; and let
them not rejoice over me.

35:24 Ps 9:4; 43:1

25 Let them not say in their hearts, Ah, so would we have it: let them not
say, We have swallowed him up.

35:25 Ps 56:1 Lam 2:16

26 Let them be ashamed and brought to confusion together that rejoice at
mine hurt: let them be clothed with shame and dishonour that magnify
themselves against me.

35:26 Ps 38:16; 40:14

27 Let them shout for joy, and be glad, that favour my righteous cause:
yea, let them say continually, Let the LORD be magnified, which hath
pleasure in the prosperity of his servant.

35:27 Ps 40:16; 70:4 149:4, 5

28 And my tongue shall speak of thy righteousness *and* of thy praise all the
day long.

35:28 Ps 51:14, 15 71:15, 24

I. THE EVIL DEEDS OF THE WICKED

To the chief Musician, A Psalm of David the servant of the LORD

36 THE transgression of the wicked saith within my heart, *that there is*
no fear of God before his eyes.
2 For he flattereth himself in his own eyes, until his iniquity be found to
be hateful.
3 The words of his mouth *are* iniquity and deceit: he hath left off to be
wise, *and* to do good.
4 He deviseth mischief upon his bed; he setteth himself in a way *that is*
not good; he abhorreth not evil.

☆36:1 Rom 3:18
36:2 Deut 29:19 Ps 10:11
36:3 Ps 10:7 Jer 4:22
36:4 Prov 4:16 Isa 65:2 Mic 2:1

II. THE STEADFAST LOVE AND FAITHFULNESS OF GOD

5 Thy mercy, O LORD, *is* in the heavens; *and* thy faithfulness *reacheth*
unto the clouds.
6 Thy righteousness *is* like the great mountains; thy judgments *are* a great
deep: O LORD, thou preservest man and beast.
7 How excellent *is* thy lovingkindness, O God! therefore the children of
men put their trust under the shadow of thy wings.
8 They shall be abundantly satisfied with the fatness of thy house; and
thou shalt make them drink of the river of thy pleasures.
9 For with thee *is* the fountain of life: in thy light shall we see light.
10 O continue thy lovingkindness unto them that know thee; and thy
righteousness to the upright in heart.
11 Let not the foot of pride come against me, and let not the hand of the
wicked remove me.

36:5 Ps 57:10 103:11; 108:4
36:6 Job 11:8 Ps 104:14, 15 145:16, 17 Rom 11:33
36:7 Ruth 2:12 Ps 91:4 139:17, 18
36:8 Ps 46:4 Isa 25:6 Rev 22:1
☆36:9 1 Pet 2:9
36:10 Ps 24:5

12 There are the workers of iniquity fallen: they are cast down, and shall
not be able to rise.

36:12 Ps 140:10 Isa 26:14

36:1ff David goes beyond his own troubles to pray for the preservation of all the saints as well as of himself (36:10–11). Running through the Psalm is the lovingkindness, faithfulness, and righteousness of God. Let God's saints take courage and let the wicked repent and turn from their evil ways.

36:9 *In thy light shall we see light.* The divine light shines in Scripture, which is the written Word of God. In addition, light is seen in the face of Jesus Christ, who is the light of the world. When we see God in glory we shall see light in perfection; thus, there is no need for the sun or the moon in the New Jerusalem, for God will be its light.

I. THE FAITHFUL AND WISE WITNESS OF AN AGED SAINT

A. THE RIGHTEOUS VINDICATED; THE WICKED DESTROYED

A Psalm of David

37:1☆ Ps 73:3; Prov 3:31; 23:17, 18

37 FRET not thyself because of evildoers, neither be thou envious against the workers of iniquity.

37:2 Job 14:2; Ps 90:5, 6; Prov 24:19

2 For they shall soon be cut down like the grass, and wither as the green herb.

37:3 Deut 30:20; Ps 62:8

3 Trust in the LORD, and do good; *so* shalt thou dwell in the land, and verily thou shalt be fed.

37:4 Job 22:26–28; Ps 145:19; Isa 58:14

4 Delight thyself also in the LORD; and he shall give thee the desires of thine heart.

37:5☆ Ps 55:22; Prov 16:3; 1 Pet 5:7

5 Commit thy way unto the LORD; trust also in him; and he shall bring *it* to pass.

37:6 Isa 58:8, 10; Mic 7:9

6 And he shall bring forth thy righteousness as the light, and thy judgment as the noonday.

37:7 Ps 40:1; 62:5; Jer 12:1

7 Rest in the LORD, and wait patiently for him: fret not thyself because of him who prospereth in his way, because of the man who bringeth wicked devices to pass.

37:8 Eph 4:31; Col 3:8

8 Cease from anger, and forsake wrath: fret not thyself in any wise to do evil.

37:9 Ps 25:13

9 For evildoers shall be cut off: but those that wait upon the LORD, they shall inherit the earth.

37:10 Job 24:24

10 For yet a little while, and the wicked *shall* not *be;* yea, thou shalt diligently consider his place, and it *shall* not *be.*

37:11 Mt 5:3, 5

11 But the meek shall inherit the earth; and shall delight themselves in the abundance of peace.

B. THE GOOD AND THE EVIL CONTRASTED

37:12 Job 18:20; Ps 2:4; 31:13

12 The wicked plotteth against the just, and gnasheth upon him with his teeth.

13 The Lord shall laugh at him: for he seeth that his day is coming.

37:14 Ps 11:2; 35:10

14 The wicked have drawn out the sword, and have bent their bow, to cast down the poor and needy, *and* to slay such as be of upright conversation.

37:15 Ps 9:16; 46:9

15 Their sword shall enter into their own heart, and their bows shall be broken.

37:16 Prov 15:16; 16:8

16 A little that a righteous man hath *is* better than the riches of many wicked.

37:17 Ps 10:15; 145:14; Ezek 30:21

17 For the arms of the wicked shall be broken: but the LORD upholdeth the righteous.

37:18 Ps 1:6

18 The LORD knoweth the days of the upright: and their inheritance shall be for ever.

37:19 Job 5:20; Ps 33:18, 19

19 They shall not be ashamed in the evil time: and in the days of famine they shall be satisfied.

37:1 This is a teaching Psalm which has no prayer or praise in it. It speaks about an issue that is not easily answered: Since God has promised blessings to the good, how then do we see some sinners who live in prosperity and some saints who experience nothing but adversity? The first counsel of David is for the righteous not to be discontented by the success of the wicked. To be fretful and envious is itself wrong and thus sin.

37:5 Anxiety is sin in the heart of the believer. It is forbidden by Jesus in Matt. 6:25; Luke 12:22, 29; and John 6:27. Anxiety may be overcome by (1) putting our trust in God (Jer. 17:7; Dan. 3:15–18), (2) turning our cares over to the Lord (55:22; Prov. 16:3; 1 Pet. 5:7), and (3) thanking God in advance of the answers to our petitions (Phil. 4:6).

20 But the wicked shall perish, and the enemies of the LORD *shall be* as the
fat of lambs: they shall consume; into smoke shall they consume away.
21 The wicked borroweth, and payeth not again: but the righteous
sheweth mercy, and giveth.
22 For *such as be* blessed of him shall inherit the earth; and *they that be*
cursed of him shall be cut off.

37:20 Ps 68:2; 73:27
37:21 Ps 112:5, 9
37:22 Job 5:3; Prov 3:33

C. THE SECURITY OF THE GODLY WHO TRUST THE LORD

23 The steps of a *good* man are ordered by the LORD: and he delighteth in
his way.
24 Though he fall, he shall not be utterly cast down: for the LORD
upholdeth *him with* his hand.
25 I have been young, and *now* am old; yet have I not seen the righteous
forsaken, nor his seed begging bread.
26 *He is* ever merciful, and lendeth; and his seed *is* blessed.
27 Depart from evil, and do good; and dwell for evermore.
28 For the LORD loveth judgment, and forsaketh not his saints; they are
preserved for ever: but the seed of the wicked shall be cut off.
29 The righteous shall inherit the land, and dwell therein for ever.
30 The mouth of the righteous speaketh wisdom, and his tongue talketh of
judgment.
31 The law of his God *is* in his heart; none of his steps shall slide.
32 The wicked watcheth the righteous, and seeketh to slay him.
33 The LORD will not leave him in his hand, nor condemn him when he is
judged.
34 Wait on the LORD, and keep his way, and he shall exalt thee to inherit
the land: when the wicked are cut off, thou shalt see *it*.
35 I have seen the wicked in great power, and spreading himself like a
green bay tree.
36 Yet he passed away, and, lo, he *was* not: yea, I sought him, but he could
not be found.
37 Mark the perfect *man*, and behold the upright: for the end of *that* man
is peace.
38 But the transgressors shall be destroyed together: the end of the wicked
shall be cut off.
39 But the salvation of the righteous *is* of the LORD: *he is* their strength in
the time of trouble.
40 And the LORD shall help them, and deliver them: he shall deliver them
from the wicked, and save them, because they trust in him.

37:23 Ps 40:2; 147:11
37:24 Ps 145:14; 147:6; Prov 24:15, 16; Mic 7:8
☆**37:25** Isa 41:17; Heb 13:5
☆**37:26** Ps 147:13
37:27 Ps 34:14
37:28 Ps 11:7; 30:23; 33:5; Prov 2:22
37:30 Mt 12:35; Ps 40:8; 49:2; 119:11; Isa 51:7
37:32 Ps 10:8; 37:14
37:33 Ps 37:22; 109:31; 2 Pet 2:9
37:34 Ps 27:14; 37:9
37:35 Job 5:3, 18:6; 20:5
37:37 Ps 7:10; Isa 57:1, 2
37:38 Ps 1:4; 73:18
37:39 Ps 3:8; 9:9; 62:1
37:40 1 Chron 5:20; Ps 22:3, 4; 34:22; Dan 3:17; 6:23

I. A PENITENTIAL PSALM: A PLEA FOR THE LORD'S MERCY

A. A DESCRIPTION OF THE PENITENT'S PLIGHT

A Psalm of David, to bring to remembrance

38 O LORD, rebuke me not in thy wrath: neither chasten me in thy
hot displeasure.

☆**38:1** Ps 6:1

37:25, 26 More than five thousand promises are to be found in the Scriptures. Many of them include God's promise to provide for his people's material needs (e.g., Phil. 4:19; Eph. 3:20). Our estimate of our material needs may differ from God's. And any one Christian's needs will differ from all others. But every believer may claim God's promises for the supply of his legitimate material needs in his own particular situation. However, this should not lead to the generalization that no believer will ever have to beg bread. Some interpret these verses differently; they hold that they constitute a promise to those who are charitable and liberal to the poor, that they will never bring themselves to poverty by their charity.

38:1ff This is a penitential Psalm in which David remembers his sins and afflictions. Grief is expressed

38:2 Job 6:4; Ps 32:4 **38:3** Ps 6:2; 31:9, 10; 40:12; Isa 1:5, 6

2 For thine arrows stick fast in me, and thy hand presseth me sore.

3 *There is* no soundness in my flesh because of thine anger; neither *is there any* rest in my bones because of my sin.

4 For mine iniquities are gone over mine head: as an heavy burden they are too heavy for me.

38:5☆ Ps 42:9; 69:5

5 My wounds stink *and* are corrupt because of my foolishness.

6 I am troubled; I am bowed down greatly; I go mourning all the day long.

38:7 Ps 102:3, 4; Lam 1:13

7 For my loins are filled with a loathsome *disease:* and *there is* no soundness in my flesh.

38:8☆ Job 3:24; Ps 22:1; Lam 5:17

8 I am feeble and sore broken: I have roared by reason of the disquietness of my heart.

B. THE CERTAINTY THAT THE LORD HEARS THE PENITENT

38:9 Ps 6:6; 10:17 **38:10** Ps 6:7

9 Lord, all my desire *is* before thee; and my groaning is not hid from thee.

10 My heart panteth, my strength faileth me: as for the light of mine eyes, it also is gone from me.

38:11 Lk 23:49

11 My lovers and my friends stand aloof from my sore; and my kinsmen stand afar off.

38:12 Ps 35:20; 54:3; 140:5 **38:13** Ps 39:9

12 They also that seek after my life lay snares *for me:* and they that seek my hurt speak mischievous things, and imagine deceits all the day long.

13 But I, as a deaf *man,* heard not; and *I was* as a dumb man *that* openeth not his mouth.

14 Thus I was as a man that heareth not, and in whose mouth *are* no reproofs.

C. THE CONFIDENCE OF FORGIVENESS FOR THE PENITENT

38:15 Ps 17:6; 37:9 **38:16** Ps 13:4; 35:26 **38:17** Ps 13:2 **38:18**☆ Ps 32:5; 2 Cor 7:9, 10 **38:19** Ps 35:19 **38:20** Ps 35:12; 109:4, 5; 1 Jn 3:12 **38:21** Ps 22:19; 35:22 **38:22** Ps 27:1; 40:13, 17

15 For in thee, O LORD, do I hope: thou wilt hear, O Lord my God.

16 For I said, *Hear me,* lest *otherwise* they should rejoice over me: when my foot slippeth, they magnify *themselves* against me.

17 For I *am* ready to halt, and my sorrow *is* continually before me.

18 For I will declare mine iniquity; I will be sorry for my sin.

19 But mine enemies *are* lively, *and* they are strong: and they that hate me wrongfully are multiplied.

20 They also that render evil for good are mine adversaries; because I follow *the thing that* good *is.*

21 Forsake me not, O LORD: O my God, be not far from me.

22 Make haste to help me, O Lord my salvation.

---

as sickness and pain reminds him of what he has done; these help to keep him humble before God. He longs for deliverance, confesses his transgressions, and waits for God to help him. This is the Psalm for all believers who, like David, have come upon a time of great difficulty occasioned by their own mistakes.

38:5 David is suffering from bodily afflictions such as those suffered by Job. The difference lay in the fact that David's were caused by his own foolishness. Under the *burden of these outward afflictions,* his sense of guilt becomes a heavy burden—which is far worse because sin separates a man from God, whereas physical affliction calls forth the mercies of God.

38:8 *by reason of the disquietness of my heart,* or, "because of the pains in my heart."† In the Scriptures the word for "heart" is never used for that organ of the body. It always has to do with the mental and volitional part of man. Disquietness of heart or pains in the heart do not bespeak a physical problem but a spiritual one having to do with the soul of man.

38:18 There can be no forgiveness without repentance. Some people preach what might be called "cheap grace" by bypassing the necessity for genuine repentance and/or leaving the impression that faith without repentance is sufficient. True faith is preceded by conviction of sin which leads to godly sorrow for the dishonor sin brings to God and the harm it does to the sinner. Contrition is followed by confession that pleads for forgiveness. Whoever genuinely repents and seeks Christ by faith will be found of him.

I. A MEDITATION ON THE SHORTNESS AND VANITY OF LIFE

A. LIFE IS BUT A SHADOW

To the chief Musician, even to Jeduthun, A Psalm of David

39 I SAID, I will take heed to my ways, that I sin not with my tongue:
I will keep my mouth with a bridle, while the wicked is before me.
2 I was dumb with silence, I held my peace, *even* from good; and my
sorrow was stirred.
3 My heart was hot within me, while I was musing the fire burned: *then*
spake I with my tongue,
4 LORD, make me to know mine end, and the measure of my days, what it
is: that I may know how frail I *am.*
5 Behold, thou hast made my days *as* an handbreadth; and mine age *is* as
nothing before thee: verily every man at his best state *is* altogether vanity.
Se'lah.
6 Surely every man walketh in a vain shew: surely they are disquieted in
vain: he heapeth up *riches*, and knoweth not who shall gather them.
7 And now, Lord, what wait I for? my hope *is* in thee.
8 Deliver me from all my transgressions: make me not the reproach of the
foolish.
9 I was dumb, I opened not my mouth; because thou didst *it.*
10 Remove thy stroke away from me: I am consumed by the blow of thine
hand.
11 When thou with rebukes dost correct man for iniquity, thou makest his
beauty to consume away like a moth: surely every man *is* vanity. Se'lah.

☆**39:1** Ps 34:13; 141:3 Jas 3:2, 5–12
39:2 Ps 38:13–16 Jer 20:9
☆**39:4** Ps 78:39; 90:12 103:15
39:5 Job 14:2 Ps 49:10; 62:9 89:47; 144:4 Jas 1:10, 11 1 Pet 1:24
39:7 Ps 38:15
39:8 Ps 51:9; 79:4, 9
39:9 2 Sam 16:10 Job 2:10
39:10 Job 9:34 Ps 32:4
39:11 Job 13:27, 28 Ps 90:7 Isa 50:9

B. THE TRAVELER'S PRAYER FOR MERCY

12 Hear my prayer, O LORD, and give ear unto my cry; hold not thy peace
at my tears: for I *am* a stranger with thee, *and* a sojourner, as all my fathers
were.
13 O spare me, that I may recover strength, before I go hence, and be no
more.

☆**39:12** 2 Chron 29:15 Ps 102:1 119:19 Heb 11:13 1 Pet 2:11
39:13 Job 10:20; 14:6

I. DOING THE WILL OF GOD

A. PATIENT WAITING

To the chief Musician, A Psalm of David

40 I WAITED patiently for the LORD; and he inclined unto me, and
heard my cry.
2 He brought me up also out of an horrible pit, out of the miry clay, and
set my feet upon a rock, *and* established my goings.

☆**40:1** Ps 27:14; 34:15
40:2 Ps 27:5; 69:1, 2 Jer 38:6

39:1ff This may be thought of as a funeral Psalm in which David remembers the shortness of life and the imminent advent of death to all. He cries to be spared before death overtakes him and he is no more in this present world.

39:4 Death is the end of life and the end of all labor and enjoyments. It marks the end of our time of probation. Men then receive recompense and retribution. For the wicked man it marks the end of all joys; for the godly man it marks the end of all grief. Let all men know that our days on earth are few and, when compared with eternity, only a flicker of an eyelash.

39:12 All men are mere sojourners on this planet, guests who came into the world with nothing and leave it the same way—empty-handed. This knowledge should wean a man from the world and take away his affection for it. There is another country and another citizenship for those who trust in God. It is not the city of man but the city of God; it is built on an everlasting foundation that can never be shaken or moved. Whoever dies without having attained citizenship in this commonwealth has lost everything.

40:1ff David thanks God for divine deliverance. By the Spirit he looks forward to a greater deliverance through the work of Christ in redemption (40:6–10). It is followed by the prayers he prays for mercy and grace, knowing that his works will never help him. God, and God alone, is his salvation.

40:3 Ps 32:7; 64:9
40:4 Job 37:24; Ps 84:12
40:5 Job 5:9; Ps 136:4; 139:17, 18; Isa 55:8

3 And he hath put a new song in my mouth, *even* praise unto our God:
many shall see *it*, and fear, and shall trust in the LORD.
4 Blessed *is* that man that maketh the LORD his trust, and respecteth not
the proud, nor such as turn aside to lies.
5 Many, O LORD my God, *are* thy wonderful works *which* thou hast done,
and thy thoughts *which are* to us-ward: they cannot be reckoned up in order
unto thee: *if* I would declare and speak *of them*, they are more than can be
numbered.

B. EMPTY SACRIFICES

40:6 1 Sam 15:22; Jer 7:22, 23; Mic 6:6–8; Heb 10:5–7
40:8☆ Ps 37:31; 2 Cor 3:3; Jn 4:34; Rom 7:22
40:9 Ps 22:25; 119:13
40:10 Ps 89:1; Acts 20:20, 27

6 Sacrifice and offering thou didst not desire; mine ears hast thou opened:
burnt offering and sin offering hast thou not required.
7 Then said I, Lo, I come: in the volume of the book *it is* written of me,
8 I delight to do thy will, O my God: yea, thy law *is* within my heart.
9 I have preached righteousness in the great congregation: lo, I have not
refrained my lips, O LORD, thou knowest.
10 I have not hid thy righteousness within my heart; I have declared thy
faithfulness and thy salvation: I have not concealed thy lovingkindness and
thy truth from the great congregation.

C. THE RESCUING LORD

40:11☆ Ps 43:3; 61:7
40:12 Ps 18:5; 38:4; 73:26; 116:3
40:13 Ps 22:19; 71:12
40:14 Ps 35:4, 26; 70:2, 3
40:16 Ps 35:27; 70:4
40:17 Ps 40:5; 70:5; 86:1; 1 Pet 5:7

11 Withhold not thou thy tender mercies from me, O LORD: let thy
lovingkindness and thy truth continually preserve me.
12 For innumerable evils have compassed me about: mine iniquities have
taken hold upon me, so that I am not able to look up; they are more than
the hairs of mine head: therefore my heart faileth me.
13 Be pleased, O LORD, to deliver me: O LORD, make haste to help me.
14 Let them be ashamed and confounded together that seek after my soul
to destroy it; let them be driven backward and put to shame that wish me
evil.
15 Let them be desolate for a reward of their shame that say unto me, Aha,
aha.
16 Let all those that seek thee rejoice and be glad in thee: let such as love
thy salvation say continually, The LORD be magnified.
17 But I *am* poor and needy; *yet* the Lord thinketh upon me: thou *art* my
help and my deliverer; make no tarrying, O my God.

I. THE REMEMBRANCE OF THE POOR
A. GOD BLESSES THOSE WHO HELP THE POOR

To the chief Musician, A Psalm of David

41:1☆ Ps 37:19; 82:3, 4; Prov 14:21
41:2 Ps 27:12; 37:22, 28

41 BLESSED *is* he that considereth the poor: the LORD will deliver
him in time of trouble.
2 The LORD will preserve him, and keep him alive; *and* he shall be blessed
upon the earth: and thou wilt not deliver him unto the will of his enemies.

40:8 This verse was quoted by Christ as applying to himself (see John 4:34).
40:11 *David is overcome by the* number of his iniquities. They were more than the hairs on his head. Even if they had been few he would have been in an awful state, for he was both an adulterer and a murderer. These are awful sins. Yet there is mercy with the Lord so that this wicked one can seek him and find forgiveness, for God is the helper and the deliverer of the worst of men and the vilest of sinners who come to him.
41:1ff God is a compassionate friend. He supports and comforts his saints on sickbeds and when faced with the troubles of life. David's integrity is vindicated, his false friends are overcome, and he experiences help from the God who is from everlasting to everlasting.

3 The LORD will strengthen him upon the bed of languishing: thou wilt
make all his bed in his sickness.

☆41:3 Ps 6:6

B. THE HATRED OF FALSE FRIENDS

4 I said, LORD, be merciful unto me: heal my soul; for I have sinned
against thee.
5 Mine enemies speak evil of me, When shall he die, and his name perish?
6 And if he come to see *me*, he speaketh vanity: his heart gathereth
iniquity to itself; *when* he goeth abroad, he telleth *it*.
7 All that hate me whisper together against me: against me do they devise
my hurt.
8 An evil disease, *say they*, cleaveth fast unto him: and *now* that he lieth he
shall rise up no more.
9 Yea, mine own familiar friend, in whom I trusted, which did eat of my
bread, hath lifted up *his* heel against me.
10 But thou, O LORD, be merciful unto me, and raise me up, that I may
requite them.

41:4 Ps 5:4; 6:2; 103:3
41:5 Ps 38:12
41:6 Ps 12:2; Prov 26:24–26
41:8 Ps 71:10, 11
☆41:9 Job 19:19; Ps 55:12, 13, 20; Jer 20:10; Jn 13:18
41:10 Ps 3:3

C. THE LORD PRESERVES THE HONEST

11 By this I know that thou favourest me, because mine enemy doth not
triumph over me.
12 And as for me, thou upholdest me in mine integrity, and settest me
before thy face for ever.
13 Blessed *be* the LORD God of Israel from everlasting, and to everlasting.
Amen, and Amen.

41:11 Ps 37:23; 147:11
41:12 Job 36:7; Ps 18:32; 21:6; 37:17
41:13 Ps 72:18, 19; 106:48

BOOK II (PSALMS 42—72)

I. A THIRST FOR GOD

A. THE SEPARATED SOUL THAT THIRSTS FOR GOD

To the chief Musician, Maschil, for the sons of Korah

42 AS the hart panteth after the water brooks, so panteth my soul after
thee, O God.
2 My soul thirsteth for God, for the living God: when shall I come and
appear before God?
3 My tears have been my meat day and night, while they continually say
unto me, Where *is* thy God?
4 When I remember these *things*, I pour out my soul in me: for I had gone
with the multitude, I went with them to the house of God, with the voice of
joy and praise, with a multitude that kept holyday.
5 Why art thou cast down, O my soul? and *why* art thou disquieted in me?
hope thou in God: for I shall yet praise him *for* the help of his countenance.

☆42:1 Ps 63:1
42:2 Ps 43:4; 84:2; 143:6; Jer 10:10; Rom 9:26
42:3 Ps 79:10; 80:5; Joel 2:17
42:4 Job 30:16; Ps 62:8; 71:14; Isa 30:29; Lam 3:24; Mt 26:38

B. THE EXPECTATION OF GOD'S DELIVERANCE

6 *O my God, my soul is cast down within me*: therefore will I remember
thee from the land of Jordan, and of the Her′mon-ites, from the hill Mi′zar.

42:6 Ps 61:2

41:3 *thou wilt make all his bed in his sickness,* i.e., "He nurses them when they are sick, and soothes their pains and worries."†

41:9 *mine . . . friend . . . hath lifted up his heel against me.* This verse suggests Jesus' betrayal by Judas Iscariot. Jesus himself quoted this verse as he prophesied his own betrayal (John 13:18).

42:1ff Here the psalmist experiences a sense of separation from God, due to his transgressions. But in this separation his desire turns toward God for help. He depends upon God, his rock, and looks with expectation to that moment when his disquieted soul will once more praise the God who is his only hope and help.

42:7☆ Ps 88:7; Jonah 2:3
42:8 Ps 16:7; 57:3; 77:6; 149:4, 5; Job 35:10
42:9☆ Ps 17:9; 18:2; 38:6

7 Deep calleth unto deep at the noise of thy waterspouts: all thy waves
and thy billows are gone over me.
8 *Yet* the LORD will command his lovingkindness in the daytime, and in
the night his song *shall be* with me, *and* my prayer unto the God of my life.
9 I will say unto God my rock, Why hast thou forgotten me? why go I
mourning because of the oppression of the enemy?
10 *As* with a sword in my bones, mine enemies reproach me; while they
say daily unto me, Where *is* thy God?
11 Why art thou cast down, O my soul? and why art thou disquieted
within me? hope thou in God: for I shall yet praise him, *who is* the health of
my countenance, and my God.

I. THE PSALMIST'S PRAYER OF FAITH FOR GOD TO DEFEND HIM

43:1☆ 1 Sam 24:15; Ps 26:1; 35:24
43:2 Ps 28:7; 42:9; 44:9
43:3 Ps 36:9; 42:4, 5; 84:1
43:4 Ps 26:6; 33:2; 71:22
43:5 Ps 42:11

43 JUDGE me, O God, and plead my cause against an ungodly
nation: O deliver me from the deceitful and unjust man.
2 For thou *art* the God of my strength: why dost thou cast me off? why go
I mourning because of the oppression of the enemy?
3 O send out thy light and thy truth: let them lead me; let them bring me
unto thy holy hill, and to thy tabernacles.
4 Then will I go unto the altar of God, unto God my exceeding joy: yea,
upon the harp will I praise thee, O God my God.
5 Why art thou cast down, O my soul? and why art thou disquieted within
me? hope in God: for I shall yet praise him, *who is* the health of my
countenance, and my God.

I. DELIVERANCE FROM AFFLICTION
A. THE REMINDER OF GOD'S PAST MERCIES

44:1☆ Ex 12:26, 27; Deut 32:7; Josh 3:10; 2 Sam 7:10, 11; Ps 78:2, 3, 12, 55; 80:8; 135:10–12; Isa 51:9
44:3☆ Deut 4:37; Josh 24:12; Ps 77:15
44:4 Ps 74:12
44:5 Ps 60:12; 108:11
44:6 Ps 33:16, 17
44:7 Ps 53:5; 136:24
44:8 Ps 30:12; 34:2

To the chief Musician for the sons of Korah, Maschil

44 WE have heard with our ears, O God, our fathers have told us, *what*
work thou didst in their days, in the times of old.
2 *How* thou didst drive out the heathen with thy hand, and plantedst
them; *how* thou didst afflict the people, and cast them out.
3 For they got not the land in possession by their own sword, neither did
their own arm save them: but thy right hand, and thine arm, and the light
of thy countenance, because thou hadst a favour unto them.
4 Thou art my King, O God: command deliverances for Jacob.
5 Through thee will we push down our enemies: through thy name will we
tread them under that rise up against us.
6 For I will not trust in my bow, neither shall my sword save me.
7 But thou hast saved us from our enemies, and hast put them to shame
that hated us.
8 In God we boast all the day long, and praise thy name for ever. Se'lah.

42:7 *Deep calleth unto deep at the noise of thy watersprouts,* i.e., "floods of sorrow pour upon me like a thundering cataract."†

42:9 *God, my rock.* God is a sure foundation on which to build, a rock of shelter, the rock of ages in whom is everlasting strength. To this rock David had access without fear and in confidence. And he could be sure of a gracious audience; God, the rock, is his friend.

43:1ff The psalmist takes his refuge in the God he trusts, the one on whom he calls to vindicate him by defending his cause. His desire is to come to the altar of God and to stand before the One in whom he hopes.

44:1ff This is a Psalm for all seasons and for all people. It makes little difference whether the Spirit wrote this looking to the Babylonian captivity, the suffering of the Jews under Antiochus Epiphanes, or the future sufferings of the early Church. God's people suffer in all ages and should raise their prayers to a faithful God for deliverance on the basis of God's steadfast, unchanging love.

44:3 It was God who planted Israel in Canaan. He gave his people victory over the inhabitants of the land. However great the victories were, they could not be attributed to the Israelites but to their God.

B. THE REMINDER OF PRESENT DIFFICULTIES

9 But thou hast cast off, and put us to shame; and goest not forth with our
armies.
10 Thou makest us to turn back from the enemy: and they which hate us
spoil for themselves.
11 Thou hast given us like sheep *appointed* for meat; and hast scattered us
among the heathen.
12 Thou sellest thy people for nought, and dost not increase *thy wealth* by
their price.
13 Thou makest us a reproach to our neighbours, a scorn and a derision to
them that are round about us.
14 Thou makest us a byword among the heathen, a shaking of the head
among the people.
15 My confusion *is* continually before me, and the shame of my face hath
covered me,
16 For the voice of him that reproacheth and blasphemeth; by reason of
the enemy and avenger.

☆**44:9** Ps 43:2; 60:10; 74:1
44:10 Lev 26:33; Josh 7:8, 12; Ps 89:42
44:11 Lev 26:33; Deut 4:27; 28:64; Ps 106:27; Ezek 20:23, 24
44:12 Isa 52:3, 4
44:13 Ps 79:4; 80:6
44:14 Ps 17:6; 109:25; Jer 24:9
44:15 Ps 109:25

C. THE PRAYER FOR PRESENT HELP

17 All this is come upon us; yet have we not forgotten thee, neither have
we dealt falsely in thy covenant.
18 Our heart is not turned back, neither have our steps declined from thy
way;
19 Though thou hast sore broken us in the place of dragons, and covered
us with the shadow of death.
20 If we have forgotten the name of our God, or stretched out our hands
to a strange god;
21 Shall not God search this out? for he knoweth the secrets of the heart.
22 Yea, for thy sake are we killed all the day long; we are counted as sheep
for the slaughter.
23 Awake, why sleepest thou, O Lord? arise, cast *us* not off for ever.
24 Wherefore hidest thou thy face, *and* forgettest our affliction and our
oppression?
25 For our soul is bowed down to the dust: our belly cleaveth unto the
earth.
26 Arise for our help, and redeem us for thy mercies' sake.

44:17 Ps 119:61, 83, 109, 141, 153, 176
44:18 Job 23:11; Ps 119:51, 157
44:19 Job 3:5; 30:29; Ps 51:8; 94:5
44:20 Ps 78:11; 81:9
44:21 Ps 139:1, 2; Jer 17:10
44:22 Isa 53:7; Rom 8:36
44:23 Ps 7:6; 77:7; 78:65
44:24 Job 13:24; Ps 42:9; 88:14; Lam 5:20
44:25 Ps 119:25
Ps 6:4; 35:2

I. THE MARRIAGE OF THE KING

A. THE DESCRIPTION OF THE KING (A TYPE OF CHRIST)

To the chief Musician upon Shoshannim, for the sons of Korah, Maschil, A Song of loves

45 MY heart is inditing a good matter: I speak of the things which I
have made touching the king: my tongue *is* the pen of a ready
writer.
2 Thou art fairer than the children of men: grace is poured into thy lips:
therefore God hath blessed thee for ever.

☆**45:1** Ezra 7:6
45:2 Ps 21:6; Lk 4:22

44:9 The God who brought them into the land and gave them victory would keep them, but only if they remained faithful to him. Here we learn that God cast them off and abased them. Again and again in the history of the two kingdoms, their kings and armies were put to shame by the enemy because they had forsaken their rock.

45:1 This is a Psalm that celebrates the marriage of a king. It has messianic implications, especially in 45:6. While this verse applies first to some ancient monarch, it is picked up in Hebrews and applied to Jesus Christ "But unto the Son he saith, Thy throne, O God, is for ever and ever" (Heb. 1:8).

45:3 Isa 9:6 3 Gird thy sword upon *thy* thigh, O *most* mighty, with thy glory and thy
majesty.
45:4 Rev 6:2 4 And in thy majesty ride prosperously because of truth and meekness *and*
righteousness; and thy right hand shall teach thee terrible things.
45:5 Ps 120:4 5 Thine arrows *are* sharp in the heart of the king's enemies; *whereby* the
Isa 5:28 people fall under thee.
45:6 Ps 93:2; 98:8, 9 6 Thy throne, O God, *is* for ever and ever: the sceptre of thy kingdom *is* a
Heb 1:8, 9 right sceptre.
45:7 Ps 11:7; 21:6 7 Thou lovest righteousness, and hatest wickedness: therefore God, thy
33:5 God, hath anointed thee with the oil of gladness above thy fellows.
45:8 Song 1:3 8 All thy garments *smell* of myrrh, and aloes, *and* cassia, out of the ivory
4:13, 14 palaces, whereby they have made thee glad.
45:9☆ 1 Kgs 2:19; 9:28 9 Kings' daughters *were* among thy honourable women: upon thy right
Song 6:8 Isa 13:12 hand did stand the queen in gold of O'phir.

B. THE BRIDE AND THE NUPTIALS (CHRIST AND THE CHURCH)

45:10 Deut 21:13 10 Hearken, O daughter, and consider, and incline thine ear; forget also
Isa 54:5 thine own people, and thy father's house;
Eph 5:33 1 Pet 3:6 11 So shall the king greatly desire thy beauty: for he *is* thy Lord; and
worship thou him.
45:12☆ Ps 22:29 12 And the daughter of Tyre *shall be there* with a gift; *even* the rich among
72:10, 11 the people shall intreat thy favour.
45:13 Isa 61:10 13 The king's daughter *is* all glorious within: her clothing *is* of wrought
gold.
45:14 Song 1:4 14 She shall be brought unto the king in raiment of needlework: the
Ezek 16:9–13 virgins her companions that follow her shall be brought unto thee.
15 With gladness and rejoicing shall they be brought: they shall enter into
the king's palace.
16 Instead of thy fathers shall be thy children, whom thou mayest make
princes in all the earth.
45:17☆ Ps 138:4 17 I will make thy name to be remembered in all generations: therefore
Mal 1:11 shall the people praise thee for ever and ever.

I. GOD, OUR REFUGE AND STRENGTH

A. GOD, OUR REFUGE

To the chief Musician for the sons of Korah, A Song upon Alamoth

46:1☆ Ps 9:9; 14:6 **46** GOD *is* our refuge and strength, a very present help in trouble.
62:7, 8; 145:18 2 Therefore will not we fear, though the earth be removed, and
46:2 Ps 18:7; 23:4 though the mountains be carried into the midst of the sea;
46:3 Ps 93:3, 4 3 *Though* the waters thereof roar *and* be troubled, *though* the mountains
shake with the swelling thereof. Se'lah.

B. GOD, OUR STRENGTH

46:4☆ Ps 87:3 Isa 60:14 4 *There is* a river, the streams whereof shall make glad the city of God, the
Rev 3:12; 22:1 holy *place* of the tabernacles of the most High.

45:9 *honourable women,* i.e., "concubines."†
45:12 *Tyre* is pictured here as bringing gifts to a bride (Israel). Tyre was a wealthy maritime nation which, under Hiram, assisted David and Solomon in their numerous building projects.
45:17 The royal bridegroom (Christ) will be praised forever. His father has given him a name that is above every name and his people shall extol that name by word and deed for endless generations.
46:1ff The theme of this Psalm is our hope and trust in God. In this Psalm we see God's power, providence, and presence among his people in bad times as well as in good ones. We learn of what he has done for us and will do in the future. It was said of Luther that when bad news came his way he would say: "Let us sing Psalm 46." So may we in bad times do the same today.
46:4 *There is a river,* i.e., the waters of Siloam which went softly by Jerusalem and served as a defense of the city in Hezekiah's day.

[5]God *is* in the midst of her; she shall not be moved: God shall help her,
and that right early.
[6]The heathen raged, the kingdoms were moved: he uttered his voice, the
earth melted.
[7]The LORD of hosts *is* with us; the God of Jacob *is* our refuge. Se'lah.

46:5 Isa 12:6; 41:14 Ezek 43:7 Lk 1:54
46:6 Ps 2:1 Amos 9:5 Mic 1:4
46:7 Num 14:9 Ps 9:9

C. GOD, THE GIVER OF VICTORY

[8]Come, behold the works of the LORD, what desolations he hath made in
the earth.
[9]He maketh wars to cease unto the end of the earth; he breaketh the bow,
and cutteth the spear in sunder; he burneth the chariot in the fire.
[10]Be still, and know that I *am* God: I will be exalted among the heathen,
I will be exalted in the earth.
[11]The LORD of hosts *is* with us; the God of Jacob *is* our refuge. Se'lah.

☆46:8 Ps 66:5 Jer 51:43
46:9 Isa 2:4; 9:5 Mic 4:3
☆46:10 Ps 100:3 Isa 2:11, 17

I. THE PSALM OF THE ASCENDED KING

A. GOD SUBDUES THE NATIONS

To the chief Musician, A Psalm for the sons of Korah

47 O CLAP your hands, all ye people; shout unto God with the voice
of triumph.
[2]For the LORD most high *is* terrible; *he is* a great King over all the earth.
[3]He shall subdue the people under us, and the nations under our feet.
[4]He shall choose our inheritance for us, the excellency of Jacob whom he
loved. Se'lah.

☆47:1 Ps 98:8, 9 106:47
47:2 Deut 7:21 Ps 66:3 Mal 1:14
47:3 Ps 18:47
47:4 1 Pet 1:4

B. GOD ASCENDS TO SIT ON HIS THRONE

[5]God is gone up with a shout, the LORD with the sound of a trumpet.
[6]Sing praises to God, sing praises: sing praises unto our King, sing
praises.
[7]For God *is* the King of all the earth: sing ye praises with understanding.
[8]God reigneth over the heathen: God sitteth upon the throne of his
holiness.
[9]The princes of the people are gathered together, *even* the people of the
God of Abraham: for the shields of the earth *belong* unto God: he is greatly
exalted.

47:5 Ps 68:18, 25, 33
47:6 Ps 68:4; 89:18 Zech 14:9 1 Cor 14:15
☆47:8 1 Chron 16:31 Ps 22:28
47:9 Ps 72:11 102:21, 22 Isa 49:7, 23 Rom 4:11, 12

I. ZION, THE RESIDENCE OF THE KING

A. ZION, THE CITY OF THE KING

A Song and Psalm for the sons of Korah

48 GREAT *is* the LORD, and greatly to be praised in the city of our
God, *in* the mountain of his holiness.

☆48:1 1 Chron 16:25 Ps 87:1; 96:4 145:3 Zech 8:3

46:8 *When God is pleased to use his sword he can make havoc among the nations. No power is so strong that he cannot abase it.*
46:10 Let the enemies of God be still and know that he is God. Let the friends of God also be still, see his deliverance, and know that he alone is able to conquer and overcome the enemy, including that last enemy, death.
47:1ff The purpose of this Psalm is to stir up praise to our God and to excite the people of God to sing those praises. The God we praise is *King of all the earth* who . . . *sitteth upon the throne of his holiness.* He is a great God and should be praised.
47:8 God who is the Creator and the God of all nature is also the God who reigns over the heathen. Although they do not know him or obey him, he determines their destiny and directs their paths. All the heathen are born within his dominion and are ruled by the true God who sits upon the throne of his holiness.
48:1 Zion is Jerusalem, the city of the great King. In covenant with its people, he lives and reigns there and defeats its enemies. The divine dominion over this city is established forever. Let all men praise the God of Zion, who is the guide of the city and its people forever.

48:2 Ps 50:2; Lam 2:15; Mt 5:35

[2]Beautiful for situation, the joy of the whole earth, *is* mount Zion, *on* the sides of the north, the city of the great King.

B. ZION ESTABLISHED FOREVER

48:3 Ps 46:7

[3]God is known in her palaces for a refuge.
[4]For, lo, the kings were assembled, they passed by together.
[5]They saw *it*, *and* so they marvelled; they were troubled, *and* hasted away.

48:6 Isa 13:8; **48:7** Jer 18:17; **48:8** Ps 87:5

[6]Fear took hold upon them there, *and* pain, as of a woman in travail.
[7]Thou breakest the ships of Tarshish with an east wind.
[8]As we have heard, so have we seen in the city of the LORD of hosts, in the city of our God: God will establish it for ever. Se'lah.

C. THE PEOPLE PRAISE THE GOD OF ZION

48:9 Ps 26:3; 40:10

[9]We have thought of thy lovingkindness, O God, in the midst of thy temple.

48:10 Josh 7:9; Mal 1:11; **48:11** Ps 97:8

[10]According to thy name, O God, so *is* thy praise unto the ends of the earth: thy right hand is full of righteousness.
[11]Let mount Zion rejoice, let the daughters of Judah be glad, because of thy judgments.
[12]Walk about Zion, and go round about her: tell the towers thereof.

48:13 Ps 78:5–7; **48:14** Ps 23:4; Isa 58:11

[13]Mark ye well her bulwarks, consider her palaces; that ye may tell *it* to the generation following.
[14]For this God *is* our God for ever and ever: he will be our guide *even* unto death.

I. THE VANITY OF WEALTH

A. THE CALL FOR RICH AND POOR TO LISTEN

To the chief Musician, A Psalm for the sons of Korah

49:1☆ Ps 78:1

49 HEAR this, all *ye* people; give ear, all *ye* inhabitants of the world:
[2]Both low and high, rich and poor, together.

49:3 Ps 39:30; 119:130; **49:4** 2 Kgs 3:15; Ps 78:23

[3]My mouth shall speak of wisdom; and the meditation of my heart *shall be* of understanding.
[4]I will incline mine ear to a parable: I will open my dark saying upon the harp.

B. THE INADEQUACIES OF WEALTH

49:5 Ps 23:4; 27:1; **49:6☆** Ps 52:7; Prov 11:28; Mark 10:24

[5]Wherefore should I fear in the days of evil, *when* the iniquity of my heels shall compass me about?
[6]They that trust in their wealth, and boast themselves in the multitude of their riches;

49:7 Job 36:18; Mt 25:8, 9

[7]None *of them* can by any means redeem his brother, nor give to God a ransom for him:

49:8 Ps 16:10; 89:48; Mt 16:26

[8](For the redemption of their soul *is* precious, and it ceaseth for ever:)
[9]That he should still live for ever, *and* not see corruption.

49:1 *Most of the Psalms speak about* praying and praising God. This one is devoted to preaching and teaching. Its purpose is to convince worldly men that it is folly to set their hearts on material things that perish. They should seek a better world.

49:6 *They that trust in their wealth.* This Psalm speaks of the deceptive nature of wealth. Wealthy but worldly people put their trust in wealth, boast of their possessions, and suppose they can keep it forever. They fail to realize that wealth cannot keep them or their closest relatives and friends from dying, and that it cannot affect their state after death.

10 For he seeth *that* wise men die, likewise the fool and the brutish person
perish, and leave their wealth to others.
11 Their inward thought *is, that* their houses *shall continue* for ever, *and*
their dwelling places to all generations; they call *their* lands after their own
names.
12 Nevertheless man *being* in honour abideth not: he is like the beasts *that*
perish.
13 This their way *is* their folly: yet their posterity approve their sayings.
Se'lah.

49:10 Ps 39:6; Eccles 2:16, 18, 20–23; Lk 12:20, 21
49:11 Deut 3:14
49:13 Jer 17:11; 49:18, 19

C. THE GLORIES OF THE RIGHTEOUS IN THE WORLD TO COME

14 Like sheep they are laid in the grave; death shall feed on them; and the
upright shall have dominion over them in the morning; and their beauty
shall consume in the grave from their dwelling.
15 But God will redeem my soul from the power of the grave: for he shall
receive me. Se'lah.
16 Be not thou afraid when one is made rich, when the glory of his house
is increased;
17 For when he dieth he shall carry nothing away: his glory shall not
descend after him.
18 Though while he lived he blessed his soul: and *men* will praise thee,
when thou doest well to thyself.
19 He shall go to the generation of his fathers; they shall never see light.
20 Man *that is* in honour, and understandeth not, is like the beasts *that*
perish.

49:14 Ps 9:17; Dan 7:18; Mal 4:3; 1 Cor 6:2; Rev 2:26
49:15 Gen 5:21–24; Ps 16:10, 11; 56:13; 73:24
49:16 Ps 37:7
49:17 Ps 17:14; 1 Tim 6:7
49:18 Deut 29:19; Ps 10:3; Lk 12:19
49:19 Job 33:29, 30
☆**49:20**

I. THE TRUE WORSHIP OF GOD

A. GOD IS THE TRUE AND FAIR JUDGE

A Psalm of Asaph

50 THE mighty God, *even* the LORD, hath spoken, and called the earth
from the rising of the sun unto the going down thereof.
2 Out of Zion, the perfection of beauty, God hath shined.
3 Our God shall come, and shall not keep silence: a fire shall devour
before him, and it shall be very tempestuous round about him.
4 He shall call to the heavens from above, and to the earth, that he may
judge his people.
5 Gather my saints together unto me; those that have made a covenant
with me by sacrifice.
6 And the heavens shall declare his righteousness: for God *is* judge
himself. Se'lah.

☆**50:1** Josh 22:22; Ps 113:3
50:2 Deut 33:2; Ps 48:2; 80:1
50:3 Lev 10:2; Ps 18:12, 13; 97:3; Dan 7:10
50:4 Deut 32:1
50:5 Ex 24:7; Ps 30:4; 37:28
50:6 Ps 96:13; 97:6

B. ANIMAL SACRIFICE MEANS NOTHING; THE LORD JUDGES THE HEART

7 *Hear, O my people, and* I will speak; O Israel, and I will testify against
thee: I *am* God, *even* thy God.
8 I will not reprove thee for thy sacrifices or thy burnt offerings, *to have
been* continually before me.

50:7 Ex 20:5; Ps 81:8
50:8 Ps 40:8

49:20 *Man that is in honour and understandeth not,* i.e., "Man without insight." It is uncertain whether this phrase was part of the original text.†

50:1ff This is not a Psalm of praise and prayer. It is designed to instruct, reprove, and admonish. Carnal Jews who practiced the externals of religion without inward faith and practical action are rebuked. The threat of judgment hangs over the heads of the disobedient. Let us all take heed and find God's true salvation.

50:9 Ps 69:31
50:10☆ Ps 104:24
50:12 Ex 19:5; Deut 10:14; Ps 24:1
50:13 Hos 6:6
50:14 Deut 23:21; Ps 22:25; 69:30, 31; 81:7; 91:15; 107:6, 13; Hos 14:2; Rom 12:1; Heb 13:15

9 I will take no bullock out of thy house, *nor* he goats out of thy folds.
10 For every beast of the forest *is* mine, *and* the cattle upon a thousand
hills.
11 I know all the fowls of the mountains: and the wild beasts of the field
are mine.
12 If I were hungry, I would not tell thee: for the world *is* mine, and the
fulness thereof.
13 Will I eat the flesh of bulls, or drink the blood of goats?
14 Offer unto God thanksgiving; and pay thy vows unto the most High:
15 And call upon me in the day of trouble: I will deliver thee, and thou
shalt glorify me.

C. GOD WILL JUDGE HYPOCRISY

50:16 Isa 29:13
50:17 Neh 9:26; Rom 2:21, 22
50:18 Rom 1:32; 1 Tim 5:22
50:19 Ps 10:7; 36:3
50:20 Job 19:18; Mt 10:21
50:21 Ps 90:8; Eccles 8:11; Isa 42:14
50:22 Ps 7:2; 19:17

16 But unto the wicked God saith, What hast thou to do to declare my
statutes, or *that* thou shouldest take my covenant in thy mouth?
17 Seeing thou hatest instruction, and castest my words behind thee.
18 When thou sawest a thief, then thou consentedst with him, and hast
been partaker with adulterers.
19 Thou givest thy mouth to evil, and thy tongue frameth deceit.
20 Thou sittest *and* speakest against thy brother; thou slanderest thine
own mother's son.
21 These *things* hast thou done, and I kept silence; thou thoughtest that I
was altogether *such an one* as thyself: *but* I will reprove thee, and set *them* in
order before thine eyes.
22 Now consider this, ye that forget God, lest I tear *you* in pieces, and
there be none to deliver.

D. THE WORTH OF TRUE PRAISE

50:23 Ps 91:16

23 Whoso offereth praise glorifieth me: and to him that ordereth *his*
conversation *aright* will I shew the salvation of God.

I. DAVID'S PRAYER OF REPENTANCE

A. DAVID'S CONFESSION OF SIN

51:1☆ Ps 4:1; Isa 43:25; 44:22; Acts 3:19; Col 2:14
51:2 Isa 4:4; Jer 33:8; Ezek 36:33; Acts 22:16; Heb 9:13, 14; 1 Jn 1:7, 9
51:3 Isa 59:12
51:4 Gen 20:6; 2 Sam 12:13; Lk 15:21; Rom 3:4
51:5 Ps 58:3; Job 14:4; Eph 2:3
51:6 Prov 2:6; Jas 1:5

To the chief Musician, A Psalm of David, when Nathan the prophet came unto him, after he had gone in to Bath-sheba

51 HAVE mercy upon me, O God, according to thy lovingkindness:
according unto the multitude of thy tender mercies blot out my
transgressions.
2 Wash me throughly from mine iniquity, and cleanse me from my sin.
3 For I acknowledge my transgressions: and my sin *is* ever before me.
4 Against thee, thee only, have I sinned, and done *this* evil in thy sight:
that thou mightest be justified when thou speakest, *and* be clear when thou
judgest.
5 Behold, I was shapen in iniquity; and in sin did my mother conceive me.
6 Behold, thou desirest truth in the inward parts: and in the hidden *part*
thou shalt make me to know wisdom.

50:10 God does not need the animal sacrifices of his people. He has command over the beasts of the forest, and the cattle on a thousand hills belong to him. He owns everything and has dominion over everything. They are under his eye and within his reach. They wait on him and are at his disposal, so he can make any use of them that he desires.

51:1ff This Psalm lays down the biblical requirements for confession and cleansing from sin. David's repentance included (1) a godly sorrow for his transgressions, (2) confession of his sins, (3) his determination to commit these sins no more, (4) forgiveness from God, (5) restoration, (6) rejoicing, and (7) a readiness to tell others of the grace of God.

B. DAVID'S PETITION FOR CLEANSING AND A NEW HEART

[7]Purge me with hyssop, and I shall be clean: wash me, and I shall be
whiter than snow.
[8]Make me to hear joy and gladness; *that* the bones *which* thou hast
broken may rejoice.
[9]Hide thy face from my sins, and blot out all mine iniquities.
[10]Create in me a clean heart, O God; and renew a right spirit within me.
[11]Cast me not away from thy presence; and take not thy holy spirit from
me.
[12]Restore unto me the joy of thy salvation; and uphold me *with thy* free
spirit.
[13]*Then* will I teach transgressors thy ways; and sinners shall be converted
unto thee.
[14]Deliver me from bloodguiltiness, O God, thou God of my salvation:
and my tongue shall sing aloud of thy righteousness.
[15]O Lord, open thou my lips; and my mouth shall shew forth thy praise.

☆**51:7** Ex 12:22 Isa 1:18 1 Jn 1:7, 9 **51:9** Jer 16:17 **51:10** Ps 78:37 Mt 5:8 Acts 15:9 Eph 2:10 ☆**51:11** Eph 4:30 **51:12** Ps 13:5 2 Cor 3:17 **51:13** Ps 22:27 Acts 19:21, 22 **51:14** 2 Sam 12:9 Ps 9:14; 25:5 71:15

C. GOD'S ACCEPTANCE OF A BROKEN AND CONTRITE HEART

[16]For thou desirest not sacrifice; else would I give *it:* thou delightest not
in burnt offering.
[17]The sacrifices of God *are* a broken spirit: a broken and a contrite heart,
O God, thou wilt not despise.

51:16 1 Sam 15:22 Ps 40:6 **51:17** Ps 34:18

D. DAVID'S PETITION FOR ISRAEL

[18]Do good in thy good pleasure unto Zion: build thou the walls of
Jerusalem.
[19]Then shalt thou be pleased with the sacrifices of righteousness, with
burnt offering and whole burnt offering: then shall they offer bullocks upon
thine altar.

51:18 Ps 69:35 102:16; 147:2 Isa 51:3 **51:19** Ps 4:5 66:13, 15

I. THE END OF BOASTERS OF EVIL DEEDS

A. THE SINS OF THE WICKED

To the chief Musician, Maschil, A Psalm of David, when Doeg the Edomite came and told Saul, and said unto him, David is come to the house of Ahimelech

52 WHY boastest thou thyself in mischief, O mighty man? the
goodness of God *endureth* continually.
[2]Thy tongue deviseth mischiefs; like a sharp razor, working deceitfully.
[3]Thou lovest evil more than good; *and* lying rather than to speak
righteousness. Se′lah.
[4]Thou lovest all devouring words, O *thou* deceitful tongue.

☆**52:1** Ps 94:4 **52:2** Ps 5:9; 57:4 59:7 **52:3** Ps 36:4; 58:3 Jer 9:5 **52:4** Ps 120:3

51:7 *purge me with hyssop,* i.e., "sprinkle me with the cleansing blood." (See Exod. 12:22; Heb. 9:18–22.)† Hyssop was an edible plant. Its leaves and heads were used as a spice or condiment. As employed here it does not mean ingestion of the spice. Rather, the phrase here is used as in Exod. 12:22, where the plant was dipped in the blood of an animal then used to sprinkle the blood on the lintels and doorposts. (See also Lev. 14:4–8; Num. 19:17, 18.)

51:11 The work of the Holy Spirit in the Old Testament differs from that in the New Testament. The Spirit came and went from people as in the case of Samson. When David sinned and repented he prayed that God would not take away the Holy Spirit, who had come upon him when he was chosen to be king. In this age, believers are sealed by the Spirit, who can be quenched or made to sorrow, but who does not leave the believer once he has been converted.

52:1ff This Psalm has to do with the murders committed by Doeg the Edomite. He slew eighty-five priests, including Ahimelech. David later executed Doeg for his treachery. Saul, of course, was behind the slaying of the priests and shared Doeg's guilt. David pictures the acts of the wicked and the judgment that falls upon them, and he offers praise for the righteous. (See 1 Sam. 22 for the details of the executions.)

B. THE DESTINY OF THE WICKED

52:5 Prov 2:22; Ps 27:13; Isa 22:18, 19
52:6 Job 22:19; Ps 37:34
52:7 Ps 10:6; 49:6

5 God shall likewise destroy thee for ever, he shall take thee away, and pluck thee out of *thy* dwelling place, and root thee out of the land of the living. Se'lah.
6 The righteous also shall see, and fear, and shall laugh at him:
7 Lo, *this is* the man *that* made not God his strength; but trusted in the abundance of his riches, *and* strengthened himself in his wickedness.

C. THE LORD'S PROTECTION OF THE RIGHTEOUS

52:8 Ps 13:5; 128:3; Jer 11:16
52:9 Ps 30:12; 54:6

8 But I *am* like a green olive tree in the house of God: I trust in the mercy of God for ever and ever.
9 I will praise thee for ever, because thou hast done *it:* and I will wait on thy name; for *it is* good before thy saints.

I. THE SINS AND THE DOOM OF WICKED MEN

A. THE FOOLISHNESS OF THE ATHEIST

To the chief Musician upon Mahalath, Maschil, A Psalm of David

53:1☆ Ps 14:1–4
53:2 Ps 33:13–15

53 THE fool hath said in his heart, *There is* no God. Corrupt are they, and have done abominable iniquity: *there is* none that doeth good.
2 God looked down from heaven upon the children of men, to see if there were *any* that did understand, that did seek God.

B. THE DOOM OF THE WICKED

53:3 Rom 3:10, 12
53:4 Jer 4:22
53:5 Lev 26:17, 36; Ps 44:7; Prov 28:1; Jer 6:30; 8:1, 2; Ezek 6:5

3 Every one of them is gone back: they are altogether become filthy; *there is* none that doeth good, no, not one.
4 Have the workers of iniquity no knowledge? who eat up my people *as* they eat bread: they have not called upon God.
5 There were they in great fear, *where* no fear was: for God hath scattered the bones of him that encampeth *against* thee: thou hast put *them* to shame, because God hath despised them.

C. THE PRAYER FOR THE SALVATION OF ISRAEL

53:6 Ps 14:7

6 Oh that the salvation of Israel *were come* out of Zion! When God bringeth back the captivity of his people, Jacob shall rejoice, *and* Israel shall be glad.

I. THE GOD WHO HELPS THE DISTRESSED

A. THE PSALMIST'S COMPLAINT

To the chief Musician on Neginoth, Maschil, A Psalm of David, when the Ziphims came and said to Saul, Doth not David hide himself with us?

54:1☆ 2 Chron 20:6; Ps 20:1
54:2 Ps 17:6
54:3 1 Sam 20:1; Ps 36:1; 40:14; 86:14; 140:1, 4

54 SAVE me, O God, by thy name, and judge me by thy strength.
2 Hear my prayer, O God; give ear to the words of my mouth.
3 For strangers are risen up against me, and oppressors seek after my soul: they have not set God before them. Se'lah.

53:1 *fool.* See note on 14:1. The word in the Hebrew is *nabal* (*"senseless, foolish, bereft of any sense of* ethical or religious values"). It implies that such a person is ignoble. Some scholars think the similarities between this Psalm and Ps. 14 indicate that Ps. 53 was used in the Northern Kingdom along with the other Psalms of Book II and reflects linguistic and local peculiarities.

54:1 *by thy name,* i.e., "by thy great power." This Psalm recounts the treachery of the Zithites, who betrayed David to Saul on two occasions (1 Sam. 23:19; 26:1). The actions of the wicked will be forever remembered against them as a warning to others who are tempted to follow in their evil ways.

B. THE GOD WHO HELPS AND DELIVERS

4 Behold, God *is* mine helper: the Lord *is* with them that uphold my soul.
5 He shall reward evil unto mine enemies: cut them off in thy truth.
6 I will freely sacrifice unto thee: I will praise thy name, O LORD; for *it is*
good.
7 For he hath delivered me out of all trouble: and mine eye hath seen *his*
desire upon mine enemies.

54:4 Ps 37:17, 24, 40; 41:12; Isa 41:10
☆**54:5** Ps 94:23; 96:13
54:6 Ps 50:14; 116:17
54:7 Ps 34:6; 59:10

I. A PSALM FOR THOSE BETRAYED BY FRIENDS

A. DAVID'S ANGUISH AND DISTRESS

To the chief Musician on Neginoth, Maschil, A Psalm of David

55 GIVE ear to my prayer, O God; and hide not thyself from my
supplication.
2 Attend unto me, and hear me: I mourn in my complaint, and make a
noise;
3 Because of the voice of the enemy, because of the oppression of the
wicked: for they cast iniquity upon me, and in wrath they hate me.
4 My heart is sore pained within me: and the terrors of death are fallen
upon me.
5 Fearfulness and trembling are come upon me, and horror hath over-
whelmed me.
6 And I said, Oh that I had wings like a dove! *for then* would I fly away,
and be at rest.
7 Lo, *then* would I wander far off, *and* remain in the wilderness. Se'lah.
8 I would hasten my escape from the windy storm *and* tempest.

☆**55:1** Ps 27:9; 61:1
55:2 1 Sam 1:16; Ps 77:3; 86:6, 7; Isa 38:14
55:3 2 Sam 16:7, 8; Ps 17:9; 71:11
55:4 Ps 116:3
55:5 Job 21:6; Ezek 7:18
☆**55:6** Job 3:13
55:8 Isa 25:4

B. THE TREACHERY OF DAVID'S FRIEND

9 Destroy, O Lord, *and* divide their tongues: for I have seen violence and
strife in the city.
10 Day and night they go about it upon the walls thereof: mischief also
and sorrow *are* in the midst of it.
11 Wickedness *is* in the midst thereof: deceit and guile depart not from her
streets.
12 For *it was* not an enemy *that* reproached me; then I could have borne *it:*
neither *was it* he that hated me *that* did magnify *himself* against me; then I
would have hid myself from him:
13 But *it was* thou, a man mine equal, my guide, and mine acquaintance.
14 We took sweet counsel together, *and* walked unto the house of God in
company.
15 Let death seize upon them, *and* let them go down quick into hell: for
wickedness *is* in their dwellings, *and* among them.

55:9 Gen 11:9; Ps 11:5
55:11 Ps 5:9; 10:7; Jer 6:7
☆**55:13** Ps 41:9
55:15 Num 16:30, 33; Prov 6:15; Isa 47:11; 1 Thess 5:3

C. DAVID GIVES HIS BURDEN TO THE LORD

16 As for me, I will call upon God; and the LORD shall save me.
17 Evening, and morning, and at noon, will I pray, and cry aloud: and he
shall hear my voice.

55:16 Ps 57:2, 3
55:17 Ps 5:3; 88:13; 141:2; Dan 6:10; Acts 3:1

54:5 David need not fear his enemies, for God will judge and repay them for their wickedness. He prays, not with malice but with faith, that God will do what he says about sinners who refuse to repent.
55:1ff Many commentators think this Psalm sprang from the rebellion of Absalom against his father David. In that episode, Ahithophel dealt treacherously with King David. Some liken the death of Ahithophel to the death of Judas Iscariot; they both hanged themselves.
55:6 Here David the warrior speaks the language of a dove, which flies low, seeks shelter, and wants peace. It is the voice of an escapist who wants to flee from what life has brought, rather than face and overcome it.
55:13 Here David may have been thinking of Ahithophel, who was numbered among the conspirators with Absalom. David had esteemed him as a bosom friend, who has now deserted him and betrayed him.

55:18 Ps 103:4
55:19 Ps 36:1; 90:2; 93:2
55:20 Num 30:2; Ps 7:3, 4; 89:34
55:21☆ Ps 12:2; 28:3; Prov 5:3, 4
55:22 Ps 37:5; 112:6; 1 Pet 5:7
55:23☆ Ps 5:6; 56:3, 4; 73:18; Prov 10:27; Ezek 28:8

18 He hath delivered my soul in peace from the battle *that was* against me:
for there were many with me.
19 God shall hear, and afflict them, even he that abideth of old. Se'lah.
Because they have no changes, therefore they fear not God.
20 He hath put forth his hands against such as be at peace with him: he
hath broken his covenant.
21 *The words* of his mouth were smoother than butter, but war *was* in his
heart: his words were softer than oil, yet *were* they drawn swords.
22 Cast thy burden upon the LORD, and he shall sustain thee: he shall
never suffer the righteous to be moved.
23 But thou, O God, shalt bring them down into the pit of destruction:
bloody and deceitful men shall not live out half their days; but I will trust
in thee.

I. THE PSALM OF THE DESOLATE WANDERER

A. THE PRAYER FOR MERCY

To the chief Musician upon Jonath-elem-rechokim, Michtam of David, when the Philistines took him in Gath

56:1☆ Ps 17:9; 35:1, 25
56:3 Ps 11:1; 56:10, 11; Heb 13:6

56 BE merciful unto me, O God: for man would swallow me up; he
fighting daily oppresseth me.
2 Mine enemies would daily swallow *me* up: for *they be* many that fight
against me, O thou most High.
3 What time I am afraid, I will trust in thee.
4 In God I will praise his word, in God I have put my trust; I will not fear
what flesh can do unto me.

B. THE ACTIONS OF HIS ENEMIES

56:5 Ps 41:7; 2 Pet 3:15, 16
56:6 Ps 17:11; 59:3; 140:2
56:7 Ps 36:12; 55:23; Prov 19:5

5 Every day they wrest my words: all their thoughts *are* against me for
evil.
6 They gather themselves together, they hide themselves, they mark my
steps, when they wait for my soul.
7 Shall they escape by iniquity? in *thine* anger cast down the people, O
God.

C. HE PUTS HIS TRUST IN GOD

56:8 Ps 39:12; 139:3; Mal 3:16
56:9 Ps 41:11; 118:6; Rom 8:31
56:12 Ps 50:14, 15
56:13☆ Job 33:30; Ps 33:19; 86:13; 116:8, 9

8 Thou tellest my wanderings: put thou my tears into thy bottle: *are they*
not in thy book?
9 When I cry *unto thee*, then shall mine enemies turn back: this I know;
for God *is* for me.
10 In God will I praise *his* word: in the LORD will I praise *his* word.
11 In God have I put my trust: I will not be afraid what man can do unto
me.
12 Thy vows *are* upon me, O God: I will render praises unto thee.
13 For thou hast delivered my soul from death: *wilt* not *thou deliver* my
feet from falling, that I may walk before God in the light of the living?

55:21 David's enemy was a smooth talker who pretended friendship, when he was really engaged in mischief. He desired to kiss and kill David, even as *Judas Iscariot did with Jesus.*

55:23 In his overpowering providence God would bring David's enemies down to the bottomless pit of destruction.

56:1ff It appears that in almost every instance of suffering and difficulty David composed Psalms to reiterate the malice of those who attacked him and to recount his dependence on God for deliverance through prayer. Here as elsewhere when God answers his prayer, he expresses his thanks to God, his benefactor and deliverer.

56:13 God did not bring his people out of Egypt to slay them. Neither did he call David to the kingship and then desert him before the covenant promise was fulfilled.

I. GOD DELIVERS DAVID FROM KING SAUL

A. DAVID SURROUNDED BY LIONS

To the chief Musician, Al-taschith, Michtam of David, when he fled from Saul in the cave

57 BE merciful unto me, O God, be merciful unto me: for my soul ☆**57:1** Ruth 2:12
trusteth in thee: yea, in the shadow of thy wings will I make my Ps 36:7; 91:4
refuge, until *these* calamities be overpast. Isa 26:20
2 I will cry unto God most high; unto God that performeth *all things* for **57:2**
me. Ps 138:8
3 He shall send from heaven, and save me *from* the reproach of him that **57:3**
would swallow me up. Se'lah. God shall send forth his mercy and his truth. Ps 18:16; 25:10 56:2; 144:5, 7
4 My soul *is* among lions: *and* I lie *even among* them that are set on fire, **57:4** Ps 58:6; 64:3
even the sons of men, whose teeth *are* spears and arrows, and their tongue Prov 30:13, 14
a sharp sword.
5 Be thou exalted, O God, above the heavens; *let* thy glory *be* above all the **57:5**
earth. Ps 108:5
6 They have prepared a net for my steps; my soul is bowed down: they ☆**57:6**
have digged a pit before me, into the midst whereof they are fallen Ps 10:9; 35:7 140:5
themselves. Se'lah. Prov 26:27

B. DAVID'S CONFIDENCE IN GOD

7 My heart is fixed, O God, my heart is fixed: I will sing and give praise. **57:7**
8 Awake up, my glory; awake, psaltery and harp: I *myself* will awake Ps 108:1-5 112:7
early. **57:8** Ps 150:3
9 I will praise thee, O Lord, among the people: I will sing unto thee **57:9**
among the nations. Ps 108:3
10 For thy mercy *is* great unto the heavens, and thy truth unto the clouds. **57:10**
11 Be thou exalted, O God, above the heavens: *let* thy glory *be* above all Ps 36:5
the earth.

I. THE DEPRAVITY AND PUNISHMENT OF THE WICKED

A. THE SINS OF THE WICKED

To the chief Musician, Al-taschith, Michtam of David

58 DO ye indeed speak righteousness, O congregation? do ye judge ☆**58:1**
uprightly, O ye sons of men? Ps 82:2; 94:20 Isa 10:1
2 Yea, in heart ye work wickedness; ye weigh the violence of your hands ☆**58:2**
in the earth.
3 The wicked are estranged from the womb: they go astray as soon as they **58:3** Ps 53:3
be born, speaking lies. Isa 48:8
4 Their poison *is* like the poison of a serpent: *they are* like the deaf adder **58:4** Deut 32:33 Ps 81:11; 140:3
that stoppeth her ear; Jer 8:17

57:1ff Like Psalm 56, this one reflects a similar deliverance from trouble or temptation followed by thanksgiving to the God of steadfast love whom David exalts.
57:6 Saul had set a net for David from which there seemed to be no escape. A cave was David's only refuge. He believed that God would let the enemy fall into the pit he had dug for him. And he did. *Selah* appears 71 times in Psalms and twice in Habakkuk. Some think it was a lifting of the voice in singing a benediction, others that it was the playing of instrumental music in an interlude or postlude. The latter view has support from the Septuagint which translates *selah* as *diapsalma.*
58:1ff Some have conjectured that this Psalm was penned by David at a time preceding the effort of Saul to kill him. Saul had recourse to the law and had David condemned in his absence and pronounced a traitor. The elders of Israel, anxious to gain Saul's favor, agreed to do what Saul wanted. David then wrote the Psalm.
58:2 *ye weigh the violence of your hands in the earth,* i.e., "All your dealings are crooked: you give 'justice' in exchange for bribes."†

5 Which will not hearken to the voice of charmers, charming never so
wisely.

B. THE PRAYER FOR GOD TO JUDGE THE WICKED

6 Break their teeth, O God, in their mouth: break out the great teeth of
the young lions, O LORD.
7 Let them melt away as waters *which* run continually: *when* he bendeth
his bow to shoot his arrows, let them be as cut in pieces.
8 As a snail *which* melteth, let *every one of them* pass away: *like* the
untimely birth of a woman, *that* they may not see the sun.
9 Before your pots can feel the thorns, he shall take them away as with a
whirlwind, both living, and in *his* wrath.
10 The righteous shall rejoice when he seeth the vengeance: he shall wash
his feet in the blood of the wicked.
11 So that a man shall say, Verily *there is* a reward for the righteous: verily
he is a God that judgeth in the earth.

58:6 Job 4:10; Ps 3:7
58:7 Ps 64:3; Isa 13:7; Ezek 21:7
58:8 Job 3:16
58:9 Job 27:21; Prov 10:25
58:10 Ps 32:11; 64:10; 68:22, 23; 91:8; 107:42
58:11 Ps 9:8; 18:20; 67:4; Isa 3:10; Lk 6:23, 35

I. THE PSALM OF RETRIBUTION (IMPRECATORY PSALM)

A. A PRAYER FOR GOD TO PUNISH TREACHEROUS MEN

To the chief Musician, Al-taschith, Michtam of David; when Saul sent, and they watched the house to kill him

59 DELIVER me from mine enemies, O my God: defend me from
them that rise up against me.
2 Deliver me from the workers of iniquity, and save me from bloody men.
3 For, lo, they lie in wait for my soul: the mighty are gathered against me;
not *for* my transgression, nor *for* my sin, O LORD.
4 They run and prepare themselves without *my* fault: awake to help me,
and behold.
5 Thou therefore, O LORD God of hosts, the God of Israel, awake to visit
all the heathen: be not merciful to any wicked transgressors. Se'lah.
6 They return at evening: they make a noise like a dog, and go round
about the city.
7 Behold, they belch out with their mouth: swords *are* in their lips: for
who, *say they,* doth hear?
8 But thou, O LORD, shalt laugh at them; thou shalt have all the heathen
in derision.

59:1☆ Ps 20:1; 143:9
59:2 Ps 14:4; 28:3; 94:16; 139:19
59:3 Ps 7:3, 4; 56:6; 69:4
59:4 Ps 35:19, 23
59:5 Ps 9:5; 84:8; Jer 18:23
59:6☆
59:7☆ Job 22:13; Ps 10:11; 73:11; 94:47
59:8 Ps 2:4; 37:13

B. A PRAYER FOR GOD TO DESTROY THE ENEMY NATIONS

9 *Because of* his strength will I wait upon thee: for God *is* my defence.
10 The God of my mercy shall prevent me: God shall let me see *my desire*
upon mine enemies.
11 Slay them not, lest my people forget: scatter them by thy power; and
bring them down, O Lord our shield.
12 *For* the sin of their mouth *and* the words of their lips let them even be
taken in their pride: and for cursing and lying *which* they speak.

59:9 Ps 9:9
59:10 Ps 54:7
59:11 Deut 4:9; Ps 106:27; 144:6
59:12 Ps 10:7; 83:18; Prov 12:13; Zeph 3:11

59:1ff This Psalm, like some of those preceding it, registers *David's* complaints against those who hate and malign him. He calls upon God to defeat the enemy and ends with praise to his deliverer. This and other similar Psalms reveal the intimacy of David's relationship to God. He always brought his problems to God, rather than trusting in himself for deliverance. God was David's first resort, not the one on whom he called in a last extremity. So should God be the first resort of the believer today.

59:6, 7 The enemy comes howling, prowling, bellowing, and snarling (as the RSV has it). This picturesque language befits the situation.

13 Consume *them* in wrath, consume *them,* that they *may* not *be:* and let
them know that God ruleth in Jacob unto the ends of the earth. Se'lah.
14 And at evening let them return; *and* let them make a noise like a dog,
and go round about the city.
15 Let them wander up and down for meat, and grudge if they be not
satisfied.

C. THE SONG OF PRAISE AND THANKSGIVING TO GOD

16 But I will sing of thy power; yea, I will sing aloud of thy mercy in the
morning: for thou hast been my defence and refuge in the day of my
trouble.
17 Unto thee, O my strength, will I sing: for God *is* my defence, *and* the
God of my mercy.

☆**59:16** 2 Sam 22:3; Ps 21:13; 46:1; 101:1
59:17 Ps 59:9, 10

I. A PRAYER FOR ISRAEL'S DELIVERANCE

A. ISRAEL'S DANGER

To the chief Musician upon Shushan-eduth, Michtam of David, to teach; when he strove with Aram-naharaim and with Aram-zobah, when Joab returned, and smote of Edom in the valley of salt twelve thousand

60 O GOD, thou hast cast us off, thou hast scattered us, thou hast
been displeased; O turn thyself to us again.
2 Thou hast made the earth to tremble; thou hast broken it: heal the
breaches thereof; for it shaketh.
3 Thou hast shewed thy people hard things: thou hast made us to drink
the wine of astonishment.
4 Thou hast given a banner to them that fear thee, that it may be
displayed because of the truth. Se'lah.
5 That thy beloved may be delivered; save *with* thy right hand, and hear
me.

☆**60:1** Ps 44:9; 79:5; 80:3
60:2 2 Chron 7:14; Ps 18:7; Isa 30:26
60:3 Ps 66:12
☆**60:4** Ps 11:12; 13:2; 17:7; 20:5

B. THE CLAIM OF GOD'S PROMISE

6 God hath spoken in his holiness; I will rejoice, I will divide She'chem,
and mete out the valley of Suc'coth.
7 Gilead *is* mine, and Ma-nas'seh *is* mine; E'phra-im also *is* the strength
of mine head; Judah *is* my lawgiver;
8 Moab *is* my washpot; over Edom will I cast out my shoe: Philistia,
triumph thou because of me.

60:6 Gen 33:17; 49:10; Josh 13:31; 17:7; Ps 89:35
60:8 2 Sam 8:1, 2, 14

C. THE PETITION FOR DIVINE ASSISTANCE

9 Who will bring me *into* the strong city? who will lead me into Edom?
10 *Wilt* not thou, O God, *which* hadst cast us off? and *thou,* O God, *which*
didst not go out with our armies?
11 Give us help from trouble: for vain *is* the help of man.
12 Through God we shall do valiantly: for he *it is that* shall tread down
our enemies.

60:9 Ps 44:9
60:11 Ps 146:3
☆**60:12** Num 24:15–19; Ps 44:5; 118:16; Isa 63:3

59:16 In the midst of his distress David would sing his song of praise to God. He would sing out loud when the morning dawns and so fit himself for the events of that new day.

60:1ff This Psalm apparently was penned after David's mighty victories over the Syrians and Edomites. His kingship has reached its highest point. David is as devout in prosperity as he was in adversity. He speaks of his prayers which not only were offered, but were abundantly answered. This is a national, not a personal, Psalm.

60:4 *that it may be displayed because of the truth,* i.e., "all who love truth will rally to it."†

60:12 However valiantly David and his people fight, the

I. IN THE SHELTER OF GOD'S WINGS

A. GOD, THE PSALMIST'S REFUGE

To the chief Musician upon Neginah, A Psalm of David

61:1☆ Ps 64:1; 86:6
61:2 Ps 18:2; 77:3; 94:22
61:3 Ps 62:7; Prov 18:10
61:4 Ps 17:8; 23:6; 27:4; 91:4

61 HEAR my cry, O God; attend unto my prayer.
2From the end of the earth will I cry unto thee, when my heart is overwhelmed: lead me to the rock *that* is higher than I.
3For thou hast been a shelter for me, *and* a strong tower from the enemy.
4I will abide in thy tabernacle for ever: I will trust in the covert of thy wings. Se'lah.

B. PRAISE TO GOD FOR HEARING HIS VOWS

61:5 Ps 56:12; 86:11; Mal 2:5; 4:2
61:6 Ps 21:4
61:7 Ps 40:11; 41:12
61:8 Judg 5:3; Ps 30:4; 65:1; 71:22

5For thou, O God, hast heard my vows: thou hast given *me* the heritage of those that fear thy name.
6Thou wilt prolong the king's life: *and* his years as many generations.
7He shall abide before God for ever: O prepare mercy and truth, *which* may preserve him.
8So will I sing praise unto thy name for ever, that I may daily perform my vows.

I. FAITH WAITS ON GOD THE ROCK

To the chief Musician, to Jeduthun, A Psalm of David

62:1☆ Ps 33:20; 37:39
62:2 Ps 59:17; 89:26
62:3 Ps 28:3; 55:21

62 TRULY my soul waiteth upon God: from him *cometh* my salvation.
2He only *is* my rock and my salvation; *he is* my defence; I shall not be greatly moved.
3How long will ye imagine mischief against a man? ye shall be slain all of you: as a bowing wall *shall ye be, and as* a tottering fence.
4They only consult to cast *him* down from his excellency: they delight in lies: they bless with their mouth, but they curse inwardly. Se'lah.

II. FAITH REFUSES TO FEAR

5My soul, wait thou only upon God; for my expectation *is* from him.
6He only *is* my rock and my salvation: *he is* my defence; I shall not be moved.

III. THE EXHORTATION TO TRUST GOD ALL THE TIME

62:7 Ps 46:1
62:8 Ps 37:5; 52:8; Isa 26:4; Lam 2:19
62:9 Isa 40:15

7In God *is* my salvation and my glory: the rock of my strength, *and* my refuge, *is* in God.
8Trust in him at all times; ye people, pour out your heart before him: God *is* a refuge for us. Se'lah.
9Surely men of low degree *are* vanity, *and* men of high degree *are* a lie: to be laid in the balance, they *are* altogether *lighter* than vanity.

---

battle is the Lord's, not theirs. Every victory, as well as all valor, are God's gifts, and these trophies shall be laid at God's feet and for his glory.

61:1ff Like many others, this Psalm begins with a troubled heart that finds its expression in tears and prayers but ends with songs of praise. Probably David had been in flight either from Saul or from Absalom, and this experience brought him closer to God and provided encouragement for singing songs in the night.

62:1ff This Psalm is devoted to faith which is tried, the confidence of faith in God in the midst of the trial, and an exhortation for faith that is called upon to persevere. It appears to be a general treatment of a theme for which we have no knowledge of any particular difficulty which caused it to be written.

10 Trust not in oppression, and become not vain in robbery: if riches increase, set not your heart *upon them.*
11 God hath spoken once; twice have I heard this; that power *belongeth* unto God.
12 Also unto thee, O Lord, *belongeth* mercy: for thou renderest to every man according to his work.

62:10 Ps 49:6; Isa 30:12, 13; 61:8; Mk 10:24; Lk 12:15; 1 Tim 6:10
62:12 Ps 86:5; 103:8; 130:7; 1 Cor 3:8

I. THE PRAYER OF THE THIRSTY SOUL

A. DAVID'S THIRST FOR GOD

A Psalm of David, when he was in the wilderness of Judah

63 O GOD, thou *art* my God; early will I seek thee: my soul thirsteth for thee, my flesh longeth for thee in a dry and thirsty land, where no water is;
2 To see thy power and thy glory, so *as* I have seen thee in the sanctuary.
3 Because thy lovingkindness *is* better than life, my lips shall praise thee.
4 Thus will I bless thee while I live: I will lift up my hands in thy name.
5 My soul shall be satisfied as *with* marrow and fatness; and my mouth shall praise *thee* with joyful lips:

☆**63:1** Ps 42:2; 84:2; 143:6; Mt 5:6
63:2 Ps 27:4
63:3 Ps 69:16
63:4 Ps 28:2; 104:33; 146:2
63:5 Ps 36:8; 71:23

B. GOD HELPS THOSE WHO THIRST FOR HIM

6 When I remember thee upon my bed, *and* meditate on thee in the *night* watches.
7 Because thou hast been my help, therefore in the shadow of thy wings will I rejoice.
8 My soul followeth hard after thee: thy right hand upholdeth me.
9 But those *that* seek my soul, to destroy *it,* shall go into the lower parts of the earth.
10 They shall fall by the sword: they shall be a portion for foxes.
11 But the king shall rejoice in God; every one that sweareth by him shall glory: but the mouth of them that speak lies shall be stopped.

☆**63:6** Ps 4:4; 16:7; 119:55
63:7 Ps 17:8
63:8 Num 32:12; Ps 18:35
63:9 Ps 40:14
63:10 Ezek 35:4, 5
63:11 Job 5:16; Ps 21:1; 107:42

I. A PRAYER FOR HELP FROM SLANDERERS

A. THE COMPLAINT OF THE PSALMIST

To the chief Musician, A Psalm of David

64 HEAR my voice, O God, in my prayer: preserve my life from fear of the enemy.
2 Hide me from the secret counsel of the wicked; from the insurrection of the workers of iniquity:
3 Who whet their tongue like a sword, *and* bend *their bows to shoot* their arrows, *even* bitter words:

☆**64:1** Ps 56:6; 59:2; 140:1
64:3 Ps 140:3

63:1ff *Just as Paul wrote some of his finest prose in* prison, so David wrote some of his finest Psalms in the wilderness when he was fleeing and desolate. Psalm 63 is an optimistic paean of praise from a soul that finds its best refuge from the heat of the day and the wants of the wilderness under the shadow of God's wings.

63:6 We must not simply think about God; we must meditate on him, not transiently but constantly. David may have been in exile and slept on the ground or in different beds every night. But whether he slept on the ground with a stone for a pillow or on a bed, his thoughts centered on his God who was with him. He also spoke of *night watches,* which probably refers to those kept at the tabernacle by the Levites and in which he had participated. Special times of intense concentration and praise of God benefit the soul.

64:1ff This is the Psalm of one who has enemies, persecutors, and slanderers whose darts have penetrated his very soul. What occasioned the Psalm is not known, but we can suspect that this and other Psalms like it reflect the fulfillment of divine judgment rendered against David for his sin with Bath-sheba. The consequence of that transgression was that he would smart for his sin all the days of his life. And he did.

64:4 Ps 10:8; 11:2
4That they may shoot in secret at the perfect: suddenly do they shoot at
him, and fear not.

64:5 Job 22:13 Ps 140:5
5They encourage themselves *in* an evil matter: they commune of laying
snares privily; they say, Who shall see them?

64:6☆ Ps 49:11
6They search out iniquities; they accomplish a diligent search: both the
inward *thought* of every one *of them,* and the heart, *is* deep.

B. GOD'S JUDGMENT OF THE WICKED

64:7 Ps 7:12, 13
7But God shall shoot at them *with* an arrow; suddenly shall they be
wounded.

64:8 Job 22:19 Ps 9:3 Prov 18:6, 7 Jer 18:16
8So they shall make their own tongue to fall upon themselves: all that see
them shall flee away.

64:9 Ps 40:3
9And all men shall fear, and shall declare the work of God; for they shall
wisely consider his doing.

64:10☆ Ps 11:1; 32:11
10The righteous shall be glad in the LORD, and shall trust in him; and all
the upright in heart shall glory.

I. GOD'S POWER AND GOODNESS

A. PRAISE TO GOD WHO ANSWERS PRAYER

To the chief Musician, A Psalm and Song of David

65:1☆ Ps 86:9; 116:18 145:21
65 PRAISE waiteth for thee, O God, in Sion: and unto thee shall the
vow be performed.
2O thou that hearest prayer, unto thee shall all flesh come.

65:3 Ps 38:4; 40:12 79:9 Heb 9:14
3Iniquities prevail against me: *as for* our transgressions, thou shalt purge
them away.

65:4☆ Ps 33:12; 36:8 84:4
4Blessed *is the man whom* thou choosest, and causest to approach *unto*
thee, that he may dwell in thy courts: we shall be satisfied with the goodness
of thy house, *even* of thy holy temple.

B. THE GOODNESS OF GOD'S CREATIVE POWER AND BOUNTY

65:5☆ Ps 45:4; 48:10 85:4
5*By* terrible things in righteousness wilt thou answer us, O God of our
salvation; *who art* the confidence of all the ends of the earth, and of them
that are afar off *upon* the sea:

65:6 Ps 93:1; 95:4
6Which by his strength setteth fast the mountains; *being* girded with
power:

65:7 Ps 89:9 Isa 17:12, 13 Mt 8:26
7Which stilleth the noise of the seas, the noise of their waves, and the
tumult of the people.

65:8 Ps 139:9, 10 Isa 24:16
8They also that dwell in the uttermost parts are afraid at thy tokens: thou
makest the outgoings of the morning and evening to rejoice.

65:9 Lev 26:4 Job 5:10 Ps 46:4 104:13, 14, 24
9Thou visitest the earth, and waterest it: thou greatly enrichest it with the
river of God, *which* is full of water: thou preparest them corn, when thou
hast so provided for it.

64:6 *the inward thought of every one of them, and the heart, is deep,* i.e., "they spend long hours with their endless evil thoughts and plans."†

64:10 Again and again David in the Psalms ends with a note of rejoicing and praise. His undying optimism derives from his knowledge of God's grace, which *justifies the worst of men through faith* and guarantees that their end will be good.

65:1ff The chief end of man is to glorify God. He does this in part by acknowledging the power and goodness of God, manifested in nature and over man. The years are crowned by the divine bounty so that flocks and valleys shout and sing together for joy. Men should do the same.

65:4 Access to God is a privilege of the saints made possible by the Holy Spirit through the work of Christ (Eph. 2:18). Believers are to come to God boldly and expect to receive mercy and help. The universal priesthood of all believers means that we need no intermediaries who stand between us and God. We have immediate and direct access to him.

65:5 *By terrible things in righteousness wilt thou answer us,* i.e., "You will defend us from our enemies."†

10 Thou waterest the ridges thereof abundantly: thou settlest the furrows
thereof: thou makest it soft with showers: thou blessest the springing
thereof.
11 Thou crownest the year with thy goodness; and thy paths drop fatness.
12 They drop *upon* the pastures of the wilderness: and the little hills rejoice
on every side.
13 The pastures are clothed with flocks; the valleys also are covered over
with corn; they shout for joy, they also sing.

65:10 Deut 32:2; Ps 72:6
65:11 Job 38:26, 27; Joel 2:22
65:13 Ps 98:8; 144:13; Isa 30:23; 55:12

I. SINGING GOD'S PRAISES
A. PRAISE FOR THE DELIVERANCE OF ISRAEL

To the chief Musician, A Song or Psalm

66 MAKE a joyful noise unto God, all ye lands:
2 Sing forth the honour of his name: make his praise glorious.
3 Say unto God, How terrible *art thou in* thy works! through the greatness
of thy power shall thine enemies submit themselves unto thee.
4 All the earth shall worship thee, and shall sing unto thee; they shall sing
to thy name. Se'lah.
5 Come and see the works of God: *he is* terrible *in his* doing toward the
children of men.
6 He turned the sea into dry *land:* they went through the flood on foot:
there did we rejoice in him.
7 He ruleth by his power for ever; his eyes behold the nations: let not the
rebellious exalt themselves. Se'lah.
8 O bless our God, ye people, and make the voice of his praise to be
heard:
9 Which holdeth our soul in life, and suffereth not our feet to be moved.
10 For thou, O God, hast proved us: thou hast tried us, as silver is tried.
11 Thou broughtest us into the net; thou laidst affliction upon our loins.
12 Thou hast caused men to ride over our heads; we went through fire and
through water: but thou broughtest us out into a wealthy *place.*

☆**66:1** Ps 98:4; 100:1
66:2 Ps 81:1
66:3 Ps 18:44; 47:2; 65:5
66:4 Ps 22:27; 67:4; 86:9
66:5 Ps 46:8
66:6 Ex 14:21; Josh 3:15, 16; Ps 105:43
66:7 Ps 11:4; 145:13
66:8 Ps 98:4
66:9 Ps 30:3; 121:3, 4
66:10 Ps 17:3; Zech 13:9; Mal 3:3; 1 Pet 1:7
66:11 Lam 1:13
☆**66:12** Ps 18:19; Isa 43:2; 51:23

B. PERSONAL PRAISE OF THE PSALMIST FOR GOD'S HELP

13 I will go into thy house with burnt offerings: I will pay thee my vows,
14 Which my lips have uttered, and my mouth hath spoken, when I was in
trouble.
15 I will offer unto thee burnt sacrifices of fatlings, with the incense of
rams; I will offer bullocks with goats. Se'lah.
16 Come *and* hear, all ye that fear God, and I will declare what he hath
done for my soul.
17 I cried unto him with my mouth, and he was extolled with my tongue.
18 If I regard iniquity in my heart, the Lord will not hear *me:*
19 *But* verily God hath heard *me;* he hath attended to the voice of my
prayer.
20 Blessed *be* God, which hath not turned away my prayer, nor his mercy
from me.

66:13 Ps 22:25; Jer 17:26
66:15 Num 6:14; Ps 51:19
66:16 Ps 34:11; 71:15, 24
☆**66:18** Job 36:21; Ps 18:41; Prov 1:28; 28:9; Isa 1:15; Jas 4:3
66:19 Ps 116:1, 2
66:20 Ps 22:24; 68:35

66:1ff Thanksgiving is the main theme of this Psalm. Let the men of Israel thank God for national deliverances. Indeed let all lands and all the earth praise the divine name. Let every individual who knows God and has been helped by him bring praise to his name for what he has provided for them.

66:12 *Thou hast caused men to ride over our heads,* i.e., "You sent troops to ride across our broken bodies."†

66:18 Unconfessed sin (regarding iniquity in the heart) is one of the reasons believers do not obtain answers to their petitions. The first question to be asked when one prays is: "Is there any known, unconfessed sin in my life?"

I. A MISSIONARY PSALM

To the chief Musician on Neginoth, A Psalm or Song

67 GOD be merciful unto us, and bless us; *and* cause his face to shine
upon us; Se'lah.
2 That thy way may be known upon earth, thy saving health among all
nations.
3 Let the people praise thee, O God; let all the people praise thee.
4 O let the nations be glad and sing for joy: for thou shalt judge the
people righteously, and govern the nations upon earth. Se'lah.
5 Let the people praise thee, O God; let all the people praise thee.
6 *Then* shall the earth yield her increase; *and* God, *even* our own God,
shall bless us.
7 God shall bless us; and all the ends of the earth shall fear him.

67:1☆ Num 6:25; Ps 4:6; 80:3, 7, 19
67:2 Acts 18:25; Tit 2:11
67:3 Ps 66:4
67:4 Ps 96:10, 13; 98:9
67:5 Ps 67:3
67:6 Lev 26:4; Ps 22:27; 115:12; Ezek 34:27; Zech 8:12

I. THE GOD OF THE UNIVERSE

A. GOD DELIVERS ISRAEL FROM EGYPT

To the chief Musician, A Psalm or Song of David

68 LET God arise, let his enemies be scattered: let them also that hate
him flee before him.
2 As smoke is driven away, *so* drive *them* away: as wax melteth before the
fire, *so* let the wicked perish at the presence of God.
3 But let the righteous be glad; let them rejoice before God: yea, let them
exceedingly rejoice.
4 Sing unto God, sing praises to his name: extol him that rideth upon the
heavens by his name JAH, and rejoice before him.
5 A father of the fatherless, and a judge of the widows, *is* God in his holy
habitation.
6 God setteth the solitary in families: he bringeth out those which are
bound with chains: but the rebellious dwell in a dry *land.*

68:1☆ Num 10:35; Ps 12:5
68:2 Ps 37:20; Isa 9:18; Hos 13:3; Mic 1:4
68:3 Ps 32:11; 97:12
68:4 Ps 40:3; 68:33
68:5 Deut 10:18; Ps 146:9
68:6 Ps 69:33; 107:10, 14, 34, 40; Acts 12:7; 16:26

B. GOD SUSTAINS ISRAEL IN THE WILDERNESS

7 O God, when thou wentest forth before thy people, when thou didst
march through the wilderness; Se'lah:
8 The earth shook, the heavens also dropped at the presence of God: *even*
Si'nai itself *was moved* at the presence of God, the God of Israel.
9 Thou, O God, didst send a plentiful rain, whereby thou didst confirm
thine inheritance, when it was weary.
10 Thy congregation hath dwelt therein: thou, O God, hast prepared of
thy goodness for the poor.

68:7 Ex 13:21; Judg 5:4
68:8☆ Ex 19:18; Judg 5:4, 5; Ps 77:16–18
68:9 Deut 11:11; Ps 65:9; 78:24; 107:9; Ezek 34:26

C. GOD GIVES CANAANLAND TO ISRAEL

11 The Lord gave the word: great *was* the company of those that published
it.

68:11 Ex 15:20; Judg 5:19, 30; 1 Sam 18:6; 30:24

67:1ff This Psalm and all of Scripture witnesses to the missionary nature of biblical faith. God wishes to bless all the nations of the earth and desires that his glorious salvation be proclaimed to all people irrespective of *race, color, or creed.*

68:1ff This Psalm seems to be based on the bringing of the ark from the house of Obed-edom to the city of Jerusalem (2 Sam. 6:12). It is historically oriented and speaks of God's work of delivering his people from Egypt, his support of them in the wilderness, the conquest of Canaan and the establishment of the kingdom—with Jerusalem as its capital, where God is established in his sanctuary. It ends with praise to the God of the whole earth.

68:8 No people and no nation has seen the manifested presence of the glory of God or heard the divine voice as did Israel. The earth itself shook and the mountains moved. The commandments of God dropped as rain from heaven to anoint men and earth. This glorious God was Israel's God.

12 Kings of armies did flee apace: and she that tarried at home divided the
spoil.
13 Though ye have lien among the pots, *yet shall ye be as* the wings of a
dove covered with silver, and her feathers with yellow gold.
14 When the Almighty scattered kings in it, it was *white* as snow in
Sal'mon.

☆68:12
☆68:14 Josh 10:10

D. GOD IS THE GOD OF MOUNT ZION

15 The hill of God *is as* the hill of Ba'shan; an high hill *as* the hill of
Ba'shan.
16 Why leap ye, ye high hills? *this is* the hill *which* God desireth to dwell
in; yea, the LORD will dwell *in it* for ever.
17 The chariots of God *are* twenty thousand, *even* thousands of angels: the
Lord *is* among them, *as in* Si'nai, in the holy *place.*
18 Thou hast ascended on high, thou hast led captivity captive: thou hast
received gifts for men; yea, *for* the rebellious also, that the LORD God might
dwell *among them.*

68:15 Deut 12:4, 5; Ps 36:6; 87:1, 2
68:17 Deut 33:2; 2 Kgs 6:17; Hab 3:8; Dan 7:10
☆68:18 Ps 47:5; Eph 4:8; 1 Tim 1:13

E. GOD IS THE GOD OF SALVATION

19 Blessed *be* the Lord, *who* daily loadeth us *with benefits, even* the God of
our salvation. Se'lah.
20 *He that is* our God *is* the God of salvation; and unto GOD the Lord
belong the issues from death.
21 But God shall wound the head of his enemies, *and* the hairy scalp of
such an one as goeth on still in his trespasses.
22 The Lord said, I will bring again from Ba'shan, I will bring *my people*
again from the depths of the sea:
23 That thy foot may be dipped in the blood of *thine* enemies, *and* the
tongue of thy dogs in the same.

68:19 Ps 55:22; 65:5; Isa 46:4
☆68:20 Ps 56:13
68:21 Ps 110:6; Heb 3:13
68:22 Amos 9:1–3
68:23 1 Kgs 21:19; Ps 58:10; Jer 15:3

F. GOD IS THE GOD OF THE SANCTUARY

1. The Temple Procession

24 They have seen thy goings, O God; *even* the goings of my God, my
King, in the sanctuary.
25 The singers went before, the players on instruments *followed* after;
among *them were* the damsels playing with timbrels.
26 Bless ye God in the congregations, *even* the Lord, from the fountain of
Israel.
27 There *is* little Benjamin *with* their ruler, the princes of Judah *and* their
council, the princes of Zeb'u-lun, *and* the princes of Naph'ta-li.

☆68:24 Ps 63:2
68:25 Ex 15:20; 1 Chron 13:8
68:26 Deut 33:28; Ps 22:22, 23
68:27 Judg 5:13, 14; 1 Sam 9:21

2. The Kings of the Earth Acknowledge God

28 Thy God hath commanded thy strength: strengthen, O God, that which
thou hast wrought for us.

68:28 Ps 29:11; 44:4

68:12 *at home,* i.e., "among the sheepfolds." *she . . . divideth the spoil.* The victorious army brought back the spoils of battle which were then shared by the wives of the soldiers.

68:14 *Salmon* ("Zalmon"), a mountain near Shechem, where God may have used a snowstorm to rout Israel's enemies (Judg. 9:48).

68:18 *received gifts for men,* see Eph. 4:8.

68:20 If, after the fall of Adam, God had absented himself from earth, there could and would have been no salvation. The presence of God makes eternal salvation possible. Whoever has him for their God has salvation, and this means that death has been conquered. God has altered the property of death to make resurrection possible. Death, man's last enemy, shall be destroyed.

68:24 Whatever the place of worship, it becomes the sanctuary for God Almighty. When we come, we should enter its gates prayerfully and silently. The word from Habakkuk should be observed at all times: "But the LORD is in his holy temple: let all the earth keep silence before him" (2:20). And when we speak, let it be in songs of praise or for proclaiming of the Word of God.

68:29 Ps 72:10; Isa 18:7
68:30☆ Ps 89:10
68:31 Isa 19:19, 21; Zeph 3:10

29 Because of thy temple at Jerusalem shall kings bring presents unto thee.
30 Rebuke the company of spearmen, the multitude of the bulls, with the
calves of the people, *till every one* submit himself with pieces of silver:
scatter thou the people *that* delight in war.
31 Princes shall come out of Egypt; E-thi-o′pi-a shall soon stretch out her
hands unto God.

3. Singing Praise to the God of the Whole Earth

68:32 Ps 102:21, 22
68:33 Deut 10:14; Ps 18:10; 29:4; 104:3
68:34 Ps 150:1
68:35 Deut 10:17; Ps 29:11; 47:2; Isa 40:29; 2 Cor 1:3, 4

32 Sing unto God, ye kingdoms of the earth; O sing praises unto the Lord;
Se′lah:
33 To him that rideth upon the heavens of heavens, *which were* of old; lo,
he doth send out his voice, *and that* a mighty voice.
34 Ascribe ye strength unto God: his excellency *is* over Israel, and his
strength *is* in the clouds.
35 O God, *thou art* terrible out of thy holy places: the God of Israel *is* he
that giveth strength and power unto *his* people. Blessed *be* God.

I. A MESSIANIC PSALM: THE SUFFERING SERVANT

A. THE PSALMIST'S PLIGHT AND PRAYER

To the chief Musician upon Shoshannim, A Psalm of David

69:1☆ Ps 32:6; Jon 2:3
69:3 Ps 6:6; 119:82, 123; Isa 38:14
69:4 Ps 35:11; 59:3; Jer 15:10; Jn 15:25
69:5 Ps 44:21
69:6 2 Sam 12:14
69:7 Isa 50:6; Jer 15:15
69:8 Job 19:13–15; Ps 31:11; 38:11
69:9☆ Ps 119:139; Jn 2:17
69:10 Ps 35:13
69:11 1 Kgs 20:31; Ps 35:13
69:12 Job 30:9

69 SAVE me, O God; for the waters are come in unto *my* soul.
2 I sink in deep mire, where *there is* no standing: I am come into
deep waters, where the floods overflow me.
3 I am weary of my crying: my throat is dried: mine eyes fail while I wait
for my God.
4 They that hate me without a cause are more than the hairs of mine head:
they that would destroy me, *being* mine enemies wrongfully, are mighty:
then I restored *that* which I took not away.
5 O God, thou knowest my foolishness; and my sins are not hid from thee.
6 Let not them that wait on thee, O Lord GOD of hosts, be ashamed for
my sake: let not those that seek thee be confounded for my sake, O God of
Israel.
7 Because for thy sake I have borne reproach; shame hath covered my
face.
8 I am become a stranger unto my brethren, and an alien unto my
mother's children.
9 For the zeal of thine house hath eaten me up; and the reproaches of
them that reproached thee are fallen upon me.
10 When I wept, *and chastened* my soul with fasting, that was to my
reproach.
11 I made sackcloth also my garment; and I became a proverb to them.
12 They that sit in the gate speak against me; and I *was* the song of the
drunkards.

68:30 *till every one submit himself with pieces of silver,* i.e., "submissive tax in hand." An alternate rendering of this could be, "Trample upon those who lust after the tribute of smaller nations, and who delight in aggressive wars."†

69:1ff Some messianic implications are to be found in this Psalm. Obviously its first application has to do with some experience in the life of David. But it also has typical reference to Jesus, for Matt. 27:34, 48 constitutes a literal fulfillment of 69:21. But the entire Psalm does not refer to Jesus; David, in 69:5, is confessing his sins, and Jesus did not sin. Yet all representations of Jesus in the Scriptures are valuable in certain respects, but not in all, for every human being who typified Jesus fell short of the One they typified.

69:9 *the zeal of thine house hath eaten me up,* i.e., "Zeal for thy house has consumed me" (RSV, NASB)—quoted by Jesus in John 2:17.

B. THE CONTINUING PRAYER FOR DIVINE HELP

13 But as for me, my prayer *is* unto thee, O LORD, *in* an acceptable time:
O God, in the multitude of thy mercy hear me, in the truth of thy salvation.
14 Deliver me out of the mire, and let me not sink: let me be delivered
from them that hate me, and out of the deep waters.
15 Let not the waterflood overflow me, neither let the deep swallow me up,
and let not the pit shut her mouth upon me.
16 Hear me, O LORD; for thy lovingkindness *is* good: turn unto me
according to the multitude of thy tender mercies.
17 And hide not thy face from thy servant; for I am in trouble: hear me
speedily.
18 Draw nigh unto my soul, *and* redeem it: deliver me because of mine
enemies.
19 Thou hast known my reproach, and my shame, and my dishonour:
mine adversaries *are* all before thee.

69:13 Ps 32:6; Isa 49:8; 2 Cor 6:2
69:14 Ps 144:7
69:15 Num 16:33; Ps 124:4, 5
69:16 Ps 25:16; 51:1; 63:3; 106:45; 109:21
69:17 Ps 27:9; 31:9; 143:7
69:18 Ps 49:15; 119:134
69:19 Ps 22:6, 7; Isa 53:3

C. THE PRAYER OF IMPRECATION

20 Reproach hath broken my heart; and I am full of heaviness: and I
looked *for some* to take pity, but *there was* none; and for comforters, but I
found none.
21 They gave me also gall for my meat; and in my thirst they gave me
vinegar to drink.
22 Let their table become a snare before them: and *that which should have*
been for *their* welfare, *let it become* a trap.
23 Let their eyes be darkened, that they see not; and make their loins
continually to shake.
24 Pour out thine indignation upon them, and let thy wrathful anger take
hold of them.
25 Let their habitation be desolate; *and* let none dwell in their tents.
26 For they persecute *him* whom thou hast smitten; and they talk to the
grief of those whom thou hast wounded.
27 Add iniquity unto their iniquity: and let them not come into thy
righteousness.
28 Let them be blotted out of the book of the living, and not be written
with the righteous.

69:20 Jer 23:9
69:21 Deut 29:18; Mt 27:48; Jn 19:29
☆**69:22** 1. Thess 5:3
☆**69:23** Isa 6:9, 10; Dan 5:6
☆**69:24** Jer 10:25; Ezek 20:8
☆**69:25** Lk 13:35; Acts 1:20
☆**69:26** 2 Chron 28:9; Isa 53:4
☆**69:27** Neh 4:5; Rom 1:28
☆**69:28** Ex 32:33; Lk 10:20; Rev 3:5; 13:8; 20:15

D. THE PSALMIST'S PRAISE TO GOD

29 But I *am* poor and sorrowful: let thy salvation, O God, set me up on
high.
30 I will praise the name of God with a song, and will magnify him with
thanksgiving.
31 *This* also shall please the LORD better than an ox *or* bullock that hath
horns and hoofs.
32 The humble shall see *this, and* be glad: and your heart shall live that
seek God.
33 For the LORD heareth the poor, and despiseth not his prisoners.
34 Let the heaven and earth praise him, the seas, and every thing that
moveth therein.

69:29 Ps 59:1; 70:5
69:30 Ps 28:7; 50:14, 15
69:31 Ps 50:13, 14
69:32 Ps 22:26; 34:2
69:33 Ps 12:5
69:34 Ps 148:1–13; Isa 44:23; 49:13

69:22–28 These verses are imprecatory, but one commentator has observed that they are not a prayer of David uttered to place a curse on the enemies. Rather, they are prophecies of the destruction of the persecutors of Jesus (for this is a messianic Psalm). Its larger reference has to do with the Jewish nation, which rejected the Messiah. The imprecations here were fulfilled when Jerusalem was destroyed in A.D. 70 by the forces of Rome under Titus and Vespasian. In his history of the Jews, Josephus describes the awful conditions surrounding the siege and the dispersion of the Jews when the war ended.

69:35 Ps 147:2 Isa 44:26 Obad 17 **69:36** Ps 25:13; 27:29 102:28

35 For God will save Zion, and will build the cities of Judah: that they
may dwell there, and have it in possession.
36 The seed also of his servants shall inherit it: and they that love his name
shall dwell therein.

I. A PETITION FOR HELP AGAINST PERSECUTORS

To the chief Musician, A Psalm of David, to bring to remembrance

70:1 Ps 40:13–17

70 *MAKE haste,* O God, to deliver me; make haste to help me, O
LORD.
2 Let them be ashamed and confounded that seek after my soul: let them
be turned backward, and put to confusion, that desire my hurt.
3 Let them be turned back for a reward of their shame that say, Aha, aha.
4 Let all those that seek thee rejoice and be glad in thee: and let such as
love thy salvation say continually, Let God be magnified.

70:5 Ps 141:1

5 But I *am* poor and needy: make haste unto me, O God: thou *art* my help
and my deliverer; O LORD, make no tarrying.

I. THE SONG AND PRAYER OF AN AGED SAINT

A. HIS PRAYER FOR GOD'S HELP

71:1☆ Ps 31:1–3

71 IN thee, O LORD, do I put my trust: let me never be put to
confusion.
2 Deliver me in thy righteousness, and cause me to escape: incline thine
ear unto me, and save me.

71:3 Deut 33:27 Ps 18:2; 44:4 **71:4** Ps 140:1, 4 **71:5** Ps 22:9–11; 39:7 Jer 17:7, 13, 17 **71:6** Ps 22:9, 10 34:1 Isa 46:3 **71:7** Ps 61:3 **71:8** Ps 63:5 **71:9**☆ Ps 92:14 Isa 46:4 **71:10** Ps 31:13 Mt 27:1 **71:11** Ps 3:2; 7:2 **71:12** Ps 22:9–11 35:33; 70:5 **71:13** Ps 35:4, 26 109:29

3 Be thou my strong habitation, whereunto I may continually resort: thou
hast given commandment to save me; for thou *art* my rock and my fortress.
4 Deliver me, O my God, out of the hand of the wicked, out of the hand
of the unrighteous and cruel man.
5 For thou *art* my hope, O Lord GOD: *thou art* my trust from my youth.
6 By thee have I been holden up from the womb: thou art he that took me
out of my mother's bowels: my praise *shall be* continually of thee.
7 I am as a wonder unto many; but thou *art* my strong refuge.
8 Let my mouth be filled *with* thy praise *and with* thy honour all the day.
9 Cast me not off in the time of old age; forsake me not when my strength
faileth.
10 For mine enemies speak against me; and they that lay wait for my soul
take counsel together,
11 Saying, God hath forsaken him: persecute and take him; for *there is*
none to deliver *him.*
12 O God, be not far from me: O my God, make haste for my help.
13 Let them be confounded *and* consumed that are adversaries to my soul;
let them be covered *with* reproach and dishonour that seek my hurt.

B. HIS SONG OF PRAISE FOR THE CERTAINTY OF DELIVERANCE

71:14 Ps 130:7 **71:15** Ps 35:28; 40:5 96:2

14 But I will hope continually, and will yet praise thee more and more.
15 My mouth shall shew forth thy righteousness *and* thy salvation all the
day; for I know not the numbers *thereof.*

71:1ff This Psalm is for general use. It was written *toward the end of the life of the author, who may have* been David. Afflictions attend later life as well as youth; elderly people have as much need as ever for the help of God the deliverer. It ends as so many Psalms do, with the assurance that God has helped in bygone days and is to be praised for past and present mercies.

71:9 He who was brought forth from his mother's womb by God (71:6) need not fear that God will desert him when age overtakes him and death awaits him. Body, mind, sight, voice, and limbs begin to fail but the God of the aged is not far away. The holy angels gather to take the soul into the presence of God; and when the river of death is crossed, time will be replaced by eternity.

16 I will go in the strength of the Lord GOD: I will make mention of thy
righteousness, *even* of thine only.
17 O God, thou hast taught me from my youth: and hitherto have I
declared thy wondrous works.
18 Now also when I am old and greyheaded, O God, forsake me not; until
I have shewed thy strength unto *this* generation, *and* thy power to every one
that is to come.
19 Thy righteousness also, O God, *is* very high, who hast done great
things: O God, who *is* like unto thee!
20 *Thou,* which hast shewed me great and sore troubles, shalt quicken me
again, and shalt bring me up again from the depths of the earth.
21 Thou shalt increase my greatness, and comfort me on every side.
22 I will also praise thee with the psaltery, *even* thy truth, O my God: unto
thee will I sing with the harp, O thou Holy One of Israel.
23 My lips shall greatly rejoice when I sing unto thee; and my soul, which
thou hast redeemed.
24 My tongue also shall talk of thy righteousness all the day long: for they
are confounded, for they are brought unto shame, that seek my hurt.

71:16 Ps 106:2
☆**71:17** Deut 4:5; 6:7 Ps 26:7
71:18 Ps 22:31 78:4, 6
☆**71:19** Deut 3:24 Ps 35:10; 57:10 Lk 1:49
71:20 Ps 23:4; 60:3 119:25 Hos 6:2
71:21 Isa 49:13
71:22 Ps 33:2; 89:18 147:7
71:23 Ps 5:11; 103:4 132:16
71:24 Ps 35:28

I. A PRAYER FOR THE KING (SOLOMON AND JESUS)

A. THE PETITION FOR RIGHTEOUSNESS, POWER, AND PEACE

A Psalm for Solomon

72 GIVE the king thy judgments, O God, and thy righteousness unto
the king's son.
2 He shall judge thy people with righteousness, and thy poor with
judgment.
3 The mountains shall bring peace to the people, and the little hills, by
righteousness.
4 He shall judge the poor of the people, he shall save the children of the
needy, and shall break in pieces the oppressor.

☆**72:1** 1 Kgs 3:9 Ps 24:5
72:2 Ps 82:3 Isa 9:7; 11:2–5
72:3 Isa 9:5, 6 Mic 4:3, 4 Zech 9:10
72:4 Isa 11:4

B. THE PETITION FOR LONG LIFE

5 They shall fear thee as long as the sun and moon endure, throughout all
generations.
6 He shall come down like rain upon the mown grass: as showers *that*
water the earth.
7 In his days shall the righteous flourish; and abundance of peace so long
as the moon endureth.

72:5 Ps 89:36, 37
☆**72:6** Deut 32:2 Ps 65:10 Hos 6:3
72:7 Ps 92:12

C. THE PETITION FOR DOMINION

8 He shall have dominion also from sea to sea, and from the river unto the
ends of the earth.

☆**72:8** Ex 23:31 Zech 9:10

71:17 He who from his youth has known and served God still lives to praise God and testify of his saving grace. All such can be assured that their prayers for the presence, power, and keeping grace of God will be answered. He will not leave nor forsake them.

71:19 At the hour of death and before the saints breathe their last, their parting words will be, "Thou hast done great things." All glory be to such a God!

72:1ff This is a messianic Psalm that finds fulfillment in Jesus the true Messiah and in his kingdom, over which God's ideal King will rule. The Messiah reigns to the ends of the earth; his kingdom is an eternal kingdom that shall extend to "the ends of the earth" (72:8); "all nations shall serve him" (72:11); "his name shall endure forever" (72:17). The King himself is eternal, all powerful, and knows all things. Since what Solomon said goes far beyond any human possibility, it is logical to conclude that its true fulfillment comes in Jesus Christ.

72:6 *He.* The reference seems to look beyond Solomon's son to Jesus the Messiah.

72:8 We can and should pray that Christ will have

72:9 Isa 49:23; Mic 7:17
72:10 Ps 45:12; 68:29; Isa 42:4, 10; 60:6
72:11 Ps 86:9; 138:4; Isa 49:23

9 They that dwell in the wilderness shall bow before him; and his enemies
shall lick the dust.
10 The kings of Tarshish and of the isles shall bring presents: the kings of
She'ba and Se'ba shall offer gifts.
11 Yea, all kings shall fall down before him: all nations shall serve him.

D. THE COMPASSION OF THE KING

72:12 Job 29:12
72:13 Prov 19:17; 28:8
72:14 Ps 116:15

12 For he shall deliver the needy when he crieth; the poor also, and *him*
that hath no helper.
13 He shall spare the poor and needy, and shall save the souls of the
needy.
14 He shall redeem their soul from deceit and violence: and precious shall
their blood be in his sight.

E. THE CERTAINTY OF AN HONORED NAME FOREVER

72:15 Isa 60:6
72:16 Job 5:25
72:17 Gen 12:3; 22:18; Ps 89:36; 135:13; Lk 1:48

15 And he shall live, and to him shall be given of the gold of She'ba:
prayer also shall be made for him continually; *and* daily shall he be praised.
16 There shall be an handful of corn in the earth upon the top of the
mountains; the fruit thereof shall shake like Lebanon: and *they* of the city
shall flourish like grass of the earth.
17 His name shall endure for ever: his name shall be continued as long as
the sun: and *men* shall be blessed in him: all nations shall call him blessed.

F. THE BENEDICTION

72:18☆ Ex 15:11; Ps 41:13; 106:48; 136:4
72:19 Num 14:20, 21; Neh 9:5

18 Blessed *be* the LORD God, the God of Israel, who only doeth wondrous
things.
19 And blessed *be* his glorious name for ever: and let the whole earth be
filled *with* his glory; Amen, and Amen.
20 The prayers of David the son of Jesse are ended.

BOOK III (PSALMS 73—89)

I. THE PROSPERITY OF THE WICKED AND THEIR END

A. ENVYING THE WICKED WHO PROSPER

73:1☆ Ps 24:3, 4; 51:10; Mt 5:8
73:2 Ps 94:18
73:3 Ps 37:1, 7; Prov 23:17, 18; Jer 12:1
73:4☆ Ps 10:5

A Psalm of Asaph

73 TRULY God *is* good to Israel, *even* to such as are of a clean heart.
2 But as for me, my feet were almost gone; my steps had well nigh
slipped.
3 For I was envious at the foolish, *when* I saw the prosperity of the
wicked.
4 For *there are* no bands in their death: but their strength *is* firm.

---

dominion from sea to sea. In principle, this is already true. In actuality it remains to come to pass. This is what we pray for when we say, "Thy kingdom come."

72:18 The Old Testament does not present us with the full-orbed doctrine of the Trinity. But we can safely assert that when we say "blessed be the LORD," we are praising the one God in three persons—the Father, the Son, and the Holy Spirit. Thus Christian churches sing the "Doxology" and the "Gloria Patri," both of which glorify the triune God.

73:1ff Psalms 73–83 carry the name of Asaph in the titles. Asaph was appointed by David over the service of song and by Solomon in the temple service. Whether he wrote these Psalms or whether they are Psalms *for* Asaph we do not know. Psalm 73 speaks of the conflict the psalmist encountered when facing the temptation to envy the prosperity of the wicked. It ends with a note of assurance that God delivers the righteous and allows those whose hearts are far from him to perish.

73:4 *there are no bands in their death,* i.e., "all through life their road is smooth."†

5 They *are* not in trouble *as other* men; neither are they plagued like *other*
men.
6 Therefore pride compasseth them about as a chain; violence covereth
them *as* a garment.
7 Their eyes stand out with fatness: they have more than heart could wish.
8 They are corrupt, and speak wickedly *concerning* oppression: they speak
loftily.
9 They set their mouth against the heavens, and their tongue walketh
through the earth.

73:5 Job 21:9, 10
73:6 Ps 109:18
73:7 Job 15:27, 28
73:8 Ps 1:1; 17:10 Jude 16

B. THE CONFUSION OF THE RIGHTEOUS

10 Therefore his people return hither: and waters of a full *cup* are wrung
out to them.
11 And they say, How doth God know? and is there knowledge in the
most High?
12 Behold, these *are* the ungodly, who prosper in the world; they increase
in riches.
13 Verily I have cleansed my heart *in* vain, and washed my hands in
innocency.
14 For all the day long have I been plagued, and chastened every morning.

73:11 Job 22:13
73:12 Ps 49:6 Jer 49:31 Ezek 23:42
73:13 Job 21:15; 34:9 35:2, 3 Ps 26:6
73:14 Ps 38:5, 6 118:18

C. THE RESOLUTION OF THE PROBLEM

15 If I say, I will speak thus; behold, I should offend *against* the generation
of thy children.
16 When I thought to know this, it *was* too painful for me;
17 Until I went into the sanctuary of God; *then* understood I their end.
18 Surely thou didst set them in slippery places: thou castedst them down
into destruction.
19 How are they *brought* into desolation, as in a moment! they are utterly
consumed with terrors.
20 As a dream when *one* awaketh; *so*, O Lord, when thou awakest, thou
shalt despise their image.

73:16 Eccles 8:16, 17
☆**73:17** Ps 27:4; 77:13
73:18 Ps 36:12
73:19 Num 16:21 Isa 47:11

D. THE END OF THE RIGHTEOUS—DELIVERANCE

21 Thus my heart was grieved, and I was pricked in my reins.
22 So foolish *was* I, and ignorant: I was *as* a beast before thee.
23 Nevertheless I *am* continually with thee: thou hast holden *me* by my
right hand.
24 Thou shalt guide me with thy counsel, and afterward receive me *to*
glory.
25 Whom have I in heaven *but thee?* and *there is* none upon earth *that* I
desire beside thee.
26 My flesh and my heart faileth: *but* God *is* the strength of my heart, and
my portion for ever.
27 For, lo, they that are far from thee shall perish: thou hast destroyed all
them that go a whoring from thee.
28 But *it is* good for me to draw near to God: I have put my trust in the
Lord GOD, that I may declare all thy works.

73:21 Acts 2:37
73:22 Ps 49:20; 92:6 Eccles 3:18
73:23 Ps 16:8
73:24 Gen 5:24 Ps 32:8; 48:14 49:15 Isa 58:11
73:26 Ps 16:5; 38:10 84:2; 119:81
73:27 Ex 34:15 Ps 37:20 Hos 9:1
☆**73:28** Ps 40:5 Heb 10:22 Jas 4:8

73:17 The psalmist cannot understand how to reconcile the prosperity of the wicked with the justice of God. If there is no life after death, there can be no reconciliation of this problem. But when the writer went into God's sanctuary for meditation, instruction, the reading of the Word of God, and prayer, he saw the end of the wicked and knew that they were ripening for ruin.

73:28 Those who draw near to God will find that God draws near to them, but it originates from the fact that God is the divine initiator who makes it possible for us to draw near to him.

I. THE DEVASTATION OF MOUNT ZION

A. THE PRAYER FOR HELP AGAINST THE ENEMY

Maschil of Asaph

74 O GOD, why hast thou cast *us* off for ever? *why* doth thine anger
smoke against the sheep of thy pasture?
2 Remember thy congregation, *which* thou hast purchased of old; the rod
of thine inheritance, *which* thou hast redeemed; this mount Zion, wherein
thou hast dwelt.
3 Lift up thy feet unto the perpetual desolations; *even* all *that* the enemy
hath done wickedly in the sanctuary.
4 Thine enemies roar in the midst of thy congregations; they set up their
ensigns *for* signs.
5 *A man* was famous according as he had lifted up axes upon the thick
trees.
6 But now they break down the carved work thereof at once with axes and
hammers.
7 They have cast fire into thy sanctuary, they have defiled *by casting down*
the dwelling place of thy name to the ground.
8 They said in their hearts, Let us destroy them together: they have
burned up all the synagogues of God in the land.
9 We see not our signs: *there is* no more any prophet: neither *is there*
among us any that knoweth how long.
10 O God, how long shall the adversary reproach? shall the enemy
blaspheme thy name for ever?
11 Why withdrawest thou thy hand, even thy right hand? pluck *it* out of
thy bosom.

74:1☆ Deut 29:20; Ps 44:9; 89:46; 100:3
74:2 Deut 32:6, 9; Ps 68:16; Jer 10:16
74:3 Ps 79:1; Isa 61:4
74:4 Lam 2:7
74:5 1 Kgs 6:18, 29, 32, 35; Jer 46:22
74:7 2 Kgs 25:9
74:8 Ps 83:4
74:9 Lev 24:16; Ps 78:43; 79:12; Ezek 7:26; Amos 8:11
74:11 Ps 59:13; Lam 2:3

B. THE BELIEF IN GOD'S SOVEREIGN POWER

12 For God *is* my King of old, working salvation in the midst of the earth.
13 Thou didst divide the sea by thy strength: thou brakest the heads of the
dragons in the waters.
14 Thou brakest the heads of leviathan in pieces, *and* gavest him *to be* meat
to the people inhabiting the wilderness.
15 Thou didst cleave the fountain and the flood: thou driedst up mighty
rivers.
16 The day *is* thine, the night also *is* thine: thou hast prepared the light
and the sun.
17 Thou hast set all the borders of the earth: thou hast made summer and
winter.

74:12 Ps 44:4
74:13 Ex 14:21; Job 41:1; Isa 51:9
74:14☆
74:15 Ex 14:21, 22; 17:5; 6; Josh 3:13, 14; Isa 48:21
74:16 Gen 1:14–18; Ps 136:7, 8
74:17 Gen 8:22; Ps 147:16–18

C. THE CLOSING PETITION FOR DIVINE HELP

18 Remember this, *that* the enemy hath reproached, O LORD, and *that* the
foolish people have blasphemed thy name.
19 O deliver not the soul of thy turtledove unto the multitude *of the*
wicked: forget not the congregation of thy poor for ever.

74:18 Deut 32:6; Ps 53:1
74:19 Song 2:14

74:1ff Twelve Psalms bear the superscription *Asaph* (50, 73—83). Most of them were composed during the *time of David. Ps. 74, which describes the* destruction of Jerusalem by Nebuchadnezzar, presents a difficulty. Either it constitutes predictive prophecy—in which event it would have been written by the same Asaph who wrote Psalms in David's day—or it was written by another Asaph living at a later time. The Asaph of David's day was a son of Berechiah, of the family of Gershom. He was the "choir director" for Solomon as well as for David (see 1 Chron. 6:39; 15:17; 16:5; 2 Chron. 5:12). If this Asaph did not compose Ps. 74, we do not know which other Asaph it was.

74:14 *Thou breakest the heads of leviathan,* i.e., "You crushed the sea-god's heads."† *leviathan,* "the sea-monster," is used as a symbol of evil throughout the Bible.

20 Have respect unto the covenant: for the dark places of the earth are full
of the habitations of cruelty.
21 O let not the oppressed return ashamed: let the poor and needy praise
thy name.
22 Arise, O God, plead thine own cause: remember how the foolish man
reproacheth thee daily.
23 Forget not the voice of thine enemies: the tumult of those that rise up
against thee increaseth continually.

☆**74:20** Gen 17:7; Ps 106:45; 143:3
74:21 Ps 35:10; Isa 41:17
74:22 Ps 43:1; Isa 3:13; Ezek 20:35, 36
74:23 Ps 65:7

I. THE GOD WHO JUDGES RULERS

A. THE INVOCATION OF PRAISE

To the chief Musician, Al-taschith, A Psalm or Song of Asaph

75 UNTO thee, O God, do we give thanks, *unto thee* do we give
thanks: for *that* thy name is near thy wondrous works declare.

☆**75:1** Ps 44:1; 71:17

B. THE CERTAINTY OF GOD'S JUDGMENT

2 When I shall receive the congregation I will judge uprightly.
3 The earth and all the inhabitants thereof are dissolved: I bear up the
pillars of it. Se'lah.

75:2 Ps 9:7, 8; Isa 11:4
75:3 1 Sam 2:8; Ps 46:6; Isa 24:19

C. PROMOTION COMES ONLY FROM GOD

4 I said unto the fools, Deal not foolishly: and to the wicked, Lift not up
the horn:
5 Lift not up your horn on high: speak *not with* a stiff neck.
6 For promotion *cometh* neither from the east, nor from the west, nor
from the south.
7 But God *is* the judge: he putteth down one, and setteth up another.
8 For in the hand of the LORD *there is* a cup, and the wine is red; it is full
of mixture; and he poureth out of the same: but the dregs thereof, all the
wicked of the earth shall wring *them* out, *and* drink *them.*

75:5 1 Sam 2:3; Ps 94:4
75:6 1 Sam 2:7; Ps 113:6–8; 147:6; Dan 2:21
75:8 Ps 11:6; Jer 25:15; Obad 16

D. THE CLOSING WORD OF PRAISE

9 But I will declare for ever; I will sing praises to the God of Jacob.
10 All the horns of the wicked also will I cut off; *but* the horns of the
righteous shall be exalted.

75:9 Ps 40:10
75:10 Ps 89:17; 148:14

I. A HYMN OF THANKSGIVING FOR DELIVERANCE

To the chief Musician on Neginoth, A Psalm or Song of Asaph

76 IN Judah *is* God known: his name *is* great in Israel.
2 In Salem also is his tabernacle, and his dwelling place in Zion.

☆**76:1**
76:2 Ps 48:2, 3; 132:13; 135:21

74:20 The psalmist begs God to have respect for the covenant he had made with Israel. That covenant was conditional: disobedience would bring dispersion; obedience would bring the eventual fulfillment of all the promises. There were many in the diaspora who had broken faith with the covenant, but there were others, however small a minority, who had not broken the covenant and still loved God with their whole hearts. This is true today. Some Jews who have found Christ to be the true Messiah look for the restoration of Israel in the days to come. God is ready and willing to fulfill the covenant promises as soon as Israel repents.

75:1ff It is thought that this Psalm refers to the time when David, after the death of Saul, came into his kingship. Either David wrote it himself and had it delivered to Asaph, song leader of the temple, or it was crafted by Asaph, using the substance of a speech made by David.

76:1ff This song features a great victory experienced by Israel. Which victory, we do not know; many differences of opinion exist among the commentators. The song celebrates the mighty power of God before whom no enemy of his people will be victorious.

76:3 Ps 46:9

[3]There brake he the arrows of the bow, the shield, and the sword, and the
battle. Se'lah.
[4]Thou *art* more glorious *and* excellent than the mountains of prey.

76:5 Isa 10:12

[5]The stouthearted are spoiled, they have slept their sleep: and none of the
men of might have found their hands.

76:6 Ex 15:1, 21 Ps 78:53

[6]At thy rebuke, O God of Jacob, both the chariot and horse are cast into
a dead sleep.

76:7 Ps 89:7 Nah 1:6 Rev 6:17

[7]Thou, *even* thou, *art* to be feared: and who may stand in thy sight when
once thou art angry?

76:8 1 Chron 16:30 Ezek 38:20

[8]Thou didst cause judgment to be heard from heaven; the earth feared,
and was still,

76:9 Ps 9:7–9; 72:4

[9]When God arose to judgment, to save all the meek of the earth. Se'lah.
[10]Surely the wrath of man shall praise thee: the remainder of wrath shalt
thou restrain.

76:11☆ Ps 50:14

[11]Vow, and pay unto the LORD your God: let all that be round about him
bring presents unto him that ought to be feared.

76:12 Ps 47:2

[12]He shall cut off the spirit of princes: *he is* terrible to the kings of the
earth.

I. THE REMEMBRANCE OF GOD'S PAST MERCIES

A. THE CRY FOR HELP

To the chief Musician, to Jeduthun, A Psalm of Asaph

77:1☆ Ps 3:4

77 I CRIED unto God with my voice, *even* unto God with my voice;
and he gave ear unto me.

77:2 Job 11:13 Ps 50:15; 88:9 Isa 26:9

[2]In the day of my trouble I sought the Lord: my sore ran in the night,
and ceased not: my soul refused to be comforted.

77:3 Ps 43:5; 61:2 142:2, 3

[3]I remembered God, and was troubled: I complained, and my spirit was
overwhelmed. Se'lah.
[4]Thou holdest mine eyes waking: I am so troubled that I cannot speak.

B. A RECOLLECTION OF GOD'S MIRACLES

77:5 Ps 143:5 Isa 51:9

[5]I have considered the days of old, the years of ancient times.

77:6 Ps 42:8

[6]I call to remembrance my song in the night: I commune with mine own
heart: and my spirit made diligent search.

77:7 Ps 44:9

[7]Will the Lord cast off for ever? and will he be favourable no more?

77:8 Ps 89:49 2 Pet 3:9

[8]Is his mercy clean gone for ever? doth *his* promise fail for evermore?

77:9 Ps 25:6 Isa 49:14, 15

[9]Hath God forgotten to be gracious? hath he in anger shut up his tender
mercies? Se'lah.

77:10 Ps 31:22 44:2, 3

[10]And I said, This *is* my infirmity: *but I will remember* the years of the
right hand of the most High.

77:11☆ Ps 105:5, 6

[11]I will remember the works of the LORD: surely I will remember thy
wonders of old.

76:11 This is a call for all Israelites to submit themselves to their God and to become his loyal subjects. They are to vow to be his and pay what they vowed. When this happens, the people of God will be fully cared for by God.

77:1ff What occasioned the cry for help is not stated in this Psalm. Thus we may assume that it has a general purpose for all people of all ages who suffer severe testings and turn to God for solace and help. It is good for sufferers to recall God's past mercies in the firm conviction that he who delivered Israel in its many difficulties is the same God who will help his people today when they call upon him. This is an intensely personal Psalm. The word "I" is prominent: I cried; I remembered; I am troubled; I commune; I will remember; I will meditate. Conversation with God has room for personal dialogue and the use of personal pronouns.

77:11 It is important for God's people to remember what he has done before. His deeds of yesterday give believers reason to be sure that he can do great things again. God does not discontinue his works of mercy and grace for any believer.

12 I will meditate also of all thy work, and talk of thy doings.
13 Thy way, O God, *is* in the sanctuary: who *is so* great a God as *our* God?
14 Thou *art* the God that doest wonders: thou hast declared thy strength
among the people.

77:13 Ex 15:11; Ps 86:8
77:14 Ps 72:18; 106:8

C. THE MEMORY OF DELIVERANCE FROM EGYPT

15 Thou hast with *thine* arm redeemed thy people, the sons of Jacob and
Joseph. Se'lah.
16 The waters saw thee, O God, the waters saw thee; they were afraid: the
depths also were troubled.
17 The clouds poured out water: the skies sent out a sound: thine arrows
also went abroad.
18 The voice of thy thunder *was* in the heaven: the lightnings lightened the
world: the earth trembled and shook.
19 Thy way *is* in the sea, and thy path in the great waters, and thy
footsteps are not known.
20 Thou leddest thy people like a flock by the hand of Moses and Aaron.

77:15 Ex 6:6; Deut 9:29; Ps 74:2
77:16 Ex 14:21; Ps 114:3; Hab 3:8–10
77:17 Judg 5:4; Ps 68:33
77:18 Judg 5:4; Ps 97:4
77:19 Isa 51:10
☆77:20 Ex 13:21; Ps 78:52; Isa 63:11, 12

I. GOD'S DEALINGS WITH HIS PEOPLE ISRAEL

A. LEARNING LESSONS FROM THE PAST

Maschil of Asaph

78 GIVE ear, O my people, *to* my law: incline your ears to the words
of my mouth.
2 I will open my mouth in a parable: I will utter dark sayings of old:
3 Which we have heard and known, and our fathers have told us.
4 We will not hide *them* from their children, shewing to the generation to
come the praises of the LORD, and his strength, and his wonderful works
that he hath done.
5 For he established a testimony in Jacob, and appointed a law in Israel,
which he commanded our fathers, that they should make them known to
their children:
6 That the generation to come might know *them, even* the children *which*
should be born; *who* should arise and declare *them* to their children:
7 That they might set their hope in God, and not forget the works of God,
but keep his commandments:
8 And might not be as their fathers, a stubborn and rebellious generation;
a generation *that* set not their heart aright, and whose spirit was not stedfast
with God.

☆78:1 Isa 55:3
78:2 Ps 44:1; Mt 13:34, 35
☆78:4 Deut 11:19; Job 15:17–19; Ps 22:30; Isa 38:19; Joel 1:3
78:5 Deut 6:4–9; Ps 147:19
78:6 Deut 11:19
78:7 Deut 4:2, 9; Josh 22:5
☆78:8

B. ISRAEL'S TRANSGRESSIONS

1. The Sins of the Ephraimites

9 The children of E'phra-im, *being* armed, *and* carrying bows, turned back
in the day of battle.

☆78.9 Ex 32:9; Deut 9:7, 24; Ps 51:10

77:20 *In Israel the shepherd always* leads the flocks. He never drives them. They follow him. Christ is our shepherd and he goes before the sheep. If they follow him they will never lose the way nor be separated from the flock.

78:1ff This song is to be a constant reminder to Israel of their sins and of the consequences that always followed when the judgments of God fell on them. It records the fact that God was merciful and delivered his people again and again, for they did not learn from these experiences never to repeat their transgressions. Those who do not learn from past history repeat the mistakes of their forebears. This song, then, should be in the forefront of the thinking of God's people today, lest they fall into the same trap as their spiritual ancestors.

78:4 When we teach "our children the knowledge of God, we repay our parents some of the debt we owe to them for teaching us."*

78:8 Children are told not to follow in the footsteps of parents who are not devoted to God. Reason and experience teach such children the lesson that they should avoid the errors of their ancestors and not follow their example. Good tradition, not bad tradition, is to be accepted and followed.

78:9 *The children of Ephraim . . . turned back.*

78:10 2 Kgs 18:12 Jer 32:23 **78:11**☆ Ps 106:13

10 They kept not the covenant of God, and refused to walk in his law;
11 And forgat his works, and his wonders that he had shewed them.
12 Marvellous things did he in the sight of their fathers, in the land of
Egypt, *in* the field of Zo'an.

78:13 Ex 14:21; 15:18

13 He divided the sea, and caused them to pass through; and he made the
waters to stand as an heap.

78:14 Ex 13:21

14 In the daytime also he led them with a cloud, and all the night with a
light of fire.

78:15 Ex 17:5, 6 1 Cor 10:4

15 He clave the rocks in the wilderness, and gave *them* drink as *out of* the
great depths.

78:16 Num 20:8, 10, 11

16 He brought streams also out of the rock, and caused waters to run
down like rivers.

2. Grumbling over the Manna

78:17 Isa 63:10 Heb 3:16 **78:18** Num 11:4, 5 1 Cor 10:9, 10 **78:19** Ex 16:3 Num 21:5

17 And they sinned yet more against him by provoking the most High in
the wilderness.
18 And they tempted God in their heart by asking meat for their lust.
19 Yea, they spake against God; they said, Can God furnish a table in the
wilderness?
20 Behold, he smote the rock, that the waters gushed out, and the streams
overflowed; can he give bread also? can he provide flesh for his people?

78:21 Num 11:1

21 Therefore the LORD heard *this,* and was wroth; so a fire was kindled
against Jacob, and anger also came up against Israel;

78:22 Deut 9:23 Heb 3:18 **78:23** Mal 3:10 **78:24**☆ Ex 16:4 Jn 6:30, 31

22 Because they believed not in God, and trusted not in his salvation:
23 Though he had commanded the clouds from above, and opened the
doors of heaven,
24 And had rained down manna upon them to eat, and had given them of
the corn of heaven.
25 Man did eat angels' food: he sent them meat to the full.

78:26 Num 11:31

26 He caused an east wind to blow in the heaven: and by his power he
brought in the south wind.

78:27 Ex 16:13 Ps 105:40

27 He rained flesh also upon them as dust, and feathered fowls like as the
sand of the sea:
28 And he let *it* fall in the midst of their camp, round about their
habitations.

78:29 Num 11:19, 20

29 So they did eat, and were well filled: for he gave them their own desire;
30 They were not estranged from their lust. But while their meat *was* yet in
their mouths,

78:31 Num 11:33, 34

31 The wrath of God came upon them, and slew the fattest of them, and
smote down the chosen *men* of Israel.

78:32☆ Num 14:10, 11 **78:33** Num 14:29, 34, 35

32 For all this they sinned still, and believed not for his wondrous works.
33 Therefore their days did he consume in vanity, and their years in
trouble.

Probably this refers to the incident that occurred in Eli's time in which the Philistines defeated the well-armed Ephraimites and captured the ark (1 Sam. 4:10, 11). The Ephraimites, in whose region Shiloh was, lacked a martial spirit due to their violation of God's law and their covenant with him.

78:11 *They forgat his works,* i.e., they did not remember what God had done for Israel in the wilderness. His many miracles should have encouraged them and strengthened them against the Philistines. Let all believers know today that what God did yesterday he can and will do again for his people.

78:24 God through angels provided manna for his people in the wilderness (food as given by the ministry of angels, 78:25). They ate the bread of the mighty which all could digest and by which all were strengthened. But they quarreled with God and demanded meat. He gave them quails, and they died for their disobedience.

78:32 The judgments of God against unbelief did not reform the Israelites. They continued their waywardness and God continued his judgments. They never seemed to learn that it pays to obey God. Those who go on sinning must expect to go on hurting and remain troubled and discomforted.

3. Israel's Lack of Heart Faith

34 When he slew them, then they sought him: and they returned and
inquired early after God.

78:34 Hos 5:15

35 And they remembered that God *was* their rock, and the high God their
redeemer,

78:35 Deut 9:26; 32:4 Isa 41:14

36 Nevertheless they did flatter him with their mouth, and they lied unto
him with their tongues.

78:36 Ezek 33:31

37 For their heart was not right with him, neither were they stedfast in his
covenant.

38 But he, *being* full of compassion, forgave *their* iniquity, and destroyed
them not: yea, many a time turned he his anger away, and did not stir up all
his wrath.

78:38 Ex 34:5, 6 Num 14:19

39 For he remembered that they *were but* flesh; a wind that passeth away,
and cometh not again.

78:39 Job 7:7 Jas 4:14

40 How oft did they provoke him in the wilderness, *and* grieve him in the
desert!

78:40 Ps 106:43 Eph 4:30

41 Yea, they turned back and tempted God, and limited the Holy One of
Israel.

☆**78:41** 2 Kgs 19:22

42 They remembered not his hand, *nor* the day when he delivered them
from the enemy.

78:42 Judg 8:34

43 How he had wrought his signs in Egypt, and his wonders in the field of
Zo'an:

☆**78:43** Ex 7:3

44 And had turned their rivers into blood; and their floods, that they could
not drink.

78:44 Ex 7:20 Ps 105:29

45 He sent divers sorts of flies among them, which devoured them; and
frogs, which destroyed them.

78:45 Ex 8:6, 24 Ps 105:30, 31

46 He gave also their increase unto the caterpiller, and their labour unto
the locust.

78:46 Ex 10:14

47 He destroyed their vines with hail, and their sycomore trees with frost.

78:47 Ex 9:23 Ps 105:32

48 He gave up their cattle also to the hail, and their flocks to hot
thunderbolts.

78:48 Ex 9:19

49 He cast upon them the fierceness of his anger, wrath, and indignation,
and trouble, by sending evil angels *among them.*

78:49 Ex 15:7

50 He made a way to his anger; he spared not their soul from death, but
gave their life over to the pestilence;

51 And smote all the firstborn in Egypt; the chief of *their* strength in the
tabernacles of Ham:

78:51 Ex 12:29, 30 Ps 105:36

52 But made his own people to go forth like sheep, and guided them in the
wilderness like a flock.

78:52 Ps 77:20

53 And he led them on safely, so that they feared not: but the sea
overwhelmed their enemies.

78:53 Ex 14:19, 20, 27, 28 Ps 106:11

54 And he brought them to the border of his sanctuary, *even to* this
mountain, *which* his right hand had purchased.

78:54 Ex 15:17

55 He cast out the heathen also before them, and divided them an
inheritance by line, and made the tribes of Israel to dwell in their tents.

78:55 Josh 23:4, 5 Ps 44:1, 2 105:10, 11

4. *Israel's Rebellion* in the Promised Land

56 Yet they tempted and provoked the most high God, and kept not his
testimonies:

78:41 This might better be translated: "Again and again they put God to the test; they vexed the Holy One of Israel." Israel's repeated refusals to let God be God provoked him. (Num. 14:22 says, "they have tempted me these ten times".) They confessed and were pardoned, only to tempt God again. This sort of conduct is not uncommon among many believers in every age.

78:43 *the field of Zoan,* i.e., "Tanis," an ancient Egyptian city. In the period 1085–715 B.C. Tanis-Zoan was the capital of the Pharaohs.

78:57 Hos 7:16
78:58 Lev 26:1; Deut 32:16, 21; 1 Kgs 14:9, 22, 23; Isa 65:3
78:59 Lev 26:30; Deut 32:19; Amos 6:98
78:60 1 Sam 4:11; Jer 7:12–14; 26:6
78:61☆ 1 Sam 4:17
78:62 Judg 20:21; 1 Sam 4:10
78:63 Num 11:1; Jer 7:34; 16:9; Lam 2:21
78:64 1 Sam 22:18; Job 27:15
78:65 Ps 44:23; Isa 42:13
78:66 1 Sam 5:6

57 But turned back, and dealt unfaithfully like their fathers: they were turned aside like a deceitful bow.
58 For they provoked him to anger with their high places, and moved him to jealousy with their graven images.
59 When God heard *this,* he was wroth, and greatly abhorred Israel:
60 So that he forsook the tabernacle of Shi′loh, the tent *which* he placed among men;
61 And delivered his strength into captivity, and his glory into the enemy's hand.
62 He gave his people over also unto the sword; and was wroth with his inheritance.
63 The fire consumed their young men; and their maidens were not given to marriage.
64 Their priests fell by the sword; and their widows made no lamentation.
65 Then the Lord awaked as one out of sleep, *and* like a mighty man that shouteth by reason of wine.
66 And he smote his enemies in the hinder parts: he put them to a perpetual reproach.

C. GOD'S CHOICE OF JUDAH AND DAVID

78:68 Ps 87:1, 2
78:69 1 Kgs 6:1–38
78:70☆ 1 Sam 16:10–12
78:71 2 Sam 5:2; 7:8; 1 Kgs 9:4; 1 Chron 11:2

67 Moreover he refused the tabernacle of Joseph, and chose not the tribe of E′phra-im:
68 But chose the tribe of Judah, the mount Zion which he loved.
69 And he built his sanctuary like high *palaces,* like the earth which he hath established for ever.
70 He chose David also his servant, and took him from the sheepfolds:
71 From following the ewes great with young he brought him to feed Jacob his people, and Israel his inheritance.
72 So he fed them according to the integrity of his heart; and guided them by the skilfulness of his hands.

I. THE DESTRUCTION OF JERUSALEM

A. THE CONQUEST BY THE ENEMY

A Psalm of Asaph

79:1☆ Ps 74:2–7; Jer 26:18; Lam 1:10; Mic 3:12
79:2 Deut 28:26; Jer 7:33; 16:4
79:3 Jer 14:16
79:4 Ps 44:13; 80:6

79 O GOD, the heathen are come into thine inheritance; thy holy temple have they defiled; they have laid Jerusalem on heaps.
2 The dead bodies of thy servants have they given *to be* meat unto the fowls of the heaven, the flesh of thy saints unto the beasts of the earth.
3 Their blood have they shed like water round about Jerusalem; and *there was* none to bury *them.*
4 We are become a reproach to our neighbours, a scorn and derision to them that are round about us.

78:61 God allowed Israel's enemy to seize the ark of the covenant and carry it away from Shiloh. The ark, which betokened the presence of God, was no longer in their midst. God allowed his own glory to be disgraced by being abandoned into the hands of infidels. Israel had forsaken God; he would now forsake them.

78:70 God chose David to recover the fortunes of Israel. He was not an educated, scholarly, or military man. He was just a shepherd boy. God uses the least of all to deliver his people that glory might come to his own name. Jesus was just a carpenter whose words and deeds transformed the world.

79:1ff This song is thought by many to be a prophetical statement concerning the ravaging of Jerusalem and the destruction of the temple by the Chaldeans under Nebuchadnezzar. Jer. 10:25 picks up 79:6, 7. The song has the same sort of schematic arrangement as the Lamentations of Jeremiah.

B. THE PRAYER FOR DIVINE DELIVERANCE

5 How long, LORD? wilt thou be angry for ever? shall thy jealousy burn
like fire?
6 Pour out thy wrath upon the heathen that have not known thee, and
upon the kingdoms that have not called upon thy name.
7 For they have devoured Jacob, and laid waste his dwelling place.
8 O remember not against us former iniquities: let thy tender mercies
speedily prevent us: for we are brought very low.
9 Help us, O God of our salvation, for the glory of thy name: and deliver
us, and purge away our sins, for thy name's sake.
10 Wherefore should the heathen say, Where *is* their God? let him be
known among the heathen in our sight *by* the revenging of the blood of thy
servants *which is* shed.
11 Let the sighing of the prisoner come before thee; according to the
greatness of thy power preserve thou those that are appointed to die;
12 And render unto our neighbours sevenfold into their bosom their
reproach, wherewith they have reproached thee, O Lord.
13 So we thy people and sheep of thy pasture will give thee thanks for
ever: we will shew forth thy praise to all generations.

☆**79:5** Ps 74:1, 9, 10; 89:46
79:6 Jer 10:25; Zeph 3:8; 2 Thess 1:8
79:7 Ps 53:4
79:8 Ps 106:6; 142:6; Isa 26:5; 64:9
☆**79:9** Chron 14:11; Ps 25:11; Jer 14:7
79:10 Ps 115:2
79:11 Ps 102:20
79:12 Gen 4:15; Lev 26:21, 28; Ps 74:10, 22; 119:164; Prov 6:31
79:13 Ps 95:7; 100:3; Isa 43:21

I. A PETITION FOR ISRAEL'S NATIONAL DELIVERANCE

A. THE NATIONAL PRAYER FOR HELP

To the chief Musician upon Shoshannim-Eduth, A Psalm of Asaph

80 GIVE ear, O Shepherd of Israel, thou that leadest Joseph like a
flock; thou that dwellest *between* the cherubims, shine forth.
2 Before E'phra-im and Benjamin and Ma-nas'seh stir up thy strength,
and come *and* save us.
3 Turn us again, O God, and cause thy face to shine; and we shall be
saved.

☆**80:1** Ex 25:22; Ps 23:1; 77:20; 99:1
80:2 Ps 35:23
80:3 Num 6:24–26; Ps 31:16; 60:1

B. THE NATIONAL CRISIS

4 O LORD God of hosts, how long wilt thou be angry against the prayer of
thy people?
5 Thou feedest them with the bread of tears; and givest them tears to
drink in great measure.
6 Thou makest us a strife unto our neighbours: and our enemies laugh
among themselves.
7 Turn us again, O God of hosts, and cause thy face to shine; and we shall
be saved.

80:4 Ps 79:5; 84:8
80:5 Ps 102:9
80:6 Ps 44:13

79:5 *Wilt thou be angry forever?* God was angry and delivered his people into the Babylonian captivity. He was angry and delivered the temple over to complete destruction in A.D. 70 under Titus and Vespasian. He has allowed two millennia to pass without reversing the judgment. But his anger will some day give way to restoration and peace, when his people Israel turn to him in repentance and confession (which must always precede restoration).

79:9 *Help us . . . for the glory of thy name.* Will not God's glory be diminished and his omnipotence questioned if he cannot deliver his people from their degradation? So it would appear from the history of Israel. The nation seems to have been relegated to the dustbin of history. Yet the dry bones shall someday live again, and God's glory will glisten as the sun.

80:1 This Psalm constitutes a prayer for divine deliverance from Israel's calamities. What the particular calamity is we are not told. Scripture does not always provide us with a detailed history of the people of God, who undoubtedly experienced many difficulties. The psalmist expresses hope and confidence in the power of God to help and to deliver Israel out of its greatest distresses.

C. THE NATION, A DYING VINE

80:8 2 Chron 20:7; Ps 44:2; Isa 5:2, 7; Jer 2:21; 11:17; Ezek 17:6, 23; Amos 9:15 **80:9** Ex 23:28; Isa 5:2; Hos 14:5 **80:11** Ps 72:8 **80:12** Ps 89:40; Isa 5:5 **80:13** Jer 5:6

8 Thou hast brought a vine out of Egypt: thou hast cast out the heathen,
and planted it.
9 Thou preparedst *room* before it, and didst cause it to take deep root, and
it filled the land.
10 The hills were covered with the shadow of it, and the boughs thereof
were like the goodly cedars.
11 She sent out her boughs unto the sea, and her branches unto the river.
12 Why hast thou *then* broken down her hedges, so that all they which
pass by the way do pluck her?
13 The boar out of the wood doth waste it, and the wild beast of the field
doth devour it.

D. THE PRAYER FOR NATIONAL REVIVAL

80:14 Ps 90:13; Isa 63:15 **80:16** 2 Chron 36:19; Ps 39:11; 76:6; Jer 52:13 **80:17☆** Ps 89:21 **80:18** Ps 71:20; Isa 50:5

14 Return, we beseech thee, O God of hosts: look down from heaven, and
behold, and visit this vine;
15 And the vineyard which thy right hand hath planted, and the branch
that thou madest strong for thyself.
16 *It is* burned with fire, *it is* cut down: they perish at the rebuke of thy
countenance.
17 Let thy hand be upon the man of thy right hand, upon the son of man
whom thou madest strong for thyself.
18 So will not we go back from thee: quicken us, and we will call upon thy
name.
19 Turn us again, O LORD God of hosts, cause thy face to shine; and we
shall be saved.

I. THE PSALM FOR THE NEW MOON

A. THE SONG OF PRAISE

To the chief Musician upon Gittith, A Psalm of Asaph

81:1☆ Ps 46:1; 59:16; 66:1; 95:1, 2 **81:2** Ps 108:2; 144:9; 149:3 **81:3** Lev 23:24; Num 10:10 **81:5** Ex 11:4

81 SING aloud unto God our strength: make a joyful noise unto the
God of Jacob.
2 Take a psalm, and bring hither the timbrel, the pleasant harp with the
psaltery.
3 Blow up the trumpet in the new moon, in the time appointed, on our
solemn feast day.
4 For this *was* a statute for Israel, *and* a law of the God of Jacob.
5 This he ordained in Joseph *for* a testimony, when he went out through
the land of Egypt: *where* I heard a language *that* I understood not.

B. THE MERCIES OF GOD

81:6 Isa 9:4; 10:27 **81:7☆** Ex 2:23; 17:5–7; 19:19; Ps 50:15; 95:8 **81:8** Ps 50:7; 95:7

6 I removed his shoulder from the burden: his hands were delivered from
the pots.
7 Thou calledst in trouble, and I delivered thee; I answered thee in the
secret place of thunder: I proved thee at the waters of Mer'i-bah. Se'lah.
8 Hear, O my people, and I will testify unto thee: O Israel, if thou wilt
hearken unto me;

80:17 *the man of thy right hand,* i.e., "the man you love." *the son of man,* i.e., "the son of your choice."†
81:1ff This Psalm was not composed as a result of some particular historical crisis or momentous event. Rather, it was written for use on special feast occasions, such as the new moon in general, or for the feast of trumpets. On special occasions, Psalms are to be used either to give glory to God or to receive instructions from him.
81:7 *the secret place of thunder,* i.e., "Mount Sinai."

9 There shall no strange god be in thee; neither shalt thou worship any
strange god.
10 I *am* the LORD thy God, which brought thee out of the land of Egypt:
open thy mouth wide, and I will fill it.

☆**81:9** Ex 20:3; Isa 43:12
81:10 Ex 20:2; Ps 78:25; 103:5; 107:9

C. GOD'S YEARNING OVER HIS WAYWARD PEOPLE

11 But my people would not hearken to my voice; and Israel would none
of me.
12 So I gave them up unto their own hearts' lust: *and* they walked in their
own counsels.
13 Oh that my people had hearkened unto me, *and* Israel had walked in
my ways!
14 I should soon have subdued their enemies, and turned my hand against
their adversaries.
15 The haters of the LORD should have submitted themselves unto him:
but their time should have endured for ever.
16 He should have fed them also with the finest of the wheat: and with
honey out of the rock should I have satisfied thee.

81:11 Ex 32:1
81:12 Acts 7:42; Rom 1:24, 26
81:13 Deut 5:29; Ps 128:1; Isa 48:18; Jer 7:23
81:14 Ps 18:47; Amos 1:8
81:15 Ps 66:3
81:16 Deut 32:13, 14; Ps 147:14

I. A REBUKE TO UNJUST JUDGES AND MAGISTRATES

A Psalm of Asaph

82 GOD standeth in the congregation of the mighty; he judgeth
among the gods.
2 How long will ye judge unjustly, and accept the persons of the wicked?
Se'lah.
3 Defend the poor and fatherless: do justice to the afflicted and needy.
4 Deliver the poor and needy: rid *them* out of the hand of the wicked.
5 They know not, neither will they understand; they walk on in darkness:
all the foundations of the earth are out of course.
6 I have said, Ye *are* gods; and all of you *are* children of the most High.
7 But ye shall die like men, and fall like one of the princes.
8 Arise, O God, judge the earth: for thou shalt inherit all nations.

☆**82:1** Ps 58:11; Isa 3:13
82:2 Deut 1:17; Ps 58:1, 2; Prov 18:5
82:3 Deut 24:17; Isa 11:4; Jer 22:16
82:4 Job 29:12
82:5 Isa 59:9; Jer 4:22
82:6 Ps 89:26; Jn 10:34–36
82:7 Ps 49:12; 83:11
82:8 Ps 2:8; 12:5; 96:13; Rev 11:15

I. A PSALM ABOUT ISRAEL'S ENEMIES

A. THE PETITION FOR GOD TO JUDGE THEIR ENEMIES

A Song or Psalm of Asaph

83 KEEP not thou silence, O God: hold not thy peace, and be not still,
O God.
2 For, lo, thine enemies make a tumult: and they that hate thee have lifted
up the head.
3 They have taken crafty counsel against thy people, and consulted
against thy hidden ones.

☆**83:1** Ps 28:1; 109:1
83:2 Ps 2:1; Isa 17:12
83:3 Ps 31:20; 64:1, 2; Zech 1:21

81:9 *There shall no strange god be in thee,* i.e., "You shall not have an idol in your home."†
82:1 *he judgeth among the gods,* i.e., "He pronounces judgment on the judges."† This Psalm instructs those in power (whether ecclesiastical or civil power) how to conduct themselves with respect to the temptations of the office of the magistracy. What is said would apply not only to Israel but to all the nations of the earth.
83:1ff This is the last of the Psalms connected with the name of Asaph. It refers by name to some of Israel's inveterate enemies and pleads with God to judge them. The closing section (83:9–18) constitutes a prayer of imprecation against the enemies. Whether this practice is proper in the age instituted by Christ is the subject of much controversy—what was done in the Old Testament may be forbidden in the New. One thing is clear: both the Old and the New Testaments bind God's people of all ages to the commandment that they must love their neighbors as they love themselves.

83:4 Esth 3:5, 6; Ps 74:8
83:5 Ps 2:2; Dan 6:7
83:6 Gen 25:12–16; 2 Chron 20:1, 10; Ps 137:7
83:7 2 Chron 20:10; 1 Sam 4:1; 15:2; Ezek 27:2, 3, 9
83:8 Deut 2:9

4 They have said, Come, and let us cut them off from *being* a nation; that
the name of Israel may be no more in remembrance.
5 For they have consulted together with one consent: they are confederate
against thee:
6 The tabernacles of Edom, and the Ish′ma-el-ites; of Moab, and the
Ha′gar-enes;
7 Ge′bal, and Ammon, and Am′a-lek; the Philistines with the inhabitants
of Tyre;
8 Assur also is joined with them: they have holpen the children of Lot.
Se′lah.

B. THE PETITION FOR GOD TO CONFOUND THEIR ENEMIES

83:9☆ Judg 4:22, 23; 7:22
83:10☆
83:11☆ Judg 7:25; 8:21
83:12☆ 2 Chron 20:11
83:13 Isa 17:13; 40:24; Jer 13:24, 25
83:14 Deut 32:22; Isa 9:18
83:15 Job 9:17; Ps 58:9
83:16 Ps 109:29; 132:18
83:17 Ps 70:2, 3
83:18 Ps 97:9; Isa 45:21

9 Do unto them as *unto* the Mid′i-an-ites; as *to* Sis′e-ra, as *to* Ja′bin, at the
brook of Ki′son:
10 *Which* perished at En–dor: they became *as* dung for the earth.
11 Make their nobles like O′reb, and like Ze′eb: yea, all their princes as
Ze′bah, and as Zal-mun′na:
12 Who said, Let us take to ourselves the houses of God in possession.
13 O my God, make them like a wheel; as the stubble before the wind.
14 As the fire burneth a wood, and as the flame setteth the mountains on
fire;
15 So persecute them with thy tempest, and make them afraid with thy
storm.
16 Fill their faces with shame; that they may seek thy name, O LORD.
17 Let them be confounded and troubled for ever; yea, let them be put to
shame, and perish:
18 That *men* may know that thou, whose name alone *is* JEHOVAH, *art* the
most high over all the earth.

I. THE PSALM OF THE COURTYARD OF THE LIVING GOD

A. THE JOY OF WORSHIP

84:1☆ Ps 27:5
84:2 Ps 42:1, 2; 63:1
84:3 Ps 43:4
84:4 Ps 65:4

To the chief Musician upon Gittith, A Psalm for the sons of Korah

84 HOW amiable *are* thy tabernacles, O LORD of hosts!
2 My soul longeth, yea, even fainteth for the courts of the LORD:
my heart and my flesh crieth out for the living God.
3 Yea, the sparrow hath found an house, and the swallow a nest for
herself, where she may lay her young, *even* thine altars, O LORD of hosts,
my King, and my God.
4 Blessed *are* they that dwell in thy house: they will be still praising thee.
Se′lah.

B. THE DIVINE REFRESHMENT FOR WORSHIPPERS

84:5 Ps 81:1; 86:11
84:6☆ Ps 107:35; Joel 2:23

5 Blessed *is* the man whose strength *is* in thee; in whose heart *are* the ways
of them.
6 *Who* passing through the valley of Ba′ca make it a well; the rain also
filleth the pools.

83:9–12 This is an imprecatory prayer in which the psalmist calls on God to destroy the enemies of Israel, just as he had on other occasions.

84:1ff The author of this Psalm is not named nor do the contents state specifically what circumstances caused it to be written. It is a song well suited to the worship of God on the sabbath, when the people gather to hear the Word of God, to praise him for the privilege of collective worship, and to celebrate the ordinances or sacraments of the faith.

84:6 *valley of Baca* ("the valley of weeping"), a normally dry valley where balsam trees grew in profusion.

[7]They go from strength to strength, *every one of them* in Zion appeareth before God.
[8]O LORD God of hosts, hear my prayer: give ear, O God of Jacob. Se'lah.
[9]Behold, O God our shield, and look upon the face of thine anointed.

84:7 Deut 16:16; 2 Chron 3:18; Prov 4:18; Isa 40:31; Jn 1:16
84:8 Ps 59:5; 81:1
☆84:9 Gen 15:1; 2 Sam 19:21; Ps 115:9–11; 132:17

C. THE BLESSEDNESS OF A DAY IN GOD'S TEMPLE

[10]For a day in thy courts *is* better than a thousand. I had rather be a doorkeeper in the house of my God, than to dwell in the tents of wickedness.
[11]For the LORD God *is* a sun and shield: the LORD will give grace and glory: no good *thing* will he withhold from them that walk uprightly.
[12]O LORD of hosts, blessed *is* the man that trusteth in thee.

84:10 1 Chron 23:5; Ps 27:4
☆84:11 Ps 34:10; Isa 60:19, 20; Mal 4:2; Rev 21:23
84:12 Ps 40:4

I. THE PSALM OF RELEASE FROM CAPTIVITY

A. THE END OF GOD'S ANGER

To the chief Musician, A Psalm for the sons of Korah

85 LORD, thou hast been favourable unto thy land: thou hast brought back the captivity of Jacob.
[2]Thou hast forgiven the iniquity of thy people, thou hast covered all their sin. Se'lah.
[3]Thou hast taken away all thy wrath: thou hast turned *thyself* from the fierceness of thine anger.

☆85:1 Jer 30:18; Ezek 39:25; Joel 3:1
85:2 Num 14:19; Jer 31:34; Ps 32:1
85:3 Ex 32:12; Ps 78:38; Jonah 3:9

B. THE PRAYER FOR RENEWAL

[4]Turn us, O God of our salvation, and cause thine anger toward us to cease.
[5]Wilt thou be angry with us for ever? wilt thou draw out thine anger to all generations?
[6]Wilt thou not revive us again: that thy people may rejoice in thee?
[7]Shew us thy mercy, O LORD, and grant us thy salvation.

85:4 Ps 80:3, 7
85:5 Ps 79:5; 80:4
85:6 Ps 149:2; Hab 3:2

C. THE LOVING LORD'S FAITHFULNESS

[8]I will hear what God the LORD will speak: for he will speak peace unto his people, and to his saints: but let them not turn again to folly.
[9]Surely his salvation *is* nigh them that fear him; that glory may dwell in our land.
[10]Mercy and truth are met together; righteousness and peace have kissed *each other.*
[11]Truth shall spring out of the earth; and righteousness shall look down from heaven.
[12]Yea, the LORD shall give *that which is* good; and our land shall yield her *increase.*
[13]Righteousness shall go before him; and shall set *us* in the way of his steps.

85:8 Ps 29:11; 78:57; Hag 2:9; 2 Pet 2:21
85:9 Ps 34:18; 84:11; Isa 46:13; Jn 1:14
85:10 Ps 89:4; Prov 3:3; Isa 32:17
85:11 Isa 45:8
85:12 Lev 26:4; Zech 8:12; Jas 1:17
85:13 Ps 89:14

84:9 *thine anointed,* i.e., "your king."
84:11 *the LORD God is a sun,* i.e., "God is the source from which we get light, life, and fruitfulness." *walk uprightly,* i.e., "walk along his paths."
85:1 Some commentators think this Psalm was composed after the return of Israel to the land of promise following the Babylonian captivity The times were dark and dismal, for the consequences of Israel's sins were not fully over. In view of the faithfulness of Israel's God, prayer is made to turn away his anger and find solace and relief in his great salvation.

I. A PSALM OF PETITION AND PENITENCE

A. DAVID'S PETITION FOR HELP

A Prayer of David

86:1☆ Ps 31:2 **86:2** Ps 4:3; 25:20 31:14 **86:3** Ps 88:9 **86:4** Ps 25:1 **86:5** Neh 9:17 Ps 103:8; 130:4 Joel 2:13 **86:7** Ps 50:14, 15 77:2

86 BOW down thine ear, O LORD, hear me: for I *am* poor and needy.
2 Preserve my soul; for I *am* holy: O thou my God, save thy
servant that trusteth in thee.
3 Be merciful unto me, O Lord: for I cry unto thee daily.
4 Rejoice the soul of thy servant: for unto thee, O Lord, do I lift up my
soul.
5 For thou, Lord, *art* good, and ready to forgive; and plenteous in mercy
unto all them that call upon thee.
6 Give ear, O LORD, unto my prayer; and attend to the voice of my
supplications.
7 In the day of my trouble I will call upon thee: for thou wilt answer me.

B. DAVID'S ADORATION OF THE LORD

86:8☆ Ex 15:11 Deut 3:24 1 Kgs 8:23 **86:9** Isa 66:23 Rev 15:3, 4 **86:10** Deut 32:39 Isa 44:6, 8 Mk 12:29 1 Cor 8:4

8 Among the gods *there is* none like unto thee, O Lord; neither *are there*
any works like unto thy works.
9 All nations whom thou hast made shall come and worship before thee,
O Lord; and shall glorify thy name.
10 For thou *art* great, and doest wondrous things: thou *art* God alone.

C. DAVID'S PETITION AND THANKSGIVING

86:11 Ps 25:5 Jer 32:39 **86:12** Ps 111:1 **86:13** Ps 30:3

11 Teach me thy way, O LORD; I will walk in thy truth: unite my heart to
fear thy name.
12 I will praise thee, O Lord my God, with all my heart: and I will glorify
thy name for evermore.
13 For great *is* thy mercy toward me: and thou hast delivered my soul
from the lowest hell.

D. THE ASSURANCE OF GOD'S LOVINGKINDNESS

86:14 Ps 54:3 **86:15** Ps 86:5 **86:16** Ps 68:35 **86:17** Ps 112:10 118:13; 119:122

14 O God, the proud are risen against me, and the assemblies of violent
men have sought after my soul; and have not set thee before them.
15 But thou, O Lord, *art* a God full of compassion, and gracious,
longsuffering, and plenteous in mercy and truth.
16 O turn unto me, and have mercy upon me; give thy strength unto thy
servant, and save the son of thine handmaid.
17 Shew me a token for good; that they which hate me may see *it,* and be
ashamed: because thou, LORD, hast holpen me, and comforted me.

I. A PSALM OF PRAISE FOR JERUSALEM (ZION)

A Psalm or Song for the sons of Korah

87:1☆ Ps 78:68, 69 Isa 28:16

87 HIS foundation *is* in the holy mountains.
2 The LORD loveth the gates of Zion more than all the dwellings
of Jacob.

86:1ff This is thought to be a general prayer of David for use in times of affliction. Thus it is ageless and especially useful to believers in any time of trouble and in personal sorrow, grief, and dismay.
86:8 *There is none like unto thee, O LORD.* David is not saying that there are other gods. Rather, all other so-called gods are false gods. None of them is wise, mighty, and good. Nor do their works support the claims of their adherents—that they are true gods. The God of Israel alone does great works (86:10).
87:1 This short Psalm is to the praise of Jerusalem, which is called the city of God. It was written at a time

3 Glorious things are spoken of thee, O city of God. Se'lah.
4 I will make mention of Rahab and Babylon to them that know me:
behold Philistia, and Tyre, with E-thi-o'pi-a; this *man* was born there.
5 And of Zion it shall be said, This and that man was born in her: and the
highest himself shall establish her.
6 The LORD shall count, when he writeth up the people, *that* this *man* was
born there. Se'lah.
7 As well the singers as the players on instruments *shall be there:* all my
springs *are* in thee.

87:3 Ps 46:4; 48:8
☆**87:4** Ps 45:12; 68:31 Isa 19:23–25
87:5 Ps 48:8
87:6 Isa 4:2–4
87:7 Ps 30:11; 36:9

I. A PSALM FOR INVALIDS

A. PRAYER FOR THE PSALMIST'S HOPELESS CASE

A Song or Psalm for the sons of Korah, to the chief Musician upon Mahalath Leannoth, Maschil of Heman the Ezrahite

88 O LORD God of my salvation, I have cried day *and* night before
thee:
2 Let my prayer come before thee: incline thine ear unto my cry;
3 For my soul is full of troubles: and my life draweth nigh unto the grave.
4 I am counted with them that go down into the pit: I am as a man *that*
hath no strength:
5 Free among the dead, like the slain that lie in the grave, whom thou
rememberest no more: and they are cut off from thy hand.
6 Thou hast laid me in the lowest pit, in darkness, in the deeps.
7 Thy wrath lieth hard upon me, and thou hast afflicted *me* with all thy
waves. Se'lah.
8 Thou hast put away mine acquaintance far from me; thou hast made me
an abomination unto them: *I am* shut up, and I cannot come forth.
9 Mine eye mourneth by reason of affliction: LORD, I have called daily
upon thee, I have stretched out my hands unto thee.

☆**88:1** Ps 22:2; 24:5 Lk 18:7
88:2 Ps 18:6; 86:1
88:3 Ps 107:18 116:3
88:4 Ps 28:1; 143:7
88:5 Ps 31:12 Isa 53:8
88:6 Ps 32:4; 42:7 69:15; 143:3 Lam 3:55
☆**88:8** Job 19:19; 30:10 Ps 31:11 Jer 32:2
☆**88:9** Job 11:13 Ps 6:7; 22:2 143:6

B. THE PSALMIST'S QUERIES

10 Wilt thou shew wonders to the dead? shall the dead arise *and* praise
thee? Se'lah.
11 Shall thy lovingkindness be declared in the grave? *or* thy faithfulness in
destruction?
12 Shall thy wonders be known in the dark? and thy righteousness in the
land of forgetfulness?
13 But unto thee have I cried, O LORD; and in the morning shall my
prayer prevent thee.
14 LORD, why castest thou off my soul? *why* hidest thou thy face from me?

88:10 Ps 6:5 Isa 38:18
88:12 Job 10:20, 21
88:13 Ps 5:3; 119:147
88:14 Job 13:24 Ps 13:1

---

when the city lay in ruins (according to some), and it *was designed to encourage* faith and hope for its restoration to its pristine glory. Others think it was written when the city was flourishing and thus expressed the joy of the people for its greatness.

87:4 *Rahab,* which is the name of a mythological monster, is used here as a symbol for Egypt. The word means "the haughty," "arrogant." (See Isa. 30:7.)

88:1ff This is one of the penitential Psalms. Mourning and woe comprise its contents. It is unrelieved and does not mention any comfort or joy. It speaks of the dark night of the soul as the penitent sinner asks why God has hidden his face from him. It is a Psalm we all need at certain times in our journey toward the celestial city, for it graphically represents the way we all feel on occasion.

88:8, 9 The psalmist is shut up a prisoner under the divine wrath. Sinking under the weight of his sins, he does not see any possibility of getting out of them. He weeps as he prays. He has not grasped what the New Testament so graphically portrays—that if we confess our sins, God is faithful and just and forgives our sins. Mourning should then give way to rejoicing, for our sins are cast behind the back of God to be remembered against us no more. Let not the forgiven sinner dwell in his thought life on those things God has chosen to forget.

C. THE PSALMIST'S LONELY LAMENT

88:15 Job 6:4; 31:23
88:16 Isa 13:13; Lam 1:12
88:17 Ps 22:12, 16
88:18☆ Job 19:13; Ps 38:11

15 I *am* afflicted and ready to die from *my* youth up: *while* I suffer thy
terrors I am distracted.
16 Thy fierce wrath goeth over me; thy terrors have cut me off.
17 They came round about me daily like water; they compassed me about
together.
18 Lover and friend hast thou put far from me, *and* mine acquaintance
into darkness.

I. GOD'S DAVIDIC COVENANT; A MESSIANIC PROMISE

A. THE LORD WHO IS FAITHFUL AND MERCIFUL

89:1☆ Ps 40:10; 59:16; 89:5, 8, 24, 33, 49
89:2 Ps 36:5; 103:17, 18
89:3 2 Sam 7:16; Ps 132:11; Isa 9:7; Lk 1:31–33
89:6☆ Ps 29:1; 96:4
89:7☆ Ps 47:2; 96:4
89:8 Ps 35:10
89:9 Ps 65:7; 107:29; 113:5
89:10☆ Ps 18:14; Isa 30:7; 51:9
89:11 Gen 1:1; 1 Chron 29:11; Ps 24:1
89:13 Ps 118:16
89:14 Num 10:10; Ps 97:2; 98:6

Maschil of Ethan the Ezrahite

89 I WILL sing of the mercies of the LORD for ever: with my mouth
will I make known thy faithfulness to all generations.
2 For I have said, Mercy shall be built up for ever: thy faithfulness shalt
thou establish in the very heavens.
3 I have made a covenant with my chosen, I have sworn unto David my
servant,
4 Thy seed will I establish for ever, and build up thy throne to all
generations. Se'lah.
5 And the heavens shall praise thy wonders, O LORD: thy faithfulness also
in the congregation of the saints.
6 For who in the heaven can be compared unto the LORD? *who* among the
sons of the mighty can be likened unto the LORD?
7 God is greatly to be feared in the assembly of the saints, and to be had
in reverence of all *them that are* about him.
8 O LORD God of hosts, who *is* a strong LORD like unto thee? or to thy
faithfulness round about thee?
9 Thou rulest the raging of the sea: when the waves thereof arise, thou
stillest them.
10 Thou hast broken Rahab in pieces, as one that is slain; thou hast
scattered thine enemies with thy strong arm.
11 The heavens *are* thine, the earth also *is* thine: *as for* the world and the
fulness thereof, thou hast founded them.
12 The north and the south thou hast created them: Ta'bor and Hermon
shall rejoice in thy name.
13 Thou hast a mighty arm: strong is thy hand, *and* high is thy right hand.
14 Justice and judgment *are* the habitation of thy throne: mercy and truth
shall go before thy face.
15 Blessed *is* the people that know the joyful sound: they shall walk, O
LORD, in the light of thy countenance.

88:18 Dolefully the psalmist closes his lament without a cheerful note or any expression of hope that he will be delivered from his difficulties. The Psalm might be called an unfinished symphony, of which his words are no more than the overture.

89:1ff This Psalm deals with the Davidic covenant and *the throne promised to his heirs forever.* 89:39 reaffirms the divine promise of a dynasty that will go on forever, a throne to the end of time. This messianic Psalm looks forward, of course, to Jesus as the heir of David. After the fall of Jerusalem in 587 B.C., no throne existed and no king sat on a throne. This does not mean that the plan or the purpose of God changed. An unbroken line of David's male heirs continued. The temporary suspension of the throne and the kingdom awaited the coming of Jesus, who now sits on the throne of his father David—a throne which is gloriously heavenly but which will be manifested on earth when the Messiah comes the second time.

89:6 *the sons of the mighty,* i.e., "the mightiest angels."†

89:7 *the assembly of the saints,* or, "the assembly of the angelic powers," or, "the assembly of the holy ones."†

89:10 *Rahab,* i.e., "Egypt."

16 In thy name shall they rejoice all the day: and in thy righteousness shall
they be exalted.
17 For thou *art* the glory of their strength: and in thy favour our horn shall
be exalted.
18 For the LORD *is* our defence; and the Holy One of Israel *is* our king.

B. THE LORD'S PROMISE TO DAVID AND HIS DESCENDANTS

19 Then thou spakest in vision to thy holy one, and saidst, I have laid help
upon *one that is* mighty; I have exalted *one* chosen out of the people.
20 I have found David my servant; with my holy oil have I anointed him:
21 With whom my hand shall be established: mine arm also shall
strengthen him.
22 The enemy shall not exact upon him; nor the son of wickedness afflict
him.
23 And I will beat down his foes before his face, and plague them that hate
him.
24 But my faithfulness and my mercy *shall be* with him: and in my name
shall his horn be exalted.
25 I will set his hand also in the sea, and his right hand in the rivers.
26 He shall cry unto me, Thou *art* my father, my God, and the rock of my
salvation.
27 Also I will make him *my* firstborn, higher than the kings of the earth.
28 My mercy will I keep for him for evermore, and my covenant shall
stand fast with him.
29 His seed also will I make *to endure* for ever, and his throne as the days
of heaven.
30 If his children forsake my law, and walk not in my judgments;
31 If they break my statutes, and keep not my commandments;
32 Then will I visit their transgression with the rod, and their iniquity with
stripes.
33 Nevertheless my lovingkindness will I not utterly take from him, nor
suffer my faithfulness to fail.
34 My covenant will I not break, nor alter the thing that is gone out of my
lips.
35 Once have I sworn by my holiness that I will not lie unto David.
36 His seed shall endure for ever, and his throne as the sun before me.
37 It shall be established for ever as the moon, and *as* a faithful witness in
heaven. Se'lah.

C. THE GREATNESS OF THE LORD'S PROMISE DESPITE DISTRESS

38 But thou hast cast off and abhorred, thou hast been wroth with thine
anointed.
39 Thou hast made void the covenant of thy servant: thou hast profaned
his crown *by casting it* to the ground.
40 Thou hast broken down all his hedges; thou hast brought his strong
holds to ruin.
41 All that pass by the way spoil him: he is a reproach to his neighbours.

89:16 Ps 105:3
89:17 Ps 44:3; 75:10; 148:14
89:18 Ps 47:9
☆**89:19** 2 Sam 17:10; 1 Kgs 11:34; Ps 78:70
89:20 1 Sam 16:13; Acts 13:22
89:21 Ps 18:32, 35
89:22 2 Sam 7:10, 11; Ps 125:3
89:23 2 Sam 7:9
89:24 Ps 132:17
89:25 Ps 72:8
89:26 2 Sam 7:14; 22:47; 1 Chron 22:10
89:27 Ps 2:7; 72:11; Rev 19:1, 5, 16
89:28 Isa 55:3
89:29 1 Kgs 2:4; Isa 9:7; Jer 33:17
89:30 2 Sam 7:14
89:33 2 Sam 7:15
89:34 Num 23:19; Deut 7:9; Jer 33:20, 21
89:35 Ps 60:6, 7; 89:29
89:37 Ps 72:5
89:38 1 Chron 28:9; Ps 44:9
89:39 Ps 78:59; Lam 2:7; 5:16
89:40 Ps 80:12; Lam 2:2, 5
89:41 Ps 44:13; 79:4

89:19 God made his will known to men in ages past by visions and other means. This was true in both the Old and New Testaments (Num. 12:6; Acts 16:9). Sometimes visions came at night, or while people were in trances. Sometimes they were not understood by the recipient. False prophets also claimed to have had visions. Among those who experienced dreams were (1) Abraham (Gen. 15:1), (2) Moses (Exod. 3:2, 3), (3) Samuel (1 Sam. 3:2–15), (4) Paul (Acts 9:3, 6, 12; 16:9), (5) Peter (Acts 10:9–17), (6) John (Rev. 1:2ff). *to thy holy one,* or, "to your saint." This apparently is a reference to Samuel, who was sent to anoint David as king.

89:42 Ps 13:2; 80:6

42 Thou hast set up the right hand of his adversaries; thou hast made all his enemies to rejoice.

89:43 Ps 44:10

43 Thou hast also turned the edge of his sword, and hast not made him to stand in the battle.

89:44 Ezek 28:7

44 Thou hast made his glory to cease, and cast his throne down to the ground.

89:45 Ps 44:15, 16 102:23

45 The days of his youth hast thou shortened: thou hast covered him with shame. Se′lah.

89:46 Ps 13:1; 79:5

46 How long, LORD? wilt thou hide thyself for ever? shall thy wrath burn like fire?

89:47 Job 7:7; 14:1 Ps 39:5; 6 Eccles 1:2; 2:11

47 Remember how short my time is: wherefore hast thou made all men in vain?

89:48 Ps 22:29 49:9, 15 Heb 11:5

48 What man *is he that* liveth, and shall not see death? shall he deliver his soul from the hand of the grave? Se′lah.

89:49☆

49 Lord, where *are* thy former lovingkindnesses, *which* thou swarest unto David in thy truth?

89:50 Ps 69:9, 19

50 Remember, Lord, the reproach of thy servants; *how* I do bear in my bosom *the reproach of* all the mighty people;

89:51 Ps 74:9, 10

51 Wherewith thine enemies have reproached, O LORD; wherewith they have reproached the footsteps of thine anointed.

89:52 Ps 41:13 106:48

52 Blessed *be* the LORD for evermore. Amen, and Amen.

BOOK IV (PSALMS 90—106)

I. GOD'S ETERNITY; MAN'S MORTALITY

A. THE GOD WHO IS FOREVER

A Prayer of Moses the man of God

90:1☆ Deut 33:27 Ezek 11:16 **90:2** Gen 1:1 Ps 102:24, 25, 27 Prov 8:22–26

90 LORD, thou hast been our dwelling place in all generations.
2 Before the mountains were brought forth, or ever thou hadst formed the earth and the world, even from everlasting to everlasting, thou *art* God.

B. MAN WHO IS BORN TO DIE

90:3 Job 34:14, 15

3 Thou turnest man to destruction; and sayest, Return, ye children of men.

90:4 Ps 39:5 2 Pet 3:8

4 For a thousand years in thy sight *are but* as yesterday when it is past, and *as* a watch in the night.

90:5 Job 14:2; 20:8 27:20 Isa 40:6 Mt 6:30 Jas 1:11

5 Thou carriest them away as with a flood; they are *as* a sleep: in the morning *they are* like grass *which* groweth up.

6 In the morning it flourisheth, and groweth up; in the evening it is cut down, and withereth.

90:7 Ps 39:11

7 For we are consumed by thine anger, and by thy wrath are we troubled.

89:49 *thy truth,* i.e., "thy faithful pledge." The Hebrew word *emunah* ("truth") speaks of God and truth. God keeps his word. Christ is called "the truth" (John 14:6; 7:18). The Holy Spirit is labeled the "Spirit of truth" (John 14:17). The Word of God itself is thus defined: "*thy word is truth*" (John 17:17). God's truth should be known, believed, and practiced. It should also be handled rightly and with care.

90:1ff This prayer of Moses seems to refer to what happened on the journey of Israel from Egypt to Canaan. God had sentenced his people to thirty-eight years of wandering because of their unbelief, murmuring, and rebellion. Moses' prayer was one they could well have used daily in their tents and in the tabernacle services. It would be a prayer of instruction for the new generation of Israelites who would enter the land after their sinning fathers had died in the wilderness. In Exodus we find the hymn of praise (Exod. 15) composed and sung by Moses and the people after their deliverance from the Egyptians. It is mentioned in Rev. 15:3. At the end of Moses' life he composed another song of instruction found in Deut. 32. Ps. 90 is different in that it is a prayer and as such can be used by all today.

8 Thou hast set our iniquities before thee, our secret *sins* in the light of thy
countenance.
9 For all our days are passed away in the wrath: we spend our years as a
tale *that is told.*
10 The days of our years *are* threescore years and ten; and if by reason of
strength *they be* fourscore years, yet *is* their strength labour and sorrow; for
it is soon cut off, and we fly away.
11 Who knoweth the power of thine anger? even according to thy fear, *so*
is thy wrath.
12 So teach *us* to number our days, that we may apply *our* hearts unto
wisdom.

90:8 Ps 50:21; Jer 16:17; Eccles 12:14
90:9 Ps 78:33
90:10 Ps 78:39; Eccles 12:2–7
90:11 Ps 76:7
☆**90:12** Ps 39:4; Prov 2:1–6

C. THE PRAYER FOR GOD TO HELP MORTAL MEN

13 Return, O LORD, how long? and let it repent thee concerning thy
servants.
14 O satisfy us early with thy mercy; that we may rejoice and be glad all
our days.
15 Make us glad according to the days *wherein* thou hast afflicted us, *and*
the years *wherein* we have seen evil.
16 Let thy work appear unto thy servants, and thy glory unto their
children.
17 And let the beauty of the LORD our God be upon us: and establish thou
the work of our hands upon us; yea, the work of our hands establish thou it.

90:13 Deut 32:36; Ps 80:14; 106:45; Jonah 3:9
90:14 Ps 36:8; 103:5; Jer 31:14
90:15 Ps 31:10; 86:4
90:16 Ps 44:1; Hab 3:2
90:17 Isa 26:12; 1 Cor 3:7

I. SHELTERED IN THE SHADOW OF THE ALMIGHTY

A. GOD'S PEOPLE ARE SAFE

91 HE that dwelleth in the secret place of the most High shall abide
under the shadow of the Almighty.
2 I will say of the LORD, *He is* my refuge and my fortress: my God; in him
will I trust.
3 Surely he shall deliver thee from the snare of the fowler, *and* from the
noisome pestilence.
4 He shall cover thee with his feathers, and under his wings shalt thou
trust: his truth *shall be thy* shield and buckler.
5 Thou shalt not be afraid for the terror by night; *nor* for the arrow *that*
flieth by day;
6 *Nor* for the pestilence *that* walketh in darkness; *nor* for the destruction
that wasteth at noonday.

☆**91:1** Ps 31:20; Isa 25:4; 32:2
91:2 Ps 18:2; 142:5; Jer 16:19
91:3 2 Chron 20:9; Ps 124:7
91:4 Ps 35:2; 57:1; 63:7; Isa 51:1–6
91:5 Job 5:19–23; Ps 23:4
91:6 Job 5:22

B. GOD'S ANGELS PROTECT THEM

7 A thousand shall fall at thy side, and ten thousand at thy right hand; *but*
it shall not come nigh thee.
8 Only with thine eyes shalt thou behold and see the reward of the wicked.
9 Because thou hast made the LORD, *which is* my refuge, *even* the most
High, thy habitation;

☆**91:7** Gen 7:23
91:8 Ps 37:34; 58:10

90:12 Let a man consider that his days are few in number and that he has little time to arrange the affairs of life before death overtakes him. The shortness and uncertainty of life will give way to death and eternity. While there is time, let a man seek the instruction of God by his Spirit so that his heart will incline to wisdom—which is the practice of serious godliness.

91:1ff The authorship of this Psalm is not stated. Some think it relates to the numbering of Israel by David contrary to the will of God. It speaks of "the pestilence that walketh in darkness" (91:6). It has for its central message the certainty that God is our deliverer so that we need not fear. It is a Psalm having particular relevance to the present disordered age.

91:7 "When death rides in triumph, and diseases rage, so that thousands and ten thousands fall . . . and the sight of their fall is enough to frighten thee . . . yet it shall not come nigh thee, the death shall not, the fear of death shall not."* This is the promise of God to the righteous as they see the fall of the wicked.

91:10 Prov 12:21
[10]There shall no evil befall thee, neither shall any plague come nigh thy
dwelling.
91:11 Ps 34:7; Mt 4:6; Lk 4:9–11
[11]For he shall give his angels charge over thee, to keep thee in all thy
ways.
[12]They shall bear thee up in *their* hands, lest thou dash thy foot against a
stone.
91:13 Judg 14:6; Dan 6:22; Lk 10:19
[13]Thou shalt tread upon the lion and adder: the young lion and the
dragon shalt thou trample under feet.

C. GOD PROMISES HE WILL RESCUE HIS PEOPLE

91:14 Ps 9:10; 145:20
[14]Because he hath set his love upon me, therefore will I deliver him: I will
set him on high, because he hath known my name.
91:15 1 Sam 2:30; Ps 50:15; Jn 12:26
[15]He shall call upon me, and I will answer him: I *will be* with him in
trouble; I will deliver him, and honour him.
91:16☆ Deut 6:2; Ps 21:4; 50:23
[16]With long life will I satisfy him, and shew him my salvation.

I. A SONG FOR THE SABBATH DAY

A. SING GOD'S PRAISES ON THE SABBATH

A Psalm or Song for the sabbath day

92:1☆ Ps 147:1
92 *IT is a* good *thing* to give thanks unto the LORD, and to sing praises
unto thy name, O most High:
92:2☆ Ps 59:16
[2]To shew forth thy lovingkindness in the morning, and thy faithfulness
every night,
92:3 1 Sam 10:5; 1 Chron 13:8; Neh 12:27
[3]Upon an instrument of ten strings, and upon the psaltery; upon the
harp with a solemn sound.
92:4 Ps 106:47
[4]For thou, LORD, hast made me glad through thy work: I will triumph in
the works of thy hands.

B. NOTE THE END OF THE WICKED

92:5 Ps 36:6; 40:5; 139:17; Rom 11:33; Rev 15:3
[5]O LORD, how great are thy works! *and* thy thoughts are very deep.
92:6 Ps 49:10
[6]A brutish man knoweth not; neither doth a fool understand this.
92:7 Ps 37:38
[7]When the wicked spring as the grass, and when all the workers of
iniquity do flourish; *it is* that they shall be destroyed for ever:
92:8 Ps 113:5
[8]But thou, LORD, *art most* high for evermore.
92:9 Ps 37:20; 68:1
[9]For, lo, thine enemies, O LORD, for, lo, thine enemies shall perish; all
the workers of iniquity shall be scattered.

C. NOTE THE BLESSEDNESS OF THE RIGHTEOUS

92:10 Ps 23:5; 45:7; 75:10
[10]But my horn shalt thou exalt like *the horn of* an unicorn: I shall be
anointed with fresh oil.
92:11 Ps 54:7
[11]Mine eye also shall see *my desire* on mine enemies, *and* mine ears shall
hear *my desire* of the wicked that rise up against me.
92:12 Jer 17:8; Ezek 31:3; Hos 14:5, 6
[12]The righteous shall flourish like the palm tree: he shall grow like a cedar
in Lebanon.
92:13 Isa 60:21
[13]Those that be planted in the house of the LORD shall flourish in the
courts of our God.
92:14 Isa 37:31; Jn 15:2; Jas 3:18
[14]They shall still bring forth fruit in old age; they shall be fat and
flourishing;

91:16 Even as sin and death go hand in hand, so do life and salvation.
92:1, 2 This Psalm was used on the sabbath for praising the God who blesses the righteous and judges the wicked. Praise him for his love in the morning, and when evening comes, thank him for his faithfulness.

15 To shew that the LORD *is* upright: *he is* my rock, and *there is* no unrighteousness in him.

[☆92:15 Job 34:10; Ps 24:8; Rom 9:14]

I. JEHOVAH, THE KING OF THE OCEAN WAVES

93 THE LORD reigneth, he is clothed with majesty; the LORD is clothed with strength, *wherewith* he hath girded himself: the world also is stablished, that it cannot be moved.

[93:1 Isa 51:9]

2 Thy throne *is* established of old: thou *art* from everlasting.

3 The floods have lifted up, O LORD, the floods have lifted up their voice; the floods lift up their waves.

[93:2 Lam 5:19; 93:3 Ps 98:7, 8]

4 The LORD on high *is* mightier than the noise of many waters, *yea, than* the mighty waves of the sea.

[93:4 Ps 65:7]

5 Thy testimonies are very sure: holiness becometh thine house, O LORD, for ever.

[☆93:5 1 Cor 3:17]

I. A PSALM ABOUT OPPRESSORS

A. SEEKING GOD'S VENGEANCE ON THE OPPRESSORS

94 O LORD God, to whom vengeance belongeth; O God, to whom vengeance belongeth, shew thyself.

2 Lift up thyself, thou judge of the earth: render a reward to the proud.

3 LORD, how long shall the wicked, how long shall the wicked triumph?

4 *How long* shall they utter *and* speak hard things? *and* all the workers of iniquity boast themselves?

5 They break in pieces thy people, O LORD, and afflict thine heritage.

6 They slay the widow and the stranger, and murder the fatherless.

7 Yet they say, The LORD shall not see, neither shall the God of Jacob regard *it*.

[☆94:1 Deut 32:35; Isa 35:4; Nah 1:2; Rom 12:19; 94:3 Job 20:5; 94:4 Ps 31:18; 52:1; 94:5 Isa 3:15; 94:6 Job 22:13; Isa 10:2]

8 Understand, ye brutish among the people: and *ye* fools, when will ye be wise?

9 He that planted the ear, shall he not hear? he that formed the eye, shall he not see?

[94:9 Ex 4:11; Prov 20:12]

10 He that chastiseth the heathen, shall not he correct? he that teacheth man knowledge, *shall not he know?*

11 The LORD knoweth the thoughts of man, that they *are* vanity.

12 Blessed *is* the man whom thou chastenest, O LORD, and teachest him out of thy law;

13 That thou mayest give him rest from the days of adversity, until the pit be digged for the wicked.

[94:11 Job 11:11; 1 Cor 3:20; ☆94:12 Deut 8:5; Ps 9:15; Prov 3:11, 12; Heb 12:5, 6]

14 For the LORD will not cast off his people, neither will he forsake his inheritance.

15 But judgment shall return unto righteousness: and all the upright in heart shall follow it.

[94:14 1 Sam 12:22; Rom 11:2; 94:15 Isa 42:3; Mic 7:9]

92:15 *my rock.* "I have chosen him for my rock on which to build, in the clefts of which to take shelter, on the top of which to set my feet. I have found him a rock, strong and steadfast, and his word as firm as a rock."*

93:5 The promises of God cannot be broken. He reigns in truth and holiness. All the saints may rely on God's Word.

94:1ff Those who use this Psalm ask the Lord to avenge them against their enemies. God indeed is the one *to whom vengeance belongeth.* In the New Testament Jesus sustained this notion: "Shall not God avenge his own elect, which cry day and night unto him . . . ?" (Luke 18:7). The deeds of the wicked are such that they deserve the wrath of God and will experience it at last.

94:12 God uses the instruments of trouble to chasten those who love him; such people are blessed whether they realize it or not. They are under divine discipline, and are taught, reformed, and improved.

B. SEEKING GOD'S HELP AGAINST THE OPPRESSORS

94:16 Num 10:35; Isa 28:21; 33:10
94:17 Ps 124:1, 2
94:18 Ps 73:2
94:19 Isa 57:18, 66:13
94:20☆ Ps 58:2
94:21 Ex 23:7; Mt 27:4
94:23 Ps 140:9, 11

16 Who will rise up for me against the evildoers? *or* who will stand up for
me against the workers of iniquity?
17 Unless the LORD *had been* my help, my soul had almost dwelt in
silence.
18 When I said, My foot slippeth; thy mercy, O LORD, held me up.
19 In the multitude of my thoughts within me thy comforts delight my
soul.
20 Shall the throne of iniquity have fellowship with thee, which frameth
mischief by a law?
21 They gather themselves together against the soul of the righteous, and
condemn the innocent blood.
22 But the LORD is my defence; and my God *is* the rock of my refuge.
23 And he shall bring upon them their own iniquity, and shall cut them off
in their own wickedness; *yea*, the LORD our God shall cut them off.

I. GOD IS OUR ROCK AND SHEPHERD

A. THE SONG OF PRAISE AND WORSHIP TO GOD

95:1☆ Ps 66:1
95:2 Mic 6:6–8; Eph 5:19; Jas 5:13
95:4 Ps 135:5, 6
95:5 Gen 1:9, 10; Jonah 1:9
95:6 Isa 17:7; Dan 6:10; Hos 8:14
95:7 Heb 3:7–11; 15; 4:7

95 O COME, let us sing unto the LORD: let us make a joyful noise to
the rock of our salvation.
2 Let us come before his presence with thanksgiving, and make a joyful
noise unto him with psalms.
3 For the LORD *is* a great God, and a great King above all gods.
4 In his hand *are* the deep places of the earth: the strength of the hills *is*
his also.
5 The sea *is* his, and he made it: and his hands formed the dry *land*.
6 O come, let us worship and bow down: let us kneel before the LORD our
maker.
7 For he *is* our God; and we *are* the people of his pasture, and the sheep
of his hand. To day if ye will hear his voice,

B. THE MEMORY OF ISRAEL'S UNBELIEF

95:8☆ Num 20:13; Deut 6:16
95:9 Num 14:22
95:10 Acts 7:36; 13:18; Heb 3:17
95:11 Deut 1:35; Heb 4:3, 5

8 Harden not your heart, as in the provocation, *and* as *in* the day of
temptation in the wilderness:
9 When your fathers tempted me, proved me, and saw my work.
10 Forty years long was I grieved with *this* generation, and said, It *is* a
people that do err in their heart, and they have not known my ways:
11 Unto whom I sware in my wrath that they should not enter into my
rest.

I. THE NEW SONG TO THE LORD, THE KING

A. THE CALL TO WORSHIP

96:1☆

96 O SING unto the LORD a new song: sing unto the LORD, all the
earth.

94:20 *which frameth mischief by a law.* These words mean that the wicked have their evil intentions legalized by legislation. Thus they can convict the righteous *innocent* as *malefactors* under their wicked statutes.
95:1ff This is an evangelistic Psalm, part of which is quoted in Heb. 3:10, 17 and 4:3, 5. Only those who have experienced God's salvation through the gospel can make a joyful noise to God. The unconverted are warned not to harden their hearts, else they will never enter the rest of God.

95:8 The elders of Israel hardened their hearts at Meribah when they quarreled with Moses and with God. For this they were shut out from entering Canaan. Let no believer harden his heart and be shut out of his everlasting rest.
96:1ff This Psalm was delivered into the hand of Asaph and his brethren by David its author (1 Chron. 16:7). It is then repeated in the book of 1 Chronicles. It was sung in connection with the bringing of the ark to Jerusalem, where it was placed in the midst of the tent

2 Sing unto the LORD, bless his name; shew forth his salvation from day
to day.
3 Declare his glory among the heathen, his wonders among all people.
4 For the LORD *is* great, and greatly to be praised: he *is* to be feared above
all gods.
5 For all the gods of the nations *are* idols: but the LORD made the
heavens.
6 Honour and majesty *are* before him: strength and beauty *are* in his
sanctuary.

96:3 Ps 145:12
96:5 1 Chron 16:26; Isa 42:5

B. THE CALL TO THE NATIONS TO PRAISE GOD

7 Give unto the LORD, O ye kindreds of the people, give unto the LORD
glory and strength.
8 Give unto the LORD the glory *due unto* his name: bring an offering, and
come into his courts.
9 O worship the LORD in the beauty of holiness: fear before him, all the
earth.
10 Say among the heathen *that* the LORD reigneth: the world also shall be
established that it shall not be moved: he shall judge the people righteously.

96:8 Ps 115:1
96:9 1 Chron 16:29; 2 Chron 20:21
☆**96:10** Ps 58:11; 67:4

C. THE WITNESS OF NATURE THAT GOD IS JUDGE

11 Let the heavens rejoice, and let the earth be glad; let the sea roar, and
the fulness thereof.
12 Let the field be joyful, and all that *is* therein: then shall all the trees of
the wood rejoice
13 Before the LORD: for he cometh, for he cometh to judge the earth: he
shall judge the world with righteousness, and the people with his truth.

☆**96:11** Isa 49:13
☆**96:12** Isa 35:1; 44:23; 55:12, 13
☆**96:13**

I. JEHOVAH IS KING

A. JEHOVAH IS KING OVER ALL

97 THE LORD reigneth; let the earth rejoice; let the multitude of isles
be glad *thereof*.
2 Clouds and darkness *are* round about him: righteousness and judgment
are the habitation of his throne.
3 A fire goeth before him, and burneth up his enemies round about.
4 His lightnings enlightened the world: the earth saw, and trembled.
5 The hills melted like wax at the presence of the LORD, at the presence of
the Lord of the whole earth.
6 The heavens declare his righteousness, and all the people see his glory.

☆**97:1** Isa 42:10, 12
97:2 Ex 19:9; Deut 4:11; 1 Kgs 8:12
97:3 Heb 12:29
97:4 Ps 77:18
97:5 Josh 3:11; Amos 9:5
97:6 Isa 6:3

B. THE WHOLE EARTH WITNESSES TO HIS MAJESTY

7 Confounded be all they that serve graven images, that boast themselves
of idols: worship him, all *ye* gods.
8 Zion heard, and was glad; and the daughters of Judah rejoiced because
of thy judgments, O LORD.

97:7 Jer 10:14; Heb 1:6
97:8 Ex 18:11; Zeph 3:14

David had erected to house it. The Psalm has a missionary aspect and looks forward to the incarnation of Christ when it speaks about declaring "God's glory among the heathen, his wonders among all people" (96:3).

96:10–13 If all nature can celebrate the reign of the glorious God, should not all men at least follow nature and do the same?

97:1ff This Psalm obviously looks far beyond its immediate purpose. It prophetically portrays the truth con-cerning the Lord's Christ, who will fulfill in himself all that is contained here.

97:9☆ 9 For thou, LORD, *art* high above all the earth: thou art exalted far above
all gods.

C. THE LORD PROTECTS AND RESCUES HIS PEOPLE

97:10 Prov 8:13 10 Ye that love the LORD, hate evil: he preserveth the souls of his saints;
Dan 3:28 he delivereth them out of the hand of the wicked.
Rom 12:9 97:11 Job 22:28 11 Light is sown for the righteous, and gladness for the upright in heart.
97:12 12 Rejoice in the LORD, ye righteous; and give thanks at the remembrance
Ps 32:11 of his holiness.

I. LET THE EARTH REJOICE; THE LORD IS KING

A. THE SONG OF VICTORY

A Psalm

98:1☆ Ex 15:6 **98** O SING unto the LORD a new song; for he hath done marvellous
Isa 52:10 things: his right hand, and his holy arm, hath gotten him the
victory.
98:2 2 The LORD hath made known his salvation: his righteousness hath he
Lk 1:54, 72 Rom 3:25 openly shewed in the sight of the heathen.
3 He hath remembered his mercy and his truth toward the house of Israel:
all the ends of the earth have seen the salvation of our God.
4 Make a joyful noise unto the LORD, all the earth: make a loud noise, and
rejoice, and sing praise.
5 Sing unto the LORD with the harp; with the harp, and the voice of a
psalm.
98:6 Num 10:10 6 With trumpets and sound of cornets make a joyful noise before the
2 Chron 15:14 LORD, the King.

B. THE EARTH AND ALL NATURE PRAISE THE KING

98:7 7 Let the sea roar, and the fulness thereof; the world, and they that dwell
Ps 24:1 therein.
98:8 8 Let the floods clap *their* hands: let the hills be joyful together
98:9☆ 9 Before the LORD; for he cometh to judge the earth: with righteousness
Isa 55:12 shall he judge the world, and the people with equity.

I. PRAISE TO THE EXALTED KING OF GLORY

99:1☆ Ex 25:22 1 Sam 4:4

A. LET THE EARTH'S RULERS EXALT THE LORD

99:2 Isa 12:6 **99** THE LORD reigneth; let the people tremble: he sitteth *between* the
99:3 cherubims; let the earth be moved.
Deut 28:58 2 The LORD *is* great in Zion; and he *is* high above all the people.
Josh 24:19 1 Sam 2:2 3 Let them praise thy great and terrible name; *for* it *is* holy.
99:4 Ps 17:2 4 The king's strength also loveth judgment; thou dost establish equity,
Jer 23:5 thou executest judgment and righteousness in Jacob.
99:5☆ Ps 34:3; 118:28 5 Exalt ye the LORD our God, and worship at his footstool; *for* he *is* holy.

97:9 *all gods,* i.e., "all counterfeit gods or idols."
98:1 This Psalm is a prophecy of the coming Messiah. He will set up his kingdom and bring even the Gentiles into it. Therefore let the righteous praise their God and let all nature join in the refrain.
98:9 *he cometh to judge the earth.* This reference to the coming judgment looks to the second advent of Jesus Christ. 2 Tim. 4:1, 1 Pet. 4:5, and Rev. 19:11 all point to this.
99:1 This Psalm includes the notion of the Messiah's kingdom but is more directly related to the old dispensation under which the Israelites lived. They were not to neglect the regimen under which they functioned or the ordinances they were given.
99:5 *he is holy.* Holiness sums up all of God's moral perfections. Therefore all flesh should worship him.

B. THE ILLUSTRATIONS OF MOSES, AARON, AND SAMUEL

6 Moses and Aaron among his priests, and Samuel among them that call
upon his name; they called upon the LORD, and he answered them.
7 He spake unto them in the cloudy pillar: they kept his testimonies, and
the ordinance *that* he gave them.
8 Thou answeredst them, O LORD our God: thou wast a God that
forgavest them, though thou tookest vengeance of their inventions.
9 Exalt the LORD our God, and worship at his holy hill; for the LORD our
God *is* holy.

☆**99:6** Ex 15:25; 1 Sam 7:9; 12:18
☆**99:7** Ex 33:9; Num 12:5
99:8 Num 14:20; 20:12

I. THE EXHORTATION FOR ALL MEN TO PRAISE THE LORD

A Psalm of praise

100 MAKE a joyful noise unto the LORD, all ye lands.
2 Serve the LORD with gladness: come before his presence with
singing.
3 Know ye that the LORD he *is* God: *it is* he *that* hath made us, and not we
ourselves; *we are* his people, and the sheep of his pasture.
4 Enter into his gates with thanksgiving, *and* into his courts with praise:
be thankful unto him, *and* bless his name.
5 For the LORD *is* good; his mercy *is* everlasting; and his truth *endureth* to
all generations.

☆**100:1**
100:2 Deut 12:11, 12; 28:47
100:3 1 Kgs 18:39; Isa 40:11; Ezek 34:30, 31; Mk 14:27; Jn 10:11
100:5 Ps 25:8; Jer 33:11; Nah 1:7

I. A RULER OF INTEGRITY

A. THE DESIRE FOR A HOLY RULE

A Psalm of David

101 I WILL sing of mercy and judgment: unto thee, O LORD, will I
sing.
2 I will behave myself wisely in a perfect way. O when wilt thou come
unto me? I will walk within my house with a perfect heart.
3 I will set no wicked thing before mine eyes: I hate the work of them that
turn aside; *it* shall not cleave to me.
4 A froward heart shall depart from me: I will not know a wicked *person*.
5 Whoso privily slandereth his neighbour, him will I cut off: him that hath
an high look and a proud heart will not I suffer.

☆**101:1** Ps 145:7
☆**101:3** Deut 15:9
101:4 Prov 11:20
101:5 Prov 6:16–19

B. THE DESIRE FOR A GODLY PEOPLE

6 Mine eyes *shall be* upon the faithful of the land, that they may dwell
with me: he that walketh in a perfect way, he shall serve me.
7 He that worketh deceit shall not dwell within my house: he that telleth
lies shall not tarry in my sight.

99:6, 7 Moses and Aaron worshipped God in their earnest prayers and by their holy lives.
100:1 This verse calls for all the earth to make *a joyful noise unto the LORD.* This envisions the gospel age and the preaching of the good news to all men everywhere. All peoples are urged to enter his courts, accept and thank him for his salvation, and remember that he is forever the same in his steadfastness.
101:1ff This Psalm is David's solemn vow to God that he will use his royal power for the glory of the God who gave him that power. There will be terror for those who do evil, and praise for those who do good. Such should be the case in connection with government today in its attitude toward the wicked and the righteous.
101:3 What we hear and see can be the greatest source of temptation that leads to evil. Here the eye is mentioned. The good man shuts his eye from seeing evil (Isa. 33:15).

101:8☆ Ps 46:4; 75:10

8 I will early destroy all the wicked of the land; that I may cut off all
wicked doers from the city of the LORD.

I. THE PRAYER OF A CAPTIVE EXILE

A. THE PSALMIST'S DISTRESS

A Prayer of the afflicted, when he is overwhelmed, and poureth out his complaint before the LORD

102:1☆ Ex 2:23; 1 Sam 9:16

102 HEAR my prayer, O LORD, and let my cry come unto thee.
2 Hide not thy face from me in the day *when* I am in trouble;
incline thine ear unto me: in the day *when* I call answer me speedily.

102:3☆ Ezra 10:6; Job 30:30; Jas 4:14 — **102:4**☆

3 For my days are consumed like smoke, and my bones are burned as an
hearth.
4 My heart is smitten, and withered like grass; so that I forget to eat my
bread.

102:5☆ Lam 4:8 — **102:6** Zeph 2:14 — **102:8** 2 Sam 16:5; Isa 65:15; Lk 23:11; Acts 26:11 — **102:9** Job 27:21

5 By reason of the voice of my groaning my bones cleave to my skin.
6 I am like a pelican of the wilderness: I am like an owl of the desert.
7 I watch, and am as a sparrow alone upon the house top.
8 Mine enemies reproach me all the day; *and* they that are mad against me
are sworn against me.
9 For I have eaten ashes like bread, and mingled my drink with weeping,
10 Because of thine indignation and thy wrath: for thou hast lifted me up,
and cast me down.
11 My days *are* like a shadow that declineth; and I am withered like grass.

102:12☆ Ex 3:15; Lam 5:19

12 But thou, O LORD, shalt endure for ever; and thy remembrance unto all
generations.

B. GOD WILL HELP THE DESTITUTE

102:13 Isa 60:10; Zech 1:12

13 Thou shalt arise, *and* have mercy upon Zion: for the time to favour her,
yea, the set time, is come.
14 For thy servants take pleasure in her stones, and favour the dust
thereof.

102:15 1 Kgs 8:41, 42 — **102:16** Isa 60:1, 2 — **102:17** Neh 1:6 — **102:18** Deut 31:19; 1 Cor 10:11 — **102:19** Deut 26:15

15 So the heathen shall fear the name of the LORD, and all the kings of the
earth thy glory.
16 When the LORD shall build up Zion, he shall appear in his glory.
17 He will regard the prayer of the destitute, and not despise their prayer.
18 This shall be written for the generation to come: and the people which
shall be created shall praise the LORD.
19 For he hath looked down from the height of his sanctuary; from heaven
did the LORD behold the earth;

102:20☆ — **102:21** Isa 49:22; 23; 60:3; Zech 8:20–23

20 To hear the groaning of the prisoner; to loose those that are appointed
to death;
21 To declare the name of the LORD in Zion, and his praise in Jerusalem;

101:8 "David would do his utmost to destroy all the wicked . . . He would do it early; he would lose no time and spare no pains; he would be forward and zealous in promoting the reformation of manners and suppression of vice."*

102:1ff *102:25 and 26 of this Psalm are quoted in Heb. 1:10–12. In Hebrews they are applied to Jesus Christ;* therefore, some think this Psalm to be of the messianic variety. In any event, the psalmist was in great affliction. He finds solace in the eternal God of comfort as he faithfully believes in and looks for deliverance.

102:3–5 The psalmist speaks of his body as being emaciated. He was nothing but skin and bones (102:5). So bad was his condition that he forgot to eat his bread (102:4).

102:12 Men are dying creatures, but God is an everliving, everlasting God. Their lives are transient, God's is permanent. Friend and foe alike die but God does not. The good man who loves God can counter sorrow and death with the pleasing thought of the unchangeable God who gives him blessedness forever.

102:20 All men are doomed to die but God has set free those who hear and believe the gospel. The groaning of the prisoner turns to shouts of praise.

22 When the people are gathered together, and the kingdoms, to serve the
LORD.

C. GOD WILL PRESERVE HIS PEOPLE

23 He weakened my strength in the way; he shortened my days.
24 I said, O my God, take me not away in the midst of my days: thy years
are throughout all generations.
25 Of old hast thou laid the foundation of the earth: and the heavens *are*
the work of thy hands.
26 They shall perish, but thou shalt endure: yea, all of them shall wax old
like a garment; as a vesture shalt thou change them, and they shall be
changed:
27 But thou *art* the same, and thy years shall have no end.
28 The children of thy servants shall continue, and their seed shall be
established before thee.

102:24 Isa 38:10; Hab 1:12
☆**102:25** Gen 1:1; Neh 9:6; Heb 1:10–12
102:26 Mt 24:35; 2 Pet 3:10; Rev 20:11
102:27 Mal 3:6; Jas 1:17

I. A COMMAND TO BLESS THE LORD

A. THE CALL TO BLESS HIM

A Psalm of David

103 BLESS the LORD, O my soul: and all that is within me, *bless* his
holy name.
2 Bless the LORD, O my soul, and forget not all his benefits:

☆**103:1** Ezek 39:7
103:2 Deut 8:11

B. THE REASONS FOR BLESSING HIM

3 Who forgiveth all thine iniquities; who healeth all thy diseases;
4 Who redeemeth thy life from destruction; who crowneth thee with
lovingkindness and tender mercies;
5 Who satisfieth thy mouth with good *things; so that* thy youth is renewed
like the eagle's.
6 The LORD executeth righteousness and judgment for all that are
oppressed.
7 He made known his ways unto Moses, his acts unto the children of
Israel.
8 The LORD *is* merciful and gracious, slow to anger, and plenteous in
mercy.
9 He will not always chide: neither will he keep *his anger* for ever.
10 He hath not dealt with us after our sins; nor rewarded us according to
our iniquities.
11 For as the heaven is high above the earth, *so* great is his mercy toward
them that fear him.
12 As far as the east is from the west, *so* far hath he removed our
transgressions from us.
13 Like as a father pitieth *his* children, *so* the LORD pitieth them that fear
him.

☆**103:3** Ex 34:7; Jer 30:17
103:4 Ps 49:15
103:5 Isa 40:31
103:7 Ex 33:13
103:8 Num 14:18; Neh 1:3; 9:17; Joel 2:13; Jonah 4:2
103:9 Jer 3:12
103:10 Lam 3:22
☆**103:12** Isa 38:17; Heb 9:26
103:13 Mal 3:17

102:25 God is the source of all being and has all power and dominion. He speaks and it comes to pass. God and his children shall endure forever.

103:1ff This song of praise is general in nature. The psalmist praises the God who pities his children, vindicates them, and forgives their sins. The love of God is everlasting and his throne is forever established in the heavens. Let angels, men, and the hosts of heaven bless the name of this great God.

103:3 By the forgiveness of our sins, we are restored to the favor of God. And all that we lost in Adam we shall regain at last, so that Paradise itself is regained and restored.

103:12 So far are our transgressions removed from us that they shall never be laid to our charge, nor shall they be used in judgment against us. They shall be sought for and not found.

103:14 Gen 3:19; Eccles 12:7 **103:15** Jas 1:10, 11; 1 Pet 1:24

14 For he knoweth our frame; he remembereth that we *are* dust.
15 *As for* man, his days *are* as grass: as a flower of the field, so he
flourisheth.
16 For the wind passeth over it, and it is gone; and the place thereof shall
know it no more.

C. THE LORD'S LOVE IS EVERLASTING

103:17 Deut 5:10

17 But the mercy of the LORD *is* from everlasting to everlasting upon them
that fear him, and his righteousness unto children's children;
18 To such as keep his covenant, and to those that remember his
commandments to do them.

D. LET EVERYONE AND EVERYTHING BLESS THE LORD

103:19 Dan 4:17

19 The LORD hath prepared his throne in the heavens; and his kingdom
ruleth over all.

103:20☆ Mt 6:10; Heb 1:14 **103:21** Lk 2:13

20 Bless the LORD, ye his angels, that excel in strength, that do his
commandments, hearkening unto the voice of his word.
21 Bless ye the LORD, all *ye* his hosts; *ye* ministers of his, that do his
pleasure.
22 Bless the LORD, all his works in all places of his dominion: bless the
LORD, O my soul.

I. A PSALM TO JEHOVAH, THE GOD OF CREATION

A. THE FORMATION OF THE HEAVENS AND THE EARTH

104:1☆ Isa 40:22; Dan 7:9

104 BLESS the LORD, O my soul. O LORD my God, thou art very
great; thou art clothed with honour and majesty.
2 Who coverest *thyself* with light as *with* a garment: who stretchest out the
heavens like a curtain:

104:3 Amos 9:6 **104:4** 2 Kgs 2:11; 6:17; Heb 1:7 **104:5** Job 38:4 **104:6** Gen 1:2

3 Who layeth the beams of his chambers in the waters: who maketh the
clouds his chariot: who walketh upon the wings of the wind:
4 Who maketh his angels spirits; his ministers a flaming fire:
5 *Who* laid the foundations of the earth, *that* it should not be removed for
ever.
6 Thou coveredst it with the deep as *with* a garment: the waters stood
above the mountains.

104:7 Ps 18:15; 29:3 **104:8☆** **104:9** Jer 5:22

7 At thy rebuke they fled; at the voice of thy thunder they hasted away.
8 They go up by the mountains; they go down by the valleys unto the
place which thou hast founded for them.
9 Thou hast set a bound that they may not pass over; that they turn not
again to cover the earth.

B. GOD'S PROVISION FOR BEASTS, BIRDS, AND MAN

104:10 Isa 41:18

10 He sendeth the springs into the valleys, *which* run among the hills.
11 They give drink to every beast of the field: the wild asses quench their
thirst.

103:20 The angels are mighty in strength. One of them slew 185,000 Assyrian soldiers in one night. They are ministers to the saints to help them.

104:1ff This Psalm is noted for its poetic beauty, the splendor of its ideas, its flight of fancy, and its wonderful language. In it the greatness, majesty, and sovereign control of God are celebrated. He is the God of nature as well as the God of man. This is manifested in his works of creation and providence with respect to all creatures. Let all men bless and praise and rejoice in such a great God.

104:8 There are evidences of sea life on the tops of some of the highest mountains, which suggests that at one time they were submerged under the waters. God makes mountains to rise and fall according to his good pleasure.

12 By them shall the fowls of the heaven have their habitation, *which* sing
among the branches.
104:12 Mt 8:20

13 He watereth the hills from his chambers: the earth is satisfied with the
fruit of thy works.

14 He causeth the grass to grow for the cattle, and herb for the service of
man: that he may bring forth food out of the earth;
☆**104:14** Gen 1:29; Job 28:5

15 And wine *that* maketh glad the heart of man, *and* oil to make *his* face to
shine, and bread *which* strengtheneth man's heart.
104:15 Judg 9:13; 19:5, 8; Prov 31:6; Eccles 10:19; Lk 7:46

16 The trees of the LORD are full *of sap;* the cedars of Lebanon, which he
hath planted;

17 Where the birds make their nests: *as for* the stork, the fir trees *are* her
house.
104:17 Lev 11:19

18 The high hills *are* a refuge for the wild goats; *and* the rocks for the
conies.
104:18 Lev 11:5; Prov 30:26

C. THE CREATION OF THE SUN AND MOON

19 He appointed the moon for seasons: the sun knoweth his going down.
104:19 Gen 1:14

20 Thou makest darkness, and it is night: wherein all the beasts of the
forest do creep *forth.*
104:20 Isa 45:7; 56:9

21 The young lions roar after their prey, and seek their meat from God.
104:21 Joel 1:20

22 The sun ariseth, they gather themselves together, and lay them down in
their dens.
104:22 Job 37:8

23 Man goeth forth unto his work and to his labour until the evening.
104:23 Gen 3:19

24 O LORD, how manifold are thy works! in wisdom hast thou made them
all: the earth is full of thy riches.
104:24 Jer 10:12; 51:15

D. THE CREATION OF THE SEAS AND ALL THAT IS IN THEM

25 *So is* this great and wide sea, wherein *are* things creeping innumerable,
both small and great beasts.
☆**104:25**

26 There go the ships: *there is* that leviathan, *whom* thou hast made to play
therein.
104:26 Job 41:1

27 These wait all upon thee; that thou mayest give *them* their meat in due
season.
104:27 Ps 136:25

28 *That* thou givest them they gather: thou openest thine hand, they are
filled with good.
104:28 Ps 145:16

29 Thou hidest thy face, they are troubled: thou takest away their breath,
they die, and return to their dust.
104:29 Gen 3:19; Deut 31:17; Job 10:9

E. PRAISE TO THE GOD OF CREATION

30 Thou sendest forth thy spirit, they are created: and thou renewest the
face of the earth.
104:30 Ezek 37:9

31 The glory of the LORD shall endure for ever: the LORD shall rejoice in
his works.
104:31 Gen 1:31

32 He looketh on the earth, and it trembleth: he toucheth the hills, and
they smoke.
104:32 Ex 19:18; Judg 5:5

33 I will sing unto the LORD as long as I live: I will sing praise to my God
while I have my being.

34 My meditation of him shall be sweet: I will be glad in the LORD.
104:34 Ps 9:2

104:14 The fruitfulness of the earth is sufficient to feed all animal and human life. Men have despoiled God's creation and disbalanced nature by their depredations.

104:25 The seas contain food and plant life in abundance. Again, men have abused God's gift; they have polluted the waters and overfished the seas. If people used these resources properly, there would be food aplenty. Men do not lack for want of God's provision but from their lack of stewardship of those resources.

104:35 Ps 37:10

35 Let the sinners be consumed out of the earth, and let the wicked be no
more. Bless thou the LORD, O my soul. Praise ye the LORD.

I. A PSALM TO THE COVENANT GOD OF ISRAEL

A. THE COMMAND TO SING THE LORD'S PRAISES

105:1☆ 1 Chron 16:8–22, 34
105:2 Ps 98:5
105:4 Ps 27:8

105 O GIVE thanks unto the LORD; call upon his name: make known
his deeds among the people.
2 Sing unto him, sing psalms unto him: talk ye of all his wondrous works.
3 Glory ye in his holy name: let the heart of them rejoice that seek the
LORD.
4 Seek the LORD, and his strength: seek his face evermore.

B. GOD'S COVENANT WITH ABRAHAM

105:5 1 Chron 16:13
105:7 Isa 26:9
105:8 Gen 22:16–18 Deut 7:9 Lk 1:72 Gal 3:17
105:9☆
105:10 Gen 28:13–15 Josh 23:4
105:12 Gen 34:30 Heb 11:9
105:14☆ Gen 12:17 20:7; 35:5
105:15☆

5 Remember his marvellous works that he hath done; his wonders, and
the judgments of his mouth;
6 O ye seed of Abraham his servant, ye children of Jacob his chosen.
7 He *is* the LORD our God: his judgments *are* in all the earth.
8 He hath remembered his covenant for ever, the word *which* he com-
manded to a thousand generations.
9 Which *covenant* he made with Abraham, and his oath unto Isaac;
10 And confirmed the same unto Jacob for a law, *and* to Israel *for* an
everlasting covenant:
11 Saying, Unto thee will I give the land of Canaan, the lot of your
inheritance:
12 When they were *but* a few men in number; yea, very few, and strangers
in it.
13 When they went from one nation to another, from *one* kingdom to
another people;
14 He suffered no man to do them wrong: yea, he reproved kings for their
sakes;
15 *Saying*, Touch not mine anointed, and do my prophets no harm.

C. GOD SENDS JOSEPH TO EGYPT

105:16 Lev 26:26 Isa 3:1 Ezek 4:16
105:17☆ Gen 37:28, 36 Acts 7:9
105:19 Ps 66:10
105:20 Gen 41:14

16 Moreover he called for a famine upon the land: he brake the whole staff
of bread.
17 He sent a man before them, *even* Joseph, *who* was sold for a servant:
18 Whose feet they hurt with fetters: he was laid in iron:
19 Until the time that his word came: the word of the LORD tried him.
20 The king sent and loosed him; *even* the ruler of the people, and let him
go free.

105:1ff This hymn of praise presents an overview of the God of history who accomplishes the divine purpose through his people, Israel. The psalmist talks of God's promise to Abraham, the role of Joseph in the preservation of a people, their captivity in Egypt followed by Moses' divinely sent plagues, the exodus, and, at last, the entrance into the land of promise. For God's mercies, preservation, and fulfillment of his promises, let all the people praise the Lord.

105:9 The psalmist speaks of God's covenant made with the patriarchs and passed on to Israel from generation to generation. It was an everlasting covenant that finds its great fulfillment in Jesus Christ, who sits upon the throne of his father David to order and establish it forever.

105:14 *He suffered no man to do them wrong*, i.e., "He would not let one thing be done to them apart from his decision."†

105:15 The prophets of God are precious to him; he protects them even from kings, as when he caused Jeroboam's hand to wither when it was stretched forth against God's prophet (1 Kings 13:1–5).

105:17 Joseph was sold into captivity. But God was behind the nefarious act of his brothers and *sent a man before them, even Joseph, who was sold for a servant*. Joseph himself knew that God had sent him (Gen. 45:5).

21 He made him lord of his house, and ruler of all his substance:
22 To bind his princes at his pleasure; and teach his senators wisdom.

D. GOD BRINGS JACOB TO EGYPT

23 Israel also came into Egypt; and Jacob sojourned in the land of Ham.
24 And he increased his people greatly; and made them stronger than their **105:24** Ex 1:7, 9
enemies.
25 He turned their heart to hate his people, to deal subtilly with his **105:25** Acts 7:19
servants.

E. MOSES GOES TO DELIVER ISRAEL

26 He sent Moses his servant; *and* Aaron whom he had chosen. ☆**105:26** Ex 3:10
27 They shewed his signs among them, and wonders in the land of Ham. **105:27** Ex 8:10
28 He sent darkness, and made it dark; and they rebelled not against his Ps 78:43–51
word.
29 He turned their waters into blood, and slew their fish.
30 Their land brought forth frogs in abundance, in the chambers of their
kings.
31 He spake, and there came divers sorts of flies, *and* lice in all their coasts.
32 He gave them hail for rain, *and* flaming fire in their land.
33 He smote their vines also and their fig trees; and brake the trees of their
coasts.
34 He spake, and the locusts came, and caterpillers, and that without
number,
35 And did eat up all the herbs in their land, and devoured the fruit of
their ground.
36 He smote also all the firstborn in their land, the chief of all their **105:36** Ex 12:30
strength.
37 He brought them forth also with silver and gold: and *there was* not one
feeble *person* among their tribes.
38 Egypt was glad when they departed: for the fear of them fell upon
them.

F. GOD'S PROVISION FOR ISRAEL IN THE WILDERNESS

39 He spread a cloud for a covering; and fire to give light in the night. **105:39** Neh 9:12 Isa 4:5
40 *The people* asked, and he brought quails, and satisfied them with the **105:40** Num 11:31 Jn 6:31
bread of heaven.
41 He opened the rock, and the waters gushed out; they ran in the dry **105:41** 1 Cor 10:4
places *like* a river.
42 For he remembered his holy promise, *and* Abraham his servant.

G. ISRAEL ENTERS THE PROMISED LAND

43 And he brought forth his people with joy, *and* his chosen with gladness: **105:43** Ex 15:1
44 And gave them the lands of the heathen: and they inherited the labour **105:44** Josh 13:7
of the people;
45 That they might observe his statutes, and keep his laws. Praise ye the ☆**105:45** Deut 4:40
LORD.

105:26 God delivered Israel from Egypt (1) by human instrumentalities (Moses and Aaron), (2) by overcoming Pharaoh's stubborn opposition, (3) by events that enabled Israel to gain wealth, respect, and joy.

105:45 After recounting what God had done for Israel, the psalmist had only one response to make: Praise the Lord.

I. THE MERCY OF GOD TOWARD HIS SINFUL PEOPLE

A. THE PSALMIST'S PETITION FOR MERCY

106:1☆ 1 Chron 16:34, 41
106 PRAISE ye the LORD. O give thanks unto the LORD; for *he is* good: for his mercy *endureth* for ever.
2 Who can utter the mighty acts of the LORD? *who* can shew forth all his praise?
106:3 Ps 15:2
3 Blessed *are* they that keep judgment, *and* he that doeth righteousness at all times.
106:4 Ps 44:3
4 Remember me, O LORD, with the favour *that thou bearest unto* thy people: O visit me with thy salvation;
106:5 Ps 1:3
5 That I may see the good of thy chosen, that I may rejoice in the gladness of thy nation, that I may glory with thine inheritance.

B. ISRAEL'S REBELLION AT THE RED SEA

106:6 2 Chron 30:7 Ezra 9:7 Neh 1:7 Zech 1:4
6 We have sinned with our fathers, we have committed iniquity, we have done wickedly.
106:7 Judg 3:7
7 Our fathers understood not thy wonders in Egypt; they remembered not the multitude of thy mercies; but provoked *him* at the sea, *even* at the Red sea.
106:8 Ezek 20:9
8 Nevertheless he saved them for his name's sake, that he might make his mighty power to be known.
106:9 Ex 14:21 Isa 63:11–13
9 He rebuked the Red sea also, and it was dried up: so he led them through the depths, as through the wilderness.
10 And he saved them from the hand of him that hated *them*, and redeemed them from the hand of the enemy.
106:11 Ex 15:5
11 And the waters covered their enemies: there was not one of them left.
12 Then believed they his words; they sang his praise.

C. ISRAEL'S REBELLION IN THE WILDERNESS

13 They soon forgat his works; they waited not for his counsel:
106:14 Num 11:4
14 But lusted exceedingly in the wilderness, and tempted God in the desert.
106:15☆ Ps 78:29–31
15 And he gave them their request; but sent leanness into their soul.
106:16☆
16 They envied Moses also in the camp, *and* Aaron the saint of the LORD.
106:17 Num 16:32
17 The earth opened and swallowed up Da'than, and covered the company of A-bi'ram.
18 And a fire was kindled in their company; the flame burned up the wicked.

D. ISRAEL'S IDOLATROUS OX AT HOREB

106:19 Acts 7:41 Rom 1:23
19 They made a calf in Ho'reb, and worshipped the molten image.
20 Thus they changed their glory into the similitude of an ox that eateth grass.
106:21 Deut 10:21
21 They forgat God their saviour, which had done great things in Egypt;

106:1ff This is the first of what have been called the "Hallelujah Psalms." The word *Hallelujah* is the inscription. Other "Hallelujah Psalms" are 111–113, 117, 135, and 146–150. (See note on Ps. 111:11ff.)
106:15 The children of Israel were unhappy in the wilderness journey when they had only manna to eat. They longed for meat. Indeed they insisted on having it. And God sent them what they demanded but the consequence was spiritually deadening. God *sent leanness into their soul*, or, "sent a plague to punish them." In return for meat they got spiritual poverty. So also for the Christian today: if God's servant insists on his own way when God has decided differently, only disaster will result.
106:16 *the saint of the LORD,* i.e., "the man anointed," or, "the holy one of Jehovah (Yahweh)."†

22Wondrous works in the land of Ham, *and* terrible things by the Red sea.
23Therefore he said that he would destroy them, had not Moses his chosen stood before him in the breach, to turn away his wrath, lest he should destroy *them*.

106:23 Ex 32:10–14

E. ISRAEL'S REFUSAL TO ENTER THE PROMISED LAND

24Yea, they despised the pleasant land, they believed not his word:
25But murmured in their tents, *and* hearkened not unto the voice of the LORD.
26Therefore he lifted up his hand against them, to overthrow them in the wilderness:
27To overthrow their seed also among the nations, and to scatter them in the lands.

106:24 Jer 3:19
106:26 Heb 3:11

F. THE SIN OF BAAL WORSHIP AT PEOR

28They joined themselves also unto Ba'al-pe'or, and ate the sacrifices of the dead.
29Thus they provoked *him* to anger with their inventions: and the plague brake in upon them.
30Then stood up Phin'e-has, and executed judgment: and *so* the plague was stayed.
31And that was counted unto him for righteousness unto all generations for evermore.

☆**106:28** Hos 9:10
106:30 Num 25:7–13

G. ISRAEL'S SIN AT MERIBAH

32They angered *him* also at the waters of strife, so that it went ill with Moses for their sakes:
33Because they provoked his spirit, so that he spake unadvisedly with his lips.

106:32 Ps 78:40

H. ISRAEL'S ADULTERY IN CANAAN

34They did not destroy the nations, concerning whom the LORD commanded them:
35But were mingled among the heathen, and learned their works.
36And they served their idols: which were a snare unto them.
37Yea, they sacrificed their sons and their daughters unto devils,
38And shed innocent blood, *even* the blood of their sons and of their daughters, whom they sacrificed unto the idols of Canaan: and the land was polluted with blood.
39Thus were they defiled with their own works, and went a whoring with their own inventions.

☆**106:34** Judg 1:21, 27–36
106:37 Num 35:33; 2 Kgs 17:17
106:39 Hos 4:12

I. GOD'S PUNISHMENT OF ISRAEL AND HIS MERCY

40Therefore was the wrath of the LORD kindled against his people, insomuch that he abhorred his own inheritance.

106:40 Judg 2:12–14

106:28 *ate the sacrifices of the dead,* i.e., "ate sacrifices offered to lifeless gods." Israel offered such sacrifices again and again. It was a recurring sin, which often brought judgment.

106:34 God's indictment against Israel was substantial. They (1) did not destroy the nations in the land as God had told them to do; (2) took over the idolatry of the heathen nations; (3) married among the heathen; and (4) offered up their children as human sacrifices. Since they would not repent, judgment had to overtake them.

106:41 Neh 9:27 41 And he gave them into the hand of the heathen; and they that hated
them ruled over them.
42 Their enemies also oppressed them, and they were brought into
subjection under their hand.
106:43 Judg 6:6 Ps 81:12 43 Many times did he deliver them; but they provoked *him* with their
counsel, and were brought low for their iniquity.
106:44☆ 44 Nevertheless he regarded their affliction, when he heard their cry:
106:45 Lev 26:42 45 And he remembered for them his covenant, and repented according to
106:46 2 Chron 30:9 the multitude of his mercies.
Ezra 9:9 46 He made them also to be pitied of all those that carried them captives.

J. THE SONG OF PRAISE TO THE LORD GOD

106:47 Ps 147:2 47 Save us, O LORD our God, and gather us from among the heathen, to
give thanks unto thy holy name, *and* to triumph in thy praise.
106:48 Ps 41:13 48 Blessed *be* the LORD God of Israel from everlasting to everlasting: and
let all the people say, Amen. Praise ye the LORD.

BOOK V (PSALMS 107—150)

I. HYMN OF PRAISE TO GOD, THE DELIVERER

A. THE COMMAND TO THINK THE LORD

107:1☆ 107 O GIVE thanks unto the LORD, for *he is* good: for his mercy
endureth for ever.
107:2 Isa 35:9, 10 2 Let the redeemed of the LORD say *so*, whom he hath redeemed from the
hand of the enemy;
107:3 Neh 1:9 Ezek 20:34 3 And gathered them out of the lands, from the east, and from the west,
from the north, and from the south.

B. GOD'S DELIVERANCE IN THE DESERT

107:4 Josh 5:6 4 They wandered in the wilderness in a solitary way; they found no city to
dwell in.
107:5 Ps 77:3 5 Hungry and thirsty, their soul fainted in them.
107:6☆ 6 Then they cried unto the LORD in their trouble, *and* he delivered them
out of their distresses.
107:7 Jer 31:9 7 And he led them forth by the right way, that they might go to a city of
habitation.
8 Oh that *men* would praise the LORD *for* his goodness, and *for* his
wonderful works to the children of men!
107:9 Mt 5:6 Lk 1:53 9 For he satisfieth the longing soul, and filleth the hungry soul with
goodness.

C. GOD'S DELIVERANCE FROM THE PRISON

107:10 Mic 7:8 Lk 1:79 10 Such as sit in darkness and in the shadow of death, *being* bound in
affliction and iron;

106:44 Despite the punishment visited on Israel by their God, he did not forget them in their sufferings. Nor has he forgotten Israel today. God waits for their repentance and turning to him.

107:1 The recurring sequence expressed in this Psalm is as follows: (1) men ought to praise God for his goodness and his delivering mercies; (2) men soon forget what they ought to remember; (3) men turn from God to sin; (4) God employs judgment to bring them to repentance; (5) men sense their need for deliverance and call upon God; (6) God delivers them; (7) they then praise God for his deliverance.

107:6 *Then they cried unto the LORD* is a phrase that appears in 107:6, 13, 19 and 28. They would not have needed to cry unto the Lord had they not sinned and fallen into disrepute under the judgment of God. This is a prayer that no believer ought to have to pray, and he will not need to do so if his heart and walk are right before God.

11Because they rebelled against the words of God, and contemned the counsel of the most High: 107:11 Num 15:31 Prov 1:25
12Therefore he brought down their heart with labour; they fell down and *there was* none to help. 107:12 Ps 22:11
13Then they cried unto the LORD in their trouble, *and* he saved them out of their distresses.
14He brought them out of darkness and the shadow of death, and brake their bands in sunder. 107:14 Nah 1:13 Acts 12:7
15Oh that *men* would praise the LORD *for* his goodness, and *for* his wonderful works to the children of men!
16For he hath broken the gates of brass, and cut the bars of iron in sunder. 107:16 Isa 45:1, 2

D. GOD'S DELIVERANCE FROM ILLNESS

17Fools because of their transgression, and because of their iniquities, are afflicted. ☆107:17 Isa 65:6, 7 Ezek 24:23
18Their soul abhorreth all manner of meat; and they draw near unto the gates of death. 107:18 Job 33:19–22 Ps 9:13
19Then they cry unto the LORD in their trouble, *and* he saveth them out of their distresses.
20He sent his word, and healed them, and delivered *them* from their destructions. 107:20 2 Kgs 20:5 Mt 8:8
21Oh that *men* would praise the LORD *for* his goodness, and *for* his wonderful works to the children of men!
22And let them sacrifice the sacrifices of thanksgiving, and declare his works with rejoicing. 107:22 Lev 7:12 Ps 73:28

E. GOD'S DELIVERANCE FROM THE STORMS AT SEA

23They that go down to the sea in ships, that do business in great waters; 107:23 Jonah 1:3
24These see the works of the LORD, and his wonders in the deep.
25For he commandeth, and raiseth the stormy wind, which lifteth up the waves thereof. 107:25 Ps 93:3, 4
26They mount up to the heaven, they go down again to the depths: their soul is melted because of trouble.
27They reel to and fro, and stagger like a drunken man, and are at their wit's end. 107:27 Isa 24:20
28Then they cry unto the LORD in their trouble, and he bringeth them out of their distresses.
29He maketh the storm a calm, so that the waves thereof are still. 107:29 Mt 8:26 Lk 8:24
30Then are they glad because they be quiet; so he bringeth them unto their desired haven.
31Oh that *men* would praise the LORD *for* his goodness, and *for* his wonderful works to the children of men!
32Let them exalt him also in the congregation of the people, and praise him in the assembly of the elders. 107:32 Ps 22:22; 25 Isa 25:1

F. GOD'S BLESSINGS ON THE EARTH

33He turneth rivers into a wilderness, and the watersprings into dry ground; ☆107:33 Isa 50:2

107:17 Sometimes believers become ill as a direct result of their sins. "They prejudice their bodily health by intemperance and endanger their lives by indulging their appetites."* The doing of these things is sin.

107:33 The Lord blesses the earth. How much more does he wish to bless his people if they will but heed and obey him.

107:34 Gen 19:24, 25

34 A fruitful land into barrenness, for the wickedness of them that dwell
therein.

107:35 Isa 35:6, 7; 41:18

35 He turneth the wilderness into a standing water, and dry ground into
watersprings.
36 And there he maketh the hungry to dwell, that they may prepare a city
for habitation;

107:37 2 Kgs 19:29; Amos 9:14

37 And sow the fields, and plant vineyards, which may yield fruits of
increase.

107:38 Gen 12:2; Ex 1:7

38 He blesseth them also, so that they are multiplied greatly; and suffereth
not their cattle to decrease.

G. GOD'S CONTINUAL LOVINGKINDNESS

107:39 Ezek 5:11

39 Again, they are minished and brought low through oppression,
affliction, and sorrow.

107:40 Job 12:21, 24

40 He poureth contempt upon princes, and causeth them to wander in the
wilderness, *where there is* no way.

107:41 1 Sam 2:8; Job 42:12–14

41 Yet setteth he the poor on high from affliction, and maketh *him* families
like a flock.

107:42 Job 22:19; Rom 3:19

42 The righteous shall see *it*, and rejoice: and all iniquity shall stop her
mouth.

107:43☆ Hos 14:9

43 Whoso *is* wise, and will observe these *things*, even they shall understand
the lovingkindness of the LORD.

I. A PSALM OF FAITH IN GOD (CF. 57:7–11; 60:5–12)

A. PRAISE TO GOD FOR HIS LOVINGKINDNESS

A Song or Psalm of David

108:1☆ Ps 57:7–11

108 O GOD, my heart is fixed: I will sing and give praise, even with
my glory.
2 Awake, psaltery and harp: I *myself* will awake early.
3 I will praise thee, O LORD, among the people: and I will sing praises
unto thee among the nations.
4 For thy mercy *is* great above the heavens: and thy truth *reacheth* unto
the clouds.
5 Be thou exalted, O God, above the heavens: and thy glory above all the
earth;
6 That thy beloved may be delivered: save *with* thy right hand, and answer
me.

B. CLAIMING GOD'S PROMISES

7 God hath spoken in his holiness; I will rejoice, I will divide She′chem,
and mete out the valley of Suc′coth.
8 Gilead *is* mine; Ma-nas′seh *is* mine; E′phra-im also *is* the strength of
mine head; Judah *is* my lawgiver;

108:9☆

9 Moab *is* my washpot; over Edom will I cast out my shoe; over Philistia
will I triumph.

107:43 *Experience is a great* teacher. He who is wise will learn his lessons well from what happens to him when he sins and to others who do likewise. If we lay these teachings up, mind them, and retain them in our hearts, life will be more pleasant and the rod of chastening less needful.

108:1ff This is a Psalm of praise and prayer. It combines parts of Pss. 57 and 60 with minor variations. They are put together in new form to be sung in public worship or private devotions for the believer's comfort and for glorifying God.

108:9 *Moab is my washpot; over Edom will I cast out my shoe,* i.e., "Moab and Edom are despised."†

C. CALLING UPON GOD FOR HELP

10 Who will bring me into the strong city? who will lead me into Edom?
11 *Wilt* not *thou*, O God, *who* hast cast us off? and wilt not thou, O God,
go forth with our hosts?
12 Give us help from trouble: for vain *is* the help of man.
13 Through God we shall do valiantly: for he *it is that* shall tread down
our enemies.

108:11 Ps 44:9

I. A PSALM OF VENGEANCE ON ENEMIES

A. THE PSALMIST'S SAD ESTATE

To the chief Musician, A Psalm of David

109 HOLD not thy peace, O God of my praise;
2 For the mouth of the wicked and the mouth of the deceitful
are opened against me: they have spoken against me with a lying tongue.
3 They compassed me about also with words of hatred; and fought
against me without a cause.
4 For my love they are my adversaries: but I *give myself unto* prayer.
5 And they have rewarded me evil for good, and hatred for my love.

☆**109:1** Deut 10:21 Ps 83:1
109:3 Ps 69:4
109:4 Ps 38:20
109:5 Mt 5:44 Jn 7:7

B. THE PSALMIST'S DEMAND FOR RETRIBUTION

6 Set thou a wicked man over him: and let Satan stand at his right hand.
7 When he shall be judged, let him be condemned: and let his prayer
become sin.
8 Let his days be few; *and* let another take his office.
9 Let his children be fatherless, and his wife a widow.
10 Let his children be continually vagabonds, and beg: let them seek *their*
bread also out of their desolate places.
11 Let the extortioner catch all that he hath; and let the strangers spoil his
labour.
12 Let there be none to extend mercy unto him: neither let there be any to
favour his fatherless children.
13 Let his posterity be cut off; *and* in the generation following let their
name be blotted out.
14 Let the iniquity of his fathers be remembered with the LORD; and let
not the sin of his mother be blotted out.
15 Let them be before the LORD continually, that he may cut off the
memory of them from the earth.
16 Because that he remembered not to shew mercy, but persecuted the
poor and needy man, that he might even slay the broken in heart.
17 As he loved cursing, so let it come unto him: as he delighted not in
blessing, so let it be far from him.
18 As he clothed himself with cursing like as with his garment, so let it
come into his bowels like water, and like oil into his bones.
19 Let it be unto him as the garment *which* covereth him, and for a girdle
wherewith he is girded continually.

☆**109:6** Zech 3:1
☆**109:7** Ps 1:5 Prov 28:9
☆**109:8** Acts 1:20
☆**109:9** Ex 22:24 Job 30:5–8 Jer 18:21
☆**109:10**
☆**109:11** Isa 1:7 Lam 5:2
☆**109:12** Ps 21:10 Prov 10:7 Isa 9:17
☆**109:13**
☆**109:14** Neh 4:5 Isa 65:6, 7
☆**109:15** Jer 16:17
109:16 Ps 37:32
109:17 Mt 7:2
109:18 Ps 73:6
109:19 Ezek 7:27

109:1ff This Psalm is to be sung with the conviction that the God of righteousness will, in the future, destroy the enemies of Christ and of his church. Those who trust in God will inherit his great salvation if they keep close to him. 109:8 is picked up by the Holy Spirit in Acts 1:20 and applied to Judas Iscariot. This indicates that David, whether he realized it or not, was speaking prophetically concerning that which would take place long after his own death.

109:6–15 The imprecations here are very terrible. Woe to the man against whom God himself says "Amen" to these imprecations. If what is prayed for were to come to pass, such a man would either repent and be converted or look for the end of life—perhaps by suicide.

109:20 Isa 3:11 2 Tim 4:14

20 *Let* this *be* the reward of mine adversaries from the LORD, and of them
that speak evil against my soul.

C. THE PSALMIST'S PLEA FOR GOD'S ASSISTANCE

109:21☆ Ps 25:11 Ezek 36:22 109:22 Ps 40:17 Prov 18:14

21 But do thou for me, O GOD the Lord, for thy name's sake: because thy
mercy *is* good, deliver thou me.
22 For I *am* poor and needy, and my heart is wounded within me.
23 I am gone like the shadow when it declineth: I am tossed up and down
as the locust.

109:24 Heb 12:12 109:25 Lam 2:15

24 My knees are weak through fasting; and my flesh faileth of fatness.
25 I became also a reproach unto them: *when* they looked upon me they
shaked their heads.
26 Help me, O LORD my God: O save me according to thy mercy:

109:27 Job 37:7

27 That they may know that this *is* thy hand; *that* thou, LORD, hast done
it.

109:28 2 Sam 16:11, 12

28 Let them curse, but bless thou: when they arise, let them be ashamed;
but let thy servant rejoice.

109:29 Job 8:22 Ps 35:26

29 Let mine adversaries be clothed with shame, and let them cover
themselves with their own confusion, as with a mantle.
30 I will greatly praise the LORD with my mouth; yea, I will praise him
among the multitude.

109:31 Ps 16:8; 37:33

31 For he shall stand at the right hand of the poor, to save *him* from those
that condemn his soul.

I. A MESSIANIC PSALM ABOUT THE SON OF DAVID
A. THE MESSIAH KING

A Psalm of David

110:1☆ Mt 22:44 Lk 20:42, 43 Acts 2:34, 35 Eph 1:20, 22 Heb 1:13 110:2 Ps 45:6 Dan 7:13, 14 110:3 Judg 5:2 Ps 96:9 1 Chron 16:29

110 THE LORD said unto my Lord, Sit thou at my right hand, until I
make thine enemies thy footstool.
2 The LORD shall send the rod of thy strength out of Zion: rule thou in the
midst of thine enemies.
3 Thy people *shall be* willing in the day of thy power, in the beauties of
holiness from the womb of the morning: thou hast the dew of thy youth.

B. THE MESSIAH PRIEST

110:4 Heb 6:20; 7:21 110:5 Ps 76:12 Rom 2:5 Rev 6:17

4 The LORD hath sworn, and will not repent, Thou *art* a priest for ever
after the order of Mel-chiz'e-dek.
5 The Lord at thy right hand shall strike through kings in the day of his
wrath.

C. THE MESSIAH CONQUEROR

110:6 Joel 3:12 Ps 68:21

6 He shall judge among the heathen, he shall fill *the places* with the dead
bodies; he shall wound the heads over many countries.
7 He shall drink of the brook in the way: therefore shall he lift up the
head.

109:21 This hard-pressed and bedeviled suppliant prays for mercy. He needs someone to act on his behalf. He asks for help without trying to inform God as to what he should do. The curses of wicked men are impotent, whereas the blessings of God are omnipotent. He who has God for his helper need not fear the worst that men can do.

110:1ff This is a messianic Psalm that is used two ways in the New Testament. Jesus himself confounded his critics and made his claim to deity in Matt. 22:44 by the use of 110:1. Heb. 5:6 quotes 110:4 to endorse the eternal priesthood of Jesus. The whole Psalm looks with expectation to the day in which Christ will reign over all the nations of the earth.

I. HALLELUJAH TO THE LORD

A. THANKS BE TO GOD FOR HIS MIRACLES

111 PRAISE ye the LORD. I will praise the LORD with *my* whole
heart, in the assembly of the upright, and *in* the congregation.
2 The works of the LORD *are* great, sought out of all them that have
pleasure therein.
3 His work *is* honourable and glorious: and his righteousness endureth for
ever.

☆111:1 Ps 92:5; 138:1
111:3 Ps 96:6; 145:5

B. THE MIRACLES OF GOD DESCRIBED

4 He hath made his wonderful works to be remembered: the LORD *is*
gracious and full of compassion.
5 He hath given meat unto them that fear him: he will ever be mindful of
his covenant.
6 He hath shewed his people the power of his works, that he may give
them the heritage of the heathen.
7 The works of his hands *are* verity and judgment; all his commandments
are sure.
8 They stand fast for ever and ever, *and are* done in truth and uprightness.
9 He sent redemption unto his people: he hath commanded his covenant
for ever: holy and reverend *is* his name.

111:4 Ps 86:15; 103:8
111:5 Ps 103:8, 9 Mt 6:31–33
111:7 Ps 19:7–9 Rev 15:3, 4
111:8 Ps 19:9 119:160 Isa 40:8 Mt 5:18
☆111:9 Ps 99:3 Lk 1:68

C. THE CONCLUDING WORD OF PRAISE

10 The fear of the LORD *is* the beginning of wisdom: a good understanding
have all they that do *his commandments:* his praise endureth for ever.

111:10 Prov 1:7, 9 3:4, 5; 9:10 145:1, 2

I. GOD'S BLESSING ON THOSE WHO KEEP HIS COMMANDMENTS

112 PRAISE ye the LORD. Blessed *is* the man *that* feareth the LORD,
that delighteth greatly in his commandments.
2 His seed shall be mighty upon earth: the generation of the upright shall
be blessed.
3 Wealth and riches *shall be* in his house: and his righteousness endureth
for ever.
4 Unto the upright there ariseth light in the darkness: *he is* gracious, and
full of compassion, and righteous.
5 A good man sheweth favour, and lendeth: he will guide his affairs with
discretion.
6 Surely he shall not be moved for ever: the righteous shall be in
everlasting remembrance.
7 He shall not be afraid of evil tidings: his heart is fixed, trusting in the
LORD.

☆112:1 Ps 1:1, 2; 128:1
112:2 Ps 25:13
112:3 Prov 3:16, 17 8:18
112:4 Job 11:17 Ps 97:11
112:5 Ps 37:21, 26
112:6 Ps 15:5; 55:22 Prov 10:7
112:7 Ps 56:4 Prov 1:33

111:1ff Pss. 111—113 are all songs of praise; each is titled "Hallelujah." The word "hallelujah" means "praise the Lord." It is used in the Bible only in songs of praise and appears exclusively in the books of Psalms and Revelation (Rev. 19:1–6, where it appears four times—the word "alleluia" in Revelation is a transliteration from the Hebrew text). Other Hebrew words for praise, *hillel* and *hallel,* appear many times in the Old Testament. The word "hallelu-jah," the highest form of praise, occurs only about fifteen times in the Old Testament, all in the Psalms. God's people are to sing the "Hallelujah Psalms" with hearts disposed to God.

111:9 *holy and reverend* [awesome] *is his name.* The name of God is holy and worthy of all respect. Let no one take his name in vain. Those who do, sin against God. Unfortunately, this sin is prevalent among men everywhere.

112:1 This Psalm speaks of the happiness of the saints. Such happiness brings glory to God. Whatever we have by way of godly pleasure, he must have by way of praise.

112:8 Ps 56:10, 11 Prov 3:24–26
112:9 2 Cor 9:9 Ps 148:14
112:10 Ps 58:7 Prov 10:28 Mt 8:12 Lk 13:28

8 His heart *is* established, he shall not be afraid, until he see *his desire*
upon his enemies.
9 He hath dispersed, he hath given to the poor; his righteousness endureth
for ever; his horn shall be exalted with honour.
10 The wicked shall see *it*, and be grieved; he shall gnash with his teeth,
and melt away: the desire of the wicked shall perish.

I. A PSALM OF PRAISE TO THE LORD OUR GOD

113:1☆ Ps 34:22; 135:1
113:2 Dan 2:20
113:3 Ps 50:1
113:4 Ps 8:1; 97:9
113:5 Ps 89:6; 103:19
113:6 Ps 11:4 Isa 57:15
113:7 1 Sam 2:8 Ps 107:41
113:8 Job 36:7
113:9 1 Sam 2:5 Isa 54:1

113 PRAISE ye the LORD. Praise, O ye servants of the LORD, praise
the name of the LORD.
2 Blessed be the name of the LORD from this time forth and for evermore.
3 From the rising of the sun unto the going down of the same the LORD's
name *is* to be praised.
4 The LORD *is* high above all nations, *and* his glory above the heavens.
5 Who *is* like unto the LORD our God, who dwelleth on high,
6 Who humbleth *himself* to behold *the things that are* in heaven, and in the
earth!
7 He raiseth up the poor out of the dust, *and* lifteth the needy out of the
dunghill;
8 That he may set *him* with princes, *even* with the princes of his people.
9 He maketh the barren woman to keep house, *and to be* a joyful mother
of children. Praise ye the LORD.

I. A PSALM ABOUT THE BIRTH OF A NATION

114:1☆ Ex 13:3
114:2 Ex 29:45, 46 Ps 78:68, 69
114:3 Ex 14:21 Josh 3:13, 14 Ps 77:16
114:4 Ps 29:5, 6 Hab 3:6
114:5 Hab 3:8
114:7 Ps 96:9
114:8 Ex 17:5, 6 Deut 8:15

114 WHEN Israel went out of Egypt, the house of Jacob from a
people of strange language;
2 Judah was his sanctuary, *and* Israel his dominion.
3 The sea saw *it*, and fled: Jordan was driven back.
4 The mountains skipped like rams, *and* the little hills like lambs.
5 What *ailed* thee, O thou sea, that thou fleddest? thou Jordan, *that* thou
wast driven back?
6 Ye mountains, *that* ye skipped like rams; *and* ye little hills, like lambs?
7 Tremble, thou earth, at the presence of the Lord, at the presence of the
God of Jacob;
8 Which turned the rock *into* a standing water, the flint into a fountain of
waters.

I. A HALLELUJAH TO THE GLORY OF GOD

A. THE CALL TO PRAISE

115:1☆ Ps 29:2 Isa 48:11 Ezek 36:22, 32
115:2 Ps 79:10

115 NOT unto us, O LORD, not unto us, but unto thy name give
glory, for thy mercy, *and* for thy truth's sake.
2 Wherefore should the heathen say, Where *is* now their God?

113:1 This Psalm begins and ends with the word *"Hallelujah." The purpose of the Psalm* is to promote and forward the best of all works, which is to praise God.

114:1ff This Psalm celebrates the deliverance of Israel from Egypt. The deliverance was to be held in everlasting remembrance, and this Psalm is part of the eternal commemoration. This song was generally sung by the Israelites, along with other "Hallelujah Psalms," as part of their praise at the close of the Passover meal.

115:1ff In the Hebrew this Psalm is a separate song. The Septuagint joins it to Ps. 114, as does the vulgar Latin. Its refrain is similar to that of Ps. 114: we are to give all glory to God, not to ourselves. The songs end with *Hallelujah,* although it is not titled "Hallelujah."

B. IDOLS ARE OF NO USE

3 But our God *is* in the heavens: he hath done whatsoever he hath
pleased.
4 Their idols *are* silver and gold, the work of men's hands.
5 They have mouths, but they speak not: eyes have they, but they see not:
6 They have ears, but they hear not: noses have they, but they smell not:
7 They have hands, but they handle not: feet have they, but they
walk not: neither speak they through their throat.
8 They that make them are like unto them; *so is* every one that trusteth in
them.

☆**115:3** Ps 103:19; Dan 4:35
115:4 2 Kgs 19:18; Ps 115:4–8; 135:15–18; Jer 10:25

C. ISRAEL MUST TRUST THE LORD

9 O Israel, trust thou in the LORD: he *is* their help and their shield.
10 O house of Aaron, trust in the LORD: he *is* their help and their shield.
11 Ye that fear the LORD, trust in the LORD: he *is* their help and their
shield.

115:9 Ps 33:20; 62:8
115:11 Ps 103:11; 135:20

D. JEHOVAH WILL BLESS ISRAEL; LET HER PRAISE HIM

12 The LORD hath been mindful of us: he will bless *us;* he will bless the
house of Israel; he will bless the house of Aaron.
13 He will bless them that fear the LORD, *both* small and great.
14 The LORD shall increase you more and more, you and your children.
15 Ye *are* blessed of the LORD which made heaven and earth.
16 The heaven, *even* the heavens, *are* the LORD'S: but the earth hath he
given to the children of men.
17 The dead praise not the LORD, neither any that go down into silence.
18 But we will bless the LORD from this time forth and for evermore.
Praise the LORD.

115:12 Ps 98:3; 128:1, 4
115:13 Ps 103:11; 112:1
115:14 Deut 1:11
115:15 Gen 1:1; 14:19; Ps 134:3; Rev 14:7
115:16 Ps 8:6; 89:11
115:17 Ps 6:5; 31:17
115:18 Ps 113:2

I. PERSONAL THANKSGIVING FOR GOD'S DELIVERANCE

A. THE PSALMIST'S PERSONAL TESTIMONY

116 I LOVE the LORD, because he hath heard my voice *and* my
supplications.
2 Because he hath inclined his ear unto me, therefore will I call upon *him*
as long as I live.
3 The sorrows of death compassed me, and the pains of hell gat hold upon
me: I found trouble and sorrow.
4 Then called I upon the name of the LORD; O LORD, I beseech thee,
deliver my soul.
5 Gracious *is* the LORD, and righteous; yea, our God *is* merciful.
6 The LORD preserveth the simple: I was brought low, and he helped me.
7 Return unto thy rest, O my soul; for the LORD hath dealt bountifully
with thee.
8 For thou hast delivered my soul from death, mine eyes from tears, *and*
my feet from falling.
9 I will walk before the LORD in the land of the living.

☆**116:1** Ps 18:1; 66:19
116:2 Ps 17:6; 31:2
116:3 Ps 18:4–6
116:5 Ex 34:6
116:6 Ps 142:6; Prov 1:4
116:7 Ps 13:6; Mt 11:29
116:8 Ps 49:15

115:3 *he hath done whatsoever he hath pleased.* God is sovereign and he does what he pleases. All believers need to do is discover what God is pleased to do, accept it, and thank him for it. He was pleased to send Jesus Christ his Son to make atonement for the sins of men. Had he not been pleased to do so, salvation would not have been possible.

116:1 This is a Psalm of thanksgiving for God's great deliverances. What occasioned it we do not know, but its content applies to all believers.

B. THE PSALMIST TO PAY WHAT HE HAS VOWED

116:10 Ps 88:7

10 I believed, therefore have I spoken: I was greatly afflicted:
11 I said in my haste, All men *are* liars.

116:12☆ 2 Chron 32:25; 1 Thess 3:9

12 What shall I render unto the LORD *for* all his benefits toward me?
13 I will take the cup of salvation, and call upon the name of the LORD.

116:14 Ps 22:25; 50:14

14 I will pay my vows unto the LORD now in the presence of all his people.

116:15☆ Ps 72:14

15 Precious in the sight of the LORD *is* the death of his saints.

116:16 Ps 143:12

16 O LORD, truly I *am* thy servant; I *am* thy servant, *and* the son of thine
handmaid: thou hast loosed my bonds.
17 I will offer to thee the sacrifice of thanksgiving, and will call upon the
name of the LORD.

116:18 Ps 96:8

18 I will pay my vows unto the LORD now in the presence of all his people,
19 In the courts of the LORD's house, in the midst of thee, O Jerusalem.
Praise ye the LORD.

I. ALL NATIONS ARE TO PRAISE THE LORD

117:1 Rom 15:11; **117:2** Ps 100:5

117 O PRAISE the LORD, all ye nations: praise him, all ye people.
2 For his merciful kindness is great toward us: and the truth of
the LORD *endureth* for ever. Praise ye the LORD.

I. A VICTORY PSALM TO EVERLASTING MERCY

A. GOD'S LOVINGKINDNESS IS FOREVER

118:1☆ Ps 136

118 O GIVE thanks unto the LORD; for *he is* good: because his mercy
endureth for ever.
2 Let Israel now say, that his mercy *endureth* for ever.
3 Let the house of Aaron now say, that his mercy *endureth* for ever.

118:4☆

4 Let them now that fear the LORD say, that his mercy *endureth* for ever.

B. GOD ANSWERS PRAYER

118:5 Ps 18:19; **118:6** Job 19:27; Heb 13:6; **118:7** Ps 54:7; **118:8☆** 2 Chron 32:7, 8; Isa 57:13; Jer 17:5

5 I called upon the LORD in distress: the LORD answered me, *and set me* in
a large place.
6 The LORD *is* on on my side; I will not fear: what can man do unto me?
7 The LORD taketh my part with them that help me: therefore shall I see
my desire upon them that hate me.
8 *It is* better to trust in the LORD than to put confidence in man.
9 *It is* better to trust in the LORD than to put confidence in princes.

C. GOD GIVES THE VICTORY

118:10 Ps 18:40

10 All nations compassed me about: but in the name of the LORD will I
destroy them.

116:12 *What shall I render unto the LORD for all his benefits?* There is no way that we can repay God for what he has done for us. We do need to surrender ourselves to him and seek to glorify his name. But when all of these things have been done, we are still an infinity away from equaling what he has done for us.
116:15 Paraphrased: "His loved ones are very pre*cious to him and he does not lightly let them die.*" See context for the validity of this paraphrase.†
118:1ff The authorship, the time, and the circumstances of this Psalm are not known specifically. Many attribute it to David. At least a segment of it has messianic implications. 118:22, 23 are picked up in whole or in part or are referred to in Matt. 21:42, Mark 12:10, Luke 20:17, Acts 4:11, Eph. 2:20, and 1 Pet. 2:4, 7. The Psalm is one of thanksgiving to a mighty, wise, prayer-answering God, who delivers the suppliant. It ends with a doxology.
118:4 Love that is not steadfast is not genuine love. It may be feeling or emotion but it is not constituted with the reality of true love.
118:8 It is hardly to be supposed that there is a real choice between placing confidence in God or in man. The nature of trust implies the assurance that it will not be breached. Only God can be trusted absolutely.

11 They compassed me about; yea, they compassed me about: but in the
name of the LORD I will destroy them.
12 They compassed me about like bees; they are quenched as the fire of
thorns: for in the name of the LORD I will destroy them.
13 Thou hast thrust sore at me that I might fall: but the LORD helped me.
14 The LORD *is* my strength and song, and is become my salvation.

118:12 Deut 1:44
118:13 Ps 86:17
118:14 Ex 15:2; Isa 12:2

D. THE LORD'S STRONG ARM HAS DONE IT

15 The voice of rejoicing and salvation *is* in the tabernacles of the
righteous: the right hand of the LORD doeth valiantly.
16 The right hand of the LORD is exalted: the right hand of the LORD
doeth valiantly.
17 I shall not die, but live, and declare the works of the LORD.
18 The LORD hath chastened me sore: but he hath not given me over unto
death.
19 Open to me the gates of righteousness: I will go into them, *and* I will
praise the LORD:
20 This gate of the LORD, into which the righteous shall enter.
21 I will praise thee: for thou hast heard me, and art become my salvation.

118:15 Ps 89:13; Lk 1:51
118:17 Hab 1:12
118:18 Jer 31:18; 1 Cor 11:32; 2 Cor 6:9
118:19 Isa 26:2
118:20 Ps 15:1, 2

E. THE REJECTED STONE BECOMES THE CAPSTONE

22 The stone *which* the builders refused is become the head *stone* of the
corner.
23 This is the LORD's doing; *it is* marvellous in our eyes.
24 This *is* the day *which* the LORD hath made; we will rejoice and be glad
in it.
25 Save now, I beseech thee, O LORD: O LORD, I beseech thee, send now
prosperity.
26 Blessed *be* he that cometh in the name of the LORD: we have blessed
you out of the house of the LORD.

118:22 Mt 21:42; Mk 12:10, 11; Lk 20:17; Acts 4:11; 1 Pet 2:7
118:25 Ps 122:6, 7
118:26 Mt 21:9; Mk 11:9; Lk 13:35; Jn 12:13

F. THE CLOSING DOXOLOGY TO GOD

27 God *is* the LORD, which hath shewed us light: bind the sacrifice with
cords, *even* unto the horns of the altar.
28 Thou *art* my God, and I will praise thee: *thou art* my God, I will exalt
thee.
29 O give thanks unto the LORD; for *he is* good: for his mercy *endureth* for
ever.

118:27 Isa 25:1; 1 Pet 2:9
☆**118:29**

I. UNDYING DEVOTION TO THE WORD OF GOD WRITTEN

A. BLESSINGS ON THOSE WHO LOVE GOD'S WORD

א ALEPH

119 BLESSED *are* the undefiled in the way, who walk in the law of
the LORD.

☆**119:1** Prov 11:20; 13:6; Ezek 11:20; Mic 4:2

118:29 The love, mercy, and goodness of God last forever. For this the believer should give thanks every day of his life.
119:1ff This Psalm is divided into twenty-two segments arranged according to the Hebrew alphabet. It is more than twice as long as any other Psalm and is among the brightest of them all. It has been compared with Proverbs as being "a chest of gold, not a chain of gold links,"* for the various segments of the Psalm are pious declarations that stand by themselves without reference to the other parts. The alphabetic arrangement has occasioned some to say that it is like our ABC's. On the whole, the Psalm exalts the law of God and sets forth the excellency and glories of divine revelation.

119:2 Deut 4:29; 10:12; 11:13; 30:2; Ps 25:10
119:3 1 Jn 3:9; 15:18
119:4 Deut 4:13; Neh 9:13
119:5 2 Chron 7:17; Prov 4:26

2 Blessed *are* they that keep his testimonies, *and that* seek him with the
whole heart.
3 They also do no iniquity: they walk in his ways.
4 Thou hast commanded *us* to keep thy precepts diligently.
5 O that my ways were directed to keep thy statutes!
6 Then shall I not be ashamed, when I have respect unto all thy
commandments.
7 I will praise thee with uprightness of heart, when I shall have learned thy
righteous judgments.

119:8 Ps 71:9, 18

8 I will keep thy statutes: O forsake me not utterly.

ב BETH

B. PERSONAL HOLINESS THROUGH THE WORD

119:9 1 Kgs 8:25; 2 Chron 6:16

9 Wherewithal shall a young man cleanse his way? by taking heed *thereto*
according to thy word.
10 With my whole heart have I sought thee: O let me not wander from thy
commandments.

119:11☆ Lk 2:19, 51

11 Thy word have I hid in mine heart, that I might not sin against thee.
12 Blessed *art* thou, O LORD: teach me thy statutes.

119:13 Ps 40:9

13 With my lips have I declared all the judgments of thy mouth.
14 I have rejoiced in the way of thy testimonies, as *much as* in all riches.

119:15 Isa 58:2

15 I will meditate in thy precepts, and have respect unto thy ways.
16 I will delight myself in thy statutes: I will not forget thy word.

ג GIMEL

C. A PRAYER FOR OPEN EYES

17 Deal bountifully with thy servant, *that* I may live, and keep thy word.

119:18☆

18 Open thou mine eyes, that I may behold wondrous things out of thy
law.

119:19 1 Chron 29:15; Heb 11:13

19 I *am* a stranger in the earth: hide not thy commandments from me.
20 My soul breaketh for the longing *that it hath* unto thy judgments at all
times.

119:21 Deut 27:26; Ps 37:22

21 Thou hast rebuked the proud *that are* cursed, which do err from thy
commandments.

119:11 The Bible is the inspired and inerrant Word of God. Apologists give solid and sound reasons for believing the Bible to be true. Among them are these: (1) the writers of the Old Testament claimed that what they said is the Word of God. "Thus saith the Lord" or its equivalent appears more than two thousand times (2 Sam. 23:1–3; Isa. 8:1, 11; Jer. 1:9; 5:14; 7:27; 13:12; Ezek. 3:4; Mic. 5:10; Hab. 2:2; etc.); (2) the apostles accepted all of the Scriptures as the infallible Word of God (2 Tim. 3:16; 2 Pet. 1:21; 1 Cor. 14:37; 1 Thess. 2:13; Gal. 1:11, 12); (3) Jesus Christ affirmed the Word of God to be trustworthy (John 10:35; Matt. 5:18; etc); (4) fulfilled prophecy shows the Bible to be true (Deut. 28:63–65; 28:37; Luke 21:24; Nah. 3:1, 4–6; Zeph. 2:13, 14; Isa. 13:19–22; Jer. 51:37; Ezek. 29:15; 30:6; Jer. 46:19, 20); (5) archeology confirms the truthfulness of the Scriptures; and (6) the pragmatic test establishes the fact that the Bible does what it says it will do in human experience (see 34:8; John 7:17). The proper approach to the study of the Word of God is comprehended in these four words: (1) *admit,* i.e., to allow the Word of God to enter heart and mind; (2) *submit,* i.e., to assent to God's truth and to use it; (3) *commit,* i.e., to let his Word possess the believer by hiding it in his heart; and (4) *transmit,* i.e., to pass it on to others so that it can become real in their lives too.

119:18 Methods of Bible study include (1) book study: master one book at a time—who wrote it, what its purpose is, what its outline is, and how it relates to the remainder of the Scriptures; (2) topical study: track down words such as *love, grace, faith, prayer,* and *assurance;* (3) biographical study: look into the lives of God's saints to discover what lessons can be learned from their experiences—Moses, Abraham, Sarah, Saul, Mary, Paul, and, most of all, Jesus; and (4) other methods: the study of great passages of Scripture (e.g., Rom. 8; 1 Cor. 13; Heb. 12; John 1) or smaller segments of a book on an intensive basis; comparison of passage to passage; etc.

22 Remove from me reproach and contempt; for I have kept thy testimo-
nies.
23 Princes also did sit *and* speak against me: *but* thy servant did meditate
in thy statutes.
24 Thy testimonies also *are* my delight *and* my counsellors.

ד DALETH

D. GETTING INSTRUCTIONS FROM THE WORD

25 My soul cleaveth unto the dust: quicken thou me according to thy **119:25** Ps 44:25
word.
26 I have declared my ways, and thou heardest me: teach me thy statutes.
27 Make me to understand the way of thy precepts: so shall I talk of thy
wondrous works.
28 My soul melteth for heaviness: strengthen thou me according unto thy **119:28** Ps 22:14; 1 Pet 5:10
word.
29 Remove from me the way of lying: and grant me thy law graciously. ☆**119:29**
30 I have chosen the way of truth: thy judgments have I laid *before me.*
31 I have stuck unto thy testimonies: O LORD, put me not to shame. **119:31** Deut 11:22
32 I will run the way of thy commandments, when thou shalt enlarge my
heart.

ה HE

E. A PRAYER TO FOLLOW GOD'S WORD

33 Teach me, O LORD, the way of thy statutes; and I shall keep it *unto the* **119:33** 1 Chron 22:12; Ezek 44:24
end.
34 Give me understanding, and I shall keep thy law; yea, I shall observe it
with *my* whole heart.
35 Make me to go in the path of thy commandments; for therein do I **119:35** Ps 25:4; 112:1
delight.
36 Incline my heart unto thy testimonies, and not to covetousness. **119:36** Lk 12:15; Heb 13:5
37 Turn away mine eyes from beholding vanity; *and* quicken thou me in **119:37** Ps 71:20; Isa 33:15
thy way.
38 Stablish thy word unto thy servant, who *is devoted* to thy fear. **119:38** 2 Sam 7:25
39 Turn away my reproach which I fear: for thy judgments *are* good.
40 Behold, I have longed after thy precepts: quicken me in thy righteous- **119:40** Ps 102:39
ness.

ו VAU

F. GOD'S WORDS ARE OUR ONLY HOPE

41 Let thy mercies come also unto me, O LORD, *even* thy salvation,
according to thy word.
42 So shall I have wherewith to answer him that reproacheth me: for I
trust in thy word.
43 And take not the word of truth utterly out of my mouth; for I have
hoped in thy judgments.
44 So shall I keep thy law continually for ever and ever. ☆**119:44** Acts 26:1, 2

119:29 The kings of Israel were supposed to write out a copy of the law for their own use (Deut. 17:18). The Psalmist here wants the law to be inscribed on his heart, for the Word of God before him should be the Word of God in him.

119:44 It is important to have the Word of God before me and in me, but unless I keep the Word of God (i.e., follow it and execute its commandments in my life) it profits me nothing.

45 And I will walk at liberty: for I seek thy precepts.
46 I will speak of thy testimonies also before kings, and will not be ashamed.
47 And I will delight myself in thy commandments, which I have loved.
48 My hands also will I lift up unto thy commandments, which I have loved; and I will meditate in thy statutes.

ז ZAIN

G. GOD'S WORD, THE SOURCE OF COMFORT

119:49☆ 49 Remember the word unto thy servant, upon which thou hast caused me
Job 6:10 Rom 15:14 to hope.
50 This *is* my comfort in my affliction: for thy word hath quickened me.
119:51 51 The proud have had me greatly in derision: *yet* have I not declined from
Job 23:11 Jer 20:7 thy law.
119:52 Ps 103:18 52 I remembered thy judgments of old, O LORD; and have comforted
myself.
119:53 53 Horror hath taken hold upon me because of the wicked that forsake thy
Ex 32:19 Neh 13:25 law.
119:54☆ 54 Thy statutes have been my songs in the house of my pilgrimage.
119:55 55 I have remembered thy name, O LORD, in the night, and have kept thy
Ps 42:8; 63:6 92:2 law.
Isa 26:9 Acts 16:25 56 This I had, because I kept thy precepts.

ח CHETH

H. A RESOLVE TO OBEY THE WORD OF GOD

119:57☆ Ps 16:5 57 *Thou art* my portion, O LORD: I have said that I would keep thy words.
119:58 58 I intreated thy favour with *my* whole heart: be merciful unto me
Ps 41:4 according to thy word.
119:59 59 I thought on my ways, and turned my feet unto thy testimonies.
Mk 14:72 Lk 15:17 60 I made haste, and delayed not to keep thy commandments.
119:61 61 The bands of the wicked have robbed me: *but* I have not forgotten thy
Ps 140:5 law.
62 At midnight I will rise to give thanks unto thee because of thy righteous judgments.
119:63 63 I *am* a companion of all *them* that fear thee, and of them that keep thy
Ps 101:6 precepts.
119:64 64 The earth, O LORD, is full of thy mercy: teach me thy statutes.
Ps 33:5

ט TETH

I. AFFLICTION TEACHES US TO ATTEND TO GOD'S WORD

65 Thou hast dealt well with thy servant, O LORD, according unto thy word.
119:66 66 Teach me good judgment and knowledge: for I have believed thy
Phil 1:9 commandments.

119:49 The hope of the believer is founded on the Word of God. There is no other basis for hope in life. **119:54** The wise traveler along the pathway of life sings songs in the night. They are borrowed from the Word of God. For the psalmist the words of God are as familiar to him as any of the songs men generally sing. **119:57** The psalmist has chosen God as his portion, not money, fame, or any other worldly satisfaction; therefore, he thinks of God's ways and hastens to keep his commandments. He refuses to forget God's law.

67 Before I was afflicted I went astray: but now have I kept thy word.
68 Thou *art* good, and doest good; teach me thy statutes.
69 The proud have forged a lie against me: *but* I will keep thy precepts
with *my* whole heart.
70 Their heart is as fat as grease; *but* I delight in thy law.
71 *It is* good for me that I have been afflicted; that I might learn thy
statutes.
72 The law of thy mouth *is* better unto me than thousands of gold and
silver.

☆**119:67** Jer 31:18, 19; Heb 12:5–11
119:68 Deut 30:5; Ps 86:5; 125:4
119:70 Isa 6:10; Jer 5:28
119:71 Prov 8:10, 11, 19

י JOD

J. FELLOWSHIP WITH OTHERS AROUND GOD'S WORD

73 Thy hands have made me and fashioned me: give me understanding,
that I may learn thy commandments.
74 They that fear thee will be glad when they see me; because I have
hoped in thy word.
75 I know, O LORD, that thy judgments *are* right, and *that* thou in
faithfulness hast afflicted me.
76 Let, I pray thee, thy merciful kindness be for my comfort, according to
thy word unto thy servant.
77 Let thy tender mercies come unto me, that I may live: for thy law *is* my
delight.
78 Let the proud be ashamed; for they dealt perversely with me without a
cause: *but* I will meditate in thy precepts.
79 Let those that fear thee turn unto me, and those that have known thy
testimonies.
80 Let my heart be sound in thy statutes; that I be not ashamed.

☆**119:73** Job 31:15; Ps 139:15, 16
119:74 Ps 35:27
119:75 Heb 12:10

כ CAPH

K. OBEDIENCE TO THE WORD OCCASIONS GOD'S HELP

81 My soul fainteth for thy salvation: *but* I hope in thy word.
82 Mine eyes fail for thy word, saying, When wilt thou comfort me?
83 For I am become like a bottle in the smoke; *yet* do I not forget thy
statutes.
84 How many *are* the days of thy servant? when wilt thou execute
judgment on them that persecute me?
85 The proud have digged pits for me, which *are* not after thy law.
86 All thy commandments *are* faithful: they persecute me wrongfully; help
thou me.
87 They had almost consumed me upon earth; but I forsook not thy
precepts.
88 *Quicken me after thy lovingkindness*; so shall I keep the testimony of
thy mouth.

☆**119:81**
119:82 Isa 38:14; Lam 2:11
119:83 Job 30:30
119:84 Ps 39:4; Rev 6:10
119:85 Ps 35:19; 57:6; Jer 18:22

119:67 While the Psalmist lived in prosperity, peace, and plenty he wandered away from God. Then he went back and kept the Word of God and recovered from his wanderings or sins.
119:73 God, the Creator, has made us by his power and intends that his creatures glorify him.
119:81 The psalmist's soul faints and his eyes fail, so he longs for God's salvation. The hope of that salvation springs from the Word of God. He is saved that he might keep the testimony of God's mouth, i.e., make it his portion and confidence. His God quickens him; otherwise he could not love God and keep his commandments.

ל LAMED

L. THE LORD'S WORD NEVER CHANGES

119:89☆ Isa 40:8 Mt 24:35 1 Pet 1:25 **119:90** Ps 89:1, 2 104:2–4; 148:6 Jer 31:35

89 For ever, O LORD, thy word is settled in heaven.
90 Thy faithfulness *is* unto all generations: thou hast established the earth,
and it abideth.
91 They continue this day according to thine ordinances: for all *are* thy
servants.
92 Unless thy law *had been* my delights, I should then have perished in
mine affliction.
93 I will never forget thy precepts: for with them thou hast quickened me.
94 I *am* thine, save me; for I have sought thy precepts.

119:95 Ps 40:14 Isa 32:7

95 The wicked have waited for me to destroy me: *but* I will consider thy
testimonies.
96 I have seen an end of all perfection: *but* thy commandment *is* exceeding
broad.

מ MEM

M. THE PSALMIST'S LOVE OF GOD'S WORD

119:97☆

97 O how love I thy law! it *is* my meditation all the day.

119:98 Deut 4:6

98 Thou through thy commandments hast made me wiser than mine
enemies: for they *are* ever with me.
99 I have more understanding than all my teachers: for thy testimonies *are*
my meditation.

119:100 Job 32:7–9

100 I understand more than the ancients, because I keep thy precepts.
101 I have refrained my feet from every evil way, that I might keep thy
word.

119:102 Deut 17:20 Josh 23:6 Ps 19:10 Prov 24:13, 14

102 I have not departed from thy judgments: for thou hast taught me.
103 How sweet are thy words unto my taste! *yea, sweeter* than honey to my
mouth!
104 Through thy precepts I get understanding: therefore I hate every false
way.

נ NUN

N. THE WORD IS A LIGHT TO THE PATH

119:105☆ Prov 6:23

105 Thy word *is* a lamp unto my feet, and a light unto my path.
106 I have sworn, and I will perform *it*, that I will keep thy righteous
judgments.
107 I am afflicted very much: quicken me, O LORD, according unto thy
word.

119:108 Hos 14:2 Heb 13:15

108 Accept, I beseech thee, the freewill offerings of my mouth, O LORD,
and teach me thy judgments.

119:89 The Word of God is unchangeable, as are all *his counsels.* Not one word spoken by God shall fail. Before a single letter of the alphabet in any single word of God can be changed or abridged, heaven and earth would first have to pass away. The Word of God is eternal.

119:97 Whoever does not love the Word of God does not love the Giver of that Word. And he who refuses to meditate on the Word is either lost or backslidden.

119:105 The Word of God is a lamp and a light. It is light to the eyes so that we can see, and it searches us out to discover whether indeed we are blind or we really see. It is also a guide to the people of God so their feet will not go astray, that is, that they may walk the pathway of life and stay on the path, never departing from it.

109 My soul *is* continually in my hand: yet do I not forget thy law.
110 The wicked have laid a snare for me: yet I erred not from thy precepts.
111 Thy testimonies have I taken as an heritage for ever: for they *are* the
rejoicing of my heart.
112 I have inclined mine heart to perform thy statutes alway, *even unto* the
end.

119:109 Job 13:14
119:110 Ps 91:3; 140:5
119:111 Deut 33:4

ס SAMECH

O. GOD'S WORD, A REFUGE AND A SHIELD

113 I hate *vain* thoughts: but thy law do I love.
114 Thou *art* my hiding place and my shield: I hope in thy word.
115 Depart from me, ye evildoers: for I will keep the commandments of
my God.
116 Uphold me according unto thy word, that I may live: and let me not be
ashamed of my hope.
117 Hold thou me up, and I shall be safe: and I will have respect unto thy
statutes continually.
118 Thou hast trodden down all them that err from thy statutes: for their
deceit *is* falsehood.
119 Thou puttest away all the wicked of the earth *like* dross: therefore I
love thy testimonies.
120 My flesh trembleth for fear of thee; and I am afraid of thy judgments.

119:113 1 Kgs 18:21 Jas 1:8; 4:8
119:114 Ps 31:20; 61:4 84:9
119:115 Ps 6:8; 139:19 Mt 7:23
☆**119:116** Ps 25:2, 20 31:1, 17 Rom 5:5; 9:33 Phil 1:20
119:117 Ps 12:5 Prov 29:25
119:119 Isa 1:22, 25 Ezek 22:18, 19
119:120 Job 4:14 Hab 3:16

ע AIN

P. THE PSALMIST HAS OBEYED GOD'S LAW

121 I have done judgment and justice: leave me not to mine oppressors.
122 Be surety for thy servant for good: let not the proud oppress me.
123 Mine eyes fail for thy salvation, and for the word of thy righteousness.
124 Deal with thy servant according unto thy mercy, and teach me thy
statutes.
125 I *am* thy servant; give me understanding, that I may know thy
testimonies.
126 *It is* time for *thee,* LORD, to work: *for* they have made void thy law.
127 Therefore I love thy commandments above gold; yea, above fine gold.
128 Therefore I esteem all *thy* precepts *concerning* all *things to be* right; *and*
I hate every false way.

119:121 2 Sam 8:15 Job 29:14
119:124 Ps 51:1; 106:45 109:26
☆**119:125** Ps 116:16
119:126 Jer 18:23 Ezek 31:11
119:128 Ps 19:8

פ PE

Q. A PRAYER FOR GRACE TO OBEY GOD'S WORD

129 Thy testimonies *are* wonderful: therefore doth my soul keep them.
130 The entrance of thy words giveth light; it giveth understanding unto
the simple.
131 I opened my mouth, and panted: for I longed for thy commandments.

☆**119:130**

119:116 Hope in God's Word is the confidence that he will do what he has said he will do. Believing this, the Christian need never be ashamed of that confidence or be disappointed that any of God's promises will not come to pass.

119:125 The psalmist is God's servant. Therefore he has work to do for his master. He prays to be taught to do that work and to do it well.

119:130 We first begin to see and to see rightly when we begin to study the Word of God. It is milk to the beginner and meat to the mature.

119:132 Ps 25:16 **119:133** Ps 19:13 **119:134** Ps 142:6 **119:135** Num 6:25 Ps 67:1 **119:136** Jer 9:1, 18 14:17 Lam 3:48

132 Look thou upon me, and be merciful unto me, as thou usest to do unto
those that love thy name.
133 Order my steps in thy word: and let not any iniquity have dominion
over me.
134 Deliver me from the oppression of man: so will I keep thy precepts.
135 Make thy face to shine upon thy servant; and teach me thy statutes.
136 Rivers of waters run down mine eyes, because they keep not thy law.

צ TZADDI

R. GOD'S LAWS AND JUSTICE ARE FAIR

119:137 Ezra 9:15 Jer 12:1 Dan 9:7, 14 **119:139** Ps 69:9 **119:140☆** Ps 12:6 **119:141** Ps 22:6 **119:144** Ps 19:9

137 Righteous *art* thou, O LORD, and upright *are* thy judgments.
138 Thy testimonies *that* thou hast commanded *are* righteous and very
faithful.
139 My zeal hath consumed me, because mine enemies have forgotten thy
words.
140 Thy word *is* very pure: therefore thy servant loveth it.
141 I *am* small and despised: *yet* do not I forget thy precepts.
142 Thy righteousness *is* an everlasting righteousness, and thy law *is* the
truth.
143 Trouble and anguish have taken hold on me: *yet* thy commandments
are my delights.
144 The righteousness of thy testimonies *is* everlasting: give me understanding, and I shall live.

ק KOPH

S. A PETITION FOR GOD'S SALVATION

119:146 Ps 3:7 **119:147☆** Ps 108:2 **119:151** Ps 34:18 Isa 50:8 **119:152** Lk 21:33

145 I cried with *my* whole heart; hear me, O LORD: I will keep thy statutes.
146 I cried unto thee; save me, and I shall keep thy testimonies.
147 I prevented the dawning of the morning, and cried: I hoped in thy
word.
148 Mine eyes prevent the *night* watches, that I might meditate in thy
word.
149 Hear my voice according unto thy lovingkindness: O LORD, quicken
me according to thy judgment.
150 They draw nigh that follow after mischief: they are far from thy law.
151 Thou *art* near, O LORD; and all thy commandments *are* truth.
152 Concerning thy testimonies, I have known of old that thou hast
founded them for ever.

ר RESH

T. DESPITE ADVERSITY, THE PSALMIST KEPT GOD'S LAW

119:153☆ Hos 4:6 **119:154** Ps 35:1 Mic 7:9

153 Consider mine affliction, and deliver me: for I do not forget thy law.
154 Plead my cause, and deliver me: quicken me according to thy word.

119:140 The love of the Word of God is evidence of *love for the author* of that Word. That Word is pure because it bears the image of God's holiness and has for its purpose to make us partakers of God's holiness.

119:147 Before the dawning of the morning the psalmist's heart is seeking after God. Before the business of the day and its distractions, while the mind is fresh, the psalmist converses with his God. When evening comes he finds that God has been with him all the day.

119:153 In the midst of affliction the believer's first resource is God. Whoever is afflicted, let him pray. Where else can one turn, and who can help him better than his God?

155 Salvation *is* far from the wicked: for they seek not thy statutes.
156 Great *are* thy tender mercies, O LORD: quicken me according to thy
judgments.
157 Many *are* my persecutors and mine enemies; *yet* do I not decline from
thy testimonies.
158 I beheld the transgressors, and was grieved; because they kept not thy
word.
159 Consider how I love thy precepts: quicken me, O LORD, according to
thy lovingkindness.
160 Thy word *is* true *from* the beginning: and every one of thy righteous
judgments *endureth* for ever.

119:156 2 Sam 24:14
119:158 Ps 139:21; Isa 24:16

ש SCHIN

U. PRAISE FOR GOD'S LAW SEVEN TIMES A DAY

161 Princes have persecuted me without a cause: but my heart standeth in
awe of thy word.
162 I rejoice at thy word, as one that findeth great spoil.
163 I hate and abhor lying: *but* thy law do I love.
164 Seven times a day do I praise thee because of thy righteous judgments.
165 Great peace have they which love thy law: and nothing shall offend
them.
166 LORD, I have hoped for thy salvation, and done thy commandments.
167 My soul hath kept thy testimonies; and I love them exceedingly.
168 I have kept thy precepts and thy testimonies: for all my ways *are*
before thee.

119:161 1 Sam 26:18
119:162 1 Sam 30:16; Isa 9:3
119:163 Ps 31:6; Prov 13:5
☆**110:164**
119:165 Prov 3:23; Isa 26:3; 1 Jn 2:10
119:166 Gen 49:18
119:168 Ps 139:3; Prov 5:21

ת TAU

V. THE CLOSING LITANY OF PRAYER AND PRAISE

169 Let my cry come near before thee, O LORD: give me understanding
according to thy word.
170 Let my supplication come before thee: deliver me according to thy
word.
171 My lips shall utter praise, when thou hast taught me thy statutes.
172 My tongue shall speak of thy word: for all thy commandments *are*
righteousness.
173 Let thine hand help me; for I have chosen thy precepts.
174 I have longed for thy salvation, O LORD; and thy law *is* my delight.
175 Let my soul live, and it shall praise thee; and let thy judgments help
me.
176 I have gone astray like a lost sheep; seek thy servant; for I do not
forget thy commandments.

119:169 Job 16:18; Ps 18:6
119:170 Ps 22:20; 31:2; 140:6
119:171 Isa 2:3; Mic 4:2
119:172 Ps 51:14
119:173 Josh 24:22; Lk 10:42
119:175 Isa 55:3
☆**119:176** Isa 53:6; Jer 50:6; Mt 18:12; Lk 15:4

119:164 *Seven times a day* has been taken literally by some interpreters. Rabbi Solomon took this to mean that God was to be praised in the morning twice before reading the Ten Commandments and once following the reading. In the evening God was to be praised twice before reading the Law and twice afterward.

119:176 *like a lost sheep.* Everywhere in the Scriptures sheep are spoken of as stupid or dumb. Men, like sheep, go astray. The loving shepherd searches and finds the lost sheep. It is fitting that the longest Psalm celebrating the Word of God should end on a note of lostness with a plea for God to rescue the lost.

I. A PETITION FOR DIVINE HELP
A. FROM LYING TONGUES

A Song of degrees

120:1ff☆ Ps 18:6; 66:14; 102:2 **120:2** Prov 12:22 **120:3** Ps 52:4; Zeph 3:13 **120:4**☆ Ps 45:15; 140:10; Prov 25:18

120 IN my distress I cried unto the LORD, and he heard me.
2 Deliver my soul, O LORD, from lying lips, *and* from a deceitful
tongue.
3 What shall be given unto thee? or what shall be done unto thee, thou
false tongue?
4 Sharp arrows of the mighty, with coals of juniper.

B. FROM THOSE WHO HATE PEACE

120:5☆ Ps 35:20; Jer 2:10; 49:28; Ezek 27:13; 38:2, 3 **120:7** Ps 109:4

5 Woe is me, that I sojourn in Me'sech, *that* I dwell in the tents of Ke'dar!
6 My soul hath long dwelt with him that hateth peace.
7 I *am for* peace: but when I speak, they *are* for war.

I. THE TRAVELER'S PSALM: THE LORD IS MY KEEPER

A Song of degrees

121:1☆ Ps 87:1 **121:2** Ps 124:8 **121:3** Ps 66:9 **121:5** Ps 91:4 **121:6** Isa 49:10; Rev 7:16 **121:7** Ps 91:10–12

121 I WILL lift up mine eyes unto the hills, from whence cometh my help.
2 My help *cometh* from the LORD, which made heaven and earth.
3 He will not suffer thy foot to be moved: he that keepeth thee will not
slumber.
4 Behold, he that keepeth Israel shall neither slumber nor sleep.
5 The LORD *is* thy keeper: the LORD *is* thy shade upon thy right hand.
6 The sun shall not smite thee by day, nor the moon by night.
7 The LORD shall preserve thee from all evil: he shall preserve thy soul.
8 The LORD shall preserve thy going out and thy coming in from this time
forth, and even for evermore.

I. THE PEACE OF JERUSALEM
A. ATTENDING THE TEMPLE OF THE LORD

A Song of degrees of David

122:1☆ Ps 42:4; Isa 2:3; Mic 4:2; Zech 8:21

122 I WAS glad when they said unto me, Let us go into the house of the LORD.
2 Our feet shall stand within thy gates, O Jerusalem.

120:1ff Psalms 120–134 have been placed together under the label "songs of degrees," or "songs of ascents," as the RSV has it. Following Ps. 119, the longest of all the Psalms, these fifteen Psalms are the shortest. Two of them have only three verses. These Psalms were written by different people. They may have been sung together with a musical pause at the end of each. Some think they were used as the singers climbed the fifteen steps from the outward court of the *temple to the inner court.* The Psalms have one feature called an "ascent" or "climax." For example, in Ps. 121:1 the text reads "From whence cometh my help?" The next verse rises to a higher pitch saying, "My help cometh from the LORD." Some of these Psalms are personal. Others refer to the corporate body of believers.

120:4 *with coals of juniper,* i.e., "with coals of the broom tree,"† a big shrub with white flowers whose root makes excellent charcoal.

120:5 *Meshech . . . Kedar.* Cf. Gen. 10:2; 25:13. The reference here is to two ethnic groups of barbarous strangers in which an Israelite is either living far from home or in a place where his people have surrendered their faith in God's truth.

121:1 This has been called the traveler's or soldier's Psalm. Whoever calls on his God before he goes will find that God is with him on the journey.

122:1 Three times a year the people came to Jerusalem for their solemn feasts. Their hearts were glad when friends and neighbors would joyfully say, *Let us go into the house of the LORD.*

3 Jerusalem is builded as a city that is compact together:
4 Whither the tribes go up, the tribes of the LORD, unto the testimony of
Israel, to give thanks unto the name of the LORD.
5 For there are set thrones of judgment, the thrones of the house of David.

122:4 Deut 16:16 Ps 84:5
122:5 Deut 17:8 2 Chron 19:8

B. PRAYING FOR THE PEACE OF JERUSALEM

6 Pray for the peace of Jerusalem: they shall prosper that love thee.
7 Peace be within thy walls, *and* prosperity within thy palaces.
8 For my brethren and companions' sakes, I will now say, Peace *be* within
thee.
9 Because of the house of the LORD our God I will seek thy good.

122:6 Ps 102:14 Jer 29:7
122:7 Isa 62:6 Jer 17:27
122:8 Ps 133:1
122:9 1 Sam 25:6

I. THE PATIENCE OF THE SAINTS

A. LOOKING TO JEHOVAH

A Song of degrees

123 UNTO thee lift I up mine eyes, O thou that dwellest in the
heavens.
2 Behold, as the eyes of servants *look* unto the hand of their masters, *and*
as the eyes of a maiden unto the hand of her mistress; so our eyes *wait* upon
the LORD our God, until that he have mercy upon us.

☆**123:1** Ps 11:4; 141:8
123:2 Mal 1:6

B. PRAYING FOR MERCY

3 Have mercy upon us, O LORD, have mercy upon us: for we are
exceedingly filled with contempt.
4 Our soul is exceedingly filled with the scorning of those that are at ease,
and with the contempt of the proud.

123:3 Neh 4:4 Job 12:5 Ps 4:1; 51:1 79:4; 119:22 Amos 6:1

I. DELIVERANCE FROM SUDDEN DANGER

A. THE LORD IS ON OUR SIDE

A Song of degrees of David

124 IF *it had* not *been* the LORD who was on our side, now may Israel
say;
2 If *it had* not *been* the LORD who was on our side, when men rose up
against us:
3 Then they had swallowed us up quick, when their wrath was kindled
against us:
4 Then the waters had overwhelmed us, the stream had gone over our
soul:
5 Then the proud waters had gone over our soul.

☆**124:1** Ps 94:17
124:2 Ps 56:1; 138:7
124:4 Job 22:11 Ps 18:16; 69:2 144:7

B. LET JEHOVAH BE BLESSED

6 Blessed *be* the LORD, who hath not given us *as* a prey to their teeth.
7 Our soul is escaped as a bird out of the snare of the fowlers: the snare is
broken, and we are escaped.
8 Our help *is* in the name of the LORD, who made heaven and earth.

124:6 Prov 30:14
124:7 Ps 91:3; 141:10 Prov 6:5 2 Cor 11:33 Heb 11:34

123:1 Some think this Psalm was written when God's people were captives in Babylon. It may be useful to us today when the church is beset by persecution and/or languishes from apostasy and the coldness of the backslidden.

124:1 Without God there is no ultimate hope for deliverance from ruin or from the brink of disaster. God in his goodness makes a way of escape for his own people.

I. THE LORD SURROUNDS AND PROTECTS HIS PEOPLE

A Song of degrees

125:1☆ Ps 46:5
125 THEY that trust in the LORD *shall be* as mount Zion, *which*
cannot be removed, *but* abideth for ever.

125:2 Zech 2:5
2 *As* the mountains *are* round about Jerusalem, so the LORD *is* round
about his people from henceforth even for ever.

125:3 1 Sam 24:10; Prov 22:8; Isa 14:5
3 For the rod of the wicked shall not rest upon the lot of the righteous;
lest the righteous put forth their hands unto iniquity.

125:4 Job 23:11; Ps 7:10; 94:15; 119:68
4 Do good, O LORD, unto *those that be* good, and to *them that are* upright
in their hearts.

125:5 Gal 6:16
5 As for such as turn aside unto their crooked ways, the LORD shall lead
them forth with the workers of iniquity: *but* peace *shall be* upon Israel.

I. GOD'S DELIVERANCE FROM CAPTIVITY

A Song of degrees

126:1☆ Jer 29:14; Acts 12:9
126 WHEN the LORD turned again the captivity of Zion, we were like
them that dream.

126:2 1 Sam 12:24; Job 8:21; Ps 51:14; Lk 1:49
2 Then was our mouth filled with laughter, and our tongue with singing:
then said they among the heathen, The LORD hath done great things for
them.

126:3 Zeph 3:14
3 The LORD hath done great things for us; *whereof* we are glad.

126:4 Isa 35:6; 43:19
4 Turn again our captivity, O LORD, as the streams in the south.

126:5 Ps 80:5; Lam 1:2; Isa 51:11; Gal 6:9
5 They that sow in tears shall reap in joy.
6 He that goeth forth and weepeth, bearing precious seed, shall doubtless
come again with rejoicing, bringing his sheaves *with him.*

I. A PSALM FOR THE FAMILY

A Song of degrees for Solomon

127:1☆ Ps 78:69
127 EXCEPT the LORD build the house, they labour in vain that
build it: except the LORD keep the city, the watchman waketh *but*
in vain.

127:2 Gen 3:17; Job 11:18, 19; Eccles 5:12
2 *It is* vain for you to rise up early, to sit up late, to eat the bread of
sorrows: *for* so he giveth his beloved sleep.

127:3 Deut 28:4
3 Lo, children *are* an heritage of the LORD: *and* the fruit of the womb *is*
his reward.

127:4 Ps 112:2
4 As arrows *are* in the hand of a mighty man; so *are* children of the youth.
5 Happy *is* the man that hath his quiver full of them: they shall not be
ashamed, but they shall speak with the enemies in the gate.

I. A PSALM OF FAMILY BLESSEDNESS

A. THE BLESSEDNESS OF THE SAINTS

A Song of degrees

128:1☆ Ps 119:3
128 BLESSED *is* every one that feareth the LORD; that walketh in his
ways.

125:1 Of this we can be sure: it is well for the righteous and ill for the wicked.

126:1 This Psalm may have reference to the deliverance of Israel from the captivity. When Israel's liberation came from God, the weeping of the afflicted turned to shouts of joy.

127:1 Men seek to found a family and to ensure the continuance of their family names. To do this is good in itself, but if it is done apart from God, their labors to this end are futile.

128:1ff This Psalm is thought to have been sung at Israelite wedding ceremonies. It emphasizes marriage and children, which are a heritage of the Lord.

B. THE BLESSEDNESS OF THE HOME

2 For thou shalt eat the labour of thine hands: happy *shalt* thou *be,* and *it*
shall be well with thee.
3 Thy wife *shall be* as a fruitful vine by the sides of thine house: thy
children like olive plants round about thy table.
4 Behold, that thus shall the man be blessed that feareth the LORD.

128:2 Eccles 8:12
128:3 Ps 52:8

C. THE BLESSEDNESS OF THE NATION ISRAEL

5 The LORD shall bless thee out of Zion: and thou shalt see the good of
Jerusalem all the days of thy life.
6 Yea, thou shalt see thy children's children, *and* peace upon Israel.

128:5 Ps 122:9; 134:3
128:6 Gen 48:11; Prov 17:6

I. A PRAYER AGAINST THOSE WHO AFFLICT ISRAEL

A Song of degrees

129 MANY a time have they afflicted me from my youth, may Israel
now say:
2 Many a time have they afflicted me from my youth: yet they have not
prevailed against me.
3 The plowers plowed upon my back: they made long their furrows.
4 The LORD *is* righteous: he hath cut asunder the cords of the wicked.
5 Let them all be confounded and turned back that hate Zion.
6 Let them be as the grass *upon* the housetops, which withereth afore it
groweth up:
7 Wherewith the mower filleth not his hand; nor he that bindeth sheaves
his bosom.
8 Neither do they which go by say, The blessing of the LORD *be* upon you:
we bless you in the name of the LORD.

☆**129:1** Ex 1:11; Judg 3:8; Jer 22:21; Hos 2:15; 11:1
129:2 Jer 15:20; Mt 16:17; 2 Cor 4:8, 9
129:3 Ps 140:5
129:5 Ps 71:13; Mic 4:11
129:6 2 Kgs 19:26; Ps 37:2
129:8 Ps 118:26

I. WAITING ON THE LORD WITH HOPE

A. THE CRY FOR HELP

A Song of degrees

130 OUT of the depths have I cried unto thee, O LORD.
2 Lord, hear my voice: let thine ears be attentive to the voice of
my supplications.

B. EXPECTANT WAITING

3 If thou, LORD, shouldest mark iniquities, O Lord, who shall stand?
4 But *there is* forgiveness with thee, that thou mayest be feared.
5 I wait for the LORD, my soul doth wait, and in his word do I hope.
6 My soul *waiteth* for the Lord more than they that watch for the
morning: *I say, more than* they that watch for the morning.

C. LET ISRAEL HOPE IN THE LORD

7 Let Israel hope in the LORD: for with the LORD *there is* mercy, and with
him *is* plenteous redemption.
8 And he shall redeem Israel from all his iniquities.

☆**130:1** Ps 42:7; 69:2
130:2 Neh 1:6, 11; Ps 28:2; 64:1
130:3 Neh 9:17; Ps 76:7; 86:5; Jer 33:8, 9; Dan 9:9; Mal 3:2; Rev 6:17
130:5 Ps 40:1; 119:74, 81; Isa 8:17
130:6 Ps 63:6
130:7 Ps 103:4; Rom 3:24; Eph 1:7
130:8 Lk 1:68; Tit 2:14

129:1 This Psalm appears to have been penned after the Babylonian captivity had begun. It emphasizes Israel's tribulations even as far back as the time spent in Egypt.

130:1 Men can anticipate no help apart from God, but no one is beyond God's help if he will call on him. Let whoever is helpless call to God, who will throw out a lifeline.

131:1☆
2 Sam 22:28
Job 42:3
Isa 2:12
Zeph 3:11
Prov 30:13
Rom 12:16
131:2
Ps 62:1
Mt 18:3
1 Cor 14:20

I. THE PSALM OF THE HUMBLE AND QUIET HEART

A Song of degrees of David

131 LORD, my heart is not haughty, nor mine eyes lofty: neither do
I exercise myself in great matters, or in things too high for me.
[2]Surely I have behaved and quieted myself, as a child that is weaned of
his mother: my soul *is* even as a weaned child.
[3]Let Israel hope in the LORD from henceforth and for ever.

I. DAVID BRINGS BACK THE ARK

A. DAVID'S SOLEMN PROMISE

132:1☆
132:2
1 Kgs 8:17
1 Chron 22:7
Acts 7:46
Isa 49:26

A Song of degrees

132 LORD, remember David, *and* all his afflictions:
[2]How he sware unto the LORD, *and* vowed unto the mighty
God of Jacob;
[3]Surely I will not come into the tabernacle of my house, nor go up into
my bed;
[4]I will not give sleep to mine eyes, *or* slumber to mine eyelids,
[5]Until I find out a place for the LORD, an habitation for the mighty *God*
of Jacob.

B. THE FULFILLMENT OF THE PROMISE

132:6☆
Gen 35:19
1 Sam 7:1
132:7
1 Chron 28:2
Ps 5:7; 99:5
132:8
Num 10:35
2 Chron 6:41
Ps 78:61
132:9
Job 29:14
Ps 149:5

[6]Lo, we heard of it at Eph′ra-tah: we found it in the fields of the wood.
[7]We will go into his tabernacles: we will worship at his footstool.
[8]Arise, O LORD, into thy rest; thou, and the ark of thy strength.
[9]Let thy priests be clothed with righteousness; and let thy saints shout
for joy.

C. DAVID CLAIMS THE LORD'S PROMISES TO HIM AND TO ZION

132:11
2 Sam 7:12–16
2 Chron 6:16
132:12
Lk 1:32
Acts 2:30
132:13
Ps 78:68
132:14
Mt 23:21
132:15
Ps 107:9
147:14
132:17☆
132:18
Job 8:22
Ps 21:3; 35:26
109:29

[10]For thy servant David's sake turn not away the face of thine anointed.
[11]The LORD hath sworn *in* truth unto David; he will not turn from it; Of
the fruit of thy body will I set upon thy throne.
[12]If thy children will keep my covenant and my testimony that I shall
teach them, their children shall also sit upon thy throne for evermore.
[13]For the LORD hath chosen Zion; he hath desired *it* for his habitation.
[14]This *is* my rest for ever: here will I dwell; for I have desired it.
[15]I will abundantly bless her provision: I will satisfy her poor with bread.
[16]I will also clothe her priests with salvation: and her saints shall shout
aloud for joy.
[17]There will I make the horn of David to bud: I have ordained a lamp for
mine anointed.
[18]His enemies will I clothe with shame: but upon himself shall his crown
flourish.

131:1 The humility of David is expressed by the absence of a proud heart, of the "haughty look," and of *vain ambition* to attain things beyond their reach. The psalmist is like a child satisfied and content at its mother's breast. Contrariwise, the proud are always fretful and discontented, restless and unsatisfied.

132:1 This Psalm has been attributed by some to Solomon and was to be sung at the dedication of the temple, which he built as charged by his father. God refused David permission to build the temple. Solomon, having done what God had commended, begs God to accept his labors and occupy his dwelling place.

132:6 *Ephratah,* meaning "fruitful land," was usually used for Bethlehem (Gen. 35:19) but here appears to be Kirjath-jearim ("Jaar") (1 Sam. 7:1, 2). *Lo, we heard of it at Ephrathah,* i.e., "First the ark was in Ephrathah."

132:17 *a lamp,* i.e., "a mighty son," or, "a progeny."†

I. BROTHERLY HARMONY

A Song of degrees of David

133 BEHOLD, how good and how pleasant *it is* for brethren to dwell together in unity!
2 *It is* like the precious ointment upon the head, that ran down upon the
beard, *even* Aaron's beard: that went down to the skirts of his garments;
3 As the dew of Hermon, *and as the dew* that descended upon the
mountains of Zion: for there the LORD commanded the blessing, *even* life
for evermore.

133:1 Gen 13:8; Heb 13:1
☆**133:2** Ex 30:25, 30; 39:24; Lev 8:12
133:3 Prov 19:12; Deut 4:48; 28:8; Ps 21:4; 42:8; 48:2

I. WATCHMEN IN THE NIGHT

A Song of degrees

134 BEHOLD, bless ye the LORD, all *ye* servants of the LORD, which by night stand in the house of the LORD.
2 Lift up your hands *in* the sanctuary, and bless the LORD.
3 The LORD that made heaven and earth bless thee out of Zion.

134:1 Deut 10:8; 1 Chron 9:33; 2 Chron 29:11
134:2 Ps 28:2

I. PRAISE TO THE LORD BY HIS SERVANTS

A. LET HIS SERVANTS PRAISE HIM

135 PRAISE ye the LORD. Praise ye the name of the LORD; praise *him*, O ye servants of the LORD.
2 Ye that stand in the house of the LORD, in the courts of the house of our
God,
3 Praise the LORD; for the LORD *is* good: sing praises unto his name; for
it is pleasant.
4 For the LORD hath chosen Jacob unto himself, *and* Israel for his peculiar
treasure.

☆**135:1** Ps 113:1
135:2 Ps 116:19
135:3 Ps 68:4; 100:5
135:4 Ex 19:5; Deut 7:6; 10:15; 1 Pet 2:9

B. THE GREATNESS OF THE LORD AND HIS DELIVERANCE

5 For I know that the LORD *is* great, and *that* our Lord *is* above all gods.
6 Whatsoever the LORD pleased, *that* did he in heaven, and in earth, in the
seas, and all deep places.
7 He causeth the vapours to ascend from the ends of the earth; he maketh
lightnings for the rain; he bringeth the wind out of his treasuries.
8 Who smote the firstborn of Egypt, both of man and beast.
9 *Who* sent tokens and wonders into the midst of thee, O Egypt, upon
Pharaoh, and upon all his servants.
10 Who smote great nations, and slew mighty kings;
11 Sihon king of the Am′or-ites, and Og king of Ba′shan, and all the
kingdoms of Canaan:
12 And gave their land *for* an heritage, an heritage unto Israel his people.

135:5 Ps 48:1; 97:9
☆**135:6** Ps 115:3
135:7 Job 38:25, 26; Jer 51:16; Zech 10:1
135:8 Ps 78:51
135:9 Deut 6:22
135:10 Ps 136:17–21
135:11 Num 21:33–35; Deut 29:7; Josh 12:7–24

C. GOD WILL VINDICATE HIS SERVANTS

13 Thy name, O LORD, *endureth* for ever; *and* thy memorial, O LORD,
throughout all generations.

135:13 Ex 3:15

133:2 The *precious ointment* was used for anointing the priests.

135:1 This is one of the "Hallelujah Psalms." It ends as it begins, with "Hallelujah" to a sovereign God who delivers his people and shames idolatry. Let all Israel, the house of the priesthood, and all who dwell in Jerusalem say "Hallelujah" to our God.

135:6 Here the Psalmist stresses the sovereignty of God over men and all creation. He is beholden to no one but himself and what he does is good and holy.

135:14 Deut 32:36 Ps 106:45 14 For the LORD will judge his people, and he will repent himself
concerning his servants.

D. IDOL MAKERS BECOME LIKE THEIR IDOLS

135:15☆ Ps 115:4–8 15 The idols of the heathen *are* silver and gold, the work of men's hands.
16 They have mouths, but they speak not; eyes have they, but they see not;
17 They have ears, but they hear not; neither is there *any* breath in their
mouths.
18 They that make them are like unto them: *so is* every one that trusteth in
them.

E. LET ALL ISRAEL BLESS JEHOVAH

19 Bless the LORD, O house of Israel: bless the LORD, O house of Aaron:
135:20 Ps 118:4 20 Bless the LORD, O house of Levi: ye that fear the LORD, bless the LORD.
135:21 Ps 132:14 21 Blessed be the LORD out of Zion, which dwelleth at Jerusalem. Praise
ye the LORD.

I. PRAISE AND THANKSGIVING TO JEHOVAH

A. THE CALL TO THANKSGIVING

136:1☆ 1 Chron 16:41 2 Chron 20:21 Ps 107:1 **136** O GIVE thanks unto the LORD; for *he is* good: for his mercy
endureth for ever.
136:2 Deut 10:17 2 O give thanks unto the God of gods: for his mercy *endureth* for ever.
3 O give thanks to the Lord of lords: for his mercy *endureth* for ever.

B. PRAISE TO THE CREATOR GOD

136:4 Job 9:10 Ps 72:18 4 To him who alone doeth great wonders: for his mercy *endureth* for ever.
136:5 Prov 3:19 Jer 10:12; 51:15 5 To him that by wisdom made the heavens: for his mercy *endureth* for
ever.
136:6☆ Ps 24:2 6 To him that stretched out the earth above the waters: for his mercy
endureth for ever.
136:7 Ps 74:16 7 To him that made great lights: for his mercy *endureth* for ever:
136:8 Gen 1:16 8 The sun to rule by day: for his mercy *endureth* for ever:
9 The moon and stars to rule by night: for his mercy *endureth* for ever.

C. PRAISE TO THE DELIVERER OF ISRAEL

136:10 Ex 12:29 Ps 78:51 10 To him that smote Egypt in their firstborn: for his mercy *endureth* for
ever:
136:11 Ex 12:51; 13:3 Deut 9:29 Ps 44:3 Jer 32:17, 21 11 And brought out Israel from among them: for his mercy *endureth* for
ever:
12 With a strong hand, and with a stretched out arm: for his mercy
endureth for ever.
136:13 Ex 14:21 Ps 78:13 13 To him which divided the Red sea into parts: for his mercy *endureth* for
ever:
136:14 Ps 106:9 14 And made Israel to pass through the midst of it: for his mercy *endureth*
for ever:

135:15 The gods the heathen worship are men's creations. They have no power in themselves, only *what their makers give them.* Thus these gods have no power either to help or to hurt anyone. Whoever worships such gods is stupid and senseless.

136:1ff This is one of the most unusual Psalms in that there is the constant refrain, "for his mercy endureth for ever." The repetition serves a useful purpose—each time it appears it calls forth a response to a particular blessing of God that marks the history of the people of God. The Psalm is excellently put together for a responsive reading in the congregation. The reader speaks of the blessing, then the congregation repeats the refrain.

136:6 *stretched out the earth above the waters,* i.e., "separated the earth from the oceans."†

15 But overthrew Pharaoh and his host in the Red sea: for his mercy
endureth for ever.
16 To him which led his people through the wilderness: for his mercy
endureth for ever.
17 To him which smote great kings: for his mercy *endureth* for ever:
18 And slew famous kings: for his mercy *endureth* for ever:
19 Sihon king of the Am′or-ites: for his mercy *endureth* for ever:
20 And Og the king of Ba′shan: for his mercy *endureth* for ever:
21 And gave their land for an heritage: for his mercy *endureth* for ever:
22 *Even* an heritage unto Israel his servant: for his mercy *endureth* for ever.

136:16 Ex 13:18; Deut 8:15
136:17 Ps 135:10–12
136:22 Ps 105:6; Isa 41:8; 45:4

D. PRAISE TO THE GOD OF LOVINGKINDNESS

23 Who remembered us in our low estate: for his mercy *endureth* for ever:
24 And hath redeemed us from our enemies: for his mercy *endureth* for
ever.
25 Who giveth food to all flesh: for his mercy *endureth* for ever.
26 O give thanks unto the God of heaven: for his mercy *endureth* for ever.

136:23 Ps 9:12; 106:45
136:24 Judg 6:9
136:25 Ps 104:27; 145:15
136:26 2 Chron 36:23; Ezra 5:11

I. A SONG OF THE CAPTIVE EXILES IN BABYLON
A. THE EXILES CANNOT FORGET ZION

137 BY the rivers of Babylon, there we sat down, yea, we wept, when
we remembered Zion.
2 We hanged our harps upon the willows in the midst thereof.
3 For there they that carried us away captive required of us a song; and
they that wasted us *required of us* mirth, *saying,* Sing us *one* of the songs of
Zion.
4 How shall we sing the LORD's song in a strange land?
5 If I forget thee, O Jerusalem, let my right hand forget *her cunning.*
6 If I do not remember thee, let my tongue cleave to the roof of my
mouth; if I prefer not Jerusalem above my chief joy.

☆**137:1** Neh 1:4; Ezek 1:1, 3
137:2 Lev 23:40; Job 30:31; Isa 44:4; Ezek 26:13
137:3 2 Chron 29:27; Neh 12:46; Ps 80:6

B. THE EXILES PRAY FOR GOD TO AVENGE THEM

7 Remember, O LORD, the children of Edom in the day of Jerusalem; who
said, Rase *it,* rase *it, even* to the foundation thereof.
8 O daughter of Babylon, who art to be destroyed; happy *shall he be,* that
rewardeth thee as thou hast served us.
9 Happy *shall he be,* that taketh and dasheth thy little ones against the
stones.

137:7 Ps 83:4–8; Jer 49:7–22; Ezek 25:12–14; Amos 1:11; Obad 10–14
137:8 Isa 13:1–22; 47:1–15; Jer 50:1–46; 51:1–64
☆**137:9** 2 Kgs 8:12

I. THE COVENANT GOD WHO IS FAITHFUL
A. DAVID PRAISES THE FAITHFULNESS OF GOD

A Psalm of David

138 I WILL praise thee with my whole heart: before the gods will I
sing praise unto thee.

☆**138:1** Ps 111:1

137:1ff This is a song of mournful melody commemorating the captivity of Israel in Babylon. The Septuagint indicates that the author was Jeremiah, although this is uncertain. The song is one of the last to have been composed for inclusion in sacred writ. The canon of the Old Testament was ready to be closed, but not before this lamentation was written. The song is an expression of longing to return to Jerusalem, the golden city of David's day, the city of the Messiah, outside of whose gates he will be crucified.

137:9 *Happy shall he be, that taketh and dasheth thy little ones against the stones.* Perhaps this could be paraphrased, "Blessed is he who invades and sacks your city."†

138:1ff This is a general Psalm of remembrance, penned by David without particular reference to any specific incident in his life. It is a panoramic view of a lifetime filled with evidences of God's unbroken faithful-

138:2 Ps 5:7 Isa 42:21
2 I will worship toward thy holy temple, and praise thy name for thy
lovingkindness and for thy truth: for thou hast magnified thy word above
all thy name.

138:3 Ps 28:7
3 In the day when I cried thou answeredst me, *and* strengthenedst me *with*
strength in my soul.

B. THE KINGS OF THE EARTH SHALL PRAISE GOD

138:4 Ps 102:15
4 All the kings of the earth shall praise thee, O LORD, when they hear the
words of thy mouth.
5 Yea, they shall sing in the ways of the LORD: for great *is* the glory of the
LORD.

138:6 Ps 101:5 113:4–7 Prov 3:34 Jas 4:6
6 Though the LORD *be* high, yet hath he respect unto the lowly: but the
proud he knoweth afar off.

C. DAVID IS CERTAIN OF GOD'S POWER TO SAVE HIM

138:7☆ Ex 15:12 Ezra 9:8, 9 Ps 20:6; 23:4 Isa 5:25
7 Though I walk in the midst of trouble, thou wilt revive me: thou shalt
stretch forth thine hand against the wrath of mine enemies, and thy right
hand shall save me.

138:8☆ Job 10:3 Ps 27:9; 71:9 100:3 Phil 1:6
8 The LORD will perfect *that which* concerneth me: thy mercy, O LORD,
endureth for ever: forsake not the works of thine own hands.

I. THE GLORY OF THE ALL-SEEING GOD

A. THE GOD WHO KNOWS ALL

To the chief Musician, A Psalm of David

139:1☆ Ps 44:21 **139:2** Ps 94:11
139 O LORD, thou hast searched me, and known *me.*
2 Thou knowest my downsitting and mine uprising, thou
understandest my thought afar off.

139:3 Job 14:16
3 Thou compassest my path and my lying down, and art acquainted *with*
all my ways.

139:4 Heb 4:13
4 For *there is* not a word in my tongue, *but,* lo, O LORD, thou knowest it
altogether.
5 Thou hast beset me behind and before, and laid thine hand upon me.

139:6 Job 42:3 Rom 11:33
6 *Such* knowledge *is* too wonderful for me; it is high, I cannot *attain* unto
it.

B. THE GOD WHO IS EVERYWHERE

139:7☆ Jer 23:24
7 Whither shall I go from thy spirit? or whither shall I flee from thy
presence?

139:8 Prov 15:11 Amos 9:2–4
8 If I ascend up into heaven, thou *art* there: if I make my bed in hell,
behold, thou *art there.*

---

ness. He has experienced a life filled with trouble but his life has been preserved and deliverance has come time and again. The steadfast love of God does not change, whatever the circumstances of life. *before the gods,* i.e., "before the armies of angels." The same Hebrew word is used here as in Ps. 8:5.†

138:7, 8 Although David was a great and a good man, *he walked in the midst* of trouble. God comforted him and delivered him. He believed that his sovereign God knew what was best for him and made those things come to pass. He prayed that God would not stop until he had done what he intended in David's life.

139:1ff Verses 1, 2, 4, and 6 speak of God's omniscience, i.e., that he is all-knowing. 139:7–13 speaks of God's omnipresence, i.e., that God is everywhere at the same time, thereby making it impossible to flee from his presence. 139:15, 16 deals with God's foreknowledge of men before their conception.

139:7ff The psalmist stresses the omnipresence of God in these verses—he is everywhere. But God is not to be identified with creation as though he were a part of it. Pantheism has no place in the Scriptures. God created the universe and he sustains it, but he is independent of it and cannot be thought of as a part of it.

9 *If* I take the wings of the morning, *and* dwell in the uttermost parts of
the sea;
10 Even there shall thy hand lead me, and thy right hand shall hold me.
11 If I say, Surely the darkness shall cover me; even the night shall be light
about me.
12 Yea, the darkness hideth not from thee; but the night shineth as the
day: the darkness and the light *are* both alike *to thee*.

139:10 Ps 23:2, 3
139:11 Job 22:13
139: 12 Job 34:22; 1 Jn 1:5

C. THE GOD OF CREATION WHO MADE US

13 For thou hast possessed my reins: thou hast covered me in my mother's
womb.
14 I will praise thee; for I am fearfully *and* wonderfully made: marvellous
are thy works; and *that* my soul knoweth right well.
15 My substance was not hid from thee, when I was made in secret, *and*
curiously wrought in the lowest parts of the earth.
16 Thine eyes did see my substance, yet being unperfect; and in thy book
all *my members* were written, *which* in continuance were fashioned, when *as*
yet there was none of them.

☆**139:13** Ps 119:73
139:15 Job 10:8–10; Eccles 11:5
139:16 Job 14:5; Ps 56:8

D. THE GOD WHO THINKS ABOUT US AND SEARCHES US

17 How precious also are thy thoughts unto me, O God! how great is the
sum of them!
18 *If* I should count them, they are more in number than the sand: when
I awake, I am still with thee.
19 Surely thou wilt slay the wicked, O God: depart from me therefore, ye
bloody men.
20 For they speak against thee wickedly, *and* thine enemies take *thy name*
in vain.
21 Do not I hate them, O LORD, that hate thee? and am not I grieved with
those that rise up against thee?
22 I hate them with perfect hatred: I count them mine enemies.
23 Search me, O God, and know my heart: try me, and know my thoughts:
24 And see if *there be any* wicked way in me, and lead me in the way
everlasting.

☆**139:17**
139:19 Isa 11:4
139:20 Ex 20:7; Deut 5:11; Jude 15
139:21 Ps 26:5; 119:158
139:23 Ps 26:2; Prov 17:3; 1 Thess 2:4
139:24 Ps 5:8; 16:11; Jer 25:5

I. DELIVERANCE FROM ONE'S ENEMIES

A. PETITION FOR DELIVERANCE FROM ENEMIES

To the chief Musician, A Psalm of David

140 DELIVER me, O LORD, from the evil man: preserve me from the
violent man;
2 Which imagine mischiefs in *their* heart; continually are they gathered
together *for* war.
3 They have sharpened their tongues like a serpent; adders' poison *is*
under their lips. Se'lah.

☆**140:1**
140:2 Ps 56:6; Prov 6:14; Isa 59:4; Hos 7:15
140:3 Rom 3:13; Jas 3:8

139:13ff Man is a unique and marvelous being whose secrets have not yet been uncovered by science. The complexity of the human frame defies analysis and what has been learned about it is as nothing compared to what is still unknown. There is no place for the evolutionary hypothesis to explain man's origins. He was a direct and immediate creation by his Maker.

139:17 *How precious are thy thoughts unto me,* i.e., "I can't even count how many times a day your thoughts turn towards me."†

140:1ff This and the four Psalms that follow were written by David and apparently refer to his experiences when Saul was persecuting him and seeking to kill him. Ps. 142 speaks about the time when David was in a cave. Probably these Psalms were all composed at that time. Ps. 143 constitutes a cry for deliverance, a prayer for retribution, and an expression of confidence in God.

4 Keep me, O LORD, from the hands of the wicked; preserve me from the
violent man; who have purposed to overthrow my goings.

140:5 Job 18:9 Ps 35:7; 57:6

5 The proud have hid a snare for me, and cords; they have spread a net by
the wayside; they have set gins for me. Se'lah.

B. VENGEANCE AGAINST ONE'S ENEMIES

140:6 Esth 9:25 Ps 112:10 116:1

6 I said unto the LORD, Thou *art* my God: hear the voice of my
supplications, O LORD.
7 O GOD the Lord, the strength of my salvation, thou hast covered my
head in the day of battle.
8 Grant not, O LORD, the desires of the wicked: further not his wicked
device; *lest* they exalt themselves. Se'lah.
9 *As for* the head of those that compass me about, let the mischief of their
own lips cover them.

140:10 Ps 11:6 Mt 3:10 **140:11** Ps 34:21 1 Kgs 8:45, 49 Ps 18:27; 35:10

10 Let burning coals fall upon them: let them be cast into the fire; into
deep pits, that they rise not up again.
11 Let not an evil speaker be established in the earth: evil shall hunt the
violent man to overthrow *him.*
12 I know that the LORD will maintain the cause of the afflicted, *and* the
right of the poor.

140:13 Ps 16:11; 17:15 97:12

13 Surely the righteous shall give thanks unto thy name: the upright shall
dwell in thy presence.

I. A PRAYER TO BE KEPT FROM SIN

A. THE APPEAL TO THE LORD

A Psalm of David

141:1☆ Ps 70:5 **141:2** Ex 29:41; 30:8 Dan 9:21 Rev 5:8; 8:3, 4

141 LORD, I cry unto thee: make haste unto me; give ear unto my
voice, when I cry unto thee.
2 Let my prayer be set forth before thee *as* incense; *and* the lifting up of
my hands *as* the evening sacrifice.

B. THE PRAYER TO BE KEPT FROM TEMPTATIONS

141:3 Ps 39:1 Prov 13:3; 21:23 **141:4** Ps 119:36 Prov 23:6 Mal 3:15 **141:5** Ps 23:5; 35:14 Prov 19:25; 27:6 Gal 6:1 **141:6** Ps 53:5 **141:7☆**

3 Set a watch, O LORD, before my mouth; keep the door of my lips.
4 Incline not my heart to *any* evil thing, to practise wicked works with
men that work iniquity: and let me not eat of their dainties.
5 Let the righteous smite me; *it shall be* a kindness: and let him reprove
me; *it shall be* an excellent oil, *which* shall not break my head: for yet my
prayer also *shall be* in their calamities.
6 When their judges are overthrown in stony places, they shall hear my
words; for they are sweet.
7 Our bones are scattered at the grave's mouth, as when one cutteth and
cleaveth *wood* upon the earth.

C. LOOKING TO GOD FOR HELP

141:8 Ps 11:1

8 But mine eyes *are* unto thee, O GOD the Lord: in thee is my trust; leave
not my soul destitute.

141:1ff When we are persecuted, maligned, and hated, *how then shall we live?* In this Psalm David asks to be delivered from doing anything contrary to the will of God, for he knows the end of the wicked and does not wish to follow in their ways. In the conclusion he affirms that God is his refuge who will deliver him from the snares which the enemy has set for him.

141:7 *Our bones are* scattered at the grave's mouth, or, "When their leaders are condemned, and their bones are strewn across the ground" (TLB), or, "As a rock which one cleaves and shatters on the land, so shall their bones be strewn at the mouth of Sheol" (RSV).

9 Keep me from the snares *which* they have laid for me, and the gins of the
workers of iniquity.
10 Let the wicked fall into their own nets, whilst that I withal escape.

141:9 Ps 91:3
141:10 Ps 57:6

I. DAVID'S PRAYER IN THE CAVE OF ADULLAM
A. HE IMPLORES GOD'S MERCY AND DESCRIBES HIS PLIGHT

Maschil of David; A Prayer when he was in the cave

142 I CRIED unto the LORD with my voice; with my voice unto the
LORD did I make my supplication.
2 I poured out my complaint before him; I shewed before him my trouble.
3 When my spirit was overwhelmed within me, then thou knewest my
path. In the way wherein I walked have they privily laid a snare for me.
4 I looked on *my* right hand, and beheld, but *there was* no man that would
know me: refuge failed me; no man cared for my soul.

☆142:1 Ps 30:8
☆142:4 Ps 88:8, 18; Jer 30:17

B. HE CRIES FOR GOD TO RELEASE HIM

5 I cried unto thee, O LORD: I said, Thou *art* my refuge *and* my portion in
the land of the living.
6 Attend unto my cry; for I am brought very low: deliver me from my
persecutors; for they are stronger than I.
7 Bring my soul out of prison, that I may praise thy name: the righteous
shall compass me about; for thou shalt deal bountifully with me.

142:5 Ps 91:2, 9
142:6 Ps 18:17; 79:8
142:7 Ps 13:6

I. A PRAYER IN THE HOUR OF DARKNESS
A. THE PSALMIST'S COMPLAINT AND LONGING

A Psalm of David

143 HEAR my prayer, O LORD, give ear to my supplications: in thy
faithfulness answer me, *and* in thy righteousness.
2 And enter not into judgment with thy servant: for in thy sight shall no
man living be justified.
3 For the enemy hath persecuted my soul; he hath smitten my life down
to the ground; he hath made me to dwell in darkness, as those that have
been long dead.

☆143:1
143:2 1 Kgs 8:46; Job 14:3; 22:4; Eccles 7:20
143:3 Lam 3:6

B. THE PRAYER FOR DELIVERANCE

4 Therefore is my spirit overwhelmed within me; my heart within me is
desolate.
5 I remember the days of old; I meditate on all thy works; I muse on the
work of thy hands.
6 I stretch forth my hands unto thee: my soul *thirsteth* after thee, as a
thirsty land. Se'lah.
7 Hear me speedily, O LORD: my spirit faileth: hide not thy face from me,
lest I be like unto them that go down into the pit.

143:5 Ps 77:5, 10, 11
143:6 Job 11:13; Ps 63:1
143:7 Ps 69:17; 88:4; Jer 8:18; Lam 1:22

142:1ff David is trapped in a cave as a prisoner. Outside, the enemy waits to destroy him. As a forlorn prisoner he pleads with God to deliver him. He asks to be safely brought out of his prison. This prayer and the same kind of prayer said by God's people then and in every age will surely be heard and answered.

142:4 David's best friends had forsaken him. Their doors were shut to him and no bed was available on which to lay his head. This was even more true of Jesus, who was forsaken by the Father when he *alone* endured the winepress of the wrath of God for our salvation. We who belong to Christ are never alone. He is with us and will be with us through all the days of this life's journey.

143:1 David in affliction prayed to God. He did this much and often. Perseverance in prayer is a necessity.

143:8 Ps 32:8
[8]Cause me to hear thy lovingkindness in the morning; for in thee do I
trust: cause me to know the way wherein I should walk; for I lift up my soul
unto thee.
143:9 Ps 59:1
[9]Deliver me, O LORD, from mine enemies: I flee unto thee to hide me.
143:10 Neh 9:20 Ps 23:3; 119:12
[10]Teach me to do thy will; for thou *art* my God: thy spirit *is* good; lead
me into the land of uprightness.

C. WAITING FOR GOD TO FULFILL HIS PROMISE

[11]Quicken me, O LORD, for thy name's sake: for thy righteousness' sake
bring my soul out of trouble.
143:12 Ps 52:5; 116:16
[12]And of thy mercy cut off mine enemies, and destroy all them that afflict
my soul: for I *am* thy servant.

I. THE PSALM FOR THE SOLDIER

A. GOD IS THE SOLDIER'S TOWER OF STRENGTH

A Psalm of David

144:1☆ Ps 18:2 144:2 Ps 84:9 144:3 Ps 8:4
144 BLESSED *be* the LORD my strength, which teacheth my hands to
war, *and* my fingers to fight:
[2]My goodness, and my fortress; my high tower, and my deliverer; my
shield, and *he* in whom I trust; who subdueth my people under me.
[3]LORD, what *is* man, that thou takest knowledge of him! *or* the son of
144:4 Job 8:9; 14:2 Ps 39:11 109:23
man, that thou makest account of him!
[4]Man is like to vanity: his days *are* as a shadow that passeth away.

B. HE PLEADS FOR GOD TO SAVE HIM

144:5 Ex 19:18 Ps 18:9 Isa 64:1
[5]Bow thy heavens, O LORD, and come down: touch the mountains, and
they shall smoke.
144:6 Hab 3:11 Zech 9:14
[6]Cast forth lightning, and scatter them: shoot out thine arrows, and
destroy them.
144:7 Ps 18:44 69:1, 14
[7]Send thine hand from above; rid me, and deliver me out of great waters,
from the hand of strange children;
144:8 Deut 32:40 Ps 12:2; 41:6 Isa 44:20
[8]Whose mouth speaketh vanity, and their right hand *is* a right hand of
falsehood.
144:9 Ps 40:3
[9]I will sing a new song unto thee, O God: upon a psaltery *and* an
instrument of ten strings will I sing praises unto thee.
144:10 2 Sam 18:7 Ps 140:7
[10]*It is he* that giveth salvation unto kings: who delivereth David his
servant from the hurtful sword.

C. HE PRAYS FOR GOD TO BLESS THE LAND

[11]Rid me, and deliver me from the hand of strange children, whose
mouth speaketh vanity, and their right hand *is* a right hand of falsehood:
144:12 2 Kgs 25:10, 11 Ps 33:12; 60:2 92:12–14; 128:3 Song 4:4; 7:4 Prov 3:9; 10 Isa 24:11 Jer 14:2 Amos 5:3
[12]That our sons *may be* as plants grown up in their youth; *that* our
daughters *may be* as corner stones, polished *after* the similitude of a palace:
[13]*That* our garners *may be* full, affording all manner of store: *that* our
sheep may bring forth thousands and ten thousands in our streets:
[14]*That* our oxen *may be* strong to labour; *that there be* no breaking in, nor
going out; that *there be* no complaining in our streets.

144:1ff This is the Psalm of a warrior who has been victorious with the help of God. This God is a high tower, a fortress, a shield, and a deliverer. However strong the warrior, he must pray and seek the face and the help of God. When victory comes he promises to sing a new song to the God "who delivereth David his servant from the hurtful sword," (144:10).

15 Happy *is that* people, that is in such a case: *yea,* happy *is that* people,
whose God *is* the LORD.

I. OUR GREAT GOD

A. THE GREATNESS OF OUR GOD

David's Psalm of praise

145 I WILL extol thee, my God, O king; and I will bless thy name for
ever and ever.
2 Every day will I bless thee; and I will praise thy name for ever and ever.
3 Great *is* the LORD, and greatly to be praised; and his greatness *is*
unsearchable.
4 One generation shall praise thy works to another, and shall declare thy
mighty acts.
5 I will speak of the glorious honour of thy majesty, and of thy wondrous
works.
6 And *men* shall speak of the might of thy terrible acts: and I will declare
thy greatness.
7 They shall abundantly utter the memory of thy great goodness, and shall
sing of thy righteousness.

B. THE MERCY AND MAJESTY OF GOD

8 The LORD *is* gracious, and full of compassion; slow to anger, and of
great mercy.
9 The LORD *is* good to all: and his tender mercies *are* over all his works.
10 All thy works shall praise thee, O LORD; and thy saints shall bless thee.
11 They shall speak of the glory of thy kingdom, and talk of thy power;
12 To make known to the sons of men his mighty acts, and the glorious
majesty of his kingdom.

C. THE PERFECTIONS AND WONDROUS WORKS OF GOD

13 Thy kingdom *is* an everlasting kingdom, and thy dominion *endureth*
throughout all generations.
14 The LORD upholdeth all that fall, and raiseth up all *those that be* bowed
down.
15 The eyes of all wait upon thee; and thou givest them their meat in due
season.
16 Thou openest thine hand, and satisfiest the desire of every living thing.
17 The LORD *is* righteous in all his ways, and holy in all his works.
18 The LORD *is* nigh unto all them that call upon him, to all that call upon
him in truth.
19 He will fulfil the desire of them that fear him: he also will hear their cry,
and will save them.
20 The LORD preserveth all them that love him: but all the wicked will he
destroy.
21 My mouth shall speak the praise of the LORD: and let all flesh bless his
holy name for ever and ever.

☆**145:1** Ps 34:1
145:3 Job 11:7; Ps 71:6; 147:5; Isa 40:28; Rom 11:33
145:4 Isa 38:19
☆**145:5** Ps 119:27
☆**145:6** Deut 10:21; 32:3
☆**145:7** Ps 51:14; Isa 63:7
145:8 Ex 34:6
145:9 Ps 100:5; Nah 1:7; Mt 19:17; Mk 10:18
145:10 Ps 19:1; 68:26
145:12 Ps 105:1; Isa 2:10, 19, 21
145:13 2 Pet 1:11
145:14 Ps 37:24
145:15 Ps 104:27
145:17 Ps 116:5
☆**145:18** Deut 4:7; Jn 4:24
145:19 Ps 10:17; Prov 15:29; 1 Jn 5:14
145:20 Ps 31:23; 37:38
145:21 Ps 71:8; 150:6

145:1ff The last six Psalms are songs of praise. The last five of the six begin and end with hallelujahs, setting them off as being among the "Hallelujah Psalms." But Ps. 145 is clearly a song of praise to God in which David enlarges on the subject of God's greatness, grace, mercy, and goodness. It affirms that God will destroy the wicked and preserve those who love him. Let all true believers, then, praise the Lord.

145:5–7 Men are to give glory to God for his great works, and then for his great goodness.

145:18 If we do not call, God will not answer. But he is near to those who wish to call on him and whoever calls will find that they are within reach of his help. God indeed is closer than our very breath.

I. THE LORD GOD, OUR GREAT PROTECTOR
A. THE FUTILITY OF TRUSTING MEN

146:1☆
146:2 Ps 63:4; 104:33
146:3 Ps 60:11; 118:8, 9; Isa 2:22
146:4 Eccles 12:7

146 PRAISE ye the LORD. Praise the LORD, O my soul.
[2]While I live will I praise the LORD: I will sing praises unto my
God while I have any being.
[3]Put not your trust in princes, *nor* in the son of man, in whom *there is* no
help.
[4]His breath goeth forth, he returneth to his earth; in that very day his
thoughts perish.

B. THE WISDOM OF TRUSTING GOD, THE PROTECTOR

146:5 Ps 71:5
146:6 Ps 117:2; Acts 14:15
146:7 Ps 68:6; Isa 61:1
146:8 Ps 11:7; Mt 9:30; Jn 9:7
146:9 Ex 22:21; Lev 19:34; Deut 10:18
146:10☆ Ex 15:18; Ps 10:16

[5]Happy *is he* that *hath* the God of Jacob for his help, whose hope *is* in the
LORD his God:
[6]Which made heaven, and earth, the sea, and all that therein *is*: which
keepeth truth for ever:
[7]Which executeth judgment for the oppressed: which giveth food to the
hungry. The LORD looseth the prisoners:
[8]The LORD openeth *the eyes of* the blind: the LORD raiseth them that are
bowed down: the LORD loveth the righteous:
[9]The LORD preserveth the strangers; he relieveth the fatherless and
widow: but the way of the wicked he turneth upside down.
[10]The LORD shall reign for ever, *even* thy God, O Zion, unto all
generations. Praise ye the LORD.

I. GOD'S WATCH-CARE OVER HIS PEOPLE
A. GOD'S POWER AND LEADING MANIFEST

147:1☆
147:2 Deut 30:3; Ps 51:18; 102:16; Isa 11:12; 56:8; Ezek 39:28
147:3 Job 5:18; Isa 30:26; Ezek 34:16
147:4☆ Gen 15:5; Isa 40:26
147:6 Ps 37:24

147 PRAISE ye the LORD: for *it is* good to sing praises unto our
God; for *it is* pleasant; *and* praise is comely.
[2]The LORD doth build up Jerusalem: he gathereth together the outcasts
of Israel.
[3]He healeth the broken in heart, and bindeth up their wounds.
[4]He telleth the number of the stars; he calleth them all by *their* names.
[5]Great *is* our Lord, and of great power: his understanding *is* infinite.
[6]The LORD lifteth up the meek: he casteth the wicked down to the
ground.

B. GOD'S BOUNTY IN NATURE

147:7 Ps 95:1, 2
147:8 Job 5:10; 26:8; 38:26

[7]Sing unto the LORD with thanksgiving; sing praise upon the harp unto
our God:
[8]Who covereth the heaven with clouds, who prepareth rain for the earth,
who maketh grass to grow upon the mountains.
[9]He giveth to the beast his food, *and* to the young ravens which cry.

146:1 Praising the Lord includes trusting him. We are not to trust the sons of men or princes, for they are finite. But the Lord reigns for ever. He helps all who hope in him, executing justice on their behalf, caring for the widows and orphans, opening the eyes of the *blind, and setting the prisoners* free. These are excellent reasons for singing Hallelujah to our God.

146:10 Despite the enmity of Satan and the attacks of men, our God *shall* reign forever. His kingdom shall continue in endless glory, however strong the adversaries. Thus believers can shout Hallelujah!

147:1ff This Psalm supplies the believer with a number of reasons for praising the Lord. He is the God of might who has worked in history for the benefit of his people Israel; he is the sustainer of life who meets the needs of his people. Let Jerusalem, yea, all the people of Zion, join together in songs of praise to God.

147:4 God made the stars, knows them by number to the last one, and has dominion over them. But one of his children is more important than all the luminaries of the heavens—for Christ did not die for the stars but for human beings.

10He delighteth not in the strength of the horse: he taketh not pleasure in
the legs of a man.
11The LORD taketh pleasure in them that fear him, in those that hope in
his mercy.

147:10 1 Sam 16:7 Ps 33:17

C. ZION COMMANDED TO PRAISE GOD

12Praise the LORD, O Jerusalem; praise thy God, O Zion.
13For he hath strengthened the bars of thy gates; he hath blessed thy
children within thee.
14He maketh peace *in* thy borders, *and* filleth thee with the finest of the
wheat.
15He sendeth forth his commandment *upon* earth: his word runneth very
swiftly.
16He giveth snow like wool: he scattereth the hoarfrost like ashes.
17He casteth forth his ice like morsels: who can stand before his cold?
18He sendeth out his word, and melteth them: he causeth his wind to
blow, *and* the waters flow.
19He sheweth his word unto Jacob, his statutes and his judgments unto
Israel.
20He hath not dealt so with any nation: and *as for his* judgments, they
have not known them. Praise ye the LORD.

147:13 Neh 3:3; 7:3 Ps 37:26
147:14 Deut 32:14 Isa 54:13 60:17, 18
147:15 Job 37:12 Ps 104:4
147: 18 Ps 107:25
☆147:19 Deut 33:3, 4 Mal 4:4
147:20 Deut 4:7, 8 Ps 79:6 Jer 10:25

I. LET THE HEAVENS AND THE EARTH PRAISE THE LORD

A. LET THE HEAVENS AND ANGELS PRAISE THE LORD

148 PRAISE ye the LORD. Praise ye the LORD from the heavens:
praise him in the heights.
2Praise ye him, all his angels: praise ye him, all his hosts.
3Praise ye him, sun and moon: praise him, all ye stars of light.
4Praise him, ye heavens of heavens, and ye waters that *be* above the
heavens.
5Let them praise the name of the LORD: for he commanded, and they
were created.
6He hath also stablished them for ever and ever: he hath made a decree
which shall not pass.

B. LET THE WHOLE EARTH PRAISE THE LORD

7Praise the LORD from the earth, ye dragons, and all deeps:
8Fire, and hail; snow, and vapour; stormy wind fulfilling his word:
9Mountains, and all hills; fruitful trees, and all cedars:
10Beasts, and all cattle; creeping things, and flying fowl:
11Kings of the earth, and all people; princes, and all judges of the earth:
12Both young men, and maidens; old men, and children:
13Let them praise the name of the LORD: for his name alone is excellent;
his glory *is* above the earth and heaven.

☆148:1 Job 16:19 Ps 102:19 Mt 21:9
148:2 Ps 103:20, 21
148:4 Gen 1:7 Deut 10:14 1 Kgs 8:27 Neh 9:6
148:5 Gen 1:1
148:6 Job 38:33 Jer 31:35, 36 33:20, 25
148:7 Gen 1:21 Ps 74:13 Hab 3:10
148:8 Job 37:12 Ps 18:12
148:9 Isa 44:23 49:13; 55:12
148:10 Hos 2:18
148:11 Ps 102:15
☆148:13 Ps 8:1; 113:4 Rev 5:12

147:19 The Word of God was given to Israel and was preserved by Israel for all people, for "the God of the whole earth shall he be called" (Isa. 54:5).

148:1ff This song tells us who shall sing their hallelujahs to the Lord. The angelic hosts are called to praise him. So are the sun, moon, and myriad of stars that dot the heavens. Let the monsters of the deep, mountains and fruit trees, hail, fire, and snow sing the divine praises. Let the young and the old, the kings and all the rulers of the earth resound his praises. Above all, let his people Israel sing forth in praise to their God. So shall his people do the same at all times, under all circumstances and through all the ages.

148:13 The name of God is above every other name. That name which represents his person is the only name worthy of the praise of nature and men. If the dumb can praise this God, how much more those who have been given voices and tongues with which to say Hallelujah!

148:14 Deut 10:21; 1 Sam 2:1; Jer 17:14; Eph 2:17

[14]He also exalteth the horn of his people, the praise of all his saints; *even*
of the children of Israel, a people near unto him. Praise ye the LORD.

I. A SONG FOR VICTORIOUS ISRAEL

A. LET ISRAEL PRAISE THE LORD

149:1☆ Ps 33:3; 89:5
149:2 Judg 8:23; Ps 47:6
149:3 Ex 15:20; 2 Sam 6:14
149:4 Job 35:10; Ps 35:27; Isa 61:3

149 PRAISE ye the LORD. Sing unto the LORD a new song, *and* his
praise in the congregation of saints.
[2]Let Israel rejoice in him that made him: let the children of Zion be
joyful in their King.
[3]Let them praise his name in the dance: let them sing praises unto him
with the timbrel and harp.
[4]For the LORD taketh pleasure in his people: he will beautify the meek
with salvation.
[5]Let the saints be joyful in glory: let them sing aloud upon their beds.

B. LET GOD PUNISH THE NATIONS

149:6 Ps 66:17; Ezek 25:17; Mic 5:15
149:8 Nah 3:10
149:9 Ps 112:9; Ezek 28:26

[6]*Let* the high *praises* of God *be* in their mouth, and a twoedged sword in
their hand;
[7]To execute vengeance upon the heathen, *and* punishments upon the
people;
[8]To bind their kings with chains, and their nobles with fetters of iron;
[9]To execute upon them the judgment written: this honour have all his
saints. Praise ye the LORD.

I. THE FINAL DOXOLOGY: LET EVERYTHING ALIVE PRAISE THE LORD

150:1☆ Ps 19:1; 73:17; 102:19
150:2 Deut 3:24
150:3 Ps 98:6

150 PRAISE ye the LORD. Praise God in his sanctuary: praise him in
the firmament of his power.
[2]Praise him for his mighty acts: praise him according to his excellent
greatness.
[3]Praise him with the sound of the trumpet: praise him with the psaltery
and harp.
[4]Praise him with the timbrel and dance: praise him with stringed
instruments and organs.
[5]Praise him upon the loud cymbals: praise him upon the high sounding
cymbals.
[6]Let every thing that hath breath praise the LORD. Praise ye the LORD.

149:1ff If Ps. 148 was praise directed toward God as the Creator, this Psalm is praise to God who is also the Redeemer. It looks first toward God's redeemed in the Old Testament, but it is apparent that the theme of God as Redeemer extends to all ages, particularly to the church since the day of Pentecost.

150:1 *in the firmament of his power,* i.e., "in the heavens he made with mighty power."† The Psalter closes with suggestions of how, and with what instruments, God's faithful can praise his holy name. We are to praise him in the church and in the streets. We are to use every instrument from the trumpet and saxophone to the harp and all the stringed instruments, including the violin and piano. We are to use the drums that thunder and cymbals that clang. "Let everything that hath breath praise the LORD. Praise ye the LORD" (150:6).

THE PROVERBS

Authorship, date, and background Proverbs is an anthology of wise sayings. Many, if not most of them, were written by Solomon, who was widely known for having composed three thousand proverbs and one thousand and five songs. The sayings of Solomon which are included in this book are a sample of the many he wrote. In addition, some of the sayings came from other ancient sources. Moreover, scribes in Hezekiah's day copied down some of the ancient sayings for inclusion in this book. Many of these were from the lips of Solomon. The last two chapters of Proverbs were written by Agur and Lemuel, about whom we have little or no knowledge. Proverbs is called "wisdom literature," a genre of writing which was common to the ancient Near East. Some have thought there is a relationship between the Egyptian "Wisdom of Amenemope" and Proverbs. There are many parallels with 22:17—24:22.

Rationalist critics have concluded that nothing in Proverbs can be dated earlier than 350 B.C., and later material was added in the second century. There is no solid evidence for this. W. F. Albright wrote: "We may freely admit that the book of Proverbs was not edited in its present form until about the fifth century B.C. without assuming that any material of post-exilic date is included in the book. But the contents of Proverbs is considerably older, and it is entirely possible that aphorisms and even longer sections go back into the Bronze Age in substantially their present form."

Characteristics and content At the heart of Proverbs lies the dictum that "the fear of the LORD is the beginning of knowledge" (1:7). The book is theological, stressing the sovereignty of God, his omniscience, his creative activity, his rulership over the moral order, and the certainty that he will judge men's actions.

Proverbs ranges widely over the activities of men, leaving virtually no area of human life untouched. Social relationships are grappled with: social evils, concern for the poor, laziness, poverty, and wealth are discussed. Family relationships are covered: children and parents, and the importance of friendship are dealt with. The tongue, personal habits, attitudes, and the concept of life itself are examined. Wisdom is contrasted with foolishness and distinctions drawn about simple fools, hardened fools, arrogant fools, and brutish ones.

King Lemuel of Massa ends the book with his observations about the ideal wife. It is one of the most tasteful descriptions of how such a woman conducts herself in a fitting manner. Such a wife is an example to all brides. At the heart of this wife's life and thinking lies the true reason for her greatness: "a woman that feareth the LORD, she shall be praised" (31:30).

Outline

I. The introduction: authorship, purpose, and theme (1:1–6)
II. Wisdom and folly contrasted and compared (1:7—9:18)
III. Ethical observations (10:1—22:16)
IV. The words of the wise (22:17—24:34)
V. Solomon's proverbs collected by Hezekiah's aides (25:1—29:27)
VI. The messages of Agur (30:1–33)
VII. The sayings of King Lemuel (31:1–31).

I. THE INTRODUCTION: AUTHORSHIP, PURPOSE, AND THEME (1:1–6)

1:1☆ 1 Kgs 4:32; Prov 25:1; Eccles 1:1; 12:9
1:2☆ Deut 4:5, 6; Prov 4:5; 7:4
1:3 Prov 2:9; 19:20
1:4☆ Ps 19:7; 119:30; Prov 8:4; 9:4
1:5–6☆ Ps 78:2; 119:98; Prov 2:10, 11; 9:9; 12:1; Eccles 9:11

1 THE proverbs of Solomon the son of David, king of Israel;
2To know wisdom and instruction; to perceive the words of understanding;
3To receive the instruction of wisdom, justice, and judgment, and equity;
4To give subtilty to the simple, to the young man knowledge and discretion.
5A wise *man* will hear, and will increase learning; and a man of understanding shall attain unto wise counsels:
6To understand a proverb, and the interpretation; the words of the wise, and their dark sayings.

II. WISDOM AND FOLLY CONTRASTED AND COMPARED (1:7—9:18)

A. THE ADVANTAGES OF WISDOM

1. It Keeps Men from Wicked Companions

1:7 Prov 9:10; 15:33; Eccles 12:13
1:8, 9 Ex 20:12; Prov 6:20
1:10☆ Ps 1:1; Prov 7:21; 13:20
1:11 Prov 1:18
1:15 Ps 1:1; 26:4; Prov 4:14; 2 Cor 6:17
1:16☆ Prov 4:16; Isa 59:7
1:18 Ps 7:15; Prov 5:22; 9:17
1:19 Prov 15:27; 28:25

7¶The fear of the LORD *is* the beginning of knowledge: *but* fools despise wisdom and instruction.
8My son, hear the instruction of thy father, and forsake not the law of thy mother:
9For they *shall be* an ornament of grace unto thy head, and chains about thy neck.
10¶My son, if sinners entice thee, consent thou not.
11If they say, Come with us, let us lay wait for blood, let us lurk privily for the innocent without cause:
12Let us swallow them up alive as the grave; and whole, as those that go down into the pit:
13We shall find all precious substance, we shall fill our houses with spoil:
14Cast in thy lot among us; let us all have one purse:
15My son, walk not thou in the way with them; refrain thy foot from their path:
16For their feet run to evil, and make haste to shed blood.
17Surely in vain the net is spread in the sight of any bird.
18And they lay wait for their *own* blood; they lurk privily for their *own* lives.
19So *are* the ways of every one that is greedy of gain; *which* taketh away the life of the owners thereof.

1:1 The major portion of the book is Solomonic. Agur and Lemuel are other contributors. The book, as we know it, was put together several centuries after the death of Solomon.

1:2 *To know wisdom and instruction.* God gave Solomon the gift of wisdom. It was this gift that accounts for Solomon's greatness. The book of Proverbs will help us to entertain right notions of things, to distinguish between truth and falsehood, and to discern *between good and evil. The apprehension* of these things will enable us to mature in spirituality and to guard against mistakes. We can be instructed in wisdom by listening to and understanding the divine wisdom given by God to Solomon.

1:4 The sayings were written for the least educated, the simpleminded, all of whom could understand the meaning. If the simple can understand, so can the well-educated and the learned.

1:5, 6 The sayings will make the wise and good wiser and better.

1:10 *if sinners entice thee, consent thou not.* Sinners love to have company. Even the fallen angels became tempters as soon as they had sinned. Tempters do not argue or threaten; they use flattery and smooth talk. They make promises they cannot fulfill. But no one can legitimately say, "the devil made me do it." Each must choose to do or not to do for himself.

1:16 Sin is downhill all the way. The longer sinners continue their wicked ways, the faster they run and the more they make haste.

2. It Is Spurned by Fools

20¶Wisdom crieth without; she uttereth her voice in the streets:
21She crieth in the chief place of concourse, in the openings of the gates:
in the city she uttereth her words, *saying,*
22How long, ye simple ones, will ye love simplicity? and the scorners
delight in their scorning, and fools hate knowledge?
23Turn you at my reproof: behold, I will pour out my spirit unto you, I
will make known my words unto you.
24¶Because I have called, and ye refused; I have stretched out my hand,
and no man regarded;
25But ye have set at nought all my counsel, and would none of my
reproof:
26I also will laugh at your calamity; I will mock when your fear cometh;
27When your fear cometh as desolation, and your destruction cometh as
a whirlwind; when distress and anguish cometh upon you.
28Then shall they call upon me, but I will not answer; they shall seek me
early, but they shall not find me:
29For that they hated knowledge, and did not choose the fear of the
LORD:
30They would none of my counsel: they despised all my reproof.
31Therefore shall they eat of the fruit of their own way, and be filled with
their own devices.
32For the turning away of the simple shall slay them, and the prosperity
of fools shall destroy them.
33But whoso hearkeneth unto me shall dwell safely, and shall be quiet
from fear of evil.

☆**1:20** Prov 8:1–5; 9:3
1:22 Prov 9:4; 14:15
1:23 Joel 2:28
☆**1:24** Prov 15:32; Isa 65:12; 66:4
1:25 2 Chron 36:16; Ps 107:11
☆**1:26** Ps 2:4
1:27 Prov 3:25; 10:25
☆**1:28** Job 27:9; Ps 18:41; Ezek 8:18
1:29 Job 21:14; Prov 8:4
1:30 Ps 81:11; Jer 8:9
☆**1:31** Job 4:8; Prov 5:22; 22:8
1:32 Jer 2:19
1:33 Ps 23:4; 25:13; Prov 3:24–26

3. It Gives Sense to Avoid Evil Men and Adulteresses

2 MY son, if thou wilt receive my words, and hide my commandments
with thee;
2So that thou incline thine ear unto wisdom, *and* apply thine heart to
understanding;
3Yea, if thou criest after knowledge, *and* liftest up thy voice for
understanding;
4If thou seekest her as silver, and searchest for her as *for* hid treasures;
5Then shalt thou understand the fear of the LORD, and find the
knowledge of God.
6For the LORD giveth wisdom: out of his mouth *cometh* knowledge and
understanding.
7He layeth up sound wisdom for the righteous: *he is* a buckler to them
that walk uprightly.

☆**2:1** Prov 3:1; 4:10
2:3 Job 28:12; Prov 1:7; 3:14; Mt 13:44
☆**2:6** Job 32:8; Prov 8:7; Jas 1:5
2:7 1 Sam 2:9; Ps 121:5; Prov 30:5

1:20 Wisdom is not silent in the midst of evil. She *makes her voice known* so that sinners can never say, "Nobody told me"—and thus claim innocence.
1:24 *I have called, and ye refused.* The neglect of wisdom is a serious fault. To ignore the counsel of wisdom is to eat the fruit of that refusal and thus be unable to dwell safely.
1:26 Those who have laughed at God and mocked him will discover a time comes when God will laugh at them and mock them for their insolence and their haughty refusal to hear him and be helped by him.
1:28 The door to heaven is open but there comes a time when it will be shut to sinners. Then when they cry, their prayers will not be heard because when God called they did not answer.
1:31 All men's wages will be according to their works, and they choose their own doom by those works.
2:1 Solomon says that those who are willing to be taught will obtain from God the knowledge and grace they want. The attainment of this is a great advantage and will preserve them from a variety of snares that would otherwise overtake and destroy them. We are instructed how to obtain wisdom and how to use it.
2:6 *out of his mouth.* God speaks by his law and his prophets and apostles. Men have the written Word of the living God, and it is preached to them by God's ministers. It is not for lack of a word from God that men are lost; it is because of the rejection of that word.

8 He keepeth the paths of judgment, and preserveth the way of his saints.
9 Then shalt thou understand righteousness, and judgment, and equity;
yea, every good path.
10 ¶When wisdom entereth into thine heart, and knowledge is pleasant
unto thy soul;
11 Discretion shall preserve thee, understanding shall keep thee:
12 To deliver thee from the way of the evil *man,* from the man that
speaketh froward things;
13 Who leave the paths of uprightness, to walk in the ways of darkness;
14 Who rejoice to do evil, *and* delight in the frowardness of the wicked;
15 Whose ways *are* crooked, and *they* froward in their paths:
16 To deliver thee from the strange woman, *even* from the stranger *which*
flattereth with her words;
17 Which forsaketh the guide of her youth, and forgetteth the covenant of
her God.
18 For her house inclineth unto death, and her paths unto the dead.
19 None that go unto her return again, neither take they hold of the paths
of life.
20 That thou mayest walk in the way of good *men,* and keep the paths of
the righteous.
21 For the upright shall dwell in the land, and the perfect shall remain in
it.
22 But the wicked shall be cut off from the earth, and the transgressors
shall be rooted out of it.

B. EVERYDAY BLESSINGS OF WISDOM

1. Wisdom's Excellent Consequences

3 MY son, forget not my law; but let thine heart keep my command-
ments:
2 For length of days, and long life, and peace, shall they add to thee.
3 Let not mercy and truth forsake thee: bind them about thy neck; write
them upon the table of thine heart:
4 So shalt thou find favour and good understanding in the sight of God
and man.
5 ¶Trust in the LORD with all thine heart; and lean not unto thine own
understanding.
6 In all thy ways acknowledge him, and he shall direct thy paths.
7 ¶Be not wise in thine own eyes: fear the LORD, and depart from evil.
8 It shall be health to thy navel, and marrow to thy bones.
9 Honour the LORD with thy substance, and with the firstfruits of all thine
increase:

2:9 Prov 1:2–6
2:10☆ Prov 14:33
2:11 Ps 82:5; Prov 4:19; 6:12; Jn 3:19, 20
2:14 Prov 10:23; Hab 1:15
2:15 Deut 32:5
2:16☆ Prov 6:24; 23:27
2:18 Prov 5:5
2:19☆
2:20☆ Prov 13:20
2:21 Ps 37:9, 29; Prov 10:30
2:23 Deut 28:63; Ps 37:38; 52:5; Prov 10:30
3:1 Ex 20:6; Deut 30:16; Ps 91:16; 119:93; Prov 4:5; 9:11; 10:27
3:3 Prov 6:21; 7:3; 8:13; Hos 4:1; 2 Cor 3:3
3:4 1 Sam 2:26; Ps 37:3, 5; Prov 8:35; 22:19; Jer 9:23, 24; Lk 2:52
3:5☆
3:6 1 Chron 28:9; Prov 16:3
3:7 Job 1:1; 28:28; Prov 4:21; 8:13; 16:6
3:9☆ Ex 23:19; Prov 11:24; 19:17; Joel 2:24; Mal 3:10

2:10 Whoever gives himself over to wisdom will be possessed by it. It will enter his heart, and as yeast leavens bread it will suffuse his being. It will be pleasant to his soul, and he will be kept or preserved by it.
2:16 True wisdom will save a man from *the strange woman* (an adulteress), whose flattery is false, whose sexual promiscuity violates her sacred marriage vows, and whose relation to God is defiled for she "forgetteth *the covenant of her God*" (2:17).
2:19 *None that go unto her return again,* i.e., "None of these men will ever be the same again"†
2:20 No one can do well who has not first ceased to do evil. There is a way that is good, and the good man follows the example of those who have walked in the paths of righteousness. Then his life will be an example for those who come after him.
3:5 Those who have true wisdom will by faith put their confidence in the wisdom, power, and goodness of God. They will trust that he will do what is best for them. They will acknowledge God in all their ways—by prayer (3:6) they will seek divine guidance and look for heavenly advice from the Author of wisdom. When they do this, God will direct their paths. He will bring them at last to their Canaan rest.
3:9 We must honor God with our souls, bodies, and material goods. The more God gives us of material things, the more we should work to honor him.

[10]So shall thy barns be filled with plenty, and thy presses shall burst out with new wine.
[11]¶My son, despise not the chastening of the LORD; neither be weary of his correction:
[12]For whom the LORD loveth he correcteth; even as a father the son *in whom* he delighteth.
[13]¶Happy *is* the man *that* findeth wisdom, and the man *that* getteth understanding.
[14]For the merchandise of it *is* better than the merchandise of silver, and the gain thereof than fine gold.
[15]She *is* more precious than rubies: and all the things thou canst desire are not to be compared unto her.
[16]Length of days *is* in her right hand; *and* in her left hand riches and honour.
[17]Her ways *are* ways of pleasantness, and all her paths *are* peace.
[18]She *is* a tree of life to them that lay hold upon her: and happy *is every one* that retaineth her.

3:11 Deut 8:5; Job 5:17; Ps 94:12; Prov 13:24; Heb 12:5, 6
☆**3:13** Job 28:17; Prov 8:10, 34; 16:16
3:16 Ps 21:4; Prov 3:2; 4:10; 8:18; 16:7; 22:4
3:18 Gen 2:9; Prov 11:30; Rev 2:7

2. Wisdom's Safety

[19]The LORD by wisdom hath founded the earth; by understanding hath he established the heavens.
[20]By his knowledge the depths are broken up, and the clouds drop down the dew.
[21]¶My son, let not them depart from thine eyes: keep sound wisdom and discretion:
[22]So shall they be life unto thy soul, and grace to thy neck.
[23]Then shalt thou walk in thy way safely, and thy foot shall not stumble.
[24]When thou liest down, thou shalt not be afraid: yea, thou shalt lie down, and thy sleep shall be sweet.
[25]Be not afraid of sudden fear, neither of the desolation of the wicked, when it cometh.
[26]For the LORD shall be thy confidence, and shall keep thy foot from being taken.

☆**3:19** Job 26:7–13; Prov 8:27, 28
3:20 Gen 7:11; Job 38:11
3:21 Prov 3:2; 4:21; 9:11
3:22 Deut 32:47; Prov 1:9; 4:22
3:23 Ps 37:23; 91:11; Prov 4:12; 10:9
3:24 1 Sam 2:9; Job 5:21; 11:19; Ps 3:5; 91:5; Prov 1:33; 6:22

3. Wisdom's Prohibitions

[27]¶Withhold not good from them to whom it is due, when it is in the power of thine hand to do *it*.
[28]Say not unto thy neighbour, Go, and come again, and to morrow I will give; when thou hast it by thee.
[29]Devise not evil against thy neighbour, seeing he dwelleth securely by thee.
[30]¶Strive not with a man without cause, if he have done thee no harm.
[31]¶Envy thou not the oppressor, and choose none of his ways.

3:27 Deut 24:15; Rom 13:8
☆**3:28**
☆**3:29** Ps 35:20; 55:20; Prov 14:22
☆**3:30** Prov 18:6; 26:17; Rom 12:18
☆**3:31** Ps 37:11; 73:3; Prov 23:17; 24:1, 19

3:13 Although wisdom comes from God, attaining it requires work. And it can be increased day by day. The seeker will sell all he has to attain wisdom. It turns out to be a great bargain which, after being purchased, must be retained and sustained. It produces happiness and long life. It is like the perfect tree of life such as is described in Eden.

3:19 God made the heavens that are flawless, set in their places, orderly, and suffering from no wear or tear. The sea does not overrun its banks, and all nature responds to the Creator's laws of nature.

3:28ff Wise people practice neighborly love in charity and justice. They will not hurt their neighbors nor will they be quarrelsome or contentious. Envy will not characterize their lives. And they will be honored, whereas fools will experience shame.

3:30 We are to live at peace with our neighbors as much as possible. Frivolous complaints are to be avoided, and no provocations should be given to those who have done us no wrong. Whoever acts without just cause is a peacebreaker, not a peacemaker.

3:32 Ps 25:14; Prov 6:16; 11:20
[32] For the froward *is* abomination to the LORD: but his secret *is* with the
righteous.

3:33 Deut 11:28; Job 8:6; Mal 2:2
[33] The curse of the LORD *is* in the house of the wicked: but he blesseth the
habitation of the just.

3:34 Isa 57:15; Jas 4:6; 1 Pet 5:5
[34] Surely he scorneth the scorners: but he giveth grace unto the lowly.
[35] The wise shall inherit glory: but shame shall be the promotion of fools.

C. A FATHER'S ADVICE TO HIS SON
1. Seek Wisdom
a. Learn to Be Wise

4:1 Prov 1:8; 5:1; 6:20
4 HEAR, ye children, the instruction of a father, and attend to know
understanding.
[2] For I give you good doctrine, forsake ye not my law.

4:3☆
[3] For I was my father's son, tender and only *beloved* in the sight of my
mother.

4:4 Prov 3:1; 4:10; 9:11
[4] He taught me also, and said unto me, Let thine heart retain my words:
keep my commandments, and live.
[5] Get wisdom, get understanding: forget *it* not; neither decline from the
words of my mouth.

4:6 Prov 2:16; 3:26; 8:14, 17; 2 Thess 2:10
[6] Forsake her not, and she shall preserve thee: love her, and she shall keep
thee.

4:7 Ps 119:104; Prov 18:15; 23:23
[7] Wisdom *is* the principal thing; *therefore* get wisdom: and with all thy
getting get understanding.

4:8 Prov 1:9; 3:22, 35
[8] Exalt her, and she shall promote thee: she shall bring thee to honour,
when thou dost embrace her.
[9] She shall give to thine head an ornament of grace: a crown of glory shall
she deliver to thee.

4:10 Prov 2:1; 3:16; 9:11; 10:27; 22:4
[10] Hear, O my son, and receive my sayings; and the years of thy life shall
be many.

b. Wisdom and Folly Contrasted

[11] I have taught thee in the way of wisdom; I have led thee in right paths.

4:12 Ps 37:23; 91:11
[12] When thou goest, thy steps shall not be straitened; and when thou
runnest, thou shalt not stumble.

4:13 Prov 3:18, 22; 16:22; Jn 6:63
[13] Take fast hold of instruction; let *her* not go: keep her; for she *is* thy life.

4:14 Ps 1:1; Prov 1:15
[14] ¶Enter not into the path of the wicked, and go not in the way of evil
men.

4:15 Job 11:14
[15] Avoid it, pass not by it, turn from it, and pass away.

4:16☆ Ps 36:4; Mic 2:1
[16] For they sleep not, except they have done mischief; and their sleep is
taken away, unless they cause *some* to fall.

4:17 Ps 14:4; Prov 20:17
[17] For they eat the bread of wickedness, and drink the wine of violence.

4:18☆ 2 Sam 23:4
[18] But the path of the just *is* as the shining light, that shineth more and
more unto the perfect day.

4:19 Job 18:5; Isa 59:9; Jn 1:4, 5
[19] The way of the wicked *is* as darkness: they know not at what they
stumble.

4:3 Solomon was taught well by his father. He continued in the things he had been taught. We are puzzled by the fact that Solomon, the wisest king Israel ever *had, failed signally in teaching* wisdom to his own successor. It would appear that Solomon himself forsook wisdom in his later years, and Rehoboam learned wrong things from his father's conduct, especially as it related to the number of wives and concubines he assembled.

4:16 The good man will shun those who are mischievous. By nature they are malicious, violent, and spiteful. They scheme and spend long hours of the night in thinking up mischief for the sake of mischief. Stay clear of such people.

4:18 Those who live rightly are like light that shines brighter all the time. And like the noonday sun, the righteous will arrive at the end of their journey in the perfect day.

c. Specific Injunctions to Follow

20 ¶My son, attend to my words; incline thine ear unto my sayings.
21 Let them not depart from thine eyes; keep them in the midst of thine
heart.
22 For they *are* life unto those that find them, and health to all their flesh.
23 ¶Keep thy heart with all diligence; for out of it *are* the issues of life.
24 Put away from thee a froward mouth, and perverse lips put far from
thee.
25 Let thine eyes look right on, and let thine eyelids look straight before
thee.
26 Ponder the path of thy feet, and let all thy ways be established.
27 Turn not to the right hand nor to the left: remove thy foot from evil.

4:20 Prov 2:1; 5:1 7:1; 22:17
4:22 Prov 3:8, 22 4:10
4:23 Lk 6:45
4:24 Job 11:14
☆4:25 Job 31:1 Mt 6:22
4:26 Prov 5:21; 15:3 Eph 5:15 Heb 12:13
4:27 Deut 5:32; 28:14

2. Marriage
a. Warning against Adultery

5 MY son, attend unto my wisdom, *and* bow thine ear to my under-
standing:
2 That thou mayest regard discretion, and *that* thy lips may keep
knowledge.
3 ¶For the lips of a strange woman drop *as* an honeycomb, and her mouth
is smoother than oil:
4 But her end is bitter as wormwood, sharp as a twoedged sword.
5 Her feet go down to death; her steps take hold on hell.
6 Lest thou shouldest ponder the path of life, her ways are moveable, *that*
thou canst not know *them*.
7 Hear me now therefore, O ye children, and depart not from the words of
my mouth.
8 Remove thy way far from her, and come not nigh the door of her house:
9 Lest thou give thine honour unto others, and thy years unto the cruel:
10 Lest strangers be filled with thy wealth; and thy labours *be* in the house
of a stranger;
11 And thou mourn at the last, when thy flesh and thy body are consumed,
12 And say, How have I hated instruction, and my heart despised reproof;
13 And have not obeyed the voice of my teachers, nor inclined mine ear to
them that instructed me!
14 I was almost in all evil in the midst of the congregation and assembly.

5:1 Prov 4:1, 20 7:24; 22:17
5:2 Prov 4:26; 27:23
☆5:3 Ps 55:21 Prov 5:20; 7:5
5:4 Eccles 7:26
5:5 Prov 2:18; 7:27 9:18
5:6 Prov 3:23 2 Pet 2:14
5:7 Prov 3:1; 7:24
5:8 Prov 7:25; 9:14 2 Tim 2:22
☆5:11 Prov 3:35; 9:13
5:12 Prov 1:22, 25 12:1
5:13 Prov 1:8 Lk 15:18
5:14 Prov 6:23

b. The Joys of Marriage and Evil Consequences of Adultery

15 ¶Drink waters out of thine own cistern, and running waters out of thine
own well.
16 Let thy fountains be dispersed abroad, *and* rivers of waters in the
streets.
17 Let them be only thine own, and not strangers' with thee.
18 Let thy fountain be blessed: and rejoice with the wife of thy youth:

5:15 Prov 5:18 Eccles 9:9 Song 4:15
5:16 Prov 5:18
☆5:18 Prov 18:22 19:14 Eccles 9:9 Mal 2:14

4:25 The eyes of the righteous look straight ahead to the good rather than backward to the bad. They are like "Pilgrim" (in *Pilgrim's Progress*) whose back was to the world, his face was looking up to heaven, and his hands were holding his Bible.

5:3 *of a strange woman,* i.e., "of a prostitute."† Herein the reader is warned to flee from fornication, adultery, and all uncleanness. These sins are attractive and the immediate satisfaction tempting. But the end is death, not life, and the consequences disastrous.

5:11 *when thy flesh and thy body are consumed,* referring to venereal disease.

5:18 It is better to marry than burn. Let every man have his own wife. Let him be ravished by her and remain faithful to her. An extramarital liaison is folly. Solomon here is endorsing monogamous marriage, the biblical ideal. How he strayed so far from the ideal remains forever a mystery.

5:19 Song 4:5; 7:3
5:20 Prov 2:16; 5:3; 7:5; 22:14
5:21 Job 14:16; Ps 7:15; 9:15; 119:168; Prov 15:13
5:22 Num 32:23; Prov 1:31, 32
5:23 Prov 10:21; 14:32

19 *Let her be as* the loving hind and pleasant roe; let her breasts satisfy
thee at all times; and be thou ravished always with her love.
20 And why wilt thou, my son, be ravished with a strange woman, and
embrace the bosom of a stranger?
21 For the ways of man *are* before the eyes of the LORD, and he pondereth
all his goings.
22 ¶His own iniquities shall take the wicked himself, and he shall be
holden with the cords of his sins.
23 He shall die without instruction; and in the greatness of his folly he
shall go astray.

3. Advice against Guaranteeing a Debt

6:1☆ Prov 17:18; 22:26; 27:13
6:2 Prov 11:15; 20:16
6:5 Ps 91:3; 124:7; Prov 1:17

6 MY son, if thou be surety for thy friend, *if* thou hast stricken thy hand
with a stranger,
2 Thou art snared with the words of thy mouth, thou art taken with the
words of thy mouth.
3 Do this now, my son, and deliver thyself, when thou art come into the
hand of thy friend; go, humble thyself, and make sure thy friend.
4 Give not sleep to thine eyes, nor slumber to thine eyelids.
5 Deliver thyself as a roe from the hand *of the hunter*, and as a bird from
the hand of the fowler.

4. Laziness Condemned

6:6☆ Prov 10:26; 13:4; 30:24, 25
6:8 Prov 10:5
6:10 Prov 24:33, 34
6:11 Prov 23:19

6 ¶Go to the ant, thou sluggard; consider her ways, and be wise:
7 Which having no guide, overseer, or ruler,
8 Provideth her meat in the summer, *and* gathereth her food in the
harvest.
9 How long wilt thou sleep, O sluggard? when wilt thou arise out of thy
sleep?
10 *Yet* a little sleep, a little slumber, a little folding of the hands to sleep:
11 So shall thy poverty come as one that travelleth, and thy want as an
armed man.

5. Watch Out for Liars

6:12☆ Prov 4:27; 8:13; 10:27; 16:27
6:14 Prov 10:32; 17:11; Mic 2:1
6:15 Ps 73:18; Prov 24:22; Jer 19:11

12 ¶A naughty person, a wicked man, walketh with a froward mouth.
13 He winketh with his eyes, he speaketh with his feet, he teacheth with his
fingers;
14 Frowardness *is* in his heart, he deviseth mischief continually; he soweth
discord.
15 Therefore shall his calamity come suddenly; suddenly shall he be
broken without remedy.

6. Six Things God Hates

6:16☆ Gen 6:5; Prov 1:16; 6:14; 19:5, 9; 21:4; 24:2; 28:17; 30:21; Isa 1:15
6:17☆

16 ¶These six *things* doth the LORD hate: yea, seven *are* an abomination
unto him:
17 A proud look, a lying tongue, and hands that shed innocent blood,

---

6:1 Solomon warns against binding one's self as a surety even for a friend. This is one way by which many *friendships have been ruined*. He suggests that the arrangement be cancelled as quickly as possible, especially if the cost will be greater than the bondsman can afford to pay.

6:6 The sluggard should watch the ant and learn a lesson from lower life that will help him to attain a higher life than he now has.

6:12 The wicked man is a crafty schemer who hides his wickedness by professing the good. He is subtle and cunning, yet has evil designs in heart and mind. The Scriptures condemn all such connivers.

6:16–19 Herein are listed the seven deadly sins, any one of which is enough to condemn a person. Most of the wicked are guilty of all seven and others as well.

[18]An heart that deviseth wicked imaginations, feet that be swift in
running to mischief,
[19]A false witness *that* speaketh lies, and he that soweth discord among
brethren.

7. Strong Warnings against Adultery

[20]¶My son, keep thy father's commandment, and forsake not the law of
thy mother:
[21]Bind them continually upon thine heart, *and* tie them about thy neck.
[22]When thou goest, it shall lead thee; when thou sleepest, it shall keep
thee; and *when* thou awakest, it shall talk with thee.
[23]For the commandment *is* a lamp; and the law *is* light; and reproofs of
instruction *are* the way of life:
[24]To keep thee from the evil woman, from the flattery of the tongue of a
strange woman.
[25]Lust not after her beauty in thine heart; neither let her take thee with
her eyelids.
[26]For by means of a whorish woman *a man is brought* to a piece of bread:
and the adulteress will hunt for the precious life.
[27]Can a man take fire in his bosom, and his clothes not be burned?
[28]Can one go upon hot coals, and his feet not be burned?
[29]So he that goeth in to his neighbour's wife; whosoever toucheth her
shall not be innocent.
[30]*Men* do not despise a thief, if he steal to satisfy his soul when he is
hungry;
[31]But *if* he be found, he shall restore sevenfold; he shall give all the
substance of his house.
[32]*But* whoso committeth adultery with a woman lacketh understanding:
he *that* doeth it destroyeth his own soul.
[33]A wound and dishonour shall he get; and his reproach shall not be
wiped away.
[34]For jealousy *is* the rage of a man: therefore he will not spare in the day
of vengeance.
[35]He will not regard any ransom; neither will he rest content, though
thou givest many gifts.

☆**6:20** Prov 1:7
6:21 Prov 3:3; 6:21; 7:1; 19:20; 23:22
6:22 Prov 3:23; 4:12; 10:9
6:23 Ps 119:105; Prov 13:9
6:24 Prov 2:16; 5:3; 7:15, 21; 23:26
6:25 2 Kgs 9:30; Job 31:1; Prov 21:4; Jer 2:24; Mt 5:28
6:26 Prov 5:9, 10; 7:27; 29:3
6:28 Prov 9:18
6:29 Prov 16:5; Jer 5:8; Ezek 22:11
6:31 Ex 22:7; 2 Sam 12:7; Mt 18:25
6:32 Prov 7:7, 22, 23; 9:14, 16
6:33 Ps 51:8; Prov 18:3
☆**6:34** Lev 20:10; Prov 27:4; Song 8:6

8. The Folly of Yielding to an Adulteress

7 MY son, keep my words, and lay up my commandments with thee.
[2]Keep my commandments, and live; and my law as the apple of
thine eye.
[3]Bind them upon thy fingers, write them upon the table of thine heart.
[4]Say unto wisdom, Thou *art* my sister; and call understanding *thy*
kinswoman:
[5]That they may keep thee from the strange woman, from the stranger
which flattereth with her words.
[6]¶*For at the window of my* house I looked through my casement,

7:1 Prov 2:1; 3:1; 4:1
7:2 Ps 17:8; Prov 4:4; 9:11; 10:27; 16:22
☆**7:3** Deut 6:8; Prov 3:3; 6:21
7:4 Prov 4:6
7:5 Prov 4:24; 22:14

6:20 The commandments spoken of here are the Word of God which is a light as well as a law. Mother and father alike are bound by it and should teach it to their children. It is to be remembered, thought about, and practiced when walking, lying down, and rising in the morning. No part of any day is good if the Word of God is not present and active.

6:34 Adultery is one of the gravest sins a man can commit. The adulterer destroys his own soul and faces the justice of both God and of man. The husband whose wife has been violated has been affronted and wounded. His anger is a righteous anger. The wronged husband will accept no ransom; he will not be bought off. Theft can be atoned for by a ransom, but the law demands the death of persons guilty of adultery.

7:3 *Bind them upon thy fingers,* i.e., "Write them down."†

7:7☆ Prov 1:22; 6:32 8:5, 22:3 — 7 And beheld among the simple ones, I discerned among the youths, a
young man void of understanding,
7:8 Prov 4:14, 15 5:8; 7:12, 27 — 8 Passing through the street near her corner; and he went the way to her
house,
9 In the twilight, in the evening, in the black and dark night:
7:10 Gen 38:14, 15 Isa 3:16; 23:16 — 10 And, behold, there met him a woman *with* the attire of an harlot, and
subtil of heart.
7:11 Prov 9:13; 23:28 — 11 (She *is* loud and stubborn; her feet abide not in her house:
12 Now *is she* without, now in the streets, and lieth in wait at every
corner.)
13 So she caught him, and kissed him, *and* with an impudent face said
unto him,
14 I have peace offerings with me; this day have I payed my vows.
15 Therefore came I forth to meet thee, diligently to seek thy face, and I
have found thee.
7:16 Ps 45:8 Prov 31:22 Ezek 27:7 — 16 I have decked my bed with coverings of tapestry, with carved *works*,
with fine linen of Egypt.
17 I have perfumed my bed with myrrh, aloes, and cinnamon.
7:18☆ — 18 Come, let us take our fill of love until the morning: let us solace
ourselves with loves.
7:19☆ — 19 For the goodman *is* not at home, he is gone a long journey:
20 He hath taken a bag of money with him, *and* will come home at the day
appointed.
7:21 Prov 5:3; 6:24 — 21 With her much fair speech she caused him to yield, with the flattering of
her lips she forced him.
22 He goeth after her straightway, as an ox goeth to the slaughter, or as a
fool to the correction of the stocks;
7:23 Prov 1:17 Eccles 9:12 — 23 Till a dart strike through his liver; as a bird hasteth to the snare, and
knoweth not that it *is* for his life.
7:24 Prov 4:1; 5:7 8:32 — 24 ¶Hearken unto me now therefore, O ye children, and attend to the
words of my mouth.
7:25 Prov 4:23; 5:8 6:25 — 25 Let not thine heart decline to her ways, go not astray in her paths.
26 For she hath cast down many wounded: yea, many strong *men* have
been slain by her.
7:27☆ Prov 2:18; 5:5 9:18 — 27 Her house *is* the way to hell, going down to the chambers of death.

D. THE PERSONIFICATION OF WISDOM

1. The Voice of Wisdom Presents Its Case

8:1☆ Job 19:7 Prov 1:20, 21 9:3 — 8 DOTH not wisdom cry? and understanding put forth her voice?
2 She standeth in the top of high places, by the way in the places of
the paths.

7:7ff Many of the Proverbs are addressed to youth, warning them of life's pitfalls. They state that the youth will be tempted, but if he seeks and finds wisdom he will avoid sin and say "no" to the temptress.

7:18 *let us take our fill of love.* "Of *love,* does she say? Of *lust,* she means, brutish lust; but it is a pity that the name of love should be thus abused. True love is from heaven; this is from hell."*

7:19 This adulteress is not a common prostitute. She is *a wife, who no doubt had the respect* of her neighbors and the love of her husband. She engages in seduction. Bad as she is, one must also fault her "lover," who along with her betrays her husband and by his conduct is no less guilty in the crime. She breaks faith with her husband and violates her marriage vows.

7:27 The house of pleasure is the way to hell. Her bedroom goes down to the chambers of death and everlasting darkness. "The cup of fornication must shortly be exchanged for the cup of trembling; and the flames of lust, if not quenched by repentance and mortification, will burn in the lowest hell. Therefore stand in awe and sin not."*

8:1 God has made known to man all he needs for salvation and the conduct of his life. Man knows these things from the works of creation, the common rules of good and evil, and in the revelation of God given through Moses and the prophets. Wisdom everywhere calls men to a life of righteousness. Thus wisdom cannot be compared to wealth; it is better than all the precious jewels men can own. He who is wise will walk in the way of righteousness and in the paths of justice.

3 She crieth at the gates, at the entry of the city, at the coming in at the
doors.
4 Unto you, O men, I call; and my voice *is* to the sons of man.
5 O ye simple, understand wisdom: and, ye fools, be ye of an understand-
ing heart.
6 Hear; for I will speak of excellent things; and the opening of my lips
shall be right things.
7 For my mouth shall speak truth; and wickedness *is* an abomination to
my lips.
8 All the words of my mouth *are* in righteousness; *there is* nothing
froward or perverse in them.
9 They *are* all plain to him that understandeth, and right to them that find
knowledge.
10 Receive my instruction, and not silver; and knowledge rather than
choice gold.
11 For wisdom *is* better than rubies; and all the things that may be desired
are not to be compared to it.
12 I wisdom dwell with prudence, and find out knowledge of witty
inventions.
13 The fear of the LORD *is* to hate evil: pride, and arrogancy, and the evil
way, and the froward mouth, do I hate.
14 Counsel *is* mine, and sound wisdom: I *am* understanding; I have
strength.
15 By me kings reign, and princes decree justice.
16 By me princes rule, and nobles, *even* all the judges of the earth.
17 I love them that love me; and those that seek me early shall find me.
18 Riches and honour *are* with me; *yea*, durable riches and righteousness.
19 My fruit *is* better than gold, yea, than fine gold; and my revenue than
choice silver.
20 I lead in the way of righteousness, in the midst of the paths of
judgment:
21 That I may cause those that love me to inherit substance; and I will fill
their treasures.

2. Wisdom Has Existed Forever

22 The LORD possessed me in the beginning of his way, before his works of
old.
23 I was set up from everlasting, from the beginning, or ever the earth was.
24 When *there were* no depths, I was brought forth; when *there were* no
fountains abounding with water.
25 Before the mountains were settled, before the hills was I brought forth:
26 While as yet he had not made the earth, nor the fields, nor the highest
part of the dust of the world.
27 When he prepared the heavens, I *was* there: when he set a compass
upon the face of the depth:
28 When he established the clouds above: when he strengthened the
fountains of the deep:

8:4 Ps 19:7; Prov 1:4, 20
8:8 Ps 12:6:
8:9 Ps 25:12; Prov 14:6; 15:14; 17:24; 18:15
☆**8:10** Ps 119:72, 127; Prov 2:4; 3:13; 8:19; Eccles 7:11
☆**8:11** Prov 3:14, 15; 16:16; 20:15
8:12 Ex 31:3; Prov 3:13; 4:5
8:13 Prov 3:7; 15:9; 16:6; Isa 13:11
8:14 Prov 10:21, 31; 19:20; Isa 1:26; Rom 13:1
8:17 1 Sam 2:30; Ps 91:14; Prov 2:4, 5; 4:6; Jn 14:21; Jas 1:5
☆**8:18** Ps 112:3; Prov 3:16; 22:4; Mt 6:33; Jas 2:5
8:20 Ps 23:3; 25:4; 32:8; Prov 6:22; Isa 2:3
8:21 Prov 3:19
☆**8:22** Job 28:27; Ps 104:24; Prov 3:19; Jn 1:1; Col 1:17; 2:3; Rev 3:14
8:23 Jn 17:5, 24
8:24 Gen 1:9; Job 38:16; Prov 3:20
8:25 Ps 90:2
8:27 Job 26:10; 38:6; Ps 33:6; 104:5; 136:5; Prov 3:19; Jer 10:12; Heb 1:2

8:10, 11 Wisdom must be accepted as well as taught. It is to be preferred above silver or gold. It is better than the brightest gem. He who has everything else the world can offer but does not have wisdom has nothing.
8:18 Sometimes those who have wisdom also have wealth. But the fruit of wisdom is righteousness, which is infinitely better than silver or gold.
8:22 From this verse onward wisdom is personified. Wisdom is looked upon as an attribute of God and must therefore be reckoned as part of man's inheritance from the Creator. Without wisdom, life is shortchanged. In 1 Cor. 1:24 Christ is called "the wisdom of God." Some commentators do not think there are any Christological references in this verse, but this would not change the Pauline statement that Christ is the wisdom of God.

29 When he gave to the sea his decree, that the waters should not pass his
commandment: when he appointed the foundations of the earth:
30 Then I was by him, *as* one brought up *with him:* and I was daily *his*
delight, rejoicing always before him;
31 Rejoicing in the habitable part of his earth; and my delights *were* with
the sons of men.
32 Now therefore hearken unto me, O ye children: for blessed *are they that*
keep my ways.

3. The Invitation to Seek It

33 Hear instruction, and be wise, and refuse it not.
34 Blessed *is* the man that heareth me, watching daily at my gates, waiting
at the posts of my doors.
35 For whoso findeth me findeth life, and shall obtain favour of the LORD.
36 But he that sinneth against me wrongeth his own soul: all they that hate
me love death.

4. The Invitation to Wisdom's Banquet

9 WISDOM hath builded her house, she hath hewn out her seven pillars:
2 She hath killed her beasts; she hath mingled her wine; she hath also
furnished her table.
3 She hath sent forth her maidens: she crieth upon the highest places of
the city,
4 Whoso *is* simple, let him turn in hither: *as for* him that wanteth
understanding, she saith to him,
5 Come, eat of my bread, and drink of the wine *which* I have mingled.
6 Forsake the foolish, and live; and go in the way of understanding.
7 He that reproveth a scorner getteth to himself shame: and he that
rebuketh a wicked *man getteth* himself a blot.
8 Reprove not a scorner, lest he hate thee: rebuke a wise man, and he will
love thee.
9 Give *instruction* to a wise *man*, and he will be yet wiser: teach a just *man*,
and he will increase in learning.
10 The fear of the LORD *is* the beginning of wisdom: and the knowledge of
the holy *is* understanding.
11 For by me thy days shall be multiplied, and the years of thy life shall be
increased.
12 If thou be wise, thou shalt be wise for thyself: but *if* thou scornest, thou
alone shalt bear *it*.

8:32☆ Ps 119:1, 2; Prov 5:7; 29:18
8:33 Prov 4:1; 5:1; 7:24; Isa 55:3
8:34 Ps 27:4; Prov 1:21; 2:3; Jas 1:22
8:35 Prov 3:4; 4:22; 12:2; Jn 17:3
8:36☆ Prov 1:31, 32; 5:12, 32; 15:32
9:1☆ Eph 2:20; Heb 3:5, 6; 1 Pet 2:5
9:2 Isa 25:6; Mt 22:2
9:3 Prov 1:20; 8:1; Mt 22:3
9:4 Ps 19:7; Prov 8:5
9:5 Song 5:1
9:6 Prov 3:22; 4:22; 9:11; 16:22
9:7 Ps 141:5; Prov 10:8; 15:12; 23:9
9:9 Prov 1:5; 25:12
9:10☆ Job 28:28; Ps 111:10; Prov 1:7; 15:33
9:11 Prov 3:2, 16; 9:6; 10:27
9:12 Job 22:2; Ezek 18:4; Gal 6:5

8:32 The best sermon includes a word of exhortation or the drawing of the net. All listeners here are called to hear and diligently obey the word of wisdom with all their hearts. Happy are those who embrace wisdom.
8:36 The sermon ends with a final word of warning *that those who reject wisdom are left to ruin and doom.* Whoever sins against wisdom sins against the Author of wisdom. In this gospel age it is to sin against Jesus Christ, who is wisdom, the wisdom of God incarnated in the flesh. Whoever hates Christ hates wisdom, and whoever hates wisdom loves death.
9:1 Wisdom here is designated by the female gender. She is a queen who is great and generous. Those who become her disciples will sit down to a sumptuous feast. "Heaven is the house which Wisdom has built to entertain all her guests that are called to the marriage-supper of the Lamb; that is her Father's house, where there are many mansions, and whither she has gone to prepare places for us."*
9:10 True wisdom consists in the fear of God. It comes about when the head is filled with knowledge of the things of God given to us by revelation. This knowledge has come to men through the prophets and apostles who spoke as they were moved by the Holy Spirit.

5. The Invitation of Folly

13 ¶A foolish woman *is* clamorous: *she is* simple, and knoweth nothing.
14 For she sitteth at the door of her house, on a seat in the high places of
the city,
15 To call passengers who go right on their ways:
16 Whoso *is* simple, let him turn in hither: and *as for* him that wanteth
understanding, she saith to him,
17 Stolen waters are sweet, and bread *eaten* in secret is pleasant.
18 But he knoweth not that the dead *are* there; *and that* her guests *are* in
the depths of hell.

III. ETHICAL OBSERVATIONS (10:1—22:16)

A. WISE AND FOOLISH PRACTICES COMPARED

1. Righteous and Wicked Acts Contrasted

10 THE proverbs of Solomon. A wise son maketh a glad father: but a
foolish son *is* the heaviness of his mother.
2 Treasures of wickedness profit nothing: but righteousness delivereth
from death.
3 The LORD will not suffer the soul of the righteous to famish: but he
casteth away the substance of the wicked.
4 He becometh poor that dealeth *with* a slack hand: but the hand of the
diligent maketh rich.
5 He that gathereth in summer *is* a wise son: *but* he that sleepeth in
harvest *is* a son that causeth shame.
6 Blessings *are* upon the head of the just: but violence covereth the mouth
of the wicked.
7 The memory of the just *is* blessed: but the name of the wicked shall rot.
8 The wise in heart will receive commandments: but a prating fool shall
fall.
9 He that walketh uprightly walketh surely: but he that perverteth his
ways shall be known.
10 He that winketh with the eye causeth sorrow: but a prating fool shall
fall.
11 The mouth of a righteous *man is* a well of life: but violence covereth the
mouth of the wicked.
12 Hatred stirreth up strifes: but love covereth all sins.
13 In the lips of him that hath understanding wisdom is found: but a rod
is for the back of him that is void of understanding.
14 Wise *men* lay up knowledge: but the mouth of the foolish *is* near
destruction.
15 The rich man's wealth *is* his strong city: the destruction of the poor *is*
their poverty.
16 The labour of the righteous *tendeth* to life: the fruit of the wicked to sin.

☆9:13 Prov 5:4; 7:11
9:15 Prov 7:25; 23:26
9:17 Prov 20:17 30:20
9:18 Prov 2:18; 5:5 7:27
10:1 Prov 15:20 17:25; 29:3, 15
☆10:2 Ps 49:6, 7 Prov 11:4; 21:6 Eccles 2:4
10:3 Ps 34:9, 10 37:25 Mt 6:33
10:4 Prov 6:6
☆10:5
☆10:5
10:6 Prov 9:11; 28:20
10:7 Ps 9:5, 6 109:13; 112:6
10:8 Prov 9:8 Mt 7:24
10:9 Ps 23:4 Prov 3:23; 26:27 Isa 33:15, 16 Mt 10:26
10:10 Prov 6:13
10:11 Ps 37:20 Prov 13:14 18:4; 20:5
☆10:12 Prov 17:9 1 Cor 13:4–7
10:13 Prov 10:31; 26:3
10:14 Prov 13:3; 18:7 Jas 3:2, 5
10:15 Ps 52:7 Prov 18:11; 19:7
10:16 Prov 11:18, 19

9:13ff Verses 13–18 describe the feast of folly in which the guests wrong themselves, wrong God, and wrong their fellow-men by sitting down at the foolish woman's (i.e., the prostitute's) wicked table.

10:2 Whoever grows rich unjustly cannot profit from it in the long run. Riches will not deliver a man from death or from judgment, and he will leave it all behind him. He cannot send any of it ahead. Heaven is a bank for the believers, whereas hell is bankrupt and offers naught but insecurity.

10:5 Two sons from the same family may live different sorts of life. One is idle, lazy, shiftless, sleepy, and neglectful. Such a one is unwise. But another improves his opportunities and makes provision in the fall for the coming winter. He is a wise son who brings honor to his parents.

10:12 Those who exhibit hatred stir up trouble and are the devil's accomplices. Those who love do not publicly flaunt the errors of others nor do they regard the sins of others with pleasure. Love excuses every offense that springs from mistakes and is committed inadvisedly. Love covers a multitude of sins (1 Pet. 4:8).

10:17 Prov 6:23; 12:1; 22:17
10:18 Prov 26:24
10:19 Job 11:2; Prov 18:21; Eccles 5:3
10:21 Prov 12:18; 15:4; Hos 4:6
10:22☆ Gen 24:35; 26:12; Deut 8:18; Prov 8:21

17 He *is in* the way of life that keepeth instruction: but he that refuseth reproof erreth.

18 He that hideth hatred *with* lying lips, and he that uttereth a slander, *is* a fool.

19 In the multitude of words there wanteth not sin: but he that refraineth his lips *is* wise.

20 The tongue of the just *is as* choice silver: the heart of the wicked *is* little worth.

21 The lips of the righteous feed many: but fools die for want of wisdom.

22 The blessing of the LORD, it maketh rich, and he addeth no sorrow with it.

2. The Fear of the Lord Prolongs One's Days

10:23 Prov 2:14; 15:21
10:24 Job 15:21; Ps 145:19; Prov 1:27; 15:8; Isa 66:4; Mt 5:6
10:25 Ps 15:1–5; 125:1; Prov 12:3; Mt 7:24, 25
10:27 Job 22:16; Ps 55:23; Prov 3:2; 9:11; 14:27
10:28 Job 11:20; Prov 11:7, 23
10:29 Prov 21:15
10:30 Ps 37:25; 125:1; Prov 2:22
10:31 Ps 37:30; Prov 10:13; 11:13
10:32 Prov 6:12; Eccles 12:10

23 *It is* as sport to a fool to do mischief: but a man of understanding hath wisdom.

24 The fear of the wicked, it shall come upon him: but the desire of the righteous shall be granted.

25 As the whirlwind passeth, so *is* the wicked no *more:* but the righteous *is* an everlasting foundation.

26 As vinegar to the teeth, and as smoke to the eyes, so *is* the sluggard to them that send him.

27 The fear of the LORD prolongeth days: but the years of the wicked shall be shortened.

28 The hope of the righteous *shall be* gladness: but the expectation of the wicked shall perish.

29 The way of the LORD *is* strength to the upright: but destruction *shall be* to the workers of iniquity.

30 The righteous shall never be removed: but the wicked shall not inhabit the earth.

31 The mouth of the just bringeth forth wisdom: but the froward tongue shall be cut out.

32 The lips of the righteous know what is acceptable: but the mouth of the wicked *speaketh* frowardness.

3. Differing Actions of Good and Bad Men

11:1☆ Deut 25:13–16; Prov 16:11
11:2 Prov 16:18; 18:12; 29:23
11:3 Prov 13:6; 21:7; 22:12
11:4 Prov 10:2; Ezek 7:19; 1 Tim 4:8; 6:7
11:5 Prov 3:6; 5:22
11:6 Ps 7:15, 16; 9:15

11 A FALSE balance *is* abomination to the LORD: but a just weight *is* his delight.

2 *When* pride cometh, then cometh shame: but with the lowly *is* wisdom.

3 The integrity of the upright shall guide them: but the perverseness of transgressors shall destroy them.

4 Riches profit not in the day of wrath: but righteousness delivereth from death.

5 The righteousness of the perfect shall direct his way: but the wicked shall fall by his own wickedness.

6 The righteousness of the upright shall deliver them: but transgressors shall be taken in *their own* naughtiness.

10:22 *he addeth no sorrow with it,* i.e., "*All our work adds nothing to it.*"† *Most men* have their eyes on worldly wealth and are mistaken in what they desire and how to attain it. True wealth that has no sorrow in it is the blessing of God. This blessing constitutes man's true riches. We need to be diligent in seeking God's blessing and diligent in the pursuit of our duties, which are fructified under the blessing of the Lord.

11:1 When it comes to money, even Christians are tempted to engage in shady practices and to justify minor infractions of the law, for these do not constitute felonies that would land them in jail. But God desires fair and honest dealings in all things. The weight that favors the seller by half an ounce is an abomination to God and is especially obnoxious because it pretends to weigh the goods most exactly.

7 When a wicked man dieth, *his* expectation shall perish: and the hope of
unjust *men* perisheth.
8 The righteous is delivered out of trouble, and the wicked cometh in his
stead.
9 An hypocrite with *his* mouth destroyeth his neighbour: but through
knowledge shall the just be delivered.
10 When it goeth well with the righteous, the city rejoiceth: and when the
wicked perish, *there is* shouting.
11 By the blessing of the upright the city is exalted: but it is overthrown by
the mouth of the wicked.

4. Quarreling and Gossip

12 He that is void of wisdom despiseth his neighbour: but a man of
understanding holdeth his peace.
13 A talebearer revealeth secrets: but he that is of a faithful spirit
concealeth the matter.
14 Where no counsel *is*, the people fall: but in the multitude of counsellors
there is safety.
15 He that is surety for a stranger shall smart *for it:* and he that hateth
suretiship is sure.
16 A gracious woman retaineth honour: and strong *men* retain riches.
17 The merciful man doeth good to his own soul: but *he that is* cruel
troubleth his own flesh.
18 The wicked worketh a deceitful work: but to him that soweth righteous-
ness *shall be* a sure reward.
19 As righteousness *tendeth* to life: so he that pursueth evil *pursueth it* to
his own death.
20 They that are of a froward heart *are* abomination to the LORD: but *such
as are* upright in *their* way *are* his delight.
21 *Though* hand *join* in hand, the wicked shall not be unpunished: but the
seed of the righteous shall be delivered.
22 *As* a jewel of gold in a swine's snout, *so is* a fair woman which is
without discretion.
23 The desire of the righteous *is* only good: *but* the expectation of the
wicked *is* wrath.

5. The Grace of Liberality

24 There is that scattereth, and yet increaseth; and *there is* that withhold-
eth more than is meet, but *it tendeth* to poverty.
25 The liberal soul shall be made fat: and he that watereth shall be
watered also himself.
26 He that withholdeth corn, the people shall curse him: but blessing *shall
be* upon the head of him that selleth *it*.

11:7 Prov 10:28; 11:23; 14:32
11:8 Ps 22:8; 51:14, 15
11:10 Prov 28:28; Eccles 10:5
11:11 Prov 14:34
☆**11:12** Prov 10:14; 13:3; 18:7
11:13 Ps 15:3; Prov 19:11; 20:19; 1 Tim 5:13
11:14 Prov 15:22; 20:18; 24:6
☆**11:15** Prov 6:1; 27:13
11:16 Prov 31:28, 30
11:17 Mt 5:7; 25:34–36
11:18 Hos 10:12; Gal 16:8, 9
11:19 Prov 10:16; 19:23; 21:16; Rom 6:23; Jas 1:15
11:20 Ps 75:5; Prov 13:6; 21:29
11:21 Prov 16:5
☆**11:22** Ezek 16:15; Nah 3:4; 1 Pet 3:3
11:23 Prov 10:28; Rom 2:8, 9
☆**11:24** Prov 3:9, 10; Mt 5:7; 2 Cor 9:6, 7
☆**11:26** Gen 41:56, 57; Amos 8:4

11:12 Gossips tell their stories from house to house without checking their facts to see whether they are false or true. They make mischief and sow discord. Let the rule of thumb be: "Is it true? Is it kind? Is it necessary?" If it is not, then keep silent.

11:15 Charity begins at home, even though it does not end there. A good father who is interested in his family's future will not place his estate in jeopardy by acting as surety for a stranger.

11:22 A woman whose conversation and life are not under grace and the Christian faith is likened to a pig whose snout is bedecked with a jewel of gold. Beauty without virtue is like this, unless it is clothed with the righteousness of God.

11:24 God blesses the giving hand and makes it a getting hand. He is no man's debtor. Whoever sows liberally for the glory of God will reap liberally and experience a spiritual blessing that cannot be bought with money.

11:26 The believer whose farm has yielded much wheat will not hold it in the granery for a higher price at a time there is drought and the poor are suffering from the lack of food. It is good charity to help keep prices down by selling one's excess grain during a time of famine when extortion becomes easy.

11:27 Prov 17:11

27 He that diligently seeketh good procureth favour: but he that seeketh mischief, it shall come unto him.

11:28 Ps 1:2, 3; 92:12 Jer 17:7, 8 Mk 10:24, 25 1 Tim 6:17

28 He that trusteth in his riches shall fall; but the righteous shall flourish as a branch.

11:29 Prov 14:19 15:27

29 He that troubleth his own house shall inherit the wind: and the fool *shall be* servant to the wise of heart.

11:30 Prov 3:18 Jas 5:20

30 The fruit of the righteous *is* a tree of life; and he that winneth souls *is* wise.

11:31 2 Sam 22:21

31 Behold, the righteous shall be recompensed in the earth: much more the wicked and the sinner.

6. Knowledge Must Be Taught

12:1☆ Prov 1:5; 9:9 25:12

12 WHOSO loveth instruction loveth knowledge: but he that hateth reproof *is* brutish.

12:2 Prov 3:4 8:35, 36

2 A good *man* obtaineth favour of the LORD: but a man of wicked devices will he condemn.

12:3 Ps 15:1–5 Prov 10:25; 11:5

3 A man shall not be established by wickedness: but the root of the righteous shall not be moved.

12:4☆ Prov 14:1 19:13; 21:9 27:15; 31:10 1 Cor 11:7

4 A virtuous woman *is* a crown to her husband: but she that maketh ashamed *is* as rottenness in his bones.

12:5 Prov 16:23 Mt 12:34; 15:18

5 The thoughts of the righteous *are* right: *but* the counsels of the wicked *are* deceit.

12:6 Ps 12:5; 35:11 Prov 14:3; 31:8

6 The words of the wicked *are* to lie in wait for blood: but the mouth of the upright shall deliver them.

12:7 Prov 11:21 14:11 Isa 3:10, 11 Mt 7:24–27

7 The wicked are overthrown, and *are* not: but the house of the righteous shall stand.

12:8 Eccles 8:1

8 A man shall be commended according to his wisdom: but he that is of a perverse heart shall be despised.

7. Hard Work Is a Boon

12:9☆ Lk 14:11

9 *He that is* despised, and hath a servant, *is* better than he that honoureth himself, and lacketh bread.

12:10 Gen 33:13

10 A righteous *man* regardeth the life of his beast: but the tender mercies of the wicked *are* cruel.

12:11 Prov 9:6; 14:24

11 He that tilleth his land shall be satisfied with bread: but he that followeth vain *persons is* void of understanding.

12:12 Prov 1:18, 19 11:24, 25; 21:10

12 The wicked desireth the net of evil *men:* but the root of the righteous yieldeth *fruit.*

12:13 Prov 11:8; 13:5 25:18

13 The wicked is snared by the transgression of *his* lips: but the just shall come out of trouble.

12:14 Prov 12:24, 27 13:11; 14:11 24:12 Isa 3:10

14 A man shall be satisfied with good by the fruit of *his* mouth: and the recompence of a man's hands shall be rendered unto him.

8. The Wise and the Foolish Contrasted

12:15 Prov 14:12 16:2; 21:2

15 The way of a fool *is* right in his own eyes: but he that hearkeneth unto counsel *is* wise.

12:1 *reproof* is a discipline valued by those who seek a good education. Whoever hates reproof is void of common sense, is foolish, and lacks genuine understanding. We should not be like the ox that kicks against the goad.

12:4 A good man can have a bad wife. His peace of mind and public reputation can be damaged by such a woman. Yet he is bound by oath until death parts them. Let those who marry consider the matter carefully, lest they marry in haste and repent at leisure. A good wife can have a bad husband and suffer just as much as the good man with the bad wife.

12:9 How easy it is to put on a good act while away from home, pretending to be what we are not and impressing others with our high estate. Better is the man who is content with lesser fame but whose home is blessed with food and raiment and who has hired someone to help him.

16 A fool's wrath is presently known: but a prudent *man* covereth shame.
17 *He that* speaketh truth sheweth forth righteousness: but a false witness
deceit.
18 There is that speaketh like the piercings of a sword: but the tongue of
the wise *is* health.
19 The lip of truth shall be established for ever: but a lying tongue *is* but
for a moment.
20 Deceit *is* in the heart of them that imagine evil: but to the counsellors
of peace *is* joy.
21 There shall no evil happen to the just: but the wicked shall be filled
with mischief.
22 Lying lips *are* abomination to the LORD: but they that deal truly *are* his
delight.
23 A prudent man concealeth knowledge: but the heart of fools proclaim-
eth foolishness.
24 The hand of the diligent shall bear rule: but the slothful shall be under
tribute.
25 Heaviness in the heart of man maketh it stoop: but a good word
maketh it glad.
26 The righteous *is* more excellent than his neighbour: but the way of the
wicked seduceth them.
27 The slothful *man* roasteth not that which he took in hunting: but the
substance of a diligent man *is* precious.
28 In the way of righteousness *is* life: and *in* the pathway *thereof there is* no
death.

9. A Good Man's Way of Life

13 A WISE son *heareth* his father's instruction: but a scorner heareth
not rebuke.
2 A man shall eat good by the fruit of *his* mouth: but the soul of the
transgressors *shall eat* violence.
3 He that keepeth his mouth keepeth his life: *but* he that openeth wide his
lips shall have destruction.
4 The soul of the sluggard desireth, and *hath* nothing: but the soul of the
diligent shall be made fat.
5 A righteous *man* hateth lying: but a wicked *man* is loathsome, and
cometh to shame.
6 Righteousness keepeth *him that is* upright in the way: but wickedness
overthroweth the sinner.
7 There is that maketh himself rich, yet *hath* nothing: *there is* that maketh
himself poor, yet *hath* great riches.

☆**12:16** Prov 19:11; 29:11
12:17 Prov 12:13; 14:3, 23; 25:18
12:18 Ps 57:4; Prov 8:6, 7; 15:4
12:19 Job 20:5; Prov 19:9; Zech 1:4
12:20 Prov 2:10; 26:24–26
☆**12:21** Ps 121:7; Prov 1:33; 1 Pet 3:13
12:22 Eccles 5:2; Isa 19:21
12:23 Prov 10:14; 13:16
12:24 Prov 12:11; 14:11; 22:29
12:25 Prov 15:13; 17:22
12:26 Prov 6:21; 12:15; 18:15
12:27 Prov 10:4; 13:4
☆**12:28** Prov 8:35; 9:11; Ezek 18:9, 20; Rom 5:21
13:1 Prov 10:1; 15:20
13:3 Prov 10:19; 18:7, 21; 20:19; 21:23; Jas 3:2
☆**13:4** Prov 12:11, 24; 14:11; 22:29
13:5 Prov 3:35; 12:5, 13
13:6 Ps 15:3; 119:163; Prov 2:20–22; 6:15; 11:3
☆**13:7** Prov 11:24; Lk 12:20, 21; 2 Cor 6:10; Jas 2:5

12:16 *a prudent man covereth shame,* i.e., a man who has been insulted by a fool should not pick up the insult, for the insult will do him no harm but anger, resentment, and heat will do what the insult in itself cannot do.
12:21 The surest protection against evil and temptation is the life of piety. The pious will not be overcome by temptation, and they will work for good. On the other hand, the wicked delight in mischief, from which comes their misery and the absence of divine protection when the storms of life assail them.
12:28 The proverbist concludes again by assuring men that true religion has right reason and equity on its side. Therefore, righteousness provides satisfaction and leaves one pleasant and comfortable. In this way of righteousness, there is life and not death.
13:4 Misery and shame attend the lazy; happiness and honor come to the diligent. Choose wisely and well!
13:7 He who has little pretends to have much and lives as though he did. This hurts the family and brings reproach on God whom he professes to believe in. The other man has much, but pretends that he has little. He lives a miserly life and chooses to bury his wealth rather than use it. His pretense shows lack of gratitude to God as he fails to use what God has given—an injustice to his loved ones who suffer under his meanness, and a lack of charity toward the poor whom he could easily help. Both attitudes are wrong.

8 The ransom of a man's life *are* his riches: but the poor heareth not
rebuke.
9 The light of the righteous rejoiceth: but the lamp of the wicked shall be
put out.
10 Only by pride cometh contention: but with the well advised *is* wisdom.
11 Wealth *gotten* by vanity shall be diminished: but he that gathereth by
labour shall increase.

13:9 Job 18:5; 29:3 Ps 19:7, 8 Prov 4:18; 24:20
13:10 Prov 12:15 17:14; 19:20
13:11☆

10. The Source of Hope

12 Hope deferred maketh the heart sick: but *when* the desire cometh, *it is*
a tree of life.
13 Whoso despiseth the word shall be destroyed: but he that feareth the
commandment shall be rewarded.
14 The law of the wise *is* a fountain of life, to depart from the snares of
death.
15 Good understanding giveth favour: but the way of transgressors *is*
hard.
16 Every prudent *man* dealeth with knowledge: but a fool layeth open *his*
folly.
17 A wicked messenger falleth into mischief: but a faithful ambassador *is*
health.
18 Poverty and shame *shall be to* him that refuseth instruction: but he that
regardeth reproof shall be honoured.
19 The desire accomplished is sweet to the soul: but *it is* abomination to
fools to depart from evil.
20 He that walketh with wise *men* shall be wise: but a companion of fools
shall be destroyed.
21 Evil pursueth sinners: but to the righteous good shall be repayed.
22 A good *man* leaveth an inheritance to his children's children: and the
wealth of the sinner *is* laid up for the just.
23 Much food *is in* the tillage of the poor: but there is *that is* destroyed for
want of judgment.
24 He that spareth his rod hateth his son: but he that loveth him
chasteneth him betimes.
25 The righteous eateth to the satisfying of his soul: but the belly of the
wicked shall want.

13:12☆ Prov 10:28
13:13 2 Chron 36:16 Prov 1:25, 30
13:14 Prov 8:8 10:11, 21
13:15 Ps 111:10 Prov 3:4; 8:35
13:16 Prov 16:1, 9 27:1
13:17 Prov 26:6
13:18 Prov 15:5, 32 23:12
13:19 Prov 13:12
13:20☆ Prov 2:20
13:21 Ps 32:10 Prov 11:31 Isa 3:10; 47:11
13:22 Ezra 9:12 Ps 37:25 Prov 28:8
13:24☆ Prov 19:18 22:15; 23:13 Heb 12:6
13:25☆ Ps 34:10 Prov 10:3

11. The Righteous and Unrighteous Contrasted

14 EVERY wise woman buildeth her house: but the foolish plucketh it
down with her hands.

14:1 Prov 12:4; 21:9 27:15; 31:10

13:11 The wealth of the man who got it wickedly has a curse attached to it, and he who has secured his wealth wrongly is likely to spend it in equally sinful ways. It will be taken from him at last. Wealth of honest men, accumulated by industry and honesty, will increase, and this man gives to him who has need and is blessed by God.

13:12 *Hope.* There can be no hope unless there is also *a desire for that which one wants.* Along with desire there must be expectancy. The absence of either of these elements means true hope is not present. *when the desire cometh, it is a tree of life,* i.e., "but when dreams come true at last, there is life and joy" (TLB), or, "but a desire fulfilled is a tree of life" (RSV).

13:20 A man is known by the company he keeps. Good men do not keep company with bad men (that is, make them their intimate friends) lest they be contaminated. The wise will walk with the wise and each will improve the other. To consort with evildoers is a form of debauchery.

13:24 Parents are enjoined to (1) love their children (Tit. 2:4), (2) bring them to Christ (Matt.19:13, 14), (3) train them up for God (22:6; Eph. 1:4), (4) instruct them in God's Word (Deut. 4:9; 11:19; Isa 38:19), (5) bless them (Gen. 48:15; Heb. 11:21), (6) discipline them (13:24), (7) provide for them (2 Cor. 12:14; 1 Tim. 5:8), and (8) not treat them shabbily or provoke them (Eph. 6:4; Col. 3:21).

13:25 Paraphrased: "The good man eats to live, while the evil man lives to eat."†

2 He that walketh in his uprightness feareth the LORD: but *he that is*
perverse in his ways despiseth him.
3 In the mouth of the foolish *is* a rod of pride: but the lips of the wise shall
preserve them.
4 Where no oxen *are*, the crib *is* clean: but much increase *is* by the
strength of the ox.
5 A faithful witness will not lie: but a false witness will utter lies.
6 A scorner seeketh wisdom, and *findeth it* not: but knowledge *is* easy
unto him that understandeth.
7 Go from the presence of a foolish man, when thou perceivest not *in him*
the lips of knowledge.
8 The wisdom of the prudent *is* to understand his way: but the folly of
fools *is* deceit.
9 Fools make a mock at sin: but among the righteous *there is* favour.
10 The heart knoweth his own bitterness; and a stranger doth not
intermeddle with his joy.
11 The house of the wicked shall be overthrown: but the tabernacle of the
upright shall flourish.
12 There is a way which seemeth right unto a man, but the end thereof *are*
the ways of death.
13 Even in laughter the heart is sorrowful; and the end of that mirth *is*
heaviness.
14 The backslider in heart shall be filled with his own ways: and a good
man *shall be satisfied* from himself.
15 The simple believeth every word: but the prudent *man* looketh well to
his going.
16 A wise *man* feareth, and departeth from evil: but the fool rageth, and is
confident.
17 *He that is* soon angry dealeth foolishly: and a man of wicked devices is
hated.
18 The simple inherit folly: but the prudent are crowned with knowledge.
19 The evil bow before the good; and the wicked at the gates of the
righteous.

12. Poverty

20 The poor is hated even of his own neighbour: but the rich *hath* many
friends.
21 He that despiseth his neighbour sinneth: but he that hath mercy on the
poor, happy *is* he.
22 Do they not err that devise evil? but mercy and truth *shall be* to them
that devise good.
23 In all labour there is profit: but the talk of the lips *tendeth* only to
penury.
24 The crown of the wise *is* their riches: *but* the foolishness of fools *is* folly.

☆**14:2** Ps 23:2, 3; 92:15
☆**14:3** Prov 24:7, 9; 26:9
14:5 Prov 14:25; 19:9; Rev 3:14
14:6 Prov 9:7, 8; 15:12, 14
14:7 Prov 9:6; 23:9
14:8 Prov 1:22; 10:8; 12:15; 18:2; 28:26
14:9 Ps 16:3; Prov 10:23
14:11 Prov 12:7, 11; 13:11; 22:29
14:12 Prov 16:25; Rom 6:21
14:13 Eccles 2:1
14:14 Prov 1:31; 12:14, 21
☆**14:15**
14:16 Prov 22:3; 27:12
14:17 Prov 12:16; 14:29; 19:19; 22:24, 25
14:18 Prov 3:35; 14:24; 16:22
14:19 1 Sam 2:36; Prov 11:29
☆**14:20** Prov 10:15; 19:4, 7
14:21 Ps 41:1; Prov 19:17; 28:8
14:22 Prov 12:2; Gal 6:7
14:23 Prov 12:11, 24; 14:11; 20:13; 28:19
14:24 Prov 14:18; 16:22

14:2 Grace and sin are here painted in their true colors. When grace reigns, there is reverence of God; when sin reigns, God is despised. The good man walks in uprightness; the wicked man walks in perversities.
14:3 It is better to be thought wise by being silent than to open the mouth and leave no doubt about one's folly.
14:15 It is foolish to believe all the stories that float around, however probable they may appear. Those who believe everything they hear forget that "all men, in some sense, are liars in comparison with God, all of whose words we can believe with an implicit faith, for he cannot lie."*
14:20 The world frowns on the poor, who are thought to be hardly worthy of respect. When God is our friend, he will not desert us if we are poor. Better poverty with the friendship of God than riches without it. On the other hand, everyone wishes to be a friend of the rich. Governed by self-interest, the friends of the rich expect to get something out of that friendship. Whoever makes the world his god will seek those who have most of this world's goods.

14:25 Prov 14:5, 21:28 **14:26** Ps 34:7 Prov 3:7, 8, 24–26; 18:10 19:23 **14:27** Prov 13:14 **14:28**☆ 1 Kgs 4:20 Jer 31:27 **14:29** Prov 16:32 19:11; 29:11 Jas 1:19 **14:31** Ps 12:5 Prov 14:21 17:5; 22:2, 16 Eccles 5:8 **14:32** Ps 14:6 2 Cor 1:9 **14:33** Prov 1:20; 8:4 **14:34** Deut 4:6 28:1, 15 Ps 107:34

25 A true witness delivereth souls: but a deceitful *witness* speaketh lies.
26 In the fear of the LORD *is* strong confidence: and his children shall have
a place of refuge.
27 The fear of the LORD *is* a fountain of life, to depart from the snares of
death.
28 In the multitude of people *is* the king's honour: but in the want of
people *is* the destruction of the prince.
29 *He that is* slow to wrath *is* of great understanding: but *he that is* hasty
of spirit exalteth folly.
30 A sound heart *is* the life of the flesh: but envy the rottenness of the
bones.
31 He that oppresseth the poor reproacheth his Maker: but he that
honoureth him hath mercy on the poor.
32 The wicked is driven away in his wickedness: but the righteous hath
hope in his death.
33 Wisdom resteth in the heart of him that hath understanding: but *that
which is* in the midst of fools is made known.
34 Righteousness exalteth a nation: but sin *is* a reproach to any people.
35 The king's favour *is* toward a wise servant: but his wrath is *against* him
that causeth shame.

13. The Use of the Tongue

15:1☆ Judg 8:1–3 1 Sam 25:10–13 Prov 15:18 25:10, 15 **15:2** Prov 15:28 16:21 Eccles 12:10 **15:3** 1 Chron 29:17 Job 31:4; 34:21 Ps 139:8 Prov 5:21 Heb 4:13 **15:5** 1 Sam 2:25 Prov 10:1; 13:1 23:22 **15:6** Ps 112:3 Prov 8:21 **15:7** Ps 37:30 Prov 10:20 **15:8** Prov 15:29 21:27 Isa 1:11 **15:9, 10** Ps 1:6; 146:8, 9 Prov 4:18 **15:11**☆ 1 Sam 16:7 2 Chron 6:30 Job 26:6 Ps 139:1 Acts 1:24 **15:12** Prov 9:7; 13:1 19:25; 24:9

15 A SOFT answer turneth away wrath: but grievous words stir up
anger.
2 The tongue of the wise useth knowledge aright: but the mouth of fools
poureth out foolishness.
3 The eyes of the LORD *are* in every place, beholding the evil and the
good.
4 A wholesome tongue *is* a tree of life: but perverseness therein *is* a breach
in the spirit.
5 A fool despiseth his father's instruction: but he that regardeth reproof is
prudent.
6 In the house of the righteous *is* much treasure: but in the revenues of the
wicked is trouble.
7 The lips of the wise disperse knowledge: but the heart of the foolish
doeth not so.
8 The sacrifice of the wicked *is* an abomination to the LORD: but the
prayer of the upright *is* his delight.
9 The way of the wicked *is* an abomination unto the LORD: but he loveth
him that followeth after righteousness.
10 Correction *is* grievous unto him that forsaketh the way: *and* he that
hateth reproof shall die.
11 Hell and destruction *are* before the LORD: how much more then the
hearts of the children of men?
12 A scorner loveth not one that reproveth him: neither will he go unto the
wise.

14:28 A king who has no people is like a soldier who has no sword, a jockey who has no horse, or a driver who has no automobile.

15:1 "Reason will be better spoken, and a righteous cause better pleaded, with meekness than with passion; hard arguments do best with soft words."* Soft and temperate speech is the mark of the sanctified heart. When men speak softly, the listener is not apt to take offense. Upbraiding people and calling them foul names produces anger. If people are offended when our speech is peaceable and mild, that is unfortunate. We cannot help it. But if they are offended because we are caustic, bitter, and contumacious, we have no one to blame but ourselves.

15:11 *Hell and destruction* in the Hebrew is *Sheol and Abaddon. Abaddon* means destruction and is the name given to the fallen angel and king of the abyss in Rev. 9:11. For *Sheol* see note to Deut. 32:22.

14. The Glad Heart

13 A merry heart maketh a cheerful countenance: but by sorrow of the
heart the spirit is broken.
14 The heart of him that hath understanding seeketh knowledge: but the
mouth of fools feedeth on foolishness.
15 All the days of the afflicted *are* evil: but he that is of a merry heart *hath*
a continual feast.
16 Better *is* little with the fear of the LORD than great treasure and trouble
therewith.
17 Better *is* a dinner of herbs where love is, than a stalled ox and hatred
therewith.
18 A wrathful man stirreth up strife: but *he that is* slow to anger appeaseth
strife.
19 The way of the slothful *man is* as an hedge of thorns: but the way of the
righteous *is* made plain.
20 A wise son maketh a glad father: but a foolish man despiseth his
mother.

☆**15:13** Prov 17:22; 27:19; Eccles 8:1
15:14 Prov 12:26; 18:15
15:16 Ps 37:16; Prov 16:8; 28:6
15:17 Ps 133:1–3; Prov 17:1
☆**15:18** Prov 14:29; 16:28; 26:21; Eccles 10:4
15:19 Prov 22:13; 26:13
15:20 Prov 10:1; 29:3; 30:17

15. The Value of Counsel and Advice

21 Folly *is* joy to *him that is* destitute of wisdom: but a man of understand-
ing walketh uprightly.
22 Without counsel purposes are disappointed: but in the multitude of
counsellors they are established.
23 A man hath joy by the answer of his mouth: and a word *spoken* in due
season, how good *is it!*
24 The way of life *is* above to the wise, that he may depart from hell
beneath.
25 The LORD will destroy the house of the proud: but he will establish the
border of the widow.
26 The thoughts of the wicked *are* an abomination to the LORD: but *the*
words of the pure *are* pleasant words.
27 He that is greedy of gain troubleth his own house; but he that hateth
gifts shall live.
28 The heart of the righteous studieth to answer: but the mouth of the
wicked poureth out evil things.
29 The LORD *is* far from the wicked: but he heareth the prayer of the
righteous.
30 The light of the eyes rejoiceth the heart: *and* a good report maketh the
bones fat.
31 The ear that heareth the reproof of life abideth among the wise.

15:22 Prov 11:14; 24:6
15:23 Prov 12:14; 24:26; 25:11
15:24 Ps 139:24; Jer 21:8; Col 3:1, 2
☆**15:25** Ps 68:5; 146:9; Prov 14:11
15:26 Ps 64:6
15:27 Ex 23:8; Deut 16:19; Prov 20:21; 28:16
15:28 Prov 10:19, 32; 13:16; 16:23; 1 Pet 3:15
15:29 Ps 145:18; Prov 1:28; 15:8
15:30 Prov 13:9; 17:22; 25:25
☆**15:31** Prov 8:33; 13:18; 15:5; 23:12

15:13 A cheerful spirit that radiates the grace of God is a great ornament of religion. It gives lustre to the beauty of holiness. On the other hand, a melancholy believer is beset by a tyrannical master who breaks the spirit and renders one less fit in the service of God.
15:18 Anger may be sinful or justifiable, depending on the circumstances. In any event, the Scriptures say we are to be slow to anger. Sinful anger is a work of the flesh (Gal. 5:20). Examples of those who displayed sinful anger include: (1) Cain (Gen. 4:5, 6), (2) Balaam (Num. 22:27), (3) Jonah (Jon. 4:4), Herod (Matt. 2:16), and the Jews (Luke 4:28). Those who showed justifiable anger include (1) our Lord (Mark 3:5), (2) Moses (Exod. 11:8), (3) Nehemiah (Neh. 5:6). In Eph. 5:26 anger is validated; however, a caution is inserted—godly anger can become sinful if we nurse a grudge.
15:25 The proud magnify themselves and suppose they are autonomous beings. God delights to abase the proud; he ordinarily accomplishes this through his general providence. Pride is a sin that ruins many. The same God cares for and establishes the house of the poor widow who cannot defend herself. God protects the weak—his people—but he also delights in the rich who do not evidence pride but walk in obedience to the divine will.
15:31 The wise man will accept reproof and will associate with those who by their counsel and lives enable him to see what is wrong with him.

32 He that refuseth instruction despiseth his own soul: but he that heareth
reproof getteth understanding.
33 The fear of the LORD *is* the instruction of wisdom; and before honour *is*
humility.

B. THE FEAR OF GOD AND OBEDIENCE

1. Doing Things God's Way

16 THE preparations of the heart in man, and the answer of the
tongue, *is* from the LORD.
2 All the ways of a man *are* clean in his own eyes; but the LORD weigheth
the spirits.
3 Commit thy works unto the LORD, and thy thoughts shall be estab-
lished.
4 The LORD hath made all *things* for himself: yea, even the wicked for the
day of evil.
5 Every one *that is* proud in heart *is* an abomination to the LORD: *though*
hand *join* in hand, he shall not be unpunished.
6 By mercy and truth iniquity is purged: and by the fear of the LORD *men*
depart from evil.
7 When a man's ways please the LORD, he maketh even his enemies to be
at peace with him.
8 Better *is* a little with righteousness than great revenues without right.
9 A man's heart deviseth his way: but the LORD directeth his steps.
10 A divine sentence *is* in the lips of the king: his mouth transgresseth not
in judgment.
11 A just weight and balance *are* the LORD'S: all the weights of the bag *are*
his work.

2. Wisdom Is Better than Gold

12 *It is* an abomination to kings to commit wickedness: for the throne is
established by righteousness.
13 Righteous lips *are* the delight of kings; and they love him that speaketh
right.
14 The wrath of a king *is as* messengers of death: but a wise man will
pacify it.
15 In the light of the king's countenance *is* life; and his favour *is* as a cloud
of the latter rain.
16 How much better *is it* to get wisdom than gold! and to get understand-
ing rather to be chosen than silver!
17 The highway of the upright *is* to depart from evil: he that keepeth his
way preserveth his soul.
18 Pride *goeth* before destruction, and an haughty spirit before a fall.
19 Better *it is to be* of an humble spirit with the lowly, than to divide the
spoil with the proud.

15:33 Job 28:28; Ps 34:11; Prov 1:7
16:1☆ Prov 16:9; 19:21; 20:24
16:2 Prov 21:2; 24:12
16:3 Ps 10:5; 19:11; 37:5; 55:22; Prov 3:6
16:4 Job 38:23; Eccles 3:11; Isa 43:7; 54:16
16:5 Prov 6:16, 17; 8:13; 11:21; Isa 3:11
16:6 Job 1:8; Prov 8:13; 14:27
16:7☆ 2 Chron 17:10; Prov 29:25
16:8 Prov 15:16; 21:6; Ps 37:16; 1 Tim 6:8
16:9☆ Ps 37:23; Prov 16:1; 19:21; 20:24
16:10 1 Kgs 3:28; Prov 20:8; 28:16; 29:4
16:11 Ps 37:28; 50:6; Prov 11:1
16:12 Prov 14:34; 25:5; 29:14
16:13 Prov 14:35; 22:11
16:14 Prov 19:12; 20:2; Eccles 10:4; Dan 3:13
16:16 Ps 119:127; Prov 3:14; 8:10, 19
16:18☆ Jer 49:16
16:19 Ps 147:6; Isa 57:15

16:1 Man is free to think and to act as he chooses. He can make his plans and determine to execute them. But God is the one who disposes. Man cannot go ahead on his own without divine assistance and the blessing of God. *God can nullify man's intentions and desires. For* example, Balaam determined in his heart to curse Israel, but the words from his tongue blessed them according to God's intentions.

16:7 God delights to turn our enemies into our friends. He controls the hearts and the spirits of men and works irresistibly upon them to acccomplish good for his people. It was God who made Abimelech to be Isaac's friend, and he moved the heart of Esau to be at peace with his brother Jacob.

16:9 He is no fool who, when he makes his plans for today or tomorrow, takes into account the divine factor that, "If the Lord will, we shall live, and do this, or that" (James 4:15).

16:18 Pride is a besetting sin that must be dealt with. Only two possibilities exist for it to be defeated: repentance or ruin.

20 He that handleth a matter wisely shall find good: and whoso trusteth in
the LORD, happy *is* he.
21 The wise in heart shall be called prudent: and the sweetness of the lips
increaseth learning.
22 Understanding *is* a wellspring of life unto him that hath it: but the
instruction of fools *is* folly.
23 The heart of the wise teacheth his mouth, and addeth learning to his
lips.
24 Pleasant words *are as* an honeycomb, sweet to the soul, and health to
the bones.

16:20 Ps 2:12; 34:8 Jer 17:7
16:21 Prov 8:14 10:13; 15:2 16:23
16:22 Prov 3:22 14:18, 24, 27
16:23 Ps 37:30 Prov 12:5 15:18, 28
16:24 Prov 4:22 15:26; 17:22 24:13

3. The Broad Road That Leads to Death

25 There is a way that seemeth right unto a man, but the end thereof *are*
the ways of death.
26 He that laboureth laboureth for himself; for his mouth craveth it of
him.
27 An ungodly man diggeth up evil: and in his lips *there is* as a burning
fire.
28 A froward man soweth strife: and a whisperer separateth chief friends.
29 A violent man enticeth his neighbour, and leadeth him into the way *that*
is not good.
30 He shutteth his eyes to devise froward things: moving his lips he
bringeth evil to pass.
31 The hoary head *is* a crown of glory, *if* it be found in the way of
righteousness.
32 *He that is* slow to anger *is* better than the mighty; and he that ruleth his
spirit than he that taketh a city.
33 The lot is cast into the lap; but the whole disposing thereof *is* of the
LORD.

16:26 Prov 14:23 Eccles 6:7
16:27 Jas 3:6
16:28 Prov 6:14, 19 18:8; 26:20
16:29 Prov 1:10 2:11, 12; 3:31 17:4
16:31 Mt 5:36
16:32 Prov 14:29 15:18; 19:11
☆**16:33** Num 26:55 Josh 18:5, 10

4. Good and Evil Speech

17 BETTER *is* a dry morsel, and quietness therewith, than an house
full of sacrifices *with* strife.
2 A wise servant shall have rule over a son that causeth shame, and shall
have part of the inheritance among the brethren.
3 The fining pot *is* for silver, and the furnace for gold: but the LORD trieth
the hearts.
4 A wicked doer giveth heed to false lips; *and* a liar giveth ear to a
naughty tongue.
5 Whoso mocketh the poor reproacheth his Maker: *and* he that is glad at
calamities shall not be unpunished.
6 Children's children *are* the crown of old men; and the glory of children
are their fathers.
7 Excellent speech becometh not a fool: much less do lying lips a prince.

☆**17:1** Ps 37:16 Prov 15:17; 21:9
17:3 1 Chron 29:17 Ps 26:2
17:4 Prov 1:10; 16:29
17:5 Job 31:29 Prov 14:31 24:17 Obad 17
17:6 Gen 48:11 Ps 127:3–5 Prov 13:22
17:7 Prov 12:22; 24:7

16:33 *The lot is cast into the lap.* Providence governs the result. The Westminster Confession defines providence this way: "God, the great Creator of all things, doth uphold, direct, dispose, and govern all creatures, actions and things, from the greatest even to the least, by His most wise and holy providence, according to His infallible foreknowledge, and the free and immutable counsel of His own will, to the praise of the glory of His wisdom, power, justice, goodness and mercy." Illustrations of God's providence include: preserving and providing for all creatures; determining the length of our days; ordaining the conditions and circumstances of men; directing the events of life; power over nature such as storms, hail, snow and frost; stopping the evil designs of men; and ordering even the smallest matters. Sometimes God's providence is dark and mysterious (Ps. 73:16; 77:19; Rom. 11:33).

17:1 "Love will sweeten a *dry morsel,* but strife will sour and embitter a house *full of sacrifices.* A little of the leaven of malice will leaven all the enjoyments."*

8 A gift *is as* a precious stone in the eyes of him that hath it: whitherso-
ever it turneth, it prospereth.
9 He that covereth a transgression seeketh love; but he that repeateth a
matter separateth *very* friends.
10 A reproof entereth more into a wise man than an hundred stripes into
a fool.
11 An evil *man* seeketh only rebellion: therefore a cruel messenger shall be
sent against him.
12 Let a bear robbed of her whelps meet a man, rather than a fool in his
folly.

17:8☆ Prov 21:14; Isa 1:23; Amos 5:12
17:9 Prov 10:12; 1 Cor 13:5
17:10 Prov 9:8; 13:1
17:11☆ Prov 10:32; 19:25
17:12 Prov 29:9; Hos 13:8

5. The Price of Wisdom

13 Whoso rewardeth evil for good, evil shall not depart from his house.
14 The beginning of strife *is as* when one letteth out water: therefore leave
off contention, before it be meddled with.
15 He that justifieth the wicked, and he that condemneth the just, even
they both *are* abomination to the LORD.
16 Wherefore *is there* a price in the hand of a fool to get wisdom, seeing *he
hath* no heart *to it?*
17 A friend loveth at all times, and a brother is born for adversity.
18 A man void of understanding striketh hands, *and* becometh surety in
the presence of his friend.
19 He loveth transgression that loveth strife: *and* he that exalteth his gate
seeketh destruction.
20 He that hath a froward heart findeth no good: and he that hath a
perverse tongue falleth into mischief.
21 He that begetteth a fool *doeth it* to his sorrow: and the father of a fool
hath no joy.
22 A merry heart doeth good *like* a medicine: but a broken spirit drieth
the bones.
23 A wicked *man* taketh a gift out of the bosom to pervert the ways of
judgment.
24 Widsom *is* before him that hath understanding; but the eyes of a fool
are in the ends of the earth.
25 A foolish son *is* a grief to his father, and bitterness to her that bare him.
26 Also to punish the just *is* not good, *nor* to strike princes for equity.
27 He that hath knowledge spareth his words: *and* a man of understanding
is of an excellent spirit.
28 Even a fool, when he holdeth his peace, is counted wise: *and* he that
shutteth his lips *is esteemed* a man of understanding.

17:13 Prov 13:21; Jer 18:20
17:14 Prov 20:3; 25:8
17:15 Prov 24:24
17:17 Ruth 1:16; Prov 18:24
17:18 Prov 6:1; 11:15; 22:26
17:19 Prov 13:2; 29:22, 23
17:21 Prov 10:1; 17:25; 19:13
17:22 Prov 15:13
17:23 Ex 23:8; Eccles 7:7
17:24 Prov 3:21; 4:7
17:25 Prov 10:1
17:26 Prov 18:5
17:27 Job 13:5; Prov 10:19; Jas 1:19

6. Foolish and Wise Words

18 THROUGH desire a man, having separated himself, seeketh *and*
intermeddleth with all wisdom.
2 A fool hath no delight in understanding, but that his heart may discover
itself.

18:1 Prov 1:31
18:2 Prov 1:29; 23:23

17:8 *gift,* i.e., "bribe" (NIV, RSV). *It is quite true that a bribe may bring about prosperity*. But nowhere do the Scriptures encourage bribery. In fact, this act is called a sin.
17:11 *a cruel messenger shall be sent against him,* i.e., "they shall be severely punished." To render evil for evil is a fault, but to render evil for good is of the *devil.* The man who renders evil for good commits a heinous crime and shall reap as he has sown. The punishment shall equal the crime and shall affect not only the culprit but also his whole house, perhaps for generations. David rewarded Uriah evil for his service to the king; as a result, the sword never departed from David's house.

3 When the wicked cometh, *then* cometh also contempt, and with
ignominy reproach.
4 The words of a man's mouth *are as* deep waters, *and* the wellspring of
wisdom *as* a flowing brook.
5 *It is* not good to accept the person of the wicked, to overthrow the
righteous in judgment.
6 A fool's lips enter into contention, and his mouth calleth for strokes.
7 A fool's mouth *is* his destruction, and his lips *are* the snare of his soul.
8 The words of a talebearer *are* as wounds, and they go down into the
innermost parts of the belly.
9 He also that is slothful in his work is brother to him that is a great
waster.
10 The name of the LORD *is* a strong tower: the righteous runneth into it,
and is safe.
11 The rich man's wealth *is* his strong city, and as an high wall in his own
conceit.
12 Before destruction the heart of man is haughty, and before honour *is*
humility.
13 He that answereth a matter before he heareth *it*, it *is* folly and shame
unto him.
14 The spirit of a man will sustain his infirmity; but a wounded spirit who
can bear?
15 The heart of the prudent getteth knowledge; and the ear of the wise
seeketh knowledge.
16 A man's gift maketh room for him, and bringeth him before great men.
17 *He that is* first in his own cause *seemeth* just; but his neighbour cometh
and searcheth him.
18 The lot causeth contentions to cease, and parteth between the mighty.
19 A brother offended *is harder to be won* than a strong city: and *their*
contentions *are* like the bars of a castle.
20 A man's belly shall be satisfied with the fruit of his mouth; *and* with the
increase of his lips shall he be filled.
21 Death and life *are* in the power of the tongue: and they that love it shall
eat the fruit thereof.
22 *Whoso* findeth a wife findeth a good *thing*, and obtaineth favour of the
LORD.
23 The poor useth intreaties; but the rich answereth roughly.
24 A man *that hath* friends must shew himself friendly: and there is a
friend *that* sticketh closer than a brother.

7. The Poor and Lending to Them

19 BETTER *is* the poor that walketh in his integrity, than *he that is*
perverse in his lips, and is a fool.
2 Also, *that* the soul *be* without knowledge, *it is* not good; and he that
hasteth with *his* feet sinneth.
3 The foolishness of man perverteth his way: and his heart fretteth against
the LORD.

18:4 Prov 20:5
18:5 Prov 17:15 24:23
18:6 Prov 10:14; 13:3
☆**18:7**
18:8 Lev 19:16 Prov 11:13
18:10 2 Sam 22:2 Ps 18:2; 61:3 91:2 Prov 29:25
18:11 Ps 49:6 Prov 10:15
18:12 Prov 11:2 16:18; 29:23
18:13 Prov 20:25 Jn 7:51
18:15 Prov 12:26 15:14; 23:23
18:16 Gen 32:20 1 Sam 25:27 Prov 17:8
☆**18:17**
18:18 Prov 16:33
18:19 2 Cor 6:3
18:21 Prov 13:3 Mt 12:37
18:22 Prov 12:4 19:14; 31:10–31
18:23 2 Chron 10:13 Prov 19:7 Jas 2:3
☆**18:24** Prov 14:20 19:4, 6
19:1 Prov 11:18 13:7; 20:7
19:2 Prov 18:13 20:25
19:3 Isa 8:21

18:7 An ungoverned and ungovernable tongue is a mischievous tongue. Whoever has one is a fool. By our words we are justified or condemned. Let our speech be seasoned with salt and give to every man a restrained, careful, and solicitous word.
18:17 The plaintiff in any case of law speaks only that which will help his case. Let him be examined by the defendant who can present his side. A judge has two ears to hear both sides before judgment is pronounced.
18:24 Sometimes a friend will be of more help than a brother. Jesus Christ is the sinner's best friend, and he sticks closer to us than any brother.

4Wealth maketh many friends; but the poor is separated from his
neighbour.
5A false witness shall not be unpunished, and *he that* speaketh lies shall
not escape.
6Many will intreat the favour of the prince: and every man *is* a friend to
him that giveth gifts.
7All the brethren of the poor do hate him: how much more do his friends
go far from him? he pursueth *them with* words, *yet* they *are* wanting *to him.*
8He that getteth wisdom loveth his own soul: he that keepeth under-
standing shall find good.
9A false witness shall not be unpunished, and *he that* speaketh lies shall
perish.
10Delight is not seemly for a fool; much less for a servant to have rule
over princes.
11The discretion of a man deferreth his anger; and *it is* his glory to pass
over a transgression.
12The king's wrath *is* as the roaring of a lion; but his favour *is* as dew
upon the grass.
13A foolish son *is* the calamity of his father: and the contentions of a wife
are a continual dropping.
14House and riches *are* the inheritance of fathers: and a prudent wife *is*
from the LORD.
15Slothfulness casteth into a deep sleep; and an idle soul shall suffer
hunger.
16He that keepeth the commandment keepeth his own soul; *but* he that
despiseth his ways shall die.
17He that hath pity upon the poor lendeth unto the LORD; and that which
he hath given will he pay him again.

8. Counsel and Instruction

18Chasten thy son while there is hope, and let not thy soul spare for his
crying.
19A man of great wrath shall suffer punishment: for if thou deliver *him,*
yet thou must do it again.
20Hear counsel, and receive instruction, that thou mayest be wise in thy
latter end.
21*There are* many devices in a man's heart; nevertheless the counsel of the
LORD, that shall stand.
22The desire of a man *is* his kindness: and a poor man *is* better than a
liar.
23The fear of the LORD *tendeth* to life: and *he that hath it* shall abide
satisfied; he shall not be visited with evil.
24A slothful *man* hideth his hand in *his* bosom, and will not so much as
bring it to his mouth again.

19:4 Prov 14:20; 18:24
19:5 Ex 23:1; Deut 19:16–19; Prov 19:9
19:6 Prov 18:16; 29:26
19:7 Ps 38:11; Prov 4:20; 18:23
19:8 Prov 16:20; 8:35, 36
19:9 Prov 19:5
19:10 Prov 26:1; Eccles 10:6
19:11 Prov 14:29; 16:32; Col 4:6
19:12 Gen 27:28; Prov 16:14, 15; 20:2
19:13 Prov 12:4; 15:20; 17:25; 21:9, 19
19:14 Prov 18:22
19:15☆ Prov 6:9; 16:26; 24:33
19:16 Prov 16:17; Lk 10:28; 11:28
19:17☆ Deut 15:7; Prov 14:31; 28:27; Lk 6:38
19:18 Prov 13:24; Heb 12:6
19:19 Prov 12:16; 14:17; 15:18; Eccles 7:9
19:20 Prov 4:1; 8:33; 12:15; 18:15
19:21☆ Prov 16:1, 9
19:23 Ps 25:13; Prov 14:27; 22:3; 1 Tim 4:8
19:24☆

19:15 Indolence stupifies a man and makes him careless about his affairs. It is as if he is cast into a deep sleep, dreaming away the hours when he should have been busily at work. Idleness brings a man to poverty and want. That is why those who will not labor are not to eat. This is no indictment against anyone *who is industrious yet lacks* work to do. Provision for such a one is made by the charity of those who have more of this world's goods than they need to keep themselves.

19:17 This verse speaks of charity, which springs from a heart of compassion. The poor and the hungry should be objects of our care and concern. When we aid such people it is as if we have made a loan to God himself. But it is not here spoken of as a loan without interest. Rather, the Word says that God will repay all we give, with interest. Thus, charity is a wise investment that pays off well in this life or in the life to come.

19:21 The counsels of God stand sure. Whoever seeks to annul what God has intended will be defeated in due season.

19:24 The NIV and RSV translate the phrase *in his bosom,* as *in the dish.* In either event the conclusion is the same: a slothful man would rather starve than stir.

25 Smite a scorner, and the simple will beware: and reprove one that hath
understanding, *and* he will understand knowledge.
26 He that wasteth *his* father, *and* chaseth away *his* mother, *is* a son that
causeth shame, and bringeth reproach.
27 Cease, my son, to hear the instruction *that causeth* to err from the words
of knowledge.
28 An ungodly witness scorneth judgment: and the mouth of the wicked
devoureth iniquity.
29 Judgments are prepared for scorners, and stripes for the back of fools.

19:25 Prov 9:7, 8 19:29; 21:11
19:26 Prov 20:20
19:28 Job 15:16 Prov 6:12
19:29 Prov 9:12 19:9, 25; 26:3

9. Honesty Better than Cheating

20 WINE *is* a mocker, strong drink *is* raging: and whosoever is
deceived thereby is not wise.
2 The fear of a king *is* as the roaring of a lion: *whoso* provoketh him to
anger sinneth *against* his own soul.
3 *It is* an honour for a man to cease from strife: but every fool will be
meddling.
4 The sluggard will not plow by reason of the cold; *therefore* shall he beg
in harvest, and *have* nothing.
5 Counsel in the heart of man *is like* deep water; but a man of under-
standing will draw it out.
6 Most men will proclaim every one his own goodness: but a faithful man
who can find?
7 The just *man* walketh in his integrity: his children *are* blessed after him.
8 A king that sitteth in the throne of judgment scattereth away all evil
with his eyes.
9 Who can say, I have made my heart clean, I am pure from my sin?
10 Divers weights, *and* divers measures, both of them *are* alike abomina-
tion to the LORD.
11 Even a child is known by his doings, whether his work *be* pure, and
whether *it be* right.
12 The hearing ear, and the seeing eye, the LORD hath made even both of
them.
13 Love not sleep, lest thou come to poverty; open thine eyes, *and* thou
shalt be satisfied with bread.
14 *It is* naught, *it is* naught, saith the buyer: but when he is gone his way,
then he boasteth.

☆**20:1** Prov 31:4 Isa 5:22; 56:12
20:2 1 Kgs 2:23 Prov 16:14 19:12
20:3 Prov 14:29 16:32; 19:11
20:5 Prov 18:4
20:6 Prov 12:1 Prov 25:14 Mt 6:2 Lk 18:8, 11
20:7 Ps 37:26; 112:2
20:8 Prov 16:12 18:13; 23:23 29:14
20:9 2 Chron 6:36 Job 14:4
☆**20:10** Prov 11:1; 20:23
20:11 Mt 7:16 Prov 21:8
20:12 Ex 4:11
20:13 Prov 6:9, 10 19:15; 24:32, 33
☆**20:14**

10. The Evil of a Fortune Gotten by Cheating

15 There is gold, and a multitude of rubies: but the lips of knowledge *are*
a precious jewel.
16 Take his garment that is surety *for* a stranger: and take a pledge of him
for a strange woman.

20:15 Prov 3:13–15
20:16 Ex 22:26 Prov 6:1–5

20:1 Everywhere the Scriptures forbid drunkeness, which makes men unfit for society. Their speech often becomes abusive and their actions stupid. Alcohol makes a fool out of a man; it is a deceiver. Nowhere do the Scriptures speak of alcoholism as a disease. It is a sin, for God forbids drunkeness. It is one of several diseases that men bring upon themselves. He who does not drink will never become an alcoholic. Abstinence is a surer guarantee than temperance, although the use of wine is not prohibited in the Scriptures.

20:10 *Divers weights, and divers measures,* i.e., "every kind of cheating."†

20:14 The sinful nature of man can be seen in his buying and selling. The seller overvalues his goods and the buyer underestimates their value. The latter presses the seller as hard as he can to drive a hard bargain. When the buyer pushes the seller down to the lowest price at which he will sell and still make a profit, he goes home to crow about the excellent bargain he got. The rapacious nature of men is such that the one wants as much as he can get and the other wants to buy at the lowest possible price. The principle of neighbor-love would dictate a fair price to buy at and a fair profit for the seller.

20:17 Prov 5:4; 9:17, 18; 15:27; 20:10, 21; 23:8
20:18 Prov 11:14; 15:22; Lk 14:31
20:19 Ps 15:3; Prov 11:13; 6:28
20:20 Ex 21:17; Lev 20:9; Prov 19:26; 30:11; Mt 15:4
20:21 Prov 15:27; 28:16
20:22☆ Ps 27:14; Prov 17:23; 24:28, 29; Mt 5:39; Rom 12:17
20:23☆ Prov 11:1; 20:10
20:24 Gen 50:20; 1 Kgs 12:15; Ps 37:23
20:25 Eccles 5:4, 5
20:26 Prov 20:8, 30
20:27☆ Prov 21:2
20:28 Prov 29:14
20:29 Prov 16:31

17 Bread of deceit *is* sweet to a man; but afterwards his mouth shall be
filled with gravel.
18 *Every* purpose is established by counsel: and with good advice make
war.
19 He that goeth about *as* a talebearer revealeth secrets: therefore meddle
not with him that flattereth with his lips.
20 Whoso curseth his father or his mother, his lamp shall be put out in
obscure darkness.
21 An inheritance *may be* gotten hastily at the beginning; but the end
thereof shall not be blessed.
22 Say not thou, I will recompense evil; *but* wait on the LORD, and he shall
save thee.
23 Divers weights *are* an abomination unto the LORD; and a false balance
is not good.
24 Man's goings *are* of the LORD; how can a man then understand his own
way?
25 *It is* a snare to the man *who* devoureth *that which is* holy, and after vows
to make inquiry.
26 A wise king scattereth the wicked, and bringeth the wheel over them.
27 The spirit of man *is* the candle of the LORD, searching all the inward
parts of the belly.
28 Mercy and truth preserve the king: and his throne is upholden by
mercy.
29 The glory of young men *is* their strength: and the beauty of old men *is*
the gray head.
30 The blueness of a wound cleanseth away evil: so *do* stripes the inward
parts of the belly.

11. Men Are Known by Their Actions

21:1 Ezra 6:21, 22; Prov 16:1, 9
21:2 Prov 16:2; 24:11, 12; Lk 16:15
21:3 Ps 50:8, 9; Prov 15:8
21:4☆ Prov 6:17; 30:13; Lk 11:34
21:5 Prov 14:23; 28:19, 20
21:6 Prov 10:2; 13:11

21 THE king's heart *is* in the hand of the LORD, *as* the rivers of water:
he turneth it whithersoever he will.
2 Every way of a man *is* right in his own eyes: but the LORD pondereth the
hearts.
3 To do justice and judgment *is* more acceptable to the LORD than
sacrifice.
4 An high look, and a proud heart, *and* the plowing of the wicked, *is* sin.
5 The thoughts of the diligent *tend* only to plenteousness; but of every one
that is hasty only to want.
6 The getting of treasures by a lying tongue *is* a vanity tossed to and fro of
them that seek death.
7 The robbery of the wicked shall destroy them; because they refuse to do
judgment.

20:22 Every believer will, at some time or other, be wrongly treated and thus have a legitimate grievance against the one who has done evil to him. How then shall he act? Herein we learn that it is wrong to recompense evil with evil. We must never do anything for which we cannot in good faith pray to God for help. Rather, we should wait for the Lord and let him reward the evildoer.

20:23 See note to 20:10.

20:27 The spirit God placed in man gives him light so that he can gauge the rightness of his thoughts and motives and by volition make prudent decisions. Through man's spirit, when regenerated, there lies the possibility of attaining the purposes for which God created him.

21:4 Pride is a grave sin everywhere condemned in the Scriptures (6:16, 17; 16:5; 1 Sam. 2:3; Ps. 131:1; 101:5). Pride is said to be a besetting sin of: (1) false teachers (1 Tim. 6:3, 4), (2) the wicked (Hab. 2:4, 5; Rom. 1:30), (3) Satan (1 Tim. 3:6), and (4) lovers of this world (1 John 2:16). Pride produces anger, quarrelsomeness toward others, and deceiving of self (21:24; 28:25; Jer. 49:16). It lead to punishment, debasement, and disgrace (11:2; 29:23; Zeph. 2:10-11). God resists the proud (James 4:6; 1 Pet. 5:5) and sends judgment on them.

8 The way of man *is* froward and strange: but *as for* the pure, his work *is*
right.
9 *It is* better to dwell in a corner of the housetop, than with a brawling
woman in a wide house.
10 The soul of the wicked desireth evil: his neighbour findeth no favour in
his eyes.
11 When the scorner is punished, the simple is made wise: and when the
wise is instructed, he receiveth knowledge.
12 The righteous *man* wisely considereth the house of the wicked: *but God*
overthroweth the wicked for *their* wickedness.

12. The Acts of the Godly

13 Whoso stoppeth his ears at the cry of the poor, he also shall cry himself,
but shall not be heard.
14 A gift in secret pacifieth anger: and a reward in the bosom strong
wrath.
15 *It is* joy to the just to do judgment: but destruction *shall be* to the
workers of iniquity.
16 The man that wandereth out of the way of understanding shall remain
in the congregation of the dead.
17 He that loveth pleasure *shall be* a poor man: he that loveth wine and oil
shall not be rich.
18 The wicked *shall be* a ransom for the righteous, and the transgressor for
the upright.
19 *It is* better to dwell in the wilderness, than with a contentious and an
angry woman.
20 *There is* treasure to be desired and oil in the dwelling of the wise; but a
foolish man spendeth it up.
21 He that followeth after righteousness and mercy findeth life, righteous-
ness, and honour.
22 A wise *man* scaleth the city of the mighty, and casteth down the
strength of the confidence thereof.
23 Whoso keepeth his mouth and his tongue keepeth his soul from
troubles.
24 Proud *and* haughty scorner *is* his name, who dealeth in proud wrath.
25 The desire of the slothful killeth him; for his hands refuse to labour.
26 He coveteth greedily all the day long: but the righteous giveth and
spareth not.
27 The sacrifice of the wicked *is* abomination: how much more, *when* he
bringeth it with a wicked mind?
28 A false witness shall perish: but the man that heareth speaketh
constantly.

21:8 Prov 20:11
21:9 Prov 19:13; 21:19
21:11 Prov 9:9; 15:14; 19:25
☆**21:13** Prov 24:11, 12; Mt 18:30–34; Lk 16:19–31; 1 Jn 3:17
21:14 Prov 17:8; 19:6
21:15 Prov 10:29; 28:5
21:16 Ps 49:14; 125:4, 5
21:17 Prov 23:19–21
☆**21:18** Prov 11:8; Isa 43:3, 4
21:19 Prov 19:13; 21:9
☆**21:20** Prov 8:21; Eccles 5:19, 20
21:21 Prov 2:10, 21; 3:16; 11:19
21:22 2 Sam 5:6–9; Prov 24:5; Eccles 9:15
21:23 Prov 13:3; 18:7, 21; Jas 3:2
21:24 Ps 1:1; Prov 13:1; 14:6; 19:29
☆**21:25** Ps 37:26; 112:5; Prov 10:4; 12:24
☆**21:26**
21:27 Ps 50:9; Prov 15:8
21:28 Prov 19:9

21:13 *Some believers are* lacking in charity. They close their ears to the cry of the poor, refusing to give them a hearing, turning them away from their doors, and forbidding them to come near. They shut up their bowels of compassion. God says that such people will come to a place where they have needs and they shall not be heard either. Just retribution comes at last. God will be deaf to the entreaties of those who are deaf to the entreaties of the poor.
21:18 *The wicked shall be a ransom for the righteous,* i.e., "The wicked will finally lose; the righteous will finally win."†
21:20 *There is a treasure to be desired and oil in the dwelling of the wise,* i.e., "The wise man saves for the future."†
21:25, 26 The slothful refuse to work even though they are able to do so. Though they refuse to work, their hearts do not cease to covet riches and pleasures. They expect everybody to do for them what they will not do for themselves. The righteous and the industrious work to feed themselves and freely give of their surplus for the aid of the poor. Nowhere do the Scriptures say believers are to feed the slothful; they are enjoined to help those who are genuinely poor through no fault of their own or lack of desire to labor.

21:29 Prov 11:20
21:30 Eccles 9:11; Isa 8:9; 14:27; Acts 5:38, 39
21:31 Ps 20:7; Isa 31:1–3; 1 Cor 15:57
22:1☆
22:2 Job 31:15; Prov 14:31; 29:13
22:3 Prov 14:15; 27:12
22:4 Prov 3:16; 4:4
22:5 Prov 13:9, 15
22:6☆ Ps 78:4; Eph 6:4
22:7 Prov 22:15; Jas 2:6
22:8 Job 4:8; Hos 8:7; 10:13; Prov 24:16
22:9 Prov 19:17; Lk 14:13; 2 Cor 9:6
22:10 Prov 24:9
22:11 Ps 24:4; Prov 14:35; 16:15; 22:29; Mt 5:8
22:13 Prov 26:13; Rom 12:11
22:14 Prov 5:3; 23:26; Eccles 7:26
22:15☆ Prov 13:24; 23:14
22:16☆ Job 20:19; Prov 14:31; 28:3; Zech 7:9
22:17 Prov 1:7; 2:1, 2; 8:33

29 A wicked man hardeneth his face: but *as for* the upright, he directeth
his way.
30 *There is* no wisdom nor understanding nor counsel against the LORD.
31 The horse *is* prepared against the day of battle: but safety *is* of the
LORD.

13. Choosing a Good Name

22 A *GOOD* name *is* rather to be chosen than great riches, *and* loving
favour rather than silver and gold.
2 The rich and poor meet together: the LORD *is* the maker of them all.
3 A prudent *man* foreseeth the evil, and hideth himself: but the simple
pass on, and are punished.
4 By humility *and* the fear of the LORD *are* riches, and honour, and life.
5 Thorns *and* snares *are* in the way of the froward: he that doth keep his
soul shall be far from them.
6 Train up a child in the way he should go: and when he is old, he will not
depart from it.
7 The rich ruleth over the poor, and the borrower *is* servant to the lender.
8 He that soweth iniquity shall reap vanity: and the rod of his anger shall
fail.
9 He that hath a bountiful eye shall be blessed; for he giveth of his bread
to the poor.
10 Cast out the scorner, and contention shall go out; yea, strife and
reproach shall cease.
11 He that loveth pureness of heart, *for* the grace of his lips the king *shall*
be his friend.
12 The eyes of the LORD preserve knowledge, and he overthroweth the
words of the transgressor.
13 The slothful *man* saith, *There is* a lion without, I shall be slain in the
streets.
14 The mouth of strange women *is* a deep pit: he that is abhorred of the
LORD shall fall therein.
15 Foolishness *is* bound in the heart of a child; *but* the rod of correction
shall drive it far from him.
16 He that oppresseth the poor to increase his *riches, and* he that giveth to
the rich, *shall* surely *come* to want.

IV. THE WORDS OF THE WISE (22:17—24:34)

A. LISTENING TO WISE ADVICE

17 Bow down thine ear, and hear the words of the wise, and apply thine
heart unto my knowledge.
18 For *it is* a pleasant thing if thou keep them within thee; they shall
withal be fitted in thy lips.

22:1 What good are wealth and position to the man who suffers from a bad reputation and who can find no one who loves him?

22:6 Parents and instructors are enjoined to train up their children. They are to be catechized, they are to be disciplined, they are to be shown the way they ought to go, *not the way they might seek to go of their own devising.* One hopes they will never depart from the way of righteousness they have been taught, but if they do, the parents and instructors at least will know they have done their duty and used the means.

22:15 Delinquency and youthful rebellion come naturally to young people because of original sin. They must be taught virtue and be provided with correction and discipline. No youngster has ever had to be taught to lie, cheat, or steal. They must be taught not to.

22:16 It is evil enough to leave the poor in their poverty. It is far worse to oppress them and take from them what little they have. Oppression that seeks to bring more wealth to the oppressor at the expense of the defenseless poor is contrary to the commandments of God. These wicked people will bribe the wealthy to curry their favor and to gain position and more wealth. Such sinners will come to want, whether it be in this life or in the life to come.

19 That thy trust may be in the LORD, I have made known to thee this day,
even to thee.
20 Have not I written to thee excellent things in counsels and knowledge,
21 That I might make thee know the certainty of the words of truth; that
thou mightest answer the words of truth to them that send unto thee?
22 Rob not the poor, because he *is* poor: neither oppress the afflicted in
the gate:
23 For the LORD will plead their cause, and spoil the soul of those that
spoiled them.
24 Make no friendship with an angry man; and with a furious man thou
shalt not go:
25 Lest thou learn his ways, and get a snare to thy soul.
26 Be not thou *one* of them that strike hands, *or* of them that are sureties
for debts.
27 If thou hast nothing to pay, why should he take away thy bed from
under thee?
28 Remove not the ancient landmark, which thy fathers have set.
29 Seest thou a man diligent in his business? he shall stand before kings;
he shall not stand before mean *men*.

☆**22:23**
22:24 Prov 1:15; 14:7 29:22
22:26 Ex 22:26 Prov 6:1–5 20:16
☆**22:28** Deut 19:14 27:17 Prov 23:10, 11
22:29 Prov 27:18

B. GLUTTONY

23 WHEN thou sittest to eat with a ruler, consider diligently what *is*
before thee:
2 And put a knife to thy throat, if thou *be* a man given to appetite.
3 Be not desirous of his dainties: for they *are* deceitful meat.
4 Labour not to be rich: cease from thine own wisdom.
5 Wilt thou set thine eyes upon that which is not? for *riches* certainly
make themselves wings; they fly away as an eagle toward heaven.
6 Eat thou not the bread of *him that hath* an evil eye, neither desire thou
his dainty meats:
7 For as he thinketh in his heart, so *is* he: Eat and drink, saith he to thee;
but his heart *is* not with thee.
8 The morsel *which* thou hast eaten shalt thou vomit up, and lose thy
sweet words.
9 Speak not in the ears of a fool: for he will despise the wisdom of thy
words.
10 Remove not the old landmark; and enter not into the fields of the
fatherless:
11 For their redeemer *is* mighty; he shall plead their cause with thee.
12 Apply thine heart unto instruction, and thine ears to the words of
knowledge.
13 Withhold not correction from the child: for *if* thou beatest him with the
rod, he shall not die.
14 Thou shalt beat him with the rod, and shalt deliver his soul from hell.

23:1 Ps 141:4 Prov 23:6 Eccles 7:7 Dan 1:5
23:4 Prov 15:27 27:23, 24; 28:20 Mt 6:19 1 Tim 6:17
23:6 Prov 1:15; 4:14 23:1
23:9 Prov 14:7; 24:7 26:4
23:10 Deut 19:14 27:17 Job 19:25 Prov 22:28 Jer 22:3 Zech 7:10
23:12 Prov 2:2; 5:1 22:17
☆**23:13** Prov 13:24 19:18; 29:15 1 Cor 5:5
☆**23:14**

22:23 Those who oppress the poor will discover that God is the friend of the poor and will avenge them. At the least God will repay oppressors in spiritual judgment as their souls are cursed. Thus such oppressors end up murdering themselves. The ultimate solution is not to legislate morality with the idea of forcing the rich to act in a certain way, but to change their inner lives by regeneration, which will profoundly change their outer lives as well.

22:28 *ancient landmark.* These were markers that set off one man's property from another. To move them was to steal land from a neighbor. Obviously there would have been no need for such a provision if no one were guilty of this sin.

23:13, 14 There is a difference between proper corporal punishment and child abuse. The latter is forever forbidden by the Scriptures. The former is appropriate when necessary. But it must always be done with a tender heart and never in a spurt of anger, in heartless revenge, or with the notion of doing physical damage to the child.

C. WISDOM, A FATHER'S DESIRE FOR HIS SON

15 My son, if thine heart be wise, my heart shall rejoice, even mine.
16 Yea, my reins shall rejoice, when thy lips speak right things.
17 Let not thine heart envy sinners: but *be thou* in the fear of the LORD all
the day long.
18 For surely there is an end; and thine expectation shall not be cut off.
19 Hear thou, my son, and be wise, and guide thine heart in the way.
20 Be not among winebibbers; among riotous eaters of flesh:
21 For the drunkard and the glutton shall come to poverty: and drowsi-
ness shall clothe *a man* with rags.
22 Hearken unto thy father that begat thee, and despise not thy mother
when she is old.
23 Buy the truth, and sell *it* not; *also* wisdom, and instruction, and
understanding.
24 The father of the righteous shall greatly rejoice: and he that begetteth a
wise *child* shall have joy of him.
25 Thy father and thy mother shall be glad, and she that bare thee shall
rejoice.
26 My son, give me thine heart, and let thine eyes observe my ways.
27 For a whore *is* a deep ditch; and a strange woman *is* a narrow pit.
28 She also lieth in wait as *for* a prey, and increaseth the transgressors
among men.
29 Who hath woe? who hath sorrow? who hath contentions? who hath
babbling? who hath wounds without cause? who hath redness of eyes?
30 They that tarry long at the wine; they that go to seek mixed wine.
31 Look not thou upon the wine when it is red, when it giveth his colour in
the cup, *when* it moveth itself aright.
32 At the last it biteth like a serpent, and stingeth like an adder.
33 Thine eyes shall behold strange women, and thine heart shall utter
perverse things.
34 Yea, thou shalt be as he that lieth down in the midst of the sea, or as he
that lieth upon the top of a mast.
35 They have stricken me, *shalt thou say, and* I was not sick; they have
beaten me, *and* I felt *it* not: when shall I awake? I will seek it yet again.

23:15 Prov 4:1; 10:1; 15:20; 27:11; 29:3
23:17☆ Ps 19:11; 37:1; 73:3; Prov 24:1, 14, 19
23:18☆
23:19
Prov 20:1; 23:29
23:22 Prov 13:1; 15:5; Deut 21:18
23:23 Prov 4:7; 15:14; 18:15; Mt 13:44
23:24 Prov 10:1; 23:15
23:26☆ Prov 6:26; 22:14; Eccles 7:26
23:29 Prov 20:1; 23:19; Isa 5:11, 22
23:31 Song 7:9
23:32 Ps 140:3; Isa 28:3, 7; 1 Cor 15:55, 56; Rev 9:5
23:35 Isa 56:12

D. WISDOM IN THE BALANCE

24 BE not thou envious against evil men, neither desire to be with
them.
2 For their heart studieth destruction, and their lips talk of mischief.
3 Through wisdom is an house builded; and by understanding it is
established:
4 And by knowledge shall the chambers be filled with all precious and
pleasant riches.
5 A wise man *is* strong; yea, a man of knowledge increaseth strength.
6 For by wise counsel thou shalt make thy war: and in multitude of
counsellors *there is* safety.
7 Wisdom *is* too high for a fool: he openeth not his mouth in the gate.
8 He that deviseth to do evil shall be called a mischievous person.

24:1 Ps 1:1; 37:3; Prov 1:15; 23:17; 24:19
24:2 Ps 10:7; Jer 22:17
24:5 Prov 21:22; Eccles 7:19; 9:16
24:6 Prov 11:14; 20:18
24:7 Prov 14:6; 17:16, 24
24:8 Prov 6:14; 14:22

23:17, 18 No believer should envy a sinner his liberty to sin or his wealth. He will pay for it dearly and be cast off at last. He is to be pitied, not envied.

23:26 *give me thine heart.* If the heart is right, the outward actions will be appropriate. Whoever loves God with his whole heart is free to do whatever he pleases; he will always seek to do that which pleases God, on whom his heart's affections are set.

9 The thought of foolishness *is* sin: and the scorner *is* an abomination to
men.
10 *If* thou faint in the day of adversity, thy strength *is* small.
11 If thou forbear to deliver *them that are* drawn unto death, and *those that*
are ready to be slain;
12 If thou sayest, Behold, we knew it not; doth not he that pondereth the
heart consider *it?* and he that keepeth thy soul, doth *not* he know *it?* and
shall *not* he render to *every* man according to his works?

24:9 Isa 55:7; 59:7
☆**24:10** Job 4:5 Heb 12:3
24:11 1 Sam 16:7 Ps 82:4 Prov 21:2 Eccles 5:8 Isa 58:6, 7

E. ADVICE TO A SON

13 My son, eat thou honey, because *it is* good; and the honeycomb, *which*
is sweet to thy taste:
14 So *shall* the knowledge of wisdom *be* unto thy soul: when thou hast
found *it,* then there shall be a reward, and thy expectation shall not be cut
off.
15 Lay not wait, O wicked *man,* against the dwelling of the righteous; spoil
not his resting place:
16 For a just *man* falleth seven times, and riseth up again: but the wicked
shall fall into mischief.
17 Rejoice not when thine enemy falleth, and let not thine heart be glad
when he stumbleth:
18 Lest the LORD see *it,* and it displease him, and he turn away his wrath
from him.
19 Fret not thyself because of evil *men,* neither be thou envious at the
wicked:
20 For there shall be no reward to the evil *man;* the candle of the wicked
shall be put out.
21 My son, fear thou the LORD and the king: *and* meddle not with them
that are given to change:
22 For their calamity shall rise suddenly; and who knoweth the ruin of
them both?

24:13 Ps 19:10 Prov 25:16
24:15 Job 5:19 Ps 10:9–12 37:24 Prov 6:15 14:32; 24:21, 22 Mic 7:8
☆**24:16**
24:17 Ps 35:15 Rom 11:18–21
☆**24:19** Job 15:31 Prov 13:9; 24:1
☆**24:20**
24:21 Prov 24:15, 16 Rom 13:4 1 Pet 2:17

F. ADDITIONAL PROVERBS

23 These *things* also *belong* to the wise. *It is* not good to have respect of
persons in judgment.
24 He that saith unto the wicked, Thou *art* righteous; him shall the people
curse, nations shall abhor him:
25 But to them that rebuke *him* shall be delight, and a good blessing shall
come upon them.
26 *Every man* shall kiss *his* lips that giveth a right answer.

☆**24:23** Prov 18:5; 28:21
☆**24:24**
24:26 Job 6:25 Prov 15:23 25:12; 27:5

24:10 Days of adversity are bound to come to all. Some are discouraged by adversity. Their hands hang down, their knees knock, and they cannot work. Some even quail as adversity approaches, and long before it reaches them they have fainted. They cross bridges before they come to them. Believers are to be of good courage with the assurance that God strengthens their hearts. They need not faint in the hour of adversity.
24:16 The righteous man may fall seven times or seventy times seven and still rise again, because of his repentance and God's forgiveness. But the wicked man who falls only once is lost forever, because he refuses to repent.
24:19, 20 Believers are not to be fretful over the success of the wicked nor are they to envy their success or wealth. There is a payday some day. The wicked will receive their just deserts. Their candles may shine brightly now, but they will be put out when the day of judgment comes, if not before.
24:23, 24 Those who sit in judgment are required to give their opinions and pass sentence according to the law and on the basis of the true merits of the case. Compassion and sympathy have no place in judgment; 24:24 says that kings and judges who make decisions on the basis of what a man is rather than on what he has done pervert justice. And when the wicked are declared to be righteous by judicial fiat rather than from what they really are, kings and judges will be abhorred by the nations and cursed by the people as betrayers of their public trust.

27 Prepare thy work without, and make it fit for thyself in the field; and
afterwards build thine house.

24:28 Prov 20:22; 25:18; Mt 5:39; Rom 12:17

28 Be not a witness against thy neighbour without cause; and deceive *not*
with thy lips.
29 Say not, I will do so to him as he hath done to me: I will render to the
man according to his work.

24:29☆

24:30 Job 4:8; Prov 6:6; Isa 5:6, 7

30 I went by the field of the slothful, and by the vineyard of the man void
of understanding;
31 And, lo, it was all grown over with thorns, *and* nettles had covered the
face thereof, and the stone wall thereof was broken down.

24:32 Prov 6:10; 12:24; 23:21

32 Then I saw, *and* considered *it* well: I looked upon *it, and* received
instruction.
33 *Yet* a little sleep, a little slumber, a little folding of the hands to sleep:
34 So shall thy poverty come *as* one that travelleth; and thy want as an
armed man.

V. SOLOMON'S PROVERBS COLLECTED BY HEZEKIAH'S AIDES (25:1—29:27)

A. STANDING BEFORE THE KING

25:1☆ Prov 1:1

25 THESE *are* also proverbs of Solomon, which the men of Hez-e-
ki'ah king of Judah copied out.

25:2☆ Deut 29:29; Ezra 6:1; Rom 11:33

2 *It is* the glory of God to conceal a thing: but the honour of kings *is* to
search out a matter.
3 The heaven for height, and the earth for depth, and the heart of kings *is*
unsearchable.

25:4☆ Prov 20:8; Ezek 22:18; Mal 3:2, 3

4 Take away the dross from the silver, and there shall come forth a vessel
for the finer.

25:5☆

5 Take away the wicked *from* before the king, and his throne shall be
established in righteousness.

25:6 Ps 131:1; Prov 25:27; 27:2; Mt 12:39; Lk 14:7

6 Put not forth thyself in the presence of the king, and stand not in the
place of great *men:*
7 For better *it is* that it be said unto thee, Come up hither; than that thou
shouldest be put lower in the presence of the prince whom thine eyes have
seen.

25:8 Prov 17:14; 18:6; Mt 5:25

8 Go not forth hastily to strive, lest *thou know not* what to do in the end
thereof, when thy neighbour hath put thee to shame.

25:9☆

9 Debate thy cause with thy neighbour *himself;* and discover not a secret
to another:
10 Lest he that heareth *it* put thee to shame, and thine infamy turn not
away.

25:11 Prov 15:23

11 A word fitly spoken *is like* apples of gold in pictures of silver.

25:12 Prov 15:31; 26:23

12 *As* an earring of gold, and an ornament of fine gold, *so is* a wise
reprover upon an obedient ear.

24:29 Vengeance belongs to God, not to man. If a righteous man seeks to execute vengeance on his enemy, he takes the work out of God's hands. This implies malice on the part of the one who does this.
25:1 *These are also proverbs of Solomon.* See 1 Kings 4:32. *Hezekiah lived 200 years after Solomon.*
25:2 God, who knows all things, has chosen not to reveal to men the reasons why he acts as he does. Paul says: "O the depth of the riches both of the wisdom and knowledge of God! how unsearchable are his judgments, and his ways past finding out!" (Rom. 11:33).

25:4, 5 When wicked people are removed from the nation, it is like silver that has been purified by fire and the dross removed. When kings or presidents abandon the wicked, it will go far in improving the morality of the nation. And the reformation of heads of state and the legislatures of the people will promote the reformation of the entire nation.
25:9 Before seeking redress at the hands of a court, try to settle the problem with your neighbor privately. This is especially true when the dispute contains a secret that should not be made public. End it privately so that it may not be disclosed to the public eye.

13 As the cold of snow in the time of harvest, *so is* a faithful messenger to
them that send him: for he refresheth the soul of his masters.
14 Whoso boasteth himself of a false gift *is like* clouds and wind without
rain.

B. TREATMENT OF NEIGHBORS AND ENEMIES

15 By long forbearing is a prince persuaded, and a soft tongue breaketh
the bone.
16 Hast thou found honey? eat so much as is sufficient for thee, lest thou
be filled therewith, and vomit it.
17 Withdraw thy foot from thy neighbour's house; lest he be weary of
thee, and *so* hate thee.
18 A man that beareth false witness against his neighbour *is* a maul, and a
sword, and a sharp arrow.
19 Confidence in an unfaithful man in time of trouble *is like* a broken
tooth, and a foot out of joint.
20 *As* he that taketh away a garment in cold weather, *and as* vinegar upon
nitre, so *is* he that singeth songs to an heavy heart.
21 If thine enemy be hungry, give him bread to eat; and if he be thirsty,
give him water to drink:
22 For thou shalt heap coals of fire upon his head, and the LORD shall
reward thee.
23 The north wind driveth away rain: so *doth* an angry countenance a
backbiting tongue.
24 *It is* better to dwell in the corner of the housetop, than with a brawling
woman and in a wide house.
25 *As* cold waters to a thirsty soul, so *is* good news from a far country.
26 A righteous man falling down before the wicked *is as* a troubled
fountain, and a corrupt spring.
27 *It is* not good to eat much honey: so *for men* to search their own glory
is not glory.
28 He that *hath* no rule over his own spirit *is like* a city *that is* broken
down, *and* without walls.

☆**25:15** Prov 15:1; Eccles 10:4
25:16 Prov 25:27
25:18 Ps 57:4; Prov 12:18; 24:28; Jer 9:8
25:19 Job 6:15
☆**25:20** Prov 27:14
25:21 Ex 23:4; 2 Kgs 6:22; 2 Chron 28:15; Mt 5:44; 6:6; Rom 12:20
25:23 Prov 13:3; 26:20
☆**25:24** Prov 19:13; 21:9; 27:15
25:25 2 Cor 7:7; 1 Thess 3:5–8
25:26 Ezek 34:18
25:27 Prov 25:16
25:28 2 Chron 32:5; Prov 16:32

C. THE ARGUMENTS OF A FOOL

26 AS snow in summer, and as rain in harvest, so honour is not seemly
for a fool.
2 As the bird by wandering, as the swallow by flying, so the curse
causeless shall not come.
3 A whip for the horse, a bridle for the ass, and a rod for the fool's back.
4 Answer not a fool according to his folly, lest thou also be like unto him.
5 Answer a fool according to his folly, lest he be wise in his own conceit.

☆**26:1** 1 Sam 12:17; Prov 26:8
☆**26:2** Num 23:8; 2 Sam 16:12; Ps 109:28
26:3 Ps 32:9; Prov 10:13
26:4 Prov 23:9; 29:8

25:15 *In dealing with others,* two things are stressed as important: (1) *patience,* by which we wait for the right opportunity to make our case and then give time for consideration of it; (2) *mildness,* by which we make our case without provoking the person with whom we are dealing, and do so without using hard words or undue passion.
25:20 *vinegar upon nitre,* i.e., "vinegar upon an open wound" (RSV).
25:24 This counsel is not to be understood as putting women down. It is addressed to both men and women. Whoever is married to a brawling and contentious spouse is likely to be better off single than married. There are occasions when it is right to say: "Blessed be the man or woman who has never married, but who lives in a garret."
26:1 "It is too common a thing for honor to be given to fools, who are utterly unworthy of it and unfit for it."* It does them more hurt than good and lowers the value of honor for those who deserve it.
26:2 Men curse others for no good reason and think thereby to gain their point and bind the conscience of the one cursed. Whoever is cursed without cause need never fear such imprecations. They are like birds who fly overhead without ever landing on the head of the innocent.

26:6 Prov 13:17; 25:13

6 He that sendeth a message by the hand of a fool cutteth off the feet, *and*
drinketh damage.

26:7 Ps 50:16, 17; Prov 17:7

7 The legs of the lame are not equal: so *is* a parable in the mouth of fools.
8 As he that bindeth a stone in a sling, so *is* he that giveth honour to a
fool.

26:9 Eccles 12:11

9 *As* the thorn goeth up into the hand of a drunkard, so *is* a parable in the
mouth of fools.
10 The great *God* that formed all *things* both rewardeth the fool, and
rewardeth transgressors.

26:11☆ Ex 8:15; 2 Pet 2:22

11 As a dog returneth to his vomit, *so* a fool returneth to his folly.

26:12 Prov 3:7; 28:11; 29:20

12 Seest thou a man wise in his own conceit? *there is* more hope of a fool
than of him.

D. THE LAZY AND THE LYING

26:13 Prov 15:19; 22:13

13 The slothful *man* saith, *There is* a lion in the way; a lion *is* in the streets.

26:14 Prov 6:9; 19:15

14 *As* the door turneth upon his hinges, so *doth* the slothful upon his bed.

26:15 Prov 12:27; 19:24; Eccles 4:5

15 The slothful hideth his hand in *his* bosom; it grieveth him to bring it
again to his mouth.

26:16 Prov 12:15

16 The sluggard *is* wiser in his own conceit than seven men that can render
a reason.

26:17 Prov 3:30; 18:6; 20:3

17 He that passeth by, *and* meddleth with strife *belonging* not to him, *is*
like one that taketh a dog by the ears.

26:18 Prov 24:12, 28

18 As a mad *man* who casteth firebrands, arrows, and death,

26:19☆

19 So *is* the man *that* deceiveth his neighbour, and saith, Am not I in
sport?

26:20☆ Prov 16:28; 22:10; Jas 3:6

20 Where no wood is, *there* the fire goeth out: so where *there is* no
talebearer, the strife ceaseth.

26:21 Prov 10:12; 15:18; 29:22; 30:33

21 *As* coals *are* to burning coals, and wood to fire; so *is* a contentious man
to kindle strife.

26:22 Ps 141:4; Prov 18:8; 20:19

22 The words of a talebearer *are* as wounds, and they go down into the
innermost parts of the belly.

26:23 Mt 23:28; Lk 11:39

23 Burning lips and a wicked heart *are like* a potsherd covered with silver
dross.

26:24 Ps 12:2; 28:3; 41:6; Prov 12:20; Jer 12:6

24 He that hateth dissembleth with his lips, and layeth up deceit within
him;
25 When he speaketh fair, believe him not: for *there are* seven abomina-
tions in his heart.
26 *Whose* hatred is covered by deceit, his wickedness shall be shewed
before the *whole* congregation.

26:27☆ Ps 7:15

27 Whoso diggeth a pit shall fall therein: and he that rolleth a stone, it will
return upon him.

26:28 Prov 6:24; 28:23; 29:5

28 A lying tongue hateth *those that are* afflicted by it; and a flattering
mouth worketh ruin.

26:11 This earthy illustration should caution the listener to follow its instructions. A dog will vomit and then return to eat what it has just thrown up. So is the man who sins, becomes aware of what he has done, and, as it were, vomits it up. He then returns to do the very thing that caused him to sin in the first place. Peter applies this adage (2 Peter 2:22) to those have known the way of righteousness but have turned away from it. John assures the reader that God will spue such people out of his mouth (Rev. 3:16).

26:19 He who for jest employs fraud or falsehood against his neighbor commits a sin. "He that sins in jest must repent in earnest, or his sin will be his ruin."*

26:20ff A *talebearer* is a bearer of falsehoods and a malicious retailer of gossip, however true the facts may be. He feeds the fires of contention with fuel and enjoys the blaze. Those he attacks with his gossip are *wounded* just as though they had been struck by a spear that pierced their innermost parts.

26:27 The wicked will discover that the pit they dig for others is the pit they fall into themselves. And he who starts a stone rolling to the hurt of his neighbor will be crushed by the stone he first moved.

E. WISDOM FOR TOMORROW

27 BOAST not thyself of to morrow; for thou knowest not what a day
may bring forth.
2 Let another man praise thee, and not thine own mouth; a stranger, and
not thine own lips.
3 A stone *is* heavy, and the sand weighty; but a fool's wrath *is* heavier
than them both.
4 Wrath *is* cruel, and anger *is* outrageous; but who *is* able to stand before
envy?
5 Open rebuke *is* better than secret love.
6 Faithful *are* the wounds of a friend; but the kisses of an enemy *are*
deceitful.
7 The full soul loatheth an honeycomb; but to the hungry soul every bitter
thing is sweet.
8 As a bird that wandereth from her nest, so *is* a man that wandereth from
his place.
9 Ointment and perfume rejoice the heart: so *doth* the sweetness of a
man's friend by hearty counsel.
10 Thine own friend, and thy father's friend, forsake not; neither go into
thy brother's house in the day of thy calamity: *for* better *is* a neighbour *that*
is near than a brother far off.
11 My son, be wise, and make my heart glad, that I may answer him that
reproacheth me.
12 A prudent *man* foreseeth the evil, *and* hideth himself; *but* the simple
pass on, *and* are punished.
13 Take his garment that is surety for a stranger, and take a pledge of him
for a strange woman.
14 He that blesseth his friend with a loud voice, rising early in the
morning, it shall be counted a curse to him.
15 A continual dropping in a very rainy day and a contentious woman are
alike.
16 Whosoever hideth her hideth the wind, and the ointment of his right
hand, *which* bewrayeth *itself*.

F. A MAN'S EYES ARE NEVER SATISFIED

17 Iron sharpeneth iron; so a man sharpeneth the countenance of his
friend.
18 Whoso keepeth the fig tree shall eat the fruit thereof: so he that waiteth
on his master shall be honoured.
19 As in water face *answereth* to face, so the heart of man to man.
20 Hell and destruction are never full; so the eyes of man are never
satisfied.

☆**27:1** Mt 6:34; Lk 12:19, 20; Jas 4:13–16
27:2 Prov 25:27; 2 Cor 10:12, 18
27:4 Prov 6:34
27:5 Prov 24:26; 25:12; 28:23
☆**27:6** Ps 141:5; Mt 26:49
☆**27:8** 1 Sam 26:19; Prov 21:16; Heb 11:13
27:9 Prov 15:5
☆**27:10** 1 Kgs 12:6; 2 Chron 10:6; Prov 17:17; 18:24
27:11 Prov 10:1; 23:15
27:12 Prov 22:3
27:13 Prov 6:1–5; 20:16
27:14 Prov 26:18, 19
27:15 Prov 19:13; 21:9; 25:24
☆**27:17**
27:18 Lk 12:42; 2 Tim 2:6
27:20 Prov 30:15; Eccles 1:8–11; 5:10; Hab 2:5

27:1 Nowhere do the Scriptures forbid us to prepare for tomorrow. They do forbid us to presume upon tomorrow, for we know not what the day will bring forth. As in the parable of the rich fool, we may presume that we can take our ease, eat, drink, and be merry for many years. But before the morrow comes, God has sent the angel of death to bring the soul into his presence. Moreover, God in his wisdom has kept us from knowing the future, lest we be unprepared for what it will bring when it comes. Here the lack of knowledge is a blessing, not a curse.

27:6 It is better to be reproved by a friend than to be kissed deceitfully by an enemy, as in the case of Judas Iscariot, who betrayed Jesus with a kiss.

27:8 Some people are not happy with the slot the Lord has placed them in and seek to flee from that haven for another. They are like a bird that deserts its nest and wanders about, while the eggs or young ones perish. The grass always looks greener in the other man's yard until you get there.

27:10 A neighbor who helps you is better than a brother far removed and disinterested in your welfare.

27:17 Men, by talking amiably with each other, are "filed, made smooth, and bright, and fit for business."*

27:21
1 Sam 18:7, 8
2 Sam 14:25
Ps 12:6
Prov 17:3
Zech 13:9
Lk 6:26
27:22☆
Prov 23:35
26:11
Jer 5:3
27:23
Job 19:9
Ps 89:39
Jer 13:18
Ezek 34:12
Jn 10:3

21 *As* the fining pot for silver, and the furnace for gold; so *is* a man to his
praise.
22 Though thou shouldest bray a fool in a mortar among wheat with a
pestle, *yet* will not his foolishness depart from him.
23 Be thou diligent to know the state of thy flocks, *and* look well to thy
herds.
24 For riches *are* not for ever: and doth the crown *endure* to every
generation?
25 The hay appeareth, and the tender grass sheweth itself, and herbs of the
mountains are gathered.
26 The lambs *are* for thy clothing, and the goats *are* the price of the field.
27 And *thou shalt have* goats' milk enough for thy food, for the food of thy
household, and *for* the maintenance for thy maidens.

G. THE WICKED AND THE GODLY

28:1☆
Lev 26:17, 36
Ps 27:1, 2
28:2
1 Kgs 16:8–28
2 Kgs 15:8–15
Hos 7:7; 8:4
13:11
28:3
Mt 18:28
28:4
Rom 1:32
Eph 5:11
28:5
Ps 92:6, 7
Prov 2:9; 21:15
Isa 6:10
28:6☆
Prov 12:9
15:16; 16:8, 19
28:7
Prov 2:1
23:25, 26; 29:3
28:8
Ex 22:25
Deut 23:19, 20
Prov 19:17
28:9
Ps 66:18; 109:7
Prov 15:8
Isa 1:15, 16
28:10
Ps 7:15; 9:15
Prov 26:27
Mt 5:19; 18:6
23:15
Heb 6:12
28:11
Prov 18:23
25:27; 26:12
28:12
Eccles 10:5, 6
28:13☆
Job 31:33
Ps 32:1–11
1 Jn 1:6–9

28 THE wicked flee when no man pursueth: but the righteous are bold
as a lion.
2 For the transgression of a land many *are* the princes thereof: but by a
man of understanding *and* knowledge the state *thereof* shall be prolonged.
3 A poor man that oppresseth the poor *is like* a sweeping rain which
leaveth no food.
4 They that forsake the law praise the wicked: but such as keep the law
contend with them.
5 Evil men understand not judgment: but they that seek the LORD
understand all *things.*
6 Better *is* the poor that walketh in his uprightness, than *he that is* perverse
in his ways, though he *be* rich.
7 Whoso keepeth the law *is* a wise son: but he that is a companion of
riotous *men* shameth his father.
8 He that by usury and unjust gain increaseth his substance, he shall
gather it for him that will pity the poor.
9 He that turneth away his ear from hearing the law, even his prayer *shall
be* abomination.
10 Whoso causeth the righteous to go astray in an evil way, he shall fall
himself into his own pit: but the upright shall have good *things* in
possession.
11 The rich man *is* wise in his own conceit; but the poor that hath
understanding searcheth him out.
12 When righteous *men* do rejoice, *there is* great glory: but when the
wicked rise, a man is hidden.
13 He that covereth his sins shall not prosper: but whoso confesseth and
forsaketh *them* shall have mercy.

27:22 After gentle means have been tried for the fool, one must then resort to rough and severe methods. He must then be pulverized with a pounding instrument. Force is called for when men will not be ruled by reason. Yet some are so incurably bad that they resist refining in the furnace, and they must at last be cut off.
28:1 The wicked are secretly terrified that they may be exposed for what they really are, and thus they run away when no one is pursuing them.
28:6 This is a paradox of Scripture; of such, there are many examples. The truth is proclaimed that an honest, godly poor man is better than a dishonest, wealthy bad one. How can this be, except when we think of eternity, not this present life? But the Scriptures here certainly refer to this life as well. When a rich man scolded Aristides about his poverty, the Athenian statesman answered him by saying: "Thy riches do thee more hurt than my poverty does me."
28:13 It is folly to indulge oneself in sin. It is even worse to hide one's transgressions as though they could be excused by denying them, by disguising them, or by blaming others for them. Sooner or later, sins will be made public, for there is nothing hidden that will not be revealed. Whoever sins is benefited best by confessing those sins to God and reforming his life, thus having his conscience eased. This will prevent his ruin, which otherwise is certain.

14 Happy *is* the man that feareth alway: but he that hardeneth his heart
shall fall into mischief.
15 *As* a roaring lion, and a ranging bear; *so is* a wicked ruler over the poor
people.
16 The prince that wanteth understanding *is* also a great oppressor: *but* he
that hateth covetousness shall prolong *his* days.
17 A man that doeth violence to the blood of *any* person shall flee to the
pit; let no man stay him.
18 Whoso walketh uprightly shall be saved: but *he that is* perverse *in his*
ways shall fall at once.
19 He that tilleth his land shall have plenty of bread: but he that followeth
after vain *persons* shall have poverty enough.
20 A faithful man shall abound with blessings: but he that maketh haste to
be rich shall not be innocent.
21 To have respect of persons *is* not good: for for a piece of bread *that*
man will transgress.
22 He that hasteth to be rich *hath* an evil eye, and considereth not that
poverty shall come upon him.
23 He that rebuketh a man afterwards shall find more favour than he that
flattereth with the tongue.
24 Whoso robbeth his father or his mother, and saith, *It is* no transgres-
sion; the same *is* the companion of a destroyer.
25 He that is of a proud heart stirreth up strife: but he that putteth his
trust in the LORD shall be made fat.
26 He that trusteth in his own heart is a fool: but whoso walketh wisely, he
shall be delivered.
27 He that giveth unto the poor shall not lack: but he that hideth his eyes
shall have many a curse.
28 When the wicked rise, men hide themselves: but when they perish, the
righteous increase.

H. GOOD MEN IN AUTHORITY

29 HE, that being often reproved hardeneth *his* neck, shall suddenly be
destroyed, and that without remedy.
2 When the righteous are in authority, the people rejoice: but when the
wicked beareth rule, the people mourn.
3 Whoso loveth wisdom rejoiceth his father: but he that keepeth company
with harlots spendeth *his* substance.
4 The king by judgment establisheth the land: but he that receiveth gifts
overthroweth it.
5 A man that flattereth his neighbour spreadeth a net for his feet.
6 In the transgression of an evil man *there is* a snare: but the righteous
doth sing and rejoice.

☆**28:14** Rom 2:5; Phil 2:12
28:15 Prov 19:12; Mt 2:16; 1 Pet 5:8
28:16 Eccles 10:16; Isa 3:12
28:17 Gen 9:6; Ex 21:14; Prov 6:16–19; 28:24
28:19 Prov 12:11; 14:4; 23:19–21
28:20 Prov 13:11; 23:4; Mt 25:21
28:21 Ezek 13:19
☆**28:23** Ps 141:5; Prov 29:5, 6; Mt 18:15
28:24 Prov 19:26; 20:20
28:25 2 Pet 2:3
28:26 Job 28:28; Prov 3:5
☆**28:27** Prov 11:24; 19:17
☆**29:1** 1 Sam 2:25; 2 Chron 36:16; Prov 1:24, 25; 13:18; 15:31, 32
29:2 Esth 8:15, 16; Prov 11:10; 28:12, 28
29:3 Prov 6:26; 10:1; 28:7; Lk 15:13
29:4 Prov 8:15; 15:27; 29:14
29:5 Ps 5:9; Prov 28:23

28:14 Sin always leads to one of two things. Either the sinner turns to God for pardon and restoration or he hardens his heart. When the hardening reaches a certain point, that person puts himself beyond the possibility of forgiveness. Unremedied sin constitutes a most precarious state for anyone.

28:23 It has been said that flattery will get a man everything. The flatterer is a liar and ill serves the person he flatters. He harms his friend and hurts himself. Flattery also demeans the person flattered because it supposes that he is an easy victim to this vice. He who tells his friend the truth keeps his integrity, because he has done his duty and helped that friend, whether what he has done is accepted or rejected.

28:27 Whoever covers his eyes to keep from seeing and helping the poor will be cursed. Whoever gives—whether from his poverty or abundance—will not suffer for it. Rather, God will make what he had in the first place go farther.

29:1 The obstinate, criminally minded person who rejects the reproof of parents, friends, and officers of the law hardens his heart and crosses the point of no return. God says such a person shall be suddenly destroyed when he is unprepared for it. For such a person there is no remedy. "Whoever sins against the preventing remedy should not expect any recovering remedy."*

29:7 Ps 41:1 Prov 28:27 31:8, 9
29:8 Prov 13:2; 17:19 Jas 3:13–18
29:9 Prov 26:4
29:11 Prov 14:17, 29 19:11
29:12 1 Kgs 12:14
29:13 Job 3:19 Mt 5:45
29:14☆ Ps 72:4 Prov 16:12; 29:4
29:16☆ Ps 37:34–38
29:18☆ Ex 32:25 Ps 1:1, 2; 74:9 119:2, 3
29:20 Prov 26:12 Eccles 7:9 Jas 1:19
29:22 Prov 22:24
29:23 Prov 15:33; 22:4 Dan 4:30 Mt 23:12 Jas 4:6
29:24 Lev 5:1 Ps 50:18 Prov 1:10, 11
29:25 Gen 12:11–13 20:11, 12 Prov 16:7 Lk 12:4
29:26☆ Isa 49:4 Acts 24:24, 25 1 Cor 2:6–8
29:27 Ps 69:4 139:21, 22 Mt 10:22; 24:9 2 Cor 6:14–18

7 The righteous considereth the cause of the poor: *but* the wicked
regardeth not to know *it*.
8 Scornful men bring a city into a snare: but wise *men* turn away wrath.
9 *If* a wise man contendeth with a foolish man, whether he rage or laugh,
there is no rest.
10 The bloodthirsty hate the upright: but the just seek his soul.
11 A fool uttereth all his mind: but a wise *man* keepeth it in till afterwards.
12 If a ruler hearken to lies, all his servants *are* wicked.
13 The poor and the deceitful man meet together: the LORD lighteneth
both their eyes.
14 The king that faithfully judgeth the poor, his throne shall be established
for ever.
15 The rod and reproof give wisdom: but a child left *to himself* bringeth his
mother to shame.
16 When the wicked are multiplied, transgression increaseth: but the
righteous shall see their fall.
17 Correct thy son, and he shall give thee rest; yea, he shall give delight
unto thy soul.
18 Where *there is* no vision, the people perish: but he that keepeth the law,
happy *is* he.
19 A servant will not be corrected by words: for though he understand he
will not answer.
20 Seest thou a man *that is* hasty in his words? *there is* more hope of a fool
than of him.
21 He that delicately bringeth up his servant from a child shall have him
become *his* son at the length.
22 An angry man stirreth up strife, and a furious man aboundeth in
transgression.
23 A man's pride shall bring him low: but honour shall uphold the humble
in spirit.
24 Whoso is partner with a thief hateth his own soul: he heareth cursing,
and bewrayeth *it* not.
25 The fear of man bringeth a snare: but whoso putteth his trust in the
LORD shall be safe.
26 Many seek the ruler's favour; but *every* man's judgment *cometh* from
the LORD.
27 An unjust man *is* an abomination to the just: and *he that is* upright in
the way *is* abomination to the wicked.

29:14 Judgment should be based on law and equity. Equity is "a body of legal doctrines and rules developed to enlarge, supplement, or override a narrow rigid system of law" (*Webster's Ninth New Collegiate Dictionary*). Thus the believer who sometimes does what is contrary to the will of God will be declared *innocent by reason of his heart's intention, rather than the deed itself.*

29:16 "The more sinners there are the more sin there is."* This leads to more transgressions and more injustice. The more a nation sins, the closer it is to the judgment of God. Let the righteous be patient, for God will bring an end to the power and dignity of the wicked.

29:18 *Where there is no vision,* (i.e., "where there is no prophet to expound the word of God," or "where there is no priest or Levite to teach the word of God," or, "where the word of God is scarce") there the people are stripped of their armor and opened to every evil device and false wind of doctrine. They are destroyed because of the lack of true knowledge.

29:26 Men seek to gain their own ends by currying the friendship and favor of those who rule over them. True justice and genuine favor come from God, not from men. Let the Christian seek God's favor, not man's.

VI. THE MESSAGES OF AGUR (30:1–33)

A. EVERY WORD OF GOD PROVES TRUE

30 THE words of A'gur the son of Ja'keh, *even* the prophecy: the man
spake unto Ith'i-el, even unto Ith'i-el and U'cal,
[2]Surely I *am* more brutish than *any* man, and have not the understanding
of a man.
[3]I neither learned wisdom, nor have the knowledge of the holy.
[4]Who hath ascended up into heaven, or descended? who hath gathered
the wind in his fists? who hath bound the waters in a garment? who hath
established all the ends of the earth? what *is* his name, and what *is* his son's
name, if thou canst tell?
[5]Every word of God *is* pure: he *is* a shield unto them that put their trust
in him.
[6]Add thou not unto his words, lest he reprove thee, and thou be found a
liar.
[7]Two *things* have I required of thee; deny me *them* not before I die:
[8]Remove far from me vanity and lies: give me neither poverty nor riches;
feed me with food convenient for me:
[9]Lest I be full, and deny *thee*, and say, Who *is* the LORD? or lest I be
poor, and steal, and take the name of my God *in vain*.

☆**30:1**
30:2 Job 42:3–6; Ps 49:10
30:4 Ex 15:10; Job 26:8; 38:8, 9; Ps 24:2; 68:18; 135:7; Isa 45:18; Rev 19:12
☆**30:5** Ps 3:3; 12:6; 18:30; 84:11; Prov 2:7, 8
30:6 Deut 4:2; 12:32; Rev 22:18
30:7 1 Kgs 3:5; Ps 27:4
30:8 Ps 119:29, 37; Prov 23:5; Mt 6:11–13
30:9 Deut 8:12; 31:20; Neh 9:25; Hos 13:6

B. NUMERICAL SAYINGS

[10]Accuse not a servant unto his master, lest he curse thee, and thou be
found guilty.
[11]*There is* a generation *that* curseth their father, and doth not bless their
mother.
[12]*There is* a generation *that are* pure in their own eyes, and *yet* is not
washed from their filthiness.
[13]*There is* a generation, O how lofty are their eyes! and their eyelids are
lifted up.
[14]*There is* a generation, whose teeth *are as* swords, and their jaw teeth *as*
knives, to devour the poor from off the earth, and the needy from *among*
men.
[15]The horseleach hath two daughters, *crying*, Give, give. There are three
things that are never satisfied, *yea*, four *things* say not, *It is* enough:
[16]The grave; and the barren womb; the earth *that* is not filled with water;
and the fire *that* saith not, *It is* enough.
[17]The eye *that* mocketh at *his* father, and despiseth to obey *his* mother,
the ravens of the valley shall pick it out, and the young eagles shall eat it.
[18]There be three *things which* are too wonderful for me, yea, four which I
know not:

30:10 Eccles 7:21
30:11 Ex 21:17; Prov 20:20
30:13 Job 29:17; Ps 57:4; Lk 18:11
☆**30:14**
30:15 Gen 30:1, 2; Prov 27:20
30:17 Gen 9:22; Prov 19:26; 20:20
30:18 Job 39:27; 42:3; Ps 139:6

30:1 *The words of Agur.* We know nothing about Agur except what the Scriptures say, nor do the names of *Ithiel* and *Ucal* appear elsewhere. Some scholars think Ithiel and Ucal are not names. By rearranging the Hebrew text without changing the consonants, they make the verse read: "I have wearied myself, O God, I have wearied myself, O God, and am consumed."
30:5 *Every word of God is pure.* The least of the words of God have neither falsehood nor corruption in them. They are as silver purified seven times (Ps. 12:6). The words of God are also sure. They do not change. They are completely dependable. They are sufficient. They are all we need and nothing need be or can be added to them. Moreover, they will accomplish the purpose for which they were intended when men yield to them, obey them, and make them the guiding light of life.
30:14 The Old Testament so said and it is true today that we shall always have the poor and they shall never cease out of the land. We can either love or hate the poor and either help or hurt them. Here the Scriptures portray those who hate the poor as having teeth of iron and steel, like swords and knives. They consume the poor, cutting the meat from their bodies and eating it. This accusation may go beyond poverty and include the condemnation of evil tongues, which slice men into pieces by slander and false reports.

19 The way of an eagle in the air; the way of a serpent upon a rock; the
way of a ship in the midst of the sea; and the way of a man with a maid.

30:20☆ Prov 7:13

20 Such *is* the way of an adulterous woman; she eateth, and wipeth her
mouth, and saith, I have done no wickedness.

30:21 1 Sam 25:25; Ps 14:1; Prov 17:7, 21

21 For three *things* the earth is disquieted, and for four *which* it cannot
bear:
22 For a servant when he reigneth; and a fool when he is filled with meat;
23 For an odious *woman* when she is married; and an handmaid that is
heir to her mistress.

30:24 Lev 11:5; Job 12:7–9; Ps 104:18; Prov 6:6–8; Joel 1:6

24 There be four *things which are* little upon the earth, but they *are*
exceeding wise:
25 The ants *are* a people not strong, yet they prepare their meat in the
summer;
26 The conies *are but* a feeble folk, yet make they their houses in the rocks;
27 The locusts have no king, yet go they forth all of them by bands;
28 The spider taketh hold with her hands, and is in kings' palaces.

30:29 Mic 5:8; Prov 20:2

29 There be three *things* which go well, yea, four are comely in going:
30 A lion *which is* strongest among beasts, and turneth not away for any;
31 A greyhound; an he goat also; and a king, against whom *there is* no
rising up.

30:32☆ Job 21:5; 40:4; Prov 17:27, 28; Mic 7:16
30:33 Prov 15:18; 16:28; 26:21; 29:22

32 If thou hast done foolishly in lifting up thyself, or if thou hast thought
evil, *lay* thine hand upon thy mouth.
33 Surely the churning of milk bringeth forth butter, and the wringing of
the nose bringeth forth blood: so the forcing of wrath bringeth forth strife.

VII. THE SAYINGS OF KING LEMUEL (31:1–31)

A. WINE AND WOMEN

31:1☆

31 THE words of king Lem'u-el, the prophecy that his mother taught
him.

31:2☆ 1 Sam 1:11; Isa 49:15
31:3 Deut 17:17; 1 Kgs 11:1; Prov 5:9; 7:26
31:4 Prov 20:1; Eccles 10:16, 17; Isa 5:22, 23; 28:7; Hos 4:11
31:5 Deut 16:19; Prov 17:15
31:6 Job 3:20; Isa 38:15
31:8 Job 29:12–17; Ps 82:3–5; Prov 24:11

2 What, my son? and what, the son of my womb? and what, the son of my
vows?
3 Give not thy strength unto women, nor thy ways to that which
destroyeth kings.
4 *It is* not for kings, O Lem'u-el, *it is* not for kings to drink wine; nor for
princes strong drink:
5 Lest they drink, and forget the law, and pervert the judgment of any of
the afflicted.
6 Give strong drink unto him that is ready to perish, and wine unto those
that be of heavy hearts.
7 Let him drink, and forget his poverty, and remember his misery no
more.
8 Open thy mouth for the dumb in the cause of all such as are appointed
to destruction.

30:20 The Scriptures always condemn adultery. Nowhere is there a word that condones such conduct. Here the Scriptures speak of the adulteress who has profaned her husband's bed by her vile conduct and who uses every device to conceal her treachery. So good is her coverup that it would be easier to track the *flight of an eagle than to discover her* sin. She presents herself to the world as a model of chastity and in effect calls evil good. She publicly parades her virtue and swears she has done no evil.

30:32 He who has done foolishly should not seek to justify it. By silence, confession to God, and determination to right any wrong, he will appease those whom he has offended.

31:1 *king Lemuel. Lemuel* means "devoted to God." Nothing is known about him except what the text says. Rabbinic tradition equates Lemuel with Solomon. Modern scholars reject this.

31:2 In 31:2-9 Lemuel's mother speaks a word of counsel to her beloved son. She warns him to stay away from fornication and other sexual sins, to stay sober (31:4, 5), to do good with his wealth by helping those who are poor, and to use his kingly power (31:8, 9) in the pursuit of justice.

9 Open thy mouth, judge righteously, and plead the cause of the poor and
needy.

B. THE TRULY GOOD WIFE

10 ¶Who can find a virtuous woman? for her price *is* far above rubies.
11 The heart of her husband doth safely trust in her, so that he shall have
no need of spoil.
12 She will do him good and not evil all the days of her life.
13 She seeketh wool, and flax, and worketh willingly with her hands.
14 She is like the merchants' ships; she bringeth her food from afar.
15 She riseth also while it is yet night, and giveth meat to her household,
and a portion to her maidens.
16 She considereth a field, and buyeth it: with the fruit of her hands she
planteth a vineyard.
17 She girdeth her loins with strength, and strengtheneth her arms.
18 She perceiveth that her merchandise *is* good: her candle goeth not out
by night.
19 She layeth her hands to the spindle, and her hands hold the distaff.
20 She stretcheth out her hand to the poor; yea, she reacheth forth her
hands to the needy.
21 She is not afraid of the snow for her household: for all her household
are clothed with scarlet.
22 She maketh herself coverings of tapestry; her clothing *is* silk and
purple.
23 Her husband is known in the gates, when he sitteth among the elders of
the land.
24 She maketh fine linen, and selleth *it;* and delivereth girdles unto the
merchant.
25 Strength and honour *are* her clothing; and she shall rejoice in time to
come.
26 She openeth her mouth with wisdom; and in her tongue *is* the law of
kindness.
27 She looketh well to the ways of her household, and eateth not the bread
of idleness.
28 Her children arise up, and call her blessed; her husband *also*, and he
praiseth her.
29 Many daughters have done virtuously, but thou excellest them all.
30 Favour *is* deceitful, and beauty *is* vain: *but* a woman *that* feareth the
LORD, she shall be praised.
31 Give her of the fruit of her hands; and let her own works praise her in
the gates.

31:9 Lev 19:15; Isa 1:17
☆**31:10** Ruth 3:11; Prov 8:11; 12:4; 19:14
31:11 1 Pet 3:1, 2
31:13 Gen 18:6; 24:18–20; 29:9, 10
31:19 Deut 15:11; Job 31:16; Prov 22:9; Rom 12:13
31:22 Ps 45:13, 14; Ezek 16:9, 10; 1 Pet 3:3
31:23 Job 29:7
31:25 Prov 14:26
☆**31:26** Prov 11:16; 12:18; 16:21, 24; 19:20
31:27 Prov 6:6–11; Rom 12:11
31:28 2 Tim 1:5
31:30 Ps 147:11; Prov 1:7; 8:13; 11:16
31:31 Ps 128:2, 3; Prov 14:1

31:10 From this verse to the end of the chapter we are given the portrait of the ideal wife. Each of the twenty-two verses begins with a letter of the Hebrew alphabet, as do some of the Psalms. What is taught in these verses is repeated in condensed form in 1 Tim. 2:9, 10 and 1 Pet. 3:1–6. A mother has the unique opportunity of performing two invaluable services for her children—the keeping of the true faith in the family and the passing on of that same faith to succeeding generations. This passage is a mirror by which the godly woman may dress and adorn herself, bringing honor and happiness to the family so blessed with such a wife and mother.

31:26 A good mother and wife is known not only for what she does but for what she says. A mother's knee is a good place for children to hear the Word of God and find Jesus Christ as their Savior.

ECCLESIASTES
OR THE PREACHER

Authorship, date, and background Ecclesiastes, meaning "The Preacher," is the title assigned to this book in the Septuagint. The Hebrew title is *Qoheleh,* which is derived from a root Hebrew word meaning "assembly, congregation." The Hebrew title is the feminine abstract noun which may have meant "the office or function of a speaker in the assembly." Ecclesiastes was part of the Megilloth (scrolls) which included Ruth, Esther, The Song of Solomon, and Lamentations. Ecclesiastes was read publicly at the Feast of Tabernacles. Some conservative scholars such as E. W. Hengstenberg, F. Delitzsch, H. C. Leupold, and E. J. Young think it was composed in the fifth century B.C. G. L. Archer assigns it to the tenth century B.C. and accepts the Solomonic authorship for a variety of reasons. The book itself opens with the statement "The words of the Preacher, the son of David, king in Jerusalem" (KJV and RSV). Some scholars from Luther's time onward have assumed that the book reflects Solomonic wisdom but was written centuries after his death (ca. 430–400 B.C. or later).

In this instance the date and the authorship are not vital questions relative to one's belief in the truthfulness of the Word of God. The book itself cannot be said to determine both the date and the authorship without question. This is one of the rare cases where even conservative scholars are tentative in their findings.

Characteristics and content Ecclesiastes is not an easy book to interpret. It constitutes a series of philosophical presuppositions about life and death put together in a fashion which suggests a compilation of ideas that do not form a connected whole. The vocabulary is difficult and the style is somewhat disjointed. At the same time the book is definitely marked by an unvarying theme which is treated in an amazing variety of ways. Basically the message is that life is futile when it is based upon earthly ambitions and desires. When man refuses to rise above himself and find the meaning of life in a transcendent God, it leads to meaninglessness and frustration.

The Preacher speaks about human wisdom, education, power, servants, wealth, pleasure, religion, temperance, and length of days, among other subjects. He concludes that all is in vain. None brings true satisfaction and all men alike go down to the grave. He who lives for any other purpose than the glory of God is doomed to disappointment. God and his will are the highest good for those who seek the best in life and desire the highest possible fulfillment.

Outline

I. The first sermon: the futility of human wisdom (1:1—2:26)
II. The second sermon: life's disappointments (3:1—5:20)
III. The third sermon: the futility of wealth and fame (6:1—8:17)
IV. The fourth sermon: God will take care of life's unfairness (9:1—12:8)
V. Conclusion: living in the light of eternity (12:9–14)

I. THE FIRST SERMON: THE FUTILITY OF HUMAN WISDOM (1:1—2:26)

A. THE BASIC THEME: THE FUTILITY OF IT ALL

1:1☆ Eccles 1:12
1:2 Ps 39:5, 6; 62:9; 144:4; Rom 8:20
1:2☆

1 THE words of the Preacher, the son of David, king in Jerusalem.
2 Vanity of vanities, saith the Preacher, vanity of vanities; all *is*
vanity.

1:1 *The words of the Preacher, the son* [or, "descendant"] *of David, king in Jerusalem,* i.e., "Solomon." The writer uses the name *Koheleth* or *Qoheleth,* a word traditionally rendered "The Preacher." The word means "the gatherer" and may refer to a gatherer of people or of wise sayings and proverbs. Since the name Solomon is not used, some believe that the author was not Solomon but someone else who profited from Solomon's experiences and who may have incorporated some of his words in a work written after Solomon's death.

1:2 *all is vanity,* i.e., "life is useless and empty when lived outside of fellowship with God and apart from the divine will." The solution is found in 12:13, 14.

B. THE FUTILITY OF IT ALL DEMONSTRATED

1. The Cycle of Life Merely Repeats Itself

3 What profit hath a man of all his labour which he taketh under the sun?
4 *One* generation passeth away, and *another* generation cometh: but the
earth abideth for ever.

1:3 Ps 19:4–6 Eccles 2:11 3:9; 5:16

5 The sun also ariseth, and the sun goeth down, and hasteth to his place
where he arose.
6 The wind goeth toward the south, and turneth about unto the north; it
whirleth about continually, and the wind returneth again according to his
circuits.

1:6 Eccles 11:5

7 All the rivers run into the sea; yet the sea *is* not full; unto the place from
whence the rivers come, thither they return again.
8 All things *are* full of labour; man cannot utter *it:* the eye is not satisfied
with seeing, nor the ear filled with hearing.

1:8 Prov 27:20 Eccles 4:8 6:10; 9:5

9 The thing that hath been, it *is that* which shall be; and that which is
done *is* that which shall be done: and *there is* no new *thing* under the sun.

☆**1:9**

10 Is there *any* thing whereof it may be said, See, this *is* new? it hath been
already of old time, which was before us.
11 *There is* no remembrance of former *things;* neither shall there be *any*
remembrance of *things* that are to come with *those* that shall come after.

1:11 Eccles 2:16; 9:5

2. Wisdom Increases Distress

12 I the Preacher was king over Israel in Jerusalem.
13 And I gave my heart to seek and search out by wisdom concerning all
things that are done under heaven: this sore travail hath God given to the
sons of man to be exercised therewith.
14 I have seen all the works that are done under the sun; and, behold, all
is vanity and vexation of spirit.

1:12 Eccles 1:12 7:27; 12:8–10
1:13 Eccles 1:17 3:10, 11; 7:25 8:17
1:14 Eccles 2:11 4:4; 6:9

15 *That which is* crooked cannot be made straight: and that which is
wanting cannot be numbered.

☆**1:15**

16 I communed with mine own heart, saying, Lo, I am come to great
estate, and have gotten more wisdom than all *they* that have been before me
in Jerusalem: yea, my heart had great experience of wisdom and know-
edge.

1:16 1 Kgs 3:12 4:30; 10:23 Eccles 2:9 12:12

17 And I gave my heart to know wisdom, and to know madness and folly:
I perceived that this also is vexation of spirit.
18 For in much wisdom *is* much grief: and he that increaseth knowledge
increaseth sorrow.

☆**1:18**

1:9 *there is no new thing under the sun.* Properly understood, this is correct. We know many things today which were unknown to our ancestors. They are *new to us, yet not new to nature* or to providence. Computer knowledge existed before it was discovered by man. What we do know is as nothing compared to what can be known and will be known in the days ahead. When we come to theology and philosophy, it appears that there is nothing new to be said. Every vagary, every cult, every "new" viewpoint can be traced back to someone who said the same thing centuries ago. When men reflect on the doctrine of God, every "new" idea has its origin in theism, atheism, or agnosticism. There may arise new syntheses of old ideas but no new ideas.

1:15 *That which is crooked cannot be made straight.* Solomon was disappointed to discover that what he found to be crooked he could not make straight. Spiritually, we can say that philosophy and politics cannot make bad men good, nor will learning restore to men the rectitude that Adam had in the Garden of Eden before he sinned. Even justification and regeneration will not result in the perfection of men in this life. That awaits glorification, when, by the return of Christ, the crooked will become straight.

1:18 Getting wisdom is a long and tedious task. Remembering it is equally difficult. The more we know, the more we know we do not know. Thus there is no end to the task of learning wisdom. Wisdom increases grief because the more we know, the more we learn of things that are calamitous.

3. Pleasure and Wealth Are Futile

2:1☆ Prov 14:13; Eccles 7:4, 6; 8:15
2:2☆
2:3 Judg 9:13; Prov 20:1; 23:29–35; Eccles 1:17; 6:12; 8:15; 12:13
2:4 1 Kgs 7:1–12; Song 8:10, 11
2:5 Neh 2:8; Song 4:16; 5:1
2:6 Neh 2:14; 3:15, 16
2:7 Gen 14:14; 15:3; 2 Sam 19:35; 1 Kgs 4:23; 9:28; 10:10, 14, 21; Ezra 2:58
2:9 1 Chron 29:25; Eccles 1:16
2:10 Gen 6:2; Judg 14:2; Eccles 3:22; 5:18; 6:2; 9:9
2:11☆ Eccles 1:3, 14; 2:22; 3:9; 5:16

2 I SAID in mine heart, Go to now, I will prove thee with mirth,
therefore enjoy pleasure: and, behold, this also *is* vanity.
2 I said of laughter, *It is* mad: and of mirth, What doeth it?
3 I sought in mine heart to give myself unto wine, yet acquainting mine
heart with wisdom; and to lay hold on folly, till I might see what *was* that
good for the sons of men, which they should do under the heaven all the
days of their life.
4 I made me great works; I builded me houses; I planted me vineyards:
5 I made me gardens and orchards, and I planted trees in them of all *kind*
of fruits:
6 I made me pools of water, to water therewith the wood that bringeth
forth trees:
7 I got *me* servants and maidens, and had servants born in my house; also
I had great possessions of great and small cattle above all that were in
Jerusalem before me:
8 I gathered me also silver and gold, and the peculiar treasure of kings and
of the provinces: I gat me men singers and women singers, and the delights
of the sons of men, *as* musical instruments, and that of all sorts.
9 So I was great, and increased more than all that were before me in
Jerusalem: also my wisdom remained with me.
10 And whatsoever mine eyes desired I kept not from them, I withheld not
my heart from any joy; for my heart rejoiced in all my labour: and this was
my portion of all my labour.
11 Then I looked on all the works that my hands had wrought, and on the
labour that I had laboured to do: and, behold, all *was* vanity and vexation
of spirit, and *there was* no profit under the sun.

4. The Wise Man and the Fool Both Must Die

2:12 Eccles 1:9, 10, 17; 7:25
2:13☆ Ps 49:10; Prov 4:5–7; 17:24; Eccles 3:19; 6:6; 7:2, 11, 12, 19; 9:2, 3, 18; 1 Jn 2:11
2:15 1 Kgs 3:12; Eccles 2:16; 6:8, 11

12 ¶And I turned myself to behold wisdom, and madness, and folly: for
what *can* the man *do* that cometh after the king? *even* that which hath been
already done.
13 Then I saw that wisdom excelleth folly, as far as light excelleth
darkness.
14 The wise man's eyes *are* in his head; but the fool walketh in darkness:
and I myself perceived also that one event happeneth to them all.
15 Then said I in my heart, As it happeneth to the fool, so it happeneth
even to me; and why was I then more wise? Then I said in my heart, that
this also *is* vanity.

2:1 By personal experience Solomon found that pleasure does not satisfy the heart except momentarily. In fact, before the end of his days pleasure had wrought ruin—with his many wives and concubines, his heart was turned away from God. No one can wear more than one pair of shoes at a time nor can anyone eat more than his stomach will hold. Overindulgence produces satiety; satiety makes pleasure useless. Why should we not accept this truth by the witness of those who have tried it, rather than having to discover it by *personal experience?*

2:2ff Solomon tried everything: laughter, wine, works, slaves, herds, silver, gold, singers, and concubines. Everything ended in vexation of spirit. The moral is plain: only God can fill the void in a man's heart and give him lasting satisfaction and inward joy.

2:11 When God ended his six days of creation, he saw that what he had done was good and he rested from his work. When Solomon surveyed what he had done he was far from satisfied. It was *vanity and vexation of spirit.* There was no profit either in his labors to acquire many things, nor in his attempt to gratify his every desire. He had everything, only to end up bankrupt.

2:13 Solomon knows that it is better to have wisdom than folly. One brings light, the other darkness. But some things happen alike to the wise and to the foolish. And at the end both die, to be remembered no more. After the death of the wise and the foolish, men rarely will have learned enough from the wise to keep them from repeating the follies of the foolish. In this sense the wise are remembered no more, for succeeding generations refuse to take their wisdom seriously.

16 For *there is* no remembrance of the wise more than of the fool for ever;
seeing that which now *is* in the days to come shall all be forgotten. And how
dieth the wise *man?* as the fool.

2:16 Eccles 1:11; 9:5

17 Therefore I hated life; because the work that is wrought under the sun
is grievous unto me: for all *is* vanity and vexation of spirit.

2:17 Num 11:15 Eccles 4:2

5. The Dead Leave Everything Behind

18 ¶Yea, I hated all my labour which I had taken under the sun: because
I should leave it unto the man that shall be after me.
19 And who knoweth whether he shall be a wise *man* or a fool? yet shall he
have rule over all my labour wherein I have laboured, and wherein I have
shewed myself wise under the sun. This *is* also vanity.

☆2:18 Ps 39:6; 49:10 Eccles 2:11 1 Cor 3:10

☆2:19

20 Therefore I went about to cause my heart to despair of all the labour
which I took under the sun.
21 For there is a man whose labour *is* in wisdom, and in knowledge, and in
equity; yet to a man that hath not laboured therein shall he leave it *for* his
portion. This also *is* vanity and a great evil.
22 For what hath man of all his labour, and of the vexation of his heart,
wherein he hath laboured under the sun?
23 For all his days *are* sorrows, and his travail grief; yea, his heart taketh
not rest in the night. This is also vanity.

2:20 Job 5:7; 14:1 Ps 127:2 Eccles 1:18 5:17

24 ¶*There is* nothing better for a man, *than* that he should eat and drink,
and *that* he should make his soul enjoy good in his labour. This also I saw,
that it *was* from the hand of God.
25 For who can eat, or who else can hasten *hereunto*, more than I?
26 For *God* giveth to a man that *is* good in his sight wisdom, and
knowledge, and joy: but to the sinner he giveth travail, to gather and to
heap up, that he may give to *him that is* good before God. This also *is* vanity
and vexation of spirit.

2:24 Prov 2:6; 13:22 Eccles 2:3 3:12, 13, 22 5:18; 6:12 8:15; 9:7 1 Tim 6:17

II. THE SECOND SERMON: LIFE'S DISAPPOINTMENTS (3:1—5:20)

A. THE SENSIBLE ATTITUDE TOWARD LIFE

1. A Right Time for Everything

3 TO every *thing there is* a season, and a time to every purpose under the
heaven:
2 A time to be born, and a time to die; a time to plant, and a time to pluck
up *that which is* planted;
3 A time to kill, and a time to heal; a time to break down, and a time to
build up;
4 A time to weep, and a time to laugh; a time to mourn, and a time to
dance;
5 A time to cast away stones, and a time to gather stones together; a time
to embrace, and a time to refrain from embracing;

☆3:1

3:2 Gen 17:21 1 Sam 2:5 Job 7:1 Ps 52:5 Heb 9:27

3:4 Ex 15:20 Ps 126:2 Rom 12:15

2:18, 19 Men often wait with pleasure for the advent of new rulers over them. They think things will change and conditions will get better. Who knows for sure whether the next king, president, or premier will be wise or foolish? He will take over all his predecessor left behind and may use them foolishly rather than wisely. Some commentators suggest that Solomon looked with trepidation upon his son Rehoboam, to whom the kingship would come, expecting him to be foolish rather than wise. So the end of Solomon's labors would indeed be futility and vanity.

3:1ff Here Solomon contrasts various activities in life: birth and death, getting and losing, etc. Some changes spring from the will of God alone; others depend on the will of man, but both are determined by the immutable counsel of God. Everything in earth is changeable. Only in heaven is there an unchangeable estate. He who has heaven for his hope can endure all changes, for he knows that some day he will inherit the unchangeable.

6A time to get, and a time to lose; a time to keep, and a time to cast
away;
7A time to rend, and a time to sew; a time to keep silence, and a time to
speak;
8A time to love, and a time to hate; a time of war, and a time of peace.

2. A Man Should Enjoy the Gifts of God

9What profit hath he that worketh in that wherein he laboureth?
10I have seen the travail, which God hath given to the sons of men to be
exercised in it.
11He hath made every *thing* beautiful in his time: also he hath set the
world in their heart, so that no man can find out the work that God maketh
from the beginning to the end.
12I know that *there is* no good in them, but for *a man* to rejoice, and to do
good in his life.
13And also that every man should eat and drink, and enjoy the good of all
his labour, it *is* the gift of God.
14I know that, whatsoever God doeth, it shall be for ever: nothing can be
put to it, nor any thing taken from it: and God doeth *it,* that *men* should
fear before him.
15That which hath been is now; and that which is to be hath already
been; and God requireth that which is past.

3. A Man Should Make the Best of This Life

16¶And moreover I saw under the sun the place of judgment, *that*
wickedness *was* there; and the place of righteousness, *that* iniquity *was*
there.
17I said in mine heart, God shall judge the righteous and the wicked: for
there is a time there for every purpose and for every work.
18I said in mine heart concerning the estate of the sons of men, that God
might manifest them, and that they might see that they themselves are
beasts.
19For that which befalleth the sons of men befalleth beasts; even one
thing befalleth them: as the one dieth, so dieth the other; yea, they have all
one breath; so that a man hath no preeminence above a beast: for all *is*
vanity.
20All go unto one place; all are of the dust, and all turn to dust again.
21Who knoweth the spirit of man that goeth upward, and the spirit of the
beast that goeth downward to the earth?
22Wherefore I perceive that *there is* nothing better, than that a man
should rejoice in his own works; for that *is* his portion: for who shall bring
him to see what shall be after him?

3:7 Amos 5:13
3:8 Ps 101:3; Prov 5
3:9 Eccles 1:3; 2:11; 5:16
3:10 Eccles 1:13; 2:26
3:11☆ Gen 1:31; Deut 32:4; Job 5:9; Eccles 8:17; Rom 11:33
3:12 Eccles 2:24
3:13 Eccles 5:19
3:14 Ps 76:10; Prov 19:21; 21:30; Eccles 5:7; 7:18; 8:12, 13; 12:13
3:15 Eccles 1:9; 6:10
3:16 Eccles 4:1; 5:8; 8:9
3:17 Gen 18:25; Ps 96:13; 98:9; Eccles 3:1; 8:6; Mt 16:27; Rom 2:6–10
3:18 Ps 49:12, 20; 73:22
3:19☆
3:20 Gen 3:19; Ps 103:14; Eccles 12:7; Dan 12:2
3:21☆ Eccles 12:7
3:22 Eccles 2:18, 24; 6:12; 8:7; 10:14; Mt 6:34; Phil 4:4, 5

3:11 God has made all things beautiful. Nature and providence work together in ways beyond men's ability to search them out. At last it will be seen that every*thing will have been done properly* and at the right time. This will be the wonder of eternity, when men see then what they see only imperfectly now. Let us therefore wait with patience for this unveiling.

3:19 Men and beasts all die but their ends are different. So also wicked and righteous men all die, yet their ends are different.

3:21 In 3:19 we read that beasts and men both die. All are of dust and to dust return. Yet there is a difference. The souls of beasts die with their bodies. The soul of a beast is like that of a candle that is blown out. It has ended to rise no more. It goes downward to the earth. The spirit of a man goes upwards to meet the Father and Maker of spirits. In the judgment to come the fixed state of those spirits will be determined; some will go to everlasting blessedness and others to eternal separation from the God who made them all.

B. LIFE'S DISAPPOINTMENTS

1. The Oppression and Sadness of Life

4 SO I returned, and considered all the oppressions that are done under
the sun: and behold the tears of *such as were* oppressed, and they had
no comforter; and on the side of their oppressors *there was* power; but they
had no comforter.
2 Wherefore I praised the dead which are already dead more than the
living which are yet alive.
3 Yea, better *is he* than both they, which hath not yet been, who hath not
seen the evil work that is done under the sun.

☆4:1 Deut 28:33; Ps 10:9, 10; Prov 28:3, 15, 16; Eccles 3:16; 5:8; Isa 5:7; Lam 1:9; 2 Tim 4:16, 17
4:2 Job 3:11–26; Eccles 2:17
4:3 Eccles 6:3

2. Walking Alone Is Worse than Having a Partner

4 ¶Again, I considered all travail, and every right work, that for this a man
is envied of his neighbour. This *is* also vanity and vexation of spirit.
5 The fool foldeth his hands together, and eateth his own flesh.
6 Better *is* an handful *with* quietness, than both the hands full *with* travail
and vexation of spirit.
7 ¶Then I returned, and I saw vanity under the sun.
8 There is one *alone*, and *there is* not a second; yea, he hath neither child
nor brother: yet *is there* no end of all his labour; neither is his eye satisfied
with riches; neither *saith he*, For whom do I labour, and bereave my soul of
good? This *is* also vanity, yea, it *is* a sore travail.
9 ¶Two *are* better than one; because they have a good reward for their
labour.
10 For if they fall, the one will lift up his fellow: but woe to him *that is*
alone when he falleth; for *he hath* not another to help him up.
11 Again, if two lie together, then they have heat: but how can one be
warm *alone?*
12 And if one prevail against him, two shall withstand him; and a
threefold cord is not quickly broken.

4:4 Eccles 1:14; 2:21; Jas 4:5
4:5 Prov 6:10; 15:16, 17; 16:8; 24:33; Isa 9:20
☆4:7
4:8 Prov 27:20; Eccles 1:8; 2:21; 5:10; Mt 11:28
☆4:9
☆4:10
☆4:11 1 Kgs 1:1
☆4:12

3. Political Fame Does Not Last

13 ¶Better *is* a poor and a wise child than an old and foolish king, who will
no more be admonished.
14 For out of prison he cometh to reign; whereas also *he that is* born in his
kingdom becometh poor.
15 I considered all the living which walk under the sun, with the second
child that shall stand up in his stead.

☆4:13 Eccles 7:19; 9:15
4:14 Gen 41:14, 41–43

4:1 Solomon expresses great distress over the condition of the oppressed. The oppressors have power, misplaced power, used for evil purposes. The oppressed have nothing to look forward to and think death is preferable to a life of bondage. Good men, however, should not think this way nor wish they had never been born. Those who love God, whatever their outward state, can glorify him; and they will be happy at last and forever. While there is life, there is hope. No man living is ever beyond the reach of hope.

4:7 Some people dote on themselves and think only of adding to what they have. They live alone and die alone. There is no purpose to their labor except to get more. They are worldlings who have enough to live well but whose eyes are never satisfied. They deny themselves the comforts of life and despise pleasure. But at the same time, they have barren souls and empty hearts. This is vanity.

4:9–12 Solomon compares the monastic life to that of life in fellowship with others. There is no state of perfection in the lives of those who live alone. And no one really loves God who does not also love others as well as God. The best of life is a threefold cord that cannot be broken: it consists in two people who help each other in love and who fellowship with God.

4:13 Being a king himself, Solomon knew something about the vanity of life for those in the highest places. However grave, dignified, and powerful a monarch may be, if he is a fool (and some kings are fools), he is worse off than a wise young man who has no wealth and power. Wisdom is to be preferred above all else, for true wisdom always leads to God and to salvation.

4:16 Eccles 1:14

16 *There is* no end of all the people, *even* of all that have been before them:
they also that come after shall not rejoice in him. Surely this also *is* vanity
and vexation of spirit.

C. THE FUTILITY OF SELF-AGGRANDIZEMENT

1. Counsel against Certain Sins

5:1☆ Ex 3:5; 30:18–20; 1 Sam 15:22; Prov 15:8; 21:27; Eccles 10:14; Isa 1:12; Mt 6:7

5 KEEP thy foot when thou goest to the house of God, and be more
ready to hear, than to give the sacrifice of fools: for they consider not
that they do evil.
2 Be not rash with thy mouth, and let not thine heart be hasty to utter *any*
thing before God: for God *is* in heaven, and thou upon earth: therefore let
thy words be few.
3 For a dream cometh through the multitude of business; and a fool's
voice *is known* by multitude of words.

5:4 Num 30:2; Ps 50:14; 66:13, 14; 76:11; Isa 19:21; Mt 5:33
5:5 Prov 20:25; Acts 5:4
5:6 Lev 4:2, 22; Num 15:25; Eccles 3:14; 7:18; 8:12, 13; 12:13; Hos 14:4, 5; 1 Cor 11:10

4 When thou vowest a vow unto God, defer not to pay it; for *he hath* no
pleasure in fools: pay that which thou hast vowed.
5 Better *is it* that thou shouldest not vow, than that thou shouldest vow
and not pay.
6 Suffer not thy mouth to cause thy flesh to sin; neither say thou before
the angel, that it *was* an error: wherefore should God be angry at thy voice,
and destroy the work of thine hands?
7 For in the multitude of dreams and many words *there are* also *divers*
vanities: but fear thou God.

2. Oppressors and Covetous Reap as They Sow

5:8 Ex 2:25; Ps 12:5; Eccles 4:1; Ezek 18:18; 1 Pet 4:12

8 If thou seest the oppression of the poor, and violent perverting of
judgment and justice in a province, marvel not at the matter: for *he that is*
higher than the highest regardeth; and *there be* higher than they.
9 ¶Moreover the profit of the earth is for all: the king *himself* is served by
the field.

5:10☆ Eccles 2:10, 11

10 He that loveth silver shall not be satisfied with silver; nor he that loveth
abundance with increase: this *is* also vanity.

5:11☆ Eccles 2:9
5:12☆ Prov 3:24; Jer 31:26
5:13 Eccles 6:2; Lk 12:16–21; 1 Tim 6:9, 10

11 When goods increase, they are increased that eat them: and what good
is there to the owners thereof, saving the beholding *of them* with their eyes?
12 The sleep of a labouring man *is* sweet, whether he eat little or much:
but the abundance of the rich will not suffer him to sleep.
13 There is a sore evil *which* I have seen under the sun, *namely,* riches kept
for the owners thereof to their hurt.
14 But those riches perish by evil travail: and he begetteth a son, and *there*
is nothing in his hand.

5:15☆ Job 1:21; Ps 49:17; 1 Tim 6:7

15 As he came forth of his mother's womb, naked shall he return to go as
he came, and shall take nothing of his labour, which he may carry away in
his hand.

5:1 The Spirit of God drives men from the world that they may be driven to God. In our worship of God in his house we should behave rightly, take no false step, keep our minds fixed on God, and offer the proper sacrifices.

5:10 Whoever loves money and sets his heart on it will *never have* enough. He always wants more. Worldly abundance will never satisfy spiritual desires. (See also note on 1 Tim. 6:10.)

5:11 "The more men have, the better house they must keep, the more servants they must employ, the more guests they must entertain, the more they must give to the poor, and the more they will have hanging on them, for where *the carcase is the eagles will be* (Matt. 24:28)."*

5:12 The tired laborer on a common diet sleeps better at night than the overfed, overindulged rich man whose worries are carried to his bed where he turns and twists in sleepless concern for the morrow (Luke 12:17).

5:15 The more one has, the more he has to lose. And some lose it all, if not in this life, then at death and in the life to come. We go out the way we came into the world—empty-handed. The end is the same for all: earth to earth, ashes to ashes, dust to dust.

16And this also *is* a sore evil, *that* in all points as he came, so shall he go:
and what profit hath he that hath laboured for the wind?
17All his days also he eateth in darkness, and *he hath* much sorrow and
wrath with his sickness.

5:16 Prov 11:29; Eccles 1:3; 2:11; 3:9; Hos 8:7
5:17 Eccles 2:23

3. Man Should Accept and Enjoy What God Gives

18¶Behold *that* which I have seen: *it is* good and comely *for one* to eat and
to drink, and to enjoy the good of all his labour that he taketh under the
sun all the days of his life, which God giveth him: for it *is* his portion.
19Every man also to whom God hath given riches and wealth, and hath
given him power to eat thereof, and to take his portion, and to rejoice in his
labour; this *is* the gift of God.
20For he shall not much remember the days of his life; because God
answereth *him* in the joy of his heart.

☆**5:18** Eccles 2:10, 24; 9:7; 1 Tim 6:17
☆**5:19** 2 Chron 1:12; Eccles 3:13; 6:2
5:20 Deut 28:8–12; Isa 64:5; Rom 5:1–5

III. THE THIRD SERMON: THE FUTILITY OF WEALTH AND FAME (6:1—8:17)

A. MAN'S MOST AMBITIOUS DESIRES ARE THWARTED

6 THERE is an evil which I have seen under the sun, and it *is* common
among men:
2A man to whom God hath given riches, wealth, and honour, so that he
wanteth nothing for his soul of all that he desireth, yet God giveth him not
power to eat thereof, but a stranger eateth it: this *is* vanity, and it *is* an evil
disease.
3If a man beget an hundred *children*, and live many years, so that the
days of his years be many, and his soul be not filled with good, and also *that*
he have no burial; I say, *that* an untimely birth *is* better than he.
4For he cometh in with vanity, and departeth in darkness, and his name
shall be covered with darkness.
5Moreover he hath not seen the sun, nor known *any thing:* this hath more
rest than the other.
6¶Yea, though he live a thousand years twice *told*, yet hath he seen no
good: do not all go to one place?
7All the labour of man *is* for his mouth, and yet the appetite is not filled.
8For what hath the wise more than the fool? what hath the poor, that
knoweth to walk before the living?
9¶Better *is* the sight of the eyes than the wandering of the desire: this *is*
also vanity and vexation of spirit.

6:1 Eccles 5:13
☆**6:2** 1 Kgs 3:13; Ps 17:14; 73:7; Lk 12:19, 20
☆**6:3** Job 3:16; Eccles 4:3; Isa 14:20; Jer 8:2; Mt 26:24
6:6 Eccles 2:14
☆**6:7** Prov 16:26
6:8 Eccles 2:15
6:9 Prov 30:15, 16; Eccles 1:14; 11:9

5:18 We are not to starve ourselves because we are covetous or kill ourselves with overwork to amass a fortune. Let us use well what we have, serve God with it, care for our families, and make good use of our resources.

5:19 Contrary to what some believers think, we are to accept with gratitude what God has given us, enjoy those things, and find satisfaction in the labor of our hands. All things come from our God, and what we give him is only a part of what he has given us.

6:2 Riches, wealth, and honor are gifts from God. Unlike sunshine, which is given for all men to enjoy, God does not give riches, wealth, and honor to all men. In his providence he gives them to some and not to others, at his good pleasure. Some of those who have received these gifts from God do not make good use of them. Some never get enjoyment or satisfaction from such gifts.

6:3 Solomon asserts that a stillborn baby is better off than a wealthy man who does not enjoy the wealth and honor God has given him. Though such a man were to live two thousand years, he would end up in the same place as the stillborn child. It is the place to which all go, the wealthy and the poor, the learned and unlearned, the short-lived and the long-lived. The dust of all the dead is mingled together and there is no distinction.

6:7 A little provision will allow men to live comfortably. Whoever earns an honest living, lives decently, and is diligent is better off than the wealthy man who is full of complaints and exhibits a haughty spirit.

10 That which hath been is named already, and it is known that it *is* man:
neither may he contend with him that is mightier than he.
11 ¶Seeing there be many things that increase vanity, what *is* man the
better?
12 For who knoweth what *is* good for man in *this* life, all the days of his
vain life which he spendeth as a shadow? for who can tell a man what shall
be after him under the sun?

B. ADVICE TO THOSE WHO LIVE IN A SINFUL WORLD

1. Choosing the Better

7 A GOOD name *is* better than precious ointment; and the day of death
than the day of one's birth.
2 *It is* better to go to the house of mourning, than to go to the house of
feasting: for that *is* the end of all men; and the living will lay *it* to his heart.
3 Sorrow *is* better than laughter: for by the sadness of the countenance the
heart is made better.
4 The heart of the wise *is* in the house of mourning; but the heart of fools
is in the house of mirth.
5 *It is* better to hear the rebuke of the wise, than for a man to hear the
song of fools.
6 For as the crackling of thorns under a pot, so *is* the laughter of the fool:
this also *is* vanity.
7 ¶Surely oppression maketh a wise man mad; and a gift destroyeth the
heart.
8 Better *is* the end of a thing than the beginning thereof: *and* the patient in
spirit *is* better than the proud in spirit.
9 Be not hasty in thy spirit to be angry: for anger resteth in the bosom of
fools.

2. Wisdom Is Better than Wealth

10 Say not thou, What is *the cause* that the former days were better than
these? for thou dost not inquire wisely concerning this.
11 ¶Wisdom *is* good with an inheritance: and *by it there is* profit to them
that see the sun.
12 For wisdom *is* a defence, *and* money *is* a defence: but the excellency of
knowledge *is, that* wisdom giveth life to them that have it.
13 Consider the work of God: for who can make *that* straight, which he
hath made crooked?
14 In the day of prosperity be joyful, but in the day of adversity consider:

6:10☆ Gen 3:17–19; Job 9:32; 40:2; Prov 21:30; Eccles 1:9; 3:15; Isa 45:7
6:11 Hos 12:1
6:12 Lam 3:24–27; Mic 6:8
7:1 Prov 22:1; Eccles 4:2; 7:8; Isa 56:5; Heb 11:2
7:2☆ Ps 90:12; Eccles 2:16; 3:19, 20; 9:2, 3; Amos 6:3–6
7:3☆ Eccles 2:2; 2 Cor 7:10
7:5 Ps 141:5; Prov 6:23; 13:18; 15:31, 32; 25:12; Eccles 9:17
7:6 Ps 58:9; Eccles 2:2
7:7 Ex 23:8; Deut 16:19; Prov 17:23; Eccles 4:1; 5:8; Isa 33:15
7:8 Prov 14:29; 16:32; Eccles 7:1; Lk 21:19; Gal 5:22; Eph 4:2; Jas 5:8
7:9☆ Prov 14:17; 16:32; Mk 6:19, 24; Jas 1:19
7:10☆
7:11 Prov 8:10, 11
7:12 Prov 3:18; 8:35; Eccles 9:18; Jn 12:50; 17:3
7:13 Eccles 1:15; 3:11; 8:17; Rom 9:15, 19
7:14☆ Deut 8:5; 26:11; Eccles 3:22; 9:7; 11:9

6:10 Our lot in life is set for us by the counsel of God. Some are born into homes of wealth, others into homes of poverty. Some are black, some brown, some white, and others yellow. Some are born in remote areas, others in crowded cities. What cannot be altered should be accepted. It is better to reconcile ourselves to these things cheerfully and acquiesce than to quarrel with God. Wisdom makes a virtue of necessity, and what pleases God should please us.

7:2 How can a visit to a house of mourning be better than going to a house of feasting? A funeral is better than a festival, because the former is more apt to make us think of the ultimate issues of life, whereas a festival will bring pleasure without serious thought to life's final question: "What happens to me when I die?"

7:3 Sorrow concentrates one's mind on the things that are most important, whereas laughter and gaiety are an escape mechanism, used to avoid thinking about important matters.

7:9 Anger is passion lacking in wisdom and grace. We should not become angry quickly nor should we remain angry long. When we do get angry, to let the anger settle in our frames is to act like fools.

7:10 Why do people assume that yesterday was better than today? Why complain about the badness of the times without complaining of the badness of our own hearts? Would not the times get better if men's hearts got better? And are not complaints about our times a quarrel against God, who oversees all of life and who is to be found and worshipped regardless of the times?

7:14 God sends good times and bad ones. Rejoice when they are good and give serious thought to life when times are bad. God may have rich blessings and good health enclosed in ragged boxes. Adversity can be good food for those who think through why God allowed it to take place.

God also hath set the one over against the other, to the end that man
should find nothing after him.

3. The Middle Way Is Better

15 All *things* have I seen in the days of my vanity: there is a just *man* that
perisheth in his righteousness, and there is a wicked *man* that prolongeth *his*
life in his wickedness.
16 Be not righteous over much; neither make thyself over wise: why
shouldest thou destroy thyself?
17 Be not over much wicked, neither be thou foolish: why shouldest thou
die before thy time?
18 *It is* good that thou shouldest take hold of this; yea, also from this
withdraw not thine hand: for he that feareth God shall come forth of them
all.

4. Wisdom versus Folly

19 Wisdom strengtheneth the wise more than ten mighty *men* which are in
the city.
20 For *there is* not a just man upon earth, that doeth good, and sinneth
not.
21 Also take no heed unto all words that are spoken; lest thou hear thy
servant curse thee:
22 For oftentimes also thine own heart knoweth that thou thyself likewise
hast cursed others.
23 ¶All this have I proved by wisdom: I said, I will be wise; but it *was* far
from me.
24 That which is far off, and exceeding deep, who can find it out?
25 I applied mine heart to know and to search, and to seek out wisdom,
and the reason *of things*, and to know the wickedness of folly, even of
foolishness *and* madness:

5. A Wicked Woman and Sinful Men

26 And I find more bitter than death the woman, whose heart *is* snares and
nets, *and* her hands *as* bands: whoso pleaseth God shall escape from her;
but the sinner shall be taken by her.
27 Behold, this have I found, saith the preacher, *counting* one by one, to
find out the account:
28 Which yet my soul seeketh, but I find not: one man among a thousand
have I found; but a woman among all those have I not found.
29 Lo, this only have I found, that God hath made man upright; but they
have sought out many inventions.

☆7:15 Job 22:16; Prov 10:27; Eccles 6:12; 8:12–14; 9:9; Rom 12:3
7:18 Ps 25:12–14; Prov 4:25–27; Eccles 3:14; 5:7; 8:12, 13; 12:13
☆7:20 1 Kgs 8:46; 2 Chron 6:36; Ps 143:2; Prov 20:9; Rom 3:23
☆7:21
☆7:23
7:24 Deut 30:11–14; Job 11:7; 37:23; Rom 11:33; 1 Tim 6:16
7:25 Eccles 1:7; 10:13; Jer 12:1, 2; 2 Pet 2:3–9; 3:3–9
7:26 Prov 5:4; 6:23, 24; 7:23; 22:14
7:28 1 Kgs 11:3
☆7:29 Gen 1:27

7:15 *We may not understand* but we should not be offended when the rich prosper, while the godly encounter great and grave misfortunes. Wisdom will help us understand how to reconcile the calamities of life with the wisdom, holiness, goodness, and faithfulness of our God.
7:20 All men function and act according to their nature (a good tree brings forth good fruit), yet the righteous are not perfectly free from sin in this life. Nevertheless, they have the promise of forgiveness and restoration if they confess their sins (1 John 1:9).
7:21 It is better to close our eyes to injuries, as though we did not see them. Nor are we to be overly concerned to discover what people think of us, for this knowledge will either feed our pride or stir up our anger. If we are approved of God, our consciences are at rest and we need not heed what men say about us.
7:23ff Wise as Solomon was, he had to admit and lament his own inadequacy. He left no stone unturned to find wisdom, but he hardly scratched the surface in his search.
7:29 Only Adam was upright when he came out of God's hands, but he became marred and "unmade" by his own choice. All men follow in the footsteps of their first parent and exhibit the same imperfection.

C. MAKING THE BEST OF AN IMPERFECT WORLD
1. Obeying Rulers

8 WHO *is* as the wise *man?* and who knoweth the interpretation of a
thing? a man's wisdom maketh his face to shine, and the boldness of
his face shall be changed.
2 I *counsel thee* to keep the king's commandment, and *that* in regard of the
oath of God.
3 Be not hasty to go out of his sight: stand not in an evil thing; for he
doeth whatsoever pleaseth him.
4 Where the word of a king *is, there is* power: and who may say unto him,
What doest thou?
5 Whoso keepeth the commandment shall feel no evil thing: and a wise
man's heart discerneth both time and judgment.
6 ¶Because to every purpose there is time and judgment, therefore the
misery of man *is* great upon him.
7 For he knoweth not that which shall be: for who can tell him when it
shall be?
8 *There is* no man that hath power over the spirit to retain the spirit;
neither *hath he* power in the day of death: and *there is* no discharge in *that*
war; neither shall wickedness deliver those that are given to it.

8:1☆ Ex 34:29, 30 Deut 28:50 Eph 6:19 2 Tim 4:17
8:2☆ Ex 22:11 2 Sam 21:7 Eccles 10:4 Ezek 17:18
8:4 Job 9:12 Prov 19:12; 20:2 Dan 4:35 Rom 9:20
8:5 Ex 1:17–21 Prov 12:21 Eccles 10:2 12:14 Lk 12:56, 57 1 Cor 2:14, 15
8:6 Eccles 3:1, 17, 22; 6:12; 7:14 9:12
8:8 Deut 20:5–8 Ps 49:7–9 Eccles 8:13 Heb 9:27

2. The Wicked Will Be Punished at Last

9 All this have I seen, and applied my heart unto every work that is done
under the sun: *there is* a time wherein one man ruleth over another to his
own hurt.
10 And so I saw the wicked buried, who had come and gone from the
place of the holy, and they were forgotten in the city where they had so
done: this *is* also vanity.
11 Because sentence against an evil work is not executed speedily,
therefore the heart of the sons of men is fully set in them to do evil.
12 ¶Though a sinner do evil an hundred times, and his *days* be prolonged,
yet surely I know that it shall be well with them that fear God, which fear
before him:
13 But it shall not be well with the wicked, neither shall he prolong *his*
days, *which are* as a shadow; because he feareth not before God.

8:9 Eccles 1:11 2:16; 4:1, 16 5:8; 9:5, 15
8:11☆ Ex 34:6 Job 21:11–15 Ps 86:15 Jer 48:11 Rom 2:4, 5 2 Pet 3:9
8:12 Deut 4:40 1 Kgs 2:5–9 Ps 37:11 Prov 1:33 Eccles 7:15
8:13 Eccles 6:12; 8:8 Isa 3:11

3. The Paradox of Providence

14 There is a vanity which is done upon the earth; that there be just *men*,
unto whom it happeneth according to the work of the wicked; again, there
be wicked *men*, to whom it happeneth according to the work of the
righteous: I said that this also *is* vanity.

8:14☆ Job 21:7 Ps 73:3, 12 Eccles 2:14 7:15 Jer 12:1 Mal 3:15

8:1 The wise man is a good man because he knows God, keeps his commandments, and glorifies him. Like Moses' face, the face of the good man shines—for the light of the glory of God transfigures him.

8:2 Men live under authority. They are to obey rulers. This is not an absolute commandment, for Solomon *knew that he had sworn to* rule over Israel in the fear of the Lord. Such rulers are not be feared by the people. But if the rulers do not fear God and require of men what God has forbidden, they must be resisted.

8:11 This verse suggests that it is good to execute sentences against the guilty quickly as a deterrent rather than to let them suppose they will never be punished. When sentences are deferred, the wicked take heart and work further evil. Thus they abuse the patience of God and fail to see that when vengeance does come it will be even more severe.

8:14 Solomon knew that sometimes providence smiled on the wicked and allowed them to become prosperous and successful. While the righteous were being laughed at and censured, the wicked were being applauded and preferred. He did not charge God with sin but the world with vanity, because of its twisted sense of values.

15 Then I commended mirth, because a man hath no better thing under
the sun, than to eat, and to drink, and to be merry: for that shall abide with
him of his labour the days of his life, which God giveth him under the sun.

8:15
Eccles 2:24
3:12, 13; 5:18
1 Tim 6:17

4. God's Ways Cannot Be Known by Man

16 ¶When I applied mine heart to know wisdom, and to see the business
that is done upon the earth: (for also *there is that* neither day nor night
seeth sleep with his eyes:)
17 Then I beheld all the work of God, that a man cannot find out the work
that is done under the sun: because though a man labour to seek *it* out, yet
he shall not find *it;* yea further; though a wise *man* think to know *it*, yet
shall he not be able to find *it*.

☆**8:16**
Eccles 1:13, 14
3:11
Isa 40:28
☆**8:17**

IV. THE FOURTH SERMON: GOD WILL TAKE CARE OF LIFE'S UNFAIRNESS (9:1—12:8)

A. DOING THE BEST YOU CAN

1. Death Comes to the Good and the Bad; Enjoy Life while You Can

9 FOR all this I considered in my heart even to declare all this, that the
righteous, and the wise, and their works, *are* in the hand of God: no
man knoweth either love or hatred *by* all *that is* before them.
2 All *things come* alike to all: *there is* one event to the righteous, and to the
wicked; to the good and to the clean, and to the unclean; to him that
sacrificeth, and to him that sacrificeth not: as *is* the good, so *is* the sinner;
and he that sweareth, as *he* that feareth an oath.
3 This *is* an evil among all *things* that are done under the sun, that *there is*
one event unto all: yea, also the heart of the sons of men is full of evil, and
madness *is* in their heart while they live, and after that *they go* to the dead.
4 ¶For to him that is joined to all the living there is hope: for a living dog
is better than a dead lion.
5 For the living know that they shall die: but the dead know not any
thing, neither have they any more a reward; for the memory of them is
forgotten.
6 Also their love, and their hatred, and their envy, is now perished;
neither have they any more a portion for ever in any *thing* that is done
under the sun.
7 ¶Go thy way, eat thy bread with joy, and drink thy wine with a merry
heart; for God now accepteth thy works.

☆**9:1**
Deut 33:3
1 Sam 2:9
Ps 37:5, 6
Prov 16:3
Eccles 9:6
10:14
9:2
Job 9:22
Eccles 2:14
3:19; 6:6; 7:2
Mal 3:5, 18
☆**9:5**
Job 7:8–10
14:21
Ps 88:12
Eccles 1:11
2:16; 8:10
Isa 26:14
Heb 9:27
9:6
Eccles 2:10
3:22
9:7
Eccles 2:24
Lk 11:41
Acts 10:35

8:16, 17 Whoever seeks to discover the reasons why God acts as he does will never find the answers. Men should "be contentedly and piously ignorant of the meaning of God's proceedings in the government of the world."* However industriously men labor in seeking answers, they will never find the key that unlocks the door to this cosmic mystery.

9:1 Solomon, wise as he was, found it difficult to understand how providence made little difference between the good and the bad as to the conveniences of life. But he did grasp the truth that the good are in the tender and loving hands of God, while the wicked are sure to reap as they have sowed.

9:5 *the dead know not any thing.* These statements are Solomon's discouraged opinion, and do not reflect a knowledge of God's truth on these points. From 9:10 some have adopted the notion that the dead know nothing until the resurrection, and that their souls sleep. The Bible is a book of progressive revelation, and this helps us understand this passage. God does not reveal everything at once. The Old Testament does not have a fully developed doctrine of the condition of the soul upon death. Paul, for example, teaches that it is better to be with Christ, which can only mean in conscious fellowship. In cases like this, the hermeneutical principle is that the Old Testament is to be interpreted in the light of the New Testament. Clear passages take precedence over the obscure. And no single part of the Bible is to be interpreted without reference to the totality of God's revelation. Finally, Scripture interprets Scripture. This is the analogy of faith principle.

9:8☆ Ps 23:5; Rev 3:4
9:9☆

8 Let thy garments be always white; and let thy head lack no ointment.
9 Live joyfully with the wife whom thou lovest all the days of the life of
thy vanity, which he hath given thee under the sun, all the days of thy
vanity: for that *is* thy portion in *this* life, and in thy labour which thou
takest under the sun.

9:10 Gen 37:35; Job 21:13; Eccles 9:5; 11:6; Rom 12:11; Col 3:23

10 Whatsoever thy hand findeth to do, do *it* with thy might; for *there is* no
work, nor device, nor knowledge, nor wisdom, in the grave, whither thou
goest.

2. Chance Happens to All Men

9:11☆ Deut 8:17, 18; 1 Sam 6:9; 2 Chron 20:15; Ps 76:5; Amos 2:14, 15; Zech 4:6
9:12 Eccles 8:7; Isa 24:18; Hos 9:8; Lk 21:34, 35

11 I returned, and saw under the sun, that the race *is* not to the swift, nor
the battle to the strong, neither yet bread to the wise, nor yet riches to men
of understanding, nor yet favour to men of skill; but time and chance
happeneth to them all.
12 For man also knoweth not his time: as the fishes that are taken in an
evil net, and as the birds that are caught in the snare; so *are* the sons of men
snared in an evil time, when it falleth suddenly upon them.

3. Wisdom Is Better than Strength

9:15 2 Sam 20:22; Eccles 2:16; 4:13; 8:10
9:16 Eccles 7:12, 19
9:17 Eccles 7:5; 10:12
9:18 Josh 7:1–26; 2 Kgs 21:2–17; Eccles 9:16; Heb 12:15, 16

13 ¶This wisdom have I seen also under the sun, and it *seemed* great unto
me:
14 *There was* a little city, and few men within it; and there came a great
king against it, and besieged it, and built great bulwarks against it:
15 Now there was found in it a poor wise man, and he by his wisdom
delivered the city; yet no man remembered that same poor man.
16 Then said I, Wisdom *is* better than strength: nevertheless the poor
man's wisdom *is* despised, and his words are not heard.
17 The words of wise *men are* heard in quiet more than the cry of him that
ruleth among fools.
18 Wisdom *is* better than weapons of war: but one sinner destroyeth much
good.

B. THE UNCERTAINTY OF LIFE AND THE STUPIDITY OF FOLLY

1. Folly versus Wisdom

10:1☆ Ex 30:25
10:3 Prov 13:16; 18:2
10:4 1 Sam 25:24–33; Prov 25:15; Eccles 8:3
10:6 Esth 3:1; Prov 28:12; 29:2; Jas 2:3–5

10 DEAD flies cause the ointment of the apothecary to send forth a
stinking savour: *so doth* a little folly him that is in reputation for
wisdom *and* honour.
2 A wise man's heart *is* at his right hand; but a fool's heart at his left.
3 Yea also, when he that is a fool walketh by the way, his wisdom faileth
him, and he saith to every one *that* he *is* a fool.
4 If the spirit of the ruler rise up against thee, leave not thy place; for
yielding pacifieth great offences.
5 There is an evil *which* I have seen under the sun, as an error *which*
proceedeth from the ruler:
6 Folly is set in great dignity, and the rich sit in low place.

9:8 *White* garments were worn on festive occasions; *oil* on the head produced a cooling and refreshing effect.

9:9 To live joyfully with one's wife is good advice. It *was too bad that Solomon did not follow this advice*, for he multiplied wives and concubines. They were the source of his downfall.

9:11 From the human perspective we should remember the uncertainty and contingency of the future. Who knows what the morrow will bring forth? God knows; we do not. And our times are in his hands. Therefore, let us do with all our might what we are supposed to do. Humanly speaking, things never turn out quite the way we anticipated or hoped for.

10:1 A good reputation gained by great labor may be lost with a little folly. Believers should abstain from all appearances of evil lest they ruin their testimony. Solomon's description is graphic: dead flies in perfume give forth "a stinking savor."

7 I have seen servants upon horses, and princes walking as servants upon
the earth.
8 He that diggeth a pit shall fall into it; and whoso breaketh an hedge, a
serpent shall bite him.
9 Whoso removeth stones shall be hurt therewith; *and* he that cleaveth
wood shall be endangered thereby.
10 If the iron be blunt, and he do not whet the edge, then must he put to
more strength: but wisdom *is* profitable to direct.
11 Surely the serpent will bite without enchantment; and a babbler is no
better.

2. The Empty Talk of the Fool

12 The words of a wise man's mouth *are* gracious; but the lips of a fool
will swallow up himself.
13 The beginning of the words of his mouth *is* foolishness: and the end of
his talk *is* mischievous madness.
14 A fool also is full of words: a man cannot tell what shall be; and what
shall be after him, who can tell him?
15 The labour of the foolish wearieth every one of them, because he
knoweth not how to go to the city.

3. Concluding Admonitions

16 ¶Woe to thee, O land, when thy king *is* a child, and thy princes eat in
the morning!
17 Blessed *art* thou, O land, when thy king *is* the son of nobles, and thy
princes eat in due season, for strength, and not for drunkenness!
18 ¶By much slothfulness the building decayeth; and through idleness of
the hands the house droppeth through.
19 ¶A feast is made for laughter, and wine maketh merry: but money
answereth all *things*.
20 ¶Curse not the king, no not in thy thought; and curse not the rich in thy
bedchamber: for a bird of the air shall carry the voice, and that which hath
wings shall tell the matter.

C. HOW TO LIVE YOUR LIFE

1. Doing Good Things

11 CAST thy bread upon the waters: for thou shalt find it after many
days.
2 Give a portion to seven, and also to eight; for thou knowest not what
evil shall be upon the earth.

10:7 Esth 6:8 Prov 19:10 30:22
10:8 Judg 9:53–57 Esth 7:10 Ps 7:15 Prov 26:27 Amos 5:19
☆**10:10**
☆**10:11**
10:12 Prov 10:14, 32 22:11 Eccles 7:25 Lk 4:22 Eph 4:29 Col 4:6
☆**10:14** Prov 15:2 Eccles 3:22 5:3; 6:12; 7:14 8:7
☆**10:16** 2 Chron 13:7 Prov 20:1, 2 Isa 3:4, 12; 5:11
☆**10:17**
☆**10:18** Prov 24:30–34 2 Pet 1:5–10
10:19 Judg 9:13 Ps 104:15 Eccles 2:3; 7:12
☆**10:20** Ex 22:28 Acts 23:5
11:1 Deut 15:7–11 Prov 11:24, 25 19:17 Isa 32:20 Mt 10:42 Lk 14:14 2 Cor 9:8 Heb 6:10
☆**11:2** Neh 8:10 Ps 112:9 Prov 6:16 Mic 5:5 Lk 17:4 1 Tim 6:18, 19

10:10 Wisdom teaches us to look before we leap. Cutting wood with an axe is always easier if we sharpen the blade before we begin. We save work and escape from harm if we meditate before we speak and act. By advance preparation we save ourselves from having to do remedial work in the long run.
10:11 *Surely the serpent will bite without enchantment,* or, "If the serpent bites before it is charmed, there is no advantage to the charmer."†
10:14 *A fool also is full of words.* The Scriptures do not forbid talking, only the foolish and unwise use of speech. Right speaking is a powerful force for good, an ally of true wisdom. The wrong use of speech is forbidden and the consequences of such use made plain.
10:16, 17 Israel experienced what Solomon discusses here. Rulers like Absalom and Rehoboam lacked the virtues essential to good rulership and were self-willed and dissolute.
10:18 *Slothfulness* produces home problems and spiritual degeneration.
10:20 Prudence keeps men from saying things that may be true but are unwise to make public. What you say may be made known at a time when you wish you had never spoken the words. One instance of this is found in 2 Kings 6:2, TLB: "Elisha, the prophet, tells the king of Israel even the words you speak in the privacy of your bedroom!"
11:2 *Give a portion to seven, and also to eight,* i.e., "Divide your gifts among many."† This is a Hebrew idiom indicating an indefinite number. A climactic use of numbers was a common poetic device in the Near East.

[3]If the clouds be full of rain, they empty *themselves* upon the earth: and
if the tree fall toward the south, or toward the north, in the place where the
tree falleth, there it shall be.

11:4☆

[4]He that observeth the wind shall not sow; and he that regardeth the
clouds shall not reap.

11:5 Ps 139:13–16; Eccles 1:15; 3:10; 8:17; Jn 3:8

[5]As thou knowest not what *is* the way of the spirit, *nor* how the bones *do*
grow in the womb of her that is with child: even so thou knowest not the
works of God who maketh all.

11:6 Eccles 9:10

[6]In the morning sow thy seed, and in the evening withhold not thine
hand: for thou knowest not whether shall prosper, either this or that, or
whether they both *shall be* alike good.

11:7 Eccles 6:5; 7:11

[7]¶Truly the light *is* sweet, and a pleasant *thing it is* for the eyes to behold
the sun:

11:8 Eccles 9:7; 12:1

[8]But if a man live many years, *and* rejoice in them all; yet let him
remember the days of darkness; for they shall be many. All that cometh *is*
vanity.

2. Every Life Must Account to God

11:9 Num 15:39; Job 31:7; Ps 81:12; Eccles 2:10; 3:17; 12:4; Acts 24:25; Rom 14:10

[9]¶Rejoice, O young man, in thy youth; and let thy heart cheer thee in the
days of thy youth, and walk in the ways of thine heart, and in the sight of
thine eyes: but know thou, that for all these *things* God will bring thee into
judgment.

11:10☆ 2 Cor 7:1; 2 Tim 2:22

[10]Therefore remove sorrow from thy heart, and put away evil from thy
flesh: for childhood and youth *are* vanity.

3. The Command to Live for the Creator

12:1☆ Deut 8:18; 2 Sam 19:35; Neh 4:14; Ps 63:6; 119:55; Eccles 11:8; Hos 7:9

12 REMEMBER now thy Creator in the days of thy youth, while the
evil days come not, nor the years draw nigh, when thou shalt say, I
have no pleasure in them;

12:2 Isa 13:10; Ezek 32:7, 8; Joel 3:5; Mt 24:29

[2]While the sun, or the light, or the moon, or the stars, be not darkened,
nor the clouds return after the rain:

12:3 Gen 27:1; 1 Sam 3:2; Ps 35:14; 38:6

[3]In the day when the keepers of the house shall tremble, and the strong
men shall bow themselves, and the grinders cease because they are few, and
those that look out of the windows be darkened,

12:4 2 Sam 19:35; Rev 18:22

[4]And the doors shall be shut in the streets, when the sound of the
grinding is low, and he shall rise up at the voice of the bird, and all the
daughters of musick shall be brought low;

12:5 Gen 50:10; Job 17:13; Zech 4:2, 3

[5]Also *when* they shall be afraid of *that which is* high, and fears *shall be* in
the way, and the almond tree shall flourish, and the grasshopper shall be a
burden, and desire shall fail: because man goeth to his long home, and the
mourners go about the streets:

12:7☆ Gen 3:19; Ps 104:29; Eccles 3:20, 21; Lk 23:46; Acts 7:59; Heb 12:9, 23

[6]Or ever the silver cord be loosed, or the golden bowl be broken, or the
pitcher be broken at the fountain, or the wheel broken at the cistern.

[7]Then shall the dust return to the earth as it was: and the spirit shall
return unto God who gave it.

12:8 Eccles 1:2

[8]¶Vanity of vanities, saith the preacher; all *is* vanity.

11:4 *Paraphrased: "If you wait for perfect conditions, you will never get anything done."*†

11:10 Life is filled with its ups and downs. All men experience both. But the downs can be lessened and their effects softened when God's people obey him. When life's difficulties cannot be avoided, God's grace makes it possible to endure what cannot be changed.

12:1ff Here is an excellent portrayal of the changes brought on by old age—its effects on mind and body, the gradual deterioration which overtakes us all.

12:7 The body perishes but the spirit returns to the God who made it and gave it. He will judge it.

V. CONCLUSION: LIVING IN THE LIGHT OF ETERNITY (12:9–14)

A. THE PREACHER'S INTENTION

9And moreover, because the preacher was wise, he still taught the people
knowledge; yea, he gave good heed, and sought out, *and* set in order many
proverbs.
10The preacher sought to find out acceptable words: and *that which was*
written *was* upright, *even* words of truth.

12:9
1 Kgs 4:32
Prov 10:1; 25:1

☆**12:10**

B. MASTERING THE TEACHING OF THE PREACHER

11The words of the wise *are* as goads, and as nails fastened *by* the masters
of assemblies, *which* are given from one shepherd.
12And further, by these, my son, be admonished: of making many books
there is no end; and much study *is* a weariness of the flesh.

12:11
Ezra 9:8
Eccles 7:5
10:12
Isa 22:23
Acts 2:37
2 Cor 10:4

12:12
1 Kgs 4:32, 33
Lk 16:29–31
2 Pet 1:19–21

C. THE CONCLUSION: THE CHIEF DUTIES OF MAN

13¶Let us hear the conclusion of the whole matter: Fear God, and keep
his commandments: for this *is* the whole *duty* of man.
14For God shall bring every work into judgment, with every secret thing,
whether *it be* good, or whether *it be* evil.

☆**12:13**
Deut 6:2; 10:12
Eccles 3:14
5:7; 8:5
Mic 6:8

☆**12:14**
Eccles 3:17
11:9
Mt 10:26
Rom 2:16
1 Cor 4:5

12:10 Truth can be taught in a compelling fashion or in such a way that the listener does not profit from it. Truth should be made palatable and clothed in garments of beauty.

12:13 The Preacher sums up the whole matter of one's philosophy of life. Every notion has its opposing notion and when life has been searched, no final answers are available from that search. Worldly wisdom is not enough. There is a revelation which comes from God and not from outward observation. All of life may be comprehended in this dictum—*Fear God, and keep his commandments.* This is the entire duty of man. At any time and under all circumstances, the best that man can do is to trust God.

12:14 One of the best inducements to live the good life lies in the fact that God will bring every work into judgment. All the secrets of men's hearts will be revealed to determine the goodness and the badness of them. Some of the righteous will enter into life empty-handed; others will be richly rewarded with many crowns.

THE SONG OF SOLOMON

Authorship, date, and background The Song of Songs is the first of the five Megilloth (or Scrolls) including the books of Ruth, Lamentations, Ecclesiastes, and Esther. It was read publicly every year at the Passover celebration. Substantial differences of opinion exist even among conservative scholars about the authorship and the interpretation of the book. The opening verse of the book ascribes the authorship to Solomon, whose reign is dated 970–930 B.C. Scholars such as F. Delitzsch, J. H. Raven, J. E. Steinmueller, E. J. Young and G. L. Archer accept the Solomonic authorship. Once that is done, the dating of the book falls into place as a tenth century B.C. product. The language agrees with that of Ecclesiastes and many have assumed that the same person wrote both books.

The text indicates that the Davidic kingdom was still intact. The author was acquainted with the flora and fauna of the entire country. He had poetic gifts and used them to the fullest. Because the book dealt with intimate marital details, an old rabbinical requirement forbade the reading of it until a Jew had attained the age of thirty. Apparently similar type songs were read as a *wasf* at wedding ceremonies in the Near East, according to some interpreters, but whether this was customary of The Song of Songs at Jewish weddings is questionable.

Characteristics and content Virtually all scholars agree that Solomon is involved in the story. They differ as to whether Solomon and the shepherd hero are the same person. Some think the Shulamite maiden marries Solomon and teaches him the values of monogamous love, which he gladly accepts over against the corrupt splendor of his own court; others think the shepherd hero is the man the Shulamite maiden loves and from whom she is separated when taken to Solomon's harem. When Solomon cannot win her love, she is permitted to return to her shepherd lover, whom she marries. Conservative scholars like G. L. Archer and S. J. Schultz opt for opposing viewpoints.

Most interpreters agree that there is more to the book than the story of love and marriage. The bridegroom is regarded by some as a type of God, who loves Israel, his bride. Many think the story typifies the New Testament revelation of Jesus Christ as the bridegroom and the Church as his bride. This would follow the idea of the shepherd, which Jesus calls himself in John 10 when he speaks of the shepherd's giving his life for the sheep.

Certainly this is the most explicit book in the Bible having to do with sex and marriage. E. J. Young comments that "the eye of faith, as it beholds this picture of exalted human love, will be reminded of the one love that is above all earthly and human affections—even the love of the Son of God for lost humanity."

Outline

I. The bride and her beloved (1:1—2:7)
II. The lovers seek and find each other (2:8—3:5)
III. The bridegroom in pursuit of his bride (3:6—4:16)
IV. The painful interlude (5:1—7:9)
V. The reunion and consummation of their love (7:10—8:14)

I. THE BRIDE AND HER BELOVED (1:1—2:7)

A. INTRODUCTION

1:1 1 Kgs 4:32
1:2☆ Ps 63:3–5; Isa 55:1, 2; Song 1:4; 4:10

1 THE song of songs, which *is* Solomon's.
2 Let him kiss me with the kisses of his mouth: for thy love *is* better
than wine.

1:2 The bride desires the kisses of the bridegroom. They are more to be desired than wine. She waits for her lover to draw near to her. She will not put herself forward. The king has drawn her into his chambers, where she awaits him. Some take this to mean that Jesus Christ is the one who draws us to him with the bands of love. By the Spirit the unwilling are made willing.

B. THE BRIDE WAITS WITH EXPECTANCY

3 Because of the savour of thy good ointments thy name *is as* ointment
poured forth, therefore do the virgins love thee.
4 Draw me, we will run after thee: the king hath brought me into his
chambers: we will be glad and rejoice in thee, we will remember thy love
more than wine: the upright love thee.
5 I *am* black, but comely, O ye daughters of Jerusalem, as the tents of
Ke′dar, as the curtains of Solomon.
6 Look not upon me, because I *am* black, because the sun hath looked
upon me: my mother's children were angry with me; they made me the
keeper of the vineyards; *but* mine own vineyard have I not kept.
7 Tell me, O thou whom my soul loveth, where thou feedest, where thou
makest *thy flock* to rest at noon: for why should I be as one that turneth
aside by the flocks of thy companions?

C. THE BRIDE AND GROOM COME TOGETHER

8 If thou know not, O thou fairest among women, go thy way forth by the
footsteps of the flock, and feed thy kids beside the shepherds' tents.
9 I have compared thee, O my love, to a company of horses in Pharaoh's
chariots.
10 Thy cheeks are comely with rows *of jewels*, thy neck with chains *of gold*.
11 We will make thee borders of gold with studs of silver.
12 ¶While the king *sitteth* at his table, my spikenard sendeth forth the
smell thereof.
13 A bundle of myrrh *is* my well-beloved unto me; he shall lie all night
betwixt my breasts.
14 My beloved *is* unto me *as* a cluster of camphire in the vineyards of En-
ge′di.
15 Behold, thou *art* fair, my love; behold, thou *art* fair; thou *hast* doves'
eyes.
16 Behold, thou *art* fair, my beloved, yea, pleasant: also our bed *is* green.
17 The beams of our house *are* cedar, *and* our rafters of fir.

2 I AM the rose of Shar′on, *and* the lily of the valleys.
2 As the lily among thorns, so *is* my love among the daughters.
3 As the apple tree among the trees of the wood, so *is* my beloved among
the sons. I sat down under his shadow with great delight, and his fruit *was*
sweet to my taste.

1:3 Prov 27:9 Eccles 7:1 Song 4:10 Jn 12:3
1:4 Ps 45:14, 15 Song 2:3–5
☆**1:5** Ps 90:17 Song 2:7, 14 4:3; 6:4
1:6 Song 8:11
☆**1:7** Gen 37:16 Ps 18:1 Isa 40:11 Song 3:1–4 8:13
1:8 Song 5:9; 6:1
1:9 2 Chron 1:16, 17 Isa 31:1
☆**1:10** Gen 24:53 Num 31:50 Isa 3:18–21 Song 5:13
1:12 Song 4:13, 14 Mk 14:3 Phil 4:18
☆**1:13** Ps 45:8 Jn 19:39
1:14 1 Sam 23:29 Song 4:13
☆**1:15** Song 1:16 2:10, 13; 4:1
1:17 2 Chron 3:5 Jer 22:14 Ezek 41:16
☆**2:1** Isa 33:9; 35:2 Hos 14:5
☆**2:2**
☆**2:3** Judg 9:15 Song 1:13, 16 8:5 Isa 4:2 Jonah 4:5–8

1:5 *I am black,* i.e., she had been exposed to weathering by her nomadic wanderings. The sun had tanned her; she had borne the heat of the day. Still she was beautiful and likened herself in a figure to the furnishings of Solomon's royal palace, which were sumptuous and rich.

1:7 The bride loves the groom with all her heart. He is the shepherd who feeds the flock and makes them rest when the sun is at its zenith. They walk through green pastures and stay beside the still waters. Believers love the shepherd who tends his sheep. Indeed he gave his life for the sheep. He gives his people rest and comfort, and he watches over them with care and concern.

1:10, 13 The bride is lovely and decorated with precious jewels. Believers become beautiful as God bejewels them for his glory. As the bride here has regard for her king, so the believers reverence Christ. Even as her lover lies between her breasts, so Christ's people have him close to their hearts.

1:15 The bride beholds the beauty of her lover, whose couch is lovely and whose house is made of sweet-smelling wood. She calls it "ours," for as husband and wife they will share all things together. There is no "mine" and "yours" where true love exists; it is always "ours."

2:1 Although the lover is probably speaking about herself, some commentators have thought this verse has christological implications. If so, Jesus, the Son of the Highest, the bright and morning star, is the *rose of Sharon, and the lily of the valleys.* These are beautiful pictures of the fragrant beauty and glory of the Redeemer.

2:2 He is *the* lily; she is as a lily. The groom does not think less of her because she is a lily among thorns. The church of Jesus Christ now lies among the thorns, but will be transplanted into the paradise where there are no thorns, no briers.

2:3 The bride sits down near her lover, under the shade of his shadow, sheltered from the scorching sun, cooled and rested. The apples are sweet which have dropped from the tree for her to consume.

4 He brought me to the banqueting house, and his banner over me *was*
love.
5 Stay me with flagons, comfort me with apples: for I *am* sick of love.
6 His left hand *is* under my head, and his right hand doth embrace me.
7 I charge you, O ye daughters of Jerusalem, by the roes, and by the hinds
of the field, that ye stir not up, nor awake *my* love, till he please.

II. THE LOVERS SEEK AND FIND EACH OTHER (2:8—3:5)

A. THE BRIDE PAYS HOMAGE BY DAY

8 ¶The voice of my beloved! behold, he cometh leaping upon the
mountains, skipping upon the hills.
9 My beloved is like a roe or a young hart: behold, he standeth behind our
wall, he looketh forth at the windows, shewing himself through the lattice.
10 My beloved spake, and said unto me, Rise up, my love, my fair one,
and come away.
11 For, lo, the winter is past, the rain is over *and* gone;
12 The flowers appear on the earth; the time of the singing *of birds* is
come, and the voice of the turtle is heard in our land;
13 The fig tree putteth forth her green figs, and the vines *with* the tender
grape give a *good* smell. Arise, my love, my fair one, and come away.
14 ¶O my dove, *that art* in the clefts of the rock, in the secret *places* of the
stairs, let me see thy countenance, let me hear thy voice; for sweet *is* thy
voice, and thy countenance *is* comely.
15 Take us the foxes, the little foxes, that spoil the vines: for our vines *have*
tender grapes.
16 ¶My beloved *is* mine, and I *am* his: he feedeth among the lilies.
17 Until the day break, and the shadows flee away, turn, my beloved, and
be thou like a roe or a young hart upon the mountains of Be'ther.

B. THE BRIDE PAYS HOMAGE BY NIGHT

3 BY night on my bed I sought him whom my soul loveth: I sought him,
but I found him not.
2 I will rise now, and go about the city in the streets, and in the broad
ways I will seek him whom my soul loveth: I sought him, but I found him
not.
3 The watchmen that go about the city found me: *to whom I said*, Saw ye
him whom my soul loveth?
4 *It was* but a little that I passed from them, but I found him whom my
soul loveth: I held him, and would not let him go, until I had brought him
into my mother's house, and into the chamber of her that conceived me.
5 I charge you, O ye daughters of Jerusalem, by the roes, and by the hinds
of the field, that ye stir not up, nor awake *my* love, till he please.

2:4☆ Ps 63:2–5 Song 1:4; 5:1 Jn 15:9–15
2:5 Song 5:8; 7:8
2:6 Prov 4:8 Song 8:3 Isa 54:5–10
2:7 Gen 49:21 Song 3:5; 5:8 8:14 Hab 3:19
2:8☆ 2 Sam 6:16 Song 2:17 Isa 52:7
2:9☆ Judg 5:28 Prov 6:5 Song 2:17; 3:5 8:14
2:10☆
2:12 Gen 15:9 Ps 74:19
2:13 Isa 18:5 Hos 14:6 Mt 24:32 Lk 13:6, 7
2:14 Ps 68:13 Song 5:2; 6:9 Jer 48:28 Mt 10:16
2:15 Song 2:13; 7:12
2:16☆ Ps 48:14; 63:1 Song 4:5 6:2, 3; 7:10
2:17 Song 2:8, 9; 4:6
3:1☆ Ps 130:1, 2 Song 1:7; 5:6
3:2 Jer 5:1 Lk 14:21–23
3:3 Song 5:7 Ezek 33:2–9
3:4☆ Song 8:2

2:4 The groom has brought her into the banqueting house, but the food is less important than his banner over her, which is love. She exhibits strong and passionate love for her beloved, whose hand supports her head as he presses her to his heart.

2:8–10 The bride rejoices in the groom, who comes *bounding to her like a stag. He gazes* through the windows and speaks his word of love: "Rise up and come away."

2:16 *My beloved is mine, and I am his.* She has title to her beloved, both possession and tenure, for what God has joined together let not man put asunder. But she is also his. So also we are Christ's and Christ is ours, joined together in an unbroken and unbreakable relationship.

3:1 This is probably a song in which the bride relates a dream. Her waking and sleeping hours are always filled with thoughts of her beloved.

3:4 She who had sought him so eagerly has now found him. She does not want to lose him. So she holds him fast even as those who met Jesus in the resurrection took hold of his feet. She wanted to be with her lover forever.

III. THE BRIDEGROOM IN PURSUIT OF HIS BRIDE (3:6—4:16)

A. THE ARRIVAL OF THE BRIDEGROOM

6 ¶Who *is* this that cometh out of the wilderness like pillars of smoke,
perfumed with myrrh and frankincense, with all powders of the merchant?
7 Behold his bed, which is Solomon's; threescore valiant men *are* about it,
of the valiant of Israel.
8 They all hold swords, *being* expert in war: every man *hath* his sword
upon his thigh because of fear in the night.
9 King Solomon made himself a chariot of the wood of Lebanon.
10 He made the pillars thereof *of* silver, the bottom thereof *of* gold, the
covering of it *of* purple, the midst thereof being paved *with* love, for the
daughters of Jerusalem.
11 Go forth, O ye daughters of Zion, and behold king Solomon with the
crown wherewith his mother crowned him in the day of his espousals, and
in the day of the gladness of his heart.

3:6 Ex 13:21, 22 Deut 8:2 Song 1:13 4:12–14 Rev 5:8; 18:13
☆**3:7**
3:8 Ps 45:3; 91:5 Jer 50:9
☆**3:11** Isa 62:5 Jer 2:2 Hos 2:19

B. THE BRIDE ACCEPTS THE MARRIAGE PROPOSAL

4 BEHOLD, thou *art* fair, my love; behold, thou *art* fair; thou *hast*
doves' eyes within thy locks: thy hair *is* as a flock of goats, that appear
from mount Gilead.
2 Thy teeth *are* like a flock *of sheep that are even* shorn, which came up
from the washing; whereof every one bear twins, and none *is* barren among
them.
3 Thy lips *are* like a thread of scarlet, and thy speech *is* comely: thy
temples *are* like a piece of a pomegranate within thy locks.
4 Thy neck *is* like the tower of David builded for an armoury, whereon
there hang a thousand bucklers, all shields of mighty men.
5 Thy two breasts *are* like two young roes that are twins, which feed
among the lilies.
6 Until the day break, and the shadows flee away, I will get me to the
mountain of myrrh, and to the hill of frankincense.
7 Thou *art* all fair, my love; *there is* no spot in thee.
8 ¶Come with me from Lebanon, *my* spouse, with me from Lebanon: look
from the top of A-ma′na, from the top of She′nir and Hermon, from the
lions' dens, from the mountains of the leopards.
9 Thou hast ravished my heart, my sister, *my* spouse; thou hast ravished
my heart with one of thine eyes, with one chain of thy neck.
10 How fair is thy love, my sister, *my* spouse! how much better is thy love
than wine! and the smell of thine ointments than all spices!
11 Thy lips, O *my* spouse, drop *as* the honeycomb: honey and milk *are*
under thy tongue; and the smell of thy garments *is* like the smell of
Lebanon.

☆**4:1** Ps 45:11 Song 1:15 Ezek 16:14 Mic 7:14
☆**4:3** Prov 10:13, 20, 21; 16:21–24 Song 5:13, 16
☆**4:4** Neh 3:19 Song 7:4
4:5 Song 2:16 6:2, 3; 7:3
4:8 Deut 3:9 1 Kgs 4:33 2 Kgs 5:12 1 Chron 5:23 Song 5:1 Isa 62:5
4:9 Gen 41:42 Ezek 16:11
4:11 Gen 27:27 Prov 24:13, 14 Song 7:9 Hos 14:6

3:7 *bed,* i.e., "litter," or "palanquin." Solomon here is *a type of Christ, for his wisdom,* wealth, and the building of the temple. Surrounded by the holy angels, Christ is our resting place. The church, which is made up of the people of God, have their rest and safety in their Redeemer. The effect of righteousness is quietness and peace forever (Isa. 32:17).

3:11 Solomon was crowned with gold by his mother on his wedding day. Jesus was crowned with thorns on his way to Golgotha. He will be crowned King of kings and Lord of lords when he comes in his kingdom. Conversion is the coronation day for sinners who become saints; it is the day when they are espoused to their Redeemer, and they are presented to the Father as chaste virgins, who have had their garments made white in the blood of the Lamb. It is the day of gladness, for Satan has been defeated and the angels of heaven rejoice over one sinner who repents.

4:1 Christ the bridegroom is espoused to his church. This church is described as beautiful. Its inner beauty is manifested in bright images, strong shades, and bold comparisons.

4:3 *like a piece of pomegranate,* i.e., "matched loveliness." *within thy locks,* i.e., "behind your veil."†

4:4 *Thy neck is like the tower of David,* i.e., "Your neck is stately."†

4:12 Gen 29:3; Prov 5:15–18; Hos 6:3
12 A garden inclosed *is* my sister, *my* spouse; a spring shut up, a fountain
sealed.
4:13 Ex 30:23; Ps 45:8; Song 1:12; 3:6; 4:6; Jn 15:1–3
13 Thy plants *are* an orchard of pomegranates, with pleasant fruits;
camphire, with spikenard,
14 Spikenard and saffron; calamus and cinnamon, with all trees of
frankincense; myrrh and aloes, with all the chief spices:
4:15 Zech 14:8; Jn 4:10, 14; 7:38; Rev 22:1
15 A fountain of gardens, a well of living waters, and streams from
Lebanon.
4:16☆ Song 1:13; 2:3; 4:13; 2 Cor 9:10–15; 2 Pet 3:18
16 ¶Awake, O north wind; and come, thou south; blow upon my garden,
that the spices thereof may flow out. Let my beloved come into his garden,
and eat his pleasant fruits.

IV. THE PAINFUL INTERLUDE (5:1—7:9)

A. THE BRIDE'S DISTRESSING DREAM

5:1☆ Prov 9:5; Song 1:13; 4:9; 6:2; Isa 55:1; Jn 3:29
5 I AM come into my garden, my sister, *my* spouse: I have gathered my
myrrh with my spice; I have eaten my honeycomb with my honey; I
have drunk my wine with my milk: eat, O friends; drink, yea, drink
abundantly, O beloved.
5:2☆ Song 2:14
2 I sleep, but my heart waketh: *it is* the voice of my beloved that
knocketh, *saying*, Open to me, my sister, my love, my dove, my undefiled:
for my head is filled with dew, *and* my locks with the drops of the night.
5:3 Gen 19:2; Lk 11:7
3 I have put off my coat; how shall I put it on? I have washed my feet;
how shall I defile them?
4 My beloved put in his hand by the hole *of the door*, and my bowels were
moved for him.
5:5 Song 5:13
5 I rose up to open to my beloved; and my hands dropped *with* myrrh,
and my fingers *with* sweet smelling myrrh, upon the handles of the lock.
5:6 Prov 1:28; Song 3:1; 5:2; 6:1
6 I opened to my beloved; but my beloved had withdrawn himself, *and*
was gone: my soul failed when he spake: I sought him, but I could not find
him; I called him, but he gave me no answer.
5:7 Song 3:3
7 The watchmen that went about the city found me, they smote me, they
wounded me; the keepers of the walls took away my veil from me.
5:8 Song 2:7; 3:5
8 I charge you, O daughters of Jerusalem, if ye find my beloved, that ye
tell him, that I *am* sick of love.
5:9☆ Song 6:1
9 ¶What *is* thy beloved more than *another* beloved, O thou fairest among
women? what *is* thy beloved more than *another* beloved, that thou dost so
charge us?
5:10☆ 1 Sam 16:12; Ps 45:2
10 My beloved *is* white and ruddy, the chiefest among ten thousand.

4:16 The bride invites her beloved into her garden to enjoy the best entertainment it can afford him. She calls it *his* garden, for she and all she has belong to him. So believers call nothing their own; all belongs to Christ now and forever.

5:1 The groom responds to the bride's invitation. He has come into *his* garden, gathered *his* fruits, and eaten from *his* honeycomb. He invites the bride to share with him in that which he has freely given to her.

5:2 Speaking for the church, the bride in her dream is troubled like the churches of the Revelation, which were rebuked for their weaknesses and commended for their strengths. God's people are not always what they should be. But when they waken from their slumber, Christ returns to the hearts that were asleep when they should have been on guard and alive to the service of the bridegroom.

5:9 Speaking of his beloved and analogically of the Church, the Spirit through Solomon describes the bride as the fairest among women. The church—the bride of Christ—is the world's most wonderful society of the redeemed. The communion of saints is the finest community of people, who exhibit holiness and show forth the praise of God, the Author of everlasting salvation.

5:10 The sons and daughters of the bridegroom love him who enjoys incomparable perfections and unparalled worth. His beauty is internal rather than external, because there was no form, or comeliness, in the one who was crucified to save his bride (Isa. 53:2). The description here of the finest possible specimen of manhood is infinitely surpassed in the excellency of the divine being, who is true God and true man.

11 His head *is as* the most fine gold, his locks *are* bushy, *and* black as a
raven.
12 His eyes *are* as *the eyes* of doves by the rivers of waters, washed with
milk, *and* fitly set.
13 His cheeks *are* as a bed of spices, *as* sweet flowers: his lips *like* lilies,
dropping sweet smelling myrrh.
14 His hands *are as* gold rings set with the beryl: his belly *is as* bright ivory
overlaid *with* sapphires.
15 His legs *are as* pillars of marble, set upon sockets of fine gold: his
countenance *is* as Lebanon, excellent as the cedars.
16 His mouth *is* most sweet: yea, he *is* altogether lovely. This *is* my
beloved, and this *is* my friend, O daughters of Jerusalem.

6 WHITHER is thy beloved gone, O thou fairest among women?
whither is thy beloved turned aside? that we may seek him with thee.
2 My beloved is gone down into his garden, to the beds of spices, to feed
in the gardens, and to gather lilies.
3 I *am* my beloved's, and my beloved *is* mine: he feedeth among the lilies.

B. THE BRIDEGROOM'S INNER THOUGHTS

4 ¶Thou *art* beautiful, O my love, as Tir'zah, comely as Jerusalem, terrible
as *an army* with banners.
5 Turn away thine eyes from me, for they have overcome me: thy hair *is* as
a flock of goats that appear from Gilead.
6 Thy teeth *are* as a flock of sheep which go up from the washing, whereof
every one beareth twins, and *there is* not one barren among them.
7 As a piece of a pomegranate *are* thy temples within thy locks.
8 There are threescore queens, and fourscore concubines, and virgins
without number.
9 My dove, my undefiled is *but* one; she *is* the *only* one of her mother, she
is the choice *one* of her that bare her. The daughters saw her, and blessed
her; *yea*, the queens and the concubines, and they praised her.
10 ¶Who *is* she *that* looketh forth as the morning, fair as the moon, clear as
the sun, *and* terrible as *an army* with banners?
11 I went down into the garden of nuts to see the fruits of the valley, *and*
to see whether the vine flourished, *and* the pomegranates budded.
12 Or ever I was aware, my soul made me *like* the chariots of Am-min'a-
dib.
13 Return, return, O Shu'lam-ite; return, return, that we may look upon
thee. What will ye see in the Shu'lam-ite? As it were the company of two
armies.

5:12 Song 1:15; 4:1
5:13 Song 2:1; 5:5; 6:2
5:14 Ex 24:10; 28:18, 20; Job 28:16; Isa 54:11; Ezek 1:16; Dan 10:6
5:15 1 Kgs 4:33; Song 7:4
☆**5:16**
5:16 2 Sam 1:23; Song 7:9
☆**6:1**
☆**6:2** Song 1:7; 2:1; 4:16; 5:1, 13
6:3 Song 2:16; 4:5; 7:10
☆**6:4** 1 Kgs 14:17; Ps 48:2; 50:2; Song 6:10
6:5 Song 4:1
☆**6:7**
6:8 1 Kgs 11:3; Song 1:3
6:9 Gen 30:13; Song 2:14; 5:2
☆**6:10** Job 31:26; Song 6:4; Mt 17:2; Rev 1:16
6:11 Song 4:13; 7:12
☆**6:12**
☆**6:13** Gen 32:2; Judg 21:21; 2 Sam 17:24

5:16 This one whom the bride has described in verses 10–15 is her beloved and her friend. She has abandoned herself to him, and on him her heart's affection is set. So Christ loves those who love him, and to those who once were his enemies he now is their friend. Such are the wonders of God's grace!
6:1, 2 In her dream the bride wonders where her beloved has gone. Now she sees that he is not on the streets of a crowded city but has gone into his garden for privacy and retirement. It is also her garden, for their relationship is mutual: she is his and he is hers. The knot has been tied and cannot be loosed.
6:4 *Tirzah,* the capital of the Northern Kingdom until Omri built Samaria (1 Kings 16:15–24). In this verse, the beauty of Tirzah is compared to that of Jerusalem. *Thou art . . . terrible as an army with banners,* i.e., "you capture my heart."†
6:7 *As a piece of pomegranate are thy temples,* see note on 4:3.
6:10 *terrible as an army with banners,* i.e., "so utterly captivating."†
6:12 *the chariots of Ammi-nadib,* i.e., "the chariots of my princely people." Another possible translation is, "terrible desire to sit beside my beloved in his chariot."†
6:13 *Shulamite,* probably came from Shulem (likely a variant of Shunem), a town in the Plain of Esdraelon (see 1 Sam. 28:4 and 2 Kings 4:8). *As it were the company of two armies,* i.e., "as upon a dance before two armies," or, "you dance so beautifully."†

7:1ff☆ Ps 45:13

7 HOW beautiful are thy feet with shoes, O prince's daughter! the joints of thy thighs *are* like jewels, the work of the hands of a cunning workman.

2 Thy navel *is like* a round goblet, *which* wanteth not liquor: thy belly *is like* an heap of wheat set about with lilies.

7:3 Song 4:5

3 Thy two breasts *are* like two young roes *that are* twins.

7:4 Num 21:26 Song 4:4

4 Thy neck *is* as a tower of ivory; thine eyes *like* the fishpools in Hesh'bon, by the gate of Bath-rab'bim: thy nose *is* as the tower of Lebanon which looketh toward Damascus.

7:5 Isa 35:2

5 Thine head upon thee *is* like Carmel, and the hair of thine head like purple; the king *is* held in the galleries.

6 How fair and how pleasant art thou, O love, for delights!

7 This thy stature is like to a palm tree, and thy breasts to clusters *of grapes*.

7:8 Song 2:5

8 I said, I will go up to the palm tree, I will take hold of the boughs thereof: now also thy breasts shall be as clusters of the vine, and the smell of thy nose like apples;

7:9 Prov 23:31 Song 5:16

9 And the roof of thy mouth like the best wine for my beloved, that goeth *down* sweetly, causing the lips of those that are asleep to speak.

V. THE REUNION AND CONSUMMATION OF THEIR LOVE (7:10—8:14)

A. THE BRIDE LONGING FOR HER LOVER

7:10☆ Ps 45:11 Song 2:16; 6:3

10 I *am* my beloved's, and his desire *is* toward me.

11 Come, my beloved, let us go forth into the field; let us lodge in the villages.

12 Let us get up early to the vineyards; let us see if the vine flourish, *whether* the tender grape appear, *and* the pomegranates bud forth: there will I give thee my loves.

7:13☆ Gen 30:14 Song 2:3 4:13, 16

13 The mandrakes give a smell, and at our gates *are* all manner of pleasant *fruits*, new and old, *which* I have laid up for thee, O my beloved.

8:1☆

8 O THAT thou *wert* as my brother, that sucked the breasts of my mother! *when* I should find thee without, I would kiss thee; yea, I should not be despised.

8:2☆ Song 3:4

2 I would lead thee, *and* bring thee into my mother's house, *who* would instruct me: I would cause thee to drink of spiced wine of the juice of my pomegranate.

8:3 Song 2:6

3 His left hand *should be* under my head, and his right hand should embrace me.

8:4 Song 2:7; 3:5

4 I charge you, O daughters of Jerusalem, that ye stir not up, nor awake *my* love, until he please.

B. THE HAPPY ENDING

8:5 Song 2:3; 3:6

5 Who *is* this that cometh up from the wilderness, leaning upon her beloved? I raised thee up under the apple tree: there thy mother brought thee forth: there she brought thee forth *that* bare thee.

7:1ff The groom describes the beauties of his spouse in ten particulars. She has honored him and he will now honor her. So Christ honors those who are married to him; he gives them his praise.

7:10 Just as a husband's desire is toward his beloved wife, so the desire of Christ is toward his people. Between them there is a blessed communion unmarked by discord or disaffection. The church needs nothing more than its bridegroom.

7:13 *mandrakes* were supposed to produce feelings of sexual love (cf. Gen. 30:14–16). They were also associated with magic.

8:1 The Shulamite bride wishes that her husband were her brother because it was indelicate in that culture for a married couple to express their love publicly, but not so for a sister and brother.

8:2 *my mother's house,* i.e., "my childhood home."†

6¶Set me as a seal upon thine heart, as a seal upon thine arm: for love *is*
strong as death; jealousy *is* cruel as the grave: the coals thereof *are* coals of
fire, *which hath* a most vehement flame.
7Many waters cannot quench love, neither can the floods drown it: if a
man would give all the substance of his house for love, it would utterly be
contemned.
8¶We have a little sister, and she hath no breasts: what shall we do for
our sister in the day when she shall be spoken for?
9If she *be* a wall, we will build upon her a palace of silver: and if she *be*
a door, we will inclose her with boards of cedar.
10I *am* a wall, and my breasts like towers: then was I in his eyes as one
that found favour.
11Solomon had a vineyard at Ba'al–ha'mon; he let out the vineyard unto
keepers; every one for the fruit thereof was to bring a thousand *pieces* of
silver.
12My vineyard, which *is* mine, *is* before me: thou, O Solomon, *must have*
a thousand, and those that keep the fruit thereof two hundred.
13Thou that dwellest in the gardens, the companions hearken to thy
voice: cause me to hear *it*.
14¶Make haste, my beloved, and be thou like to a roe or to a young hart
upon the mountains of spices.

8:6 Prov 6:34 Isa 49:16 Jer 22:24 Hag 2:23
☆**8:7**
8:8 Ezek 16:7
☆**8:9** 1 Kgs 6:15
☆**8:10**
☆**8:11** Eccles 2:4 Song 1:6; 8:12 Isa 7:23 Mt 21:33
8:13 Song 1:7
8:14 Song 2:7, 9, 17 4:6

8:7 True love is indestructible. It is a valiant, victorious passion. It is constant and rocklike and will not give way to desertion of the beloved by fair means or foul, by life or by death (Rom. 8:38). Water will quench a fire, but it cannot quench love. Floods will drown people and strike terror to the heart, but they will not overwhelm love. Life and all the comforts of this world will not seduce the believer from his love of Christ.

8:9 *If she be a wall,* i.e., "If she has no breasts."† A wall is symbolic of resistance to invasion. The brothers look at their sister as one who resists those who would assault her innocence.

8:10 *I am a wall,* i.e., "I am tall." *my breasts like towers,* i.e., "I am full-breasted."†

8:11 *Baal-hamon.* Evidently the grapes from this vineyard were of exceptional quality. The location is unknown to us today. Possibly the reference here is not to a real vineyard. If this is the case, it was a poetic expression. The vineyard which is so fruitful is a type of the church of Christ. And, as in 8:12, the members of Christ's body are the keepers of the vineyard.

THE BOOK OF THE PROPHET
ISAIAH

Authorship, date, and background The author of this book was Isaiah (whose name means "Yahweh is salvation"), the son of Amoz. He lived in Jerusalem, was a student of international affairs, was well educated, and was on familiar terms with the royal court. He prophesied during the reigns of Uzziah, Jotham, Ahaz, and Hezekiah, and, according to tradition, was sawn in pieces during the kingship of Manasseh. His ministry extended over a period of more than fifty years (ca. 740–681 B.C.) and concerned itself largely with Judah, although references are made to Samaria. He lived through the days when Assyria under either Shalmaneser V or Sargon II conquered Samaria and brought an end to the Northern Kingdom comprising ten of the tribes of Israel.

The authorship of Isaiah has been questioned by rationalist scholars since the late eighteenth century. Chapters 40—66 have been thought by these scholars to have been written by someone other than Isaiah, a Deutero-Isaiah or second Isaiah. Underlying this viewpoint is the opinion that future events cannot be predicted in advance of their happening. Conservatives have always agreed that under the aegis of the Holy Spirit the Bible does contain predictive prophecy so that in principle the authorship of the second half of Isaiah cannot be questioned on this basis. A strong case can be made for Isaiahic authorship on the grounds of the book's unity, style, use of words, and internal evidences for a pre-exilic date, and for its composition in Palestine rather than Babylon. The New Testament consistently witnesses to the authorship of the latter part of the book by Isaiah the prophet and not someone else. The strongest affirmation is found in John 12:38–41. Indeed if Isaiah did not write chapters 40—66, the testimony of the New Testament is untrue and the biblical doctrine of scriptural infallibility or inerrancy falls to the ground. Bible-believing Christians have always assented to Isaiahic authorship.

Characteristics and content Isaiah has been and still is the most universally cherished prophetical book in the Old Testament. The New Testament alludes to it more than 250 times and portions of the book are quoted expressly at least fifty times. It is, perhaps, the richest book of the Old Testament in theological matters concerning God, creation and providence, man, sin, redemption, resurrection, judgment, and the coming Messiah. It is panoramic in its sweep, carrying the reader to the end of the age, when history will be consummated. The immediate message of Isaiah is to show that salvation is based upon the doctrine of grace originating in the power of God the Redeemer, not in man or his good works. God is holy and will not put up with unholiness in his covenant people. The person and work of Jesus the Messiah is detailed more fully here than in any other Old Testament book. Isaiah speaks of the Messiah as the virgin-born child of God, of Jesus as the suffering Messiah, who by his substitutionary atonement makes salvation possible, and of Jesus as the eternal God who is the Prince of Peace.

Among the prophecies contained in the book are: the pronouncement of the doom of Samaria (the Northern Kingdom), the fall of Assyria (the nation which brings Samaria to its knees), and the judgment of God on the surrounding nations of Babylon, Philistia, Moab, Ethiopia, Edom, Arabia, Tyre, and Jerusalem (which is to go into captivity under Nebuchadnezzar, spelled Nebu-chadrezzar in this version, and be returned to the land after the seventy-year period has elapsed).

From chapter 40 to the end of the book Isaiah speaks a word of comfort. He looks to the Messiah to bring Israel back to the land and to bring light to the Gentiles. God is the God of the whole earth, and salvation includes Jew and Gentile. He distinguishes between true and false worship and paints a sweet picture of the restoration and peace of Zion when the people of God will worship the Lord in the beauty of holiness and in obedience to the divine will. These latter chapters may be divided into three segments: the purpose of peace, the Prince of Peace, and the program of peace. Isaiah distinguishes national Israel from the Church with the promise that this nation will someday be brought into being again in the land where its people will worship the living God.

Isaiah closes his prophecy on a solemn note once he depicts the glory of Zion. Just as God saves so God also judges the wicked and dispenses divine punishment upon them. The fateful word is spoken: "For by fire and by his sword will the LORD plead with all flesh, and the slain of the LORD shall be many" (66:16). Let all who do not now know God be warned of their end if they do not repent and receive salvation through the blood of the Lamb.

Outline

I. The messenger and his message (1:1—6:13)
II. Immanuel: present and future prospects (7:1—12:6)
III. Prophecies concerning the heathen nations (13:1—23:18)
IV. Israel in relation to the world (24:1—27:13)
V. Zion's hopes (28:1—35:10)
VI. Judgment delayed for Jerusalem (36:1—39:8)
VII. God's assurance of Israel's future deliverance (40:1—56:8)
VIII. The establishment of God's universal kingdom (56:9—66:24)

I. THE MESSENGER AND HIS MESSAGE (1:1—6:13)

A. INTRODUCTION

1 THE vision of Isaiah the son of Amoz, which he saw concerning Judah ☆1:1 2 Kgs 15:1, 13
and Jerusalem in the days of Uz-zi'ah, Jo'tham, Ahaz, *and* Hez-e-ki'ah, 18:1
kings of Judah. Isa 2:1; 40:9

B. JUDAH'S JUDGMENT BY GOD

1. Judah's Sins

2Hear, O heavens, and give ear, O earth: for the LORD hath spoken, I ☆1:2
have nourished and brought up children, and they have rebelled against me. Deut 32:1 Jer 3:22
3The ox knoweth his owner, and the ass his master's crib: *but* Israel doth Isa 65:2
not know, my people doth not consider. Mic 1:2 ☆1:3 Jer 8:7
4Ah sinful nation, a people laden with iniquity, a seed of evildoers, ☆1:4
children that are corrupters: they have forsaken the LORD, they have Song 2:7, 9, 17 4:6
provoked the Holy One of Israel unto anger, they are gone away backward. Isa 5:24
5Why should ye be stricken any more? ye will revolt more and more: the ☆1:5
whole head is sick, and the whole heart faint. Ps 38:3
6From the sole of the foot even unto the head *there is* no soundness in it;
but wounds, and bruises, and putrifying sores: they have not been closed,
neither bound up, neither mollified with ointment.
7Your country *is* desolate, your cities *are* burned with fire: your land, 1:7
strangers devour it in your presence, and *it is* desolate, as overthrown by Lev 26:33 Jer 44:6
strangers.
8And the daughter of Zion is left as a cottage in a vineyard, as a lodge in
a garden of cucumbers, as a besieged city.

1:1 A prophet is one who has been given the gift of foretelling events yet future. All of the Old Testament prophets had this gift and used it. Men have seen the fulfillment of Old Testament prophecy in history, and certainly so at the time of Christ when many of the Old Testament prophecies were fulfilled. The members of the Trinity cooperate in the bestowal of the prophetic gift. In the New Testament the prophetic gift consists mostly of instruction in the holy faith with less emphasis on predictive prophecy, although there is some of that. At best, predictive prophecy is rare in our age and the gift of prophecy, without which no one should be a minister of the gospel, consists in the ability to understand and expound the Word of God.

1:2,3 Isaiah accuses Judah of ingratitude. The ox and the ass are wiser than Judah, for each of them dutifully knows and serves its master. But Judah obstinately chose to rebel against its master. The nation lacked understanding, for it refused to consider its obligations to God its creator.

1:4 Judah's rebellion was national in scope. Corruption had penetrated deep into the fabric of national life. The nation had forsaken God, and the Holy One of Israel was now prepared to forsake the nation.

1:5 Sennacherib of Assyria attacked Judah in 701 B.C., laying waste to the countryside. Only Jerusalem was spared (2 Kings 18:13–16). Here (1:5–9) Isaiah describes the consequences of the invasion. Sadly, Judah learned nothing of a continuing nature from the experience, for the Captivity was to come a century later.

1:9☆ 9Except the LORD of hosts had left unto us a very small remnant, we
Isa 10:20–22; 11:11, 16 should have been as Sodom, *and* we should have been like unto Go-
Rom 9:29 mor'rah.

2. God Demands Holiness, not Sacrifices

1:10☆ 10¶Hear the word of the LORD, ye rulers of Sodom; give ear unto the law
Ezek 16:46 of our God, ye people of Go-mor'rah.
1:11 11To what purpose *is* the multitude of your sacrifices unto me? saith the
Jer 6:20 Mal 1:10 LORD: I am full of the burnt offerings of rams, and the fat of fed beasts;
and I delight not in the blood of bullocks, or of lambs, or of he goats.
1:12 12When ye come to appear before me, who hath required this at your
1 Chron 23:31 Jer 7:9, 10 hand, to tread my courts?
1:13☆ 13Bring no more vain oblations; incense is an abomination unto me; the
new moons and sabbaths, the calling of assemblies, I cannot away with; *it*
is iniquity, even the solemn meeting.
14Your new moons and your appointed feasts my soul hateth: they are a
trouble unto me; I am weary to bear *them.*
1:15☆ 15And when ye spread forth your hands, I will hide mine eyes from you:
Isa 59:2 Mic 3:4 yea, when ye make many prayers, I will not hear: your hands are full of
blood.
1:16 16¶Wash you, make you clean; put away the evil of your doings from
Ps 26:6 Isa 52:11 before mine eyes; cease to do evil;
Jer 25:5 1:17 17Learn to do well; seek judgment, relieve the oppressed, judge the
Jer 22:3 fatherless, plead for the widow.

3. Judah's Choice: Obedience or Death

1:18☆ 18Come now, and let us reason together, saith the LORD: though your sins
Ps 51:7 Isa 43:26; 44:22 be as scarlet, they shall be as white as snow; though they be red like
Rev 7:14 crimson, they shall be as wool.
1:19☆ 19If ye be willing and obedient, ye shall eat the good of the land:
Deut 30:15, 16 20But if ye refuse and rebel, ye shall be devoured with the sword: for the
mouth of the LORD hath spoken *it.*

4. God Promises Redemption after Judgment

1:21☆ 21¶How is the faithful city become an harlot! it was full of judgment;
righteousness lodged in it; but now murderers.

1:9 Sodom and Gomorrah had been destroyed because not even ten righteous men could be found among the people. But in Judah there is still a small, faithful remnant who are not iniquitous, whom God has reserved for mercy. This tiny remnant will be preserved and kept alive from the calamity that will overtake Judah as a whole.

1:10 Isaiah likens the ungodly to Sodom and Gomorrah. As such they can expect the same sort of judgment for their transgressions. The prophet urges them to hear the Word of God and to obey its teaching so that the upcoming judgment may be averted.

1:13 Vain oblations (offerings) were sacrifices without spiritual content. Judah preserved and honored religious forms and practices without real love for God.

***1:15** when ye make many prayers, I will not hear.* There are times when God closes his eyes, hides his face, and refuses to listen to our prayers. This silence of God will remain until there is repentance, confession, and restoration to fellowship. When our prayers are not heard, we can be sure we are backslidden. God refuses to hear the prayers of the wicked even though they are accompanied by religious ceremonies and costly sacrifices. Hypocrisy is especially hated by God, who beheld the pretended zeal of Israel for the law, the temple, and the offerings, when in their hearts they were as ravenous wolves. The evils pictured here were fully manifested later when Israel killed Jesus and his followers while pretending to love God.

1:18 Here an appeal is made to right reason. God is saying that if only his people would think straight they would cleanse themselves from their defilements. Once they did this, they would be welcomed into covenant and communion with the true God.

1:19 God's covenant blessings for Israel were contingent upon obedience to him. A formal relationship was not sufficient.

1:21 Judah and Jerusalem had at one time been faithful to God. Degeneracy had set in so that righteousness had disappeared and injustice had flourished. Judah became a debauched adulteress in whose borders even murderers went unpunished.

22 Thy silver is become dross, thy wine mixed with water:
23 Thy princes *are* rebellious, and companions of thieves: every one loveth
gifts, and followeth after rewards: they judge not the fatherless, neither
doth the cause of the widow come unto them.

1:23 Ex 23:8; Jer 5:28; Ezek 22:7; Mic 7:3

24 Therefore saith the Lord, the LORD of hosts, the mighty One of Israel,
Ah, I will ease me of mine adversaries, and avenge me of mine enemies:
25 ¶And I will turn my hand upon thee, and purely purge away thy dross,
and take away all thy tin:

1:25 Ezek 22:19–22; Mal 3:3

26 And I will restore thy judges as at the first, and thy counsellors as at the
beginning: afterward thou shalt be called, The city of righteousness, the
faithful city.

☆1:26 Isa 33:5; Zech 8:3

27 Zion shall be redeemed with judgment, and her converts with righ-
teousness.
28 ¶And the destruction of the transgressors and of the sinners *shall be*
together, and they that forsake the LORD shall be consumed.

☆1:28 Ps 9:5; 2 Thess 1:8, 9

29 For they shall be ashamed of the oaks which ye have desired, and ye
shall be confounded for the gardens that ye have chosen.
30 For ye shall be as an oak whose leaf fadeth, and as a garden that hath
no water.
31 And the strong shall be as tow, and the maker of it as a spark, and they
shall both burn together, and none shall quench *them.*

1:31 Isa 33:11–14; Mt 3:12

C. IMMEDIATE JUDGMENT; FUTURE GLORY

1. God Will Restore Jerusalem at Last

2 THE word that Isaiah the son of Amoz saw concerning Judah and
Jerusalem.

☆2:1

2 And it shall come to pass in the last days, *that* the mountain of the
LORD's house shall be established in the top of the mountains, and shall be
exalted above the hills; and all nations shall flow unto it.

2:2 Isa 66:20; Mic 4:1, 2

3 And many people shall go and say, Come ye, and let us go up to the
mountain of the LORD, to the house of the God of Jacob; and he will teach
us of his ways, and we will walk in his paths: for out of Zion shall go forth
the law, and the word of the LORD from Jerusalem.

2:3 Isa 51:4, 5

4 And he shall judge among the nations, and shall rebuke many people:
and they shall beat their swords into plowshares, and their spears into
pruninghooks: nation shall not lift up sword against nation, neither shall
they learn war any more.

☆2:4 Isa 11:6–9; Hos 2:18; Joel 3:10; Zech 9:10

5 O house of Jacob, come ye, and let us walk in the light of the LORD.

2:5 Isa 60:1, 2, 19, 20; 1 Jn 1:5, 7

2. Judgment Will Precede Redemption

a. God Has Rejected Judah

6 ¶Therefore thou hast forsaken thy people the house of Jacob, because
they be replenished from the east, and *are* soothsayers like the Philistines,
and they please themselves in the children of strangers.

☆2:6 2 Kgs 1:2

1:26 Isaiah already forsees Judah's decline and God's abandonment of his people. But he also foresees a great future, one which has not come to this day. But it surely will.

1:28 Judah's evil is so great that chastening and correction will not avail. These transgressors must be destroyed and consumed.

2:1ff This passage is prophetic and looks to the day when Christ will set up his church in the world. The gospel will be professed and preached to all the earth. The Christian faith, founded on the Rock—Christ Jesus—will overcome all opposition. The gates of hell will not prevail against it. The vision foresees the day when men will war no more and their weapons will be beaten into plowshares and pruninghooks. This will occur when the Son of Man returns in glory and great power.

2:4 *beat their swords into plowshares, and their spears into pruninghooks,* i.e., "will convert their weapons of war into implements of peace."†

2:6 The rejection of Israel is here stated (see Rom. 11:12–15). The nation will be dispersed to the four quarters of the earth. Yet before the end of the age, God will gather his chosen people together again when they turn in faith to the Messiah.

7 Their land also is full of silver and gold, neither *is there any* end of their
treasures; their land is also full of horses, neither *is there any* end of their
chariots:
2:8 Ps 115:4–8 Isa 44:17
8 Their land also is full of idols; they worship the work of their own
hands, that which their own fingers have made:
9 And the mean man boweth down, and the great man humbleth himself:
therefore forgive them not.
2:10☆ Rev 6:15, 16
10 ¶Enter into the rock, and hide thee in the dust, for fear of the LORD,
and for the glory of his majesty.
2:11 Isa 13:11
11 The lofty looks of man shall be humbled, and the haughtiness of men
shall be bowed down, and the LORD alone shall be exalted in that day.

b. The Proud and Haughty Will Be Humbled

2:12☆ Job 40:11, 12 Mal 4:1
12 For the day of the LORD of hosts *shall be* upon every *one that is* proud
and lofty, and upon every *one that is* lifted up; and he shall be brought low:
2:13 Isa 10:33, 34 Zech 11:2
13 And upon all the cedars of Lebanon, *that are* high and lifted up, and
upon all the oaks of Ba′shan,
14 And upon all the high mountains, and upon all the hills *that are* lifted
up,
15 And upon every high tower, and upon every fenced wall,
2:16 Isa 23:1, 14
16 And upon all the ships of Tarshish, and upon all pleasant pictures.
17 And the loftiness of man shall be bowed down, and the haughtiness of
men shall be made low: and the LORD alone shall be exalted in that day.
2:18☆ Isa 21:9 Mic 1:7
18 And the idols he shall utterly abolish.
19 And they shall go into the holes of the rocks, and into the caves of the
2:19 Ps 18:7 Hag 2:6, 7
earth, for fear of the LORD, and for the glory of his majesty, when he ariseth
to shake terribly the earth.
2:20 Isa 30:22
20 In that day a man shall cast his idols of silver, and his idols of gold,
which they made *each one* for himself to worship, to the moles and to the
bats;
21 To go into the clefts of the rocks, and into the tops of the ragged rocks,
for fear of the LORD, and for the glory of his majesty, when he ariseth to
shake terribly the earth.
2:22 Ps 8:4; 144:3, 4 Jer 17:5
22 Cease ye from man, whose breath *is* in his nostrils: for wherein is he to
be accounted of?

c. All Classes of People Will Suffer Judgment

3:1☆ Ezek 4:16
3 FOR, behold, the Lord, the LORD of hosts, doth take away from
Jerusalem and from Judah the stay and the staff, the whole stay of
bread, and the whole stay of water,
3:2 Isa 9:14, 15
2 The mighty man, and the man of war, the judge, and the prophet, and
the prudent, and the ancient,
3 The captain of fifty, and the honourable man, and the counsellor, and
the cunning artificer, and the eloquent orator.
3:4☆ Eccles 10:16
4 And I will give children *to be* their princes, and babes shall rule over
them.

2:10 The terror, glory, and majesty of God is such that Judeans will "enter into the rock" (as expanded in verse 19) to go into "the caves of the earth" where *they hope they will not be found. They will* "hide in the dust" (i.e., in holes in the ground) where they hope they may escape the avenging wrath of an angry God.

2:12 *The day of the LORD of hosts* has come. The divine patience has been exhausted; judgment and wrath replace love and mercy.

2:18 The idols in which Judah trusted shall be swept away. If the idols could not protect themselves against the vengeance of God, how could they deliver those who worshipped them?

3:1 *the stay and the staff,* i.e., everything the Judeans looked upon as a means of support.

3:4 This is a promise that Judah's future rulers will be youthful and inexperienced, adding to the national problems.

5 And the people shall be oppressed, every one by another, and every one ☆3:5
by his neighbour: the child shall behave himself proudly against the Jer 9:3–8
ancient, and the base against the honourable. Mic 7:3–6
6 When a man shall take hold of his brother of the house of his father,
saying, Thou hast clothing, be thou our ruler, and *let* this ruin *be* under thy
hand:
7 In that day shall he swear, saying, I will not be an healer; for in my **3:7**
house *is* neither bread nor clothing: make me not a ruler of the people. Ezek 34:4
8 For Jerusalem is ruined, and Judah is fallen: because their tongue and **3:8**
their doings *are* against the LORD, to provoke the eyes of his glory. Isa 65:3, 5
9 ¶The shew of their countenance doth witness against them; and they ☆**3:9**
declare their sin as Sodom, they hide *it* not. Woe unto their soul! for they Gen 13:13; Prov 8:36
have rewarded evil unto themselves.
10 Say ye to the righteous, that *it shall be* well *with him:* for they shall eat ☆**3:10**
the fruit of their doings. Deut 28:1–14
11 Woe unto the wicked! *it shall be* ill *with him:* for the reward of his hands **3:11**
shall be given him. Deut 28:15–68
12 ¶*As for* my people, children *are* their oppressors, and women rule over
them. O my people, they which lead thee cause *thee* to err, and destroy the
way of thy paths.
13 ¶The LORD standeth up to plead, and standeth to judge the people. **3:13**
14 The LORD will enter into judgment with the ancients of his people, and Hos 4:1; Mic 6:2
the princes thereof: for ye have eaten up the vineyard; the spoil of the poor **3:14** Job 24:9, 14
is in your houses. Ps 10:9; 14:4
15 What mean ye *that* ye beat my people to pieces, and grind the faces of Ezek 18:12; Jas 2:6
the poor? saith the Lord GOD of hosts. ☆**3:15** Ps 94:5
16 ¶Moreover the LORD saith, Because the daughters of Zion are haughty, ☆**3:16**
and walk with stretched forth necks and wanton eyes, walking and mincing
as they go, and making a tinkling with their feet:
17 Therefore the Lord will smite with a scab the crown of the head of the
daughters of Zion, and the LORD will discover their secret parts.
18 In that day the Lord will take away the bravery of *their* tinkling ☆**3:18–23**
ornaments *about their feet,* and *their* cauls, and *their* round tires like the
moon,
19 The chains, and the bracelets, and the mufflers,
20 The bonnets, and the ornaments of the legs, and the headbands, and
the tablets, and the earrings,
21 The rings, and nose jewels,
22 The changeable suits of apparel, and the mantles, and the wimples, and
the crisping pins,
23 The glasses, and the fine linen, and the hoods, and the vails.

3:5 Anarchic conditions exist in which neighbor oppresses neighbor. The base assault the honorable, and the young no longer honor their fathers, mothers, or elders. They are insolent.

3:9 Like the unveiled face of a prostitute, the faces of the wicked Judeans manifest their sins. But they do not blush. Instead, they glory in their shameless lack of virtue. They cannot cease from their sins.

3:10 "Let the righteous man know that he shall not be lost in the crowd of sinners; *the Judge of all the earth will not slay the righteous with the wicked* (Gen. 18:25). Those who do not share the common iniquity will not share the common calamity."*

3:15 It was bad enough for some people to be poor. But then the poor were ground as wheat is ground in a mill. Their land was not only seized—their persons were abused, their faces crushed and bleeding from their wounds.

3:16 The men of Judah are not alone in their wickedness. They are joined by the women who are haughty and wanton. They lack what Paul later enjoins in 1 Tim. 2:9, that "women adorn themselves in modest apparel, with shamefacedness and sobriety; not with braided hair, or gold, or pearls, or costly array."

3:18–23 Fashions alter but the principle remains. The excess of finery and ornaments described in these verses shall perish with the user. The hearts of these women centered more on these outward adornments than on the worship and love of God. Whatever usurps our love to God is an idol.

3:24 Esth 2:12; Isa 15:3; 1 Pet 3:3

24 And it shall come to pass, *that* instead of sweet smell there shall be stink; and instead of a girdle a rent; and instead of well set hair baldness; and instead of a stomacher a girding of sackcloth; *and* burning instead of beauty.

3:25 Isa 65:12; Lam 2:10

25 Thy men shall fall by the sword, and thy mighty in the war.

26 And her gates shall lament and mourn; and she *being* desolate shall sit upon the ground.

4:1☆ Isa 54:4

4 AND in that day seven women shall take hold of one man, saying, We will eat our own bread, and wear our own apparel: only let us be called by thy name, to take away our reproach.

d. Messiah Will Revive Israel Later

4:2☆ Ex 32:32; Ps 72:16; Isa 28:6; 62:12; Joel 2:32; Obad 17; Lk 10:20

2 In that day shall the branch of the LORD be beautiful and glorious, and the fruit of the earth *shall be* excellent and comely for them that are escaped of Israel.

3 And it shall come to pass, *that he that is* left in Zion, and *he that* remaineth in Jerusalem, shall be called holy, *even* every one that is written among the living in Jerusalem:

4 When the Lord shall have washed away the filth of the daughters of Zion, and shall have purged the blood of Jerusalem from the midst thereof by the spirit of judgment, and by the spirit of burning.

4:5 Num 9:15–23

5 And the LORD will create upon every dwelling place of mount Zion, and upon her assemblies, a cloud and smoke by day, and the shining of a flaming fire by night: for upon all the glory *shall be* a defence.

4:6☆ Ps 27:5; Isa 32:1, 2

6 And there shall be a tabernacle for a shadow in the daytime from the heat, and for a place of refuge, and for a covert from storm and from rain.

D. GOD WILL SEND JUDAH INTO CAPTIVITY

1. The Parable of the Vineyard

5:1 Ps 80:8; Jer 12:10

5 NOW will I sing to my wellbeloved a song of my beloved touching his vineyard. My wellbeloved hath a vineyard in a very fruitful hill:

5:2 Jer 2:21; Mk 11:13

2 And he fenced it, and gathered out the stones thereof, and planted it with the choicest vine, and built a tower in the midst of it, and also made a winepress therein: and he looked that it should bring forth grapes, and it brought forth wild grapes.

3 And now, O inhabitants of Jerusalem, and men of Judah, judge, I pray you, betwixt me and my vineyard.

5:4☆ Jer 7:25, 26; Mt 23:37

4 What could have been done more to my vineyard, that I have not done in it? wherefore, when I looked that it should bring forth grapes, brought it forth wild grapes?

5:5☆ Lam 1:15; Lk 21:24; Rev 11:2

5 And now go to; I will tell you what I will do to my vineyard: I will take away the hedge thereof, and it shall be eaten up; *and* break down the wall thereof, and it shall be trodden down:

4:1 The day will come when men will be few in number because of war, and women will need protectors in times of anarchy.

4:2ff In the Old Testament, Christ is called *the branch.* That term is used here in the Hebrew. It refers to the Messianic king who comes from David's loins. The *Hebrew word tsemach means "sprout."* In Jer. 23:5 and 33:15 it is called *righteous Branch* and is the personal name for the Messiah in Zech. 3:8 and 6:12. In Isaiah he is *the branch of the Lord;* in Jeremiah he is David's "righteous Branch." In Zechariah he is *the man . . . BRANCH.*

4:6 When Messiah has come and God's Israel is right with him, he shall be a shade for them against the heat of the day and a refuge from storms and rain. God is the refuge for his people in all seasons.

5:4 Isaiah compares Judah to a vineyard. God has cared for the vineyard but it has produced wild grapes, which speaks of Judah's lack of gratitude and persistent disobedience.

5:5 God had erected protecting fences around Judah. This protection had not produced good vintage, so the fences will be destroyed and the grape arbors trampled down by cattle and sheep.

6 And I will lay it waste: it shall not be pruned, nor digged; but there shall
come up briers and thorns: I will also command the clouds that they rain
no rain upon it.

5:6 Jer 14:1–22; 25:11

2. The Seven Sins of Judah
a. Greed

7 For the vineyard of the LORD of hosts *is* the house of Israel, and the men
of Judah his pleasant plant: and he looked for judgment, but behold
oppression; for righteousness, but behold a cry.

☆**5:7**

8 ¶Woe unto them that join house to house, *that* lay field to field, till *there*
be no place, that they may be placed alone in the midst of the earth!

☆**5:8** Jer 22:13–17; Mic 2:2

9 In mine ears *said* the LORD of hosts, Of a truth many houses shall be
desolate, *even* great and fair, without inhabitant.

☆**5:9** Mt 23:38

10 Yea, ten acres of vineyard shall yield one bath, and the seed of an
homer shall yield an ephah.

☆**5:10** Hag 1:6; 2:16

b. Drunken Indulgence

11 ¶Woe unto them that rise up early in the morning, *that* they may follow
strong drink; that continue until night, *till* wine inflame them!

☆**5:11** Prov 23:29, 30; Isa 28:1, 3, 7, 8

12 And the harp, and the viol, the tabret, and pipe, and wine, are in their
feasts: but they regard not the work of the LORD, neither consider the
operation of his hands.

5:12 Ps 28:5

13 ¶Therefore my people are gone into captivity, because *they have* no
knowledge: and their honourable men *are* famished, and their multitude
dried up with thirst.

5:13 Hos 4:6

14 Therefore hell hath enlarged herself, and opened her mouth without
measure: and their glory, and their multitude, and their pomp, and he that
rejoiceth, shall descend into it.

☆**5:14**

15 And the mean man shall be brought down, and the mighty man shall be
humbled, and the eyes of the lofty shall be humbled:
16 But the LORD of hosts shall be exalted in judgment, and God that is
holy shall be sanctified in righteousness.

5:16 Isa 33:5, 10

17 Then shall the lambs feed after their manner, and the waste places of
the fat ones shall strangers eat.

5:17 Zeph 2:6

c. Mocking the Holy One of Israel

18 Woe unto them that draw iniquity with cords of vanity, and sin as it
were with a cart rope:

☆**5:18** Jer 23:10–14

19 That say, Let him make speed, *and* hasten his work, that we may see *it*:
and let the counsel of the Holy One of Israel draw nigh and come, that we
may know *it!*

5:19 2 Pet 3:3, 4

5:7 *he looked for judgment, but behold oppression; for righteousness, but behold a cry.* Here is an example of serious punning often used by the prophets: the Hebrew words for "justice" and "bloodshed" sound very much alike, as do those for "righteousness" and "cry."†

5:8–10 Judah's greed will be repaid by God, for its houses will go untenanted and its fields will yield little grain. The God of the whole earth will exercise retributive justice against a wicked people.

5:11 Generally people wait until the end of a day's work before they turn to alcohol and end up in a drunken stupor. These sinners have made drinking their major business and start to imbibe from early morning to late night.

5:14 Hell is personified and described as a monster licking its chops with the expectancy of devouring the inhabitants of Jerusalem.

5:18 *cart rope.* The figure is "like a bullock on a rope," or "with cords of falsehood."†

d. Immorality

5:20 Job 17:12 Prov 17:15 20¶Woe unto them that call evil good, and good evil; that put darkness
for light, and light for darkness; that put bitter for sweet, and sweet for
bitter!

e. Pride

5:21 Prov 3:7 Rom 12:16 1 Cor 3:18–20 21 Woe unto *them that are* wise in their own eyes, and prudent in their
own sight!

f. Intemperance

5:22 Isa 56:12 Hab 2:15 22 Woe unto *them that are* mighty to drink wine, and men of strength to
mingle strong drink:

g. Injustice

5:23 Mic 3:11 Jas 5:6 23 Which justify the wicked for reward, and take away the righteousness
of the righteous from him!

3. God Will Smash Judah

5:24☆ Isa 30:12 24 Therefore as the fire devoureth the stubble, and the flame consumeth
the chaff, *so* their root shall be as rottenness, and their blossom shall go up
as dust: because they have cast away the law of the LORD of hosts, and
despised the word of the Holy One of Israel.
5:25 2 Kgs 22:17 Isa 9:12, 17, 21 10:4; 66:15 25 Therefore is the anger of the LORD kindled against his people, and he
hath stretched forth his hand against them, and hath smitten them: and the
hills did tremble, and their carcases *were* torn in the midst of the streets.
For all this his anger is not turned away, but his hand *is* stretched out still.
5:26☆ Isa 13:2, 3 26¶And he will lift up an ensign to the nations from far, and will hiss unto
them from the end of the earth: and, behold, they shall come with speed
swiftly:
5:27 Joel 2:7, 8 27 None shall be weary nor stumble among them; none shall slumber nor
sleep; neither shall the girdle of their loins be loosed, nor the latchet of their
shoes be broken:
5:28☆ Jer 4:13 28 Whose arrows *are* sharp, and all their bows bent, their horses' hoofs
shall be counted like flint, and their wheels like a whirlwind:
5:29☆ Isa 42:22 Zeph 3:3 29 Their roaring *shall be* like a lion, they shall roar like young lions: yea,
they shall roar, and lay hold of the prey, and shall carry *it* away safe, and
none shall deliver *it.*
5:30☆ Jer 4:23–28 6:23 Joel 2:10 30 And in that day they shall roar against them like the roaring of the sea:
and if *one* look unto the land, behold darkness *and* sorrow, and the light is
darkened in the heavens thereof.

E. GOD CALLS ISAIAH
1. God's Holiness

6:1☆ Jn 12:41 6 IN the year that king Uz-zi'ah died I saw also the Lord sitting upon a
throne, high and lifted up, and his train filled the temple.

5:24 The ruin of Judah and Jerusalem will be just, for they have refused to submit themselves to God and his law. They have despised and disregarded the Word of *the Holy One of Israel. What worse crime could* they commit?

5:26 God will *lift up an ensign* to strong pagan nations to punish his people. This was probably a reference to Assyria.

5:28–30 The nations God will use to bring judgment against Judah and Jerusalem have bent bows and sharp arrows. Their horses' hoofs and the chariots' wheels are like the whirlwind. They roar like lions and growl as they consume their carcasses. Light gives way to darkness and distress.

6:1 Isaiah here recalls the awful death of King Uzziah from leprosy, contracted when he violated the law of God and offered burnt incense (2 Chron. 26:16ff). Israel's king died but Israel's God lives forever.

2 Above it stood the seraphims: each one had six wings; with twain he ☆6:2 Rev 4:8
covered his face, and with twain he covered his feet, and with twain he did
fly.
3 And one cried unto another, and said, Holy, holy, holy, *is* the LORD of 6:3 Ps 72:19
hosts: the whole earth *is* full of his glory.
4 And the posts of the door moved at the voice of him that cried, and the
house was filled with smoke.

2. Isaiah's Confession and Cleansing

5 ¶Then said I, Woe *is* me! for I am undone; because I *am* a man of ☆6:5 Lk 5:8 Jer 9:3–8
unclean lips, and I dwell in the midst of a people of unclean lips: for mine
eyes have seen the King, the LORD of hosts.
6 Then flew one of the seraphims unto me, having a live coal in his hand,
which he had taken with the tongs from off the altar:
7 And he laid *it* upon my mouth, and said, Lo, this hath touched thy lips; ☆6:7 Isa 40:2 Jer 1:9 Jn 1:7
and thine iniquity is taken away, and thy sin purged.

3. Isaiah's Call to Preach

8 Also I heard the voice of the Lord, saying, Whom shall I send, and who ☆6:8 Mt 13:14 Lk 8:10 Acts 26:19 Rom 11:8
will go for us? Then said I, Here *am* I; send me.
9 ¶And he said, Go, and tell this people, Hear ye indeed, but understand
not; and see ye indeed, but perceive not.
10 Make the heart of this people fat, and make their ears heavy, and shut ☆6:10 Jer 5:21
their eyes; lest they see with their eyes, and hear with their ears, and
understand with their heart, and convert, and be healed.
11 Then said I, Lord, how long? And he answered, Until the cities be 6:11 Lev 26:31 Mic 3:12
wasted without inhabitant, and the houses without man, and the land be
utterly desolate,
12 And the LORD have removed men far away, and *there be* a great 6:12 Jer 4:29
forsaking in the midst of the land.
13 ¶But yet in it *shall be* a tenth, and *it* shall return, and shall be eaten: as ☆6:13 Job 14:7
a teil tree, and as an oak, whose substance *is* in them, when they cast *their*
leaves: so the holy seed *shall be* the substance thereof.

II. IMMANUEL: PRESENT AND FUTURE PROSPECTS (7:1—12:6)

A. JUDAH'S DELIVERANCE FROM REZIN AND PEKAH

1. The Military Alliance against Judah

7 AND it came to pass in the days of Ahaz the son of Jo'tham, the son 7:1 2 Kgs 16:1
of Uz-zi'ah, king of Judah, *that* Re'zin the king of Syria, and Pe'kah the

6:2 *seraphims,* i.e., "angels of fire," which in the Hebrew means something which is burning and dazzling. The word also appears in 6:6. Isaiah applies it to angelic beings. It is used nowhere else in the Scriptures, and the Bible gives no explanation of the term. The Jews thought them to be a higher order of celestial beings, since Isaiah pictures them as worshipping and glorifying God. They acted as agents and spokesmen for God and may possibly be related to the cherubim. They appear to be moral beings of some sort.

6:5 Isaiah's vision of the glory of God brought terror to his heart. He was painfully aware of his lostness and uncleanness, when measured against the holiness and purity of God.

6:7 The terror of Isaiah was replaced by a sense of comfort and consolation when the angel assured him that his guilt was gone, his sins forgiven, and his standing with God made right. Renewing grace is God's response to the penitent heart.

6:8 The question, *Who will go for us?,* was not addressed to Isaiah alone. It was addressed to God's people in all ages. But Isaiah had listening ears and he promptly responded—he was willing to go. The words "for us" suggest a council among the Godhead, who is triune, consisting of the Father, the Son, and the Holy Spirit.

6:10 Apparently God's patience with their chronic rebellion was finally exhausted.

6:13 God is frequently the God of the remnant. Here a few people who are righteous and are left after the fall of judgment will be the stump from which God will raise up a new nation.

son of Rem-a-li′ah, king of Israel, went up toward Jerusalem to war against
it, but could not prevail against it.
2 And it was told the house of David, saying, Syria is confederate with
E′phra-im. And his heart was moved, and the heart of his people, as the
trees of the wood are moved with the wind.

2. God's Promise of Deliverance to Ahaz

7:3☆ 3 Then said the LORD unto Isaiah, Go forth now to meet Ahaz, thou, and
She′ar–ja′shub thy son, at the end of the conduit of the upper pool in the
highway of the fuller's field;
7:4 4 And say unto him, Take heed, and be quiet; fear not, neither be
Ex 14:13 Isa 10:24; 35:4 fainthearted for the two tails of these smoking firebrands, for the fierce
Lam 3:26 anger of Re′zin with Syria, and of the son of Rem-a-li′ah.
5 Because Syria, E′phra-im, and the son of Rem-a-li′ah, have taken evil
counsel against thee, saying,
7:6☆ 6 Let us go up against Judah, and vex it, and let us make a breach therein
for us, and set a king in the midst of it, *even* the son of Ta′be-al:
7:7 7 Thus saith the Lord GOD, It shall not stand, neither shall it come to
Ps 2:4–6 pass.
7:8☆ 8 For the head of Syria *is* Damascus, and the head of Damascus *is* Re′zin;
Isa 17:1–3 and within threescore and five years shall E′phra-im be broken, that it be
not a people.
7:9☆ 9 And the head of E′phra-im *is* Sa-ma′ri-a, and the head of Sa-ma′ri-a *is*
2 Chron 20:20 Isa 30:12–14 Rem-a-li′ah's son. If ye will not believe, surely ye shall not be established.

3. God's Sign to Ahaz: Immanuel, a Double Fulfillment

10 ¶Moreover the LORD spake again unto Ahaz, saying,
7:11☆ 11 Ask thee a sign of the LORD thy God; ask it either in the depth, or in
2 Kgs 19:29 Isa 37:30 the height above.
12 But Ahaz said, I will not ask, neither will I tempt the LORD.
13 And he said, Hear ye now, O house of David; *Is it* a small thing for you
to weary men, but will ye weary my God also?
7:14☆ 14 Therefore the Lord himself shall give you a sign; Behold, a virgin shall
Isa 8:8, 10 Mt 1:23 conceive, and bear a son, and shall call his name Im-man′u-el.

7:3 *Ahaz* will be found at the aqueduct, where he has gone to check the water supply. Israel and Syria formed an alliance against Judah, and in the event of war and especially if there were a siege, Jerusalem would need adequate water supplies.

7:6 Since Ahaz refused to join the alliance of Israel (Ephraim) and Syria against Assyria, they decided to depose Ahaz and place their own puppet on his throne.

7:8 *shall Ephraim be broken.* Samaria, the capital of Ephraim, fell to the Assyrian armies in 722 B.C., thirteen years after this oracle. This ended the Northern Kingdom.†

7:9 *If ye will not believe.* Evidently Ahaz was weak in his faith in God. Isaiah plainly told him that his future was assured if he trusted in God.

7:11 *ask it either in the depth, or in the height above, i.e.,* "ask anything you like, in heaven or on earth."†

7:14 *a virgin shall conceive, and bear a son.* Before we can understand this verse, we need to consider two Hebrew words. One is *bethulah* and the other *almah.* The former means virgin, and the latter an unmarried female. *Almah* is used here. Its use in this context covers two cases. One has to do with the wife of Isaiah and her newborn son (Isa. 8:1–4). Isaiah's wife was a virgin until she was married. She was no longer a virgin when married. Of course, one supposes that an unmarried female is a virgin. The second case covers that of the virgin Mary. She was a virgin before the conception of Jesus. And she remained a virgin then, because Joseph was not the father of Jesus. The Holy Spirit was. Stated another way, Isaiah's wife was no longer a virgin when she conceived; Mary was still a virgin *after* she conceived, for she had not yet known a male. Interestingly, the Septuagint translates *almah* by the use of the Greek word *parthenos* which means virgin. And Matthew uses the word *parthenos* for Mary's case. The word *almah* thus covers both births involved in this prophecy and we learn that Maher-shalal-hash-baz, the son of Isaiah, had a human mother and father and his birth was a natural one. Jesus, on the other hand, had a human mother but not a human father. His birth was supernatural. *Almah* allows for both prophetic words.

15 Butter and honey shall he eat, that he may know to refuse the evil, and
choose the good.

7:15 Isa 8:4; 17:3

16 For before the child shall know to refuse the evil, and choose the good,
the land that thou abhorrest shall be forsaken of both her kings.

☆7:16

17 ¶The LORD shall bring upon thee, and upon thy people, and upon thy
father's house, days that have not come from the day that E'phra-im
departed from Judah; *even* the king of Assyria.

7:17 1 Kgs 12:16, 17 Isa 10:5, 6

18 And it shall come to pass in that day, *that* the LORD shall hiss for the fly
that *is* in the uttermost part of the rivers of Egypt, and for the bee that *is* in
the land of Assyria.

☆7:18

19 And they shall come, and shall rest all of them in the desolate valleys,
and in the holes of the rocks, and upon all thorns, and upon all bushes.

7:19 Jer 16:16

20 In the same day shall the Lord shave with a razor that is hired, *namely,*
by them beyond the river, by the king of Assyria, the head, and the hair of
the feet: and it shall also consume the beard.

7:20 Isa 24:1 Ezek 5:1–4

21 And it shall come to pass in that day, *that* a man shall nourish a young
cow, and two sheep;

☆7:21 Jer 39:10

22 And it shall come to pass, for the abundance of milk *that* they shall give
he shall eat butter: for butter and honey shall every one eat that is left in
the land.

23 And it shall come to pass in that day, *that* every place shall be, where
there were a thousand vines at a thousand silverlings, it shall *even* be for
briers and thorns.

24 With arrows and with bows shall *men* come thither; because all the land
shall become briers and thorns.

25 And *on* all hills that shall be digged with the mattock, there shall not
come thither the fear of briers and thorns: but it shall be for the sending
forth of oxen, and for the treading of lesser cattle.

B. THE WAR AND THE LAST DAYS' DELIVERER

1. The First Fulfillment: Maher-Shalal-Hash-Baz

8 MOREOVER the LORD said unto me, Take thee a great roll, and write
in it with a man's pen concerning Ma'her-shal'al-hash'-baz.

☆8:1 Hab 2:2

2 And I took unto me faithful witnesses to record, U-ri'ah the priest, and
Zech-a-ri'ah the son of Je-ber-e-chi'ah.

8:2 2 Kgs 16:10, 11, 15, 16

3 And I went unto the prophetess; and she conceived, and bare a son.
Then said the LORD to me, Call his name Ma'her-shal'al-hash'-baz.

☆8:3

4 For before the child shall have knowledge to cry, My father, and my
mother, the riches of Damascus and the spoil of Sa-ma'ri-a shall be taken
away before the king of Assyria.

7:16 *For before the child shall know to refuse the evil, and choose the good,* i.e., "By the time this child is weaned." *shall be forsaken of both her kings,* i.e., "the kings of Israel and Syria (implied) will both be dead," or, "the lands will be deserted (of their kings)."†

7:18 Paraphrased: "At that time the Lord will whistle for the army of Upper Egypt, and of Assyria too, to swarm down upon you like flies and destroy you, like bees to sting and kill." "Upper Egypt" refers to the powerful twenty-fifth Ethiopian Dynasty which would soon arise.†

7:21ff Judah is pictured as being desolate and poverty-stricken. Its population will be greatly reduced; meat will be scarce; curds and honey will be its food.

8:1 Maher-shalal-hash-baz, meaning, "Your enemies will soon be destroyed," or, literally, "plundering and despoiling (will) come quickly."†

8:3 God gave Ahaz a sign that has a double fulfillment. Here the first fulfillment is stated. The prophetess, who probably was virgin at the time 7:14 was spoken, gives birth to a son in a normal marriage relationship. His name is Maher-shalal-hash-baz (meaning "the spoil speeds, the prey hastes," RSV footnote). Some hold that this boy was a type of the messianic Immanuel, who was born of the virgin Mary and fathered by the Holy Spirit. (See note on 7:14.)

2. The Flooding River

5 ¶The LORD spake also unto me again, saying,
8:6☆ 6 Forasmuch as this people refuseth the waters of Shi-lo'ah that go softly,
Isa 30:12 and rejoice in Re'zin and Rem-a-li'ah's son;
8:7 7 Now therefore, behold, the Lord bringeth up upon them the waters of
Isa 7:14 the river, strong and many, *even* the king of Assyria, and all his glory: and
17:12, 13 Amos 8:8; 9:5 he shall come up over all his channels, and go over all his banks:
8 And he shall pass through Judah; he shall overflow and go over, he shall
reach *even* to the neck; and the stretching out of his wings shall fill the
breadth of thy land, O Im-man'u-el.

3. The Rock of Stumbling

8:9☆ 9 ¶Associate yourselves, O ye people, and ye shall be broken in pieces;
Dan 2:34, 35 Rom 8:31 and give ear, all ye of far countries: gird yourselves, and ye shall be broken
in pieces; gird yourselves, and ye shall be broken in pieces.
8:10☆ 10 Take counsel together, and it shall come to nought; speak the word,
and it shall not stand: for God *is* with us.
8:11 11 ¶For the LORD spake thus to me with a strong hand, and instructed me
Ezek 2:8 that I should not walk in the way of this people, saying,
8:12 12 Say ye not, A confederacy, to all *them to* whom this people shall say, A
1 Pet 3:13–15 confederacy; neither fear ye their fear, nor be afraid.
8:13☆ 13 Sanctify the LORD of hosts himself; and *let* him *be* your fear, and *let*
him *be* your dread.
8:14☆ 14 And he shall be for a sanctuary; but for a stone of stumbling and for a
Isa 25:4 Ezek 11:16 rock of offence to both the houses of Israel, for a gin and for a snare to the
Lk 2:34 Rom 9:32, 33 inhabitants of Jerusalem.
1 Pet 2:8 15 And many among them shall stumble, and fall, and be broken, and be
snared, and be taken.
8:16☆ 16 Bind up the testimony, seal the law among my disciples.
Isa 50:4
Dan 12:4

4. The Command to Trust God, Not Witches and Mediums

8:17 17 And I will wait upon the LORD, that hideth his face from the house of
Deut 31:17 Isa 30:18; 54:8 Jacob, and I will look for him.
Hab 2:3 8:18 18 Behold, I and the children whom the LORD hath given me *are* for signs
Heb 2:13 and for wonders in Israel from the LORD of hosts, which dwelleth in mount
Zion.
8:19 19 ¶And when they shall say unto you, Seek unto them that have familiar
Lev 20:6 2 Kgs 21:6 spirits, and unto wizards that peep, and that mutter: should not a people
seek unto their God? for the living to the dead?
8:20☆ 20 To the law and to the testimony: if they speak not according to this
word, *it is* because *there is* no light in them.

8:6 *refuseth the waters of Shiloah that go softly,* i.e., "are planning to refuse my gentle care." The waters of Shiloah are known as Ain Silwan and are located southwest of Mount Moriah. Here Shiloah's quiet waters are contrasted with the turbulent waters of Euphrates' mighty flood (implied in 8:7). Because Samaria has rejected Shiloah, which symbolizes God's rule, she will be overwhelmed by the king of Assyria, who will come from beyond the Euphrates.
8:9 *O ye people,* i.e., "O Syria and Israel."
8:10 *God is with us,* i.e., "Immanuel."
8:13, 14 *let him be your fear.* The fear of the Lord cancels out the fear of men. His greatness eclipses all the pomp and pretense of the enemy. He becomes a sanctuary for those who trust in him.
8:16 *Bind up the testimony.* God graciously entrusted his revelation to the Jews who must preserve it safely for the comfort of God's faithful people as they go through the approaching times of trouble, difficulty, and distress.
8:20 Isaiah directs the attention of the people to the oracles of God. Whoever turns away from their light, turns away from the Father of lights.

21 And they shall pass through it, hardly bestead and hungry: and it shall
come to pass, that when they shall be hungry, they shall fret themselves,
and curse their king and their God, and look upward.
22 And they shall look unto the earth; and behold trouble and darkness,
dimness of anguish; and *they shall be* driven to darkness.

8:22 Jer 13:16; Amos 5:18, 20; Zeph 1:14, 15

5. The Promise of the Coming Messiah

9 NEVERTHELESS the dimness *shall* not *be* such as *was* in her
vexation, when at the first he lightly afflicted the land of Zeb′u-lun and
the land of Naph′ta-li, and afterward did more grievously afflict *her by* the
way of the sea, beyond Jordan, in Galilee of the nations.
2 The people that walked in darkness have seen a great light: they that
dwell in the land of the shadow of death, upon them hath the light shined.
3 Thou hast multiplied the nation, *and* not increased the joy: they joy
before thee according to the joy in harvest, *and* as *men* rejoice when they
divide the spoil.
4 For thou hast broken the yoke of his burden, and the staff of his
shoulder, the rod of his oppressor, as in the day of Mid′i-an.
5 For every battle of the warrior *is* with confused noise, and garments
rolled in blood; but *this* shall be with burning *and* fuel of fire.
6 For unto us a child is born, unto us a son is given: and the government
shall be upon his shoulder: and his name shall be called Wonderful,
Counsellor, The mighty God, The everlasting Father, The Prince of Peace.
7 Of the increase of *his* government and peace *there shall be* no end, upon
the throne of David, and upon his kingdom, to order it, and to establish it
with judgment and with justice from henceforth even for ever. The zeal of
the LORD of hosts will perform this.

☆**9:1**
9:2 Mt 4:15, 16
9:3 Isa 26:15; 35:10; 66:10
9:4 Isa 49:26
☆**9:6** Deut 10:17; Neh 9:32; Isa 26:3, 12; Mt 28:18; Lk 2:11; 1 Cor 15:25
☆**9:7** Dan 2:44; Lk 1:32, 33

C. THE DESTRUCTION OF SAMARIA (EPHRAIM-ISRAEL)
1. Israel, the Braggart and Hypocrite

8 ¶The Lord sent a word into Jacob, and it hath lighted upon Israel.
9 And all the people shall know, *even* E′phra-im and the inhabitant of Sa-
ma′ri-a, that say in the pride and stoutness of heart,
10 The bricks are fallen down, but we will build with hewn stones: the
sycomores are cut down, but we will change *them into* cedars.
11 Therefore the LORD shall set up the adversaries of Re′zin against him,
and join his enemies together;
12 The Syrians before, and the Philistines behind; and they shall devour

9:8 Mal 1:4
☆**9:11** Ps 79:7; Jer 10:25

9:1 In 2 Kings 15:29 we see that Tiglath-pileser took Ephraim, Zebulun, and Naphtali from Israel. Isaiah looks to that day when God will revisit Israel and restore her. There are three promises made here: (1) of a great and glorious light (9:2), (2) of economic plenty and universal joy (9:3), and (3) of glorious enlargement and freedom from the enemy (9:4, 5).

9:6 *For unto us a child is born.* This verse has been seen by some as a prophecy about the birth of Hezekiah. But it expresses hope for a future deliverance. 9:1 speaks about what will happen in a more distant future. Thus the prophecy speaks about the birth of the Messiah King, which finds its fulfillment in Jesus Christ as the God-man. He is given the title *The everlasting Father* (literally, "Father of Eternity," in the sense that he made all things). Creation, of course, was the work of the Trinity: the Father, the Son, and the Holy Spirit. The title *Prince of Peace* bespeaks the one who brings spiritual peace to the sinful heart through regeneration. The Messiah is also called *Wonderful, Counsellor* or better," Wonderful Counsellor," which might also be translated "Supernatural Counsellor." He came to bring us the words of everlasting life, and he will come to rule in power and with wisdom at his second advent. He is the mighty God, a title used in Isa. 10:21 for Yahweh. He has all power to do all things and to accomplish what God intended. This constellation of names clearly indicates the Messiah is God himself, the second person of the Trinity.

9:7 *The zeal of the LORD of hosts will perform this.* The God who has all power in his hand and all men at his beck and call will preserve the throne of David until the Prince of Peace is seated on it. He will overcome all opposition.

9:11 *adversaries of Rezin,* i.e., "your enemies," or, "Rezin's enemies," in some ancient versions.†

Israel with open mouth. For all this his anger is not turned away, but his
hand *is* stretched out still.

9:13 Jer 5:3; Hos 7:10

13¶For the people turneth not unto him that smiteth them, neither do
they seek the LORD of hosts.
14Therefore the LORD will cut off from Israel head and tail, branch and
rush, in one day.

9:15☆

15The ancient and honourable, he *is* the head; and the prophet that
teacheth lies, he *is* the tail.

9:16 Mt 15:14

16For the leaders of this people cause *them* to err; and *they that are* led of
them *are* destroyed.

2. The Evil Consequences of Sin

9:17 Isa 32:6; Amos 8:13; Mt 12:34

17Therefore the Lord shall have no joy in their young men, neither shall
have mercy on their fatherless and widows: for every one *is* an hypocrite
and an evildoer, and every mouth speaketh folly. For all this his anger is
not turned away, but his hand *is* stretched out still.

9:18 Mal 4:1

18¶For wickedness burneth as the fire: it shall devour the briers and
thorns, and shall kindle in the thickets of the forest, and they shall mount
up *like* the lifting up of smoke.

9:19 Joel 2:3; Mic 7:2, 6

19Through the wrath of the LORD of hosts is the land darkened, and the
people shall be as the fuel of the fire: no man shall spare his brother.
20And he shall snatch on the right hand, and be hungry; and he shall eat
on the left hand, and they shall not be satisfied: they shall eat every man the
flesh of his own arm:

9:21 Isa 11:13

21Ma-nas′seh, E′phra-im; and E′phra-im, Ma-nas′seh: *and* they together
shall be against Judah. For all this his anger is not turned away, but his
hand *is* stretched out still.

3. Those Who Mistreat the Poor and Fatherless Shall Be Punished

10:1☆ Ps 94:20; Isa 59:13, 14

10 WOE unto them that decree unrighteous decrees, and that write
grievousness *which* they have prescribed.
2To turn aside the needy from judgment, and to take away the right from
the poor of my people, that widows may be their prey, and *that* they may
rob the fatherless!

10:3 Isa 13:6; Lk 19:43, 44

3And what will ye do in the day of visitation, and in the desolation *which*
shall come from far? to whom will ye flee for help? and where will ye leave
your glory?

10:4 Isa 34:3; 66:16

4Without me they shall bow down under the prisoners, and they shall fall
under the slain. For all this his anger is not turned away, but his hand *is*
stretched out still.

D. THE PROPHECY CONCERNING ASSYRIA AND GOD'S FUTURE KINGDOM

1. Assyria Is God's Whip; It Too Will Be Judged Afterwards

a. Assyria, the Whip, Will Suffer God's Vengeance

10:5☆ Isa 13:5; Jer 51:20

5¶O Assyrian, the rod of mine anger, and the staff in their hand is mine
indignation.

9:15 *he is the tail.* The prophet who teaches lies is here demoted to the lowest position. He is not the head *but the tail, which is insignificant when* compared to the head. A dog can live without a tail but not without a head.

10:1 God's indictment against his people includes the charges that (1) they have legislated wicked laws and issued iniquitous decrees; (2) they have perverted justice; and (3) they have enriched themselves at the expense of the most unfortunate of the people: the poor, the widowed, and the orphans. Therefore, God's anger is just and his judgment is according to righteousness.

10:5 *O Assyrian, the rod of mine anger.* God used this wicked nation to humble sinful Israel and Judah. Assyria, in turn, would be punished by a righteous God.

6 I will send him against an hypocritical nation, and against the people of
my wrath will I give him a charge, to take the spoil, and to take the prey,
and to tread them down like the mire of the streets.
7 Howbeit he meaneth not so, neither doth his heart think so; but *it is* in
his heart to destroy and cut off nations not a few.
8 For he saith, *Are* not my princes altogether kings?
9 *Is* not Cal′no as Car′che-mish? *is* not Ha′math as Ar′pad? *is* not Sa-
ma′ri-a as Damascus?
10 As my hand hath found the kingdoms of the idols, and whose graven
images did excel them of Jerusalem and of Sa-ma′ri-a;
11 Shall I not, as I have done unto Sa-ma′ri-a and her idols, so do to
Jerusalem and her idols?
12 Wherefore it shall come to pass, *that* when the Lord hath performed his
whole work upon mount Zion and on Jerusalem, I will punish the fruit of
the stout heart of the king of Assyria, and the glory of his high looks.
13 For he saith, By the strength of my hand I have done *it,* and by my
wisdom; for I am prudent: and I have removed the bounds of the people,
and have robbed their treasures, and I have put down the inhabitants like a
valiant *man:*
14 And my hand hath found as a nest the riches of the people: and as one
gathereth eggs *that are* left, have I gathered all the earth; and there was
none that moved the wing, or opened the mouth, or peeped.
15 Shall the axe boast itself against him that heweth therewith? *or* shall the
saw magnify itself against him that shaketh it? as if the rod should shake
itself against them that lift it up, *or* as if the staff should lift up *itself, as if it*
were no wood.
16 Therefore shall the Lord, the Lord of hosts, send among his fat ones
leanness; and under his glory he shall kindle a burning like the burning of
a fire.
17 And the light of Israel shall be for a fire, and his Holy One for a flame:
and it shall burn and devour his thorns and his briers in one day;
18 And shall consume the glory of his forest, and of his fruitful field, both
soul and body: and they shall be as when a standardbearer fainteth.
19 And the rest of the trees of his forest shall be few, that a child may write
them.

10:7 Gen 50:20; Mic 4:11, 12; Acts 2:23, 24
10:10 2 Kgs 19:17, 18
☆**10:11**
10:12 Jer 50:18
10:13 2 Kgs 19:22–24; Isa 37:24–27; Dan 4:30
☆**10:15** Isa 29:16
☆**10:17** Isa 27:4; 30:33; 31:9; 33:12; 37:23; Jer 4:4
10:19 Isa 21:17

b. A Remnant of God's People Will Be Saved

20 ¶And it shall come to pass in that day, *that* the remnant of Israel, and
such as are escaped of the house of Jacob, shall no more again stay upon
him that smote them; but shall stay upon the LORD, the Holy One of Israel,
in truth.
21 The remnant shall return, *even* the remnant of Jacob, unto the mighty
God.

☆**10:20** Isa 17:7, 8

10:11 Proud Assyria boasted that it had conquered and overcome other nations: *Calno, Arpad, Hamath, Carchemish* and *Samaria.* Will not Assyria do to Judah and Jerusalem (and its idols) what it has done to other nations? When Assyria had completed its work under the stern eye of God (whom it does not know), it would be judged in turn by the God of Israel.

10:15 *the axe.* Sennacherib is the axe in the hand of God, accomplishing what God wanted done. But this profane babbler supposes that he has done it by his own might, little realizing that when God had finished using him to punish Israel, God would then destroy the destroyer. We learn here that even the wicked become instruments in the hands of God, executing God's righteous judgments even when they are unaware of what they really are doing.

10:17 The God whose light shines as a beacon for those who believe will become a light of destroying fire against those who trifle against his Word and dare to disobey him.

10:20ff Assyria will not be victorious over all the people of Judah. God will save a remnant. But these verses show the inexorable march of the Assyrians toward Jerusalem. None of the cities mentioned is more than three hours away from Zion.

10:22 Isa 28:22 Rom 9:27, 28
22 For though thy people Israel be as the sand of the sea, *yet* a remnant of
them shall return: the consumption decreed shall overflow with righteous-
ness.
23 For the Lord GOD of hosts shall make a consumption, even deter-
mined, in the midst of all the land.
10:24 Ex 5:14–16
24 ¶Therefore thus saith the Lord GOD of hosts, O my people that dwellest
in Zion, be not afraid of the Assyrian: he shall smite thee with a rod, and
shall lift up his staff against thee, after the manner of Egypt.
10:25 Isa 17:14
25 For yet a very little while, and the indignation shall cease, and mine
anger in their destruction.
10:26 Ex 14:16, 27 Judg 7:25 Isa 37:36–38
26 And the LORD of hosts shall stir up a scourge for him according to the
slaughter of Mid′i-an at the rock of O′reb: and *as* his rod *was* upon the sea,
so shall he lift it up after the manner of Egypt.
10:27☆ Isa 14:25
27 And it shall come to pass in that day, *that* his burden shall be taken
away from off thy shoulder, and his yoke from off thy neck, and the yoke
shall be destroyed because of the anointing.
28 He is come to A-i′ath, he is passed to Mig′ron; at Mich′mash he hath
laid up his carriages:
29 They are gone over the passage: they have taken up their lodging at
Ge′ba; Ra′mah is afraid; Gib′e-ah of Saul is fled.
30 Lift up thy voice, O daughter of Gal′lim: cause it to be heard unto
La′ish, O poor An′a-thoth.
31 Mad-me′nah is removed; the inhabitants of Ge′bim gather themselves
to flee.
10:32 Isa 19:16 Zech 2:9
32 As yet shall he remain at Nob that day: he shall shake his hand *against*
the mount of the daughter of Zion, the hill of Jerusalem.
10:33 Isa 37:24 Ezek 31:2, 3 Amos 2:9
33 Behold, the Lord, the LORD of hosts, shall lop the bough with terror:
and the high ones of stature *shall* be hewn down, and the haughty shall be
humbled.
34 And he shall cut down the thickets of the forest with iron, and Lebanon
shall fall by a mighty one.

2. The Coming Messianic Age

a. The New Branch from the Old Root

11:1☆ Jer 23:5 Zech 6:12 Rev 5:5
11 AND there shall come forth a rod out of the stem of Jesse, and a
Branch shall grow out of his roots:
11:2 Isa 61:1 Jn 1:32 Eph 1:17
2 And the spirit of the LORD shall rest upon him, the spirit of wisdom and
understanding, the spirit of counsel and might, the spirit of knowledge and
of the fear of the LORD;
11:3 Jn 2:24, 25
3 And shall make him of quick understanding in the fear of the LORD:
and he shall not judge after the sight of his eyes, neither reprove after the
hearing of his ears:
11:4 Isa 30:28 2 Thess 2:8
4 But with righteousness shall he judge the poor, and reprove with equity
for the meek of the earth: and he shall smite the earth with the rod of his
mouth, and with the breath of his lips shall he slay the wicked.
5 And righteousness shall be the girdle of his loins, and faithfulness the
girdle of his reins.
11:6☆ Isa 65:25
6 The wolf also shall dwell with the lamb, and the leopard shall lie down

---

10:27 *because of the anointing.* Some see here a reference to the Messiah, the Anointed One.†

11:1 out of the stem of Jesse . . . a Branch . . . out of his roots. Jesse, the father of David, is likened to a tree that was felled. From the stump would come a new shoot. So God's covenant with David will be fulfilled. The Shoot or new *Branch* is none other than Jesus Christ, the Messiah.

11:6 This prophetic word will be fulfilled at the end of the age, with the return of the Messiah as King of kings. The Messiah is our peace, who breaks down all the walls that separate one people from another. All enmities shall be slain and lasting friendship shall come between Jew and Gentile, who will be members of the one flock. It will be a glorious age.

with the kid; and the calf and the young lion and the fatling together; and
a little child shall lead them.
[7]And the cow and the bear shall feed; their young ones shall lie down
together: and the lion shall eat straw like the ox.
[8]And the sucking child shall play on the hole of the asp, and the weaned
child shall put his hand on the cockatrice' den.
[9]They shall not hurt nor destroy in all my holy mountain: for the earth
shall be full of the knowledge of the LORD, as the waters cover the sea.

☆**11:9** Isa 45:6; Ezek 34:25; Hos 2:18; Hab 2:14

b. Messiah Will Regather Israel

[10]¶And in that day there shall be a root of Jesse, which shall stand for an
ensign of the people; to it shall the Gentiles seek: and his rest shall be
glorious.

☆**11:10** Lk 2:32; Jn 3:14, 15; Rom 15:12

[11]And it shall come to pass in that day, *that* the Lord shall set his hand
again the second time to recover the remnant of his people, which shall be
left, from Assyria, and from Egypt, and from Path'ros, and from Cush, and
from E'lam, and from Shi'nar, and from Ha'math, and from the islands of
the sea.

11:11 Isa 60:9; Zech 10:10

[12]And he shall set up an ensign for the nations, and shall assemble the
outcasts of Israel, and gather together the dispersed of Judah from the four
corners of the earth.

☆**11:12** Zeph 3:10

[13]The envy also of E'phra-im shall depart, and the adversaries of Judah
shall be cut off: E'phra-im shall not envy Judah, and Judah shall not vex
E'phra-im.

11:13 Ezek 37:16, 17, 22

[14]But they shall fly upon the shoulders of the Philistines toward the west;
they shall spoil them of the east together: they shall lay their hand upon
Edom and Moab; and the children of Ammon shall obey them.
[15]And the LORD shall utterly destroy the tongue of the Egyptian sea; and
with his mighty wind shall he shake his hand over the river, and shall smite
it in the seven streams, and make *men* go over dryshod.

☆**11:15** Isa 51:10

[16]And there shall be an highway for the remnant of his people, which
shall be left, from Assyria; like as it was to Israel in the day that he came up
out of the land of Egypt.

☆**11:16** Ex 14:26-29; Isa 19:23

c. A Psalm of Praise for God the Savior

12 AND in that day thou shalt say, O LORD, I will praise thee: though
thou wast angry with me, thine anger is turned away, and thou
comfortedst me.

☆**12:1** Isa 40:1

[2]Behold, God *is* my salvation; I will trust, and not be afraid: for the
LORD JEHOVAH *is* my strength and *my* song; he also is become my
salvation.

☆**12:2** Ps 118:14; Isa 26:3; 62:11

11:9 This earth presently does not have the knowledge of the Lord from north to south, or from east to west. But the day is coming when all that would hinder or prevent the knowledge of God from sweeping over all creation will be destroyed. Then shall the fullness of God's knowledge reign from sea to sea and shore to shore.

11:10 *a root of Jesse,* i.e., "the royal dynasty of David." Possibly the meaning is, "the Heir of David's royal line."†

11:12 A remnant of the Jews will be gathered by God from the ends of the earth. They will be united with the Gentiles, over whom the flag of God will fly. This will come about by the powerful working of the Holy Spirit with and through the Word of God.

11:15 *the Egyptian sea,* i.e., "the Red Sea." *the river,* i.e., "the Euphrates."† The sea of Egypt referred to here is the Gulf of Suez. God is said to provide a passageway for the safe return of his people as he did during the Exodus.

11:16 Even as God dried up the Red Sea for Israel to pass through dry shod, so God will bring Jews and Gentiles together. He will remove all obstructions, break down every barrier, and even lead the blind by a way they know not. The insuperable will yield to the divine power.

12:1 God often has good reason to be angry with us, his people, but we never have reason to be angry with him nor the right to speak other than well of him.

12:2 Since God is our salvation and guarantees that we shall inherit eternal life, we can also trust him completely for all of our temporal concerns.

3Therefore with joy shall ye draw water out of the wells of salvation.
4And in that day shall ye say, Praise the LORD, call upon his name,
declare his doings among the people, make mention that his name is
exalted.
5Sing unto the LORD; for he hath done excellent things: this *is* known in
all the earth.
6Cry out and shout, thou inhabitant of Zion: for great *is* the Holy One of
Israel in the midst of thee.

12:3 Jer 2:13
12:4 Ps 145:4
12:5☆ Ps 98:1; Isa 44:23
12:6☆ Isa 54:1; Zeph 3:14, 15–17

III. PROPHECIES CONCERNING THE HEATHEN NATIONS (13:1—23:18)

A. THE PROPHECY ABOUT BABYLON

1. The Promised Destruction of Babylon

13 THE burden of Babylon, which Isaiah the son of Amoz did see.
2Lift ye up a banner upon the high mountain, exalt the voice
unto them, shake the hand, that they may go into the gates of the nobles.
3I have commanded my sanctified ones, I have also called my mighty
ones for mine anger, *even* them that rejoice in my highness.
4The noise of a multitude in the mountains, like as of a great people; a
tumultuous noise of the kingdoms of nations gathered together: the LORD
of hosts mustereth the host of the battle.
5They come from a far country, from the end of heaven, *even* the LORD,
and the weapons of his indignation, to destroy the whole land.
6¶Howl ye; for the day of the LORD *is* at hand; it shall come as a
destruction from the Almighty.
7Therefore shall all hands be faint, and every man's heart shall melt:
8And they shall be afraid: pangs and sorrows shall take hold of them;
they shall be in pain as a woman that travaileth: they shall be amazed one
at another; their faces *shall be as* flames.
9Behold, the day of the LORD cometh, cruel both with wrath and fierce
anger, to lay the land desolate: and he shall destroy the sinners thereof out
of it.
10For the stars of heaven and the constellations thereof shall not give
their light: the sun shall be darkened in his going forth, and the moon shall
not cause her light to shine.
11And I will punish the world for *their* evil, and the wicked for their
iniquity; and I will cause the arrogancy of the proud to cease, and will lay
low the haughtiness of the terrible.
12I will make a man more precious than fine gold; even a man than the
golden wedge of O'phir.

13:1☆
13:2 Isa 45:1–3
13:3☆
13:4☆ Isa 5:30
13:5 Isa 5:26
13:6☆ Isa 34:2, 8; Ezek 30:3; Amos 5:18
13:7 Ezek 21:7
13:8 Isa 21:3, 26:17
13:9 Isa 66:15, 16
13:10☆ Mt 24:29
13:11 Dan 5:22, 23
13:12 Isa 6:11, 12

12:5, 6 God's people are called upon to sing God's praises for the glorious things he has done—and all the more because he has come into their midst and revealed himself as the Holy One of Israel.

13:1 Isaiah receives God's revelation in which the doom of Babylon is predicted. Babylon will do wrong against God's people at God's command, but God will then execute judgment on the very nation that he used to avenge himself against Judah and Jerusalem.

13:3 God will use the Medes and the Persians under Darius and Cyrus to ruin the Babylonian monarchy. *Darius and Cyrus are called God's sanctified* ones, for they were called to this service and set apart for it, by the providence of God, to accomplish the divine purpose.

13:4 It will be no mob that will overthrow Babylon. The troops will come in ordered array from a far country. They will not be rude barbarians but model soldiers who are well ordered and militarily able to be used by God to scourge and destroy Babylon.

13:6 Men may have their day, but they frequently fail to see that God will have his day, which is coming soon. Whoever puts his own day above God's or supposes that God cannot or will not reward nations according to their works, will shortly discover his error and perish in the midst of his secular splendor.

13:10 The light from the stars of heaven will not be seen because they will be clouded and overcast. The light of the sun will be lost to men amid foul weather. The armies of Babylon will be like men in trouble on the sea when there is neither sun, moon, nor stars to guide them. The God of nature has power to use nature against whomever he pleases.

[13]Therefore I will shake the heavens, and the earth shall remove out of
her place, in the wrath of the LORD of hosts, and in the day of his fierce
anger.

☆13:13 Hag 2:6

[14]And it shall be as the chased roe, and as a sheep that no man taketh up:
they shall every man turn to his own people, and flee every one into his own
land.

13:14 1 Kgs 22:17 Mt 9:36

[15]Every one that is found shall be thrust through; and every one that is
joined *unto them* shall fall by the sword.

13:15 Jer 51:3, 4

[16]Their children also shall be dashed to pieces before their eyes; their
houses shall be spoiled, and their wives ravished.

☆13:16 Ps 137:8, 9 Hos 10:14

[17]Behold, I will stir up the Medes against them, which shall not regard
silver; and *as for* gold, they shall not delight in it.

☆13:17 Jer 51:11

[18]*Their* bows also shall dash the young men to pieces; and they shall have
no pity on the fruit of the womb; their eye shall not spare children.

13:18 2 Chron 36:17

[19]¶And Babylon, the glory of kingdoms, the beauty of the Chal'dees'
excellency, shall be as when God overthrew Sodom and Go-mor'rah.

13:19 Gen 19:24 Rev 18:11–16, 19

[20]It shall never be inhabited, neither shall it be dwelt in from generation
to generation: neither shall the Arabian pitch tent there; neither shall the
shepherds make their fold there.

☆13:20 Jer 51:37–43

[21]But wild beasts of the desert shall lie there; and their houses shall be
full of doleful creatures; and owls shall dwell there, and satyrs shall dance
there.

☆13:21 Isa 34:11–15 Zeph 2:14 Isa 32:14; 34:13

[22]And the wild beasts of the islands shall cry in their desolate houses, and
dragons in *their* pleasant palaces: and her time *is* near to come, and her
days shall not be prolonged.

2. Jeering the King of Babylon

14 FOR the LORD will have mercy on Jacob, and will yet choose
Israel, and set them in their own land: and the strangers shall be
joined with them, and they shall cleave to the house of Jacob.

☆14:1 Ps 102:13 Isa 41:8, 9 49:13, 15 Zech 2:11, 12

[2]And the people shall take them, and bring them to their place: and the
house of Israel shall possess them in the land of the LORD for servants and
handmaids: and they shall take them captives, whose captives they were;
and they shall rule over their oppressors.

☆14:2 Isa 45:14 Dan 7:18, 27

[3]And it shall come to pass in the day that the LORD shall give thee rest
from thy sorrow, and from thy fear, and from the hard bondage wherein
thou wast made to serve.

14:3 Ezra 9:8, 9 Jer 30:10

[4]¶That thou shalt take up this proverb against the king of Babylon, and
say, How hath the oppressor ceased! the golden city ceased!

13:13 Earthquakes will shake Babylon; its armies will be fearful and run to escape from the impending judgment. Amid blood and horror the sword will destroy.

13:16 Even as the Babylonians had cruelly killed Judean infants, so *shall their own infants* be dashed against the stones. And their houses, which had been filled with the loot gathered from Jerusalem, shall be plundered and spoiled.

13:17 *the Medes* were an ancient Aryan (Iranian) people who lived southwest of the Caspian Sea. They joined forces with the Babylonians (Chaldeans) in the destruction of Nineveh (612 B.C.). Later they were incorporated into the Persian Empire which, under Cyrus, overcame and destroyed Babylon (539 B.C.).

13:20 Isaiah prophesied that Babylon would "never be inhabited." It never has been. Its ruins have been uncovered and its majesty and greatness confirmed. On the basis of this prophecy, it is proper to conclude that the Babylon of Rev. 17 is not a literal Babylon. It is probably a political and ecclesiastical confederacy, of which the Old Testament Babylon is a type or example.

13:21 *satyrs,* i.e., "demons" which in ancient mythology were part goat, part man.

14:1 God determined that he would free his people from Babylon after their captivity had reached its full course. Then it would be necessary to destroy the oppressor to free the oppressed. The yoke of repression would be broken and the prisoners set free.

14:2 God promises the great reversal in which his people would return to their own land. Israel's people would take their captors captive and rule over those who had oppressed them.

5 The LORD hath broken the staff of the wicked, *and* the sceptre of the
rulers.
14:6 Isa 47:6 6 He who smote the people in wrath with a continual stroke, he that ruled
the nations in anger, is persecuted, *and* none hindereth.
14:7 Ps 98:1–9 7 The whole earth is at rest, *and* is quiet: they break forth into singing.
8 Yea, the fir trees rejoice at thee, *and* the cedars of Lebanon, *saying,* Since
thou art laid down, no feller is come up against us.
9 Hell from beneath is moved for thee to meet *thee* at thy coming: it
stirreth up the dead for thee, *even* all the chief ones of the earth; it hath
raised up from their thrones all the kings of the nations.
14:10 Ezek 32:21 10 All they shall speak and say unto thee, Art thou also become weak as
we? art thou become like unto us?
11 Thy pomp is brought down to the grave, *and* the noise of thy viols: the
worm is spread under thee, and the worms cover thee.
14:12☆ Lk 10:18 Rev 9:1 12 How art thou fallen from heaven, O Lu'ci-fer, son of the morning! *how*
art thou cut down to the ground, which didst weaken the nations!
14:13☆ Ezek 28:2 13 For thou hast said in thine heart, I will ascend into heaven, I will exalt
my throne above the stars of God: I will sit also upon the mount of the
congregation, in the sides of the north:
14:14 2 Thess 2:4 14 I will ascend above the heights of the clouds; I will be like the most
High.
14:15–17☆ 15 Yet thou shalt be brought down to hell, to the sides of the pit.
16 They that see thee shall narrowly look upon thee, *and* consider thee,
saying, Is this the man that made the earth to tremble, that did shake
kingdoms;
17 *That* made the world as a wilderness, and destroyed the cities thereof;
that opened not the house of his prisoners?
18 All the kings of the nations, *even* all of them, lie in glory, every one in
his own house.
14:19 Isa 5:25 19 But thou art cast out of thy grave like an abominable branch, *and as* the
raiment of those that are slain, thrust through with a sword, that go down
to the stones of the pit; as a carcase trodden under feet.

14:12 The Scriptures give Satan *(Lucifer)* many different names, such as (1) father of liars (John 8:44), (2) the prince of the power of the air (Eph. 2:2), (3) the adversary (1 Pet. 5:8), and (4) the dragon, that old serpent, which is the Devil, and Satan (Rev. 20:2). His origin is not clear, but light is provided in Isa. 14:12–15, Ezek. 28:12–19, and Luke 10:18. Satan is: (1) evil (1 John 3:8), (2) deceptive, foxy and adroit (Rev. 12:9; 2 Cor. 11:3, 13–15), and (3) the great enemy who rules this world and has many helpers (Eph. 6:12; Luke 8:30; 11:15). But Christ has already defeated Satan in principle (John 12:31). He will be cast into the lake of fire at the end of time (Rev. 20:10). He works to: (1) tempt and seduce the people of God (1 Thess. 3:5; 2 Cor. 2:11); (2) blind men's eyes to the truth of God (2 Cor. 4:3, 4); (3) destroy the Word of God (Mark 4:15); (4) take up his abode in men's hearts (John 13:27); (5) accuse believers before God (Rev. 12:10); and (6) stop God's servants from doing God's will (1 Thess. 2:18; 1 Pet. 5:8). Believers are told to: (1) resist the devil (James 4:7); (2) watch and pray (Matt. 26:41); and (3) use the shield of faith to stop Satan's fiery darts (Eph. 6:16).

In this passage (14:12) Satan is called *Lucifer, son of the morning.* The phrase has two references, one to the king of Babylon (14:4), and the other to Satan, which goes far beyond anything pictured of a mere human king or ruler. Perhaps the best interpretation is to see the king of Babylon as a tool in the hands of Satan himself, who leads and directs this monarch in his evildoings. The "Daystar" or "Son of dawn," which is the morning star, quickly is lost to sight when the sun rises. The Babylonian king is like this. He will shortly be removed from his place, eclipsed, as it were. Since the Babylonians worshipped Ishtar, later equated with Venus, an astral deity, it may be this was the reason why the Spirit led Isaiah to use a figure of speech for the Babylonian ruler.

14:13 *the stars of God,* i.e., "the angels." *I will sit also upon the mount of the congregation, in the sides of the north,* i.e., "I will preside on the Mount of Assembly (or, "on the slopes of Mount Saphon") far away in the north" (Ps. 48:2).†

14:15–17 Satan and all the wicked will at last be brought down to hell (sheol). When Satan is seen by hell's inhabitants, they will be astonished that the one who had such great power and used it so wickedly could have such an abominable end. He who shook kingdoms and made the earth tremble will be helpless and confined.

20 Thou shalt not be joined with them in burial, because thou hast
destroyed thy land, *and* slain thy people: the seed of evildoers shall never be
renowned.
21 Prepare slaughter for his children for the iniquity of their fathers; that **14:21**
they do not rise, nor possess the land, nor fill the face of the world with Ex 20:5
cities. Isa 13:16
22 For I will rise up against them, saith the LORD of hosts, and cut off
from Babylon the name, and remnant, and son, and nephew, saith the
LORD.
23 I will also make it a possession for the bittern, and pools of water: and ☆**14:23**
I will sweep it with the besom of destruction, saith the LORD of hosts.

B. THE CRUSHING OF ASSYRIA

24 ¶The LORD of hosts hath sworn, saying, Surely as I have thought, so ☆**14:24**
shall it come to pass; and as I have purposed, *so* shall it stand: Job 23:13 Isa 46:11
25 That I will break the Assyrian in my land, and upon my mountains ☆**14:25**
tread him under foot: then shall his yoke depart from off them, and his Isa 9:4 Nah 1:13
burden depart from off their shoulders.
26 This *is* the purpose that is purposed upon the whole earth: and this *is*
the hand that is stretched out upon all the nations.
27 For the LORD of hosts hath purposed, and who shall disannul *it?* and ☆**14:27**
his hand *is* stretched out, and who shall turn it back? Isa 43:13 Dan 4:31, 35

C. THE FALL OF PHILISTIA

28 In the year that king Ahaz died was this burden. **14:28** 2 Kgs 16:20
29 ¶Rejoice not thou, whole Palestina, because the rod of him that smote ☆**14:29**
thee is broken: for out of the serpent's root shall come forth a cockatrice,
and his fruit *shall be* a fiery flying serpent.
30 And the firstborn of the poor shall feed, and the needy shall lie down in **14:30**
safety: and I will kill thy root with famine, and he shall slay thy remnant. Isa 8:21; 11:4
31 Howl, O gate; cry, O city; thou, whole Palestina, *art* dissolved: for there ☆**14:31**
shall come from the north a smoke, and none *shall be* alone in his appointed Isa 3:26 Jer 1:14
times.
32 What shall *one* then answer the messengers of the nation? That the ☆**14:32**
LORD hath founded Zion, and the poor of his people shall trust in it. Isa 25:4

D. THE MESSAGE ABOUT MOAB
1. A Description of Moab's Destruction

15 THE burden of Moab. Because in the night Ar of Moab is laid ☆**15:1**
waste, *and* brought to silence; because in the night Kir of Moab is
laid waste, *and* brought to silence;

14:23 God will destroy Babylon. The broom ("besom") with which he sweeps is a broom of destruction, not a broom that clears away the dirt and restores a room to its pristine state.
14:24, 25 God is also going to destroy Assyria. Because he is the sovereign ruler of the universe, his plans and purposes cannot be thwarted, and what he intends to do will be done. No one and nothing can keep it from coming to pass.
14:27 God is determined to be the enemy of his people's enemies. All the powers of heaven and hell are challenged to change the counsel of God—only to fail in their vain attempts.
14:29 *him that smote thee,* i.e., "Shalmaneser V of Assyria."†
14:31 *there shall come from the north a smoke,* i.e., "a perfectly trained army (Sargon of Assyria) is coming down".†
14:32 *The LORD had founded Zion,* therefore the Philistines must fall. Zion is a refuge for God's people, who are afflicted but can never be removed. Thus they need not fear what man can do.
15:1 See note on Ezek. 25:9 for information about the Moabites. God said that the chief cities of Moab would be taken by surprise in one night. Evidently the people thought they dwelt securely, so they lived in luxury and indulged themselves.

15:2☆ Jer 48:37
[2]He is gone up to Ba′jith, and to Di′bon, the high places, to weep: Moab
shall howl over Nebo, and over Med′e-ba: on all their heads *shall be*
baldness, *and* every beard cut off.
15:3 Isa 22:4 Jer 48:38 Jonah 3:6–8
[3]In their streets they shall gird themselves with sackcloth: on the tops of
their houses, and in their streets, every one shall howl, weeping abundantly.
[4]And Hesh′bon shall cry, and E-le-a′leh: their voice shall be heard *even*
unto Ja′haz: therefore the armed soldiers of Moab shall cry out; his life
shall be grievous unto him.
15:5 Jer 31:5
[5]My heart shall cry out for Moab; his fugitives *shall flee* unto Zo′ar, an
heifer of three years old: for by the mounting up of Lu′hith with weeping
shall they go it up; for in the way of Hor-o-na′im they shall raise up a cry
of destruction.
15:6 Jer 48:34 Joel 1:10–12
[6]For the waters of Nim′rim shall be desolate: for the hay is withered
away, the grass faileth, there is no green thing.
15:7 Jer 48:36
[7]Therefore the abundance they have gotten, and that which they have
laid up, shall they carry away to the brook of the willows.
[8]For the cry is gone round about the borders of Moab; the howling
thereof unto Eg′la-im, and the howling thereof unto Be′er-e′lim.
15:9 2 Kgs 17:25 Jer 50:17
[9]For the waters of Di′mon shall be full of blood: for I will bring more
upon Di′mon, lions upon him that escapeth of Moab, and upon the
remnant of the land.

2. Moab's Sins: Pride, Arrogance, and Insolence

16:1☆ 2 Kgs 3:4; 14:7 Isa 42:11
16 SEND ye the lamb to the ruler of the land from Se′la to the
wilderness, unto the mount of the daughter of Zion.
16:2☆ Num 21:13
[2]For it shall be, *that,* as a wandering bird cast out of the nest, *so* the
daughters of Moab shall be at the fords of Arnon.
[3]Take counsel, execute judgment; make thy shadow as the night in the
midst of the noonday; hide the outcasts; bewray not him that wandereth.
16:4 Isa 9:6, 7; 54:14 Lk 1:32, 33
[4]Let mine outcasts dwell with thee, Moab; be thou a covert to them from
the face of the spoiler: for the extortioner is at an end, the spoiler ceaseth,
the oppressors are consumed out of the land.
[5]And in mercy shall the throne be established: and he shall sit upon it in
truth in the tabernacle of David, judging, and seeking judgment, and
hasting righteousness.
16:6☆ Jer 48:29 Zeph 2:8, 10
[6]¶We have heard of the pride of Moab; *he is* very proud: *even* of his
haughtiness, and his pride, and his wrath: *but* his lies *shall* not *be* so.
16:7 2 Kgs 3:25 Jer 48:31
[7]Therefore shall Moab howl for Moab, every one shall howl: for the
foundations of Kir–har′e-seth shall ye mourn; surely *they are* stricken.
[8]For the fields of Hesh′bon languish, *and* the vine of Sib′mah: the lords
of the heathen have broken down the principal plants thereof, they are
come *even* unto Ja′zer, they wandered *through* the wilderness: her branches
are stretched out, they are gone over the sea.

15:2 City after city is named and its destruction foretold. Assyria will wreak great devastation upon all of Moab; nothing pertaining to them shall be left untouched.

16:1 Refugees from Moab had escaped to Edom, *which had Sela for its capital. They entreat Judah* to help them so that they can resettle in that land. They send the lamb as a token of sacrifice or tribute.

16:2ff Isaiah warns the Moabites to treat the true people of God well. He assures them that God is still interested in Israel and will restore it. The throne of David will have a king who is interested in seeking justice and doing righteousness.

16:6 Beginning with this verse, Isaiah brings to light God's indictment of the sins of Moab, concluding that they will not take his advice. Therefore God's judgment will come upon them. It will be irreversible, for God will not hear them when they cry. Verse 14 predicts that the disaster will come in three years. Moab will be brought into contempt, and many will be slain. Those who remain will be few and feeble.

9¶Therefore I will bewail with the weeping of Ja′zer the vine of Sib′mah
I will water thee with my tears, O Hesh′bon, and E-le-a′leh: for the
shouting for thy summer fruits and for thy harvest is fallen.

16:9 Jer 48:32

10And gladness is taken away, and joy out of the plentiful field; and in
the vineyards there shall be no singing, neither shall there be shouting: the
treaders shall tread out no wine in *their* presses; I have made *their vintage*
shouting to cease.

16:10 Isa 24:7, 8 Jer 48:33 Amos 5:17

11Wherefore my bowels shall sound like an harp for Moab, and mine
inward parts for Kir–ha′resh.

16:11 Isa 15:5

12¶And it shall come to pass, when it is seen that Moab is weary on the
high place, that he shall come to his sanctuary to pray; but he shall not
prevail.

16:12 1 Kgs 18:26–29

13This *is* the word that the LORD hath spoken concerning Moab since
that time.

16:13 Isa 25:10 Jer 48:42

14But now the LORD hath spoken, saying, Within three years, as the years
of an hireling, and the glory of Moab shall be contemned, with all that great
multitude; and the remnant *shall be* very small *and* feeble.

E. THE MESSAGE TO SYRIA (DAMASCUS) AND EPHRAIM (SAMARIA)

1. Damascus and Ephraim's Destruction; a Remnant to Remain

17 THE burden of Damascus. Behold, Damascus is taken away from
being a city, and it shall be a ruinous heap.

☆17:1 Isa 10:9; 25:2 Mic 1:6

2The cities of Ar′o-er *are* forsaken: they shall be for flocks, which shall lie
down, and none shall make *them* afraid.

17:2 Mic 4:4 Zeph 2:6

3The fortress also shall cease from E′phra-im, and the kingdom from
Damascus, and the remnant of Syria: they shall be as the glory of the
children of Israel, saith the LORD of hosts.

17:3 Isa 8:4 Hos 9:11

4And in that day it shall come to pass, *that* the glory of Jacob shall be
made thin, and the fatness of his flesh shall wax lean.

☆17:4

5And it shall be as when the harvestman gathereth the corn, and reapeth
the ears with his arm; and it shall be as he that gathereth ears in the valley
of Reph′a-im.

17:5 Jer 51:33

6¶Yet gleaning grapes shall be left in it, as the shaking of an olive tree,
two *or* three berries in the top of the uppermost bough, four *or* five in the
outmost fruitful branches thereof, saith the LORD God of Israel.

17:6 Deut 4:27 Isa 24:13

7At that day shall a man look to his Maker, and his eyes shall have
respect to the Holy One of Israel.

☆17:7 Isa 10:20 Hos 6:1

8And he shall not look to the altars, the work of his hands, neither shall
respect *that* which his fingers have made, either the groves, or the images.

☆17:8 Ex 34:13 Isa 27:9; 30:22

2. The Consequences of the Invasion

9¶In that day shall his strong cities be as a forsaken bough, and an
uppermost branch, which they left because of the children of Israel: and
there shall be desolation.

☆17:9–11

17:1 Syria, which had Damascus for its capital, was in league with Ephraim (i.e., the Northern Kingdom of Israel) against Judah. Verses 1–6 and 9–11 foretell the destruction of the strong cities of both nations.
17:4 In mercy God will remember Ephraim and he graciously promises that a remnant of that nation will be preserved. Good will come out of these adversities.
17:7, 8 The afflictions God will send on Ephraim will cause the godly remnant to turn from their transgressions, seek the mercy of God, and destroy their idols. Ephraim had idols and they offered worship to the sun at some of their altars. Any affliction God sends that separates us from our sins and makes us reject the vanity of this world is a boon to us and an indicator of the grace of God toward repentant sinners.
17:9–11 These verses foretell the awful destruction that will be executed on the land of Israel (Ephraim). The strongest of their cities will be pillaged and left desolate.

17:10 Deut 32:4, 18, 30, 31; Isa 30:29; 62:11

10 Because thou hast forgotten the God of thy salvation, and hast not been mindful of the rock of thy strength, therefore shalt thou plant pleasant plants, and shalt set it with strange slips:

17:11 Hos 10:13

11 In the day shalt thou make thy plant to grow, and in the morning shalt thou make thy seed to flourish: *but* the harvest *shall be* a heap in the day of grief and of desperate sorrow.

17:12☆ Jer 6:23

12 ¶Woe to the multitude of many people, *which* make a noise like the noise of the seas; and to the rushing of nations, *that* make a rushing like the rushing of mighty waters!

17:13 Ps 1:4; Isa 29:5

13 The nations shall rush like the rushing of many waters: but *God* shall rebuke them, and they shall flee far off, and shall be chased as the chaff of the mountains before the wind, and like a rolling thing before the whirlwind.

17:14 2 Kgs 19:35; Isa 41:11, 12

14 And behold at eveningtide trouble; *and* before the morning he *is* not. This *is* the portion of them that spoil us, and the lot of them that rob us.

F. THE DOWNFALL OF ETHIOPIA

18 WOE to the land shadowing with wings, which *is* beyond the rivers of E-thi-o'pi-a:

2 That sendeth ambassadors by the sea, even in vessels of bulrushes upon the waters, *saying,* Go, ye swift messengers, to a nation scattered and peeled, to a people terrible from their beginning hitherto; a nation meted out and trodden down, whose land the rivers have spoiled!

18:3 Ps 49:1; Mic 1:2

3 All ye inhabitants of the world, and dwellers on the earth, see ye, when he lifteth up an ensign on the mountains; and when he bloweth a trumpet, hear ye.

4 For so the LORD said unto me, I will take my rest, and I will consider in my dwelling place like a clear heat upon herbs, *and* like a cloud of dew in the heat of harvest.

18:5 Ezek 17:6–10

5 For afore the harvest, when the bud is perfect, and the sour grape is ripening in the flower, he shall both cut off the sprigs with pruning hooks, and take away *and* cut down the branches.

18:6 Isa 56:9; Ezek 39:17–20

6 They shall be left together unto the fowls of the mountains, and to the beasts of the earth: and the fowls shall summer upon them, and all the beasts of the earth shall winter upon them.

18:7☆ Zech 14:16, 17

7 In that time shall the present be brought unto the LORD of hosts of a people scattered and peeled, and from a people terrible from their beginning hitherto; a nation meted out and trodden under foot, whose land the rivers have spoiled, to the place of the name of the LORD of hosts, the mount Zion.

G. THE PROPHECY ABOUT EGYPT

1. The Fall of Egypt

19:1☆ Josh 2:11; Ps 104:3; Jer 43:12; Mt 26:64

19 THE burden of Egypt. Behold, the LORD rideth upon a swift cloud, and shall come into Egypt: and the idols of Egypt shall be moved at his presence, and the heart of Egypt shall melt in the midst of it.

17:12ff These verses foretell the failure of the Assyrian attack against Judah. At this point Judah is not yet ripe for ruin. That will come later, when Nebuchadnezzar *acts as God's scourge against that nation. Chronologically,* chapter seventeen should be read after chapter nine, for the destruction of Damascus (which is stated in this chapter) came to pass in the reign of Ahaz (2 Kings 16:9).

18:7 This verse speaks of a future time when the Ethiopians (dealt with in this chapter) will bring their presents to Zion, which is the place where the name of the Lord of hosts is enshrined. Ps. 68:31, Isa. 45:14, and Zeph. 3:10 speak of the conversion of the Ethiopians and their participation in the kingdom of God at the end of the age.

19:1 *the LORD rideth upon a swift cloud.* Baal, the Canaanite god, was a god of fertility who was said to ride on the clouds. This figure of speech is picked up

2And I will set the Egyptians against the Egyptians: and they shall fight
every one against his brother, and every one against his neighbour; city
against city, *and* kingdom against kingdom.

☆**19:2** Judg 7:22 Mt 10:21, 36

3And the spirit of Egypt shall fail in the midst thereof; and I will destroy
the counsel thereof: and they shall seek to the idols, and to the charmers,
and to them that have familiar spirits, and to the wizards.

19:3 Isa 8:19

4And the Egyptians will I give over into the hand of a cruel lord; and a
fierce king shall rule over them, saith the Lord, the LORD of hosts.

☆**19:4** Isa 20:4 Ezek 29:19

5And the waters shall fail from the sea, and the river shall be wasted and
dried up.

☆**19:5** Ezek 30:12

6And they shall turn the rivers far away; *and* the brooks of defence shall
be emptied and dried up: the reeds and flags shall wither.

19:6 Ex 7:18

7The paper reeds by the brooks, by the mouth of the brooks, and every
thing sown by the brooks, shall wither, be driven away, and be no *more.*
8The fishers also shall mourn, and all they that cast angle into the brooks
shall lament, and they that spread nets upon the waters shall languish.
9Moreover they that work in fine flax, and they that weave networks,
shall be confounded.
10And they shall be broken in the purposes thereof, all that make sluices
and ponds for fish.
11¶Surely the princes of Zo'an *are* fools, the counsel of the wise
counsellors of Pharaoh is become brutish: how say ye unto Pharaoh, I *am*
the son of the wise, the son of ancient kings?

☆**19:11** Gen 41:38, 39 1 Kgs 4:30 Acts 7:22

12Where *are* they? where *are* thy wise *men?* and let them tell thee now,
and let them know what the LORD of hosts hath purposed upon Egypt.

☆**19:12** Rom 9:17

13The princes of Zo'an are become fools, the princes of Noph are
deceived; they have also seduced Egypt, *even they that are* the stay of the
tribes thereof.

19:13 Jer 46:14, 19

14The LORD hath mingled a perverse spirit in the midst thereof: and they
have caused Egypt to err in every work thereof, as a drunken *man*
staggereth in his vomit.

19:14 Isa 3:12

15Neither shall there be *any* work for Egypt, which the head or tail,
branch or rush, may do.

2. God's Ultimate Deliverance of Egypt

16In that day shall Egypt be like unto women: and it shall be afraid and
fear because of the shaking of the hand of the LORD of hosts, which he
shaketh over it.

19:16 Jer 51:30 Heb 10:31

17And the land of Judah shall be a terror unto Egypt, every one that
maketh mention thereof shall be afraid in himself, because of the counsel of
the LORD of hosts, which he hath determined against it.

19:17 Dan 4:35

---

and used of the *Lord God, who does bring fertility* to the land and who blesses his faithful people and executes judgment upon the wicked.

19:2 Even as God destroyed Assyria, so he would also pass judgment against Egypt. Judah had trusted in the power of Egypt to help her in the attacks of the enemy from the north, but Egypt proved to be a road of reed. Egypt will be weakened and brought low; she will be contemptible among the nations.

19:4 Egypt will be given over to one of their own kings, who will be a cruel lord—tyrannous and oppressive. The people of Egypt will experience the same barbarous treatment the Israelites experienced years before.

19:5ff The Nile River was important to Egypt's defense against invaders. Now it will be dried up, the fish will die, and people who depended on fish for food will be deprived of that staple in their diet. The loss of water will affect the production of flax and cotton, leaving the economy of the nation in shambles.

19:11 *Zoan.* See note on Num. 13:22.

19:12 What God has purposed, no man can thwart. The doom of Egypt is certain. Confusion will come; Egypt will stagger and act as a vomiting drunk. See also 19:17.

19:18–19☆ Judg 1:22; Mt 10:31?

18 ¶In that day shall five cities in the land of Egypt speak the language of Canaan, and swear to the LORD of hosts; one shall be called, The city of destruction.

19:19 Gen 28:18 Josh 22:10, 26, 27

19 In that day shall there be an altar to the LORD in the midst of the land of Egypt, and a pillar at the border thereof to the LORD.

19:20 Isa 43:3, 11 45:15, 21; 49:25

20 And it shall be for a sign and for a witness unto the LORD of hosts in the land of Egypt: for they shall cry unto the LORD because of the oppressors, and he shall send them a saviour, and a great one, and he shall deliver them.

19:21 Isa 56:7

21 And the LORD shall be known to Egypt, and the Egyptians shall know the LORD in that day, and shall do sacrifice and oblation; yea, they shall vow a vow unto the LORD, and perform *it.*

19:22 Deut 32:39 Isa 27:13 Heb 12:11

22 And the LORD shall smite Egypt: he shall smite and heal *it:* and they shall return *even* to the LORD, and he shall be intreated of them, and shall heal them.

19:23☆ Isa 11:16

23 ¶In that day shall there be a highway out of Egypt to Assyria, and the Assyrian shall come into Egypt, and the Egyptian into Assyria, and the Egyptians shall serve with the Assyrians.

19:24☆

24 In that day shall Israel be the third with Egypt and with Assyria, *even* a blessing in the midst of the land:

19:25☆ Hos 2:23

25 Whom the LORD of hosts shall bless, saying, Blessed *be* Egypt my people, and Assyria the work of my hands, and Israel mine inheritance.

3. Egypt's Immediate Conquest by Assyria

20:1☆

20 IN the year that Tartan came unto Ash′dod, (when Sar′gon the king of Assyria sent him,) and fought against Ash′dod, and took it;

20:2☆ 1 Sam 19:24 Mic 1:8

2 At the same time spake the LORD by Isaiah the son of Amoz, saying, Go and loose the sackcloth from off thy loins, and put off thy shoe from thy foot. And he did so, walking naked and barefoot.

20:3 Isa 8:18; 43:3

3 And the LORD said, Like as my servant Isaiah hath walked naked and barefoot three years *for* a sign and wonder upon Egypt and upon E-thi-o′-pi-a;

20:4 Isa 19:4; 47:2, 3

4 So shall the king of Assyria lead away the Egyptians prisoners, and the E-thi-o′pi-ans captives, young and old, naked and barefoot, even with *their* buttocks uncovered, to the shame of Egypt.

20:5 Isa 31:3 Jer 9:23, 24

5 And they shall be afraid and ashamed of E-thi-o′pi-a their expectation, and of Egypt their glory.

20:6☆

6 And the inhabitant of this isle shall say in that day, Behold, such *is* our expectation, whither we flee for help to be delivered from the king of Assyria: and how shall we escape?

19:18, 19 Despite the upcoming judgment God still has a spiritual concern for Egypt. It will become a base nation and prosperity is not promised. But God's blessing will be to bring true religion to the people. By grace he will call them to salvation. Indeed, this passage predicts a time when Egypt will call upon God and worship him at an altar erected in that nation. Josephus states that Onian IV appealed to this text when he built an altar at Leontopolis in 154 B.C.

19:23 *Assyria,* now Iraq.

19:24, 25 This beautiful promise remains to be fulfilled *at the end of the age.* God here promises that the feuds and enmities of Egyptians, Assyrians, and Israelites will end someday. They will be joined together in love for the Messiah and, like a three-fold cord, will not easily be broken. These united people will be a blessing and will be blessed of God. However, at this point in history, Egypt is about to be conquered by Assyria, as forecast following God's great promise (chapter 20).

19:25 *the LORD of hosts shall bless* Egypt and Assyria because of their friendship for Israel.

20:1 *Ashdod,* a Philistine city allied with Egypt against Assyria. The city was taken by Sargon's commander in 711 B.C., and was besieged again by Sennacherib and other attackers.

20:2 Isaiah was called by God to remove his outer clothing and go, as it were, undressed and barefoot. When compared with the dress of others, he would have been ridiculed for his appearance and jeered at by the young. Yet this was a sign from God to Egypt, which was to be conquered by Assyria.

20:6 *the inhabitant of this isle,* i.e., "the Philistines."

H. THE FALL OF BABYLON AT THE HAND OF MEDO-PERSIA

21 THE burden of the desert of the sea. As whirlwinds in the south
pass through; *so* it cometh from the desert, from a terrible land.
2 A grievous vision is declared unto me; the treacherous dealer dealeth
treacherously, and the spoiler spoileth. Go up, O E′lam: besiege, O Me′-
di-a; all the sighing thereof have I made to cease.

21:1 Isa 13:20–22 Jer 51:41 Zech 9:14

3 Therefore are my loins filled with pain: pangs have taken hold upon me,
as the pangs of a woman that travaileth: I was bowed down at the hearing
of it; I was dismayed at the seeing *of it.*

21:3 Ps 48:6 1 Thess 5:3

4 My heart panted, fearfulness affrighted me: the night of my pleasure
hath he turned into fear unto me.

21:4 Deut 28:67

5 Prepare the table, watch in the watchtower, eat, drink: arise, ye princes,
and anoint the shield.

☆**21:5** Jer 51:39, 57

6 For thus hath the Lord said unto me, Go, set a watchman, let him
declare what he seeth.
7 And he saw a chariot *with* a couple of horsemen, a chariot of asses, *and*
a chariot of camels; and he hearkened diligently with much heed:

☆**21:7**

8 And he cried, A lion: My lord, I stand continually upon the watchtower
in the daytime, and I am set in my ward whole nights:
9 And, behold, here cometh a chariot of men, *with* a couple of horsemen.
And he answered and said, Babylon is fallen, is fallen; and all the graven
images of her gods he hath broken unto the ground.

21:8 Isa 13:19 46:1, 2 Jer 50:2 Hab 2:1 Rev 14:8

☆**21:9**

10 O my threshing, and the corn of my floor: that which I have heard of
the LORD of hosts, the God of Israel, have I declared unto you.

21:10 Jer 51:33

I. THE MESSAGE TO EDOM

11 ¶The burden of Du′mah. He calleth to me out of Se′ir, Watchman, what
of the night? Watchman, what of the night?
12 The watchman said, The morning cometh, and also the night: if ye will
inquire, inquire ye: return, come.

☆**21:11** Gen 32:3

J. THE FATE OF ARABIA

13 ¶The burden upon Arabia. In the forest in Arabia shall ye lodge, O ye
travelling companies of Ded′a-nim.
14 The inhabitants of the land of Te′ma brought water to him that was
thirsty, they prevented with their bread him that fled.
15 For they fled from the swords, from the drawn sword, and from the
bent bow, and from the grievousness of war.
16 For thus hath the Lord said unto me, Within a year, according to the
years of an hireling, and all the glory of Ke′dar shall fail:

☆**21:13**

21:15 Isa 13:14, 15

☆**21:16**

21:1 This prophecy refers to Babylon (see 21:9).
21:5 This refers to the bacchanalian feast that preceded Babylon's demise. More details of the feast are seen in Daniel 5, as this prophecy was fulfilled when Cyrus captured the city.
21:7 *a chariot . . . of horsemen . . . of asses . . . of camels.* Possibly the meaning is that the asses and camels were paired for the attack. The city fell to the Medes and Persians, perhaps represented by these paired riders.†
21:9 Babylon is pictured here as fallen. Her day of conquest and power is vanished irretrievably. Her idols could not protect her; they have been ground to dust.
21:11 *Dumah,* i.e., "Edom."
21:13 *Arabia,* meaning "desert," is a large peninsula with a landed area of approximately one million square miles. Its Arab inhabitants are of Abrahamic extraction. They speak of their area as the "island of the Arabs," because the peninsula is surrounded by water on three sides. Today Saudi Arabia is the largest of the nations in the area, along with Yemen, South Yemen, Oman, and Jordan in the far north. On the eastern edge are Kuwait, Qatar, and the United Arab Emirates. The economic and political importance of the region derives from the discovery of the immense deposits of oil in recent years. *Dedanim.* The Dedanites were a mercantile people who traded with Tyre and Damascus.
21:16 This prophecy was literally fulfilled within the time span stated by Isaiah. *Within a year.* The Dead Sea manuscript reads, "within three years, as the years of an hireling."† (See 16:14.)

21:17 Isa 10:19 17 And the residue of the number of archers, the mighty men of the
children of Ke′dar, shall be diminished: for the LORD God of Israel hath
spoken *it.*

K. JERUSALEM'S COMING DESTRUCTION
1. The Fall of Jerusalem

22:1☆ Jer 21:13 22 THE burden of the valley of vision. What aileth thee now, that thou
art wholly gone up to the housetops?
22:2 Isa 23:7 2 Thou that art full of stirs, a tumultuous city, a joyous city: thy slain *men*
Jer 14:18 *are* not slain with the sword, nor dead in battle.
3 All thy rulers are fled together, they are bound by the archers: all that
are found in thee are bound together, *which* have fled from far.
22:4 Jer 9:1 4 Therefore said I, Look away from me; I will weep bitterly, labour not to
comfort me, because of the spoiling of the daughter of my people.
22:5 Isa 37:3 5 For *it is* a day of trouble, and of treading down, and of perplexity by the
Lam 2:2 Lord GOD of hosts in the valley of vision, breaking down the walls, and of
crying to the mountains.
22:6 Isa 21:2 6 And E′lam bare the quiver with chariots of men *and* horsemen, and Kir
uncovered the shield.
7 And it shall come to pass, *that* thy choicest valleys shall be full of
chariots, and the horsemen shall set themselves in array at the gate.
22:8☆ 8 ¶And he discovered the covering of Judah, and thou didst look in that
day to the armour of the house of the forest.
22:9 2 Kgs 25:4 9 Ye have seen also the breaches of the city of David, that they are many:
and ye gathered together the waters of the lower pool.
10 And ye have numbered the houses of Jerusalem, and the houses have ye
broken down to fortify the wall.
22:11☆ 11 Ye made also a ditch between the two walls for the water of the old
pool: but ye have not looked unto the maker thereof, neither had respect
unto him that fashioned it long ago.
22:12☆ Isa 32:11 12 And in that day did the Lord GOD of hosts call to weeping, and to
Joel 1:13 mourning, and to baldness, and to girding with sackcloth:
22:13 Isa 5:11, 22 13 And behold joy and gladness, slaying oxen, and killing sheep, eating
56:12 flesh, and drinking wine: let us eat and drink; for to morrow we shall die.
1 Cor 15:32 14 And it was revealed in mine ears by the LORD of hosts, Surely this
iniquity shall not be purged from you till ye die, saith the Lord GOD of
hosts.

2. Faithful Eliakim to Replace Wicked Shebna

22:15☆ 2 Chron 16:14 15 ¶Thus saith the Lord GOD of hosts, Go, get thee unto this treasurer,
Mt 27:60 *even* unto Sheb′na, which *is* over the house, *and say,*

22:1 *The valley of vision,* i.e., "Jerusalem." Isaiah had pronounced divine judgment on nations surrounding Judah. These had either been spiteful enemies or deceitful friends to the people of God. Now Judah is to hear about the vision of God given to Isaiah against Judah itself and Jerusalem.

22:8 *house of the forest.* See 1 Kings 7:2; 10:17; 2 Chron. 9:16. This was an armory or treasure house located in or near Jerusalem. It is spoken of here as the place where the weapons of war were stored.

22:11 Judah did everything it could to defend itself against the enemy. But one thing it failed to do: look to the God who had chosen Abraham and his descendants to be his people.

22:12ff God's judgment against Judah was designed to humble the proud, bring them to repentance, and constrain them to trust in God as their only hope. Had Judah repented immediately, God would have delivered them from their enemies. But they persisted in their wrongful behavior; therefore, they must die in their sins.

22:15 Shebna, a high official, was a crooked stick. God pronounces judgment against him, saying that he will lose his position and die. The fulfillment of this prophetic word should have warned king and people and turned them to God in repentance.

16 What hast thou here? and whom hast thou here, that thou hast hewed
thee out a sepulchre here, *as* he that heweth him out a sepulchre on high,
and that graveth an habitation for himself in a rock?
17 Behold, the LORD will carry thee away with a mighty captivity, and will
surely cover thee.
18 He will surely violently turn and toss thee *like* a ball into a large
country: there shalt thou die, and there the chariots of thy glory *shall be* the
shame of thy lord's house.
19 And I will drive thee from thy station, and from thy state shall he pull — **22:19** Ezek 17:24
thee down.
20 ¶And it shall come to pass in that day, that I will call my servant E-li'a- — ☆**22:20** Isa 36:3
kim the son of Hil-ki'ah:
21 And I will clothe him with thy robe, and strengthen him with thy girdle, — **22:21** Gen 45:8
and I will commit thy government into his hand: and he shall be a father to
the inhabitants of Jerusalem, and to the house of Judah.
22 And the key of the house of David will I lay upon his shoulder; so he — ☆**22:22**
shall open, and none shall shut; and he shall shut, and none shall open.
23 And I will fasten him *as* a nail in a sure place; and he shall be for a — **22:23** Job 36:7 Zech 10:4
glorious throne to his father's house.
24 And they shall hang upon him all the glory of his father's house, the
offspring and the issue, all vessels of small quantity, from the vessels of
cups, even to all the vessels of flagons.
25 In that day, saith the LORD of hosts, shall the nail that is fastened in the — ☆**22:25** Esth 9:24, 25 Isa 46:11
sure place be removed, and be cut down, and fall; and the burden that *was*
upon it shall be cut off: for the LORD hath spoken *it*.

L. THE MESSAGE TO TYRE
1. Its Fall Predicted

23 THE burden of Tyre. Howl, ye ships of Tarshish; for it is laid — ☆**23:1** Josh 19:29 Ezek 26:1–28
waste, so that there is no house, no entering in: from the land of
Chit'tim it is revealed to them.
2 Be still, ye inhabitants of the isle; thou whom the merchants of Zi'don, — **23:2** Isa 47:5 Ezek 27:3–23
that pass over the sea, have replenished.
3 And by great waters the seed of Si'hor, the harvest of the river, *is* her
revenue; and she is a mart of nations.
4 Be thou ashamed, O Zi'don: for the sea hath spoken, *even* the strength — **23:4** Gen 10:15, 19 Jer 47:4
of the sea, saying, I travail not, nor bring forth children, neither do I
nourish up young men, *nor* bring up virgins.
5 As at the report concerning Egypt, *so* shall they be sorely pained at the — **23:5** Josh 2:9–11
report of Tyre.
6 Pass ye over to Tarshish; howl, ye inhabitants of the isle.
7 *Is* this your joyous *city*, whose antiquity *is* of ancient days? her own feet — **23:7** Isa 32:13
shall carry her afar off to sojourn.

22:20 *Eliakim.* His name means "God will establish." Eliakim was among those who stood against Sheba, a worldling. Eliakim represented those who loved God and did his will. God gave him power to open and shut and made him a "strong and steady peg . . . [who] will be an honor to his family name" (22:23, 24, TLB). He is a type of Christ, which is fulfilled in Rev. 3:7, where Christ has the key of David and opens and shuts, just as Eliakim did.

22:22 *the key of the house of David . . . upon his shoulder.* Paraphrased: "I will give him responsibility over all my people" (TLB). The key is a symbol of the royal authority which Jesus has, and which is called "the key of David" in Rev. 3:7.

22:25 Spiritually speaking, we here learn that Jesus is a nail in a sure place. Everything derives from him, hangs on him, and depends on him for its continuance. Whoever trusts in him cannot perish or fall to the ground.

23:1 *Tyre* was originally a colony of the mother-city, Sidon. *ships of Tarshish* is a term used in the Old Testament for merchant ships. Tarshish probably refers to a city of Tartesus, which was located on the Guadalquivir River in Spain. It had been colonized by Tyrians. See note on 1 Kings 10:22 for further information.

23:8☆ 8 Who hath taken this counsel against Tyre, the crowning *city,* whose
merchants *are* princes, whose traffickers *are* the honourable of the earth?
23:9 9 The LORD of hosts hath purposed it, to stain the pride of all glory, *and*
Isa 5:13 Dan 4:37 to bring into contempt all the honourable of the earth.
10 Pass through thy land as a river, O daughter of Tarshish: *there is* no
more strength.
23:11 11 He stretched out his hand over the sea, he shook the kingdoms: the
Isa 50:2 Zech 9:3, 4 LORD hath given a commandment against the merchant *city,* to destroy the
strong holds thereof.
23:12 12 And he said, Thou shalt no more rejoice, O thou oppressed virgin,
Rev 18:22 daughter of Zi′don: arise, pass over to Chit′tim; there also shalt thou have
no rest.
23:13☆ 13 Behold the land of the Chal-de′ans; this people was not, *till* the
Isa 13:21 Assyrian founded it for them that dwell in the wilderness: they set up the
towers thereof, they raised up the palaces thereof; *and* he brought it to ruin.
14 Howl, ye ships of Tarshish: for your strength is laid waste.

2. Tyre's Restoration after Seventy Years

23:15 15 And it shall come to pass in that day, that Tyre shall be forgotten
Jer 25:11 seventy years, according to the days of one king: after the end of seventy
years shall Tyre sing as an harlot.
16 Take an harp, go about the city, thou harlot that hast been forgotten;
make sweet melody, sing many songs, that thou mayest be remembered.
23:17☆ 17 ¶And it shall come to pass after the end of seventy years, that the LORD
will visit Tyre, and she shall turn to her hire, and shall commit fornication
with all the kingdoms of the world upon the face of the earth.
18 And her merchandise and her hire shall be holiness to the LORD; it
shall not be treasured nor laid up; for her merchandise shall be for them
that dwell before the LORD, to eat sufficiently, and for durable clothing.

IV. ISRAEL IN RELATION TO THE WORLD (24:1—27:13)

A. GOD WILL MAKE JUDAH A WASTELAND

1. Description of the Chaos

24:1ff☆ 24 BEHOLD, the LORD maketh the earth empty, and maketh it waste,
and turneth it upside down, and scattereth abroad the inhabitants
thereof.
24:2 2 And it shall be, as with the people, so with the priest; as with the
Lev 25:36, 37 Deut 23:19, 20 servant, so with his master; as with the maid, so with her mistress; as with
the buyer, so with the seller; as with the lender, so with the borrower; as
with the taker of usury, so with the giver of usury to him.
3 The land shall be utterly emptied, and utterly spoiled: for the LORD
hath spoken this word.

23:8 See note on Ezek. 26:2 for information about Tyre and this prophetic word spoken by Isaiah.
23:13 God will use the Chaldeans, i.e., Nebuchadnezzar, to bring about the destruction of Tyre.
23:17 After seventy years God will allow Tyre to rise *from the dust for a season. The island of Tyre itself was* later destroyed under the assault by Alexander the Great, and it has remained a desolation for the centuries since then. But mainland Tyre continued to exist, although it had been assaulted by foreign nations again and again. It was still there in Jesus' day, and he made reference to Tyre and Sidon several times (e.g., Matt. 11:21; Luke 10:13). In Acts 21:3 Paul landed at Tyre and went up from there to Jerusalem, before going to Rome.
24:1ff *the LORD maketh the earth empty, and maketh it waste.* A change of focus takes place as Isaiah turns from prophesying about individual nations and now makes reference to the whole earth. The use of the word *world* in verse 4 indicates that Isaiah's sermon, in apocalyptic form, foresees a guilty world in chaos due to God's judgment.

4 The earth mourneth *and* fadeth away, the world languisheth *and* fadeth
away, the haughty people of the earth do languish.
5 The earth also is defiled under the inhabitants thereof; because they
have transgressed the laws, changed the ordinance, broken the everlasting
covenant.
6 Therefore hath the curse devoured the earth, and they that dwell therein
are desolate: therefore the inhabitants of the earth are burned, and few men
left.
7 The new wine mourneth, the vine languisheth, all the merryhearted do
sigh.
8 The mirth of tabrets ceaseth, the noise of them that rejoice endeth, the
joy of the harp ceaseth.
9 They shall not drink wine with a song; strong drink shall be bitter to
them that drink it.
10 The city of confusion is broken down: every house is shut up, that no
man may come in.
11 *There is* a crying for wine in the streets; all joy is darkened, the mirth of
the land is gone.
12 In the city is left desolation, and the gate is smitten with destruction.
13 ¶When thus it shall be in the midst of the land among the people, *there
shall be* as the shaking of an olive tree, *and* as the gleaning grapes when the
vintage is done.

24:4 Gen 3:17; Num 35:33
☆**24:5**
24:6 Isa 34:5; Zech 5:3, 4
24:7 Joel 1:10, 12
24:8 Jer 16:9
24:9 Isa 5:11, 22
24:10 Gen 1:2
24:11 Isa 32:13
24:12 Isa 45:2
☆**24:13** Isa 17:6

2. The Remnant That Praises God

14 They shall lift up their voice, they shall sing for the majesty of the
LORD, they shall cry aloud from the sea.
15 Wherefore glorify ye the LORD in the fires, *even* the name of the LORD
God of Israel in the isles of the sea.

☆**24:14** Isa 12:6; 52:8
☆**24:15** Isa 42:4, 10, 12; Jer 5:1

3. The Judgment Will Give Way to a New Age

16 ¶From the uttermost part of the earth have we heard songs, *even* glory
to the righteous. But I said, My leanness, my leanness, woe unto me! the
treacherous dealers have dealt treacherously; yea, the treacherous dealers
have dealt very treacherously.
17 Fear, and the pit, and the snare, *are* upon thee, O inhabitant of the
earth.
18 And it shall come to pass, *that* he who fleeth from the noise of the fear
shall fall into the pit; and he that cometh up out of the midst of the pit shall
be taken in the snare: for the windows from on high are open, and the
foundations of the earth do shake.
19 The earth is utterly broken down, the earth is clean dissolved, the earth
is moved exceedingly.
20 The earth shall reel to and fro like a drunkard, and shall be removed
like a cottage; and the transgression thereof shall be heavy upon it; and it
shall fall, and not rise again.

☆**24:16**
24:18 Gen 7:10–12; Ps 46:2
24:19 Num 16:31, 32
☆**24:20** Isa 19:14; 43:27

24:5 Judah is guilty of at least three sins: (1) it has committed crimes against the laws of nature in the land; (2) it has sinned against the statutes of revealed religion, i.e., the laws of God; and (3) it has broken the contract it made with God.

24:13, 14 As in other times of judgment, a remnant remains faithful to God. These lift their voices in praise to God and sing for joy. Despite the catastrophic circumstances, the true people of God here and always find their consolation and deliverance in the God they worship.

24:15, 16 Songs of praise are raised to the righteous One, who sent the fire that consumes the wicked but not the righteous. Fire consumes the dross and refines the gold. For the people of God, the fire purifies—so that they may be pure and spotless before him, in the glory of the new world.

24:20 *it shall fall and not rise again.* In place of the earth as we now know it there will be new heavens and a new earth wherein dwells nothing but righteousness. The final abode of the righteous is the New Jerusalem, which comes down from God out of heaven.

24:21 Ps 76:12

21 And it shall come to pass in that day, *that* the LORD shall punish the host of the high ones *that are* on high, and the kings of the earth upon the earth.

24:22 Isa 10:4

22 And they shall be gathered together, *as* prisoners are gathered in the pit, and shall be shut up in the prison, and after many days shall they be visited.

24:23☆ Mic 4:7 Rev 21:23

23 Then the moon shall be confounded, and the sun ashamed, when the LORD of hosts shall reign in mount Zion, and in Jerusalem, and before his ancients gloriously.

B. A HYMN OF PRAISE

1. For God's Past Righteous Judgments

25:1 Ex 15:2 Ps 40:5 Eph 1:11

25 O LORD, thou *art* my God; I will exalt thee, I will praise thy name; for thou hast done wonderful *things; thy* counsels of old *are* faithfulness *and* truth.

25:2 Isa 17:1

2 For thou hast made of a city an heap; *of* a defenced city a ruin: a palace of strangers to be no city; it shall never be built.

3 Therefore shall the strong people glorify thee, the city of the terrible nations shall fear thee.

25:4 Isa 32:2

4 For thou hast been a strength to the poor, a strength to the needy in his distress, a refuge from the storm, a shadow from the heat, when the blast of the terrible ones *is* as a storm *against* the wall.

25:5 Jer 51:54–56

5 Thou shalt bring down the noise of strangers, as the heat in a dry place; *even* the heat with the shadow of a cloud: the branch of the terrible ones shall be brought low.

2. For Future Salvation Which Is Sure to Come

25:6☆

6 ¶And in this mountain shall the LORD of hosts make unto all people a feast of fat things, a feast of wines on the lees, of fat things full of marrow, of wines on the lees well refined.

7 And he will destroy in this mountain the face of the covering cast over all people, and the vail that is spread over all nations.

25:8:☆ Ps 69:9 Isa 65:19 1 Cor 15:54 1 Pet 4:14 Rev 21:4

8 He will swallow up death in victory; and the Lord GOD will wipe away tears from off all faces; and the rebuke of his people shall he take away from off all the earth: for the LORD hath spoken *it.*

25:9 Isa 30:18 35:1, 2, 10; 40:9

9 ¶And it shall be said in that day, Lo, this *is* our God; we have waited for him, and he will save us: this *is* the LORD; we have waited for him, we will be glad and rejoice in his salvation.

10 For in this mountain shall the hand of the LORD rest, and Moab shall be trodden down under him, even as straw is trodden down for the dunghill.

25:11 Isa 16:6

11 And he shall spread forth his hands in the midst of them, as he that swimmeth spreadeth forth *his hands* to swim: and he shall bring down their pride together with the spoils of their hands.

25:12 Isa 26:5

12 And the fortress of the high fort of thy walls shall he bring down, lay low, *and* bring to the ground, *even* to the dust.

24:23 When Christ reigns in glory, the brightness of *his shining will be such that the light of the moon and of* the sun will appear as nothing. The moon will be confounded and the sun ashamed. Some of the nations surrounding Israel worshipped the sun and the moon. These pretended deities will be ashamed that they ever received homage from their deluded worshippers.

25:6 *a feast* set by God himself, comes as a victory banquet on Mount Zion. This is yet in the future.

25:8 *He will swallow up death in victory.* One of the chief consequences of Christ's death on Calvary is the death of death (see 1 Cor. 15:54). It will be abolished forever and all tears will be washed away. This is the happy prospect for all believers.

C. THE HYMN THAT WILL BE SUNG "IN THAT DAY"

1. The Lord, the Deliverer of His People

26 IN THAT day shall this song be sung in the land of Judah; We
have a strong city; salvation will *God* appoint *for* walls and
bulwarks.
☆26:1 Isa 12:1; 31:9 60:18

2 Open ye the gates, that the righteous nation which keepeth the truth
may enter in.
26:2 Isa 45:25

3 Thou wilt keep *him* in perfect peace, *whose* mind *is* stayed *on thee:*
because he trusteth in thee.
26:3 Isa 57:19

4 Trust ye in the LORD for ever: for in the LORD JEHOVAH *is* everlasting
strength:
☆26:4 Isa 50:10

5 ¶For he bringeth down them that dwell on high; the lofty city, he layeth
it low; he layeth it low, *even* to the ground; he bringeth it *even* to the dust.

6 The foot shall tread it down, *even* the feet of the poor, *and* the steps of
the needy.
26:6 Isa 29:19

7 The way of the just *is* uprightness: thou, most upright, dost weigh the
path of the just.
26:7 Ps 25:4, 5 Isa 42:16

8 Yea, in the way of thy judgments, O LORD, have we waited for thee; the
desire of *our* soul *is* to thy name, and to the remembrance of thee.
26:8 Isa 12:4

9 With my soul have I desired thee in the night; yea, with my spirit within
me will I seek thee early: for when thy judgments *are* in the earth, the
inhabitants of the world will learn righteousness.
26:9 Ps 63:1; 77:2 Hos 5:15

2. The Lord Will Destroy Wrongdoers

10 Let favour be shewed to the wicked, *yet* will he not learn righteousness;
in the land of uprightness will he deal unjustly, and will not behold the
majesty of the LORD.
26:10 Isa 22:12, 13 Jn 5:37, 38

11 LORD, *when* thy hand is lifted up, they will not see: *but* they shall see,
and be ashamed for *their* envy at the people; yea, the fire of thine enemies
shall devour them.

12 ¶LORD, thou wilt ordain peace for us: for thou also hast wrought all our
works in us.
☆26:12

13 O LORD our God, *other* lords beside thee have had dominion over us:
but by thee only will we make mention of thy name.
☆26:13 Isa 2:8

14 *They are* dead, they shall not live; *they are* deceased, they shall not rise:
therefore hast thou visited and destroyed them, and made all their memory
to perish.
26:14 Hab 2:19

15 Thou hast increased the nation, O LORD, thou hast increased the
nation: thou art glorified: thou hadst removed *it* far *unto* all the ends of the
earth.
26:15 Isa 54:2

26:1ff *in that day,* yes, even today, whoever experiences the delivering mercies of the God of grace shall sing their song. To those who sing this song there is given the promise of perfect peace, because the minds of such people remain fixed on God as they put their trust in him alone. His guidance and his government constitute their strongholds, whatever the circumstances of life may be.

26:4 *the* LORD *JEHOVAH is everlasting strength,* translated "we have an everlasting Rock" (NASB) and "the LORD God is an everlasting rock" (RSV). God indeed is the Rock of ages, the only foundation upon which to build one's house. Any house built on that foundation will stand against any storm. From this Rock believers receive everlasting strength.

26:12 *peace.* The word "peace" is used variously in the Scriptures. The root itself suggests prosperity and well-being such as Israel enjoyed under King Solomon (1 Kings 4:20, 25), also an earthly blessedness, wholeness, and right relations, which believers will enjoy forever under Messiah's rule (Mic. 4:3, 4). A second meaning for the word is absence of war. This kind of peace for the world will come only after Christ's Second Advent. Until then, there will be wars and rumors of wars (Matt. 24:6–14). For believers, the word "peace" has two further meanings: (1) that spiritual peace that comes from justification or having been made right with God through Jesus Christ. This is peace *with* God (Rom. 5:1); and (2) the peace *of* God, which is described as passing all understanding (Phil. 4:7). This has to do with the inner life of utter tranquility despite external trouble and difficulties.

26:13 *other lords beside thee,* i.e., other gods whom they worship in place of the true God.

3. The Prayer of God's People Answered

26:16 Hos 5:15
16 LORD, in trouble have they visited thee, they poured out a prayer *when*
thy chastening *was* upon them.
26:17 Jn 16:21
17 Like as a woman with child, *that* draweth near the time of her delivery,
is in pain, *and* crieth out in her pangs; so have we been in thy sight, O
LORD.
26:18 Isa 33:11
18 We have been with child, we have been in pain, we have as it were
brought forth wind; we have not wrought any deliverance in the earth;
neither have the inhabitants of the world fallen.
26:19☆ Ezek 37:1–14 Dan 12:2 Eph 5:14
19 Thy dead *men* shall live, *together with* my dead body shall they arise.
Awake and sing, ye that dwell in dust: for thy dew *is as* the dew of herbs,
and the earth shall cast out the dead.

4. The Appeal to Trust God until Deliverance Comes

26:20 Ps 30:5
20 ¶Come, my people, enter thou into thy chambers, and shut thy doors
about thee: hide thyself as it were for a little moment, until the indignation
be overpast.
26:21 Job 16:18 Mic 1:3
21 For, behold, the LORD cometh out of his place to punish the inhabi-
tants of the earth for their iniquity: the earth also shall disclose her blood,
and shall no more cover her slain.

27:1☆ Job 3:8 Ps 74:14
27 IN that day the LORD with his sore and great and strong sword
shall punish leviathan the piercing serpent, even leviathan that
crooked serpent; and he shall slay the dragon that *is* in the sea.

D. THE ASSURANCE OF ISRAEL'S DELIVERANCE

1. Israel Shall Take Root and Blossom

27:2–6☆
2 In that day sing ye unto her, A vineyard of red wine.
27:3 Jn 10:28
3 I the LORD do keep it; I will water it every moment: lest *any* hurt it, I
will keep it night and day.
27:4 2 Sam 23:6 Isa 33:12 Rom 5:1
4 Fury *is* not in me: who would set the briers *and* thorns against me in
battle? I would go through them, I would burn them together.
5 Or let him take hold of my strength, *that* he may make peace with me;
and he shall make peace with me.
27:6 Isa 35:1, 2
6 He shall cause them that come of Jacob to take root: Israel shall
blossom and bud, and fill the face of the world with fruit.

2. Israel's Exile Will Correct Her

27:7 Isa 10:12, 17 Hos 13:15
7 ¶Hath he smitten him, as he smote those that smote him? *or* is he slain
according to the slaughter of them that are slain by him?
27:8☆
8 In measure, when it shooteth forth, thou wilt debate with it: he stayeth
his rough wind in the day of the east wind.

26:19 Isaiah clearly believed in the bodily resurrection of the righteous and the wicked dead. Those who are "in the graves shall hear his voice, and shall come forth; they that have done good, unto the resurrection of life; and they that have done evil, unto the resurrection of damnation" (John 5:28, 29).
27:1 *leviathan* was a mythological monster of the sea which, as a symbol of evil, must be slain.
27:2–6 God contends with his people when they sin *but is reconciled to them when they repent*. The divine anger can be reversed only by humiliation and prayer on the part of the transgressor. God wants his people to be at peace with him and they should be persuaded to do so for three reasons: (1) God gives them time and space to repent—he does not cut them off forever; (2) it is vain to think one can win a contest with him, for no one is a match for Omnipotence; (3) God's way is the only sure way to reconciliation. If we take God's course, he is willing to be reconciled and we will be reconciled to him.
27:8 God dealt out afflictions to Israel just as a wise physician prescribes medicine for pneumonia. But divine judgment and Israel's afflictions are mixed with mercy, for his people will eventually return to him for pardon and cleansing.

9 By this therefore shall the iniquity of Jacob be purged; and this *is* all the 27:9
fruit to take away his sin; when he maketh all the stones of the altar as Dan 11:35
chalkstones that are beaten in sunder, the groves and images shall not stand Isa 17:8
up.
10 Yet the defenced city *shall be* desolate, *and* the habitation forsaken, and
left like a wilderness: there shall the calf feed, and there shall he lie down,
and consume the branches thereof.
11 When the boughs thereof are withered, they shall be broken off: the 27:11
women come, *and* set them on fire: for it *is* a people of no understanding: Deut 32:18, 28
therefore he that made them will not have mercy on them, and he that Isa 43:1, 7
formed them will shew them no favour.

3. Israel Will Be Regathered to Mount Zion

12 ¶And it shall come to pass in that day, *that* the LORD shall beat off from ☆27:12
the channel of the river unto the stream of Egypt, and ye shall be gathered Deut 30:3, 4
one by one, O ye children of Israel. Isa 11:11
13 And it shall come to pass in that day, *that* the great trumpet shall be 27:13
blown, and they shall come which were ready to perish in the land of Zech 14:16
Assyria, and the outcasts in the land of Egypt, and shall worship the LORD Mt 24:31
in the holy mount at Jerusalem. Rev 11:15

V. ZION'S HOPES: TRUE ONES AND FALSE ONES (28:1—35:10)

A. GOD'S JUDGMENT AGAINST DRUNKARDS AND SCOFFERS

1. Woe to the Drunkards

28 WOE to the crown of pride, to the drunkards of E'phra-im, whose ☆28:1ff
glorious beauty *is* a fading flower, which *are* on the head of the fat
valleys of them that are overcome with wine!
2 Behold, the Lord hath a mighty and strong one, *which* as a tempest of 28:2
hail *and* a destroying storm, as a flood of mighty waters overflowing, shall Isa 8:7; 30:28
cast down to the earth with the hand. Nah 1:8
3 The crown of pride, the drunkards of E'phra-im, shall be trodden under
feet:
4 And the glorious beauty, which *is* on the head of the fat valley, shall be 28:4
a fading flower, *and* as the hasty fruit before the summer; which *when* he Hos 9:10
that looketh upon it seeth, while it is yet in his hand he eateth it up. Nah 3:12
5 In that day shall the LORD of hosts be for a crown of glory, and for a 28:5
diadem of beauty, unto the residue of his people, Isa 41:16
6 And for a spirit of judgment to him that sitteth in judgment, and for 28:6
strength to them that turn the battle to the gate. 2 Chron 32:6–8
7 ¶But they also have erred through wine, and through strong drink are ☆28:7
out of the way; the priest and the prophet have erred through strong drink, Hab 2:15, 16
they are swallowed up of wine, they are out of the way through strong
drink; they err in vision, they stumble *in* judgment.
8 For all tables are full of vomit *and* filthiness, *so that there is* no place ☆28:8
clean. Jer 48:26

27:12 The anger of God against his people will not last forever. When they turn to the Messiah in faith, they will be regathered from the ends of the earth to be brought back to their ancestral lands. They will then worship God with hearts that are right and deeds that correspond to their profession.

28:1ff The Ephraimites (Samaria or the Northern Kingdom) are reproved here for their sins: pride, drunkenness, security, and sensuality.

28:7, 8 Drunkenness was not simply the preoccupation of princes and people. It was common to priests and prophets as well. Instead of truth, righteousness, and purity there was vomit and filthiness, so low had the religious leaders fallen.

2. God Promises Death to Scoffers

28:9☆ Heb 5:12, 13

9¶Whom shall he teach knowledge? and whom shall he make to
understand doctrine? *them that are* weaned from the milk, *and* drawn from
the breasts.
10For precept *must be* upon precept, precept upon precept; line upon line,
line upon line; here a little, *and* there a little:

28:11 Isa 33:19; 1 Cor 14:21

11For with stammering lips and another tongue will he speak to this
people.

28:12 Jer 6:16; Mt 11:28, 29

12To whom he said, This *is* the rest *wherewith* ye may cause the weary to
rest; and this *is* the refreshing: yet they would not hear.

28:13 Mt 21:44

13But the word of the LORD was unto them precept upon precept, precept
upon precept; line upon line, line upon line; here a little, *and* there a little;
that they might go, and fall backward, and be broken, and snared, and
taken.
14¶Wherefore hear the word of the LORD, ye scornful men, that rule this
people which *is* in Jerusalem.

28:15☆ Isa 28:18

15Because ye have said, We have made a covenant with death, and with
hell are we at agreement; when the overflowing scourge shall pass through,
it shall not come unto us: for we have made lies our refuge, and under
falsehood have we hid ourselves;

28:16☆ Ps 118:22; Mt 21:42; Acts 4:11; Eph 2:20

16¶Therefore thus saith the Lord GOD, Behold, I lay in Zion for a
foundation a stone, a tried stone, a precious corner *stone,* a sure founda-
tion; he that believeth shall not make haste.

28:17 Isa 61:8; Amos 7:7–9

17Judgment also will I lay to the line, and righteousness to the plummet:
and the hail shall sweep away the refuge of lies, and the waters shall
overflow the hiding place.
18¶And your covenant with death shall be disannulled, and your
agreement with hell shall not stand; when the overflowing scourge shall
pass through, then ye shall be trodden down by it.
19From the time that it goeth forth it shall take you: for morning by
morning shall it pass over, by day and by night: and it shall be a vexation
only *to* understand the report.

28:20☆

20For the bed is shorter than that *a man* can stretch himself *on it:* and the
covering narrower than that he can wrap himself *in it.*

28:21☆ 2 Sam 5:20; Lk 19:41–44

21For the LORD shall rise up as *in* mount Per'a-zim, he shall be wroth as
in the valley of Gibeon, that he may do his work, his strange work; and
bring to pass his act, his strange act.

28:9ff Isaiah hoped to teach the people the truth, but in their wretched stupidity they were unteachable. They continued as they were. They did not rectify their errors, their hearts were unchanged, and their lives were unreformed. Since Samaria would not hear the comfortable word of God, they would hear the dreadful roar of his rod as it was applied to them.

28:15 *We have made a covenant with death, and with hell.* Judah thinks itself to be secure because of its alliance with Egypt against Assyria. But this is only a covenant with death and the netherworld.

28:16 *foundation . . . stone* or *corner stone* can only be Christ. He is referred to as a stone who protects, delivers, and judges. It may be said that (1) Christ the Rock was smitten for our transgressions (Exod. 17:6; Num. 20:8); (2) Christ is the Rock that demolishes the last world power (Dan. 2:34); (3) Christ's stone becomes a great mountain that will cover the whole earth (Dan. 2:35); (4) Christ is the precious cornerstone (1 Pet. 2:6); and (5) "the Stone that some will stumble over, and the Rock that will make them fall" (1 Pet. 2:8, TLB; Rom. 9:32, 33; 1 Cor. 1:23).

28:20 That which Samaria trusted in would never fulfill their needs or their expectations. Isaiah likens their dilemma to that of a tall man trying to sleep in a short bed. He is forced to assume a fetal position and cannot find the rest he desires. He also has a blanket that will not cover him, so he never is warm on a cold night. The shame of Samaria's nakedness will equal that of Adam and Eve, who had only fig leaves to cover their private parts. This is ever the plight of those who refuse to build upon Jesus Christ as their only sure foundation: they stand naked and ashamed.

28:21 God will rise up against Israel as he rose up against the Philistines in David's time at Mt. Perazim (2 Sam. 5:20) and in Joshua's time in the valley of Gibeon (Josh. 10:1ff). The destruction he wrought among Israel's enemies on these occasions is an example of the same destruction he will rain upon his own people.

22 Now therefore be ye not mockers, lest your bands be made strong: for
I have heard from the Lord GOD of hosts a consumption, even determined
upon the whole earth.

3. The Illustration of the Farmer

23 ¶Give ye ear, and hear my voice; hearken, and hear my speech. ☆28:23–29
24 Doth the plowman plow all day to sow? doth he open and break the
clods of his ground?
25 When he hath made plain the face thereof, doth he not cast abroad the
fitches, and scatter the cummin, and cast in the principal wheat and the
appointed barley and the rie in their place?
26 For his God doth instruct him to discretion, *and* doth teach him.
27 For the fitches are not threshed with a threshing instrument, neither is **28:27**
a cart wheel turned about upon the cummin; but the fitches are beaten out Amos 1:3
with a staff, and the cummin with a rod.
28 Bread *corn* is bruised; because he will not ever be threshing it, nor
break *it with* the wheel of his cart, nor bruise it *with* his horsemen.
29 This also cometh forth from the LORD of hosts, *which* is wonderful in **28:29**
counsel, *and* excellent in working. Rom 11:33

B. THE JUDGMENT ON JERUSALEM

1. God Will Destroy Jerusalem

29 WOE to A′ri-el, to A′ri-el, the city *where* David dwelt! add ye year ☆**29:1**
to year; let them kill sacrifices. 2 Sam 5:9
2 Yet I will distress A′ri-el, and there shall be heaviness and sorrow: and **29:2**
it shall be unto me as A′ri-el. Lam 2:5
3 And I will camp against thee round about, and will lay siege against thee **29:3**
with a mount, and I will raise forts against thee. Lk 19:43, 44
4 And thou shalt be brought down, *and* shalt speak out of the ground, and
thy speech shall be low out of the dust, and thy voice shall be, as of one that
hath a familiar spirit, out of the ground, and thy speech shall whisper out of
the dust.

2. God Will Destroy Jerusalem's Foes Too

5 Moreover the multitude of thy strangers shall be like small dust, and the **29:5**
multitude of the terrible ones *shall be* as chaff that passeth away: yea, it Isa 17:14 41:15, 16
shall be at an instant suddenly. 1 Thess 5:3
6 Thou shalt be visited of the LORD of hosts with thunder, and with **29:6**
earthquake, and great noise, with storm and tempest, and the flame of Lk 21:11 Rev 11:13, 19
devouring fire.
7 ¶And the multitude of all the nations that fight against A′ri-el, even all **29:7**
that fight against her and her munition, and that distress her, shall be as a Zech 12:9
dream of a night vision.
8 It shall even be as when an hungry *man* dreameth, and, behold, he ☆**29:8**
eateth; but he awaketh, and his soul is empty: or as when a thirsty man Isa 54:17
dreameth, and, behold, he drinketh; but he awaketh, and, behold, *he is*
faint, and his soul hath appetite: so shall the multitude of all the nations be,
that fight against mount Zion.

28:23–29 As farmers use different instruments to produce their crops, so God will employ particular judgments to produce the righteousness he demands from his people.
29:1 *to Ariel,* i.e., "to Jerusalem."

29:8 The Assyrians expected to conquer Jerusalem without difficulty. They fell into the sleep of death, as their dreams turned into a nightmare of disappointment and failure.

3. God Cannot Be Deceived by False Faith

9¶Stay yourselves, and wonder; cry ye out, and cry: they are drunken,
but not with wine; they stagger, but not with strong drink.

29:10☆ Rom 11:8; 2 Thess 2:9–12

10For the LORD hath poured out upon you the spirit of deep sleep, and
hath closed your eyes: the prophets and your rulers, the seers hath he
covered.

29:11☆ Dan 12:4

11And the vision of all is become unto you as the words of a book that is
sealed, which *men* deliver to one that is learned, saying, Read this, I pray
thee: and he saith, I cannot; for it *is* sealed:

29:12☆

12And the book is delivered to him that is not learned, saying, Read this,
I pray thee: and he saith, I am not learned.

29:13☆ Ezek 33:31; Mk 7:6, 7

13¶Wherefore the Lord said, Forasmuch as this people draw near *me* with
their mouth, and with their lips do honour me, but have removed their
heart far from me, and their fear toward me is taught by the precept of
men:

29:14 Isa 44:25; 1 Cor 1:19

14Therefore, behold, I will proceed to do a marvellous work among this
people, *even* a marvellous work and a wonder: for the wisdom of their wise
men shall perish, and the understanding of their prudent *men* shall be hid.

29:15 Ps 10:11, 13; Isa 47:10

15Woe unto them that seek deep to hide their counsel from the LORD, and
their works are in the dark, and they say, Who seeth us? and who knoweth
us?

29:16 Isa 45:9; Rom 9:19–21

16Surely your turning of things upside down shall be esteemed as the
potter's clay: for shall the work say of him that made it, He made me not?
or shall the thing framed say of him that framed it, He had no understand-
ing?
17*Is* it not yet a very little while, and Lebanon shall be turned into a
fruitful field, and the fruitful field shall be esteemed as a forest?

29:18☆ Isa 32:3

18¶And in that day shall the deaf hear the words of the book, and the eyes
of the blind shall see out of obscurity, and out of darkness.

29:19 Isa 14:30, 32; Mt 5:5; Jas 2:5

19The meek also shall increase *their* joy in the LORD, and the poor among
men shall rejoice in the Holy One of Israel.
20For the terrible one is brought to nought, and the scorner is consumed,
and all that watch for iniquity are cut off:

29:21 Amos 5:10, 12

21That make a man an offender for a word, and lay a snare for him that
reproveth in the gate, and turn aside the just for a thing of nought.

4. Israel Will Praise the Holy One at Last

29:22 Isa 41:8

22Therefore thus saith the LORD, who redeemed Abraham, concerning
the house of Jacob, Jacob shall not now be ashamed, neither shall his face
now wax pale.

29:10 Strangely enough, the God who called upon his people to open their eyes poured out upon them a spirit of deep sleep and closed their eyes (Isa. 51:9; 52:1). "This was the way of righteous judgment, a punishment for loving darkness rather than light. Romans 11:8 says the same thing about Israel in Paul's day and today: 'God has given Israel the spirit of slumber.' "

29:11, 12 *God sent Isaiah to his people. He saw the* vision and uttered the prophecy. But this made no difference to the people of God. It was as if they had a book that was sealed and they could not read it, or as if the illiterate were given a book. Because their hearts were wrong, they could not understand what God had said in any event. Even if the book were open and they could read, they still would have been blind to its real meaning.

29:13 God charges his people with hypocrisy; theirs was a religion of the lip, not of the heart. They worshipped God according to their own inventions, not from what God himself required of them in his revelation.

29:18 Despite Israel's transgressions, the day will come when their ignorance will turn to intelligence, their deafness to hearing and their blindness to sight. Whoever rightly uses the Word of God will not be ignorant and will both hear and see as he ought.

23 But when he seeth his children, the work of mine hands, in the midst of
him, they shall sanctify my name, and sanctify the Holy One of Jacob, and
shall fear the God of Israel.
24 They also that erred in spirit shall come to understanding, and they that **29:24**
murmured shall learn doctrine. Isa 30:21; 41:20

C. THE FUTILITY OF TRUSTING PHARAOH

1. Trusting Egypt Instead of God

30 WOE to the rebellious children, saith the LORD, that take counsel, **30:1**
but not of me; and that cover with a covering, but not of my spirit, Isa 8:11, 12
that they may add sin to sin:
2 That walk to go down into Egypt, and have not asked at my mouth; to ☆**30:2**
strengthen themselves in the strength of Pharaoh, and to trust in the Isa 8:19; 31:1
shadow of Egypt!
3 Therefore shall the strength of Pharaoh be your shame, and the trust in **30:3**
the shadow of Egypt *your* confusion. Isa 36:6 Jer 42:18, 22
4 For his princes were at Zo'an, and his ambassadors came to Ha'nes.
5 They were all ashamed of a people *that* could not profit them, nor be an **30:5**
help nor profit, but a shame, and also a reproach. Isa 31:3 Jer 2:36

2. Egypt's Promises Are Worthless

6 The burden of the beasts of the south: into the land of trouble and **30:6**
anguish, from whence *come* the young and old lion, the viper and fiery Deut 8:15
flying serpent, they will carry their riches upon the shoulders of young
asses, and their treasures upon the bunches of camels, to a people *that* shall
not profit *them.*
7 For the Egyptians shall help in vain, and to no purpose: therefore have ☆**30:7**
I cried concerning this, Their strength *is* to sit still. Isa 51:9

3. God Cannot Be Deceived by False Faith

8 ¶Now go, write it before them in a table, and note it in a book, that it
may be for the time to come for ever and ever:
9 That this *is* a rebellious people, lying children, children *that* will not hear
the law of the LORD:
10 Which say to the seers, See not; and to the prophets, Prophesy not unto **30:10**
us right things, speak unto us smooth things, prophesy deceits: 1 Kgs 22:8, 13 Jer 6:14
11 Get you out of the way, turn aside out of the path, cause the Holy One Ezek 13:7 Amos 2:12
of Israel to cease from before us. 2 Tim 4:3, 4 ☆**30:11**
12 Wherefore thus saith the Holy One of Israel, Because ye despise this **30:12**
word, and trust in oppression and perverseness, and stay thereon: Isa 5:24; 59:13
13 Therefore this iniquity shall be to you as a breach ready to fall, swelling
out in a high wall, whose breaking cometh suddenly at an instant.

30:2 Hezekiah was seeking a defensive alliance with Ethiopia's Egyptian dynasty against Sennacherib of Assyria. Israel sought the arm of the flesh rather than faith in God. They did not even consult God. The sin was that they had greater confidence in Egypt than in God. Isaiah told them that (1) strength lies in returning and waiting on God to help them (30:15); (2) Egypt's promises are worthless (30:7); and (3) God is both willing and able to be gracious to his people if they will turn to him in repentance and faith so that he can bless them (30:18).

30:7 *Their strength is to sit still,* literally, "Rahab who sits still" (RSV). This is an allusion to a sea monster or demonic power. Isaiah says that Egypt, like Rahab, is arrogant, sits still, and will not help her allies. Judah is silly to trust such a "friend."

30:11 Isaiah and every true prophet "were continually telling them (Judah) of the Holy One of Israel, what an enemy he is to sin and how severely he will reckon with sinners; and this they could not endure to hear of."*

30:14☆ 14 And he shall break it as the breaking of the potters' vessel that is
Ps 2:9 broken in pieces; he shall not spare: so that there shall not be found in the
Jer 19:10, 11 bursting of it a sherd to take fire from the hearth, or to take water *withal* out
of the pit.
30:15 15 For thus saith the Lord GOD, the Holy One of Israel; In returning and
Isa 28:12; 32:17 rest shall ye be saved; in quietness and in confidence shall be your strength:
and ye would not.
30:16 16 But ye said, No; for we will flee upon horses; therefore shall ye flee:
Isa 31:1, 3 and, We will ride upon the swift; therefore shall they that pursue you be
swift.
30:17☆ 17 One thousand *shall flee* at the rebuke of one; at the rebuke of five shall
Deut 32:30 ye flee: till ye be left as a beacon upon the top of a mountain, and as an
ensign on an hill.

4. God's Blessings on a Repentant People

30:18 18 ¶And therefore will the LORD wait, that he may be gracious unto you,
Isa 25:9 and therefore will he be exalted, that he may have mercy upon you: for the
2 Pet 3:9, 15 LORD *is* a God of judgment: blessed *are* all they that wait for him.
30:19 19 For the people shall dwell in Zion at Jerusalem: thou shalt weep no
Isa 25:8; 65:24 more: he will be very gracious unto thee at the voice of thy cry; when he
shall hear it, he will answer thee.
30:20☆ 20 And *though* the Lord give you the bread of adversity, and the water of
Ps 80:5 affliction, yet shall not thy teachers be removed into a corner any more, but
thine eyes shall see thy teachers:
30:21 21 And thine ears shall hear a word behind thee, saying, This *is* the way,
Isa 35:8, 9 walk ye in it, when ye turn to the right hand, and when ye turn to the left.
30:22 22 Ye shall defile also the covering of thy graven images of silver, and the
Ex 32:2, 4 ornament of thy molten images of gold: thou shalt cast them away as a
menstruous cloth; thou shalt say unto it, Get thee hence.
30:23 23 Then shall he give the rain of thy seed, that thou shalt sow the ground
Ps 65:9–13 withal; and bread of the increase of the earth, and it shall be fat and
plenteous: in that day shall thy cattle feed in large pastures.
30:24 24 The oxen likewise and the young asses that ear the ground shall eat
Mt 3:12 clean provender, which hath been winnowed with the shovel and with the
fan.
30:25 25 And there shall be upon every high mountain, and upon every high hill,
Isa 41:18 rivers *and* streams of waters in the day of the great slaughter, when the
towers fall.
30:26☆ 26 Moreover the light of the moon shall be as the light of the sun, and the
Isa 33:24 light of the sun shall be sevenfold, as the light of seven days, in the day that
Hos 6:1, 2 the LORD bindeth up the breach of his people, and healeth the stroke of
their wound.

30:14 The ruin of Judah would be like a vessel broken into such small pieces that nothing of the vessel would be left. Not a *shard* (which is a small but visible piece) would be left.

30:17 When sin enters a life, it debilitates its victim and renders him helpless against the enemy of the soul. The sinner becomes so weak that a single enemy will *rout a thousand of them with ease*. The power of God departs from the sinner's life, as happened to Samson who, when God was gone, became so insensate that he was not even aware of the divine departure.

30:20 Mercy is in store, and God waits to bless the penitent who come to him for healing. Until the people of God become penitent and turn to him, they will eat the *bread of adversity* and drink *the water of affliction*. They will survive on coarse food and drink puddle water. Retribution always has in it the possibility that the sufferer will learn from this and turn to God for deliverance. And God waits with patience for his people to repent.

30:26 So great are the mercies of God that the penitent will discover that the light of the moon is equal to the light of the sun, and the light of the sun will increase sevenfold. In deliverance, God heals the wounds, removes the distresses, and sends innumerable blessings to his people.

5. God's Anger against Israel's Enemies

27 ¶Behold, the name of the LORD cometh from far, burning *with* his
anger, and the burden *thereof is* heavy: his lips are full of indignation, and
his tongue as a devouring fire:

30:27 Isa 66:15

28 And his breath, as an overflowing stream, shall reach to the midst of the
neck, to sift the nations with the sieve of vanity: and *there shall be* a bridle
in the jaws of the people, causing *them* to err.

30:28 2 Kgs 19:28 Isa 8:7, 8

29 Ye shall have a song, as in the night *when* a holy solemnity is kept; and
gladness of heart, as when one goeth with a pipe to come into the mountain
of the LORD, to the mighty One of Israel.
30 And the LORD shall cause his glorious voice to be heard, and shall shew
the lighting down of his arm, with the indignation of *his* anger, and *with* the
flame of a devouring fire, *with* scattering, and tempest, and hailstones.
31 For through the voice of the LORD shall the Assyrian be beaten down,
which smote with a rod.
32 And *in* every place where the grounded staff shall pass, which the LORD
shall lay upon him, *it* shall be with tabrets and harps: and in battles of
shaking will he fight with it.

30:32 1 Sam 18:6 Jer 31:4

33 For To'phet *is* ordained of old; yea, for the king it is prepared; he hath
made *it* deep *and* large: the pile thereof *is* fire and much wood; the breath
of the LORD, like a stream of brimstone, doth kindle it.

30:33 Gen 19:24 Isa 34:9

6. The Folly of Trusting Egypt

31 WOE to them that go down to Egypt for help; and stay on horses,
and trust in chariots, because *they are* many; and in horsemen,
because they are very strong; but they look not unto the Holy One of Israel,
neither seek the LORD!

☆**31:1** Ps 20:7 Isa 10:17 Hos 11:9 Hab 1:12

2 Yet he also *is* wise, and will bring evil, and will not call back his words:
but will arise against the house of the evildoers, and against the help of
them that work iniquity.

31:2 Num 23:19 Jer 44:29 Rom 16:27

3 Now the Egyptians *are* men, and not God; and their horses flesh, and
not spirit. When the LORD shall stretch out his hand, both he that helpeth
shall fall, and he that is holpen shall fall down, and they all shall fail
together.

31:3 Jer 15:6 Ezek 28:9

7. God Calls His People to Trust Him

4 For thus hath the LORD spoken unto me, Like as the lion and the young
lion roaring on his prey, when a multitude of shepherds is called forth
against him, *he* will not be afraid of their voice, nor abase himself for the
noise of them: so shall the LORD of hosts come down to fight for mount
Zion, and for the hill thereof.

31:4 Deut 32:11 Isa 42:13

5 As birds flying, so will the LORD of hosts defend Jerusalem; defending
also he will deliver *it; and* passing over he will preserve it.

☆**31:5**

31:1 *It would have been proper* for Israel to seek the help of Egypt and make an alliance with that nation if God had so commanded. But God forbade such an alliance and considered such action an indicator of Israel's lack of confidence in the Lord God. Israel here not only sought help from Egypt, it failed to seek the help of God. This was a tragic mistake and a sign of lack of faith in Jehovah. The basic principle applies to the believer today. If we live in contempt of divine laws, that is, if we fail to do what God has commanded us to do, then the woes of God will be our lot. We are to seek the face of God in everything and at all times, and do it first. If we are sick, we should consult a physician, but not before we have first consulted the Great Physician.

31:5 God will send a single angel to destroy the Assyrian army and save Jerusalem. Though Jerusalem deserved to be destroyed as well, the angel would draw his sword only against the besiegers. Despite this deliverance, Jerusalem would continue its wicked ways. Later, God used Nebuchadnezzar to execute judgment against Jerusalem and to begin the seventy-year Babylonian captivity. All this could have been avoided if Jerusalem had repented.

31:6 Isa 55:7; Jer 3:10, 14, 22

6¶Turn ye unto *him from* whom the children of Israel have deeply
revolted.
7For in that day every man shall cast away his idols of silver, and his
idols of gold, which your own hands have made unto you *for* a sin.

31:8 Isa 10:12; 14:2

8¶Then shall the Assyrian fall with the sword, not of a mighty man; and
the sword, not of a mean man, shall devour him: but he shall flee from the
sword, and his young men shall be discomfited.

31:9 Isa 13:2

9And he shall pass over to his strong hold for fear, and his princes shall
be afraid of the ensign, saith the LORD, whose fire *is* in Zion, and his
furnace in Jerusalem.

D. GOD'S BLESSING ON THOSE WHO TRUST HIM

1. God Will Deliver His People at Last

32:1☆ Jer 23:5; Ezek 37:24; Zech 9:9
32:2 Isa 25:4; 35:6

32 BEHOLD, a king shall reign in righteousness, and princes shall rule
in judgment.
2And a man shall be as an hiding place from the wind, and a covert from
the tempest; as rivers of water in a dry place, as the shadow of a great rock
in a weary land.
3And the eyes of them that see shall not be dim, and the ears of them that
hear shall hearken.

32:4 Isa 29:24

4The heart also of the rash shall understand knowledge, and the tongue
of the stammerers shall be ready to speak plainly.
5The vile person shall be no more called liberal, nor the churl said *to be*
bountiful.

32:6 Isa 10:2; 59:7, 13

6For the vile person will speak villany, and his heart will work iniquity, to
practise hypocrisy, and to utter error against the LORD, to make empty the
soul of the hungry, and he will cause the drink of the thirsty to fail.

32:7 Isa 5:23; Jer 5:26–28; Mic 7:3
32:8 2 Cor 9:6–11

7The instruments also of the churl *are* evil: he deviseth wicked devices to
destroy the poor with lying words, even when the needy speaketh right.
8But the liberal deviseth liberal things; and by liberal things shall he
stand.

2. Calamity Will Be Followed by Restoration

32:9 Isa 47:8

9¶Rise up, ye women that are at ease; hear my voice, ye careless
daughters; give ear unto my speech.

32:10 Isa 5:5, 6

10Many days and years shall ye be troubled, ye careless women: for the
vintage shall fail, the gathering shall not come.
11Tremble, ye women that are at ease; be troubled, ye careless ones: strip
you, and make you bare, and gird *sackcloth* upon *your* loins.
12They shall lament for the teats, for the pleasant fields, for the fruitful
vine.

32:13 Isa 5:5, 6, 10, 17

13Upon the land of my people shall come up thorns *and* briers; yea, upon
all the houses of joy *in* the joyous city:

32:14 Isa 24:12

14Because the palaces shall be forsaken; the multitude of the city shall be
left; the forts and towers shall be for dens for ever, a joy of wild asses, a
pasture of flocks;

32:1 *a king shall reign in righteousness.* The Old Testament saints looked for and prayed for a king whose chief attribute would be to rule in righteousness. Despite oppression and the series of weak and unworthy monarchs, the godly people in Israel looked for a day when a truly righteous king would reign. So also do Christians look and pray for peace, but this will never materialize until the Prince of Peace comes back to rule and reign in righteousness.

15 Until the spirit be poured upon us from on high, and the wilderness be ☆32:15
a fruitful field, and the fruitful field be counted for a forest. Ps 107–35 Isa 11:2
16 Then judgment shall dwell in the wilderness, and righteousness remain Joel 2:28 32:16
in the fruitful field. Isa 33:5
17 And the work of righteousness shall be peace; and the effect of ☆32:17
righteousness quietness and assurance for ever. Isa 2:4 Jas 3:18
18 And my people shall dwell in a peaceable habitation, and in sure 32:18
dwellings, and in quiet resting places; Hos 2:18–23
19 When it shall hail, coming down on the forest; and the city shall be low
in a low place.
20 Blessed *are* ye that sow beside all waters, that send forth *thither* the feet 32:20
of the ox and the ass. Isa 30:23

3. Gentile Destroyers Will Themselves Be Destroyed

33 WOE to thee that spoilest, and thou *wast* not spoiled; and dealest ☆33:1
treacherously, and they dealt not treacherously with thee! when Jer 25:12–14 Hab 2:8
thou shalt cease to spoil, thou shalt be spoiled; *and* when thou shalt make
an end to deal treacherously, they shall deal treacherously with thee.
2 O LORD, be gracious unto us; we have waited for thee: be thou their arm 33:2
every morning, our salvation also in the time of trouble. Isa 25:9; 40:10
3 At the noise of the tumult the people fled; at the lifting up of thyself the 33:3
nations were scattered. Jer 25:30, 31
4 And your spoil shall be gathered *like* the gathering of the caterpiller: as ☆33:4
the running to and fro of locusts shall he run upon them.
5 The LORD is exalted; for he dwelleth on high: he hath filled Zion with ☆33:5
judgment and righteousness. Ps 97:9
6 And wisdom and knowledge shall be the stability of thy times, *and* 33:6
strength of salvation: the fear of the LORD *is* his treasure. Ps 112:1–3 Isa 51:6

4. Assyria Grinds Down God's People

7 Behold, their valiant ones shall cry without: the ambassadors of peace
shall weep bitterly.
8 The highways lie waste, the wayfaring man ceaseth: he hath broken the
covenant, he hath despised the cities, he regardeth no man.
9 The earth mourneth *and* languisheth: Lebanon is ashamed *and* hewn 33:9
down: Shar′on is like a wilderness; and Ba′shan and Carmel shake off *their* Isa 10:34; 24:4 35:2
fruits.

5. God Will Destroy Israel's Enemy

10 Now will I rise, saith the LORD; now will I be exalted; now will I lift up 33:10
myself. Ps 12:5 Isa 2:19

32:15 God promises that *the spirit* [will] *be poured upon us from on high.* Thus in Luke 11:13 Jesus asks, "how much more shall your heavenly Father give the Holy Spirit to them that ask him?" Every believer is sealed and indwelt by the Spirit from the moment of justification and regeneration, so something more is promised to the believer. This undoubtedly refers to the Pauline teaching in which we are commanded to be filled with the Holy Spirit (Eph. 5:18). The infilling of the Spirit guarantees to the believer endowment with gifts and enduement with divine power.

32:17 *and assurance for ever.* This is the doctrine of assurance, which means the believer is firmly convinced he has been saved and will be kept by faith through the knowledge of the Word of God, to which the Holy Spirit bears his witness to the believer's heart. Assurance derives from the promises of God and is the product of faith given by the Spirit. The believer can be certain of (1) salvation (12:2; John 3:17; Acts 16:30, 31), (2) eternal life (1 John 5:13), (3) peace with God (Rom. 5:1), (4) glorious resurrection body (Phil. 3:21), (5) an eternal kingdom (Heb. 12:28), and (6) a crown of life (2 Tim. 4:7, 8; James 1:12).

33:1 *to thee that spoilest,* i.e., "to the Assyrians."

33:4, 5 Judah gathered the spoils left for them after the deaths of the Assyrian soldiers, who were slain by the angel of God. In this "the LORD is exalted." He will have the praise for what happened, for Judah had nothing to do with the victory.

33:11 Isa 26:18

11 Ye shall conceive chaff, ye shall bring forth stubble: your breath, *as* fire, shall devour you.

33:12 2 Sam 23:6, 7; Isa 10:17

12 And the people shall be *as* the burnings of lime: *as* thorns cut up shall they be burned in the fire.

33:13 Isa 49:1

13 ¶Hear, ye *that are* far off, what I have done; and, ye *that are* near, acknowledge my might.

33:14 Isa 1:28; 30:27; Heb 12:29

14 The sinners in Zion are afraid; fearfulness hath surprised the hypocrites. Who among us shall dwell with the devouring fire? who among us shall dwell with everlasting burnings?

33:15☆ Ps 24:3, 4; Isa 58:6–11

15 He that walketh righteously, and speaketh uprightly; he that despiseth the gain of oppressions, that shaketh his hands from holding of bribes, that stoppeth his ears from hearing of blood, and shutteth his eyes from seeing evil;

33:16 Isa 49:10

16 He shall dwell on high: his place of defence *shall be* the munitions of rocks: bread shall be given him; his waters *shall be* sure.

6. A Vision of Jerusalem at Peace under Messiah

33:17☆ Isa 6:5

17 Thine eyes shall see the king in his beauty: they shall behold the land that is very far off.

18 Thine heart shall meditate terror. Where *is* the scribe? where *is* the receiver? where *is* he that counted the towers?

33:19 Deut 28:49, 50

19 Thou shalt not see a fierce people, a people of a deeper speech than thou canst perceive; of a stammering tongue, *that thou canst* not understand.

33:20☆ Ps 46:5

20 Look upon Zion, the city of our solemnities: thine eyes shall see Jerusalem a quiet habitation, a tabernacle *that* shall not be taken down; not one of the stakes thereof shall ever be removed, neither shall any of the cords thereof be broken.

33:21 Isa 48:18

21 But there the glorious LORD *will be* unto us a place of broad rivers *and* streams; wherein shall go no galley with oars, neither shall gallant ship pass thereby.

33:22 Isa 49:25, 26; Zech 9:9; Jas 4:12

22 For the LORD *is* our judge, the LORD *is* our lawgiver, the LORD *is* our king; he will save us.

23 Thy tacklings are loosed; they could not well strengthen their mast, they could not spread the sail: then is the prey of a great spoil divided; the lame take the prey.

33:24 Mic 7:18, 19; 1 Jn 1:7–9

24 And the inhabitant shall not say, I am sick: the people that dwell therein *shall be* forgiven *their* iniquity.

33:15 The good man speaks what is true and right and does so with honest intention. He does not think one thing and say another. His word can be trusted, and he need not take an oath in the name of God for anyone to trust what he says. He despises ill-gotten gain, accepts no bribe, refuses to hear whatever tends to bloodshed and cruelty, and keeps his eyes from seeing evil.

33:17 While the phrase "the king in his beauty" refers *directly to Hezekiah after the defeat* of the Assyrians, it also intimates the coming Messiah. By the eye of faith we can see the King of kings in his beauty, which is the beauty of holiness, a holiness that becomes ours by grace through the sacrifice of the Savior.

33:20 Isaiah was surely speaking about the deliverance of Judah from the threat presented by Sennacherib. Judah *was* delivered and the city and temple *were* safe—for a time. The day was to come when something would occur which was worse than that threatened by Sennacherib. Jerusalem and the temple were destroyed by Nebuchadnezzar; both were rebuilt only to be destroyed again in A.D. 70. And while Jerusalem has more recently been brought back to a place of magnificence, the temple has never been restored. This passage, then, has a future fulfillment, whether or not Isaiah was aware of it when he wrote these words. Ezekiel prophesied the rebuilding of the temple; that remains to be accomplished. It will happen before the end of this age.

E. GOD'S JUDGMENT AGAINST THE GENTILE NATIONS

1. The Description of the Judgment

34 COME near, ye nations, to hear; and hearken, ye people: let the
earth hear, and all that is therein; the world, and all things that
come forth of it.
[34:1 Deut 32:1]
2 For the indignation of the LORD *is* upon all nations, and *his* fury upon
all their armies: he hath utterly destroyed them, he hath delivered them to
the slaughter.
[☆34:2]
3 Their slain also shall be cast out, and their stink shall come up out of
their carcases, and the mountains shall be melted with their blood.
[34:3 Ezek 35:6]
4 And all the host of heaven shall be dissolved, and the heavens shall be
rolled together as a scroll: and all their host shall fall down, as the leaf
falleth off from the vine, and as a falling *fig* from the fig tree.
[34:4 Joel 2:31; Mt 24:29; 2 Pet 3:10; Rev 6:12–14]

2. The Illustration of Edom

5 For my sword shall be bathed in heaven: behold, it shall come down
upon I-du-me'a, and upon the people of my curse, to judgment.
[34:5 Isa 24:6]
6 The sword of the LORD is filled with blood, it is made fat with fatness,
and with the blood of lambs and goats, with the fat of the kidneys of rams:
for the LORD hath a sacrifice in Boz'rah, and a great slaughter in the land of
I-du-me'a.
[☆34:6 Isa 63:1]
7 And the unicorns shall come down with them, and the bullocks with the
bulls; and their land shall be soaked with blood, and their dust made fat
with fatness.
8 For *it is* the day of the LORD's vengeance, *and* the year of recompences
for the controversy of Zion.
[34:8 Isa 13:6; 63:4]
9 And the streams thereof shall be turned into pitch, and the dust thereof
into brimstone, and the land thereof shall become burning pitch.
10 It shall not be quenched night nor day; the smoke thereof shall go up
for ever: from generation to generation it shall lie waste; none shall pass
through it for ever and ever.
[34:10 Isa 1:31; Ezek 29:11; Mal 1:3, 4; Rev 14:11; 19:3]
11 ¶But the cormorant and the bittern shall possess it; the owl also and the
raven shall dwell in it: and he shall stretch out upon it the line of confusion,
and the stones of emptiness.
[34:11 Lam 2:8]
12 They shall call the nobles thereof to the kingdom, but none *shall be*
there, and all her princes shall be nothing.
13 And thorns shall come up in her palaces, nettles and brambles in the
fortresses thereof: and it shall be an habitation of dragons, *and* a court for
owls.
[☆34:13 Jer 9:11; 10:22]
14 The wild beasts of the desert shall also meet with the wild beasts of the
island, and the satyr shall cry to his fellow; the screech owl also shall rest
there, and find for herself a place of rest.
[34:14 Isa 13:21]

34:2 God is enraged against the nations; they are fatally doomed because they are the enemies of God's people and of the church God has founded.
34:6 God is sometimes pictured for us as a beneficent being who is never angry and who refuses to use the sword to accomplish his purposes. However, both the Old and New Testaments speak of God who executes vengeance and whose sword drips with blood. In the Revelation of St. John, Christ is pictured as having a sharp sword that comes from his mouth. He uses it to smite the nations. His robe is dipped in blood. God has used men and nations in days past to execute judgment, but the time will come when God will directly execute vengeance himself.
34:13 Edom is an example of God's judgment against the nations. That land would become a habitation for poisonous dragons. The place that had been the court for princes would be occupied by owls or ostriches. Such is the verdict of a holy God against unholy nations that spurn his grace and laugh at his laws.

15There shall the great owl make her nest, and lay, and hatch, and gather
under her shadow: there shall the vultures also be gathered, every one with
her mate.
34:16☆ 16¶Seek ye out of the book of the LORD, and read: no one of these shall
Isa 40:5 fail, none shall want her mate: for my mouth it hath commanded, and his
spirit it hath gathered them.
17And he hath cast the lot for them, and his hand hath divided it unto
them by line: they shall possess it for ever, from generation to generation
shall they dwell therein.

F. GOD'S PROMISE TO RESTORE ISRAEL TO ZION

35:1☆ **35** THE wilderness and the solitary place shall be glad for them; and
Isa 41:18, 19 51:3; 55:12, 13 the desert shall rejoice, and blossom as the rose.
35:2☆ 2It shall blossom abundantly, and rejoice even with joy and singing: the
Isa 25:9; 60:13 66:10, 14 glory of Lebanon shall be given unto it, the excellency of Carmel and
Shar'on, they shall see the glory of the LORD, *and* the excellency of our
God.
35:3 3¶Strengthen ye the weak hands, and confirm the feeble knees.
Job 4:3, 4 35:4 4Say to them *that are* of a fearful heart, Be strong, fear not: behold, your
Ps 145:19 Isa 63:4 God will come *with* vengeance, *even* God *with* a recompence; he will come
and save you.
35:5 5Then the eyes of the blind shall be opened, and the ears of the deaf shall
Jn 9:6, 7 be unstopped.
35:6 6Then shall the lame *man* leap as an hart, and the tongue of the dumb
Lk 11:14 Jn 7:38 Acts 3:7, 8 sing: for in the wilderness shall waters break out, and streams in the desert.
35:7 7And the parched ground shall become a pool, and the thirsty land
Mt 7:13, 14 springs of water: in the habitation of dragons, where each lay, *shall be* grass
with reeds and rushes.
8And an highway shall be there, and a way, and it shall be called The way
of holiness; the unclean shall not pass over it; but it *shall be* for those: the
wayfaring men, though fools, shall not err *therein.*
35:9 9No lion shall be there, nor *any* ravenous beast shall go up thereon, it
Isa 51:10 shall not be found there; but the redeemed shall walk *there:*
35:10☆ 10And the ransomed of the LORD shall return, and come to Zion with
Rev 21:4 songs and everlasting joy upon their heads: they shall obtain joy and
gladness, and sorrow and sighing shall flee away.

34:16 *the book of the* LORD. Here is the clearest evidence that God has foretold many things that will happen. Prophetic Scriptures may be compared with the events themselves. This comparison will validate the claim that whatever has been prophesied must, of necessity, take place sooner or later.

35:1, 2 Chapter 34 presented a dark and dreadful picture of confusion, judgment, and dismay. Now Isaiah forecasts what will happen to the wilderness and the dry land in the providence of a forgiving God. There *shall come (1) gladness and rejoicing, (2) a blooming* desert, (3) beauty (after aridity and sterility), (4) glory and majesty, and (5) *the glory of the* LORD.

35:5ff These verses go far beyond what occurred in Hezekiah's flourishing kingdom after the Assyrian threat had disappeared. It looks to a future age not yet come. God will manifest himself through signs and wonders. The blind shall see, the lame shall leap, and the dumb shall talk. Streams shall flow in the desert where they are least expected. Uncleanness shall disappear and holiness prevail. No wild beasts shall disturb this paradise. The redeemed of God who have been ransomed shall be there. They shall come to Zion with joy and gladness and their songs will redound to the Redeemer's praise.

35:10 This prophetic word of Isaiah's has a future reference not yet experienced by the Church; Christ was yet to come when these words were written. There is the promise of a heavenly Zion, the New Jerusalem, the city of God that will not be built by human hands. There is no night there, no sorrow, and no sighing. Joy and gladness prevail.

VI. JUDGMENT DELAYED FOR JERUSALEM (36:1—39:8)

A. JERUSALEM'S DELIVERANCE FROM SENNACHERIB

1. Sennacherib's Challenge

a. The Demand for Judah's Capitulation

36 NOW it came to pass in the fourteenth year of king Hez-e-ki'ah,
that Sen-nach'e-rib king of Assyria came up against all the defenced
cities of Judah, and took them.

☆36:1

2And the king of Assyria sent Rab'sha-keh from La'chish to Jerusalem
unto king Hez-e-ki'ah with a great army. And he stood by the conduit of
the upper pool in the highway of the fuller's field.

☆36:2 2 Kgs 18:17—20:11; 2 Chron 32:9–24

3Then came forth unto him E-li'a-kim, Hil-ki'ah's son, which was over
the house, and Sheb'na the scribe, and Jo'ah, A'saph's son, the recorder.

4¶And Rab'sha-keh said unto them, Say ye now to Hez-e-ki'ah, Thus
saith the great king, the king of Assyria, What confidence *is* this wherein
thou trustest?

36:4 2 Kgs 18:19

5I say, *sayest thou,* (but *they are but* vain words) *I have* counsel and
strength for war: now on whom dost thou trust, that thou rebellest against
me?

36:5 2 Kgs 18:7

6Lo, thou trustest in the staff of this broken reed, on Egypt; whereon if a
man lean, it will go into his hand, and pierce it: so *is* Pharaoh king of Egypt
to all that trust in him.

36:6 Ps 146:3; Ezek 29:6, 7

7But if thou say to me, We trust in the LORD our God: *is it* not he, whose
high places and whose altars Hez-e-ki'ah hath taken away, and said to
Judah and to Jerusalem, Ye shall worship before this altar?

☆36:7 Deut 12:2–5; 2 Kgs 18:4, 5

8Now therefore give pledges, I pray thee, to my master the king of
Assyria, and I will give thee two thousand horses, if thou be able on thy
part to set riders upon them.

36:8 Isa 30:2–5, 7; 31:3

9How then wilt thou turn away the face of one captain of the least of my
master's servants, and put thy trust on Egypt for chariots and for
horsemen?

10And am I now come up without the LORD against this land to destroy
it? the LORD said unto me, Go up against this land, and destroy it.

☆36:10 1 Kgs 13:18

b. The Message to the Common People to Surrender

11¶Then said E-li'a-kim and Sheb'na and Jo'ah unto Rab'sha-keh, Speak,
I pray thee, unto thy servants in the Syrian language; for we understand *it:*
and speak not to us in the Jews' language, in the ears of the people that *are*
on the wall.

☆36:11 Ezra 4:7; Dan 2:4

12¶But Rab'sha-keh said, Hath my master sent me to thy master and to
thee to speak these words? *hath he* not *sent me* to the men that sit upon the
wall, that they may eat their own dung, and drink their own piss with you?

13Then Rab'sha-keh stood, and cried with a loud voice in the Jews'
language, and said, Hear ye the words of the great king, the king of Assyria.

36:13 2 Chron 32:18

36:1 Sennacherib took the fortified cities but not Jerusalem. That effort was about to come and God would intervene on behalf of Zion. 2 Kings 18 should be consulted here.

36:2 *Rabshakeh,* i.e., the chief officer of the Assyrian army.

36:7 Sennacherib's ambassador seeks to undercut King Hezekiah by saying that his religious reforms, in which he destroyed pagan high places and practices, were an insult to the gods, a sacrilege. The implication is that even Judah's God is displeased. Little did he understand true religion.

36:10 Rabshakeh claimed to have been sent by God to take Jerusalem. He was not really *for* God; he was *against* him. Many saints have been killed by those who claim or think they are doing God a service. Sometimes true believers have fallen into this error and have justified actions that God never approved and the Holy Spirit never originated.

36:11 *Speak . . . in the Syrian language,* i.e., "talk to us in Aramaic." Aramaic was the language used in international diplomacy at this time †

36:14 Isa 37:10

14 Thus saith the king, Let not Hez-e-ki'ah deceive you: for he shall not be able to deliver you.

15 Neither let Hez-e-ki'ah make you trust in the LORD, saying, The LORD will surely deliver us: this city shall not be delivered into the hand of the king of Assyria.

36:16☆ Zech 3:10

16 Hearken not to Hez-e-ki'ah: for thus saith the king of Assyria, Make *an agreement* with me *by* a present, and come out to me: and eat ye every one of his vine, and every one of his fig tree, and drink ye every one the waters of his own cistern;

17 Until I come and take you away to a land like your own land, a land of corn and wine, a land of bread and vineyards.

18 *Beware* lest Hez-e-ki'ah persuade you, saying, The LORD will deliver us. Hath any of the gods of the nations delivered his land out of the hand of the king of Assyria?

36:19☆ 2 Kgs 17:6 Isa 10:9–11 37:13 Jer 49:23

19 Where *are* the gods of Ha'math and Ar'phad? where *are* the gods of Seph-ar-va'im? and have they delivered Sa-ma'ri-a out of my hand?

36:20☆ 1 Kgs 20:23, 28

20 Who *are they* among all the gods of these lands, that have delivered their land out of my hand, that the LORD should deliver Jerusalem out of my hand?

21 But they held their peace, and answered him not a word: for the king's commandment was, saying, Answer him not.

22 ¶Then came E-li'a-kim, the son of Hil-ki'ah, that *was* over the household, and Sheb'na the scribe, and Jo'ah, the son of A'saph, the recorder, to Hez-e-ki'ah with their clothes rent, and told him the words of Rab'sha-keh.

2. God's Response to Sennacherib's Demands

a. Hezekiah's Distress

37:1☆ 2 Kgs 19:1–37

37 AND it came to pass, when king Hez-e-ki'ah heard *it,* that he rent his clothes, and covered himself with sackcloth, and went into the house of the LORD.

2 And he sent E-li'a-kim, who *was* over the household, and Sheb'na the scribe, and the elders of the priests covered with sackcloth, unto Isaiah the prophet the son of Amoz.

37:3 Isa 22:5 26:17, 18

3 And they said unto him, Thus saith Hez-e-ki'ah, This day *is* a day of trouble, and of rebuke, and of blasphemy: for the children are come to the birth, and *there is* not strength to bring forth.

37:4☆ Isa 1:9 10:20–22

4 It may be the LORD thy God will hear the words of Rab'sha-keh, whom the king of Assyria his master hath sent to reproach the living God, and will reprove the words which the LORD thy God hath heard: wherefore lift up *thy* prayer for the remnant that is left.

36:16 Rabshakeh's appeal was enticing: capitulate to Assyria and you will be free. You will have all the food and drink you want. This promise of liberty was deceptive, for Judah would be led into the basest captivity and slavery.

36:19, 20 It was quite true that the gods of other nations had not been able to deliver their worshippers from the power of Assyria. What Assyria did not realize was that in this instance they were waging war against *the true God who had delivered* his people on numerous occasions and who could and would deliver them now. But Sennacherib, who has conquered other countries and overcome the gods they worshipped, does not fear the God of Israel. He challenges Israel and their God to keep him from taking the city of Jerusalem. Hezekiah's dilemma provided God's opportunity, for the king had recourse to the mighty power of God by prayer.

37:1 This chapter is the same as 2 Kings 19:1–37. In all probability the Kings' account was taken from the prophecy of Isaiah.

37:4 Hezekiah sent his representatives to Isaiah, seeking his help from the prophet. They represented the king as saying: "It may be that the LORD *thy* God will hear the words of Rabshakeh . . . ." Why did the king not say "The LORD *our* God?" Isaiah's God was the king's God too. One would have expected the monarch to have a better spiritual understanding than he appeared to have.

b. God's Promise of Deliverance

5 So the servants of king Hez-e-ki'ah came to Isaiah.
6 ¶And Isaiah said unto them, Thus shall ye say unto your master, Thus ☆37:6 Isa 7:4; 35:4
saith the LORD, Be not afraid of the words that thou hast heard, wherewith
the servants of the king of Assyria have blasphemed me.
7 Behold, I will send a blast upon him, and he shall hear a rumour, and
return to his own land; and I will cause him to fall by the sword in his own
land.

c. Assyria's Arrogant Attitude

8 ¶So Rab'sha-keh returned, and found the king of Assyria warring 37:8 Isa 20:5
against Lib'nah: for he had heard that he was departed from La'chish.
9 And he heard say concerning Tir'ha-kah king of E-thi-o'pi-a, He is come ☆37:9
forth to make war with thee. And when he heard *it,* he sent messengers to
Hez-e-ki'ah, saying,
10 Thus shall ye speak to Hez-e-ki'ah king of Judah, saying, Let not thy
God, in whom thou trustest, deceive thee, saying, Jerusalem shall not be
given into the hand of the king of Assyria.
11 Behold, thou hast heard what the kings of Assyria have done to all 37:11 Isa 10:9–11
lands by destroying them utterly; and shalt thou be delivered?
12 Have the gods of the nations delivered them which my fathers have 37:12 Gen 11:31 2 Kgs 17:6
destroyed, *as* Go'zan, and Ha'ran, and Re'zeph, and the children of Eden
which *were* in Te-las'sar?
13 Where *is* the king of Ha'math, and the king of Ar'phad, and the king of
the city of Seph-ar-va'im, He'na, and I'vah?

d. Hezekiah's Prayer to God for Help

14 ¶And Hez-e-ki'ah received the letter from the hand of the messengers,
and read it: and Hez-e-ki'ah went up unto the house of the LORD, and
spread it before the LORD.
15 And Hez-e-ki'ah prayed unto the LORD, saying, ☆37:15
16 O LORD of hosts, God of Israel, that dwellest *between* the cherubims, 37:16 Ex 25:22 Ps 17:6; 74:22 80:1; 86:10 Jer 10:12
that *art* the God, *even* thou alone, of all the kingdoms of the earth: thou
hast made heaven and earth.
17 Incline thine ear, O LORD, and hear; open thine eyes, O LORD, and see:
and hear all the words of Sen-nach'e-rib, which hath sent to reproach the
living God.
18 Of a truth, LORD, the kings of Assyria have laid waste all the nations,
and their countries.
19 And have cast their gods into the fire: for they *were* no gods, but the 37:19 Isa 17:8; 26:14
work of men's hands, wood and stone: therefore they have destroyed them.
20 Now therefore, O LORD our God, save us from his hand, that all the 37:20 1 Kgs 18:36, 37 Isa 33:22 Ezek 36:23
kingdoms of the earth may know that thou *art* the LORD, *even* thou only.

37:6 Sennacherib had reviled Hezekiah and in so doing he also reviled the God of Hezekiah. Thus God orders Isaiah to tell Hezekiah's servants that Sennacherib has reviled the Lord of glory through his subordinates who have reflected their king's views.

37:9 *Tirhakah,* known also as Taharkah, was leading an army (probably from the south). He was the next to the last king of the Twenty-fifth (or Ethiopian) Dynasty in Egypt.

37:15 Hezekiah does what he should have done in the first place. He seeks the face of God in prayer, asking for divine help. Even before he received the gladsome word from Isaiah, he should have been praying directly to God.

e. God's Second Response: Sennacherib Will Be Crushed

37:21☆ 21 ¶Then Isaiah the son of Amoz sent unto Hez-e-ki′ah, saying, Thus saith
the LORD God of Israel, Whereas thou hast prayed to me against Sen-
nach′e-rib king of Assyria:
37:22 22 This *is* the word which the LORD hath spoken concerning him; The
Lam 2:13 Zeph 3:14 virgin, the daughter of Zion, hath despised thee, *and* laughed thee to scorn;
the daughter of Jerusalem hath shaken her head at thee.
37:23☆ 23 Whom hast thou reproached and blasphemed? and against whom hast
Isa 5:15, 21 Ezek 39:7 thou exalted *thy* voice, and lifted up thine eyes on high? *even* against the
Hab 1:12 Holy One of Israel.
37:24 24 By thy servants hast thou reproached the Lord, and hast said, By the
Isa 14:8 multitude of my chariots am I come up to the height of the mountains, to
the sides of Lebanon; and I will cut down the tall cedars thereof, *and* the
choice fir trees thereof: and I will enter into the height of his border, *and* the
forest of his Carmel.
25 I have digged, and drunk water; and with the sole of my feet have I
dried up all the rivers of the besieged places.
37:26 26 Hast thou not heard long ago, *how* I have done it; *and* of ancient times,
Isa 25:2 Acts 2:23 that I have formed it? now have I brought it to pass, that thou shouldest be
4:27, 28 to lay waste defenced cities *into* ruinous heaps.
37:27 27 Therefore their inhabitants *were* of small power, they were dismayed
Ps 129:6 Isa 40:7 and confounded: they were *as* the grass of the field, and *as* the green herb,
as the grass on the housetops, and *as corn* blasted before it be grown up.
37:28☆ 28 But I know thy abode, and thy going out, and thy coming in, and thy
Ps 139:1 rage against me.
37:29☆ 29 Because thy rage against me, and thy tumult, is come up into mine ears,
Isa 30:28 Ezek 38:4 therefore will I put my hook in thy nose, and my bridle in thy lips, and I
will turn thee back by the way by which thou camest.
37:30☆ 30 And this *shall be* a sign unto thee, Ye shall eat *this* year such as groweth
Lev 25:5, 11 of itself; and the second year that which springeth of the same: and in the
third year sow ye, and reap, and plant vineyards, and eat the fruit thereof.
37:31 31 And the remnant that is escaped of the house of Judah shall again take
Isa 10:20; 27:36 root downward, and bear fruit upward:
37:32 32 For out of Jerusalem shall go forth a remnant, and they that escape out
2 Kgs 19:31 of mount Zion: the zeal of the LORD of hosts shall do this.
33 Therefore thus saith the LORD concerning the king of Assyria, He shall
not come into this city, nor shoot an arrow there, nor come before it with
shields, nor cast a bank against it.
34 By the way that he came, by the same shall he return, and shall not
come into this city, saith the LORD.
37:35 35 For I will defend this city to save it for mine own sake, and for my
2 Kgs 20:6 Isa 48:9, 11 servant David's sake.

37:21 *Whereas thou hast prayed to me.* Had Hezekiah not prayed, God would not have answered. We learn how valuable prayer is and what power is released when we pray. The Scriptures are filled with illustrations of the value of prayer; this should encourage every believer's heart today, for the God of Hezekiah is the God of every believer today.

37:23 God's people may not be perfect, but when scorners attack his people, it constitutes an attack against himself. God himself said that Sennacherib mocked and reviled him. He haughtily raised his voice and lifted his eyes against the holy God of the universe. Therefore he had to be dealt with.

37:28, 29 God knew Sennacherib's every thought and design. He regarded the arrogance of this tyrant as directed against himself. So God put the divine hook in his nose and his bridle in his lips. He did it so quickly that Sennacherib had no time to shoot a single arrow over the city walls, or to gather his troops before its gate, or build a mound for his soldiers to enter the city over the walls. Sennacherib came, saw, and was conquered by God.

37:30 *in the third year sow ye, and reap,* i.e., "two years from now you will be living in luxury again."† The third harvest from then would yield a bumper crop.

f. The Fulfillment of God's Promise

[36]Then the angel of the LORD went forth, and smote in the camp of the Assyrians a hundred and fourscore and five thousand: and when they arose early in the morning, behold, they *were* all dead corpses.

[37]¶So Sen-nach'e-rib king of Assyria departed, and went and returned, and dwelt at Nin'e-veh.

[38]And it came to pass, as he was worshipping in the house of Nis'roch his god, that A-dram'me-lech and Sha-re'zer his sons smote him with the sword; and they escaped into the land of Ar-me'ni-a: and E'sar-had'don his son reigned in his stead.

37:36 2 Kgs 19:35; Isa 10:12, 33, 34
☆**37:37** Gen 10:11; Jonah 3:3; Zeph 2:13
37:38 Gen 8:4

B. HEZEKIAH'S ILLNESS AND HEALING

1. Hezekiah's Prayer and God's Response

38 IN those days was Hez-e-ki'ah sick unto death. And Isaiah the prophet the son of Amoz came unto him, and said unto him, Thus saith the LORD, Set thine house in order: for thou shalt die, and not live.

[2]Then Hez-e-ki'ah turned his face toward the wall, and prayed unto the LORD,

[3]And said, Remember now, O LORD, I beseech thee, how I have walked before thee in truth and with a perfect heart, and have done *that which is* good in thy sight. And Hez-e-ki'ah wept sore.

[4]¶Then came the word of the LORD to Isaiah, saying,

[5]Go, and say to Hez-e-ki'ah, Thus saith the LORD, the God of David thy father, I have heard thy prayer, I have seen thy tears: behold, I will add unto thy days fifteen years.

[6]And I will deliver thee and this city out of the hand of the king of Assyria: and I will defend this city.

[7]And this *shall be* a sign unto thee from the LORD, that the LORD will do this thing that he hath spoken;

[8]Behold, I will bring again the shadow of the degrees, which is gone down in the sun dial of Ahaz, ten degrees backward. So the sun returned ten degrees, by which degrees it was gone down.

☆**38:1** 2 Kgs 20:1–6
☆**38:2**
38:3 2 Kgs 18:5, 6; Neh 13:14; Ps 6:6–8
38:5 2 Kgs 18:2, 13
38:6 Isa 31:5
☆**38:7** Isa 7:11, 14
38:8 2 Kgs 20:9–11

2. Hezekiah's Poem of Praise

[9]¶The writing of Hez-e-ki'ah king of Judah, when he had been sick, and was recovered of his sickness:

☆**38:9**

37:37 Sennacherib fled home in shame, leaving his dead troops behind him. His highest expectations had been dashed, and fear filled his heart that the angel who destroyed his army might also destroy him. But the worst was yet to come: Sennacherib's own sons, who should have been guarding their father, slew him as he worshipped before Nisroch (whose protection he *sought but whose* "power" could not keep him safe from his own children).

38:1 See note on 2 Kings 20:1 for information about this incident.

38:2 This incident reminds us of Israel in the wilderness when they demanded meat—which was not according to the will of God. The Psalmist says, "He gave them their request; but sent leanness into their soul." So here Hezekiah should have accepted the will of God. With tears and many prayers he pleaded for an extension of his life. He got what he wanted, but the cost was high. Manasseh was born, succeeded to the throne, and became a bad king.

38:7 Nowhere else in the Scriptures is it stated that anyone should have a certain number of years to live. In Hezekiah's case the promise of God was confirmed to the king by a miracle. "The sign was the going back of the shadow upon the sun-dial. The sun is a faithful measurer of time, and *rejoices as a strong man to run a race;* but he that set that clock a going can set it back when he pleases, and make it return; for the Father of all lights is the director of them."*

38:9 Beginning here we read Hezekiah's thanksgiving-song. He might have used some of the Psalms written by David, but he preferred to devise his own. He wished to express his love and devotion to God, stating them not in the words of others but with his own words. He put it in writing that he might return to it from time to time by way of remembrance. Unfortunately we are told that "Hezekiah gave no return for the benefit he received" (2 Chron. 32:25). "Thanksgiving is good, but thanksliving is better."*

38:10 Ps 102:24
10 I said in the cutting off of my days, I shall go to the gates of the grave:
I am deprived of the residue of my years.

38:11 Ps 27:13
11 I said, I shall not see the LORD, *even* the LORD, in the land of the living:
I shall behold man no more with the inhabitants of the world.

38:12 Job 4:20; 2 Cor 5:1
12 Mine age is departed, and is removed from me as a shepherd's tent: I
have cut off like a weaver my life: he will cut me off with pining sickness:
from day *even* to night wilt thou make an end of me.
13 I reckoned till morning, *that,* as a lion, so will he break all my bones:
from day *even* to night wilt thou make an end of me.

38:14 Ps 119:123; Ezek 7:16
14 Like a crane *or* a swallow, so did I chatter: I did mourn as a dove: mine
eyes fail *with looking* upward: O LORD, I am oppressed; undertake for me.

38:15 Job 7:11
15 What shall I say? he hath both spoken unto me, and himself hath done
it: I shall go softly all my years in the bitterness of my soul.

38:16 Ps 39:13; 119:71, 75
16 O Lord, by these *things men* live, and in all these *things is* the life of my
spirit: so wilt thou recover me, and make me to live.

38:17☆ Isa 43:25; Jer 31:34; Jonah 2:6
17 Behold, for peace I had great bitterness: but thou hast in love to my
soul *delivered it* from the pit of corruption: for thou hast cast all my sins
behind thy back.

38:18☆ Ps 6:5
18 For the grave cannot praise thee, death can *not* celebrate thee: they that
go down into the pit cannot hope for thy truth.

38:19 Ps 78:5–7; 119:175
19 The living, the living, he shall praise thee, as I *do* this day: the father to
the children shall make known thy truth.

38:20 Ps 33:1–3; 116:17–19; 146:2
20 The LORD *was ready* to save me: therefore we will sing my songs to the
stringed instruments all the days of our life in the house of the LORD.
21 For Isaiah had said, Let them take a lump of figs, and lay *it* for a
plaister upon the boil, and he shall recover.
22 Hez-e-ki'ah also had said, What *is* the sign that I shall go up to the
house of the LORD?

C. HEZEKIAH'S GREAT MISTAKE
1. The Display of His Riches

39:1☆ 2 Kgs 20:12–19
39 AT that time Me-ro'dach-bal'a-dan, the son of Bal'a-dan, king of
Babylon, sent letters and a present to Hez-e-ki'ah: for he had heard
that he had been sick, and was recovered.

39:2 2 Kgs 18:15, 16; 2 Chron 32:25, 31
2 And Hez-e-ki'ah was glad of them, and shewed them the house of his
precious things, the silver, and the gold, and the spices, and the precious
ointment, and all the house of his armour, and all that was found in his
treasures: there was nothing in his house, nor in all his dominion, that Hez-
e-ki'ah, shewed them not.

39:3 Jer 5:15
3 ¶Then came Isaiah the prophet unto king Hez-e-ki'ah, and said unto
him, What said these men? and from whence came they unto thee? And
Hez-e-ki'ah said, They are come from a far country unto me, *even* from
Babylon.

38:17 When we cast our sins behind our backs, God remembers them and we smart because of them. But when we repent honestly and acknowledge our transgressions, God pardons us and casts our sins behind his back and remembers them no more. "The pardon does not make the sin not to have been, or not to have *been sin, but not to be punished as it deserves.*"*

38:18 *For the grave cannot praise thee.* The meaning is unclear. Perhaps Hezekiah was unaware of the blessedness of the future life for those who trust in God (57:1, 2). Or perhaps his meaning is, "Dead bodies cannot praise you."†

39:1 *Merodach-baladan,* the Babylonian king, reigned from 721–710 B.C., and also for about nine months in 703 B.C. Under the rule of Sargon II, the Assyrian king, he entered Babylon and made himself king. In 710 B.C. Sargon swept into Babylon and was not opposed by Merodach-baladan to the day of his death. When Sargon died, Merodach-baladan revolted again in 703 B.C. and remained king until Sennacherib defeated him and his rebels, at which time Merodach-baladan retreated to his homeland. He died in Elam, and was known as a smart and ambitious ruler.

4Then said he, What have they seen in thine house? And Hez-e-ki′ah
answered, All that *is* in mine house have they seen: there is nothing among
my treasures that I have not shewed them.

2. God's Message of Doom, but Peace in Hezekiah's Time

5Then said Isaiah to Hez-e-ki′ah, Hear the word of the LORD of hosts:
6Behold, the days come, that all that *is* in thine house, and *that* which thy
fathers have laid up in store until this day, shall be carried to Babylon:
nothing shall be left, saith the LORD.
7And of thy sons that shall issue from thee, which thou shalt beget, shall
they take away; and they shall be eunuchs in the palace of the king of
Babylon.
8Then said Hez-e-ki′ah to Isaiah, Good *is* the word of the LORD which
thou hast spoken. He said moreover, For there shall be peace and truth in
my days.

☆39:6 2 Kgs 24:13 Jer 20:5
39:8 2 Chron 34:28

VII. GOD'S ASSURANCE OF ISRAEL'S FUTURE DELIVERANCES (40:1—56:8)

A. THE LORD, THE COMFORTER

1. God's Messenger to Come

40 COMFORT ye, comfort ye my people, saith your God.
2Speak ye comfortably to Jerusalem, and cry unto her, that her
warfare is accomplished, that her iniquity is pardoned: for she hath
received of the LORD's hand double for all her sins.
3¶The voice of him that crieth in the wilderness, Prepare ye the way of
the LORD, make straight in the desert a highway for our God.
4Every valley shall be exalted, and every mountain and hill shall be made
low: and the crooked shall be made straight, and the rough places plain:
5And the glory of the LORD shall be revealed, and all flesh shall see *it*
together: for the mouth of the LORD hath spoken *it*.
6The voice said, Cry. And he said, What shall I cry? All flesh *is* grass, and
all the goodliness thereof *is* as the flower of the field:
7The grass withereth, the flower fadeth: because the spirit of the LORD
bloweth upon it: surely the people *is* grass.
8The grass withereth, the flower fadeth: but the word of our God shall
stand for ever.
9¶O Zion, that bringest good tidings, get thee up into the high mountain;
O Jerusalem, that bringest good tidings, lift up thy voice with strength; lift
it up, be not afraid; say unto the cities of Judah, Behold your God!
10Behold, the Lord GOD will come with strong *hand*, and his arm shall
rule for him: behold, his reward *is* with him, and his work before him.

☆40:1 Isa 49:13 2 Cor 1:4
40:2 Isa 53:5, 6, 11 Zech 9:12
☆40:3 Mal 3:1 Mt 3:3
40:4 Ezek 17:24
40:5 Hab 2:14
40:6 Job 14:2
40:7 Jas 1:10, 11
☆40:8 Mt 5:18
40:10 Isa 59:16 Rev 22:12

39:6ff God was angry with Hezekiah because of the *pride of his heart.* The message was designed to mortify the king, convince him of his foolishness, and take from him the very things he had been proud to display to the Babylonians. God graciously suspended the fulfillment of the prophetic word until after Hezekiah's death. The king was grateful, and yet he recognized the rightness of God's judgment.

40:1 Chapters 40—66 were written later in Isaiah's life; they are predictive prophecy. Liberal scholars believe that these chapters were written by one or more prophets *after* the events took place rather than before. Since many of these prophecies relate to the end of the age, it is difficult, if not impossible, to argue successfully for such views.

40:3 The alarm given here by Isaiah is picked up in the New Testament and applied to John the Baptist, who was called by God to prepare the way for the Messiah. He preached repentance to all Judah and Jerusalem and thus "made ready a people prepared for the Lord" (Luke 1:17).

40:8 Whatever God says is of eternal value and can neither be untrue or left undone. All of the Bible is the Word of God and will stand forever. This word can do for us what we cannot do for ourselves. Its perpetuity is the surest guarantee of our eternity and of our happiness as well. The things that are not seen but must be believed are eternal.

40:11☆ Ezek 34:12–14, 23, 31; Jn 10:11, 14–16

11 He shall feed his flock like a shepherd: he shall gather the lambs with
his arm, and carry *them* in his bosom, *and* shall gently lead those that are
with young.

2. God's Mighty Power

40:12 Isa 48:13

12 ¶Who hath measured the waters in the hollow of his hand, and meted
out heaven with the span, and comprehended the dust of the earth in a
measure, and weighed the mountains in scales, and the hills in a balance?

40:13☆ Rom 11:34

13 Who hath directed the Spirit of the LORD, or *being* his counsellor hath
taught him?

40:14 Col 2:3

14 With whom took he counsel, and *who* instructed him, and taught him in
the path of judgment, and taught him knowledge, and shewed to him the
way of understanding?

40:15 Isa 17:13

15 Behold, the nations *are* as a drop of a bucket, and are counted as the
small dust of the balance: behold, he taketh up the isles as a very little
thing.

16 And Lebanon *is* not sufficient to burn, nor the beasts thereof sufficient
for a burnt offering.

40:17 Isa 29:7

17 All nations before him *are* as nothing; and they are counted to him less
than nothing, and vanity.

3. Idols and the Living God Compared

40:18 Ex 8:10; Isa 46:5; Mic 7:18

18 ¶To whom then will ye liken God? or what likeness will ye compare
unto him?

40:19 Ps 115:4–8; Hab 2:18, 19

19 The workman melteth a graven image, and the goldsmith spreadeth it
over with gold, and casteth silver chains.

40:20 Isa 46:7

20 He that *is* so impoverished that he hath no oblation chooseth a tree *that*
will not rot; he seeketh unto him a cunning workman to prepare a graven
image, *that* shall not be moved.

40:21☆ Isa 51:13; Rom 1:19

21 Have ye not known? have ye not heard? hath it not been told you from
the beginning? have ye not understood from the foundations of the earth?

40:22 Ps 104:2

22 *It is* he that sitteth upon the circle of the earth, and the inhabitants
thereof *are* as grasshoppers; that stretcheth out the heavens as a curtain,
and spreadeth them out as a tent to dwell in:

40:23 Ps 107:40; Jer 25:18–27

23 That bringeth the princes to nothing; he maketh the judges of the earth
as vanity.

40:24 Isa 17:13

24 Yea, they shall not be planted; yea, they shall not be sown: yea, their
stock shall not take root in the earth: and he shall also blow upon them,
and they shall wither, and the whirlwind shall take them away as stubble.

40:11 Isaiah's description of the good shepherd applies in type to Jesus (see also Gen. 49:24; Ezek. 34:23; 37:24). In the New Testament, Jesus, although a carpenter and never a shepherd who kept sheep, is called: (1) the good shepherd who gives his life for the sheep (John 10:11, 14); (2) the great shepherd who is making the sheep like himself (Heb. 13:20; Mic. 5:4); (3) the chief Shepherd who will reward his people in glory (1 Pet. 5:4).

40:13 The wisdom of the triune God is unsearchable. No one can give either information or direction to *wisdom that belongs to God alone*. "As none can do what God has done and does, so none can assist him in the doing of it or suggest anything to him which he thought not of."*

40:21 Christians begin with God or Spirit as the ultimate reality. All other things are created by him, including matter. Marxists begin with matter and deny spirit. They are materialists. The passage here supposes that all men either know by nature that there is a God or they have been taught by their fathers. This great God has command over all his creation. He sits above the circle of the earth (implying that it is round or circular) and all animals and men are as grasshoppers to him. The heavens do not collapse. They are stretched out and kept stretched by him. Princes and judges who exercise authority and have magisterial might in their hands are controlled by God. He humbles them, tames them, and makes them as vanity (40:23, 24). All men need to do is glance into the sky at night and remember that God knows each star by its own name. How much more then does he know each one of us and particularly those who belong to him by faith in his Son.

[25]To whom then will ye liken me, or shall I be equal? saith the Holy One.
[26]Lift up your eyes on high, and behold who hath created these *things,* **40:26** Ps 147:4 Isa 42:5
that bringeth out their host by number: he calleth them all by names by the
greatness of his might, for that *he is* strong in power; not one faileth.

4. God's Faithfulness and Empowerment

[27]Why sayest thou, O Jacob, and speakest, O Israel, My way is hid from **40:27** Job 34:5, 6 Isa 54:8
the LORD, and my judgment is passed over from my God?
[28]¶Hast thou not known? hast thou not heard, *that* the everlasting God, ☆**40:28** Ps 90:2; 147:5
the LORD, the Creator of the ends of the earth, fainteth not, neither is
weary? *there is* no searching of his understanding.
[29]He giveth power to the faint; and to *them that have* no might he **40:29** Jer 31:25
increaseth strength.
[30]Even the youths shall faint and be weary, and the young men shall **40:30** Jer 9:21
utterly fall:
[31]But they that wait upon the LORD shall renew their strength; they shall **40:31** 2 Cor 4:8–10, 16 Heb 12:3
mount up with wings as eagles; they shall run, and not be weary; *and* they
shall walk, and not faint.

B. ISRAEL, THE CHOSEN SERVANT OF GOD

1. The Sovereignty of God over the Nations

41 KEEP silence before me, O islands; and let the people renew their ☆**41:1** Hab 2:20
strength: let them come near; then let them speak: let us come near
together to judgment.
[2]Who raised up the righteous *man* from the east, called him to his foot, ☆**41:2** 2 Chron 36:23 Isa 46:11
gave the nations before him, and made *him* rule over kings? he gave *them* as
the dust to his sword, *and* as driven stubble to his bow.
[3]He pursued them, *and* passed safely; *even* by the way *that* he had not
gone with his feet.
[4]Who hath wrought and done *it,* calling the generations from the ☆**41:4** Isa 44:7; 48:12 Rev 1:8, 17, 18
beginning? I the LORD, the first, and with the last; I *am* he.
[5]The isles saw *it,* and feared; the ends of the earth were afraid, drew near, **41:5** Josh 5:1 Ezek 26:15, 16
and came.
[6]They helped every one his neighbour; and *every one* said to his brother, **41:6** Joel 3:9–11
Be of good courage.
[7]So the carpenter encouraged the goldsmith, *and* he that smootheth with ☆**41:7**
the hammer him that smote the anvil, saying, It *is* ready for the sodering:
and he fastened it with nails, *that* it should not be moved.

2. Israel Is the Object of His Sovereign Choice

[8]But thou, Israel, *art* my servant, Jacob whom I have chosen, the seed of **41:8** Isa 51:2 Jas 2:23
Abraham my friend.

40:28 *God is almighty.* He is everlasting and exists from eternity to eternity. He created the earth from end to end. His understanding cannot be plumbed or its depth discovered by finite men. This God is the helper of his people. He gives strength to the faint and powerless (40:29). He helps those who best help themselves by reliance on him. When we wait on him, we get new strength so that we can soar through life like eagles. We walk and run through life toward heaven as the athlete who heads for the tape. Those who aspire to heaven shall neither be weary nor faint.
41:1 The providence of God is dynamically related to the omnipotence of God. (For a note on the meaning of the term "providence" see Prov 16:33.)
41:2 *the man from the east.* Doubtless Cyrus the Great of Persia. (See 44:28.)†
41:4 God is the first and the last. He is the alpha and the omega. This is picked up in the Revelation of St. John and applied to Jesus, who, like the Father and the Spirit, is from eternity to eternity.
41:7 Few people in the modern civilized world make graven images. Rather, they either substitute atheism (which is even worse than the worship of false gods) or secularism, by which they exalt man to the role and position of God as master of his own fate or the captain of his soul.

41:9☆ Deut 7:6 Isa 11:11

9 *Thou* whom I have taken from the ends of the earth, and called thee
from the chief men thereof, and said unto thee, Thou *art* my servant; I have
chosen thee, and not cast thee away.

41:10☆ Deut 31:6 Ps 89:13 Rom 8:31

10 ¶Fear thou not; for I *am* with thee: be not dismayed; for I *am* thy God:
I will strengthen thee; yea, I will help thee; yea, I will uphold thee with the
right hand of my righteousness.

3. God Will Give Israel the Victory

41:11☆ Isa 29:5, 7, 8

11 Behold, all they that were incensed against thee shall be ashamed and
confounded: they shall be as nothing; and they that strive with thee shall
perish.

41:12 Job 20:7–9

12 Thou shalt seek them, and shalt not find them, *even* them that
contended with thee: they that war against thee shall be as nothing, and as
a thing of nought.

41:13 Isa 45:1

13 For I the LORD thy God will hold thy right hand, saying unto thee,
Fear not; I will help thee.

41:14☆ Isa 43:14

14 Fear not, thou worm Jacob, *and* ye men of Israel; I will help thee, saith
the LORD, and thy redeemer, the Holy One of Israel.

41:15 Mic 4:13

15 Behold, I will make thee a new sharp threshing instrument having
teeth: thou shalt thresh the mountains, and beat *them* small, and shalt make
the hills as chaff.

41:16 Isa 35:10

16 Thou shalt fan them, and the wind shall carry them away, and the
whirlwind shall scatter them: and thou shalt rejoice in the LORD, *and* shalt
glory in the Holy One of Israel.

4. God Will Bless and Prosper His People

41:17☆ Isa 30:19 42:16; 44:3

17 *When* the poor and needy seek water, and *there is* none, *and* their
tongue faileth for thirst, I the LORD will hear them, I the God of Israel will
not forsake them.

41:18 Ps 107:35 Isa 30:25

18 I will open rivers in high places, and fountains in the midst of the
valleys: I will make the wilderness a pool of water, and the dry land springs
of water.

41:19 Isa 55:13

19 I will plant in the wilderness the cedar, the shittah tree, and the myrtle,
and the oil tree; I will set in the desert the fir tree, *and* the pine, and the box
tree together:

41:20 Job 12:7–9

20 That they may see, and know, and consider, and understand together,
that the hand of the LORD hath done this, and the Holy One of Israel hath
created it.

5. God Is the One Who Prophesies the Future

21 Produce your cause, saith the LORD; bring forth your strong *reasons,*
saith the King of Jacob.

41:9 Israel is the servant of God. Through it came the Messiah; to it was given the revelation of God, the Old Testament; to it was entrusted the task of preserving that revelation; and to it was given the vision of taking that word to the ends of the earth for the salvation of men. In Abraham shall all the nations of the world be blessed (Gen. 12:3). This is the first statement of the *great commission.*

41:10 *with the right hand of my righteousness,* i.e., "with my victorious right hand."†

41:11 God's people always have been, and always will be, surrounded by enemies. God commands his people to fight the good fight with the promise of victory over their foes. But there is no relief from this warfare until death.

41:14 *thou worm Jacob* is really a term of compassion and love. Anyone can trample the worm on the ground. God will assist his helpless worm, Jacob-Israel, and he will also assist all believers who, like Jacob, are worms in need of divine help.

41:17ff These verses speak of the strange and surprising things God does. They are designed to inform God's people of his favor and power and to assure them that nothing happens without his knowledge and nothing can take place that he cannot control or direct.

22 Let them bring *them* forth, and shew us what shall happen: let them
shew the former things, what they *be*, that we may consider them, and know
the latter end of them; or declare us things for to come.

41:22 Isa 43:9; 45:21

23 Shew the things that are to come hereafter, that we may know that ye
are gods: yea, do good, or do evil, that we may be dismayed, and behold *it*
together.

41:23 Jer 10:5 Jn 13:19

24 Behold, ye *are* of nothing, and your work of nought: an abomination *is*
he that chooseth you.

41:24 1 Cor 8:4

25 I have raised up *one* from the north, and he shall come: from the rising
of the sun shall he call upon my name: and he shall come upon princes as
upon morter, and as the potter treadeth clay.

41:25 Jer 50:3 Mic 7:10

26 Who hath declared from the beginning, that we may know? and
beforetime, that we may say, *He is* righteous? yea, *there is* none that
sheweth, yea, *there is* none that declareth, yea, *there is* none that heareth
your words.

☆**41:26** Isa 44:7

27 The first *shall say* to Zion, Behold, behold them: and I will give to
Jerusalem one that bringeth good tidings.

41:27 Isa 40:9

28 For I beheld, and *there was* no man; even among them, and *there was*
no counsellor, that, when I asked of them, could answer a word.

41:28 Isa 63:5

29 Behold, they *are* all vanity; their works *are* nothing: their molten
images *are* wind and confusion.

41:29 Jer 5:13

C. GOD'S SERVANTS: THE IDEAL AND THE SINFUL

1. The Mission of the Servant

42 BEHOLD my servant, whom I uphold; mine elect, *in whom* my soul
delighteth; I have put my spirit upon him: he shall bring forth
judgment to the Gentiles.

☆**42:1** Isa 11:2; 53:11 Mt 3:17 12:18–21

2 He shall not cry, nor lift up, nor cause his voice to be heard in the street.
3 A bruised reed shall he not break, and the smoking flax shall he not
quench: he shall bring forth judgment unto truth.

42:3 Ps 72:2, 4

4 He shall not fail nor be discouraged, till he have set judgment in the
earth: and the isles shall wait for his law.

42:4 Isa 24:15; 66:19

2. The Servant, a Light to Guide the Nations to God

5 ¶Thus saith God the LORD, he that created the heavens, and stretched
them out; he that spread forth the earth, and that which cometh out of it;
he that giveth breath unto the people upon it, and spirit to them that walk
therein:

42:5 Job 33:4 Ps 104:2 Isa 45:18

6 I the LORD have called thee in righteousness, and will hold thine hand,

☆**42:6** Jer 23:5, 6 Lk 2:32

41:26 No idol can predict the future. God has declared in advance many events, and the fulfillment of his prophetic word establishes his omniscience as well as his power to fulfill what he has declared will be.

42:1 *Behold my servant.* Not Cyrus, as in chapter 41, but Christ. This prophetic word has two applications. The first relates to Israel as the servant of God. The second and more important is its reference to Jesus Christ, as Matt. 12:18–20 expressly states. Jesus is the servant of the Father. He was elected by the Father and made his covenant of redemption with the Father. The Father had confidence in his Son that he would execute his mission on Calvary and make atonement for the sins of men. The Father delights in his Son and supports him in his office as mediator. The Father gave the Son the Holy Spirit without measure. As in the life and ministry of Jesus, so in the lives of all of God's people, the fullness of the Holy Spirit is of the greatest significance and importance. The greatest leaders of the Old Testament were Spirit-filled. So were the early apostles. And so ought we to be filled with the Spirit.

42:6 *give thee for a covenant of the people,* i.e., "I have given you to my people as the personal confirmation of my covenant with them."† Since the Father has given us Christ, so has he also given us all of the covenantal blessings that attend the work of the mediator. This Christ is a light to open the eyes of the Gentiles. Thus Jesus is the cosmic Christ, the man for all seasons and for all people. He is more than redeemer for Israel. The Gospel is for the Gentiles as well. Redemption is liberty to the captives, that is, to those who sit in darkness and under the shadow of death for their sins. Christ brings us the prisoners from the prisonhouse into freedom and liberty, delivered from the law and set free to follow Christ the Lord.

and will keep thee, and give thee for a covenant of the people, for a light of the Gentiles;

42:7 Isa 35:5; 61:1 — 7To open the blind eyes, to bring out the prisoners from the prison, *and* them that sit in darkness out of the prison house.

42:8 Ex 3:15; 20:3–5 — 8I am the LORD: that *is* my name: and my glory will I not give to another, neither my praise to graven images.

9Behold, the former things are come to pass, and new things do I declare: before they spring forth I tell you of them.

3. The New Song to the Lord

42:10 Ps 33:3 — 10¶Sing unto the LORD a new song, *and* his praise from the end of the earth, ye that go down to the sea, and all that is therein; the isles, and the inhabitants thereof.

42:11☆ — 11Let the wilderness and the cities thereof lift up *their voice,* the villages *that* Ke′dar doth inhabit: let the inhabitants of the rock sing, let them shout from the top of the mountains.

42:12☆ — 12Let them give glory unto the LORD, and declare his praise in the islands.

4. God Will Not Forsake Israel: Idolaters Will Be Turned Away

42:13 Isa 59:17; 66:14–16 — 13The LORD shall go forth as a mighty man, he shall stir up jealousy like a man of war: he shall cry, yea, roar; he shall prevail against his enemies.

14I have long time holden my peace; I have been still, *and* refrained myself: *now* will I cry like a travailing woman; I will destroy and devour at once.

42:15 Ezek 38:19, 20; Nah 1:4–6 — 15I will make waste mountains and hills, and dry up all their herbs; and I will make the rivers islands, and I will dry up the pools.

42:16☆ Ps 94:14; Isa 40:4; Lk 1:78, 79; Eph 5:8 — 16And I will bring the blind by a way *that* they knew not; I will lead them in paths *that* they have not known: I will make darkness light before them, and crooked things straight. These things will I do unto them, and not forsake them.

42:17 Ps 97:7; Isa 44:9, 11 — 17¶They shall be turned back, they shall be greatly ashamed, that trust in graven images, that say to the molten images, Ye *are* our gods.

5. The Servant Nation: Blind and Deaf

42:18 Isa 35:5 — 18Hear, ye deaf; and look, ye blind, that ye may see.

42:19☆ Isa 44:26 — 19Who *is* blind, but my servant? or deaf, as my messenger *that* I sent? who *is* blind as *he that is* perfect, and blind as the LORD's servant?

42:20 Jer 6:10 — 20Seeing many things, but thou observest not; opening the ears, but he heareth not.

21The LORD is well pleased for his righteousness' sake; he will magnify the law, and make *it* honourable.

42:22☆ Isa 24:18 — 22But this *is* a people robbed and spoiled; *they are* all of them snared in holes, and they are hid in prison houses: they are for a prey, and none delivereth; for a spoil, and none saith, Restore.

42:11 *the cities thereof.* These cities were occupied by nomads of the Syrian desert. They would observe how God would be glorified when he returned his people *from exile.*

42:12 Whoever is joined to the church by faith should give glory to the God who has redeemed him. The chief end of man is to glorify God and to enjoy him forever.

42:16 The unconverted are blind; salvation brings sight and light and life. Then and only then, are the crooked things made straight, the way made plain, and the yoke made easy.

42:19 God had called Israel to be his messenger, but that select nation had become scandalously blind and deaf. They were obstinate and unbelieving, but God's purposes would still not be thwarted.

42:22 What happened to Israel demonstrated to the world the glory of God's law, which was executed even against his elect nation when it became apostate.

23Who among you will give ear to this? *who* will hearken and hear for the
time to come?
24Who gave Jacob for a spoil, and Israel to the robbers? did not the
LORD, he against whom we have sinned? for they would not walk in his
ways, neither were they obedient unto his law.
25Therefore he hath poured upon him the fury of his anger, and the
strength of battle: and it hath set him on fire round about, yet he knew not;
and it burned him, yet he laid *it* not to heart.

42:24 Isa 10:5; 48:18
42:25 Isa 5:25

D. THE RETURN FROM THE BABYLONIAN CAPTIVITY
1. God's Grace and Israel's Redemption
a. God Has Ransomed His People

43 BUT now thus saith the LORD that created thee, O Jacob, and he
that formed thee, O Israel, Fear not: for I have redeemed thee, I
have called *thee* by thy name; thou *art* mine.
2When thou passest through the waters, I *will be* with thee; and through
the rivers, they shall not overflow thee: when thou walkest through the fire,
thou shalt not be burned; neither shall the flame kindle upon thee.
3For I *am* the LORD thy God, the Holy One of Israel, thy Saviour: I gave
Egypt *for* thy ransom, E-thi-o'pi-a and Se'ba for thee.
4Since thou wast precious in my sight, thou hast been honourable, and I
have loved thee: therefore will I give men for thee, and people for thy life.
5Fear not: for I *am* with thee: I will bring thy seed from the east, and
gather thee from the west;
6I will say to the north, Give up; and to the south, Keep not back: bring
my sons from far, and my daughters from the ends of the earth;
7*Even* every one that is called by my name: for I have created him for my
glory, I have formed him; yea, I have made him.
8¶Bring forth the blind people that have eyes, and the deaf that have ears.

☆43:1 Isa 44:2, 21, 22, 23, 24; 45:3, 4
43:2 Deut 31:6, 8; Isa 8:7, 8; Dan 3:25, 27
☆43:3
43:4 Isa 63:9
43:5 Isa 49:12; Jer 30:10, 11
43:6 Ps 107:3; 2 Cor 6:17, 18
☆43:7 Ps 100:3; Isa 46:13; Eph 2:10
43:8 Ezek 12:2

b. Israel, a Witness to the World

9Let all the nations be gathered together, and let the people be
assembled: who among them can declare this, and shew us former things?
let them bring forth their witnesses, that they may be justified: or let them
hear, and say, *It is* truth.
10Ye *are* my witnesses, saith the LORD, and my servant whom I have
chosen; that ye may know and believe me, and understand that I *am* he:
before me there was no God formed, neither shall there be after me.
11I, *even* I, *am* the LORD; and beside me *there is* no saviour.

☆43:11 Hos 13:4

43:1 This chapter looks toward the deliverance of God's people from captivity. But it also looks through that and beyond it to the great work of man's redemption by the Lord Jesus. God has gone to great lengths to provide salvation for the lost world of men. His love is *such that even* while they are sinners, he continues to care for them and urge upon them the necessity for repentance.

43:3 *Egypt for thy ransom, Ethiopia and Sheba for thee.* God gave these nations over to Cyrus by divine promise as consolation for the loss of the Israelites. They were conquered by Cambyses, the son of Cyrus. Once again this account indicates how God is the God of all history and that all the nations are under his control.

43:7 God created man (1) for his own glory, (2) for his own pleasure (Rev. 4:11), (3) for fellowship with himself; even as man was made to have fellowship with other men (1 John 1:7), so was he made to have fellowship with his Creator. The catechism has caught this refrain from the Scriptures in its first question: "What is the chief end of man?" The answer is: "To glorify God and to enjoy him forever." When believers glorify God, they have fulfilled their main purpose in life. And when they do this, they enjoy God, which is life's greatest blessing.

43:11 *beside me there is no saviour.* Comparative religionists think there are many ways to heaven. Christianity claims to be the only road to God and salvation. Therefore, it is unique, pronouncing adverse judgment on all ethnic religions and the many cults which men have founded. Once the uniqueness of the Christian faith is denied, syncretism takes over and the cardinal teachings of the Bible lose their force and are emptied of their content.

43:12 Ps 81:9

12 I have declared, and have saved, and I have shewed, when *there was* no strange *god* among you: therefore ye *are* my witnesses, saith the LORD, that I *am* God.

43:13 Job 9:12; Ps 90:2

13 Yea, before the day *was* I *am* he; and *there is* none that can deliver out of my hand: I will work, and who shall let it?

c. The Lord, the Redeemer, Will Return His People from Babylon

43:14☆ Isa 41:14

14 ¶Thus saith the LORD, your redeemer, the Holy One of Israel; For your sake I have sent to Babylon, and have brought down all their nobles, and the Chal-de'ans, whose cry *is* in the ships.

43:15 Isa 44:6

15 I *am* the LORD, your Holy One, the creator of Israel, your King.

43:16 Ex 14:21, 22; Josh 3:15, 16; Ps 77:19

16 Thus saith the LORD, which maketh a way in the sea, and a path in the mighty waters;

43:17 Ps 76:5, 6

17 Which bringeth forth the chariot and horse, the army and the power; they shall lie down together, they shall not rise: they are extinct, they are quenched as tow.

43:18 Jer 16:14

18 ¶Remember ye not the former things, neither consider the things of old.

43:19 Deut 8:15; 2 Cor 5:17

19 Behold, I will do a new thing; now it shall spring forth; shall ye not know it? I will even make a way in the wilderness, *and* rivers in the desert.

43:20 Isa 41:17, 18

20 The beast of the field shall honour me, the dragons and the owls: because I give waters in the wilderness, *and* rivers in the desert, to give drink to my people, my chosen.

43:21 Ps 102:18

21 This people have I formed for myself; they shall shew forth my praise.

d. Israel's Ingratitude

43:22☆ Mic 6:3

22 ¶But thou hast not called upon me, O Jacob; but thou hast been weary of me, O Israel.

43:23 Ex 30:34; Mal 1:6–8

23 Thou hast not brought me the small cattle of thy burnt offerings; neither hast thou honoured me with thy sacrifices. I have not caused thee to serve with an offering, nor wearied thee with incense.

43:24 Jer 6:20; Mal 2:17

24 Thou hast bought me no sweet cane with money, neither hast thou filled me with the fat of thy sacrifices: but thou hast made me to serve with thy sins, thou hast wearied me with thine iniquities.

43:25 Isa 55:7; Jer 31:34; Ezek 36:22

25 I, *even* I, *am* he that blotteth out thy transgressions for mine own sake, and will not remember thy sins.

26 Put me in remembrance: let us plead together: declare thou, that thou mayest be justified.

43:27 Isa 51:2

27 Thy first father hath sinned, and thy teachers have transgressed against me.

43:28 Lam 2:2, 6; Ezek 5:15

28 Therefore I have profaned the princes of the sanctuary, and have given Jacob to the curse, and Israel to reproaches.

43:14 God assures his despondent people in Babylon that they will return to the land from which they had been taken and that the power of the oppressor will be broken. He reminds them of the things he had done when he brought them out of Egypt (43:16). He who *did great things can and will shortly* do a great thing for his people. It behooves all believers to set up "stones of remembrance" concerning God's former blessings—with the expectation that present difficulties will also yield to the same great God.

43:22 Lacking gratitude for God's former mercies, God's people do not call on him for deliverance from their present plight. They have sinned against God and show no signs of being willing to repent. This is illustrated in Ezek. 8:18 where God says his people have sinned and refused to repent: "though they cry in mine ears with a loud voice, yet will I not hear them." It behooves us in our day to remember that any call to God for help must be preceded by cleansing the heart from defilement through repentance and confession. Then will God hear and help.

e. The Future Conversion of Israel, God's Servant-Nation

44 YET now hear, O Jacob my servant; and Israel, whom I have
chosen:

44:1 Jer 30:10

2Thus saith the LORD that made thee, and formed thee from the womb,
which will help thee; Fear not, O Jacob, my servant; and thou, Jes'u-run,
whom I have chosen.
3For I will pour water upon him that is thirsty, and floods upon the dry
ground: I will pour my spirit upon thy seed, and my blessing upon thine
offspring:
4And they shall spring up *as* among the grass, as willows by the water
courses.
5One shall say, I *am* the LORD's; and another shall call *himself* by the
name of Jacob; and another shall subscribe *with* his hand unto the LORD,
and surname *himself* by the name of Israel.

☆44:3 Isa 61:9 Joel 2:28

2. God's Judgment against Polytheism

a. The Lord Is the First and the Last

6Thus saith the LORD the King of Israel, and his redeemer the LORD of
hosts; I *am* the first, and I *am* the last; and beside me *there is* no God.
7And who, as I, shall call, and shall declare it, and set it in order for me,
since I appointed the ancient people? and the things that are coming, and
shall come, let them shew unto them.
8Fear ye not, neither be afraid: have not I told thee from that time, and
have declared *it?* ye *are* even my witnesses. Is there a God beside me? yea,
there is no God; I know not *any*.

☆44:6 Isa 41:21; 45:5, 6, 21; Rev 1:8, 17
☆44:7
☆44:8 Deut 4:35, 39; Isa 30:29

b. The Evils of Idol Worship

9¶They that make a graven image *are* all of them vanity; and their
delectable things shall not profit; and they *are* their own witnesses; they see
not, nor know; that they may be ashamed.
10Who hath formed a god, or molten a graven image *that* is profitable for
nothing?
11Behold, all his fellows shall be ashamed: and the workmen, they *are* of
men: let them all be gathered together, let them stand up; *yet* they shall
fear, *and* they shall be ashamed together.
12The smith with the tongs both worketh in the coals, and fashioneth it
with hammers, and worketh it with the strength of his arms: yea, he is
hungry, and his strength faileth: he drinketh no water, and is faint.

☆44:9 Ps 97:7
☆44:10 Jer 10:5; Hab 2:18; Acts 19:26
☆44:11

44:3 *I will pour my Spirit upon thy seed.* God waters dry ground with his Spirit. The Spirit was given without measure to Jesus and by measure to those who are in Jesus. Every believer is sealed and indwelt by the Spirit upon conversion. But not all believers have the fullness of the Spirit. Being filled with the Spirit is the blessing of blessings; from it God's people derive their power for witness and service. Every great evangelist who has won multitudes to Christ has had the infilling of the Holy Spirit.

44:6 The Redeemer is the first and the last. He is self-existent and self-sufficient. He is from everlasting, that is, before there were any worlds. And he shall be when the world is no more.

44:7, 8 No one could foretell what would happen in the years ahead except God who, by his prophet, announced many things hundreds of years before they came to pass. God challenges anyone who thinks himself to be god or prophet to do this. Thus Scripture itself avers that the prophetic word offers the clearest evidence to the unbelieving mind that God is God.

44:9 Idolatry is more than the making of images that men worship. It often consists, not in graven images, but in the mind and heart, when God is put out and in his place other things are substituted. Men sometimes worship the intellect, or place the material things of life above the spiritual. Whatever crowds out God is idolatry. A sophisticated, secular, and sensate culture needs to be aware of this newer form of idolatry.

44:10, 11 Whoever makes graven images or who imagines them in heart and mind should let them stand and plead their case. It will then be seen that they are like a mirage in the desert.

44:13 Ps 115:5-7 Isa 41:7

13The carpenter stretcheth out *his* rule; he marketh it out with a line; he fitteth it with planes, and he marketh it out with the compass, and maketh it after the figure of a man, according to the beauty of a man; that it may remain in the house.

14He heweth him down cedars, and taketh the cypress and the oak, which he strengtheneth for himself among the trees of the forest: he planteth an ash, and the rain doth nourish *it.*

44:15 2 Chron 25:14

15Then shall it be for a man to burn: for he will take thereof, and warm himself; yea, he kindleth *it,* and baketh bread; yea, he maketh a god, and worshippeth *it;* he maketh it a graven image, and falleth down thereto.

16He burneth part thereof in the fire; with part thereof he eateth flesh; he roasteth roast, and is satisfied: yea, he warmeth *himself,* and saith, Aha, I am warm, I have seen the fire:

44:17 1 Kgs 18:26, 28 Isa 45:20

17And the residue thereof he maketh a god, *even* his graven image: he falleth down unto it, and worshippeth *it,* and prayeth unto it, and saith, Deliver me; for thou *art* my god.

44:18 Ps 81:12 Isa 6:9, 10 29:10 Jer 10:8, 14

18They have not known nor understood: for he hath shut their eyes, that they cannot see; *and* their hearts, that they cannot understand.

44:19☆ Deut 27:15

19And none considereth in his heart, neither *is there* knowledge nor understanding to say, I have burned part of it in the fire; yea, also I have baked bread upon the coals thereof; I have roasted flesh, and eaten *it:* and shall I make the residue thereof an abomination? shall I fall down to the stock of a tree?

44:20 Ps 102:9 Hos 4:12

20He feedeth on ashes: a deceived heart hath turned him aside, that he cannot deliver his soul, nor say, *Is there* not a lie in my right hand?

c. *God Has Redeemed Jacob*

21¶Remember these, O Jacob and Israel; for thou *art* my servant: I have formed thee; thou *art* my servant: O Israel, thou shalt not be forgotten of me.

44:22 Ps 51:1, 9 Isa 55:7 Acts 3:19 1 Pet 1:18, 19

22I have blotted out, as a thick cloud, thy transgressions, and, as a cloud, thy sins: return unto me; for I have redeemed thee.

44:23 Ps 69:34 98:7, 8

23Sing, O ye heavens; for the LORD hath done *it:* shout, ye lower parts of the earth: break forth into singing, ye mountains, O forest, and every tree therein: for the LORD hath redeemed Jacob, and glorified himself in Israel.

3. God Uses Heathen Nations and Converts Whom He Pleases

a. *God Has Chosen Cyrus as His Shepherd*

44:24☆ Isa 40:22

24Thus saith the LORD, thy redeemer, and he that formed thee from the womb, I *am* the LORD that maketh all *things;* that stretcheth forth the heavens alone; that spreadeth abroad the earth by myself;

44:25 1 Cor 1:20, 27

25That frustrateth the tokens of the liars, and maketh diviners mad; that turneth wise *men* backward, and maketh their knowledge foolish;

44:26 Jer 32:15, 44

26That confirmeth the word of his servant, and performeth the counsel of his messengers; that saith to Jerusalem, Thou shalt be inhabited; and to the

---

44:19 From the wood of the same tree men make idols, cook their food, or warm their houses. Then they fall down before a piece of wood, imagining they have *created a god. Whoever can make a god* is greater than the god he makes, for he existed before the god he just made. Succeeding generations should consider that the image before which they bow was created by some ancestor and thus was made in time, not in and for eternity.

44:24 No greater claims can be made than those contained in this verse. God made all things at first and continues to make things at his pleasure. "All being, power, life, motion, and perfection, are from God."* He had no need for anyone to advise him or assist him. The extent of his power is boundless. And nothing is too hard for the One who made the world. Every fetus is God's creation; thus, all human life comes from him and belongs to him from the moment of conception.

cities of Judah, Ye shall be built, and I will raise up the decayed places
thereof:
27 That saith to the deep, Be dry, and I will dry up thy rivers:
28 That saith of Cyrus, *He is* my shepherd, and shall perform all my
pleasure: even saying to Jerusalem, Thou shalt be built; and to the temple,
Thy foundation shall be laid.

44:27 Isa 50:2
☆**44:28** 2 Chron 36:22, 23; Isa 14:32

b. God Will Enable Cyrus to Crush Kings

45 THUS saith the LORD to his anointed, to Cyrus, whose right hand
I have holden, to subdue nations before him; and I will loose the
loins of kings, to open before him the two leaved gates; and the gates shall
not be shut;
2 I will go before thee, and make the crooked places straight: I will break
in pieces the gates of brass, and cut in sunder the bars of iron:
3 And I will give thee the treasures of darkness, and hidden riches of
secret places, that thou mayest know that I, the LORD, which call *thee* by
thy name, *am* the God of Israel.
4 For Jacob my servant's sake, and Israel mine elect, I have even called
thee by thy name: I have surnamed thee, though thou hast not known me.
5 I *am* the LORD, and *there is* none else, *there is* no God beside me: I
girded thee, though thou hast not known me:
6 That they may know from the rising of the sun, and from the west, that
there is none beside me. I *am* the LORD, and *there is* none else.
7 I form the light, and create darkness: I make peace, and create evil: I the
LORD do all these *things*.
8 Drop down, ye heavens, from above, and let the skies pour down
righteousness: let the earth open, and let them bring forth salvation, and let
righteousness spring up together; I the LORD have created it.

☆**45:1** Ps 73:23; Jer 51:11, 20, 24
45:2 Isa 40:4; Jer 51:30
☆**45:3** Isa 49:1
45:4 Isa 43:1; Acts 17:23
45:6 Mal 1:11
☆**45:7** Ps 104:20; Amos 3:6
45:8 Ps 72:6; 85:11; Isa 61:11

c. Woe to Him Who Strives against His Creator

9 Woe unto him that striveth with his Maker! *Let* the potsherd *strive* with
the potsherds of the earth. Shall the clay say to him that fashioneth it, What
makest thou? or thy work, He hath no hands?

☆**45:9** Rom 9:20, 21

44:28 Isaiah prophesied that the temple would be rebuilt under Cyrus. This prophecy was made one hundred and fifty years prior to the fulfillment. Cyrus' decree was given approximately 538 B.C. (Ezra 1:1, 2; 6:3). The building was to become known as the second temple and was used by the Jews until Jerusalem fell in A.D. 70. This temple was desecrated by Antiochus Epiphanes in 168 B.C., an event predicted by Daniel (Dan. 9:27; 11:31). Herod the Great and his successors improved this temple. Jesus worshipped and taught in it (Mark 14:49) and predicted its destruction (Matt. 24:2; Mark 13:2; Luke 21:6). The veil or curtain of the temple was rent in two when Christ died (Matt. 27:51). Non-Jews were never permitted to enter its inner courts (Acts 21:27–30).

45:1 In 44:28 and here Cyrus was known in history as Cyrus II, the Great (559–530 B.C.). He founded the Achaemenid Persian Empire, which lasted for two centuries, until the time of Alexander the Great (331 B.C.). In October 539 B.C. the Medo-Persians under the command of Ugbaru captured Babylon. A few days later the king, Cyrus, entered the city and assumed the rulership. Isaiah's prophecy is predictive, since it was written before 687 B.C. The critical view disallows predictive prophecy and thus dates the latter half of Isaiah *after* rather than *before* Cyrus' day, attributing the material to someone other than Isaiah. Those who hold to the supernatural see no problem with respect to the Holy Spirit's power to predict events in advance of their occurrence.

45:3 The gold and silver became Cyrus's, not because he extracted them from the earth but because he had seized the riches of those who had hidden treasures. God would give Cyrus this wealth in order to show him that God is the Lord of all. Whether or not Cyrus came to know God in a personal way is not said. In any event, Cyrus was God's instrument to bring about the rebuilding of the temple in Jerusalem.

45:7 *I make peace and create evil.* God is not the author of evil (i.e., sin). The NASB says God is "the One causing well-being and creating calamity." The RSV says, "I make weal and woe." God does bring about calamity but does not author moral evil.

45:9 No one has the right or the reason to tell God how he should make man or, after the fact, to question what God has done. "Shall we impeach God's wisdom, or question his power, who are ourselves so curiously, so wonderfully made?"*

10 Woe unto him that saith unto *his* father, What begettest thou? or to the woman, What hast thou brought forth?

45:11 Ezek 39:7

11 Thus saith the LORD, the Holy One of Israel, and his Maker, Ask me of things to come concerning my sons, and concerning the work of my hands command ye me.

45:12 Neh 9:6 Jer 27:5

12 I have made the earth, and created man upon it: I, *even* my hands, have stretched out the heavens, and all their host have I commanded.

45:13☆ 2 Chron 36:22, 23 Isa 52:3

13 I have raised him up in righteousness, and I will direct all his ways: he shall build my city, and he shall let go my captives, not for price nor reward, saith the LORD of hosts.

d. The Future Conversion of the Heathen

45:14 Isa 14:1, 2 49:23 1 Cor 14:25

14 Thus saith the LORD, The labour of Egypt, and merchandise of E-thi-o′pi-a and of the Sa-be′ans, men of stature, shall come over unto thee, and they shall be thine: they shall come after thee; in chains they shall come over, and they shall fall down unto thee, they shall make supplication unto thee, *saying,* Surely God *is* in thee; and *there is* none else, *there is* no God.

15 Verily thou *art* a God that hidest thyself, O God of Israel, the Saviour.

45:16 Isa 44:11

16 They shall be ashamed, and also confounded, all of them: they shall go to confusion together *that are* makers of idols.

45:17 Isa 51:6

17 *But* Israel shall be saved in the LORD with an everlasting salvation: ye shall not be ashamed nor confounded world without end.

45:18☆ Gen 1:2, 26 Ps 115:16 Isa 42:5

18 For thus saith the LORD that created the heavens; God himself that formed the earth and made it; he hath established it, he created it not in vain, he formed it to be inhabited: I *am* the LORD; and *there is* none else.

45:19 2 Chron 15:2 Isa 43:12 Jer 29:13, 14

19 I have not spoken in secret, in a dark place of the earth: I said not unto the seed of Jacob, Seek ye me in vain: I the LORD speak righteousness, I declare things that are right.

45:20☆ Isa 44:18, 19 46:6, 7 Jer 10:5

20 ¶Assemble yourselves and come; draw near together, ye *that are* escaped of the nations: they have no knowledge that set up the wood of their graven image, and pray unto a god *that* cannot save.

45:21 Isa 43:3, 11 44:7

21 Tell ye, and bring *them* near; yea, let them take counsel together: who hath declared this from ancient time? *who* hath told it from that time? *have* not I the LORD? and *there is* no God else beside me; a just God and a Saviour; *there is* none beside me.

45:22☆ Num 21:8, 9 Isa 52:10 Mic 7:7

22 Look unto me, and be ye saved, all the ends of the earth: for I *am* God, and *there is* none else.

45:23 Rom 14:11

23 I have sworn by myself, the word is gone out of my mouth *in* righteousness, and shall not return, That unto me every knee shall bow, every tongue shall swear.

24 Surely, shall *one* say, in the LORD have I righteousness and strength: *even* to him shall *men* come; and all that are incensed against him shall be ashamed.

45:25 Isa 53:11

25 In the LORD shall all the seed of Israel be justified, and shall glory.

45:13 *I have raised him up,* i.e., "I have raised up Cyrus." The reference probably is also to Christ in the *more distant future.† This is another illustration* of a double fulfillment of the prophetic word.

45:18 God alone created all things, including the planet Earth, on which man is stationed. The maker can rightfully demand that his creation obey him and walk according to his commandments.

45:20 This was written to convince idolaters of their folly in bowing before gods who cannot help them, while neglecting the true God, who can.

45:22 In 45:20 we read about awful idolatry. In 45:22 God bespeaks his loving concern and extends a universal call to all men, indicating that all need to be saved and that all who come to him will be saved.

E. THE JUDGMENT ON BABYLON

1. Babylon's Idols Helpless against an Omnipotent God

46 BEL boweth down, Nebo stoopeth, their idols were upon the
beasts, and upon the cattle: your carriages *were* heavy loaden; *they*
are a burden to the weary *beast*.

☆46:1 Isa 21:9; Jer 43:12, 13; 51:44

2 They stoop, they bow down together; they could not deliver the burden,
but themselves are gone into captivity.

3 ¶Hearken unto me, O house of Jacob, and all the remnant of the house
of Israel, which are borne *by me* from the belly, which are carried from the
womb:

☆46:3 Isa 10:21, 22

4 And *even* to *your* old age I *am* he; and *even* to hoar hairs will I carry *you:*
I have made, and I will bear; even I will carry, and will deliver *you*.

☆46:4

5 ¶To whom will ye liken me, and make *me* equal, and compare me, that
we may be like?

46:5 Isa 40:18, 25

6 They lavish gold out of the bag, and weigh silver in the balance, *and* hire
a goldsmith; and he maketh it a god: they fall down, yea, they worship.

☆46:6 Isa 44:12–17

7 They bear him upon the shoulder, they carry him, and set him in his
place, and he standeth; from his place shall he not remove: yea, *one* shall
cry unto him, yet can he not answer, nor save him out of his trouble.

☆46:7 Isa 40:20; Jer 10:5

8 Remember this, and shew yourselves men: bring *it* again to mind, O ye
transgressors.

9 Remember the former things of old: for I *am* God, and *there is* none
else; I *am* God, and *there is* none like me,

☆46:9 Isa 41:26, 27; 42:9

10 Declaring the end from the beginning, and from ancient times *the things*
that are not *yet* done, saying, My counsel shall stand, and I will do all my
pleasure:

46:10 Acts 5:39

11 Calling a ravenous bird from the east, the man that executeth my
counsel from a far country: yea, I have spoken *it*, I will also bring it to pass;
I have purposed *it*, I will also do it.

46:11 Num 23:19

12 ¶Hearken unto me, ye stouthearted, that *are* far from righteousness:
13 I bring near my righteousness: it shall not be far off, and my salvation
shall not tarry: and I will place salvation in Zion for Israel my glory.

46:12 Zech 7:11, 12
46:13 Isa 51:5; 61:3

2. God's Judgment against Arrogant Babylon

47 COME down, and sit in the dust, O virgin daughter of Babylon, sit
on the ground: *there is* no throne, O daughter of the Chal-de'ans:
for thou shalt no more be called tender and delicate.

47:1 Jer 48:18

2 Take the millstones, and grind meal; uncover thy locks, make bare the
leg, uncover the thigh, pass over the rivers.

☆47:2 Gen 24:65; 1 Cor 11:5

3 Thy nakedness shall be uncovered, yea, thy shame shall be seen: I will
take vengeance, and I will not meet *thee as* a man.

47:3 Isa 63:4

4 *As for* our redeemer, the LORD of hosts *is* his name, the Holy One of
Israel.

46:1 *Bel . . . Nebo. Bell*-Marduk was Babylon's greatest god. *Nebo* was the god of writing and patron of Borsippa.

46:3, 4 Israel is God's creation. From birth to old age those of Israel who trust in him will be preserved, not by their own power, but by the grace of the all-powerful God.

46:6, 7 Is it not strange that the idols that men make are fixed in their places and cannot move except they be carried by their worshippers? Meanwhile, the idolators refuse to bow before the true God, who is omnipresent and who does not need to be carried on the shoulders of those who trust in him?

46:9 God reminds the reader that it is not in the power of any creature to control him. God is omnipotent and what he chooses to do will be done according to the divine purpose. If this were not true, then he would not be God.

47:2 *uncover thy locks,* i.e., "put off your veil." In ancient Babylonia (and in many eastern lands today) only harlots were permitted to go without veils.†

47:5 Lam 2:10 Dan 2:37

5 Sit thou silent, and get thee into darkness, O daughter of the Chalde'ans: for thou shalt no more be called, The lady of kingdoms.

47:6 Deut 28:50 Zech 1:15

6 I was wroth with my people, I have polluted mine inheritance, and given them into thine hand: thou didst shew them no mercy; upon the ancient hast thou very heavily laid thy yoke.

7 ¶And thou saidst, I shall be a lady for ever: *so* that thou didst not lay these *things* to thy heart, neither didst remember the latter end of it.

3. Babylon's False Sense of Security

47:8 Isa 22:13 32:9, 11 Rev 18:7

8 Therefore hear now this, *thou that art* given to pleasures, that dwellest carelessly, that sayest in thine heart, I *am,* and none else beside me; I shall not sit *as* a widow, neither shall I know the loss of children:

47:9 Isa 13:16 1 Thess 5:2, 3 Rev 18:8, 10, 23

9 But these two *things* shall come to thee in a moment in one day, the loss of children, and widowhood: they shall come upon thee in their perfection for the multitude of thy sorceries, *and* for the great abundance of thine enchantments.

47:10☆ Ps 52:7 Isa 5:21 Ezek 8:12

10 ¶For thou hast trusted in thy wickedness: thou hast said, None seeth me. Thy wisdom and thy knowledge, it hath perverted thee; and thou hast said in thine heart, I *am,* and none else beside me.

47:11 Jer 51:8, 43

11 ¶Therefore shall evil come upon thee; thou shalt not know from whence it riseth: and mischief shall fall upon thee; thou shalt not be able to put it off: and desolation shall come upon thee suddenly, *which* thou shalt not know.

4. Babylon Is Helpless before God's Judgment

12 Stand now with thine enchantments, and with the multitude of thy sorceries, wherein thou hast laboured from thy youth; if so be thou shalt be able to profit, if so be thou mayest prevail.

47:13☆ Isa 8:19

13 Thou art wearied in the multitude of thy counsels. Let now the astrologers, the stargazers, the monthly prognosticators, stand up, and save thee from *these things* that shall come upon thee.

47:14 Jer 51:30, 32, 58 Nah 1:10

14 Behold, they shall be as stubble; the fire shall burn them; they shall not deliver themselves from the power of the flame: *there shall* not *be* a coal to warm at, *nor* fire to sit before it.

15 Thus shall they be unto thee with whom thou hast laboured, *even* thy merchants, from thy youth: they shall wander every one to his quarter; none shall save thee.

F. GOD'S DEALING WITH HIS SINFUL PEOPLE

1. God's Prediction of the Captivity has been Fulfilled

48:1 Isa 45:23; 52:1 Rom 2:17

48 HEAR ye this, O house of Jacob, which are called by the name of Israel, and are come forth out of the waters of Judah, which swear by the name of the LORD, and make mention of the God of Israel, *but* not in truth, nor in righteousness.

2 For they call themselves of the holy city, and stay themselves upon the God of Israel; The LORD of hosts *is* his name.

47:10 *Babylon supposed herself* to have wisdom and knowledge. We can know where and when the sun will rise but we cannot know what the day will bring. Babylon with all its wisdom and knowledge could not foresee, and even if she had known it, could not prevent the ruin to which she had been assigned by the righteous judgment of God. Man proposes; God disposes.

47:13 Those who study the stars, prepare horoscopes, and prognosticate daily events are cheats, and their arts are a sham. Some people rely on such things, while they leave their Bible unread.

3 I have declared the former things from the beginning; and they went
forth out of my mouth, and I shewed them; I did *them* suddenly, and they
came to pass.

☆**48:3** Josh 21:45; Isa 42:9

4 Because I knew that thou *art* obstinate, and thy neck *is* an iron sinew,
and thy brow brass;

48:4 Ezek 2:4

5 I have even from the beginning declared *it* to thee; before it came to
pass I shewed *it* thee: lest thou shouldest say, Mine idol hath done them,
and my graven image, and my molten image, hath commanded them.

48:5 Jer 44:15–18

6 Thou hast heard, see all this; and will not ye declare *it?* I have shewed
thee new things from this time, even hidden things, and thou didst not
know them.

☆**48:6** Isa 43:19

7 They are created now, and not from the beginning; even before the day
when thou heardest them not; lest thou shouldest say, Behold, I knew them.

2. The Honor of God's Name Upheld by the Captivity

8 Yea, thou heardest not; yea, thou knewest not; yea, from that time *that*
thine ear was not opened: for I knew that thou wouldest deal very
treacherously, and wast called a transgressor from the womb.

48:8 Deut 9:7, 24; Ps 58:3

9 ¶For my name's sake will I defer mine anger, and for my praise will I
refrain for thee, that I cut thee not off.

48:9 Ps 103:8–10

10 Behold, I have refined thee, but not with silver; I have chosen thee in
the furnace of affliction.

☆**48:10** 1 Kgs 8:51; Ezek 22:18–22

11 For mine own sake, *even* for mine own sake, will I do *it:* for how should
my name be polluted? and I will not give my glory unto another.

☆**48:11** Deut 32:26, 27; Ps 106:8; Isa 42:8

3. Cyrus Will Perform God's Will against Babylon

12 ¶Hearken unto me, O Jacob and Israel, my called; I *am* he; I *am* the
first, I also *am* the last.

48:12 Deut 32:39

13 Mine hand also hath laid the foundation of the earth, and my right
hand hath spanned the heavens: *when* I call unto them, they stand up
together.

48:13 Ps 102:25

14 All ye, assemble yourselves, and hear; which among them hath declared
these *things?* The LORD hath loved him: he will do his pleasure on Babylon,
and his arm *shall be on* the Chal-de'ans.

48:14 Jer 50:21–29

15 I, *even* I, have spoken; yea, I have called him: I have brought him, and
he shall make his way prosperous.

48:15 Isa 41:2; 45:1, 2

16 ¶Come ye near unto me, hear ye this; I have not spoken in secret from
the beginning; from the time that it was, there *am* I: and now the Lord
GOD, and his Spirit, hath sent me.

☆**48:16** Isa 45:19

4. Israel's Flight from Babylon to Return Home

17 Thus saith the LORD, thy Redeemer, the Holy One of Israel; I *am* the
LORD thy God which teacheth thee to profit, which leadeth thee by the way
that thou shouldest go.

48:17 Ps 32:8; Isa 41:14

48:3 God had foretold the Babylonian captivity, and what he said has come true.
48:6 God gave the captives information concerning Cyrus and the exact time of their release from their Babylonian captivity.
48:10 Silver is refined until all the dross is gone. God's people will at last be fully refined and perfected. God uses affliction to refine us in the here and now, but the process will not be completed until death, at which time all believers will be glorified. In this life sanctification is designed to make God's people purer day by day as the dross becomes less and less.
48:11 God will release his people from their captivity, not because they are worthy of release (for he owes them nothing) but because he does not want his name to be polluted by the triumph of heathen Babylonia.
48:16 The Spirit is here spoken of as a person. He has divine authority to send the prophets. Whoever God sends, the Spirit sends, and the words the prophets speak are the Spirit's words.

48:18 Deut 5:29 Ps 119:165 Amos 5:24
48:19 Gen 12:17

18 O that thou hadst hearkened to my commandments! then had thy peace
been as a river, and thy righteousness as the waves of the sea:
19 Thy seed also had been as the sand, and the offspring of thy bowels like
the gravel thereof; his name should not have been cut off nor destroyed
from before me.

48:20 Isa 52:9 Jer 31:10

20 ¶Go ye forth of Babylon, flee ye from the Chal-de'ans, with a voice of
singing declare ye, tell this, utter it *even* to the end of the earth; say ye, The
LORD hath redeemed his servant Jacob.

48:21☆ Ps 78:15, 16 Mt 1:20, 21

21 And they thirsted not *when* he led them through the deserts: he caused
the waters to flow out of the rock for them: he clave the rock also, and the
waters gushed out.
22 *There is* no peace, saith the LORD, unto the wicked.

5. Messiah's Call and Commission

49:1☆

49 LISTEN, O isles, unto me; and hearken, ye people, from far; The
LORD hath called me from the womb; from the bowels of my
mother hath he made mention of my name.

49:2 Isa 51:16 Heb 4:12 Rev 1:16

2 And he hath made my mouth like a sharp sword; in the shadow of his
hand hath he hid me, and made me a polished shaft; in his quiver hath he
hid me;
3 And said unto me, Thou *art* my servant, O Israel, in whom I will be
glorified.
4 Then I said, I have laboured in vain, I have spent my strength for
nought, and in vain: *yet* surely my judgment *is* with the LORD, and my work
with my God.

49:5 Isa 12:2

5 ¶And now, saith the LORD that formed me from the womb *to be* his
servant, to bring Jacob again to him, Though Israel be not gathered, yet
shall I be glorious in the eyes of the LORD, and my God shall be my
strength.

49:6☆ Ps 37:28 Acts 13:47 26:23

6 And he said, It is a light thing that thou shouldest be my servant to raise
up the tribes of Jacob, and to restore the preserved of Israel: I will also give
thee for a light to the Gentiles, that thou mayest be my salvation unto the
end of the earth.

49:7☆ Ps 22:6–8 Isa 53:3

7 Thus saith the LORD, the Redeemer of Israel, *and* his Holy One, to him
whom man despiseth, to him whom the nation abhorreth, to a servant of
rulers, Kings shall see and arise, princes also shall worship, because the
LORD that is faithful, *and* the Holy One of Israel, and he shall choose thee.

6. God's Deliverance of His People

49:8☆ Ps 69:13 Isa 26:3; 42:7 44:26 Lk 4:18 2 Cor 6:2

8 Thus saith the LORD, In an acceptable time have I heard thee, and in a
day of salvation have I helped thee: and I will preserve thee, and give thee
for a covenant of the people, to establish the earth, to cause to inherit the
desolate heritages;

48:21 Israel should call to remembrance the providences and miracles of God performed for his people in past times and be assured that he is able to do similar mighty deeds on their behalf now.

49:1 The God who delivered Israel from captivity now speaks to the Gentiles concerning the Christ whom *the Father called* from the day of his birth to be the Redeemer of men. Jesus was fitted and qualified for the office to which he was called by his Father. Let men of all colors, creeds, and persuasions heed the call of God who offers them salvation.

49:6 The servant-king, the Messiah, has a twofold work: (1) he will come to restore the preserved of Israel who must respond to the gospel; and (2) he will be a light to the Gentiles by providing a gospel which will go to the ends of the earth. This is a missionary verse.

49:7 The Messiah, who should be received and accepted by all, will be humiliated and rejected, suffering a shameful death—for the purpose of procuring salvation.

49:8 The despised and rejected Son of God will be owned by his Father. He shall be the one who guarantees that the covenant of salvation and peace between God and man will prevail.

9 That thou mayest say to the prisoners, Go forth; to them that *are* in
darkness, Shew yourselves. They shall feed in the ways, and their pastures
shall be in all high places.
10 They shall not hunger nor thirst; neither shall the heat nor sun smite **49:10**
them: for he that hath mercy on them shall lead them, even by the springs Ps 23:2
of water shall he guide them. Rev 7:16
11 And I will make all my mountains a way, and my highways shall be
exalted.
12 Behold, these shall come from far: and, lo, these from the north and
from the west; and these from the land of Si'nim.
13 ¶Sing, O heavens; and be joyful, O earth; and break forth into singing, **49:13**
O mountains: for the LORD hath comforted his people, and will have mercy Isa 54:7, 8, 10
upon his afflicted. Rev 12:12

7. God's Continuing Love for His People

14 But Zion said, The LORD hath forsaken me, and my Lord hath ☆**49:14**
forgotten me.
15 Can a woman forget her sucking child, that she should not have
compassion on the son of her womb? yea, they may forget, yet will I not
forget thee.
16 Behold, I have graven thee upon the palms of *my* hands; thy walls *are* ☆**49:16**
continually before me. Song 8:6
17 Thy children shall make haste; thy destroyers and they that made thee
waste shall go forth of thee.
18 ¶Lift up thine eyes round about, and behold: all these gather them- **49:18**
selves together, *and* come to thee. *As* I live, saith the LORD, thou shalt Isa 45:23
surely clothe thee with them all, as with an ornament, and bind them *on*
thee, as a bride *doeth.*
19 For thy waste and thy desolate places, and the land of thy destruction, **49:19**
shall even now be too narrow by reason of the inhabitants, and they that Ps 56:1, 2 Isa 1:7
swallowed thee up shall be far away. Zech 10:10
20 The children which thou shalt have, after thou hast lost the other, shall **49:20**
say again in thine ears, The place *is* too strait for me: give place to me that Isa 54:1–3
I may dwell.
21 Then shalt thou say in thine heart, who hath begotten me these, seeing **49:21**
I have lost my children, and am desolate, a captive, and removing to and Lam 1:1
fro? and who hath brought up these? Behold, I was left alone; these, where
had they *been?*

8. Israel Restored and Gentiles Converted

22 Thus saith the Lord GOD, Behold, I will lift up mine hand to the **49:22**
Gentiles, and set up my standard to the people: and they shall bring thy Isa 11:10, 12 14:2
sons in *their* arms, and thy daughters shall be carried upon *their* shoulders. ☆**49:23**
23 And kings shall be thy nursing fathers, and their queens thy nursing Ps 25:3; 72:9 Isa 60:14, 16

49:14 The God of Zion never forsakes his people, unless they first forsake him. Those who trust in him shall never be forsaken despite external difficulties, violence against them, and even death.

49:16 Even as one ties a string on a finger to call to remembrance some duty to be discharged, so God guarantees never to forget what he has promised.

49:23 *they . . . that wait for me.* God's timing is not man's timing. Believers must always wait for the Lord. Thousands of years elapsed between the time of God's promise of a redeemer to Adam (Gen. 3:15) and the fulfillment of that promise. A long time has elapsed since the promise of Christ's Second Advent was prophesied in the New Testament. However much people may scoff because two thousand years have gone by and Jesus has not yet come, those who wait for that coming *shall not be ashamed.*

mothers: they shall bow down to thee with *their* face toward the earth, and
lick up the dust of thy feet; and thou shalt know that I *am* the LORD: for
they shall not be ashamed that wait for me.
24 ¶Shall the prey be taken from the mighty, or the lawful captive
delivered?
49:25 Jer 50:33, 34 — 25 But thus saith the LORD, Even the captives of the mighty shall be taken
away, and the prey of the terrible shall be delivered: for I will contend with
him that contendeth with thee, and I will save thy children.
49:26☆ Isa 14:4 Ezek 39:7 — 26 And I will feed them that oppress thee with their own flesh; and they
shall be drunken with their own blood, as with sweet wine: and all flesh
shall know that I the LORD *am* thy Saviour and thy Redeemer, the mighty
One of Jacob.

9. The Sinful Servant Nation and the Obedient Servant

a. Israel, the Lord's Adulterous Wife

50:1☆ Deut 32:30 Isa 59:2 Jer 3:8 — **50** THUS saith the LORD, Where *is* the bill of your mother's divorce-
ment, whom I have put away? or which of my creditors *is it* to
whom I have sold you? Behold, for your iniquities have ye sold yourselves,
and for your transgressions is your mother put away.
50:2☆ Gen 18:14 Ex 14:21 Josh 3:16 — 2 Wherefore, when I came, *was there* no man? when I called, *was there*
none to answer? Is my hand shortened at all, that it cannot redeem? or have
I no power to deliver? behold, at my rebuke I dry up the sea, I make the
rivers a wilderness: their fish stinketh, because *there is* no water, and dieth
for thirst.
50:3 Rev 6:12 — 3 I clothe the heavens with blackness, and I make sackcloth their covering.

b. Messiah, the Obedient Servant

50:4 Ps 5:3 Jer 31:25 — 4 The Lord GOD hath given me the tongue of the learned, that I should
know how to speak a word in season to *him that is* weary: he wakeneth
morning by morning, he wakeneth mine ear to hear as the learned.
50:5 Mt 26:39 Heb 5:8 — 5 ¶The Lord GOD hath opened mine ear, and I was not rebellious, neither
turned away back.
50:6☆ Mk 15:19 — 6 I gave my back to the smiters, and my cheeks to them that plucked off
the hair: I hid not my face from shame and spitting.
50:7☆ Ezek 3:8, 9 — 7 ¶For the Lord GOD will help me; therefore shall I not be confounded:
therefore have I set my face like a flint, and I know that I shall not be
ashamed.
50:8 Rom 8:33, 34 — 8 *He is* near that justifieth me; who will contend with me? let us stand
together: who *is* mine adversary? let him come near to me.
50:9 Isa 54:17 — 9 Behold, the Lord GOD will help me; who *is* he *that* shall condemn me?
lo, they all shall wax old as a garment; the moth shall eat them up.

49:26 God's judgment against Babylon will show all men that although Israel seems cast down they have a Redeemer. So also may the church be assured that it too will be delivered from the attacks of its enemies by *the omnipotent God of the whole earth.*
50:1 The questions posed in this verse are rhetorical. Israel never has been divorced by God and never will be. Although estranged from God by her sin, she is still beloved of him.
50:2 *Is my hand shortened . . . that it cannot redeem?* The captivity occurred, not because God was unable to save his people, but because of his people's sins. God, who is sovereign, could easily have delivered Israel, and he will do so at the end of the age.
50:6 Messiah shall be smitten, scourged, have his hair pulled out, and be made the offscouring of the world—all for the salvation of those who come to him by faith.
50:7 Christ set his face like a flint toward Jerusalem and Calvary (see Luke 9:51). He went about his work as mediator with constancy and resolution. He was not to be discouraged nor would he fail to accomplish what he had set out to do.

c. The Command to Trust the Lord

10¶Who *is* among you that feareth the LORD, that obeyeth the voice of his servant, that walketh *in* darkness, and hath no light? let him trust in the name of the LORD, and stay upon his God. ☆50:10 Eph 5:8

11Behold, all ye that kindle a fire, that compass *yourselves* about with sparks: walk in the light of your fire, and in the sparks *that* ye have kindled. This shall ye have of mine hand; ye shall lie down in sorrow. 50:11 Isa 65:13–15

G. ISRAEL ENCOURAGED TO TRUST AND HOPE IN GOD
1. Trust God; Do Not Fear Men
a. God's Mercy Bestowed on Abraham's Seed

51 HEARKEN to me, ye that follow after righteousness, ye that seek the LORD: look unto the rock *whence* ye are hewn, and to the hole of the pit *whence* ye are digged. ☆51:1 Gen 12:1 17:15–17 Heb 11:11, 12

2Look unto Abraham your father, and unto Sarah *that* bare you: for I called him alone, and blessed him, and increased him.

3For the LORD shall comfort Zion: he will comfort all her waste places; and he will make her wilderness like Eden, and her desert like the garden of the LORD; joy and gladness shall be found therein, thanksgiving, and the voice of melody. 51:3 Gen 2:8 Isa 41:19

b. Fear Not People; Trust the God of Israel

4¶Hearken unto me, my people; and give ear unto me, O my nation: for a law shall proceed from me, and I will make my judgment to rest for a light of the people. ☆51:4 Ps 78:1 Isa 42:4

5My righteousness *is* near; my salvation is gone forth, and mine arms shall judge the people; the isles shall wait upon me, and on mine arm shall they trust. 51:5 Isa 46:13

6Lift up your eyes to the heavens, and look upon the earth beneath: for the heavens shall vanish away like smoke, and the earth shall wax old like a garment, and they that dwell therein shall die in like manner: but my salvation shall be for ever, and my righteousness shall not be abolished. 51:6 Ps 102:25, 26 2 Pet 3:10

7¶Hearken unto me, ye that know righteousness, the people in whose heart *is* my law; fear ye not the reproach of men, neither be ye afraid of their revilings. 51:7 Ps 37:30, 31 Mt 5:11 Acts 5:40, 41

8For the moth shall eat them up like a garment, and the worm shall eat them like wool: but my righteousness shall be for ever, and my salvation from generation to generation. ☆51:8 Isa 14:11

c. Prayer for Israel's Redemption

9¶Awake, awake, put on strength, O arm of the LORD; awake, as in the ancient days, in the generations of old. *Art* thou not it that hath cut Rahab, *and* wounded the dragon? ☆51:9 Deut 4:34

10*Art* thou not it which hath dried the sea, the waters of the great deep; that hath made the depths of the sea a way for the ransomed to pass over? 51:10 Ex 14:21, 22 Isa 63:11, 12

50:10 Whoever is disconsolate and walks in darkness is encouraged to continue to trust God and rely upon him for deliverance, which is certain to come.
51:1 *ye that follow after righteousness,* i.e., "you who are anxious to be both justified and sanctified." *look to the rock whence ye are hewn,* i.e., look back at such things as the stones of memorial set up after crossing the Jordan—and be encouraged. Right tradition is a valuable resource, for it assures us that what God has done in the past he can do again today.
51:4 Law and gospel function together. The law condemns; the gospel saves. The word of salvation through grace shall shine as a light before all peoples.
51:8 Righteousness and salvation shall be forever; no one can alter, abridge, or abolish them.
51:9 *Rahab . . . the dragon,* i.e., "Egypt, the dragon."†

51:11☆ Isa 61:7 Rev 21:4
11 Therefore the redeemed of the LORD shall return, and come with
singing unto Zion; and everlasting joy *shall be* upon their head: they shall
obtain gladness and joy; *and* sorrow and mourning shall flee away.

d. God Will Deliver Israel

51:12 Ps 118:6
12 I, *even* I, *am* he that comforteth you: who *art* thou, that thou shouldest
be afraid of a man *that* shall die, and of the son of man *which* shall be made
as grass;
51:13☆ Deut 8:11 Job 9:8
13 And forgettest the LORD thy maker, that hath stretched forth the
heavens, and laid the foundations of the earth; and hast feared continually
every day because of the fury of the oppressor, as if he were ready to
destroy? and where *is* the fury of the oppressor?
51:14 Isa 49:10
14 The captive exile hasteneth that he may be loosed, and that he should
not die in the pit, nor that his bread should fail.
51:15 Ps 107:25
15 But I *am* the LORD thy God, that divided the sea, whose waves roared:
The LORD of hosts *is* his name.
51:16 Ex 33:22 Deut 18:18
16 And I have put my words in thy mouth, and I have covered thee in the
shadow of mine hand, that I may plant the heavens, and lay the founda-
tions of the earth, and say unto Zion, Thou *art* my people.

2. The Call for Israel to Wake Up and Turn to God
a. Israel Has Drunk of the Cup of the Lord's Fury

51:17☆ Jer 25:15
17 ¶Awake, awake, stand up, O Jerusalem, which hast drunk at the hand
of the LORD the cup of his fury; thou hast drunken the dregs of the cup of
trembling, *and* wrung *them* out.
51:18 Ps 142:4
18 *There is* none to guide her among all the sons *whom* she hath brought
forth; neither *is there any* that taketh her by the hand of all the sons *that* she
hath brought up.
19 These two *things* are come unto thee; who shall be sorry for thee?
desolation, and destruction, and the famine, and the sword: by whom shall
I comfort thee?
51:20 Isa 66:15 Jer 14:16
20 Thy sons have fainted, they lie at the head of all the streets, as a wild
bull in a net: they are full of the fury of the LORD, the rebuke of thy God.
21 ¶Therefore hear now this, thou afflicted, and drunken, but not with
wine:
51:22 Jer 50:34
22 Thus saith thy Lord the LORD, and thy God *that* pleadeth the cause of
his people, Behold, I have taken out of thine hand the cup of trembling,
even the dregs of the cup of my fury; thou shalt no more drink it again:
51:23 Jer 25:15–17, 26, 28
23 But I will put it into the hand of them that afflict thee; which have said
to thy soul, Bow down, that we may go over: and thou hast laid thy body as
the ground, and as the street, to them that went over.

51:11 When the redeemed of the Lord are released from their captivity, it is proper for them to come singing like birds freed from their cages. And when the spirits of just men are released from their bodily *prisons, they come to the heavenly Zion* with songs in their hearts, making melody to the Lord. In the hereafter our heads will be crowned with immortal glory and we will enjoy all of the promised blessings we do not have in this vale of tears.

51:13 *hast feared continually.* The only thing we have to fear is fear. God's people who fear have placed themselves in bondage to Satan, who is the author of fears. The timorous imagine the worst, expect the worst, and tremble at every shaking leaf. God has not given his people a spirit of timidity (2 Tim. 1:7—"fear" in the KJV but "timidity" in the NASB and RSV, and "cowardice" in Nestle and Marshall's *Interlinear*). In him there is deliverance from all our fears, cowardice, and timidity.

51:17 Israel has drunk the cup of God's wrath. So the Messiah drank of that cup, which made it possible for God to free sinners from his wrath.

b. Captive Jerusalem Will Be Freed for God's Glory

52 AWAKE, awake; put on thy strength, O Zion; put on thy beautiful garments, O Jerusalem, the holy city: for henceforth there shall no more come into thee the uncircumcised and the unclean.

☆**52:1** Ex 28:2, 40; Neh 11:1; Isa 48:2; 61:10

2 Shake thyself from the dust; arise, *and* sit down, O Jerusalem: loose thyself from the bands of thy neck, O captive daughter of Zion.

3 For thus saith the LORD, Ye have sold yourselves for nought; and ye shall be redeemed without money.

52:3 Ps 44:12; Isa 63:4

4 For thus saith the Lord GOD, My people went down aforetime into Egypt to sojourn there; and the Assyrian oppressed them without cause.

5 Now therefore, what have I here, saith the LORD, that my people is taken away for nought? they that rule over them make them to howl, saith the LORD; and my name continually every day *is* blasphemed.

☆**52:5** Ezek 36:20, 23

6 Therefore my people shall know my name: therefore *they shall know* in that day that I *am* he that doth speak: behold, *it is* I.

c. Captive Israelites Rejoice in God's Deliverance

7 ¶How beautiful upon the mountains are the feet of him that bringeth good tidings, that publisheth peace; that bringeth good tidings of good, that publisheth salvation; that saith unto Zion, Thy God reigneth!

☆**52:7** Ps 93:1; Rom 10:15

8 Thy watchmen shall lift up the voice; with the voice together shall they sing: for they shall see eye to eye, when the LORD shall bring again Zion.

52:8 Isa 62:6

9 ¶Break forth into joy, sing together, ye waste places of Jerusalem: for the LORD hath comforted his people, he hath redeemed Jerusalem.

52:9 Ps 98:4; Isa 61:4

10 The LORD hath made bare his holy arm in the eyes of all the nations; and all the ends of the earth shall see the salvation of our God.

52:10 Ps 98:1–3; Lk 3:6

11 ¶Depart ye, depart ye, go ye out from thence, touch no unclean *thing;* go ye out of the midst of her; be ye clean, that bear the vessels of the LORD.

52:11 Isa 1:16; 2 Cor 6:17

12 For ye shall not go out with haste, nor go by flight: for the LORD will go before you; and the God of Israel *will be* your rereward.

52:12 Ex 12:11, 33; 14:19, 20; Isa 26:7

H. GOD DELIVERS ISRAEL THROUGH A SUFFERING SERVANT

1. The Humiliation of the Servant

13 ¶Behold, my servant shall deal prudently, he shall be exalted and extolled, and be very high.

☆**52:13** Phil 2:9

14 As many were astonied at thee; his visage was so marred more than any man, and his form more than the sons of men:

52:14 Ps 22:6, 7; Rom 15:21

52:1 In 51:9 the people of God call upon him to awaken and put forth the divine strength. Here God calls for the saints of Zion to awake and put on *their* strength. They are to bestir themselves, to stop being sluggish, and to get busy doing what they are supposed to be doing. Believers should take this counsel seriously every day of this pilgrim journey. Nothing is so provoking as sleeping saints who refuse to waken from their lethargy and who therefore do not commend the faith of Christ to others.

52:5 God's people have tainted his glory due to their sins. They have injured him.

52:7 God's deliverance of his people from Babylon was a type and figure of Jesus Christ's redemption of man. Whoever bears tidings of redemption does the work of God. The gospel is good news, even the best news, for the God of Zion reigns, rules, and forgives the sins of the repentant.

52:12 Whoever does the will of God and walks in his light will find that God goes before him to prepare the way and stands behind him to protect him from all assaults.

52:13 *my servant.* The Servant of the Lord, as the term is used here, is the Messiah, our Lord Jesus. This passage was so interpreted by Christ himself, by the writers of the New Testament, and by orthodox Christianity ever since. Commissioned and qualified by the Father, Jesus Christ was the servant of his Father. He humbled himself that he might be exalted; every knee should bow before him and every tongue confess his name.

52:15☆
15 So shall he sprinkle many nations; the kings shall shut their mouths at
him: for *that* which had not been told them shall they see; and *that* which
they had not heard shall they consider.

2. The Servant: Despised and Rejected by Men

53:1ff☆ 53:1 Jn 12:38 Rom 10:16 53:2 Isa 11:1

53 WHO hath believed our report? and to whom is the arm of the
LORD revealed?
2 For he shall grow up before him as a tender plant, and as a root out of
a dry ground: he hath no form nor comeliness; and when we shall see him,
there is no beauty that we should desire him.

53:3 Ps 22:6 Lk 18:31–33

3 He is despised and rejected of men; a man of sorrows, and acquainted
with grief: and we hid as it were *our* faces from him; he was despised, and
we esteemed him not.

3. The Servant: God's Messiah Redeemer

53:4 Mt 8:17 Jn 19:7

4 ¶Surely he hath borne our griefs, and carried our sorrows: yet we did
esteem him stricken, smitten of God, and afflicted.

53:5☆ 1 Cor 15:3 Heb 5:8; 9:28 1 Pet 2:24, 25

5 But he *was* wounded for our transgressions, *he was* bruised for our
iniquities: the chastisement of our peace *was* upon him; and with his stripes
we are healed.

53:6☆

6 All we like sheep have gone astray; we have turned every one to his own
way; and the LORD hath laid on him the iniquity of us all.

4. Man Views the Servant's Death as a Failure

53:7 Mt 27:12–14 Lk 23:9 Acts 8:32, 33

7 He was oppressed, and he was afflicted, yet he opened not his mouth: he
is brought as a lamb to the slaughter, and as a sheep before her shearers is
dumb, so he openeth not his mouth.

53:8☆

8 He was taken from prison and from judgment: and who shall declare his
generation? for he was cut off out of the land of the living: for the
transgression of my people was he stricken.

53:9 Mt 27:57–60 1 Pet 2:22

9 And he made his grave with the wicked, and with the rich in his death;
because he had done no violence, neither *was any* deceit in his mouth.

5. God Regards the Servant's Death as a Glorious Triumph

53:10☆ Ps 22:30 Jn 1:29

10 ¶Yet it pleased the LORD to bruise him; he hath put *him* to grief: when
thou shalt make his soul an offering for sin, he shall see *his* seed, he shall
prolong *his* days, and the pleasure of the LORD shall prosper in his hand.

52:15 *So shall he sprinkle many nations,* or, "So shall he startle many nations." The meaning of the Hebrew word is uncertain.†

53:1ff This chapter is not looked upon by most Jews as pertaining to the Messiah. They think of it in terms of the nation Israel. The use of *he, his,* and *him* makes it difficult to suppose that Isaiah in this passage means anyone other than the Messiah. The New Testament makes this clear, but Jews generally refuse to accept the New Testament as having authority.

53:5 See note on 1 Pet. 2:24 regarding the doctrine of *the substitutionary or vicarious atonement of Jesus Christ. 53:5, 6 clearly* says that Jesus Christ died in the place of sinners.

53:6 Like sheep, men also go astray. They are ready to follow the examples of evil men. Like sheep, lost sinners cannot find their way back home. Christ is the Good Shepherd who finds the lost sheep and brings them back to the fold.

53:8 Isaiah foretold Christ's death by judicial murder. Other aspects of his work on Calvary which the Scriptures teach are (1) its necessity for our redemption (Acts 17:3; Luke 24:46); (2) its ordination by God (Acts 2:23); (3) its voluntary action by Jesus himself (Matt. 26:53; John 10:17, 18); and (4) its acceptability to the Father as a true and saving sacrifice (Eph. 5:2; 1 Thess. 5:10). Among the many fulfillments connected with the death of Jesus are the following: (1) his hands and his feet would be pierced (Ps. 22:14–17); (2) he would be offered gall and vinegar (Ps. 69:21); (3) he would be crucified with other malefactors (53:9, 12); (4) his bones would not be broken (Ps. 34:20); (5) the soldiers would cast lots for his garments (Ps. 22:18); and (6) he would be buried with a rich man (53:9).

53:10 *he shall prolong his days,* i.e., "he shall live again."†

11 He shall see of the travail of his soul, *and* shall be satisfied: by his
knowledge shall my righteous servant justify many; for he shall bear their
iniquities.

12 Therefore will I divide him *a portion* with the great, and he shall divide
the spoil with the strong; because he hath poured out his soul unto death:
and he was numbered with the transgressors; and he bare the sin of many,
and made intercession for the transgressors.

53:11 Jn 10:14–18; Rom 5:18, 19
☆**53:12** Mt 26:38, 39, 42; Lk 22:37; 2 Cor 5:21; Phil 2:9–11

I. GOD'S SALVATION FOR JEW AND GENTILE
1. The Servant's Death Brings Blessings to Israel
a. Israel's Enlargement

54 SING, O barren, thou *that* didst not bear; break forth into singing,
and cry aloud, thou *that* didst not travail with child: for more *are*
the children of the desolate than the children of the married wife, saith the
LORD.

2 Enlarge the place of thy tent, and let them stretch forth the curtains of
thine habitations: spare not, lengthen thy cords, and strengthen thy stakes;

3 For thou shalt break forth on the right hand and on the left; and thy
seed shall inherit the Gentiles, and make the desolate cities to be inhabited.

54:1 Isa 62:4; Gal 4:27
54:3 Gen 28:14; Isa 14:1, 2

b. The Lord's Abandoned Wife Restored

4 Fear not; for thou shalt not be ashamed: neither be thou confounded;
for thou shalt not be put to shame: for thou shalt forget the shame of thy
youth, and shalt not remember the reproach of thy widowhood any more.

5 For thy Maker *is* thine husband; the LORD of hosts *is* his name; and thy
Redeemer the Holy One of Israel; The God of the whole earth shall he be
called.

6 For the LORD hath called thee as a woman forsaken and grieved in
spirit, and a wife of youth, when thou wast refused, saith thy God.

7 For a small moment have I forsaken thee; but with great mercies will I
gather thee.

8 In a little wrath I hid my face from thee for a moment; but with
everlasting kindness will I have mercy on thee, saith the LORD thy
Redeemer.

☆**54:5** Hos 2:19
54:6 Isa 62:4
54:7 Isa 11:12
54:8 Isa 49:10, 13; 60:10

c. God's Kindness Will Never Leave Israel

9 For this *is as* the waters of Noah unto me: for *as* I have sworn that the
waters of Noah should no more go over the earth; so have I sworn that I
would not be wroth with thee, nor rebuke thee.

10 For the mountains shall depart, and the hills be removed; but my
kindness shall not depart from thee, neither shall the covenant of my peace
be removed, saith the LORD that hath mercy on thee.

54:9 Gen 9:9–11; Ezek 39:29
☆**54:10** 2 Sam 23:5; Ps 89:34; 102:25, 26

53:12 He who bore the sins of the world will win an incontestable victory and will exercise a universal dominion over all things. Because Christ conquered, his redeemed become more than conquerors through him who loved them and gave himself for them.

54:5 *The God of the whole earth shall he be called.* In the Old Testament God was known primarily as the God of Israel. But the partition wall between Israel and the Gentiles is being taken down. Thus he is the God of the whole earth, even of Athens, where there was a statue to the unknown God. In Christ there is no east or west.

54:10 The steadfast love and the peace of God are greater and stronger than the strongest parts of the visible creation. The unimaginable removal of the everlasting mountains and the perpetual hills would not diminish the character of God nor lessen his love and peace.

d. The Heritage of the Israel of God

54:11
Isa 28:16

11 ¶O thou afflicted, tossed with tempest, *and* not comforted, behold, I will
lay thy stones with fair colours, and lay thy foundations with sapphires.
12 And I will make thy windows of agates, and thy gates of carbuncles,
and all thy borders of pleasant stones.

54:13☆
Isa 66:12
Jer 31:34

13 And all thy children *shall be* taught of the LORD; and great *shall be* the
peace of thy children.

54:14
Isa 9:4, 7

14 In righteousness shalt thou be established: thou shalt be far from
oppression; for thou shalt not fear: and from terror; for it shall not come
near thee.

54:15
Isa 41:11–16

15 Behold, they shall surely gather together, *but* not by me: whosoever
shall gather together against thee shall fall for thy sake.
16 Behold, I have created the smith that bloweth the coals in the fire, and
that bringeth forth an instrument for his work; and I have created the
waster to destroy.

54:17
Isa 29:8

17 ¶No weapon that is formed against thee shall prosper; and every
tongue *that* shall rise against thee in judgment thou shalt condemn. This *is*
the heritage of the servants of the LORD, and their righteousness *is* of me,
saith the LORD.

2. The Servant Brings Blessing to the Gentiles

a. God's Everlasting Covenant

55:1☆
Ps 63:1
Lam 5:4
Mt 10:8
Jn 4:14

55 HO, every one that thirsteth, come ye to the waters, and he that
hath no money; come ye, buy, and eat; yea, come, buy wine and
milk without money and without price.

55:2
Ps 22:26
Eccles 6:2

2 Wherefore do ye spend money for *that which is* not bread? and your
labour for *that which* satisfieth not? hearken diligently unto me, and eat ye
that which is good, and let your soul delight itself in fatness.

55:3☆
Acts 13:34
Rom 10:5

3 Incline your ear, and come unto me: hear, and your soul shall live; and
I will make an everlasting covenant with you, *even* the sure mercies of
David.
4 Behold, I have given him *for* a witness to the people, a leader and
commander to the people.

55:5
Zech 8:22

5 Behold, thou shalt call a nation *that* thou knowest not, and nations *that*
knew not thee shall run unto thee because of the LORD thy God, and for the
Holy One of Israel; for he hath glorified thee.

b. Repentant Sinners Told to Seek the Lord

55:6
Ps 32:6
2 Cor 6:1, 2

6 ¶Seek ye the LORD while he may be found, call ye upon him while he is
near:

55:7☆
Isa 1:16; 44:22

7 Let the wicked forsake his way, and the unrighteous man his thoughts:
and let him return unto the LORD, and he will have mercy upon him; and to
our God, for he will abundantly pardon.

54:13 In the church age those who have been born again of the Spirit are children; they will be taught by the same Spirit. The God who adopts them will also see that they are educated in the things of God.

55:1 Whoever is thirsty is invited to come. In its larger *context, this obviously is the invitation to come* to Christ. He is the fountain opened for our sins, and the rock smitten for our salvation. Whoever thirsts and drinks of him finds that there are living waters and healing power in the Savior's blood.

55:3 *everlasting covenant . . . the sure mercies of David.* See 2 Sam. 7 for the terms of God's covenant with David, here remembered.†

55:7 A pardon is a remission of the penalty for one's transgression. Only God can issue a pardon, while the assurance of the pardon may be communicated to men by the agents of God. In order to receive a pardon the guilty one must (1) acknowledge his guilt and transgression (Ps. 51:3, 4; Luke 15:18; 18:13); (2) forsake his wickedness, i.e., repent (Acts 3:19; 17:30); and (3) turn to God who alone can grant the pardon (55:6; 1 Thess. 1:9; Acts 26:20). God's mercy is always available and a pardon assured when men repent and turn to God (55:7; Jer. 33:3, 8; Luke 24:47).

8 ¶For my thoughts *are* not your thoughts, neither *are* your ways my
ways, saith the LORD.

☆55:8 Isa 65:2

9 For *as* the heavens are higher than the earth, so are my ways higher than
your ways, and my thoughts than your thoughts.

55:9 Ps 103:11

c. God's Word Is Effective

10 For as the rain cometh down, and the snow from heaven, and returneth
not thither, but watereth the earth, and maketh it bring forth and bud, that
it may give seed to the sower, and bread to the eater:

55:10 2 Cor 9:10

11 So shall my word be that goeth forth out of my mouth: it shall not
return unto me void, but it shall accomplish that which I please, and it shall
prosper *in the thing* whereto I sent it.

☆55:11 Isa 46:10

d. The Redeemed Will Live in Joy

12 For ye shall go out with joy, and be led forth with peace: the mountains
and the hills shall break forth before you into singing, and all the trees of
the field shall clap *their* hands.

55:12 1 Chron 16:33; Jer 29:11

13 Instead of the thorn shall come up the fir tree, and instead of the brier
shall come up the myrtle tree: and it shall be to the LORD for a name, for an
everlasting sign *that* shall not be cut off.

55:13 Jer 33:9

e. God Has Opened His Arms to the Gentiles

56 THUS saith the LORD, Keep ye judgment, and do justice: for my
salvation *is* near to come, and my righteousness to be revealed.

☆56:1 Ps 85:9; Isa 1:17

2 Blessed *is* the man *that* doeth this, and the son of man *that* layeth hold
on it; that keepeth the sabbath from polluting it, and keepeth his hand from
doing any evil.

☆56:2 Ex 31:13–17; Ps 119:1, 2; Ezek 20:12, 20

3 ¶Neither let the son of the stranger, that hath joined himself to the
LORD, speak, saying, The LORD hath utterly separated me from his people:
neither let the eunuch say, Behold, I *am* a dry tree.

56:3 Acts 8:27, 37

4 For thus saith the LORD unto the eunuchs that keep my sabbaths, and
choose *the things* that please me, and take hold of my covenant;
5 Even unto them will I give in mine house and within my walls a place
and a name better than of sons and of daughters: I will give them an
everlasting name, that shall not be cut off.

56:5 Isa 2:2, 3; 26:1; 62:2

6 Also the sons of the stranger, that join themselves to the LORD, to serve
him, and to love the name of the LORD, to be his servants, every one that
keepeth the sabbath from polluting it, and taketh hold of my covenant;
7 Even them will I bring to my holy mountain, and make them joyful in
my house of prayer: their burnt offerings and their sacrifices *shall be*

☆56:6

☆56:7 Isa 65:25; Mic 4:1, 2; Mk 11:17; Rom 12:1; Heb 13:15

55:8 God's ways and thoughts are immutable, i.e., unchangeable. He is the same yesterday, today, and forever.

55:11 The word that comes from the mouth of God is efficacious in nature and among men. Whatever it is sent to do, it will do. The promises of mercy and grace will not lack anything in their fulfillment. But the word is sent on different errands. The same word that is a savor of life unto life for some is the savor of death unto death for others. It convinces the conscience and softens the heart in some; it sears the conscience and hardens the heart in others. It is therefore either the converting or the condemning word, leading to heaven or to hell.

56:1, 2 God solemnly charges those who know him to follow the line of duty, as a response to the fact that we benefit from all the gospel promises.

56:6 We are to remember the sabbath day to keep it holy. Whoever is glad to sanctify the Lord's day, not as a legalistic regulation but in the proper spirit, shall experience the assistance, acceptance, and comfort of God. Since the church is the house of God, all his people should assemble on the Lord's day.

56:7 All believers are called to a life of private and family prayer and devotion to God. Public prayer is also required (Heb. 10:25). God has promised to answer the public prayers of his people (2 Chron. 7:14; Matt. 18:19), and the Scriptures contain numerous examples of saints who engaged in public prayer.

accepted upon mine altar; for mine house shall be called an house of prayer
for all people.

56:8 Jn 10:16

8 The Lord GOD which gathereth the outcasts of Israel saith, Yet will I
gather *others* to him, beside those that are gathered unto him.

VIII. THE ESTABLISHMENT OF GOD'S UNIVERSAL KINGDOM (56:9—66:24)

A. ISRAEL'S EVIL RULERS CONDEMNED

1. Israel's Wicked Leaders

56:9 Jer 12:9

9 ¶All ye beasts of the field, come to devour, *yea,* all ye beasts in the
forest.

56:10 Jer 14:13, 14; Ezek 3:17

10 His watchmen *are* blind: they are all ignorant, they *are* all dumb dogs,
they cannot bark; sleeping, lying down, loving to slumber.

56:11 Jer 22:17; Mic 3:5, 11

11 Yea, *they are* greedy dogs *which* can never have enough, and they *are*
shepherds *that* cannot understand: they all look to their own way, every one
for his gain, from his quarter.

56:12 Lk 12:19, 20

12 Come ye, *say they,* I will fetch wine, and we will fill ourselves with
strong drink; and to morrow shall be as this day, *and* much more abundant.

2. God's Care for the Godly

57:1☆ 2 Kgs 22:19, 20; Ps 12:1

57 THE righteous perisheth, and no man layeth *it* to heart: and
merciful men *are* taken away, none considering that the righteous is
taken away from the evil *to come.*

57:2☆ Isa 26:7

2 He shall enter into peace: they shall rest in their beds, *each one* walking
in his uprightness.

3. The Evil of Children Offered as Human Sacrifices

3 ¶But draw near hither, ye sons of the sorceress, the seed of the adulterer
and the whore.

4 Against whom do ye sport yourselves? against whom make ye a wide
mouth, *and* draw out the tongue? *are* ye not children of transgression, a
seed of falsehood,

57:5☆ Ps 106:37, 38; Jer 2:20; 7:31

5 Enflaming yourselves with idols under every green tree, slaying the
children in the valleys under the clifts of the rocks?

57:6 Jer 5:9, 29; 7:18; Hab 2:19

6 Among the smooth *stones* of the stream *is* thy portion; they, they *are* thy
lot: even to them hast thou poured a drink offering, thou hast offered a
meat offering. Should I receive comfort in these?

4. Israel's Adulterous Idolatry

57:7 Ezek 16:16, 28

7 Upon a lofty and high mountain hast thou set thy bed: even thither
wentest thou up to offer sacrifice.

8 Behind the doors also and the posts hast thou set up thy remembrance:
for thou hast discovered *thyself to another* than me, and art gone up; thou
hast enlarged thy bed, and made thee *a covenant* with them; thou lovedst
their bed where thou sawest *it.*

57:9 Ezek 23:16, 40

9 And thou wentest to the king with ointment, and didst increase thy
perfumes, and didst send thy messengers far off, and didst debase *thyself*
even unto hell.

57:1, 2 God providentially takes the righteous out of this world through death. Thus they are removed from the calamities of life and enter into their eternal rest. To die in the Lord is great gain.

57:5 Those who professed to worship God but had turned to idols burned with lust and performed sexual sins. They also slew their own children as a sacrifice to idols in the valley of Hinnom and in the darkness of solitary places where they thought God could not see them.

10Thou art wearied in the greatness of thy way; *yet* saidst thou not, There
is no hope: thou hast found the life of thine hand; therefore thou wast not
grieved.
11And of whom hast thou been afraid or feared, that thou hast lied, and
hast not remembered me, nor laid *it* to thy heart? have not I held my peace
even of old, and thou fearest me not?

57:10 Jer 2:25
☆57:11 Prov 29:25 Jer 2:32

5. Idols Cannot Save Anyone

12I will declare thy righteousness, and thy works; for they shall not profit
thee.
13¶When thou criest, let thy companies deliver thee; but the wind shall
carry them all away; vanity shall take *them:* but he that putteth his trust in
me shall possess the land, and shall inherit my holy mountain;
14And shall say, Cast ye up, cast ye up, prepare the way, take up the
stumblingblock out of the way of my people.

57:12 Mic 3:1–4
☆57:13 Ps 37:3, 9 Jer 30:14
57:14 Isa 62:10

6. Refreshment for the Penitent; No Peace for the Wicked

15For thus saith the high and lofty One that inhabiteth eternity, whose
name *is* Holy; I dwell in the high and holy *place,* with him also *that is* of a
contrite and humble spirit, to revive the spirit of the humble, and to revive
the heart of the contrite ones.
16For I will not contend for ever, neither will I be always wroth: for the
spirit should fail before me, and the souls *which* I have made.
17For the iniquity of his covetousness was I wroth, and smote him: I hid
me, and was wroth, and he went on frowardly in the way of his heart.
18I have seen his ways, and will heal him: I will lead him also, and restore
comforts unto him and to his mourners.
19I create the fruit of the lips; Peace, peace to *him that is* far off, and to
him that is near, saith the LORD; and I will heal him.
20But the wicked *are* like the troubled sea, when it cannot rest, whose
waters cast up mire and dirt.
21*There is* no peace, saith my God, to the wicked.

57:15 Deut 33:27 Ps 34:18 Isa 66:1
57:16 Mic 7:18
57:17 Isa 1:4
57:18 Isa 53:5; 61:1–3
57:19 Isa 26:12 Eph 2:17
57:20 Job 18:5–14
☆57:21 Isa 48:22

7. True and False Worship
a. Good and Bad Fasting

58 CRY aloud, spare not, lift up thy voice like a trumpet, and shew my
people their transgression, and the house of Jacob their sins.
2Yet they seek me daily, and delight to know my ways, as a nation that
did righteousness, and forsook not the ordinance of their God: they ask of
me the ordinances of justice; they take delight in approaching to God.
3¶Wherefore have we fasted, *say they,* and thou seest not? *wherefore* have
we afflicted our soul, and thou takest no knowledge? Behold, in the day of
your fast ye find pleasure, and exact all your labours.

58:2 Isa 29:13 Jer 7:9, 10 Titus 1:16
☆58:3 Zech 7:5, 6 Lk 18:12

57:11 Because God has not immediately sentenced the wicked to their just deserts, they suppose that they do not need to fear the lawgiver. Because of the divine silence, they think they will forever escape divine wrath. God laughs in the heavens and challenges them to find their deliverance in their idols when they are in need of help. The wind will blow their idols in every direction.

57:13 *let thy companies deliver thee,* i.e., "let your idol-gods help you." The Israelites are to remember that there is no salvation in these false gods.

57:21 *There is no peace . . . to the wicked.* The wicked cannot be on good terms with God; there is no reconciliation with him. Whoever continues in his sins will find no rest in this life or in the life to come. God assures us that this is so simply because he says so.

58:3 All the fasting in the world will be of no value unless the heart is right with God. Performing such ceremonies while living in sin will avail nothing. True fasting must honor and please God. No fasting and an obedient heart are much better than great fasting and a disobedient walk.

58:4 1 Kgs 21:9, 10

4 Behold, ye fast for strife and debate, and to smite with the fist of
wickedness: ye shall not fast as *ye do this* day, to make your voice to be
heard on high.
5 Is it such a fast that I have chosen? a day for a man to afflict his soul? *is*
it to bow down his head as a bulrush, and to spread sackcloth and ashes
under him? wilt thou call this a fast, and an acceptable day to the LORD?

58:6 Neh 5:10–12

6 *Is* not this the fast that I have chosen? to loose the bands of wickedness,
to undo the heavy burdens, and to let the oppressed go free, and that ye
break every yoke?

58:7 Deut 22:1–4; Ezek 18:7, 16; Lk 3:11; Heb 13:2

7 *Is it* not to deal thy bread to the hungry, and that thou bring the poor
that are cast out to thy house? when thou seest the naked, that thou cover
him; and that thou hide not thyself from thine own flesh?

b. The Blessings for the Righteous

58:8 Ps 85:13; Jer 30:17

8 ¶Then shall thy light break forth as the morning, and thine health shall
spring forth speedily: and thy righteousness shall go before thee; the glory
of the LORD shall be thy rereward.

58:9☆

9 Then shalt thou call, and the LORD shall answer; thou shalt cry, and he
shall say, Here I *am.* If thou take away from the midst of thee the yoke, the
putting forth of the finger, and speaking vanity;

58:10☆ Deut 15:7

10 And *if* thou draw out thy soul to the hungry, and satisfy the afflicted
soul; then shall thy light rise in obscurity, and thy darkness *be* as the
noonday:

58:11 Ps 107:9; Song 4:15; Jn 4:14

11 And the LORD shall guide thee continually, and satisfy thy soul in
drought, and make fat thy bones: and thou shalt be like a watered garden,
and like a spring of water, whose waters fail not.

58:12 Ezek 36:10; Amos 9:11

12 And *they that shall be* of thee shall build the old waste places: thou shalt
raise up the foundations of many generations; and thou shalt be called, The
repairer of the breach, The restorer of paths to dwell in.

c. The Reward for Sabbath Observance

58:13☆ Ps 84:2, 10; Jer 17:21–27

13 If thou turn away thy foot from the sabbath, *from* doing thy pleasure on
my holy day; and call the sabbath a delight, the holy of the LORD,
honourable; and shalt honour him, not doing thine own ways, nor finding
thine own pleasure, nor speaking *thine own* words:

58:14 Deut 32:13

14 Then shalt thou delight thyself in the LORD; and I will cause thee to
ride upon the high places of the earth, and feed thee with the heritage of
Jacob thy father: for the mouth of the LORD hath spoken *it.*

8. Israel's Sins Cut Them Off from God

a. Israel's Sins Recounted

59:1☆ Jer 32:17; Ezek 8:18

59 BEHOLD, the LORD's hand is not shortened, that it cannot save;
neither his ear heavy, that it cannot hear:

58:9, 10 There is a right and a wrong way of fasting. The kind of fasting God wants is twofold: (1) they are to commit no acts of violence and fraud; (2) they are to abound in acts of charity by giving freely and cheerfully, plentifully and largely.

58:13 *The sabbath,* according to the Scriptures, was *set apart for the worship of God. Men were to abstain* from business activities and from personal pleasure and recreation. These principles have been largely abandoned among Christians today. But there is reason to suppose that faithfully keeping one day a week for the Lord will result in the same blessings being poured out on the faithful as promised here. Profaning the Lord's Day has resulted in spiritual decline, resulting in the withdrawal of the blessing of God. (See Neh. 13:17, 18).

59:1 The worshippers who have fasted and prayed to God for deliverance want to know why their prayers have not been answered and their fasting has gone unnoticed. Isaiah assures these inquirers that it is not because God is deaf or because he no longer has the power to deliver. Their iniquities have separated them from God and he will not listen to them nor will he help them. The only cure for this folly is repentance and confession, which is always followed by restoration.

2 But your iniquities have separated between you and your God, and your sins have hid *his* face from you, that he will not hear.

59:2 Isa 1:15

3 For your hands are defiled with blood, and your fingers with iniquity; your lips have spoken lies, your tongue hath muttered perverseness.

59:3 Jer 2:30, 34 Hos 4:2

4 None calleth for justice, nor *any* pleadeth for truth: they trust in vanity, and speak lies; they conceive mischief, and bring forth iniquity.

59:4 Ps 7:14

5 They hatch cockatrice' eggs, and weave the spider's web: he that eateth of their eggs dieth, and that which is crushed breaketh out into a viper.

☆**59:5**

6 Their webs shall not become garments, neither shall they cover themselves with their works: their works *are* works of iniquity, and the act of violence *is* in their hands.

59:6 Jer 6:7

7 Their feet run to evil, and they make haste to shed innocent blood: their thoughts *are* thoughts of iniquity; wasting and destruction *are* in their paths.

☆**59:7** Prov 1:16 Mk 7:21, 22 Rom 3:15–17

8 The way of peace they know not; and *there is* no judgment in their goings: they have made them crooked paths: whosoever goeth therein shall not know peace.

b. Israel's Confession of Sin

9 ¶Therefore is judgment far from us, neither doth justice overtake us: we wait for light, but behold obscurity; for brightness, *but* we walk in darkness.

59:9 Isa 5:30

10 We grope for the wall like the blind, and we grope as if *we had* no eyes: we stumble at noonday as in the night; *we are* in desolate places as dead *men*.

59:10 Deut 28:29 Lam 3:6

11 We roar all like bears, and mourn sore like doves: we look for judgment, but *there is* none; for salvation, *but* it is far off from us.

59:11 Ezek 7:16

12 For our transgressions are multiplied before thee, and our sins testify against us: for our transgressions *are* with us; and *as for* our iniquities, we know them;

☆**59:12** Ezra 9:6 Hos 5:5

13 In transgressing and lying against the LORD, and departing away from our God, speaking oppression and revolt, conceiving and uttering from the heart words of falsehood.

59:13 Mt 10:33

14 And judgment is turned away backward, and justice standeth afar off: for truth is fallen in the street, and equity cannot enter.

59:14 Hab 1:4

c. God Steps in to Redeem Zion

15 Yea, truth faileth; and he *that* departeth from evil maketh himself a prey: and the LORD saw *it*, and it displeased him that *there was* no judgment.

59:15 Isa 1:21–23 5:23

16 ¶And he saw that *there was* no man, and wondered that *there was* no intercessor: therefore his arm brought salvation unto him; and his righteousness, it sustained him.

59:16 Ezek 22:30

17 For he put on righteousness as a breastplate, and an helmet of salvation upon his head; and he put on the garments of vengeance *for* clothing, and was clad with zeal as a cloak.

59:17 Eph 6:14

18 *According to their* deeds, accordingly he will repay, fury to his adversaries, recompence to his enemies; to the islands he will repay recompence.

59:5 *cockatrice eggs* are snakes or adders, which are poisonous.

59:7 Their feet run to commit evil because their thoughts are iniquitous, and as a man "thinketh in his heart, so is he" (Prov. 23:7). What we do speaks more loudly than what we say.

59:12ff Israel confesses that its people have broken faith with God, who now contends with them for their transgressions. God has done rightly, for they have acted wickedly. God who sees everything sees iniquity immediately, and because he is pure he takes immediate offense, for all wickedness is ultimately directed against him.

59:19 Isa 30:28

19 So shall they fear the name of the LORD from the west, and his glory
from the rising of the sun. When the enemy shall come in like a flood, the
Spirit of the LORD shall lift up a standard against him.

59:20 Ezek 18:30, 31 Acts 2:38 Rom 11:26, 27
59:21☆ Isa 44:3 Jer 31:31–34

20 ¶And the Redeemer shall come to Zion, and unto them that turn from
transgression in Jacob, saith the LORD.
21 As for me, this *is* my covenant with them, saith the LORD; My spirit
that *is* upon thee, and my words which I have put in thy mouth, shall not
depart out of thy mouth, nor out of the mouth of thy seed, nor out of the
mouth of thy seed's seed, saith the LORD, from henceforth and for ever.

B. ZION'S FUTURE GLORY

1. Zion, the Light That Shines

60:1☆ Eph 5:14

60 ARISE, shine; for thy light is come, and the glory of the LORD is
risen upon thee.

60:2 Col 1:13

2 For, behold, the darkness shall cover the earth, and gross darkness the
people: but the LORD shall arise upon thee, and his glory shall be seen upon
thee.

60:3 Isa 2:3

3 And the Gentiles shall come to thy light, and kings to the brightness of
thy rising.

2. Gentiles Will Worship Israel's God

4 Lift up thine eyes round about, and see: all they gather themselves
together, they come to thee: thy sons shall come from far, and thy
daughters shall be nursed at *thy* side.

60:5 Ps 34:5 Isa 61:6

5 Then thou shalt see, and flow together, and thine heart shall fear, and be
enlarged; because the abundance of the sea shall be converted unto thee,
the forces of the Gentiles shall come unto thee.

60:6 Ps 72:10

6 The multitude of camels shall cover thee, the dromedaries of Mid'i-an
and E'phah; all they from She'ba shall come: they shall bring gold and
incense; and they shall shew forth the praises of the LORD.

60:7☆

7 All the flocks of Ke'dar shall be gathered together unto thee, the rams of
Ne-bai'oth shall minister unto thee: they shall come up with acceptance on
mine altar, and I will glorify the house of my glory.
8 Who *are* these *that* fly as a cloud, and as the doves to their windows?

60:9 Isa 49:22

9 Surely the isles shall wait for me, and the ships of Tarshish first, to bring
thy sons from far, their silver and their gold with them, unto the name of
the LORD thy God, and to the Holy One of Israel, because *he* hath glorified
thee.

3. Millennial Glory; Anti-Semites Will Bow before Israel

60:10 Isa 49:23

10 And the sons of strangers shall build up thy walls, and their kings shall
minister unto thee: for in my wrath I smote thee, but in my favour have I
had mercy on thee.

60:11 Isa 26:2

11 Therefore thy gates shall be open continually: they shall not be shut
day nor night; that *men* may bring unto thee the forces of the Gentiles, and
that their kings *may be* brought.

59:21 The Spirit and the Word go together. All the words spoken by clergymen will not profit anyone *unless these words are empowered by the work of the* Holy Spirit. The Spirit does his work by the Word and in agreement with it. Everything we say must be tried against the written Word of God. Then will it have the power of the Spirit working through it.

60:1 Although this chapter speaks about Zion's future glory, it may also be taken to have meaning for the church. Christ the light has come, and the glory of God is upon us who are in his Son. And people from every nation, kindred, and tongue shall be told of Christ, who is the light of the world that shines in the midst of pagan darkness. Converted Gentiles will know and worship Israel's God.

60:7 *Kedar . . . Nebaioth* were tribes of nomadic peoples springing from the loins of Ishmael.

[12]For the nation and kingdom that will not serve thee shall perish; yea,
those nations shall be utterly wasted.
[13]The glory of Lebanon shall come unto thee, the fir tree, the pine tree,
and the box together, to beautify the place of my sanctuary; and I will
make the place of my feet glorious.
[14]The sons also of them that afflicted thee shall come bending unto thee;
and all they that despised thee shall bow themselves down at the soles of
thy feet; and they shall call thee, The city of the LORD, The Zion of the
Holy One of Israel.

☆60:12 Zech 14:17
60:13 Ps 132:7
60:14 Isa 1:26; 14:1, 2 Rev 3:9

4. The Lord Will Be the Light of His People

[15]Whereas thou hast been forsaken and hated, so that no man went
through *thee,* I will make thee an eternal excellency, a joy of many
generations.
[16]Thou shalt also suck the milk of the Gentiles, and shalt suck the breast
of kings: and thou shalt know that I the LORD *am* thy Saviour and thy
Redeemer, the mighty One of Jacob.
[17]For brass I will bring gold, and for iron I will bring silver, and for wood
brass, and for stones iron: I will also make thy officers peace, and thine
exactors righteousness.
[18]Violence shall no more be heard in thy land, wasting nor destruction
within thy borders; but thou shalt call thy walls Salvation, and thy gates
Praise.
[19]The sun shall be no more thy light by day; neither for brightness shall
the moon give light unto thee: but the LORD shall be unto thee an
everlasting light, and thy God thy glory.
[20]Thy sun shall no more go down; neither shall thy moon withdraw itself:
for the LORD shall be thine everlasting light, and the days of thy mourning
shall be ended.
[21]Thy people also *shall be* all righteous: they shall inherit the land for
ever, the branch of my planting, the work of my hands, that I may be
glorified.
[22]A little one shall become a thousand, and a small one a strong nation:
I the LORD will hasten it in his time.

☆60:15 Isa 65:18 Jer 30:17
60:16 Isa 43:3, 11 63:16
60:18 Isa 26:1
☆60:19 Isa 9:2 Zech 2:5 Rev 21:23
60:20 Rev 21:4
60:21 Ps 37:22 Isa 45:24, 25
60:22 Isa 51:2

5. The Glad News of Salvation

a. The Command to Preach the Good News

61 THE Spirit of the Lord GOD *is* upon me; because the LORD hath
anointed me to preach good tidings unto the meek; he hath sent me
to bind up the brokenhearted, to proclaim liberty to the captives, and the
opening of the prison to *them that are* bound;

☆61:1 Isa 49:9 Lk 4:18, 19

60:12 Any nation or kingdom or peoples who do not submit themselves to the *Messiah,* who has been promised to Israel, shall perish eternally. Vengeance will come upon those who do not obey Messiah's gospel (see 2 Thess. 1:8).
60:15 The persecution and hatred of the Jews, who are still God's people and in whom he has an interest, will some day cease.
60:19 The day is coming when we shall need the sun and the moon no more. In the New Jerusalem, Jesus is the light of the city. There is no night there. Just as God was the light of the world before he created the sun and the moon, so shall the triune God be the light and moon of the universe when the end of time comes and sin has been eradicated from the cosmos.
61:1, 2 In the synagogue, Jesus quoted from these verses and applied them to himself (Luke 4:18, 19). For him to break off the quotation in the middle of 61:2 was odd, were it not for one important fact. The reason is plain enough. He said, "To preach the acceptable year of the Lord," and stopped. He stated that this passage had now been fulfilled. And it was, by his first advent. The remainder of 61:2, *the day of vengeance,* is yet future. That day will arrive when the times of the Gentiles have been fulfilled and the Lord returns in glory at his Second Advent. The remainder of the verse, which Jesus did not quote, will be fulfilled, inexorably and in God's time.

61:2 Mt 5:4
[2]To proclaim the acceptable year of the LORD, and the day of vengeance
of our God; to comfort all that mourn;
61:3 Ps 23:5 Jer 17:7, 8
[3]To appoint unto them that mourn in Zion, to give unto them beauty for
ashes, the oil of joy for mourning, the garment of praise for the spirit of
heaviness; that they might be called trees of righteousness, the planting of
the LORD, that he might be glorified.

b. Zion to Be Rebuilt at Last

61:4 Ezek 36:33 Amos 9:14
[4]¶And they shall build the old wastes, they shall raise up the former
desolations, and they shall repair the waste cities, the desolations of many
generations.
61:5 Isa 14:2
[5]And strangers shall stand and feed your flocks, and the sons of the alien
shall be your plowmen and your vinedressers.
61:6 Isa 66:21
[6]But ye shall be named the Priests of the LORD: *men* shall call you the
Ministers of our God: ye shall eat the riches of the Gentiles, and in their
glory shall ye boast yourselves.
61:7 Zech 9:12
[7]¶For your shame *ye shall have* double; and *for* confusion they shall
rejoice in their portion: therefore in their land they shall possess the
double: everlasting joy shall be unto them.
61:8 Gen 17:7 Isa 5:16
[8]For I the LORD love judgment, I hate robbery for burnt offering; and I
will direct their work in truth, and I will make an everlasting covenant with
them.
[9]And their seed shall be known among the Gentiles, and their offspring
among the people: all that see them shall acknowledge them, that they *are*
the seed *which* the LORD hath blessed.

c. The Hymn of Praise to God

61:10 Isa 51:3; 52:1
[10]I will greatly rejoice in the LORD, my soul shall be joyful in my God;
for he hath clothed me with the garments of salvation, he hath covered me
with the robe of righteousness, as a bridegroom decketh *himself* with
ornaments, and as a bride adorneth *herself* with her jewels.
[11]For as the earth bringeth forth her bud, and as the garden causeth the
things that are sown in it to spring forth; so the Lord GOD will cause
righteousness and praise to spring forth before all the nations.

6. Zion, Restored and Glorified

a. Israel, the Bride of the Lord

62:1 Isa 46:13
62 FOR Zion's sake will I not hold my peace, and for Jerusalem's sake
I will not rest, until the righteousness thereof go forth as brightness,
and the salvation thereof as a lamp *that* burneth.
62:2 Isa 56:5
[2]And the Gentiles shall see thy righteousness, and all kings thy glory:
and thou shalt be called by a new name, which the mouth of the LORD shall
name.
62:3 Zech 9:16 1 Thess 2:19
[3]Thou shalt also be a crown of glory in the hand of the LORD, and a royal
diadem in the hand of thy God.
62:4☆ Isa 54:6, 7 Jer 32:41 Zeph 3:17, 18
[4]Thou shalt no more be termed Forsaken; neither shall thy land any
more be termed Desolate: but thou shalt be called Heph'zi-bah, and thy
land Beu'lah: for the LORD delighteth in thee, and thy land shall be
married.

62:4 *Hephzi-bah,* i.e., "My delight is in her." *Beulah,* i.e., "married." God at last returns Israel to himself as his wife. 61:10 says that Israel has been "clothed . . . with the garments of salvation," and God "hath covered me with the robe of righteousness, as a bridegroom decketh himself with ornaments." The adulterous wife has been redeemed and once again is the pure bride in whom her husband delights.

[5]¶For *as* a young man marrieth a virgin, *so* shall thy sons marry thee: and
as the bridegroom rejoiceth over the bride, *so* shall thy God rejoice over
thee.

b. God's Rest for His People

[6]I have set watchmen upon thy walls, O Jerusalem, *which* shall never hold
their peace day nor night: ye that make mention of the LORD, keep not
silence,
[7]And give him no rest, till he establish, and till he make Jerusalem a
praise in the earth.

☆**62:6** Jer 14:21; Ezek 33:7; Zeph 3:19, 20; Lk 18:1–8

[8]The LORD hath sworn by his right hand, and by the arm of his strength,
Surely I will no more give thy corn *to be* meat for thine enemies; and the
sons of the stranger shall not drink thy wine, for the which thou hast
laboured:

62:8 Lev 26:16; Deut 28:31, 33

[9]But they that have gathered it shall eat it, and praise the LORD; and they
that have brought it together shall drink it in the courts of my holiness.

62:9 Isa 65:13, 21–23

c. The Favor of God on the Lord's Redeemed

[10]¶Go through, go through the gates; prepare ye the way of the people;
cast up, cast up the highway; gather out the stones; lift up a standard for
the people.
[11]Behold, the LORD hath proclaimed unto the end of the world, Say ye to
the daughter of Zion, Behold, thy salvation cometh; behold, his reward *is*
with him, and his work before him.

62:11 Isa 49:6; Zech 9:9

[12]And they shall call them, The holy people, The redeemed of the LORD:
and thou shalt be called, Sought out, A city not forsaken.

☆**62:12** Deut 7:6; 1 Pet 2:9

d. God's Vengeance on Israel's Enemies

63 WHO *is* this that cometh from Edom, with dyed garments from
Boz'rah? this *that is* glorious in his apparel, travelling in the
greatness of his strength? I that speak in righteousness, mighty to save.

☆**63:1** Jer 49:13; Zeph 3:17

[2]Wherefore *art thou* red in thine apparel, and thy garments like him that
treadeth in the winefat?

63:2 Rev 19:13, 15

[3]I have trodden the winepress alone; and of the people *there was* none
with me: for I will tread them in mine anger, and trample them in my fury;
and their blood shall be sprinkled upon my garments, and I will stain all
my raiment.

☆**63:3** Isa 22:5; Mic 7:10

[4]For the day of vengeance *is* in mine heart, and the year of my redeemed
is come.

63:4 Jer 51:6

[5]And I looked, and *there was* none to help; and I wondered that *there was*
none to uphold: therefore mine own arm brought salvation unto me; and
my fury, it upheld me.

62:6 *watchmen,* i.e., "intercessors."
62:12 *they shall call them, The holy people.* Israel, the chosen people of God, had become unholy through their transgressions. They had wandered far from God and had been dispersed around the earth. Now they have been regathered to their homeland and redeemed from their sins. Once more God, who is both righteous and just, is able to call them "the holy people." It is all of grace and not of works. God's original intention for Israel after thousands of years has been fulfilled at last.
63:1 Isaiah here predicts God's judgment on Edom, a people who had acted treacherously against Judah at the time of its overthrow. Judah's foe will now suffer retribution. *Bozrah,* an ancient city of Edom. It was militarily strong and was practically impregnable.
63:3 *I have trodden the winepress alone.* The reference here is to Jesus Christ, who experienced the wrath of God for sinners at Calvary and thus triumphed over principalities and powers. He was deserted by all, including his own disciples. The day is coming, however, when an angel from heaven will put in the sickle, gather the grapes, and thrust them into "the great winepress of the wrath of God" (Rev. 14:19).

6 And I will tread down the people in mine anger, and make them drunk in my fury, and I will bring down their strength to the earth.

C. ISRAEL REMEMBERS GOD'S MERCY AND PLEADS FOR DELIVERANCE

1. Israel, God's Very Own

63:7 1 Kgs 8:66; Ps 25:6, 7; 86:5; Eph 2:4

7 I will mention the lovingkindnesses of the LORD, *and* the praises of the LORD, according to all that the LORD hath bestowed on us, and the great goodness toward the house of Israel, which he hath bestowed on them according to his mercies, and according to the multitude of his lovingkindnesses.

63:8 Ex 6:7

8 For he said, Surely they *are* my people, children *that* will not lie: so he was their Saviour.

63:9☆ Ex 23:20–23; Judg 10:16

9 In all their affliction he was afflicted, and the angel of his presence saved them: in his love and in his pity he redeemed them; and he bare them, and carried them all the days of old.

2. God's Deliverance under Moses

63:10☆ Ps 78:40; Eph 4:30

10 ¶But they rebelled, and vexed his holy Spirit: therefore he was turned to be their enemy, *and* he fought against them.

63:11☆ Num 11:17, 25, 29; Isa 51:9, 10

11 Then he remembered the days of old, Moses, *and* his people, *saying,* Where *is* he that brought them up out of the sea with the shepherd of his flock? where *is* he that put his holy Spirit within him?

63:12 Ex 6:6; 14:21, 22

12 That led *them* by the right hand of Moses with his glorious arm, dividing the water before them, to make himself an everlasting name?

63:13 Jer 31:9

13 That led them through the deep, as an horse in the wilderness, *that* they should not stumble?

63:14☆ Josh 21:44

14 As a beast goeth down into the valley, the Spirit of the LORD caused him to rest: so didst thou lead thy people, to make thyself a glorious name.

3. Judah Beseeches God for Help

63:15 Ps 80:14; 123:1; Jer 31:20

15 ¶Look down from heaven, and behold from the habitation of thy holiness and of thy glory: where *is* thy zeal and thy strength, the sounding of thy bowels and of thy mercies toward me? are they restrained?

63:16 Isa 41:8

16 Doubtless thou *art* our father, though Abraham be ignorant of us, and Israel acknowledge us not: thou, O LORD, *art* our father, our redeemer; thy name *is* from everlasting.

63:17☆ Isa 29:13, 14

17 ¶O LORD, why hast thou made us to err from thy ways, *and* hardened our heart from thy fear? Return for thy servants' sake, the tribes of thine inheritance.

63:9 *the angel of his presence.* Some understand this to be a created angel, one of the highest if not the highest one who stands before God. Others say this refers to Jesus Christ, who is the eternal Word, the angel of the covenant, God's messenger to the world. He is the angel of God's face, for he is the express image of his person (Heb. 1:3). The glory of God shines in the face of Jesus Christ.

63:10 In all ages and at all times men are saved when *they come under conviction of sin by the Holy Spirit* and in faith are regenerated by him. Here we are told that Israel rebelled against the work of the Holy Spirit and by that rebellion vexed or grieved the Holy Spirit. In the New Testament, believers are commanded, "Grieve not the holy Spirit of God, whereby ye are sealed unto the day of redemption" (Eph. 4:30). So we learn that it is possible for the saints of God to grieve the Holy Spirit. They are saints because they have been sealed.

63:11 God had put his Holy Spirit upon Moses. Neh. 9:20 declares that God gave Israel the Holy Spirit to instruct them. In Isa. 63:14 we read that the Holy Spirit gave rest to the people of Israel. The Holy Spirit, the third person of the Trinity, was gloriously at work in the Old Testament. This work of the Holy Spirit before Pentecost is often overlooked by believers.

63:14 Israel in the wilderness was given places of rest from time to time by Moses, who worked under the direction of the Holy Spirit.

63:17 *Return for thy servants' sake.* Those who are God's need him; from him alone they expect their deliverance.

18The people of thy holiness have possessed *it* but a little while: our
adversaries have trodden down thy sanctuary.
19We are *thine:* thou never barest rule over them; they were not called by
thy name.

63:18 Ps 74:3-7
63:19 Lam 3:43-45

4. Prayer for Help against the Gentiles

64 OH that thou wouldest rend the heavens, that thou wouldest come
down, that the mountains might flow down at thy presence,
2As *when* the melting fire burneth, the fire causeth the waters to boil, to
make thy name known to thine adversaries, *that* the nations may tremble at
thy presence!
3When thou didst terrible things *which* we looked not for, thou camest
down, the mountains flowed down at thy presence.
4For since the beginning of the world *men* have not heard, nor perceived
by the ear, neither hath the eye seen, O God, beside thee, *what* he hath
prepared for him that waiteth for him.

64:1 Ex 19:18; Judg 5:5; Nah 1:5
64:2 Ps 99:1
64:3 Ps 65:5
☆64:4 Isa 40:31; 1 Cor 2:9

5. The Confession of Sin

5Thou meetest him that rejoiceth and worketh righteousness, *those that*
remember thee in thy ways: behold, thou art wroth; for we have sinned: in
those is continuance, and we shall be saved.
6But we are all as an unclean *thing*, and all our righteousnesses *are* as
filthy rags; and we all do fade as a leaf; and our iniquities, like the wind,
have taken us away.
7And *there is* none that calleth upon thy name, that stirreth up himself to
take hold of thee: for thou hast hid thy face from us, and hast consumed us,
because of our iniquities.

☆64:6 Ps 90:5, 6; Isa 1:30; 48:1
64:7 Deut 31:18; Isa 1:15

6. Appeal for Divine Help

8But now, O LORD, thou *art* our father; we *are* the clay, and thou our
potter; and we all *are* the work of thy hand.
9¶Be not wroth very sore, O LORD, neither remember iniquity for ever:
behold, see, we beseech thee, we *are* all thy people.
10Thy holy cities are a wilderness, Zion is a wilderness, Jerusalem a
desolation.
11Our holy and our beautiful house, where our fathers praised thee, is
burned up with fire: and all our pleasant things are laid waste.
12Wilt thou refrain thyself for these *things*, O LORD? wilt thou hold thy
peace, and afflict us very sore?

☆64:8 Ps 100:3; Isa 45:9
64:9 Ps 79:13; Mic 7:18
64:11 Ps 74:5-7
☆64:12 Ps 83:1

64:4 Believers can be assured that as they wait for God, he is at work on their behalf to accomplish good for them.
64:6 *filthy rags,* literally, "filthy as a menstruating woman's rags."†
64:8 *thou art our father.* The concept of God as our father, that is, the father of believers, is found in the Old Testament and expanded considerably in the New Testament. In our relationship to God, he is our father and we are his children. We may not always walk as we should, and we may act foolishly and carelessly, but God is still our father. He is our father by creation, for he has made us. But he is especially our father by covenant, for he has redeemed us, and, by his death, Christ has restored the relationship which was broken and lost because of our sins.
64:12 Infidelity was one of the sins of the later Jews who no longer made idols of wood and stone. When Jesus stood and cried to them, they did not hear and they refused to answer (John 7:37). They remained unmoved by his warnings and had no confidence in his reasonings.

D. GOD'S MERCY FOR SPIRITUAL ISRAEL

1. God's Judgment against Unspiritual Israel

65:1☆ Hos 1:10

65 I am sought of *them that* asked not *for me;* I am found of *them that*
sought me not: I said, Behold me, behold me, unto a nation *that*
was not called by my name.

65:2☆ Ps 81:11, 12; Rom 10:21

2 I have spread out my hands all the day unto a rebellious people, which
walketh in a way *that was* not good, after their own thoughts;

65:3 Job 2:5

3 A people that provoketh me to anger continually to my face; that
sacrificeth in gardens, and burneth incense upon altars of brick;

65:4 Lev 11:7

4 Which remain among the graves, and lodge in the monuments, which
eat swine's flesh, and broth of abominable *things is in* their vessels;

65:5 Mt 9:11

5 Which say, Stand by thyself, come not near to me; for I am holier than
thou. These *are* a smoke in my nose, a fire that burneth all the day.

65:6 Ps 50:3, 21; Isa 42:14

6 Behold, *it is* written before me: I will not keep silence, but will
recompense, even recompense into their bosom,

65:7 Jer 13:25; Ezek 20:27, 28; Hos 2:13

7 Your iniquities, and the iniquities of your fathers together, saith the
LORD, which have burned incense upon the mountains, and blasphemed me
upon the hills: therefore will I measure their former work into their bosom.

2. God Will Save Spiritual Israel and Destroy Apostates

8 ¶Thus saith the LORD, As the new wine is found in the cluster, and *one*
saith, Destroy it not; for a blessing *is* in it: so will I do for my servants'
sakes, that I may not destroy them all.

65:9☆ Amos 9:11–15

9 And I will bring forth a seed out of Jacob, and out of Judah an inheritor
of my mountains: and mine elect shall inherit it, and my servants shall
dwell there.

65:10☆ Josh 7:24; Isa 33:9

10 And Shar′on shall be a fold of flocks, and the valley of A′chor a place
for the herds to lie down in, for my people that have sought me.

65:11 Isa 1:4, 28

11 ¶But ye *are* they that forsake the LORD, that forget my holy mountain,
that prepare a table for that troop, and that furnish the drink offering unto
that number.

65:12 2 Chron 36:15, 16; Prov 1:24

12 Therefore will I number you to the sword, and ye shall all bow down to
the slaughter: because when I called, ye did not answer; when I spake, ye
did not hear; but did evil before mine eyes, and did choose *that* wherein I
delighted not.

65:13 Isa 5:13

13 Therefore thus saith the Lord GOD, Behold, my servants shall eat, but
ye shall be hungry: behold, my servants shall drink, but ye shall be thirsty:
behold, my servants shall rejoice, but ye shall be ashamed:

65:14 Mt 8:12; Lk 13:28

14 Behold, my servants shall sing for joy of heart, but ye shall cry for
sorrow of heart, and shall howl for vexation of spirit.

65:15 Jer 24:9

15 And ye shall leave your name for a curse unto my chosen: for the Lord
GOD shall slay thee, and call his servants by another name:

65:16 Isa 45:23

16 That he who blesseth himself in the earth shall bless himself in the God
of truth; and he that sweareth in the earth shall swear by the God of truth;

65:1, 2 *of them,* i.e., "of people," or "those." Some believe that this verse as well as the next applies to *Israelites rather than to the nations.*† *These verses are quoted by Paul* in Romans: "I was found of them that sought me not; I was made manifest unto them that asked not after me. . . . All day long I have stretched forth my hands unto a disobedient and gainsaying people" (Rom. 10:20, 21). This is the love of God, manifested toward sinners who neither seek God nor call on him. Yet God reaches out to such people for he continues to love sinners, bad as they are and rebellious as they continue to be.

65:9, 10 Israel is back in the land of Palestine today, but not in peace and safety. God here promises a time when Jews will not only occupy the land, but will do so without danger or fear, and in abundant material as well as spiritual blessing.

because the former troubles are forgotten, and because they are hid from
mine eyes.

3. Happiness in the Messianic New Age

17¶For, behold, I create new heavens and a new earth: and the former ☆65:17 2 Pet 3:13
shall not be remembered, nor come into mind.
18But be ye glad and rejoice for ever *in that* which I create: for, behold, I 65:18 Ps 98 Isa 35:10
create Jerusalem a rejoicing, and her people a joy.
19And I will rejoice in Jerusalem, and joy in my people: and the voice of 65:19 Jer 32:41
weeping shall be no more heard in her, nor the voice of crying.
20There shall be no more thence an infant of days, nor an old man that 65:20 Eccles 8:12, 13
hath not filled his days: for the child shall die an hundred years old; but the
sinner *being* an hundred years old shall be accursed.
21And they shall build houses, and inhabit *them;* and they shall plant 65:21 Deut 32:46, 47 Ps 92:12–14 Amos 9:14
vineyards, and eat the fruit of them.
22They shall not build, and another inhabit; they shall not plant, and
another eat: for as the days of a tree *are* the days of my people, and mine
elect shall long enjoy the work of their hands.
23They shall not labour in vain, nor bring forth for trouble; for they *are* 65:23 Isa 61:9
the seed of the blessed of the LORD, and their offspring with them.
24And it shall come to pass, that before they call, I will answer; and while ☆65:24 Ps 91:15 Dan 10:12
they are yet speaking, I will hear.
25The wolf and the lamb shall feed together, and the lion shall eat straw ☆65:25 Gen 3:14 Isa 11:6, 9
like the bullock: and dust *shall be* the serpent's meat. They shall not hurt
nor destroy in all my holy mountain, saith the LORD.

E. GOD'S FINAL JUDGMENTS

1. The Ultimate Doom of Sinners

66 THUS saith the LORD, The heaven *is* my throne, and the earth *is* ☆66:1 Ps 11:4 Mt 5:34, 35 Jn 4:20, 21 Acts 7:48–50
my footstool: where *is* the house that ye build unto me? and where
is the place of my rest?
2For all those *things* hath mine hand made, and all those *things* have 66:2 Ps 34:18 Lk 18:13, 14
been, saith the LORD: but to this *man* will I look, *even* to *him that is* poor
and of a contrite spirit, and trembleth at my word.
3He that killeth an ox *is as if* he slew a man; he that sacrificeth a lamb, *as
if* he cut off a dog's neck; he that offereth an oblation, *as if he offered*
swine's blood; he that burneth incense, *as if* he blessed an idol. Yea, they
have chosen their own ways, and their soul delighteth in their abominations.
4I also will choose their delusions, and will bring their fears upon them; 66:4 Prov 1:31, 32 10:24 Jer 7:13, 30
because when I called, none did answer; when I spake, they did not hear:
but they did evil before mine eyes, and chose *that* in which I delighted not.

65:17 This verse seems to be quite in accord with John's great vision of the new heaven and the new earth (Rev. 21:1).
65:24, 25 How great is God; he answers the prayers of people before they have prayed them, and while they then pray, gives them what they want before they have finished their prayers. 65:25 assures us that what all good men want will come at last. The ideal age, the utopia men dream of, will come when Messiah returns in power and glory. The wolf and the lamb will feed together. The lion will eat straw as does the ox. Peace will reign and war shall be no more. All men will live in peace with each other.
66:1 Great as the temple was, it is as nothing when compared with heaven—there rests the throne of God. Heaven is the site of his glory and of his government. He sits exalted in the highest dignity and dominion. From there he rules all the affairs of the cosmos. The earth is the footstool on which God stands. If this is true, then by comparison the temple is small indeed.

2. The Rebirth of Israel

66:5☆ Ps 38:20; Mt 5:10–12; Jn 9:34

5¶Hear the word of the LORD, ye that tremble at his word; Your brethren
that hated you, that cast you out for my name's sake, said, Let the LORD be
glorified: but he shall appear to your joy, and they shall be ashamed.

66:6 Joel 3:7

6A voice of noise from the city, a voice from the temple, a voice of the
LORD that rendereth recompence to his enemies.
7Before she travailed, she brought forth; before her pain came, she was
delivered of a man child.
8Who hath heard such a thing? who hath seen such things? Shall the
earth be made to bring forth in one day? *or* shall a nation be born at once?
for as soon as Zion travailed, she brought forth her children.

66:9 Isa 37:3

9Shall I bring to the birth, and not cause to bring forth? saith the LORD:
shall I cause to bring forth, and shut *the womb?* saith thy God.

3. The Prosperity of the New Age

66:10☆ Ps 122:6; Rom 15:10

10Rejoice ye with Jerusalem, and be glad with her, all ye that love her:
rejoice for joy with her, all ye that mourn for her:
11That ye may suck, and be satisfied with the breasts of her consolations;
that ye may milk out, and be delighted with the abundance of her glory.

66:12 Isa 48:18; 60:5

12For thus saith the LORD, Behold, I will extend peace to her like a river,
and the glory of the Gentiles like a flowing stream: then shall ye suck, ye
shall be borne upon *her* sides, and be dandled upon *her* knees.
13As one whom his mother comforteth, so will I comfort you; and ye
shall be comforted in Jerusalem.

66:14 Prov 3:8; Zech 10:7

14And when ye see *this*, your heart shall rejoice, and your bones shall
flourish like an herb: and the hand of the LORD shall be known toward his
servants, and *his* indignation toward his enemies.

4. The Punishment of the Wicked

15For, behold, the LORD will come with fire, and with his chariots like a
whirlwind, to render his anger with fury, and his rebuke with flames of fire.

66:16☆ Ezek 38:22

16For by fire and by his sword will the LORD plead with all flesh: and the
slain of the LORD shall be many.

66:17 Lev 11:7

17They that sanctify themselves, and purify themselves in the gardens
behind one *tree* in the midst, eating swine's flesh, and the abomination, and
the mouse, shall be consumed together, saith the LORD.

5. Jew and Gentile Together Glorify God

66:18☆

18For I *know* their works and their thoughts: it shall come, that I will
gather all nations and tongues; and they shall come, and see my glory.

66:19 1 Chron 16:24; Isa 42:12

19And I will set a sign among them, and I will send those that escape of
them unto the nations, *to* Tarshish, Pul, and Lud, that draw the bow, *to*
Tu'bal, and Ja'van, *to* the isles afar off, that have not heard my fame,

---

66:5 Israel in general would not hear God, but in all generations there have been the few who tremble at the Word of God. To them there is comfort, help, and forgiveness in the Redeemer.

66:10 *Israel and the church together are objects* of God's love and are recipients of his great salvation. We are to pray for the peace of Jerusalem, which means the restoration of Israel. And we are to pray for the church of Christ—his bride and thus his pride and joy. Israel and the church together will live forever in the New Jerusalem, the heavenly fulfillment of the type manifested in the Jerusalem of Israel on earth.

66:16 At the time of the final judgment, God will satisfy his wrath by fire and sword. He will cut off and send to the lake of fire the impenitent, upon whom judgment comes for their rejection of God's gracious offer of eternal life.

66:18 Jewish and Gentile believers of all ages will be gathered to see the glory of God the Redeemer. This will occur at the end of the age, when all things will be delivered into the hands of the Father by Jesus Christ the Redeemer.

neither have seen my glory; and they shall declare my glory among the
Gentiles.
20 And they shall bring all your brethren *for* an offering unto the LORD
out of all nations upon horses, and in chariots, and in litters, and upon
mules, and upon swift beasts, to my holy mountain Jerusalem, saith the
LORD, as the children of Israel bring an offering in a clean vessel into the
house of the LORD.
21 And I will also take of them for priests *and* for Levites, saith the LORD.

66:20 Isa 2:2; 43:5, 6 49:22; 52:11 60:4

66:21 Isa 61:6 1 Pet 2:5, 9

6. Heaven for the Righteous; Hell for the Wicked

22 For as the new heavens and the new earth, which I will make, shall
remain before me, saith the LORD, so shall your seed and your name
remain.
23 And it shall come to pass, *that* from one new moon to another, and
from one sabbath to another, shall all flesh come to worship before me,
saith the LORD.
24 And they shall go forth, and look upon the carcases of the men that
have transgressed against me: for their worm shall not die, neither shall
their fire be quenched; and they shall be an abhorring unto all flesh.

☆**66:22** Jn 10:27–29 2 Pet 3:13

66:23 Isa: 27:13

66:24 Isa 1:31 Dan 12:2

66:22 Paradise was lost by the sin of Adam in the Garden of Eden. The whole cosmos was affected by his transgression. For millennia God has been working out his great plan of salvation. And now the end of the age has come. The work of Christ has been fully finished. The new heavens and the new earth have come. Their pristine glory has been recovered. Paradise has been regained, and sin shall reign no more. God is all in all, and eternity for the saints of God has begun.

THE BOOK OF THE PROPHET
JEREMIAH

Authorship, date, and background This book is named after the prophet Jeremiah (whose name means "Yahweh establishes"), who was born in Anathoth. His father, Hilkiah (not to be confused with Hilkiah the high priest who was associated with the discovery of the Law in the temple in 2 Kings 22–23), was a member of the priestly class. Jeremiah was undoubtedly of the line of Abiathar, who also lived in the territory of Benjamin, and not of the line of Zadok, which started under Solomon in Jerusalem. He was born ca. 652–648 B.C. and began his ministry in 627 B.C. when he was about twenty years of age. He was God's prophet to Judah in its last days before the captivity (627–586 B.C.). He was a reluctant prophet who suffered greatly for his bold pronouncements of coming judgment. Yet he had been called of God before he was born (see 1:4–10). Baruch was his faithful secretary to whom he dictated much of the book we have.

The Septuagint version of this book differs from the Hebrew text in two important regards: the arrangement is different and the Hebrew is approximately 2700 words longer. The text in our English Bibles comes from the Hebrew, which is not arranged chronologically. Baruch probably added details about Jeremiah's ministry as seen by the observation, "Then took Jeremiah another roll, and gave it to Baruch the scribe, the son of Neriah; who wrote therein from the mouth of Jeremiah all the words of the book which Jehoiakim king of Judah had burned in the fire: and there were added besides unto them many like words" (36:32). Rationalistic scholars claim that parts of the book were not dictated by Jeremiah or written by Baruch. There is no adequate evidence for this assumption. In its written form the entire book can be ascribed to Baruch.

Jeremiah's ministry began when Josiah, who was king, began a reform movement which was not continued by his successors. Jeremiah prophesied under the kingships of Jehoahaz, Jehoiakim, Jehoiachin, and Zedekiah. The latter was to witness the defeat of Judah and the execution of his kin. He was blinded and sent off to Babylonia when Nebuchadnezzar (called Nebuchadrezzar in the King James Version) seized and razed Jerusalem. The Northern Kingdom had already fallen and Judah was now declining.

The period prior to the captivity which began in 586 B.C. was a triangular struggle for world supremacy by Assyria, Babylon, and Egypt. Babylonia was able to crush the Assyrian army. In 605 B.C. at Carchemish, Babylon defeated the Egyptians too. Judah was caught in the middle of the warfare since it was in the pathway between Africa and the Middle East. The fall of Judah and the seventy years' captivity were a direct result of Judah's apostasy and refusal to repent.

Characteristics and content Jeremiah is known to us as the weeping prophet. He speaks his word for God against a background of deceptive prophets who, for the most part, tell the people of Judah the exact opposite of what Jeremiah says. Jeremiah claims to be God's true prophet over against false prophets like Hananiah, who is judged and killed at last by God. Jeremiah wishes to remain silent and prophesy no more. But God's word is like a burning fire and he cannot contain himself. Yet he is threatened by what happens to other true prophets. Uriah is one of them. He flees to Egypt to escape the wrath of King Jehoiakim. Uriah is seized in Egypt and brought back to King Jehoiakim "who slew him with a sword and cast his dead body into the graves of the common people" (26:20–23).

Jeremiah faithfully delivers God's word of doom and judgment to Judah. Nothing moves him from doing this over and over again. He suffers in solitude, agonizes over the gross sins of his countrymen, and feels keenly the awfulness of judgment which is sure to come. God promises Jeremiah deliverance. When Babylonia seizes Judah, Jeremiah is not taken captive to Babylon. After the captivity begins, he goes to Egypt to continue his prophetic ministry among a remnant. So far as we know, he dies there among a people who still are unwilling to repent and turn to God for deliverance.

Outline

I. Jeremiah's call from God and his message (1:1—20:18)
II. Prophecies under Jehoiakim and Zedekiah (21:1—39:18)
III. Prophecies after the fall of Jerusalem (40:1—45:5)

IV. Prophecies against the heathen nations and cities (46:1—51:64)
V. The appendix (52:1–34)

I. JEREMIAH'S CALL FROM GOD AND HIS MESSAGE (1:1—20:18)

A. GOD CALLS AND COMMISSIONS THE PROPHET

1. The Introduction

1 THE words of Jer-e-mi'ah the son of Hil-ki'ah, of the priests that *were* **1:1**
in An'a-thoth in the land of Benjamin: 1 Kgs 13:2; 2 Kgs 21:24
2To whom the word of the LORD came in the days of Jo-si'ah the son of 2 Chron 36:12, 21
A'mon king of Judah, in the thirteenth year of his reign. Ezra 1:1
3It came also in the days of Je-hoi'a-kim the son of Jo-si'ah king of Jer 3:6; 36:2; Dan 9:2
Judah, unto the end of the eleventh year of Zed-e-ki'ah the son of Jo-si'ah Mt 2:17; 16:14; 27:9
king of Judah, unto the carrying away of Jerusalem captive in the fifth **1:3**
month. 2 Kgs 23:34; Jer 25:1; 39:2

2. God Calls Jeremiah

4¶Then the word of the LORD came unto me, saying, ☆**1:4**
5Before I formed thee in the belly I knew thee; and before thou camest ☆**1:5**
forth out of the womb I sanctified thee, *and* I ordained thee a prophet unto Ps 139:15, 16; Isa 49:1, 5
the nations. Jer 25:15–26
6Then said I, Ah, Lord GOD! behold, I cannot speak: for I *am* a child. ☆**1:6** Ex 4:10
7¶But the LORD said unto me, Say not, I *am* a child: for thou shalt go to ☆**1:7**
all that I shall send thee, and whatsoever I command thee thou shalt speak. Ezek 2:3, 4
8Be not afraid of their faces: for I *am* with thee to deliver thee, saith the **1:8**
LORD. Ezek 2:6
9Then the LORD put forth his hand, and touched my mouth. And the **1:9**
LORD said unto me, Behold, I have put my words in thy mouth. Ex 4:11–16; Deut 18:18
10See, I have this day set thee over the nations and over the kingdoms, to **1:10**
root out, and to pull down, and to destroy, and to throw down, to build, Isa 44:26–28; Jer 24:6; 31:28
and to plant.

3. The Vision of the Branch and the Boiling Pot

11¶Moreover the word of the LORD came unto me, saying, Jer-e-mi'ah, **1:11**
what seest thou? And I said, I see a rod of an almond tree. Jer 24:3; Amos 7:8
12Then said the LORD unto me, Thou hast well seen: for I will hasten my ☆**1:12**
word to perform it. Deut 32:35
13And the word of the LORD came unto me the second time, saying, What **1:13**
seest thou? And I said, I see a seething pot; and the face thereof *is* toward Zech 4:2
the north.

1:4 The word of the Lord came to Jeremiah. It was not Jeremiah's word, nor was it a delusion. Not every one who claims to speak for God has the true message of God. There are false prophets as well as true ones. Jeremiah was to be accused of being a false prophet, but the supernatural works he performed were proofs to all that he was genuine.

1:5 God's sovereign direction of Jeremiah's life tells us something of the divine operation of God's will. God had a master plan for Jeremiah before the prophet was conceived in his mother's womb. God's call to the prophetic office was effectual; Jeremiah responded to the sovereign call. God gave Jeremiah all he needed to fulfill his ministry. Jeremiah's excuses to avoid fulfilling God's call for his life were silly and unworthy. Moreover, Jeremiah was not able to keep from prophesying even when he decided to remain silent (20:9).

1:6, 7 Jeremiah either was lacking in confidence or lacking in a willingness to become a prophet when God called him. His excuse was that he was only a youth (twenty years of age). A tender age is no reason to refuse to speak for God. Samuel was a mere child when he conveyed God's message to Eli.

1:12 *for I will hasten* ["watch over"] *my word to perform it,* i.e., "I will surely carry out my threats of punishment." There is a word play here between *shaqedh* ("almond") in 1:11 and *shoqedh* ("watching").†

1:14 Isa 41:25; Jer 4:6; 10:22

14 Then the LORD said unto me, Out of the north an evil shall break forth upon all the inhabitants of the land.

1:15 Isa 22:7; Jer 25:9

15 For, lo, I will call all the families of the kingdoms of the north, saith the LORD; and they shall come, and they shall set every one his throne at the entering of the gates of Jerusalem, and against all the walls thereof round about, and against all the cities of Judah.

1:16 Isa 2:8; 37:19; Jer 7:9; 10:3–5; 19:4

16 And I will utter my judgments against them touching all their wickedness, who have forsaken me, and have burned incense unto other gods, and worshipped the works of their own hands.

1:17☆ Ezek 3:16–18

17 ¶Thou therefore gird up thy loins, and arise, and speak unto them all that I command thee: be not dismayed at their faces, lest I confound thee before them.

1:18☆

18 For, behold, I have made thee this day a defenced city, and an iron pillar, and brasen walls against the whole land, against the kings of Judah, against the princes thereof, against the priests thereof, and against the people of the land.

1:19☆ Jer 20:11

19 And they shall fight against thee; but they shall not prevail against thee; for I *am* with thee, saith the LORD, to deliver thee.

B. THE WICKEDNESS OF ISRAEL

1. Israel's Earlier Faithfulness

2 MOREOVER the word of the LORD came to me, saying,

2:2 Isa 58:1; Jer 11:6; Ezek 16:8

2 Go and cry in the ears of Jerusalem, saying, Thus saith the LORD; I remember thee, the kindness of thy youth, the love of thine espousals, when thou wentest after me in the wilderness, in a land *that was* not sown.

2:3 Ex 19:5, 6; Deut 7:6; 14:2; Isa 41:11; Jer 30:16

3 Israel *was* holiness unto the LORD, *and* the firstfruits of his increase: all that devour him shall offend; evil shall come upon them, saith the LORD.

2. Israel's Unfaithfulness

2:4 2 Kgs 17:15; Jer 8:19; Mic 6:3

4 Hear ye the word of the LORD, O house of Jacob, and all the families of the house of Israel:

5 ¶Thus saith the LORD, What iniquity have your fathers found in me, that they are gone far from me, and have walked after vanity, and are become vain?

2:6 Deut 8:15; 32:10

6 Neither said they, Where *is* the LORD that brought us up out of the land of Egypt, that led us through the wilderness, through a land of deserts and of pits, through a land of drought, and of the shadow of death, through a land that no man passed through, and where no man dwelt?

2:7☆ Deut 8:7–9; 11:10–12; Jer 3:2; 16:18

7 And I brought you into a plentiful country, to eat the fruit thereof and the goodness thereof; but when ye entered, ye defiled my land, and made mine heritage an abomination.

2:8☆ Jer 10:21; 23:13; Hab 2:18; Mal 2:6, 7

8 The priests said not, Where *is* the LORD? and they that handle the law

---

1:17–19 In 1:17–19 God informs Jeremiah about his responsibilities. He is told to gird up his loins, i.e., to free himself from anything that would hinder him in his work for God. He is to declare the whole counsel of God. Every word from God is weighty; nothing is to be left out. He is to appear against kings, princes, and *priests, thus he has much to fear. But he is not to be* dismayed, for God will be with him. "The fear of God is the best antidote against the fear of man."* And he who has the world for his enemy but God for his friend is safe and secure. God prophesies that Jeremiah will be assaulted by those to whom he preaches, but he is guaranteed that the enemy will not overcome him. God will deliver him.

2:7 The land of Canaan was a good land, and Israel was well cared for. However, they defiled the land and made it an abomination in the sight of God. Instead of conserving and improving what they were given, they despoiled it.

2:8 God tells Jeremiah that he is against the priests who practice their profession but do not know the God they say they represent. He says the kings have transgressed against him and the prophets are false prophets who speak for Baal rather than for him. Through Jeremiah God takes on the whole political and religious establishment as a voice in the wilderness.

knew me not: the pastors also transgressed against me, and the prophets
prophesied by Ba'al, and walked after *things that* do not profit.
9 ¶Wherefore I will yet plead with you, saith the LORD, and with your
children's children will I plead.
10 For pass over the isles of Chit'tim, and see; and send unto Ke'dar, and
consider diligently, and see if there be such a thing.
11 Hath a nation changed *their* gods, which *are* yet no gods? but my
people have changed their glory for *that which* doth not profit.
12 Be astonished, O ye heavens, at this, and be horribly afraid, be ye very
desolate, saith the LORD.
13 For my people have committed two evils; they have forsaken me the
fountain of living waters, *and* hewed them out cisterns, broken cisterns, that
can hold no water.

2:10 Ps 106:20; 120:5; Isa 23:12; 37:19; Jer 16:20; 49:28; Rom 1:23
☆**2:11**
☆**2:13** Ps 36:9; Jer 17:13; Jn 4:14

3. The Consequences of Israel's Sins

14 *Is* Israel a servant? *is* he a homeborn *slave?* why is he spoiled?
15 The young lions roared upon him, *and* yelled, and they made his land
waste: his cities are burned without inhabitant.
16 Also the children of Noph and Ta-hap'a-nes have broken the crown of
thy head.
17 Hast thou not procured this unto thyself, in that thou hast forsaken the
LORD thy God, when he led thee by the way?
18 And now what hast thou to do in the way of Egypt, to drink the waters
of Si'hor? or what hast thou to do in the way of Assyria, to drink the waters
of the river?
19 Thine own wickedness shall correct thee, and thy backslidings shall
reprove thee: know therefore and see that *it is* an evil *thing* and bitter, that
thou hast forsaken the LORD thy God, and that my fear *is* not in thee, saith
the Lord GOD of hosts.

2:15 Jer 4:7
2:16 Jer 44:1; Hos 9:6
☆**2:17** Deut 32:10; Jer 4:18
2:19 Ps 36:1; Isa 3:9; Jer 3:8; 5:24; Hos 11:7; Amos 8:10

4. The Guilt Cannot Be Washed Away

20 ¶For of old time I have broken thy yoke, *and* burst thy bands; and thou
saidst, I will not transgress; when upon every high hill and under every
green tree thou wanderest, playing the harlot.
21 Yet I had planted thee a noble vine, wholly a right seed: how then art
thou turned into the degenerate plant of a strange vine unto me?
22 For though thou wash thee with nitre, and take thee much soap, *yet*
thine iniquity is marked before me, saith the Lord GOD.
23 How canst thou say, I am not polluted, I have not gone after Ba'al-im?
see thy way in the valley, know what thou hast done: *thou art* a swift
dromedary traversing her ways;
24 A wild ass used to the wilderness, *that* snuffeth up the wind at her
pleasure; in her occasion who can turn her away? all they that seek her will
not weary themselves; in her month they shall find her.

☆**2:20** Deut 12:2; Isa 57:5; Jer 32:6; 17:2
2:21 Ex 15:17; Ps 80:8; Isa 5:2, 4
2:22 Jer 4:14
☆**2:23** Prov 30:12; Jer 7:31

2:11 What Israel did was unique. No other nation ever changed its allegiance to its gods, yet Israel, who had the true God who helped them and provided for them, changed its God. "The zeal and constancy of idolaters should shame Christians out of their coldness and inconstancy."*

2:13 Israel forsook the God of living waters and replaced him with cisterns incapable of holding water. Whoever makes an idol of wealth, pleasure, or honor has dug a cistern that will hold no water.

2:17 Israel had no one to blame but itself for the catastrophe it faced.

2:20 *every high hill.* Israel's idolatrous worship of Baal took place at "high places." Israel took over this heathen custom from their neighbors, and even in her worship of Yahweh the people adopted the idolatrous practices of Baal worship.

2:23 *the valley* probably refers to the Valley of Hinnom, where the people of the Molech cult sacrificed children. This valley was located southwest of Jerusalem.

2:25 Deut 32:16; Jer 18:12
25 Withhold thy foot from being unshod, and thy throat from thirst: but
thou saidst, There is no hope: no; for I have loved strangers, and after them
will I go.

2:26☆ Isa 26:16
26 As the thief is ashamed when he is found, so is the house of Israel
ashamed; they, their kings, their princes, and their priests, and their
prophets,

2:27☆
27 Saying to a stock, Thou *art* my father; and to a stone, Thou hast
brought me forth: for they have turned *their* back unto me, and not *their*
face: but in the time of their trouble they will say, Arise, and save us.

2:28☆ Deut 32:37; 2 Kgs 17:30, 31; Isa 45:20; Jer 11:12, 13
28 But where *are* thy gods that thou hast made thee? let them arise, if they
can save thee in the time of thy trouble: for *according to* the number of thy
cities are thy gods, O Judah.

2:29 Dan 9:11
29 Wherefore will ye plead with me? ye all have transgressed against me,
saith the LORD.

2:30☆ Neh 9:26; Isa 1:5; Jer 5:3; 7:28; 26:20–24
30 In vain have I smitten your children; they received no correction: your
own sword hath devoured your prophets, like a destroying lion.

5. Punishment Is at Hand

2:31 Deut 32:15
31 ¶O generation, see ye the word of the LORD. Have I been a wilderness
unto Israel? a land of darkness? wherefore say my people, We are lords; we
will come no more unto thee?

2:32☆ Isa 17:10; Jer 3:21; Hos 8:14
32 Can a maid forget her ornaments, *or* a bride her attire? yet my people
have forgotten me days without number.
33 Why trimmest thou thy way to seek love? therefore hast thou also
taught the wicked ones thy ways.

2:34 2 Kgs 21:16; Jer 7:6; 19:4
34 Also in thy skirts is found the blood of the souls of the poor innocents:
I have not found it by secret search, but upon all these.

2:35 Jer 25:31
35 Yet thou sayest, Because I am innocent, surely his anger shall turn from
me. Behold, I will plead with thee, because thou sayest, I have not sinned.

2:36 2 Chron 28:16, 20, 21; Hos 12:1; 1 Jn 1:8, 10
36 Why gaddest thou about so much to change thy way? thou also shalt be
ashamed of Egypt, as thou wast ashamed of Assyria.

2:37 Jer 37:7–10
37 Yea, thou shalt go forth from him, and thine hands upon thine head:
for the LORD hath rejected thy confidences, and thou shalt not prosper in
them.

6. God's People Refuse to Repent

3:1☆ Deut 24:4; Jer 4:1; Ezek 16:26, 28, 29; Zech 1:3
3 THEY say, If a man put away his wife, and she go from him, and
become another man's, shall he return unto her again? shall not that
land be greatly polluted? but thou hast played the harlot with many lovers;
yet return again to me, saith the LORD.

2:26, 27 So evil has Israel become that its kings, princes, priests, and prophets worship wood and stone. Yet when they find no deliverance from their idols, they cry to Jehovah. God mocks them in 2:28, telling them to find help from the idols they worship, for he will not help them. The realities of life overtake them as they discover that their gods cannot help them and the God they have deserted *will* not help them. This is ever the plight of those who turn away from the true God.

2:28 Polytheism abounded among the heathen. God *accuses Israel of inventing gods and challenges* them to see whether their new gods could deliver them.

2:30 God sent prophets to warn his people of their sins. They killed God's messengers with rage and fury precisely because the prophets were faithful to their calling. The sinful people turned from them as one would from a plague.

2:32 Israel had deliberately banished God from their minds and hearts so that they forgot the God who had begotten them, and they no longer remembered his former mercies. This they did for days without number, i.e., over a long period of time, during which their children and their children's children were without true religious instruction.

3:1 *They say,* i.e., "There is a law" (Deut. 24:1–4). Paradoxically, God knew the captivity was about to begin. He knew what Judah would do, yet 3:1–5 reveals the mercy of God, who urged the people to repent and turn to him with the promise that the imminent judgment could still be averted. At the very least, judgment would have been delayed, as was Nineveh's, had they repented. Morever, once again the Scriptures make plain that ultimate judgment cannot be averted when disobedience is the way of life.

[2]Lift up thine eyes unto the high places, and see where thou hast not been
lien with. In the ways hast thou sat for them, as the Arabian in the
wilderness; and thou hast polluted the land with thy whoredoms and with
thy wickedness.
[3]Therefore the showers have been withholden, and there hath been no
latter rain; and thou hadst a whore's forehead, thou refusedst to be
ashamed.
[4]Wilt thou not from this time cry unto me, My father, thou *art* the guide
of my youth?
[5]Will he reserve *his anger* for ever? will he keep *it* to the end? Behold,
thou hast spoken and done evil things as thou couldest.

☆3:2 Deut 12:2; Jer 2:7, 20; Ezek 16:25
3:3 Jer 6:15; 14:3–6

C. THE EXAMPLE OF EXILED SAMARIA (THE NORTHERN KINGDOM)
1. The Illustration of the Ten Tribes

[6]¶The LORD said also unto me in the days of Jo-si′ah the king, Hast thou
seen *that* which backsliding Israel hath done? she is gone up upon every
high mountain and under every green tree, and there hath played the harlot.
[7]And I said after she had done all these *things*, Turn thou unto me. But
she returned not. And her treacherous sister Judah saw *it*.
[8]And I saw, when for all the causes whereby backsliding Israel com-
mitted adultery I had put her away, and given her a bill of divorce; yet her
treacherous sister Judah feared not, but went and played the harlot also.
[9]And it came to pass through the lightness of her whoredom, that she
defiled the land, and committed adultery with stones and with stocks.
[10]And yet for all this her treacherous sister Judah hath not turned unto
me with her whole heart, but feignedly, saith the LORD.
[11]And the LORD said unto me, The backsliding Israel hath justified
herself more than treacherous Judah.
[12]¶Go and proclaim these words toward the north, and say, Return, thou
backsliding Israel, saith the LORD; *and* I will not cause mine anger to fall
upon you: for I *am* merciful, saith the LORD, *and* I will not keep *anger* for
ever.
[13]Only acknowledge thine iniquity, that thou hast transgressed against
the LORD thy God, and hast scattered thy ways to the strangers under every
green tree, and ye have not obeyed my voice, saith the LORD.
[14]Turn, O backsliding children, saith the LORD; for I am married unto
you: and I will take you one of a city, and two of a family, and I will bring
you to Zion:
[15]And I will give you pastors according to mine heart, which shall feed
you with knowledge and understanding.
[16]And it shall come to pass, when ye be multiplied and increased in the
land, in those days, saith the LORD, they shall say no more, The ark of the

☆3:6 Jer 17:2; Ezek 23:4–10
3:8 Isa 50:1; Ezek 16:46, 47; 23:11
3:9 Isa 57:6; Jer 2:7, 27
3:10 Jer 12:2
☆3:11 Ezek 16:51
☆3:12 Ps 86:15; Jer 31:20; 33:26
☆3:13 Deut 12:2; 30:1–3; Jer 14:20
3:14 Jer 50:4, 5; Hos 2:19
☆3:15 Jer 23:4; Acts 20:28
3:16 Isa 65:17

3:2 *as the Arabian in the wilderness,* i.e., "like a Bedouin in the desert," who was free to attack anyone *who wandered into his area, so Israel* has committed adultery by embracing the gods of the land as her lovers.

3:6 God warns men and nations, and in so doing often refers to actual historical incidents to illustrate what will happen if they disobey him. God warns Judah here, illustrating the warning by pointing out what has happened to Samaria, which God has already judged. Men and nations, however, learn little from history and repeat the mistakes of earlier generations. In the New Testament Peter offers a warning and mentions what happened to Sodom and Gomorrah, and also to Balaam (2 Pet. 2:1–6).

3:11–13 God declares that faithless Israel (the Northern Kingdom of Samaria) was less guilty than Judah. Although they have been dispersed, he sends them a message of hope—that he will have mercy on them and cease to be angry if they will repent.

3:15 However great sinners men become, God still entreats them to turn from their wicked ways. Despite the multitude and the enormity of his people's transgressions, God holds out gracious promises to them if they will repent. *I will give you pastors according to mine heart,* i.e., "I will see that you have ministers and magistrates who will serve me and act justly." Any nation will be blessed that has for its ministers and rulers those whose lives are patterned after the heart of God.

covenant of the LORD: neither shall it come to mind: neither shall they remember it; neither shall they visit *it;* neither shall *that* be done any more.

3:17 Jer 12:15, 16; 16:19; 17:12; Ezek 43:7

17 At that time they shall call Jerusalem the throne of the LORD; and all the nations shall be gathered unto it, to the name of the LORD, to Jerusalem: neither shall they walk any more after the imagination of their evil heart.

3:18 Isa 60:9; Jer 16:14, 15; 31:8; 50:4, 5; Hos 1:11

18 In those days the house of Judah shall walk with the house of Israel, and they shall come together out of the land of the north to the land that I have given for an inheritance unto your fathers.

3:19 Isa 63:16

19 But I said, How shall I put thee among the children, and give thee a pleasant land, a goodly heritage of the hosts of nations? and I said, Thou shalt call me, My father; and shalt not turn away from me.

3:20☆

20 ¶Surely *as* a wife treacherously departeth from her husband, so have ye dealt treacherously with me, O house of Israel, saith the LORD.

3:21 Isa 15:2; Jer 2:32

21 A voice was heard upon the high places, weeping *and* supplications of the children of Israel: for they have perverted their way, *and* they have forgotten the LORD their God.

3:22 Hos 6:1; 14:4

22 Return, ye backsliding children, *and* I will heal your backslidings. Behold, we come unto thee; for thou *art* the LORD our God.

3:23☆ Ps 3:8; 121:1, 2; Jer 17:14

23 Truly in vain *is salvation hoped for* from the hills, *and from* the multitude of mountains: truly in the LORD our God *is* the salvation of Israel.

24 For shame hath devoured the labour of our fathers from our youth; their flocks and their herds, their sons and their daughters.

3:25 Jer 22:21; Ezra 9:7

25 We lie down in our shame, and our confusion covereth us: for we have sinned against the LORD our God, we and our fathers, from our youth even unto this day, and have not obeyed the voice of the LORD our God.

4:1☆ Jer 7:3, 7; 35:15; Joel 2:12

4 IF thou wilt return, O Israel, saith the LORD, return unto me: and if thou wilt put away thine abominations out of my sight, then shalt thou not remove.

4:2 Deut 10:20; Isa 65:16; Jer 9:24; 1 Cor 1:31

2 And thou shalt swear, The LORD liveth, in truth, in judgment, and in righteousness; and the nations shall bless themselves in him, and in him shall they glory.

2. Judah Is Promised a Similar Judgment

a. The Judgment That Comes from the North

4:3 Hos 10:12; Mt 13:7, 22

3 ¶For thus saith the LORD to the men of Judah and Jerusalem, Break up your fallow ground, and sow not among thorns.

4:4 Deut 10:16; Isa 30:27; Jer 9:25, 26; 21:12; Mk 9:43, 48; Rom 2:28, 29

4 Circumcise yourselves to the LORD, and take away the foreskins of your heart, ye men of Judah and inhabitants of Jerusalem: lest my fury come forth like fire, and burn that none can quench *it,* because of the evil of your doings.

4:5 Josh 10:20; Jer 6:1; Hos 8:1

5 Declare ye in Judah, and publish in Jerusalem; and say, Blow ye the trumpet in the land: cry, gather together, and say, Assemble yourselves, and let us go into the defenced cities.

4:6☆ Jer 1:14, 15; 6:1, 22

6 Set up the standard toward Zion: retire, stay not: for I will bring evil from the north, and a great destruction.

3:20 As an adulterous wife leaves her husband for another man, so has *the house of Israel* committed spiritual adultery by forsaking the God to whom they have been espoused. However bad physical adultery may be, spiritual adultery is far worse.

3:23 *in vain is salvation hoped for from the hills.* Israel can expect no help from the worship of idols on the high places, whereas they can find help and salvation in the true God of Israel.

4:1 The word *if* is found many times in the Scriptures. If dispersed Israel (the ten tribes) repented by turning away from their idols and turning to God, he would help them. But if they do not, then there is no help. Always and ever God says to the heathen that "if you come unto me you will be saved."

4:6 *from the north,* i.e., "from Babylon."

7 The lion is come up from his thicket, and the destroyer of the Gentiles is
on his way; he is gone forth from his place to make thy land desolate; *and*
thy cities shall be laid waste, without an inhabitant.
8 For this gird you with sackcloth, lament and howl: for the fierce anger
of the LORD is not turned back from us.
9 And it shall come to pass at that day, saith the LORD, *that* the heart of
the king shall perish, and the heart of the princes; and the priests shall be
astonished, and the prophets shall wonder.
10 Then said I, Ah, Lord GOD! surely thou hast greatly deceived this
people and Jerusalem, saying, Ye shall have peace; whereas the sword
reacheth unto the soul.
11 At that time shall it be said to this people and to Jerusalem, A dry wind
of the high places in the wilderness toward the daughter of my people, not
to fan, nor to cleanse,
12 *Even* a full wind from those *places* shall come unto me: now also will I
give sentence against them.
13 Behold, he shall come up as clouds, and his chariots *shall be* as a
whirlwind: his horses are swifter than eagles. Woe unto us! for we are
spoiled.
14 O Jerusalem, wash thine heart from wickedness, that thou mayest be
saved. How long shall thy vain thoughts lodge within thee?
15 For a voice declareth from Dan, and publisheth affliction from mount
E′phra-im.
16 Make ye mention to the nations; behold, publish against Jerusalem,
that watchers come from a far country, and give out their voice against the
cities of Judah.
17 As keepers of a field, are they against her round about; because she
hath been rebellious against me, saith the LORD.
18 Thy way and thy doings have procured these *things* unto thee; this *is*
thy wickedness, because it is bitter, because it reacheth unto thine heart.
19 ¶My bowels, my bowels! I am pained at my very heart; my heart
maketh a noise in me; I cannot hold my peace, because thou hast heard, O
my soul, the sound of the trumpet, the alarm of war.
20 Destruction upon destruction is cried; for the whole land is spoiled:
suddenly are my tents spoiled, *and* my curtains in a moment.
21 How long shall I see the standard, *and* hear the sound of the trumpet?
22 For my people *is* foolish, they have not known me; they *are* sottish
children, and they have none understanding: they *are* wise to do evil, but to
do good they have no knowledge.
23 I beheld the earth, and, lo, *it was* without form, and void; and the
heavens, and they *had* no light.
24 I beheld the mountains, and, lo, they trembled, and all the hills moved
lightly.
25 I beheld, and, lo, *there was* no man, and all the birds of the heavens
were fled.
26 I beheld, and, lo, the fruitful place *was* a wilderness, and all the cities
thereof were broken down at the presence of the LORD, *and* by his fierce
anger.

☆**4:7** Isa 1:7; 6:11 Jer 2:15; 5:6 25:9, 38
4:8 Isa 5:25; 10:4 Jer 6:26
4:9 Jer 48:41
4:10 2 Thess 2:11 14:13
4:13 Deut 28:49 Isa 66:15 Lam 4:19
4:14 Isa 1:16 Jer 13:27 Jas 4:8
☆**4:15**
4:16 Jer 5:15 Ezek 21:22
4:17 2 Kgs 25:1 Jer 5:23
4:18 Jer 2:17, 19
☆**4:19** Isa 21:3; 22:4 Hab 3:16
4:20 Jer 10:20 Ezek 7:26
4:22 Jer 5:21; 10:8 13:23 Rom 16:19
4:23 Isa 24:19
4:24 Isa 5:25 Ezek 38:20
4:25 Jer 9:10; 12:4 Zeph 1:3

4:7 *A lion* is used as a metaphor for Nebuchadnezzar of Babylon, who later was to destroy Jerusalem.
4:15 *Dan* was in the far north of Palestine, and enemy invaders from the north and east could be seen as they moved from the east through the Fertile Crescent.
4:19 Jeremiah was not called the weeping prophet for nothing. The prophet foresees the ruthless advance of Nebuchadnezzar and his armies who will, as it were, disembowel Judah and destroy Jerusalem; this knowledge brings anguish he can hardly bear. His heart is torn and his language defies anyone to surpass it for vividness and horror at the approaching doom of Judah.

27 For thus hath the LORD said, The whole land shall be desolate; yet will
I not make a full end.
28 For this shall the earth mourn, and the heavens above be black:
because I have spoken *it*, I have purposed *it*, and will not repent, neither
will I turn back from it.
29 The whole city shall flee for the noise of the horsemen and bowmen;
they shall go into thickets, and climb up upon the rocks: every city *shall be*
forsaken, and not a man dwell therein.
30 And *when* thou *art* spoiled, what wilt thou do? Though thou clothest
thyself with crimson, though thou deckest thee with ornaments of gold,
though thou rentest thy face with painting, in vain shalt thou make thyself
fair; *thy* lovers will despise thee, they will seek thy life.
31 For I have heard a voice as of a woman in travail, *and* the anguish as of
her that bringeth forth her first child, the voice of the daughter of Zion, *that*
bewaileth herself, *that* spreadeth her hands, *saying*, Woe *is* me now! for my
soul is wearied because of murderers.

b. The Fruitless Search for a Righteous Man

5 RUN ye to and fro through the streets of Jerusalem, and see now, and
know, and seek in the broad places thereof, if ye can find a man, if
there be *any* that executeth judgment, that seeketh the truth; and I will
pardon it.
2 And though they say, The LORD liveth; surely they swear falsely.
3 O LORD, *are* not thine eyes upon the truth? thou hast stricken them, but
they have not grieved; thou hast consumed them, *but* they have refused to
receive correction: they have made their faces harder than a rock; they have
refused to return.
4 Therefore I said, Surely these *are* poor; they are foolish: for they know
not the way of the LORD, *nor* the judgment of their God.
5 I will get me unto the great men, and will speak unto them; for they
have known the way of the LORD, *and* the judgment of their God: but these
have altogether broken the yoke, *and* burst the bonds.
6 Wherefore a lion out of the forest shall slay them, *and* a wolf of the
evenings shall spoil them, a leopard shall watch over their cities: every one
that goeth out thence shall be torn in pieces: because their transgressions
are many, *and* their backslidings are increased.
7 ¶How shall I pardon thee for this? thy children have forsaken me, and
sworn by *them that are* no gods: when I had fed them to the full, they then
committed adultery, and assembled themselves by troops in the harlots'
houses.
8 They were *as* fed horses in the morning: every one neighed after his
neighbour's wife.
9 Shall I not visit for these *things*? saith the LORD: and shall not my soul
be avenged on such a nation as this?

4:27 Jer 5:10, 18; 12:11, 12; 30:11; 46:28
4:28☆ Num 23:19; Isa 5:30; 50:3; Jer 23:20; 30:24; Hos 4:3; Joel 2:30, 31
4:29 Isa 2:19–21; Jer 16:16
4:30 2 Kgs 9:30; Jer 22:20, 22; Ezek 23:9, 10, 22
4:31 Jer 13:21; Lam 1:17
5:1☆ Gen 18:26, 32; 2 Chron 16:9
5:2 Tit 1:16
5:3 Jer 7:26, 28; 8:5; 19:15; Ezek 3:8; Zeph 3:2
5:4 Isa 27:11; Jer 4:22; Hos 4:6
5:5 Jer 2:20; Mic 3:1
5:6☆ Jer 30:14, 15; Hos 13:7; Hab 1:8
5:7 Deut 32:21; Josh 23:7; Jer 2:11; Zeph 1:5; Gal 4:8
5:8 Jer 29:23; Ezek 22:11
5:9 Jer 9:9

4:28 God who foreknows everything knows that Judah will not repent. Therefore he has passed judgment on that nation and will not relent or turn back. So certain is the destruction of Jerusalem that not even God himself can now save it, unless he were to break his word and annul his judgment.

5:1 God is willing to suspend his judgment and recall his edict to destroy Jerusalem if just one man can be found in the streets of the city who does right. God would have delivered Sodom had there been but ten righteous men found in its confines. So he would deliver Jerusalem if there were a few people whose hearts were right. The melancholy answer is that there are none who could be found. Judah, therefore, is doomed.

5:6 God is angry with Judah because its *transgressions are many,* i.e., they were of many kinds and often repeated. They were also apostates who committed spiritual adultery with the worship of idols, a worship due to God alone. They also were guilty of physical adulteries. 5:7, 8 graphically depict their vile affections, their scandalous conduct, and brutish lusts. How could God be God and not pronounce definitive judgment upon such a people?

10 ¶Go ye up upon her walls, and destroy; but make not a full end: take
away her battlements; for they *are* not the LORD's.

5:10 Jer 4:27

c. God Will Consume Judah

11 For the house of Israel and the house of Judah have dealt very
treacherously against me, saith the LORD.
12 They have belied the LORD, and said, *It is* not he; neither shall evil
come upon us; neither shall we see sword nor famine:
13 And the prophets shall become wind, and the word *is* not in them: thus
shall it be done unto them.
14 Wherefore thus saith the LORD God of hosts, Because ye speak this
word, behold, I will make my words in thy mouth fire, and this people
wood, and it shall devour them.
15 Lo, I will bring a nation upon you from far, O house of Israel, saith the
LORD; it *is* a mighty nation, it *is* an ancient nation, a nation whose language
thou knowest not, neither understandest what they say.
16 Their quiver *is* as an open sepulchre, they *are* all mighty men.
17 And they shall eat up thine harvest, and thy bread, *which* thy sons and
thy daughters should eat: they shall eat up thy flocks and thine herds: they
shall eat up thy vines and thy fig trees: they shall impoverish thy fenced
cities, wherein thou trustedst, with the sword.

5:11 Jer 3:6, 7
5:12 2 Chron 36:16; Jer 43:1-4
☆**5:13** Jer 14:13, 15
5:14 Jer 23:29
☆**5:15** Deut 28:49; Isa 5:26; 28:11
5:16 Isa 5:28, 13:18
5:17 Lev 26:16; Deut 28:31, 33; Jer 8:16; Hos 8:14

d. Judgment, the Result of Stubbornness and Rebellion

18 Nevertheless in those days, saith the LORD, I will not make a full end
with you.
19 ¶And it shall come to pass, when ye shall say, Wherefore doeth the
LORD our God all these *things* unto us? then shalt thou answer them, Like
as ye have forsaken me, and served strange gods in your land, so shall ye
serve strangers in a land *that is* not yours.
20 Declare this in the house of Jacob, and publish it in Judah, saying,
21 Hear now this, O foolish people, and without understanding; which
have eyes, and see not; which have ears, and hear not:
22 Fear ye not me? saith the LORD: will ye not tremble at my presence,
which have placed the sand *for* the bound of the sea by a perpetual decree,
that it cannot pass it: and though the waves thereof toss themselves, yet can
they not prevail; though they roar, yet can they not pass over it?
23 But this people hath a revolting and a rebellious heart; they are
revolted and gone.
24 Neither say they in their heart, Let us now fear the LORD our God, that
giveth rain, both the former and the latter, in his season: he reserveth unto
us the appointed weeks of the harvest.
25 ¶Your iniquities have turned away these *things*, and your sins have
withholden good *things* from you.
26 For among my people are found wicked *men:* they lay wait, as he that
setteth snares; they set a trap, they catch men.
27 As a cage is full of birds, so *are* their houses full of deceit: therefore
they are become great, and waxen rich.

☆**5:18**
5:19 Deut 29:24–26; 28:48; 1 Kgs 9:8, 9; Jer 16:10–13
5:21 Isa 43:8; Ezek 12:2; Mt 13:14
5:22 Deut 28:58; Job 38:8–11; Ps 104:9; 119:120; Jer 10:7
5:23 Gen 8:22; Ps 78:8; 147:8; Jer 4:17; Joel 2:23; Mt 5:45
5:25 Jer 2:17; 4:18
5:26 Ps 10:9; Jer 18:22

5:13 Paraphrased: " 'God's prophets,' they say, 'are windbags full of words with no divine authority. Their claims of doom will fall upon themselves, not us!' "† Judah will refuse to listen to God's true prophets; it will love the false ones who support its wrong views.
5:15 *an ancient nation.* The kingdom of Babylonia, being revived in Jeremiah's time (about 626 B.C.), had a long and illustrious history. The old Babylonian Empire lasted from about 1900 B.C. to 1550 B.C. (the days of the Hebrew patriarchs), and earlier kingdoms had ruled on Babylonian soil as early as 3000 B.C.†
5:18 *I will not make a full end with you.* God looks beyond the soon-to-come captivity under Nebuchadnezzar; it will not mean the end of his people. God is compassionate—the enemy will lay waste to Judah but will not eliminate her completely. There is mercy in store for Judah; a return to the land left desolate will come later. If God will not make a full end of Judah, we can be sure that the enemy cannot do so.

5:28 Deut 32:15 Isa 1:23 Jer 7:6; 22:3 Zech 7:10

[28]They are waxen fat, they shine: yea, they overpass the deeds of the
wicked: they judge not the cause, the cause of the fatherless, yet they
prosper; and the right of the needy do they not judge.
[29]Shall I not visit for these *things?* saith the LORD: shall not my soul be
avenged on such a nation as this?

5:30 Jer 23:14 Hos 6:10 **5:31**☆ Jer 14:14 Mic 2:11

[30]¶A wonderful and horrible thing is committed in the land;
[31]The prophets prophesy falsely, and the priests bear rule by their means;
and my people love *to have it* so: and what will ye do in the end thereof?

e. The Faithful Remnant Ordered to Flee

6:1☆ Jer 1:14; 4:6

6 O YE children of Benjamin, gather yourselves to flee out of the midst
of Jerusalem, and blow the trumpet in Te-ko′a, and set up a sign of fire
in Beth-hac′ce-rem: for evil appeareth out of the north, and great
destruction.

6:2 Deut 28:56 **6:3** 2 Kgs 25:1 Jer 4:17 Lk 19:43 **6:4** Jer 6:23 **6:5** Isa 32:14 Jer 52:13

[2]I have likened the daughter of Zion to a comely and delicate *woman.*
[3]The shepherds with their flocks shall come unto her; they shall pitch
their tents against her round about; they shall feed every one in his place.
[4]Prepare ye war against her; arise, and let us go up at noon. Woe unto us!
for the day goeth away, for the shadows of the evening are stretched out.
[5]Arise, and let us go by night, and let us destroy her palaces.

f. God's Encouragement to the Invaders

6:6 Deut 20:19, 20

[6]¶For thus hath the LORD of hosts said, Hew ye down trees, and cast a
mount against Jerusalem: this *is* the city to be visited; she *is* wholly
oppression in the midst of her.

6:7☆ Jer 30:12, 13 Ezek 7:11, 23 Jas 3:10–12

[7]As a fountain casteth out her waters, so she casteth out her wickedness:
violence and spoil is heard in her; before me continually *is* grief and
wounds.

6:8 Jer 7:28; 17:23 Hos 9:12 **6:9** Jer 8:3, 16:16 49:9 Obad 5, 6

[8]Be thou instructed, O Jerusalem, lest my soul depart from thee; lest I
make thee desolate, a land not inhabited.
[9]¶Thus saith the LORD of hosts, They shall throughly glean the remnant
of Israel as a vine: turn back thine hand as a grapegatherer into the baskets.
[10]To whom shall I speak, and give warning, that they may hear? behold,
their ear *is* uncircumcised, and they cannot hearken: behold, the word of
the LORD is unto them a reproach; they have no delight in it.

6:11 Job 32:18, 19 Jer 7:20; 9:21 15:6

[11]Therefore I am full of the fury of the LORD; I am weary with holding
in: I will pour it out upon the children abroad, and upon the assembly of
young men together: for even the husband with the wife shall be taken, the
aged with *him that is* full of days.

6:12 Deut 28:30 Jer 8:10; 38:22

[12]And their houses shall be turned unto others, *with their* fields and wives
together: for I will stretch out my hand upon the inhabitants of the land,
saith the LORD.

5:31 Among those who called themselves prophets, Jeremiah was one of the few true prophets. As a class, the prophets were false; they were not from God, but were influential even though uninspired. So it is today, too.

6:1 Jerusalem at this point seems safe enough from external danger. God warns the people of Benjamin in *whose territory part of Jerusalem* lay to flee from the city and escape the coming tragedy. *blow the trumpet in Tekoa.* This city was ten miles south of Jerusalem and was built on a site 2,700 feet above sea level. From there the Mount of Olives is visible. It was a good place from which warnings could be given to the inhabitants of Jerusalem. *set up a sign of fire in Beth-haccerem.* This city (its name means "house of the vine-yard") was located on a high hill between Bethlehem and Jerusalem. It was high enough above seal level for signaling near Jerusalem. Thus Tekoa, ten miles away, and this city halfway between would both be signaling stations for Jerusalem in times of danger.

6:7ff Among the charges lodged against Judah and Jerusalem are (1) oppression (6:7), (2) contempt for the Word of God (6:10–12), (3) worldliness (6:13), (4) treachery on the part of their prophets (6:14), (5) unashamedness for their sins (6:15), and (6) obstinacy (6:18, 19). So God gave them up to judgment.

13 For from the least of them even unto the greatest of them every one *is*
given to covetousness; and from the prophet even unto the priest every one
dealeth falsely.

6:13 Isa 56:11; 57:17 Jer 22:17 Mic 3:5, 11

14 They have healed also the hurt *of the daughter* of my people slightly,
saying, Peace, peace; when *there is* no peace.

6:14 Jer 8:11, 12 Ezek 13:10

15 Were they ashamed when they had committed abomination? nay, they
were not at all ashamed, neither could they blush: therefore they shall fall
among them that fall: at the time *that* I visit them they shall be cast down,
saith the LORD.

6:15 Jer 3:3; 8:12

g. Judah Refuses to Repent

16 Thus saith the LORD, Stand ye in the ways, and see, and ask for the old
paths, where *is* the good way, and walk therein, and ye shall find rest for
your souls. But they said, We will not walk *therein.*

6:16 Jer 18:15; 31:21 Mt 11:29

17 Also I set watchmen over you, *saying,* Hearken to the sound of the
trumpet. But they said, We will not hearken.

6:17 Isa 21:11; 58:1 Jer 25:4 Ezek 3:17

18 ¶Therefore hear, ye nations, and know, O congregation, what *is* among
them.

6:18 Prov 1:31 Isa 1:2 Jer 8:9; 22:29

19 Hear, O earth: behold, I will bring evil upon this people, *even* the fruit
of their thoughts, because they have not hearkened unto my words, nor to
my law, but rejected it.

20 To what purpose cometh there to me incense from She'ba, and the
sweet cane from a far country? your burnt offerings *are* not acceptable, nor
your sacrifices sweet unto me.

☆6:20 Ps 40:6; 50:7–9 Isa 1:11; 60:6 66:3 Amos 5:21

21 Therefore thus saith the LORD, Behold, I will lay stumblingblocks
before this people, and the fathers and the sons together shall fall upon
them; the neighbour and his friend shall perish.

6:21 Isa 8:14 9:14–17 Jer 9:21, 22

h. The Invader Will Suddenly Destroy Jerusalem

22 Thus saith the LORD, Behold, a people cometh from the north country,
and a great nation shall be raised from the sides of the earth.

6:22 Jer 1:15; 10:22

23 They shall lay hold on bow and spear; they *are* cruel, and have no
mercy; their voice roareth like the sea; and they ride upon horses, set in
array as men for war against thee, O daughter of Zion.

☆6:23 Isa 5:30 Jer 4:29; 50:42

24 We have heard the fame thereof: our hands wax feeble: anguish hath
taken hold of us, *and* pain, as of a woman in travail.

6:24 Isa 28:19 Jer 4:19–21

25 Go not forth into the field, nor walk by the way; for the sword of the
enemy *and* fear *is* on every side.

6:25 Jer 12:12; 14:18

26 ¶O daughter of my people, gird *thee* with sackcloth, and wallow thyself
in ashes: make thee mourning, *as for* an only son, most bitter lamentation:
for the spoiler shall suddenly come upon us.

6:26 Jer 4:8 Amos 8:10 Mic 1:10

27 I have set thee *for* a tower *and* a fortress among my people, that thou
mayest know and try their way.

6:27 Jer 1:18; 15:20

28 They *are* all grievous revolters, walking with slanders: *they are* brass
and iron; they *are* all corrupters.

6:28 Ezek 22:18

29 The bellows are burned, the lead is consumed of the fire; the founder
melteth in vain: for the wicked are not plucked away.

6:20 There was no lack of religious ceremonies among the people of Judah. Rather, they were hypocrites whose ceremonies lacked hearts in tune with God. Despite the ceremonies, Judah has rejected God.

6:23 The Chaldeans are described as a great nation, a warlike people, a barbarous group of cut-throats who are cruel and lacking in mercy. Riding on horses and formidable with bow and spear, they frighten their enemies and their voice roars like the sea. This description should have constrained Judah to turn to God for deliverance. Instead, they hardened their hearts and became easy prey for the enemy.

30 Reprobate silver shall *men* call them, because the LORD hath rejected
them.

D. THE REASONS FOR THE IMPENDING EXILE
1. The First Charge: Idolatry and Immorality

7 THE word that came to Jer-e-mi'ah from the LORD, saying,
2 Stand in the gate of the LORD's house, and proclaim there this
word, and say, Hear the word of the LORD, all *ye of* Judah, that enter in at
these gates to worship the LORD.
3 Thus saith the LORD of hosts, the God of Israel, Amend your ways and
your doings, and I will cause you to dwell in this place.
4 Trust ye not in lying words, saying, The temple of the LORD, The temple
of the LORD, The temple of the LORD, *are* these.
5 For if ye throughly amend your ways and your doings; if ye throughly
execute judgment between a man and his neighbour;
6 *If* ye oppress not the stranger, the fatherless, and the widow, and shed
not innocent blood in this place, neither walk after other gods to your hurt:
7 Then will I cause you to dwell in this place, in the land that I gave to
your fathers, for ever and ever.
8 ¶Behold, ye trust in lying words, that cannot profit.
9 Will ye steal, murder, and commit adultery, and swear falsely, and burn
incense unto Ba'al, and walk after other gods whom ye know not;
10 And come and stand before me in this house, which is called by my
name, and say, We are delivered to do all these abominations?
11 Is this house, which is called by my name, become a den of robbers in
your eyes? Behold, even I have seen *it*, saith the LORD.
12 But go ye now unto my place which *was* in Shi'loh, where I set my name
at the first, and see what I did to it for the wickedness of my people Israel.
13 And now, because ye have done all these works, saith the LORD, and I
spake unto you, rising up early and speaking, but ye heard not; and I called
you, but ye answered not;
14 Therefore will I do unto *this* house, which is called by my name,
wherein ye trust, and unto the place which I gave to you and to your
fathers, as I have done to Shi'loh.
15 And I will cast you out of my sight, as I have cast out all your brethren,
even the whole seed of E'phra-im.
16 Therefore pray not thou for this people, neither lift up cry nor prayer
for them, neither make intercession to me: for I will not hear thee.
17 ¶Seest thou not what they do in the cities of Judah and in the streets of
Jerusalem?

6:30☆ Ps 119:119; Isa 1:22
7:1☆
7:2☆ Jer 17:19
7:3 Jer 4:1; 18:11; 26:13
7:4 Mic 3:11
7:5 Isa 1:19; Jer 21:12; 22:3
7:6 Ex 22:21–24; Deut 6:14, 15; 8:19; Jer 5:28; 13:10
7:7 Deut 4:40
7:9☆ Jer 11:13, 17; 19:4
7:10 Ezek 23:39
7:11 Isa 56:7; Jer 29:23; Mt 21:13; Mk 11:17; Lk 19:46
7:12☆ Josh 18:1, 10; Jer 26:6
7:13 1 Kgs 9:7; Jer 4:1, 2; 18:11; 26:13
7:15 Deut 6:14, 15; 8:19; 2 Kgs 17:23
7:16☆ Deut 4:40; Jer 11:14; 15:1

6:30 God did not reject Judah without first using every proper means to reform them. They now had reached the point of "no return"; they were like reprobate silver.
7:1, 2 Revelation is one way God discloses his message to men. This was accomplished through the ministry of prophets, to whom God communicated what he wanted said. The phrase "thus saith the LORD" or its equivalent appears throughout the Old Testament. Jeremiah, for example, frequently uses this phrase as a means by which we can know that the message is God's message and not Jeremiah's. The essence of revelation is that the message has come directly from God himself.
7:9 The Judeans were superstitious. They sinned every sin and worshipped Baal, but thought that they were safe because they had the temple in their midst. But not even the temple in their midst could save them so long as they kept on committing these awful sins against the true God.
7:12 *Shiloh* was the city where a sanctuary was erected to Israel's God; it was destroyed by the Philistines (cf. 1 Sam. 4:10). Even as God had destroyed Samaria's sanctuary, so also would he destroy Jerusalem.
7:16 God forbids Jeremiah to pray for Jerusalem. It is beyond prayer, for the decree to destroy has gone forth against a people who have sinned unto death. God will not hear any prayers on their behalf.

18 The children gather wood, and the fathers kindle the fire, and the
women knead *their* dough, to make cakes to the queen of heaven, and to
pour out drink offerings unto other gods, that they may provoke me to
anger.
19 Do they provoke me to anger? saith the LORD: *do they* not *provoke*
themselves to the confusion of their own faces?
20 Therefore thus saith the Lord GOD; Behold, mine anger and my fury
shall be poured out upon this place, upon man, and upon beast, and upon
the trees of the field, and upon the fruit of the ground; and it shall burn,
and shall not be quenched.
21 ¶Thus saith the LORD of hosts, the God of Israel; Put your burnt
offerings unto your sacrifices and eat flesh.
22 For I spake not unto your fathers, nor commanded them in the day that
I brought them out of the land of Egypt, concerning burnt offerings or
sacrifices:
23 But this thing commanded I them, saying, Obey my voice, and I will be
your God, and ye shall be my people: and walk ye in all the ways that I
have commanded you, that it may be well unto you.
24 But they hearkened not, nor inclined their ear, but walked in the
counsels *and* in the imagination of their evil heart, and went backward, and
not forward.
25 Since the day that your fathers came forth out of the land of Egypt unto
this day I have even sent unto you all my servants the prophets, daily rising
up early and sending *them:*
26 Yet they hearkened not unto me, nor inclined their ear, but hardened
their neck: they did worse than their fathers.
27 Therefore thou shalt speak all these words unto them; but they will not
hearken to thee: thou shalt also call unto them; but they will not answer
thee.
28 But thou shalt say unto them, This *is* a nation that obeyeth not the
voice of the LORD their God, nor receiveth correction: truth is perished,
and is cut off from their mouth.
29 ¶Cut off thine hair, *O Jerusalem,* and cast *it* away, and take up a
lamentation on high places; for the LORD hath rejected and forsaken the
generation of his wrath.
30 For the children of Judah have done evil in my sight, saith the LORD:
they have set their abominations in the house which is called by my name,
to pollute it.
31 And they have built the high places of To'phet, which *is* in the valley of
the son of Hin'nom, to burn their sons and their daughters in the fire;
which I commanded *them* not, neither came it into my heart.

☆**7:18** Deut 32:16; Jer 11:17; 44:17
7:19 Job 35:6; Jer 9:19
☆**7:20** Jer 8:13
7:21 Isa 1:11; Jer 6:20; 14:12; Hos 8:13; Amos 5:21
7:22 1 Sam 15:22; Ps 51:16; Hos 6:6
7:23 Ex 15:26; 19:5, 6; Lev 26:12; Deut 6:3; Isa 3:10; Jer 11:4; 38:20
☆**7:24** Ps 81:11; Jer 11:8; Ezek 20:8, 13, 16, 21
☆**7:25**
7:26 Jer 16:12; 17:23; Mt 23:32
7:27 Isa 65:12; Jer 26:2; Ezek 2:7
7:28 Jer 11:10
7:29 Isa 15:2; 22:12; Jer 6:30; 14:19; 16:6; Mic 1:16
☆**7:30** 2 Kgs 21:4; 2 Chron 33:4, 5, 7; Jer 32:34
☆**7:31** 2 Kgs 16:17; 23:10; Ps 106:38; Jer 19:5

7:18 *the queen of heaven,* a name by which Ishtar, the Mesopotamian goddess of love and war, was known. *After the fall of Jerusalem* the refugees who fled to Egypt continued to worship her (chapter 44). A papyrus dating from the fifth century B.C., found at Hermopolis in Egypt, mentions the "Queen of Heaven" among the gods honored by the Jewish community.†

7:20 Human life, animal life, and plant life will all be affected by God's judgment. This judgment would differ from the flood only in its extent (i.e., this one would be limited).

7:24 Judah refused to learn anything from experience. They set their own will against God's will. They spurned the law of God. They walked *in the imagination of their evil heart.* They *went backward, and not forward.* They said they would obey God, then did the opposite. God sent his prophets to warn them and to threaten them, but they were as deaf to the prophets as they were to the law of God. And so judgment fell and the righteousness of God was sustained.

7:25 If the punishment meted out to Judah seemed greater than the iniquities, it should be remembered that God exercised patience and he sent servants and prophets again and again to warn Judah of the impending tragedy for an unrepentant people.

7:30 Judah had defiled the temple of God, and in so doing defiled the God of the temple.

7:31 *I commanded them not.* Human sacrifices are everywhere forbidden in the Scriptures. God never even allowed for the possibility of such a thing.

32 ¶Therefore, behold, the days come, saith the LORD, that it shall no
more be called To'phet, nor the valley of the son of Hin'nom, but the valley
of slaughter: for they shall bury in To'phet, till there be no place.
33 And the carcases of this people shall be meat for the fowls of the
heaven, and for the beasts of the earth; and none shall fray *them* away.
34 Then will I cause to cease from the cities of Judah, and from the streets
of Jerusalem, the voice of mirth, and the voice of gladness, the voice of the
bridegroom, and the voice of the bride: for the land shall be desolate.

8 AT that time, saith the LORD, they shall bring out the bones of the
kings of Judah, and the bones of his princes, and the bones of the
priests, and the bones of the prophets, and the bones of the inhabitants of
Jerusalem, out of their graves:
2 And they shall spread them before the sun, and the moon, and all the
host of heaven, whom they have loved, and whom they have served, and
after whom they have walked, and whom they have sought, and whom they
have worshipped: they shall not be gathered, nor be buried; they shall be
for dung upon the face of the earth.
3 And death shall be chosen rather than life by all the residue of them that
remain of this evil family, which remain in all the places whither I have
driven them, saith the LORD of hosts.

2. The Second Charge: the Stubborn Refusal to Repent

4 ¶Moreover thou shalt say unto them, Thus saith the LORD; Shall they
fall, and not arise? shall he turn away, and not return?
5 Why *then* is this people of Jerusalem slidden back by a perpetual
backsliding? they hold fast deceit, they refuse to return.
6 I hearkened and heard, *but* they spake not aright: no man repented him
of his wickedness, saying, What have I done? every one turned to his
course, as the horse rusheth into the battle.
7 Yea, the stork in the heaven knoweth her appointed times; and the
turtle and the crane and the swallow observe the time of their coming; but
my people know not the judgment of the LORD.
8 How do ye say, We *are* wise, and the law of the LORD *is* with us? Lo,
certainly in vain made he *it;* the pen of the scribes *is* in vain.
9 The wise *men* are ashamed, they are dismayed and taken: lo, they have
rejected the word of the LORD; and what wisdom *is* in them?
10 Therefore will I give their wives unto others, *and* their fields to them
that shall inherit *them:* for every one from the least even unto the greatest is
given to covetousness, from the prophet even unto the priest every one
dealeth falsely.
11 For they have healed the hurt of the daughter of my people slightly,
saying, Peace, peace; when *there is* no peace.
12 Were they ashamed when they had committed abomination? nay, they
were not at all ashamed, neither could they blush: therefore shall they fall
among them that fall: in the time of their visitation they shall be cast down,
saith the LORD.

7:32 Jer 19:6, 7
7:33 Deut 28:26; Ps 79:2; Jer 12:9
7:34 Isa 1:7; 24:7; Jer 4:27; 16:9; Ezek 26:13; Hos 2:11
8:1 Ezek 6:5
8:1ff☆
8:2 2 Kgs 23:5; Jer 22:19; 36:30; Zeph 1:5; Acts 7:42
8:3 Deut 30:1, 4; Job 3:21, 22; Jonah 4:3; Rev 9:6
8:4 Prov 24:16; Jer 7:24, 27; 9:6; Mic 7:8
8:6 Job 39:21–25; Ps 74:2; Mal 3:16
8:7☆ Prov 6:6–8; Song 2:12; Isa 1:3
8:8 Jer 4:22; Rom 1:22; 2:17
8:9☆ Jer 6:15; 1 Cor 1:27
8:10 Deut 28:30; Isa 56:11; Jer 6:12, 13
8:11☆ Jer 6:14; 14:13, 14; Lam 2:14; Ezek 13:10
8:12 Deut 32:35; Isa 3:9; 9:14; Jer 6:15; Zeph 3:5

8:1ff In this chapter Jeremiah specifies how awful the destructive judgment of God will be for this wicked people. But he also shows that the judgment is righteous. The God of holiness and love is also the God *of justice and judgment* for those who sin against his holiness and decline his love.
8:7 By instinct birds know the times and seasons—when to fly south and when to return home in the spring, when to mate and when to produce little ones. God's people have no regard for instinct, reason, or revelation. They go their merry way that leads to death.
8:9 Some people do not have the Word of God. Judah was fortunate in that it had the word, but it rejected what it had. And greater light, when rejected, brings greater judgment.
8:11 False priests and prophets assured the people that all was well. Thus they aided the situation *slightly.* They put a bandaid over what they thought was a superficial wound, when it was really a malignant cancer.

13 ¶I will surely consume them, saith the LORD: *there shall be* no grapes on
the vine, nor figs on the fig tree, and the leaf shall fade; and *the things that*
I have given them shall pass away from them.
14 Why do we sit still? assemble yourselves, and let us enter into the
defenced cities, and let us be silent there: for the LORD our God hath put us
to silence, and given us water of gall to drink, because we have sinned
against the LORD.
15 We looked for peace, but no good *came; and* for a time of health, and
behold trouble!
16 The snorting of his horses was heard from Dan: the whole land
trembled at the sound of the neighing of his strong ones; for they are come,
and have devoured the land, and all that is in it; the city, and those that
dwell therein.
17 For, behold, I will send serpents, cockatrices, among you, which *will*
not *be* charmed, and they shall bite you, saith the LORD.
18 ¶*When* I would comfort myself against sorrow, my heart *is* faint in me.
19 Behold the voice of the cry of the daughter of my people because of
them that dwell in a far country: *Is* not the LORD in Zion? *is* not her king
in her? Why have they provoked me to anger with their graven images, *and*
with strange vanities?
20 The harvest is past, the summer is ended, and we are not saved.
21 For the hurt of the daughter of my people am I hurt; I am black;
astonishment hath taken hold on me.
22 *Is there* no balm in Gilead; *is there* no physician there? why then is not
the health of the daughter of my people recovered?

3. The Third Charge: They Are Faithless Liars Who Must Be Punished

9 OH that my head were waters, and mine eyes a fountain of tears, that
I might weep day and night for the slain of the daughter of my people!
2 Oh that I had in the wilderness a lodging place of wayfaring men; that
I might leave my people, and go from them! for they *be* all adulterers, an
assembly of treacherous men.
3 And they bend their tongues *like* their bow *for* lies: but they are not
valiant for the truth upon the earth; for they proceed from evil to evil, and
they know not me, saith the LORD.
4 Take ye heed every one of his neighbour, and trust ye not in any
brother: for every brother will utterly supplant, and every neighbour will
walk with slanders.
5 And they will deceive every one his neighbour, and will not speak the
truth: they have taught their tongue to speak lies, *and* weary themselves to
commit iniquity.
6 Thine habitation *is* in the midst of deceit; through deceit they refuse to
know me, saith the LORD.

8:13 Mt 21:19
8:14 Deut 29:18; Ps 69:21; Jer 3:25; 4:5; 9:15; 14:20
8:15 Jer 14:19
☆**8:16** Judg 5:22
☆**8:17** Num 21:6; Deut 32:24; Ps 58:4, 5; Isa 22:4
8:19 Deut 32:2; Ps 31:6; Isa 13:4, 5; Jer 9:16
8:21 Jer 4:19; 9:1; 14:17
☆**8:22** Gen 37:25; Jer 30:13; 46:11
☆**9:1** Jer 8:18; 13:17
9:2 Ps 55:6, 7; 120:5, 6
9:3 Ps 64:3; Isa 59:4; Jer 9:8; Hos 4:1
☆**9:4** Gen 27:35; Prov 10:18; Jer 12:6
9:5 Mic 6:12
9:6 Jer 5:27; 11:10; 13:10

8:16 *The snorting of his horses was heard from Dan,* i.e., the report of the invaders' presence in the far north is known by the neighing of their horses—a sign of the immense strength of the advancing cavalry troops.

8:17 The people knew about men who could charm poisonous snakes so they would not bite. The advancing armies cannot be charmed, so their bite will kill off the resisting Israelites.

8:22 *balm.* Gilead produced a medicinal balm noted for its curative powers. Israel's sickness, however, could not be cured by any medicine. Its problem was spiritual, not physical.

9:1 Jeremiah spoke about sin and judgment, but he did so with a broken heart. He neither rejoiced at iniquity nor was he glad for the calamities that were to take place.

9:4 So low had the moral state of God's people become that no one could trust his neighbor. They are characterized as slanderers, liars, cheaters, oppressors, and deceivers. When this state of affairs is common to a people, society cannot function properly and life is disordered, uncertain, and on the road to ruin. When such conditions exist in churches, their spirituality is dead and they no longer have power. A dead church is like a body without a soul; it is a corpse.

9:7 Isa 1:25 Jer 6:27 Mal 3:3
9:8 Ps 28:3 Jer 5:26
9:9 Isa 1:24 Jer 5:9, 29
9:10 Jer 4:24, 25 12:4 Ezek 29:11 33:28 Hos 4:3
9:11 Isa 25:2; 34:13 Jer 26:9
9:12 Jer 23:10, 16 Hos 14:9
9:13 2 Chron 7:19, 20 Ps 89:30 Jer 5:19; 22:9
9:14☆ Jer 2:8; 7:24 11:8 Rom 1:21–24 1 Pet 1:18
9:15 Deut 29:18 Jer 8:14; 23:15
9:16 Lev 26:33 Deut 28:64 Jer 13:24; 44:27 Ezek 5:2, 12
9:17 Isa 22:4 Jer 9:1; 14:17 Amos 5:16
9:19 Deut 28:29 Jer 4:13 7:15, 29; 15:1
9:21 2 Chron 36:17 Jer 6:11; 18:21
9:22 Ps 83:10 Isa 5:25 Jer 8:2; 16:4
9:23☆ 1 Kgs 20:10, 11 Ps 49:6–9 Eccles 9:11 Ezek 28:3–7

7 Therefore thus saith the LORD of hosts, Behold, I will melt them, and try
them; for how shall I do for the daughter of my people?
8 Their tongue *is as* an arrow shot out; it speaketh deceit: *one* speaketh
peaceably to his neighbour with his mouth, but in heart he layeth his wait.
9 ¶Shall I not visit them for these *things?* saith the LORD: shall not my
soul be avenged on such a nation as this?
10 For the mountains will I take up a weeping and wailing, and for the
habitations of the wilderness a lamentation, because they are burned up, so
that none can pass through *them;* neither can *men* hear the voice of the
cattle; both the fowl of the heavens and the beast are fled; they are gone.
11 And I will make Jerusalem heaps, *and* a den of dragons; and I will
make the cities of Judah desolate, without an inhabitant.
12 ¶Who *is* the wise man, that may understand this? and *who is he* to
whom the mouth of the LORD hath spoken, that he may declare it, for what
the land perisheth *and* is burned up like a wilderness, that none passeth
through?
13 And the LORD saith, Because they have forsaken my law which I set
before them, and have not obeyed my voice, neither walked therein;
14 But have walked after the imagination of their own heart, and after
Ba′al-im, which their fathers taught them:
15 Therefore thus saith the LORD of hosts, the God of Israel; Behold, I will
feed them, *even* this people, with wormwood, and give them water of gall to
drink.
16 I will scatter them also among the heathen, whom neither they nor their
fathers have known: and I will send a sword after them, till I have
consumed them.
17 ¶Thus saith the LORD of hosts, Consider ye, and call for the mourning
women, that they may come; and send for cunning *women,* that they may
come:
18 And let them make haste, and take up a wailing for us, that our eyes
may run down with tears, and our eyelids gush out with waters.
19 For a voice of wailing is heard out of Zion, How are we spoiled! we are
greatly confounded, because we have forsaken the land, because our
dwellings have cast *us* out.
20 Yet hear the word of the LORD, O ye women, and let your ear receive
the word of his mouth, and teach your daughters wailing, and every one her
neighbour lamentation.
21 For death is come up into our windows, *and* is entered into our palaces,
to cut off the children from without, *and* the young men from the streets.

4. The Conclusion: Wisdom's Reward and Idolatry's Penalty

22 Speak, Thus saith the LORD, Even the carcases of men shall fall as dung
upon
the open field, and as the handful after the harvestman, and none shall
gather *them.*
23 ¶Thus saith the LORD, Let not the wise *man* glory in his wisdom,

---

9:14 God's people have committed a double sin. They have left their first love, the God of Abraham. This sin is bad enough. But the vacuum created by the absence of *the true God led to the active* pursuit of Baalim; many others gods were substituted in place of Jehovah. Man is incurably religious; few can stand the absence of anything religious. Thus there is a tendency to fill the gap with gods of man's own creation, a lamentable state of affairs and one that calls forth the judgment of a righteous God.

9:23 Men will always glory in something. When they do not glory in God, to what then do they turn? Here, *wisdom, might,* and *riches* become the triad of human achievements in which men take pride and in which they glory. True glory consists in the knowledge and understanding of God, whose attributes are love, justice, and righteousness, a triad of attributes not to be found among this apostate people.

neither let the mighty *man* glory in his might, let not the rich *man* glory in
his riches:
24 But let him that glorieth glory in this, that he understandeth and
knoweth me, that I *am* the LORD which exercise lovingkindness, judgment,
and righteousness, in the earth: for in these *things* I delight, saith the LORD.
25 ¶Behold, the days come, saith the LORD, that I will punish all *them*
which are circumcised with the uncircumcised;
26 Egypt, and Judah, and Edom, and the children of Ammon, and Moab,
and all *that are* in the utmost corners, that dwell in the wilderness: for all
these nations *are* uncircumcised, and all the house of Israel *are* uncircum-
cised in the heart.

10 HEAR ye the word which the LORD speaketh unto you, O house of
Israel:
2 Thus saith the LORD, Learn not the way of the heathen, and be not
dismayed at the signs of heaven; for the heathen are dismayed at them.
3 For the customs of the people *are* vain: for *one* cutteth a tree out of the
forest, the work of the hands of the workman, with the axe.
4 They deck it with silver and with gold; they fasten it with nails and with
hammers, that it move not.
5 They *are* upright as the palm tree, but speak not: they must needs be
borne, because they cannot go. Be not afraid of them; for they cannot do
evil, neither also *is it* in them to do good.
6 Forasmuch as *there is* none like unto thee, O LORD; thou *art* great, and
thy name *is* great in might.
7 Who would not fear thee, O King of nations? for to thee doth it
appertain: forasmuch as among all the wise *men* of the nations, and in all
their kingdoms, *there is* none like unto thee.
8 But they are altogether brutish and foolish: the stock *is* a doctrine of
vanities.
9 Silver spread into plates is brought from Tarshish, and gold from
U'phaz, the work of the workman, and of the hands of the founder: blue
and purple *is* their clothing: they *are* all the work of cunning *men*.
10 But the LORD *is* the true God, he *is* the living God, and an everlasting
king: at his wrath the earth shall tremble, and the nations shall not be able
to abide his indignation.
11 Thus shall ye say unto them, The gods that have not made the heavens
and the earth, *even* they shall perish from the earth, and from under these
heavens.
12 He hath made the earth by his power, he hath established the world by
his wisdom, and hath stretched out the heavens by his discretion.
13 When he uttereth his voice, *there is* a multitude of waters in the
heavens, and he causeth the vapours to ascend from the ends of the earth;
he maketh lightnings with rain, and bringeth forth the wind out of his
treasures.

9:24 Ex 34:6, 7; Ps 36:5, 7; 44:8; Isa 61:8; Mic 7:18; 1 Cor 1:31; 2 Cor 10:17; Gal 6:14
☆**9:25** Lev 26:41; Jer 4:4; Ezek 44:7; Rom 2:8, 9, 28, 29
☆**9:26**
☆**10:1**
10:2 Lev 18:3; Isa 44:9–20; 47:12–14
10:4 Isa 40:19; 41:7
☆**10:5** Isa 41:23, 24; 46:1, 7
10:6 Deut 33:26; Ps 48:1; 96:4; Isa 12:6; Jer 10:16
10:7 Ps 22:28; Dan 2:27, 28; 1 Cor 1:19, 20
☆**10:9** Ps 115:4
☆**10:10** Ps 10:16; 29:10; 76:7; Isa 65:16
10:11 Ps 96:5; Isa 2:18; Zeph 2:11
10:12 Job 9:8; 38:4–7; Ps 148:4, 5; Isa 40:22; 45:18; Jer 51:15
10:13 Job 36:27–29; Ps 29:3–9; 135:7

9:25, 26 Circumcision was practiced by heathen peoples as well as by Israelites. Among the heathen it was a physical matter. Among the Israelites the rite of circumcision was both physical and spiritual. Circumcision without spiritual motivation and the covenant implications meant no more than circumcision meant to the heathen.

10:1 Some think that this chapter was written after the first captivity, in the time of Jeconiah or Jehoiachin. Jeremiah warns the captives against embracing the astrology and idolatry of their conquerors.

10:5 Idols have no power in fact, only in fancy. Shun them in favor of God who can speak, walk, and do what he pleases.

10:9 *Uphaz,* for which *Ophir* is a more modern reading. If so, this would place it in southwest Arabia.

10:10 Idols are all counterfeits or pretenders. The Lord God is genuine, as is evidenced by his works that endorse and enforce his words

10:14☆

14 Every man is brutish in *his* knowledge: every founder is confounded by
the graven image: for his molten image *is* falsehood, and *there is* no breath
in them.

10:15 Isa 41:24; Jer 8:12; 14:22

15 They *are* vanity, *and* the work of errors: in the time of their visitation
they shall perish.

10:16 Deut 32:9; Isa 45:7; Jer 31:35; 32:18; 51:19; 10:12

16 The portion of Jacob *is* not like them: for he *is* the former of all *things;*
and Israel *is* the rod of his inheritance: The LORD of hosts *is* his name.

10:17 Ezek 12:3–12

17 ¶Gather up thy wares out of the land, O inhabitant of the fortress.
18 For thus saith the LORD, Behold, I will sling out the inhabitants of the
land at this once, and will distress them, that they may find *it so.*

10:19 Jer 4:31; Mic 7:9

19 ¶Woe is me for my hurt! my wound is grievous: but I said, Truly this *is*
a grief, and I must bear it.

10:20 Isa 51:18; Jer 4:20; 31:15; Lam 1:5; 2:4

20 My tabernacle is spoiled, and all my cords are broken: my children are
gone forth of me, and they *are* not: *there is* none to stretch forth my tent
any more, and to set up my curtains.

10:21☆ Jer 23:2

21 For the pastors are become brutish, and have not sought the LORD:
therefore they shall not prosper, and all their flocks shall be scattered.

10:22☆ Jer 9:11; 49:33

22 Behold, the noise of the bruit is come, and a great commotion out of the
north country, to make the cities of Judah desolate, *and* a den of dragons.

10:23☆ Prov 20:24; Isa 26:7

23 ¶O LORD, I know that the way of man *is* not in himself: *it is* not in man
that walketh to direct his steps.

10:24 Ps 6:1

24 O LORD, correct me, but with judgment; not in thine anger, lest thou
bring me to nothing.

10:25☆ Ps 79:6; Jer 8:16; 50:7; Zeph 1:6; 3:8

25 Pour out thy fury upon the heathen that know thee not, and upon the
families that call not on thy name: for they have eaten up Jacob, and
devoured him, and consumed him, and made his habitation desolate.

5. The Broken Covenant and the Linen Loincloth

a. Judah Has Broken the Covenant

11:1 Ex 19:5; Deut 27:26; Jer 17:5; Gal 3:10

11 THE word that came to Jer-e-mi′ah from the LORD, saying,
2 Hear ye the words of this covenant, and speak unto the men of
Judah, and to the inhabitants of Jerusalem;

11:2☆ **11:3☆**

3 And say thou unto them, Thus saith the LORD God of Israel; Cursed *be*
the man that obeyeth not the words of this covenant,

11:4 Ex 24:3, 7; Deut 4:20; 1 Kgs 8:51; Jer 31:32; Zech 8:8

4 Which I commanded your fathers in the day *that* I brought them forth
out of the land of Egypt, from the iron furnace, saying, Obey my voice, and
do them, according to all which I command you: so shall ye be my people,
and I will be your God:

10:14 The world of Jeremiah's day contained few, if any, atheists. The heathen had a superfluity of gods. They made graven images to these gods and bowed before and worshipped them. The Scriptures picture the difference between the gods made by the hands of men and the God who by his hands made man and the universe, and who holds all things together by divine power. The contrast is so startling that one is left to ponder how anyone could choose false gods in place of the one true God.

10:21 The shepherds (i.e., the rulers and priests) had no eye for God. They neither saw that judgment was about to fall, nor did they expect deliverance could or would come from the hand of the true God.

10:22 This invasion, which comes from the north, is noted by the peoples to the north of Judah. It refers, of course, to Nebuchadnezzar's armies moving southward to attack Judah.

10:23 Neither men nor nations can "go it" alone. The affairs of both are directed and determined by providence, not by their own will and wisdom. Those who look to God will be directed properly.

10:25 This is an imprecatory prayer asking God to execute his divine wrath against the enemies of Israel. Christians today have the right to ask God to pull down the strongholds of Satan and to destroy the enemies of the true faith.

11:2 God's covenant with Israel had one unchanging requirement—obedience to him.

11:3 Jeremiah here speaks of how Israel has broken its covenant with God (see note on Deut. 29:1). Israel's failure can only mean judgment and dispersion, according to what God promised when he made the covenant.

5 That I may perform the oath which I have sworn unto your fathers, to
give them a land flowing with milk and honey, as *it is* this day. Then
answered I, and said, So be it, O LORD.

6 Then the LORD said unto me, Proclaim all these words in the cities of
Judah, and in the streets of Jerusalem, saying, Hear ye the words of this
covenant, and do them.

7 For I earnestly protested unto your fathers in the day *that* I brought
them up out of the land of Egypt, *even* unto this day, rising early and
protesting, saying, Obey my voice.

8 Yet they obeyed not, nor inclined their ear, but walked every one in the
imagination of their evil heart: therefore I will bring upon them all the
words of this covenant, which I commanded *them* to do; but they did *them*
not.

9 And the LORD said unto me, A conspiracy is found among the men of
Judah, and among the inhabitants of Jerusalem.

10 They are turned back to the iniquities of their forefathers, which
refused to hear my words; and they went after other gods to serve them: the
house of Israel and the house of Judah have broken my covenant which I
made with their fathers.

11 ¶Therefore thus saith the LORD, Behold, I will bring evil upon them,
which they shall not be able to escape; and though they shall cry unto me,
I will not hearken unto them.

12 Then shall the cities of Judah and inhabitants of Jerusalem go, and cry
unto the gods unto whom they offer incense: but they shall not save them at
all in the time of their trouble.

13 For *according to* the number of thy cities were thy gods, O Judah; and
according to the number of the streets of Jerusalem have ye set up altars to
that shameful thing, *even* altars to burn incense unto Ba'al.

14 Therefore pray not thou for this people, neither lift up a cry or prayer
for them: for I will not hear *them* in the time that they cry unto me for their
trouble.

15 What hath my beloved to do in mine house, *seeing* she hath wrought
lewdness with many, and the holy flesh is passed from thee? when thou
doest evil, then thou rejoicest.

16 The LORD called thy name, A green olive tree, fair, *and* of goodly fruit:
with the noise of a great tumult he hath kindled fire upon it, and the
branches of it are broken.

17 For the LORD of hosts, that planted thee, hath pronounced evil against
thee, for the evil of the house of Israel and of the house of Judah, which
they have done against themselves to provoke me to anger in offering
incense unto Ba'al.

b. Judah's Doom Is Inevitable

18 ¶And the LORD hath given me knowledge *of it*, and I know *it:* then thou
shewedst me their doings.

11:5 Ex 13:5; Deut 7:12; Jer 32:22
11:6 Jer 3:12; 7:2
11:7 Ex 15:26; 2 Chron 36:15; Jer 7:25; 11:4
☆**11:8** Lev 26:14–43; Jer 7:24, 9:14; 35:15; Ezek 20:8
11:9 Ezek 22:25
11:10 Deut 9:7; Judg 2:11–13; Jer 3:6–9; 13:10; Ezek 16:59
☆**11:11** Jer 6:19; 25:35
11:12 Deut 32:37; Jer 44:17
11:13 Jer 2:28; 7:9, 10
☆**11:14** Ps 66:18; Jer 7:16; 14:11; Hos 5:6
11:16 Ps 52:8; 83:2; Isa 27:11; Jer 21:14
11:17 Jer 2:21; 32:29
11:18 1 Sam 23:11, 12; 2 Kgs 6:9, 10; Ezek 8:6

11:8 Whoever turns away his ear from hearing the word of God, i.e., the law of God, will find that his prayers to God are an abomination and the ear of God is closed to his prayers. In 11:13 we are told that Judah had as many gods as they had cities and even streets. So great is their apostasy that God cannot be God and let them go unpunished. The corruption of Judah has made its doom inevitable.

11:11 There is a time when it is too late. God will not hear any prayers by Judah for deliverance. The sentence must be executed. So also after the final judgment at the end of the age; whoever pleads for mercy then will find that it is too late.

11:14 Jeremiah was God's chosen prophet, yet God will not hear any prayer from his lips for mercy on Judah. God forbids him to pray for divine help, because it is too late.

11:19☆ Ps 52:5; 83:4; 109:13

19 But I *was* like a lamb *or* an ox *that* is brought to the slaughter; and I knew not that they had devised devices against me, *saying*, Let us destroy the tree with the fruit thereof, and let us cut him off from the land of the living, that his name may be no more remembered.

11:20 Ps 7:9; Jer 17:10; 20:12

20 But, O LORD of hosts, that judgest righteously, that triest the reins and the heart, let me see thy vengeance on them: for unto thee have I revealed my cause.

11:21 2 Chron 36:17; Jer 1:1; 12:5, 6; 18:21; 20:10; 26:8; 38:4

21 Therefore thus saith the LORD of the men of An′a-thoth, that seek thy life, saying, Prophesy not in the name of the LORD, that thou die not by our hand:

11:22☆

22 Therefore thus saith the LORD of hosts, Behold, I will punish them: the young men shall die by the sword; their sons and their daughters shall die by famine:

11:23 Jer 6:9; 23:12; Hos 9:7; Mic 7:4

23 And there shall be no remnant of them: for I will bring evil upon the men of An′a-thoth, *even* the year of their visitation.

12:1☆ Ezra 9:15; Job 13:3; Jer 5:27, 28; 11:20; Hab 1:4

12 RIGHTEOUS *art* thou, O LORD, when I plead with thee: yet let me talk with thee of *thy* judgments: Wherefore doth the way of the wicked prosper? *wherefore* are all they happy that deal very treacherously?

12:2 Isa 29:13; Ezek 17:5–10; 33:31; Tit 1:16

2 Thou hast planted them, yea, they have taken root: they grow, yea, they bring forth fruit: thou *art* near in their mouth, and far from their reins.

12:3 Ps 7:9; 139:1–4; Jer 11:20

3 But thou, O LORD, knowest me: thou hast seen me, and tried mine heart toward thee: pull them out like sheep for the slaughter, and prepare them for the day of slaughter.

12:4 Jer 5:31; Hos 4:3; Joel 1:10–17

4 How long shall the land mourn, and the herbs of every field wither, for the wickedness of them that dwell therein? the beasts are consumed, and the birds; because they said, He shall not see our last end.

12:5☆

5 ¶If thou hast run with the footmen, and they have wearied thee, then how canst thou contend with horses? and *if* in the land of peace, *wherein* thou trustedst, *they wearied thee*, then how wilt thou do in the swelling of Jordan?

12:6 Gen 37:4–11; Ps 69:8; Prov 26:25

6 For even thy brethren, and the house of thy father, even they have dealt treacherously with thee; yea, they have called a multitude after thee: believe them not, though they speak fair words unto thee.

12:7 Jer 7:29; 11:15; Hos 11:1–4

7 I have forsaken mine house, I have left mine heritage; I have given the dearly beloved of my soul into the hand of her enemies.

12:8 Hos 9:15; Amos 6:8

8 Mine heritage is unto me as a lion in the forest; it crieth out against me: therefore have I hated it.

12:9 2 Kgs 24:2; Isa 56:9; Jer 7:33, 15:3; 34:20

9 Mine heritage *is* unto me *as* a speckled bird, the birds round about *are* against her; come ye, assemble all the beasts of the field, come to devour.

12:10 Ps 80:8–16; Isa 5:1–7; Lam 1:10

10 Many pastors have destroyed my vineyard, they have trodden my portion under foot, they have made my pleasant portion a desolate wilderness.

11:19 Jeremiah, God's prophet, now experiences persecution by the very people he has come to help. Judah not only laughs at his words and spurns his counsel, the people also damage his person. God's prophets (then and now) can expect from men the same sort of treatment the Messiah was accorded by *recalcitrant sinners*.

11:22 Jeremiah was warned by his enemies not to prophesy in the name of the Lord. God here promises that he will judge and punish those who said this. Yet God did not deliver Jeremiah from his difficulties; he supported and sustained him in the midst of them (as he later did for Paul, whose sufferings are enumerated in 2 Cor. 11).

12:1 *when I plead with thee,* i.e., "when I plead my case with thee" (NASB and RSV). Jeremiah is upset about the prosperity of the wicked, so he reasons with God concerning his judgments.

12:5 God says Jeremiah's trials will become greater, not less. Instead of running against men (*If thou hast run with the footmen*) he will now have to race against horses, a figure of speech used to mean political and religious bigwigs.

11 They have made it desolate, *and being* desolate it mourneth unto me;
the whole land is made desolate, because no man layeth *it* to heart.
12 The spoilers are come upon all high places through the wilderness: for
the sword of the LORD shall devour from the *one* end of the land even to the
other end of the land: no flesh shall have peace.
13 They have sown wheat, but shall reap thorns: they have put themselves
to pain, *but* shall not profit: and they shall be ashamed of your revenues
because of the fierce anger of the LORD.
14 ¶Thus saith the LORD against all mine evil neighbours, that touch the
inheritance which I have caused my people Israel to inherit; Behold, I will
pluck them out of their land, and pluck out the house of Judah from among
them.
15 And it shall come to pass, after that I have plucked them out I will
return, and have compassion on them, and will bring them again, every
man to his heritage, and every man to his land.
16 And it shall come to pass, if they will diligently learn the ways of my
people, to swear by my name, The LORD liveth; as they taught my people to
swear by Ba'al; then shall they be built in the midst of my people.
17 But if they will not obey, I will utterly pluck up and destroy that nation,
saith the LORD.

12:11 Jer 4:20, 27; 25:11
☆12:12 Isa 34:6; Jer 47:6; Amos 9:4
12:13 Isa 55:2; Jer 4:26; 17:10; 25:37, 38
12:14 Jer 2:3; 49:1; 50:11, 12; Zeph 2:8–10; Zech 2:8
12:15 Isa 11:11–16; Jer 49:6, 39
12:16 Josh 23:7; Isa 49:6; Jer 3:17; 4:2; 5:7; 16:19
☆12:17 Ps 2:8–12; Isa 60:12

c. God's Warning to Judah; the Ruined Loincloth

13 THUS saith the LORD unto me, Go and get thee a linen girdle, and
put it upon thy loins, and put it not in water.
2 So I got a girdle according to the word of the LORD, and put *it* on my
loins.
3 And the word of the LORD came unto me the second time, saying,
4 Take the girdle that thou hast got, which *is* upon thy loins, and arise, go
to Eu-phra'tes, and hide it there in a hole of the rock.
5 So I went, and hid it by Eu-phra'tes, as the LORD commanded me.
6 And it came to pass after many days, that the LORD said unto me, Arise,
go to Eu-phra'tes, and take the girdle from thence, which I commanded
thee to hide there.
7 Then I went to Eu-phra'tes, and digged, and took the girdle from the
place where I had hid it: and, behold, the girdle was marred, it was
profitable for nothing.
8 Then the word of the LORD came unto me, saying,
9 Thus saith the LORD, After this manner will I mar the pride of Judah,
and the great pride of Jerusalem.
10 This evil people, which refuse to hear my words, which walk in the
imagination of their heart, and walk after other gods, to serve them, and to
worship them, shall even be as this girdle, which is good for nothing.
11 For as the girdle cleaveth to the loins of a man, so have I caused to
cleave unto me the whole house of Israel and the whole house of Judah,

☆13:1 Jer 13:11
13:2 Isa 20:2
13:4 Jer 51:63
13:5 Ex 39:42, 43; 40:16
13:8 Lev 26:19; Isa 2:10–17; 23:9
13:11 Ex 19:5, 6; Deut 32:10, 11; Ps 81:11; Isa 43:21; Jer 7:24; 33:9

12:12 *the sword of the LORD.* The primary function of God's sword is to protect his people from the enemy. But when the people of God become his enemy, the sword originally designed for their protection becomes the sword which will be used against them for their apostasy.

12:17 God here promises that any nation that will not listen to him and obey him will be destroyed at last. This all-embracing statement should be understood to include the lesser as well as the greater. Thus any family, any particular person, and even any church that will not be ruled by God will be destroyed by God. Whoever will not be ruled by the grace of God will be destroyed by the justice of God.

13:1 The *linen girdle* here is parabolic. Israel was the linen girdle worn by God with pleasure and as a witness of his people's fidelity to him. But the girdle has become useless and can no longer be worn. It must be cast off. So shall the people of God be cast off, for their iniquities have separated them from their Redeemer, who cannot put up with a spoiled and degenerate people.

saith the LORD; that they might be unto me for a people, and for a name,
and for a praise, and for a glory: but they would not hear.
13:12☆ 12¶Therefore thou shalt speak unto them this word; Thus saith the LORD
God of Israel, Every bottle shall be filled with wine: and they shall say unto
thee, Do we not certainly know that every bottle shall be filled with wine?
13:13 13Then shalt thou say unto them, Thus saith the LORD, Behold, I will fill
Ps 60:3; 75:8 Jer 25:27 all the inhabitants of this land, even the kings that sit upon David's throne,
and the priests, and the prophets, and all the inhabitants of Jerusalem, with
drunkenness.
13:14 14And I will dash them one against another, even the fathers and the sons
Isa 27:11 Jer 6:21; 16:5 19:9–11 together, saith the LORD: I will not pity, nor spare, nor have mercy, but
destroy them.
13:15 15¶Hear ye, and give ear; be not proud: for the LORD hath spoken.
Prov 16:5 13:16 16Give glory to the LORD your God, before he cause darkness, and before
Ps 96:8 Isa 5:30; 59:9 your feet stumble upon the dark mountains, and, while ye look for light, he
Amos 5:18 turn it into the shadow of death, *and* make *it* gross darkness.
13:17☆ 17But if ye will not hear it, my soul shall weep in secret places for *your*
Jer 9:1; 23:1, 2 Mal 2:2 pride; and mine eye shall weep sore, and run down with tears, because the
Lk 19:41, 42 LORD's flock is carried away captive.
13:18☆ 18Say unto the king and to the queen, Humble yourselves, sit down: for
2 Kgs 24:12, 15 your principalities shall come down, *even* the crown of your glory.
13:19☆ 19The cities of the south shall be shut up, and none shall open *them:*
Judah shall be carried away captive all of it, it shall be wholly carried away
captive.
13:20 20Lift up your eyes, and behold them that come from the north: where *is*
Jer 1:15; 6:22 13:17; 23:2 the flock *that* was given thee, thy beautiful flock?
Hab 1:6 13:21 21What wilt thou say when he shall punish thee? for thou hast taught
Isa 13:8 Jer 4:31; 38:22 them *to be* captains, *and* as chief over thee: shall not sorrows take thee, as
a woman in travail?
13:22 22¶And if thou say in thine heart, Wherefore come these things upon me?
Jer 2:17–19 9:2–9 For the greatness of thine iniquity are thy skirts discovered, *and* thy heels
made bare.
13:23 23Can the E-thi-o'pi-an change his skin, or the leopard his spots? *then*
Prov 27:22 Jer 4:22 may ye also do good, that are accustomed to do evil.
Mt 19:24 13:24 24Therefore will I scatter them as the stubble that passeth away by the
Lev 26:33 wind of the wilderness.
Ps 9:17 Jer 2:32; 9:16 25This *is* thy lot, the portion of thy measures from me, saith the LORD;
18:17 Ezek 5:2, 12 because thou hast forgotten me, and trusted in falsehood.
13:26☆ 26Therefore will I discover thy skirts upon thy face, that thy shame may
Lam 1:8 appear.
13:27 27I have seen thine adulteries and thy neighings, the lewdness of thy
Prov 1:22 Jer 2:20; 5:7, 8 whoredom, *and* thine abominations on the hills in the fields. Woe unto thee,
11:15 O Jerusalem! wilt thou not be made clean? when *shall it* once *be?*

13:12 Everything gets what it is fitted for. God's people have become a vessel fit for destruction. Their sins have made them objects of God's wrath, not his mercy.
13:17 The little word *if* keeps rising on the lips of God. If Judah will not hear God, they must pay the price of *their failure.*
13:18 *Say unto the king and to the queen,* i.e., to King Jehoiachin and his mother Nehashta.†
13:19 *the cities of the south shall be shut up.* The meaning of this is unclear. Some think it refers to the cities of Egypt that lay to the south of Judah and from which they could expect neither help nor access. Others think it refers to the cities of Judah that lay to the south in Canaan. They will be besieged by the enemy, deserted by their inhabitants, and no one can go in or go out of them.
13:26 *Therefore I will discover thy skirts upon thy face.* If a wind blows one's garment face high, the person is left exposed, naked in open view to all. God will expose his people's nakedness to public view. All the world will see their adulteries and harlotries.

6. The Coming Judgment and Future Restoration of Judah
a. Judgment Cannot Be Averted

14 THE word of the LORD that came to Jer-e-mi'ah concerning the
dearth.
2 Judah mourneth, and the gates thereof languish; they are black unto the
ground; and the cry of Jerusalem is gone up.
3 And their nobles have sent their little ones to the waters: they came to
the pits, *and* found no water; they returned with their vessels empty; they
were ashamed and confounded, and covered their heads.
4 Because the ground is chapt, for there was no rain in the earth, the
plowmen were ashamed, they covered their heads.
5 Yea, the hind also calved in the field, and forsook *it*, because there was
no grass.
6 And the wild asses did stand in the high places, they snuffed up the wind
like dragons; their eyes did fail, because *there was* no grass.
7 ¶O LORD, though our iniquities testify against us, do thou *it* for thy
name's sake: for our backslidings are many; we have sinned against thee.
8 O the hope of Israel, the saviour thereof in time of trouble, why
shouldest thou be as a stranger in the land, and as a wayfaring man *that*
turneth aside to tarry for a night?
9 Why shouldest thou be as a man astonied, as a mighty man *that* cannot
save? yet thou, O LORD, *art* in the midst of us, and we are called by thy
name; leave us not.
10 ¶Thus saith the LORD unto this people, Thus have they loved to
wander, they have not refrained their feet, therefore the LORD doth not
accept them; he will now remember their iniquity, and visit their sins.
11 Then said the LORD unto me, Pray not for this people for *their* good.
12 When they fast, I will not hear their cry; and when they offer burnt
offering and an oblation, I will not accept them: but I will consume them
by the sword, and by the famine, and by the pestilence.
13 ¶Then said I, Ah, Lord GOD! behold, the prophets say unto them, Ye
shall not see the sword, neither shall ye have famine; but I will give you
assured peace in this place.
14 Then the LORD said unto me, The prophets prophesy lies in my name:
I sent them not, neither have I commanded them, neither spake unto them:
they prophesy unto you a false vision and divination, and a thing of nought,
and the deceit of their heart.
15 Therefore thus saith the LORD concerning the prophets that prophesy
in my name, and I sent them not, yet they say, Sword and famine shall not
be in this land; By sword and famine shall those prophets be consumed.
16 And the people to whom they prophesy shall be cast out in the streets
of Jerusalem because of the famine and the sword; and they shall have none

☆**14:1ff**
14:2 Jer 11:11; Zech 7:13
14:3 2 Sam 15:30; 1 Kgs 18:5
14:4 Joel 1:11, 19, 20
14:6 Job 39:5, 6
☆**14:7** Isa 59:12; Hos 5:5
14:8 Ps 9:9; Isa 43:3; 63:8; Jer 17:13
14:9 Num 11:23; Ps 46:5; Isa 50:2; 63:19; Jer 8:19; 15:16
14:10 Ps 119:101; Jer 2:25; 44:21–23
14:11 Jer 7:16; 11:14
14:12 Isa 1:15; Jer 8:13
☆**14:13** Jer 5:12; 6:14; 8:11; 23:17
14:14 Jer 5:31; 23:16, 25, 26; 27:9, 10
14:15 Ezek 14:10
14:16 Ps 79:2, 3; Prov 1:31; Jer 7:33; 15:2, 3

14:1ff The world is always one harvest away from famine. If the earth did not give forth a harvest for a single year, many of the world's people would starve. The Scriptures plainly state that on occasion God sends famine by way of judicial judgment against sinners and with the intention of directing their thoughts to him in repentance for their transgressions. Famine may be penal, but it is also therapeutic. Lack of food is not as bad as lack of devotion to God or disobedience to his commandments. When food is lacking, it is an incentive for starving people to look to God for help.

14:7 Here Jeremiah prays for the people, and so would move them to pray for themselves. He confesses their sins, knowing that sinners deserve every judgment that comes to them. Most sinners plead that it is not their fault or they could not help themselves. True repentance includes an acknowledgement and acceptance of true guilt.

14:13 Where there are true prophets of God, there will always be false prophets as well. Here the false prophets reassure the people that the ax will not fall and the famine will disappear. But God declares that these false prophets are liars. He did not send them nor did he give them a message of hope. He did not speak to them, nor was he speaking through them. These false prophets will be consumed by the sword and famine (14:15).

to bury them, them, their wives, nor their sons, nor their daughters: for I
will pour their wickedness upon them.

14:17☆ Jer 8:21; 9:1 Lam 2:13

[17]¶Therefore thou shalt say this word unto them; Let mine eyes run down
with tears night and day, and let them not cease: for the virgin daughter of
my people is broken with a great breach, with a very grievous blow.

14:18☆ Jer 6:25 Lam 1:20 Ezek 7:15

[18]If I go forth into the field, then behold the slain with the sword! and if
I enter into the city, then behold them that are sick with famine! yea, both
the prophet and the priest go about into a land that they know not.

14:19 Job 30:26 Jer 8:15; 30:13 1 Thess 5:3

[19]Hast thou utterly rejected Judah? hath thy soul lothed Zion? why hast
thou smitten us, and *there is* no healing for us? we looked for peace, and
there is no good; and for the time of healing, and behold trouble!

14:20 Ps 32:5 Jer 3:25

[20]We acknowledge, O LORD, our wickedness, *and* the iniquity of our
fathers: for we have sinned against thee.

14:21 Ps 25:11 Jer 3:17; 14:7 17:12

[21]Do not abhor *us*, for thy name's sake, do not disgrace the throne of thy
glory: remember, break not thy covenant with us.

14:22 1 Kgs 17:1 Isa 41:29 Jer 5:24; 10:3 Lam 3:26

[22]Are there *any* among the vanities of the Gentiles that can cause rain? or
can the heavens give showers? *art* not thou he, O LORD our God? therefore
we will wait upon thee: for thou hast made all these *things*.

b. The Prayers of Moses and Samuel Could Not Save Judah

15:1☆ Ex 32:11–14 1 Sam 7:9 Ps 99:6; 106:23 Jer 10:18; 52:3 Ezek 14:14, 20

15 THEN said the LORD unto me, Though Moses and Samuel stood
before me, *yet* my mind *could* not *be* toward this people: cast *them*
out of my sight, and let them go forth.

15:2 Jer 14:12 24:10; 43:11 Ezek 5:2, 12

[2]And it shall come to pass, if they say unto thee, Whither shall we go
forth? then thou shalt tell them, Thus saith the LORD; Such as *are* for death,
to death; and such as *are* for the sword, to the sword; and such as *are* for
the famine, to the famine; and such as *are* for the captivity, to the captivity.

15:3☆ Lev 26:16, 22, 25 Deut 28:26 Isa 18:6 Ezek 14:21

[3]And I will appoint over them four kinds, saith the LORD: the sword to
slay, and the dogs to tear, and the fowls of the heaven, and the beasts of the
earth, to devour and destroy.

15:4 2 Kgs 23:26, 27 24:3, 4 Jer 24:9; 29:18

[4]And I will cause them to be removed into all kingdoms of the earth,
because of Ma-nas'seh the son of Hez-e-ki'ah king of Judah, for *that* which
he did in Jerusalem.

15:5 Ps 69:20 Jer 13:14

[5]For who shall have pity upon thee, O Jerusalem? or who shall bemoan
thee? or who shall go aside to ask how thou doest?

15:6 Isa 1:4 Jer 6:11 7:16, 24 Zeph 1:4

[6]Thou hast forsaken me, saith the LORD, thou art gone backward:
therefore will I stretch out my hand against thee, and destroy thee; I am
weary with repenting.

15:7 Jer 18:21; 51:2 Hos 9:12–16

[7]And I will fan them with a fan in the gates of the land; I will bereave
them of children, I will destroy my people, *since* they return not from their
ways.

15:8 Isa 3:25, 26; 4:1

[8]Their widows are increased to me above the sand of the seas: I have
brought upon them against the mother of the young men a spoiler at
noonday: I have caused *him* to fall upon it suddenly, and terrors upon the
city.

14:17, 18 Jeremiah is the prophet with a broken heart. He weeps over the ruin of his country. He sees what Judah does not see—that they will perish and that famine will come.

15:1 *Moses and Samuel* were looked upon as great prophets of God in the Old Testament. Their intercession for Israel was responded to by God on a number of occasions. Thus they were known as special favorites of God to whom he responded by granting their many prayer requests. Now God says that even if Moses and Samuel were alive and offered intercessory prayer for Judah, he would not hear them. And if he would not grant them their petitions, it was foolish to suppose that he would answer the prayers of apostate hypocrites. Judgment was inescapable; the verdict against the sinners was irrevocable.

15:3 God will harness men and nature against his people. The sword, dogs, birds, and beasts will consume the guilty.

9She that hath borne seven languisheth: she hath given up the ghost; her
sun is gone down while *it was* yet day: she hath been ashamed and
confounded: and the residue of them will I deliver to the sword before their
enemies, saith the LORD.
10¶Woe is me, my mother, that thou hast borne me a man of strife and a
man of contention to the whole earth! I have neither lent on usury, nor men
have lent to me on usury; *yet* every one of them doth curse me.
11The LORD said, Verily it shall be well with thy remnant; verily I will
cause the enemy to entreat thee *well* in the time of evil and in the time of
affliction.
12Shall iron break the northern iron and the steel?
13Thy substance and thy treasures will I give to the spoil without price,
and *that* for all thy sins, even in all thy borders.
14And I will make *thee* to pass with thine enemies into a land *which* thou
knowest not: for a fire is kindled in mine anger, *which* shall burn upon you.

c. God Will Deliver Jeremiah

15¶O LORD, thou knowest: remember me, and visit me, and revenge me
of my persecutors; take me not away in thy longsuffering: know that for thy
sake I have suffered rebuke.
16Thy words were found, and I did eat them; and thy word was unto me
the joy and rejoicing of mine heart: for I am called by thy name, O LORD
God of hosts.
17I sat not in the assembly of the mockers, nor rejoiced; I sat alone
because of thy hand: for thou hast filled me with indignation.
18Why is my pain perpetual, and my wound incurable, *which* refuseth to
be healed? wilt thou be altogether unto me as a liar, *and as* waters *that* fail?
19¶Therefore thus saith the LORD, If thou return, then will I bring thee
again, *and* thou shalt stand before me: and if thou take forth the precious
from the vile, thou shalt be as my mouth: let them return unto thee; but
return not thou unto them.
20And I will make thee unto this people a fenced brasen wall: and they
shall fight against thee, but they shall not prevail against thee: for I *am* with
thee to save thee and to deliver thee, saith the LORD.
21And I will deliver thee out of the hand of the wicked, and I will redeem
thee out of the hand of the terrible.

7. Jeremiah to Remain Unmarried

16 THE word of the LORD came also unto me, saying,
2Thou shalt not take thee a wife, neither shalt thou have sons or
daughters in this place.

15:9 1 Sam 2:5; Isa 47:9; Amos 8:9
☆**15:10** Deut 23:19; Job 3:3; Jer 1:18, 19; 20:7, 8, 14
15:11 Isa 41:10
15:12 Jer 17:3; 20:5
☆**15:13**
☆**15:14** Deut 28:64; Jer 16:13; 17:4
15:15 Ps 69:7–9; Jer 20:8
☆**15:15ff**
15:16 Job 23:12; Ps 119:103; Jer 14:9
15:17 Job 6:15, 20; 34:6; Ps 102:7; Jer 13:17; 16:8; 30:12, 15; 2 Cor 6:17
☆**15:19** Ezek 44:23
15:20 Jer 1:8, 18, 19; Ps 46:7; Isa 41:10; Ezek 3:9
15:21 Ps 37:40; Isa 49:26; Jer 39:11, 12
☆**16:1ff**

15:10ff Jeremiah begins a lamentation or complaint. He argues his innocence and notes that he was regarded as a man of strife and contention. He was looked upon with contempt. Yet he had prayed and pleaded for his people.

15:13, 14 God's judgment will make both those who die and those who survive aware that Jeremiah the prophet spoke the truth, but it would be learned too late to help them.

15:15ff The prophet pleads with God for mercy and relief from the venomous persecutions, slanders, and physical abuse of his enemies.

15:19ff In Jeremiah's dark night of the soul, God speaks comfortable words to his servant. He tells Jeremiah to recover from his depression, to be faithful in service, and to obey what God orders him to do. If he does this, his mind will be at rest, he will continue to be useful to God, and he will have the strength and courage to face all difficulties. God will be his protector and deliverer.

16:1ff The situation is so bad that God cautions Jeremiah to remain celibate and not think of having a family. He is not to go into mourning nor is he to go into the house of feasting. The reason for this is plain. God's people have done worse than their fathers (16:12). Since Manasseh, the son of Hezekiah, was one of the worst kings of Judah, it is almost inconceivable to suppose that those who came after could have done worse. But they did. And judgment was about to fall.

3 For thus saith the LORD concerning the sons and concerning the daughters that are born in this place, and concerning their mothers that bare them, and concerning their fathers that begat them in this land;

16:4 Ps 79:2; Isa 18:6; Jer 15:2, 3; 34:20

4 They shall die of grievous deaths; they shall not be lamented; neither shall they be buried; *but* they shall be as dung upon the face of the earth: and they shall be consumed by the sword, and by famine; and their carcases shall be meat for the fowls of heaven, and for the beasts of the earth.

16:5 Ps 25:6; Isa 27:11; Jer 12:12; Ezek 24:16–23

5 For thus saith the LORD, Enter not into the house of mourning, neither go to lament nor bemoan them: for I have taken away my peace from this people, saith the LORD, *even* lovingkindness and mercies.

16:6 Deut 14:1; Ezek 9:6

6 Both the great and the small shall die in this land: they shall not be buried, neither shall *men* lament for them, nor cut themselves, nor make themselves bald for them:

16:7 Ezek 24:17

7 Neither shall *men* tear *themselves* for them in mourning, to comfort them for the dead; neither shall *men* give them the cup of consolation to drink for their father or for their mother.

16:8 Eccles 7:2–4; Isa 22:12–14; Jer 15:17

8 Thou shalt not also go into the house of feasting, to sit with them to eat and to drink.

16:9 Jer 7:34; 25:10; Hos 2:11

9 For thus saith the LORD of hosts, the God of Israel; Behold, I will cause to cease out of this place in your eyes, and in your days, the voice of mirth, and the voice of gladness, the voice of the bridegroom, and the voice of the bride.

16:10☆ Deut 29:24, 25; 1 Kgs 9:8, 9; Jer 5:19; 13:22

10 ¶And it shall come to pass, when thou shalt shew this people all these words, and they shall say unto thee, Wherefore hath the LORD pronounced all this great evil against us? or what *is* our iniquity? or what *is* our sin that we have committed against the LORD our God?

16:11 Neh 9:26–29; Ps 106:35–41; 1 Pet 4:3

11 Then shalt thou say unto them, Because your fathers have forsaken me, saith the LORD, and have walked after other gods, and have served them, and have worshipped them, and have forsaken me, and have not kept my law;

16:12 Jer 7:24; 9:14; 3:10; Mark 7:21

12 And ye have done worse than your fathers; for, behold, ye walk every one after the imagination of his evil heart, that they may not hearken unto me:

16:13 Deut 4:26, 27; 28:36; Jer 5:19; 15:14

13 Therefore will I cast you out of this land into a land that ye know not, *neither* ye nor your fathers; and there shall ye serve other gods day and night; where I will not shew you favour.

16:14☆ Deut 15:15; Ps 106:47; Isa11:11–16; 14:1; 43:18, 19; Jer 23:7, 8; Hos 3:4, 5

14 ¶Therefore, behold, the days come, saith the LORD, that it shall no more be said, The LORD liveth, that brought up the children of Israel out of the land of Egypt;

16:15☆

15 But, The LORD liveth, that brought up the children of Israel from the land of the north, and from all the lands whither he had driven them: and I will bring them again into their land that I gave unto their fathers.

16:16 Isa 2:21; Amos 4:2, 9:1–3; Hab 1:14, 15

16 ¶Behold, I will send for many fishers, saith the LORD, and they shall fish them; and after will I send for many hunters, and they shall hunt them from every mountain, and from every hill, and out of the holes of the rocks.

16:17 Ps 90:8; Jer 23:24; 32:19; Lk 12:2; 1 Cor 4:5; Heb 4:13

17 For mine eyes *are* upon all their ways: they are not hid from my face, neither is their iniquity hid from mine eyes.

16:10 *One would hope that the remnant* in Babylon would have known why God's judgment had fallen on them. But if they were to ask Jeremiah why it had happened, he was to tell them the truth, however much it hurt them. They were there in Babylon because of Judah's transgressions, and if some of them were innocent, it yet remains true that the innocent sometimes suffer for the sins of the guilty.

16:14, 15 God gives his dispersed people a word of hope and encouragement. The days will come when he who sent his people into Babylon will bring them back to the land from which they were taken. It will constitute one of the wonders of their great God.

18And first I will recompense their iniquity and their sin double; because
they have defiled my land, they have filled mine inheritance with the
carcases of their detestable and abominable things.
19O LORD, my strength, and my fortress, and my refuge in the day of
affliction, the Gentiles shall come unto thee from the ends of the earth, and
shall say, Surely our fathers have inherited lies, vanity, and *things* wherein
there is no profit.
20Shall a man make gods unto himself, and they *are* no gods?
21Therefore, behold, I will this once cause them to know, I will cause
them to know mine hand and my might; and they shall know that my name
is The LORD.

16:18 Num 35:34, Jer 2:7; 3:9, Rev 18:6
16:19 Ps 18:1, 2, Isa 25:4, Jer 3:17; 4:2, Nah 1:7
16:20 Ps 115:4–8, Jer 5:7, Hos 8:4–6
☆**16:21** Ps 33:18, Isa 43:3, Amos 5:8

8. Trust in Man Denounced
a. Judah's Only Hope Is God

17 THE sin of Judah *is* written with a pen of iron, *and* with the point
of a diamond: *it is* graven upon the table of their heart, and upon
the horns of your altars;
2Whilst their children remember their altars and their groves by the green
trees upon the high hills.
3O my mountain in the field, I will give thy substance *and* all thy
treasures to the spoil, *and* thy high places for sin, throughout all thy
borders.
4And thou, even thyself, shalt discontinue from thine heritage that I gave
thee; and I will cause thee to serve thine enemies in the land which thou
knowest not; for ye have kindled a fire in mine anger, *which* shall burn for
ever.
5¶Thus saith the LORD; Cursed *be* the man that trusteth in man, and
maketh flesh his arm, and whose heart departeth from the LORD.
6For he shall be like the heath in the desert, and shall not see when good
cometh; but shall inhabit the parched places in the wilderness, *in* a salt land
and not inhabited.
7Blessed *is* the man that trusteth in the LORD, and whose hope the
LORD is.
8For he shall be as a tree planted by the waters, and *that* spreadeth out
her roots by the river, and shall not see when heat cometh, but her leaf shall
be green; and shall not be careful in the year of drought, neither shall cease
from yielding fruit.
9¶The heart *is* deceitful above all *things*, and desperately wicked: who can
know it?
10I the LORD search the heart, *I* try the reins, even to give every man
according to his ways, *and* according to the fruit of his doings.

☆**17:1** Job 19:24, Prov 3:3; 7:3, 2 Cor 3:3
17:2 Ex 34:13, Isa 39:4–6, Jer 3:6; 15:13, 20:5
☆**17:3**
☆**17:4** Deut 28:48, Isa 5:25, Jer 7:20; 12:7, 15:14
☆**17:5** Ps 146:3, Isa 30:1; 31:3, Ezek 29:6, 7
17:6 Deut 29:23, Jer 48:6
☆**17:7** Ps 34:8; 40:4, 84:12
☆**17:8** Ps 1:3; 92:12–14
☆**17:9** Eccles 9:3, Mt 13:15, Mk 2:17, Rom 1:21
☆**17:10** 1 Sam 16:7, Jer 11:20, Rom 8:27

16:21 *I will cause them to know,* i.e., "I will make them know."

17:1 *a pen of iron,* i.e., an instrument used to chisel a message permanently on a rock. Israel's sins are of such a nature that they cannot be erased. They are indelibly manifested and must be punished, for there is no repentance.

17:3, 4 Because Judah is wedded to its sins, God's judgment is established as right, and the sentence pronounced against his people is ratified.

17:5 Whoever puts his trust in man is, by that decision, rejecting God.

17:7, 8 Trust in God is compared with trust in man. The contrast is between a well-watered field and an arid one. Take your choice! The reason for man not to trust man is that the unregenerate are frail, false, and deceitful by nature. Even the regenerate man is not perfected until the time of glorification, so that trust in God is always better than trust in man.

17:9, 10 All of us have some wickedness in our hearts of which we are unaware. We think better of ourselves than we should. This often cheats men of salvation, for they think themsleves to be good and suppose that God will accept them as they are. We who do not know our own hearts cannot know the hearts of others either. But God knows the hearts of all and sees what we cover over or fail to detect. God is the only one who can judge; he alone truly knows what lies in our hearts.

17:11☆ 11 *As* the partridge sitteth *on eggs*, and hatcheth *them* not; *so* he that
getteth riches, and not by right, shall leave them in the midst of his days,
and at his end shall be a fool.
17:12 12 ¶A glorious high throne from the beginning *is* the place of our
Jer 14:21 sanctuary.
17:13 13 O LORD, the hope of Israel, all that forsake thee shall be ashamed, *and*
Jer 14:8 they that depart from me shall be written in the earth, because they have
forsaken the LORD, the fountain of living waters.
17:14 14 Heal me, O LORD, and I shall be healed; save me, and I shall be saved:
Deut 10:21 Ps 54:1 for thou *art* my praise.
Jer 33:6 17:15 15 ¶Behold, they say unto me, where *is* the word of the LORD? let it come
Isa 5:19 Amos 5:18 now.
16 As for me, I have not hastened from *being* a pastor to follow thee:
neither have I desired the woeful day; thou knowest: that which came out
of my lips was *right* before thee.
17:17 17 Be not a terror unto me: thou *art* my hope in the day of evil.
Jer 16:19 Nah 1:7 18 Let them be confounded that persecute me, but let not me be
17:18 Ps 35:4, 26 confounded: let them be dismayed, but let not me be dismayed: bring upon
Jer 20:11 them the day of evil, and destroy them with double destruction.

b. Keeping the Sabbath

19 ¶Thus said the LORD unto me; Go and stand in the gate of the children
of the people, whereby the kings of Judah come in, and by the which they
go out, and in all the gates of Jerusalem;
17:20 20 And say unto them, Hear ye the word of the LORD, ye kings of Judah,
Jer 19:3, 4 and all Judah, and all the inhabitants of Jerusalem, that enter in by these
gates:
17:21☆ 21 Thus saith the LORD; Take heed to yourselves, and bear no burden on
Ex 16:23–29 20:8–10 the sabbath day, nor bring *it* in by the gates of Jerusalem;
Num 15:32–36 Neh 13:15–21 22 Neither carry forth a burden out of your houses on the sabbath day,
Isa 56:2; 58:13 Ezek 20:12 neither do ye any work, but hallow ye the sabbath day, as I commanded
Zech 1:4 Mk 4:24 your fathers.
Jn 5:9–12 17:23 23 But they obeyed not, neither inclined their ear, but made their neck
Jer 7:26; 19:15 stiff, that they might not hear, nor receive instruction.
17:24☆ Ex 15:26 24 And it shall come to pass, if ye diligently hearken unto me, saith the
20:8–11 Deut 11:13 LORD, to bring in no burden through the gates of this city on the sabbath
Ezek 20:20 day, but hallow the sabbath day, to do no work therein;
17:25 2 Sam 7:16 25 Then shall there enter into the gates of this city kings and princes
Ps 132:13, 14 sitting upon the throne of David, riding in chariots and on horses, they, and
Jer 22:4 Lk 1:32 their princes, the men of Judah, and the inhabitants of Jerusalem: and this
city shall remain for ever.
17:26 26 And they shall come from the cities of Judah, and from the places
Ps 107:22 Jer 33:11 about Jerusalem, and from the land of Benjamin, and from the plain, and
from the mountains, and from the south, bringing burnt offerings, and
sacrifices, and meat offerings, and incense, and bringing sacrifices of praise,
17:27 unto the house of the LORD.
Jer 39:8 Ezek 20:47 27 But if ye will not hearken unto me to hallow the sabbath day, and not
Amos 2:5 to bear a burden, even entering in at the gates of Jerusalem on the sabbath

---

17:11 *Let all men learn to get their wealth honestly and to use it charitably, for then they lay up treasure in heaven.*

17:21 *bear no burden on the sabbath.* Works of mercy and necessity were permitted on the sabbath, but Israel was breaking the sabbath by doing what was not related to mercy or necessity. The sabbath was God's gift to man, given for his good. When men break the sabbath they will in turn be broken. Judgment must follow sabbath-breaking.

17:24 Once again God uses the word *if* (so also in 17:27). There is attached to the first *if* the promise of divine blessing and to the second *if* the promise of a fire that shall devour the palaces of Jerusalem.

day; then will I kindle a fire in the gates thereof, and it shall devour the
palaces of Jerusalem, and it shall not be quenched.

9. The Sign of the Potter's Work

a. The First Sign: the Potter and the Clay

18 THE word which came to Jer-e-mi'ah from the LORD, saying,
2 Arise, and go down to the potter's house, and there I will cause 18:2 Jer 19:1, 2
thee to hear my words.
3 Then I went down to the potter's house, and, behold, he wrought a work
on the wheels.
4 And the vessel that he made of clay was marred in the hand of the ☆18:4
potter: so he made it again another vessel, as seemed good to the potter to
make *it*.
5 Then the word of the LORD came to me, saying,
6 O house of Israel, cannot I do with you as this potter? saith the LORD. 18:6 Isa 45:9; 64:8 Rom 9:21
Behold, as the clay *is* in the potter's hand, so *are* ye in mine hand, O house
of Israel.
7 *At what* instant I shall speak concerning a nation, and concerning a ☆18:7 Jer 1:10
kingdom, to pluck up, and to pull down, and to destroy *it;*
8 If that nation, against whom I have pronounced, turn from their evil, I 18:8 Jer 7:3–7 Ezek 18:21
will repent of the evil that I thought to do unto them.
9 And *at what* instant I shall speak concerning a nation, and concerning a 18:9 Jer 31:28 Amos 9:11–15
kingdom, to build and to plant *it;*
10 If it do evil in my sight, that it obey not my voice, then I will repent of 18:10 1 Sam 2:30 Jer 7:24–28 Ezek 33:18
the good, wherewith I said I would benefit them.
11 ¶Now therefore go to, speak to the men of Judah, and to the 18:11 2 Kgs 17:13 Isa 1:16–19 Jer 4:6; 11:11 Acts 28:20
inhabitants of Jerusalem, saying, Thus saith the LORD; Behold, I frame evil
against you, and devise a device against you: return ye now every one from
his evil way, and make your ways and your doings good.
12 And they said, There is no hope: but we will walk after our own 18:12 Deut 29:19 Jer 2:25; 16:12
devices, and we will every one do the imagination of his evil heart.
13 Therefore thus saith the LORD; Ask ye now among the heathen, who 18:13 Jer 2:10, 11 23:14 Hos 6:10
hath heard such things: the virgin of Israel hath done a very horrible thing.
14 Will *a man* leave the snow of Lebanon *which cometh* from the rock of
the field? *or* shall the cold flowing waters that come from another place be
forsaken?
15 Because my people hath forgotten me, they have burned incense to 18:15 Isa 62:10 Jer 2:32; 6:16 7:9; 44:17
vanity, and they have caused them to stumble in their ways *from* the ancient
paths, to walk in paths, *in* a way not cast up;
16 To make their land desolate, *and* a perpetual hissing; every one that 18:16 Jer 25:9; 48:27 50:13 Ezek 33:28, 29
passeth thereby shall be astonished, and wag his head.
17 I will scatter them as with an east wind before the enemy; I will shew 18:17 Jer 13:24
them the back, and not the face, in the day of their calamity.

18:4 Just as clay in the potter's hand is malleable and can be fashioned into whatever form the potter desires, so God can do the same with men who are as clay to be fashioned by his hand. In Romans Paul picks up this theme and enlarges upon it. The theology of the sovereignty of God in relation to free will, predestination, and foreknowledge has in it an element of mystery that remains to be disclosed to us in eternity.

18:7 This verse and those that follow are important not only to Israel but to all nations, for the principles expounded relate to all nations in general. In the realm of common grace God can and does bless some nations that act in accord with divine standards. God can and does fashion kingdoms and nations as it pleases him, but he never acts capriciously. He works according to his fixed rules of equity and goodness. Any nation that turns to God can be raised up from their ruins, even as the potter can make a new vessel from the clay that was marred in his hands. So also with individuals.

18:18☆ Ps 52:2 Jer 2:8; 5:13 8:8; 11:19 18:11; 20:10

18 ¶Then said they, Come, and let us devise devices against Jer-e-mi′ah;
for the law shall not perish from the priest, nor counsel from the wise, nor
the word from the prophet. Come, and let us smite him with the tongue,
and let us not give heed to any of his words.
19 Give heed to me, O LORD, and hearken to the voice of them that
contend with me.

18:20 Ps 35:7; 57:6 Jer 5:26

20 Shall evil be recompensed for good? for they have digged a pit for my
soul. Remember that I stood before thee to speak good for them, *and* to
turn away thy wrath from them.

18:21 Ps 109:9–20 Jer 9:21; 11:22 14:16

21 Therefore deliver up their children to the famine, and pour out their
blood by the force of the sword; and let their wives be bereaved of their
children, and *be* widows; and let their men be put to death; *let* their young
men *be* slain by the sword in battle.

18:22 Ps 140:5 Jer 6:26

22 Let a cry be heard from their houses, when thou shalt bring a troop
suddenly upon them: for they have digged a pit to take me, and hid snares
for my feet.

18:23☆ Jer 6:15, 21 7:20; 17:4

23 Yet, LORD, thou knowest all their counsel against me to slay *me:*
forgive not their iniquity, neither blot out their sin from thy sight, but let
them be overthrown before thee; deal *thus* with them in the time of thine
anger.

b. The Second Sign: the Smashed Jar

19:1☆ Num 11:16 Josh 15:8 Jer 7:31, 32 18:2

19 THUS saith the LORD, Go and get a potter's earthen bottle, and
take of the ancients of the people, and of the ancients of the priests;
2 And go forth unto the valley of the son of Hin′nom, which *is* by the
entry of the east gate, and proclaim there the words that I shall tell thee,

19:3 1 Sam 3:11

3 And say, Hear ye the word of the LORD, O kings of Judah, and
inhabitants of Jerusalem; Thus saith the LORD of hosts, the God of Israel;
Behold, I will bring evil upon this place, the which whosoever heareth, his
ears shall tingle.

19:4 2 Kgs 21:6, 16 Isa 65:11 Jer 2:34; 7:6, 9 11:13; 17:13 Dan 11:31

4 Because they have forsaken me, and have estranged this place, and have
burned incense in it unto other gods, whom neither they nor their fathers
have known, nor the kings of Judah, and have filled this place with the
blood of innocents;

19:5 2 Kgs 7:17 Ps 106:37, 38 Jer 32:35

5 They have built also the high places of Ba′al, to burn their sons with fire
for burnt offerings unto Ba′al, which I commanded not, nor spake *it*, neither
came *it* into my mind:
6 Therefore, behold, the days come, saith the LORD, that this place shall
no more be called To′phet, nor The valley of the son of Hin′nom, but The
valley of slaughter.

19:7 Ps 33:10, 11 79:2, 3 Isa 28:17, 18 Jer 16:4

7 And I will make void the counsel of Judah and Jerusalem in this place;
and I will cause them to fall by the sword before their enemies, and by the
hands of them that seek their lives: and their carcases will I give to be meat
for the fowls of the heaven, and for the beasts of the earth.

18:18 Jeremiah has faithfully proclaimed the word he received from God. Now he becomes the object of hatred both with respect to his person and to the word he has spoken. The enemies of God plot to do him harm, to offset his influence, and to subtly undermine his counsel. In 18:9–19 Jeremiah prays earnestly that God will overrule the plans of the enemy and wreak vengeance upon them. This prayer comes just before the intense persecution starts.

18:23 Jeremiah did not need to pray as he did, that God would not forgive their iniquity nor blot out their sin. So long as they remained unrepentant, God could not forgive them or blot out their sins.

19:1ff Undoubtedly Jeremiah spoke forth the Word of God more times than those that are recorded in the Scriptures. In this incident one can ask the question why it was that the leaders of state and church would be willing to go with Jeremiah to listen to a message that would likely follow Jeremiah's normal pattern. Perhaps some of them did regard him as a genuine prophet and prevailed on the others to accompany them.

8 And I will make this city desolate, and an hissing; every one that passeth thereby shall be astonished and hiss because of all the plagues thereof.

19:8 1 Kgs 9:8 2 Chron 7:21 Jer 18:16

9 And I will cause them to eat the flesh of their sons and the flesh of their daughters, and they shall eat every one the flesh of his friend in the siege and straitness, wherewith their enemies, and they that seek their lives, shall straiten them.

19:9 Deut 28:53, 55 Ezek 5:10 Lam 4:10

10 Then shalt thou break the bottle in the sight of the men that go with thee,

☆**19:10**

11 And shalt say unto them, Thus saith the LORD of hosts; Even so will I break this people and this city, as *one* breaketh a potter's vessel, that cannot be made whole again: and they shall bury *them* in To'phet, till *there be* no place to bury.

19:11 Ps 2:9 Isa 30:14 Jer 7:32 Rev 2:27

12 Thus will I do unto this place, saith the LORD, and to the inhabitants thereof, and *even* make this city as To'phet:

13 And the houses of Jerusalem, and the houses of the kings of Judah, shall be defiled as the place of To'phet, because of all the houses upon whose roofs they have burned incense unto all the host of heaven, and have poured out drink offerings unto other gods.

19:13 Deut 4:19 2 Kgs 17:16 Jer 8:2, 32:29 52:13 Ezek 20:28 Zeph 1:5

14 Then came Jer-e-mi'ah from To'phet, whither the LORD had sent him to prophesy; and he stood in the court of the LORD'S house; and said to all the people,

☆**19:14** Jer 26:2

15 Thus saith the LORD of hosts, the God of Israel; Behold, I will bring upon this city and upon all her towns all the evil that I have pronounced against it, because they have hardened their necks, that they might not hear my words.

19:15 Neh 9:17, 29 Jer 7:26; 17:23

c. Jeremiah's Call to Preach Reinforced

20 NOW Pash'ur the son of Im'mer the priest, who *was* also chief governor in the house of the LORD, heard that Jer-e-mi'ah prophesied these things.

20:1 1 Chron 24:14 Ezra 2:37, 38

2 Then Pash'ur smote Jer-e-mi'ah the prophet, and put him in the stocks that *were* in the high gate of Benjamin, which *was* by the house of the LORD.

☆**20:2** 1 Kgs 22:27 2 Chron 16:10 24:21 Job 13:27 Jer 1:19; 37:13 38:7 Zech 14:10

3 And it came to pass on the morrow, that Pash'ur brought forth Jer-e-mi'ah out of the stocks. Then said Jer-e-mi'ah unto him, The LORD hath not called thy name Pash'ur, but Ma'gor–mis'sa-bib.

4 For thus saith the LORD, Behold, I will make thee a terror to thyself, and to all thy friends: and they shall fall by the sword of their enemies, and thine eyes shall behold *it:* and I will give all Judah into the hand of the king of Babylon, and he shall carry them captive into Babylon, and shall slay them with the sword.

20:4 Jer 29:21 39:6, 7 Ezek 26:21

5 Moreover I will deliver all the strength of this city, and all the labours thereof, and all the precious things thereof, and all the treasures of the kings of Judah will I give into the hand of their enemies, which shall spoil them, and take them, and carry them to Babylon.

20:5 2 Kgs 20:17 2 Chron 36:10 Jer 15:13; 17:3 27:21, 22

19:10 Jeremiah had taken a potter's vessel with him, one that was whole and had hardened. Now he breaks that vessel, which will then be irrepairable and impossible to be reshaped. The message is plain: God will break Judah and Jerusalem the way Jeremiah broke the potter's vessel.

19:14 When Jeremiah had finished speaking at Tophet, he repeated to the people in the court of the Lord's house what he had told their leaders. His message was refused and his person abused.

20:2 Jeremiah has become known in history as the "weeping prophet." His heart was broken by the apostasy and impenitence of the age. He himself suffered persecution for his faithful but unpopular preaching. He stands as a superb example of a prophet who preached God's Word to a people who refused to hear that Word, consciously and maliciously rejecting it.

20:6☆ Jer 14:14, 15; Lam 2:14

6 And thou, Pash'ur, and all that dwell in thine house shall go into
captivity: and thou shalt come to Babylon, and there thou shalt die, and
shalt be buried there, thou, and all thy friends, to whom thou hast
prophesied lies.

20:7 Ps 22:7; Lam 3:14; Ezek 3:14; Mic 3:8
20:8 2 Chron 36:16; Jer 6:10

7 ¶O LORD, thou hast deceived me, and I was deceived: thou art stronger
than I, and hast prevailed: I am in derision daily, every one mocketh me.
8 For since I spake, I cried out, I cried violence and spoil; because the
word of the LORD was made a reproach unto me, and a derision, daily.

20:9☆ Ps 39:3; Jer 4:19; Acts 4:20

9 Then I said, I will not make mention of him, nor speak any more in his
name. But *his word* was in mine heart as a burning fire shut up in my bones,
and I was weary with forbearing, and I could not *stay*.

20:10 1 Kgs 19:2; 22:27; Neh 6:6–13; Ps 41:9; Jer 18:18

10 ¶For I heard the defaming of many, fear on every side. Report, *say they*,
and we will report it. All my familiars watched for my halting, *saying*,
Peradventure he will be enticed, and we shall prevail against him, and we
shall take our revenge on him.

20:11 Deut 32:35, 36; Jer 1:8; 15:20

11 But the LORD *is* with me as a mighty terrible one: therefore my
persecutors shall stumble, and they shall not prevail: they shall be greatly
ashamed; for they shall not prosper: *their* everlasting confusion shall never
be forgotten.

20:12 Ps 7:9; 17:3; 59:10, 62:8; 139:23; Jer 11:20; 17:103
20:13 Ps 34:6; 69:33; Jer 15:21

12 But, O LORD of hosts, that triest the righteous, *and* seest the reins and
the heart, let me see thy vengeance on them: for unto thee have I opened
my cause.
13 Sing unto the LORD, praise ye the LORD: for he hath delivered the soul
of the poor from the hand of evildoers.

20:14☆ Job 3:3–6

14 ¶Cursed *be* the day wherein I was born: let not the day wherein my
mother bare me be blessed.
15 Cursed *be* the man who brought tidings to my father, saying, A man
child is born unto thee; making him very glad.
16 And let that man be as the cities which the LORD overthrew, and
repented not: and let him hear the cry in the morning, and the shouting at
noontide;

20:17 Job 3:10, 11, 16; 10:18, 19
20:18 Job 3:20; 14:1; Ps 102:3; Jer 15:10; 1 Cor 4:9–13

17 Because he slew me not from the womb; or that my mother might have
been my grave, and her womb *to be* always great *with me*.
18 Wherefore came I forth out of the womb to see labour and sorrow, that
my days should be consumed with shame?

II. PROPHECIES UNDER JEHOIAKIM AND ZEDEKIAH (21:1—39:18)

A. NEBUCHADREZZAR, GOD'S INSTRUMENT AGAINST JERUSALEM

1. Advice for Zedekiah

21:1 2 Kgs 25:18–21; 1 Chron 9:12; Jer 29:25, 29; 37:3

21 THE word which came unto Jer-e-mi'ah from the LORD, when king
Zed-e-ki'ah sent unto him Pash'ur the son of Mel-chi'ah, and Zeph-
a-ni'ah the son of Ma-a-sei'ah the priest, saying,

20:6 Pashur was a legitimate priest but still a false *prophet. Jeremiah pronounces* definitive judgment on him, which will end in his death. In every age there are priests and ministers of God who are false prophets. Each must be tested against the Scriptures to find which are false and which are true ministers of God.

20:9 *nor speak any more in his name.* Humanly speaking, Jeremiah would have preferred to remain silent since his message was rejected and his person attacked. Princes, priests, and people laughed at his warnings. Yet it was impossible for him to stop preaching, because God's Word was like a fire burning in his bones and he could not contain it or himself.

20:14 In this passage Jeremiah either was familiar with the book of Job or entertained much the same notions as that suffering saint did.

2 Inquire, I pray thee, of the LORD for us; for Neb-u-chad-rez′zar king of Babylon maketh war against us; if so be that the LORD will deal with us according to all his wondrous works, that he may go up from us.

3 ¶Then said Jer-e-mi′ah unto them, Thus shall ye say to Zed-e-ki′ah:

4 Thus saith the LORD God of Israel; Behold, I will turn back the weapons of war that *are* in your hands, wherewith ye fight against the king of Babylon, and *against* the Chal-de′ans, which besiege you without the walls, and I will assemble them into the midst of this city.

5 And I myself will fight against you with an outstretched hand and with a strong arm, even in anger, and in fury, and in great wrath.

6 And I will smite the inhabitants of this city, both man and beast: they shall die of a great pestilence.

7 And afterward, saith the LORD, I will deliver Zed-e-ki′ah king of Judah, and his servants, and the people, and such as are left in this city from the pestilence, from the sword, and from the famine, into the hand of Neb-u-chad-rez′zar king of Babylon, and into the hand of their enemies, and into the hand of those that seek their life: and he shall smite them with the edge of the sword; he shall not spare them, neither have pity, nor have mercy.

8 ¶And unto this people thou shalt say, Thus saith the LORD; Behold, I set before you the way of life, and the way of death.

9 He that abideth in this city shall die by the sword, and by the famine, and by the pestilence: but he that goeth out, and falleth to the Chal-de′ans that besiege you, he shall live, and his life shall be unto him for a prey.

10 For I have set my face against this city for evil, and not for good, saith the LORD: it shall be given into the hand of the king of Babylon, and he shall burn it with fire.

11 ¶And touching the house of the king of Judah, *say*, Hear ye the word of the LORD;

12 O house of David, thus saith the LORD; Execute judgment in the morning, and deliver *him that is* spoiled out of the hand of the oppressor, lest my fury go out like fire, and burn that none can quench *it*, because of the evil of your doings.

13 Behold, I *am* against thee, O inhabitant of the valley, *and* rock of the plain, saith the LORD; which say, Who shall come down against us? or who shall enter into our habitations?

14 But I will punish you according to the fruit of your doings, saith the LORD: and I will kindle a fire in the forest thereof, and it shall devour all things round about it.

2. Kings and False Prophets

a. Wicked Kings and Messiah, the True King

22 THUS saith the LORD; Go down to the house of the king of Judah, and speak there this word,

2 And say, Hear the word of the LORD, O king of Judah, that sittest upon

☆**21:2** 2 Kgs 25:1, 2; Ps 44:1–4
21:3 Jer 32:5; 33:5; 37:8–10; 38:17, 18; 39:3; Lam 2:5, 7; Zech 14:2
21:5 Isa 5:25; 63:10; Jer 6:12
21:6 Jer 14:12; 32:24
21:7 2 Chron 36:17; Jer 13:14; Ezek 7:9; Hab 1:6–10
21:8 Deut 30:15, 19
☆**21:9** Jer 38:2; 39:18
21:10 2 Chron 36:19; Jer 32:28, 29; 39:8; 44:11, 27; 52:13
21:12 Isa 1:17; Jer 4:5; 7:5, 20; 17:4; 22:3; Ezek 20:47, 48; Nah 1:6; Zech 7:9, 10
21:13 2 Sam 5:6, 7; Ps 125:2; Lam 4:12; Obad 3, 4
☆**21:14** 2 Chron 36:19; Jer 52:13
☆**22:1**
22:2 Isa 9:7; Jer 17:25; 22:4, 20; Lk 1:32

21:2 *the LORD will deal with us.* King Zedekiah doubtless had in mind God's deliverances of Jerusalem from Sennacherib, king of Assyria, in the days of Hezekiah (Isa. 36–37). But Zedekiah's hopes were dashed. He was Judah's last ruler before the exile of 597 B.C.†

21:9 Jeremiah here foretells the fall of Judah at the hands of Nebuchadnezzar. He tells the people to surrender to Babylon and warns that whoever fails to do so will perish. This word from God was regarded as treason by the Judean leaders who punished Jeremiah for his preaching.

21:14 *the fruits of your doing,* i.e., according to the merit of what you have done. Every act bears fruit. The fruit of Judah's doing was evil, and the judgment of God was the retribution for transgression.

22:1 Jeremiah is commanded to preach to the king again. Kings have power over their subjects and God has power over the king. The king refused to acknowledge God's power over him, otherwise he would have repented and turned from his wicked ways. In the Christian era many believers refuse to let Jesus be Lord of their lives and thus live autonomously. Sooner or later this must bring judgment.

the throne of David, thou, and thy servants, and thy people that enter in by these gates:

22:3 Ex 22:21–24 Ps 72:4 Jer 7:6; 19:4 21:12; 22:17

3 Thus saith the LORD; Execute ye judgment and righteousness, and deliver the spoiled out of the hand of the oppressor: and do no wrong, do no violence to the stranger, the fatherless, nor the widow, neither shed innocent blood in this place.

4 For if ye do this thing indeed, then shall there enter in by the gates of this house kings sitting upon the throne of David, riding in chariots and on horses, he, and his servants, and his people.

22:5☆ Amos 6:8 Heb 6:13

5 But if ye will not hear these words, I swear by myself, saith the LORD, that this house shall become a desolation.

22:6 Isa 6:11 Jer 7:34

6 For thus saith the LORD unto the king's house of Judah; thou *art* Gilead unto me, *and* the head of Lebanon: *yet* surely I will make thee a wilderness, *and* cities *which* are not inhabited.

22:7 Isa 10:3–6, 33, 34 Jer 4:6, 7

7 And I will prepare destroyers against thee, every one with his weapons: and they shall cut down thy choice cedars, and cast *them* into the fire.

22:8☆ Deut 29:24–26 1 Kgs 9:8, 9 2 Chron 7:20, 22 Jer 16:10

8 And many nations shall pass by this city, and they shall say every man to his neighbour, Wherefore hath the LORD done thus unto this great city?

22:9☆ 2 Chron 34:25 Jer 11:3

9 Then they shall answer, Because they have forsaken the covenant of the LORD their God, and worshipped other gods, and served them.

10 ¶Weep ye not for the dead, neither bemoan him: *but* weep sore for him that goeth away: for he shall return no more, nor see his native country.

22:11☆

11 For thus saith the LORD touching Shal'lum the son of Jo-si'ah king of Judah, which reigned instead of Jo-si'ah his father, which went forth out of this place; He shall not return thither any more:

22:12☆ 2 Kgs 23:34

12 But he shall die in the place whither they have led him captive, and shall see this land no more.

22:13☆ Jer 17:11 Hab 2:9

13 ¶Woe unto him that buildeth his house by unrighteousness, and his chambers by wrong; *that* useth his neighbour's service without wages, and giveth him not for his work;

22:14 Isa 5:8, 9 Hab 1:4

14 That saith, I will build me a wide house and large chambers, and cutteth him out windows; and *it is* cieled with cedar, and painted with vermilion.

22:15 2 Kgs 23:25 Jer 21:12; 42:6

15 Shalt thou reign, because thou closest *thyself* in cedar? did not thy father eat and drink, and do judgment and justice, *and* then *it was* well with him?

22:16 Ps 72:1–4, 12, 13 Jer 9:24

16 He judged the cause of the poor and needy; then *it was* well *with him: was* not this to know me? saith the LORD.

22:17 Jer 6:13; 8:10 Lk 12:15–20

17 But thine eyes and thine heart *are* not but for thy covetousness, and for to shed innocent blood, and for oppression, and for violence, to do *it.*

18 Therefore thus saith the LORD concerning Je-hoi'a-kim the son of Jo-si'ah king of Judah; They shall not lament for him, *saying,* Ah my brother! or, Ah sister! they shall not lament for him, *saying,* Ah lord! or, Ah his glory!

22:5 God still offers Judah an opportunity to turn from their wicked ways, even though he knows they will not do so. Never could they say they did not have many opportunities to reform themselves and mend their *ways. God is long-suffering.*

22:8, 9 When men and nations wonder why Judah and Jerusalem were devastated, the answer will be this: they broke their covenant with God, and they worshipped and served other gods. God had two choices. Either he could disregard their apostasy and do nothing, or he could punish them for their transgressions. As God, he could not choose the former and at the same time retain his own justice and integrity.

22:11 *Shallum,* i.e., "Jehoahaz," who succeeded his father (Josiah). Jehoahaz reigned for three months in the year 609 B.C.†

22:12 *the place,* i.e., "Egypt."

22:13 *him.* King Jehoiakim is the one referred to here. See 22:18. He was chosen by the Egyptians to replace Jehoahaz, whom they took back to Egypt with them. He ruled from 609–598 B.C.†

19 He shall be buried with the burial of an ass, drawn and cast forth
beyond the gates of Jerusalem.

22:19 Jer 36:30

20 ¶Go up to Lebanon, and cry; and lift up thy voice in Ba′shan, and cry
from the passages: for all thy lovers are destroyed.

22:20 Deut 32:49

21 I spake unto thee in thy prosperity; *but* thou saidst, I will not hear. This
hath been thy manner from thy youth, that thou obeyedst not my voice.

☆**22:21**

22 The wind shall eat up all thy pastors, and thy lovers shall go into
captivity: surely then shalt thou be ashamed and confounded for all thy
wickedness.

22:22 Jer 30:14

23 O inhabitant of Lebanon, that makest thy nest in the cedars, how
gracious shalt thou be when pangs come upon thee, the pain as of a woman
in travail!

24 *As* I live, saith the LORD, though Co-ni′ah the son of Je-hoi′a-kim king
of Judah were the signet upon my right hand, yet would I pluck thee
thence;

☆**22:24** 2 Kgs 24:15, 16; Jer 21:7; 34:20, 21; Hag 2:23

25 And I will give thee into the hand of them that seek thy life, and into
the hand *of them* whose face thou fearest, even into the hand of Neb-u-
chad-rez′zar king of Babylon, and into the hand of the Chal-de′ans.

26 And I will cast thee out, and thy mother that bare thee, into another
country, where ye were not born; and there shall ye die.

27 But to the land whereunto they desire to return, thither shall they not
return.

28 *Is* this man Co-ni′ah a despised broken idol? *is he* a vessel wherein *is* no
pleasure? wherefore are they cast out, he and his seed, and are cast into a
land which they know not?

22:28 Jer 15:1; Hos 8:8

29 O earth, earth, earth, hear the word of the LORD.

☆**22:29** Jer 6:19; Mic 1:2

30 Thus saith the LORD, Write ye this man childless, a man *that* shall not
prosper in his days: for no man of his seed shall prosper, sitting upon the
throne of David, and ruling any more in Judah.

☆**22:30** Jer 36:30; Mt 1:12

23

WOE be unto the pastors that destroy and scatter the sheep of my
pasture! saith the LORD.

☆**23:1** Isa 56:9–12; Jer 10:21; 50:6; Ezek 13:3; 34:2; Zech 11:17

2 Therefore thus saith the LORD God of Israel against the pastors that
feed my people; Ye have scattered my flock, and driven them away, and
have not visited them: behold, I will visit upon you the evil of your doings,
saith the LORD.

23:2 Ex 32:34; Jer 44:22

3 And I will gather the remnant of my flock out of all countries whither I
have driven them, and will bring them again to their folds; and they shall
be fruitful and increase.

☆**23:3** Isa11:11–16; Jer 31:7, 8; 32:37

4 And I will set up shepherds over them which shall feed them: and they
shall fear no more, nor be dismayed, neither shall they be lacking, saith the
LORD.

23:4 Jer 3:15; 31:10; Jn 6:39; 10:28; 1 Pet 1:5

22:21 Prosperity often leads to indulgence, softness, and a turning away from dependence on God—especially if one is raised in luxury and has never known times of indigence, sacrifice, and hard work.

22:24 *Coniah.* Coniah is an abbreviation—perhaps a disparaging nickname for Jeconiah, or Jehoiachin, his other names. His name means, "The Lord will establish my throne!"†

22:29 Let all the earth hear the word of the Lord. If God will judge his own people whom he loves and is about to cast off, how much more will he sentence those who are not his people and who reject his grace. Let all men know that God is righteous and just.

22:30 *no man of his seed shall* [sit] *upon the throne of David.* This man's grandson, Zerubbabel, was briefly governor, but not king.†

23:1 *Woe be unto the pastors,* i.e., woe to the shepherds of church and state who fail to discharge their responsibilities faithfully and fully under God.

23:3 When human shepherds fail, God is still in charge and interested in his sheep. Though they have been scattered by the failure of their shepherds, God will bring them back to the fold where they will be safe and satisfied.

23:5☆ Isa 9:6; 11:1–5; 53:2; Jer 33:15, 16; Zech 3:8; 6:12, 13; Mt 1:21–23; Rom 3:21, 22; 1 Cor 1:30
23:6☆
23:7 Isa 43:18, 19; Jer 16:14, 15

5¶Behold, the days come, saith the LORD, that I will raise unto David a
righteous Branch, and a King shall reign and prosper, and shall execute
judgment and justice in the earth.
6In his days Judah shall be saved, and Israel shall dwell safely: and this
is his name whereby he shall be called, THE LORD OUR RIGHTEOUS-
NESS.
7Therefore, behold, the days come, saith the LORD, that they shall no
more say, The LORD liveth, which brought up the children of Israel out of
the land of Egypt;
8But, The LORD liveth, which brought up and which led the seed of the
house of Israel out of the north country, and from all countries whither I
had driven them; and they shall dwell in their own land.

b. The Punishment for False Prophets

23:9☆ Hab 3:16
23:10 Ps 107:34; Jer 5:7, 8; 9:10; 12:4; Hos 4:2, 3
23:11☆ Jer 6:13; 7:9–10; 8:10
23:12 Ps 35:6; Isa 8:22; Jer 13:16; Jn 12:35
23:13 1 Kgs 18:18–21; Jer 2:8
23:14 Isa 1:9, 10; Jer 5:30, 32; 29:23; Ezek 13:22, 23; Mt 11:24
23:15 Deut 29:18; Jer 8:14; 9:15
23:16☆ Jer 14:14; Ezek 13:2, 3, 6; Mt 7:15; 2 Cor 11:13–15; Gal 1:8, 9; 1 Jn 4:1

9¶Mine heart within me is broken because of the prophets; all my bones
shake; I am like a drunken man, and like a man whom wine hath overcome,
because of the LORD, and because of the words of his holiness.
10For the land is full of adulterers; for because of swearing the land
mourneth; the pleasant places of the wilderness are dried up, and their
course is evil, and their force *is* not right.
11For both prophet and priest are profane; yea, in my house have I found
their wickedness, saith the LORD.
12Wherefore their way shall be unto them as slippery *ways* in the
darkness: they shall be driven on, and fall therein: for I will bring evil upon
them, *even* the year of their visitation, saith the LORD.
13And I have seen folly in the prophets of Sa-ma′ri-a; they prophesied in
Ba′al, and caused my people Israel to err.
14I have seen also in the prophets of Jerusalem an horrible thing: they
commit adultery, and walk in lies: they strengthen also the hands of
evildoers, that none doth return from his wickedness: they are all of them
unto me as Sodom, and the inhabitants thereof as Go-mor′rah.
15Therefore thus saith the LORD of hosts concerning the prophets;
Behold, I will feed them with wormwood, and make them drink the water
of gall: for from the prophets of Jerusalem is profaneness gone forth into all
the land.
16Thus saith the LORD of hosts, Hearken not unto the words of the
prophets that prophesy unto you: they make you vain: they speak a vision
of their own heart, *and* not out of the mouth of the LORD.

23:5, 6 Messiah is here called *a righteous Branch,* a true shoot from the stock of King David. David's descendants had become kings of injustice in some cases; now the people look for the coming of a righteous king who will come as the Lord's anointed or Messiah. *in the earth,* or, "throughout the land." The phrase *THE LORD OUR RIGHTEOUSNESS* can be translated, "JESUS OUR RIGHTEOUSNESS." The word *LORD* here is "Yahweh"; in this context, it can only mean Jesus the Messiah. Thus Jesus is God, or Yahweh. And Jesus is our righteousness—his righteousness is imputed to us. We have no righteousness in ourselves, only his righteousness. This same righteousness is imparted to us subsequent to our salvation so that at last we will be righteous in ourselves, or like unto Jesus.

23:9 *because of the words of his holiness,* literally, "from the face of the word of his holiness." The judgment that awaited Judah was decreed by a holy God whose word had been forsaken.

23:11 Priests and prophets are here condemned. The priests profaned the ordinances of God when their walk did not agree with their talk. They were hypocrites. The prophets claimed to prophesy in the name of God, but at the same time (11:14) they committed adultery and walked in lies. God was saying, "What you are speaks so loudly that I cannot hear what you say nor can I hear you when you pray."

23:16 False prophets are an abomination to God. There were a number of them who contradicted what Jeremiah preached and who plotted against him. Today there are many false prophets whose advertisements will be found in newspapers around the world. They undercut and malign the Christian faith and offer substitutes which please darkened minds and assuage the fears of those who have enjoyed some light. They have no horns and carry no pitchforks, but they do the work of Satan and keep many people from coming to the knowledge of Jesus Christ.

17 They say still unto them that despise me, The LORD hath said, Ye shall
have peace; and they say unto every one that walketh after the imagination
of his own heart, No evil shall come upon you.
18 For who hath stood in the counsel of the LORD, and hath perceived and
heard his word? who hath marked his word, and heard *it?*
19 Behold, a whirlwind of the LORD is gone forth in fury, even a grievous
whirlwind: it shall fall grievously upon the head of the wicked.
20 The anger of the LORD shall not return, until he have executed, and till
he have performed the thoughts of his heart: in the latter days ye shall
consider it perfectly.
21 I have not sent these prophets, yet they ran: I have not spoken to them,
yet they prophesied.
22 But if they had stood in my counsel, and had caused my people to hear
my words, then they should have turned them from their evil way, and from
the evil of their doings.
23 *Am* I a God at hand, saith the LORD, and not a God afar off?
24 Can any hide himself in secret places that I shall not see him? saith the
LORD. Do not I fill heaven and earth? saith the LORD.
25 I have heard what the prophets said, that prophesy lies in my name,
saying, I have dreamed, I have dreamed.
26 How long shall *this* be in the heart of the prophets that prophesy lies?
yea, *they are* prophets of the deceit of their own heart;
27 Which think to cause my people to forget my name by their dreams
which they tell every man to his neighbour, as their fathers have forgotten
my name for Ba'al.
28 The prophet that hath a dream, let him tell a dream; and he that hath
my word, let him speak my word faithfully. What *is* the chaff to the wheat?
saith the LORD.
29 *Is* not my word like as a fire? saith the LORD; and like a hammer *that*
breaketh the rock in pieces?
30 Therefore, behold, I *am* against the prophets, saith the LORD, that steal
my words every one from his neighbour.
31 Behold, I *am* against the prophets, saith the LORD, that use their
tongues, and say, He saith.
32 Behold, I *am* against them that prophesy false dreams, saith the LORD,
and do tell them, and cause my people to err by their lies, and by their
lightness; yet I sent them not, nor commanded them: therefore they shall
not profit this people at all, saith the LORD.
33 ¶And when this people, or the prophet, or a priest, shall ask thee,
saying, What *is* the burden of the LORD? thou shalt then say unto them,
What burden? I will even forsake you, saith the LORD.
34 And *as for* the prophet, and the priest, and the people, that shall say,
The burden of the LORD, I will even punish that man and his house.
35 Thus shall ye say every one to his neighbour, and every one to his
brother, What hath the LORD answered? and, What hath the LORD spoken?

23:17 Jer 5:12; 8:11 Amos 9:10 Mic 2:11; 3:11
23:19 Jer 30:23 Amos 1:14
☆**23:20** Isa 55:11 Jer 30:24 Zech 1:5, 6
23:21 Jer 14:14
23:22 Jer 35:15 Zech 1:4 1 Thess 1:9, 10
☆**23:23** Ps 139:1–10 Jn 1:3, 4
23:24 Job 22:13, 14 Ps 139:7–12 Isa 29:15, 16
23:25 Jer 8:6; 29:8
23:26 1 Tim 4:1, 2
23:27 Deut 13:1–3 Judg 3:12
23:28 1 Cor 3:12, 13
23:29 Jer 5:14; 20:9 2 Cor 10:4, 5
23:30 Ezek 13:8
23:32 Lam 2:14
☆**23:33** Isa 13:1 Jer 12:7 Nah 1:1 Hab 1:1 Zech 9:1
23:34 Lam 2:14 Zech 13:3
23:35 Jer 33:3; 42:4

23:20 *in the latter days,* i.e., after Jerusalem falls and you are captive in Babylon, you will see straight and know why all this has happened.
23:23 God is all-knowing and is everywhere at the same time. He is transcendent in that he is over all. At the same time, he is imminent in that he is here among us on the earth. He is far off but he is also near. God's power on earth is equal to his power in heaven; he rules over both in his sovereignty. Let no one suppose that he can escape the all-seeing eye and the all-hearing ear of God.
23:33 Good and bad prophets used the phrase *the burden of the LORD,* but it meant something different to false prophets. They said it was something heavy placed on them by God which they never deserved or wanted. They often used it in jest, whereas the true prophets knew it was a word of doom for those to whom they spoke God's Word.

23:36 2 Kgs 19:4 Jer 10:10 2 Pet 3:16

36 And the burden of the LORD shall ye mention no more: for every man's
word shall be his burden; for ye have perverted the words of the living God,
of the LORD of hosts our God.
37 Thus shalt thou say to the prophet, What hath the LORD answered
thee? and, What hath the LORD spoken?

23:38☆ Jer 7:14, 15 Ezek 8:18

38 But since ye say, The burden of the LORD; therefore thus saith the
LORD; Because ye say this word, The burden of the LORD, and I have sent
unto you, saying, Ye shall not say, The burden of the LORD;
39 Therefore, behold, I, even I, will utterly forget you, and I will forsake
you, and the city that I gave you and your fathers, *and cast you* out of my
presence:

23:40 Jer 20:11 Ezek 5:14, 15

40 And I will bring an everlasting reproach upon you, and a perpetual
shame, which shall not be forgotten.

c. The Baskets of Good and Bad Figs

24:1☆ 2 Kgs 24:10–16 2 Chron 36:10 Jer 27:19–21 29:1, 2

24 THE LORD shewed me, and, behold, two baskets of figs *were* set
before the temple of the LORD, after that Neb-u-chad-rez′zar king
of Babylon had carried away captive Jec-o-ni′ah the son of Je-hoi′a-kim
king of Judah, and the princes of Judah, with the carpenters and smiths,
from Jerusalem, and had brought them to Babylon.

24:2 Jer 29:17

2 One basket *had* very good figs, *even* like the figs *that are* first ripe: and
the other basket *had* very naughty figs, which could not be eaten, they were
so bad.
3 Then said the LORD unto me, What seest thou, Jer-e-mi′ah? And I said,
Figs; the good figs, very good; and the evil, very evil, that cannot be eaten,
they are so evil.

24:4 Nah 1:7 Zech 13:9

4 ¶Again the word of the LORD came unto me, saying,
5 Thus saith the LORD, the God of Israel; Like these good figs, so will I
acknowledge them that are carried away captive of Judah, whom I have
sent out of this place into the land of the Chal-de′ans for *their* good.

24:6 Jer 29:10; 31:4 32:37, 41; 33:7 Ezek 11:17

6 For I will set mine eyes upon them for good, and I will bring them again
to this land: and I will build them, and not pull *them* down; and I will plant
them, and not pluck *them* up.

24:7 Jer 31:33; 32:40 Zech 8:8 Heb 8:10

7 And I will give them an heart to know me, that I *am* the LORD: and they
shall be my people, and I will be their God: for they shall return unto me
with their whole heart.

24:8☆ Jer 29:17; 39:5 44:26–30 Ezek 12:13

8 ¶And as the evil figs, which cannot be eaten, they are so evil; surely thus
saith the LORD, So will I give Zed-e-ki′ah the king of Judah, and his princes,
and the residue of Jerusalem, that remain in this land, and them that dwell
in the land of Egypt:

24:9☆ 1 Kgs 9:7 Ps 44:13, 14 Isa 65:15 Jer 15:4; 29:18 34:17

9 And I will deliver them to be removed into all the kingdoms of the earth
for *their* hurt, *to be* a reproach and a proverb, a taunt and a curse, in all
places whither I shall drive them.

23:38 God here forbids the people to speak of his Word as the "burden of the LORD." For their failure to speak respectfully of his Word, God will unburden himself of the burden by placing it on their backs in *judgment. Thus, they will no longer jest* of his Word as a burden.

24:1 The sign of the *two baskets of figs* indicates that Judah was divided into two groups of people. Some were so evil that they would experience the avenging sword of God, the righteous Judge. The others were experiencing suffering designed for their good. It was a correcting rod rather than an avenging one. God distinguishes between the precious and the vile. The good ones will be brought back to the land and restored to their inheritance. God "will plant them, and not pluck them up" (24:6).

24:8–10 The bad figs are those who will be sent to Babylon when Jerusalem is destroyed. They will suffer from sword, pestilence, and famine, so that those already in Babylon would be far better off than those who remained in Jerusalem.

10 And I will send the sword, the famine, and the pestilence, among them,
till they be consumed from off the land that I gave unto them and to their
fathers.

24:10 Isa 51:19; Jer 27:8; Ezek 5:12–17

3. God's Vengeance against the Nations
a. Judah's Captivity and Babylon's Fall

25 THE word that came to Jer-e-mi'ah concerning all the people of
Judah in the fourth year of Je-hoi'a-kim the son of Jo-si'ah king of
Judah, that *was* the first year of Neb-u-chad-rez'zar king of Babylon;
2 The which Jer-e-mi'ah the prophet spake unto all the people of Judah,
and to all the inhabitants of Jerusalem, saying,
3 From the thirteenth year of Jo-si'ah the son of A'mon king of Judah,
even unto this day, that *is* the three and twentieth year, the word of the
LORD hath come unto me, and I have spoken unto you, rising early and
speaking; but ye have not hearkened.
4 And the LORD hath sent unto you all his servants the prophets, rising
early and sending *them;* but ye have not hearkened, nor inclined your ear to
hear.
5 They said, Turn ye again now every one from his evil way, and from the
evil of your doings, and dwell in the land that the LORD hath given unto
you and to your fathers for ever and ever:
6 And go not after other gods to serve them, and to worship them, and
provoke me not to anger with the works of your hands; and I will do you no
hurt.
7 Yet ye have not hearkened unto me, saith the LORD; that ye might
provoke me to anger with the works of your hands to your own hurt.
8 ¶Therefore thus saith the LORD of hosts; Because ye have not heard my
words,
9 Behold, I will send and take all the families of the north, saith the LORD,
and Neb-u-chad-rez'zar the king of Babylon, my servant, and will bring
them against this land, and against the inhabitants thereof, and against all
these nations round about, and will utterly destroy them, and make them
an astonishment, and an hissing, and perpetual desolations.
10 Moreover I will take from them the voice of mirth, and the voice of
gladness, the voice of the bridegroom, and the voice of the bride, the sound
of the millstones, and the light of the candle.
11 And this whole land shall be a desolation, *and* an astonishment; and
these nations shall serve the king of Babylon seventy years.

☆**25:1** 2 Kgs 24:1, 2; Jer 36:1; 46:2
☆**25:2** Jer 1:2; 7:25, 26; 11:7, 8; 26:5; 36:2, 3
☆**25:3**
25:5 Gen 17:8–10; Isa 55:6, 7; Jer 4:1; 7:7; 35:15
25:6 Deut 6:14; 8:19; 2 Kgs 17:35
25:7 2 Kgs 17:17; 21:15; Jer 7:19; 32:30–33
25:8 Jer 27:6; 43:10
☆**25:9**
25:10 Isa 24:8–11; Jer 16:9; Ezek 26:13
☆**25:11** Dan 9:2; Zech 7:5

25:1 *in the fourth year of Jehoiakim,* i.e., 605 B.C. Daniel 1:1 says it was the third year of Jehoiakim's reign. He was using Babylonian dating, which varied from that of Judah.

25:2, 3 Jeremiah addressed this message to all the people of Judah. He had been prophesying for twenty-three years, and his warnings had been disregarded. In this sense he was an unsuccessful prophet. Other prophets' ministries led to repentance and restoration. The difference did not lie in the prophet but in the sovereignty of God. No blame can be attached to Jeremiah for the failure of Judah to repent. Neither his message nor his preaching style was at fault; the fault lay in the hearts of the Judeans whose hearts were hardened.

25:9 *Nebuchadrezzar* is said here to be the servant of God. God uses good and evil nations and rulers to do his bidding. The sword of judgment against Judah will be Nebuchadnezzar.

25:11 God sentenced Judah to *seventy years* of captivity in Babylon. Some think the seventy years began in 605 B.C., when the first deportation occurred (2 Kings 24:10–15); others commence with 586 B.C., when the temple was destroyed and the last deportation took place. In the former view, the captivity terminated in 538 B.C., when Cyrus issued his decree for the return of the remnant to the land (Ezra 1:1–3). In the latter view, the terminal date would be 516 B.C., when the second temple was finished. Seventy, however, may simply be a round number (ten times seven). If so, it is unnecessary to press for the exact length of time the people of Judah spent in servitude in Babylon.

25:12☆ Ezra 1:1 Isa 13:14 Jer 29:10, 50, 51

12 ¶And it shall come to pass, when seventy years are accomplished, *that* I
will punish the king of Babylon, and that nation, saith the LORD, for their
iniquity, and the land of the Chal-de'ans, and will make it perpetual
desolations.

25:13 Jer 36:4, 29, 32

13 And I will bring upon that land all my words which I have pronounced
against it, *even* all that is written in this book, which Jer-e-mi'ah hath
prophesied against all the nations.

25:14 Jer 27:7

14 For many nations and great kings shall serve themselves of them also:
and I will recompense them according to their deeds, and according to the
works of their own hands.

b. God's Wrath on the Nations

25:15 Jer 51:7

15 ¶For thus saith the LORD God of Israel unto me; Take the wine cup of
this fury at my hand, and cause all the nations, to whom I send thee, to
drink it.
16 And they shall drink, and be moved, and be mad, because of the sword
that I will send among them.

25:17 Jer 1:10

17 Then took I the cup at the LORD's hand, and made all the nations to
drink, unto whom the LORD had sent me:
18 *To wit,* Jerusalem, and the cities of Judah, and the kings thereof, and
the princes thereof, to make them a desolation, an astonishment, an hissing,
and a curse; as *it is* this day;

25:19 Jer 46:2–28 Lam 4:21

19 Pharaoh king of Egypt, and his servants, and his princes, and all his
people;
20 And all the mingled people, and all the kings of the land of Uz, and all
the kings of the land of the Philistines, and Ash'ke-lon, and Az'zah, and
Ekron, and the remnant of Ash'dod,

25:21 Jer 48:1–47 49:1–22 Amos 1:13–15 2:1–3
25:22 Jer 47:4 Zech 9:2–4
25:23 Jer 49:7, 8

21 Edom, and Moab, and the children of Ammon,
22 And all the kings of Tyrus, and all the kings of Zi'don, and the kings of
the isles which *are* beyond the sea,
23 De'dan, and Te'ma, and Buz, and all *that are* in the utmost corners,
24 And all the kings of Arabia, and all the kings of the mingled people that
dwell in the desert,

25:25 Jer 49:34

25 And all the kings of Zimri, and all the kings of E'lam, and all the kings
of the Medes,

25:26 Jer 50:9; 51:41

26 And all the kings of the north, far and near, one with another, and all
the kingdoms of the world, which *are* upon the face of the earth: and the
king of She'shach shall drink after them.
27 Therefore thou shalt say unto them, Thus saith the LORD of hosts, the
God of Israel; Drink ye, and be drunken, and spue, and fall, and rise no
more, because of the sword which I will send among you.
28 And it shall be, if they refuse to take the cup at thine hand to drink,
then shalt thou say unto them, Thus saith the LORD of hosts; Ye shall
certainly drink.

25:29 Prov 11:31 1 Pet 4:17

29 For, lo, I begin to bring evil on the city which is called by my name,
and should ye be utterly unpunished? Ye shall not be unpunished: for I will
call for a sword upon all the inhabitants of the earth, saith the LORD of
hosts.

25:12 *when seventy years are accomplished, that I will punish the king of Babylon.* This event is further described in Dan. 5. The troops of Cyrus the Great entered Babylon in 539 B.C. and killed Belshazzar, the last Babylonian ruler.† Babylon then sank into the sands of time to be seen no more in the history of man.

c. The Fierce Anger of the Lord

30 Therefore prophesy thou against them all these words, and say unto
them, The LORD shall roar from on high, and utter his voice from his holy
habitation; he shall mightily roar upon his habitation; he shall give a shout,
as they that tread *the grapes,* against all the inhabitants of the earth.

25:30 Joel 2:11 Amos 1:2

31 A noise shall come *even* to the ends of the earth; for the LORD hath a
controversy with the nations, he will plead with all flesh; he will give them
that are wicked to the sword, saith the LORD.

25:31 Isa 66:16

32 Thus saith the LORD of hosts, Behold, evil shall go forth from nation to
nation, and a great whirlwind shall be raised up from the coasts of the
earth.

25:32 Isa 30:30 34:2, 3

33 And the slain of the LORD shall be at that day from *one* end of the earth
even unto the *other* end of the earth: they shall not be lamented, neither
gathered, nor buried; they shall be dung upon the ground.

25:33 Isa 5:25 Jer 16:4 Ezek 39:4, 7

34 ¶Howl, ye shepherds, and cry; and wallow yourselves *in the ashes,* ye
principal of the flock: for the days of your slaughter and of your dispersions
are accomplished; and ye shall fall like a pleasant vessel.

25:34 Isa 34:7 Jer 50:27

35 And the shepherds shall have no way to flee, nor the principal of the
flock to escape.

36 A voice of the cry of the shepherds, and an howling of the principal of
the flock, *shall be heard:* for the LORD hath spoiled their pasture.

37 And the peaceable habitations are cut down because of the fierce anger
of the LORD.

38 He hath forsaken his covert, as the lion: for their land is desolate
because of the fierceness of the oppressor, and because of his fierce anger.

25:38 Jer 4:7; 5:6 Hos 5:14 13:7, 8

4. Jeremiah Arrested and Released

26 IN the beginning of the reign of Je-hoi'a-kim the son of Jo-si'ah
king of Judah came this word from the LORD, saying,

☆26:1

2 Thus saith the LORD; Stand in the court of the LORD's house, and speak
unto all the cities of Judah, which come to worship in the LORD's house, all
the words that I command thee to speak unto them; diminish not a word:

26:2 Deut 4:2 Jer 7:2; 19:14 42:4 Acts 20:20, 27

3 If so be they will hearken, and turn every man from his evil way, that I
may repent me of the evil, which I purpose to do unto them because of the
evil of their doings.

26:3 Isa 1:16–19 Jer 36:3–7

4 And thou shalt say unto them, Thus saith the LORD; If ye will not
hearken to me, to walk in my law, which I have set before you,

26:4 Lev 26:14 1 Kgs 9:6 Isa 1:20 Jer 17:27; 22:5 44:10, 23

5 To hearken to the words of my servants the prophets, whom I sent unto
you, both rising up early, and sending *them,* but ye have not hearkened;

26:5 Ezra 9:11 Jer 25:4

6 Then will I make this house like Shi'loh, and will make this city a curse
to all the nations of the earth.

26:6 Ps 78:60, 61 Jer 7:12, 14 25:8

7 So the priests and the prophets and all the people heard Jer-e-mi'ah
speaking these words in the house of the LORD.

26:7 Jer 5:31; 11:19 Lam 4:13, 14 Mic 3:11 Mt 23:34, 35

8 ¶Now it came to pass, when Jer-e-mi'ah had made an end of speaking
all that the LORD had commanded *him* to speak unto all the people, that the
priests and the prophets and all the people took him, saying, Thou shalt
surely die.

26:1 This chapter paints the picture of Jeremiah's ministry in four segments: (1) he was a faithful preacher (1–6); (2) he was a persecuted preacher—by the priests and other prophets (7–11); (3) he was a brave preacher who kept speaking despite the persecution (12–15); (4) he was wonderfully protected by God through the prudence of the rulers and the elders (16–19).

26:9☆
9 Why hast thou prophesied in the name of the LORD, saying, This house shall be like Shi'loh, and this city shall be desolate without an inhabitant? And all the people were gathered against Jer-e-mi'ah in the house of the LORD.

26:10 Acts 21:31, 32
10 ¶When the princes of Judah heard these things, then they came up from the king's house unto the house of the LORD, and sat down in the entry of the new gate of the LORD's *house.*

26:11☆ Jer 18:23; 38:4 Mt 26:66 Acts 6:11–14
11 Then spake the priests and the prophets unto the princes and to all the people, saying, This man *is* worthy to die; for he hath prophesied against this city, as ye have heard with your ears.

12 ¶Then spake Jer-e-mi'ah unto all the princes and to all the people, saying, The LORD sent me to prophesy against this house and against this city all the words that ye have heard.

26:13 Jer 7:3, 5; 18:11
13 Therefore now amend your ways and your doings, and obey the voice of the LORD your God; and the LORD will repent him of the evil that he hath pronounced against you.

14 As for me, behold, I *am* in your hand: do with me as seemeth good and meet unto you.

26:15 Num 35:33
15 But know ye for certain, that if ye put me to death, ye shall surely bring innocent blood upon yourselves, and upon this city, and upon the inhabitants thereof: for of a truth the LORD hath sent me unto you to speak all these words in your ears.

26:16 Jer 36:19, 25 38:7, 13 Acts 5:34–39 23:9, 29; 25:25 26:31
16 ¶Then said the princes and all the people unto the priests and to the prophets; This man *is* not worthy to die: for he hath spoken to us in the name of the LORD our God.

17 Then rose up certain of the elders of the land, and spake to all the assembly of the people, saying,

26:18 Mic 1:1
18 Mi'cah the Mo'ras-thite prophesied in the days of Hez-e-ki'ah king of Judah, and spake to all the people of Judah, saying, Thus saith the LORD of hosts; Zion shall be plowed *like* a field, and Jerusalem shall become heaps, and the mountain of the house as the high places of a forest.

26:19 2 Chron 29:6–11; 32:26 Isa 37:1, 15–20
19 Did Hez-e-ki'ah king of Judah and all Judah put him at all to death? did he not fear the LORD, and besought the LORD, and the LORD repented him of the evil which he had pronounced against them? Thus might we procure great evil against our souls.

20 And there was also a man that prophesied in the name of the LORD, U-ri'jah the son of Shem-a-i'ah of Kir'jath–je'a-rim, who prophesied against this city and against this land according to all the words of Jer-e-mi'ah:

26:21☆ 1 Kgs 19:2–4 2 Chron 16:10 Jer 36:26 Mt 10:23, 28
21 And when Je-hoi'a-kim the king, with all his mighty men, and all the princes, heard his words, the king sought to put him to death: but when U-ri'jah heard it, he was afraid, and fled, and went into Egypt;

26:22☆ Jer 36:12
22 And Je-hoi'a-kim the king sent men into Egypt, *namely,* El-na'than the son of Ach'bor, and *certain* men with him into Egypt.

26:23☆ Jer 2:30
23 And they fetched forth U-ri'jah out of Egypt, and brought him unto Je-hoi'a-kim the king, who slew him with the sword, and cast his dead body into the graves of the common people.

26:9 Jeremiah cited *Shiloh* as an example of how God destroyed a sanctuary erected in his honor. God would also destroy the temple at Jerusalem even though the false prophets said the temple was inviolable.

26:11 Jeremiah once again has pronounced God's sentence against Judah. The leaders, including the religious establishment comprising the false priests and prophets, urge the princes and the people to sentence Jeremiah to death. This threat does not deter the prophet from continuing to speak the Word of the Lord.

26:20ff Jeremiah escaped with his life. Here we are told of another righteous prophet, Urijah, who suffered martyrdom. He fled to Egypt but Jehoiakim had him brought back. He slew Urijah and cast his body into a common burial ground without respect or decency. God lets some of his people be martyred while others die a natural death. The reasons are not disclosed this side of eternity. God's ways are not our ways.

24 Nevertheless the hand of A-hi'kam the son of Sha'phan was with Jer-e-mi'ah, that they should not give him into the hand of the people to put him to death.

5. Jeremiah Warns Judah, Rebukes Hananiah, and Counsels about Babylon

a. Jeremiah Warns That Nebuchadrezzar Will Conquer

27 IN the beginning of the reign of Je-hoi'a-kim the son of Jo-si'ah king of Judah came this word unto Jer-e-mi'ah from the LORD, saying,

2 Thus saith the LORD to me; Make thee bonds and yokes, and put them upon thy neck,

3 And send them to the king of Edom, and to the king of Moab, and to the king of the Ammonites, and to the king of Tyrus, and to the king of Zi'don, by the hand of the messengers which come to Jerusalem unto Zed-e-ki'ah king of Judah;

4 And command them to say unto their masters, Thus saith the LORD of hosts, the God of Israel; Thus shall ye say unto your masters;

5 I have made the earth, the man and the beast that *are* upon the ground, by my great power and by my outstretched arm, and have given it unto whom it seemed meet unto me.

6 And now have I given all these lands into the hand of Neb-u-chad-nez'zar the king of Babylon, my servant; and the beasts of the field have I given him also to serve him.

7 And all nations shall serve him, and his son, and his son's son, until the very time of his land come: and then many nations and great kings shall serve themselves of him.

8 And it shall come to pass, *that* the nation and kingdom which will not serve the same Neb-u-chad-nez'zar the king of Babylon, and that will not put their neck under the yoke of the king of Babylon, that nation will I punish, saith the LORD, with the sword, and with the famine, and with the pestilence, until I have consumed them by his hand.

9 Therefore hearken not ye to your prophets, nor to your diviners, nor to your dreamers, nor to your enchanters, nor to your sorcerers, which speak unto you, saying, Ye shall not serve the king of Babylon:

10 For they prophesy a lie unto you, to remove you far from your land; and that I should drive you out, and ye should perish.

11 But the nations that bring their neck under the yoke of the king of Babylon, and serve him, those will I let remain still in their own land, saith the LORD; and they shall till it, and dwell therein.

12 I spake also to Zed-e-ki'ah king of Judah according to all these words,

☆**26:24** 2 Kgs 22:12–14; Jer 1:18, 19; 39:14; 40:5, 6
☆**27:1**
☆**27:2** Jer 28:10, 13; 30:8
27:3 Jer 25:21, 22
27:5 Deut 9:29; Ps 115:15, 16; 146:5, 6; Jer 10:12; 32:17; 51:15
☆**27:6** Jer 21:7; 22:25; 28:14; 43:10; Ezek 29:18–20
☆**27:7** Isa 14:4–6; Jer 25:12; 44:30
27:8 Jer 24:10; 29:17; 42:15, 16; Ezek 14:21; 17:19–21
27:9 Deut 18:10; Isa 8:19; Mal 3:5
27:10 Jer 23:25
☆**27:11** Jer 21:9; 38:2; 40:9–12; 42:10, 11
☆**27:12**

26:24 *Ahikam* was a prominent official in the government. He was the father of Gedaliah, who was appointed governor of the land by Nebuchadnezzar following the destruction of Jerusalem. Ahikam protected Jeremiah from being put to death. *the son of Shaphan,* "the royal secretary," implied. (See 2 Kings 22:12.)

27:1 *reign of Jehoiakim.* Some manuscripts read "Zedekiah," which is correct according to 27:3 and 12.

27:2 Jeremiah has pleaded with the people of Judah to repent by turning to God and keeping his commandments. When this fails, he urges Judah to give themselves over to the providence of God and submit tamely to the yoke of Nebuchadnezzar. Their becoming tributaries would prevent the greater calamity. The land would not be laid waste by fire and sword. If they sacrificed their liberties they would save their lives. Once again the counsel of Jeremiah is rejected.

27:6, 7 Nebuchadnezzar was an idolater, yet God in his providence gave him vast domains. Bad people may be used by God to do good things. Thus, Nebuchadnezzar is called God's servant, used by him to chastise the nations and God's own people Judah. But Babylon's time would run out, and judgment would fall on that wicked nation.

27:11, 12 God declares that Babylon will rule; it is inescapable. And since it is the divine will, it is better for Judah to give in—to bend and not break. Those who refuse to bend will break, but if they bend they will be preserved in their own lands.

saying, Bring your necks under the yoke of the king of Babylon, and serve
him and his people, and live.

27:13 Jer 38:23; Ezek 18:31

13 Why will ye die, thou and thy people, by the sword, by the famine, and
by the pestilence, as the LORD hath spoken against the nation that will not
serve the king of Babylon?

27:14 2 Chron 11:13–15; Ezek 13:22

14 Therefore hearken not unto the words of the prophets that speak unto
you, saying, Ye shall not serve the king of Babylon: for they prophesy a lie
unto you.

27:15 2 Chron 25:16; Jer 23:21, 25; 29:9

15 For I have not sent them, saith the LORD, yet they prophesy a lie in my
name; that I might drive you out, and that ye might perish, ye, and the
prophets that prophesy unto you.

27:16☆ 2 Kgs 24:13; 2 Chron 36:7, 10; Jer 28:3

16 Also I spake to the priests and to all this people, saying, Thus saith the
LORD; Hearken not to the words of your prophets that prophesy unto you,
saying, Behold, the vessels of the LORD's house shall now shortly be
brought again from Babylon: for they prophesy a lie unto you.
17 Hearken not unto them; serve the king of Babylon, and live: wherefore
should this city be laid waste?

27:18 1 Kgs 18:24

18 But if they *be* prophets, and if the word of the LORD be with them, let
them now make intercession to the LORD of hosts, that the vessels which
are left in the house of the LORD, and *in* the house of the king of Judah, and
at Jerusalem, go not to Babylon.

27:19 1 Kgs 7:15; 2 Kgs 25:13, 17; Jer 22:28; 24:1; 52:17–23

19 ¶For thus saith the LORD of hosts concerning the pillars, and concern-
ing the sea, and concerning the bases, and concerning the residue of the
vessels that remain in this city,
20 Which Neb-u-chad-nez′zar king of Babylon took not, when he carried
away captive Jec-o-ni′ah the son of Je-hoi′a-kim king of Judah from
Jerusalem to Babylon, and all the nobles of Judah and Jerusalem;
21 Yea, thus saith the LORD of hosts, the God of Israel, concerning the
vessels that remain *in* the house of the LORD, and *in* the house of the king
of Judah and of Jerusalem;

27:22 Ezra 5:13–15; 7:9; Jer 29:10; 32:5; 34:2, 3

22 They shall be carried to Babylon, and there shall they be until the day
that I visit them, saith the LORD; then will I bring them up, and restore
them to this place.

b. Jeremiah Denounces Hananiah and Prophesies His Death

28:1☆ Jer 27:12

28 AND it came to pass the same year, in the beginning of the reign of
Zed-e-ki′ah king of Judah, in the fourth year, *and* in the fifth
month, *that* Han-a-ni′ah the son of A′zur the prophet, which *was* of Gibeon,
spake unto me in the house of the LORD, in the presence of the priests and
of all the people, saying,
2 Thus speaketh the LORD of hosts, the God of Israel, saying, I have
broken the yoke of the king of Babylon.

27:16 Judah's false prophet forecast that the temple vessels taken to Babylon would be brought back shortly. They would not. It was customary for conquerers to seize the gods of the nations they defeated. They brought them back to their own places of worship. Since the temple in Jerusalem did not have idols, the vessels of the temple were taken back. Jeremiah *prophesied that whatever* was left in Jerusalem would shortly be seized and taken to Babylon.

28:1 *Hananiah* was a false prophet. There have always been and always will be false prophets who counterfeit the real thing. The problem is to determine which prophet is the true one and which is the false one. The people of Hananiah's time probably found him more to their liking than Jeremiah, who prophesied bad news. At this critical junction point, Jeremiah prophesied Hananiah's death. When it occurred, the people should have been convinced, but they were not (28:1–17). It is important to see that God, who is self-consistent, may say one thing at one time in history and the opposite at another time. The false prophets of Jeremiah's day said God would protect Jerusalem and keep the temple unscathed. This had been God's promise when Sennacherib invaded the country (Isa. 37:6, 7). Now God said through Jeremiah that Nebuchadnezzar would triumph, the city would be captured, and the temple torn down (see 32:26–35).

3 Within two full years will I bring again into this place all the vessels of
the LORD'S house, that Neb-u-chad-nez'zar king of Babylon took away
from this place, and carried them to Babylon:
4 And I will bring again to this place Jec-o-ni'ah the son of Je-hoi'a-kim
king of Judah, with all the captives of Judah, that went into Babylon, saith
the LORD: for I will break the yoke of the king of Babylon.
5 ¶Then the prophet Jer-e-mi'ah said unto the prophet Han-a-ni'ah in the
presence of the priests, and in the presence of all the people that stood in
the house of the LORD,
6 Even the prophet Jer-e-mi'ah said, Amen: the LORD do so: the LORD
perform thy words which thou hast prophesied, to bring again the vessels of
the LORD'S house, and all that is carried away captive, from Babylon into
this place.
7 Nevertheless hear thou now this word that I speak in thine ears, and in
the ears of all the people;
8 The prophets that have been before me and before thee of old
prophesied both against many countries, and against great kingdoms, of
war, and of evil, and of pestilence.
9 The prophet which prophesieth of peace, when the word of the prophet
shall come to pass, *then* shall the prophet be known, that the LORD hath
truly sent him.
10 ¶Then Han-a-ni'ah the prophet took the yoke from off the prophet Jer-
e-mi'ah's neck, and brake it.
11 And Han-a-ni'ah spake in the presence of all the people, saying, Thus
saith the LORD; Even so will I break the yoke of Neb-u-chad-nez'zar king of
Babylon from the neck of all nations within the space of two full years. And
the prophet Jer-e-mi'ah went his way.
12 ¶Then the word of the LORD came unto Jer-e-mi'ah *the prophet,* after
that Han-a-ni'ah the prophet had broken the yoke from off the neck of the
prophet Jer-e-mi'ah, saying,
13 Go and tell Han-a-ni'ah, saying, Thus saith the LORD; Thou hast
broken the yokes of wood; but thou shalt make for them yokes of iron.
14 For thus saith the LORD of hosts, the God of Israel; I have put a yoke
of iron upon the neck of all these nations, that they may serve Neb-u-chad-
nez'zar king of Babylon; and they shall serve him: and I have given him the
beasts of the field also.
15 ¶Then said the prophet Jer-e-mi'ah unto Han-a-ni'ah the prophet, Hear
now, Han-a-ni'ah; The LORD hath not sent thee; but thou makest this
people to trust in a lie.
16 Therefore thus saith the LORD; Behold, I will cast thee from off the face
of the earth: this year thou shalt die, because thou hast taught rebellion
against the LORD.
17 So Han-a-ni'ah the prophet died the same year in the seventh month.

c. Jeremiah Tells the People of Judah They Will Be Safer in Babylon

29 NOW these *are* the words of the letter that Jer-e-mi'ah the prophet
sent from Jerusalem unto the residue of the elders which were

28:3 2 Chron 36:10; Jer 27:16; Dan 1:2
☆**28:4** 2 Kgs 25:27; Jer 22:10; 27:8
28:5 Ps 41:13; Jer 11:5; 17:16
28:7 1 Kgs 22:28
28:8 1 Kgs 14:15; 17:1; 22:17; Isa 5:5–7; Joel 1:20; Amos 1:2; Nah 1:2
☆**28:9** Deut 18:22
☆**28:10** 1 Kgs 22:11, 24; Jer 27:2
28:11 Jer 14:15; 27:10
28:12 Jer 1:2
28:13 Ps 107:16
28:14 Deut 28:48; Jer 25:11; 27:6, 8
28:15 Jer 29:31; Ezek 13:2, 3, 22; 22:28; Lam 2:14
28:16 Gen 7:4; Deut 6:15; 13:5; 1 Kgs 13:34; Jer 20:6; 29:32
29:1 2 Kgs 24:12; Jer 22:24–28; 24:1; 27:20

28:4 *Jeconiah,* or, "Jehoiachin."
28:9 In the final analysis, any prophet will be a true prophet if and when his predictions are fulfilled. If they are not, he is a false prophet and should be disregarded. By this test Hananiah proved to be a false prophet.
28:10 Hananiah affronted Jeremiah by removing the yoke-bars from his neck and breaking them. Jeremiah did not protest, revile him, or use force to prevent him from doing this. He suffered in silence. But in verse 19 the judgment of God is pronounced against this false prophet and his death sentence assigned in that very year. Who then was the true prophet? And why did Judah not heed Jeremiah's word after Hananiah died?

carried away captives, and to the priests, and to the prophets, and to all the
people whom Neb-u-chad-nez'zar had carried away captive from Jerusalem
to Babylon;
2 (After that Jec-o-ni'ah the king, and the queen, and the eunuchs, the
princes of Judah and Jerusalem, and the carpenters, and the smiths, were
departed from Jerusalem;)
3 By the hand of El'a-sah the son of Sha'phan, and Gem-a-ri'ah the son of
Hil-ki'ah, (whom Zed-e-ki'ah king of Judah sent unto Babylon to Neb-u-
chad-nez'zar king of Babylon) saying,

29:4☆ Jer 24:5

4 Thus saith the LORD of hosts, the God of Israel, unto all that are carried
away captives, whom I have caused to be carried away from Jerusalem unto
Babylon;
5 Build ye houses, and dwell *in them;* and plant gardens, and eat the fruit
of them;

29:6 Jer 16:1–4

6 Take ye wives, and beget sons and daughters; and take wives for your
sons, and give your daughters to husbands, that they may bear sons and
daughters; that ye may be increased there, and not diminished.

29:7 Ezra 6:10; Dan 4:27; 1 Tim 2:1, 2

7 And seek the peace of the city whither I have caused you to be carried
away captives, and pray unto the LORD for it: for in the peace thereof shall
ye have peace.

29:8 Jer 14:14; 23:21, 25, 27; 27:9; 28:15

8 ¶For thus saith the LORD of hosts, the God of Israel; Let not your
prophets and your diviners, that *be* in the midst of you, deceive you, neither
hearken to your dreams which ye cause to be dreamed.

29:9 Jer 27:15; 29:31

9 For they prophesy falsely unto you in my name: I have not sent them,
saith the LORD.

29:10 2 Chron 36:21–23; Jer 24:6, 7; Dan 9:2; Zeph 2:7; Zech 7:5
29:11 Ps 40:5; Isa 40:9–11; Jer 23:5, 6; 30:9, 10, 18–22; 31:17; Hos 2:15
29:12☆ Ps 145:19; Jer 33:3
29:13 Deut 4:29; Jer 24:7
29:14 Deut 30:1–10; Isa 43:5, 6; Jer 12:15; 16:14, 15; 30:3; 32:37–41
29:16 Jer 24:3, 8–10; 32:24; 38:2, 3, 17–23

10 ¶For thus saith the LORD, That after seventy years be accomplished at
Babylon I will visit you, and perform my good word toward you, in causing
you to return to this place.
11 For I know the thoughts that I think toward you, saith the LORD,
thoughts of peace, and not of evil, to give you an expected end.
12 Then shall ye call upon me, and ye shall go and pray unto me, and I
will hearken unto you.
13 And ye shall seek me, and find *me,* when ye shall search for me with all
your heart.
14 And I will be found of you, saith the LORD: and I will turn away your
captivity, and I will gather you from all the nations, and from all the places
whither I have driven you, saith the LORD; and I will bring you again into
the place whence I caused you to be carried away captive.
15 ¶Because ye have said, The LORD hath raised us up prophets in
Babylon;
16 *Know* that thus saith the LORD of the king that sitteth upon the throne
of David, and of all the people that dwelleth in this city, *and* of your
brethren that are not gone forth with you into captivity;
17 Thus saith the LORD of hosts; Behold, I will send upon them the sword,
the famine, and the pestilence, and will make them like vile figs, that cannot
be eaten, they are so evil.

29:4ff God has Jeremiah send a letter to the prisoners in Babylon in which he counters two wrong notions: (1) False prophets told them the captivity would be short. *Jeremiah says they will be there a long time and they should build houses, marry, raise families, and pray for* the land to which they were exiled; (2) Discouragement might make them think the captivity would last forever. It would be long—seventy years (29:10), but when the people sought God with their whole hearts (29:13) they would find him. Sin brought on the exile, but when sin was repented of, confessed, and forsaken, God's purpose would be realized and they would return to the land.

29:12ff God promises to return his people to their land *after the captivity. He will hear their prayers for this* return. But is it necessary to plead with God to do what he has already promised to do? Should not their prayers be those of thanksgiving to God as they wait with expectancy for the answer to the divine promise?

18 And I will persecute them with the sword, with the famine, and with the
pestilence, and will deliver them to be removed to all the kingdoms of the
earth, to be a curse, and an astonishment, and an hissing, and a reproach,
among all the nations whither I have driven them:
19 Because they have not hearkened to my words, saith the LORD, which I
sent unto them by my servants the prophets, rising up early and sending
them; but ye would not hear, saith the LORD.
20 ¶Hear ye therefore the word of the LORD, all ye of the captivity, whom
I have sent from Jerusalem to Babylon:
21 Thus saith the LORD of hosts, the God of Israel, of Ahab the son of
Kol-a-i'ah, and of Zed-e-ki'ah the son of Ma-a-sei'ah, which prophesy a lie
unto you in my name; Behold, I will deliver them into the hand of Neb-u-
chad-rez'zar king of Babylon; and he shall slay them before your eyes.
22 And of them shall be taken up a curse by all the captivity of Judah
which *are* in Babylon, saying, The LORD make thee like Zed-e-ki'ah and
like Ahab, whom the king of Babylon roasted in the fire;
23 Because they have committed villany in Israel, and have committed
adultery with their neighbours' wives, and have spoken lying words in my
name, which I have not commanded them; even I know, and *am* a witness,
saith the LORD.
24 ¶*Thus* shalt thou also speak to Shem-a-i'ah the Ne-hel'a-mite, saying,
25 Thus speaketh the LORD of hosts, the God of Israel, saying, Because
thou hast sent letters in thy name unto all the people that *are* at Jerusalem,
and to Zeph-a-ni'ah the son of Ma-a-sei'ah the priest, and to all the priests,
saying,
26 The LORD hath made thee priest in the stead of Je-hoi'a-da the priest,
that ye should be officers in the house of the LORD, for every man *that is*
mad, and maketh himself a prophet, that thou shouldest put him in prison,
and in the stocks.
27 Now therefore why hast thou not reproved Jer-e-mi'ah of An'a-thoth,
which maketh himself a prophet to you?
28 For therefore he sent unto us *in* Babylon, saying, This *captivity is* long:
build ye houses, and dwell *in them;* and plant gardens, and eat the fruit of
them.
29 And Zeph-a-ni'ah the priest read this letter in the ears of Jer-e-mi'ah
the prophet.
30 ¶Then came the word of the LORD unto Jer-e-mi'ah, saying,
31 Send to all them of the captivity, saying, Thus saith the LORD
concerning Shem-a-i'ah the Ne-hel'a-mite; Because that Shem-a-i'ah hath
prophesied unto you, and I sent him not, and he caused you to trust in a lie:
32 Therefore thus saith the LORD; Behold, I will punish Shem-a-i'ah the
Ne-hel'a-mite, and his seed: he shall not have a man to dwell among this
people; neither shall he behold the good that I will do for my people, saith
the LORD; because he hath taught rebellion against the LORD.

29:18 Isa 65:15 Jer 25:9; 42:18 Lam 2:15, 16

29:19 Jer 6:19; 26:5 35:15

29:20 Jer 24:5 Ezek 11:9

29:21 Jer 14:14, 15 Lam 2:14

29:22 Isa 65:15

29:23 2 Sam 13:12 Prov 5:21 Jer 5:8; 7:11 16:17; 23:14

☆**29:24**

29:25 2 Kgs 25:18 Jer 21:1; 37:3 52:24

29:26 Deut 13:1–5 Jer 20:1, 2 Hos 9:7 Zech 13:1–5 Jn 10:20 Acts 16:24 26:24, 25 2 Cor 5:13

29:27 Jer 1:1

☆**29:31** Jer 14:14, 15 28:15 Ezek 13:8, 16, 22, 23

29:32 Deut 13:5 1 Sam 2:30–34 Jer 22:30 28:16; 36:31

29:24 There was no lack of false prophets in Judah. Here Shemaiah opposes Jeremiah and occasions the prophecy by Jeremiah that he and his family will perish so that not one of them will be alive to witness the return of Judah to the land after the captivity. *Shemaiah the Nehelamite,* or, "Shemaiah the dreamer." Nehelem was Shemaiah's home town, the name of which means "Dreamer." This seems to be another of the frequent puns in the prophetic books.†

29:31 *I sent him not.* God's people need to be careful that what they do is what God wants them to do. Some missionaries and ministers have not been called and sent by God. So also there are people God has called and wants to send, but they refuse to go.

B. GOD'S FUTURE PLAN FOR ISRAEL'S RESTORATION

1. God's New Covenant

a. Israel Restored and the Heathen Judged

30 THE word that came to Jer-e-mi'ah from the LORD, saying,

2 Thus speaketh the LORD God of Israel, saying, Write thee all the words that I have spoken unto thee in a book.

3 For, lo, the days come, saith the LORD, that I will bring again the captivity of my people Israel and Judah, saith the LORD: and I will cause them to return to the land that I gave to their fathers, and they shall possess it.

4 ¶And these *are* the words that the LORD spake concerning Israel and concerning Judah.

5 For thus saith the LORD; We have heard a voice of trembling, of fear, and not of peace.

6 Ask ye now, and see whether a man doth travail with child? wherefore do I see every man with his hands on his loins, as a woman in travail, and all faces are turned into paleness?

7 Alas! for that day *is* great, so that none *is* like it: it *is* even the time of Jacob's trouble; but he shall be saved out of it.

8 For it shall come to pass in that day, saith the LORD of hosts, *that* I will break his yoke from off thy neck, and will burst thy bonds, and strangers shall no more serve themselves of him:

9 But they shall serve the LORD their God, and David their king, whom I will raise up unto them.

10 ¶Therefore fear thou not, O my servant Jacob, saith the LORD; neither be dismayed, O Israel: for, lo, I will save thee from afar, and thy seed from the land of their captivity; and Jacob shall return, and shall be in rest, and be quiet, and none shall make *him* afraid.

11 For I *am* with thee, saith the LORD, to save thee: though I make a full end of all nations whither I have scattered thee, yet will I not make a full end of thee: but I will correct thee in measure, and will not leave thee altogether unpunished.

12 For thus saith the LORD, Thy bruise *is* incurable, *and* thy wound *is* grievous.

13 *There is* none to plead thy cause, that thou mayest be bound up: thou hast no healing medicines.

14 All thy lovers have forgotten thee; they seek thee not; for I have wounded thee with the wound of an enemy, with the chastisement of a cruel one, for the multitude of thine iniquity; *because* thy sins were increased.

15 Why criest thou for thine affliction? thy sorrow *is* incurable for the multitude of thine iniquity: *because* thy sins were increased, I have done these things unto thee.

16 Therefore all they that devour thee shall be devoured; and all thine adversaries, every one of them, shall go into captivity; and they that spoil thee shall be a spoil, and all that prey upon thee will I give for a prey.

30:2☆ Jer 25:13; 36:4, 28, 32; Hab 2:2
30:3☆ Ps 53:6; Jer 3:18; 16:15; 23:7, 8; 25:13; 29:10; 30:18; 36:4, 28; Ezek 20:42; 36:24; Hab 2:2; Zeph 3:20
30:5 Isa 5:30; Jer 6:25; Amos 5:16–18
30:6 Jer 4:31; 6:24; 22:23
30:7 Isa 2:12; Jer 2:27; 50:19; Lam 1:12; Dan 9:12; Joel 2:11
30:8 Isa 9:4; Ezek 34:27
30:9☆ Ezek 34:23, 24; 37:24; Hos 3:5; Lk 1:69; Acts 2:30; 13:23, 24
30:10 Isa 35:9; 43:5; 44:2; Jer 23:3; 29:14; 46:27, 28; Mic 4:4
30:11☆ Jer 1:8, 19; 4:27; 5:10, 18; 10:24; 46:28
30:13 Jer 14:19; 46:11
30:14 Jer 22:20, 22
30:16 Isa 14:2; Jer 2:3; 10:25

30:2, 3 Jeremiah was not simply a prophet of gloom and doom. Here he is ordered to put into a book the Word of God, promising that he will restore his people to the land from which they have been taken. When they read the book they will know how exactly every word of promise has been fulfilled to the letter and how great is the truth of God, which cannot be broken, annulled, or destroyed.

30:9 *David their king.* The Messiah, David's greater Son, whom God has raised up for them.

30:11 Even as the calamities they have suffered came from God (30:15), so will their deliverance come from the same God, when he has finished his work of punishment. God will also punish the nations that have punished his people.

17 For I will restore health unto thee, and I will heal thee of thy wounds,
saith the LORD; because they called thee an Outcast, *saying,* This *is* Zion,
whom no man seeketh after.
18 ¶Thus saith the LORD; Behold, I will bring again the captivity of
Jacob's tents, and have mercy on his dwellingplaces; and the city shall be
builded upon her own heap, and the palace shall remain after the manner
thereof.
19 And out of them shall proceed thanksgiving and the voice of them that
make merry: and I will multiply them, and they shall not be few; I will also
glorify them, and they shall not be small.
20 Their children also shall be as aforetime, and their congregation shall
be established before me, and I will punish all that oppress them.
21 And their nobles shall be of themselves, and their governor shall
proceed from the midst of them; and I will cause him to draw near, and he
shall approach unto me: for who *is* this that engaged his heart to approach
unto me? saith the LORD.
22 And ye shall be my people, and I will be your God.
23 Behold, the whirlwind of the LORD goeth forth with fury, a continuing
whirlwind: it shall fall with pain upon the head of the wicked.
24 The fierce anger of the LORD shall not return, until he have done *it,* and
until he have performed the intents of his heart: in the latter days ye shall
consider it.

30:17 Ps 107:20; Isa 56:8; Jer 8:22; 33:6, 24
30:18 1 Chron 29:1, 19; Ps 48:3; 122:7; Jer 31:38–40
30:19 Isa 12:1; 51:3; 55:5; 60:9; Jer 17:26; 33:11
30:20 Isa 54:14
☆**30:21** Ex 3:5; Num 16:5
30:22 Ex 6:7; Jer 32:38; Hos 2:23; Zech 13:9
30:23 Jer 23:19, 20

b. Ephraim and Judah Restored and Blessed

31 AT the same time, saith the LORD, will I be the God of all the
families of Israel, and they shall be my people.
2 Thus saith the LORD, The people *which were* left of the sword found
grace in the wilderness; *even* Israel, when I went to cause him to rest.
3 The LORD hath appeared of old unto me, *saying,* Yea, I have loved thee
with an everlasting love: therefore with lovingkindness have I drawn thee.
4 Again I will build thee, and thou shalt be built, O virgin of Israel: thou
shalt again be adorned with thy tabrets, and shalt go forth in the dances of
them that make merry.
5 Thou shalt yet plant vines upon the mountains of Sa-ma′ri-a: the
planters shall plant, and shall eat *them* as common things.
6 For there shall be a day, *that* the watchman upon the mount E′phra-im
shall cry, Arise ye, and let us go up to Zion unto the LORD our God.
7 For thus saith the LORD; Sing with gladness for Jacob, and shout among
the chief of the nations: publish ye, praise ye, and say, O LORD, save thy
people, the remnant of Israel.
8 Behold, I will bring them from the north country, and gather them from
the coasts of the earth, *and* with them the blind and the lame, the woman
with child and her that travaileth with child together: a great company shall
return thither.
9 They shall come with weeping, and with supplications will I lead them:
I will cause them to walk by the rivers of waters in a straight way, wherein

☆**31:1** Gen 17:7, 8; Jer 30:22; Rom 11:26–28
31:2 Ex 33:14; Josh 1:13
31:3 Deut 4:37; 7:8; Ps 25:6
31:4 Isa 30:32; Jer 24:6; 33:7
31:5 Ps 107:37; Isa 65:21; Ezek 28:26
31:7 Ps 14:7; 28:9; Isa 37:31; 61:9; Jer 20:13; 23:3
31:8 Deut 30:64; Isa 40:11; 43:6; Ezek 34:16; Mic 4:6
☆**31:9** Isa 49:10; 63:13

30:21 *their governor shall proceed from the midst of them.* This verse probably refers to the restoration after the Babylonian captivity (the rulers of the Maccabean period were priests as well as kings) as well as to the final restoration under Christ.†

31:1 Chapter 31 divides into three parts: (1) verses 1–22 have to do with Ephraim or the Northern Kingdom, which was destroyed by Sennacherib in the eighth century B.C.; (2) verses 23–26 relate to Judah or the Southern Kingdom, whose people are in Babylon; (3) verses 27–40 speak about both kingdoms as one unity.

31:9 Ephraim and Manasseh were the sons of Joseph. Ephraim (the Northern Kingdom) is not worthy to be called a son, but God will own him as a first-born, as one belonging to God and never again a servant of men.

they shall not stumble: for I am a father to Israel, and E′phra-im *is* my
firstborn.
10 ¶Hear the word of the LORD, O ye nations, and declare *it* in the isles
afar off, and say, He that scattered Israel will gather him, and keep him, as
a shepherd *doth* his flock.
11 For the LORD hath redeemed Jacob, and ransomed him from the hand
of *him that was* stronger than he.
12 Therefore they shall come and sing in the height of Zion, and shall flow
together to the goodness of the LORD, for wheat, and for wine, and for oil,
and for the young of the flock and of the herd: and their soul shall be as a
watered garden; and they shall not sorrow any more at all.
13 Then shall the virgin rejoice in the dance, both young men and old
together: for I will turn their mourning into joy, and will comfort them, and
make them rejoice from their sorrow.
14 And I will satiate the soul of the priests with fatness, and my people
shall be satisfied with my goodness, saith the LORD.
15 ¶Thus saith the LORD; A voice was heard in Ra′mah, lamentation, *and*
bitter weeping; Rahel weeping for her children refused to be comforted for
her children, because they *were* not.
16 Thus saith the LORD; Refrain thy voice from weeping, and thine eyes
from tears: for thy work shall be rewarded, saith the LORD; and they shall
come again from the land of the enemy.
17 And there is hope in thine end, saith the LORD, that thy children shall
come again to their own border.
18 I have surely heard E′phra-im bemoaning himself *thus;* Thou hast
chastised me, and I was chastised, as a bullock unaccustomed *to the yoke:*
turn thou me, and I shall be turned; for thou *art* the LORD my God.
19 Surely after that I was turned, I repented; and after that I was
instructed, I smote upon *my* thigh: I was ashamed, yea, even confounded,
because I did bear the reproach of my youth.
20 *Is* E′phra-im my dear son? *is he* a pleasant child? for since I spake
against him, I do earnestly remember him still: therefore my bowels are
troubled for him; I will surely have mercy upon him, saith the LORD.
21 Set thee up waymarks, make thee high heaps: set thine heart toward the
highway, *even* the way *which* thou wentest: turn again, O virgin of Israel,
turn again to these thy cities.
22 ¶How long wilt thou go about, O thou backsliding daughter? for the
LORD hath created a new thing in the earth, A woman shall compass a man.
23 Thus saith the LORD of hosts, the God of Israel; As yet they shall use
this speech in the land of Judah and in the cities thereof, when I shall bring
again their captivity; The LORD bless thee, O habitation of justice, *and*
mountain of holiness.
24 And there shall dwell in Judah itself, and in all the cities thereof
together, husbandmen, and they *that* go forth with flocks.
25 For I have satiated the weary soul, and I have replenished every
sorrowful soul.

31:10 Isa 40:11; 66:19
31:12 Isa 2:2; 35:10; 58:11; 60:20; 65:19; Hos 2:22; Joel 3:18; Mic 4:1; Jn 16:22
31:13 Ps 30:11; Isa 51:11; 61:3; Zech 8:4, 5
31:14 Jer 50:19
31:15☆ Ps 77:2; Jer 10:20
31:16☆ Isa 25:8; 30:19; Jer 30:3; Ezek 11:17
31:17 Jer 29:11
31:18☆ Job 5:17; Ps 80:3, 7, 19; 94:12; Jer 17:14; Hos 4:16
31:19 Ezek 36:31; Lk 18:13
31:20 Isa 55:7; Hos 11:8; 14:4
31:21 Isa 48:20; 52:11
31:22☆
31:23 Ps 48:1; 87:1; Isa 1:26
31:24 Ezek 36:10; Zech 8:4–8
31:25 Ps 107:9; Jn 4:14

31:15 *Rahel* (Rachel) was the mother of Joseph (and the grandmother of Ephraim and Manasseh) and Benjamin. She is weeping because her children have *been taken into exile.* 31:16, 17 indicate that they will return to their habitations later on. The Northern Kingdom was captured and dispossessed by the Assyrians in 722 B.C. The people of this kingdom were largely descended from Rachel. This prophecy is also cited in Matt. 2:17 with respect to Herod's slaughter of the innocents at the time of Christ's birth.

31:16 *for thy work shall be rewarded,* i.e., "for I have heard your prayers."†

31:18 Ephraim repents and turns to God. The term Ephraim is used of a single person to represent all of the ten tribes. The people shall be as one man; they will glorify God singlemindedly and with one voice. The people acknowledge God as their God and pray for restoration. God will answer this prayer.

31:22 *a woman shall compass a man,* i.e., "a woman shall court a suitor," or, "Israel will search for God."†

26 Upon this I awaked, and beheld; and my sleep was sweet unto me.
27 ¶Behold, the days come, saith the LORD, that I will sow the house of
Israel and the house of Judah with the seed of man, and with the seed of
beast.
28 And it shall come to pass, *that* like as I have watched over them, to
pluck up, and to break down, and to throw down, and to destroy, and to
afflict; so will I watch over them to build, and to plant, saith the LORD.
29 In those days they shall say no more, The fathers have eaten a sour
grape, and the children's teeth are set on edge.
30 But every one shall die for his own iniquity: every man that eateth the
sour grape, his teeth shall be set on edge.
31 ¶Behold, the days come, saith the LORD, that I will make a new
covenant with the house of Israel, and with the house of Judah:
32 Not according to the covenant that I made with their fathers in the day
that I took them by the hand to bring them out of the land of Egypt; which
my covenant they brake, although I was an husband unto them, saith the
LORD:
33 But this *shall be* the covenant that I will make with the house of Israel;
After those days, saith the LORD, I will put my law in their inward parts,
and write it in their hearts; and will be their God, and they shall be my
people.
34 And they shall teach no more every man his neighbour, and every man
his brother, saying, Know the LORD: for they shall all know me, from the
least of them unto the greatest of them, saith the LORD: for I will forgive
their iniquity, and I will remember their sin no more.
35 ¶Thus saith the LORD, which giveth the sun for a light by day, *and* the
ordinances of the moon and of the stars for a light by night, which divideth
the sea when the waves thereof roar; The LORD of hosts *is* his name:
36 If those ordinances depart from before me, saith the LORD, *then* the
seed of Israel also shall cease from being a nation before me for ever.
37 Thus saith the LORD; If heaven above can be measured, and the
foundations of the earth searched out beneath, I will also cast off all the
seed of Israel for all that they have done, saith the LORD.
38 ¶Behold, the days come, saith the LORD, that the city shall be built to
the LORD from the tower of Ha-nan'e-el unto the gate of the corner.
39 And the measuring line shall yet go forth over against it upon the hill
Ga'reb, and shall compass about to Go'ath.

☆**31:26** Prov 3:24; Zech 4:1
31:27 Ezek 36:9–11; Hos 2:23
31:28 Dan 9:14
☆**31:29** Ezek 18:2; Lam 5:7
☆**31:30** Deut 24:16; Isa 3:11; Ezek 18:4, 20
☆**31:31** Jer 32:40; Ezek 37:26; Lk 22:20; 1 Cor 11:25; Heb 8:8–12
☆**31:32** Deut 1:31; 5:2, 3; Isa 63:12
☆**31:33** Heb 10:16, 17
31:34 Isa 11:9; 43:25; Jer 50:20; Mic 7:18; 1 Thess 4:9; 1 Jn 2:27
31:35 Gen 1:14–18; Ps 19:1–6; 136:7–9
31:36 Ps 89:36, 37; Isa 54:9, 10; Jer 33:20–26; Amos 9:8, 9
31:37 Isa 40:12; Jer 33:22, 24–26; Rom 11:2–5, 26, 27
☆**31:38** 2 Chron 26:9; Neh 3:1; 12:39; Zech 14:10

31:26 When Jeremiah perceives that both Ephraim and Judah will be brought back by God and be blessed, he was overcome with joy; and his sleep was sweet because his heart's yearning would be brought to pass even though he would not live to see it.

31:29, 30 Whoever eats sour grapes shall have his *own teeth set on edge*—i.e., one reaps the consequences of his own sins. But Israel had complained that their teeth were set on edge by their father's sins. God may well deliver nations but he will not by that act overlook an individual's sins. At any rate, verse 30 makes plain the fact that children are not held responsible for their fathers' sins; each is on his own.

31:31 Here Jeremiah speaks of the new contract or covenant between God and his people. In Rom. 11:26–36 Paul refers to this covenant (see also Heb. 8:8–12). The law was written on tables of stone; the new covenant will be written on the hearts of men. It is not new in the sense that is was totally divorced from the old contract. Rather, it was the fuller disclosure of God's progressive revelation, which marked an advance in which he would bestow on men what they could not earn by their own good works. It was more of grace than they had fully understood before this.

31:32 *my covenant they brake.* Some versions read, "a covenant they broke, even though I cared for them as a husband does his wife." (See Heb. 8:9b.)†

31:33 *in their hearts,* i.e., rather than upon tablets of stone, as were the Ten Commandments. *I . . . will be their God, and they shall be my people.* In 17:1 we read that their sin was inscribed on their hearts, so that they wanted above all to disobey. This change seems to describe an experience very much like, if not the same as, the new birth.†

31:38 The day will come, however long it may be in coming, that Jerusalem will be built again and be safe from all attacks. That has not happened yet, but it will come to pass.

31:40 2 Kgs 23:6; Neh 3:28; Joel 3:17; Zech 14:20

40 And the whole valley of the dead bodies, and of the ashes, and all the
fields unto the brook of Kidron, unto the corner of the horse gate toward
the east, *shall be* holy unto the LORD; it shall not be plucked up, nor thrown
down any more for ever.

2. The Sign of Israel's Restoration: Jeremiah's Land Purchase

32:1 2 Kgs 25:1, 2; Jer 39:1, 2

32 THE word that came to Jer-e-mi'ah from the LORD in the tenth
year of Zed-e-ki'ah king of Judah, which *was* the eighteenth year of
Neb-u-chad-rez'zar.

32:2☆

2 For then the king of Babylon's army besieged Jerusalem: and Jer-e-
mi'ah the prophet was shut up in the court of the prison, which *was* in the
king of Judah's house.

32:3 Jer 21:4–7; 26:8, 9; 34:2, 3

3 For Zed-e-ki'ah king of Judah had shut him up, saying, Wherefore dost
thou prophesy, and say, Thus saith the LORD, Behold, I will give this city
into the hand of the king of Babylon, and he shall take it;

32:4 2 Kgs 25:4–7; Jer 37:17; 39:4–7

4 And Zed-e-ki'ah king of Judah shall not escape out of the hand of the
Chal-de'ans, but shall surely be delivered into the hand of the king of
Babylon, and shall speak with him mouth to mouth, and his eyes shall
behold his eyes;

32:5 Ezek 12:12, 13; 17:9, 10, 15

5 And he shall lead Zed-e-ki'ah to Babylon, and there shall he be until I
visit him, saith the LORD: though ye fight with the Chal-de'ans, ye shall not
prosper.

32:6☆ Lev 25:25; Ruth 4:3, 4

32:7☆

6 ¶And Jer-e-mi'ah said, The word of the LORD came unto me, saying,
7 Behold, Ha-nam'e-el the son of Shal'lum thine uncle shall come unto
thee, saying, Buy thee my field that *is* in An'a-thoth: for the right of
redemption *is* thine to buy *it.*

32:8 1 Sam 9:16, 17; 10:3–7

8 So Ha-nam'e-el mine uncle's son came to me in the court of the prison
according to the word of the LORD, and said unto me, Buy my field, I pray
thee, that *is* in An'a-thoth, which *is* in the country of Benjamin: for the
right of inheritance *is* thine, and the redemption *is* thine; buy *it* for thyself.
Then I knew that this *was* the word of the LORD.

32:9 Gen 23:16; 24:22

9 And I bought the field of Ha-nam'e-el my uncle's son, that *was* in An'a-
thoth, and weighed him the money, *even* seventeen shekels of silver.

32:10 Ruth 4:1, 9; Isa 8:1, 2

10 And I subscribed the evidence, and sealed *it,* and took witnesses, and
weighed *him* the money in the balances.
11 So I took the evidence of the purchase, *both* that which was sealed
according to the law and custom, and that which was open:
12 And I gave the evidence of the purchase unto Ba'ruch the son of Ne-
ri'ah, the son of Ma-a-sei'ah, in the sight of Ha-nam'e-el mine uncle's *son,*
and in the presence of the witnesses that subscribed the book of the
purchase, before all the Jews that sat in the court of the prison.
13 ¶And I charged Ba'ruch before them, saying,

32:14☆

14 Thus saith the LORD of hosts, the God of Israel; Take these evidences,
this evidence of the purchase, both which is sealed, and this evidence which
is open; and put them in an earthen vessel, that they may continue many
days.

32:2 *in the court of the prison, which was in the king of Judah's house,* i.e., "in the dungeon beneath."†

32:6, 7 We do not know how the Holy Spirit conveyed the knowledge of God's will to Jeremiah. It is important to observe that this revelation was followed by outward, external, confirming evidence, according to 32:8. So Jeremiah says: "Then I knew for sure that the message I had heard was really from the Lord."† The purpose of the purchase was to signal the fact that God would restore his people to the land after the captivity even though Jeremiah himself would not be among the returnees.

32:14 *an earthen vessel,* "a pottery jar." This guaranteed their preservation. The Dead Sea Scrolls were preserved for two thousand years in large jars like this.

15 For thus saith the LORD of hosts, the God of Israel; Houses and fields
and vineyards shall be possessed again in this land.
16 ¶Now when I had delivered the evidence of the purchase unto Ba'ruch
the son of Ne-ri'ah, I prayed unto the LORD, saying,
17 Ah Lord GOD! behold, thou hast made the heaven and the earth by thy
great power and stretched out arm, *and* there is nothing too hard for thee:
18 Thou shewest lovingkindness unto thousands, and recompensest the
iniquity of the fathers into the bosom of their children after them: the
Great, the Mighty God, the LORD of hosts, *is* his name,
19 Great in counsel, and mighty in work: for thine eyes *are* open upon all
the ways of the sons of men: to give every one according to his ways, and
according to the fruit of his doings:
20 Which hast set signs and wonders in the land of Egypt, *even* unto this
day, and in Israel, and among *other* men; and hast made thee a name, as at
this day;
21 And hast brought forth thy people Israel out of the land of Egypt with
signs, and with wonders, and with a strong hand, and with a stretched out
arm, and with great terror;
22 And hast given them this land, which thou didst swear to their fathers
to give them, a land flowing with milk and honey;
23 And they came in, and possessed it; but they obeyed not thy voice,
neither walked in thy law; they have done nothing of all that thou
commandedst them to do: therefore thou hast caused all this evil to come
upon them:
24 Behold the mounts, they are come unto the city to take it: and the city
is given into the hand of the Chal-de'ans, that fight against it, because of the
sword, and of the famine, and of the pestilence: and what thou hast spoken
is come to pass; and, behold, thou seest *it*.
25 And thou hast said unto me, O Lord GOD, Buy thee the field for
money, and take witnesses; for the city is given into the hand of the Chal-
de'ans.
26 ¶Then came the word of the LORD unto Jer-e-mi'ah, saying,
27 Behold, I *am* the LORD, the God of all flesh: is there any thing too hard
for me?
28 Therefore thus saith the LORD; Behold, I will give this city into the
hand of the Chal-de'ans, and into the hand of Neb-u-chad-rez'zar king of
Babylon, and he shall take it:
29 And the Chal-de'ans, that fight against this city, shall come and set fire
on this city, and burn it with the houses, upon whose roofs they have
offered incense unto Ba'al, and poured out drink offerings unto other gods,
to provoke me to anger.
30 For the children of Israel and the children of Judah have only done evil
before me from their youth: for the children of Israel have only provoked
me to anger with the work of their hands, saith the LORD.
31 For this city hath been to me *as* a provocation of mine anger and of my
fury from the day that they built it even unto this day; that I should remove
it from before my face,

32:15 Jer 30:18; 31:5, 12; 33:12, 13; Amos 9:14, 15; Zech 3:10
☆**32:16** Gen 32:9–12; Jer 12:1; Phil 4:6, 7
32:17 Gen 18:14; 2 Kgs 19:15; Ps 102:25; Isa 40:26–29; Jer 27:5
32:18 Ex 34:6, 7; Deut 7:9, 10; 1 Kgs 16:1–3; Ps 50:1; 145:3; Jer 10:16; 20:11; 31:35; Mt 23:32–36
☆**32:19** Job 34:21; Ps 62:12; Isa 28:29; Jer 17:10; 21:14; 23:24; Mt 16:27; Jn 5:29
32:20 Ps 78:43; 105:27; Isa 63:12, 14; Dan 9:15
32:21 Deut 4:34; 26:8; 1 Chron 17:21
32:22 Ex 13:5; Deut 1:8; Ps 105:9–11; Jer 11:5
32:23 Ezra 9:7; Ps 44:2, 3; 78:54, 55; Jer 2:7; 44:10; Lam 1:18; Dan 9:11, 12
32:24 Josh 23:15, 16; Ezek 14:21; Zech 1:6
32:27 Num 16:22; 27:16; Mt 19:26
32:28 Jer 19:7–12; 34:2, 3
32:29 2 Chron 36:19; Jer 19:13; 21:10; 39:8; 44:17–19, 25; 52:13
32:31 1 Kgs 11:7, 8; 2 Kgs 21:4–7, 15; 23:27; 24:3, 4; Jer 5:9–11; 6:6, 7; Mt 23:37

32:16ff Jeremiah lays hold of God in prayer. He has purchased some land; but since he knows the destruction of Jerusalem is at hand, he asks God why he should have bought the land. Beginning with verse 26 God responds to Jeremiah's question. His people are guilty and judgment has come, but God is gracious. Later on, he will restore his people to the land from which he dispossessed them; therefore, Jeremiah's purchase certifies God's promise of the restoration.

32:19 God sovereignly orders his purposes and plans. They are called: (1) wonderful and wise (Isa. 28:29), (2) great and mighty (32:19), (3) immutable or unalterable (Heb. 6:16), (4) just the way he planned it (Eph. 3:11), and (5) unbreakable (Isa. 14:27). Evildoers neither understand God's plans and purposes nor do they respect or accept them.

32:32 Ezra 9:7 Isa 1:23 Jer 2:26 44:17, 21
32:33 2 Chron 36:15, 16 Jer 25:3; 26:5 35:15
32:35 Lev 18:21 20:2–5 2 Chron 28:2, 3 33:6 Acts 7:43
32:37 Deut 30:3 Isa 11:11–16 Jer 23:6 Ezek 11:17 34:25, 28 Amos 9:14, 15 Hos 1:11 Zech 14:11
32:39 Deut 11:18–21 Ezek 37:25 Jn 17:21 Acts 4:32
32:40☆ Isa 55:3
32:41 Deut 30:9 Isa 65:19 Jer 31:28 Amos 9:15
32:42 Jer 31:28 Zech 8:14, 15
32:43 Ezek 37:11–14

32 Because of all the evil of the children of Israel and of the children of
Judah, which they have done to provoke me to anger, they, their kings, their
princes, their priests, and their prophets, and the men of Judah, and the
inhabitants of Jerusalem.
33 And they have turned unto me the back, and not the face: though I
taught them, rising up early and teaching *them,* yet they have not hearkened
to receive instruction.
34 But they set their abominations in the house, which is called by my
name, to defile it.
35 And they built the high places of Ba′al, which *are* in the valley of the
son of Hin′nom, to cause their sons and their daughters to pass through *the*
fire unto Mo′lech; which I commanded them not, neither came it into my
mind, that they should do this abomination, to cause Judah to sin.
36 ¶And now therefore thus saith the LORD, the God of Israel, concerning
this city, whereof ye say, It shall be delivered into the hand of the king of
Babylon by the sword, and by the famine, and by the pestilence;
37 Behold, I will gather them out of all countries, whither I have driven
them in mine anger, and in my fury, and in great wrath; and I will bring
them again unto this place, and I will cause them to dwell safely:
38 And they shall be my people, and I will be their God:
39 And I will give them one heart, and one way, that they may fear me for
ever, for the good of them, and of their children after them:
40 And I will make an everlasting covenant with them, that I will not turn
away from them, to do them good; but I will put my fear in their hearts,
that they shall not depart from me.
41 Yea, I will rejoice over them to do them good, and I will plant them in
this land assuredly with my whole heart and with my whole soul.
42 For thus saith the LORD; Like as I have brought all this great evil upon
this people, so will I bring upon them all the good that I have promised
them.
43 And fields shall be bought in this land, whereof ye say, *It is* desolate
without man or beast; it is given into the hand of the Chal-de′ans.
44 Men shall buy fields for money, and subscribe evidences, and seal *them,*
and take witnesses in the land of Benjamin, and in the places about
Jerusalem, and in the cities of Judah, and in the cities of the mountains, and
in the cities of the valley, and in the cities of the south: for I will cause their
captivity to return, saith the LORD.

3. Jerusalem's Restoration under the Branch (the Son of David)

33:2 Ex 3:15
33:3☆ Ps 50:15 Isa 48:6; 55:6, 7

33 MOREOVER the word of the LORD came unto Jer-e-mi′ah the
second time, while he was yet shut up in the court of the prison,
saying,
2 Thus saith the LORD the maker thereof, the LORD that formed it, to
establish it; the LORD *is* his name;
3 Call unto me, and I will answer thee, and shew thee great and mighty
things, which thou knowest not.

32:40 *God will make an everlasting* covenant with his people in the future, and nothing will alter it because God will put fear into their hearts that they may not sin against him. This is the only sure way that they will not apostatize.

33:3 Again and again the Scriptures teach that God is willing and ready to answer those who will turn to him in believing faith. In this instance Jeremiah looks beyond the captivity, foresees the return to the land, and promises that Jerusalem will come to life again. God's people will once more experience the divine blessings of abundance, prosperity, and security. The impossible will become a reality because God is God.

4For thus saith the LORD, the God of Israel, concerning the houses of this
city, and concerning the houses of the kings of Judah, which are thrown
down by the mounts, and by the sword;
5They come to fight with the Chal-de'ans, but *it is* to fill them with the
dead bodies of men, whom I have slain in mine anger and in my fury, and
for all whose wickedness I have hid my face from this city.
6Behold, I will bring it health and cure, and I will cure them, and will
reveal unto them the abundance of peace and truth.
7And I will cause the captivity of Judah and the captivity of Israel to
return, and will build them, as at the first.
8And I will cleanse them from all their iniquity, whereby they have
sinned against me; and I will pardon all their iniquities, whereby they have
sinned, and whereby they have transgressed against me.
9¶And it shall be to me a name of joy, a praise and an honour before all
the nations of the earth, which shall hear all the good that I do unto them:
and they shall fear and tremble for all the goodness and for all the
prosperity that I procure unto it.
10Thus saith the LORD; Again there shall be heard in this place, which ye
say *shall be* desolate without man and without beast, *even* in the cities of
Judah, and in the streets of Jerusalem, that are desolate, without man, and
without inhabitant, and without beast,
11The voice of joy, and the voice of gladness, the voice of the bridegroom,
and the voice of the bride, the voice of them that shall say, Praise the LORD
of hosts: for the LORD *is* good; for his mercy *endureth* for ever: *and* of them
that shall bring the sacrifice of praise into the house of the LORD. For I will
cause to return the captivity of the land, as at the first, saith the LORD.
12Thus saith the LORD of hosts; Again in this place, which is desolate
without man and without beast, and in all the cities thereof, shall be an
habitation of shepherds causing *their* flocks to lie down.
13In the cities of the mountains, in the cities of the vale, and in the cities
of the south, and in the land of Benjamin, and in the places about
Jerusalem, and in the cities of Judah, shall the flocks pass again under the
hands of him that telleth *them,* saith the LORD.
14Behold, the days come, saith the LORD, that I will perform that good
thing which I have promised unto the house of Israel and to the house of
Judah.
15In those days, and at that time, will I cause the Branch of righteousness
to grow up unto David; and he shall execute judgment and righteousness in
the land.
16In those days shall Judah be saved, and Jerusalem shall dwell safely:
and this *is the name* wherewith she shall be called, The LORD our
righteousness.
17¶For thus saith the LORD; David shall never want a man to sit upon the
throne of the house of Israel;

33:4 Isa 32:13, 14
33:5 Jer 21:10
33:6 Isa 66:12; Jer 17:14; Gal 5:22, 23
33:7 Ps 85:1; Jer 30:18; Amos 9:14, 15
☆**33:8** Ps 51:2; Jer 50:20; Heb 9:11–14
33:9 Ps 40:3; Isa 62:2, 4; Jer 16:19; 24:6; Hos 3:5
33:10 Isa 35:10
☆**33:11**
33:12 Ezek 34:12–14; Zeph 2:6, 7
33:14 Hag 2:6–9
☆**33:15** Ps 72:1–5; Isa 11:1–5
33:16 Isa 45:24, 25; Jer 23:6; 2 Cor 5:21; Phil 3:9
☆**33:17** 1 Kgs 2:4; Ps 89:29–37

33:8 *The removal of guilt* and cleansing from sin is not for those who have died in their sins; they are lost forever. The cleansing is for those who repent and seek forgiveness, especially for those of Judah and Israel participating in the restoration.

33:11 *they shall bring the sacrifice of praise.* This seems to mean spiritual sacrifices (not animal offerings), thanksgivings, or what Hosea calls "the calves of our lips" (Hos. 14:2). "The Jews say that in the days of the Messiah all sacrifices shall cease but *the sacrifice of praise,* and to those days this promise has a further reference."*

33:15 *the Branch of righteousness to grow up unto David.* This refers to Christ the rightful king, who is not an usurper. "He grows up unto David," i.e., he descends from David's loins according to the biblical promise. And he is the seed with whom the covenant of God is established and fixed forever.

33:17 *David shall never want a man to sit upon the throne of the house of Israel.* This refers to the previous verse, which speaks of the time, in those days, i.e., "at the end of the age." There can be no doubt that the Davidic Covenant promised an unending line for David. The line continued even though the royal authority was suspended. Jesus was born of the royal line of David. Luke 1:32 makes clear that Jesus was the fulfillment of

33:18 Deut 18:1 Ezek 44:15 Heb 13:15

18 Neither shall the priests the Levites want a man before me to offer
burnt offerings, and to kindle meat offerings, and to do sacrifice continu-
ally.
19 ¶And the word of the LORD came unto Jer-e-mi'ah, saying,

33:20 2 Sam 23:5 2 Chron 21:7 Ps 104:19–23 Isa 54:9

20 Thus saith the LORD, If ye can break my covenant of the day, and my
covenant of the night, and that there should not be day and night in their
season;
21 *Then* may also my covenant be broken with David my servant, that he
should not have a son to reign upon his throne; and with the Levites the
priests, my ministers.

33:22 Gen 22:17

22 As the host of heaven cannot be numbered, neither the sand of the sea
measured: so will I multiply the seed of David my servant, and the Levites
that minister unto me.
23 Moreover the word of the LORD came to Jer-e-mi'ah, saying,

33:24☆ Neh 4:2–4 Ps 44:13, 14 Isa 11:13 Jer 3:7, 8, 10, 18 Ezek 36:2

24 Considerest thou not what this people have spoken, saying, The two
families which the LORD hath chosen, he hath even cast them off? thus they
have despised my people, that they should be no more a nation before
them.

33:25 Gen 49:10 Ezek 39:25 Hos 2:23

25 Thus saith the LORD; If my covenant *be* not with day and night, *and if*
I have not appointed the ordinances of heaven and earth;
26 Then will I cast away the seed of Jacob, and David my servant, *so* that
I will not take *any* of his seed *to be* rulers over the seed of Abraham, Isaac,
and Jacob: for I will cause their captivity to return, and have mercy on
them.

C. THE FALL OF JUDAH

1. God's Condemnation of Zedekiah for Breaking His Pledge

34:1 Jer 1:15 Dan 2:37, 38

34 THE word which came unto Jer-e-mi'ah from the LORD, when Neb-
u-chad-nez'zar king of Babylon, and all his army, and all the
kingdoms of the earth of his dominion, and all the people, fought against
Jerusalem, and against all the cities thereof, saying,

34:2☆ 2 Chron 36:11, 12 Jer 37:1–4

2 Thus saith the LORD, the God of Israel; Go and speak to Zed-e-ki'ah
king of Judah, and tell him, Thus saith the LORD; Behold, I will give this
city into the hand of the king of Babylon, and he shall burn it with fire:

34:3 2 Kgs 25:4–7 Jer 21:7

3 And thou shalt not escape out of his hand, but shalt surely be taken, and
delivered into his hand; and thine eyes shall behold the eyes of the king of
Babylon, and he shall speak with thee mouth to mouth, and thou shalt go to
Babylon.
4 Yet hear the word of the LORD, O Zed-e-ki'ah king of Judah; Thus saith
the LORD of thee, Thou shalt not die by the sword:

34:5☆ 2 Chron 16:14

5 *But* thou shalt die in peace: and with the burnings of thy fathers, the

---

the promise to David and that he was ordained by the Father to occupy David's throne, which had been vacant for centuries. Since the eternal Son of God came, there is no need for other sons of David to come; the throne God promised is an eternal throne on which the Son of God now sits in the heavenlies. He will someday sit on its earthly counterpart on this planet.

33:24 The question has come whether God's covenant with Israel has been abrogated. The answer is No. It remains and will be brought back in history by the King-Messiah, who will be a descendant of David and will occupy his throne and reign forever.

34:2 God marvelously protected his prophet Jeremiah from harm and danger. By divine providence, Jeremiah has access to King Zedekiah. One would have supposed that Zedekiah would never have allowed Jeremiah to come into his presence nor would he have listened to him.

34:5 *so shall they burn odours for thee,* or, "with the burnings of his fathers." In his death they will accord him "with the respect usually shown to their kings, especially to those who had done good in Israel . . . . [I]n his captivity he had conducted himself so well towards his own people that they were willing to do him this honour . . . If Zedekiah had continued in his prosperity, perhaps he would have grown worse and would have departed at last without being desired; but his afflictions wrought such a change in him that his death was looked upon as a great loss. It is better to live and die penitent in a prison than to live and die impenitent in a palace."*

former kings which were before thee, so shall they burn *odours* for thee; and
they will lament thee, *saying,* Ah lord! for I have pronounced the word,
saith the LORD.
6 Then Jer-e-mi'ah the prophet spake all these words unto Zed-e-ki'ah
king of Judah in Jerusalem,
7 When the king of Babylon's army fought against Jerusalem, and against
all the cities of Judah that were left, against La'chish, and against A-ze'kah:
for these defenced cities remained of the cities of Judah.

34:7 Josh 10:3, 10; 2 Kgs 14:19; 2 Chron 11:5–10

8 ¶*This is* the word that came unto Jer-e-mi'ah from the LORD, after that
the king Zed-e-ki'ah had made a covenant with all the people which *were* at
Jerusalem, to proclaim liberty unto them;

34:8 Lev 25:39–46; Neh 5:1–13

9 That every man should let his manservant, and every man his maidser-
vant, *being* an Hebrew or an Hebrewess, go free; that none should serve
himself of them *to wit,* of a Jew his brother.

34:9 Gen 14:13

10 Now when all the princes, and all the people, which had entered into
the covenant, heard that every one should let his manservant, and every one
his maidservant, go free, that none should serve themselves of them any
more, then they obeyed, and let *them* go.
11 But afterward they turned, and caused the servants and the handmaids,
whom they had let go free, to return, and brought them into subjection for
servants and for handmaids.

☆34:11 Ps 78:34–36; Hos 6:4

12 ¶Therefore the word of the LORD came to Jer-e-mi'ah from the LORD,
saying,
13 Thus saith the LORD, the God of Israel; I made a covenant with your
fathers in the day that I brought them forth out of the land of Egypt, out of
the house of bondmen, saying,

34:13 Deut 5:2, 3, 27; Jer 31:32

14 At the end of seven years let ye go every man his brother an Hebrew,
which hath been sold unto thee; and when he hath served thee six years,
thou shalt let him go free from thee: but your fathers hearkened not unto
me, neither inclined their ear.

34:14 Ex 21:2; 1 Kgs 9:22; 2 Kgs 17:13, 14

15 And ye were now turned, and had done right in my sight, in proclaim-
ing liberty every man to his neighbour; and ye had made a covenant before
me in the house which is called by my name:

34:15 Neh 10:29

16 But ye turned and polluted my name, and caused every man his
servant, and every man his handmaid, whom he had set at liberty at their
pleasure, to return, and brought them into subjection, to be unto you for
servants and for handmaids.

34:16 Ex 20:7; 1 Sam 15:11; Ezek 18:24

17 Therefore thus saith the LORD; Ye have not hearkened unto me, in
proclaiming liberty, every one to his brother, and every man to his
neighbour: behold, I proclaim a liberty for you, saith the LORD, to the
sword, to the pestilence, and to the famine; and I will make you to be
removed into all the kingdoms of the earth.

☆34:17 Lev 26:34, 35; Deut 28:25, 64; Mt 7:2

18 And I will give the men that have transgressed my covenant, which
have not performed the words of the covenant which they had made before
me, when they cut the calf in twain, and passed between the parts thereof,
19 The princes of Judah, and the princes of Jerusalem, the eunuchs, and
the priests, and all the people of the land, which passed between the parts
of the calf;

34:18 Gen 15:10; Hos 6:7; Mic 7:1–5

34:11 Zedekiah and those who had servants set them free. Then they changed their minds and brought the victims back into slavery. This occurred when the siege was temporarily lifted, causing them to become bold and to turn back to their sins. These were Hebrew slaves, not Gentiles; they should have been freed on the seventh year.

34:17 "That is not said to be done which does not last."* Because Zedekiah and the slaveholders reversed their stand, God gave them liberty to choose their punishment: sword, famine, or pestilence.

34:20 1 Sam 17:46; Jer 19:7
34:21 2 Kgs 25:18–21; Ezek 17:16
34:22 Jer 44:22

20 I will even give them into the hand of their enemies, and into the hand
of them that seek their life: and their dead bodies shall be for meat unto the
fowls of the heaven, and to the beasts of the earth.
21 And Zed-e-ki'ah king of Judah and his princes will I give into the hand
of their enemies, and into the hand of them that seek their life, and into the
hand of the king of Babylon's army, which are gone up from you.
22 Behold, I will command, saith the LORD, and cause them to return to
this city; and they shall fight against it, and take it, and burn it with fire:
and I will make the cities of Judah a desolation without an inhabitant.

2. The Illustration of the Faithful Rechabites

35:1☆ 2 Kgs 23:34–36; Dan 1:1
35:2☆ 1 Kgs 6:5, 6, 8; 1 Chron 2:55

35 THE word which came unto Jer-e-mi'ah from the LORD in the days
of Je-hoi'a-kim the son of Jo-si'ah king of Judah, saying,
2 Go unto the house of the Re'chab-ites, and speak unto them, and bring
them into the house of the LORD, into one of the chambers, and give them
wine to drink.
3 Then I took Ja-az-a-ni'ah the son of Jer-e-mi'ah, the son of Hab-a-zi-
ni'ah, and his brethren, and all his sons, and the whole house of the
Re'chab-ites;
4 And I brought them into the house of the LORD, into the chamber of the
sons of Ha'nan, the son of Ig-da-li'ah, a man of God, which *was* by the
chamber of the princes, which *was* above the chamber of Ma-a-sei'ah
the son of Shal'lum, the keeper of the door:

35:5☆ 2 Cor 2:9
35:6☆ Lev 10:9; Num 6:2–4; 2 Kgs 10:15, 23; 1 Chron 2:55; Lk 1:15
35:7 Ex 20:12; 1 Chron 16:19; Heb 11:9
35:8 Prov 4:1, 2, 10; 6:20; Col 3:20
35:9 Ps 37:16; 1 Tim 6:6

5 And I set before the sons of the house of the Re'chab-ites pots full of
wine, and cups, and I said unto them, Drink ye wine.
6 But they said, We will drink no wine: for Jon'a-dab the son of Re'chab
our father commanded us, saying, Ye shall drink no wine, *neither* ye, nor
your sons for ever:
7 Neither shall ye build house, nor sow seed, nor plant vineyard, nor have
any: but all your days ye shall dwell in tents; that ye may live many days in
the land where ye *be* strangers.
8 Thus have we obeyed the voice of Jon'a-dab the son of Re'chab our
father in all that he hath charged us, to drink no wine all our days, we, our
wives, our sons, nor our daughters;
9 Nor to build houses for us to dwell in: neither have we vineyard, nor
field, nor seed:
10 But we have dwelt in tents, and have obeyed, and done according to all
that Jon'a-dab our father commanded us.

35:11 2 Kgs 24:1, 2; Dan 1:1, 2
35:13 Isa 28:9–12

11 But it came to pass, when Neb-u-chad-rez'zar king of Babylon came up
into the land, that we said, Come, and let us go to Jerusalem for fear of the
army of the Chal-de'ans, and for fear of the army of the Syrians: so we
dwell at Jerusalem.
12 ¶Then came the word of the LORD unto Jer-e-mi'ah, saying,
13 Thus saith the LORD of hosts, the God of Israel; Go and tell the men of
Judah and the inhabitants of Jerusalem, Will ye not receive instruction to
hearken to my words? saith the LORD.

35:1 *in the days of Jehoiakim,* This is apparently an early message of Jeremiah, and is not here in its chronological order with the other messages.†

35:2 *Rechabites. They were a seminomadic* people who descended from the Kenites. They refused to drink alcoholic beverages and never were urbanized.

35:5, 6 Jeremiah placed wine before the Rechabites, but they refused to drink any of it because their ancestor, Jonadab, had told them never to do it. Jeremiah was testing them with regard to the wine, and they passed the test. God used that illustration to show that he had given his people Israel instructions which they had abandoned. If the Rechabites were able to keep the pledge of abstinence, Israel could have remained faithful to their covenant with God. Since Israel had not done so, God pronounces judgment on them (35:16, 17).

[14]The words of Jon'a-dab the son of Re'chab, that he commanded his
sons not to drink wine, are performed; for unto this day they drink none,
but obey their father's commandment: notwithstanding I have spoken unto
you, rising early and speaking; but ye hearkened not unto me.
[15]I have sent also unto you all my servants the prophets, rising up early
and sending *them*, saying, Return ye now every man from his evil way, and
amend your doings, and go not after other gods to serve them, and ye shall
dwell in the land which I have given to you and to your fathers: but ye have
not inclined your ear, nor hearkened unto me.
[16]Because the sons of Jon'a-dab the son of Re'chab have performed the
commandment of their father, which he commanded them; but this people
hath not hearkened unto me:
[17]Therefore thus saith the LORD God of hosts, the God of Israel; Behold,
I will bring upon Judah and upon all the inhabitants of Jerusalem all the
evil that I have pronounced against them: because I have spoken unto
them, but they have not heard; and I have called unto them, but they have
not answered.
[18]¶And Jer-e-mi'ah said unto the house of the Re'chab-ites, Thus saith
the LORD of hosts, the God of Israel; Because ye have obeyed the
commandment of Jon'a-dab your father, and kept all his precepts, and
done according unto all that he hath commanded you:
[19]Therefore thus saith the LORD of hosts, the God of Israel; Jon'a-dab the
son of Re'chab shall not want a man to stand before me for ever.

35:14 2 Chron 36:15; Isa 30:9
35:15 Deut 6:14; Jer 29:19; Ezek 18:30–32; Acts 26:20
35:16 Mal 1:6
35:17 Prov 1:24, 25; Mic 3:12; Lk 13:34, 35; Rom 10:21
☆**35:18** Ex 20:12; Jer 15:19; Eph 6:1–3

3. Jehoiakim Arrogantly Burns the Scroll

36 AND it came to pass in the fourth year of Je-hoi'a-kim the son of
Jo-si'ah king of Judah, *that* this word came unto Jer-e-mi'ah from
the LORD, saying,
[2]Take thee a roll of a book, and write therein all the words that I have
spoken unto thee against Israel, and against Judah, and against all the
nations, from the day I spake unto thee, from the days of Jo-si'ah, even
unto this day.
[3]It may be that the house of Judah will hear all the evil which I purpose
to do unto them; that they may return every man from his evil way; that I
may forgive their iniquity and their sin.
[4]Then Jer-e-mi'ah called Ba'ruch the son of Ne-ri'ah: and Ba'ruch wrote
from the mouth of Jer-e-mi'ah all the words of the LORD, which he had
spoken unto him, upon a roll of a book.
[5]And Jer-e-mi'ah commanded Ba'ruch, saying, I *am* shut up; I cannot go
into the house of the LORD:
[6]Therefore go thou, and read in the roll, which thou hast written from my
mouth, the words of the LORD in the ears of the people in the LORD's house
upon the fasting day: and also thou shalt read them in the ears of all Judah
that come out of their cities.
[7]It may be they will present their supplication before the LORD, and will
return every one from his evil way: for great *is* the anger and the fury that
the LORD *hath* pronounced against this people.

☆**36:1** Jer 25:1–3; 45:1
36:2 Jer 1:2, 3, 5, 9, 10; 25:9–29; 47–51; Zech 5:1, 2
36:3 Isa 55:7; Jer 18:8, 11; 26:3; Mk 4:12; Acts 3:19
☆**36:4** Jer 32:12; Ezek 2:9
☆**36:5** Jer 32:2
36:6 Zech 8:19
36:7 1 Kgs 8:33; 2 Kgs 22:13; Jer 26:3

35:18 Because of the obedience of the Rechabites to the command of Jonadab, God said they would never lack a man to stand before him. If they obeyed Jonadab, how much more would they obey the Lord God.
36:1 *In the fourth year of Jehoiakim.* Probably in the summer of 605 B.C., shortly after Nebuchadnezzar's victory over the Egyptian army at Carchemish.†
36:4 We are not told why Jeremiah did not write down the words given him by God. Baruch was his secretary. Perhaps Baruch was a gifted amanuensis. This would have made a considerable difference in the finished product.
36:5 The king had debarred Jeremiah from going to the house of the Lord. By doing this he thought he could silence the prophet. But Jeremiah sent Baruch in his stead. He read the Word of God to the people for Jeremiah.

8 And Ba'ruch the son of Ne-ri'ah did according to all that Jer-e-mi'ah the
prophet commanded him, reading in the book the words of the LORD in the
LORD'S house.

36:9ff☆
9 And it came to pass in the fifth year of Je-hoi'a-kim the son of Jo-si'ah
king of Judah, in the ninth month, *that* they proclaimed a fast before the
LORD to all the people in Jerusalem, and to all the people that came from
the cities of Judah unto Jerusalem.

36:10 Jer 26:10
10 Then read Ba'ruch in the book the words of Jer-e-mi'ah in the house of
the LORD, in the chamber of Gem-a-ri'ah the son of Sha'phan the scribe, in
the higher court, at the entry of the new gate of the LORD'S house, in the
ears of all the people.

11 ¶When Mi-chai'ah the son of Gem-a-ri'ah, the son of Sha'phan, had
heard out of the book all the words of the LORD,

36:12 Jer 26:22
12 Then he went down into the king's house, into the scribe's chamber:
and, lo, all the princes sat there, *even* E-lish'a-ma the scribe, and Del-a-i'ah
the son of Shem-a-i'ah, and El-na'than the son of Ach'bor, and Gem-a-ri'ah
the son of Sha'phan, and Zed-e-ki'ah the son of Han-a-ni'ah, and all the
princes.

36:13 2 Kgs 22:9, 10
13 Then Mi-chai'ah declared unto them all the words that he had heard,
when Ba'ruch read the book in the ears of the people.

14 Therefore all the princes sent Je-hu'di the son of Neth-a-ni'ah, the son
of Shel-e-mi'ah, the son of Cu'shi, unto Ba'ruch, saying, Take in thine hand
the roll wherein thou hast read in the ears of the people, and come. So
Ba'ruch the son of Ne-ri'ah took the roll in his hand, and came unto them.

15 And they said unto him, Sit down now, and read it in our ears. So
Ba'ruch read *it* in their ears.

36:16 Amos 7:10, 11; Acts 24:25
16 Now it came to pass, when they had heard all the words, they were
afraid both one and other, and said unto Ba'ruch, We will surely tell the
king of all these words.

17 And they asked Ba'ruch, saying, Tell us now, How didst thou write all
these words at his mouth?

36:18 Jer 43:2, 3
18 Then Ba'ruch answered them, He pronounced all these words unto me
with his mouth, and I wrote *them* with ink in the book.

36:19 1 Kgs 17:3; 18:4; Jer 26:20–24
19 Then said the princes unto Ba'ruch, Go, hide thee, thou and Jer-e-
mi'ah; and let no man know where ye be.

20 ¶And they went in to the king into the court, but they laid up the roll in
the chamber of E-lish'a-ma the scribe, and told all the words in the ears of
the king.

36:21 2 Kgs 22:9, 10; 2 Chron 34:18; Ezek 2:4, 5
21 So the king sent Je-hu'di to fetch the roll: and he took it out of E-lish'a-
ma the scribe's chamber. And Je-hu'di read it in the ears of the king, and in
the ears of all the princes which stood beside the king.

36:22 Amos 3:15
22 Now the king sat in the winterhouse in the ninth month: and *there was
a fire* on the hearth burning before him.

36:23 Prov 1:29, 30; Isa 5:18, 19; 28:14, 22
23 And it came to pass, *that* when Je-hu'di had read three or four leaves,
he cut it with the penknife, and cast *it* into the fire that *was* on the hearth,
until all the roll was consumed in the fire that *was* on the hearth.

36:24 2 Kgs 19:1, 2; Ps 36:1; Isa 26:10, 11; Acts 5:34–39
24 Yet they were not afraid, nor rent their garments, *neither* the king, nor
any of his servants that heard all these words.

36:9ff *One would* suppose that the calling for a fast was a sign of genuine repentance, which would be pleasing to God. Jehoiakim's actions, however, spoke louder than his words. Baruch, Jeremiah's secretary, took the words of the prophet and read them to the people. When Jehoiakim heard of this, he had Baruch brought before him. When Baruch read one scroll, the king cut off piece after piece and threw the pieces into the fire until the entire scroll was destroyed. The king and his servants were unafraid; they refused to tear their garments as a sign of repentance (36:24). Jehoiakim was not the least bit repentant.

[25]Nevertheless El-na'than and Del-a-i'ah and Gem-a-ri'ah had made
intercession to the king that he would not burn the roll: but he would not
hear them.
[26]But the king commanded Je-rah'me-el the son of Ham'me-lech, and
Ser-a-i'ah the son of Az'ri-el, and Shel-e-mi'ah the son of Ab'de-el, to take
Ba'ruch the scribe and Jer-e-mi'ah the prophet: but the LORD hid them.
[27]¶Then the word of the LORD came to Jer-e-mi'ah, after that the king
had burned the roll, and the words which Ba'ruch wrote at the mouth of
Jer-e-mi'ah, saying,
[28]Take thee again another roll, and write in it all the former words that
were in the first roll, which Je-hoi'a-kim the king of Judah hath burned.
[29]And thou shalt say to Je-hoi'a-kim king of Judah, Thus saith the LORD;
Thou hast burned this roll, saying, Why hast thou written therein, saying,
The king of Babylon shall certainly come and destroy this land, and shall
cause to cease from thence man and beast?
[30]Therefore thus saith the LORD of Je-hoi'a-kim king of Judah; He shall
have none to sit upon the throne of David: and his dead body shall be cast
out in the day to the heat, and in the night to the frost.
[31]And I will punish him and his seed and his servants for their iniquity;
and I will bring upon them, and upon the inhabitants of Jerusalem, and
upon the men of Judah, all the evil that I have pronounced against them;
but they hearkened not.
[32]¶Then took Jer-e-mi'ah another roll, and gave it to Ba'ruch the scribe,
the son of Ne-ri'ah; who wrote therein from the mouth of Jer-e-mi'ah all
the words of the book which Je-hoi'a-kim king of Judah had burned in the
fire: and there were added besides unto them many like words.

☆**36:26** 1 Kgs 19:1–3, 10, 14; Jer 15:20, 21
☆**36:28** Jer 28:13, 14; 44:28; Zech 1:5, 6
36:29 Deut 29:19; Isa 30:10, 11; 45:9; Jer 25:8–11; 26:9
☆**36:30** 2 Kgs 24:12–15; Jer 22:30
36:31 Deut 28:15–19; Prov 29:1; Jer 19:15
36:32 Ex 34:1

4. The Imprisonment of Jeremiah

37 AND king Zed-e-ki'ah the son of Jo-si'ah reigned instead of Co-
ni'ah the son of Je-hoi'a-kim, whom Neb-u-chad-rez'zar king of
Babylon made king in the land of Judah.
[2]But neither he, nor his servants, nor the people of the land, did hearken
unto the words of the LORD, which he spake by the prophet Jer-e-mi'ah.
[3]And Zed-e-ki'ah the king sent Je-hu'cal the son of Shel-e-mi'ah and
Zeph-a-ni'ah the son of Ma-a-sei'ah the priest to the prophet Jer-e-mi'ah
saying, Pray now unto the LORD our God for us.
[4]Now Jer-e-mi'ah came in and went out among the people: for they had
not put him into prison.

☆**37:1** 2 Kgs 24:17; 1 Chron 3:15, 16; 2 Chron 36:9, 10; Jer 22:24, 28; Ezek 17:12–21
☆**37:2** 2 Kgs 24:18–20; 2 Chron 36:12; Prov 29:12
37:3 Jer 2:26, 27; 21:1, 2; 52:24

36:26 Where and how God hid Jeremiah and Baruch we are not told. God's providence working on behalf of his servants was greater and more effective than the orders and enmity of the king.

36:28 The Word of the Lord cannot be destroyed. When Jehoiakim burned that Word, Jeremiah, at the command of God, had another scroll prepared. And God added words to those that had been burned by Jehoiakim. One of the miracles of the ages is the preservation of the Word of God, a feat that defies human understanding and leaves man without excuse.

36:30 *He shall have none to sit upon the throne.* A three-month interregnum by his son Jehoiachin (also called Coniah and Jeconiah) evidently did not qualify as "sitting on the throne," under the meaning of permanence implied in the Hebrew expression used here.†

37:1 *Coniah* was the son of Jehoiakim. His name as king was Jehoiachin. He reigned for less than four months. How his father Jehoiakim died is not stated in the Scriptures. Jehoiachin was taken to Babylon, where he lived for at least thirty-seven years. Nebuchadnezzar appointed Zedekiah to be king in Judah after Jehoiachin was taken to Babylon. Zedekiah was his uncle, the brother of Jehoiakim, and the son of Josiah, as was Jehoiakim. Zedekiah revolted against Nebuchadnezzar, was defeated, and, after his eyes were put out, was sent down to Babylon as a prisoner.

37:2 Even though they did not hearken unto the words of the Lord, this does not mean that there were no true followers of God left in the land. There always has been a remnant left among an apostate people so that the gospel is not eliminated and the fire is not quenched. The faithful remnant was exactly that—a small number of true believers.

5 Then Pharaoh's army was come forth out of Egypt: and when the Chal-
de'ans that besieged Jerusalem heard tidings of them, they departed from
Jerusalem.
6 ¶Then came the word of the LORD unto the prophet Jer-e-mi'ah, saying,
7 Thus saith the LORD, the God of Israel; Thus shall ye say to the king of
Judah, that sent you unto me to inquire of me; Behold, Pharaoh's army,
which is come forth to help you, shall return to Egypt into their own land.
8 And the Chal-de'ans shall come again, and fight against this city, and
take it, and burn it with fire.
9 Thus saith the LORD; Deceive not yourselves, saying, The Chal-de'ans
shall surely depart from us: for they shall not depart.
10 For though ye had smitten the whole army of the Chal-de'ans that fight
against you, and there remained *but* wounded men among them, *yet* should
they rise up every man in his tent, and burn this city with fire.
11 ¶And it came to pass, that when the army of the Chal-de'ans was
broken up from Jerusalem for fear of Pharaoh's army,
12 Then Jer-e-mi'ah went forth out of Jerusalem to go into the land of
Benjamin, to separate himself thence in the midst of the people.
13 And when he was in the gate of Benjamin, a captain of the ward *was*
there, whose name *was* I-ri'jah, the son of Shel-e-mi'ah, the son of Han-a-
ni'ah; and he took Jer-e-mi'ah the prophet, saying, Thou fallest away to the
Chal-de'ans.
14 Then said Jer-e-mi'ah, *It is* false; I fall not away to the Chal-de'ans. But
he hearkened not to him: so I-ri'jah took Jer-e-mi'ah, and brought him to
the princes.
15 Wherefore the princes were wroth with Jer-e-mi'ah, and smote him, and
put him in prison in the house of Jonathan the scribe: for they had made
that the prison.
16 ¶When Jer-e-mi'ah was entered into the dungeon, and into the cabins,
and Jer-e-mi'ah had remained there many days;
17 Then Zed-e-ki'ah the king sent, and took him out: and the king asked
him secretly in his house, and said, Is there *any* word from the LORD? And
Jer-e-mi'ah said, There is: for, said he, thou shalt be delivered into the hand
of the king of Babylon.
18 Moreover Jer-e-mi'ah said unto king Zed-e-ki'ah, What have I offended
against thee, or against thy servants, or against this people, that ye have put
me in prison?
19 Where *are* now your prophets which prophesied unto you, saying, The
king of Babylon shall not come against you, nor against this land?
20 Therefore hear now, I pray thee, O my lord the king: let my supplica-
tion, I pray thee, be accepted before thee; that thou cause me not to return
to the house of Jonathan the scribe, lest I die there.
21 Then Zed-e-ki'ah the king commanded that they should commit Jer-e-
mi'ah into the court of the prison, and that they should give him daily a

37:5 Ezek 17:15, 16
37:7 Isa 30:1–3; 31:1–3; Jer 21:1, 2; Ezek 17:17
37:8☆ Jer 34:22
37:9 Jer 29:8; Obad 3; Eph 5:6
37:10 Lev 26:36–38; Isa 30:17; Joel 2:11
37:12 Jer 32:8
37:13 Jer 18:18; 20:10; Zech 14:10; Acts 24:5–9, 13
37:14 Ps 27:12; Jer 40:4–6; Mt 5:11, 12
37:15☆ Jer 18:23; 38:6; Mt 21:35; Acts 5:18
37:17 Jer 21:7; 38:14-16, 24–27; Ezek 12:12, 13; 17:19–21
37:18 1 Sam 24:9; 26:18; Jn 10:32; Acts 25:8, 10, 11
37:19 Deut 32:37, 38
37:20☆ Jer 38:26
37:21☆ Job 5:20; Ps 33:18, 19; Isa 33:16; Jer 52:6

37:8 God ordained that Jerusalem would be set on fire by the Babylonians. So certain was this that 37:10 declares that even if Judah defeated the Babylonians and only injured enemy soldiers who lay in their tents, the wounded still would destroy Jerusalem and burn it.

37:15 God nowhere declares that his prophets will be protected against the onslaughts of those who spurn his Word. Jeremiah is seized by the apostates and imprisoned after he has been beaten. His life will be preserved, but his body will suffer. It is better to suffer at the hands of men while engaged in the work of God than to suffer at the hands of God for refusing to do his work.

37:20 Jeremiah implores the king not to send him back to the house of Jonathan lest he die there. When speaking as a mouthpiece for God, Jeremiah was bold. When asking something for himself, he was modest, humble, and uncomplaining. He did not claim that his role as God's messenger entitled him to special treatment. When the apostle Paul appealed to the Roman government, he did so as a Roman citizen. He did not make an appeal on the basis of his role as God's servant, nor did he claim that he should not be bound by Roman law.

37:21 *the court of the prison,* i.e., "in the palace prison."†

piece of bread out of the bakers' street, until all the bread in the city were
spent. Thus Jer-e-mi'ah remained in the court of the prison.

5. Jeremiah Rescued from the Miry Cistern

38 THEN Sheph-a-ti'ah the son of Mat'tan, and Ged-a-li'ah the son of Pash'ur, and Ju'cal the son of Shel-e-mi'ah, and Pash'ur the son of Mal-chi'ah, heard the words that Jer-e-mi'ah had spoken unto all the people, saying, 38:1 Jer 21:8
2 Thus saith the LORD, He that remaineth in this city shall die by the sword, by the famine, and by the pestilence: but he that goeth forth to the Chal-de'ans shall live; for he shall have his life for a prey, and shall live. 38:2 Jer 21:9; 42:17
3 Thus saith the LORD, This city shall surely be given into the hand of the king of Babylon's army, which shall take it. 38:3 Jer 21:10 32:3–5
4 Therefore the princes said unto the king, We beseech thee, let this man be put to death: for thus he weakeneth the hands of the men of war that remain in this city, and the hands of all the people, in speaking such words unto them: for this man seeketh not the welfare of this people, but the hurt. ☆38:4 1 Kgs 18:17, 18 Jer 26:11 Amos 7:10 Acts 16:20, 21
5 Then Zed-e-ki'ah the king said, Behold, he *is* in your hand: for the king *is* not *he that* can do *any* thing against you. 38:5 1 Sam 15:24 29:9
6 Then took they Jer-e-mi'ah, and cast him into the dungeon of Mal-chi'ah the son of Ham'me-lech, that *was* in the court of the prison: and they let down Jer-e-mi'ah with cords. And in the dungeon *there was* no water, but mire: so Jer-e-mi'ah sunk in the mire. ☆38:6 Ps 40:2 69:1, 2, 14 Jer 37:15, 16 Zech 9:11
7 ¶Now when E'bed-me'lech the E-thi-o'pi-an, one of the eunuchs which was in the king's house, heard that they had put Jer-e-mi'ah in the dungeon; the king then sitting in the gate of Benjamin;
8 E'bed-me'lech went forth out of the king's house, and spake to the king, saying, 38:8 Job 29:7
9 My lord the king, these men have done evil in all that they have done to Jer-e-mi'ah the prophet, whom they have cast into the dungeon; and he is like to die for hunger in the place where he is: for *there is* no more bread in the city. 38:9 Jer 37:21
10 Then the king commanded E'bed-me'lech the E-thi-o'pi-an, saying, Take from hence thirty men with thee, and take up Jer-e-mi'ah the prophet out of the dungeon, before he die.
11 So E'bed-me'lech took the men with him, and went into the house of the king under the treasury, and took thence old cast clouts and old rotten rags, and let them down by cords into the dungeon to Jer-e-mi'ah.
12 And E'bed-me'lech the E-thi-o'pi-an said unto Jer-e-mi'ah, Put now *these* old cast clouts and rotten rags under thine armholes under the cords. And Jer-e-mi'ah did so.
13 So they drew up Jer-e-mi'ah with cords and took him up out of the dungeon: and Jer-e-mi'ah remained in the court of the prison. 38:13 Jer 37:21 39:14, 15

38:4 The Judeans thought Jeremiah was guilty of betrayal and treason when he advocated surrender to Nebuchadnezzar. His enemies sought to kill him, but God saved him. Yet he was thrown into an empty cistern with a muddy bottom, into which he sank (38:6, 11–13). Nowhere do the Scriptures say God's faithful servants will escape persecution. Sometimes they even suffer death. Heb. 11:32–37 speaks of suffering. But God promises grace and strength to put up with whatever occurs so that believers can triumph in the midst of adversity (Phil. 4:6, 7, 19; 2 Cor. 1:3–7; 9:8; Eph. 3:20).

38:6 Jeremiah here sinks into the mire at the bottom of the cistern. Humanly speaking, he has no bread and no hope for deliverance. He is left to perish. God intervenes in the person of Ebed-melech, an Ethiopian, who petitions the king for his release. Jeremiah is then lifted from the cistern and placed in the court of the prison (38:13).

38:14☆ 1 Kgs 22:16 Jer 21:1, 2 37:17

14¶Then Zed-e-ki′ah the king sent, and took Jer-e-mi′ah the prophet unto
him into the third entry that *is* in the house of the LORD: and the king said
unto Jer-e-mi′ah, I will ask thee a thing; hide nothing from me.

38:15 Jer 42:2–5, 20 Lk 22:67, 68

15Then Jer-e-mi′ah said unto Zed-e-ki′ah, If I declare *it* unto thee, wilt
thou not surely put me to death? and if I give thee counsel, wilt thou not
hearken unto me?
16So Zed-e-ki′ah the king sware secretly unto Jer-e-mi′ah saying, *As* the
LORD liveth, that made us this soul, I will not put thee to death, neither will
I give thee into the hand of these men that seek thy life.

38:17 2 Kgs 25:27–30 Ps 80:7, 14 Jer 21:8–10 27:12, 17

17Then said Jer-e-mi′ah unto Zed-e-ki′ah, Thus saith the LORD, the God
of hosts, the God of Israel; If thou wilt assuredly go forth unto the king of
Babylon's princes, then thy soul shall live, and this city shall not be burned
with fire; and thou shalt live, and thine house:

38:18 2 Kgs 25:4–10 Jer 27:8; 37:8

18But if thou wilt not go forth to the king of Babylon's princes, then shall
this city be given into the hand of the Chal-de′ans, and they shall burn it
with fire, and thou shalt not escape out of their hand.

38:19 Isa 51:12, 13 57:11 Jer 39:9 Jn 12:42

19And Zed-e-ki′ah the king said unto Jer-e-mi′ah, I am afraid of the Jews
that are fallen to the Chal-de′ans, lest they deliver me into their hand, and
they mock me.

38:20 Isa 55:3 Jer 7:23 11:4, 8; 26:13

20But Jer-e-mi′ah said, They shall not deliver *thee*. Obey, I beseech thee,
the voice of the LORD, which I speak unto thee: so it shall be well unto thee,
and thy soul shall live.

38:21☆ Jer 6:12; 8:10 43:6

21But if thou refuse to go forth, this *is* the word that the LORD hath
shewed me:
22And, behold, all the women that are left in the king of Judah's house
shall be brought forth to the king of Babylon's princes, and those *women*
shall say, Thy friends have set thee on, and have prevailed against thee: thy
feet are sunk in the mire, *and* they are turned away back.

38:23 2 Kgs 25:7 Jer 39:6; 41:10

23So they shall bring out all thy wives and thy children to the Chal-
de′ans: and thou shalt not escape out of their hand, but shalt be taken by
the hand of the king of Babylon: and thou shalt cause this city to be burned
with fire.
24¶Then said Zed-e-ki′ah unto Jer-e-mi′ah, Let no man know of these
words, and thou shalt not die.
25But if the princes hear that I have talked with thee, and they come unto
thee, and say unto thee, Declare unto us now what thou hast said unto the
king, hide it not from us, and we will not put thee to death; also what the
king said unto thee:

38:26 Jer 37:15, 16, 20

26Then thou shalt say unto them, I presented my supplication before the
king, that he would not cause me to return to Jonathan's house, to die there.

38:27 1 Sam 10:15, 16; 16:2–5

27Then came all the princes unto Jer-e-mi′ah, and asked him: and he told
them according to all these words that the king had commanded. So they
left off speaking with him; for the matter was not perceived.

38:28 Ps 23:4 Jer 37:20, 21 39:13, 14

28So Jer-e-mi′ah abode in the court of the prison until the day that
Jerusalem was taken: and he was *there* when Jerusalem was taken.

38:14 Zedekiah could not resist sending for Jeremiah, presumably hoping that this time the prophet would *bring him some good word*. If there ever was a temptation for a prophet to dilute his message, this was the time. Instead, Jeremiah assured the king that Nebuchadnezzar would burn the city unless Zedekiah surrendered to the Babylonian monarch. Zedekiah refused to heed Jeremiah's counsel. So Nebuchadnezzar sieged the city and took it. He then put out Zedekiah's eyes and shipped him off to Babylon.

38:21 God had shown Jeremiah what the alternatives were for the king. If he chose to obey God, he was told what the consequences would be. And if he disobeyed, he knew what God said would happen. God makes the alternatives plain to us by revealing them in the Word of God.

6. Jerusalem Surrenders and Zedekiah Is Captured

39 IN the ninth year of Zed-e-ki′ah king of Judah, in the tenth month,
came Neb-u-chad-rez′zar king of Babylon and all his army against
Jerusalem, and they besieged it.
2 *And* in the eleventh year of Zed-e-ki′ah, in the fourth month, the ninth
day of the month, the city was broken up.
3 And all the princes of the king of Babylon came in, and sat in the
middle gate, *even* Ner′gal–sha-re′zer, Sam′gar–ne′bo, Sar-se′chim, Rab′-sa-
ris, Ner′gal–sha-re′zer, Rab′–mag, with all the residue of the princes of the
king of Babylon.
4 ¶And it came to pass, *that* when Zed-e-ki′ah the king of Judah saw them,
and all the men of war, then they fled, and went forth out of the city by
night, by the way of the king's garden, by the gate betwixt the two walls:
and he went out the way of the plain.
5 But the Chal-de′ans' army pursued after them, and overtook Zed-e-ki′ah
in the plains of Jericho: and when they had taken him, they brought him up
to Neb-u-chad-nez′zar king of Babylon to Rib′lah in the land of Ha′math,
where he gave judgment upon him.
6 Then the king of Babylon slew the sons of Zed-e-ki′ah in Rib′lah before
his eyes: also the king of Babylon slew all the nobles of Judah.
7 Moreover he put out Zed-e-ki′ah's eyes, and bound him with chains, to
carry him to Babylon.
8 ¶And the Chal-de′ans burned the king's house, and the houses of the
people, with fire, and brake down the walls of Jerusalem.
9 ¶Then Neb′u-zar–a′dan the captain of the guard carried away captive
into Babylon the remnant of the people that remained in the city, and those
that fell away, that fell to him, with the rest of the people that remained.
10 But Neb′u-zar–a′dan the captain of the guard left of the poor of the
people, which had nothing, in the land of Judah, and gave them vineyards
and fields at the same time.
11 ¶Now Neb-u-chad-rez′zar king of Babylon gave charge concerning Jer-
e-mi′ah to Neb′u-zar–a′dan the captain of the guard, saying,
12 Take him, and look well to him, and do him no harm; but do unto him
even as he shall say unto thee.
13 So Neb′u-zar–a′dan the captain of the guard sent, and Neb-u-shas′ban,
Rab′–sa-ris, and Ner′gal-sha-re′zer, Rab′–mag, and all the king of
Babylon's princes;
14 Even they sent, and took Jer-e-mi′ah out of the court of the prison, and
committed him unto Ged-a-li′ah the son of A-hi′kam the son of Sha′phan,
that he should carry him home: so he dwelt among the people.
15 ¶Now the word of the LORD came unto Jer-e-mi′ah, while he was shut
up in the court of the prison, saying,
16 Go and speak to E′bed–me′lech the E-thi-o′pi-an, saying, Thus saith
the LORD of hosts, the God of Israel; Behold, I will bring my words upon

☆**39:1** 2 Kgs 25:1–12
☆**39:2**
39:3 Jer 21:3, 4
39:4 2 Kgs 25:4; Isa 30:15, 16; Jer 52:7; Amos 2:14
39:5 Jer 32:4, 5; 52:9; Lam 4:20; 52:8
39:6 Jer 24:8–10; 34:18–21; 52:10
39:7 2 Kgs 25:7; Jer 52:11; Ezek 12:13
39:8 2 Kgs 25:9, 10; Neh 1:3
39:9 2 Kgs 25:11, 20; Jer 52:12–16, 26
39:10 2 Kgs 25:12
☆**39:11** Job 5:15, 16; Ps 105:14, 15; Prov 16:7; 1:1; Jer 1:8; 15:20, 21
☆**39:12**
39:14 2 Kgs 22:12, 14; Jer 26:24; 40:1–6
☆**39:16** Jer 21:10; Dan 9:12; Zech 1:6

39:1, 2 The siege of Jerusalem began in the ninth year and the tenth month of Zedekiah. During the siege no one could enter or leave the city. Famine began as supplies ran low. Verse 2 indicates that the walls were breached by the enemy in the eleventh year of Zedekiah and the fourth month and ninth day of that month. Thus the siege was long and exhausting.

39:11, 12 Apparently, Nebuchadnezzar was acquainted with the role and activities of Jeremiah. He must have known that the prophet told Judah to submit to the Babylonians. This would have won him the king's favor. God protected his faithful servant.

39:16 *Ebed-melech the Ethiopian* had been responsible for delivering Jeremiah from incarceration in the cistern. God did not forget the work of Ebed-Melech. Jeremiah was commanded by God to tell him that he would be saved from the sword because "thou hast put thy trust in me" (39:18). Ebed-melech was a stranger to God's covenant made with Israel, for he was not a Jew. But he was no stranger to the covenant of grace, based on his personal faith in God. This covenant is available to Jew and Gentile alike.

this city for evil, and not for good; and they shall be *accomplished* in that day before thee.

39:17 Ps 41:1, 2; 50:14, 15

17 But I will deliver thee in that day, saith the LORD: and thou shalt not be given into the hand of the men of whom thou *art* afraid.

39:18 Ps 34:22; Jer 17:7, 8

18 For I will surely deliver thee, and thou shalt not fall by the sword, but thy life shall be for a prey unto thee: because thou hast put thy trust in me, saith the LORD.

III. PROPHECIES AFTER THE FALL OF JERUSALEM (40:1—45:5)

A. JEREMIAH'S MINISTRY TO THE PALESTINIAN REMNANT

1. Jeremiah Lives at Mizpah under Governor Gedaliah

40:1☆ Jer 31:15

40 THE word that came to Jer-e-mi′ah from the LORD, after that Neb′u-zar-a′dan the captain of the guard had let him go from Ra′mah, when he had taken him being bound in chains among all that were carried away captive of Jerusalem and Judah, which were carried away captive unto Babylon.

40:2 Deut 29:24–28; Jer 22:8, 9; 50:7; Dan 9:11; Rom 2:5

2 And the captain of the guard took Jer-e-mi′ah, and said unto him, The LORD thy God hath pronounced this evil upon this place.

3 Now the LORD hath brought *it,* and done according as he hath said: because ye have sinned against the LORD, and have not obeyed his voice, therefore this thing is come upon you.

40:4☆ Gen 20:15; Jer 39:11, 12

4 And now, behold, I loose thee this day from the chains which *were* upon thine hand. If it seem good unto thee to come with me into Babylon, come; and I will look well unto thee: but if it seem ill unto thee to come with me into Babylon, forbear: behold, all the land *is* before thee: whither it seemeth good and convenient for thee to go, thither go.

40:5 2 Kgs 25:23

5 Now while he was not yet gone back, *he said,* Go back also to Ged-a-li′ah the son of A-hi′kam the son of Sha′phan, whom the king of Babylon hath made governor over the cities of Judah, and dwell with him among the people: or go wheresoever it seemeth convenient unto thee to go. So the captain of the guard gave him victuals and a reward, and let him go.

6 Then went Jer-e-mi′ah unto Ged-a-li′ah the son of A-hi′kam to Mizpah; and dwelt with him among the people that were left in the land.

40:7 2 Kgs 25:23, 24; Jer 39:10; 52:16

7 ¶Now when all the captains of the forces which *were* in the fields, *even* they and their men, heard that the king of Babylon had made Ged-a-li′ah the son of A-hi′kam governor in the land, and had committed unto him men, and women, and children, and of the poor of the land, of them that were not carried away captive to Babylon;

40:8 2 Kgs 25:23; Jer 41:1

8 Then they came to Ged-a-li′ah to Mizpah, even Ish′ma-el the son of Neth-a-ni′ah, and Jo-ha′nan and Jonathan the sons of Ka-re′ah, and Ser-a-i′ah the son of Tan′hu-meth, and the sons of E′phai the Ne-toph′a-thite, and Jez-a-ni′ah the son of a Ma-ach′a-thite, they and their men.

40:9 2 Kgs 25:24; Jer 27:11

9 And Ged-a-li′ah the son of A-hi′kam the son of Sha′phan sware unto them and to their men, saying, Fear not to serve the Chal-de′ans: dwell in the land, and serve the king of Babylon, and it shall be well with you.

40:1 Jerusalem has been overthrown. Many of the people have been taken to Babylon, where they will remain for seventy years, until the time according to the prophetic word is fulfilled. But some of the people were left behind in the land. Chapters 40–44 depict the history of these people, their calamities, and their blindness to the commands of God.

40:4 Nebuzar-adan suggests that Jeremiah go to Babylon. Jeremiah, who is free to make his own choice, elects to remain with those left in the land. He stays with Gedaliah, who is now the governor of Judah. He lives at Mizpah, the location of which is uncertain except that it was in Judah.

10 As for me, behold, I will dwell at Mizpah, to serve the Chal-de'ans,
which will come unto us: but ye, gather ye wine, and summer fruits, and oil,
and put *them* in your vessels, and dwell in your cities that ye have taken
11 Likewise when all the Jews that *were* in Moab, and among the
Ammonites, and in Edom, and that *were* in all the countries, heard that the
king of Babylon had left a remnant of Judah, and that he had set over them
Ged-a-li'ah the son of A-hi'kam the son of Sha'phan;
12 Even all the Jews returned out of all places whither they were driven,
and came to the land of Judah, to Ged-a-li'ah, unto Mizpah, and gathered
wine and summer fruits very much.
13 ¶Moreover Jo-ha'nan the son of Ka-re'ah, and all the captains of the
forces that *were* in the fields, came to Ged-a-li'ah to Mizpah,
14 And said unto him, Dost thou certainly know that Ba'a-lis the king of
the Ammonites hath sent Ish'ma-el the son of Neth-a-ni'ah to slay thee?
But Ged-a-li'ah the son of A-hi'kam believed them not.
15 Then Jo-ha'nan the son of Ka-re'ah spake to Ged-a-li'ah in Mizpah
secretly, saying, Let me go, I pray thee, and I will slay Ish'ma-el the son of
Neth-a-ni'ah, and no man shall know *it:* wherefore should he slay thee, that
all the Jews which are gathered unto thee should be scattered, and the
remnant in Judah perish?
16 But Ged-a-li'ah the son of A-hi'kam said unto Jo-ha'nan the son of Ka-
re'ah, Thou shalt not do this thing: for thou speakest falsely of Ish'ma-el.

40:10 Jer 35:19; 39:10
☆**40:11** 1 Sam 11:1; Isa 11:14; 16:4, 5
40:12 Jer 43:5
40:13 Jer 25:21; 41:10
☆**40:14**
40:15 1 Sam 26:8; 2 Sam 21:17; Jer 42:1, 2
40:16 Mt 10:16

2. Ishmael Slays Gedaliah

41 NOW it came to pass in the seventh month, that Ish'ma-el the son
of Neth-a-ni'ah the son of E-lish'a-ma, of the seed royal, and the
princes of the king, even ten men with him, came unto Ged-a-li'ah the son
of A-hi'kam to Mizpah; and there they did eat bread together in Mizpah.
2 Then arose Ish'ma-el the son of Neth-a-ni'ah, and the ten men that were
with him, and smote Ged-a-li'ah the son of A-hi'kam the son of Sha'phan
with the sword, and slew him, whom the king of Babylon had made
governor over the land.
3 Ish'ma-el also slew all the Jews that were with him, *even* with Ged-a-
li'ah, at Mizpah, the Chal-de'ans that were found there, *and* the men of war.
4 And it came to pass the second day after he had slain Ged-a-li'ah, and
no man knew *it,*
5 That there came certain from She'chem, from Shi'loh, and from Sa-
ma'ri-a, *even* fourscore men, having their beards shaven, and their clothes

☆**41:1** 2 Kgs 25:25; Jer 39:14; 40:5, 6, 8, 13, 14
41:2 2 Sam 3:27; 20:8–10; Ps 41:9; 109:5; Jn 13:18
☆**41:5** Deut 14:1; Josh 18:1; 1 Kgs 16:24; Ps 78:60; Jer 16:6

40:11 There was rest in Judah under Gedaliah, who was capable and prudent. Jews who had been dispersed all over Palestine returned to Judah and came under the care and control of Gedaliah. Verse 12 *indicates that* some degree of prosperity came, inasmuch as they gathered a goodly supply of *wine and* summer fruits.

40:14 A dark cloud hangs over the infant state under Gedaliah and a storm brews. Baalis, the king of the Ammonites, wants to destroy Gedaliah. He employs Ishmael, a Jew of royal seed, to settle in Gedaliah's territory in order to slay Gedaliah. Johanan, a friend of Gedaliah, seeks to warn him about the plot of which Gedaliah must have had some knowledge. He offers to kill Ishmael. Gedaliah, a peaceful and honorable man, refuses the offer and thinks his friend is speaking falsely about Ishmael, whom, obviously, he must have trusted. Gedaliah had more of the innocence of a dove than the wisdom of the serpent—as the outcome of the plot indicates.

41:1ff Ishmael and ten of his henchmen visit Gedaliah, eat his bread, and then assassinate him without *warning.* They did not stop there. They also slew all of the Jews and Chaldeans who were with Gedaliah at the time. For two days the crime went unnoticed by the people, for it was carried out carefully and was artfully concealed.

41:5ff Eighty Jews from various places came to Jerusalem to visit the ashes of the temple. They devoutly had shaven themselves, rent their clothes, and brought their offerings. Ishmael and his small band slew them and cast their bodies into a pit. Then they took some prisoners from among the people and went to the Ammonites.

rent, and having cut themselves, with offerings and incense in their hand, to
bring *them* to the house of the LORD.

41:6
Jer 50:4

6 And Ish'ma-el the son of Neth-a-ni'ah went forth from Mizpah to meet
them, weeping all along as he went: and it came to pass, as he met them, he
said unto them, Come to Ged-a-li'ah the son of A-hi'kam.

41:7
Isa 59:7
Ezek 22:27
33:24, 26

7 And it was *so*, when they came into the midst of the city, that Ish'ma-el
the son of Neth-a-ni'ah slew them, *and cast them* into the midst of the pit,
he, and the men that *were* with him.
8 But ten men were found among them that said unto Ish'ma-el, Slay us
not: for we have treasures in the field, of wheat, and of barley, and of oil,
and of honey. So he forbare, and slew them not among their brethren.

41:9☆
1 Sam 13:6
1 Kgs 15:17–22
2 Chron 16:1–6
Heb 11:37, 38

9 Now the pit wherein Ish'ma-el had cast all the dead bodies of the men,
whom he had slain because of Ged-a-li'ah, *was* it which Asa the king had
made for fear of Ba'a-sha king of Israel: *and* Ish'ma-el the son of Neth-a-
ni'ah filled it with *them that were* slain.

41:10
Jer 40:11, 12
43:6

10 Then Ish'ma-el carried away captive all the residue of the people that
were in Mizpah, *even* the king's daughters, and all the people that remained
in Mizpah, whom Neb'u-zar-a'dan the captain of the guard had committed
to Ged-a-li'ah the son of A-hi'kam: and Ish'ma-el the son of Neth-a-ni'ah
carried them away captive, and departed to go over to the Ammonites.

41:11☆
Jer 40:7, 8
13–16

11 ¶But when Jo-ha'nan the son of Ka-re'ah, and all the captains of the
forces that *were* with him, heard of all the evil that Ish'ma-el the son of
Neth-a-ni'ah had done,

41:12
2 Sam 2:13

12 Then they took all the men, and went to fight with Ish'ma-el the son of
Neth-a-ni'ah, and found him by the great waters that *are* in Gibeon.
13 Now it came to pass, *that* when all the people which *were* with Ish'ma-
el saw Jo-ha'nan the son of Ka-re'ah, and all the captains of the forces that
were with him, then they were glad.
14 So all the people that Ish'ma-el had carried away captive from Mizpah
cast about and returned, and went unto Jo-ha'nan the son of Ka-re'ah.

41:15
Prov 28:17

15 But Ish'ma-el the son of Neth-a-ni'ah escaped from Jo-ha'nan with
eight men, and went to the Ammonites.

41:16☆
2 Sam 19:37,
38, 40
Jer 42:8, 14
43:4–7

16 Then took Jo-ha'nan the son of Ka-re'ah, and all the captains of the
forces that *were* with him, all the remnant of the people whom he had
recovered from Ish'ma-el the son of Neth-a-ni'ah, from Mizpah, after *that*
he had slain Ged-a-li'ah the son of A-hi'kam, *even* mighty men of war, and
the women, and the children, and the eunuchs, whom he had brought again
from Gibeon:
17 And they departed, and dwelt in the habitation of Chim'ham, which is
by Beth-lehem, to go to enter into Egypt,

41:18
Isa 57:11
Lk 12:4, 5

18 Because of the Chal-de'ans: for they were afraid of them, because
Ish'ma-el the son of Neth-a-ni'ah had slain Ged-a-li'ah the son of A-hi'kam,
whom the king of Babylon made governor in the land.

41:9 King Asa fortified Mizpah to protect himself against Baasha of Israel. Ishmael filled a cistern with dead people. (See 1 Kings 15:22.) Fifty-three cisterns *have been uncovered by excavators at the site of* ancient Mizpah.†

41:11ff When Johanan learned what had happened, he and his followers pursued Ishmael. Before Ishmael rejoined the Ammonites, a battle was fought and the prisoners taken by Ishmael were released. Ishmael and seven of his followers escaped and went back to the Ammonites.

41:16ff Johanan and his company of people planned to go to Egypt. From the human perspective, this was a reasonable objective. Since Ishmael had slain some Chaldeans, Babylon would not tolerate captive peoples' slaying their comrades. Vengeance would soon come.

B. JEREMIAH EN ROUTE TO EGYPT
1. Jeremiah Warns against Going to Egypt

42 THEN all the captains of the forces, and Jo-ha′nan the son of Ka-
re′ah, Jez-a-ni′ah the son of Hosh-a-i′ah, and all the people from
the least even unto the greatest, came near,

☆42:1 Jer 40:8, 12, 13

2And said unto Jer-e-mi′ah the prophet, Let, we beseech thee, our
supplication be accepted before thee, and pray for us unto the LORD thy
God, *even* for all this remnant; (for we are left *but* a few of many, as thine
eyes do behold us:)

42:2 Deut 28:62; Isa 1:9

3That the LORD thy God may shew us the way wherein we may walk, and
the thing that we may do.

42:3 Ps 86:11; Prov 3:6; Mic 4:2

4Then Jer-e-mi′ah the prophet said unto them, I have heard *you;* behold,
I will pray unto the LORD your God according to your words; and it shall
come to pass, *that* whatsoever thing the LORD shall answer you, I will
declare *it* unto you; I will keep nothing back from you.

42:4 Ps 40:10; Jer 23:28

5Then they said to Jer-e-mi′ah, The LORD be a true and faithful witness
between us, if we do not even according to all things for the which the
LORD thy God shall send thee to us.

42:5 Jer 43:2; Mic 1:2

6Whether *it be* good, or whether *it be* evil, we will obey the voice of the
LORD our God, to whom we send thee; that it may be well with us, when we
obey the voice of the LORD our God.

42:6 Ex 24:7; Deut 5:29; Jer 7:23

7¶And it came to pass after ten days, that the word of the LORD came
unto Jer-e-mi′ah.

☆42:7 Ps 27:14

8Then called he Jo-ha′nan the son of Ka-re′ah, and all the captains of the
forces which *were* with him, and all the people from the least even to the
greatest,
9And said unto them, Thus saith the LORD, the God of Israel, unto whom
ye sent me to present your supplication before him;
10If ye will still abide in this land, then will I build you, and not pull *you*
down, and I will plant you, and not pluck *you* up: for I repent me of the evil
that I have done unto you.

☆42:10 Jer 31:28; Hos 11:8; Joel 2:13

11Be not afraid of the king of Babylon, of whom ye are afraid; be not
afraid of him, saith the LORD: for I *am* with you to save you, and to deliver
you from his hand.

42:11 Ps 46:7, 11; Isa 43:5; Jer 41:18; Rom 8:31

12And I will shew mercies unto you, that he may have mercy upon you,
and cause you to return to your own land.

42:12 Ps 106:45, 46; Prov 16:7

13¶But if ye say, We will not dwell in this land, neither obey the voice of
the LORD your God,

42:13 Isa 31:1; Jer 41:16, 17

14Saying, No; but we will go into the land of Egypt, where we shall see no
war, nor hear the sound of the trumpet, nor have hunger of bread; and
there will we dwell:

42:1ff Now Johanan and the people in general be*seech Jeremiah* to intervene with God on their behalf. They want divine approval of what they have already decided to do. Had their relationship to God been right, they could have prayed for themselves or at least have had a common prayer meeting with Jeremiah.

42:7 Johanan and other companions asked Jeremiah to seek the counsel of God for them. God was in no hurry to respond to their request. Ten days went by before Jeremiah received a word from God. The remnant was told to stay in the land, trust God, and not be afraid of Nebuchadnezzar. The perfidy of these people was manifested once again. They had solemnly sworn to obey the voice of God. But when he made his will known, they did the exact opposite, suffering the consequences.

42:10 In verses 10 and 13 Jeremiah lays before Johanan and his followers what the alternatives are. The little word *if* appears twice. He tells them what will happen if they stay in the land and what will take place if they decide to go to Egypt. But he makes it plain that it is the will of God for them to remain in the land. Since they had earlier determined to go to Egypt, what God said made no difference to them. It is an insult to God to ask for his will, when a decision has already been made before his answer comes. Whoever prays with a closed mind might just as well not pray.

42:15 Jer 44:12 15 And now therefore hear the word of the LORD, ye remnant of Judah;
Thus saith the LORD of hosts, the God of Israel; If ye wholly set your faces
to enter into Egypt, and go to sojourn there;
42:16 Jer 44:13, 27 16 Then it shall come to pass, *that* the sword, which ye feared, shall
overtake you there in the land of Egypt, and the famine, whereof ye were
afraid, shall follow close after you there in Egypt; and there ye shall die.
42:17 Jer 44:13, 14, 28 17 So shall it be with all the men that set their faces to go into Egypt to
sojourn there; they shall die by the sword, by the famine, and by the
pestilence: and none of them shall remain or escape from the evil that I will
bring upon them.
42:18 2 Chron 36:16–19 Jer 29:18, 19 39:1–9 18 For thus saith the LORD of hosts, the God of Israel; As mine anger and
my fury hath been poured forth upon the inhabitants of Jerusalem; so shall
my fury be poured forth upon you, when ye shall enter into Egypt: and ye
shall be an execration, and an astonishment, and a curse, and a reproach;
and ye shall see this place no more.
42:19 Deut 17:16 Ezek 2:5 19 ¶The LORD hath said concerning you, O ye remnant of Judah; Go ye
not into Egypt: know certainly that I have admonished you this day.
42:20☆ Ezek 14:3 20 For ye dissembled in your hearts, when ye sent me unto the LORD your
God, saying, Pray for us unto the LORD our God; and according unto all
that the LORD our God shall say, so declare unto us, and we will do *it*.
42:21 Deut 11:26 Ezek 2:7 21 And *now* I have this day declared *it* to you; but ye have not obeyed the
voice of the LORD your God, nor any *thing* for the which he hath sent me
unto you.
42:22 Jer 43:11 22 Now therefore know certainly that ye shall die by the sword, by the
famine, and by the pestilence, in the place whither ye desire to go *and* to
sojourn.

2. The Jews Migrate to Tahpanhes in Egypt

43 AND it came to pass, *that* when Jer-e-mi′ah had made an end of
speaking unto all the people all the words of the LORD their God,
for which the LORD their God had sent him to them, *even* all these words,
43:2☆ Jer 5:12, 13 36:4, 10, 32 38:4; 42:5 2 Then spake Az-a-ri′ah the son of Hosh-a-i′ah, and Jo-ha′nan the son of
Ka-re′ah, and all the proud men, saying unto Jer-e-mi′ah, Thou speakest
falsely: the LORD our God hath not sent thee to say, Go not into Egypt to
sojourn there:
3 But Ba′ruch the son of Ne-ri′ah setteth thee on against us, for to deliver
us into the hand of the Chal-de′ans, that they might put us to death, and
carry us away captives into Babylon.
43:4 Jer 42:5, 6, 10–12 4 So Jo-ha′nan the son of Ka-re′ah, and all the captains of the forces, and
all the people, obeyed not the voice of the LORD, to dwell in the land of
Judah.

42:20 Jeremiah reminds Johanan and the others that they had sworn to do whatever Jeremiah declared to be the will of God. They refused to do so when they heard what they did not like. So Jeremiah prophesies that they will die in Egypt by the sword, by pestilence, and by famine. One would suppose that the gravity of the consequences would have occasioned a change of mind. But it was not so. They went and they were punished, as Jeremiah had prophesied.

43:2 Jeremiah is accused of being a liar. Since his other prophecies about Jerusalem had been fulfilled in a literal way, it is hard to understand the depravity and obtuseness of these people in the face of all the evidence they had. They thought Jeremiah was part of a plot to have them killed by the Babylonians or sent down to Babylon as prisoners of war. Little did they dream that what they thought would happen to them if they stayed in Judea was exactly what happened to them by going down to Egypt. The Babylonians came there and defeated the Egyptians. Thus they did not escape Nebuchadnezzar. The wisdom of men is not better than the wisdom of God. It is better to obey God when all the externals seem to point in the wrong direction. His ways are not our ways, and his thoughts are higher than our thoughts. His way is always best.

5But Jo-ha'nan the son of Ka-re'ah, and all the captains of the forces,
took all the remnant of Judah, that were returned from all nations, whither
they had been driven, to dwell in the land of Judah;
6*Even* men, and women, and children, and the king's daughters, and
every person that Neb'u-zar-a'dan the captain of the guard had left with
Ged-a-li'ah the son of A-hi'kam the son of Sha'phan, and Jer-e-mi'ah the
prophet, and Ba'ruch the son of Ne-ri'ah.
7So they came into the land of Egypt: for they obeyed not the voice of
the LORD: thus came they *even* to Tah'pan-hes.

43:5 Jer 40:11, 12
43:6 Jer 40:7
☆**43:7**

C. JEREMIAH'S MINISTRY IN EGYPT

1. Chaldea to Invade Egypt

8¶Then came the word of the LORD unto Jer-e-mi'ah in Tah'pan-hes,
saying,
9Take great stones in thine hand, and hide them in the clay in the
brickkiln, which *is* at the entry of Pharaoh's house in Tah'pan-hes, in the
sight of the men of Judah;
10And say unto them, Thus saith the LORD of hosts, the God of Israel;
Behold, I will send and take Neb-u-chad-rez'zar the king of Babylon, my
servant, and will set his throne upon these stones that I have hid; and he
shall spread his royal pavilion over them.
11And when he cometh, he shall smite the land of Egypt, *and deliver* such
as are for death to death; and such *as are* for captivity to captivity; and
such *as are* for the sword to the sword.
12And I will kindle a fire in the houses of the gods of Egypt; and he shall
burn them, and carry them away captives: and he shall array himself with
the land of Egypt, as a shepherd putteth on his garment; and he shall go
forth from thence in peace.
13He shall break also the images of Beth-she'mesh, that *is* in the land of
Egypt; and the houses of the gods of the Egyptians shall he burn with fire.

43:8 Ps 139:7 Jer 44:1; 46:14 Ezek 30:18 2 Tim 2:9
☆**43:10** Ps 18:11 Jer 25:8, 9, 11 27:6; 46:13
43:11 Isa 19:1–25 44:13
43:12 Jer 46:25 Ezek 29:19 30:13

2. The Jewish Refugees to Perish in Egypt

44 THE word that came to Jer-e-mi'ah concerning all the Jews which
dwell in the land of Egypt, which dwell at Mig'dol, and at Tah'pan-
hes, and at Noph, and in the country of Path'ros, saying,
2Thus saith the LORD of hosts, the God of Israel; Ye have seen all the evil
that I have brought upon Jerusalem, and upon all the cities of Judah; and,
behold, this day they *are* a desolation, and no man dwelleth therein,
3Because of their wickedness which they have committed to provoke me
to anger, in that they went to burn incense, *and* to serve other gods, whom
they knew not, *neither* they, ye, nor your fathers.
4Howbeit I sent unto you all my servants the prophets, rising early and
sending *them*, saying, Oh, do not this abominable thing that I hate.

☆**44:1ff**
44:2 Isa 6:11 Jer 6:11 Mic 3:12
44:3 Deut 32:17 Jer 32:30–32
44:4 Jer 32:34, 35 35:15 Ezek 8:10 Zech 7:7

43:7 *they obeyed not the voice of the LORD.* In plainest speech, they did not believe what God said. Neither did Adam believe that God would do what he said if Adam ate the fruit of the tree he had been forbidden to eat. Whoever is condemned to everlasting separation from God is condemned because he refuses to obey the Word of God. Jesus said, "Him that cometh to me I will in no wise cast out" (John 6:37). Whoever refuses to come refuses to obey the voice of the Lord. So the counterpoint becomes true: "Whoever will not come to him will be cast out."

43:10 Those who fled from Judah to Egypt thought they would escape from Nebuchadnezzar. Jeremiah now prophesies that Nebuchadnezzar will attack Egypt and destroy it. The Jews will find that they have not escaped from him. God now providentially uses one bad nation to defeat another bad nation. Nebuchadnezzar will burn the houses of the gods of Egypt and he will also carry many people into captivity.

44:1ff In this passage there are no *ifs* spoken by God. He does not lay before the refugees in Egypt a choice between two opposing possibilities. This is a picture of unrelieved judgment spoken to people whose ancestors disobeyed God and who themselves refuse to repent and reform.

5 But they hearkened not, nor inclined their ear to turn from their
wickedness, to burn no incense unto other gods.

44:6 Isa 51:17–20; Jer 7:17, 34

6 Wherefore my fury and mine anger was poured forth, and was kindled
in the cities of Judah and in the streets of Jerusalem; and they are wasted
and desolate, as at this day.

44:7 Jer 9:21; Ezek 33:11

7 Therefore now thus saith the LORD, the God of hosts, the God of Israel;
Wherefore commit ye *this* great evil against your souls, to cut off from you
man and woman, child and suckling, out of Judah, to leave you none to
remain;

44:8 1 Kgs 9:7, 8; 2 Kgs 17:15–17; 2 Chron 7:19, 20; Jer 11:12, 17; 1 Cor 10:21, 22

8 In that ye provoke me unto wrath with the works of your hands, burning
incense unto other gods in the land of Egypt, whither ye be gone to dwell,
that ye might cut yourselves off, and that ye might be a curse and a
reproach among all the nations of the earth?

44:9 Jer 7:9, 10, 17, 18

9 Have ye forgotten the wickedness of your fathers, and the wickedness of
the kings of Judah, and the wickedness of their wives, and your own
wickedness, and the wickedness of your wives, which they have committed
in the land of Judah, and in the streets of Jerusalem?

44:10 Jer 6:15; 8:12

10 They are not humbled *even* unto this day, neither have they feared, nor
walked in my law, nor in my statutes, that I set before you and before your
fathers.

44:11 Lev 26:17; Jer 21:10

11 ¶Therefore thus saith the LORD of hosts, the God of Israel; Behold, I
will set my face against you for evil, and to cut off all Judah.

44:12☆ Isa 65:15; Jer 42:15–18, 22

12 And I will take the remnant of Judah, that have set their faces to go
into the land of Egypt to sojourn there, and they shall all be consumed, *and*
fall in the land of Egypt; they shall *even* be consumed by the sword *and* by
the famine: they shall die, from the least even unto the greatest, by the
sword and by the famine: and they shall be an execration, *and* an
astonishment, and a curse, and a reproach.

44:13 Jer 24:10

13 For I will punish them that dwell in the land of Egypt, as I have
punished Jerusalem, by the sword, by the famine, and by the pestilence:

44:14 Isa 10:20; Rom 9:27

14 So that none of the remnant of Judah, which are gone into the land of
Egypt to sojourn there, shall escape or remain, that they should return into
the land of Judah, to the which they have a desire to return to dwell there:
for none shall return but such as shall escape.

44:15 Jer 5:1–5

15 ¶Then all the men which knew that their wives had burned incense unto
other gods, and all the women that stood by, a great multitude, even all the
people that dwelt in the land of Egypt, in Path′ros, answered Jer-e-mi′ah,
saying,

44:16 Jer 8:6; 13:10

16 *As for* the word that thou hast spoken unto us in the name of the LORD,
we will not hearken unto thee.

44:17☆ Ex 16:3; 2 Kgs 17:16; Jer 7:18; Phil 3:19

17 But we will certainly do whatsoever thing goeth forth out of our own
mouth, to burn incense unto the queen of heaven, and to pour out drink
offerings unto her, as we have done, we, and our fathers, our kings, and our
princes, in the cities of Judah, and in the streets of Jerusalem: for *then* had
we plenty of victuals, and were well, and saw no evil.

44:18☆ Num 11:5, 6; Mal 3:13–15

18 But since we left off to burn incense to the queen of heaven, and to pour
out drink offerings unto her, we have wanted all *things,* and have been
consumed by the sword and by the famine.

44:12 The judgment is final and extensive. The least to the greatest *shall die by sword and by famine.*

44:17 *queen of heaven.* See note on 7:18.

44:18 The point is made that when these Jews had offered incense to other gods and had poured out libations to the queen of heaven, all went well. When they ceased to do these things, circumstances worked against them. Somehow they refused to realize that it was the doing of these things which had first occasioned the invasion of Judah by Nebuchadnezzar. Wicked people will always find excuses to evade guilt and justify illicit actions. Both the husbands and their wives were guilty of disobedience. They ripened each other for hell. While the women kneaded the dough for their sacrifices, the husbands kindled the fire for the offerings.

19And when we burned incense to the queen of heaven, and poured out
drink offerings unto her, did we make her cakes to worship her, and pour
out drink offerings unto her, without our men?

44:19 Num 30:6, 7

20¶Then Jer-e-mi'ah said unto all the people, to the men, and to the
women, and to all the people which had given him *that* answer, saying,
21The incense that ye burned in the cities of Judah, and in the streets of
Jerusalem, ye, and your fathers, your kings, and your princes, and the
people of the land, did not the LORD remember them, and came it *not* into
his mind?

44:21 Jer 11:13; 14:10 Ezek 8:10, 11 16:24 Hos 7:2

22So that the LORD could no longer bear, because of the evil of your
doings, *and* because of the abominations which ye have committed;
therefore is your land a desolation, and an astonishment, and a curse,
without an inhabitant, as at this day.

44:22 Isa 7:13 Jer 4:4 25:11, 18, 38 30:14

23Because ye have burned incense, and because ye have sinned against
the LORD, and have not obeyed the voice of the LORD, nor walked in his
law, nor in his statutes, nor in his testimonies; therefore this evil is
happened unto you, as at this day.

44:23 1 Kgs 9:9 Jer 7:13–15 40:3 Dan 9:11, 12

24Moreover Jer-e-mi'ah said unto all the people, and to all the women,
Hear the word of the LORD, all Judah that *are* in the land of Egypt:

44:24 Jer 43:7

25Thus saith the LORD of hosts, the God of Israel, saying; Ye and your
wives have both spoken with your mouths, and fulfilled with your hand,
saying, We will surely perform our vows that we have vowed, to burn
incense to the queen of heaven, and to pour out drink offerings unto her: ye
will surely accomplish your vows, and surely perform your vows.

44:25 Ezek 20:39 Jas 1:14, 15

26Therefore hear ye the word of the LORD, all Judah that dwell in the
land of Egypt; Behold, I have sworn by my great name, saith the LORD,
that my name shall no more be named in the mouth of any man of Judah in
all the land of Egypt, saying, The Lord GOD liveth.

44:26 Deut 32:40 Ps 50:16, 17 Heb 6:13, 18

27Behold, I will watch over them for evil, and not for good: and all the
men of Judah that *are* in the land of Egypt shall be consumed by the sword
and by the famine, until there be an end of them.

☆**44:27** Jer 1:10

28Yet a small number that escape the sword shall return out of the land of
Egypt into the land of Judah, and all the remnant of Judah, that are gone
into the land of Egypt to sojourn there, shall know whose words shall stand,
mine, or their's.

44:28 Isa 14:27 46:9, 10 Zech 1:5, 6

29¶And this *shall be* a sign unto you, saith the LORD, that I will punish
you in this place, that ye may know that my words shall surely stand
against you for evil:

44:29 Isa 40:8 Mt 24:15, 16, 32

30Thus saith the LORD; Behold, I will give Pha'raoh-hoph-ra king of
Egypt into the hand of his enemies, and into the hand of them that seek his
life; as I gave Zed-e-ki'ah king of Judah into the hand of Neb-u-chad-
rez'zar king of Babylon, his enemy, and that sought his life.

☆**44:30** 2 Kgs 25:4–7 Jer 46:25 Ezek 29:3

D. GOD'S PROMISE TO BARUCH, JEREMIAH'S SECRETARY, THROUGH THE PROPHET

45 THE word that *Jer-e-mi'ah the prophet* spake unto Ba'ruch the son
of Ne-ri'ah, when he had written these words in a book at the
mouth of Jer-e-mi'ah, in the fourth year of Je-hoi'a-kim the son of Jo-si'ah
king of Judah, saying,

☆**45:1** *Jer 25:1* 36:4, 18, 32

44:27 "To those whom God finds impenitent sinners he will be found an implacable Judge."*

44:30 *Pharaoh-hophra.* Hophra, or Apries, ruled Egypt from 588 to 568 B.C. *into the hand of . . . his enemy.* Pharaoh-hophra was killed by Amasis, one of his generals who had revolted and who was then crowned in his place.†

45:1 This message, in point of time, follows chapter 36.

45:2ff☆

2 Thus saith the LORD, the God of Israel, unto thee, O Ba'ruch;

45:3 Ps 6:6; 2 Cor 4:1, 16; Gal 6:9

3 Thou didst say, Woe is me now! for the LORD hath added grief to my
sorrow; I fainted in my sighing, and I find no rest.
4 ¶Thus shalt thou say unto him, The LORD saith thus; Behold, *that* which
I have built will I break down, and that which I have planted I will pluck
up, even this whole land.

45:5 Isa 66:16; Mt 6:25; 31, 32; Rom 12:16

5 And seekest thou great things for thyself? seek *them* not: for, behold, I
will bring evil upon all flesh, saith the LORD: but thy life will I give unto
thee for a prey in all places whither thou goest.

IV. PROPHECIES AGAINST THE HEATHEN NATIONS AND CITIES (46:1—51:64)

A. THE PROPHECIES AGAINST EGYPT

1. Nebuchadrezzar Will Defeat Necho at Carchemish

46:1 Jer 1:10; Ezek 29—32

46 THE word of the LORD which came to Jer-e-mi'ah the prophet
against the Gentiles;

46:2☆ 2 Kgs 23:29; 2 Chron 35:20

2 Against Egypt, against the army of Pharaoh–necho king of Egypt, which
was by the river Eu-phra'tes in Car'che-mish, which Neb-u-chad-rez'zar
king of Babylon smote in the fourth year of Je-hoi'a-kim the son of Jo-si'ah
king of Judah.

46:3 Joel 3:9 **46:4** Ezek 21:9–11

3 Order ye the buckler and shield, and draw near to battle.
4 Harness the horses; and get up, ye horsemen, and stand forth with *your*
helmets; furbish the spears, *and* put on the brigandines.

46:5☆ Isa 42:17; Jer 6:25; 49:29; Ezek 39:18

5 Wherefore have I seen them dismayed *and* turned away back? and their
mighty ones are beaten down, and are fled apace, and look not back: *for*
fear *was* round about, saith the LORD.

46:6☆ Isa 30:16; Dan 11:18

6 Let not the swift flee away, nor the mighty man escape; they shall
stumble, and fall toward the north by the river Eu-phra'tes.
7 Who *is* this *that* cometh up as a flood, whose waters are moved as the
rivers?

46:8 Isa 10:13

8 Egypt riseth up like a flood, and *his* waters are moved like the rivers;
and he saith, I will go up, *and* will cover the earth; I will destroy the city
and the inhabitants thereof.

46:9 Nah 3:9

9 Come up, ye horses; and rage, ye chariots; and let the mighty men come
forth; the E-thi-o'pi-ans and the Lib'y-ans that handle the shield; and the
Lyd'i-ans, that handle *and* bend the bow.

46:10 Isa 31:8; 34:6; Zeph 1:7

10 For this *is* the day of the Lord GOD of hosts, a day of vengeance, that
he may avenge him of his adversaries: and the sword shall devour, and it
shall be satiate and made drunk with their blood: for the Lord GOD of
hosts hath a sacrifice in the north country by the river Eu-phra'tes.

45:2ff Faithful Baruch, Jeremiah's secretary, is down in the dumps. Instead of thanking God that he was counted worthy to suffer for his sake, he is fretful, discontented, and speaking unadvisedly. God told him to forget seeking great things for himself because he was bringing evil on all flesh. But in his sovereign mercy, he was going to give Baruch his life as a prize of war. The preservation and continuance of life are great mercies and should be dutifully appreciated. This is good news and a comfort, especially in those moments when the things we hoped for, the great things we expected, do not materialize.

45:5 All that God promises Baruch is his life. He will not promise him riches or an honorable estate. Everything is uncertain and perishing. All things around him are being pulled down. There is no continuing city here.

46:2 *Carchemish* was located on the Euphrates River, sixty miles northeast of Aleppo. The city guarded the main ford over this river and thus was an important military site. Under the kingship of Neco II, Egypt captured the city and harassed the Babylonians. Nebuchadnezzar and his army fell on the city in May or June of 605 B.C., defeating Neco II, whose armies fled to Hamath.

46:6 The race is not always to the swift nor the battle to the strong (Eccles. 9:11). The swift will not be able to flee and the strong will not be able to triumph. God's judgment is the decisive factor.

11Go up into Gilead, and take balm, O virgin, the daughter of Egypt: in
vain shalt thou use many medicines; *for* thou shalt not be cured.

46:11 Jer 8:22; 30:13 Ezek 30:21–26 Nah 3:19

12The nations have heard of thy shame, and thy cry hath filled the land:
for the mighty man hath stumbled against the mighty, *and* they are fallen
both together.

46:12 Jer 2:36 Nah 3:8–10

2. Memphis and Thebes to Be Sacked

13¶The word that the LORD spake to Jer-e-mi′ah the prophet, how Neb-u-
chad-rez′zar king of Babylon should come *and* smite the land of Egypt.
14Declare ye in Egypt, and publish in Mig′dol, and publish in Noph and
in Tah′pan-hes: say ye, Stand fast, and prepare thee; for the sword shall
devour round about thee.

46:14 Jer 44:1 Nah 2:13

15Why are thy valiant *men* swept away? they stood not, because the LORD
did drive them.

☆**46:15** Ps 18:39 68:1, 2

16He made many to fall, yea, one fell upon another: and they said, Arise,
and let us go again to our own people, and to the land of our nativity, from
the oppressing sword.

46:16 Jer 51:9

17They did cry there, Pharaoh king of Egypt *is but* a noise; he hath passed
the time appointed.

☆**46:17** Ex 15:9, 10 1 Kgs 20:10, 11 Isa 19:11–16

18*As* I live, saith the King, whose name *is* the LORD of hosts, Surely as
Ta′bor *is* among the mountains, and as Carmel by the sea, *so* shall he come.

46:18 1 Kgs 18:42 Ps 89:12 Jer 48:15

19O thou daughter dwelling in Egypt, furnish thyself to go into captivity:
for Noph shall be waste and desolate without an inhabitant.

46:19 Isa 20:4 Ezek 30:13

20Egypt *is like* a very fair heifer, *but* destruction cometh; it cometh out of
the north.

☆**46:20** Isa 34:7 Jer 48:44 Obad 13

21Also her hired men *are* in the midst of her like fatted bullocks; for they
also are turned back, *and* are fled away together: they did not stand,
because the day of their calamity was come upon them, *and* the time of
their visitation.
22The voice thereof shall go like a serpent; for they shall march with an
army, and come against her with axes, as hewers of wood.

46:22 Isa 10:34

23They shall cut down her forest, saith the LORD, though it cannot be
searched; because they are more than the grasshoppers, and *are* innumer-
able.
24The daughter of Egypt shall be confounded; she shall be delivered into
the hand of the people of the north.
25The LORD of hosts, the God of Israel, saith; Behold, I will punish the
multitude of No, and Pharaoh, and Egypt, with their gods, and their kings;
even Pharaoh, and *all* them that trust in him:

46:25 Isa 20:5, 6 Jer 43:12, 13 Ezek 30:13–16

26And I will deliver them into the hand of those that seek their lives, and
into the hand of Neb-u-chad-rez′zar king of Babylon, and into the hand of
his servants: and afterward it shall be inhabited, as in the days of old, saith
the LORD.

46:26 Jer 44:30 Ezek 29:8–14 32:11

3. Israel Will Be Restored and the Enemy Nations Destroyed

27¶But fear not thou, O my servant Jacob, and be not dismayed, O Israel:
for, behold, I will save thee from afar off, and thy seed from the land of

☆**46:27** Isa 41:13, 14 Jer 23:3, 4

46:15 The RSV reads: "Why has Apis fled? Why did not your bull stand? Because the LORD thrust him down." *are they valiant men,* i.e., "Apis" (the sacred bull of the Egyptian god Ptah).

46:17 The RSV translates this: "Call the name of Pharaoh, king of Egypt. 'Noisy one who lets the hour go by.'"

46:20 Egypt is a calf or fair heifer not yet accustomed to the yoke. This may refer to Apis, the bull or calf that the Egyptians worshipped.

46:27 Most of the prophecies of Jeremiah are filled with woe for Israel, the object of God's wrath because of its transgressions. Here Jeremiah speaks the hopeful word that God will someday restore Israel after an end has been made to the nations who have plundered the Israelites. Israel will not be exterminated, only punished in a just measure, looking for the day of restoration.

their captivity; and Jacob shall return, and be in rest and at ease, and none
shall make *him* afraid.

46:28 Ps 46:7 Isa 43:2 Jer 10:24 Amos 9:8, 9

28 Fear thou not, O Jacob my servant, saith the LORD: for I *am* with thee;
for I will make a full end of all the nations whither I have driven thee: but
I will not make a full end of thee, but correct thee in measure; yet will I not
leave thee wholly unpunished.

B. THE PROPHECY AGAINST THE PHILISTINES

The Philistines

47:1☆ Jer 25:17, 20 Amos 1:6 Zeph 2:4
47:2 Isa 14:31

47 THE word of the LORD that came to Jer-e-mi'ah the prophet
against the Philistines, before that Pharaoh smote Ga'za.
2 Thus saith the LORD; Behold, waters rise up out of the north, and shall
be an overflowing flood, and shall overflow the land, and all that is therein;
the city, and them that dwell therein: then the men shall cry, and all the
inhabitants of the land shall howl.

47:3 Jer 8:16

3 At the noise of the stamping of the hoofs of his strong *horses,* at the
rushing of his chariots, *and at* the rumbling of his wheels, the fathers shall
not look back to *their* children for feebleness of hands;

47:4☆ Gen 10:13, 14 Isa 14:31 Amos 9:7

4 Because of the day that cometh to spoil all the Philistines, *and* to cut off
from Tyrus and Zi'don every helper that remaineth: for the LORD will spoil
the Philistines, the remnant of the country of Caph'tor.

47:5 Jer 25:19, 20 Amos 1:7, 8 Zeph 2:4, 7; 9:5
47:6☆ Jer 12:12
47:7 Mic 6:9

5 Baldness is come upon Ga'za; Ash'ke-lon is cut off *with* the remnant of
their valley: how long wilt thou cut thyself?
6 O thou sword of the LORD, how long *will it be* ere thou be quiet? put up
thyself into thy scabbard, rest, and be still.
7 How can it be quiet, seeing the LORD hath given it a charge against
Ash'ke-lon, and against the sea shore? there hath he appointed it.

C. THE PROPHECY AGAINST MOAB

The Moabites

48:1☆ Num 32:37, 38 Ezek 25:9, 10

48 AGAINST Moab thus saith the LORD of hosts, the God of Israel;
Woe unto Nebo! for it is spoiled: Kir-i-a-tha'im is confounded *and*
taken: Mis'gab is confounded and dismayed.

48:2 Isa 15:4, 5 16:13, 14

2 *There shall be* no more praise of Moab: in Hesh'bon they have devised
evil against it; come, and let us cut it off from *being* a nation. Also thou
shalt be cut down, O Mad'men; the sword shall pursue thee.
3 A voice of crying *shall be* from Hor-o-na'im, spoiling and great
destruction.
4 Moab is destroyed; her little ones have caused a cry to be heard.

48:5☆ Isa 15:5
48:7☆ Num 21:29 Jer 9:23

5 For in the going up of Lu'hith continual weeping shall go up; for in the
going down of Hor-o-na'im the enemies have heard a cry of destruction.
6 Flee, save your lives, and be like the heath in the wilderness.
7 ¶For because thou hast trusted in thy works and in thy treasures, thou

---

47:1 *before that Pharaoh smote Gaza.* In 609 B.C., the year King Josiah died.†
47:4 *Caphtor,* the island of Crete.
47:6 Jeremiah longed for peace. He asked when the withdrawn sword would be replaced in its scabbard. The desolations of war were such that peace looked more and more desirable. However, Jeremiah affirmed that war "is the sword of the LORD." With it he punishes enemies and pleads the cause of his own people.

48:1 See note on Ezek. 25:9, 10 for information on the Moabites.
48:5 Similar to the lament in Isa. 15:5.
48:7 *Chemosh* was the god of Moab. Here, as well as in 48:11, the reasons for the demise of Moab are adduced: (1) they trusted in their wealth and strength; and (2) they did not reform themselves in their days of prosperity and peace, for they were undisturbed and they were *settled on* [their] *lees,* i.e., they were corrupt and had been sensual and secure in their depravity.

shalt also be taken: and Che'mosh shall go forth into captivity *with* his
priests and his princes together.
8 And the spoiler shall come upon every city, and no city shall escape: the
valley also shall perish, and the plain shall be destroyed, as the LORD hath
spoken.
9 Give wings unto Moab, that it may flee and get away: for the cities
thereof shall be desolate, without any to dwell therein.
10 Cursed *be* he that doeth the work of the LORD deceitfully, and cursed *be*
he that keepeth back his sword from blood.
11 ¶Moab hath been at ease from his youth, and he hath settled on his
lees, and hath not been emptied from vessel to vessel, neither hath he gone
into captivity: therefore his taste remained in him, and his scent is not
changed.
12 Therefore, behold, the days come, saith the LORD, that I will send unto
him wanderers, that shall cause him to wander, and shall empty his vessels,
and break their bottles.
13 And Moab shall be ashamed of Che'mosh, as the house of Israel was
ashamed of Beth-el their confidence.
14 ¶How say ye, We *are* mighty and strong men for the war?
15 Moab is spoiled, and gone up *out of* her cities, and his chosen young
men are gone down to the slaughter, saith the King, whose name *is* the
LORD of hosts.
16 The calamity of Moab *is* near to come, and his affliction hasteth fast.
17 All ye that are about him, bemoan him; and all ye that know his name.
say, How is the strong staff broken, *and* the beautiful rod!
18 Thou daughter that dost inhabit Di'bon, come down from *thy* glory,and
sit in thirst; for the spoiler of Moab shall come upon thee, *and* he shall
destroy thy strong holds.
19 O inhabitant of Ar'o-er, stand by the way, and espy; ask him that
fleeth, and her that escapeth, *and* say, What is done?
20 Moab is confounded; for it is broken down: howl and cry; tell ye it in
Arnon, that Moab is spoiled,
21 And judgment is come upon the plain country; upon Ho'lon, and upon
Ja-ha'zah, and upon Meph'a-ath,
22 And upon Di'bon, and upon Nebo, and upon Beth-dib-la-tha'im,
23 And upon Kir-i-a-tha'im, and upon Beth-ga'mul, and upon Beth-
me'on,
24 And upon Ke'ri-oth, and upon Boz'rah, and upon all the cities of the
land of Moab, far or near.
25 The horn of Moab is cut off, and his arm is broken, saith the LORD.
26 ¶Make ye him drunken: for he magnified *himself* against the LORD:
Moab also shall wallow in his vomit, and he also shall be in derision.
27 For was not Israel a derision unto thee? was he found among thieves?
for since thou spakest of him, thou skippedst for joy.
28 O ye that dwell in Moab, leave the cities, and dwell in the rock, and be
like the dove *that maketh her nest in* the sides of the hole's mouth.
29 We have heard the pride of Moab, (he is exceeding proud) his loftiness,
and his arrogancy, and his pride, and the haughtiness of his heart.

48:8 Josh 13:10, 17, 21
48:9 Isa 16:2
☆**48:10** 1 Kgs 20:42; Jer 47:6, 7
48:11 Zech 1:15
48:13 1 Kgs 12:29; Isa 45:16; Hos 10:6
48:14 Ps 33:16, 17; Isa 10:13–16
☆**48:18** Josh 13:9, 17; Isa 47:1
48:19 Josh 12:2
48:20 Num 21:13; Isa 16:7
48:21 Josh 13:18; Isa 15:4
48:23 Josh 13:19
48:24 Amos 2:2
48:25 Ps 10:15; 75:10; Zech 1:19–21
☆**48:26** Jer 25:15, 27
48:27 Lam 2:15–17; Zeph 2:8
48:28 Ps 55:6; Song 2:14; Isa 2:19
48:29 Ps 138:6; Isa 16:6; Zeph 2:8

48:10 The Moabites had sinned against God by sinning against God's people. Their destruction is called "the work of the LORD." Whoever does the Lord's work must do it thoroughly and completely, even though it may go against the grain of "compassion for humanity."

48:18 Dibon was the place where the Moabite Stone was discovered. The site is some thirteen miles east of the Dead Sea.

48:26 Here and in verse 42 it is stated that "Moab magnified himself against the LORD." God was being mocked, so judgment had to come.

30 I know his wrath, saith the LORD, but *it shall* not *be* so; his lies shall not
so effect *it.*

48:31 Isa 15:5; 16:7, 11

31 Therefore will I howl for Moab, and I will cry out for all Moab; *mine*
heart shall mourn for the men of Kir–he′res.

48:32 Isa 16:8, 9

32 O vine of Sib′mah, I will weep for thee with the weeping of Ja′zer: thy
plants are gone over the sea, they reach *even* to the sea of Ja′zer: the spoiler
is fallen upon thy summer fruits and upon thy vintage.

48:33 Isa 16:10

33 And joy and gladness is taken from the plentiful field, and from the
land of Moab; and I have caused wine to fail from the winepresses: none
shall tread with shouting; *their* shouting *shall be* no shouting.

48:34 Gen 13:10; Isa 15:4–6

34 From the cry of Hesh′bon *even* unto E-le-a′leh, *and even* unto Ja′haz,
have they uttered their voice, from Zo′ar *even* unto Hor-o-na′im, *as* an
heifer of three years old: for the waters also of Nimrim shall be desolate.

48:35☆

35 Moreover I will cause to cease in Moab, saith the LORD, him that
offereth in the high places, and him that burneth incense to his gods.

48:36 Isa 16:11

36 Therefore mine heart shall sound for Moab like pipes, and mine heart
shall sound like pipes for the men of Kir–he′res: because the riches *that* he
hath gotten are perished.

48:37 Isa 15:2, 3

37 For every head *shall be* bald, and every beard clipped: upon all the
hands *shall be* cuttings, and upon the loins sackcloth.

48:38 Jer 25:34

38 *There shall be* lamentation generally upon all the housetops of Moab,
and in the streets thereof: for I have broken Moab like a vessel wherein *is*
no pleasure, saith the LORD.

39 They shall howl, *saying,* How is it broken down! how hath Moab turned
the back with shame! so shall Moab be a derision and a dismaying to all
them about him.

48:40 Jer 49:22

40 For thus saith the LORD; Behold, he shall fly as an eagle, and shall
spread his wings over Moab.

48:41 Jer 30:6; 49:22

41 Ke′ri-oth is taken, and the strong holds are surprised, and the mighty
men's hearts in Moab at that day shall be as the heart of a woman in her
pangs.

48:42☆ Ps 83:4; Jer 48:26

42 And Moab shall be destroyed from *being* a people, because he hath
magnified *himself* against the LORD.

48:43 Isa 24:17; Lam 3:47

43 Fear, and the pit, and the snare, *shall be* upon thee, O inhabitant of
Moab, saith the LORD.

48:44 1 Kgs 19:17; Amos 5:19

44 He that fleeth from the fear shall fall into the pit; and he that getteth up
out of the pit shall be taken in the snare: for I will bring upon it, *even* upon
Moab, the year of their visitation, saith the LORD.

48:45 Num 21:27–30; Ps 135:10, 11

45 They that fled stood under the shadow of Hesh′bon because of the
force: but a fire shall come forth out of Hesh′bon, and a flame from the
midst of Sihon, and shall devour the corner of Moab, and the crown of
the head of the tumultuous ones.

48:46 Num 21:27–30

46 Woe be unto thee, O Moab! the people of Che′mosh perisheth: for thy
sons are taken captives, and thy daughters captives.

48:47☆ Jer 12:14–17

47 ¶Yet will I bring again the captivity of Moab in the latter days, saith
the LORD. Thus far *is* the judgment of Moab.

48:35 *If God judged Israel for the worship of idols or* false gods, how could he overlook the same idolatry on the part of the Moabites, who were heathen?

48:42 *Moab shall be destroyed.* There may well have been some among the Moabites who believed in the God of Israel. Verse 47 implies this, for the fortunes of Moab would be restored in the latter days. This could not happen if all the Moabites were slain to the last man.

48:47 The judgment against Moab is not a perpetual destruction. God promises restoration in the latter days.

D. THE PROPHECIES AGAINST AMMON, EDOM, KEDAR, AND ELAM

1. The Captivity of the Ammonites

The Ammonites

49 CONCERNING the Ammonites, thus saith the LORD; Hath Israel
no sons? hath he no heir? why *then* doth their king inherit Gad, and
his people dwell in his cities?

☆49:1 1 Kgs 11:5 Ezek 25:2

2 Therefore, behold, the days come, saith the LORD, that I will cause an
alarm of war to be heard in Rab'bah of the Ammonites; and it shall be a
desolate heap, and her daughters shall be burned with fire: then shall Israel
be heir unto them that were his heirs, saith the LORD.

49:2 2 Sam 11:1 Isa 14:2 Ezek 21:28

3 Howl, O Hesh'bon, for A'i is spoiled: cry, ye daughters of Rab'bah, gird
you with sackcloth; lament, and run to and fro by the hedges; for their king
shall go into captivity, *and* his priests and his princes together.

49:3 Josh 7:2–5 8:1–29 Jer 48:2

4 Wherefore gloriest thou in the valleys, thy flowing valley, O backsliding
daughter? that trusted in her treasures, *saying,* Who shall come unto me?

49:4 Ps 62:10, 11 Ezek 28:4, 5 1 Tim 6:17

5 Behold, I will bring a fear upon thee, saith the Lord GOD of hosts, from
all those that be about thee; and ye shall be driven out every man right
forth; and none shall gather up him that wandereth.

49:5 Jer 16:16 Lam 4:15

6 And afterward I will bring again the captivity of the children of
Ammon, saith the LORD.

☆49:6 Jer 48:47; 49:39

2. The Devastation and Dispossession of the Edomites

The Edomites

7 ¶Concerning Edom, thus saith the LORD of hosts; *Is* wisdom no more in
Te'man? is counsel perished from the prudent? is their wisdom vanished?

☆49:7 Gen 36:11, 15 Amos 1:12

8 Flee ye, turn back, dwell deep, O inhabitants of De'dan; for I will bring
the calamity of Esau upon him, the time *that* I will visit him.

☆49:8 Isa 21:13 Jer 25:23

9 If grapegatherers come to thee, would they not leave *some* gleaning
grapes? if thieves by night, they will destroy till they have enough.

49:9 Isa 17:14 Jer 13:26 Obad 5

10 But I have made Esau bare, I have uncovered his secret places, and he
shall not be able to hide himself: his seed is spoiled, and his brethren, and
his neighbours, and he *is* not.

11 Leave thy fatherless children, I will preserve *them* alive; and let thy
widows trust in me.

49:11 Ps 68:5 Zech 7:10

12 For thus saith the LORD; Behold, they whose judgment *was* not to drink
of the cup have assuredly drunken; and *art* thou he *that* shall altogether go
unpunished? thou shalt not go unpunished, but thou shalt surely drink *of it.*

49:12 Jer 25:15, 28, 29 1 Pet 4:17

13 For I have sworn by myself, saith the LORD, that Boz'rah shall become
a desolation, a reproach, a waste, and a curse; and all the cities thereof shall
be perpetual wastes.

☆49:13 Isa 34:6, 9–15

14 I have heard a rumour from the LORD, and an ambassador is sent unto
the heathen, *saying,* Gather ye together, and come against her, and rise up
to the battle.

49:14 Jer 50:14 Obad 1–4

15 *For, lo,* I will make thee small among the heathen, *and* despised among
men.

49:15 Lk 1:51

49:1 See note on Ezek. 25:2 for information on the Ammonites.
49:6 As in the case of Moab (48:47), the destruction of the Ammonites is not their final obliteration. God promises to restore their fortunes at a later time.
49:7 See note on Gen. 36:9 for information on the Edomites.
49:8 *Dedan* was in Northern Arabia and was a flourishing caravan city at the time of Jeremiah and Ezekiel.†
49:13 *I have sworn by myself,* i.e., the decree has gone forth from the lips of God, who has sworn to do this by his own name, for there is no one else to whom God could take an oath because no one is higher than he. *Bozrah,* a sheep herding center in Edom.

49:16 Isa 14:13–15; Amos 9:2

16 Thy terribleness hath deceived thee, *and* the pride of thine heart, O thou that dwellest in the clefts of the rock, that holdest the height of the hill: though thou shouldest make thy nest as high as the eagle, I will bring thee down from thence, saith the LORD.

49:17 Jer 51:37; Ezek 35:7

17 Also Edom shall be a desolation: every one that goeth by it shall be astonished, and shall hiss at all the plagues thereof.

49:18 Gen 19:24, 25

18 As in the overthrow of Sodom and Go-mor'rah and the neighbour *cities* thereof, saith the LORD, no man shall abide there, neither shall a son of man dwell in it.

49:19 Isa 46:9; Jer 50:44

19 Behold, he shall come up like a lion from the swelling of Jordan against the habitation of the strong: but I will suddenly make him run away from her: and who *is* a chosen *man, that* I may appoint over her? for who *is* like me? and who will appoint me the time? and who *is* that shepherd that will stand before me?

49:20 Isa 14:24, 27; Jer 50:45

20 Therefore hear the counsel of the LORD, that he hath taken against Edom; and his purposes, that he hath purposed against the inhabitants of Te'man: Surely the least of the flock shall draw them out: surely he shall make their habitations desolate with them.

49:21 Jer 50:46

21 The earth is moved at the noise of their fall, at the cry the noise thereof was heard in the Red sea.

49:22 Isa 13:8; Jer 48:40, 41

22 Behold, he shall come up and fly as the eagle, and spread his wings over Boz'rah: and at that day shall the heart of the mighty men of Edom be as the heart of a woman in her pangs.

3. The Fate of Damascus

Damascus

49:23☆ Ex 15:15; Isa 10:9; 57:20; Jer 39:5; Amos 6:2; Nah 2:10

23 ¶Concerning Damascus. Ha'math is confounded, and Arpad: for they have heard evil tidings: they are fainthearted; *there is* sorrow on the sea; it cannot be quiet.

24 Damascus is waxed feeble, *and* turneth herself to flee, and fear hath seized on *her:* anguish and sorrows have taken her, as a woman in travail.

49:25 Jer 51:41

25 How is the city of praise not left, the city of my joy!

49:26 Jer 50:30

26 Therefore her young men shall fall in her streets, and all the men of war shall be cut off in that day, saith the LORD of hosts.

49:27 1 Kgs 15:18–20; Amos 1:3–5

27 And I will kindle a fire in the wall of Damascus, and it shall consume the palaces of Ben-ha'dad.

4. The Ravaging of Kedar and Hazor

Kedar and Hazor

49:28☆ Isa 21:16, 17

28 ¶Concerning Ke'dar, and concerning the kingdoms of Ha'zor, which Neb-u-chad-rez'zar king of Babylon shall smite, thus saith the LORD; Arise ye, go up to Ke'dar, and spoil the men of the east.

49:29

29 Their tents and their flocks shall they take away: they shall take to themselves their curtains, and all their vessels, and their camels; and they shall cry unto them, Fear *is* on every side.

49:23 *Damascus* was the capital city of Syria. Then and now it has been an important site which has suffered from one invasion after another. *Hamath,* a city on the Orontes River, more than a hundred miles from Damascus. *Arpad,* some twenty miles northwest of Aleppo.

49:28 *Kedar,* an Arab tribe which came from the loins of Ishmael and lived in the desert east of Palestine. *Hazor,* not the Hazor mentioned in Joshua and Judges (a great city north of the Sea of Galilee), but rather, a group of Arab tribes, located east of Palestine in the Arabian Desert, about which little is known.

30 ¶Flee, get you far off, dwell deep, O ye inhabitants of Ha'zor, saith the
LORD; for Neb-u-chad-rez'zar king of Babylon hath taken counsel against
you, and hath conceived a purpose against you.

49:30 Jer 25:8, 9, 24 27:6

31 Arise, get you up unto the wealthy nation, that dwelleth without care,
saith the LORD, which have neither gates nor bars, *which* dwell alone.

49:31 Judg 18:7 Isa 47:8

32 And their camels shall be a booty, and the multitude of their cattle a
spoil: and I will scatter into all winds them *that are* in the utmost corners;
and I will bring their calamity from all sides thereof, saith the LORD.

☆**49:32** Jer 9:25, 26 25:23

33 And Ha'zor shall be a dwelling for dragons, *and* a desolation for ever:
there shall no man abide there, nor *any* son of man dwell in it.

49:33 Isa 13:20–22 Zeph 2:9, 13–15

5. The Scattering of Elam

Elam

34 ¶The word of the LORD that came to Jer-e-mi'ah the prophet against
E'lam in the beginning of the reign of Zed-e-ki'ah king of Judah, saying,
35 Thus saith the LORD of hosts; Behold, I will break the bow of E'lam,
the chief of their might.

☆**49:34** Gen 10:22 2 Kgs 24:17, 18 Isa 11:11 Dan 8:2

36 And upon E'lam will I bring the four winds from the four quarters of
heaven, and will scatter them toward all those winds; and there shall be no
nation whither the outcasts of E'lam shall not come.

49:36 Ezek 5:10 Rev 7:1

37 For I will cause E'lam to be dismayed before their enemies, and before
them that seek their life: and I will bring evil upon them, *even* my fierce
anger, saith the LORD; and I will send the sword after them, till I have
consumed them:

49:37 Jer 6:19; 30:24

38 And I will set my throne in E'lam, and will destroy from thence the
king and the princes, saith the LORD.
39 ¶But it shall come to pass in the latter days, *that* I will bring again the
captivity of E'lam, saith the LORD.

E. THE PROPHECY AGAINST BABYLON

1. The Destruction of Babylon and the Return of the Jews to the Land

Babylon

50 THE word that the LORD spake against Babylon *and* against the
land of the Chal-de'ans by Jer-e-mi'ah the prophet.
2 Declare ye among the nations, and publish, and set up a standard;
publish, *and* conceal not: say, Babylon is taken, Bel is confounded, Me-
ro'dach is broken in pieces; her idols are confounded, her images are
broken in pieces.

50:2 Isa 46:1 Jer 51:31

3 For out of the north there cometh up a nation against her, which shall
make her land desolate, and none shall dwell therein: they shall remove,
they shall depart, both man and beast.

☆**50:3** Zeph 1:3

4 In those days, and in that time, saith the LORD, the children of Israel
shall come, they and the children of Judah together, going and weeping:
they shall go, and seek the LORD their God.

☆**50:4** Isa 11:12, 13 Ezra 3:12, 13 Hos 1:11 Jer 31:9

49:32 *them that are in the utmost corners,* i.e., "those who cut the corners of their hair."†

49:34ff The kingdom of Elam derived from Elam, the son of Shem. It was located in the region that is now the province of Khuzistan in Iran. The Elamites attacked Jerusalem, were among those who attacked Babylon under Cyrus, and were among the peoples sent by the Assyrians to settle in Samaria after the demise of the Northern Kingdom of Israel. God's judgment against the Elamites was not a final judgment, for they were to be restored. Several Elamites were among those who were present at Pentecost when the Holy Spirit came and multitudes were converted.

50:3 See note on Isa. 13:20 for information about the demise of Babylon.

50:4 This prophetic word concerns the regathering of Israel, a promise not yet fulfilled in history. First the people of Israel must turn to God. Then they will be returned to their land from all parts of the globe. The Jews in Israel today have returned in unbelief, and most of those who call themselves Jews still remain outside of Palestine.

50:5 Isa 55:3 Jer 6:16; 32:40
5 They shall ask the way to Zion with their faces thitherward, *saying,*
Come, and let us join ourselves to the LORD in a perpetual covenant *that*
shall not be forgotten.

50:6 Isa 53:6 Jer 13:16 Ezek 34:15, 16 Mt 9:36
6 My people hath been lost sheep: their shepherds have caused them to go
astray, they have turned them away *on* the mountains: they have gone from
mountain to hill, they have forgotten their restingplace.

50:7 Jer 17:13
7 All that found them have devoured them: and their adversaries said, We
offend not, because they have sinned against the LORD, the habitation of
justice, even the LORD, the hope of their fathers.

8 Remove out of the midst of Babylon, and go forth out of the land of the
Chal-de'ans, and be as the he goats before the flocks.

50:9☆
9 ¶For, lo, I will raise and cause to come up against Babylon an assembly
of great nations from the north country: and they shall set themselves in
array against her; from thence she shall be taken: their arrows *shall be* as of
a mighty expert man; none shall return in vain.

50:10 Jer 51:24, 35
10 And Chal-de'a shall be a spoil: all that spoil her shall be satisfied, saith
the LORD.

11 Because ye were glad, because ye rejoiced, O ye destroyers of mine
heritage, because ye are grown fat as the heifer at grass, and bellow as bulls;

50:12 Jer 22:6
12 Your mother shall be sore confounded; she that bare you shall be
ashamed: behold, the hindermost of the nations *shall be* a wilderness, a dry
land, and a desert.

50:13 Jer 18:16
13 Because of the wrath of the LORD it shall not be inhabited, but it shall
be wholly desolate: every one that goeth by Babylon shall be astonished,
and hiss at all her plagues.

50:14 Hab 2:8, 17
14 Put yourselves in array against Babylon round about: all ye that bend
the bow, shoot at her, spare no arrows: for she hath sinned against the
LORD.

50:15 Ps 137:8
15 Shout against her round about: she hath given her hand: her founda-
tions are fallen, her walls are thrown down: for it *is* the vengeance of the
LORD: take vengeance upon her; as she hath done, do unto her.

50:16 Jer 46:16
16 Cut off the sower from Babylon, and him that handleth the sickle in the
time of harvest: for fear of the oppressing sword they shall turn every one
to his people, and they shall flee every one to his own land.

50:17 2 Kgs 18:9–13 24:1, 10–12 Jer 4:7
17 Israel *is* a scattered sheep; the lions have driven *him* away: first the king
of Assyria hath devoured him; and last this Neb-u-chad-rez'zar king of
Babylon hath broken his bones.

50:18 Isa 10:12 Nah 1:1 3:7, 18, 19
18 Therefore thus saith the LORD of hosts, the God of Israel; Behold, I will
punish the king of Babylon and his land, as I have punished the king of
Assyria.

50:19 Jer 31:10
19 And I will bring Israel again to his habitation, and he shall feed on
Carmel and Ba'shan, and his soul shall be satisfied upon mount E'phra-im
and Gilead.

50:20☆ Jer 31:34 Mic 7:19
20 In those days, and in that time, saith the LORD, the iniquity of Israel
shall be sought for, and *there shall be* none; and the sins of Judah, and they
shall not be found: for I will pardon them whom I reserve.

50:9 *Jeremiah kept the* destruction of Babylon until the last, for it was the last (in terms of chronology) to experience the wrath of God. Isaiah foretold its destruction by Cyrus in graphic terms.

50:20 The day is coming when God's people, Israel, will live in perfect harmony with him. Their iniquity will be forgiven and remembered against them no more. Their sin will be as if it had never been. This same truth lies at the heart of the New Testament. For justification includes the cancelling out of the debt and its being cast behind the back of God, to be remembered no more.

21¶Go up against the land of Mer-a-tha'im, *even* against it, and against
the inhabitants of Pe'kod: waste and utterly destroy after them, saith the
LORD, and do according to all that I have commanded thee.
22A sound of battle *is* in the land, and of great destruction.
23How is the hammer of the whole earth cut asunder and broken! how is
Babylon become a desolation among the nations!
24I have laid a snare for thee, and thou art also taken, O Babylon, and
thou wast not aware: thou art found, and also caught, because thou hast
striven against the LORD.
25The LORD hath opened his armoury, and hath brought forth the
weapons of his indignation: for this *is* the work of the Lord GOD of hosts in
the land of the Chal-de'ans.
26Come against her from the utmost border, open her storehouses: cast
her up as heaps, and destroy her utterly: let nothing of her be left.
27Slay all her bullocks; let them go down to the slaughter: woe unto
them! for their day is come, the time of their visitation.
28The voice of them that flee and escape out of the land of Babylon, to
declare in Zion the vengeance of the LORD our God, the vengeance of his
temple.
29Call together the archers against Babylon: all ye that bend the bow,
camp against it round about; let none thereof escape: recompense her
according to her work; according to all that she hath done, do unto her: for
she hath been proud against the LORD, against the Holy One of Israel.
30Therefore shall her young men fall in the streets, and all her men of war
shall be cut off in that day, saith the LORD.
31Behold, I *am* against thee, *O thou* most proud, saith the Lord GOD of
hosts: for thy day is come, the time *that* I will visit thee.
32And the most proud shall stumble and fall, and none shall raise him
up: and I will kindle a fire in his cities, and it shall devour all round about
him.
33¶Thus saith the LORD of hosts; The children of Israel and the children
of Judah *were* oppressed together: and all that took them captives held
them fast; they refused to let them go.
34Their Redeemer *is* strong; the LORD of hosts *is* his name: he shall
throughly plead their cause, that he may give rest to the land, and disquiet
the inhabitants of Babylon.
35¶A sword *is* upon the Chal-de'ans, saith the LORD, and upon the
inhabitants of Babylon, and upon her princes, and upon her wise *men*.
36A sword *is* upon the liars; and they shall dote: a sword *is* upon her
mighty men; and they shall be dismayed.
37A sword *is* upon their horses, and upon their chariots, and upon all the
mingled people that *are* in the midst of her; and they shall become as
women: a sword *is* upon her treasures; and they shall be robbed.
38A drought *is* upon her waters; and they shall be dried up: for it *is* the
land of graven images, and they are mad upon *their* idols.

☆**50:21** Isa 13:20
50:22 Jer 4:19–21
50:23 Jer 51:20–24
50:24 Job 9:4; 40:2, 9 Jer 48:43
☆**50:25** Isa 13:4, 5
50:26 Isa 14:23
50:27 Ps 37:13 Ezek 7:7
50:28 Ps 149:6–9 Isa 48:20 Lam 1:10
☆**50:29** Ex 10:3 Ps 137:8
50:30 Jer 18:21
50:31 Nah 2:13
50:32 Isa 10:12–15 Jer 21:14
50:33 Isa 14:17
50:34 Isa 14:3–7 43:14 Mic 7:9
50:35 Jer 47:6
50:36 Isa 44:25
50:37 Ps 20:7, 8 Jer 25:19, 20 48:41

50:21 *Merathaim,* meaning "double rebellion," refers to southern Babylonia. *Pekod,* meaning "punishment," refers to a people in eastern Babylonia.†

50:25 When the God of hosts has a work to do, he does not lack instruments to execute his will—whether they be other people, other nations, or just himself. In the case of Babylon, God used Cyrus as his servant. God said "He shall perform all my pleasure" (Isa. 44:28).

50:29 *the Holy One of Israel* God's wrath against Babylon came from Babylon's treatment of God's people. The divine holiness hac been insulted, and the price for this must be exacted.

50:39☆ Isa 13:20
[39]Therefore the wild beasts of the desert with the wild beasts of the
islands shall dwell *there,* and the owls shall dwell therein: and it shall be no
more inhabited for ever; neither shall it be dwelt in from generation to
generation.

50:40 Lk 17:28–30; 2 Pet 2:6; Jude 7
[40]As God overthrew Sodom and Go-mor′rah and the neighbour *cities*
thereof, saith the LORD; *so* shall no man abide there, neither shall any son
of man dwell therein.

50:41 Isa 13:2–5
[41]Behold, a people shall come from the north, and a great nation, and
many kings shall be raised up from the coasts of the earth.

50:42 Isa 13:17, 18; Hab 1:8
[42]They shall hold the bow and the lance: they *are* cruel, and will not shew
mercy: their voice shall roar like the sea, and they shall ride upon horses,
every one put in array, like a man to the battle, against thee, O daughter of
Babylon.

50:43 Jer 30:6
[43]The king of Babylon hath heard the report of them, and his hands
waxed feeble: anguish took hold of him, *and* pangs as of a woman in travail.

50:44 Num 16:5; Job 41:10; Isa 46:9
[44]Behold, he shall come up like a lion from the swelling of Jordan unto
the habitation of the strong: but I will make them suddenly run away from
her: and who *is* a chosen *man, that* I may appoint over her? for who *is* like
me? and who will appoint me the time? and who *is* that shepherd that will
stand before me?
[45]Therefore hear ye the counsel of the LORD, that he hath taken against
Babylon; and his purposes, that he hath purposed against the land of the
Chal-de′ans: Surely the least of the flock shall draw them out: surely he
shall make *their* habitation desolate with them.

50:46 Jer 10:10; Ezek 26:18
[46]At the noise of the taking of Babylon the earth is moved, and the cry is
heard among the nations.

2. The Medes, God's Instrument against Babylon

51:1 Jer 4:11, 12
51 THUS saith the LORD; Behold, I will raise up against Babylon, and
against them that dwell in the midst of them that rise up against
me, a destroying wind;

51:2 Jer 15:7; Mt 3:12
[2]And will send unto Babylon fanners, that shall fan her, and shall empty
her land: for in the day of trouble they shall be against her round about.

51:3☆
[3]Against *him that* bendeth let the archer bend his bow, and against *him*
that lifteth himself up in his brigandine: and spare ye not her young men;
destroy ye utterly all her host.
[4]Thus the slain shall fall in the land of the Chal-de′ans, and *they that are*
thrust through in her streets.

51:5☆ Isa 54:7, 8; Jer 33:24–26
[5]For Israel *hath* not *been* forsaken, nor Judah of his God, of the LORD of
hosts; though their land was filled with sin against the Holy One of Israel.

51:6☆ Num 16:26
[6]Flee out of the midst of Babylon, and deliver every man his soul: be not
cut off in her iniquity; for this *is* the time of the LORD's vengeance; he will
render unto her a recompence.

51:7 Jer 25:15; Rev 14:8; 18:3
[7]Babylon *hath been* a golden cup in the LORD's hand, that made all the
earth drunken: the nations have drunken of her wine; therefore the nations
are mad.
[8]Babylon is suddenly fallen and destroyed: howl for her; take balm for
her pain, if so be she may be healed.

50:39 God ordained that Babylon would never rise again. The site is currently being uncovered and the glories of that ancient city are being recovered by archeologists. There is no evidence that it will ever rise from its present state and become important in the history of mankind. God's judgment was irreversible.

51:3 *brigandine,* i.e., his coat of armor.

51:5 Israel and Judah had been punished but not forsaken forever. Babylon, on the other hand, was both punished and forever forsaken. God's purpose for Israel looks beyond the captivity.

51:6 *deliver every man his soul,* i.e., "let every man save his life."

9 We would have healed Babylon, but she is not healed: forsake her, and
let us go every one into his own country: for her judgment reacheth unto
heaven, and is lifted up *even* to the skies.
10 The LORD hath brought forth our righteousness: come, and let us
declare in Zion the work of the LORD our God.
11 Make bright the arrows; gather the shields: the LORD hath raised up
the spirit of the kings of the Medes: for his device *is* against Babylon, to
destroy it; because it *is* the vengeance of the LORD, the vengeance of his
temple.
12 Set up the standard upon the walls of Babylon, make the watch strong,
set up the watchmen, prepare the ambushes: for the LORD hath both
devised and done that which he spake against the inhabitants of Babylon.
13 O thou that dwellest upon many waters, abundant in treasures, thine
end is come, *and* the measure of thy covetousness.
14 The LORD of hosts hath sworn by himself, *saying,* Surely I will fill thee
with men, as with caterpillers; and they shall lift up a shout against thee.
15 He hath made the earth by his power, he hath established the world by
his wisdom, and hath stretched out the heaven by his understanding.
16 When he uttereth *his* voice, *there is* a multitude of waters in the
heavens; and he causeth the vapours to ascend from the ends of the earth:
he maketh lightnings with rain, and bringeth forth the wind out of his
treasures.
17 Every man is brutish by *his* knowledge; every founder is confounded by
the graven image: for his molten image *is* falsehood, and *there is* no breath
in them.
18 They *are* vanity, the work of errors: in the time of their visitation they
shall perish.
19 The portion of Jacob *is* not like them; for he *is* the former of all things:
and *Israel is* the rod of his inheritance: the LORD of hosts *is* his name.
20 Thou *art* my battle axe *and* weapons of war: for with thee will I break
in pieces the nations, and with thee will I destroy kingdoms;
21 And with thee will I break in pieces the horse and his rider; and with
thee will I break in pieces the chariot and his rider;
22 With thee also will I break in pieces man and woman; and with thee
will I break in pieces old and young; and with thee will I break in pieces the
young man and the maid;
23 I will also break in pieces with thee the shepherd and his flock; and
with thee will I break in pieces the husbandman and his yoke of oxen; and
with thee will I break in pieces captains and rulers.
24 And I will render unto Babylon and to all the inhabitants of Chal-de'a
all their evil that they have done in Zion in your sight, saith the LORD.
25 Behold, I *am* against thee, O destroying mountain, saith the LORD,
which destroyest all the earth: and I will stretch out mine hand upon thee,
and roll thee down from the rocks, and will make thee a burnt mountain.
26 And they shall not take of thee a stone for a corner, nor a stone for
foundations; but thou shalt be desolate for ever, saith the LORD.

51:9 Jer 46:16
51:10 Isa 40:2; Mic 7:9
☆**51:11** Joel 3:9, 10
51:12 Jer 4:28
51:13 Hab 2:9–11
51:14 Nah 3:15
☆**51:15** Ps 146:5, 6; Jer 10:12–16; Rom 1:20
☆**51:16** Job 37:2–5; Ps 18:13; 135:7; Jonah 1:4
☆**51:17** Ps 73:22; Isa 44:18–20; Hab 2:18, 19
☆**51:18**
51:19 Jer 10:16
☆**51:20** Mic 4:12, 13
51:21 Ex 15:1; Isa 43:17
51:22 Isa 13:15, 16, 18
☆**51:25** Rev 8:8
☆**51:26** Isa 13:19–22

51:11 Whether the Medes knew it or not, it was God who "hath raised up the spirit of the kings of the Medes." Men seem to do what they want to do, but according to the mystery of God's providence their decisions coincide with God's decisions.

51:15–18 These verses are identical with Jer. 10:12–16. Moffatt in his translation omits these verses altogether.

51:20 *Thou,* i.e., "Cyrus," who was used of God to conquer Babylon. (See Isa. 44:28; 45:1.)†

51:25 *O destroying mountain* signifies great power. *burnt mountain* refers to an extinct volcano.

51:26 *thou shalt be desolate forever.* This complete destruction of the city of Babylon was accomplished by later Persian kings. Jeremiah here sees the long-range picture of the city's history, and does not confine himself to Cyrus.†

51:27☆ Gen 8:4; 10:3 / 2 Kgs 19:37 / Isa 13:2–5

27 Set ye up a standard in the land, blow the trumpet among the nations,
prepare the nations against her, call together against her the kingdoms of
Ar′a-rat, Min′ni, and Ash′che-naz; appoint a captain against her; cause the
horses to come up as the rough caterpillers.
28 Prepare against her the nations with the kings of the Medes, the
captains thereof, and all the rulers thereof, and all the land of his dominion.

51:29 Jer 10:10 / Amos 8:8

29 And the land shall tremble and sorrow: for every purpose of the LORD
shall be performed against Babylon, to make the land of Babylon a
desolation without an inhabitant.

51:30 Isa 13:7, 8; 45:1

30 The mighty men of Babylon have forborn to fight, they have remained
in *their* holds: their might hath failed; they became as women: they have
burned her dwellingplaces; her bars are broken.
31 One post shall run to meet another, and one messenger to meet
another, to shew the king of Babylon that his city is taken at *one* end,
32 And that the passages are stopped, and the reeds they have burned with
fire, and the men of war are affrighted.

51:33 Isa 21:10 / Joel 3:13

33 For thus saith the LORD of hosts, the God of Israel; The daughter of
Babylon *is* like a threshingfloor, *it is* time to thresh her: yet a little while,
and the time of her harvest shall come.

51:34 Job 20:15 / Ps 137:8 / Isa 24:1–3

34 Neb-u-chad-rez′zar the king of Babylon hath devoured me, he hath
crushed me, he hath made me an empty vessel, he hath swallowed me up
like a dragon, he hath filled his belly with my delicates, he hath cast me out.
35 The violence done to me and to my flesh *be* upon Babylon, shall the
inhabitant of Zion say; and my blood upon the inhabitants of Chal-de′a,
shall Jerusalem say.

51:36 Ps 140:12 / Rom 12:19

36 Therefore thus saith the LORD; Behold, I will plead thy cause, and take
vengeance for thee, and I will dry up her sea, and make her springs dry.
37 And Babylon shall become heaps, a dwellingplace for dragons, an
astonishment, and an hissing, without an inhabitant.
38 They shall roar together like lions: they shall yell as lions' whelps.

51:39 Ps 76:5 / Jer 25:27

39 In their heat I will make their feasts, and I will make them drunken,
that they may rejoice, and sleep a perpetual sleep, and not wake, saith the
LORD.
40 I will bring them down like lambs to the slaughter, like rams with he
goats.
41 How is She′shach taken! and how is the praise of the whole earth
surprised! how is Babylon become an astonishment among the nations!
42 The sea is come up upon Babylon: she is covered with the multitude of
the waves thereof.

51:43 Isa 13:20

43 Her cities are a desolation, a dry land, and a wilderness, a land wherein
no man dwelleth, neither doth *any* son of man pass thereby.

51:44 Isa 2:2 / Ezra 1:7

44 And I will punish Bel in Babylon, and I will bring forth out of his
mouth that which he hath swallowed up: and the nations shall not flow
together any more unto him: yea, the wall of Babylon shall fall.

51:45☆ Gen 19:12–16 / Isa 48:20 / Acts 2:40

45 My people, go ye out of the midst of her, and deliver ye every man his
soul from the fierce anger of the LORD.

51:46 Isa 19:2

46 And lest your heart faint, and ye fear for the rumour that shall be heard
in the land; a rumour shall both come *one* year, and after that in *another*
year *shall come* a rumour, and violence in the land, ruler against ruler.

51:27 *Ararat, Minni, and Ashchenaz.* Ararat (Assyrian *Urartu*) is located in modern Armenia; Minni (*Mannai*) is located southwest of Lake Van; Ashchenaz (*Ashguzu*) is south of Lake Urmiah.

51:45 *deliver ye every man his soul,* i.e., "Let every man save his life" (as in 51:6).

47 Therefore, behold, the days come, that I will do judgment upon the ☆51:47 Isa 21:9; 46:1, 2
graven images of Babylon: and her whole land shall be confounded, and all
her slain shall fall in the midst of her.
48 Then the heaven and the earth, and all that *is* therein, shall sing for 51:48 Isa 44:23
Babylon: for the spoilers shall come unto her from the north, saith the
LORD.
49 As Babylon *hath caused* the slain of Israel to fall, so at Babylon shall
fall the slain of all the earth.
50 Ye that have escaped the sword, go away, stand not still: remember the
LORD afar off, and let Jerusalem come into your mind.
51 We are confounded, because we have heard reproach: shame hath ☆51:51 Lam 1:10
covered our faces: for strangers are come into the sanctuaries of the LORD's
house.
52 Wherefore, behold, the days come, saith the LORD, that I will do
judgment upon her graven images: and through all her land the wounded
shall groan.
53 Though Babylon should mount up to heaven, and though she should 51:53 Job 20:6, 7
fortify the height of her strength, *yet* from me shall spoilers come unto her,
saith the LORD.
54 A sound of a cry *cometh* from Babylon, and great destruction from the
land of the Chal-de'ans:
55 Because the LORD hath spoiled Babylon, and destroyed out of her the 51:55 Ps 69:2
great voice; when her waves do roar like great waters, a noise of their voice
is uttered:
56 Because the spoiler is come upon her, *even* upon Babylon, and her 51:56 Ps 76:3; 94:1, 2
mighty men are taken, every one of their bows is broken: for the LORD God
of recompences shall surely requite.
57 And I will make drunk her princes, and her wise *men*, her captains, and 51:57 Ps 76:5, 6
her rulers, and her mighty men: and they shall sleep a perpetual sleep, and
not wake, saith the King, whose name *is* the LORD of hosts.
58 Thus saith the LORD of hosts; The broad walls of Babylon shall be 51:58 Isa 45:1, 2
utterly broken, and her high gates shall be burned with fire; and the people Hab 2:13
shall labour in vain, and the folk in the fire, and they shall be weary.
59 ¶The word which Jer-e-mi'ah the prophet commanded Ser-a-i'ah the ☆51:59
son of Ne-ri'ah, the son of Ma-a-sei'ah, when he went with Zed-e-ki'ah the
king of Judah into Babylon in the fourth year of his reign. And *this* Ser-a-
i'ah *was* a quiet prince.
60 So Jer-e-mi'ah wrote in a book all the evil that should come upon ☆51:60
Babylon, *even* all these words that are written against Babylon.
61 And Jer-e-mi'ah said to Ser-a-i'ah, When thou comest to Babylon, and
shalt see, and shalt read all these words;
62 Then shalt thou say, O LORD, thou hast spoken against this place, to 51:62 Isa 13:19–22
cut it off, that none shall remain in it, neither man nor beast, but that it Ezek 35:9
shall be desolate for ever.

51:47 God, who used Babylon to punish Judah, will now punish Babylon for its idolatry.

51:51 *for strangers have come into the sanctuaries of the LORD's house.* The Jews never allowed Gentiles to come into the sanctuary of God. There was a court of the Gentiles beyond which none of them could go. (In Acts 21 Paul was accused of bringing Gentiles into the Temple.) Only Jews went into the court of Israel, and only priests went into the court of the priests. Non-Jews and even Jews who had not gone through the rites of cleansing could not enter the holy places. To do so was a crime punishable by death. Obviously non-Jews from Babylon destroyed the sanctuaries of God.

51:59 Seraiah's capture occurred six years after this prophecy.

51:60 Here it would appear that Jeremiah wrote the prophecy concerning Babylon in a book. Nothing is said of Baruch, his secretary. Jeremiah told Seraiah to read the word of prophecy (apparently in a public manner, although it is not specifically stated) and then throw the book into the Euphrates River, where it would sink—thus signifying the destruction of Babylon.

51:63 Rev 18:21
63 And it shall be, when thou hast made an end of reading this book, *that*
thou shalt bind a stone to it, and cast it into the midst of Eu-phra′tes:
51:64 Nah 1:8, 9
64 And thou shalt say, Thus shall Babylon sink, and shall not rise from the
evil that I will bring upon her: and they shall be weary. Thus far *are* the
words of Jer-e-mi′ah.

V. THE APPENDIX (52:1–34)

A. THE REIGN OF ZEDEKIAH

(Events told about in chapter 39.)

52:1☆ 2 Kgs 8:22; 24:18–20
52 ZED-E-KI′AH *was* one and twenty years old when he began to
reign, and he reigned eleven years in Jerusalem. And his mother's
name *was* Ha-mu′tal the daughter of Jer-e-mi′ah of Lib′nah.
52:2 Jer 36:30, 31
2 And he did *that which was* evil in the eyes of the LORD, according to all
that Je-hoi′a-kim had done.
52:3 2 Chron 36:13
3 For through the anger of the LORD it came to pass in Jerusalem and
Judah, till he had cast them out from his presence, that Zed-e-ki′ah rebelled
against the king of Babylon.

B. THE SIEGE AND DESTRUCTION OF JERUSALEM

52:4 2 Kgs 25:1–7; Jer 39:1
4 ¶And it came to pass in the ninth year of his reign, in the tenth month,
in the tenth *day* of the month, *that* Neb-u-chad-rez′zar king of Babylon
came, he and all his army, against Jerusalem, and pitched against it, and
built forts against it round about.
5 So the city was besieged unto the eleventh year of king Zed-e-ki′ah.
52:6☆ Jer 38:9
6 And in the fourth month, in the ninth *day* of the month, the famine was
sore in the city, so that there was no bread for the people of the land.
52:7 Jer 39:2, 4–7
7 Then the city was broken up, and all the men of war fled, and went forth
out of the city by night by the way of the gate between the two walls, which
was by the king's garden; (now the Chal-de′ans *were* by the city round
about:) and they went by the way of the plain.
52:8 Jer 21:7; 38:23
8 ¶But the army of the Chal-de′ans pursued after the king, and overtook
Zed-e-ki′ah in the plains of Jericho; and all his army was scattered from
him.
52:9 2 Kgs 25:6; Jer 39:5
9 Then they took the king, and carried him up unto the king of Babylon to
Rib′lah in the land of Ha′math; where he gave judgment upon him.
52:10 Jer 39:6
10 And the king of Babylon slew the sons of Zed-e-ki′ah before his eyes:
he slew also all the princes of Judah in Rib′lah.
52:11 Ezek 12:13
11 Then he put out the eyes of Zed-e-ki′ah; and the king of Babylon
bound him in chains, and carried him to Babylon, and put him in prison till
the day of his death.
52:12 2 Kgs 25:8–21
12 ¶Now in the fifth month, in the tenth *day* of the month, which *was* the
nineteenth year of Neb-u-chad-rez′zar king of Babylon, came Neb′u-zar-
a′dan, captain of the guard, *which* served the king of Babylon, into
Jerusalem,

52:1 Chapter 52 is much the same as 2 Kgs. 24:18—25:30. It is an appendix showing how the prophetic word was fulfilled; it constitutes a sort of preface to the Lamentations which follow, and it serves as a key to that work.

52:6 During the siege of Jerusalem by Nebuchadnezzar the famine was severe. For what it might have been like one can read of the famine that occurred when Jerusalem was besieged by the Romans in A.D. 50, as described by Josephus in his history of the Jews.

13And burned the house of the LORD, and the king's house; and all the
houses of Jerusalem, and all the houses of the great *men,* burned he with
fire:
14And all the army of the Chal-de'ans, that *were* with the captain of the
guard, brake down all the walls of Jerusalem round about.
15Then Neb'u-zar-a'dan the captain of the guard carried away captive
certain of the poor of the people, and the residue of the people that
remained in the city, and those that fell away, that fell to the king of
Babylon, and the rest of the multitude.
16But Neb'u-zar–a'dan the captain of the guard left *certain* of the poor of
the land for vinedressers and for husbandmen.
17Also the pillars of brass that *were* in the house of the LORD, and the
bases, and the brasen sea that *was* in the house of the LORD, the Chal-
de'ans brake, and carried all the brass of them to Babylon.
18The caldrons also, and the shovels, and the snuffers, and the bowls, and
the spoons, and all the vessels of brass wherewith they ministered, took they
away.
19And the basons, and the firepans, and the bowls, and the caldrons, and
the candlesticks, and the spoons, and the cups; *that* which *was* of gold *in*
gold, and *that* which *was* of silver *in* silver, took the captain of the guard
away.
20The two pillars, one sea, and twelve brasen bulls that *were* under the
bases, which king Solomon had made in the house of the LORD: the brass of
all these vessels was without weight.
21And *concerning* the pillars, the height of one pillar *was* eighteen cubits;
and a fillet of twelve cubits did compass it; and the thickness thereof *was*
four fingers: *it was* hollow.
22And a chapiter of brass *was* upon it; and the height of one chapiter *was*
five cubits, with network and pomegranates upon the chapiters round
about, all *of* brass. The second pillar also and the pomegranates *were* like
unto these.
23And there were ninety and six pomegranates on a side; *and* all the
pomegranates upon the network *were* an hundred round about.
24¶And the captain of the guard took Ser-a-i'ah the chief priest, and
Zeph-a-ni'ah the second priest, and the three keepers of the door:
25He took also out of the city an eunuch, which had the charge of the men
of war; and seven men of them that were near the king's person, which were
found in the city; and the principal scribe of the host, who mustered the
people of the land; and threescore men of the people of the land, that were
found in the midst of the city.
26So Neb'u-zar–a'dan the captain of the guard took them, and brought
them to the king of Babylon to Rib'lah.
27And the king of Babylon smote them, and put them to death in Rib'lah
in the land of Ha'math. Thus Judah was carried away captive out of his
own land.

☆**52:13** 2 Chron 36:19; Ps 74:6–8; Jer 39:8
52:14 2 Kgs 25:10
52:17 1 Kgs 7:15–36
52:18 1 Kgs 7:40, 45
52:20 1 Kgs 7:47
52:22 1 Kgs 7:20, 42
52:24 2 Kgs 25:18; Ezra 7:1; Esth 1:14
52:27 Jer 13:19; Mic 4:10

C. THE DEPORTATION TO BABYLON

28This *is* the people whom Neb-u-chad-rez'zar carried away captive: in
the seventh year three thousand Jews and three and twenty:

52:28 2 Kgs 24:2, 3, 12–16

52:13 Before Nebuchadnezzar and his soldiers destroyed Jerusalem and burned the temple, the glory of God had departed from that sacred house. So far as we know, the Ark of the Covenant was destroyed when the temple was burned. The possibility that the ark still exists somewhere is very remote. The ark without the glory and presence of God might be archeologically significant but it would be spiritually useless. Any person or any thing which is not energized and possessed by the Spirit of God has little value.

[29]In the eighteenth year of Neb-u-chad-rez′zar he carried away captive from Jerusalem eight hundred thirty and two persons:

52:30☆ [30]In the three and twentieth year of Neb-u-chad-rez′zar Neb′u-zar–a′dan the captain of the guard carried away captive of the Jews seven hundred forty and five persons: all the persons *were* four thousand and six hundred.

D. EVIL-MERODACH'S KINDNESS TO JEHOIACHIN

52:31☆ 2 Kgs 25:27–30 Ps 3:3 [31]¶And it came to pass in the seven and thirtieth year of the captivity of Je-hoi′a-chin king of Judah, in the twelfth month, in the five and twentieth *day* of the month, *that* E′vil–me-ro′dach king of Babylon in the *first* year of his reign lifted up the head of Je-hoi′a-chin king of Judah, and brought him forth out of prison.

[32]And spake kindly unto him, and set his throne above the throne of the kings that *were* with him in Babylon,

52:33 2 Sam 9:7, 13 [33]And changed his prison garments: and he did continually eat bread before him all the days of his life.

[34]And *for* his diet, there was a continual diet given him of the king of Babylon, every day a portion until the day of his death, all the days of his life.

52:30 If this is the sum total of the number of people carried off to Babylon (4,600), then the devastation wrought by God's judgment against Judah was extensive. The number of God's people was sharply reduced. They grew in numbers in Babylon, for the Lord God made them fruitful, and the more they were persecuted or oppressed, the more they grew. Thus, the wonder of Jewish survival for the two thousand years since Pentecost must be attributed to God's grace on behalf of his people.

52:31 *Evil-merodach* was the son and successor of Nebuchadnezzar as king of the Neo-Babylonian Empire (c. 562–560). He released Jehoiachin and supplied him with food. Documents found in the ruins of Babylon indicate this to be true. Evil-merodach was assassinated by his brother-in-law, Nerglissar, who acceded to the throne in his place.

THE LAMENTATIONS OF JEREMIAH

Authorship, date, and background The book of Lamentations, until the last several centuries, was attributed to Jeremiah the prophet. Various dates and unknown authors have been assigned to the book by those who do not think Jeremiah wrote it. The book itself makes clear that the author was an eyewitness who experienced what he was describing. Jeremiah was surely the best qualified to fit the circumstances and to account for the contents of the poems. He had been predicting the captivity and the destruction of Jerusalem for forty years before it happened. Beholding the destroyed city, en route to Egypt, his soul was moved with anguish over what had happened and the memory remained with him as he wrote the poems between 586 B.C. and 538 B.C.

The book of Lamentations was one of five books included in the Megilloth (meaning *scroll* or *roll*). The Song of Songs, Ruth, Ecclesiastes, and Esther are the others of the scroll. Lamentations was read publicly on the ninth of Ab at an annual religious festival. The shortness of these five books made their public reading possible at Purim (Esther), Pentecost (Ruth), Tabernacles (Ecclesiastes), and Passover (Song of Songs), as well as the ninth of Ab. Chapters one, two, four and five have twenty-two verses. Chapter three has sixty-six. Part of the book follows an alphabetic acrostic. For example, in chapters one and two each verse starts with a Hebrew letter of the alphabet in order. This cannot be seen, of course, in the English versions. Chapter five does not use the acrostic form.

Characteristics and content Jeremiah, in writing this book, speaks of Jerusalem's former glories and present desolation. The contrast is marked. He acknowledges the righteousness of God in judgment even as the divine wrath is poured out in vengeance for sin. He accepts suffering with the knowledge that God who is the author of good and allows evil is responsive to the contrite of heart. Suffering, however, has its origin in man's transgressions and has for its ultimate purpose bringing the people of God to repentance. Jeremiah's description of the siege of Jerusalem is filled with pathos as he portrays the effect on the lives of the inhabitants. Using words like "we," "our," and "us" in the closing chapter, Jeremiah makes confession for the sins of God's people as he beseeches God to restore them to their inheritance.

Outline

I. The devastation and desolation of Jerusalem (1:1–22)
II. The reasons for God's anger (2:1–22)
III. God's mercy, Jerusalem's only hope (3:1–66)
IV. Jerusalem's lamentation and repentance (4:1–22)
V. The prayer of repentance (5:1–22)

I. THE DEVASTATION AND DESOLATION OF JERUSALEM (1:1–22)

A. JERUSALEM'S DESOLATE STATE

1 HOW doth the city sit solitary, *that was* full of people! *how* is she
become as a widow! *she that was* great among the nations, *and* princess
among the provinces, *how* is she become tributary!
2 She weepeth sore in the night, and her tears *are* on her cheeks: among

☆1:1 Isa 22:2; Jer 31:7; 40:9
☆1:2 Job 19:13, 14; Ps 77:2–6; Jer 2:25; 22:20–22; Mic 7:5

1:1 The Northern Kingdom of Israel has long since been destroyed. The Southern Kingdom of Judah is ruled by the descendants of the house of David, who are still occupying the royal throne. Judah is now following the same path her northern counterpart had followed, one that had led to divine judgment. Judah and Jerusalem are now faced with a similar judgment. The hour for reprieve has passed and destruction and captivity will come upon an apostate people.

1:2 *among all her lovers* refers to Egypt and Israel's other former allies.†

all her lovers she hath none to comfort *her:* all her friends have dealt
treacherously with her, they are become her enemies.

1:3☆ Lev 26:39; Deut 28:64–67; 2 Kgs 25:4, 5

3 Judah is gone into captivity because of affliction, and because of great
servitude: she dwelleth among the heathen, she findeth no rest: all her
persecutors overtook her between the straits.

1:4☆ Jer 9:11; 10:22; Lam 2:6, 7; Joel 1:8–13

4 The ways of Zion do mourn, because none come to the solemn feasts: all
her gates are desolate: her priests sigh, her virgins are afflicted, and she *is* in
bitterness.

1:5 Ps 90:7, 8; Ezek 8:17, 18; 9:9, 10

5 Her adversaries are the chief, her enemies prosper; for the LORD hath
afflicted her for the multitude of her transgressions: her children are gone
into captivity before the enemy.

1:6 Ps 132:13; Jer 13:18

6 And from the daughter of Zion all her beauty is departed: her princes
are become like harts *that* find no pasture, and they are gone without
strength before the pursuer.

B. JERUSALEM'S PAST MEMORIES

1:7☆ Jer 37:7; Lam 4:17

7 Jerusalem remembered in the days of her affliction and of her miseries
all her pleasant things that she had in the days of old, when her people fell
into the hand of the enemy, and none did help her: the adversaries saw her,
and did mock at her sabbaths.

1:8☆ Isa 59:2–13; Lam 1:15

8 Jerusalem hath grievously sinned; therefore she is removed: all that
honoured her despise her, because they have seen her nakedness: yea, she
sigheth, and turneth backward.

1:9☆ Ps 74:23; Isa 3:8; Jer 13:17, 18; Eccles 4:1

9 Her filthiness *is* in her skirts; she remembereth not her last end;
therefore she came down wonderfully: she had no comforter. O LORD,
behold my affliction: for the enemy hath magnified *himself.*

1:10 Ps 74:4–8; Isa 64:10, 11; Jer 51:51

10 The adversary hath spread out his hand upon all her pleasant things:
for she hath seen *that* the heathen entered into her sanctuary, whom thou
didst command *that* they should not enter into thy congregation.

1:11 1 Sam 30:12; Jer 15:19

11 All her people sigh, they seek bread; they have given their pleasant
things for meat to relieve the soul: see, O LORD, and consider; for I am
become vile.

C. JERUSALEM'S SORROW

1:12☆ Isa 13:13; Jer 4:8; 18:16; 48:27

12 *Is it* nothing to you, all ye that pass by? behold, and see if there be any
sorrow like unto my sorrow, which is done unto me, wherewith the LORD
hath afflicted *me* in the day of his fierce anger.

1:13 Job 19:6; 30:30; Ps 22:14; Jer 44:6; Hab 3:16

13 From above hath he sent fire into my bones, and it prevaileth against
them: he hath spread a net for my feet, he hath turned me back: he hath
made me desolate *and* faint all the day.

1:14☆ Prov 5:22; Isa 47:6; Jer 32:3, 5; Ezek 25:4, 7

14 The yoke of my transgressions is bound by his hand: they are wreathed,
and come up upon my neck: he hath made my strength to fall, the LORD
hath delivered me into *their* hands, *from whom* I am not able to rise up.

1:3 Israel was God's chosen people, separated from the heathen that she might not be defiled. Now she sits among those who are aliens to God. She has no rest of mind and is ordered about by tyrants.

1:4 No longer are the roads to Jerusalem lined with crowds coming to worship God or celebrate feasts. The priests, who have lost their jobs, sigh—*longing for the good old days.*

1:7 *Jerusalem* has no one to help her. When God has left his people, who can replace him?

1:8 *have seen her nakedness.* Sin leaves the sinner without adequate covering.

1:9 Jerusalem has been doomed; her fall is terrible to behold. To whom can she turn for help? Jeremiah beseeches God to look on Jerusalem's affliction—having the expectation that he will help her.

1:12 Jerusalem now sees that her plight was not brought about by accident but by design. Great as her sorrow is, the source of that sorrow is God, whose wrath has been poured out on the beloved city.

1:14 *Jerusalem's sins had placed her under a yoke,* not for service but for penance, due to her many transgressions. For believers, the yoke of Christ is easy and the burden light; but the yoke of Jerusalem's transgressions was a heavy one.

15 The LORD hath trodden under foot all my mighty *men* in the midst of
me: he hath called an assembly against me to crush my young men: the
LORD hath trodden the virgin, the daughter of Judah, *as* in a winepress.
16 For these *things* I weep; mine eye, mine eye runneth down with water,
because the comforter that should relieve my soul is far from me: my
children are desolate, because the enemy prevailed.
17 Zion spreadeth forth her hands, *and there is* none to comfort her: the
LORD hath commanded concerning Jacob, *that* his adversaries *should be*
round about him: Jerusalem is as a menstruous woman among them.

1:15 Isa 41:2; Jer 13:24; 37:10
1:16 Ps 69:20; Eccles 4:1; Lam 1:2
☆**1:17** 2 Kgs 24:2–4; Isa 1:15; Jer 4:31

D. THE RIGHTNESS OF THE LORD'S JUDGMENT

18 ¶The LORD is righteous; for I have rebelled against his commandment:
hear, I pray you, all people, and behold my sorrow: my virgins and my
young men are gone into captivity.
19 I called for my lovers, *but* they deceived me: my priests and mine elders
gave up the ghost in the city, while they sought their meat to relieve their
souls.
20 Behold, O LORD; for I *am* in distress: my bowels are troubled; mine
heart is turned within me; for I have grievously rebelled: abroad the sword
bereaveth, at home *there is* as death.
21 They have heard that I sigh: *there is* none to comfort me: all mine
enemies have heard of my trouble; they are glad that thou hast done *it:*
thou wilt bring the day *that* thou hast called, and they shall be like unto me.
22 Let all their wickedness come before thee; and do unto them, as thou
hast done unto me for all my transgressions: for my sighs *are* many, and my
heart *is* faint.

1:18 Deut 28:32, 41; 1 Sam 12:14, 15; Ps 119:75; Jer 12:1
☆**1:19** Job 19:13–19; Jer 14:15; Lam 1:2; 2:20
1:20 Isa 16:11; Jer 4:19
1:21 Ps 35:15; Isa 14:5, 6; 47:6; Jer 30:16
☆**1:22** Neh 4:4, 5; Ps 137:7, 8

II. THE REASONS FOR GOD'S ANGER (2:1–22)

A. GOD'S DESTRUCTION OF JERUSALEM

2 HOW hath the Lord covered the daughter of Zion with a cloud in his
anger, *and* cast down from heaven unto the earth the beauty of Israel,
and remembered not his footstool in the day of his anger!
2 The Lord hath swallowed up all the habitations of Jacob, and hath not
pitied: he hath thrown down in his wrath the strong holds of the daughter
of Judah; he hath brought *them* down to the ground: he hath polluted the
kingdom and the princes thereof.
3 He hath cut off in *his* fierce anger all the horn of Israel: he hath drawn
back his right hand from before the enemy, and he burned against Jacob
like a flaming fire, *which* devoureth round about.
4 He hath bent his bow like an enemy: he stood with his right hand as an
adversary, and slew all *that were* pleasant to the eye in the tabernacle of the
daughter of Zion: he poured out his fury like fire.
5 The Lord was as an enemy: he hath swallowed up Israel, he hath

2:1 Ps 99:5; 132:7; Isa 64:11; Ezek 28:14–16
2:2 Ps 21:9; 89:39, 40; Lam 3:43
2:3 Ps 75:5, 10; Isa 42:25; Jer 21:14
2:4 Job 6:4; 16:13; Jer 7:20
☆**2:5** Jer 52:13; Lam 2:2

1:17 *Zion spreadeth forth her hands,* i.e., "Zion throws up her arms in distress and despair." Her God has withdrawn from her, so she has no comforter. Her former friends have failed her. She reaches forth for help and there is none from those fickle friends. Zion is learning what the absence of God means, and God's refusal to come to her aid must lead to still further woes.

1:19 Jerusalem called to her lovers, Assyria and Egypt, but they deceived her and turned their eyes from her in the hour of adversity. Priests and elders, who should have been leading the people, died of hunger and served no one.

1:22 This is a prayer of imprecation which declares that *God will do to the enemies* of Jerusalem what he has done to Jerusalem itself. Our prayers must agree with God's Word. When God has pronounced judgment against the nations for their failure to repent and glorify him, we may pray that God's pronouncement be brought to pass.

2:5 *The LORD was as an enemy.* The God who had been their best friend has become their enemy. His love no longer is present among them and his power to overcome their foes is no longer available. Whoever chooses to live without God must suffer the consequences of that evil decision.

swallowed up all her palaces: he hath destroyed his strong holds, and hath
increased in the daughter of Judah mourning and lamentation.

2:6 Lam 1:4; Zeph 3:18

6 And he hath violently taken away his tabernacle, as *if it were of* a
garden: he hath destroyed his places of the assembly: the LORD hath caused
the solemn feasts and sabbaths to be forgotten in Zion, and hath despised
in the indignation of his anger the king and the priest.

2:7 Ps 74:3–8; Isa 64:11; Ezek 7:20–22

7 The Lord hath cast off his altar, he hath abhorred his sanctuary, he hath
given up into the hand of the enemy the walls of her palaces; they have
made a noise in the house of the LORD, as in the day of a solemn feast.

2:8 2 Kgs 21:13; Isa 34:11; Amos 7:7–9

8 The LORD hath purposed to destroy the wall of the daughter of Zion: he
hath stretched out a line, he hath not withdrawn his hand from destroying:
therefore he made the rampart and the wall to lament; they languished
together.

2:9☆ Neh 1:3; Jer 23:16

9 Her gates are sunk into the ground; he hath destroyed and broken her
bars: her king and her princes *are* among the Gentiles: the law *is* no *more;*
her prophets also find no vision from the LORD.

2:10 Job 2:13; Isa 3:26; Amos 8:3; Jonah 3:6–8

10 The elders of the daughter of Zion sit upon the ground, *and* keep
silence: they have cast up dust upon their heads; they have girded
themselves with sackcloth: the virgins of Jerusalem hang down their heads
to the ground.

B. DESIRE FOR CONSOLATION

2:11 Job 16:13; Jer 4:19; Lam 2:19

11 Mine eyes do fail with tears, my bowels are troubled, my liver is poured
upon the earth, for the destruction of the daughter of my people; because
the children and the sucklings swoon in the streets of the city.

2:12 Job 30:16; Ps 42:4

12 They say to their mothers, Where *is* corn and wine? when they swooned
as the wounded in the streets of the city, when their soul was poured out
into their mothers' bosom.

2:13 Lam 1:12

13 What thing shall I take to witness for thee? what thing shall I liken to
thee, O daughter of Jerusalem? what shall I equal to thee, that I may
comfort thee, O virgin daughter of Zion? for thy breach *is* great like the sea:
who can heal thee?

2:14☆ Ezek 22:25, 28; 23:36; Mic 3:8

14 Thy prophets have seen vain and foolish things for thee: and they have
not discovered thine iniquity, to turn away thy captivity; but have seen for
thee false burdens and causes of banishment.

2:15☆ Job 27:23; Ps 48:2; 50:2; Jer 18:16

15 All that pass by clap *their* hands at thee; they hiss and wag their head
at the daughter of Jerusalem, *saying, Is* this the city that *men* call The
perfection of beauty, The joy of the whole earth?

2:16 Ps 56:2; Lam 3:46; Obad 12–15

16 All thine enemies have opened their mouth against thee: they hiss and
gnash the teeth: they say, We have swallowed *her* up: certainly this *is* the
day that we looked for; we have found, we have seen *it.*

2:17 Deut 28:43, 44; Ps 89:42; Lam 1:5

17 The LORD hath done *that* which he had devised; he hath fulfilled his
word that he had commanded in the days of old: he hath thrown down, and
hath not pitied: and he hath caused *thine* enemy to rejoice over thee, he
hath set up the horn of thine adversaries.

2:18 Ps 119:145; Lam 2:8; Hos 7:14; Hab 2:11

18 Their heart cried unto the Lord, O wall of the daughter of Zion, let

---

2:9 God had always used prophets to whom were given visions or dreams. Now his people shall have no *more prophets and no more visions*, for they had persecuted the prophets he had sent and despised the visions he had given the prophets. Let them seek the faces of their false prophets in whom they had trusted.
2:14 As always, there will be false and true prophets. False prophets tell people what they want to hear, not what they need to hear. Their promise of good things and easy times allure those whose deeds are evil and who seek to justify themselves. Because false prophets claim to speak in the name of God, they are more welcome with their sweet words than true prophets with their stern and unyielding denouncements of the people's sins.
2:15 Jerusalem is now laid waste and depopulated.

tears run down like a river day and night: give thyself no rest; let not the
apple of thine eye cease.
19 Arise, cry out in the night: in the beginning of the watches pour out
thine heart like water before the face of the Lord: lift up thy hands toward
him for the life of thy young children, that faint for hunger in the top of
every street.
20 ¶Behold, O LORD, and consider to whom thou hast done this. Shall the
women eat their fruit, *and* children of a span long? shall the priest and the
prophet be slain in the sanctuary of the Lord?
21 The young and the old lie on the ground in the streets: my virgins and
my young men are fallen by the sword; thou hast slain *them* in the day of
thine anger; thou hast killed, *and* not pitied.
22 Thou hast called as in a solemn day my terrors round about, so that in
the day of the LORD's anger none escaped nor remained: those that I have
swaddled and brought up hath mine enemy consumed.

2:19 1 Sam 1:15; Ps 42:3, 4; Isa 51:20
☆2:20 Ex 32:11; Deut 9:26; Ps 78:64; Jer 23:11, 12; Lam 4:13, 16
2:21 2 Chron 36:17; Jer 6:11
2:22 Ps 31:13; Isa 24:17, 18; Jer 16:2–4

III. GOD'S MERCY, JERUSALEM'S ONLY HOPE (3:1–66)

A. LAMENT OVER JERUSALEM'S DOWNFALL

3 I *AM* the man *that* hath seen affliction by the rod of his wrath.
2 He hath led me, and brought *me into* darkness, but not *into* light.
3 Surely against me is he turned; he turneth his hand *against me* all the
day.
4 My flesh and my skin hath he made old; he hath broken my bones.
5 He hath builded against me, and compassed *me* with gall and travail.
6 He hath set me in dark places, as *they that be* dead of old.
7 He hath hedged me about, that I cannot get out: he hath made my chain
heavy.
8 Also when I cry and shout, he shutteth out my prayer.
9 He hath inclosed my ways with hewn stone, he hath made my paths
crooked.
10 He *was* unto me *as* a bear lying in wait, *and as* a lion in secret places.
11 He hath turned aside my ways, and pulled me in pieces: he hath made
me desolate.
12 He hath bent his bow, and set me as a mark for the arrow.
13 He hath caused the arrows of his quiver to enter into my reins.
14 I was a derision to all my people; *and* their song all the day.
15 He hath filled me with bitterness, he hath made me drunken with
wormwood.
16 He hath also broken my teeth with gravel stones, he hath covered me
with ashes.
17 And thou hast removed my soul far off from peace: I forgat prosperity.
18 And I said, My strength and my hope is perished from the LORD.

☆3:2 Isa 59:9; Jer 4:23
3:3 Ps 38:2; Isa 5:25
3:4 Ps 31:9, 10; 38:2–8; Jer 50:17
3:5 Job 19:8; Ps 69:21; Jer 23:15
3:6 Ps 88:5, 6; 143:3
3:7 Job 3:23; Jer 40:4
3:8 Job 30:20; Ps 22:2
☆3:9 Isa 63:17
3:10 Job 10:16
3:11 Job 16:12, 13; Hos 6:1
3:12 Ps 7:12, 13
3:14 Ps 22:6, 7; Lam 3:63
☆3:16 Ps 3:7; Prov 20:17
3:17 Isa 59:11; Jer 12:12
☆3:18 Job 17:15; Ezek 37:11

2:20 *Shall the women eat their . . . children?* The famine produced inhuman conditions.

3:2 The word *he* is used many times in verses 2 to 16. He, i.e. God, had brought great evils upon Jerusalem. The divine patience had been exhausted, and when that happened, divine judgment fell. It took visible form in the ways described in these verses.

3:9 *inclosed my ways with hewn stone,* i.e., "he has built a wall that I cannot go through or circle around or climb over." Whatever way Jerusalem sought to go, she was frustrated.

3:16 God has mingled gravel with bread and the teeth of the eater are broken. What is eaten is neither pleasant nor nourishing. Some interpret the phrase *he hath covered me with ashes* to mean "he has fed me with ashes." Ps. 102:9 says: "For I have eaten ashes like bread."

3:18 Jeremiah pictures Jerusalem as saying that God has ceased to be available, and he offers no encouragement to her to come to him. There is no remedy. Whatever anyone may think and no matter how backslidden the case, God is still the only never-failing help to those in trouble.

3:19 Lam 3:5, 15
19 Remembering mine affliction and my misery, the wormwood and the
gall.
3:20 Ps 42:5, 6, 11; 43:5
20 My soul hath *them* still in remembrance, and is humbled in me.

B. GOD'S FAITHFULNESS TO THE REPENTANT

3:21 Ps 130:7
3:22☆ Ps 78:38; Jer 3:12; Mal 3:6
3:24 Ps 73:26
3:25 Isa 25:9; 26:9

21 This I recall to my mind, therefore have I hope.
22 *It is of* the LORD's mercies that we are not consumed, because his
compassions fail not.
23 *They are* new every morning: great *is* thy faithfulness.
24 The LORD *is* my portion, saith my soul; therefore will I hope in him.
25 The LORD *is* good unto them that wait for him, to the soul *that* seeketh
him.
26 *It is* good that *a man* should both hope and quietly wait for the
salvation of the LORD.
27 *It is* good for a man that he bear the yoke in his youth.
28 He sitteth alone and keepeth silence, because he hath borne *it* upon
him.

3:29 Job 16:15; 40:4
3:30 Job 16:10; Isa 50:6; Mt 5:39
3:31☆ Ps 94:14; Isa 54:7–10
3:32☆ Ps 106:43–45; Hos 11:8

29 He putteth his mouth in the dust; if so be there may be hope.
30 He giveth *his* cheek to him that smiteth him: he is filled full with
reproach.
31 For the Lord will not cast off for ever:
32 But though he cause grief, yet will he have compassion according to the
multitude of his mercies.
33 For he doth not afflict willingly nor grieve the children of men.

C. GOD HELPS ONE AND HARMS THE OTHER

3:35 Prov 17:15
3:36 Jer 22:3; Hab 1:13
3:37☆
3:38 Job 2:10; Jer 32:42

34 To crush under his feet all the prisoners of the earth,
35 To turn aside the right of a man before the face of the most High,
36 To subvert a man in his cause, the Lord approveth not.
37 ¶Who *is* he *that* saith, and it cometh to pass, *when* the Lord command-
eth *it* not?
38 Out of the mouth of the most High proceedeth not evil and good?

D. JERUSALEM PLEADS FOR GOD'S MERCY

3:39☆ Mic 7:2; Heb 12:5, 6
3:40 Ps 119:59; 139:23, 24; 2 Cor 13:5
3:41 Ps 25:1; 141:2

39 Wherefore doth a living man complain, a man for the punishment of his
sins?
40 Let us search and try our ways, and turn again to the LORD.
41 Let us lift up our heart with *our* hands unto God in the heavens.

3:22 In suffering we must look to God. Here is a word of hope. Some are afflicted by the rod of God's wrath, but because of the Lord's mercies, they are not consumed. Therefore let those who are beaten by the rod of wrath turn quickly to the God of grace in the hope that restoration will take place.

3:31, 32 He who is penitent must also be patient until God's deliverance comes. While he waits, he must ever say that God is gracious and merciful. This knowledge produces hope and leads to genuine repentance.

3:37 The Babylonians *said they would destroy Jerusalem and it came* to pass. However, it did not come to pass because Nebuchadnezzar and his leaders said it, but because God commanded it and commissioned the Chaldeans to do it.

3:38 This verse does not imply that God is the author of sin. It does speak about evils such as sickness, punishments for sins, and the like. In this sense, both good and evil are ordained and appointed by God. We are to be reconciled to those evils which come upon us, not because we have sinned, but because God wishes to purify us. And if we suffer because of our transgressions, let us accept the reproof meekly, look to God in repentance, and wait for the hand of God to lift the burden and give us peace of heart.

3:39 Do sinners who are being punished for their transgressions have a right to complain? Do they have *a right to* impugn God, who has sentenced them to difficulties? A believer has every right to pour out his complaints *before* the Lord, so long as he does not say that his complaints are *against* God. Sinful men must not quarrel with God, for his ways are pure, just, holy, and according to truth.

42 We have transgressed and have rebelled: thou hast not pardoned.
43 Thou hast covered with anger, and persecuted us: thou hast slain, thou
hast not pitied.
44 Thou hast covered thyself with a cloud, that *our* prayer should not pass
through.
45 Thou hast made us *as* the offscouring and refuse in the midst of the
people.
46 All our enemies have opened their mouths against us.
47 Fear and a snare is come upon us, desolation and destruction.
48 Mine eye runneth down with rivers of water for the destruction of the
daughter of my people.
49 Mine eye trickleth down, and ceaseth not, without any intermission,
50 Till the LORD look down, and behold from heaven.
51 Mine eye affecteth mine heart because of all the daughters of my city.
52 Mine enemies chased me sore, like a bird, without cause.
53 They have cut off my life in the dungeon, and cast a stone upon me.
54 Waters flowed over mine head; *then* I said, I am cut off.
55 I called upon thy name, O LORD, out of the low dungeon.
56 Thou hast heard my voice: hide not thine ear at my breathing, at my
cry.
57 Thou drewest near in the day *that* I called upon thee: thou saidst, Fear
not.
58 O Lord, thou hast pleaded the causes of my soul; thou hast redeemed
my life.
59 O LORD, thou hast seen my wrong: judge thou my cause.
60 Thou hast seen all their vengeance *and* all their imaginations against
me.
61 Thou hast heard their reproach, O LORD, *and* all their imaginations
against me;
62 The lips of those that rose up against me, and their device against me
all the day.
63 Behold their sitting down, and their rising up; I *am* their musick.
64 ¶Render unto them a recompence, O LORD, according to the work of
their hands.
65 Give them sorrow of heart, thy curse unto them.
66 Persecute and destroy them in anger from under the heavens of the
LORD.

IV. JERUSALEM'S LAMENTATION AND REPENTANCE (4:1–22)

A. JERUSALEM'S FORMER GLORY; ITS LATTER CONDITION

4 HOW is the gold become dim! *how* is the most fine gold changed! the
stones of the sanctuary are poured out in the top of every street.
2 The precious sons of Zion, comparable to fine gold, how are they
esteemed as earthen pitchers, the work of the hands of the potter!
3 Even the sea monsters draw out the breast, they give suck to their young

☆**3:42** Neh 9:26; Jer 14:20
3:44 Lam 3:8
3:46 Lam 2:16
3:47 Isa 24:17, 18; Jer 48:43, 44
3:49 Ps 77:2; Lam 2:11
3:50 Isa 63:15
3:52 1 Sam 26:20; Ps 11:1
3:54 Jonah 2:3–5
☆**3:55**
3:56 Job 34:28; Ps 55:1; 116:12
☆**3:57** Josh 1:6; Isa 41:10, 14
3:58 Ps 34:22; Jer 50:34; 51:36
3:59 Ps 26:1; 43:1
3:61 Lam 5:1
3:62 Ps 59:7; 140:3; Ezek 36:3
3:63 Lam 3:14
3:64 Ps 28:4; Jer 51:24
3:65 Deut 2:30; Isa 6:10
☆**4:1** 2 Kgs 25:9, 10
4:2 Isa 30:14; Jer 19:1, 11
4:3 Job 39:14–16; Lam 2:12

3:42 The question is asked why bondage continues after the offenders have repented of their sins. Sins are forgiven as soon as sinners have repented and turned from their wicked ways. But the temporal consequences may continue long after a pardon has been granted. In the case of Judah, the seventy years' captivity would not be reduced even one day, in spite of the people's repentance.

3:55, 57 No matter how deep the pit into which we have fallen, God will hear us if we call upon him. Verse 57 reveals the goodness of God who quiets the fears of the anxious heart that seeks him in truth.

4:1 The stones of the temple were regarded as holy to the Lord. Now those stones lie scattered, mingled among the common stones. And the smoke of the fire when the temple burned marred the gold of the edifice.

ones: the daughter of my people *is become* cruel, like the ostriches in the
wilderness.
4 The tongue of the sucking child cleaveth to the roof of his mouth for
thirst: the young children ask bread, *and* no man breaketh *it* unto them.
5 They that did feed delicately are desolate in the streets: they that were
brought up in scarlet embrace dunghills.

4:6 Gen 19:25; Jer 20:16; Ezek 16:48

6 For the punishment of the iniquity of the daughter of my people is
greater than the punishment of the sin of Sodom, that was overthrown as in
a moment, and no hands stayed on her.

4:7 Ps 51:7

7 Her Nazarites were purer than snow, they were whiter than milk, they
were more ruddy in body than rubies, their polishing *was* of sapphire:

4:8 Ps 102:5; Lam 5:10

8 Their visage is blacker than a coal; they are not known in the streets:
their skin cleaveth to their bones; it is withered, it is become like a stick.

4:9 Lev 26:39

9 *They that be* slain with the sword are better than *they that be* slain with
hunger: for these pine away, stricken through for *want of* the fruits of the
field.

4:10 Deut 28:53–55; 2 Kgs 6:26–30; Lam 2:20

10 The hands of the pitiful women have sodden their own children: they
were their meat in the destruction of the daughter of my people.

4:11 Deut 32:22

11 The LORD hath accomplished his fury; he hath poured out his fierce
anger, and hath kindled a fire in Zion, and it hath devoured the foundations
thereof.

4:12☆ Jer 21:13

12 The kings of the earth, and all the inhabitants of the world, would not
have believed that the adversary and the enemy should have entered into
the gates of Jerusalem.

B. THE FORSAKENNESS OF JERUSALEM

4:13☆ Jer 2:30; 26:8, 9; Ezek 22:26

13 ¶For the sins of her prophets, *and* the iniquities of her priests, that have
shed the blood of the just in the midst of her,

4:14 Deut 28:28, 29; Isa 29:10; 56:10; 59:9, 10

14 They have wandered *as* blind *men* in the streets, they have polluted
themselves with blood, so that men could not touch their garments.

4:15 Lev 13:45, 46; Jer 45:5

15 They cried unto them, Depart ye; *it is* unclean; depart, depart, touch
not: when they fled away and wandered, they said among the heathen, They
shall no more sojourn *there.*

4:16 Isa 9:14–16; Jer 52:24–27

16 The anger of the LORD hath divided them; he will no more regard
them: they respected not the persons of the priests, they favoured not the
elders.

4:17☆ Jer 37:7; Lam 1:7; Ezek 29:16

17 As for us, our eyes as yet failed for our vain help: in our watching we
have watched for a nation *that* could not save *us.*

4:18 Jer 5:31; 16:16; Amos 8:2

18 They hunt our steps, that we cannot go in our streets: our end is near,
our days are fulfilled; for our end is come.

4:19 Deut 28:49; Isa 5:26–28; Jer 4:13; Hab 1:8

19 Our persecutors are swifter than the eagles of the heaven: they pursued
us upon the mountains, they laid wait for us in the wilderness.

4:20 Jer 39:5; Ezek 12:12, 13; 19:4, 8; Dan 4:12

20 The breath of our nostrils, the anointed of the LORD, was taken in their
pits, of whom we said, Under his shadow we shall live among the heathen.

4:12 The previous verse indicates that the destruction of Jerusalem was a complete destruction. Here we read that what happened to Jerusalem was a surprise to the kings of the earth. It seemed impossible for Jerusalem to be destroyed, for it was a strong and well-fortified city. The kings of the nations knew that Jerusalem was under the protection of the great King who resided in that holy city. They knew that Sennacherib had tried to seize Jerusalem and had failed dismally when the God of the Israelites delivered the city from his hands without his shooting a single arrow over its walls. They could only conclude that the success of Nebuchadnezzar in taking the city came about because God had given up Jerusalem and commissioned Nebuchadnezzar to seize it.

4:13 It was surprising that the very people who should have been a guarantee of Jerusalem's survival were the cause of its destruction. The prophets and the priests were among the chief offenders. Their sins and iniquities are spoken of here. But the people did not object. They loved "to have it so," according to Jer. 5:31. Nothing can work greater harm for a church today than for its ministers, elders, and deacons to sin against God.

4:17 *a nation.* Probably the reference is to Egypt.†

21 ¶Rejoice and be glad, O daughter of Edom, that dwellest in the land of
Uz; the cup also shall pass through unto thee; thou shalt be drunken, and
shalt make thyself naked.
22 ¶The punishment of thine iniquity is accomplished, O daughter of
Zion; he will no more carry thee away into captivity: he will visit thine
iniquity, O daughter of Edom; he will discover thy sins.

V. THE PRAYER OF REPENTANCE (5:1–22)

A. THE CONFESSION OF GUILT

5 REMEMBER, O LORD, what is come upon us: consider, and behold
our reproach.
2 Our inheritance is turned to strangers, our houses to aliens.
3 We are orphans and fatherless, our mothers *are* as widows.
4 We have drunken our water for money; our wood is sold unto us.
5 Our necks *are* under persecution: we labour, *and* have no rest.
6 We have given the hand *to* the Egyptians, *and to* the Assyrians, to be
satisfied with bread.
7 Our fathers have sinned, *and are* not; and we have borne their iniquities.
8 Servants have ruled over us: *there is* none that doth deliver *us* out of
their hand.
9 We gat our bread with *the peril of* our lives because of the sword of the
wilderness.
10 Our skin was black like an oven because of the terrible famine.
11 They ravished the women in Zion, *and* the maids in the cities of Judah.
12 Princes are hanged up by their hand: the faces of elders were not
honoured.
13 They took the young men to grind, and the children fell under the
wood.
14 The elders have ceased from the gate, the young men from their musick.
15 The joy of our heart is ceased; our dance is turned into mourning.
16 The crown is fallen *from* our head: woe unto us, that we have sinned!
17 For this our heart is faint; for these *things* our eyes are dim.
18 Because of the mountain of Zion, which is desolate, the foxes walk
upon it.

B. THE APPEAL FOR MERCY

19 Thou, O LORD, remainest for ever; thy throne from generation to
generation.
20 Wherefore dost thou forget us for ever, *and* forsake us so long time?
21 Turn thou us unto thee, O LORD, and we shall be turned; renew our
days as of old.
22 But thou hast utterly rejected us; thou art very wroth against us.

☆**4:21** Isa 34:7; Amos 1:11
4:22 Isa 40:2; Jer 49:10; Mal 1:2–4
☆**5:1** Ps 44:13–16
5:2 Isa 1:7; Hos 8:7, 8
5:3 Ex 22:24; Jer 15:8; 18:21
5:4 Isa 3:1
5:5 Neh 9:36, 37
5:7 Jer 14:20; 16:12
5:8 Neh 5:15; Ps 7:2; Zech 11:6
5:9 Jer 40:9–12
5:10 Job 30:30; Lam 4:8
5:11 Isa 13:16; Zech 14:2
☆**5:12** Isa 47:6; Lam 4:16
5:14 Isa 24:8; Jer 7:34
5:15 Jer 25:10; Amos 8:10
5:16 Job 19:9; Ps 89:39; Jer 13:18
5:17 Job 17:7; Ps 6:7; Isa 1:5; Lam 2:11
☆**5:19** Ps 45:6
5:20 Ps 13:1; 44:24
5:21 Ps 80:3; Isa 60:20–22; Jer 31:18
5:22 Ps 60:1; Isa 64:9

4:21 *O daughter of Edom.* The Edomites were always enemies of Israel. They had sided with Babylon in the months before the fall and destruction of Jerusalem. Edom rejoiced in Jerusalem's fall, but she will be punished by God in the days to come (cf. Ezek. 25:12–14; Obad. 1:11–14).

5:1ff Jeremiah pictures the calamitous condition of God's people in their captivity. They have lost their homes and they are orphans. They suffer the yoke of the oppressor; slaves rule over them. There seems to be no hope for them.

5:12 Great men suffered ignominious deaths; they were slain as though they were slaves. It is thought that perhaps their bodies were hung up (after death) to public view, for people to revile.

5:19ff Bad as the situation was in Judah, there still is a believing remnant, however small, who was calling on God to remember mercy and to deliver his people from their distress. They address God in his sovereign majesty and acknowledge that he reigns eternally. They plead for restoration as they recall better days. The last verse in the KJV differs from that in the RSV, TLB, and the NIV. The RSV and TLB make this verse a question, asking whether God has utterly rejected his people. The NIV translates it: "Restore us to yourself . . . unless you have utterly rejected us and are angry with us beyond measure" (5:21, 22).

THE BOOK OF THE PROPHET

EZEKIEL

Authorship, date, and background The author of this book was Ezekiel, whose name means "God strengthens." Buzi, of the priestly family of Zadok, was his father. Ezekiel was born ca. 621 B.C. He was raised in Jerusalem and was to become a prophet and priest of God during the most difficult period of Judah's history. The Southern Kingdom, or Judah, had been under the yoke of Assyria following the fall of the Northern Kingdom of Samaria in 722 B.C. Babylonia was to crush Assyria more than a hundred years later. In 605 B.C., after Nebuchadnezzar had defeated the Egyptians and Assyrians at Carchemish, the first deportation of Jews from Judea took place and Daniel was numbered among the victims. A second deportation followed in 597 B.C. and Ezekiel was among those sent to Babylon.

Undoubtedly Ezekiel knew both Daniel and Jeremiah. In Babylon he lived beside the Chebar Canal, was married, and had his own home. God called him to his ministry when he had been in Babylon for approximately five years. He exercised the office of prophet for around two decades. His wife died the day the siege of Jerusalem began and he was instructed by God neither to mourn nor weep. Ezekiel's statements about Jerusalem at a time he was in Babylon have occasioned liberal critics to question whether he wrote the book. Bible believers have always accepted the book as genuine and have found adequate archeological evidence to support their viewpoint.

Characteristics and content The burden of Ezekiel is one of divine judgment on Judah for its sins. In the early part of the prophecy, God commissions him to be a watchman on the wall, warning sinners to flee from God's wrath. In various ways he repeatedly warns of the coming destruction of Jerusalem, which is guilty of harlotry, of listening to false prophets, and of failing to put its trust in God.

In the severest terms Ezekiel also pronounces the judgment of God against the surrounding heathen nations. Ammon, Moab, and Philistia receive the divine sentence. Tyre is given special attention and its end is described in detail. Egypt's treachery and pride are adduced, and Ezekiel prophesies that God will use Babylonia and its king Nebuchadnezzar (Nebuchadrezzar in King James Version) to destroy her.

In the latter part of his prophecy, Ezekiel foresees the ultimate restoration of Israel, which he illustrates in his vision of the valley of dry bones. He describes the erection of a new temple in the latter days and provides detailed information about its dimensions and its auxiliary buildings and rooms. He foretells the return of the glory of God to this temple, along with the restoration of the priesthood and the reinstitution of the Levitical sacrifices. Despite Ezekiel's arraignments which are spoken in connection with the judgments of God in the earlier part of the book, a ray of hope shines through at the end. There will come a time when Israel will turn again to its God in repentance and faith and be fully restored.

Outline

I. Ezekiel's call and commission (1:1—3:27)
II. The prophecies about Judah before the captivity (4:1—24:27)
III. The prophecies against the heathen nations (25:1—32:32)
IV. The promise of Israel's restoration (33:1—39:29)
V. Israel's future in the coming kingdom age (40:1—48:35)

I. EZEKIEL'S CALL AND COMMISSION (1:1—3:27)

A. INTRODUCTION

1 NOW it came to pass in the thirtieth year, in the fourth *month*, in the
fifth *day* of the month, as I *was* among the captives by the river of
Che'bar, *that* the heavens were opened, and I saw visions of God.
2 In the fifth *day* of the month, which *was* the fifth year of king Je-hoi'a-
chin's captivity,
3 The word of the LORD came expressly unto E-ze'ki-el the priest, the son
of Bu'zi, in the land of the Chal-de'ans by the river Che'bar; and the hand
of the LORD was there upon him.

B. THE VISION OF GOD'S GLORY

4 ¶And I looked, and, behold, a whirlwind came out of the north, a great
cloud, and a fire infolding itself, and a brightness *was* about it, and out of
the midst thereof as the colour of amber, out of the midst of the fire.
5 Also out of the midst thereof *came* the likeness of four living creatures.
And this *was* their appearance; they had the likeness of a man.
6 And every one had four faces, and every one had four wings.
7 And their feet *were* straight feet; and the sole of their feet *was* like the
sole of a calf's foot: and they sparkled like the colour of burnished brass.
8 And *they had* the hands of a man under their wings on their four sides;
and they four had their faces and their wings.
9 Their wings *were* joined one to another; they turned not when they
went; they went every one straight forward.
10 As for the likeness of their faces, they four had the face of a man, and
the face of a lion, on the right side: and they four had the face of an ox on
the left side; they four also had the face of an eagle.
11 Thus *were* their faces: and their wings *were* stretched upward; two
wings of every one *were* joined one to another, and two covered their
bodies.
12 And they went every one straight forward: whither the spirit was to go,
they went; *and* they turned not when they went.
13 As for the likeness of the living creatures, their appearance *was* like
burning coals of fire, *and* like the appearance of lamps: it went up and
down among the living creatures; and the fire was bright, and out of the fire
went forth lightning.
14 And the living creatures ran and returned as the appearance of a flash
of lightning.
15 ¶Now as I beheld the living creatures, behold one wheel upon the earth
by the living creatures, with his four faces.
16 The appearance of the wheels and their work *was* like unto the colour of
a beryl: and they four had one likeness: and their appearance and their
work *was* as it were a wheel in the middle of a wheel.
17 When they went, they went upon their four sides: *and* they turned not
when they went.

☆1:1 Num 12:6; Isa 1:1; Ezek 40:2; Dan 8:1, 2; Mt 3:16; Lk 3:21; Acts 7:56; Rev 4:1; 19:11
1:4 Isa 21:1; Jer 23:19; Ezek 13:11, 13; Heb 12:29
☆1:5 Ezek 10:15–17, 20; Rev 4:6–8; 6:6
1:6 Ex 25:20; 1 Kgs 6:24–27; Ezek 10:14, 21
1:7 Ps 18:33; Dan 10:6; Rev 1:15; 2:18
1:8 Ezek 10:8, 21
1:9 Ezek 10:22
☆1:10 Ezek 10:14; Rev 4:7
1:11 Isa 6:2; Ezek 10:16, 19
1:13 Ps 104:4; Dan 10:5, 6; Rev 4:5
1:14 Zech 4:10; Mt 24:27
☆1:16 Ezek 10:9–13

1:1 *the thirtieth year.* This may have been when Ezekiel was thirty years old and thus able to enter upon the full duties of the priesthood at that age. Or it was thirty years after the beginning of the reign of Nabopolassar, who was the father of Nebuchadnezzar. He reigned nineteen years and this was the eleventh year of his son, which totals thirty years.

1:5 *four living creatures.* They were living creatures of angelic order. Men die but angels do not; they live forever. (See note on *cherubim,* Ezek. 10:1.) The mercy-seat of the ark had cherubim fastened to it. The living creatures were not men; they had the likeness or appearance of men.

1:10 The creatures were four sided, in that each had four faces made up of man, lion, ox, and eagle.

1:16 *a wheel in the middle of a wheel,* i.e., "a second wheel crosswise inside, perhaps as in a gyroscope."†

1:18 Prov 15:3; Ezek 10:9–13; Zech 4:10; Rev 4:6, 8
1:19 Ezek 10:16, 17, 19

18 As for their rings, they were so high that they were dreadful; and their
rings *were* full of eyes round about them four.
19 And when the living creatures went, the wheels went by them: and
when the living creatures were lifted up from the earth, the wheels were
lifted up.
20 Whithersoever the spirit was to go, they went, thither *was their* spirit to
go; and the wheels were lifted up over against them: for the spirit of the
living creature *was* in the wheels.
21 When those went, *these* went; and when those stood, *these* stood; and
when those were lifted up from the earth, the wheels were lifted up over
against them: for the spirit of the living creature *was* in the wheels.

1:22 Ex 24:10; Job 37:22; Ezek 10:1; Rev 4:6; 22:1

22 And the likeness of the firmament upon the heads of the living creature
was as the colour of the terrible crystal, stretched forth over their heads
above.
23 And under the firmament *were* their wings straight, the one toward the
other: every one had two, which covered on this side, and every one had
two, which covered on that side, their bodies.

1:24 Ezek 10:5; 43:2; Dan 10:6; Rev 1:15; 19:6

24 And when they went, I heard the noise of their wings, like the noise of
great waters, as the voice of the Almighty, the voice of speech, as the noise
of an host: when they stood, they let down their wings.
25 And there was a voice from the firmament that *was* over their heads,
when they stood, *and* had let down their wings.

1:26 Ex 24:10; Isa 6:1; 54:11; Ezek 10:1; 24:10; 43:6; Dan 7:9; Rev 1:13
1:27 Gen 9:13; Ezek 3:23; 8:2; 2 Thess 1:7; Rev 1:17; 4:3; 10:1
1:28☆

26 ¶And above the firmament that *was* over their heads *was* the likeness of
a throne, as the appearance of a sapphire stone: and upon the likeness of
the throne *was* the likeness as the appearance of a man above upon it.
27 And I saw as the colour of amber, as the appearance of fire round about
within it, from the appearance of his loins even upward, and from the
appearance of his loins even downward, I saw as it were the appearance of
fire, and it had brightness round about.
28 As the appearance of the bow that is in the cloud in the day of rain, so
was the appearance of the brightness round about. This *was* the appearance
of the likeness of the glory of the LORD. And when I saw *it*, I fell upon my
face, and I heard a voice of one that spake.

C. THE COMMISSIONING OF EZEKIEL

1. To Go to the Nation of Israel

2:1☆ Dan 10:11; Mt 16:13–16
2:2☆ Num 11:25, 26; Judg 13:25; Ezek 3:24; Dan 8:18
2:3☆ 1 Sam 8:7, 8; Ezra 9:7; Jer 3:25; Dan 9:5–13

2 AND he said unto me, Son of man, stand upon thy feet, and I will
speak unto thee.
2 And the spirit entered into me when he spake unto me, and set me upon
my feet, that I heard him that spake unto me.
3 And he said unto me, Son of man, I send thee to the children of Israel,
to a rebellious nation that hath rebelled against me: they and their fathers
have transgressed against me, *even* unto this very day.

1:28 *the likeness of the glory of the LORD.* God is spirit without human form. Here the glory is spoken of as a likeness. When Ezekiel saw this likeness, he fell on his face. The majesty of God produced awe in the prophet.

2:1 *Son of man.* The phrase stresses Ezekiel's humanity. Despite the many celestial visions Ezekiel had, he was nothing more than the *son of man,* i.e., a human being. Later this term came to be applied in a messianic sense to describe the one who would establish God's rule over all the earth and usher in God's messianic age (e.g., Dan. 7:9–13). This messianic usage does not appear in Ezekiel.

2:2 The third person of the Trinity appears, the Spirit of God. He will appear again and again in Ezekiel, far more than in any other Old Testament book. The Spirit came upon Ezekiel and picked him up and set him on his feet after he had fallen to the ground.

2:3 God's people are called rebellious, impudent, and stubborn. Judah and Jerusalem still stand, although some of the people are already captive in Babylon. Ezekiel will forecast the capture and destruction of Jerusalem by Nebuchadnezzar.

4 For *they are* impudent children and stiffhearted. I do send thee unto
them; and thou shalt say unto them, Thus saith the Lord GOD.
5 And they, whether they will hear, or whether they will forbear, (for they
are a rebellious house,) yet shall know that there hath been a prophet
among them.
6 ¶And thou, son of man, be not afraid of them, neither be afraid of their
words, though briers and thorns *be* with thee, and thou dost dwell among
scorpions: be not afraid of their words, nor be dismayed at their looks,
though they *be* a rebellious house.
7 And thou shalt speak my words unto them, whether they will hear, or
whether they will forbear: for they *are* most rebellious.

2:4 Isa 48:4 Jer 5:3 Ezek 3:7
2:5 Ezek 3:11, 27 33:33 Mt 10:12–15 Lk 10:10, 11 Jn 15:22 Acts 13:46
☆**2:6** 2 Sam 23:6, 7 Isa 51:12 Jer 1:8 Ezek 3:9 Mic 7:4
☆**2:7** Jer 1:7, 17 Ezek 3:17

2. To Eat the Scroll

8 But thou, son of man, hear what I say unto thee; Be not thou rebellious
like that rebellious house: open thy mouth, and eat that I give thee.
9 ¶And when I looked, behold, an hand *was* sent unto me; and, lo, a roll
of a book *was* therein;
10 And he spread it before me; and it *was* written within and without: and
there was written therein lamentations, and mourning, and woe.

☆**2:8** Jer 15:16 1 Tim 4:14–16 Rev 10:9
2:9 Jer 36:2 Dan 5:5; 10:10 Rev 5:1–5; 8:13 10:8–11

3 MOREOVER he said unto me, Son of man, eat that thou findest; eat
this roll, and go speak unto the house of Israel.
2 So I opened my mouth, and he caused me to eat that roll.
3 And he said unto me, Son of man, cause thy belly to eat, and fill thy
bowels with this roll that I give thee. Then did I eat *it;* and it was in my
mouth as honey for sweetness.

☆**3:1**
3:2 Jer 25:17 Acts 26:19
3:3 Ps 19:10 119:102, 103 Jer 6:11; 15:16 Rev 10:9, 10

3. To Speak God's Messages to Israel

4 ¶And he said unto me, Son of man, go, get thee unto the house of Israel,
and speak with my words unto them.
5 For thou *art* not sent to a people of a strange speech and of an hard
language, *but* to the house of Israel;
6 Not to many people of a strange speech and of an hard language, whose
words thou canst not understand. Surely, had I sent thee to them, they
would have hearkened unto thee.
7 But the house of Israel will not hearken unto thee; for they will not
hearken unto me: for all the house of Israel *are* impudent and hardhearted.
8 Behold, I have made thy face strong against their faces, and thy
forehead strong against their foreheads.
9 As an adamant harder than flint have I made thy forehead: fear them
not, neither be dismayed at their looks, though they *be* a rebellious house.
10 Moreover he said unto me, Son of man, all my words that I shall speak
unto thee receive in thine heart, and hear with thine ears.
11 And go, get thee to them of the captivity, unto the children of thy

☆**3:4**
3:5 Ps 81:5 Jonah 1:2; 3:2–4 Acts 26:17, 18
3:6 Isa 28:11
☆**3:7** Ezek 2:4 Lk 10:16 Jn 5:40–47 15:20
3:8 Jer 1:18
3:10 Job 22:22 Ezek 2:8 Lk 8:15 1 Thess 2:13
☆**3:11** Ezek 2:5, 7

2:6, 7 God warns Ezekiel that he will face hardships as a prophet. He is to preach whether the people listen and heed, or refuse to listen and choose to continue in their sins. God has already allowed Judah hundreds of years and has sent scores of prophets to warn them. The wonders of his grace include divine patience in the face of repeated evidences of apostasy.

2:8 God first opened Ezekiel's eyes and ears. Now he has him open his mouth and receive the exact word God wants spoken to his people.

3:1ff Ezekiel is not to speak until he has received the revelation of God. The word in his mouth was as sweet as honey.

3:4 Ezekiel is sent only to the house of Israel to speak only what God has given him.

3:7 To be forewarned is to be forearmed. God tells Ezekiel that his message will not be listened to, not because it is given by Ezekiel but because the people will not hear God.

3:11 As always, God makes it clear that his people have two options: either they hear, heed, repent, and are saved, or they refuse to hear and are judged.

people, and speak unto them, and tell them, Thus saith the Lord GOD;
whether they will hear, or whether they will forbear.

4. The Visit to the Exiles by the River Chebar

3:12☆ 12Then the spirit took me up, and I heard behind me a voice of a great
Ezek 8:3; Acts 2:2; 8:39 rushing, *saying*, Blessed *be* the glory of the LORD from his place.
3:13 13*I heard* also the noise of the wings of the living creatures that touched
2 Sam 5:24; Ezek 1:15, 24 one another, and the noise of the wheels over against them, and a noise of
10:5, 16, 17 a great rushing.
3:14☆ 14So the spirit lifted me up, and took me away, and I went in bitterness,
Job 2:13; Ezek 8:1 in the heat of my spirit; but the hand of the LORD was strong upon me.
3:15☆ 15¶Then I came to them of the captivity at Tel–a′bib, that dwelt by the
river of Che′bar, and I sat where they sat, and remained there astonished
among them seven days.

5. To Be a Watchman for Israel

3:16☆ 16And it came to pass at the end of seven days, that the word of the LORD
came unto me, saying,
3:17 17Son of man, I have made thee a watchman unto the house of Israel:
Isa 52:8; 58:1; 62:6 therefore hear the word at my mouth, and give them warning from me.
Jer 6:17; Ezek 33:7–9 18When I say unto the wicked, Thou shalt surely die; and thou givest him
3:18 not warning, nor speakest to warn the wicked from his wicked way, to save
Ezek 33:6, 8 his life; the same wicked *man* shall die in his iniquity; but his blood will I
require at thine hand.
3:19 19Yet if thou warn the wicked, and he turn not from his wickedness, nor
2 Kgs 17:13, 14; Ezek 33:3, 9 from his wicked way, he shall die in his iniquity; but thou hast delivered thy
Acts 18:6 soul.
3:20 20Again, When a righteous *man* doth turn from his righteousness, and
Ezek 18:24; 33:18 commit iniquity, and I lay a stumblingblock before him, he shall die:
Zeph 1:6 because thou hast not given him warning, he shall die in his sin, and his
righteousness which he hath done shall not be remembered; but his blood
will I require at thine hand.
3:21 21Nevertheless if thou warn the righteous *man*, that the righteous sin not,
Acts 20:31 and he doth not sin, he shall surely live, because he is warned; also thou
hast delivered thy soul.

6. God Lays Hands on Ezekiel

3:22 22¶And the hand of the LORD was there upon me; and he said unto me,
Acts 9:6 Arise, go forth into the plain, and I will there talk with thee.
3:23☆ 23Then I arose, and went forth into the plain: and, behold, the glory of
Ezek 1:28; 8:4; Acts 7:55 the LORD stood there, as the glory which I saw by the river of Che′bar: and
I fell on my face.

3:12 *a voice of a great rushing,* i.e., "accompanied by the sound of a great earthquake." In 2:2 we see that the Spirit set Ezekiel on his feet. Here the Spirit lifts him up. In 3:24 the Spirit enters into him. The work of the Spirit in Ezekiel's life is mentioned more times than in any other account in the Old Testament.
3:14 Ezekiel assumes the role of prophet with a heavy heart, embittered by the knowledge that he will not succeed among these reprobate people, and conscious that he must speak God's word.
3:15 The Spirit of God carried him to Babylon where he waited among the captives for God to tell him what to say. He had a twofold message for them when he spoke. The captives would be in Babylon a long time, and they would be joined by many others when Judah and Jerusalem had been taken and the city destroyed.
3:16ff God called Ezekiel as a watchman to sound the alarm whenever danger arose. If he failed to do so, his people would be destroyed and he would be responsible. Even if the people refused to heed his warnings when given, he was to watch, but he could not be held responsible so long as he did his job. We, like Ezekiel, are to warn men to flee from the wrath to come.
3:23, 24 The glory of God fells him; the Spirit sets him on his feet.

24 Then the spirit entered into me, and set me upon my feet, and spake
with me, and said unto me, Go, shut thyself within thine house.
25 But thou, O son of man, behold, they shall put bands upon thee, and
shall bind thee with them, and thou shalt not go out among them:
26 And I will make thy tongue cleave to the roof of thy mouth, that thou
shalt be dumb, and shalt not be to them a reprover: for they *are* a rebellious
house.
27 But when I speak with thee, I will open thy mouth, and thou shalt say
unto them, Thus saith the Lord GOD; He that heareth, let him hear; and he
that forbeareth, let him forbear: for they *are* a rebellious house.

☆**3:24** Ezek 2:2
☆**3:25** Ezek 4:8; Hos 4:17
3:26 Amos 8:11, 12
3:27 Ezek 33:22

II. THE PROPHECIES ABOUT JUDAH BEFORE THE CAPTIVITY (4:1—24:27)

A. THE APPROACHING DEVASTATION OF JERUSALEM

1. Ezekiel Draws a Picture of the Siege

4 THOU also, son of man, take thee a tile, and lay it before thee, and
pourtray upon it the city, *even* Jerusalem:
2 And lay siege against it, and build a fort against it, and cast a mount
against it; set the camp also against it, and set *battering* rams against it
round about.
3 Moreover take thou unto thee an iron pan, and set it *for* a wall of iron
between thee and the city: and set thy face against it, and it shall be
besieged, and thou shalt lay siege against it. This *shall be* a sign to the house
of Israel.

☆**4:1** Isa 20:2; Jer 6:6; 13:1; 19:1; Ezek 21:22
4:3 Isa 8:18; 20:3; Jer 39:1, 2; Ezek 12:6, 11; 24:24–27

2. The Length of God's Punishment

4 Lie thou also upon thy left side, and lay the iniquity of the house of
Israel upon it: *according* to the number of the days that thou shalt lie upon
it thou shalt bear their iniquity.
5 For I have laid upon thee the years of their iniquity, according to the
number of the days, three hundred and ninety days: so shalt thou bear the
iniquity of the house of Israel.
6 And when thou hast accomplished them, lie again on thy right side, and
thou shalt bear the iniquity of the house of Judah forty days: I have
appointed thee each day for a year.
7 Therefore thou shalt set thy face toward the siege of Jerusalem, and
thine arm *shall be* uncovered, and thou shalt prophesy against it.
8 And, behold, I will lay bands upon thee, and thou shalt not turn thee
from one side to another, till thou hast ended the days of thy siege.

4:4 Num 14:34
☆**4:5**
4:6 Dan 9:24–26; 26:11, 12; Rev 11:2, 3
☆**4:7** Ezek 21:2
☆**4:8** Ezek 3:25

3. The Famine during the Siege

9 ¶Take thou also unto thee wheat, and barley, and beans, and lentiles,
and millet, and fitches, and put them in one vessel, and make thee bread

☆**4:9** Ex 9:32; Isa 28:25

3:25ff Ezekiel is overtaken by a kind of paralysis in which he lies dumb and bound, incapable of fulfilling the prophetic office until God opens his mouth and fills it with his words.
4:1 *a tile,* i.e., a clay tablet used by the Babylonians for writing. God told Ezekiel to draw a map of Jerusalem on it, along with information about the coming siege against the city.
4:5 *three hundred and ninety days.* Some versions, such as the Septuagint, read, "190 days." If the Septuagint figure is correct, it would cover the period from 721 to 536 B.C. If the 390 figure is correct, then the period covers the time from the first apostasy under Jeroboam to the destruction of Jerusalem. It is better not to be dogmatic about the meaning of the symbol, since commentators interpret this passage differently.
4:7 *thine arm shall be uncovered,* i.e., "outstretched" to signify (as some think) dealing blows without mercy.
4:8 *I will lay bands upon thee,* i.e., God binds him in order to carry out the symbol that Jerusalem will be bound by the siege before it capitulates.
4:9ff Ezekiel is to eat only enough to remain alive, signifying that famine will overtake Jerusalem during the siege. To cook food with human dung was nau-

thereof, *according* to the number of the days that thou shalt lie upon thy
side, three hundred and ninety days shalt thou eat thereof.

4:10 Ezek 45:12

10And thy meat which thou shalt eat *shall be* by weight, twenty shekels a
day: from time to time shalt thou eat it.
11Thou shalt drink also water by measure, the sixth part of an hin: from
time to time shalt thou drink.

4:12 Isa 36:12

12And thou shalt eat it *as* barley cakes, and thou shalt bake it with dung
that cometh out of man, in their sight.

4:13 Dan 1:8; Hos 9:3

13And the LORD said, Even thus shall the children of Israel eat their
defiled bread among the Gentiles, whither I will drive them.

4:14 Lev 17:15; 22:8; Deut 14:3–5; Isa 66:17; Ezek 20:49; Acts 10:14

14Then said I, Ah Lord GOD! behold, my soul hath not been polluted; for
from my youth up even till now have I not eaten of that which dieth of
itself, or is torn in pieces; neither came there abominable flesh into my
mouth.
15Then he said unto me, Lo, I have given thee cow's dung for man's dung,
and thou shalt prepare thy bread therewith.

4:16 Lev 26:26; Isa 3:1; Lam 5:4; Ezek 5:16; 12:18, 19; 14:13

16Moreover he said unto me, Son of man, behold, I will break the staff of
bread in Jerusalem: and they shall eat bread by weight, and with care; and
they shall drink water by measure, and with astonishment:

4:17 Ezek 24:23; 33:10

17That they may want bread and water, and be astonied one with
another, and consume away for their iniquity.

4. Jerusalem's Fate
a. The Razor, the Knife, and the Fire

5:1☆ Lev 21:5; Isa 7:20; Ezek 44:20; Dan 5:27

5 AND thou, son of man, take thee a sharp knife, take thee a barber's
razor, and cause *it* to pass upon thine head and upon thy beard: then
take thee balances to weigh, and divide the *hair*.

5:2 Lev 26:33; Jer 39:1, 2; Ezek 4:1–8

2Thou shalt burn with fire a third part in the midst of the city, when the
days of the siege are fulfilled: and thou shalt take a third part, *and* smite
about it with a knife: and a third part thou shalt scatter in the wind; and I
will draw out a sword after them.

5:3 2 Kgs 25:15; Jer 39:10

3Thou shalt also take thereof a few in number, and bind them in thy
skirts.

5:4 Jer 41:12; 42:16, 17, 22

4Then take of them again, and cast them into the midst of the fire, and
burn them in the fire; *for* thereof shall a fire come forth into all the house of
Israel.

b. God Will Not Spare His People Because of Their Sins

5:5☆ 2 Kgs 17:8–20; Jer 6:6; Lam 1:1; Ezek 4:1; 16:47, 48, 51; Zech 7:11

5¶Thus saith the Lord GOD; This *is* Jerusalem: I have set it in the midst
of the nations and countries *that are* round about her.
6And she hath changed my judgments into wickedness more than the
nations, and my statutes more than the countries that *are* round about her:

5:6☆

for they have refused my judgments and my statutes, they have not walked
in them.

---

seous, so God let him change it to animal dung. *abominable flesh.* The famine will bring the Jews to a place where they will eat anything, even forbidden food, to stay alive. (*See Lev. 11 for the dietary laws Ezekiel refers to.*)

5:1ff This is a sign by which the complete destruction of Jerusalem is set forth. He divided the hair from his head and beard into three parts. It symbolized the fact that one-third of the Jews in Jerusalem would perish by fire, famine and pestilence, one-third will be slain in the warfare, and one-third will be scattered far and wide.

5:5 The various prophets who spoke about the destruction of Jerusalem were in full agreement that the *judgment* of God fell because of the people's apostasy, which included idolatry and disobedience to God's commandments.

5:6 The nation Israel has broken God's statutes, but this does not mean that all of the people have done so. There was a remnant of faithful people who kept the law of God and loved God with their whole hearts.

7 Therefore thus saith the Lord GOD; Because ye multiplied more than
the nations that *are* round about you, *and* have not walked in my statutes,
neither have kept my judgments, neither have done according to the
judgments of the nations that *are* round about you;
8 Therefore thus saith the Lord GOD; Behold, I, even I, *am* against thee,
and will execute judgments in the midst of thee in the sight of the nations.
9 And I will do in thee that which I have not done, and whereunto I will
not do any more the like, because of all thine abominations.
10 Therefore the fathers shall eat the sons in the midst of thee, and the
sons shall eat their fathers; and I will execute judgments in thee, and the
whole remnant of thee will I scatter into all the winds.
11 Wherefore, *as* I live, saith the Lord GOD; Surely, because thou hast
defiled my sanctuary with all thy detestable things, and with all thine
abominations, therefore will I also diminish *thee;* neither shall mine eye
spare, neither will I have any pity.
12 ¶A third part of thee shall die with the pestilence, and with famine shall
they be consumed in the midst of thee: and a third part shall fall by the
sword round about thee; and I will scatter a third part into all the winds,
and I will draw out a sword after them.
13 Thus shall mine anger be accomplished, and I will cause my fury to rest
upon them, and I will be comforted: and they shall know that I the LORD
have spoken *it* in my zeal, when I have accomplished my fury in them.
14 Moreover I will make thee waste, and a reproach among the nations
that *are* round about thee, in the sight of all that pass by.
15 So it shall be a reproach and a taunt, an instruction and an astonish-
ment unto the nations that *are* round about thee, when I shall execute
judgments in thee in anger and in fury and in furious rebukes. I the LORD
have spoken *it.*
16 When I shall send upon them the evil arrows of famine, which shall be
for *their* destruction, *and* which I will send to destroy you: and I will
increase the famine upon you, and will break your staff of bread:
17 So will I send upon you famine and evil beasts, and they shall bereave
thee; and pestilence and blood shall pass through thee; and I will bring the
sword upon thee. I the LORD have spoken *it.*

5:8 Jer 24:9; Ezek 5:15; 15:7; 21:3; Zech 14:2
5:9 Dan 9:12; Mt 24:21
☆**5:10** Lev 26:29; Ps 44:11; Jer 19:9; Ezek 6:8; Amos 9:9; Zech 2:6; 7:14
5:11 Jer 7:9–11; Ezek 8:5, 6, 16, 18
5:12 Jer 15:2; 44:27; Ezek 6:11, 12; 12:14; 15:2; Amos 9:9; Zech 2:6
☆**5:13** Isa 1:24; 59:17; Lam 4:11; Ezek 38:19
5:14 Ps 74:3–10; 79:1–4; Ezek 22:4
5:15 Isa 66:15, 16; Jer 22:8, 9; Ezek 25:17; 1 Cor 10:11
5:16 Deut 32:23, 24
☆**5:17** Ezek 14:21; 28:23

B. IDOLATRY LEADS TO GOD'S JUDGMENT
1. God Will Destroy the Idol Altars

6 AND the word of the LORD came unto me, saying,
2 Son of man, set thy face toward the mountains of Israel, and
prophesy against them,
3 And say, Ye mountains of Israel, hear the word of the Lord GOD; Thus
saith the Lord GOD to the mountains, and to the hills, to the rivers, and to
the valleys; Behold, I, *even* I, will bring a sword upon you, and I will
destroy your high places.

6:2 Ezek 36:1
☆**6:3** Ezek 36:4

5:10 Josephus tells how human flesh was eaten during the siege of Jerusalem, when the famine was at its height.
5:13 *zeal,* or, "jealousy" (RSV). The Hebrew word is variously translated in the Old Testament as "zeal" and "jealousy." Jealousy usually has a negative meaning. But jealousy in God and jealousy in man are not the same. Jealousy or zeal in God has to do with the exactment of exclusive devotion. God will not suffer himself to be supplanted by any other gods, nor will he permit any substitutes in place of himself.
5:17 God clearly states that what happened to Jerusalem, although accomplished by a heathen nation and people, was done by God himself through secondary agents. God can and does accomplish his aims directly or mediately through nature, men, angels, or circumstances.
6:3 The Israelites habitually resorted to idolatry. They set up groves for worship, made images, and otherwise offended the true God by substituting pagan worship for the worship of God. These idolators must die.

6:4 Lev 26:30; 2 Chron 14:5; Isa 27:9; Ezek 6:6; Mic 1:7; Zech 13:2
6:6☆

4 And your altars shall be desolate, and your images shall be broken: and
I will cast down your slain *men* before your idols.
5 And I will lay the dead carcases of the children of Israel before their
idols; and I will scatter your bones round about your altars.
6 In all your dwellingplaces the cities shall be laid waste, and the high
places shall be desolate; that your altars may be laid waste and made
desolate, and your idols may be broken and cease, and your images may be
cut down, and your works may be abolished.
7 And the slain shall fall in the midst of you, and ye shall know that I *am*
the LORD.

2. God Will Let Some People Escape the Sword

6:8☆ Isa 6:13; Jer 44:14, 28; Ezek 7:16; 14:22
6:9 Deut 30:2; Job 42:6; Ps 78:40; Isa 7:13; 43:24; Ezek 20:43; Hos 11:8

8 ¶Yet will I leave a remnant, that ye may have *some* that shall escape the
sword among the nations, when ye shall be scattered through the countries.
9 And they that escape of you shall remember me among the nations
whither they shall be carried captives, because I am broken with their
whorish heart, which hath departed from me, and with their eyes, which go
a whoring after their idols: and they shall lothe themselves for the evils
which they have committed in all their abominations.
10 And they shall know that I *am* the LORD, *and that* I have not said in
vain that I would do this evil unto them.

3. Israel Will Know God by His Judgments

6:11☆ Ezek 5:12; 7:15; 9:4; 25:6
6:12 Lam 4:11, 12; Ezek 5:13; Dan 9:7
6:13 1 Kgs 14:23; 2 Kgs 16:4; Isa 57:5–7; Ezek 20:27, 28; Hos 4:13
6:14 Isa 5:25; Ezek 14:13

11 ¶Thus saith the Lord GOD; Smite with thine hand, and stamp with thy
foot, and say, Alas for all the evil abominations of the house of Israel! for
they shall fall by the sword, by the famine, and by the pestilence.
12 He that is far off shall die of the pestilence; and he that is near shall fall
by the sword; and he that remaineth and is besieged shall die by the
famine: thus will I accomplish my fury upon them.
13 Then shall ye know that I *am* the LORD, when their slain *men* shall be
among their idols round about their altars, upon every high hill, in all the
tops of the mountains, and under every green tree, and under every thick
oak, the place where they did offer sweet savour to all their idols.
14 So will I stretch out my hand upon them, and make the land desolate,
yea, more desolate than the wilderness toward Dib'lath, in all their
habitations: and they shall know that I *am* the LORD.

C. THE MESSAGE OF THE APPROACHING END
1. The Land Is Finished

7:1☆
7:2 Ezek 11:13; Amos 8:2, 10
7:4 Ezek 11:21; 22:31; Hos 9:7

7 MOREOVER the word of the LORD came unto me, saying,
2 Also, thou son of man, thus saith the Lord GOD unto the land of
Israel; An end, the end is come upon the four corners of the land.
3 Now *is* the end *come* upon thee, and I will send mine anger upon thee,
and will judge thee according to thy ways, and will recompense upon thee
all thine abominations.
4 And mine eye shall not spare thee, neither will I have pity: but I will

6:6 Because God is zealous for his honor, those who dishonor him must suffer the consequences of their wickedness. All of man's substitutes for God will be destroyed and all their works wiped out.
6:8 In the midst of a judgment unto death, God will preserve a remnant for himself.
6:11 Ezekiel is commanded to demonstrate his sense of horror, urgency, and grief by clapping his hands and stamping his feet. Thus will the people know how *serious* he is and how certain will be the evil consequences of Israel's transgressions. When the Israelites see these things come to pass, they will know that God is the Lord.
7:1ff Ezekiel informs the Jews about the final ruin, the absolute destruction of the land.

recompense thy ways upon thee, and thine abominations shall be in the
midst of thee: and ye shall know that I *am* the LORD.
5 Thus saith the Lord GOD; An evil, an only evil, behold, is come.
6 An end is come, the end is come: it watcheth for thee; behold, it is come.
7 The morning is come unto thee, O thou that dwellest in the land: the
time is come, the day of trouble *is* near, and not the sounding again of the
mountains.
8 Now will I shortly pour out my fury upon thee, and accomplish mine
anger upon thee: and I will judge thee according to thy ways, and will
recompense thee for all thine abominations.
9 And mine eye shall not spare, neither will I have pity: I will recompense
thee according to thy ways and thine abominations *that* are in the midst of
thee; and ye shall know that I *am* the LORD that smiteth.
10 Behold the day, behold, it is come: the morning is gone forth; the rod
hath blossomed, pride hath budded.
11 Violence is risen up into a rod of wickedness: none of them *shall
remain*, nor of their multitude, nor of any of theirs: neither *shall there be*
wailing for them.
12 The time is come, the day draweth near: let not the buyer rejoice, nor
the seller mourn: for wrath *is* upon all the multitude thereof.
13 For the seller shall not return to that which is sold, although they were
yet alive: for the vision *is* touching the whole multitude thereof, *which* shall
not return; neither shall any strengthen himself in the iniquity of his life.

2. The Death and Suffering of the People

14 They have blown the trumpet, even to make all ready; but none goeth
to the battle: for my wrath *is* upon all the multitude thereof.
15 The sword *is* without, and the pestilence and the famine within: he that
is in the field shall die with the sword; and he that *is* in the city, famine and
pestilence shall devour him.
16 ¶But they that escape of them shall escape, and shall be on the
mountains like doves of the valleys, all of them mourning, every one for his
iniquity.
17 All hands shall be feeble, and all knees shall be weak *as* water.
18 They shall also gird *themselves* with sackcloth, and horror shall cover
them; and shame *shall be* upon all faces, and baldness upon all their heads.
19 They shall cast their silver in the streets, and their gold shall be
removed: their silver and their gold shall not be able to deliver them in the
day of the wrath of the LORD: they shall not satisfy their souls, neither fill
their bowels: because it is the stumblingblock of their iniquity.
20 ¶As for the beauty of his ornament, he set it in majesty: but they made
the images of their abominations *and* of their detestable things therein:
therefore have I set it far from them.
21 And I will give it into the hands of the strangers for a prey, and to the
wicked of the earth for a spoil; and they shall pollute it.
22 My face will I turn also from them, and they shall pollute my secret
place: for the robbers shall enter into it, and defile it.

7:5 2 Kgs 21:12, 13 Nah 1:9 Zech 13:7
☆**7:7** Isa 22:5 Ezek 12:23–25, 28
7:8 Isa 42:25 Ezek 9:8; 14:19 33:20; 36:19 Nah 1:6
7:10 Ps 73:8; 89:32 Isa 10:5; 59:6–8 Zeph 1:18
☆**7:11**
7:12 Isa 5:13, 14 Ezek 6:11, 12 1 Cor 7:29–31 Jas 5:8, 9
7:13 Lev 25:24–28, 31
7:14 Num 10:9 Jer 4:5
☆**7:15** Jer 14:18 Ezek 6:11, 12 12:16
7:16 Isa 38:14; 59:11 Ezek 6:8; 14:22 Nah 2:7
7:17 Isa 13:7 Ezek 21:7; 22:14 Heb 12:12
7:18 Job 21:6 Isa 15:3 Ezek 27:31 Amos 8:10
7:19 Prov 11:4 Isa 2:20; 30:22 Zeph 1:8
7:21 2 Kgs 24:13 Ps 74:2–8 Jer 7:30
7:22 Jer 18:17 Ezek 39:23, 24

7:7ff God says that the end is nearer than the Jews thought. Time has run out; their defeat is certain.

7:11ff The Jews cannot say that it was not their fault or that what happened was an accident. Their sins had brought this judgment upon them, and no one else was to blame.

7:15 God declares that his judgment will be universal and that none shall escape. Death will ride triumphantly in the city and in the countryside. No one will be safe anywhere. Whoever is marked for death will not escape. No one will wail for those who die, and resistance will do no good. Thus the sentence of judgment will be executed and doom will overtake these sinners.

3. The Defiling of the Temple

7:23 Jer 27:4; Ezek 8:17; 9:9; Hos 4:2
7:24 2 Chron 7:20; Ezek 21:31; 28:7; 33:28
7:25☆ Ezek 13:10, 16
7:26 Ps 35:26; Isa 47:11; Jer 4:20; 18:18; 37:17; Ezek 21:7; 22:26; 26:16; Mic 3:6

23 ¶Make a chain: for the land is full of bloody crimes, and the city is full of violence.

24 Wherefore I will bring the worst of the heathen, and they shall possess their houses: I will also make the pomp of the strong to cease; and their holy places shall be defiled.

25 Destruction cometh; and they shall seek peace, and *there shall be* none.

26 Mischief shall come upon mischief, and rumour shall be upon rumour; then shall they seek a vision of the prophet; but the law shall perish from the priest, and counsel from the ancients.

27 The king shall mourn, and the prince shall be clothed with desolation, and the hands of the people of the land shall be troubled: I will do unto them after their way, and according to their deserts will I judge them; and they shall know that I *am* the LORD.

D. GOD WILL ABANDON HIS TEMPLE
1. Idolatry in Jerusalem
a. The Backdrop for the Vision

8:1☆
8:2☆ Ezek 1:4, 27, 28

8 AND it came to pass in the sixth year, in the sixth *month*, in the fifth *day* of the month, *as* I sat in mine house, and the elders of Judah sat before me, that the hand of the Lord GOD fell there upon me.

2 Then I beheld, and lo a likeness as the appearance of fire: from the appearance of his loins even downward, fire; and from his loins even upward, as the appearance of brightness, as the colour of amber.

8:3 Jer 7:30; Ezek 3:12; 11:1; Dan 5:5
8:4 Ezek 1:27, 28

3 And he put forth the form of an hand, and took me by a lock of mine head; and the spirit lifted me up between the earth and the heaven, and brought me in the visions of God to Jerusalem, to the door of the inner gate that looketh toward the north; where *was* the seat of the image of jealousy, which provoketh to jealousy.

4 And, behold, the glory of the God of Israel *was* there, according to the vision that I saw in the plain.

b. The Worship of Idols and Pictures

8:5 Ps 78:58; Jer 3:2; 7:30; 32:34; Ezek 8:3; Zech 5:5
8:6 2 Kgs 23:4, 5; Ezek 5:11; 8:9, 17
8:8 Job 34:22; Isa 29:15

5 ¶Then said he unto me, Son of man, lift up thine eyes now the way toward the north. So I lifted up mine eyes the way toward the north, and behold northward at the gate of the altar this image of jealousy in the entry.

6 He said furthermore unto me, Son of man, seest thou what they do? *even* the great abominations that the house of Israel committeth here, that I should go far off from my sanctuary? but turn thee yet again, *and* thou shalt see greater abominations.

7 ¶And he brought me to the door of the court; and when I looked, behold a hole in the wall.

8 Then said he unto me, Son of man, dig now in the wall: and when I had digged in the wall, behold a door.

7:25 *they shall seek peace.* When the judgment of God falls, even sinful men will seek peace so that their lives will be saved. They will pray for it, seek it, and expect it, but it will not come. They will court their enemies to no avail. There always comes a time when the patience of God is exhausted and the door of grace is closed. It is presumption for people to assume that they may continue in their evil ways and that God will answer. Once the divine ear chooses not to hear, there can be no reversal of judgment.

8:1 *the sixth year* was the sixth year of Jehoiachin's captivity in Babylon, before the destruction of Jerusalem had taken place.

8:2ff Ezekiel sees God through the appearance of a man with girded loins like unto fire. Then the Spirit miraculously takes him to Jerusalem and to the temple, where he has a message to bring, a duty to perform. *the image of jealousy* was probably an image of a grove or an image of Baal set up in the house of God. A God who is jealous of his divine prerogatives cannot let such apostasy pass unnoticed.

9 And he said unto me, Go in, and behold the wicked abominations that
they do here.
10 So I went in and saw; and behold every form of creeping things, and
abominable beasts, and all the idols of the house of Israel, pourtrayed upon
the wall round about.

8:10 Ex 20:4; Isa 29:15

11 And there stood before them seventy men of the ancients of the house
of Israel, and in the midst of them stood Ja-az-a-ni'ah the son of Sha'phan,
with every man his censer in his hand; and a thick cloud of incense went
up.

8:11 Num 11:16, 25; 16:17, 35; Jer 19:1; Lk 10:1

12 Then said he unto me, Son of man, hast thou seen what the ancients of
the house of Israel do in the dark, every man in the chamber of his imagery?
for they say, The LORD seeth us not; the LORD hath forsaken the earth.
13 ¶He said also unto me, Turn thee yet again, *and* thou shalt see greater
abominations that they do.

☆8:12 Ezek 9:9

c. The Women Weeping for Their God, Tammuz

14 Then he brought me to the door of the gate of the LORD's house which
was toward the north; and, behold, there sat women weeping for Tam'muz.
15 ¶Then said he unto me, Hast thou seen *this*, O son of man? turn thee
yet again, *and* thou shalt see greater abominations than these.

☆8:14 Ezek 44:4; 46:9

d. The Worship of the Sun

16 And he brought me into the inner court of the LORD's house, and,
behold, at the door of the temple of the LORD, between the porch and the
altar, *were* about five and twenty men, with their backs toward the temple
of the LORD, and their faces toward the east; and they worshipped the sun
toward the east.

☆8:16 Deut 4:19; 17:3; 2 Chron 29:6; Job 31:26–28; Jer 2:27; 44:17; Ezek 23:39

e. God Will Not Pity Them

17 ¶Then he said unto me, Hast thou seen *this*, O son of man? Is it a light
thing to the house of Judah that they commit the abominations which they
commit here? for they have filled the land with violence, and have returned
to provoke me to anger: and, lo, they put the branch to their nose.
18 Therefore will I also deal in fury: mine eye shall not spare, neither will
I have pity: and though they cry in mine ears with a loud voice, *yet* will I
not hear them.

8:17 Jer 7:18, 19; Ezek 7:10, 11, 23; 9:9; Amos 3:10; Mic 2:2

☆8:18 Isa 1:15; Jer 11:11; Mic 3:4; Zech 7:13

8:12 These evildoers perform their idolatrous exercise in darkness lest they be seen. They suppose that: (1) because *they do it secretly God will not* know about it—thus they deny the omniscience of God; and (2) either God cannot deliver them or will not do so—thus they must look to some other god. They failed to see that if God had forsaken them, it was because of their own transgressions, not because God lacked either the power or the desire to save them.

8:14 *Tammuz* was a Babylonian vegetation god who went to the underworld during the dry season when vegetation withered and streams dried up. Public mourning took place when he was thought to go to the netherworld. Jewish women took part in this idolatrous worship, an indicator of the hold that idolatry had on the people in the Holy City. *women* [wept] *for Tammuz,* the god of fertility, because, according to Mesopotamian myths, he had been killed, and fertility had vanished with him.

8:16 Here the priests who were supposed to be offering true sacrifices to God are pictured as practicing abominable wickedness in God's very house. They had sunk so low that they worshipped the sun. These men who were entrusted with the true religion betrayed that trust and turned their backs toward the temple of the Lord. The jealousy of God to preserve his divine integrity could not allow this wickedness to go unpunished or overlooked.

8:18 God is offended. His wrath is released, his pity is gone, and prayer to him will not be heard.

2. God's Judgment Executed

a. Marking the Foreheads of the Innocent

9 HE cried also in mine ears with a loud voice, saying, Cause them that
have charge over the city to draw near, even every man *with* his
destroying weapon in his hand.

9:2 Ezek 10:2

2 And, behold, six men came from the way of the higher gate, which lieth
toward the north, and every man a slaughter weapon in his hand; and one
man among them *was* clothed with linen, with a writer's inkhorn by his
side: and they went in, and stood beside the brasen altar.

9:3☆ Ezek 10:4; 11:22, 23

3 And the glory of the God of Israel was gone up from the cherub,
whereupon he was, to the threshold of the house. And he called to the man
clothed with linen, which *had* the writer's inkhorn by his side;

9:4☆ Ex 12:7, 13; Ps 119:53, 136; 2 Cor 1:22; 2 Tim 2:19; Rev 7:2, 3

4 And the LORD said unto him, Go through the midst of the city, through
the midst of Jerusalem, and set a mark upon the foreheads of the men that
sigh and that cry for all the abominations that be done in the midst thereof.

b. The Death of the Guilty

9:5☆

5 ¶And to the others he said in mine hearing, Go ye after him through the
city, and smite: let not your eye spare, neither have ye pity:

9:6 Ex 12:23; 2 Chron 36:17; Ezek 5:11; 8:11, 12; Rev 9:4

6 Slay utterly old *and* young, both maids, and little children, and women:
but come not near any man upon whom *is* the mark; and begin at my
sanctuary. Then they began at the ancient men which *were* before the
house.

9:7 Ezek 7:20–22

7 And he said unto them, Defile the house, and fill the courts with the
slain: go ye forth. And they went forth, and slew in the city.

9:8 1 Chron 21:16; Ezek 11:13; Amos 7:2–6

8 ¶And it came to pass, while they were slaying them, and I was left, that
I fell upon my face, and cried, and said, Ah Lord GOD! wilt thou destroy all
the residue of Israel in thy pouring out of thy fury upon Jerusalem?

9:9☆ 2 Kgs 21:16; Ps 10:11; 94:7; Isa 29:15; Ezek 7:23; 8:12; 22:2, 3, 29; Mic 3:1–3; 7:3

9 Then said he unto me, The iniquity of the house of Israel and Judah *is*
exceeding great, and the land is full of blood, and the city full of
perverseness: for they say, The LORD hath forsaken the earth, and the
LORD seeth not.

9:10 Isa 65:6; Ezek 7:4; 24:14; Hos 9:7

10 And as for me also, mine eye shall not spare, neither will I have pity,
but I will recompense their way upon their head.
11 And, behold, the man clothed with linen, which *had* the inkhorn by his
side, reported the matter, saying, I have done as thou hast commanded me.

3. The Glory of the Lord Leaves the Temple

10:1☆ Ex 24:10; Ezek 1:22, 26; Rev 4:2, 3

10 THEN I looked, and, behold, in the firmament that was above the
head of the cherubims there appeared over them as it were a
sapphire stone, as the appearance of the likeness of a throne.

9:3 *to the threshold of,* i.e., "above the entrance." The glory of God filled the tabernacle and the Solomonic temple. Now Ezekiel sees God's glory departing from the temple. It hovered over the city and stopped for a time on the Mount of Olives. God was leaving his people, and once the glory had left, the city was defenseless against its enemies. (See 9:3; 11:23).

9:4 *the men that sigh and that cry* are the remnant who disapprove of Jerusalem's idolatry. God has them *marked for safety.*

9:5 As God's agent of death proceeds, no one is to be spared except those who have been specially marked (9:6).

9:9 *The iniquity . . . is great.* The Jews are guilty and their guilt must be atoned for. By their death the price is paid but not in full; it will remain forever without the justice of God being satisfied.

10:1 *sapphire,* literally, "lapis lazuli." Cherubim in the Scriptures are stated to be winged creatures of great beauty and power in the service of the Lord. Gen. 3:24 says that God placed the cherubim on the east side of Eden to keep Adam from eating of the tree of life and living forever. In the tabernacle, two cherubim were on either end of the lid or mercy seat of the ark of the covenant. They touched each other with the tips of their wings and bowed before the presence of God (Exod. 25:18–21). Figures of cherubim were embroidered on the veil that separated the Holy of Holies from the Holy Place (Exod. 26:31). John, in The Revelation, speaks of the cherubim as living creatures, four in

2 And he spake unto the man clothed with linen, and said, Go in between
the wheels, *even* under the cherub, and fill thine hand with coals of fire from
between the cherubims, and scatter *them* over the city. And he went in in
my sight.
3 Now the cherubims stood on the right side of the house, when the man
went in; and the cloud filled the inner court.
4 Then the glory of the LORD went up from the cherub, *and stood* over the
threshold of the house; and the house was filled with the cloud, and the
court was full of the brightness of the LORD's glory.
5 And the sound of the cherubims' wings was heard *even* to the outer
court, as the voice of the Almighty God when he speaketh.
6 And it came to pass, *that* when he had commanded the man clothed
with linen, saying, Take fire from between the wheels, from between the
cherubims; then he went in, and stood beside the wheels.
7 And *one* cherub stretched forth his hand from between the cherubims
unto the fire that *was* between the cherubims, and took *thereof,* and put *it*
into the hands of *him that was* clothed with linen: who took *it,* and went
out.
8 ¶And there appeared in the cherubims the form of a man's hand under
their wings.
9 And when I looked, behold the four wheels by the cherubims, one wheel
by one cherub, and another wheel by another cherub: and the appearance
of the wheels *was* as the colour of a beryl stone.
10 And *as for* their appearances, they four had one likeness, as if a wheel
had been in the midst of a wheel.
11 When they went, they went upon their four sides; they turned not as
they went, but to the place whither the head looked they followed it; they
turned not as they went.
12 And their whole body, and their backs, and their hands, and their
wings, and the wheels, *were* full of eyes round about, *even* the wheels that
they four had.
13 As for the wheels, it was cried unto them in my hearing, O wheel.
14 And every one had four faces: the first face *was* the face of a cherub,
and the second face *was* the face of a man, and the third the face of a lion,
and the fourth the face of an eagle.
15 And the cherubims were lifted up. This *is the living creature that I saw
by the river of Che'bar.*
16 And when the cherubims went, the wheels went by them: and when the
cherubims lifted up their wings to mount up from the earth, the same
wheels also turned not from beside them.
17 When they stood, *these* stood; and when they were lifted up, *these* lifted
up themselves *also:* for the spirit of the living creature *was* in them.
18 Then the glory of the LORD departed from off the threshold of the
house, and stood over the cherubims.
19 And the cherubims lifted up their wings, and mounted up from the
earth in my sight: when they went out, the wheels also *were* beside them,
and *every one* stood at the door of the east gate of the LORD's house; and
the glory of the God of Israel *was* over them above.

10:2 Ps 18:10–13; Isa 6:6; Ezek 1:15–21; 10:13; Rev 8:5
10:3 Ezek 8:3, 16
10:4 Ex 40:34, 35; Isa 6:1–4; Ezek 1:27, 28; 9:3; 11:22, 23
10:5 Job 40:9; Ezek 1:24; Rev 10:3
10:7 Ezek 1:8
10:9 Ezek 1:16, 17; Rev 21:18–20
10:14 1 Kgs 7:27–30, 36; Ezek 1:6, 10; 10:21; Rev 4:7
10:15 Ezek 1:3-6, 19-21
☆**10:17** Ezek 1:12
☆**10:18** Ps 18:10

number, who stand around and in the midst of the throne of God (Rev. 4:6, 7). The reference to the cherub in 28:14 is understood by many to speak of Satan, whose fall may have been described in Isa. 14:12–14.

10:17 The wheels and the cherubim are so interrelated that neither exists apart from the other.

10:18 The glory of God had filled the tabernacle built in Moses' day. When the Solomonic temple was finished, the glory of God entered the sanctuary when it was dedicated. Now the glory of God departs from the temple, never again to return. When the destroyed temple was rebuilt, the glory of God never filled it, nor was there any such manifestation of the divine presence in the temple of Jesus' day.

20 This *is* the living creature that I saw under the God of Israel by the river
of Che′bar; and I knew that they *were* the cherubims.
21 Every one had four faces apiece, and every one four wings; and the
likeness of the hands of a man *was* under their wings.
22 And the likeness of their faces *was* the same faces which I saw by the
river of Che′bar, their appearances and themselves: they went every one
straight forward.

4. The Leaders of the People Suffer Punishment

11 MOREOVER the spirit lifted me up, and brought me unto the east
gate of the LORD's house, which looketh eastward: and behold at
the door of the gate five and twenty men; among whom I saw Ja-az-a-ni′ah
the son of A′zur, and Pel-a-ti′ah the son of Be-nai′ah, princes of the people.
2 Then said he unto me, Son of man, these *are* the men that devise
mischief, and give wicked counsel in this city:
3 Which say, *It is* not near; let us build houses: this *city is* the caldron, and
we *be* the flesh.
4 ¶Therefore prophesy against them, prophesy, O son of man.
5 And the Spirit of the LORD fell upon me, and said unto me, Speak; Thus
saith the LORD; Thus have ye said, O house of Israel: for I know the things
that come into your mind, *every one of* them.
6 Ye have multiplied your slain in this city, and ye have filled the streets
thereof with the slain.
7 Therefore thus saith the Lord GOD; Your slain whom ye have laid in the
midst of it, they *are* the flesh, and this *city is* the caldron: but I will bring
you forth out of the midst of it.
8 Ye have feared the sword; and I will bring a sword upon you, saith the
Lord GOD.
9 And I will bring you out of the midst thereof, and deliver you into the
hands of strangers, and will execute judgments among you.
10 Ye shall fall by the sword; I will judge you in the border of Israel; and
ye shall know that I *am* the LORD.
11 This *city* shall not be your caldron, neither shall ye be the flesh in the
midst thereof; *but* I will judge you in the border of Israel:
12 And ye shall know that I *am* the LORD: for ye have not walked in my
statutes, neither executed my judgments, but have done after the manners
of the heathen that *are* round about you.
13 ¶And it came to pass, when I prophesied, that Pel-a-ti′ah the son of Be-
nai′ah died. Then fell I down upon my face, and cried with a loud voice,
and said, Ah Lord GOD! wilt thou make a full end of the remnant of Israel?
14 Again the word of the LORD came unto me, saying,
15 Son of man, thy brethren, *even* thy brethren, the men of thy kindred,
and all the house of Israel wholly, *are* they unto whom the inhabitants of

10:20 Ezek 1:5, 26; 10:15
10:21 Ezek 1:6, 8; 10:14; 41:18–20
10:22 Ezek 1:10, 12
11:1☆ 1 Kgs 18:12; 2 Kgs 2:16; Isa 30:1; Jer 5:5; Ezek 8:3; 43:5; Mic 2:1
11:3☆ Jer 1:13; Ezek 24:3, 6; 2 Pet 3:4
11:4 Ezek 3:4, 17; Hos 6:5
11:5☆ Ps 50:21; Isa 28:15; Jer 11:20; 17:10; Heb 4:13
11:6 Isa 1:15; Ezek 7:23; 22:2–6, 9, 12, 27; Mt 23:35
11:7☆ 2 Kgs 25:18-22; Jer 52:24-27
11:9 Deut 28:36, 49, 50; Ps 106:41; Rom 13:4
11:10 Num 34:8, 9; Josh 13:5; Ezek 6:4-7
11:12 Lev 26:40; Deut 12:30, 31; 2 Kgs 16:3–12; Ezek 8:10, 14, 16; 18:8, 9
11:13 Ezek 9:8; Amos 7:2, 5
11:15 Jer 24:1–5; Ezek 33:24

11:1 Again the Spirit places Ezekiel in a place where he can see the evils for himself. The leaders of Jerusalem feel quite safe, remain immersed in their transgressions, and think only of material things—such as building more houses. Had they taken God seriously *their thoughts would hardly rest on such matters.*
11:3 *this city is the cauldron, and we be the flesh,* i.e., "We are as safe in this city as flesh in a boiling pot; the walls of the city will be to us as *walls of brass,* and shall receive no more damage from the besiegers about it than the cauldron does from the fire under it."*
11:5 *thus saith the LORD.* The Spirit of God fell upon Ezekiel and told him to speak this phrase. The Holy Spirit is the divine author of the Scriptures. He is God. It is quite possible that many of the words of the Old Testament attributed to the Lord may have been spoken by the Holy Spirit. The Trinity is deeply involved in all aspects of the work of God. Thus, whatever the Father says, or Jesus Christ says, or the Holy Spirit says, God says.
11:7 "The bodies you have thrown there are the meat and this city is the pot, but I will drive you out of it" (NIV).

Jerusalem have said, Get you far from the LORD: unto us is this land given
in possession.
16 Therefore say, Thus saith the Lord GOD; Although I have cast them far
off among the heathen, and although I have scattered them among the
countries, yet will I be to them as a little sanctuary in the countries where
they shall come.
17 Therefore say, Thus saith the Lord GOD; I will even gather you from
the people, and assemble you out of the countries where ye have been
scattered, and I will give you the land of Israel.
18 And they shall come thither, and they shall take away all the detestable
things thereof and all the abominations thereof from thence.
19 And I will give them one heart, and I will put a new spirit within you;
and I will take the stony heart out of their flesh, and will give them an heart
of flesh:
20 That they may walk in my statutes, and keep mine ordinances, and do
them: and they shall be my people, and I will be their God.
21 But *as for them* whose heart walketh after the heart of their detestable
things and their abominations, I will recompense their way upon their own
heads, saith the Lord GOD.

5. The Glory of the Lord Leaves Jerusalem

22 ¶Then did the cherubims lift up their wings, and the wheels beside
them; and the glory of the God of Israel *was* over them above.
23 And the glory of the LORD went up from the midst of the city, and
stood upon the mountain which *is* on the east side of the city.
24 ¶Afterwards the spirit took me up, and brought me in a vision by the
Spirit of God into Chal-de'a, to them of the captivity. So the vision that I
had seen went up from me.
25 Then I spake unto them of the captivity all the things that the LORD
had shewed me.

E. THE REASONS FOR JERUSALEM'S FALL

1. The People's Refusal to Heed God

a. The Baggage of an Exile

12 THE word of the LORD also came unto me, saying,
2 Son of man, thou dwellest in the midst of a rebellious house,
which have eyes to see, and see not; they have ears to hear, and hear not:
for they *are* a rebellious house.
3 Therefore, thou son of man, prepare thee stuff for removing, and remove
by day in their sight; and thou shalt remove from thy place to another place
in their sight: it may be they will consider, though they *be* a rebellious
house.

11:16 Jer 29:7, 11
11:17 Isa 11:11–16; Jer 24:5; Ezek 20:41, 42; 28:25; Hos 1:10, 11; Amos 9:14, 15
☆**11:18** Ezek 5:11; 37:23
11:19 Deut 30:6; 2 Kgs 22:19; Jer 24:7; 32:39; Ezek 36:26; Zech 7:12; 2 Cor 3:3
11:20 Ezek 36:27; Hos 2:23
☆**11:21** Jer 16:18; Ezek 9:10; 16:43
11:22 Ezek 10:19
11:23 Ezek 8:4; Zech 14:4
☆**11:24** Ezek 8:3; 37:1; 2 Cor 12:2–4; Acts 10:16
☆**11:25** Ezek 2:7; 3:17, 27
12:2 Deut 29:4; Isa 6:9, 10; Jer 5:21; Ezek 2:6–8; Mt 13:13, 14; Jn 9:39–41
☆**12:3** Deut 5:29; Ps 18:13; Jer 26:3; Lk 20:13; 2 Tim 2:25

11:18 The captivity, which was occasioned by Israel's *idolatry, among other sins, effectually cured them* of this particular sin. Graven images, the worship of stones, sun, and moon, and other flagrant idolatries ceased to exist when Israel was restored to the land. Jesus did not accuse the scribes, Pharisees, and Sadducees of worshipping idols, although they were guilty of many other sins that brought about the destruction of Jerusalem and the temple in A.D. 70.

11:21 *as for those,* i.e., those who are presently in Jerusalem.

11:24, 25 Ezekiel, by the Spirit, is back in Chaldea with the exiles there. *the vision went up from me,* i.e., it mounted upwards and disappeared from my sight. (See note on Ps. 89:19 for information regarding visions.) Following this, Ezekiel told the exiles everything he had seen.

12:3 Ezekiel was told to carry his worldly possessions on his shoulders and start a journey. From this we learn that he obeyed God cheerfully although he was not to learn the full intent of God's purpose until the morning after he began carrying his baggage. He held his worldly possessions loosely and was ready to do anything he could to improve the spiritual state of God's people. God's servants must be willing and ready to perform difficult and inconvenient tasks so that if even one person is converted, the effort is worthwhile.

12:4
2 Kgs 25:4
Jer 39:4; 52:7

4 Then shalt thou bring forth thy stuff by day in their sight, as stuff for
removing: and thou shalt go forth at even in their sight, as they that go
forth into captivity.
5 Dig thou through the wall in their sight, and carry out thereby.

12:6
Isa 20:3
Ezek 4:3

6 In their sight shalt thou bear *it* upon *thy* shoulders, *and* carry *it* forth in
the twilight: thou shalt cover thy face, that thou see not the ground: for I
have set thee *for* a sign unto the house of Israel.

12:7
Ezek 24:18
Mt 21:6, 7
Mk 14:16
Jn 2:5–8

7 And I did so as I was commanded: I brought forth my stuff by day, as
stuff for captivity, and in the even I digged through the wall with mine
hand; I brought *it* forth in the twilight, *and* I bare *it* upon *my* shoulder in
their sight.
8 ¶And in the morning came the word of the LORD unto me, saying,

12:9
Ezek 2:5–8
17:12; 24:19

9 Son of man, hath not the house of Israel, the rebellious house, said unto
thee, What doest thou?

12:10☆
2 Kgs 9:25
Isa 13:1; 14:28
Mal 1:1

10 Say thou unto them, Thus saith the Lord GOD; This burden *concerneth*
the prince in Jerusalem, and all the house of Israel that *are* among them.

12:11
Jer 15:2, 28–30

11 Say, I *am* your sign: like as I have done, so shall it be done unto them:
they shall remove *and* go into captivity.

12:12☆
2 Kgs 25:4
Jer 39:4; 52:7

12 And the prince that *is* among them shall bear upon *his* shoulder in the
twilight, and shall go forth: they shall dig through the wall to carry out
thereby: he shall cover his face, that he see not the ground with *his* eyes.

12:13☆
Isa 24:17
Jer 39:7
Hos 7:12

13 My net also will I spread upon him, and he shall be taken in my snare:
and I will bring him to Babylon *to* the land of the Chal-de′ans; yet shall he
not see it, though he shall die there.

12:14
Ezek 5:2; 17:21

14 And I will scatter toward every wind all that *are* about him to help him,
and all his bands; and I will draw out the sword after them.
15 And they shall know that I *am* the LORD, when I shall scatter them
among the nations, and disperse them in the countries.

12:16☆
Deut 29:24–28
1 Kgs 9:6–9
Jer 22:8, 9

16 But I will leave a few men of them from the sword, from the famine,
and from the pestilence; that they may declare all their abominations
among the heathen whither they come; and they shall know that I *am* the
LORD.

b. Eating and Drinking in Despair

17 ¶Moreover the word of the LORD came to me, saying,
18 Son of man, eat thy bread with quaking, and drink thy water with
trembling and with carefulness;

12:19
Isa 6:11
Mic 7:13
Zech 7:14

19 And say unto the people of the land, Thus saith the Lord GOD of the
inhabitants of Jerusalem, *and* of the land of Israel; They shall eat their
bread with carefulness, and drink their water with astonishment, that her
land may be desolate from all that is therein, because of the violence of all
them that dwell therein.

12:20
Isa 7:23, 24
Jer 25:9
Dan 9:17

20 And the cities that are inhabited shall be laid waste, and the land shall
be desolate; and ye shall know that I *am* the LORD.

12:10 *the prince in Jerusalem,* i.e., "King Zedekiah." Not only would the king be captured and sent to Babylon, a remnant of the people would also go into the captivity and wait seventy years for their children and grandchildren to return.

12:12, 13 *that he see not the ground with his eyes* and *yet shall he not see it.* These statements apparently refer to the fact that the king's eyes were blinded before he was taken to Babylon (see Jer. 52:11).†

12:16 Some of God's people will be cut off. Others will be scattered but not cut off, that they might bear witness in their captivity to their sins and find restoration when they repented. God was not finished with Israel, for they were still the custodians of his revealed Word, and from their seed the Messiah was to come in the fullness of time.

c. God Will Execute Judgment Now

21 ¶And the word of the LORD came unto me, saying,
22 Son of man, what *is* that proverb *that* ye have in the land of Israel,
saying, The days are prolonged, and every vision faileth?
23 Tell them therefore, Thus saith the Lord GOD; I will make this proverb
to cease, and they shall no more use it as a proverb in Israel; but say unto
them, The days are at hand, and the effect of every vision.
24 For there shall be no more any vain vision nor flattering divination
within the house of Israel.
25 For I *am* the LORD: I will speak, and the word that I shall speak shall
come to pass; it shall be no more prolonged: for in your days, O rebellious
house, will I say the word, and will perform it, saith the Lord GOD.
26 ¶Again the word of the LORD came to me, saying,
27 Son of man, behold, *they of* the house of Israel say, The vision that he
seeth *is* for many days *to come*, and he prophesieth of the times *that are* far
off.
28 Therefore say unto them, Thus saith the Lord GOD; There shall none of
my words be prolonged any more, but the word which I have spoken shall
be done, saith the Lord GOD.

☆**12:22** Jer 5:12; Amos 6:3; 2 Pet 3:3, 4
12:24 1 Kgs 22:11–13; Prov 26:28; Jer 14:13–16; Zech 13:2–4
12:25 Num 14:28–34; Hab 1:5
12:27 Dan 10:14

2. Listening to False Prophets and Prophetesses

a. Ezekiel's Prophecy against False Prophets

13 AND the word of the LORD came unto me, saying,
2 Son of man, prophesy against the prophets of Israel that
prophesy, and say thou unto them that prophesy out of their own hearts,
Hear ye the word of the LORD;
3 Thus saith the Lord GOD; Woe unto the foolish prophets, that follow
their own spirit, and have seen nothing!
4 O Israel, thy prophets are like the foxes in the deserts.
5 Ye have not gone up into the gaps, neither made up the hedge for the
house of Israel to stand in the battle in the day of the LORD.
6 They have seen vanity and lying divination, saying, The LORD saith: and
the LORD hath not sent them: and they have made *others* to hope that they
would confirm the word.
7 Have ye not seen a vain vision, and have ye not spoken a lying
divination, whereas ye say, The LORD saith *it;* albeit I have not spoken?
8 Therefore thus saith the Lord GOD; Because ye have spoken vanity, and
seen lies, therefore, behold, I *am* against you, saith the Lord GOD.
9 And mine hand shall be upon the prophets that see vanity, and that
divine lies: they shall not be in the assembly of my people, neither shall

☆**13:1ff**
☆**13:2** Isa 9:15; 56:9–12; Jer 37:19; Zech 11:15; 2 Pet 2:1–3
☆**13:3**
13:5 Ps 106:23; Isa 58:12; Eph 6:13, 14; Rev: 16:14
13:6 Prov 14:15; Jer 28:15; 29:8; Mk 13:22, 23; 2 Thess 2:11
13:8 Nah 2:13
☆**13:9** Ex 32:32, 33; Ezra 2:59–63; Ps 69:28; Jer 20:3–6; Dan 12:1; Phil 4:3

12:22 The prophecies given about the coming destruction had been confirmed to the people by visions and illustrated by signs. But nothing happened, and they assumed that nothing would happen, or that if it did happen, it would be so far in the future that they did not need to concern themselves about it. They would have peace in their time. Moreover, when nothing happened they concluded that they could no longer trust the true prophets. God now tells them that what had been prophesied so far in advance would indeed come to pass, and that it would be in their days.

13:1ff Ezekiel sharply condemns false prophets, not because he is envious of them or threatened by them. Their great sin is that they have challenged God and hurt the people.

13:2 Ezekiel is now told to *prophesy against the prophets of Israel* who prophesied and were false prophets. False prophets did not arise in Israel until after the people had rejected and abused the true prophets. So it was to be in the days of the Messiah. False messiahs did not arise until after the true Messiah had been rejected. When the true preachers of the Word of God are rejected by men in our generation, then false prophets speaking smooth words and offering easy solutions will arise to replace them.

13:3 False prophets are foolish prophets, for they make fools of themselves. They claim to have been sent from God, but when their prophecies fall to the ground, they are shown up as pretenders or counterfeits.

13:9 God's hand is against the false prophets. God will seize them and bring them before the bar of divine justice, and no place will be found for them in the commonwealth of his people.

they be written in the writing of the house of Israel, neither shall they enter
into the land of Israel; and ye shall know that I *am* the Lord GOD.
13:10☆ 10¶Because, even because they have seduced my people, saying, Peace;
Jer 8:11; 50:6 and *there was* no peace; and one built up a wall, and, lo, others daubed it
1 Tim 4:1 2 Tim 3:13 with untempered *morter:*
11Say unto them which daub *it* with untempered *morter*, that it shall fall:
there shall be an overflowing shower; and ye, O great hailstones, shall fall;
and a stormy wind shall rend *it*.
12Lo, when the wall is fallen, shall it not be said unto you, Where *is* the
daubing wherewith ye have daubed *it?*
13:13 13Therefore thus saith the Lord GOD; I will even rend *it* with a stormy
Ex 9:24, 25 Ps 18:12, 13 wind in my fury; and there shall be an overflowing shower in mine anger,
Rev 11:19 16:21 and great hailstones in *my* fury to consume *it*.
13:14 14So will I break down the wall that ye have daubed with untempered
Mic 1:6 1 Cor 3:11–15 *morter*, and bring it down to the ground, so that the foundation thereof
shall be discovered, and it shall fall, and ye shall be consumed in the midst
thereof: and ye shall know that I *am* the LORD.
15Thus will I accomplish my wrath upon the wall, and upon them that
have daubed it with untempered *morter*, and will say unto you, The wall *is*
no *more*, neither they that daubed it;
13:16 16*To wit*, the prophets of Israel which prophesy concerning Jerusalem,
Isa 57:21 and which see visions of peace for her, and *there is* no peace, saith the Lord
GOD.

b. Ezekiel's Prophecy against False Prophetesses

13:17☆ 17¶Likewise, thou son of man, set thy face against the daughters of thy
Judg 4:4 2 Kgs 22:14 people, which prophesy out of their own heart; and prophesy thou against
Lk 2:36 them,
Acts 21:9 Rev 2:20 18And say, Thus saith the Lord GOD; Woe to the *women* that sew pillows
13:18☆ to all armholes, and make kerchiefs upon the head of every stature to hunt
souls! Will ye hunt the souls of my people, and will ye save the souls alive
that come unto you?
13:19 19And will ye pollute me among my people for handfuls of barley and for
Jer 23:14, 17 pieces of bread, to slay the souls that should not die, and to save the souls
alive that should not live, by your lying to my people that hear *your* lies?
20Wherefore thus saith the Lord GOD; Behold, I *am* against your pillows,
wherewith ye there hunt the souls to make *them* fly, and I will tear them
from your arms, and will let the souls go, *even* the souls that ye hunt to
make *them* fly.
13:21 21Your kerchiefs also will I tear, and deliver my people out of your hand,
Ps 91:3; 124:7 and they shall be no more in your hand to be hunted; and ye shall know
that I *am* the LORD.

13:10 False prophets like to tell people the things they wish to hear, not the things God wants them to hear. They prophesy the peace all hearts desire and fool their listeners, for there is no peace.
13:17 *prophesy out of their own heart.* This condemnation is not pronounced on the prophetesses because they are women or because women should not prophesy; rather, they are judged because they spoke what they had dreamed up in their minds. God can speak and has spoken through prophetesses, but not through counterfeits.
13:18 *sew pillows to all armholes,* "to signify that they might be easy and repose themselves, and needed not be disquieted with the apprehensions of trouble approaching."* *made kerchiefs upon the head of every stature.* "These kerchiefs were badges of liberty or triumph, intimating that they should not only be delivered from the Chaldeans, but be victorious over them."* *will ye hunt the souls of my people,* i.e., "will you influence them to do what you want them to do and thus tyrannize them for your own profit." *will ye save the souls alive that come unto you?,* i.e., they made them think they were saved while refusing to repent and mend their ways, thus they hardened their hearts.

[22]Because with lies ye have made the heart of the righteous sad, whom I
have not made sad; and strengthened the hands of the wicked, that he
should not return from his wicked way, by promising him life:
[23]Therefore ye shall see no more vanity, nor divine divinations: for I will
deliver my people out of your hand: and ye shall know that I *am* the LORD.

13:22 Amos 5:12; 2 Pet 2:18, 19
13:23 Mic 3:6; Zech 13:3

3. The Idolatry of the Elders
a. Their Hypocrisy

14 THEN came certain of the elders of Israel unto me, and sat before
me.
[2]And the word of the LORD came unto me, saying,
[3]Son of man, these men have set up their idols in their heart, and put the
stumblingblock of their iniquity before their face: should I be inquired of at
all by them?
[4]Therefore speak unto them, and say unto them, Thus saith the Lord
GOD; Every man of the house of Israel that setteth up his idols in his heart,
and putteth the stumblingblock of his iniquity before his face, and cometh
to the prophet; I the LORD will answer him that cometh according to the
multitude of his idols;
[5]That I may take the house of Israel in their own heart, because they are
all estranged from me through their idols.

☆**14:1** 2 Kgs 6:32
☆**14:3** Isa 1:15; Zeph 1:3
14:4 1 Kgs 21:20–24; 2 Kgs 1:16; Isa 66:4
14:5 Deut 32:14, 15; Jer 2:11; Hos 10:2; Zech 7:12

b. The Warning to Repent

[6]¶Therefore say unto the house of Israel, Thus saith the Lord GOD;
Repent, and turn *yourselves* from your idols; and turn away your faces from
all your abominations.
[7]For every one of the house of Israel, or of the stranger that sojourneth in
Israel, which separateth himself from me, and setteth up his idols in his
heart, and putteth the stumblingblock of his iniquity before his face, and
cometh to a prophet to inquire of him concerning me; I the LORD will
answer him by myself:
[8]And I will set my face against that man, and will make him a sign and
a proverb, and I will cut him off from the midst of my people; and ye shall
know that I *am* the LORD.
[9]And if the prophet be deceived when he hath spoken a thing, I the LORD
have deceived that prophet, and I will stretch out my hand upon him, and
will destroy him from the midst of my people Israel.
[10]And they shall bear the punishment of their iniquity: the punishment of
the prophet shall be even as the punishment of him that seeketh *unto him;*
[11]That the house of Israel may go no more astray from me, neither be
polluted any more with all their transgressions; but that they may be my
people, and I may be their God, saith the Lord GOD.

☆**14:6** 1 Sam 7:3; Neh 1:9; Isa 30:22; 55:6, 7
14:8 Isa 65:15; Jer 24:9; Rom 11:22
14:9 Jer 6:14, 15
14:11 Deut 13:11; 19:20; Isa 9:16; Ezek 44:10, 15

c. The Presence of Noah, Daniel, and Job Could Not Save the Wicked

[12]¶The word of the LORD came again to me, saying,
[13]*Son of man, when* the land sinneth against me by trespassing griev-
ously, then will I stretch out mine hand upon it, and will break the staff of

14:13 Ezek 15:8; 20:27

14:1ff Some who were thought to be spiritual leaders among the exiles inquire of the prophet concerning Jerusalem. God knows that in their private lives they are idolators and thus hypocrites. He will answer them according to their sinfulness and give them no hope. **14:3** *set up their idols in their heart.* They had come to love their idols, were wedded to them, and could not bear to surrender them or part with them.

14:6ff God still urges his people to repent. There are counterfeit prophets and counterfeit saints who shall perish together. God intends to rid himself and Israel of those who are wretched sinners, as a warning to the faithful to keep his ways and walk in his paths. In verse 11 the heart of God is stated: he wants them to be his people so he may be their God, neither going astray again nor defiling themselves.

the bread thereof, and will send famine upon it, and will cut off man and
beast from it:

14:14☆ Gen 6:8; 8:20, 21; Job 1:1, 5; Dan 10:11; Heb 11:7

14 Though these three men, Noah, Daniel, and Job, were in it, they should
deliver *but* their own souls by their righteousness, saith the Lord GOD.
15 If I cause noisome beasts to pass through the land, and they spoil it, so
that it be desolate, that no man may pass through because of the beasts:

14:16 Gen 19:29; Acts 27:24

16 *Though* these three men *were* in it, *as* I live, saith the Lord GOD, they
shall deliver neither sons nor daughters; they only shall be delivered, but
the land shall be desolate.
17 ¶Or *if* I bring a sword upon that land, and say, Sword, go through the
land; so that I cut off man and beast from it:
18 Though these three men *were* in it, *as* I live, saith the Lord GOD, they
shall deliver neither sons nor daughters, but they only shall be delivered
themselves.

14:19 Jer 14:12; Ezek 5:12

19 ¶Or *if* I send a pestilence into that land, and pour out my fury upon it
in blood, to cut off from it man and beast:
20 Though Noah, Daniel, and Job, *were* in it, *as* I live, saith the Lord GOD,
they shall deliver neither son nor daughter; they shall *but* deliver their own
souls by their righteousness.

14:21 Amos 4:6–10; Rev 6:4–8

21 For thus saith the Lord GOD; How much more when I send my four
sore judgments upon Jerusalem, the sword, and the famine, and the
noisome beast, and the pestilence, to cut off from it man and beast?

14:22☆ Ezek 36:20

22 ¶Yet, behold, therein shall be left a remnant that shall be brought forth,
both sons and daughters: behold, they shall come forth unto you, and ye
shall see their way and their doings: and ye shall be comforted concerning
the evil that I have brought upon Jerusalem, *even* concerning all that I have
brought upon it.

14:23☆

23 And they shall comfort you, when ye see their ways and their doings:
and ye shall know that I have not done without cause all that I have done
in it, saith the Lord GOD.

F. THE NECESSITY OF JUDGMENT AND PUNISHMENT

1. The Vines of the Forest

15:1☆; 15:2 Ps 80:8–16; Isa 5:1–7; Hos 10:1; Jn 15:1–6

15 AND the word of the LORD came unto me, saying,
2 Son of man, What is the vine tree more than any tree, *or than* a
branch which is among the trees of the forest?
3 Shall wood be taken thereof to do any work? or will *men* take a pin of it
to hang any vessel thereon?

15:4 Isa 27:11; Heb 6:8

4 Behold, it is cast into the fire for fuel; the fire devoureth both the ends of
it, and the midst of it is burned. Is it meet for *any* work?
5 Behold, when it was whole, it was meet for no work: how much less shall
it be meet yet for *any* work, when the fire hath devoured it, and it is burned?
6 ¶Therefore thus saith the Lord GOD; As the vine tree among the trees of

15:7 Lev 26:17; 1 Kgs 19:17; Amos 5:19; 9:1–4

the forest, which I have given to the fire for fuel, so will I give the
inhabitants of Jerusalem.
7 And I will set my face against them; they shall go out from *one* fire, and

---

14:14 The apostasy of Ezekiel's day was so acute that God said the prayers even of Israel's greatest and most holy saints—*Noah, Daniel, and Job—could not prevail.* The best that their godly intercessions could do would be to save only the intercessors themselves.

14:22, 23 Jerusalem is marked for ruin, yet in its midst are a few who are faithful to God. Thus God preserves some who are examples of divine grace. They shall go into captivity but their children will be preserved to return to the land at a later date. God insists that what he has done is not without good cause.

15:1ff No one uses the wood of the grapevine to make furniture. When its usefulness is over, it is fit only for burning. So has God given the useless sinners of Jerusalem to the fire for burning. They are good for nothing else. The punishment is both sure and required by God's holiness and his righteous judgment.

another fire shall devour them; and ye shall know that I *am* the LORD, when
I set my face against them.
8 And I will make the land desolate, because they have committed a
trespass, saith the Lord GOD.

2. The Prostitute Wife
a. Jerusalem, a Foundling

16 AGAIN the word of the LORD came unto me, saying,
2 Son of man, cause Jerusalem to know her abominations,
3 And say, Thus saith the Lord GOD unto Jerusalem; Thy birth and thy
nativity *is* of the land of Canaan; thy father *was* an Am′or-ite, and thy
mother an Hittite.
4 And *as for* thy nativity, in the day thou wast born thy navel was not cut,
neither wast thou washed in water to supple *thee;* thou wast not salted at
all, nor swaddled at all.
5 None eye pitied thee, to do any of these unto thee, to have compassion
upon thee; but thou wast cast out in the open field, to the lothing of thy
person, in the day that thou wast born.
6 ¶And when I passed by thee, and saw thee polluted in thine own blood,
I said unto thee *when thou wast* in thy blood, Live; yea, I said unto thee
when thou wast in thy blood, Live.
7 I have caused thee to multiply as the bud of the field, and thou hast
increased and waxen great, and thou art come to excellent ornaments: *thy*
breasts are fashioned, and thine hair is grown, whereas thou *wast* naked and
bare.

b. God Rescues the Foundling

8 Now when I passed by thee, behold, thy time *was*
the time of love; and I spread my skirt over thee, and covered thy
nakedness: yea, I sware unto thee, and entered into a covenant with thee,
saith the Lord GOD, and thou becamest mine.
9 Then washed I thee with water; yea, I throughly washed away thy blood
from thee, and I anointed thee with oil.
10 I clothed thee also with broidered work, and shod thee with badgers'
skin, and I girded thee about with fine linen, and I covered thee with silk.
11 I decked thee also with ornaments, and I put bracelets upon thy hands,
and a chain on thy neck.
12 And I put a jewel on thy forehead, and earrings in thine ears, and a
beautiful crown upon thine head.
13 Thus wast thou decked with gold and silver; and thy raiment *was of* fine
linen, and silk, and broidered work; thou didst eat fine flour, and honey,
and oil: and thou wast exceeding beautiful, and thou didst prosper into a
kingdom.
14 And thy renown went forth among the heathen for thy beauty: for it
was perfect through my comeliness, which I had put upon thee, saith the
Lord GOD.

☆**16:1**
16:2 Isa 58:1; Hos 8:1
16:5 Deut 32:10; Isa 49:15; Jer 9:21, 22; 22:19
☆**16:6** Ex 1:7; Deut 1:10; Ps 105:10-15
☆**16:7**
☆**16:8** Gen 22:16–18; Ex 24:7, 8; Deut 4:31; Hos 2:18-20
16:9 Ex 26:36; Ezek 26:16; 27:7, 16
16:11 Gen 24:22, 47; Pro 4:9; Isa 3:18, 19
16:12 Jer 13:18
16:13 Deut 32:13, 14; Ps 45:13, 14
16:14 Deut 4:6–8, 32–38; 1 Kgs 10:1, 24; Ps 50:2; Lam 2:15

16:1 Ezekiel is to show forth the sins of his people in detail and with specific illustrations.

16:6, 7 God took Israel in Egypt, a foundling with little or no hope, delivered them, and made them a great nation.

16:8 God looked upon Israel with kindness and tender affection. He obviously did not love them on the grounds that there was anything good in them, for often they were disobedient. Yet he called them to be his people and made a gracious covenant with them. So in this age of grace Christ has come to redeem those in whom there is no good thing. In kindness and love, the Father sent the Son to redeem us and the Holy Spirit to sanctify us.

c. The Foundling Becomes a Prostitute

16:15☆
Ezek 27:3

15 ¶But thou didst trust in thine own beauty, and playedst the harlot
because of thy renown, and pouredst out thy fornications on every one that
passed by; his it was.
16 And of thy garments thou didst take, and deckedst thy high places with
divers colours, and playedst the harlot thereupon: *the like things* shall not
come, neither shall it be *so*.

16:17
Ex 32:3, 4
Hos 2:13; 10:1

17 Thou hast also taken thy fair jewels of my gold and of my silver, which
I had given thee, and madest to thyself images of men, and didst commit
whoredom with them,
18 And tookest thy broidered garments, and coveredst them: and thou
hast set mine oil and mine incense before them.
19 My meat also which I gave thee, fine flour, and oil, and honey,
wherewith I fed thee, thou hast even set it before them for a sweet savour:
and *thus* it was, saith the Lord GOD.

16:20
Ex 13:2, 12
Ps 106: 37, 38
Jer 7:31

16:21
2 Kgs 17:17
21:6

20 Moreover thou hast taken thy sons and thy daughters, whom thou hast
borne unto me, and these hast thou sacrificed unto them to be devoured. *Is
this* of thy whoredoms a small matter,
21 That thou hast slain my children, and delivered them to cause them to
pass through *the fire* for them?
22 And in all thine abominations and thy whoredoms thou hast not
remembered the days of thy youth, when thou wast naked and bare, *and*
wast polluted in thy blood.
23 And it came to pass after all thy wickedness, (woe, woe unto thee! saith
the Lord GOD;)

16:24
2 Kgs 21:3–7
23:5-7
Ps 78:58
Isa 57:5–7

24 *That* thou hast also built unto thee an eminent place, and hast made
thee an high place in every street.
25 Thou hast built thy high place at every head of the way, and hast made
thy beauty to be abhorred, and hast opened thy feet to every one that
passed by, and multiplied thy whoredoms.

16:26
Jer 7:18, 19

26 Thou hast also committed fornication with the Egyptians thy neigh-
bours, great of flesh; and hast increased thy whoredoms, to provoke me to
anger.

16:27
Isa 9:12

27 Behold, therefore I have stretched out my hand over thee, and have
diminished thine ordinary *food*, and delivered thee unto the will of them
that hate thee, the daughters of the Philistines, which are ashamed of thy
lewd way.

16:28
Judg 10:6
2 Kgs 16:7–18
2 Chron
28:16–23
Hos 10:6

16:30
Prov 7:11–13
9:13
Isa 3:9
Rev 17:1–6

16:31☆
Isa 52:3
Hos 12:11

28 Thou hast played the whore also with the Assyrians, because thou wast
unsatiable; yea, thou hast played the harlot with them, and yet couldest not
be satisfied.
29 Thou hast moreover multiplied thy fornication in the land of Canaan
unto Chal-de′a; and yet thou wast not satisfied herewith.
30 How weak is thine heart, saith the Lord GOD, seeing thou doest all
these *things*, the work of an imperious whorish woman;
31 In that thou buildest thine eminent place in the head of every way, and

---

16:15 In his covenant with Israel, God married this people as a man weds the woman who becomes his wife. The bride proved herself to be unfaithful and broke the marriage covenant, only to be cast away as an adulterous spouse. Beautiful Israel, who under David and Solomon became world-renowned, became so enamoured with its neighbors that it joined them in their pagan worship and took over their pagan life-styles. It has scorned and broken its covenant of marriage with the true God.

16:31 God charges his people with a greater sin than that of the harlot, who expects to be paid for the service she renders. God says Israel plays the harlot, but pays those with whom she engages in adultery. No one solicited God's people to engage in harlotry (16:34). This people, as the wife of God, solicited others and paid them for their services. This was how low Israel had sunk from her former pristine and holy state, when she was the virgin bride of a covenant-keeping God.

makest thine high place in every street; and hast not been as an harlot, in
that thou scornest hire;
32 *But as* a wife that committeth adultery, *which* taketh strangers instead
of her husband!
33 They give gifts to all whores: but thou givest thy gifts to all thy lovers,
and hirest them, that they may come unto thee on every side for thy
whoredom.
34 And the contrary is in thee from *other* women in thy whoredoms,
whereas none followeth thee to commit whoredoms: and in that thou givest
a reward, and no reward is given unto thee, therefore thou art contrary.

16:33 Hos 8:9, 10 Joel 3:3 Lk 15:30

d. God Judges the Prostitute's Adultery

35 ¶Wherefore, O harlot, hear the word of the LORD:
36 Thus saith the Lord GOD; Because thy filthiness was poured out, and
thy nakedness discovered through thy whoredoms with thy lovers, and with
all the idols of thy abominations, and by the blood of thy children, which
thou didst give unto them;
37 Behold, therefore I will gather all thy lovers, with whom thou hast
taken pleasure, and all *them* that thou hast loved, with all *them* that thou
hast hated; I will even gather them round about against thee, and will
discover thy nakedness unto them, that they may see all thy nakedness.
38 And I will judge thee, as women that break wedlock and shed blood are
judged; and I will give thee blood in fury and jealousy.
39 And I will also give thee into their hand, and they shall throw down
thine eminent place, and shall break down thy high places: they shall strip
thee also of thy clothes, and shall take thy fair jewels, and leave thee naked
and bare.
40 They shall also bring up a company against thee, and they shall stone
thee with stones, and thrust thee through with their swords.
41 And they shall burn thine houses with fire, and execute judgment upon
thee in the sight of many women: and I will cause thee to cease from
playing the harlot, and thou also shalt give no hire any more.
42 So will I make my fury toward thee to rest, and my jealousy shall
depart from thee, and I will be quiet, and will be no more angry.
43 Because thou hast not remembered the days of thy youth, but hast
fretted me in all these *things;* behold, therefore I also will recompense thy
way upon *thine* head, saith the Lord GOD: and thou shalt not commit this
lewdness above all thine abominations.

☆**16:35ff**

16:36 Jer 19:5 Ezek 20:31 23:37

16:37 Isa 47:3 Nah 3:5, 6

16:38 Ps 79:3, 5 Zeph 1:17 Rev 16:6

16:40 2 Kgs 25:9 Jer 39:8

16:42 2 Sam 24:25 Isa 40:1, 2 54:9, 10

16:43 Ps 78:42 Isa 63:10

e. The Evil Is Worse than Sodom and Samaria

44 ¶Behold, every one that useth proverbs shall use *this* proverb against
thee, saying, As *is* the mother, *so is* her daughter.
45 Thou *art* thy mother's daughter, that lotheth her husband and her
children; and thou *art* the sister of thy sisters, which lothed their husbands
and their children: your mother *was* an Hittite, and your father an Am'or-
ite.

☆**16:44ff**

16:45 Isa 1:4 Zech 11:8

16:35ff Jerusalem is accused of two violations of the law of God. She was guilty of idolatry (or breaking the first two commandments of the ten). She was guilty also of breaking the first two commandments of the second table of the law by the murder of her own innocent infants. Because of these transgressions of the law (which means they had repudiated the law-giver), judgment shall fall. So verse 43 speaks of God's requiting these people for their sins, based on his justice.

16:44ff God shows how judgment had fallen on such as the people of Sodom and Samaria. And if judgment fell on them, how much more must judgment fall on Jerusalem, for she has committed more and worse sins than those whom God had destroyed earlier (16:52).

16:46 Gen 13:11–13; Deut 32:32; Jer 3:8–11

46 And thine elder sister *is* Sa-ma'ri-a, she and her daughters that dwell at thy left hand: and thy younger sister, that dwelleth at thy right hand, *is* Sodom and her daughters.

16:47 1 Kgs 16:31; 2 Kgs 21:9; Jn 15:21, 22; 1 Cor 5:1

47 Yet hast thou not walked after their ways, nor done after their abominations: but, as *if that were* a very little *thing*, thou wast corrupted more than they in all thy ways.

16:48 Mt 11:23, 24

48 *As* I live, saith the Lord GOD, Sodom thy sister hath not done, she nor her daughters, as thou hast done, thou and thy daughters.

16:49 Gen 13:10; Ps 138:6; Isa 22:13; Lk 12:16–20

49 Behold, this was the iniquity of thy sister Sodom, pride, fulness of bread, and abundance of idleness was in her and in her daughters, neither did she strengthen the hand of the poor and needy.

16:50 Gen 19:24, 25

50 And they were haughty, and committed abomination before me: therefore I took them away as I saw *good*.

16:51 Jer 3:8–11; Mt 12:41, 42; Rom 3:9–20

51 Neither hath Sa-ma'ri-a committed half of thy sins; but thou hast multiplied thine abominations more than they, and hast justified thy sisters in all thine abominations which thou hast done.

52 Thou also, which hast judged thy sisters, bear thine own shame for thy sins that thou hast committed more abominable than they: they are more righteous than thou: yea, be thou confounded also, and bear thy shame, in that thou hast justified thy sisters.

16:53 Isa 19:24, 25

53 When I shall bring again their captivity, the captivity of Sodom and her daughters, and the captivity of Sa-ma'ri-a and her daughters, then *will I bring again* the captivity of thy captives in the midst of them:

16:54 Jer 2:26

54 That thou mayest bear thine own shame, and mayest be confounded in all that thou hast done, in that thou art a comfort unto them.

f. God Promises Restoration

55 When thy sisters, Sodom and her daughters, shall return to their former estate, and Sa-ma'ri-a and her daughters shall return to their former estate, then thou and thy daughters shall return to your former estate.

56 For thy sister Sodom was not mentioned by thy mouth in the day of thy pride,

16:57 2 Kgs 16:5–7; 2 Chron 28:5, 6, 18–23; Hos 2:10; 7:1

57 Before thy wickedness was discovered, as at the time of *thy* reproach of the daughters of Syria, and all *that are* round about her, the daughters of the Philistines, which despise thee round about.

58 Thou hast borne thy lewdness and thine abominations, saith the LORD.

16:59☆ Isa 24:5; Jer 32:38–41

59 For thus saith the Lord GOD; I will even deal with thee as thou hast done, which hast despised the oath in breaking the covenant.

16:60☆

60 ¶Nevertheless I will remember my covenant with thee in the days of thy youth, and I will establish unto thee an everlasting covenant.

61 Then thou shalt remember thy ways, and be ashamed, when thou shalt receive thy sisters, thine elder and thy younger: and I will give them unto thee for daughters, but not by thy covenant.

16:62☆ Jer 24:7

62 And I will establish my covenant with thee; and thou shalt know that I *am* the LORD:

16:63 Ezra 9:6; Ps 39:9; Dan 9:7, 8; Rom 3:19

63 That thou mayest remember, and be confounded, and never open thy mouth any more because of thy shame, when I am pacified toward thee for all that thou hast done, saith the Lord GOD.

16:59, 60 Israel's apostasy is so great that judgment must be executed. But God will never forget his covenant with his people. Grace and lovingkindness will prevail, and a future restoration is in God's plan for Israel. Someday the nation will be regathered to its ancestral land.

16:62 Here the promise of a reestablished covenant is repeated (see 16:60). God will be glorified, for they will know him as God and as One faithful to his covenant promises. In other instances God said, "You shall know that I am the LORD," by way of designating himself as the requiter of their sins. But here it is said in mercy for their comfort, because they would be redeemed.

3. The Eagles and the Cedar Tree
a. The Riddle Presented

17 AND the word of the LORD came unto me, saying,
2Son of man, put forth a riddle, and speak a parable unto the ☆**17:2**
house of Israel; Ezek 20:49; 24:3
3And say, Thus saith the Lord GOD; A great eagle with great wings, ☆**17:3**
longwinged, full of feathers, which had divers colours, came unto Lebanon, Jer 48:40 Dan 4:22
and took the highest branch of the cedar:
4He cropped off the top of his young twigs, and carried it into a land of ☆**17:4**
traffick; he set it in a city of merchants.
5He took also of the seed of the land, and planted it in a fruitful field; he **17:5**
placed *it* by great waters, *and* set it *as* a willow tree. Deut 8:7–9 Isa 44:4 Jer 37:1
6And it grew, and became a spreading vine of low stature, whose
branches turned toward him, and the roots thereof were under him: so it
became a vine, and brought forth branches, and shot forth sprigs.
7There was also another great eagle with great wings and many feathers: ☆**17:7**
and, behold, this vine did bend her roots toward him, and shot forth her Ezek 31:4
branches toward him, that he might water it by the furrows of her
plantation.
8It was planted in a good soil by great waters, that it might bring forth
branches, and that it might bear fruit, that it might be a goodly vine.

b. The Riddle Explained

9Say thou, Thus saith the Lord GOD; Shall it prosper? shall he not pull
up the roots thereof, and cut off the fruit thereof, that it wither? it shall
wither in all the leaves of her spring, even without great power or many
people to pluck it up by the roots thereof.
10Yea, behold, *being* planted, shall it prosper? shall it not utterly wither, **17:10**
when the east wind toucheth it? it shall wither in the furrows where it grew. Ezek 19:12–14 Hos 13:15
11¶Moreover the word of the LORD came unto me, saying, Mt 21:19
12Say now to the rebellious house, Know ye not what these *things mean?* **17:12**
tell *them*, Behold, the king of Babylon is come to Jerusalem, and hath taken 2 Kgs 24:10–17 2 Chron 36:13
the king thereof, and the princes thereof, and led them with him to Jer 22:24–28
Babylon;
13And hath taken of the king's seed, and made a covenant with him, and ☆**17:13**
hath taken an oath of him: he hath also taken the mighty of the land:
14That the kingdom might be base, that it might not lift itself up, *but* that **17:14**
by keeping of his covenant it might stand. Jer 27:12–17 38:17
15But he rebelled against him in sending his ambassadors into Egypt, that **17:15**
they might give him horses and much people. Shall he prosper? shall he Deut 29:12–15 2 Kgs 24:20
escape that doeth such *things?* or shall he break the covenant, and be 2 Chron 36:13 Jer 38:18, 23
delivered?

17:2ff This chapter concerns itself with Zedekiah, who had been set up as king over what was left of Judah after Nebuchadnezzar had destroyed the city and burned the temple. Zedekiah plotted with the Egyptians against Nebuchadnezzar—this was a treacherous violation of his oath of allegiance which he had sworn in the name of Jehovah. Nebuchadnezzar caught up with Zedekiah, slew his sons before his eyes, blinded the king, and brought him to Babylon in fetters.

17:3 Riddles and parables are effective tools in preaching because they drive home truths in a manner designed to interest the listener and compel his attention. This illustration of the two eagles and the cedar is stated and the interpretation explained so no one could misunderstand what God had in mind.

17:4 Nebuchadnezzar had come to Judah, captured Jehoiachin (who was eighteen years old and had reigned for three months), and took him and some of the princes to Babylon. This act is represented by the first eagle who crops the top, tender branch from the cedar tree and carries it to a land of traffic, that is, to Babylon.

17:7 The second eagle, which has great wings and many feathers, is Egypt, with whom Zedekiah contracted an alliance in defiance of his agreement with Nebuchadnezzar. Expecting to escape from the grip of Nebuchadnezzar, Zedekiah made Egypt a vassel. God says he shall pay the price of his perfidy, be blinded, and be brought to Babylon in chains.

17:13 *with him,* i.e., "with Zedekiah."

17:16 Jer 52:11 Hos 10:4

[16]*As* I live, saith the Lord GOD, surely in the place *where* the king *dwelleth*
that made him king, whose oath he despised, and whose covenant he brake,
even with him in the midst of Babylon he shall die.

17:17 Isa 36:6 Jer 37:7

[17]Neither shall Pharaoh with *his* mighty army and great company make
for him in the war, by casting up mounts, and building forts, to cut off
many persons:

17:18 1 Chron 29:24 2 Chron 30:8

[18]Seeing he despised the oath by breaking the covenant, when, lo, he had
given his hand, and hath done all these *things*, he shall not escape.
[19]Therefore thus saith the Lord GOD; *As* I live, surely mine oath that he
hath despised, and my covenant that he hath broken, even it will I
recompense upon his own head.
[20]And I will spread my net upon him, and he shall be taken in my snare,
and I will bring him to Babylon, and will plead with him there for his
trespass that he hath trespassed against me.

17:21 2 Kgs 25:5, 11 Jer 48:44 Amos 9:1–10

[21]And all his fugitives with all his bands shall fall by the sword, and they
that remain shall be scattered toward all winds: and ye shall know that I
the LORD have spoken *it*.

17:22☆ Ps 72:16; 80:15 Isa 27:6 Zech 3:8 4:12–14

[22]¶Thus saith the Lord GOD; I will also take of the highest branch of the
high cedar, and will set *it;* I will crop off from the top of his young twigs a
tender one, and will plant *it* upon an high mountain and eminent:
[23]In the mountain of the height of Israel will I plant it: and it shall bring
forth boughs, and bear fruit, and be a goodly cedar: and under it shall dwell
all fowl of every wing; in the shadow of the branches thereof shall they
dwell.

17:24 Isa 37:12, 13 55:12 Amos 9:11 1 Cor 1:27, 28

[24]And all the trees of the field shall know that I the LORD have brought
down the high tree, have exalted the low tree, have dried up the green tree,
and have made the dry tree to flourish: I the LORD have spoken and have
done *it*.

G. THE GOD WHO IS JUST AND RIGHTEOUS

1. The Sinner Shall Die

18:2☆ Jer 31:29 Mt 23:36 Rom 9:20

18 THE word of the LORD came unto me again, saying,
[2]What mean ye, that ye use this proverb concerning the land of
Israel, saying, The fathers have eaten sour grapes, and the children's teeth
are set on edge?
[3]*As* I live, saith the Lord GOD, ye shall not have *occasion* any more to use
this proverb in Israel.

18:4 Num 16:22 27:16 Isa 57:16 Zech 12:1 Rom 6:23

[4]Behold, all souls are mine; as the soul of the father, so also the soul of
the son is mine: the soul that sinneth, it shall die.

2. The Righteous Shall Live

18:5☆ **18:6** Deut 4:19 Mt 5:28 1 Cor 6:9–11 10:20

[5]¶But if a man be just, and do that which is lawful and right,
[6]*And* hath not eaten upon the mountains, neither hath lifted up his eyes
to the idols of the house of Israel, neither hath defiled his neighbour's wife,
neither hath come near to a menstruous woman,

17:22ff With the end of the Davidic kingdom what will happen to the covenant God made with David, that there should be a king on the throne forever? Verses *22–24 refer to the Messiah King, Jesus Christ,* who shall come as a root from a dry ground to sit on the throne of his father David to order and to establish it forever.

18:2ff *The fathers have eaten sour grapes and the children's teeth are set on edge,* i.e., to punish children for their fathers' sins is as absurd as saying that children shall have their teeth set on edge for the grapes their fathers have eaten when the children have eaten none. God answers that accusation by making it plain that each one stands on his own feet. The soul, be it the father or the son, belongs to God and the soul that sins shall die.

18:5 Whoever is just shall live, and his state of grace is known by the way he lives. He who is saved obeys God's laws and shows by that action that he is indeed one of God's people.

7 And hath not oppressed any, *but* hath restored to the debtor his pledge,
hath spoiled none by violence, hath given his bread to the hungry, and hath
covered the naked with a garment;
8 He *that* hath not given forth upon usury, neither hath taken any
increase, *that* hath withdrawn his hand from iniquity, hath executed true
judgment between man and man,
9 Hath walked in my statutes, and hath kept my judgments, to deal truly;
he *is* just, he shall surely live, saith the Lord GOD.

18:7 Lev 19:13; 1 Sam 12:3, 4; Mt 25:35–40; Lk 3:11
☆**18:8** Ex 22:25; Zech 8:16
18:9 Hab 2:4; Rom 1:17

3. A Righteous Man's Wicked Son Shall Die

10 If he beget a son *that is* a robber, a shedder of blood, and *that* doeth the
like to *any* one of these *things*,
11 And that doeth not any of those *duties*, but even hath eaten upon the
mountains, and defiled his neighbour's wife,
12 Hath oppressed the poor and needy, hath spoiled by violence, hath not
restored the pledge, and hath lifted up his eyes to the idols, hath committed
abomination,
13 Hath given forth upon usury, and hath taken increase: shall he then
live? he shall not live; he hath done all these abominations; he shall surely
die; his blood shall be upon him.

☆**18:10ff**
18:12 2 Kgs 21:11; Hos 12:7; Amos 4:1
☆**18:13**

4. A Sinful Man's Righteous Son Shall Live

14 ¶Now, lo, *if* he beget a son, that seeth all his father's sins which he hath
done, and considereth, and doeth not such like,
15 *That* hath not eaten upon the mountains, neither hath lifted up his eyes
to the idols of the house of Israel, hath not defiled his neighbour's wife,
16 Neither hath oppressed any, hath not withholden the pledge, neither
hath spoiled by violence, *but* hath given his bread to the hungry, and hath
covered the naked with a garment,
17 *That* hath taken off his hand from the poor, *that* hath not received usury
nor increase, hath executed my judgments, hath walked in my statutes; he
shall not die for the iniquity of his father, he shall surely live.
18 *As for* his father, because he cruelly oppressed, spoiled his brother by
violence, and did *that* which *is* not good among his people, lo, even he shall
die in his iniquity.
19 ¶Yet say ye, Why? doth not the son bear the iniquity of the father?
When the son hath done that which is lawful and right, *and* hath kept all
my statutes, and hath done them, he shall surely live.
20 The soul that sinneth, it shall die. The son shall not bear the iniquity of
the father, neither shall the father bear the iniquity of the son: the
righteousness of the righteous shall be upon him, and the wickedness of the
wicked shall be upon him.

☆**18:14** 2 Chron 29:6–10; 34:21; Prov 17:21; Mt 23:32
18:16 Job 31:16; Ps 41:1
18:19 Zech 1:3–6
18:20 Deut 24:16; 1 Kgs 14:13; Isa 53:11; Mt 16:27; Rom 2:6–9

5. The Repentant Sinner Shall Live

21 But if the wicked will turn from all his sins that he hath committed, and
keep all my statutes, and do that which is lawful and right, he shall surely
live, he shall not die.

☆**18:21**

18:8 *He that hath not given forth upon usury,* i.e., "if he does not lend money on interest" (NASB).
18:10ff Those who break the laws of God show by their actions that they are not the people of God. They shall die.
18:13 *Hath given forth upon usury,* i.e., "He lends money on interest" (NASB).
18:14 Two cases are given for our edification. A wicked son of a pious father shall die for his iniquity; his father's faith cannot save him. So also, a wicked man's righteous son shall not die for his father's transgressions. He shall be saved because he has followed the Lord, even though his father has not done so.
18:21 Some men who live wicked lives turn from their wicked ways shortly before death and find forgiveness. Their sins will be remembered against them no more.

18:22 Ps 18:20–24 Mic 7:19
18:23 Ps 147:11 2 Pet 3:9
18:24 1 Sam 15:11 Prov 21:16 Gal 3:3, 4

22 All his transgressions that he hath committed, they shall not be
mentioned unto him: in his righteousness that he hath done he shall live.
23 Have I any pleasure at all that the wicked should die? saith the Lord
GOD: *and* not that he should return from his ways, and live?
24 ¶But when the righteous turneth away from his righteousness, and
committeth iniquity, *and* doeth according to all the abominations that the
wicked *man* doeth, shall he live? All his righteousness that he hath done
shall not be mentioned: in his trespass that he hath trespassed, and in his
sin that he hath sinned, in them shall he die.

6. God's Ways Are Just

18:25☆ Gen 18:25 Deut 32:4 Zeph 3:5 Mal 3:13–15

25 ¶Yet ye say, The way of the Lord is not equal. Hear now, O house of
Israel; Is not my way equal? are not your ways unequal?
26 When a righteous *man* turneth away from his righteousness, and
committeth iniquity, and dieth in them; for his iniquity that he hath done
shall he die.
27 Again, when the wicked *man* turneth away from his wickedness that he
hath committed, and doeth that which is lawful and right, he shall save his
soul alive.
28 Because he considereth, and turneth away from all his transgressions
that he hath committed, he shall surely live, he shall not die.
29 Yet saith the house of Israel, The way of the Lord is not equal. O house
of Israel, are not my ways equal? are not your ways unequal?

7. God Commands Sinners to Turn and Live

18:30☆ Ezek 14:6; 33:11 Hos 12:6
18:31 Ps 51:10 Jer 32:39 Acts 3:19 Rom 8:13 Jas 4:8

30 Therefore I will judge you, O house of Israel, every one according to his
ways, saith the Lord GOD. Repent, and turn *yourselves* from all your
transgressions; so iniquity shall not be your ruin.
31 ¶Cast away from you all your transgressions, whereby ye have
transgressed; and make you a new heart and a new spirit: for why will ye
die, O house of Israel?
32 For I have no pleasure in the death of him that dieth, saith the Lord
GOD: wherefore turn *yourselves*, and live ye.

H. DIRGE FOR THE LEADERS OF ISRAEL
1. King Jehoahaz

19:1☆ 2 Kgs 25:5–7 2 Chron 36:3–10 Jer 22:10–12, 28–30
19:2☆
19:3 2 Kgs 23:31–34 2 Chron 36:1–4

19 MOREOVER take thou up a lamentation for the princes of Israel,
2 And say, What *is* thy mother? A lioness: she lay down among
lions, she nourished her whelps among young lions.
3 And she brought up one of her whelps: it became a young lion, and it
learned to catch the prey; it devoured men.
4 The nations also heard of him; he was taken in their pit, and they
brought him with chains unto the land of Egypt.

God's grace can be effectual the hour before death, even though the sinner may enter into life empty-handed.

18:25 Sinful men usually charge God with being unjust. The Scriptures do teach that God's ways are not our ways, but it also says that whatever God does is right (Rom. 9:20–24). At the last judgment, every mouth will be stopped and every tongue will have to confess that God's ways are righteous and just and in accordance with truth (Rev. 19:2).

18:30ff God urges men to repent for four reasons: (1) repentance is the only way to escape eternal separation from God; (2) whoever will not repent shall surely perish; (3) God does not delight in the death of the wicked; (4) he who repents will live forever.

19:1 Jehoahaz, Jehoiachin, and Zedekiah were three of the last four kings of Judah before the coming of the Messiah, who was to occupy the throne of his father David forever. The fourth king was Jehoiakim, who was king between the time of Jehoahaz and Jehoiachin. We don't know why he is omitted here.

19:2 Jehoahaz reigned for three months, then was deposed by the Egyptian Pharaoh and taken to Egypt where he died.

2. King Jehoiachin

[5]Now when she saw that she had waited, *and* her hope was lost, then she took another of her whelps, *and* made him a young lion.
[6]And he went up and down among the lions, he became a young lion, and learned to catch the prey, *and* devoured men.
[7]And he knew their desolate palaces, and he laid waste their cities; and the land was desolate, and the fulness thereof, by the noise of his roaring.
[8]Then the nations set against him on every side from the provinces, and spread their net over him: he was taken in their pit.
[9]And they put him in ward in chains, and brought him to the king of Babylon: they brought him into holds, that his voice should no more be heard upon the mountains of Israel.

☆19:5 2 Kgs 24:8–12; 2 Chron 36:9, 10
19:9 2 Kgs 24:15

3. King Zedekiah

[10]¶Thy mother *is* like a vine in thy blood, planted by the waters: she was fruitful and full of branches by reason of many waters.
[11]And she had strong rods for the sceptres of them that bare rule, and her stature was exalted among the thick branches, and she appeared in her height with the multitude of her branches.
[12]But she was plucked up in fury, she was cast down to the ground, and the east wind dried up her fruit: her strong rods were broken and withered; the fire consumed them.
[13]And now she *is* planted in the wilderness, in a dry and thirsty ground.
[14]And fire is gone out of a rod of her branches, *which* hath devoured her fruit, so that she hath no strong rod *to be* a sceptre to rule. This *is* a lamentation, and shall be for a lamentation.

☆19:10 Ps 80:8–11
19:12 Hos 13:15; Mt 3:10; Jn 15:6
19:13 2 Kgs 24:12–16
☆19:14

I. ISRAEL'S FAILURE

1. The Elders Wait for Ezekiel's Instructions

20 AND it came to pass in the seventh year, in the fifth *month*, the tenth *day* of the month, *that* certain of the elders of Israel came to inquire of the LORD, and sat before me.

☆20:1 Ezek 8:1, 11, 12

2. Israel's Defilement with Egyptian Gods

[2]Then came the word of the LORD unto me, saying,
[3]Son of man, speak unto the elders of Israel, and say unto them, Thus saith the Lord GOD; Are ye come to inquire of me? *As* I live, saith the Lord GOD, I will not be inquired of by you.
[4]Wilt thou judge them, son of man, wilt thou judge *them?* cause them to know the abominations of their fathers:

20:4 Ezek 16:2; 22:2

19:5 Jehoiachin (also called Jeconiah) reigned three months, after which he was taken to Babylon, where he lived at least thirty-seven years.

19:10 Zedekiah reigned eleven years. He was enthroned by Nebuchadnezzar and made a covenant with him, which he broke. Nebuchadnezzar took him prisoner, blinded him, and carried him in chains to Babylon, where he died in prison.

19:14 *fire is gone out of a rod of her branches.* Jerusalem is burned with fire, and Zedekiah, by rebelling against Nebuchadnezzar, was the occasion for the mischief—i.e., the fire that consumed Jerusalem was set by Zedekiah, who was a rod of Judah's branch.

20:1 Some of the elders of Judah come to discuss matters with Ezekiel. God graciously speaks to them through Ezekiel. God states the divine case against them, showing how graciously he had treated them and how they and their fathers had dealt treacherously with him. Yet God would still have mercy and would cause a remnant to repent. At that time he would return them to the land from which they were to be dispossessed. *in the seventh year,* i.e., "six years after King Jeconiah was captured."†

20:5☆ Ezek 6:2–9; 33:3 Deut 7:6; 14:2 Jer 33:24 Mk 13:20

5¶And say unto them, Thus saith the Lord GOD; In the day when I chose
Israel, and lifted up mine hand unto the seed of the house of Jacob, and
made myself known unto them in the land of Egypt, when I lifted up mine
hand unto them, saying, I *am* the LORD your God;
6In the day *that* I lifted up mine hand unto them, to bring them forth of
the land of Egypt into a land that I had espied for them, flowing with milk
and honey, which *is* the glory of all lands:

20:7 Deut 29:16, 18

7Then said I unto them, Cast ye away every man the abominations of his
eyes, and defile not yourselves with the idols of Egypt: I *am* the LORD your
God.

20:8 Isa 63:10

8But they rebelled against me, and would not hearken unto me: they did
not every man cast away the abominations of their eyes, neither did they
forsake the idols of Egypt: then I said, I will pour out my fury upon them,
to accomplish my anger against them in the midst of the land of Egypt.

3. Israel's Rebellion in the Wilderness

20:9 Ex 32:11–14 Num 14:13 Deut 9:28 32:26, 27

9But I wrought for my name's sake, that it should not be polluted before
the heathen, among whom they *were*, in whose sight I made myself known
unto them, in bringing them forth out of the land of Egypt.
10¶Wherefore I caused them to go forth out of the land of Egypt, and
brought them into the wilderness.

20:11 Ex 20:1–23, 33 Lev 18:5 Neh 9:13, 14

11And I gave them my statutes, and shewed them my judgments, which *if*
a man do, he shall even live in them.
12Moreover also I gave them my sabbaths, to be a sign between me and
them, that they might know that I *am* the LORD that sanctify them.

20:13 Num 14:11 Isa 56:6

13But the house of Israel rebelled against me in the wilderness: they
walked not in my statutes, and they despised my judgments, which *if* a man
do, he shall even live in them; and my sabbaths they greatly polluted: then
I said, I would pour out my fury upon them in the wilderness, to consume
them.
14But I wrought for my name's sake, that it should not be polluted before
the heathen, in whose sight I brought them out.
15Yet also I lifted up my hand unto them in the wilderness, that I would
not bring them into the land which I had given *them*, flowing with milk and
honey, which *is* the glory of all lands;

20:16 Ezek 11:21 14:3–7

16Because they despised my judgments, and walked not in my statutes,
but polluted my sabbaths: for their heart went after their idols.

20:17 Jer 4:27; 5:18 Nah 1:8, 9

17Nevertheless mine eye spared them from destroying them, neither did I
make an end of them in the wilderness.

20:18☆ Deut 4:3, 4 Ps 78:6, 8

18But I said unto their children in the wilderness, Walk ye not in the
statutes of your fathers, neither observe their judgments, nor defile
yourselves with their idols:

20:19 Ex 6:7; 20:2

19I *am* the LORD your God; walk in my statutes, and keep my judgments,
and do them;
20And hallow my sabbaths; and they shall be a sign between me and you,
that ye may know that I *am* the LORD your God.

20:5ff God's charges against Israel cover three periods of their history. While in Egypt, they had turned from him (20:5–9); therefore, God's deliverance from Egypt was all of grace and not of works. Second, they sinned against God in the wilderness, which occasioned his refusal to let them enter Canaan for forty years (20:10–26). Third, they continued their sinful ways after God brought them into Canaan and blessed them with every material blessing (20:27–32). Therefore, God will no longer hear them when they call on him.

20:18 Among the duties of children to parents are the following: (1) being taught by parents (Prov. 1:7–9); (2) honoring parents (Exod. 20:12; Heb. 12:9); (3) obeying parents (Prov. 6:20; Eph. 6:1); (4) providing for aged parents (1 Tim. 5:4). Children are told not to imitate bad parents (20:18).

21 Notwithstanding the children rebelled against me: they walked not in
my statutes, neither kept my judgments to do them, which *if* a man do, he
shall even live in them; they polluted my sabbaths: then I said, I would
pour out my fury upon them, to accomplish my anger against them in the
wilderness.

20:21 Num 25:1–3

22 Nevertheless I withdrew mine hand, and wrought for my name's sake,
that it should not be polluted in the sight of the heathen, in whose sight I
brought them forth.

20:22 Job 13:21 Ps 78:38 Isa 48:9–11

23 I lifted up mine hand unto them also in the wilderness, that I would
scatter them among the heathen, and disperse them through the countries;
24 Because they had not executed my judgments, but had despised my
statutes, and had polluted my sabbaths, and their eyes were after their
fathers' idols.

20:23 Deut 28:64–68 32:26, 27 Jer 15:4

25 Wherefore I gave them also statutes *that were* not good, and judgments
whereby they should not live;
26 And I polluted them in their own gifts, in that they caused to pass
through *the fire* all that openeth the womb, that I might make them
desolate, to the end that they might know that I *am* the LORD.

20:25 Ps 81:12 Rom 1:21–25, 28 2 Thess 2:9–11
20:26 Rom 11:8

4. Israel's Idolatry in the Land of Promise

27 ¶Therefore, son of man, speak unto the house of Israel, and say unto
them, Thus saith the Lord GOD; Yet in this your fathers have blasphemed
me, in that they have committed a trespass against me.
28 *For* when I had brought them into the land, *for* the which I lifted up
mine hand to give it to them, then they saw every high hill, and all the thick
trees, and they offered there their sacrifices, and there they presented the
provocation of their offering: there also they made their sweet savour, and
poured out there their drink offerings.
29 Then I said unto them, What *is* the high place whereunto ye go? And
the name thereof is called Ba'mah unto this day.

20:27 1 Kgs 14:23
☆**20:29**

5. God Will Not Listen to Them

30 Wherefore say unto the house of Israel, Thus saith the Lord GOD; Are
ye polluted after the manner of your fathers? and commit ye whoredom
after their abominations?
31 For when ye offer your gifts, when ye make your sons to pass through
the fire, ye pollute yourselves with all your idols, even unto this day: and
shall I be inquired of by you, O house of Israel? *As* I live, saith the Lord
GOD, I will not be inquired of by you.

20:30 Judg 2:19
20:31 Ps 106:37–39

6. God Will Judge and Purge Israel

32 And that which cometh into your mind shall not be at all, that ye say,
We will be as the heathen, as the families of the countries, to serve wood
and stone.
33 ¶*As* I live, saith the Lord GOD, surely with a mighty hand, and with a
stretched out arm, and with fury poured out, will I rule over you:
34 And I will bring you out from the people, and will gather you out of the
countries wherein ye are scattered, with a mighty hand, and with a
stretched out arm, and with fury poured out.

☆**20:33ff**
20:34 Lam 2:4

20:29 *Bamah.* A hilltop area where sacrifices were made to the gods.†
20:33ff Herein the coming judgment of God on his people is stated. He will separate himself from them and later regather them.

20:35☆ Deut 32:10; 1 Cor 10:5–10

35 And I will bring you into the wilderness of the people, and there will I
plead with you face to face.

36 Like as I pleaded with your fathers in the wilderness of the land of
Egypt, so will I plead with you, saith the Lord GOD.

37 And I will cause you to pass under the rod, and I will bring you into the
bond of the covenant:

20:38 Ps 95:11; Ezek 34:17–22; Heb 4:3

38 And I will purge out from among you the rebels, and them that
transgress against me: I will bring them forth out of the country where they
sojourn, and they shall not enter into the land of Israel: and ye shall know
that I *am* the LORD.

20:39 Isa 1:12–15

39 As for you, O house of Israel, thus saith the Lord GOD; Go ye, serve ye
every one his idols, and hereafter *also*, if ye will not hearken unto me: but
pollute ye my holy name no more with your gifts, and with your idols.

7. The Obedient Will Know the Lord

20:40☆ Ezek 43:12, 27

40 For in mine holy mountain, in the mountain of the height of Israel,
saith the Lord GOD, there shall all the house of Israel, all of them in the
land, serve me: there will I accept them, and there will I require your
offerings, and the firstfruits of your oblations, with all your holy things.

20:41 Isa 27:12, 13; Amos 9:14

41 I will accept you with your sweet savour, when I bring you out from the
people, and gather you out of the countries wherein ye have been scattered;
and I will be sanctified in you before the heathen.

42 And ye shall know that I *am* the LORD, when I shall bring you into the
land of Israel, into the country *for* the which I lifted up mine hand to give
it to your fathers.

20:43 Zech 12:10–14; Lk 18:13; 2 Cor 7:11

43 And there shall ye remember your ways, and all your doings, wherein
ye have been defiled; and ye shall lothe yourselves in your own sight for all
your evils that ye have committed.

44 And ye shall know that I *am* the LORD, when I have wrought with you
for my name's sake, not according to your wicked ways, nor according to
your corrupt doings, O ye house of Israel, saith the Lord GOD.

8. Ezekiel's Prophecy against the Negeb

20:45ff☆

45 ¶Moreover the word of the LORD came unto me, saying,

20:46 Jer 13:19

46 Son of man, set thy face toward the south, and drop *thy word* toward
the south, and prophesy against the forest of the south field;

20:47 Isa 9:18

47 And say to the forest of the south, Hear the word of the LORD; Thus
saith the Lord GOD; Behold, I will kindle a fire in thee, and it shall devour
every green tree in thee, and every dry tree: the flaming flame shall not be
quenched, and all faces from the south to the north shall be burned therein.

20:48☆ Jer 17:27

48 And all flesh shall see that I the LORD have kindled it: it shall not be
quenched.

20:49☆ Mt 13:12, 13; Jn 16:25

49 Then said I, Ah Lord GOD! they say of me, Doth he not speak
parables?

20:35 *the wilderness of the people,* i.e., the desert judgment hall (the Syro-Arabian deserts), peopled by nomadic tribes. This desert would be traversed in returning to Israel from Babylon.†

20:40ff In due time God's people will know he is Lord, *and those who are obedient* to their God will be blessed—not for their works, because they are impure—but for God's own name's sake.

20:45ff Beginning here and going on in the next chapter, God directs attention to Judah and Jerusalem (the south) against whom he pronounces judgment. Fire will come upon them and not be quenched. So harsh is the judgment and so disturbing to the elders that they express their distaste for it, as is indicated by Ezekiel's complaint to God (20:49).

20:49 *Doth he not speak parables?* "This was the language either of their ignorance or infidelity, or of their malice and ill-will to the prophet. It is common for those who will not be wrought upon by the word to pick quarrels with it; it is either too plain or too obscure, too fine or too homely, too common or too singular; something or other is amiss in it."*

J. THE UNSHEATHED SWORD
1. God's Sword Is in His Hand

21 AND the word of the LORD came unto me, saying, ☆21:1
2 Son of man, set thy face toward Jerusalem, and drop *thy word*
toward the holy places, and prophesy against the land of Israel,
3 And say to the land of Israel, Thus saith the LORD; Behold, I *am* against 21:3
thee, and will draw forth my sword out of his sheath, and will cut off from Isa 57:1 Jer 21:13
thee the righteous and the wicked. Nah 2:13; 3:5
4 Seeing then that I will cut off from thee the righteous and the wicked, 21:4
therefore shall my sword go forth out of his sheath against all flesh from the Jer 12:12 Ezek 7:2
south to the north:
5 That all flesh may know that I the LORD have drawn forth my sword out 21:5
of his sheath: it shall not return any more. 1 Sam 3:12 Neh 1:9
6 Sigh therefore, thou son of man, with the breaking of *thy* loins; and with
bitterness sigh before their eyes.
7 And it shall be, when they say unto thee, Wherefore sighest thou? that 21:7
thou shalt answer, For the tidings; because it cometh: and every heart shall Isa 13:7 Ezek 7:26
melt, and all hands shall be feeble, and every spirit shall faint, and all knees
shall be weak *as* water: behold, it cometh, and shall be brought to pass,
saith the Lord GOD.

2. The Sharpening of the Sword for Judgment

8 ¶Again the word of the LORD came unto me, saying, ☆21:8ff
9 Son of man, prophesy, and say, Thus saith the LORD; Say, A sword, a ☆21:9
sword is sharpened, and also furbished: Ps 110:5, 6 Isa 34:5, 6
10 It is sharpened to make a sore slaughter; it is furbished that it may
glitter: should we then make mirth? it contemneth the rod of my son, *as*
every tree.
11 And he hath given it to be furbished, that it may be handled: this sword
is sharpened, and it is furbished, to give it into the hand of the slayer.
12 Cry and howl, son of man: for it shall be upon my people, it *shall be* 21:12
upon all the princes of Israel: terrors by reason of the sword shall be upon Joel 1:13
my people: smite therefore upon *thy* thigh.
13 Because *it is* a trial, and what if *the sword* contemn even the rod? it shall
be no *more*, saith the Lord GOD.
14 Thou therefore, son of man, prophesy, and smite *thine* hands together,
and let the sword be doubled the third time, the sword of the slain: it *is* the
sword of the great *men that are* slain, which entereth into their privy
chambers.
15 I have set the point of the sword against all their gates, that *their* heart 21:15
may faint, and *their* ruins be multiplied: ah! *it is* made bright, *it is* wrapped Josh 2:11 2 Sam 17:10
up for the slaughter. Jer 17:27
16 Go thee one way or other, *either* on the right hand, *or* on the left,
whithersoever thy face *is* set.
17 *I will also smite mine* hands together, and I will cause my fury to rest: 21:17
I the LORD have said *it*. Ezek 5:13

21:1ff Picking up from where he left off in the last chapter, God foretells the coming disaster on Jerusalem. Ezekiel is to announce the judgment with sighs and a broken heart. The sword of judgment is about to be unsheathed, and nothing can stop this from being done.
21:8ff Jerusalem has despised the rod God used to chasten its people. Now the sword will slaughter them. God will clap his hands and satisfy his anger.
21:9 *a sword is sharpened* and will cut, wound, or kill. It is a sharp and victorious sword against which no one can stand. If it had temporarily rusted in its scabbard, it is now polished and gleaming, flashing like lightning in the sunshine (21:10).

3. God Uses the Sword of Babylon

21:18ff☆
18¶The word of the LORD came unto me again, saying,
21:19 Deut 3:11 Amos 1:14
19Also, thou son of man, appoint thee two ways, that the sword of the
king of Babylon may come: both twain shall come forth out of one land:
and choose thou a place, choose *it* at the head of the way to the city.
20Appoint a way, that the sword may come to Rab′bath of the Ammon-
ites, and to Judah in Jerusalem the defenced.
21:21☆ Prov 16:33; 21:1 Hos 4:12 Zech 10:2
21For the king of Babylon stood at the parting of the way, at the head of
the two ways, to use divination: he made *his* arrows bright, he consulted
with images, he looked in the liver.
21:22 Ezek 4:2; 26:9
22At his right hand was the divination for Jerusalem, to appoint captains,
to open the mouth in the slaughter, to lift up the voice with shouting, to
appoint *battering* rams against the gates, to cast a mount, *and* to build a
fort.
21:23 Num 5:15 Ezek 17:16, 18
23And it shall be unto them as a false divination in their sight, to them
that have sworn oaths: but he will call to remembrance the iniquity, that
they may be taken.
24Therefore thus saith the Lord GOD; Because ye have made your
iniquity to be remembered, in that your transgressions are discovered, so
that in all your doings your sins do appear; because, *I say*, that ye are come
to remembrance, ye shall be taken with the hand.

4. God Punishes King Zedekiah

21:25 Ps 37:13 Ezek 7:2–7
25¶And thou, profane wicked prince of Israel, whose day is come, when
iniquity *shall have* an end,
21:26☆ Ps 75:7 Jer 13:18
26Thus saith the Lord GOD; Remove the diadem, and take off the crown:
this *shall* not *be* the same: exalt *him that is* low, and abase *him that is* high.
21:27 Ps 2:6 Jer 23:56 Hag 2:21, 22
27I will overturn, overturn, overturn, it: and it shall be no *more*, until he
come whose right it is; and I will give it *him*.

5. God Uses the Sword against the Ammonites

21:28☆ Jer 12:12 Zeph 2:8–10
28¶And thou, son of man, prophesy and say, Thus saith the Lord GOD
concerning the Ammonites, and concerning their reproach; even say thou,
The sword, the sword *is* drawn: for the slaughter *it is* furbished, to consume
because of the glittering:
21:29 Jer 27:9 Ezek 13:6–9
29Whiles they see vanity unto thee, whiles they divine a lie unto thee, to
bring thee upon the necks of *them that are* slain, of the wicked, whose day
is come, when their iniquity *shall have* an end.
21:30 Jer 47:6, 7 Ezek 25:5
30Shall I cause *it* to return into his sheath? I will judge thee in the place
where thou wast created, in the land of thy nativity.
21:31 Ps 18:15 Nah 1:6 Hab 1:6, 10
31And I will pour out mine indignation upon thee, I will blow against
thee in the fire of my wrath, and deliver thee into the hand of brutish men,
and skilful to destroy.
21:32 Mal 4:1 Mt 3:10
32Thou shalt be for fuel to the fire; thy blood shall be in the midst of the
land; thou shalt be no *more* remembered: for I the LORD have spoken *it*.

21:18ff Babylon will be the agent God uses to accomplish Jerusalem's ruin. This state of affairs will continue until the coming of the Lord's Messiah, when God will give his Son dominion. There shall be no more kings on David's throne until Christ sits upon that throne.
21:21 *looked in the liver.* Inspecting the livers of sacrifices was a very common type of divination by which ancients thought they could obtain information from the gods.† Nebuchadnezzar is here spoken of as using divination to get directions about besieging Jerusalem or marching against Rabbah.
21:28ff After God has finished the overthrow of Jerusalem, Babylon will destroy the Ammonites, who had delighted in the afflictions that had come to the covenant people of God. (See note on 25:2 for further information concerning the Ammonites.)

K. JERUSALEM'S TRANSGRESSIONS
1. God's Accusation against Jerusalem

22 MOREOVER the word of the LORD came unto me, saying,
2 Now, thou son of man, wilt thou judge, wilt thou judge the
bloody city? yea, thou shalt shew her all her abominations.
3 Then say thou, Thus saith the Lord GOD, The city sheddeth blood in the
midst of it, that her time may come, and maketh idols against herself to
defile herself.
4 Thou art become guilty in thy blood that thou hast shed; and hast
defiled thyself in thine idols which thou hast made; and thou hast caused
thy days to draw near, and art come *even* unto thy years: therefore have I
made thee a reproach unto the heathen, and a mocking to all countries.
5 *Those that be* near, and *those that be* far from thee, shall mock thee,
which art infamous *and* much vexed.
6 Behold, the princes of Israel, every one were in thee to their power to
shed blood.
7 In thee have they set light by father and mother: in the midst of thee
have they dealt by oppression with the stranger: in thee have they vexed the
fatherless and the widow.
8 Thou hast despised mine holy things, and hast profaned my sabbaths.
9 In thee are men that carry tales to shed blood: and in thee they eat upon
the mountains: in the midst of thee they commit lewdness.
10 In thee have they discovered their fathers' nakedness: in thee have they
humbled her that was set apart for pollution.
11 And one hath committed abomination with his neighbour's wife; and
another hath lewdly defiled his daughter in law; and another in thee hath
humbled his sister, his father's daughter.
12 In thee have they taken gifts to shed blood; thou hast taken usury and
increase, and thou hast greedily gained of thy neighbours by extortion, and
hast forgotten me, saith the Lord GOD.
13 ¶Behold, therefore I have smitten mine hand at thy dishonest gain
which thou hast made, and at thy blood which hath been in the midst of
thee.
14 Can thine heart endure, or can thine hands be strong, in the days that
I shall deal with thee? I the LORD have spoken *it*, and will do *it*.
15 And I will scatter thee among the heathen, and disperse thee in the
countries, and will consume thy filthiness out of thee.
16 And thou shalt take thine inheritance in thyself in the sight of the
heathen, and thou shalt know that I *am* the LORD.

2. The Heat of God's Wrath in Judgment

17 And the word of the LORD came unto me, saying,
18 Son of man, the house of Israel is to me become dross: all they *are*
brass, and tin, and iron, and lead, in the midst of the furnace; they are *even*
the dross of silver.
19 Therefore thus saith the Lord GOD; Because ye are all become dross,
behold, therefore I will gather you into the midst of Jerusalem.
20 *As* they gather silver, and brass, and iron, and lead, and tin, into the

☆**22:1**
22:3 Ezek 23:37, 45; Zeph 3:3
22:4 2 Kgs 21:16; Ps 44:13, 14; Ezek 5:14, 15; Dan 9:16
22:6 Isa 1:23; Mic 3:1–3, 9-11; Zech 3:3
22:7 Ex 22:22; 23:9; Deut 27:19; Prov 22:22, 23
22:9 Judg 20:6; Hos 4:2, 10, 14
22:10 Lev 18:8, 19; Deut 27:20–23; Amos 2:7; 1 Cor 5:1
22:11 Lev 18:15; 2 Sam 13:14
22:12 Lev 19:13; 25:36; Deut 27:25; Ps 106:21
☆**22:13** Num 24:10; Prov 28:8; Isa 33:15; Amos 2:6–8
22:15 Deut 4:27; Zech 7:14
22:16 Ezek 6:4–7
☆**22:17**
22:18 Ps 119:119; Prov 17:3; Isa 1:25; 48:10

22:1ff Jerusalem's sins are specified explicitly. God must therefore judge them, and he will scatter them among the nations. Their filthiness must be removed from them, and at last they would know that God is the Lord. The Jews should have been asking, "Why has God not cut us off years ago?" They should have noted and heeded the long-suffering patience of their loving God.

22:17ff God put Jerusalem into the smelting pot so that it might be purified. Instead, what remains is dross—it is worthless.

midst of the furnace, to blow the fire upon it, to melt *it;* so will I gather *you*
in mine anger and in my fury, and I will leave *you there,* and melt you.
21 Yea, I will gather you, and blow upon you in the fire of my wrath, and
ye shall be melted in the midst thereof.

22:22 Ezek 20:8, 33; Hos 5:10

22 As silver is melted in the midst of the furnace, so shall ye be melted in
the midst thereof; and ye shall know that I the LORD have poured out my
fury upon you.

3. The Extent of the Apostasy

22:23☆
22:24 2 Chron 28:22; Isa 9:13; Jer 2:30; Zeph 3:2
22:25 Jer 2:34; 15:8; Hos 6:9

23 ¶And the word of the LORD came unto me, saying,
24 Son of man, say unto her, Thou *art* the land that is not cleansed, nor
rained upon in the day of indignation.
25 *There is* a conspiracy of her prophets in the midst thereof, like a roaring
lion ravening the prey; they have devoured souls; they have taken the
treasure and precious things; they have made her many widows in the midst
thereof.

22:26 Lev 10:10; 1 Sam 2:12–17; Hag 2:11–14

26 Her priests have violated my law, and have profaned mine holy things:
they have put no difference between the holy and profane, neither have they
shewed *difference* between the unclean and the clean, and have hid their
eyes from my sabbaths, and I am profaned among them.
27 Her princes in the midst thereof *are* like wolves ravening the prey, to
shed blood, *and* to destroy souls, to get dishonest gain.

22:28 Jer 23:25–32; Ezek 13:6

28 And her prophets have daubed them with untempered *morter,* seeing
vanity, and divining lies unto them, saying, Thus saith the Lord GOD, when
the LORD hath not spoken.

22:29 Isa 5:7; Amos 3:10; Jas 5:4
22:30 Ps 106:23; Isa 59:16; 63:5; Jer 5:1; Ezek 13:5
22:31 Isa 10:5; Ezek 7:3–9; 16:43; Rom 2:8, 9

29 The people of the land have used oppression, and exercised robbery,
and have vexed the poor and needy: yea, they have oppressed the stranger
wrongfully.
30 And I sought for a man among them, that should make up the hedge,
and stand in the gap before me for the land, that I should not destroy it:
but I found none.
31 Therefore have I poured out mine indignation upon them; I have
consumed them with the fire of my wrath: their own way have I recom-
pensed upon their heads, saith the Lord GOD.

L. THE PROSTITUTION OF AHOLAH (SAMARIA) & AHOLIBAH (JERUSALEM)

1. The Background Information

23:2 Jer 3:7–10

23 THE word of the LORD came again unto me, saying,
2 Son of man, there were two women, the daughters of one
mother:
3 And they committed whoredoms in Egypt; they committed whoredoms
in their youth: there were their breasts pressed, and there they bruised the
teats of their virginity.

2. Aholah's Idolatry and Whoredom

23:4☆ 2 Kgs 15:19; 16:7; 17:3; Hos 5:13; 8:9, 10; 10:6

4 And the names of them *were* A-ho′lah the elder, and A-hol′i-bah her
sister: and they were mine, and they bare sons and daughters. Thus *were*
their names; Sa-ma′ri-a *is* A-ho′lah, and Jerusalem A-hol′i-bah.

22:23ff All classes of people in Jerusalem have turned away from God and are guilty: prince, prophets, priests, and citizens. God sought to find someone who would intercede for Jerusalem, but there was none. No one would speak a good word for Jerusalem or offer a prayer for its deliverance. The end has come.

23:4 *Aholah* (*Oholah* in some versions) means "her own tent." It was a symbolic name for Samaria and the ten tribes known as the Northern Kingdom. *Aholibah* (*Oholibah* in some versions) means "my tent is in her." It was a symbolic name for Judah and Jerusalem.

5 And A-ho'lah played the harlot when she was mine; and she doted on ☆23:5
her lovers, on the Assyrians *her* neighbours,
6 *Which were* clothed with blue, captains and rulers, all of them desirable
young men, horsemen riding upon horses.
7 Thus she committed her whoredoms with them, with all them *that were* 23:7
the chosen men of Assyria, and with all on whom she doted: with all their Hos 5:3; 6:10
idols she defiled herself.
8 Neither left she her whoredoms *brought* from Egypt: for in her youth 23:8
they lay with her, and they bruised the breasts of her virginity, and poured Ex 32:4; 1 Kgs 12:28
their whoredom upon her. 2 Kgs 17:16
9 Wherefore I have delivered her into the hand of her lovers, into the hand 23:9
of the Assyrians, upon whom she doted. Ezek 16:37; Hos 11:5
10 These discovered her nakedness: they took her sons and her daughters, Rev 17:12–16
and slew her with the sword: and she became famous among women; for
they had executed judgment upon her.

3. Aholibah's Greater Sins

11 And when her sister A-hol'i-bah saw *this*, she was more corrupt in her ☆23:11
inordinate love than she, and in her whoredoms more than her sister in *her* Jer 3:8–11
whoredoms.
12 She doted upon the Assyrians *her* neighbours, captains and rulers
clothed most gorgeously, horsemen riding upon horses, all of them
desirable young men.
13 Then I saw that she was defiled, *that* they *took* both one way, 23:13
14 And *that* she increased her whoredoms: for when she saw men Hos 12:1, 2
pourtrayed upon the wall, the images of the Chal-de'ans pourtrayed with 23:14 Ezek 8:10
vermilion,
15 Girded with girdles upon their loins, exceeding in dyed attire upon
their heads, all of them princes to look to, after the manner of the
Babylonians of Chal-de'a, the land of their nativity:
16 And as soon as she saw them with her eyes, she doted upon them, and 23:16
sent messengers unto them into Chal-de'a. Prov 6:25; Mt 5:28
17 And the Babylonians came to her into the bed of love, and they defiled 2 Pet 2:14
her with their whoredom, and she was polluted with them, and her mind 23:17 2 Kgs 24:17
was alienated from them.
18 So she discovered her whoredoms, and discovered her nakedness: then 23:18
my mind was alienated from her, like as my mind was alienated from her Deut 32:19; Ps 78:59
sister. 106:40; Jer 8:12
19 Yet she multiplied her whoredoms, in calling to remembrance the days
of her youth, wherein she had played the harlot in the land of Egypt.
20 For she doted upon their paramours, whose flesh *is as* the flesh of asses, 23:20
and whose issue *is like* the issue of horses. Ezek 17:15
21 Thus thou calledst to remembrance the lewdness of thy youth, in 23:21
bruising thy teats by the Egyptians for the paps of thy youth. Jer 3:9

4. *Babylon,* God's Instrument of Wrath against Aholibah (Jerusalem)

22 ¶Therefore, O A-hol'i-bah, thus saith the Lord GOD; Behold, I will ☆23:22
raise up thy lovers against thee, from whom thy mind is alienated, and I Isa 10:5, 6
will bring them against thee on every side; Hab 1:6–10

23:5ff The sin of Samaria (Israel) was her entangling alliances and conformity to the religion and life-style, first of Assyria (2 Kings 15:19–29) and then of Egypt (2 Kings 17:3–6).

23:11ff The Southern Kingdom (Judah-Aholibah) also made alliances with Assyria (Isa. 7:1–25), Babylon (2 Kings 24:1), and Egypt (Isa. 30–31).

23:22ff God depicts the rottenness of Judah and Jerusalem, and he describes the indignities that kingdom will experience at the hands of a nation she

23:23 Gen 25:18 2 Kgs 20:14–17 Job 1:17

23 The Babylonians, and all the Chal-de′ans, Pe′kod, and Sho′a, and Ko′a,
and all the Assyrians with them: all of them desirable young men, captains
and rulers, great lords and renowned, all of them riding upon horses.

23:24 Jer 39:5, 6

24 And they shall come against thee with chariots, wagons, and wheels,
and with an assembly of people, *which* shall set against thee buckler and
shield and helmet round about: and I will set judgment before them, and
they shall judge thee according to their judgments.
25 And I will set my jealousy against thee, and they shall deal furiously
with thee: they shall take away thy nose and thine ears; and thy remnant
shall fall by the sword: they shall take thy sons and thy daughters; and thy
residue shall be devoured by the fire.

23:26 Isa 3:16–24

26 They shall also strip thee out of thy clothes, and take away thy fair
jewels.
27 Thus will I make thy lewdness to cease from thee, and thy whoredom
brought from the land of Egypt: so that thou shalt not lift up thine eyes
unto them, nor remember Egypt any more.

23:28 Jer 21:7–10

28 For thus saith the Lord GOD; Behold, I will deliver thee into the hand
of them whom thou hatest, into the hand *of them* from whom thy mind is
alienated:

23:29 Deut 28:48 2 Sam 13:15

29 And they shall deal with thee hatefully, and shall take away all thy
labour, and shall leave thee naked and bare: and the nakedness of thy
whoredoms shall be discovered, both thy lewdness and thy whoredoms.
30 I will do these *things* unto thee, because thou hast gone a whoring after
the heathen, *and* because thou art polluted with their idols.

23:31 1 Kgs 21:8–14 2 Kgs 21:13 Dan 9:12

31 Thou hast walked in the way of thy sister; therefore will I give her cup
into thine hand.

23:32☆ Ps 60:3 Ezek 5:14, 15

32 Thus saith the Lord GOD; Thou shalt drink of thy sister's cup deep and
large: thou shalt be laughed to scorn and had in derision; it containeth
much.

23:33 Jer 25:15, 16, 27

33 Thou shalt be filled with drunkenness and sorrow, with the cup of
astonishment and desolation, with the cup of thy sister Sa-ma′ri-a.

23:34 Ps 75:8 Isa 51:17

34 Thou shalt even drink it and suck *it* out, and thou shalt break the
sherds thereof, and pluck off thine own breasts: for I have spoken *it*, saith
the Lord GOD.

23:35 1 Kgs 14:9 Neh 9:26 Hos 13:6

35 Therefore thus saith the Lord GOD; Because thou hast forgotten me,
and cast me behind thy back, therefore bear thou also thy lewdness and thy
whoredoms.

5. God's Judgment on Aholah and Aholibah

23:36☆ Isa 58:1 Jer 1:10 Mt 23:13–35

36 ¶The LORD said moreover unto me; Son of man, wilt thou judge
A-ho′lah and A-hol′i-bah? yea, declare unto them their abominations;
37 That they have committed adultery, and blood *is* in their hands, and
with their idols have they committed adultery, and have also caused their
sons, whom they bare unto me, to pass for them through *the fire*, to devour
them.

23:38 2 Kgs 21:4, 7 Neh 13:17, 18 Jer 17:27

38 Moreover this they have done unto me: they have defiled my sanctuary
in the same day, and have profaned my sabbaths.

---

had made her lover—Babylon. She had cast God behind her back (23:35); therefore, God would render judgment for her transgressions.

23:32 *Thou shalt drink of thy sister's cup deep and large.* Judah has walked in the same steps as Samaria, committing equally heinous sins. Thus she must expect none other than Samaria's fate.

23:36ff God speaks about Aholibah and Aholah as one nation. Yet the Northern Kingdom had gone into captivity long before this. The remnant left in Samaria drifted toward Judah gradually, so that the two sisters had, in effect, become one again. Therefore, this judgment of the Lord includes not only Judah and Jerusalem but also the remnant of Samaria conjoined with Judah.

39 For when they had slain their children to their idols, then they came the
same day into my sanctuary to profane it; and, lo, thus have they done in
the midst of mine house.
40 And furthermore, that ye have sent for men to come from far, unto
whom a messenger *was* sent; and, lo, they came: for whom thou didst wash
thyself, paintedst thy eyes, and deckedst thyself with ornaments,
41 And satest upon a stately bed, and a table prepared before it,
whereupon thou hast set mine incense and mine oil.
42 And a voice of a multitude being at ease *was* with her: and with the
men of the common sort *were* brought Sa-be'ans from the wilderness, which
put bracelets upon their hands, and beautiful crowns upon their heads.
43 Then said I unto *her that was* old in adulteries, Will they now commit
whoredoms with her, and she *with them?*
44 Yet they went in unto her, as they go in unto a woman that playeth the
harlot: so went they in unto A-ho'lah and unto A-hol'i-bah, the lewd
women.
45 ¶And the righteous men, they shall judge them after the manner of
adulteresses, and after the manner of women that shed blood; because they
are adulteresses, and blood *is* in their hands.
46 For thus saith the Lord GOD; I will bring up a company upon them,
and will give them to be removed and spoiled.
47 And the company shall stone them with stones, and dispatch them with
their swords; they shall slay their sons and their daughters, and burn up
their houses with fire.
48 Thus will I cause lewdness to cease out of the land, that all women may
be taught not to do after your lewdness.
49 And they shall recompense your lewdness upon you, and ye shall bear
the sins of your idols: and ye shall know that I *am* the Lord GOD.

23:39 Jer 7:9–11
23:40 2 Kgs 9:30; 20:13–15; Ezek 16:13–16
23:41 Esth 1:6; Jer 44:17
23:42 Gen 24:30; Amos 6:3–6
23:43 Ezra 9:7
23:47 Jer 24:9; 29:18
23:49 Isa 59:18; Ezek 9:10

M. THE STORY OF THE BOILING POT

24 AGAIN in the ninth year, in the tenth month, in the tenth *day* of
the month, the word of the LORD came unto me, saying,
2 Son of man, write thee the name of the day, *even* of this same day: the
king of Babylon set himself against Jerusalem this same day.
3 And utter a parable unto the rebellious house, and say unto them, Thus
saith the Lord GOD; Set on a pot, set *it* on, and also pour water into it:
4 Gather the pieces thereof into it, *even* every good piece, the thigh, and
the shoulder; fill *it* with the choice bones.
5 Take the choice of the flock, and burn also the bones under it, *and* make
it boil well, and let them seethe the bones of it therein.
6 ¶Wherefore thus saith the Lord GOD; Woe to the bloody city, to the pot
whose scum *is* therein, and whose scum is not gone out of it! bring it out
piece by piece; let no lot fall upon it.
7 For her blood is in the midst of her; she set it upon the top of a rock;
she poured it not upon the ground, to cover it with dust;
8 That it might cause fury to come up to take vengeance; I have set her
blood upon the top of a rock, that it should not be covered.
9 Therefore thus saith the Lord GOD; Woe to the bloody city! I will even
make the pile for fire great.

☆24:1
24:2 2 Kgs 25:1; Jer 39:1; 52:4; Hab 2:2, 3
☆24:3 Jer 1:13, 14
24:4 Mic 3:2, 3
24:5 Jer 52:10; 24–27
☆24:6 2 Kgs 24:3, 4; Nah 3:1; Rev 11:7, 8; 17:6; 18:24
24:7 Lev 17:13; Deut 12:16
24:8 Isa 26:21; Jer 22:8, 9
24:9 Hab 2:12; Lk 13:34, 35; Rev 14:20; 16:6, 19

24:1 This word from God to Ezekiel took place on the same day that Nebuchadnezzar's siege of Jerusalem began.
24:3 The flesh in the pot is a sign of the miseries Jerusalem must justly suffer for her transgressions.
24:6 *let no lot fall upon it.* All the meat in the pot will be taken out and eaten. There is therefore no need to cast lots to decide which pieces shall be brought out first.

10 Heap on wood, kindle the fire, consume the flesh, and spice it well, and
let the bones be burned.

24:11 Mal 4:1

11 Then set it empty upon the coals thereof, that the brass of it may be
hot, and may burn, and *that* the filthiness of it may be molten in it, *that* the
scum of it may be consumed.

24:12 Jer 6:28–30; Dan 9:13, 14; Hos 12:1
24:13 Ezek 8:18; Rom 2:8, 9

12 She hath wearied *herself* with lies, and her great scum went not forth
out of her: her scum *shall be* in the fire.
13 In thy filthiness *is* lewdness: because I have purged thee, and thou wast
not purged, thou shalt not be purged from thy filthiness any more, till I
have caused my fury to rest upon thee.

24:14☆ Ps 33:9; Isa 55:11

14 I the LORD have spoken *it:* it shall come to pass, and I will do *it;* I will
not go back, neither will I spare, neither will I repent; according to thy
ways, and according to thy doings, shall they judge thee, saith the Lord
GOD.

N. THE PARABLE INVOLVING THE DEATH OF EZEKIEL'S WIFE

15 ¶Also the word of the LORD came unto me, saying,

24:16☆ Job 23:2; Song 7:10; Jer 22:10

16 Son of man, behold, I take away from thee the desire of thine eyes with
a stroke: yet neither shalt thou mourn nor weep, neither shall thy tears run
down.

24:17 Lev 21:10–12; 2 Sam 15:30; Jer 16:7

17 Forbear to cry, make no mourning for the dead, bind the tire of thine
head upon thee, and put on thy shoes upon thy feet, and cover not *thy* lips,
and eat not the bread of men.
18 So I spake unto the people in the morning: and at even my wife died;
and I did in the morning as I was commanded.
19 ¶And the people said unto me, Wilt thou not tell us what these *things*
are to us, that thou doest *so?*

24:20 Ps 27:4; 84:1; Jer 16:3, 4; Dan 11:31

20 Then I answered them, The word of the LORD came unto me, saying,
21 Speak unto the house of Israel, Thus saith the Lord GOD; Behold, I will
profane my sanctuary, the excellency of your strength, the desire of your
eyes, and that which your soul pitieth; and your sons and your daughters
whom ye have left shall fall by the sword.
22 And ye shall do as I have done: ye shall not cover *your* lips, nor eat the
bread of men.
23 And your tires *shall be* upon your heads, and your shoes upon your
feet: ye shall not mourn nor weep; but ye shall pine away for your
iniquities, and mourn one toward another.

24:24 Ezek 4:3; Lk 11:29, 30; Jn 13:19; 14:29
24:25☆ Ps 48:2; 122:1–9; Jer 7:4; 11:22
24:26 1 Sam 4:12; Job 1:15–19; Ezek 33:21, 22

24 Thus E-ze'ki-el is unto you a sign: according to all that he hath done
shall ye do: and when this cometh, ye shall know that I *am* the Lord GOD.
25 Also, thou son of man, *shall it* not *be* in the day when I take from them
their strength, the joy of their glory, the desire of their eyes, and that
whereupon they set their minds, their sons and their daughters,
26 *That* he that escapeth in that day shall come unto thee, to cause *thee* to
hear *it* with *thine* ears?

24:14 The ruin of Jerusalem did not indicate that every last soul in that city was under the judgment of God. There were some who were faithful to God; yet when catastrophe does take place, the innocent often suffer *along with the malefactors. In war, particularly, the* righteous suffer with the wicked. If they die, their suffering will be over and they will be with Christ. If they survive, God will provide for them and help them.

24:16 Prophets, like other men, were entitled to marry and to enjoy that state. Death comes to all, and one spouse dies before the other. God takes Ezekiel's wife from him by death and orders the prophet not to show his sorrow. This would be most unusual for one whose mate had been taken from him. This event symbolized for Jerusalem that God was going to take from the residents of that city all that was dearest to them. If God's faithful servant is afflicted, how much more will a generation of rebels be punished!

24:25ff When Jerusalem is ruined and the refugees arrive in Babylon as captives of Nebuchadnezzar, Ezekiel will be free to open his mouth and speak to them for God.

27 In that day shall thy mouth be opened to him which is escaped, and
thou shalt speak, and be no more dumb: and thou shalt be a sign unto
them; and they shall know that I *am* the LORD.

24:27 Ex 6:11, 12; Ps 51:15; Eph 6:19

III. THE PROPHECIES AGAINST THE HEATHEN NATIONS (25:1—32:32)

A. AMMON

25 THE word of the LORD came again unto me, saying,
2 Son of man, set thy face against the Ammonites, and prophesy
against them;
3 And say unto the Ammonites, Hear the word of the Lord GOD; Thus
saith the Lord GOD; Because thou saidst, Aha, against my sanctuary, when
it was profaned; and against the land of Israel, when it was desolate; and
against the house of Judah, when they went into captivity;
4 Behold, therefore I will deliver thee to the men of the east for a
possession, and they shall set their palaces in thee, and make their dwellings
in thee: they shall eat thy fruit, and they shall drink thy milk.
5 And I will make Rab'bah a stable for camels, and the Ammonites a
couchingplace for flocks: and ye shall know that I *am* the LORD.
6 For thus saith the Lord GOD; Because thou hast clapped *thine* hands,
and stamped with the feet, and rejoiced in heart with all thy despite against
the land of Israel;
7 Behold, therefore I will stretch out mine hand upon thee, and will
deliver thee for a spoil to the heathen; and I will cut thee off from the
people, and I will cause thee to perish out of the countries: I will destroy
thee; and thou shalt know that I *am* the LORD.

☆**25:2**
25:3 Ps 70:2, 3; Ezek 21:28; 26:2; 36:2
25:4 Deut 28:33, 51; Judg 6:3, 33; Isa 1:7
25:5 2 Sam 12:26; Jer 49:2; Zeph 2:14, 15
25:6 Job 27:23; Obad 12
25:7 Amos 1:14, 15

B. MOAB

8 ¶Thus saith the Lord GOD; Because that Moab and Se'ir do say, Behold,
the house of Judah *is* like unto all the heathen;
9 Therefore, behold, I will open the side of Moab from the cities, from his
cities *which are* on his frontiers, the glory of the country, Beth–jesh'i-moth,
Ba'al–me'on, and Kir-i-a-tha'im,
10 Unto the men of the east with the Ammonites, and will give them in
possession, that the Ammonites may not be remembered among the
nations.
11 And I will execute judgments upon Moab; and they shall know that I
am the LORD.

☆**25:9** Num 32:37, 38; Josh 13:17–20; 1 Chron 5:8; Jer 48:23

C. EDOM

12 ¶Thus saith the Lord GOD; Because that Edom hath dealt against the
house of Judah by taking vengeance, and hath greatly offended, and
revenged himself upon them;
13 Therefore thus saith the Lord GOD; *I will also stretch out mine* hand
upon Edom, and will cut off man and beast from it; and I will make it
desolate from Te'man; and they of De'dan shall fall by the sword.

☆**25:12**
25:13 Gen 36:34; Jer 49:7; Mal 1:3, 4

25:2 *the Ammonites* were the descendants of Lot's younger daughter, who (by incest) bore her father a son, Benammi. This lad fathered the Ammonites, who became deadly enemies of the true people of God. (See Gen. 19:33–38).

25:9 *Moab.* The Moabites descended from Lot's elder daughter, who (by incest) bore Moab by her father. The Moabites and the Ammonites were forbidden to enter the congregation of Israel until the tenth generation. (See Gen. 19:33–38; Deut. 23:3).

25:12 *Edom.* See note on Gen 36:9 for information regarding the Edomites.

25:14 Ezek 34:11 Nah 1:2–4 Heb 10:30, 31

14 And I will lay my vengeance upon Edom by the hand of my people
Israel: and they shall do in Edom according to mine anger and according to
my fury; and they shall know my vengeance, saith the Lord GOD.

D. PHILISTIA

25:15☆ Isa 14:29–31 Joel 3:4 Amos 1:6–8 Zeph 2:4–7 Zech 9:5–8 **25:16** 1 Sam 30:14 Jer 47:4 Zeph 2:5

15 ¶Thus saith the Lord GOD; Because the Philistines have dealt by
revenge, and have taken vengeance with a despiteful heart, to destroy *it* for
the old hatred;
16 Therefore thus saith the Lord GOD; Behold, I will stretch out mine
hand upon the Philistines, and I will cut off the Cher'e-thims and destroy
the remnant of the sea coast.
17 And I will execute great vengeance upon them with furious rebukes;
and they shall know that I *am* the LORD, when I shall lay my vengeance
upon them.

E. TYRE

1. God Will Destroy Tyre

26:2☆ 2 Sam 5:11 Isa 23:1 Jer 25:22 Joel 3:4 **26:3** Jer 50:42; 51:42 Lk 21:25

26 AND it came to pass in the eleventh year, in the first *day* of the
month, *that* the word of the LORD came unto me, saying,
2 Son of man, because that Tyrus hath said against Jerusalem, Aha, she is
broken *that was* the gates of the people: she is turned unto me: I shall be
replenished, *now* she is laid waste:
3 Therefore thus saith the Lord GOD; Behold, I *am* against thee, O Tyrus,
and will cause many nations to come up against thee, as the sea causeth his
waves to come up.

26:4 Isa 23:11 Amos 1:10

4 And they shall destroy the walls of Tyrus, and break down her towers:
I will also scrape her dust from her, and make her like the top of a rock.
5 It shall be *a place for* the spreading of nets in the midst of the sea: for I
have spoken *it*, saith the Lord GOD: and it shall become a spoil to the
nations.

26:6 Jer 47:4; 49:2

6 And her daughters which *are* in the field shall be slain by the sword; and
they shall know that I *am* the LORD.

2. Nebuchadrezzar Will Be God's Instrument of Destruction

26:7 Dan 2:37, 47 Nah 2:3, 4 **26:8** Jer 6:6; 32:24 52:4

7 ¶For thus saith the Lord GOD; Behold, I will bring upon Tyrus Neb-u-
chad-rez'zar king of Babylon, a king of kings, from the north, with horses,
and with chariots, and with horsemen, and companies, and much people.
8 He shall slay with the sword thy daughters in the field: and he shall
make a fort against thee, and cast a mount against thee, and lift up the
buckler against thee.
9 And he shall set engines of war against thy walls, and with his axes he
shall break down thy towers.

26:10 Jer 39:3

10 By reason of the abundance of his horses their dust shall cover thee: thy
walls shall shake at the noise of the horsemen, and of the wheels, and of the
chariots, when he shall enter into thy gates, as men enter into a city wherein
is made a breach.

25:15 The Philistines descended from Mizraim and *were constant opponents of God's people.* They worshipped Dagon and other gods. In the Maccabean age they were finally exterminated, according to the prophetic word.

26:2 Isaiah predicted the fall of Tyre long before Ezekiel's time (see Isa. 23). Nebuchadnezzar was God's instrument to bring about Tyre's downfall. The new Tyre was built on an island that lay a half mile offshore. Nebuchadnezzar besieged mainland Tyre for thirteen years before it capitulated. Alexander the Great (332 B.C.) finished the work begun by Nebuchadnezzar. Unable to take the island by ships, he built a stone causeway from the mainland to the island. From that day forward its glory was gone and the prophetic Word of God was fulfilled (26:4, 5, 15, 21; 27:36; 28:2–9).

11 With the hoofs of his horses shall he tread down all thy streets: he shall
slay thy people by the sword, and thy strong garrisons shall go down to the
ground.
12 And they shall make a spoil of thy riches, and make a prey of thy
merchandise: and they shall break down thy walls, and destroy thy pleasant
houses: and they shall lay thy stones and thy timber and thy dust in the
midst of the water.
13 And I will cause the noise of thy songs to cease; and the sound of thy
harps shall be no more heard.
14 And I will make thee like the top of a rock: thou shalt be *a place* to
spread nets upon; thou shalt be built no more: for I the LORD have spoken
it, saith the Lord GOD.

3. The Dirge of the Seaport Rulers over Tyre

15 ¶Thus saith the Lord GOD to Tyrus; Shall not the isles shake at the
sound of thy fall, when the wounded cry, when the slaughter is made in the
midst of thee?
16 Then all the princes of the sea shall come down from their thrones, and
lay away their robes, and put off their broidered garments: they shall clothe
themselves with trembling; they shall sit upon the ground, and shall
tremble at *every* moment, and be astonished at thee.
17 And they shall take up a lamentation for thee, and say to thee, How art
thou destroyed, *that wast* inhabited of seafaring men, the renowned city,
which wast strong in the sea, she and her inhabitants, which cause their
terror *to be* on all that haunt it!
18 Now shall the isles tremble in the day of thy fall; yea, the isles that *are*
in the sea shall be troubled at thy departure.

4. Tyre Shall Be Inhabited No More

19 For thus saith the Lord GOD; When I shall make thee a desolate city,
like the cities that are not inhabited; when I shall bring up the deep upon
thee, and great waters shall cover thee;
20 When I shall bring thee down with them that descend into the pit, with
the people of old time, and shall set thee in the low parts of the earth, in
places desolate of old, with them that go down to the pit, that thou be not
inhabited; and I shall set glory in the land of the living;
21 I will make thee a terror, and thou *shalt be* no *more:* though thou be
sought for, yet shalt thou never be found again, saith the Lord GOD.

5. The Sad Dirge for Tyre
a. Tyre's Splendor and Wealth

27 THE word of the LORD came again unto me, saying,
2 Now, thou son of man, take up a lamentation for Tyrus;
3 And say unto Tyrus, O thou that art situate at the entry of the sea, *which
art* a merchant of the people for many isles, Thus saith the Lord GOD; O
Tyrus, thou hast said, I *am* of perfect beauty.

26:11 Isa 5:28; 26:5 Hab 1:8
26:12 2 Chron 32:27 Isa 23:8, 18 Dan 11:8 Amos 5:11
26:13 Isa 24:8, 9 Amos 6:5 Jas 5:1–5 Rev 18:22, 23
☆**26:14** Deut 13:16 Job 12:14 Isa 14:27
26:15 Jer 49:21 Heb 12:26, 27
26:16 Ps 35:26 Jonah 3:6 1 Pet 3:4
26:17 Isa 14:12 Jer 48:39; 50:23 Mic 2:4
26:18 Isa 23:5–7, 10–15
26:19 Isa 8:7, 8 Dan 9:26; 11:40 Rev 17:15
☆**26:20** Ps 88:6 Jonah 2:2, 6 Zech 2:8
☆**27:2** Jer 7:20 9:10; 17–20

26:14 *I will make thee like the top of a rock.* Certain aspects of verses 12 and 14 exceed the actual damage done to Tyre by Nebuchadnezzar, and foreshadow what happened to the island settlement later as a result of the conquest by Alexander the Great.†
26:20 *the land of the living* is a type of heaven, where men see the goodness of God and enjoy felicity. Tyre is not to be numbered among those in the land of the living.
27:2 God orders Ezekiel to raise a lamentation over Tyre at a time when it was highly prosperous and there was no reason to suppose it would decay and disappear as a significant city of commerce. Pride and a sense of security against all enemies caused its ruin.

4 Thy borders *are* in the midst of the seas, thy builders have perfected thy beauty.

27:5 Deut 3:9; 1 Kgs 5:1, 6; Song 4:8; Isa 14:8

5 They have made all thy *ship* boards of fir trees of Se′nir: they have taken cedars from Lebanon to make masts for thee.

27:6 Num 21:33; Jer 22:20; Zech 11:2

6 *Of* the oaks of Ba′shan have they made thine oars; the company of the Ashurites have made thy benches *of* ivory, *brought* out of the isles of Chit′tim.

27:7 Ex 25:4; 1 Kgs 10:28; Prov 7:16; Jer 10:9

7 Fine linen with broidered work from Egypt was that which thou spreadest forth to be thy sail; blue and purple from the isles of E-li′shah was that which covered thee.

27:8 Gen 10:18; 1 Kgs 9:27; 1 Chron 1:16

8 The inhabitants of Zi′don and Ar′vad were thy mariners: thy wise *men*, O Tyrus, *that* were in thee, were thy pilots.

9 The ancients of Ge′bal and the wise *men* thereof were in thee thy calkers: and all the ships of the sea with their mariners were in thee to occupy thy merchandise.

b. Tyre's Military Might

27:10☆ Ezek 38:5

10 They of Persia and of Lud and of Phut were in thine army, thy men of war: they hanged the shield and helmet in thee; they set forth thy comeliness.

27:11☆

11 The men of Ar′vad with thine army *were* upon thy walls round about, and the Gam′ma-dims were in thy towers: they hanged their shields upon thy walls round about; they have made thy beauty perfect.

c. Tyre's Commercial Wealth

12 Tarshish *was* thy merchant by reason of the multitude of all *kind of* riches; with silver, iron, tin, and lead, they traded in thy fairs.

27:13☆ Gen 10:2, 3; 1 Chron 1:5, 7; Isa 66:19; Dan 8:21; 10:20; Rev 18:13

13 Ja′van, Tu′bal, and Me′shech, they *were* thy merchants: they traded the persons of men and vessels of brass in thy market.

27:14☆ 1 Kgs 10:22

14 They of the house of To-gar′mah traded in thy fairs with horses and horsemen and mules.

15 The men of De′dan *were* thy merchants; many isles *were* the merchandise of thine hand: they brought thee *for* a present horns of ivory and ebony.

27:16 Ezek 16:13, 18

16 Syria *was* thy merchant by reason of the multitude of the wares of thy making: they occupied in thy fairs with emeralds, purple, and broidered work, and fine linen, and coral, and agate.

27:17 Judg 11:33; 1 Kgs 5:9; Ezra 3:7; Acts 12:20

17 Judah, and the land of Israel, they *were* thy merchants: they traded in thy market wheat of Min′nith, and Pan′nag, and honey, and oil, and balm.

27:18 Gen 14:15; Ezek 47:16–18

18 Damascus *was* thy merchant in the multitude of the wares of thy making, for the multitude of all riches; in the wine of Hel′bon, and white wool.

27:19☆

19 Dan also and Ja′van going to and fro occupied in thy fairs: bright iron, cassia, and calamus, were in thy market.

20 De′dan *was* thy merchant in precious clothes for chariots.

27:21 Gen 25:13; Isa 21:13; 60:7; Gal 4:25

21 Arabia, and all the princes of Ke′dar, they occupied with thee in lambs, and rams, and goats: in these *were they* thy merchants.

27:10 *Persia and of Lud and of Phut*. These were three cities of ancient North Africa.†

27:11 *Arvad with thine army*, should be translated "Arvad and Helech." Helech was a region in ancient Cilicia known from Assyrian records as *Hilakku*.†

27:13, 14 *Javan, Tubal, and Meshech . . . Togarmah*. Regions of Asia Minor, now in Turkey.†

27:19 The text here is uncertain. The NIV says, "they exchanged wrought iron, cassia and calamus for your wares."

22 The merchants of She′ba and Ra′a-mah, they *were* thy merchants: they
occupied in thy fairs with chief of all spices, and with all precious stones,
and gold.
23 Ha′ran, and Can′neh, and Eden, the merchants of She′ba, Asshur, *and*
Chil′mad, *were* thy merchants.
24 These *were* thy merchants in all sorts *of things*, in blue clothes, and
broidered work, and in chests of rich apparel, bound with cords, and made
of cedar, among thy merchandise.
25 The ships of Tarshish did sing of thee in thy market: and thou wast
replenished, and made very glorious in the midst of the seas.

27:22 Gen 10:7; 43:11; 1 Kgs 10:2; Ezek 38:13
27:23 2 Kgs 19:12; Isa 37:12; Amos 1:5; 6:2

d. The Total Destruction of Tyre

26 ¶Thy rowers have brought thee into great waters: the east wind hath
broken thee in the midst of the seas.
27 Thy riches, and thy fairs, thy merchandise, thy mariners, and thy pilots,
thy calkers, and the occupiers of thy merchandise, and all thy men of war,
that *are* in thee, and in all thy company which *is* in the midst of thee, shall
fall into the midst of the seas in the day of thy ruin.
28 The suburbs shall shake at the sound of the cry of thy pilots.
29 And all that handle the oar, the mariners, *and* all the pilots of the sea,
shall come down from their ships, they shall stand upon the land;
30 And shall cause their voice to be heard against thee, and shall cry
bitterly, and shall cast up dust upon their heads, they shall wallow
themselves in the ashes:
31 And they shall make themselves utterly bald for thee, and gird them
with sackcloth, and they shall weep for thee with bitterness of heart *and*
bitter wailing.
32 And in their wailing they shall take up a lamentation for thee, and
lament over thee, *saying*, What *city is* like Tyrus, like the destroyed in the
midst of the sea?
33 When thy wares went forth out of the seas, thou filledst many people;
thou didst enrich the kings of the earth with the multitude of thy riches and
of thy merchandise.
34 In the time *when* thou shalt be broken by the seas in the depths of the
waters thy merchandise and all thy company in the midst of thee shall fall.
35 All the inhabitants of the isles shall be astonished at thee, and their
kings shall be sore afraid, they shall be troubled in *their* countenance.
36 The merchants among the people shall hiss at thee; thou shalt be a
terror, and never *shalt be* any more.

☆**27:26** Ps 48:7; Jer 18:17; Acts 27:14, 41; Rev 17:15
27:29 Rev 18:17–19
27:30 1 Sam 4:12; 2 Sam 1:2; Isa 23:1–6; Jonah 3:6; Mic 1:10
27:31 Isa 16:9; Ezek 7:18
27:32 Lam 2:13; Rev 18:18
27:34 Zech 9:3, 4
27:36 Ps 37:10, 36; Jer 49:17; Zeph 2:15

F. TYRE AND SIDON
1. Tyre's Sin of Pride

28 THE word of the LORD came again unto me, saying,
2 Son of man, say unto the prince of Tyrus, Thus saith the Lord
GOD; *Because thine heart is* lifted up, and thou hast said, I *am* a God, I sit
in the seat of God, in the midst of the seas; yet thou *art* a man, and not
God, though thou set thine heart as the heart of God:

☆**28:2** Ps 82:6, 7; Dan 2:20–23; 5:11, 12; 2 Thess 2:4

27:26 Tyre is pictured here as overtaken by an east wind, which refers to Nebuchadnezzar. He begins the work of destruction that will be furthered by Alexander the Great at a later date.
28:2 *in the midst of the seas.* Tyre was an island fortress just a half mile off the Phoenician coast. It was so strongly fortified that for thirteen years it was able to withstand the siege by Nebuchadnezzar. It was almost impregnable.

28:3☆ Gen 10:7; 43:11 ...
28:4 Prov 18:11; 23:4, 5; Zech 9:2–4
28:5 Job 31:24, 25; Ps 52:7; Hos 12:7, 8
28:6 Ex 9:17; 1 Cor 10:22; Jas 1:11
28:7 Dan 7:7; Hab 1:6–8
28:10 1 Sam 17:26, 36; Acts 7:51; Phil 3:3
28:12☆
28:13 Gen 2:8; Ex 28:17–20; 39:10–21; Isa 51:3; 54:11, 12
28:14☆ Ex 25:17–20; Ezek 20:40; Dan 2:37, 38; 5:18–23; Rev 18:16
28:15 Isa 14:12; Rom 7:9
28:16☆ Ezek 8:17; Hab 2:8, 17

3 Behold, thou *art* wiser than Daniel; there is no secret that they can hide
from thee:
4 With thy wisdom and with thine understanding thou hast gotten thee
riches, and hast gotten gold and silver into thy treasures:
5 By thy great wisdom *and* by thy traffick hast thou increased thy riches,
and thine heart is lifted up because of thy riches:
6 Therefore thus saith the Lord GOD; Because thou hast set thine heart as
the heart of God;
7 Behold, therefore I will bring strangers upon thee, the terrible of the
nations: and they shall draw their swords against the beauty of thy wisdom,
and they shall defile thy brightness.
8 They shall bring thee down to the pit, and thou shalt die the deaths of
them that are slain in the midst of the seas.
9 Wilt thou yet say before him that slayeth thee, I *am* God? but thou *shalt
be* a man, and no God, in the hand of him that slayeth thee.
10 Thou shalt die the deaths of the uncircumcised by the hand of
strangers: for I have spoken *it*, saith the Lord GOD.

2. Ezekiel Weeps over Tyre's Fate

11 ¶Moreover the word of the LORD came unto me, saying,
12 Son of man, take up a lamentation upon the king of Tyrus, and say
unto him, Thus saith the Lord GOD; Thou sealest up the sum, full of
wisdom, and perfect in beauty.
13 Thou hast been in Eden the garden of God; every precious stone *was*
thy covering, the sardius, topaz, and the diamond, the beryl, the onyx, and
the jasper, the sapphire, the emerald, and the carbuncle, and gold: the
workmanship of thy tabrets and of thy pipes was prepared in thee in the
day that thou wast created.
14 Thou *art* the anointed cherub that covereth; and I have set thee *so:* thou
wast upon the holy mountain of God; thou hast walked up and down in the
midst of the stones of fire.
15 Thou *wast* perfect in thy ways from the day that thou wast created, till
iniquity was found in thee.
16 By the multitude of thy merchandise they have filled the midst of thee
with violence, and thou hast sinned: therefore I will cast thee as profane out
of the mountain of God: and I will destroy thee, O covering cherub, from
the midst of the stones of fire.

28:3 *wiser than Daniel.* The king of Tyre must have known about the wisdom and greatness of Daniel in Babylon. He prided himself on being wiser than Daniel, from whom no secret could be hidden. He was puffed up, pretending to be a god.

28:12 *take up a lamentation upon the king of Tyrus.* In this passage (28:11–19) some descriptive phrases apply to a human king of Tyre, and some seem to apply to Satan. Therefore great care must be taken to apply these verses with discernment.† The note on John 8:44 lists various names that describe Satan. Isa. 14:12ff describes the origin and fall of Satan. As an angel, Satan is a created being. In Isa. 14:12 he is called *Lucifer,* which means "light bearer." In Ezekiel, which describes the king of Tyre as a historical personage and a type of Satan, descriptive words appear that can only apply to Satan: "full of wisdom, and perfect in beauty" (28:12); the "anointed cherub that covereth" (28:14); perfect in all he did from the day he was created by God until iniquity was found in him (28:15). His heart was filled with pride because of his beauty (28:17). This created being of wisdom, beauty, and perfection revolted against the Creator and fell. Isa. 14:13, 14 speaks of Satan's five "I wills" which brought about his downfall (see also Luke 10:18). In the Isaiah passage the primary reference is to the king of Babylon. But no human monarch could speak the language of Isa. 14:13, 14. Thus the human king is the tool of Satan, in whose hand he is directed to make claims Satan himself made and to represent ambitions that were Satan's.

28:14 *thou hast walked up and down in the midst of the stones of fire.* Probably a symbol of the angels.†

28:16 The cherub here appears to refer to Satan who is to be judged (28:16–19) and then cast into the lake of fire (Rev. 20:10). The king of Tyre thought of himself as a guardian angel for his people, but if so, he was a fallen angel and ultimately the destroyer of his people.

17 Thine heart was lifted up because of thy beauty, thou hast corrupted
thy wisdom by reason of thy brightness: I will cast thee to the ground, I will
lay thee before kings, that they may behold thee.

28:17 Isa 19:11 Jer 8:9

18 Thou hast defiled thy sanctuaries by the multitude of thine iniquities,
by the iniquity of thy traffick; therefore will I bring forth a fire from the
midst of thee, it shall devour thee, and I will bring thee to ashes upon the
earth in the sight of all them that behold thee.

28:18 Amos 1:9, 10 Mal 4:3

19 All they that know thee among the people shall be astonished at thee:
thou shalt be a terror, and never *shalt* thou *be* any more.

28:19 Jer 51:64 Rev 18:21

3. The Prophecy of Doom for Sidon

20 ¶Again the word of the LORD came unto me, saying,
21 Son of man, set thy face against Zi′don, and prophesy against it,
22 And say, Thus saith the Lord GOD: Behold, I *am* against thee, O
Zi′don; and I will be glorified in the midst of thee: and they shall know that
I *am* the LORD, when I shall have executed judgments in her, and shall be
sanctified in her.

☆**28:20**

28:21 Gen 10:15–19 Isa 23:2–4, 12 Jer 25:22; 27:3 Joel 3:4–8

23 For I will send into her pestilence, and blood into her streets; and the
wounded shall be judged in the midst of her by the sword upon her on
every side; and they shall know that I *am* the LORD.
24 ¶And there shall be no more a pricking brier unto the house of Israel,
nor *any* grieving thorn of all *that are* round about them, that despised them;
and they shall know that I *am* the Lord GOD.

☆**28:24** Num 33:35 Josh 23:13

25 Thus saith the Lord GOD; When I shall have gathered the house of
Israel from the people among whom they are scattered, and shall be
sanctified in them in the sight of the heathen, then shall they dwell in their
land that I have given to my servant Jacob.

28:25 Ps 106:47 Isa 11:12, 13 Jer 23:8

26 And they shall dwell safely therein, and shall build houses, and plant
vineyards; yea, they shall dwell with confidence, when I have executed
judgments upon all those that despise them round about them; and they
shall know that I *am* the LORD their God.

28:26 Jer 32:15, 43, 44 Amos 9:13, 14

G. EGYPT
1. God's Judgment on Egypt and Its Pharaoh
a. Pharaoh's Sin of Pride

29 IN the tenth year, in the tenth *month*, in the twelfth *day* of the
month, the word of the LORD came unto me, saying,
2 Son of man, set thy face against Pharaoh king of Egypt, and prophesy
against him, and against all Egypt:
3 Speak, and say, Thus saith the Lord GOD; Behold, I *am* against thee,
Pharaoh king of Egypt, the great dragon that lieth in the midst of his rivers,
which hath said, My river *is* mine own, and I have made *it* for myself.
4 But I will put hooks in thy jaws, and I will cause the fish of thy rivers to
stick unto thy scales, and I will bring thee up out of the midst of thy rivers,
and all the fish of thy rivers shall stick unto thy scales.

☆**29:2** Isa 19:1–17 Jer 43:8–13 46:2–16 Joel 3:19
29:3 Ps 74:13 Isa 27:1
29:4 2 Kgs 19:28 Isa 37:29 Ezek 38:4

28:20ff Zidon (Sidon) was a neighbor of Tyre and was also the object of God's wrath. She too would be destroyed.
28:24ff Again and again God promised to regather and restore his people Israel. The ultimate fulfillment of this promise will take place at the end of the age. Premillennialists hold that this will be especially true in the millennium, after the return of Christ.
29:2 Egypt and Israel were interlocked in their history in many ways. Abraham had gone to Egypt in a time of famine. Egypt depended on the Nile, which overflowed its banks and deposited rich soil. It was a productive country that sheltered him. Joseph was a slave and a premier in Egypt and brought his people there. God delivered his people from their bondage in Egypt. Later Israel made alliances with Egypt against common enemies. Jesus was taken to Egypt, and out of Egypt God called his Son. At the end of the age Israel will be a third partner with Egypt and Assyria, and God will say, "Blessed is Egypt my people" (Isa. 19:25).

29:5 Jer 7:33; 34:20

5 And I will leave thee *thrown* into the wilderness, thee and all the fish of
thy rivers: thou shalt fall upon the open fields; thou shalt not be brought
together, nor gathered: I have given thee for meat to the beasts of the field
and to the fowls of the heaven.

b. God Will Destroy Egypt

29:6 Isa 36:6; Jer 2:36
29:7 Prov 25:19; Jer 37:5–11; Ezek 17:15–17

6 And all the inhabitants of Egypt shall know that I *am* the LORD, because
they have been a staff of reed to the house of Israel.
7 When they took hold of thee by thy hand, thou didst break, and rend all
their shoulder: and when they leaned upon thee, thou brakest, and madest
all their loins to be at a stand.
8 ¶Therefore thus saith the Lord GOD; Behold, I will bring a sword upon
thee, and cut off man and beast out of thee.

29:9☆ Prov 18:12; 29:23

9 And the land of Egypt shall be desolate and waste; and they shall know
that I *am* the LORD: because he hath said, The river *is* mine, and I have
made *it*.

c. The Forty Year Judgment: Egypt's Future Lowly Estate

10 Behold, therefore I *am* against thee, and against thy rivers, and I will
make the land of Egypt utterly waste *and* desolate, from the tower of Sy-
e′ne even unto the border of E-thi-o′pi-a.

29:11 Jer 43:11, 12; Dan 9:2
29:12 Jer 25:15–19; 27:6–11

11 No foot of man shall pass through it, nor foot of beast shall pass
through it, neither shall it be inhabited forty years.
12 And I will make the land of Egypt desolate in the midst of the countries
that are desolate, and her cities among the cities *that are* laid waste shall be
desolate forty years: and I will scatter the Egyptians among the nations,
and will disperse them through the countries.
13 ¶Yet thus saith the Lord GOD; At the end of forty years will I gather
the Egyptians from the people whither they were scattered:

29:14 Isa 11:11; Jer 44:1

14 And I will bring again the captivity of Egypt, and will cause them to
return *into* the land of Path′ros, into the land of their habitation; and they
shall be there a base kingdom.

29:15 Dan 11:42, 43; Nah 3:8, 9; Zech 10:11

15 It shall be the basest of the kingdoms; neither shall it exalt itself any
more above the nations: for I will diminish them, that they shall no more
rule over the nations.

29:16 Isa 30:1–3; 64:9; Hos 5:13; 8:13; 9:9

16 And it shall be no more the confidence of the house of Israel, which
bringeth *their* iniquity to remembrance, when they shall look after them:
but they shall know that I *am* the Lord GOD.

d. God Gives Egypt to Nebuchadrezzar as His Wages

29:17☆ Ezek 24:1; 30:20
29:18☆ Jer 25:9; 27:6; Ezek 26:7–12

17 ¶And it came to pass in the seven and twentieth year, in the first *month*,
in the first *day* of the month, the word of the LORD came unto me, saying,
18 Son of man, Neb-u-chad-rez′zar king of Babylon caused his army to
serve a great service against Tyrus: every head *was* made bald, and every
shoulder *was* peeled: yet had he no wages, nor his army, for Tyrus, for the
service that he had served against it:

29:9 This prophetic promise of the overthrow of Egypt was fulfilled when Nebuchadnezzar invaded that nation in 572 and 568 B.C. It was reduced to nothing more than a base kingdom. Following the conquest of Egypt by Cambyses, the Persian (ca. 524 B.C.), Egypt, for the most part, has been under the control of foreign powers. Today it is small among the nations in its power and influence.

29:17 Ezekiel here refers to the twenty-seventh year of Jehoiachin's captivity.

29:18 *yet had he no wage.* Nebuchadnezzar laid siege to Tyre for thirteen years (587–574 B.C.) before it fell. His reward for his trouble was negligible. So God gave him Egypt to make up for what he did not get from the sack of Tyre.

19 Therefore thus saith the Lord GOD; Behold, I will give the land of
Egypt unto Neb-u-chad-rez′zar king of Babylon; and he shall take her
multitude, and take her spoil, and take her prey; and it shall be the wages
for his army.
20 I have given him the land of Egypt *for* his labour wherewith he served
against it, because they wrought for me, saith the Lord GOD.
21 In that day will I cause the horn of the house of Israel to bud forth, and
I will give thee the opening of the mouth in the midst of them; and they
shall know that I *am* the LORD.

29:19 Jer 43:10–13; Ezek 30:10–12
29:20 Isa 10:6, 7; 45:1–3
29:21 1 Sam 2:10; Ps 92:10; Amos 3:7, 8; Lk 21:15

2. Egypt's Approaching Doom

a. Egypt's Terrible Day Has Come

30 THE word of the LORD came again unto me, saying,
2 Son of man, prophesy and say, Thus saith the Lord GOD; Howl
ye, Woe worth the day!
3 For the day *is* near, even the day of the LORD *is* near, a cloudy day; it
shall be the time of the heathen.
4 And the sword shall come upon Egypt, and great pain shall be in E-thi-
o′pi-a, when the slain shall fall in Egypt, and they shall take away her
multitude, and her foundations shall be broken down.
5 E-thi-o′pi-a, and Libya, and Lyd′i-a, and all the mingled people, and
Chub, and the men of the land that is in league, shall fall with them by the
sword.

30:2 Isa 13:6; 65:14; Joel 1:5, 11, 13, 15; Jas 5:1
☆30:3
☆30:5 Isa 18:1; 20:4; Jer 25:20, 24; Nah 3:8, 9

b. Egypt's Allies Shall Fall

6 Thus saith the LORD; They also that uphold Egypt shall fall; and the
pride of her power shall come down: from the tower of Sy-e′ne shall they
fall in it by the sword, saith the Lord GOD.
7 And they shall be desolate in the midst of the countries *that are* desolate,
and her cities shall be in the midst of the cities *that are* wasted.
8 And they shall know that I *am* the LORD, when I have set a fire in Egypt,
and *when* all her helpers shall be destroyed.
9 In that day shall messengers go forth from me in ships to make the
careless E-thi-o′pi-ans afraid, and great pain shall come upon them, as in
the day of Egypt: for, lo, it cometh.

30:6 Isa 20:3–6
30:8 Ps 58:11; Amos 1:4, 7, 10–14; Nah 1:5, 6
30:9 Isa 23:6; Jer 49:21; Zech 11:2, 3

c. Nebuchadrezzar Is Coming

10 Thus saith the Lord GOD; I will also make the multitude of Egypt to
cease by the hand of Neb-u-chad-rez′zar king of Babylon.
11 He and his people with him, the terrible of the nations, shall be brought
to destroy the land: and they shall draw their swords against Egypt, and fill
the land with the slain.
12 And I will make the rivers dry, and sell the land into the hand of the
wicked: and I will make the land waste, and all that is therein, by the hand
of strangers: I the LORD have spoken *it*.

30:12 Ezek 29:3, 9

d. The Destruction of Egypt's Strongholds

13 Thus saith the Lord GOD; I will also destroy the idols, and I will cause
their images to cease out of Noph; and there shall be no more a prince of
the land of Egypt: and I will put a fear in the land of Egypt.

☆30:13 Isa 2:18; Jer 44:1; 46:14; Hos 9:6

30:3 *the day of the LORD is near,* i.e., the day of God's judgment against Egypt, not the end of the age.
30:5 The neighbors of Egypt, here specified, will also suffer from the invasion of Nebuchadnezzar.

30:13–19 Ezekiel elaborates on the defeat of Egypt by mentioning the names of major cities and strongholds taken by the Babylonians.

30:14 Ps 78:12, 43 Isa 19:11, 13 Nah 3:8

14 And I will make Path'ros desolate, and will set fire in Zo'an, and will
execute judgments in No.
15 And I will pour my fury upon Sin, the strength of Egypt; and I will cut
off the multitude of No.
16 And I will set fire in Egypt: Sin shall have great pain, and No shall be
rent asunder, and Noph *shall have* distresses daily.

30:17 Gen 41:45

17 The young men of A'ven and of Pi–be'seth shall fall by the sword: and
these *cities* shall go into captivity.

30:18 Lev 26:13 Jer 43:8–13 46:20–26

18 At Te-haph'ne-hes also the day shall be darkened, when I shall break
there the yokes of Egypt: and the pomp of her strength shall cease in her:
as for her, a cloud shall cover her, and her daughters shall go into captivity.

30:19 Num 33:4 Ps 9:16 Ezek 5:8, 15

19 Thus will I execute judgments in Egypt: and they shall know that I *am*
the LORD.

e. God Will Break the Arms of Pharaoh

30:20☆ Ezek 26:1

20 ¶And it came to pass in the eleventh year, in the first *month*, in the
seventh *day* of the month, *that* the word of the LORD came unto me, saying,

30:21☆ Ps 10:15; 37:17 Jer 30:13; 46:11 Nah 3:16

21 Son of man, I have broken the arm of Pharaoh king of Egypt; and, lo,
it shall not be bound up to be healed, to put a roller to bind it, to make it
strong to hold the sword.

30:22 2 Kgs 24:7 Jer 37:7 46:1–12; 21–25

22 Therefore thus saith the Lord GOD; Behold, I *am* against Pharaoh king
of Egypt, and will break his arms, the strong, and that which was broken;
and I will cause the sword to fall out of his hand.
23 And I will scatter the Egyptians among the nations, and will disperse
them through the countries.

30:24 Isa 10:5, 6 45:1, 5 Zech 10:12

24 And I will strengthen the arms of the king of Babylon, and put my
sword in his hand: but I will break Pharaoh's arms, and he shall groan
before him with the groanings of a deadly wounded *man*.

30:25 Josh 8:18 1 Chron 21:16 Ps 9:16

25 But I will strengthen the arms of the king of Babylon, and the arms of
Pharaoh shall fall down; and they shall know that I *am* the LORD, when I
shall put my sword into the hand of the king of Babylon, and he shall
stretch it out upon the land of Egypt.
26 And I will scatter the Egyptians among the nations, and disperse them
among the countries; and they shall know that I *am* the LORD.

3. The Allegory of the Cedar of Lebanon
a. Egypt Is Like a Great Cedar of Lebanon

31:1☆

31 AND it came to pass in the eleventh year, in the third *month*, in the
first *day* of the month, *that* the word of the LORD came unto me,
saying,

31:2 Isa 10:33, 34 Dan 4:20–23 Nah 3:8, 9

2 Son of man, speak unto Pharaoh king of Egypt, and to his multitude;
Whom art thou like in thy greatness?

31:3☆

3 ¶Behold, the Assyrian *was* a cedar in Lebanon with fair branches, and
with a shadowing shroud, and of an high stature; and his top was among
the thick boughs.

31:4 Ezek 17:5, 8 Rev 17:1, 15

4 The waters made him great, the deep set him up on high with her rivers
running round about his plants, and sent out her little rivers unto all the
trees of the field.

30:20 *This took* place three months before the fall of Jerusalem.
30:21 A few months before Jerusalem was taken, Nebuchadnezzar took time off to defeat the Egyptian force that sought to relieve the besieged Jerusalem. This was that which broke the arm of Pharaoh; later both arms of Pharaoh would be broken.
31:1 This was a month before Jerusalem fell.
31:3 Egypt is likened to a great cedar in Lebanon. This probably refers to the Assyrian empire under Sennacherib that was great in extent, wealth, and power. It was unrivaled in its days.

5 Therefore his height was exalted above all the trees of the field, and his
boughs were multiplied, and his branches became long because of the
multitude of waters, when he shot forth.
6 All the fowls of heaven made their nests in his boughs, and under his
branches did all the beasts of the field bring forth their young, and under
his shadow dwelt all great nations.
7 Thus was he fair in his greatness, in the length of his branches: for his
root was by great waters.
8 The cedars in the garden of God could not hide him: the fir trees were
not like his boughs, and the chesnut trees were not like his branches; nor
any tree in the garden of God was like unto him in his beauty.
9 I have made him fair by the multitude of his branches: so that all the
trees of Eden, that *were* in the garden of God, envied him.

31:5 Ps 1:3
31:6 Ezek 17:23; Dan 4:12, 21; Mt 13:23
31:8 Gen 2:8, 9; 13:10; Ps 80:10; Isa 51:3

b. The Cedar Tree (Egypt) Will Fall into Hell

10 ¶Therefore thus saith the Lord GOD; Because thou hast lifted up thyself
in height, and he hath shot up his top among the thick boughs, and his
heart is lifted up in his height;
11 I have therefore delivered him into the hand of the mighty one of the
heathen; he shall surely deal with him: I have driven him out for his
wickedness.
12 And strangers, the terrible of the nations, have cut him off, and have
left him: upon the mountains and in all the valleys his branches are fallen,
and his boughs are broken by all the rivers of the land; and all the people
of the earth are gone down from his shadow, and have left him.
13 Upon his ruin shall all the fowls of the heaven remain, and all the
beasts of the field shall be upon his branches:
14 To the end that none of all the trees by the waters exalt themselves for
their height, neither shoot up their top among the thick boughs, neither
their trees stand up in their height, all that drink water: for they are all
delivered unto death, to the nether parts of the earth, in the midst of the
children of men, with them that go down to the pit.
15 Thus saith the Lord GOD; In the day when he went down to the grave
I caused a mourning: I covered the deep for him, and I restrained the floods
thereof, and the great waters were stayed: and I caused Lebanon to mourn
for him, and all the trees of the field fainted for him.
16 I made the nations to shake at the sound of his fall, when I cast him
down to hell with them that descend into the pit: and all the trees of Eden,
the choice and best of Lebanon, all that drink water, shall be comforted in
the nether parts of the earth.
17 They also went down into hell with him unto *them that be* slain with the
sword; and *they that were* his arm, *that* dwelt under his shadow in the midst
of the heathen.
18 ¶To whom art thou thus like in glory and in greatness among the trees
of Eden? yet shalt thou be brought down with the trees of Eden unto the
nether parts of the earth: thou shalt lie in the midst of the uncircumcised
with *them that be* slain by the sword. This *is* Pharaoh and all his multitude,
saith the Lord GOD.

31:10 2 Chron 32:25; Isa 14:13, 14; Dan 5:20
☆**31:10ff**
31:11 Deut 18:12; Dan 5:18, 19; Nah 3:18
31:12 Dan 4:14; Hab 1:6
31:13 Isa 18:6; Rev 19:17, 18
31:14 Num 16:30–33; Ps 63:9; Jonah 2:2, 6; Eph 4:9; 2 Pet 2:6
31:15 Nah 2:8–10; Rev 18:9–11, 16, 19
☆**31:16** Isa 14:8; Hag 2:7; Heb 12:26, 27; Rev 18:9
☆**31:17** Ps 9:17; Dan 4:11, 12; Nah 3:17
31:18 Ps 52:7; Jer 9:25, 26; Mt 13:19

31:10ff Even as Egypt was likened to Assyria in its zenith, so now Egypt is likened to Assyria in its fall. So great will be the fall of Egypt that the nations will quake at the sounds of the fall (31:16). Egypt will go down to sheol, to the nether parts of the earth.

31:16, 17 Other nations that rejoiced at the fall of Egypt would themselves go the same route at a later date.

4. The Mourning for Pharaoh, King of Egypt

a. God's Vengeance on the Pharaoh

32 AND it came to pass in the twelfth year, in the twelfth month, in
the first *day* of the month, *that* the word of the LORD came unto me,
saying,

32:2☆ Jer 46:7, 8 Nah 2:11–13

2Son of man, take up a lamentation for Pharaoh king of Egypt, and say
unto him, Thou art like a young lion of the nations, and thou *art* as a whale
in the seas: and thou camest forth with thy rivers, and troubledst the waters
with thy feet, and fouledst their rivers.

32:3☆

3Thus saith the Lord GOD; I will therefore spread out my net over thee
with a company of many people; and they shall bring thee up in my net.

32:4 1 Sam 17:44–46 Isa 34:2–7 Jer 8:2

4Then will I leave thee upon the land, I will cast thee forth upon the open
field, and will cause all the fowls of the heaven to remain upon thee, and I
will fill the beasts of the whole earth with thee.
5And I will lay thy flesh upon the mountains, and fill the valleys with thy
height.

32:6 Ex 7:17 Isa 34:3, 7 Rev 14:20; 16:6

6I will also water with thy blood the land wherein thou swimmest, *even* to
the mountains; and the rivers shall be full of thee.

32:7☆ Ex 10:21–23 Prov 13:9 Amos 8:9

7And when I shall put thee out, I will cover the heaven, and make the
stars thereof dark; I will cover the sun with a cloud, and the moon shall not
give her light.

32:8☆ Gen 1:14

8All the bright lights of heaven will I make dark over thee, and set
darkness upon thy land, saith the Lord GOD.

b. The Sword of Babylon Will Fall on Egypt

32:9☆ Ex 15:14–16 Jer 25:15–26 Rev 18:10–15

9I will also vex the hearts of many people, when I shall bring thy
destruction among the nations, into the countries which thou hast not
known.
10Yea, I will make many people amazed at thee, and their kings shall be
horribly afraid for thee, when I shall brandish my sword before them; and
they shall tremble at *every* moment, every man for his own life, in the day
of thy fall.
11¶For thus saith the Lord GOD; The sword of the king of Babylon shall
come upon thee.
12By the swords of the mighty will I cause thy multitude to fall, the
terrible of the nations, all of them: and they shall spoil the pomp of Egypt,
and all the multitude thereof shall be destroyed.
13I will destroy also all the beasts thereof from beside the great waters;
neither shall the foot of man trouble them any more, nor the hoofs of beasts
trouble them.

32:15☆ Ex 7:5; 14:4, 18 Ps 83:17, 18 Ezek 8:7

14Then will I make their waters deep, and cause their rivers to run like oil,
saith the Lord GOD.
15When I shall make the land of Egypt desolate, and the country shall be

---

32:2 God orders Ezekiel to begin a lamentation over Egypt. (Such compassion by the bearer of a sad message of judgment might possibly cause Egypt to change its ways.) God does not delight in the death of *the wicked.*

32:3 *I will spread my net over thee,* i.e., a sovereign God, no matter how big and how strong a nation, has a net big enough to cover it, strong enough to keep it enclosed and unbroken. In this instance the net is the Chaldeans.

32:7, 8 This probably refers to the darkness that came upon Egypt in the contest between Moses and Pharaoh. The remembrance of this past event might bring some sense to Egypt in the present difficulty and cause her to repent, lest a similar judgment fall on her.

32:9 The judgment on Egypt will cause surrounding nations to tremble. Aware of their own sins, they are no less worthy of similar punishment at the hands of God.

32:15 When God strips Egypt bare, it will demonstrate that it was *the LORD* who caused this. It is unfortunate that nations who refuse to acknowledge God must learn the lesson the hard way and when it is too late.

destitute of that whereof it was full, when I shall smite all them that dwell
therein, then shall they know that I *am* the LORD.
16 This *is* the lamentation wherewith they shall lament her: the daughters
of the nations shall lament her: they shall lament for her, *even* for Egypt,
and for all her multitude, saith the Lord GOD.

32:16 2 Sam 3:33, 34; 2 Chron 35:25; Jer 9:17

c. Egypt Will Join Other Nations in Hell

17 It came to pass also in the twelfth year, in the fifteenth *day* of the
month, *that* the word of the LORD came unto me, saying,
18 Son of man, wail for the multitude of Egypt, and cast them down, *even*
her, and the daughters of the famous nations, unto the nether parts of the
earth, with them that go down into the pit.
19 Whom dost thou pass in beauty? go down, and be thou laid with the
uncircumcised.
20 They shall fall in the midst of *them that are* slain by the sword: she is
delivered to the sword: draw her and all her multitudes.
21 The strong among the mighty shall speak to him out of the midst of hell
with them that help him: they are gone down, they lie uncircumcised, slain
by the sword.
22 Asshur *is* there and all her company: his graves *are* about him: all of
them slain, fallen by the sword:
23 Whose graves are set in the sides of the pit, and her company is round
about her grave: all of them slain, fallen by the sword, which caused terror
in the land of the living.
24 There *is* E'lam and all her multitude round about her grave, all of them
slain, fallen by the sword, which are gone down uncircumcised into the
nether parts of the earth, which caused their terror in the land of the living;
yet have they borne their shame with them that go down to the pit.
25 They have set her a bed in the midst of the slain with all her multitude:
her graves *are* round about him: all of them uncircumcised, slain by the
sword: though their terror was caused in the land of the living, yet have
they borne their shame with them that go down to the pit: he is put in the
midst of *them that be* slain.
26 There *is* Me'shech, Tu'bal, and all her multitude: her graves *are* round
about him: all of them uncircumcised, slain by the sword, though they
caused their terror in the land of the living.
27 And they shall not lie with the mighty *that are* fallen of the uncircum-
cised, which are gone down to hell with their weapons of war: and they
have laid their swords under their heads, but their iniquities shall be upon
their bones, though *they were* the terror of the mighty in the land of the
living.
28 Yea, thou shalt be broken in the midst of the uncircumcised, and shalt
lie with *them that are* slain with the sword.
29 There *is* Edom, her kings, and all her princes, which with their might
are laid by *them that were* slain by the sword: they shall lie with the
uncircumcised, and with them that go down to the pit.
30 There *be* the princes of the north, all of them, and all the Zi-do'ni-ans,
which are gone down with the slain; with their terror they are ashamed of
their might; and they lie uncircumcised with *them that be* slain by the
sword, and bear their shame with them that go down to the pit.

☆**32:18** Jer 1:10; Hos 6:5
32:19 Jer 9:25, 26
32:20 Ps 28:3; Prov 24:11; Jer 22:19
32:21 Isa 14:9–12; Lk 16:23, 24
32:22 Ps 83:8–10; Isa 37:36–38; Nah 1:7–12
32:24 Gen 10:22; Job 28:13; Ps 52:5; Jer 49:32–39
32:25 Ps 139:8
32:26 Gen 10:2; Isa 66:19
☆**32:27** Prov 14:32; Isa 14:18, 19; Jn 8:24
32:29 Isa 34:5–15; Jer 49:7–22; Ezek 25:13
32:30 Jer 1:15; 25:26; Ezek 28:21–23; 38:15

32:18 Egypt will go down to the pit. She will join other nations there who will welcome her with pomp and ceremony. "Hell from beneath is moved for thee to meet thee at thy coming" (Isa. 14:9). The nations are like graves set in a row. And among those mentioned as having come there before Egypt are Elam, Meshech, Tubal, and Edom.

32:27 *their iniquities shall be upon their bones,* i.e., "whose shields are upon their bones," (RSV).

31 Pharaoh shall see them, and shall be comforted over all his multitude,
even Pharaoh and all his army slain by the sword, saith the Lord GOD.
32 For I have caused my terror in the land of the living: and he shall be
laid in the midst of the uncircumcised with *them that are* slain with the
sword, *even* Pharaoh and all his multitude, saith the Lord GOD.

IV. THE PROMISE OF ISRAEL'S RESTORATION (33:1—39:29)

A. THE RECOMMISSIONING OF EZEKIEL

1. God Appoints Ezekiel as a Watchman

33 AGAIN the word of the LORD came unto me, saying,
2 Son of man, speak to the children of thy people, and say unto
them, When I bring the sword upon a land, if the people of the land take a
man of their coasts, and set him for their watchman:
3 If when he seeth the sword come upon the land, he blow the trumpet,
and warn the people;
4 Then whosoever heareth the sound of the trumpet, and taketh not
warning; if the sword come, and take him away, his blood shall be upon his
own head.
5 He heard the sound of the trumpet, and took not warning; his blood
shall be upon him. But he that taketh warning shall deliver his soul.
6 But if the watchman see the sword come, and blow not the trumpet, and
the people be not warned; if the sword come, and take *any* person from
among them, he is taken away in his iniquity; but his blood will I require at
the watchman's hand.
7 ¶So thou, O son of man, I have set thee a watchman unto the house of
Israel; therefore thou shalt hear the word at my mouth, and warn them
from me.
8 When I say unto the wicked, O wicked *man*, thou shalt surely die; if
thou dost not speak to warn the wicked from his way, that wicked *man* shall
die in his iniquity; but his blood will I require at thine hand.
9 Nevertheless, if thou warn the wicked of his way to turn from it; if he do
not turn from his way, he shall die in his iniquity; but thou hast delivered
thy soul.

2. God Gives Ezekiel His Message

10 Therefore, O thou son of man, speak unto the house of Israel; Thus ye
speak, saying, If our transgressions and our sins *be* upon us, and we pine
away in them, how should we then live?
11 Say unto them, *As* I live, saith the Lord GOD, I have no pleasure in the
death of the wicked; but that the wicked turn from his way and live: turn
ye, turn ye from your evil ways; for why will ye die, O house of Israel?

32:31 Lam 2:13; Ezek 31:16
32:32☆
33:2 2 Sam 18:24, 25; 2 Kgs 9:17; Jer 12:12
33:3 Neh 4:18–20; Hos 8:1; Joel 2:1
33:4 Jer 6:17; Ezek 18:13; Zech 1:4; Acts 18:6
33:5 Ex 9:19–21, 25; 2 Kgs 8:10; Ps 95:7; Heb 11:7
33:6 Isa 56:10; Ezek 3:18, 20; 34:10
33:7☆ Isa 62:6, 7; Jer 26:2; Acts 5:20
33:8 Ezek 18:4, 13, 18–20; Acts 20:26, 27
33:9 Ezek 3:19, 21; Acts 13:40–46; Gal 5:19–21
33:10 Lev 26:39; Isa 49:14; Jer 2:25; Ezek 24:23; 37:11
33:11☆ Ezek 18:23, 30–32; Hos 11:8; Acts 3:19; 1 Tim 2:4; 2 Pet 3:9

32:32 "Here is a plain allusion to the final and everlasting ruin of impenitent sinners, of those who are uncircumcised in heart; they are slain by the sword of divine justice; their iniquity is upon them, and with it they bear their shame."*

33:7 God has set Ezekiel as a watchman to warn the *city of its impending destruction if the people refuse* to repent. When the watchman has given the warning, he has discharged his trust. He has not only delivered his own soul, he has also earned his wages. But if he fails to warn the wicked to flee from their wicked ways, his own soul is required of him. This role of watchman belongs to princes and presidents, to statesmen and public servants. It belongs especially to ministers of the gospel, who are called upon to warn sinners to flee to Christ for salvation and everlasting life.

33:11 "It is certain that God has no delight in the ruin of sinners, nor does he desire it. If they destroy themselves, he will glorify himself in it, but he has no pleasure in it, but would rather they should turn and live, for his goodness is that attribute of his which is most his glory, which is most his delight. He would rather sinners should turn and live than go on and die. He has said it, he has sworn it, that by these two immutable things, in both of which it is impossible for God to lie, we might have strong consolation."*

[12]Therefore, thou son of man, say unto the children of thy people, The
righteousness of the righteous shall not deliver him in the day of his
transgression: as for the wickedness of the wicked, he shall not fall thereby
in the day that he turneth from his wickedness; neither shall the righteous
be able to live for his *righteousness* in the day that he sinneth.
[13]When I shall say to the righteous, *that* he shall surely live; if he trust to
his own righteousness, and commit iniquity, all his righteousnesses shall not
be remembered; but for his iniquity that he hath committed, he shall die for
it.
[14]Again, when I say unto the wicked, Thou shalt surely die; if he turn
from his sin, and do that which is lawful and right;
[15]*If* the wicked restore the pledge, give again that he had robbed, walk in
the statutes of life, without committing iniquity; he shall surely live, he shall
not die.
[16]None of his sins that he hath committed shall be mentioned unto him:
he hath done that which is lawful and right; he shall surely live.
[17]¶Yet the children of thy people say, The way of the Lord is not equal:
but as for them, their way is not equal.
[18]When the righteous turneth from his righteousness, and committeth
iniquity, he shall even die thereby.
[19]But if the wicked turn from his wickedness, and do that which is lawful
and right, he shall live thereby.
[20]¶Yet ye say, The way of the Lord is not equal. O ye house of Israel, I
will judge you every one after his ways.

33:12 2 Chron 7:14 Ezek 3:20 18:21, 24 Mt 21:28–31 Rom 3:25
33:13 Ezek 18:26 Heb 10:38 2 Pet 2:20, 21
33:14 Isa 55:7 Ezek 18:27 Hos 14:1, 4 Mic 6:8
33:15 Lev 6:4, 5 Num 5:6–8 Ezek 20:11 Lk 19:8
33:16 Isa 1:18; 43:25 Ezek 18:22 Rom 5:16, 21 1 Jn 2:1–3
☆33:17 Ezek 18:24–29

3. The News of Jerusalem's Downfall

[21]¶And it came to pass in the twelfth year of our captivity, in the tenth
month, in the fifth *day* of the month, *that* one that had escaped out of
Jerusalem came unto me, saying, The city is smitten.
[22]Now the hand of the LORD was upon me in the evening, afore he that
was escaped came; and had opened my mouth, until he came to me in the
morning; and my mouth was opened, and I was no more dumb.

☆33:21 Jer 39:1, 2 Ezek 24:1, 2, 26
33:22 Ezek 3:26, 27 24:27 Lk 1:64

4. God Will Send Desolation upon the Remnant

[23]Then the word of the LORD came unto me, saying,
[24]Son of man, they that inhabit those wastes of the land of Israel speak,
saying, Abraham was one, and he inherited the land: but we *are* many; the
land is given us for inheritance.
[25]Wherefore say unto them, Thus saith the Lord GOD; Ye eat with the
blood, and lift up your eyes toward your idols, and shed blood: and shall ye
possess the land?
[26]Ye stand upon your sword, ye work abomination, and ye defile every
one his neighbour's wife: and shall ye possess the land?
[27]Say thou thus unto them, Thus saith the Lord GOD; *As* I live, surely
they that *are* in the wastes shall fall by the sword, and him that *is* in the
open field will I give to the beasts to be devoured, and they that *be* in the
forts and in the caves shall die of the pestilence.

☆33:23
33:24 Isa 51:1, 2 Jer 39:10 Acts 7:5 Rom 4:12; 9:7
33:25 Lev 17:10–14 Deut 12:16, 23 Jer 7:9, 10
33:26 Mic 2:1, 2 Zeph 3:3
33:27 Isa 2:19 Jer 15:2–4 Ezek 5:12–14

33:17 The ways of God are just; the ways of sinners are not. In the end, all who dispute with God will discover that he is right and they are wrong.

33:21 Beginning here Ezekiel turns from a message of disaster and judgment to a word of promise for Israel in the far-off future. God opens his sealed mouth so that he can speak publicly again.

33:23ff The Jews who remained in the land after the destruction of Jerusalem claimed that if a single individual, Abraham, was given the whole land, they had a right to it. Ezekiel responds by saying that the right to the land depends on obedience, and then he lists their sins (33:25, 26).

33:28 Jer 44:22; Ezek 6:14; 36:34; Mic 7:13
33:29 Ezek 23:33, 35

28 For I will lay the land most desolate, and the pomp of her strength shall
cease; and the mountains of Israel shall be desolate, that none shall pass
through.
29 Then shall they know that I *am* the LORD, when I have laid the land
most desolate because of all their abominations which they have com-
mitted.

5. The Remnant Hears but Refuses to Pay Attention to Ezekiel

33:30☆ Ezek 14:3; 29:13
33:31 Ps 78:36, 37; Isa 29:13; Mt 13:22; Lk 12:15; Jas 2:14–16; 1 Jn 3:18
33:32 Mk 6:20
33:33 Ezek 2:5; 33:29

30 ¶Also, thou son of man, the children of thy people still are talking
against thee by the walls and in the doors of the houses, and speak one to
another, every one to his brother, saying, Come, I pray you, and hear what
is the word that cometh forth from the LORD.
31 And they come unto thee as the people cometh, and they sit before thee
as my people, and they hear thy words, but they will not do them: for with
their mouth they shew much love, *but* their heart goeth after their
covetousness.
32 And, lo, thou *art* unto them as a very lovely song of one that hath a
pleasant voice, and can play well on an instrument: for they hear thy words,
but they do them not.
33 And when this cometh to pass, (lo, it will come,) then shall they know
that a prophet hath been among them.

B. PROPHECY ABOUT THE LEADERS (SHEPHERDS) OF ISRAEL
1. The Shepherds Are Faithless; They Do Not Tend the Sheep

34:2☆ 2 Sam 5:2; Jer 10:21; 23:1; Mic 3:1–3; Jn 10:11; 21:15–17
34:3 Isa 56:11; Zech 11:5, 16; 22:27
34:4 Zech 11:15, 16; Mt 9:36; 18:12, 13; 1 Pet 5:3
34:5 1 Kgs 22:17; Jer 10:21; 23:2; Zech 10:2
34:6 Ps 142:4; Jer 5:1; 1 Pet 2:25
34:8 1 Sam 2:29, 30; Ps 72:12–14; Zech 10:3; Acts 20:29

34 AND the word of the LORD came unto me, saying,
2 Son of man, prophesy against the shepherds of Israel, prophesy,
and say unto them, Thus saith the Lord GOD unto the shepherds; Woe *be*
to the shepherds of Israel that do feed themselves! should not the shepherds
feed the flocks?
3 Ye eat the fat, and ye clothe you with the wool, ye kill them that are fed:
but ye feed not the flock.
4 The diseased have ye not strengthened, neither have ye healed that
which was sick, neither have ye bound up *that which was* broken, neither
have ye brought again that which was driven away, neither have ye sought
that which was lost; but with force and with cruelty have ye ruled them.
5 And they were scattered, because *there is* no shepherd: and they became
meat to all the beasts of the field, when they were scattered.
6 My sheep wandered through all the mountains, and upon every high
hill: yea, my flock was scattered upon all the face of the earth, and none did
search or seek *after them*.
7 ¶Therefore, ye shepherds, hear the word of the LORD;
8 *As* I live, saith the Lord GOD, surely because my flock became a prey,
and my flock became meat to every beast of the field, because *there was* no
shepherd, neither did my shepherds search for my flock, but the shepherds
fed themselves, and fed not my flock;
9 Therefore, O ye shepherds, hear the word of the LORD;
10 Thus saith the Lord GOD; Behold, I *am* against the shepherds; and I
will require my flock at their hand, and cause them to cease from feeding

---

33:30ff *The people are hypocrites who put on a good show of outward religion. They pretend really to listen to the prophet, but inwardly they think him to be merely entertaining. They hear what he says, but they refuse to heed him.*

34:2 This prophecy against the shepherds of Israel is an indictment against the princes and magistrates, the priests and Levites, and the Sanhedrin. They did not feed the sheep, i.e., the people under their charge. Their primary interest was to improve their own condition, not that of the sheep. They were willing to shear the sheep, not to feed them. They left the sheep exposed to the wintry blasts—minus their wool and bereft of adequate food, both material and spiritual.

the flock; neither shall the shepherds feed themselves any more; for I will
deliver my flock from their mouth, that they may not be meat for them.

2. God Will Seek the Lost Sheep and Save Them

11¶For thus saith the Lord GOD; Behold, I, *even* I, will both search my
sheep, and seek them out.
12As a shepherd seeketh out his flock in the day that he is among his
sheep *that are* scattered; so will I seek out my sheep, and will deliver them
out of all places where they have been scattered in the cloudy and dark day.
13And I will bring them out from the people, and gather them from the
countries, and will bring them to their own land, and feed them upon
the mountains of Israel by the rivers, and in all the inhabited places of the
country.
14I will feed them in a good pasture, and upon the high mountains of
Israel shall their fold be: there shall they lie in a good fold, and *in* a fat
pasture shall they feed upon the mountains of Israel.
15I will feed my flock, and I will cause them to lie down, saith the Lord
GOD.
16I will seek that which was lost, and bring again that which was driven
away, and will bind up *that which was* broken, and will strengthen that
which was sick: but I will destroy the fat and the strong; I will feed them
with judgment.

☆**34:11** Ezek 11:17; 20:41; Mt 13:11, 12; Jn 10:16
34:12 Jer 23:3; 31:10; Ezek 30:3; Joel 2:2; Lk 19:10
34:13 Isa 30:25; Ps 23:1–3; Ezek 36:29, 30
34:14 Isa 49:26; Mt 18:11; Lk 5:32; Jn 10:9
34:16 Isa 10:16; 49:26

3. God Will Judge between the Fat Shepherds and the Scrawny Sheep

17And *as for* you, O my flock, thus saith the Lord GOD; Behold, I judge
between cattle and cattle, between the rams and the he goats.
18*Seemeth it* a small thing unto you to have eaten up the good pasture,
but ye must tread down with your feet the residue of your pastures? and to
have drunk of the deep waters, but ye must foul the residue with your feet?
19And *as for* my flock, they eat that which ye have trodden with your feet;
and they drink that which ye have fouled with your feet.
20¶Therefore thus saith the Lord GOD unto them; Behold, I, *even* I, will
judge between the fat cattle and between the lean cattle.
21Because ye have thrust with side and with shoulder, and pushed all the
diseased with your horns, till ye have scattered them abroad;
22Therefore will I save my flock, and they shall no more be a prey; and I
will judge between cattle and cattle.

34:17 Ezek 20:38; Zech 10:3; Mal 4:1; Mt 25:32
34:18 Num 16:9, 13; Mt 23:13, 14; Lk 11:52
34:21 Dan 8:4; Lk 13:14–16
34:22 Ps 72:12–14; Jer 23:2, 3; Zech 11:7–9

4. The New Shepherd, My Servant, David

23And I will set up one shepherd over them, and he shall feed them, *even*
my servant David; he shall feed them, and he shall be their shepherd.
24And I the LORD will be their God, and my servant David a prince
among them; I the LORD have spoken *it*.

☆**34:23** Isa 40:11; Jer 23:4–6; 30:9; Jn 10:11; Heb 13:20
34:24 Jer 30:9; Ezek 37:24, 25

34:11 The Lord is the chief Shepherd. He has a concern for and an interest in his sheep. They will be scattered far and wide, but the Shepherd will search for and find his sheep. He will restore them to their land and sustain them by providing for them. This verse has both an immediate and a long-range prophetic element. There was to be an immediate return of the remnant to Palestine, and at the end of the age there would be the full and final fulfillment of the divine promise, marked by the Second Advent of Jesus Christ as the glorious victor over sin and death.

34:23 This is a specific reference to Jesus the Messiah, the son of David. Here he is called *my servant David.* David, however, died long before this prophetic word was spoken. Yet it refers to the Davidic covenant, in which God promised that there should always be one of David's descendants on the throne of David. In his sermon in Acts 2, Peter makes it clear that Jesus now sits on the throne of his father David and will come at last to rule and reign over the whole earth. *one shepherd.* Jesus, the Davidic king, will reunite Israel and Judah into one kingdom as it was during the reigns of David and Solomon.

5. God's New Peace Pact

34:25 Isa 11:6–9; Jer 33:16; Ezek 37:26; Hos 2:18

25 And I will make with them a covenant of peace, and will cause the evil
beasts to cease out of the land: and they shall dwell safely in the wilderness,
and sleep in the woods.

34:26 Gen 12:2; Deut 28:12; Isa 32:15; 44:3; Zech 8:13; Mal 3:10

26 And I will make them and the places round about my hill a blessing;
and I will cause the shower to come down in his season; there shall be
showers of blessing.

34:27 Lev 26:13; Ps 85:12; Isa 52:2, 3; Jn 15:5–8

27 And the tree of the field shall yield her fruit, and the earth shall yield
her increase, and they shall be safe in their land, and shall know that I *am*
the LORD, when I have broken the bands of their yoke, and delivered them
out of the hand of those that served themselves of them.

34:28 Jer 30:10; Ezek 39:26

28 And they shall no more be a prey to the heathen, neither shall the beast
of the land devour them; but they shall dwell safely, and none shall make
them afraid.

34:29☆ Isa 53:2; 60:21; Ezek 36:6, 15, 29; Zech 3:8; 6:12

29 And I will raise up for them a plant of renown, and they shall be no
more consumed with hunger in the land, neither bear the shame of the
heathen any more.

34:30 Ps 46:7, 11; Ezek 36:28; 37:27

30 Thus shall they know that I the LORD their God *am* with them, and *that*
they, *even* the house of Israel, *are* my people, saith the Lord GOD.

34:31 Ps 100:2; Mic 7:14; Jn 10:11

31 And ye my flock, the flock of my pasture, *are* men, *and* I *am* your God,
saith the Lord GOD.

C. EDOM AND ISRAEL CONTRASTED

1. The Prophecy against Mount Seir (Edom)

35:2☆ Gen 36:6–8; Deut 2:5; Josh 24:4; Ezek 25:12

35 MOREOVER the word of the LORD came unto me, saying,
2 Son of man, set thy face against mount Se′ir, and prophesy
against it,

35:3 Jer 49:13, 17, 18; Ezek 25:13

3 And say unto it, Thus saith the Lord GOD; Behold, O mount Se′ir, I *am*
against thee, and I will stretch out mine hand against thee, and I will make
thee most desolate.

35:4 Ps 137:7; Ezek 6:6; Amos 1:11; Obad 10; Mal 1:2–4

4 I will lay thy cities waste, and thou shalt be desolate, and thou shalt
know that I *am* the LORD.
5 Because thou hast had a perpetual hatred, and hast shed *the blood of* the
children of Israel by the force of the sword in the time of their calamity, in
the time *that their* iniquity *had* an end:

35:6 Ezek 32:6

6 Therefore, *as* I live, saith the Lord GOD, I will prepare thee unto blood,
and blood shall pursue thee: sith thou hast not hated blood, even blood
shall pursue thee.

35:7 Ezek 25:13

7 Thus will I make mount Se′ir most desolate, and cut off from it him that
passeth out and him that returneth.

35:8 Isa 34:5, 6; Ezek 31:12; 32:4, 5

8 And I will fill his mountains with his slain *men:* in thy hills, and in thy
valleys, and in all thy rivers, shall they fall that are slain with the sword.

35:9 Jer 49:13; Ezek 25:13

9 I will make thee perpetual desolations, and thy cities shall not return:
and ye shall know that I *am* the LORD.

35:10 Ps 48:1–3; Ezek 36:2, 5

10 Because thou hast said, These two nations and these two countries shall
be mine, and we will possess it; whereas the LORD was there:

35:11 Ps 9:16; 137:7; Ezek 25:14; Amos 1:11

11 Therefore, *as* I live, saith the Lord GOD, I will even do according to
thine anger, and according to thine envy which thou hast used out of thy
hatred against them; and I will make myself known among them, when I
have judged thee.

34:29 *And I will raise up for them a plant of renown,* i.e., "I will provide for them a land renowned for its crops" (NIV).

35:2 *Seir,* i.e., "Edom." See note on Gen. 36:9 for information on the Edomites.

12 And thou shalt know that I *am* the LORD, *and that* I have heard all thy
blasphemies which thou hast spoken against the mountains of Israel,
saying, They are laid desolate, they are given us to consume.
13 Thus with your mouth ye have boasted against me, and have multiplied
your words against me: I have heard *them.*
14 Thus saith the Lord GOD; When the whole earth rejoiceth, I will make
thee desolate.
15 As thou didst rejoice at the inheritance of the house of Israel, because it
was desolate, so will I do unto thee: thou shalt be desolate, O mount Se′ir,
and all I-du-me′a, *even* all of it: and they shall know that I *am* the LORD.

35:12 Ps 83:12; Jer 50:7; Ezek 36:2
35:13 Isa 10:13, 14; Ezek 36:3; Dan 11:36
35:14 Isa 44:23, 49:13; Jer 51:48
☆**35:15** Isa 34:5, 6; Lam 4:21; Obad 12, 15

2. Israel's Glorious Future

a. God Will Judge Israel's Enemies

36 ALSO, thou son of man, prophesy unto the mountains of Israel,
and say, Ye mountains of Israel, hear the word of the LORD:
2 Thus saith the Lord GOD; Because the enemy hath said against you,
Aha, even the ancient high places are ours in possession:
3 Therefore prophesy and say, Thus saith the Lord GOD; Because they
have made *you* desolate, and swallowed you up on every side, that ye might
be a possession unto the residue of the heathen, and ye are taken up in the
lips of talkers, and *are* an infamy of the people:
4 Therefore, ye mountains of Israel, hear the word of the Lord GOD; thus
saith the Lord GOD to the mountains, and to the hills, to the rivers, and to
the valleys, to the desolate wastes, and to the cities that are forsaken, which
became a prey and derision to the residue of the heathen that *are* round
about;
5 Therefore thus saith the Lord GOD; Surely in the fire of my jealousy
have I spoken against the residue of the heathen, and against all I-du-me′a,
which have appointed my land into their possession with the joy of all *their*
heart, with the despiteful minds, to cast it out for a prey.
6 Prophesy therefore concerning the land of Israel, and say unto the
mountains, and to the hills, to the rivers, and to the valleys, Thus saith the
Lord GOD; Behold, I have spoken in my jealousy and in my fury, because
ye have borne the shame of the heathen:
7 Therefore thus saith the Lord GOD; I have lifted up mine hand, Surely
the heathen that *are* about you, they shall bear their shame.

b. Good Things in Store for Israel

8 ¶But ye, O mountains of Israel, ye shall shoot forth your branches, and
yield your fruit to my people of Israel; for they are at hand to come.
9 For, behold, I *am* for you, and I will turn unto you, and ye shall be tilled
and sown:
10 And I will multiply men upon you, all the house of Israel, *even* all of it:
and the cities shall be inhabited, and the wastes shall be builded:
11 *And I will multiply* upon you man and beast; and they shall increase
and bring fruit: and I will settle you after your old estates, and will do

☆**36:1** Ezek 6:2, 3; 37:22
36:2 Deut 32:13; Ps 78:69; Isa 58:14; Ezek 35:10
36:3 Jer 2:15; 51:34; Lam 2:16; Ezek 35:13
36:4 Deut 11:11; Ps 79:4; Jer 48:27; Ezek 34:28
36:5 Isa 66:15, 16; Jer 50:11; Ezek 35:15
36:6 Ps 123:4; Ezek 34:29
☆**36:8** Isa 27:6; Ezek 17:22, 23; 34:26–29; Hos 2:21–23; Amos 9:13–15; Heb 10:37
36:9 Lev 26:9; Ps 46:11; Ezek 28:26; 34:14
36:10 Isa 27:6; 49:17–22; Jer 31:27, 28; Ezek 37:21, 22
36:11 Jer 30:18; Ezek 16:55

35:15 The major sin of Edom was that it rejoiced over the desolation of Israel. This was an insult to God, who continued to love Israel and to remember his covenant with that nation. Therefore Edom shall be destroyed and other nations will rejoice over its destruction, as Edom did over that of Israel.

36:1ff Canaan, Israel's land, has been emptied of its people. It has been occupied by enemies of Israel, who had been reproached by these peoples. God proclaims that he will judge those who have taken over his land and he will later return mountains, hills, ravines, and valleys to those in whom he delights.

36:8ff Herein God promises the return of Canaan to his people Israel. It will flourish and be fruitful. This promise, which has been partially fulfilled, will completely come to pass in the future.

better *unto you* than at your beginnings: and ye shall know that I *am* the
LORD.

36:12 Jer 32:44; Ezek 34:13, 14; 47:14

[12]Yea, I will cause men to walk upon you, *even* my people Israel; and
they shall possess thee, and thou shalt be their inheritance, and thou shalt
no more henceforth bereave them *of men.*
[13]Thus saith the Lord GOD; Because they say unto you, Thou *land*
devourest up men, and hast bereaved thy nations;
[14]Therefore thou shalt devour men no more, neither bereave thy nations
any more, saith the Lord GOD.

36:15 Isa 54:4; Jer 18:15; Ezek 22:4; 34:29

[15]Neither will I cause *men* to hear in thee the shame of the heathen any
more, neither shalt thou bear the reproach of the people any more, neither
shalt thou cause thy nations to fall any more, saith the Lord GOD.

c. God Has Punished Israel for Idolatry

36:16☆

36:17 Jer 2:7

36:18 2 Chron 34:21, 25; Lam 2:4; 4:11; Ezek 22:18–20

36:19 Deut 28:64; Ezek 22:15; Amos 9:9; Rom 2:6; Rev 20:12–15

36:20 Isa 52:5; Jer 33:24; Ezek 12:16; Rom 2:24

36:21 Isa 48:9; Ezek 20:44

[16]¶Moreover the word of the LORD came unto me, saying,
[17]Son of man, when the house of Israel dwelt in their own land, they
defiled it by their own way and by their doings: their way was before me as
the uncleanness of a removed woman.
[18]Wherefore I poured my fury upon them for the blood that they had
shed upon the land, and for their idols *wherewith* they had polluted it:
[19]And I scattered them among the heathen, and they were dispersed
through the countries: according to their way and according to their doings
I judged them.
[20]And when they entered unto the heathen, whither they went, they
profaned my holy name, when they said to them, These *are* the people of
the LORD, and are gone forth out of his land.
[21]¶But I had pity for mine holy name, which the house of Israel had
profaned among the heathen, whither they went.

d. God Will Bring Israel Back

36:22 Deut 9:5–7; Ps 106:8; 115:1, 2

36:23 Ps 126:2; Ezek 20:41; 39:7

36:24 Deut 30:3–5; Isa 43:5, 6; Ezek 34:13; 37:21

36:25☆ Isa 52:15; Zech 13:1; Jn 3:5; Tit 3:5, 6; Heb 10:22

36:26 Ps 51:10; Ezek 11:19; 2 Cor 5:17

36:27 Isa 59:21; Ezek 11:20; 37:14

[22]Therefore say unto the house of Israel, Thus saith the Lord GOD; I do
not *this* for your sakes, O house of Israel, but for mine holy name's sake,
which ye have profaned among the heathen, whither ye went.
[23]And I will sanctify my great name, which was profaned among the
heathen, which ye have profaned in the midst of them; and the heathen
shall know that I *am* the LORD, saith the Lord GOD, when I shall be
sanctified in you before their eyes.
[24]For I will take you from among the heathen, and gather you out of all
countries, and will bring you into your own land.
[25]¶Then will I sprinkle clean water upon you, and ye shall be clean: from
all your filthiness, and from all your idols, will I cleanse you.
[26]A new heart also will I give you, and a new spirit will I put within you:
and I will take away the stony heart out of your flesh, and I will give you an
heart of flesh.
[27]And I will put my spirit within you, and cause you to walk in my
statutes, and ye shall keep my judgments, and do *them.*

36:16ff The downfall of Israel enabled pagan nations to speak scornfully of Israel and its God. Israel has *become the refuse of the nations and her enemies* taunt them by saying that their God can hardly be worthy of devotion, for he has been unable to keep them from these disasters. Because of this, God has concern for his holy name (36:21).

36:25 God will cleanse his people from the pollution of sin. They will be delivered from the guilt, penalty, and power of sin. He will also give them a new heart and an inward change, which will enable them to see and think correctly. It will replace the heart of stone. It will be a soft and tender heart (36:26), brought about by renewing grace. And they will then walk according to the will and commandments of God, for they will have the Spirit of God in his fullness. By reason of his sanctifying power (36:27), they will be empowered to live holy lives.

28 And ye shall dwell in the land that I gave to your fathers; and ye shall
be my people, and I will be your God.
29 I will also save you from all your uncleannesses: and I will call for the
corn, and will increase it, and lay no famine upon you.
30 And I will multiply the fruit of the tree, and the increase of the field,
that ye shall receive no more reproach of famine among the heathen.
31 Then shall ye remember your own evil ways, and your doings that *were*
not good, and shall lothe yourselves in your own sight for your iniquities
and for your abominations.
32 Not for your sakes do I *this,* saith the Lord GOD, be it known unto you:
be ashamed and confounded for your own ways, O house of Israel.

36:28 Jer 30:22 Ezek 14:11 37:23, 27 2 Cor 6:16–18
36:29 Ezek 34:27, 29 Hos 2:21–23 Mt 6:33
36:30 Lev 26:4 Deut 29:23–28 Joel 2:17, 26
36:31 Ezek 6:9 16:61–63; 20:43
36:32 Deut 9:5 Ezra 9:6 Dan 9:18, 19

e. God Will Rebuild the Ruins

33 Thus saith the Lord GOD; In the day that I shall have cleansed you
from all your iniquities I will also cause *you* to dwell in the cities, and the
wastes shall be builded.
34 And the desolate land shall be tilled, whereas it lay desolate in the sight
of all that passed by.
35 And they shall say, This land that was desolate is become like the
garden of Eden; and the waste and desolate and ruined cities *are become*
fenced, *and* are inhabited.
36 Then the heathen that are left round about you shall know that I the
LORD build the ruined *places, and* plant that that was desolate: I the LORD
have spoken *it,* and I will do *it.*

36:33 Isa 58:12 Zech 8:7, 8
☆**36:35** Isa 51:3 Joel 2:3
36:36 Hos 14:4–7 Mic 7:15–17 Mt 24:35

f. God Will Multiply His People

37 Thus saith the Lord GOD; I will yet *for* this be inquired of by the house
of Israel, to do *it* for them; I will increase them with men like a flock.
38 As the holy flock, as the flock of Jerusalem in her solemn feasts; so shall
the waste cities be filled with flocks of men: and they shall know that I *am*
the LORD.

36:37 1 Kgs 8:62, 63 2 Chron 35:7–9 Zech 11:17 Jn 10:9, 16

D. ISRAEL'S TRIUMPH AND RESTORATION

1. The Valley of Dry Bones: a Sign of Israel Made Alive

37 THE hand of the LORD was upon me, and carried me out in the
spirit of the LORD, and set me down in the midst of the valley which
was full of bones,
2 And caused me to pass by them round about: and, behold, *there were*
very many in the open valley; and, lo, *they were* very dry.
3 And he said unto me, Son of man, can these bones live? And I answered,
O Lord GOD, thou knowest.
4 Again he said unto me, Prophesy upon these bones, and say unto them,
O ye dry bones, hear the word of the LORD.
5 Thus saith the Lord GOD unto these bones; Behold, I will cause breath
to enter into you, and ye shall live:
6 And I will lay sinews upon you, and will bring up flesh upon you, and
cover you with skin, and put breath in you, and ye shall live; and ye shall
know that I *am* the LORD.
7 So I prophesied as I was commanded: and as I prophesied, there was a
noise, and behold a shaking, and the bones came together, bone to his bone.

☆**37:1** Jer 7:32—8:2 Ezek 33:22; 40:1 Acts 8:39
37:3 Deut 32:29 1 Sam 2:6 Isa 26:19 Jn 6:5, 6 Rom 4:17
37:4 Num 20:8 Isa 42:18 Jer 22:29
37:5 Ps 104:29, 30 Jn 20:22 Rom 8:2 Eph 2:5
37:6 Joel 2:27
37:7 Jer 13:5–7

36:35 The promise of God—that Canaan will become as Eden was before Adam's fall and expulsion—staggers the imagination. It seems like an impossible dream. But God has spoken and so shall it be.

37:1ff Such a desolate scene! A valley filled with fleshless bones (skeletons) of people slain in battle and left for birds to eat the flesh. This is a vision of how Israel will be after God's judgment has taken place.

8 And when I beheld, lo, the sinews and the flesh came up upon them, and
the skin covered them above: but *there was* no breath in them.

37:9 Ps 104:30; Hos 13:14

9 Then said he unto me, Prophesy unto the wind, prophesy, son of man,
and say to the wind, thus saith the Lord GOD; Come from the four winds,
O breath, and breathe upon these slain, that they may live.

37:10 Jer 30:19; Rev 11:11; 20:4, 5

10 So I prophesied as he commanded me, and the breath came into them,
and they lived, and stood up upon their feet, an exceeding great army.

37:11☆ Num 17:12, 13; Ps 141:7; Isa 49:14

11 ¶Then he said unto me, Son of man, these bones are the whole house of
Israel: behold, they say, Our bones are dried, and our hope is lost: we are
cut off for our parts.

37:12 Deut 32:39; Isa 26:19; Ezek 36:24; Hos 13:14; Amos 9:14, 15

12 Therefore prophesy and say unto them, Thus saith the Lord GOD;
Behold, O my people, I will open your graves, and cause you to come up
out of your graves, and bring you into the land of Israel.
13 And ye shall know that I *am* the LORD, when I have opened your
graves, O my people, and brought you up out of your graves,

37:14 Ezek 11:19; 36:27; Joel 2:28, 29

14 And shall put my spirit in you, and ye shall live, and I shall place you
in your own land: then shall ye know that I the LORD have spoken *it,* and
performed *it,* saith the LORD.

2. The Sign of the Two Sticks: Israel and Judah Rejoined

37:15☆

15 ¶The word of the LORD came again unto me, saying,

37:16 1 Kgs 12:16–20; 2 Chron 11:11–17

16 Moreover, thou son of man, take thee one stick, and write upon it, For
Judah, and for the children of Israel his companions: then take another
stick, and write upon it, For Joseph, the stick of E′phra-im, and *for* all the
house of Israel his companions:

37:17 Isa 11:13; 50:4; Hos 1:11; Zeph 3:9

17 And join them one to another into one stick; and they shall become one
in thine hand.

37:18 Ezek 20:49; 24:19

18 ¶And when the children of thy people shall speak unto thee, saying,
Wilt thou not shew us what thou *meanest* by these?
19 Say unto them, Thus saith the Lord GOD; Behold, I will take the stick
of Joseph, which *is* in the hand of E′phra-im, and the tribes of Israel his
fellows, and will put them with him, *even* with the stick of Judah, and make
them one stick, and they shall be one in mine hand.
20 ¶And the sticks whereon thou writest shall be in thine hand before their
eyes.

37:21 Isa 43:5, 6; Jer 29:14; Ezek 39:27

21 And say unto them, Thus saith the Lord GOD; Behold, I will take the
children of Israel from among the heathen, whither they be gone, and will
gather them on every side, and bring them into their own land:

37:22 Isa 11:13; Jer 50:4; Ezek 34:23, 24; Hos 1:11

22 And I will make them one nation in the land upon the mountains of
Israel; and one king shall be king to them all: and they shall be no more
two nations, neither shall they be divided into two kingdoms any more at
all:

37:23 Isa 2:18; Ezek 11:18; 36:25; Hos 14:8; Zech 13:1, 2; 14:21

23 Neither shall they defile themselves any more with their idols, nor with
their detestable things, nor with any of their transgressions: but I will save
them out of all their dwellingplaces, wherein they have sinned, and will
cleanse them: so shall they be my people, and I will be their God.

37:11 The dry bones represent dead Israel. 37:11–14 prophesies that God will restore Israel, i.e., bring back life to the dry bones. This prophecy remains to be fulfilled. It is guaranteed, for God has spoken and does not change.

37:15ff The Davidic kingdom was divided into two kingdoms after the death of Solomon. That division was never overcome. No reunion took place. Here God promises that the Northern and the Southern kingdoms will be rejoined in peace, harmony, and good will. The two will become one nation before God—undefiled and full of the knowledge of God.

24 And David my servant *shall be* king over them; and they all shall have
one shepherd: they shall also walk in my judgments, and observe my
statutes, and do them.
25 And they shall dwell in the land that I have given unto Jacob my
servant, wherein your fathers have dwelt; and they shall dwell therein, *even*
they, and their children, and their children's children for ever: and my
servant David *shall be* their prince for ever.
26 Moreover I will make a covenant of peace with them; it shall be an
everlasting covenant with them: and I will place them, and multiply them,
and will set my sanctuary in the midst of them for evermore.
27 My tabernacle also shall be with them: yea, I will be their God, and
they shall be my people.
28 And the heathen shall know that I the LORD do sanctify Israel, when
my sanctuary shall be in the midst of them for evermore.

3. The Prophecy about Gog and Magog

a. The Gathering of the Armies; Gog's Evil Intent

38 AND the word of the LORD came unto me, saying,
2 Son of man, set thy face against Gog, the land of Ma'gog, the
chief prince of Me'shech and Tu'bal, and prophesy against him,
3 And say, Thus saith the Lord GOD; Behold, I *am* against thee, O Gog,
the chief prince of Me'shech and Tu'bal:
4 And I will turn thee back, and put hooks into thy jaws, and I will bring
thee forth, and all thine army, horses and horsemen, all of them clothed
with all sorts *of armour, even* a great company *with* bucklers and shields, all
of them handling swords:
5 Persia, E-thi-o'pi-a, and Libya with them; all of them with shield and
helmet:
6 Go'mer, and all his bands; the house of To-gar'mah of the north
quarters, and all his bands: *and* many people with thee.
7 Be thou prepared, and prepare for thyself, thou, and all thy company
that are assembled unto thee, and be thou a guard unto them.
8 ¶After many days thou shalt be visited: in the latter years thou shalt
come into the land *that is* brought back from the sword, *and is* gathered out
of many people, against the mountains of Israel, which have been always
waste: but it is brought forth out of the nations, and they shall dwell safely
all of them.
9 Thou shalt ascend and come like a storm, thou shalt be like a cloud to
cover the land, thou, and all thy bands, and many people with thee.

☆**37:24** Isa 40:11; Jer 30:9; Ezek 34:23, 24; Hos 3:5
37:25 Isa 11:1
37:26 Isa 55:3; Jer 30:19; Ezek 43:7; Hos 2:18–23; Heb 13:20, 21
37:27 Lev 26:11, 12; Hos 2:23; Jn 1:14; 2 Cor 6:16
37:28 Ex 31:13; Ezek 20:12; 36:23; Jn 17:17–19; Eph 5:26
☆**38:2** Ezek 39:1, 9; Rev 20:8, 9
38:4 Isa 43:17; Ezek 39:2; Dan 11:40
☆**38:5** Gen 10:6, 7; 1 Chron 1:8; Ezek 27:10; 30:4, 5; Nah 3:9
☆**38:6** Gen 10:2, 3; 1 Chron 1:5; Ezek 27:14
38:8 Isa 11:11; Ezek 34:13; 36:24; Amos 9:14, 15
38:9 Isa 5:28; Jer 4:13; Dan 11:40; Joel 2:2

37:24ff These verses have been interpreted variously. Some think the promises made here to Israel are to be fulfilled in the church, which they believe to be the new Israel. Others hold that there must be a literal fulfillment of this prophecy, that Israel and the church are two separate entities, with different destinies. Still others think that while Jews and Gentiles comprise the one body—the church—yet Israel will literally be regathered, Christ will rule over them, and the temple will be rebuilt. Much depends on whether one is a premillennialist, an amillennialist, or a postmillennialist. (See the note on Rev. 20:2 for information on the various millennial views. See also the note on 43:19.)

38:2 Chapters 38 and 39 picture, at the end of the age, an attack on Israel by a collusion of wicked powers. They will be defeated by God and Israel will be delivered. Magog is headed up by Gog. That nation, along with Meshech and Tubal, derive from those who were the sons of Japheth in Gen. 10:2. They have been identified with the Russians, the Scythians, Goths, and Cretans but such identifications are not certain. Gog and Magog are mentioned in Rev. 20:8 as leaders in the final rebellion against God. The size and fearsomeness of the battle can be seen from the statistics connected with it. The weapons of war left after the battle will provide fuel for seven years, and it will take seven months to finish burying the dead. Some premillennialists think there are two battles described here—one at the end of the tribulation and the other at the end of the millennium.

38:5, 6 Other nations involved in this titanic struggle are allied with those mentioned in verse 2. They seem to be people from Iran, Ethiopia, Turkey, and the Ukraine.

38:10 Ps 36:4; Mic 2:1
38:11 Prov 3:29, 30; Isa 37:24, 25; Zech 2:4, 5; Rom 3:15
38:12 Isa 10:6; Ezek 29:19
38:13☆ Isa 10:5–7; Ezek 32:2; Nah 2:11–13

10 Thus saith the Lord GOD; It shall also come to pass, *that* at the same
time shall things come into thy mind, and thou shalt think an evil thought:
11 And thou shalt say, I will go up to the land of unwalled villages; I will
go to them that are at rest, that dwell safely, all of them dwelling without
walls, and having neither bars nor gates,
12 To take a spoil, and to take a prey; to turn thine hand upon the
desolate places *that are now* inhabited, and upon the people *that are*
gathered out of the nations, which have gotten cattle and goods, that dwell
in the midst of the land.
13 She'ba, and De'dan, and the merchants of Tarshish, with all the young
lions thereof, shall say unto thee, Art thou come to take a spoil? hast thou
gathered thy company to take a prey? to carry away silver and gold, to take
away cattle and goods, to take a great spoil?

b. Gog's Attack against God's Land

38:14☆ Jer 23:5, 6; Zech 2:5, 8
38:15 Ps 83:18; Isa 8:13; Ezek 28:22; 36:23
38:16☆

14 ¶Therefore, son of man, prophesy and say unto Gog, Thus saith the
Lord GOD; In that day when my people of Israel dwelleth safely, shalt thou
not know *it?*
15 And thou shalt come from thy place out of the north parts, thou, and
many people with thee, all of them riding upon horses, a great company,
and a mighty army:
16 And thou shalt come up against my people of Israel, as a cloud to cover
the land; it shall be in the latter days, and I will bring thee against my land,
that the heathen may know me, when I shall be sanctified in thee, O Gog,
before their eyes.

c. God Will Defeat Gog

38:17☆ Isa 5:26–30; Dan 11:40–45; Zech 12:2–8
38:18 Ps 18:7, 8; Nah 1:2
38:19 Ezek 36:5, 6; Joel 3:16; Hag 2:6, 7; Heb 12:26–29
38:20 Jer 4:24; Nah 1:5, 6; Zech 14:4, 5
38:21 Judg 7:22; 2 Chron 20:23; Hag 2:22
38:22 Ps 11:6; Zech 14:12–15; Rev 16:21
38:23 Ezek 36:23; 37:28; Rev 15:3, 4; 19:1–6

17 Thus saith the Lord GOD; *Art* thou he of whom I have spoken in old
time by my servants the prophets of Israel, which prophesied in those days
many years that I would bring thee against them?
18 And it shall come to pass at the same time when Gog shall come
against the land of Israel, saith the Lord GOD, *that* my fury shall come up
in my face.
19 For in my jealousy *and* in the fire of my wrath have I spoken, Surely in
that day there shall be a great shaking in the land of Israel;
20 So that the fishes of the sea, and the fowls of the heaven, and the beasts
of the field, and all creeping things that creep upon the earth, and all the
men that *are* upon the face of the earth, shall shake at my presence, and the
mountains shall be thrown down, and the steep places shall fall, and every
wall shall fall to the ground.
21 And I will call for a sword against him throughout all my mountains,
saith the Lord GOD; every man's sword shall be against his brother.
22 And I will plead against him with pestilence and with blood; and I will
rain upon him, and upon his bands, and upon the many people that *are*
with him, an overflowing rain, and great hailstones, fire, and brimstone.
23 Thus will I magnify myself, and sanctify myself; and I will be known in
the eyes of many nations, and they shall know that I *am* the LORD.

38:13 *Sheba and Dedan* are Arab peoples.
38:14 *when my people of Israel dwelleth safely.* God will have returned Israel to the land, and their safety will have come from God their protector, who is a wall of fire around them.
38:16 *in the latter days,* i.e., "in the latter years of history," an expression which does not, in Hebrew usage, necessarily mean "the end times."†
38:17ff In this final battle God will personally engage the enemy and defeat Gog and his allies. By this he will show his omnipotence and his holiness. The heathen will learn from this that God is God.

d. God's Vast Graveyard for Gog's Army

39 THEREFORE, thou son of man, prophesy against Gog, and say,
Thus saith the Lord GOD; Behold, I *am* against thee, O Gog, the
chief prince of Me'shech and Tu'bal:
2 And I will turn thee back, and leave but the sixth part of thee, and will
cause thee to come up from the north parts, and will bring thee upon the
mountains of Israel:
3 And I will smite thy bow out of thy left hand, and will cause thine
arrows to fall out of thy right hand.
4 Thou shalt fall upon the mountains of Israel, thou, and all thy bands,
and the people that *is* with thee: I will give thee unto the ravenous birds of
every sort, and *to* the beasts of the field to be devoured.
5 Thou shalt fall upon the open field: for I have spoken *it,* saith the Lord
GOD.
6 And I will send a fire on Ma'gog, and among them that dwell carelessly
in the isles: and they shall know that I *am* the LORD.
7 So will I make my holy name known in the midst of my people Israel;
and I will not *let them* pollute my holy name any more: and the heathen
shall know that I *am* the LORD, the Holy One in Israel.
8 ¶Behold, it is come, and it is done, saith the Lord GOD; this *is* the day
whereof I have spoken.
9 And they that dwell in the cities of Israel shall go forth, and shall set on
fire and burn the weapons, both the shields and the bucklers, the bows and
the arrows, and the handstaves, and the spears, and they shall burn them
with fire seven years:
10 So that they shall take no wood out of the field, neither cut down *any*
out of the forests; for they shall burn the weapons with fire: and they shall
spoil those that spoiled them, and rob those that robbed them, saith the
Lord GOD.
11 ¶And it shall come to pass in that day, *that* I will give unto Gog a place
there of graves in Israel, the valley of the passengers on the east of the sea:
and it shall stop the *noses* of the passengers: and there shall they bury Gog
and all his multitude: and they shall call *it* The valley of Ha'mon-gog.
12 And seven months shall the house of Israel be burying of them, that
they may cleanse the land.
13 Yea, all the people of the land shall bury *them;* and it shall be to them
a renown the day that I shall be glorified, saith the Lord GOD.
14 And they shall sever out men of continual employment, passing
through the land to bury with the passengers those that remain upon the
face of the earth, to cleanse it: after the end of seven months shall they
search.
15 And the passengers *that* pass through the land, when *any* seeth a man's
bone, then shall he set up a sign by it, till the buriers have buried it in the
valley of Ha'mon-gog.
16 And also the name of the city *shall be* Ha-mo'nah. Thus shall they
cleanse the land.

☆39:1 Ezek 38:2–4; Nah 2:13; 3:5
39:2 Ezek 38:15; Dan 11:40
39:3 Ps 46:9; 76:3; Jer 21:4, 5; Ezek 30:21–24; Hos 1:5
39:4 Isa 14:24, 25; Ezek 29:5; 32:4, 5
39:6 Jer 25:22; Ezek 30:8, 16; 38:22; Amos 1:4–10; Nah 1:6
39:7 Ex 20:7; Isa 6:9, 14; Ezek 20:39
39:9 Ps 46:9; Zech 9:10
39:10 Isa 14:2; Mic 5:8; Hab 2:8; Mt 7:2
39:11 Num 11:34; Ezek 47:18
39:13 Jer 33:9; Ezek 28:22; Zeph 3:19, 20; 1 Pet 1:7

e. The Birds and Animals Gathered for a Sacrificial Feast

17 ¶And, thou son of man, thus saith the Lord GOD; Speak unto every
feathered fowl, and to every beast of the field, Assemble yourselves, and

39:17 Isa 34:6, 7; Jer 46:10; Zeph 1:7; Rev 19:17, 18

39:1ff God reiterates the certainty of the complete destruction of Gog and his partners in crime. He illustrates how vast is the destruction of the enemy in three ways: (1) their armaments will be used for fuel for seven years; (2) it will take seven months to bury all of the dead; (3) the fowls of the air will feast on the flesh of the unburied dead.

come; gather yourselves on every side to my sacrifice that I do sacrifice for
you, *even* a great sacrifice upon the mountains of Israel, that ye may eat
flesh, and drink blood.

39:18 Deut 32:14; Ps 22:12; Jer 51:40; Amos 4:1

18 Ye shall eat the flesh of the mighty, and drink the blood of the princes
of the earth, of rams, of lambs, and of goats, of bullocks, all of them fatlings
of Ba′shan.
19 And ye shall eat fat till ye be full, and drink blood till ye be drunken, of
my sacrifice which I have sacrificed for you.

39:20 Ps 75:5, 6; Ezek 38:4; Hag 2:22
39:21☆ Ex 9:16; 14:4; Isa 34:7; Ezek 38:16, 23

20 Thus ye shall be filled at my table with horses and chariots, with mighty
men, and with all men of war, saith the Lord GOD.
21 And I will set my glory among the heathen, and all the heathen shall see
my judgment that I have executed, and my hand that I have laid upon
them.
22 So the house of Israel shall know that I *am* the LORD their God from
that day and forward.

39:23 Isa 59:2; Jer 22:8, 9; Ezek 36:18, 19

23 ¶And the heathen shall know that the house of Israel went into
captivity for their iniquity: because they trespassed against me, therefore
hid I my face from them, and gave them into the hand of their enemies: so
fell they all by the sword.

39:24 2 Kgs 17:7; Jer 2:17, 19; 4:18; Ezek 36:19

24 According to their uncleanness and according to their transgressions
have I done unto them, and hid my face from them.

f. God Brings Israel Home; They Will Know He Is Lord

39:25☆ Jer 33:7; Ezek 34:13; 36:10; Hos 1:11
39:26 Ezek 34:25–28; Dan 9:16; Mic 4:4

25 Therefore thus saith the Lord GOD; Now will I bring again the
captivity of Jacob, and have mercy upon the whole house of Israel, and will
be jealous for my holy name;
26 After that they have borne their shame, and all their trespasses whereby
they have trespassed against me, when they dwelt safely in their land, and
none made *them* afraid.

39:27 Ezek 28:25, 26; 37:21

27 When I have brought them again from the people, and gathered them
out of their enemies' lands, and am sanctified in them in the sight of many
nations;

39:28 Deut 30:3, 4; Neh 1:8–10; Amos 9:9; Rom 9:6–8; 11:1–7
39:29☆ Isa 32:15; Ezek 37:14; Joel 2:28; Acts 2:17

28 Then shall they know that I *am* the LORD their God, which caused them
to be led into captivity among the heathen: but I have gathered them unto
their own land, and have left none of them any more there.
29 Neither will I hide my face any more from them: for I have poured out
my spirit upon the house of Israel, saith the Lord GOD.

V. ISRAEL'S FUTURE IN THE COMING KINGDOM AGE (40:1—48:35)

A. THE REBUILT TEMPLE AREA

1. Introduction

40:1☆ 2 Kgs 25:1–7; Jer 39:1–9

40 IN the five and twentieth year of our captivity, in the beginning of
the year, in the tenth *day* of the month, in the fourteenth year after

---

39:21ff The wicked nations will see the glory of God manifested and know that what happened to Israel was the doing of God, as recompense for their transgressions. Israel will also learn the lesson the hard way—*that the One who has done all this is the Lord their God.*

39:25 Behind the sin, the shame, and the judgments of God, one discerns the merciful face of a tender and loving father whose intention toward Israel is to restore their fortunes. God will have wiped out the memory of their sins, and they will fear no more.

39:29 The indwelling of the Holy Spirit is the sure guarantee of the presence and the blessing of God. The Spirit of God had departed from Israel, but God promises here that his Spirit will be poured out on the revived and quickened house of Israel in the latter days, when Israel turns to God in repentance and in faith looks to Jesus, the true Messiah, for salvation. (See the note on Eph. 1:13 for information on the sealing of the Holy Spirit.)

40:1 The remainder of Ezekiel's prophecy was given to him in visions by God, who brought him to the land of

that the city was smitten, in the selfsame day the hand of the LORD was
upon me, and brought me thither.
2In the visions of God brought he me into the land of Israel, and set me
upon a very high mountain, by which *was* as the frame of a city on the
south.
3And he brought me thither, and, behold, *there was* a man, whose
appearance *was* like the appearance of brass, with a line of flax in his hand,
and a measuring reed; and he stood in the gate.

40:2 Ps 48:2; Ezek 17:23; 20:40; Mic 4:1; Rev 21:10
☆40:3 Dan 10:5, 6; Zech 2:1, 2; Rev 11:1; 21:15

2. The Eastern Wall

4And the man said unto me, Son of man, behold with thine eyes, and
hear with thine ears, and set thine heart upon all that I shall shew thee; for
to the intent that I might shew *them* unto thee *art* thou brought hither:
declare all that thou seest to the house of Israel.
5And behold a wall on the outside of the house round about, and in the
man's hand a measuring reed of six cubits *long* by the cubit and an hand
breadth: so he measured the breadth of the building, one reed; and the
height, one reed.
6¶Then came he unto the gate which looketh toward the east, and went
up the stairs thereof, and measured the threshold of the gate, *which was* one
reed broad; and the other threshold *of the gate, which was* one reed broad.
7And *every* little chamber *was* one reed long, and one reed broad; and
between the little chambers *were* five cubits; and the threshold of the gate
by the porch of the gate within *was* one reed.
8He measured also the porch of the gate within, one reed.
9Then measured he the porch of the gate, eight cubits; and the posts
thereof, two cubits; and the porch of the gate *was* inward.
10And the little chambers of the gate eastward *were* three on this side, and
three on that side; they three *were* of one measure: and the posts had one
measure on this side and on that side.
11And he measured the breadth of the entry of the gate, ten cubits; *and*
the length of the gate, thirteen cubits.
12The space also before the little chambers *was* one cubit *on this side,* and
the space *was* one cubit on that side: and the little chambers *were* six cubits
on this side, and six cubits on that side.
13He measured then the gate from the roof of *one* little chamber to the
roof of another: the breadth *was* five and twenty cubits, door against door.
14He made also posts of threescore cubits, even unto the post of the court
round about the gate.
15And from the face of the gate of the entrance unto the face of the porch
of the inner gate *were* fifty cubits.
16And *there were* narrow windows to the little chambers, and to their
posts within the gate round about, and likewise to the arches: and windows
were round about inward: and upon *each* post *were* palm trees.

40:4 Jer 26:2; Ezek 43:10; 44:5
☆40:5 Ezek 42:20
☆40:6 Ezek 8:16; 11:1; 43:1
40:7 1 Kgs 6:5–10; 2 Chron 31:11; Jer 35:4
40:14 Ex 27:9; 1 Chron 28:6; Ps 100:4; Isa 62:4; Ezek 42:1
40:16 1 Kgs 6:4; Ezek 41:26; 1 Cor 13:12

Israel for this purpose. Detailed instructions are given for the rebuilding of the temple and for its services. Israel and God will be in full fellowship with each other, and Israel's national life will be reconstructed without interruption or discord (see note to Ezek. 43:19).

40:3 *there was a man.* This was not an angel but Christ himself via a theophany. His brass appearance denotes brightness and strength. In Rev. 1:15 Jesus is pictured as having feet of brass.

40:5 A wall separates the temple from the world and is under the divine protection of God. Christians have bodies that are temples of the Holy Spirit, and as such are also to be separated from the world and under the protection of God.

40:6ff These verses describe the large gateway on the east. There were three side rooms that served as guardrooms to control the use of the passageway.

3. The Passageway to the Court; the Thirty Rooms

40:17 1 Chron 9:26; 2 Chron 31:11; Ezek 46:21; Rev 11:2
40:18 Ezek 46:1, 2
40:19☆

17 Then brought he me into the outward court, and, lo, *there were* chambers, and a pavement made for the court round about: thirty chambers *were* upon the pavement.

18 And the pavement by the side of the gates over against the length of the gates *was* the lower pavement.

19 Then he measured the breadth from the forefront of the lower gate unto the forefront of the inner court without, an hundred cubits eastward and northward.

4. The Northern Gate of the Outer Court

20 ¶And the gate of the outward court that looked toward the north, he measured the length thereof, and the breadth thereof.

21 And the little chambers thereof *were* three on this side and three on that side; and the posts thereof and the arches thereof were after the measure of the first gate: the length thereof *was* fifty cubits, and the breadth five and twenty cubits.

40:22 1 Kgs 6:29–35; 7:36; 2 Chron 3:5; Rev 7:9
40:23 Ex 27:9–18; 38:9–12

22 And their windows, and their arches, and their palm trees, *were* after the measure of the gate that looketh toward the east; and they went up unto it by seven steps; and the arches thereof *were* before them.

23 And the gate of the inner court *was* over against the gate toward the north, and toward the east; and he measured from gate to gate an hundred cubits.

5. The Southern Gate of the Outer Court

40:24 Ezek 46:9

24 ¶After that he brought me toward the south, and behold a gate toward the south: and he measured the posts thereof and the arches thereof according to these measures.

25 And *there were* windows in it and in the arches thereof round about, like those windows: the length *was* fifty cubits, and the breadth five and twenty cubits.

26 And *there were* seven steps to go up to it, and the arches thereof *were* before them: and it had palm trees, one on this side, and another on that side, upon the posts thereof.

27 And *there was* a gate in the inner court toward the south: and he measured from gate to gate toward the south an hundred cubits.

6. The Inner Court Gates and Walls

40:28☆

28 And he brought me to the inner court by the south gate: and he measured the south gate according to these measures;

29 And the little chambers thereof, and the posts thereof, and the arches thereof, according to these measures: and *there were* windows in it and in the arches thereof round about: *it was* fifty cubits long, and five and twenty cubits broad.

30 And the arches round about *were* five and twenty cubits long, and five cubits broad.

40:19ff Ezekiel describes the gates on the north and the south. *They are much the same* as the east gate. What is significant is that there is no gate facing the west. Josephus states that there was no west gate in the second temple, although 1 Chron. 9:24 and 26:8 speak about gates facing westward in Solomon's temple. Since the sun rises in the east and sets in the west, this may explain the absence of a west gate—for the sun will never set on this temple or that kingdom.

40:28 Inside the three outer gates on the east, north, and south, lay the inner court. Inside the inner court were three more gates which led to the temple. A wall surrounded the temple area, and the three inner gates made entrance into the temple area possible.

31 And the arches thereof *were* toward the utter court; and palm trees *were*
upon the posts thereof: and the going up to it *had* eight steps.
32 ¶And he brought me into the inner court toward the east: and he
measured the gate according to these measures.
33 And the little chambers thereof, and the posts thereof, and the arches
thereof, *were* according to these measures: and *there were* windows therein
and in the arches thereof round about: *it was* fifty cubits long, and five and
twenty cubits broad.
34 And the arches thereof *were* toward the outward court; and palm trees
were upon the posts thereof, on this side, and on that side: and the going up
to it *had* eight steps.
35 ¶And he brought me to the north gate, and measured *it* according to
these measures;
36 The little chambers thereof, the posts thereof, and the arches thereof,
and the windows to it round about: the length *was* fifty cubits, and the
breadth five and twenty cubits.
37 And the posts thereof *were* toward the outer court; and palm trees *were*
upon the posts thereof, on this side, and on that side: and the going up to
it *had* eight steps.

7. The Tables for Preparing the Sacrifices

38 And the chambers and the entries thereof *were* by the posts of the gates,
where they washed the burnt offering.
39 ¶And in the porch of the gate *were* two tables on this side, and two
tables on that side, to slay thereon the burnt offering and the sin offering
and the trespass offering.
40 And at the side without, as one goeth up to the entry of the north gate,
were two tables; and on the other side, which *was* at the porch of the gate,
were two tables.
41 Four tables *were* on this side, and four tables on that side, by the side of
the gate; eight tables, whereupon they slew *their sacrifices.*
42 And the four tables *were* of hewn stone for the burnt offering, of a cubit
and an half long, and a cubit and an half broad, and one cubit high:
whereupon also they laid the instruments wherewith they slew the burnt
offering and the sacrifice.
43 And within *were* hooks, an hand broad, fastened round about: and
upon the tables *was* the flesh of the offering.

8. The Building for the Priests

44 ¶And without the inner gate *were* the chambers of the singers in the
inner court, which *was* at the side of the north gate; and their prospect *was*
toward the south: one at the side of the east gate *having* the prospect
toward the north.
45 And he said unto me, This chamber, whose prospect *is* toward the
south, *is* for the priests, the keepers of the charge of the house.
46 And the chamber whose prospect *is* toward the north *is* for the priests,
the keepers of the charge of the altar: these *are* the sons of Za'dok among
the sons of Levi, which come near to the LORD to minister unto him.
47 So he measured the court, an hundred cubits long, and an hundred
cubits broad, foursquare; and the altar *that was* before the house.

40:35 Ezek 44:4; 47:2
☆**40:38** 1 Kgs 6:8; 1 Chron 28:12; Ezek 41:10; 42:13; Neh 13:5, 9
40:39 Lev 1:2-17; 4:2, 3; 5:6; 6:6; 7:1, 2; Ezek 46:2
40:42 Ex 20:25
☆**40:44** 1 Chron 6:31, 32; 16:41-43; 25:1-7
40:45 Lev 8:35; Num 3:27-32; 18:5; 1 Chron 9:23; Mal 2:4-7
40:46 1 Kgs 2:35; Ezek 43:19; 48:11

40:38 Outside the inner gates on the north side were the tables for sacrifice.
40:44 On the north and south sides of the temple walls, toward the west, were the priests' chambers. The chamber facing south housed the priests who had charge of the temple, and the one facing north housed the priests who had charge of the altar. That was why the places for the sacrifices were on the north side.

9. The Entry Hall to the Temple

40:48 1 Kgs 6:3 2 Chron 3:17 Jer 52:17–23 Rev 3:12

48 ¶And he brought me to the porch of the house, and measured *each* post
of the porch, five cubits on this side, and five cubits on that side: and the
breadth of the gate *was* three cubits on this side, and three cubits on that
side.
49 The length of the porch *was* twenty cubits, and the breadth eleven
cubits; and *he brought me* by the steps whereby they went up to it: and *there*
were pillars by the posts, one on this side, and another on that side.

B. THE REBUILT TEMPLE

1. The Nave and the Most Holy Place

41:1☆ Ezek 40:2, 3, 17 Zech 6:12, 13 Eph 2:20–22 Rev 11:1, 2 21:3, 15
41:2 1 Kgs 6:2, 17

41 AFTERWARD he brought me to the temple, and measured the
posts, six cubits broad on the one side, and six cubits broad on the
other side, *which was* the breadth of the tabernacle.
2 And the breadth of the door *was* ten cubits; and the sides of the door
were five cubits on the one side, and five cubits on the other side: and he
measured the length thereof, forty cubits: and the breadth, twenty cubits.
3 Then went he inward, and measured the post of the door, two cubits;
and the door, six cubits; and the breadth of the door, seven cubits.

41:4 Ex 26:33, 34 1 Kgs 6:20 2 Chron 3:8 Heb 9:3–8

4 So he measured the length thereof, twenty cubits; and the breadth,
twenty cubits, before the temple: and he said unto me, This *is* the most holy
place.

2. The Surrounding Rooms

41:5 1 Kgs 6:5

5 After he measured the wall of the house, six cubits; and the breadth of
every side chamber, four cubits, round about the house on every side.

41:6 1 Kgs 6:6, 10

6 And the side chambers *were* three, one over another, and thirty in order;
and they entered into the wall which *was* of the house for the side chambers
round about, that they might have hold, but they had not hold in the wall
of the house.

41:7 1 Kgs 6:8

7 And *there was* an enlarging, and a winding about still upward to the side
chambers: for the winding about of the house went still upward round
about the house: therefore the breadth of the house *was still* upward, and so
increased *from* the lowest *chamber* to the highest by the midst.

41:8 Ezek 40:5 Rev 21:16

8 I saw also the height of the house round about: the foundations of the
side chambers *were* a full reed of six great cubits.
9 The thickness of the wall, which *was* for the side chamber without, *was*
five cubits: and *that* which *was* left *was* the place of the side chambers that
were within.

41:10 Ezek 40:17

10 And between the chambers *was* the wideness of twenty cubits round
about the house on every side.
11 And the doors of the side chambers *were* toward *the place that was* left,
one door toward the north, and another door toward the south: and the
breadth of the place that was left *was* five cubits round about.

41:1 *The description of the new temple* shows that it is different from Solomon's temple. There is no reason to suppose that it should be identical with the first temple. Architecture changes from age to age. Some of the details are difficult for us to understand, and the meaning of this or that is variously understood by exegetes. Architects and builders in Ezekiel's day would have understood the details without difficulty. Nowhere in the account does the vision reveal the time frame when this prophetic word concerning the temple will be fulfilled.

3. Measurements: the West Building, the Temple, and Inner Court

12 Now the building that *was* before the separate place at the end toward
the west *was* seventy cubits broad; and the wall of the building *was* five
cubits thick round about, and the length thereof ninety cubits.
13 So he measured the house, an hundred cubits long; and the separate
place, and the building, with the walls thereof, an hundred cubits long;
14 Also the breadth of the face of the house, and of the separate place
toward the east, an hundred cubits.

41:12 Ezek 42:1 Rev 21:27 22:14, 15
41:13 Ezek 40:47

4. The Details about the Interior of the Temple

15 And he measured the length of the building over against the separate
place which *was* behind it, and the galleries thereof on the one side and on
the other side, an hundred cubits, with the inner temple, and the porches of
the court;
16 The door posts, and the narrow windows, and the galleries round about
on their three stories, over against the door, cieled with wood round about,
and from the ground up to the windows, and the windows *were* covered;
17 To that above the door, even unto the inner house, and without, and by
all the wall round about within and without, by measure.
18 And *it was* made with cherubims and palm trees, so that a palm tree
was between a cherub and a cherub; and *every* cherub had two faces;
19 So that the face of a man *was* toward the palm tree on the one side, and
the face of a young lion toward the palm tree on the other side: *it was* made
through all the house round about.
20 From the ground unto above the door *were* cherubims and palm trees
made, and *on* the wall of the temple.
21 The posts of the temple *were* squared, *and* the face of the sanctuary; the
appearance *of the one* as the appearance *of the other.*
22 The altar of wood *was* three cubits high, and the length thereof two
cubits; and the corners thereof, and the length thereof, and the walls
thereof, *were* of wood: and he said unto me, This *is* the table that *is* before
the LORD.
23 And the temple and the sanctuary had two doors.
24 And the doors had two leaves *apiece,* two turning leaves; two *leaves* for
the one door, and two leaves for the other *door.*
25 And *there were* made on them, on the doors of the temple, cherubims
and palm trees, like as *were* made upon the walls; and *there were* thick
planks upon the face of the porch without.
26 And *there were* narrow windows and palm trees on the one side and on
the other side, on the sides of the porch, and *upon* the side chambers of the
house, and thick planks.

41:15 1 Kgs 6:4, 15 Isa 6:4 Zech 3:7
41:17 1 Kgs 6:29, 32 2 Chron 3:5 Ezek 10:18
41:19 Ezek 1:10; 10:14
41:21 1 Kgs 6:33
41:22 Ex 25:23, 30 30:1–3, 8 Ezek 44:16 Mal 1:7, 12 Rev 8:3
41:23 1 Kgs 6:31–35
41:24 1 Kgs 6:34
41:26 Ezek 40:7–12

C. THE BUILDINGS FOR THE PRIESTS

42 THEN he brought me forth into the outer court, the way toward
the north: and he brought me into the chamber that *was* over
against the separate place, and which *was* before the building toward the
north.
2 Before the length of an hundred cubits *was* the north door, and the
breadth *was* fifty cubits.
3 Over against the twenty *cubits* which *were* for the inner court, and over
against the pavement which *was* for the outer court, *was* gallery against
gallery in three *stories.*

☆42:1 Ezek 40:2, 3, 17 41:9, 12–15
42:2 Ezek 41:13
42:3 Ezek 40:17 41:10

42:1ff To the north of the temple in the inner court are two blocks of buildings, three stories high. One block is twice the length of the other. They are for the storing of priestly garments and for the priests on duty.

42:4 Ezek 46:19

4 And before the chambers *was* a walk of ten cubits breadth inward, a way of one cubit; and their doors toward the north.

5 Now the upper chambers *were* shorter: for the galleries were higher than these, than the lower, and than the middlemost of the building.

42:6 1 Kgs 6:8 Ezek 41:6

6 For they *were* in three *stories,* but had not pillars as the pillars of the courts: therefore *the building* was straitened more than the lowest and the middlemost from the ground.

42:7 Ezek 41:13, 14

7 And the wall that *was* without over against the chambers, toward the outer court on the forepart of the chambers, the length thereof *was* fifty cubits.

8 For the length of the chambers that *were* in the outer court *was* fifty cubits: and, lo, before the temple *were* an hundred cubits.

42:9 Ezek 44:5; 46:19

9 And from under these chambers *was* the entry on the east side, as one goeth into them from the utter court.

10 The chambers *were* in the thickness of the wall of the court toward the east, over against the separate place, and over against the building.

11 And the way before them *was* like the appearance of the chambers which *were* toward the north, as long as they, *and* as broad as they: and all their goings out *were* both according to their fashions, and according to their doors.

12 And according to the doors of the chambers that *were* toward the south *was* a door in the head of the way, *even* the way directly before the wall toward the east, as one entereth into them.

42:13 Lev 6:25, 29 7:6; 10:13–17 Num 18:9, 10

13 ¶Then said he unto me, The north chambers *and* the south chambers, which *are* before the separate place, they *be* holy chambers, where the priests that approach unto the LORD shall eat the most holy things: there shall they lay the most holy things, and the meat offering, and the sin offering, and the trespass offering; for the place *is* holy.

42:14 Ex 29:4–9 Isa 61:10 Ezek 22:26 Zech 3:4, 5

14 When the priests enter therein, then shall they not go out of the holy *place* into the outer court, but there they shall lay their garments wherein they minister; for they *are* holy; and shall put on other garments, and shall approach to *those things* which *are* for the people.

D. THE MEASUREMENTS OF THE TEMPLE AREA

15 Now when he had made an end of measuring the inner house, he brought me forth toward the gate whose prospect *is* toward the east, and measured it round about.

42:16 Ezek 40:3, 5 45:2 Zech 2:5 Rev 11:1, 2

16 He measured the east side with the measuring reed, five hundred reeds, with the measuring reed round about.

17 He measured the north side, five hundred reeds, with the measuring reed round about.

18 He measured the south side, five hundred reeds, with the measuring reed.

19 ¶He turned about to the west side, *and* measured five hundred reeds with the measuring reed.

20 He measured it by the four sides: it had a wall round about, five hundred *reeds* long, and five hundred broad, to make a separation between the sanctuary and the profane place.

E. THE GLORY OF GOD RETURNS TO THE TEMPLE

1. The Glory of the Lord Fills the Temple

43:1 Ezek 10:19 40:6; 44:1; 46:1

43 AFTERWARD he brought me to the gate, *even* the gate that looketh toward the east:

[2]And, behold, the glory of the God of Israel came from the way of the
east: and his voice *was* like a noise of many waters: and the earth shined
with his glory.
[3]And *it was* according to the appearance of the vision which I saw, *even*
according to the vision that I saw when I came to destroy the city: and the
visions *were* like the vision that I saw by the river Che′bar; and I fell upon
my face.
[4]And the glory of the LORD came into the house by the way of the gate
whose prospect *is* toward the east.
[5]So the spirit took me up, and brought me into the inner court; and,
behold, the glory of the LORD filled the house.
[6]And I heard *him* speaking unto me out of the house; and the man stood
by me.

2. The Lord's Message about the Temple's Holiness

[7]¶And he said unto me, Son of man, the place of my throne, and the
place of the soles of my feet, where I will dwell in the midst of the children
of Israel for ever, and my holy name, shall the house of Israel no more
defile, *neither* they, nor their kings, by their whoredom, nor by the carcases
of their kings in their high places.
[8]In their setting of their threshold by my thresholds, and their post by my
posts, and the wall between me and them, they have even defiled my holy
name by their abominations that they have committed: wherefore I have
consumed them in mine anger.
[9]Now let them put away their whoredom, and the carcases of their kings,
far from me, and I will dwell in the midst of them for ever.
[10]¶Thou son of man, shew the house to the house of Israel, that they may
be ashamed of their iniquities: and let them measure the pattern.
[11]And if they be ashamed of all that they have done, shew them the form
of the house, and the fashion thereof, and the goings out thereof, and the
comings in thereof, and all the forms thereof, and all the ordinances
thereof, and all the forms thereof, and all the laws thereof: and write *it* in
their sight, that they may keep the whole form thereof, and all the
ordinances thereof, and do them.
[12]This *is* the law of the house; Upon the top of the mountain the whole
limit thereof round about *shall be* most holy. Behold, this *is* the law of the
house.

3. Measurements of the Burnt Offering Altar

[13]¶And these *are* the measures of the altar after the cubits: The cubit *is* a
cubit and an hand breadth; even the bottom *shall be* a cubit, and the
breadth a cubit, and the border thereof by the edge thereof round about
shall be a span: and this *shall be* the higher place of the altar.
[14]And from the bottom *upon* the ground *even* to the lower settle *shall be*
two cubits, and the breadth one cubit; and from the lesser settle *even* to the
greater settle *shall be* four cubits, and the breadth *one* cubit.
[15]So the altar *shall be* four cubits; and from the altar and upward *shall be*
four horns.

☆**43:2** Isa 6:3; Ezek 10:4, 18, 19; 11:23; Hab 2:14; 3:3; Rev 1:15
43:3 Jer 1:10; Ezek 1:4, 27, 28; 3:23
43:4 Ezek 44:2
43:5 1 Kgs 8:10, 11; 2 Chron 5:14; Hag 2:7–9; 2 Cor 12:2–4
☆**43:6** Ezek 1:26; 40:3
43:7 Lev 26:30; Ps 74:8; Jer 16:18; Ezek 6:4–7; 37:26–28
43:8 2 Kgs 21:4–7; 2 Chron 33:4, 7; Ezek 8:3
43:9 Ezek 18:30, 31
43:10 Ezek 40:4
43:11 Ezek 11:20; 36:27; 44:5
43:12 Ezek 40:2
43:13 Ex 27:1–8; 2 Chron 4:1
43:14 Ezek 45:19
43:15 Ex 27:2; Lev 9:9; 1 Kgs 1:49, 50; Ps 118:27

43:2 The glory of God had departed from the temple (9:3) and from Jerusalem, leaving Judah at the mercy of its enemies. Here the glory returns from the east—the direction to which it went when God's presence was leaving Jerusalem. This return prophesied by Ezekiel refers to the fact that someday God will come to reside among his people once again.

43:6ff The Lord reminds his people of their former iniquities and tells them to repent and reform. He promises them that they *shall* be as they *should* be, and they will not defile his holy name anymore. He will dwell in them and with them, and he commands them to observe his laws and ordinances.

43:16 Ex 27:1; 38:1, 2 Ezra 3:3
43:17 Neh 9:4 Ezek 40:6

16 And the altar *shall be* twelve *cubits* long, twelve broad, square in the
four squares thereof.
17 And the settle *shall be* fourteen *cubits* long and fourteen broad in the
four squares thereof; and the border about it *shall be* half a cubit; and
the bottom thereof *shall be* a cubit about; and his stairs shall look toward
the east.

4. Details for Consecrating the Altar

43:18 Ex 40:29 Lev 1:5, 11 Heb 9:21, 22
43:19☆ 1 Kgs 2:35 Ezek 40:46 44:15 Heb 7:27
43:20 Lev 8:15; 9:9

18 ¶And he said unto me, Son of man, thus saith the Lord GOD; These *are*
the ordinances of the altar in the day when they shall make it, to offer burnt
offerings thereon, and to sprinkle blood thereon.
19 And thou shalt give to the priests the Levites that be of the seed of
Za'dok, which approach unto me, to minister unto me, saith the Lord GOD,
a young bullock for a sin offering.
20 And thou shalt take of the blood thereof, and put *it* on the four horns
of it, and on the four corners of the settle, and upon the border round
about: thus shalt thou cleanse and purge it.

43:21 Ex 29:14 Lev 4:11, 12 Heb 13:11
43:22 Ex 29:15–18 Lev 8:18–21
43:23 Ex 29:1

21 Thou shalt take the bullock also of the sin offering, and he shall burn it
in the appointed place of the house, without the sanctuary.
22 And on the second day thou shalt offer a kid of the goats without
blemish for a sin offering; and they shall cleanse the altar, as they did
cleanse *it* with the bullock.
23 When thou hast made an end of cleansing *it,* thou shalt offer a young
bullock without blemish, and a ram out of the flock without blemish.

43:24 Lev 2:13 Num 18:19 Num 18:19 Mk 9:49, 50 Col 4:6
43:25 Ex 29:35–37 Lev 8:33, 35

24 And thou shalt offer them before the LORD, and the priests shall cast
salt upon them, and they shall offer them up *for* a burnt offering unto the
LORD.
25 Seven days shalt thou prepare every day a goat *for* a sin offering: they
shall also prepare a young bullock, and a ram out of the flock, without
blemish.
26 Seven days shall they purge the altar and purify it; and they shall
consecrate themselves.

43:27 Lev 3:1; 9:1 17:5 Ezek 20:40 Hos 8:13 Rom 12:1 1 Pet 2:5

27 And when these days are expired, it shall be, *that* upon the eighth day,
and *so* forward, the priests shall make your burnt offerings upon the altar,
and your peace offerings; and I will accept you, saith the Lord GOD.

F. THE REGULATIONS ABOUT THE USE OF THE TEMPLE

1. The Prince and the East Gate

44:1☆ Ezek 40:6
44:2☆ Ezek 43:4

44 THEN he brought me back the way of the gate of the outward
sanctuary which looketh toward the east; and it *was* shut.
2 Then said the LORD unto me; This gate shall be shut, it shall not be
opened, and no man shall enter in by it; because the LORD, the God of
Israel, hath entered in by it, therefore it shall be shut.

43:19 Chapters 40—48 of Ezekiel's prophecies are filled with difficulties for interpreters, whether they be millennialists or nonmillennialists. The prophecies appear to speak of the kingdom age, for nothing remotely resembling these prophecies has as yet appeared. Some take these prophecies literally, others figuratively. Perplexing indeed is the question of *whether there will be a literal restoration* of animal sacrifices, which were done away with by Christ's atoning work at Calvary. Some think these offerings will serve as a memorial, corresponding to the Lord's Supper of this present age. Others, knowing that the Old Testament sacrifices have been superseded, consider these prophecies to be a description in Old Testament terms of the principle that Christ's blood will avail wholly during the kingdom age. Amillennialists, who think there will be no thousand-year kingdom age, do not look for any other fulfillment of these prophecies, assuming that the Church is the new Israel.

44:1–3 The east gate is shut once the Lord has entered it and his glory has rested on the temple and the holy place. Verse 3 mentions a prince, but who this is is not stated explicitly. In Ezek. 45:22 the prince makes a sacrifice for himself and for the people. In Ezek. 46:16 he is said to have sons. Therefore it cannot be Jesus Christ. Some think this is the high priest of God or the second in command after the high priest. Either way, he is God's representative.

3 *It is* for the prince; the prince, he shall sit in it to eat bread before the
LORD; he shall enter by the way of the porch of *that* gate, and shall go out
by the way of the same.

2. Only the Circumcised to Enter the Sanctuary

4 ¶Then brought he me the way of the north gate before the house: and I
looked, and, behold, the glory of the LORD filled the house of the LORD:
and I fell upon my face.
5 And the LORD said unto me, Son of man, mark well, and behold with
thine eyes, and hear with thine ears all that I say unto thee concerning all
the ordinances of the house of the LORD, and all the laws thereof; and mark
well the entering in of the house, with every going forth of the sanctuary.
6 And thou shalt say to the rebellious, *even* to the house of Israel, Thus
saith the Lord GOD; O ye house of Israel, let it suffice you of all your
abominations,
7 In that ye have brought *into my sanctuary* strangers, uncircumcised in
heart, and uncircumcised in flesh, to be in my sanctuary, to pollute it, *even*
my house, when ye offer my bread, the fat and the blood, and they have
broken my covenant because of all your abominations.
8 And ye have not kept the charge of mine holy things: but ye have set
keepers of my charge in my sanctuary for yourselves.

3. The Unfaithful Levites Excluded from Ministry

9 ¶Thus saith the Lord GOD; No stranger, uncircumcised in heart, nor
uncircumcised in flesh, shall enter into my sanctuary, of any stranger that *is*
among the children of Israel.
10 And the Levites that are gone away far from me, when Israel went
astray, which went astray away from me after their idols; they shall even
bear their iniquity.
11 Yet they shall be ministers in my sanctuary, *having* charge at the gates
of the house, and ministering to the house: they shall slay the burnt offering
and the sacrifice for the people, and they shall stand before them to
minister unto them.
12 Because they ministered unto them before their idols, and caused the
house of Israel to fall into iniquity; therefore have I lifted up mine hand
against them, saith the Lord GOD, and they shall bear their iniquity.
13 And they shall not come near unto me, to do the office of a priest unto
me, nor to come near to any of my holy things, in the most holy *place:* but
they shall bear their shame, and their abominations which they have
committed.
14 But I will make them keepers of the charge of the house, for all the
service thereof, and for all that shall be done therein.

4. The Ministry of the Faithful Sons of Zadok

15 ¶But the priests the Levites, the sons of Za'dok, that kept the charge of
my sanctuary when the children of Israel went astray from me, they shall

44:3 Ex 24:9–11; Deut 12:7, 17, 18; Ezek 37:25; 46:2, 8; Zech 6:12, 13
☆**44:4** Isa 6:3, 4; Ezek 1:28; 3:23; Hag 2:7; Rev 15:8
44:5 Deut 12:32; 32:46; Ezek 40:4; 43:10, 11
44:6 Ezek 2:5–7; 3:9; 1 Pet 4:3
44:7 Gen 17:14; Ex 12:43–49; Jer 4:4; 9:26; Heb 8:9
44:8 Num 18:7; Acts 7:53; 1 Tim 6:13
44:9 Ps 50:16; Joel 3:17; Zech 14:21; Tit 1:5–9
44:10 Num 18:23; 2 Kgs 23:8, 9; Ezek 22:26
44:11 Num 3:5–37; 4:1–33; 16:8, 9; 18:2, 6
44:12 2 Kgs 16:10–16; Ezek 14:3, 4; Hos 4:6, 5:1
44:13 Num 18:3; 2 Kgs 23:9; Ezek 16:61, 63
44:14 Num 18:4, 6; 1 Chron 23:28, 32; Ezek 40:45
☆**44:15** Num 18:7; Jer 33:18–22; Ezek 48:11; Zech 3:7

44:4ff In earlier times the Jews had profaned the temple by allowing admittance to it by some who were uncircumcised either in heart or in flesh or both. Here the uncircumcised in heart and flesh are forbidden to enter the sanctuary. This would not exclude non-Jews, only those who had not submitted to the laws of the sanctuary. Priests who had defiled God's sanctuary are here demoted to the more ordinary work of Levites, who are not of the priestly order.

44:15 *Zadok,* the son of Ahitub, became the progenitor of the legitimate priesthood after the line of Eli had been extinguished. His name appears for the first time in 2 Sam. 8:17. He descended from the priestly line of Aaron, Eleazar, and Phinehas. The Scriptures do not tell us where his father or some of his earlier ancestors served as priests. Zadok himself served under David and crowned Solomon as king. 1 Chron. 12:26–28 indicates that he served as a military leader in his younger days and was described as "a young man mighty of valour."

come near to me to minister unto me, and they shall stand before me to
offer unto me the fat and the blood, saith the Lord GOD:
16 They shall enter into my sanctuary, and they shall come near to my
table, to minister unto me, and they shall keep my charge.
17 ¶And it shall come to pass, *that* when they enter in at the gates of the
inner court, they shall be clothed with linen garments; and no wool shall
come upon them, whiles they minister in the gates of the inner court, and
within.
18 They shall have linen bonnets upon their heads, and shall have linen
breeches upon their loins; they shall not gird *themselves* with any thing that
causeth sweat.
19 And when they go forth into the outer court, *even* into the outer court
to the people, they shall put off their garments wherein they ministered, and
lay them in the holy chambers, and they shall put on other garments; and
they shall not sanctify the people with their garments.
20 Neither shall they shave their heads, nor suffer their locks to grow long;
they shall only poll their heads.
21 Neither shall any priest drink wine, when they enter into the inner
court.
22 Neither shall they take for their wives a widow, nor her that is put
away: but they shall take maidens of the seed of the house of Israel, or a
widow that had a priest before.
23 And they shall teach my people *the difference* between the holy and
profane, and cause them to discern between the unclean and the clean.
24 And in controversy they shall stand in judgment; *and* they shall judge it
according to my judgments: and they shall keep my laws and my statutes in
all mine assemblies; and they shall hallow my sabbaths.
25 And they shall come at no dead person to defile themselves: but for
father, or for mother, or for son, or for daughter, for brother, or for sister
that hath had no husband, they may defile themselves.
26 And after he is cleansed, they shall reckon unto him seven days.
27 And in the day that he goeth into the sanctuary, unto the inner court, to
minister in the sanctuary, he shall offer his sin offering, saith the Lord GOD.
28 And it shall be unto them for an inheritance: I *am* their inheritance:
and ye shall give them no possession in Israel: I *am* their possession.
29 They shall eat the meat offering, and the sin offering, and the trespass
offering; and every dedicated thing in Israel shall be theirs.
30 And the first of all the firstfruits of all *things,* and every oblation of all,
of every *sort* of your oblations, shall be the priest's: ye shall also give unto
the priest the first of your dough, that he may cause the blessing to rest in
thine house.
31 The priests shall not eat of any thing that is dead of itself, or torn,
whether it be fowl or beast.

G. THE LAND ALLOTTED TO THE PRINCE AND THE PRIESTS

45 MOREOVER, when ye shall divide by lot the land for inheritance,
ye shall offer an oblation unto the LORD, an holy portion of the

44:16 Ezek 41–22; Mal 1:17, 12
44:17 Ex 28:39–43; 39:27–29; Rev 19:8
44:18 Ex 28:40, 42
44:19 Lev 16:23, 24; Ezek 42:14; 46:20; Mt 23:17–19; 1 Cor 3:5, 6
44:20☆ Lev 21:5
44:21 Lev 10:8, 9
44:22 Lev 21:7, 13–15
44:23☆ Lev 10:10; Deut 33:10; Ezek 22:26; Hos 4:6; Mal 2:6
44:24 Deut 17:8, 9; 21:5; 2 Chron 19:8–10; Ezek 20:12, 20
44:25 Lev 21:1–3; Mt 8:21, 22; 2 Cor 5:16
44:26 Num 19:13–19; Heb 9:13, 14
44:27 Num 6:9–11
44:28☆ Num 18:20; Deut 10:9; Josh 13:33; 1 Pet 5:2–4
44:29 Lev 27:21, 28; Num 18:9, 14, 15; Josh 13:14
44:30 Num 18:12; 2 Chron 31:4–6, 10; Neh 10:35–37; Mal 3:10
44:31 Lev 22:8; Deut 14:21; Ezek 4:14
45:1☆ Josh 13:7; 14:2; Ps 16:5, 6; Ezek 47:21; 48:8, 9

44:20ff The priests were subject to certain regulations regarding their persons and their marital state. The use *of wine before entering the inner court* was also forbidden.
44:23 *between the holy and profane,* i.e., between good and evil, the lawful and the unlawful.
44:28 The priests who serve at the altar must live upon the altar. They are to have no other job or source of income except what they get from their priestly service. They have no need of farm lands, nor should they be entangled with the affairs of this life.
45:1ff The temple is to be protected by being located within a larger land area measuring some eight square miles. Evidently housing for the priests was related to this provision. The portion for the prince was approximately eight more miles outside the sacred area.

land: the length *shall be* the length of five and twenty thousand *reeds,* and the breadth *shall be* ten thousand. This *shall be* holy in all the borders thereof round about.

2 Of this there shall be for the sanctuary five hundred *in length,* with five hundred *in breadth,* square round about; and fifty cubits round about for the suburbs thereof.

45:2 Ezek 42:16–20

3 And of this measure shalt thou measure the length of five and twenty thousand, and the breadth of ten thousand: and in it shall be the sanctuary *and* the most holy *place.*

45:3 Ezek 48:10

4 The holy *portion* of the land shall be for the priests the ministers of the sanctuary, which shall come near to minister unto the LORD: and it shall be a place for their houses, and an holy place for the sanctuary.

45:4 Num 16:5 Ezek 40:45 44:13, 14 48:10, 11

5 And the five and twenty thousand of length, and the ten thousand of breadth, shall also the Levites, the ministers of the house, have for themselves, for a possession for twenty chambers.

45:5 Ezek 48:12–14

6 ¶And ye shall appoint the possession of the city five thousand broad, and five and twenty thousand long, over against the oblation of the holy *portion:* it shall be for the whole house of Israel.

45:6 Ezek 48:15, 16

7 ¶And *a portion shall be* for the prince on the one side and on the other side of the oblation of the holy *portion,* and of the possession of the city, before the oblation of the holy *portion,* and before the possession of the city, from the west side westward, and from the east side eastward: and the length *shall be* over against one of the portions, from the west border unto the east border.

45:7 Ezek 46:16–18 48:21, 22

8 In the land shall be his possession in Israel: and my princes shall no more oppress my people; and *the rest of* the land shall they give to the house of Israel according to their tribes.

45:8 Isa 11:3–5 Jer 23:5, 6 Ezek 22:27 46:18

H. VARIOUS OTHER REGULATIONS

1. Honest Scales and Money

9 ¶Thus saith the Lord GOD; Let it suffice you, O princes of Israel: remove violence and spoil, and execute judgment and justice, take away your exactions from my people, saith the Lord GOD.

☆**45:9** Jer 6:7; 22:3 Nah 5:1–5 Zech 8:16

10 Ye shall have just balances, and a just ephah, and a just bath.

45:10 Lev 19:35, 36 Deut 25:13–15 Prov 11:1; 16:11 Mic 6:10, 11

11 The ephah and the bath shall be of one measure, that the bath may contain the tenth part of an homer, and the ephah the tenth part of an homer: the measure thereof shall be after the homer.

12 And the shekel *shall be* twenty gerahs: twenty shekels, five and twenty shekels, fifteen shekels, shall be your maneh.

45:12 Ex 30:13 Lev 27:25 Num 3:47

2. Meal (Meat) Offerings

13 This *is* the oblation that ye shall offer; the sixth part of an ephah of an homer of wheat, and ye shall give the sixth part of an ephah of an homer of barley:

☆**45:13**

14 Concerning the ordinance of oil, the bath of oil, *ye shall offer* the tenth part of a bath out of the cor, *which is* an homer of ten baths; for ten baths *are* an homer:

☆**45:14**

45:9ff Religious and civil authorities are to be concerned with fair and just dealings between people. Weights and measures are not to be tampered with—that people not be cheated. These regulations presuppose the fact that perfection will not yet have come and that sin would still be possible. In a perfected society no laws are needed to prevent wrongdoing.

45:13–17 The people will pay an oblation (i.e., a religious offering) to the prince, who will then provide the sacrifices for public worship.

45:15 Lev 1:4; 6:30 Prov 3:9, 10 Dan 9:24
45:17 Lev 23:1–44 1 Kgs 8:62–64 Ezek 43:27 46:4–12

15 And one lamb out of the flock, out of two hundred, out of the fat
pastures of Israel; for a meat offering, and for a burnt offering, and for
peace offerings, to make reconciliation for them, saith the Lord GOD.
16 All the people of the land shall give this oblation for the prince in
Israel.
17 And it shall be the prince's part *to give* burnt offerings, and meat
offerings, and drink offerings, in the feasts, and in the new moons, and in
the sabbaths, in all solemnities of the house of Israel: he shall prepare the
sin offering, and the meat offering, and the burnt offering, and the peace
offerings, to make reconciliation for the house of Israel.

3. Offerings on Certain Holy Days

45:18☆ Ex 12:2 Lev 16:16, 20 22:20 Heb 9:14
45:19 Lev 16:18–20 Ezek 43:20
45:20 Lev 4:27 Ps 19:12 Rom 16:18, 19 Heb 5:2
45:21 Ex 1:24 Lev 23:5–8 Num 9:2, 3 28:16, 17
45:22 Lev 4:14 Mt 20:28 26:26–28 2 Cor 5:21
45:23 Lev 23:8 Num 28:16–25 Job 42:8 Heb 10:8–12
45:24 Num 28:12–15 Ezek 46:5–7
45:25☆ Lev 23:33–36 Num 29:12–38

18 Thus saith the Lord GOD; In the first *month,* in the first *day* of the
month, thou shalt take a young bullock without blemish, and cleanse the
sanctuary:
19 And the priest shall take of the blood of the sin offering, and put *it*
upon the posts of the house, and upon the four corners of the settle of the
altar, and upon the posts of the gate of the inner court.
20 And so thou shalt do the seventh *day* of the month for every one that
erreth, and for *him that is* simple: so shall ye reconcile the house.
21 In the first *month,* in the fourteenth day of the month, ye shall have the
passover, a feast of seven days; unleavened bread shall be eaten.
22 And upon that day shall the prince prepare for himself and for all the
people of the land a bullock *for* a sin offering.
23 And seven days of the feast he shall prepare a burnt offering to the
LORD, seven bullocks and seven rams without blemish daily the seven days;
and a kid of the goats daily *for* a sin offering.
24 And he shall prepare a meat offering of an ephah for a bullock, and an
ephah for a ram, and an hin of oil for an ephah.
25 In the seventh *month,* in the fifteenth day of the month, shall he do the
like in the feast of the seven days, according to the sin offering, according to
the burnt offering, and according to the meat offering, and according to the
oil.

4. Sabbath and New Moon Offerings; the Duties of the Prince

46:1☆ Ex 20:9, 10 Isa 66:23 Ezek 44:1, 2
46:2 Ezek 44:3 Jn 10:1–3

46 THUS saith the Lord GOD; The gate of the inner court that looketh
toward the east shall be shut the six working days; but on the
sabbath it shall be opened, and in the day of the new moon it shall be
opened.
2 And the prince shall enter by the way of the porch of *that* gate without,
and shall stand by the post of the gate, and the priests shall prepare his
burnt offering and his peace offerings, and he shall worship at the threshold
of the gate: then he shall go forth; but the gate shall not be shut until the
evening.

45:18 *In the first month, in the first day of the month,* the beginning of the new year, they are to offer a sacrifice for the cleansing of the sanctuary. The Jews dated the new year from around the middle of March.
45:25 *This event is the feast of tabernacles.*
46:1ff Ezekiel here speaks about public worship services on the sabbath, the new moon, and the daily offerings. If this time frame refers to the millennium subsequent to the Second Advent of Christ, the effects of sin will still be evident, for the Jews are here forbidden to bring blemished animals for sacrifice. However, such sacrifices would be memorial in nature rather than actually atoning, for the work of Christ is a finished work and needs no repeating. If these things occur before the Second Advent, as some think, a different picture emerges. For those who hold these chapters (40–48) to be figurative and apply them to the church in a nonliteral sense, there are great problems. We will have to wait patiently until the time when the meaning of Ezekiel's prophecies are made plain to us.

3 Likewise the people of the land shall worship at the door of this gate
before the LORD in the sabbaths and in the new moons.
4 And the burnt offering that the prince shall offer unto the LORD in the
sabbath day *shall be* six lambs without blemish, and a ram without blemish.
5 And the meat offering *shall be* an ephah for a ram, and the meat offering
for the lambs as he shall be able to give, and an hin of oil to an ephah.
6 And in the day of the new moon *it shall be* a young bullock without
blemish, and six lambs, and a ram: they shall be without blemish.
7 And he shall prepare a meat offering, an ephah for a bullock, and an
ephah for a ram, and for the lambs according as his hand shall attain unto,
and an hin of oil to an ephah.
8 And when the prince shall enter, he shall go in by the way of the porch
of *that* gate, and he shall go forth by the way thereof.
9 ¶But when the people of the land shall come before the LORD in the
solemn feasts, he that entereth in by the way of the north gate to worship
shall go out by the way of the south gate: and he that entereth by the way
of the south gate shall go forth by the way of the north gate: he shall not
return by the way of the gate whereby he came in, but shall go forth over
against it.
10 And the prince in the midst of them, when they go in, shall go in; and
when they go forth, shall go forth.

46:3 Lk 1:10; Jn 10:9; Heb 10:19–22
46:4 Ezek 45:17
46:5 Ezek 45:24
46:7 Deut 16:17
46:8 Ezek 44:1–3; Col 1:18
46:9 Ex 23:14–17; Deut 16:16; Ps 84:7; Heb 10:38; 2 Pet 2:20, 21
46:10 2 Chron 6:3; 7:4; Ps 42:4

5. Summary of the Rules Governing Sacrifices

11 And in the feasts and in the solemnities the meat offering shall be an
ephah to a bullock, and an ephah to a ram, and to the lambs as he is able
to give, and an hin of oil to an ephah.
12 Now when the prince shall prepare a voluntary burnt offering or peace
offerings voluntarily unto the LORD, *one* shall then open him the gate that
looketh toward the east, and he shall prepare his burnt offering and his
peace offerings, as he did on the sabbath day: then he shall go forth; and
after his going forth *one* shall shut the gate.
13 Thou shalt daily prepare a burnt offering unto the LORD *of* a lamb of
the first year without blemish: thou shalt prepare it every morning.
14 And thou shalt prepare a meat offering for it every morning, the sixth
part of an ephah, and the third part of an hin of oil, to temper with the fine
flour; a meat offering continually by a perpetual ordinance unto the LORD.
15 Thus shall they prepare the lamb, and the meat offering, and the oil,
every morning *for* a continual burnt offering.

46:11 Ezek 45:17
46:12 Lev 23:38; 2 Chron 29:31; Ezek 44:3; 45:17
46:13 Ex 29:38; Num 28:3, 4; Isa 50:4; Dan 8:11–13
46:14 Ex 29:42; Num 28:5, 6

6. The Prince and Rules for Land Ownership

16 ¶Thus saith the Lord GOD; If the prince give a gift unto any of his sons,
the inheritance thereof shall be his sons'; it *shall be* their possession by
inheritance.
17 But if he give a gift of his inheritance to one of his servants, then it shall
be his to the year of liberty; after it shall return to the prince: but his
inheritance shall be his sons' for them.
18 Moreover the prince shall not take of the people's inheritance by
oppression, to thrust them out of their possession; *but* he shall give his sons
inheritance out of his own possession: that my people be not scattered
every man from his possession.

☆**46:17** Lev 25:10; Mt 25:14–29; Lk 19:25, 26; Gal 4:30, 31
46:18 Isa 11:3, 4; Ezek 45:8; Mic 2:1, 2

46:17 *the year of liberty* refers to the year of jubilee (see Lev. 25:13–15).

7. The Rooms for Boiling the Sacrifices

46:19☆ Lev 2:4–7; 2 Chron 35:13; Ezek 42:9; 44:19

19¶After he brought me through the entry, which *was* at the side of the
gate, into the holy chambers of the priests, which looked toward the north:
and, behold, there *was* a place on the two sides westward.
20Then said he unto me, This *is* the place where the priests shall boil the
trespass offering and the sin offering, where they shall bake the meat
offering; that they bear *them* not out into the outer court, to sanctify the
people.
21Then he brought me forth into the outer court, and caused me to pass
by the four corners of the court; and, behold, in every corner of the court
there was a court.
22In the four corners of the court *there were* courts joined of forty *cubits*
long and thirty broad: these four corners *were* of one measure.
23And *there was* a row *of building* round about in them, round about them
four, and *it was* made with boiling places under the rows round about.

46:24 Lev 44:10, 11; 1 Pet 5:2

24Then said he unto me, these *are* the places of them that boil, where the
ministers of the house shall boil the sacrifice of the people.

I. THE HEALING WATER OF THE GREAT RIVER FLOWING FROM THE TEMPLE

47:1☆ Ps 46:4; Joel 2:13; Zech 13:1; Rev 22:1, 17

47 AFTERWARD he brought me again unto the door of the house;
and, behold, waters issued out from under the threshold of the
house eastward: for the forefront of the house *stood toward* the east, and the
waters came down from under from the right side of the house, at the south
side of the altar.

47:2 Ezek 44:1–4

2Then brought he me out of the way of the gate northward, and led me
about the way without unto the outer gate by the way that looketh
eastward; and, behold, there ran out waters on the right side.

47:3 Ezek 40:3; Zech 2:1; Rev 11:1; 21:15

3And when the man that had the line in his hand went forth eastward, he
measured a thousand cubits, and he brought me through the waters; the
waters *were* to the ancles.
4Again he measured a thousand, and brought me through the waters; the
waters *were* to the knees. Again he measured a thousand, and brought me
through; the waters *were* to the loins.

47:5 Isa 11:9; Hab 2:14

5Afterward he measured a thousand; *and it was* a river that I could not
pass over: for the waters were risen, waters to swim in, a river that could
not be passed over.

47:6 Ezek 40:4; 44:5
47:7 Isa 60:21; 61:3; Rev 22:2
47:8 Deut 3:17; Isa 35:6, 7; 41:17–19; 44:3; Jer 31:9

6¶And he said unto me, Son of man, hast thou seen *this?* Then he brought
me, and caused me to return to the brink of the river.
7Now when I had returned, behold, at the bank of the river *were* very
many trees on the one side and on the other.
8Then said he unto me, These waters issue out toward the east country,

---

46:19ff This is the first mention of the buildings in which the flesh of the offerings is to be boiled. The flesh is holy and is to be eaten by the priests. None is to be taken from there into the outer court.

47:1ff Ezekiel sees a river flowing eastward and having *its source from the temple.* It becomes a deep river with banks lined with trees, and it will sweeten the Dead Sea so that marine life will live in its waters. Some think this vision has a mystical and spiritual meaning and is not to be taken literally. Others think it is to be taken literally, otherwise the remainder of the visions must also be regarded spiritually and this presents many difficulties. Curiously, the river referred to here corresponds to the one described in Rev. 22:1, 2 ("a pure river of water of life, clear as crystal, proceeding out of the throne of God and of the Lamb"). Jesus said, "He that believeth on me, as the scripture hath said, out of his belly shall flow rivers of living water" (John 7:38). In all of these instances, the language describes the blessings of God which refresh the soul and provide what the believer needs to become all that he should be.

and go down into the desert, and go into the sea: *which being* brought forth
into the sea, the waters shall be healed.
9 And it shall come to pass, *that* every thing that liveth, which moveth,
whithersoever the rivers shall come, shall live: and there shall be a very
great multitude of fish, because these waters shall come thither: for they
shall be healed; and every thing shall live whither the river cometh.
10 And it shall come to pass, *that* the fishers shall stand upon it from En-
ge'di even unto En-eg'la-im; they shall be a *place* to spread forth nets; their
fish shall be according to their kinds, as the fish of the great sea, exceeding
many.
11 But the miry places thereof and the marishes thereof shall not be
healed; they shall be given to salt.
12 And by the river upon the bank thereof, on this side and on that side,
shall grow all trees for meat, whose leaf shall not fade, neither shall the fruit
thereof be consumed: it shall bring forth new fruit according to his months,
because their waters they issued out of the sanctuary: and the fruit thereof
shall be for meat, and the leaf thereof for medicine.

47:9 Isa 12:3 Zech 2:11 8:21–23 Jn 4:14 7:37, 38 Rev 21:6
47:10 2 Chron 20:2 Ps 104:25 Mt 13:47 Lk 5:5–9
47:12 Gen 2:9 Ps 1:3 Jer 17:8 Rev 22:2

J. INSTRUCTIONS FOR DIVIDING THE LAND

13 ¶Thus saith the Lord God; This *shall be* the border, whereby ye shall
inherit the land according to the twelve tribes of Israel: Joseph *shall have
two* portions.
14 And ye shall inherit it, one as well as another: *concerning* the which I
lifted up mine hand to give it unto your fathers: and this land shall fall unto
you for inheritance.
15 And this *shall be* the border of the land toward the north side, from the
great sea, the way of Heth'lon, as men go to Ze'dad;
16 Ha'math, Be-ro'thah, Sib'ra-im, which *is* between the border of
Damascus and the border of Ha'math; Ha'zar-hat'ti-con, which *is* by the
coast of Hau'ran.
17 And the border from the sea shall be Ha'zar–e'nan, the border of
Damascus, and the north northward, and the border of Ha'math. And *this
is* the north side.
18 And the east side ye shall measure from Hau'ran, and from Damascus,
and from Gilead, and from the land of Israel *by* Jordan, from the border
unto the east sea. And *this is* the east side.
19 And the south side southward, from Ta'mar *even* to the waters of strife
in Ka'desh, the river to the great sea. And *this is* the south side southward.
20 The west side also *shall be* the great sea from the border, till a man
come over against Ha'math. This *is* the west side.
21 So shall ye divide this land unto you according to the tribes of Israel.
22 ¶And it shall come to pass, *that* ye shall divide it by lot for an
inheritance unto you, and to the strangers that sojourn among you, which
shall beget children among you: and they shall be unto you as born in the
country among the children of Israel; they shall have inheritance with you
among the tribes of Israel.
23 And it shall come to pass, *that* in what tribe the stranger sojourneth,
there shall ye give *him* his inheritance, saith the Lord God.

☆**47:13** Gen 48:5 Num 34:1–13 1 Chron 5:1 Ezek 48:4, 5
47:14 Gen 12:7 Deut 1:8 Ezek 20:5, 6
47:15 Num 34:7–9 Ezek 48:1
47:16 Num 13:21 1 Kgs 8:65 Amos 6:14 Zech 9:2
47:17 Num 34:9 Ezek 48:1
47:18 Gen 13:10, 11 Num 34:10–12 Judg 10:8 Job 40:23
47:19 Num 34:3–5 Deut 32:51 Isa 27:12
47:20 Num 34:6
47:22 Isa 14:1; 56:6, 7 Acts 11:18 Rom 10:12 Eph 2:12–14 Col 3:11

47:13ff The land of Canaan is here guaranteed to the covenant people of God, and its boundaries are set. It shall be divided among the tribes of Israel, and provision is made for aliens who will share their land. At the very least, this typifies the heavenly Canaan, a better country, mentioned in Heb. 11:16. In this Canaan all distinctions are broken down, for there is neither Jew nor Gentile. All are members of the body of Christ.

K. THE DIVISION OF THE LAND

1. The Allocations to the Tribes of Israel

48:1☆ Ex 1:1; Josh 19:40–48; 2 Sam 24:2; 1 Kgs 12:28, 29

48 NOW these *are* the names of the tribes. From the north end to the
coast of the way of Heth'lon, as one goeth to Ha'math, Ha'zar-
e'nan, the border of Damascus northward, to the coast of Ha'math; for
these are his sides east *and* west; a *portion for* Dan.

48:2 Gen 30:12, 13; Josh 19:24–31

2 And by the border of Dan, from the east side unto the west side, a
portion for Asher.

48:3 Gen 30:7, 8; Josh 19:32–39

3 And by the border of Asher, from the east side even unto the west side,
a *portion for* Naph'ta-li.

48:4 Gen 30:22–24; 41:51; 48:5, 14–20; Josh 13:29–31; 17:1–11

4 And by the border of Naph'ta-li, from the east side unto the west side,
a *portion for* Ma-nas'seh.
5 And by the border of Ma-nas'seh, from the east side unto the west side,
a *portion for* E'phra-im.

48:5 Josh 13:15–23; 15:1–63; 16:5–10; 17:8–10, 14–18; 19:9

6 And by the border of E'phra-im, from the east side even unto the west
side, a *portion for* Reuben.
7 And by the border of Reuben, from the east side unto the west side, a
portion for Judah.

2. The Land for the Priests and Levites

48:8☆ Ezek 45:1–6; Zech 2:11, 12; 2 Cor 6:16; Rev 21:3, 22

8 ¶And by the border of Judah, from the east side unto the west side, shall
be the offering which ye shall offer of five and twenty thousand *reeds in*
breadth, and *in* length as one of the *other* parts, from the east side unto the
west side: and the sanctuary shall be in the midst of it.
9 The oblation that ye shall offer unto the LORD *shall be* of five and twenty
thousand in length, and of ten thousand in breadth.

48:10 Ezek 44:28; 45:4

10 And for them, *even* for the priests, shall be *this* holy oblation; toward
the north five and twenty thousand *in length,* and toward the west ten
thousand in breadth, and toward the east ten thousand in breadth, and
toward the south five and twenty thousand in length: and the sanctuary of
the LORD shall be in the midst thereof.

48:11 Ezek 44:10–15

11 It shall be for the priests that are sanctified of the sons of Za'dok;
which have kept my charge, which went not astray when the children of
Israel went astray, as the Levites went astray.
12 And *this* oblation of the land that is offered shall be unto them a thing
most holy by the border of the Levites.
13 And over against the border of the priests the Levites *shall have* five and
twenty thousand in length, and ten thousand in breadth: all the length *shall
be* five and twenty thousand, and the breadth ten thousand.

48:14 Lev 25:32–34; Mal 3:8–10

14 And they shall not sell of it, neither exchange, nor alienate the firstfruits
of the land: for *it is* holy unto the LORD.

3. The General Use of Some of the Land

48:15 Ezek 42:20; 45:6

15 ¶And the five thousand, that are left in the breadth over against the five
and twenty thousand, shall be a profane *place* for the city, for dwelling, and
for suburbs: and the city shall be in the midst thereof.

48:16 Rev 21:16

16 And these *shall be* the measures thereof; the north side four thousand
and five hundred, and the south side four thousand and five hundred, and

---

48:1ff The land north of the temple will be allotted to the seven tribes of Dan, Asher, Naphtali, Manasseh, Ephraim, Reuben, and Judah.

48:8ff See Ezek. 45:1–8, which also describes the area of Canaan devoted to sacred activities. Included are the sanctuary, the portion for the priests and for the Levites, the city, and the area assigned to the prince.

on the east side four thousand and five hundred, and the west side four
thousand and five hundred.
17 And the suburbs of the city shall be toward the north two hundred and
fifty, and toward the south two hundred and fifty, and toward the east two
hundred and fifty, and toward the west two hundred and fifty.
18 And the residue in length over against the oblation of the holy *portion*
shall be ten thousand eastward, and ten thousand westward: and it shall be
over against the oblation of the holy *portion;* and the increase thereof shall
be for food unto them that serve the city.
19 And they that serve the city shall serve it out of all the tribes of Israel.
20 All the oblation *shall be* five and twenty thousand by five and twenty
thousand: ye shall offer the holy oblation foursquare, with the possession of
the city.

4. The Land for the Prince

21 ¶And the residue *shall be* for the prince, on the one side and on the
other of the holy oblation, and of the possession of the city, over against the
five and twenty thousand of the oblation toward the east border, and
westward over against the five and twenty thousand toward the west
border, over against the portions for the prince: and it shall be the holy
oblation; and the sanctuary of the house *shall be* in the midst thereof.
22 Moreover from the possession of the Levites, and from the possession
of the city, *being* in the midst *of that* which is the prince's, between the
border of Judah and the border of Benjamin, shall be for the prince.

48:21 Ezek 34:24; 45:7

5. Other Tribal Distribution of Land

23 As for the rest of the tribes, from the east side unto the west side,
Benjamin *shall have* a *portion.*
24 And by the border of Benjamin, from the east side unto the west side,
Simeon *shall have* a *portion.*
25 And by the border of Simeon, from the east side unto the west side,
Is'sa-char a *portion.*
26 And by the border of Is'sa-char, from the east side unto the west side,
Zeb'u-lun a *portion.*
27 And by the border of Zeb'u-lun, from the east side unto the west side,
Gad a *portion.*
28 And by the border of Gad, at the south side southward, the border shall
be even from Ta'mar *unto* the waters of strife *in* Ka'desh, *and* to the river
toward the great sea.
29 This *is* the land which ye shall divide by lot unto the tribes of Israel for
inheritance, and these *are* their portions, saith the Lord GOD.

☆48:23 Gen 35:16–19 Josh 18:21–28
48:24 Gen 29:33 49:5–7 Josh 19:1–9
48:25 Gen 30:14–18 Josh 19:17–23
48:26 Gen 30:19, 20 Josh 19:10–16
48:27 Gen 30:10, 11 Josh 13:24–28 Ezek 47:19, 20
48:29 Num 34:2, 13 Ezek 47:13–23

6. The City Name: the City of God

30 ¶And these *are* the goings out of the city on the north side, four
thousand and five hundred measures.
31 And the gates of the city *shall be* after the names of the tribes of Israel:
three gates northward; one gate of Reuben, one gate of Judah, one gate of
Levi.
32 And at the east side four thousand and five hundred: and three gates;
and one gate of Joseph, one gate of Benjamin, one gate of Dan.

48:30 Rev 21:12, 13

48:23ff The land south of the sacred area will be given to the five tribes of Benjamin, Simeon, Issachar, Zebulun, and Gad. The arrangement differs from that described in Joshua 13–17.

33 And at the south side four thousand and five hundred measures: and three gates; one gate of Simeon, one gate of Is'sa-char, one gate of Zeb'u-lun.

48:35☆ Isa 12:6; 24:23 Jer 23:6 Joel 3:21 Zech 2:10 Rev 21:3; 22:3

34 At the west side four thousand and five hundred, *with* their three gates; one gate of Gad, one gate of Asher, one gate of Naph'ta-li.
35 *It was* round about eighteen thousand *measures:* and the name of the city from *that* day *shall be,* The LORD *is* there.

48:35 *The LORD is there,* literally, "Jehovah-Shammah." Where God is, nothing else is needed; where God is, all we need is there, too. Israel here is promised that God will dwell among his people. What is promised for Israel in time and on this earth is but a token of the still greater promise that, in eternity, all the people of God shall dwell in the New Jerusalem. However dimly we perceive what is revealed here, and however defective may be our interpretations, the reality remains and is described for us in Heb. 12:22: "But ye are come unto mount Sion, and unto the city of the living God, the heavenly Jerusalem, and to an innumerable company of angels." This is the believer's hope and expectation.

THE BOOK OF DANIEL

Authorship, date, and background Daniel, the subject of this book, was born to a Judean noble family shortly before Josiah's reformation in 621 B.C. His name means "God is my judge." He was among the first group of Jewish captives taken to Babylon by Nebuchadnezzar in 605 B.C. He lived and ministered in Babylon for a period of approximately sixty years under the kingships of Nebuchadnezzar, Belshazzar, Darius the Mede (Gubaru), and Cyrus. The book was written in Babylon and contains a large segment in the Aramaic tongue, whereas the other Old Testament books were written in the Hebrew tongue.

For a variety of reasons, liberal scholars beginning with Prophyry (ca. A.D. 260) think the book was written in 165 B.C., which means that the prophetic portions, for the most part, were inscribed after, rather than before, the events took place, and the author most certainly could not have been Daniel. From the earliest days, however, Daniel was regarded as the author, although he may have been aided by a scribe, and the date of the composition was set in the sixth century B.C. Recent evidences, and particularly the Dead Sea Scrolls, reinforce the view of the early church and Jewish tradition about Daniel's authorship and the sixth century B.C. composition date.

Daniel wrote to convince his fellow captives that their stay in Babylon was in accord with the plan of God and that it was possible to have a living faith in God despite the captivity. He demonstrated the superiority of Jehovah God over the idols of Babylon and assured the Jews that Babylon, the agent of God's judgment, would itself disappear.

Characteristics and content Daniel develops a view of history which began with the Jews in captivity and stretches from there to the end of the age. His apocalyptic vision, which has its origin in Nebuchadnezzar's dream, forecasts the rise and fall of four world-empires along with the rise and permanence of God's eternal and universal kingdom. God's direct intervention in the affairs of men and nations may be seen in the miraculous deliverance of Daniel's three colleagues who land in the fiery furnace when they refuse to worship the golden image set up by the king; later Daniel himself is miraculously delivered after being cast into the lions' den.

In the latter part of the book Daniel writes about the beast vision of a lion, a bear, a leopard, and a fourth beast with ten horns. Additional details are given in the vision of the ram and the goat along with the prophetic interpretation. Then follows the seventy weeks and the end times. No one can develop a prophetic scheme without reference to the seminal work of Daniel. This book and the Revelation of John in the New Testament have much in common.

Outline

I. DANIEL AND HIS FRIENDS IN BABYLON (1:1—6:28)

A. THE CAPTURE AND TRAINING OF THE JEWISH YOUTHS

1. Nebuchadnezzar's Victory over Jehoiakim

1 IN the third year of the reign of Je-hoi'a-kim king of Judah came Neb-
u-chad-nez'zar king of Babylon unto Jerusalem, and besieged it.
2 And the Lord gave Je-hoi'a-kim king of Judah into his hand, with part

☆1:1 Gen 10:10; 2 Kgs 24:1, 2, 13; 2 Chron 36:5–7; Jer 25:1; 52:12, 28–30; Dan 2:37, 38; 5:2; Zech 5:11

1:1 Babylonia defeated Judah and took it captive. God ordained this because of Judah's idolatry. God preserved his people in Babylon and showed them the evils of idolatry. Thus they were prepared to return to Judea, as the people through whom the Messiah would come.

of the vessels of the house of God: which he carried into the land of Shi′nar
to the house of his god; and he brought the vessels into the treasure house
of his god.

2. The Four Youths Chosen for the King's Service

1:3☆ 3 ¶And the king spake unto Ash′pe-naz the master of his eunuchs, that he
2 Kgs 24:14 Isa 39:7 should bring *certain* of the children of Israel, and of the king's seed, and of
Dan 5:7, 11, 30 9:1 the princes;
1:4☆ 4 Children in whom *was* no blemish, but well favoured, and skilful in all
wisdom, and cunning in knowledge, and understanding science, and such as
had ability in them to stand in the king's palace, and whom they might
teach the learning and the tongue of the Chal-de′ans.
1:5☆ 5 And the king appointed them a daily provision of the king's meat, and
1 Sam 16:22 Dan 1:19 of the wine which he drank: so nourishing them three years, that at the end
thereof they might stand before the king.
1:6☆ 6 Now among these were of the children of Judah, Daniel, Han-a-ni′ah,
Ezek 14:14, 20 28:3 Mish′a-el, and Az-a-ri′ah:
Mt 24:15 7 Unto whom the prince of the eunuchs gave names: for he gave unto
1:7☆ Dan 2:49 Daniel *the name* of Bel-te-shaz′zar; and to Han-a-ni′ah, of Sha′drach; and
3:12–30; 4:8 to Mish′a-el, of Me′shach; and to Az-a-ri′ah, of A-bed′–ne-go.

3. The Test of Their True Faith

1:8☆ 8 ¶But Daniel purposed in his heart that he would not defile himself with
Lev 11:47 Deut 32:38 the portion of the king's meat, nor with the wine which he drank: therefore
Ezek 4:13, 14 Hos 9:3 he requested of the prince of the eunuchs that he might not defile himself.
1:9 9 Now God had brought Daniel into favour and tender love with the
Ezra 7:27, 28 Neh 1:11 prince of the eunuchs.
Ps 106:46 Prov 16:7 10 And the prince of the eunuchs said unto Daniel, I fear my lord the king,
who hath appointed your meat and your drink: for why should he see your
faces worse liking than the children which *are* of your sort? then shall ye
make *me* endanger my head to the king.
11 Then said Daniel to Mel′zar, whom the prince of the eunuchs had set
over Daniel, Han-a-ni′ah, Mish′a-el, and Az-a-ri′ah,
1:12☆ 12 Prove thy servants, I beseech thee, ten days; and let them give us pulse
to eat, and water to drink.
13 Then let our countenances be looked upon before thee, and the
countenance of the children that eat of the portion of the king's meat: and
as thou seest, deal with thy servants.

1:3 *the master of the eunuchs* was the one in charge of the palace slaves.
1:4 *the tongue of the Chaldeans* was Aramaic and part of Daniel is in Aramaic. The Hebrew men received instruction in such subjects as history, astronomy, and mathematics. Magic and alchemy were also among the courses of study.
1:5–7 Nebuchadnezzar sought to make Babylonians—loyal to him and to his court—out of the young Jewish captives. He did this by adopting a threefold plan: (1) new Babylonian names were given them to identify them with Babylonia; (2) they were enrolled in a three-year program of indigenization; and (3) they were *given the finest Babylonian food.* Daniel complied with the program except where it conflicted with the law of God. God blessed his faithfulness and caused him to prosper in an alien environment.
1:6 The four Hebrew young men all had "jah" or "el" in their names. Both of these are names for God. Their names were changed when they got to Babylon, and their Babylonian names seem to have had connections to some of the deities worshipped by these pagans. However, the meaning of the names is uncertain and there are differences of opinion as to which deities were represented.
1:8 Though the Babylonians had changed Daniel's name, they could not change his nature. He was an Israelite and would be so all the days of his life. It would have been an offense for him to eat meat that was not kosher, although that would not apply to wine. In any event these were his convictions at that time. Later (in 10:2) we are told that Daniel refused to eat any flesh or drink any wine for a particular time. Thus he was used to eating flesh and drinking wine. Whether he had worked out arrangements for the flesh to be kosher is not stated.
1:12 *pulse,* i.e., vegetables.

14So he consented to them in this matter, and proved them ten days.
15And at the end of ten days their countenances appeared fairer and
fatter in flesh than all the children which did eat the portion of the king's
meat.
16Thus Mel'zar took away the portion of their meat, and the wine that
they should drink; and gave them pulse.

4. The Reward of Their Faith

17¶As for these four children, God gave them knowledge and skill in all
learning and wisdom: and Daniel had understanding in all visions and
dreams.
18Now at the end of the days that the king had said he should bring them
in, then the prince of the eunuchs brought them in before Neb-u-chad-
nez'zar.
19And the king communed with them; and among them all was found
none like Daniel, Han-a-ni'ah, Mish'a-el, and Az-a-ri'ah: therefore stood
they before the king.
20And in all matters of wisdom *and* understanding, that the king inquired
of them, he found them ten times better than all the magicians *and*
astrologers that *were* in all his realm.
21And Daniel continued *even* unto the first year of king Cyrus.

B. DANIEL INTERPRETS NEBUCHADNEZZAR'S DREAM

1. Nebuchadnezzar Forgets His Awful Dream

2 AND in the second year of the reign of Neb-u-chad-nez'zar Neb-u-
chad-nez'zar dreamed dreams, wherewith his spirit was troubled, and
his sleep brake from him.
2Then the king commanded to call the magicians, and the astrologers,
and the sorcerers, and the Chal-de'ans, for to shew the king his dreams. So
they came and stood before the king.
3And the king said unto them, I have dreamed a dream, and my spirit
was troubled to know the dream.
4Then spake the Chal-de'ans to the king in Syr'i-ack, O king, live for
ever: tell thy servants the dream, and we will shew the interpretation.
5The king answered and said to the Chal-de'ans, The thing is gone from
me: if ye will not make known unto me the dream, with the interpretation
thereof, ye shall be cut in pieces, and your houses shall be made a dunghill.
6But if ye shew the dream, and the interpretation thereof, ye shall receive

1:15 Ex 23:25; Prov 10:22
☆**1:17** 1 Kgs 3:12, 28; Job 32:8; Dan 1:20; 2:21; 7:1; 8:1
1:19 Gen 41:46; 1 Kgs 17:1; Prov 22:29; Jer 15:1; Dan 1:5
☆**1:20** Num 14:22; Isa 19:3; Dan 1:17; 2:2; 4:18; 5:7
☆**1:21** Dan 6:28; 10:1
☆**2:1** Gen 40:5–8; 41:1; Job 33:15–17; Dan 2:3; 4:5; 6:18
☆**2:2**
☆**2:4** Ezra 4:7; Isa 36:11
2:5 Deut 13:16; Ezra 6:11; Dan 2:12; 3:29
☆**2:6** Dan 2:48; 5:7, 16, 29

1:17 In their academic pursuits God gave these Israelites knowledge and skill. They were, of course, diligent in their studies and intent on learning, yet God gave them an uncommon capacity that enabled them to surpass others in the classroom. The source of their intellectual gifts was the Father of lights, who gives men *the minds to grasp* and employ difficult subjects.

1:20 The Hebrew men were ten times better than the others in their classes. This was obvious when they were questioned by the king. The magicians and astrologers could not hold a candle to these young men.

1:21 Kings came and went, but Daniel lived on and served until he was well into his eighties. Despite the many testings and conspiracies against him, God delivered him from them all. We are not told anything about his departure from this life.

2:1 Unknown to Nebuchadnezzar his dreams came from God, not from natural causes. They troubled him so much that he could not sleep. But he was even more perplexed by the fact that he could not recall what the dreams were, so he resorted to diviners and soothsayers to discover the truth about his dreams.

2:2 *Chaldeans,* or "astrologers" (TLB). The word Chaldeans may be used for the Neo-Babylonians, who established an empire in Mesopotamia under Nabopolassar, or for wise men (astrologers), who were noted for their astral studies.

2:4 The book of Daniel was written in Hebrew and Aramaic. The Aramaic section begins with this verse and continues through 7:28.

2:6 Nebuchadnezzar promised his wise men that if they told him the content of his dreams and the interpretation, he would reward them beyond their wildest dreams. With this promise, they would do all they could to satisfy the king. If they could not do so, it would not be for lack of intention, but of power.

of me gifts and rewards and great honour: therefore shew me the dream,
and the interpretation thereof.

2:7 Dan 2:26; 4:8 5:12
2:8☆ Isa 41:23 Dan 3:15

7 They answered again and said, Let the king tell his servants the dream,
and we will shew the interpretation of it.
8 The king answered and said, I know of certainty that ye would gain the
time, because ye see the thing is gone from me.
9 But if ye will not make known unto me the dream, *there is but* one
decree for you: for ye have prepared lying and corrupt words to speak
before me, till the time be changed: therefore tell me the dream, and I shall
know that ye can shew me the interpretation thereof.

2:10☆

10 ¶The Chal-de′ans answered before the king, and said, There is not a
man upon the earth that can shew the king's matter: therefore *there is* no
king, lord, nor ruler, *that* asked such things at any magician, or astrologer,
or Chal-de′an.

2:11 Gen 41:39 Ex 29:45 1 Kgs 8:27 Isa 57:15 Dan 5:11
2:12 Ps 76:10 Dan 2:5; 3:13

11 And *it is* a rare thing that the king requireth, and there is none other
that can shew it before the king, except the gods, whose dwelling is not with
flesh.
12 For this cause the king was angry and very furious, and commanded to
destroy all the wise *men* of Babylon.
13 And the decree went forth that the wise *men* should be slain; and they
sought Daniel and his fellows to be slain.

2. Daniel's Offer to Interpret the Dream and His Prayer for Help

14 ¶Then Daniel answered with counsel and wisdom to A′ri-och the
captain of the king's guard, which was gone forth to slay the wise *men* of
Babylon:

2:16☆
2:18 Gen 18:28 Esth 4:15 Ps 50:15 Isa 37:4 Ezek 36:27 Dan 2:23
2:19 Num 12:6 2 Kgs 6:8–12 Job 33:15, 16 Dan 7:2, 7
2:20☆ 1 Chron 29:11, 12 Job 12:13 Ps 103:1, 2 Dan 2:21–23 Mt 6:13
2:21 1 Sam 2:7, 8 1 Kgs 3:9, 10 4:29 Ps 75:6, 7 Jas 1:5

15 He answered and said to A′ri-och the king's captain, Why *is* the decree
so hasty from the king? Then A′ri-och made the thing known to Daniel.
16 Then Daniel went in, and desired of the king that he would give him
time, and that he would shew the king the interpretation.
17 Then Daniel went to his house, and made the thing known to Han-a-
ni′ah, Mish′a-el, and Az-a-ri′ah, his companions:
18 That they would desire mercies of the God of heaven concerning this
secret; that Daniel and his fellows should not perish with the rest of the
wise *men* of Babylon.
19 ¶Then was the secret revealed unto Daniel in a night vision. Then
Daniel blessed the God of heaven.
20 Daniel answered and said, Blessed be the name of God for ever and
ever: for wisdom and might are his:
21 And he changeth the times and the seasons: he removeth kings, and
setteth up kings: he giveth wisdom unto the wise, and knowledge to them
that know understanding:

2:10 The Chaldeans tell the king that no one can recreate forgotten dreams; it is unfair to demand this of them. Nebuchadnezzar furiously orders all the magicians of Babylon to be executed without exception. Thus he includes the four Hebrew servants, although they have had no part in the proceedings. This tyrant shows his true colors; he speaks death when he cannot speak sense. The only fault the magicians committed was that they cannot serve the king, although they wanted very much to do so.

2:16 When Daniel came into the presence of the king, he made no pretense that he then had the answer to the king's dream. He only sought for time to get the answer. His method to get a word from God was by means of prayer. He was joined in prayer by his friends. The Scripture says the secret was "revealed unto Daniel in a night vision" (2:19). Daniel's prayer is not recorded, but his thanksgiving for the answer to his prayer is. He gave all the glory to God.

2:20ff This prayer is a model of what thanksgiving is all about. Daniel praises God, who has wisdom and might, who sets up and pulls down kings, who changes times and seasons according to the divine will. This God of his fathers—and his God too—has given him wisdom, prudence, and knowledge; for this he expresses his thanks.

22 He revealeth the deep and secret things: he knoweth what *is* in the darkness, and the light dwelleth with him.

23 I thank thee, and praise thee, O thou God of my fathers, who hast given me wisdom and might, and hast made known unto me now what we desired of thee: for thou hast *now* made known unto us the king's matter.

2:22 Gen 37:5-9 Job 12:22; 26:6 Ps 139:12 Isa 45:7 Dan 2:19, 28 1 Jn 1:5
2:23 Gen 31:42 Ex 3:15 Ps 21:2, 4 Dan 2:21

3. Daniel Glorifies God before Nebuchadnezzar

24 ¶Therefore Daniel went in unto A'ri-och, whom the king had ordained to destroy the wise *men* of Babylon: he went and said thus unto him; Destroy not the wise *men* of Babylon: bring me in before the king, and I will shew unto the king the interpretation.

25 Then A'ri-och brought in Daniel before the king in haste, and said thus unto him, I have found a man of the captives of Judah, that will make known unto the king the interpretation.

26 The king answered and said to Daniel, whose name *was* Bel-te-shaz'zar, Art thou able to make known unto me the dream which I have seen, and the interpretation thereof?

27 Daniel answered in the presence of the king, and said, The secret which the king hath demanded cannot the wise *men,* the astrologers, the magicians, the soothsayers, shew unto the king;

28 But there is a God in heaven that revealeth secrets, and maketh known to the king Neb-u-chad-nez'zar what shall be in the latter days. Thy dream, and the visions of thy head upon thy bed, are these;

29 As for thee, O king, thy thoughts came *into thy mind* upon thy bed what should come to pass hereafter: and he that revealeth secrets maketh known to thee what shall come to pass.

30 But as for me, this secret is not revealed to me for *any* wisdom that I have more than any living, but for *their* sakes that shall make known the interpretation to the king, and that thou mightest know the thoughts of thy heart.

☆**2:24** Dan 2:12, 13 Acts 27:24
2:25 Gen 41:14 Prov 24:11 Dan 1:6; 5:13 6:13
2:27 Dan 2:2, 10, 11 5:7, 8
☆**2:28** Gen 40:8; 41:16 Isa 41:21 Dan 2:22, 45 Hos 3:5
2:30 Gen 41:16 Ps 139:2 Isa 43:3 Dan 1:17 Acts 3:12 1 Cor 3:21–23

4. Daniel Tells Nebuchadnezzar What His Dream Was

31 ¶Thou, O king, sawest, and behold a great image. This great image, whose brightness *was* excellent, stood before thee; and the form thereof *was* terrible.

32 This image's head *was* of fine gold, his breast and his arms of silver, his belly and his thighs of brass,

33 His legs of iron, his feet part of iron and part of clay.

34 Thou sawest till that a stone was cut out without hands, which smote the image upon his feet *that were* of iron and clay, and brake them to pieces.

35 Then was the iron, the clay, the brass, the silver, and the gold, broken to pieces together, and became like the chaff of the summer threshingfloors; and the wind carried them away, that no place was found for them: and the stone that smote the image became a great mountain, and filled the whole earth.

☆**2:31**
2:34 Dan 8:25 Zech 4:6
2:35 Ps 1:4 Isa 17:13 Hos 13:3

2:24 Daniel follows protocol and goes to Arioch to ask for an audience with the king, to whom he will reveal not only his dream but also the interpretation.

2:28 Daniel dares to tell the king the truth. No magician can get to know what the king's dream was, and neither could Daniel himself. He bears testimony to the God in heaven who is the revealer of secrets. By doing this he cuts across all the idols of Nebuchadnezzar's kingdom and proclaims the superiority of the God of Abraham. He is careful to say that what his God has done is to show the king what will take place in advance of the happenings. Why God chose to disclose the secret to Nebuchadnezzar, we are not told.

2:31ff We are not told how Nebuchadnezzar could know that this really was the dream he had dreamed. He must have been satisfied, for Daniel proceeded without interruption to tell the king he would give him the meaning of the dream which, after all, is more important than the dream itself.

5. Daniel Explains the Meaning of the Dream

2:36ff☆ 36¶This *is* the dream; and we will tell the interpretation thereof before the
king.
2:37 37Thou, O king, *art* a king of kings: for the God of heaven hath given thee
1 Kgs 4:24 a kingdom, power, and strength, and glory.
Ezra 7:12
Isa 10:8; 47:5 38And wheresoever the children of men dwell, the beasts of the field and
Jer 27:6, 7
Ezek 26:7 the fowls of the heaven hath he given into thine hand, and hath made thee
Hos 8:10
Rev 1:5; 17:14 ruler over them all. Thou *art* this head of gold.
2:38
Ps 50:10 39And after thee shall arise another kingdom inferior to thee, and another
2:39☆ third kingdom of brass, which shall bear rule over all the earth.
2:40☆ 40And the fourth kingdom shall be strong as iron: forasmuch as iron
breaketh in pieces and subdueth all *things:* and as iron that breaketh all
these, shall it break in pieces and bruise.
41And whereas thou sawest the feet and toes, part of potters' clay, and
part of iron, the kingdom shall be divided; but there shall be in it of the
strength of the iron, forasmuch as thou sawest the iron mixed with miry
clay.
42And *as* the toes of the feet *were* part of iron, and part of clay, *so* the
kingdom shall be partly strong, and partly broken.
43And whereas thou sawest iron mixed with miry clay, they shall mingle
themselves with the seed of men: but they shall not cleave one to another,
even as iron is not mixed with clay.
2:44☆ 44And in the days of these kings shall the God of heaven set up a
Gen 49:10
Ps 2:9; 21:8, 9 kingdom, which shall never be destroyed: and the kingdom shall not be left
145:13
Isa 9:6, 7 to other people, *but* it shall break in pieces and consume all these kingdoms,
Ezek 37:25 and it shall stand for ever.
Mic 4:7
2:45 45Forasmuch as thou sawest that the stone was cut out of the mountain
Gen 41:28, 32
Deut 10:17 without hands, and that it brake in pieces the iron, the brass, the clay, the
2 Sam 7:22 silver, and the gold; the great God hath made known to the king what shall
Dan 2:29
Rev 1:19; 4:1 come to pass hereafter: and the dream *is* certain, and the interpretation
thereof sure.
2:46☆
Lev 26:31 46¶Then the king Neb-u-chad-nez'zar fell upon his face, and worshipped
Dan 3:5, 7 Daniel, and commanded that they should offer an oblation and sweet
Acts 10:25
Rev 19:10; 22:8 odours unto him.

2:36ff Except for the part of Nebuchadnezzar's dream that has not yet been fulfilled, the rest is easily explained. The four metals stand for four great empires: (1) Nebuchadnezzar's Babylonian Empire (2:37, 38); (2) the Medo-Persian Empire (represented by the silver breast and arms, and the leopard—2:32, 39; 7:6); (3) the Grecian Empire under Alexander the Great and his successors (2:39); and (4) the Roman Empire, which was the greatest of them all (2:40). The Roman Empire was to be sectioned into the Eastern and Western Empires (the two legs). Then ten toes are mentioned; about this there are differences of opinion. Some think the Roman Empire will be restored at the close of this age in the form of a confederacy of ten nations, represented by the ten toes. The confederacy will be led by the Beast or world conqueror. According to this view, the Rock (Christ) will conquer (2:35). Others hold that the Rock struck its blow by the death and resurrection of Christ, whose kingdom is filling the whole earth. *Christ's kingdom certainly is here now in a spiritual* form as he reigns in the hearts of his people. The final consummation awaits Christ's Second Advent.

2:39 *another kingdom,* or, "another world power." This refers to the Medo-Persian Empire, whose first great ruler was Cyrus. *another third kingdom,* or, "yet a third great power." The reference is to the Greek Empire, founded by Alexander the Great.†

2:40 *the fourth kingdom.* Apparently the Roman Empire.†

2:44 See note on 2:36. History knows of no fulfillment of this prophecy to date. Some think the "ten toes" of the image lends itself to the millennial interpretation and is yet future. The kingdom of God, which exists spiritually at present, will then exist literally, and Christ, the Rock, will defeat the enemy who has taken over the ten kingdoms and who exercises world rule and political supremacy.

2:46 Nebuchadnezzar is so impressed by what Daniel has told him that he bows before him in an act of worship. He commands that oblations and sweet odours be made to him. He can be excused, for he knows no better, and what happened was unique and supernatural and thus worthy of adulation. He confesses that Daniel's God is the God of gods and the Lord of kings because he has revealed these mysteries. There is a difference between confessing that God is God and coming to him in faith for salvation. Nebuchadnezzar had "head" knowledge but not believing faith that would bring him into the kingdom.

47The king answered unto Daniel, and said, Of a truth *it is,* that your God
is a God of gods, and a Lord of kings, and a revealer of secrets, seeing thou
couldest reveal this secret.
48Then the king made Daniel a great man, and gave him many great gifts,
and made him ruler over the whole province of Babylon, and chief of the
governors over all the wise *men* of Babylon.
49Then Daniel requested of the king, and he set Sha′drach, Me′shach, and
A-bed′–ne-go, over the affairs of the province of Babylon: but Daniel *sat* in
the gate of the king.

2:47 Deut 10:17; Dan 3:15; 4:25; Amos 3:7
☆2:48 Gen 41:39–43; Dan 2:6; 3:1, 12, 30; 5:16
☆2:49 Esth 2:19, 21; Dan 3:12–30; Amos 5:15

C. THE GOLD STATUE AND THE FIERY FURNACE

1. The Statue and the Command to Worship It

3 NEB-U-CHAD-NEZ′ZAR the king made an image of gold, whose
height *was* threescore cubits, *and* the breadth thereof six cubits: he set
it up in the plain of Du′ra, in the province of Babylon.
2Then Neb-u-chad-nez′zar the king sent to gather together the princes,
the governors, and the captains, the judges, the treasurers, the counsellors,
the sheriffs, and all the rulers of the provinces, to come to the dedication
of the image which Neb-u-chad-nez′zar the king had set up.
3Then the princes, the governors, and captains, the judges, the treasurers,
the counsellors, the sheriffs, and all the rulers of the provinces, were
gathered together unto the dedication of the image that Neb-u-chad-nez′zar
the king had set up; and they stood before the image that Neb-u-chad-
nez′zar had set up.
4Then an herald cried aloud, To you it is commanded, O people, nations,
and languages,
5*That* at what time ye hear the sound of the cornet, flute, harp, sackbut,
psaltery, dulcimer, and all kinds of musick, ye fall down and worship the
golden image that Neb-u-chad-nez′zar the king hath set up:
6And whoso falleth not down and worshippeth shall the same hour be
cast into the midst of a burning fiery furnace.
7Therefore at that time, when all the people heard the sound of the
cornet, flute, harp, sackbut, psaltery, and all kinds of musick, all the people,
the nations, and the languages, fell down *and* worshipped the golden image
that Neb-u-chad-nez′zar the king had set up.

☆3:1 Isa 46:6; Jer 16:20; Dan 2:31; Hab 2:19
☆3:2 Dan 3:3, 27; 6:1–7
3:4 Isa 40:9; 58:1; Dan 3:7; 4:1; Rev 18:2
3:5 Dan 3:7, 10
☆3:6 Dan 3:11, 15, 21; 6:7; Mt 13:42; Rev 9:2; 14:11
☆3:7

2. Shadrach, Meshach, and Abednego: Their Trial for Disobedience

8¶Wherefore at that time certain Chal-de′ans came near, and accused the
Jews.

3:8 Ezra 4:12–16; Esth 3:8, 9; Dan 6:12, 13

2:48, 49 Daniel now rises to the heights and becomes one of the chief rulers of the kingdom under the king himself. He secures the advancement of his three friends to high positions, for they can help him in his own labors and he can trust them.

3:1, 2 *Nebuchadnezzar* learned nothing from his earlier dream and his acknowledgement that Daniel's God was the God of gods. He now erects an image, perhaps of himself, to be worshipped. It was covered with gold and stood around ninety feet high. Idolators are always seeking new gods to be worshipped. The leaders of the nation gathered for the dedication of the image and the worship of it.

3:6 There was no religious freedom either for natives or foreigners. All are required to bow down and worship before the golden image. Anyone who refuses to do so for any reason whatever will be cast into a burning fiery furnace. Under such threats it would take someone of strong conviction to refrain from engaging in idolatrous worship. For those who already worshipped idols it was no problem to worship just another statue. But for the Hebrews, who had always been forbidden to bow before any idol and commanded to worship God alone, it was different. Is it better to bow than to perish? What difference does it make to follow the instructions when you deny what you are doing in your heart? Life is more valuable than death. But not to Daniel's three friends.

3:7 We are left to ponder what happened. Why were the three friends of Daniel present? It is quite obvious that there were many Jews in the kingdom; either they bowed down and prostituted their faith, or they were not present when the idol was dedicated. Certainly Daniel was not present, and he was not put into the fiery furnace. All the people present did bow, but not Daniel's close friends.

9 They spake and said to the king Neb-u-chad-nez'zar, O king, live for ever.

3:10 Esth 3:12–14 Dan 3:4–6

10 Thou, O king, hast made a decree, that every man that shall hear the sound of the cornet, flute, harp, sackbut, psaltery, and dulcimer, and all kinds of musick, shall fall down and worship the golden image:

11 And whoso falleth not down and worshippeth, *that* he should be cast into the midst of a burning fiery furnace.

12 There are certain Jews whom thou hast set over the affairs of the province of Babylon, Sha'drach, Me'shach, and A-bed'–ne-go; these men, O king, have not regarded thee: they serve not thy gods, nor worship the golden image which thou hast set up.

3:13☆ Dan 2:12; 3:19

13 ¶Then Neb-u-chad-nez'zar in *his* rage and fury commanded to bring Sha'drach, Me'shach, and A-bed'–ne-go. Then they brought these men before the king.

3:14 Ex 21:13, 14 Isa 46:1 Dan 3:1; 4:8

14 Neb-u-chad-nez'zar spake and said unto them, *Is it* true, O Sha'drach, Me'shach, and A-bed'–ne-go, do not ye serve my gods, nor worship the golden image which I have set up?

3:15 Ex 5:2 Isa 36:18–20 Dan 2:47

15 Now if ye be ready that at what time ye hear the sound of the cornet, flute, harp, sackbut, psaltery, and dulcimer, and all kinds of musick, ye fall down and worship the image which I have made; *well:* but if ye worship not, ye shall be cast the same hour into the midst of a burning fiery furnace; and who *is* that God that shall deliver you out of my hands?

3:16 Dan 1:7; 3:12

16 Sha'drach, Me'shach, and A-bed'–ne-go, answered and said to the king, O Neb-u-chad-nez'zar, we *are* not careful to answer thee in this matter.

3:17☆ 1 Sam 17:37 Ps 27:1, 2 Isa 26:3, 4 Jer 1:8

17 If it be *so,* our God whom we serve is able to deliver us from the burning fiery furnace, and he will deliver *us* out of thine hand, O king.

3:18 Josh 24:15 1 Kgs 19:14 Dan 3:28 Lk 12:3–9 Rev 12:11

18 But if not, be it known unto thee, O king, that we will not serve thy gods, nor worship the golden image which thou hast set up.

3. Nebuchadnezzar Sentences Them to the Fiery Furnace

3:19 Lev 26:18–28 Dan 3:13

19 ¶Then was Neb-u-chad-nez'zar full of fury, and the form of his visage was changed against Sha'drach, Me'shach, and A-bed'–ne-go: *therefore* he spake, and commanded that they should heat the furnace one seven times more than it was wont to be heated.

20 And he commanded the most mighty men that *were* in his army to bind Sha'drach, Me'shach, and A-bed'–ne-go, *and* to cast *them* into the burning fiery furnace.

3:21☆

21 Then these men were bound in their coats, their hosen, and their hats, and their *other* garments, and were cast into the midst of the burning fiery furnace.

3:22 Dan 2:15

22 Therefore because the king's commandment was urgent, and the furnace exceeding hot, the flame of the fire slew those men that took up Sha'drach, Me'shach, and A-bed'–ne-go.

3:13 Nebuchadnezzar got angry easily. When he learns that the three Jews did not bow when the music was played, he is enraged and has them brought before him. He gives them a last chance: bow now and be free; refuse to bow and be consumed by the fiery furnace. He asks the Jews what god is able to deliver *them from such an ordeal?*

3:17 The Jews are made of sterner stuff and stand for God. They affirm that God is able to deliver them, and they believe that he will do so. Strongly defying the king, they say that even if God does not choose to deliver them, they would rather die than obey. They must obey their God, not men; they prefer to suffer than to sin. In a weak and effeminate age is it not difficult to find such heroes as these?

3:21 So great was the anger of the king that he had the three Hebrews bound before being cast into the fiery furnace, which was heated seven times more than usual. Ordinarily they would have died quickly and been transported into paradise, where they would enjoy everlasting life. Bad as such a death would be, it would not be comparable to "the second death" to which unbelievers go (Rev. 20:6). There the fires of hell torture but do not kill.

23 And these three men, Sha'drach, Me'shach, and A-bed'-ne-go, fell
down bound into the midst of the burning fiery furnace.

4. God's Supernatural Deliverance

24 Then Neb-u-chad-nez'zar the king was astonied, and rose up in haste,
and spake, and said unto his counsellors, Did not we cast three men bound
into the midst of the fire? They answered and said unto the king, True, O
king.
25 He answered and said, Lo, I see four men loose, walking in the midst of
the fire, and they have no hurt; and the form of the fourth is like the Son of
God.

☆**3:25** Ps 91:3–9; Jer 1:8, 19

26 ¶Then Neb-u-chad-nez'zar came near to the mouth of the burning fiery
furnace, *and* spake, and said, Sha'drach, Me'shach, and A-bed'-ne-go, ye
servants of the most high God, come forth, and come *hither.* Then
Sha'drach, Me'shach, and A-bed'-ne-go, came forth of the midst of the fire.

3:26 Deut 4:20; 1 Kgs 8:51; Dan 3:17; 4:2

27 And the princes, governors, and captains, and the king's counsellors,
being gathered together, saw these men, upon whose bodies the fire had no
power, nor was an hair of their head singed, neither were their coats
changed, nor the smell of fire had passed on them.

3:27 Dan 3:21; Heb 11:34

5. Nebuchadnezzar Submits to God

28 *Then* Neb-u-chad-nez'zar spake, and said, Blessed *be* the God of
Sha'drach, Me'shach, and A-bed'-ne-go, who hath sent his angel, and
delivered his servants that trusted in him, and have changed the king's
word, and yielded their bodies, that they might not serve nor worship any
god, except their own God.

☆**3:28** Ps 34:7, 8; Isa 37:36; Dan 3:25; 6:22; Acts 5:19; 12:7

29 Therefore I make a decree, That every people, nation, and language,
which speak any thing amiss against the God of Sha'drach, Me'shach, and
A-bed'-ne-go, shall be cut in pieces, and their houses shall be made a
dunghill: because there is no other God that can deliver after this sort.

☆**3:29** Ezra 6:11; Dan 3:12, 15

30 ¶Then the king promoted Sha'drach, Me'shach, and A-bed'-ne-go, in
the province of Babylon.

3:30 Dan 2:49; 3:12

D. NEBUCHADNEZZAR'S HUMILIATION

1. Nebuchadnezzar's Terrifying Dream

4 NEB-U-CHAD-NEZ'ZAR the king, unto all people, nations, and
languages, that dwell in all the earth; Peace be multiplied unto you.
2 I thought it good to shew the signs and wonders that the high God hath
wrought toward me.
3 How great *are* his signs! and how mighty *are* his wonders! his kingdom

☆**4:1**
4:2 Dan 3:26; 4:17, 24, 25, 34
4:3 Deut 4:34; Ps 77:19; Isa 25:1; Dan 2:44; 4:34; 6:26

3:25 A fourth person appeared in the fiery furnace with Meshach, Shadrach, and Abednego. Nebuchadnezzar said, *the fourth is like the Son of God.* This may have been a theophany, an appearance of Jesus Christ in the Old Testament. Spiritually, the lesson is plain. When in difficulty, God's people have the help of Jesus, who has promised to go with them and help them (Heb. 2:18). Christ's great promise is that he will never forsake his own (Matt. 28:20; Heb. 13:5).

3:28 Only a miracle could have kept these faithful Jews from death in the furnace. Nebuchadnezzar seems to have felt that it was an angel sent by God who performed the miracle. The king knew that what had happened was a supernatural event, and it should have occasioned his own repentance, but his later conduct seems to rule this out. For the true believer, the incident illustrates God's watchful care over faithful servants.

3:29 Nebuchadnezzar turns from one extreme to another. Now he orders death for anyone who speaks against the God of the Hebrews. This kind of evangelization is foreign to the Scriptures, and multitudes who would keep from vilifying the name of God to save their lives would hardly be converts to the true faith.

4:1 This chapter is a record of a formal statement of the king, a public paper that was part of the nation's archives.

is an everlasting kingdom, and his dominion *is* from generation to
generation.

4:4☆ Ps 30:6; Isa 47:7, 8; Zeph 1:12
4:5 Job 7:13, 14; Dan 4:10, 13
4:6 Gen 41:8; Dan 2:2
4:7 Isa 44:25; Jer 27:9, 10; Dan 2:7; 2 Tim 3:8, 9
4:8☆ Num 11:17; Isa 63:11; Dan 1:7; 4:9, 18

4 I Neb-u-chad-nez′zar was at rest in mine house, and flourishing in my
palace:
5 I saw a dream which made me afraid, and the thoughts upon my bed
and the visions of my head troubled me.
6 Therefore made I a decree to bring in all the wise *men* of Babylon before
me, that they might make known unto me the interpretation of the dream.
7 Then came in the magicians, the astrologers, the Chal-de′ans, and the
soothsayers: and I told the dream before them; but they did not make
known unto me the interpretation thereof.
8 ¶But at the last Daniel came in before me, whose name *was* Bel-te-
shaz′zar, according to the name of my god, and in whom *is* the spirit of the
holy gods: and before him I told the dream, *saying*,

2. Nebuchadnezzar Asks Daniel to Interpret the Dream

4:9☆ Gen 11:6–8; 41:38; Ezek 28:3; Dan 1:20; 2:4, 5, 47, 48; 4:8; 5:11
4:12 Jer 27:6, 7; Ezek 31:7; Mt 13:32; Lk 13:19
4:13 Deut 33:2; Ps 89:7; Dan 8:13
4:14 Jer 51:5, 6; Ezek 31:10–14; Mt 3:10; 7:19; Rev 10:3; 18:2
4:15 Job 14:7–9

9 O Bel-te-shaz′zar, master of the magicians, because I know that the
spirit of the holy gods *is* in thee, and no secret troubleth thee, tell me the
visions of my dream that I have seen, and the interpretation thereof.
10 Thus *were* the visions of mine head in my bed; I saw, and behold a tree
in the midst of the earth, and the height thereof *was* great.
11 The tree grew, and was strong, and the height thereof reached unto
heaven, and the sight thereof to the end of all the earth:
12 The leaves thereof *were* fair, and the fruit thereof much, and in it *was*
meat for all: the beasts of the field had shadow under it, and the fowls of
the heaven dwelt in the boughs thereof, and all flesh was fed of it.
13 I saw in the visions of my head upon my bed, and, behold, a watcher
and an holy one came down from heaven;
14 He cried aloud, and said thus, Hew down the tree, and cut off his
branches, shake off his leaves, and scatter his fruit: let the beasts get away
from under it, and the fowls from his branches:
15 Nevertheless leave the stump of his roots in the earth, even with a band
of iron and brass, in the tender grass of the field; and let it be wet with the
dew of heaven, and *let* his portion *be* with the beasts in the grass of the
earth:

4:16 1 Chron 29:30; Isa 6:10; Dan 4:23–25; 7:25; Heb 1:11
4:17 Ex 9:16; 1 Sam 2:8; Ps 9:16; Dan 4:25; 11:21
4:18 Gen 41:8; 1 Kgs 14:2, 3; Dan 4:7; 5:8

16 Let his heart be changed from man's, and let a beast's heart be given
unto him: and let seven times pass over him.
17 This matter *is* by the decree of the watchers, and the demand by the
word of the holy ones: to the intent that the living may know that the most
High ruleth in the kingdom of men, and giveth it to whomsoever he will,
and setteth up over it the basest of men.
18 This dream I king Neb-u-chad-nez′zar have seen. Now thou, O Bel-te-
shaz′zar, declare the interpretation thereof, forasmuch as all the wise *men* of
my kingdom are not able to make known unto me the interpretation: but
thou *art* able; for the spirit of the holy gods *is* in thee.

4:4 Nebuchadnezzar died when he was around forty-five years of age. The madness that came upon him occurred about nine years before his death. Seven of those years were spent in an animal-like state of mind. *It may well be that God sent this judgment upon him* for his conduct in the affair of the Hebrews whom he committed to the fiery furnace or for his other depredations. He was at ease, quite prosperous, and satisfied with himself when he dreamed yet another dream.

4:8 Daniel does not appear in this incident immediately. Nebuchadnezzar, of course, remembers what Daniel did for him in past years, when he had interpreted his first dream. So he shares his dream with Daniel. This time, however, Nebuchadnezzar remembers very clearly the contents of his dream; but its meaning escapes him. So he needs Daniel again.

4:9 *the spirit of the holy gods is in thee.* Nebuchadnezzar was a polytheist, thus he could recognize the gods working through Daniel. He was certainly not a monotheist.

3. Daniel Interprets the Dream and Warns the King

19¶Then Daniel, whose name *was* Bel-te-shaz'zar, was astonied for one
hour, and his thoughts troubled him. The king spake, and said, Bel-te-
shaz'zar, let not the dream, or the interpretation thereof, trouble thee. Bel-
te-shaz'zar answered and said, My lord, the dream *be* to them that hate
thee, and the interpretation thereof to thine enemies.
20The tree that thou sawest, which grew, and was strong, whose height
reached unto the heaven, and the sight thereof to all the earth;
21Whose leaves *were* fair, and the fruit thereof much, and in it *was* meat
for all; under which the beasts of the field dwelt, and upon whose branches
the fowls of the heaven had their habitation:
22It *is* thou, O king, that art grown and become strong: for thy greatness
is grown, and reacheth unto heaven, and thy dominion to the end of the
earth.
23And whereas the king saw a watcher and an holy one coming down
from heaven, and saying, Hew the tree down, and destroy it; yet leave the
stump of the roots thereof in the earth, even with a band of iron and brass,
in the tender grass of the field; and let it be wet with the dew of heaven, and
let his portion *be* with the beasts of the field, till seven times pass over him;
24This *is* the interpretation, O king, and this *is* the decree of the most
High, which is come upon my lord the king:
25That they shall drive thee from men, and thy dwelling shall be with the
beasts of the field, and they shall make thee to eat grass as oxen, and they
shall wet thee with the dew of heaven, and seven times shall pass over thee,
till thou know that the most High ruleth in the kingdom of men, and giveth
it to whomsoever he will.
26And whereas they commanded to leave the stump of the tree roots; thy
kingdom shall be sure unto thee, after that thou shalt have known that the
heavens do rule.
27Wherefore, O king, let my counsel be acceptable unto thee, and break
off thy sins by righteousness, and thine iniquities by shewing mercy to the
poor; if it may be a lengthening of thy tranquillity.

4. Nebuchadnezzar's Punishment Exacted

28¶All this came upon the king Neb-u-chad-nez'zar.
29At the end of twelve months he walked in the palace of the kingdom of
Babylon.
30The king spake, and said, Is not this great Babylon, that I have built for
the house of the kingdom by the might of my power, and for the honour of
my majesty?
31While the word *was* in the king's mouth, there fell a voice from heaven,
saying, O king Neb-u-chad-nez'zar, to thee it is spoken; The kingdom is
departed from thee.

☆**4:19** 1 Sam 3:17; 2 Sam 18:32; 1 Kgs 18:7; Dan 7:15, 28; 8:27
4:22 Jer 27:6, 7; Dan 2:37, 38
☆**4:24**
4:25 Job 40:11, 12; Ps 75:7; 107:40; Jer 27:5; Dan 4:17, 33; 5:21
4:26 Dan 4:31
☆**4:27** Gen 41:33–37; 2 Sam 12:7; 1 Kgs 21:29; Ps 41:1–3; 119:46; Prov 28:13; Isa 55:6, 7; Jonah 3:9
☆**4:28** Num 23:19; Zech 1:6
4:29 2 Pet 3:9
4:30 Hab 2:4

4:19 Daniel is astonished, fearful, trembling. He knows the meaning of the dream without having to spend time in prayer. *God has already revealed it to him.* He does not desire to tell the king the truth, for the punishment God is bringing to Nebuchadnezzar is terrifying even to Daniel. Moreover, he feels a sense of compassion and concern for a king he had served for years.

4:24 The meaning of the dream is simple. God has decreed that the king will be driven from his throne, separated from men, and will live among the beasts of the field. The sentence will last seven years. But he will return to his throne and kingdom, which shall be kept for him. The reason for the punishment sent by God is explained in verses 29, 30.

4:27 Daniel was a missionary to Nebuchadnezzar. Here he implores the king to repent and mend his ways. He makes it clear that God may well spare him from the fulfillment of the vision if he does so. It was to no avail—4:28–30 shows that he remained a self-willed, egotistical, autonomous ruler who would not submit himself to God or ask for pardon and mercy. He reaped what he had sown.

4:28ff Here the patience of God is manifested. For twelve months Nebuchadnezzar had the opportunity to repent and mend his ways. When he did not, the judgment of God overtook him at last. He became an animal in the shape of a man.

32 And they shall drive thee from men, and thy dwelling *shall be* with the
beasts of the field: they shall make thee to eat grass as oxen, and seven
times shall pass over thee, until thou know that the most High ruleth in the
kingdom of men, and giveth it to whomsoever he will.
33 The same hour was the thing fulfilled upon Neb-u-chad-nez'zar: and he
was driven from men, and did eat grass as oxen, and his body was wet with
the dew of heaven, till his hairs were grown like eagles' *feathers,* and his
nails like birds' *claws.*

4:33 Dan 4:25; 5:21

5. Nebuchadnezzar Restored upon Repentance

34 And at the end of the days I Neb-u-chad-nez'zar lifted up mine eyes
unto heaven, and mine understanding returned unto me, and I blessed the
most High, and I praised and honoured him that liveth for ever, whose
dominion *is* an everlasting dominion, and his kingdom *is* from generation
to generation:
35 And all the inhabitants of the earth *are* reputed as nothing: and he
doeth according to his will in the army of heaven, and *among* the
inhabitants of the earth: and none can stay his hand, or say unto him, What
doest thou?
36 At the same time my reason returned unto me; and for the glory of my
kingdom, mine honour and brightness returned unto me; and my counsel-
lors and my lords sought unto me; and I was established in my kingdom,
and excellent majesty was added unto me.
37 Now I Neb-u-chad-nez'zar praise and extol and honour the King of
heaven, all whose works *are* truth, and his ways judgment: and those that
walk in pride he is able to abase.

4:34☆ 1 Sam 13:14; Ps 102:24; 145:13; Jer 10:10; Dan 4:2; 5:18, 21; Rev 4:10; 10:6
4:35 Job 42:2; Isa 43:13; Dan 6:27; Acts 4:28
4:36 2 Chron 33:12, 13; Prov 22:4; Dan 4:22, 34; Mt 6:33; 2 Cor 4:17
4:37 Ex 18:11; 1 Sam 2:3; Mt 11:25; Acts 17:24; Rev 15:3; 16:7; 19:1, 2

E. BELSHAZZAR'S FEAST AND DEFIANCE OF GOD

1. Belshazzar Drinks from the Temple Cups

5 BEL-SHAZ'ZAR the king made a great feast to a thousand of his
lords, and drank wine before the thousand.
2 Bel-shaz'zar, whiles he tasted the wine, commanded to bring the golden
and silver vessels which his father Neb-u-chad-nez'zar had taken out of the
temple which *was* in Jerusalem; that the king, and his princes, his wives,
and his concubines, might drink therein.
3 Then they brought the golden vessels that were taken out of the temple
of the house of God which *was* at Jerusalem; and the king, and his princes,
his wives, and his concubines, drank in them.
4 They drank wine, and praised the gods of gold, and of silver, of brass, of
iron, of wood, and of stone.

5:1☆ Esth 1:3; Isa 22:12–14
5:2 2 Kgs 24:13; 2 Chron 36:10, 18; Ezra 1:7–11; Jer 27:7; Dan 1:2; 3:1; Hab 2:19

2. The Handwriting on the Plaster Wall

5 In the same hour came forth fingers of a man's hand, and wrote over
against the candlestick upon the plaister of the wall of the king's palace:
and the king saw the part of the hand that wrote.
6 Then the king's countenance was changed, and his thoughts troubled

5:6 Ps 69:23; Dan 7:28; Nah 2:10

4:34 *at the end of the days,* i.e., "at the end of seven years." It is not clear here whether Nebuchadnezzar has now become a monotheist and is worshipping the *one true God, or whether he is acknowledging* the great power of Daniel's God as one of many. If the former is true, then he had become a follower of Yahweh and a true believer.

5:1 *Belshazzar.* Until recently the historicity of Belshazzar was questioned by rationalist critics. However, recent discoveries prove he was a real person; he was the Chaldean ruler who was reigning when Darius the Mede captured Babylon. Belshazzar's father, Nabonidus, made him coregent and commander of the army whenever Nabonidus was absent in military adventures. When Daniel interpreted the writing on the wall, Belshazzar made him the third ruler in the kingdom, i.e., after his father and himself, but before the crown prince, his son.

him, so that the joints of his loins were loosed, and his knees smote one
against another.
7 The king cried aloud to bring in the astrologers, the Chal-de'ans, and the
soothsayers. *And* the king spake, and said to the wise *men* of Babylon,
Whosoever shall read this writing, and shew me the interpretation thereof,
shall be clothed with scarlet, and *have* a chain of gold about his neck, and
shall be the third ruler in the kingdom.
8 Then came in all the king's wise *men:* but they could not read the
writing, nor make known to the king the interpretation thereof.
9 Then was king Bel-shaz'zar greatly troubled, and his countenance was
changed in him, and his lords were astonied.

3. Belshazzar Calls for Daniel

10 ¶*Now* the queen, by reason of the words of the king and his lords, came
into the banquet house: *and* the queen spake and said, O king, live for ever:
let not thy thoughts trouble thee, nor let thy countenance be changed:
11 There is a man in thy kingdom, in whom *is* the spirit of the holy gods;
and in the days of thy father light and understanding and wisdom, like the
wisdom of the gods, was found in him; whom the king Neb-u-chad-nez'zar
thy father, the king, *I say*, thy father, made master of the magicians,
astrologers, Chal-de'ans, *and* soothsayers;
12 Forasmuch as an excellent spirit, and knowledge, and understanding,
interpreting of dreams, and shewing of hard sentences, and dissolving of
doubts, were found in the same Daniel, whom the king named Bel-te-
shaz'zar: now let Daniel be called, and he will shew the interpretation.
13 Then was Daniel brought in before the king. *And* the king spake and
said unto Daniel, *Art* thou that Daniel, which *art* of the children of the
captivity of Judah, whom the king my father brought out of Jewry?
14 I have even heard of thee, that the spirit of the gods *is* in thee, and *that*
light and understanding and excellent wisdom is found in thee.
15 And now the wise *men*, the astrologers, have been brought in before me,
that they should read this writing, and make known unto me the interpreta-
tion thereof: but they could not shew the interpretation of the thing:
16 And I have heard of thee, that thou canst make interpretations, and
dissolve doubts: now if thou canst read the writing, and make known to me
the interpretation thereof, thou shalt be clothed with scarlet, and *have* a
chain of gold about thy neck, and shalt be the third ruler in the kingdom.

4. Daniel Interprets the Writing on the Wall

17 ¶Then Daniel answered and said before the king, Let thy gifts be to
thyself, and give thy rewards to another; yet I will read the writing unto the
king, and make known to him the interpretation.
18 O thou king, the most high God gave Neb-u-chad-nez'zar thy father a
kingdom, and majesty, and glory, and honour:

5:7 Gen 41:42–44 Isa 44:25 Ezek 16:11 Dan 5:11, 16, 29; 6:2, 3
5:9 Job 18:11–14 Ps 18:14 Isa 21:2–4 Jer 6:24 Dan 5:6 Mt 2:3
☆**5:10** Dan 3:9; 6:6
☆**5:11** Gen 41:11–15 2 Sam 14:17 Dan 2:47 4:8, 9; 5:14 Acts 16:16
5:12 Dan 5:14; 6:3
5:13 Dan 1:1; 2:25
5:15 Isa 47:12 Dan 5:8
☆**5:17** 2 Kgs 5:16
☆**5:18** Deut 32:8 Ps 7:17; 47:2 92:8 Dan 2:37 4:2, 17; 5:21

5:10 *the queen.* Probably the widow of Nebuchadnezzar. The queen learns of Belshazzar's predicament about the handwriting on the wall. She commends Daniel to him, expresses her judgment of his religious faith, and tells him how Nebuchadnezzar had been helped by him in interpreting dreams. She says he has "light and understanding and wisdom, like the wisdom of the gods." He calls for Daniel to come.
5:11 *king Nebuchadnezzar thy father.* The Aramaic word for "father" can also mean "predecessor" (in this instance, fifth removed).† Nabonidus, not Nebuchadnezzar, was Belshazzar's father. But Nebuchadnezzar might have been Belshazzar's grandfather on his mother's side. The terms "father" and "son" do not mean the same thing in near-eastern terms. Thus, for example, Jesus is called the son of David, even though he was many generations removed from David.
5:17–23 Daniel needs and wants no rewards for interpreting Belshazzar's sign. He does speak very specifically about the king's sins. First he recounts what the sins of Nebuchadnezzar were and assigns the same sins to his successor: "[Thou] hast lifted up thyself against the Lord of heaven." What greater sins can one commit?

5:19 Prov 16:14 Dan 2:12; 3:6 11:3

19 And for the majesty that he gave him, all people, nations, and
languages, trembled and feared before him: whom he would he slew; and
whom he would he kept alive; and whom he would he set up; and whom he
would he put down.

5:20 Ex 9:17 Prov 16:5, 18 Isa 14:13–15 Jer 13:18 Dan 4:30 Lk 18:14
5:21 Ex 9:14–16 Ps 83:17, 18 Ezek 17:24

20 But when his heart was lifted up, and his mind hardened in pride, he
was deposed from his kingly throne, and they took his glory from him:
21 And he was driven from the sons of men; and his heart was made like
the beasts, and his dwelling *was* with the wild asses: they fed him with grass
like oxen, and his body was wet with the dew of heaven; till he knew that
the most high God ruled in the kingdom of men, and *that* he appointeth
over it whomsoever he will.

5:22 Ex 10:3 2 Chron 33:23 36:12 Acts 4:8–13
5:23 2 Kgs 14:10 Job 12:10 Jer 50:29 Dan 5:3, 4 Hab 2:18, 19 1 Cor 8:4

22 And thou his son, O Bel-shaz′zar, hast not humbled thine heart, though
thou knewest all this;
23 But hast lifted up thyself against the Lord of heaven; and they have
brought the vessels of his house before thee, and thou, and thy lords, thy
wives, and thy concubines, have drunk wine in them; and thou hast praised
the gods of silver, and gold, of brass, iron, wood, and stone, which see not,
nor hear, nor know: and the God in whose hand thy breath *is*, and whose
are all thy ways, hast thou not glorified:
24 Then was the part of the hand sent from him; and this writing was
written.

5:25☆

25 ¶And this *is* the writing that was written, MEʹNE, MEʹNE, TEʹKEL,
U-PHARʹSIN.

5:26 Job 14:14 Isa 13:6, 17 Jer 25:11 Acts 15:18
5:27 Job 31:6 Ps 62:9
5:28☆ Isa 21:2; 45:1, 2 Dan 5:31; 6:28

26 This *is* the interpretation of the thing: MEʹNE; God hath numbered thy
kingdom, and finished it.
27 TEʹKEL; Thou art weighed in the balances, and art found wanting.
28 PEʹRES; Thy kingdom is divided, and given to the Medes and Persians.

5. Daniel Honored and Belshazzar Slain

5:30☆ Isa 21:4–9 Jer 51:11, 31, 39, 57
5:31☆ Dan 6:1; 9:1

29 Then commanded Bel-shaz′zar, and they clothed Daniel with scarlet,
and *put* a chain of gold about his neck, and made a proclamation
concerning him, that he should be the third ruler in the kingdom.
30 In that night was Bel-shaz′zar the king of the Chal-deʹans slain.
31 And Darius the Meʹdi-an took the kingdom, *being* about threescore and
two years old.

F. DANIEL IN THE LIONS' DEN

1. The Plot to Unseat Daniel

6:1☆ Esth 1:1
6:2 Ezra 4:22 Esth 7:4 Dan 2:48, 49 5:16, 29 Mt 18:23 Lk 16:2

6 IT pleased Darius to set over the kingdom an hundred and twenty
princes, which should be over the whole kingdom;
2 And over these three presidents; of whom Daniel *was* first: that the

---

5:25 MENE was the Aramaic term for the weight known as a *maneh* and comes from the verb "to number." TEKEL is Aramaic for the weight known as a *shekel* and is related to the verb meaning "to weigh." UPHARSIN (*Parsin* in TLB, RSV, NIV) is the Aramaic plural of the half-*maneh* weight and is related to the verb meaning "to divide."

5:28 God has chosen to give Belshazzar's kingdom to the Medes and the Persians. The judgment is certain and its fulfillment imminent—it takes place that night.

***5:30** Xenophon and Herodotus, ancient historians,* wrote about the fall of Babylon. The Euphrates River ran through the center of the city. The Medo-Persian armies strategically diverted the river from its normal channel. Then, while the Babylonians, assuming they were safe, were engaged in carousing and revelry, two Babylonian deserters directed the conquering hosts into the city via the dry bed of the river. The defenders were helpless, and that very night Belshazzar was slain as the invaders overran the city.

5:31 *Darius the Median.* Darius was made "king," or governor, over Chaldea after the defeat of Belshazzar by Cyrus the Great. "Darius the Mede is not to be confused with Darius the Persian mentioned in Ezra, Haggai, and Zechariah, nor with the one mentioned in Neh. 12:22."† It seems quite likely that Darius was also known under the name of Gubaru (not to be confused with Ugbaru, who apparently was the general under Cyrus who conquered Babylon and died shortly thereafter).

6:1 Daniel had the unique capacity of commending himself to kings, a gift that came from God, who used

princes might give accounts unto them, and the king should have no
damage.
3 Then this Daniel was preferred above the presidents and princes,
because an excellent spirit *was* in him; and the king thought to set him over
the whole realm.
4 ¶Then the presidents and princes sought to find occasion against Daniel
concerning the kingdom; but they could find none occasion nor fault;
forasmuch as he *was* faithful, neither was there any error or fault found in
him.
5 Then said these men, We shall not find any occasion against this Daniel,
except we find *it* against him concerning the law of his God.
6 Then these presidents and princes assembled together to the king, and
said thus unto him, King Darius, live for ever.
7 All the presidents of the kingdom, the governors, and the princes, the
counsellors, and the captains, have consulted together to establish a royal
statute, and to make a firm decree, that whosoever shall ask a petition of
any God or man for thirty days, save of thee, O king, he shall be cast into
the den of lions.
8 Now, O king, establish the decree, and sign the writing, that it be not
changed, according to the law of the Medes and Persians, which altereth
not.
9 Wherefore king Darius signed the writing and the decree.

2. The Success of the Plot: Daniel in the Lions' Den

10 ¶Now when Daniel knew that the writing was signed, he went into his
house; and his windows being open in his chamber toward Jerusalem, he
kneeled upon his knees three times a day, and prayed, and gave thanks
before his God, as he did aforetime.
11 Then these men assembled, and found Daniel praying and making
supplication before his God.
12 Then they came near, and spake before the king concerning the king's
decree; Hast thou not signed a decree, that every man that shall ask *a
petition* of any God or man within thirty days, save of thee, O king, shall be
cast into the den of lions? The king answered and said, The thing *is* true,
according to the law of the Medes and Persians, which altereth not.
13 Then answered they and said before the king, That Daniel, which *is* of
the children of the captivity of Judah, regardeth not thee, O king, nor the
decree that thou hast signed, but maketh his petition three times a day.

6:3 Gen 41:40; Prov 22:29; Eccles 2:13; Dan 5:12
6:4 Gen 43:18; Ps 37:12, 13; Prov 29:27; Lk 20:20; 23:14, 15; Phil 2:15
6:5 1 Sam 24:17; Jn 19:6, 7; Acts 24:13–16
6:7 Ps 62:4; 64:2–6; Dan 6:16; Mt 12:14
6:8 Esth 3:12; 8:10; Isa 10:1; Dan 6:12, 13; Mt 24:35
☆**6:9** Ps 62:9, 10; 118:9
☆**6:10** 1 Kgs 8:48, 49; 2 Chron 6:38; Ps 34:1; Dan 9:4–19; Col 3:17; 1 Thess 5:17, 18
6:11 Ps 37:32, 33; Dan 6:6
6:12 Esth 1:19; Dan 3:8–12; 6:8
6:13 Esth 3:8; Dan 3:12; Acts 5:29; 17:7

him to accomplish some of the divine purposes. He served pagan monarchs with fidelity but did so without compromising his own faith. He followed the footsteps of Joseph, who served the Pharaoh with faithful regard to the king's interests. In a complex world today most believers are called upon to labor amid secular and ungodly people who do not know their God. This is permissible, so long as they do not compromise their convictions and their convictions square with the Word of God. Darius was delighted with Daniel, knowing full well that he would protect the king's interests and serve him well. Daniel became the number one man in the kingdom—after the monarch himself. But this gave rise to envy and hatred on the part of those who did not share Daniel's faith in God.

6:9 Some have said that no king would dare do what is reported in 6:7–9. Thus they think the account to be legendary. Not so. The new Persian rulers of Babylon thought to consolidate their reign by allowing for no gods other than their own. The unity of the empire would be advanced by getting rid of all the local or regional deities. Wordly wisdom could justify such action on purely political grounds.

6:10 The decree of Darius ran counter to the law of God. The age-old question arose: Shall I obey God or Caesar, when Caesar's law contradicts the law of God? For some this might have required a long time to wrestle with the implications. But Daniel was an old and seasoned warrior. He was so committed that he had no second thoughts; he simply continued his daily devotions in the sight of all, even three times a day. Undoubtedly those who plotted against him did so with the knowledge that Daniel would act exactly the way he did. They knew their man and understood how deep his reverence was for God and his obedience to the law of God.

6:14☆ Mk 6:26

14 Then the king, when he heard *these* words, was sore displeased with himself, and set *his* heart on Daniel to deliver him: and he laboured till the going down of the sun to deliver him.

6:15 Esth 8:8 Ps 94:20, 21 Dan 6:8, 12

15 Then these men assembled unto the king, and said unto the king, Know, O king, that the law of the Medes and Persians *is*, That no decree nor statute which the king establisheth may be changed.

6:16☆ Job 5:19 Ps 37:39, 40 Jer 38:5 Dan 6:20

16 Then the king commanded, and they brought Daniel, and cast *him* into the den of lions. *Now* the king spake and said unto Daniel, Thy God whom thou servest continually, he will deliver thee.

6:17 Lam 3:53 Mt 27:66 Acts 12:4

17 And a stone was brought, and laid upon the mouth of the den; and the king sealed it with his own signet, and with the signet of his lords; that the purpose might not be changed concerning Daniel.

3. The Miraculous Delivery of Daniel

6:18 2 Sam 12:16, 17 Rev 18:22

18 ¶Then the king went to his palace, and passed the night fasting: neither were instruments of musick brought before him: and his sleep went from him.

19 Then the king arose very early in the morning, and went in haste unto the den of lions.

6:20☆ Jer 32:17 Dan 3:17 Hos 12:6

20 And when he came to the den, he cried with a lamentable voice unto Daniel: *and* the king spake and said to Daniel, O Daniel, servant of the living God, is thy God, whom thou servest continually, able to deliver thee from the lions?

21 Then said Daniel unto the king, O king, live for ever.

6:22☆ Num 20:16 Ps 91:11–13 Acts 12:11 2 Tim 4:17 Heb 11:33

22 My God hath sent his angel, and hath shut the lions' mouths, that they have not hurt me: forasmuch as before him innocency was found in me; and also before thee, O king, have I done no hurt.

6:23 Ps 118:8 Isa 26:3 Dan 3:17, 28

23 Then was the king exceeding glad for him, and commanded that they should take Daniel up out of the den. So Daniel was taken up out of the den, and no manner of hurt was found upon him, because he believed in his God.

6:24☆ Deut 19:18, 19 Prov 11:8 Isa 38:13

24 ¶And the king commanded, and they brought those men which had accused Daniel, and they cast *them* into the den of lions, them, their children, and their wives; and the lions had the mastery of them, and brake all their bones in pieces or ever they came at the bottom of the den.

4. Darius Bows before Daniel's God

6:25 Ezra 1:1, 2 Ps 93:1, 2 Dan 3:29; 4:1 6:20 Hos 1:10 1 Pet 1:2

25 ¶Then king Darius wrote unto all people, nations, and languages, that dwell in all the earth; Peace be multiplied unto you.

26 I make a decree, That in every dominion of my kingdom men tremble and fear before the God of Daniel: for he *is* the living God, and stedfast for ever, and his kingdom *that* which shall not be destroyed, and his dominion *shall be even* unto the end.

6:14 Darius knew he had been taken in by the plotters, but there was nothing he could do, for his word was pledged and must be carried out.

6:16 Daniel was cast into the lions' den when he was an old man (probably over eighty). The incident reveals again his undying devotion to God and his refusal to compromise conscience for temporal gain or advantage.

6:20 After a sleepless night of fasting, Darius hastens to the lions' den to see what has happened during the night. He asks the question, "Is thy God able to deliver thee?" For Daniel that was no problem. He believed that his God could deliver him. Whether God chose to deliver him or let him die and go to paradise depended on the will of God, not on the divine ability to stop the lions' mouths. Any believer who is in the will of God can rest comfortably, knowing that whatever God does for him will work for good.

6:22 Daniel attributes his deliverance to an angel of God who sealed shut the mouths of the lions.

6:24 Cheaters never prosper and false witnesses never triumph. The enemies who planned the death of Daniel now die in his place, along with their families. They had mocked God when they mocked his servant, thus God rewarded them appropriately. What they intended for Daniel they themselves received.

27 He delivereth and rescueth, and he worketh signs and wonders in heaven and in earth, who hath delivered Daniel from the power of the lions.
28 So this Daniel prospered in the reign of Darius, and in the reign of Cyrus the Persian.

II. DANIEL'S TWO DREAMS (7:1—8:27)

A. THE VISION OF THE FOUR HUGE ANIMALS

1. The Four Beasts

7 IN the first year of Bel-shaz'zar king of Babylon Daniel had a dream and visions of his head upon his bed: then he wrote the dream, *and* told the sum of the matters.
2 Daniel spake and said, I saw in my vision by night, and, behold, the four winds of the heaven strove upon the great sea.
3 And four great beasts came up from the sea, diverse one from another.
4 The first *was* like a lion, and had eagle's wings: I beheld till the wings thereof were plucked, and it was lifted up from the earth, and made stand upon the feet as a man, and a man's heart was given to it.
5 And behold another beast, a second, like to a bear, and it raised up itself on one side, and *it had* three ribs in the mouth of it between the teeth of it: and they said thus unto it, Arise, devour much flesh.
6 After this I beheld, and lo another, like a leopard, which had upon the back of it four wings of a fowl; the beast had also four heads; and dominion was given to it.
7 After this I saw in the night visions, and behold a fourth beast, dreadful and terrible, and strong exceedingly; and it had great iron teeth: it devoured and brake in pieces, and stamped the residue with the feet of it: and it *was* diverse from all the beasts that *were* before it; and it had ten horns.
8 I considered the horns, and, behold, there came up among them another little horn, before whom there were three of the first horns plucked up by the roots: and, behold, in this horn *were* eyes like the eyes of man, and a mouth speaking great things.

2. The Ancient of Days: Messiah's Enthronement

9 I beheld till the thrones were cast down, and the Ancient of days did sit, whose garment *was* white as snow, and the hair of his head like the pure wool: his throne *was like* the fiery flame, *and* his wheels *as* burning fire.
10 A fiery stream issued and came forth from before him: thousand thousands ministered unto him, and ten thousand times ten thousand stood before him: the judgment was set, and the books were opened.
11 I beheld then because of the voice of the great words which the horn

☆**6:28**
☆**7:1** Num 12:6; Job 33:14–16; Dan 1:7; 2:1, 26–28; 4:5–9; Jer 36:4; Joel 2:28
7:2 Rev 7:1
7:3 Rev 13:1
☆**7:4**
☆**7:5**
7:7 Rev 12:3; 13:1
☆**7:8**
☆**7:9** Ezek 1:13; 10:2, 6; Mic 5:2; Mk 9:3; Rev 1:14
☆**7:10** Ps 50:3; 97:3; Isa 30:27; Dan 7:22, 26; 12:1; Mt 25:31; Rev 5:11; 20:11–15
☆**7:11** Rev 19:20; 20:10

6:28 *So this Daniel prospered.* God brought forth good out of evil.
7:1 Daniel speaks now of a dream or vision he had received during the reign of Belshazzar. Chronologically this chapter fits after chapter four and before chapters five and six.
7:4 *a lion, and had eagle's wings.* Archeologists have found winged lions among the ruins of Nimrud and Babylon. Here they symbolize the Babylonian empire.
7:5 *another beast,* i.e., "the second animal." The total vision comprised four animals, of which the first was the winged lion. There is also a bear, a leopard, and the fourth animal too dreadful to be described. These animals have been thought to represent either Babylon, Media, Persia, and Greece or Babylon, Medo-Persia, Greece, and Rome.
7:8 *little horn.* Horns symbolize power. Here they are applied to kings. Some interpret the fourth kingdom to be Greece and identify the little horn as Antiochus Epiphanes, the Seleucid ruler who tried to halt Jewish worship. Others identify the fourth kingdom as Rome and think the little horn refers to a future antichrist.
7:9–14 These verses refer to the *Son of Man*—Jesus Christ—who sits on the throne of an eternal kingdom. Before him all nations bow. The vision is general, however, not specific. The details cannot be extracted from it.

spake: I beheld *even* till the beast was slain, and his body destroyed, and
given to the burning flame.
12 As concerning the rest of the beasts, they had their dominion taken
away: yet their lives were prolonged for a season and time.
7:13☆ 13 I saw in the night visions, and, behold, *one* like the Son of man came
with the clouds of heaven, and came to the Ancient of days, and they
brought him near before him.
7:14 14 And there was given him dominion, and glory, and a kingdom, that all
Ps 2:6–8; 72:17 people, nations, and languages, should serve him: his dominion *is* an
102:22 Dan 7:27 everlasting dominion, which shall not pass away, and his kingdom *that*
Eph 1:20–22 Heb 12:28 which shall not be destroyed.
Rev 1:6

3. The Angel's Interpretation of Daniel's Dream

7:15 15 I Daniel was grieved in my spirit in the midst of *my* body, and the
Dan 4:19; 7:28 visions of my head troubled me.
7:16 16 I came near unto one of them that stood by, and asked him the truth of
Dan 8:13–16 10:5, 6, 11, 12 all this. So he told me, and made me know the interpretation of the things.
Zech 1:8–11 17 These great beasts, which are four, *are* four kings, *which* shall arise out
Rev 5:5 7:13, 14 of the earth.
7:18 18 But the saints of the most High shall take the kingdom, and possess the
Dan 7:22, 25, 27 2 Tim 2:11, 12 kingdom for ever, even for ever and ever.
Rev 2:26, 27 19 Then I would know the truth of the fourth beast, which was diverse
20:4 from all the others, exceeding dreadful, whose teeth *were of* iron, and his
nails *of* brass; *which* devoured, brake in pieces, and stamped the residue
with his feet;
20 And of the ten horns that *were* in his head, and *of* the other which came
up, and before whom three fell; even *of* that horn that had eyes, and a
mouth that spake very great things, whose look *was* more stout than his
fellows.
7:21 21 I beheld, and the same horn made war with the saints, and prevailed
Rev 13:7 against them;
7:22 22 Until the Ancient of days came, and judgment was given to the saints
Dan 7:10 1 Cor 6:2, 3 of the most High; and the time came that the saints possessed the kingdom.
7:23☆ 23 Thus he said, The fourth beast shall be the fourth kingdom upon earth,
which shall be diverse from all kingdoms, and shall devour the whole earth,
and shall tread it down, and break it in pieces.
7:24☆ 24 And the ten horns out of this kingdom *are* ten kings *that* shall arise:
and another shall rise after them; and he shall be diverse from the first, and
he shall subdue three kings.
7:25☆ 25 And he shall speak *great* words against the most High, and shall wear
Dan 4:2; 11:36 12:7, 14 out the saints of the most High, and think to change times and laws: and
Rev 12:14 13:6, 7 they shall be given into his hand until a time and times and the dividing of
time.

7:13 *the Son of man came.* Daniel here refers to the coming of the Lord Jesus at the end of the age. "The Son of man" is a title later applied to the Messiah and is so used in the New Testament. The Second Coming of Christ is prophesied repeatedly in the Old Testament. Christ himself spoke of his Second Advent (Matt. 25:31; John 14:3). So did the apostles (Acts 2:30, 1 Tim. 6:14) and the angels who spoke God's message to the disciples at the time of the ascension (Acts 1:10, 11).

7:23 *the fourth kingdom,* or, "the fourth world power." Usually believed to be a revived Roman Empire—see 2:40.†

7:24 The visions of the *ten horns* and ten toes are parallel. 7:27 shows that the world ruler of the end of this age will suffer final defeat by Christ. The little horn of this verse, which defeats three of the ten kings, should not be confused with the "little horn" of Dan. 8:9, which is to emerge from the third kingdom (the Greek empire, established by Alexander the Great). The horn mentioned here will emerge from the fourth kingdom (the latter-day Roman empire). *another shall rise,* i.e., "another king shall rise." This probably refers to the future Antichrist of 2 Thess. 2:3, 4.

7:25 *change times and laws,* i.e., "change all laws, morals, and customs." Perhaps the meaning is, "change right to wrong and wrong to right."†

26 But the judgment shall sit, and they shall take away his dominion, to
consume and to destroy *it* unto the end.
27 And the kingdom and dominion, and the greatness of the kingdom
under the whole heaven, shall be given to the people of the saints of the
most High, whose kingdom *is* an everlasting kingdom, and all dominions
shall serve and obey him.
28 Hitherto *is* the end of the matter. As for me Daniel, my cogitations
much troubled me, and my countenance changed in me: but I kept the
matter in my heart.

7:26 Rev 17:14; 19:2
7:27 Ps 2:6–12; 22:27; 86:9; 145:13; Isa 60:12; Dan 2:44; 4:34; 7:14, 18, 22; Rev 11:1; 20:4
☆7:28 Lk 2:19, 51

B. THE VISION OF THE RAM AND THE BUCK (HE) GOAT

1. The Ram and the Buck (He) Goat and the Little Horn

8 IN the third year of the reign of king Bel-shaz′zar a vision appeared
unto me, *even unto* me Daniel, after that which appeared unto me at
the first.
2 And I saw in a vision; and it came to pass, when I saw, that I *was* at
Shu′shan *in* the palace, which *is* in the province of E′lam; and I saw in a
vision, and I was by the river of U′la-i.
3 Then I lifted up mine eyes, and saw, and, behold, there stood before the
river a ram which had *two* horns: and the *two* horns *were* high; but one *was*
higher than the other, and the higher came up last.
4 I saw the ram pushing westward, and northward, and southward; so
that no beasts might stand before him, neither *was there any* that could
deliver out of his hand; but he did according to his will, and became great.
5 And as I was considering, behold, an he goat came from the west on the
face of the whole earth, and touched not the ground: and the goat *had* a
notable horn between his eyes.
6 And he came to the ram that had *two* horns, which I had seen standing
before the river, and ran unto him in the fury of his power.
7 And I saw him come close unto the ram, and he was moved with choler
against him, and smote the ram, and brake his two horns: and there was no
power in the ram to stand before him, but he cast him down to the ground,
and stamped upon him: and there was none that could deliver the ram out
of his hand.
8 Therefore the he goat waxed very great: and when he was strong, the
great horn was broken; and for it came up four notable ones toward the
four winds of heaven.
9 And out of one of them came forth a little horn, which waxed exceeding
great, toward the south, and toward the east, and toward the pleasant *land*.

☆8:1 Num 12:6; Esth 1:2; 2:8; Neh 1:1
☆8:2 Gen 10:22; 14:1; Isa 11:11; Jer 25:25; Ezek 32:34; Dan 7:2, 15
☆8:3 Dan 8:20
8:4 Deut 33:17; 1 Kgs 22:11; Ezek 34:21; Mic 5:8
☆8:5 Dan 8:8, 21; 11:3
☆8:8 2 Chron 26:16; Dan 5:20; 7:2; Rev 7:1
☆8:9 Dan 8:23; 11:16, 41

7:28 Daniel kept in mind all that God had revealed to him. He kept the vision in his heart, not to keep it *from* us but to keep it *for* us. It has been given to us in the Scriptures, which we are to treasure up in our hearts. However much the vision may puzzle us, we can be assured that God is working out his own plan through the church, a plan men cannot annul, abridge, change, or destroy.

8:1 Chronologically this chapter precedes chapter five. The vision came in the last year of Belshazzar's reign. The vision that came to him previously came while he was asleep. This one came when he was awake.

8:2 *Shushan* was one of the several capitals of the empire at this time.

8:3 *two horns.* These represent Media and Persia (cf. 8:20).

8:5 *he goat,* i.e., "Greece" (cf. 8:21). *a notable horn,* i.e., "Alexander the Great."

8:8 *and for it came up four notable ones,* i.e., "in its place grew four good-sized horns." The four principal successors of Alexander the Great were Ptolemy I of Egypt, Seleucus of Babylonia, Antigonus of Syria and Asia Minor, and Antipater of Macedonia and Greece.†

8:9ff Daniel here returns to the ram and he-goat visions, which have to do with the second and third of the four great kingdoms. Earlier in chapter 2, they are the silver and brass or bronze kingdoms; in 7:5, 6 they are the bear and leopard kingdoms. The two kingdoms are Medo-Persia and Greece. The little horn, growing slowly at first, is said by some to be Antiochus Epiphanes (175–164 B.C.) who in 168 B.C., profaned the temple and tried to crush Jewish religion altogether. They also say Antiochus is a type of the last world

8:10☆ 2 Kgs 19:22, 23; 2 Chron 32:15–17; Isa 37:23; Jer 48:26, 42; Ezek 46:14; Dan 7:7; 8:7; 11:31; Rev 12:4

10 And it waxed great, *even* to the host of heaven; and it cast down *some*
of the host and of the stars to the ground, and stamped upon them.

8:11☆

11 Yea, he magnified *himself* even to the prince of the host, and by him the
daily *sacrifice* was taken away, and the place of his sanctuary was cast
down.

8:12☆ Isa 59:14

12 And an host was given *him* against the daily *sacrifice* by reason of
transgression, and it cast down the truth to the ground; and it practised,
and prospered.

8:13 Deut 33:2; Ps 74:10; 79:5; Isa 63:18; Dan 4:13, 23; 12:6, 8; Lk 10:22; 21:24; Heb 10:29; Rev 6:10; 11:2

13 ¶Then I heard one saint speaking, and another saint said unto that
certain *saint* which spake, How long *shall be* the vision *concerning* the daily
sacrifice, and the transgression of desolation, to give both the sanctuary and
the host to be trodden under foot?

8:14☆ Dan 7:25; 12:7, 11; Rev 11:2, 3; 12:14; 13:5

14 And he said unto me, Unto two thousand and three hundred days; then
shall the sanctuary be cleansed.

2. Gabriel Explains the Dream

8:15 Dan 7:13; 10:16, 18

15 ¶And it came to pass, when I, *even* I Daniel, had seen the vision, and
sought for the meaning, then, behold, there stood before me as the
appearance of a man.

8:16 Dan 9:21; Lk 1:19, 26

16 And I heard a man's voice between *the banks of* U'la-i, which called,
and said, Gabriel, make this *man* to understand the vision.

8:17 Gen 17:3; Ezek 1:28; 6:2; 44:4; Dan 2:46; 8:19; 11:35, 40

17 So he came near where I stood: and when he came, I was afraid, and
fell upon my face: but he said unto me, Understand, O son of man: for at
the time of the end *shall be* the vision.

8:18 Ezek 2:2; Dan 10:9, 10, 16, 18; Lk 9:32

18 Now as he was speaking with me, I was in a deep sleep on my face
toward the ground: but he touched me, and set me upright.

8:19 Dan 8:15–17

19 And he said, Behold, I will make thee know what shall be in the last
end of the indignation: for at the time appointed the end *shall be*.

20 The ram which thou sawest having *two* horns *are* the kings of Me'di-a
and Persia.

21 And the rough goat *is* the king of Grecia: and the great horn that *is*
between his eyes *is* the first king.

22 Now that being broken, whereas four stood up for it, four kingdoms
shall stand up out of the nation, but not in his power.

8:23☆

23 And in the latter time of their kingdom, when the transgressors are
come to the full, a king of fierce countenance, and understanding dark
sentences, shall stand up.

8:24☆ Dan 8:11–13; 12:7; Rev 13:3–9; 16:6; 17:12–17

24 And his power shall be mighty, but not by his own power: and he shall
destroy wonderfully, and shall prosper, and practise, and shall destroy the
mighty and the holy people.

8:25 Job 34:20; Dan 2:34, 45

25 And through his policy also he shall cause craft to prosper in his hand;

---

dictator (the beast of the Revelation) who is yet to come. Thus both Antiochus (the type) and the beast (antitype) are said to be the small or little horn. *the pleasant land,* i.e., "the glorious land," or, "the land of Israel." Israel was attacked by Antiochus IV Epiphanes, with a further fulfillment of this prophecy indicated for the future. (See 8:17, 19, 23.)†

8:10 *host of heaven . . . and of the stars,* i.e., "the *people of God and . . . some of their leaders.*"† (See 8:24.)

8:11 *the prince,* i.e., "the commander." (cf. Josh. 5:13–15.)†

8:12 Paraphrased: "But the army of heaven was restrained from destroying him for this transgression. As a result, truth and righteousness perished, and evil triumphed and prospered." The Hebrew text is obscure.†

8:14 *two thousand and three hundred days,* literally, "two thousand and three hundred evenings and mornings"—1,150 days.

8:23 The literal description here is of one who possesses great shrewdness and intelligence—one who understands riddles and is skilled in intrigues. This is probably a reference to Antiochus Epiphanes and further future fulfillment by the Antichrist at the end of human history.†

8:24 *not by his own power.* He was assisted by his allies, by a man of the Jews, and by God, who had ordained what was to take place.

and he shall magnify *himself* in his heart, and by peace shall destroy many:
he shall also stand up against the Prince of princes; but he shall be broken
without hand.
26 And the vision of the evening and the morning which was told *is* true:
wherefore shut thou up the vision; for it *shall be* for many days.
27 And I Daniel fainted, and was sick *certain* days; afterward I rose up,
and did the king's business; and I was astonished at the vision, but none
understood *it*.

☆8:26

8:27 Dan 7:28; 8:17 Hab 3:16

III. DANIEL'S PRAYER AND THE VISION OF THE SEVENTY WEEKS (9:1–27)

A. THE PRAYER AND THE VISION

9 IN the first year of Darius the son of A-has-u-e'rus, of the seed of the
Medes, which was made king over the realm of the Chal-de'ans;
2 In the first year of his reign I Daniel understood by books the number of
the years, whereof the word of the LORD came to Jer-e-mi'ah the prophet,
that he would accomplish seventy years in the desolations of Jerusalem.
3 ¶And I set my face unto the Lord God, to seek by prayer and
supplications, with fasting, and sackcloth, and ashes:
4 And I prayed unto the LORD my God, and made my confession, and
said, O Lord, the great and dreadful God, keeping the covenant and mercy
to them that love him, and to them that keep his commandments;
5 We have sinned, and have committed iniquity, and have done wickedly,
and have rebelled, even by departing from thy precepts and from thy
judgments:
6 Neither have we hearkened unto thy servants the prophets, which spake
in thy name to our kings, our princes, and our fathers, and to all the people
of the land.
7 O Lord, righteousness *belongeth* unto thee, but unto us confusion of
faces, as at this day; to the men of Judah, and to the inhabitants of
Jerusalem, and unto all Israel, *that are* near, and *that are* far off, through all
the countries whither thou hast driven them, because of their trespass that
they have trespassed against thee.
8 O Lord, to us *belongeth* confusion of face, to our kings, to our princes,
and to our fathers, because we have sinned against thee.
9 To the Lord our God *belong* mercies and forgivenesses, though we have
rebelled against him;
10 Neither have we obeyed the voice of the LORD our God, to walk in his
laws, which he set before us by his servants the prophets.
11 Yea, all Israel have transgressed thy law, even by departing, that they
might not obey thy voice; therefore the curse is poured upon us, and the
oath that *is* written in the law of Moses the servant of God, because we
have sinned against him.

9:1 Dan 5:31; 11:1
☆9:2 2 Chron 36:21 Ezra 1:1 Jer 25:11; 29:10 Mic 3:12 Zech 7:5
☆9:3
9:4 Deut 7:9, 21 Neh 9:32 Nah 1:2–7 Jas 2:5 1 Jn 5:2, 3
9:5 Ps 119:176 Isa 53:6 Lam 1:18, 20 Dan 9:11
9:6 Jer 44:4, 5, 21
9:7 Ezra 9:6, 7 Ps 44:15 Jer 2:26, 27 3:25; 23:6 33:16 Dan 9:18
☆9:9 Neh 9:17 Ps 106:43 130:4 Dan 9:5, 6
9:10 2 Kgs 17:13–15 18:12

8:26 *God has fixed the length of time during* which the daily sacrifice would cease. That *the vision of the evening and morning* was true simply confirms the fact—however unlikely it seemed—that God would allow his sanctuary to be profaned.

9:2 Daniel obviously had a copy of the prophecy of Jeremiah and understood its content. Jeremiah 29:10 expressly foretold the seventy years' captivity. The time of the captivity was now nearing its end. During the captivity the holy city of Jerusalem would lie desolate.

9:3 Fearing that the sins of the people might cause God to defer deliverance, Daniel earnestly pleaded with him to end the captivity.

9:9 Two conditions exist that make possible the forgiveness of sins by God: (1) God's own mercy permits it—God is holy and righteous, but he is also merciful, which caused him to vindicate the claims of his character and at the same time provide a way of forgiveness for the sinner; and (2) the sacrifice of Jesus is the ground of forgiveness, for "without shedding of blood there is no remission" (Heb. 9:22). God's forgiveness of sins is not based on the character, the teaching, or the example of Jesus. It is based on his shed blood (Eph. 1:7).

12 And he hath confirmed his words, which he spake against us, and
against our judges that judged us, by bringing upon us a great evil: for
under the whole heaven hath not been done as hath been done upon
Jerusalem.
13 As *it is* written in the law of Moses, all this evil is come upon us: yet
made we not our prayer before the LORD our God, that we might turn from
our iniquities, and understand thy truth.
14 Therefore hath the LORD watched upon the evil, and brought it upon
us: for the LORD our God *is* righteous in all his works which he doeth: for
we obeyed not his voice.
15 And now, O Lord our God, that hast brought thy people forth out of
the land of Egypt with a mighty hand, and hast gotten thee renown, as at
this day; we have sinned, we have done wickedly.
16 ¶O Lord, according to all thy righteousness, I beseech thee, let thine
anger and thy fury be turned away from thy city Jerusalem, thy holy
mountain: because for our sins, and for the iniquities of our fathers,
Jerusalem and thy people *are become* a reproach to all *that are* about us.
17 Now therefore, O our God, hear the prayer of thy servant, and his
supplications, and cause thy face to shine upon thy sanctuary that is
desolate, for the Lord's sake.
18 O my God, incline thine ear, and hear; open thine eyes, and behold our
desolations, and the city which is called by thy name: for we do not present
our supplications before thee for our righteousnesses, but for thy great
mercies.
19 O Lord, hear; O Lord, forgive; O Lord, hearken and do; defer not, for
thine own sake, O my God: for thy city and thy people are called by thy
name.

B. GABRIEL'S INTERPRETATION OF THE DREAM

20 ¶And whiles I *was* speaking, and praying, and confessing my sin and
the sin of my people Israel, and presenting my supplication before the
LORD my God for the holy mountain of my God;
21 Yea, whiles I *was* speaking in prayer, even the man Gabriel, whom I
had seen in the vision at the beginning, being caused to fly swiftly, touched
me about the time of the evening oblation.
22 And he informed *me*, and talked with me, and said, O Daniel, I am now
come forth to give thee skill and understanding.
23 At the beginning of thy supplications the commandment came forth,
and I am come to shew *thee;* for thou *art* greatly beloved: therefore
understand the matter, and consider the vision.
24 Seventy weeks are determined upon thy people and upon thy holy city,
to finish the transgression, and to make an end of sins, and to make

9:12 Ps 82:2–7 Isa 44:26 Jer 44:2–6 Zech 1:6
9:13☆ Lev 26:14–45 Deut 28:15–68 Isa 9:13 Jer 2:30; 5:3 Dan 9:11
9:14☆ Jer 31:28; 44:27 Dan 9:7
9:15 Deut 5:15 Neh 9:10 Jer 32:20 2 Cor 1:10
9:16 Ps 87:1-3 Ezek 5:14 Dan 9:20 Joel 3:17 Zech 8:3 Mt 23:31, 32
9:17 Num 6:24–26 Ps 80:3, 7, 19 Lam 5:18
9:18 Ps 80:14 Isa 37:17 Jer 7:12; 36:7 Ezek 36:22
9:19 Ps 44:23 74:10, 11
9:20 Ps 145:18 Isa 6:5; 58:9 Dan 9:3; 10:12
9:21☆ Ex 29:39 1 Kgs 18:36 Ezra 9:4 Dan 8:16 Acts 12:7 Heb 1:7
9:22 Dan 8:16; 10:21 Zech 1:9, 14 Rev 4:1
9:23 Mt 24:15
9:24☆ Lev 25:8 Num 14:34 2 Chron 29:24 Isa 51:6, 8 53:10 Rom 3:21; 5:10 2 Cor 5:18–20

9:13, 14 What had happened was due to the sins of God's people, and the punishment continued because of failure to pray with humble, penitent, and obedient hearts.
9:21 *the man Gabriel,* i.e., the angel Gabriel who appeared in human form.
9:24 *Seventy weeks,* or, "four hundred and ninety years." There have been many different interpretations of this prophecy of the seventy weeks. One thing is quite apparent. Each week *(heptad)* must comprise a period of seven years, making a total of 490 years. Daniel breaks down this period into three sections: the first comprises seven weeks, or forty-nine years; the second section comprises a period of sixty-two weeks, or four hundred and thirty-four years; and the third section comprises one week, or seven years. Some say that the seventy weeks follow each other without interruption. This view encounters difficulties. The Hebrew text says that after the sixty-nine weeks (9:26) the anointed one is to be cut off (this refers, of course, to Christ). In addition, using the figure of 490 years, none of the three dates when decrees were issued (538, 457, and 445 B.C.) comes out to fit the date for the cutting off of the anointed one. Some say that sixty-nine weeks elapsed and the Messiah was cut off. Then there is an interruption and the seventieth week takes place during the period of the great tribulation. The early church fathers held this view. Some who hold that view today believe that the New Testament church age was an unrevealed mystery in the Old Testament, so

reconciliation for iniquity, and to bring in everlasting righteousness, and to
seal up the vision and prophecy, and to anoint the most Holy.
25 Know therefore and understand, *that* from the going forth of the
commandment to restore and to build Jerusalem unto the Messiah the
Prince *shall be* seven weeks, and threescore and two weeks: the street shall
be built again, and the wall, even in troublous times.
26 And after threescore and two weeks shall Messiah be cut off, but not
for himself: and the people of the prince that shall come shall destroy the
city and the sanctuary; and the end thereof *shall be* with a flood, and unto
the end of the war desolations are determined.
27 And he shall confirm the covenant with many for one week: and in the
midst of the week he shall cause the sacrifice and the oblation to cease, and
for the overspreading of abominations he shall make *it* desolate, even until
the consummation, and that determined shall be poured upon the desolate.

☆**9:25** Ezra 4:24 6:1–15 Neh 2:1–8; 3:1 Isa 9:6 Jn 1:41; 4:25

9:26 Isa 53:8 Nah 1:8 Mt 24:2 Mk 9:12; 13:2 Lk 19:43, 44 24:26

☆**9:27** Isa 10:23, 28:22 Dan 11:31 Mt 24:15 Mk 13:14 Lk 21:20

IV. THE VISION OF THE LATTER DAYS (10:1—12:13)

A. AN ANGEL APPEARS TO DANIEL

10 IN the third year of Cyrus king of Persia a thing was revealed unto
Daniel, whose name was called Bel-te-shaz'zar; and the thing *was*
true, but the time appointed *was* long: and he understood the thing, and
had understanding of the vision.
2 In those days I Daniel was mourning three full weeks.
3 I ate no pleasant bread, neither came flesh nor wine in my mouth,
neither did I anoint myself at all, till three whole weeks were fulfilled.
4 And in the four and twentieth day of the first month, as I was by the
side of the great river, which *is* Hid'de-kel;

☆**10:1** Dan 1:17, 21 2:21; 6:28

10:2 Ezra 9:4 Neh 1:4

☆**10:3**

10:4 Ezek 1:3 Dan 8:2

---

that this age constitutes a parenthesis until the beginning of the seventieth week in the future. Still others who hold to the deferment of the seventieth week say that the New Testament church was often alluded to in the Old Testament. 9:25 indicates that the sixty-nine weeks started from the time the command to rebuild the temple was given. This may refer to the divine decree or one of three historical edicts: (1) the decree of King Cyrus in 538 B.C. (Ezra 1:1–4); (2) Artaxerxes' order to Ezra in 457 B.C. to erect the walls of Jerusalem (see Ezra 7:6, 7; 9:9); or (3) the command for Nehemiah in 445 B.C. to finish rebuilding the walls, which Ezra had not yet done. The first date does not come near the time of Christ's ministry. The third date is too late, unless a lunar calendar is used. The second date, using solar years, is the only one that comes out correctly. It places the commencement of Christ's ministry at A.D. 27. Ezra and Nehemiah indicate that Jerusalem was rebuilt in forty-nine troubled years. That period is followed by the sixty-two weeks, after which the Messiah is cut off. One's view of the last week depends on one's whole scheme of prophetic interpretation. Herbert C. Leupold, in his *Exposition of Daniel* (Baker Book House, 1969), holds that the passage uses numbers symbolically (as in 12:11, 12), and that it "covers the whole period of time from Daniel to the consummation of all things"(p. 405).

9:25 *seven weeks, and threescore and two weeks.* This totals four hundred eighty three years, instead of the four hundred ninety years mentioned in 9:24, leaving seven years unaccounted for at the time of Messiah's death. For their future fulfillment, see 9:27 and the Revelation. Or, consider the destruction of Jerusalem in A.D. 70 by Titus and the subsequent slaughter of one million Jews during the following three and a half years as at least a partial fulfillment of this prophecy.†

9:27 In the Old and New Testaments what is described as the "abomination of desolation" (in the Hebrew and the Greek) appears in 9:27; 11:31; 12:11; Matt. 24:15; and Mark 13:14. It has three different fulfillments. The first occurred under Antiochus Epiphanes in 168 B.C. when the temple was desecrated, the services suspended, a statute of Zeus set up, and the Holy of Holies profaned. A pig was also offered as a sacrifice. The second fulfillment occurred in A.D. 70 under Titus and Vespasian when Roman legions sacked the city, burned the temple, and defiled the sanctuary. The third fulfillment is yet future; it will come during the time of the great tribulation. Dan. 9 is regarded by some as a rather comprehensive description of the New Testament Antichrist. *he shall cause the sacrifice and the oblation to cease,* Antiochus Eipinanes, the conquerer, did precisely this. Moreover, in A.D. 70 the temple was itself destroyed and sacrifices ended to this very hour.

10:1 Daniel attested to the truth of the vision he had. It came during the reign of Cyrus, for whom he worked and with whom he was well acquainted.

10:3 In their youth Daniel and his friends ate vegetables and drank only water. Here we note that Daniel's lifestyle had changed. He was eating meat and drinking wine. But even now he would not consume pork, which was forbidden.

10:5 Jer 10:9; Ezek 9:2; Dan 12:6, 7; Rev 1:13; 15:6

5 Then I lifted up mine eyes, and looked, and behold a certain man
clothed in linen, whose loins *were* girded with fine gold of U'phaz:
6 His body also *was* like the beryl, and his face as the appearance of
lightning, and his eyes as lamps of fire, and his arms and his feet like in
colour to polished brass, and the voice of his words like the voice of a
multitude.

10:7☆ 2 Kgs 6:17; Ezek 12:18; Acts 9:7; Heb 12:21
10:8 Gen 32:34; Ex 3:3; Dan 7:28; 8:27; Hab 3:16; Rev 1:17
10:9 Gen 15:12; Dan 8:18

7 And I Daniel alone saw the vision: for the men that were with me saw
not the vision; but a great quaking fell upon them, so that they fled to hide
themselves.
8 Therefore I was left alone, and saw this great vision, and there remained
no strength in me: for my comeliness was turned in me into corruption, and
I retained no strength.
9 Yet heard I the voice of his words: and when I heard the voice of his
words, then was I in a deep sleep on my face, and my face toward the
ground.
10 ¶And, behold, an hand touched me, which set me upon my knees and
upon the palms of my hands.

10:11☆ Job 4:14, 15; Ezek 2:1; Dan 8:16, 17; Mk 16:8

11 And he said unto me, O Daniel, a man greatly beloved, understand the
words that I speak unto thee, and stand upright: for unto thee am I now
sent. And when he had spoken this word unto me, I stood trembling.

B. THE ANGEL ENCOURAGES DANIEL

10:12 Dan 9:20–23; 10:2, 3, 19; Acts 10:30, 31
10:13☆ Dan 10:21; 12:1; Zech 3:1; Eph 6:12; Jude 9; Rev 12:7
10:14 Dan 2:28; 8:26; 12:4, 9; Hos 3:5; 2 Thess 3:1; Heb 2:3
10:15 Ezek 24:27; 33:22; Lk 1:20
10:16 Ex 4:10; Josh 5:14; Isa 6:7; Jer 1:9; Dan 7:15; 8:17, 27; 10:8, 9
10:17 Ex 24:10, 11; Isa 6:1–5; Mt 22:43, 44
10:18 Isa 35:3, 4
10:19 Josh 1:6–9; Isa 35:4; 43:1; Dan 10:12
10:20☆ Dan 8:21; 11:2

12 Then said he unto me, Fear not, Daniel: for from the first day that thou
didst set thine heart to understand, and to chasten thyself before thy God,
thy words were heard, and I am come for thy words.
13 But the prince of the kingdom of Persia withstood me one and twenty
days: but, lo, Michael, one of the chief princes, came to help me; and I
remained there with the kings of Persia.
14 Now I am come to make thee understand what shall befall thy people
in the latter days: for yet the vision *is* for *many* days.
15 And when he had spoken such words unto me, I set my face toward the
ground, and I became dumb.
16 And, behold, *one* like the similitude of the sons of men touched my lips:
then I opened my mouth, and spake, and said unto him that stood before
me, O my lord, by the vision my sorrows are turned upon me, and I have
retained no strength.
17 For how can the servant of this my lord talk with this my lord? for as
for me, straightway there remained no strength in me, neither is there
breath left in me.
18 Then there came again and touched me *one* like the appearance of a
man, and he strengthened me,
19 And said, O man greatly beloved, fear not: peace *be* unto thee, be
strong, yea, be strong. And when he had spoken unto me, I was
strengthened, and said, Let my lord speak; for thou hast strengthened me.
20 Then said he, Knowest thou wherefore I come unto thee? and now will
I return to fight with the prince of Persia: and when I am gone forth, lo, the
prince of Grecia shall come.

10:7 The companions of Daniel did not see the vision. Yet something caused them to quake with fear and fly *from the scene.*

10:11 *I have been sent.* Angels are God's messengers who go where they are sent and speak what they have been told to say. They are utterly faithful, so what the receiver of the message hears can be regarded as trustworthy.

10:13 *the prince of the kingdom of Persia.* Nations were thought to have a guardian angel watching over them. Israel regarded Michael as its guardian angel. Here he came to the aid of Daniel.

10:20, 21 The angel who came to Daniel had been detained by a superior, evil angel. After coming to Daniel, he returned to fight against the prince of Persia. But he needed help, which was given to him in the person of Michael, who is more powerful than he. Michael was the prince of the people of Israel.

21 But I will shew thee that which is noted in the scripture of truth: and
there is none that holdeth with me in these things, but Michael your prince.

10:21
Dan 12:1, 4

C. THE INTERPRETATION OF DANIEL'S VISION

1. From the Persian Empire to Alexander's Death

11 ALSO I in the first year of Darius the Mede, *even* I, stood to
confirm and to strengthen him.

☆**11:1**
Dan 5:31; 9:1

2 And now will I shew thee the truth. Behold, there shall stand up yet
three kings in Persia; and the fourth shall be far richer than *they* all: and by
his strength through his riches he shall stir up all against the realm of
Grecia.

☆**11:2**
Dan 8:21, 26
10:1, 20, 21

3 And a mighty king shall stand up, that shall rule with great dominion,
and do according to his will.

☆**11:3**
Dan 5:19
8:4, 5, 21
11:16, 36

4 And when he shall stand up, his kingdom shall be broken, and shall be
divided toward the four winds of heaven; and not to his posterity, nor
according to his dominion which he ruled: for his kingdom shall be plucked
up, even for others beside those.

11:4
Jer 49:36
Ezek 37:9
Dan 7:2; 8:8
Zech 2:6
Lk 12:20
Rev 7:1

2. Wars between the Ptolemaic and Seleucid Empires

5 ¶And the king of the south shall be strong, and *one* of his princes; and
he shall be strong above him, and have dominion; his dominion *shall be* a
great dominion.

☆**11:5**
Dan 11:9, 11, 14, 25, 40

6 And in the end of years they shall join themselves together; for the
king's daughter of the south shall come to the king of the north to make an
agreement: but she shall not retain the power of the arm; neither shall he
stand, nor his arm: but she shall be given up, and they that brought her,
and he that begat her, and he that strengthened her in *these* times.

☆**11:6**
Dan 11:7, 13, 15, 40

7 But out of a branch of her roots shall *one* stand up in his estate, which
shall come with an army, and shall enter into the fortress of the king of the
north, and shall deal against them, and shall prevail:

☆**11:7**
Dan 11:19, 38, 39

8 And shall also carry captives into Egypt their gods, with their princes,
and with their precious vessels of silver and of gold; and he shall continue
more years than the king of the north.

11:8
Isa 37:19
46:1, 2
Jer 43:12, 13

9 So the king of the south shall come into *his* kingdom, and shall return
into his own land.
10 But his sons shall be stirred up, and shall assemble a multitude of great
forces: and *one* shall certainly come, and overflow, and pass through: then
shall he return, and be stirred up, *even* to his fortress.

11:10
Isa 8:8
Jer 46:7, 8
51:42
Dan 11:26, 40

11 And the king of the south shall be moved with choler, and shall come
forth and fight with him, *even* with the king of the north: and he shall set
forth a great multitude; but the multitude shall be given into his hand.
12 *And* when he hath taken away the multitude, his heart shall be lifted

---

11:1ff This chapter outlines the history of the Near East for the last few centuries prior to the birth of Jesus. The data make the period complicated. Any good book on the history of this period will be helpful to the reader. (See also Ezra 4:24; 6:1, 22.)
11:2 *the fourth.* Perhaps this refers to Xerxes (486–465 B.C.), who launched an all-out effort against Greece.†
11:3 *do according to his will,* i.e., "and accomplish everything he sets out to do." This doubtless was Alexander the Great.†
11:5 *the king of the south,* i.e., "Ptolemy II."
11:6 *shall join themselves together.* In 252 B.C. Ptolemy II of Egypt gave his daughter Berenice in marriage to Antiochus II of Syria to conclude a treaty of peace between their two lands. *the king of the north,* i.e., "the king of Syria," and so also throughout this passage. These prophecies seem to have been fulfilled many years later in the Seleucid wars between Egypt and Syria.†
11:7 *out of a branch of her roots,* i.e., "when her brother." Berenice, murdered in Antioch by Antiochus II's former wife Laodice, was the sister of Ptolemy III, who now ascended the Egyptian throne and declared war against the Seleucids to avenge his sister's murder.†

up; and he shall cast down *many* ten thousands: but he shall not be
strengthened *by it.*
11:13☆ 13 For the king of the north shall return, and shall set forth a multitude
Dan 4:16; 12:7 greater than the former, and shall certainly come after certain years with a
great army and with much riches.
11:14☆ 14 And in those times there shall many stand up against the king of the
south: also the robbers of thy people shall exalt themselves to establish the
vision; but they shall fall.
11:15☆ 15 So the king of the north shall come, and cast up a mount, and take the
Jer 6:6 Ezek 4:2; 17:17 most fenced cities: and the arms of the south shall not withstand, neither
his chosen people, neither *shall there be any* strength to withstand.
11:16 16 But he that cometh against him shall do according to his own will, and
Josh 1:5 Dan 5:19; 8:9 none shall stand before him: and he shall stand in the glorious land, which
11:3, 36, 41 by his hand shall be consumed.
11:17☆ 17 He shall also set his face to enter with the strength of his whole
2 Kgs 12:17 Ezek 4:3, 7 kingdom, and upright ones with him; thus shall he do: and he shall give
Lk 9:51; 11:23 Rom 8:31 him the daughter of women, corrupting her: but she shall not stand *on his*
side, neither be for him.
11:18☆ 18 After this shall he turn his face unto the isles, and shall take many: but
Gen 10:5 Zeph 2:11 a prince for his own behalf shall cause the reproach offered by him to cease;
without his own reproach he shall cause *it* to turn upon him.
11:19 19 Then shall he turn his face toward the fort of his own land: but he shall
Ps 27:2; 37:36 Jer 46:6 stumble and fall, and not be found.
Ezek 26:21 **11:20**☆ 20 Then shall stand up in his estate a raiser of taxes *in* the glory of the
kingdom: but within few days he shall be destroyed, neither in anger, nor in
battle.

3. Persecution of Israel by Antiochus IV

11:21☆ 21 And in his estate shall stand up a vile person, to whom they shall not
give the honour of the kingdom: but he shall come in peaceably, and obtain
the kingdom by flatteries.
11:22☆ 22 And with the arms of a flood shall they be overflown from before him,
and shall be broken; yea, also the prince of the covenant.
23 And after the league *made* with him he shall work deceitfully: for he
shall come up, and shall become strong with a small people.
11:24 24 He shall enter peaceably even upon the fattest places of the province;
Num 13:20 Neh 9:25 and he shall do *that* which his fathers have not done, nor his fathers'
Ezek 34:14 fathers; he shall scatter among them the prey, and spoil, and riches: *yea*,
and he shall forecast his devices against the strong holds, even for a time.
25 And he shall stir up his power and his courage against the king of the

---

11:13 *the king of the north,* i.e., "the Syrian king." Possibly Antiochus III the Great, who was later defeated by the Romans at Magnesia.†
11:14 *to establish the vision,* i.e., "thus fulfilling prophecy."†
11:15 *take the most fenced cities.* Antiochus defeated Ptolemy's army at Panion (198 B.C.). Following this *victory, Seleucid control of Palestine was complete.*
11:17 *give him the daughter of women,* i.e., "give him a daughter in marriage." Antiochus' daughter, Cleopatra, was married off to the Egyptian king. Antiochus wanted to control Egypt but failed to accomplish this aim.
11:18 *a prince.* Probably the Roman consul Scipio, who defeated Antiochus at Magnesia near Smyrna in 190 B.C.
11:20 *in his estate,* or, "in his place." Seleucus IV, successor to Antiochus III, sent Heliodorus to rob and desecrate the temple in Jerusalem.†
11:21 *And in his estate shall stand up a vile person,* or, "Next to come to power will be an evil man not directly in line for royal succession." This may refer to Antiochus IV Epiphanes who, when his brother Seleucus was assassinated, ingratiated himself with the Romans and took over.†
11:22 *the prince of the covenant,* i.e., "a leader of the priests." Probably Jason, treacherously removed by the Hellenist Menelaus.†

south with a great army; and the king of the south shall be stirred up to
battle with a very great and mighty army; but he shall not stand: for they
shall forecast devices against him.
26 Yea, they that feed of the portion of his meat shall destroy him, and his
army shall overflow: and many shall fall down slain.
27 And both these kings' hearts *shall be* to do mischief, and they shall
speak lies at one table; but it shall not prosper: for yet the end *shall be* at
the time appointed.
28 Then shall he return into his land with great riches; and his heart *shall
be* against the holy covenant; and he shall do *exploits*, and return to his own
land.
29 At the time appointed he shall return, and come toward the south; but
it shall not be as the former, or as the latter.
30 ¶For the ships of Chit'tim shall come against him: therefore he shall be
grieved, and return, and have indignation against the holy covenant: so
shall he do; he shall even return, and have intelligence with them that
forsake the holy covenant.
31 And arms shall stand on his part, and they shall pollute the sanctuary
of strength, and shall take away the daily *sacrifice*, and they shall place the
abomination that maketh desolate.
32 And such as do wickedly against the covenant shall he corrupt by
flatteries: but the people that do know their God shall be strong, and do
exploits.
33 And they that understand among the people shall instruct many: yet
they shall fall by the sword, and by flame, by captivity, and by spoil, *many*
days.
34 Now when they shall fall, they shall be holpen with a little help: but
many shall cleave to them with flatteries.
35 And *some* of them of understanding shall fall, to try them, and to purge,
and to make *them* white, *even* to the time of the end: because *it is* yet for a
time appointed.
36 And the king shall do according to his will; and he shall exalt himself,
and magnify himself above every god, and shall speak marvellous things
against the God of gods, and shall prosper till the indignation be
accomplished: for that that is determined shall be done.
37 Neither shall he regard the God of his fathers, nor the desire of women,
nor regard any god: for he shall magnify himself above all.
38 But in his estate shall he honour the God of forces: and a god whom his
fathers knew not shall he honour with gold, and silver, and with precious
stones, and pleasant things.
39 Thus shall he do in the most strong holds with a strange god, whom he
shall acknowledge *and* increase with glory: and he shall cause them to rule
over many, and shall divide the land for gain.

☆**11:27** Ps 64:6; Jer 9:3–5; Dan 11:35, 40; Hab 2:3; Acts 17:31
☆**11:30**
☆**11:31** Ezek 24:21, 24; Dan 8:11–13; 9:27; 12:11; Mt 24:15; Mk 13:14
☆**11:32** Dan 11:21, 34; Zech 9:13–16; 10:3–6; 2 Tim 2:1–3; Rev 12:7–11
11:33 Zech 8:20–23; Mt 24:9; Jn 16:2; Heb 11:36–38; Rev 1:9; 6:9; 7:14
11:34 Dan 11:21, 32; Mt 7:15; Rom 16:18; Rev 2:20; 13:11–14
11:35 Deut 8:16; Prov 17:3; Dan 12:10; Zech 13:9; Rev 14:15; 17:17
11:36 Deut 10:17; Ps 136:2; Isa 10:25; 14:13; 26:20; Dan 2:47; 5:20; 7:8, 11; 8:11; 9:27; 11:3; Acts 4:28; Rev 10:7; 13:5, 6
☆**11:37**
☆**11:38**

11:27 *both these kings.* This probably refers to Antiochus IV and Ptolemy IV.†
11:30 *ships of Chittim,* i.e., "Roman warships," or, "ships from Cyprus."
11:31 *pollute the sanctuary,* by offering swine on the altar. This event was fulfilled in 168–167 B.C. *place the abomination that maketh desolate,* i.e., "worshipping idols (a statute of Zeus) inside the temple."
11:32 *shall he corrupt by flatteries,* i.e., "He will flatter those who hate the things of God." Menelaus, the High Priest, conspired with Antiochus against the Jews, who were loyal to God's laws. *but the people that do know their God,* perhaps the valiant Maccabees and their sympathizers. However, a further fulfillment may lie in the future.†
11:37 *the desire of women,* i.e., "the god beloved of women," which was probably Tammuz-Adonis, whose worship was popular among women—cf. Ezek. 8:14.†
11:38 *forces,* i.e., "the Fortress god"† which probably was Jupiter Capitolinus (Zeus) for whom he built a temple at Antioch.

4. The Antitype of Antiochus in the Last Days

11:40☆ Jer 4:13; Dan 11:27, 35; 12:4, 9; Zech 9:14

40 And at the time of the end shall the king of the south push at him: and
the king of the north shall come against him like a whirlwind, with chariots,
and with horsemen, and with many ships; and he shall enter into the
countries, and shall overflow and pass over.

11:41 Jer 48:47; 49:6

41 He shall enter also into the glorious land, and many *countries* shall be
overthrown: but these shall escape out of his hand, *even* Edom, and Moab,
and the chief of the children of Ammon.

42 He shall stretch forth his hand also upon the countries: and the land of
Egypt shall not escape.

11:43 Ezek 30:4, 5; Nah 3:9

43 But he shall have power over the treasures of gold and of silver, and
over all the precious things of Egypt; and the Lib′y-ans and the E-thi-o′pi-
ans *shall be* at his steps.

44 But tidings out of the east and out of the north shall trouble him:
therefore he shall go forth with great fury to destroy, and utterly to make
away many.

45 And he shall plant the tabernacles of his palace between the seas in the
glorious holy mountain; yet he shall come to his end, and none shall help
him.

5. Tribulation and Resurrection unto Life and Death

12:1☆ Jer 30:7; Ezek 5:9; Dan 7:10; 9:12; 10:21; 12:4; Mk 13:19

12 AND at that time shall Michael stand up, the great prince which
standeth for the children of thy people: and there shall be a time of
trouble, such as never was since there was a nation *even* to that same time:
and at that time thy people shall be delivered, every one that shall be found
written in the book.

12:2 Isa 26:19; Ezek 37:12–14; Jn 5:28, 29
12:3☆ Isa 53:11; Dan 11:33, 35; 12:10; Jn 5:35
12:4 Isa 8:16; 11:9; Dan 8:17, 26; 11:33; 12:9, 13

2 And many of them that sleep in the dust of the earth shall awake, some
to everlasting life, and some to shame *and* everlasting contempt.

3 And they that be wise shall shine as the brightness of the firmament;
and they that turn many to righteousness as the stars for ever and ever.

4 But thou, O Daniel, shut up the words, and seal the book, *even* to the
time of the end: many shall run to and fro, and knowledge shall be
increased.

6. Sealing the Prophecies for Future Fulfillment

5 ¶Then I Daniel looked, and, behold, there stood other two, the one on
this side of the bank of the river, and the other on that side of the bank of
the river.

12:6 Ezek 9:2; Dan 8:13, 16; 10:5; 12:8; Zech 1:12, 13; Mt 24:3; Mk 13:4
12:7☆ Ezek 20:5; Dan 7:25; 8:24; Lk 21:24; Rev 10:7; 11:7–15; 12:14

6 And *one* said to the man clothed in linen, which *was* upon the waters of
the river, How long *shall it be to* the end of these wonders?

7 And I heard the man clothed in linen, which *was* upon the waters of the
river, when he held up his right hand and his left hand unto heaven, and
sware by him that liveth for ever that *it shall be* for a time, times, and an
half; and when he shall have accomplished to scatter the power of the holy
people, all these *things* shall be finished.

11:40 *at the time of the end.* The prophecy takes a turn here. Antiochus IV fades from view and the Antichrist of *the last days becomes the center of attention* from this point on.†
12:1 God had deputed Michael to help his people, and they will need his help. He supplies it to those whose names are "written in the book," i.e., the book of life in which the redeemed are listed by name.
12:3 Whoever leads men to Christ will share in the glory of those they have helped to heaven. Only God can save, but the people who lead them to Christ will have a rich reward. They shall be burning and shining lights, and the memory of their service to God will never be eclipsed. The stars will fall from heaven as do the leaves of the trees in the autumn, whereas those who turn many to righteousness shall shine on forever.
12:7 *a time, times, and an half,* or, "three and a half years."

8 And I heard, but I understood not: then said I, O my Lord, what *shall be*
the end of these *things?*
9 And he said, Go thy way, Daniel: for the words *are* closed up and sealed
till the time of the end.
10 Many shall be purified, and made white, and tried; but the wicked shall
do wickedly: and none of the wicked shall understand; but the wise shall
understand.
11 And from the time *that* the daily *sacrifice* shall be taken away, and the
abomination that maketh desolate set up, *there shall be* a thousand two
hundred and ninety days.
12 Blessed *is* he that waiteth, and cometh to the thousand three hundred
and five and thirty days.
13 But go thou thy way till the end *be:* for thou shalt rest, and stand in thy
lot at the end of the days.

12:10
Isa 32:6, 7
Dan 12:3
Hos 14:9
Rev 3:18
9:20, 21; 16:11
22:11
☆**12:11**
Dan 9:27; 11:31
Mt 24:15
Mk 13:14
Rev 11:2; 12:6
13:5
12:12
Dan 8:14
Rev 11:2
12:13
Ps 16:5
Rev 16:5

12:11 *a thousand two hundred and ninety days.* Three and a half years (12:7) and thirty extra days.

HOSEA

Authorship, date, and background The author, Hosea (whose name means "salvation") was the son of Beeri. The name itself is identical with that of Hoshea and derives originally from the name of Joshua. Hosea lived during the eighth century B.C. His ministry can be dated from 753 B.C. to around 723 B.C. He was a prophet in the Northern Kingdom during the reign of Jeroboam and overlapped with Isaiah, Micah, and Amos. It was a time of great prosperity and gross religious apostasy. The Northern Kingdom had been delivered from its vassalage to Syria, which had declined under Benhadad III. Its territory had been expanded to include Damascus, and control of the caravan trade routes brought about the rise of a successful mercantile class. This widened the gap between the rich and the poor even as the mercantile class could now afford the luxuries previously known only by the nobility.

Prosperity brought with it spiritual decline. The Canaanite religion of Baal worship had penetrated Israelite life. It was the most degenerate of all the cults of the area. Baal and his female consort Asherat and the goddess Anat (also known as Ashtoreth or Asherah) were fertility deities often worshipped in the form of bulls and cows. Jeroboam I had set up two golden calves, one at Bethel and one at Dan, for the people of the Northern Kingdom to worship. Drunkenness, prostitution, and violence attended their cultic practices, which were all contrary to the covenant they had with God. God called Hosea to his ministry during the closing days of the Northern Kingdom before the Assyrian invasion of 722 B.C.

Characteristics and content Hosea marries a woman of harlotries who proves unfaithful even after her marriage to the prophet. God uses this to demonstrate the relation of Israel to himself. He is the faithful husband; Israel is the faithless and adulterous wife. Even as Hosea tenderly deals with his faithless wife and recovers her from her life of sin, so a loving and tender God calls Israel to repent of her adultery and return to her God. Hosea's three children are named Jezreel (as a sign of God's punishment of King Jehu's dynasty for their murders), Lo-ruhamah (meaning "no more mercy" to be extended to the Northern Kingdom), and Lo-ammi (meaning "not mine" or that God has rejected the apostate kingdom of Israel).

All of the tragic consequences experienced by Hosea in his marital disasters are used as signs of Israel's harlotry and departure from the covenant promises made with God years before. He pronounces divine judgment in the name of God and assures Israel that it will experience captivity and its cities will be destroyed. Its wealth will be taken from the people and their prayers will not be heard. Hosea, however, looks far beyond Israel's present apostasy as he forecasts the time when Israel, because of God's continuing love and faithfulness, will repent and will be restored when the anger of God will be gone forever.

Outline

I. Hosea's marriage: its meaning for Israel (1:1—3:5)
II. God's indictment of Israel (4:1—6:3)
III. Israel's sin and its coming judgment (6:4—10:15)
IV. God's design in judgment and mercy (11:1—14:9)

I. HOSEA'S MARRIAGE: ITS MEANING FOR ISRAEL (1:1—3:5)

A. INTRODUCTION

1:1☆ 1 Kgs 13:1–34; 2 Kgs 15:32–38; 16:1; 18:1; 2 Chron 10:12–16; 26:1–23; *Mic 1:1*

1 THE word of the LORD that came unto Ho-se'a, the son of Be-e'ri, in
the days of Uz-zi'ah, Jo'tham, Ahaz, *and* Hez-e-ki'ah, kings of Judah,
and in the days of Jer-o-bo'am the son of Jo'ash, king of Israel.

1:1 Hosea is the first of the twelve minor prophets. The books of the twelve have sometimes been considered to be but one book. These prophets are called *minor* because the amount of material contained in each is considerably less than that of the major prophets such as Isaiah, Jeremiah, and Ezekiel. The first nine proph-

B. HOSEA'S MARRIAGE WITH GOMER, A WHORE

[2]The beginning of the word of the LORD by Ho-se'a. And the LORD said
to Ho-se'a, Go, take unto thee a wife of whoredoms and children of
whoredoms: for the land hath committed great whoredom, *departing* from
the LORD.

☆1:2
Hos 3:1

[3]So he went and took Go'mer the daughter of Dib'la-im; which
conceived, and bare him a son.
[4]And the LORD said unto him, Call his name Jez're-el; for yet a little
while, and I will avenge the blood of Jez're-el upon the house of Jehu, and
will cause to cease the kingdom of the house of Israel.

☆1:4
Josh 17:16
Judg 6:33
2 Kgs 9:14–36
10:1–28
2 Chron 22:8, 9

[5]And it shall come to pass at that day, that I will break the bow of Israel
in the valley of Jez're-el.

☆1:5

[6]¶And she conceived again, and bare a daughter. And *God* said unto him,
Call her name Lo–ru-ha'mah: for I will no more have mercy upon the house
of Israel; but I will utterly take them away.

☆1:6

[7]But I will have mercy upon the house of Judah, and will save them by
the LORD their God, and will not save them by bow, nor by sword, nor by
battle, by horses, nor by horsemen.

☆1:7
Ps 44:3–7
Isa 30:18

[8]¶Now when she had weaned Lo–ru-ha'mah, she conceived, and bare a
son.
[9]Then said *God*, Call his name Lo–am'mi: for ye *are* not my people, and
I will not be your *God*.

☆1:9

C. THE ULTIMATE REUNION OF ISRAEL AND JUDAH PROMISED

[10]¶Yet the number of the children of Israel shall be as the sand of the sea,
which cannot be measured nor numbered; and it shall come to pass, *that* in
the place where it was said unto them, Ye *are* not my people, *there* it shall
be said unto them, *Ye are* the sons of the living God.

☆1:10
Gen 22:17
Isa 63:16; 64:8
Jer 33:22

[11]Then shall the children of Judah and the children of Israel be gathered
together, and appoint themselves one head, and they shall come up out of
the land: for great *shall be* the day of Jez're-el.

☆1:11
Jer 30:21
Hos 3:5

D. GOMER, A PICTURE OF ISRAEL
1. Her Adultery

2 SAY ye unto your brethren, Am'mi; and to your sisters, Ru-ha'mah.
[2]Plead with your mother, plead: for she *is* not my wife, neither *am* I

☆2:1
Hos 1:4, 5, 11

---

esied before the captivity; the last three wrote after the captivity was over. Jeremiah and Ezekiel repeat some of the material contained in Hosea, with which they were familiar. It was the word of the Lord which came to Hosea that he spoke and wrote in the book.

1:2 *hath committed great whoredom.* Hosea's marriage to a prostitute served as the background for his message. Just as Gomer was unfaithful to Hosea, so Israel was unfaithful to God.

1:4 *avenge the blood of Jezreel.* Jehu was party to the deaths of Joram of Israel, Ahaziah of Judah, and Jezebel the wife of King Ahab (2 Kings 9). His desire to exterminate the Baalites was no justification for his murderous acts, and God, in turn, punished the house of Jehu. God simply commanded him to execute the family of Ahab. (See 1 Kings 21:21; 2 Kings 10:11.)

1:5 *break the bow of Israel in the valley of Jezreel,* a prediction of the Assyrian conquest of Israel twenty-five years later.†

1:6 *Lo-ruhamah,* i.e., "not pitied," or "not having obtained mercy."

1:7 *I will have mercy upon the house of Judah.* Shortly after defeating Israel, the Assyrian Emperor Sennacherib invaded Judah and besieged Jerusalem. He was driven off by special intervention of God's angel (Isa. 36–37).†

1:9 *Lo-ammi,* i.e., "not my people."

1:10 Even as Hosea prophesied judgment against Israel, so he also looked to that future day when she would be restored to a position of blessing and honor. The new name *sons of the living God* indicates that this indeed will come to pass.

1:11 This is a word of promise from God, that Judah and Israel (the Northern Kingdom) shall be brought together again. It was fulfilled in part in Jesus' day when people from Galilee (which part of the country belonged to the Northern Kingdom) along with people from Judea came to know Christ and embraced the gospel. Eleven of the twelve disciples were Galileans. At the end of the age all Israel, north and south, shall be living together in harmony and love.

2:1 Israel's sins include idolatry (or serving other gods) and spiritual whoredom (or prostitution)—2:1, 2, 5, 8.

her husband: let her therefore put away her whoredoms out of her sight,
and her adulteries from between her breasts;

2:3☆ Isa 20:2, 3; 32:13, 14 · Jer 14:3 · Ezek 16:7, 22, 29 · Hos 13:15 · Amos 8:11–13

3 Lest I strip her naked, and set her as in the day that she was born, and
make her as a wilderness, and set her like a dry land, and slay her with
thirst.
4 And I will not have mercy upon her children; for they *be* the children of
whoredoms.

2:5 Jer 2:25; 3:1, 2 · Ezek 23:16, 17, 40–45

5 For their mother hath played the harlot: she that conceived them hath
done shamefully: for she said, I will go after my lovers, that give *me* my
bread and my water, my wool and my flax, mine oil and my drink.

2. The Divine Judgment

2:6 Job 19:8

6 ¶Therefore, behold, I will hedge up thy way with thorns, and make a
wall, that she shall not find her paths.

2:7 2 Chron 28:20–22 · Jer 2:2; 3:1 · Ezek 23:4 · Hos 2:5; 5:13

7 And she shall follow after her lovers, but she shall not overtake them;
and she shall seek them, but shall not find *them:* then shall she say, I will go
and return to my first husband; for then *was it* better with me than now.

2:8 Hos 2:13; 8:4; 13:2

8 For she did not know that I gave her corn, and wine, and oil, and
multiplied her silver and gold, *which* they prepared for Ba'al.
9 Therefore will I return, and take away my corn in the time thereof, and
my wine in the season thereof, and will recover my wool and my flax *given*
to cover her nakedness.

2:10 Ezek 16:37 · Hos 2:3

10 And now will I discover her lewdness in the sight of her lovers, and
none shall deliver her out of mine hand.

2:11 Jer 7:34; 16:9

11 I will also cause all her mirth to cease, her feast days, her new moons,
and her sabbaths, and all her solemn feasts.

2:12 Jer 5:17; 8:13

12 And I will destroy her vines and her fig trees, whereof she hath said,
These *are* my rewards that my lovers have given me: and I will make them
a forest, and the beasts of the field shall eat them.

2:13 Jer 7:9 · Ezek 23:40–42 · Hos 4:13; 11:2

13 And I will visit upon her the days of Ba'al-im, wherein she burned
incense to them, and she decked herself with her earrings and her jewels,
and she went after her lovers, and forgat me, saith the LORD.

3. Her Promised Recovery

2:14☆ Ezek 20:33–38

14 ¶Therefore, behold, I will allure her, and bring her into the wilderness,
and speak comfortably unto her.

2:15☆ Josh 7:26 · Isa 65:10 · Jer 2:1–3 · Ezek 16:8, 22

15 And I will give her her vineyards from thence, and the valley of A'chor
for a door of hope: and she shall sing there, as in the days of her youth, and
as in the day when she came up out of the land of Egypt.

2:16☆ Isa 54:5 · Hos 2:7

16 And it shall be at that day, saith the LORD, *that* thou shalt call me I'shi;
and shalt call me no more Ba'al-i.

2:18☆ Lev 26:5, 6 · Isa 2:4 · Jer 33:16 · Ezek 34:25; 39:1–10 · Mic 4:3

17 For I will take away the names of Ba'al-im out of her mouth, and they
shall no more be remembered by their name.
18 And in that day will I make a covenant for them with the beasts of the
field, and with the fowls of heaven, and *with* the creeping things of the

---

2:3 God threatens to take away their prosperity and abandon them to ruin because of their sins (2:3, 4, 6, 7, 9–13).

2:14 *I will allure her. God still loves faithless* Israel. God will take his people away from Canaan and the worship of the baalim. He will take them to the wilderness, where he will speak tenderly to them.

2:15 *The valley of Achor for a door of hope.* There is no hope for Israel in Canaan. Exile (or *Achor,* meaning "trouble") is the only way by which she will be restored to favor with God.

2:16 *call me Ishi* ("my husband") instead of *Baal,* meaning "my Lord." Baal was a tainted word because it applied to idols, so it would no longer be used in reference to the true God.†

2:18–20 God here promises to renew his covenant with them, a covenant they had broken by reason of their infidelity.

ground: and I will break the bow and the sword and the battle out of the
earth, and will make them to lie down safely.
19 And I will betroth thee unto me for ever; yea, I will betroth thee unto
me in righteousness, and in judgment, and in lovingkindness, and in
mercies.
20 I will even betroth thee unto me in faithfulness: and thou shalt know
the LORD.
21 And it shall come to pass in that day, I will hear, saith the LORD, I will
hear the heavens, and they shall hear the earth;
22 And the earth shall hear the corn, and the wine, and the oil; and they
shall hear Jez're-el.
23 And I will sow her unto me in the earth; and I will have mercy upon her
that had not obtained mercy; and I will say to *them which were* not my
people, Thou *art* my people; and they shall say, *Thou art* my God.

2:20 Jer 31:34; Hos 6:6; 13:4
☆**2:21** Isa 55:10; Jer 31:27; Zech 8:12
2:23 Hos 1:6, 9

4. Her Recovery Effected

3 THEN said the LORD unto me, Go yet, love a woman beloved of *her*
friend, yet an adulteress, according to the love of the LORD toward the
children of Israel, who look to other gods, and love flagons of wine.
2 So I bought her to me for fifteen *pieces* of silver, and *for* an homer of
barley, and an half homer of barley:
3 And I said unto her, Thou shalt abide for me many days; thou shalt not
play the harlot, and thou shalt not be for *another* man: so *will* I also *be* for
thee.
4 For the children of Israel shall abide many days without a king, and
without a prince, and without a sacrifice, and without an image, and
without an ephod, and *without* teraphim:
5 Afterward shall the children of Israel return, and seek the LORD their
God, and David their king; and shall fear the LORD and his goodness in the
latter days.

3:1 2 Sam 6:19; 1 Chron 16:3; Song 2:5
☆**3:2** Gen 31:41; 34:12; Ruth 4:10
☆**3:3**
☆**3:4** Judg 17:5; 18:17–24; 2 Kgs 23:24
☆**3:5** Isa 55:3, 4; Jer 50:4, 5; Ezek 34:24; Amos 9:11; Acts 15:16–18

II. GOD'S INDICTMENT OF ISRAEL (4:1—6:3)
A. ISRAEL'S ADULTERY

4 HEAR the word of the LORD, ye children of Israel: for the LORD hath
a controversy with the inhabitants of the land, because *there is* no
truth, nor mercy, nor knowledge of God in the land.
2 By swearing, and lying, and killing, and stealing, and committing
adultery, they break out, and blood toucheth blood.
3 Therefore shall the land mourn, and every one that dwelleth therein
shall languish, with the beasts of the field, and with the fowls of heaven;
yea, the fishes of the sea also shall be taken away.
4 Yet let no man strive, nor reprove another: for thy people *are* as they
that strive with the priest.

☆**4:1** Isa 50:4; Jer 7:28; Hos 12:2; Mic 6:2
☆**4:2**
4:3 Isa 24:4; 33:9
4:4 Deut 17:12; Ezek 3:26; Amos 5:10, 13

2:21ff God promises at last to bless his people with plenty, so that they shall lack nothing anymore. *had not obtained mercy.* See note on 1:6. *not my people.* See note on 1:9.

3:2 *I bought her to me,* i.e., I bought her back. The prophet Hosea courted his adulterous wife, seeking reconciliation and beseeching her to leave her wickedness and return to him. This allegorically applied to God's pursuit of Israel, who had played the harlot. In a further spiritual sense all we who have been separated from God and are adulterers and adulteresses have been bought back by God. Hosea paid fifteen pieces of silver, an homer of barley, and an half homer of barley for his wife's redemption. God paid for our return to him by the blood of Jesus shed on Calvary.

3:3, 4 Israel's exile is symbolized in these verses. *ephod.* See note on Judg. 8:27. *teraphim.* See note on Gen. 31:19.

3:5 A happy reformation of Israel will take place in the latter days. *David their king.* Christ was "the Greater David."

4:1, 2 God's indictment against Israel is manifold. They certainly sinned boldly and extensively. They were guilty of unfaithfulness, unkindness, lack of the knowledge of God, swearing, lying, stealing, murder, and adultery. There were few sins left for them to commit.

4:5 Ezek 14:3, 7; Hos 5:5

5 Therefore shalt thou fall in the day, and the prophet also shall fall with
thee in the night, and I will destroy thy mother.

4:6 Hos 4:14; Zech 11:8, 9, 15–17

6 ¶My people are destroyed for lack of knowledge: because thou hast
rejected knowledge, I will also reject thee, that thou shalt be no priest to
me: seeing thou hast forgotten the law of thy God, I will also forget thy
children.

4:7 Hos 2:16; 10:1; 13:6; Rom 1:21–23

7 As they were increased, so they sinned against me: *therefore* will I
change their glory into shame.

4:8☆

8 They eat up the sin of my people, and they set their heart on their
iniquity.

4:9 Isa 24:2; Jer 5:31; Mt 15:13, 14

9 And there shall be, like people, like priest: and I will punish them for
their ways, and reward them their doings.
10 For they shall eat, and not have enough: they shall commit whoredom,
and shall not increase: because they have left off to take heed to the LORD.

4:11 Isa 5:12; 28:7

11 Whoredom and wine and new wine take away the heart.

4:12☆ 1 Chron 10:13; Isa 19:3; Ezek 21:21

12 ¶My people ask counsel at their stocks, and their staff declareth unto
them: for the spirit of whoredoms hath caused *them* to err, and they have
gone a whoring from under their God.

4:13 Jer 2:20; 3:6; Ezek 6:13; Hos 2:13; 11:2

13 They sacrifice upon the tops of the mountains, and burn incense upon
the hills, under oaks and poplars and elms, because the shadow thereof *is*
good: therefore your daughters shall commit whoredom, and your spouses
shall commit adultery.

4:14 Deut 23:17

14 I will not punish your daughters when they commit whoredom, nor
your spouses when they commit adultery: for themselves are separated with
whores, and they sacrifice with harlots: therefore the people *that* doth not
understand shall fall.
15 ¶Though thou, Israel, play the harlot, *yet* let not Judah offend; and
come not ye unto Gilgal, neither go ye up to Beth–a'ven, nor swear, The
LORD liveth.

4:16 Ps 23:2, 3; 78:8; Isa 5:17; 7:25

16 For Israel slideth back as a backsliding heifer: now the LORD will feed
them as a lamb in a large place.

4:17☆

17 E'phra-im *is* joined to idols: let him alone.

4:18☆

18 Their drink is sour: they have committed whoredom continually: her
rulers *with* shame do love, Give ye.

4:19☆ Hos 12:1; 13:15; Zech 5:9–11

19 The wind hath bound her up in her wings, and they shall be ashamed
because of their sacrifices.

B. GOD ABANDONS ISRAEL TO JUDGMENT

5:1☆

5 HEAR ye this, O priests; and hearken, ye house of Israel; and give ye
ear, O house of the king; for judgment *is* toward you, because ye have
been a snare on Mizpah, and a net spread upon Ta'bor.
2 And the revolters are profound to make slaughter, though I *have been* a
rebuker of them all.

4:8 The priests were greedy for gain derived from their office, but their hearts were not in their duties. Moreover, they encouraged the people in their sins, becoming partakers of the same. They helped to keep up that which they should have beaten down. Thus they were guilty of promoting evil and being accessories to sins.
4:12 *counsel at their stocks, and their staff declareth unto them,* i.e., they have guidance from false gods and they have taken over the arts of sorcerers whose predictions were based on how their staffs landed on the ground when thrown or allowed to fall.
4:17 *Ephraim is joined to idols,* i.e., is in love with them, has an addiction for them. The nation is beyond repentance; leave it alone.
4:18 *her rulers with shame do love,* i.e., "their rulers dearly love shameful ways" (NIV).
4:19 *The wind hath bound her up,* i.e., "A whirlwind will sweep them away" (NIV). The Assyrian invasion came about twenty years later and the nation of Ephraim disappeared.†
5:1 Priests and all other classes of society are called to answer the charges against them. This is repeated in different form in 5:8.

3 I know E'phra-im, and Israel is not hid from me: for now, O E'phra-im,
thou committest whoredom, *and* Israel is defiled.
4 They will not frame their doings to turn unto their God: for the spirit of
whoredoms *is* in the midst of them, and they have not known the LORD.
5 And the pride of Israel doth testify to his face: therefore shall Israel and
E'phra-im fall in their iniquity; Judah also shall fall with them.
6 They shall go with their flocks and with their herds to seek the LORD;
but they shall not find *him;* he hath withdrawn himself from them.
7 They have dealt treacherously against the LORD: for they have begotten
strange children: now shall a month devour them with their portions.
8 Blow ye the cornet in Gib'e-ah, *and* the trumpet in Ra'mah: cry aloud *at*
Beth–a'ven, after thee, O Benjamin.
9 E'phra-im shall be desolate in the day of rebuke: among the tribes of
Israel have I made known that which shall surely be.
10 The princes of Judah were like them that remove the bound: *therefore* I
will pour out my wrath upon them like water.
11 E'phra-im *is* oppressed *and* broken in judgment, because he willingly
walked after the commandment.
12 Therefore *will* I *be* unto E'phra-im as a moth, and to the house of Judah
as rottenness.
13 When E'phra-im saw his sickness, and Judah *saw* his wound, then went
E'phra-im to the Assyrian, and sent to king Ja'reb: yet could he not heal
you, nor cure you of your wound.
14 For I *will be* unto E'phra-im as a lion, and as a young lion to the house
of Judah: I, *even* I, will tear and go away; I will take away, and none shall
rescue *him.*

C. GOD'S PROMISED RESPONSE TO REPENTANCE

15 I will go *and* return to my place, till they acknowledge their offence, and
seek my face: in their affliction they will seek me early.

6 COME, and let us return unto the LORD: for he hath torn, and he will
heal us; he hath smitten, and he will bind us up.
2 After two days will he revive us: in the third day he will raise us up, and
we shall live in his sight.
3 Then shall we know, *if* we follow on to know the LORD: his going forth
is prepared as the morning; and he shall come unto us as the rain, as the
latter *and* former rain unto the earth.

III. ISRAEL'S SIN AND ITS COMING JUDGMENT (6:4—10:15)

A. ISRAEL HAS BROKEN THE COVENANT

4 ¶O E'phra-im, what shall I do unto thee? O Judah, what shall I do unto
thee? for your goodness *is* as a morning cloud, and as the early dew it goeth
away.

☆**5:3** Amos 5:12; Heb 4:13
☆**5:4** Hos 4:6, 14
☆**5:5** 2 Kgs 17:19, 20; Ezek 23:31–35
5:6 Ezek 8:6
5:7 Hos 2:4
5:9 Isa 28:1–4; 37:3; Hos 9:11–17; Amos 3:14, 15
☆**5:10** Deut 27:17; Ps 32:6; 93:3, 4; Prov 22:28; Ezek 7:8
5:12 Ps 39:11; Isa 51:8
☆**5:13**
5:14 Ps 7:2; Hos 13:7
☆**6:1** Isa 30:26; 61:1; Jer 50:4; Zeph 2:1–3
6:2 Ps 30:5; 1 Cor 15:4
6:3 Deut 32:2; Isa 2:3; 5:6; Hos 14:5; Mic 4:2
☆**6:4** Ps 78:34–37; Hos 13:3

5:3, 4 The charge is that of spiritual prostitution or harlotry. They have turned from God, are confirmed in their ways, and delight in what they are doing. They have broken their marriage vows, i.e., their covenant with God.

5:5 Judah is like Ephraim in her sins. The ten tribes will be carried captive to Assyria and lose their identity, whereas Judah will fall but will rise again after punishment.

5:10 *like them that remove the bound,* i.e., they are like thieves who change boundary markers to gain additional land.

5:13 Both kingdoms, when contended with by God, seek relief by making heathen alliances. But this would bring disappointment because only God can heal sicknesses.

6:1 The plea to turn to the Lord comes either from the lips of Hosea or from people who see the need to seek help from God for their sins.

6:4ff Both Ephraim and Judah have wobbled in their ways (6:4, 5) and have been faithless to their covenant with God (6:6, 7). They are like knotty timber and rough stone, which need to be hewed into proper shape to become useful.

6:5 Isa 49:2 Heb 4:12 [5]Therefore have I hewed *them* by the prophets; I have slain them by the
words of my mouth: and thy judgments *are as* the light *that* goeth forth.
6:6 Mt 9:13; 12:7 [6]For I desired mercy, and not sacrifice; and the knowledge of God more
than burnt offerings.
6:7☆ [7]But they like men have transgressed the covenant: there have they dealt
treacherously against me.
[8]Gilead *is* a city of them that work iniquity, *and is* polluted with blood.
6:9 Jer 7:9 Hos 4:2 [9]And as troops of robbers wait for a man, *so* the company of priests
murder in the way by consent: for they commit lewdness.
[10]I have seen an horrible thing in the house of Israel: there *is* the
whoredom of E′phra-im, Israel is defiled.
6:11 Jer 51:33 Joel 3:13 [11]Also, O Judah, he hath set an harvest for thee, when I returned the
captivity of my people.

7:1☆ Jer 51:9 Ezek 24:13 Hos 7:13 7 WHEN I would have healed Israel, then the iniquity of E′phra-im was
discovered, and the wickedness of Sa-ma′ri-a: for they commit
falsehood; and the thief cometh in, *and* the troop of robbers spoileth
without.
[2]And they consider not in their hearts *that* I remember all their
wickedness: now their own doings have beset them about; they are before
my face.
7:3 Hos 7:5 Mic 7:3 [3]They make the king glad with their wickedness, and the princes with
their lies.
7:4 Jer 9:2; 23:10 Jas 4:4 [4]They *are* all adulterers, as an oven heated by the baker, *who* ceaseth
from raising after he hath kneaded the dough, until it be leavened.
7:5 Prov 20:1 Isa 5:11, 22, 23 28:1 [5]In the day of our king the princes have made *him* sick with bottles of
wine; he stretched out his hand with scorners.
7:6 Ps 21:9 Dan 3:6 [6]For they have made ready their heart like an oven, whiles they lie in
wait: their baker sleepeth all the night; in the morning it burneth as a
flaming fire.
7:7☆ [7]They are all hot as an oven, and have devoured their judges; all their
kings are fallen: *there is* none among them that calleth unto me.
7:8☆ [8]E′phra-im, he hath mixed himself among the people; E′phra-im is a cake
not turned.
7:9 Isa 57:1–11 [9]Strangers have devoured his strength, and he knoweth *it* not: yea, gray
hairs are here and there upon him, yet he knoweth not.
[10]And the pride of Israel testifieth to his face: and they do not return to
the LORD their God, nor seek him for all this.
7:11☆ [11]¶E′phra-im also is like a silly dove without heart: they call to Egypt,
they go to Assyria.
7:12 Job 19:6 Ezek 12:13 [12]When they shall go, I will spread my net upon them; I will bring them
down as the fowls of the heaven; I will chastise them, as their congregation
hath heard.
7:13☆ [13]Woe unto them! for they have fled from me: destruction unto them!

6:7 Even as Adam broke his covenant with God and died, so has Ephraim violated the conditions of its agreement with God, and therefore must lose the benefits that accrue to those who keep the covenant.

7:1ff God was eager and anxious to heal Ephraim's cancer, which appeared to be fatal, but Ephraim refused to seek his aid. The princes are liars (7:3); they *are adulterers (7:4); drunkenness is epidemic*; and their unclean hearts are heated ovens that only increase their desire to sin (7:5–7).

7:7 *all their kings are fallen,* i.e., they kill their own kings. This happened to Zechariah, Shallum, and Pekahiah.

7:8 *Ephraim mixes himself with the peoples,* i.e., they associated with and adopted heathen peoples and customs. *a cake not turned,* i.e., like a pancake that is burned on one side and uncooked on the other and is therefore worthless altogether.

7:11 *they call to Egypt, they go to Assyria.* The royal court of Israel was torn between supporters of a pro-Egyptian and those of a pro-Assyrian alliance. Hosea viewed this as evidence of Israel's failure to trust God.

7:13 The NIV translates one segment, "I long to redeem them but they speak lies against me." God will not save those who refuse to bend their knees before him. Indeed, he cannot save them without their repen-

because they have transgressed against me: though I have redeemed them,
yet they have spoken lies against me.
14 And they have not cried unto me with their heart, when they howled
upon their beds: they assemble themselves for corn and wine, *and* they
rebel against me.
15 Though I have bound *and* strengthened their arms, yet do they imagine
mischief against me.
16 They return, *but* not to the most High: they are like a deceitful bow:
their princes shall fall by the sword for the rage of their tongue: this *shall be*
their derision in the land of Egypt.

7:15 Ps 2:1; Nah 1:9
7:16 Hos 8:13; 9:3, 6; Lk 8:13

B. GOD'S JUDGMENT PRONOUNCED

1. God's Sentence upon Them

8 *SET* the trumpet to thy mouth. *He shall come* as an eagle against the
house of the LORD, because they have transgressed my covenant, and
trespassed against my law.
2 Israel shall cry unto me, My God, we know thee.
3 Israel hath cast off *the thing that is* good: the enemy shall pursue him.
4 They have set up kings, but not by me: they have made princes, and I
knew *it* not: of their silver and their gold have they made them idols, that
they may be cut off.
5 ¶Thy calf, O Sa-ma′ri-a, hath cast *thee* off; mine anger is kindled against
them: how long *will it be* ere they attain to innocency?
6 For from Israel *was* it also: the workman made it; therefore it *is* not
God: but the calf of Sa-ma′ri-a shall be broken in pieces.
7 For they have sown the wind, and they shall reap the whirlwind: it hath
no stalk: the bud shall yield no meal: if so be it yield, the strangers shall
swallow it up.
8 Israel is swallowed up: now shall they be among the Gentiles as a vessel
wherein *is* no pleasure.
9 For they are gone up to Assyria, a wild ass alone by himself: E′phra-im
hath hired lovers.
10 Yea, though they have hired among the nations, now will I gather them,
and they shall sorrow a little for the burden of the king of princes.
11 Because E′phra-im hath made many altars to sin, altars shall be unto
him to sin.
12 I have written to him the great things of my law, *but* they were counted
as a strange thing.
13 They sacrifice flesh *for* the sacrifices of mine offerings, and eat *it; but* the
LORD accepteth them not; now will he remember their iniquity, and visit
their sins: they shall return to Egypt.
14 For Israel hath forgotten his Maker, and buildeth temples; and Judah
hath multiplied fenced cities: but I will send a fire upon his cities, and it
shall devour the palaces thereof.

☆**8:1** Jer 48:40; Hab 1:8
8:5 Jer 13:27
☆**8:7** Job 38:1; Nah 1:3; Zech 7:14; 9:14
8:8 Isa 30:14; Jer 48:38
8:9 Job 39:5–8; Jer 2:24; Ezek 16:33
8:10 Hos 10:10
8:13 Hos 7:2; 9:9; 1 Cor 4:5
8:14 2 Sam 7:2; 1 Kgs 7:1–12; 2 Kgs 18:13; Neh 1:1; Jer 17:27; Dan 4:29; 8:2; Hos 2:13; 4:6

2. Israel's Wealth to Evaporate

9 REJOICE not, O Israel, for joy, as *other* people: for thou hast gone a
whoring from thy God, thou hast loved a reward upon every cornfloor.

☆**9:1** Isa 17:11; 22:12, 13

---

tance, for this would be a violation of the divine nature. He can urge men everywhere to repent, but unless they do he cannot save them.

8:1 Hosea sets forth the particular sins of Israel in 8:1, 3, 12, 14. They are (1) the breaking of the covenant, (2) breaking the commandments of God, (3) despising the writings, and (4) forgetting their God.

8:7ff As a consequence of their sins they shall reap the whirlwind, their foreign alliances will be their disappointment (8:6, 8, 10), their sacrifices will do them no good (8:13), and their cities (which are their home bases) will be laid in ashes (8:14). God will not be mocked.

9:1ff Israel has no cause for rejoicing, for her sins have found her out. Her land will not produce enough food, nor will it be their habitation. They will be taken

2The floor and the winepress shall not feed them, and the new wine shall
fail in her.

9:3 Ezek 4:13 Dan 1:8 Acts 10:14

3They shall not dwell in the LORD's land; but E'phra-im shall return to
Egypt, and they shall eat unclean *things* in Assyria.

9:4 Ex 29:40 Lev 22:4–9 23:13 Hag 2:14

4They shall not offer wine *offerings* to the LORD, neither shall they be
pleasing unto him: their sacrifices *shall be* unto them as the bread of
mourners; all that eat thereof shall be polluted: for their bread for their
soul shall not come into the house of the LORD.

9:5 Hos 2:11 Joel 1:13

5What will ye do in the solemn day, and in the day of the feast of the
LORD?

9:6☆ Prov 24:31 Isa 5:6; 7:23 Hos 10:8

6For, lo, they are gone because of destruction: Egypt shall gather them
up, Mem'phis shall bury them: the pleasant *places* for their silver, nettles
shall possess them: thorns *shall be* in their tabernacles.

9:7☆ Isa 10:3 Jer 10:15 Jer 29:26 Lam 2:14 Ezek 7:2–7 13:3, 10 Amos 8:2

7The days of visitation are come, the days of recompence are come; Israel
shall know *it:* the prophet *is* a fool, the spiritual man *is* mad, for the
multitude of thine iniquity, and the great hatred.
8The watchman of E'phra-im *was* with my God: *but* the prophet *is* a
snare of a fowler in all his ways, *and* hatred in the house of his God.

9:9☆ Isa 24:4, 5; 31:6 Hos 7:2; 8:13

9They have deeply corrupted *themselves*, as in the days of Gib'e-ah:
therefore he will remember their iniquity, he will visit their sins.

3. Israel's People to Be Few in Number

9:10☆ Num 13:21–23 25:1–9 Josh 22:17, 18 Jer 24:2 Mic 7:1

10I found Israel like grapes in the wilderness; I saw your fathers as the
firstripe in the fig tree at her first time: *but* they went to Ba'al–pe'or, and
separated themselves unto *that* shame; and *their* abominations were
according as they loved.

9:11 Hos 4:7

11*As for* E'phra-im, their glory shall fly away like a bird, from the birth,
and from the womb, and from the conception.
12Though they bring up their children, yet will I bereave them, *that there
shall* not *be* a man *left:* yea, woe also to them when I depart from them!

9:13☆

13E'phra-im, as I saw Tyrus, *is* planted in a pleasant place: but E'phra-im
shall bring forth his children to the murderer.
14Give them, O LORD: what wilt thou give? give them a miscarrying
womb and dry breasts.

9:15☆ Hos 5:2 Amos 4:4; 5:5

15All their wickedness *is* in Gilgal: for there I hated them: for the
wickedness of their doings I will drive them out of mine house, I will love
them no more: all their princes *are* revolters.

9:16 Ezek 24:21

16E'phra-im is smitten, their root is dried up, they shall bear no fruit: yea,
though they bring forth, yet will I slay *even* the beloved *fruit* of their womb.

---

from the land and live in Assyria, where their kosher laws will be defunct and they will eat unclean food. They shall lack the proper sacrifices, they shall have no altar, and there will be no priests to officiate. It will be a living death for them.

9:6 *Memphis shall bury them.* They will flee to a refuge that will turn out to be a place of death. They expected life by their flight from God, only to discover they had inherited death instead.

9:7 *The day of God's judgment is at hand and will not be delayed.* They will see that their false prophets were fools and know that the word of the true prophets has come to pass. Israel has followed in the steps of their fathers and committed the same kinds of sins.

9:9 *in the days of Gibeah.* See Judg. 19:14ff.

9:10 *but they went to Baal Peor,* i.e., they forsook the true God and consecrated themselves to Baalpeor, who was the god of Peor, a city of Moab where fertility rites and Baal-worship abounded. The Moabites invited the Israelites to their temple. However, Baal-worship had started among the Israelites long before this (see Num. 23; Judg. 2:11–13).

9:13 Mothers will anguish in pain as their children are born. They will nurse them only to have the cruel enemy put them to the sword. Then they will say that the womb that bears no fruit is better than the one that does.

9:15 *Gilgal,* the town where Baal-worship flourished (4:15; 12:11), and where the monarchy, hated of God, was instituted (1 Sam. 11:15).

17 My God will cast them away, because they did not hearken unto him:
and they shall be wanderers among the nations.

4. Israel's Idol Altars to Crumble

10 ISRAEL *is* an empty vine, he bringeth forth fruit unto himself:
according to the multitude of his fruit he hath increased the altars;
according to the goodness of his land they have made goodly images.
2 Their heart is divided; now shall they be found faulty: he shall break
down their altars, he shall spoil their images.
3 For now they shall say, We have no king, because we feared not the
LORD; what then should a king do to us?
4 They have spoken words, swearing falsely in making a covenant: thus
judgment springeth up as hemlock in the furrows of the field.
5 The inhabitants of Sa-ma′ri-a shall fear because of the calves of Beth–
a′ven: for the people thereof shall mourn over it, and the priests thereof *that*
rejoiced on it, for the glory thereof, because it is departed from it.
6 It shall be also carried unto Assyria *for* a present to king Ja′reb: E′phra-
im shall receive shame, and Israel shall be ashamed of his own counsel.
7 *As for* Sa-ma′ri-a, her king is cut off as the foam upon the water.
8 The high places also of A′ven, the sin of Israel, shall be destroyed: the
thorn and the thistle shall come up on their altars; and they shall say to the
mountains, Cover us; and to the hills, Fall on us.

☆**10:1** 1 Kgs 14:23; Isa 5:1–7; Ezek 15:1–5; Hos 8:11; 12:11
☆**10:2** 1 Kgs 18:21; Hos 10:8; Mic 5:13; Zeph 1:5
10:3 Hos 3:4; 13:11; Mic 4:9
10:4 Ezek 17:13–19; Rom 1:31
☆**10:5** 1 Kgs 12:28–32; 2 Chron 11:15; Hos 10:6
10:6 Hos 10:5
10:8 Hos 5:8; 9:6; 10:5

5. Israel's Forts Will Fall

9 O Israel, thou hast sinned from the days of Gib′e-ah: there they stood:
the battle in Gib′e-ah against the children of iniquity did not overtake
them.
10 *It is* in my desire that I should chastise them; and the people shall be
gathered against them, when they shall bind themselves in their two
furrows.
11 And E′phra-im *is as* an heifer *that is* taught, *and* loveth to tread out *the
corn;* but I passed over upon her fair neck: I will make E′phra-im to ride;
Judah shall plow, *and* Jacob shall break his clods.
12 Sow to yourselves in righteousness, reap in mercy; break up your fallow
ground: for *it is* time to seek the LORD, till he come and rain righteousness
upon you.
13 Ye have plowed wickedness, ye have reaped iniquity; ye have eaten the
fruit of lies: because thou didst trust in thy way, in the multitude of thy
mighty men.
14 Therefore shall a tumult arise among thy people, and all thy fortresses
shall be spoiled, as Shal′man spoiled Beth–ar′bel in the day of battle: the
mother was dashed in pieces upon *her* children.
15 So shall Beth–el do unto you because of your great wickedness: in a
morning shall the king of Israel utterly be cut off.

☆**10:9**
☆**10:11** Deut 28:48; Jer 28:14
10:12 Prov 11:18; Isa 32:20
10:13 Ps 33:16; Eccles 9:11
☆**10:14** 2 Kgs 17:6; 18:9, 10

10:1, 2 The more they experienced the providence of God, the more prodigal they became in making and serving idols. They halted between two opinions, so God would destroy their idols.
10:5 These idolaters shall tremble and fear, for God will shake them as he shakes the earth. In that hour of judgment they will ask the mountains to cover them and the hills to fall on them (10:8), but it will do no good for they refuse to repent and seek the face of God.
10:9 *the days of Gibeah.* See Judg. 19, 20.
10:11 Ephraim is likened to a fair and lovely heifer trained to tread out the corn. She loved her work. But now Ephraim must be yoked and Judah will plow. Thus Ephraim's lot will be far worse than that of Judah.
10:14 *Shalman.* Probably Salaman, king of Moab, who invaded Gilead around 740 B.C.†

IV. GOD'S DESIGN IN JUDGMENT AND MERCY (11:1—14:9)

A. ASSYRIA WILL TAKE ISRAEL CAPTIVE

11:1☆ Ex 4:22 Hos 2:15 12:9, 13; 13:4 Mt 2:15
11:2 Judg 10:6 1 Kgs 18:19 Isa 65:7 Jer 18:15 Hos 2:13 13:1, 2
11:3☆
11:4☆ Ex 16:32 Jer 31:2, 3
11:5☆
11:6 Ps 80:11–16 Isa 9:14; 18:5
11:7 Jer 8:5 Hos 4:16

11 WHEN Israel *was* a child, then I loved him, and called my son out
of Egypt.
2 *As* they called them, so they went from them: they sacrificed unto Ba′al-
im, and burned incense to graven images.
3 I taught E′phra-im also to go, taking them by their arms; but they knew
not that I healed them.
4 I drew them with cords of a man, with bands of love: and I was to them
as they that take off the yoke on their jaws, and I laid meat unto them.
5 ¶He shall not return into the land of Egypt, but the Assyrian shall be his
king, because they refused to return.
6 And the sword shall abide on his cities, and shall consume his branches,
and devour *them*, because of their own counsels.
7 And my people are bent to backsliding from me: though they called
them to the most High, none at all would exalt *him*.

B. GOD STILL LOVES ISRAEL

11:8☆ Gen 14:8 Deut 29:23 Hos 6:4; 7:1
11:9 Ex 32:10–14 Deut 13:17 Isa 5:24; 12:6 41:14 Jer 31:1–3 Hos 11:12

8 How shall I give thee up, E′phra-im? *how* shall I deliver thee, Israel? how
shall I make thee as Ad′mah? *how* shall I set thee as Ze-bo′im? mine heart
is turned within me, my repentings are kindled together.
9 I will not execute the fierceness of mine anger, I will not return to
destroy E′phra-im: for I *am* God, and not man; the Holy One in the midst
of thee: and I will not enter into the city.

C. GOD WILL RESTORE ISRAEL

11:10 Ps 2:11 Isa 31:4 Isa 66:2, 5 Jer 5:22; 25:30 33:9 Hos 3:5; 6:1–3 Joel 3:16 Amos 1:2; 3:4
11:11 Isa 11:11; 60:8 Hos 7:11 Zech 10:10
11:12 Hos 11:9

10 They shall walk after the LORD: he shall roar like a lion: when he shall
roar, then the children shall tremble from the west.
11 They shall tremble as a bird out of Egypt, and as a dove out of the land
of Assyria: and I will place them in their houses, saith the LORD.

D. ISRAEL'S UNFAITHFULNESS RESTATED; HER CAPTIVITY IS COMING

12 E′phra-im compasseth me about with lies, and the house of Israel with
deceit: but Judah yet ruleth with God, and is faithful with the saints.

12:1☆ Gen 41:6 Jer 22:22 Ezek 17:10 Hos 8:7

12 E′PHRA-IM feedeth on wind, and followeth after the east wind: he
daily increaseth lies and desolation; and they do make a covenant
with the Assyrians, and oil is carried into Egypt.

11:1 This statement has a double meaning. God called his son, Jacob (or the people of Israel), out of Egypt. Jesus, the Messiah, was also called out of Egypt—the second fulfillment of this prophetic word (see Matt. 2:15).

11:3 *I taught Ephraim* ("Israel"). When Israel grew up, she deserted the Lord, who had raised her, and substituted the Baals for the Lord.

11:4 *I drew them,* i.e., "he brought them into his *service by mild and gentle methods.*"*

11:5 The Northern Kingdom, also known as Israel, lasted for two centuries after the division of the kingdom following Solomon's death. Hosea prophesied its downfall. This took place in 722 B.C. under the leadership of Shalmaneser V and Sargon. Israel never recovered from the expulsion of its people as Judah did after her Babylonian captivity. The Scriptures do promise the regathering of all of Israel into a single realm in the last days (14:4–8; Isa. 11:13). Some hold that the prophecy of the restoration of the Northern Kingdom has been fulfilled, at least in part, with the filling in of the vacant ranks by Gentile believers who have become God's people.

11:8 *Admah . . . Zeboim,* cities of the plain that perished with Sodom and Gomorrah (Deut. 29:23).

12:1 *Ephraim feedeth . . . and followeth after the east wind,* i.e., places vain hopes on the assistance of men, which is like following the east wind that is good for neither man nor beast.

E. THE LAWSUIT AGAINST JUDAH (JACOB)

[2]The LORD hath also a controversy with Judah, and will punish Jacob
according to his ways; according to his doings will he recompense him.
[3]¶He took his brother by the heel in the womb, and by his strength he
had power with God:
[4]Yea, he had power over the angel, and prevailed: he wept, and made
supplication unto him: he found him *in* Beth–el, and there he spake with
us;
[5]Even the LORD God of hosts; the LORD *is* his memorial.
[6]Therefore turn thou to thy God: keep mercy and judgment, and wait on
thy God continually.

☆12:2 Hos 4:1
12:3 Gen 25:26; Rom 9:11
12:4 Gen 28:13–15; 32:24–30; 35:10–15
12:5 Ex 3:15
12:6 Mic 7:7

F. EPHRAIM'S (ISRAEL'S) SINS RESTATED

[7]¶*He is* a merchant, the balances of deceit *are* in his hand: he loveth to
oppress.
[8]And E'phra-im said, Yet I am become rich, I have found me out
substance: *in* all my labours they shall find none iniquity in me that *were*
sin.
[9]And I *that am* the LORD thy God from the land of Egypt will yet make
thee to dwell in tabernacles, as in the days of the solemn feast.
[10]I have also spoken by the prophets, and I have multiplied visions, and
used similitudes, by the ministry of the prophets.
[11]*Is there* iniquity *in* Gilead? surely they are vanity: they sacrificed
bullocks in Gilgal; yea, their altars *are* as heaps in the furrows of the fields.
[12]And Jacob fled into the country of Syria, and Israel served for a wife,
and for a wife he kept *sheep*.
[13]And by a prophet the LORD brought Israel out of Egypt, and by a
prophet was he preserved.
[14]E'phra-im provoked *him* to anger most bitterly: therefore shall he leave
his blood upon him, and his reproach shall his Lord return unto him.

☆12:7 Prov 11:1; Hos 7:14; Amos 8:5; Mic 6:11
12:8 Ps 62:10; Hos 13:6; Zech 11:5
☆12:9 Lev 23:42
12:10 1 Kgs 13:1; 2 Kgs 17:13; Isa 20:2–5; Jer 25:4; Ezek 17:2; 20:49; Amos 7:14
☆12:12 Gen 28:5; 29:20
12:13 Ex 12:50; 14:19–22; Isa 63:11, 12
12:14 2 Sam 1:16; 1 Kgs 2:33, 34; 2 Kgs 17:7–18; Ezek 18:13; 23:2–10; 24:7, 8; 33:5

G. ISRAEL'S DOOM IMPENDING

13 WHEN E'phra-im spake trembling, he exalted himself in Israel; but
when he offended in Ba'al, he died.
[2]And now they sin more and more, and have made them molten images
of their silver, *and* idols according to their own understanding, all of it the
work of the craftsmen: they say of them, Let the men that sacrifice kiss the
calves.
[3]Therefore they shall be as the morning cloud, and as the early dew that
passeth away, as the chaff *that* is driven with the whirlwind out of the floor,
and as the smoke out of the chimney.

☆13:1 Hos 8:6
13:2 1 Kgs 19:18; Isa 44:17–20; 46:6; Jer 10:2–5; Hos 8:6
13:3 Ps 68:2; Isa 17:13; Hos 6:4

12:2ff Hosea refers to Jacob, from whom Israel descended. Jacob had three great experiences. One was when he caught the heel of his brother in the womb and demonstrated conquering strength. The second was when he wrestled with the angel and secured the blessing. The third was his encounter with God at Bethel, where the covenant made with Abraham was repeated and renewed. Jacob's God should be Ephraim's God. He exhorts them to turn to the God of their father Jacob.

12:7 Ephraim not only farmed the land, he also was a successful merchant. But he used fraud and force to accomplish his ends. His weights and balances were false ones. He took pride in his oppression and loved to engage in it. He thought that what success he had gained came from his own efforts. God was left out of the picture.

12:9 God became angry with Ephraim because of his sins. He must pay for them dearly. He will live again in tents because his cities will be destroyed.

12:12 *Israel served for a wife.* Jacob served Laban in order to secure Rachel as his wife. He was deceived and married Leah and then served another seven years in order to marry Rachel too.

13:1ff Hosea reproves Ephraim for idolatry, a sin forbidden by the second commandment: "Thou shalt not make unto thee any graven image. . . ." They did not believe that there is no savior but God.

13:4 Ex 20:3 Isa 43:11 45:21, 22
13:5☆ Deut 2:7; 8:15 32:10
13:6 Hos 2:13; 4:6 8:14
13:9ff☆
13:10 2 Kgs 17:4 Hos 8:4
13:11☆ 1 Sam 8:7 1 Kgs 14:7–10 Hos 10:7
13:12 Isa 25:8 Deut 32:34, 35 Rom 2:5
13:13 Mic 4:9, 10
13:14 Ezek 37:12, 13 1 Cor 15:55 Phil 3:21
13:15 Jer 51:36 Hos 12:1
13:16 2 Kgs 15:16

[4]Yet I *am* the LORD thy God from the land of Egypt, and thou shalt
know no god but me: for *there is* no saviour beside me.
[5]I did know thee in the wilderness, in the land of great drought.
[6]According to their pasture, so were they filled; they were filled, and their
heart was exalted; therefore have they forgotten me.
[7]Therefore I will be unto them as a lion: as a leopard by the way will I
observe *them:*
[8]I will meet them as a bear *that is* bereaved *of her whelps*, and will rend
the caul of their heart, and there will I devour them like a lion: the wild
beast shall tear them.
[9]¶O Israel, thou hast destroyed thyself; but in me *is* thine help.
[10]I will be thy king: where *is any other* that may save thee in all thy cities?
and thy judges of whom thou saidst, Give me a king and princes?
[11]I gave thee a king in mine anger, and took *him* away in my wrath.
[12]The iniquity of E′phra-im *is* bound up; his sin *is* hid.
[13]The sorrows of a travailing woman shall come upon him: he *is* an
unwise son; for he should not stay long in *the place of* the breaking forth of
children.
[14]I will ransom them from the power of the grave; I will redeem them
from death: O death, I will be thy plagues; O grave, I will be thy
destruction: repentance shall be hid from mine eyes.
[15]¶Though he be fruitful among *his* brethren, an east wind shall come, the
wind of the LORD shall come up from the wilderness, and his spring shall
become dry, and his fountain shall be dried up: he shall spoil the treasure
of all pleasant vessels.
[16]Sa-ma′ri-a shall become desolate; for she hath rebelled against her
God: they shall fall by the sword: their infants shall be dashed in pieces,
and their women with child shall be ripped up.

H. GOD'S PROMISE OF FORGIVENESS AND BLESSING IF ISRAEL REPENTS

1. The Call to Return to the Lord

14:1ff☆
14:2 Mic 7:18, 19 Rom 11:27
14:3☆ Ps 68:5 Mic 5:10–14

14 O ISRAEL, return unto the LORD thy God; for thou hast fallen by
thine iniquity.
[2]Take with you words, and turn to the LORD: say unto him, Take away
all iniquity, and receive *us* graciously: so will we render the calves of our
lips.
[3]Asshur shall not save us; we will not ride upon horses: neither will we
say any more to the work of our hands, *Ye are* our gods: for in thee the
fatherless findeth mercy.

13:5ff Ephraim is accused of pride, luxury, and lack of discipline. Prosperity was the root of these sins.

13:9ff God will destroy Ephraim and the blame rests on their own heads. They are guilty, and God now has no compassion on them (13:14). The east wind, which is a destroying wind, will come. Ephraim will be parched and dried up, her people will fall by the sword, their pregnant women will be ripped open, and their babes dashed to pieces. The wrath of God toward sinners is terrible to behold, but the righteous need not fear, for as a remnant they shall be saved by a God of love.

13:11 *I gave . . . a king . . . and took him away.* Probably an allusion to the kings of Israel who were assassinated during her last tempestuous years—Zechariah, Shallum, and Pekahiah.†

14:1ff Chapter 14 is entirely different from the rest of this prophecy. All that precedes it is made up of rebukes for sins and threatenings of the outpouring of the wrath of God. Now God exhorts the people of Israel to repent, promising them mercy if they will do so. In judgment he will wound them so that when they repent he will be able to heal them. 14:9 repeats the refrain found everywhere in the writings of the prophets: "For the ways of the LORD are right, and the just shall walk in them: but the transgressors shall fall therein." In the end there are only two ways one can walk. One road leads to life eternal; the other leads to everlasting death.

14:3 Hosea calls on Israel to acknowledge that she cannot be saved by dependence upon or association with such nations as Assyria or Egypt. If there is to be deliverance, it must come from God, for Israel is an helpless orphan.

2. The Promise of God's Blessing

4I will heal their backsliding, I will love them freely; for mine anger is
turned away from him.
5I will be as the dew unto Israel: he shall grow as the lily, and cast forth
his roots as Lebanon.
6His branches shall spread, and his beauty shall be as the olive tree, and
his smell as Lebanon.
7They that dwell under his shadow shall return; they shall revive *as* the
corn, and grow as the vine: the scent thereof *shall be* as the wine of
Lebanon.
8E'phra-im *shall say*, What have I to do any more with idols? I have
heard *him*, and observed him: I *am* like a green fir tree. From me is thy fruit
found.

14:4 Isa 57:18; Jer 3:22; Zeph 3:17
14:5 Song 2:1
14:6 Ps 52:8; Jer 11:16
14:7 Ps 91:1; Isa 32:1, 2
☆14:8 Isa 41:19; Hos 14:3

3. The Postscript

9Who *is* wise, and he shall understand these *things?* prudent, and he shall
know them? for the ways of the LORD *are* right, and the just shall walk in
them: but the transgressors shall fall therein.

☆14:9 Job 34:10–12; Ps 19:7, 8; Prov 1:5, 6; 4:18; Isa 1:28; Jer 9:12; Rom 9:32

14:8 *from me is thy fruit found,* i.e., the fruit *for* us, the fruit *in* us, and the fruit *by* us has its source in God, the author of good.

14:9 The truly wise are those whc hear, understand, and agree that God's ways are right; then they walk in those ways.

JOEL

Authorship, date, and background Joel, whose name means "Yahweh is God," was the son of Pethuel and is the author of the book which goes by his name. Nothing is known about him or his father. He was from Jerusalem and was well acquainted with the city and the land of Judah. The book cannot be dated either from internal or external evidences and scholars have varied in their suggestions from a pre-exilic date earlier than 800 B.C. to a post-exilic date as late as 350 B.C. The fact that Joel mentioned Edom, Egypt, Philistia, and Phoenicia as contemporary nations at the time of the writing has occasioned conservative scholars to prefer the early date for the composition of the book. Some similarities with the prophecies of Amos, whose work has been dated in the eighth century B.C., suggest to some a similar time frame.

The background against which the book was written was a locust invasion which devastated the land, leaving behind hunger and destitution for both man and beast. Such invasions were not uncommon, although they usually did not come from the north. Joel used the invasion to call his people to repentance and prayer for divine forgiveness. He looked upon the invasion as a divine judgment against the nation.

Characteristics and content Joel writes beautifully and descriptively of an actual locust invasion and likens it to the invasion of any army from the north. He calls the locusts a vast army and goes on to describe the starving priests, the bare fields, the stricken farmers, and the weeping vinedressers. He calls for the priests to dress in sackcloth, and recommends a fast and the assembling of themselves at the temple to plead with God for help. From there Joel addresses himself to the future. A portion of his prophecy about the outpouring of God's Spirit on all flesh, with sons and daughters prophesying and old men dreaming dreams, is picked up by Peter in his discourse at Pentecost. But the remaining portion of the prophecy was not fulfilled at Pentecost and thus many commentators think it awaits fulfillment at the end of the present age or what Joel calls "the day of the LORD." At that time Joel prophesies "wonders in the heavens and in the earth, blood, and fire, and pillars of smoke. The sun shall be turned into darkness and the moon into blood before the great and terrible day of the LORD come" (2:30, 31).

In chapter three, Joel, like so many of the other prophets, foresees future prosperity for Judah and Jerusalem. This will be a divine deliverance by the power of God following severe judgments. When this happens, Joel promises that by his power God will insure that "Judah shall dwell for ever, and Jerusalem from generation to generation" (3:20).

Outline

I. The locust plague (1:1—2:27)
II. The Day of the Lord: God's final triumph (2:28—3:21)

1:1 Acts 2:16
1:2☆ Job 12:12; 15:10; Jer 30:7; Joel 1:14
1:3☆ Ex 10:2; Deut 6:4–9
1:4☆ Isa 33:4; Jer 51:14; Joel 2:25; Nah 3:15

I. THE LOCUST PLAGUE (1:1—2:27)

A. THE DEVASTATION WROUGHT BY THE LOCUSTS

1 THE word of the LORD that came to Jo'el the son of Pe-thu'el.
2 Hear this, ye old men, and give ear, all ye inhabitants of the land.
Hath this been in your days, or even in the days of your fathers?
3 Tell ye your children of it, and *let* your children *tell* their children, and
their children another generation.
4 That which the palmerworm hath left hath the locust eaten; and that

---

1:2 *Joel is about to speak of something* not known in previous experience or recorded in books of history. The old men of the nation are challenged to declare whether they have ever experienced or known of any devastation like that which is about to take place.

1:3 What is going to take place will be so unusual and so breathtaking that all generations to come will stand astonished.

1:4 There are a variety of locusts, four of which are mentioned here. Their swarms could reach millions if not billions.

which the locust hath left hath the cankerworm eaten; and that which the
cankerworm hath left hath the caterpiller eaten.
5 Awake, ye drunkards, and weep; and howl, all ye drinkers of wine,
because of the new wine; for it is cut off from your mouth.
6 For a nation is come up upon my land, strong, and without number, ☆1:6
whose teeth *are* the teeth of a lion, and he hath the cheek teeth of a great Joel 1:4
lion.
7 He hath laid my vine waste, and barked my fig tree: he hath made it ☆1:7
clean bare, and cast *it* away; the branches thereof are made white. Amos 4:9

B. THE LOCUSTS, A SIGN OF COMING JUDGMENT BY THE ASSYRIANS AND CHALDEANS

8 ¶Lament like a virgin girded with sackcloth for the husband of her
youth.
9 The meat offering and the drink offering is cut off from the house of the 1:9
LORD; the priests, the LORD's ministers, mourn. Hos 9:4 Joel 1:13; 2:14
10 The field is wasted, the land mourneth; for the corn is wasted: the new
wine is dried up, the oil languisheth.
11 Be ye ashamed, O ye husbandmen; howl, O ye vinedressers, for the 1:11
wheat and for the barley; because the harvest of the field is perished. Ezra 9:3 Amos 5:16
12 The vine is dried up, and the fig tree languisheth; the pomegranate tree, ☆1:12
the palm tree also, and the apple tree, *even* all the trees of the field, are Song 2:3 Joel 1:7
withered: because joy is withered away from the sons of men. Hab 3:17, 18 Hag 2:19
13 ¶Gird yourselves, and lament, ye priests: howl, ye ministers of the ☆1:13
altar: come, lie all night in sackcloth, ye ministers of my God: for the meat 1 Kgs 21:27 Jer 4:8
offering and the drink offering is withholden from the house of your God.
14 Sanctify ye a fast, call a solemn assembly, gather the elders *and* all the ☆1:14
inhabitants of the land *into* the house of the LORD your God, and cry unto
the LORD,
15 Alas for the day! for the day of the LORD *is* at hand, and as a ☆1:15
destruction from the Almighty shall it come. Isa 13:9 Ezek 7:2–13 Joel 2:1
16 Is not the meat cut off before our eyes, *yea,* joy and gladness from the 1:16
house of our God? Isa 3:7 Amos 4:6, 7
17 The seed is rotten under their clods, the garners are laid desolate, the ☆1:17
barns are broken down; for the corn is withered. Isa 17:10, 11
18 How do the beasts groan! the herds of cattle are perplexed, because ☆1:18
they have no pasture; yea, the flocks of sheep are made desolate.
19 O LORD, to thee will I cry: for the fire hath devoured the pastures of the 1:19
wilderness, and the flame hath burned all the trees of the field. Ps 50:15; 91:15 Mic 7:7

1:6 *a nation,* not a nation of human beings, but an unimaginable army of locusts who constitute a nation. They are numberless and have teeth like lions to destroy.

1:7 *The locusts ate everything that was edible, including the bark from the trees, which stand in whiteness against the clear sky.*

1:12 *The vine is dried up.* The workers labor, but the fields bring forth no fruit. This is only one of the signs of a future disaster. Joel calls for the priests to prepare their hearts in private for their public duty of seeking God's help.

1:13 In good times the people brought their offerings to the priests from the produce taken from the fields. Now there is nothing for the priests to eat. The earth is barren and the crops, if any, scanty.

1:14 Joel makes it clear that the only hope the people have is to turn to God for help. They must fast, meet in solemn assembly, and, of course, be ready to admit that what has happened came as a result of their transgressions.

1:15 *the day of the LORD is at hand,* by which is meant either the present judgment against Judah and Jerusalem, or that and another judgment at the end of the age. *Alas for the day,* for it will be terrible. Destruction will come and it has come from the hand of God himself.

1:17 The caterpillars have destroyed the corn; the garners are empty; the seed they plant does not produce its fruitage.

1:18 The cattle perish for lack of grass; their groans should touch the hearts of the people on whom this judgment has fallen—for their transgression.

1:20 1 Kgs 17:7; 18:5 Ps 104:21 Joel 1:18

20 The beasts of the field cry also unto thee: for the rivers of waters are
dried up, and the fire hath devoured the pastures of the wilderness.

C. THE FUTURE DAY OF THE LORD: A RECKONING

2:1☆ Joel 1:15 2:11, 15, 31 3:14 Zeph 1:16
2:2 Dan 9:12 Joel 1:2 2:5, 10, 11, 15, 31
2:3 Gen 2:8 Ps 50:3 Isa 51:3 Amos 7:4
2:4☆ Rev 9:7
2:5☆ Isa 5:24; 30:30 Nah 2:3, 4 3:2, 3
2:6 Jer 30:6
2:7 Isa 5:26–29
2:9 Ex 10:6 Jer 9:21 Jn 10:1
2:10☆ Ps 18:7 Isa 13:10 Joel 2:31; 3:15 Nah 1:5 Mt 24:29; 27:51 Acts 2:20
2:11 Ps 46:6 Isa 42:13 Joel 2:1; 3:16

2 BLOW ye the trumpet in Zion, and sound an alarm in my holy
mountain: let all the inhabitants of the land tremble: for the day of the
LORD cometh, for *it is* nigh at hand;
2 A day of darkness and of gloominess, a day of clouds and of thick
darkness, as the morning spread upon the mountains: a great people and a
strong; there hath not been ever the like, neither shall be any more after it,
even to the years of many generations.
3 A fire devoureth before them; and behind them a flame burneth: the
land *is* as the garden of Eden before them, and behind them a desolate
wilderness; yea, and nothing shall escape them.
4 The appearance of them *is* as the appearance of horses; and as
horsemen, so shall they run.
5 Like the noise of chariots on the tops of mountains shall they leap, like
the noise of a flame of fire that devoureth the stubble, as a strong people set
in battle array.
6 Before their face the people shall be much pained: all faces shall gather
blackness.
7 They shall run like mighty men; they shall climb the wall like men of
war; and they shall march every one on his ways, and they shall not break
their ranks:
8 Neither shall one thrust another; they shall walk every one in his path:
and *when* they fall upon the sword, they shall not be wounded.
9 They shall run to and fro in the city; they shall run upon the wall, they
shall climb up upon the houses; they shall enter in at the windows like a
thief.
10 The earth shall quake before them; the heavens shall tremble: the sun
and the moon shall be dark, and the stars shall withdraw their shining:
11 And the LORD shall utter his voice before his army: for his camp *is* very
great: for *he is* strong that executeth his word: for the day of the LORD *is*
great and very terrible; and who can abide it?

D. THE CALL TO TURN TO THE LORD

2:12 Deut 4:29, 30
2:13 Ex 34:6 Num 14:18 Ps 106:45 Amos 7:2–6
2:14☆ Hag 2:19
2:15☆ Joel 2:1

12 ¶Therefore also now, saith the LORD, Turn ye *even* to me with all your
heart, and with fasting, and with weeping, and with mourning:
13 And rend your heart, and not your garments, and turn unto the LORD
your God: for he *is* gracious and merciful, slow to anger, and of great
kindness, and repenteth him of the evil.
14 Who knoweth *if* he will return and repent, and leave a blessing behind
him; *even* a meat offering and a drink offering unto the LORD your God?
15 ¶Blow the trumpet in Zion, sanctify a fast, call a solemn assembly:

2:1 *the day of the LORD* is yet future, coming at the end of the age. The prophets saw the ranges of mountains, but they could not see the valleys in between. Therefore, they had no way of knowing how soon the Lord's judgment would fall.

2:4, 5 The locusts appear like war horses, rumbling *chariots, and brands of burning fire that* destroys without leaving anything behind.

2:10 *The sun and the moon shall be dark.* Multitudes of locusts clouded sun and moon. And in the last days before the Second Advent of Christ a similar or worse situation will prevail.

2:14 Joel sees the judgment coming, but urges repentance and a turning to God in the hope that God might turn the curse and the disaster into blessing. We cannot deny that, had the people heeded Joel's advice, the judgment would have been at least delayed. The same might be said for any nation today that will turn to God.

2:15 *Blow the trumpet in Zion* is the prophet's clear call to humiliation, fasting, prayer, and a complete turning to God for mercy. This was not uncommon; in 2 Chron. 20 we see what happened when this course of action was pursued.

16Gather the people, sanctify the congregation, assemble the elders,
gather the children, and those that suck the breasts: let the bridegroom go
forth of his chamber, and the bride out of her closet.
17Let the priests, the ministers of the LORD, weep between the porch and
the altar, and let them say, Spare thy people, O LORD, and give not thine
heritage to reproach, that the heathen should rule over them: wherefore
should they say among the people, Where *is* their God?

2:17 Ps 44:13; 79:10 Isa 37:20 Mic 7:10

E. THE FORGIVENESS OF GOD AND HIS OUTPOURED BLESSING

18¶Then will the LORD be jealous for his land, and pity his people.
19Yea, the LORD will answer and say unto his people, Behold, I will send
you corn, and wine, and oil, and ye shall be satisfied therewith: and I will
no more make you a reproach among the heathen:
20But I will remove far off from you the northern *army*, and will drive
him into a land barren and desolate, with his face toward the east sea, and
his hinder part toward the utmost sea, and his stink shall come up, and his
ill savour shall come up, because he hath done great things.
21¶Fear not, O land; be glad and rejoice: for the LORD will do great
things.
22Be not afraid, ye beasts of the field: for the pastures of the wilderness
do spring, for the tree beareth her fruit, the fig tree and the vine do yield
their strength.
23Be glad then, ye children of Zion, and rejoice in the LORD your God:
for he hath given you the former rain moderately, and he will cause to come
down for you the rain, the former rain, and the latter rain in the first *month*.
24And the floors shall be full of wheat, and the fats shall overflow with
wine and oil.
25And I will restore to you the years that the locust hath eaten, the
cankerworm, and the caterpiller, and the palmerworm, my great army
which I sent among you.
26And ye shall eat in plenty, and be satisfied, and praise the name of the
LORD your God, that hath dealt wondrously with you: and my people shall
never be ashamed.
27And ye shall know that I *am* in the midst of Israel, and *that* I *am* the
LORD your God, and none else: and my people shall never be ashamed.

2:18 Deut 32:36 Isa 60:10
2:19 Ezek 34:29 39:29
2:20 Deut 11:24 Jer 1:14, 15 Zech 14:8
2:23 Ps 28:6; 72:6 95:1–3 Hos 6:3 Zech 10:1 Phil 3:1 1 Thess 5:16
☆**2:25**
2:26 Ps 67:5–7 Isa 45:17 Rom 10:11
2:27 Lev 26:11, 12 Isa 45:5, 6, 18 Ezek 39:22, 28 Joel 3:17, 21

II. THE DAY OF THE LORD: GOD'S FINAL TRIUMPH (2:28—3:21)

A. THE OUTPOURING OF GOD'S SPIRIT

28¶And it shall come to pass afterward, *that* I will pour out my spirit
upon all flesh; and your sons and your daughters shall prophesy, your old
men shall dream dreams, your young men shall see visions:
29And also upon the servants and upon the handmaids in those days will
I pour out my spirit.
30And I will shew wonders in the heavens and in the earth, blood, and
fire, and pillars of smoke.
31The sun shall be turned into darkness, and the moon into blood, before
the great and the terrible day of the LORD come.

☆**2:28** Isa 32:15 Acts 2:16–18
2:29 1 Cor 12:13
2:31 Joel 2:1, 10 3:15

2:25 This is a promise of restoration following repentance. There is yet a period of time to come when blessing and abundance will reign.

2:28 *I will pour out my spirit upon all flesh.* God had poured out his Spirit upon numbers of people in the Old Testament age. The promise of a future fulfillment may be seen in what happened at Pentecost. Peter stated that what happened then was a fulfillment of Joel's prophecy (Acts 2:17–21). Some also believe there will be another fulfillment of this prophecy afterward, i.e., "in the last days," when there will be miraculous signs and frightening physical and meteoric phenomena.

2:32 Isa 4:2; Acts 2:21; Rom 10:13; 11:26

32 And it shall come to pass, *that* whosoever shall call on the name of the
LORD shall be delivered: for in mount Zion and in Jerusalem shall be
deliverance, as the LORD hath said, and in the remnant whom the LORD
shall call.

B. GOD'S RESTORATION OF JUDAH AND HIS JUDGMENT ON HER ENEMIES

3:1☆

3:2☆ Isa 66:18; Joel 3:12, 14; Zeph 3:8

3:3 Obad 11; Nah 3:10

3:4☆

3 FOR, behold, in those days, and in that time, when I shall bring again
the captivity of Judah and Jerusalem,
2 I will also gather all nations, and will bring them down into the valley of
Je-hosh'a-phat, and will plead with them there for my people and *for* my
heritage Israel, whom they have scattered among the nations, and parted
my land.
3 And they have cast lots for my people; and have given a boy for an
harlot, and sold a girl for wine, that they might drink.
4 Yea, and what have ye to do with me, O Tyre, and Zi'don, and all the
coasts of Palestine? will ye render me a recompence? and if ye recompense
me, swiftly *and* speedily will I return your recompence upon your own
head;

3:5 2 Kgs 12:18; Dan 5:2, 3

5 Because ye have taken my silver and my gold, and have carried into
your temples my goodly pleasant things:
6 The children also of Judah and the children of Jerusalem have ye sold
unto the Grecians, that ye might remove them far from their border.
7 Behold, I will raise them out of the place whither ye have sold them, and
will return your recompence upon your own head:
8 And I will sell your sons and your daughters into the hand of the
children of Judah, and they shall sell them to the Sa-be'ans, to a people far
off: for the LORD hath spoken *it*.

3:9☆ Isa 34:1; Jer 46:3; 51:27; Zech 14:2, 3

3:10 Isa 2:4; Mic 4:3

3:12 Ps 76:8, 9; Isa 3:13; Joel 3:2, 14; Rev 19:11

3:13 Hos 6:11; Mt 13:39; Mk 4:29

3:14☆ Isa 34:2–8; Ezek 38:8–23; Joel 2:1; 3:2, 12

3:15☆ Joel 12:10, 31

9 ¶Proclaim ye this among the Gentiles; Prepare war, wake up the mighty
men, let all the men of war draw near; let them come up:
10 Beat your plowshares into swords, and your pruninghooks into spears:
let the weak say, I *am* strong.
11 Assemble yourselves, and come, all ye heathen, and gather yourselves
together round about: thither cause thy mighty ones to come down, O
LORD.
12 Let the heathen be wakened, and come up to the valley of Je-hosh'a-
phat: for there will I sit to judge all the heathen round about.
13 Put ye in the sickle, for the harvest is ripe: come, get you down; for the
press is full, the fats overflow; for their wickedness *is* great.
14 Multitudes, multitudes in the valley of decision: for the day of the
LORD *is* near in the valley of decision.
15 The sun and the moon shall be darkened, and the stars shall withdraw
their shining.

3:1 Though the present circumstances appear horrendous and unending, they will not be everlasting. God will restore Judah and Jerusalem according to his covenant promise. It will take place, though no one can date the time with precision.

3:2 *valley of Jehoshaphat,* or, "valley where Jehovah judges."† The name *Jehoshaphat* means "Yahweh has judged." Joel's word is that the coming judgment is a reality and will be measured out to the godless people in that very valley.

3:4ff The nations have wasted the people of God. They have stolen God's gold and silver; they have sold his people into slavery. God will not stand for this forever. These nations will be destroyed and their children delivered over to Judah.

3:9ff God warns the nations to prepare for war against him. He will follow through on his challenge, and they will see who comes out victorious.

3:14 Judgment day is coming. It will be a day of decision. Multitudes will be there to hear their sentence pronounced and their doom sealed.

3:15 Before the end of time the kingdom of nature will be shaken and changed. The light from sun, moon, and stars will be withdrawn. The earth and the sky will shake. In Rev. 8:12 a similar sort of catastrophe is forecast.

[16]The LORD also shall roar out of Zion, and utter his voice from
Jerusalem; and the heavens and the earth shall shake: but the LORD *will be*
the hope of his people, and the strength of the children of Israel.
[17]So shall ye know that I *am* the LORD your God dwelling in Zion, my
holy mountain: then shall Jerusalem be holy, and there shall no strangers
pass through her any more.

3:16 Ps 18:2; 19:21 Prov 18:10 Hos 11:10 Joel 12:10 Amos 1:2; 3:8 Zech 12:5–9
☆3:17 Isa 11:9 Ezek 20:40 Zech 8:3

C. GOD'S BLESSING ON ISRAEL AND ALL OF THE REDEEMED FOREVER

[18]¶And it shall come to pass in that day, *that* the mountains shall drop
down new wine, and the hills shall flow with milk, and all the rivers of
Judah shall flow with waters, and a fountain shall come forth of the house
of the LORD, and shall water the valley of Shit'tim.
[19]Egypt shall be a desolation, and Edom shall be a desolate wilderness,
for the violence *against* the children of Judah, because they have shed
innocent blood in their land.
[20]But Judah shall dwell for ever, and Jerusalem from generation to
generation.
[21]For I will cleanse their blood *that* I have not cleansed: for the LORD
dwelleth in Zion.

☆3:18 Ex 3:8 Isa 55:12, 13 Amos 9:13
☆3:19 Amos 1:11 Obad 10
3:20 Ezek 37:25 Amos 9:15
3:21 Isa 4:4 Ezek 36:25, 29 Mt 27:25

3:17 The time is coming when all men and nations will know that God is Lord, that Zion is his holy mountain, and Jerusalem the city of our God. Only the righteous shall pass through that city.
3:18 In that day yet to come the waters will enrich the parched earth, the mountains will yield wine, the hills will flow with milk, and the comforts all men yearn for will be theirs. The paradise lost by Adam will be restored by Jesus Christ.
3:19 Edom and Egypt will be made a desolation. Israel, spiritually revived and right with God, will be favored, and blessed with perpetuity.

AMOS

Authorship, date, and background Amos, the author of this book, was one of the twelve minor prophets. No identification is given concerning his parentage. His name means "burden" or "burden-bearer." He was from Tekoa, which was approximately five miles south of Bethlehem. Amos was a herdsman and a dresser of sycamore trees. He prophesied around the middle of the eighth century B.C. and was a contemporary of Isaiah, Micah, and Hosea. Although he came from the Southern Kingdom of Judah, God called him from his pastoral duties to speak to the Northern Kingdom of Samaria. At that time, during the reign of Jeroboam II, a large and financially successful mercantile class had come into being in Samaria. They were prosperous and corrupt. The rich got richer and the poor got poorer. Luxury and ease was a contemporary phenomenon among the wealthy who then oppressed the poorer people by seizing their lands (it was God's intention that the people of Israel should be small independent landowners), by making serfs of these people, and selling them into bondage.

At the same time, the Canaanite religion had overtaken the Northern Kingdom, with all of its wicked features such as ritual prostitution, orgies, its fertility cult with four annual feasts, accompanied by drunkenness, idolatrous worship, and debilitating violence. Two years before the earthquake, about which we know little, God called Amos to be his prophet, and a strange prophet he was: he had no priestly background nor was he a learned scholar; his parents, unnamed, were among the common people. God's ways are not man's ways.

Characteristics and content Amos comes to Samaria with a message of divine judgment against the surrounding nations. It is a delight to the people of Samaria who remembered their suffering under Damascus, the Philistines, Tyre, Moab, Ammon, and Edom. He pronounces God's judgment on his own nation of Judah for their disobedience and their rejection of the Law of God. Samaria is delighted with this message since they traditionally resented their southern relatives. Then Amos speaks the word of judgment against Samaria. He says they have sinned, and God is about to judge them by sending divine retribution upon them. He catalogs their sins of sumptuous living, bribery, neglect of the poor, drunkenness, and even their ritual sacrifices which have no internal significance since their hearts are far removed from God. He announces the divine judgment which will follow their impenitence, a judgment which will be fulfilled not too many years after Amos completes his short ministry for God among this people. His visions of a vast swarm of locusts, a great fire, a plumbline, a basket full of ripe fruit, and the smitten temple and slain people are used to dramatize the coming destruction which will be their lot because of their transgressions.

Amos, like so many of the other prophets, paints a brighter and more hopeful picture toward the end of his diatribe (see 9:11–15). Amos' first prophecy of judgment was fulfilled shortly and thereafter Samaria disappeared from history. And to this day Amos' glorious promise of Israel's return to the land has not yet taken place. But it will—in the latter days.

Outline

I. The Lord's judgment on the nations (1:1—2:16)
II. God's judgment against Israel expanded (3:1—6:14)
III. The five visions and the promise of restoration (7:1—9:10)
IV. The promise of the restoration of Israel (9:11–15)

I. THE LORD'S JUDGMENT ON THE NATIONS (1:1—2:16)

A. THE PRELUDE

1:1☆ *2 Sam 14:2* 2 Chron 11:6

1 *THE words of* Amos, who was among the herdmen of Te-ko'a, which
he saw concerning Israel in the days of Uz-zi'ah king of Judah, and in

---

1:1 Some think that Amos was a cattle-dealer; others that he was a poor shepherd who watched over flocks of his own. He was a gatherer of wild figs, which was a poor employment. Why God chose Amos to be his

the days of Jer-o-bo′am the son of Jo′ash king of Israel, two years before
the earthquake.
2And he said, The LORD will roar from Zion, and utter his voice from
Jerusalem; and the habitations of the shepherds shall mourn, and the top of
Carmel shall wither.

1:2
Prov 20:2
Isa 42:13
Jer 12:4; 14:2
25:30
Joel 1:9–13, 16–18; 3:16
Zech 14:5

B. THE JUDGMENT AGAINST DAMASCUS

3Thus saith the LORD; For three transgressions of Damascus, and for
four, I will not turn away *the punishment* thereof; because they have
threshed Gilead with threshing instruments of iron:
4But I will send a fire into the house of Haz′a-el, which shall devour the
palaces of Ben–ha′dad.
5I will break also the bar of Damascus, and cut off the inhabitant from
the plain of A′ven, and him that holdeth the sceptre from the house of
Eden: and the people of Syria shall go into captivity unto Kir, saith the
LORD.

☆1:3
Isa 8:4
Amos 1:6, 9, 11, 13; 2:1, 4, 6

☆1:5
Jer 50:36; 51:30
Lam 2:9
Nah 3:13

C. THE JUDGMENT AGAINST GAZA (THE PHILISTINES)

6¶Thus saith the LORD; For three transgressions of Ga′za, and for four, I
will not turn away *the punishment* thereof; because they carried away
captive the whole captivity, to deliver *them* up to Edom:
7But I will send a fire on the wall of Ga′za, which shall devour the palaces
thereof:
8And I will cut off the inhabitant from Ash′dod, and him that holdeth the
sceptre from Ash′ke-lon, and I will turn mine hand against Ekron: and the
remnant of the Philistines shall perish, saith the Lord GOD.

☆1:6
1 Sam 6:17
2 Chron 28:16
Ezek 35:5
Amos 1:9, 11
☆1:7

1:8
Isa 14:29–31
Jer 47:1–7
Ezek 25:16
Zeph 2:4–7

D. THE JUDGMENT AGAINST TYRE

9¶Thus saith the LORD; For three transgressions of Tyrus, and for four, I
will not turn away *the punishment* thereof; because they delivered up the
whole captivity to Edom, and remembered not the brotherly covenant:
10But I will send a fire on the wall of Tyrus, which shall devour the
palaces thereof.

1:9
2 Sam 5:11
1 Kgs 5:1
9:11–14
Isa 23:1–18
Zech 9:2–4

E. THE JUDGMENT AGAINST EDOM

11¶Thus saith the LORD; For three transgressions of Edom, and for four,
I will not turn away *the punishment* thereof; because he did pursue his
brother with the sword, and did cast off all pity, and his anger did tear
perpetually, and he kept his wrath for ever:
12But I will send a fire upon Te′man, which shall devour the palaces of
Boz′rah.

1:11
Gen 27:40
Num 20:14–21
Isa 34:1–17
63:1–3
Jer 49:7–22
Ezek 25:12–14
☆1:12
Gen 36:11
Jer 49:7, 20

prophet we do not know. Humanly speaking, he would appear to be a very ordinary person. But God who calls also endows, and to whatever occupation God calls anyone, God will give him what he needs for his ministry. Amos was called to exercise his prophetic office in the Northern Kingdom. Coming from Tekoa, he was a native of Judea. The earthquake mentioned here is spoken of in Zech. 14:5. Josephus mentions it and alludes to Uzziah's sin in intruding into the priestly office (2 Chron. 26:16) as the reason for the earthquake.

1:3 *For three transgressions . . . and for four.* Damascus is guilty of many transgressions. Three and four add up to seven, the perfect number, which suggests that this nation has filled up the measure of iniquities and thus is ripe for ruin. The same "three . . . and for four" is used by Amos for the iniquities of the other nations who are also facing the judgment of God.

1:5 *the people of Syria shall go . . . unto Kir.* Kir was the district to which the captives of Damascus went (2 Kings 16:9) after the victory of Pul, the king of Assyria. "Decreeing that the Syrians should go back to Kir as slaves was like saying to the Israelites that they must go back to Egypt as slaves, for the Syrians had made their exodus from Kir and now were free (see 9:7)."†

1:6, 7 Gaza was a commercial city. Slaves were bought and sold there. Here many Israelites are sold into slavery to Edom, their ancient enemy.

1:12 *Teman . . . Bozrah.* Teman was in the north of Edom, and Bozrah in the south. The entire country was to be devastated.†

F. THE JUDGMENT AGAINST AMMON

1:13 Jer 49:1–6; Hos 13:16

13¶Thus saith the LORD; For three transgressions of the children of
Ammon, and for four, I will not turn away *the punishment* thereof; because
they have ripped up the women with child of Gilead, that they might
enlarge their border:

1:14☆ Ps 83:15; Job 39:25; Isa 9:5; 30:30; Dan 11:40; Amos 2:2; Zech 7:14
1:15 Jer 49:3

14But I will kindle a fire in the wall of Rab′bah, and it shall devour the
palaces thereof, with shouting in the day of battle, with a tempest in the day
of the whirlwind:
15And their king shall go into captivity, he and his princes together, saith
the LORD.

G. THE JUDGMENT AGAINST MOAB

2:1☆ Isa 15:1–9; 16:1–14; Zech 2:8, 9
2:2 Isa 9:5; Jer 48:24, 41, 45

2 THUS saith the LORD; For three transgressions of Moab, and for four,
I will not turn away *the punishment* thereof; because he burned the
bones of the king of Edom into lime:
2But I will send a fire upon Moab, and it shall devour the palaces of
Kir′i-oth: and Moab shall die with tumult, with shouting, *and* with the
sound of the trumpet:
3And I will cut off the judge from the midst thereof, and will slay all the
princes thereof with him, saith the LORD.

H. THE JUDGMENT AGAINST GOD'S COVENANT NATIONS

1. Judah

2:4☆ Lev 26:14, 15; Judg 2:17–20; 2 Kgs 17:19; Hos 6:11; Amos 3:2
2:5 Jer 17:27; 37:8–10; Hos 8:14

4¶Thus saith the LORD; For three transgressions of Judah, and for four, I
will not turn away *the punishment* thereof; because they have despised the
law of the LORD, and have not kept his commandments, and their lies
caused them to err, after the which their fathers have walked:
5But I will send a fire upon Judah, and it shall devour the palaces of
Jerusalem.

2. Israel

2:6☆ Joel 3:3, 6; Amos 5:11; 8:4–6; Mic 3:2, 3
2:7 Lev 18:8, 15; Prov 28:21; Ezek 22:11; Hos 4:14
2:8☆ Ex 22:26; Deut 24:12–17; Amos 4:1
2:9☆ Josh 11:21, 22; Ezek 17:9; Mal 4:1

6¶Thus saith the LORD; For three transgressions of Israel, and for four, I
will not turn away *the punishment* thereof; because they sold the righteous
for silver, and the poor for a pair of shoes;
7That pant after the dust of the earth on the head of the poor, and turn
aside the way of the meek: and a man and his father will go in unto the
same maid, to profane my holy name:
8And they lay *themselves* down upon clothes laid to pledge by every altar,
and they drink the wine of the condemned *in* the house of their god.
9¶Yet destroyed I the Am′or-ite before them, whose height *was* like the
height of the cedars, and he *was* strong as the oaks; yet I destroyed his fruit
from above, and his roots from beneath.

1:14 *Rabbah,* literally, "the great city," was the capital of the Ammonite nation. Its modern name is Amman; it is now the capital city of the Hashemite Kingdom of Jordan.

2:1 God's moral law pertains to all nations, not to Israel alone. Here a Gentile nation (Moab) commits atrocity against another Gentile nation (Edom).

2:4 The other nations Amos condemned sinned against other nations and many peoples. In accusing Judah of sinfulness, he charges this nation for contempt of God's laws—despising them as well as flaunting their disobedience against them. Any rejection of God's law is a rejection of the lawgiver.

2:6 There were few, if any, of the sins of the pagan nations that Israel itself did not commit. The sacred was overtaken by the secular so that the true faith was virtually abandoned by all except a small minority, who lived amid a licentious and apostate population.

2:8 *lay themselves down upon clothes,* i.e., "clothing stolen from their debtors" (TLB). Under Mosaic law, it was illegal to keep pledged clothing of debtors overnight. (See Exod. 22:26.)

2:9 *Amorite.* God dispossessed the Amorites from their land and gave it to Israel. The Amorites were expelled because of their sins. Amos says that Israel is now guilty of the same sins that the Amorites committed.

10 Also I brought you up from the land of Egypt, and led you forty years
through the wilderness, to possess the land of the Am'or-ite.
11 And I raised up of your sons for prophets, and of your young men for
Nazarites. *Is it* not even thus, O ye children of Israel? saith the LORD.
12 But ye gave the Nazarites wine to drink; and commanded the prophets,
saying, Prophesy not.
13 Behold, I am pressed under you, as a cart is pressed *that is* full of
sheaves.
14 Therefore the flight shall perish from the swift, and the strong shall not
strengthen his force, neither shall the mighty deliver himself:
15 Neither shall he stand that handleth the bow; and *he that is* swift of
foot shall not deliver *himself:* neither shall he that rideth the horse deliver
himself.
16 And *he that is* courageous among the mighty shall flee away naked in
that day, saith the LORD.

2:10 Num 14:34; Deut 2:7; 8:2–4
☆**2:11** Num 6:1–21; 1 Sam 3:20; 19:20; 1 Kgs 17:1; 22:8
☆**2:12** Jer 11:21; Amos 7:13, 16
2:13 Joel 13:13
2:14 Isa 30:16, 17; Jer 9:23; Amos 9:1–3
2:15 Ps 33:16, 17; Isa 31:3
2:16 Judg 4:17

II. GOD'S JUDGMENT AGAINST ISRAEL EXPANDED (3:1—6:14)

A. ISRAEL'S SPECIAL RELATION TO GOD

3 HEAR this word that the LORD hath spoken against you, O children of
Israel, against the whole family which I brought up from the land of
Egypt, saying,
2 You only have I known of all the families of the earth: therefore I will
punish you for all your iniquities.
3 Can two walk together, except they be agreed?
4 Will a lion roar in the forest, when he hath no prey? will a young lion cry
out of his den, if he have taken nothing?
5 Can a bird fall in a snare upon the earth, where no gin *is* for him? shall
one take up a snare from the earth, and have taken nothing at all?
6 Shall a trumpet be blown in the city, and the people not be afraid? shall
there be evil in a city, and the LORD hath not done *it?*
7 Surely the Lord GOD will do nothing but, he revealeth his secret unto his
servants the prophets.
8 The lion hath roared, who will not fear? the Lord GOD hath spoken,
who can but prophesy?

B. SAMARIA'S SINS

9 ¶Publish in the palaces at Ash'dod, and in the palaces in the land of
Egypt, and say, Assemble yourselves upon the mountains of Sa-ma'ri-a,
and behold the great tumults in the midst thereof, and the oppressed in the
midst thereof.

☆**3:1** Jer 8:3; 33:24–26; Ezek 37:16
☆**3:2** Ex 19:5, 6; Deut 7:6
☆**3:3** Gen 5:22; 6:9; Lev 26:23, 24
☆**3:4** Ps 104:21; Hos 11:10
3:6 Isa 14:24–27; Jer 4:5; Ezek 33:3; Hos 5:8; Zeph 1:16; Acts 2:23; 4:28
3:7 Gen 18:17; Dan 9:22–27; Jn 15:15; Rev 4:1
☆**3:8** Jer 20:9; 1 Cor 9:16
☆**3:9** Amos 4:1; 6:1

2:11 *men for Nazarites.* See note on Judg. 13:5.
2:12 Israel seduced Nazarites to break their vow not to drink wine. Satan and his cohorts sought to corrupt young minds that were set on looking toward heaven to join them in mirth, pleasure, and drunkenness. They also threatened the prophets and ordered them not to prophesy. They hated the prophets' messages and did what they could to suppress those who had this gift.
3:1 This word is spoken to the whole family of Israel, not just to the northern tribes.
3:2 *You only have I known.* God bypassed all the other nations of the earth and chose Israel alone to be his people. This choice obligated the chosen nation to serve the One who chose them faithfully. Every privilege carries with it a corresponding responsibility.
3:3 If two people are at variance, harmony cannot prevail. "Where there is not friendship there can be no fellowship."* God and his people must first be friends, but sin makes this impossible.
3:4 God's threats and providences are not bugbears designed to frighten his people. They are warnings designed to bring sinners to their senses.
3:8 Once God has spoken to a prophet, the prophet can only prophesy. The prophetic impulse is like a fire in the bones.
3:9–15 These verses are directed specifically to Samaria (the Northern Kingdom). There is riot in the streets; the prisons are filled with innocent people; the courts of justice are ruled by injustice; the treasuries are replenished by violence and robbery.

3:10 Ps 14:4; Amos 5:7; 6:12; Hab 2:8–11; Zeph 1:9; Zech 5:3, 4; Jas 5:3, 4
3:11☆
3:12☆ 1 Sam 17:34–37

10 For they know not to do right, saith the LORD, who store up violence
and robbery in their palaces.
11 Therefore thus saith the Lord GOD; An adversary *there shall be* even
round about the land; and he shall bring down thy strength from thee, and
thy palaces shall be spoiled.
12 Thus saith the LORD; As the shepherd taketh out of the mouth of the
lion two legs, or a piece of an ear; so shall the children of Israel be taken
out that dwell in Sa-ma′ri-a in the corner of a bed, and in Damascus *in* a
couch.

3:13 Ezek 2:7

13 Hear ye, and testify in the house of Jacob, saith the Lord GOD, the God
of hosts,

3:14 Amos 4:4; 5:5, 6; 7:10, 13

14 That in the day that I shall visit the transgressions of Israel upon him I
will also visit the altars of Beth–el: and the horns of the altar shall be cut
off, and fall to the ground.

3:15 Judg 3:20; 1 Kgs 22:39; Jer 36:22

15 And I will smite the winter house with the summer house; and the
houses of ivory shall perish, and the great houses shall have an end, saith
the LORD.

4:1☆ Deut 32:14, 15; Ps 22:12

4 HEAR this word, ye kine of Ba′shan, that *are* in the mountain of Sa-
ma′ri-a, which oppress the poor, which crush the needy, which say to
their masters, Bring, and let us drink.

4:2☆ Isa 37:29; Jer 16:16; Ezek 29:4; 38:4

2 The Lord GOD hath sworn by his holiness, that, lo, the days shall come
upon you, that he will take you away with hooks, and your posterity with
fishhooks.

4:3 2 Kgs 25:4; Ezek 12:5, 12

3 And ye shall go out at the breaches, every *cow at that which is* before her;
and ye shall cast *them* into the palace, saith the LORD.

C. ISRAEL'S FAILURE TO REPENT

4:4☆

4 ¶Come to Beth–el, and transgress; at Gilgal multiply transgression; and
bring your sacrifices every morning, *and* your tithes after three years:

4:5☆ Lev 7:13; 22:18–21; Hos 9:1, 10

5 And offer a sacrifice of thanksgiving with leaven, and proclaim *and*
publish the free offerings: for this liketh you, O ye children of Israel, saith
the Lord GOD.

4:6☆ Lev 26:26; Deut 28:38; Isa 3:1; Jer 14:18
4:7☆ 1 Kgs 8:35, 36; Zech 14:17

6 ¶And I also have given you cleanness of teeth in all your cities, and want
of bread in all your places: yet have ye not returned unto me, saith the
LORD.
7 And also I have withholden the rain from you, when *there were* yet three
months to the harvest: and I caused it to rain upon one city, and caused it
not to rain upon another city: one piece was rained upon, and the piece
whereupon it rained not withered.

3:11, 12 Samaria shall be invaded and destroyed. The citizenry shall be taken captive by the hands of the enemy. Let this be told to all, for God the Lord has spoken, the God of Israel, who has the right to pass judgment and the power to execute it.

4:1 *ye kine* ["fat cows"] *of Bashan.* Amos derides the women of Israel, likening them to fat cows. Bashan was a fruitful, grain-producing region.

4:2 *hooks* "in your noses," implied.† Assyrian reliefs portray prisoners who have hooks in their lips.

4:4, 5 In effect God says, "Multiply your transgressions by multiplying your sacrifices. It will do you no good for I regard them as an abomination inasmuch as your hearts are not right with me. What you do will only fill up the measure of your iniquity, and then will judgment be executed."

4:6 Over and over again God sent Samaria famine, blight, pestilence, and the like in order to warn them to repent and turn from their wicked ways. In chapter 4 God's words "you did not return to me" appear five times. Samaria paid no attention to God's warnings. The arraignment is concluded by the statement that since Samaria (Israel) refused to repent, the nation must now prepare to meet God, who will send the divine judgment upon them by means of the Assyrian invaders. The Assyrians will destroy the Northern Kingdom, and it will rise no more.

4:7ff God tried everything to get the attention of Samaria so that they would repent. Nothing worked. He sent famine (4:6); he sent drought (4:7); he sent blight and mildew (4:9); he sent pestilence (4:10); he overthrew some and spared others (4:11). Nothing moved them, so the last word from God is this: "Prepare to meet thy God, O Israel." This is the God of anger, judgment, and unyielding retribution.

8 So two *or* three cities wandered unto one city, to drink water; but they
were not satisfied: yet have ye not returned unto me, saith the LORD.
9 I have smitten you with blasting and mildew: when your gardens and
your vineyards and your fig trees and your olive trees increased, the
palmerworm devoured *them:* yet have ye not returned unto me, saith the
LORD.
10 I have sent among you the pestilence after the manner of Egypt: your
young men have I slain with the sword, and have taken away your horses;
and I have made the stink of your camps to come up unto your nostrils: yet
have ye not returned unto me, saith the LORD.
11 I have overthrown *some* of you, as God overthrew Sodom and Go-
mor'rah, and ye were as a firebrand plucked out of the burning: yet have ye
not returned unto me, saith the LORD.
12 Therefore thus will I do unto thee, O Israel: *and* because I will do this
unto thee, prepare to meet thy God, O Israel.
13 For, lo, he that formeth the mountains, and createth the wind, and
declareth unto man what *is* his thought, that maketh the morning darkness,
and treadeth upon the high places of the earth, The LORD, The God of
hosts, *is* his name.

D. THE SONG OF GRIEF OVER ISRAEL

5 HEAR ye this word which I take up against you, *even* a lamentation, O
house of Israel.
2 The virgin of Israel is fallen; she shall no more rise: she is forsaken upon
her land; *there is* none to raise her up.
3 For thus saith the Lord GOD; The city that went out *by* a thousand shall
leave an hundred, and that which went forth *by* an hundred shall leave ten,
to the house of Israel.

E. GOD'S CALL FOR ISRAEL TO REPENT

4 ¶For thus saith the LORD unto the house of Israel, Seek ye me, and ye
shall live:
5 But seek not Beth–el, nor enter into Gilgal, and pass not to Be'er–
she'ba: for Gilgal shall surely go into captivity, and Beth–el shall come to
nought.
6 Seek the LORD, and ye shall live; lest he break out like fire in the house
of Joseph, and devour *it*, and *there be* none to quench *it* in Beth–el.
7 Ye who turn judgment to wormwood, and leave off righteousness in the
earth,
8 *Seek him* that maketh the seven stars and O-ri'on, and turneth the
shadow of death into the morning, and maketh the day dark with night:
that calleth for the waters of the sea, and poureth them out upon the face of
the earth: The LORD *is* his name:
9 That strengtheneth the spoiled against the strong, so that the spoiled
shall come against the fortress.
10 They hate him that rebuketh in the gate, and they abhor him that
speaketh uprightly.

4:8 1 Kgs 18:5; Isa 41:17, 18; Jer 14:3, 4; Ezek 4:16; Mic 6:14; Hag 1:6
4:9 Deut 28:22, 42; 1 Kgs 8:37; Joel 2:25; Amos 7:1, 2
4:10 Ex 9:3–6; 12:29, 30; Lev 26:25; Deut 28:26; Jer 11:22; 18:21; Isa 9:13; Amos 8:3
4:11 Gen 19:24, 25; Jer 23:14
4:12 Isa 47:3; Ezek 13:5; Amos 5:4–15
4:13 Deut 32:13; Job 38:4–11; Ps 135:7; 139:2; Dan 2:28, 30; Amos 5:8; 8:9; Hab 3:19
☆**5:1** Jer 9:10; Ezek 19:1, 14; Mic 2:4
5:2 Amos 7:2–5
☆**5:4** Deut 4:29; 30:1–8; 32:46, 47; Amos 5:6
☆**5:5**
5:6 Ex 22:6; Deut 4:24; Amos 5:4
5:7 Amos 2:3; 5:12; 6:12
5:8 Gen 7:11–20; Job 9:9; 12:22; 37:13; 38:31–34; Amos 9:6; Mt 4:16; Lk 1:79
5:9 Amos 2:14; Mic 5:11
5:10 Jer 17:16, 17; Amos 5:15; Jn 7:7; 8:45–47

5:1 Chapters 3, 4, and 5 begin with this phrase: "Hear ye this word." God is serious and demands that they attend to his word.
5:4 There still is time. Despite their great evils God waits for them to seek his face in repentance, so that they may live.
5:5ff The sins of Samaria were many. They turned to idols (5:5); they executed injustice (5:7); they persecuted God's faithful priests and people (5:10); they trod on the poor (5:11).

5:11 Deut 28:30; Isa 65:21, 23; Mic 6:15

11Forasmuch therefore as your treading *is* upon the poor, and ye take
from him burdens of wheat: ye have built houses of hewn stone, but ye
shall not dwell in them; ye have planted pleasant vineyards, but ye shall not
drink wine of them.

5:12 Ps 26:9, 10; Isa 1:23; Mic 3:11; 7:3

12For I know your manifold transgressions and your mighty sins: they
afflict the just, they take a bribe, and they turn aside the poor in the gate
from their right.

13Therefore the prudent shall keep silence in that time: for it *is* an evil
time.

5:14☆

14Seek good, and not evil, that ye may live: and so the LORD, the God of
hosts, shall be with you, as ye have spoken.

5:15 1 Kgs 20:31; Ps 34:14; 97:10; Joel 2:14; Jonah 3:9

15Hate the evil, and love the good, and establish judgment in the gate: it
may be that the LORD God of hosts will be gracious unto the remnant of
Joseph.

5:16 Isa 15:2–5; Amos 8:3, 10; Joel 1:8, 11; Mic 1:8, 2:4

16Therefore the LORD, the God of hosts, the Lord, saith thus; Wailing
shall be in all streets; and they shall say in all the highways, Alas! alas! and
they shall call the husbandman to mourning, and such as are skilful of
lamentation to wailing.

5:17 Isa16:10; 32:10–12

17And in all vineyards *shall be* wailing: for I will pass through thee, saith
the LORD.

5:18☆ Isa 5:30; Jer 30:7; Zeph 1:14; 2 Pet 3:10

18Woe unto you that desire the day of the LORD! to what end *is* it for
you? the day of the LORD *is* darkness, and not light.

5:19 Job 20:24; Amos 9:1, 2

19As if a man did flee from a lion, and a bear met him; or went into the
house, and leaned his hand on the wall, and a serpent bit him.

5:20 Amos 5:18

20*Shall* not the day of the LORD *be* darkness, and not light? even very
dark, and no brightness in it?

5:21☆ Prov 15:8; 21:27; Isa 1:11–16; Jer 14:12; Hos 5:6

21I hate, I despise your feast days, and I will not smell in your solemn
assemblies.

5:22 Lev 6:9–23; 7:11–21

22Though ye offer me burnt offerings and your meat offerings, I will not
accept *them:* neither will I regard the peace offerings of your fat beasts.

23Take thou away from me the noise of thy songs; for I will not hear the
melody of thy viols.

5:24 Jer 22:3; Amos 5:7; Mic 6:8

24But let judgment run down as waters, and righteousness as a mighty
stream.

25Have ye offered unto me sacrifices and offerings in the wilderness forty
years, O house of Israel?

26But ye have borne the tabernacle of your Mo′loch and Chi′un your
images, the star of your god, which ye made to yourselves.

27Therefore will I cause you to go into captivity beyond Damascus, saith
the LORD, whose name *is* The God of hosts.

F. THE DOOM OF EXILE FOR THOSE WHO LIVE IN LUXURY

6:1 Judg 18:7; Isa 32:9–11

6 WOE to them *that are* at ease in Zion, and trust in the mountain of Sa-
ma′ri-a, *which are* named chief of the nations, to whom the house of
Israel came!

5:14 Judgment is about to fall on Israel, yet God continues to hold forth the olive branch of peace. He implores his people to seek good and not evil, to "Hate the evil, and love the good" (5:15). Although the hour is late, God is still ready to reverse the forces of judgment and bring peace and safety to his people. Sad to say, they spurned the last-minute appeals and were destroyed. Today God speaks the same word of hope to the most awful sinners, assuring them that before the clock strikes twelve he will save them, if they will repent.

5:18 *Woe unto you that desire the day of the LORD.* Israel regarded this "day" as a time when their enemies would be overcome and Israel would be vindicated before the world as God's elect people. Amos' bad news is that God's elect people must face judgment.

5:21ff God hated Samaria's feast-days, their solemn assemblies, their offerings, their songs, and their melodies. "To obey is better than to sacrifice and to hearken than the fat of rams" (1 Sam. 15:22). But they refused to do this; so he would not listen to them. God desired justice and righteousness to be among them.

2 Pass ye unto Cal′neh, and see; and from thence go ye to Ha′math the
great: then go down to Gath of the Philistines: *be they* better than these
kingdoms? or their border greater than your border?
3 Ye that put far away the evil day, and cause the seat of violence to come
near;
4 That lie upon beds of ivory, and stretch themselves upon their couches,
and eat the lambs out of the flock, and the calves out of the midst of the
stall;
5 That chant to the sound of the viol, *and* invent to themselves instru-
ments of musick, like David;
6 That drink wine in bowls, and anoint themselves with the chief
ointments: but they are not grieved for the affliction of Joseph.
7 ¶Therefore now shall they go captive with the first that go captive, and
the banquet of them that stretched themselves shall be removed.
8 The Lord GOD hath sworn by himself, saith the LORD the God of hosts,
I abhor the excellency of Jacob, and hate his palaces: therefore will I deliver
up the city with all that is therein.
9 And it shall come to pass, if there remain ten men in one house, that
they shall die.
10 And a man's uncle shall take him up, and he that burneth him, to bring
out the bones out of the house, and shall say unto him that *is* by the sides
of the house, *Is there* yet *any* with thee? and he shall say, No. Then shall he
say, Hold thy tongue: for we may not make mention of the name of the
LORD.
11 For, behold, the LORD commandeth, and he will smite the great house
with breaches, and the little house with clefts.
12 ¶Shall horses run upon the rock? will *one* plow *there* with oxen? for ye
have turned judgment into gall, and the fruit of righteousness into hemlock:
13 Ye which rejoice in a thing of nought, which say, Have we not taken to
us horns by our own strength?
14 But, behold, I will raise up against you a nation, O house of Israel, saith
the LORD the God of hosts; and they shall afflict you from the entering in
of Ha′math unto the river of the wilderness.

6:2 Gen 10:10; 1 Sam 17:23; 2 Kgs 17:24, 30; 19:13; Isa 10:9
6:3 Amos 5:18; 9:10
6:4 Ezek 34:2, 3
6:5 1 Chron 15:16; 23:5
☆**6:7**
☆**6:8** Lev 26:11; Zech 11:8
6:10 1 Sam 31:12; Amos 5:13; 8:3
6:12 Amos 5:7, 11, 12
☆**6:14** Num 34:7, 8; 2 Kgs 14:25

III. THE FIVE VISIONS AND THE PROMISE OF RESTORATION (7:1—9:10)

A. THE VISION OF THE SWARM OF LOCUSTS

7 THUS hath the Lord GOD shewed unto me; and, behold, he formed
grasshoppers in the beginning of the shooting up of the latter growth;
and, lo, *it was* the latter growth after the king's mowings.
2 And it came to pass, *that* when they had made an end of eating the grass
of the land, then I said, O Lord GOD, forgive, I beseech thee: by whom
shall Jacob arise? for he *is* small.
3 The LORD repented for this: It shall not be, saith the LORD.

☆**7:1** Ex 10:12–16; Nah 3:15–17
7:2 Ex 10:15; Num 14:17–19; Isa 37:4; Jer 14:7; 42:2; Ezek 9:8; Rev 9:4
7:3 Deut 32:36; Hos 11:8

6:7 *at ease,* i.e., full of pride, self-satisfied, and secure. Many of the people supposed they were safe and that God would preserve them as he had often done before. They thought no judgment could overtake the elect nation.

6:8 *I abhor the excellency of Jacob.* God gave to his people everything the human heart could desire. They belonged to the congregation of Israel; they were called the chief of the nations; they had the temple, the altar, and the priesthood. This people followed the forms of worship, but denied its power. They were hypocrites, who did not practice what was preached to them by God. Therefore, God loathes, hates, detests, despises, and execrates them. His judgment against their wickedness must follow.

6:14 God can easily bring to pass whatever he needs to do to correct, chastise, or even destroy a nation. He now will raise up a nation, Assyria, to do what he wants done to Israel, and no one can stop him.

7:1 God shows Amos his intention to send grasshoppers over Israel. The prophet prays for God not to do this. God agrees not to send the grasshoppers, saying, "It shall not be."

B. THE FIRE THAT BURNED UP THE WATER

7:4☆ Isa 66:15, 16; Amos 2:5

4 ¶Thus hath the Lord GOD shewed unto me: and, behold, the Lord GOD called to contend by fire, and it devoured the great deep, and did eat up a part.

5 Then said I, O Lord GOD, cease, I beseech thee: by whom shall Jacob arise? for he *is* small.

7:6 Amos 7:3

6 The LORD repented for this: This also shall not be, saith the Lord GOD.

C. THE VISION OF THE PLUMBLINE

7:7☆

7 ¶Thus he shewed me: and, behold, the Lord stood upon a wall *made* by a plumbline, with a plumbline in his hand.

7:8 Isa 28:17; 34:11; Amos 8:2

8 And the LORD said unto me, Amos, what seest thou? And I said, A plumbline. Then said the Lord, Behold, I will set a plumbline in the midst of my people Israel: I will not again pass by them any more:

7:9 2 Kgs 15:8–10; Amos 3:14; 5:5; 7:13; 8:14

9 And the high places of Isaac shall be desolate, and the sanctuaries of Israel shall be laid waste; and I will rise against the house of Jer-o-bo′am with the sword.

7:10☆ 1 Kgs 12:31; 18:17; 2 Kgs 14:23, 24; Lk 23:2

10 ¶Then Am-a-zi′ah the priest of Beth–el sent to Jer-o-bo′am king of Israel, saying, Amos hath conspired against thee in the midst of the house of Israel: the land is not able to bear all his words.

11 For thus Amos saith, Jer-o-bo′am shall die by the sword, and Israel shall surely be led away captive out of their own land.

7:12 1 Sam 9:9; 2 Chron 16:10

12 Also Am-a-zi′ah said unto Amos, O thou seer, go, flee thee away into the land of Judah, and there eat bread, and prophesy there:

7:13☆ 1 Kgs 12:29, 32; 13:1; Amos 2:12; Acts 4:17, 18; 5:28, 40

13 But prophesy not again any more at Beth–el: for it *is* the king's chapel, and it *is* the king's court.

7:14☆ 1 Kgs 20:35; 2 Kgs 2:3–7; 2 Chron 16:7

14 ¶Then answered Amos, and said to Am-a-zi′ah, I *was* no prophet, neither *was* I a prophet's son; but I *was* an herdman, and a gatherer of sycomore fruit:

7:15 Jer 1:7; Ezek 2:3, 4

15 And the LORD took me as I followed the flock, and the LORD said unto me, Go, prophesy unto my people Israel.

7:16 Isa 31:10; Amos 7:13; Mic 2:6

16 ¶Now therefore hear thou the word of the LORD: Thou sayest, Prophesy not against Israel, and drop not *thy word* against the house of Isaac.

7:17 Isa 13:16; Jer 14:16; 20:6; Hos 4:13, 14

17 Therefore thus saith the LORD; Thy wife shall be an harlot in the city, and thy sons and thy daughters shall fall by the sword, and thy land shall be divided by line; and thou shalt die in a polluted land: and Israel shall surely go into captivity forth of his land.

D. THE VISION OF THE BASKET OF RIPE FRUIT

8:1☆ **8:2** Isa 28:4; Jer 24:1–3; Amos 7:8

8 THUS hath the Lord GOD shewed unto me: and behold a basket of summer fruit.

2 And he said, Amos, what seest thou? And I said, A basket of summer

---

7:4 God shows Amos a judgment by fire. Again he beseeches God, and God agrees that it shall not be.

7:7 Now God gives Amos a vision of a plumb line, an instrument used by surveyers, masons, and bricklayers. God will stand on the walls of Israel and cause *them to be crushed* and ruined. Multitudes will die and the royal house will be destroyed (7:8, 9).

7:10 *Amos hath conspired,* i.e., "Amos is a traitor." The prophet came from Tekoa in Judah and was thus a "foreigner." His message was unwelcome. Amos was accused of being a troublemaker and was informed that he should leave Bethel.

7:13 *at Beth-el,* i.e., "in the capital." (See note on Gen. 28:19.)

7:14 Amos adds insult to injury by stating that he is only a layman, a herdsman, and a fruit picker. To suppose that such a common person would have a message from God for Israel was thought to be ridiculous.

8:1 God shows Amos a basket of summer fruit. It signifies that Israel is ripe for ruin. There shall be universal desolation over all the land.

fruit. Then said the LORD unto me, The end is come upon my people of
Israel; I will not again pass by them any more.
3 And the songs of the temple shall be howlings in that day, saith the Lord
GOD: *there shall be* many dead bodies in every place; they shall cast *them*
forth with silence.
4 ¶Hear this, O ye that swallow up the needy, even to make the poor of
the land to fail,
5 Saying, When will the new moon be gone, that we may sell corn? and
the sabbath, that we may set forth wheat, making the ephah small, and the
shekel great, and falsifying the balances by deceit?
6 That we may buy the poor for silver, and the needy for a pair of shoes;
yea, and sell the refuse of the wheat?
7 The LORD hath sworn by the excellency of Jacob, Surely I will never
forget any of their works.
8 Shall not the land tremble for this, and every one mourn that dwelleth
therein? and it shall rise up wholly as a flood; and it shall be cast out and
drowned, as *by* the flood of Egypt.
9 And it shall come to pass in that day, saith the Lord GOD, that I will
cause the sun to go down at noon, and I will darken the earth in the clear
day:
10 And I will turn your feasts into mourning, and all your songs into
lamentation; and I will bring up sackcloth upon all loins, and baldness
upon every head; and I will make it as the mourning of an only *son,* and the
end thereof as a bitter day.
11 ¶Behold, the days come, saith the Lord GOD, that I will send a famine
in the land, not a famine of bread, nor a thirst for water, but of hearing the
words of the LORD:
12 And they shall wander from sea to sea, and from the north even to the
east, they shall run to and fro to seek the word of the LORD, and shall not
find *it.*
13 In that day shall the fair virgins and young men faint for thirst.
14 They that swear by the sin of Sa-ma'ri-a, and say, Thy God, O Dan,
liveth; and, The manner of Be'er–she'ba liveth; even they shall fall, and
never rise up again.

E. THE SMITTEN TEMPLE AND THE SLAIN PEOPLE

9 I SAW the Lord standing upon the altar: and he said, Smite the lintel
of the door, that the posts may shake: and cut them in the head, all of
them; and I will slay the last of them with the sword: he that fleeth of them
shall not flee away, and he that escapeth of them shall not be delivered.
2 Though they dig into hell, thence shall mine hand take them; though
they climb up to heaven, thence will I bring them down:

☆**8:3** Hos 10:5, 6 Amos 5:23
☆**8:4** Amos 2:6, 7 5:11
8:5 Ex 20:8–10 Neh 13:15–21 Hos 12:7
8:7 Deut 33:26–29 Ps 10:11; 47:4 68:34 Hos 7:2; 8:13
8:8 Ps 18:7; 114:3–7 Isa 8:7, 8 Jer 4:24–26 46:8 Amos 8:10; 9:5 Hag 2:6, 7
8:9 Ex 10:21–23 Amos 4:13; 5:8 Mic 3:6 Mt 24:29; 27:45 Mk 15:33 Lk 23:44
8:10 Isa 15:2, 3 Ezek 7:18 Amos 5:23 6:4–7
☆**8:11**
8:12 Ezek 20:3, 31
8:13 Isa 41:17 Lam 1:18, 2:21 Hos 2:3
8:14 1 Kgs 12:28, 29 2 Kgs 10:29 Hos 8:5
9:1 2 Chron 18:18 Zeph 2:14
☆**9:2** Job 26:6 Ps 139:7–10 Isa 14:13–16 Lk 10:18

8:3 Israel raised up temples for their idols. They went to them singing their ribald songs, rising up to commit sexual sins, and going *forth to cheat the* poor, short-change the buyers of their wares, and commit every conceivable abomination. God will turn their singing into mourning, as dead bodies are scattered over the landscape as seed is sown in the spring. The fruit of their evil deeds is likened to a basket full of ripe fruit (8:1, 2), ready to be consumed, as they will be, because of their failure to repent and turn to their God.

8:4ff God now discloses what the sins of Israel are. They have no reverence for God; they have only the forms of godliness, not the substance; they cheat; they treat the poor barbarously and without mercy. They must be punished, and God has taken an oath by himself to do so. He will bring ruin upon them. It will come when they do not expect it and it will turn their laughter into mourning. Even their songs shall become howlings.

8:11 The worst of all punishments will come upon Israel. There will be a famine of the Word of God, not of bread and water. No prophets will be sent to them and no visions from God given to guide them. They shall run to and fro, trying to find a word from God, but they will not find it (8:12). The parable is simple: When they had the pure Word of God they rejected it; now they will have nothing from God to reject.

9:2 God is omnipresent. Those who seek to flee from God and to escape the judgment even by seeking refuge in hell cannot hide from his angry hands.

9:3 Job 34:22; Ps 139:9–11; Jer 16:16; 23:23, 24
9:4 Lev 26:33, 36–39; Deut 28:63–65; Jer 24:6; 44:11
9:5 Ps 46:6; Isa 64:1; Rev 20:11
9:6 Ps 104:3, 6, 13
9:7☆ 2 Chron 14:9, 12; Isa 20:4; 43:3
9:8 Deut 4:31; 6:15; 1 Kgs 13:34; Jer 5:10; 33:24–26; Hos 9:11–17; Joel 2:32; Amos 7:17
9:9 Lev 26:33; Deut 28:64

3 And though they hide themselves in the top of Carmel, I will search and
take them out thence; and though they be hid from my sight in the bottom
of the sea, thence will I command the serpent, and he shall bite them:
4 And though they go into captivity before their enemies, thence will I
command the sword, and it shall slay them: and I will set mine eyes upon
them for evil, and not for good.
5 And the Lord GOD of hosts *is* he that toucheth the land, and it shall
melt, and all that dwell therein shall mourn: and it shall rise up wholly like
a flood; and shall be drowned, as *by* the flood of Egypt.
6 *It is* he that buildeth his stories in the heaven, and hath founded his
troop in the earth; he that calleth for the waters of the sea, and poureth
them out upon the face of the earth: The LORD *is* his name.
7 *Are* ye not as children of the E-thi-o′pi-ans unto me, O children of
Israel? saith the LORD. Have not I brought up Israel out of the land of
Egypt? and the Philistines from Caph′tor, and the Syrians from Kir?
8 Behold, the eyes of the Lord GOD *are* upon the sinful kingdom, and I
will destroy it from off the face of the earth; saving that I will not utterly
destroy the house of Jacob, saith the LORD.
9 For, lo, I will command, and I will sift the house of Israel among all
nations, like as *corn* is sifted in a sieve, yet shall not the least grain fall upon
the earth.
10 All the sinners of my people shall die by the sword, which say, The evil
shall not overtake nor prevent us.

IV. THE PROMISE OF THE RESTORATION OF ISRAEL (9:11–15)

9:11☆ Ps 143:5; Isa 9:6, 7; 11:1–10; 16:5; 63:11; Lam 5:21; Ezek 21:25–27
9:13 Lev 26:5; Isa 55:13; Ezek 36:35; Hos 2:21–23; Joel 3:18, 20; Jn 4:35
9:14 Ps 53:6; Isa 61:4; Jer 30:3; 31:38–40; Ezek 36:33–36; 37:25–28
9:15☆

11 In that day will I raise up the tabernacle of David that is fallen, and
close up the breaches thereof; and I will raise up his ruins, and I will build
it as in the days of old:
12 That they may possess the remnant of Edom, and of all the heathen,
which are called by my name, saith the LORD that doeth this.
13 Behold, the days come, saith the LORD, that the plowman shall overtake
the reaper, and the treader of grapes him that soweth seed; and the
mountains shall drop sweet wine, and all the hills shall melt.
14 And I will bring again the captivity of my people of Israel, and they
shall build the waste cities, and inhabit *them;* and they shall plant
vineyards, and drink the wine thereof; they shall also make gardens, and
eat the fruit of them.
15 And I will plant them upon their land, and they shall no more be pulled
up out of their land which I have given them, saith the LORD thy God.

Whoever flees to the uttermost parts of the heavens will find they are not beyond the reach of God's avenging hand. Wherever they are and wherever they flee to, they will not escape. God catches up with the wicked at last. And what he did to Israel in that day he will do to those who spurn his grace and mock his law today, tomorrow, or till time shall be no more.

9:7 Israel thought she was specially favored, since God had delivered her from bondage in Egypt. God reminds her that he also delivered the Philistines from Caphtor and the Syrians *from Kir. God is concerned with all nations*, not just Israel, chosen as she was.

9:11 *In that day,* or, "at that time." Amos salted his message of impending judgment with a word of hope and comfort for the future. The day would come when God would restore his people to their land. James quotes this passage in Acts 15:16, 17. Some think Amos prophesied that the reinstatement of the house of David to a place of power will come after the Second Coming of Christ, when Jesus will sit upon the throne of David, as promised in Luke 1:32.

9:15 When the restoration of God's people takes place, paradise will have been regained. God promises that never again will there be any judgment against *them*. Cities will be rebuilt; the land will flourish and bring forth its fruit; even the mountains will drip sweet wine. God has sworn and will not change. Hope deferred will have come at last.

OBADIAH

Authorship, date, and background Three of the minor prophets addressed themselves to a single nation in each book: Obadiah spoke about Edom, Habakkuk about Chaldea, and Nahum about Assyria. This book, whose author was Obadiah (which means "servant of Yahweh"), provides no information about the prophet beyond his name. We know nothing of his background. Nor is it possible to date the book with precision. Apparently Obadiah had in mind a time when Jerusalem was invaded and Edom did nothing to assist her. Whether this was the destruction of Jerusalem in 586 B.C. or one of the earlier invasions, we do not know. (Read, for example, of an invasion by Shishak in the time of Jeroboam, recorded in 1 Kings 14:25, 26; or of an invasion by the Philistines and Arabians in the days of Jehoram as recorded in 2 Chron 21:16, 17; or of the invasion by Joash of Israel in the days of Amaziah as recorded in 2 Kings 14:13, 14; or of the final invasion of Jerusalem under Nebuchadnezzar as told in 2 Kings 24:1ff.) Some conservative scholars date the book as early as the ninth century B.C.; others date it after the fall of Jerusalem under Nebuchadnezzar.

The prophecy was spoken against Edom, whose people descended from Esau, Jacob's brother. Enmity existed between their offspring for generations. The Edomites lived in fortified cities that were almost impregnable; Sela (Petra), Teman, and Bozrah were among their strongholds. Sela was located along an important caravan route and was carved out of rock. During the Exodus from Egypt the Edomites forbade the Israelites to pass through their land. This and other actions were included in the condemnation heaped upon Edom by Obadiah as a prophet of God.

Characteristics and content Obadiah points to the treachery and pride of Edom as besetting sins. He makes it plain that God does not stand by idly when his chosen people are being destroyed and their brother, Edom, does nothing to help them. Indeed the Edomites helped the enemies of Israel, and this is an act that a just God will not overlook. So God, through Obadiah, pronounces divine judgment upon this people and foretells the nation's destruction. Edom shall drink the cup of the wrath of God.

At the same time, Obadiah contrasts the end of Edom with God's providential watchcare over his people Israel. Mount Zion will be established in the future; they shall have their lands restored to them and they will have the Lord as their ruler. And in the end Mount Esau, which represents the Edomites and their power, shall someday be subject to Mount Zion or the sons and daughters of the brother they are mistreating.

Outline

I. God's judgment on Edom (1–14)
II. The coming day of the Lord's vengeance (15–21)

I. GOD'S JUDGMENT ON EDOM (1–14)

A. EDOM'S FALL PREDICTED

THE vision of O-ba-di'ah. Thus saith the Lord GOD concerning Edom; We
have heard a rumour from the LORD, and an ambassador is sent among the
heathen, Arise ye, and let us rise up against her in battle.
2 Behold, I have made thee small among the heathen: thou art greatly
despised.
3 ¶The pride of thine heart hath deceived thee, thou that dwellest in the
clefts of the rock, whose habitation *is* high; that saith in his heart, Who
shall bring me down to the ground?

☆**1:1** Isa 34:5–15; 63:1–6; Jer 49:7–22; Ps 137:7; Ezek 25:12–14; Amos 1:11, 12
1:2 Num 24:15–19
☆**1:3** Prov 16:18; Jer 49:15, 16

---

1 *Edom.* A nation southeast of Israel, including Petra, the city hewn from rocks. Her southern boundary was on the Gulf of Agaba.† (See note on Gen. 36:9 for information on the Edomites.)

3, 4 Edom proudly thought itself impregnable; however, God would bring about its destruction and prove Edom to be wrong.

1:4 Job 39:26–30 Isa 14:12–15 Jer 51:53 Amos 9:2

[4]Though thou exalt *thyself* as the eagle, and though thou set thy nest among the stars, thence will I bring thee down, saith the LORD.

B. THE REASON FOR THE JUDGMENT EXPLAINED

1:5 Jer 49:9, 10

[5]If thieves came to thee, if robbers by night, (how art thou cut off!) would they not have stolen till they had enough? if the grapegatherers came to thee, would they not leave *some* grapes?

1:6☆

[6]How are *the things* of Esau searched out! *how* are his hidden things sought up!

1:7 Ps 55:12–14 Isa 19:11–14 Jer 4:30

[7]All the men of thy confederacy have brought thee *even* to the border: the men that were at peace with thee have deceived thee, *and* prevailed against thee; *they that eat* thy bread have laid a wound under thee: *there is* none understanding in him.

1:8☆ Job 5:12–14 Isa 19:3, 13, 14 29:14

[8]Shall I not in that day, saith the LORD, even destroy the wise *men* out of Edom, and understanding out of the mount of Esau?

1:9 Jer 49:20–22 Amos 2:16

[9]And thy mighty *men,* O Te'man, shall be dismayed, to the end that every one of the mount of Esau may be cut off by slaughter.

1:10☆ Num 20:14–22 Ps 83:5–8 109:29 Ezek 7:18 25:12–14

[10]¶For *thy* violence against thy brother Jacob shame shall cover thee, and thou shalt be cut off for ever.

1:11 2 Kgs 25:8–21 2 Chron 36:19, 20 Jer 52:12–30

[11]In the day that thou stoodest on the other side, in the day that the strangers carried away captive his forces, and foreigners entered into his gates, and cast lots upon Jerusalem, even thou *wast* as one of them.

1:12 Ps 22:17 Mic 4:11

[12]But thou shouldest not have looked on the day of thy brother in the day that he became a stranger; neither shouldest thou have rejoiced over the children of Judah in the day of their destruction; neither shouldest thou have spoken proudly in the day of distress.

1:13 2 Kgs 24:13–16 2 Chron 36:18

[13]Thou shouldest not have entered into the gate of my people in the day of their calamity; yea, thou shouldest not have looked on their affliction in the day of their calamity, nor have laid *hands* on their substance in the day of their calamity;

[14]Neither shouldest thou have stood in the crossway, to cut off those of his that did escape; neither shouldest thou have delivered up those of his that did remain in the day of distress.

II. THE COMING DAY OF THE LORD'S VENGEANCE (15–21)

A. THE JUDGMENT AGAINST THE HEATHEN

1:15☆ Jer 9:25, 26 25:15 Joel 1:15

[15]For the day of the LORD *is* near upon all the heathen: as thou hast done, it shall be done unto thee: thy reward shall return upon thine own head.

1:16☆

[16]For as ye have drunk upon my holy mountain, *so* shall all the heathen drink continually, yea, they shall drink, and they shall swallow down, and they shall be as though they had not been.

---

6 *Esau.* Esau (Edom) and Jacob (Israel) were brothers. They were rivals and later their descendants became enemies. *searched out,* i.e. "pillaged."

8 *even destroy the wise men.* Edom was noted for her *wise men. Eliphaz,* the wisest of Job's three friends, was from Teman, five miles east of Petra, in Edom.

10ff The sins of Edom are laid bare. They committed violence against Jacob and his people. They failed to help their kin in the day of calamity. They looked upon their kin's calamities with pleasure and satisfaction. They insulted them, robbed them, and murdered them. They allied themselves with the enemies of their kin. They even refused to help the refugees, returning them to the enemy. Thus, they brought about their own destruction, for whoever strikes at God's people strikes at God.

15, 16 The day of God's judgment has come for Edom, as it will come for all the nations in the end. Edom, by way of retribution, would experience the same calamities she created. She must drink the cup of trembling.

B. ISRAEL DELIVERED AND REGATHERED

17¶But upon mount Zion shall be deliverance, and there shall be holiness;
and the house of Jacob shall possess their possessions.
18And the house of Jacob shall be a fire, and the house of Joseph a flame,
and the house of Esau for stubble, and they shall kindle in them, and
devour them; and there shall not be *any* remaining of the house of Esau; for
the LORD hath spoken *it*.
19And *they of* the south shall possess the mount of Esau; and *they of* the
plain the Philistines: and they shall possess the fields of E'phra-im, and the
fields of Sa-ma'ri-a: and Benjamin *shall possess* Gilead.
20And the captivity of this host of the children of Israel *shall possess* that
of the Canaanites, *even* unto Zar'e-phath; and the captivity of Jerusalem,
which *is* in Seph'a-rad, shall possess the cities of the south.
21And saviours shall come up on mount Zion to judge the mount of Esau;
and the kingdom shall be the LORD'S.

☆**1:17** Isa 14:1, 2; Joel 3:19–21; Amos 9:11–15
☆**1:18** Isa 31:9; Amos 1:11, 12; Zech 12:6
☆**1:19** Num 24:15–19; Isa 11:13; Jer 31:5; 32:44; Ezek 36:6–12; 47:13–20; Mic 7:14
☆**1:20** 1 Kgs 17:9
1:21 Ps 22:28; Isa 19:20; Mic 4:7; Zech 9:11–17; Lk 1:32, 33; Rev 11:15; 19:6

---

17 Not all the children of Jacob will be destroyed. There will be a remnant; ultimately a regathered, restored, and triumphant Israel will occupy all the possessions promised to them by God in the covenant.
18 Israel came from Jacob and Edom from Esau, Jacob's brother. God promised that Israel would be saved and Edom destroyed.
19 Here Obadiah indicates what the realm of Israel shall include and what territories held by other nations shall be part of its inheritance. The Negev formerly belonged to Esau.
20 Halah (see 2 Kings 17:6; 18:11 and 1 Chron. 5:26) was one of the places where the prisoners taken by Assyria were brought. Apparently it must have been within reach of Nineveh. *Sepharad* was another place to which captives from the Northern Kingdom were exiled. Where it is we do not know. Many conjectural identifications are without substance.

JONAH

Authorship, date, and background The authorship of this book is not plainly stated, but there is no good reason to suppose that it was not Jonah. The use of the third person is no problem since the same approach appears in the Pentateuch of Moses as well as profane literature including the writings of Julius Caesar. Jonah was the son of Amittai (whose name means "dove"), and according to 2 Kings 14:25 he lived in Gath-hepher, which was near Nazareth, in the eighth century B.C. Hosea and Amos were contemporaries and Jeroboam II was king.

The book is about Nineveh, which was the capital city of the Assyrian empire which existed for three centuries. It was a militaristic monarchy cordially detested by the surrounding nations and guilty of depraved and brutal conduct. God was to use it to punish Samaria, but this nation itself was to disappear from the face of the earth at a later time. Nineveh's insolence and pride were an offense to God, whose judgment was to be visited upon the country unless it repented. God ordered Jonah to preach the necessity of repentance to Nineveh with the promise of sudden judgment if the nation failed to respond.

Liberal scholars have always denied that Jonah is history; rather, they argue that it is fiction, not fact. They do so because they do not generally accept the supernatural, not the least of which is the great fish that swallowed Jonah, who is a type of Christ, who spent three days and three nights in the earth. Moreover, the plant that grew and protected Jonah from the heat and the worm which destroyed the plant are unacceptable to those who deny the miraculous. For conservatives, these facts present no problem.

Characteristics and content Jonah receives his prophetic call from God to minister to the people of Nineveh. He is a disobedient prophet who seeks to flee from God's presence by taking a sea voyage in the opposite direction from Nineveh. The omnipresence of God is manifested, for Jonah discovers he cannot flee from the divine presence. Following the episode of the three days and nights in the fish's belly, Jonah repents, is restored, and is recommissioned to take the same message to the same people as God had originally called him to do. He goes to Nineveh and a citywide revival occurs, reaching to the monarch himself. Jonah is unhappy about the success of his crusade and manifests anger with God. God reproves the prophet by making clear that he cares for all men everywhere and that whoever repents of sin will find mercy from the true God. The repentance of Nineveh leads to the survival of the nation for another century and is suggestive of the same need among nations today and the same promise of forgiveness by God to those who will repent.

Outline

I. God's commission and Jonah's refusal (1:1–17)
II. Jonah's repentance and deliverance (2:1–10)
III. Jonah's obedience and Nineveh's repentance (3:1–10)
IV. Jonah's anger and God's explanation (4:1–11)

1:1☆ 2 Kgs 14:25; Mt 12:39–41; 16:4; Lk 11:29, 30, 32
1:2☆ 2 Kgs 19:36; Ezra 9:6; Isa 58:1; Jer 1:7–10; Hos 7:2; Jonah 3:3; Nah 1:1

I. GOD'S COMMISSION AND JONAH'S REFUSAL (1:1–17)

A. GOD CALLS JONAH

1 NOW the word of the LORD came unto Jonah the son of A-mit'ta-i,
saying,
2 Arise, go to Nin'e-veh, that great city, and cry against it; for their
wickedness *is come up* before me.

1:1 *Jonah, the son of Amittai,* was a prophet in Israel during the kingship of Jeroboam II (2 Kings 14:25).
1:2 It was an honor for Jonah to be chosen by God to represent him as a prophet at Nineveh. It was to Jonah's dishonor that he should refuse to go.

B. JONAH REFUSES AND RUNS AWAY

[3]But Jonah rose up to flee unto Tarshish from the presence of the LORD,
and went down to Joppa; and he found a ship going to Tarshish: so he paid
the fare thereof, and went down into it, to go with them unto Tarshish from
the presence of the LORD.
[4]¶But the LORD sent out a great wind into the sea, and there was a
mighty tempest in the sea, so that the ship was like to be broken.
[5]Then the mariners were afraid, and cried every man unto his god, and
cast forth the wares that *were* in the ship into the sea, to lighten *it* of them.
But Jonah was gone down into the sides of the ship; and he lay, and was
fast asleep.
[6]So the shipmaster came to him, and said unto him, What meanest thou,
O sleeper? arise, call upon thy God, if so be that God will think upon us,
that we perish not.
[7]And they said every one to his fellow, Come, and let us cast lots, that we
may know for whose cause this evil *is* upon us. So they cast lots, and the lot
fell upon Jonah.
[8]Then said they unto him, Tell us, we pray thee, for whose cause this evil
is upon us; What *is* thine occupation? and whence comest thou? what *is* thy
country? and of what people *art* thou?
[9]And he said unto them, I *am* an Hebrew; and I fear the LORD, the God
of heaven, which hath made the sea and the dry *land*.
[10]Then were the men exceedingly afraid, and said unto him, Why hast
thou done this? For the men knew that he fled from the presence of the
LORD, because he had told them.
[11]¶Then said they unto him, What shall we do unto thee, that the sea may
be calm unto us? for the sea wrought, and was tempestuous.
[12]And he said unto them, Take me up, and cast me forth into the sea; so
shall the sea be calm unto you: for I know that for my sake this great
tempest *is* upon you.
[13]Nevertheless the men rowed hard to bring *it* to the land; but they could
not: for the sea wrought, and was tempestuous against them.
[14]Wherefore they cried unto the LORD, and said, We beseech thee, O
LORD, we beseech thee, let us not perish for this man's life, and lay not
upon us innocent blood: for thou, O LORD, hast done as it pleased thee.
[15]So they took up Jonah, and cast him forth into the sea: and the sea
ceased from her raging.
[16]Then the men feared the LORD exceedingly, and offered a sacrifice unto
the LORD, and made vows.
[17]¶Now the LORD had prepared a great fish to swallow up Jonah. And
Jonah was in the belly of the fish three days and three nights.

☆**1:3** Gen 3:8; 4:16; 2 Chron 2:16; 9:21; Isa 23:6; Acts 9:36
1:5 1 Kgs 18:26; Isa 44:17–20; Acts 27:18, 19, 38
1:6 Ps 107:28; Jer 2:28
☆**1:7** Judg 20:9, 10; Esth 3:7; Prov 16:33
1:8 Gen 47:3
☆**1:9** Gen 1:9, 10; Ezra 1:2; 5:11; Neh 1:4; 9:6
☆**1:11**
1:12 Jn 11:50
☆**1:14**
1:15 Ps 89:9; Mk 4:34
1:16 Gen 28:20; Ps 66:13, 14
☆**1:17** Jonah 1:1; 2:1

1:3 *unto Tarshish,* probably Tartessus, located in southwest Spain. (See also note on 1 Kings 10:22.)
1:7 Like most criminals Jonah refuses to admit his guilt—until he is detected by the use of the lot. He could have saved them the trouble by a quick confession; in his heart he knew he was wrong.
1:9 *I am an Hebrew,* i.e., "I am a Jew."
1:11 The seamen note that Jonah is a prophet, so they ask him what the solution is for their problem. It was he who suggested that they toss him overboard. This they were loath to do unless direst necessity required it.
1:14ff Before throwing Jonah overboard, the seamen pleaded for God's mercy that they might be held guiltless. They perceived that what they experienced had come from the hand of God. God used Jonah for good in this incident, for the seamen acknowledged that Jonah's God was the true God, and they feared him with great fear.
1:17 Christ compares his own death and entombment to that of Jonah (Matt. 12:40). As Jonah was in the belly of the fish (*kētos* in the Greek, meaning "sea monster") three days and three nights, so Jesus would be three days and three nights in the grave. And as Jonah was delivered from his tomb, so Jesus would come forth from the grave alive. Some theorize that Jonah actually died in the belly of the fish and was raised from the dead. Since he was as good as dead in the tomb of the fish, the typical meaning is not damaged by his having been kept alive in the fish's belly during the entombment. Whether God created a whale, other fish, or sea animal is immaterial. The God who created all things must have the power and the right to make a unique specimen for a special purpose if it is his will to do so. Certainly nothing in the narrative gives credence to the idea that Jonah's imprisonment was not historical (Matt. 12:39, 40).

II. JONAH'S REPENTANCE AND DELIVERANCE (2:1–10)

2 THEN Jonah prayed unto the LORD his God out of the fish's belly,
2And said, I cried by reason of mine affliction unto the LORD, and
he heard me; out of the belly of hell cried I, *and* thou heardest my voice.
3For thou hadst cast me into the deep, in the midst of the seas; and the
floods compassed me about: all thy billows and thy waves passed over me.
4Then I said, I am cast out of thy sight; yet I will look again toward thy
holy temple.
5The waters compassed me about, *even* to the soul: the depth closed me
round about, the weeds were wrapped about my head.
6I went down to the bottoms of the mountains; the earth with her bars
was about me for ever: yet hast thou brought up my life from corruption, O
LORD my God.
7When my soul fainted within me I remembered the LORD: and my
prayer came in unto thee, into thine holy temple.
8They that observe lying vanities forsake their own mercy.
9But I will sacrifice unto thee with the voice of thanksgiving; I will pay
that that I have vowed. Salvation *is* of the LORD.
10¶And the LORD spake unto the fish, and it vomited out Jonah upon the
dry *land.*

III. JONAH'S OBEDIENCE AND NINEVEH'S REPENTANCE (3:1–10)

3 AND the word of the LORD came unto Jonah the second time, saying,
2Arise, go unto Nin′e-veh, that great city, and preach unto it the
preaching that I bid thee.
3So Jonah arose, and went unto Nin′e-veh, according to the word of the
LORD. Now Nin′e-veh was an exceeding great city of three days' journey.
4And Jonah began to enter into the city a day's journey, and he cried,
and said, Yet forty days, and Nin′e-veh shall be overthrown.
5¶So the people of Nin′e-veh believed God, and proclaimed a fast, and
put on sackcloth, from the greatest of them even to the least of them.

2:1☆ Ps 130:1; Jonah 1:17
2:2☆ Ps 18:4–6; 22:24
2:3 Ps 42:7
2:4☆ 1 Kgs 8:38; Ps 5:7; Ps 77:1–7; Isa 38:10–14
2:5 Lam 3:54
2:6 Ps 30:3; 65:6; Isa 38:17; 40:12
2:7 2 Chron 30:27; Ps 18:6; 142:3
2:8☆
2:9☆ Lev 27:1–33; Deut 23:21; Ps 3:8; Ps 50:14; 68:20; Hos 14:2; Acts 4:12; Rom 12:1; Rev 7:10
2:10☆
3:1☆
3:2 Jer 1:17; Ezek 2:7; 3:17; Mt 3:8
3:3☆ Jonah 1:2; 4:11
3:4☆ 2 Kgs 20:1, 6; 2 Chron 20:3; Ezra 8:21; Dan 9:3; Mt 12:41; Lk 11:32
3:5☆

2:1 It took three days and three nights for God to gain Jonah's attention. *Then,* as a result of his affliction, Jonah began to pray.

2:2 Suppose God had refused to hear Jonah's prayers? The glory of grace is that no matter how bad we are and how far we have strayed, when we turn to God penitently he guarantees that he will hear our prayers. God listened to Jonah!

2:4 Jonah now admits that he is out of favor with God, and his prayer is one of confession for his delinquency.

2:8 Those who follow the road of disobedience, as he had done by fleeing from the presence of God, *forsake their own mercy*—i.e., they have turned away from the true God of mercy to idols who cannot help them. Whatever is not of God is idolatry, which is a substitute for God.

2:9 *Jonah swears that he will be faithful to God if he is delivered,* and he offers thanksgiving for God's mercies. The great deliverer is God and God alone. He is the author of salvation.

2:10 Imprisoned for his sin, Jonah now is set free because he has repented and God has been gracious. God spoke to the fish and Jonah was *vomited* out of its belly.

3:1 Jonah's life as depicted here falls naturally into five parts: (1) Jonah commissioned (1:2); (2) Jonah disobedient (1:3); (3) Jonah repentant (2:1–7); (4) Jonah delivered (2:10); and (5) Jonah recommissioned (3:1–3).

3:3 *city of three days' journey,* i.e., "so large it would take three days to walk through it." The Hebrew text makes no distinction between the city proper—the walls of which were only about eight miles in circumference, accommodating a population of about 175,000 persons—and the administrative district of Nineveh, which was about thirty to sixty miles across.†

3:4 *yet forty days, and Nineveh shall be overthrown.* This word by Jonah has an implied condition—"unless Nineveh repents." Nineveh did repent and was not overthrown, much to Jonah's displeasure. But a hundred years later she was overthrown when she returned to the old state of affairs.

3:5 The people of Nineveh believed God because they believed Jonah's words. Their response indicated their seriousness. They not only prayed, they also fasted and donned the garments of penitent sinners.

6 For word came unto the king of Nin'e-veh, and he arose from his ☆3:6
throne, and he laid his robe from him, and covered *him* with sackcloth, and
sat in ashes.
7 And he caused *it* to be proclaimed and published through Nin'e-veh by **3:7** 2 Chron 30:1–10
the decree of the king and his nobles, saying, Let neither man nor beast, Esth 1:22
herd nor flock, taste any thing: let them not feed, nor drink water: 8:10–14 Dan 3:4–7
8 But let man and beast be covered with sackcloth, and cry mightily unto **3:8** Ps 130:1, 2
God: yea, let them turn every one from his evil way, and from the violence Isa 1:16–19
that *is* in their hands. Jonah 1:6, 14 Acts 3:19
9 Who can tell *if* God will turn and repent, and turn away from his fierce **3:9** 2 Sam 12:22
anger, that we perish not? Joel 2:14
10 ¶And God saw their works, that they turned from their evil way; and **3:10** 1 Kgs 21:27–29
God repented of the evil, that he had said that he would do unto them; and Jer 18:8
he did *it* not. Amos 7:3, 6 Jonah 4:2 Lk 11:32

IV. JONAH'S ANGER AND GOD'S EXPLANATION (4:1–11)

4 BUT it displeased Jonah exceedingly, and he was very angry. ☆4:1
2 And he prayed unto the LORD, and said, I pray thee, O LORD, *was* ☆4:2 Ex 34:6
not this my saying, when I was yet in my country? Therefore I fled before Ps 78:38
unto Tarshish: for I knew that thou *art* a gracious God, and merciful, slow Jer 20:7
to anger, and of great kindness, and repentest thee of the evil. Hos 11:8, 9
3 Therefore now, O LORD, take, I beseech thee, my life from me; for *it is* ☆4:3 1 Kgs 19:4
better for me to die than to live. Job 6:8, 9
4 ¶Then said the LORD, Doest thou well to be angry?
5 So Jonah went out of the city, and sat on the east side of the city, and ☆4:5
there made him a booth, and sat under it in the shadow, till he might see
what would become of the city.
6 And the LORD God prepared a gourd, and made *it* to come up over
Jonah, that it might be a shadow over his head, to deliver him from his
grief. So Jonah was exceeding glad of the gourd.
7 But God prepared a worm when the morning rose the next day, and it **4:7** Joel 1:12
smote the gourd that it withered.
8 And it came to pass, when the sun did arise, that God prepared a **4:8** Isa 49:10
vehement east wind; and the sun beat upon the head of Jonah, that he Ezek 19:12
fainted, and wished in himself to die, and said, *It is* better for me to die Hos 13:15
than to live. Rev 7:16
9 And God said to Jonah, Doest thou well to be angry for the gourd? And ☆4:9
he said, I do well to be angry, *even* unto death.
10 Then said the LORD, Thou hast had pity on the gourd, for the which

---

3:6ff The king of Nineveh endorsed prayer to Jonah's God, insisted on fasting and garments of penitence, and ordered his people to turn away from their sins and perform works of righteousness. Otherwise Nineveh would perish. The Ninevites chose the better of the two alternatives: pray and repent, or perish.

4:1 Jonah was perhaps the only evangelist who ever was angry that his preaching brought his listeners to repentance. How could he be angry when more than 120,000 people responded to his preaching?

4:2 *thou art a gracious God.* As a loyal Israelite, Jonah wanted Nineveh destroyed. He tried to run away because he feared his message might save the Ninevites and keep God from destroying the kingdom. Jonah apparently did not see that God's love goes far beyond national distinctions and takes in even the most unseemly.

4:3 Jonah preferred to die rather than see his promise of judgment fail to be executed.

4:5 Jonah is so angry that he leaves the city and sulks, while he waits for the destruction—which will not take place.

4:9 *Doest thou well to be angry?* God patiently reasons with Jonah to correct him and to humble him. His recovery from the fish's belly did not teach him as much as he should have learned, not the least of which is that God's ways are not our ways and his thoughts are not our thoughts.

thou hast not laboured, neither madest it grow; which came up in a night,
and perished in a night:

4:11☆ Jonah 3:10

11 And should not I spare Nin'e-veh, that great city, wherein are more
than sixscore thousand persons that cannot discern between their right
hand and their left hand; and *also* much cattle?

4:11 Jonah was more concerned with the plant that died than he was with the death of Nineveh. God tells him that the divine concern for the city is greater than the concern for a mere plant.

MICAH

Authorship, date, and background Micah, the author of this book, came from Moresheth, which was located some twenty-five miles southwest of Jerusalem. His name means "who is like Yahweh?" Nothing is said about his ancestry. He prophesied during the reigns of Jotham, Ahaz, and Hezekiah (742 to 687 B.C.). His ministry began earlier than 722 B.C. since his prophecy included a statement about the destruction of Samaria, which had not yet occurred. During the reign of Hezekiah his ministry overlapped with that of the prophet Isaiah, who overshadowed him. Micah witnessed the fall of Samaria. But whether he lived to witness his own nation of Judah surrounded by Sennacherib is not known. In 701 B.C, when Jerusalem was threatened, a remarkable delivery was experienced by God's power as recorded in the books of Kings and Chronicles and in the prophecy of Isaiah.

Micah prophesied during turbulent times. Samaria was wealthy and its mercantile class exploited the poor and lived in luxury themselves. Judah prospered as well, and sin abounded. When Hezekiah ascended to the throne in Judah, a revival took place. The king reversed the policy of appeasing Assyria, and heathen cult worship in the temple under Ahaz was abolished. Heathen altars, the asherim, and sacred pillars were demolished. All of this may have delayed the judgment of God against Judah as announced by Micah, but it did not cancel it out. The hearts of the people were corrupted, and genuine repentance and lasting reformation of life did not come.

Characteristics and content Micah announces that God is about to reduce Samaria to a heap of ruins for its transgressions and the failure of its people to repent. Its idols and images are to be destroyed by God and the nation sent off into captivity. He also pronounces divine judgment on Jerusalem, displaying his personal grief by removing his robe and walking barefoot.

The sins of Jerusalem are manifold. Widows are evicted from their homes; travelers are robbed. The rights of inheritance are disregarded. False prophets lead the people astray. Judges accept bribes and priests teach for money. At the same time Micah announces a return of a remnant from captivity in Babylon. Zion indeed will someday be restored. Micah foresees a ruler in the future whose birthplace will be Bethlehem, a prophecy which is to be spoken of in the New Testament and applied to Jesus the Messiah.

Micah lays down the dictum that God requires men "to do justly, and to love mercy, and to walk humbly with thy God" (6:8). But this they do not do and so judgment must come. He concludes his prophetic message by a gleam of hope: God will someday gather his people together in the land of promise from among all the nations of the world to which they have gone, and he will establish them securely in their own land. In his concluding prayer of praise, Micah proclaims, "Who is a God like unto thee, that pardoneth iniquity. . . . He will turn again, he will have compassion upon us; he will subdue our iniquities; and thou wilt cast all their sins into the depths of the sea. Thou wilt perform the truth to Jacob, and the mercy to Abraham, which thou hast sworn unto our fathers from the days of old" (7:18–20).

Outline

I. God's sentence against Samaria and Jerusalem (1:1—2:13)
II. The imminent judgment and Messiah's future reign (3:1—5:15)
III. God's blessing will follow after the divine punishment (6:1—7:20)

I. GOD'S SENTENCE AGAINST SAMARIA AND JERUSALEM (1:1—2:13)

A. INTRODUCTION

1:1☆ Jer 26:18 1 THE word of the LORD that came to Mi'cah the Mo'ras-thite in the
days of Jo'tham, Ahaz, *and* Hez-e-ki'ah, kings of Judah, which he saw
concerning Sa-ma'ri-a and Jerusalem.

B. GOD'S ANGER AGAINST SAMARIA AND JERUSALEM

1:2☆ Deut 32:1 2 Hear, all ye people; hearken, O earth, and all that therein is: and let the
Ps 50:7 Lord GOD be witness against you, the Lord from his holy temple.
Jer 6:19 1:3 3 For, behold, the LORD cometh forth out of his place, and will come
Isa 26:21 64:1–3 down, and tread upon the high places of the earth.
1:4 Ps 97:5 4 And the mountains shall be molten under him, and the valleys shall be
Amos 9:5 cleft, as wax before the fire, *and* as the waters *that are* poured down a steep
place.
1:5☆ 2 Chron 34:3, 4 5 For the transgression of Jacob *is* all this, and for the sins of the house of
Israel. What *is* the transgression of Jacob? *is it* not Sa-ma'ri-a? and what *are*
the high places of Judah? *are they* not Jerusalem?
1:6☆ Jer 51:25 6 Therefore I will make Sa-ma'ri-a as an heap of the field, *and* as plantings
Lam 4:1 Ezek 13:14 of a vineyard: and I will pour down the stones thereof into the valley, and
I will discover the foundations thereof.
1:7 Lev 26:30 7 And all the graven images thereof shall be beaten to pieces, and all the
Deut 9:21; 23:18 Joel 3:3 hires thereof shall be burned with the fire, and all the idols thereof will I lay
desolate: for she gathered *it* of the hire of an harlot, and they shall return to
the hire of an harlot.
1:8 Job 30:29 8 Therefore I will wail and howl, I will go stripped and naked: I will make
Isa 13:21, 22 20:2–4; 32:11 a wailing like the dragons, and mourning as the owls.
1:9 9 For her wound *is* incurable; for it is come unto Judah; he is come unto
Isa 1:5, 6; 3:26 Jer 15:18 the gate of my people, *even* to Jerusalem.
30:11–15 10 ¶Declare ye *it* not at Gath, weep ye not at all: in the house of Aph'rah
Mic 1:11 roll thyself in the dust.
1:11☆ Mic 1:8 11 Pass ye away, thou inhabitant of Sa'phir, having thy shame naked: the
inhabitant of Za'a-nan came not forth in the mourning of Beth–e'zel; he
shall receive of you his standing.
1:12 Job 30:26 12 For the inhabitant of Ma'roth waited carefully for good: but evil came
Isa 59:9–11 Jer 8:15; 14:19 down from the LORD unto the gate of Jerusalem.
1:13 Josh 10:3; 15:39 13 O thou inhabitant of La'chish, bind the chariot to the swift beast: she *is*
Amos 2:14 the beginning of the sin to the daughter of Zion: for the transgressions of
Israel were found in thee.

1:1 *which he saw.* Again God uses visions to acquaint his prophet with the word he wants expounded. Many times God spoke; other times he used visions and dreams. Micah saw what the future held in store for Samaria and Jerusalem, i.e., the Northern and the Southern Kingdoms.

1:2 *Hear, all you people.* This was designed to get the attention of the multitudes. If God has a mouth that speaks, we should have ears that hear. God is speaking from his holy temple.

1:5 *Micah was an all-embracing prophet who spoke of* God's coming judgment upon the Northern and the Southern Kingdoms of Judah and Samaria. But there was one important difference between the judgments that fell on these kingdoms. Israel (Samaria) fell in 722 B.C. Jerusalem was destroyed in 586 B.C.—135 years after the fall of Israel. The kings of Israel were all bad—the nation was ripe for judgment long before Judah became ready for similar judgment. God is always patient, extending the time limits for repentance; then the door of hope is shut and the avenging angel of God is sent to execute God's wrath.

1:6 See 2 Kings 17:1–18 for the literal fulfillment of the prophecy that the Northern Kingdom of Israel would be taken into captivity by Assyria.

1:11 *Saphir* (or, "Shaphir"). In the Hebrew there is frequent word play in 1:10–14. Micah bitterly declaims *each* town, demonstrating their failures by the use of puns. *Saphir* sounds like the Hebrew word for "beauty," here contrasted with their shame; *Zaanan* sounds like the verb meaning "to go forth," here contrasted with the fear of its inhabitants to venture outside; *Beth-ezel* sounds like a word for "foundation," which had been taken away from them.†

14 Therefore shalt thou give presents to Mor'esh-eth–gath: the houses of
Ach'zib *shall be* a lie to the kings of Israel.
15 Yet will I bring an heir unto thee, O inhabitant of Ma-re'shah: he shall
come unto A-dul'lam the glory of Israel.
16 Make thee bald, and poll thee for thy delicate children; enlarge thy
baldness as the eagle; for they are gone into captivity from thee.

1:14 Josh 15:44
1:15 Josh 15:35; 2 Chron 11:7
1:16 Deut 28:32, 41; 2 Kgs 17:6; Isa 22:12; Jer 7:29

C. GOD'S REASONING EXPLAINED

1. Their Sins

2 WOE to them that devise iniquity, and work evil upon their beds!
when the morning is light, they practise it, because it is in the power of
their hand.
2 And they covet fields, and take *them* by violence; and houses, and take
them away: so they oppress a man and his house, even a man and his
heritage.

☆2:1 Prov 6:12–14; Isa 32:7; Hos 7:6, 7; Rom 1:30
2:2 Prov 3:27

2. Their Sentence

3 Therefore thus saith the LORD; Behold, against this family do I devise
an evil, from which ye shall not remove your necks; neither shall ye go
haughtily: for this time *is* evil.
4 In that day shall *one* take up a parable against you, and lament with a
doleful lamentation, *and* say, We be utterly spoiled: he hath changed the
portion of my people: how hath he removed *it* from me! turning away he
hath divided our fields.
5 Therefore thou shalt have none that shall cast a cord by lot in the
congregation of the LORD.
6 Prophesy ye not, *say they to them that* prophesy: they shall not prophesy
to them, *that* they shall not take shame.
7 ¶O *thou that art* named the house of Jacob, is the spirit of the LORD
straitened? *are* these his doings? do not my words do good to him that
walketh uprightly?
8 Even of late my people is risen up as an enemy: ye pull off the robe with
the garment from them that pass by securely as men averse from war.
9 The women of my people have ye cast out from their pleasant houses;
from their children have ye taken away my glory for ever.
10 Arise ye, and depart; for this *is* not *your* rest: because it is polluted, it
shall destroy *you*, even with a sore destruction.
11 If a man walking in the spirit and falsehood do lie, *saying*, I will
prophesy unto thee of wine and of strong drink; he shall even be the
prophet of this people.

2:3 Deut 28:32–35; Isa 2:11, 12; 28:14–18; Jer 11:8
2:4 Isa 14:4; Jer 6:12; 8:10; Hab 2:6
2:5 Deut 32:8; Josh 18:4, 10
☆2:6 Isa 30:10; Jer 26:8, 9; Amos 2:12
2:7 Jer 15:16; Rom 7:13
2:8 Isa 9:21; Jer 12:8; Mic 3:2, 3; 7:2, 3
2:9 Mt 23:14; Mk 12:40
2:10 Lev 18:24–28; Ps 106:38
2:11 Mic 3:5, 11

3. God's Future Mercy

12 I will surely assemble, O Jacob, all of thee; I will surely gather the
remnant of Israel; I will put them together as the sheep of Boz'rah, as the

☆2:12 Isa11:11

2:1 Micah begins here to characterize the sinful people. They are covetous. They spend their time thinking and planning to accomplish their evil desires. When they should be sleeping, they devise iniquity on their beds. When morning comes, they carry out the plans they developed in the darkness of the night. However gross their sins, they practice them openly. Even as they devised all manner of evil, so God now will devise punishment for such haughty sinners.

2:6 Prophets and seers were an annoyance to these sinners. They rebuke those who speak words they do not wish to hear and admonish them to keep these things to themselves.

2:12 This verse concerning the return of the people of God to their homeland was partially fulfilled after the seventy years of captivity. But there was no return of the ten tribes of the Northern Kingdom, nor has there been since they were removed from the land by the Assyrian invasion. Moreover, the return of some of the people of Judah from Babylon was reversed after the time of Jesus Christ, when the last dispersion occurred (A.D. 70). The day is coming when all Israel flock in the midst of their fold: they shall make great noise by reason of *the multitude of* men.

13 The breaker is come up before them: they have broken up, and have passed through the gate, and are gone out by it: and their king shall pass before them, and the LORD on the head of them.

II. THE IMMINENT JUDGMENT AND MESSIAH'S FUTURE REIGN (3:1—5:15)

A. THE LEADERS CONDEMNED AND JERUSALEM'S DESTRUCTION PROPHESIED

3 AND I said, Hear, I pray you, O heads of Jacob, and ye princes of the house of Israel; *Is it* not for you to know judgment?

2 Who hate the good, and love the evil; who pluck off their skin from off them, and their flesh from off their bones;

3 Who also eat the flesh of my people, and flay their skin from off them; and they break their bones, and chop them in pieces, as for the pot, and as flesh within the caldron.

4 Then shall they cry unto the LORD, but he will not hear them: he will even hide his face from them at that time, as they have behaved themselves ill in their doings.

5 ¶Thus saith the LORD concerning the prophets that make my people err, that bite with their teeth, and cry, Peace; and he that putteth not into their mouths, they even prepare war against him.

6 Therefore night *shall be* unto you, that ye shall not have a vision; and it shall be dark unto you, that ye shall not divine; and the sun shall go down over the prophets, and the day shall be dark over them.

7 Then shall the seers be ashamed, and the diviners confounded: yea, they shall all cover their lips; for *there is* no answer of God.

8 ¶But truly I am full of power by the spirit of the LORD, and of judgment, and of might, to declare unto Jacob his transgression, and to Israel his sin.

9 Hear this, I pray you, ye heads of the house of Jacob, and princes of the house of Israel, that abhor judgment, and pervert all equity.

10 They build up Zion with blood, and Jerusalem with iniquity.

11 The heads thereof judge for reward, and the priests thereof teach for hire, and the prophets thereof divine for money: yet will they lean upon the LORD, and say, *Is* not the LORD among us? none evil can come upon us.

12 Therefore shall Zion for your sake be plowed *as* a field, and Jerusalem shall become heaps, and the mountain of the house as the high places of the forest.

3:1☆ Deut 16:18; Ps 14:4
3:2 Ezek 22:27
3:3 Ps 14:4; 27:2; Mic 3:2
3:4 Deut 31:17; Jer 33:5
3:5 Isa 9:15; Jer 6:14; 14:14, 15; 28:15–17
3:6 Ps 74:9; Isa 8:20–22; 29:10; 59:10; Amos 8:9, 10
3:7 1 Sam 28:6, 15; Amos 8:11; Zech 13:4
3:8☆ Isa 58:1; 61:1, 2; Ezek 16:2; Mt 3:7–12
3:9 Deut 27:19; Prov 17:15; Isa 1:23
3:10 Jer 22:13–17; Ezek 22:25–28; Hab 2:9–12
3:11☆ Isa 48:2; Jer 7:8–12; Hos 4:18; Mic 7:3
3:12☆ Jer 9:11; 26:18; Mic 1:6

---

will be regathered. This is still in the future. Most of the prophets who spoke of the judgment of God against his people also include a word of hope for the future prospects of the sons and daughters of Jacob at the end of the age.

3:1 Princes and prophets are servants of God who are called to do his will. God will reprove the greatest of men and those in highest authority when they disobey his commandments. Micah is a faithful prophet who speaks the word of reproof against the princes, i.e., the leaders, of God's people. This bold prophet rebukes the ringleaders in sin. Sometimes prophets spoke of sin in general terms, but Micah is very specific. He enumerates exactly what their sins are. Thus they would have no excuse to claim ignorance of what they had done wrong. And they couldn't claim they were not responsible for what they were doing.

3:8 Most of the prophets spoke with the hope that those who listened would repent and seek the face of the Lord. Micah was no exception. Here he makes the widest of claims. He speaks of the Spirit of God who is with him, who speaks through him, and who endues him with power, judgment, and might. In the Spirit, his one aim is to tell Jacob (Judah and Jerusalem) and Israel (Samaria) what their sins are. Before the illness can be treated, it must be diagnosed.

3:11 *none evil can come upon us.* These sinners think that God is with them despite their transgressions. Therefore they rest in the false comfort that nothing can touch them, and that the God who delivered them in the past will keep them from harm now. How wrong they were!

3:12 Instead of safety and comfort, Zion shall *be ploughed as a field,* i.e., their buildings in the sacred city will be destroyed and the city will lose its identity.

B. ZION'S FUTURE RESTORATION PROMISED

1. Future Peace and Prosperity

4 BUT in the last days it shall come to pass, *that* the mountain of the
house of the LORD shall be established in the top of the mountains,
and it shall be exalted above the hills; and people shall flow unto it.
2 And many nations shall come, and say, Come, and let us go up to the
mountain of the LORD, and to the house of the God of Jacob; and he will
teach us of his ways, and we will walk in his paths: for the law shall go forth
of Zion, and the word of the LORD from Jerusalem.
3 ¶And he shall judge among many people, and rebuke strong nations
afar off; and they shall beat their swords into plowshares, and their spears
into pruninghooks: nation shall not lift up a sword against nation, neither
shall they learn war any more.
4 But they shall sit every man under his vine and under his fig tree; and
none shall make *them* afraid: for the mouth of the LORD of hosts hath
spoken *it*.
5 For all people will walk every one in the name of his god, and we will
walk in the name of the LORD our God for ever and ever.

☆**4:1** Ps 22:27; 86:9 Dan 2:28; 10:14 Mic 3:12 Zeph 3:9, 10
☆**4:2** Deut 6:1 Ps 25:8–12 Isa 2:3; 42:1–4 Jer 31:6 Hos 6:3 Zech 8:20–23 Acts 1:8 Rom 15:19
☆**4:3** Ps 82:8; 98:9 Isa 11:3–5
4:4 Lev 26:6 Isa 1:20; 40:5 58:14
☆**4:5** 2 Kgs 17:29, 34 Jer 2:10, 11

2. God Will Bring His People Back

6 In that day, saith the LORD, will I assemble her that halteth, and I will
gather her that is driven out, and her that I have afflicted;
7 And I will make her that halted a remnant, and her that was cast far off
a strong nation: and the LORD shall reign over them in mount Zion from
henceforth, even for ever.
8 ¶And thou, O tower of the flock, the strong hold of the daughter of
Zion, unto thee shall it come, even the first dominion; the kingdom shall
come to the daughter of Jerusalem.
9 Now why dost thou cry out aloud? *is there* no king in thee? is thy
counsellor perished? for pangs have taken thee as a woman in travail.
10 Be in pain, and labour to bring forth, O daughter of Zion, like a woman
in travail: for now shalt thou go forth out of the city, and thou shalt dwell
in the field, and thou shalt go *even* to Babylon: there shalt thou be
delivered; there the LORD shall redeem thee from the hand of thine
enemies.
11 ¶Now also many nations are gathered against thee, that say, Let her be
defiled, and let our eye look upon Zion.
12 But they know not the thoughts of the LORD, neither understand they
his counsel: for he shall gather them as the sheaves into the floor.

☆**4:6** Isa 35:3–7 Zeph 3:19
4:7 Isa 9:6, 7; 24:23
4:8 Ps 48:12 Dan 7:18 Zech 9:10
4:9 Jer 4:21; 8:19
☆**4:10** 2 Kgs 20:18 2 Chron 36:20 Hos 2:14 Mic 7:8–12
4:11 Isa 5:25–30 52:15
☆**4:12** Ps 147:19, 20 Isa 55:8

4:1 In the midst of the certainty of doom and disaster, Micah injects a futuristic note of hope. God has not cast off his people forever. While they wait for restoration, salvation will come to the Gentiles.

4:2 *the law shall go forth of Zion.* This awaits the day when Zion is restored and will be the means of blessing all nations and peoples.

4:3 the peace that men dream of and many seek will never come until the end of the age and the victory of the Messiah over Satan. Then peace will come, the armaments of war will be eliminated, and what can be salvaged will be used for peaceful purposes.

4:5 *For all people will walk every one in the name of his god.* All people are religious, and yet they love, worship, and implore different gods. But the true people of God will not only profess faith in God; they will also walk in his ways. Then their walk will be as good as their talk.

4:6 The people of God are afflicted, scattered, helpless, and lonely. But God will regather them and all will be well.

4:10 Micah envisions the Babylonian captivity. That captivity (586–537 B.C.) was two centuries away, but Micah and Isaiah predicted the event long before it happened. Predictive prophecy enhances the reliability of the Word of God.

4:12 Jerusalem will be destroyed. But the destroyers have their own purpose in mind. They do not know that providence works in such a way that God's purpose is quite different from theirs. The enemies of Jerusalem will themselves be smitten by God after they have done his will. Unknown to evil men today, God uses their wicked intentions and deeds to work out his ultimate purposes for the world, with his own glory in view.

4:13 2 Sam 8:10, 11; Isa 18:7; 41:15, 16; 60:9; Jer 51:33; Mic 5:8–15; Rom 15:25–28

13 Arise and thresh, O daughter of Zion: for I will make thine horn iron,
and I will make thy hoofs brass: and thou shalt beat in pieces many people:
and I will consecrate their gain unto the LORD, and their substance unto the
Lord of the whole earth.

5:1 Job 16:10; Jer 5:7; Lam 3:30

5 NOW gather thyself in troops, O daughter of troops: he hath laid siege
against us: they shall smite the judge of Israel with a rod upon the
cheek.

3. The Coming King and Israel's Rebirth

5:2☆ Ps 102:25; Prov 8:22, 23; Jer 30:21; Zech 9:9; Mt 2:6; Jn 1:1–3; 7:42
5:3 Isa 10:20–22; Mic 4:10; 5:7, 8; 7:13
5:4 Ps 72:8; Isa 52:10; Mic 7:14

2 But thou, Beth-lehem Eph′ra-tah, *though* thou be little among the
thousands of Judah, *yet* out of thee shall he come forth unto me *that is* to be
ruler in Israel; whose goings forth *have been* from of old, from everlasting.
3 Therefore will he give them up, until the time *that* she which travaileth
hath brought forth: then the remnant of his brethren shall return unto the
children of Israel.
4 ¶And he shall stand and feed in the strength of the LORD, in the majesty
of the name of the LORD his God; and they shall abide: for now shall he be
great unto the ends of the earth.

5:5☆ Isa 8:7, 8; 37:31–36; Jer 33:15
5:6 Gen 10:8–11; 2 Kgs 19:32–35; Isa 14:2; 37:36, 37; Nah 2:11–13
5:7☆ Deut 32:2; Ps 72:6

5 And this *man* shall be the peace, when the Assyrian shall come into our
land: and when he shall tread in our palaces, then shall we raise against him
seven shepherds, and eight principal men.
6 And they shall waste the land of Assyria with the sword, and the land of
Nimrod in the entrances thereof: thus shall he deliver *us* from the Assyrian,
when he cometh into our land, and when he treadeth within our borders.
7 And the remnant of Jacob shall be in the midst of many people as a dew
from the LORD, as the showers upon the grass, that tarrieth not for man,
nor waiteth for the sons of men.

5:8 Gen 49:9; Zech 9:15
5:10☆
5:11 Isa 2:12–17; Ezek 38:11; Hos 10:14; Amos 5:9
5:12☆ Deut 18:10–12

8 ¶And the remnant of Jacob shall be among the Gentiles in the midst of
many people as a lion among the beasts of the forest, as a young lion
among the flocks of sheep: who, if he go through, both treadeth down, and
teareth in pieces, and none can deliver.
9 Thine hand shall be lifted up upon thine adversaries, and all thine
enemies shall be cut off.
10 And it shall come to pass in that day, saith the LORD, that I will cut off
thy horses out of the midst of thee, and I will destroy thy chariots:
11 And I will cut off the cities of thy land, and throw down all thy strong
holds:
12 And I will cut off witchcrafts out of thine hand; and thou shalt have no
more soothsayers:

5:2 This verse is not only prophetic, it has important implications in other ways. Micah says the Messiah will be born in Bethlehem, and that he will come from the Davidic line. From Matt. 2:5 it appears that the Jews thought Micah's prophecy to be genuine. The prophecy also states that the Messiah is alive *from everlasting.* The Hebrew word translated *goings-forth* points to the times when God "went forth" to make known his truth to his people, or to redeem them from peril or bondage. The Messiah will go forth to provide eternal redemption.

5:5 Assyrian. The area of ancient Assyria is now known as Iraq.†

5:7 Micah speaks of those few people of Israel who are a remnant. On them, in the latter days, will the Spirit be poured out and they shall be saved (Rom. 9:27). They shall be a blessing among many peoples and are as welcome as the dew of the morning.

5:10 *in that day.* The seed that is planted today will germinate and become the plant of tomorrow. Everything in history has been designed by God to bring about the ultimate triumph of right over wrong, of God over Satan. There are two histories, one known and the other unknown. There is secular (profane) history and sacred history. Beyond the pale of men's knowledge lies sacred history, which works through secular history looking to the eschatological moment when God will unveil himself with the return of Jesus Christ, bringing in the Kingdom.

5:12, 13 Some of the greatest evils among the Jews sprang from the practice of sorcery and witchcraft. These shall be no longer; and the idols, which normally attended these evil practices, shall have disappeared.

13 Thy graven images also will I cut off, and thy standing images out of
the midst of thee; and thou shalt no more worship the work of thine hands.

5:13 Isa 2:8, 18, 19

14 And I will pluck up thy groves out of the midst of thee: so will I destroy
thy cities.

5:14 Ex 34:13

15 And I will execute vengeance in anger and fury upon the heathen, such
as they have not heard.

5:15 Ps 149:7; Isa 1:24; 65:12

III. GOD'S BLESSING WILL FOLLOW AFTER THE DIVINE PUNISHMENT (6:1—7:20)

A. GOD'S CASE AGAINST HIS PEOPLE

6 HEAR ye now what the LORD saith; Arise, contend thou before the
mountains, and let the hills hear thy voice.

☆6:1

2 Hear ye, O mountains, the LORD's controversy, and ye strong founda-
tions of the earth: for the LORD hath a controversy with his people, and he
will plead with Israel.

6:2 Hos 4:1; 12:2

3 O my people, what have I done unto thee? and wherein have I wearied
thee? testify against me.

6:3 Jer 2:5, 31

4 For I brought thee up out of the land of Egypt, and redeemed thee out
of the house of servants; and I sent before thee Moses, Aaron, and Miriam.

6:4 Ex 20:1, 2; Ps 77:20

5 O my people, remember now what Balak king of Moab consulted, and
what Ba'laam the son of Be'or answered him from Shit'tim unto Gilgal;
that ye may know the righteousness of the LORD.

6:5 Num 22:5, 6

6 ¶Wherewith shall I come before the LORD, *and* bow myself before the
high God? shall I come before him with burnt offerings, with calves of a
year old?

6:6 Lev 1:3, 6:9–13

7 Will the LORD be pleased with thousands of rams, *or* with ten thousands
of rivers of oil? shall I give my firstborn *for* my transgression, the fruit of
my body *for* the sin of my soul?

☆6:7 Lev 18:21; 20:1–5; Ps 50:9; Isa 40:16

8 He hath shewed thee, O man, what *is* good; and what doth the LORD
require of thee, but to do justly, and to love mercy, and to walk humbly
with thy God?

☆6:8 Lev 26:41; Deut 10:12, 13; Isa 57:15

9 The LORD's voice crieth unto the city, and *the man of* wisdom shall see
thy name: hear ye the rod, and who hath appointed it.

☆6:9

10 ¶Are there yet the treasures of wickedness in the house of the wicked,
and the scant measure *that is* abominable?

6:10 Prov 10:2; 11:1; 20:10, 23; 21:6; Jer 5:26, 27; Amos 3:10

11 Shall I count *them* pure with the wicked balances, and with the bag of
deceitful weights?

6:11 Mic 6:10

12 For the rich men thereof are full of violence, and the inhabitants
thereof have spoken lies, and their tongue *is* deceitful in their mouth.

6:12 Isa 3:10

6:1 Micah has been talking about a glorious future, but he returns to assail the people for what they were at that moment. He orders them to hear and heed. They are a rebellious people who have dishonored God. God's mercies have been many and should have caused them to remain faithful, but they have apostasized.

6:7 The Jews became so debased they offered human sacrifices. This was part of Moloch worship. Such practices were forbidden by God (see 2 Kings 16:3; 21:2, 6; Jer. 7:31; 19:4–6).

6:8 Those who have been redeemed must prove their faith by their works. They must (1) *do justly* (i.e., render to all their due according to their obligations), (2) *love mercy* (i.e., not only perform acts of mercy but delight in mercy and rejoice in every opportunity to do mercy), and (3) *walk humbly* before their God (i.e., fulfill all the duties of the first table of the law and the second table of the law by way of justice and mercy). Some have supposed that God requires only a virtuous life for salvation. The setting in which this verse appears says quite the opposite. God is not speaking to the heathen. He is addressing his covenant people, who represent a special segment of mankind. In Micah's day, the problem was that the people had a dead faith which did not lead to living a holy life. The emphasis here is on the fruits of true faith as opposed to the nonfruit of an empty and hypocritical profession of faith. In the New Testament, James says almost the same thing.

6:9 God had just commended justice and mercy to his people. Beginning here, he shows how they have done the exact opposite. This is why he has a controversy with his people and why judgment must be pronounced.

13 Therefore also will I make *thee* sick in smiting thee, in making *thee* desolate because of thy sins.

14 Thou shalt eat, but not be satisfied; and thy casting down *shall be* in the midst of thee; and thou shalt take hold, but shalt not deliver; and *that* which thou deliverest will I give up to the sword.

15 Thou shalt sow, but thou shalt not reap; thou shalt tread the olives, but thou shalt not anoint thee with oil; and sweet wine, but shalt not drink wine.

16 ¶For the statutes of Omri are kept, and all the works of the house of Ahab, and ye walk in their counsels; that I should make thee a desolation, and the inhabitants thereof an hissing: therefore ye shall bear the reproach of my people.

B. SIN CONFESSED AND MERCY HOPED FOR

7 WOE is me! for I am as when they have gathered the summer fruits, as the grapegleanings of the vintage: *there is* no cluster to eat: my soul desired the firstripe fruit.

2 The good *man* is perished out of the earth: and *there is* none upright among men: they all lie in wait for blood; they hunt every man his brother with a net.

3 ¶That they may do evil with both hands earnestly, the prince asketh, and the judge *asketh* for a reward; and the great *man*, he uttereth his mischievous desire: so they wrap it up.

4 The best of them *is* as a brier: the most upright *is sharper* than a thorn hedge: the day of thy watchmen *and* thy visitation cometh; now shall be their perplexity.

5 ¶Trust ye not in a friend, put ye not confidence in a guide: keep the doors of thy mouth from her that lieth in thy bosom.

6 For the son dishonoureth the father, the daughter riseth up against her mother, the daughter in law against her mother in law; a man's enemies *are* the men of his own house.

7 Therefore I will look unto the LORD; I will wait for the God of my salvation: my God will hear me.

8 ¶Rejoice not against me, O mine enemy: when I fall, I shall arise; when I sit in darkness, the LORD *shall be* a light unto me.

9 I will bear the indignation of the LORD, because I have sinned against him, until he plead my cause, and execute judgment for me: he will bring me forth to the light, *and* I shall behold his righteousness.

10 Then *she that is* mine enemy shall see *it*, and shame shall cover her which said unto me, Where is the LORD thy God? mine eyes shall behold her: now shall she be trodden down as the mire of the streets.

11 *In* the day that thy walls are to be built, *in* that day shall the decree be far removed.

6:13 Lev 26:16; Isa 1:5, 6; Jer 14:18; Acts 12:23
6:14 Lev 26:26; Isa 9:20; 30:6
6:15 Deut 28:38–40; Isa 62:8, 9
6:16☆ 1 Kgs 16:29–33; Jer 18:15, 16; Ezek 8:17, 18
7:1☆ Ps 12:1; Isa 28:4; 57:1; Hos 9:10; Mic 3:10
7:3 Prov 4:16, 17; Jer 3:5; Mic 3:11
7:4 Isa 10:3; 22:5; 55:13; Jer 8:12; 10:15; Ezek 2:6; Nah 1:10; Lk 21:25
7:5☆ Jer 9:4, 5; Mt 10:16
7:6☆ Mt 10:36
7:7☆ Ps 4:3; 34:5, 6; 38:15; 50:15; Hab 3:17–19
7:8 Prov 24:15, 16; Isa 9:2; 50:11; Amos 9:11
7:9 Ps 37:6; Jer 50:34; 51:35, 36; Mic 7:8
7:10 Isa 25:10–12; 51:23; Zech 10:5
7:11 Amos 9:11

6:16 *statutes of Omri.* These refer to the statutes that required and enforced the worship of Baal. 1 Kings 16:25–32, 18:19–40 describe the life of Omri and Elijah's victory over his son Ahab.

7:1 At a time when religion is at low ebb, what shall be the refuge for the saints? How shall they conduct themselves? In this chapter Micah says that believers (1) must have an eye to God (7:7); (2) must courageously bear up under the insults and insolences of the enemy (7:8–10); (3) must bow before God, accepting his rebukes for their own sins (7:9); (4) must expect trouble in this life and make the best of it (7:11–13); (5) must encourage themselves with God's gracious promises (7:14, 15); (6) must foresee the ruin of the enemies who seem to triumph over them at the moment (7:16, 17); (7) must live triumphantly in the mercy and grace of God, who is faithful to his covenant promises (7:18–20).

7:5, 6 Every man is treacherous so that no one can be trusted. The family has ceased to be a family. Discontent, friction, hatred, and abuse are the order of the day.

7:7 When conditions are as bad as those just described, what can a child of faith do? Micah's personal response to this question is that he will look to God, wait for his salvation, and know that God will hear him.

[12]*In* that day *also* he shall come even to thee from Assyria, and *from* the
fortified cities, and from the fortress even to the river, and from sea to sea,
and *from* mountain to mountain.
[13]Notwithstanding the land shall be desolate because of them that dwell
therein, for the fruit of their doings.
[14]¶Feed thy people with thy rod, the flock of thine heritage, which dwell
solitarily *in* the wood, in the midst of Carmel: let them feed *in* Ba'shan and
Gilead, as in the days of old.
[15]According to the days of thy coming out of the land of Egypt will I
shew unto him marvellous *things*.
[16]¶The nations shall see and be confounded at all their might: they shall
lay *their* hand upon *their* mouth, their ears shall be deaf.
[17]They shall lick the dust like a serpent, they shall move out of their holes
like worms of the earth: they shall be afraid of the LORD our God, and shall
fear because of thee.
[18]Who *is* a God like unto thee, that pardoneth iniquity, and passeth by
the transgression of the remnant of his heritage? he retaineth not his anger
for ever, because he delighteth *in* mercy.
[19]He will turn again, he will have compassion upon us; he will subdue
our iniquities; and thou wilt cast all their sins into the depths of the sea.
[20]Thou wilt perform the truth to Jacob, *and* the mercy to Abraham,
which thou hast sworn unto our fathers from the days of old.

7:12 Isa 11:16 19:23–25
7:13 Mic 6:13
7:14 Lev 27:32 Ps 77:5–11 110:2 Amos 9:11 Mal 3:4
7:15 Ex 3:20 14:16–31
7:16 Mic 3:7
7:17 Gen 3:14, 15 Josh 2:9–11 Ps 9:20; 72:9
☆**7:18** Ex 34:7 Num 14:18, 19 Ps 65:3 Jer 4:2; 32:41 Eph 2:4, 5 Jas 2:13
7:19 Jer 50:20 Hos 14:4
7:20 Gen 24:27 32:10 Deut 7:8, 12

7:18ff Micah ends his book on a joyful note. God is ready and able to pardon sin. Pardon is the foundation on which all other covenant promises and mercies rest. He will renew his favors to those who come to him in repentance. He will turn again and will have compassion. Our sins will be cast into the deepest part of the deepest sea, to be remembered against us no more. This message applies to every backslidden believer today and tomorrow. We are to confess our sins, flee from them, and live according to God's commandments; then all will be well.

NAHUM

Authorship, date, and background Three of the minor prophets addressed themselves to particular heathen nations and their destruction by God's fiat: Obadiah spoke about Edom; Habakkuk pronounced judgment on Chaldea; and Nahum announced the downfall and disappearance of Assyria and its capital Nineveh. Nahum's name means "consolation," "comfort," or "relief." The prophet himself came from Elkosh, the site of which is unknown except that it was undoubtedly in Judea. Apart from what is contained in the book itself, nothing else is known about Nahum.

The book can be dated with reasonable accuracy. From the text it is apparent that Thebes (i.e., No or No-Amon) has been sacked by Ashurbanipal of Assyria around 663 B.C. The sack and end of the Assyrian empire is to take place shortly. Since this event occurred in 612 B.C, when the Medes and Chaldeans destroyed Nineveh, Nahum's ministry can be dated after 663 B.C. and before 612 B.C. In all probability, Nahum's prophecy was written shortly after the sack of Thebes but before Thebes began to rise again in 654 B.C.

Under the preaching of Jonah, the judgment of God against Nineveh had been suspended because of the nation's repentance. Now there is impending judgment unrelieved by any possibility of repentance. The nation was now ripe for ruin by God. The prophecies of Jonah and Nahum, separated by more than a century and a half, illustrate the mercy and the patience of God in dealing with sinful nations.

Characteristics and content Nahum's prophecy burns with the white heat of anger against a cruel enemy of God's people. This ruthless military power which has conquered and overthrown other nations will now itself be conquered and overthrown. Judah can rejoice that at last the indignation of God has found expression in the disappearance of a nation which has kept her in a state of vassalage for many years. Nahum sees God as the sovereign ruler of the nations whose omnipotence cannot be thwarted. Yet God is slow to anger, but he will not keep his anger from resulting in judgment forever.

In this instance the coming judgment of God is to be final. Judah will never again need to fear this nation. His graphic picture of Nineveh's overflow includes the siege against the city, its conquest, and its utter and complete ruination by the invading hosts. The Ninevites justly deserve this judgment because they are ruthless plunderers and have been commercial exploiters of many peoples. When the end of Nineveh comes, no one will offer any lamentations over its demise; they will look upon the ruins with utter contempt. Worst of all, in the light of God's numerous pronouncements of judgment upon his own people, one difference between them and the Assyrians is made plain. Nahum repeats the fact that Judah will leave behind a remnant, whereas there will be no remnant left after the ruination of Nineveh—it will perish from the earth forever.

Outline

I. A psalm of God's power and deliverance of his people (1:1–14)
II. The siege and destruction of Nineveh the oppressor (1:15—2:13)
III. The reason for the fall of Nineveh (3:1–19)

I. A PSALM OF GOD'S POWER AND DELIVERANCE OF HIS PEOPLE (1:1–14)

1:1☆ Isa 13:1; Ezek 40:2; Zeph 2:13; Rev 1:1

1 THE burden of Nin'e-veh. The book of the vision of Nahum the El'kosh-ite.

1:1 *Nineveh* was located on the Tigris River. It was the capital of Assyria, a mighty nation which appeared to be indestructible. Yet Nahum predicted its downfall, and his prediction was fulfilled minutely. Under the preaching of Jonah (ca. 770 B.C.) Nineveh repented, and judgment was averted for more than a century. It was not until 612 B.C. that the Chaldeans and Medes laid siege to Nineveh for two years before it yielded.

[2]God *is* jealous, and the LORD revengeth; the LORD revengeth, and *is*
furious; the LORD will take vengeance on his adversaries, and he reserveth
wrath for his enemies.
[3]The LORD *is* slow to anger, and great in power, and will not at all acquit
the wicked: the LORD *hath* his way in the whirlwind and in the storm, and
the clouds *are* the dust of his feet.
[4]He rebuketh the sea, and maketh it dry, and drieth up all the rivers;
Ba'shan languisheth, and Carmel, and the flower of Lebanon languisheth.
[5]The mountains quake at him, and the hills melt, and the earth is burned
at his presence, yea, the world, and all that dwell therein.
[6]Who can stand before his indignation? and who can abide in the
fierceness of his anger? his fury is poured out like fire, and the rocks are
thrown down by him.
[7]The LORD *is* good, a strong hold in the day of trouble; and he knoweth
them that trust in him.
[8]But with an overrunning flood he will make an utter end of the place
thereof, and darkness shall pursue his enemies.
[9]What do ye imagine against the LORD? he will make an utter end:
affliction shall not rise up the second time.
[10]For while *they be* folden together *as* thorns, and while they are drunken
as drunkards, they shall be devoured as stubble fully dry.
[11]There is *one* come out of thee, that imagineth evil against the LORD, a
wicked counsellor.
[12]Thus saith the LORD; Though *they be* quiet, and likewise many, yet thus
shall they be cut down, when he shall pass through. Though I have afflicted
thee, I will afflict thee no more.
[13]For now will I break his yoke from off thee, and will burst thy bonds in
sunder.
[14]And the LORD hath given a commandment concerning thee, *that* no
more of thy name be sown: out of the house of thy gods will I cut off the
graven image and the molten image: I will make thy grave; for thou art vile.

☆**1:2** Ex 20:5; Deut 4:24; 32:35; Rom 12:19
☆**1:3** Ex 34:5–7; Job 38:1; Ps 18:7–15; 50:3, 145:8; Joel 2:13
1:4 Ps 104:7; Isa 33:9; Mt 8:26
1:5 2 Sam 22:8, 9; Ps 68:8; 97:5; Isa 2:12–18; Jer 4:24
☆**1:6** Ps 76:7; Mal 3:2; Rev 6:17
1:7 1 Chron 16:34; Ezra 3:11; Ps 25:8; 100:5; 1 Jn 4:8–10
1:8 Gen 6:17; Isa 8:7, 8
☆**1:9** Job 9:4; Ps 2:1–4; 21:11; Prov 21:30; Acts 5:39
1:10 Isa 9:18; 10:17; Mal 4:1; Rev 14:10, 11
1:13 Ps 107:14; Isa 9:4; Jer 2:20
1:14 Nah 3:4–6

II. THE SIEGE AND DESTRUCTION OF NINEVEH THE OPPRESSOR (1:15—2:13)

[15]Behold upon the mountains the feet of him that bringeth good tidings,
that publisheth peace! O Judah, keep thy solemn feasts, perform thy vows:
for the wicked shall no more pass through thee; he is utterly cut off.

2 HE that dasheth in pieces is come up before thy face: keep the
munition, watch the way, make *thy* loins strong, fortify *thy* power
mightily.

1:15 Ps 107:15, 21, 22; Isa 29:7, 8; 40:9; 52:7; Lk 2:10, 14; Rom 10:15–17
☆**2:1** Isa 10:12; 37:36, 37; Zeph 2:13–15

The destruction was so great that when Xenophon passed by the site two centuries later, the local people could not even tell him its name. Later, Alexander *fought the* battle of Arbela (331 B.C.) near the site. In 1885 the site was identified and the ruins were uncovered. Archeologists have confirmed the biblical account of its destruction from their examination of the ruins.

1:2 God is a God whose justice is inflexible. He is a jealous God—jealous for his own honor, for his land, and for those who worship him.

1:3 Though slow to anger, God does get angry, and when he does, his power over his enemies is irresistible. The wind and the storm bear witness to his might. Seas, rivers, and mountains are controlled by him and demonstrate his strength.

1:6 When God manifests his anger in action, he is a consuming fire. Decades before, the Ninevites learned that he was slow to anger and merciful, but now they will find him implacable in his judgment against them.

1:9ff These verses seem to point to Sennacherib and his defeat and to the affirmation of another judgment to follow a century later, when Nineveh would be finished off. The army will be decimated (1:10). Judgment shall come upon the king, who will be cut off, his lineage destroyed, and his gods defeated (1:14). The yoke of this kingdom will be lifted and the oppressed people set free (1:13). The good news of Nineveh's defeat and retreat will be welcomed, and joy inexpressible will abound everywhere (1:15).

2:1 Let Nineveh arm itself to the teeth; it will do no good. Nebuchadnezzar will dash everything to pieces.

2:2 [2]For the LORD hath turned away the excellency of Jacob, as the
Hos 2:14–23; 11:11 excellency of Israel: for the emptiers have emptied them out, and marred
their vine branches.
2:3☆ [3]The shield of his mighty men is made red, the valiant men *are* in scarlet:
the chariots *shall be* with flaming torches in the day of his preparation, and
the fir trees shall be terribly shaken.
2:4 [4]The chariots shall rage in the streets, they shall justle one against
Nah 3:2 another in the broad ways: they shall seem like torches, they shall run like
the lightnings.
[5]He shall recount his worthies: they shall stumble in their walk; they
shall make haste to the wall thereof, and the defence shall be prepared.
[6]The gates of the rivers shall be opened, and the palace shall be dissolved.
2:7☆ [7]And Huz′zab shall be led away captive, she shall be brought up, and her
maids shall lead *her* as with the voice of doves, tabering upon their breasts.
2:8 [8]But Nin′e-veh *is* of old like a pool of water: yet they shall flee away.
Nah 3:3 Stand, stand, *shall they cry;* but none shall look back.
2:9 [9]Take ye the spoil of silver, take the spoil of gold: for *there is* none end of
Gen 14:21, 24; Ex 15:9 the store *and* glory out of all the pleasant furniture.
2 Chron 25:13; Isa 33:4 [10]She is empty, and void, and waste: and the heart melteth, and the knees
2:10☆ Lev 26:33 smite together, and much pain *is* in all loins, and the faces of them all
Isa 24:1; 34:10; Jer 4:23 gather blackness.
[11]Where *is* the dwelling of the lions, and the feedingplace of the young
lions, where the lion, *even* the old lion, walked, *and* the lion's whelp, and
none made *them* afraid?
[12]The lion did tear in pieces enough for his whelps, and strangled for his
lionesses, and filled his holes with prey, and his dens with ravin.
2:13☆ [13]Behold, I *am* against thee, saith the LORD of hosts, and I will burn her
Ps 46:9 chariots in the smoke, and the sword shall devour thy young lions: and I
will cut off thy prey from the earth, and the voice of thy messengers shall no
more be heard.

III. THE REASON FOR THE FALL OF NINEVEH (3:1–19)

A. ITS CRUEL MILITARISM AND OPPRESSION

3:1☆ Ezek 22:2–5; 24:6–9 **3** WOE to the bloody city! it *is* all full of lies *and* robbery; the prey
departeth not;
Zeph 3:13 [2]The noise of a whip, and the noise of the rattling of the wheels, and of
3:2 Nah 2:4 the pransing horses, and of the jumping chariots.
3:3 [3]The horseman lifteth up both the bright sword and the glittering spear:
Nah 2:3, 6, 8 and *there is* a multitude of slain, and a great number of carcases; and *there*
is none end of *their* corpses; they stumble upon their corpses:

This chapter predicts the events of the year 612 B.C., when Nebuchadnezzar, aided by the Medes sacked Nineveh, which had appeared to be impregnable.

2:3 Beginning here, Nahum describes the awfulness of the conquest. The shields of the armies and their uniforms are red with blood. Their chariots are lit with flaming torches as they come in the night. The trees shake. The chariots rage in the streets of the city, for the river gates are opened to allow the invaders to penetrate the stronghold.

2:7ff *The queen will fall into the hands* of the invaders. Although she was secluded and shut up, she shall be exposed to the enemy. She and her maidens shall be made light of. The people of the city will be unable to repel the invaders (2:8), and the wealth of the city will be seized and possessed by the victors (2:9).

2:10ff These verses depict the utter and complete ruin of Nineveh. However much like a lion Nineveh had been, a stronger lion has come and will dash to pieces all who stand in the way.

2:13 *I am against thee.* The Ninevites miscalculated their situation. A powerful nation of warriors, they supposed that no combination of hostile powers could overcome them. That was true, except for the fact that God entered the picture and declared judgment upon them. With God against it, Nineveh did not have a chance for survival.

3:1 Nahum reflects the biblical teaching that men reap as they sow. Cause and effect will prevail so that the timeless principles of justice and equity have their day. Sin always produces its own harvest of ruination.

4 Because of the multitude of the whoredoms of the wellfavoured harlot,
the mistress of witchcrafts, that selleth nations through her whoredoms, and
families through her witchcrafts.

☆3:4 Rev 17:1-6; 18:2, 3

5 Behold, I *am* against thee, saith the LORD of hosts; and I will discover
thy skirts upon thy face, and I will shew the nations thy nakedness, and the
kingdoms thy shame.

☆3:5 Rev 18:3-7

6 And I will cast abominable filth upon thee, and make thee vile, and will
set thee as a gazingstock.

3:6 Job 30:19; Lam 3:15

7 And it shall come to pass, *that* all they that look upon thee shall flee
from thee, and say, Nin′e-veh is laid waste: who will bemoan her? whence
shall I seek comforters for thee?

3:7 Isa 51:19

B. THE RIGHTNESS OF THE DIVINE JUDGMENT

8 Art thou better than populous No, that was situate among the rivers,
that had the waters round about it, whose rampart *was* the sea, *and* her wall
was from the sea?

☆3:8 Jer 46:25; Ezek 30:14–16

9 E-thi-o′pi-a and Egypt *were* her strength, and *it was* infinite; Put and
Lu′bim were thy helpers.

3:9 Isa 20:5, 6; Jer 46:9

10 Yet *was* she carried away, she went into captivity: her young children
also were dashed in pieces at the top of all the streets: and they cast lots for
her honourable men, and all her great men were bound in chains.

☆3:10 2 Kgs 8:12; Ps 137:9; Hos 13:16; Nah 3:8; Mt 2:16–18

11 Thou also shalt be drunken: thou shalt be hid, thou also shalt seek
strength because of the enemy.

3:11 Isa 29:9; 49:26; Jer 25:15–27; 51:57

12 All thy strong holds *shall be like* fig trees with the firstripe figs: if they
be shaken, they shall even fall into the mouth of the eater.

☆3:12ff

13 Behold, thy people in the midst of thee *are* women: the gates of thy
land shall be set wide open unto thine enemies: the fire shall devour thy
bars.

3:13 Isa 19:16; Jer 50:37; 51:30

14 Draw thee waters for the siege, fortify thy strong holds: go into clay,
and tread the morter, make strong the brickkiln.

3:14 2 Chron 32:3, 4, 11; Isa 8:9, 10; 22:9–11; 37:25; Nah 2:1

15 There shall the fire devour thee; the sword shall cut thee off, it shall eat
thee up like the cankerworm: make thyself many as the cankerworm, make
thyself many as the locusts.

3:15 Isa 66:15, 16

16 Thou hast multiplied thy merchants above the stars of heaven: the
cankerworm spoileth, and fleeth away.

17 Thy crowned *are* as the locusts, and thy captains as the great
grasshoppers, which camp in the hedges in the cold day, *but* when the sun
ariseth they flee away, and their place is not known where they *are*.

☆3:17

3:4 Nineveh has already been accused of being a city of blood, full of lies and guilty of robbery and rapine. Now Nineveh is accused of being a mistress of adulteries and witchcrafts. By this Nahum means that Nineveh taught her conquered peoples to worship her gods and to join the Ninevites in their idolatrous practices.

3:5 Because of Nineveh's adulteries and witchcraft, God is against her. Her ruin is not only prophesied; it is also guaranteed. No pity will be shown her. She will be made miserable and contemptible, a laughing stock to all who pass her by. God will make of her an example and a warning to all nations for all time.

3:8 *Art thou better than populous No* [Thebes]? Thebes (also known as *No-Amon*) was a great city located four hundred miles south of Cairo. The prophet probably has in mind the destruction of Thebes by Ashurbanipal (663 B.C.). He says, in effect, that if Thebes—the capital of one of Egypt's greatest dynasties—could be destroyed, why not Nineveh?

3:10 Thebes thought she was impregnable, but she was not. She was carried away. Her children were slain. Lots were cast for the honorable men to see which of the conquerors would take them for their slaves. Nineveh is likened to this.

3:12ff Nineveh's walls shall be like paper. Shake them and they will fall. Their troops are like frail women. Their city gates are open to the enemy and the gates themselves burned. Store up water for the day of the siege and make more bricks to support your walls. The fire will devour you and the sword will cut you off (3:14). The situation is hopeless.

3:17, 18 Kings and princes cannot deliver them. Their nobles are fast asleep and their shepherds slumber. While they sleep, the flock is scattered to be gathered no more.

3:18
Jer 50:18
Ezek 32:22, 23
3:19☆
Job 27:23
Jer 30:13–15
46:11
Ezek 25:6
30:21, 22
Nah 2:2

18 Thy shepherds slumber, O king of Assyria: thy nobles shall dwell *in the*
dust: thy people is scattered upon the mountains, and no man gathereth
them.
19 *There is* no healing of thy bruise; thy wound is grievous: all that hear
the bruit of thee shall clap the hands over thee: for upon whom hath not
thy wickedness passed continually?

3:19 The end has come; Nineveh will be no more forever. Evil always pays its dividends.

HABAKKUK

Authorship, date, and background The prophet Habakkuk, whose name is derived from a Hebrew root meaning "to embrace," was the author of this book. Apart from his name and the fact that he was called a prophet, nothing else is known about him. He lived and prophesied during the closing years of the seventh century B.C. and the early years of the sixth century. The date for the book has been assigned to a period between 605 and 589 B.C. by conservative scholars. Nahum the prophet in his book had announced the doom of Assyria. Obadiah had pronounced divine judgment on Edom. Habakkuk was the third prophet whose ministry was limited to a single gentile nation. He pronounced God's judgment on Chaldea, one of whose great monarchs was Nebuchadnezzar. Nineveh had been destroyed by Nabopolassar, the father of Nebuchadnezzar. His son reigned from 605 B.C. to 562 B.C. At the battle of Carchemish Nebuchadnezzar defeated the Egyptians and re-established Babylon as the seat and center of world power in that era.

Nebuchadnezzar was God's instrument to execute divine judgment on Judah, bringing about the Babylonian captivity of seventy years. The people of Judah were guilty of violence, injustice, and of a refusal to obey the demands of the Torah (the Law). Habakkuk was disturbed about the conditions and wondered how soon it would be before the judgment of God would fall on his people.

Characteristics and content Habakkuk engages in a conversation with God about the evils of Judah. When he learns that God will use the Chaldeans to punish his people, Habakkuk has serious reservations about the justice of using a nation whose sins are greater than those of Judah to punish that nation. Habakkuk announces God's prophecy that the Chaldeans are coming and will wreak vengeance on Judah. They will spread their terror, seize Judah's possessions, take the people captive and destroy Jerusalem. God says evil does not go on forever unpunished.

Habakkuk asks God how he can use a more sinful nation to punish a less sinful one. God announces that he will punish the Chaldeans after they have been used by him to punish the people of Judah. Habakkuk argues that Chaldea is greedy, covetous, cruel, and idolatrous. Because of this, Chaldea will be destroyed by God, but only after that nation has been used to punish Judah. Then it is that Habakkuk makes known to all men the good news that the just shall live by their faith (2:2–4). This theme is mentioned by Isaiah and is picked up in the New Testament in Romans, Galatians, and Hebrews. The prophet announces his own faith in God even though trouble besets him, the trees give forth no fruit, and the earth produces no food. He concludes by saying that if all these evils come upon him, "yet I will rejoice in the LORD, I will rejoice in the God of my salvation. The Lord God is my strength, and he will make my feet like hinds' feet, and he will make me to walk upon mine high places" (3:18, 19).

Outline

I. Why does God allow oppression and injustice in Jewish life? (1:1–4)
II. God will use the Chaldeans to punish Jewish sinners (1:5–11)
III. Why will God allow the more wicked to punish the less wicked? (1:12–2:1)
IV. God will punish the Chaldeans later (2:2–20)
V. Habakkuk's prayer and psalm of praise (3:1–19)

I. WHY DOES GOD ALLOW OPPRESSION AND INJUSTICE IN JEWISH LIFE? (1:1–4)

1 THE burden which Ha-bak′kuk the prophet did see.
2 O LORD, how long shall I cry, and thou wilt not hear! *even* cry out
unto thee *of* violence, and thou wilt not save!
3 Why dost thou shew me iniquity, and cause *me* to behold grievance? for
spoiling and violence *are* before me: and there are *that* raise up strife and
contention.
4 Therefore the law is slacked, and judgment doth never go forth: for the
wicked doth compass about the righteous; therefore wrong judgment
proceedeth.

II. GOD WILL USE THE CHALDEANS TO PUNISH JEWISH SINNERS (1:5–11)

5 ¶Behold ye among the heathen, and regard, and wonder marvellously:
for *I* will work a work in your days, *which* ye will not believe, though it be
told *you.*
6 For, lo, I raise up the Chal-de′ans, *that* bitter and hasty nation, which
shall march through the breadth of the land, to possess the dwellingplaces
that are not theirs.
7 They *are* terrible and dreadful: their judgment and their dignity shall
proceed of themselves.
8 Their horses also are swifter than the leopards, and are more fierce than
the evening wolves: and their horsemen shall spread themselves, and their
horsemen shall come from far; they shall fly as the eagle *that* hasteth to eat.
9 They shall come all for violence: their faces shall sup up *as* the east
wind, and they shall gather the captivity as the sand.
10 And they shall scoff at the kings, and the princes shall be a scorn unto
them: they shall deride every strong hold; for they shall heap dust, and
take it.
11 Then shall *his* mind change, and he shall pass over, and offend,
imputing this his power unto his god.

III. WHY WILL GOD ALLOW THE MORE WICKED TO PUNISH THE LESS WICKED? (1:12—2:1)

12 ¶*Art* thou not from everlasting, O LORD my God, mine Holy One? we
shall not die. O LORD, thou hast ordained them for judgment; and, O
mighty God, thou hast established them for correction.

1:1☆ Gen 46:2; Num 22:9, 31; 2 Chron 18:6; Isa 13:1; Ezek 1:4
1:2☆ Ps 13:1–4; 22:1, 2; Jer 14:9; Lam 3:8, 9
1:3 Ps 55:9–11; Prov 13:2; 15:17; 18:6, 7; 22:16; 29:8; Jer 22:17
1:4☆ Deut 16:19; 2 Kgs 24:1–5; 2 Chron 36:4–8; Ps 11:3; 119:126; Ezek 22:26; Hab 1:3; Mk 7:9
1:5 Isa 28:21
1:6☆ Deut 28:49–57; 2 Kgs 24:2, 10–20; 25:1–23; 2 Chron 36:6–13; Isa 48:14; Jer 21:3, 4; Dan 9:1
1:7 Jer 39:5–9
1:8 Deut 28:49; Isa 5:26–30; Lam 4:19
1:9☆ 2 Kgs 24:14, 15; 25:11, 12; 2 Chron 36:18, 20; Jer 34:22
1:10☆ 2 Kgs 25:6, 7; 2 Chron 36:6; Isa 37:13; Jer 32:24; 33:4, 5; 52:4–7, 10, 11; Ezek 26:7–11
1:11 Hab 1:16
1:12☆ Deut 32:4, 30, 31; 1 Sam 2:2; 2 Kgs 19:25; Ps 18:2; Isa 10:5–7; 37:26; Jer 25:8–14

1:1 Sometimes God uses people to do his bidding without giving us any knowledge of who they are, where they came from, and whose sons and daughters they were. We know virtually nothing about Habakkuk except that he was a prophet of God.
1:2 Habakkuk cried for help and nothing happened. His soul was vexed because he identified with the oppressed who suffered from the iniquity and violence of their oppressors.
1:4 When laws on the statute books are not enforced, it is as though there were no laws. Injustice prevails and justice ceases to exist. The law is debased or passed over as underserving of notice. This state of affairs was recognized and denounced by Habakkuk.
1:6 *the Chaldeans* were a tribe of people in southern Babylon. Under Nabopolassar, they won their independence from Assyria. Later, under Nebuchadnezzar, they took over all of western Asia, including Judea, which fell in 586 B.C.
1:9 *gather the captivity as the sand,* i.e., they shall take a vast number of prisoners.
1:10 *a scorn . . . deride every strong hold,* i.e., "every fort will fall before their attack." The conquering armies laugh at their victims—at their kings and rulers who are weak and helpless against them. Their defenses are such that a little sand thrown against the walls will create a rampart over which the soldiers can enter the city and destroy it.
1:12 The people of Judah indeed have offended their God, but he is the everlasting God, who will keep his people. His covenant promises are pillows on which to rest one's head. Despite chastisement God will have a people in the world, for the gates of hell cannot prevail against his people.

[13]*Thou art* of purer eyes than to behold evil, and canst not look on
iniquity: wherefore lookest thou upon them that deal treacherously, *and*
holdest thy tongue when the wicked devoureth *the man that is* more
righteous than he?
[14]And makest men as the fishes of the sea, as the creeping things, *that
have* no ruler over them?
[15]They take up all of them with the angle, they catch them in their net,
and gather them in their drag: therefore they rejoice and are glad.
[16]Therefore they sacrifice unto their net, and burn incense unto their
drag; because by them their portion *is* fat, and their meat plenteous.
[17]Shall they therefore empty their net, and not spare continually to slay
the nations?

2 I WILL stand upon my watch, and set me upon the tower, and will
watch to see what he will say unto me, and what I shall answer when I
am reproved.

IV. GOD WILL PUNISH THE CHALDEANS LATER (2:2–20)

A. THE CHALDEANS ARE ROBBERS

[2]And the LORD answered me, and said, Write the vision, and make *it*
plain upon tables, that he may run that readeth it.
[3]For the vision *is* yet for an appointed time, but at the end it shall speak,
and not lie: though it tarry, wait for it; because it will surely come, it will
not tarry.
[4]Behold, his soul *which* is lifted up is not upright in him: but the just shall
live by his faith.
[5]¶Yea also, because he transgresseth by wine, *he is* a proud man, neither
keepeth at home, who enlargeth his desire as hell, and *is* as death, and
cannot be satisfied, but gathereth unto him all nations, and heapeth unto
him all people:
[6]Shall not all these take up a parable against him, and a taunting proverb
against him, and say, Woe to him that increaseth *that which is* not his! how
long? and to him that ladeth himself with thick clay!

☆1:13 Job 15:15; Ps 5:4; 11:7; Hab 1:4; 1 Pet 1:15, 16
☆1:14
1:15 Jer 16:16; Ezek 29:4, 5
1:16 Jer 7:18; 44:17, 18; Hab 1:11
☆1:17
☆2:1 2 Kgs 9:17; 2 Chron 20:24; Isa 21:8
☆2:2 Deut 27:8; Isa 8:1; Jer 36:2; Rev 1:19; 14:13
☆2:3 Dan 8:17–19; 9:24–27; 10:1, 14; 2 Thess 2:6–14
☆2:4 Ps 10:4; 49:17–20; Prov 3:6; 16:3; Rom 1:17; Gal 3:11; Heb 10:38
☆2:5
2:6 Prov 22:16; Isa14:4, 5, 10; Jer 29:22; 50:13, 34, 35; Mic 2:4, 5; Hab 2:9, 12, 15, 19

1:13 Wickedness may prosper for a season, but a holy God does not approve of sin, no matter who commits it and how long it lasts. (Note must be taken of the fact that at Calvary, when Jesus Christ became sin for us, the face of the Father was turned from his Son, for he could not look upon sin.) The prophet wants to know why it is that a holy God permits the triumph of any enemy who is more wicked than the people he is about to overcome.

1:14 Providence has delivered the weaker over to the stronger, so that Judah is made like the fishes of the sea. As fishermen have every advantage over the fishes, so the Chaldeans have every advantage over Judah and will take them as fishermen take fish.

1:17 Habakkuk concludes this chapter by asking God whether he will let the Chaldeans go ahead with their wicked designs. Shall the nations and their wealth be given over to the fish nets of the Chaldeans? How will God respond to such a question? Habakkuk leaves it in the hands of his God.

2:1 The prophet assumes the stance of a sentinel who waits to see what God will say. He is willing to listen attentively to the divine words and accept the divine verdict. His whole attitude is one of patience, constancy, and holy resolution in the midst of trouble. No matter how dark the days, the believer must not waver, give way to doubts, or distrust his God.

2:2 God's message must be written down to prove that what he says will have taken place and to make his word easily known to all who can read. The writing must be legible and the characters large.

2:3 Even though what God has said may not occur as quickly as what might be hoped for, it will take place in the appointed time. God is in no hurry.

2:4 *the just shall live by his faith.* This is one Old Testament instance of the clear teaching that men are justified by faith and not by works. This idea is restated in the New Testament (Rom. 1:17; Gal. 3:11; and Heb. 10:38, 39) as proof that believers are saved by grace through faith alone. The Jewish Talmud states that the prophet Habakkuk reduced the 613 Mosaic commandments down to one: "The righteous shall live by his faith." This indeed is true.

2:5 *hell.* See note on Deut. 32:22 for *Sheol,* the underworld abode. Judah's enemy is charged with the lust of the flesh, the lust of the eye, and the pride of life (see 1 John 2:16). Sensual and voluptuous, he is a proud, covetous, and greedy man. He never has enough, and his vain ambitions drive him ever onward to further depredations and conquests.

7 Shall they not rise up suddenly that shall bite thee, and awake that shall
vex thee, and thou shalt be for booties unto them?

2:8☆ Isa13:16–18; 33:1; Jer 27:7, 8; 50:10, 34–46

8 Because thou hast spoiled many nations, all the remnant of the people
shall spoil thee; because of men's blood, and *for* the violence of the land, of
the city, and of all that dwell therein.

B. THE CHALDEANS ARE COVETOUS

2:9☆ Ps 10:3–11; 52:7; Prov 18:11, 12
2:10 Num 35:30
2:11 Josh 24:27; Lk 19:40

9 ¶Woe to him that coveteth an evil covetousness to his house, that he
may set his nest on high, that he may be delivered from the power of evil!
10 Thou hast consulted shame to thy house by cutting off many people,
and hast sinned *against* thy soul.
11 For the stone shall cry out of the wall, and the beam out of the timber
shall answer it.

C. THE CHALDEANS ARE HARDHEARTED

2:12 Mic 3:10; Hab 2:9, 15, 19
2:13 Deut 28:20
2:14☆ Ps 22:27; 86:9; Isa 6:3; Zech 14:9; Rev 11:15; 15:3, 4
2:15☆ Hos 7:5; Hab 2:9, 12, 19
2:16☆ Isa 51:21–23; Jer 25:15, 16; Rev 14:10; 18:6
2:17 Lev 26:16, 17; Deut 28:25, 28, 29, 66–68

12 ¶Woe to him that buildeth a town with blood, and stablisheth a city by
iniquity!
13 Behold, *is it* not of the LORD of hosts that the people shall labour in the
very fire, and the people shall weary themselves for very vanity?
14 For the earth shall be filled with the knowledge of the glory of the
LORD, as the waters cover the sea.
15 ¶Woe unto him that giveth his neighbour drink, that puttest thy bottle
to *him,* and makest *him* drunken also, that thou mayest look on their
nakedness!
16 Thou art filled with shame for glory: drink thou also, and let thy
foreskin be uncovered: the cup of the LORD's right hand shall be turned
unto thee, and shameful spewing *shall be* on thy glory.
17 For the violence of Lebanon shall cover thee, and the spoil of beasts,
which made them afraid, because of men's blood, and for the violence of the
land, of the city, and of all that dwell therein.

D. THE CHALDEANS WORSHIP IDOLS

2:18☆ 1 Kgs 18:26–27; Isa 42:17; Jer 2:28; 50:2
2:19 Ex 32:2–4; Isa 40:19; 46:6; Jer 10:4, 5; Acts 17:29
2:20 Ps 46:10; Zeph 1:7; Zech 2:13

18 ¶What profiteth the graven image that the maker thereof hath graven it;
the molten image, and a teacher of lies, that the maker of his work trusteth
therein, to make dumb idols?
19 Woe unto him that saith to the wood, Awake; to the dumb stone, Arise,
it shall teach! Behold, it *is* laid over with gold and silver, and *there is* no
breath at all in the midst of it.
20 But the LORD *is* in his holy temple: let all the earth keep silence before
him.

2:8 Habakkuk is assured that at last he who has plundered the nations will himself be plundered. What he has taken by violence will be taken from him by violence. Later on, the Medes and Persians will do to Babylon what no other people could do. And it would be done in like vicious and violent manner.

2:9ff So covetous is Chaldea that she wants more and more until her kingdom is elevated to the heights of heaven. She will pay any price and commit any deed to accomplish this objective.

2:14 God must be honored as the God of equitable justice and invincible power. The defeat of Chaldea by this omnipotent God will manifest the divine glory, and the earth will be filled with the knowledge of it.

2:15, 16 Drunkards are indicted—both those who solicit their neighbors to get drunk and those who get drunk themselves. Belshazzar was drunk (Dan. 5:1) when his kingdom was seized by his enemies. God's punishment for this sin is to make such people drink the cup of God's fury. They shall be shamed and made victims of hissing and desolation.

2:18ff Chaldea was idolatrous. They had many gods, both graven and molten; they beautified and adorned them; they trusted in them and prayed to them; and they supposed that Chaldea's greatness lay in their affection to these idols (who cannot walk, talk, give revelations, or even breathe). God will strike idolaters as dumb and silent as their idols. Thus shall all the world stand silent before God in awe and admiration, as they offer praise without words.

V. HABAKKUK'S PRAYER AND PSALM OF PRAISE (3:1–19)

A. A PRAYER FOR MERCY

3 A PRAYER of Ha-bak'kuk the prophet upon Shi-gi'o-noth.
2 O LORD, I have heard thy speech, *and* was afraid: O LORD, revive
thy work in the midst of the years, in the midst of the years make known;
in wrath remember mercy.

B. GOD SAVES THE RIGHTEOUS AND CONDEMNS THE WICKED

3 God came from Te'man, and the Holy One from mount Paran. Se'lah.
His glory covered the heavens, and the earth was full of his praise.
4 And *his* brightness was as the light; he had horns *coming* out of his
hand: and there *was* the hiding of his power.
5 Before him went the pestilence, and burning coals went forth at his feet.
6 He stood, and measured the earth: he beheld, and drove asunder the
nations; and the everlasting mountains were scattered, the perpetual hills
did bow: his ways *are* everlasting.
7 I saw the tents of Cu'shan in affliction: *and* the curtains of the land of
Mid'i-an did tremble.
8 Was the LORD displeased against the rivers? *was* thine anger against the
rivers? *was* thy wrath against the sea, that thou didst ride upon thine horses
and thy chariots of salvation?
9 Thy bow was made quite naked, *according* to the oaths of the tribes, *even*
thy word. Se'lah. Thou didst cleave the earth with rivers.
10 The mountains saw thee, *and* they trembled: the overflowing of the
water passed by: the deep uttered his voice, *and* lifted up his hands on high.
11 The sun *and* moon stood still in their habitation: at the light of thine
arrows they went, *and* at the shining of thy glittering spear.
12 Thou didst march through the land in indignation, thou didst thresh the
heathen in anger.
13 Thou wentest forth for the salvation of thy people, *even* for salvation
with thine anointed; thou woundedst the head out of the house of the
wicked, by discovering the foundation unto the neck. Se'lah.
14 Thou didst strike through with his staves the head of his villages: they
came out as a whirlwind to scatter me: their rejoicing *was* as to devour the
poor secretly.
15 Thou didst walk through the sea with thine horses, *through* the heap of
great waters.

☆**3:1**
☆**3:2**
Num 14:17–19
Ps 6:1–3
78:38, 39
Ps 119:120
Isa 66:2
Jer 10:7
Lam 3:32
Hab 3:16
Heb 11:7
☆**3:3**
Ex 24:15–17
Deut 5:24
Ps 48:10; 113:4
148:13
Isa 6:3
Rev 5:13, 14
3:4
Ex 14:20
Job 26:14
Ps 18:12; 104:1
Prov 18:10
1 Tim 6:16
3:5
Ex 12:29, 30
Deut 32:24, 25
3:6
Josh 10:40–42
Neh 9:22–25
Ps 135:10
☆**3:7**
Gen 10:6
25:1–4
Num 31:2
1 Chron 1:5–9, 32
3:8
Ex 14:21, 22
Josh 3:12–17
2 Kgs 2:11, 12
3:10
Ps 93:3; 96:11
3:11
Josh 10:12–14
Isa 38:8
3:12
Hab 3:6
3:13
Ps 18:38; 68:21
110:6
3:14
Judg 7:22
2 Chron 20:22–24
Dan 11:40
3:15
Hab 3:8

3:1 *Shigionoth,* the meaning of which is obscure but which some have said means "mournful dirge." Nevertheless, the prayer of Habakkuk is one of triumph, and he may have sung it before the Lord.
3:2 God has answered Habakkuk's earlier petition for understanding. He has heard God's speech. Fear comes over him—as it had to Moses, Isaiah, and Daniel, among others, who had similar experiences. He prays for a quickening revival, a revelation of God himself to sight and sense, and an exhibition of mercy in the midst of wrath. God's people, who are under the anger of God, must not despair of his mercy which is their last and only plea.
3:3 *from Teman . . . from mount Paran.* Teman was a district of Edom. The language that Habakkuk uses to describe the coming of God to deliver his people is similar to that used to describe Israel's deliverance from Egypt.
3:3ff In these verses Habakkuk draws attention to earlier manifestations of God's works among his people. Such recollections serve God's people and bring to memory that what he did in ages past he can do today. He mentions the glory of God as displayed on Mount Sinai, the plagues that Egypt suffered before releasing Israel from its bondage (3:5), the conquest of Caanan and the expulsion of the heathen (3:6), the dividing of the Red Sea and the Jordan (3:8, 15), the sun that stood still (3:11), and the victories of Israel in Caanan over their enemies. The God who performed these deeds does not sleep.
3:7 *Cushan,* a Bedouin tribe near Edom, as was Midian. Nothing more is known about this tribe.

3:16☆ Isa 6:5

16 ¶When I heard, my belly trembled; my lips quivered at the voice:
rottenness entered into my bones, and I trembled in myself, that I might
rest in the day of trouble: when he cometh up unto the people, he will
invade them with his troops.

3:17☆ Deut 28:15–19; Jer 14:2–6; Joel 1:10, 12; Amos 4:9; Hag 2:16, 17; Mt 21:19, 20
3:18☆ Ex 15:2; 1 Sam 2:1; Ps 25:5; 27:1; 33:1; 149:2; Isa 12:2; Zech 10:7; Phil 4:4
3:19 Ps 18:2, 3; 46:1; Phil 14:13

C. HABAKKUK HAS FAITH DESPITE ALL ADVERSITY

17 ¶Although the fig tree shall not blossom, neither *shall* fruit *be* in the
vines; the labour of the olive shall fail, and the fields shall yield no meat;
the flock shall be cut off from the fold, and *there shall be* no herd in the
stalls:
18 Yet I will rejoice in the LORD, I will joy in the God of my salvation.
19 The LORD God *is* my strength, and he will make my feet like hinds' *feet*,
and he will make me to walk upon mine high places. To the chief singer on
my stringed instruments.

3:16 This verse represents Habakkuk in trembling and in triumph. Body, bones, and lips are affected. His steps totter and he can hardly walk. But there is still a future triumph ahead. For believers there is the certainty that in heaven there will be no more trembling, no more punishments, no more dark nights of the soul. It will be everlasting triumphs for endless ages.

3:17 Habakkuk demonstrates his supreme faith in God when he declares that even if the fruit trees, the fig trees, the olive trees, and vines produced no crops, or if the fields yielded no harvest and the animals died and there were no flocks in the stalls, he still would trust in God. Outward circumstances would never cause him to leave God, his first love. Verses 17 and 18 have been widely quoted in biblical literature.

3:18 The joy of the Lord is ever the believer's portion, and it is never out of season. Just as Jesus is the man for all seasons, so is joy to those who love God. Verse 19 indicates that those who trust God will find their strength in him, and he will give speed to their feet and success to their undertakings.

ZEPHANIAH

Authorship, date, and background Zephaniah, whose name means "he whom Yahweh has hidden, or protected," is the author of this book. He was the great-great-grandson of King Hezekiah and thus of royal blood. He was a prince as well as a prophet. He resided in Jerusalem and prophesied during the reign of Josiah (640–609 B.C.). The prophecies of the book were spoken sometime before 621 B.C. since the reform movement of Josiah (621 B.C.) had not yet occurred. Indeed, Zephaniah may have urged reform on King Josiah.

Judah had experienced revival in Hezekiah's day. Yet Isaiah the prophet had revealed that Judah would be taken into captivity in Babylon under the Chaldeans. Zephaniah must have been familiar with this prophecy. Manasseh followed his father Hezekiah and was responsible for the erection of altars to Baal. He worshipped the hosts of heaven and made asherim. The people followed him and idolatry existed everywhere. The sins of Judah were as gross as the sins of the inhabitants of Canaan whom God dispossessed of their lands. The Assyrians took evil Manasseh captive to Babylon. He repented and was returned to his kingship, but he was not successful in reversing the evils he had inaugurated. His son Amon followed him and resorted to his father's old ways. He was assassinated when he had been king for less than two years.

Zephaniah's ministry was cast within the context of the evils of his day. God used him to shock the Judeans in their complacency and to point out their sins to them. He warned them of the impending judgment of God as well as the final day of reckoning at the Day of the Lord.

Characteristics and content Zephaniah opens his book with the announcement of the final day of judgment. Judah is to be included in this judgment for she has trusted in her riches and been idolatrous. In the immediate future her houses will be destroyed and her goods taken. Repentance is urged upon the people. Then Zephaniah speaks of God's impending judgment on the surrounding nations. He will destroy Gaza and the Philistines. Moab and Ammon shall experience what happened to Sodom and Gomorrah. Ethiopia and the Assyrians and Nineveh will experience the wrath of God.

Zephaniah concentrates on the sins of Jerusalem, a city of violence and crime. She will not listen to God's voice; no one can tell her anything; she refuses correction; she does not trust in God nor seek him. Her leaders, her prophets and her judges, are guilty before God. Zephaniah does not stop with the promise of God's vengeance against Judah. He looks beyond that age to a time when God will restore the fortunes of his people. Blessings are promised, not only to the remnant from Judah, but also to the whole Israel of the Lord. At that time Jerusalem will be blessed; the Lord will disperse his people's enemies and the Lord himself, the King of Israel, will live among them. He glowingly ends his prophecy by asserting that God would reverse their captivity: "At that time I will bring you again, even in the time that I gather you: for I will make you a name and a praise among all people of the earth, when I turn back your captivity before your eyes, saith the LORD" (3:20).

Outline

I. The coming day of his judgment (1:1—3:7)
II. The assurance of God's coming kingdom (3:8–20)

I. THE COMING DAY OF HIS JUDGMENT (1:1—3:7)

A. GOD'S JUDGMENT ON JUDAH AND JERUSALEM

1. The Nature of the Punishment

1 THE word of the LORD which came unto Zeph-a-ni'ah the son of
Cu'shi, the son Ged-a-li'ah, the son of Am-a-ri'ah, the son of Hiz-ki'ah,
in the days of Jo-si'ah the son of A'mon, king of Judah.

☆1:1 2 Kgs 22:1-23:28 2 Chron 34:1-35:26

1:1 *Zephaniah* is the last of the minor prophets before the Babylonian captivity and is placed last in the canon before the post-captivity prophets. His name means "the Lord hides," and his great-great-grandfather was

1:2☆ 2 Kgs 22:15–20; Isa 6:11; Ezek 33:27–29
1:3☆ Isa 6:11, 12; Jer 4:25; 9:10; Ezek 29:11; Hos 4:3
1:4☆ 2 Kgs 21:12–15; 23:4–7; 2 Chron 34:3–7
1:5☆ Lev 20:2–5; 1 Kgs 11:33; 2 Kgs 21:3–5; Acts 7:42
1:6 Ps 10:4; Isa 43:22; Rom 3:11
1:7☆ Ps 46:10; 76:8; Isa 34:6; Ezek 39:17–21; Hab 2:20; Zech 2:13
1:8☆ Isa 10:12; 24:21–23
1:9☆ Neh 5:15
1:10☆ 2 Chron 33:14; Neh 3:3; 12:39

2 I will utterly consume all *things* from off the land, saith the LORD.
3 I will consume man and beast; I will consume the fowls of the heaven, and the fishes of the sea, and the stumblingblocks with the wicked; and I will cut off man from off the land, saith the LORD.
4 I will also stretch out mine hand upon Judah, and upon all the inhabitants of Jerusalem; and I will cut off the remnant of Ba'al from this place, *and* the name of the Chem'a-rims with the priests;
5 And them that worship the host of heaven upon the housetops; and them that worship *and* that swear by the LORD, and that swear by Mal'cham;
6 And them that are turned back from the LORD; and *those* that have not sought the LORD, nor inquired for him.
7 Hold thy peace at the presence of the Lord GOD: for the day of the LORD *is* at hand: for the LORD hath prepared a sacrifice, he hath bid his guests.
8 And it shall come to pass in the day of the LORD's sacrifice, that I will punish the princes, and the king's children, and all such as are clothed with strange apparel.
9 In the same day also will I punish all those that leap on the threshold, which fill their masters' houses with violence and deceit.
10 And it shall come to pass in that day, saith the LORD, *that there shall be* the noise of a cry from the fish gate, and an howling from the second, and a great crashing from the hills.

1:11☆ Ezek 22:12; Hos 12:7, 8
1:12☆ Jer 16:16; Amos 9:1–3; Obad 6
1:13 Deut 28:30; Isa 5:8, 9; Amos 5:11

11 Howl, ye inhabitants of Mak'tesh, for all the merchant people are cut down; all they that bear silver are cut off.
12 And it shall come to pass at that time, *that* I will search Jerusalem with candles, and punish the men that are settled on their lees: that say in their heart, The LORD will not do good, neither will he do evil.
13 Therefore their goods shall become a booty, and their houses a desolation: they shall also build houses, but not inhabit *them;* and they shall plant vineyards, but not drink the wine thereof.

2. The Nearness of the Day

1:14☆ Ezek 7:16–18
1:15 Isa 59:10; Joel 2:2

14 The great day of the LORD *is* near, *it is* near, and hasteth greatly, *even* the voice of the day of the LORD: the mighty man shall cry there bitterly.
15 That day *is* a day of wrath, a day of trouble and distress, a day of wasteness and desolation, a day of darkness and gloominess, a day of clouds and thick darkness,

---

King Hizkiah (Hezekiah). Samaria (Israel or Ephraim) had been destroyed a century earlier. His ministry revolved around Judah and Jerusalem.

1:2, 3 *I will utterly consume all things.* Thus begins the prophet, who predicts that Judah and Jerusalem will be destroyed by God. Man, beasts, birds, and fish will be destroyed in this holocaust.

1:4 The reason for the judgment is idolatry. It had extended to the point where the priests were deeply involved in the apostasy.

1:5 *that swear by the LORD, and that swear by Malcham. Malcham,* also known as "Milcom," "Molech," and "Moloch," seems to be identical to the god Baal in his role as the "king-god." At this point the Jews have *one foot in heaven and one foot in hell;* they profess to love God and also Malcham (Moloch). They swear allegiance to the service of both God and idols. God will have none of this.

1:7 Zephaniah here speaks of a prophecy that has a double fulfillment. The first one occurred when Nebuchadnezzar conquered Judah. At the end of the age, the final day of his judgment will come. *The LORD has prepared a sacrifice,* i.e., the destruction of the people who had rebelled against him.

1:8 *clothed with strange apparel,* i.e., showing their desire for foreign gods and foreign ways, and their contempt for the Lord.†

1:9 *those that leap on the threshold,* i.e., follow a foreign custom associated with idols.

1:10 *the fish gate,* located on the northern end of the Tyrophoeon Valley.

1:11 *Maktesh,* a low part of Jerusalem where goldsmiths and merchants lived.

1:12 *lees,* dregs, or sediment in wine, here meaning that they are intoxicated with their pleasures—secure, easy, and fearing nothing and no one.

1:14ff This is a description of the evil that is coming upon Judah and Jerusalem in the hour of God's wrath against that nation for its sins.

16 A day of the trumpet and alarm against the fenced cities, and against the high towers.

17 And I will bring distress upon men, that they shall walk like blind men, because they have sinned against the LORD: and their blood shall be poured out as dust, and their flesh as the dung.

18 Neither their silver nor their gold shall be able to deliver them in the day of the LORD's wrath; but the whole land shall be devoured by the fire of his jealousy: for he shall make even a speedy riddance of all them that dwell in the land.

1:16 Isa 2:12–15; Jer 4:19; Hos 5:8
1:17 Deut 28:28, 29; Ps 79:3; 83:10; Isa 59:10; Jer 8:2; 9:22; Lam 4:14; Mt 15:13, 14
☆**1:18** Deut 32:21–25; Ps 49:6–9; Zeph 3:8

3. The Summons to Repentance

2 GATHER yourselves together, yea, gather together, O nation not desired;

2 Before the decree bring forth, *before* the day pass as the chaff, before the fierce anger of the LORD come upon you, before the day of the LORD's anger come upon you.

3 Seek ye the LORD, all ye meek of the earth, which have wrought his judgment; seek righteousness, seek meekness: it may be ye shall be hid in the day of the LORD's anger.

☆**2:1** 2 Chron 20:4; Neh 8:1; 9:1; Esther 4:16; Isa 1:4, 10–15; Joel 2:12
2:2 Ezek 33:11; Zeph 1:18; Rom 2:4; 2 Pet 3:9
2:3 2 Kgs 22:18, 19; 2 Chron 7:14, 15; Ps 25:8, 9; Mic 6:8; Zeph 3:12

B. GOD'S JUDGMENT ON THE SURROUNDING NATIONS

1. Gaza and the Philistines Judged

4 ¶For Ga'za shall be forsaken, and Ash'ke-lon a desolation: they shall drive out Ash'dod at the noon day, and Ekron shall be rooted up.

5 Woe unto the inhabitants of the sea coast, the nation of the Cher'e-thites! the word of the LORD *is* against you; O Canaan, the land of the Philistines, I will even destroy thee, that there shall be no inhabitant.

6 And the sea coast shall be dwellings *and* cottages for shepherds, and folds for flocks.

7 And the coast shall be for the remnant of the house of Judah; they shall feed thereupon: in the houses of Ash'ke-lon shall they lie down in the evening: for the LORD their God shall visit them and turn away their captivity.

☆**2:4** Jer 25:19, 20; 47:1–7; Amos 1:6–8; Zech 9:5
☆**2:5** Isa 14:29, 31
2:6 Isa 14:30
2:7 Ps 85:1–3; Isa 11:11; Jer 31:7; Amos 9:14; Mic 5:3; Zeph 3:20

2. Moab and Ammon Judged

8 I have heard the reproach of Moab, and the revilings of the children of Ammon, whereby they have reproached my people, and magnified *themselves* against their border.

9 Therefore *as* I live, saith the LORD of hosts, the God of Israel, Surely Moab shall be as Sodom, and the children of Ammon as Go-mor'rah, *even* the breeding of nettles, and saltpits, and a perpetual desolation: the residue of my people shall spoil them, and the remnant of my people shall possess them.

10 This shall they have for their pride, because they have reproached and magnified *themselves* against the people of the LORD of hosts.

☆**2:8** Ps 83:4–8; Ezek 36:2; Zeph 2:10
2:10 Isa 16:6–10; Jer 48:28–31; Dan 5:20, 21; Obad 3, 4; Zeph 2:8

1:18 *Neither their silver nor their gold* will ransom them from the imminent judgment of God. They have hoarded these metals for use in the day of adversity, but it will do them no good.

2:1 *Gather yourselves together.* Zephaniah calls the shameful nation to a national assembly for the purpose of fasting, prayer, and seeking the face of God in repentance in order to avert judgment.

2:4ff Judgment is coming upon the peoples of Gaza, Ashkelon, Ashdod, and Ekron. There was a fifth group known as Gath, but some think this region was under the control of Judah at this time.

2:5 *Cherethites,* i.e., Cretans.

2:8ff The Moabites and Ammonites are guilty of the same provocations. They reviled and reproached God's people and rejoiced in their misfortunes. They are worthy of God's judgment, and he *will be terrible unto them* (2:11).

2:11 Joel 2:11

11 The LORD *will be* terrible unto them: for he will famish all the gods of
the earth; and *men* shall worship him, every one from his place, *even* all the
isles of the heathen.

3. Ethiopia and Assyria Judged

2:12☆ Isa 20:3, 4; 43:3
2:13☆ Nah 3:7
2:14 Lev 11:13–19; Deut 14:11–18; Ps 102:6; Isa 14:23; 34:11
2:15 1 Kgs 9:7, 8; Isa 10:12–14; 22:2–7; Lam 2:15, 16; Mt 27:39

12 ¶Ye E-thi-o'pi-ans also, ye *shall be* slain by my sword.
13 And he will stretch out his hand against the north, and destroy Assyria;
and will make Nin'e-veh a desolation, *and* dry like a wilderness.
14 And flocks shall lie down in the midst of her, all the beasts of the
nations: both the cormorant and the bittern shall lodge in the upper lintels
of it; *their* voice shall sing in the windows; desolation *shall be* in the
thresholds: for he shall uncover the cedar work.
15 This *is* the rejoicing city that dwelt carelessly, that said in her heart, I
am, and *there is* none beside me: how is she become a desolation, a place
for beasts to lie down in! every one that passeth by her shall hiss, *and* wag
his hand.

C. THE WOE UPON SINFUL JERUSALEM

3:1 Jer 6:6
3:2☆ Ps 78:22; Jer 32:33
3:3 Ps 10:8–10; Prov 28:15; Ezek 22:6–12
3:4 Ezek 22:28; Hos 4:6–5; Mal 2:7–9
3:5 Jer 3:3; 6:15; 8:12
3:6 Isa 10:1–33; 15:1–9; 16:1–14; Nah 2:2; Zeph 2:4, 5

3 WOE to her that is filthy and polluted, to the oppressing city!
2 She obeyed not the voice; she received not correction; she trusted
not in the LORD; she drew not near to her God.
3 Her princes within her *are* roaring lions; her judges *are* evening wolves;
they gnaw not the bones till the morrow.
4 Her prophets *are* light *and* treacherous persons: her priests have
polluted the sanctuary, they have done violence to the law.
5 The just LORD *is* in the midst thereof; he will not do iniquity: every
morning doth he bring his judgment to light, he faileth not; but the unjust
knoweth no shame.
6 I have cut off the nations: their towers are desolate; I made their streets
waste, that none passeth by: their cities are destroyed, so that there is no
man, that there is none inhabitant.
7 I said, Surely thou wilt fear me, thou wilt receive instruction; so their
dwelling should not be cut off, howsoever I punished them: but they rose
early, *and* corrupted all their doings.

II. THE ASSURANCE OF GOD'S COMING KINGDOM (3:8–20)

A. THE CALL TO PATIENT WAITING

3:8☆ Ezek 38:14–23; Zeph 1:18

8 ¶Therefore wait ye upon me, saith the LORD, until the day that I rise up
to the prey: for my determination *is* to gather the nations, that I may

---

2:12 The Ethiopians or Arabians had at times been a terror to Israel (see 2 Chron. 14:9). Justice will now catch up with them, and *my sword* (i.e., the sword of the Lord) will slay them.

2:13ff Definitive judgment is also expressed against Nineveh. People will shake their heads in disbelief at the catastrophe. "Nothing seemed more improbable than that the capital of so vast an empire, a city of sixty miles around with walls one hundred feet high and so thick that three chariots could go abreast on them, and with 1,500 towers, should be so totally destroyed that its site is with difficulty discovered" (*Jamieson, Fausset and Brown's Commentary on the Whole Bible,* Zondervan, 1957).

3:2 Jerusalem is guilty of four sins: (1) God has given her the law and sent his prophets but she has not obeyed his voice; (2) God has disciplined her with the Word and with a rod but she has not received correction; (3) she has made alliances with other nations and refused to trust the Lord; and (4) God has given her tokens of his presence and established the ordinances by which she could have communion with him, but she has not drawn near to God. Unless and until she changes her ways, there is no hope of deliverance, and judgment must fall.

3:8 *Therefore wait ye upon me,* i.e., "wait for me." The Old Testament prophesied the consolation of Israel. For hundreds of years faithful Jews waited for the fulfillment of this promise. It came when Jesus was born. Thus Luke wrote of Simeon as one of those who was "waiting for the consolation of Israel" (Luke 2:25).

assemble the kingdoms, to pour upon them mine indignation, *even* all my
fierce anger: for all the earth shall be devoured with the fire of my jealousy.
9For then will I turn to the people a pure language, that they may all call
upon the name of the LORD, to serve him with one consent.
10From beyond the rivers of E-thi-o'pi-a my suppliants, *even* the daughter
of my dispersed, shall bring mine offering.
11In that day shalt thou not be ashamed for all thy doings, wherein thou
hast transgressed against me: for then I will take away out of the midst of
thee them that rejoice in thy pride, and thou shalt no more be haughty
because of my holy mountain.
12I will also leave in the midst of thee an afflicted and poor people, and
they shall trust in the name of the LORD.
13The remnant of Israel shall not do iniquity, nor speak lies; neither shall
a deceitful tongue be found in their mouth: for they shall feed and lie down,
and none shall make *them* afraid.

☆3:9 Isa 19:18
3:10 Isa 11:11
☆3:11 Num 16:3 Isa 11:9 48:1,2; 54:4 Dan 9:16, 20 Mt 3:9 Rom 2:17–20 9:33 1 Pet 2:6
3:12 Nah 1:7 Zeph 2:3 1 Pet 1:21
3:13 Lev 26:6 Hos 2:18

B. THE CALL FOR GLADNESS AND REJOICING

14¶Sing, O daughter of Zion; shout, O Israel; be glad and rejoice with all
the heart, O daughter of Jerusalem.
15The LORD hath taken away thy judgments, he hath cast out thine
enemy: the king of Israel, *even* the LORD, *is* in the midst of thee: thou shalt
not see evil any more.
16In that day it shall be said to Jerusalem, Fear thou not: *and to* Zion, Let
not thine hands be slack.
17The LORD thy God in the midst of thee *is* mighty; he will save, he will
rejoice over thee with joy; he will rest in his love, he will joy over thee with
singing.
18I will gather *them that are* sorrowful for the solemn assembly, *who* are of
thee, *to whom* the reproach of it *was* a burden.
19Behold, at that time I will undo all that afflict thee: and I will save her
that halteth, and gather her that was driven out; and I will get them praise
and fame in every land where they have been put to shame.
20At that time will I bring you *again,* even in the time that I gather you:
for I will make you a name and a praise among all people of the earth, when
I turn back your captivity before your eyes, saith the LORD.

3:15 Ps 21:1–7 24:1–10 Isa 33:22
3:16 Isa 35:3, 4 43:1–4 Hag 2:4, 5 Heb 12:12, 13
☆3:17 Isa 63:1 Heb 7:25
☆3:18
3:19 Isa 61:7 Ezek 39:26–29
3:20 Zeph 2:7

3:9 *a pure language,* i.e., "pure speech," that which honors the name of God. Purity of worship replaces idolatrous worship, and God is glorified. This will not take place until after the Second Advent of Jesus Christ.

3:11ff This description goes far beyond anything known to God's people. It will be characteristic of a millennial age, according to premillenarians.

3:17, 18 God is love (1 John 4:8). The nature of God's love is described in the Scriptures as being: (1) sovereign (Deut. 7:7; 10:15), (2) everlasting (Jer. 31:3), (3) inextinguishable (Rom. 8:39), and (4) never-failing (Isa. 49:15, 16). The full measure of God's love is revealed in his sending Jesus Christ, his only Son, to death on Calvary's cross for sinners. God's love becomes ours upon redemption, for "the love of God is shed abroad in our hearts by the Holy Ghost which is given unto us" (Rom. 5:5).

HAGGAI

Authorship, date, and background Haggai, the author of this book, was probably born in Babylon during the captivity and returned to Jerusalem with the remnant in 539–538 B.C. The name Haggai is derived from a word meaning "festival," which suggests he may have been born at the time of some Israelite feast. Nothing is known about his family background nor is the name of his father given. He was a contemporary of Zechariah, with whom he shared the common goal to finish the rebuilding of the temple.

The Jewish remnant that returned from Babylon was small in number. Many of those who remained in Babylon had become well-to-do and preferred their present prosperity to an uncertain future in the land their fathers had left in the captivity. Others had fallen away from their faith in the God of Abraham as a result of the captivity. This meant that those who did return to the land had religious aspirations and were interested in the rebuilding of the temple which was central to their worship. Unfortunately they had a hard time at first. But when they prospered economically, their interests shifted from spiritual to material things at a time when they had done no more than finish laying the foundations of the temple. After that, further construction ceased for fifteen years, due in part to the evil intentions of their hostile neighbors.

Haggai's prophecies were given in the year 520 B.C. and consisted of four oracles spoken over a period of four months. They were addressed to the forty thousand immigrants who had returned to the land under the edict of King Cyrus of Persia after the fall of the Chaldean state. The return was led by Zerubbabel the governor and Joshua the high priest. Following Haggai's prophecies, the work on the temple was resumed in 520 B.C. and the construction of it was completed in 516 or 515 B.C.

Characteristics and content Haggai's first prophecy is directed toward the Jews who are building more elaborate homes while neglecting the temple. They are urged to rebuild the temple and are promised the help and blessing of God in material things if they meet their spiritual obligations.

In the second message Haggai encourages Zerubbabel and Joshua concerning the presence of the Lord in their midst. He promises them that God will fill his new house with his glory and that its splendor will be greater than that of the first temple.

In the third oracle Haggai says God's people are unclean. Therefore, God is withholding his blessing from them because of their disobedience. If the people will repent and do what God wants, he will bless them and the earth will yield a bountiful harvest.

Haggai's last oracle is addressed to Zerubbabel, who is like a signet ring upon God's finger. He has been specially chosen by God for his work and God will honor him. But this will take place after God has shaken the heavens and the earth and overthrown and destroyed the strength of the kingdoms of the nations (2:22). Since these things did not happen at that time, they are to be regarded as awaiting fulfillment by David's descendants, of whom Zerubbabel is a representative.

Outline

I. The first message: rebuild God's temple! (1:1–15)
II. The second message: the second temple will be greater than the first (2:1–9)
III. The third message: the reasons why they were not blessed (2:10–19)
IV. The fourth message: God will triumph at last (2:20–23)

I. THE FIRST MESSAGE: REBUILD GOD'S TEMPLE! (1:1–15)

A. GOD'S ANSWER TO THE OBJECTORS

1 IN the second year of Darius the king, in the sixth month, in the first
day of the month, came the word of the LORD by Hag'ga-i the prophet
unto Ze-rub'ba-bel the son of She-al'ti-el, governor of Judah, and to Joshua
the son of Jos'e-dech, the high priest, saying,
2Thus speaketh the LORD of hosts, saying, This people say, The time is
not come, the time that the LORD's house should be built.
3Then came the word of the LORD by Hag'ga-i the prophet, saying,
4*Is it* time for you, O ye, to dwell in your cieled houses, and this house *lie*
waste?
5Now therefore thus saith the LORD of hosts; Consider your ways.
6Ye have sown much, and bring in little; ye eat, but ye have not enough;
ye drink, but ye are not filled with drink; ye clothe you, but there is none
warm; and he that earneth wages earneth wages *to put it* into a bag with
holes.
7¶Thus saith the LORD of hosts; Consider your ways.
8Go up to the mountain, and bring wood, and build the house; and I will
take pleasure in it, and I will be glorified, saith the LORD.
9Ye looked for much, and, lo, *it came* to little; and when ye brought *it*
home, I did blow upon it. Why? saith the LORD of hosts. Because of mine
house that *is* waste, and ye run every man unto his own house.
10Therefore the heaven over you is stayed from dew, and the earth is
stayed *from* her fruit.
11And I called for a drought upon the land, and upon the mountains, and
upon the corn, and upon the new wine, and upon the oil, and upon *that*
which the ground bringeth forth, and upon men, and upon cattle, and upon
all the labour of the hands.

☆**1:1** Ezra 2:2; 3:8; 4:1–3, 24; 5:1, 2; 6:6–14; Neh 12:1–7
☆**1:2**
☆**1:4**
1:6 Lev 26:14–20; Deut 28:15–19, 22, 24, 30–34; Hag 1:9; 2:16
1:8 Ezra 3:7–13
1:9 Hag 1:6
1:10 Deut 28:24; 1 Kgs 8:35, 36; 17:1; Joel 1:18–20
1:11 Lev 26:18–22; Deut 28:22–24; Jer 14:1–6

B. THE PEOPLE ARE MOVED BY GOD TO REBUILD

12¶Then Ze-rub'ba-bel the son of She-al'ti-el, and Joshua the son of Jos'e-
dech, the high priest, with all the remnant of the people, obeyed the voice of
the LORD their God, and the words of Hag'ga-i the prophet, as the LORD
their God had sent him, and the people did fear before the LORD.
13Then spake Hag'ga-i the LORD's messenger in the LORD's message unto
the people, saying, I *am* with you, saith the LORD.
14And the LORD stirred up the spirit of Ze-rub'ba-bel the son of She-al'ti-
el, governor of Judah, and the spirit of Joshua the son of Jos'e-dech, the

☆**1:12** Ps 112:1; Eccles 12:13; Isa 50:10; Hag 1:1
1:13 2 Chron 20:15–17; Ps 46:7; Isa 8:9, 10; 43:2; Hag 2:4, 5
1:14, 15 Ezra 3:1; 4:24; 5:2; Neh 4:6; 11:2; Hag 1:1; 2:10

1:1 *Haggai* and *Zerubbabel* were among the exiles who had returned from Babylon to rebuild the temple in Jerusalem. Haggai directed his message to church and state. Zerubbabel was the political head of state, and Joshua was the *chief religious leader. Both were* held responsible for the failure of the returned remnant to finish building the temple.

1:2 Haggai appeared on the scene some eighteen years after the return of the remnant from Babylon. The rebuilding of the temple was neglected by its friends as it later was to be retarded by its enemies. Haggai had a message from God to Zerubbabel and Joshua: begin rebuilding the house of God. Note that God chose to work indirectly through the prophet rather than addressing them directly. God often sends messages to his people through other sources and by indirection makes his will known. Since we no longer have writing prophets, in this age one must be very careful to test any spirits who say they are bringing a word of knowledge from God.

1:4ff God replies to the question as to whether it was time to rebuild the temple when the people lacked food. God said they had time to build themselves houses and to plant crops. Why didn't they have time to build God's house? God who is over nature stopped the course of nature as a direct response to their failure to finish the temple.

1:12 Zerubbabel and Joshua got the message. Their response was prompt. They got things going in the finishing of the temple. The spirits of the two leaders were stirred up by God, and they began to obey the divine mandate. The people were also quickened by God to finish the job.

high priest, and the spirit of all the remnant of the people; and they came
and did work in the house of the LORD of hosts, their God,
15 In the four and twentieth day of the sixth month, in the second year of
Darius the king.

II. THE SECOND MESSAGE: THE SECOND TEMPLE WILL BE GREATER THAN THE FIRST (2:1–9)

2:1☆ 2 IN the seventh *month,* in the one and twentieth *day* of the month, came
the word of the LORD by the prophet Hag'ga-i, saying,
2 Speak now to Ze-rub'ba-bel the son of She-al'ti-el, governor of Judah,
and to Joshua the son of Jos'e-dech, the high priest, and to the residue of
the people, saying,
3 Who *is* left among you that saw this house in her first glory? and how do
ye see it now? *is it* not in your eyes in comparison of it as nothing?
4 Yet now be strong, O Ze-rub'ba-bel, saith the LORD; and be strong, O
Joshua, son of Jos'e-dech, the high priest; and be strong, all ye people of the
land, saith the LORD, and work: for I *am* with you, saith the LORD of hosts:
5 *According to* the word that I covenanted with you when ye came out of
Egypt, so my spirit remaineth among you: fear ye not.
6 For thus saith the LORD of hosts; Yet once, it *is* a little while, and I will
shake the heavens, and the earth, and the sea, and the dry *land;*
7 And I will shake all nations, and the desire of all nations shall come:
and I will fill this house with glory, saith the LORD of hosts.
8 The silver *is* mine, and the gold *is* mine, saith the LORD of hosts.
9 The glory of this latter house shall be greater than of the former, saith
the LORD of hosts: and in this place will I give peace, saith the LORD of
hosts.

III. THE THIRD MESSAGE: THE REASONS WHY THEY WERE NOT BLESSED (2:10–19)

10 In the four and twentieth *day* of the ninth *month,* in the second year of
Darius, came the word of the LORD by Hag'ga-i the prophet, saying,
11 Thus saith the LORD of hosts; Ask now the priests *concerning* the law,
saying,

2:3 Ezra 3:12
2:4☆ Deut 31:23; Josh 6:6–9; Hag 1:13; 1 Cor 16:13; Eph 6:10–12; 2 Tim 2:1
2:5☆ Ex 29:45, 46; 2 Chron 20:15–17; Hag 2:4; Mt 28:5; Jn 14:15–17; Acts 27:24
2:6☆ Isa 13:10; 34:4; Ezek 38:20; Mt 24:29; Mk 13:24, 25; Lk 21:25, 26; Rev 6:12–17
2:7☆ 1 Kgs 8:11; Ps 80:1; Rom 15:9–13; Gal 3:8, 9
2:8 Ps 84:8; Isa 9:6; Lk 2:14
2:9☆
2:10 Hag 1:14
2:11☆

2:1 Chapter 2 contains three sermons by Haggai. Sermon one declares that the new temple, inferior to that of Solomon's temple, will be spiritually greater than that of Solomon (2:1–9). Sermon two indicates that because of their response to finish the temple, God will bless them in material things in great measure (2:10–19). Sermon three assures faithful Zerubbabel that his work will be remembered and appreciated, for he will be numbered among the ancestral line of the Messiah, whose kingdom will have no end (2:20–23).
2:4 *I am with you.* God had withheld his blessing from them while they tarried in finishing the house of God. But now that they obeyed, God is with them to bless them, help them, and reward them for their obedience to his command.
2:5 *so my spirit remaineth among you.* This was the surest guarantee that the work of God would succeed and that the people of God could proceed without fear.
2:6 *I will shake the heavens and the earth.* God will employ physical phenomena and political upheavals to fully execute the divine will. This earthly confusion will be evidence that God is about to act.
2:7 *the desire of all nations.* Commentators differ as to the meaning of this phrase. Some hold that it refers to the Messiah, who is the desire of all people. He will establish his church and kingdom, and all the wealth of the nations shall be poured into them. Others hold that the word translated *desire* should be "treasures" or "wealth" of all nations, which will fill God's house. Some regard this as being literally fulfilled in the millennial kingdom.
2:9 *will I give peace,* i.e., peace with God through Christ who, five hundred years later, came often to this temple. Moreover, the second temple—externally inferior to Solomon's temple—would be greater in spiritual glory, because of the presence of the Word of God incarnate, Jesus Christ.
2:11 *Ask now the priests concerning the law,* i.e., in order to illustrate the answer from the law. If they do, people will see that: (1) sacred things cannot communicate holiness to things they touch; (2) anyone unclean will contaminate anything he touches.

12 If one bear holy flesh in the skirt of his garment, and with his skirt do
touch bread, or pottage, or wine, or oil, or any meat, shall it be holy? And
the priests answered and said, No.

2:12 Ex 29:37 Ezek 44:19

13 Then said Hag′ga-i, If *one that is* unclean by a dead body touch any of
these, shall it be unclean? And the priests answered and said, It shall be
unclean.

2:13 Lev 11:28, 40 22:4–6 Num 19:11, 12, 22

14 Then answered Hag′ga-i, and said, So *is* this people, and so *is* this
nation before me, saith the LORD; and so *is* every work of their hands; and
that which they offer there *is* unclean.

2:14 Prov 21:4, 24 Isa 1:11–15 Tit 1:15

15 And now, I pray you, consider from this day and upward, from before
a stone was laid upon a stone in the temple of the LORD:

2:15 Ezra 4:24

16 Since those *days* were, when *one* came to an heap of twenty *measures,*
there were *but* ten: when *one* came to the pressfat for to draw out fifty
vessels out of the press, there were *but* twenty.

2:16 Hag 1:9

17 I smote you with blasting and with mildew and with hail in all the
labours of your hands; yet ye *turned* not to me, saith the LORD.
18 Consider now from this day and upward, from the four and twentieth
day of the ninth *month, even* from the day that the foundation of the LORD's
temple was laid, consider *it.*

☆2:18 Hag 2:10

19 Is the seed yet in the barn? yea, as yet the vine, and the fig tree, and the
pomegranate, and the olive tree, hath not brought forth: from this day will
I bless *you.*

☆2:19

IV. THE FOURTH MESSAGE: GOD WILL TRIUMPH AT LAST (2:20–23)

20 ¶And again the word of the LORD came unto Hag′ga-i in the four and
twentieth *day* of the month, saying,
21 Speak to Ze-rub′ba-bel, governor of Judah, saying, I will shake the
heavens and the earth;

☆2:21 Hag 2:6

22 And I will overthrow the throne of kingdoms, and I will destroy the
strength of the kingdoms of the heathen; and I will overthrow the chariots,
and those that ride in them; and the horses and their riders shall come
down, every one by the sword of his brother.
23 In that day, saith the LORD of hosts, will I take thee, O Ze-rub′ba-bel,
my servant, the son of She-al′ti-el, saith the LORD, and will make thee as a
signet: for I have chosen thee, saith the LORD of hosts.

2:18 *the four and twentieth day of the ninth month* (Kislev), equivalent to early December.

2:19 *from this day will I bless you.* God favors those who turn to the way of duty. Those who do God's bidding will never lack God's blessing.

2:21 *Zerubbabel.* He was heir to the throne of David and thus is listed in the line of David (Matt. 1:12; Luke 3:27). He was active in building the new temple, and God promised to give him a house. He was chosen of God and said to be "as a signet" (2:23; a "signet" is a small, official seal). Jeconiah had been as a signet on God's right hand but was removed from that relationship (Jer. 22:24). Jesus Christ is the signet on God's right hand. All power is given to him and is derived from him.

ZECHARIAH

Authorship, date, and background Zechariah, the author of this book, whose name means "God has remembered," was the son of Berechiah and the grandson of Iddo. The latter returned from Babylon with Zerubbabel and Joshua and was in the priestly line. Zechariah may well be the one mentioned by Nehemiah in 12:16. He was a contemporary of Haggai and had similar interests in the rebuilding of the temple. His prophetic ministry began in 520 B.C.

The historical situation is the same as that described for Haggai. Those who returned to Jerusalem were among the poorer people of the captivity. The wealthier ones stayed behind. The conditions around Jerusalem and the utter desolation created apathy among the refugees, who were more interested in scratching a living from the unproductive soil than in rebuilding the temple. The book of Zechariah is readily divisible into two distinct and quite different segments (chapters 1–8 and chapters 9–14). The first segment is historical and deals with the situation in Jerusalem at the time of its writing. The second half is apocalyptic, having to do with prophecy and the end of the age. Conservative scholars have always refused to accept the liberal critics' hypothesis that the second half was written by someone other than Zechariah, although it is probably true that the latter portion of the book was written later in his life.

Characteristics and content Zechariah's first emphasis is on the rebuilding of the temple. He urges the people to complete the unfinished task which has been interrupted for some years. He says God will bless his people if they will obey him and finish rebuilding. Beginning with 1:7, Zechariah speaks of a series of night visions he has received from God. The vision of the red horse shows that God is watching over Judah. The vision of the four animal horns and the four blacksmiths indicates the defeat of Judah's enemies. The measuring line vision reveals what the expanded city of Jerusalem will be like. The dirty-clothed Joshua, reclothed in clean garments, portrays the removal of sin and the spiritual reformation of God's people. The gold lampstand whose oil is supplied by two olive trees assures Zerubbabel that God by his Spirit will accomplish his purpose. The scroll flying through the air evidences God's curse on stealing and lying. The vision of the ephah depicts the removal of sin from Judah to Babylon. The vision of the four chariots bespeaks God's sovereign control as he patrols the four corners of the earth.

Zechariah follows up the visions with a section devoted to the consecration of Joshua, who is thought to be a type of Messiah (the Branch), and one having to do with fasting as a reminder to the people of the fall of Jerusalem.

Beginning with chapter 9, Zechariah looks to the future. He pronounces God's judgment on the surrounding nations and foresees the prospects of a triumphant king over Jerusalem. God ultimately will save and protect his own people. Faithless shepherds will be destroyed by judgment. But God will punish his people first for their refusal to accept and follow the true Shepherd. Even this abandonment of his people by God is part of the divine plan. Someday Jerusalem will be restored and victorious. Before that happens Jerusalem will be rent, many will die, but the coming of the Shephered will rescue the city, and the remnant will acknowledge that the Lord is God. The Mount of Olives will be split and the Lord will become the King of the entire earth. All those who survive will go to Jerusalem to worship the Lord the King, and they will keep the Feast of Tabernacles. Jerusalem will become the capital city for all the nations of the world.

Outline

I. The messages during the buidling of the temple (1:1—8:23)
II. The messages following the rebuilding of the temple (9:1—14:21)

I. THE MESSAGES DURING THE BUILDING OF THE TEMPLE (1:1—8:23)

A. MESSAGE ONE: GOD'S CALL FOR REPENTANCE

1 IN the eighth month, in the second year of Darius, came the word of
the LORD unto Zech-a-ri'ah, the son of Ber-e-chi'ah, the son of Id'do
the prophet, saying,
2 The LORD hath been sore displeased with your fathers.
3 Therefore say thou unto them, Thus saith the LORD of hosts; Turn ye
unto me, saith the LORD of hosts, and I will turn unto you, saith the LORD
of hosts.
4 Be ye not as your fathers, unto whom the former prophets have cried,
saying, Thus saith the LORD of hosts; Turn ye now from your evil ways,
and *from* your evil doings: but they did not hear, nor hearken unto me,
saith the LORD.
5 Your fathers, where *are* they? and the prophets, do they live for ever?
6 But my words and my statutes, which I commanded my servants the
prophets, did they not take hold of your fathers? and they returned and
said, Like as the LORD of hosts thought to do unto us, according to our
ways, and according to our doings, so hath he dealt with us.

B. MESSAGE TWO: THE EIGHT VISIONS

1. The Man on the Red Horse among the Myrtles

7 ¶Upon the four and twentieth day of the eleventh month, which *is* the
month Se'bat, in the second year of Darius, came the word of the LORD
unto Zech-a-ri'ah, the son of Ber-e-chi'ah, the son of Id'do the prophet,
saying,
8 I saw by night, and behold a man riding upon a red horse, and he stood
among the myrtle trees that *were* in the bottom; and behind him *were there*
red horses, speckled, and white.
9 Then said I, O my lord, what *are* these? And the angel that talked with
me said unto me, I will shew thee what these *be*.
10 And the man that stood among the myrtle trees answered and said,
These *are they* whom the LORD hath sent to walk to and fro through the
earth.
11 And they answered the angel of the LORD that stood among the myrtle
trees, and said, We have walked to and fro through the earth, and, behold,
all the earth sitteth still, and is at rest.
12 ¶Then the angel of the LORD answered and said, O LORD of hosts, how

☆**1:1** Ezra 5:1; Neh 12:4, 16
☆**1:2** 2 Kgs 23:26; 2 Chron 36:16
☆**1:3** 2 Chron 15:4; Neh 9:28; Isa 31:6; Joel 2:12
1:4 2 Chron 24:19; 29:6–10; 36:15; Ezra 9:7; Jer 11:6–8; 36:23, 24; Zech 1:3
☆**1:5** Deut 28:45; Jer 12:16; Amos 9:10; Jn 8:52
☆**1:6**
☆**1:7**
☆**1:8** Neh 8:15; Isa 41:19; 55:13
☆**1:9**
1:10 Job 2:1, 2; Zech 1:19; 4:4, 5, 13; 6:4
☆**1:11** Zech 1:15; 1 Thess 5:3
1:12 2 Chron 36:21; Ps 74:10; 69:5; Isa 64:9–12; Jer 25:11, 12; Dan 9:2; Rev 6:10

1:1 Nine of the minor prophets prophesied before the destruction of Jerusalem. The other three—Haggai, Zechariah and Malachi—prophesied after the captivity ended. The three appear last in the canon of the Old Testament. *Zechariah came after Haggai and before Malachi. the word of the LORD unto Zechariah.* That word was the real thing, not just fancy. The Holy Spirit of God was behind it.

1:2 Before Zechariah talked of mercy, he spoke about repentance. It was law before gospel. God was displeased with the Jews' forefathers; he had a complaint against them.

1:3 He urges the returnees to turn to God, so that God can turn to them. He does so in the name of God. He goes on to urge them to become penitent, by calling attention to the misdeeds of their forebears (1:4) and warning them not to follow their wicked example.

1:5, 6 Prophets and people of the past had died, but the Word of God lives forever. What the prophets prophesied and what God threatened came to pass. Since God had done what he threatened, they should pay attention to present prophesies directed to them.

1:7 *Sebat.* Equivalent to January/February.

1:8 There were riders on the other horses even as there was a rider on the first red horse.

1:9 Some think the rider on the red horse was Christ, who earlier had appeared to Joshua with his sword drawn (Josh. 5:13, 14).

1:11 The report of the other angels is given to the angel rider on the red horse that the whole world is at peace and is prosperous. However, Jerusalem is surrounded by oppressive enemies and is suffering from internal dissension.

long wilt thou not have mercy on Jerusalem and on the cities of Judah,
against which thou hast had indignation these threescore and ten years?

1:13 Isa 40:1, 2 Zech 1:17

13 And the LORD answered the angel that talked with me *with* good words
and comfortable words.

1:14☆ Zech 1:17

14 So the angel that communed with me said unto me, Cry thou, saying,
Thus saith the LORD of hosts; I am jealous for Jerusalem and for Zion with
a great jealousy.
15 And I am very sore displeased with the heathen *that are* at ease: for I
was but a little displeased, and they helped forward the affliction.

1:16 Ezra 6:14, 15 Isa 12:1 54:8–10 Zech 2:10

16 Therefore thus saith the LORD; I am returned to Jerusalem with
mercies: my house shall be built in it, saith the LORD of hosts, and a line
shall be stretched forth upon Jerusalem.

1:17 Isa 52:9; 54:8

17 Cry yet, saying, Thus saith the LORD of hosts; My cities through
prosperity shall yet be spread abroad; and the LORD shall yet comfort Zion,
and shall yet choose Jerusalem.

2. The Four Horns and the Four Carpenters

1:18☆

18 ¶Then lifted I up mine eyes, and saw, and behold four horns.

1:19 1 Kgs 22:11

19 And I said unto the angel that talked with me, What *be* these? And he
answered me, These *are* the horns which have scattered Judah, Israel, and
Jerusalem.
20 And the LORD shewed me four carpenters.

1:21 Zech 1:18, 19 9:12–16 10:3–5; 12:2–6

21 Then said I, What come these to do? And he spake, saying, These *are*
the horns which have scattered Judah, so that no man did lift up his head:
but these are come to fray them, to cast out the horns of the Gentiles, which
lifted up *their* horn over the land of Judah to scatter it.

3. The Measuring Line

2:1 Ezek 40:3, 5 47:4

2 I LIFTED up mine eyes again, and looked, and behold a man with a
measuring line in his hand.

2:2 Jer 31:39 Rev 21:15–17

2 Then said I, Whither goest thou? And he said unto me, To measure
Jerusalem, to see what *is* the breadth thereof, and what *is* the length thereof.
3 And, behold, the angel that talked with me went forth, and another
angel went out to meet him,

2:4☆ Ezek 38:11 Jer 1:6 Dan 1:17 1 Tim 4:12

4 And said unto him, Run, speak to this young man, saying, Jerusalem
shall be inhabited *as* towns without walls for the multitude of men and
cattle therein:

2:5☆ Ps 46:7–11 Isa 60:18, 19 Zech 2:10, 11

5 For I, saith the LORD, will be unto her a wall of fire round about, and
will be the glory in the midst of her.

2:6☆ Num 16:26 Deut 28:64 Isa 48:20 Jer 3:18; 31:10 Rev 18:4

6 ¶Ho, ho, *come forth,* and flee from the land of the north, saith the LORD:
for I have spread you abroad as the four winds of the heaven, saith the
LORD.

1:14ff God is jealous for Jerusalem and Zion. He is angry with the nations who plotted evil (1:14, 15). He has come back to Jerusalem with compassion and is determined that the temple, the city, and his people shall prosper.

1:18ff The four horns are enemy nations. They are overcome by God, who sends carpenters (or smiths) to cut off the horns that are pointed at Judah. This will nullify their power.

2:4 This prophecy, about a Jerusalem too large to be contained within its walls and to be indwelt by God's glory, is yet future. 2:11 indicates that many Gentile peoples will have come to the knowledge of God (see Rom. 11:13–25).

2:5 *a wall of fire.* Jerusalem will be as safe as God can make it. God is a consuming fire, and his fire will surround the city and protect it against any and all enemies.

2:6, 7 Cyrus' decree, which allowed the Jews to return to Palestine, brought back a remnant; however, many chose to remain in the land of their captivity. Here they are urged to return to Jerusalem, where the temple is being rebuilt. God would regather the dispersed people and comfort them in the land from which their fathers had been taken as captives.

7Deliver thyself, O Zion, that dwellest *with* the daughter of Babylon.
8For thus saith the LORD of hosts; After the glory hath he sent me unto
the nations which spoiled you: for he that toucheth you toucheth the apple
of his eye.
9For, behold, I will shake mine hand upon them, and they shall be a spoil
to their servants: and ye shall know that the LORD of hosts hath sent me.
10¶Sing and rejoice, O daughter of Zion: for, lo, I come, and I will dwell
in the midst of thee, saith the LORD.
11And many nations shall be joined to the LORD in that day, and shall be
my people: and I will dwell in the midst of thee, and thou shalt know that
the LORD of hosts hath sent me unto thee.
12And the LORD shall inherit Judah his portion in the holy land, and shall
choose Jerusalem again.
13Be silent, O all flesh, before the LORD: for he is raised up out of his holy
habitation.

2:7
☆2:8 Deut 32:10 Isa 60:7–14 Zech 1:17
2:9 Isa 10:32 11:15; 14:2 19:16 Jer 27:7
2:10 Zech 9:9
2:11 Ex 19:5,6 Deut 32:9 Isa 52:15 Mic 4:2
☆2:13 Deut 26:15 2 Chron 30:27 Ps 46:10 Hab 2:20 Zeph 1:7

4. Joshua, the high priest

3 AND he shewed me Joshua the high priest standing before the angel of
the LORD, and Satan standing at his right hand to resist him.
2And the LORD said unto Satan, The LORD rebuke thee, O Satan; even
the LORD that hath chosen Jerusalem rebuke thee: *is* not this a brand
plucked out of the fire?
3Now Joshua was clothed with filthy garments, and stood before the
angel.
4And he answered and spake unto those that stood before him, saying,
Take away the filthy garments from him. And unto him he said, Behold, I
have caused thine iniquity to pass from thee, and I will clothe thee with
change of raiment.
5And I said, Let them set a fair mitre upon his head. So they set a fair
mitre upon his head, and clothed him with garments. And the angel of the
LORD stood by.
6And the angel of the LORD protested unto Joshua, saying,
7Thus saith the LORD of hosts; If thou wilt walk in my ways, and if thou
wilt keep my charge, then thou shalt also judge my house, and shalt also
keep my courts, and I will give thee places to walk among these that stand
by.
8Hear now, O Joshua the high priest, thou, and thy fellows that sit before
thee: for they *are* men wondered at: for, behold, I will bring forth my
servant the BRANCH.
9For behold the stone that I have laid before Joshua; upon one stone
shall be seven eyes: behold, I will engrave the graving thereof, saith the
LORD of hosts, and I will remove the iniquity of that land in one day.

☆3:1 Ezra 5:2 Job 1:6–12 2:1–8 Hag 1:1 Zech 6:11
3:2 2 Chron 6:6 Zech 2:12
3:3 Ezra 9:15 Isa 64:6 Dan 9:18
☆3:4 Isa 43:25; 61:10 Zech 3:9 Mt 22:11–13 Lk 15:22 Rev 7:14
3:5 Ex 28:37–40 Lev 8:9 Ezek 44:18
3:7 1 Kgs 3:14 Isa 62:9 Ezek 44:8
☆3:8 Isa 4:2; 8:18 11:1; 53:2 Jer 33:15 Ezek 12:11 24:24 Zech 6:12
☆3:9

2:8 This passage evidently refers to the Messiah, here seen as one of the *Godhead.*†

2:13 *Be silent . . . before the LORD.* We must let God go his own way. We must not tell him what he should do or quarrel with him about what he has done. We are to be still, knowing that he is God and seeing his salvation.

3:1 *Joshua the high priest* was the son of Jehozadak (see 1 Chron. 6:14; the KJV refers to Jehozadak as Josedech in the books of Haggai and Zechariah). He is a type of Christ, as was the Joshua who succeeded Moses in the leadership of Israel.

3:4 *filthy garments.* These reflect the sins of the people, which were atoned for by Christ on Calvary. Thus, believers today are clothed in the garments of Christ's righteousness, their own clothing being nothing more than filthy rags, as described here.

3:8 *the BRANCH,* i.e., the Christ. At Christ's first advent the Jews were blinded; they could not see him as the Messiah. At the end of the age Israel will receive him by faith and will submit to his rulership. Until that happens, Christ is building his spiritual body, the church, as indicated in 6:12–15.

3:9 *the stone.* Christ is not only the BRANCH; he is also the stone, the foundation of all good things. This is the stone the builders rejected which has become the cornerstone (see Matt. 21:42; 1 Pet. 2:7). Having won the victory by his atoning death at Calvary, he will purge his people from all their transgressions.

3:10 1 Kgs 4:25 Mic 4:4

10 In that day, saith the LORD of hosts, shall ye call every man his neighbour under the vine and under the fig tree.

5. The Gold Candlestick (Lampstand) and the Two Olive Trees

4 AND the angel that talked with me came again, and waked me, as a man that is wakened out of his sleep,

4:2☆ Ex 25:31, 37 37:17–24 Zech 5:2 Rev 4:5

2 And said unto me, What seest thou? And I said, I have looked, and behold a candlestick all *of* gold, with a bowl upon the top of it, and his seven lamps thereon, and seven pipes to the seven lamps, which *are* upon the top thereof:

4:3 Zech 4:11, 12, 14 Rev 11:4

3 And two olive trees by it, one upon the right *side* of the bowl, and the other upon the left *side* thereof.

4 So I answered and spake to the angel that talked with me, saying, What *are* these, my lord?

5 Then the angel that talked with me answered and said unto me, Knowest thou not what these be? And I said, No, my lord.

4:6☆ 2 Chron 14:11 Ezra 3:1, 2 Isa 11:2–4 Hag 2:4, 5 Eph 6:17

6 Then he answered and spake unto me, saying, This *is* the word of the LORD unto Ze-rub'ba-bel, saying, Not by might, nor by power, but by my spirit, saith the LORD of hosts.

4:7☆ Ezra 3:11–13 6:15–17 Rev 5:9–13

7 Who *art* thou, O great mountain? before Ze-rub'ba-bel *thou shalt become* a plain: and he shall bring forth the headstone *thereof with* shoutings, *crying,* Grace, grace unto it.

8 Moreover the word of the LORD came unto me, saying,

4:9 Ezra 3:8–10 5:16 Zech 6:12, 13

9 The hands of Ze-rub'ba-bel have laid the foundation of this house; his hands shall also finish it; and thou shalt know that the LORD of hosts hath sent me unto you.

4:10 Amos 7:2, 7, 8 Hag 2:3 Zech 3:9

10 For who hath despised the day of small things? for they shall rejoice, and shall see the plummet in the hand of Ze-rub'ba-bel *with* those seven; they *are* the eyes of the LORD, which run to and fro through the whole earth.

11 ¶Then answered I, and said unto him, What *are* these two olive trees upon the right *side* of the candlestick and upon the left *side* thereof?

12 And I answered again, and said unto him, What *be these* two olive branches which through the two golden pipes empty the golden *oil* out of themselves?

13 And he answered me and said, Knowest thou not what these *be?* And I said, No, my lord.

4:14☆ Ex 29:7 Isa 61:1–3 Dan 9:24–26

14 Then said he, These *are* the two anointed ones, that stand by the Lord of the whole earth.

4:2 In the vision of the candlestick and the two olive trees, Christ is the candlestick. He is for us the center of our unity, not Jerusalem or any one place. In verse four Zechariah calls the angel, "my lord," which refers to deity, even Jesus Christ.

4:6 *Zerubbabel.* Governor of Judah, who was given the responsibility for rebuilding the temple. (See Hag. 1:1; 2:23).† *Not by might, nor by power, but by my spirit.* Human might or power is different from the might and power of the Holy Spirit. The former is external and visible, the other is invisible and apparent only to the eyes of faith. The Spirit of God influenced Cyrus to release the captives. God worked secretly in the hearts of the captives to accept the decree of Cyrus and return to the land. God's way and will are often carried on successfully when they are working silently, operating without external human force or devices.

4:7 *he shall bring forth the headstone,* i.e., "he will finish building this temple." *crying, Grace,* or, "with mighty shouts, 'How beautiful it is!' " or, "The Lord bless it!" or, "All this was done by grace alone."†

4:14 *the two* anointed ones are Joshua and Zerubbabel—the first having charge of the spiritual side of Jerusalem's life and the other the political or ruling aspect of the restored nation. State and church leaders should be God's anointed, doing his work for his glory and for the good of the people.

6. The Flying Scroll

5 THEN I turned, and lifted up mine eyes, and looked, and behold a
flying roll.
2 And he said unto me, What seest thou? And I answered, I see a flying
roll; the length thereof *is* twenty cubits, and the breadth thereof ten cubits.
3 Then said he unto me, This *is* the curse that goeth forth over the face of
the whole earth: for every one that stealeth shall be cut off *as* on this side
according to it: and every one that sweareth shall be cut off *as* on that side
according to it.
4 I will bring it forth, saith the LORD of hosts, and it shall enter into the
house of the thief, and into the house of him that sweareth falsely by my
name: and it shall remain in the midst of his house, and shall consume it
with the timber thereof and the stones thereof.

☆**5:1** Jer 36:1–6; Ezek 2:9, 10; Rev 10:2, 8–11
5:3 Ex 20:15; Deut 27:15–26; 28:15; Prov 29:24; Isa 24:6; Jer 26:6
5:4 Lev 14:34–45; Deut 7:26; Jer 2:26; Hab 2:9–11; Mal 3:5

7. The Ephah and the Flight to Babylon

5 ¶Then the angel that talked with me went forth, and said unto me, Lift
up now thine eyes, and see what *is* this that goeth forth.
6 And I said, What *is* it? And he said, This *is* an ephah that goeth forth.
He said moreover, This *is* their resemblance through all the earth.
7 And, behold, there was lifted up a talent of lead: and this *is* a woman
that sitteth in the midst of the ephah.
8 And he said, This *is* wickedness. And he cast it into the midst of the
ephah; and he cast the weight of lead upon the mouth thereof.
9 Then lifted I up mine eyes, and looked, and, behold, there came out two
women, and the wind *was* in their wings; for they had wings like the wings
of a stork: and they lifted up the ephah between the earth and the heaven.
10 Then said I to the angel that talked with me, Whither do these bear the
ephah?
11 And he said unto me, To build it an house in the land of Shi′nar: and
it shall be established, and set there upon her own base.

☆**5:5**
5:6 Lev 19:36; Amos 8:5
5:8 Hos 12:7; Mic 6:11
5:9 Lev 11:13–19; Deut 14:11–18; Ps 104:17; Jer 8:7
☆**5:11** Isa 11:11; Dan 1:2

8. The Four Chariots and God's Judgment

6 AND I turned, and lifted up mine eyes, and looked, and, behold, there
came four chariots out from between two mountains; and the
mountains *were* mountains of brass.
2 In the first chariot *were* red horses; and in the second chariot black
horses;
3 And in the third chariot white horses; and in the fourth chariot grisled
and bay horses.
4 Then I answered and said unto the angel that talked with me, What *are*
these, my lord?
5 And the angel answered and said unto me, These *are* the four spirits of
the heavens, which go forth from standing before the Lord of all the earth.

☆**6:1** Zech 6:5
6:5 Dan 7:2; 11:4; Zech 6:1; Mt 24:31; Rev 7:1

5:1ff The flying scroll, thirty by fifteen feet, is unrolled. It symbolizes bitter things, namely the terrible judgment of God against sinners. It covers the earth and is directed against those who steal and those who swear rashly and profanely.
5:5 The ephah was a measure. In it sits a woman and along with her a leaden weight. The woman is pressed to death and carried away to some far country. Some think this refers to the final dispersion of the Jews following the destruction of Jerusalem in A.D. 70 by Titus and Vespasian.
5:11 *the land of Shinar,* i.e., "Babylon," which had, by the time of Zechariah, become a symbol, the center of world idolatry and wickedness. Iniquity was symbolically taken from Judah to Babylon.
6:1ff The four chariots of divine judgment are sent abroad to execute God's vengeance. *the north country* seems to picture God's judgment against Babylon, which was overthrown by the Persians. It may also refer to the end of Babylon in the New Testament (see Rev. 11:15; 18:21). *have quieted my spirit* (6:8) means that the judgment of God has been executed and his anger assuaged.

6:6 Jer 1:14, 15; 25:9; Ezek 1:4; Dan 11:5, 6, 9, 40

6 The black horses which *are* therein go forth into the north country; and
the white go forth after them; and the grisled go forth toward the south
country.
7 And the bay went forth, and sought to go that they might walk to and
fro through the earth: and he said, Get you hence, walk to and fro through
the earth. So they walked to and fro through the earth.

6:8 Zech 1:15

8 Then cried he upon me, and spake unto me, saying, Behold, these that
go toward the north country have quieted my spirit in the north country.

9. Sequel: Joshua, the Type of the Man to Come

6:10☆ Ezra 7:14–16; 8:26–30; Ps 21:3; Song 3:11; Zech 3:1
6:11☆

9 ¶And the word of the LORD came unto me, saying,
10 Take of *them of* the captivity, *even* of Hel′da-i, of To-bi′jah, and of Je-
dai′ah, which are come from Babylon, and come thou the same day, and go
into the house of Jo-si′ah the son of Zeph-a-ni′ah;
11 Then take silver and gold, and make crowns, and set *them* upon the
head of Joshua the son of Jos′e-dech, the high priest;

6:12☆ Isa 4:2, 3; 11:1; Jer 23:5, 6; Zech 3:8; 4:6–9

12 And speak unto him, saying, Thus speaketh the LORD of hosts, saying,
Behold the man whose name *is* The BRANCH; and he shall grow up out of
his place, and he shall build the temple of the LORD:

6:13☆ Ps 110:4; Isa 9:6; 11:10; Dan 7:13, 14; Heb 3:1; 4:14–16; 10:12, 13

13 Even he shall build the temple of the LORD; and he shall bear the glory,
and shall sit and rule upon his throne; and he shall be a priest upon his
throne: and the counsel of peace shall be between them both.
14 And the crowns shall be to He′lem, and to To-bi′jah, and to Je-dai′ah,
and to Hen the son of Zeph-a-ni′ah, for a memorial in the temple of the
LORD.

6:15 Isa 56:6–8; 60:10; Zech 3:7

15 And they *that are* far off shall come and build in the temple of the
LORD, and ye shall know that the LORD of hosts hath sent me unto you.
And *this* shall come to pass, if ye will diligently obey the voice of the LORD
your God.

C. MESSAGE THREE:
1. The Question about Extra Fasts

7:1☆

7 AND it came to pass in the fourth year of king Darius, *that* the word
of the LORD came unto Zech-a-ri′ah in the fourth *day* of the ninth
month, *even* in Chis′leu;

7:2☆ Zech 8:21

2 When they had sent unto the house of God She-re′zer and Re′gem-
me′lech, and their men, to pray before the LORD,

7:3☆ Ezra 3:10–12

3 *And* to speak unto the priests which *were* in the house of the LORD of
hosts, and to the prophets, saying, Should I weep in the fifth month,
separating myself, as I have done these so many years?

6:10 Some Jews who remained in Babylon have come with offerings of gold and silver. They are met, not by a priest, but by God's prophet.

6:11 A crown is placed on Joshua's head. He was the spiritual leader. Zerubbabel, the secular or political leader, was not crowned.

***6:12** The crowning of Joshua typifies the crowning of* the BRANCH, i.e., the Messiah, who is priest and king. *he shall grow up out of his place,* i.e., "He shall grow up for himself," by his own energy and exalted in his own strength.

6:13 Even as the high priest Joshua rebuilt the temple in Jerusalem, so shall the BRANCH, Jesus Christ, build the spiritual temple—the church. Its people constitute God's temple, according to 1 Cor. 3:16.

7:1 *Chisleu* (also, "Chislev," or "Kislev") in this instance is equivalent to late November. *fourth year,* 518 B.C.

7:2 *they,* the delegation that came from Bethel to inquire about keeping national fasts.

7:3 *Should I weep . . . separating myself . . . ?,* i.e., "Should I follow the custom of fasting and mourning during the month of August each year, as I have been doing so long?" This annual event commemorated the destruction of Jerusalem in 587 B.C.

2. The Four Part Answer
a. The Deceitfulness of Their Fasts

4¶Then came the word of the LORD of hosts unto me, saying,
5Speak unto all the people of the land, and to the priests, saying, When
ye fasted and mourned in the fifth and seventh *month,* even those seventy
years, did ye at all fast unto me, *even* to me?
6And when ye did eat, and when ye did drink, did not ye eat *for
yourselves,* and drink *for yourselves?*
7Should ye not *hear* the words which the LORD hath cried by the former
prophets, when Jerusalem was inhabited and in prosperity, and the cities
thereof round about her, when *men* inhabited the south and the plain?

b. God Scatters Them for Their Oppression

8¶And the word of the LORD came unto Zech-a-ri'ah, saying,
9Thus speaketh the LORD of hosts, saying, Execute true judgment, and
shew mercy and compassions every man to his brother:
10And oppress not the widow, nor the fatherless, the stranger, nor the
poor; and let none of you imagine evil against his brother in your heart.
11But they refused to hearken, and pulled away the shoulder, and stopped
their ears, that they should not hear.
12Yea, they made their hearts *as* an adamant stone, lest they should hear
the law, and the words which the LORD of hosts hath sent in his spirit by
the former prophets: therefore came a great wrath from the LORD of hosts.
13Therefore it is come to pass, *that* as he cried, and they would not hear;
so they cried, and I would not hear, saith the LORD of hosts:
14But I scattered them with a whirlwind among all the nations whom they
knew not. Thus the land was desolate after them, that no man passed
through nor returned: for they laid the pleasant land desolate.

c. God's Promise to Restore His People

8 AGAIN the word of the LORD of hosts came *to me,* saying,
2Thus saith the LORD of hosts; I was jealous for Zion with great
jealousy, and I was jealous for her with great fury.
3Thus saith the LORD; I am returned unto Zion, and will dwell in the
midst of Jerusalem: and Jerusalem shall be called a city of truth; and the
mountain of the LORD of hosts the holy mountain.
4Thus saith the LORD of hosts; There shall yet old men and old women
dwell in the streets of Jerusalem, and every man with his staff in his hand
for very age.
5And the streets of the city shall be full of boys and girls playing in the
streets thereof.
6Thus saith the LORD of hosts; If it be marvellous in the eyes of the
remnant of this people in these days, should it also be marvellous in mine
eyes? saith the LORD of hosts.

☆7:5 Isa 1:11, 12; Zech 1:12; Mt 5:16–18; 6:2, 5, 16; 23:5
7:7 Deut 34:3; Jer 17:26; 22:21; Zech 1:4
7:8 2 Sam 9:7; Mic 6:8; Zech 8:16
7:10 Ex 22:22; Deut 24:14–18; Prov 22:22, 23; Zech 8:17
7:11 Neh 9:29; Ps 58:4, 5; Isa 6:10; Jer 8:5; Acts 7:57; Heb 10:38, 39
☆7:12 2 Chron 36:16; Neh 9:30; Jer 17:1; 26:19; Ezek 3:9; Dan 9:11, 12; Zech 1:4
☆7:13 Prov 1:24–28; 21:13; Isa 1:15; 50:2; Jer 11:10, 14
7:14 Lev 26:22; Deut 28:64; Isa 17:13; Jer 12:10; 44:6
☆8:1
8:4 Isa 65:20–22; Lam 2:20
8:5 Jer 30:19, 20; Zech 2:4
8:6 Jer 32:17, 27

7:5 The rites they performed were useless, for they were not done to glorify God.
7:12 The words sent by God through the prophets were not the words of the prophets; they were the words of God. And these words were sent to the prophets immediately by his Spirit. When the people of Israel despised the Word of God they affronted God the sender and resisted the Holy Spirit, who gave the words to the prophets.
7:13 When the people turned a deaf ear to the words of God, God turned a deaf ear to their prayers. Why should God answer the prayers of those who profess to own his name but despise and disannul his Word?
8:1ff God intends to restore Jerusalem to its former glory. This was accomplished in part and to a lower degree in the Maccabean period many years before the birth of Christ. The full glory of which this prophecy speaks awaits the return of Christ and the establishment of the millennial kingdom, according to the premillennial viewpoint.

8:7☆ Ps 107:2, 3 Amos 9:14, 15

7 Thus saith the LORD of hosts; Behold, I will save my people from the east country, and from the west country;

8:8 Zech 10:10

8 And I will bring them, and they shall dwell in the midst of Jerusalem: and they shall be my people, and I will be their God, in truth and in righteousness.

8:9 Ezra 5:1; 6:14

9 ¶Thus saith the LORD of hosts; Let your hands be strong, ye that hear in these days these words by the mouth of the prophets, which *were* in the day *that* the foundation of the house of the LORD of hosts was laid, that the temple might be built.

8:10 Isa 19:2 Amos 3:6; 9:4 Hag 1:6–11 2:16–19

10 For before these days there was no hire for man, nor any hire for beast; neither *was there any* peace to him that went out or came in because of the affliction: for I set all men every one against his neighbour.

11 But now I *will* not *be* unto the residue of this people as in the former days, saith the LORD of hosts.

8:12 Gen 27:28 1 Kgs 17:1 Hag 1:10

12 For the seed *shall be* prosperous; the vine shall give her fruit, and the ground shall give her increase, and the heavens shall give their dew; and I will cause the remnant of this people to possess all these *things.*

8:13 Deut 28:37 Ps 72:17 Jer 29:18 Dan 9:11 Mic 5:7 Zech 10:6–9 14:11

13 And it shall come to pass, *that* as ye were a curse among the heathen, O house of Judah, and house of Israel; so will I save you, and ye shall be a blessing: fear not, *but* let your hands be strong.

8:13ff☆

8:14 Jer 4:28 29:11–14 Mic 4:10–13

14 For thus saith the LORD of hosts; As I thought to punish you, when your fathers provoked me to wrath, saith the LORD of hosts, and I repented not:

15 So again have I thought in these days to do well unto Jerusalem and to the house of Judah: fear ye not.

8:16☆ Zech 8:3

16 ¶These *are* the things that ye shall do; speak ye every man the truth to his neighbour; execute the judgment of truth and peace in your gates:

8:17☆ Jer 4:2 Zech 5:3, 4 7:10 Mal 3:5

17 And let none of you imagine evil in your hearts against his neighbour; and love no false oath: for all these *are things* that I hate, saith the LORD.

d. The Strong Nations Will Come to Jerusalem

18 ¶And the word of the LORD of hosts came unto me, saying,

8:19 Esth 8:17 Isa 12:1 Zech 7:3–5; 8:16 Lk 1:74, 75

19 Thus saith the LORD of hosts; The fast of the fourth *month,* and the fast of the fifth, and the fast of the seventh, and the fast of the tenth, shall be to the house of Judah joy and gladness, and cheerful feasts; therefore love the truth and peace.

8:20☆ Zech 2:11 14:16

20 Thus saith the LORD of hosts; *It shall* yet *come to pass,* that there shall come people, and the inhabitants of many cities:

21 And the inhabitants of one *city* shall go to another, saying, Let us go speedily to pray before the LORD, and to seek the LORD of hosts: I will go also.

8:22 Isa 49:6, 22, 23 52:15; 60:3–12

22 Yea, many people and strong nations shall come to seek the LORD of hosts in Jerusalem, and to pray before the LORD.

8:7 God will return his people from wherever they have been dispersed, east or west; and Jerusalem will be their home.

8:13ff Despite economic distress, the danger of traveling away from home, and the hatred of their enemies, God will restore them and bless them. Judah will also, in turn, be a blessing to all nations (8:13). Therefore they need not fear; they can act confidently and with strength.

8:16, 17 God commands his people be truthful, to act justly, to maintain clean hearts, and to keep from making false oaths.

8:20ff The inhabitants from many cities and people from many different nations will head for Jerusalem to seek the favor of God. This will transpire, not by human inventions and desires, but by the operation of divine truth and grace through the power of the Spirit. Thus shall the Jews be a blessing to all nations, for they will have seen and heard that God is with them. It is obvious that this prophecy has not yet been fulfilled. The day is coming when Jerusalem will become the leading city for the worship of God; at that time, Jewish Christians will be leaders in world evangelization.

23 Thus saith the LORD of hosts; In those days *it shall come to pass,* that
ten men shall take hold out of all languages of the nations, even shall take
hold of the skirt of him that is a Jew, saying, We will go with you: for we
have heard *that* God *is* with you.

II. THE MESSAGES FOLLOWING THE REBUILDING OF THE TEMPLE (9:1—14:21)

A. THE KING WHO IS REJECTED

1. The King Is Coming!

9 THE burden of the word of the LORD in the land of Ha'drach, and
Damascus *shall be* the rest thereof: when the eyes of man, as of all the
tribes of Israel, *shall be* toward the LORD.
2 And Ha'math also shall border thereby; Tyrus, and Zi'don, though it be
very wise.
3 And Tyrus did build herself a strong hold, and heaped up silver as the
dust, and fine gold as the mire of the streets.
4 Behold, the Lord will cast her out, and he will smite her power in the
sea; and she shall be devoured with fire.
5 Ash'ke-lon shall see *it,* and fear; Ga'za also *shall see it,* and be very
sorrowful, and Ekron; for her expectation shall be ashamed; and the king
shall perish from Ga'za, and Ash'ke-lon shall not be inhabited.
6 And a bastard shall dwell in Ash'dod, and I will cut off the pride of the
Philistines.
7 And I will take away his blood out of his mouth, and his abominations
from between his teeth: but he that remaineth, even he, *shall be* for our
God, and he shall be as a governor in Judah, and Ekron as a Jeb'u-site.
8 And I will encamp about mine house because of the army, because of
him that passeth by, and because of him that returneth: and no oppressor
shall pass through them any more: for now have I seen with mine eyes.
9 ¶Rejoice greatly, O daughter of Zion; shout, O daughter of Jerusalem:
behold, thy King cometh unto thee: he *is* just, and having salvation; lowly,
and riding upon an ass, and upon a colt the foal of an ass.
10 And I will cut off the chariot from E'phra-im, and the horse from
Jerusalem, and the battle bow shall be cut off: and he shall speak peace
unto the heathen: and his dominion *shall be* from sea *even* to sea, and from
the river *even* to the ends of the earth.

2. The Kingly Agenda

a. The Victories of the King

11 As for thee also, by the blood of thy covenant I have sent forth thy
prisoners out of the pit wherein *is* no water.

8:23 Isa 45:14; 60:14
☆**9:1** Gen 14:15; Amos 1:3–5; 3:12
9:2 Num 13:21; 1 Kgs 17:9; 2 Kgs 25:21; Isa 23:1–18; Ezek 28:3–5; 12:21–26
9:3 Josh 19:29; 1 Kgs 10:27; Isa 23:8; Ezek 27:33
9:4 Isa 23:1–7; Ezek 27:26–36; 28:16, 18; Joel 3:8
9:5 Jer 47:4–7; Zeph 2:4
☆**9:8** Isa 54:14; Zech 14:11
☆**9:9** Ps 97:6–8; Isa 9:6, 7; 12:6; 57:15; Jer 23:5, 6; Zeph 3:5; Zech 2:10; Mt 11:29
☆**9:10** Ps 72:17; Isa 57:18, 19; Mic 4:2–10; 5:4; Rev 11:15
☆**9:11** Ex 24:8; Ps 69:33; Lk 4:18; Heb 9:10–26; 10:29

9:1ff *when the eyes of man, as of all the tribes of Israel, shall be toward the LORD.* This is better rendered as: "*For to the* LORD *belong the cities of Aram [man],* even as all the tribes of Israel" (RSV). Zechariah then pronounces divine judgment on Syria (Damascus), Hamath (which was north of Damascus and had done similar deeds), Tyre and Sidon, and the Philistines. Alexander the Great was used by God to fulfill some of these prophecies.

9:8 Alexander the Great was influenced by the appearance of the high priest, Jaddus. He protected the Jews and treated them with favor, even while he was destroying surrounding nations and peoples. Thus the Jews were protected by God.

9:9 This is a prediction of Christ's triumphal entry into Jerusalem on Palm Sunday. As king, he was to be acclaimed by the people who shouted, "Hosanna to the son of David" (see Matt. 21:9). This event demonstrated the fickleness of the people, for the crucifixion followed shortly thereafter.

9:10 *from the river even to the ends of the earth,* or, "to the ends of the land" of Palestine. Either interpretation is possible from the Hebrew text, but many other passages indicate Christ's universal rule.†

9:11 The covenant of God with Abraham was sealed by the blood of circumcision. The Mosaic covenant of law was sealed by the blood of animal sacrifices. The covenant of the Father with his Son was sealed by the blood of Jesus Christ at Calvary. Without the shedding of blood there is no remission of sin (Heb. 9:22).

12¶Turn you to the strong hold, ye prisoners of hope: even to day do I
declare *that* I will render double unto thee;
13When I have bent Judah for me, filled the bow with E′phra-im, and
raised up thy sons, O Zion, against thy sons, O Greece, and made thee as
the sword of a mighty man.
14And the LORD shall be seen over them, and his arrow shall go forth as
the lightning: and the Lord GOD shall blow the trumpet, and shall go with
whirlwinds of the south.
15The LORD of hosts shall defend them; and they shall devour, and
subdue with sling stones; and they shall drink, *and* make a noise as through
wine; and they shall be filled like bowls, *and* as the corners of the altar.
16And the LORD their God shall save them in that day as the flock of his
people: for *they shall be as* the stones of a crown, lifted up as an ensign
upon his land.
17For how great *is* his goodness, and how great *is* his beauty! corn shall
make the young men cheerful, and new wine the maids.

b. The King Brings His People Back

10 ASK ye of the LORD rain in the time of the latter rain; *so* the LORD
shall make bright clouds, and give them showers of rain, to every
one grass in the field.
2For the idols have spoken vanity, and the diviners have seen a lie, and
have told false dreams; they comfort in vain: therefore they went their way
as a flock, they were troubled, because *there was* no shepherd.
3Mine anger was kindled against the shepherds, and I punished the
goats: for the LORD of hosts hath visited his flock the house of Judah, and
hath made them as his goodly horse in the battle.
4Out of him came forth the corner, out of him the nail, out of him the
battle bow, out of him every oppressor together.
5¶And they shall be as mighty *men,* which tread down *their enemies* in the
mire of the streets in the battle: and they shall fight, because the LORD *is*
with them, and the riders on horses shall be confounded.
6And I will strengthen the house of Judah, and I will save the house of
Joseph, and I will bring them again to place them; for I have mercy upon
them: and they shall be as though I had not cast them off: for I *am* the
LORD their God, and will hear them.
7And *they of* E′phra-im shall be like a mighty *man,* and their heart shall
rejoice as through wine: yea, their children shall see *it,* and be glad; their
heart shall rejoice in the LORD.
8I will hiss for them, and gather them; for I have redeemed them: and
they shall increase as they have increased.
9And I will sow them among the people: and they shall remember me in
far countries; and they shall live with their children, and turn again.

9:12 Isa 40:2; 52:2; 61:7; Joel 3:16
9:13☆ Dan 11:32–34; Joel 3:6–8; Mic 4:2, 3
9:14 Josh 6:4, 5; Ps 18:14; Isa 18:3; 27:13; 30:30
9:15 Zech 10:5; 12:6
9:16 Ps 27:4; Isa 40:10; 62:3; Jer 31:12, 14; Ezek 34:22–26; Hag 2:23
10:1☆ Deut 11:14; Job 36:27–31; Prov 16:15; Jer 10:13; Hos 6:3; Joel 2:23, 24
10:2 Jer 23:25–27; Ezek 21:29; 34:5, 8; Mic 3:6–11; Mt 9:36
10:3☆ Isa 10:12; Ezek 34:2, 7, 12; Zech 11:5-8
10:4 Zech 9:10
10:5☆ 2 Sam 22:8; Zech 9:13; 12:8
10:6☆ Isa 54:8; Zech 1:16; 8:11
10:7☆ Isa 38:19; 54:13
10:8 Isa 5:26; 7:18, 19; Jer 33:22; Ezek 36:11
10:9 Deut 30:1–4; 1 Kgs 8:47, 48; Jer 51:50; Ezek 6:9

9:13 The mention of Greece as a future power in the world has caused some to suppose that chapters 9–14 were not written by Zechariah. Once predictive prophecy is accepted, this poses no problem. Greece was defeated by the Jews during the Maccabean period (*2nd century B.C.*).

10:1 If there was no rain, times were bad for the people. The former rain came at seed-time in the autumn; the latter rain fell in the spring. God chose to send the rains with reference to the spiritual state of his people. They were called upon to pray for the rain. And they were to pray to God, not to the sun and the stars, as did the heathen. Implicit in this command is the fact mentioned by James—ye have not because ye ask not, or ye ask amiss (James 4:2, 3).

10:3 The hand of God is over his people in all things, both good and bad. God's anger was displayed in the Babylonian captivity; now his pleasure is expressed, as he chooses to bless his people who love and serve him.

10:5 Whoever has God with him shall triumph. The enemy will be confounded.

10:6, 7 God owns all his people, the twelve tribes of Israel, and he is with his people in mercy and will save them.

10 I will bring them again also out of the land of Egypt, and gather them
out of Assyria; and I will bring them into the land of Gilead and Lebanon;
and *place* shall not be found for them.
11 And he shall pass through the sea with affliction, and shall smite the
waves in the sea, and all the deeps of the river shall dry up: and the pride
of Assyria shall be brought down, and the sceptre of Egypt shall depart
away.
12 And I will strengthen them in the LORD; and they shall walk up and
down in his name, saith the LORD.

3. The King Is Rejected
a. The Shepherd King Is Rejected

11 OPEN thy doors, O Lebanon, that the fire may devour thy cedars.
2 Howl, fir tree; for the cedar is fallen; because the mighty are
spoiled: howl, O ye oaks of Ba′shan; for the forest of the vintage is come
down.
3 ¶*There is* a voice of the howling of the shepherds; for their glory is
spoiled: a voice of the roaring of young lions; for the pride of Jordan is
spoiled.
4 Thus saith the LORD my God; Feed the flock of the slaughter;
5 Whose possessors slay them, and hold themselves not guilty: and they
that sell them say, Blessed *be* the LORD; for I am rich: and their own
shepherds pity them not.
6 For I will no more pity the inhabitants of the land, saith the LORD: but,
lo, I will deliver the men every one into his neighbour's hand, and into the
hand of his king: and they shall smite the land, and out of their hand I will
not deliver *them.*
7 And I will feed the flock of slaughter, *even* you, O poor of the flock. And
I took unto me two staves; the one I called Beauty, and the other I called
Bands; and I fed the flock.
8 Three shepherds also I cut off in one month; and my soul lothed them,
and their soul also abhorred me.
9 Then said I, I will not feed you: that that dieth, let it die; and that that
is to be cut off, let it be cut off; and let the rest eat every one the flesh of
another.
10 ¶And I took my staff, *even* Beauty, and cut it asunder, that I might
break my covenant which I had made with all the people.
11 And it was broken in that day: and so the poor of the flock that waited
upon me knew that it *was* the word of the LORD.
12 And I said unto them, If ye think good, give *me* my price; and if not,
forbear. So they weighed for my price thirty *pieces* of silver.
13 And the LORD said unto me, Cast it unto the potter: a goodly price that

10:10 Isa 11:11–16; 49:19–21; 54:2, 3; Mic 7:11, 12
☆**10:11** Ps 66:10–12; Isa 11:15, 16; 19:5–7; Zeph 2:13; Ezek 30:13
☆**10:12** Isa 2:5; Mic 4:5
☆**11:1** Ezek 31:3
11:3 Jer 2:15; 25:34–36; 50:44
☆**11:5** Jer 50:7; Ezek 34:2–6, 18–21; Hos 12:8; 1 Tim 6:9
11:6 Isa 9:19–21; Jer 13:14; Zech 8:10; 14:13
☆**11:7** Lev 27:32; Ps 27:4; 90:17; 133:1; Ezek 37:16–23; Zech 11:10, 14; Jn 17:21–23
11:8 Hos 5:7
11:9 Ps 69:22–28; Jer 15:2, 3
☆**11:12** 1 Kgs 3:5; Mt 26:15; 27:9, 10; Jn 13:2, 27–30
☆**11:13** Mt 27:3–10, 12; Acts 1:18, 19

10:11 *the sea,* i.e., "the Sea of Egypt." This is a reference to the Red Sea, through which the people of Israel were miraculously brought when God first delivered them out of slavery.†

10:12 God will strengthen those who are his people, for he is both their strength and their righteousness. *they shall walk up and down in his name,* i.e., by what they do they shall bring glory to the name of their God.

11:1 *Open your doors.* Even as the Jews refused to open their doors to Christ, so shall they have to open their doors to judgment for this act.

11:5 In Jesus' day, chief priests and elders will be tyrants over the people, devouring their houses and fleecing the sheep rather than feeding them.

11:7ff God will send the good shepherd for the sheep; but when the shepherd is rejected, the result will be disastrous for those who reject the shepherd. The staff *Beauty* (or, *Grace*) represents the covenant which will be broken because of transgressions. It was conditioned by obedience, so that disobedience annuls the covenant.

11:12 *thirty pieces of silver,* the price of a slave (Exod. 21:32).

11:13 *cast them to the potter.* The thirty pieces of silver were as nothing compared to the worth of the One for whom the money was paid. Therefore cast it to the potter to buy some clay with it. Judas Iscariot placed a very low value on the Lord Jesus (see Matt.

I was prised at of them. And I took the thirty *pieces* of silver, and cast them
to the potter in the house of the LORD.

11:14 Zech 11:6

14 Then I cut asunder mine other staff, *even* Bands, that I might break the
brotherhood between Judah and Israel.

b. The Worthless Shepherd Takes the Good Shepherd's Place

11:15 Jer 2:26, 27 Ezek 13:3 Zech 11:17
11:16 :☆ Jer 23:2, 22 Ezek 34:2–6

15 ¶And the LORD said unto me, Take unto thee yet the instruments of a
foolish shepherd.
16 For, lo, I will raise up a shepherd in the land, *which* shall not visit those
that be cut off, neither shall seek the young one, nor heal that that is
broken, nor feed that that standeth still: but he shall eat the flesh of the fat,
and tear their claws in pieces.

11:17☆ Zech 10:2 11:15

17 Woe to the idol shepherd that leaveth the flock! the sword *shall be* upon
his arm, and upon his right eye: his arm shall be clean dried up, and his
right eye shall be utterly darkened.

B. THE REJECTED KING IS ENTHRONED AT LAST

1. The Repentance of Israel

a. Israel's Enemies Crushed

12:1☆ Gen 2:7 Job 26:7 Ps 102:23, 26 104:2 Isa 57:16 Jer 51:15 Heb 1:10–12
12:2☆ Ps 75:8 Isa 51:17, 22, 23 Jer 49:12
12:3 Dan 2:34, 35, 44, 45 Mt 21:44 Lk 20:18

12 THE burden of the word of the LORD for Israel, saith the LORD,
which stretcheth forth the heavens, and layeth the foundation of the
earth, and formeth the spirit of man within him.
2 Behold, I will make Jerusalem a cup of trembling unto all the people
round about, when they shall be in the siege both against Judah *and* against
Jerusalem.
3 ¶And in that day will I make Jerusalem a burdensome stone for all
people: all that burden themselves with it shall be cut in pieces, though all
the people of the earth be gathered together against it.
4 In that day, saith the LORD, I will smite every horse with astonishment,
and his rider with madness: and I will open mine eyes upon the house of
Judah, and will smite every horse of the people with blindness.
5 And the governors of Judah shall say in their heart, The inhabitants of
Jerusalem *shall be* my strength in the LORD of hosts their God.

b. Israel Empowered by God

12:6 Isa 10:16–18 Obad 18
12:7 Isa 2:11–17 Amos 9:11 Zech 4:6; 11:11
12:8 Gen 22:15–17 Ex 14:19 Lev 26:8 Ps 82:6 Mic 7:8 Zech 9:14, 15

6 ¶In that day will I make the governors of Judah like an hearth of fire
among the wood, and like a torch of fire in a sheaf; and they shall devour
all the people round about, on the right hand and on the left: and
Jerusalem shall be inhabited again in her own place, *even* in Jerusalem.
7 The LORD also shall save the tents of Judah first, that the glory of the
house of David and the glory of the inhabitants of Jerusalem do not
magnify *themselves* against Judah.
8 In that day shall the LORD defend the inhabitants of Jerusalem; and he
that is feeble among them at that day shall be as David; and the house of
David *shall be* as God, as the angel of the LORD before them.

27:3–9). Some who profess Jesus today seem to value him no higher and live as though he is worth only a few small coins.

11:16, 17 *For their punishment, those who reject the* true shepherd will have a false shepherd, who will do the exact opposite of what the true shepherd would do—he will tear and devour the flock.

12:1 Zechariah emphasizes the threefold work of the Creator: the heavens, which he might still be expanding; the earth, which has strong foundations and will not be moved by men; and the spirits (*ruach,* meaning "spirit" or "wind," not *nephesh,* meaning "animal soul") of men.

12:2ff In that day (which is still future) Jerusalem will be besieged by enemy powers, and God will deliver his people from that assault. The strength of those who defend Jerusalem will come from the God of power, who is omnipotent and who himself will intervene in the person of his Son.

9¶And it shall come to pass in that day, *that* I will seek to destroy all the
nations that come against Jerusalem.

c. Israel's Sorrow for Piercing Their King

10And I will pour upon the house of David, and upon the inhabitants of
Jerusalem, the spirit of grace and of supplications: and they shall look upon
me whom they have pierced, and they shall mourn for him, as one
mourneth for *his* only *son,* and shall be in bitterness for him, as one that is
in bitterness for *his* firstborn.
11In that day shall there be a great mourning in Jerusalem, as the
mourning of Ha-dad-rim′mon in the valley of Me-gid′don.
12And the land shall mourn, every family apart; the family of the house
of David apart, and their wives apart; the family of the house of Nathan
apart, and their wives apart;
13The family of the house of Levi apart, and their wives apart; the family
of Shim′e-i apart, and their wives apart;
14All the families that remain, every family apart, and their wives apart.

d. The Fountain of Cleansing for Israel

13 IN that day there shall be a fountain opened to the house of David
and to the inhabitants of Jerusalem for sin and for uncleanness.
2¶And it shall come to pass in that day, saith the LORD of hosts, *that* I
will cut off the names of the idols out of the land, and they shall no more be
remembered: and also I will cause the prophets and the unclean spirit to
pass out of the land.
3And it shall come to pass, *that* when any shall yet prophesy, then his
father and his mother that begat him shall say unto him, Thou shalt not
live; for thou speakest lies in the name of the LORD: and his father and his
mother that begat him shall thrust him through when he prophesieth.
4And it shall come to pass in that day, *that* the prophets shall be ashamed
every one of his vision, when he hath prophesied; neither shall they wear a
rough garment to deceive:
5But he shall say, I *am* no prophet, I *am* an husbandman; for man taught
me to keep cattle from my youth.
6And *one* shall say unto him, What *are* these wounds in thine hands?
Then he shall answer, *Those* with which I was wounded *in* the house of my
friends.

2. Israel Refined, Liberated, and Victorious

a. Israel Purged and Purified

7¶Awake, O sword, against my shepherd, and against the man *that is* my
fellow, saith the LORD of hosts: smite the shepherd, and the sheep shall be
scattered: and I will turn mine hand upon the little ones.

☆**12:9**
☆**12:10** Ps 22:16, 17; Isa 32:15; Joel 2:28, 29; Jn 19:34–37; Heb 12:2; Rev 1:7
☆**12:11** Jer 6:26; Amos 8:10; Mt 24:30; 26:75
☆**13:1** Lev 15:2; Num 19:9–22; Job 9:30, 31; Ps 51:2, 7
13:2 Ex 23:13; Deut 12:3; Josh 23:7; 1 Kgs 22:22; Jer 8:10–12; Hos 2:17; Zech 10:2
13:3 Deut 13:6–11; Jer 23:25
13:4 2 Kgs 1:8; Isa 20:2; Jer 2:26; 6:15; 8:9; Mic 3:6, 7; Mt 3:4; 11:8, 9; Mk 1:6
13:5 Amos 7:14
☆**13:6**
13:7 Isa 9:6; 40:11; 53:4, 5, 10; Hos 12:3–5; Zech 11:4, 7

12:9 *I will seek to destroy all the nations,* i.e., they will be baffled, broken, and destroyed. What they sought to do to Jerusalem will be done to them. The word *seek* does not mean that God may lack the power to do this. Rather, he is earnest and intent on doing this because he is jealous for Zion.
12:10 At the end of the age Israel will turn to the Messiah (Rom. 11:26). The Israelites will mourn for him and weep bitterly over the One whom their fathers pierced.
12:11 *the mourning of Hadad-rimmon in the valley of Megiddon.* The grieving was for King Josiah (see 2 Chron. 35:24, 25).
13:1 *there shall be a fountain opened.* That fountain is the Lamb of God who takes away the sin of the world. By faith the sinner receives the remission of his sins and the fountain of blood now becomes the fountain of life.
13:6 *these wounds in thine hands.* Evidently self-inflicted cuts, as practiced by false prophets. (See 1 Kings 18:28.) *Those with which I was wounded in the house of my friends.* Some think this is a reference to Christ; others believe this refers to a false prophet who is lying about the reasons for his scars.†

13:8☆ Zech 11:6–9
8And it shall come to pass, *that* in all the land, saith the LORD, two parts
therein shall be cut off *and* die; but the third shall be left therein.
13:9 Zech 12:10
9And I will bring the third part through the fire, and will refine them as
silver is refined, and will try them as gold is tried: they shall call on my
name, and I will hear them: I will say, It *is* my people: and they shall say,
The LORD *is* my God.

b. Jerusalem Liberated by the Lord

14:1☆ Isa 2:12 Mal 4:1 Rev 16:14 14:2☆
14 BEHOLD, the day of the LORD cometh, and thy spoil shall be
divided in the midst of thee.
2For I will gather all nations against Jerusalem to battle; and the city
shall be taken, and the houses rifled, and the women ravished; and half of
the city shall go forth into captivity, and the residue of the people shall not
be cut off from the city.
3Then shall the LORD go forth, and fight against those nations, as when
he fought in the day of battle.
14:4☆ Ezek 47:1–10 Zech 4:7
4¶And his feet shall stand in that day upon the mount of Olives, which *is*
before Jerusalem on the east, and the mount of Olives shall cleave in the
midst thereof toward the east and toward the west, *and there shall be* a very
great valley; and half of the mountain shall remove toward the north, and
half of it toward the south.
14:5☆ Isa 29:6
5And ye shall flee *to* the valley of the mountains; for the valley of the
mountains shall reach unto A'zal: yea, ye shall flee, like as ye fled from
before the earthquake in the days of Uz-zi'ah king of Judah: and the LORD
my God shall come, *and* all the saints with thee.
14:6☆ Isa 60:1–3 Acts 2:16, 19
6And it shall come to pass in that day, *that* the light shall not be clear, *nor*
dark:
14:7 Amos 8:9 Rev 21:23; 22:5
7But it shall be one day which shall be known to the LORD, not day, nor
night: but it shall come to pass, *that* at evening time it shall be light.
14:8 Lk 24:47 Jn 4:10, 14
8And it shall be in that day, *that* living waters shall go out from
Jerusalem; half of them toward the former sea, and half of them toward the
hinder sea: in summer and in winter shall it be.

c. The King Triumphant over All the Earth

14:9☆ Deut 6:4 Zech 9:9 14:16, 17
9And the LORD shall be king over all the earth: in that day shall there be
one LORD, and his name one.
14:10 Josh 15:32 21:17 2 Kgs 14:13 2 Chron 25:23 Neh 12:39 Jer 31:8
10All the land shall be turned as a plain from Ge'ba to Rimmon south of
Jerusalem: and it shall be lifted up, and inhabited in her place, from
Benjamin's gate unto the place of the first gate, unto the corner gate, and
from the tower of Ha-nan'e-el unto the king's winepresses.
14:11 Jer 31:40 Rev 22:3
11And *men* shall dwell in it, and there shall be no more utter destruction;
but Jerusalem shall be safely inhabited.

13:8 This may be a prophetic word with a double fulfillment. The first fulfillment came with the destruction of Jerusalem in A.D. 70, when unbelieving Jews were cut off (for true believers had already fled the city). It is also a future promise for the end of the age, when once again Jerusalem will be surrounded and only those who are righteous will be delivered.

14:1, 2 The second coming of the Lord Jesus is here predicted; he will save Jerusalem from complete destruction.

14:4 At the end of the age, Jesus will come again to deliver Jerusalem. The Mount of Olives will be split in two, so the saved may have a passageway of escape.

14:5 *for the valley of the mountains shall reach unto Azal,* apparently a hamlet on the eastern outskirts of Jerusalem. *all the saints,* literally, "his holy ones."†

14:6 At the coming of Christ, cosmic disturbances will occur so that sun, moon, and stars will no longer be seen by men.

14:9 This verse guarantees that the petition "Thy kingdom come" will be answered. At the end of the age Christ's kingdom will extend from shore to shore and the prayer for the unity of believers will prevail (John 17:21).

12¶And this shall be the plague wherewith the LORD will smite all the
people that have fought against Jerusalem; Their flesh shall consume away
while they stand upon their feet, and their eyes shall consume away in their
holes, and their tongue shall consume away in their mouth.
13And it shall come to pass in that day, *that* a great tumult from the LORD
shall be among them; and they shall lay hold every one on the hand of his
neighbour, and his hand shall rise up against the hand of his neighbour.
14And Judah also shall fight at Jerusalem; and the wealth of all the
heathen round about shall be gathered together, gold, and silver, and
apparel, in great abundance.

☆**14:14** Zech 14:1

15And so shall be the plague of the horse, of the mule, of the camel, and
of the ass, and of all the beasts that shall be in these tents, as this plague.

d. The Nations Conquered and Israel Sacred to the Lord

16¶And it shall come to pass, *that* every one that is left of all the nations
which came against Jerusalem shall even go up from year to year to worship
the King, the LORD of hosts, and to keep the feast of tabernacles.

14:16 Lev 23:34–44 Isa 60:6–9 66:18–21

17And it shall be, *that* whoso will not come up of *all* the families of the
earth unto Jerusalem to worship the King, the LORD of hosts, even upon
them shall be no rain.

14:17 1 Kgs 17:1 Jer 14:3–6

18And if the family of Egypt go not up, and come not, that *have* no *rain;*
there shall be the plague, wherewith the LORD will smite the heathen that
come not up to keep the feast of tabernacles.
19This shall be the punishment of Egypt, and the punishment of all
nations that come not up to keep the feast of tabernacles.
20In that day shall there be upon the bells of the horses, HOLINESS
UNTO THE LORD; and the pots in the LORD's house shall be like the
bowls before the altar.
21Yea, every pot in Jerusalem and in Judah shall be holiness unto the
LORD of hosts: and all they that sacrifice shall come and take of them, and
seethe therein: and in that day there shall be no more the Canaanite in the
house of the LORD of hosts.

☆**14:20** Ex 28:36; 39:30 Lev 6:28 Ezek 46:20–24 Rev 20:6

14:21 Deut 12:7, 12 Neh 8:10 Zech 7:6 Rom 14:6, 7 1 Cor 10:31 1 Tim 4:3–5

14:14 The plunder from the nations defeated in the battle for Jerusalem will accrue to the people of God. They will be enriched by the spoils.

14:20 *HOLINESS UNTO THE LORD.* This phrase was engraved on a golden plate worn by the high priest on his forehead (see Exod. 28:36; 39:30). This phrase will be written on horses, furniture, and the like at the end of the age, when Christ is triumphant. But it will be fully manifested by the saints, who are living temples, and the spiritual priests, who will be wholly sanctified.

MALACHI

Authorship, date, and background Malachi, the author of this book, was the last of the writing prophets. His name means "my messenger," and for this reason some have supposed that the author was an unknown and unnamed prophet. The book itself was written after the times of Haggai and Zechariah. This is clearly so because the rebuilt temple was standing, sacrifices were brought to the altar, and the people were subject to the authority of a Persian governor. Therefore the book can be dated somewhere between 450 and 425 B.C.

The people in the land were discouraged. Times were hard. They experienced drought and famine, causing them to wonder whether God cared for them. A spirit of apathy, indifference, and spiritual backsliding existed. The refugees had been in the land for almost a hundred years. The walls of Jerusalem had been rebuilt as well as the temple. The wicked seemed to prosper while those who walked penitently and kept God's commandments did not. Moveover, the kingdom they were expecting had not yet come and they wondered whether it ever would. It was against this backdrop that Malachi began his prophetic ministry.

Characteristics and content Malachi intensely loves his people. He represents great spiritual dynamism, and his words are backed by the conviction that he speaks with the authority of God. His words are God's words. His book is dialogic. He employs questions and answers to discuss the themes he has in mind. Always the justice of God is under discussion and Malachi appeals to reason and uses logic to make his case.

Malachi arraigns the people for neglecting God. They are disloyal to God and do not keep his commandments. He uses Edom as an illustration to show that cruelty and unfaithfulness do not go unpunished forever. God does judge according to righteousness. God's people have not yet learned the lessons God wanted to teach them by the captivity. They are offering blemished sacrifices at the altar. God's name is not revered. Even the priests are unfaithful in discharging the duties of their office.

Malachi is angry because the people have intermarried with women from heathen nations. These wives have introduced idolatry. Divorce is common. Malachi insists that all the sacrifices avail nothing when the hearts of the offerers are not right with their God. God has become wearied with this people. He must shortly do something about their adulteries, sorceries, lying, failure to bring their tithes to the storehouse, and the injustices they heap on widows, orphans, and strangers. God has his own book of remembrance in which he includes the names of those who walk according to his commandments. Contrary to what the people think, God knows who they are who fear him. They will be saved in the day of God's wrath when the others are destroyed.

The great and terrible day of the Lord is pending. This divine judgment will be delayed for a season so that a time of mercy may follow which will be marked by the coming of the prophet Elijah. This, of course, refers to the advent of the Messiah whose forerunner is Elijah, i.e., John the Baptist (see Mt 11:10, 14). At some undisclosed time in the future, another Elijah will appear just prior to what Malachi describes as "the coming of the great and dreadful day of the LORD" (4:5), when history will be consummated.

Outline

I. God's love for Israel (1:1–5)
II. Israel's disobedience: the sins of the priests (1:6–14)
III. God rebukes and warns his priests (2:1–9)
IV. The treachery of Judah (2:10–17)
V. God's judgments on sinners and rewards for the righteous (3:1—4:6)

I. GOD'S LOVE FOR ISRAEL (1:1–5)

1 THE burden of the word of the LORD to Israel by Mal'a-chi.
2 I have loved you, saith the LORD. Yet ye say, Wherein hast thou
loved us? *Was* not Esau Jacob's brother? saith the LORD: yet I loved Jacob,
3 And I hated Esau, and laid his mountains and his heritage waste for the
dragons of the wilderness.
4 Whereas Edom saith, We are impoverished, but we will return and build
the desolate places; thus saith the LORD of hosts, They shall build, but I
will throw down; and they shall call them, The border of wickedness, and,
The people against whom the LORD hath indignation for ever.
5 And your eyes shall see, and ye shall say, The LORD will be magnified
from the border of Israel.

☆1:1 Isa 13:1 Zech 9:1
☆1:2 Rom 9:13
1:4 Isa 9:9
1:5 Ps 35:27 58:10, 11 Mic 5:4

II. ISRAEL'S DISOBEDIENCE: THE SINS OF THE PRIESTS (1:6–14)

6 ¶A son honoureth *his* father, and a servant his master: if then I *be* a
father, where *is* mine honour? and if I *be* a master, where *is* my fear? saith
the LORD of hosts unto you, O priests, that despise my name. And ye say,
Wherein have we despised thy name?
7 Ye offer polluted bread upon mine altar; and ye say, Wherein have we
polluted thee? In that ye say, The table of the LORD *is* contemptible.
8 And if ye offer the blind for sacrifice, *is it* not evil? and if ye offer the
lame and sick, *is it* not evil? offer it now unto thy governor; will he be
pleased with thee, or accept thy person? saith the LORD of hosts.
9 And now, I pray you, beseech God that he will be gracious unto us: this
hath been by your means: will he regard your persons? saith the LORD of
hosts.
10 Who *is there* even among you that would shut the doors *for nought?*
neither do ye kindle *fire* on mine altar for nought. I have no pleasure in you,
saith the LORD of hosts, neither will I accept an offering at your hand.
11 For from the rising of the sun even unto the going down of the same my
name *shall be* great among the Gentiles; and in every place incense *shall be*
offered unto my name, and a pure offering: for my name *shall be* great
among the heathen, saith the LORD of hosts.
12 ¶But ye have profaned it, in that ye say, The table of the LORD *is*
polluted; and the fruit thereof, *even* his meat, *is* contemptible.
13 Ye said also, Behold, what a weariness *is it!* and ye have snuffed at it,
saith the LORD of hosts; and ye brought *that which was* torn, and the lame,
and the sick; thus ye brought an offering: should I accept this of your
hand? saith the LORD.

1:6 Ex 20:12 Deut 1:31 Prov 30:11, 17 Isa 1:2 Jer 31:9 Mal 2:1–10
1:7 Lev 21:6, 8 Deut 15:21
☆1:8 Lev 22:19–25 Mal 1:14
1:9 Jer 27:18 Joel 1:13, 14 2:12–14
☆1:10 Isa 1:13 Jer 6:20 14:10, 12 Amos 5:21–24
1:11 Ps 50:1; 141:2 Isa 45:6; 60:6 66:19, 20 Jer 10:6, 7
1:13 Lev 6:4 22:19–23 Isa 43:22; 61:8

1:1 *burden,* indicates that what was spoken was of *great importance. For believers* it was a light burden. For scoffers it was a reproach.

1:2 God said he loved Israel; why then were there no outward evidences of that love? God replied that he loved Jacob and hated Esau. Yet they were brothers. Hatred for Esau sprang from Esau's rejection of God. Jacob was the one with whom the covenant made with Abraham was continued. The outward sign of God's favor toward Israel was marked by his judgment against Edom, which was judged by God and wasted. Verse 4 reveals that God's attitude toward Edom is one of perpetual anger.

1:8 Who would bring blind, lame, or sick sacrifices to offer to a great King? Some Israelites did this, and God was offended. But perhaps we who no longer offer animal sacrifices sin as much by the failure to give ourselves wholly over to Jesus Christ as Lord.

1:10ff Priests and people alike offended God with their sacrifices. Torn, lame, and sick animals were brought for sacrifice. The priests were indolent and served only for what they got out of their service. To them their work was drudgery. They brought to God offerings that they never would have given to a queen or king. Should not the great God then be offended? They needed to act in accord with right principles, in a right manner, and have a right end in mind.

1:14 Ps 47:2; 68:35; Zeph 2:11; Zech 14:9; Mal 1:13

14 But cursed *be* the deceiver, which hath in his flock a male, and voweth,
and sacrificeth unto the Lord a corrupt thing: for I *am* a great King, saith
the LORD of hosts, and my name *is* dreadful among the heathen.

III. GOD REBUKES AND WARNS HIS PRIESTS (2:1–9)

2:1☆ Lev 26:14–17; Deut 28:15-20

2 AND now, O ye priests, this commandment *is* for you.
2 If ye will not hear, and if ye will not lay *it* to heart, to give glory
unto my name, saith the LORD of hosts, I will even send a curse upon you,
and I will curse your blessings: yea, I have cursed them already, because ye
do not lay *it* to heart.
3 Behold, I will corrupt your seed, and spread dung upon your faces, *even*
the dung of your solemn feasts; and *one* shall take you away with it.

2:4 Num 3:45; 18:21

4 And ye shall know that I have sent this commandment unto you, that
my covenant might be with Levi, saith the LORD of hosts.

2:5 Num 25:7, 8, 13

5 My covenant was with him of life and peace; and I gave them to him *for*
the fear wherewith he feared me, and was afraid before my name.

2:6 Ps 37:30; Ps 119:142

6 The law of truth was in his mouth, and iniquity was not found in his
lips: he walked with me in peace and equity, and did turn many away from
iniquity.

2:7 Lev 10:11; Num 27:21; Deut 17:8–11; Ezra 7:10; Neh 8:2–8

7 For the priest's lips should keep knowledge, and they should seek the
law at his mouth: for he *is* the messenger of the LORD of hosts.

2:8 Neh 13:29; Isa 9:16; Jer 18:15; Ezek 44:10

8 But ye are departed out of the way; ye have caused many to stumble at
the law; ye have corrupted the covenant of Levi, saith the LORD of hosts.

2:9 Deut 1:17

9 Therefore have I also made you contemptible and base before all the
people, according as ye have not kept my ways, but have been partial in the
law.

IV. THE TREACHERY OF JUDAH (2:10–17)

2:10☆ Ex 19:4–6; Josh 24:3; Isa 63:16; Jer 9:4; Mal 2:4, 14, 15

10 Have we not all one father? hath not one God created us? why do we
deal treacherously every man against his brother, by profaning the
covenant of our fathers?

2:11 Lev 20:26; Ezra 9:1, 2; Jer 3:7–9; Ezek 18:13

11 ¶Judah hath dealt treacherously, and an abomination is committed in
Israel and in Jerusalem; for Judah hath profaned the holiness of the LORD
which he loved, and hath married the daughter of a strange god.

2:12 Lev 18:29; Num 15:30, 31

12 The LORD will cut off the man that doeth this, the master and the
scholar, out of the tabernacles of Jacob, and him that offereth an offering
unto the LORD of hosts.

2:13 Isa 1:11–15; Jer 11:14; 14:12

13 And this have ye done again, covering the altar of the LORD with tears,
with weeping, and with crying out, insomuch that he regardeth not the
offering any more, or receiveth *it* with good will at your hand.

2:14 Mal 2:11

14 ¶Yet ye say, Wherefore? Because the LORD hath been witness between
thee and the wife of thy youth, against whom thou hast dealt treacherously:
yet *is* she thy companion, and the wife of thy covenant.

2:1ff The priests were accused of despising God and failing to perform their functions properly. They failed to teach correctly or act in accord with the will of God. They broke the agreement God made with Levi when he was chosen for the sacred office of the priesthood. These priests corrupted that office (2:8). The externals of religion were practiced, but "heart" religion was defiled, so that the externals were of no value.

2:10ff Corrupt conduct always springs from the use of corrupt principles. Marriage is the issue in this passage. Judah is married to a strange god because the men have married pagan women, who have brought their pagan gods into the home and seduced the nation. Moreover, true marriage is a covenant relationship between a man and a woman. The third party to the marriage is God. Since marriage is permanent and the Adamic principle of one woman and one man's living together is correct, divorce is something God disapproves of and hates. Divine judgment is rendered against a man who is faithless to the wife of his youth (2:15, 16).

15 And did not he make one? Yet had he the residue of the spirit. And
wherefore one? That he might seek a godly seed. Therefore take heed to
your spirit, and let none deal treacherously against the wife of his youth.
16 For the LORD, the God of Israel, saith that he hateth putting away: for
one covereth violence with his garment, saith the LORD of hosts: therefore
take heed to your spirit, that ye deal not treacherously.
17 ¶Ye have wearied the LORD with your words. Yet ye say, Wherein have
we wearied *him*? When ye say, Every one that doeth evil *is* good in the sight
of the LORD, and he delighteth in them; or, Where *is* the God of judgment?

2:15 Ex 20:14; Lev 20:10; Hos 1:10; Mal 2:14
2:16 Deut 24:1; Mt 5:31; 19:6–8
☆**2:17** Isa 5:19; 43:22, 24; Jer 17:15; Zeph 1:12

V. GOD'S JUDGMENT ON SINNERS AND REWARDS FOR THE RIGHTEOUS (3:1—4:6)

A. THE PROMISED COMING OF GOD'S MESSENGER

3 BEHOLD, I will send my messenger, and he shall prepare the way
before me: and the Lord, whom ye seek, shall suddenly come to his
temple, even the messenger of the covenant, whom ye delight in: behold, he
shall come, saith the LORD of hosts.
2 But who may abide the day of his coming? and who shall stand when he
appeareth? for he *is* like a refiner's fire, and like fullers' soap:
3 And he shall sit *as* a refiner and purifier of silver: and he shall purify the
sons of Levi, and purge them as gold and silver, that they may offer unto
the LORD an offering in righteousness.
4 Then shall the offering of Judah and Jerusalem be pleasant unto the
LORD, as in the days of old, and as in former years.
5 And I will come near to you to judgment; and I will be a swift witness
against the sorcerers, and against the adulterers, and against false swearers,
and against those that oppress the hireling in *his* wages, the widow, and the
fatherless, and that turn aside the stranger *from his right,* and fear not me,
saith the LORD of hosts.

☆**3:1** Isa 63:9
3:2 Isa 4:4; Ezek 22:14; Zech 13:9; Mt 3:10–12
3:3 Ps 51:19; Ezek 22:18–22; Dan 12:10
3:4 2 Chron 7:1–3; Ps 51:17–19; Jer 2:2; Zech 8:3
3:5 Ex 22:22–24; Deut 5:11; 18:10; 27:19; Jer 5:2; 7:9; Ezek 22:9–11

B. HOW PEOPLE ROB GOD

6 For I *am* the LORD, I change not; therefore ye sons of Jacob are not
consumed.
7 ¶Even from the days of your fathers ye are gone away from mine
ordinances, and have not kept *them.* Return unto me, and I will return unto
you, saith the LORD of hosts. But ye said, Wherein shall we return?
8 ¶Will a man rob God? Yet ye have robbed me. But ye say, Wherein have
we robbed thee? In tithes and offerings.

☆**3:6**
3:7 Zech 1:3
☆**3:8** Lev 5:15, 16; Neh 13:11

2:17 *Where is the God of Judgment?* Retributive justice is the punishing or rewarding of the individual according to what he deserves. Distributive justice means sharing on the basis of the best interests of society; this form of justice does not derive from the Scriptures. Nor does social justice, which is based upon humanistic egalitarianism. Whatever God does is just; he makes no mistakes as he distributes justice. God rightly condemns those who practice evil and pronounce that what they do is good. It is just for God to reward such appropriately, for they have wearied him by their conduct.

3:1 God promises the coming of the Messiah and his forerunner, John the Baptist. Messiah will be a comfort to the afflicted who trust in him and a terror to the evildoers who shall be judged and rewarded properly for their transgressions.

3:6 *ye sons of Jacob are not consumed.* God and his promises are immutable. Even the redeemed have no claim to the mercy of God, and they could also be consumed as the wicked are. But the God of grace and compassion has redeemed his people and will keep them for himself. Through the merits of the Messiah, God can declare righteous those who are worthy of death but who turn to him for help. Salvation is by grace and grace alone.

3:8 Tithing—giving God a tenth of one's income—was established as part of the Mosaic system and was deeply ingrained in the Hebrew tradition. But tithing existed long before the time of Moses (e.g., Abraham paid tithes to Melchizedek in Gen. 14:20). Malachi insists that to fail to tithe is to rob God of what rightfully belongs to him. And as a result, the divine blessing is withheld from those who refuse to give God his due. Tithing is not commanded in the New Testament as a legal requirement, but the Christian under grace can

[9]Ye *are* cursed with a curse: for ye have robbed me, *even* this whole nation.

3:10 Ps 78:23–29 Ezek 34:26

[10]Bring ye all the tithes into the storehouse, that there may be meat in mine house, and prove me now herewith, saith the LORD of hosts, if I will not open you the windows of heaven, and pour you out a blessing, that *there shall* not *be room* enough *to receive it.*

3:11 Joel 1:4; 2:25

[11]And I will rebuke the devourer for your sakes, and he shall not destroy the fruits of your ground; neither shall your vine cast her fruit before the time in the field, saith the LORD of hosts.

3:12 Deut 8:7–10 Ps 72:17 Isa 61:9; 62:4 Zech 8:23

[12]And all nations shall call you blessed: for ye shall be a delightsome land, saith the LORD of hosts.

C. GOD'S DIFFERENT TREATMENT OF GOOD MEN AND BAD

[13]¶Your words have been stout against me, saith the LORD. Yet ye say, What have we spoken *so much* against thee?

3:14☆ Ps 73:8–13 Isa 58:3 Jer 7:10 Zeph 1:12

[14]Ye have said, It *is* vain to serve God: and what profit *is it* that we have kept his ordinance, and that we have walked mournfully before the LORD of hosts?

[15]And now we call the proud happy; yea, they that work wickedness are set up; yea, *they that* tempt God are even delivered.

3:16 Isa 4:31 Dan 12:1

[16]¶Then they that feared the LORD spake often one to another: and the LORD hearkened, and heard *it,* and a book of remembrance was written before him for them that feared the LORD, and that thought upon his name.

3:17 Neh 13:22 1 Pet 1:13–16

[17]And they shall be mine, saith the LORD of hosts, in that day when I make up my jewels; and I will spare them, as a man spareth his own son that serveth him.

3:18☆ Ps 58:10, 11 Amos 5:15

[18]Then shall ye return, and discern between the righteous and the wicked, between him that serveth God and him that serveth him not.

4:1☆ Ps 21:9, 10 Isa 5:24 9:18,19 Mal 3:2, 3 Mt 3:12

4 FOR, behold, the day cometh, that shall burn as an oven; and all the proud, yea, and all that do wickedly, shall be stubble: and the day that cometh shall burn them up, saith the LORD of hosts, that it shall leave them neither root nor branch.

4:2☆ 2 Sam 23:4 Ps 103:3 Prov 4:18 Isa 30:26; 35:6 53:5 Jer 30:17, 33:6

[2]¶But unto you that fear my name shall the Sun of righteousness arise with healing in his wings; and ye shall go forth, and grow up as calves of the stall.

4:3 Josh 10:24, 25 Ezek 28:18 Mic 5:8; 7:10

[3]And ye shall tread down the wicked; for they shall be ashes under the soles of your feet in the day that I shall do *this,* saith the LORD of hosts.

---

hardly do less than the Jew under law. Tithing is the outward sign of an inward commitment that all one has belongs to God, who is entitled to a return on the divine investment in any individual. (See note on 1 Cor. 16:2.)

3:14 *what profit is it that we have kept his ordinance . . . ?* The implication of this is plain. If we cannot expect to get anything from serving God, why then serve him? This was to be the attitude of the Sadducees in Jesus' day, who denied the resurrection. If there is no resurrection of the dead, and no heaven or hell, *why should we serve God in this life only?* If obedience to the commandments of God yields nothing by way of commendation or reward, it is a waste of time. While we are not saved by obeying commandments—for obedience is not meritorious—yet obedience that follows justification and regeneration is pleasing in the sight of the One who has redeemed us and is rewarded at the believer's judgment.

3:18 In this world it is difficult to distinguish between the saved and the lost, the good and the bad. Appearances are deceptive and evil men oftentimes look more like saints than the saints do. "At the bar of Christ, in the last judgment, it will be easy to *discern between the righteous and the wicked;* for then every man's character will be both perfected and perfectly discovered; every man will then appear in his true colors, and his disguises will be taken off."*

4:1 *the day cometh,* i.e., the great and terrible day of the Lord when the wicked will be identified and their eternal estate will be determined. It is a day of wrath for them; the devouring fire will consume them.

4:2 *the Sun of righteousness.* This refers to Jesus, the light of the world, the light of men, the light of the glory of God.

D. THE EPILOGUE
1. The Command to Obey God's Laws

4¶Remember ye the law of Moses my servant, which I commanded unto
him in Ho'reb for all Israel, *with* the statutes and judgments.

☆4:4 Ex 20:3; Deut 4:5, 6

2. The Coming of Elijah before the Judgment Day

5¶Behold, I will send you E-li'jah the prophet before the coming of the
great and dreadful day of the LORD:
6And he shall turn the heart of the fathers to the children, and the heart
of the children to their fathers, lest I come and smite the earth with a curse.

☆4:5 Mt 11:14; Mk 9:11–13; Lk 1:17
4:6 Deut 29:19; Isa 24:6; Mt 11:21; Lk 1:17; Rev 19:15

4:4 The law of Moses is here identified as being the Word of God. Moses was simply the purveyor of the law; God was the author of it. He commands obedience to all of his commandments, for in the keeping of them there is much gain. We are not saved by works but by grace. But saving faith is never alone; it is always accompanied by good works, which include obedience to the law of God.

4:5 Malachi predicts that Elijah will come before *the great and dreadful day of the LORD.* This prophecy has two fulfillments. The first occurred with the birth of Jesus, whose forerunner, John the Baptist, is said to be the representation of Elijah (see Matt. 11:14; Luke 1:17; 9:8, 19; John 1:21). The final coming of Elijah is evidently portrayed in Rev. 11:3–6. Elijah, along with Moses, appeared at the Transfiguration (see Matt. 17:1–5; Mark 9:2–13; Luke 9:28–30). *I will send you Elijah the prophet,* i.e., "one like the prophet Elijah." (Compare with Matt. 17:10–12; Luke 1:17.)

BETWEEN THE TESTAMENTS

William Kerr

THERE is a period of some four centuries between the close of the Old Testament and the opening of the New. During this period God's voice in divine revelation was stilled. No canonical books were written, though there were fifteen books produced which have been called the Apocrypha. Neither the Jews nor Christ nor the writers of the New Testament recognized the Apocrypha as canonical, though the Roman Catholic Church at the Council of Trent in A.D. 1546 declared them as canonical (with the exception of 1 and 2 Esdras and the Prayer of Manasseh).

In addition to the literary activity that resulted in the Apocrypha, other important developments helped form the religious and cultural background of the New Testament.

The political history of the time falls into several periods of governmental dominion by foreign powers:

(1) The Persians governed the Jews from the time of the return from the Babylonian Captivity to 332 B.C.

(2) The Grecians brought the Jews under their domination with the conquest of the Persians by Alexander the Great. This opened up Palestine to the effects of Greek culture by Hellenization (332- 301 B.C.).

(3) The Ptolemaic or Egyptian period from 301-198 B.C. was a time when much Hellenization permeated Judaism and its lifestyle.

(4) The Syrian period began with Antiochus III who defeated the Egyptians in 198 B.C., and took control over Palestine. His successor Antiochus IV, who was known as Epiphanes (the manifested one) but was nicknaned Epimanes (the madman), sought to Hellenize the Jews completely and endeavored to destroy the religious practices of Judaism. He ordered pigs sacrificed on Jewish altars, and when a reprobate Jewish priest sought to do so, the Jews revolted and the Maccabean wars broke out. The fierce fighting zeal and military skill of the Maccabees finally drove the Syrians out of Palestine.

(5) The Maccabean or Hasmonean period continued from 163 B.C. to 63 B.C. when Rome conquered Palestine.

(6) The Roman period was a time when Rome ruled Palestine through either procurators or rulers such as the Herodians. In 37 B.C. Herod the Great was placed as king and ruled until 4 B.C. It was during his reign that Christ was born and the slaughter of the infants at Bethlehem took place. Herod had three sons who followed him as rulers: Archelaus ruled over Jerusalem from 4 B.C. to A.D. 6, after which Judea was ruled by Roman procurators (from A.D. 41-44, however, King Herod Agrippa 1 ruled over Judea); Herod Antipas ruled over Galilee and Perea from 4 B.C. to A.D. 39; Philip ruled east and north of the sea of Galilee from 4 B.C. to A.D. 34.

During the Roman period great power was concentrated in the hands of the high priest, who, for all practical purposes, was the political leader of the Jews. The Roman period ended about A.D. 135.

The *religious* developments during the four centuries between the Testaments saw the translation of the Septuagint (from about 250-150 B.C.), the rise of the synagogue, and the establishment of the various religious sects: The Pharisees, the Sadducees, and Essenes.

The Pharisees were the *legalists* of the day. They were devoted to the law of Moses and sought to adapt and apply it to the varying conditions and experiences of life. They had a firm belief in the supernatural, angels, the immortality of the soul, the doctrines of the future life, future rewards and punishments, and the resurrection. When Jerusalem fell, the Pharisees kept Judaism alive because they were devoted to the law of Moses; the fall of the city could destroy neither the law nor the Pharisees and so both were preserved.

The Sadducees were the *rationalists* of the day. Their beliefs were governed by a skeptical attitude toward religion. They believed in the literal interpretation of the law of Moses but did not allow it to have much effect on their lives. They denied the existence of angels, immortality, rewards, punishments, and the future life. They were materialistic and had an earthly outlook. Since they were connected primarily with the temple, its destruction brought about their gradual disappearance.

The Essenes were the *mystics* of their times. Some scholars have identified them with the Qumran community of the Dead Sea Scrolls, though there are some problems connected with such an identification. The Dead Sea Scrolls, however, are vitally important for our understanding of this type of communal life and teachings. A monastic community, the Essenes emphasized withdrawal from the world. They shared property in common and ate at a common table. They were vegetarians and their economy was based on labor in the fields. They abhorred filth in any form and their white apparel signified purity.

These sects made significant impact on Judaism and its faith. The Sadducees were politically the most powerful party during New Testament times.

The *moral* conditions during these years were especially horrendous. Orgiastic practices in heathen worship, divorce, abortion, infanticide, prostitution, seduction, and adultery characterized the Gentile world. Despair was rampant and the need for a Savior was a desperate necessity.

The Greeks, the Romans, and the Jews, with their important positions of leadership during these four centuries, made their own contributions to the world into which Christ came and through which Christianity spread.

The Greeks, the framers of classical expression and civilization, contributed in a most unusual way since it was into their language that the Old Testament was translated and was spread among the Jews through their synagogue worship. And when God gave his revelation through the New Testament, it was written in the Greek language, for Greek was the language of commerce during this time.

The Romans left the legacy of law and order and a great highway system—some five main highways leading out from Rome to the ends of the Empire. Along these highways, the gospel was taken to various parts of that great Empire.

The Jews made a fourfold contribution: a belief in one God, the Scriptures in the common language of Greek, the synagogue as the place of public worship, and a strong faith in God. These all made a strong impact upon the heathen mind and many became proselytes to Judaism.

During these centuries between the Testaments, in varied ways, God prepared the world for the coming of Christ: "But when the fullness of the time was come, God sent forth his Son, made of a woman, made under the law" (Gal. 4:4).

INTRODUCTION TO THE NEW TESTAMENT

William Kerr

The divine revelation given in the New Testament is the record of God's redemptive activity as it culminates in the incarnation, crucifixion, and resurrection of Christ and the spread of the gospel throughout the Roman Empire. The New Testament contains twenty-seven books, each written under the superintendence of the Holy Spirit by certain of the apostles or those in close relationship to the apostles.

These books relate the story of Christ's first advent, the origin of the church, the doctrinal and ethical teachings of the Christian faith, and the prophetic consummation of world history. These events may be summarized under four key words: REVELATION—The Gospels

The four Gospels provide a fourfold portrait of the birth, life, ministry, death, and resurrection of Christ. Christ is here revealed as the God-man, who came to fulfill messianic prophecy and bring salvation to mankind. These four books are historical in nature. EXPANSION—The Acts

After the death and resurrection of Christ, the apostles were told to wait for the coming of the Holy Spirit. The record of that event and the origin of the church at that time is found in this book. Subsequently, the apostles began to preach the gospel, with the main emphasis on the resurrection of Christ, throughout the then-known world. So dynamic was this new faith that the apostles were named the men who turned the world upside down. INSTRUCTION—The Epistles

Since the gospel must not only be preached but be preserved, it was necessary to give instruction concerning its doctrinal and ethical content. This was the task of the letters written by various apostles either to local churches or individuals.

The following books are doctrinal or ecclesiastical letters: Romans, 1 and 2 Corinthians, Galatians, Ephesians, Philippians, Colossians, 1 and 2 Thessalonians, Hebrews, James, 1 and 2 Peter, Jude, and 1 John. In addition, there are six letters written to individuals: 1 and 2 Timothy, Titus, Philemon, 2 and 3 John. The epistles deal with such subjects as sin, condemnation, salvation, justification, sanctification, and the second coming; and the epistles address church problems such as doctrinal errors, the ethical conduct of the believer in relationship to the state, issues of domestic life, and leadership in the local church. CONSUMMATION—The Book of Revelation

Alongside this program of instruction is God's plan for the direction of history toward its final consummation. This prophetic plan is laid down in the book of Revelation. In it, God's plans for the church, the Jews, and the world are revealed as now working toward their completion. This book gives God's ending to the story of human civilization. It is a triumphant conclusion in which redeemed man is seen in glory, Christ is made King over all, and all of the creation, with the believer, is freed from the bondage of corruption.

As the inspired record of divine revelation, the precepts and principles of the New Testament govern the life of the believer both inside and outside the bounds of the local church. Together with the Old Testament, they comprise the Scriptures, which are "profitable for doctrine, for reproof, for correction, for instruction in righteousness: That the man of God may be perfect, thoroughly furnished unto all good works" (2 Tim. 3:16, 17).

INTRODUCTION TO THE GOSPELS

William Kerr

The Gospels give a fourfold portrait of the life and ministry of Christ. Many ask the question: "Why four Gospels?" The answer is not difficult to find, since it is contained in the accounts themselves. Their contents clearly reveal that the four basic needs of mankind were met in the Savior: the political, the governmental, the intellectual, and the spiritual.

These needs were exemplified in the basic needs of the people of that day: (1) the Jews desired a king: Matthew, therefore, presents Jesus as the *King*; (2) the Romans were vitally interested in good government and in one who could accomplish great deeds: Mark presents Jesus as the worker of deeds and miracles, as the *Servant*; (3) the Greeks sought after wisdom, knowledge, and understanding: in Luke's Gospel is seen the scholarly and accurate presentation of Jesus as the Wisdom of God incarnate, the *Man*; (4) the world at large needed a satisfying and sufficient Savior who could meet its spiritual needs: John presents Jesus as the very *God.* In this One, who is Deity, the world finds the satisfying and sufficient Savior, Christ as God.

Corresponding to this fourfold picture, which produced a full-orbed, unique, and unified view of Christ, a relationship is shown between the prophecies of the Old Testament concerning Christ and their fulfillment in his coming. In two Old Testament prophecies, the promised Messiah is revealed as the longed for *King* of the Jews (Jer. 23:5; Zech. 9:9). In Matthew 27:37 Christ is presented thus: "This is Jesus the King of the Jews." Christ as *Servant* is seen in Isaiah 42:1 and Zechariah 3:8. Mark shows the fulfillment of these verses in Mark 10:45: "For even the Son of Man came not to be ministered unto, but to minister, and give his life a ransom for many." Prophesying concerning the humanity of the Messiah, Zechariah proclaimed: "Behold the man whose name is the Branch; and he shall grow out of his place, and he shall build the temple of the Lord" (6:12). Luke, who presents Christ as the *Man,* uses an Old Testament title for the Messiah portraying Christ's humanity: "For the Son of Man is come to seek and to save that which was lost" (19:10). John, presenting Christ as truly *God* because of the miracles he wrought, writes: "And many other signs truly did Jesus...that ye might believe that Jesus is the Christ, the Son of God; and that believing you might have life through his name" (20:30,31). The prophetic promise of the Messiah's deity is given in Isaiah 40:9.

Though there is a fourfold picture, with a distinctive emphasis and destination for each Gospel, given in the four Gospels, yet three of them—Matthew, Mark, and Luke—are strikingly similar in subject matter and literary expression. Thus, the name Synoptic (presenting a similar point of view) Gospels is given to these Gospels. In seeking to explain both the similarities and differences (for these also exist), scholars have postulated a number of theories by which they attempt to solve what they call "the Synoptic problem." That there were both written and oral sources available to the writers of the Gospels (some were eyewitnesses to some of the events) is probable. It must be kept in mind, however, that any theory must not neglect the agency of the Holy Spirit, who superintended, guided, and controlled the revelation to the writers, so that the product is the inspired record of the words of God in the language, style, and personality of each Gospel writer.

THE NEW TESTAMENT

THE GOSPEL ACCORDING TO
ST. MATTHEW

Authorship, date, and background The titles attached to the four Gospels, "According to Matthew," "According to Mark," "According to Luke," and "According to John," were not part of the original Gospels. These titles were added later in accord with the tradition of the church that Matthew, Mark, Luke, and John were the authors of these books. Although Matthew is not named in the first Gospel itself and no claim is made in the text for him as the author, the early church agreed that he was the author. Other explanations in support of unknown or known individuals who might have authored the book do not hold up.

Matthew Levi was a tax collector or publican. He was called by Jesus to be one of the Twelve. Virtually nothing is known about him following the resurrection. How he lived, where he witnessed, and how he died is unknown. But his imperishable monument is the Gospel according to Matthew. The Jews disliked the tax collectors, who paid the Roman government for the right to collect taxes and then extracted as much as they could from the taxpayers. They were regarded as swindlers. For Jesus to eat dinner with one of them was looked upon with great disapproval by the religious leaders of the Jews. Matthew was literate, a good businessman and bookkeeper whose records would be accurate.

No precise date can be assigned for the writing of this Gospel, although conservative scholars usually assign it to the period between A.D. 50 and 60. Nor is the place where it was written certain. Many think it was composed at Antioch. It addressed itself to both Jews and Gentiles who had become Christians. The Jewish aspect is quite plain, and the fact that the Gospel was tied in closely to the Old Testament distinguishes it from the other Gospels. Matthew and Mark are so similar in the details common to both of them that some scholars think Matthew was indebted to Mark for portions of what he wrote. This supposes that Mark was written before Matthew. If the reverse is true, then Mark owed a great deal to Matthew.

Scholars have also sought to uncover the common sources from which all of the Gospel writers got their information, and have asked why there are four Gospels. It is of no compelling concern to Christians whether Matthew got his information firsthand by his own knowledge, or from others, or from oral tradition, or from the Holy Spirit directly. The Holy Spirit, in any event, is the true author of all Scripture and if he chose to have four Gospels written for different people but containing some materials which are similar, it must be left at that. While there may have been questions about the authorship, the date, and the sources of the information, there never has been any doubt about Matthew's authenticity and its canonicity (that is, its being a part of the Word of God).

Characteristics and content Matthew's Gospel tells the story of the life of Jesus, although in a technical sense, it is not really a biography. It was designed rather for teaching, and treats the entire drama of redemption, going back to the Old Testament to demonstrate that Jesus is the promised Messiah and that everything predicted about the Messiah has been fulfilled in his life, death, resurrection, and ministry. He traces the lineage of Jesus back to Abraham, with whom God made a covenant. He details Jesus' virgin birth, his childhood, and the divine-human natures of his person. Jesus is the Son of David, the King of the Jews, the promised Messiah. His Kingdom is not of this world, but he has a Kingdom which has come and which will be fully realized in the future in the New Jerusalem. The phrase "the Kingdom of Heaven" *or* "the Kingdom of God" is important in his teaching.

The Gospel records in detail five of Jesus' *most important* discourses: the Sermon on the Mount (chapters 5—7); the commissioning of the Twelve to take the gospel abroad (chapter 10); the parables of the kingdom (chapter 13); the teaching about the Christian community, the church (Matthew is the only Gospel in which the word for church, *ekklesia,* is used, chapter 18); and the prophecies in the Mount of Olives discourse about the closing days of the age (chapters 24, 25). The familiar events in the last week of Jesus' life are emphasized, including the incident in the Garden of Gethsemane, the betrayal by Judas, the Last Supper, the appearances before Caiaphas, the Sanhedrin, and Pontius Pilate, followed by his crucifixion, burial and resurrection. Matthew concludes his account with the Great Commission, which constitutes the marching orders to the church for that generation and for all succeeding generations until Jesus comes again. His description about baptism "in the name of the Father and of the Son and of the Holy Ghost" (28:19) is among the clearest statements in Scripture about the doctrine of the Trinity and the fact that there are three persons in one essence.

Outline

I. Jesus, his origin and infancy (1:1—2:23)
II. The beginnings of Jesus' ministry (3:1—4:25)
III. The principles of the kingdom: the Sermon on the Mount (5:1—7:29)
IV. The mighty works of Jesus (8:1—9:34)
V. The Twelve sent and forewarned (9:35—10:42)
VI. The claims of Jesus (11:1—12:50)
VII. Seven parables of the Kingdom (13:1-52)
VIII. Jesus rejected and John beheaded (13:53—14:12)
IX. Jesus leaves Herod's dominion (14:13—17:27)
X. Jesus' teaching on humility and forgiveness (18:1-35)
XI. Jesus en route to Jerusalem (19:1—20:34)
XII. The last week in Jerusalem (21:1—28:10)
XIII. The post-resurrection events (28:11-20)

I. JESUS: HIS ORIGIN AND INFANCY (1:1—2:23)

A. THE MESSIAH'S GENEALOGY (CF. LK 3:23-38)

1:1 Gen 22:18; 2 Sam 7:12-14; Ps 89:3, 4; Ps 132:11; Isa; 9:6; 11:1; Mt 22:42; Lk 3:23-28; Jn 7:42; Acts 2:30; Rom 1:3; Gal 3:16; Rev 22:16
1:3 Ruth 4:18; 1 Chron 2:5, 9
1:4 Num 1:2-15
1:5☆ Josh 6:25; Heb 11:31
1:6 1 Sam 16:1; 2 Sam 12:24
1:7 1 Chron 3:10-14
1:10 2 Kgs 20:21
1:11 2 Kgs 25:11; Jer 27:20; 52:11; Dan 1:1
1:12 Ezra 3:2; Neh 12:1; Hag 1:1

1 THE book of the generation of Jesus Christ, the son of David, the son of Abraham.
2 Abraham begat Isaac; and Isaac begat Jacob; and Jacob begat Judas and his brethren;
3 And Judas begat Pha'res and Za'ra of Tha'mar; and Pha'res begat Es'rom; and Es'rom begat A'ram;
4 And A'ram begat A-min'a-dab; and A-min'a-dab begat Na-as'son; and Na-as'son begat Sal'mon;
5 And Sal'mon begat Bo'oz of Ra'chab; and Bo'oz begat O'bed of Ruth; and O'bed begat Jesse;
6 And Jesse begat David the king; and David the king begat Solomon of her *that had been the wife* of U-ri'as;
7 And Solomon begat Ro-bo'am; and Ro-bo'am begat A-bi'a; and A-bi'a begat Asa;
8 And Asa begat Jos'a-phat; and Jos'a-phat begat Joram; and Joram begat O-zi'as;
9 And O-zi'as begat Jo'a-tham; and Jo'a-tham begat A'chaz; and A'chaz begat Ez-e-ki'as;
10 And Ez-e-ki'as begat Ma-nas'ses; and Ma-nas'ses begat A'mon; and A'mon begat Jo-si'as;
11 And Jo-si'as begat Jech-o-ni'as and his brethren, about the time they were carried away to Babylon:
12 And after they were brought to Babylon, Jech-o-ni'as begat Sa-la'thi-el; and Sa-la'thi-el begat Zo-rob'a-bel;
13 And Zo-rob'a-bel begat A-bi'ud; and A-bi'ud begat E-li'a-kim; and E-li'a-kim begat Azor;

1:5 The line from which Jesus came was not totally Jewish. There were female Gentiles who were married Jewish males. *Thamar* was apparently a Canaanite. th, the wife of *Booz* and the great-grandmother of King David, was a Moabitess. Most commentators think *Rachab* was the Gentile harlot of Josh. 2:1 (see Heb. 11:31). Bathsheba is not mentioned by name. She is called the wife, or widow, of *Urias,* who was a Hittite.

14 And Azor begat Sa'doc; and Sa'doc begat A'chim; and A'chim begat
E-li'ud;
15 And E-li'ud begat E-le-a'zar; and E-le-a'zar begat Mat'than; and
Mat'than begat Jacob;
16 And Jacob begat Joseph the husband of Mary, of whom was born
Jesus, who is called Christ.
17 So all the generations from Abraham to David *are* fourteen genera-
tions; and from David until the carrying away into Babylon *are* fourteen
generations; and from the carrying away into Babylon unto Christ *are*
fourteen generations.

☆**1:16**
Gen 3:15
Isa 9:6; 53:2
Mt 27:17, 22
Lk 2:11
Jn 3:14; 4:25
Rom 9:5
1 Tim 3:16
1:17
2 Kgs 24:14
Jer 27:20

B. THE MESSIAH'S BIRTH (CF. LK 1:26–35; LK 2:1–7)

18 ¶Now the birth of Jesus Christ was on this wise: When as his mother
Mary was espoused to Joseph, before they came together, she was found
with child of the Holy Ghost.
19 Then Joseph her husband, being a just *man*, and not willing to make
her a publick example, was minded to put her away privily.
20 But while he thought on these things, behold, the angel of the Lord
appeared unto him in a dream, saying, Joseph, thou son of David, fear not
to take unto thee Mary thy wife: for that which is conceived in her is of the
Holy Ghost.
21 And she shall bring forth a son, and thou shalt call his name JESUS:
for he shall save his people from their sins.
22 Now all this was done, that it might be fulfilled which was spoken of
the Lord by the prophet, saying,
23 Behold, a virgin shall be with child, and shall bring forth a son, and
they shall call his name Em-man'u-el, which being interpreted is, God with
us.
24 Then Joseph being raised from sleep did as the angel of the Lord had
bidden him, and took unto him his wife:
25 And knew her not till she had brought forth her firstborn son: and he
called his name JESUS.

1:18
Lk 1:27, 35
Gal 4:4
Heb 10:5
☆**1:19**
Deut 24:1
☆**1:20**
Lk 1:35
☆**1:21**
Dan 9:24
Lk 1:31; 2:11, 21
Jn 1:29
Acts 5:31; 13:23
Heb 7:25
Rev 1:5
☆**1:23**
Isa 7:14; 9:6
Jn 1:14
1 Tim 3:16

1:16 Two genealogies of Jesus appear in the Gospels, one in Matthew and one in Luke. The differences can be explained by the fact that Matthew records the genealogy of Joseph as the legal, not the natural, father of Jesus. Luke traces the genealogy of Jesus through Mary, his mother, which accounts for an almost completely different set of ancestors from Heli to David (Luke 3:23–31). It is assumed that Heli was *Joseph's father-in-law. Mary's name* is not mentioned before Heli's because Jews did not trace genealogy through a female.

1:19 *her husband*, i.e., "her fiancé." *a just man*, i.e., "a man of stern principle."† A Jewish betrothal could be broken only by a divorce; an engaged girl who was pregnant by some other man was stoned to death as an adulteress. Joseph was about to put Mary away quietly, in order to avoid public scandal.

1:20 *while he thought on these things*. In his perplexity Joseph did not wish to make a decision in haste. It is better to consider a matter beforehand than to take time to repent later. He did not yet know the divine facts in the case, and 1:19 makes it clear that the thought of putting Mary away meant he believed her to be guilty of adultery. But he did not want to make her a public example. He must have suffered, thinking his beloved to be one who had broken faith with him. When God's angel told him what to do, he was prompt in his obedience and took Mary to wife. The blessed virgin was protected—so that men said, "Is he not the son of the carpenter?" rather than, "Is he not the son of a *harlot?*"

1:21 *Jesus* is the Greek equivalent of the Hebrew *Jehoshua*. It means "*Jehovah is salvation.*" The Son of God, born of Mary, is Jehovah God the Savior.

1:23 The birth of Jesus was a literal fulfillment of Isa. 7:14. The Greek word for virgin, *parthenos*, is found in the standard Greek translation of Isaiah. Jesus' uniqueness consisted in the fact that he had no human father. He was conceived in the womb of Mary, who had never known a man, by the supernatural work of the Holy Spirit. By the Holy Spirit he was born the sinless God-man.

C. THE VISIT OF THE WISE MEN (MAGI OR ASTROLOGERS)

2:1☆ 1 Kgs 4:30 Lk 2:4
2:2 a) Jer 23:5; 30:9 Zech 9:9 Mt 27:11 Lk 19:38; 23:38 b) Num 24:15–19 Isa 60:3 Rev 22:16
2:3☆
2:4 Ps 2:1 Mal 2:7
2:5☆ Jn 7:42 Rev 2:27
2:6 Mic 5:2
2:11☆ Ps 2:12; 22:29 72:10 Isa 49:7; 60:6 Jn 5:23
2:12 Job 33:14, 15 Mt 1:20; 2:19, 20

2 NOW when Jesus was born in Bethlehem of Judæa in the days of
Herod the king, behold, there came wise men from the east to
Jerusalem,
2 Saying, Where is he that is born King of the Jews? for we have seen his
star in the east, and are come to worship him.
3 When Herod the king had heard *these things*, he was troubled, and all
Jerusalem with him.
4 And when he had gathered all the chief priests and scribes of the people
together, he demanded of them where Christ should be born.
5 And they said unto him, In Bethlehem of Judæa: for thus it is written by
the prophet,
6 And thou Bethlehem, *in* the land of Juda, art not the least among the
princes of Juda: for out of thee shall come a Governor, that shall rule my
people Israel.
7 Then Herod, when he had privily called the wise men, inquired of them
diligently what time the star appeared.
8 And he sent them to Bethlehem, and said, Go and search diligently for
the young child; and when ye have found *him*, bring me word again, that I
may come and worship him also.
9 When they had heard the king, they departed; and, lo, the star, which
they saw in the east, went before them, till it came and stood over where the
young child was.
10 When they saw the star, they rejoiced with exceeding great joy.
11 ¶And when they were come into the house, they saw the young child
with Mary his mother, and fell down, and worshipped him: and when they
had opened their treasures, they presented unto him gifts; gold, and
frankincense, and myrrh.
12 And being warned of God in a dream that they should not return to
Herod, they departed into their own country another way.

D. THE FLIGHT INTO EGYPT

13 And when they were departed, behold, the angel of the Lord appeareth
to Joseph in a dream, saying, Arise, and take the young child and his
mother, and flee into Egypt, and be thou there until I bring thee word: for
Herod will seek the young child to destroy him.

2:1 *Herod* was the son of Antipater, who wormed his way into the confidence of Julius Caesar. The Romans made him procurator of Judea in 47 B.C. and elevated him to the kingship in 37 B.C., when the last reigning descendant of the Maccabean dynasty, Antigonus, was executed. Herod craftily managed to stay in power despite the changing government of Rome. He was so evil that Augustus said of him, "I would rather be Herod's dog than his son." Herod improved the temple in Jerusalem and was still king when Jesus was born in 5 or 4 B.C. Herod died shortly after the murder of the innocent infants of Bethlehem. *wise men from the east.* The term for "wise men," or "astrologers," is *magoi, the Greek form of magav*, an old Persian word. These men constituted a priestly class that originated in Media. They were expert in dreams, omens, and prophesying. These visitors doubtlessly came from Persia or Media; having heard of the promise of Messiah in Judea and having seen the new and brilliant star, they were guided by it to the birthplace of Jesus. Their worship prefigured the later submission of many Gentiles to Christ, the Jewish Messiah.

2:3 Herod had good reason to be alarmed about the rumor of the birth of Messiah. He and all the Jews supposed that Messiah would come to be king. This would mean the end of Herod's reign, and he had no intention whatever of permitting anyone to usurp his kingdom.

2:5 *the prophet*, see Mic. 5:2.

2:11 The wise men, or astrologers, saw Jesus sometime after his birth, for the family is now in a house. King Herod, according to 2:16, ordered all male infants two years of age and under to be slaughtered, for he wished to be assured that among them the infant Jesus was slain. Presumably the astrologers gave Herod the information that led to this slaughter. (See note to 2:16.)

14When he arose, he took the young child and his mother by night, and departed into Egypt: ☆2:14

15And was there until the death of Herod: that it might be fulfilled which was spoken of the Lord by the prophet, saying, Out of Egypt have I called my son. ☆2:15 Ex 4:22, 23 Hos 11:1

16¶Then Herod, when he saw that he was mocked of the wise men, was exceeding wroth, and sent forth, and slew all the children that were in Bethlehem, and in all the coasts thereof, from two years old and under, according to the time which he had diligently inquired of the wise men. ☆2:16

17Then was fulfilled that which was spoken by Jeremy the prophet, saying,

18In Ra′ma was there a voice heard, lamentation, and weeping, and great mourning, Rachel weeping *for* her children, and would not be comforted, because they are not. 2:18 Jer 31:15

E. THE RETURN TO NAZARETH (CF. MK 1:9; LK 1:26)

19¶But when Herod was dead, behold, an angel of the Lord appeareth in a dream to Joseph in Egypt,

20Saying, Arise, and take the young child and his mother, and go into the land of Israel: for they are dead which sought the young child's life.

21And he arose, and took the young child and his mother, and came into the land of Israel.

22But when he heard that Ar-che-la′us did reign in Judæa in the room of his father Herod, he was afraid to go thither: notwithstanding, being warned of God in a dream, he turned aside into the parts of Galilee: ☆2:22

23And he came and dwelt in a city called Nazareth: that it might be fulfilled which was spoken by the prophets, He shall be called a Nazarene. 2:23 Judg 13:5 Isa 11:1 Lk 2:39 Jn 1:45, 46 Acts 4:10; 24:5

II. THE BEGINNINGS OF JESUS' MINISTRY (3:1—4:25)

A. THE PREACHING OF JOHN THE BAPTIST (CF. MK 1:1–8; LK 3:2–17; JN 1:6–8, 19–28)

3 IN those days came John the Baptist, preaching in the wilderness of Judæa, 3:1 Mal 3:1 Mk 1:2–13 Lk 3:1–22 Jn 1:6–33

2And saying, Repent ye: for the kingdom of heaven is at hand. ☆3:2 Dan 2:44 Mt 4:17; 10:7

2:14 *by night,* i.e., that very night. No legions of angels were sent to protect the infant Jesus; Joseph and Mary fled to Egypt. Just as there was no room for Messiah in the inn, there was no room for him in the land of Judea.

2:15 Just as Isa. 7:14 had a double fulfillment, so this verse represents a similar situation. God called Israel out of Egypt, as recorded in Hos. 11:1. The verse speaks of Israel as God's son. Here Matthew picks up this prophetic word and assigns it to Jesus—the second fulfillment. The parents of Jesus took him to Egypt and remained there until Herod died. Their return with Jesus is said by Matthew to be the fulfillment of the Hosean prophecy.

A number of prophecies concerning the earthly career of Jesus are stated in the New Testament to be fulfillments of Old Testament prophecies. Among them are the following: (1) he would spend part of his childhood in Egypt (Hos. 11:1; Matt. 2:15); (2) he would suffer and make atonement for sins (Isa. 53:4–6; 2 Cor. 5:21); (3) he would ride into Jerusalem on the back of a donkey (Zech. 9:9; Matt. 21:2, 4, 5); (4) he would be offered a pain-killer in his agony on the cross (Ps. 69:21; Matt. 27:34); (5) he would suffer no broken bones, contrary to the usual procedure connected with crucifixion (Ps. 34:20; Exod. 12:46; John 19:33, 36); (6) men would gamble over his garment (Ps. 22:18; Matt. 27:35); (7) he would utter certain words in his dying agony (Ps. 22:1; Mark 15:34); (8) he would rise again from the dead (Ps. 16:9, 10; Acts 2:31).

2:16 Apparently the wise men told Herod the date they had first seen Christ's natal star. This pinpointed the birthdate of the Messiah and gave Herod some idea of the age of the infant. Herod slaughtered all the children two years old and under to be sure he killed the Messiah. It does not mean that Jesus was two years old at this time, only that Herod knew the child could not be more than two.

2:22 *Archelaus* was the son and heir of Herod the Great; his mother was Malthace, a Samaritan woman. Caesar Augustus made him ethnarch (not king) of Samaria, Judea, and Idumea. He was the worst of Herod's sons. The people suffered under him for nine years before he was banished to Vienna by Augustus. After his deportation, Judea was under the rule of Roman procurators until A.D. 41.

3:2 *is at hand,* i.e., "is coming soon," or, "has arrived."†

3:3☆ Isa 40:3; Lk 1:76
3 For this is he that was spoken of by the prophet E-sai'as, saying, The
voice of one crying in the wilderness, Prepare ye the way of the Lord, make
his paths straight.
3:4 Lev 11:22; 2 Kgs 1:8; Zech 13:4
4 And the same John had his raiment of camel's hair, and a leathern girdle
about his loins; and his meat was locusts and wild honey.
5 Then went out to him Jerusalem, and all Judæa, and all the region
round about Jordan,
3:6 Acts 19:4
6 And were baptized of him in Jordan, confessing their sins.
3:7☆ Mt 12:34; 23:33; Jn 8:44; Rom 5:9; 1 Thess 1:10; 1 Jn 3:8, 10
7 ¶But when he saw many of the Pharisees and Sad'du-cees come to his
baptism, he said unto them, O generation of vipers, who hath warned you
to flee from the wrath to come?
8 Bring forth therefore fruits meet for repentance:
3:9 Jn 8:33, 39; Acts 13:26; Rom 4:1
9 And think not to say within yourselves, We have Abraham to *our* father:
for I say unto you, that God is able of these stones to raise up children unto
Abraham.
3:10 Mt 7:19; Jn 15:6; Heb 6:8
10 And now also the axe is laid unto the root of the trees: therefore every
tree which bringeth not forth good fruit is hewn down, and cast into the
fire.
3:11☆ Jn 1:26, 33; Acts 1:5; 2:3, 4; Tit 3:5
11 I indeed baptize you with water unto repentance: but he that cometh
after me is mightier than I, whose shoes I am not worthy to bear: he shall
baptize you with the Holy Ghost, and *with* fire:
3:12 Mal 3:2, 3; 4:1; Mt 13:30
12 Whose fan *is* in his hand, and he will throughly purge his floor, and
gather his wheat into the garner; but he will burn up the chaff with
unquenchable fire.

B. JOHN'S BAPTISM OF JESUS (CF. MK 1:9–11; LK 3:21, 22)

3:13 Mk 1:9–11; Lk 3:21, 22; Jn 1:31–34
13 ¶Then cometh Jesus from Galilee to Jordan unto John, to be baptized
of him.
14 But John forbad him, saying, I have need to be baptized of thee, and
comest thou to me?
3:15☆
15 And Jesus answering said unto him, Suffer *it to be so* now: for thus it
becometh us to fulfil all righteousness. Then he suffered him.
3:16☆ Isa 11:2
16 And Jesus, when he was baptized, went up straightway out of the

3:3 *Esaias*, i.e., Isaiah.
3:7 The *Sadducees* were one of the leading Jewish sects of Jesus' day. Their name is thought to be derived from Zadok, a high priest during David's reign. They came mostly from the priestly nobility, whereas the *Pharisees* came from all classes of people. The Sadducees and the Pharisees disliked each other and disagreed in theological matters. The Sadducees objected strenuously to the oral law that the Pharisees accepted and practiced (it was known as "the tradition of the elders"). They accepted the written law of Moses alone. In their theology they were known for what they rejected, such as (1) the bodily resurrection of the dead; (2) future punishments and rewards on the day of judgment; (3) the reality of angels and spirits; and (4) overruling divine providence as against unconditional free will. Though less numerous than the Pharisees, they were equally opposed to Jesus. Jesus refuted the Sadducees on several occasions, although not as often as he denounced the Pharisees (16:1–4, 6–12; 22:23–33). The Pharisees were the most influential sect of the day. They believed in rigid separation from anything non-Jewish. Their theology included (1) the most careful keeping of the law; (2) a belief in the immortality of the soul, the resurrection of the body, and retribution in the afterlife; (3) a belief in the reality of angels and spirits; (4) a belief that God would deliver Israel and restore her earlier glory; and (5) a belief in the doctrine of providence along with free will. Overriding all of this was their belief that Jews earned merit by keeping all the major and minor points of the law, which countered the doctrine of justification by faith. They hated Jesus because he did what they rejected (e.g., 9:3, 11, 14; Luke 5:21). Jesus said they were legalists; he condemned their hypocrisy with vigor (e.g., 6:2, 5, 16; 12:34; 23:33; Mark 7:6).
3:11 *he shall baptize you with the Holy Ghost, and with fire.* This prophetic word was literally fulfilled at Pentecost, when the Holy Spirit infilled all of the believers present, and the cloven tongues like as of fire rested on them (Acts 2:1–4). The Pentecost event marked the beginning of the church. It also conveyed a divine enduement on the early disciples, by which their ministries became a significant force in the spreading of the gospel.
3:15 *fulfill all righteousness,* i.e., Although he did not need baptism (for he was without sin), Jesus insisted on being baptized, for this act was by God's divine appointment.
3:16 See note on Luke 3:22 for Jesus' baptism.

water: and, lo, the heavens were opened unto him, and he saw the Spirit of
God descending like a dove, and lighting upon him:
17 And lo a voice from heaven, saying, This is my beloved Son, in whom
I am well pleased.

3:17 Mt 12:18; 17:5 Mk 9:7 Isa 42:1 Lk 9:35 Jn 12:28

C. THE TEMPTATIONS IN THE WILDERNESS (CF. MK 1:12, 13; LK 4:1–13)

4 THEN was Jesus led up of the Spirit into the wilderness to be tempted
of the devil.
2 And when he had fasted forty days and forty nights, he was afterward
an hungred.
3 And when the tempter came to him, he said, If thou be the Son of God,
command that these stones be made bread.
4 But he answered and said, It is written, Man shall not live by bread
alone, but by every word that proceedeth out of the mouth of God.
5 Then the devil taketh him up into the holy city, and setteth him on a
pinnacle of the temple,
6 And saith unto him, If thou be the Son of God, cast thyself down: for it
is written, He shall give his angels charge concerning thee: and in *their*
hands they shall bear thee up, lest at any time thou dash thy foot against a
stone.
7 Jesus said unto him, It is written again, Thou shalt not tempt the Lord
thy God.
8 Again, the devil taketh him up into an exceeding high mountain, and
sheweth him all the kingdoms of the world, and the glory of them;
9 And saith unto him, All these things will I give thee, if thou wilt fall
down and worship me.
10 Then saith Jesus unto him, Get thee hence, Satan: for it is written,
Thou shalt worship the Lord thy God, and him only shalt thou serve.
11 Then the devil leaveth him, and, behold, angels came and ministered
unto him.

☆**4:1** 1 Kgs 18:12 Ezek 3:14 Mk 1:12, 13 Lk 4:1–13 Acts 8:39 Heb 4:15
4:2 Ex 34:28
☆**4:3**
4:4 Deut 8:3 Eph 6:17
4:6 Ps 91:11
4:7 Deut 6:16
4:10 Deut 6:13
4:11 Heb 1:14 Jas 4:7

D. THE BEGINNING OF THE GALILEAN MINISTRY (CF. MK 1:14, 15; LK 4:14, 15; JN 4:43–45)

12 ¶Now when Jesus had heard that John was cast into prison, he
departed into Galilee;
13 And leaving Nazareth, he came and dwelt in Ca-per′na-um, which is
upon the sea coast, in the borders of Zab′u-lon and Neph′tha-lim:
14 That it might be fulfilled which was spoken by E-sai′as the prophet,
saying,
15 The land of Zab′u-lon, and the land of Neph′tha-lim, *by* the way of the
sea, beyond Jordan, Galilee of the Gentiles;
16 The people which sat in darkness saw great light; and to them which sat
in the region and shadow of death light is sprung up.
17 ¶From that time Jesus began to preach, and to say, Repent: for the
kingdom of heaven is at hand.

☆**4:12** Mark 1:14 Lk 3:19, 20 Jn 4:1–3
☆**4:13**
4:15, 16 Isa 9:1–2; 42:6, 7 Lk 2:32
☆**4:17** Mt 10:7

4:1 The temptation represents a fight to the death between Jesus and Satan, between the seed of the woman and the seed of the serpent. Jesus is tempted, his heel bruised; the serpent is repulsed, his head broken.

4:3 Satan purposed to have Jesus despair of his Father's goodness, to presume upon his Father's power, and to deny his Father's honor by giving it to Satan. It is the same battle Christians wage today—against the lust of the flesh, the lust of the eye, and the vainglory of life (see 1 John 2:16).

4:12, 13 From this point on, Capernaum was Jesus' home in Galilee. It was the hometown of Simon and Andrew (Mark 1:29), located at the north end of the Sea of Galilee. The international highway ran through Capernaum; hence, the tax collector's office was located there (9:9; Mark 2:13, 14).

4:17 *is at hand,* i.e., "is near," or, "has arrived."† The phrase *the kingdom of heaven* is synonymous with the phrase used in Mark and Luke, "the kingdom of God."

E. THE CALL OF JAMES AND JOHN (CF. MK 1:16–20; LK 5:1–11)

4:18 Mk 1:16–20 Lk 5:1–11

18 ¶And Jesus, walking by the sea of Galilee, saw two brethren, Simon called Peter, and Andrew his brother, casting a net into the sea: for they were fishers.

4:19 Mt 16:18 Jn 1:42

19 And he saith unto them, Follow me, and I will make you fishers of men.

4:20 Mk 10:28 Lk 18:28

20 And they straightway left *their* nets, and followed him.

21 And going on from thence, he saw other two brethren, James *the son* of Zeb′e-dee, and John his brother, in a ship with Zeb′e-dee their father, mending their nets; and he called them.

22 And they immediately left the ship and their father, and followed him.

4:23 Mt 9:35 Mk 1:39 Lk 4:15

23 ¶And Jesus went about all Galilee, teaching in their synagogues, and preaching the gospel of the kingdom, and healing all manner of sickness and all manner of disease among the people.

4:24☆

24 And his fame went throughout all Syria: and they brought unto him all sick people that were taken with divers diseases and torments, and those which were possessed with devils, and those which were lunatick, and those that had the palsy; and he healed them.

25 And there followed him great multitudes of people from Galilee, and *from* De-cap′o-lis, and *from* Jerusalem, and *from* Judæa, and *from* beyond Jordan.

III. THE PRINCIPLES OF THE KINGDOM: THE SERMON ON THE MOUNT (5:1—7:29 CF. LK 6:20–49)

A. THE CHARACTER OF CHRISTIAN DISCIPLESHIP

1. The Beatitudes (Bliss or Blessedness) (Cf. Lk 6:20–23)

5:1☆ Lk 6:20–23
5:2☆
5:3 Ps 37:11; 51:17 Isa 57:15; 66:2

5 AND seeing the multitudes, he went up into a mountain: and when he was set, his disciples came unto him:

2 And he opened his mouth, and taught them, saying,

3 Blessed *are* the poor in spirit: for theirs is the kingdom of heaven.

5:4 Isa 61:2, 3 Jn 16:20 2 Cor 1:7 Jas 4:9, 10 Rev 21:4

4 Blessed *are* they that mourn: for they shall be comforted.

5:5 1 Pet 3:4

5 Blessed *are* the meek: for they shall inherit the earth.

6 Blessed *are* they which do hunger and thirst after righteousness: for they shall be filled.

5:7 Ps 41:1 Mt 6:14 Heb 6:10 Jas 2:13

7 Blessed *are* the merciful: for they shall obtain mercy.

5:8 1 Cor 13:12 Heb 12:14 1 Jn 3:2, 3

8 Blessed *are* the pure in heart: for they shall see God.

9 Blessed *are* the peacemakers: for they shall be called the children of God.

5:10 2 Cor 4:17 2 Tim 2:12 1 Pet 3:13, 14

10 Blessed *are* they which are persecuted for righteousness' sake: for theirs is the kingdom of heaven.

11 Blessed are ye, when *men* shall revile you, and persecute *you*, and shall say all manner of evil against you falsely, for my sake.

Jesus' use of the Hebrew, or Aramaic, phrase *kingdom of heaven* is a respectful equivalent to the name of God, which Jews were careful not to employ. Mark (1:15) and Luke use the same phrase, but in a form more familiar to a Gentile audience—"kingdom of God."

4:24 Those possessed by demons were not lunatics. Mark 1:32 and Luke 6:17, 18 distinguish between *demon possession and bodily ailments. Jesus ad*dressed demons who inhabited men and ordered them to leave (8:32; 17:18; Mark 1:25, 34; 9:25). In Luke 8:32 the demons left the possessed and entered a herd of swine. In Matt. 8:31 and Mark 9:26 the demons are identified as separate from the persons they have possessed. Demons are part of the spiritual hierarchy of evil led by Satan.

5:1, 2 Many suppose that Jesus delivered the Sermon on the Mount (chapters 5–7) at one time and in one place. Others believe that these three chapters are a collection of Jesus' teaching given at different times and under differing circumstances. There is no reason to suppose that Jesus did not repeat many segments of *his teaching* on a number of occasions, just as ministers preach the same sermon many times in different places. There is, however, nothing in the text to indicate that this set of sayings was not given at one time.

12Rejoice, and be exceeding glad: for great *is* your reward in heaven: for
so persecuted they the prophets which were before you.

5:12 2 Chron 36:16; Mt 23:37; Acts 7:52; 1 Thess 2:15; Jas 5:10; Heb 11:32–38

2. Believers as Salt and Light

13¶Ye are the salt of the earth: but if the salt have lost his savour,
wherewith shall it be salted? it is thenceforth good for nothing, but to be
cast out, and to be trodden under foot of men.
14Ye are the light of the world. A city that is set on an hill cannot be hid.
15Neither do men light a candle, and put it under a bushel, but on a
candlestick; and it giveth light unto all that are in the house.
16Let your light so shine before men, that they may see your good works,
and glorify your Father which is in heaven.

☆5:13

☆5:14 Phil 2:15

5:16 Jn 15:8; 1 Cor 14:25; 1 Pet 2:12

B. JESUS AND THE MOSAIC LAW

1. The Righteousness Demanded

17¶Think not that I am come to destroy the law, or the prophets: I am not
come to destroy, but to fulfil.
18For verily I say unto you, Till heaven and earth pass, one jot or one
tittle shall in no wise pass from the law, till all be fulfilled.
19Whosoever therefore shall break one of these least commandments, and
shall teach men so, he shall be called the least in the kingdom of heaven:
but whosoever shall do and teach *them*, the same shall be called great in the
kingdom of heaven.
20For I say unto you, That except your righteousness shall exceed *the
righteousness* of the scribes and Pharisees, ye shall in no case enter into the
kingdom of heaven.

☆5:17 Rom 10:4; Gal 3:24

☆5:18 Lk 16:17

5:19 Jas 2:10

5:20 Rom 10:3

2. The Sixth Commandment

21¶Ye have heard that it was said by them of old time, Thou shalt not
kill; and whosoever shall kill shall be in danger of the judgment:
22But I say unto you, That whosoever is angry with his brother without a
cause shall be in danger of the judgment: and whosoever shall say to his
brother, Raca, shall be in danger of the council: but whosoever shall say,
Thou fool, shall be in danger of hell fire.

☆5:21 Ex 20:13; Deut 5:17

☆5:22 1 Jn 3:15

5:13, 14 A handful of salt goes a long way. The gospel is as salt, quick and powerful; and Christians are also salt. In 5:14 Christ and his people are called the light of the world. In darkness even the light of a match makes a great difference. Believers are the light by what they say and how they live.

5:17 Jesus in the flesh was subject to the law of God. He met the demands of the ceremonial law of circumcision, the presentation, and his baptism by John (3:15). *In all things* Jesus was obedient to the law of his Father (John 8:46; 1 Pet. 2:21–23). But he never put himself into bondage to the legalism that the Pharisees created by the extravagant interpretations of the law. He also declared himself to be "Lord even of the sabbath" (12:8).

Christ's people are no longer required to keep the ceremonial law, which has been made obsolete by the cross (see Eph. 2:15; Col. 2:14). Christians, however, have never been excused from keeping the moral law of God, the Ten Commandments. They obey them, not to merit salvation, but as a token of lives transformed by the grace of God. Christians, like Jesus, are not to be lawless.

5:18 *till all be fulfilled*, i.e., "until its purpose is achieved" (TLB), or, "until all things be accomplished."

5:21, 22 Christ never abrogated the law of murder. He did teach that the believer's righteousness should exceed that of the scribes and Pharisees. They taught that you could hate your enemy in your heart, for there was no sin until you killed him physically. But Christ said that "heart murder" precedes the actual act. The heart-murderer is already guilty before God even if the fear of retribution restrains him from committing the overt act. Evil in the heart is the root of all outward acts of sin; God condemns both the attitude and the action. *without a cause*. This phrase has been relegated to a footnote in the RSV and the NIV, even though it appears in some ancient Greek New Testament manuscripts. Anger for a right cause is not forbidden in Scripture, as the KJV translation clarifies. God is said to be capable of anger; Jonathan Edwards preached a sermon titled "Sinners in the Hands of an Angry God."

23 Therefore if thou bring thy gift to the altar, and there rememberest that thy brother hath ought against thee;

24 Leave there thy gift before the altar, and go thy way; first be reconciled to thy brother, and then come and offer thy gift.

5:25
Prov 25:8
Lk 12:58

25 Agree with thine adversary quickly, whiles thou art in the way with him; lest at any time the adversary deliver thee to the judge, and the judge deliver thee to the officer, and thou be cast into prison.

26 Verily I say unto thee, Thou shalt by no means come out thence, till thou hast paid the uttermost farthing.

3. The Seventh Commandment (Cf. 19:9; Mk 10:11; Lk 16:18)

5:27☆
Ex 20:14
Deut 5:18
5:28☆
Heb 13:4

27 ¶Ye have heard that it was said by them of old time, Thou shalt not commit adultery:

28 But I say unto you, That whosoever looketh on a woman to lust after her hath committed adultery with her already in his heart.

5:29☆
Mt 18:9
Mk 9:43–47

29 And if thy right eye offend thee, pluck it out, and cast *it* from thee: for it is profitable for thee that one of thy members should perish, and not *that* thy whole body should be cast into hell.

5:30
Mt 18:8

30 And if thy right hand offend thee, cut it off, and cast *it* from thee: for it is profitable for thee that one of thy members should perish, and not *that* thy whole body should be cast into hell.

5:31☆
Deut 24:1
Jer 3:1
Mk 10:2
5:32
Rom 7:3
1 Cor 7:10

31 It hath been said, Whosoever shall put away his wife, let him give her a writing of divorcement:

32 But I say unto you, That whosoever shall put away his wife, saving for the cause of fornication, causeth her to commit adultery: and whosoever shall marry her that is divorced committeth adultery.

4. The Taking of Oaths

5:33
Num 30:1
Deut 23:23
5:34
Isa 66:1
Jas 5:12
5:35
Ps 48:2
Isa 66:1

33 ¶Again, ye have heard that it hath been said by them of old time, Thou shalt not forswear thyself, but shalt perform unto the Lord thine oaths:

34 But I say unto you, Swear not at all; neither by heaven; for it is God's throne:

35 Nor by the earth; for it is his footstool: neither by Jerusalem; for it is the city of the great King.

36 Neither shalt thou swear by thy head, because thou canst not make one hair white or black.

5:37
Col 4:6

37 But let your communication be, Yea, yea; Nay, nay: for whatsoever is more than these cometh of evil.

5:38☆
Lev 24:20
Lk 6:27–35
5:39
Prov 20:22
Isa 50:6
Rom 12:17
1 Cor 6:7
1 Thess 5:15
1 Pet 3:9

5. The Law of Retaliation

38 ¶Ye have heard that it hath been said, An eye for an eye, and a tooth for a tooth:

39 But I say unto you, That ye resist not evil: but whosoever shall smite thee on thy right cheek, turn to him the other also.

5:27, 28 Jesus defined "heart adultery" and physical adultery. Adultery is committed when a man looks on a woman with the intent to commit adultery. The Jews of Jesus' day said only the overt act was adultery; a heart filled with adulterous thoughts was still innocent. Jesus' *explanation did not change* the law of God. He only stated what lay at the heart of the moral law relative to adultery even in the Old Testament and thereby condemned those whose interpretation opened the door to heart adultery.

5:29 Jesus was not telling us to pluck out our eyes or cut off our hands. Yet sin is so dangerous that "it is better to lose the eye and the hand that thus offend than to give way to sin, and perish eternally in it."*

5:31 See notes on Deut. 24:1 and Mark 10:5 on divorce.

5:38 This was the law of retaliation, which an injured man might insist on. The principle is that the retaliation should equal the crime. Thus, the rule existed to prevent men from exacting a greater punishment than was warranted by the injury done.

40 And if any man will sue thee at the law, and take away thy coat, let him
have *thy* cloak also.
41 And whosoever shall compel thee to go a mile, go with him twain.
42 Give to him that asketh thee, and from him that would borrow of thee **5:42**
turn not thou away. Deut 15:8
43 ¶Ye have heard that it hath been said, Thou shalt love thy neighbour, **5:43**
and hate thine enemy. Lev 19:18 Deut 23:6

6. The Law of Love

44 But I say unto you, Love your enemies, bless them that curse you, do ☆**5:44**
good to them that hate you, and pray for them which despitefully use you, Lk 23:34 Acts 7:60
and persecute you; Rom 12:14 1 Pet 2:23
45 That ye may be the children of your Father which is in heaven: for he
maketh his sun to rise on the evil and on the good, and sendeth rain on the
just and on the unjust.
46 For if ye love them which love you, what reward have ye? do not even
the publicans the same?
47 And if ye salute your brethren only, what do ye more *than others?* do
not even the publicans so?
48 Be ye therefore perfect, even as your Father which is in heaven is ☆**5:48**
perfect. Lev 19:1 Col 1:28 1 Pet 1:15

C. RELIGIOUS PRACTICES

1. Almsgiving (Gifts to the Poor)

6 TAKE heed that ye do not your alms before men, to be seen of them: ☆**6:1**
otherwise ye have no reward of your Father which is in heaven. 2 Cor 9:9
2 Therefore when thou doest *thine* alms, do not sound a trumpet before **6:2**
thee, as the hypocrites do in the synagogues and in the streets, that they Mt 23:5
may have glory of men. Verily I say unto you, They have their reward.
3 But when thou doest alms, let not thy left hand know what thy right
hand doeth:
4 That thine alms may be in secret: and thy Father which seeth in secret **6:4**
himself shall reward thee openly. Mt 6:6, 18

2. Prayer (Cf. Lk 11:1–4)

5 ¶And when thou prayest, thou shalt not be as the hypocrites *are:* for **6:5**
they love to pray standing in the synagogues and in the corners of the Lk 18:11, 12
streets, that they may be seen of men. Verily I say unto you, They have their
reward.
6 But thou, when thou prayest, enter into thy closet, and when thou hast **6:6**
shut thy door, pray to thy Father which is in secret; and thy Father which Jer 17:10
seeth in secret shall reward thee openly.

5:44 Jesus corrected the misapprehension the Jews had about the law of love. He made it clear that love exists for enemies as well as friends, for foreigners as well as fellow Jews. Later Paul reiterated the command to love one's enemies, saying that Jesus died for us when we were his enemies.

5:48 The word *perfect* (*teleios*) comes from *telos*, which means "end," "goal," or, "limit." It signifies "attaining to the end—complete maturity." Here, however, the comparison is made between God and his children; hence, the meaning must be expanded to include more than "maturity." This perfection must then be a God-like quality—one of disinterested love and kindness even for those who do not deserve it—that is possible for us to attain. This sort of perfectness is not equivalent to absolute sinlessness; it concerns a matter of one's intention or attitude to do right. Believers can enjoy the grace from God to maintain an attitude of kindly benevolence and sincere desire for the wellbeing of others.

6:1 In this and the following verses Jesus talks about the three great Christian duties: almsgiving, prayer, and fasting. Prayer has to do with our souls, fasting with our bodies, and almsgiving with our substance. These duties are to be performed rightly, i.e., from the inward man, which seeks the approval of God and not the applause of men.

6:7 1 Kgs 18:26

7 But when ye pray, use not vain repetitions, as the heathen *do:* for they
think that they shall be heard for their much speaking.
8 Be not ye therefore like unto them: for your Father knoweth what things
ye have need of, before ye ask him.

6:9☆ Mt 23:9; Lk 11:2; Rom 8:15, 16 **6:10** Ps 103:20 **6:11** Prov 30:8 **6:13☆** Lk 22:40, 46; Jn 17:15; 1 Cor 10:13; Jas 1:13; 2 Pet 2:9; Rev 3:10 **6:14** Mt 18:35; Mk 11:25; Eph 4:32; Col 3:13

9 After this manner therefore pray ye: Our Father which art in heaven,
Hallowed be thy name.
10 Thy kingdom come. Thy will be done in earth, as *it is* in heaven.
11 Give us this day our daily bread.
12 And forgive us our debts, as we forgive our debtors.
13 And lead us not into temptation, but deliver us from evil: For thine is
the kingdom, and the power, and the glory, for ever. Amen.
14 For if ye forgive men their trespasses, your heavenly Father will also
forgive you:
15 But if ye forgive not men their trespasses, neither will your Father
forgive your trespasses.

3. Fasting

6:16 Isa 58:5, 6

16 ¶Moreover when ye fast, be not, as the hypocrites, of a sad counte-
nance: for they disfigure their faces, that they may appear unto men to fast.
Verily I say unto you, They have their reward.
17 But thou, when thou fastest, anoint thine head, and wash thy face;
18 That thou appear not unto men to fast, but unto thy Father which is in
secret: and thy Father, which seeth in secret, shall reward thee openly.

4. Worldliness

a. Wealth

6:19 Prov 23:4, 5; Heb 13:5 **6:20** Mt 19:21; Lk 12:33, 34

19 ¶Lay not up for yourselves treasures upon earth, where moth and rust
doth corrupt, and where thieves break through and steal:
20 But lay up for yourselves treasures in heaven, where neither moth nor
rust doth corrupt, and where thieves do not break through nor steal:
21 For where your treasure is, there will your heart be also.

b. Light or darkness

6:22 Lk 11:34 **6:23** Rom 1:21; 2 Cor 3:15; 4:4; Eph 4:17, 18

22 The light of the body is the eye: if therefore thine eye be single, thy
whole body shall be full of light.
23 But if thine eye be evil, thy whole body shall be full of darkness. If
therefore the light that is in thee be darkness, how great *is* that darkness!

c. God or Mammon (money)

6:24☆ Lk 16:13; Jas 4:4; 1 Jn 2:15

24 ¶No man can serve two masters: for either he will hate the one, and
love the other; or else he will hold to the one, and despise the other. Ye
cannot serve God and mammon.

6:9ff This is the model prayer. It begins as all prayer should, with adoration of God Almighty and his interests. It is followed by requests for the forgiveness of sins and petitions for daily needs. It has been the most widely used prayer among Christians everywhere. *Some have thought there is a legalistic strain in the phrase forgive us our debts, as we forgive our debtors.* But forgiveness of our sins is never granted by our furnishing God with merit of any sort, not even that of forgiving others. Our refusal to forgive others is itself a sin, and when we do not forgive others, we have not repented of our own sin, and hence cannot find forgiveness for that of which we have not repented.

6:13 *from evil*, i.e., "from the evil one." Some ancient manuscripts do not have *For thine is the kingdom, and the power, and the glory, for ever. Amen.*

6:24 *mammon*, i.e., wealth, property, or money. Being wealthy is neither bad nor good; how one uses his wealth is what makes the difference. Under the Lordship of Christ, it is good; not under the Lordship of Christ, it becomes an impediment, a handicap to one's Christian life.

d. *Faith versus anxiety (Cf. Lk 12:22–31)*

25 Therefore I say unto you, Take no thought for your life, what ye shall
eat, or what ye shall drink; nor yet for your body, what ye shall put on. Is
not the life more than meat, and the body than raiment?

☆**6:25** Lk 12:22–31 Phil 4:6, 19 1 Pet 5:7

26 Behold the fowls of the air: for they sow not, neither do they reap, nor
gather into barns; yet your heavenly Father feedeth them. Are ye not much
better than they?

6:26 Job 38:41 Ps 39:5, 6

27 Which of you by taking thought can add one cubit unto his stature?
28 And why take ye thought for raiment? Consider the lilies of the field,
how they grow; they toil not, neither do they spin:
29 And yet I say unto you, That even Solomon in all his glory was not
arrayed like one of these.

6:29 1 Kgs 10:4–7

30 Wherefore, if God so clothe the grass of the field, which to day is, and
to morrow is cast into the oven, *shall he* not much more *clothe* you, O ye of
little faith?

6:30 Mt 8:26; 14:31; 16:8

31 Therefore take no thought, saying, What shall we eat? or, What shall we
drink? or, Wherewithal shall we be clothed?

6:31 Ps 23:1

32 (For after all these things do the Gentiles seek:) for your heavenly
Father knoweth that ye have need of all these things.
33 But seek ye first the kingdom of God, and his righteousness; and all
these things shall be added unto you.

6:33 Ps 34:9; 37:25 Mk 10:29, 30

34 Take therefore no thought for the morrow: for the morrow shall take
thought for the things of itself. Sufficient unto the day *is* the evil thereof.

☆**6:34**

D. JESUS' CONCLUDING OBSERVATIONS

1. Judging Others (Cf. Lk 6:37–42)

7 JUDGE not, that ye be not judged.
2 For with what judgment ye judge, ye shall be judged: and with
what measure ye mete, it shall be measured to you again.

☆**7:1** Lk 6:37, 38 Rom 2:1–3; 14:4 1 Cor 4:5 Jas 4:11

3 And why beholdest thou the mote that is in thy brother's eye, but
considerest not the beam that is in thine own eye?

7:3 Lk 6:41, 42

4 Or how wilt thou say to thy brother, Let me pull out the mote out of
thine eye; and, behold, a beam *is* in thine own eye?
5 Thou hypocrite, first cast out the beam out of thine own eye; and then
shalt thou see clearly to cast out the mote out of thy brother's eye.
6 ¶Give not that which is holy unto the dogs, neither cast ye your pearls
before swine, lest they trample them under their feet, and turn again and
rend you.

2. Getting Things from God and the Golden Rule (Cf. Lk 11:9–13)

7 ¶Ask, and it shall be given you; seek, and ye shall find; knock, and it
shall be opened unto you:

☆**7:7** Mt 21:22 Mk 11:24 Lk 11:9–13 Jn 14:13, 14 15:7; 16:23 Jas 1:5, 6 1 Jn 3:21, 22; 5:14, 15

6:25 Anxiety is one of the worst maladies Christians experience. (See note on Ps. 37:5.)

6:34 *Sufficient unto the day is the evil thereof*, i.e., "Live one day at a time" (TLB).

7:1 This command against judging does not mean we should never judge. It does mean that we should (1) first judge ourselves; (2) never judge rashly; (3) not make our decisions binding on all; (4) never infer the worst (as we are apt to do); (5) never judge a person on the basis of a single act; (6) never judge the hearts of others, for only God knows the heart.

7:7 God speaks to believers through the written Word; believers speak to God through prayer. Effective prayer must follow the laws or principles that undergird it: (1) a right relationship to God through Jesus Christ. God promises to answer the prayers of believers. He does not promise to answer the prayers of unbelievers, although he may do so by common grace; (2) a genuine desire to secure from God the petition addressed to him (1 Sam. 1:10, 11; 2 Kings 19:14–19; Luke 11:5–10); (3) a confidence in God that leads to asking in simple trust (7:7–11; James 4:2); (4) a faith that believes that God is able and willing to answer (Heb. 11:1; 1 John 5:14, 15); and (5) the confident acceptance of the answer before it has come (Mark 11:24).

8 For every one that asketh receiveth; and he that seeketh findeth; and to
him that knocketh it shall be opened.
9 Or what man is there of you, whom if his son ask bread, will he give him
a stone?
10 Or if he ask a fish, will he give him a serpent?
11 If ye then, being evil, know how to give good gifts unto your children,
how much more shall your Father which is in heaven give good things to
them that ask him?
7:12☆ Lk 6:31 Rom 13:8–10 Gal 5:14
12 Therefore all things whatsoever ye would that men should do to you, do
ye even so to them: for this is the law and the prophets.

3. The Narrow versus the Broad Way

7:13 Lk 13:24
13 ¶Enter ye in at the strait gate: for wide *is* the gate, and broad *is* the way,
that leadeth to destruction, and many there be which go in thereat:
7:14 Jn 14:6
14 Because strait *is* the gate, and narrow *is* the way, which leadeth unto
life, and few there be that find it.

4. False Prophets

7:15☆ Deut 13:1–4 Jer 23:16 Acts 20:29 Rom 16:17 2 Pet 2:1 1 Jn 4:1
15 ¶Beware of false prophets, which come to you in sheep's clothing, but
inwardly they are ravening wolves.
16 Ye shall know them by their fruits. Do men gather grapes of thorns, or
figs of thistles?
7:16–20 Mt 12:33 Lk 6:43–49 Jas 3:12
17 Even so every good tree bringeth forth good fruit; but a corrupt tree
bringeth forth evil fruit.
18 A good tree cannot bring forth evil fruit, neither *can* a corrupt tree
bring forth good fruit.
19 Every tree that bringeth not forth good fruit is hewn down, and cast
into the fire.
20 Wherefore by their fruits ye shall know them.

5. The Two Builders

7:21☆ Lk 6:46 Jas 1:22
21 ¶Not every one that saith unto me, Lord, Lord, shall enter into the
kingdom of heaven; but he that doeth the will of my Father which is in
heaven.
7:22 Acts 19:13–15
22 Many will say to me in that day, Lord, Lord, have we not prophesied in
thy name? and in thy name have cast out devils? and in thy name done
many wonderful works?
7:23 Mt 25:11, 12, 41 Lk 13:24–27
23 And then will I profess unto them, I never knew you: depart from me,
ye that work iniquity.
7:24 2 Tim 2:19 Jas 1:22–24
24 ¶Therefore whosoever heareth these sayings of mine, and doeth them, I
will liken him unto a wise man, which built his house upon a rock:

7:12 *whatsoever ye would that men should do to you, do ye even so to them.* This is the Golden Rule. We ought to live by it. There is a four-way test by which we can make decisions as to what we should do and how we should think. We must ask, (1) Is it the truth?; (2) Is it fair to all concerned?; (3) Will it build good will?; and (4) Will it be beneficial to all concerned? *this is the law and the prophets; i.e., "this is the teaching of the* law of Moses in a nutshell."†

7:15 Scripture abounds with warnings against false prophets. They are called treacherous, covetous, crafty, drunken, immoral, and profane. These liars who pretend to be what they are not should be shunned. Their counsel is not to be followed.

7:21 The title *Lord* (*kyrios*) is applied to Jesus Christ nearly seven hundred times in the New Testament. When related to the words *Jesus* and *Christ*, these three terms tell us the following: As Jesus, he is the Savior; as Christ, he is the anointed one of God; as Lord, he is the master of our lives. The word *kyrios* was used as the equivalent of *Yahweh* in the ancient Greek translation of the Old Testament. It is so used in the New Testament, too. Thus, Jesus Christ is identified with Yahweh in the use of *kyrios ("Lord")*. Jesus the Christ is Yahweh, or God.

25 And the rain descended, and the floods came, and the winds blew, and
beat upon that house; and it fell not: for it was founded upon a rock.
26 And every one that heareth these sayings of mine, and doeth them not,
shall be likened unto a foolish man, which built his house upon the sand:
27 And the rain descended, and the floods came, and the winds blew, and
beat upon that house; and it fell: and great was the fall of it.
28 And it came to pass, when Jesus had ended these sayings, the people
were astonished at his doctrine:
29 For he taught them as *one* having authority, and not as the scribes.

7:28 Isa 50:4 Mt 13:54 Mk 1:22; 6:2 Lk 4:32 Jn 7:46
☆**7:29**

IV. THE MIGHTY WORKS OF JESUS (8:1—9:34)

A. THE CLEANSING OF THE LEPER (CF. MK 1:40–45; LK 5:12–16)

8 WHEN he was come down from the mountain, great multitudes
followed him.
2 And, behold, there came a leper and worshipped him, saying, Lord, if
thou wilt, thou canst make me clean.
3 And Jesus put forth *his* hand, and touched him, saying, I will; be thou
clean. And immediately his leprosy was cleansed.
4 And Jesus saith unto him, See thou tell no man; but go thy way, shew
thyself to the priest, and offer the gift that Moses commanded, for a
testimony unto them.

☆**8:1**
8:2 Lev 14:3 Mt 9:18; 15:25 Mk 1:40–44 Lk 5:12–14 Jn 9:38
8:4 Mk 1:43, 44 Lk 5:14; 17:14

B. HEALING THE CAPTAIN'S SERVANT (CF. LK 7:1–10)

5 ¶And when Jesus was entered into Ca-per'na-um, there came unto him
a centurion, beseeching him,
6 And saying, Lord, my servant lieth at home sick of the palsy, grievously
tormented.
7 And Jesus saith unto him, I will come and heal him.
8 The centurion answered and said, Lord, I am not worthy that thou
shouldest come under my roof: but speak the word only, and my servant
shall be healed.
9 For I am a man under authority, having soldiers under me: and I say to
this *man*, Go, and he goeth; and to another, Come, and he cometh; and to
my servant, Do this, and he doeth *it*.
10 When Jesus heard *it*, he marvelled, and said to them that followed,
Verily I say unto you, I have not found so great faith, no, not in Israel.
11 And I say unto you, That many shall come from the east and west, and
shall sit down with Abraham, and Isaac, and Jacob, in the kingdom of
heaven.
12 But the children of the kingdom shall be cast out into outer darkness:
there shall be weeping and gnashing of teeth.
13 And Jesus said unto the centurion, Go thy way; and as thou hast
believed, *so* be it done unto thee. And his servant was healed in the selfsame
hour.

☆**8:5** Lk 7:1–10
8:9 Ps 107:20
8:11 Isa 2:2; 11:10 Mal 1:11 Lk 13:28, 29 Acts 10:45 11:18; 14:27 Rom 15:9 Eph 3:6 Rev 5:9, 7:9
8:12 Mt 13:41, 42 21:43

7:29 *not as the scribes.* These leaders only quoted others; they did not presume to present any fresh revelation.†

8:1ff Matthew presents Christ as Savior—his credentials are his miracles. The miracles testify to his person and his office. The scope of his miracles shows the magnitude as well as the breadth of his power. He is (1) the master over disease (8:1–17; 9:27–34); (2) the master over nature (8:26, 27); (3) the master over death (John 11:13, 43, 44; see also Matt. 9:18, 23–25; Luke 7:12–15); and (4) the master over devils or demons (Mark 5:12, 13; see also Matt. 8:28–32; 9:32, 33; 15:22–28; 17:14–18; Mark 1:23–27).

8:5ff The centurion was a Gentile, yet he had faith in Christ. The clinching word was this: "As thou hast believed, so be it done unto thee" (8:13). The servant was healed immediately.

C. HEALING PETER'S MOTHER-IN-LAW (CF. MK 1:29–35; LK 4:28–41)

8:14 Mk 1:29–34 Lk 4:38–41

14 ¶And when Jesus was come into Peter's house, he saw his wife's mother
laid, and sick of a fever.
15 And he touched her hand, and the fever left her: and she arose, and
ministered unto them.
16 ¶When the even was come, they brought unto him many that were
possessed with devils: and he cast out the spirits with *his* word, and healed
all that were sick:

8:17☆ 1 Pet 2:24

17 That it might be fulfilled which was spoken by E-sai'as the prophet,
saying, Himself took our infirmities, and bare *our* sicknesses.

D. WOULD-BE FOLLOWERS (CF. LK 9:57–62)

8:19 Lk 9:57–60
8:20☆ Dan 7:13, 14 Mt 24:27; 26:24 Jn 1:11 Acts 7:56
8:22 Mt 9:9 Mk 2:14 Lk 9:59 Jn 1:43; 21:19
8:22☆

18 ¶Now when Jesus saw great multitudes about him, he gave command-
ment to depart unto the other side.
19 And a certain scribe came, and said unto him, Master, I will follow thee
whithersoever thou goest.
20 And Jesus saith unto him, The foxes have holes, and the birds of the air
have nests; but the Son of man hath not where to lay *his* head.
21 And another of his disciples said unto him, Lord, suffer me first to go
and bury my father.
22 But Jesus said unto him, Follow me; and let the dead bury their dead.

E. THE LORD OF NATURE (CF. MK 4:36–41; LK 8:22–25)

8:23 Mk 4:35–41 Lk 8:22–25

23 ¶And when he was entered into a ship, his disciples followed him.
24 And, behold, there arose a great tempest in the sea, insomuch that the
ship was covered with the waves: but he was asleep.
25 And his disciples came to *him*, and awoke him, saying, Lord, save us:
we perish.

8:26 Job 38:8–11 Ps 65:7; 89:9 107:29 Prov 30:4 Phil 4:6

26 And he saith unto them, Why are ye fearful, O ye of little faith? Then
he arose, and rebuked the winds and the sea; and there was a great calm.
27 But the men marvelled, saying, What manner of man is this, that even
the winds and the sea obey him!

F. THE CONQUEROR OF DEMONS (CF. MK 5:1–20; LK 8:26–39)

8:28 Mk 5:1–20 Lk 8:26–39
8:29☆ Mk 1:23, 24 Lk 4:33, 34 2 Pet 2:4

28 ¶And when he was come to the other side into the country of the
Ger'ge-senes, there met him two possessed with devils, coming out of the
tombs, exceeding fierce, so that no man might pass by that way.
29 And, behold, they cried out, saying, What have we to do with thee,

---

8:17 Healing is included in the work of Jesus Christ as redeemer. Indeed, everything the Christian has is to be found in Christ's redemption. Therefore, it does not follow that we are sick because we sin. Nor does it follow that God intends to heal every sick person and remove every malady. That God heals today cannot be denied. Certainly prayer is effective, and while some think the gift of healing is not given today, it cannot be *simply ruled out.*

8:20 *Son of man.* Jesus referred to himself as the Son of man more than eighty times in the New Testament Gospels. This term describes his office as the Messiah, but he avoided the word "Messiah" because the people of his day attached to it connotations that were improper. (The people thought of the Messiah as an irresistible military conqueror who would smite Rome and restore the political empire of King David.) In its messianic connotation the term "Son of man" was first used in Dan. 7:13, where it was applied to a heavenly figure whose everlasting rulership over all is given to him by the Ancient of days. Jesus gave this title its full messianic and redemptive significance.

8:22 The command *Follow me* takes precedence over all else in our lives.

8:29 Even devils (demons) know that Jesus is the Christ, yet they hate him. The demon who called Jesus the Son of God defiantly said he wanted nothing to do with the Savior. He also spoke a word of dread and fear. The demon asked, "Art thou come hither to torment us before the time?" He knew what many

Jesus, thou Son of God? art thou come hither to torment us before the
time?
30 And there was a good way off from them an herd of many swine
feeding.
31 So the devils besought him, saying, If thou cast us out, suffer us to go
away into the herd of swine.
32 And he said unto them, Go. And when they were come out, they went
into the herd of swine: and, behold, the whole herd of swine ran violently
down a steep place into the sea, and perished in the waters.
33 And they that kept them fled, and went their ways into the city, and
told every thing, and what was befallen to the possessed of the devils.
34 And, behold, the whole city came out to meet Jesus: and when they saw
him, they besought *him* that he would depart out of their coasts.

8:30 Deut 14:8
8:34 Lk 5:8

G. THE FORGIVER OF SINS (CF. MK 2:1–12; LK 5:17–26)

9 AND he entered into a ship, and passed over, and came into his own
city.
2 And, behold, they brought to him a man sick of the palsy, lying on a
bed: and Jesus seeing their faith said unto the sick of the palsy; Son, be of
good cheer; thy sins be forgiven thee.
3 And, behold, certain of the scribes said within themselves, This *man*
blasphemeth.
4 And Jesus knowing their thoughts said, Wherefore think ye evil in your
hearts?
5 For whether is easier, to say, *Thy* sins be forgiven thee; or to say, Arise,
and walk?
6 But that ye may know that the Son of man hath power on earth to
forgive sins, (then saith he to the sick of the palsy,) Arise, take up thy bed,
and go unto thine house.
7 And he arose, and departed to his house.
8 But when the multitudes saw *it*, they marvelled, and glorified God,
which had given such power unto men.

☆**9:2** Mk 2:2–12 Lk 5:17–26
9:3 Mt 8:10 Eph 1:7
9:4 Mt 12:25 Lk 6:8; 9:47 11:17
9:5 Acts 5:31
9:8 Mt 15:31 Mk 2:12 Lk 7:16

H. THE CALLING OF MATTHEW (CF. MK 2:13–17; LK 5:27–32)

9 ¶And as Jesus passed forth from thence, he saw a man, named Matthew,
sitting at the receipt of custom: and he saith unto him, Follow me. And he
arose, and followed him.
10 ¶And it came to pass, as Jesus sat at meat in the house, behold, many
publicans and sinners came and sat down with him and his disciples.
11 And when the Pharisees saw *it*, they said unto his disciples, Why eateth
your Master with publicans and sinners?
12 But when Jesus heard *that*, he said unto them, They that be whole need
not a physician, but they that are sick.
13 But go ye and learn what *that* meaneth, I will have mercy, and not
sacrifice: for I am not come to call the righteous, but sinners to repentance.

9:9 Mt 10:3 Mk 2:13–17; 3:18 Lk 5:27–32; 6:15 15:1, 2 Acts 1:14
☆**9:10**
9:11 Mt 11:19 Mk 2:16 Lk 5:30; 15:2
9:13 Prov 21:3 Hos 6:6 Mic 6:6–8 Mt 12:7; 18:11 Lk 19:9, 10 1 Tim 1:15

---

unbelievers do not know. There is a time when the wicked will be tormented. The demon wanted to avoid that time as long as possible.

9:2 *thy sins be forgiven thee.* Jesus had the power to forgive sins, not just to declare that they had been forgiven. God alone can forgive sins. If Jesus could do this, he was God.

9:10 *publicans and sinners,* i.e., "tax-collectors and sinners." The sinners were ordinary people who did not keep all the minute prescriptions of the ceremonial laws—especially those dealing with food and social customs—that the Pharisees prized so highly. The Pharisees criticized Jesus for eating and drinking with both kinds of people, and for befriending them as well. It was against this self-righteousness that Jesus told the story about the Pharisee and the tax collector who went to the temple to pray (Luke 18:9–14).

I. THE QUESTION ABOUT FASTING (CF. MK 2:18–22; LK 5:33–39)

9:14 Mk 2:18–22 Lk 5:33–39 18:12 **9:15** Jn 3:29 Acts 13:2; 14:23

14¶Then came to him the disciples of John, saying, Why do we and the Pharisees fast oft, but thy disciples fast not?
15And Jesus said unto them, Can the children of the bridechamber mourn, as long as the bridegroom is with them? but the days will come, when the bridegroom shall be taken from them, and then shall they fast.
16No man putteth a piece of new cloth unto an old garment, for that which is put in to fill it up taketh from the garment, and the rent is made worse.

9:17☆

17Neither do men put new wine into old bottles: else the bottles break, and the wine runneth out, and the bottles perish: but they put new wine into new bottles, and both are preserved.

J. RAISING THE DEAD (CF. MK 5:21–43; LK 8:40–56)

9:18☆ Mk 5:22–43 Lk 8:41–56

18¶While he spake these things unto them, behold, there came a certain ruler, and worshipped him, saying, My daughter is even now dead: but come and lay thy hand upon her, and she shall live.
19And Jesus arose, and followed him, and *so did* his disciples.
20¶And, behold, a woman, which was diseased with an issue of blood twelve years, came behind *him*, and touched the hem of his garment:
21For she said within herself, If I may but touch his garment, I shall be whole.

9:22 Mt 9:29; 15:28 Mk 10:52 Lk 7:50; 17:19 18:42 **9:23** 2 Chron 35:25 Jer 9:17, 18 **9:24** Jn 11:11–13 Acts 20:10 **9:26** Mt 4:24 Mk 1:28, 45 Lk 4:14; 5:15 7:17

22But Jesus turned him about, and when he saw her, he said, Daughter, be of good comfort; thy faith hath made thee whole. And the woman was made whole from that hour.
23And when Jesus came into the ruler's house, and saw the minstrels and the people making a noise,
24He said unto them, Give place: for the maid is not dead, but sleepeth. And they laughed him to scorn.
25But when the people were put forth, he went in, and took her by the hand, and the maid arose.
26And the fame hereof went abroad into all that land.

K. MAKING THE BLIND SEE AND THE DUMB TALK

9:27 Mt 15:22; 20:30 Mk 10:47 Lk 18:38

27¶And when Jesus departed thence, two blind men followed him, crying, and saying, *Thou* Son of David, have mercy on us.
28And when he was come into the house, the blind men came to him: and Jesus saith unto them, Believe ye that I am able to do this? They said unto him, Yea, Lord.
29Then touched he their eyes, saying, According to your faith be it unto you.

9:30 Ps 146:8 Lk 5:14 **9:31** Mk 7:36 **9:32** Lk 11:14, 15

30And their eyes were opened; and Jesus straitly charged them, saying, See *that* no man know *it*.
31But they, when they were departed, spread abroad his fame in all that country.
32¶As they went out, behold, they brought to him a dumb man possessed with a devil.
33And when the devil was cast out, the dumb spake: and the multitudes marvelled, saying, It was never so seen in Israel.

9:17 *bottles*, i.e., "wineskins."
9:18 The raising of the dead is one of the Bible's rarest miracles. Of the various miracles performed by Jesus, this was the one he employed the fewest times. There have been no empirically verified evidences for this sort of miracle in our generation. This does not rule out miracles; it only means some kinds of miracles are more common than others.

34 But the Pharisees said, He casteth out devils through the prince of the
devils.

9:34 Mt 12:24 Mk 3:22 Lk 11:15 Jn 7:20

V. THE TWELVE SENT AND FOREWARNED (9:35—10:42)

A. THE NEED FOR LABORERS

35 And Jesus went about all the cities and villages, teaching in their
synagogues, and preaching the gospel of the kingdom, and healing every
sickness and every disease among the people.
36 ¶But when he saw the multitudes, he was moved with compassion on
them, because they fainted, and were scattered abroad, as sheep having no
shepherd.
37 Then saith he unto his disciples, The harvest truly *is* plenteous, but the
labourers *are* few;
38 Pray ye therefore the Lord of the harvest, that he will send forth
labourers into his harvest.

9:35 Mt 4:23
9:37 Lk 10:2 Jn 4:35
☆**9:38** Acts 13:2 2 Thess 3:1

B. THE TWELVE AND THEIR MISSION (CF. MK 6:7–13; LK 9:1–6)

10 AND when he had called unto *him* his twelve disciples, he gave
them power *against* unclean spirits, to cast them out, and to heal all
manner of sickness and all manner of disease.
2 Now the names of the twelve apostles are these; The first, Simon, who is
called Peter, and Andrew his brother; James *the son* of Zeb′e-dee, and John
his brother;
3 Philip, and Bartholomew; Thomas, and Matthew the publican; James
the son of Al-phæ′us, and Leb-bæ′us, whose surname was Thad-dæ′us;
4 Simon the Canaanite, and Judas Iscariot, who also betrayed him.
5 These twelve Jesus sent forth, and commanded them, saying, Go not
into the way of the Gentiles, and into *any* city of the Sa-mar′i-tans enter ye
not:
6 But go rather to the lost sheep of the house of Israel.
7 And as ye go, preach, saying, The kingdom of heaven is at hand.
8 Heal the sick, cleanse the lepers, raise the dead, cast out devils: freely ye
have received, freely give.
9 Provide neither gold, nor silver, nor brass in your purses,
10 Nor scrip for *your* journey, neither two coats, neither shoes, nor yet
staves: for the workman is worthy of his meat.
11 And into whatsoever city or town ye shall enter, inquire who in it is
worthy; and there abide till ye go thence.
12 And when ye come into an house, salute it.
13 And if the house be worthy, let your peace come upon it: but if it be not
worthy, let your peace return to you.
14 And whosoever shall not receive you, nor hear your words, when ye
depart out of that house or city, shake off the dust of your feet.

10:1 Mk 3:13; 6:7 Lk 6:13; 9:1
10:2 Jn 1:42
☆**10:4** Jn 13:26
10:5 2 Kgs 17:24 Jn 4:9
10:6 Isa 53:6 Jer 50:6, 17 Mt 15:24 Acts 3:25, 26 13:46
☆**10:7**
☆**10:8** Mk 6:12
10:9, 10 Mk 6:8–11 Lk 9:3–5; 10:7 22:35 Acts 13:51; 18:6 1 Cor 9:7–10 1 Tim 5:17, 18
10:14 Acts 13:51

9:38 Jesus urged us to pray that God will send forth laborers into the harvest fields. Thus, there are some things that do not happen because believers have not prayed. Moreover, the command indicates that if we do pray, we can be sure that God will affirmatively answer this prayer. The power of prayer is entrusted to us for the fulfilling of the Great Commission.

10:4 *Simon the Canaanite* better rendered as "Simon the Zealot" (NASB). "Zealot" is a word derived from the Greek name *Kananaios*, which in turn was derived from the Aramaic word *kan'an*, meaning "zealous," or "zealot." Some translators have used the word Cananaean or Zealot. Maybe Simon was a former member of the radical segment of the Zealots who endeavored to overthrow Roman power by revolutionary means.

10:7, 8 *is at hand*, or, "has arrived," or, "is near." Jesus sent forth the twelve to preach the gospel. He gave his followers power to raise the dead, cast out demons, and the like. These signs of the kingdom were meant to show the multitudes that the message of the disciples was from God and should be believed.

10:15 Mt 11:23, 24; 2 Pet 2:6; Jude 7

15 Verily I say unto you, It shall be more tolerable for the land of Sodom
and Go-mor′rha in the day of judgment, than for that city.

C. CHRIST'S SUFFERING SERVANTS (CF. MK 13:9–13; LK 21:12–19)

10:16 Mk 13:8–13; Lk 21:12–19; 1 Cor 14:20
10:17 Acts 5:40
10:18 Acts 12:1; 24:10
10:19 Ex 4:12; Jer 1:7; Lk 12:11, 12
10:20☆ 2 Sam 23:2; Acts 4:8; 6:10
10:21 Mic 7:6

16 ¶Behold, I send you forth as sheep in the midst of wolves: be ye
therefore wise as serpents, and harmless as doves.
17 But beware of men: for they will deliver you up to the councils, and
they will scourge you in their synagogues;
18 And ye shall be brought before governors and kings for my sake, for a
testimony against them and the Gentiles.
19 But when they deliver you up, take no thought how or what ye shall
speak: for it shall be given you in that same hour what ye shall speak.
20 For it is not ye that speak, but the Spirit of your Father which speaketh
in you.
21 And the brother shall deliver up the brother to death, and the father the
child: and the children shall rise up against *their* parents, and cause them to
be put to death.

10:22 Gal 6:9

22 And ye shall be hated of all *men* for my name's sake: but he that
endureth to the end shall be saved.

10:23 Mt 16:28; Acts 14:6

23 But when they persecute you in this city, flee ye into another: for verily
I say unto you, Ye shall not have gone over the cities of Israel, till the Son
of man be come.

D. THE ENCOURAGEMENT FOR SUFFERING SERVANTS (CF. LK 12:2–9)

10:24 Lk 6:40; Jn 13:16; 15:20
10:25☆ Mt 9:34
10:26 Lk 12:1–9
10:27 Lk 12:3
10:28☆ Isa 8:13; Jer 1:8; Heb 10:31
10:29 Lk 12:6
10:30 Lk 21:18; Acts 27:34
10:32 Lk 12:8; Rom 10:9; Rev 3:5
10:33 Lk 9:26; 2 Tim 2:12

24 The disciple is not above *his* master, nor the servant above his lord.
25 It is enough for the disciple that he be as his master, and the servant as
his lord. If they have called the master of the house Be-el′ze-bub, how much
more *shall they call* them of his household?
26 Fear them not therefore: for there is nothing covered, that shall not be
revealed; and hid, that shall not be known.
27 What I tell you in darkness, *that* speak ye in light: and what ye hear in
the ear, *that* preach ye upon the housetops.
28 And fear not them which kill the body, but are not able to kill the soul:
but rather fear him which is able to destroy both soul and body in hell.
29 Are not two sparrows sold for a farthing? and one of them shall not fall
on the ground without your Father.
30 But the very hairs of your head are all numbered.
31 Fear ye not therefore, ye are of more value than many sparrows.
32 Whosoever therefore shall confess me before men, him will I confess
also before my Father which is in heaven.
33 But whosoever shall deny me before men, him will I also deny before
my Father which is in heaven.

10:20 Jesus promised that when his followers were haled before magistrates and kings, the Spirit of their Father would be with them. The Spirit would give them words to say—this was the surest guarantee that they would say the right thing at the right time and that their *words would be accompanied by the power of the* Spirit. Their testimony would be effective.

10:25 *Beelzebub*, a Greek word derived from the Philistine deity *Be-el-zebul* ("lord of the flies"). (See note on 2 Kings 1:2.) In the New Testament the name Beelzebub comes from an Aramaic form meaning "lord of the high house" or "lord of the temple." In Jesus' day the people believed that Beelzebub was the leader of the demons. Thus, we can assume it is simply another name for Satan. Jesus was accused by the Pharisees of being a co-worker with Beelzebub in casting out demons from people (12:24, 27; Mark 3:22; Luke 11:15, 18, 19).

10:28 The Scriptures teach four things about *hell*, or *gehenna*: (1) it is a prepared place (25:41); (2) it is a place which endures forever (25:46; Isa. 33:14; Rev. 20:10); (3) it is a place of suffering (Mark 9:47–49); (4) it is a place of fire and sulphur (Rev. 14:10; 20:15).

E. THE SERVANT'S CROSS

34 Think not that I am come to send peace on earth: I came not to send
peace, but a sword.
35 For I am come to set a man at variance against his father, and the
daughter against her mother, and the daughter in law against her mother in
law.
36 And a man's foes *shall be* they of his own household.
37 He that loveth father or mother more than me is not worthy of me: and
he that loveth son or daughter more than me is not worthy of me.
38 And he that taketh not his cross, and followeth after me, is not worthy
of me.
39 He that findeth his life shall lose it: and he that loseth his life for my
sake shall find it.

☆**10:34** Lk 12:51–53
☆**10:35** Mt 10:21
10:36 Mic 7:6
10:37 Lk 14:26
10:38 Mt 16:24; Mk 8:34; Lk 9:23; 14:27
10:39 Mt 16:25; Mk 8:35; Lk 9:24; 17:33; Jn 12:25

F. THE SERVANT'S REWARD

40 ¶He that receiveth you receiveth me, and he that receiveth me receiveth
him that sent me.
41 He that receiveth a prophet in the name of a prophet shall receive a
prophet's reward; and he that receiveth a righteous man in the name of a
righteous man shall receive a righteous man's reward.
42 And whosoever shall give to drink unto one of these little ones a cup of
cold *water* only in the name of a disciple, verily I say unto you, he shall in
no wise lose his reward.

☆**10:40** Mt 18:5; Mk 9:37; Lk 9:48; 10:16; Jn 12:44; 13:20; Gal 4:14
10:41 2 Kgs 4:8
10:42 Mt 25:40; Mk 9:41; Heb 6:10, 11

VI. THE CLAIMS OF JESUS (11:1—12:50)

A. JESUS' RESPONSE TO JOHN'S LAST MESSAGE (CF. LK 7:18–35)

11 AND it came to pass, when Jesus had made an end of commanding
his twelve disciples, he departed thence to teach and to preach in
their cities.
2 Now when John had heard in the prison the works of Christ, he sent two
of his disciples,
3 And said unto him, Art thou he that should come, or do we look for
another?
4 Jesus answered and said unto them, Go and shew John again those
things which ye do hear and see:
5 The blind receive their sight, and the lame walk, the lepers are cleansed,
and the deaf hear, the dead are raised up, and the poor have the gospel
preached to them.
6 And blessed is *he*, whosoever shall not be offended in me.

☆**11:1**
11:2 Mt 14:3; Lk 7:18–35
☆**11:3** Num 24:17; Deut 18:15; Mal 3:1; Jn 6:14
11:5 Isa 42:7; 61:1; Lk 4:18, 19; Jn 5:36; Jas 2:5
11:6 Mt 13:57; 1 Pet 2:8

10:34, 35 Jesus and his gospel are great dividers. Families are rent asunder when some believe and others do not. Whoever puts even the dearest loved one before the Son of God is not worthy of the Savior. We are not to expect temporal peace and outward prosperity. Instead, there is the sword, which is always the symbol of division, disaffection, and even judgment.
10:40 Jesus assures us that some who hear us will reject our message, but others will receive it. Whoever honors Christ's ambassadors honors him, and whoever dishonors his ambassadors dishonors him. There is a suitable reward for those who serve Christ faithfully.
11:1 *to teach and to preach in their cities.* Luke 10:1 remarks, "The Lord appointed other seventy also, and sent them two and two before his face into every city and place, whither he himself would come."
11:3 *Art thou he that should come, or do we look for another?* John had baptized Jesus. He had seen the endorsement of Jesus as Messiah by the Father and the Holy Spirit. Now he is in jail, despondent, and without the help of the Messiah whom he had announced to all men. Doubtless he expected the Messiah to deliver him. Thus he sends his disciples with the question addressed to Jesus, so that he might be reassured that indeed he is the Messiah. Jesus performed miracles before the disciples and sent them back to tell John that his credentials showed he was indeed the Messiah. Shortly thereafter John was killed, and Jesus was moving steadily toward Jerusalem—for his own date with destiny at Calvary.

7 ¶And as they departed, Jesus began to say unto the multitudes concerning John, What went ye out into the wilderness to see? A reed shaken with the wind?

8 But what went ye out for to see? A man clothed in soft raiment? behold, they that wear soft *clothing* are in kings' houses.

11:9 Lk 1:76

9 But what went ye out for to see? A prophet? yea, I say unto you, and more than a prophet.

11:10 Isa 40:3; Mal 3:1; Mk 1:2

10 For this is *he*, of whom it is written, Behold, I send my messenger before thy face, which shall prepare thy way before thee.

11:11☆

11 Verily I say unto you, Among them that are born of women there hath not risen a greater than John the Baptist: notwithstanding he that is least in the kingdom of heaven is greater than he.

11:12 Lk 16:16

12 And from the days of John the Baptist until now the kingdom of heaven suffereth violence, and the violent take it by force.

13 For all the prophets and the law prophesied until John.

11:14 Mal 4:5; Mt 17:11–13; Mk 9:11–13; Lk 1:17; Jn 1:23

14 And if ye will receive *it*, this is E-li'as, which was for to come.

11:15 Mt 13:9, 43; Mk 4:9, 23; Lk 8:8; Rev 2:7, 11, 17, 29; 3:6, 13, 22; 13:9

15 He that hath ears to hear, let him hear.

16 ¶But whereunto shall I liken this generation? It is like unto children sitting in the markets, and calling unto their fellows,

17 And saying, We have piped unto you, and ye have not danced; we have mourned unto you, and ye have not lamented.

11:18☆ Mt 3:4; Lk 1:15

18 For John came neither eating nor drinking, and they say, He hath a devil.

11:19 Mt 9:10, 11; Lk 15:2

19 The Son of man came eating and drinking, and they say, Behold a man gluttonous, and a winebibber, a friend of publicans and sinners. But wisdom is justified of her children.

B. THE REBUKE TO THE IMPENITENT CITIES (CF. LK 10:12–15)

11:20 Lk 10:12–15

20 ¶Then began he to upbraid the cities wherein most of his mighty works were done, because they repented not:

11:21☆ Mk 8:22, 23; Lk 6:17, 18; 9:10, 11; 10:13–15

21 Woe unto thee, Cho-ra'zin! woe unto thee, Beth-sa'i-da! for if the mighty works, which were done in you, had been done in Tyre and Si'don, they would have repented long ago in sackcloth and ashes.

11:22 Ezek 26:19, 20; Mt 10:15

22 But I say unto you, It shall be more tolerable for Tyre and Si'don at the day of judgment, than for you.

11:23 Isa 14:13, 15; Ezek 31:14; 32:18, 24; Rev 1:18

23 And thou, Ca-per'na-um, which art exalted unto heaven, shalt be brought down to hell: for if the mighty works, which have been done in thee, had been done in Sodom, it would have remained until this day.

24 But I say unto you, That it shall be more tolerable for the land of Sodom in the day of judgment, than for thee.

C. JESUS REVEALS HIS FATHER AND EXTENDS HIS INVITATION (CF. LK 10:21, 22)

11:25 Lk 10:21–22; 1 Cor 1:27; 2:7, 8; 2 Cor 3:14; 4:6; Eph 1:17, 18; 3:3, 4

25 ¶At that time Jesus answered and said, I thank thee, O Father, Lord of heaven and earth, because thou hast hid these things from the wise and prudent, and hast revealed them unto babes.

11:11 Jesus said that the lesser in the kingdom of heaven are greater than John the Baptist. While this statement is enigmatic, it seems that what is meant is this: as great and good as John was, he was still in the flesh, full of infirmity and imperfections, whereas the lowest saint in the kingdom of heaven is already glorified and "greater" than any saint still on earth.

Dispensationalists think this refers to the position of John the Baptist under the old dispensation, which has been superseded since the crucifixion and resurrection of Jesus and the outpouring of the Holy Spirit. The saints in the new dispensation occupy a higher position than that of John under the old one.

11:18 *He hath a devil.* Those who reject the gospel will use every excuse possible to justify their disbelief. John came as a mourner who neither ate nor drank, and he was rejected. Jesus came eating and drinking, and they rejected him. Unbelievers are perverse. When they spurn the grace of God, they want everyone to follow in their footsteps and join them in hell.

11:21 *Tyre and Sidon*, cities destroyed by God for their wickedness. *Sidon* is called "Sodom" in 11:23.†

26 Even so, Father: for so it seemed good in thy sight.
27 All things are delivered unto me of my Father: and no man knoweth
the Son, but the Father; neither knoweth any man the Father, save the Son,
and *he* to whomsoever the Son will reveal *him.*
28 ¶Come unto me, all *ye* that labour and are heavy laden, and I will give
you rest.
29 Take my yoke upon you, and learn of me; for I am meek and lowly in
heart: and ye shall find rest unto your souls.
30 For my yoke *is* easy, and my burden is light.

11:27 Mt 28:18; Jn 1:18; 3:35; 6:46; 10:15; 17:2, 26; 1 Cor 15:27
☆11:29 Jer 6:16; Jn 13:15; Eph 4:20; Phil 2:5–8; 1 Pet 2:21; 1 Jn 2:6; 5:3

D. PLUCKING WHEAT ON THE SABBATH (CF. MK 2:23–28; LK 6:1–5)

12 AT that time Jesus went on the sabbath day through the corn; and
his disciples were an hungred, and began to pluck the ears of corn,
and to eat.
2 But when the Pharisees saw *it,* they said unto him, Behold, thy disciples
do that which is not lawful to do upon the sabbath day.
3 But he said unto them, Have ye not read what David did, when he was
an hungred, and they that were with him;
4 How he entered into the house of God, and did eat the shewbread,
which was not lawful for him to eat, neither for them which were with him,
but only for the priests?
5 Or have ye not read in the law, how that on the sabbath days the priests
in the temple profane the sabbath, and are blameless?
6 But I say unto you, That in this place is *one* greater than the temple.
7 But if ye had known what *this* meaneth, I will have mercy, and not
sacrifice, ye would not have condemned the guiltless.
8 For the Son of man is Lord even of the sabbath day.

12:1 Deut 23:25; Mk 2:23–28; Lk 6:1–5
12:2 Ex 20:10; Deut 5:14; Mt 12:10; Lk 13:14; 14:3; Jn 5:10; 7:23; 9:16
☆12:3 1 Sam 21:6
☆12:4 Ex 25:30; 29:32, 33; Lev 24:5, 9
☆12:5 Num 28:9; Jn 7:22
☆12:6 Mal 3:1; Mt 12:41, 42; Lk 11:31, 32; Jn 2:19–21
12:7 1 Sam 15:22; Hos 6:6; Mic 6:6–8

E. HEALING ON THE SABBATH (CF. MK 3:1–6; LK 6:1–11)

9 And when he was departed thence, he went into their synagogue:
10 ¶And, behold, there was a man which had *his* hand withered. And they
asked him, saying, Is it lawful to heal on the sabbath days? that they might
accuse him.
11 And he said unto them, What man shall there be among you, that shall
have one sheep, and if it fall into a pit on the sabbath day, will he not lay
hold on it, and lift *it* out?
12 How much then is a man better than a sheep? Wherefore it is lawful to
do well on the sabbath days.

12:9 Mk 3:1–6; Lk 6:6–11
12:10 Lk 13:14; 14:3; Jn 9:16
☆12:11 Deut 22:4; Lk 14:5
☆12:12 Mt 10:31

11:29 Believers have a yoke for their necks and a crown for their heads. One signifies identification with Christ in his death and the sufferings attendant thereto; the other signifies participation in Christ's glory, when the believers shall wear crowns on their heads and enjoy everlasting blessedness. Becoming a Christian does not deliver anyone from suffering, but such is a *light affliction* (*2 Cor. 4:17*) *compared to* the glory that shall be revealed.

12:3–5 In response to his critics, Jesus often referred to the Old Testament Scriptures to explain and justify his conduct. He referred to two incidents: (1) David and his followers ate the bread which was reserved for the priests (1 Sam. 21:1–6) and said human need comes before ceremonial regulations; (2) the priests worked on the sabbath by offering sacrifices. If they could break one law to keep another, so Jesus could breach the sabbath law in the larger interests of the kingdom of God.

12:4 See note on Mark 2:25 regarding *shewbread.*

12:6 *in this place is one greater than the temple.* The glory of God had rested on the tabernacle and on the Solomonic temple; in Jesus dwelt all the fullness of the Godhead bodily. Since Jesus as God was present among them, the temple took on new significance. Without that presence it was a barren and useless heap of stones.

12:11 This verse asks a rhetorical question. To the Pharisees, the implied answer would be, "Of course we would."†

12:12 The Jews performed works of necessity and mercy on the sabbath. They watered and fed their animals and rescued those that fell into pits. They thought more of their property than they did of suffering humanity. Jewish respect for the law turned into legalism, in which the spirit was deadened and immeasurable harm was wrought in the heart. Legalism is still alive today. There are many whose legalism is no better than that of the contemptible Pharisees, who used the law as a club to assume power over others.

12:14 Mt 26:4 Mk 14:1 Lk 22:2 Jn 5:18 Jn 7:30, 44 11:53

13 Then saith he to the man, Stretch forth thine hand. And he stretched *it*
forth; and it was restored whole, like as the other.
14 ¶Then the Pharisees went out, and held a council against him, how they
might destroy him.

F. A MULTITUDE OF HEALINGS (CF. MK 3:7–12; LK 6:17–19)

12:15 Mk 3:7 Heb 4:13

15 But when Jesus knew *it*, he withdrew himself from thence: and great
multitudes followed him, and he healed them all;
16 And charged them that they should not make him known:
17 That it might be fulfilled which was spoken by E-sai′as the prophet,
saying,

12:18–21☆ Isa 42:1–4

18 Behold my servant, whom I have chosen; my beloved, in whom my soul
is well pleased: I will put my spirit upon him, and he shall shew judgment
to the Gentiles.
19 He shall not strive, nor cry; neither shall any man hear his voice in the
streets.
20 A bruised reed shall he not break, and smoking flax shall he not
quench, till he send forth judgment unto victory.
21 And in his name shall the Gentiles trust.

G. THE PRINCE OF DEVILS VERSUS THE SON OF DAVID
(CF. MK 3:20–30; LK 11:14–23)

12:22 Mk 3:20–30 Lk 11:14–23

22 ¶Then was brought unto him one possessed with a devil, blind, and
dumb: and he healed him, insomuch that the blind and dumb both spake
and saw.
23 And all the people were amazed, and said, Is not this the son of David?

12:24☆ Mt 9:34 **12:25** Ps 139:2 Mt 9:4 Jn 2:25 Gal 5:15

24 But when the Pharisees heard *it*, they said, This *fellow* doth not cast out
devils, but by Be-el′ze-bub the prince of the devils.
25 And Jesus knew their thoughts, and said unto them, Every kingdom
divided against itself is brought to desolation; and every city or house
divided against itself shall not stand:
26 And if Satan cast out Satan, he is divided against himself; how shall
then his kingdom stand?

12:27 Mt 9:34

27 And if I by Be-el′ze-bub cast out devils, by whom do your children cast
them out? therefore they shall be your judges.

12:28 Lk 1:33 17:20, 21 Heb 12:28 **12:30** Mk 9:40 Lk 9:50; 11:23 **12:31, 32☆** Mt 11:19 Lk 12:10 Jn 7:12 1 Tim 1:13 Heb 10:26 6:4–6 1 Jn 5:16

28 But if I cast out devils by the Spirit of God, then the kingdom of God
is come unto you.
29 Or else how can one enter into a strong man's house, and spoil his
goods, except he first bind the strong man? and then he will spoil his house.
30 He that is not with me is against me; and he that gathereth not with me
scattereth abroad.
31 ¶Wherefore I say unto you, All manner of sin and blasphemy shall be
forgiven unto men: but the blasphemy *against* the *Holy* Ghost shall not be
forgiven unto men.
32 And whosoever speaketh a word against the Son of man, it shall be

---

12:18–21 Christ as God was equal in power and glory with the Father (John 17:5, 24; Phil. 2:6). As the God-man, *the mediator, he received power and glory from* the Father (Heb. 8:6; 9:15; 12:24). The Father *put [his] Spirit upon him.* Christ had the Spirit without measure (John 3:34). He was filled with the Spirit (Luke 4:1). And he offered himself on Calvary by the eternal Spirit (Heb. 9:14).

12:24 The Pharisees believed in miracles and regarded what Jesus did as miraculous. But they attributed the miracle to Beelzebub, i.e., Satan. By this accusation they blasphemed, because they attributed to Satan what was the true work of God. They posited that Jesus was in league with Satan himself and had derived his power from him.

12:31, 32 See note on Mark 3:29 regarding blasphemy of the Holy Spirit.

forgiven him: but whosoever speaketh against the Holy Ghost, it shall not
be forgiven him, neither in this world, neither in the *world* to come.
33 Either make the tree good, and his fruit good; or else make the tree
corrupt, and his fruit corrupt: for the tree is known by *his* fruit.

12:33 Mt 7:15–20 Lk 6:43–45

34 O generation of vipers, how can ye, being evil, speak good things? for
out of the abundance of the heart the mouth speaketh.

12:34 Mt 3:7; 23:33

35 A good man out of the good treasure of the heart bringeth forth good
things: and an evil man out of the evil treasure bringeth forth evil things.
36 But I say unto you, That every idle word that men shall speak, they
shall give account thereof in the day of judgment.

☆**12:36** Eph 5:4

37 For by thy words thou shalt be justified, and by thy words thou shalt be
condemned.

H. ASKING FOR A SIGN: THE RETURN OF THE UNCLEAN SPIRIT (CF. LK 11:29–32)

38 ¶Then certain of the scribes and of the Pharisees answered, saying,
Master, we would see a sign from thee.
39 But he answered and said unto them, An evil and adulterous generation
seeketh after a sign; and there shall no sign be given to it, but the sign of the
prophet Jonas:

12:38 Mt 16:1–4 Mk 8:11, 12 Lk 11:16, 29–32 Jn 2:18 1 Cor 1:22
12:39 Jn 4:48

40 For as Jonas was three days and three nights in the whale's belly; so
shall the Son of man be three days and three nights in the heart of the earth.

☆**12:40** Jonah 1:17

41 The men of Nin′e-veh shall rise in judgment with this generation, and
shall condemn it: because they repented at the preaching of Jonas; and,
behold, a greater than Jonas *is* here.

12:41 Jonah 3:5 Rom 9:5

42 The queen of the south shall rise up in the judgment with this
generation, and shall condemn it: for she came from the uttermost parts of
the earth to hear the wisdom of Solomon; and, behold, a greater than
Solomon *is* here.

12:42 1 Kgs 10:1 2 Chron 9:1 Mt 12:6

43 When the unclean spirit is gone out of a man, he walketh through dry
places, seeking rest, and findeth none.

☆**12:43** Lk 11:24–26 1 Pet 5:8

44 Then he saith, I will return into my house from whence I came out; and
when he is come, he findeth *it* empty, swept, and garnished.
45 Then goeth he, and taketh with himself seven other spirits more wicked
than himself, and they enter in and dwell there: and the last *state* of that
man is worse than the first. Even so shall it be also unto this wicked
generation.

12:45 2 Pet 2:20

I. JESUS' TRUE FAMILY (CF. MK 3:31–35; LK 8:19–21)

46 ¶While he yet talked to the people, behold, *his* mother and his brethren
stood without, desiring to speak with him.
47 Then one said unto him, Behold, thy mother and thy brethren stand
without, desiring to speak with thee.
48 But he answered and said unto him that told him, Who is my mother?
and who are my brethren?

12:46 Mk 3:31–35; 6:3 Lk 8:19–21 Jn 7:3–5 Acts 1:14 1 Cor 9:5 Gal 1:19

12:36 What we say tells others what we really think. Idle or careless words will be judged. Words depend upon the intended meaning, and upon the heart intention for their goodness or badness. (See note on 2 Cor. 5:10 for a look at Christ's judgment.)

12:40 Jonah is a type of Christ. The difference was this: Jonah was imprisoned for his own sins; Christ was imprisoned in hell for our sins. Some who think the Book of Jonah is not factual disregard Jesus' words as support for the historicity of Jonah's imprisonment. But since Jesus mentions Jonah in connection with the queen of Sheba, a historical figure, we must assume that the Book of Jonah is historical fact. Nothing in the Book of Jonah occasions any reason to suppose that it is fictional.

12:43 *walketh through dry places*, i.e., "goes into the deserts."†

49 And he stretched forth his hand toward his disciples, and said, Behold my mother and my brethren!

12:50 Jn 14:23; 15:14 Col 3:11 Heb 2:11

50 For whosoever shall do the will of my Father which is in heaven, the same is my brother, and sister, and mother.

VII. SEVEN PARABLES OF THE KINGDOM (13:1–52)

A. (1) THE PARABLE OF THE SOWER

1. The Story Itself (Cf. Mk 4:1–9; Lk 8:4–8)

13:1 Mk 4:1–20 Lk 8:4–15

13 THE same day went Jesus out of the house, and sat by the sea side. 2 And great multitudes were gathered together unto him, so that he went into a ship, and sat; and the whole multitude stood on the shore.

13:3☆

3 And he spake many things unto them in parables, saying, Behold, a sower went forth to sow;

4 And when he sowed, some *seeds* fell by the way side, and the fowls came and devoured them up:

5 Some fell upon stony places, where they had not much earth: and forthwith they sprung up, because they had no deepness of earth:

6 And when the sun was up, they were scorched; and because they had no root, they withered away.

7 And some fell among thorns; and the thorns sprung up, and choked them:

8 But other fell into good ground, and brought forth fruit, some an hundredfold, some sixtyfold, some thirtyfold.

9 Who hath ears to hear, let him hear.

2. Why Jesus Used Parables (Cf. Mk 4:10–12; Lk 8:9, 10)

13:10☆

10 And the disciples came, and said unto him, Why speakest thou unto them in parables?

13:11 Mt 11:25; 16:17 1 Cor 2:10 Col 1:26, 27 1 Jn 2:27

11 He answered and said unto them, Because it is given unto you to know the mysteries of the kingdom of heaven, but to them it is not given.

13:12 Mk 4:25 Lk 19:26

12 For whosoever hath, to him shall be given, and he shall have more abundance: but whosoever hath not, from him shall be taken away even that he hath.

13:13 Jer 5:21

13 Therefore speak I to them in parables: because they seeing see not; and hearing they hear not, neither do they understand.

13:14 Isa 6:9, 10 Ezek 12:2 Jn 12:39, 40 Acts 28:26, 27 Rom 11:8 2 Cor 3:14

14 And in them is fulfilled the prophecy of E-sai'as, which saith, By hearing ye shall hear, and shall not understand; and seeing ye shall see, and shall not perceive:

15 For this people's heart is waxed gross, and *their* ears are dull of hearing, and their eyes they have closed; lest at any time they should see with *their* eyes, and hear with *their* ears, and should understand with *their* heart, and should be converted, and I should heal them.

16 But blessed *are* your eyes, for they see: and your ears, for they hear.

13:17 Lk 10:23, 24 Jn 8:56 Heb 11:13 1 Pet 1:10–12

17 For verily I say unto you, That many prophets and righteous *men* have desired to see *those things* which ye see, and have not seen *them;* and to hear *those things* which ye hear, and have not heard *them.*

13:3 *A parable, or illustration, contains an earthly story* with a heavenly meaning. It is spoken in terms of the language and figures of that day. No parable should be pressed beyond the central meaning, which is easily discerned. The details cannot be properly understood apart from the central thought.

13:10ff *Why speakest thou unto them in parables?* Jesus responded to the inquiry of his disciples. He said that the disciples could find the explanation of parables simply by asking him. But to those who rejected his person, the spiritual meaning of the parables would be unclear. To such people, parables were interesting fables but had no other meaning.

3. The Parable of the Sower Explained (Cf. Mk 4:13–20; Lk 8:11–15)

18 ¶Hear ye therefore the parable of the sower.
19 When any one heareth the word of the kingdom, and understandeth *it*
not, then cometh the wicked *one*, and catcheth away that which was sown in
his heart. This is he which received seed by the way side.
20 But he that received the seed into stony places, the same is he that
heareth the word, and anon with joy receiveth it;
21 Yet hath he not root in himself, but dureth for a while: for when
tribulation or persecution ariseth because of the word, by and by he is
offended.
22 He also that received seed among the thorns is he that heareth the
word; and the care of this world, and the deceitfulness of riches, choke the
word, and he becometh unfruitful.
23 But he that received seed into the good ground is he that heareth the
word, and understandeth *it;* which also beareth fruit, and bringeth forth,
some an hundredfold, some sixty, some thirty.

☆**13:18**
☆**13:19** Ezek 11:19; 2 Cor 4:3, 4; Eph 4:17, 18
13:21 Col 2:7
13:22 Jer 4:3; Ezek 33:31; Mt 19:23; Eph 2:2; 1 Tim 6:9, 10, 17; 2 Tim 4:4, 10
☆**13:23** Gen 26:12

B. (2) THE GOOD SEED AND THE TARES (CF. MK 4:18, 19)

24 ¶Another parable put he forth unto them, saying, The kingdom of
heaven is likened unto a man which sowed good seed in his field:
25 But while men slept, his enemy came and sowed tares among the wheat,
and went his way.
26 But when the blade was sprung up, and brought forth fruit, then
appeared the tares also.
27 So the servants of the householder came and said unto him, Sir, didst
not thou sow good seed in thy field? from whence then hath it tares?
28 He said unto them, An enemy hath done this. The servants said unto
him, Wilt thou then that we go and gather them up?
29 But he said, Nay; lest while ye gather up the tares, ye root up also the
wheat with them.
30 Let both grow together until the harvest: and in the time of harvest I
will say to the reapers, Gather ye together first the tares, and bind them in
bundles to burn them: but gather the wheat into my barn.

13:24 Mk 4:26–29
☆**13:30** Mt 3:12

D. (3) THE MUSTARD SEED (CF. MK 4:30–32; LK 13:18, 19)

31 ¶Another parable put he forth unto them, saying, The kingdom of
heaven is like to a grain of mustard seed, which a man took, and sowed in
his field:
32 Which indeed is the least of all seeds: but when it is grown, it is the
greatest among herbs, and becometh a tree, so that the birds of the air come
and lodge in the branches thereof.

☆**13:31** Gen 1:11, 12; Ps 104:12; Ezek 17:22, 23; 31:6; Dan 4:12, 21; Mk 4:30–32; Lk 13:18, 19
☆**13:32**

13:18ff *This illustration was easily grasped* by Jesus' listeners. They were familiar with the rocky soil they had to cultivate.

13:19 *the wicked one*, i.e., "Satan."

13:23 *beareth fruit, and bringeth forth, some an hundredfold, some sixty, some thirty*, i.e., "produces a crop many times greater than the amount planted—thirty, sixty, or even a hundred times as much."†

13:30 The parable of the wheat and the tares teaches us that there are always true and false believers in the church. We cannot always distinguish between the false and the true. The presence of false believers brings harm to Christ's Body, but harm may also come from human efforts to remove the false from the true. Unbelievers, of course, should be excluded if they can be positively identified. But, as the illustration makes plain, the final separation is made by the judge of all, the Lord Jesus, who makes no mistakes.

13:31, 32 This parable's central teaching is the growth and spread of the gospel throughout the world. Just as the tiny mustard seed becomes a giant tree (see note on 17:20), so the gospel, which begins slowly, will flourish in the end. The existence of the Christian church all around the globe represents a partial fulfillment of this prophetic word.

D. (4) LEAVEN IN THE BREAD (CF. LK 13:20, 21)

13:33☆ Lev 7:13; 23:17 Mt 16:6, 12 Lk 13:20, 21 1 Cor 5:6–8 Gal 5:8, 9 **13:34, 35☆** Ps 78:2, 3 Mk 4:34 Jn 10:6; 16:25 Rom 16:25 1 Cor 2:7 Eph 3:9 Col 1:26

33 ¶Another parable spake he unto them; The kingdom of heaven is like
unto leaven, which a woman took, and hid in three measures of meal, till
the whole was leavened.
34 All these things spake Jesus unto the multitude in parables; and
without a parable spake he not unto them:
35 That it might be fulfilled which was spoken by the prophet, saying, I
will open my mouth in parables; I will utter things which have been kept
secret from the foundation of the world.

E. THE PARABLE OF THE GOOD SEED AND THE TARES EXPLAINED

13:36 Mt 15:15 **13:38** Mk 16:15 Lk 24:27 Jn 8:44 Rom 10:18 Col 1:6 1 Jn 3:7, 8, 10 **13:39** Joel 3:13 Rev 14:15 **13:41** Mt 24:31 25:31–46 **13:42** Mt 8:12; 13:50 22:13 **13:43** Judg 5:31 Prov 4:18 Dan 12:3

36 Then Jesus sent the multitude away, and went into the house: and his
disciples came unto him, saying, Declare unto us the parable of the tares of
the field.
37 He answered and said unto them, He that soweth the good seed is the
Son of man;
38 The field is the world; the good seed are the children of the kingdom;
but the tares are the children of the wicked *one;*
39 The enemy that sowed them is the devil; the harvest is the end of the
world; and the reapers are the angels.
40 As therefore the tares are gathered and burned in the fire; so shall it be
in the end of this world.
41 The Son of man shall send forth his angels, and they shall gather out of
his kingdom all things that offend, and them which do iniquity;
42 And shall cast them into a furnace of fire: there shall be wailing and
gnashing of teeth.
43 Then shall the righteous shine forth as the sun in the kingdom of their
Father. Who hath ears to hear, let him hear.

F. (5) THE TREASURE IN THE FIELD

13:44☆ 1 Cor 6:20 Phil 3:7

44 ¶Again, the kingdom of heaven is like unto treasure hid in a field; the
which when a man hath found, he hideth, and for joy thereof goeth and
selleth all that he hath, and buyeth that field.

G. (6) THE PEARL MERCHANT

13:45☆ **13:46☆**

45 ¶Again, the kingdom of heaven is like unto a merchant man, seeking
goodly pearls:
46 Who, when he had found one pearl of great price, went and sold all that
he had, and bought it.

13:33 Yeast, or leaven, is generally used in an evil sense. It refers to (1) the doctrines of the Pharisees and Sadducees (16:6, 12); (2) ungodly professors of the true faith (1 Cor. 5:6, 7); (3) false teachers (Gal. 5:8, 9); and (4) malice and evil (1 Cor. 5:8). Leaven here suggests its silent permeating power that requires only a small amount in the dough to be effective. Leaven, or yeast, was generally forbidden in the Old Testament except for use with thank-offerings (Lev. 7:13) and with the presentation of the first-fruits of wheat (Lev. 23:17).
13:34, 35 The meaning of Jesus' stories was apparently unclear both to the multitudes and to his own disciples. For Mark tells us, "When he was alone with his disciples, he would explain his meaning to them" (Mark 4:34, TLB).
13:44 The central teaching of this illustration is that the gospel has such value that a person will give up anything and everything to possess that which is the greatest of all things (16:26). Some believe that the discoverer of the treasure is Christ, who gave his all to purchase the church.
13:45, 46 The stories of the pearl and the hidden treasure are similar. When a pearl merchant finds a pearl of real value at a low price, he will sell all he has and buy the one pearl. Salvation is comparable to the pearl of great price, yet it costs us nothing! Jesus paid it all. In the case of the pearl, it may be that Jesus is referring to himself—he is the purchaser; he paid all he had to buy the church for himself. Finding treasure or a pearl means nothing unless what is found is appropriated. Salvation is no blessing until it is appropriated on Christ's terms. Water and bread are valueless until eaten and drunk. An anchor that does not reach the bottom might just as well not be dropped.

H. (7) THE FISHING NET

47 ¶Again, the kingdom of heaven is like unto a net, that was cast into the ☆13:47 Mt 22:10
sea, and gathered of every kind:
48 Which, when it was full, they drew to shore, and sat down, and
gathered the good into vessels, but cast the bad away.
49 So shall it be at the end of the world: the angels shall come forth, and ☆13:49
sever the wicked from among the just,
50 And shall cast them into the furnace of fire: there shall be wailing and 13:50 Mt 8:12
gnashing of teeth.
51 Jesus saith unto them, Have ye understood all these things? They say
unto him, Yea, Lord.
52 Then said he unto them, Therefore every scribe *which is* instructed unto ☆13:52
the kingdom of heaven is like unto a man *that is* an householder, which
bringeth forth out of his treasure *things* new and old.

VIII. JESUS REJECTED AND JOHN BEHEADED (13:53—14:12)

A. JESUS' SECOND REJECTION (CF. MK 6:1–6; LK 4:16–30)

53 ¶And it came to pass, *that* when Jesus had finished these parables, he 13:53 Mt 2:23 Mk 6:1–6 Lk 3:23; 4:16–24
departed thence.
54 And when he was come into his own country, he taught them in their ☆13:54
synagogue, insomuch that they were astonished, and said, Whence hath this
man this wisdom, and *these* mighty works?
55 Is not this the carpenter's son? is not his mother called Mary? and his ☆13:55 Ps 69:8 Mt 12:46 Mk 15:40 Jn 6:42
brethren, James, and Joses, and Simon, and Judas?
56 And his sisters, are they not all with us? Whence then hath this *man* all
these things?
57 And they were offended in him. But Jesus said unto them, A prophet is 13:57 Ps 6 Isa 53:2, 3 Jn 4:44
not without honour, save in his own country, and in his own house.
58 And he did not many mighty works there because of their unbelief.

B. THE BEHEADING OF JOHN THE BAPTIST (CF. MK 6:14–29; LK 9:7–9)

14 AT that time Herod the tetrarch heard of the fame of Jesus, ☆14:1 Mk 6:14–29 Lk 9:7–9 3:19, 20
2 And said unto his servants, This is John the Baptist; he is risen
from the dead; and therefore mighty works do shew forth themselves in
him.

13:47ff The net represents the kingdom of God. When cast into the sea, it catches a mixed company of fishes. So it is with the kingdom of God. Good and bad are caught in its net; at the end of the age, the good will be separated from the bad. This story clearly makes impossible the idea that all people will be saved at last.
13:49 *world,* or, "age."
13:52 *bringeth forth out of his treasure things new and old.* Paraphrased: "from the Old Testament as well as from the New." The paraphrase is, of course, highly anacronistic!†
13:54 *into his own country.* Everyone knew that Jesus performed mighty deeds and spoke words of wisdom. Since he did not have the benefit of advanced education, they wondered how he was able to think and speak as he did. And they wondered where he got the power to perform miracles. They were puzzled because Jesus came from a common family. Joseph was a humble carpenter; his mother was a simple village girl. The only adequate explanation is that Jesus was of divine origin; he was the Son of God. Certainly his knowledge of the Scriptures startled the learned men of his day; he was but twelve years of age when he first talked with the doctors in the temple (Luke 2:41–52).
13:55 See note on Mark 6:3 regarding the family of Jesus.
14:1 This Herod was Herod Antipas. He was the son of Herod the Great, by Malthace, a Samaritan woman. He was born ca. 20 B.C. He ruled over Galilee and Perea. Apparently he believed in the resurrection of the dead, a doctrine affirmed by the Pharisees and denied by the Sadducees. Herod thought Jesus was a resurrected John performing greater miracles than ever before and bringing him more trouble. He was reproached by his own guilty conscience. Jesus was indeed a greater problem; he knew that Herod would do to him what he had done to John. Jesus went away so that Herod could not touch him. Sometimes God's servants should flee rather than remain and be martyred.

14:3☆ 3¶For Herod had laid hold on John, and bound him, and put *him* in
prison for He-ro′di-as′ sake, his brother Philip's wife.
14:4 4For John said unto him, It is not lawful for thee to have her.
Lev 18:16; 20:21 5And when he would have put him to death, he feared the multitude,
Eph 5:11 2 Tim 4:2 because they counted him as a prophet.
14:5 Mt 21:26 6But when Herod's birthday was kept, the daughter of He-ro′di-as
Lk 20:6 danced before them, and pleased Herod.
7Whereupon he promised with an oath to give her whatsoever she would
ask.
8And she, being before instructed of her mother, said, Give me here John
Baptist's head in a charger.
9And the king was sorry: nevertheless for the oath's sake, and them
which sat with him at meat, he commanded *it* to be given *her*.
10And he sent, and beheaded John in the prison.
11And his head was brought in a charger, and given to the damsel: and
she brought *it* to her mother.
12And his disciples came, and took up the body, and buried it, and went
and told Jesus.

IX. JESUS LEAVES HEROD'S DOMINION (14:13—17:27)

A. FEEDING THE FIVE THOUSAND (CF. MK 6:30–44; LK 9:10–17; JN 6:1–13)

14:13 Mk 6:30–45 13¶When Jesus heard *of it*, he departed thence by ship into a desert place
Lk 9:10–17 apart: and when the people had heard *thereof*, they followed him on foot
Jn 6:1–13 out of the cities.
14:14 Mt 9:36 14And Jesus went forth, and saw a great multitude, and was moved with
Mk 1:41 Heb 2:17, 18 compassion toward them, and he healed their sick.
4:15; 5:1–3 15¶And when it was evening, his disciples came to him, saying, This is a
desert place, and the time is now past; send the multitude away, that they
may go into the villages, and buy themselves victuals.
14:16☆ 16But Jesus said unto them, They need not depart; give ye them to eat.
2 Kgs 4:42–44 17And they say unto him, We have here but five loaves, and two fishes.
18He said, Bring them hither to me.
14:19 19And he commanded the multitude to sit down on the grass, and took
Mt 15:35–38 the five loaves, and the two fishes, and looking up to heaven, he blessed,
Lk 22:19 and brake, and gave the loaves to *his* disciples, and the disciples to the
multitude.
20And they did all eat, and were filled: and they took up of the fragments
that remained twelve baskets full.
21And they that had eaten were about five thousand men, beside women
and children.

B. JESUS WALKING ON THE WATER (CF. MK 6:45–52; JN 6:15–21)

14:22☆ 22¶And straightway Jesus constrained his disciples to get into a ship, and
to go before him unto the other side, while he sent the multitudes away.

14:3 See note on Luke 1:57 regarding John the Baptist and his life. See also note on Mark 6:17 about Philip, the brother of Herod Antipas.

14:16 *give ye them to eat. Earlier Jesus had given his disciples* power to cast out demons, raise the dead, and heal the sick. Here he instructs them to feed the hungry. They had missed this opportunity and stood about puzzled and hesitant. They surely represent believers of our day who have the power of the Holy Spirit available to them but who do not take advantage of that power for the glory of God and the progress of the gospel.

14:22 Jesus sent his disciples ahead of him by ship. A storm overtook them. Earlier, in another storm, they had trusted Jesus when he was present—although asleep in the back of the boat. Now they were to learn that they could trust him when he was not with them. The Master was training them to walk by faith, not by sight.

23 And when he had sent the multitudes away, he went up into a
mountain apart to pray: and when the evening was come, he was there
alone.
24 But the ship was now in the midst of the sea, tossed with waves: for the
wind was contrary.
25 And in the fourth watch of the night Jesus went unto them, walking on
the sea.
26 And when the disciples saw him walking on the sea, they were troubled,
saying, It is a spirit; and they cried out for fear.
27 But straightway Jesus spake unto them, saying, Be of good cheer; it is I;
be not afraid.
28 And Peter answered him and said, Lord, if it be thou, bid me come
unto thee on the water.
29 And he said, Come. And when Peter was come down out of the ship, he
walked on the water, to go to Jesus.
30 But when he saw the wind boisterous, he was afraid; and beginning to
sink, he cried, saying, Lord, save me.
31 And immediately Jesus stretched forth *his* hand, and caught him, and
said unto him, O thou of little faith, wherefore didst thou doubt?
32 And when they were come into the ship, the wind ceased.
33 Then they that were in the ship came and worshipped him, saying, Of a
truth thou art the Son of God.
34 ¶And when they were gone over, they came into the land of Gen-nes′a-
ret.
35 And when the men of that place had knowledge of him, they sent out
into all that country round about, and brought unto him all that were
diseased;
36 And besought him that they might only touch the hem of his garment:
and as many as touched were made perfectly whole.

C. TRADITIONS VERSUS GOD'S COMMANDMENTS (CF. MK 7:1–23)

15 THEN came to Jesus scribes and Pharisees, which were of Jerusa-
lem, saying,
2 Why do thy disciples transgress the tradition of the elders? for they wash
not their hands when they eat bread.
3 But he answered and said unto them, Why do ye also transgress the
commandment of God by your tradition?
4 For God commanded, saying, Honour thy father and mother: and, He
that curseth father or mother, let him die the death.
5 But ye say, Whosoever shall say to *his* father or *his* mother, *It is* a gift,
by whatsoever thou mightest be profited by me;
6 And honour not his father or his mother, *he shall be free*. Thus have ye
made the commandment of God of none effect by your tradition.
7 *Ye* hypocrites, well did E-sai′as prophesy of you, saying,

14:23 Mk 6:46–56 Jn 6:15–21
14:25 Job 9:8
☆**14:28**
14:32 Ps 107:29
14:33 Ps 2:7 Mt 16:16; 26:63 Mk 1:1 Lk 4:41 Jn 1:49; 6:69 11:27 Acts 8:37 Rom 1:4
15:1 Mk 7:1–23
☆**15:2** Lk 11:37, 38 Gal 1:14
15:4 Ex 20:12; 21:17 Lev 19:2; 20:9 Deut 5:16; 27:16 Prov 20:20 30:17 Eph 6:2
☆**15:5**
☆**15:7**

14:28ff Peter wanted to be with Jesus, so he asked permission to walk on the water. He began to look at the waves, forgot to keep looking at Jesus, and began to sink as terror overtook him. He turned to the right source for help, appealing to Jesus to save him. Jesus did so, but rebuked him for his lack of faith. Are not believers caught up in similar situations when they start their pilgrim journey? They are filled with joy and hope, until caught up in a terrifying situation from which there appears to be no deliverance. Then faith is tested in the fire and proved to be true or false.

15:2 God commanded only the priests to wash before eating (Lev. 22:1–16). The teachers of the law broadened this command and applied it to all Jews. This is legalism at work. Jesus censured them by showing that they had expanded the commandment about honoring parents and in so doing made it different from the intention of the Lawgiver. This is not an uncommon practice among some believers today who make their commandments—not found in Scripture—normative for all.

15:5 *It is a gift*, i.e., "It is dedicated to God."

15:7, 8 There is a world of difference between profession and possession, between external acts and

15:8 Ezek 33:31

8 This people draweth nigh unto me with their mouth, and honoureth me with *their* lips; but their heart is far from me.

15:9 Col 2:8, 18, 22; 1 Tim 1:6, 7; Tit 1:13, 14

9 But in vain they do worship me, teaching *for* doctrines the commandments of men.

10 ¶And he called the multitude, and said unto them, Hear, and understand:

15:11☆ Acts 10:15; Rom 14:14; 1 Tim 4:4

11 Not that which goeth into the mouth defileth a man; but that which cometh out of the mouth, this defileth a man.

12 Then came his disciples, and said unto him, Knowest thou that the Pharisees were offended, after they heard this saying?

15:13 Isa 60:21; 61:3; Jn 15:2; 1 Cor 3:9

13 But he answered and said, Every plant, which my heavenly Father hath not planted, shall be rooted up.

15:14 Isa 9:16; Mal 2:8; Mt 23:16; Lk 6:39

14 Let them alone: they be blind leaders of the blind. And if the blind lead the blind, both shall fall into the ditch.

15 Then answered Peter and said unto him, Declare unto us this parable.

15:16 Mt 16:9

16 And Jesus said, Are ye also yet without understanding?

17 Do not ye yet understand, that whatsoever entereth in at the mouth goeth into the belly, and is cast out into the draught?

15:18 Jas 3:6

18 But those things which proceed out of the mouth come forth from the heart; and they defile the man.

15:19 Prov 6:14; Jer 17:9; Gal 5:19–21

19 For out of the heart proceed evil thoughts, murders, adulteries, fornications, thefts, false witness, blasphemies:

20 These are *the things* which defile a man: but to eat with unwashen hands defileth not a man.

D. JESUS AT TYRE AND SIDON (CF. MK 7:24–30)

15:21 Mk 7:24–30

21 ¶Then Jesus went thence, and departed into the coasts of Tyre and Si'don.

22 And, behold, a woman of Canaan came out of the same coasts, and cried unto him, saying, Have mercy on me, O Lord, *thou* Son of David; my daughter is grievously vexed with a devil.

23 But he answered her not a word. And his disciples came and besought him, saying, Send her away; for she crieth after us.

15:24 Isa 53:6; Mt 10:5, 6; Acts 3:25, 26; 13:46

24 But he answered and said, I am not sent but unto the lost sheep of the house of Israel.

25 Then came she and worshipped him, saying, Lord, help me.

15:26 Mt 7:6; Eph 2:12

26 But he answered and said, It is not meet to take the children's bread, and to cast *it* to dogs.

15:27☆

27 And she said, Truth, Lord: yet the dogs eat of the crumbs which fall from their masters' table.

15:28☆

28 Then Jesus answered and said unto her, O woman, great *is* thy faith: be it unto thee even as thou wilt. And her daughter was made whole from that very hour.

---

internal power. Many who say the right words do not possess in their hearts what they speak with their tongues. This harsh word was directed against the Pharisees, who knew they were guilty of hypocrisy.

15:11 *that which cometh out of the mouth, this defileth a man.* "We are polluted, not by the meat we eat with unwashen hands, but by the words we speak from an *unsanctified heart."* The soul is not morally polluted* by the kind or quality of the food we eat or by the conditions of our hands when we eat it.

15:27 *Truth, Lord: yet the dogs eat of the crumbs which fall from their masters' table.* The statement Jesus made to the Canaanite woman could have produced silence, denial, and discouragement (15:26). Yet she persevered. Jesus had left her an opening when he said: "It is not meet to take the children's bread, and cast it to dogs." She was not one of the Israelites and thus a "dog," but even dogs can eat the crumbs that fall from the children's plates to the ground. Then Jesus commended the mother's faith and healed the mother's daughter. The God of the whole earth shall he be called, for Jews and Gentiles alike can claim him and his promises.

15:28 Jesus healed people instantaneously. And the healings were permanent. He spoke and it was done. Sometimes he laid hands on the victims of disease or demon possession. Sometimes people touched the hem of his garment and were healed. In this instance

E. HEALING THE MULTITUDES (CF. MK 7:31–37)

29 And Jesus departed from thence, and came nigh unto the sea of
Galilee; and went up into a mountain, and sat down there.
30 And great multitudes came unto him, having with them *those that were*
lame, blind, dumb, maimed, and many others, and cast them down at Jesus'
feet; and he healed them:
31 Insomuch that the multitude wondered, when they saw the dumb to
speak, the maimed to be whole, the lame to walk, and the blind to see: and
they glorified the God of Israel.

15:29 Mk 7:31
☆**15:30** Isa 35:5, 6; Mt 4:23; 11:5; Lk 7:22
☆**15:31**

F. FEEDING THE FOUR THOUSAND (CF. MK 8:1–9)

32 ¶Then Jesus called his disciples *unto him*, and said, I have compassion
on the multitude, because they continue with me now three days, and have
nothing to eat: and I will not send them away fasting, lest they faint in the
way.
33 And his disciples say unto him, Whence should we have so much bread
in the wilderness, as to fill so great a multitude?
34 And Jesus saith unto them, How many loaves have ye? And they said,
Seven, and a few little fishes.
35 And he commanded the multitude to sit down on the ground.
36 And he took the seven loaves and the fishes, and gave thanks, and
brake *them*, and gave to his disciples, and the disciples to the multitude.
37 And they did all eat, and were filled: and they took up of the broken
meat that was left seven baskets full.
38 And they that did eat were four thousand men, beside women and
children.
39 And he sent away the multitude, and took ship, and came into the
coasts of Mag'da-la.

15:32 Ps 103:13; 111:4, 5; Mk 1:41; 8:1, 10; Heb 2:17; 4:15; 5:1–3
15:33 Num 11:21, 22; 2 Kgs 4:43
15:36 1 Sam 9:13; Mt 14:19; Lk 22:19
15:37 Ps 104:28; 145:15
15:39 Mk 8:10

G. THE DEMAND FOR SIGNS IN THE SKIES (CF. MK 8:11–21)

16 THE Pharisees also with the Sad'du-cees came, and tempting
desired him that he would shew them a sign from heaven.
2 He answered and said unto them, When it is evening, ye say, *It will be*
fair weather: for the sky is red.
3 And in the morning, *It will be* foul weather to day: for the sky is red and
lowring. O *ye* hypocrites, ye can discern the face of the sky; but can ye not
discern the signs of the times?
4 A wicked and adulterous generation seeketh after a sign; and there shall
no sign be given unto it, but the sign of the prophet Jonas. And he left
them, and departed.

☆**16:1** Mt 12:38; Mk 8:11–21; Lk 11:16; 1 Cor 1:22
16:2 Isa 7:14; Lk 12:54–56
☆**16:4** Mt 12:39

Jesus simply spoke the word of healing and it took place. He used his power according to his good pleasure.

15:30, 31 This is an account of Christ's wholesale curing. Any and all came to him for help. In his goodness Jesus admitted rich and poor, young and old to his ministrations. He never complained of crowds, nor looked with contempt upon those who were needy. He was as interested in peasants as in princes. Such was his power that he healed all sorts and manners of sicknesses. Nothing baffled him and no disease went untreated. "Unto him shall the gathering of the people be" (Gen. 49:10); and no soul seeking salvation will be spurned, looked down upon, or rejected.

16:1 Wonder of wonders! The Pharisees and Sadducees were wholly in disagreement with each other on virtually every matter. But they were companions in crime and friends in their opposition to Jesus Christ. No matter how diverse are the views of those who cling to error, they will always get together to persecute those who hold the truth.

16:4 The Pharisees and Sadducees were persistent in asking for a supernatural sign from heaven to confirm Jesus' claim to be the Messiah. They had already dismissed his miracles. Here Jesus says that no sign would be given them except the sign of Jonah. He refused to give them a sign then, but it may be inferred that the mention of Jonah pointed toward his own death and resurrection as the great sign of the future. But even this sign, the greatest of them all, was not accepted by many Sadducees and Pharisees, as we learn later in the Book of Acts.

5 And when his disciples were come to the other side, they had forgotten
to take bread.

16:6 Mt 7:15; Lk 12:1; Rom 16:17, 18; Phil 3:2; Col 2:8; 2 Pet 3:17

6 ¶Then Jesus said unto them, Take heed and beware of the leaven of the
Pharisees and of the Sad′du-cees.
7 And they reasoned among themselves, saying, *It is* because we have
taken no bread.
8 *Which* when Jesus perceived, he said unto them, O ye of little faith, why
reason ye among yourselves, because ye have brought no bread?

16:9 Mt 14:19; 15:36

9 Do ye not yet understand, neither remember the five loaves of the five
thousand, and how many baskets ye took up?
10 Neither the seven loaves of the four thousand, and how many baskets
ye took up?

16:11 Lk 12:1

11 How is it that ye do not understand that I spake *it* not to you
concerning bread, that ye should beware of the leaven of the Pharisees and
of the Sad′du-cees?
12 Then understood they how that he bade *them* not beware of the leaven
of bread, but of the doctrine of the Pharisees and of the Sad′du-cees.

H. PETER'S CONFESSION (CF. MK 8:27–30; LK 9:18–21)

16:13 Mk 8:27–30; Lk 9:18–21
16:14 Mal 4:5; Mt 14:2; Lk 9:7–9
16:16☆ Mt 1:16; 14:33; Jn 6:69; 11:27; 20:31; Acts 8:37; 9:20; Heb 1:5, 6; 1 Jn 4:15; 5:5
16:17 1 Cor 2:10; Gal 1:16
16:18☆ Isa 28:16; Jn 1:42; Acts 9:31; 1 Cor 3:11; Eph 2:20–22; 4:15, 16; 1 Pet 2:4, 5
16:19☆ Jn 20:23

13 ¶When Jesus came into the coasts of Cæs-a-re′a Phi-lip′pi, he asked his
disciples, saying, Whom do men say that I the Son of man am?
14 And they said, Some *say that thou art* John the Baptist: some, E-li′as;
and others, Jeremias, or one of the prophets.
15 He saith unto them, But whom say ye that I am?
16 And Simon Peter answered and said, Thou art the Christ, the Son of
the living God.
17 And Jesus answered and said unto him, Blessed art thou, Simon Bar-
jo′na: for flesh and blood hath not revealed *it* unto thee, but my Father
which is in heaven.
18 And I say also unto thee, That thou art Peter, and upon this rock I will
build my church; and the gates of hell shall not prevail against it.
19 And I will give unto thee the keys of the kingdom of heaven: and
whatsoever thou shalt bind on earth shall be bound in heaven: and
whatsoever thou shalt loose on earth shall be loosed in heaven.

16:16 *Christ* is the Greek equivalent of the Hebrew *Messiah* (see John 1:41: "We have found the Messias"). The word means that Jesus is the anointed one, the promised redeemer who will save men from sin.
16:18 This verse has been used to support the notion that the church is founded on Peter. Such a view overlooks an important element in the Greek text. Christ was making a play on words: He first said, "thou art Peter" (Greek, *petros*—which means rock or "rock-man"), and then he said, "upon this rock" (Greek, *petra*—which also means rock but is morphologically feminine). Two views of Christ's play on words have been advanced. One is that when he said, "upon this rock I will build my church," he pointed to himself as being that rock—and on that he would build the church. The other view is that Christ's statement indicates that the rock was Peter's confession that Jesus was the Christ, the Son of the living God—and on that he would build his church. In either case it was Christ upon whom the church was built. In Eph. 2:20 Paul says that the church is "built upon the foundation of the apostles and prophets, Jesus Christ himself being the chief cornerstone." Whatever may have been the role of the apostles and prophets, Jesus, the chief cornerstone, was the one on whom the church was founded. Because Christ is the all-powerful one, *the gates of hell shall not prevail against it* (the church). All authority belongs to the ascended Christ, who reigns in glory over the church.
16:19 *the keys of the kingdom*, here given to Peter, were also given to all the apostles and to the church for all ages. The power of the keys does not allow the possessor to forgive sins himself or by his word. The phrase *shall be bound . . . shall be loosed* is actually "shall have been bound . . . shall have been loosed." It is heaven itself that does the binding and the loosing. Apostles and ministers of the gospel can announce the binding and loosing but not initiate them. In 18:18 and John 20:23 Christ bestows the power of the keys to all the apostles, not to Peter alone. Peter did use this power in Acts 2 when he proclaimed the good news and assured the hearers that their sins would be forgiven if they repented. But he did not say nor could he say, "I forgive your sins." Only God can do that.

20Then charged he his disciples that they should tell no man that he was
Jesus the Christ.

I. JESUS' FIRST PREDICTION OF HIS DEATH (CF. MK 8:31—9:1; LK 9:22–27)

21¶From that time forth began Jesus to shew unto his disciples, how that he must go unto Jerusalem, and suffer many things of the elders and chief priests and scribes, and be killed, and be raised again the third day. **16:21** Mk 8:31—9:1 Lk 9:22–27
22Then Peter took him, and began to rebuke him, saying, Be it far from
thee, Lord: this shall not be unto thee.
23But he turned, and said unto Peter, Get thee behind me, Satan: thou art an offence unto me: for thou savourest not the things that be of God, but those that be of men. ☆**16:23** Rom 8:7
24¶Then said Jesus unto his disciples, If any *man* will come after me, let him deny himself, and take up his cross, and follow me. ☆**16:24** 1 Thess 3:3 2 Tim 3:12
25For whosoever will save his life shall lose it: and whosoever will lose his
life for my sake shall find it.
26For what is a man profited, if he shall gain the whole world, and lose his own soul? or what shall a man give in exchange for his soul? ☆**16:26** Ps 49:7–9
27For the Son of man shall come in the glory of his Father with his angels; and then he shall reward every man according to his works. **16:27** Ps 62:12 Prov 24:11, 12 Jer 17:10 Mt 25:31 Rom 2:6 2 Cor 5:10 1 Pet 1:17 Jude 14, 15 Rev 22:12
28Verily I say unto you, There be some standing here, which shall not
taste of death, till they see the Son of man coming in his kingdom.

J. THE TRANSFIGURATION (CF. MK 9:2–13; LK 9:28–36)

17 AND after six days Jesus taketh Peter, James, and John his brother, and bringeth them up into an high mountain apart, **17:1** Mk 9:2–8 Lk 9:28–36
2And was transfigured before them: and his face did shine as the sun, and his raiment was white as the light. ☆**17:2**
3And, behold, there appeared unto them Moses and E-li'as talking with
him.
4Then answered Peter, and said unto Jesus, Lord, it is good for us to be
here: if thou wilt, let us make here three tabernacles; one for thee, and one
for Moses, and one for E-li'as.
5While he yet spake, behold, a bright cloud overshadowed them: and behold a voice out of the cloud, which said, This is my beloved Son, in whom I am well pleased; hear ye him. **17:5** Deut 18:15 Isa 42:1 Mk 1:11 Lk 3:22 Acts 3:22 Heb 12:25 2 Pet 1:17, 18
6And when the disciples heard *it*, they fell on their face, and were sore
afraid.

16:23 In 16:17 Jesus says to Peter, "Blessed art thou." Now he rebukes him pointedly. Jesus had informed his disciples about his coming death. Peter, perhaps innocently, attempted to deter Jesus from fulfilling his unique mission. Jesus regarded any interference with the will of his Father as satanic in origin. In effect, he says to Peter, "Get away from me, you Satan!"

16:24 Self-denial does not entail denying things to oneself; rather, it means the radical giving up of self to Christ. It means being crucified with Christ, i.e., the death of the old ego (Gal. 2:20). The believer is dead to the world, dead to the old life, dead to self, and alive to God (cf. Rom. 6:6–13; Col. 3:1–4). Taking up one's cross means nothing less than embracing the instrument of death to self and to all that self means.

16:26 This verse should be understood two ways: (1) its meaning in terms of this present world, and (2) its meaning in terms of the world to come. However much of this world's goods a man gains, it is of no advantage to him if he dies. We come into this world with nothing and we leave the same way—with nothing. Jesus stated that the loss of the immortal soul after death cannot be compensated for by the wealth of the whole world. The urgent choice is always between the *worth* of the soul in time and eternity against the *worthlessness* of the world, if not in time, then certainly in eternity.

17:2 See note on Mark 9:2 regarding the revelation of Christ's glory, the Transfiguration.

7 And Jesus came and touched them, and said, Arise, and be not afraid.
8 And when they had lifted up their eyes, they saw no man, save Jesus
only.
17:9☆ 9 And as they came down from the mountain, Jesus charged them, saying,
Mk 9:9–13 Tell the vision to no man, until the Son of man be risen again from the
dead.
17:10☆ 10 And his disciples asked him, saying, Why then say the scribes that
Mal 4:5 E-li′as must first come?
17:11☆ 11 And Jesus answered and said unto them, E-li′as truly shall first come,
Lk 1:17 and restore all things.
17:12 12 But I say unto you, That E-li′as is come already, and they knew him
Mt 14:3 not, but have done unto him whatsoever they listed. Likewise shall also the
Son of man suffer of them.
13 Then the disciples understood that he spake unto them of John the
Baptist.

K. DELIVERING THE DEMON-POSSESSED BOY (CF. MK 9:14–29; LK 9:37–43)

17:14 14 ¶And when they were come to the multitude, there came to him a
Mk 9:14–29 Lk 9:37–43 *certain* man, kneeling down to him, and saying,
15 Lord, have mercy on my son: for he is lunatick, and sore vexed: for
ofttimes he falleth into the fire, and oft into the water.
16 And I brought him to thy disciples, and they could not cure him.
17 Then Jesus answered and said, O faithless and perverse generation, how
long shall I be with you? how long shall I suffer you? bring him hither to
me.
18 And Jesus rebuked the devil; and he departed out of him: and the child
was cured from that very hour.
19 Then came the disciples to Jesus apart, and said, Why could not we cast
him out?
17:20☆ Mt 21:21 20 And Jesus said unto them, Because of your unbelief: for verily I say
Mk 11:22, 23 unto you, If ye have faith as a grain of mustard seed, ye shall say unto this
Lk 17:6 Jn 11:40 mountain, Remove hence to yonder place; and it shall remove; and nothing
1 Cor 13:2 shall be impossible unto you.
17:21☆ 21 Howbeit this kind goeth not out but by prayer and fasting.

L. JESUS' SECOND PREDICTION OF HIS DEATH (CF. MK 9:30–32; LK 9:43–45)

17:22 Mt 16:21 20:17–19 22 ¶And while they abode in Galilee, Jesus said unto them, The Son of
Mk 9:30–32 10:33, 34 man shall be betrayed into the hands of men:
Lk 9:22, 43–45 18:31–33 23 And they shall kill him, and the third day he shall be raised again. And
24:6, 7 they were exceeding sorry.

17:9 Why did Jesus tell his three disciples not to disclose to others what had happened at the Transfiguration? Had they done so, Jesus' death on the cross would have appeared to be wholly out of accord with *the vision. But subsequent to his resurrection* they were free to tell of the Transfiguration—the resurrection and Christ's subsequent glory would be the proof positive to explain what happened on the mount of Transfiguration.

17:10 *Elias [Elijah] must first come,* i.e., "Elijah must return before the Messiah comes."†

17:11 See note on Mal. 4:5 regarding Elijah.

17:20 *faith as a grain of mustard seed.* This seed was the smallest planted by the Jews of Jesus' day, yet the bush grew to be eight to twelve feet high and birds made their nests in its branches. Surely the smallest amount of faith will be richly rewarded, for even small faith is real faith. *nothing shall be impossible,* i.e., "anything consonant with the will of God and sought for his glory is possible."

17:21 This verse is not present in many ancient manuscripts.

M. THE TEMPLE TAX IN THE FISH'S MOUTH

24¶And when they were come to Ca-per'na-um, they that received tribute
money came to Peter, and said, Doth not your master pay tribute?
25He saith, Yes. And when he was come into the house, Jesus prevented
him, saying, What thinkest thou, Simon? of whom do the kings of the earth
take custom or tribute? of their own children, or of strangers?
26Peter saith unto him, Of strangers. Jesus saith unto him, Then are the
children free.
27Notwithstanding, lest we should offend them, go thou to the sea, and
cast an hook, and take up the fish that first cometh up; and when thou hast
opened his mouth, thou shalt find a piece of money: that take, and give
unto them for me and thee.

☆**17:24** Mk 12:14–17
17:27 Mt 18:6–9; 1 Cor 8:13; 10:32

X. JESUS' TEACHING ON HUMILITY AND FORGIVENESS (18:1–35)

A. HUMILITY (CF. MK 9:33–37; LK 9:46–48)

18 AT the same time came the disciples unto Jesus, saying, Who is the
greatest in the kingdom of heaven?
2And Jesus called a little child unto him, and set him in the midst of
them,
3And said, Verily I say unto you, Except ye be converted, and become as
little children, ye shall not enter into the kingdom of heaven.
4Whosoever therefore shall humble himself as this little child, the same is
greatest in the kingdom of heaven.
5And whoso shall receive one such little child in my name receiveth me.
6But whoso shall offend one of these little ones which believe in me, it
were better for him that a millstone were hanged about his neck, and *that*
he were drowned in the depth of the sea.
7¶Woe unto the world because of offences! for it must needs be that
offences come; but woe to that man by whom the offence cometh!
8Wherefore if thy hand or thy foot offend thee, cut them off, and cast
them from thee: it is better for thee to enter into life halt or maimed, rather
than having two hands or two feet to be cast into everlasting fire.
9And if thine eye offend thee, pluck it out, and cast *it* from thee: it is
better for thee to enter into life with one eye, rather than having two eyes to
be cast into hell fire.

18:1 Mk 9:33–50; Lk 9:46–48; 22:24
☆**18:3** Mt 19:14; Mk 10:14; Lk 18:16, 17; 1 Cor 14:20; 1 Pet 2:2
18:4 Mt 20:27; 1 Pet 5:5, 6
18:5 Mt 10:42
☆**18:6** Lk 17:1–3; 1 Cor 8:12, 13
☆**18:7**
18:8 Mt 5:29, 30
☆**18:9**

B. THE LOST SHEEP (CF. LK 15:4–7)

10Take heed that ye despise not one of these little ones; for I say unto
you, That in heaven their angels do always behold the face of my Father
which is in heaven.

18:10 Ps 34:7; Lk 1:19; Acts 12:15; Heb 1:14

17:24 *Doth not your master pay tribute?* Every free Jewish male over twenty years of age paid the yearly half-shekel temple tax (cf. Exod. 30:11–16). The Greek coin equivalent to the Hebrew half-shekel was the double drachma (didrachma); the "piece of money" referred to in 17:27 is a stater, worth two didrachmas.
18:3 *become as little children,* who are harmless, inoffensive, and not malicious. Christ's disciples are to imitate the virtues of a child, shunning the vices of adults whose values mark them off as lacking moral excellence.
18:6 *shall offend,* i.e., "shall cause to stumble."
18:7 *because of offenses,* literally, "because of occasions of stumbling."
18:9 The word translated *hell* here is *gehenna* (spelled *geenna* in the Greek), which is the Aramaic form of the Hebrew *Gehinnom,* meaning "the Valley of Hinnom." *Gehenna* is the word used to describe the place to which unrepentant sinners go. Its fire is unquenchable and the torment unending. In the Old Testament the Valley of Hinnom (Topheth) was the place where infants were immolated and where the repulsive idol of Molech was worshipped. These perversions occurred during the reigns of Ahaz and Manasseh. King Josiah converted the area into a city dump where fire smoldered continually. It became a fitting symbol for hell, or the lake of fire. Bible readers are confused when translators use the English word *hell* for both *hades* and *gehenna* (as, e.g., the King James does). The RSV, when using the word hell, does indicate in footnotes when it is Gehenna.

18:11☆ 11For the Son of man is come to save that which was lost.
18:12 Lk 15:3–7 12How think ye? if a man have an hundred sheep, and one of them be
gone astray, doth he not leave the ninety and nine, and goeth into the
mountains, and seeketh that which is gone astray?
13And if so be that he find it, verily I say unto you, he rejoiceth more of
that *sheep*, than of the ninety and nine which went not astray.
14Even so it is not the will of your Father which is in heaven, that one of
these little ones should perish.

C. THE TREATMENT OF SINNERS
1. Discipline in the Church

18:15 Lk 17:3 Gal 6:1 2 Thess 3:15 Jas 5:19, 20 15¶Moreover if thy brother shall trespass against thee, go and tell him his
fault between thee and him alone: if he shall hear thee, thou hast gained thy
brother.
18:16 Deut 19:15 2 Cor 13:1 Heb 10:28 16But if he will not hear *thee, then* take with thee one or two more, that in
the mouth of two or three witnesses every word may be established.
18:17☆ Rom 16:17 1 Cor 6:1–8 1 Tim 5:20 17And if he shall neglect to hear them, tell *it* unto the church: but if he
neglect to hear the church, let him be unto thee as an heathen man and a
publican.
18:18 Mt 16:19 Jn 20:23 18Verily I say unto you, Whatsoever ye shall bind on earth shall be bound
in heaven: and whatsoever ye shall loose on earth shall be loosed in heaven.
18:19 Jas 5:16 1 Jn 3:21, 22 19Again I say unto you, That if two of you shall agree on earth as
touching any thing that they shall ask, it shall be done for them of my
Father which is in heaven.
18:20 Mt 28:20 20For where two or three are gathered together in my name, there am I in
the midst of them.

2. The Formula for Forgiveness

18:21 Lk 17:4 21¶Then came Peter to him, and said, Lord, how oft shall my brother sin
against me, and I forgive him? till seven times?
18:22☆ Col 3:13 22Jesus saith unto him, I say not unto thee, Until seven times: but, Until
seventy times seven.
18:23☆ Mt 25:19 23¶Therefore is the kingdom of heaven likened unto a certain king, which
would take account of his servants.
18:24☆ 24And when he had begun to reckon, one was brought unto him, which
owed him ten thousand talents.

18:11 This verse is not present in several ancient manuscripts.
18:17 *let him be unto thee as an heathen man and a publican*, i.e., "let him be excommunicated." In addition to ordaining the church, God also ordained its government and order. Church discipline is the gift of God and excommunication is the means whereby discipline is to be enforced. The rules are simple enough: (1) a Christian who has something against his brother should first confront him privately; (2) if this does not effect a positive result, the offended party is to go to the offender accompanied by two or three witnesses; (3) if the first two steps do not work, the offended brother is to take the matter to the church. If the guilty brother will not repent and refuses to accept discipline, he is to be excommunicated. This action *cuts him off from the fellowship and the ordinances or* sacraments. Churches are to (1) maintain sound doctrine; (2) maintain order (Titus 1:5; 1 Cor. 11:34); and (3) rebuke and deal with offenders (1 Tim. 5:20; 2 Tim. 4:2). Believers are to accept the church's correction and should submit to its discipline (Heb. 13:17; 2 Cor. 10:8; 13:10). The purpose of excommunication is to bring the guilty to repentance. The penalty is incidental to restoration and is often the very means by which repentance takes place.
18:22 *Until seventy times seven.* On what basis does Jesus say we should forgive anyone this many times? God has forgiven us and will forgive us an unlimited number of times. We are commanded to forgive those who have sinned against us just as many times as God has forgiven us.
18:23ff The basic teaching of this illustration is the absolute necessity of forgiveness. The unmerciful debtor owed the king a great sum of money, and his debt was forgiven him. Then this man refused to forgive a fellow servant's debt, which was insignificant when compared to the debt the king had forgiven him. He unmercifully pressed for payment and jailed the man who owed him this small sum. The lesson is plain: we have been forgiven our sins, which is the heaviest of all debts; therefore, we should forgive others, whose debts are small by comparison.
18:24ff *ten thousand talents.* This is hyperbole for effect. The sum of money involved was unimaginable; it could never be repaid. So is the debt of the sinner to

25 But forasmuch as he had not to pay, his lord commanded him to be
sold, and his wife, and children, and all that he had, and payment to be
made.
26 The servant therefore fell down, and worshipped him, saying, Lord,
have patience with me, and I will pay thee all.
27 Then the lord of that servant was moved with compassion, and loosed
him, and forgave him the debt.
28 But the same servant went out, and found one of his fellowservants,
which owed him an hundred pence: and he laid hands on him, and took
him by the throat, saying, Pay me that thou owest.
29 And his fellowservant fell down at his feet, and besought him, saying,
Have patience with me, and I will pay thee all.
30 And he would not: but went and cast him into prison, till he should pay
the debt.
31 So when his fellowservants saw what was done, they were very sorry,
and came and told unto their lord all that was done.
32 Then his lord, after that he had called him, said unto him, O thou
wicked servant, I forgave thee all that debt, because thou desiredst me:
33 Shouldest not thou also have had compassion on thy fellowservant,
even as I had pity on thee?
34 And his lord was wroth, and delivered him to the tormentors, till he
should pay all that was due unto him.
35 So likewise shall my heavenly Father do also unto you, if ye from your
hearts forgive not every one his brother their trespasses.

18:25 Ex 21:2; Lev 25:39; 2 Kgs 4:1; Neh 5:5
☆**18:28**
18:33 Mt 7:2; Eph 4:32; 5:2; Col 3:13
18:34 Mark 11:25; Jas 2:13

XI. JESUS EN ROUTE TO JERUSALEM (19:1—20:34)

A. JESUS ON MARRIAGE AND DIVORCE (CF. MK 10:1–12)

19 AND it came to pass, *that* when Jesus had finished these sayings, he
departed from Galilee, and came into the coasts of Judæa beyond
Jordan;
2 And great multitudes followed him; and he healed them there.
3 ¶The Pharisees also came unto him, tempting him, and saying unto him,
Is it lawful for a man to put away his wife for every cause?
4 And he answered and said unto them, Have ye not read, that he which
made *them* at the beginning made them male and female,
5 And said, For this cause shall a man leave father and mother, and shall
cleave to his wife: and they twain shall be one flesh?
6 Wherefore they are no more twain, but one flesh. What therefore God
hath joined together, let not man put asunder.
7 They say unto him, Why did Moses then command to give a writing of
divorcement, and to put her away?
8 He saith unto them, Moses because of the hardness of your hearts
suffered you to put away your wives: but from the beginning it was not so.
9 And I say unto you, Whosoever shall put away his wife, except *it be* for
fornication, and shall marry another, committeth adultery: and whoso
marrieth her which is put away doth commit adultery.
10 ¶His disciples say unto him, If the case of the man be so with *his* wife,
it is not good to marry.

☆**19:3** Mk 10:2–12
19:4 Gen 1:27; 5:2
19:5 Gen 2:24; Mal 2:15; 1 Cor 6:16; Eph 5:31
19:7 Deut 24:1; Mt 5:31, 32
19:9 Lk 16:18; 1 Cor 7:10, 11
☆**19:10**

God, yet God is able to forgive the person who is most indebted to him. Then the most indebted, forgiven sinner should have mercy on anyone who owes him a token debt, especially when balanced against his own incalculable one.

18:28 *an hundred pence*, approximately $1,500-$2,500.

19:3 See note on Mark 10:5 regarding divorce.

19:10 The disciples of Jesus introduced the notion that it might be better for no one to marry. This was

19:11 1 Cor 7:7–9, 17
19:12 1 Cor 7:32, 34

11 But he said unto them, All *men* cannot receive this saying, save *they* to
whom it is given.
12 For there are some eunuchs, which were so born from *their* mother's
womb: and there are some eunuchs, which were made eunuchs of men: and
there be eunuchs, which have made themselves eunuchs for the kingdom of
heaven's sake. He that is able to receive *it*, let him receive *it*.

B. JESUS BLESSES LITTLE CHILDREN (CF. MK 10:13–16; LK 18:15–17)

19:13 Mk 10:13–16 Lk 18:15–17
19:14 Mt 18:3

13 ¶Then were there brought unto him little children, that he should put
his hands on them, and pray: and the disciples rebuked them.
14 But Jesus said, Suffer little children, and forbid them not, to come unto
me: for of such is the kingdom of heaven.
15 And he laid *his* hands on them, and departed thence.

C. THE RICH YOUNG MAN (CF. MK 10:17–31; LK 18:18–30)

19:16☆ Mk 10:17–31 Lk 10:25 18:18–30
19:17☆
19:18 Ex 20:12–17 Deut 5:16–21
19:19 Lev 19:18 Mt 15:4; 22:39 Mk 12:31 Rom 13:9 Gal 5:14 Jas 2:8
19:21 Lk 12:33 Acts 2:45 4:34, 35 1 Tim 6:18
19:23 Job 31:24–28 Mt 13:22 1 Cor 1:26 1 Tim 6:9
19:24☆
19:26 Gen 18:14 Job 42:2 Jer 32:17 Zech 8:6
19:27☆ Mt 4:20 Lk 5:11

16 ¶And, behold, one came and said unto him, Good Master, what good
thing shall I do, that I may have eternal life?
17 And he said unto him, Why callest thou me good? *there is* none good
but one, *that is*, God: but if thou wilt enter into life, keep the command-
ments.
18 He saith unto him, Which? Jesus said, Thou shalt do no murder, Thou
shalt not commit adultery, Thou shalt not steal, Thou shalt not bear false
witness,
19 Honour thy father and *thy* mother: and, Thou shalt love thy neighbour
as thyself.
20 The young man saith unto him, All these things have I kept from my
youth up: what lack I yet?
21 Jesus said unto him, If thou wilt be perfect, go *and* sell that thou hast,
and give to the poor, and thou shalt have treasure in heaven: and come *and*
follow me.
22 But when the young man heard that saying, he went away sorrowful:
for he had great possessions.
23 ¶Then said Jesus unto his disciples, Verily I say unto you, That a rich
man shall hardly enter into the kingdom of heaven.
24 And again I say unto you, It is easier for a camel to go through the eye
of a needle, than for a rich man to enter into the kingdom of God.
25 When his disciples heard *it*, they were exceedingly amazed, saying, Who
then can be saved?
26 But Jesus beheld *them*, and said unto them, With men this is impossi-
ble; but with God all things are possible.
27 ¶Then answered Peter and said unto him, Behold, we have forsaken all,
and followed thee; what shall we have therefore?

---

mischievous. Jesus said only that it is good for some not to marry, but let each one decide for himself whether he has the gift of continence. Whoever does not have the gift of continence should marry and bear the crosses of that estate, rather than burn with lust.

19:16ff Here was a man who was concerned about his *spiritual condition, who believed in* eternal life, who knew his life lacked meaning, and who sought to know what to do in order to secure eternal life. When Jesus told him to keep the commandments, he proudly asserted that he had done so from his youth. He was mistaken, but Jesus took him at his word and advanced the question that was to uncover his basic problem. Jesus told him to sell his worldly possessions, give the money to the poor, and follow him. The rich young ruler left sorrowfully, for he valued his worldly possessions more than he valued Jesus. Whatever comes between us and Jesus is what will keep us from eternal life.

19:17 See note on Mark 10:18.

19:24 *for a camel to go through the eye of a needle.* This figure of speech (hyperbole) indicates how difficult it is for a rich person who prides himself on his material possessions to repent and accept Christ as his Savior. (See also Mark 10:25 and Luke 18:25.)

19:27 *we have forsaken all, and followed thee; what shall we have therefore?* The disciples indeed had left

[28]And Jesus said unto them, Verily I say unto you, That ye which have
followed me, in the regeneration when the Son of man shall sit in the throne
of his glory, ye also shall sit upon twelve thrones, judging the twelve tribes
of Israel.
[29]And every one that hath forsaken houses, or brethren, or sisters, or
father, or mother, or wife, or children, or lands, for my name's sake, shall
receive an hundredfold, and shall inherit everlasting life.
[30]But many *that are* first shall be last; and the last *shall be* first.

☆19:28 Lk 22:28–30 1 Cor 6:2, 3 Rev 2:26

19:30 Mt 20:16

D. THE WORKERS IN THE HARVEST FIELD

20 FOR the kingdom of heaven is like unto a man *that is* an
householder, which went out early in the morning to hire labourers
into his vineyard.
[2]And when he had agreed with the labourers for a penny a day, he sent
them into his vineyard.
[3]And he went out about the third hour, and saw others standing idle in
the marketplace,
[4]And said unto them; Go ye also into the vineyard, and whatsoever is
right I will give you. And they went their way.
[5]Again he went out about the sixth and ninth hour, and did likewise.
[6]And about the eleventh hour he went out, and found others standing
idle, and saith unto them, Why stand ye here all the day idle?
[7]They say unto him, Because no man hath hired us. He saith unto them,
Go ye also into the vineyard; and whatsoever is right, *that* shall ye receive.
[8]So when even was come, the lord of the vineyard saith unto his steward,
Call the labourers, and give them *their* hire, beginning from the last unto
the first.
[9]And when they came that *were hired* about the eleventh hour, they
received every man a penny.
[10]But when the first came, they supposed that they should have received
more; and they likewise received every man a penny.
[11]And when they had received *it*, they murmured against the goodman of
the house,
[12]Saying, These last have wrought *but* one hour, and thou hast made
them equal unto us, which have borne the burden and heat of the day.
[13]But he answered one of them, and said, Friend, I do thee no wrong:
didst not thou agree with me for a penny?
[14]Take *that* thine *is*, and go thy way: I will give unto this last, even as
unto thee.

☆20:1 Song 1:6; 8:11, 12

☆20:2

☆20:3

20:8 Lev 19:13

20:12 Lk 1:11

all they had to follow Jesus, but it was not really very much. Peter may have been saying that leaving all put Christ in debt to them. He wanted to know what they would get for doing so. Jesus himself forsook all for the *joy of the cross. Moses looked to the recompense of* the reward. Moses was human and so are we. Ideally we leave all because of what Jesus has done for us. We do not forsake all for the reward—although there will be a reward for leaving everything to follow Jesus. But if there were no reward, we still should leave all and follow the Master.

19:28 *in the regeneration*, i.e., in the Second Advent of Jesus Christ when there will be a regeneration of the heavens and the earth. Whoever is a partaker of the regeneration of grace for salvation will be a partaker of the regeneration in glory, when Paradise will be regained.

20:1ff In this illustration, each laborer, no matter how long he worked, received the same pay. God's grace has nothing to do with our years of service or the labor of our hands. The dying thief was just as well off as a person who has been a believer for many years. The sinner who comes to God at the eleventh hour is just as blessed as the one who came at daybreak.

20:2 *a penny*, i.e., "a denarius," the payment for a day's labor, equivalent to $45-$60 in 1984.

20:3 *the third hour*, i.e., "six in the morning." This was the time daily work began. The owner of the estate hired some laborers at this time. He returned and hired others at nine o'clock, at noon, at three o'clock, and finally hired some at five o'clock. Those who had worked since six in the morning appear to be cheated, unless one understands the nature of the grace of God as illustrated in this parable.

20:15 Rom 9:21
20:16 Mt 19:30

15 Is it not lawful for me to do what I will with mine own? Is thine eye
evil, because I am good?
16 So the last shall be first, and the first last: for many be called, but few
chosen.

E. JESUS' THIRD PREDICTION OF HIS DEATH (CF. MK 10:32–34; LK 18:31–34)

20:17 Mk 10:32–34 Lk 18:31–33
20:19 Mt 16:21; 27:2 Jn 18:28 Acts 2:23; 3:13 4:27

17 ¶And Jesus going up to Jerusalem took the twelve disciples apart in the
way, and said unto them,
18 Behold, we go up to Jerusalem: and the Son of man shall be betrayed
unto the chief priests and unto the scribes, and they shall condemn him to
death,
19 And shall deliver him to the Gentiles to mock, and to scourge, and to
crucify *him:* and the third day he shall rise again.

F. THE AMBITION OF THE SONS (JOHN AND JAMES) OF ZEBEDEE (CF. MK 10:35–45)

20:20☆ Mt 4:21; 27:56 Mk 10:35–45 15:40
20:21 Mt 19:28 Jas 4:3
20:22 Mt 26:39 Mk 14:36 Jn 18:11
20:23 Acts 12:2 Rom 8:17 Rev 1:9
20:24 Lk 22:24
20:25☆
20:26 Mt 23:11 Mk 9:35 1 Pet 5:3
20:27 Mt 18:4
20:28 Lk 22:27 Jn 11:51 13:4, 5, 14 Phil 2:7 1 Tim 2:6 Tit 2:14 1 Pet 1:19

20 ¶Then came to him the mother of Zeb'e-dee's children with her sons,
worshipping *him*, and desiring a certain thing of him.
21 And he said unto her, What wilt thou? She saith unto him, Grant that
these my two sons may sit, the one on thy right hand, and the other on the
left, in thy kingdom.
22 But Jesus answered and said, Ye know not what ye ask. Are ye able to
drink of the cup that I shall drink of, and to be baptized with the baptism
that I am baptized with? They say unto him, We are able.
23 And he saith unto them, Ye shall drink indeed of my cup, and be
baptized with the baptism that I am baptized with: but to sit on my right
hand, and on my left, is not mine to give, but *it shall be given to them* for
whom it is prepared of my Father.
24 And when the ten heard *it*, they were moved with indignation against
the two brethren.
25 But Jesus called them *unto him*, and said, Ye know that the princes of
the Gentiles exercise dominion over them, and they that are great exercise
authority upon them.
26 But it shall not be so among you: but whosoever will be great among
you, let him be your minister;
27 And whosoever will be chief among you, let him be your servant:
28 Even as the Son of man came not to be ministered unto, but to
minister, and to give his life a ransom for many.

G. JESUS RESTORES SIGHT TO TWO BLIND MEN (CF. MK 10:46–52; LK 18:35–43)

20:29☆ Mk 10:46–52 Lk 18:35–43

29 And as they departed from Jericho, a great multitude followed him.
30 ¶And, behold, two blind men sitting by the way side, when they heard
that Jesus passed by, cried out, saying, Have mercy on us, O Lord, *thou* Son
of David.

20:20 *See the note on Mark 10:35 regarding* the petition of James, John, and their mother for status and power in Jesus' coming kingdom.
20:25ff Christ here contrasts the ambition of the unregenerate man who covets power, glory, and self-aggrandizement with that of the converted man who does not live for self, but for God. The saved man seeks to glorify God and is characterized by self-sacrificing love. Jesus came not to be served but to serve; the servant of Christ should also seek to serve God and others.
20:29ff See note on Mark 10:46 for information about this incident.

31And the multitude rebuked them, because they should hold their peace:
but they cried the more, saying, Have mercy on us, O Lord, *thou* Son of
David.
32And Jesus stood still, and called them, and said, What will ye that I
shall do unto you?
33They say unto him, Lord, that our eyes may be opened.
34So Jesus had compassion *on them*, and touched their eyes: and
immediately their eyes received sight, and they followed him.

XII. THE LAST WEEK IN JERUSALEM (21:1—28:10)

A. THE TRIUMPHAL ENTRY (CF. MK 11:1–11; LK 19:29–44; JN 12:12–19)

21 AND when they drew nigh unto Jerusalem, and were come to
Beth'pha-ge, unto the mount of Olives, then sent Jesus two
disciples,
2Saying unto them, Go into the village over against you, and straightway
ye shall find an ass tied, and a colt with her: loose *them*, and bring *them*
unto me.
3And if any *man* say ought unto you, ye shall say, The Lord hath need of
them; and straightway he will send them.
4All this was done, that it might be fulfilled which was spoken by the
prophet, saying,
5Tell ye the daughter of Sion, Behold, thy King cometh unto thee, meek,
and sitting upon an ass, and a colt the foal of an ass.
6And the disciples went, and did as Jesus commanded them,
7And brought the ass, and the colt, and put on them their clothes, and
they set *him* thereon.
8And a very great multitude spread their garments in the way; others cut
down branches from the trees, and strawed *them* in the way.
9And the multitudes that went before, and that followed, cried, saying,
Hosanna to the Son of David: Blessed *is* he that cometh in the name of the
Lord; Hosanna in the highest.
10And when he was come into Jerusalem, all the city was moved, saying,
Who is this?
11And the multitude said, This is Jesus the prophet of Nazareth of
Galilee.

☆**21:1** Zech 14:4; Mk 11:1–10; Lk 19:28–40; Jn 12:12–19
☆**21:2**
21:3 Ps 24:1
21:5 Zech 9:9
☆**21:9** Ps 118:26; Mt 22:42; Mk 12:35–37; Rom 1:3
21:11 Mt 2:23; Lk 7:16; Jn 6:14; 7:40; 9:17

B. THE CLEANSING OF THE TEMPLE (CF. MK 11:15–19; LK 19:45–48; JN 2:13–22)

12¶And Jesus went into the temple of God, and cast out all them that sold
and bought in the temple, and overthrew the tables of the moneychangers,
and the seats of them that sold doves,

☆**21:12** Deut 14:24–26; Mk 11:15–19; Lk 19:45–48; Jn 2:13–16

21:1ff See note on Luke 19:28 regarding the triumphal entry into Jerusalem.

21:2 Jesus instructed his two unnamed disciples to find and bring to him two animals, an ass and her colt. The prophetic word would not have been fulfilled if they had brought only one ass (see Zech. 9:9). Some people who profess to be believers stumble over prophecy (by which events are predicted long before they happen). Perhaps the greatest of all prophecies (compositely speaking) is the one which speaks of Christ's Second Advent, something which has not yet occurred. The church universal has always accepted this as true. Thus, prophecy for all other predicted events should be equally true.

21:9 The word *hosanna*, which means "save, we beseech thee," is used six times in the Gospels.

21:12 According to John 2, Jesus used a whip to drive out the money changers. No mention of a whip is made here. "Tradition says that his face shone, and beams of light darted from his blessed eyes, which astonished these market-people and compelled them to yield to his command; if so, the scripture was fulfilled, Prov. 20:8, 'A King that sitteth in the throne of judgment scattereth away all evil with his eyes.' "*

21:13 13 And said unto them, It is written, My house shall be called the house of
Isa 56:7 Jer 7:11 prayer; but ye have made it a den of thieves.
21:14 Isa 35:5, 6 14 And the blind and the lame came to him in the temple; and he healed
them.
21:15 Ps 8:2 15 And when the chief priests and scribes saw the wonderful things that he
did, and the children crying in the temple, and saying, Hosanna to the Son
of David; they were sore displeased,
16 And said unto him, Hearest thou what these say? And Jesus saith unto
them, Yea; have ye never read, Out of the mouth of babes and sucklings
thou hast perfected praise?
21:17 Mk 11:11 17 ¶And he left them, and went out of the city into Bethany; and he
Jn 11:18 lodged there.

C. THE WITHERING OF THE FIG TREE (CF. MK 11:12–14, 20–25)

21:18 Mk 11:12–14 18 Now in the morning as he returned into the city, he hungered.
21:19☆ 19 And when he saw a fig tree in the way, he came to it, and found nothing
thereon, but leaves only, and said unto it, Let no fruit grow on thee
henceforward for ever. And presently the fig tree withered away.
20 And when the disciples saw *it*, they marvelled, saying, How soon is the
fig tree withered away!
21:21☆ Mt 17:20 21 Jesus answered and said unto them, Verily I say unto you, If ye have
Lk 17:6 1 Cor 13:2 faith, and doubt not, ye shall not only do this *which is done* to the fig tree,
Jas 1:6 but also if ye shall say unto this mountain, Be thou removed, and be thou
cast into the sea; it shall be done.
21:22☆ Mt 7:7 22 And all things, whatsoever ye shall ask in prayer, believing, ye shall
Mt 11:24 Lk 11:9 Jas 5:16 1 Jn 3:22; 5:14 receive.

D. THE JEWISH LEADERS QUESTION JESUS' AUTHORITY (CF. MK 11:27–33; LK 20:1–8)

21:23 Mk 11:26–33 23 ¶And when he was come into the temple, the chief priests and the
Lk 20:1–8 elders of the people came unto him as he was teaching, and said, By what
Acts 4:7; 7:27 authority doest thou these things? and who gave thee this authority?
21:24 Job 5:13 24 And Jesus answered and said unto them, I also will ask you one thing,
which if ye tell me, I in like wise will tell you by what authority I do these
things.
21:25☆ 25 The baptism of John, whence was it? from heaven, or of men? And they
reasoned with themselves, saying, If we shall say, From heaven; he will say
unto us, Why did ye not then believe him?
21:26 Mt 14:5 26 But if we shall say, Of men; we fear the people; for all hold John as a
Mk 6:20 prophet.
27 And they answered Jesus, and said, We cannot tell. And he said unto
them, Neither tell I you by what authority I do these things.

21:19 *he saw a fig tree.* This type of fig tree produced fruit before or at the same time the leaves came out. Thus, if the tree were good, there should be fruit with the leaves. The fuller meaning of Jesus' statement is directed to the Jews who had nothing but leaves, no *fruit. Since the fig tree symbolized Israel* (Hos. 9:10; Joel 1:7), this curse pronounced judgment upon Israel.
21:21 After cursing the fig tree, Jesus informed his disciples that if they had faith and did not doubt, greater things than the cursing of this tree could be done by them through prayer. Doubt is the enemy of faith, and James says that he whose faith wavereth will not receive anything of the Lord (James 1:6, 7).
21:22 See note to Matt. 7:7 on the principles of prayer and faith.
21:25 Jesus' question about the baptism of John was very relevant; it implied that John's authority was divine and so was his own. If his enemies denied John's authority they would risk offending the people who believed John had divine authority. And if they affirmed his authority, then they should regard Jesus as having divine authority because John declared that Jesus did come from God and had authority. Jesus had them on the horns of a dilemma.

E. THE PARABLE OF THE TWO SONS

28 ¶But what think ye? A *certain* man had two sons; and he came to the
first, and said, Son, go work to day in my vineyard.
29 He answered and said, I will not: but afterward he repented, and went.
30 And he came to the second, and said likewise. And he answered and
said, I *go*, sir: and went not.
31 Whether of them twain did the will of *his* father? They say unto him,
The first. Jesus saith unto them, Verily I say unto you, That the publicans
and the harlots go into the kingdom of God before you.
32 For John came unto you in the way of righteousness, and ye believed
him not; but the publicans and the harlots believed him: and ye, when ye
had seen *it*, repented not afterward, that ye might believe him.

☆**21:28**

21:32 Mt 3:2; Lk 3:3, 12; 7:29, 30

F. THE PARABLE OF THE WICKED HUSBANDMEN (CF. MK 12:1–12; LK 20:9–19)

33 ¶Hear another parable: There was a certain householder, which planted
a vineyard, and hedged it round about, and digged a winepress in it, and
built a tower, and let it out to husbandmen, and went into a far country:
34 And when the time of the fruit drew near, he sent his servants to the
husbandmen, that they might receive the fruits of it.
35 And the husbandmen took his servants, and beat one, and killed
another, and stoned another.
36 Again, he sent other servants more than the first: and they did unto
them likewise.
37 But last of all he sent unto them his son, saying, They will reverence my
son.
38 But when the husbandmen saw the son, they said among themselves,
This is the heir; come, let us kill him, and let us seize on his inheritance.
39 And they caught him, and cast *him* out of the vineyard, and slew *him*.
40 When the lord therefore of the vineyard cometh, what will he do unto
those husbandmen?
41 They say unto him, He will miserably destroy those wicked men, and
will let out *his* vineyard unto other husbandmen, which shall render him the
fruits in their seasons.
42 Jesus saith unto them, Did ye never read in the scriptures, The stone
which the builders rejected, the same is become the head of the corner: this
is the Lord's doing, and it is marvellous in our eyes?
43 Therefore say I unto you, The kingdom of God shall be taken from you,
and given to a nation bringing forth the fruits thereof.
44 And whosoever shall fall on this stone shall be broken: but on
whomsoever it shall fall, it will grind him to powder.
45 And when the chief priests and Pharisees had heard his parables, they
perceived that he spake of them.
46 But when they sought to lay hands on him, they feared the multitude,
because they took him for a prophet.

☆**21:33** Mk 12:1–12; Lk 20:9–19

21:35 2 Chron 36:15, 16; Mt 23:34; Acts 7:52; 1 Thess 2:15

21:37 Gal 4:4

21:38 Jn 11:53; Acts 4:27; 1 Thess 2:15

21:41 Lk 21:24; Acts 13:46; Heb 2:3

☆**21:42** Ps 118:22, 23; Isa 28:16; Acts 4:11; Eph 2:20; 1 Pet 2:6, 7

21:44 Isa 8:14, 15; Dan 2:44, 45

21:46 Jn 7:40–44

21:28ff Only Matthew records this parable in connection with the questioning of Jesus' authority by the chief priests and the elders. The story of the two sons in the vineyard was meant to show the spiritual stupidity of the ecclesiastical leaders who refused to say that John's baptism was of God; even the lowly publicans and the harlots knew the story and accepted it as true.

21:33 See note to Luke 20:9 on the wicked husbandmen.

21:42 This verse, taken from Psalm 118:22, refers to a stone for the temple that was discarded when no place could be found for it. Then it was discovered that it was the chief cornerstone of the building. The rejection of the stone by the builders exemplifies the abuse to the son of the owner by the husbandmen and the abuse heaped on Jesus by the Jews when he came to them from his Father.

G. THE PARABLE OF THE WEDDING FEAST (CF. LK 14:15–24)

22:1 Lk 14:15–24
22 AND Jesus answered and spake unto them again by parables, and
said,
22:2☆
2 The kingdom of heaven is like unto a certain king, which made a
marriage for his son,
3 And sent forth his servants to call them that were bidden to the
wedding: and they would not come.
4 Again, he sent forth other servants, saying, Tell them which are bidden,
Behold, I have prepared my dinner: my oxen and *my* fatlings *are* killed, and
all things *are* ready: come unto the marriage.
5 But they made light of *it*, and went their ways, one to his farm, another
to his merchandise:
6 And the remnant took his servants, and entreated *them* spitefully, and
slew *them*.
22:7 Dan 9:26
7 But when the king heard *thereof*, he was wroth: and he sent forth his
armies, and destroyed those murderers, and burned up their city.
22:8 Acts 13:46
8 Then saith he to his servants, The wedding is ready, but they which were
bidden were not worthy.
9 Go ye therefore into the highways, and as many as ye shall find, bid to
the marriage.
10 So those servants went out into the highways, and gathered together all
as many as they found, both bad and good: and the wedding was furnished
with guests.
11 ¶And when the king came in to see the guests, he saw there a man
which had not on a wedding garment:
22:12 Rom 3:19
12 And he saith unto him, Friend, how camest thou in hither not having a
wedding garment? And he was speechless.
22:13 Mt 8:12; 25:30
13 Then said the king to the servants, Bind him hand and foot, and take
22:14 Mt 24:22; 2 Pet 1:10; Rev 17:14
him away, and cast *him* into outer darkness; there shall be weeping and
gnashing of teeth.
14 For many are called, but few *are* chosen.

H. THE JEWISH LEADERS AND JESUS: QUESTIONS AND ANSWERS

1. Paying Taxes to Rome (Cf. Mk 12:13–17; Lk 20:19–26)

22:15 Mk 12:13–17; Lk 20:20–26
15 ¶Then went the Pharisees, and took counsel how they might entangle
him in *his* talk.
22:16☆
16 And they sent out unto him their disciples with the He-ro′di-ans,
saying, Master, we know that thou art true, and teachest the way of God in
truth, neither carest thou for any *man:* for thou regardest not the person of
men.
22:17 Mt 17:24
17 Tell us therefore, What thinkest thou? Is it lawful to give tribute unto
Cæsar, or not?
18 But Jesus perceived their wickedness, and said, Why tempt ye me, *ye*
hypocrites?
19 Shew me the tribute money. And they brought unto him a penny.
20 And he saith unto them, Whose *is* this image and superscription?
22:21☆ Rom 13:7
21 They say unto him, Cæsar's. Then saith he unto them, Render therefore

---

***22:2** See note to Luke 14:16 about the parable of the* marriage feast.

22:16 The Herodians are mentioned here and in Mark 3:6; 12:13. They were a political party that attached itself to Herod's dynasty. Archelaus, Herod's son, became the ethnarch of Judea but was deposed (ca. A.D. 7) and replaced by Roman governors. The Herodians wanted the return of the Herodian dynasty to Judea. Both the Herodians and the Pharisees joined forces against Jesus, whom they considered their greatest enemy. Their alliance was one of convenience; their sole purpose was to dispose of Jesus.

22:21 God's due takes precedence over Caesar's due when one is forced to choose between them.

unto Cæsar the things which are Cæsar's; and unto God the things that are
God's.
22 When they had heard *these words*, they marvelled, and left him, and
went their way.

22:22 Job 5:12, 13

2. The Sadducees and the Resurrection (Cf. Mk 12:18–27; Lk 20:27–38)

23 ¶The same day came to him the Sad'du-cees, which say that there is no
resurrection, and asked him,
24 Saying, Master, Moses said, If a man die, having no children, his
brother shall marry his wife, and raise up seed unto his brother.
25 Now there were with us seven brethren: and the first, when he had
married a wife, deceased, and, having no issue, left his wife unto his
brother:
26 Likewise the second also, and the third, unto the seventh.
27 And last of all the woman died also.
28 Therefore in the resurrection whose wife shall she be of the seven? for
they all had her.
29 Jesus answered and said unto them, Ye do err, not knowing the
scriptures, nor the power of God.
30 For in the resurrection they neither marry, nor are given in marriage,
but are as the angels of God in heaven.
31 But as touching the resurrection of the dead, have ye not read that
which was spoken unto you by God, saying,
32 I am the God of Abraham, and the God of Isaac, and the God of
Jacob? God is not the God of the dead, but of the living.
33 And when the multitude heard *this*, they were astonished at his
doctrine.

☆**22:23** Mk 12:18–27 Lk 10:27–40 Acts 23:8 1 Cor 15:12
22:24 Gen 38:8 Deut 25:5
☆**22:25**
22:29 Jn 20:9
☆**22:32** Ex 3:6, 15 Acts 7:32
☆**22:33** Mt 7:28

3. The Pharisees and the Most Important Commandment (Cf. Mk 12:28–34)

34 ¶But when the Pharisees had heard that he had put the Sad'du-cees to
silence, they were gathered together.
35 Then one of them, *which was* a lawyer, asked *him a question*, tempting
him, and saying,
36 Master, which *is* the great commandment in the law?
37 Jesus said unto him, Thou shalt love the Lord thy God with all thy
heart, and with all thy soul, and with all thy mind.
38 This is the first and great commandment.
39 And the second *is* like unto it, Thou shalt love thy neighbour as thyself.
40 On these two commandments hang all the law and the prophets.

22:34 Mk 12:28–31
22:35 Lk 10:25
22:37 Deut 6:5 10:12, 13; 30:6
22:38 Lev 19:18 Mt 7:12 Rom 13:9 Gal 5:14 Jas 2:8

4. Jesus' Unanswerable Question (Cf. Mk 12:35–37; Lk 20:41–44)

41 ¶While the Pharisees were gathered together, Jesus asked them,
42 Saying, What think ye of Christ? whose son is he? They say unto him,
The Son of David.

22:41 Mk 12:35–37 Lk 20:41–44

22:23 See note on Luke 20:27 for information about the Sadducees and the resurrection.
22:25 See note to Deut. 25:5–10 for levirate marriage.
22:32 When God spoke to Moses he said, "I *am* the God of Abraham . . . Isaac, and . . . Jacob." He did not say, "I *was*." Therefore Abraham, Isaac, and Jacob were alive, even though they had died and their bodies were buried years before God said this. This proves that the soul of a believer is immortal, and it implies the resurrection of the body at some later date. The Sadducees were theological liberals who denied what the Bible clearly taught. They were confounded by Jesus.
22:33 Since the multitudes were astonished by the teaching of Jesus, they must not have been properly instructed by the scribes, and they themselves must have been unfamiliar with the Scriptures. Wherever the Word of God is not available, there will be theological error.

22:43☆ 2 Sam 23:2 Acts 2:30 2 Pet 1:20, 21
22:44 Ps 110:1 Mt 26:64 Mk 16:19 Acts 2:34 1 Cor 15:25 Heb 1:13; 10:12
22:46 Lk 14:6; 20:40

43 He saith unto them, How then doth David in spirit call him Lord, saying,

44 The LORD said unto my Lord, Sit thou on my right hand, till I make thine enemies thy footstool?

45 If David then call him Lord, how is he his son?

46 And no man was able to answer him a word, neither durst any *man* from that day forth ask him any more *questions*.

I. PHARISAISM

1. The Sins of the Pharisees (Cf. Mk 12:38–40; Lk 20:45–47)

23:2☆ Ezra 7:6, 25 Neh 8:1–4 Lk 11:46 Acts 15:10 Rom 2:17–23 Gal 6:13

23 THEN spake Jesus to the multitude, and to his disciples,

2 Saying, The scribes and the Pharisees sit in Moses' seat:

3 All therefore whatsoever they bid you observe, *that* observe and do; but do not ye after their works: for they say, and do not.

4 For they bind heavy burdens and grievous to be borne, and lay *them* on men's shoulders; but they *themselves* will not move them with one of their fingers.

23:5☆ Num 15:37–40 Mt 6:1, 2 Mk 12:38–40 Lk 20:46, 47

5 But all their works they do for to be seen of men: they make broad their phylacteries, and enlarge the borders of their garments,

6 And love the uppermost rooms at feasts, and the chief seats in the synagogues,

23:9 Mal 1:6
23:11 Mt 20:26 Mk 9:35 10:43–45 Lk 9:48
23:12 Job 22:29 Prov 15:33 29:23 Dan 4:37 Lk 14:11; 18:14 Jas 4:6 1 Pet 5:5, 6

7 And greetings in the markets, and to be called of men, Rabbi, Rabbi.

8 But be not ye called Rabbi: for one is your Master, *even* Christ; and all ye are brethren.

9 And call no *man* your father upon the earth: for one is your Father, which is in heaven.

10 Neither be ye called masters: for one is your Master, *even* Christ.

11 But he that is greatest among you shall be your servant.

12 And whosoever shall exalt himself shall be abased; and he that shall humble himself shall be exalted.

2. The Woes Pronounced against the Pharisees

23:13☆ Lk 11:39–52

13 ¶But woe unto you, scribes and Pharisees, hypocrites! for ye shut up the kingdom of heaven against men: for ye neither go in *yourselves*, neither suffer ye them that are entering to go in.

14 Woe unto you, scribes and Pharisees, hypocrites! for ye devour widows' houses, and for a pretence make long prayer: therefore ye shall receive the greater damnation.

15 Woe unto you, scribes and Pharisees, hypocrites! for ye compass sea and land to make one proselyte, and when he is made, ye make him twofold more the child of hell than yourselves.

22:43 See note to Mark 12:35, 36 (wherein Jesus asserts his deity).

23:2ff Nowhere else in the Gospels does Jesus speak so scorchingly about men as he does about the scribes and Pharisees here. He recognized the legitimacy of the office they held, but he made it clear that bad people can occupy good offices. The Pharisees boasted of the orthodoxy of their teaching and the goodness of their works. But what they said and what they did were not in agreement. Their talk was better than their walk. Jesus says they are hypocrites; good people should not follow their practices.

23:5 *phylacteries,* or "prayer boxes," were small leather cases containing strips of vellum on which were written the words from Exod. 13:1–16; Deut. 6:4–9; 11:13–21. Two such cases (called *tephillim,* "prayers") were carried, one on the forehead, and the other on the arm, in literal compliance with Exod. 13:16; Deut. 6:8; 11:18. *borders,* or "fringes," were the four tassels, one at each corner of the cloak, that symbolized religious devotion (Num. 15:38–41). Jesus said that all of this was done for the purpose of parading their piety before men—and he condemned the practice.

23:13ff The eight "woes" pronounced against the scribes and Pharisees appear only in this Gospel. They are hypocrites, i.e., stage-players in religion. Their condition is woeful: living, their religion is vain; dying, their ruin is great.

16 Woe unto you, *ye* blind guides, which say, Whosoever shall swear by
the temple, it is nothing; but whosoever shall swear by the gold of the
temple, he is a debtor!
17 *Ye* fools and blind: for whether is greater, the gold, or the temple that
sanctifieth the gold?
18 And, Whosoever shall swear by the altar, it is nothing; but whosoever
sweareth by the gift that is upon it, he is guilty.
19 *Ye* fools and blind: for whether *is* greater, the gift, or the altar that
sanctifieth the gift?
20 Whoso therefore shall swear by the altar, sweareth by it, and by all
things thereon.
21 And whoso shall swear by the temple, sweareth by it, and by him that
dwelleth therein.
22 And he that shall swear by heaven, sweareth by the throne of God, and
by him that sitteth thereon.
23 Woe unto you, scribes and Pharisees, hypocrites! for ye pay tithe of
mint and anise and cummin, and have omitted the weightier *matters* of the
law, judgment, mercy, and faith: these ought ye to have done, and not to
leave the other undone.
24 *Ye* blind guides, which strain at a gnat, and swallow a camel.
25 Woe unto you, scribes and Pharisees, hypocrites! for ye make clean the
outside of the cup and of the platter, but within they are full of extortion
and excess.
26 *Thou* blind Pharisee, cleanse first that *which is* within the cup and
platter, that the outside of them may be clean also.
27 Woe unto you, scribes and Pharisees, hypocrites! for ye are like unto
whited sepulchres, which indeed appear beautiful outward, but are within
full of dead *men's* bones, and of all uncleanness.
28 Even so ye also outwardly appear righteous unto men, but within ye are
full of hypocrisy and iniquity.
29 Woe unto you, scribes and Pharisees, hypocrites! because ye build the
tombs of the prophets, and garnish the sepulchres of the righteous,
30 And say, If we had been in the days of our fathers, we would not have
been partakers with them in the blood of the prophets.
31 Wherefore ye be witnesses unto yourselves, that ye are the children of
them which killed the prophets.
32 Fill ye up then the measure of your fathers.
33 *Ye* serpents, *ye* generation of vipers, how can ye escape the damnation
of hell?
34 ¶Wherefore, behold, I send unto you prophets, and wise men, and
scribes: and *some* of them ye shall kill and crucify; and *some* of them shall
ye scourge in your synagogues, and persecute *them* from city to city:
35 That upon you may come all the righteous blood shed upon the earth,

☆**23:16** Isa 56:10; Mt 5:33–35; 15:14
23:19 Ex 29:37; 30:29
23:21 1 Kgs 8:12, 13; 2 Chron 6:1; Ps 26:8; 132:14
23:22 Ps 11:4; Acts 7:48, 49
23:23 1 Sam 15:22; Hos 6:6; Mic 6:8; Mt 9:13; 12:7
23:25 Mk 7:4; Tit 1:15
23:27 Lk 11:44; Acts 23:3
23:31 Acts 7:51
23:32 Gen 15:16; 1 Thess 2:16
23:33 Mt 3:7; 12:34; Lk 3:7
23:34 Acts 5:40; 7:58; 22:19; 2 Cor 11:23–25
☆**23:35** Gen 4:8; 1 Jn 3:12; Rev 18:24

23:16 The scribes and Pharisees were condemned by Jesus for permitting men to violate their vows. Taking an oath by the temple was subject to exemption; but if it was taken by the gold of the temple, it was binding. Jesus said that the gold was sanctified by the temple, not the temple by the gold. Taking an oath by the temple, he said, is binding because the oath is taken by the one who lives in it (God). Moreover, Jesus said no one can break a commandment on the ground that to keep it would violate an oath. Wicked men would then take many oaths in order to invalidate the commandments of God.

23:35 *Zecharias,* the author of the Old Testament Book of Zechariah. Some have argued that the Zechariah here is the one mentioned in 2 Chron. 24:20. This Zechariah was murdered (his father was said to be Jehoiada the priest). Since the Book of 2 Chron. appears last in the Hebrew Bible (and Luke says nothing about Zechariah's ancestry), the phrase *from the blood of righteous Abel unto the blood of Zecharias* means no more than "from the first to the last murder in the Old Testament."

from the blood of righteous Abel unto the blood of Zach-a-ri'as son of Bar-
a-chi'as, whom ye slew between the temple and the altar.
36 Verily I say unto you, All these things shall come upon this generation.

3. Jesus' Lament over Jerusalem (Cf. Lk 13:34, 35)

23:37
Deut 32:11
Lk 13:34, 35

37 O Jerusalem, Jerusalem, *thou* that killest the prophets, and stonest them
which are sent unto thee, how often would I have gathered thy children
together, even as a hen gathereth her chickens under *her* wings, and ye
would not!

23:38
Ezek 10:4, 18, 19
23:39
Ps 118:26
Mt 21:9

38 Behold, your house is left unto you desolate.
39 For I say unto you, Ye shall not see me henceforth, till ye shall say,
Blessed *is* he that cometh in the name of the Lord.

J. THE OLIVET DISCOURSE (CF. MK 13; LK 21)

1. Predictions about the End of the Age (Cf. Mk 13:3–13; Lk 21:5–19)

24:1
Mk 13:1–13
Lk 21:5–19
24:2☆
1 Kgs 9:8
Jer 7:14; 26:18
Mic 3:12
Lk 19:44
24:3☆
1 Thess 5:1

24 AND Jesus went out, and departed from the temple: and his
disciples came to *him* for to shew him the buildings of the temple.
2 And Jesus said unto them, See ye not all these things? verily I say unto
you, There shall not be left here one stone upon another, that shall not be
thrown down.
3 ¶And as he sat upon the mount of Olives, the disciples came unto him
privately, saying, Tell us, when shall these things be? and what *shall be* the
sign of thy coming, and of the end of the world?

24:4
Jer 29:8
2 Thess 2:3
1 Jn 4:1
24:5
Jer 14:14; 23:21
Jn 5:43

4 And Jesus answered and said unto them, Take heed that no man deceive
you.
5 For many shall come in my name, saying, I am Christ; and shall deceive
many.
6 And ye shall hear of wars and rumours of wars: see that ye be not
troubled: for all *these things* must come to pass, but the end is not yet.
7 For nation shall rise against nation, and kingdom against kingdom: and
there shall be famines, and pestilences, and earthquakes, in divers places.

24:9
Acts 7:59; 12:1
24:10
2 Tim 4:10, 16
24:11
Acts 20:29
2 Cor 11:13
1 Tim 4:1
2 Pet 2:1
24:12☆
2 Tim 3:1–5
24:13
Mt 10:22
Rev 2:7
24:14☆
Mk 13:14–23
Lk 21:20–24
Rom 10:18
Col 1:6, 23

8 All these *are* the beginning of sorrows.
9 Then shall they deliver you up to be afflicted, and shall kill you: and ye
shall be hated of all nations for my name's sake.
10 And then shall many be offended, and shall betray one another, and
shall hate one another.
11 And many false prophets shall rise, and shall deceive many.
12 And because iniquity shall abound, the love of many shall wax cold.
13 But he that shall endure unto the end, the same shall be saved.
14 And this gospel of the kingdom shall be preached in all the world for a
witness unto all nations; and then shall the end come.

24:2 Both the Old and New Testament contain prophecy. Some of the New Testament prophecies, such as the destruction of Jerusalem, have already taken place. Others await fulfillment. The Olivet Discourse of Jesus (chapters 23–25) and the Book of Revelation contain much prophecy which yet remains to be fulfilled.
24:3 In this instance Jesus' disciples asked him two questions: (1) *when shall these things be?*, i.e., the destruction of the temple buildings; (2) *what shall be the sign of thy coming, and of the end of the world?* Matthew did not record all that Jesus said on this question. *world,* literally, "age."

24:12 *the love of many shall wax cold.* Many, but not all, will grow cold during the period of tribulation. But all, at one time, had love and were hot in their affection for the things of God. No one can become cold who has not first been hot, and no one can lose love who has not first had it. This is a serious warning to all as the end of the age approaches.
24:14 The coming of the Lord is here related to the preaching of the gospel to all the world. So long as Jesus tarries, the Great Commission has not been fully carried out. Let the church be about its business with diligence.

2. The Great Tribulation (Cf. Mk 13:14–23; Lk 21:20–24)

15 When ye therefore shall see the abomination of desolation, spoken of
by Daniel the prophet, stand in the holy place, (whoso readeth, let him
understand:)
16 Then let them which be in Judæa flee into the mountains:
17 Let him which is on the housetop not come down to take any thing out
of his house:
18 Neither let him which is in the field return back to take his clothes.
19 And woe unto them that are with child, and to them that give suck in
those days!
20 But pray ye that your flight be not in the winter, neither on the sabbath
day:
21 For then shall be great tribulation, such as was not since the beginning
of the world to this time, no, nor ever shall be.
22 And except those days should be shortened, there should no flesh be
saved: but for the elect's sake those days shall be shortened.
23 Then if any man shall say unto you, Lo, here *is* Christ, or there; believe
it not.
24 For there shall arise false Christs, and false prophets, and shall shew
great signs and wonders; insomuch that, if *it were* possible, they shall
deceive the very elect.
25 Behold, I have told you before.
26 Wherefore if they shall say unto you, Behold, he is in the desert; go not
forth: behold, *he is* in the secret chambers; believe *it* not.
27 For as the lightning cometh out of the east, and shineth even unto the
west; so shall also the coming of the Son of man be.
28 For wheresoever the carcase is, there will the eagles be gathered
together.

☆**24:15** Dan 9:27; 11:31 12:11
☆**24:17**
24:21 Dan 12:1 Joel 2:2 Rev 3:10; 7:14
24:22 Isa 65:8, 9
24:24 2 Thess 2:9 1 Jun 4:1–3 Rev 13:13, 14
24:28 Job 39:30 Lk 17:37 Rev 19:17, 18

3. The Coming of the Lord (Cf. Mk 13:24–27; Lk 21:25–28)

29 Immediately after the tribulation of those days shall the sun be
darkened, and the moon shall not give her light, and the stars shall fall from
heaven, and the powers of the heavens shall be shaken:
30 And then shall appear the sign of the Son of man in heaven: and then
shall all the tribes of the earth mourn, and they shall see the Son of man
coming in the clouds of heaven with power and great glory.
31 And he shall send his angels with a great sound of a trumpet, and they
shall gather together his elect from the four winds, from one end of heaven
to the other.

24:29 Isa 13:10 Ezek 32:7, 8 Joel 2:31; 3:15 Mk 13:24–37 Lk 21:25–36 Acts 2:20 Rev 6:12
24:30 Dan 7:13 Zech 12:10–14 Rev 1:7
☆**24:31** 1 Cor 15:52 1 Thess 4:16 Rev 11:15

24:15 *the abomination of desolation.* The Greek phrase used here is nearly an exact rendering of Dan. 9:27 in the Septuagint (the Greek version of the Old Testament). The first fulfillment of this prophecy occurred in 165 B.C., when Antiochus IV (Epiphanes) sacrificed a sow on the altar before the temple of Jerusalem. Here Jesus is speaking of a future event. Some think this was fulfilled in A.D. 70, when Jerusalem was destroyed by the Romans. Others believe this prophecy remains to be fulfilled at the end of the age. Those who hold the latter view usually tie the words of Daniel and Jesus to those of Paul in 2 Thess. 2:8–12, in which he speaks about the man of sin. Paul definitely relates it to the second coming of Jesus. (See note on Dan. 9:27.)

24:17 *housetop,* i.e., "rooftop." Rooftops, being flat, were used as porches at that time. (See Acts 10:9.)†

24:31 *a great sound of a trumpet.* The sound of the trumpet is connected with many events in the history of Israel: (1) at the giving of the law (Exod. 19:13, 16); (2) in the calling of assemblies (Num. 10:2); (3) in the praise of God (Ps. 81:3); (4) in offering sacrifices (Num. 10:10); (5) in proclaiming the year of jubilee (Lev. 25:9). It is spoken of in the New Testament in 1 Cor. 15:52 and 1 Thess. 4:16. When the last trumpet sounds, "sinners shall fall as sacrifices to divine justice, and the saints shall enter upon their eternal jubilee."*

4. The Lesson from the Fig Tree (Cf. Mk 13:28–31; Lk 21:29–33)

32 Now learn a parable of the fig tree; When his branch is yet tender, and
putteth forth leaves, ye know that summer *is* nigh:
24:33 Mt 16:28 Jas 5:9
33 So likewise ye, when ye shall see all these things, know that it is near,
even at the doors.
24:34☆ **24:35** Ps 102:25–27 Isa 51:6 Mt 5:18 Heb 1:10–12
34 Verily I say unto you, This generation shall not pass, till all these things
be fulfilled.
35 Heaven and earth shall pass away, but my words shall not pass away.

5. The Time of the Lord's Coming (Cf. Mk 13:32–37; Lk 21:34–36)

24:36 Acts 1:7 1 Thess 5:2 2 Pet 3:10 **24:37** Gen 6:3; 7:1 Lk 17:26 1 Pet 3:20
36 ¶But of that day and hour knoweth no *man*, no, not the angels of
heaven, but my Father only.
37 But as the days of No'e *were*, so shall also the coming of the Son of man
be.
38 For as in the days that were before the flood they were eating and
drinking, marrying and giving in marriage, until the day that No'e entered
into the ark,
39 And knew not until the flood came, and took them all away; so shall
also the coming of the Son of man be.
24:40 Lk 17:34–36
40 Then shall two be in the field; the one shall be taken, and the other left.
41 Two *women shall be* grinding at the mill; the one shall be taken, and the
other left.
24:42 Lk 12:29; 21:36 1 Thess 5:6 Rev 3:3, 16:15
42 ¶Watch therefore: for ye know not what hour your Lord doth come.
43 But know this, that if the goodman of the house had known in what
watch the thief would come, he would have watched, and would not have
suffered his house to be broken up.
44 Therefore be ye also ready: for in such an hour as ye think not the Son
of man cometh.

6. Wise and Faithful Servants (Cf. Lk 12:42–46)

24:45 Lk 12:40–47 1 Cor 4:2 Heb 3:5
45 Who then is a faithful and wise servant, whom his lord hath made ruler
over his household, to give them meat in due season?
46 Blessed *is* that servant, whom his lord when he cometh shall find so
doing.
47 Verily I say unto you, That he shall make him ruler over all his goods.
48 But and if that evil servant shall say in his heart, My lord delayeth his
coming;
49 And shall begin to smite *his* fellowservants, and to eat and drink with
the drunken;
50 The lord of that servant shall come in a day when he looketh not for
him, and in an hour that he is not aware of,
24:51 Mt 25:30
51 And shall cut him asunder, and appoint *him* his portion with the
hypocrites: there shall be weeping and gnashing of teeth.

7. The Parable of the Ten Bridesmaids

25:1☆ Isa 61:10 Mt 9:15 Jn 3:29 Rev 19:7 21:2, 9
25 THEN shall the kingdom of heaven be likened unto ten virgins,
which took their lamps, and went forth to meet the bridegroom.

24:34 A *generation* in the Old Testament was measured as forty years. There is a question about whether *Jesus was talking about the generation* of people who were alive then, or the generation of people who would be living at the time of the Second Advent. If the former is correct, then Jesus was saying that his Second Advent would come not more than forty years after his death and resurrection. In the sense that Jerusalem was destroyed in A.D. 70, Christ's contemporaries *did* live to the fulfillment of *these things.* In the latter case, however, the generation refers to those living at the time of the beginning of the signs characterizing the end times—they will live to see the fulfillment of them all.

25:1ff This illustration teaches Christians that they must be watchful and ready for the coming of the Lord. The foolish virgins were careless, assuming they had plenty of time to get ready when the event approached.

2 And five of them were wise, and five *were* foolish.
3 They that *were* foolish took their lamps, and took no oil with them:
4 But the wise took oil in their vessels with their lamps.
5 While the bridegroom tarried, they all slumbered and slept.
6 And at midnight there was a cry made, Behold, the bridegroom cometh;
go ye out to meet him.
7 Then all those virgins arose, and trimmed their lamps.
8 And the foolish said unto the wise, Give us of your oil; for our lamps are
gone out.
9 But the wise answered, saying, *Not so;* lest there be not enough for us
and you: but go ye rather to them that sell, and buy for yourselves.
10 And while they went to buy, the bridegroom came; and they that were
ready went in with him to the marriage: and the door was shut.
11 Afterward came also the other virgins, saying, Lord, Lord, open to us.
12 But he answered and said, Verily I say unto you, I know you not.
13 Watch therefore, for ye know neither the day nor the hour wherein the
Son of man cometh.

25:5 1 Thess 4:16; 5:6; 2 Pet 3:4-9
25:7 Lk 12:35-40
25:10 Lk 13:24, 25
25:13 Mt 24:42; Mk 13:33; Rev 16:15

8. The Parable of the Loaned Money

14 ¶For *the kingdom of heaven is* as a man travelling into a far country,
who called his own servants, and delivered unto them his goods.
15 And unto one he gave five talents, to another two, and to another one;
to every man according to his several ability; and straightway took his
journey.
16 Then he that had received the five talents went and traded with the
same, and made *them* other five talents.
17 And likewise he that *had received* two, he also gained other two.
18 But he that had received one went and digged in the earth, and hid his
lord's money.
19 After a long time the lord of those servants cometh, and reckoneth with
them.
20 And so he that had received five talents came and brought other five
talents, saying, Lord, thou deliveredst unto me five talents: behold, I have
gained beside them five talents more.
21 His lord said unto him, Well done, *thou* good and faithful servant: thou
hast been faithful over a few things, I will make thee ruler over many
things: enter thou into the joy of thy lord.
22 He also that had received two talents came and said, Lord, thou
deliveredst unto me two talents: behold, I have gained two other talents
beside them.
23 His lord said unto him, Well done, good and faithful servant; thou hast
been faithful over a few things, I will make thee ruler over many things:
enter thou into the joy of thy lord.
24 Then he which had received the one talent came and said, Lord, I knew
thee that thou art an hard man, reaping where thou hast not sown, and
gathering where thou hast not strawed:
25 And I was afraid, and went and hid thy talent in the earth: lo, *there*
thou hast *that is* thine.

☆**25:14**
25:15 Rom 12:6; Eph 4:11; 1 Pet 4:10
25:21 Mt 24:46, 47; Lk 12:42-44; 22:28-30; 2 Tim 2:12

25:14ff This illustration teaches that God gives talents or abilities to men according to his good pleasure. Whether many or few, they are to be used properly. The servant with one talent failed to use properly what he had been given, then charged his master with greediness and cruelty. Christ's response to this senseless charge was that if the servant knew the master was rapacious, the least he could have done was put out the money at interest. All of us are responsible to use our "talents" with care and zeal.

26 His lord answered and said unto him, *Thou* wicked and slothful servant,
thou knewest that I reap where I sowed not, and gather where I have not
strawed:
27 Thou oughtest therefore to have put my money to the exchangers, and
then at my coming I should have received mine own with usury.
28 Take therefore the talent from him, and give *it* unto him which hath ten
talents.
29 For unto every one that hath shall be given, and he shall have
abundance: but from him that hath not shall be taken away even that which
he hath.
30 And cast ye the unprofitable servant into outer darkness: there shall be
weeping and gnashing of teeth.

9. The Judgment by the Son of Man

31 ¶When the Son of man shall come in his glory, and all the holy angels
with him, then shall he sit upon the throne of his glory:
32 And before him shall be gathered all nations: and he shall separate
them one from another, as a shepherd divideth *his* sheep from the goats:
33 And he shall set the sheep on his right hand, but the goats on the left.
34 Then shall the King say unto them on his right hand, Come, ye blessed
of my Father, inherit the kingdom prepared for you from the foundation of
the world:
35 For I was an hungred, and ye gave me meat: I was thirsty, and ye gave
me drink: I was a stranger, and ye took me in:
36 Naked, and ye clothed me: I was sick, and ye visited me: I was in
prison, and ye came unto me.
37 Then shall the righteous answer him, saying, Lord, when saw we thee
an hungred, and fed *thee?* or thirsty, and gave *thee* drink?
38 When saw we thee a stranger, and took *thee* in? or naked, and clothed
thee?
39 Or when saw we thee sick, or in prison, and came unto thee?
40 And the King shall answer and say unto them, Verily I say unto you,
Inasmuch as ye have done *it* unto one of the least of these my brethren, ye
have done *it* unto me.
41 Then shall he say also unto them on the left hand, Depart from me, ye
cursed, into everlasting fire, prepared for the devil and his angels:
42 For I was an hungred, and ye gave me no meat: I was thirsty, and ye
gave me no drink:
43 I was a stranger, and ye took me not in: naked, and ye clothed me not:
sick, and in prison, and ye visited me not.
44 Then shall they also answer him, saying, Lord, when saw we thee an
hungred, or athirst, or a stranger, or naked, or sick, or in prison, and did
not minister unto thee?
45 Then shall he answer them, saying, Verily I say unto you, Inasmuch as
ye did *it* not to one of the least of these, ye did *it* not to me.
46 And these shall go away into everlasting punishment: but the righteous
into life eternal.

25:29 Lk 8:18; Jn 15:2; 1 Cor 15:10
25:30 Mt 8:12; Lk 13:28
25:31 Zech 14:5; Acts 1:11; 3:20; 17:31; 1 Thess 4:16; 2 Thess 1:7; Rev 1:7
25:32 Ezek 20:34–38; 34:17; Mt 13:49; Rom 14:10; 2 Cor 5:10; Jude 15; Rev 20:12
25:34 Lk 12:32; Rom 8:17; 1 Cor 2:9; 6:9; Gal 5:21; Heb 11:16; Jas 2:5; Rev 21:7
25:35 Isa 58:7; 2 Tim 1:16; Heb 13:2, 3; Jas 2:15
25:40 Prov 14:31; 19:17; Heb 6:10
25:41 Mt 13:41; 2 Pet 2:4; Jude 6
25:45 Prov 17:5; Zech 2:8; Acts 9:5
25:46☆ Dan 12:2; Mt 19:29; Jn 3:15, 36; 5:29; Acts 13:46, 48; 24:15; Rom 2:7, 8; 6:23; Gal 6:8; 1 Jn 5:11

25:46 Eternal punishment, or eternal death, results from the failure to seek the face of God and to embrace Jesus Christ as Savior (Rom. 6:16, 21; 8:13). It differs from physical death, which saved and unsaved alike experience. It comes in its final form at the last judgment (see note on Rev. 20:11, 12). It is variously designated in Scripture as (1) "shame and everlasting contempt" (Dan. 12:2); (2) "destruction" (Rom. 9:22); (3) God's terrible anger (1 Thess. 1:10); (4) "second death" (Rev. 2:11); and (5) the place "where their worm dieth not, and the fire is not quenched" (Mark 9:48). Christ alone is the one through whom men may escape this awful end (John 3:16; 8:51; Acts 4:12).

K. JESUS' TRIAL AND SENTENCING

1. The Plot of the Jewish Officials (Cf. Mk 14:1, 2, 10, 11; Lk 22:1–6)

26 AND it came to pass, when Jesus had finished all these sayings, he
said unto his disciples,
2 Ye know that after two days is *the feast of* the passover, and the Son of
man is betrayed to be crucified.
3 Then assembled together the chief priests, and the scribes, and the elders
of the people, unto the palace of the high priest, who was called Cai'a-phas,
4 And consulted that they might take Jesus by subtilty, and kill *him.*
5 But they said, Not on the feast *day*, lest there be an uproar among the
people.

26:1 Mk 14:1, 2; Lk 22:1, 2
26:3 Ps 2:2; Jn 11:47, 48; Acts 4:25, 26

2. Mary of Bethany Anoints Jesus (Cf. Mk 14:3–9; Jn 12:1-8)

6 ¶Now when Jesus was in Bethany, in the house of Simon the leper,
7 There came unto him a woman having an alabaster box of very precious
ointment, and poured it on his head, as he sat *at meat.*
8 But when his disciples saw *it*, they had indignation, saying, To what
purpose *is* this waste?
9 For this ointment might have been sold for much, and given to the poor.
10 When Jesus understood *it*, he said unto them, Why trouble ye the
woman? for she hath wrought a good work upon me.
11 For ye have the poor always with you; but me ye have not always.
12 For in that she hath poured this ointment on my body, she did *it* for my
burial.
13 Verily I say unto you, Wheresoever this gospel shall be preached in the
whole world, *there* shall also this, that this woman hath done, be told for a
memorial of her.

26:6 Mk 14:3–9; Jn 12:1–8
26:7 Mt 21:17; Jn 11:1
26:11 Deut 15:11; Jn 17:11

3. Judas Iscariot Accepts a Bribe

14 ¶Then one of the twelve, called Judas Iscariot, went unto the chief
priests,
15 And said *unto them*, What will ye give me, and I will deliver him unto
you? And they covenanted with him for thirty pieces of silver.
16 And from that time he sought opportunity to betray him.

☆**26:14** Mt 10:4; Mk 14:10–16; Lk 22:3–13; Jn 13:2
26:15 Zech 11:12; Mt 27:3

4. The Passover Supper

a. The Preparation (Cf. Mk 14:12–16; Lk 22:7–13)

17 ¶Now the first *day* of the *feast of* unleavened bread the disciples came to
Jesus, saying unto him, Where wilt thou that we prepare for thee to eat the
passover?
18 And he said, Go into the city to such a man, and say unto him, The
Master saith, My time is at hand; I will keep the passover at thy house with
my disciples.

26:17 Ex 12:6; Lev 23:5, 6

26:14 *Judas Iscariot.* The name *Judas* is the Greek form of Judah; *Iscariot* may have been the Hellenized form for the town of Kerioth. He was the only disciple from Judea; the others were from Galilee. The Judeans looked down on the Galileans. In the lists of the disciples, Judas' name always appears last. He was covetous and dishonest. He sold Jesus to his enemies for a few pieces of silver. Jesus knew Judas would betray him even before he chose him as a disciple. Here we have the mystery of God's foreknowledge and Judas' free will. Jesus said that it would have been "far better for that one if he had never been born" (26:24, TLB). Some have argued that Judas did not partake of the bread and the wine at the Last Supper. The apparent discrepancy in the two accounts of Judas' death have been reconciled by the fact that Matthew's statement means no more than that he went away in despair and suffocated. In the Book of Acts, Luke adds that he fell on his face and burst open, spilling out his bowels. (See Matt. 27:3–10; Acts 1:16–20). Judas' life stands as a severe warning to those who would betray Christ (e.g., see Heb. 6:6).

19 And the disciples did as Jesus had appointed them; and they made
ready the passover.

b. The Celebration (Cf. Mk 14:17–21; Lk 22:14–18; Jn 13:1–30)

26:20 Mk 14:17–21 Lk 22:14, 21–23 Jn 13:21–30

20 Now when the even was come, he sat down with the twelve.
21 And as they did eat, he said, Verily I say unto you, that one of you shall
betray me.
22 And they were exceeding sorrowful, and began every one of them to say
unto him, Lord, is it I?

26:23 Ps 41:9

23 And he answered and said, He that dippeth *his* hand with me in the
dish, the same shall betray me.

26:24 Gen 3:15 Isa 53:8 Dan 9:26 Mt 26:31, 54, 56 Mk 9:12 Lk 24:25–27, 46 Jn 17:12 Acts 17:2, 3 26:22, 23 1 Cor 15:3 1 Pet 1:10, 11

24 The Son of man goeth as it is written of him: but woe unto that man by
whom the Son of man is betrayed! it had been good for that man if he had
not been born.
25 Then Judas, which betrayed him, answered and said, Master, is it I? He
said unto him, Thou hast said.

c. The Institution of the Lord's Supper (Cf. Mk 14:22–25; Lk 22:19–24)

26:26☆ Mk 14:22–26 Lk 22:19, 20, 39 1 Cor 10:16 11:23

26 ¶And as they were eating, Jesus took bread, and blessed *it*, and brake *it*,
and gave *it* to the disciples, and said, Take, eat; this is my body.
27 And he took the cup, and gave thanks, and gave *it* to them, saying,
Drink ye all of it;

26:28☆ Ex 24:8 Lev 17:11 Jer 31:31 Rom 5:15 Heb 9:22

26:29 Acts 10:41

28 For this is my blood of the new testament, which is shed for many for
the remission of sins.
29 But I say unto you, I will not drink henceforth of this fruit of the vine,
until that day when I drink it new with you in my Father's kingdom.

d. Jesus Predicts Peter's Denial (Cf. Mk 14:27–31; Lk 22:31–34; Jn 14—17)

30 And when they had sung an hymn, they went out into the mount of
Olives.

26:31 Mt 28:7 Mark 14:27–31 16:7 Lk 22:31–34 Jn 13:36–38 16:32

31 Then saith Jesus unto them, All ye shall be offended because of me this
night: for it is written, I will smite the shepherd, and the sheep of the flock
shall be scattered abroad.
32 But after I am risen again, I will go before you into Galilee.
33 Peter answered and said unto him, Though all *men* shall be offended
because of thee, *yet* will I never be offended.

26:34☆ Mt 26:75 Mk 14:30 Lk 22:34 Jn 13:38

34 Jesus said unto him, Verily I say unto thee, That this night, before the
cock crow, thou shalt deny me thrice.
35 Peter said unto him, Though I should die with thee, yet will I not deny
thee. Likewise also said all the disciples.

5. Jesus in Gethsemane's Garden
a. His Agony (Cf. Mk 14:32–42; Lk 22:39–46; Jn 18:1)

26:36 Mk 14:32–42 Lk 22:39–46 Jn 18:1

36 ¶Then cometh Jesus with them unto a place called Geth-sem'a-ne, and
saith unto the disciples, Sit ye here, while I go and pray yonder.

26:26 See note on Mark 14:22 regarding the Eucharist, or Lord's Supper.

26:28 *At the heart of the gospel* is the forgiveness of sins. The apostles, standing before the hostile high priest, said God exalted Jesus so that the people of Israel could have their sins forgiven (Acts 5:31); in Antioch of Pisidia Paul said, "In this man Jesus, there is forgiveness for your sins" (Acts 13:38, TLB). Forgiveness of sins is a divine, not a human, prerogative: "If we confess our sins to him, he can be depended on to forgive us. . ." (1 John 1:9, TLB). When God forgives sins they are forgotten, cast behind God's back forever. He forgives *all* our sins save one—the only unforgivable sin is blaspheming the Holy Spirit (12:31; Mark 3:29; 1 John 5:16), who is the only one who can bring about repentance and faith.

26:34 See note on Mark 14:30 for information about the crowing of the cock.

37 And he took with him Peter and the two sons of Zeb′e-dee, and began
to be sorrowful and very heavy.
38 Then saith he unto them, My soul is exceeding sorrowful, even unto
death: tarry ye here, and watch with me.
39 And he went a little further, and fell on his face, and prayed, saying, O
my Father, if it be possible, let this cup pass from me: nevertheless not as I
will, but as thou *wilt*.
40 And he cometh unto the disciples, and findeth them asleep, and saith
unto Peter, What, could ye not watch with me one hour?
41 Watch and pray, that ye enter not into temptation: the spirit indeed *is*
willing, but the flesh *is* weak.
42 He went away again the second time, and prayed, saying, O my Father,
if this cup may not pass away from me, except I drink it, thy will be done.
43 And he came and found them asleep again: for their eyes were heavy.
44 And he left them, and went away again, and prayed the third time,
saying the same words.
45 Then cometh he to his disciples, and saith unto them, Sleep on now,
and take *your* rest: behold, the hour is at hand, and the Son of man is
betrayed into the hands of sinners.
46 Rise, let us be going: behold, he is at hand that doth betray me.

b. His Betrayal and Arrest (Cf. Mk 14:43–50; Lk 22:47–53; Jn 18:1–11)

47 ¶And while he yet spake, lo, Judas, one of the twelve, came, and with
him a great multitude with swords and staves, from the chief priests and
elders of the people.
48 Now he that betrayed him gave them a sign, saying, Whomsoever I
shall kiss, that same is he: hold him fast.
49 And forthwith he came to Jesus, and said, Hail, master; and kissed him.
50 And Jesus said unto him, Friend, wherefore art thou come? Then came
they, and laid hands on Jesus, and took him.
51 And, behold, one of them which were with Jesus stretched out *his* hand,
and drew his sword, and struck a servant of the high priest's, and smote off
his ear.
52 Then said Jesus unto him, Put up again thy sword into his place: for all
they that take the sword shall perish with the sword.
53 Thinkest thou that I cannot now pray to my Father, and he shall
presently give me more than twelve legions of angels?
54 But how then shall the scriptures be fulfilled, that thus it must be?
55 In that same hour said Jesus to the multitudes, Are ye come out as
against a thief with swords and staves for to take me? I sat daily with you
teaching in the temple, and ye laid no hold on me.
56 But all this was done, that the scriptures of the prophets might be
fulfilled. Then all the disciples forsook him, and fled.

26:38 Jn 12:27
☆**26:39** Mt 20:22; Jn 5:30; 6:38; Heb 5:7
26:41 Eph 6:18; 1 Pet 5:8
26:45 Jn 12:23–27; 13:1, 31
26:47 Mk 14:43–52; Lk 22:47–53; Jn 18:1–12; Acts 1:16
☆**26:49**
26:50 Ps 41:9; 55:12, 13
26:52 Gen 9:6; Rev 13:10
26:53 2 Kgs 6:16, 17; Ps 91:11; Dan 7:10
26:55 Mk 12:35; 14:49; Lk 4:20; 19:47; 20:1; 21:37; Jn 7:14, 28; 8:20; 18:20
26:56 Isa 53:7; Lam 4:20; Dan 9:26; Jn 18:15

26:39 The *cup* of which Matthew speaks has been the subject of much discussion. One school of thought says that Jesus prayed for some other way to save men than for him to die. But because Calvary was God's only way, Jesus accepted it without hesitation or qualification, for he prayed: "I want your will, not mine" (26:39, TLB). Others hold that Jesus always prayed according to the will of the Father. In his humanity he feared that Satan would kill him in the Garden of Gethsemane before he made atonement on the cross. Thus, he was prepared to die in the garden, if the Father so willed. His prayer was answered; he was able to go to Calvary. A third, very likely view is that Jesus, knowing what suffering eternal death meant, shrank from the imminent experience of burdening himself with the sins of the world, because the Father would turn his face from him when he became sin for us. In this view, the *cup* meant separation from the Father; he later said, "My God, my God, why hast thou forsaken me?" (27:46). He left the garden victoriously.

26:49 *kissed*, i.e., "embraced and kissed," the greeting still used among men in Eastern lands.† (See note on Mark 14:45 for information about Judas Iscariot and his betrayal of Jesus.)

6. Jesus' Appearance before Caiaphas (Cf. Mk 14:53–65; Lk 22:54; Jn 18:12–14, 19–25)

26:57☆ Mk 14:53–65

57 ¶And they that had laid hold on Jesus led *him* away to Cai'a-phas the
high priest, where the scribes and the elders were assembled.

26:58 Lk 22:54, 55

58 But Peter followed him afar off unto the high priest's palace, and went
in, and sat with the servants, to see the end.

26:59☆

59 Now the chief priests, and elders, and all the council, sought false
witness against Jesus, to put him to death;

26:60 Deut 19:15; 1 Kgs 21:10; Ps 27:12

60 But found none: yea, though many false witnesses came, *yet* found they
none. At the last came two false witnesses,

26:61 Mt 27:40; Jn 2:19; Acts 6:14

61 And said, This *fellow* said, I am able to destroy the temple of God, and
to build it in three days.

26:62 Mt 27:12

62 And the high priest arose, and said unto him, Answerest thou nothing?
what *is it which* these witness against thee?

26:63 Lev 5:1

63 But Jesus held his peace. And the high priest answered and said unto
him, I adjure thee by the living God, that thou tell us whether thou be the
Christ, the Son of God.

26:64 Ps 110:1; Dan 7:13; Acts 7:55; 1 Thess 4:16; Rev 1:7

64 Jesus saith unto him, Thou hast said: nevertheless I say unto you,
Hereafter shall ye see the Son of man sitting on the right hand of power,
and coming in the clouds of heaven.

26:65 Lev 24:16; 2 Kgs 18:37; 19:1; Jn 19:7; Acts 3:15; 7:52

65 Then the high priest rent his clothes, saying, He hath spoken blas-
phemy; what further need have we of witnesses? behold, now ye have heard
his blasphemy.

66 What think ye? They answered and said, He is guilty of death.

26:67 Job 30:10; Isa 50:6; 53:3; Mic 5:1; Mt 27:30; Lk 18:32; 22:63–65

67 Then did they spit in his face, and buffeted him; and others smote *him*
with the palms of their hands,

68 Saying, Prophesy unto us, thou Christ, Who is he that smote thee?

7. Peter's Denial (Cf. Mk 14:66–72; Lk 22:55–63; Jn 18:15–18, 25–27)

26:69☆ Mk 14:66–72; Lk 22:55–62; Jn 18:25–27

69 ¶Now Peter sat without in the palace: and a damsel came unto him,
saying, Thou also wast with Jesus of Galilee.

70 But he denied before *them* all, saying, I know not what thou sayest.

71 And when he was gone out into the porch, another *maid* saw him, and
said unto them that were there, This *fellow* was also with Jesus of Nazareth.

26:57 *Caiaphas, the high priest,* was son-in-law of Annas, who had previously served as high priest. Valerius Gratus, the predecessor of Pontius Pilate, had appointed him to the office. He stayed in office until A.D. 37, when he was removed by Vitellius. Caiaphas pretended to be religious and patriotic. He hated Christ and recommended the action that led to Calvary (John 11:49–53). Judas Iscariot was a pawn in his hands (Matt. 26:3ff). Jesus was silent before Caiaphas until he demanded in the name of God to know whether Jesus was the Christ (26:63). Jesus said that he was (26:64). Unable to convict Jesus by the testimony of perjurers, Caiaphas now accused Jesus of blasphemy. As a result, Jesus was condemned to be crucified.

26:59 *the council,* i.e., "the Jewish Supreme Court," or, "Sanhedrin," was the highest ecclesiastical and political body among the Jews. The origin of this body *is obscure. The Sanhedrin in Jerusalem* was generally referred to as the Great Sanhedrin. It had seventy-one members, called "elders," who usually were chosen from among the chief priests and the scribes. Exactly how they were chosen is unknown. Tradition has it that prospective candidates had to be learned, humble, and popular with the people. The Sanhedrin was led by a president. The high priest, Caiaphas, seems to have been the Sanhedrin's presiding officer during the trial of Jesus, but this does not indicate that the high priest was generally the president.

The Little Sanhedrin had twenty-three members and judged cases other than those reserved for the highest body. If the lower courts could not arrive at a decision, the case was referred to the supreme court of justice. Cases of life and death came before the Little Sanhedrin, although important cases went to the highest court. Decisions of the Great Sanhedrin were binding. This court met in the chambers of the Hall of Hewn Stone in Jerusalem. They sat in a semicircle so that all could see each other. In cases involving life or death, the younger members voted first so they could not be influenced by their elders. No fewer than twenty-three members could be present when such a case arose. If a verdict was reached by a majority of one, the number of court members had to be increased. Only when the full court was in session could a man be declared guilty by a majority of one.

26:69ff See note on Mark 14:71 regarding Peter's denial of Christ.

E. THE SERVANT'S CROSS

34 Think not that I am come to send peace on earth: I came not to send
peace, but a sword.
35 For I am come to set a man at variance against his father, and the
daughter against her mother, and the daughter in law against her mother in
law.
36 And a man's foes *shall be* they of his own household.
37 He that loveth father or mother more than me is not worthy of me: and
he that loveth son or daughter more than me is not worthy of me.
38 And he that taketh not his cross, and followeth after me, is not worthy
of me.
39 He that findeth his life shall lose it: and he that loseth his life for my
sake shall find it.

☆**10:34** Lk 12:51–53
☆**10:35** Mt 10:21
10:36 Mic 7:6
10:37 Lk 14:26
10:38 Mt 16:24; Mk 8:34; Lk 9:23; 14:27
10:39 Mt 16:25; Mk 8:35; Lk 9:24; 17:33; Jn 12:25

F. THE SERVANT'S REWARD

40 ¶He that receiveth you receiveth me, and he that receiveth me receiveth
him that sent me.
41 He that receiveth a prophet in the name of a prophet shall receive a
prophet's reward; and he that receiveth a righteous man in the name of a
righteous man shall receive a righteous man's reward.
42 And whosoever shall give to drink unto one of these little ones a cup of
cold *water* only in the name of a disciple, verily I say unto you, he shall in
no wise lose his reward.

☆**10:40** Mt 18:5; Mk 9:37; Lk 9:48; 10:16; Jn 12:44; 13:20; Gal 4:14
10:41 2 Kgs 4:8
10:42 Mt 25:40; Mk 9:41; Heb 6:10, 11

VI. THE CLAIMS OF JESUS (11:1—12:50)

A. JESUS' RESPONSE TO JOHN'S LAST MESSAGE (CF. LK 7:18–35)

11 AND it came to pass, when Jesus had made an end of commanding
his twelve disciples, he departed thence to teach and to preach in
their cities.
2 Now when John had heard in the prison the works of Christ, he sent two
of his disciples,
3 And said unto him, Art thou he that should come, or do we look for
another?
4 Jesus answered and said unto them, Go and shew John again those
things which ye do hear and see:
5 The blind receive their sight, and the lame walk, the lepers are cleansed,
and the deaf hear, the dead are raised up, and the poor have the gospel
preached to them.
6 And blessed is *he*, whosoever shall not be offended in me.

☆**11:1**
11:2 Mt 14:3; Lk 7:18–35
☆**11:3** Num 24:17; Deut 18:15; Mal 3:1; Jn 6:14
11:5 Isa 42:7; 61:1; Lk 4:18, 19; Jn 5:36; Jas 2:5
11:6 Mt 13:57; 1 Pet 2:8

10:34, 35 Jesus and his gospel are great dividers. Families are rent asunder when some believe and others do not. Whoever puts even the dearest loved one before the Son of God is not worthy of the Savior. We are not to expect temporal peace and outward prosperity. Instead, there is the sword, which is always the symbol of division, disaffection, and even judgment.
10:40 Jesus assures us that some who hear us will reject our message, but others will receive it. Whoever honors Christ's ambassadors honors him, and whoever dishonors his ambassadors dishonors him. There is a suitable reward for those who serve Christ faithfully.
11:1 *to teach and to preach in their cities.* Luke 10:1 remarks, "The Lord appointed other seventy also, and sent them two and two before his face into every city and place, whither he himself would come."
11:3 *Art thou he that should come, or do we look for another?* John had baptized Jesus. He had seen the endorsement of Jesus as Messiah by the Father and the Holy Spirit. Now he is in jail, despondent, and without the help of the Messiah whom he had announced to all men. Doubtless he expected the Messiah to deliver him. Thus he sends his disciples with the question addressed to Jesus, so that he might be reassured that indeed he is the Messiah. Jesus performed miracles before the disciples and sent them back to tell John that his credentials showed he was indeed the Messiah. Shortly thereafter John was killed, and Jesus was moving steadily toward Jerusalem—for his own date with destiny at Calvary.

7 ¶And as they departed, Jesus began to say unto the multitudes concerning John, What went ye out into the wilderness to see? A reed shaken with the wind?

8 But what went ye out for to see? A man clothed in soft raiment? behold, they that wear soft *clothing* are in kings' houses.

11:9 Lk 1:76

9 But what went ye out for to see? A prophet? yea, I say unto you, and more than a prophet.

11:10 Isa 40:3 Mal 3:1 Mk 1:2

10 For this is *he*, of whom it is written, Behold, I send my messenger before thy face, which shall prepare thy way before thee.

11:11☆

11 Verily I say unto you, Among them that are born of women there hath not risen a greater than John the Baptist: notwithstanding he that is least in the kingdom of heaven is greater than he.

11:12 Lk 16:16

12 And from the days of John the Baptist until now the kingdom of heaven suffereth violence, and the violent take it by force.

13 For all the prophets and the law prophesied until John.

11:14 Mal 4:5 Mt 17:11–13 Mk 9:11–13 Lk 1:17 Jn 1:23

14 And if ye will receive *it*, this is E-li'as, which was for to come.

11:15 Mt 13:9, 43 Mk 4:9, 23 Lk 8:8 Rev 2:7, 11, 17, 29; 3:6, 13, 22 13:9

15 He that hath ears to hear, let him hear.

16 ¶But whereunto shall I liken this generation? It is like unto children sitting in the markets, and calling unto their fellows,

17 And saying, We have piped unto you, and ye have not danced; we have mourned unto you, and ye have not lamented.

11:18☆ Mt 3:4 Lk 1:15

18 For John came neither eating nor drinking, and they say, He hath a devil.

11:19 Mt 9:10, 11 Lk 15:2

19 The Son of man came eating and drinking, and they say, Behold a man gluttonous, and a winebibber, a friend of publicans and sinners. But wisdom is justified of her children.

B. THE REBUKE TO THE IMPENITENT CITIES (CF. LK 10:12–15)

11:20 Lk 10:12–15

20 ¶Then began he to upbraid the cities wherein most of his mighty works were done, because they repented not:

11:21☆ Mk 8:22, 23 Lk 6:17, 18; 9:10, 11; 10:13–15

21 Woe unto thee, Cho-ra'zin! woe unto thee, Beth-sa'i-da! for if the mighty works, which were done in you, had been done in Tyre and Si'don, they would have repented long ago in sackcloth and ashes.

11:22 Ezek 26:19, 20 Mt 10:15

22 But I say unto you, It shall be more tolerable for Tyre and Si'don at the day of judgment, than for you.

11:23 Isa 14:13, 15 Ezek 31:14 32:18, 24 Rev 1:18

23 And thou, Ca-per'na-um, which art exalted unto heaven, shalt be brought down to hell: for if the mighty works, which have been done in thee, had been done in Sodom, it would have remained until this day.

24 But I say unto you, That it shall be more tolerable for the land of Sodom in the day of judgment, than for thee.

C. JESUS REVEALS HIS FATHER AND EXTENDS HIS INVITATION (CF. LK 10:21, 22)

11:25 Lk 10:21–22 1 Cor 1:27 2:7, 8 2 Cor 3:14; 4:6 Eph 1:17, 18 3:3, 4

25 ¶At that time Jesus answered and said, I thank thee, O Father, Lord of heaven and earth, because thou hast hid these things from the wise and prudent, and hast revealed them unto babes.

11:11 Jesus said that the lesser in the kingdom of heaven are greater than John the Baptist. While this statement is enigmatic, it seems that what is meant is this: as great and good as John was, he was still in the flesh, full of infirmity and imperfections, whereas the lowest saint in the kingdom of heaven is already glorified and "greater" than any saint still on earth.

Dispensationalists think this refers to the position of John the Baptist under the old dispensation, which has been superseded since the crucifixion and resurrection of Jesus and the outpouring of the Holy Spirit. The saints in the new dispensation occupy a higher position than that of John under the old one.

11:18 *He hath a devil.* Those who reject the gospel will use every excuse possible to justify their disbelief. John came as a mourner who neither ate nor drank, and he was rejected. Jesus came eating and drinking, and they rejected him. Unbelievers are perverse. When they spurn the grace of God, they want everyone to follow in their footsteps and join them in hell.

11:21 *Tyre and Sidon,* cities destroyed by God for their wickedness. *Sidon* is called "Sodom" in 11:23.†

H. (7) THE FISHING NET

[47]¶Again, the kingdom of heaven is like unto a net, that was cast into the
sea, and gathered of every kind:

☆13:47 Mt 22:10

[48]Which, when it was full, they drew to shore, and sat down, and
gathered the good into vessels, but cast the bad away.
[49]So shall it be at the end of the world: the angels shall come forth, and
sever the wicked from among the just,

☆13:49

[50]And shall cast them into the furnace of fire: there shall be wailing and
gnashing of teeth.

13:50 Mt 8:12

[51]Jesus saith unto them, Have ye understood all these things? They say
unto him, Yea, Lord.
[52]Then said he unto them, Therefore every scribe *which is* instructed unto
the kingdom of heaven is like unto a man *that is* an householder, which
bringeth forth out of his treasure *things* new and old.

☆13:52

VIII. JESUS REJECTED AND JOHN BEHEADED (13:53—14:12)

A. JESUS' SECOND REJECTION (CF. MK 6:1–6; LK 4:16–30)

[53]¶And it came to pass, *that* when Jesus had finished these parables, he
departed thence.

13:53 Mt 2:23 Mk 6:1–6 Lk 3:23; 4:16–24

[54]And when he was come into his own country, he taught them in their
synagogue, insomuch that they were astonished, and said, Whence hath this
man this wisdom, and *these* mighty works?

☆13:54

[55]Is not this the carpenter's son? is not his mother called Mary? and his
brethren, James, and Joses, and Simon, and Judas?
[56]And his sisters, are they not all with us? Whence then hath this *man* all
these things?

☆13:55 Ps 69:8 Mt 12:46 Mk 15:40 Jn 6:42

[57]And they were offended in him. But Jesus said unto them, A prophet is
not without honour, save in his own country, and in his own house.
[58]And he did not many mighty works there because of their unbelief.

13:57 Ps 6 Isa 53:2, 3 Jn 4:44

B. THE BEHEADING OF JOHN THE BAPTIST (CF. MK 6:14–29; LK 9:7–9)

14 AT that time Herod the tetrarch heard of the fame of Jesus,
[2]And said unto his servants, This is John the Baptist; he is risen
from the dead; and therefore mighty works do shew forth themselves in
him.

☆14:1 Mk 6:14–29 Lk 9:7–9 3:19, 20

13:47ff The net represents the kingdom of God. When cast into the sea, it catches a mixed company of fishes. So it is with the kingdom of God. Good and bad are caught in its net; at the end of the age, the good will be separated from the bad. This story clearly makes impossible the idea that all people will be saved at last.
13:49 *world,* or, "age."
13:52 *bringeth forth out of his treasure things new and old.* Paraphrased: "from the Old Testament as well as from the New." The paraphrase is, of course, highly anacronistic!†
13:54 *into his own country.* Everyone knew that Jesus performed mighty deeds and spoke words of wisdom. Since he did not have the benefit of advanced education, they wondered how he was able to think and speak as he did. And they wondered where he got the power to perform miracles. They were puzzled because Jesus came from a common family. Joseph was a humble carpenter; his mother was a simple village girl. The only adequate explanation is that Jesus was of divine origin; he was the Son of God. Certainly his knowledge of the Scriptures startled the learned men of his day; he was but twelve years of age when he first talked with the doctors in the temple (Luke 2:41–52).
13:55 See note on Mark 6:3 regarding the family of Jesus.
14:1 This Herod was Herod Antipas. He was the son of Herod the Great, by Malthace, a Samaritan woman. He was born ca. 20 B.C. He ruled over Galilee and Perea. Apparently he believed in the resurrection of the dead, a doctrine affirmed by the Pharisees and denied by the Sadducees. Herod thought Jesus was a resurrected John performing greater miracles than ever before and bringing him more trouble. He was reproached by his own guilty conscience. Jesus was indeed a greater problem; he knew that Herod would do to him what he had done to John. Jesus went away so that Herod could not touch him. Sometimes God's servants should flee rather than remain and be martyred.

14:3☆ 3¶For Herod had laid hold on John, and bound him, and put *him* in
prison for He-ro′di-as′ sake, his brother Philip's wife.
14:4 4For John said unto him, It is not lawful for thee to have her.
Lev 18:16; 20:21 Eph 5:11 5And when he would have put him to death, he feared the multitude,
2 Tim 4:2 because they counted him as a prophet.
14:5 Mt 21:26 6But when Herod's birthday was kept, the daughter of He-ro′di-as
Lk 20:6 danced before them, and pleased Herod.
7Whereupon he promised with an oath to give her whatsoever she would
ask.
8And she, being before instructed of her mother, said, Give me here John
Baptist's head in a charger.
9And the king was sorry: nevertheless for the oath's sake, and them
which sat with him at meat, he commanded *it* to be given *her*.
10And he sent, and beheaded John in the prison.
11And his head was brought in a charger, and given to the damsel: and
she brought *it* to her mother.
12And his disciples came, and took up the body, and buried it, and went
and told Jesus.

IX. JESUS LEAVES HEROD'S DOMINION (14:13—17:27)

A. FEEDING THE FIVE THOUSAND (CF. MK 6:30–44; LK 9:10–17; JN 6:1–13)

14:13 Mk 6:30–45 13¶When Jesus heard *of it*, he departed thence by ship into a desert place
Lk 9:10–17 apart: and when the people had heard *thereof*, they followed him on foot
Jn 6:1–13 out of the cities.
14:14 Mt 9:36 14And Jesus went forth, and saw a great multitude, and was moved with
Mk 1:41 Heb 2:17, 18 compassion toward them, and he healed their sick.
4:15; 5:1–3 15¶And when it was evening, his disciples came to him, saying, This is a
desert place, and the time is now past; send the multitude away, that they
may go into the villages, and buy themselves victuals.
14:16☆ 16But Jesus said unto them, They need not depart; give ye them to eat.
2 Kgs 4:42–44 17And they say unto him, We have here but five loaves, and two fishes.
18He said, Bring them hither to me.
14:19 19And he commanded the multitude to sit down on the grass, and took
Mt 15:35–38 Lk 22:19 the five loaves, and the two fishes, and looking up to heaven, he blessed,
and brake, and gave the loaves to *his* disciples, and the disciples to the
multitude.
20And they did all eat, and were filled: and they took up of the fragments
that remained twelve baskets full.
21And they that had eaten were about five thousand men, beside women
and children.

B. JESUS WALKING ON THE WATER (CF. MK 6:45–52; JN 6:15–21)

14:22☆ 22¶And straightway Jesus constrained his disciples to get into a ship, and
to go before him unto the other side, while he sent the multitudes away.

14:3 See note on Luke 1:57 regarding John the Baptist and his life. See also note on Mark 6:17 about Philip, the brother of Herod Antipas.

14:16 *give ye them to eat.* Earlier Jesus had given his disciples power to cast out demons, raise the dead, and heal the sick. Here he instructs them to feed the hungry. They had missed this opportunity and stood about puzzled and hesitant. They surely represent believers of our day who have the power of the Holy Spirit available to them but who do not take advantage of that power for the glory of God and the progress of the gospel.

14:22 Jesus sent his disciples ahead of him by ship. A storm overtook them. Earlier, in another storm, they had trusted Jesus when he was present—although asleep in the back of the boat. Now they were to learn that they could trust him when he was not with them. The Master was training them to walk by faith, not by sight.

3. The Parable of the Sower Explained (Cf. Mk 4:13–20; Lk 8:11–15)

18¶Hear ye therefore the parable of the sower. ☆13:18
19When any one heareth the word of the kingdom, and understandeth *it* ☆13:19
not, then cometh the wicked *one*, and catcheth away that which was sown in Ezek 11:19 2 Cor 4:3, 4
his heart. This is he which received seed by the way side. Eph 4:17, 18
20But he that received the seed into stony places, the same is he that
heareth the word, and anon with joy receiveth it;
21Yet hath he not root in himself, but dureth for a while: for when 13:21
tribulation or persecution ariseth because of the word, by and by he is Col 2:7
offended.
22He also that received seed among the thorns is he that heareth the 13:22
word; and the care of this world, and the deceitfulness of riches, choke the Jer 4:3 Ezek 33:31
word, and he becometh unfruitful. Mt 19:23 Eph 2:2
23But he that received seed into the good ground is he that heareth the 1 Tim 6:9, 10, 17
word, and understandeth *it;* which also beareth fruit, and bringeth forth, 2 Tim 4:4, 10 ☆13:23
some an hundredfold, some sixty, some thirty. Gen 26:12

B. (2) THE GOOD SEED AND THE TARES (CF. MK 4:18, 19)

24¶Another parable put he forth unto them, saying, The kingdom of 13:24
heaven is likened unto a man which sowed good seed in his field: Mk 4:26–29
25But while men slept, his enemy came and sowed tares among the wheat,
and went his way.
26But when the blade was sprung up, and brought forth fruit, then
appeared the tares also.
27So the servants of the householder came and said unto him, Sir, didst
not thou sow good seed in thy field? from whence then hath it tares?
28He said unto them, An enemy hath done this. The servants said unto
him, Wilt thou then that we go and gather them up?
29But he said, Nay; lest while ye gather up the tares, ye root up also the
wheat with them.
30Let both grow together until the harvest: and in the time of harvest I ☆13:30
will say to the reapers, Gather ye together first the tares, and bind them in Mt 3:12
bundles to burn them: but gather the wheat into my barn.

D. (3) THE MUSTARD SEED (CF. MK 4:30–32; LK 13:18, 19)

31¶Another parable put he forth unto them, saying, The kingdom of ☆13:31
heaven is like to a grain of mustard seed, which a man took, and sowed in Gen 1:11, 12 Ps 104:12
his field: Ezek 17:22, 23 31:6
32Which indeed is the least of all seeds: but when it is grown, it is the Dan 4:12, 21
greatest among herbs, and becometh a tree, so that the birds of the air come Mk 4:30–32 Lk 13:18, 19
and lodge in the branches thereof. ☆13:32

13:18ff *This illustration was easily grasped by Jesus'* listeners. They were familiar with the rocky soil they had to cultivate.
13:19 *the wicked one*, i.e., "Satan."
13:23 *beareth fruit, and bringeth forth, some an hundredfold, some sixty, some thirty*, i.e., "produces a crop many times greater than the amount planted—thirty, sixty, or even a hundred times as much."†
13:30 The parable of the wheat and the tares teaches us that there are always true and false believers in the church. We cannot always distinguish between the false and the true. The presence of false believers brings harm to Christ's Body, but harm may also come from human efforts to remove the false from the true. Unbelievers, of course, should be excluded if they can be positively identified. But, as the illustration makes plain, the final separation is made by the judge of all, the Lord Jesus, who makes no mistakes.
13:31, 32 This parable's central teaching is the growth and spread of the gospel throughout the world. Just as the tiny mustard seed becomes a giant tree (see note on 17:20), so the gospel, which begins slowly, will flourish in the end. The existence of the Christian church all around the globe represents a partial fulfillment of this prophetic word.

D. (4) LEAVEN IN THE BREAD (CF. LK 13:20, 21)

13:33☆
Lev 7:13; 23:17
Mt 16:6, 12
Lk 13:20, 21
1 Cor 5:6–8
Gal 5:8, 9
13:34, 35☆
Ps 78:2, 3
Mk 4:34
Jn 10:6; 16:25
Rom 16:25
1 Cor 2:7
Eph 3:9
Col 1:26

33 ¶Another parable spake he unto them; The kingdom of heaven is like
unto leaven, which a woman took, and hid in three measures of meal, till
the whole was leavened.
34 All these things spake Jesus unto the multitude in parables; and
without a parable spake he not unto them:
35 That it might be fulfilled which was spoken by the prophet, saying, I
will open my mouth in parables; I will utter things which have been kept
secret from the foundation of the world.

E. THE PARABLE OF THE GOOD SEED AND THE TARES EXPLAINED

13:36
Mt 15:15

36 Then Jesus sent the multitude away, and went into the house: and his
disciples came unto him, saying, Declare unto us the parable of the tares of
the field.
37 He answered and said unto them, He that soweth the good seed is the
Son of man;

13:38
Mk 16:15
Lk 24:27
Jn 8:44
Rom 10:18
Col 1:6
1 Jn 3:7, 8, 10
13:39
Joel 3:13
Rev 14:15
13:41
Mt 24:31
25:31–46
13:42
Mt 8:12; 13:50
22:13
13:43
Judg 5:31
Prov 4:18
Dan 12:3

38 The field is the world; the good seed are the children of the kingdom;
but the tares are the children of the wicked *one;*
39 The enemy that sowed them is the devil; the harvest is the end of the
world; and the reapers are the angels.
40 As therefore the tares are gathered and burned in the fire; so shall it be
in the end of this world.
41 The Son of man shall send forth his angels, and they shall gather out of
his kingdom all things that offend, and them which do iniquity;
42 And shall cast them into a furnace of fire: there shall be wailing and
gnashing of teeth.
43 Then shall the righteous shine forth as the sun in the kingdom of their
Father. Who hath ears to hear, let him hear.

F. (5) THE TREASURE IN THE FIELD

13:44☆
1 Cor 6:20
Phil 3:7

44 ¶Again, the kingdom of heaven is like unto treasure hid in a field; the
which when a man hath found, he hideth, and for joy thereof goeth and
selleth all that he hath, and buyeth that field.

G. (6) THE PEARL MERCHANT

13:45☆
13:46☆

45 ¶Again, the kingdom of heaven is like unto a merchant man, seeking
goodly pearls:
46 Who, when he had found one pearl of great price, went and sold all that
he had, and bought it.

13:33 Yeast, or leaven, is generally used in an evil sense. It refers to (1) the doctrines of the Pharisees and Sadducees (16:6, 12); (2) ungodly professors of the true faith (1 Cor. 5:6, 7); (3) false teachers (Gal. 5:8, 9); and (4) malice and evil (1 Cor. 5:8). Leaven here suggests its silent permeating power that requires only a small amount in the dough to be effective. Leaven, or yeast, was generally forbidden in the Old Testament except for use with thank-offerings (Lev. 7:13) and with the presentation of the first-fruits of wheat (Lev. 23:17).
13:34, 35 *The meaning* of Jesus' stories was apparently unclear both to the multitudes and to his own disciples. For Mark tells us, "When he was alone with his disciples, he would explain his meaning to them" (Mark 4:34, TLB).
13:44 The central teaching of this illustration is that the gospel has such value that a person will give up anything and everything to possess that which is the greatest of all things (16:26). Some believe that the discoverer of the treasure is Christ, who gave his all to purchase the church.
13:45, 46 The stories of the pearl and the hidden treasure are similar. When a pearl merchant finds a pearl of real value at a low price, he will sell all he has and buy the one pearl. Salvation is comparable to the pearl of great price, yet it costs us nothing! Jesus paid it all. In the case of the pearl, it may be that Jesus is referring to himself—he is the purchaser; he paid all he had to buy the church for himself. Finding treasure or a pearl means nothing unless what is found is appropriated. Salvation is no blessing until it is appropriated on Christ's terms. Water and bread are valueless until eaten and drunk. An anchor that does not reach the bottom might just as well not be dropped.

[35]And they crucified him, and parted his garments, casting lots: that it
might be fulfilled which was spoken by the prophet, They parted my
garments among them, and upon my vesture did they cast lots.
[36]And sitting down they watched him there;
[37]And set up over his head his accusation written, THIS IS JESUS THE
KING OF THE JEWS.
[38]Then were there two thieves crucified with him, one on the right hand,
and another on the left.
[39]¶And they that passed by reviled him, wagging their heads,
[40]And saying, Thou that destroyest the temple, and buildest *it* in three
days, save thyself. If thou be the Son of God, come down from the cross.
[41]Likewise also the chief priests mocking *him*, with the scribes and elders,
said,
[42]He saved others; himself he cannot save. If he be the King of Israel, let
him now come down from the cross, and we will believe him.
[43]He trusted in God; let him deliver him now, if he will have him: for he
said, I am the Son of God.
[44]The thieves also, which were crucified with him, cast the same in his
teeth.

27:35 Ps 22:18
☆**27:37**
☆**27:38** Isa 53:12
27:39 Job 16:4; Ps 22:7, 8 109:25; Lam 2:15
27:40 Mt 26:61; Jn 2:19

3. Jesus' Voluntary Death (Cf. Mk 15:33–41; Lk 23:44–49; Jn 19:28–37)

[45]Now from the sixth hour there was darkness over all the land unto the
ninth hour.
[46]And about the ninth hour Jesus cried with a loud voice, saying, E'li,
E'li, la'ma sa-bach'tha-ni? that is to say, My God, my God, why hast thou
forsaken me?
[47]Some of them that stood there, when they heard *that*, said, This *man*
calleth for E-li'as.
[48]And straightway one of them ran, and took a spunge, and filled *it* with
vinegar, and put *it* on a reed, and gave him to drink.
[49]The rest said, Let be, let us see whether E-li'as will come to save him.
[50]¶Jesus, when he had cried again with a loud voice, yielded up the ghost.

27:45 Isa 50:3; Amos 8:9; Mk 15:33–41; Lk 23:44–49
27:46 Ps 22:1
27:48 Ps 69:21; Jn 19:29, 30
☆**27:50**

4. Salvation Accomplished

[51]And, behold, the veil of the temple was rent in twain from the top to
the bottom; and the earth did quake, and the rocks rent;

☆**27:51** Ex 26:31–33; 2 Chron 3:14; Ps 18:7; Heb 6:9; 9:12; 10:19, 20

27:37 Each Gospel records something about the sign that hung over the cross of Jesus. A convicted criminal usually carried a sign on the way to his execution. On it was inscribed the crime of which he was guilty. When the execution took place, the sign was hung around the neck of the victim or nailed to the cross. Jesus' crime was insubordination to Rome. The full inscription (for no Gospel writer gives the charge in its entirety) seems *to have been: "This is Jesus of Nazareth, the King of* the Jews." According to John 19:20, it was written in Hebrew (the language of the day), Greek (the universal language of the day), and Latin (the legal language of the ruling nation, Rome). Differences in the Gospel accounts may be explained by the following facts: Matthew recorded the inscription from Aramaic (*THIS IS JESUS THE KING OF THE JEWS*), Mark and Luke from Latin ("THE KING OF THE JEWS" in Mark; "THIS IS THE KING OF THE JEWS" in Luke), and John from Greek ("JESUS OF NAZARETH THE KING OF THE JEWS"). While the accounts are not identical, they faithfully represent the differences of the versions which were tacked on the cross.

27:38 See note on Luke 23:33 as to the different deaths of the two thieves and Jesus.

27:50 Christ was not killed by Satan or the Roman soldiers. He affirmed that no man could take his life. He had the power to lay it down and to take it up again. His atoning death was a voluntary sacrifice. He laid down his own life. His was a free choice in obedience to the will of the Father. (See John 10:14–18.)

27:51 The rending of the curtain that sealed off the Holy of Holies meant that (1) full atonement had been made (Heb. 10:19, 20); (2) Christ offered his blood on the mercy-seat of the Holy of Holies, going through the rent veil, and later in the heavenly sanctuary after the resurrection where he is now seated at the right hand of the Father (Heb. 9:12, 24); (3) the high priestly ministry of Jesus made a human priesthood forever unnecessary between man and God (Heb. 7:23–28); (4) all Christians have immediate access to God the Father, without any intermediaries except Christ himself (Rom. 5:2; Eph. 2:18; 3:21).

27:52☆ Ps 69:20
52And the graves were opened; and many bodies of the saints which slept
arose,
53And came out of the graves after his resurrection, and went into the
holy city, and appeared unto many.
27:54 Ex 20:18–20
54Now when the centurion, and they that were with him, watching Jesus,
saw the earthquake, and those things that were done, they feared greatly,
saying, Truly this was the Son of God.
55And many women were there beholding afar off, which followed Jesus
from Galilee, ministering unto him:
27:56 Lk 8:2
56Among which was Mary Magdalene, and Mary the mother of James
and Joses, and the mother of Zeb'e-dee's children.

5. Jesus' Burial (Cf. Mk 15:42–47; Lk 23:50–56; Jn 19:38–42)

27:57 Mk 15:42–47 Lk 23:50–56 Jn 19:38–42
57When the even was come, there came a rich man of Ar-i-ma-thæ'a,
named Joseph, who also himself was Jesus' disciple:
58He went to Pilate, and begged the body of Jesus. Then Pilate com-
manded the body to be delivered.
59And when Joseph had taken the body, he wrapped it in a clean linen
cloth,
27:60 Isa 53:9
60And laid it in his own new tomb, which he had hewn out in the rock:
and he rolled a great stone to the door of the sepulchre, and departed.
61And there was Mary Magdalene, and the other Mary, sitting over
against the sepulchre.

6. Sealing the Tomb and Posting the Guards

27:62 Ps 2:1–6
62¶Now the next day, that followed the day of the preparation, the chief
priests and Pharisees came together unto Pilate,
27:63 Mt 16:21; 17:23 20:19 Mk 8:31; 10:34 Lk 9:22; 18:33 Jn 2:19 2 Cor 6:8
63Saying, Sir, we remember that that deceiver said, while he was yet alive,
After three days I will rise again.
64Command therefore that the sepulchre be made sure until the third day,
lest his disciples come by night, and steal him away, and say unto the
people, He is risen from the dead: so the last error shall be worse than the
first.
65Pilate said unto them, Ye have a watch: go your way, make *it* as sure as
ye can.
27:66☆ Dan 6:17
66So they went, and made the sepulchre sure, sealing the stone, and
setting a watch.

M. JESUS' RESURRECTION (CF. MK 16:1–8; LK 24:1–11; JN 20:1–18)

28:1 Mt 27:56 Mk 16:1–11 Lk 24:1–11 Jn 20:1, 2, 11–18
28 IN the end of the sabbath, as it began to dawn toward the first *day*
of the week, came Mary Magdalene and the other Mary to see the
sepulchre.
2And, behold, there was a great earthquake: for the angel of the Lord
descended from heaven, and came and rolled back the stone from the door,
and sat upon it.
28:3 Dan 7:9; 10:5, 6 Rev 1:16
3His countenance was like lightning, and his raiment white as snow:
4And for fear of him the keepers did shake, and became as dead *men*.

***27:52** Matthew alone records* this miracle of the resurrection of some dead believers during Christ's passion and resurrection. We do not know how many were raised, nor do we know whether they died later and were reburied or whether they ascended into heaven in their bodies with Jesus in his ascension. As it is translated in the KJV, RSV, and NIV, 27:53 makes it appear that these dead came out of their graves after the Lord's resurrection, then went into Jerusalem and appeared to many believers.

27:66 *sealing the stone.* This was done by stringing a cord across the rock, then sealing the cord at each end with clay.†

5And the angel answered and said unto the women, Fear not ye: for I
know that ye seek Jesus, which was crucified.

28:5 Rev 1:17, 18

6He is not here: for he is risen, as he said. Come, see the place where the
Lord lay.

☆28:6 Mt 12:40; 16:21 17:23; 20:19

7And go quickly, and tell his disciples that he is risen from the dead; and,
behold, he goeth before you into Galilee; there shall ye see him: lo, I have
told you.

28:7 Mt 26:32 Mk 16:7

8And they departed quickly from the sepulchre with fear and great joy;
and did run to bring his disciples word.
9¶And as they went to tell his disciples, behold, Jesus met them, saying,
All hail. And they came and held him by the feet, and worshipped him.
10Then said Jesus unto them, Be not afraid: go tell my brethren that they
go into Galilee, and there shall they see me.

28:10 Jn 20:17 Rom 8:29 Heb 2:11

XIII. THE POST-RESURRECTION EVENTS (28:11–20)

A. THE BRIBING OF THE GUARDS

11¶Now when they were going, behold, some of the watch came into the
city, and shewed unto the chief priests all the things that were done.
12And when they were assembled with the elders, and had taken counsel,
they gave large money unto the soldiers,
13Saying, Say ye, His disciples came by night, and stole him *away* while
we slept.
14And if this come to the governor's ears, we will persuade him, and
secure you.
15So they took the money, and did as they were taught: and this saying is
commonly reported among the Jews until this day.

B. THE GREAT COMMISSION

16¶Then the eleven disciples went away into Galilee, into a mountain
where Jesus had appointed them.
17And when they saw him, they worshipped him: but some doubted.
18And Jesus came and spake unto them, saying, All power is given unto
me in heaven and in earth.

28:18 Dan 7:14 Mt 26:64 Rom 14:9 Eph 1:19–22 Phil 2:9 Col 2:10 1 Pet 3:22

19¶Go ye therefore, and teach all nations, baptizing them in the name of
the Father, and of the Son, and of the Holy Ghost:

☆28:19 Isa 49:6; 52:10 Mal 1:11 Mk 16:15, 16 Lk 24:47 Acts 2:38, 41, 42 8:16 Rom 6:3 Gal 3:27

20Teaching them to observe all things whatsoever I have commanded
you: and, lo, I am with you alway, *even* unto the end of the world. Amen.

☆28:20 Mt 1:23; 18:20 Jn 14:17–20 Acts 18:10 Heb 13:5

28:6 Christ's resurrection is the fulfillment of Old Testament prophecy (Ps. 16:10) and of Jesus' own statements (20:19; John 10:18). While there is no record of his having been seen by nonbelievers, it is attested to in a variety of ways: (1) by the eleven apostles (Acts 1:3); he thus "proved to them in many ways that it was really he himself. . ." (TLB); (2) by the apostle Paul (Acts 9:3–8; 1 Cor. 15:8; Gal. 1:12); (3) by the five hundred Christian brothers (1 Cor. 15:6); and (4) by Thomas the doubter who had to see for himself (John 20:24–29). According to Paul in 1 Cor. 15, the Christian faith stands or falls on the bodily resurrection of Jesus, for it guarantees that (1) Jesus was truly the Son of God (Rom. 1:4); (2) God the Father accepted what Jesus did at Calvary on the basis of the resurrection (Rom. 4:25); (3) the risen Christ pleads for his people before the Father (Rom. 8:34); (4) believers have the hope of eternal life (1 Pet. 1:3–5); and (5) believers will also rise and have resurrected bodies like that of Jesus (1 Cor. 15:49; Phil. 3:21; 1 John 3:2).

28:19 Jesus' command here is warrant for water baptism, which has been accepted and practiced by the church through the ages. It replaced circumcision as the sign and seal of the covenant of grace. While virtually all Christians agree on the need for water baptism, they differ widely on all other aspects of it. Some believe that immersion constitutes the only mode of baptism; others hold to affusion (pouring) or aspersion (sprinkling). Some baptize infants on the grounds that it replaces the rite of circumcision. Others refuse to baptize until the individual is old enough to make a credible personal profession of faith. Some call baptism a sacrament, which conveys grace; others call it a symbol. According to Jesus, baptism is to be administered in the name of the Father, the Son, and the Holy Spirit. Modern critics claim this verse states something Jesus never said, and that it represents later church tradition. They do this because the book of Acts speaks of Jesus' baptism as though the rite did not include the Trinitarian formula. Evangelicals accept this verse as Jesus' words and agree that the Trinitarian formula was spoken by the Son of God himself. (See note on Acts 2:38.)

28:20 *world,* or, "age."

THE GOSPEL ACCORDING TO
SAINT MARK

Authorship, date, and background Tradition has identified John Mark as the author of the second Gospel. The text itself does not mention him by name. Mark (his Roman name; John, his Jewish name) came from a well-to-do family. His mother, Mary, was a friend of the apostles (Acts 12). Some think Mary's home was the site of the Last Supper and the home in which the disciples gathered at Pentecost. It was definitely the place in which the Christians gathered to pray for the release of Peter from prison and where he came when he was set free (Acts 12:12ff.). Barnabas was Mark's cousin and a fellow missionary.

Acts 12:25 states that Paul and Barnabas ministered in Antioch, and when they left that city they were accompanied by Mark as their assistant. Acts 13:1–5 details how Paul and Barnabas were called by the Holy Spirit and sent by the church on their first missionary journey. When Paul and Barnabas landed at Perga, John deserted them and returned to Jerusalem (Acts 13:13). Whatever the reason for the desertion, Paul was disillusioned with Mark (John). Later, when Barnabas and Paul were at Antioch following the Jerusalem conference, they agreed to go on a preaching mission to Turkey. Barnabas wanted to take Mark with them. Paul dissented. This broke up the team. Barnabas took Mark and went to Cyprus. Paul took Silas and went to Syria and Cilicia (Acts 15:34–41). Some time afterwards, Paul and Mark were reconciled. Paul paid tribute to him and described him as his traveling companion (Col 4:10; Philemon 1:24; 2 Tim 4:11).

The Apostle Peter spoke of Mark as his son in 1 Peter 5:13. This is important because the names of Mark and Peter have been connected together with the Gospel of Mark. Mark had not been a follower or companion of Jesus; he was too young at the time. But he was closely associated with Peter, and his Gospel is thought to be an account of what Peter preached everywhere. It was the earlier oral tradition of the church which Mark put into written form either before or after Peter's death. Many scholars think the Gospel was composed in Rome. Most certainly it was written before the fall of Jerusalem in A.D. 70 and perhaps as early as A.D. 50. Many scholars think it was the first Gospel to be written, and that Matthew and Luke used Mark as one of their chief sources for their own writings. Perhaps all of them had access to the oral traditions which included much of the same material. Since some scholars still regard Matthew's Gospel as the earliest, Mark may have been indebted to him or both of them to others. The date is not so important. What is important is that all of the Gospels were produced under the aegis of the Holy Spirit who got written what God wanted written. Certainly Mark's Gospel was intended for non-Jewish believers and was written in a Roman context.

Characteristics and content Mark's Gospel is not a biography. Nothing is said about the birth, the genealogy, or the early life of Jesus. Mark concentrates on the public ministry of Jesus. He does this in narrative style, paying attention to details in an action-packed, vivid, and colorful account of Jesus' last years. He does not concentrate so much on what Jesus said as on what he did. He pictures Jesus as the Son of God and the mighty overcomer of disease, demons, and death. The Greek word translated "straightway," "immediately," "at once," "soon" is used more than forty times in Mark.

Mark explains Jewish customs for his non-Jewish readers. This indicates that the Gospel was intended for a non-Jewish audience. He does not hide the miracles of Jesus nor does he downplay the gospel story itself. Mark starts by declaring, "the beginning of the gospel of Jesus Christ, the Son of God" (1:1). The effect of his writing is sharpened and reinforced by the use of active rather than passive verbs. Much of what he says sounds as though it could have been taken from Peter's preaching, the substance of which he tries to preserve for the reader. While Mark's Gospel has not been thought of as being theologically oriented, it is full of basic doctrine. Almost from the beginning he makes it clear that Jesus is pressing toward his goal—the cross of Calvary and the salvation of men through faith in him.

The ending of Mark's Gospel (16:9–20) is not found in the two oldest manuscripts. It is included in later manuscripts, and in other early manuscripts it appears with variations and partial omissions. Without the ending, the Gospel seems to conclude very abruptly. This is the only major textual problem for the book. Parts of that ending have been used to support snake handling and other odd actions. Its use in the Gospel cannot be understood apart from the promise that those who take the gospel to the ends of the earth will have the protection of God.

Outline

I. The opening events of Christ's ministry (1:1–13)
II. Jesus' early Galilean ministry (1:14—3:6)
III. The second phase of Jesus' Galilean ministry (3:7—7:23)
IV. The third phase of Jesus' Galilean ministry (7:24—9:50)
V. From Galilee to Jerusalem (10:1–52)
VI. The Jerusalem ministry of Jesus: Passion week (11:1—16:8)
VII. The post-resurrection appearances of Jesus (16:9–20)

I. THE OPENING EVENTS OF CHRIST'S MINISTRY (1:1–13)

A. THE MINISTRY OF JOHN THE BAPTIST (CF. MT 3:1–12; LK 3:2–17; JN 1:6–8, 19–28)

1 THE beginning of the gospel of Jesus Christ, the Son of God;
2 As it is written in the prophets, Behold, I send my messenger before
thy face, which shall prepare thy way before thee.
3 The voice of one crying in the wilderness, Prepare ye the way of the
Lord, make his paths straight.
4 John did baptize in the wilderness, and preach the baptism of repen-
tance for the remission of sins.
5 And there went out unto him all the land of Judæa, and they of
Jerusalem, and were all baptized of him in the river of Jordan, confessing
their sins.
6 And John was clothed with camel's hair, and with a girdle of a skin
about his loins; and he did eat locusts and wild honey;
7 And preached, saying, There cometh one mightier than I after me, the
latchet of whose shoes I am not worthy to stoop down and unloose.
8 I indeed have baptized you with water: but he shall baptize you with the
Holy Ghost.

B. THE BAPTISM OF JESUS (CF. MT 3:13–17; LK 3:21, 22)

9 And it came to pass in those days, that Jesus came from Nazareth of
Galilee, and was baptized of John in Jordan.

☆**1:1** Ps 2:7; Mt 3:1–6, 11; Lk 1:35; 3:1–6, 16; Jn 1:34; Rom 8:3; 1 Jn 4:15
☆**1:2, 3** Isa 40:3; Mal 3:1; Jn 1:23
☆**1:4** Acts 19:4
☆**1:6** Lev 11:22
☆**1:7** Jn 1:15; Acts 13:25
☆**1:8** Isa 44:3; Joel 2:28; Acts 2:4; 10:45; 11:15, 16; 1 Cor 12:13
1:9 Mt 3:13–17; Lk 3:21, 22; Jn 1:32–34

1:1 Mark begins with the gospel of Jesus Christ, who had John the Baptist as his forerunner and herald. Mark says nothing about Jesus' ancestry and genealogy to Abraham or to Adam. He says nothing about the birth of Jesus Christ. Nor does he do what John did—give us information about the pre-incarnate Christ, the *Logos (or, Word). Mark was not an apostle, and much* of what he says appears in Matthew or in Luke. His testimony, when added to that of the apostles, gives added witness to the truth of the Old and New Testaments. Whether his Gospel preceded or followed Matthew's is of no great significance.

1:2 *my messenger,* i.e., John the Baptist. See note on Luke 1:57 for information about the life of John.

1:4 *for the remission of sins,* i.e., "so that God could forgive them." The baptism of John, which certainly contained the need for repentance and the promise of the forgiveness of sins, was not full Christian baptism. The Christian church did not yet exist; John did not baptize in the name of the Trinity. He had never baptized with the Holy Spirit, who had not yet been given and whose age or dispensation had not yet begun (see John 7:39). In Acts 18:23—19:7 Paul and Apollos came across several disciples of John who had been baptized before Jesus' death. Paul and Apollos rebaptized them in the name of Jesus and laid hands on them to receive the gift of the Holy Spirit.

1:6 Jesus remarked that John came neither eating nor drinking—he came clothed in camel's hair, practicing mortification of the flesh. Men said he had a demon. Jesus came eating and drinking, and they said he was a wine-bibber and a glutton. It makes no difference what way the righteous come or how they conduct themselves—they will be misunderstood and rejected. See Matt. 11:18, 19 for the words of Jesus.

1:7 *the latchet of whose shoes I am not worthy to . . . unloose,* i.e., "I am not even worthy to be his slave."

1:8 *with water,* or, "in water." The Greek word is not

1:10☆ 10 And straightway coming up out of the water, he saw the heavens
opened, and the Spirit like a dove descending upon him:
1:11 Mt 3:17 11 And there came a voice from heaven, *saying*, Thou art my beloved Son,
Lk 3:22 in whom I am well pleased.

C. THE DESERT TEMPTATION OF JESUS (CF. MT 4:1–11; LK 4:1–13)

1:12☆ Mt 4:1–11 12 And immediately the spirit driveth him into the wilderness.
Lk 4:1–13 13 And he was there in the wilderness forty days, tempted of Satan; and
1 Tim 3:16 1:13☆ was with the wild beasts; and the angels ministered unto him.

II. JESUS' EARLY GALILEAN MINISTRY (1:14—3:6)

A. THE FIRST GALILEAN PREACHING (CF. MT 4:12–17; LK 4:14, 15; JN 4:43–45)

1:14 14 Now after that John was put in prison, Jesus came into Galilee,
Mt 4:12, 17, 23 Lk 4:14, 15 preaching the gospel of the kingdom of God,
1:15 Dan 2:44; 9:24, 25 15 And saying, The time is fulfilled, and the kingdom of God is at hand:
repent ye, and believe the gospel.
Gal 4:4
Eph 1:10
1 Tim 2:6
Tit 1:3

B. CALLING THE FIRST FOUR DISCIPLES (CF. MT 4:18–22; LK 5:1–11; JN 1:40–42)

1:16 16 Now as he walked by the sea of Galilee, he saw Simon and Andrew his
Mt 4:18–22 Lk 5:1–11 brother casting a net into the sea: for they were fishers.
Jn 1:35–42 17 And Jesus said unto them, Come ye after me, and I will make you to
become fishers of men.
1:18 18 And straightway they forsook their nets, and followed him.
Mt 19:27 19 And when he had gone a little further thence, he saw James the *son* of
Zeb'e-dee, and John his brother, who also were in the ship mending their
nets.
20 And straightway he called them: and they left their father Zeb'e-dee in
the ship with the hired servants, and went after him.

C. CASTING OUT THE DEMON AT CAPERNAUM (CF. LK 4:31–37)

1:21☆ 21 And they went into Ca-per'na-um; and straightway on the sabbath day
Lk 4:31–41 he entered into the synagogue, and taught.
1:22 22 And they were astonished at his doctrine: for he taught them as one
Mt 7:28 that had authority, and not as the scribes.

---

clear on this controversial point. *with the Holy Ghost,* or, "in God's Holy Spirit." The Greek is not clear on the precise meaning of the phrase.†

1:10 See note to Luke 3:22 on the baptism of Jesus by John.

1:12, 13 See note to Luke 4:1, 2 on the temptation of Jesus. *Angels* are sent to do God's will or communicate it to men and women. The Hebrew (*mal'akh*) and Greek (*angellos*) words mean "messenger." Angels constitute a high order of beings who stand in the presence of God. The term "angel" includes the wicked ones who, along with Satan, fell from their first *estate. In Rev. 1–3 the term seems* to apply to pastors—God's messengers to the congregations of the seven churches in Asia. On occasion, in the Old Testament, God himself appears in angelic form (Gen. 16:7–14; 22:11–19; Exod. 3:2–4; Judg. 2:1; 6:1–14; 13:3. See Exod. 24:10 for note on *theophany*). It may be said that angels (1) are created beings (Neh. 9:6; Col. 1:16); (2) are innumerable (Heb. 12:22; Rev. 5:11); (3) are above the laws of matter, i.e., can pass through closed doors and iron gates (Acts 12:7); (4) are ministering spirits (Heb. 1:14); (5) differ in rank and power (they are divided into such classes as angels, archangels, principalities, and powers. See Col. 1:16; Dan. 10:12–21); (6) are more intelligent than men (2 Sam. 14:20); and (7) excel in power (2 Sam. 24:16; 2 Kings 19:35; Ps. 103:20; Matt. 28:2, 4; 2 Pet. 2:11; Rev. 20:1–3).

1:21 This is Jesus' first contact with a demon-possessed person. No appeal is made to him to do anything either by the man who was possessed or by those attending the synagogue to which he had gone on the sabbath day. The demon himself challenged Jesus, who promptly exorcised him by saying, "Hold thy peace, and come out of him." The demon did so, and with marked dispatch. The bystanders got the message: even the demons obey the Son of God.

23 And there was in their synagogue a man with an unclean spirit; and he cried out,

24 Saying, Let *us* alone; what have we to do with thee, thou Jesus of Nazareth? art thou come to destroy us? I know thee who thou art, the Holy One of God.

1:24 Mt 8:29 Jn 6:69 Acts 3:14 Jas 2:19

25 And Jesus rebuked him, saying, Hold thy peace, and come out of him.

26 And when the unclean spirit had torn him, and cried with a loud voice, he came out of him.

1:26 Mk 9:20

27 And they were all amazed, insomuch that they questioned among themselves, saying, What thing is this? what new doctrine *is* this? for with authority commandeth he even the unclean spirits, and they do obey him.

28 And immediately his fame spread abroad throughout all the region round about Galilee.

D. HEALING PETER'S MOTHER-IN-LAW (CF. MT 8:14–17; LK 4:18–31)

29 And forthwith, when they were come out of the synagogue, they entered into the house of Simon and Andrew, with James and John.

1:29 Mt 8:14–17 Lk 4:18–31

30 But Simon's wife's mother lay sick of a fever, and anon they tell him of her.

31 And he came and took her by the hand, and lifted her up; and immediately the fever left her, and she ministered unto them.

☆**1:30, 31**

E. THE EVENING HEALINGS (CF. MT 8:16, 17; LK 4:40, 41)

32 And at even, when the sun did set, they brought unto him all that were diseased, and them that were possessed with devils.

1:32 Mt 8:16, 17 Lk 4:40, 41

33 And all the city was gathered together at the door.

34 And he healed many that were sick of divers diseases, and cast out many devils; and suffered not the devils to speak, because they knew him.

1:34 Mk 3:12 Acts 16:16, 17

F. EVANGELIZING GALILEE

35 And in the morning, rising up a great while before day, he went out, and departed into a solitary place, and there prayed.

☆**1:35** Lk 4:42–44 Heb 5:7

36 And Simon and they that were with him followed after him.

37 And when they had found him, they said unto him, All *men* seek for thee.

38 And he said unto them, Let us go into the next towns, that I may preach there also: for therefore came I forth.

1:38 Isa 61:1

39 And he preached in their synagogues throughout all Galilee, and cast out devils.

1:39 Mt 4:23

G. THE CLEANSING OF THE LEPER (CF. MT 8:1–4; LK 5:12–16)

40 And there came a leper to him, beseeching him, and kneeling down to *him, and saying unto him,* If thou wilt, thou canst make me clean.

☆**1:40** Jer 32:17 Mt 8:2–4 Lk 5:12–16

1:30, 31 Jesus was Peter's guest. When he found Peter's mother-in-law sick of a fever, he healed her. Wherever Christ comes, he comes to do good. And he is sure to be of help to those who are kind enough to entertain him. She was able to minister immediately after the healing, without a period of convalescence.

1:35 As God, Jesus was prayed to; as man, he prayed to his Father in heaven. If Jesus needed to pray, so do we. He prayed long before daybreak. He chose a solitary place where no one could observe him and where there was no danger of distraction. And when he was finished praying, he went back to his work. Prayer does not excuse us from our ordinary duties; rather, it should help us meet those obligations and provide us with the power to make them not only bearable but a delight.

1:40 See note to Matt. 8:1 on this incident and its fuller meaning.

1:41 41 And Jesus, moved with compassion, put forth *his* hand, and touched
Heb 2:17; 4:15 him, and saith unto him, I will; be thou clean.
42 And as soon as he had spoken, immediately the leprosy departed from
him, and he was cleansed.
43 And he straitly charged him, and forthwith sent him away;
1:44 44 And saith unto him, See thou say nothing to any man: but go thy way,
Lev 14:1–32 shew thyself to the priest, and offer for thy cleansing those things which
Moses commanded, for a testimony unto them.
1:45 45 But he went out, and began to publish *it* much, and to blaze abroad the
Mk 3:7; 6:31–34 matter, insomuch that Jesus could no more openly enter into the city, but
was without in desert places: and they came to him from every quarter.

H. HEALING THE PARALYZED MAN (CF. MT 9:1–8; LK 5:17–26)

2:1☆ 2 AND again he entered into Ca-per'na-um, after *some* days; and it was
Mt 9:1–8 Lk 5:17–26 noised that he was in the house.
2:2 2 And straightway many were gathered together, insomuch that there was
Eph 2:17 Heb 2:3 no room to receive *them,* no, not so much as about the door: and he
preached the word unto them.
3 And they come unto him, bringing one sick of the palsy, which was
borne of four.
4 And when they could not come nigh unto him for the press, they
uncovered the roof where he was: and when they had broken *it* up, they let
down the bed wherein the sick of the palsy lay.
2:5 5 When Jesus saw their faith, he said unto the sick of the palsy, Son, thy
Ps 103:3 sins be forgiven thee.
6 But there were certain of the scribes sitting there, and reasoning in their
hearts,
2:7☆ 7 Why doth this *man* thus speak blasphemies? who can forgive sins but
Ps 130:4 Isa 43:25 God only?
Rom 8:33 2:8 8 And immediately when Jesus perceived in his spirit that they so
Heb 4:13 reasoned within themselves, he said unto them, Why reason ye these things
in your hearts?
9 Whether is it easier to say to the sick of the palsy, *Thy* sins be forgiven
thee; or to say, Arise, and take up thy bed, and walk?
10 But that ye may know that the Son of man hath power on earth to
forgive sins, (he saith to the sick of the palsy,)
11 I say unto thee, Arise, and take up thy bed, and go thy way into thine
house.
2:12 12 And immediately he arose, took up the bed, and went forth before them
Mt 9:33 all; insomuch that they were all amazed, and glorified God, saying, We
never saw it on this fashion.

I. THE CALL OF LEVI (MATTHEW) (CF. MT 4:9–13; LK 5:27–32)

2:13 13 And he went forth again by the sea side; and all the multitude resorted
Mt 9:9–13 Lk 5:27–32 unto him, and he taught them.
14 And as he passed by, he saw Levi the *son* of Al-phæ'us sitting at the
receipt of custom, and said unto him, Follow me. And he arose and
followed him.
15 And it came to pass, that, as Jesus sat at meat in his house, many
publicans and sinners sat also together with Jesus and his disciples: for
there were many, and they followed him.

2:1ff See note to Luke 5:17.

2:7 The scribes asked the right question about Jesus and the forgiveness of sins. If God alone can do this, Jesus either was God or was guilty of blasphemy. They concluded wrongly, however, that Jesus was not God.

16And when the scribes and Pharisees saw him eat with publicans and 2:16
sinners, they said unto his disciples, How is it that he eateth and drinketh Isa 65:5
with publicans and sinners?
17When Jesus heard *it*, he saith unto them, They that are whole have no 2:17
need of the physician, but they that are sick: I came not to call the Mt 18:11
righteous, but sinners to repentance. Lk 19:9, 10 1 Tim 1:15

J. THE FASTING CONTROVERSY (CF. MT 9:14–17; LK 5:33–39)

18And the disciples of John and of the Pharisees used to fast: and they ☆2:18
come and say unto him, Why do the disciples of John and of the Pharisees Mt 9:14–17
fast, but thy disciples fast not? Lk 5:33–39
19And Jesus said unto them, Can the children of the bridechamber fast, 2:19
while the bridegroom is with them? as long as they have the bridegroom Isa 54:5
with them, they cannot fast. Jn 3:29 Rev 19:7
20But the days will come, when the bridegroom shall be taken away from
them, and then shall they fast in those days.
21No man also seweth a piece of new cloth on an old garment: else the ☆2:21
new piece that filled it up taketh away from the old, and the rent is made
worse.
22And no man putteth new wine into old bottles: else the new wine doth ☆2:22
burst the bottles, and the wine is spilled, and the bottles will be marred: but Gal 3:1–3
new wine must be put into new bottles.

K. THE SABBATH CONTROVERSY (CF. MT 12:1–8; LK 6:1–5)

23And it came to pass, that he went through the corn fields on the 2:23
sabbath day; and his disciples began, as they went, to pluck the ears of Deut 23:25 Mt 12:1–8
corn. Lk 6:1–5
24And the Pharisees said unto him, Behold, why do they on the sabbath
day that which is not lawful?
25And he said unto them, Have ye never read what David did, when he ☆2:25
had need, and was an hungred, he, and they that were with him? Ex 25:30 29:32, 33
26How he went into the house of God in the days of A-bi′a-thar the high Lev 24:9 1 Sam 21:1–6
priest, and did eat the shewbread, which is not lawful to eat but for the ☆2:26
priests, and gave also to them which were with him? ☆2:27
27And he said unto them, The sabbath was made for man, and not man Ex 23:12 Deut 5:14
for the sabbath: Jn 7:21–24 2:28
28Therefore the Son of man is Lord also of the sabbath. Col 2:16, 17

2:18 Fasting was practiced in Jesus' day, and it was done by the apostles (Acts 13:1–3). The early Christians, however, did not fast regularly as a Christian duty. When asked by his disciples why he did not fast, Jesus said that fasting was an expression of sorrow and was not in keeping with the joy his disciples shared with him, like the joy of a wedding feast. In Matt. 6:16–18 Jesus was critical of fasting that was ostentatious and that looked for the approval of men. He endorsed secret fasting only, which sought to glorify God. Present-day Christians might well engage in fasting from time to time.
2:21, 22 See note on Luke 5:36 regarding new wine and cloth patches.
2:25ff In obedience to Lev. 24:5–9 the priests prepared twelve loaves of bread every week, laying them before the Lord on the table on the sabbath (cf. Exod. 25:30; 35:13; 39:36). When the fresh loaves were laid on the table, the priests could eat the old loaves if they wished to do so. But no one else was allowed to eat the sacred bread.

2:26 Rationalist critics have said Jesus was mistaken here when he referred to Abiathar. In 1 Sam. 21:1–6 it states that Ahimelech, the father of Abiathar, gave the sacred bread to David. But according to Mark, all Jesus said is that the incident took place *in the days of Abiathar the high priest,* who served conjointly with his father before his father died. There is no error of fact. *shewbread,* i.e., "bread of the presence."
2:27 God rested on the seventh day, according to Gen. 2:2. This is the first mention of the sabbath in Scripture. In Israel the seventh day (Saturday) was the sabbath and as such was incorporated into the Mosaic law (Exod. 20:9–11). The Jews became litigious about the sabbath, adding all sorts of restrictions and regulations that made matters cumbersome. They even figured exactly how far one could travel on the sabbath before it became work and a violation of the law. The phrase "a sabbath day's journey" is illustrative of this legalism. Jesus provided them and us with two principles relative to work on the sabbath: (1) *the sabbath was made for man, and not man for the sabbath* (see

L. THE SABBATH HEALING OF THE DEFORMED HAND (CF. MT 12:9–14; LK 6:6–11)

3:1☆ Mt 12:9–16 Lk 6:6–11, 17–19
3 AND he entered again into the synagogue; and there was a man there
which had a withered hand.
2 And they watched him, whether he would heal him on the sabbath day;
that they might accuse him.
3 And he saith unto the man which had the withered hand, Stand forth.
4 And he saith unto them, Is it lawful to do good on the sabbath days, or
to do evil? to save life, or to kill? But they held their peace.
5 And when he had looked round about on them with anger, being grieved
for the hardness of their hearts, he saith unto the man, Stretch forth thine
hand. And he stretched *it* out: and his hand was restored whole as the
other.
3:6 Mt 22:16
6 And the Pharisees went forth, and straightway took counsel with the
He-ro′di-ans against him, how they might destroy him.

III. THE SECOND PHASE OF JESUS' GALILEAN MINISTRY (3:7—7:23)

A. THE SPREADING NEWS OF JESUS' MIRACLES (CF. MT 12:15–21; LK 6:17–19)

3:7 Mt 12:15–21 Lk 6:17–19
7 But Jesus withdrew himself with his disciples to the sea: and a great
multitude from Galilee followed him, and from Judæa,
8 And from Jerusalem, and from I-du-mæ′a, and *from* beyond Jordan;
and they about Tyre and Si′don, a great multitude, when they had heard
what great things he did, came unto him.
9 And he spake to his disciples, that a small ship should wait on him
because of the multitude, lest they should throng him.
10 For he had healed many; insomuch that they pressed upon him for to
touch him, as many as had plagues.
3:11☆ Mk 1:24, 25, 34 Lk 4:41 Acts 16:16, 17
11 And unclean spirits, when they saw him, fell down before him, and
cried, saying, Thou art the Son of God.
12 And he straitly charged them that they should not make him known.

B. THE SUMMONING OF THE TWELVE (CF. MT 10:1–4; LK 6:12–16)

3:13 Mt 10:2–4 Lk 6:12–16
13 And he goeth up into a mountain, and calleth *unto him* whom he
would: and they came unto him.
3:14 Lk 9:1
14 And he ordained twelve, that they should be with him, and that he
might send them forth to preach,
15 And to have power to heal sicknesses, and to cast out devils:
3:16 Jn 1:42
16 And Simon he surnamed Peter;
17 And James the *son* of Zeb′e-dee, and John the brother of James; and he
surnamed them Bo-a-ner′ges, which is, The sons of thunder:
18 And Andrew, and Philip, and Bartholomew, and Matthew, and
Thomas, and James the *son* of Al-phæ′us, and Thad-dæ′us, and Simon the
Canaanite,

---

also Matt. 12:1–8; Luke 6:1–5); and (2) works of mercy and of necessity are permissible on the sabbath. To pluck grain for food was a necessity, and to save the life of an animal from a hole was a work of mercy. So was the healing of a sick person. Incidentally, the priests were exempted from this rule in any event—they *had* to work on the sabbath.

3:1ff The only question here was whether it was right or wrong to heal on the sabbath day. Such an "act of mercy" was not forbidden, but those who hated Jesus wished to use this healing against him. They called it an "act of work" on the sabbath day, which they said was wrong.

3:11 *unclean spirits,* i.e., "demons." These demons knew about Jesus Christ and were aware of his divine sonship; nevertheless, they were not and cannot be saved. People may and do profess faith in all doctrines of the Christian faith without being regenerated.

19And Judas Iscariot, which also betrayed him: and they went into an house. ☆3:19

C. RISING RESISTANCE AND THE QUESTION ABOUT SATAN (CF. MT 12:22–45; LK 11:14–23)

20And the multitude cometh together again, so that they could not so much as eat bread. **3:20** Mk 6:31
21And when his friends heard *of it*, they went out to lay hold on him: for they said, He is beside himself.
22¶And the scribes which came down from Jerusalem said, He hath Be-el′ze-bub, and by the prince of the devils casteth he out devils. ☆**3:22** Mt 9:34; 10:25 12:22–32 Lk 11:14–23 Jn 8:48, 52 10:20
23And he called them *unto him*, and said unto them in parables, How can Satan cast out Satan?
24And if a kingdom be divided against itself, that kingdom cannot stand.
25And if a house be divided against itself, that house cannot stand.
26And if Satan rise up against himself, and be divided, he cannot stand, but hath an end. **3:26** Mt 4:10
27No man can enter into a strong man's house, and spoil his goods, except he will first bind the strong man; and then he will spoil his house. **3:27** Isa 49:24, 25
28Verily I say unto you, All sins shall be forgiven unto the sons of men, and blasphemies wherewith soever they shall blaspheme:
29But he that shall blaspheme against the Holy Ghost hath never forgiveness, but is in danger of eternal damnation: ☆**3:29** Lk 12:10 1 Jn 5:16
30Because they said, He hath an unclean spirit.

D. CHRIST'S TRUE BROTHERS (CF. MT 12:46–50; LK 8:19–21)

31¶There came then his brethren and his mother, and, standing without, sent unto him, calling him. **3:31** Mt 12:46–50 13:55 Mk 6:3 Lk 8:19–21 Jn 7:3–5
32And the multitude sat about him, and they said unto him, Behold, thy mother and thy brethren without seek for thee.
33And he answered them, saying, Who is my mother, or my brethren?
34And he looked round about on them which sat about him, and said, Behold my mother and my brethren! **3:34** Rom 8:29 Heb 2:11
35For whosoever shall do the will of God, the same is my brother, and my sister, and mother. ☆**3:35** Jn 7:16, 17

E. JESUS TEACHES BY USING PARABLES

1. The Sower Sows His Seed (Cf. Mt 13:1–9; Lk 8:4–8)

4 AND he began again to teach by the sea side: and there was gathered unto him a great multitude, so that he entered into a ship, and sat in the sea; and the whole multitude was by the sea on the land. **4:1** Mt 13:1–23 Lk 8:4–15
2And he taught them many things by parables, and said unto them in his doctrine,

---

3:19 Jesus had many followers. The twelve whom he chose were to become the apostles in the church after Pentecost. They were closest to him. From the beginning he knew that Judas Iscariot would betray him, and he was chosen in accord with the plan of God from whom nothing is hidden. Judas was later replaced by Matthias (Acts 1:26). Paul was also called by God to be an apostle.
3:22 *Beelzebub.* See note to Matt. 10:25 on Satan, here called Beelzebub.
3:29 Blaspheming the Holy Spirit is the unpardonable sin. It consists in the constant, conscious, deliberate, and malicious rejection of the Spirit's witness to Christ's deity and his power to save. Inasmuch as only the Holy Spirit can convince and convert sinners, any final rejection of his witness and wooing makes it impossible for such a person to be saved.
3:35 We may claim as our brothers and sisters those who are related to us by the blood of Christ, through which we all are adopted into the family of God. Such people are closer to us than relatives and earthly family members who do not know the Savior.

4:3☆

3 Hearken; Behold, there went out a sower to sow:

4 And it came to pass, as he sowed, some fell by the way side, and the fowls of the air came and devoured it up.

5 And some fell on stony ground, where it had not much earth; and immediately it sprang up, because it had no depth of earth:

6 But when the sun was up, it was scorched; and because it had no root, it withered away.

7 And some fell among thorns, and the thorns grew up, and choked it, and it yielded no fruit.

8 And other fell on good ground, and did yield fruit that sprang up and increased; and brought forth, some thirty, and some sixty, and some an hundred.

4:9 Mk 4:23

9 And he said unto them, He that hath ears to hear, let him hear.

2. The Reason for the Story, and Its Explanation (Cf. Mt 13:10–23; Lk 8:9–15)

10 And when he was alone, they that were about him with the twelve asked of him the parable.

4:11, 12☆ Isa 6:9; 44:18 Jer 5:21 Jn 12:39, 40 Acts 28:26, 27 Rom 11:8 1 Cor 2:10

11 And he said unto them, Unto you it is given to know the mystery of the kingdom of God: but unto them that are without, all *these* things are done in parables:

12 That seeing they may see, and not perceive; and hearing they may hear, and not understand; lest at any time they should be converted, and *their* sins should be forgiven them.

13 And he said unto them, Know ye not this parable? and how then will ye know all parables?

4:14 Eph 3:8 Jas 1:18 1 Pet 1:23–25 **4:15☆** 2 Cor 4:4 1 Pet 5:8

14 ¶The sower soweth the word.

15 And these are they by the way side, where the word is sown; but when they have heard, Satan cometh immediately, and taketh away the word that was sown in their hearts.

16 And these are they likewise which are sown on stony ground; who, when they have heard the word, immediately receive it with gladness;

17 And have no root in themselves, and so endure but for a time: afterward, when affliction or persecution ariseth for the word's sake, immediately they are offended.

18 And these are they which are sown among thorns; such as hear the word,

4:19 Prov 23:4, 5 Lk 18:24 1 Tim 6:9, 10, 17 1 Jn 2:15, 16 **4:20** Jn 15:5

19 And the cares of this world, and the deceitfulness of riches, and the lusts of other things entering in, choke the word, and it becometh unfruitful.

20 And these are they which are sown on good ground; such as hear the word, and receive *it*, and bring forth fruit, some thirtyfold, some sixty, and some an hundred.

4:3ff The elements in each part of the parable are the same—the seed, the sower, and the soil. However, it is always the same seed and the same sower. Only the soil is different. This means that four kinds of people hear the good news, but only one of the four responds in such a way as to produce acceptable fruit.

4:11, 12 *This verse clearly* says that Jesus used illustrations or parables for the purpose of hiding the truth, not to reveal it. The words of Jesus summarize what Isaiah said in Isa. 6:9, 10 as it relates Israel's rejection of Isaiah's message. At that time, Israel's unwillingness to repent and accept God's forgiveness was the result of its rejection of the Word of God mediated through Isaiah. This pattern was being duplicated in Christ's ministry when the Jews rejected his teaching, as the account in Matt. 13:13–15 makes clear.

4:15 Among the works of Satan are the following: (1) he seeks to destroy the preached Word of God; (2) he blinds men's eyes (2 Cor. 4:3, 4); (3) he tempts the people of God (1 Cor. 7:5; 2 Cor. 2:11; 1 Thess. 3:5); (4) he molests and harasses God's servants in countless ways (1 Thess. 2:18; 1 Pet. 5:8); (5) he enters into men and becomes incarnate in them to use them as his tools (John 13:27; Matt. 12:27, 28, 43–45); and (6) he accuses men before God (Job 1:8–11; Rev. 12:10).

3. The Parable of the Candlestick (Cf. Mt 5:15; Lk 8:16; 11:33)

21¶And he said unto them, Is a candle brought to be put under a bushel,
or under a bed? and not to be set on a candlestick?
22For there is nothing hid, which shall not be manifested; neither was any
thing kept secret, but that it should come abroad.
23If any man have ears to hear, let him hear.
24And he said unto them, Take heed what ye hear: with what measure ye
mete, it shall be measured to you: and unto you that hear shall more be
given.
25For he that hath, to him shall be given: and he that hath not, from him
shall be taken even that which he hath.

☆**4:21** Mt 5:15; Lk 8:16–18; 11:33
4:22 Mt 10:26; Lk 12:2
4:23 Mt 11:15; 13:43
4:25 Mt 13:12; 25:29; Lk 6:38; 19:26; 2 Cor 9:6

4. The Parable of the Growing Grain

26¶And he said, So is the kingdom of God, as if a man should cast seed
into the ground;
27And should sleep, and rise night and day, and the seed should spring
and grow up, he knoweth not how.
28For the earth bringeth forth fruit of herself; first the blade, then the ear,
after that the full corn in the ear.
29But when the fruit is brought forth, immediately he putteth in the
sickle, because the harvest is come.

☆**4:26, 27** 1 Cor 3:6, 7
4:28, 29 Mt 9:37, 38; Lk 10:2; Jn 4:35; 1 Cor 15:36–38; Rev 14:15

5. The Parable of the Mustard Seed (Cf. Mt 13:31, 32; Lk 13:18, 19)

30¶And he said, Whereunto shall we liken the kingdom of God? or with
what comparison shall we compare it?
31*It is* like a grain of mustard seed, which, when it is sown in the earth, is
less than all the seeds that be in the earth:
32But when it is sown, it groweth up, and becometh greater than all herbs,
and shooteth out great branches; so that the fowls of the air may lodge
under the shadow of it.
33And with many such parables spake he the word unto them, as they
were able to hear *it*.
34But without a parable spake he not unto them: and when they were
alone, he expounded all things to his disciples.

☆**4:30** Mt 13:31, 32; Lk 13:18, 19
4:31, 32 Gen 1:11, 12; Ps 104:12; Ezek 17:22, 23; 37:6; Dan 4:12, 21; Acts 2:41; 4:4; 5:14
4:33 Mt 13:34, 35
4:34 Jn 10:6; 16:25

F. THE MINISTRY AROUND THE LAKE OF GALILEE

1. The Calming of the Waves (Cf. Mt 8:23–27; Lk 8:22–25)

35And the same day, when the even was come, he saith unto them, Let us
pass over unto the other side.
36And when they had sent away the multitude, they took him even as he
was in the ship. And there were also with him other little ships.
37And there arose a great storm of wind, and the waves beat into the ship,
so that it was now full.
38And he was in the hinder part of the ship, asleep on a pillow: and they
awake him, and say unto him, Master, carest thou not that we perish?

4:35 Mt 8:23–27; Lk 8:22–25
☆**4:38**

4:21 *candle,* or, "lamp."

4:26ff The central teaching of this illustration is the law of growth. After planting, the seed may not sprout for some time. The kingdom of God is like that. Beginning small in Jerusalem, it now extends around the whole earth. God alone knows how to bring forth an abundant harvest from the gospel seed.

4:30ff See note on Matt. 13:31, 32 for the explanation of this parable.

4:38 However much we may sympathize with the fear and distress of the disciples, it remains clear that they did not yet understand the true nature of Jesus and his unfailing concern for them. The question about whether he cared about their welfare was a statement of doubt and lack of faith. Let it never be said of us—who have the full and final revelation of God—that we question for a single moment the solicitude of Jesus for us or doubt his power to help us in times of difficulty.

4:39☆ Job 38:11 Ps 65:7; 89:9 93:4

39 And he arose, and rebuked the wind, and said unto the sea, Peace, be
still. And the wind ceased, and there was a great calm.
40 And he said unto them, Why are ye so fearful? how is it that ye have no
faith?

4:41 Ps 33:8, 9

41 And they feared exceedingly, and said one to another, What manner of
man is this, that even the wind and the sea obey him?

2. Deliverance from Demons (Cf. Mt 8:28–34; Lk 8:26–29)

5:1☆ Mt 8:28–34 Lk 8:26–39

5 AND they came over unto the other side of the sea, into the country of
the Gad'a-renes.
2 And when he was come out of the ship, immediately there met him out
of the tombs a man with an unclean spirit,
3 Who had *his* dwelling among the tombs; and no man could bind him,
no, not with chains:
4 Because that he had been often bound with fetters and chains, and the
chains had been plucked asunder by him, and the fetters broken in pieces:
neither could any *man* tame him.
5 And always, night and day, he was in the mountains, and in the tombs,
crying, and cutting himself with stones.
6 But when he saw Jesus afar off, he ran and worshipped him,

5:7, 8 Lk 8:28 Acts 16:17 Heb 7:1

7 And cried with a loud voice, and said, What have I to do with thee,
Jesus, *thou* Son of the most high God? I adjure thee by God, that thou
torment me not.
8 For he said unto him, Come out of the man, *thou* unclean spirit.

5:9☆

9 And he asked him, What *is* thy name? And he answered, saying, My
name *is* Legion: for we are many.
10 And he besought him much that he would not send them away out of
the country.

5:11☆ Deut 14:8 Isa 65:4

11 Now there was there nigh unto the mountains a great herd of swine
feeding.
12 And all the devils besought him, saying, Send us into the swine, that we
may enter into them.

5:13 Job 1:12; 2:6 12:16 Mt 28:18 Lk 4:36 Col 2:10 Heb 2:8

13 And forthwith Jesus gave them leave. And the unclean spirits went out,
and entered into the swine: and the herd ran violently down a steep place
into the sea, (they were about two thousand;) and were choked in the sea.
14 And they that fed the swine fled, and told *it* in the city, and in the
country. And they went out to see what it was that was done.

5:15 1 Jn 3:8

15 And they come to Jesus, and see him that was possessed with the devil,
and had the legion, sitting, and clothed, and in his right mind: and they
were afraid.
16 And they that saw *it* told them how it befell to him that was possessed
with the devil, and *also* concerning the swine.

5:17 Job 21:14; 22:17 Lk 5:8

17 And they began to pray him to depart out of their coasts.

5:18 Ps 116:12

18 And when he was come into the ship, he that had been possessed with
the devil prayed him that he might be with him.
19 Howbeit Jesus suffered him not, but saith unto him, Go home to thy

---

4:39 *be still,* i.e., "be muzzled," as one would muzzle a dog to keep it from barking and biting.

5:1ff See note to Luke 8:29.

5:9 *Legion,* i.e., the largest military unit of the Roman army, numbering some three to six thousand men. Its use here simply means that many more than one demon inhabited this man.

5:11 If those who owned the *swine* were Jews, they were in violation of the Mosaic law. There is nothing to indicate that the people who owned the swine were Gentiles. When Jesus commanded the demons to enter the swine, it was suitable for evil spirits to occupy unclean rather than clean animals. Nowhere in Scripture is it ever said that demons occupied clean animals. Some would cavil that Jesus had no right to let the demons enter the swine, who then died in the waters. Since he was creator of all things, he owned them and could dispose of them according to his will.

friends, and tell them how great things the Lord hath done for thee, and
hath had compassion on thee.
20 And he departed, and began to publish in De-cap'o-lis how great things
Jesus had done for him: and all *men* did marvel.

5:20 Isa 63:7; 116:16; 1 Tim 1:13, 14

3. Healing the Woman with the Hemorrhage and Raising Jairus' Daughter (Cf. Mt 9:18–26; Lk 8:40–56)

21 And when Jesus was passed over again by ship unto the other side,
much people gathered unto him: and he was nigh unto the sea.
22 And, behold, there cometh one of the rulers of the synagogue, Ja-i'rus
by name; and when he saw him, he fell at his feet,
23 And besought him greatly, saying, My little daughter lieth at the point
of death: *I pray thee*, come and lay thy hands on her, that she may be
healed; and she shall live.
24 And *Jesus* went with him; and much people followed him, and
thronged him.
25 And a certain woman, which had an issue of blood twelve years,
26 And had suffered many things of many physicians, and had spent all
that she had, and was nothing bettered, but rather grew worse,
27 When she had heard of Jesus, came in the press behind, and touched his
garment.
28 For she said, If I may touch but his clothes, I shall be whole.
29 And straightway the fountain of her blood was dried up; and she felt in
her body that she was healed of that plague.
30 And Jesus, immediately knowing in himself that virtue had gone out of
him, turned him about in the press, and said, Who touched my clothes?
31 And his disciples said unto him, Thou seest the multitude thronging
thee, and sayest thou, Who touched me?
32 And he looked round about to see her that had done this thing.
33 But the woman fearing and trembling, knowing what was done in her,
came and fell down before him, and told him all the truth.
34 And he said unto her, Daughter, thy faith hath made thee whole; go in
peace, and be whole of thy plague.
35 While he yet spake, there came from the ruler of the synagogue's *house*
certain which said, Thy daughter is dead: why troublest thou the Master
any further?
36 As soon as Jesus heard the word that was spoken, he saith unto the
ruler of the synagogue, Be not afraid, only believe.
37 And he suffered no man to follow him, save Peter, and James, and John
the brother of James.
38 And he cometh to the house of the ruler of the synagogue, and seeth the
tumult, and them that wept and wailed greatly.
39 And when he was come in, he saith unto them, Why make ye this ado,
and weep? the damsel is not dead, but sleepeth.

5:21 Mt 9:1, 18–26; Lk 8:40–56
☆**5:22**
5:23 Mk 6:5; 7:32; 8:23; 16:18; Lk 4:40; 13:13; Acts 6:6; 9:17; 28:8
☆**5:25**
5:27 Mk 3:10; Acts 19:11, 12
☆**5:30** Lk 6:19
5:34 Mk 10:52; Lk 7:50; 17:19; 18:42; Acts 14:9
5:36 Jn 11:25, 40
☆**5:38**
5:39 Jn 11:11

5:22 See note to Luke 8:41 on Jairus and his daughter.

5:25ff Here was a woman whose plight defies description. She was an outcast because of her sickness. She could not come into the temple; she could not participate in the religious ceremonies; she could not touch other persons without making them ceremonially unclean. She could not even live with her husband. But she was healed when she touched the hem of Jesus' garment. He made her come forward and stated that she was healed because of her faith, not because she touched his garment. Moreover, he wanted the crowd to know that she was no longer an outcast. Her ceremonial defilement had been removed. So we who are unclean by our sins are made whole in Jesus Christ and the defilement disappears.

5:30 *virtue,* i.e., "power." Jesus attributed her healing to her faith, which was manifested by her touching of the Lord's garment.

5:38 *them that wept and wailed greatly.* These were professional mourners who were paid for their services by the family.

5:40 Acts 9:40

40 And they laughed him to scorn. But when he had put them all out, he
taketh the father and the mother of the damsel, and them that were with
him, and entereth in where the damsel was lying.

5:41, 42 Ps 33:9 Lk 7:14

41 And he took the damsel by the hand, and said unto her, Tal′i-tha cu′mi;
which is, being interpreted, Damsel, I say unto thee, arise.
42 And straightway the damsel arose, and walked; for she was *of the age* of
twelve years. And they were astonished with a great astonishment.

5:43 Mt 12:16; 17:9 Mk 3:12; 5:19 Lk 5:14

43 And he charged them straitly that no man should know it; and
commanded that something should be given her to eat.

4. Christ's Second Rejection by His Home Town (Cf. Mt 13:53–58; Lk 4:16–30)

6:1☆ Mt 13:53–58 9:35 Lk 4:16, 22, 24
6:2, 3☆ Ps 69:8 Isa 53:2, 3 Mt 11:6 Jn 6:42

6 AND he went out from thence, and came into his own country; and
his disciples follow him.
2 And when the sabbath day was come, he began to teach in the
synagogue: and many hearing *him* were astonished, saying, From whence
hath this *man* these things? and what wisdom *is* this which is given unto
him, that even such mighty works are wrought by his hands?
3 Is not this the carpenter, the son of Mary, the brother of James, and
Joses, and of Juda, and Simon? and are not his sisters here with us? And
they were offended at him.

6:4 Jn 4:44

4 But Jesus said unto them, A prophet is not without honour, but in his
own country, and among his own kin, and in his own house.
5 And he could there do no mighty work, save that he laid his hands upon
a few sick folk, and healed *them.*
6 And he marvelled because of their unbelief. And he went round about
the villages, teaching.

5. The Sending Out of the Twelve (Cf. Mt 10:1–15; Lk 9:1–6)

6:7☆ Mt 10:1, 9–14 11:1 Lk 9:1–6 10:1–11
6:8☆

7 ¶And he called *unto him* the twelve, and began to send them forth by
two and two; and gave them power over unclean spirits;
8 And commanded them that they should take nothing for *their* journey,
save a staff only; no scrip, no bread, no money in *their* purse:
9 But *be* shod with sandals; and not put on two coats.
10 And he said unto them, In what place soever ye enter into an house,
there abide till ye depart from that place.

6:11☆ Acts 13:51; 18:6 Heb 10:31

11 And whosoever shall not receive you, nor hear you, when ye depart
thence, shake off the dust under your feet for a testimony against them.
Verily I say unto you, It shall be more tolerable for Sodom and Go-mor′rha
in the day of judgment, than for that city.

6:1 *in his own country,* i.e., Nazareth.
6:3 Jesus is called a *carpenter,* a "carpenter's son" (Matt. 13:55), and "Joseph's son" (Luke 4:22). Calling him *the son of Mary* was probably intended as a slur, since men were commonly called the sons of their fathers, not of their mothers. In this verse Jesus' sisters are mentioned, but their names are not given. The names of his brothers are stated: *James, Joses, Juda, and Simon (see John 7:3–10;* Acts 1:14). In Gal. 1:19, Paul mentions James as the Lord's brother (the same James of Acts 12:17; 15:13–21; and 1 Cor. 15:7). From this, it has been assumed that his brothers did not believe in him until after his resurrection. The plain statements of the New Testament lead to the conclusion that the sisters and brothers of Jesus were the children of Joseph and Mary. Later theories that these were children of Joseph by an earlier marriage or that they were cousins of Jesus have no merit. *they were offended at him,* i.e., "he was like a rock over which they stumbled."
6:7 Jesus sent forth the twelve two by two. This meant that his own ministry was increased sixfold. If everyone who is converted to Christ would win one other person in a year, it would not be long before the church would be the largest group of people on the earth.
6:8 *scrip,* i.e., a wallet used to carry food or small articles.
6:11 *shake off the dust,* i.e., break off any relationship and refuse to accept responsibility for whatever happens after that.

12 And they went out, and preached that men should repent. ☆6:12
13 And they cast out many devils, and anointed with oil many that were 6:13
sick, and healed *them*. Jas 5:14

6. The Beheading of John the Baptist (Cf. Mt 14:1–12; Lk 9:7–9)

14 And king Herod heard *of him;* (for his name was spread abroad:) and ☆6:14
he said, That John the Baptist was risen from the dead, and therefore Mt 14:1–12
mighty works do shew forth themselves in him. Lk 9:7–9
15 Others said, That it is E-li'as. And others said, That it is a prophet, or 6:15
as one of the prophets. Mt 16:14
16 But when Herod heard *thereof,* he said, It is John, whom I beheaded: he
is risen from the dead.
17 For Herod himself had sent forth and laid hold upon John, and bound ☆6:17
him in prison for He-ro'di-as' sake, his brother Philip's wife: for he had Lev 18:15, 16; 20:21
married her. Lk 3:19; 2 Tim 4:2
18 For John had said unto Herod, It is not lawful for thee to have thy Heb 13:4
brother's wife.
19 Therefore He-ro'di-as had a quarrel against him, and would have killed
him; but she could not:
20 For Herod feared John, knowing that he was a just man and an holy,
and observed him; and when he heard him, he did many things, and heard
him gladly.
21 And when a convenient day was come, that Herod on his birthday 6:21
made a supper to his lords, high captains, and chief *estates* of Galilee; Gen 40:20
22 And when the daughter of the said He-ro'di-as came in, and danced, 6:22
and pleased Herod and them that sat with him, the king said unto the Esth 5:3, 6; 7:2
damsel, Ask of me whatsoever thou wilt, and I will give *it* thee.
23 And he sware unto her, Whatsoever thou shalt ask of me, I will give *it*
thee, unto the half of my kingdom.
24 And she went forth, and said unto her mother, What shall I ask? And
she said, The head of John the Baptist.
25 And she came in straightway with haste unto the king, and asked, ☆6:25
saying, I will that thou give me by and by in a charger the head of John the
Baptist.
26 And the king was exceeding sorry; *yet* for his oath's sake, and for their ☆6:26
sakes which sat with him, he would not reject her.
27 And immediately the king sent an executioner, and commanded his 6:27
head to be brought: and he went and beheaded him in the prison. Rev 6:9
28 And brought his head in a charger, and gave it to the damsel: and the
damsel gave it to her mother.
29 And when his disciples heard *of it,* they came and took up his corpse, 6:29
and laid it in a tomb. Acts 8:2

7. Feeding the Five Thousand (Cf. Mt 14:13-21; Lk 9:10-17; Jn 6:1–13)

30 And the apostles gathered themselves together unto Jesus, and told him 6:30 Mt 14:13–22; Lk 9:10–17
all things, both what they had done, and what they had taught. Jn 6:1–15

6:12 Repentance is emphasized throughout the New Testament. The four Gospels constantly reiterate this theme. So do the Book of Acts (Acts 2:38; 17:30; 20:21) and the Epistles (Rom. 2:4; 2 Cor. 7:9, 10; 2 Pet. 3:9).

6:14 See note on Luke 1:57 about John the Baptist.

6:17 The Philip mentioned here was the brother of Herod Antipas, the tetrarch of Galilee and son of Herod the Great and Mariamne (the daughter of Simon the high priest). He is not to be confused with the Philip who was the tetrarch of Ituraea (Luke 3:1).

6:25 *give me by and by in a charger,* i.e., bring me the head of John on a platter as soon as possible.

6:26 *for his oath's sake.* He who took an oath did that which was irreversible. This was true in pagan nations and among the Jews.

6:31 Mk 3:20

31 And he said unto them, Come ye yourselves apart into a desert place, and rest a while: for there were many coming and going, and they had no leisure so much as to eat.

32 And they departed into a desert place by ship privately.

33 And the people saw them departing, and many knew him, and ran afoot thither out of all cities, and outwent them, and came together unto him.

6:34 Ps 145:8, 9; Isa 61:1; Mt 9:36; Heb 5:1–3

34 And Jesus, when he came out, saw much people, and was moved with compassion toward them, because they were as sheep not having a shepherd: and he began to teach them many things.

35 And when the day was now far spent, his disciples came unto him, and said, This is a desert place, and now the time *is* far passed:

36 Send them away, that they may go into the country round about, and into the villages, and buy themselves bread: for they have nothing to eat.

6:37☆ Num 11:13, 22; 2 Kgs 4:43; Mt 15:33; Mk 8:4

37 He answered and said unto them, Give ye them to eat. And they say unto him, Shall we go and buy two hundred pennyworth of bread, and give them to eat?

38 He saith unto them, How many loaves have ye? go and see. And when they knew, they say, Five, and two fishes.

39 And he commanded them to make all sit down by companies upon the green grass.

40 And they sat down in ranks, by hundreds, and by fifties.

6:41 1 Sam 9:13; Mt 26:26; 1 Tim 4:4, 5

41 And when he had taken the five loaves and the two fishes, he looked up to heaven, and blessed, and brake the loaves, and gave *them* to his disciples to set before them; and the two fishes divided he among them all.

42 And they did all eat, and were filled.

43 And they took up twelve baskets full of the fragments, and of the fishes.

6:44☆

44 And they that did eat of the loaves were about five thousand men.

8. Jesus Walking on the Water (Cf. Mt 14:22–32; Jn 6:15–21)

45 And straightway he constrained his disciples to get into the ship, and to go to the other side before unto Beth-sa′i-da, while he sent away the people.

46 And when he had sent them away, he departed into a mountain to pray.

6:47 Mt 14:23–36; Jn 6:16–21

47 And when even was come, the ship was in the midst of the sea, and he alone on the land.

6:48☆

48 And he saw them toiling in rowing; for the wind was contrary unto them: and about the fourth watch of the night he cometh unto them, walking upon the sea, and would have passed by them.

49 But when they saw him walking upon the sea, they supposed it had been a spirit, and cried out:

50 For they all saw him, and were troubled. And immediately he talked with them, and saith unto them, Be of good cheer: it is I; be not afraid.

51 And he went up unto them into the ship; and the wind ceased: and they were sore amazed in themselves beyond measure, and wondered.

6:52 Mk 16:14

52 For they considered not *the miracle* of the loaves: for their heart was hardened.

6:37 *two hundred pennyworth*, i.e., "a year's wages."† (See the note on Matt. 14:16 for the explanation of the phrase, *Give ye them to eat.*)

6:44 *five thousand men*. This does not mean the crowd was only male. Women and children were not counted here so that many more than five thousand must have been fed.

6:48 In the Graeco-Roman system of calculation, the night watch was divided into four segments of three hours each (from six o'clock in the evening to six o'clock in the morning). Jesus appeared here in the *fourth watch*, i.e., between three and six in the morning.

9. The Miracles at Gennesaret (Cf. Mt 14:34–36)

53 And when they had passed over, they came into the land of Gen-nes′a- **6:53** Mt 14:34–36
ret, and drew to the shore. Jn 6:24, 25
54 And when they were come out of the ship, straightway they knew him,
55 And ran through that whole region round about, and began to carry ☆**6:55**
about in beds those that were sick, where they heard he was.
56 And whithersoever he entered, into villages, or cities, or country, they **6:56**
laid the sick in the streets, and besought him that they might touch if it Mk 5:28 Acts 5:15
were but the border of his garment: and as many as touched him were made
whole.

10. Jesus Rebukes the Pharisees for Hypocrisy (Cf. Mt 15:1–20)

7 THEN came together unto him the Pharisees, and certain of the ☆**7:1**
scribes, which came from Jerusalem. Mt 15:1–20
2 And when they saw some of his disciples eat bread with defiled, that is **7:2**
to say, with unwashen, hands, they found fault. Lk 11:38
3 For the Pharisees, and all the Jews, except they wash *their* hands oft, eat ☆**7:3**
not, holding the tradition of the elders. Gal 1:14 Col 2:8
4 And *when they come* from the market, except they wash, they eat not.
And many other things there be, which they have received to hold, *as* the
washing of cups, and pots, brasen vessels, and of tables.
5 Then the Pharisees and scribes asked him, Why walk not thy disciples ☆**7:5**
according to the tradition of the elders, but eat bread with unwashen
hands?
6 He answered and said unto them, Well hath E-sai′as prophesied of you ☆**7:6, 7**
hypocrites, as it is written, This people honoureth me with *their* lips, but Isa 29:13 Tit 1:16
their heart is far from me.
7 Howbeit in vain do they worship me, teaching *for* doctrines the
commandments of men.
8 For laying aside the commandment of God, ye hold the tradition of
men, *as* the washing of pots and cups: and many other such like things ye
do.
9 And he said unto them, Full well ye reject the commandment of God, **7:9**
that ye may keep your own tradition. Isa 24:4, 5
10 For Moses said, Honour thy father and thy mother; and, Whoso **7:10**
curseth father or mother, let him die the death: Ex 20:12; 21:17 Lev 20:19
11 But ye say, If a man shall say to his father or mother, *It is* Corban, that Deut 5:16 Prov 20:20
is to say, a gift, by whatsoever thou mightest be profited by me; *he shall be* 1 Tim 5:8 ☆**7:11**
free. Lev 1:2 (Heb)
12 And ye suffer him no more to do ought for his father or his mother;
13 Making the word of God of none effect through your tradition, which
ye have delivered: and many such like things do ye.
14 ¶And when he had called all the people *unto him,* he said unto them,
Hearken unto me every one *of you,* and understand:

6:55 The news of Jesus' presence brought multitudes for exactly the same reason multitudes come to healing meetings today. They have deep physical needs for which they have had no relief, and when they hear of a healer, they flock to him, hoping that something will happen to them.

7:1 See note on Matt. 3:7 about the Pharisees.

7:3 *wash their hands,* i.e., "wash with the fist," or, "sprinkle their arms to the elbows."†

7:5 *unwashen hands.* This does not necessarily mean their hands were dirty, only that they had not been washed in accordance with the religious rules and therefore were ceremonially unclean.

7:6ff See note on Matt. 15:7, 8 for information about this incident.

7:11 *Corban.* Some Jews vowed money to God and were declared to be free from using any of it for the support of their needy parents. It was simply an excuse to violate the commandment to honor father and mother.

7:15 Acts 10:14, 15 1 Cor 8:8 1 Tim 4:4
15 There is nothing from without a man, that entering into him can defile
him: but the things which come out of him, those are they that defile the
man.
7:16☆
16 If any man have ears to hear, let him hear.
7:17 Mk 2:1, 2; 3:20 9:28
17 And when he was entered into the house from the people, his disciples
asked him concerning the parable.
18 And he saith unto them, Are ye so without understanding also? Do ye
not perceive, that whatsoever thing from without entereth into the man, *it*
cannot defile him;
7:19 Lk 11:41 Acts 10:15; 11:9
19 Because it entereth not into his heart, but into the belly, and goeth out
into the draught, purging all meats?
7:20☆ Rom 14:1–12 Col 2:16
20 And he said, That which cometh out of the man, that defileth the man.
7:21 Gal 5:19 Tit 1:15
21 For from within, out of the heart of men, proceed evil thoughts,
adulteries, fornications, murders,
22 Thefts, covetousness, wickedness, deceit, lasciviousness, an evil eye,
blasphemy, pride, foolishness:
23 All these evil things come from within, and defile the man.

IV. THE THIRD PHASE OF JESUS' GALILEAN MINISTRY (7:24—9:50)

A. THE JOURNEY TOWARD TYRE AND SIDON: HEALING THE SYROPHOENICIAN WOMAN'S DAUGHTER (CF. MT 15:21–28)

7:24 Mt 15:21–28
24 ¶And from thence he arose, and went into the borders of Tyre and
Si′don, and entered into an house, and would have no man know *it:* but he
could not be hid.
25 For a *certain* woman, whose young daughter had an unclean spirit,
heard of him, and came and fell at his feet:
26 The woman was a Greek, a Sy-ro-phe-ni′cian by nation; and she
besought him that he would cast forth the devil out of her daughter.
7:27 Mt 10:5, 6 Acts 13:46 Rom 9:4 Eph 2:11, 12
27 But Jesus said unto her, Let the children first be filled: for it is not meet
to take the children's bread, and to cast *it* unto the dogs.
28 And she answered and said unto him, Yes, Lord: yet the dogs under the
table eat of the children's crumbs.
7:29 Mt 9:29
29 And he said unto her, For this saying go thy way; the devil is gone out
of thy daughter.
7:30☆ Josh 21:45
30 And when she was come to her house, she found the devil gone out, and
her daughter laid upon the bed.

B. HEALING THE DEAF AND DUMB MAN (CF. MT 15:19–31)

7:31 Mt 15:29–31
31 ¶And again, departing from the coasts of Tyre and Si′don, he came
unto the sea of Galilee, through the midst of the coasts of De-cap′o-lis.
32 And they bring unto him one that was deaf, and had an impediment in
his speech; and they beseech him to put his hand upon him.
7:33☆ Mk 8:23 Jn 9:6
33 And he took him aside from the multitude, and put his fingers into his
ears, and he spit, and touched his tongue;

7:16 This verse is not present in some reliable ancient manuscripts.
7:20 The locus of sin is the heart, not the stomach. *What one eats does not* make him a sinner. But what comes out from within him (i.e., from his heart) is what defiles him. The sins Jesus speaks about are not external to us but internal and spring from the heart: murder, theft, fornication, adultery, pride, etc.
7:30 This demon was exorcised by Jesus from a distance. He never saw the girl nor did he touch her. Yet his divine power over demons was effective whether the victims were near him or far away. His word was sufficient.
7:33ff Jesus confounds all his critics because he breaks all the rules and heals in strange and unusual ways. Here, he pokes his finger in the ears of the deaf-mute, then spits on his finger and touches the man's tongue. The man is instantly and perfectly healed, to the amazement of the mob.

34 And looking up to heaven, he sighed, and saith unto him, Eph′pha-tha,
that is, Be opened.
35 And straightway his ears were opened, and the string of his tongue was
loosed, and he spake plain.
36 And he charged them that they should tell no man: but the more he
charged them, so much the more a great deal they published *it;*
37 And were beyond measure astonished, saying, He hath done all things
well: he maketh both the deaf to hear, and the dumb to speak.

7:34 Isa 35:5, 6; Mt 11:5; Mk 6:41; Jn 11:41; 17:1
7:36 Mk 5:43

C. FEEDING THE FOUR THOUSAND (CF. MT 15:32–39)

8 IN those days the multitude being very great, and having nothing to
eat, Jesus called his disciples *unto him,* and saith unto them,
2 I have compassion on the multitude, because they have now been with
me three days, and have nothing to eat:
3 And if I send them away fasting to their own houses, they will faint by
the way: for divers of them came from far.
4 And his disciples answered him, From whence can a man satisfy these
men with bread here in the wilderness?
5 And he asked them, How many loaves have ye? And they said, Seven.
6 And he commanded the people to sit down on the ground: and he took
the seven loaves, and gave thanks, and brake, and gave to his disciples to
set before *them;* and they did set *them* before the people.
7 And they had a few small fishes: and he blessed, and commanded to set
them also before *them.*
8 So they did eat, and were filled: and they took up of the broken *meat*
that was left seven baskets.
9 And they that had eaten were about four thousand: and he sent them
away.
10 ¶And straightway he entered into a ship with his disciples, and came
into the parts of Dal-ma-nu′tha.

8:1 Mt 15:32–38
☆**8:2** Ps 111:4, 5; 145:9; Mk 1:41; Heb 2:17; 4:15; 5:1–3
8:4 Num 11:21, 22; 2 Kgs 4:42, 43
8:5 Mk 6:38
8:6 1 Tim 4:4, 5
8:7 Mt 14:19
☆**8:8**
☆**8:10** Mt 15:39—16:12

D. THE JEWISH LEADERS DEMAND A SIGN FROM HEAVEN (CF. MT 16:1–10)

11 And the Pharisees came forth, and began to question with him, seeking
of him a sign from heaven, tempting him.
12 And he sighed deeply in his spirit, and saith, Why doth this generation
seek after a sign? verily I say unto you, There shall no sign be given unto
this generation.
13 And he left them, and entering into the ship again departed to the other
side.
14 ¶Now *the disciples* had forgotten to take bread, neither had they in the
ship with them more than one loaf.
15 And he charged them, saying, Take heed, beware of the leaven of the
Pharisees, and *of* the leaven of Herod.

☆**8:11** Mt 12:38; 16:1–10; Lk 11:16; Jn 6:30; 1 Cor 1:22
8:15 Lk 12:1

8:2 A great multitude had gathered to listen to Jesus. They remained with him for three days without food. This tells us something about the zeal of those who are moved by the Word of God and would rather do without food than miss what the master would tell them. The common people, unlike the religious leaders, appreciated Jesus and listened to him. He fed them out of compassion and concern for those who sustain hardships for his sake and for the sake of the gospel.

8:8 *seven baskets.* In the feeding of the five thousand the baskets were much smaller than those mentioned here. These were large, like the one used to let Paul down the wall in his escape from Damascus (Acts 9:25).

8:10 *Dalmanutha* seems to have been a town on the west shore of the Sea of Galilee. Its precise location is unknown. The ruins near modern Mejdel (Magdala) may be the location. Some ancient manuscripts of Mark substitute Magaden, or Magdala, in place of Dalmanutha.

8:11 *tempting him,* i.e., "testing him." They said in effect, "If we see the sign, then we will believe in you." (See note to Matt. 16:4 about this request for a sign from heaven.)

16 And they reasoned among themselves, saying, *It is* because we have no
bread.
8:17 Mk 6:52 17 And when Jesus knew *it,* he saith unto them, Why reason ye, because ye
have no bread? perceive ye not yet, neither understand? have ye your heart
yet hardened?
8:18 Ezek 12:2 18 Having eyes, see ye not? and having ears, hear ye not? and do ye not
remember?
8:19 Mt 14:20; Mk 6:43, 44; Lk 9:17; Jn 6:13 19 When I brake the five loaves among five thousand, how many baskets
full of fragments took ye up? They say unto him, Twelve.
8:20 Mt 15:37; Mk 8:8, 9 20 And when the seven among four thousand, how many baskets full of
fragments took ye up? And they said, Seven.
21 And he said unto them, How is it that ye do not understand?

E. HEALING THE BLIND MAN NEAR BETHSAIDA

22 ¶And he cometh to Beth-sa′i-da; and they bring a blind man unto him,
and besought him to touch him.
8:23 Mk 7:33; Jn 9:6 23 And he took the blind man by the hand, and led him out of the town;
and when he had spit on his eyes, and put his hands upon him, he asked
him if he saw ought.
24 And he looked up, and said, I see men as trees, walking.
25 After that he put *his* hands again upon his eyes, and made him look up:
and he was restored, and saw every man clearly.
8:26 Mt 8:4 26 And he sent him away to his house, saying, Neither go into the town,
nor tell *it* to any in the town.

F. PETER'S GREAT CONFESSION (CF. MT 16:13–20; LK 9:18–21)

8:27 Mt 16:13–20; Lk 9:18–21 27 ¶And Jesus went out, and his disciples, into the towns of Cæs-a-re′a
Phi-lip′pi: and by the way he asked his disciples, saying unto them, Whom
do men say that I am?
8:28 Mt 14:2 28 And they answered, John the Baptist: but some *say,* E-li′as; and others,
One of the prophets.
8:29☆ Jn 6:69; 11:27 29 And he saith unto them, But whom say ye that I am? And Peter
answereth and saith unto him, Thou art the Christ.
30 And he charged them that they should tell no man of him.

G. JESUS PREDICTS HIS DEATH, RESURRECTION, AND COMING AGAIN (CF. MT 16:21–28; LK 9:22–27)

8:31 Mt 16:21–28; 17:22, 23; Lk 9:22–27 31 And he began to teach them, that the Son of man must suffer many
things, and be rejected of the elders, and *of* the chief priests, and scribes,
and be killed, and after three days rise again.
8:32☆ 32 And he spake that saying openly. And Peter took him, and began to
rebuke him.
8:33 Rom 8:7 33 But when he had turned about and looked on his disciples, he rebuked
Peter, saying, Get thee behind me, Satan: for thou savourest not the things
that be of God, but the things that be of men.
8:34 Mt 10:38; Lk 14:27 34 ¶And when he had called the people *unto him* with his disciples also, he
said unto them, Whosoever will come after me, let him deny himself, and
take up his cross, and follow me.

8:29 See note on Matt. 16:18.
8:32 *he spake that saying openly.* In this case, Jesus did not speak obliquely, parabolically, or indirectly. He was plain and explicit. However prejudiced the disciples might have been, they could not then misunderstand what he was saying to them. Peter, out of a misplaced love, wanted to shield the Savior from this horrible fate. Jesus rebuked him strongly and emphatically.

35 For whosoever will save his life shall lose it; but whosoever shall lose
his life for my sake and the gospel's, the same shall save it.
36 For what shall it profit a man, if he shall gain the whole world, and lose
his own soul?
37 Or what shall a man give in exchange for his soul?
38 Whosoever therefore shall be ashamed of me and of my words in this
adulterous and sinful generation; of him also shall the Son of man be
ashamed, when he cometh in the glory of his Father with the holy angels.

8:35 Lk 17:33 Jn 12:25 Rev 12:11

8:38 Mt 10:33 Lk 12:9 Rom 1:16 2 Thess 1:7 2 Tim 1:8; 2:12 Heb 11:16

9 AND he said unto them, Verily I say unto you, That there be some of
them that stand here, which shall not taste of death, till they have seen
the kingdom of God come with power.

9:1 Mt 16:28; 24:30 25:31 Lk 9:27; 22:18

H. THE TRANSFIGURATION (CF. MT 17:1–8; LK 9:28–36)

2 ¶And after six days Jesus taketh *with him* Peter, and James, and John,
and leadeth them up into an high mountain apart by themselves: and he
was transfigured before them.
3 And his raiment became shining, exceeding white as snow; so as no
fuller on earth can white them.
4 And there appeared unto them E-li'as with Moses: and they were
talking with Jesus.
5 And Peter answered and said to Jesus, Master, it is good for us to be
here: and let us make three tabernacles; one for thee, and one for Moses,
and one for E-li'as.
6 For he wist not what to say; for they were sore afraid.
7 And there was a cloud that overshadowed them: and a voice came out of
the cloud, saying, This is my beloved Son: hear him.
8 And suddenly, when they had looked round about, they saw no man any
more, save Jesus only with themselves.
9 And as they came down from the mountain, he charged them that they
should tell no man what things they had seen, till the Son of man were risen
from the dead.
10 And they kept that saying with themselves, questioning one with
another what the rising from the dead should mean.
11 ¶And they asked him, saying, Why say the scribes that E-li'as must first
come?
12 And he answered and told them, E-li'as verily cometh first, and
restoreth all things; and how it is written of the Son of man, that he must
suffer many things, and be set at nought.
13 But I say unto you, That E-li'as is indeed come, and they have done
unto him whatsoever they listed, as it is written of him.

☆**9:2** Mt 17:1–13 Lk 9:28–36

9:3 Dan 7:9 Mt 28:3

9:7 Ex 40:34 2 Pet 1:17, 18 Heb 1:2; 2:3 12:25

☆**9:11** Mal 4:5 Mt 11:14

9:12, 13 Gen 3:15 Ps 22:6, 7 Isa 50:6; 53:2, 3 Dan 9:26 Mt 11:13, 14 Lk 1:17; 23:11 Jn 3:14

I. HEALING A DEMON-POSSESSED BOY (CF. MT 17:14–21; LK 9:37–43)

14 ¶And when he came to *his* disciples, he saw a great multitude about
them, and the scribes questioning with them.
15 And straightway *all the* people, when they beheld him, were greatly
amazed, and running to *him* saluted him.

9:14 Mt 17:14–21 Lk 9:37–43

9:2 The account of Christ's glory appears in the first three Gospels. Each description contains unique details. The event probably occurred on Mount Hermon. Moses and Elijah appeared in person and three of Jesus' disciples witnessed their presence (Luke 9:32). Christ's radiance was only a foretaste of his glory, but the event strengthened the disciples. They heard the voice of God from heaven (9:7). The sudden disappearance of Elijah and Moses, leaving only Jesus, meant that in him Old Testament prophecy and law were fulfilled. Peter never forgot that moment. He drew attention to the fact that he was an eyewitness of Christ's splendor and glory (2 Pet. 1:16–18).

9:11 *Elias [Elijah] must first come.* See note on Mal. 4:5 about Elijah.

16 And he asked the scribes, What question ye with them?
17 And one of the multitude answered and said, Master, I have brought unto thee my son, which hath a dumb spirit;
18 And wheresoever he taketh him, he teareth him: and he foameth, and gnasheth with his teeth, and pineth away: and I spake to thy disciples that they should cast him out; and they could not.
9:19 19 He answereth him, and saith, O faithless generation, how long shall I be
Jn 4:48 with you? how long shall I suffer you? bring him unto me.
9:20 20 And they brought him unto him: and when he saw him, straightway the
Mk 1:26 spirit tare him; and he fell on the ground, and wallowed foaming.
21 And he asked his father, How long is it ago since this came unto him? And he said, Of a child.
22 And ofttimes it hath cast him into the fire, and into the waters, to destroy him: but if thou canst do any thing, have compassion on us, and help us.
9:23☆ 23 Jesus said unto him, If thou canst believe, all things *are* possible to him
Mk 11:22–24 Lk 17:6 that believeth.
Jn 11:40 Acts 14:9 24 And straightway the father of the child cried out, and said with tears,
9:24 Eph 2:8 Lord, I believe; help thou mine unbelief.
9:25 25 When Jesus saw that the people came running together, he rebuked the
Acts 10:38 foul spirit, saying unto him, *Thou* dumb and deaf spirit, I charge thee, come out of him, and enter no more into him.
26 And *the spirit* cried, and rent him sore, and came out of him: and he was as one dead; insomuch that many said, He is dead.
27 But Jesus took him by the hand, and lifted him up; and he arose.
28 And when he was come into the house, his disciples asked him privately, Why could not we cast him out?
9:29☆ 29 And he said unto them, This kind can come forth by nothing, but by prayer and fasting.

J. JESUS AGAIN PREDICTS HIS DEATH AND RESURRECTION (CF. MT 17:22, 23; LK 9:43–45)

9:30 30 ¶And they departed thence, and passed through Galilee; and he would
Mt 17:22, 23 Lk 9:43–45 not that any man should know *it*.
9:31 Mt 16:21 31 For he taught his disciples, and said unto them, The Son of man is
Mk 8:31 delivered into the hands of men, and they shall kill him; and after that he is
Lk 9:22 killed, he shall rise the third day.
32 But they understood not that saying, and were afraid to ask him.

K. JESUS TEACHES HIS DISCIPLES ABOUT HUMILITY (CF. MT 18:1–5; LK 9:46–48)

9:33 Mt 18:1–11 33 ¶And he came to Ca-per'na-um: and being in the house he asked them,
Lk 9:46–50 What was it that ye disputed among yourselves by the way?
9:34 Prov 13:10 34 But they held their peace: for by the way they had disputed among
Lk 22:24, 26 9:35 themselves, who *should be* the greatest.
Mt 20:26, 27 23:11 35 And he sat down, and called the twelve, and saith unto them, If any
Mk 10:43, 44 man desire to be first, *the same* shall be last of all, and servant of all.

9:23 *all things are possible to him that believeth.* This statement should not be extended beyond its immediate frame of reference. All men must die. Scripture nowhere promises eternal physical life. And we cannot ask God in faith to change our sex or the color of our skin. The key point in Jesus' statement is "to him that believeth." Faith always rests on the will of God. To claim that which is not the will of God "by faith" is wrong. It is presumption, not faith.

9:29 *This kind can come forth by nothing, but by prayer,* i.e., "Cases like this require prayer."† *and fasting,* which appears in some manuscripts, is not included in the most ancient.

36 And he took a child, and set him in the midst of them: and when he had
taken him in his arms, he said unto them,
37 Whosoever shall receive one of such children in my name, receiveth me:
and whosoever shall receive me, receiveth not me, but him that sent me.
38 ¶And John answered him, saying, Master, we saw one casting out devils
in thy name, and he followeth not us: and we forbad him, because he
followeth not us.
39 But Jesus said, Forbid him not: for there is no man which shall do a
miracle in my name, that can lightly speak evil of me.
40 For he that is not against us is on our part.
41 For whosoever shall give you a cup of water to drink in my name,
because ye belong to Christ, verily I say unto you, he shall not lose his
reward.
42 And whosoever shall offend one of *these* little ones that believe in me, it
is better for him that a millstone were hanged about his neck, and he were
cast into the sea.
43 And if thy hand offend thee, cut it off: it is better for thee to enter into
life maimed, than having two hands to go into hell, into the fire that never
shall be quenched:
44 Where their worm dieth not, and the fire is not quenched.
45 And if thy foot offend thee, cut it off: it is better for thee to enter halt
into life, than having two feet to be cast into hell, into the fire that never
shall be quenched:
46 Where their worm dieth not, and the fire is not quenched.
47 And if thine eye offend thee, pluck it out: it is better for thee to enter
into the kingdom of God with one eye, than having two eyes to be cast into
hell fire:
48 Where their worm dieth not, and the fire is not quenched.
49 For every one shall be salted with fire, and every sacrifice shall be salted
with salt.
50 Salt *is* good: but if the salt have lost his saltness, wherewith will ye
season it? Have salt in yourselves, and have peace one with another.

9:37 Mt 10:40 Mk 10:16 Jn 13:20
☆**9:38** Num 11:26–29
☆**9:39** 1 Cor 12:3
9:40 Mt 12:30
9:41 Mt 10:42
☆**9:42** Lk 17:1–3
☆**9:43** Deut 13:6–10 Mt 5:29, 30 Rom 8:12, 13 Col 3:5 Heb 12:1
☆**9:44, 46**
☆**9:47**
9:48 Isa 66:24 2 Thess 1:9
☆**9:49** Lev 2:13 Ezek 43:24
9:50 Mt 5:13 Lk 14:34 Rom 12:18 Eph 4:29 Col 4:6 1 Thess 5:13 Heb 12:14

V. FROM GALILEE TO JERUSALEM (10:1–52)

A. JESUS IN JUDEA

10 AND he arose from thence, and cometh into the coasts of Judæa by
the farther side of Jordan: and the people resort unto him again;
and, as he was wont, he taught them again.

☆**10:1**

9:38ff Jesus rebuked sectarianism here. The fact that someone is not a member of a specific denomination does not mean he cannot love Christ, honor him, and do his work. Largeness of spirit is in accord with Jesus' viewpoint, even though we may have differing beliefs in secondary matters.

9:39 *that can lightly speak evil of me,* i.e., "that will quickly turn against me."

9:42 *whosoever shall offend one of these little ones that believe in me,* i.e., "whoever causes one of these little ones who believe in me to lose faith."

9:43ff See note on Matt. 5:29.

9:44, 46 Verses 44 and 46 (which are identical with verse 48) are not in the best ancient manuscripts.

9:47 Jesus here contrasts the kingdom of God with hell, or *gehenna.* Scripture teaches that the inhabitants of hell include (1) the devil, the beast, and the false prophet (Rev. 19:20; 20:10); (2) the fallen angels (2 Pet. 2:4); (3) the wicked (Ps. 9:17); (4) anyone whose name is not written in the Lamb's book of life (Rev. 20:15); and (5) those who refuse to do the will of God (Matt. 7:21). A denial of the existence or reality of hell constitutes a repudiation of the teaching of Scripture, a denial of the teaching of the Lord Jesus, and an undermining of the reality of heaven, which is hell's opposite. Scripture is crystal clear on this matter: people will go to hell unless they accept Jesus Christ as their Savior.

9:49 *For every one shall be salted with fire.* Numerous explanations have been given for this phrase. Many commentators perceive this as an allusion to Lev. 2:13, which states that cereal offerings are to be offered with the salt of the covenant (that is the literal translation). Salt is a preservative and fire is often used as a purifier. Moffatt translates this verse: "Everyone has to be consecrated by the fire of the discipline."

10:1 *And he arose from thence,* i.e., "Then he left Capernaum." Mentioned here so quietly, this was his final farewell to Galilee. He never returned until after his death and resurrection.†

B. JESUS ON MARRIAGE AND DIVORCE (CF. MT 19:3–12)

10:2 [2]¶And the Pharisees came to him, and asked him, Is it lawful for a man
Mt 19:3–12 to put away *his* wife? tempting him.
[3]And he answered and said unto them, What did Moses command you?
10:4 [4]And they said, Moses suffered to write a bill of divorcement, and to put
Deut 24:1–3 Mt 5:31 *her* away.
10:5☆ [5]And Jesus answered and said unto them, For the hardness of your heart
he wrote you this precept.
10:6 [6]But from the beginning of the creation God made them male and
Gen 1:27; 2:24 female.
[7]For this cause shall a man leave his father and mother, and cleave to his
wife;
10:8 [8]And they twain shall be one flesh: so then they are no more twain, but
1 Cor 6:16 Eph 5:31 one flesh.
[9]What therefore God hath joined together, let not man put asunder.
[10]And in the house his disciples asked him again of the same *matter.*
10:11 [11]And he saith unto them, Whosoever shall put away his wife, and marry
Mt 5:32 Lk 16:18 another, committeth adultery against her.
Rom 7:2, 3 [12]And if a woman shall put away her husband, and be married to
another, she committeth adultery.

C. JESUS BLESSING THE LITTLE CHILDREN (CF. MT 19:13–15; LK 18:15–17)

10:13 [13]¶And they brought young children to him, that he should touch them:
Mt 19:13–15 Lk 18:15–17 and *his* disciples rebuked those that brought *them.*
[14]But when Jesus saw *it,* he was much displeased, and said unto them,
Suffer the little children to come unto me, and forbid them not: for of such
is the kingdom of God.
10:15 [15]Verily I say unto you, Whosoever shall not receive the kingdom of God
Mt 18:3 1 Cor 14:20 as a little child, he shall not enter therein.
1 Pet 2:2 **10:16** [16]And he took them up in his arms, put *his* hands upon them, and blessed
Isa 40:11 them.

D. THE PERIL OF RICHES: THE WEALTHY YOUNG MAN (CF. MT 19:16–30; LK 18:18–30)

10:17☆ [17]¶And when he was gone forth into the way, there came one running,
Mt 19:16–30 Lk 18:18–30 and kneeled to him, and asked him, Good Master, what shall I do that I
may inherit eternal life?
10:18☆ [18]And Jesus said unto him, Why callest thou me good? *there is* none good
but one, *that is,* God.
10:19 [19]Thou knowest the commandments, Do not commit adultery, Do not
Ex 20:12–17 Deut 5:16–20 kill, Do not steal, Do not bear false witness, Defraud not, Honour thy
Rom 13:9 father and mother.
10:20 Jas 2:10 [20]And he answered and said unto him, Master, all these have I observed
10:21 Mt 6:19, 20 from my youth.
Lk 12:33 [21]Then Jesus beholding him loved him, and said unto him, One thing
Acts 2:44, 45 1 Tim 6:17–19 thou lackest: go thy way, sell whatsoever thou hast, and give to the poor,

---

10:5ff *The teachings of* Jesus on divorce are found here and in Matt. 5:27–32; 19:3–9; and Luke 16:18. Paul states that his teaching on divorce comes from Jesus (1 Cor. 7:10, 11). Except for Matt. 5:32 and 19:9, divorce is everywhere forbidden except for adultery. (See notes on Gen. 2:24 and Deut. 24:1.)

10:17 See note on Matt. 19:16 for information about the question of the rich young ruler and Jesus' person-to-person evangelism.

10:18 The rich young ruler called Jesus "good." Jesus said only God can be called good. The implication is plain: "If you call me good, call me God, for that is who I am."

and thou shalt have treasure in heaven: and come, take up the cross, and
follow me.
22 And he was sad at that saying, and went away grieved: for he had great
possessions.
23 ¶And Jesus looked round about, and saith unto his disciples, How
hardly shall they that have riches enter into the kingdom of God!
24 And the disciples were astonished at his words. But Jesus answereth ☆10:24
again, and saith unto them, Children, how hard is it for them that trust in Ps 52:7
riches to enter into the kingdom of God!
25 It is easier for a camel to go through the eye of a needle, than for a rich ☆10:25
man to enter into the kingdom of God.
26 And they were astonished out of measure, saying among themselves,
Who then can be saved?
27 And Jesus looking upon them saith, With men *it is* impossible, but not 10:27
with God: for with God all things are possible. Jer 32:17 Heb 7:25
28 ¶Then Peter began to say unto him, Lo, we have left all, and have 10:28
followed thee. Mk 1:18
29 And Jesus answered and said, Verily I say unto you, There is no man
that hath left house, or brethren, or sisters, or father, or mother, or wife, or
children, or lands, for my sake, and the gospel's,
30 But he shall receive an hundredfold now in this time, houses, and 10:30
brethren, and sisters, and mothers, and children, and lands, with persecu- Acts 14:22 1 Thess 3:3
tions; and in the world to come eternal life. 2 Tim 3:12
31 But many *that are* first shall be last; and the last first. 10:31
Mt 20:16 Lk 13:30

E. JESUS PREDICTS HIS DEATH AND RESURRECTION THE THIRD TIME (CF. MT 20:17–19; LK 18:31–34)

32 ¶And they were in the way going up to Jerusalem; and Jesus went 10:32
before them: and they were amazed; and as they followed, they were afraid Mt 20:17–19
And he took again the twelve, and began to tell them what things should Lk 18:31–34
happen unto him,
33 *Saying,* Behold, we go up to Jerusalem; and the Son of man shall be 10:33
delivered unto the chief priests, and unto the scribes; and they shall Mt 16:21; 26:67 27:30
condemn him to death, and shall deliver him to the Gentiles: Mk 8:31; 9:31 14:65
34 And they shall mock him, and shall scourge him, and shall spit upon Lk 9:22
him, and shall kill him: and the third day he shall rise again. 1 Cor 15:3, 4

F. THE WISH OF THE AMBITIOUS SONS OF ZEBEDEE (CF. MT 20:20–28)

35 ¶And James and John, the sons of Zeb'e-dee, come unto him, saying, ☆10:35
Master, we would that thou shouldest do for us whatsoever we shall desire. Mt 20:20–28
36 And he said unto them, What would ye that I should do for you?
37 They said unto him, Grant unto us that we may sit, one on thy right
hand, and the other on thy left hand, in thy glory.

10:24 *for them that trust in riches.* Some of the ancient manuscripts do not contain these words.†

10:25 *eye of a needle* probably refers to a Jerusalem gate that was so narrow it was difficult for a loaded camel to pass through.

10:35ff In Matt. 20:21 the mother of James and John asks for her sons to be seated on the left and the right hands of Jesus in his kingdom. Here James and John make the request for themselves. We can assume that both the mother and the sons asked the same petition of Jesus and received the same sort of reply. We learn that prayer can be used and abused. Some of us do not use it and others use it by abusing it. Jesus bypassed the petition by saying it is not part of his role to make this decision. It belongs to his Father, to whom he is obedient and from whom he will not wrest what is not his to do. The petition was based on a serious sinful inclination—the desire for power and status. Such desires reflect a lack of true sanctification and display a spirit of worldliness.

10:38 Lk 12:50
38 But Jesus said unto them, Ye know not what ye ask: can ye drink of the
cup that I drink of? and be baptized with the baptism that I am baptized
with?

10:39 Acts 12:2 Rev 1:9
39 And they said unto him, We can. And Jesus said unto them, Ye shall
indeed drink of the cup that I drink of; and with the baptism that I am
baptized withal shall ye be baptized:

10:40 Jas 4:3
40 But to sit on my right hand and on my left hand is not mine to give; but
it shall be given to them for whom it is prepared.
41 And when the ten heard *it,* they began to be much displeased with
James and John.

10:42☆ Lk 22:25, 26
42 But Jesus called them *to him,* and saith unto them, Ye know that they
which are accounted to rule over the Gentiles exercise lordship over them;
and their great ones exercise authority upon them.

10:43 Mk 9:35 Lk 9:48
43 But so shall it not be among you: but whosoever will be great among
you, shall be your minister:
44 And whosoever of you will be the chiefest, shall be servant of all.

10:45 Jn 13:14 Phil 2:7 1 Tim 2:5, 6 Tit 2:14
45 For even the Son of man came not to be ministered unto, but to
minister, and to give his life a ransom for many.

G. THE HEALING OF BLIND BARTIMAEUS (CF. MT 20:29–34; LK 18:35–43)

10:46☆ Mt 20:29–34 Lk 18:35–43
46 ¶And they came to Jericho: and as he went out of Jericho with his
disciples and a great number of people, blind Bar-ti-mæ′us, the son of Ti-
mæ′us, sat by the highway side begging.

10:47 Isa 11:1 Jer 23:5, 6 Rom 1:3 Rev 22:16
47 And when he heard that it was Jesus of Nazareth, he began to cry out,
and say, Jesus, *thou* Son of David, have mercy on me.
48 And many charged him that he should hold his peace: but he cried the
more a great deal, *Thou* Son of David, have mercy on me.
49 And Jesus stood still, and commanded him to be called. And they call
the blind man, saying unto him, Be of good comfort, rise; he calleth thee.
50 And he, casting away his garment, rose, and came to Jesus.
51 And Jesus answered and said unto him, What wilt thou that I should do
unto thee? The blind man said unto him, Lord, that I might receive my
sight.

10:52 Isa 35.5 Mt 9:22
52 And Jesus said unto him, Go thy way; thy faith hath made thee whole.
And immediately he received his sight, and followed Jesus in the way.

VI. THE JERUSALEM MINISTRY OF JESUS: PASSION WEEK (11:1—16:8)

A. THE PALM SUNDAY ENTRY (CF. MT 21:1–11; LK 19:29–44; JN 12:12–19)

11:1☆ Mt 21:1–9 Lk 19:29–40 Jn 12:12–19 Acts 1:12
11 AND when they came nigh to Jerusalem, unto Beth′pha-ge and
Bethany, at the mount of Olives, he sendeth forth two of his
disciples,
2 And saith unto them, Go your way into the village over against you: and

10:42 See note on Matt. 20:25.
10:46ff The story of Bartimaeus is found in Matt. *20:29–34 and* Luke 18:35–43. Some have assumed that there are real discrepancies between these accounts. In the *Encyclopedia of Bible Difficulties* (Zondervan, 1982) Gleason L. Archer harmonizes the accounts quite satisfactorily (pp. 332, 333).
11:1 *Bethphage* (meaning "place of unripe figs") was a village on the Mount of Olives near or on the road from Jericho to Jerusalem. It was probably less than a mile from Jerusalem and might, therefore, be considered a suburb. Bethany (probably meaning "house of dates or figs") was about two miles southeast of Jerusalem (John 11:18). Lazarus and his sisters, Martha and Mary, lived there (John 11:1). (See note on Luke 19:28 for additional information on the triumphal entry of Jesus into Jerusalem.)

as soon as ye be entered into it, ye shall find a colt tied, whereon never man
sat; loose him, and bring *him.*
3 And if any man say unto you, Why do ye this? say ye that the Lord hath
need of him; and straightway he will send him hither.
4 And they went their way, and found the colt tied by the door without in
a place where two ways met; and they loose him.
5 And certain of them that stood there said unto them, What do ye,
loosing the colt?
6 And they said unto them even as Jesus had commanded: and they let
them go.
7 And they brought the colt to Jesus, and cast their garments on him; and **11:7** Zech 9:9
he sat upon him.
8 And many spread their garments in the way: and others cut down
branches off the trees, and strawed *them* in the way.
9 And they that went before, and they that followed, cried, saying, **11:9** Ps 118:25, 26
Hosanna; Blessed *is* he that cometh in the name of the Lord:
10 Blessed *be* the kingdom of our father David, that cometh in the name of
the Lord: Hosanna in the highest.
11 And Jesus entered into Jerusalem, and into the temple: and when he **11:11** Mt 21:10, 17
had looked round about upon all things, and now the eventide was come,
he went out unto Bethany with the twelve.

B. THE FRUITLESS FIG TREE CURSED (CF. MT 21:18–22)

12 ¶And on the morrow, when they were come from Bethany, he was ☆**11:12–14** Mt 21:18, 19
hungry:
13 And seeing a fig tree afar off having leaves, he came, if haply he might
find anything thereon: and when he came to it, he found nothing but
leaves; for the time of figs was not *yet.*
14 And Jesus answered and said unto it, No man eat fruit of thee hereafter
for ever. And his disciples heard *it.*

C. THE CLEANSING OF THE TEMPLE (CF. MT 21:12–17; LK 19:45–48; JN 2:13–22)

15 ¶And they come to Jerusalem: and Jesus went into the temple, and ☆**11:15** Mt 21:12–17 Lk 19:45–48 Jn 2:13–17
began to cast out them that sold and bought in the temple, and overthrew
the tables of the moneychangers, and the seats of them that sold doves;
16 And would not suffer that any man should carry *any* vessel through the
temple.
17 And he taught, saying unto them, Is it not written, My house shall be **11:17** Isa 56:7 Jer 7:11
called of all nations the house of prayer? but ye have made it a den of
thieves.
18 And the scribes and chief priests heard *it,* and sought how they might **11:18** Mt 21:46 Mk 12:12 Lk 4:32; 20:19 Jn 7:1
destroy him: for they feared him, because all the people was astonished at
his doctrine.
19 *And when even was come, he went out of the city.*

11:12 In the account by Matthew we are told that the fig tree withered at once and would never again bear fruit (Matt. 21:18). Christ has power over all of nature, including the trees of the field.

11:15ff Multitudes gathered at Jerusalem each year to offer animal sacrifices. Coming from afar, they had to buy the animals at the temple site. Animal vendors offered ritually clean animals for a price. Money merchants were there to exchange currencies so that the Jews of the dispersion could pay the annual half-shekel poll tax. These transactions took place in the court of the Gentiles where non-Jews were allowed to worship. The bazaarlike atmosphere made worship virtually impossible, voiding God's Word that his house was to be a house of prayer for all nations (Isa. 56:7).

D. EXHORTATION AND CONTROVERSY

1. The Power of Faith

11:20 Mt 21:20–22

[20]¶And in the morning, as they passed by, they saw the fig tree dried up
from the roots.
[21]And Peter calling to remembrance saith unto him, Master, behold, the
fig tree which thou cursedst is withered away.

11:22 Mt 17:20 Lk 17:6

[22]And Jesus answering saith unto them, Have faith in God.
[23]For verily I say unto you, That whosoever shall say unto this mountain,
Be thou removed, and be thou cast into the sea; and shall not doubt in his
heart, but shall believe that those things which he saith shall come to pass;
he shall have whatsoever he saith.

11:24☆ Mt 7:7 Lk 11:9 Jn 14:12–14 15:7; 16:24 Jas 1:5–8 **11:25** Mt 6:14, 15 Eph 4:32 Col 3:13 **11:26☆** Mt 21:23–27 Lk 20:1–8

[24]Therefore I say unto you, What things soever ye desire, when ye pray,
believe that ye receive *them,* and ye shall have *them.*
[25]And when ye stand praying, forgive, if ye have ought against any: that
your Father also which is in heaven may forgive you your trespasses.
[26]But if ye do not forgive, neither will your Father which is in heaven
forgive your trespasses.

2. The Challenge to Jesus' Authority (Cf. Mt 21:23–27; Lk 20:1–8)

11:27☆

[27]¶And they come again to Jerusalem: and as he was walking in the
temple, there come to him the chief priests, and the scribes, and the elders,
[28]And say unto him, By what authority doest thou these things? and who
gave thee this authority to do these things?
[29]And Jesus answered and said unto them, I will also ask of you one
question, and answer me, and I will tell you by what authority I do these
things.
[30]The baptism of John, was *it* from heaven, or of men? answer me.
[31]And they reasoned with themselves, saying, If we shall say, From
heaven; he will say, Why then did ye not believe him?

11:32 Mt 14:5 Mk 6:20 **11:33** Job 5:12, 13

[32]But if we shall say, Of men; they feared the people: for all *men* counted
John, that he was a prophet indeed.
[33]And they answered and said unto Jesus, We cannot tell. And Jesus
answering saith unto them, Neither do I tell you by what authority I do
these things.

3. The Parable of the Wicked Tenant Farmers (Cf. Mt 21:33–46; Lk 20:9–19)

12:1☆ Isa 5:1, 2 Mt 21:33–46 Lk 20:9–19

12 AND he began to speak unto them by parables. A *certain* man
planted a vineyard, and set an hedge about *it,* and digged *a place for*
the winefat, and built a tower, and let it out to husbandmen, and went into
a far country.
[2]And at the season he sent to the husbandmen a servant, that he might
receive from the husbandmen of the fruit of the vineyard.
[3]And they caught *him,* and beat him, and sent *him* away empty.
[4]And again he sent unto them another servant; and at him they cast
stones, and wounded *him* in the head, and sent *him* away shamefully
handled.

11:24ff See notes on Matt. 7:7 for the principles which govern prayer.
11:26 The best manuscripts do not have this verse. A nearly identical version of it appears in Matt. 6:15.
11:27 Christ was teaching here as he walked. This followed the custom known to the Greeks as peripatetic schools in which the philosophers did the same. His authority was questioned. See here note to Matt. 21:25 on this subject.
12:1ff See note on Luke 20:9 for information on the parable of the tenant farmers.

5 And again he sent another; and him they killed, and many others;
beating some, and killing some.
6 Having yet therefore one son, his wellbeloved, he sent him also last unto
them, saying, They will reverence my son.
7 But those husbandmen said among themselves, This is the heir; come,
let us kill him, and the inheritance shall be ours.
8 And they took him, and killed *him,* and cast *him* out of the vineyard.
9 What shall therefore the lord of the vineyard do? he will come and
destroy the husbandmen, and will give the vineyard unto others.
10 And have ye not read this scripture; The stone which the builders
rejected is become the head of the corner:
11 This was the Lord's doing, and it is marvellous in our eyes?
12 And they sought to lay hold on him, but feared the people: for they
knew that he had spoken the parable against them: and they left him, and
went their way.

12:5 2 Chron 24:21; 36:15, 16; Neh 9:26; Mt 23:34–37; Acts 7:52; 1 Thess 2:15
12:6 Rom 8:3; Gal 4:4
12:7 Acts 4:27
12:8 Acts 2:23
12:9 Acts 28:23–29
☆**12:10, 11** Ps 118:22, 23; Rom 9:33; Eph 2:20; 1 Pet 2:5–7
12:12 Mt 11:18; Jn 7:26, 30, 44

4. Paying Taxes to the Emperor (Cf. Mt 22:15–22; Lk 20:20–26)

13 ¶And they send unto him certain of the Pharisees and of the He-ro′di-
ans, to catch him in *his* words.
14 And when they were come, they say unto him, Master, we know that
thou art true, and carest for no man: for thou regardest not the person of
men, but teachest the way of God in truth: Is it lawful to give tribute to
Cæsar, or not?
15 Shall we give, or shall we not give? But he, knowing their hypocrisy,
said unto them, Why tempt ye me? bring me a penny, that I may see *it.*
16 And they brought *it.* And he saith unto them, Whose *is* this image and
superscription? And they said unto him, Cæsar's.
17 And Jesus answering said unto them, Render to Cæsar the things that
are Caesar's, and to God the things that are God's. And they marvelled at
him.

☆**12:13** Mt 22:15–40, 46; Lk 20:20–40
☆**12:14**
☆**12:17**

5. The Sadducees and the Resurrection (Cf. Mt 22:23–33; Lk 20:27–38)

18 ¶Then come unto him the Sad′du-cees, which say there is no resurrec-
tion; and they asked him, saying,
19 Master, Moses wrote unto us, If a man's brother die, and leave *his* wife
behind him, and leave no children, that his brother should take his wife, and
raise up seed unto his brother.
20 Now there were seven brethren: and the first took a wife, and dying left
no seed.
21 And the second took her, and died, neither left he any seed: and the
third likewise.
22 And the seven had her, and left no seed: last of all the woman died also.
23 *In the resurrection therefore, when they shall rise,* whose wife shall she
be of them? for the seven had her to wife.

☆**12:18** Mt 22:23–33; Lk 20:27–38; Acts 23:8; 1 Cor 15:12
12:19 Gen 38:8; Deut 25:5

12:10 *The stone which the builders rejected.* This word comes from Ps. 118:22, 23. While we cannot be sure, tradition has it that when the temple was being constructed (all of the stones were hewed out beforehand and assembled on the site of the temple), there was one stone for which there appeared to be no place. It was discarded. Later it was found to be the chief cornerstone.

12:13 *Herodians.* See note on Matt. 22:16.
12:14 See note to Luke 20:20 for information on paying taxes to Caesar and to God.
12:17 God's due takes precedence over Caesar's due when one is forced to choose between them.
12:18 See note on Luke 20:27 for information about the Sadducees and the resurrection.

12:24☆ Dan 12:2 Rom 4:17 1 Tim 1:7 2 Pet 1:19

24 And Jesus answering said unto them, Do ye not therefore err, because ye know not the scriptures, neither the power of God?

12:25 1 Cor 15:42, 49, 52 1 Jn 3:2

25 For when they shall rise from the dead, they neither marry, nor are given in marriage; but are as the angels which are in heaven.

12:26☆ Ex 3:6 Lk 20:37

26 And as touching the dead, that they rise: have ye not read in the book of Moses, how in the bush God spake unto him, saying, I *am* the God of Abraham, and the God of Isaac, and the God of Jacob?

12:27 Mt 22:32 Lk 20:38

27 He is not the God of the dead, but the God of the living: ye therefore do greatly err.

6. The Most Important Commandment (Cf. Mt 22:34–40)

12:28☆

28 ¶And one of the scribes came, and having heard them reasoning together, and perceiving that he had answered them well, asked him, Which is the first commandment of all?

12:29☆ Deut 6:4, 5

29 And Jesus answered him, The first of all the commandments *is,* Hear, O Israel; The Lord our God is one Lord:

12:30 Lk 10:27

30 And thou shalt love the Lord thy God with all thy heart, and with all thy soul, and with all thy mind, and with all thy strength: this *is* the first commandment.

12:31 Lev 19:18 Rom 13:9 Gal 5:14 Jas 2:8

31 And the second *is* like, *namely* this, Thou shalt love thy neighbour as thyself. There is none other commandment greater than these.

12:32 Deut 4:35, 39 Isa 45:5, 6, 14 46:9 1 Cor 8:4–6

32 And the scribe said unto him, Well, Master, thou hast said the truth: for there is one God; and there is none other but he:

12:33 1 Sam 15:22 Hos 6:6 Mic 6:6–8

33 And to love him with all the heart and with all the understanding, and with all the soul, and with all the strength, and to love *his* neighbour as himself, is more than all whole burnt offerings and sacrifices.

12:34 Mt 22:46 Lk 14:6; 20:40

34 And when Jesus saw that he answered discreetly, he said unto him, Thou art not far from the kingdom of God. And no man after that durst ask him *any question.*

7. Who Is the Son of David? (Cf. Mt 22:41–46; Lk 20:41–44)

12:35☆ Mt 22:41–46 Lk 20:41–44

35 ¶And Jesus answered and said, while he taught in the temple, How say the scribes that Christ is the Son of David?

12:24 *ye know not the Scriptures.* Jesus here asserts that the Old Testament teaches about the resurrection, and those who read the Scriptures should have known it. We are responsible for all that the Bible contains whether we know all of it or not. Many people have Bibles that might as well have blank pages, for they are never read.
12:26 Jesus provides an interpretation we might easily miss. The difference is between "I am" and "I was." The verb tense makes all the difference in the world. "I was" would have meant that Abraham and the fathers were dead; "I am" means they are alive and God is still their God.
12:28 *scribes.* See note on 2 Sam. 8:17 regarding scribes in the Old Testament. In the New Testament we are told what they did and how they felt: (1) they were often Pharisees (Acts 23:9); (2) they were the doctors of the Old Testament law (Matt. 22:35); (3) they were Old Testament experts (12:35; Matt. 2:4; 17:10); (4) *they were filled with pride* (12:38); (5) they sat on Moses' seat (Matt. 23:2); (6) Jesus condemned them (Matt. 23:15); (7) they helped to secure Christ's condemnation (Luke 23:10); and (8) they persecuted the New Testament saints (Acts 4:5, 18, 21; 6:12).
12:29ff The twofold law of love (love toward God, and love toward all men including enemies) governs all Christian conduct. Even love is governed by other commandments; it works in concert with righteousness, holiness, and justice. Love is governed by (1) principles—love will do nothing that is expressly forbidden (e.g., it is never loving to commit adultery or tell a lie, however compelling the circumstances might appear to be); and (2) expediency, which dictates the surrendering of that which might cause a brother to stumble; thus Paul refused to eat meat that had been offered to idols, not because it was wrong to do so, but because it would offend a weaker brother.
12:35 Christ here states that the scribes were defective in their teaching when they refused to explain what David meant when he called the Son of David Lord. The scribes did teach that the Messiah was to be the Son of David. Well and good. But they did not explain how and why David called that Son "Lord." Obviously, by calling him Lord, David meant that the Son of David was the Son of God and as such was worthy of being his Lord. The Messiah is God, if David is to be believed—a truth not taught by the scribes. This incident is another one in which Jesus himself claimed to be God. Christ as God is David's Lord. Christ as man is David's Son. Rev. 22:16 indicates that Christ as God was David's root and as man was David's offspring.

36For David himself said by the Holy Ghost, The LORD said to my Lord,
Sit thou on my right hand, till I make thine enemies thy footstool.
37David therefore himself calleth him Lord; and whence is he *then* his
son? And the common people heard him gladly.

☆12:36 2 Sam 23:2 Ps 110:1 1 Cor 15:25 Heb 1:13 2 Pet 1:21
12:37 Rom 1:3; 9:5 Rev 22:16

8. Jesus' Warning about the Teachers of Religion (Cf. Mt 23:1–12; Lk 20:45–47)

38¶And he said unto them in his doctrine, Beware of the scribes, which
love to go in long clothing, and *love* salutations in the marketplaces,
39And the chief seats in the synagogues, and the uppermost rooms at
feasts:
40Which devour widows' houses, and for a pretence make long prayers:
these shall receive greater damnation.

☆12:38 Mt 23:1–10, 14 Lk 20:45–47
12:39 Lk 11:43

9. The Poor Widow's Gift

41¶And Jesus sat over against the treasury, and beheld how the people
cast money into the treasury: and many that were rich cast in much.
42And there came a certain poor widow, and she threw in two mites,
which make a farthing.
43And he called *unto him* his disciples, and saith unto them, Verily I say
unto you, That this poor widow hath cast more in, than all they which have
cast into the treasury:
44For all *they* did cast in of their abundance; but she of her want did cast
in all that she had, *even* all her living.

12:41 2 Kgs 12:9 Lk 21:1–4 Jn 8:20
12:43 Lk 8:43, 44 2 Cor 8:12

E. THE MOUNT OF OLIVES DISCOURSE

1. The Course of History: The Signs of the End Times (Cf. Mt 24:1–14; Lk 21:5–19)

13 AND as he went out of the temple, one of his disciples saith unto
him, Master, see what manner of stones and what buildings *are*
here!
2And Jesus answering said unto him, Seest thou these great buildings?
there shall not be left one stone upon another, that shall not be thrown
down.
3And as he sat upon the mount of Olives over against the temple, Peter
and James and John and Andrew asked him privately,
4Tell us, when shall these things be? and what *shall be* the sign when all
these things shall be fulfilled?
5And Jesus answering them began to say, Take heed lest any *man* deceive
you:
6For many shall come in my name, saying, I am *Christ;* and shall deceive
many.
7And when ye shall hear of wars and rumours of wars, be ye not
troubled: for *such things* must needs be; but the end *shall* not *be* yet.
8For nation shall rise against nation, and kingdom against kingdom: and
there shall be earthquakes in divers places, and there shall be famines and
troubles: these *are* the beginnings of sorrows.

☆13:1 Mt 24:1–51 Lk 21:5–36
13:2 Lk 19:43, 44
☆13:7

12:36 *The LORD said to my Lord.* The first use of LORD means "God"; the second *Lord means "Messiah."*
12:38 *in his doctrine,* i.e., in his teaching, which, of course, was doctrinal. He accused the scribes of hypocrisy.
13:1ff See note on Matt. 24:2 regarding the Olivet Discourse.

13:7 *the end shall not be yet.* Jesus nowhere taught that he would return the second time shortly after his ascension. The time lag is indeterminate. So believers should live as though he were coming today; and yet at the same time, they should make proper preparations for their earthly life as though he were not coming for a long time.

13:9 Mt 10:17–22

9 ¶But take heed to yourselves: for they shall deliver you up to councils; and in the synagogues ye shall be beaten: and ye shall be brought before rulers and kings for my sake, for a testimony against them.

13:10 Rom 10:18

10 And the gospel must first be published among all nations.

13:11☆ Lk 12:11, 12; 21:14, 15; Acts 2:4; 4:8, 31

11 But when they shall lead *you,* and deliver you up, take no thought beforehand what ye shall speak, neither do ye premeditate: but whatsoever shall be given you in that hour, that speak ye: for it is not ye that speak, but the Holy Ghost.

13:12 Mic 7:6

12 Now the brother shall betray the brother to death, and the father the son; and children shall rise up against *their* parents, and shall cause them to be put to death.

13:13 Jn 15:18–21; 2 Tim 4:7, 8; Heb 3:6, 14; Rev 2:10

13 And ye shall be hated of all *men* for my name's sake: but he that shall endure unto the end, the same shall be saved.

2. The Great Tribulation (Cf. Mt 24:15–28; Lk 21:20–24)

13:14☆ Dan 9:27; 11:31; 12:11; Mt 24:15

14 ¶But when ye shall see the abomination of desolation, spoken of by Daniel the prophet, standing where it ought not, (let him that readeth understand,) then let them that be in Judæa flee to the mountains:

15 And let him that is on the housetop not go down into the house, neither enter *therein,* to take any thing out of his house:

16 And let him that is in the field not turn back again for to take up his garment.

13:17 Lk 23:29

17 But woe to them that are with child, and to them that give suck in those days!

18 And pray ye that your flight be not in the winter.

13:19 Jer 30:7; Dan 12:1; Joel 2:2; Rev 3:10

19 For *in* those days shall be affliction, such as was not from the beginning of the creation which God created unto this time, neither shall be.

13:20☆

20 And except that the Lord had shortened those days, no flesh should be saved: but for the elect's sake, whom he hath chosen, he hath shortened the days.

13:21 Lk 17:23

21 And then if any man shall say to you, Lo, here *is* Christ; or, lo, *he is* there; believe *him* not:

13:22 Mt 7:15; 24:24; 2 Thess 2:9

22 For false Christs and false prophets shall rise, and shall shew signs and wonders, to seduce, if *it were* possible, even the elect.

13:23 2 Pet 3:17

23 But take ye heed: behold, I have foretold you all things.

3. The Second Coming of the Son of Man (Cf. Mt 24:29–31; Lk 21:25–28)

13:24☆ Isa 13:10; Ezek 32:7, 8; Joel 2:31; 3:15; Zech 1:15; Acts 2:20; Rev 6:12

24 ¶But in those days, after that tribulation, the sun shall be darkened, and the moon shall not give her light,

13:25☆

25 And the stars of heaven shall fall, and the powers that are in heaven shall be shaken.

13:26 Dan 7:13; Mt 16:27; Acts 1:11; 1 Thess 4:16; 2 Thess 1:7; Rev 1:7

26 And then shall they see the Son of man coming in the clouds with great power and glory.

13:11 Christ's followers will suffer persecution and be called upon to speak to their own defense. The Holy Spirit will supply them with words in the hour of their need. Their own wisdom and resolution will be helped by the Spirit. None of us is capable in himself of doing and saying the right things under such circumstances.
13:14 *standing where it ought not,* i.e., "standing in the temple."† (See note on Dan. 9:27 about the defiling of the sanctuary.)
13:20 God has his elect, for he knows who are his own. They will be preserved despite the seductive approaches of the enemy of souls. Yet Jesus warns even the elect to take heed and be careful; he has warned them ahead of time what dangers lie ahead and how they will be exposed to the wiles of the devil.
13:24, 25 The disruption of sun, moon, and stars will take place before the second coming of Jesus. This should assure all believers who remain alive until Christ's coming that Christ has not come and will not come until these disturbances of nature occur first.

27And then shall he send his angels, and shall gather together his elect
from the four winds, from the uttermost part of the earth to the uttermost
part of heaven.

13:27 Deut 30:3, 4

4. The Lesson of the Fig Tree (Cf. Mt 24:32–35; Lk 21:29–33)

28Now learn a parable of the fig tree; When her branch is yet tender, and
putteth forth leaves, ye know that summer is near:
29So ye in like manner, when ye shall see these things come to pass, know
that it is nigh, *even* at the doors.
30Verily I say unto you, that this generation shall not pass, till all these
things be done.
31Heaven and earth shall pass away: but my words shall not pass away.

13:31 Isa 40:8; 51:6 Ps 102:25–27

5. The Command to Watch for the Coming of the Lord
(Cf. Mt 24:32–35; Lk 21:29–33)

32¶But of that day and *that* hour knoweth no man, no, not the angels
which are in heaven, neither the Son, but the Father.
33Take ye heed, watch and pray: for ye know not when the time is.
34*For the Son of man is* as a man taking a far journey, who left his house,
and gave authority to his servants, and to every man his work, and
commanded the porter to watch.
35Watch ye therefore: for ye know not when the master of the house
cometh, at even, or at midnight, or at the cockcrowing, or in the morning:
36Lest coming suddenly he find you sleeping.
37And what I say unto you I say unto all, Watch.

13:32 Acts 1:7
13:33 Rom 13:11 Eph 6:17, 18 Col 4:2 1 Thess 5:6
13:34 Mt 25:14 Lk 19:9
☆**13:35–37** Lk 12:39, 40 2 Pet 3:1–18 Rev 3:3

F. JESUS' LAST DAYS (14:1—15:47)
1. The Plot to Put Jesus to Death (Cf 26:1–5; Lk 22:1–6)

14 AFTER two days was *the feast of* the passover, and of unleavened
bread: and the chief priests and the scribes sought how they might
take him by craft, and put *him* to death.
2But they said, Not on the feast *day,* lest there be an uproar of the people.

☆**14:1** Mt 26:1–5 Lk 22:1, 2 Jn 11:55–57

2. The Anointing of Jesus in Bethany (Cf. Mt 26:6–13; Jn 12:1–8)

3¶And being in Bethany in the house of Simon the leper, as he sat at
meat, there came a woman having an alabaster box of ointment of
spikenard very precious; and she brake the box, and poured *it* on his head.
4And there were some that had indignation within themselves, and said,
Why was this waste of the ointment made?

☆**14:3** Mt 26:6–13 Lk 7:37–39 Jn 12:1–8

13:35–37 *God's people are enjoined to be watchful.* The Greek word *grēgoreō* means to "be awake," "keep awake," "be alert and on guard," or "watch out." We are to be courageous (1 Cor. 16:13), prayerful (Luke 21:36; Eph. 6:18), and thankful (Col. 4:2). Blessings await those who watch (Rev. 16:15). Above all we are to look for the coming of the Lord, since we know not the day nor the hour (Mt. 24:42; 25:13).

14:1 *the passover* was celebrated on the fourteenth day of Nisan (March-April). All males over age twelve were to go to Jerusalem for this observance. The Passover commemorated Israel's deliverance from Egypt the night the angel of death passed through the land and slew the firstborn of every household except those whose doors had been sprinkled with blood. It looked forward to Calvary and the shed blood of Christ. The Passover was followed by the seven-day festival of unleavened bread, when no yeast was used. The festival commemorated Israel's flight from Egypt. Passover and the festival of unleavened bread were generally celebrated as one festival. (See also note on Exod. 12:11.)

14:3 See note on Luke 7:36ff for information about the various Marys.

14:5☆ 5 For it might have been sold for more than three hundred pence, and
have been given to the poor. And they murmured against her.
6 And Jesus said, Let her alone; why trouble ye her? she hath wrought a
good work on me.
14:7 Deut 15:11 7 For ye have the poor with you always, and whensoever ye will ye may
do them good: but me ye have not always.
14:8 Mk 16:1 8 She hath done what she could: she is come aforehand to anoint my body
Lk 24:1 to the burying.
Jn 19:40 9 Verily I say unto you, Wheresoever this gospel shall be preached
throughout the whole world, *this* also that she hath done shall be spoken of
for a memorial of her.

3. Judas' Arrangement to Betray Jesus

14:10☆ Mt 26:14–16 10 ¶And Judas Iscariot, one of the twelve, went unto the chief priests, to
Lk 22:3–6 betray him unto them.
Jn 6:71 **14:11** 11 And when they heard *it,* they were glad, and promised to give him
Zech 11:12 1 Tim 6:10 money. And he sought how he might conveniently betray him.
Jude 11

4. The Last Supper

a. The Preparations (Cf. Mt 26:17–19; Lk 22:7–13)

14:12 Deut 16:5 12 ¶And the first day of unleavened bread, when they killed the passover,
Mt 26:17–19 his disciples said unto him, Where wilt thou that we go and prepare that
Lk 22:7–13 1 Cor 5:7, 8 thou mayest eat the passover?
14:13☆ 13 And he sendeth forth two of his disciples, and saith unto them, Go ye
into the city, and there shall meet you a man bearing a pitcher of water:
follow him.
14:14 Ex 12:8 14 And wheresoever he shall go in, say ye to the goodman of the house,
Lev 23:5 The Master saith, Where is the guestchamber, where I shall eat the passover
with my disciples?
15 And he will shew you a large upper room furnished *and* prepared: there
make ready for us.
16 And his disciples went forth, and came into the city, and found as he
had said unto them: and they made ready the passover.

b. The Celebration (Cf. Mt 26:20–25; Lk 22:14–18; Jn 13)

14:17 Mt 26:20–30 17 And in the evening he cometh with the twelve.
Lk 22:14–23 18 And as they sat and did eat, Jesus said, Verily I say unto you, One of
Jn 13:21–30 you which eateth with me shall betray me.
19 And they began to be sorrowful, and to say unto him one by one, *Is* it
I? and another *said, Is* it I?
20 And he answered and said unto them, *It is* one of the twelve, that
dippeth with me in the dish.
14:21 Ps 22:1–21 21 The Son of man indeed goeth, as it is written of him: but woe to that
Isa 53:3–8 man by whom the Son of man is betrayed! good were it for that man if he
had never been born.

14:5 The cost of the ointment would have equaled the yearly pay of a lower-class worker. Matthew says that "his disciples . . . had indignation." Judas Iscariot was not alone in his objections to the use of the expensive aromatic ointment. The tension between helping the poor and spending on one's self that which could have been given to the poor remains with us in this and in all ages. Jesus endorsed Mary's act. Each believer, under the Holy Spirit, is responsible for what he or she does with what God has given.

14:10 See note on Matt. 26:14 regarding Judas Iscariot.

14:13 See note to Luke 22:10 on the man carrying the jar of water.

c. The Institution of the Lord's Supper (Cf. Mt 26:26–29; Lk 22:19–24)

22 ¶And as they did eat, Jesus took bread, and blessed, and brake *it*, and
gave to them, and said, Take, eat: this is my body.
23 And he took the cup, and when he had given thanks, he gave *it* to them:
and they all drank of it.
24 And he said unto them, This is my blood of the new testament, which
is shed for many.
25 Verily I say unto you, I will drink no more of the fruit of the vine, until
that day that I drink it new in the kingdom of God.

☆**14:22** 1 Cor 10:16; 11:23–26
14:24 Heb 9:13–15

5. The Prediction of Peter's Denial (Cf. Mt 36:30–35; LK 22:31–34; Jn 13:36–38)

26 ¶And when they had sung an hymn, they went out into the mount of
Olives.
27 And Jesus saith unto them, All ye shall be offended because of me this
night: for it is written, I will smite the shepherd, and the sheep shall be
scattered.
28 But after that I am risen, I will go before you into Galilee.
29 But Peter said unto him, Although all shall be offended, yet *will* not I.
30 And Jesus saith unto him, Verily I say unto thee, That this day, *even* in
this night, before the cock crow twice, thou shalt deny me thrice.
31 But he spake the more vehemently, If I should die with thee, I will not
deny thee in any wise. Likewise also said they all.

☆**14:26**
14:27 Zech 13:7; Mt 26:31–35; Lk 22:31–34; Jn 13:36–38
14:28 Mk 16:7
☆**14:30**

6. Jesus in Gethsemane's Garden
a. His Deep Distress (Cf. Mt 26:36–46; Lk 22:39–46)

32 And they came to a place which was named Geth-sem'a-ne: and he
saith to his disciples, Sit ye here, while I shall pray.
33 And he taketh with him Peter and James and John, and began to be
sore amazed, and to be very heavy;
34 And saith unto them, My soul is exceeding sorrowful unto death: tarry
ye here, and watch.
35 And he went forward a little, and fell on the ground, and prayed that,
if it were possible, the hour might pass from him.
36 And he said, Abba, Father, all things *are* possible unto thee; take away
this cup from me: nevertheless not what I will, but what thou wilt.

14:32 Mt 26:36–46; Lk 22:39–46; Jn 18:1
14:33 Mt 17:1; Mk 9:2; Lk 9:28
14:35 Jn 12:27; Heb 5:7
☆**14:36** Mt 20:22; Jn 5:30; 6:38; 18:11; Rom 8:15; Gal 4:6

14:22ff The Lord's Supper, or Eucharist, was instituted by Christ and is recorded in the three synoptic Gospels. Paul states specifically that the Supper was instituted by Christ (1 Cor. 11:23ff). It was the fulfillment of the type, the Passover meal celebrated according to Exod. 12:21–28, and referred to by Paul in 1 Cor. 5:7, 8. It is to be celebrated by the church *until the return of the Lord. Paul urges self-examination* on the part of every communicant in the meal. Only professing Christians should sit at the table of the Lord. Those who do not discern the Lord's body bring judgment upon themselves, according to 1 Cor. 11:27–30. Some churches believe in the real presence of Christ in the elements; some believe in his spiritual presence; others hold merely to symbolic presence. Roman Catholics hold to transubstantiation, Lutherans to consubstantiation, Presbyterians to spiritual presence, and Baptists to symbolic presence. One's view is determined by how he interprets the words, "this is my body," and "this is my blood." Some celebrate the Lord's Supper daily, some weekly, some monthly, and some quarterly. People living sinful lives should not be permitted to participate in the Supper.

14:26 Jesus and his disciples sang. Probably they used Psalms of rejoicing and praise. Christ and his disciples surrounded by their enemies were not afraid to fulfill the duty of singing Psalms. Paul and Silas did the same when in prison at Philippi (Acts 16:25).

14:30 *twice*. The various Gospel accounts contain slight differences related to the crowing of the cock, the number of times Peter denied the Lord, and whether he denied Christ again after the first crowing of the cock. The explanation of the seeming discrepancies is rather detailed; the best reconciliation can be found in Gleason L. Archer's *Encyclopedia of Biblical Difficulties* (Zondervan, 1982, pp. 339–341). The NIV notes that the word *twice* does not appear in some early manuscripts.

14:36 *this cup*. See note on Matt. 26:39 for the meaning of the cup.

14:37☆
37 And he cometh, and findeth them sleeping, and saith unto Peter, Simon, sleepest thou? couldest not thou watch one hour?

14:38 Rom 7:23 Gal 5:17
38 Watch ye and pray, lest ye enter into temptation. The spirit truly *is* ready, but the flesh *is* weak.

39 And again he went away, and prayed, and spake the same words.

40 And when he returned, he found them asleep again, (for their eyes were heavy,) neither wist they what to answer him.

41 And he cometh the third time, and saith unto them, Sleep on now, and take *your* rest: it is enough, the hour is come; behold, the Son of man is betrayed into the hands of sinners.

42 Rise up, let us go; lo, he that betrayeth me is at hand.

b. Jesus Betrayed and Arrested (Cf. Mt 26:47–56; Lk 22:47–53; Jn 18:1–11)

14:43 Mt 26:47–56 Lk 22:47–53 Jn 18:2–11
43 ¶And immediately, while he yet spake, cometh Judas, one of the twelve, and with him a great multitude with swords and staves, from the chief priests and the scribes and the elders.

14:44☆
44 And he that betrayed him had given them a token, saying, Whomsoever I shall kiss, that same is he; take him, and lead *him* away safely.

14:45☆ Jn 20:16
45 And as soon as he was come, he goeth straightway to him, and saith, Master, master; and kissed him.

46 ¶And they laid their hands on him, and took him.

14:47☆ Jn 18:10
47 And one of them that stood by drew a sword, and smote a servant of the high priest, and cut off his ear.

48 And Jesus answered and said unto them, Are ye come out, as against a thief, with swords and *with* staves to take me?

14:49☆ Ps 22:6–18 Isa 53:7–9 Dan 9:26 Lk 24:44
49 I was daily with you in the temple teaching, and ye took me not: but the scriptures must be fulfilled.

14:50 Ps 88:8 Jn 16:32
50 And they all forsook him, and fled.

51 And there followed him a certain young man, having a linen cloth cast about *his* naked *body;* and the young men laid hold on him:

52 And he left the linen cloth, and fled from them naked.

7. Jesus before the High Priest and the Court (Cf. Mt 26:57–68; Jn 18:12–14, 19–25)

14:53 Mt 26:57–68 Lk 22:54, 63–71 Jn 18:12–14, 19–24
53 ¶And they led Jesus away to the high priest: and with him were assembled all the chief priests and the elders and the scribes.

14:54 Mt 26:3 Jn 18:18
54 And Peter followed him afar off, even into the palace of the high priest: and he sat with the servants, and warmed himself at the fire.

14:55 Dan 6:4 1 Pet 3:16
55 And the chief priests and all the council sought for witness against Jesus to put him to death; and found none.

14:56 Ps 35:11 Prov 6:16–19 19:5
56 For many bare false witness against him, but their witness agreed not together.

14:37 Jesus did not ask his closest friends to watch with him all night—only for a single hour. And they failed him miserably in this momentous hour.

14:44 *kiss,* the usual oriental greeting even to this day.†

14:45 The betrayal of Jesus by Judas Iscariot defies explanation. He had been with Jesus for two and a half years. He had watched him and was aware of his sinless life. He had heard the Savior's words of grace. He had seen him perform matchless miracles beyond anything ever known to man. He had eaten with him, prayed with him, and heard him tell of his coming death and resurrection. None of this affected him sufficiently to alter his malign intentions or to keep him from selling the Son of God for thirty pieces of silver. He served as the treasurer and was a thief. He knew all about hell, yet never turned from his sins to receive the gift of life.

14:47 *one of them,* i.e., "Peter." (See John 18:10.)†

14:49 *but the scriptures must be fulfilled.* Jesus had a special awareness of the necessity for every prophetic word of the Old Testament to be fulfilled. He left nothing undone in his life to keep any scripture from being fulfilled.

57 And there arose certain, and bare false witness against him, saying,
58 We heard him say, I will destroy this temple that is made with hands,
and within three days I will build another made without hands.
59 But neither so did their witness agree together.
60 And the high priest stood up in the midst, and asked Jesus, saying,
Answerest thou nothing? what *is it which* these witness against thee?
61 But he held his peace, and answered nothing. Again the high priest
asked him, and said unto him, Art thou the Christ, the Son of the Blessed?
62 And Jesus said, I am: and ye shall see the Son of man sitting on the
right hand of power, and coming in the clouds of heaven.
63 Then the high priest rent his clothes, and saith, What need we any
further witnesses?
64 Ye have heard the blasphemy: what think ye? And they all condemned
him to be guilty of death.
65 And some began to spit on him, and to cover his face, and to buffet
him, and to say unto him, Prophesy: and the servants did strike him with
the palms of their hands.

8. Peter's Great Denial (Cf. Mt 26:69–75; Lk 22:55–62; Jn 18:15–18, 25–27)

66 ¶And as Peter was beneath in the palace, there cometh one of the maids
of the high priest:
67 And when she saw Peter warming himself, she looked upon him, and
said, And thou also wast with Jesus of Nazareth.
68 But he denied, saying, I know not, neither understand I what thou
sayest. And he went out into the porch; and the cock crew.
69 And a maid saw him again, and began to say to them that stood by,
This is *one* of them.
70 And he denied it again. And a little after, they that stood by said again
to Peter, Surely thou art *one* of them: for thou art a Galilæan, and thy
speech agreeth *thereto*.
71 But he began to curse and to swear, *saying*, I know not this man of
whom ye speak.
72 And the second time the cock crew. And Peter called to mind the word
that Jesus said unto him, Before the cock crow twice, thou shalt deny me
thrice. And when he thought thereon, he wept.

9. Jesus before Pilate the Roman Governor (Cf. Mt 27:11–26; Lk 23:3–25; Jn 18:29–40)

a. Pilate Interrogates Jesus

15 AND straightway in the morning the chief priests held a consulta-
tion with the elders and scribes and the whole council, and bound
Jesus, and carried *him* away, and delivered *him* to Pilate.

14:58 Mk 15:29, 30; Jn 2:19
☆**14:61** Isa 53:7; 1 Pet 2:23
14:62 Ps 110:1; Dan 7:13; Mt 16:27; 24:30; Mk 8:38; 13:26; Acts 1:11; 1 Thess 4:16; 2 Thess 1:7; Rev 1:7; 22:20
14:63 Lev 24:15, 16; Jn 19:7; Acts 6:11
14:65 Isa 50:6; 53:5
14:66 Mt 26:69–75; Lk 22:55–62; Jn 18:15–18, 25–27
☆**14:68**
14:70 Acts 2:7
☆**14:71** Prov 29:25; 1 Cor 10:12
14:72 2 Cor 7:10
☆**15:1** Ps 2:2; Mt 27:1–26; Lk 22:66–23:3, 15–25; Jn 18:28–40; Acts 4:27

14:61 *answered nothing.* This was a fulfillment of Isa. 53:7: "He openeth not his mouth."

14:68 *the cock crew.* These words are not found in some of the best manuscripts.

14:71 It was bad enough that Peter denied his Lord. It was still worse that he did so by taking an oath in the name of God. He perjured himself when he testified to that which he knew was untrue. It was a sad spectacle, but it had one positive aspect—the glory of God's grace was made greater by the fact that Peter was restored and became an ardent witness after Pentecost. This fact opens the door of hope to all sinners, no matter what they have done or how bad they are.

15:1 *Pilate* was the Roman procurator (governor) over the territory formerly ruled by Herod's son, Archelaus. Judea, Idumea, and Samaria were part of that territory. Nothing is known of Pontius Pilate's origins, although procurators usually came from the Roman equestrian class. Pilate's rule began about the time John the Baptist started preaching. Under Rome the people enjoyed much freedom. Pilate was responsible for the financial administration of the territory and the collection of taxes. The Sanhedrin exercised great power, except that it did not have the right to impose a death sentence without an appeal to the procurator, who also carried out executions. Pilate and the Jews were constantly at odds with each other. Pilate was weak, rude, overbearing, and willful. He intended to release

15:2 1 Tim 6:13
2 And Pilate asked him, Art thou the King of the Jews? And he answering
said unto him, Thou sayest *it.*
3 And the chief priests accused him of many things: but he answered
nothing.
4 And Pilate asked him again, saying, Answerest thou nothing? behold
how many things they witness against thee.
15:5 Isa 53:7 Jn 19:9 1 Pet 2:23
5 But Jesus yet answered nothing; so that Pilate marvelled.

b. Barabbas Released and Jesus to Be Crucified

6 Now at *that* feast he released unto them one prisoner, whomsoever they
desired.
15:7☆
7 And there was *one* named Ba-rab′bas, *which lay* bound with them that
had made insurrection with him, who had committed murder in the
insurrection.
8 And the multitude crying aloud began to desire *him to do* as he had ever
done unto them.
15:9 Ps 2:6 Jer 23:5, 6 Mic 5:2 Lk 1:31–33 Acts 3:13, 14
9 But Pilate answered them, saying, Will ye that I release unto you the
King of the Jews?
10 For he knew that the chief priests had delivered him for envy.
11 But the chief priests moved the people, that he should rather release Ba-
rab′bas unto them.
12 And Pilate answered and said again unto them, What will ye then that
I shall do *unto him* whom ye call the King of the Jews?
13 And they cried out again, Crucify him.
14 Then Pilate said unto them, Why, what evil hath he done? And they
cried out the more exceedingly, Crucify him.
15:15 Prov 29:25
15 ¶And *so* Pilate, willing to content the people, released Ba-rab′bas unto
them, and delivered Jesus, when he had scourged *him,* to be crucified.

10. The Suffering of the Savior
a. Jesus Crowned, Beaten, and Spat On (Cf. Mt 27:27–31)

15:16 Mt 27:27–31 Jn 19:1–3, 16
16 And the soldiers led him away into the hall, called Præ-to′ri-um; and
they call together the whole band.
17 And they clothed him with purple, and platted a crown of thorns, and
put it about his *head,*
18 And began to salute him, Hail, King of the Jews!
19 And they smote him on the head with a reed, and did spit upon him,
and bowing *their* knees worshipped him.
20 And when they had mocked him, they took off the purple from him,
and put his own clothes on him, and led him out to crucify him.

b. Jesus Hanging on the Cross (Cf. Mt 27:32–44; Lk 23:32–43; Jn 19:17–24)

15:21 Mt 27:32–44 Lk 23:26–43 Jn 19:17–24 Rom 16:13
21 And they compel one Simon a Cy-re′ni-an, who passed by, coming out
of the country, the father of Alexander and Rufus, to bear his cross.

Jesus, but was outsmarted by the Jews. He finally capitulated to their demands that Jesus be crucified. *Any sense of justice* and moral rectitude was put aside in favor of personal and political considerations. After ten years' service he was removed from the procuratorship.

15:7 *Barabbas* was a well-known revolutionary who probably led the revolt mentioned in Luke 23:18, 19, 25. In John 18:40 he is called a "robber" (Greek, *lēstēs*), a word used by Josephus the historian to describe rebels against Roman authority. The same word is used to describe the two thieves crucified on either side of Jesus. We know nothing more about Barabbas than is found in Scripture. Some manuscripts call him "Jesus Barabbas." Origen, a church father, said this name occurred in some old copies of the Gospel of Matthew.

22 And they bring him unto the place Gol′go-tha, which is, being
interpreted, The place of a skull.
23 And they gave him to drink wine mingled with myrrh: but he received
it not.
24 And when they had crucified him, they parted his garments, casting lots
upon them, what every man should take.
25 And it was the third hour, and they crucified him.
26 And the superscription of his accusation was written over, THE KING
OF THE JEWS.
27 And with him they crucify two thieves; the one on his right hand, and
the other on his left.
28 And the scripture was fulfilled, which saith, And he was numbered with
the transgressors.
29 And they that passed by railed on him, wagging their heads, and saying,
Ah, thou that destroyest the temple, and buildest *it* in three days,
30 Save thyself, and come down from the cross.
31 Likewise also the chief priests mocking said among themselves with the
scribes, He saved others; himself he cannot save.
32 Let Christ the King of Israel descend now from the cross, that we may
see and believe. And they that were crucified with him reviled him.

c. Jesus Giving Himself Over to Death (Cf. Mt 27:45–50; Lk 23:44–49; Jn 19:28–37)

33 And when the sixth hour was come, there was darkness over the whole
land until the ninth hour.
34 And at the ninth hour Jesus cried with a loud voice, saying, E-lo′i,
E-lo′i, la′ma sa-bach′tha-ni? which is, being interpreted, My God, my God,
why hast thou forsaken me?
35 And some of them that stood by, when they heard *it,* said, Behold, he
calleth E-li′as.
36 And one ran and filled a spunge full of vinegar, and put *it* on a reed,
and gave him to drink, saying, Let alone; let us see whether E-li′as will
come to take him down.
37 And Jesus cried with a loud voice, and gave up the ghost.
38 And the veil of the temple was rent in twain from the top to the bottom.
39 ¶And when the centurion, which stood over against him, saw that he so
cried out, and gave up the ghost, he said, Truly this man was the Son of
God.
40 There were also women looking on afar off: among whom was Mary
Magdalene, and Mary the mother of James the less and of Joses, and Sa-
lo′me;
41 (Who also, when he was in Galilee, followed him, and ministered unto
him;) and many other women which came up with him unto Jerusalem.

☆15:22
☆15:23 Ps 69:21
15:24 Ps 22:18
15:25 Jn 19:14
☆15:26 Ps 2:6 Jer 23:5 Lk 1:31–33
☆15:27
☆15:28 Lk 22:37
15:29, 30 Ps 22:7 Mk 14:58 Jn 2:19 Acts 6:14
15:32 Heb 12:2, 3
15:33 Mt 27:45–56 Lk 23:44–49 Jn 19:28–30
☆15:34 Ps 22:1
15:36 Ps 69:21
☆15:38 Ex 26:31–33 Eph 2:14 Heb 6:19 10:19, 20
15:40 Ps 38:11 Lk 8:2

15:22 *Golgotha.* See note on John 19:17.
15:23 This concoction may have been offered to dull the pain, but Jesus refused this escape from his sufferings.
15:26 See note on Matt. 27:37 for information on the superscriptions on Jesus' cross.
15:27 See note on Luke 23:33 about the deaths of Jesus and the two thieves.
15:28 This verse does not appear in most of the best ancient manuscripts. The quotation is from Isa. 53:12.
15:34 *Eloi, Eloi, lama sabachthani.* Jesus spoke in Aramaic. The onlookers, who spoke Greek and Latin, misunderstood his first two words (*Eloi, Eloi*) and thought he was calling for the prophet Elijah.† Jesus died in the darkness, for the light of God's countenance was withdrawn from his Son and from the earth. Jesus was made sin for us (2 Cor. 5:21); he endured the wrath of God and the absence of the Father for the first and last time. Thus he cried out in his suffering and distress, *My God, my God, why hast thou forsaken me?*
15:38 *vail,* i.e., "curtain." A heavy curtain hung in front of the Holy of Holies, a place in the temple reserved by God for himself; the curtain separated him from sinful mankind. Now it was split from above, showing that Christ's death for man's sin had opened up access to the holy God.†

d. Jesus Laid in the Rock-Hewn Tomb (Cf. Mt 27:57–61; Lk 23:50–56; Jn 19:38–42)

15:42, 43☆ Deut 21:22, 23 Mt 27:57–61 Lk 2:25 23:50–56 Jn 19:38–42

42¶And now when the even was come, because it was the preparation,
that is, the day before the sabbath,
43Joseph of Ar-i-ma-thæ'a, an honourable counsellor, which also waited
for the kingdom of God, came, and went in boldly unto Pilate, and craved
the body of Jesus.
44And Pilate marvelled if he were already dead: and calling *unto him* the
centurion, he asked him whether he had been any while dead.
45And when he knew *it* of the centurion, he gave the body to Joseph.

15:46 Isa 53:9 Acts 13:29

46And he bought fine linen, and took him down, and wrapped him in the
linen, and laid him in a sepulchre which was hewn out of a rock, and rolled
a stone unto the door of the sepulchre.
47And Mary Magdalene and Mary *the mother* of Joses beheld where he
was laid.

G. THE GLORIOUS RESURRECTION (CF. MT 28:1–10; LK 24:1–11; JN 20:1–18)

16:1 Mt 28:1–8 Lk 24:1–10 Jn 20:1, 11–13

16 AND when the sabbath was past, Mary Magdalene, and Mary the
mother of James, and Sa-lo'me, had bought sweet spices, that they
might come and anoint him.
2And very early in the morning the first *day* of the week, they came unto
the sepulchre at the rising of the sun.

16:3☆ Mt 27:60 Mk 15:46

3And they said among themselves, Who shall roll us away the stone from
the door of the sepulchre?
4And when they looked, they saw that the stone was rolled away: for it
was very great.

16:5 John 20:11, 12 Acts 1:10; 10:30

5And entering into the sepulchre, they saw a young man sitting on the
right side, clothed in a long white garment; and they were affrighted.

16:6☆ Acts 2:23–32 Rom 1:3, 4 1 Cor 15:4, 12–20 2 Cor 5:15 1 Pet 1:3 Rev 1:18

6And he saith unto them, Be not affrighted: Ye seek Jesus of Nazareth,
which was crucified: he is risen; he is not here: behold the place where they
laid him.

16:7 Mt 26:32 Mk 14:28 Jn 21:1

7But go your way, tell his disciples and Peter that he goeth before you
into Galilee: there shall ye see him, as he said unto you.
8And they went out quickly, and fled from the sepulchre; for they
trembled and were amazed: neither said they any thing to any *man;* for
they were afraid.

VII. THE POST-RESURRECTION APPEARANCES OF JESUS (16:9–20)

16:9☆ Mt 28:9, 10 Lk 24:11 Jn 20:11–18

9¶Now when *Jesus* was risen early the first *day* of the week, he appeared
first to Mary Magdalene, out of whom he had cast seven devils.

15:43 *Joseph of Arimathaea* was a member of the Sanhedrin. He placed the body of Jesus in his own unused tomb. He was one of the few who was looking for the kingdom of God, and indeed may have been a believer in Jesus Christ. His conduct set him apart from the scribes, Pharisees, Sadducees, and hypocrites.

16:3 *The three women who came to anoint the body of* Jesus with spices speak here about the problem of moving the stone that closed over Jesus' tomb. It was a large stone and they did not have the power to move it. How they expected to solve the problem is not stated. Moreover, they must have had a defective understanding of Jesus' message. He had told his followers that he would rise from the dead on the third day. In that event, there would be no need for more unguents to anoint his body. The empty tomb was indeed a surprise to them.

16:6 See note on Matt. 28:6 regarding the resurrection of Jesus.

16:9ff *Some scholars think* 16:9–20 does not belong to the original Markan text because it is absent in the two oldest manuscripts (Codex Sinaiticus and Codex Vaticanus); however, evangelicals generally accept this passage as authentic.

10*And* she went and told them that had been with him, as they mourned
and wept.
11And they, when they had heard that he was alive, and had been seen of
her, believed not.
12¶After that he appeared in another form unto two of them, as they
walked, and went into the country.
13And they went and told *it* unto the residue: neither believed they them.
14¶Afterward he appeared unto the eleven as they sat at meat, and
upbraided them with their unbelief and hardness of heart, because they
believed not them which had seen him after he was risen.
15And he said unto them, Go ye into all the world, and preach the gospel
to every creature.
16He that believeth and is baptized shall be saved; but he that believeth
not shall be damned.
17And these signs shall follow them that believe; In my name shall they
cast out devils; they shall speak with new tongues;
18They shall take up serpents; and if they drink any deadly thing, it shall
not hurt them; they shall lay hands on the sick, and they shall recover.
19¶So then after the Lord had spoken unto them, he was received up into
heaven, and sat on the right hand of God.
20And they went forth, and preached every where, the Lord working with
them, and confirming the word with signs following. Amen.

16:12 Lk 24:13–33; 1 Cor 15:35–45
16:13 Lk 24:33–35
16:14 Lk 24:36; Jn 20:19–23; 1 Cor 15:5
☆**16:15** Mt 28:16–20; Col 1:23
16:16 Jn 3:18, 36; 12:48; Acts 2:38; 16:31; Rom 10:9; 1 Pet 3:21
☆**16:17** Lk 10:17; Acts 2:4; 19:6; 1 Cor 12:10
16:18 Acts 5:16; 9:17; 28:5
16:19 Lk 24:50, 51; Rom 8:34; Heb 1:3; Rev 3:21

16:15 Christ delivers the Great Commission four other times in the New Testament (Matt. 28:18–20; Luke 24:44–49; John 20:21; and Acts 1:8). The evangelization of the entire world is the church's primary mission. Before Christ returns to earth the gospel must have been preached to all the world. The world will never be totally Christianized, however, since not all people will believe. But it must be *evangelized*—all must hear the good news.

16:17 *new tongues.* Some ancient manuscripts omit "new." This text specifically enjoins the followers of Jesus to cast out demons in his name. This would be impossible if there were no such thing as demon possession. The Bible would then be inaccurate. Some scholars do not think the latter part of chapter 16 is in the autograph. Nevertheless, in Acts 16:18 we read that Paul cast out a demon in the name of Jesus Christ. That act by Paul serves to enforce what is said here; even if this verse was not in the original text, the principle enunciated in it is consistent with the Pauline practice.

THE GOSPEL ACCORDING TO

SAINT LUKE

Authorship, date, and background The Gospel according to Luke and The Acts of the Apostles were obviously written by the same person. The unvarying tradition of the early church assigned the authorship to Luke, called the beloved physician (Col 4:14) by the apostle Paul. Luke was not an apostle nor did he personally witness most of the events he wrote about. At the time of the writing there were already in existence many garbled accounts of the life of Jesus, both oral and perhaps written. Luke intended to write about Jesus only after having carefully checked the sources to make sure of their accuracy. He was a companion of Paul and had the benefit not only of the witness of other apostles who were with Jesus from the beginning, but from Paul, who had received his knowledge of the gospel by special revelation directly from God.

Luke was a Gentile Christian converted in Antioch less than fifteen years after Pentecost. The "we" of Acts 16:10 indicates that Luke joined Paul at Troas. He may have been a leader of the church at Philippi, rejoining Paul when he returned to that city on his third missionary journey (Acts 20:6). Luke was well-educated, wrote flawless Greek, was a physician, and was well versed in the culture of the Roman world. He was with Paul when the latter wrote 2 Timothy, for he wrote, "Only Luke is with me" (2 Tim 4:11). Luke was no armchair historian. He was a missionary as well as the church's first historian, for Luke's Gospel and The Acts of the Apostles are peerless historical works.

The place where this Gospel was composed is unknown, although it was somewhere in the Hellenic world outside Palestine. The date is also uncertain. Some scholars think it was written before the fall of Jerusalem in A.D. 70, and others during the period from A.D. 80 to 90. Probably A.D. 60 is the best approximate date for the writing of the book. It was addressed to Theophilus, a wealthy citizen of Antioch who also held a government position. He may or may not have been a Christian at this point, for the Gospel seems directed to convince him of the truth of Jesus' messiahship and his divinity. Apparently Luke expected Theophilus to distribute this writing widely. In any event, it was intended for all people everywhere, even though specifically directed to Theophilus.

Characteristics and content Luke's Gospel has been called "the most beautiful book ever written." In its pages Luke traces the ancestry of Jesus back to Adam, who is a son of God. He has all humanity in view and makes clear God's interest in all men everywhere. He writes in an orderly and precise fashion, but behind the human author lies the Holy Spirit who inspired Luke to put on paper what God wanted written. Thus, while Luke uses some material similar to that found in Mark and Matthew, his purpose is different; each Gospel fills a need not met by the others. Non-Jews in particular would find Luke's Gospel best suited to their needs.

Luke contains material not found in any other Gospel. The stories of the rich man and Lazarus and of the lost son are told with great skill. The account of Jesus' post-resurrection appearance at Emmaus is one of the enthralling stories. The birth of Christ is beatified by hymns which are well known in the Church: the *Magnificat* of Mary (1:46–55), the *Benedictus* of John's father Zacharias (1:67–79), the *Gloria in Excelsis* chanted by the angels (2:14), and the *Nunc Dimittis* spoken by Simeon when he cradled Jesus in his arms (2:25–32).

Luke writes doctrinally to show that Jesus is God incarnate, that he came to seek and to save the lost. More references to the person and work of the Holy Spirit appear in Luke's book than there are in the first two Gospels together. He supplies more information about faithful women believers than any other Gospel writer and praises them without demeaning them in any sense. Luke identifies himself with the lower classes, even though he himself was of upper class origin. He says a great deal about poverty and wealth and pictures Jesus as a champion of the poor and distressed. Luke also writes about a number of persons whose names do not appear elsewhere in the Gospels: Zacharias, Elizabeth, Simeon, Anna, Zacchaeus, and Cleopas. The good Samaritan, the rich man who gloated over his wealth, and the sharp accountant who looked after himself, as well as the self-righteous Pharisee who pointed to the tax collector and thanked God he was not like him, are part of the larger canvas, in the middle of which stands the God-man Jesus, who is the Savior of the world.

Outline

I. Jesus' background and early life (1:1—2:52)
II. The ministry of John the Baptist (3:1–20)
III. The opening events of Jesus' ministry (3:21—4:13)
IV. Jesus in Galilee (4:14—9:50)
V. The journey from Galilee to Jerusalem (9:51—19:44)
VI. Jesus' last week in Jerusalem (19:45—23:56)
VII. The resurrection and later appearances of Jesus (24:1–53)

I. JESUS' BACKGROUND AND EARLY LIFE (1:1—2:52)

A. PREFACE

1 FORASMUCH as many have taken in hand to set forth in order a
declaration of those things which are most surely believed among us,
2 Even as they delivered them unto us, which from the beginning were
eyewitnesses, and ministers of the word;
3 It seemed good to me also, having had perfect understanding of all
things from the very first, to write unto thee in order, most excellent The-
oph'i-lus,
4 That thou mightest know the certainty of those things, wherein thou
hast been instructed.

1:1, 2 Jn 15:27; Acts 1:21, 22; 1 Tim 3:16; Heb 2:3; 1 Pet 5:1; 2 Pet 1:16; 1 Jn 1:1–4
☆**1:3** Acts 1:1; 11:4
1:4 Jn 20:31; Acts 18:25; Rom 15:4; 2 Pet 1:12

B. THE PROMISE OF JOHN THE BAPTIST'S BIRTH

5 ¶THERE was in the days of Herod, the king of Judæa, a certain priest
named Zach-a-ri'as, of the course of A-bi'a: and his wife *was* of the
daughters of Aaron, and her name *was* Elisabeth.
6 And they were both righteous before God, walking in all the command-
ments and ordinances of the Lord blameless.
7 And they had no child, because that Elisabeth was barren, and they
both were *now* well stricken in years.
8 And it came to pass, that while he executed the priest's office before
God in the order of his course,
9 According to the custom of the priest's office, his lot was to burn incense
when he went into the temple of the Lord.
10 And the whole multitude of the people were praying without at the time
of incense.
11 And there appeared unto him an angel of the Lord standing on the
right side of the altar of incense.
12 And when Zach-a-ri'as saw *him,* he was troubled, and fear fell upon
him.
13 But the angel said unto him, Fear not, Zach-a-ri'as: for thy prayer is

☆**1:5** 1 Chron 24:10, 19; Neh 12:4; Mt 2:1
☆**1:6** 2 Kgs 20:3; Phil 3:6
1:7 1 Sam 1:5
1:8 2 Chron 8:14; 31:2
☆**1:9** Ex 30:7, 8
☆**1:10** Lev 16:17
☆**1:11, 12** Dan 10:8; Lk 2:19; Acts 10:4; Rev 1:17
☆**1:13** Gen 25:21; 1 Sam 1:19; Lk 1:60–63

1:3 *to write unto thee in order,* i.e., "to pass the summary on to you." *most excellent Theophilus.* The name means "one who loves God."†
1:5 Elisabeth came from a priestly family in the line of Aaron. The Levitical priesthood had its beginnings with Aaron and included his descendants. Many descendants of Levi were not eligible for the priesthood. According to Mosaic law only the "sons of Aaron" could be priests (Exod. 28:1; Lev. 1:3; Num. 3:10). Thus both Elisabeth and Zacharias were from the line of Aaron. *Herod.* See note to Matt. 2:1 on Herod the Great.
1:6 *they were both righteous before God.* Like Abraham their father, they had been justified by their faith, and they were regenerated. They also walked in accordance with the law of God and were well pleasing to him. Like Abraham and Sarah, they had no children. This was in the will of God, who later gave them John, the forerunner of Jesus.
1:9 *his lot.* This was probably decided by throwing dice or something similar.†
1:10 See note on Exod. 30:1 for information concerning the incense offering.
1:11 *an angel.* This was Gabriel (1:19).
1:13 *thy prayer is heard.* No doubt he and Elisabeth had prayed for children for a long time. Their prayers

heard; and thy wife Elisabeth shall bear thee a son, and thou shalt call his
name John.
14 And thou shalt have joy and gladness; and many shall rejoice at his
birth.

1:15 Num 6:3 Judg 13:4 Jer 1:5 Mt 11:11 Gal 1:15
1:16 Mal 4:5, 6
1:17☆ Isa 40:3 Mal 4:5 Mt 11:14 Mk 9:12 Rom 9:5
1:18 Gen 17:17
1:19☆ Dan 8:16 9:21–23 Heb 1:14
1:20 Ezek 3:26; 24:27

15 For he shall be great in the sight of the Lord, and shall drink neither
wine nor strong drink; and he shall be filled with the Holy Ghost, even
from his mother's womb.
16 And many of the children of Israel shall he turn to the Lord their God.
17 And he shall go before him in the spirit and power of E-li'as, to turn the
hearts of the fathers to the children, and the disobedient to the wisdom of
the just; to make ready a people prepared for the Lord.
18 And Zach-a-ri'as said unto the angel, Whereby shall I know this? for I
am an old man, and my wife well stricken in years.
19 And the angel answering said unto him, I am Gabriel, that stand in the
presence of God; and am sent to speak unto thee, and to shew thee these
glad tidings.
20 And, behold, thou shalt be dumb, and not able to speak, until the day
that these things shall be performed, because thou believest not my words,
which shall be fulfilled in their season.
21 And the people waited for Zach-a-ri'as, and marvelled that he tarried so
long in the temple.
22 And when he came out, he could not speak unto them: and they
perceived that he had seen a vision in the temple: for he beckoned unto
them, and remained speechless.
23 And it came to pass, that, as soon as the days of his ministration were
accomplished, he departed to his own house.
24 And after those days his wife Elisabeth conceived, and hid herself five
months, saying,

1:25 Gen 30:23

25 Thus hath the Lord dealt with me in the days wherein he looked on *me*,
to take away my reproach among men.

C. THE ANNOUNCEMENT OF JESUS' BIRTH TO MARY (CF. MT 1:18–25)

1:26 Mt 2:23
1:27☆ Isa 7:14 Mt 1:18 Lk 2:4
1:28☆
1:31 Mt 1:21, 25 Lk 2:21 Gal 4:4
1:32 2 Sam 7:11 Ps 132:11 Isa 9:6, 7; 16:5 Jer 23:5 Lk 1:35, 36 Phil 2:10 1 Tim 6:15

26 And in the sixth month the angel Gabriel was sent from God unto a
city of Galilee, named Nazareth,
27 To a virgin espoused to a man whose name was Joseph, of the house of
David; and the virgin's name *was* Mary.
28 And the angel came in unto her, and said, Hail, *thou that art* highly
favoured, the Lord *is* with thee: blessed *art* thou among women.
29 And when she saw *him*, she was troubled at his saying, and cast in her
mind what manner of salutation this should be.
30 And the angel said unto her, Fear not, Mary: for thou hast found
favour with God.
31 And, behold, thou shalt conceive in thy womb, and bring forth a son,
and shalt call his name JESUS.
32 He shall be great, and shall be called the Son of the Highest: and the
Lord God shall give unto him the throne of his father David:

---

were heard, even though the answer was delayed in accordance with the plan of God. Delay is not denial.

***1:17** See note on Mal. 4:5 for information about Elias (Elijah). to turn the hearts of the fathers to the children, and the disobedient to the wisdom of the just,* i.e., "He will soften adult hearts to become like little children's, and will change disobedient minds to the wisdom of faith" (TLB).

1:19 Gabriel, Michael, and Satan are the only angels named in the Bible. Satan, of course, was a fallen angel; the other two, archangels of God.

1:27 *a virgin espoused.* This arrangement was so binding that it could be broken only by divorce.

1:28 *blessed art thou among women* is not in some of the best ancient manuscripts.

33 And he shall reign over the house of Jacob for ever; and of his kingdom
there shall be no end.
34 Then said Mary unto the angel, How shall this be, seeing I know not a
man?
35 And the angel answered and said unto her, The Holy Ghost shall come
upon thee, and the power of the Highest shall overshadow thee: therefore
also that holy thing which shall be born of thee shall be called the Son of
God.
36 And, behold, thy cousin Elisabeth, she hath also conceived a son in her
old age: and this is the sixth month with her, who was called barren.
37 For with God nothing shall be impossible.
38 And Mary said, Behold the handmaid of the Lord; be it unto me
according to thy word. And the angel departed from her.

D. MARY'S VISIT TO ELIZABETH

39 And Mary arose in those days, and went into the hill country with
haste, into a city of Juda;
40 And entered into the house of Zach-a-ri'as, and saluted Elisabeth.
41 And it came to pass, that, when Elisabeth heard the salutation of Mary,
the babe leaped in her womb; and Elisabeth was filled with the Holy
Ghost:
42 And she spake out with a loud voice, and said, Blessed *art* thou among
women, and blessed *is* the fruit of thy womb.
43 And whence *is* this to me, that the mother of my Lord should come to
me?
44 For, lo, as soon as the voice of thy salutation sounded in mine ears, the
babe leaped in my womb for joy.
45 And blessed *is* she that believed: for there shall be a performance of
those things which were told her from the Lord.

E. MARY'S SONG OF JOY

46 And Mary said, My soul doth magnify the Lord,
47 And my spirit hath rejoiced in God my Saviour.
48 For he hath regarded the low estate of his handmaiden: for, behold,
from henceforth all generations shall call me blessed.
49 For he that is mighty hath done to me great things; and holy *is* his
name.
50 And his mercy *is* on them that fear him from generation to generation.
51 He hath shewed strength with his arm; he hath scattered the proud in
the imagination of their hearts.
52 He hath put down the mighty from *their* seats, and exalted them of low
degree.

1:33 Dan 2:44; 7:14, 18, 27 Mic 4:7 Mt 28:18 Jn 12:34 Heb 1:8
☆**1:35** Mt 14:33; 26:63 Mk 1:1 Jn 1:34; 20:31 Rom 1:4
☆**1:36**
1:37 Gen 18:14 Jer 32:17 Rom 4:21
☆**1:38**
1:39 Josh 20:7; 21:9, 11
☆**1:41** Lk 1:67 Acts 6:3
1:42 Judg 5:24
1:43 Lk 2:11
1:46 1 Sam 2:1–10 Ps 34:2, 3
☆**1:47** 1 Tim 1:1; 2:3 Tit 1:3; 2:10; 3:4 Jude 25
1:48 1 Sam 1:11 Ps 138:6 Mal 3:12 Lk 11:27
1:50 Gen 17:7 Ex 20:6 Ps 103:17
1:51 Ps 33:10; 98:1 118:15 Isa 40:10 1 Pet 5:5
1:52 1 Sam 2:6 Job 5:11

1:35 The virgin birth of Jesus is important for three reasons: (1) it relates to the authority of the Word of God, which clearly asserts it; (2) it undergirds the supernatural and miraculous—something that is offensive to the natural mind; and (3) any denial of the doctrine is destructive of the whole fabric of the Christian faith, for it weakens or destroys the reality of the Incarnation (God manifest in the flesh), without which the faith cannot possibly survive.

1:36 *cousin*, literally, "relative."

1:38 God does not violate the integrity of the human person. The Holy Spirit would not have come upon Mary without her consent. This verse indicates that Mary had responded positively to the message of the angel Gabriel and was willing to be the *handmaid of the Lord*.

1:41 Elisabeth was filled with the Holy Spirit. So were Mary, Zacharias, and John the Baptist, of whom it had been said the Holy Spirit would fill him while he was still in his mother's womb. All believers should be filled with the Holy Spirit.

1:47 *rejoiced in God my Saviour*. This statement refutes the view of those who hold that Mary was born without original sin. If she had been, she would not have needed a Savior. Here Mary speaks about Jesus Christ as God her Savior. We are left with the question of how a sinful woman could bear a sinless son. It was a miraculous generation by the Holy Spirit.

1:53 Ps 34:10; 107:9

53 He hath filled the hungry with good things; and the rich he hath sent empty away.

1:54 Ps 98:3 Jer 31:3, 20

54 He hath holpen his servant Israel, in remembrance of *his* mercy;

1:55 Gen 17:9 Ps 132:11 Gal 3:16

55 As he spake to our fathers, to Abraham, and to his seed for ever.

56 And Mary abode with her about three months, and returned to her own house.

1:57☆

57 Now Elisabeth's full time came that she should be delivered; and she brought forth a son.

F. THE BIRTH OF JOHN THE BAPTIST

58 And her neighbours and her cousins heard how the Lord had shewed great mercy upon her; and they rejoiced with her.

1:59☆ Gen 17:12 Lev 12:3 Lk 2:21 Phil 13:5

59 And it came to pass, that on the eighth day they came to circumcise the child; and they called him Zach-a-ri′as, after the name of his father.

1:60☆

60 And his mother answered and said, Not *so;* but he shall be called John.

61 And they said unto her, There is none of thy kindred that is called by this name.

1:62☆

62 And they made signs to his father, how he would have him called.

63 And he asked for a writing table, and wrote, saying, His name is John. And they marvelled all.

64 And his mouth was opened immediately, and his tongue *loosed,* and he spake, and praised God.

65 And fear came on all that dwelt round about them: and all these sayings were noised abroad throughout all the hill country of Judæa.

1:66 Lk 2:19 Acts 11:21

66 And all they that heard *them* laid *them* up in their hearts, saying, What manner of child shall this be! And the hand of the Lord was with him.

G. THE SONG OF ZACHARIAS (THE BENEDICTUS)

1:67☆ Joel 2:28

67 And his father Zach-a-ri′as was filled with the Holy Ghost, and prophesied, saying,

1:68☆ Lk 2:38 Acts 1:6 Heb 9:12

68 Blessed *be* the Lord God of Israel; for he hath visited and redeemed his people,

1:69☆ 1 Sam 2:1, 10 Ps 18:2; 132:17 Ezek 29:21

69 And hath raised up an horn of salvation for us in the house of his servant David;

1:70 Jer 23:5; 30:10 Dan 9:24 Acts 3:21 Rom 1:2–4

70 As he spake by the mouth of his holy prophets, which have been since the world began:

1:71 Ps 106:10

71 That we should be saved from our enemies, and from the hand of all that hate us;

1:57 Jesus said, "Of all men ever born, none shines more brightly than John the Baptist" (Matt. 11:11, TLB), yet little is known about his life. Aside from Scripture, only Josephus, the Jewish historian, says anything about him. Scripture tells us he was the son of Elisabeth and Zacharias. He was six months older than Jesus. He was born in an unnamed town in the hill country of Judah (1:39). Little is said of his early life. He was the forerunner who announced the coming of the Messiah, and his ministry was prophetic. He preached about the coming kingdom, stressing repentance and confession of sin. He baptized Jesus. Herod *imprisoned him (ca.* A.D. *28) because* he preached against Herod's marriage to his brother Philip's wife, Herodias. Herodias and her daughter Salome forced Herod to behead John (Mark 6:14ff).

1:59, 60 Circumcision was performed on the eighth day after the birth of the male. At that time the child was named. He was named John, which means "God is gracious." Circumcision was the sign of the old covenant, just as baptism is the sign of the new covenant.

1:62 *made signs to his father.* Zacharias was apparently stone deaf, as well as speechless, and had not heard what his wife had said.†

1:67 Zacharias was filled with the Holy Spirit, as Elisabeth had been earlier. John, his son, was filled with the Holy Spirit from his mother's womb according to the prophetic word spoken by the angel Gabriel (1:15). The whole family was Spirit-filled.

1:68 *he hath visited and redeemed his people.* This was God's self-disclosure, for no one could know God unless he chose to make himself known.

1:69 *horn of salvation* is "a mighty work" (Goodspeed), "a deliverer of victorious power" (New English Bible).

72 To perform the mercy *promised* to our fathers, and to remember his
holy covenant;
73 The oath which he sware to our father Abraham,
74 That he would grant unto us, that we being delivered out of the hand of
our enemies might serve him without fear,
75 In holiness and righteousness before him, all the days of our life.
76 And thou, child, shalt be called the prophet of the Highest: for thou
shalt go before the face of the Lord to prepare his ways;
77 To give knowledge of salvation unto his people by the remission of
their sins,
78 Through the tender mercy of our God; whereby the dayspring from on
high hath visited us,
79 To give light to them that sit in darkness and *in* the shadow of death, to
guide our feet into the way of peace.
80 And the child grew, and waxed strong in spirit, and was in the deserts
till the day of his shewing unto Israel.

☆1:72, 73 Lev 26:42; Ps 105:8; 106:45; Mic 7:20; Gen 12:3; Heb 6:13
1:74 Rom 6:18; Heb 9:14
1:75 Jer 32:39; Eph 4:24
1:76 Isa 40:3; Mal 3:1; Mt 11:10
1:77 Jer 31:34; Mk 1:4
1:78 Eph 5:14; 2 Pet 1:19
1:79 Isa 9:2; Mt 4:16
1:80 Lk 2:40

H. THE BIRTH OF JESUS CHRIST (CF. MT 1:18–25)

2 AND it came to pass in those days, that there went out a decree from
Cæsar Augustus, that all the world should be taxed.
2 (*And* this taxing was first made when Cy-re′ni-us was governor of Syria.)
3 And all went to be taxed, every one into his own city.
4 And Joseph also went up from Galilee, out of the city of Nazareth, into
Judæa, unto the city of David, which is called Bethlehem; (because he was
of the house and lineage of David:)
5 To be taxed with Mary his espoused wife, being great with child.
6 And so it was, that, while they were there, the days were accomplished
that she should be delivered.
7 And she brought forth her firstborn son, and wrapped him in swaddling
clothes, and laid him in a manger; because there was no room for them in
the inn.

2:1 Mt 1:18–25
☆2:2
2:4 1 Sam 16:1; Mic 5:2; Mt 1:16; Lk 1:27; Jn 7:42
☆2:5
☆2:6
☆2:7 Mt 1:25; Gal 4:4

I. THE ANGELS AND THE SHEPHERDS

8 And there were in the same country shepherds abiding in the field,
keeping watch over their flock by night.
9 And, lo, the angel of the Lord came upon them, and the glory of the
Lord shone round about them: and they were sore afraid.

2:9 Lk 1:11; 24:4; Acts 5:19; 12:7

1:73 *The oath,* i.e., God swore to Abraham that he would keep the divine convenant; and since there was no one by whom God could swear who was greater than himself, he swore by himself. (See note to Heb. 6:16 on the immutability of God).

2:2 The statement about *Cyrenius* (Quirinius) as *governor of Syria* has been widely questioned by critics of the Bible. In the *Zondervan Pictorial Encyclopedia of the Bible* (Zondervan), E. M. Blaiklock accepts the Lukan account and felicitously explains away the adverse criticism (Vol. 5, pp. 5, 6). Luke was an able historian; even apart from the superintendence of the Holy Spirit he would not have made this sort of error.

2:5 *his espoused wife.* Mary and Joseph were betrothed but not yet married. This was a legal arrangement that could be broken by divorce. Thus, betrothal was not the same as engagement in modern America, where an engagement can be broken without any legal involvement. Mary's pregnancy would have been construed as adultery and she could have been stoned to death. God protected her in her innocence and used Joseph as her shield against any charge of misconduct. (See note on Matt. 1:19.)

2:6 *that she should be delivered.* Jesus was born in the fullness of time. His year of birth was predicted by Daniel (Dan. 2:44). It came at a time when there was universal peace, for the Roman temple of Janus was shut for the first time, as a sign of peace without war. Judah was under Roman control, so that the sceptre had departed from Israel. And Greek was the universal language. At this moment, the Prince of Peace was born.

2:7 *swaddling clothes,* i.e., clean cloths wrapped around the newborn child according to the custom of that day. A *manger* was a feeding trough for animals. If Jesus was born in a cave (as some suppose), it was probably cut out of a rock wall.

2:10☆ Mt 28:19; Acts 13:47; Col 1:23
2:11 Isa 9:6; Mt 1:16, 21; 16:16, 20; Jn 4:42; 11:27; 20:31; Acts 2:36; 10:36; Phil 2:11
2:13 Gen 28:12; Ps 103:20; Rev 5:11
2:14☆ Isa 57:19; Eph 2:14, 18; Col 1:20; 2 Thess 2:16

10 And the angel said unto them, Fear not: for, behold, I bring you good
tidings of great joy, which shall be to all people.
11 For unto you is born this day in the city of David a Saviour, which is
Christ the Lord.
12 And this *shall be* a sign unto you; Ye shall find the babe wrapped in
swaddling clothes, lying in a manger.
13 And suddenly there was with the angel a multitude of the heavenly host
praising God, and saying,
14 Glory to God in the highest, and on earth peace, good will toward men.
15 And it came to pass, as the angels were gone away from them into
heaven, the shepherds said one to another, Let us now go even unto
Bethlehem, and see this thing which is come to pass, which the Lord hath
made known unto us.
16 And they came with haste, and found Mary, and Joseph, and the babe
lying in a manger.
17 And when they had seen *it,* they made known abroad the saying which
was told them concerning this child.
18 And all they that heard *it* wondered at those things which were told
them by the shepherds.
19 But Mary kept all these things, and pondered *them* in her heart.
20 And the shepherds returned, glorifying and praising God for all the
things that they had heard and seen, as it was told unto them.

J. THE INFANT JESUS
1. The Circumcision

2:21☆ Gen 17:12; Lev 12:3; Mt 1:21

21 And when eight days were accomplished for the circumcising of the
child, his name was called JESUS, which was so named of the angel before
he was conceived in the womb.

2. The Presentation in the Temple

2:22 Lev 12:2–6
2:23 Ex 13:2, 12
2:24 Lev 12:8
2:25☆ Isa 40:1; Mk 15:43

22 And when the days of her purification according to the law of Moses
were accomplished, they brought him to Jerusalem, to present *him* to the
Lord;
23 (As it is written in the law of the Lord, Every male that openeth the
womb shall be called holy to the Lord;)
24 And to offer a sacrifice according to that which is said in the law of the
Lord, A pair of turtledoves, or two young pigeons.
25 And, behold, there was a man in Jerusalem, whose name *was* Simeon;

2:10 Scripture clearly teaches that not all men will be saved. But all men are to be reached with the good news. Thus the gospel is universal. The primacy of missionary outreach to all people may be seen from (1) the universal message at the birth of Jesus ("the Savior you have given to the world," 2:30–32, TLB); (2) the missionary thrust of Christ's model prayer ("your will be done here on earth, just as it is in heaven," Matt. 6:10, TLB); (3) Jesus' first convert, who became a missionary immediately ("Andrew . . . brought Peter to meet Jesus," John 1:41, 42, TLB); and (4) the first apostolic sermon—a missionary call ("to each one of *you . . . and to your children and* even to those in distant lands," Acts 2:39, TLB). The Great Commission, given by Jesus five times, expresses the Savior's concern for all men everywhere (Matt. 28:18–20; Mark 16:15; Luke 24:45–49; John 20:21; and Acts 1:8).
2:14 The angels chant their hallelujah song of praise. God gets the honor and men gain the joy of the Savior's birth. The visit of the angel caused them to go posthaste to Bethlehem. They spoke the language of faith (2:15–17)—for they did not say, "Let us go to see *if.*" After they found the Savior's family, they spread the good news abroad for all to hear. If the world did not receive it, it was not for lack of knowledge but of desire.
2:21 It was supposed that the one who came to be circumcised was, by this ceremony, admitted into the covenant of God. But Christ was always God's beloved Son. He did not need circumcision—the cutting away of the flesh—because although he was made after the likeness of sinful flesh, he himself was without sin.
2:25 *Simeon* is nowhere else mentioned in the Bible. He was righteous and devout. He was waiting with expectancy for the coming of the Messiah. And best of all, he was taught, led, and filled by the Holy Spirit. *the consolation of Israel,* i.e., "the Messiah."†

and the same man *was* just and devout, waiting for the consolation of
Israel: and the Holy Ghost was upon him.
26 And it was revealed unto him by the Holy Ghost, that he should not see
death, before he had seen the Lord's Christ.
27 And he came by the Spirit into the temple: and when the parents
brought in the child Jesus, to do for him after the custom of the law,
28 Then took he him up in his arms, and blessed God, and said,

3. The Song of Simeon

29 Lord, now lettest thou thy servant depart in peace, according to thy
word:
30 For mine eyes have seen thy salvation,
31 Which thou hast prepared before the face of all people;
32 A light to lighten the Gentiles, and the glory of thy people Israel.
33 And Joseph and his mother marvelled at those things which were
spoken of him.
34 And Simeon blessed them, and said unto Mary his mother, Behold, this
child is set for the fall and rising again of many in Israel; and for a sign
which shall be spoken against;
35 (Yea, a sword shall pierce through thy own soul also,) that the thoughts
of many hearts may be revealed.

4. The Adoration of Anna

36 And there was one Anna, a prophetess, the daughter of Pha-nu'el, of
the tribe of A'ser: she was of a great age, and had lived with an husband
seven years from her virginity;
37 And she *was* a widow of about fourscore and four years, which
departed not from the temple, but served *God* with fastings and prayers
night and day.
38 And she coming in that instant gave thanks likewise unto the Lord, and
spake of him to all them that looked for redemption in Jerusalem.
39 And when they had performed all things according to the law of the
Lord, they returned into Galilee, to their own city Nazareth.
40 And the child grew, and waxed strong in spirit, filled with wisdom: and
the grace of God was upon him.

K. JESUS AS A BOY IN THE TEMPLE

41 Now his parents went to Jerusalem every year at the feast of the
passover.
42 And when he was twelve years old, they went up to Jerusalem after the
custom of the feast.
43 And when they had fulfilled the days, as they returned, the child Jesus
tarried behind in Jerusalem; and Joseph and his mother knew not *of it*.

2:26 Ps 89:48; Jn 8:51; Heb 11:5
2:27 Rev 1:10
2:29 Gen 46:30; 1 Cor 15:54; Phil 1:23; Rev 14:13
2:30 Isa 52:10; Acts 4:12
2:32 Isa 9:2; 42:6,7; 49:6; Acts 13:47; 26:23
☆**2:34** Isa 8:14; Hos 14:9; Acts 24:5, 14; 28:22; 1 Cor 1:23; 1 Pet 2:7, 8, 12
☆**2:35** Ps 42:10; 1 Cor 11:19
☆**2:36**
2:37 Acts 21:9; 26:7; 1 Tim 5:5, 9
☆**2:38** Lam 3:25, 26; Mk 15:43; Lk 24:21
2:39 Mt 2:23
☆**2:41** Deut 16:1–6

2:34, 35 Simeon speaks a prophetic word to Mary, who rejoiced (yet with trembling) over the birth of her son. He is *for the fall and rising again of many in Israel.* Her son shall be a suffering servant, and a sword shall pass through her own soul too. This prophetic word was fulfilled when she beheld him on the cross.

2:36 *Anna* was a prophetess whose work was comparable to that of the male prophets. She belonged to the tribe of Asher, which had been taken from the land of Palestine in the Assyrian captivity. While the tribe never returned officially to Palestine, her family had come back and had remembered their genealogy. She probably was more than one hundred years old when Jesus was brought to the temple for the presentation. Anna was a devout and saintly woman who joined in praise to God for Jesus, whom she looked upon as the Messiah.

2:38 *looked for redemption in Jerusalem,* i.e., "for the coming of the Savior."†

2:41ff Luke alone records the incident of the boy Jesus in the temple. He sat among the teachers of the law, who were amazed at his understanding and responses. From this point onward the boyhood of Jesus is clothed in silence.

44 But they, supposing him to have been in the company, went a day's journey; and they sought him among *their* kinsfolk and acquaintance.

45 And when they found him not, they turned back again to Jerusalem, seeking him.

2:46 Isa 11:1–4

46 And it came to pass, that after three days they found him in the temple, sitting in the midst of the doctors, both hearing them, and asking them questions.

2:47☆ Mt 7:28; Mk 1:22; Jn 7:15

47 And all that heard him were astonished at his understanding and answers.

2:48 Mt 12:26; Lk 4:22

48 And when they saw him, they were amazed: and his mother said unto him, Son, why hast thou thus dealt with us? behold, thy father and I have sought thee sorrowing.

2:49☆ Jn 2:16; 4:34; 6:38; 8:29

49 And he said unto them, How is it that ye sought me? wist ye not that I must be about my Father's business?

2:50 Lk 9:45; 18:34

50 And they understood not the saying which he spake unto them.

2:51 Dan 7:28

51 And he went down with them, and came to Nazareth, and was subject unto them: but his mother kept all these sayings in her heart.

2:52☆ 1 Sam 2:26

52 And Jesus increased in wisdom and stature, and in favour with God and man.

II. THE MINISTRY OF JOHN THE BAPTIST (3:1–20; CF. MT 3:1–12; MK 1:1–8; JN 1:6–8, 19–28)

3:1☆ Mt 3:1–12; Mk 1:1–8

3 NOW in the fifteenth year of the reign of Ti-be'ri-us Cæsar, Pontius Pilate being governor of Judæa, and Herod being tetrarch of Galilee, and his brother Philip tetrarch of I-tu-ræ'a and of the region of Trach-o-ni'tis, and Ly-sa'ni-as the tetrarch of Ab-i-le'ne,

3:2☆ Jn 11:49; 18:13; Acts 4:6

2 An'nas and Cai'a-phas being the high priests, the word of God came unto John the son of Zach-a-ri'as in the wilderness.

3:3☆ Mal 4:6; Mt 3:1; Mk 1:4; Lk 1:77; Acts 13:24; 19:4

3 And he came into all the country about Jordan, preaching the baptism of repentance for the remission of sins;

3:4☆ Isa 40:3; Mt 3:3; Mk 1:3; Jn 1:23

4 As it is written in the book of the words of E-sai'as the prophet, saying, The voice of one crying in the wilderness, Prepare ye the way of the Lord, make his paths straight.

3:5 Isa 40:4

5 Every valley shall be filled, and every mountain and hill shall be brought low; and the crooked shall be made straight, and the rough ways *shall be* made smooth;

3:6 Ps 98:2; Isa 40:5; 52:10; Jn 1:14

6 And all flesh shall see the salvation of God.

3:7 Mt 3:7; Jn 8:44

7 Then said he to the multitude that came forth to be baptized of him, O generation of vipers, who hath warned you to flee from the wrath to come?

2:47 John Calvin remarked that Jesus gave the doctors of the law a taste of his divine wisdom and knowledge, which was then drawn in again until the beginning of his public ministry at age thirty.

2:49ff *wist ye not* . . . Even at this tender age Jesus had a preternatural knowledge about himself and his role as Savior of the world. What he said made an indelible impression on the mind and heart of Mary, for she "kept all these sayings in her heart."

2:52 In his humanity Jesus, who was true man and *true God, developed by way of human* wisdom, human stature, and human associations.

3:1 Tiberius was the adopted son of Caesar Augustus. He reigned from A.D. 14–37. *Pilate,* see note to Mark 15:1.

3:2 *the word of God came unto John.* The word of God had come to the prophets of old. It now comes to John. But we are not told how the word came to him. Whether he got it through his father, from an angel, in a dream, by a vision, or through a voice from heaven, we do not know. In any event, God made his word known to John, who began to preach that word in the power of the Holy Spirit.

3:3 *preaching the baptism of repentance for remission of sins.* John assured the listeners that their sins would be pardoned and their lives changed if they repented. They were to sin no more. If they refused to repent, they would be ruined.

3:4 *the voice of one crying in the wilderness.* Thus, Isa. 40:3 was fulfilled to the letter. The proud were to be humbled; the humble were to be enriched; sinners were to be converted; difficulties were to be removed; all flesh was to see the salvation of the Lord.

[8]Bring forth therefore fruits worthy of repentance, and begin not to say
within yourselves, We have Abraham to *our* father: for I say unto you, That
God is able of these stones to raise up children unto Abraham.
[9]And now also the axe is laid unto the root of the trees: every tree
therefore which bringeth not forth good fruit is hewn down, and cast into
the fire.
[10]And the people asked him, saying, What shall we do then?
[11]He answereth and saith unto them, He that hath two coats, let him
impart to him that hath none; and he that hath meat, let him do likewise.
[12]Then came also publicans to be baptized, and said unto him, Master,
what shall we do?
[13]And he said unto them, Exact no more than that which is appointed
you.
[14]And the soldiers likewise demanded of him, saying, And what shall we
do? And he said unto them, Do violence to no man, neither accuse *any*
falsely; and be content with your wages.
[15]And as the people were in expectation, and all men mused in their
hearts of John, whether he were the Christ, or not;
[16]John answered, saying unto *them* all, I indeed baptize you with water;
but one mightier than I cometh, the latchet of whose shoes I am not worthy
to unloose: he shall baptize you with the Holy Ghost and with fire:
[17]Whose fan *is* in his hand, and he will throughly purge his floor, and will
gather the wheat into his garner; but the chaff he will burn with fire
unquenchable.
[18]And many other things in his exhortation preached he unto the people.
[19]But Herod the tetrarch, being reproved by him for He-ro'di-as his
brother Philip's wife, and for all the evils which Herod had done,
[20]Added yet this above all, that he shut up John in prison.

3:8 Acts 26:20
3:9 Mt 3:10; 7:19 Jn 15:2, 6
3:10 Acts 2:37
3:11 Jas 2:15 1 Jn 3:17
☆**3:12** Mt 21:32
3:13 Mic 6:8 Lk 19:8
3:14 Ex 23:1 Lev 19:11
3:15 Jn 1:19, 20
☆**3:16** Mt 3:11 Mk 1:7, 8 Jn 1:26, 33 1 Cor 12:13
3:17 Mic 4:12 Mt 13:20
☆**3:19, 20** Mt 14:3 Mk 6:17 Jn 3:24

III. THE OPENING EVENTS OF JESUS' MINISTRY (3:21—4:13)

A. JESUS' BAPTISM (CF. MT 3:13–17; MK 1:9–11)

[21]Now when all the people were baptized, it came to pass, that Jesus also
being baptized, and praying, the heaven was opened,
[22]And the Holy Ghost descended in a bodily shape like a dove upon him,
and a voice came from heaven, which said, Thou art my beloved Son; in
thee I am well pleased.

3:21 Mt 3:13–17 Mk 1:9–11 Jn 1:32
☆**3:22** Mt 3:17

B. JESUS' GENEALOGY

[23]And Jesus himself began to be about thirty years of age, being (as was
supposed) the son of Joseph, which was *the son* of He'li,

☆**3:23** Num 4:3, 35, 39, 47 Mt 1:1–17; 13:55 Jn 6:42

3:12 *publicans* were tax collectors who were hated by their fellow Jews.
3:16 *the latchet of whose shoes I am not worthy to unloose*, i.e., "I am not worthy of being his slave."† *he shall baptize.* John said he baptized with water but Jesus would baptize with the Holy Spirit and with fire. This prophecy was fulfilled at Pentecost when the Holy Spirit descended following the ascension of Jesus into heaven. The firelike cloven tongues were a one-time external act that proved that the Spirit had come. The infilling of the Holy Spirit remains for believers throughout the present age.
3:20 Luke mentions the imprisonment of John before he mentions the baptism of Jesus by John. He does this to finish the story about John, although his imprisonment occurred one year after the baptism of Jesus.
3:22 This incident in the life of Jesus marks the obvious presence of the Trinity. The Father spoke by acknowledging Jesus as his Son. The Holy Spirit alighted on Jesus in the form of a dove. This event marked the beginning of the public ministry of Jesus.
3:23–38 Luke traces Jesus' genealogy through Mary, whereas Matthew traces it through Joseph, his legal father. Joseph is called the son of Heli in Luke, in accordance with Jewish legal custom; this means he was the husband of Heli's daughter. Luke carefully notes that Jesus was not really Joseph's son after the

[24]Which was *the son* of Mat′that, which was *the son* of Levi, which was *the son* of Mel′chi, which was *the son* of Jan′na, which was *the son* of Joseph,
[25]Which was *the son* of Mat-ta-thi′as, which was *the son* of Amos, which was *the son* of Na′um, which was *the son* of Es′li, which was *the son* of Nag′ge,
[26]Which was *the son* of Ma′ath, which was *the son* of Mat-ta-thi′as, which was *the son* of Sem′e-i, which was *the son* of Joseph, which was *the son* of Juda,
[27]Which was *the son* of Jo-an′na, which was *the son* of Rhe′sa, which was *the son* of Zo-rob′a-bel, which was *the son* of Sa-la′thi-el, which was *the son* of Ne′ri,
[28]Which was *the son* of Mel′chi, which was *the son* of Ad′di, which was *the son* of Co′sam, which was *the son* of El-mo′dam, which was *the son* of Er,
[29]Which was *the son* of Jo′se, which was *the son* of E-li-e′zer, which was *the son* of Jo′rim, which was *the son* of Mat′that, which was *the son* of Levi,
[30]Which was *the son* of Simeon, which was *the son* of Juda, which was *the son* of Joseph, which was *the son* of Jo′nan, which was *the son* of E-li′a-kim,
3:31 2 Sam 5:14; 1 Chron 3:5; Zech 12:12
[31]Which was *the son* of Me′le-a, which was *the son* of Me′nan, which was *the son* of Mat′ta-tha, which was *the son* of Nathan, which was *the son* of David,
3:32☆ Ruth 4:18; 1 Chron 2:10
[32]Which was *the son* of Jesse, which was *the son* of O′bed, which was *the son* of Bo′oz, which was *the son* of Sal′mon, which was *the son* of Na-as′son,
[33]Which was *the son* of A-min′a-dab, which was *the son* of A′ram, which was *the son* of Es′rom, which was *the son* of Pha′res, which was *the son* of Juda,
3:34 Gen 11:24, 26
[34]Which was *the son* of Jacob, which was *the son* of Isaac, which was *the son* of Abraham, which was *the son* of Tha′ra, which was *the son* of Na′chor,
[35]Which was *the son* of Sa′ruch, which was *the son* of Ra′gau, which was *the son* of Pha′lec, which was *the son* of He′ber, which was *the son* of Sa′la,
3:36 Gen 11:10, 12
[36]Which was *the son* of Ca-i′nan, which was *the son* of Ar-phax′ad, which was *the son* of Sem, which was *the son* of No′e, which was *the son* of La′mech,
[37]Which was *the son* of Ma-thu′sa-la, which was *the son* of E′noch, which was *the son* of Ja′red, which was *the son* of Ma-le′le-el, which was *the son* of Ca-i′nan,
3:38 Gen 1:26, 27; 2:7; 5:1, 2; Isa 64:8
[38]Which was *the son* of Enos, which was *the son* of Seth, which was *the son* of Adam, which was *the son* of God.

C. JESUS' TEMPTATION IN THE BARREN WILDERNESS (CF. MT 4:1–11; MK 1:12, 13)

4:1☆ Isa 11:2; 61:1; Mt 4:1–11; Mk 1:12, 13; Lk 2:27; Jn 1:33; 3:34
4:2☆ Ex 34:28; 1 Kgs 19:8; Heb 2:18; 4:15

4 AND Jesus being full of the Holy Ghost returned from Jordan, and was led by the Spirit into the wilderness,
[2]Being forty days tempted of the devil. And in those days he did eat nothing: and when they were ended, he afterward hungered.
[3]And the devil said unto him, If thou be the Son of God, command this stone that it be made bread.

---

flesh. For Luke, a Greek, to trace Mary's genealogy is quite appropriate—he always showed an interest in the *women who followed Jesus. Matthew* traces the genealogy of Jesus to Abraham, while Luke takes it all the way back to Adam.

3:32 *Salmon,* i.e., "Solomon."

4:1 Here Jesus is said to have been led by the Holy Spirit. As the people of God, we have the same right to be led by the Spirit. When we have been so led, we can rest in the confidence that we are safe in the will of God and that we will be sustained and helped by the divine power that is available to us.

4:2 Jesus was tempted by the devil, but he never sinned. (See Matt. 4:1; Mark 1:12, 13; 2 Cor. 5:21; Heb. 4:15; 1 John 3:5). It was possible for Christ to be tempted without sinning. In his humanity he could have sinned but did not. In his deity, however, it was impossible for him to sin.

[4]And Jesus answered him, saying, It is written, That man shall not live by ☆4:4 Deut 8:3
bread alone, but by every word of God. Eph 6:17
[5]And the devil, taking him up into an high mountain, shewed unto him
all the kingdoms of the world in a moment of time.
[6]And the devil said unto him, All this power will I give thee, and the 4:6
glory of them: for that is delivered unto me; and to whomsoever I will I Jn 12:31; 14:30 1 Jn 5:19
give it. Rev 13:2, 7
[7]If thou therefore wilt worship me, all shall be thine.
[8]And Jesus answered and said unto him, Get thee behind me, Satan: for 4:8
it is written, Thou shalt worship the Lord thy God, and him only shalt thou Deut 6:13; 10:20
serve.
[9]And he brought him to Jerusalem, and set him on a pinnacle of the 4:9
temple, and said unto him, If thou be the Son of God, cast thyself down Mt 4:5 1 Pet 5:8
from hence:
[10]For it is written, He shall give his angels charge over thee, to keep thee:
[11]And in *their* hands they shall bear thee up, lest at any time thou dash 4:11
thy foot against a stone. Ps 91:11
[12]And Jesus answering said unto him, It is said, Thou shalt not tempt the 4:12
Lord thy God. Deut 6:16
[13]And when the devil had ended all the temptation, he departed from ☆4:13
him for a season. Jn 14:30 Heb 4:15 Jas 4:7

IV. JESUS IN GALILEE (4:14—9:50)

A. BEGINNING OF JESUS' GALILEAN MINISTRY (CF. MT 4:12–17; MK 1:14, 15; JN 4:43–45)

[14]¶And Jesus returned in the power of the Spirit into Galilee: and there ☆4:14
went out a fame of him through all the region round about. Mt 4:12–17 Mk 1:14, 15 Jn 4:43–45 Acts 10:37

B. HIS FIRST REJECTION AT NAZARETH

[15]And he taught in their synagogues, being glorified of all. 4:15
[16]¶And he came to Nazareth, where he had been brought up: and, as his Isa 52:13 4:16
custom was, he went into the synagogue on the sabbath day, and stood up Mt 2:23 13:54–58
for to read. Mk 6:1–6 Acts 13:14
[17]And there was delivered unto him the book of the prophet E-sai'as.
And when he had opened the book, he found the place where it was written,
[18]The Spirit of the Lord *is* upon me, because he hath anointed me to 4:18
preach the gospel to the poor; he hath sent me to heal the brokenhearted, Isa 61:1–2 Dan 9:24
to preach deliverance to the captives, and recovering of sight to the blind,
to set at liberty them that are bruised, ☆4:19
[19]To preach the acceptable year of the Lord. Lev 25:8–10 2 Cor 6:2

4:4 In this threefold temptation certain truths are evident: (1) Jesus would make no compact with the devil; (2) he would perform no miracles until he began preaching, for miracles ratified his doctrine; (3) he would work no miracles for himself because he came to suffer, not to please himself; (4) he gladly put off the proof of his being the Son of God until later rather than to do what was not fit and proper at that time; (5) he would not act independent from his Father.

4:13 The devil was put to flight. He had emptied his quiver of all his tricks, and had failed signally. Christ emerged the conqueror; the devil retired to work out other plans to entrap and defeat Jesus.

4:14ff Jesus, filled with the power of the Spirit, now begins his offensive warfare against the hosts of darkness. He taught publicly, centered his work in the synagogues, and kept the sabbath. The net result was that he preached and was persecuted.

4:19 *to preach the acceptable year of the Lord,* i.e., "to give blessings to all who come to him."† When Jesus closed the Book of Isaiah, he stopped before adding "and the day of vengeance of our God" (Isa. 61:2). Jesus finished by speaking of "the time of God's favor,"† which meant his own incarnation and atoning death on the cross. But the wrath of God awaits Christ's Second Advent; it is yet future. This was a purposeful omission on Jesus' part and may have puzzled his audience.

20 And he closed the book, and he gave *it* again to the minister, and sat
down. And the eyes of all them that were in the synagogue were fastened on
him.
21 And he began to say unto them, This day is this scripture fulfilled in
your ears.

4:22☆ Ps 45:2 Lk 2:47 Jn 1:16; 6:42 **4:23** Mt 4:13; 11:23 Mk 1:21–28 2:1–12 Jn 4:46–54 **4:24** Mt 13:57 Mk 6:4 Jn 4:44 **4:25, 26** 1 Kgs 17:9; 18:1 Jas 5:17

22 And all bare him witness, and wondered at the gracious words which
proceeded out of his mouth. And they said, Is not this Joseph's son?
23 And he said unto them, Ye will surely say unto me this proverb,
Physician, heal thyself: whatsoever we have heard done in Ca-per'na-um,
do also here in thy country.
24 And he said, Verily I say unto you, No prophet is accepted in his own
country.
25 But I tell you of a truth, many widows were in Israel in the days of
E-li'as, when the heaven was shut up three years and six months, when
great famine was throughout all the land;
26 But unto none of them was E-li'as sent, save unto Sar-ep'ta, *a city* of
Si'don, unto a woman *that was* a widow.

4:27 2 Kgs 5:14

27 And many lepers were in Israel in the time of El-i-se'us the prophet;
and none of them was cleansed, saving Na'a-man the Syrian.

4:28☆

28 And all they in the synagogue, when they heard these things, were filled
with wrath,

4:29 Num 15:35 Acts 7:58 Heb 13:12

29 And rose up, and thrust him out of the city, and led him unto the brow
of the hill whereon their city was built, that they might cast him down
headlong.

4:30 Jn 8:59; 10:39

30 But he passing through the midst of them went his way,

C. HIS MIRACLES AT CAPERNAUM (4:31–44)
1. Casting Out a Demon (Cf. Mk 1:21–28)

4:31 Mt 4:13–16 8:14–17 Mk 1:21–34 **4:32**☆ Mt 7:28, 29 Tit 2:15

31 And came down to Ca-per'na-um, a city of Galilee, and taught them on
the sabbath days.
32 And they were astonished at his doctrine: for his word was with power.
33 ¶And in the synagogue there was a man, which had a spirit of an
unclean devil, and cried out with a loud voice,

4:34 Isa 49:7 Dan 9:24 Lk 1:35

34 Saying, Let *us* alone; what have we to do with thee, *thou* Jesus of
Nazareth? art thou come to destroy us? I know thee who thou art; the Holy
One of God.

4:35 Lk 4:39, 41

35 And Jesus rebuked him, saying, Hold thy peace, and come out of him.
And when the devil had thrown him in the midst, he came out of him, and
hurt him not.

4:36☆

36 And they were all amazed, and spake among themselves, saying, What
a word *is* this! for with authority and power he commandeth the unclean
spirits, and they come out.

4:22 *Is not this Joseph's son*? The listeners have heard things they never heard before. They were so impressed that they found it difficult to believe that a son of Joseph could say and do these things. God, through Joseph, had covered Mary's virgin birth with dignity and kept her from scandal, public disgrace, and humiliation. What the God-man said and did was the *product of his being both God and man and offspring* of the Holy Spirit.

4:28 From the beginning we hear how "he came unto his own, and his own received him not" (John 1:11). He escaped from their wrath because his hour had not yet come. The Jews could not stand hearing that God was interested in the Gentiles and would save some of them too.

4:32 *his word was with power*. The word translated "power" is *exousia* ("authority") in the Greek text. Jesus had the authority of absolute truth, for he was God. And his words were absolute truth as well. The Jewish scribes and rabbis appealed to the traditions of their human forefathers. But Jesus' authority went beyond that of the rabbis and scribes. It came from God and his words were final. From them there was no appeal.

4:36 Christ cast out devils with authority and power, not with tricks and gimmicks. He muzzled demons and always delivered people from them, so that the victims were left unhurt.

37 And the fame of him went out into every place of the country round
about.

4:37 Mic 5:4

2. Healing Peter's Mother-in-law (Cf. Mt 8:14–17; Mk 1:29–34)

38 ¶And he arose out of the synagogue, and entered into Simon's house.
And Simon's wife's mother was taken with a great fever; and they besought
him for her.

4:38 Mt 8:14–17 Mk 1:29–34

39 And he stood over her, and rebuked the fever; and it left her: and
immediately she arose and ministered unto them.

4:39 Ps 103:3

3. Casting Out Demons (Cf. Mt 8:16, 17; Mk 1:32–34)

40 ¶Now when the sun was setting, all they that had any sick with divers
diseases brought them unto him; and he laid his hands on every one of
them, and healed them.

4:40 Mt 8:16, 17 Mk 1:32–34

41 And devils also came out of many, crying out, and saying, Thou art
Christ the Son of God. And he rebuking *them* suffered them not to speak:
for they knew that he was Christ.

☆**4:41** Mk 3:11

42 And when it was day, he departed and went into a desert place: and the
people sought him, and came unto him, and stayed him, that he should not
depart from them.

4:42 Mt 4:23 Mk 1:35–39

43 And he said unto them, I must preach the kingdom of God to other
cities also: for therefore am I sent.

4:43 Mk 1:14, 15 Acts 10:38 Rom 15:8

44 And he preached in the synagogues of Galilee.

D. THE CALLING OF SIMON, JAMES, AND JOHN (CF. MT 4:18–22; MK 1:16–20)

5 AND it came to pass, that, as the people pressed upon him to hear the
word of God, he stood by the lake of Gen-nes'a-ret,

☆**5:1** Mt 4:18–22 Mk 1:16–20

2 And saw two ships standing by the lake: but the fishermen were gone
out of them, and were washing *their* nets.
3 And he entered into one of the ships, which was Simon's, and prayed
him that he would thrust out a little from the land. And he sat down, and
taught the people out of the ship.
4 Now when he had left speaking, he said unto Simon, Launch out into
the deep, and let down your nets for a draught.

5:4 Jn 21:6

5 And Simon answering said unto him, Master, we have toiled all the
night, and have taken nothing: nevertheless at thy word I will let down the
net.

☆**5:5** Jn 21:3

6 And when they had this done, they inclosed a great multitude of fishes:
and their net brake.
7 And they beckoned unto *their* partners, which were in the other ship,
that they should come and help them. And they came, and filled both the
ships, so that they began to sink.
8 When Simon Peter saw *it*, he fell down at Jesus' knees, saying, Depart
from me; for I am a sinful man, O Lord.

5:8 2 Sam 6:9 Job 42:5, 6 Dan 8:17

4:41 Demons know fully well that Jesus Christ is God. But they will not bow down and worship him, at least now. They tremble at what the future has in store for them (James 2:19), but this does not change them. Scripture does not tell us whether it is possible, even now, for demons to change their minds and receive Christ, or whether their condition has become so fixed that they are beyond redemption.

5:1 *Genneseret*, i.e., the Sea of Galilee.

5:5 Life has its risks. Simon and his fellow fishermen toiled all night and caught nothing. Some work all night while others sleep. However hard one's vocation, it is good to see men diligent in their work. Yet even the diligent are often disappointed. This should not discourage the believer who is called upon to endure hardness and be a good soldier for Jesus Christ. When things go wrong, believers still have hope and help from their God. Peter obeyed the command of Jesus and caught a great multitude of fishes.

9 For he was astonished, and all that were with him, at the draught of the
fishes which they had taken:

5:10 Ezek 47:9, 10

10 And so *was* also James, and John, the sons of Zeb′e-dee, which were
partners with Simon. And Jesus said unto Simon, Fear not; from hence-
forth thou shalt catch men.

5:11☆ Mt 19:27; Lk 18:28; Phil 3:7, 8

11 And when they had brought their ships to land, they forsook all, and
followed him.

E. JESUS' MIRACLES

1. The Cleansing of the Leper (Cf. Mt 8:1–4; Mk 1:40–45)

5:12☆ Gen 18:14; Jer 32:17, 27; Mt 8:1–4; Mk 1:40–48; Heb 7:25

12 ¶And it came to pass, when he was in a certain city, behold a man full
of leprosy: who seeing Jesus fell on *his* face, and besought him, saying,
Lord, if thou wilt, thou canst make me clean.
13 And he put forth *his* hand, and touched him, saying, I will: be thou
clean. And immediately the leprosy departed from him.

5:14☆ Lev 13:1; 14:4, 10, 21, 22

14 And he charged him to tell no man: but go, and shew thyself to the
priest, and offer for thy cleansing, according as Moses commanded, for a
testimony unto them.

5:15 Mt 4:25; Mk 3:7; Jn 6:2

15 But so much the more went there a fame abroad of him: and great
multitudes came together to hear, and to be healed by him of their
infirmities.

5:16 Mt 14:23; Mk 6:46

16 ¶And he withdrew himself into the wilderness, and prayed.

2. The Paralyzed Man Healed and Forgiven (Cf. Mt 9:1–8; Mk 2:1–12)

5:17☆ Mt 9:1–8; Mk 2:1–12

17 And it came to pass on a certain day, as he was teaching, that there
were Pharisees and doctors of the law sitting by, which were come out of
every town of Galilee, and Judæa, and Jerusalem: and the power of the
Lord was *present* to heal them.
18 ¶And, behold, men brought in a bed a man which was taken with a
palsy: and they sought *means* to bring him in, and to lay *him* before him.
19 And when they could not find by what *way* they might bring him in
because of the multitude, they went upon the housetop, and let him down
through the tiling with *his* couch into the midst before Jesus.

5:20 Acts 5:31

5:21☆ Ex 34:7; Ps 32:5; 103:3; Isa 1:18; 43:25; Dan 9:9

20 And when he saw their faith, he said unto him, Man, thy sins are
forgiven thee.
21 And the scribes and the Pharisees began to reason, saying, Who is this
which speaketh blasphemies? Who can forgive sins, but God alone?

5:11 *they forsook all.* Christ called Peter, James, and John. So powerful and effective was that call that they surrendered everything to the Lordship of Jesus. It was an all-or-nothing decision, and they left all to follow him, not knowing where it would lead them or what they might be called upon to do or to suffer.

5:12 Leprosy was a common disease among the Jews. It was transmissible and incurable at that time. Lepers were considered unclean, were cut off from their people, could not occupy the office of the priesthood, could not associate with clean people, and were obliged to shout out that they were unclean (Lev. 13:45). The priests acted as the physicians to diagnose the disease and to watch it carefully. Leprosy from the biblical perspective is representative of sin, which cuts men off from God until cleansed. Jesus is the only cure for the leprosy of sin.

5:14 Jesus was not a schismatic. He gave the priests no reason to accuse him of dividing the Jews by separating them from the temple or the synagogue. Here he commanded the healed leper to show himself to the priest and get clearance, since he was no longer leprous. That such a man could be made whole was nothing short of a miracle. The priest, upon seeing this, should have known that Jesus was no mere man.

5:17 *Pharisees and doctors of the law,* i.e., Jews of position and authority who heard of the fame of Jesus and came to carp. The power of the Lord was present to help these critics too. Is it not surprising that those who saw others healed would turn away from the Son of God?

5:21 Who can forgive sins, but God alone? Jesus had the power on earth to forgive sins and his healings were proof of that power. The scribes and Pharisees asked the right question here. If God alone can forgive sins and Jesus did this, then he must be God. Jesus' claim to be God eventually led to his crucifixion.

22 But when Jesus perceived their thoughts, he answering said unto them,
What reason ye in your hearts?
23 Whether is easier, to say, Thy sins be forgiven thee; or to say, Rise up
and walk?
24 But that ye may know that the Son of man hath power upon earth to **5:24**
forgive sins, (he said unto the sick of the palsy,) I say unto thee, Arise, and Acts 5:31
take up thy couch, and go into thine house. Col 3:13
25 And immediately he rose up before them, and took up that whereon he **5:25**
lay, and departed to his own house, glorifying God. Ps 103:1
26 And they were all amazed, and they glorified God, and were filled with
fear, saying, We have seen strange things to day.

F. THE CALLING OF LEVI (MATTHEW) (CF. MT 9:9–13; MK 2:13–17)

27 ¶And after these things he went forth, and saw a publican, named Levi, ☆**5:27**
sitting at the receipt of custom: and he said unto him, Follow me. Mt 9:9–13
28 And he left all, rose up, and followed him. Mk 2:13–17
29 And Levi made him a great feast in his own house: and there was a **5:29**
great company of publicans and of others that sat down with them. Lk 15:1
30 But their scribes and Pharisees murmured against his disciples, saying,
Why do ye eat and drink with publicans and sinners?
31 And Jesus answering said unto them, They that are whole need not a
physician: but they that are sick.
32 I came not to call the righteous, but sinners to repentance. **5:32** 1 Tim 1:15

G. FEASTING VERSUS FASTING (CF. MT 9:14–17)

33 ¶And they said unto him, Why do the disciples of John fast often, and **5:33**
make prayers, and likewise *the disciples* of the Pharisees; but thine eat and Mt 9:14–17
drink? Mk 2:18–22
34 And he said unto them, Can ye make the children of the bridechamber **5:34**
fast, while the bridegroom is with them? Mt 22:2 Lk 14:16–23
35 But the days will come, when the bridegroom shall be taken away from 2 Cor 11:2 Rev 19:7; 21:2
them, and then shall they fast in those days. ☆**5:35**
36 ¶And he spake also a parable unto them; No man putteth a piece of a Zech 13:7 Mt 6:16, 17
new garment upon an old; if otherwise, then both the new maketh a rent, Jn 7:33; 16:6, 20, 22
and the piece that was *taken* out of the new agreeth not with the old. Acts 13:2, 3 1 Cor 7:5
37 And no man putteth new wine into old bottles; else the new wine will ☆**5:36**
burst the bottles, and be spilled, and the bottles shall perish.
38 But new wine must be put into new bottles; and both are preserved.
39 No man also having drunk old *wine* straightway desireth new: for he
saith, The old is better.

5:27 *publican(s),* i.e., "tax collectors" were looked upon as extortioners by the Jews, who hated them (3:13; 18:11; 19:8). Some collectors became wealthy (19:2). Jesus was criticized for associating with them (Matt. 9:11; 11:19). Some of them responded to the preaching of John the Baptist and were baptized (3:12; 7:29; Matt. 21:32). Some of them heard Jesus and became believers (15:1; Matt. 21:31; Mark 2:15). The apostle Matthew was a tax collector (Matt. 10:3).
5:35 *shall be taken away from them* is an oblique expression referring to the death of Jesus Christ followed by his resurrection and ascension. (Nevertheless, he would send them the promised Holy Spirit, who would take his place in their hearts.)
5:36ff The parables of the new cloth and the new wine in old wineskins teach the same lesson. Any effort to mix the kingdom of God with the old legalistic Jewish system is self-defeating. The truth of this was demonstrated after Pentecost when the church and synagogue finally had to be separated, for the Judaistic community continued to trust in works of merit.

H. THE RIGHT USE OF THE SABBATH (CF. MT 12:1–14; MK 2:23—3:6)

6:1☆ Mt 12:1–8 Mk 2:23–28

6 AND it came to pass on the second sabbath after the first, that he went
through the corn fields; and his disciples plucked the ears of corn, and
did eat, rubbing *them* in *their* hands.

6:2 Ex 20:10 Mark 7:2

2 And certain of the Pharisees said unto them, Why do ye that which is
not lawful to do on the sabbath days?

6:3☆ 1 Sam 21:6

3 And Jesus answering them said, Have ye not read so much as this, what
David did, when himself was an hungred, and they which were with him;

6:4 Ex 29:23, 33 Lev 24:9

4 How he went into the house of God, and did take and eat the
shewbread, and gave also to them that were with him; which it is not lawful
to eat but for the priests alone?

5 And he said unto them, That the Son of man is Lord also of the sabbath.

6:6 Mt 12:9–14 Mk 3:1–6 Lk 13:14; 14:3 Jn 9:16

6 And it came to pass also on another sabbath, that he entered into the
synagogue and taught: and there was a man whose right hand was
withered.

7 And the scribes and Pharisees watched him, whether he would heal on
the sabbath day; that they might find an accusation against him.

6:8 1 Sam 16:7 Mt 9:4 Lk 5:22 Jn 2:24, 25 6:64; 21:17 Acts 1:24 Rev 2:23

8 But he knew their thoughts, and said to the man which had the withered
hand, Rise up, and stand forth in the midst. And he arose and stood forth.

9 Then said Jesus unto them, I will ask you one thing; Is it lawful on the
sabbath days to do good, or to do evil? to save life, or to destroy *it?*

6:9 Jn 7:23

10 And looking round about upon them all, he said unto the man, Stretch
forth thy hand. And he did so: and his hand was restored whole as the
other.

11 And they were filled with madness; and communed one with another
what they might do to Jesus.

I. JESUS CHOOSING HIS INNER CIRCLE (CF. MT 10:1–4; MK 3:13–19)

6:12☆ Mt 10:2–4; 14:23 Mk 3:13–19

12 And it came to pass in those days, that he went out into a mountain to
pray, and continued all night in prayer to God.

6:13☆ Mt 10:1

13 ¶And when it was day, he called *unto him* his disciples: and of them he
chose twelve, whom also he named apostles;

6:14 Jn 1:42

14 Simon, (whom he also named Peter,) and Andrew his brother, James
and John, Philip and Bartholomew,

15 Matthew and Thomas, James the *son* of Al-phæ'us, and Simon called
Ze-lo'tes,

6:16 Jn 14:22 Acts 1:13

16 And Judas *the brother* of James, and Judas Iscariot, which also was the
traitor.

6:1 See note to Mark 2:27 for information on the sabbath. We learn here that works of necessity excuse us for breaking ceremonial regulations. Works of mercy do the same. But some use necessity and mercy for license to do as they please; this is not allowable.
6:3 See note to Matt. 12:3 for further elaboration on *this theme.*
6:12 Jesus is in secret prayer to the Father. He is alone and he is long with God in prayer. Following this season of prayer he chose his disciples. Believers should make their decisions after, not before, prayer.
6:13 *apostles,* literally, "ones sent forth." An apostle is an ambassador or missionary serving the one who sent him. The office of apostle no longer continues, for one of the qualifications was that he must have seen the Lord Jesus face to face so as to be an eyewitness of the resurrection (24:48; Acts 1:8, 22; 1 Cor. 9:1). He had to be called or appointed by the Holy Spirit himself, for no mere man could endow anyone with this authority. The apostles performed miracles and signs that testified to their authenticity. There were more than twelve apostles, for besides the disciples, Scripture speaks of Paul, Barnabas, James, and possibly Andronicus and Junius as apostles (Acts 14:14; Rom. 16:7; 1 Cor. 15:7; Gal. 1:19).

J. THE SERMON ON THE PLAIN
1. The Beatitudes (Blessedness) (Cf. Mt 5—7)

17 ¶And he came down with them, and stood in the plain, and the
company of his disciples, and a great multitude of people out of all Judæa
and Jerusalem, and from the sea coast of Tyre and Si′don, which came to
hear him, and to be healed of their diseases;
18 And they that were vexed with unclean spirits: and they were healed.
19 And the whole multitude sought to touch him: for there went virtue out
of him, and healed *them* all.
20 ¶And he lifted up his eyes on his disciples, and said, Blessed *be ye* poor:
for yours is the kingdom of God.
21 Blessed *are ye* that hunger now: for ye shall be filled. Blessed *are ye* that
weep now: for ye shall laugh.
22 Blessed are ye, when men shall hate you, and when they shall separate
you *from their company*, and shall reproach *you*, and cast out your name as
evil, for the Son of man's sake.
23 Rejoice ye in that day, and leap for joy: for, behold, your reward *is*
great in heaven: for in the like manner did their fathers unto the prophets.
24 But woe unto you that are rich! for ye have received your consolation.
25 Woe unto you that are full! for ye shall hunger. Woe unto you that
laugh now! for ye shall mourn and weep.
26 Woe unto you, when all men shall speak well of you! for so did their
fathers to the false prophets.

☆6:17 Mt 4:25
6:19 Mt 14:36; Mk 5:30
☆6:20 Mt 5, 6, 7, 8:1; 11:5; Jas 2:5
6:21 Isa 55:1; 61:3; 1 Cor 4:11; Rev 7:14–17
6:22 Jn 9:22; 16:2; 1 Pet 2:19; 3:14; 4:14
6:23 Acts 5:41; 7:51; Col 1:24; Jas 1:2
☆6:24 Amos 6:1; Lk 12:21; 16:25; Jas 5:1
6:25 Isa 65:13; Prov 14:13
6:26 Jn 15:19; 1 Jn 4:5

2. The Law of Love (Cf. Mt 5:43–48)

27 ¶But I say unto you which hear, Love your enemies, do good to them
which hate you,
28 Bless them that curse you, and pray for them which despitefully use
you.
29 And unto him that smiteth thee on the *one* cheek offer also the other;
and him that taketh away thy cloak forbid not *to take thy* coat also.
30 Give to every man that asketh of thee; and of him that taketh away thy
goods ask *them* not again.
31 And as ye would that men should do to you, do ye also to them
likewise.
32 For if ye love them which love you, what thank have ye? for sinners also
love those that love them.
33 And if ye do good to them which do good to you, what thank have ye?
for sinners also do even the same.
34 And if ye lend *to them* of whom ye hope to receive, what thank have ye?
for sinners also lend to sinners, to receive as much again.

☆6:27 Ex 23:4; Prov 25:21; Rom 12:20
6:28 Lk 23:34; Acts 7:60
6:29 1 Cor 6:7
6:30 Deut 15:7; Prov 3:27
6:31 Phil 4:8

6:17ff Up to this point the ministry of Jesus was *generally limited to the synagogues. Now he goes* public. Multitudes come to hear him and all who need healing are healed. Today's healings in no way resemble what Jesus did. Nowadays, a few here and there and only occasionally are healed compared to those who are not healed. Moreover he had virtue in him and it went out to heal. Healers today do not have this. Jesus healed directly because he was God; healers today heal indirectly in that they must seek the power of God, which they do not have in and of themselves.

6:20ff This passage is similar to Matt. 5—7. Luke's account is an abbreviated version of Matthew's report. Probably both accounts were summaries of the Sermon on the Mount. The longer Matthean account can be read in a few minutes' time, even though Jesus undoubtedly spoke far longer. All of the Gospels together give us just a small portion of everything Jesus said and did in the nearly three years of his public ministry.

6:24 *woe unto you that are rich*, not because they are rich but because they trusted in their riches instead of trusting in God. It is the folly of fools to make anything in this world their consolation.

6:27ff Jesus here expanded on the law of love that was taught in the Old Testament. Some of his ideas on the subject were considered radically unorthodox. Paul enlarged on this theme in 1 Cor. 13.

6:35 Lev 25:35; Ps 37:26; Acts 14:17; 1 Jn 3:1 **6:36** Eph 5:1, 2

35 But love ye your enemies, and do good, and lend, hoping for nothing
again; and your reward shall be great, and ye shall be the children of the
Highest: for he is kind unto the unthankful and *to* the evil.
36 Be ye therefore merciful, as your Father also is merciful.

3. Criticism and Rebuke (Cf. Mt 7:1–5)

6:37☆ Jas 4:11 **6:38** Ps 79:12; Prov 19:17; Mk 4:24; Jas 2:13 **6:39** Mt 15:14 **6:40** Mt 10:24; Jn 13:16; 15:20 **6:41**☆ **6:42** Prov 18:17 **6:43** 1 Tim 3:1–9 **6:44** Mt 12:33 **6:45** Rom 8:5–8

37 Judge not, and ye shall not be judged: condemn not, and ye shall not be
condemned: forgive, and ye shall be forgiven:
38 Give, and it shall be given unto you; good measure, pressed down, and
shaken together, and running over, shall men give into your bosom. For
with the same measure that ye mete withal it shall be measured to you
again.
39 And he spake a parable unto them, Can the blind lead the blind? shall
they not both fall into the ditch?
40 The disciple is not above his master: but every one that is perfect shall
be as his master.
41 And why beholdest thou the mote that is in thy brother's eye, but
perceivest not the beam that is in thine own eye?
42 Either how canst thou say to thy brother, Brother, let me pull out the
mote that is in thine eye, when thou thyself beholdest not the beam that is
in thine own eye? Thou hypocrite, cast out first the beam out of thine own
eye, and then shalt thou see clearly to pull out the mote that is in thy
brother's eye.
43 For a good tree bringeth not forth corrupt fruit; neither doth a corrupt
tree bring forth good fruit.
44 For every tree is known by his own fruit. For of thorns men do not
gather figs, nor of a bramble bush gather they grapes.
45 A good man out of the good treasure of his heart bringeth forth that
which is good; and an evil man out of the evil treasure of his heart bringeth
forth that which is evil: for of the abundance of the heart his mouth
speaketh.

4. The Parable of the Two Houses (Cf. Mt 7:24–27)

6:46 Mal 1:6; Mt 25:11; Lk 13:25; Rom 2:13 **6:47**☆ **6:48**☆ Ps 125:1; Acts 14:22; 1 Cor 3:11; 2 Tim 2:19; 3:12 **6:49** Job 8:13; Prov 1:29–31; Heb 10:28–31; 2 Pet 2:20, 21

46 ¶And why call ye me, Lord, Lord, and do not the things which I say?
47 Whosoever cometh to me, and heareth my sayings, and doeth them, I
will shew you to whom he is like:
48 He is like a man which built an house, and digged deep, and laid the
foundation on a rock: and when the flood arose, the stream beat vehe-
mently upon that house, and could not shake it: for it was founded upon a
rock.
49 But he that heareth, and doeth not, is like a man that without a
foundation built an house upon the earth; against which the stream did
beat vehemently, and immediately it fell; and the ruin of that house was
great.

K. HEALING THE CENTURION'S PRIZED SLAVE (CF. MT 8:5–13)

7:1 Mt 8:5–13

7 NOW when he had ended all his sayings in the audience of the people,
he entered into Ca-per'na-um.

6:37 forgive and ye shall be forgiven, i.e., the failure to forgive others is a sin itself, and until others are forgiven, we are not forgiven.

6:41 Jesus is saying here that we who pick out the speck of dust in another's eye may have a two-by-four in our own. Before we reform others we must first reform ourselves.

6:47, 48 Jesus distinguishes between a true and false profession. The *rock*, or good foundation, symbolizes those who come to Jesus Christ for salvation. Those who build on sand have no foundation, even if their works of righteousness abound. Paul speaks of Christ Jesus as the solid foundation (1 Cor. 3:11; see also 1 Pet. 2:7, 8).

2 And a certain centurion's servant, who was dear unto him, was sick, and ☆7:2
ready to die.
3 And when he heard of Jesus, he sent unto him the elders of the Jews,
beseeching him that he would come and heal his servant.
4 And when they came to Jesus, they besought him instantly, saying, That
he was worthy for whom he should do this:
5 For he loveth our nation, and he hath built us a synagogue.
6 Then Jesus went with them. And when he was now not far from the **7:6–8**
house, the centurion sent friends to him, saying unto him, Lord, trouble not Ps 33:9 Lk 4:36
thyself: for I am not worthy that thou shouldest enter under my roof: Jn 11:43
7 Wherefore neither thought I myself worthy to come unto thee: but say
in a word, and my servant shall be healed.
8 For I also am a man set under authority, having under me soldiers, and
I say unto one, Go, and he goeth; and to another, Come, and he cometh;
and to my servant, Do this, and he doeth *it*.
9 When Jesus heard these things, he marvelled at him, and turned him ☆7:9
about, and said unto the people that followed him, I say unto you, I have Rom 3:1, 2; 9:4
not found so great faith, no, not in Israel.
10 And they that were sent, returning to the house, found the servant
whole that had been sick.

L. RAISING THE WIDOW'S SON AT NAIN

11 ¶And it came to pass the day after, that he went into a city called Nain; ☆7:11
and many of his disciples went with him, and much people.
12 Now when he came nigh to the gate of the city, behold, there was a
dead man carried out, the only son of his mother, and she was a widow:
and much people of the city was with her.
13 And when the Lord saw her, he had compassion on her, and said unto **7:13**
her, Weep not. Lam 3:32 Jn 11:33, 35
14 And he came and touched the bier: and they that bare *him* stood still. Heb 4:15 **7:14**
And he said, Young man, I say unto thee, Arise. Lk 8:54
15 And he that was dead sat up, and began to speak. And he delivered him Jn 11:43 Acts 9:40
to his mother. Rom 4:17
16 And there came a fear on all: and they glorified God, saying, That a **7:16**
great prophet is risen up among us; and, That God hath visited his people. Lk 1:65, 68 24:19
17 And this rumour of him went forth throughout all Judæa, and Jn 4:19; 6:14 9:17
throughout all the region round about. **7:17** Mt 9:26

M. ANSWERING JOHN THE BAPTIST'S LAST QUESTIONS (CF. MT 11:2–19)

7:18 Mt 11:2–30

18 And the disciples of John shewed him of all these things. **7:19** Ezek 21:27 Dan 9:24–26
19 ¶And John calling *unto him* two of his disciples sent *them* to Jesus, Mic 5:2 Zech 9:9
saying, Art thou he that should come? or look we for another? Mal 3:1–3

7:2 *centurion*, noncommissioned Roman army officer, in this case a Gentile who loved the Jews and owned a slave. He had built a synagogue for the Jews.

7:9 The centurion had faith and believed Jesus without doubt. He stood in sharp contrast with the Jews who exhibited unbelief.

7:11ff The resurrection of the widow's son appears only in the Gospel of Luke. A number of items in Luke's Gospel do not appear elsewhere. The story of Lazarus and the rich man, the parables of the lost sheep, the lost coin and the lost son, and the story of the good Samaritan are found in Luke alone. Jesus performed so many miracles of healing and deliverance from demons that if all of the stories connected with such events were recorded we would have a clear notion of the meaning of John 21:25: "And there are also many other things which Jesus did, the which, if they should be written every one, I suppose that even the world itself could not contain the books that should be written."

7:20☆

20 When the men were come unto him, they said, John Baptist hath sent us unto thee, saying, Art thou he that should come? or look we for another?

21 And in that same hour he cured many of *their* infirmities and plagues, and of evil spirits; and unto many *that were* blind he gave sight.

7:22 Isa 29:18; 35:5 42:6; 61:1 Lk 4:18 Jas 2:5

22 Then Jesus answering said unto them, Go your way, and tell John what things ye have seen and heard; how that the blind see, the lame walk, the lepers are cleansed, the deaf hear, the dead are raised, to the poor the gospel is preached.

7:23☆

23 And blessed is *he*, whosoever shall not be offended in me.

24 ¶And when the messengers of John were departed, he began to speak unto the people concerning John, What went ye out into the wilderness for to see? A reed shaken with the wind?

7:25 Mt 3:4 Mk 1:6

25 But what went ye out for to see? A man clothed in soft raiment? Behold, they which are gorgeously apparelled, and live delicately, are in kings' courts.

26 But what went ye out for to see? A prophet? Yea, I say unto you, and much more than a prophet.

7:27 Isa 40:3 Mal 3:1; 4:5

27 This is *he*, of whom it is written, Behold, I send my messenger before thy face, which shall prepare thy way before thee.

28 For I say unto you, Among those that are born of women there is not a greater prophet than John the Baptist: but he that is least in the kingdom of God is greater than he.

7:29☆ Mt 3:5 Lk 3:12 Acts 18:25; 19:3

29 And all the people that heard *him*, and the publicans, justified God, being baptized with the baptism of John.

7:30 Acts 20:27

30 But the Pharisees and lawyers rejected the counsel of God against themselves, being not baptized of him.

7:31☆

31 ¶And the Lord said, Whereunto then shall I liken the men of this generation? and to what are they like?

32 They are like unto children sitting in the marketplace, and calling one to another, and saying, We have piped unto you, and ye have not danced; we have mourned to you, and ye have not wept.

7:33 Mt 3:4 Mk 1:6 Lk 1:15

33 For John the Baptist came neither eating bread nor drinking wine; and ye say, He hath a devil.

34 The Son of man is come eating and drinking; and ye say, Behold a gluttonous man, and a winebibber, a friend of publicans and sinners!

7:35 1 Cor 1:23, 24

35 But wisdom is justified of all her children.

N. JESUS ANOINTED BY A PROSTITUTE; HER SINS FORGIVEN

7:36☆ Mt 26:6 Mk 14:3 Jn 11:2

36 ¶And one of the Pharisees desired him that he would eat with him. And he went into the Pharisee's house, and sat down to meat.

7:20 John the Baptist was in a state of depression in jail. No doubt he wondered why Jesus, his cousin and his Lord, would not come to visit him and help him. He sought for reassurance that the one he had baptized was indeed the Messiah. In response to the question of John's disciples, Jesus performed many mighty miracles and told them to report it to John. This should have given him rest of spirit and mind.

7:23 Jesus warns John the Baptist not to reject or condemn him because of a wrong idea of what he was *supposed to do and what kinds of* methods he used to accomplish his work. The divine Messiah does the right things the right way at the right time.

7:29 *all the people . . . justified God*, i.e., the worst of men, high and low, ordinary or in high position, even tax gatherers, agreed that God's way was right.

7:31ff This is a parable in which Jesus likens the Pharisees and lawyers to two groups of children. One group plays a wedding song and expects the second group to dance to their tune. The second group plays a funeral dirge, and the first group will not weep with them. The Pharisees and lawyers rejected John the Baptist because he was an ascetic. They then rejected Jesus because he acted the opposite way. No matter which way God offered them eternal life, they turned it down.

7:36ff This incident is not to be confused with a similar one that occurred in Bethany of Judea during the closing week of Jesus' life and ministry. The incident reported here occurred during Jesus' Galilean ministry. The sinful woman is unnamed, whereas in Bethany the woman is said to be Mary, the sister of Martha and Lazarus. In this incident the host is Simon the Pharisee; in Bethany it was Simon the leper. Jesus' concluding

37 And, behold, a woman in the city, which was a sinner, when she knew
that *Jesus* sat at meat in the Pharisee's house, brought an alabaster box of
ointment,
38 And stood at his feet behind *him* weeping, and began to wash his feet
with tears, and did wipe *them* with the hairs of her head, and kissed his feet,
and anointed *them* with the ointment.
39 Now when the Pharisee which had bidden him saw *it*, he spake within
himself, saying, This man, if he were a prophet, would have known who and
what manner of woman *this is* that toucheth him: for she is a sinner.
40 And Jesus answering said unto him, Simon, I have somewhat to say
unto thee. And he saith, Master, say on.
41 There was a certain creditor which had two debtors: the one owed five
hundred pence, and the other fifty.
42 And when they had nothing to pay, he frankly forgave them both. Tell
me therefore, which of them will love him most?
43 Simon answered and said, I suppose that *he*, to whom he forgave most.
And he said unto him, Thou hast rightly judged.
44 And he turned to the woman, and said unto Simon, Seest thou this
woman? I entered into thine house, thou gavest me no water for my feet:
but she hath washed my feet with tears, and wiped *them* with the hairs of
her head.
45 Thou gavest me no kiss: but this woman since the time I came in hath
not ceased to kiss my feet.
46 My head with oil thou didst not anoint: but this woman hath anointed
my feet with ointment.
47 Wherefore I say unto thee, Her sins, which are many, are forgiven; for
she loved much: but to whom little is forgiven, *the same* loveth little.
48 And he said unto her, Thy sins are forgiven.
49 And they that sat at meat with him began to say within themselves,
Who is this that forgiveth sins also?
50 And he said to the woman, Thy faith hath saved thee; go in peace.

7:37 Lk 8:2
7:38 Zech 12:10
7:39 Lk 15:2 Jn 7:52
☆7:41 Mt 18:28
7:42 Isa 1:18; 43:25 44:22
7:44 Gen 18:4 1 Tim 5:10
7:45 1 Cor 16:20 2 Cor 13:12
7:46 2 Sam 12:20 Ps 23:5 Eccles 9:8
7:47 1 Tim 1:14
7:48 Mt 9:2 Mk 2:5
7:49 Isa 53:3 Mt 9:3 Mk 2:7 Jn 1:10
7:50 Mt 9:22 Mk 5:34; 10:52 Lk 8:48

O. JESUS' HELPERS IN HIS SECOND EVANGELISTIC JOURNEY

8 AND it came to pass afterward, that he went throughout every city
and village, preaching and shewing the glad tidings of the kingdom of
God: and the twelve *were* with him,
2 And certain women, which had been healed of evil spirits and infirmi-
ties, Mary called Magdalene, out of whom went seven devils,
3 And Jo-an'na the wife of Chu'za Herod's steward, and Susanna, and
many others, which ministered unto him of their substance.

☆8:1 Mt 4:23
☆8:2 Mt 27:55, 56 Mk 16:9 Lk 23:49
8:3 Mt 14:1

P. THE PARABLE OF THE SOWER AND THE REASON FOR IT (CF. MT 13:1–17; MK 4:1–12)

4 ¶And when much people were gathered together, and were come to him
out of every city, he spake by a parable:

8:4 Mt 13:1–53 Mk 4:1–34

---

statements here are quite different from those recorded in accounts of the Bethany incident. Not a shred of evidence exists for supposing—as some do—that this sinful woman was Mary Magdalene. (Cf. note on 8:2.)

7:41ff The point of this illustration is that the more we have been forgiven, the more gratitude we should express to the Lord. Simon pronounced a wrong judgment about this sinful woman, but Jesus knew that she now had been saved by faith and was expressing her changed life in outward fashion. Her works showed the reality of her saving faith.

8:1 *village*, "of Galilee," implied.†

8:2 *Magdalene* means "of the town of Magdala." Magdala (also called Tarichaea) was a fishing village on the west bank of the Sea of Galilee. Jesus delivered Mary from demon possession. Nowhere in Scripture does it say or suggest that she was guilty of immorality or prostitution.

8:5☆

5 A sower went out to sow his seed: and as he sowed, some fell by the way
side; and it was trodden down, and the fowls of the air devoured it.
6 And some fell upon a rock; and as soon as it was sprung up, it withered
away, because it lacked moisture.
7 And some fell among thorns; and the thorns sprang up with it, and
choked it.
8 And other fell on good ground, and sprang up, and bare fruit an
hundredfold. And when he had said these things, he cried, He that hath
ears to hear, let him hear.
9 ¶And his disciples asked him, saying, What might this parable be?

8:10 Isa 6:9

10 And he said, Unto you it is given to know the mysteries of the kingdom
of God: but to others in parables; that seeing they might not see, and
hearing they might not understand.

Q. THE PARABLE OF THE SOWER EXPLAINED (CF. MT 13:18–23; MK 4:13–20)

8:11 Acts 20:27, 32; 1 Pet 1:23
8:12 2 Cor 2:11; 4:3; 2 Thess 2:10; Jas 1:23, 24; 1 Pet 5:8

11 Now the parable is this: The seed is the word of God.
12 Those by the way side are they that hear; then cometh the devil, and
taketh away the word out of their hearts, lest they should believe and be
saved.
13 They on the rock *are they*, which, when they hear, receive the word with
joy; and these have no root, which for a while believe, and in time of
temptation fall away.

8:14 Mt 19:23; 1 Tim 6:9, 10; 2 Tim 4:10

14 And that which fell among thorns are they, which, when they have
heard, go forth, and are choked with cares and riches and pleasures of *this*
life, and bring no fruit to perfection.

8:15 Ps 32:2, 5; Eph 2:4; 2 Pet 1:5–10

15 But that on the good ground are they, which in an honest and good
heart, having heard the word, keep *it*, and bring forth fruit with patience.

8:16☆ Mt 5:15; Lk 11:33; Phil 2:15, 16

16 ¶No man, when he hath lighted a candle, covereth it with a vessel, or
putteth *it* under a bed; but setteth *it* on a candlestick, that they which enter
in may see the light.

8:17 Mt 10:26; Lk 12:2

17 For nothing is secret, that shall not be made manifest; neither *any thing*
hid, that shall not be known and come abroad.

8:18 Mt 25:29; Lk 19:26; Jn 15:2

18 Take heed therefore how ye hear: for whosoever hath, to him shall be
given; and whosoever hath not, from him shall be taken even that which he
seemeth to have.

R. JESUS' TRUE RELATIVES (CF. MT 12:46–50; MK 3:31–35)

8:19☆ Mt 12:46–50; 13:55; Mk 3:31–35; Jn 7:5; Acts 1:14; 1 Cor 9:5; Gal 1:19
8:21☆ Lk 11:28

19 ¶Then came to him *his* mother and his brethren, and could not come at
him for the press.
20 And it was told him *by certain* which said, Thy mother and thy brethren
stand without, desiring to see thee.
21 And he answered and said unto them, My mother and my brethren are
these which hear the word of God, and do it.

8:5 See note on Mark 4:3 concerning the parable of the sower.
8:16 These words were spoken to the disciples and *constitute advice to those who* preach the gospel. Whoever has the gift to do so must minister the gospel. Those who do are like lighted candles. Talents are not given to be buried but traded. These gifts will either be increased by use or perish by lack of use.
8:19 Jesus had brothers and sisters. James and Judas (Jude), both writers of New Testament books, were his brothers. So were Joseph and Simon. He also had at least two sisters (Mark 6:3). Jesus was the eldest child and had a large responsibility in the well-being of his mother, brothers, and sisters before he began his public ministry.
8:21 Faithful hearers of the Word of God always become faithful doers of the work of God. Those who hear and do are closer to Jesus than mother or brothers.

S. STILLING THE STORM ON THE LAKE (CF. MT 8:23–27; MK 4:36–41)

22¶Now it came to pass on a certain day, that he went into a ship with his
disciples: and he said unto them, Let us go over unto the other side of the
lake. And they launched forth.
23But as they sailed he fell asleep: and there came down a storm of wind
on the lake; and they were filled *with water*, and were in jeopardy.
24And they came to him, and awoke him, saying, Master, master, we
perish. Then he arose, and rebuked the wind and the raging of the water:
and they ceased, and there was a calm.
25And he said unto them, Where is your faith? And they being afraid
wondered, saying one to another, What manner of man is this! for he
commandeth even the winds and water, and they obey him.

8:22 Job 28:11; 38:11; Ps 29:10; 65:7; 89:9; Mt 8:18, 23–27; Mk 4:35–41
☆8:24
8:25 Ps 33:8, 9; Mk 6:51

T. DELIVERANCE FROM DEMONS: THE MAN FROM GADARA (CF. MT 8:28–34; MK 5:1–20)

26¶And they arrived at the country of the Gad'a-renes, which is over
against Galilee.
27And when he went forth to land, there met him out of the city a certain
man, which had devils long time, and ware no clothes, neither abode in *any*
house, but in the tombs.
28When he saw Jesus, he cried out, and fell down before him, and with a
loud voice said, What have I to do with thee, Jesus, *thou* Son of God most
high? I beseech thee, torment me not.
29(For he had commanded the unclean spirit to come out of the man. For
oftentimes it had caught him: and he was kept bound with chains and in
fetters; and he brake the bands, and was driven of the devil into the
wilderness.)
30And Jesus asked him, saying, What is thy name? And he said, Legion:
because many devils were entered into him.
31And they besought him that he would not command them to go out
into the deep.
32And there was there an herd of many swine feeding on the mountain:
and they besought him that he would suffer them to enter into them. And
he suffered them.
33Then went the devils out of the man, and entered into the swine: and
the herd ran violently down a steep place into the lake, and were choked.
34When they that fed *them* saw what was done, they fled, and went and
told *it* in the city and in the country.
35Then they went out to see what was done; and came to Jesus, and
found the man, out of whom the devils were departed, sitting at the feet of
Jesus, clothed, and in his right mind: and they were afraid.
36They also which saw *it* told them by what means he that was possessed
of the devils was healed.
37¶Then the whole multitude of the country of the Gad'a-renes round
about besought him to depart from them; for they were taken with great
fear: and he went up into the ship, and returned back again.

8:26 Mt 8:28–34; Mk 5:1–20
8:28 Acts 16:16, 17; Phil 2:10, 11
☆8:29
8:31 Rev 9:1; 20:3
8:32 Lev 11:7; Deut 14:8; Job 1:12; 12:16; Rev 20:7
8:35 1 Jn 3:8; Rom 16:20
8:37 1 Sam 16:4; Job 21:14; Mk 1:24; Lk 4:34; 5:8; Acts 16:39

8:24 In this incident Jesus demonstrated his power over nature. He commanded the waves to be still, and a great calm came over the waters. The disciples were fishermen and accustomed to storms. This one was so fierce they were thoroughly frightened. The way to silence fears is to call on the Lord Jesus. This they did and were delivered. It is the devil's business to raise storms and Jesus' business to still them.

8:29ff Unclean spirits have great physical power over the bodies of those they inhabit. These spirits were so strong that they broke the chains and fetters with which this demon-possessed man was bound. When he was delivered and his mind was right, multitudes came to see him. Instead of sensing the greatness of Jesus and opening their hearts to him, they were afraid (8:37) and urged him to leave as quickly as possible. This was an insult to the Lord Jesus.

8:38 Lk 18:43 38 Now the man out of whom the devils were departed besought him that
he might be with him: but Jesus sent him away, saying,
39 Return to thine own house, and shew how great things God hath done
unto thee. And he went his way and published throughout the whole city
how great things Jesus had done unto him.

U. HEALING THE BLEEDING WOMAN AND RAISING JAIRUS' DAUGHTER (CF. MT 9:18–26; MK 5:21–43)

8:40 Mt 9:1, 18–26 Mk 5:21–43 40 And it came to pass, that, when Jesus was returned, the people *gladly*
received him: for they were all waiting for him.
8:41☆ 41 ¶And, behold, there came a man named Ja-i′rus, and he was a ruler of
the synagogue: and he fell down at Jesus' feet, and besought him that he
would come into his house:
42 For he had one only daughter, about twelve years of age, and she lay a
dying. But as he went the people thronged him.
8:43☆ Lev 15:25 43 ¶And a woman having an issue of blood twelve years, which had spent
all her living upon physicians, neither could be healed of any,
8:44 Acts 5:15; 19:12 44 Came behind *him*, and touched the border of his garment: and
immediately her issue of blood stanched.
45 And Jesus said, Who touched me? When all denied, Peter and they that
were with him said, Master, the multitude throng thee and press *thee*, and
sayest thou, Who touched me?
8:46☆ Lk 5:17; 6:19 46 And Jesus said, Somebody hath touched me: for I perceive that virtue is
gone out of me.
47 And when the woman saw that she was not hid, she came trembling,
and falling down before him, she declared unto him before all the people
for what cause she had touched him, and how she was healed immediately.
48 And he said unto her, Daughter, be of good comfort: thy faith hath
made thee whole; go in peace.
49 ¶While he yet spake, there cometh one from the ruler of the syna-
gogue's *house*, saying to him, Thy daughter is dead; trouble not the Master.
8:50 2 Chron 20:20 Mk 9:23 50 But when Jesus heard *it*, he answered him, saying, Fear not: believe
only, and she shall be made whole.
51 And when he came into the house, he suffered no man to go in, save
Peter, and James, and John, and the father and the mother of the maiden.
8:52 Jn 11:11, 13 52 And all wept, and bewailed her: but he said, Weep not; she is not dead,
but sleepeth.
53 And they laughed him to scorn, knowing that she was dead.
8:54 Lk 7:14 Jn 11:43 54 And he put them all out, and took her by the hand, and called, saying,
Maid, arise.

8:41ff Jairus was a ruler of the synagogue. He knew about Jesus and his healings, but he did not ask him to speak a healing word at a distance. He wanted him to come to his home and cure his dying daughter. As they were en route, the news came that the girl was dead. The implication was that the case was hopeless. Why bother the teacher anymore? Jesus told them to have faith, a faith that should be bold and daring. (Surely to call a physician when the patient is dead is hopeless, *but to call Christ after death* is not hopeless.) The healing of the woman with the issue of blood for twelve years undoubtedly encouraged Jairus. Jesus spoke a word to Jairus' daughter and her spirit returned to her body. There is no physical life without the spirit, for while body and spirit are separate, the body cannot exist without the spirit. The immortality of the spirit is herein posited, for it existed without the body and came back into the body.

8:43 *which had spent all her living upon physicians.* This clause is not included in some of the ancient manuscripts.†

8:46 *virtue*, i.e., "power." Here and in the parallel account in Mark 5:30 the word "virtue" is used (from the Greek *dunamis*). This power went forth from Jesus and the woman with the issue of blood was healed. There does not appear to have been any conscious volition on the part of Jesus. In 5:17 it is reported that "the Lord's healing power was upon him" (TLB), and in 6:19 it says, "healing power went out from him" (TLB). Jesus certainly healed people and expelled demons by the power of God, or the Spirit of God. (Cf. 4:18; 11:20; Matt. 12:28).

55 And her spirit came again, and she arose straightway: and he com-
manded to give her meat.
56 And her parents were astonished: but he charged them that they should
tell no man what was done.

V. THE MISSION OF THE TWELVE (CF. MT 10:1–15; MK 6:7–13)

9 THEN he called his twelve disciples together, and gave them power
and authority over all devils, and to cure diseases.
2 And he sent them to preach the kingdom of God, and to heal the sick.
3 And he said unto them, Take nothing for *your* journey, neither staves,
nor scrip, neither bread, neither money; neither have two coats apiece.
4 And whatsoever house ye enter into, there abide, and thence depart.
5 And whosoever will not receive you, when ye go out of that city, shake
off the very dust from your feet for a testimony against them.
6 And they departed, and went through the towns, preaching the gospel,
and healing every where.

W. HEROD THE GOVERNOR: THE MURDERER OF JOHN THE BAPTIST (CF. MT 14:1–12; MK 6:14–39)

7 ¶Now Herod the tetrarch heard of all that was done by him: and he was
perplexed, because that it was said of some, that John was risen from the
dead;
8 And of some, that E-li′as had appeared; and of others, that one of the
old prophets was risen again.
9 And Herod said, John have I beheaded: but who is this, of whom I hear
such things? And he desired to see him.

X. FEEDING THE FIVE THOUSAND (CF. MT 14:13–21; MK 6:30–44; JN 6:1–13)

10 ¶And the apostles, when they were returned, told him all that they had
done. And he took them, and went aside privately into a desert place
belonging to the city called Beth-sa′i-da.
11 And the people, when they knew *it*, followed him: and he received
them, and spake unto them of the kingdom of God, and healed them that
had need of healing.
12 And when the day began to wear away, then came the twelve, and said
unto him, Send the multitude away, that they may go into the towns and
country round about, and lodge, and get victuals: for we are here in a desert
place.
13 But he said unto them, Give ye them to eat. And they said, We have no

8:55 Deut 32:39; Ps 33:9
8:56 Mt 8:4; 9:30
☆**9:1** Mt 9:36–11:1; 3:13; 6:7–13
9:2 Lk 10:1, 9; Tit 2:12, 14
9:3 Ps 37:3; Lk 10:4; 22:35; 2 Tim 2:4
9:5 Acts 13:51
9:6 Lk 8:1
☆**9:7** Mt 14:1–12; Mk 6:14–29
9:8 Mt 16:14
9:9 Lk 23:8
☆**9:10** Mt 14:13–23; Mk 6:30–46; Jn 6:1–15
☆**9:13** Num 11:22; 2 Kgs 4:42, 43; Ps 78:19, 20

9:1 Jesus sends his disciples forth to preach, to heal, and to cast out devils. They receive their power from him. They are to go as they are, without a change of clothing or a second pair of shoes. Nor are they to take either money or food; rather they must trust God to care for them. And they are to stay at the home of whoever takes them in and not go elsewhere. In this manner they would learn that God takes care of his messengers and supplies their every need.

9:7 *Herod the tetrarch*, i.e., "Herod the governor."

9:10ff The four Gospels all report the feeding of the five thousand. Mark says that the grass was green, which means that the feeding took place shortly before the feast of the Passover, which falls in March-April. Jesus gave a blessing before distributing the food. The Jews usually prayed, "Blessed art thou, O Lord our God, King of the universe, who bringest forth bread from the earth." Perhaps this is what Jesus prayed. No food was wasted. Whatever was left over was gathered and kept. The type of basket was what Jews carried filled with food so that when they traveled they would not need to buy bread from pagans, for that would be unclean.

9:13 *Give ye them to eat.* Earlier Jesus had sent his disciples to preach and to heal. He gave them authority and power (Luke 9:1). Now he tells them to exercise this power to feed the hungry multitudes. The disciples had the power, but were either unaware of it or did not have the faith to meet the challenge. Their response shows the barrenness of their understanding of what they had in Jesus Christ. Since Pentecost, the Holy Spirit has empowered believers; there are few, however, who understand the possibilities or who use the power available to them.

more but five loaves and two fishes; except we should go and buy meat for all this people.

14 For they were about five thousand men. And he said to his disciples, Make them sit down by fifties in a company.

15 And they did so, and made them all sit down.

16 Then he took the five loaves and the two fishes, and looking up to heaven, he blessed them, and brake, and gave to the disciples to set before the multitude.

9:17 Ps 145:15, 16 Prov 10:22

17 And they did eat, and were all filled: and there was taken up of fragments that remained to them twelve baskets.

Y. PETER'S CONFESSION AND JESUS' PREDICTION OF HIS DEATH AND RESURRECTION (CF. MT 16:13–28; MK 8:27—9:2)

9:18☆ Mt 16:13–20 Mk 8:27–30

18 ¶And it came to pass, as he was alone praying, his disciples were with him: and he asked them, saying, Whom say the people that I am?

9:19 Mt 14:2

19 They answering said, John the Baptist; but some *say*, E-li'as; and others *say*, that one of the old prophets is risen again.

9:20☆ Jn 6:69 Rom 10:9 1 Jn 4:14, 15 5:5

20 He said unto them, But whom say ye that I am? Peter answering said, The Christ of God.

21 And he straitly charged them, and commanded *them* to tell no man that thing;

9:22 Mt 16:21–28 17:22; 20:17 Mk 8:31—9:1, 31 Lk 18:31 24:6, 7

22 Saying, The Son of man must suffer many things, and be rejected of the elders and chief priests and scribes, and be slain, and be raised the third day.

9:23☆ Mt 10:38 Lk 14:27

23 ¶And he said to *them* all, If any *man* will come after me, let him deny himself, and take up his cross daily, and follow me.

9:24 Mt 10:39

24 For whosoever will save his life shall lose it: but whosoever will lose his life for my sake, the same shall save it.

25 For what is a man advantaged, if he gain the whole world, and lose himself, or be cast away?

9:26 Mt 10:33 2 Tim 2:12

26 For whosoever shall be ashamed of me and of my words, of him shall the Son of man be ashamed, when he shall come in his own glory, and *in his* Father's, and of the holy angels.

27 But I tell you of a truth, there be some standing here, which shall not taste of death, till they see the kingdom of God.

Z. JESUS' CHANGE IN APPEARANCE (THE TRANSFIGURATION) (CF. MT 17:1–8; MK 9:2–13)

9:28☆ Mt 17:1–13 Mk 9:2–13

28 ¶And it came to pass about an eight days after these sayings, he took Peter and John and James, and went up into a mountain to pray.

9:29☆ Ex 34:29, 35

29 And as he prayed, the fashion of his countenance was altered, and his raiment *was* white *and* glistering.

9:18ff Jesus was alone and praying until his disciples came near him. When he asks them who men said he was, they respond with a number of suggestions: Elijah, John the Baptist and others. When he asks them to say who *they* think he is, Peter rises to the occasion by declaring Jesus to be "the Christ of God." This *opens the door for him* to tell them what it means to be the Christ of God. He forecasts his rejection, his death, and his resurrection; but they fail to understand, as we discover later.

9:20 See note on Matt. 16:19 regarding Peter, the church, and the keys to the kingdom.

9:23ff Jesus now tells his disciples that they are not to prevent his suffering but rather prepare for their own. They should choose the good of their souls before any other concern. They are to deny self, exercise patience, mortify themselves, and endure hardship as his followers. Their souls are at stake. Matthew and Mark speak about losing the soul. Luke speaks of a man losing himself, for the soul is the self. Jesus says that, when weighed in the balance, the whole world is not worth the price of the soul.

9:28ff For the Transfiguration account see note to Mark 9:2.

9:29 *the fashion of his countenance was altered,* i.e., "the appearance of his face became different" (NASB).

30 And, behold, there talked with him two men, which were Moses and
E-li'as:
31 Who appeared in glory, and spake of his decease which he should
accomplish at Jerusalem.
32 But Peter and they that were with him were heavy with sleep: and when
they were awake, they saw his glory, and the two men that stood with him.
33 And it came to pass, as they departed from him, Peter said unto Jesus,
Master, it is good for us to be here: and let us make three tabernacles; one
for thee, and one for Moses, and one for E-li'as: not knowing what he said.
34 While he thus spake, there came a cloud, and overshadowed them: and
they feared as they entered into the cloud.
35 And there came a voice out of the cloud, saying, This is my beloved
Son: hear him.
36 And when the voice was past, Jesus was found alone. And they kept *it*
close, and told no man in those days any of those things which they had
seen.

9:30 2 Kgs 2:11; Rom 3:21
9:31 Rom 3:21; Col 3:4; 2 Pet 1:15; 1 Jn 3:2
9:32 Dan 8:18; 10:9
9:35 Ex 23:21; Deut 18:15, 18; Mt 3:17; Acts 3:22; Heb 2:3; 2 Pet 1:16, 17

AA. THE DEMON-POSSESSED BOY DELIVERED (CF. MT 17:14–21; MK 9:14–29)

37 ¶And it came to pass, that on the next day, when they were come down
from the hill, much people met him.
38 And, behold, a man of the company cried out, saying, Master, I beseech
thee, look upon my son: for he is mine only child.
39 And, lo, a spirit taketh him, and he suddenly crieth out; and it teareth
him that he foameth again, and bruising him hardly departeth from him.
40 And I besought thy disciples to cast him out; and they could not.
41 And Jesus answering said, O faithless and perverse generation, how
long shall I be with you, and suffer you? Bring thy son hither.
42 And as he was yet a coming, the devil threw him down, and tare *him*.
And Jesus rebuked the unclean spirit, and healed the child, and delivered
him again to his father.

☆9:37 Mt 17:14–21; Mk 9:14–29
9:38 Lk 7:12

BB. JESUS' SECOND PREDICTION OF HIS DEATH AND RESURRECTION (CF. MT 17:22, 23; MK 9:30–32)

43 ¶And they were all amazed at the mighty power of God. But while they
wondered every one at all things which Jesus did, he said unto his disciples,
44 Let these sayings sink down into your ears: for the Son of man shall be
delivered into the hands of men.
45 But they understood not this saying, and it was hid from them, that
they perceived it not: and they feared to ask him of that saying.

9:43 Mt 17:22, 23; Mk 9:30–32; 2 Pet 1:16
9:44 Mt 17:22, 23; Mk 9:30–32
☆9:45 Lk 2:50; 18:34

CC. THE LESSON ON HUMILITY AND FORGIVENESS (CF. MT 18:1–6; MK 9:33–40)

46 ¶Then there arose a reasoning among them, which of them should be
greatest.

☆9:46 Mt 18; Mk 9:33–40

9:37ff The awe-inspiring experience on the mount of Transfiguration gives way to the problems and needs of everyday life, as they come back to the plains. An unnamed man's only son is torn, bruised, and possessed of an evil spirit. Jesus' other disciples had been unable to help this man, so he appeals to the Master. They should have been able to help, but they lacked faith. Jesus had given them the power to heal and to cast out demons. So Jesus brought healing and health, done in a manner that left them all wondering in amazement.

9:45 *they understood not this saying.* We, like the disciples, are often left in the dark, lacking understanding and wondering whether in fact what God has done is the right thing to do. Perhaps their inability to see and understand was due to the fact that they were expecting a kingdom under Jesus in which they would be sitting in seats of authority and lording it over everything. Indeed they began to argue about which of them would be greatest in that kingdom.

9:46 So sharp was the argument that nothing would satisfy any one of them short of being greatest in Christ's kingdom. So Jesus had to teach them the lesson of humility.

9:47☆ Mt 9:4 Jn 2:24, 25
47 And Jesus, perceiving the thought of their heart, took a child, and set
him by him,

9:48☆ Mt 10:40 23:11, 12 Lk 18:17, 22:26 Jn 12:44; 13:20
48 And said unto them, Whosoever shall receive this child in my name
receiveth me: and whosoever shall receive me receiveth him that sent me:
for he that is least among you all, the same shall be great.

9:49☆ Num 11:28
49 ¶And John answered and said, Master, we saw one casting out devils in
thy name; and we forbad him, because he followeth not with us.

9:50☆ Mt 12:30 Lk 11:23 1 Cor 12:3
50 And Jesus said unto him, Forbid *him* not: for he that is not against us
is for us.

V. THE JOURNEY FROM GALILEE TO JERUSALEM (9:51—19:44)

A. FURTHER LESSONS IN DISCIPLESHIP (CF. MT 8:18–22)

9:51 Mt 19:1, 2 8:18–22 Mk 10:1; 16:19 Lk 13:22; 17:11 18:31 19:28; 24:51 Acts 1:2
51 ¶And it came to pass, when the time was come that he should be
received up, he stedfastly set his face to go to Jerusalem,
52 And sent messengers before his face: and they went, and entered into a
village of the Sa-mar′i-tans, to make ready for him.

9:53☆
53 And they did not receive him, because his face was as though he would
go to Jerusalem.

9:54☆ 2 Kgs 1:10, 12
54 And when his disciples James and John saw *this*, they said, Lord, wilt
thou that we command fire to come down from heaven, and consume them,
even as E-li′as did?

9:55☆ Rom 10:2
55 But he turned, and rebuked them, and said, Ye know not what manner
of spirit ye are of.

9:56☆
56 For the Son of man is not come to destroy men's lives, but to save *them*.
And they went to another village.
57 ¶And it came to pass, that, as they went in the way, a certain *man* said
unto him, Lord, I will follow thee whithersoever thou goest.
58 And Jesus said unto him, Foxes have holes, and birds of the air *have*
nests; but the Son of man hath not where to lay *his* head.
59 And he said unto another, Follow me. But he said, Lord, suffer me first
to go and bury my father.

9:60 Mt 4:23
60 Jesus said unto him, Let the dead bury their dead: but go thou and
preach the kingdom of God.

9:61 1 Kgs 19:20
61 And another also said, Lord, I will follow thee; but let me first go bid
them farewell, which are at home at my house.

9:47 *perceiving the thought of their heart.* Jesus knew then, and knows now, the thoughts and intentions of every heart. Thoughts are words to him and whispers are loud cries. This omniscience should cause us to be careful about our thought lives, lest we fall into the same trap that the disciples fell into.

9:48 The lesson of being like a little child supports the thesis that even as Jesus stooped to conquer, so must his disciples be willing to be least in the kingdom.

9:49 The disciples of Jesus, the inner circle of the twelve, constituted a select group. They could bear with no activities by others that would rival their own position. So John, speaking for all, says that they forbade a man to cast out demons since he was not a *member of the special* circle.

9:50 Here Jesus says, *"He that is not against us is for* us," while in Luke 11:23 he seems to be saying the exact opposite: "He that is not with me is against me." The explanation is that both statements are true when the context is understood. In Luke 9:50 Jesus refers to those who are for him but who are not openly associated with the disciples. They are not opponents of Jesus but friends who believe in him and seek to serve him through faith and prayer. In Luke 11:23 Jesus refers to those who are not his followers in any true sense, and thus are against him. There can be no neutrality about our relationship to Jesus. Either we are for him or against him.

9:53 This was a typical case of discrimination (cf. John 4:9). The Jews called the Samaritans "half-breeds," so the Samaritans naturally hated the Jews.†

9:54 *even as Elias did.* The best ancient manuscripts do not have this phrase. But the reference to fire undoubtedly goes back to Elijah on Mount Carmel. Here John and James, whom Jesus calls the "sons of thunder," now want to become the sons of lightning. *What was right in Elijah's situation was wrong in this* one. Great discernment is required to know the difference.

9:55, 56 *Ye know not what manner of spirit . . . but to save them.* These words are not present in the best, ancient manuscripts.

[62] And Jesus said unto him, No man, having put his hand to the plough, and looking back, is fit for the kingdom of God.

B. THE SENDING OF THE SEVENTY

10 AFTER these things the Lord appointed other seventy also, and sent them two and two before his face into every city and place, whither he himself would come.

[2] Therefore said he unto them, The harvest truly *is* great, but the labourers *are* few: pray ye therefore the Lord of the harvest, that he would send forth labourers into his harvest.

[3] Go your ways: behold, I send you forth as lambs among wolves.

[4] Carry neither purse, nor scrip, nor shoes: and salute no man by the way.

[5] And into whatsoever house ye enter, first say, Peace *be* to this house.

[6] And if the son of peace be there, your peace shall rest upon it: if not, it shall turn to you again.

[7] And in the same house remain, eating and drinking such things as they give: for the labourer is worthy of his hire. Go not from house to house.

[8] And into whatsoever city ye enter, and they receive you, eat such things as are set before you:

[9] And heal the sick that are therein, and say unto them, The kingdom of God is come nigh unto you.

[10] But into whatsoever city ye enter, and they receive you not, go your ways out into the streets of the same, and say,

[11] Even the very dust of your city, which cleaveth on us, we do wipe off against you: notwithstanding be ye sure of this, that the kingdom of God is come nigh unto you.

[12] But I say unto you, that it shall be more tolerable in that day for Sodom, than for that city.

[13] Woe unto thee, Cho-ra'zin! woe unto thee, Beth-sa'i-da! for if the mighty works had been done in Tyre and Si'don, which have been done in you, they had a great while ago repented, sitting in sackcloth and ashes.

[14] But it shall be more tolerable for Tyre and Si'don at the judgment, than for you.

[15] And thou, Ca-per'na-um, which art exalted to heaven, shalt be thrust down to hell.

[16] He that heareth you heareth me; and he that despiseth you despiseth me; and he that despiseth me despiseth him that sent me.

9:62 Phil 3:13; Heb 6:4
☆**10:1** Mt 10:1; Mk 6:7
10:2 Jer 3:15; Mt 9:37, 38; Jn 4:35; 1 Cor 12:28; 2 Thess 3:1
10:3 Mt 10:16
10:4 2 Kgs 4:29; Mt 10:9; Mk 6:8; Lk 9:3
10:5 Mt 10:12
10:7 Mt 10:10, 11; 1 Cor 9:4; 10:27; Eph 5:15; 1 Tim 5:18
10:8 1 Cor 10:8
10:9 Isa 2:2; Mt 3:2; 10:7; Lk 9:2; Rom 10:8; Tit 2:11
10:11 Mt 10:14; Lk 9:5; Acts 13:51; 18:6
☆**10:12** Mt 10:15; Heb 6:4–8
☆**10:13** Ezek 3:6; Mt 11:21; Jn 3:5
☆**10:14**
☆**10:15** Gen 11:4; Deut 1:28; Isa 14:13; Jer 51:53; Ezek 26:20; 32:18; Mt 11:23
10:16 Mt 10:40; Jn 5:23; 13:20; 1 Thess 4:8

10:1 The sending of the seventy indicates the growing numbers of those who followed Jesus. Luke alone records this incident for us. The number seventy recurs often in Scripture. Seventy elders went with Moses and Aaron to see God's glory (Exod. 24:1, 9). Seventy were chosen to assist Moses in governing Israel (Num. 11:24, 25). The Sanhedrin had seventy members. Tradition has it that the Septuagint (the Greek version of the Old Testament) was translated by seventy men in seventy days.

10:12 *in that day.* This refers to the day of judgment. Other Scripture passages indicate there are to be two judgments. One is the believers' judgment. The other is the judgment of the great white throne (Rev. 20:11ff). The latter is the one referred to here, for it is the final judgment comparable to that which destroyed Sodom.

10:13, 14 Christ pronounces doom on Chorazin, Bethsaida, and Capernaum—cities where much of his evangelizing work had been done. They enjoyed greater privileges and opportunities than did Tyre and Sidon. There was reason to suppose that had Christ gone to Tyre and Sidon, they would have repented. He did come to Chorazin, Bethsaida, and Capernaum, and they did not repent except for a few. Having had the privilege of hearing Christ, their punishment shall be greater than that pronounced upon Tyre and Sidon, who did not hear Christ.

10:15 *hell* is derived from the Greek word *hades* or *haides*, meaning "not to be seen." *Hades* is the New Testament equivalent for the Old Testament *sheol*. Sheol was the general abode of the dead, both good and bad. Progressive revelation has added to our knowledge. *Hades* in the New Testament may mean an actual place, as in 16:23, or the state of death itself, as in Acts 2:27–31. When anyone speaks of people "going to hell" it does not mean the state of being dead but the everlasting abode of the wicked dead which is denominated by one of two terms: (1) the lake of fire (Rev. 20:15); (2) Gehenna (for which see the note to Matt. 18:9). Hell or hades is *not* the eternal abode of the wicked.

17 ¶And the seventy returned again with joy, saying, Lord, even the devils
are subject unto us through thy name.
18 And he said unto them, I beheld Satan as lightning fall from heaven.
19 Behold, I give unto you power to tread on serpents and scorpions, and
over all the power of the enemy: and nothing shall by any means hurt you.
20 Notwithstanding in this rejoice not, that the spirits are subject unto
you; but rather rejoice, because your names are written in heaven.
21 In that hour Jesus rejoiced in spirit, and said, I thank thee, O Father,
Lord of heaven and earth, that thou hast hid these things from the wise and
prudent, and hast revealed them unto babes: even so, Father; for so it
seemed good in thy sight.
22 All things are delivered to me of my Father: and no man knoweth who
the Son is, but the Father; and who the Father is, but the Son, and *he* to
whom the Son will reveal *him*.
23 ¶And he turned him unto *his* disciples, and said privately, Blessed *are*
the eyes which see the things that ye see:
24 For I tell you, that many prophets and kings have desired to see those
things which ye see, and have not seen *them;* and to hear those things which
ye hear, and have not heard *them*.

C. THE PARABLE OF THE GOOD SAMARITAN

25 ¶And, behold, a certain lawyer stood up, and tempted him, saying,
Master, what shall I do to inherit eternal life?
26 He said unto him, What is written in the law? how readest thou?
27 And he answering said, Thou shalt love the Lord thy God with all thy
heart, and with all thy soul, and with all thy strength, and with all thy
mind; and thy neighbour as thyself.
28 And he said unto him, Thou hast answered right: this do, and thou
shalt live.
29 But he, willing to justify himself, said unto Jesus, And who is my
neighbour?
30 And Jesus answering said, A certain *man* went down from Jerusalem to
Jericho, and fell among thieves, which stripped him of his raiment, and
wounded *him*, and departed, leaving *him* half dead.
31 And by chance there came down a certain priest that way: and when he
saw him, he passed by on the other side.
32 And likewise a Levite, when he was at the place, came and looked *on
him*, and passed by on the other side.
33 But a certain Sa-mar'i-tan, as he journeyed, came where he was: and
when he saw him, he had compassion *on him*,

10:17☆
10:18 Jn 12:31; 1 Jn 3:8; Rev 9:1; 12:8, 9
10:19 Acts 28:5
10:20 Ex 32:32; Ps 69:28; Isa 4:3; Phil 4:3; Rev 20:12
10:21 Mt 11:25; 1 Cor 1:19; 2 Cor 2:6
10:22 Mt 28:18; Jn 1:18; 3:35; 5:27; 17:2; Eph 1:21; 2:9
10:23 Mt 13:16
10:24 1 Pet 1:10
10:25 Mt 22:34–40; Mk 12:28–31
10:27 Deut 6:5; Lev 19:18
10:28 Lev 18:5; Neh 9:29; Ezek 20:11; Rom 10:5
10:29 Lk 16:15
10:30☆
10:31 Ps 38:11
10:33 Jn 4:9

10:17ff The seventy returned, declaring that their ministry was successful to the extent that even demons were subjected to them. Jesus agreed with their words about the demons and stated that he saw Satan fall as lightning from heaven. The prince of this world is cast out (John 12:31). He repeated and enlarged the commission of the seventy, who now would have power to trample down serpents and not be hurt by *scorpions or serpents. Nevertheless,* he said that having their names written down in heaven is better and greater than having power over demons.

10:30ff The story of the good Samaritan is reported only by Luke. It must be understood within the context in which it was told. An expert in Moses' law asked Jesus what he needed to do to inherit eternal life. Jesus gave him the first table of the law: love God with your whole heart. Then he added the central thrust of the second table of the law: love your neighbor as yourself. The Jews of Jesus' day considered only their fellow Jews to be neighbors. When the legal expert asked Jesus to tell him who his neighbor was, Jesus gave him the illustration of the good Samaritan. The Jews who passed by the injured man did nothing, even though he was a Jew. The Samaritan had cared for him. When pressed by Jesus, the Jew had to admit that the Samaritan loved his neighbor while the Jews did not. In this parable, Jesus did not say that the Samaritan was saved by his good works. Elsewhere he made it plain that salvation is by faith alone, not of good works (John 6:28, 29; cf. Matt. 7:22, 23).

34 And went to *him*, and bound up his wounds, pouring in oil and wine,
and set him on his own beast, and brought him to an inn, and took care of
him.
35 And on the morrow when he departed, he took out two pence, and gave
them to the host, and said unto him, Take care of him; and whatsoever thou
spendest more, when I come again, I will repay thee.
36 Which now of these three, thinkest thou, was neighbour unto him that
fell among the thieves?
37 And he said, He that shewed mercy on him. Then said Jesus unto him,
Go, and do thou likewise.

D. JESUS VISITS MARY AND MARTHA

38 ¶Now it came to pass, as they went, that he entered into a certain
village: and a certain woman named Martha received him into her house.
39 And she had a sister called Mary, which also sat at Jesus' feet, and
heard his word.
40 But Martha was cumbered about much serving, and came to him, and
said, Lord, dost thou not care that my sister hath left me to serve alone? bid
her therefore that she help me.
41 And Jesus answered and said unto her, Martha, Martha, thou art
careful and troubled about many things:
42 But one thing is needful: and Mary hath chosen that good part, which
shall not be taken away from her.

E. JESUS' TEACHING ON PRAYER (CF. MT 6:5–15)

11 AND it came to pass, that, as he was praying in a certain place,
when he ceased, one of his disciples said unto him, Lord, teach us to
pray, as John also taught his disciples.
2 And he said unto them, When ye pray, say, Our Father which art in
heaven, Hallowed be thy name. Thy kingdom come. Thy will be done, as in
heaven, so in earth.
3 Give us day by day our daily bread.
4 And forgive us our sins; for we also forgive every one that is indebted to
us. And lead us not into temptation; but deliver us from evil.
5 And he said unto them, Which of you shall have a friend, and shall go
unto him at midnight, and say unto him, Friend, lend me three loaves;
6 For a friend of mine in his journey is come to me, and I have nothing to
set before him?
7 And he from within shall answer and say, Trouble me not: the door is
now shut, and my children are with me in bed; I cannot rise and give thee.
8 I say unto you, Though he will not rise and give him, because he is his
friend, yet because of his importunity he will rise and give him as many as
he needeth.
9 And I say unto you, Ask, and it shall be given you; seek, and ye shall
find; knock, and it shall be opened unto you.
10 For every one that asketh receiveth; and he that seeketh findeth; and to
him that knocketh it shall be opened.

☆**10:35** Philem 18
10:38 Jn 11:1, 5, 19, 30, 39; 12:2
10:39 Jn 11:1, 19, 28, 45; 12:3 Acts 22:3
☆**10:40**
10:41 Mt 6:25
10:42 Ps 27:4 Phil 3:13, 14
☆**11:1** 2 Cor 3:5
11:2 Isa 11:9; 63:16 Dan 7:14
☆**11:4** Eph 4:32 1 Cor 10:13 Jas 1:13 Rev 3:10
☆**11:8** Lk 18:1
11:9 Mt 7:7; 21:22 Mk 11:24 Jn 15:7 Jas 1:6 1 Jn 3:22; 5:14

10:35 *two pence*, the equivalent of two days' wages.
10:40 Here are two sisters who act quite differently. Martha, who was busy serving, was distressed because Mary did not help her. Jesus avers that there is a need to maintain a right balance between the life of active service and that of quiet meditation and communion with the Lord. Serving Jesus a meal was not as important as sitting at his feet and learning what he had to teach.
11:1 *to pray*. See note on Matt. 7:7 about principles of prayer.
11:4 Some manuscripts add to this verse additional portions of the Lord's Prayer as recorded in Matt. 6:9–13. The words *but deliver us from evil* do not appear in the best manuscripts.
11:8 Here and in Luke 18:1–6 Jesus encourages importunity in prayer. We are never to let God go until the answers have come.

11:11 Mt 7:9
[11]If a son shall ask bread of any of you that is a father, will he give him
a stone? or if *he ask* a fish, will he for a fish give him a serpent?
11:12☆
[12]Or if he shall ask an egg, will he offer him a scorpion?
11:13 Isa 44:3 Jas 1:15
[13]If ye then, being evil, know how to give good gifts unto your children:
how much more shall *your* heavenly Father give the Holy Spirit to them
that ask him?

F. JESUS REPLIES TO THE PHARISEES' SLANDER (CF. MT 12:22–45; MK 3:20–30)

11:14 Mt 9:32; 12:22–32; 38–45 Mk 3:22–30
[14]¶And he was casting out a devil, and it was dumb. And it came to pass,
when the devil was gone out, the dumb spake; and the people wondered.
11:15☆ Mt 9:34
[15]But some of them said, He casteth out devils through Be-el′ze-bub the
chief of the devils.
11:16☆ Mt 16:1
[16]And others, tempting *him,* sought of him a sign from heaven.
11:17 Jn 2:25 Rev 2:23
[17]But he, knowing their thoughts, said unto them, Every kingdom divided
against itself is brought to desolation; and a house *divided* against a house
falleth.
[18]If Satan also be divided against himself, how shall his kingdom stand?
because ye say that I cast out devils through Be-el′ze-bub.
11:19 Mk 9:38 Lk 9:49
[19]And if I by Be-el′ze-bub cast out devils, by whom do your sons cast
them out? therefore shall they be your judges.
11:20 Ex 8:19 Jn 3:2 Acts 2:22; 10:38
[20]But if I with the finger of God cast out devils, no doubt the kingdom of
God is come upon you.
11:21☆ Eph 2:2; 6:12 1 Pet 5:8
[21]When a strong man armed keepeth his palace, his goods are in peace:
11:22☆ Isa 53:12 Col 2:15 Heb 7:25
[22]But when a stronger than he shall come upon him, and overcome him,
he taketh from him all his armour wherein he trusted, and divideth his
spoils.
[23]He that is not with me is against me: and he that gathereth not with me
scattereth.
[24]When the unclean spirit is gone out of a man, he walketh through dry
places, seeking rest; and finding none, he saith, I will return unto my house
whence I came out.
[25]And when he cometh, he findeth *it* swept and garnished.
11:26 Jn 5:14 Heb 6:4; 10:26 2 Pet 2:20
[26]Then goeth he, and taketh *to him* seven other spirits more wicked than
himself; and they enter in, and dwell there: and the last *state* of that man is
worse than the first.
11:27 Lk 1:28, 48
[27]¶And it came to pass, as he spake these things, a certain woman of the
company lifted up her voice, and said unto him, Blessed *is* the womb that
bare thee, and the paps which thou hast sucked.
11:28 Mt 7:21 Lk 8:21 Jas 1:25
[28]But he said, Yea rather, blessed *are* they that hear the word of God, and
keep it.

G. JESUS TEACHES THE MULTITUDES

1. Warning against Looking for Signs from the Heavens (Cf. Mt 12:38–42)

11:29☆ Mt 12:38–40
[29]¶And when the people were gathered thick together, he began to say,
This is an evil generation: they seek a sign; and there shall no sign be given
it, but the sign of Jonas the prophet.

11:12 *will he offer him a scorpion?* This is a hypothetical question, the answer to which is self-evident. A father will not give his son a scorpion instead of bread.

11:15 *Beelzebub,* i.e., "Satan." (See note on Matt. 10:25.)

11:16 *a sign from heaven,* i.e., something spectacular to prove that he is the Messiah.

11:21, 22 *when a strong man armed keepeth his palace.* This refers to Satan, who thinks all is well because of his armor. But that which Satan trusts in will be taken from him by One stronger than he.

11:29 See note on Matt. 12:40 about Jonah and the queen of Sheba.

30 For as Jonas was a sign unto the Nin′e-vites, so shall also the Son of
man be to this generation.

11:30 Jonah 1:17; 2:10

31 The queen of the south shall rise up in the judgment with the men of
this generation, and condemn them: for she came from the utmost parts of
the earth to hear the wisdom of Solomon; and, behold, a greater than
Solomon *is* here.

☆**11:31** 1 Kgs 10:1 Isa 9:6 Rom 9:5 Phil 2:10 Tit 2:13

32 The men of Nin′e-ve shall rise up in the judgment with this generation,
and shall condemn it: for they repented at the preaching of Jonas; and,
behold, a greater than Jonas *is* here.

☆**11:32** Jn 3:5

2. The Parable of the Lighted Candle

33 No man, when he hath lighted a candle, putteth *it* in a secret place,
neither under a bushel, but on a candlestick, that they which come in may
see the light.

11:33 Mt 5:15 Mk 4:21 Lk 8:16

34 The light of the body is the eye: therefore when thine eye is single, thy
whole body also is full of light; but when *thine eye* is evil, thy body also *is*
full of darkness.

☆**11:34** Mt 6:22

35 Take heed therefore that the light which is in thee be not darkness.
36 If thy whole body therefore *be* full of light, having no part dark, the
whole shall be full of light, as when the bright shining of a candle doth give
thee light.

3. Denunciation of the Pharisees

37 ¶And as he spake, a certain Pharisee besought him to dine with him:
and he went in, and sat down to meat.
38 And when the Pharisee saw *it*, he marvelled that he had not first washed
before dinner.

11:38 Mk 7:3

39 And the Lord said unto him, Now do ye Pharisees make clean the
outside of the cup and the platter; but your inward part is full of ravening
and wickedness.

11:39 Mt 23:25 2 Tim 3:5 Tit 1:15

40 *Ye* fools, did not he that made that which is without make that which is
within also?
41 But rather give alms of such things as ye have; and, behold, all things
are clean unto you.

11:41 Isa 58:7 Dan 4:27 Lk 12:33 Tit 1:15

42 But woe unto you, Pharisees! for ye tithe mint and rue and all manner
of herbs, and pass over judgment and the love of God: these ought ye to
have done, and not to leave the other undone.

11:42 Mt 23:23 1 Sam 15:22 Hos 6:6

43 Woe unto you, Pharisees! for ye love the uppermost seats in the
synagogues, and greetings in the markets.

11:43 Mt 23:6, 7 Mk 12:38, 39

44 Woe unto you, scribes and Pharisees, hypocrites! for ye are as graves
which appear not, and the men that walk over *them* are not aware *of them.*
45 ¶Then answered one of the lawyers, and said unto him, Master, thus
saying thou reproachest us also.
46 And he said, Woe unto you also, *ye* lawyers! for ye lade men with
burdens grievous to be borne, and ye yourselves touch not the burdens with
one of your fingers.

11:46 Mt 23:4

47 Woe unto you! for ye build the sepulchres of the prophets, and your
fathers killed them.

11:47 Mt 23:29–36 Acts 7:51, 52

11:31 *queen of the south*, i.e., "queen of Sheba."
11:32 *a greater than Jonas is here.* Nineveh repented due to the preaching of Jonah. Now Christ, who is greater, has come; but the Jewish nation to whom he is preaching will not learn from Nineveh. They refuse to repent.
11:34 *The light of the body is the eye.* When the eye is sound and the light is shining, the beholder can see where he is and can know how to walk and do his work. When the eye is blinded, the whole body is wrapped in darkness. Christ is the light who keeps shining, but the wrong inner nature of sinners keeps them from seeing the light of Christ.

11:48 Acts 8:1; 22:20
11:49 Prov 8:12, 22–31; Mt 11:19; 23:34; Lk 7:35; 1 Cor 1:24, 30; Col 2:3
11:50 1 Thess 2:15
11:51☆ Gen 4:8; 2 Chron 24:20, 21
11:52 Mt 23:13
11:53 Mk 12:13

48 Truly ye bear witness that ye allow the deeds of your fathers: for they indeed killed them, and ye build their sepulchres.

49 Therefore also said the wisdom of God, I will send them prophets and apostles, and *some* of them they shall slay and persecute:

50 That the blood of all the prophets, which was shed from the foundation of the world, may be required of this generation;

51 From the blood of Abel unto the blood of Zach-a-ri'as, which perished between the altar and the temple: verily I say unto you, It shall be required of this generation.

52 Woe unto you, lawyers! for ye have taken away the key of knowledge: ye entered not in yourselves, and them that were entering in ye hindered.

53 And as he said these things unto them, the scribes and the Pharisees began to urge *him* vehemently, and to provoke him to speak of many things:

54 Laying wait for him, and seeking to catch something out of his mouth, that they might accuse him.

4. The Warning about the Leaven of the Pharisees

12:1☆ Mt 16:6, 11, 12; Mk 8:15
12:2 Mt 10:26–33; Mk 4:22; Lk 8:17
12:5☆ Heb 10:31; Rev 1:17, 18
12:8 Rom 10:9–11; Rev 3:5
12:9 Mk 8:38; Lk 9:26; 2 Tim 2:12
12:10 Mt 12:31, 32; Mk 3:28, 29; 1 Jn 5:16

12 IN the mean time, when there were gathered together an innumerable multitude of people, insomuch that they trode one upon another, he began to say unto his disciples first of all, Beware ye of the leaven of the Pharisees, which is hypocrisy.

2 For there is nothing covered, that shall not be revealed; neither hid, that shall not be known.

3 Therefore whatsoever ye have spoken in darkness shall be heard in the light; and that which ye have spoken in the ear in closets shall be proclaimed upon the housetops.

4 And I say unto you my friends, Be not afraid of them that kill the body, and after that have no more that they can do.

5 But I will forewarn you whom ye shall fear: Fear him, which after he hath killed hath power to cast into hell; yea, I say unto you, Fear him.

6 Are not five sparrows sold for two farthings, and not one of them is forgotten before God?

7 But even the very hairs of your head are all numbered. Fear not therefore: ye are of more value than many sparrows.

8 Also I say unto you, Whosoever shall confess me before men, him shall the Son of man also confess before the angels of God:

9 But he that denieth me before men shall be denied before the angels of God.

10 And whosoever shall speak a word against the Son of man, it shall be forgiven him: but unto him that blasphemeth against the Holy Ghost it shall not be forgiven.

11:51 See note on Matt. 23:35 about Abel and Zacharias.

12:1 In warning against the hypocrisy of the Pharisees, Jesus wants his disciples to know he is opposed to the same sin among his followers. Good men must be warned against this sin, remembering that nothing is covered that will not be revealed. What is done in the darkness will be made known in the light.

12:5 *hell* (*gehenna* in the Greek). Those who do not believe in the reality of hell usually entertain one of three views which negate its existence: (1) annihilationism, which says God is too loving to permit men to suffer forever; therefore he annihilates their souls at some point after physical death; (2) restorationism, which teaches that God cannot condemn men to eternal punishment forever, so he ultimately restores them to fellowship with himself in heaven, no matter how long it takes to do so; (3) presentism, which teaches that men experience their heaven or hell here on earth during this life, with rewards or retribution meted out in the here and now. All these views are false. The Bible teaches the reality of the eternal *gehenna*, symbolized by the lake of fire.

11 And when they bring you unto the synagogues, and *unto* magistrates,
and powers, take ye no thought how or what thing ye shall answer, or what
ye shall say:
12 For the Holy Ghost shall teach you in the same hour what ye ought to
say.

12:11 Ex 4:12; Mt 10:19, 20; Mk 13:11; Lk 21:14, 15; 1 Pet 5:7

5. The Parable of the Wealthy Fool

13 ¶And one of the company said unto him, Master, speak to my brother,
that he divide the inheritance with me.
14 And he said unto him, Man, who made me a judge or a divider over
you?
15 And he said unto them, Take heed, and beware of covetousness: for a
man's life consisteth not in the abundance of the things which he
possesseth.
16 And he spake a parable unto them, saying, The ground of a certain rich
man brought forth plentifully:
17 And he thought within himself, saying, What shall I do, because I have
no room where to bestow my fruits?
18 And he said, This will I do: I will pull down my barns, and build
greater; and there will I bestow all my fruits and my goods.
19 And I will say to my soul, Soul, thou hast much goods laid up for many
years; take thine ease, eat, drink, *and* be merry.
20 But God said unto him, *Thou* fool, this night thy soul shall be required
of thee: then whose shall those things be, which thou hast provided?
21 So *is* he that layeth up treasure for himself, and is not rich toward God.

12:14 Acts 7:27
12:15 1 Tim 6:6–10; Heb 13:5
☆**12:16**
12:19 Prov 27:1; Eccles 11:9; 1 Cor 15:32; Jas 5:1–5
12:20 Job 27:8; Ps 39:5, 6; Jer 17:11; 1 Thess 5:3; Jas 4:14
12:21 Hab 2:9; 1 Tim 6:18, 19; Jas 2:5

6. Worry versus Faith or Trust

22 ¶And he said unto his disciples, Therefore I say unto you, Take no
thought for your life, what ye shall eat; neither for the body, what ye shall
put on.
23 The life is more than meat, and the body *is more* than raiment.
24 Consider the ravens: for they neither sow nor reap; which neither have
storehouse nor barn; and God feedeth them: how much more are ye better
than the fowls?
25 And which of you with taking thought can add to his stature one cubit?
26 If ye then be not able to do that thing which is least, why take ye
thought for the rest?
27 Consider the lilies how they grow: they toil not, they spin not; and yet
I say unto you, that Solomon in all his glory was not arrayed like one of
these.
28 If then God so clothe the grass, which is to day in the field, and to
morrow is cast into the oven; how much more *will he clothe* you, O ye of
little faith?

☆**12:22** Mt 6:25–33; Phil 4:6
☆**12:23**
12:24 Job 38:41; Ps 147:9
12:25 Ps 39:5
12:27 1 Kgs 10:1–10
☆**12:28**

12:16ff Worldliness concerns itself with this life and its material aspects. Christ warns against this attitude, which always involves covetousness. Scripture does not teach that wealth *per se* is evil, nor does it endorse a disregard of life's practical considerations. But when wealth becomes an end in itself it is a snare and a sin. Wealthy believers must take special precautions, since material possessions constitute a source of temptation. (See Matt. 6:20, 32–34; 19:16–24.)

12:22 Jesus had far more disciples than the twelve who comprised the inner circle. Here he speaks to a larger gathering of disciples about the problem of anxiety—a sign of a lack of faith.

12:23 God has already done for believers the greater thing—he has given them eternal life. And he who has done the greater can also do the lesser; he will provide food and drink for his people so that they need not be anxious about the things of this life.

12:28 *grass . . . cast into the oven.* Since wood was scarce, the Jews used dry grass in their ovens. Jesus was familiar with this practice and makes mention of it here.

29 And seek not ye what ye shall eat, or what ye shall drink, neither be ye of doubtful mind.

12:30 Mt 6:8; Phil 4:19

30 For all these things do the nations of the world seek after: and your Father knoweth that ye have need of these things.

31 ¶But rather seek ye the kingdom of God; and all these things shall be added unto you.

12:32 Dan 7:27; Eph 1:5

32 Fear not, little flock; for it is your Father's good pleasure to give you the kingdom.

12:33☆ Mt 6:19–21; 19:21; Acts 2:45; 4:34

33 Sell that ye have, and give alms; provide yourselves bags which wax not old, a treasure in the heavens that faileth not, where no thief approacheth, neither moth corrupteth.

34 For where your treasure is, there will your heart be also.

7. The Warning to Be Prepared

12:35 Mt 24:42–47; 25:1–13; 1 Pet 1:13

35 Let your loins be girded about, and *your* lights burning;

36 And ye yourselves like unto men that wait for their lord, when he will return from the wedding; that when he cometh and knocketh, they may open unto him immediately.

12:37 Jn 13:4

37 Blessed *are* those servants, whom the lord when he cometh shall find watching: verily I say unto you, that he shall gird himself, and make them to sit down to meat, and will come forth and serve them.

38 And if he shall come in the second watch, or come in the third watch, and find *them* so, blessed are those servants.

12:39 1 Thess 5:2; Rev 16:15

39 And this know, that if the goodman of the house had known what hour the thief would come, he would have watched, and not have suffered his house to be broken through.

12:40 Mk 13:32, 33

40 Be ye therefore ready also: for the Son of man cometh at an hour when ye think not.

8. The Parable of Faithful and Unfaithful Servants (Cf. Mt 23:45–51)

41 ¶Then Peter said unto him, Lord, speakest thou this parable unto us, or even to all?

12:42☆ Mt 24:45–51; 1 Cor 4:2; 1 Pet 5:4

42 And the Lord said, Who then is that faithful and wise steward, whom *his* lord shall make ruler over his household, to give *them their* portion of meat in due season?

43 Blessed *is* that servant, whom his lord when he cometh shall find so doing.

44 Of a truth I say unto you, that he will make him ruler over all that he hath.

45 But and if that servant say in his heart, My lord delayeth his coming; and shall begin to beat the menservants and maidens, and to eat and drink, and to be drunken;

12:46 1 Thess 5:3

46 The lord of that servant will come in a day when he looketh not for *him*, and at an hour when he is not aware, and will cut him in sunder, and will appoint him his portion with the unbelievers.

12:47 Num 15:31; Deut 25:1–3

47 And that servant, which knew his lord's will, and prepared not *himself*, neither did according to his will, shall be beaten with many *stripes*.

12:48 Lev 5:17; Jn 9:41; 15:22; 1 Tim 1:13; Jas 4:17

48 But he that knew not, and did commit things worthy of stripes, shall be beaten with few *stripes*. For unto whomsoever much is given, of him shall

12:33 *give alms.* This means to give again and again, every time God brings us into touch with someone in need.

12:42ff This parable stresses the necessity for faithfully discharging one's obligations as a servant. Jesus warns that the delay in the return of the master is no excuse for slothfulness or taking one's ease. He emphasizes the time of judgment when the returned master rewards faithfulness and fittingly punishes a lack of it.

be much required: and to whom men have committed much, of him they
will ask the more.

9. Jesus, the Great Divider

49 I am come to send fire on the earth; and what will I, if it be already
kindled?
50 But I have a baptism to be baptized with; and how am I straitened till
it be accomplished!
51 Suppose ye that I am come to give peace on earth? I tell you, Nay; but
rather division:
52 For from henceforth there shall be five in one house divided, three
against two, and two against three.
53 The father shall be divided against the son, and the son against the
father; the mother against the daughter, and the daughter against the
mother; the mother in law against her daughter in law, and the daughter in
law against her mother in law.
54 ¶And he said also to the people, When ye see a cloud rise out of the
west, straightway ye say, There cometh a shower; and so it is.
55 And when *ye see* the south wind blow, ye say, There will be heat; and it
cometh to pass.
56 *Ye* hypocrites, ye can discern the face of the sky and of the earth; but
how is it that ye do not discern this time?
57 Yea, and why even of yourselves judge ye not what is right?
58 ¶When thou goest with thine adversary to the magistrate, *as thou art* in
the way, give diligence that thou mayest be delivered from him; lest he hale
thee to the judge, and the judge deliver thee to the officer, and the officer
cast thee into prison.
59 I tell thee, thou shalt not depart thence, till thou hast paid the very last
mite.

H. JESUS' DEMAND FOR REPENTANCE

13 THERE were present at that season some that told him of the
Galilæans, whose blood Pilate had mingled with their sacrifices.
2 And Jesus answering said unto them, Suppose ye that these Galilæans
were sinners above all the Galilæans, because they suffered such things?
3 I tell you, Nay: but, except ye repent, ye shall all likewise perish.
4 Or those eighteen, upon whom the tower in Si-lo'am fell, and slew them,
think ye that they were sinners above all men that dwelt in Jerusalem?
5 I tell you, Nay: but, except ye repent, ye shall all likewise perish.
6 ¶He spake also this parable; A certain *man* had a fig tree planted in his
vineyard; and he came and sought fruit thereon, and found none.
7 Then said he unto the dresser of his vineyard, Behold, these three years
I come seeking fruit on this fig tree, and find none: cut it down; why
cumbereth it the ground?

12:50 Mk 10:38
12:51 Mt 10:34-36; Mic 7:6; Jn 7:43; 9:16; 10:19
☆**12:53**
12:54 Mt 16:2, 3
12:55 Job 37:17
12:56 Lk 21:30, 31
12:58 Prov 25:8-10; Mt 5:25, 26
☆**13:1**
13:2 Jn 9:2
13:3 Ezek 18:30
13:4 Isa 8:6; Jn 9:7, 11
☆**13:6** Isa 5:2; Mt 21:18, 19; Mk 11:12-14, 20, 21; Rom 2:4, 5; 2 Pet 3:9
13:7 Mt 3:10; Lk 3:9

12:53 Jesus affirms that the effect of gospel preaching will be divisive. It will even reach into private families and divide its members. Unbelievers in the family will be provoked, will hate, persecute, and condemn.

13:1 *Galileans, whose blood Pilate had mingled with their sacrifices.* This is all the information we have about this event. Apparently Pilate's soldiers murdered some Jews in the act of offering blood sacrifices and mixed their blood with that of their offerings. Perhaps Pilate feared an insurrection by these Jews. Such an incident may explain the hostility which existed between Pilate and Herod Antipas, tetrarch of Galilee (Luke 23:12).

13:6ff The illustration of the barren fig tree refers primarily to the nation of Israel (See Hos. 9:10; Joel 1:7). For many centuries God looked for Israel to bring forth fruit unto repentance. But nothing had happened. Now Israel has rejected God's Son. God, however, is long-suffering and will grant more time for Israel to repent and turn to him at last. But if Israel persists in her refusal to turn to God, she will be cut off.

13:8 8And he answering said unto him, Lord, let it alone this year also, till I
2 Pet 3:9 shall dig about it, and dung *it:*
9And if it bear fruit, *well:* and if not, *then* after that thou shalt cut it
down.

I. JESUS HEALS THE HANDICAPPED WOMAN

13:10 10And he was teaching in one of the synagogues on the sabbath.
Mt 4:23
13:11☆ 11¶And, behold, there was a woman which had a spirit of infirmity
eighteen years, and was bowed together, and could in no wise lift up *herself.*
12And when Jesus saw her, he called *her to him*, and said unto her,
Woman, thou art loosed from thine infirmity.
13:13 13And he laid *his* hands on her: and immediately she was made straight,
Mk 5:23 and glorified God.
13:14 14And the ruler of the synagogue answered with indignation, because that
Ex 20:8, 9 Jesus had healed on the sabbath day, and said unto the people, There are
Mt 12:9–12 Mk 3:2 six days in which men ought to work: in them therefore come and be
Lk 6:7; 14:3 Rom 10:1–4 healed, and not on the sabbath day.
13:15 15The Lord then answered him, and said, *Thou* hypocrite, doth not each
Lk 14:5 one of you on the sabbath loose his ox or *his* ass from the stall, and lead *him*
away to watering?
13:16 16And ought not this woman, being a daughter of Abraham, whom Satan
Lk 19:9 hath bound, lo, these eighteen years, be loosed from this bond on the
sabbath day?
13:17 17And when he had said these things, all his adversaries were ashamed:
Lk 18:43 and all the people rejoiced for all the glorious things that were done by him.

J. THE KINGDOM OF GOD

1. The Mustard Seed (Cf. Mt 13:31, 32; Mk 4:30–32)

13:18 18¶Then said he, Unto what is the kingdom of God like? and whereunto
Gen 1:11, 12 Ps 104:12 shall I resemble it?
Ezek 17:22, 23 37:6 19It is like a grain of mustard seed, which a man took, and cast into his
Dan 4:12, 21 garden; and it grew, and waxed a great tree; and the fowls of the air lodged
Mt 13:31, 32 Mk 4:30–32 in the branches of it.
13:19☆

2. The Leaven (Cf. Mt 13:31, 32)

13:20☆ 20And again he said, Whereunto shall I liken the kingdom of God?
Mt 13:33
13:21☆ 21It is like leaven, which a woman took and hid in three measures of
meal, till the whole was leavened.

3. Heaven's Narrow Door

13:22☆ 22And he went through the cities and villages, teaching, and journeying
Mt 9:35 Mk 6:6 toward Jerusalem.

13:11 Here was a woman who had an infirmity for eighteen years. She came to the right place at the right time, that is, to the synagogue on the sabbath. She did not ask Jesus for anything. Instead he espied her, felt compassion for her in her grievous plight, and cured her immediately and completely. The ruler of the *synagogue was very angry.* He stretched the law concerning work to include speaking a word and laying a hand on this woman. He forgot that works of mercy and necessity are permissible on the sabbath. This poor woman had greater spiritual insight than the ruler of the synagogue, for she praised and glorified God while the ruler was, in effect, condemning what Jesus Christ had done.

13:19 See note on Matt. 13:31 about the parable of the mustard seed.

13:20, 21 See note on Matt. 13:33 about the parable of the leaven.

13:22ff This passage appears only in Luke's Gospel. Salvation indeed is through a narrow door; it is through Jesus Christ alone, who is the door (John 10:7). There is no other door and no other way to eternal life. There are many substitutes and counterfeits to this door, but they all lead to darkness and everlasting separation from the true God.

23 Then said one unto him, Lord, are there few that be saved? And he said
unto them,
24 ¶Strive to enter in at the strait gate: for many, I say unto you, will seek
to enter in, and shall not be able.
25 When once the master of the house is risen up, and hath shut to the
door, and ye begin to stand without, and to knock at the door, saying,
Lord, Lord, open unto us; and he shall answer and say unto you, I know
you not whence ye are:
26 Then shall ye begin to say, We have eaten and drunk in thy presence,
and thou hast taught in our streets.
27 But he shall say, I tell you, I know you not whence ye are; depart from
me, all *ye* workers of iniquity.
28 There shall be weeping and gnashing of teeth, when ye shall see
Abraham, and Isaac, and Jacob, and all the prophets, in the kingdom of
God, and you *yourselves* thrust out.
29 And they shall come from the east, and *from* the west, and from the
north, and *from* the south, and shall sit down in the kingdom of God.
30 And, behold, there are last which shall be first, and there are first which
shall be last.

13:24 Isa 55:6; Mt 7:13, 14, 22, 23: 25:11, 12; Lk 6:46; Jn 7:34; 8:21; 13:33
13:26 Tit 1:16
13:27 Ps 6:18; Mt 25:41
13:28 Mt 8:10–12; 13:41, 42
13:29 Gen 28:14; Isa 49:6–12; 60:3; Rev 5:9; 7:9
13:30 Mt 19:30; 20:16; Mk 10:31

K. JESUS REBUKES HEROD AND WEEPS OVER JERUSALEM

31 ¶The same day there came certain of the Pharisees, saying unto him,
Get thee out, and depart hence: for Herod will kill thee.
32 And he said unto them, Go ye, and tell that fox, Behold, I cast out
devils, and I do cures to day and to morrow, and the third *day* I shall be
perfected.
33 Nevertheless I must walk to day, and to morrow, and the *day* following:
for it cannot be that a prophet perish out of Jerusalem.
34 O Jerusalem, Jerusalem, which killest the prophets, and stonest them
that are sent unto thee; how often would I have gathered thy children
together, as a hen *doth gather* her brood under *her* wings, and ye would not!
35 Behold, your house is left unto you desolate: and verily I say unto you,
Ye shall not see me, until *the time* come when ye shall say, Blessed *is* he that
cometh in the name of the Lord.

☆**13:32** Lk 24:26; Heb 2:10; 5:5, 9; 7:28
13:33 Mt 16:21; Jn 11:7–10
13:34 Mt 23:37–39; Lk 19:41–44
13:35 Lev 26:31, 32; Ps 69:25; 118:26; Prov 1:24–30; Isa 1:7; Ezek 10:4, 18, 19; Mic 3:12; Mt 21:9; Mk 11:9; Lk 19:38; 21:24; Jn 8:21; 12:12, 13

L. JESUS AT A PHARISEE'S TABLE

1. Healing on the Sabbath

14 AND it came to pass, as he went into the house of one of the chief
Pharisees to eat bread on the sabbath day, that they watched him.
2 And, behold, there was a certain man before him which had the dropsy.
3 And Jesus answering spake unto the lawyers and Pharisees, saying, Is it
lawful to heal on the sabbath day?
4 And they held their peace. And he took *him*, and healed him, and let
him go;
5 *And answered them*, saying, Which of you shall have an ass or an ox
fallen into a pit, and will not straightway pull him out on the sabbath day?
6 And they could not answer him again to these things.

☆**14:1** Mt 12:9–13; Mk 3:1–5; Lk 6:6–11; 13:10–16
☆**14:3**

13:32 *tell that fox.* Christ was not terrified by the thought that Herod sought his life. He speaks plainly and insultingly when he calls Herod a fox. The term meant that Herod was a man of low cunning. He was insignificant when compared with someone of stature, greatness, and power.

14:1 *the sabbath.* See note on Mark 2:27.

14:3 Jesus confounds his critics by asking whether it is lawful to heal on the sabbath. They would not say "yes," because then they would have nothing against him; and they would not say "no," because it obviously was not wrong and they knew it.

2. Parable of the Wedding Feast

14:7☆

7 ¶And he put forth a parable to those which were bidden, when he marked how they chose out the chief rooms; saying unto them,

8 When thou art bidden of any *man* to a wedding, sit not down in the highest room; lest a more honourable man than thou be bidden of him;

9 And he that bade thee and him come and say to thee, Give this man place; and thou begin with shame to take the lowest room.

14:10 Prov 15:33; 18:12; 25:6, 7

10 But when thou art bidden, go and sit down in the lowest room; that when he that bade thee cometh, he may say unto thee, Friend, go up higher: then shalt thou have worship in the presence of them that sit at meat with thee.

14:11 Ps 18:27; Prov 29:23; Mt 23:12; Lk 18:14; Jas 4:6; 1 Pet 5:5

11 For whosoever exalteth himself shall be abased; and he that humbleth himself shall be exalted.

12 ¶Then said he also to him that bade him, When thou makest a dinner or a supper, call not thy friends, nor thy brethren, neither thy kinsmen, nor *thy* rich neighbours; lest they also bid thee again, and a recompence be made thee.

14:13 Job 31:17

13 But when thou makest a feast, call the poor, the maimed, the lame, the blind:

14:14 Jn 5:28, 29; Acts 24:15

14 And thou shalt be blessed; for they cannot recompense thee: for thou shalt be recompensed at the resurrection of the just.

3. Parable of the Great Feast (Cf. Mt 22:1–14)

14:15 Mt 22:1–10

15 ¶And when one of them that sat at meat with him heard these things, he said unto him, Blessed *is* he that shall eat bread in the kingdom of God.

14:16☆ Rev 19:9

16 Then said he unto him, A certain man made a great supper, and bade many:

17 And sent his servant at supper time to say to them that were bidden, Come; for all things are now ready.

18 And they all with one *consent* began to make excuse. The first said unto him, I have bought a piece of ground, and I must needs go and see it: I pray thee have me excused.

19 And another said, I have bought five yoke of oxen, and I go to prove them: I pray thee have me excused.

14:20 Deut 24:15; 1 Cor 7:33

20 And another said, I have married a wife, and therefore I cannot come.

14:21 Acts 13:46

21 So that servant came, and shewed his lord these things. Then the master of the house being angry said to his servant, Go out quickly into the streets and lanes of the city, and bring in hither the poor, and the maimed, and the halt, and the blind.

22 And the servant said, Lord, it is done as thou hast commanded, and yet there is room.

23 And the lord said unto the servant, Go out into the highways and hedges, and compel *them* to come in, that my house may be filled.

14:24 Mt 8:12; 21:43; Heb 3:18, 19

24 For I say unto you, That none of those men which were bidden shall taste of my supper.

14:7 This parable appears only in Luke. Jesus rebukes the guests who strive to get the best seats and *therefore* exhibit their lack of humility. He suggests that guests should start by taking the low seats; then if they are raised higher, they will be honored. The opposite approach could lead to degradation and dishonor. He also reproves the host who has invited so many wealthy people. It should not be a common custom; they should not be proud of doing it, and they should not expect to be paid back in their own coin. Rather they are to invite the poor (14:13, 14), and they will be recompensed in the resurrection and the world to come.

14:16ff The illustration of the great supper indicates that the Jews are the invited guests who refuse to attend the banquet. Gentiles are invited in their place and attend. The call to repentance and salvation is universal—to Jew and Gentile alike.

M. THE COST OF DISCIPLESHIP

1. Parables of Erecting a Building or Waging a War

25 ¶And there went great multitudes with him: and he turned, and said unto them,

26 If any *man* come to me, and hate not his father, and mother, and wife, and children, and brethren, and sisters, yea, and his own life also, he cannot be my disciple.

☆**14:26** Mt 10:37, 38 Rev 12:11

27 And whosoever doth not bear his cross, and come after me, cannot be my disciple.

☆**14:27** Mt 16:24 Mk 8:34 Lk 9:23

28 For which of you, intending to build a tower, sitteth not down first, and counteth the cost, whether he have *sufficient* to finish *it?*

☆**14:28**

29 Lest haply, after he hath laid the foundation, and is not able to finish *it,* all that behold *it* begin to mock him,

30 Saying, This man began to build, and was not able to finish.

31 Or what king, going to make war against another king, sitteth not down first, and consulteth whether he be able with ten thousand to meet him that cometh against him with twenty thousand?

32 Or else, while the other is yet a great way off, he sendeth an ambassage, and desireth conditions of peace.

33 So likewise, whosoever he be of you that forsaketh not all that he hath, he cannot be my disciple.

14:33 Mt 19:27, 28 Lk 18:29, 30 Phil 3:7 Heb 11:26

2. Parable of the Salt

34 ¶Salt *is* good: but if the salt have lost his savour, wherewith shall it be seasoned?

☆**14:34** Mt 5:13 Mk 9:50

35 It is neither fit for the land, nor yet for the dunghill; *but* men cast it out. He that hath ears to hear, let him hear.

14:35 Mt 11:15 13:9, 43 Mk 4:9, 23 Lk 8:8 Rev 2:11

15 THEN drew near unto him all the publicans and sinners for to hear him.

2 And the Pharisees and scribes murmured, saying, This man receiveth sinners, and eateth with them.

15:1 Mt 9:10, 11 Lk 5:29, 30 19:7 Acts 11:3 Gal 2:12 1 Tim 1:15, 16

N. THREE PARABLES OF THE LOST

1. The Lost Sheep (Cf. Mt 18:10–14)

3 ¶And he spake this parable unto them, saying,

☆**15:3** Mt 18:12–14

4 What man of you, having an hundred sheep, if he lose one of them, doth not leave the ninety and nine in the wilderness, and go after that which is lost, until he find it?

15:4 Ezek 34:11, 12 Jn 10:11

5 And when he hath found *it,* he layeth *it* on his shoulders, rejoicing.

6 And when he cometh home, he calleth together *his* friends and neighbours, saying unto them, Rejoice with me; for I have found my sheep which was lost.

15:6 1 Pet 2:25

7 I say unto you, that likewise joy shall be in heaven over one sinner that repenteth, more than over ninety and nine just persons, which need no repentance.

15:7 Lk 5:32

14:26 *If any man come to me, and hate not his father, and mother,* i.e., "If anyone comes to me he must love me far more than his father and mother."† This verse, as well as Matt. 10:37, 38, says anything that removes Jesus from first place in our hearts and lives is an idol.

14:27, 28 He who would become a Christian should count the cost before he makes the decision. It is reprehensible for those who take up the Christian faith to break off and cease to persevere. We would not build a house without counting the cost; we should not embark on the journey of faith without doing the same.

14:34 *if the salt have lost its savour.* Perhaps this refers to impure salt; when wet, the salt dissolves and drains out, leaving a tasteless residue. (See Matt. 5:13.)†

15:3ff Jesus gave this parable to the Pharisees and scribes, who objected to his mingling and eating with publicans—tax collectors and sinners. Instead of criticizing, they should have rejoiced, as the angels did when a single lost sheep was brought into the fold.

2. The Lost Silver Coin

15:8☆ 8 ¶Either what woman having ten pieces of silver, if she lose one piece, doth not light a candle, and sweep the house, and seek diligently till she find *it?*

9 And when she hath found *it,* she calleth *her* friends and *her* neighbours together, saying, Rejoice with me; for I have found the piece which I had lost.

15:10 Ezek 18:23 10 Likewise, I say unto you, there is joy in the presence of the angels of God over one sinner that repenteth.

3. The Lost Son

15:11☆ 11 ¶And he said, A certain man had two sons:

15:12 Deut 21:17 12 And the younger of them said to *his* father, Father, give me the portion of goods that falleth *to me.* And he divided unto them *his* living.

13 And not many days after the younger son gathered all together, and took his journey into a far country, and there wasted his substance with riotous living.

14 And when he had spent all, there arose a mighty famine in that land; and he began to be in want.

15 And he went and joined himself to a citizen of that country; and he sent him into his fields to feed swine.

16 And he would fain have filled his belly with the husks that the swine did eat: and no man gave unto him.

17 And when he came to himself, he said, How many hired servants of my father's have bread enough and to spare, and I perish with hunger!

15:18 Lam 3:40 Lk 18:13, 14 18 I will arise and go to my father, and will say unto him, Father, I have sinned against heaven, and before thee,

19 And am no more worthy to be called thy son: make me as one of thy hired servants.

15:20☆ Gen 45:14; 46:29 20 And he arose, and came to his father. But when he was yet a great way off, his father saw him, and had compassion, and ran, and fell on his neck, and kissed him.

21 And the son said unto him, Father, I have sinned against heaven, and in thy sight, and am no more worthy to be called thy son.

15:22 Isa 61:10 Zech 3:4 Rev 6:11 22 But the father said to his servants, Bring forth the best robe, and put *it* on him; and put a ring on his hand, and shoes on *his* feet:

23 And bring hither the fatted calf, and kill *it;* and let us eat, and be merry:

15:24 Rom 11:15 Eph 2:1–5 Col 2:13 24 For this my son was dead, and is alive again; he was lost, and is found. And they began to be merry.

25 Now his elder son was in the field: and as he came and drew nigh to the house, he heard musick and dancing.

15:8ff The parables of the lost sheep and coin belong together. Jesus sometimes used duplicate stories to illustrate the same truth. In both parables the angels of heaven rejoice in the finding of the lost coin and the lost sheep. If one person is converted to Christ the angels rejoice, and so should the people of God. The publicans, or tax collectors and other sinners, may not have been numerous, but if even one of them found Christ, that should have been cause for the Pharisees and scribes to thank God.

15:11ff The three parables of chapter 15 are interrelated. In this parable the lost sheep and the lost coin are equivalent to the lost son, a human being. The shepherd and the woman now become the father. The son leaves his father's house to live in sin. He repents and returns to be received with joy by the father. The lost son's elder brother dislikes what happens even as the Pharisees and scribes do not like Gentiles coming home to God the Father. No doubt the Pharisees and scribes could see that Jesus was responding to their criticisms about his eating with publicans and sinners.

15:20 The loving father received his son (1) with eyes of mercy—for he saw him afar off; (2) with bowels of mercy—for he had compassion; (3) with feet of mercy—for he ran to greet him; (4) with arms of mercy—for he fell on his neck; (5) with lips of mercy—for he kissed him.

[26]And he called one of the servants, and asked what these things meant.
[27]And he said unto him, Thy brother is come; and thy father hath killed
the fatted calf, because he hath received him safe and sound.
[28]And he was angry, and would not go in: therefore came his father out,
and intreated him.
[29]And he answering said to *his* father, Lo, these many years do I serve
thee, neither transgressed I at any time thy commandment: and yet thou
never gavest me a kid, that I might make merry with my friends:
[30]But as soon as this thy son was come, which hath devoured thy living
with harlots, thou hast killed for him the fatted calf.
[31]And he said unto him, Son, thou art ever with me, and all that I have is
thine.
[32]It was meet that we should make merry, and be glad: for this thy
brother was dead, and is alive again; and was lost, and is found.

15:29 Mt 20:11–15
15:30 Prov 29:3
☆**15:32** Lk 15:7

O. TEACHING ABOUT WEALTH
1. The Dishonest Accountant

16 AND he said also unto his disciples, There was a certain rich man,
which had a steward; and the same was accused unto him that he
had wasted his goods.
[2]And he called him, and said unto him, How is it that I hear this of thee?
give an account of thy stewardship; for thou mayest be no longer steward.
[3]Then the steward said within himself, What shall I do? for my lord
taketh away from me the stewardship: I cannot dig; to beg I am ashamed.
[4]I am resolved what to do, that, when I am put out of the stewardship,
they may receive me into their houses.
[5]So he called every one of his lord's debtors *unto him,* and said unto the
first, How much owest thou unto my lord?
[6]And he said, An hundred measures of oil. And he said unto him, Take
thy bill, and sit down quickly, and write fifty.
[7]Then said he to another, And how much owest thou? And he said, An
hundred measures of wheat. And he said unto him, Take thy bill, and write
fourscore.
[8]And the lord commended the unjust steward, because he had done
wisely: for the children of this world are in their generation wiser than the
children of light.
[9]And I say unto you, Make to yourselves friends of the mammon of
unrighteousness; that, when ye fail, they may receive you into everlasting
habitations.
[10]He that is faithful in that which is least is faithful also in much: and he
that is unjust in the least is unjust also in much.
[11]If therefore ye have not been faithful in the unrighteous mammon, who
will commit to your trust the true *riches?*
[12]And if ye have not been faithful in that which is another man's, who
shall give you that which is your own?

☆**16:1**
16:2 Rom 14:12
16:8 Jn 12:36 Eph 5:8, 9 1 Thess 5:5
☆**16:9**
16:10 Mt 25:21 Lk 19:17
☆**16:11**

15:32 The conversion of a single soul is the raising of that soul from the dead. It pleases God and should please the whole family of God. If the angels of heaven rejoice over one sinner that repents (15:10), how much more should we rejoice who are like that sinner.
16:1ff This illustration was told in the presence of the Pharisees. The point is plain: if unsaved people will spend all their time looking to their material interests and the promotion of their own welfare, believers should use their energies and talents to advance their spiritual interests—the only ones of lasting value.
16:9 Jesus uses this parable to speak to his disciples and to us about the use of the little material means they had, and we may have. "What is it here that our Lord Jesus exhorts us to; to provide for our comfortable reception to the happiness of another world, by making good use of our possessions and enjoyments in this world."*
16:11 The truly rich are those who are rich in faith. The riches of the world are deceitful and uncertain; they are unimaginably less than the riches of glory and grace.

16:13 Mt 6:24

13 ¶No servant can serve two masters: for either he will hate the one, and
love the other; or else he will hold to the one, and despise the other. Ye
cannot serve God and mammon.

2. The Money-Loving Pharisees

16:14 Mt 23:13, 14; 1 Tim 3:2
16:15 1 Sam 16:7; 2 Chron 16:30; Ps 7:9; Prov 15:11; 21:2; Jer 17:10; Mt 23:28; Heb 4:13
16:16 Mt 11:12, 13
16:17 Isa 40:8; Mt 5:17, 18; Lk 21:33; 1 Pet 1:25
16:18☆ Mt 5:32; 19:9; Mk 10:11, 12; 1 Cor 7:10, 11

14 And the Pharisees also, who were covetous, heard all these things: and
they derided him.
15 And he said unto them, Ye are they which justify yourselves before
men; but God knoweth your hearts: for that which is highly esteemed
among men is abomination in the sight of God.
16 The law and the prophets *were* until John: since that time the kingdom
of God is preached, and every man presseth into it.
17 And it is easier for heaven and earth to pass, than one tittle of the law
to fail.
18 Whosoever putteth away his wife, and marrieth another, committeth
adultery: and whosoever marrieth her that is put away from *her* husband
committeth adultery.

3. The Rich Man and Lazarus

16:19☆
16:20 Acts 3:2
16:22☆ Ps 103:20, 21; Mt 8:11; Jn 1:18; Heb 1:14; Jas 2:5
16:23☆
16:24 Mk 9:44; Lk 3:8
16:25 Job 21:7–14; Lk 6:24, 25
16:26 2 Thess 1:9
16:28 Acts 2:40; 10:42; 18:5
16:29 Jn 5:39, 45–47; Acts 15:21; 2 Tim 3:15

19 ¶There was a certain rich man, which was clothed in purple and fine
linen, and fared sumptuously every day:
20 And there was a certain beggar named Lazarus, which was laid at his
gate, full of sores,
21 And desiring to be fed with the crumbs which fell from the rich man's
table: moreover the dogs came and licked his sores.
22 And it came to pass, that the beggar died, and was carried by the angels
into Abraham's bosom: the rich man also died, and was buried;
23 And in hell he lift up his eyes, being in torments, and seeth Abraham
afar off, and Lazarus in his bosom.
24 And he cried and said, Father Abraham, have mercy on me, and send
Lazar-us, that he may dip the tip of his finger in water, and cool my tongue;
for I am tormented in this flame.
25 But Abraham said, Son, remember that thou in thy lifetime receivedst
thy good things, and likewise Lazarus evil things: but now he is comforted,
and thou art tormented.
26 And beside all this, between us and you there is a great gulf fixed: so
that they which would pass from hence to you cannot; neither can they pass
to us, that *would come* from thence.
27 Then he said, I pray thee therefore, father, that thou wouldest send him
to my father's house:
28 For I have five brethren; that he may testify unto them, lest they also
come into this place of torment.
29 Abraham saith unto him, They have Moses and the prophets; let them
hear them.
30 And he said, Nay, father Abraham: but if one went unto them from the
dead, they will repent.

16:18 See note on Mark 10:5ff about divorce.

16:19ff Some think this is a parable; others believe it is a true story. In either event it teaches two lessons: (1) wealth, or station in life, is no guarantee of life eternal; and (2) Moses and the prophets have supplied men with all the information they need to keep them from everlasting destruction.

16:22 *into Abraham's bosom*, i.e., to be in paradise where Abraham is. This is a figurative manner of speaking.

16:23 *in hell*, i.e., in hades, which here is that part of hades where unbelievers go to await the final judgment. The rich man is conscious; he is already suffering. There is no deliverance from his estate. And he cannot communicate with the living.

31 And he said unto him, If they hear not Moses and the prophets, neither
will they be persuaded, though one rose from the dead.

16:31 Jn 12:9, 10

P. TEACHING ABOUT FORGIVENESS AND FAITH

17 THEN said he unto the disciples, It is impossible but that offences
will come: but woe *unto him,* through whom they come!
2 It were better for him that a millstone were hanged about his neck, and
he cast into the sea, than that he should offend one of these little ones.
3 ¶Take heed to yourselves: If thy brother trespass against thee, rebuke
him; and if he repent, forgive him.
4 And if he trespass against thee seven times in a day, and seven times in
a day turn again to thee, saying, I repent: thou shalt forgive him.
5 And the apostles said unto the Lord, Increase our faith.
6 And the Lord said, If ye had faith as a grain of mustard seed, ye might
say unto this sycamine tree, Be thou plucked up by the root, and be thou
planted in the sea; and it should obey you.
7 But which of you, having a servant plowing or feeding cattle, will say
unto him by and by, when he is come from the field, Go and sit down to
meat?
8 And will not rather say unto him, Make ready wherewith I may sup, and
gird thyself, and serve me, till I have eaten and drunken; and afterward
thou shalt eat and drink?
9 Doth he thank that servant because he did the things that were
commanded him? I trow not.
10 So likewise ye, when ye shall have done all those things which are
commanded you, say, We are unprofitable servants: we have done that
which was our duty to do.

17:1 Mt 18:6, 7 Mk 9:42 1 Cor 8:12
☆**17:3** Lev 19:17 Mt 18:15, 21, 22 Jas 5:19
17:6 Mt 17:20; 21:21 Mk 9:23 11:22, 23
☆**17:7**
17:10 1 Cor 9:16–18

Q. THE HEALING OF TEN LEPERS

11 ¶And it came to pass, as he went to Jerusalem, that he passed through
the midst of Sa-ma′ri-a and Galilee.
12 And as he entered into a certain village, there met him ten men that
were lepers, which stood afar off:
13 And they lifted up *their* voices, and said, Jesus, Master, have mercy on
us.
14 And when he saw *them,* he said unto them, Go shew yourselves unto
the priests. And it came to pass, that, as they went, they were cleansed.
15 And one of them, when he saw that he was healed, turned back, and
with a loud voice glorified God,
16 And fell down on *his* face at his feet, giving him thanks: and he was a
Sa-mar′i-tan.
17 And Jesus answering said, Were there not ten cleansed? but where *are*
the nine?

17:11 Lk 9:51; 13:22
☆**17:12** Lev 13:45, 46
17:14 Lev 14:3 Mt 8:4 Mk 1:43, 44 Lk 5:14
17:16 2 Kgs 17:24 Mt 10:5 Jn 8:48

17:3 To forgive those who offend us is a great duty. We must not be apt to be vengeful, or hate, or speak out of turn. Some say, "Don't get mad; get even." This is not biblical. Talk with the offender, and if he repents, forgive him freely, even to seventy times seven, or seven times a day—which suggests an indefinite number.

17:7 Whoever serves Christ must be a humble servant who admits he cannot merit any favor with God. Whoever does all he is commanded is not worthy of special notice, for he has done no more than he ought to have done. And who can do more for God than God has done for him?

17:12 The Jews supposed that leprosy was inflicted on men for punishment of a particular sin and was a mark of God's displeasure. Jesus went to be found of those lepers who sought him until he came near. The ten lepers asked Jesus for mercy without mentioning their leprosy. Jesus did not tell them they were healed. He said for them to show themselves to the priests, who would look to see whether they were unclean. While en route to see the priests, their leprosy vanished. Only one, a Samaritan, returned to give thanks and glorify God.

18 There are not found that returned to give glory to God, save this
stranger.

17:19 Mt 9:22 Lk 18:42

19 And he said unto him, Arise, go thy way: thy faith hath made thee
whole.

R. THE COMING OF THE KINGDOM OF GOD

17:20 Mt 12:28 Lk 11:20; 19:11 Jn 3:3; 18:36 Acts 1:6

20 ¶And when he was demanded of the Pharisees, when the kingdom of
God should come, he answered them and said, The kingdom of God
cometh not with observation:

17:21☆

21 Neither shall they say, Lo here! or, lo there! for, behold, the kingdom of
God is within you.

17:22 Mt 9:15 Jn 17:11

22 And he said unto the disciples, The days will come, when ye shall desire
to see one of the days of the Son of man, and ye shall not see *it*.

17:23 Mt 24:23, 26, 27 Mk 13:21 Lk 21:8

23 And they shall say to you, See here; or, see there: go not after *them*, nor
follow *them*.

17:24 1 Tim 6:15

24 For as the lightning, that lighteneth out of the one *part* under heaven,
shineth unto the other *part* under heaven; so shall also the Son of man be in
his day.

17:25 Mt 16:21 Mk 8:31 Lk 9:22

25 But first must he suffer many things, and be rejected of this generation.
26 And as it was in the days of No'e, so shall it be also in the days of the
Son of man.

17:26☆ Gen 6:12, 13 Mt 24:37–39 17:27☆

27 They did eat, they drank, they married wives, they were given in
marriage, until the day that No'e entered into the ark, and the flood came,
and destroyed them all.
28 Likewise also as it was in the days of Lot; they did eat, they drank, they
bought, they sold, they planted, they builded;

17:29 Gen 19:24–26

29 But the same day that Lot went out of Sodom it rained fire and
brimstone from heaven, and destroyed *them* all.

17:30 2 Thess 1:7

30 Even thus shall it be in the day when the Son of man is revealed.

17:31 Mt 24:17, 18 Mk 13:15, 16

31 In that day, he which shall be upon the housetop, and his stuff in the
house, let him not come down to take it away: and he that is in the field, let
him likewise not return back.
32 Remember Lot's wife.

17:33 Mt 10:39; 16:25 Mk 8:35 Lk 9:24 Jn 12:25

33 Whosoever shall seek to save his life shall lose it; and whosoever shall
lose his life shall preserve it.
34 I tell you, in that night there shall be two *men* in one bed; the one shall
be taken, and the other shall be left.

17:35 Mt 24:40, 41 1 Thess 4:17

35 Two *women* shall be grinding together; the one shall be taken, and the
other left.
36 Two *men* shall be in the field; the one shall be taken, and the other left.

17:37☆ Job 39:30 Mt 24:28

37 And they answered and said unto him, Where, Lord? And he said unto
them, Wheresoever the body *is*, thither will the eagles be gathered together.

17:21 *within you*, i.e., "among you." This means there is an already existing spiritual reality in the hearts of men. External manifestations of this inward reality flow from the actions of those who have received Christ. If they have not done so, all the externals are false. In its outward form, the kingdom of God will come with the Second Advent of Jesus.

17:26, 27 Until the time of Jesus' coming great masses of people will be fully absorbed in worldly activities and concern for the material aspects of life. They will take no precautions for the return of the Son of God, and they will not be prepared for it. Therefore the judgment will overtake them suddenly and unexpectedly, so that they will have no time or opportunity to find deliverance.

17:37 *Wheresoever the body is, thither will the eagles be gathered.* This may mean that God's people will be taken out to the execution grounds and their bodies left to the vultures.†

S. TWO PARABLES ABOUT PRAYER

1. The Godless Judge and the Persistent Widow

18 AND he spake a parable unto them *to this end,* that men ought always to pray, and not to faint;

[2]Saying, There was in a city a judge, which feared not God, neither regarded man:

[3]And there was a widow in that city; and she came unto him, saying, Avenge me of mine adversary.

[4]And he would not for a while: but afterward he said within himself, Though I fear not God, nor regard man;

[5]Yet because this widow troubleth me, I will avenge her, lest by her continual coming she weary me.

[6]And the Lord said, Hear what the unjust judge saith.

[7]And shall not God avenge his own elect, which cry day and night unto him, though he bear long with them?

[8]I tell you that he will avenge them speedily. Nevertheless when the Son of man cometh, shall he find faith on the earth?

☆**18:1** Rom 12:12 Eph 6:18 Col 4:2 1 Thess 5:17
18:4, 5 Lk 11:8
18:7 Mt 24:22 Rom 8:33 Rev 6:10
18:8 1 Tim 4:1

2. The Proud Pharisee and the Corrupt Tax Collector

[9]And he spake this parable unto certain which trusted in themselves that they were righteous, and despised others:

[10]Two men went up into the temple to pray; the one a Pharisee, and the other a publican.

[11]The Pharisee stood and prayed thus with himself, God, I thank thee, that I am not as other men *are,* extortioners, unjust, adulterers, or even as this publican.

[12]I fast twice in the week, I give tithes of all that I possess.

[13]And the publican, standing afar off, would not lift up so much as *his* eyes unto heaven, but smote upon his breast, saying, God be merciful to me a sinner.

[14]I tell you, this man went down to his house justified *rather* than the other: for every one that exalteth himself shall be abased; and he that humbleth himself shall be exalted.

☆**18:9** Rom 14:10
18:11 Isa 58:2 Mt 6:5 Rev 3:17
☆**18:12**
18:13 Ps 40:12
18:14 Job 22:29 Mt 23:12 Lk 14:11 Jas 4:6 1 Pet 5:5, 6

T. JESUS AND THE CHILDREN (CF. MT 19:13–15; MK 10:13–16)

[15]And they brought unto him also infants, that he would touch them: but when *his* disciples saw *it,* they rebuked them.

[16]But Jesus called them *unto him,* and said, Suffer little children to come unto me, and forbid them not: for of such is the kingdom of God.

[17]Verily I say unto you, Whosoever shall not receive the kingdom of God as a little child shall in no wise enter therein.

18:15 Mt 19:13–15 Mk 10:13–16
18:17 Mt 18:3 1 Cor 14:20 1 Pet 2:2

18:1ff This parable teaches us the lesson that the faithful people of God should continue steadfast in prayer when they do not receive an immediate answer.
18:9ff This story shows the difference between the self-righteous Pharisee who boasted of his good works and the cheating tax collector who knew he was wicked and who sought the mercy of God without any works of righteousness. The Greek word for "be merciful" in 18:13 is *hilaskomai,* which means "to be propitiated." Its use indicates that the tax collector was pleading for God to be merciful to him.

18:12 *I fast twice in the week.* The law of Moses required fasting one day in the year in connection with the Day of Atonement (see Lev. 16:29ff). The fasting is referred to in Acts 27:9. The Pharisee here fasted two days a week, although oral tradition did not require it. He was proud of the fact that he exceeded the requirements of the law. The Pharisees and the disciples of John the Baptist often fasted (5:33; Matt 9:14; Mark 2:18). (See note on Mark 2:18 about Christian fasting.)

U. JESUS AND THE RICH RULER (CF. MT 19:16–30; MK 10:17–31)

18:18☆ Mt 19:16–22 Mk 10:17–22
18 And a certain ruler asked him, saying, Good Master, what shall I do to
inherit eternal life?
18:19☆
19 And Jesus said unto him, Why callest thou me good? none *is* good, save
one, *that is,* God.
18:20 Ex 20:12–16 Deut 5:16–20
20 Thou knowest the commandments, Do not commit adultery, Do not
kill, Do not steal, Do not bear false witness, Honour thy father and thy
mother.
21 And he said, All these have I kept from my youth up.
18:22 Mt 6:19–21 1 Tim 6:18, 19
22 Now when Jesus heard these things, he said unto him, Yet lackest thou
one thing: sell all that thou hast, and distribute unto the poor, and thou
shalt have treasure in heaven: and come, follow me.
18:23 Ezek 33:31
23 And when he heard this, he was very sorrowful: for he was very rich.
18:24 Mt 19:23–30 Mk 10:23–31 1 Tim 6:9 Jas 2:5
24 And when Jesus saw that he was very sorrowful, he said, How hardly
shall they that have riches enter into the kingdom of God!
25 For it is easier for a camel to go through a needle's eye, than for a rich
man to enter into the kingdom of God.
26 And they that heard *it* said, Who then can be saved?
18:27 Jer 32:17
27 And he said, The things which are impossible with men are possible
with God.
18:28 Lk 5:11
28 Then Peter said, Lo, we have left all, and followed thee.
29 And he said unto them, Verily I say unto you, There is no man that
hath left house, or parents, or brethren, or wife, or children, for the
kingdom of God's sake,
18:30 Job 42:10
30 Who shall not receive manifold more in this present time, and in the
world to come life everlasting.

V. JESUS' THIRD PREDICTION OF HIS DEATH AND RESURRECTION (CF. MT 20:17–19; MK 10:32–34)

18:31 Ps 22 Isa 53 Mt 20:17–19 Mk 10:32–34 Lk 9:22, 44, 45 17:25
31 ¶Then he took *unto him* the twelve, and said unto them, Behold, we go
up to Jerusalem, and all things that are written by the prophets concerning
the Son of man shall be accomplished.
18:32 Mt 16:21; 17:22 27:2
32 For he shall be delivered unto the Gentiles, and shall be mocked, and
spitefully entreated, and spitted on:
33 And they shall scourge *him,* and put him to death: and the third day he
shall rise again.
18:34 Mk 9:32 Lk 2:50 Jn 12:16
34 And they understood none of these things: and this saying was hid
from them, neither knew they the things which were spoken.

W. HEALING OF THE BLIND BEGGAR (CF. MT 20:39–34; MK 10:46–52)

18:35☆ Mt 20:29–34 Mk 10:46–52
35 ¶And it came to pass, that as he was come nigh unto Jericho, a certain
blind man sat by the way side begging:
36 And hearing the multitude pass by, he asked what it meant.
37 And they told him, that Jesus of Nazareth passeth by.
18:38 Heb 2:17
38 And he cried, saying, Jesus, *thou* Son of David, have mercy on me.
39 And they which went before rebuked him, that he should hold his
peace: but he cried so much the more, *Thou* Son of David, have mercy on
me.

18:18ff See note on Matt. 19:16 for information on the rich young ruler and Jesus' person-to-person evangelism.

18:19 See note on Mark 10:18.

18:35 *Jericho.* There were two Jerichos. One was the site of a Canaanite city. The new Jericho was a recently built Herodian city. See also note on Mark 10:46 on blind Bartimaeus.

40And Jesus stood, and commanded him to be brought unto him: and
when he was come near, he asked him,
41Saying, What wilt thou that I shall do unto thee? And he said, Lord,
that I may receive my sight.
42And Jesus said unto him, Receive thy sight: thy faith hath saved thee.
43And immediately he received his sight, and followed him, glorifying
God: and all the people, when they saw *it,* gave praise unto God.

18:42 Mt 9:22 Lk 7:50; 17:19
18:43 Isa 35:5 Mt 9:8 Lk 19:37 Acts 4:21

X. CONVERSION OF ZACCHAEUS, THE WEALTHY TAX COLLECTOR

19 AND *Jesus* entered and passed through Jericho.
2And, behold, *there was* a man named Zac-chæ'us, which was the
chief among the publicans, and he was rich.
3And he sought to see Jesus who he was; and could not for the press,
because he was little of stature.
4And he ran before, and climbed up into a sycomore tree to see him: for
he was to pass that *way.*
5And when Jesus came to the place, he looked up, and saw him, and said
unto him, Zac-chæ'us, make haste, and come down; for to day I must abide
at thy house.
6And he made haste, and came down, and received him joyfully.
7And when they saw *it,* they all murmured, saying, That he was gone to
be guest with a man that is a sinner.
8And Zac-chæ'us stood, and said unto the Lord; Behold, Lord, the half
of my goods I give to the poor; and if I have taken any thing from any man
by false accusation, I restore *him* fourfold.
9And Jesus said unto him, This day is salvation come to this house,
forsomuch as he also is a son of Abraham
10For the Son of man is come to seek and to save that which was lost.

☆**19:1** Josh 6:26 1 Kgs 16:34 Lk 18:35
19:4 1 Kings 10:27 2 Chron 1:15
19:7 Mt 9:11; 11:19 Lk 5:30; 15:2
19:8 Ex 22:1 Num 5:7 2 Sam 12:6 Lk 3:12, 13
19:9 Mt 9:13; 15:24 18:11 Lk 5:32 Rom 4:11, 12, 16, 17 Gal 3:7 1 Tim 1:15

Y. PARABLE OF THE STEWARDSHIP OF THE NOBLEMAN'S TEN SERVANTS

11And as they heard these things, he added and spake a parable, because
he was nigh to Jerusalem, and because they thought that the kingdom of
God should immediately appear.
12He said therefore, A certain nobleman went into a far country to
receive for himself a kingdom, and to return.
13And he called his ten servants, and delivered them ten pounds, and said
unto them, Occupy till I come.
14But his citizens hated him, and sent a message after him, saying, We
will not have this *man* to reign over us.
15And it came to pass, that when he was returned, having received the
kingdom, then he commanded these servants to be called unto him, to

☆**19:11** Acts 1:6
19:12 Mt 25:14-30 Mk 13:34
19:13 1 Pet 4:10, 11
19:14 Jn 1:11

19:1 *Only Luke tells the story about Zacchaeus.* He was a Jew and a tax collector who had others working under him. He was rich, which probably means that he extorted money from the taxpayers. Nonetheless, he was curious and determined to see Jesus. He climbed a tree to do so. Without saying a word to Jesus, he was told that Jesus would stay at his house. For a Jew to enter the house of a tax collector was unheard of. The Jews were angry that Jesus would do this. Yet salvation came to this despised publican, for Jesus came to save the lost; and such was Zacchaeus.

19:11ff This story has the same intent as the parable of the talents in Matt. 25:14ff. Diligence receives its rich reward; laziness is punished. Jesus pictures himself as the nobleman who has gone away and left all to his servants. In God's kingdom there are faithful and unfaithful servants who receive their just deserts. In this story, a fatal destiny awaits those who are not truly the Lord's servants and who refuse to let him reign over them.

This parable also teaches us that the kingdom of God will not appear immediately. The king has gone into a far country to receive to himself a kingdom. Christ must first go to heaven and sit at the right hand of the Father; at the end of the age he will return. Meanwhile, the king's servants have a work to do.

whom he had given the money, that he might know how much every man
had gained by trading.
16 Then came the first, saying, Lord, thy pound hath gained ten pounds.
19:17 17 And he said unto him, Well, thou good servant: because thou hast been
Lk 16:10 faithful in a very little, have thou authority over ten cities.
18 And the second came, saying, Lord, thy pound hath gained five pounds.
19 And he said likewise to him, Be thou also over five cities.
20 And another came, saying, Lord, behold, *here is* thy pound, which I
have kept laid up in a napkin:
21 For I feared thee, because thou art an austere man: thou takest up that
thou layedst not down, and reapest that thou didst not sow.
19:22 22 And he saith unto him, Out of thine own mouth will I judge thee, *thou*
Job 15:6; Mt 12:37 wicked servant. Thou knewest that I was an austere man, taking up that I
Tit 3:11 laid not down, and reaping that I did not sow:
23 Wherefore then gavest not thou my money into the bank, that at my
coming I might have required mine own with usury?
24 And he said unto them that stood by, Take from him the pound, and
give *it* to him that hath ten pounds.
25 (And they said unto him, Lord, he hath ten pounds.)
19:26 26 For I say unto you, That unto every one which hath shall be given; and
Mt 13:12; Mk 4:25 from him that hath not, even that he hath shall be taken away from him.
Lk 8:18; **19:27** 27 But those mine enemies, which would not that I should reign over them,
Lk 19:14 bring hither, and slay *them* before me.

Z. JESUS COMES TO JERUSALEM

1. The Triumphal Entry (Cf. Mt 21:1–11; Mk 11:1–11; Jn 12:12–19)

19:28☆ 28 ¶And when he had thus spoken he went before, ascending up to
Mk 10:32; **19:29** Jerusalem.
Mt 21:1–9; Mk 11:1–10 29 And it came to pass, when he was come nigh to Beth′pha-ge and
Jn 12:12–18 Bethany, at the mount called *the mount* of Olives, he sent two of his
disciples,
30 Saying, Go ye into the village over against *you;* in the which at your
entering ye shall find a colt tied, whereon yet never man sat: loose him, and
bring *him hither.*
31 And if any man ask you, Why do ye loose *him?* thus shall ye say unto
him, Because the Lord hath need of him.
32 And they that were sent went their way, and found even as he had said
unto them.
33 And as they were loosing the colt, the owners thereof said unto them,
Why loose ye the colt?
34 And they said, The Lord hath need of him.
35 And they brought him to Jesus: and they cast their garments upon the
colt, and they set Jesus thereon.
19:36 36 And as he went, they spread their clothes in the way.
2 Kgs 9:13 37 And when he was come nigh, even now at the descent of the mount of
Olives, the whole multitude of the disciples began to rejoice and praise God
19:38 Ps 118:26 with a loud voice for all the mighty works that they had seen;
Mt 2:2; 25:34; Lk 2:14; 13:35 38 Saying, Blessed *be* the King that cometh in the name of the Lord: peace
1 Tim 1:17 in heaven, and glory in the highest.

19:28ff The triumphal entry into Jerusalem is recorded in all of the Gospels. This event was a fulfillment of the prophecy of Zech. 9:9. It took place on the first day of the week of Christ's passion, when he was to be rejected and crucified. He came into Jerusalem as king and conqueror; this was a preview of the Second Advent, when he will come in power and great glory. This triumphal entry as king was the last opportunity for the Jews to face up to his royal claims and to make their decision for or against him.

39 And some of the Pharisees from among the multitude said unto him, Master, rebuke thy disciples.

40 And he answered and said unto them, I tell you that, if these should hold their peace, the stones would immediately cry out.

19:40 Hab 2:11

2. Weeping over Jerusalem

41 ¶And when he was come near, he beheld the city, and wept over it,

42 Saying, If thou hadst known, even thou, at least in this thy day, the things *which belong* unto thy peace! but now they are hid from thine eyes.

43 For the days shall come upon thee, that thine enemies shall cast a trench about thee, and compass thee round, and keep thee in on every side,

44 And shall lay thee even with the ground, and thy children within thee; and they shall not leave in thee one stone upon another; because thou knewest not the time of thy visitation.

☆**19:41** Lk 13:34; Jn 11:35
19:43 Eccles 9:14; Isa 29:3; Jer 6:6; Ezek 4:1–3; Lk 21:6, 20
19:44 1 Kgs 9:6–9; Dan 9:26; Mic 3:12; Mt 24:2; Mk 13:2; Lk 21:6

VI. JESUS' LAST WEEK IN JERUSALEM (19:45—23:56)

A. THE SECOND CLEANSING OF THE TEMPLE (CF. MT 21:12–17; MK 11:15–19; JN 2:13–22)

45 And he went into the temple, and began to cast out them that sold therein, and them that bought;

46 Saying unto them, It is written, My house is the house of prayer: but ye have made it a den of thieves.

47 And he taught daily in the temple. But the chief priests and the scribes and the chief of the people sought to destroy him,

48 And could not find what they might do: for all the people were very attentive to hear him.

☆**19:45** Mt 21:12–16; Mk 11:11, 15–18; Jn 2:14–17
19:46 Isa 56:7; Jer 7:11
19:47 Mt 26:55; Lk 21:37; 22:53; Jn 18:20

B. JESUS' AUTHORITY QUESTIONED (CF. MT 21:23–27; MK 11:27–33)

20 AND it came to pass, *that* on one of those days, as he taught the people in the temple, and preached the gospel, the chief priests and the scribes came upon *him* with the elders,

2 And spake unto him, saying, Tell us, by what authority doest thou these things? or who is he that gave thee this authority?

3 And he answered and said unto them, I will also ask you one thing; and answer me:

4 The baptism of John, was it from heaven, or of men?

5 And they reasoned with themselves, saying, If we shall say, From heaven; he will say, Why then believed ye him not?

6 But and if we say, Of men; all the people will stone us: for they be persuaded that John was a prophet.

7 And they answered, that they could not tell whence *it was.*

20:1 Mt 21:23–27; Mk 11:26–33; Acts 4:1; 6:12
☆**20:2** Jn 2:18; Acts 4:7, 10
20:6 Mt 14:5; Lk 7:29
20:7 Rom 1:18, 21

19:41 Luke alone records the fact that Jesus' entry into Jerusalem was interrupted briefly as he stopped to weep over the city and bemoan the fact that the Jews would not surrender to his claims. His tears were a sign of Jerusalem's appointed doom that occurred in A.D. 70 as a direct consequence of the Jewish rejection of the Messiah.

19:45 Jesus loved the purity of the temple more than its wealth. This house of prayer was profaned by those who bought and sold there. This was his second cleansing of that sacred house (see John 2:13–22). See note on Mark 11:15–17 for information on this cleansing of the temple.

20:2 It is not unusual for men to question what is evident. Christ's miracles showed by what authority he did his works. They knew his authority was from heaven and not from men. Thus when Jesus asked them about John and his authority (whether it was from God or from men), they were stumped. By questioning Jesus' authority the chief priests, scribes, and elders lost their own authority, for Jesus' rights preceded theirs and their rights sprang from his.

20:8 Job 5:12, 13

[8]And Jesus said unto them, Neither tell I you by what authority I do
these things.

C. THE PARABLE OF THE WICKED TENANT FARMERS
(CF. MT 21:33–46; MK 12:1–12)

20:9☆ Isa 5:1–7 Mt 21:33–46 Mk 12:1–12
20:10 2 Kgs 17:13, 14 2 Chron 36:15, 16 Acts 7:52

[9]Then began he to speak to the people this parable; A certain man
planted a vineyard, and let it forth to husbandmen, and went into a far
country for a long time.
[10]And at the season he sent a servant to the husbandmen, that they
should give him of the fruit of the vineyard: but the husbandmen beat him,
and sent *him* away empty.
[11]And again he sent another servant: and they beat him also, and
entreated *him* shamefully, and sent *him* away empty.
[12]And again he sent a third: and they wounded him also, and cast *him*
out.

20:13 Jn 3:16 Rom 8:3 Gal 4:4
20:14 Heb 1:2

[13]Then said the lord of the vineyard, What shall I do? I will send my
beloved son: it may be they will reverence *him* when they see him.
[14]But when the husbandmen saw him, they reasoned among themselves,
saying, This is the heir: come, let us kill him, that the inheritance may be
ours.

20:15 Acts 3:15 1 Thess 2:15

[15]So they cast him out of the vineyard, and killed *him*. What therefore
shall the lord of the vineyard do unto them?
[16]He shall come and destroy these husbandmen, and shall give the
vineyard to others. And when they heard *it*, they said, God forbid.

20:17 Ps 118:22 Acts 4:11 Eph 2:20 1 Pet 2:7, 8
20:18 Isa 8:14, 15 Dan 2:34, 35

[17]And he beheld them, and said, What is this then that is written, The
stone which the builders rejected, the same is become the head of the
corner?
[18]Whosoever shall fall upon that stone shall be broken; but on whomso-
ever it shall fall, it will grind him to powder.

D. EFFORTS TO TRAP JESUS
1. Paying Taxes to Caesar (Cf. Mt 22:15–22; Mk 12:13–17)

[19]¶And the chief priests and the scribes the same hour sought to lay
hands on him; and they feared the people: for they perceived that he had
spoken this parable against them.

20:20☆ Mt 22:15–22 Mk 12:13–17

[20]And they watched *him*, and sent forth spies, which should feign
themselves just men, that they might take hold of his words, that so they
might deliver him unto the power and authority of the governor.
[21]And they asked him, saying, Master, we know that thou sayest and
teachest rightly, neither acceptest thou the person *of any*, but teachest the
way of God truly:
[22]Is it lawful for us to give tribute unto Cæsar, or no?

20:9ff This parable of the wicked farmer tenants (*husbandmen*) was applied to the Jewish nation for its rejection of God's Messiah. Jesus warned of the dire consequences of this decision—not only were they to be cast out; their inheritance was to be given over to Gentiles, who were offered the kingdom the Jews had rejected.

***20:20** Jesus' enemies wanted to* deliver him over to the power and authority of the Roman government. They could not put him to death, but the governor could. They wanted to be informers against him. They were spies who pretended to be honest men. They asked whether it was lawful for the free-born sons of Abraham to pay tribute to Caesar. If Jesus said it was wrong, they would deliver him to the Roman government for treason. If he said it was right, the Jews would be angry, for they thought the Messiah should free them from Rome's yoke. The questioners admitted that the coin they gave Jesus had Caesar's image on it. Thus he was telling them that they should have asked whether it was right to pay and receive Caesar's money and use it as an instrument of commerce. Since they did this, *they ought to pay tribute to the one who gave* them this convenience and whose money had value. Therefore render to Caesar the things that are Caesar's. But the Jews were not to be bound to Caesar's religion, for only God has the authority to say, "Give me your heart."

[23]But he perceived their craftiness, and said unto them, Why tempt ye
me?
[24]Shew me a penny. Whose image and superscription hath it? They
answered and said, Cæsar's.
[25]And he said unto them, Render therefore unto Cæsar the things which
be Cæsar's, and unto God the things which be God's.
[26]And they could not take hold of his words before the people: and they
marvelled at his answer, and held their peace.

20:25 Lk 23:2; Rom 13:7

2. The Sadducees and the Resurrection (Cf. Mt 22:15–22; Mk 12:18–27)

[27]¶Then came to *him* certain of the Sad'du-cees, which deny that there is
any resurrection; and they asked him,
[28]Saying, Master, Moses wrote unto us, If any man's brother die, having
a wife, and he die without children, that his brother should take his wife,
and raise up seed unto his brother.
[29]There were therefore seven brethren: and the first took a wife, and died
without children.
[30]And the second took her to wife, and he died childless.
[31]And the third took her; and in like manner the seven also: and they left
no children, and died.
[32]Last of all the woman died also.
[33]Therefore in the resurrection whose wife of them is she? for seven had
her to wife.
[34]And Jesus answering said unto them, The children of this world marry,
and are given in marriage:
[35]But they which shall be accounted worthy to obtain that world, and the
resurrection from the dead, neither marry, nor are given in marriage:
[36]Neither can they die any more: for they are equal unto the angels; and
are the children of God, being the children of the resurrection.
[37]Now that the dead are raised, even Moses shewed at the bush, when he
calleth the Lord the God of Abraham, and the God of Isaac, and the God
of Jacob.
[38]For he is not a God of the dead, but of the living: for all live unto him.
[39]¶Then certain of the scribes answering said, Master, thou hast well said.

☆**20:27** Mt 22:15–33; Mk 12:18–27; Acts 23:8
20:28 Gen 38:8; Deut 25:5
20:36 Rom 8:23; 1 Cor 15:42, 49, 52; 1 Jn 3:1, 2
20:37 Ex 3:6; Jn 11:25; Acts 7:32; Rom 4:17; 2 Cor 5:15; Heb 11:10, 35
☆**20:38**

3. Christ's Unanswerable Question (Cf. Mt 22:41–46; Mk 12:35–37)

[40]And after that they durst not ask him any *question at all.*
[41]And he said unto them, How say they that Christ is David's son?
[42]And David himself saith in the book of Psalms, The LORD said unto my
Lord, Sit thou on my right hand,
[43]Till I make thine enemies thy footstool.
[44]David therefore calleth him Lord, how is he then his son?

20:40 Mt 22:41–46; Mk 12:34–37
☆**20:42** Ps 110:1; Acts 2:34; 1 Cor 15:25
☆**20:44**

20:27ff *certain of the Sadducees.* The Sadducees opposed the Pharisees, but when it came to Jesus they were in league with each other to rid themselves of him. The Sadducees did not believe in the resurrection of the dead, yet they asked Jesus a question which had no significance whatever if there was no such resurrection. Their question was dishonest and had for its purpose the entrapment of Jesus. They supposed that their question could not be answered by Jesus and that this would further their cause against the doctrine of the bodily resurrection, which Jesus taught so plainly. But as usual the Son of God used Scripture to support his answer and left them confounded.

20:38 *for all live unto him.* All believers who have died physically are as alive unto the Lord.

20:42 *The LORD said unto my Lord.* The first use of LORD in this verse means "God"; the second *Lord* means "Messiah."

20:44 Jesus' question is this: If David calls his son Lord, how then can he who is Lord be David's son? The true answer is: (1) Christ as God was David's Lord; (2) Christ as man was David's son. In his human nature he was the offspring of David; in his divine nature he was the root of David. (See note on Mark 12:35.)

E. WARNING AGAINST THE RELIGIOUS TEACHERS (CF. MT 23:1–12; MK 12:38–40)

20:45 Mt 23:1–7, 13, 14 Mk 12:38–40 Lk 11:43 **20:46☆** **20:47** Lk 12:47 Jas 4:17

45 ¶Then in the audience of all the people he said unto his disciples,
46 Beware of the scribes, which desire to walk in long robes, and love greetings in the markets, and the highest seats in the synagogues, and the chief rooms at feasts;
47 Which devour widows' houses, and for a shew make long prayers: the same shall receive greater damnation.

F. THE WIDOW AND THE MITES (COPPER COINS)

21:1 Prov 3:9, 10; 11:24, 25 Mk 12:41–44 2 Cor 8:12; 9:6, 7 **21:4☆**

21 AND he looked up, and saw the rich men casting their gifts into the treasury.
2 And he saw also a certain poor widow casting in thither two mites.
3 And he said, Of a truth I say unto you, that this poor widow hath cast in more than they all:
4 For all these have of their abundance cast in unto the offerings of God: but she of her penury hath cast in all the living that she had.

G. JESUS' TEACHING ABOUT THE FUTURE

1. The Course of History (Cf. Mt 24:1–14; Mk 13:3–13)

21:5 Mk 24:1–22 Mk 13:1–23 **21:6** 1 Kgs 9:8 Mic 3:12 Lk 19:44 **21:7☆** **21:8** Lk 17:23

5 ¶And as some spake of the temple, how it was adorned with goodly stones and gifts, he said,
6 *As for* these things which ye behold, the days will come, in the which there shall not be left one stone upon another, that shall not be thrown down.
7 And they asked him, saying, Master, but when shall these things be? and what sign *will there be* when these things shall come to pass?
8 And he said, Take heed that ye be not deceived: for many shall come in my name, saying, I am *Christ;* and the time draweth near: go ye not therefore after them.
9 But when ye shall hear of wars and commotions, be not terrified: for these things must first come to pass; but the end *is* not by and by.
10 Then said he unto them, Nation shall rise against nation, and kingdom against kingdom:
11 And great earthquakes shall be in divers places, and famines, and pestilences; and fearful sights and great signs shall there be from heaven.

21:12 Mt 10:17, 18 Acts 4:3; 5:18; 12:4; 16:24; 25:23 Rev 2:10 **21:13** Phil 1:12, 13 **21:14** Mt 10:19, 20 Lk 12:11, 12 Acts 6:10 **21:15☆**

12 But before all these, they shall lay their hands on you, and persecute *you,* delivering *you* up to the synagogues, and into prisons, being brought before kings and rulers for my name's sake.
13 And it shall turn to you for a testimony.
14 Settle *it* therefore in your hearts, not to meditate before what ye shall answer:
15 For I will give you a mouth and wisdom, which all your adversaries shall not be able to gainsay nor resist.

20:46 Jesus accuses the scribes of being proud, haughty, covetous, oppressive, users of religion as a *cloak for crime. For a show they make long* prayers. Their pretended piety constituted a double iniquity, for which they must pay.

21:4 Paraphrased: "He who gives all he has is better than he who gives a tithe of a large fortune."

21:7 See note to Matt. 24:3 about these questions.

21:15 The disciples of Jesus, then and now, need not be afraid about what they will say when they stand before Jewish and pagan authorities. Christ through the Spirit will tell them what to say and their testimony will not be overthrown or disproved. They may not always be acquitted, because their persecutors, filled with hatred, will condemn them even if they can prove nothing against them. Some will be imprisoned, or beaten, or put to death. This is true today in many parts of the globe where atheistic tyrants rule.

16 And ye shall be betrayed both by parents, and brethren, and kinsfolks,
and friends; and *some* of you shall they cause to be put to death.
17 And ye shall be hated of all *men* for my name's sake.
18 But there shall not an hair of your head perish.
19 In your patience possess ye your souls.

21:16 Mic 7:6; Mt 10:21, 22; Acts 7:60; 12:2
21:17 2 Tim 3:12
21:19 Rom 2:7; 1 Pet 1:6–9

2. The Conquest of Jerusalem: Its Destruction (Cf. Mt 25:15–28; Mk 13:14–23)

20 And when ye shall see Jerusalem compassed with armies, then know
that the desolation thereof is nigh.
21 Then let them which are in Judæa flee to the mountains; and let them
which are in the midst of it depart out; and let not them that are in the
countries enter thereinto.
22 For these be the days of vengeance, that all things which are written
may be fulfilled.
23 But woe unto them that are with child, and to them that give suck, in
those days! for there shall be great distress in the land, and wrath upon this
people.
24 And they shall fall by the edge of the sword, and shall be led away
captive into all nations: and Jerusalem shall be trodden down of the
Gentiles, until the times of the Gentiles be fulfilled.

☆21:20
21:22 Isa 61:2; Dan 9:26, 27; Hos 9:7; Rom 11:25; Rev 11:2
☆21:24 Isa 63:18; Dan 8:13; Rom 11:25; Rev 11:2

3. The Coming of the Man from Heaven (Cf. Mt 23:29–31; Mk 13:24–27)

25 ¶And there shall be signs in the sun, and in the moon, and in the stars;
and upon the earth distress of nations, with perplexity; the sea and the
waves roaring;
26 Men's hearts failing them for fear, and for looking after those things
which are coming on the earth: for the powers of heaven shall be shaken.
27 And then shall they see the Son of man coming in a cloud with power
and great glory.
28 And when these things begin to come to pass, then look up, and lift up
your heads; for your redemption draweth nigh.

21:25 Mt 24:29–31; Mk 13:24–27; 2 Pet 3:10, 12
21:27 Dan 7:13; Acts 1:11; Rev 1:7, 14:14

4. The Parable of the Fig Tree (Cf. Mt 24:32–35; Mk 13:28–31)

29 And he spake to them a parable; Behold the fig tree, and all the trees;
30 When they now shoot forth, ye see and know of your own selves that
summer is now nigh at hand.
31 So likewise ye, when ye see these things come to pass, know ye that the
kingdom of God is nigh at hand.
32 Verily I say unto you, This generation shall not pass away, till all be
fulfilled.
33 Heaven and earth shall pass away: but my words shall not pass away.

21:29 Mt 24:32–35; Mk 13:28–31
21:31 Mk 1:15
21:33 Isa 40:6–8; Mt 5:18; Lk 6:17; 1 Pet 1:23–25

21:20 Jesus' prophecy about Jerusalem's destruction was literally fulfilled in A.D. 70 when Titus and the Roman legions captured it. Josephus, the Jewish historian, describes the taking of the city in some detail in his *Wars of the Jews,* Books V and VI. After A.D. 70, Jerusalem was trodden down of the Gentiles (21:24). Some think the recent return of the Jews to Israel and their control of Jerusalem marks the end of the Gentile control and the fulfillment of this prophetic word.

21:24 *until the times of the Gentiles be fulfilled,* or, "until the period of Gentile triumph ends in God's good time" (TLB). Jerusalem was to be trodden down by the Gentiles for this period of time. This implies that an end will come when Jerusalem will be restored to the Jews. Jerusalem is now in Jewish hands; this may represent the fulfillment of that prophecy in our lifetime. In Rom. 11, Paul says that Israel will set themselves against the gospel until the full number of the Gentiles have come into God's kingdom, at which time "all Israel shall be saved" (Rom. 11:26).

5. The Command to Watch and Pray (Cf. Mt 24:36–51; Mk 13:32–37)

21:34 Rom 13:12, 13; 1 Thess 5:2; 1 Pet 3:3; 16:15

34¶And take heed to yourselves, lest at any time your hearts be
overcharged with surfeiting, and drunkenness, and cares of this life, and *so*
that day come upon you unawares.
35For as a snare shall it come on all them that dwell on the face of the
whole earth.

21:36 Mt 25:13; Mk 13:33; Eph 6:13, 18; 1 Thess 5:17; 1 Jn 2:28
21:37, 38 Lk 22:39; Jn 8:1, 2

36Watch ye therefore, and pray always, that ye may be accounted worthy
to escape all these things that shall come to pass, and to stand before the
Son of man.
37And in the day time he was teaching in the temple; and at night he
went out, and abode in the mount that is called *the mount* of Olives.
38And all the people came early in the morning to him in the temple, for
to hear him.

H. PLANNING JESUS' BETRAYAL (CF. MT 26:1–5, 14–16; MK 14:1, 2, 10, 11)

22:1 Mt 26:1–5, 14–16; Mk 14:1, 2, 10, 11
22:2☆ Ps 2:2; Acts 4:27
22:3☆ Jn 13:2, 27

22 NOW the feast of unleavened bread drew nigh, which is called the
Passover.
2And the chief priests and scribes sought how they might kill him; for
they feared the people.
3¶Then entered Satan into Judas surnamed Iscariot, being of the number
of the twelve.
4And he went his way, and communed with the chief priests and
captains, how he might betray him unto them.

22:5 Zech 11:12; 1 Tim 6:10

5And they were glad, and covenanted to give him money.
6And he promised, and sought opportunity to betray him unto them in
the absence of the multitude.

I. THE LAST PASSOVER SUPPER

1. The Preparation (Cf. Mt 26:17–19; Mk 14:12–16)

22:7 Ex 12:3, 4, 17; Deut 16:1; Mt 26:17–19; Mk 14:12–16
22:8 Acts 3:1; 4:13; Gal 2:9
22:10☆ 1 Sam 10:3

7¶Then came the day of unleavened bread, when the passover must be
killed.
8And he sent Peter and John, saying, Go and prepare us the passover,
that we may eat.
9And they said unto him, Where wilt thou that we prepare?
10And he said unto them, Behold, when ye are entered into the city, there
shall a man meet you, bearing a pitcher of water; follow him into the house
where he entereth in.
11And ye shall say unto the goodman of the house, The Master saith unto
thee, Where is the guestchamber, where I shall eat the passover with my
disciples?
12And he shall shew you a large upper room furnished: there make ready.
13And they went, and found as he had said unto them: and they made
ready the passover.

2. The Celebration (Cf. Mt 26:20–25; Mk 14:17–21; Jn 13:1–30)

22:14 Mt 26:20, 26–29; Mk 14:17, 22–25

14And when the hour was come, he sat down, and the twelve apostles
with him.

22:2 The chief priests and scribes feared the people who saw in Jesus what they missed. These enemies, supposedly long on piety and learning, would do anything to kill Jesus.

22:3 See note on Matt. 26:14 regarding Judas Iscariot.

22:10 Women carried pitchers on their heads; men carried water skins. Here a man carries a pitcher. He was thus easily identifiable by Jesus' disciples. Unless this was a prearranged signal, this event again demonstrates divine prescience.

15And he said unto them, With desire I have desired to eat this passover
with you before I suffer:

☆22:15

16For I say unto you, I will not any more eat thereof, until it be fulfilled
in the kingdom of God.

22:16 Lk 14:15; Rev 19:9

17And he took the cup, and gave thanks, and said, Take this, and divide
it among yourselves:

☆22:17

3. The Institution of the Lord's Supper (Cf. Mt 26:26–29; Mk 14:22–25)

18For I say unto you, I will not drink of the fruit of the vine, until the
kingdom of God shall come.

19¶And he took bread, and gave thanks, and brake *it,* and gave unto
them, saying, This is my body which is given for you: this do in
remembrance of me.

☆22:19 1 Cor 10:16; 11:23–26

20Likewise also the cup after supper, saying, This cup *is* the new
testament in my blood, which is shed for you.

22:20 Jer 31:31; Heb 9:15–18

21¶But, behold, the hand of him that betrayeth me *is* with me on the
table.

22:21 Ps 41:9; Mt 26:20–25; Mk 14:17–21; Jn 13:21–30

22And truly the Son of man goeth, as it was determined: but woe unto
that man by whom he is betrayed!

22:22 Acts 2:23; 4:28

23And they began to inquire among themselves, which of them it was that
should do this thing.

24¶And there was also a strife among them, which of them should be
accounted the greatest.

22:24 Mk 9:34; Lk 9:46

25And he said unto them, The kings of the Gentiles exercise lordship over
them; and they that exercise authority upon them are called benefactors.

22:25 Mt 20:25–28; Mk 10:42–45

26But ye *shall* not *be* so: but he that is greatest among you, let him be as
the younger; and he that is chief, as he that doth serve.

22:26 Mt 23:11; Mk 9:35; Lk 9:48; 1 Pet 5:5

27For whether *is* greater, he that sitteth at meat, or he that serveth? *is* not
he that sitteth at meat? but I am among you as he that serveth.

22:27 Jn 13:14; Phil 2:7

28Ye are they which have continued with me in my temptations.

22:28 Heb 2:18; 4:15

29And I appoint unto you a kingdom, as my Father hath appointed unto
me;

22:29 Lk 12:32

30That ye may eat and drink at my table in my kingdom, and sit on
thrones judging the twelve tribes of Israel.

22:30 Mt 8:11; 19:28; Lk 14:15; 1 Cor 6:2; 2 Tim 2:12; Rev 3:21; 19:9

4. The Prediction of Peter's Denial (Cf. Mt 26:30–35; Mk 14:27–31)

31¶And the Lord said, Simon, Simon, behold, Satan hath desired *to have*
you, that he may sift *you* as wheat:

22:31 Amos 9:9; Mt 26:31–35; Mk 14:27–31; 1 Pet 5:8

32But I have prayed for thee, that thy faith fail not: and when thou art
converted, strengthen thy brethren.

☆22:32 Ps 51:13; Jn 17:9, 11, 15; 21:15; 2 Cor 1:3, 4

33And he said unto him, Lord, I am ready to go with thee, both into
prison, and to death.

22:33 Jn 13:37, 38

22:15 See note to Mark 14:1 and Exod. 12:11 on the *Passover.*

22:17 Churches differ about the Eucharist (the Lord's Supper). Protestants commune in two kinds; they eat the bread and drink from the cup. Roman Catholics eat the bread but usually do not drink from the cup. A greater difference relates to the presence of Jesus Christ in the elements. Jesus is the God-man and as such is in a body. If he is present he must be physically present. Thus some accept the real, literal presence of Christ in the Eucharist. Roman Catholics teach that the bread and wine become the very body and blood of Jesus. Presbyterians believe in the spiritual, not bodily, presence of Christ in the elements. Baptists believe that Christ is symbolically present. Lutherans hold to the real presence of Christ, called consubstantiation; this differs from the Roman Catholics, whose doctrine is called transubstantiation.

22:19 See note on Mark 14:22ff.

22:32 Intercessory prayer consists of asking God's help on behalf of other people. It must be in accord with the laws that govern all prayer. Such prayer includes (1) interceding for others, including kings and those in authority (1 Tim. 2:1, 2); (2) praying for ministers of the gospel (2 Cor. 1:11; Phil. 1:19); (3) praying for those who persecute us (Matt. 5:44); and (4) praying for friends (Job 42:8).

22:34☆ [34]And he said, I tell thee, Peter, the cock shall not crow this day, before
that thou shalt thrice deny that thou knowest me.
22:35 [35]And he said unto them, When I sent you without purse, and scrip, and
Mt 10:9, 10
Lk 9:3 shoes, lacked ye any thing? And they said, Nothing.
[36]Then said he unto them, But now, he that hath a purse, let him take *it*,
and likewise *his* scrip: and he that hath no sword, let him sell his garment,
and buy one.
22:37 [37]For I say unto you, that this that is written must yet be accomplished in
Isa 53:12
Mk 15:28 me, And he was reckoned among the transgressors: for the things
concerning me have an end.
[38]And they said, Lord, behold, here *are* two swords. And he said unto
them, It is enough.

J. JESUS IN GETHSEMANE'S GARDEN
1. The Agony (Cf. Mt 26:36–46; Mk 14:32–43)

22:39 [39]¶And he came out, and went, as he was wont, to the mount of Olives;
Mt 26:30, 36–46
Mk 14:26, 32–42 and his disciples also followed him.
Jn 18:1 [40]And when he was at the place, he said unto them, Pray that ye enter not
22:40
Mt 6:13 into temptation.
22:41
Mk 10:38 [41]And he was withdrawn from them about a stone's cast, and kneeled
Jn 5:30; 6:38
18:11 down, and prayed,
22:42☆ [42]Saying, Father, if thou be willing, remove this cup from me: neverthe-
less not my will, but thine, be done.
22:43 [43]And there appeared an angel unto him from heaven, strengthening him.
Mt 4:11
22:44 [44]And being in an agony he prayed more earnestly: and his sweat was as
Jn 12:27
Heb 5:7 it were great drops of blood falling down to the ground.
[45]And when he rose up from prayer, and was come to his disciples, he
found them sleeping for sorrow,
[46]And said unto them, Why sleep ye? rise and pray, lest ye enter into
temptation.

2. Betrayal and Arrest (Cf. Mt 26:47–56; Mk 14:43–50; Jn 18:1–11)

22:47☆ [47]¶And while he yet spake, behold a multitude, and he that was called
Mt 26:47–56
Mk 14:43–50 Judas, one of the twelve, went before them, and drew near unto Jesus to
Jn 18:1–11 kiss him.
[48]But Jesus said unto him, Judas, betrayest thou the Son of man with a
kiss?
[49]When they which were about him saw what would follow, they said
unto him, Lord, shall we smite with the sword?
[50]¶And one of them smote the servant of the high priest, and cut off his
right ear.
[51]And Jesus answered and said, Suffer ye thus far. And he touched his
ear, and healed him.
[52]Then Jesus said unto the chief priests, and captains of the temple, and
the elders, which were come to him, Be ye come out, as against a thief, with
swords and staves?
22:53
Gen 3:15 [53]When I was daily with you in the temple, ye stretched forth no hands
Lk 19:47
Jn 7:30 against me: but this is your hour, and the power of darkness.

22:34 See note on Mark 14:30 about the crowing of the cock.
22:42 *this cup.* See note on Matt. 26:39.
22:47 *drew near unto Jesus to kiss him.* This is still the traditional greeting among men in eastern lands.† (See the note on Mark 14:45 for information about the betrayal of Jesus.)

K. PETER'S DENIALS OF JESUS (CF. MT 26:69–75; MK 14:66–72; JN 18:15–18, 25–27)

54 ¶Then took they him, and led *him,* and brought him into the high
priest's house. And Peter followed afar off.
55 And when they had kindled a fire in the midst of the hall, and were set
down together, Peter sat down among them.
56 But a certain maid beheld him as he sat by the fire, and earnestly
looked upon him, and said, This man was also with him.
57 And he denied him, saying, Woman, I know him not.
58 And after a little while another saw him, and said, Thou art also of
them. And Peter said, Man, I am not.
59 And about the space of one hour after another confidently affirmed,
saying, Of a truth this *fellow* also was with him: for he is a Galilæan.
60 And Peter said, Man, I know not what thou sayest. And immediately,
while he yet spake, the cock crew.
61 And the Lord turned, and looked upon Peter. And Peter remembered
the word of the Lord, how he had said unto him, Before the cock crow, thou
shalt deny me thrice.
62 And Peter went out, and wept bitterly.
63 ¶And the men that held Jesus mocked him, and smote *him.*
64 And when they had blindfolded him, they struck him on the face, and
asked him, saying, Prophesy, who is it that smote thee?
65 And many other things blasphemously spake they against him.
66 ¶And as soon as it was day, the elders of the people and the chief
priests and the scribes came together, and led him into their council, saying,
67 Art thou the Christ? tell us. And he said unto them, If I tell you, ye will
not believe:
68 And if I also ask *you,* ye will not answer me, nor let *me* go.
69 Hereafter shall the Son of man sit on the right hand of the power of
God.
70 Then said they all, Art thou then the Son of God? And he said unto
them, Ye say that I am.
71 And they said, What need we any further witness? for we ourselves
have heard of his own mouth.

22:54 Mt 26:57, 58, 69–75; Mk 14:53, 54, 66–72; Jn 18:15–18, 25–27
☆**22:61** Jn 13:38
☆**22:62** 2 Cor 7:10
22:63 Isa 52:14; Mt 26:67, 68; Mk 14:65; Jn 18:22
22:66 Mt 26:63–66; 27:1; Mk 14:61–64; 15:1
22:69 Dan 7:13, 14; Acts 3:21; Heb 1:3; 8:1

L. JESUS' TRIAL BEFORE PONTIUS PILATE (CF. MT 27:11–26; MK 15:2–15; JN 18:29–40)

1. Pilate's Question

23 AND the whole multitude of them arose, and led him unto Pilate.
2 And they began to accuse him, saying, We found this *fellow*
perverting the nation, and forbidding to give tribute to Cæsar, saying that
he himself is Christ a King.
3 And Pilate asked him, saying, Art thou the King of the Jews? And he
answered him and said, Thou sayest *it.*

23:1 Mt 27:2, 11–14; Mk 15:1–5; Jn 18:28, 33–38
23:2 Mt 17:24–27; 22:21; Mk 12:17; Jn 19:12; Acts 17:7; 24:5
☆**23:3** 1 Tim 6:13

22:61 *the Lord turned, and looked upon Peter.* This look signifies certain things: (1) It was a convicting look, for Jesus was asking, "Peter, do you not know me?" (2) It was a reproving look because of Peter's sin. (3) It was a remonstrating look asking, "Did you not confess me as the Son of God? Should you not now come and witness for me?" (4) It was a compassionate look of tenderness: "Peter, how weak is thy heart?" (5) It was a directing look, encouraging Peter to go away and think of what he had done. (6) It was a loving look conveying grace, which later enabled him to repent and be restored.

22:62 *wept bitterly.* This could have been weeping because he was caught doing what was wrong, or weeping because he was sorry. The latter was the case, for the weeping was followed by repentance and restoration.

23:3 *Thou sayest it.* This is enigmatic. It might mean, "Can you prove it?" Or, "Have you any evidence?" Or, "It is as thou sayest. I am, but over Israel and not as a rival to Rome."

23:4 Jn 19:4 1 Pet 2:22 4 Then said Pilate to the chief priests and *to* the people, I find no fault in
this man.
5 And they were the more fierce, saying, He stirreth up the people,
teaching throughout all Jewry, beginning from Galilee to this place.

2. Pilate Sends Jesus to King Herod

6 When Pilate heard of Galilee, he asked whether the man were a
Galilæan.
23:7 Lk 3:1 7 And as soon as he knew that he belonged unto Herod's jurisdiction, he
sent him to Herod, who himself also was at Jerusalem at that time.
23:8 Mt 14:1 Mk 6:14 Lk 9:9 8 ¶And when Herod saw Jesus, he was exceeding glad: for he was desirous
to see him of a long *season,* because he had heard many things of him; and
he hoped to have seen some miracle done by him.
23:9 Jn 19:9 9 Then he questioned with him in many words; but he answered him
nothing.
10 And the chief priests and scribes stood and vehemently accused him.
11 And Herod with his men of war set him at nought, and mocked *him,*
and arrayed him in a gorgeous robe, and sent him again to Pilate.
23:12 Acts 4:27 12 ¶And the same day Pilate and Herod were made friends together: for
before they were at enmity between themselves.

3. Pilate's Effort to Release Jesus

13 ¶And Pilate, when he had called together the chief priests and the rulers
and the people,
14 Said unto them, Ye have brought this man unto me, as one that
perverteth the people: and, behold, I, having examined *him* before you,
have found no fault in this man touching those things whereof ye accuse
him:
23:15 Lk 9:9 15 No, nor yet Herod: for I sent you to him; and, lo, nothing worthy of
death is done unto him.
23:16☆ Jn 19:1 Acts 16:37 16 I will therefore chastise him, and release *him.*

4. Pilate Sets Barabbas Free and Delivers Jesus

23:17☆ Mt 27:15–26 Mk 15:6–15 Jn 18:39, 40 17 (For of necessity he must release one unto them at the feast.)
18 And they cried out all at once, saying, Away with this *man,* and release
23:18☆ Acts 3:14 unto us Ba-rab'bas:
19 (Who for a certain sedition made in the city, and for murder, was cast
into prison.)
20 Pilate therefore, willing to release Jesus, spake again to them.
21 But they cried, saying, Crucify *him,* crucify him.
22 And he said unto them the third time, Why, what evil hath he done? I
have found no cause of death in him: I will therefore chastise him, and let
him go.
23:23 Ex 23:2, 3 23 And they were instant with loud voices, requiring that he might be
crucified. And the voices of them and of the chief priests prevailed.
23:24 Jn 19:16 24 And Pilate gave sentence that it should be as they required.
23:25 Prov 17:15 25 And he released unto them him that for sedition and murder was cast
into prison, whom they had desired; but he delivered Jesus to their will.

23:16 If Jesus was innocent of the charges, why would Pilate chastise him before releasing him? To chastise meant to scourge; in many cases this ended in death. Pilate's moral sense was dulled by political equivocation and personal enhancement.

23:17 This verse is not present in the best, earliest manuscripts.

23:18 See note on Mark 15:7 for information about Barabbas.

M. THE CRUCIFIXION OF JESUS

1. Jesus En Route to Calvary

26 And as they led him away, they laid hold upon one Simon, a Cy-re′ni-
an, coming out of the country, and on him they laid the cross, that he might
bear *it* after Jesus.
27 ¶And there followed him a great company of people, and of women,
which also bewailed and lamented him.
28 But Jesus turning unto them said, Daughters of Jerusalem, weep not for
me, but weep for yourselves, and for your children.
29 For, behold, the days are coming, in the which they shall say, Blessed
are the barren, and the wombs that never bare, and the paps which never
gave suck.
30 Then shall they begin to say to the mountains, Fall on us; and to the
hills, Cover us.
31 For if they do these things in a green tree, what shall be done in the
dry?

☆**23:26** Mt 27:32 Mk 15:21 Jn 19:17
23:29 Lk 21:23
23:30 Isa 2:19 Hos 10:8 Rev 6:16
☆**23:31** Ezek 20:47 1 Pet 4:17

2. The Execution (Cf. Mt 27:32–44; Mk 15:21–32; Jn 19:17–24)

32 And there were also two other, malefactors, led with him to be put to
death.
33 And when they were come to the place, which is called Calvary, there
they crucified him, and the malefactors, one on the right hand, and the
other on the left.
34 ¶Then said Jesus, Father, forgive them; for they know not what they
do. And they parted his raiment, and cast lots.
35 And the people stood beholding. And the rulers also with them derided
him, saying, He saved others; let him save himself, if he be Christ, the
chosen of God.
36 And the soldiers also mocked him, coming to him, and offering him
vinegar,
37 And saying, If thou be the king of the Jews, save thyself.
38 And a superscription also was written over him in letters of Greek, and
Latin, and Hebrew, THIS IS THE KING OF THE JEWS.

23:32 Isa 53:12 Mt 27:33–44 Mk 15:22–32 Jn 19:18–24 Heb 13:12
☆**23:33**
☆**23:34** Mt 5:44 Acts 3:17; 7:60 1 Cor 2:8
23:35 Ps 22:16–18
23:36 Mt 27:48

3. The Salvation of the Criminal on the Cross

39 ¶And one of the malefactors which were hanged railed on him, saying,
If thou be Christ, save thyself and us.
40 But the other answering rebuked him, saying, Dost not thou fear God,
seeing thou art in the same condemnation?
41 And we indeed justly; for we receive the due reward of our deeds: but
this man hath done nothing amiss.

23:26 *Simon, a Cyrenian,* was a man from North Africa who was in Jerusalem, probably on business, at the time of the crucifixion. He is said to be the father of Alexander and Rufus, known to readers of Mark's Gospel. In all probability he was a displaced Jew residing in Africa.

23:31 Paraphrased: "For if such things as this are done to me, the Living Tree, what will they do to you?"†

23:33 Jesus died between two thieves. They died different deaths. One thief died with sin *in* him and *on* him; the other thief died with sin *in* him but no sin *on* him, because of his faith in Christ. Jesus had no sin *in* him but the sin of the world was laid *on* him. Thus one man died *to* sin, the second one died *in* sin, and Jesus died *for* sin. (See note on John 19:17.)

23:34ff The order in which Christ spoke his seven last sayings on the cross is as follows: (1) the word of forgiveness: "Father, forgive them; for they know not what they do" (23:34); (2) the word of salvation: "To day shalt thou be with me in paradise" (23:43); (3) the word of affection: "Woman, behold thy son"; "Behold thy mother" (John 19:26, 27); (4) the word of despair: "My God, my God, why hast thou forsaken me?" (Matt. 27:46; Mark 15:34); (5) the word of physical torment: "I thirst" (John 19:28); (6) the word of triumph: "It is finished" (John 19:30); and (7) the word of commital: "Father, into thy hands I commend my spirit" (23:46).

23:42 Heb 8:1 — 42 And he said unto Jesus, Lord, remember me when thou comest into thy
kingdom.
23:43☆ 2 Cor 12:3, 4 Rev 2:7 — 43 And Jesus said unto him, **Verily I say unto thee, To day shalt thou be
with me in paradise.**

4. Jesus Surrenders to Death (Cf. Mt 27:45–50; Mk 15:33–41; Jn 19:28–37)

23:44 Mt 27:45–51 Mk 15:33–38 Jn 19:14, 28–30 — 44 And it was about the sixth hour, and there was a darkness over all the
earth until the ninth hour.
23:45 Ex 26:33 Heb 9:8; 10:19 — 45 And the sun was darkened, and the veil of the temple was rent in the
midst.
23:46☆ Ps 31:5 — 46 ¶And when Jesus had cried with a loud voice, he said, **Father, into thy
hands I commend my spirit:** and having said thus, he gave up the ghost.
23:47 Mt 27:54–56 Mk 15:39–41 Jn 19:25 — 47 Now when the centurion saw what was done, he glorified God, saying,
Certainly this was a righteous man.
48 And all the people that came together to that sight, beholding the
things which were done, smote their breasts, and returned.
49 And all his acquaintance, and the women that followed him from
Galilee, stood afar off, beholding these things.

5. The Entombment of Jesus (Cf. Mt 27:57–61; Mk 15:42–47; Jn 19:38–42)

23:50 Mt 27:57–61 Mk 15:42–47 Lk 2:25, 38 Jn 19:38–42 — 50 ¶And, behold, *there was* a man named Joseph, a counsellor; *and he was*
a good man, and a just:
51 (The same had not consented to the counsel and deed of them;) *he was*
of Ar-i-ma-thæ'a, a city of the Jews: who also himself waited for the
kingdom of God.
52 This *man* went unto Pilate, and begged the body of Jesus.
23:53 Isa 53:9 — 53 And he took it down, and wrapped it in linen, and laid it in a sepulchre
that was hewn in stone, wherein never man before was laid.
23:54☆ — 54 And that day was the preparation, and the sabbath drew on.
23:55 Lk 8:2 — 55 And the women also, which came with him from Galilee, followed
after, and beheld the sepulchre, and how his body was laid.
23:56 Ex 20:10; 35:2 Lev 23:3 Deut 5:14 Isa 58:13, 14 Mk 16:1 — 56 And they returned, and prepared spices and ointments; and rested the
sabbath day according to the commandment.

VII. THE RESURRECTION AND LATER APPEARANCES OF JESUS (24:1–53; CF. MT 28:1–10; MK 16:1–8; JN 20:1–18)

A. THE RESURRECTION MORNING

24:1☆ Mt 28:1–8 Mk 16:1–11 Jn 20:1, 2, 10–13 — 24 NOW upon the first *day* of the week, very early in the morning,
they came unto the sepulchre, bringing the spices which they had
prepared, and certain *others* with them.
2 And they found the stone rolled away from the sepulchre.

23:43 *paradise. Paradeisos,* the word that appears in the Greek text, is actually a Persian loan word and appears only two other times in the New Testament (in *2 Cor. 12:4 and Rev. 2:7). Originally* it meant an enclosed park or a pleasure ground. In the Septuagint it was used as a term for the Garden of Eden, and in the intertestamental times it was the word for a superterrestrial place of felicity. As used here, it can mean "heaven" or "the presence of God."

23:46 *he gave up the ghost,* i.e., "he died."

23:54 *the preparation,* i.e., Friday (cf. Mark 15:42; John 19:31, 42). All necessary preparations were made in advance of the sabbath, when no work was permitted. The sabbath began at sundown on Friday, thus that day was the day of preparation. The burial of Jesus, therefore, had to be carried out before sundown on Friday.

24:1ff See note on Matt. 28:6 about the resurrection of Jesus.

3And they entered in, and found not the body of the Lord Jesus.
4And it came to pass, as they were much perplexed thereabout, behold,
two men stood by them in shining garments:

☆**24:4** Acts 1:10

5And as they were afraid, and bowed down *their* faces to the earth, they
said unto them, Why seek ye the living among the dead?

24:5 Rev 1:17, 18

6He is not here, but is risen: remember how he spake unto you when he
was yet in Galilee,
7Saying, The Son of man must be delivered into the hands of sinful men,
and be crucified, and the third day rise again.

24:6 Mt 16:21; Mk 8:31; Lk 9:22

8And they remembered his words,
9And returned from the sepulchre, and told all these things unto the
eleven, and to all the rest.

24:8 Jn 2:22

10It was Mary Magdalene, and Jo-an′na, and Mary *the mother* of James,
and other *women that were* with them, which told these things unto the
apostles.

24:10 Mt 27:56; Lk 8:3

11And their words seemed to them as idle tales, and they believed them
not.

24:11 Mk 16:11

12Then arose Peter, and ran unto the sepulchre; and stooping down, he
beheld the linen clothes laid by themselves, and departed, wondering in
himself at that which was come to pass.

24:12 Lk 24:34; Jn 20:2–10

B. THE WALK TO EMMAUS

13¶And, behold, two of them went that same day to a village called Em-
ma′us, which was from Jerusalem *about* threescore furlongs.

24:13 Mk 16:12, 13

14And they talked together of all these things which had happened.
15And it came to pass, that, while they communed *together* and reasoned,
Jesus himself drew near, and went with them.

24:15 Mt 18:20

16But their eyes were holden that they should not know him.

24:16 Lk 24:31; Jn 20:14; 21:4

17And he said unto them, What manner of communications *are* these that
ye have one to another, as ye walk, and are sad?
18And the one of them, whose name was Cle′o-pas, answering said unto
him, Art thou only a stranger in Jerusalem, and hast not known the things
which are come to pass there in these days?

24:18 Jn 19:25

19And he said unto them, What things? And they said unto him,
Concerning Jesus of Nazareth, which was a prophet mighty in deed and
word before God and all the people:

24:19 Jn 3:2; Acts 2:22

20And how the chief priests and our rulers delivered him to be con-
demned to death, and have crucified him.

24:20 Lk 23:13; Acts 13:27

21But we trusted that it had been he which should have redeemed Israel:
and beside all this, to day is the third day since these things were done.

24:21 Lk 1:68; Acts 1:6

22Yea, and certain women also of our company made us astonished,
which were early at the sepulchre;
23And when they found not his body, they came, saying, that they had
also seen a vision of angels, which said that he was alive.
24*And certain of them which were with us went to* the sepulchre, and
found *it* even so as the women had said: but him they saw not.
25Then he said unto them, O fools, and slow of heart to believe all that
the prophets have spoken:

24:25 2 Cor 4:14, 15

26Ought not Christ to have suffered these things, and to enter into his
glory?

24:26 Mt 26:24; Lk 24:7, 44; Jn 12:23, 24; 13:31, 32; Acts 17:3; Cor 15:42–44; Phil 2:6–11; Heb 2:10; 5:5

24:4 *two men.* Some have supposed there is a discrepancy here, for Matthew and Mark mention only one angel (Matt. 28:5; Mark 16:5). (Curiously, John says nothing about any angel.) But the problem is readily resolved: Matthew and Mark did not say there was *only* one angel. Luke simply gives us fuller information.

24:27
Gen 3:15
14:18–20; 26:4
49:10
Ex 3:6; 12:3–11
16:15; 17:6
Num 21:8, 9
24:17
Deut 18:15, 18
2 Sam 7:12–14
Job 19:25
Ps 2:2, 6–9, 12
8:4–6; 16:8–11
22:1–22; 31:5
34:20; 41:9
45:6, 7; 68:18
69:4, 9, 21
78:2; 89:3, 4
97:7; 110:1, 2, 4
118:22, 26
132:11
Prov 8:22–31
30:4
Isa 4:2; 6:1, 5
7:14; 8:14, 15,
18; 9:1, 2, 6, 7
11:1–10
22:22–24; 25:8,
9; 32:1–4; 35:5,
6; 40:3–11
42:1–9; 49:1–10
50:5–7; 52:10,
13; 53:1–12
61:1, 2
Jer 23:5, 6; 30:9
33:15
Ezek 34:23, 24
37: 24, 25
Dan 2:34, 35, 44,
45; 7:13
9:25, 26
Hos 11:1
Mic 5:2
Zech 3:8, 9; 6:12,
13; 9:9
11:12, 13; 12:10
13:1, 7
Mal 3:1; 4:2, 5
24:31☆
24:34
1 Cor 15:5
24:36
Mk 16:14
Jn 20:19, 20
24:39☆
1 Jn 1:1
24:40☆
24:42☆
24:43☆
Acts 10:41
24:44
Lk 24:27

27 And beginning at Moses and all the prophets, he expounded unto them
in all the scriptures the things concerning himself.
28 And they drew nigh unto the village, whither they went: and he made
as though he would have gone further.
29 But they constrained him, saying, Abide with us: for it is toward
evening, and the day is far spent. And he went in to tarry with them.
30 And it came to pass, as he sat at meat with them, he took bread, and
blessed *it,* and brake, and gave to them.
31 And their eyes were opened, and they knew him; and he vanished out
of their sight.
32 And they said one to another, Did not our heart burn within us, while
he talked with us by the way, and while he opened to us the scriptures?
33 And they rose up the same hour, and returned to Jerusalem, and found
the eleven gathered together, and them that were with them,
34 Saying, The Lord is risen indeed, and hath appeared to Simon.
35 And they told what things *were done* in the way, and how he was known
of them in breaking of bread.

C. THE APPEARANCE TO THE TEN IN JERUSALEM (CF. JN 20:19–25)

36 ¶And as they thus spake, Jesus himself stood in the midst of them, and
saith unto them, Peace *be* unto you.
37 But they were terrified and affrighted, and supposed that they had seen
a spirit.
38 And he said unto them, Why are ye troubled? and why do thoughts
arise in your hearts?
39 Behold my hands and my feet, that it is I myself: handle me, and see;
for a spirit hath not flesh and bones, as ye see me have.
40 And when he had thus spoken, he shewed them *his* hands and *his* feet.
41 And while they yet believed not for joy, and wondered, he said unto
them, Have ye here any meat?
42 And they gave him a piece of a broiled fish, and of an honeycomb.
43 And he took *it,* and did eat before them.

D. THE COMMAND TO EVANGELIZE (CF. MT 28:18–20; JN 20:21; ACTS 1:8)

44 And he said unto them, These *are* the words which I spake unto you,
while I was yet with you, that all things must be fulfilled, which were
written in the law of Moses, and *in* the prophets, and *in* the psalms,
concerning me.
45 Then opened he their understanding, that they might understand the
scriptures,

24:31 *he vanished out of their sight.* Jesus, in his resurrected body, was able to disappear at will. He could pass through doors (John 20:26) and come and go as he pleased. The angels who took on human form were able to pass through bars of iron, according to *Acts 12:7. When the angel led Peter out of the prison* the iron gate opened by itself to let them out, for Peter could not pass through otherwise. Jesus' resurrection body had different properties; so will ours.

24:39 Jesus told his disciples that he was not a spirit. He had hands and feet. He invited them to feel him. In 24:42, 43 we see that he took and ate broiled fish. Whoever denies the bodily resurrection does so against the expressed affirmation of it in Scripture.

24:40 *he shewed them his hands and his feet,* i.e., "he showed them the marks of the nails in his hands and feet."

24:42 *and of an honeycomb.* This phrase is not found in the best manuscripts.

24:43 *did eat.* The fact that Jesus ate the fish indicates that his resurrection state was not simply that of spirit. It was a different body in that it was immortal and perfect, yet he performed the normal bodily act of eating food.

46 And said unto them, Thus it is written, and thus it behoved Christ to
suffer, and to rise from the dead the third day:
47 And that repentance and remission of sins should be preached in his
name among all nations, beginning at Jerusalem.
48 And ye are witnesses of these things.
49 ¶And, behold, I send the promise of my Father upon you: but tarry ye
in the city of Jerusalem, until ye be endued with power from on high

E. THE ASCENSION (CF. MK 16:19, 20; ACTS 1:9–11)

50 ¶And he led them out as far as to Bethany, and he lifted up his hands,
and blessed them.
51 And it came to pass, while he blessed them, he was parted from them,
and carried up into heaven.
52 And they worshipped him, and returned to Jerusalem with great joy:
53 And were continually in the temple, praising and blessing God. Amen.

☆**24:46**
24:47 Isa 49:6 Jer 31:34 Dan 9:24 Hos 2:23 Mic 4:2 Mal 1:11 Acts 2:38; 5:31 10:43; 13:38 26:18
24:48 Jn 15:27
☆**24:49** Isa 44:3 Joel 2:28 Acts 2:1–4
☆**24:50**
24:51 Mk 16:19, 20 Eph 1:20; 4:8
24:53 Acts 2:46; 5:42

24:46ff Everywhere in the Bible the resurrection of Christ is treated as a bodily resurrection, destroying oft-repeated rationalized explanations such as (1) the "swoon theory," which claims Jesus died later—he did not really die on the cross; (2) the "fraud theory"—that the disciples stole his body and lied about the resurrection; (3) the "hallucination theory"—that the excited disciples saw visions but not the real Jesus; and (4) the "wrong-tomb theory"—that the disciples went to the wrong tomb. Jesus' empty tomb nullifies all of these hollow notions, for the *belief* in Christ's resurrection arose out of the *fact* of the resurrection. Moreover, the bodily resurrection of Christ was necessary in order to (1) make the forgiveness of sins possible (1 Cor. 15:17); (2) fulfill the biblical prophecies of the resurrection (24:45, 46); (3) make justification of sinners possible (Rom. 4:25; 8:34); and (4) lay a solid foundation for the Christian's hope (1 Cor. 15:19). Christ's resurrection was wrought by the power of God (Acts 2:24; Rom. 8:11; Eph. 1:19, 20) and by Christ himself (John 2:19; 10:18).

The Great Commission presented here has three parts: (1) the message they are to preach (the death and resurrection of Jesus and the promise of the forgiveness of sins upon repentance); (2) the people they are to reach (all nations, beginning at Jerusalem); and (3) the power they will have to make their work effective.

24:49 *the promise of my Father.* According to Acts 1:4, 5 the promise was the baptism of the Holy Spirit.

24:50 *as far as to Bethany.* Bethany was approximately a mile away, across the valley on the Mount of Olives.†

THE GOSPEL ACCORDING TO

SAINT JOHN

Authorship, date, and background The authorship of the fourth Gospel cannot be determined from the material in the book itself. No author is named directly. But there are enough hints to draw the conclusion that John, the son of Zebedee and Salome (who was probably the sister of Mary, the mother of Jesus), was the author. The writer was a Jew, a Palestinian, and an eyewitness who was familiar with Jewish customs and traditions. The early church regarded John as the author of this Gospel and contrary claims have scant evidence to displace this view. John was with Jesus on numerous occasions. The Lord called him and his brother the "sons of thunder" for they were prejudiced, brash, and belligerent. They were ready to reprimand the man who was casting out demons successfully, simply because he was not one of them. Jesus forbade them (Lk 9:49, 50). Moreover, they asked Jesus on one occasion: "Lord, wilt thou that we command fire to come down from heaven, and consume them?" (Lk 9:52–55). Jesus rebuked them. They had their mother intercede for them with Jesus. She asked that her sons might sit on two thrones next to his throne in his Kingdom (Mt 20:20ff.). Jesus refused this request. It was John who sat so close to Jesus at the Last Supper. And it was he who was to become known later as the apostle of love. He also authored 1, 2, and 3 John and The Revelation, which closed the canon of Scripture.

In all probability the book was written in Ephesus (Asia Minor) and can be dated in the last decade of the first century (A.D. 90–95). The date is important because this Gospel is quite different from Matthew, Mark, and Luke. These have been called the "synoptic Gospels" (meaning having the same or common views). John's work does not fit this pattern. The simplest explanation is that he was familiar with the other Gospels, and the Holy Spirit wanted him to fill in some of the gaps and to stress more specifically what the other Gospels hinted at but did not say explicitly. It was unnecessary for him to repeat what was already known and widely read. Moreover, some time had passed since the writing of the other Gospels, and the theology of the church was developing. John had something to contribute to this development.

Characteristics and content John presents Jesus as true God and true man. He repeats his witness and that of others, together with the teaching of Jesus about his deity, at least five times: (1) He "was God" (John 1:1, 2); (2) "I and the Father are one" (10:30); (3) "Before Abraham was, I am" (8:58); (4) "He that hath seen me hath seen the Father" (14:9); (5) Thomas said, "My Lord and my God!" (20:28). He also emphasizes the humanity of Jesus when he speaks of him as tired, hungry, troubled, loyal to his friends, loving, and brave. John shows that Jesus, as the God-man, was functionally subordinate to his Father, who sent him into this world. He was obedient to the Father and he always did his Father's will, even unto death on the cross. Moreover, he accomplished the Father's work, which was to bring life to sinful men.

John states his purpose for writing the book: "And many other signs truly did Jesus in the presence of his disciples, which are not written in this book: But these are written, that ye might believe that Jesus is the Christ, the Son of God; and that believing ye might have life through his name" (20:30, 31). In these verses John uses three of the words which constitute the dominant motif of the work: (1) miracles or signs; (2) faith or believing on Jesus; (3) and life, which is the result of faith in him. John thus declares that men need not believe without evidence. He presents seven miracles or signs by way of evidence and expects that as a result of the evidences, men ought to have faith in Jesus.

The seven signs or miracles designed to lead men to believe in Jesus Christ are (1) changing water into wine (2:1–11); (2) healing the government official's son (4:46–54); (3) healing the helpless disabled man (5:1–9); (4) feeding the five thousand (6:1–14); (5) walking on the water (6:16–21); (6) healing the blind man (9:1–12); (7) raising Lazarus from the dead (11:1–46). Five of these seven miracles do not appear in the other Gospels. All seven were performed publicly to help people or were for the benefit of other people.

John also records the seven "I ams" of Jesus: (1) "I am the bread of life" (6:35); (2) "I am the light of the world (8:12); (3) "I am the gate of the sheep" (10:7); (4) "I am the good shepherd" (10:11, 14); (5) "I am the resurrection and the life" (11:25); (6) "I am the way, the truth, and the life" (14:6); (7) "I am the true vine" (15:1). John's Gospel is probably the most unusual and unique of the four Gospels.

Outline

I. The introduction (1:1–51)
II. Jesus' public ministry: the seven signs (2:1—12:50)
III. Jesus in the Upper Room (13:1—17:26)
IV. Jesus arrested, tried, and crucified (18:1—19:37)
V. Jesus' burial and resurrection (19:38—20:31)
VI. The epilogue (21:1–25)

I. THE INTRODUCTION (1:1–51)

A. THE PROLOGUE

1. Jesus, the Eternal God

1 IN the beginning was the Word, and the Word was with God, and the
Word was God.
2 The same was in the beginning with God.
3 All things were made by him; and without him was not any thing made
that was made.
4 In him was life; and the life was the light of men.
5 And the light shineth in darkness; and the darkness comprehended it
not.

2. The Witness of John the Baptist

6 ¶There was a man sent from God, whose name *was* John.
7 The same came for a witness, to bear witness of the Light, that all *men*
through him might believe.
8 He was not that Light, but *was sent* to bear witness of that Light.

3. The Incarnation of Jesus and His Rejection

9 *That* was the true Light, which lighteth every man that cometh into the
world.
10 He was in the world, and the world was made by him, and the world
knew him not.
11 He came unto his own, and his own received him not.
12 But as many as received him, to them gave he power to become the sons
of God, *even* to them that believe on his name:
13 Which were born, not of blood, nor of the will of the flesh, nor of the
will of man, but of God.

☆**1:1** Gen 1:1 Isa 9:6 Jn 1:14, 18 10:30; 20:28 Rom 9:5 Phil 2:6 Col 2:9 Rev 19:13
1:2 Col 1:15
1:3 1 Cor 8:6 Col 1:16, 17 Heb 1:2
1:4 Jn 3:15, 16, 36 5:26, 39, 40 6:35, 48; 8:12 11:25; 14:6 20:31 Col 3:4 1 Jn 5:12, 20
1:5 Jn 3:19; 9:5 12:35, 36, 46
1:6 Mal 3:1
1:7 Jn 1:15; 3:26 5:33
1:8 Jn 1:20 Acts 13:25
1:9 49:6 1 Jn 2:8
1:10 Ps 33:6 1 Cor 8:6 Heb 1:2
1:11 Lk 19:14
☆**1:12** Rom 8:15, 16, 29 Eph 1:5 1 Jn 3:1, 23
1:13 Jas 1:18 1 Pet 1:23 1 Jn 3:9 5:1, 10–12

1:1 *In the beginning,* i.e., "Before anything else existed." *the Word,* or, "Christ," the wisdom and power of God and the first cause of all things, God's personal expression of himself to men. Christ was the incarnate Word, as opposed to the written Word, the Bible. The incarnate Word is eternal. The Word was with God, distinct from God, and yet in communion with the Father. The Word was identical in essence to God the Father and to God the Holy Spirit. The Word had a part in creation (Col. 1:16; Heb. 1:2; 11:3). The Word became flesh (i.e., God became man); Jesus is thus the God-man. "For in him dwelleth all the fulness of the Godhead bodily" (Col. 2:9). The incarnate Word is made known to men through the written Word, the Bible. The loss of either means the loss of the Christian faith.

1:12 *that believe on his name,* i.e., "that trust him to save them." At least four benefits come to those who are regenerated: (1) they become children of God; (2) they become "new creatures" (2 Cor. 5:17; Gal. 6:15); (3) they are given God's own character, i.e., they are "partakers of the divine nature" (2 Pet. 1:4); and (4) they share Christ's triumph and power over sin and the world (1 John 3:9; 5:4, 18).

4. John's Testimony to Jesus

14 And the Word was made flesh, and dwelt among us, (and we beheld his
glory, the glory as of the only begotten of the Father,) full of grace and
truth.
15 ¶John bare witness of him, and cried, saying, This was he of whom I
spake, He that cometh after me is preferred before me: for he was before
me.
16 And of his fulness have all we received, and grace for grace.
17 For the law was given by Moses, *but* grace and truth came by Jesus
Christ.
18 No man hath seen God at any time; the only begotten Son, which is in
the bosom of the Father, he hath declared *him.*

5. John's Claim about Himself

19 ¶And this is the record of John, when the Jews sent priests and Levites
from Jerusalem to ask him, Who art thou?
20 And he confessed, and denied not; but confessed, I am not the Christ.
21 And they asked him, What then? Art thou E-li′as? And he saith, I am
not. Art thou that prophet? And he answered, No.
22 Then said they unto him, Who art thou? that we may give an answer to
them that sent us. What sayest thou of thyself?
23 He said, I *am* the voice of one crying in the wilderness, Make straight
the way of the Lord, as said the prophet E-sai′as.
24 And they which were sent were of the Pharisees.
25 And they asked him, and said unto him, Why baptizest thou then, if
thou be not that Christ, nor E-li′as, neither that prophet?
26 John answered them, saying, I baptize with water: but there standeth
one among you, whom ye know not;
27 He it is, who coming after me is preferred before me, whose shoe's
latchet I am not worthy to unloose.

1:14☆
a) Exo 40:34, 35
Mt 1:23
Rom 1:3; 8:3
Gal 4:4
Phil 2:6–8
Col 2:9
1 Tim 3:16
Heb 2:14
1 Jn 1:1; 4:2, 3
b) Mt 17:2
Jn 2:11; 3:16, 18
11:4; 13:31, 32
2 Pet 1:16, 17
1 Jn 1:1, 2; 4:9
c) Jn 14:6
Rom 16:20, 24
Eph 4:21
1:15
Mt 3:11
Jn 1:27, 30
1:16
Eph 1:6, 23
Col 1:19; 2:9, 10
1:17☆
Ex 20:1
Rom 5:21; 6:14
Eph 4:21
1:18☆
Ex 33:20
Jn 3:16; 14:9
2 Cor 4:4, 6
Col 1:15
Heb 1:3
1 Jn 4:9
1:19☆
1:20
Lk 3:15
Jn 3:28
1:21☆
Deut 18:15
Mal 4:5
Mt 11:14
Lk 1:17
1:23
Isa 40:3
1:26☆
Mal 3:1
Mt 3:11
Mk 1:8
Lk 3:16

1:14 *the Word was made flesh,* i.e., "Christ became a human being" (TLB). This is called the "incarnation." This word in Latin means "in the flesh" (*in* means "in" or "into"; *caro* means "flesh"—see Gal. 4:4, 5; Phil. 2:6, 7). The incarnation is the act whereby the second person of the Trinity, the Son of God, took on real human flesh. He was one person with two natures—a perfectly divine nature and a perfectly human (albeit sinless) nature. As the God-man he had all the attributes of deity (Col. 1:19; Heb. 1:8–10). As man he had all the attributes of the first Adam, or humanity. His two natures are separate, distinct, and without fusion or mixture (cf. Acts 3:22; Gal. 4:4; 1 Tim. 2:5; Heb. 2:14, 17, 18; 4:15). The resurrected and ascended Lord Jesus will forever be the God-man in a body (cf. Acts 1:11). His Second Advent will also be in bodily form. *the only begotten of the Father,* i.e., "the only Son of the Father." *grace,* i.e., "God's loving-kindness."
1:17 *grace* is the unearned favor of God or "everything for nothing to those who deserve the exact opposite." It is translated from the Greek word *charis,* which can also mean "favor." Grace is an attribute of God (Exod. 22:27; 33:19; Neh. 9:17; 1 Pet. 5:10). We are (1) justified by grace (Rom. 3:24; Titus 3:7); (2) saved by grace (Eph. 1:7, 8); (3) elected by grace (Rom. 11:5, 6); (4) given faith by grace (Acts 18:27; Eph. 2:8, 9); (5) given spiritual gifts by grace (Rom. 12:6); and (6) provided with strength, comfort, and hope through grace (2 Cor. 12:9; 2 Thess. 2:16).
1:18 God is spirit. As such, he is invisible and nonmaterial. Yet Scripture says that men have beheld God or his presence (e.g., Gen. 32:30; Exod. 24:9, 10; Judg. 13:22; Isa. 6:1; Dan. 7:9). How do we explain this? God may have assumed human forms momentarily in order to communicate with men. These appearances are called "theophanies." Another explanation is that God may have sent proxies to act for him—such as created angels or the "Angel of the Lord," believed by many to be the preincarnate Christ. A third alternative is that the language of some appearances may have been symbolic, as when Isaiah evidently saw a vision (Isa. 6:1), or Num. 12:8, which suggests that Moses simply enjoyed a closer relationship with God than did the children of Israel. Since the advent of Jesus, all who have seen him have seen the Father (John 14:9). Believers, having the Scriptures and knowing Christ, need no other supernatural visions or theophanies today.
1:19 *the Jews,* i.e., "the Jewish leaders."†
1:21 The prophet referred to in this verse (also in 1:25; 6:14; 7:40; Acts 3:22, 23; 7:37) is the one spoken about by Moses in Deut. 18:15, 18. It does not refer to John the Baptist. Rather, the prophecy is about Jesus, who is also Priest and King.
1:26 *with,* or, "in." (See also 1:33.)

28 These things were done in Beth-ab'a-ra beyond Jordan, where John was
baptizing.

6. John Declares Jesus to Be the Lamb of God

29 ¶The next day John seeth Jesus coming unto him, and saith, Behold the
Lamb of God, which taketh away the sin of the world.
30 This is he of whom I said, After me cometh a man which is preferred
before me: for he was before me.
31 And I knew him not: but that he should be made manifest to Israel,
therefore am I come baptizing with water.
32 And John bare record, saying, I saw the Spirit descending from heaven
like a dove, and it abode upon him.
33 And I knew him not: but he that sent me to baptize with water, the
same said unto me, Upon whom thou shalt see the Spirit descending, and
remaining on him, the same is he which baptizeth with the Holy Ghost.
34 And I saw, and bare record that this is the Son of God.

7. The First Three Disciples

35 ¶Again the next day after John stood, and two of his disciples;
36 And looking upon Jesus as he walked, he saith, Behold the Lamb of
God!
37 And the two disciples heard him speak, and they followed Jesus.
38 Then Jesus turned, and saw them following, and saith unto them, What
seek ye? They said unto him, Rabbi, (which is to say, being interpreted,
Master,) where dwellest thou?
39 He saith unto them, Come and see. They came and saw where he dwelt,
and abode with him that day: for it was about the tenth hour.
40 One of the two which heard John *speak*, and followed him, was
Andrew, Simon Peter's brother.
41 He first findeth his own brother Simon, and saith unto him, We have
found the Mes-si'as, which is, being interpreted, the Christ.
42 And he brought him to Jesus. And when Jesus beheld him, he said,
Thou art Simon the son of Jona: thou shalt be called Ce'phas, which is by
interpretation, A stone.

8. Philip and Nathanael

43 ¶The day following Jesus would go forth into Galilee, and findeth
Philip, and saith unto him, Follow me.
44 Now Philip was of Beth-sa'i-da, the city of Andrew and Peter.
45 Philip findeth Nathanael, and saith unto him, We have found him, of
whom Moses in the law, and the prophets, did write, Jesus of Nazareth, the
son of Joseph.

1:28 Jn 3:26; 10:40
1:29 Ex 12:3; Isa 53:7; Mt 1:21; Acts 8:32; 1 Cor 5:7; Heb 1:3; 2:17; 9:28; 1 Pet 1:19; 1 Jn 2:2; 3:5; Rev 1:5; 5:6; 7:14
☆**1:30** Jn 1:15, 27
☆**1:32** Mt 3:16; Mk 1:10; Lk 3:22
1:33 Lk 3:16; Acts 1:5
1:34 Jn 1:49; 10:36; 11:27; 20:30, 31; Acts 9:20; Rom 1:4; 2 Cor 1:19; 1 Jn 1:1; 5:5, 6
☆**1:40** Mt 4:18–22; Mk 1:16; Lk 5:2–11
☆**1:41** Job 23:3; Dan 9:25; Jn 4:25
1:42 Mt 16:18; 1 Cor 15:5; 1 Pet 2:5; Rev 21:14
1:43 Jn 6:5, 6; 12:20–22
1:44 Jn 14:8
☆**1:45** Gen 3:15; 26:4; 49:10; Num 21:8, 9; Deut 18:15, 18; Ps 2; 16:8–11, 22; 110; 132:11; Isa 6:5; 7:14; 9:6; 11:1–10; 32:1–5; 42:1–9; 49:1–13; 50:6, 53; Jer 23:5, 6; 33:15; Ezek 34:23; 37:25; Dan 7:13; 9:25; Mic 5:2; Zech 3:8, 9; 6:12; 9:9; 13:1, 7; Mal 3:1, 4:5; Mt 10:3; Lk 3:23; 4:22; Jn 21:2

1:30 *for he was before me.* Since John the Baptist was *conceived before Jesus Christ* was, this statement refers to Christ's preincarnate existence as the eternal God. This may have been revealed to John by the Spirit directly or else by the Spirit's teaching through the Old Testament.

1:32 *bare record,* i.e., "bore witness." John did not do this of himself. He was sent by God. By some sign God told John that the one on whom he saw the Holy Spirit coming and remaining was the Son of God. John baptized Jesus with water but affirmed that Jesus would baptize with the Holy Spirit. Jesus gained nothing from John's water baptism that he did not already possess. By the sign of the Spirit, John was prevented from making any mistake—for the event answered the prediction. His own faith was confirmed, just as our faith is confirmed by the many answers to prayer we experience.

1:40, 41 Andrew was the first disciple of Jesus. And he was the first missionary. The Scripture says that *he first findeth his own brother Simon,* and brought him to Jesus. Simon Peter was converted; his brother was the agent God used to bring it to pass. Nothing is more beautiful than to bring our own families to Jesus Christ for salvation.

1:45 *Philip* came to Christ just as Andrew had; he did the same thing that Andrew did—he shared his faith with someone else and brought him to Jesus. He told

46 And Nathanael said unto him, Can there any good thing come out of Nazareth? Philip saith unto him, Come and see.

47 Jesus saw Nathanael coming to him, and saith of him, Behold an Israelite indeed, in whom is no guile!

48 Nathanael saith unto him, Whence knowest thou me? Jesus answered and said unto him, Before that Philip called thee, when thou wast under the fig tree, I saw thee.

1:49 Mt 21:5 Jn 1:34

49 Nathanael answered and saith unto him, Rabbi, thou art the Son of God; thou art the King of Israel.

50 Jesus answered and said unto him, Because I said unto thee, I saw thee under the fig tree, believest thou? thou shalt see greater things than these.

1:51 Gen 28:12

51 And he saith unto him, Verily, verily, I say unto you, Hereafter ye shall see heaven open, and the angels of God ascending and descending upon the Son of man.

II. JESUS' PUBLIC MINISTRY: THE SEVEN SIGNS (2:1—12:50)

A. THE FIRST SIGN: WATER TURNED INTO WINE

2:1 Jn 1:29, 35, 43

2 AND the third day there was a marriage in Cana of Galilee; and the mother of Jesus was there:

2 And both Jesus was called, and his disciples, to the marriage.

3 And when they wanted wine, the mother of Jesus saith unto him, They have no wine.

2:4☆ Eccles 3:1 Mt 12:46–49 Jn 7:6; 8:20 19:26

4 Jesus saith unto her, Woman, what have I to do with thee? mine hour is not yet come.

5 His mother saith unto the servants, Whatsoever he saith unto you, do *it*.

2:6 Mk 7:3, 4 Jn 3:25

6 And there were set there six waterpots of stone, after the manner of the purifying of the Jews, containing two or three firkins apiece.

7 Jesus saith unto them, Fill the waterpots with water. And they filled them up to the brim.

8 And he saith unto them, Draw out now, and bear unto the governor of the feast. And they bare *it*.

2:9 Jn 4:46

9 When the ruler of the feast had tasted the water that was made wine, and knew not whence it was: (but the servants which drew the water knew;) the governor of the feast called the bridegroom,

10 And saith unto him, Every man at the beginning doth set forth good wine; and when men have well drunk, then that which is worse; *but* thou hast kept the good wine until now.

2:11☆ Jn 2:23; 3:2 4:54; 6:14; 11:47 12:37

11 This beginning of miracles did Jesus in Cana of Galilee, and manifested forth his glory; and his disciples believed on him.

Nathanael, *we have found him.* The "we" is significant, for Philip came from the same town as Andrew and Peter. Already there was the nucleus for the twelve men Jesus would bring into the closest communion with himself. When Jesus told Nathanael that he had seen him under the fig tree, Nathanael's realization of Jesus' omnipresence brought him to faith in the Savior. From the beginning the great truth was made manifest: Jesus saves.

2:4 *Woman. As man, Jesus was close* to Mary his mother; as God, he was distant from her. He was both her son and her Savior. She had to learn from the beginning of his public ministry that her son had begun his office as Messiah. Yet Jesus never forgot his mother, as the tender scene at Calvary indicates. He gave her over to his disciple to care for her after his departure from this world. It is John who records both of these incidents (see 19:26).

2:11 *miracles,* or, "signs" (from the Greek word *semeion,* used in the Gospel of John to describe Christ's miracles—2:23; 3:2; 4:54; 6:2, 14; 7:31; 9:16; 11:47; 12:18). These signs were not only intended to help people; they were intended to bring men to salvation. In 20:30, 31 it says these "miracles . . . are recorded so that you will believe that he is the Messiah, the Son of God, and that believing in him you will have life" (TLB). Christ's miracles were unique in that he performed them by virtue of his inherent power; all other miracles by God were made possible by delegated power, as stated in Acts 19:11: "God gave Paul the power to do unusual miracles" (TLB).

12¶After this he went down to Ca-per'na-um, he, and his mother, and his
brethren, and his disciples: and they continued there not many days.

B. THE CLEANSING OF THE TEMPLE (CF. MT 21:12–17; MK 11:15–19; LK 19:45–48)

13¶And the Jews' passover was at hand, and Jesus went up to Jerusalem,
14And found in the temple those that sold oxen and sheep and doves, and
the changers of money sitting:
15And when he had made a scourge of small cords, he drove them all out
of the temple, and the sheep, and the oxen; and poured out the changers'
money, and overthrew the tables;
16And said unto them that sold doves, Take these things hence; make not
my Father's house an house of merchandise.
17And his disciples remembered that it was written, The zeal of thine
house hath eaten me up.
18¶Then answered the Jews and said unto him, What sign shewest thou
unto us, seeing that thou doest these things?
19Jesus answered and said unto them, Destroy this temple, and in three
days I will raise it up.
20Then said the Jews, Forty and six years was this temple in building, and
wilt thou rear it up in three days?
21But he spake of the temple of his body.
22When therefore he was risen from the dead, his disciples remembered
that he had said this unto them; and they believed the scripture, and the
word which Jesus had said.
23¶Now when he was in Jerusalem at the passover, in the feast *day*, many
believed in his name, when they saw the miracles which he did.
24But Jesus did not commit himself unto them, because he knew all *men*,
25And needed not that any should testify of man: for he knew what was
in man.

C. JESUS' TEACHING ABOUT THE NEW BIRTH: NICODEMUS

3 THERE was a man of the Pharisees, named Nic-o-de'mus, a ruler of
the Jews:
2The same came to Jesus by night, and said unto him, Rabbi, we know
that thou art a teacher come from God: for no man can do these miracles
that thou doest, except God be with him.
3Jesus answered and said unto him, Verily, verily, I say unto thee, Except
a man be born again, he cannot see the kingdom of God.

2:12 Mt 12:46–50
2:13 Ex 12:14 Num 28:16 Deut 16:1 Jn 6:4 11:55, 56
☆**2:14** Mal 3:1, 2 Mt 21:12 Mk 11:15, 16 Lk 19:45, 46
2:16 Lk 2:49 Jn 14:2
2:17 Ps 69:9
☆**2:18** Mt 12:38
2:19 Mt 26:61; 27:40 Mk 14:58 Acts 6:14
2:20 Ezra 5:16
2:21 Jn 10:38 14:2, 10; 17:21 1 Cor 3:16; 6:19 2 Cor 6:16 Eph 2:21, 22 Col 2:9 1 Pet 2:4–7
2:22 Ps 2:7; 16:10 Lk 24:8, 25, 26 Jn 12:16; 14:26 20:9
☆**2:23**
2:24 1 Sam 16:7 1 Chron 28:9 Mt 9:4 Mk 2:8 Rev 2:23
3:1 Jn 7:50; 19:39
3:2 Jn 9:33 Acts 2:22; 10:38
☆**3:3** Jn 1:13 2 Cor 5:17 Gal 6:15 Eph 2:5, 10 Jas 1:18 1 Pet 1:23 1 Jn 3:9

2:14ff Hundreds of thousands of dispersed Jews came to Jerusalem for Passover. They came from afar and could not bring animals for sacrifice. They brought *different kinds of currency, which had* to be exchanged and then used for the purchase of animals. Thus the temple site became the haunt of money changers and animal dealers.

Liberal scholars say this cleansing of the temple is the same as that recorded in the Synoptic Gospels. However, the first three Gospels speak of the second cleansing of the temple as having occurred shortly before Christ's crucifixion. If John's account is the same, he was chronologically incorrect in assigning it to the beginning of Jesus' ministry rather than to the end of it. But there were two temple cleansings. John alone speaks of the first one.

2:18 *the Jews,* i.e., "the Jewish leaders."†

2:23 *passover.* See notes to Mark 14:1 and Exod. 12:11.

3:3 A once-born person dies twice—he dies in the flesh, and he dies in the spirit. A twice-born man dies once—he dies in the flesh but his soul lives forever. Thus regeneration, or the "new birth," is the impartation of divine life to the believer's soul. All Christians must be twice-born: the first time from a mother's womb, then again by the Spirit of God to new life. The new birth comes through the redemption of Jesus Christ, whose blood was shed for this purpose (1 Pet. 1:17–23). The Holy Spirit through the Word of God convicts, converts, and regenerates the sinner.

3:5☆ Acts 2:38; Tit 3:4, 5; 1 Pet 3:21
3:6 Ezek 36:26, 27; Jn 1:13; Rom 8:15, 16; 1 Cor 15:50; Gal 4:6
3:8 Eccles 11:5; Ezek 37:5, 9, 10, 14
3:10, 11 Jn 7:16; 8:26; 12:49
3:13☆ Prov 30:4; Deut 30:12; Jn 6:38, 42; 16:28; Rom 10:6; Eph 4:9, 10
3:14☆ Num 21:8, 9; Jn 12:32
3:15 1 Jn 5:11, 12
3:16 Num 5:8; Jn 11:25, 26; Rom 5:8; 8:32; Eph 2:4, 6; 1 Jn 4:9, 10
3:17 Lk 19:9, 10; Jn 12:47
3:18 Mk 16:16; Jn 5:24; Rom 8:1
3:19 Jn 1:4, 5; 7:7; 8:12; 12:46
3:20 Eph 5:11–13
3:21 1 Jn 1:7

4 Nic-o-de′mus saith unto him, How can a man be born when he is old?
can he enter the second time into his mother's womb, and be born?
5 Jesus answered, Verily, verily, I say unto thee, Except a man be born of
water and *of* the Spirit, he cannot enter into the kingdom of God.
6 That which is born of the flesh is flesh; and that which is born of the
Spirit is spirit.
7 Marvel not that I said unto thee, Ye must be born again.
8 The wind bloweth where it listeth, and thou hearest the sound thereof,
but canst not tell whence it cometh, and whither it goeth: so is every one
that is born of the Spirit.
9 Nic-o-de′mus answered and said unto him, How can these things be?
10 Jesus answered and said unto him, Art thou a master of Israel, and
knowest not these things?
11 Verily, verily, I say unto thee, We speak that we do know, and testify
that we have seen; and ye receive not our witness.
12 If I have told you earthly things, and ye believe not, how shall ye
believe, if I tell you *of* heavenly things?
13 And no man hath ascended up to heaven, but he that came down from
heaven, *even* the Son of man which is in heaven.
14 ¶And as Moses lifted up the serpent in the wilderness, even so must the
Son of man be lifted up:
15 That whosoever believeth in him should not perish, but have eternal
life.
16 ¶For God so loved the world, that he gave his only begotten Son, that
whosoever believeth in him should not perish, but have everlasting life.
17 For God sent not his Son into the world to condemn the world; but
that the world through him might be saved.
18 ¶He that believeth on him is not condemned: but he that believeth not
is condemned already, because he hath not believed in the name of the only
begotten Son of God.
19 And this is the condemnation, that light is come into the world, and
men loved darkness rather than light, because their deeds were evil.
20 For every one that doeth evil hateth the light, neither cometh to the
light, lest his deeds should be reproved.
21 But he that doeth truth cometh to the light, that his deeds may be made
manifest, that they are wrought in God.

D. JOHN THE BAPTIST'S LAST PUBLIC WITNESS TO JESUS

3:22 Jn 4:2

22 ¶After these things came Jesus and his disciples into the land of Judæa;
and there he tarried with them, and baptized.

3:5 *born of water and of the Spirit,* i.e., "born physically and spiritually"—this paraphrase interprets "born of water" as meaning the normal process observed during every human birth. Some believe this phrase refers to water baptism.† The Roman Catholic Church, Anglo-Catholics among the Anglicans, and some Lutherans teach that new life is imparted by water baptism, or what is called "baptismal regeneration." Others hold to "believer's baptism," by which water baptism is performed as a symbol that the recipient already has been born again. Still others hold that while baptism, particularly infant baptism, does not save the recipient, it is a means of grace and constitutes a sacrament. The dying thief at Calvary was saved without water baptism, but those who insist on baptismal regeneration accept the intention for the act itself.

3:13 *which is in heaven.* This phrase clearly indicates the omnipresence of Jesus Christ; he is said to be on earth and in heaven at the same time. It has been relegated to a footnote in the RSV and the NIV. The phrase may have been dropped very early in the transmission of the text of John because of the theological problem of accepting the fact that the God-man, Jesus, could be two places at the same time.

3:14 See note on Num. 21:9. The brazen serpent was representative of Christ. Like the serpent, he was to be lifted up in death. No one was saved by the serpent, whereas all who come to Christ are saved by him. The serpent was effective only when those who had been bitten lifted their eyes to behold it. Whoever looked lived. And whoever looks to Jesus will live forever.

23¶And John also was baptizing in Æ′non near to Sa′lim, because there
was much water there: and they came, and were baptized.
24For John was not yet cast into prison.
25¶Then there arose a question between *some* of John's disciples and the
Jews about purifying.
26And they came unto John, and said unto him, Rabbi, he that was with
thee beyond Jordan, to whom thou barest witness, behold, the same
baptizeth, and all *men* come to him.
27John answered and said, A man can receive nothing, except it be given
him from heaven.
28Ye yourselves bear me witness, that I said, I am not the Christ, but that
I am sent before him.
29He that hath the bride is the bridegroom: but the friend of the
bridegroom, which standeth and heareth him, rejoiceth greatly because of
the bridegroom's voice: this my joy therefore is fulfilled.
30He must increase, but I *must* decrease.
31He that cometh from above is above all: he that is of the earth is
earthly, and speaketh of the earth: he that cometh from heaven is above all.
32And what he hath seen and heard, that he testifieth; and no man
receiveth his testimony.
33He that hath received his testimony hath set to his seal that God is true.
34For he whom God hath sent speaketh the words of God: for God
giveth not the Spirit by measure *unto him.*
35The Father loveth the Son, and hath given all things into his hand.
36He that believeth on the Son hath everlasting life: and he that believeth
not the Son shall not see life; but the wrath of God abideth on him.

E. THE MINISTRY OF JESUS IN SAMARIA

1. Jesus Goes to Sychar

4 WHEN therefore the Lord knew how the Pharisees had heard that
Jesus made and baptized more disciples than John,
2(Though Jesus himself baptized not, but his disciples,)
3He left Judæa, and departed again into Galilee.
4And he must needs go through Sa-ma′ri-a.
5Then cometh he to a city of Sa-ma′ri-a, which is called Sy′char, near to
the parcel of ground that Jacob gave to his son Joseph.
6Now Jacob's well was there. Jesus therefore, being wearied with *his*
journey, sat thus on the well: *and* it was about the sixth hour.

2. Jesus' Conversation with the Woman at the Well

7There cometh a woman of Sa-ma′ri-a to draw water: Jesus saith unto
her, Give me to drink.
8(For his disciples were gone away unto the city to buy meat.)
9Then saith the woman of Sa-ma′ri-a unto him, How is it that thou, being
a Jew, askest drink of me, which am a woman of Sa-ma′ri-a? for the Jews
have no dealings with the Sa-mar′i-tans.

3:23 Gen 14:18
3:24 Mt 4:12
3:26 Jn 1:6, 7, 34
3:27 1 Cor 4:7 Heb 5:4
3:28 Mal 3:1 Jn 1:20, 23
3:29 Isa 62:5 2 Cor 11:2 Rev 21:9
3:30 Phil 3:8, 9
3:31 Jn 1:15; 8:23 Rom 9:5 Eph 1:19–23
3:32 Jn 3:11
3:33 2 Cor 1:22 1 Jn 5:10
3:34 Mt 12:18 Lk 4:18, 19 Jn 6:63 Acts 10:38
3:35 Dan 7:14 Mt 28:18 Jn 5:20; 17:2, 24 Heb 2:8
3:36 Hab 2:4 Jn 3:16 Rom 1:17 Heb 3:18
4:4 Lk 9:52
☆**4:5** Gen 33:19 48:22 Josh 24:32
☆**4:6**
4:7 Gen 24:11
4:9 2 Kgs 17:24 Ezra 4 Mt 10:5 Jn 8:48 Acts 10:48

4:5, 6 The Samaritan village of *Sychar* (now Askar) is on the east slope of Mount Ebal, not far from Mount Gerazim. The Samaritans' temple on Mount Gerazim had been torn down by John Hyrcanus in 128 B.C. The Samaritan Passover was held on Mount Gerazim each year near the ruins of the temple. But the Samaritans probably worshipped regularly at the foot of Gerazim, near Shechem.

The Samaritans were a numerous people in Jesus' day. The Jews had no intercourse with them and hated them. They were a mixed breed of the union of Jews with Assyrians. After the fall of Samaria in 722 B.C. the land of the Northern Kingdom was repopulated by Gentiles from the Assyrian Empire. They intermarried with Jews and formed the Samaritans. The Jews of Jesus' day did not regard them as their neighbors; that is why Jesus gave the illustration of the good Samaritan (see note on Luke 10:30). The scribes and Pharisees suspected Jesus of being treasonous because he ministered to Samaritans.

4:10 Isa 12:3, 44:3; Jer 2:13; Jn 7:37–39; 1 Cor 12:13; Rev 21:6; 22:17

10 Jesus answered and said unto her, If thou knewest the gift of God, and
who it is that saith to thee, Give me to drink; thou wouldest have asked of
him, and he would have given thee living water.
11 The woman saith unto him, Sir, thou hast nothing to draw with, and the
well is deep: from whence then hast thou that living water?
12 Art thou greater than our father Jacob, which gave us the well, and
drank thereof himself, and his children, and his cattle?
13 Jesus answered and said unto her, Whosoever drinketh of this water
shall thirst again:

4:14 Jn 6:35; 7:37, 38

14 But whosoever drinketh of the water that I shall give him shall never
thirst; but the water that I shall give him shall be in him a well of water
springing up into everlasting life.

4:15 Jn 6:34

15 The woman saith unto him, Sir, give me this water, that I thirst not,
neither come hither to draw.
16 Jesus saith unto her, Go, call thy husband, and come hither.
17 The woman answered and said, I have no husband. Jesus said unto her,
Thou hast well said, I have no husband:

4:18☆

18 For thou hast had five husbands; and he whom thou now hast is not thy
husband: in that saidst thou truly.

4:19 Lk 7:16

4:20☆ Gen 12:6, 7; 33:18; Judg 9:7; Deut 12:5; 2 Chron 7:12

19 The woman saith unto him, Sir, I perceive that thou art a prophet.
20 Our fathers worshipped in this mountain; and ye say, that in Jerusalem
is the place where men ought to worship.
21 Jesus saith unto her, Woman, believe me, the hour cometh, when ye
shall neither in this mountain, nor yet at Jerusalem, worship the Father.

4:21☆ Mal 1:11; 1 Tim 2:8

4:22☆ 2 Kings 17:28–41; Isa 2:3; Acts 17:24–29; Rom 3:1, 2; 9:4, 5

22 Ye worship ye know not what: we know what we worship: for salvation
is of the Jews.
23 But the hour cometh, and now is, when the true worshippers shall
worship the Father in spirit and in truth: for the Father seeketh such to
worship him.

4:23, 24☆ Isa 57:15; 66:1, 2; 2 Cor 3:17, 18; Eph 2:18, 22; Phil 3:3

24 God *is* a Spirit: and they that worship him must worship *him* in spirit
and in truth.

4:25 Deut 18:15; Mt 1:16; Jn 1:41

25 The woman saith unto him, I know that Mes-si′as cometh, which is
called Christ: when he is come, he will tell us all things.
26 Jesus saith unto her, I that speak unto thee am *he.*

4:26 Mk 14:61, 62; Jn 8:24; 9:35–37

27 ¶And upon this came his disciples, and marvelled that he talked with
the woman: yet no man said, What seekest thou? or, Why talkest thou with
her?

4:28☆

28 The woman then left her waterpot, and went her way into the city, and
saith to the men,

4:29☆ Jn 7:26, 31

29 Come, see a man, which told me all things that ever I did: is not this the
Christ?

4:18ff The Samaritan woman at the well was sinful. She knew about the Messiah and believed he would come. Jesus did not hesitate to identify himself as the one she was looking for (4:26). Like Andrew and Philip, she received Christ and went back to the village to tell the world about Jesus. The upshot of the incident was that "many of the Samaritans of that city believed on him for the saying of the woman, which testified, He *told me all that ever I did*" (4:39).

4:20 *in this mountain,* i.e., "at Mount Gerazim."

4:21–23 God requires two responses from all believers: (1) we are to worship him in spirit and in truth (see also Matt. 4:10) and (2) we are required to glorify him in life and conduct. He has created and redeemed us so that these requirements are met when "you give him first place in your life and live as he wants you to" (Matt. 6:33, TLB).

4:24 *God is a spirit,* "for he is an infinite and eternal mind, an intelligent being, incorporeal, immaterial, invisible, and incorruptible."*

4:28–30 Upon coming to Christ for salvation, this immoral woman immediately becomes a witness, and her heart is moved to share her faith with her friends and neighbors, not just that they would rejoice with her, but that they would come to know Christ. She says that Jesus told her all things about herself, especially that she was a sinner and needed a savior. As a result of her witness, the crowd went out to see and talk with Jesus.

30 Then they went out of the city, and came unto him.
31 In the mean while his disciples prayed him, saying, Master, eat.
32 But he said unto them, I have meat to eat that ye know not of.
33 Therefore said the disciples one to another, Hath any man brought him
ought to eat?
34 Jesus saith unto them, My meat is to do the will of him that sent me,
and to finish his work.
35 Say not ye, There are yet four months, and *then* cometh harvest?
behold, I say unto you, Lift up your eyes, and look on the fields; for they
are white already to harvest.
36 And he that reapeth receiveth wages, and gathereth fruit unto life
eternal: that both he that soweth and he that reapeth may rejoice together.
37 And herein is that saying true, One soweth, and another reapeth.
38 I sent you to reap that whereon ye bestowed no labour: other men
laboured, and ye are entered into their labours.

4:34 Job 23:12; Jn 5:30, 36; 6:38; 17:4; 19:28, 30
☆**4:35** Mt 9:37, 38; Lk 10:2
4:36 Dan 12:3; 1 Cor 3:8, 9; 9:17–19; Jas 5:19, 20
4:37 Job 31:8; Mic 6:15
4:38 1 Pet 1:12

3. Many Samaritans Get Converted

39 ¶And many of the Sa-mar'i-tans of that city believed on him for the
saying of the woman, which testified, He told me all that ever I did.
40 So when the Sa-mar'i-tans were come unto him, they besought him that
he would tarry with them: and he abode there two days.
41 And many more believed because of his own word;
42 And said unto the woman, Now we believe, not because of thy saying:
for we have heard *him* ourselves, and know that this is indeed the Christ,
the Saviour of the world.

☆**4:39** Gen 49:10
4:40 Isa 42:1
4:42 Isa 49:6; Mt 1:21; Lk 2:29–31; Jn 1:29; 17:8; Acts 5:31; 13:23; Eph 2:13; Phil 3:20; 1 Tim 1:15; 1 Jn 4:14

F. THE SECOND SIGN

1. Jesus Returns to Galilee (Cf. Mt 4:12–17; Mk 1:14, 15; Lk 4:14, 15)

43 ¶Now after two days he departed thence, and went into Galilee.
44 For Jesus himself testified, that a prophet hath no honour in his own
country.
45 Then when he was come into Galilee, the Galilæans received him,
having seen all the things that he did at Jerusalem at the feast: for they also
went unto the feast.

4:43, 44 Mt 13:57; Mk 6:4; Lk 4:24
4:45 Deut 16:16; Jn 2:23; 3:2

2. The Second Sign: The Healing of the Government Official's Son

46 So Jesus came again into Cana of Galilee, where he made the water
wine. And there was a certain nobleman, whose son was sick at Ca-per'na-
um.
47 When he heard that Jesus was come out of Judæa into Galilee, he went
unto him, and besought him that he would come down, and heal his son:
for he was at the point of death.

☆**4:46** Jn 2:1, 11, 23

4:35 Jesus' followers were, as yet, immature believers *who had much to learn.* They wanted to wait between the time the barley seeds were planted and the reaping, which would come four months later. In the meantime, they would eat and drink. Jesus enlightened them by using a material fact as an illustration of a spiritual truth: the fields are already ripe unto harvest; souls out there are perishing, not in some far-off land but right where you are. Jesus' disciples had not sowed the seed; all they needed to do was harvest the crop.

4:39 Who can despise the day of small things? A single, very wicked Samaritan woman starts a revival of true religion. Many Samaritans believe on Jesus because of her testimony. As a result of her witness, Jesus spends two days in Samaria and multitudes get converted. They bear witness that the woman's testimony inspired them to believe; faith came when they met and talked with the Savior himself (4:42).

4:46 John alone reports the healing of the nobleman's son, which is the second miracle he was to perform. The nobleman said, "Come." And Jesus said, "Go." That was all that was needed. The Master could heal from a distance without even the laying on of hands. Since John's Gospel was written long after the synoptic Gospels were written, he no doubt had access to them. And perhaps this accounts for the fact that so much of John's Gospel contains things not mentioned by the other Gospel writers.

4:48 1 Cor 1:22 Heb 2:4

48 Then said Jesus unto him, Except ye see signs and wonders, ye will not
believe.
49 The nobleman saith unto him, Sir, come down ere my child die.
50 Jesus saith unto him, Go thy way; thy son liveth. And the man believed
the word that Jesus had spoken unto him, and he went his way.
51 And as he was now going down, his servants met him, and told *him,*
saying, Thy son liveth.
52 Then inquired he of them the hour when he began to amend. And they
said unto him, Yesterday at the seventh hour the fever left him.

4:53 Acts 11:14 16:34

53 So the father knew that *it was* at the same hour, in the which Jesus said
unto him, Thy son liveth: and himself believed, and his whole house.

4:54 Jn 2:11

54 This *is* again the second miracle *that* Jesus did, when he was come out
of Judæa into Galilee.

G. THE THIRD SIGN AND THE UNBELIEVING JEWS

1. The Third Sign: the Healing of the Disabled Man at Bethesda

5:1 Lev 23:1, 2 Deut 16:1 Jn 2:13

5 AFTER this there was a feast of the Jews; and Jesus went up to
Jerusalem.

5:2 Neh 3:1; 12:39

2 Now there is at Jerusalem by the sheep *market* a pool, which is called in
the Hebrew tongue Be-thes'da, having five porches.

5:3☆

3 In these lay a great multitude of impotent folk, of blind, halt, withered,
waiting for the moving of the water.

5:4☆

4 For an angel went down at a certain season into the pool, and troubled
the water: whosoever then first after the troubling of the water stepped in
was made whole of whatsoever disease he had.
5 And a certain man was there, which had an infirmity thirty and eight
years.

5:6 Ps 72:13 113:5, 6 Heb 4:13

6 When Jesus saw him lie, and knew that he had been now a long time *in
that case,* he saith unto him, Wilt thou be made whole?
7 The impotent man answered him, Sir, I have no man, when the water is
troubled, to put me into the pool: but while I am coming, another steppeth
down before me.

5:8 Mt 9:6 Mk 2:11 Lk 5:24

8 Jesus saith unto him, Rise, take up thy bed, and walk.
9 And immediately the man was made whole, and took up his bed, and
walked: and on the same day was the sabbath.

5:10 Ex 20:10 Neh 13:19 Jer 17:21 Mt 12:2 Mk 2:24; 3:4 Lk 6:2; 13:14

10 ¶The Jews therefore said unto him that was cured, It is the sabbath
day: it is not lawful for thee to carry *thy* bed.
11 He answered them, He that made me whole, the same said unto me,
Take up thy bed, and walk.
12 Then asked they him, What man is that which said unto thee, Take up
thy bed, and walk?
13 And he that was healed wist not who it was: for Jesus had conveyed
himself away, a multitude being in *that* place.

5:14 Jn 8:11

14 Afterward Jesus findeth him in the temple, and said unto him, Behold,
thou art made whole: sin no more, lest a worse thing come unto thee.
15 The man departed, and told the Jews that it was Jesus, which had made
him whole.

5:16☆

16 And therefore did the Jews persecute Jesus, and sought to slay him,
because he had done these things on the sabbath day.

5:3a In many places where the Savior went he healed all who were ailing. Here we see multitudes who were impotent, blind, halt, and withered. Yet only one of them was healed. It is, of course, possible that Jesus healed others and John mentioned only this one case. Or it may be that the others had no faith whatever in Jesus and his power to heal.

5:3b, 4 *waiting for the moving of the water.* Many of the ancient manuscripts omit this phrase and all of verse 4.

5:16 Almost from the beginning of Jesus' ministry some Jews were so legalistic that they could not bear to see a man made whole on the sabbath day. When this man who had been ill for thirty-eight years was

2. Jesus' Claim to Be God

17 ¶But Jesus answered them, My Father worketh hitherto, and I work.
18 Therefore the Jews sought the more to kill him, because he not only had
broken the sabbath, but said also that God was his Father, making himself
equal with God.
19 Then answered Jesus and said unto them, Verily, verily, I say unto you,
The Son can do nothing of himself, but what he seeth the Father do: for
what things soever he doeth, these also doeth the Son likewise.
20 For the Father loveth the Son, and sheweth him all things that himself
doeth: and he will shew him greater works than these, that ye may marvel.
21 For as the Father raiseth up the dead, and quickeneth *them;* even so the
Son quickeneth whom he will.
22 For the Father judgeth no man, but hath committed all judgment unto
the Son:
23 That all *men* should honour the Son, even as they honour the Father.
He that honoureth not the Son honoureth not the Father which hath sent
him.
24 Verily, verily, I say unto you, He that heareth my word, and believeth
on him that sent me, hath everlasting life, and shall not come into
condemnation; but is passed from death unto life.

3. The Resurrection to Life or to Judgment

25 Verily, verily, I say unto you, The hour is coming, and now is, when the
dead shall hear the voice of the Son of God: and they that hear shall live.
26 For as the Father hath life in himself; so hath he given to the Son to
have life in himself;
27 And hath given him authority to execute judgment also, because he is
the Son of man.
28 Marvel not at this: for the hour is coming, in the which all that are in
the graves shall hear his voice,
29 And shall come forth; they that have done good, unto the resurrection
of life; and they that have done evil, unto the resurrection of damnation.

4. The Father Testifies about His Son

30 I can of mine own self do nothing: as I hear, I judge: and my judgment
is just; because I seek not mine own will, but the will of the Father which
hath sent me.
31 If I bear witness of myself, my witness is not true.

5:17 Jn 9:4; 14:10
☆**5:18** Isa 9:6; Jn 1:1, 18; 10:30, 33; 20:28; Rom 9:5; Phil 2:6; Col 2:9; Tit 2:13; 2 Pet 1:1; 1 Jn 5:21
5:19 Jn 8:28; 12:49; 14:10
5:20 Mt 3:17; Jn 3:35; 14:12, 13
5:21 Lk 8:54; Jn 11:25; Rom 4:17; 8:11
5:22 Mt 11:27; Jn 3:35; 17:2; Acts 10:42; 17:31
5:23 Lk 10:16; 1 Jn 2:23
☆**5:24** Jn 3:18; 20:30, 31; Rom 10:17; Gal 3:2; 1 Jn 3:14; 5:13
5:25 Lk 15:24; Jn 4:21; 6:63, 68; Gal 2:20; Eph 2:1, 5; 5:14; Col 2:13; Rev 3:1
5:26 Jn 1:4; 6:57; 1 Jn 5:11, 12
5:27 Dan 7:13, 14; Jn 9:39; Acts 10:42; 17:31
5:29 Dan 12:2; Mt 25:31–46; Acts 24:15; 1 Cor 15:52
5:30 Mt 26:39; Jn 5:19; 6:38; 8:16
☆**5:31** Jn 8:14

---

healed, one would suppose the Jews would have sung praise to God for his healing. Instead they began immediately to persecute the one who had performed the miracle. It is difficult to understand why some were saved immediately when they listened to Jesus while others were so hard of heart that they tried to kill him.
5:18 *equal with God.* Jesus claimed a number of times to be God. In this citation the Jews understood what Jesus was saying: he made himself equal with God. Either he was guilty of blasphemy or his claim was true. If it was blasphemy, he deserved to die; if it was true, they should worship him. Either Jesus was what he claimed to be or he was the world's greatest fraud and deceiver. Thus his deity is always the dividing line between those who believe in him and those who are guilty of unbelief.
5:24 *shall not come into condemnation.* Scripture speaks of three major judgments of God: (1) the judgment of the sins of those who accept Christ—a judgment that took place once for all by the death of Jesus on the cross (Rom. 8:1); (2) the judgment of believers at the judgment seat of Christ when rewards will be handed out after we have given an accounting for our lives (Rom. 14:10; 2 Cor. 5:10); and (3) the judgment of unbelievers (the great white throne judgment), at which time the unsaved dead will be resurrected, the books will be opened, and every mouth will be stopped—the verdict will be announced with no appeal, no excuses, and no mitigating circumstances, with the lake of fire the final resting place for impenitent sinners.
5:31 In John 8:14 Jesus states that his own witness or testimony to himself *is* sufficient. But here Jesus acceded to the demands of the rabbis for some verification for his claims. The verse may well be phrased: "If I bear witness to myself without other

5:32 Jn 1:6, 7, 15
5:34 1 Jn 5:9
5:35 2 Sam 21:17; Mt 13:20; 21:25–27; Mk 1:5; 2 Pet 1:19
5:36 Jn 10:25, 37, 38; 14:11; 15:24; 1 Jn 5:9
5:37 Deut 4:12; Mt 3:17; 17:5; Jn 1:18; 8:18; 1 Tim 1:17; 2 Pet 1:17, 18; 1 Jn 4:12
5:38 Jn 8:37; 1 Jn 2:14
5:39 Isa 34:16; Lk 16:29; 24:25; Jn 5:46, 47; 7:52; Acts 13:27; 17:11; Rom 2:17
5:41 Jn 7:18
5:43 Mt 24:5
5:45 Jn 9:28; Rom 2:17
5:46 Gen 3:15; 12:3; 18:18; 22:18; 49:10; Deut 18:15, 18; Lk 24:27, 44; Acts 26:22, 23
5:47 Lk 16:31

32 ¶There is another that beareth witness of me; and I know that the
witness which he witnesseth of me is true.
33 Ye sent unto John, and he bare witness unto the truth.
34 But I receive not testimony from man: but these things I say, that ye
might be saved.
35 He was a burning and a shining light: and ye were willing for a season
to rejoice in his light.
36 ¶But I have greater witness than *that* of John: for the works which the
Father hath given me to finish, the same works that I do, bear witness of
me, that the Father hath sent me.
37 And the Father himself, which hath sent me, hath borne witness of me.
Ye have neither heard his voice at any time, nor seen his shape.
38 And ye have not his word abiding in you: for whom he hath sent, him
ye believe not.
39 ¶Search the scriptures; for in them ye think ye have eternal life: and
they are they which testify of me.
40 And ye will not come to me, that ye might have life.
41 I receive not honour from men.
42 But I know you, that ye have not the love of God in you.
43 I am come in my Father's name, and ye receive me not: if another shall
come in his own name, him ye will receive.
44 How can ye believe, which receive honour one of another, and seek not
the honour that *cometh* from God only?
45 Do not think that I will accuse you to the Father: there is *one* that
accuseth you, *even* Moses, in whom ye trust.
46 For had ye believed Moses, ye would have believed me: for he wrote of
me.
47 But if ye believe not his writings, how shall ye believe my words?

H. THE FOURTH AND FIFTH SIGNS AND SUBSEQUENT EVENTS

1. The Fourth Sign: the Feeding of the Five Thousand
(Cf. Mt 14:13–21; Mk 6:30–44; Lk 9:10–17)

6:1☆
6:2 Mt 14:14; Mk 6:35; Lk 9:12
6:6 Num 11:21, 22
6:7☆ Mk 6:37
6:9 2 Kgs 4:43, 44

6 AFTER these things Jesus went over the sea of Galilee, which is *the*
sea of Ti-be'ri-as.
2 And a great multitude followed him, because they saw his miracles
which he did on them that were diseased.
3 And Jesus went up into a mountain, and there he sat with his disciples.
4 And the passover, a feast of the Jews, was nigh.
5 ¶When Jesus then lifted up *his* eyes, and saw a great company come
unto him, he saith unto Philip, Whence shall we buy bread, that these may
eat?
6 And this he said to prove him: for he himself knew what he would do.
7 Philip answered him, Two hundred pennyworth of bread is not sufficient
for them, that every one of them may take a little.
8 One of his disciples, Andrew, Simon Peter's brother, saith unto him,
9 There is a lad here, which hath five barley loaves, and two small fishes:
but what are they among so many?

---

witnesses, it does not measure up to the legal requirement." Then Christ offered other witnesses to himself: (1) God his Father (5:36, 37); (2) John the Baptist (5:33); (3) the witnesses of his miraculous works (5:36); (4) the Word of God (5:39); (5) the prophecy of Moses (5:46; cf. Deut. 18:19). In other words, their patent unbelief was not caused by a lack of witnesses.

6:1 John carefully refrains from simply repeating what the other three Gospel writers tell us. The feeding of the five thousand is the only miracle recorded in all four Gospels. He probably wrote about this because it provides a necessary backdrop for what follows.

6:7 *two hundred pennyworth,* i.e., "200 denarii," a denarius being a full day's wage.†

10And Jesus said, Make the men sit down. Now there was much grass in
the place. So the men sat down, in number about five thousand.
11And Jesus took the loaves; and when he had given thanks, he
distributed to the disciples, and the disciples to them that were set down;
and likewise of the fishes as much as they would.
12When they were filled, he said unto his disciples, Gather up the
fragments that remain, that nothing be lost.
13Therefore they gathered *them* together, and filled twelve baskets with
the fragments of the five barley loaves, which remained over and above
unto them that had eaten.
14Then those men, when they had seen the miracle that Jesus did, said,
This is of a truth that prophet that should come into the world.

6:10 Mt 14:21 Mk 6:43, 44 Lk 9:14
6:11 1 Tim 4:4, 5
☆6:12
6:14 Gen 49:10 Deut 18:15, 18 Isa 7:14; 9:6 35:5 Mt 11:3 Jn 1:21; 7:40–42

2. The Fifth Sign: Walking on the Waves (Cf. Mt 14:22–32; Mk 6:45–52)

15¶When Jesus therefore perceived that they would come and take him by
force, to make him a king, he departed again into a mountain himself alone.
16And when even was *now* come, his disciples went down unto the sea,
17And entered into a ship, and went over the sea toward Ca-per′na-um.
And it was now dark, and Jesus was not come to them.
18And the sea arose by reason of a great wind that blew.
19So when they had rowed about five and twenty or thirty furlongs, they
see Jesus walking on the sea, and drawing nigh unto the ship: and they were
afraid.
20But he saith unto them, It is I; be not afraid.
21Then they willingly received him into the ship: and immediately the
ship was at the land whither they went.

☆6:15 Jn 18:36, 37
6:16 Mt 14:23–27 Mk 6:47–51

3. Jesus, the True Bread of Life

22¶The day following, when the people which stood on the other side of
the sea saw that there was none other boat there, save that one whereinto
his disciples were entered, and that Jesus went not with his disciples into
the boat, but *that* his disciples were gone away alone;
23(Howbeit there came other boats from Ti-be′ri-as nigh unto the place
where they did eat bread, after that the Lord had given thanks:)
24When the people therefore saw that Jesus was not there, neither his
disciples, they also took shipping, and came to Ca-per′na-um, seeking for
Jesus.
25And when they had found him on the other side of the sea, they said
unto him, Rabbi, when camest thou hither?
26Jesus answered them and said, Verily, verily, I say unto you, Ye seek
me, not because ye saw the miracles, but because ye did eat of the loaves,
and were filled.
27Labour not for the meat which perisheth, but for that meat which

☆6:27 Isa 55:2 Mt 3:17; 17:5 Mk 1:11; 9:7 Lk 3:22 Jn 1:33; 5:37 8:18 Acts 2:22 Rom 6:23 2 Pet 1:17, 18

6:12 *Gather up the fragments that remain.* If Jesus, who supplied this large amount of food, was concerned that what was left be gathered up and used for human consumption, how much more should Christians be careful not to be wasteful. Multitudes could be fed by the food thrown away in a prodigal society. "Waste not, want not" is a good maxim.

6:15 These now well-fed people would forcibly make Jesus king. Then they would not have to work by the sweat of their brows to get food. Their carnality was the impetus of this notion, plus their desire to be delivered from the yoke of the Roman oppressor. It was revolutionary zeal that prompted this effort. And they would do it whether Jesus wanted to be king or not. In his humility and self-denial, he squelched their designs; he withdrew to be by himself.

6:27 *labor not for the meat that perishes,* i.e., do not make the concerns of this present life your chief care and pursuit. Rather, they are to labor for the meat that has to do with the soul. Jesus takes their concern for endureth unto everlasting life, which the Son of man shall give unto you: for him hath God the Father sealed.

28 Then said they unto him, What shall we do, that we might work the works of God?

29 Jesus answered and said unto them, This is the work of God, that ye believe on him whom he hath sent.

30 They said therefore unto him, What sign shewest thou then, that we may see, and believe thee? what dost thou work?

31 Our fathers did eat manna in the desert; as it is written, He gave them bread from heaven to eat.

32 Then Jesus said unto them, Verily, verily, I say unto you, Moses gave you not that bread from heaven; but my Father giveth you the true bread from heaven.

33 For the bread of God is he which cometh down from heaven, and giveth life unto the world.

34 Then said they unto him, Lord, evermore give us this bread.

35 And Jesus said unto them, I am the bread of life: he that cometh to me shall never hunger; and he that believeth on me shall never thirst.

36 But I said unto you, That ye also have seen me, and believe not.

37 All that the Father giveth me shall come to me; and him that cometh to me I will in no wise cast out.

38 For I came down from heaven, not to do mine own will, but the will of him that sent me.

39 And this is the Father's will which hath sent me, that of all which he hath given me I should lose nothing, but should raise it up again at the last day.

40 And this is the will of him that sent me, that every one which seeth the Son, and believeth on him, may have everlasting life: and I will raise him up at the last day.

6:29 1 Thess 1:3; 1 Jn 3:23
6:30☆
6:31 Ex 16:4, 15; Num 11:7; Neh 9:15; Ps 78:24; 105:40; Mt 12:38; Mk 8:11; 1 Cor 10:3
6:33 Jn 6:41, 50
6:35☆ Jn 4:14; 6:48; 7:37, 38
6:37 Job 8:20; Jer 31:35–37; 33:25, 26; Jn 10:28, 29; 17:2, 24; 2 Tim 2:19; 1 Jn 2:19
6:38 Mt 26:39; Lk 22:42; Jn 4:34; 5:30
6:39 Jn 5:24; 10:28; 17:12; 18:9; Col 3:3
6:40 Jn 1:14, 18; 3:16; 12:45; 14:9–11

4. The Jews Disbelieve Jesus' Claim

41 The Jews then murmured at him, because he said, I am the bread which came down from heaven.

42 And they said, Is not this Jesus, the son of Joseph, whose father and mother we know? how is it then that he saith, I came down from heaven?

43 Jesus therefore answered and said unto them, Murmur not among yourselves.

44 No man can come to me, except the Father which hath sent me draw him: and I will raise him up at the last day.

45 It is written in the prophets, And they shall be all taught of God. Every man therefore that hath heard, and hath learned of the Father, cometh unto me.

6:41 Jn 6:33, 51, 58
6:42☆ Jn 7:27
6:44 Jer 31:3; Hos 11:4; Jn 6:65; 12:32
6:45 Isa 54:13; Jer 31:34; Mic 4:2; 1 Thess 4:9; Heb 8:10, 11

---

the bodily aspect of life and turns their attention to the spiritual side of life, i.e., the necessity to care for the soul, which does not perish as the body does.

6:30 Jesus had just fed five thousand people. Following this event he spoke to the people about the food that endures to eternal life. They asked him for a sign that they might see and believe. They did not realize that we see *after* we believe, not before. The people *reversed the divine order.* They wanted to see first and then believe. This is indicative of the old problem of faith and reason. Faith precedes reason. And faith makes us reason correctly.

6:35 Bread is not a type of Christ, but it is used figuratively to illustrate that he is life to the believer as bread is to physical life. *I am the bread of life* is to be taken no more literally than the words "I am the door," or "I am the vine." Jesus is not bread, nor a door, nor a vine. It is true, however, that whoever comes to Jesus as the bread of life will find his spiritual hunger cared for and his heart's needs fully met.

6:42 It is easy to understand why the Jews were disconcerted with the words of Jesus concerning his descent from heaven. They knew Jesus as the son of Mary and Joseph, and the family itself was certainly not notable. They had heard of angels coming down from heaven but never of a man doing so. Since they refused to accept the proofs Jesus gave them of his messiahship, they were left in the dark. Whoever sets Jesus on the level with all the sons of men thereby denies his deity and salvational work.

46 Not that any man hath seen the Father, save he which is of God, he
hath seen the Father.
47 Verily, verily, I say unto you, He that believeth on me hath everlasting
life.
48 I am that bread of life.
49 Your fathers did eat manna in the wilderness, and are dead.
50 This is the bread which cometh down from heaven, that a man may eat
thereof, and not die.
51 I am the living bread which came down from heaven: if any man eat of
this bread, he shall live for ever: and the bread that I will give is my flesh,
which I will give for the life of the world.
52 The Jews therefore strove among themselves, saying, How can this man
give us *his* flesh to eat?
53 Then Jesus said unto them, Verily, verily, I say unto you, Except ye eat
the flesh of the Son of man, and drink his blood, ye have no life in you.
54 Whoso eateth my flesh, and drinketh my blood, hath eternal life; and I
will raise him up at the last day.
55 For my flesh is meat indeed, and my blood is drink indeed.
56 He that eateth my flesh, and drinketh my blood, dwelleth in me, and I
in him.
57 As the living Father hath sent me, and I live by the Father: so he that
eateth me, even he shall live by me.
58 This is that bread which came down from heaven: not as your fathers
did eat manna, and are dead: he that eateth of this bread shall live for ever.
59 These things said he in the synagogue, as he taught in Ca-per'na-um.

5. The Doubts of Jesus' Disciples

60 Many therefore of his disciples, when they had heard *this*, said, This is
an hard saying; who can hear it?
61 When Jesus knew in himself that his disciples murmured at it, he said
unto them, Doth this offend you?
62 *What* and if ye shall see the Son of man ascend up where he was before?
63 It is the spirit that quickeneth; the flesh profiteth nothing: the words
that I speak unto you, *they* are spirit, and *they* are life.
64 But there are some of you that believe not. For Jesus knew from the
beginning who they were that believed not, and who should betray him.
65 And he said, Therefore said I unto you, that no man can come unto me,
except it were given unto him of my Father.

6. Peter's Great Confession

66 ¶From that *time* many of his disciples went back, and walked no more
with him.
67 Then said Jesus unto the twelve, Will ye also go away?

6:46 Mt 11:27 Lk 10:22 Jn 1:18; 5:37 7:29 2 Cor 4:6
6:47 Jn 3:16
6:48 Jn 6:58 Heb 10:5, 10
6:51 Jn 10:10, 11 Gal 2:20 Heb 10:10
6:52 Jn 7:43; 9:16 10:19
☆**6:53** Lev 17:10–14 Mt 26:26
6:54 Jn 6:39
6:56 Isa 57:15 Jn 14:20; 15:4 17:21–23 Rom 8:9, 10 1 Cor 3:16 6:17 2 Cor 6:16 Eph 3:17 1 Jn 4:15 Rev 3:20
6:57 Jn 5:26; 14:19 15:5 2 Pet 1:3, 4
6:58 Jn 6:31
☆**6:59** Mt 4:23
☆**6:60**
6:62 Mk 16:19 Jn 3:13 Acts 1:9 Eph 4:8
6:63 Jn 3:34 Rom 8:2 1 Cor 15:45 2 Cor 3:6 Heb 4:12
☆**6:64** Mt 10:4 Jn 13:11
6:65 Jn 6:37, 44
6:66 Lk 9:62 Heb 10:38 1 Jn 2:19

***6:53** Here Jesus is not speaking of a literal* eating of his flesh. What he says is a figure of speech designed to teach a great spiritual truth in physical terms. The Lord's Supper was not yet instituted, so it does not refer to that. It therefore was a spiritual eating and drinking, not a sacramental one.

6:59 Jesus did not proclaim his doctrine in a corner. He taught openly in the synagogue, where the religious elite had every opportunity to hear him and to gauge the truth of what he said.

6:60 Many of Jesus' disciples, i.e., those beyond the smaller select group, were offended by what Jesus said about eating his flesh. Because they thought in terms of cannibalism, it was a hard saying for them to accept (and for us too in this day). But they failed to admit they did not understand, nor did they ask Jesus to explain what he meant and to open their eyes to the truth beneath the words. He undoubtedly would have done so, if asked to.

6:64 John asserts that Jesus knew from the beginning who they were who would believe on him and who would not. He also knew who would betray him. He could infallibly distinguish between those whose love was counterfeit and those whose love was real. He knew who all of those were whom the Father had given him—past, present, and future.

68 Then Simon Peter answered him, Lord, to whom shall we go? thou hast
the words of eternal life.
69 And we believe and are sure that thou art that Christ, the Son of the
living God.
70 Jesus answered them, Have not I chosen you twelve, and one of you is
a devil?
71 He spake of Judas Iscariot *the son* of Simon: for he it was that should
betray him, being one of the twelve.

I. THE FEAST OF TABERNACLES

1. Jesus Goes to the Feast

7 AFTER these things Jesus walked in Galilee: for he would not walk in
Jewry, because the Jews sought to kill him.
2 Now the Jews' feast of tabernacles was at hand.
3 His brethren therefore said unto him, Depart hence, and go into Judæa,
that thy disciples also may see the works that thou doest.
4 For *there is* no man *that* doeth any thing in secret, and he himself
seeketh to be known openly. If thou do these things, shew thyself to the
world.
5 For neither did his brethren believe in him.
6 Then Jesus said unto them, My time is not yet come: but your time is
alway ready.
7 The world cannot hate you; but me it hateth, because I testify of it, that
the works thereof are evil.
8 Go ye up unto this feast: I go not up yet unto this feast; for my time is
not yet full come.
9 When he had said these words unto them, he abode *still* in Galilee.
10 ¶But when his brethren were gone up, then went he also up unto the
feast, not openly, but as it were in secret.
11 Then the Jews sought him at the feast, and said, Where is he?
12 And there was much murmuring among the people concerning him: for
some said, He is a good man: others said, Nay; but he deceiveth the people.
13 Howbeit no man spake openly of him for fear of the Jews.

2. Jesus Openly Teaches at the Temple

14 ¶Now about the midst of the feast Jesus went up into the temple, and
taught.
15 And the Jews marvelled, saying, How knoweth this man letters, having
never learned?
16 Jesus answered them, and said, My doctrine is not mine, but his that
sent me.

6:68☆ Mt 16:16; Jn 3:34, 5:25, 26; 6:63
6:69 Mk 1:24; Lk 4:34; Acts 3:14; 1 Jn 2:20
6:70 Mt 10:2–4; Jn 13:2, 27; 17:12
6:71 Mk 14:10
7:1 Jn 5:18; 7:19; 8:37
7:2☆ Lev. 23:23, 24; Deut 16:16; Zech 14:16
7:3 Mt 12:46; Mk 3:31, 32; Acts 1:14
7:5☆
7:6 Jn 2:4
7:7 Jn 3:19; 15:18, 19
7:8 Jn 8:20
7:11 Jn 11:56
7:12 Mt 21:45, 46; Lk 7:16; Jn 7:40–43; 9:16; 10:19
7:13 Jn 9:22, 23
7:14☆
7:15☆ Acts 4:13; 22:3; 2 Tim 3:15
7:16 Jn 8:28; 12:49; 14:10

6:68 *To whom shall we go?* Peter, acting as spokesman for the twelve, made it clear that if Jesus was not their choice, they had no other alternative. If he could not save them, then no one and nothing else could do it. Jesus is the way, the truth, and the life.

7:2 *feast of tabernacles.* This was the Old Testament festival that began on the fifteenth day of the seventh month (September-October) and lasted eight days. The *feast commemorated the wilderness* life of the Hebrews when they left Egypt. At this feast, priests drew water from the pool of Siloam and poured it out in libation upon the altar of the temple. (See 7:37–39; note on Exod. 23:16.)

7:5 At this stage, Jesus' brothers did not believe in him. If they had, they never would have said what we find recorded in 7:3, 4. His brothers were related to him by bloodline but not by "faithline." Grace does not run in the bloodline. Saved parents have unsaved children, and sometimes saved children have unsaved parents. Being born in a Christian family is a good sign, but it is no guarantee of salvation. Each of us has to make an individual decision.

7:14, 15 Jesus was an enigma to those who listened to him at the temple. The people knew he had not been a student in the schools of the prophets, nor did he have the benefit of what we might call academies, colleges, or universities. He had received the Spirit without measure (3:34), so that he did not need to receive knowledge from man or by man. He had knowledge beyond what any human being ever had or would have.

17 If any man will do his will, he shall know of the doctrine, whether it be of God, or *whether* I speak of myself.

18 He that speaketh of himself seeketh his own glory: but he that seeketh his glory that sent him, the same is true, and no unrighteousness is in him.

19 Did not Moses give you the law, and *yet* none of you keepeth the law? Why go ye about to kill me?

20 The people answered and said, Thou hast a devil: who goeth about to kill thee?

21 Jesus answered and said unto them, I have done one work, and ye all marvel.

22 Moses therefore gave unto you circumcision; (not because it is of Moses, but of the fathers;) and ye on the sabbath day circumcise a man.

23 If a man on the sabbath day receive circumcision, that the law of Moses should not be broken; are ye angry at me, because I have made a man every whit whole on the sabbath day?

24 Judge not according to the appearance, but judge righteous judgment.

25 Then said some of them of Jerusalem, Is not this he, whom they seek to kill?

26 But, lo, he speaketh boldly, and they say nothing unto him. Do the rulers know indeed that this is the very Christ?

27 Howbeit we know this man whence he is: but when Christ cometh, no man knoweth whence he is.

28 Then cried Jesus in the temple as he taught, saying, Ye both know me, and ye know whence I am: and I am not come of myself, but he that sent me is true, whom ye know not.

29 But I know him: for I am from him, and he hath sent me.

30 Then they sought to take him: but no man laid hands on him, because his hour was not yet come.

31 And many of the people believed on him, and said, When Christ cometh, will he do more miracles than these which this *man* hath done?

32 ¶The Pharisees heard that the people murmured such things concerning him; and the Pharisees and the chief priests sent officers to take him.

33 Then said Jesus unto them, Yet a little while am I with you, and *then* I go unto him that sent me.

34 Ye shall seek me, and shall not find *me:* and where I am, *thither* ye cannot come.

35 Then said the Jews among themselves, Whither will he go, that we shall not find him? will he go unto the dispersed among the Gentiles, and teach the Gentiles?

36 What *manner of* saying is this that he said, Ye shall seek me, and shall not find *me:* and where I am, *thither* ye cannot come?

3. Jesus' Sermon on the Last Day of the Feast

37 In the last day, that great *day* of the feast, Jesus stood and cried, saying, If any man thirst, let him come unto me, and drink.

7:17 Hos 6:1–3
7:18 Jn 5:41; 8:50, 54 12:43
7:19 Mt 12:14 Mk 3:6; 11:18 Jn 1:17; 7:1 Acts 7:38
7:20 Jn 8:48–52 10:20
☆**7:21, 22** Gen 17:9, 10 Lev 12:3 Jn 5:8 Acts 7:8
☆**7:23** Jn 5:10
7:24 Isa 11:3 Jn 8:15
7:27 Jn 7:41, 42 9:29
7:28 Jn 1:18; 5:43 8:14, 26, 55
7:29 Mt 11:27 Jn 3:17; 8:55 10:15; 17:25
☆**7:30**
7:32 Mt 12:14
7:33 Jn 14:19 16:5, 10, 16–18, 28
7:34 Jn 8:21; 13:33
7:35 Isa 11:12 Jn 8:22 Jas 1:1 1 Pet 1:1
7:37 Isa 55:1 Jn 4:10, 14 6:35 Rev 22:17

7:21–23 All male infants were circumcised on the eighth day after birth. If the baby was born on the sabbath, circumcision was performed the following sabbath despite the prohibition against work on that day. Jesus argued that if the Jews violated the sabbath law in order to keep the law of circumcision, it was far more reasonable to allow for healing on the sabbath day, which was more important than circumcising infants. Helping one's neighbor was the second table of the law.

7:30 *his hour was not yet come.* "His hour" is a phrase used often in John's Gospel but not in the others. The reason the multitude could not touch Jesus was not that they lacked the desire to do so, or that they talked without intending to act. Rather, God hindered them from doing what they wanted because he had a timetable of his own, and nothing could interfere with the divine plan.

7:38☆ Isa 12:3; 44:3; 58:11; Ezek 47:1–10; Joel 3:18
7:39 Joel 2:28; Jn 12:23, 24; 13:31, 32; 14:17, 18; 16:7; 20:22; Acts 2:17; 16:7; Rom 8:9; 1 Cor 15:45; 2 Cor 3:17; Phil 1:19
7:40 Deut 18:15; Jn 1:21; 6:14
7:41, 42 1 Sam 16:1; 2 Sam 7:12; Ps 132:11; Mic 5:2; Mt 1:1; 2:5–10; Lk 2:4; Jn 7:52
7:43 Jn 9:16; 10:19
7:46 Lk 4:22
7:48 1 Cor 1:20
7:50 Jn 3:1, 2; 19:39
7:51 Ex 23:1; Deut 17:2–8; 19:15–19; Prov 18:13
7:52 Isa 9:1, 2; Mt 4:14–16; Jn 1:46
7:53ff☆
8:5 Ex 20:14; Lev 18:20; 20:10; Deut 5:18; 22:22; Job 31:9–11; Mt 5:27, 28

38 He that believeth on me, as the scripture hath said, out of his belly shall flow rivers of living water.
39 (But this spake he of the Spirit, which they that believe on him should receive: for the Holy Ghost was not yet *given;* because that Jesus was not yet glorified.)
40 ¶Many of the people therefore, when they heard this saying, said, Of a truth this is the Prophet.
41 Others said, This is the Christ. But some said, Shall Christ come out of Galilee?
42 Hath not the scripture said, That Christ cometh of the seed of David, and out of the town of Bethlehem, where David was?
43 So there was a division among the people because of him.
44 And some of them would have taken him; but no man laid hands on him.
45 ¶Then came the officers to the chief priests and Pharisees; and they said unto them, Why have ye not brought him?
46 The officers answered, Never man spake like this man.
47 Then answered them the Pharisees, Are ye also deceived?
48 Have any of the rulers or of the Pharisees believed on him?
49 But this people who knoweth not the law are cursed.
50 Nic-o-de'mus saith unto them, (he that came to Jesus by night, being one of them,)
51 Doth our law judge *any* man, before it hear him, and know what he doeth?
52 They answered and said unto him, Art thou also of Galilee? Search, and look: for out of Galilee ariseth no prophet.
53 And every man went unto his own house.

J. JESUS REPROVES THE JEWS

1. The Woman Taken in Adultery

8 JESUS went unto the mount of Olives.
2 And early in the morning he came again into the temple, and all the people came unto him; and he sat down, and taught them.
3 And the scribes and Pharisees brought unto him a woman taken in adultery; and when they had set her in the midst,
4 They say unto him, Master, this woman was taken in adultery, in the very act.
5 Now Moses in the law commanded us, that such should be stoned: but what sayest thou?
6 This they said, tempting him, that they might have to accuse him. But Jesus stooped down, and with *his* finger wrote on the ground, *as though he heard them not.*

7:38 There is no direct quotation to be found in Scripture for the phrase *out of his belly shall flow rivers of living water.* "The scripture that the Lord referred to was not a particular Old Testament verse, but the general tenor of Scripture that spoke of the living waters flowing forth (see Isa. 12:3; 44:3; 58:11; Ezek. 47:1–12; Joel 3:18)." (See *A Study Guide to Translating the Gospel of John,* Philip W. Comfort, B.B.H. Distributors of Baker Book House, 1985, pp. 42, 43.) Jesus, who knew the Scriptures well, took these general references and applied them in this new context.

7:53—8:11 Most textual critics think this passage was not in John's autograph because it does not appear in any of the earliest manuscripts. However, most conservatives believe that this incident really occurred (for it is known to have been a piece of oral tradition), even though it was not part of John's original writing.

According to this story, the Jews were guilty of misapplying God's law. The Pharisees brought only the woman, not the accomplice in her crime. The law demanded that both parties be stoned, if guilty. When Jesus called for witnesses to cast the first stone, the Pharisees and the woman's other accusers disappeared. They knew their case was illegal. Perhaps one of them or several of them had used her services. When the woman was set free, Jesus told her to go and to sin no more.

7 So when they continued asking him, he lifted up himself, and said unto
them, He that is without sin among you, let him first cast a stone at her.
8 And again he stooped down, and wrote on the ground.
9 And they which heard *it*, being convicted by *their own* conscience, went
out one by one, beginning at the eldest, *even* unto the last: and Jesus was
left alone, and the woman standing in the midst.
10 When Jesus had lifted up himself, and saw none but the woman, he said
unto her, Woman, where are those thine accusers? hath no man condemned
thee?
11 She said, No man, Lord. And Jesus said unto her, Neither do I
condemn thee: go, and sin no more.

8:7 Deut 17:7
8:11 Jn 5:14

2. Jesus' Claim to Be the Light of the World

12 ¶Then spake Jesus again unto them, saying, I am the light of the world:
he that followeth me shall not walk in darkness, but shall have the light of
life.
13 The Pharisees therefore said unto him, Thou bearest record of thyself;
thy record is not true.
14 Jesus answered and said unto them, Though I bear record of myself, *yet*
my record is true: for I know whence I came, and whither I go; but ye
cannot tell whence I come, and whither I go.
15 Ye judge after the flesh; I judge no man.
16 And yet if I judge, my judgment is true: for I am not alone, but I and
the Father that sent me.
17 It is also written in your law, that the testimony of two men is true.
18 I am one that bear witness of myself, and the Father that sent me
beareth witness of me.
19 Then said they unto him, Where is thy Father? Jesus answered, Ye
neither know me, nor my Father: if ye had known me, ye should have
known my Father also.
20 These words spake Jesus in the treasury, as he taught in the temple: and
no man laid hands on him; for his hour was not yet come.

☆8:12 Isa 9:1, 2 Jn 1:4, 5, 9; 3:19 9:5; 12:35, 36, 46 2 Cor 4:6
8:14 Jn 7:28; 18:37 Rev 1:5
8:15 1 Sam 16:7
8:16 Jn 5:30 14:10, 11; 16:32
8:17 Deut 17:6; 19:15 Mt 18:16 2 Cor 13:1 Heb 10:28
8:18 Jn 5:37 2 Pet 1:17, 18 1 Jn 5:9
8:19 Jn 14:7, 9
8:20 Mk 12:41 Lk 21:1 Jn 7:30

3. The Warning against Unbelief

21 Then said Jesus again unto them, I go my way, and ye shall seek me,
and shall die in your sins: whither I go, ye cannot come.
22 Then said the Jews, Will he kill himself? because he saith, Whither I go,
ye cannot come.
23 And he said unto them, Ye are from beneath; I am from above: ye are
of this world; I am not of this world.
24 I said therefore unto you, that ye shall die in your sins: for if ye believe
not that I am *he*, ye shall die in your sins.
25 Then said they unto him, Who art thou? And Jesus saith unto them,
Even *the same* that I said unto you from the beginning.
26 I have many things to say and to judge of you: but he that sent me is
true: and I speak to the world those things which I have heard of him.
27 They understood not that he spake to them of the Father.

8:21 Jn 7:34; 13:33
8:22 Jn 7:35, 36
8:23 Jn 3:31; 15:19 17:16 1 Jn 4:5
☆8:24 Ex 3:14, 15 Jn 4:26; 8:28, 58 13:19
8:26 Jn 3:32–34 12:49; 15:15

8:12 A worthy Christian walk is characterized by certain inward and outward qualities. Some of the inward qualities are (1) purity, or walking as children of the light (1 John 1:6, 7; 2:11); (2) sincerity, or integrity and frankness (2 Cor. 4:2); (3) obedience to God (2 John 6); (4) faith, not sight (2 Cor. 5:7); and (5) living in the truth (3 John 3, 4). The outward characteristics are (1) outward honesty (Rom. 13:12, 13; 1 Thess. 4:11, 12); (2) acting carefully or prudently (Eph. 5:15, 16); (3) walking wisely (Col. 4:5, 6); and (4) manifesting love (Eph. 5:2).

8:24 Jesus asserts that he is God and that salvation depends on believing in him. Those who do not believe in him will die in their sins. And to die in one's sins is to lose all hope of eternal life.

8:28☆ Jn 3:11, 14, 15; 5:19, 8:24; 12:32; Rom 1:4

28 Then said Jesus unto them, When ye have lifted up the Son of man, then shall ye know that I am *he*, and *that* I do nothing of myself; but as my Father hath taught me, I speak these things.

8:29 Jn 4:34; 6:38; 14:10; 16:32

29 And he that sent me is with me: the Father hath not left me alone; for I do always those things that please him.

4. Abraham's True Children

30 As he spake these words, many believed on him.

8:31☆ Jn 15:7; 2 Jn 9

31 Then said Jesus to those Jews which believed on him, If ye continue in my word, *then* are ye my disciples indeed;

8:32 Rom 8:2; 2 Cor 3:17; Gal 5:1, 13; 1 Pet 2:16

32 And ye shall know the truth, and the truth shall make you free.

33 ¶They answered him, We be Abraham's seed, and were never in bondage to any man: how sayest thou, Ye shall be made free?

8:33 Lev 25:42; Mt 3:9

34 Jesus answered them, Verily, verily, I say unto you, Whosoever committeth sin is the servant of sin.

8:34 Rom 6:16; 2 Pet 2:19

8:35 Gen 21:10; Gal 4:30

35 And the servant abideth not in the house for ever: *but* the Son abideth ever.

8:36 Jn 8:32

36 If the Son therefore shall make you free, ye shall be free indeed.

8:37 Jn 7:19

37 I know that ye are Abraham's seed; but ye seek to kill me, because my word hath no place in you.

38 I speak that which I have seen with my Father: and ye do that which ye have seen with your father.

8:39☆ Mt 3:9; Rom 3:28; 9:7; Gal 3:7, 29

39 They answered and said unto him, Abraham is our father. Jesus saith unto them, If ye were Abraham's children, ye would do the works of Abraham.

40 But now ye seek to kill me, a man that hath told you the truth, which I have heard of God: this did not Abraham.

8:41 Deut 32:6; Isa 63:16; 64:8; Mal 1:6

41 Ye do the deeds of your father. Then said they to him, We be not born of fornication; we have one Father, *even* God.

8:42☆ Jn 1:14; 3:16; 5:43; 16:27; 17:8; Gal 4:4; 1 Jn 4:9; 5:1

42 Jesus said unto them, If God were your Father, ye would love me: for I proceeded forth and came from God; neither came I of myself, but he sent me.

8:43 Jn 7:17

43 Why do ye not understand my speech? *even* because ye cannot hear my word.

8:44☆ Gen 3:1, 4; Mt 12:34; 13:38; 2 Cor 11:3; 1 Jn 2:4; 3:8

44 Ye are of *your* father the devil, and the lusts of your father ye will do. He was a murderer from the beginning, and abode not in the truth, because there is no truth in him. When he speaketh a lie, he speaketh of his own: for he is a liar, and the father of it.

8:28 *lifted up,* i.e., lifted up on the cross.

8:31ff All the Jews were children of Abraham after the flesh but not all were children of Abraham according to faith. Jesus promises that faith in him will set them free. Some carnal Jews took exception to Jesus' words (8:33). As Abraham's seed they thought they were free by birthright and never were in bondage to anyone. He informs them that, as sinners, they are slaves to sin. Jesus has the power to set them free from their bondage to sin, which is the worst of all bondages. Moreover, Jesus agrees that they are descendants of *Abraham (8:37), but it avails them nothing,* for they do not have Abraham's faith.

8:39 *ye would do the works of Abraham,* i.e., they would claim their interest in the covenant God made with Abraham and his seed. This would entail faith and obedience, neither of which they had at this moment.

8:42 Jesus makes the astounding claim that they did not have God as their Father because they did not love Jesus himself. Whoever does not love Jesus is anathema (1 Cor. 16:22). The second reason they did not have God as their Father was that they did not understand Jesus' speech, which was heavenly, divine, and intelligible to those who were familiar with the voice of God in the Old Testament. In plainest words, they did not speak the language of the family of God.

8:44 *the devil,* or, "Satan," is characterized as (1) *a liar*; (2) "the prince of this world" (14:30); (3) "the god of this world" (2 Cor. 4:4); (4) "the mighty prince of the power of the air, who is at work right now in the hearts of those who are against the Lord" (Eph. 2:2, TLB); (5) "your adversary" (1 Pet. 5:8); and (6) "the dragon, that old serpent, which is the Devil, and Satan" (Rev. 20:2). Everyone is either a son of God or a son of the devil. The devil is here looked upon as having his own children to whom he is father.

45 And because I tell *you* the truth, ye believe me not.
46 Which of you convinceth me of sin? And if I say the truth, why do ye
not believe me?
47 He that is of God heareth God's words: ye therefore hear *them* not,
because ye are not of God.
48 Then answered the Jews, and said unto him, Say we not well that thou
art a Sa-mar'i-tan, and hast a devil?
49 Jesus answered, I have not a devil; but I honour my Father, and ye do
dishonour me.
50 And I seek not mine own glory: there is one that seeketh and judgeth.
51 Verily, verily, I say unto you, If a man keep my saying, he shall never
see death.
52 Then said the Jews unto him, Now we know that thou hast a devil.
Abraham is dead, and the prophets; and thou sayest, If a man keep my
saying, he shall never taste of death.
53 Art thou greater than our father Abraham, which is dead? and the
prophets are dead: whom makest thou thyself?
54 Jesus answered, If I honour myself, my honour is nothing: it is my
Father that honoureth me; of whom ye say, that he is your God:
55 Yet ye have not known him; but I know him: and if I should say, I
know him not, I shall be a liar like unto you: but I know him, and keep his
saying.
56 Your father Abraham rejoiced to see my day: and he saw *it*, and was
glad.
57 Then said the Jews unto him, Thou art not yet fifty years old, and hast
thou seen Abraham?
58 Jesus said unto them, Verily, verily, I say unto you, Before Abraham
was, I am.
59 Then took they up stones to cast at him: but Jesus hid himself, and
went out of the temple, going through the midst of them, and so passed by.

K. THE MAN WHO WAS BORN BLIND

1. The Sixth Sign: Healing the Blind Man

9 AND as *Jesus* passed by, he saw a man which was blind from *his* birth.
2 And his disciples asked him, saying, Master, who did sin, this man,
or his parents, that he was born blind?
3 Jesus answered, Neither hath this man sinned, nor his parents: but that
the works of God should be made manifest in him.
4 I must work the works of him that sent me, while it is day: the night
cometh, when no man can work.
5 As long as I am in the world, I am the light of the world.
6 When he had thus spoken, he spat on the ground, and made clay of the
spittle, and he anointed the eyes of the blind man with the clay,

8:45 Jn 18:37
8:47 1 Jn 4:6
8:49 Jn 7:20
8:50 Jn 5:41, 42
8:51 Jn 5:24; 11:25, 26
8:53 Jn 4:12
8:54 Jn 16:14; 17:1; Acts 3:13
8:55 Jn 7:29; 15:10
8:56 Gen 22:17, 18; Lk 10:24; Gal 3:8, 9, 16; Heb 11:10, 13
☆**8:58** Ex 3:14; Isa 9:6; 43:13; Mic 5:2; Jn 8:24, 28; 13:19; Col 1:17; Heb 13:8; Rev 1:8
☆**9:1** Ex 20:5; Lk 13:2; Jn 9:34; Acts 28:4
9:3 Jn 11:4
9:4 Jn 4:34; 5:19, 36; 11:9; 12:35; 17:4
9:5 Isa 9:2; 42:6; 49:6; Lk 2:32; Jn 1:5, 9; 3:19; 8:12; 12:46
9:6 Mk 7:33; 8:23

8:58 *Before Abraham was, I am.* This is one of Jesus' own statements about his eternal existence. The immediate and negative response of the listeners makes clear that such a statement presumed the uniqueness of his person. They were not ready to accept what he said, for to do so meant they would have to worship him. In the Arian controversy before the Council of Nicea (A.D. 325), Arius claimed that Jesus was a created being—that there was a time when he did not exist. Scripture, however, teaches that Jesus is the eternally preexistent one. Other verses confirm the eternity of Jesus: Isa. 9:6; John 1:1, 2.

9:1ff A common opinion, apparently shared by Jesus' disciples, was that sickness was a result of sin. Since this man was blind from birth it was obvious that his own sin had not been the cause of the "punishment." So the question was whether his blindness was a punishment for his parents' sins. Jesus said that sickness is not always the result of sin. The man was born blind so that God's power might be demonstrated through the healing. Jesus made him whole. This is the only instance in which Jesus healed someone who was blind from birth.

9:7 2 Kgs 5:14 Neh 3:15 Isa 35:5 — 7 And said unto him, Go, wash in the pool of Si-lo'am, (which is by
interpretation, Sent.) He went his way therefore, and washed, and came
seeing.
9:8 Acts 3:2, 10 — 8 ¶The neighbours therefore, and they which before had seen him that he
was blind, said, Is not this he that sat and begged?
9 Some said, This is he: others *said*, He is like him: *but* he said, I am *he*.
10 Therefore said they unto him, How were thine eyes opened?
11 He answered and said, A man that is called Jesus made clay, and
anointed mine eyes, and said unto me, Go to the pool of Si-lo'am, and
wash: and I went and washed, and I received sight.
12 Then said they unto him, Where is he? He said, I know not.

2. The Pharisees Interrogate the Blind Man

13 ¶They brought to the Pharisees him that aforetime was blind.
9:14 Jn 5:9 — 14 And it was the sabbath day when Jesus made the clay, and opened his
eyes.
15 Then again the Pharisees also asked him how he had received his sight.
He said unto them, He put clay upon mine eyes, and I washed, and do see.
9:16☆ Jn 3:2; 7:12, 43 — 16 Therefore said some of the Pharisees, This man is not of God, because
he keepeth not the sabbath day. Others said, How can a man that is a
sinner do such miracles? And there was a division among them.
9:17 Deut 18:15 Mt 21:11 Jn 4:19; 6:14 — 17 They say unto the blind man again, What sayest thou of him, that he
hath opened thine eyes? He said, He is a prophet.
18 But the Jews did not believe concerning him, that he had been blind,
and received his sight, until they called the parents of him that had received
his sight.
19 And they asked them, saying, Is this your son, who ye say was born
blind? how then doth he now see?
20 His parents answered them and said, We know that this is our son, and
that he was born blind:
21 But by what means he now seeth, we know not; or who hath opened his
eyes, we know not: he is of age; ask him: he shall speak for himself.
9:22☆ Jn 7:13; 12:42 16:2; 19:38 Acts 5:13 — 22 These *words* spake his parents, because they feared the Jews: for the
Jews had agreed already, that if any man did confess that he was Christ, he
should be put out of the synagogue.
23 Therefore said his parents, He is of age; ask him.

3. The Pharisees Interrogate the Blind Man the Second Time

9:24 Josh 7:19 — 24 Then again called they the man that was blind, and said unto him, Give
God the praise: we know that this man is a sinner.
25 He answered and said, Whether he be a sinner *or no*, I know not: one
thing I know, that, whereas I was blind, now I see.
26 Then said they to him again, What did he to thee? how opened he thine
eyes?
27 He answered them, I have told you already, and ye did not hear:
wherefore would ye hear *it* again? will ye also be his disciples?

9:16 *How can a man that is a sinner do such miracles?* This excellent question produced a division of the *house. Miracles did not move* those who were steeped in their unbelief. The blind man's eyes were opened by Jesus, but their blind hearts were darkened; and they refused the remedy by which they, too, could see spiritually.

9:22 Because of the Pharisees' views on Jesus, it was quite proper for them to disfellowship anyone who professed faith in Jesus as the Messiah. Such persons were considered apostates. The Pharisees did not think him to be the Messiah for two reasons: (1) his teachings were contrary to their traditions; (2) they expected the Messiah to come in pomp and splendor; since Jesus came in lowliness and humility, they felt he could not be the true Messiah. On the basis of his miraculous deeds, however, they should have discarded their false views and received him as the Messiah.

28 Then they reviled him, and said, Thou art his disciple; but we are
Moses' disciples.
29 We know that God spake unto Moses: *as for* this *fellow*, we know not
from whence he is.
30 The man answered and said unto them, Why herein is a marvellous
thing, that ye know not from whence he is, and *yet* he hath opened mine
eyes.
31 Now we know that God heareth not sinners: but if any man be a
worshipper of God, and doeth his will, him he heareth.
32 Since the world began was it not heard that any man opened the eyes of
one that was born blind.
33 If this man were not of God, he could do nothing.
34 They answered and said unto him, Thou wast altogether born in sins,
and dost thou teach us? And they cast him out.

9:28 Jn 5:45 Rom 2:17
9:29 Jn 1:10; 8:14
9:31 Job 27:8, 9 Ps 34:15; 66:18 145:19 Prov 15:29 Isa 1:15 Jer 11:11; 14:12 Mic 3:4 Zech 7:13
9:33 Jn 3:2
☆9:34 Jn 12:42

4. Jesus Seeks Out the Man Who Had Been Blind

35 Jesus heard that they had cast him out; and when he had found him, he
said unto him, Dost thou believe on the Son of God?
36 He answered and said, Who is he, Lord, that I might believe on him?
37 And Jesus said unto him, Thou hast both seen him, and it is he that
talketh with thee.
38 And he said, Lord, I believe. And he worshipped him.
39 ¶And Jesus said, For judgment I am come into this world, that they
which see not might see; and that they which see might be made blind.
40 And *some* of the Pharisees which were with him heard these words, and
said unto him, Are we blind also?
41 Jesus said unto them, If ye were blind, ye should have no sin: but now
ye say, We see; therefore your sin remaineth.

9:35 Mt 16:16 Mk 1:1
9:37 Jn 4:26
☆9:38
9:39 Lk 4:18, 19
9:40 Rom 2:19
9:41 Prov 26:12 Jn 15:22

L. JESUS, THE GOOD SHEPHERD

10 VERILY, verily, I say unto you, He that entereth not by the door
into the sheepfold, but climbeth up some other way, the same is a
thief and a robber.
2 But he that entereth in by the door is the shepherd of the sheep.
3 To him the porter openeth; and the sheep hear his voice: and he calleth
his own sheep by name, and leadeth them out.
4 And when he putteth forth his own sheep, he goeth before them, and the
sheep follow him: for they know his voice.
5 And a stranger will they not follow, but will flee from him: for they
know not the voice of strangers.
6 This parable spake Jesus unto them: but they understood not what
things they were which he spake unto them.

☆10:1 Isa 56:10
10:2 Acts 20:28
10:5 Prov 19:27 Gal 1:8 Eph 4:14 Col 2:8
10:6 Jn 16:25 2 Pet 2:22

9:34 *Thou wast altogether born in sins.* The man who was healed of his blindness is now cast out of the synagogue. Good men may well be denied the comfort of the church then and now. It is better to be cast out of the fellowship than to remain and surrender true convictions. What this man suffered is much the same as that suffered by the disciples of Jesus in the beginning of the church age.

9:38 *he worshipped him.* It would have been blasphemous for Jesus to accept this worship, which belongs only to God, if indeed he was not God.

10:1ff Jesus' story of the good shepherd is an allegory, not an illustration or parable. An allegory differs from a parable in one important way: *all* the details of an allegory are significant. In a parable the details are incidental to the main point. Thus, for example, in the parable of the mustard seed (Matt. 13:31, 32) the main point relates to the growth of the kingdom. The details about the seed, the tree, and the birds are incidental—no special point should be deduced from their mention. In the allegory of the good shepherd all of the details are important: Jesus is the shepherd of the sheep. He is the door. The sheep enter the kingdom through the door. Jesus, the Shepherd, died for his sheep. And whoever is not a true sheep cannot enter the door. (See note on Matt. 13:3 regarding the definition of an illustration or parable.)

7 Then said Jesus unto them again, Verily, verily, I say unto you, I am the
door of the sheep.
8 All that ever came before me are thieves and robbers: but the sheep did
not hear them.
9 I am the door: by me if any man enter in, he shall be saved, and shall go
in and out, and find pasture.
10 The thief cometh not, but for to steal, and to kill, and to destroy: I am
come that they might have life, and that they might have *it* more
abundantly.
11 I am the good shepherd: the good shepherd giveth his life for the sheep.
12 But he that is an hireling, and not the shepherd, whose own the sheep
are not, seeth the wolf coming, and leaveth the sheep, and fleeth: and the
wolf catcheth them, and scattereth the sheep.
13 The hireling fleeth, because he is an hireling, and careth not for the
sheep.
14 I am the good shepherd, and know my *sheep,* and am known of mine.
15 As the Father knoweth me, even so know I the Father: and I lay down
my life for the sheep.
16 And other sheep I have, which are not of this fold: them also I must
bring, and they shall hear my voice; and there shall be one fold, *and* one
shepherd.
17 Therefore doth my Father love me, because I lay down my life, that I
might take it again.
18 No man taketh it from me, but I lay it down of myself. I have power to
lay it down, and I have power to take it again. This commandment have I
received of my Father.
19 ¶There was a division therefore again among the Jews for these sayings.
20 And many of them said, He hath a devil, and is mad; why hear ye him?
21 Others said, These are not the words of him that hath a devil. Can a
devil open the eyes of the blind?

10:7 Jn 14:6; Eph 2:18; Heb 10:19, 20
10:8 Jer 23:1, 50:6; Ezek 34:2
10:10 Jn 5:40; Acts 20:29; 2 Pet 2:1
10:11☆ Isa 40:11; Ezek 34:11–16, 23; 37:24; Heb 13:20, 21; 1 Pet 2:25; 5:4; 1 Jn 3:16; Rev 7:17
10:12 Zech 11:16
10:14 Phil 3:10; 2 Tim 2:19
10:16☆ Isa 56:6, 7; Ezek 37:21, 22; Jn 11:52; 17:20–24; Eph 2:14; 3:6
10:17 Isa 53:6, 7; 2 Cor 5:15; Heb 2:9; 1 Jn 3:16
10:18 Jn 11:25; 19:11; Heb 5:8; 7:16
10:19 Jn 7:43; 9:16
10:20☆ Jn 7:20
10:21 Ex 4:11; Ps 146:8; Jn 9:32

M. THE DEDICATION CELEBRATION: JESUS CLAIMS TO BE THE MESSIAH

22 ¶And it was at Jerusalem the feast of the dedication, and it was winter.
23 And Jesus walked in the temple in Solomon's porch.
24 Then came the Jews round about him, and said unto him, How long
dost thou make us to doubt? If thou be the Christ, tell us plainly.
25 Jesus answered them, I told you, and ye believed not: the works that I
do in my Father's name, they bear witness of me.
26 But ye believe not, because ye are not of my sheep, as I said unto you.

10:22☆
10:23 Acts 3:11; 5:12
10:24 Lk 22:67
10:25 Jn 5:36; 10:38; 14:10, 11
10:26 Jn 8:47; 1 Jn 4:6

10:11 Christ is called *the good shepherd* here, the "great shepherd" in Heb. 13:20, and the "chief Shepherd" in 1 Pet. 5:4. The good shepherd died for his sheep, the great shepherd conforms the sheep to his image, and the chief shepherd is coming again with his reward for the sheep. The good shepherd's work is finished, the great shepherd's work is present, and the chief shepherd's work is future.

10:16 *There shall be one fold, and one shepherd.* The word for *fold* should be properly translated "flock." *Jews and Gentiles* shall be incorporated into the one church of which Christ is shepherd. Those who are united with Christ should be united in Christ. The one church is subject to the one head, Christ. It is guided and led by the one Spirit and is commanded to have love for all members of the flock while waiting for the one common destiny of all believers.

10:20 *He hath a devil, and is mad.* John does not report as many of the healings as the other Gospel writers mention. For example, he does not record any of the miracles in which Jesus cast out demons. But he does record how Jesus was accused of having a devil and being insane, of imagining things (7:20), and of speaking wildly (8:48–52).

10:22 *the feast of the dedication* started after 168 B.C. The temple had been violated by Antiochus Epiphanes, who offered a sow on the altar. When Judas Maccabeus recaptured the city, he had the temple cleansed of its idolatry. The feast, or celebration, commemorated the rededication of the temple once the defilement had been removed. The festival lasted eight days in the winter month of Chislev (December), according to the apocryphal books of the Maccabees. Dan. 11:31 mentions the profaning of the temple by Antiochus.

27 My sheep hear my voice, and I know them, and they follow me:
28 And I give unto them eternal life; and they shall never perish, neither
shall any *man* pluck them out of my hand.
29 My Father, which gave *them* me, is greater than all; and no *man* is able
to pluck *them* out of my Father's hand.
30 I and *my* Father are one.
31 Then the Jews took up stones again to stone him.
32 Jesus answered them, Many good works have I shewed you from my
Father; for which of those works do ye stone me?
33 The Jews answered him, saying, For a good work we stone thee not; but
for blasphemy; and because that thou, being a man, makest thyself God.
34 Jesus answered them, Is it not written in your law, I said, Ye are gods?
35 If he called them gods, unto whom the word of God came, and the
scripture cannot be broken;
36 Say ye of him, whom the Father hath sanctified, and sent into the
world, Thou blasphemest; because I said, I am the Son of God?
37 If I do not the works of my Father, believe me not.
38 But if I do, though ye believe not me, believe the works: that ye may
know, and believe, that the Father *is* in me, and I in him.
39 Therefore they sought again to take him: but he escaped out of their
hand,
40 And went away again beyond Jordan into the place where John at first
baptized; and there he abode.
41 And many resorted unto him, and said, John did no miracle: but all
things that John spake of this man were true.
42 And many believed on him there.

☆**10:28** Jn 6:37, 39 17:2, 3 1 Jn 5:11, 12
10:29 Jn 14:28 17:2, 6
☆**10:30** Isa 9:6 Jn 1:1; 10:38 14:8–11 17:21–24 1 Cor 8:6 Col 2:2 1 Tim 3:16 1 Jn 1:3
10:33 Lev 24:15, 16 Jn 1:1, 18 Jn 5:18; 20:28 Acts 20:28 Rom 9:5 Phil 2:6 Col 2:9 Tit 2:13 Heb 1:8, 9 2 Pet 1:1 1 Jn 5:20
10:34 Ps 82:1, 6 Lk 1:35 Jn 5:36; 8:42
☆**10:35**
10:37 Jn 15:24
10:38 Jn 14:10 17:21, 23
10:39 Jn 7:30
10:40 Jn 1:28
10:41 Jn 1:29; 3:30
10:42 Jn 7:31 8:30, 31; 11:45

N. THE SEVENTH SIGN: THE RAISING OF LAZARUS

1. The Message about Lazarus' Illness

11 NOW a certain *man* was sick, *named* Lazarus, of Bethany, the town
of Mary and her sister Martha.

11:1 Mt 21:17 Lk 10:38

10:28 *eternal life* is promised to those who receive Christ as Savior (1:12). Believers may know they have eternal life (1 John 5:13). This is the doctrine of assurance. Eternal life has a beginning but no ending. Believers are assured they will never perish. They are "kept by the power of God through faith unto salvation" (1 Pet. 1:5). Christians do die physically, but they are guaranteed a resurrection unto life eternal when mortality and corruption have been replaced by immortality and incorruption (1 Cor. 15).

10:30 Here Jesus declared he was God. In John 14:9 he said, "Anyone who has seen me has seen the Father!" (TLB). In Matt. 11:27 he said, "Only the Father knows the Son, and the Father is known only by the Son and by those to whom the Son reveals him" (TLB). *When the high priest asked, "Are you the Messiah, the* Son of God?" Jesus responded, "I am, and you will see me sitting at the right hand of God, and returning to earth in the clouds of heaven" (Mark 14:61, 62, TLB). The high priest declared this to be blasphemy, for Jesus claimed to be God (Mark 14:64). If Jesus is not God, he was a liar, an evil seducer, and the worst enemy of the souls of men.

10:35 *word of God.* The sixty-six books that make up the Bible are called the canon. The word "canon" means "rod" or "rule." The books in the canon constitute authoritative books comprising God's revelation. The canon of the Old Testament was well known in Jesus' day and included the thirty-nine books we have in our Bibles. Jesus placed his stamp of approval on the Old Testament Scriptures and called them the Word of God. He also said the Word of God *cannot be broken.* The books now in the New Testament were first separate books sent to and used by various churches in Asia Minor, Greece, and Rome. Copies were made and circulated widely. The Gospels were written to tell new believers about the content of the gospel message and to prepare them for baptism and Christian service. Gradually the twenty-seven books which presently comprise the New Testament were accepted and acknowledged to be God's Word. Lists of these canonical letters and Gospels were drawn up, possibly as a safeguard against spurious apocryphal "Gospels" *and* so-called "apostolic letters" produced by Gnostics and other heretics. The authority of a few of the New Testament books was questioned at first, but gradually all that are in our present canon were accepted as normative. Jesus' words that "scripture cannot be broken" are his witness to a Bible without error. The Lordship of Jesus requires that Christians believe what Jesus taught. He never raised a question about any part of Scripture. He went so far as to assert that even the smallest particle of the Word cannot be destroyed without the heavens and the earth first being destroyed.

11:2 Mt 26:7; Mk 14:3; Lk 7:37, 38; Jn 12:3
11:3☆
11:4 Jn 9:3

2 (It was *that* Mary which anointed the Lord with ointment, and wiped his
feet with her hair, whose brother Lazarus was sick.)
3 Therefore his sisters sent unto him, saying, Lord, behold, he whom thou
lovest is sick.
4 When Jesus heard *that*, he said, This sickness is not unto death, but for
the glory of God, that the Son of God might be glorified thereby.

2. Jesus Goes to Waken Lazarus

11:8 Jn 8:59; 10:31
11:9 Ps 97:11; 119:105, 130; Prov 4:18; 13:9; Lk 13:33; Jn 9:4
11:10 Job 12:24, 25; Jn 12:35; 1 Jn 2:11
11:11☆ Dan 12:2; Mt 9:24; Mk 5:39; Lk 8:52, 53; Acts 7:60; 1 Cor 15:51
11:16 Mt 10:3; Jn 14:5; 20:24–28; 21:2

5 Now Jesus loved Martha, and her sister, and Lazarus.
6 When he had heard therefore that he was sick, he abode two days still in
the same place where he was.
7 Then after that saith he to *his* disciples, Let us go into Judæa again.
8 *His* disciples say unto him, Master, the Jews of late sought to stone thee;
and goest thou thither again?
9 Jesus answered, Are there not twelve hours in the day? If any man walk
in the day, he stumbleth not, because he seeth the light of this world.
10 But if a man walk in the night, he stumbleth, because there is no light
in him.
11 These things said he: and after that he saith unto them, Our friend
Lazarus sleepeth; but I go, that I may awake him out of sleep.
12 Then said his disciples, Lord, if he sleep, he shall do well.
13 Howbeit Jesus spake of his death: but they thought that he had spoken
of taking of rest in sleep.
14 Then said Jesus unto them plainly, Lazarus is dead.
15 And I am glad for your sakes that I was not there, to the intent ye may
believe; nevertheless let us go unto him.
16 Then said Thomas, which is called Did′y-mus, unto his fellowdisciples,
Let us also go, that we may die with him.

3. Jesus Tells Martha about the Resurrection

11:17☆ Jn 11:39
11:20 Lk 10:38–42
11:22 Jn 9:31

17 Then when Jesus came, he found that he had *lain* in the grave four days
already.
18 Now Bethany was nigh unto Jerusalem, about fifteen furlongs off:
19 And many of the Jews came to Martha and Mary, to comfort them
concerning their brother.
20 Then Martha, as soon as she heard that Jesus was coming, went and
met him: but Mary sat *still* in the house.
21 Then said Martha unto Jesus, Lord, if thou hadst been here, my brother
had not died.
22 But I know, that even now, whatsoever thou wilt ask of God, God will
give *it* thee.

11:3 Mary and Martha send for Jesus when their brother is sick unto death. Their relationship to Jesus was more than that of friends. They believed on him, knew that he did perform miracles, and confidently sought his help in the hour of trial. Trials like sickness and death come to all people, including Christians. But they have God for their helper, as Mary and Martha had Jesus, the God-man, for their helper. It would have *been odd indeed* had they not sought Jesus' help in this situation, just as it would be odd for God's people not to seek him when they need him and his help.

11:11 Jesus said Lazarus was asleep just as we speak about those who are asleep in Jesus. The disciples misunderstood Jesus, believing Lazarus was ill and restless and that at last he had fallen asleep and was probably on the mend. But Jesus speaks forthrightly to correct their misunderstanding: "Lazarus is dead" (11:14). Jesus can raise the dead just as easily as he can heal the sick. Life and death are under the control of the Son of God.

11:17 *he had lain in the grave four days.* By this time the body was in a state of decay, and no one could question whether Lazarus was really dead. Jesus knew very well what he was doing and why he delayed coming until his friend was dead. He also had some business to attend to, especially with Martha, one of the two sisters of Lazarus. She needed to be instructed, not only about the resurrection of the dead, but, more important, that Jesus himself was and is the resurrection and the life.

23 Jesus saith unto her, Thy brother shall rise again.
24 Martha saith unto him, I know that he shall rise again in the
resurrection at the last day.
25 Jesus said unto her, I am the resurrection, and the life: he that believeth
in me, though he were dead, yet shall he live:
26 And whosoever liveth and believeth in me shall never die. Believest
thou this?
27 She saith unto him, Yea, Lord: I believe that thou art the Christ, the
Son of God, which should come into the world.

11:23 Dan 12:2 Phil 3:21 1 Thess 4:14
☆**11:24** Jn 5:28, 29 Acts 24:15
11:25 Jn 1:4; 3:36 5:21; 6:39, 40 14:6 Col 1:18; 3:4 1 Jn 1:1, 2 5:10, 11 Rev 1:17, 18
11:26 Jn 6:47–51; 8:51
11:27 Mt 16:16 Jn 4:42 6:14, 68, 69

4. Mary Pleads for Lazarus with Tears

28 And when she had so said, she went her way, and called Mary her sister
secretly, saying, The Master is come, and calleth for thee.
29 As soon as she heard *that*, she arose quickly, and came unto him.
30 Now Jesus was not yet come into the town, but was in that place where
Martha met him.
31 The Jews then which were with her in the house, and comforted her,
when they saw Mary, that she rose up hastily and went out, followed her,
saying, She goeth unto the grave to weep there.
32 Then when Mary was come where Jesus was, and saw him, she fell
down at his feet, saying unto him, Lord, if thou hadst been here, my brother
had not died.
33 When Jesus therefore saw her weeping, and the Jews also weeping
which came with her, he groaned in the spirit, and was troubled,
34 And said, Where have ye laid him? They said unto him, Lord, come and
see.
35 Jesus wept.
36 Then said the Jews, Behold how he loved him!
37 And some of them said, Could not this man, which opened the eyes of
the blind, have caused that even this man should not have died?

☆**11:35** Isa 53:3 Lk 19:41 Rom 12:15 Heb 4:15
11:37 Jn 9:6, 7

5. Lazarus Rises from the Dead

38 Jesus therefore again groaning in himself cometh to the grave. It was a
cave, and a stone lay upon it.
39 Jesus said, Take ye away the stone. Martha, the sister of him that was
dead, saith unto him, Lord, by this time he stinketh: for he hath been *dead*
four days.
40 Jesus saith unto her, Said I not unto thee, that, if thou wouldest believe,
thou shouldest see the glory of God?
41 Then they took away the stone *from the place* where the dead was laid.
And Jesus lifted up *his* eyes, and said, Father, I thank thee that thou hast
heard me.
42 And I knew that thou hearest me always: but because of the people
which stand by I said *it*, that they may believe that thou hast sent me.

11:39 Jn 11:17
☆**11:41** Mt 11:25; 27:60 Lk 24:2
☆**11:42** Jn 12:30

11:24 Martha professed to believe in the resurrection of the dead. Jesus gently took her from that conviction to the necessity for her to believe in *him.* He pressed her to tell him whether she believed him to be the Christ, the Son of God. Martha responded in the affirmative; this may have been the crucial moment in her life when she stepped from darkness into light and from the dominion of Satan to the dominion of God.
11:35 Scripture never says Jesus laughed, although we can imagine that he had a robust sense of humor and that he undoubtedly expressed his pleasure with laughter. But here the Bible records his grief over physical death. In Luke 19:41 we see Jesus weeping over the fate of Jerusalem.
11:41, 42 Jesus' prayer teaches us to (1) call God our Father when we pray, (2) praise him when we come for further mercies, and (3) rest in the certainty that God hears prayer and answers. The Father always answered Jesus' requests.

43 And when he thus had spoken, he cried with a loud voice, Lazarus,
come forth.
44 And he that was dead came forth, bound hand and foot with grave-
clothes: and his face was bound about with a napkin. Jesus saith unto them,
Loose him, and let him go.

6. The Jewish Leaders Plot Jesus' Death

45 Then many of the Jews which came to Mary, and had seen the things
which Jesus did, believed on him.
46 But some of them went their ways to the Pharisees, and told them what
things Jesus had done.
47 ¶Then gathered the chief priests and the Pharisees a council, and said,
What do we? for this man doeth many miracles.
48 If we let him thus alone, all *men* will believe on him: and the Romans
shall come and take away both our place and nation.
49 And one of them, *named* Cai'a-phas, being the high priest that same
year, said unto them, Ye know nothing at all,
50 Nor consider that it is expedient for us, that one man should die for the
people, and that the whole nation perish not.
51 And this spake he not of himself: but being high priest that year, he
prophesied that Jesus should die for that nation;
52 And not for that nation only, but that also he should gather together in
one the children of God that were scattered abroad.
53 Then from that day forth they took counsel together for to put him to
death.
54 Jesus therefore walked no more openly among the Jews; but went
thence unto a country near to the wilderness, into a city called E'phra-im,
and there continued with his disciples.
55 ¶And the Jews' passover was nigh at hand: and many went out of the
country up to Jerusalem before the passover, to purify themselves.
56 Then sought they for Jesus, and spake among themselves, as they stood
in the temple, What think ye, that he will not come to the feast?
57 Now both the chief priests and the Pharisees had given a command-
ment, that, if any man knew where he were, he should shew *it*, that they
might take him.

O. THE BANQUET AT BETHANY; MARY ANOINTS JESUS (CF. MT. 26:6–13; MK 14:3–9)

12 THEN Jesus six days before the passover came to Bethany, where
Lazarus was which had been dead, whom he raised from the dead.
2 There they made him a supper; and Martha served: but Lazarus was
one of them that sat at the table with him.

11:43 Deut 32:39; 1 Sam 2:6; Lk 7:14; 8:54; Acts 3:15; 9:40
11:44 Jn 19:40; 20:7
11:45☆ Jn 2:23; 10:42; 12:11
11:47 Ps 2:2; Mt 26:3; Mk 14:1; Jn 12:19; Acts 4:16
11:48 Dan 9:26, 27
11:49 Mt 26:3; Lk 3:1, 2; Acts 4:6
11:50 Jn 18:14
11:51 Ex 28:30; Num 27:21; Ezra 2:62, 63
11:52 Isa 49:6; Jn 10:16; Acts 13:47; Gal 3:28; Eph 2:14–19; 3:6; 1 Pet 5:9; 1 Jn 2:2
11:53 Mt 26:3, 4
11:54☆
11:55 Ex 19:10; Num 9:10; 2 Chron 30:17–19; Mt 26:1, 2; Mk 14:1; Lk 22:1; Jn 18:28
11:56 Ps 2:1; Jn 7:11; Acts 4:25–28
12:1 Jn 11:43
12:2☆ Mt 26:6–13; Mk 14:3–9

11:45ff In none of the larger meetings when numbers of men and women listened to Jesus were all of them converted. Some believed and some did not. Here many Jews believed as a result of the raising of Lazarus from the dead. Others were irritated, unsettled, and hostile. Some of these went to the Pharisees, who they knew were hostile to Jesus, and told them about the latest exploits of Jesus. A special council meeting was called, which had for its one purpose the destruction of Jesus and his ministry.

11:54 Jesus now withdraws from walking openly among the Jews. He did not go from place to place preaching the gospel and working miracles. He did not do this because he was afraid or had lost his courage; it was a mark of his displeasure against Jerusalem for its rejection of him. He removed himself and his gospel from those who had rejected both. In addition, his removal would make the cruelty and conduct of his enemies even more inexcusable, for they could no longer blame him for making public appearances and performing miracles that upset them. Moreover, his hour was not yet come. Last, his re-entrance into the fray in Jerusalem at the proper moment would be ever so remarkable and awe-inspiring, not to say glorious.

12:2ff Mary, Martha, and Lazarus of Bethany made a great feast for Jesus. Mary anointed the feet of Jesus with a costly ointment. This gave rise to the criticism of Judas Iscariot (12:5) that the money so spent would

3 Then took Mary a pound of ointment of spikenard, very costly, and
anointed the feet of Jesus, and wiped his feet with her hair: and the house
was filled with the odour of the ointment.
4 Then saith one of his disciples, Judas Iscariot, Simon's *son*, which
should betray him,
5 Why was not this ointment sold for three hundred pence, and given to
the poor?
6 This he said, not that he cared for the poor; but because he was a thief,
and had the bag, and bare what was put therein.
7 Then said Jesus, Let her alone: against the day of my burying hath she
kept this.
8 For the poor always ye have with you; but me ye have not always.
9 Much people of the Jews therefore knew that he was there: and they
came not for Jesus' sake only, but that they might see Lazarus also, whom
he had raised from the dead.
10 ¶But the chief priests consulted that they might put Lazarus also to
death;
11 Because that by reason of him many of the Jews went away, and
believed on Jesus.

P. JESUS' TRIUMPHAL ENTRY (CF. MT 21:1–11; MK 11:1–11; LK 19:29–44)

12 ¶On the next day much people that were come to the feast, when they
heard that Jesus was coming to Jerusalem,
13 Took branches of palm trees, and went forth to meet him, and cried,
Hosanna: Blessed *is* the King of Israel that cometh in the name of the Lord.
14 And Jesus, when he had found a young ass, sat thereon; as it is written,
15 Fear not, daughter of Sion; behold, thy King cometh, sitting on an ass's
colt.
16 These things understood not his disciples at the first: but when Jesus
was glorified, then remembered they that these things were written of him,
and *that* they had done these things unto him.
17 The people therefore that was with him when he called Lazarus out of
his grave, and raised him from the dead, bare record.
18 For this cause the people also met him, for that they heard that he had
done this miracle.
19 The Pharisees therefore said among themselves, Perceive ye how ye
prevail nothing? behold, the world is gone after him.

Q. JESUS' LAST PUBLIC SERMON: HOW GENTILES CAN FIND SALVATION

20 ¶And there were certain Greeks among them that came up to worship
at the feast:
21 The same came therefore to Philip, which was of Beth-sa'i-da of
Galilee, and desired him, saying, Sir, we would see Jesus.
22 Philip cometh and telleth Andrew: and again Andrew and Philip tell
Jesus.

12:3 Lk 10:38–41; Jn 11:1, 2
12:4 Jn 6:70, 71
12:6 Prov 28:20, 22; Jn 13:29; 1 Cor 5:10, 11; 6:10; Eph 5:5; 1 Tim 6:9, 10
12:7 Mt 26:10–13; Mk 14:8, 9; Jn 19:40
12:8 Deut 15:11; Mk 14:7
12:10 Prov 4:16; Lk 16:31
12:11 Mk 15:10; Jn 11:45
☆**12:12** Mt 21:4-9; Mk 11:7–10; Lk 19:35–38
12:13 Ps 118:26; 1 Tim 1:17
12:15 Zech 9:9
☆**12:16** Jn 2:22; 7:39; 12:23; 14:26
12:17 Jn 11:42
12:18 Jn 12:11
12:20 1 Kgs 8:41–43; Acts 8:27; 17:4
12:21 Jn 1:43, 44
☆**12:22**

---

have been better used to feed the poor. This was hypocritical, for he was a thief who stole from the money bag entrusted to him. Within a short time this crooked stick would sell his own soul to Satan and his master to Jewish enemies for a few pieces of silver.

12:12 See note on Luke 19:28ff for information on the triumphal entry of Jesus into Jerusalem.

12:16 The disciples, including John who wrote about this, did not understand the meaning and significance of the triumphal entry of Jesus into the holy city. In their infant spiritual state they still had much to learn—despite their having been with the teacher for more than two years. Later the Holy Spirit recalled to their memory some of these things, which then became clear to them.

12:22 *Philip.* His name was Greek, even though he was a Jew.

12:23, 24☆
Jn 13:32; 17:1
Rom 6:4, 5
1 Cor 15:36–45
Heb 2:10
Rev 5:9, 10
12:25
Mt 20:39
Lk 9:24; 17:33
12:26
1 Sam 2:30
Ps 91:15
Jn 14:3; 17:24
2 Cor 5:8
Phil 1:23
1 Thess 4:17
12:27
Lk 12:50; 22:53
12:28
Mt 3:17; 17:5
Mk 1:11; 9:7
Lk 3:22; 9:35
2 Pet 1:17, 18
12:31☆
Jn 14:30; 16:11
Eph 6:12
Col 2:15
Heb 2:14
12:32☆
Jn 3:14; 6:44
Rom 5:18
Heb 2:9
12:33
Mt 20:19
Jn 18:32
12:34
2 Sam 7:13
Ps 89:35, 36
110:4
Isa 9:7
Ezek 37:24, 25
Dan 7:14
Mic 4:7
12:35
Jer 13:16
Jn 8:12; 9:5
12:46
12:36
Lk 16:8
Jn 8:12; 12:46
Eph 5:8
1 Thess 5:5
1 Jn 2:9, 10
12:38☆
Isa 53:1
Rom 10:16
12:40☆
Isa 6:9, 10
Mt 13:14
12:41
Isa 6:1
12:42☆
Jn 7:13, 48
9:22, 23; 12:11

23 ¶And Jesus answered them, saying, The hour is come, that the Son of man should be glorified.

24 Verily, verily, I say unto you, Except a corn of wheat fall into the ground and die, it abideth alone: but if it die, it bringeth forth much fruit.

25 He that loveth his life shall lose it; and he that hateth his life in this world shall keep it unto life eternal.

26 If any man serve me, let him follow me; and where I am, there shall also my servant be: if any man serve me, him will *my* Father honour.

27 Now is my soul troubled; and what shall I say? Father, save me from this hour: but for this cause came I unto this hour.

28 Father, glorify thy name. Then came there a voice from heaven, *saying*, I have both glorified *it*, and will glorify *it* again.

29 The people therefore, that stood by, and heard *it*, said that it thundered: others said, An angel spake to him.

30 Jesus answered and said, This voice came not because of me, but for your sakes.

31 Now is the judgment of this world: now shall the prince of this world be cast out.

32 And I, if I be lifted up from the earth, will draw all *men* unto me.

33 This he said, signifying what death he should die.

34 The people answered him, We have heard out of the law that Christ abideth for ever: and how sayest thou, The Son of man must be lifted up? who is this Son of man?

35 Then Jesus said unto them, Yet a little while is the light with you. Walk while ye have the light, lest darkness come upon you: for he that walketh in darkness knoweth not whither he goeth.

36 While ye have light, believe in the light, that ye may be the children of light. These things spake Jesus, and departed, and did hide himself from them.

R. WHY PEOPLE DO NOT BELIEVE

37 ¶But though he had done so many miracles before them, yet they believed not on him:

38 That the saying of E-sai'as the prophet might be fulfilled, which he spake, Lord, who hath believed our report? and to whom hath the arm of the Lord been revealed?

39 Therefore they could not believe, because that E-sai'as said again,

40 He hath blinded their eyes, and hardened their heart; that they should not see with *their* eyes, nor understand with *their* heart, and be converted, and I should heal them.

41 These things said E-sai'as, when he saw his glory, and spake of him.

42 ¶Nevertheless among the chief rulers also many believed on him; but

---

12:24 Some Greeks, who probably were Gentile proselytes, warmly attended Jesus in what was his last public preaching assignment. To them he spoke of his approaching death and burial by the figure of a grain of wheat, which must first die and then produce new life. So he, the Savior of the world, must die and be buried, and from that death would come forth a bountiful harvest of life for those who put their trust in him.

12:31 *the prince of this world, i.e.,* "Satan." Jesus never denied that Satan has power over this present ungodly world (cf. Matt. 4:8–10; Luke 4:5–8; John 14:30; 16:11). Here, however, Jesus makes the stupendous claim that he will be victorious over Satan, terminating the devil's earthly reign. This was accomplished by the death of Jesus, which was to result in the redemption of man (12:32) and the defeat of Satan.

12:32 *from the earth,* i.e., "on the cross."

12:38 *to whom hath the arm of the Lord been revealed?* i.e., "Who will accept God's mighty miracles as proof?"† The question is from Isa. 53:1.

12:40 *He,* i.e., "God." The Greek here is a paraphrase of Isa. 6:10.†

12:42 Some of the chief rulers believed Jesus to be the Messiah, but were afraid to say so publicly. The Pharisees had controlling power and would have put them out of the synagogue. These rulers loved the applause of men more than the approval of God. Going along with the crowd is an ancient practice and a

because of the Pharisees they did not confess *him*, lest they should be put
out of the synagogue:
43 For they loved the praise of men more than the praise of God.

S. JESUS' SUMMARY OF HIS OWN TEACHING

44 ¶Jesus cried and said, He that believeth on me, believeth not on me, but
on him that sent me.
45 And he that seeth me seeth him that sent me.
46 I am come a light into the world, that whosoever believeth on me
should not abide in darkness.
47 And if any man hear my words, and believe not, I judge him not: for I
came not to judge the world, but to save the world.
48 He that rejecteth me, and receiveth not my words, hath one that
judgeth him: the word that I have spoken, the same shall judge him in the
last day.
49 For I have not spoken of myself; but the Father which sent me, he gave
me a commandment, what I should say, and what I should speak.
50 And I know that his commandment is life everlasting: whatsoever I
speak therefore, even as the Father said unto me, so I speak.

12:43 Jn 5:44
12:44 Mt 10:40 Mk 9:37 1 Pet 1:21
12:45 Jn 14:9
12:46 Jn 1:4, 5, 9 3:19; 8:12 9:5, 39
12:47 Jn 3:17; 5:45 8:15, 16
12:48 Deut 18:18, 19 Mk 16:16 Lk 10:16
12:49 Jn 3:11; 8:38 17:8
☆**12:50** Jn 6:68; 8:28

III. JESUS IN THE UPPER ROOM (13:1—17:26)

A. JESUS WASHES HIS DISCIPLES' FEET

13 NOW before the feast of the passover, when Jesus knew that his
hour was come that he should depart out of this world unto the
Father, having loved his own which were in the world, he loved them unto
the end.
2 And supper being ended, the devil having now put into the heart of
Judas Iscariot, Simon's *son*, to betray him;
3 Jesus knowing that the Father had given all things into his hands, and
that he was come from God, and went to God;
4 He riseth from supper, and laid aside his garments; and took a towel,
and girded himself.
5 After that he poureth water into a bason, and began to wash the
disciples' feet, and to wipe *them* with the towel wherewith he was girded.
6 Then cometh he to Simon Peter: and Peter saith unto him, Lord, dost
thou wash my feet?
7 Jesus answered and said unto him, What I do thou knowest not now;
but thou shalt know hereafter.
8 Peter saith unto him, Thou shalt never wash my feet. Jesus answered
him, If I wash thee not, thou hast no part with me.
9 Simon Peter saith unto him, Lord, not my feet only, but also *my* hands
and *my* head.
10 Jesus saith to him, He that is washed needeth not save to wash *his* feet,
but is clean every whit: and ye are clean, but not all.

13:1 Jn 3:35; 16:28 17:2 1 Cor 15:27
☆**13:2** Lk 22:3 Jn 6:70, 71
☆**13:4** Lk 12:37; 22:27
☆**13:5** Lk 7:44
13:8 Ps 51:2, 7 Isa 52:14, 15 Ezek 36:25 Jn 3:5 Acts 2:38 1 Cor 6:11 Eph 5:26 Tit 3:5 Heb 9:13, 14 10:22
13:10 Ex 29:4 30:18–21; 40:12 Jn 15:3

---

modern one as well. There are clergymen today who fear the establishment, who are concerned with their upward mobility, and who never want to put their retirement benefits in jeopardy.

12:50 This verse is a fitting summary of the ministry of Jesus as it approaches its end. He delivered the message given him by the Father. He kept back nothing that was profitable for men to hear. He set us an example of supreme obedience to the Father. Paul sounded the same kind of note in 2 Tim. 4:7.

13:2 Scripture says that the devil put into the heart of Judas the intention to betray the Son of God and deliver him over to sinful hands, which would lead to his crucifixion. In verse 27 we note that Satan entered into him. Judas opened his heart so that this demon of demons possessed him, body, soul, and spirit.

13:4 *girded himself*, i.e., "wrapped a towel around his loins," as the lowliest slave would dress.

13:5 Jesus washed the disciples' feet to (1) show his disciples that he loved them; (2) demonstrate the emptying of himself; (3) teach them about spiritual washing, which is much more important than the washing of feet; and (4) provide the disciples with his example so that they might also demonstrate their humility.

13:11 Jn 6:64; 13:2
11 For he knew who should betray him; therefore said he, Ye are not all
clean.
13:12 Jn 13:4
12 So after he had washed their feet, and had taken his garments, and was
set down again, he said unto them, Know ye what I have done to you?
13:13 1 Cor 8:6; 12:3
13 Ye call me Master and Lord: and ye say well; for *so* I am.
13:14☆ Lk 22:27; Rom 12:10; 1 Pet 5:5
14 If I then, *your* Lord and Master, have washed your feet; ye also ought
to wash one another's feet.
13:15 Phil 2:5–7; 1 Pet 5:3–5; 1 Jn 2:6
15 For I have given you an example, that ye should do as I have done to
you.
13:16 Mt 10:24; Lk 6:40; Jn 15:20
16 Verily, verily, I say unto you, The servant is not greater than his lord;
neither he that is sent greater than he that sent him.
13:17 Jas 1:25
17 If ye know these things, happy are ye if ye do them.
13:18 Ps 41:9; 2 Tim 2:19
18 I speak not of you all: I know whom I have chosen: but that the
scripture may be fulfilled, He that eateth bread with me hath lifted up his
heel against me.
19 Now I tell you before it come, that, when it is come to pass, ye may
believe that I am *he*.
13:20 Mt 10:40; Lk 10:16
20 Verily, verily, I say unto you, He that receiveth whomsoever I send
receiveth me; and he that receiveth me receiveth him that sent me.

B. JUDAS ISCARIOT, THE TRAITOR, GOES OUT INTO THE NIGHT (CF. MT 26:21–25; MK 14:18–21; LK 22:21–23)

13:21☆ Mt 26:20–25; Mk 14:18–21; Lk 22:21–23
21 When Jesus had thus said, he was troubled in spirit, and testified, and
said, Verily, verily, I say unto you, that one of you shall betray me.
22 Then the disciples looked one on another, doubting of whom he spake.
13:23☆ Jn 19:26; 20:2; 21:7
23 Now there was leaning on Jesus' bosom one of his disciples, whom
Jesus loved.
24 Simon Peter therefore beckoned to him, that he should ask who it
should be of whom he spake.
13:25 Jn 21:20
25 He then lying on Jesus' breast saith unto him, Lord, who is it?
13:26☆ Jn 6:71
26 Jesus answered, He it is, to whom I shall give a sop, when I have dipped
it. And when he had dipped the sop, he gave *it* to Judas Iscariot, *the son* of
Simon.
13:27☆ Lk 22:3
27 And after the sop Satan entered into him. Then said Jesus unto him,
That thou doest, do quickly.
28 Now no man at the table knew for what intent he spake this unto him.
13:29 Jn 12:6
29 For some *of them* thought, because Judas had the bag, that Jesus had
said unto him, Buy *those things* that we have need of against the feast; or,
that he should give something to the poor.
13:30 Lk 22:53
30 He then having received the sop went immediately out: and it was
night.

C. JESUS' TIME HAS COME

13:31, 32 Lk 24:26; Jn 12:23; 17:1, 5; 1 Cor 15:42; Heb 5:5
31 ¶Therefore, when he was gone out, Jesus said, Now is the Son of man
glorified, and God is glorified in him.

13:14 Some take Jesus' washing of the disciples' feet literally and practice foot washing in the church. Others hold that it is figurative and instructive, and not sacramental as is the Eucharist.

13:21 *Jesus knew from the beginning who it was that should betray him.* He knew what was in Judas Iscariot more than did Judas himself.

13:23 *leaning on Jesus' bosom.* The custom of the period was to recline around the table, leaning on the left elbow. *one of his disciples.* Most commentators believe him to be John, the writer of this book.†

13:26 *He it is, to whom I shall give a sop, when I have dipped it.* The honored guest was thus singled out in the custom of that time.†

13:27 Satan can be in only one place at a time. But he is virtually omnipresent, because he has a horde of fallen angels who do his bidding. In the case of Judas Iscariot, Scripture says that Satan himself entered into his heart and took possession of him.

32 If God be glorified in him, God shall also glorify him in himself, and
shall straightway glorify him.
33 Little children, yet a little while I am with you. Ye shall seek me: and as
I said unto the Jews, Whither I go, ye cannot come; so now I say to you.
34 A new commandment I give unto you, That ye love one another; as I
have loved you, that ye also love one another.
35 By this shall all *men* know that ye are my disciples, if ye have love one
to another.

D. PETER'S DENIAL PREDICTED (MT 26:33–35; MK 14:27–31; LK 22:31–34)

36 ¶Simon Peter said unto him, Lord, whither goest thou? Jesus answered
him, Whither I go, thou canst not follow me now; but thou shalt follow me
afterwards.
37 Peter said unto him, Lord, why cannot I follow thee now? I will lay
down my life for thy sake.
38 Jesus answered him, Wilt thou lay down thy life for my sake? Verily,
verily, I say unto thee, The cock shall not crow, till thou hast denied me
thrice.

E. WORDS OF COMFORT AND PROMISE

1. Jesus the Way, the Truth, and the Life

14 LET not your heart be troubled: ye believe in God, believe also in
me.
2 In my Father's house are many mansions: if *it were* not *so*, I would have
told you. I go to prepare a place for you.
3 And if I go and prepare a place for you, I will come again, and receive
you unto myself; that where I am, *there* ye may be also.
4 And whither I go ye know, and the way ye know.
5 Thomas saith unto him, Lord, we know not whither thou goest; and how
can we know the way?
6 Jesus saith unto him, I am the way, the truth, and the life: no man
cometh unto the Father, but by me.
7 If ye had known me, ye should have known my Father also: and from
henceforth ye know him, and have seen him.
8 Philip saith unto him, Lord, shew us the Father, and it sufficeth us.
9 Jesus saith unto him, Have I been so long time with you, and yet hast
thou not known me, Philip? he that hath seen me hath seen the Father; and
how sayest thou *then*, Shew us the Father?
10 Believest thou not that I am in the Father, and the Father in me? the
words that I speak unto you I speak not of myself: but the Father that
dwelleth in me, he doeth the works.
11 Believe me that I *am* in the Father, and the Father in me: or else believe
me for the very works' sake.

13:33 Jn 7:33, 34
13:34 Lev 19:18; Eph 5:2; 1 Thess 4:9; Heb 13:1; Jas 2:8; 1 Pet 1:22; 1 Jn 2:8; 3:11; 4:20, 21
13:35 Acts 2:44–46
13:36 Jn 14:2; 21:18; 2 Pet 1:13, 14
☆**13:37** Mt 26:33–35; Mk 14:29–31; Lk 22:33, 34
13:38 Jn 18:27
14:1 Jn 5:24; 12:44
14:2 Ps 90:1; Jn 2:16, 19–21; 14:6; 2 Cor 5:1; 1 Thess 4:17
14:3 Jn 10:38; 14:10, 11, 18, 20; 16:16, 19–22; 17:21–24
☆**14:6** Ps 16:11; Jn 1:4, 14, 16; 8:32; 10:9, 10; 11:25; Rom 5:2; Eph 2:18; Heb 10:20; 1 Jn 5:20
14:7 Jn 6:46; 8:19; 1 Jn 2:13
14:9 Jn 1:14, 18; 12:45; 2 Cor 4:4; Col 1:15; Heb 1:3
14:10 Jn 5:19; 10:38; 17:11, 21–24
☆**14:11** Jn 5:36

13:37 We can give Peter the benefit of the doubt that his intentions to lay down his life for Jesus were genuine. No doubt he correctly believed that it would be better to die with Jesus than to live without him. In the carrying out of this intention he failed miserably, and which of us could say that he would do better than Peter?

14:6 Jesus affirms, "I am the way to God; I am the truth about God; I am the life of God." And he who would know God must come to him through Jesus Christ. He is the only way, the only truth, and the only life of God. All other ways are dead-end streets or even endless roads that lead no place except to darkness and everlasting night.

14:11 *I am in the Father and the Father in me.* Whoever knows Jesus Christ as "God of God, light of light, very God of very God, begotten, not made, and as being of one substance with the Father, by whom all things were made" knows the Father. Jesus gives two reasons for this: (1) he said so and we are to believe for his word's sake; (2) his works corroborate his words, so that if his words seem unbelievable, then believe for his works' sake.

2. The Promise of Miracles in Jesus' Name

14:12☆ Acts 5:15; 19:11, 12
14:13☆ Jas 1:5; 1 Jn 3:21, 22; 5:14
14:14 Jn 15:16; 16:23
14:15☆ Jn 15:10; 1 Jn 5:3; 2 Jn 6
14:16☆ Jn 14:26; 15:26; 16:7
14:17☆ Rom 8:15, 16; 1 Cor 2:14; 1 Jn 3:24
14:18☆ Jn 14:3, 28; 20:22; Rom 8:9–11; 2 Cor 3:17, 18
14:19 Jn 6:57; 16:16; 1 Cor 15:20
14:20 Jn 10:38, 15:4, 5; 16:16, 23; 17:21–24
14:21 Prov 8:17; Jn 15:10; 16:27; 1 Jn 2:5; 2 Jn 6
14:22 Lk 6:14–16; Acts 10:40
14:23 Ps 91:1; Jn 15:10; Eph 3:17; 1 Jn 4:16; 5:3; Rev 3:20; 21:3
14:24 Jn 7:16; 14:10

12 Verily, verily, I say unto you, He that believeth on me, the works that I
do shall he do also; and greater *works* than these shall he do; because I go
unto my Father.
13 And whatsoever ye shall ask in my name, that will I do, that the Father
may be glorified in the Son.
14 If ye shall ask any thing in my name, I will do *it*.

3. The Promise of the Comforter

15 If ye love me, keep my commandments.
16 And I will pray the Father, and he shall give you another Comforter,
that he may abide with you for ever;
17 *Even* the Spirit of truth; whom the world cannot receive, because it
seeth him not, neither knoweth him: but ye know him; for he dwelleth with
you, and shall be in you.
18 I will not leave you comfortless: I will come to you.
19 Yet a little while, and the world seeth me no more; but ye see me:
because I live, ye shall live also.
20 At that day ye shall know that I *am* in my Father, and ye in me, and I
in you.
21 He that hath my commandments, and keepeth them, he it is that loveth
me: and he that loveth me shall be loved of my Father, and I will love him,
and will manifest myself to him.
22 Judas saith unto him, not Iscariot, Lord, how is it that thou wilt
manifest thyself unto us, and not unto the world?
23 Jesus answered and said unto him, If a man love me, he will keep my
words: and my Father will love him, and we will come unto him, and make
our abode with him.
24 He that loveth me not keepeth not my sayings: and the word which ye
hear is not mine, but the Father's which sent me.

14:12 *greater works than these shall he do,* i.e., in the kingdom of nature they will do greater works than Jesus did. "Christ had healed with the hem of his garment, but Peter with his shadow (Acts 5:15), Paul by the handkerchiefs that had touched him (Acts 19:12). Christ wrought miracles for two or three years in one country, but his followers have wrought miracles in his name for many ages and in divers countries. *You shall do greater works,* if there be occasion, for the glory of God."*

14:13 Great is the power of prayer and nowhere is this truth spoken more broadly and in such an all-encompassing way. Jesus says we must pray if we have need of help. We are to ask in his name, which has great power. He promises that we will receive what we ask for. And the end of all this is the glory of God the Father in and through his Son, Jesus Christ.

14:15, 16 In John 14–16 five passages are written about the Holy Spirit, and four times he is called *parakletos* ("comforter"). The verb *parakaleo,* from which the noun is formed, means "to encourage," "to exhort," or "to comfort." The noun *parakletos* refers to *someone who takes our part or intercedes* on our behalf to help us. Elsewhere in the New Testament this Greek word is translated "someone to plead for you," or, "advocate." The Holy Spirit comes from the Father (15:26) at the request of the Son (14:16) and in Jesus' name (14:26). Jesus also says he will send the Comforter. From these passages the church has deduced that the Spirit comes from the Father and the Son. (An early church controversy raged over whether the Spirit was sent by the Father or by the Father and the Son.) The Holy Spirit resides in every believer's heart (14:16, 17), teaches believers all things (14:26), leads them in the truth (16:13), speaks as directed by Jesus (16:13–15) (bearing witness to him [15:26], glorifying him (16:14), reminding Christ's disciples what Jesus taught [14:26]), and tells the disciples about the future (16:13). He will also convince the world of sin, righteousness, and judgment (16:8–11).

14:17, 18 The promise of the coming of the Holy Spirit boggles the mind. Jesus will pray the Father to send the Spirit, who will come from the Father and the Son. He will be our advocate. He is the Spirit of truth. He will abide with us and in us and never leave us. The Holy Spirit is equal in power and glory with the Lord Jesus Christ, so that the going of the Lord Jesus and the coming of the Spirit means we have nothing less and need nothing more than what we have in Jesus. Thus, the coming of the Holy Spirit is tantamount to the coming of Jesus to our hearts. Experientially speaking, to have the Spirit is to have Christ. (See *A Study Guide to Translating the Gospel of John,* Philip W. Comfort, B.B.H. Distributors of Baker Book House, 1985, pp. 165, 166.)

4. Peace of Heart and Mind

25These things have I spoken unto you, being *yet* present with you.
26But the Comforter, *which is* the Holy Ghost, whom the Father will send
in my name, he shall teach you all things, and bring all things to your
remembrance, whatsoever I have said unto you.
27Peace I leave with you, my peace I give unto you: not as the world
giveth, give I unto you. Let not your heart be troubled, neither let it be
afraid.
28Ye have heard how I said unto you, I go away, and come *again* unto
you. If ye loved me, ye would rejoice, because I said, I go unto the Father:
for my Father is greater than I.
29And now I have told you before it come to pass, that, when it is come
to pass, ye might believe.
30Hereafter I will not talk much with you: for the prince of this world
cometh, and hath nothing in me.
31But that the world may know that I love the Father; and as the Father
gave me commandment, even so I do. Arise, let us go hence.

F. THE ALLEGORY OF THE TRUE VINE

15 I AM the true vine, and my Father is the husbandman.
2Every branch in me that beareth not fruit he taketh away: and
every *branch* that beareth fruit, he purgeth it, that it may bring forth more
fruit.
3Now ye are clean through the word which I have spoken unto you.
4Abide in me, and I in you. As the branch cannot bear fruit of itself,
except it abide in the vine; no more can ye, except ye abide in me.
5I am the vine, ye *are* the branches: He that abideth in me, and I in him,
the same bringeth forth much fruit: for without me ye can do nothing.
6If a man abide not in me, he is cast forth as a branch, and is withered;
and men gather them, and cast *them* into the fire, and they are burned.
7If ye abide in me, and my words abide in you, ye shall ask what ye will,
and it shall be done unto you.
8Herein is my Father glorified, that ye bear much fruit; so shall ye be my
disciples.
9As the Father hath loved me, so have I loved you: continue ye in my
love.
10If ye keep my commandments, ye shall abide in my love; even as I have
kept my Father's commandments, and abide in his love.
11These things have I spoken unto you, that my joy might remain in you,
and *that* your joy might be full.

☆**14:26** Lk 24:49 Jn 1:33; 15:26 16:7; 20:22 1 Jn 2:20, 27
☆**14:27** Jn 16:33; 20:19 Phil 4:7 Col 3:15
14:28 1 Cor 11:3
14:29 Jn 13:19
14:30 Jn 12:31 Heb 4:15 1 Jn 3:5
14:31 Jn 10:18; 12:49 Heb 5:8
15:1 Ps 80:8 Isa 5:1–7 Jer 2:19–21 Mt 21:33 Rom 11:17 1 Cor 3:9
☆**15:2**
15:3 Jn 17:17 Eph 5:26
15:4 Jn 6:56; 14:20 Eph 2:21, 22 3:17 Col 2:7 1 Jn 4:12, 13
15:5 Hos 14:8
15:6 Mt 3:10; 7:19 Heb 6:4–6
15:7 Mt 7:7
15:8 Mt 5:15, 16
☆**15:9** Jn 3:35 17:23–26
15:10 Jn 8:29 14:15, 16, 31
15:11 Jn 16:24; 17:13 1 Jn 1:4

14:26 The Comforter or helper will teach us all things and will bring back to our memories things we have forgotten.

14:27 *my peace I give unto you.* "When Christ was *about to leave the world he made his will.* His soul he bequeathed to his Father; his body he bequeathed to Joseph, to be decently interred; his clothes fell to the soldiers; his mother he left to the care of John: but what should he leave to his poor disciples, who had left all for him? Silver and gold he had none; but he left them that which is infinitely better, *his peace. 'I leave you,* but I leave *my peace* with you. I not only give you a title to it, but put you in possession of it.' "*

15:2 Fruit trees are expected to produce fruit. Once regenerated, the Christian is also expected to bear fruit in his life and walk. Fruitlessness is abnormal. Jesus says branches that bear no fruit are lopped off. And even fruitbearing branches are pruned so that they bear more fruit. Fruitbearing glorifies God but is not an end in itself. The goal of the Christian life is a happy and loving fellowship with God.

15:9ff Jesus here speaks of love's four relationships: (1) the Father loves the Son; (2) Jesus uses the Father's love for himself as the pattern of his love for his disciples ("I have loved you even as the Father has loved me," TLB); the demonstration of this love is found in Christ's death for his friends; (3) the disciples are to love him and to abide in his love (15:10); and (4) Jesus demands that the disciples love one another (15:17). Elsewhere Scripture states that Jesus loves the church, which is his body (Eph. 5:25); it declares that nothing "can ever keep Christ's love from us" (Rom. 8:35, TLB).

12 This is my commandment, That ye love one another, as I have loved
you.
13 Greater love hath no man than this, that a man lay down his life for his
friends.
14 Ye are my friends, if ye do whatsoever I command you.
15 Henceforth I call you not servants; for the servant knoweth not what
his lord doeth: but I have called you friends; for all things that I have heard
of my Father I have made known unto you.
16 Ye have not chosen me, but I have chosen you, and ordained you, that
ye should go and bring forth fruit, and *that* your fruit should remain: that
whatsoever ye shall ask of the Father in my name, he may give it you.
17 These things I command you, that ye love one another.

G. THE WORLD'S HATRED AND PERSECUTION OF BELIEVERS

18 If the world hate you, ye know that it hated me before *it hated* you.
19 If ye were of the world, the world would love his own: but because ye
are not of the world, but I have chosen you out of the world, therefore the
world hateth you.
20 Remember the word that I said unto you, The servant is not greater
than his lord. If they have persecuted me, they will also persecute you; if
they have kept my saying, they will keep yours also.
21 But all these things will they do unto you for my name's sake, because
they know not him that sent me.
22 If I had not come and spoken unto them, they had not had sin: but now
they have no cloak for their sin.
23 He that hateth me hateth my Father also.
24 If I had not done among them the works which none other man did,
they had not had sin: but now have they both seen and hated both me and
my Father.
25 But *this cometh to pass*, that the word might be fulfilled that is written in
their law, They hated me without a cause.
26 But when the Comforter is come, whom I will send unto you from the
Father, *even* the Spirit of truth, which proceedeth from the Father, he shall
testify of me:
27 And ye also shall bear witness, because ye have been with me from the
beginning.

16 THESE things have I spoken unto you, that ye should not be
offended.
2 They shall put you out of the synagogues: yea, the time cometh, that
whosoever killeth you will think that he doeth God service.
3 And these things will they do unto you, because they have not known
the Father, nor me.
4 But these things have I told you, that when the time shall come, ye may
remember that I told you of them. And these things I said not unto you at
the beginning, because I was with you.

15:12 1 Thess 4:9; 1 Pet 4:8; 1 Jn 3:11
15:13 Jn 10:11; Rom 5:6–8; Eph 5:2
15:14 Mt 12:50
15:15 Jn 8:26
15:16 Jn 14:12, 13; 15:5
15:18☆ Jn 7:7; 1 Jn 3:1, 13
15:19 Mt 10:22; 24:9; Jn 17:14; 1 Jn 4:5, 6
15:20 Ezek 3:7; 2 Cor 4:8–10
15:21 Mk 13:13; Jn 17:25; Acts 5:41; 1 Pet 4:14
15:22 Jn 9:41; Rom 1:20; Jas 4:17
15:23 1 Jn 2:23; 2 Jn 9
15:24☆ Jn 5:36–38; 10:37, 38
15:25 Ps 35:19; 69:4
15:26 Jn 14:15–17, 26; 16:7; Acts 2:33
15:27 Lk 1:2; 24:48; Jn 19:35; 21:24; Acts 1:8; 2:32; 1 Pet 5:1; 2 Pet 1:16; 1 Jn 1:1, 2
16:2 Isa 66:5; Acts 8:1; 9:1; 26:9; Rev 6:9
16:3 Acts 3:17; Rom 16:3; 1 Cor 2:8; 1 Tim 1:13
16:4 Jn 13:19; 14:29

15:18ff There are two kinds of children: the children of God and the children of the world. Jesus says that the children of the world hate the children of God. They do so because *God's children are not of the world*; if they were, the world would love them as its own. But because God's children belong to Jesus Christ, the world hates them as it hates him. This hatred stems from ignorance, for the children of the world do not know "him that sent me."

15:24 The great sin of the children of the world is that they see Christ, deny him, and hate him; and because they do this, they also hate the one who sent him, the Father. If there were no God, atheists need not hate the God that does not exist. But the beauty of nature, the providence of God that abounds in the universe, the fact of justice, and the appearance of Jesus Christ attest to God's existence—so that those who hate God and Jesus Christ are without excuse.

H. JESUS' DEPARTURE: THE COMFORTER'S COMING AND MINISTRY

5 But now I go my way to him that sent me; and none of you asketh me,
Whither goest thou?
6 But because I have said these things unto you, sorrow hath filled your
heart.
7 Nevertheless I tell you the truth; It is expedient for you that I go away:
for if I go not away, the Comforter will not come unto you; but if I depart,
I will send him unto you.
8 And when he is come, he will reprove the world of sin, and of
righteousness, and of judgment:
9 Of sin, because they believe not on me;
10 Of righteousness, because I go to my Father, and ye see me no more;
11 Of judgment, because the prince of this world is judged.
12 I have yet many things to say unto you, but ye cannot bear them now.
13 Howbeit when he, the Spirit of truth, is come, he will guide you into all
truth: for he shall not speak of himself; but whatsoever he shall hear, *that*
shall he speak: and he will shew you things to come.
14 He shall glorify me: for he shall receive of mine, and shall shew *it* unto
you.
15 All things that the Father hath are mine: therefore said I, that he shall
take of mine, and shall shew *it* unto you.

I. THE "LITTLE WHILE"

16 A little while, and ye shall not see me: and again, a little while, and ye
shall see me, because I go to the Father.
17 Then said *some* of his disciples among themselves, What is this that he
saith unto us, A little while, and ye shall not see me: and again, a little
while, and ye shall see me: and, Because I go to the Father?
18 They said therefore, What is this that he saith, A little while? we cannot
tell what he saith.
19 Now Jesus knew that they were desirous to ask him, and said unto

16:5 Jn 7:33; 13:36 14:5
16:6 Jn 14:1
☆**16:7** Jn 14:26 Acts 2:33
☆**16:8** 1 Pet 1:2
16:9 Rom 1:18–23 3:9, 10; 14:23
16:10 Isa 42:6, 21 Acts 3:14; 7:52 1 Pet 3:18
16:11 Lk 10:18 Jn 12:31 Acts 26:18 Col 2:15 Heb 2:14
☆**16:12**
☆**16:13** Jn 14:26 1 Cor 2:10, 13 1 Jn 2:27
☆**16:14** Phil 1:19
16:15 Mt 11:27 Jn 17:10 Col 2:9, 10
16:16 Jn 14:3, 19–25

16:7 *It is expedient for you that I go away.* This refers to the ascension, which was necessary in order for Jesus to (1) make possible the coming of the Holy Spirit (16:7); (2) fulfill his own prophetic word (14:28; 16:5; 20:17); (3) make possible the further work of Jesus to prepare a place for his people and to intercede for them (14:2, 3; Heb. 8:12); (4) enter the holy place in heaven with his blood to secure eternal redemption (Heb. 9:11). The Holy Spirit could not come until the work of Jesus was completed on earth. Christ had to die, rise again, ascend into heaven, and be seated at the right hand of the Father. This would signify that his atoning work was not only complete but was completely satisfying to the demands of divine justice. Only then could the age of the Holy Spirit as the vice-regent of Jesus Christ on earth commence.
16:8 *he will reprove* ["convict"] *the world of sin, and of righteousness, and of judgment.* Sin consists in the refusal to accept Christ and his message. Righteousness by the Spirit indicates that Christ's death was not a defeat but a victory. Christ returned to the Father, who vindicated his mission and accepted what the Son had done. The Spirit's judgment indicates that the life, death, and resurrection of Jesus Christ constitute the basis on which God condemned the ruler of this world's darkness.
16:12 The revelation of God is progressive. Christ told his disciples many things not revealed in the Old Testament. But he left untold some things that were to be revealed by the Holy Spirit after his ascension. He pre-authenticated the New Testament in 16:13 ("the Holy Spirit . . . shall guide you into all truth, for he will not be presenting his own ideas, but will be passing on to you what he has heard," TLB). God's revelation was completed when the canon of Scripture was closed, and no further revelation will come. We await the coming of the revelator, Jesus Christ, and the time in heaven when we will know more than we know now.
16:13, 14 Christ introduces the ministry of the Holy Spirit. Among the works performed by the Holy Spirit are the following: (1) he exalts Christ; (2) he convicts *men of sin* (16:8); (3) he regenerates men (3:15); (4) he indwells the hearts of all believers and produces his fruit in their lives (1 Cor. 3:16; Gal. 5:22, 23); (5) he seals believers or marks them (Eph. 1:13; see also note on Eph. 4:30); (6) he leads and guides believers (Acts 8:29; 13:2, 4); (7) he prompts believers to worship, for they are "to pray in the power and strength of the Holy Spirit" (Jude 20, TLB; see also Eph. 6:18); (8) he empowers believers for testimony (Acts 1:8); (9) he enables believers to understand and discern what is taught in Scripture (1 Cor. 2:12); and (10) he quickens and gives life to believers' dead bodies in the resurrection (Rom. 8:11).

them, Do ye inquire among yourselves of that I said, A little while, and ye
shall not see me: and again, a little while, and ye shall see me?
20 Verily, verily, I say unto you, That ye shall weep and lament, but the
world shall rejoice: and ye shall be sorrowful, but your sorrow shall be
turned into joy.
21 A woman when she is in travail hath sorrow, because her hour is come:
but as soon as she is delivered of the child, she remembereth no more the
anguish, for joy that a man is born into the world.
22 And ye now therefore have sorrow: but I will see you again, and your
heart shall rejoice, and your joy no man taketh from you.
23 And in that day ye shall ask me nothing. Verily, verily, I say unto you,
Whatsoever ye shall ask the Father in my name, he will give *it* you.
24 Hitherto have ye asked nothing in my name: ask, and ye shall receive,
that your joy may be full.
25 These things have I spoken unto you in proverbs: but the time cometh,
when I shall no more speak unto you in proverbs, but I shall shew you
plainly of the Father.
26 At that day ye shall ask in my name: and I say not unto you, that I will
pray the Father for you:
27 For the Father himself loveth you, because ye have loved me, and have
believed that I came out from God.
28 I came forth from the Father, and am come into the world: again, I
leave the world, and go to the Father.
29 His disciples said unto him, Lo, now speakest thou plainly, and
speakest no proverb.
30 Now are we sure that thou knowest all things, and needest not that any
man should ask thee: by this we believe that thou camest forth from God.
31 Jesus answered them, Do ye now believe?
32 Behold, the hour cometh, yea, is now come, that ye shall be scattered,
every man to his own, and shall leave me alone: and yet I am not alone,
because the Father is with me.
33 These things I have spoken unto you, that in me ye might have peace.
In the world ye shall have tribulation: but be of good cheer; I have
overcome the world.

16:20 Mk 16:10 Lk 23:27 Jn 20:19, 20
16:21 Isa 26:16–19 Acts 13:33 Col 1:18
16:22 Jn 20:19, 20
16:23 Jn 14:20 15:16; 16:26
16:24 Jn 15:11
16:25 Jn 10:6; 16:29
16:26☆
16:27 Jn 8:42; 14:21 17:8
16:28 Jn 1:14 6:32, 46 8:42; 13:1, 3 17:11, 13
16:32 Zech 13:7 Mt 26:31 Jn 8:29
16:33☆ Jn 14:27 Acts 14:22 Rom 5:1; 8:37 1 Cor 15:27 2 Cor 2:14 Eph 2:14 Col 1:20 Rev 3:19

J. THE PRAYER OF JESUS, THE BELIEVER'S HIGH PRIEST

1. The Revelation of the Son's Glory

17:1☆ Jn 7:39 13:31, 32

17 THESE words spake Jesus, and lifted up his eyes to heaven, and
said, Father, the hour is come; glorify thy Son, that thy Son also
may glorify thee:

16:26 *ye shall ask in my name,* i.e., "then you will present your petitions over my signature." This paraphrase is a modern equivalent of this idea, otherwise obscure.†

16:33 Jesus promised that his followers would suffer persecution. Why God permits suffering and allows tribulation is a deep mystery. The Book of Job deals with the problem more fully than any other book. For the believer there are three kinds of afflictions that need *to be understood: (1) some things* happen to us simply because we are alive—such as sickness, bereavement, death, and the like; (2) some trials come from Satan by God's permission; (3) some trials and troubles are sent by God to purify his people and to conform them to the image of Jesus his Son. It is not always clear to us from which source a problem may have come. Believers should be careful not to attribute to God, or to Satan, things that happen because of their own follies and faults.

17:1 Jesus begins here a family prayer, for his disciples were part of his family. Those he had preached to he now prays for. When Jacob was dying he prayed for and blessed the twelve patriarchs (Gen. 49:1ff). When Moses was about to die, he prayed for the twelve tribes (Deut. 33:1ff). Now Jesus prays for the twelve apostles. This prayer, made by our high priest, was a preface to his redeeming death, in which he speaks of the favors and blessing he purchased through his death for his people. And the prayer is illustrative of his present intercession within the veil for his people then, now, and through the ages until he comes again.

[2]As thou hast given him power over all flesh, that he should give eternal life to as many as thou hast given him.
[3]And this is life eternal, that they might know thee the only true God, and Jesus Christ, whom thou hast sent.
[4]I have glorified thee on the earth: I have finished the work which thou gavest me to do.
[5]And now, O Father, glorify thou me with thine own self with the glory which I had with thee before the world was.

17:2 Dan 7:14; Jn 3:35; 6:37; 10:28; 1 Cor 15:25; Heb 2:8
17:3 Isa 53:11; Jer 9:24; Eph 4:13; Phil 3:8, 10; Col 1:10; 1 Thess 1:9; 2 Pet 1:2, 3, 8; 1 Jn 5:20
17:4 Jn 4:34
17:5 Jn 1:1, 2; 17:24; Phil 2:6; Col 1:15, 16; Heb 1:3

2. Christ's Plea for His Disciples

[6]I have manifested thy name unto the men which thou gavest me out of the world: thine they were, and thou gavest them me; and they have kept thy word.
[7]Now they have known that all things whatsoever thou hast given me are of thee.
[8]For I have given unto them the words which thou gavest me; and they have received *them*, and have known surely that I came out from thee, and they have believed that thou didst send me.
[9]I pray for them: I pray not for the world, but for them which thou hast given me; for they are thine.
[10]And all mine are thine, and thine are mine; and I am glorified in them.
[11]And now I am no more in the world, but these are in the world, and I come to thee. Holy Father, keep through thine own name those whom thou hast given me, that they may be one, as we *are*.
[12]While I was with them in the world, I kept them in thy name: those that thou gavest me I have kept, and none of them is lost, but the son of perdition; that the scripture might be fulfilled.
[13]And now come I to thee; and these things I speak in the world, that they might have my joy fulfilled in themselves.
[14]I have given them thy word; and the world hath hated them, because they are not of the world, even as I am not of the world.
[15]I pray not that thou shouldest take them out of the world, but that thou shouldest keep them from the evil.
[16]They are not of the world, even as I am not of the world.
[17]Sanctify them through thy truth: thy word is truth.
[18]As thou hast sent me into the world, even so have I also sent them into the world.
[19]And for their sakes I sanctify myself, that they also might be sanctified through the truth.

17:6 Jn 17:26
17:8 Jn 15:15; 16:50
17:9 1 Jn 5:19
17:10 Rom 8:29, 30; Eph 3:21
17:11 Jn 10:30; 17:21; Rom 12:4, 5; Gal 3:28
17:12 Jn 6:39; 10:28; 18:9; Acts 1:20; Heb 2:13; 1 Jn 2:19
17:13 Jn 7:33; 15:11
☆**17:14** Jn 15:19; 1 Jn 3:13
17:15 Mt 6:13; Gal 1:4; 2 Thess 3:3; 1 Jn 5:18
☆**17:17** Jn 15:3; Eph 5:26
17:18 Jn 20:21
17:19 1 Cor 1:30; Heb 2:11

3. Christ's Prayer for Future Believers

[20]Neither pray I for these alone, but for them also which shall believe on me through their word;

17:20 Acts 2:40, 41; 4:29, 31; 10:44

17:14 The Christian is not *of* the world, but Christ never said his people were not to be *in* the world. He said, "I'm not asking you to take them out of the world ... I am sending them into the world" (17:15, 18, TLB). The Christian is the salt of the earth and the light of the world. While *in* the world the believer is to have victory *over* the world. He is to "stop loving this evil world" (1 John 2:15, TLB); rather he is to "be a new and different person with a fresh newness in all you do and think" (Rom. 12:2, TLB). The major temptations of life are "the lust of the flesh, and the lust of the eyes, and the pride of life" (1 John 2:16).

17:17 Sanctification is the work of the Holy Spirit in the believer's life. The use of the written Word of God is essential to sanctification. So are the means of grace such as prayer, worship, the use of the ordinances or the sacraments, and the communion of the saints. God uses chastisement to improve the believer's character (Heb. 12:10). Equally important is the believer's use of his will, whereby he separates himself from unrighteousness (2 Cor. 6:17).

17:21☆ Jn 10:30, 38; 14:11; 17:11; Gal 3:28; Eph 4:3–6
17:22 2 Cor 4:6; Eph 3:16, 21; Col 1:27; Heb 1:3; 1 Jn 1:3; 3:24
17:23☆ Jn 10:38; 16:27; 17:11
17:24 Jn 1:14; 12:26; 17:5; 2 Cor 3:18
17:25 Jn 7:29; 15:21
17:26 Jn 15:9; 2 Cor 13:5; Eph 3:17; Col 1:27; 1 Jn 3:24

21 That they all may be one; as thou, Father, *art* in me, and I in thee, that
they also may be one in us: that the world may believe that thou hast sent
me.
22 And the glory which thou gavest me I have given them; that they may
be one, even as we are one:
23 I in them, and thou in me, that they may be made perfect in one; and
that the world may know that thou hast sent me, and hast loved them, as
thou hast loved me.
24 Father, I will that they also, whom thou hast given me, be with me
where I am; that they may behold my glory, which thou hast given me: for
thou lovedst me before the foundation of the world.
25 O righteous Father, the world hath not known thee: but I have known
thee, and these have known that thou hast sent me.
26 And I have declared unto them thy name, and will declare *it:* that the
love wherewith thou hast loved me may be in them, and I in them.

IV. JESUS ARRESTED, TRIED, AND CRUCIFIED (18:1—19:37)

A. JESUS BETRAYED AND SEIZED (CF. MT 26:47–56; MK 14:43–50; LK 22:27–53)

18:1☆ 2 Sam 15:23; 1 Kgs 2:36, 37; 15:13; 2 Kgs 23:4, 6, 12; 2 Chron 15:16; 29:16; 30:14; Jer 31:40; Mt 26:30, 36; Mk 14:26, 32; Lk 22:39
18:2 Lk 21:37, 38
18:3 Mt 26:47; Mk 14:43; Lk 22:47; Acts 1:16
18:6☆

18 WHEN Jesus had spoken these words, he went forth with his
disciples over the brook Ce′dron, where was a garden, into the
which he entered, and his disciples.
2 And Judas also, which betrayed him, knew the place: for Jesus ofttimes
resorted thither with his disciples.
3 Judas then, having received a band *of men* and officers from the chief
priests and Pharisees, cometh thither with lanterns and torches and
weapons.
4 Jesus therefore, knowing all things that should come upon him, went
forth, and said unto them, Whom seek ye?
5 They answered him, Jesus of Nazareth. Jesus saith unto them, I am *he.*
And Judas also, which betrayed him, stood with them.
6 As soon then as he had said unto them, I am *he,* they went backward,
and fell to the ground.
7 Then asked he them again, Whom seek ye? And they said, Jesus of
Nazareth.

17:21 The communion of the saints lies at the heart of Christ's prayer in this chapter. The people of God are to be united in life and experience with each other because they are united with him. The communion of the saints suggests (1) the fellowship we have with God through Jesus Christ by the Spirit (1 John 1:3); (2) fellowship by promise with the saints already in glory with whom we are also united (Heb. 12:22–24); and (3) fellowship with all other believers who are still on earth (Gal. 2:9, 10; 1 John 1:7). All believers enjoy organic unity with each other as members of the mystical body of Christ known only to God. This hidden unity must find expression in concrete forms in the churches on earth. Saints should (1) pray for one another (2 Cor. 1:11; Eph. 6:18); (2) exhort one another (Col. 3:16; Heb. 10:25); and (3) comfort and edify one another (1 Thess. 4:18; 5:11). The outward expression of inner unity is shown when the saints gather for the public worship of God, celebrate the Eucharist, and practice water baptism.
17:23 *I in them, and thou in me, that they may be made perfect in one.* This is a threefold truth: (1) believers have union with Christ—"I in them"; (2) believers have union with God through Jesus Christ—"thou in me"; (3) believers have union with each other which comes from their being in God and in Christ.
18:1 Christ is about to fulfill the third responsibility of a priest. Priests were to teach, pray, and offer sacrifices. Christ has finished both his teaching and his preaching ministries. He is about to make his soul an offering for sin. This will mark the completion of his priestly work.
18:6 *they went backward and fell to the ground.* Jesus "spoke them to the ground." He could have struck them dead. He could have summoned the angels of heaven to rescue him. He could have had the ground swallow them up as it did Korah (Num. 16:31ff). He struck these people to the ground so that they would see their need for repentance and have time to repent if they wished to do so. He also struck them down to show that no one could take his life from him. He would lay it down of himself, voluntarily and in accord with the Father's will.

[8]Jesus answered, I have told you that I am *he:* if therefore ye seek me, let
these go their way:
[9]That the saying might be fulfilled, which he spake, Of them which thou
gavest me have I lost none.
[10]Then Simon Peter having a sword drew it, and smote the high priest's
servant, and cut off his right ear. The servant's name was Mal'chus.
[11]Then said Jesus unto Peter, Put up thy sword into the sheath: the cup
which my Father hath given me, shall I not drink it?

18:9 Jn 17:12
☆**18:10** Mt 26:51 Mk 14:47 Lk 22:49, 50
18:11 Mt 20:22 26:39, 42

B. JESUS BEFORE ANNAS

[12]Then the band and the captain and officers of the Jews took Jesus, and
bound him,
[13]And led him away to An'nas first; for he was father in law to Cai'a-
phas, which was the high priest that same year.
[14]Now Cai'a-phas was he, which gave counsel to the Jews, that it was
expedient that one man should die for the people.

18:12 Mt 26:57
18:13 Lk 3:1, 2 Acts 4:6
18:14 Jn 11:50

C. PETER'S DENIAL (CF. MT 26:69–75; MK 14:66–72; LK 22:55–62)

[15]¶And Simon Peter followed Jesus, and *so did* another disciple: that
disciple was known unto the high priest, and went in with Jesus into the
palace of the high priest.
[16]But Peter stood at the door without. Then went out that other disciple,
which was known unto the high priest, and spake unto her that kept the
door, and brought in Peter.
[17]Then saith the damsel that kept the door unto Peter, Art not thou also
one of this man's disciples? He saith, I am not.
[18]And the servants and officers stood there, who had made a fire of coals;
for it was cold: and they warmed themselves: and Peter stood with them,
and warmed himself.

☆**18:15** Mt 26:58 Lk 22:54
18:16 Mt 26:69
18:18 Mk 14:54

D. ANNAS SENDS JESUS TO CAIAPHAS, THE HIGH PRIEST

[19]¶The high priest then asked Jesus of his disciples, and of his doctrine.
[20]Jesus answered him, I spake openly to the world; I ever taught in the
synagogue, and in the temple, whither the Jews always resort; and in secret
have I said nothing.
[21]Why askest thou me? ask them which heard me, what I have said unto
them: behold, they know what I said.
[22]And when he had thus spoken, one of the officers which stood by struck
Jesus with the palm of his hand, saying, Answerest thou the high priest so?
[23]Jesus answered him, If I have spoken evil, bear witness of the evil: but
if well, why smitest thou me?
[24]Now An'nas had sent him bound unto Cai'a-phas the high priest.
[25]And Simon Peter stood and warmed himself. They said therefore unto
him, Art not thou also *one* of his disciples? He denied *it*, and said, I am not.
[26]One of the servants of the high priest, being *his* kinsman whose ear
Peter cut off, saith, Did not I see thee in the garden with him?
[27]Peter then denied again: and immediately the cock crew.

18:19 Mt 26:59–68 Mk 14:55–65 Lk 22:63–71
18:20 Mt 26:55 Lk 4:15 Jn 7:14, 26, 28 8:2
18:22 Isa 50:6 Mic 5:1 Jn 19:3
18:23 Mt 5:39 Acts 23:2 Heb 12:3 1 Pet 2:21–23
☆**18:24**
18:25 Mt 26:73–75 Mk 14:70–72 Lk 22:58–60
18:27 Jn 13:38

18:10 Only John says it was Peter who did this. Matthew (26:51) and Mark (14:47) say "one of them" did this, whereas Luke identifies him as one of the disciples (22:45, 50).

18:15ff See note on Mark 14:71.

18:24 *Caiaphas.* See note on Matt. 26:57.

E. JESUS BEFORE PONTIUS PILATE THE GOVERNOR
(CF. MT 27:11–16; MK 15:2–15; LK 23:3–25)
1. Pilate Asks What Jesus Is Charged With

18:28☆ Mt 27:2; Mk 15:1; Lk 23:1; Jn 11:55; Acts 11:3

28¶Then led they Jesus from Cai'a-phas unto the hall of judgment: and it
was early; and they themselves went not into the judgment hall, lest they
should be defiled; but that they might eat the passover.
29Pilate then went out unto them, and said, What accusation bring ye
against this man?
30They answered and said unto him, If he were not a malefactor, we
would not have delivered him up unto thee.
31Then said Pilate unto them, Take ye him, and judge him according to
your law. The Jews therefore said unto him, It is not lawful for us to put
any man to death:

18:32☆ Mt 20:19; Jn 12:32, 33

32That the saying of Jesus might be fulfilled, which he spake, signifying
what death he should die.

2. Pilate Questions Jesus

18:33☆ Lk 23:3; Jn 19:12 **18:34☆**

33Then Pilate entered into the judgment hall again, and called Jesus, and
said unto him, Art thou the King of the Jews?
34Jesus answered him, Sayest thou this thing of thyself, or did others tell
it thee of me?
35Pilate answered, Am I a Jew? Thine own nation and the chief priests
have delivered thee unto me: what hast thou done?

18:36☆ Isa 9:6; Dan 2:44; 7:14; Mt 26:53; Lk 17:20, 21; Jn 6:15 **18:37** Jn 8:47; 1 Pet 1:23; 1 Jn 3:19; 4:6; Rev 1:5

36Jesus answered, My kingdom is not of this world: if my kingdom were
of this world, then would my servants fight, that I should not be delivered
to the Jews: but now is my kingdom not from hence.
37Pilate therefore said unto him, Art thou a king then? Jesus answered,
Thou sayest that I am a king. To this end was I born, and for this cause
came I into the world, that I should bear witness unto the truth. Every one
that is of the truth heareth my voice.

18:38 Jn 19:4, 6

38Pilate saith unto him, What is truth? And when he had said this, he
went out again unto the Jews, and saith unto them, I find in him no fault *at*
all.

3. The People Scream for Barabbas' Release

18:39 Mt 27:15–18, 20–23; Mk 15:6–15

39But ye have a custom, that I should release unto you one at the
passover: will ye therefore that I release unto you the King of the Jews?

18:28 *lest they should be defiled.* By Jewish law, entering the house of a Gentile was a serious offense.†

18:32 *signifying what death he should die,* i.e., "fulfill[ing] Jesus' prediction concerning the method of his execution." This prophecy is recorded in Matt. 20:19, which indicates his death by crucifixion, a practice under Roman law.† Jewish execution was by stoning (cf. 8:5; Acts 7:58, 59). Jesus, however, said, "I must be lifted up on a pole" (3:14, TLB; see also 8:28; 12:32, 34).

18:33 *the judgment hall,* i.e., "the praetorium," which was the headquarters of the high court officers and the guards. Jesus was crowned with thorns in this hall of judgment (Mark 15:16, 17).

18:34 Paraphrased: " 'King' as *you* use the word or as *the Jews use it? Jesus asked.*" An extended paraphrase of this verse would be, "Do you mean their king, or their Messiah?" Pilate was asking whether Jesus was setting up a rebel government. But the Jews were using the word "king" to mean their religious ruler, the Messiah.†

18:36 Christ is King. Someday he will reign over a visible kingdom. But this fact is incidental to the fact that his kingdom is not of this world system. He has a spiritual and eternal kingdom. He came to wrest the kingdoms of this world from their rulers and will present them to the Father at the end of time. He fights against Satan, ruler of this present world (12:31). A kingship implies three things: (1) the king must be sovereign; (2) he must have a people to rule over; and (3) he must have a territory under his control. Spiritually, Christ has all of these now. He is seated at the right hand of the Father on his throne (Acts 2:34; Heb. 1:3; Rev. 3:21), he has a people in the church who are his subjects, and the Father has given him authority. It was never in the plan of God for Christ to set up an earthly kingdom at the time of his first coming. Apart from the cross he could not have been "the Lamb slain from the foundation of the world" (Rev. 13:8); nor could he have been he who "taketh away the sin of the world" (1:29). His second coming will mark his visible glory and irresistible power as the King of kings and Lord of the whole universe (Phil. 2:10, 11; Rev. 19:16).

40 Then cried they all again, saying, Not this man, but Ba-rab'bas. Now
Ba-rab'bas was a robber.

☆18:40 Lk 23:17–19 Acts 3:14

4. Pilate Whips Jesus and Questions Him Again

19 THEN Pilate therefore took Jesus, and scourged *him.*
2 And the soldiers platted a crown of thorns, and put *it* on his
head, and they put on him a purple robe,
3 And said, Hail, King of the Jews! and they smote him with their hands.
4 Pilate therefore went forth again, and saith unto them, Behold, I bring
him forth to you, that ye may know that I find no fault in him.
5 Then came Jesus forth, wearing the crown of thorns, and the purple
robe. And *Pilate* saith unto them, Behold the man!
6 When the chief priests therefore and officers saw him, they cried out,
saying, Crucify *him,* crucify *him.* Pilate saith unto them, Take ye him, and
crucify *him:* for I find no fault in him.
7 The Jews answered him, We have a law, and by our law he ought to die,
because he made himself the Son of God.
8 ¶When Pilate therefore heard that saying, he was the more afraid;
9 And went again into the judgment hall, and saith unto Jesus, Whence
art thou? But Jesus gave him no answer.
10 Then saith Pilate unto him, Speakest thou not unto me? knowest thou
not that I have power to crucify thee, and have power to release thee?
11 Jesus answered, Thou couldest have no power *at all* against me, except
it were given thee from above: therefore he that delivered me unto thee hath
the greater sin.

☆19:1 Isa 50:6 Mt 27:26–30 Mk 15:15–19 Lk 18:32, 33
19:3 Jn 18:22
19:4 Jn 18:38 2 Cor 5:21
19:6 Acts 3:13
19:7 Lev 24:15, 16 Mt 26:63–66
19:9 Isa 53:7 Mt 27:12, 14 Acts 8:32
☆19:10
☆19:11 Acts 2:23; 3:13 Rom 13:1

5. Pilate Gives Jesus to Be Crucified

12 And from thenceforth Pilate sought to release him: but the Jews cried
out, saying, If thou let this man go, thou art not Cæsar's friend: whosoever
maketh himself a king speaketh against Cæsar.
13 ¶When Pilate therefore heard that saying, he brought Jesus forth, and
sat down in the judgment seat in a place that is called the Pavement, but in
the Hebrew, Gab'ba-tha.
14 And it was the preparation of the passover, and about the sixth hour:
and he saith unto the Jews, Behold your King!
15 But they cried out, Away with *him,* away with *him,* crucify him. Pilate
saith unto them, Shall I crucify your King? The chief priests answered, We
have no king but Cæsar.
16 Then delivered he him therefore unto them to be crucified. And they
took Jesus, and led *him* away.

19:12 Lk 23:2 Acts 17:7
☆19:13 Mt 27:19
19:16 Mt 27:26, 31 Mk 15:15 Lk 23:24

18:40 *Barabbas.* See note on Mark 15:7.

19:1 *and scourged him.* Scourging was a dreadful punishment. The Romans normally used a scourge weighted by pieces of bone and metal. Some victims died during scourging. To some, it was worse than death itself. Jesus was scourged, then forced to carry his cross, and at last fastened to the cross to die. His suffering was such that it can only bring tears to those who know him as the Lord of glory.

19:10 Pilate was disturbed that Jesus refused to answer his question. It appeared to be an affront to him who had great power and was accustomed to having people answer him quickly. Perhaps he was thinking that since he knew Jesus to be innocent and may have wished to set him free, Jesus ought to make his own defense and thus help Pilate acquit him. But Jesus would not and could not do this, for he had come to die. Boastfully and arrogantly Pilate asks Jesus a question: "Knowest thou not that I have power to crucify thee, and have power to release thee?" Jesus' reply should have shaken him to his depths, for he plainly says that no one has authority or power except it be given to him by God. Every king or tyrant must pass muster under a higher law, which says, "We can do only that which we can do justly."

19:11 *he,* thought to mean Caiaphas, the high priest, under whose direction the Jews "handed over" (*paradidomi*) Jesus to Pilate. If so, Caiaphas was responsible for Jesus' arrest and condemnation. Others think "he" refers to Judas Iscariot, who betrayed, or handed over, Jesus to the Jews.

19:13 *the judgment seat in a place that is called the pavement, but in the Hebrew, Gabbatha,* i.e., "the judgment bench on the stone-paved platform."†

F. THE CRUCIFIXION

1. The Crucifixion Itself (Cf. Mt 27:32–44; Mk 15:21–32; Lk 23:32–43)

19:17☆ Num 15:36 Heb 13:12

17 And he bearing his cross went forth into a place called *the place* of a skull, which is called in the Hebrew Gol′go-tha:

19:18☆ Gal 3:13

18 Where they crucified him, and two other with him, on either side one, and Jesus in the midst.

19:19 Isa 53:12 Mt 27:37 Mk 15:26 Lk 23:38

19 ¶And Pilate wrote a title, and put *it* on the cross. And the writing was, JESUS OF NAZARETH THE KING OF THE JEWS.

20 This title then read many of the Jews: for the place where Jesus was crucified was nigh to the city: and it was written in Hebrew, *and* Greek, *and* Latin.

21 Then said the chief priests of the Jews to Pilate, Write not, The King of the Jews; but that he said, I am King of the Jews.

22 Pilate answered, What I have written I have written.

19:23, 24 Ps 22:18

23 ¶Then the soldiers, when they had crucified Jesus, took his garments, and made four parts, to every soldier a part; and also *his* coat: now the coat was without seam, woven from the top throughout.

24 They said therefore among themselves, Let us not rend it, but cast lots for it, whose it shall be: that the scripture might be fulfilled, which saith, They parted my raiment among them, and for my vesture they did cast lots. These things therefore the soldiers did.

19:25☆ Mt 27:55, 56 Lk 8:2, 3; 24:18

25 ¶Now there stood by the cross of Jesus his mother, and his mother's sister, Mary the *wife* of Cle′o-phas, and Mary Magdalene.

19:26☆ Jn 2:4; 13:23 21:24

26 When Jesus therefore saw his mother, and the disciple standing by, whom he loved, he saith unto his mother, Woman, behold thy son!

27 Then saith he to the disciple, Behold thy mother! And from that hour that disciple took her unto his own *home*.

2. JESUS DISMISSES HIS SPIRIT (CF. MT 27:45–50; MK 15:33–41; LK 23:44–49)

19:28☆ Ps 2:1–3 22:1–21; 69:21 Isa 53 Mt 27:48–50 Mk 15:36, 37 Lk 23:36

28 ¶After this, Jesus knowing that all things were now accomplished, that the scripture might be fulfilled, saith, I thirst.

29 Now there was set a vessel full of vinegar: and they filled a spunge with vinegar, and put *it* upon hyssop, and put *it* to his mouth.

19:30☆ Lk 23:46 Heb 10:1–14

30 When Jesus therefore had received the vinegar, he said, It is finished: and he bowed his head, and gave up the ghost.

19:17 *the place of a skull, which is called in the Hebrew Golgotha.* The location of Golgotha, or Calvary, cannot be known with certainty. Two locations are possible. The first and the oldest by way of tradition is the site now within the old city of Jerusalem on which the Church of the Holy Sepulchre was built in the fourth century A.D. Those who favor this site claim it lay outside the old city walls when Christ was crucified. The other location is known as Gordon's Calvary and/or the Garden Tomb, or Golgotha. The site was suggested by one Otto Thenius in 1842 and declared in 1885 by General Charles Gordon to be the site of the crucifixion. Roman Catholics prefer the site of the Church of the Holy Sepulchre. Most Protestants prefer Gordon's site because part of it has been landscaped to resemble Joseph of Arimathea's garden. Even if the site was the one on which the Church of the Holy Sepulchre was erected, it takes quite a bit of imagination to visualize a garden tomb there today.

19:18 See note on Luke 23:33 about the three crucifixions.

19:25 Four faithful women stood beside the cross of Jesus: (1) Mary, Jesus' mother, whose presence the other Gospel writers fail to mention; (2) Mary's sister, probably the same as Salome (Mark 15:40), the wife of Zebedee and mother of John and James (Matt. 27:56); (3) Mary, Cleopas' wife, the mother of James the younger and Joses (Matt. 27:56; Mark 15:40); and (4) Mary Magdalene (Matt. 27:56; Mark 15:40).

19:26 Despite his intense suffering Jesus does not forget his mother after the flesh. His filial devotion is such that he makes provision for his mother after his death. He turns her over to John, who was to be like a son to her. When God removes one of our supports he sometimes raises up another to take its place. Sometimes it is something we never looked or hoped for. John cheerfully accepted this responsibility and Mary was assured of help all the days of her life, for John lived almost to the end of the first century.

19:28ff See note on Luke 23:34ff for the seven sayings of Christ on the cross.

19:30 *It is finished.* The work given him by the Father was now completed. Nothing more needed to be added to it and nothing could be taken away from it. *he bowed*

[31]The Jews therefore, because it was the preparation, that the bodies
should not remain upon the cross on the sabbath day, (for that sabbath day
was an high day,) besought Pilate that their legs might be broken, and *that*
they might be taken away.
[32]Then came the soldiers, and brake the legs of the first, and of the other
which was crucified with him.
[33]But when they came to Jesus, and saw that he was dead already, they
brake not his legs:
[34]But one of the soldiers with a spear pierced his side, and forthwith came
there out blood and water.
[35]And he that saw *it* bare record, and his record is true: and he knoweth
that he saith true, that ye might believe.
[36]For these things were done, that the scripture should be fulfilled, A
bone of him shall not be broken.
[37]And again another scripture saith, They shall look on him whom they
pierced.

19:31 Num 28:17; Deut 21:22, 23
19:35 Jn 20:30, 31; 21:24; 1 Jn 1:1
19:36, 37 Ex 12:46; Num 9:12; Ps 34:20; Zech 12:10; Rev 1:7

V. JESUS' BURIAL AND RESURRECTION (19:38—20:31)

A. JESUS' BODY LAID IN THE TOMB (CF. MT 27:57–61; MK 15:42–47; LK 23:50–56)

[38]¶And after this Joseph of Ar-i-ma-thæ'a, being a disciple of Jesus, but
secretly for fear of the Jews, besought Pilate that he might take away the
body of Jesus: and Pilate gave *him* leave. He came therefore, and took the
body of Jesus.
[39]And there came also Nic-o-de'mus, which at the first came to Jesus by
night, and brought a mixture of myrrh and aloes, about an hundred pound
weight.
[40]Then took they the body of Jesus, and wound it in linen clothes with
the spices, as the manner of the Jews is to bury.
[41]Now in the place where he was crucified there was a garden; and in the
garden a new sepulchre, wherein was never man yet laid.
[42]There laid they Jesus therefore because of the Jews' preparation *day;*
for the sepulchre was nigh at hand.

19:38 Mt 27:57, 58; Mk 14:42, 43; Lk 23:50–52; Jn 9:22, 23
19:39 2 Chron 16:13, 14; Mt 26:12; Mk 14:8; Jn 3:1, 2; 7:50; 12:7
19:40 Lk 23:56; Jn 11:44
19:41 Mt 27:60; Lk 23:52
19:42 Isa 53:9

B. THE RESURRECTION APPEARANCES

1. Mary, Peter, John, and the Empty Tomb (Cf. Mt 28:1–10; Mk 16:1–8; Lk 24:1–11)

20 THE first *day* of the week cometh Mary Magdalene early, when it
was yet dark, unto the sepulchre, and seeth the stone taken away
from the sepulchre.
[2]Then she runneth, and cometh to Simon Peter, and to the other disciple,
whom Jesus loved, and saith unto them, They have taken away the Lord
out of the sepulchre, and we know not where they have laid him.
[3]Peter therefore went forth, and that other disciple, and came to the
sepulchre.
[4]So they ran both together: and the other disciple did outrun Peter, and
came first to the sepulchre.

☆**20:1** Mt 28:1; Mk 16:1, 2; Lk 24:1
☆**20:2** Jn 13:23
☆**20:3** Lk 24:12

---

his head. Those who died by crucifixion raised their heads at the last to gasp for breath and then dropped them when they died. Jesus bowed his head before he died as a sign of his submission to the Father's will, and to show he gave his life by his own volition and not because he was powerless.

20:1 *The first day of the week,* i.e., "early Sunday." See note on Matt. 28:6 for information about the resurrection of Jesus.

20:2 *to the other disciple, whom Jesus loved,* i.e., John.

20:3 *that other disciple,* i.e., John.

20:5 5 And he stooping down, *and looking in,* saw the linen clothes lying; yet
Jn 19:40 went he not in.
20:6☆ 6 Then cometh Simon Peter following him, and went into the sepulchre,
Lk 24:12 and seeth the linen clothes lie,
20:7☆ 7 And the napkin, that was about his head, not lying with the linen
Jn 11:44; 19:40 clothes, but wrapped together in a place by itself.
20:8☆ 8 Then went in also that other disciple, which came first to the sepulchre,
and he saw, and believed.
20:9☆ 9 For as yet they knew not the scripture, that he must rise again from the
Ps 2:7; 16:8–11 Mt 16:21 dead.
Acts 2:25–28 13:34, 35 10 Then the disciples went away again unto their own home.

2. Mary Magdalene Sees Jesus Alive

20:11☆ 11 ¶But Mary stood without at the sepulchre weeping: and as she wept,
she stooped down, *and looked* into the sepulchre,
20:12 Mt 28:2 12 And seeth two angels in white sitting, the one at the head, and the other
Mk 16:5 Lk 24:4 at the feet, where the body of Jesus had lain.
13 And they say unto her, Woman, why weepest thou? She saith unto
them, Because they have taken away my Lord, and I know not where they
have laid him.
20:14 Mt 28:9 14 And when she had thus said, she turned herself back, and saw Jesus
Mk 16:9 Jn 21:4 standing, and knew not that it was Jesus.
15 Jesus saith unto her, Woman, why weepest thou? whom seekest thou?
She, supposing him to be the gardener, saith unto him, Sir, if thou have
borne him hence, tell me where thou hast laid him, and I will take him
away.
16 Jesus saith unto her, Mary. She turned herself, and saith unto him,
Rab-bo'ni; which is to say, Master.
20:17☆ 17 Jesus saith unto her, Touch me not; for I am not yet ascended to my
Mt 28:10 Jn 16:28 Father: but go to my brethren, and say unto them, I ascend unto my
Rom 8:29 Col 1:18 Father, and your Father; and *to* my God, and your God.
Heb 2:11 1 Pet 1:3 18 Mary Magdalene came and told the disciples that she had seen the
20:18 Mt 28:10 Lord, and *that* he had spoken these things unto her.
Mk 16:10 Lk 24:10

3. Jesus Appears to the Ten in the Evening in Jerusalem (Cf. Lk 24:36–43)

20:19 Mk 16:14 19 ¶Then the same day at evening, being the first *day* of the week, when
Lk 24:36–43 1 Cor 15:5, the doors were shut where the disciples were assembled for fear of the Jews,
42–45 came Jesus and stood in the midst, and saith unto them, Peace *be* unto you.

20:6, 7 The presence of linen clothes lying there and the head wrapping rolled up in a place by itself could indicate that Jesus miraculously came through the grave clothes when he rose from the dead.

20:8 *and believed.* What was it they believed?—that Jesus had risen from the dead and was alive forevermore.

20:9 *For as yet they knew not the scripture.* The Old Testament spoke of the resurrection (Ps. 16:10) of the Messiah. Jesus himself told his disciples he would rise from the dead (Luke 18:33). Despite this, the disciples were under a cloud, not understanding what is plain to us today but not plain to them in that day before the full revelation of God was given. After the resurrection Jesus opened their minds that they might understand the Old Testament, and he revealed to them, in all of that book, the things concerning himself (Luke 24:44, 45).

20:11ff The chronology of Christ's resurrection appearances seems to be as follows: (1) to Mary Magdalene and the other women (Matt. 28:9; Mark 16:9, 10; John 20:11–18); (2) to the disciples on the road to Emmaus (Mark 16:12; Luke 24:13–15); (3) to Peter (Luke 24:34; 1 Cor. 15:5); (4) to the ten disciples in the upper room (20:19); (5) to the eleven in the upper room with Thomas present (Mark 16:14; Luke 24:36; John 20:26); (6) to the disciples at the Sea of Tiberias (21:1–24); (7) to the eleven on a mountain in Galilee (Matt. 28:16–20); (8) to five hundred of the brethren (1 Cor. 15:6); (9) to James (1 Cor. 15:7); (10) to all of the apostles (1 Cor. 15:7); (11) to those present when he ascended into heaven (Mark 16:19; Luke 24:50, 51; Acts 1:3–12).

20:17 *Touch me not,* i.e., do not detain me. Go tell the others what you have seen. There is now a difference between the Christ of the preresurrection and the risen Lord who must ascend into heaven. Later he was touched and handled, but at this moment he was not.

[20]And when he had so said, he shewed unto them *his* hands and his side.
Then were the disciples glad, when they saw the Lord.
[21]Then said Jesus to them again, Peace *be* unto you: as *my* Father hath
sent me, even so send I you.
[22]And when he had said this, he breathed on *them*, and saith unto them,
Receive ye the Holy Ghost:
[23]Whose soever sins ye remit, they are remitted unto them; *and* whose
soever *sins* ye retain, they are retained.
[24]¶But Thomas, one of the twelve, called Did′y-mus, was not with them
when Jesus came.
[25]The other disciples therefore said unto him, We have seen the Lord. But
he said unto them, Except I shall see in his hands the print of the nails, and
put my finger into the print of the nails, and thrust my hand into his side,
I will not believe.

20:20 Jn 16:22; 1 Jn 1:1
20:21 Isa 61:1; Mt 28:18–20; Jn 17:18; 2 Tim 2:2
☆**20:22** Jn 7:37–39; 14:16–18, 26; 15:26; 16:7, 13; 1 Cor 15:45
20:23 Mt 16:19; 18:18
20:24 Jn 11:16

4. Jesus Appears to Thomas and the Ten

[26]¶And after eight days again his disciples were within, and Thomas with
them: *then* came Jesus, the doors being shut, and stood in the midst, and
said, Peace *be* unto you.
[27]Then saith he to Thomas, Reach hither thy finger, and behold my
hands; and reach hither thy hand, and thrust *it* into my side: and be not
faithless, but believing.
[28]And Thomas answered and said unto him, My Lord and my God.
[29]Jesus saith unto him, Thomas, because thou hast seen me, thou hast
believed: blessed *are* they that have not seen, and *yet* have believed.

20:26 Mic 5:5; Jn 14:27; Col 1:20
20:27 Ps 103:13; 1 Jn 1:1
☆**20:28** Jn 1:1, 18; 10:30; 14:9; Acts 20:28; Rom 9:5; Phil 2:6; Col 2:9; Tit 2:13; 2 Pet 1:1; 1 Jn 5:20
20:29 2 Cor 5:7; 1 Pet 1:8

C. JOHN'S PURPOSE FOR WRITING THIS GOSPEL

[30]¶And many other signs truly did Jesus in the presence of his disciples,
which are not written in this book:
[31]But these are written, that ye might believe that Jesus is the Christ, the
Son of God; and that believing ye might have life through his name.

20:30, 31 Lk 1:3, 4; Jn 3:15, 16; 5:24; 19:35; 21:25; 1 Jn 5:10–13

VI. THE EPILOGUE (21:1–25)

A. JESUS APPEARS TO THE DISCIPLES AT THE SEA OF TIBERIAS (GALILEE)

21 AFTER these things Jesus shewed himself again to the disciples at
the sea of Ti-be′ri-as; and on this wise shewed he *himself*.
[2]There were together Simon Peter, and Thomas called Did′y-mus, and
Nathanael of Cana in Galilee, and the *sons* of Zeb′e-dee, and two other of
his disciples.

☆**21:1** Jn 21:14
☆**21:2** Mt 4:21, 22; Jn 1:45–51

20:22 *Receive ye the Holy Ghost.* The relationship is unclear between this verse and the Pentecost event as recorded in Acts 1 and 2. We do not know if this verse means the disciples were then sealed and indwelt by the Spirit and filled later, or whether this was a promise to be fulfilled at Pentecost. There is little room for undue dogmatism here.

20:28 *my God.* A watershed question in Christian theology has to do with the deity of Jesus Christ. Is or isn't he God? Scripture states definitively that Jesus Christ is God manifest in the flesh. He is said to be eternally preexistent (1:1, 2; Isa. 9:6; Heb. 13:8; Rev. 22:13). He said that he was the only Son of God (10:30; 14:9; Matt. 11:27; Mark 14:61, 62). In the New Testament he is referred to as God in Titus 2:13 and 1 John 5:20. The following attributes of deity are assigned to him: (1) holiness (8:46; 2 Cor. 5:21; Heb. 7:26); (2) omnipresence (Matt. 18:20; 28:20); (3) omnipotence (Matt. 28:18; Heb. 1:3; Rev. 1:8); (4) immutability (Heb. 1:11, 12; 13:8); (5) divine creative activity (1:3; 1 Cor. 8:6; Col. 1:16, 17; Heb. 1:10); (6) his right to be worshipped (Matt. 2:11; 14:33; 28:9; Phil. 2:10; Heb. 1:6); (7) his right and power to forgive sins (1:29; Mark 2:5, 7, 9, 10; Luke 24:47; Acts 10:43; 1 John 1:7). Christ's deity is of the utmost importance. Its denial destroys the basic structure of the Christian faith.

21:1 *sea of Tiberias,* also known as Lake Gennesaret, Sea of Galilee, and Lake of Tiberias.

21:2 *the sons of Zebedee,* i.e., James and John.

21:3☆ 3 Simon Peter saith unto them, I go a fishing. They say unto him, We also
go with thee. They went forth, and entered into a ship immediately; and
that night they caught nothing.
4 But when the morning was now come, Jesus stood on the shore: but the
disciples knew not that it was Jesus.
5 Then Jesus saith unto them, Children, have ye any meat? They answered
him, No.
21:6☆ 6 And he said unto them, Cast the net on the right side of the ship, and ye
Lk 5:4–7 shall find. They cast therefore, and now they were not able to draw it for
the multitude of fishes.
21:7☆ 7 Therefore that disciple whom Jesus loved saith unto Peter, It is the
Jn 13:21; 21:20 Lord. Now when Simon Peter heard that it was the Lord, he girt *his* fisher's
coat *unto him*, (for he was naked,) and did cast himself into the sea.
8 And the other disciples came in a little ship; (for they were not far from
land, but as it were two hundred cubits,) dragging the net with fishes.
21:9 9 As soon then as they were come to land, they saw a fire of coals there,
Jn 6:9, 11 and fish laid thereon, and bread.
10 Jesus saith unto them, Bring of the fish which ye have now caught.
11 Simon Peter went up, and drew the net to land full of great fishes, an
hundred and fifty and three: and for all there were so many, yet was not the
net broken.
21:12 12 Jesus saith unto them, Come *and* dine. And none of the disciples durst
Acts 10:41 ask him, Who art thou? knowing that it was the Lord.
13 Jesus then cometh, and taketh bread, and giveth them, and fish
likewise.
21:14 14 This is now the third time that Jesus shewed himself to his disciples,
Jn 20:19, 26 after that he was risen from the dead.

21:15☆ Mt 26:33 Acts 20:28 Eph 4:11

B. JESUS' CONVERSATION WITH PETER

21:16 Heb 13:20, 21 1 Pet 2:25, 5:2 **21:17** 1 Chron 28:9 29:17 2 Chron 6:30 Jer 17:10 Jn 2:24, 25 13:38 Rom 8:27 1 Thess 2:4

15 ¶So when they had dined, Jesus saith to Simon Peter, Simon, *son* of
Jonas, lovest thou me more than these? He saith unto him, Yea, Lord; thou
knowest that I love thee. He saith unto him, Feed my lambs.
16 He saith to him again the second time, Simon, *son* of Jonas, lovest thou
me? He saith unto him, Yea, Lord; thou knowest that I love thee. He saith
unto him, Feed my sheep.
17 He saith unto him the third time, Simon, *son* of Jonas, lovest thou me?
Peter was grieved because he said unto him the third time, Lovest thou me?

21:3 *I go a fishing.* After the resurrection, the disciples were at a loss to know what to do. Shortly, Jesus would tell them to tarry in Jerusalem until the Holy Spirit came upon them in mighty power. In the meantime, these men, who had been busy with Jesus for almost three years, could not bear to sit by and do nothing. So they returned to what had been their trade before they became disciples of Jesus. The time for them to start their pentecostal preaching had not yet dawned.

21:6 This incident is instructive, for it was something that had happened to them before. Luke tells us how Peter, James, and John had fished all night and caught nothing. Jesus told them to cast in their nets and they *reaped a large harvest of fish* (Luke 5:1–8). Then they became followers of Jesus. Now at the end of Jesus' earthly existence the same thing happens. The disciples are fishing and again they catch nothing. Jesus appears and tells them to cast in their nets, and when they do they catch many fish. Peter, remembering the first occasion, senses immediately that it is the Lord (as John, who was there on both occasions, sees and tells him).

21:7 *Therefore that disciple whom Jesus loved,* i.e., John.

21:15 There have been differing understandings about the question "Lovest thou me more than these?" Some think it means: "Do you love me more than you love these other disciples?" Others, that it means: "Do you love me more than these other disciples love me?" And still others: "Do you love me more than your boats, nets, and fishes?" Two different Greek words are used for *love.* The first two times the word *agapaō,* which means high, devoted love, appears. When Peter refuses to use the same word, Jesus turns to the word *phileō,* a lower form of love having to do with the love of friendship. Peter accepts this word and avers that he loves Jesus this way. Peter was humbler now than earlier in his life and was making no claim to superior love.

And he said unto him, Lord, thou knowest all things; thou knowest that I
love thee. Jesus saith unto him, Feed my sheep.
18 Verily, verily, I say unto thee, When thou wast young, thou girdedst
thyself, and walkedst whither thou wouldest: but when thou shalt be old,
thou shalt stretch forth thy hands, and another shall gird thee, and carry
thee whither thou wouldest not.
19 This spake he, signifying by what death he should glorify God. And **21:19** 2 Pet 1:13, 14
when he had spoken this, he saith unto him, Follow me.
20 Then Peter, turning about, seeth the disciple whom Jesus loved **21:20** Jn 13:23–25
following; which also leaned on his breast at supper, and said, Lord, which
is he that betrayeth thee?
21 Peter seeing him saith to Jesus, Lord, and what *shall* this man *do?* ☆**21:21**
22 Jesus saith unto him, If I will that he tarry till I come, what *is that* to **21:22** Deut 29:29
thee? follow thou me. 1 Cor 4:5; 11:26
23 Then went this saying abroad among the brethren, that that disciple Rev 2:25; 3:11
should not die: yet Jesus said not unto him, He shall not die; but, If I will 22:7, 20
that he tarry till I come, what *is that* to thee?

C. JOHN'S PERSONAL WITNESS AND TESTIMONY

24 This is the disciple which testifieth of these things, and wrote these **21:24** Jn 1:14; 15:27
things: and we know that his testimony is true. 19:35
25 And there are also many other things which Jesus did, the which, if they 1 Jn 1:1–3
should be written every one, I suppose that even the world itself could not 3 Jn 12
contain the books that should be written. Amen. ☆**21:25** Jn 20:30, 31

21:21 Curious Peter, who has been told what will happen to him later in life, becomes very curious about John. He asks Jesus what will happen to John. Jesus tells him, in effect, "It is none of your business. All you need to do is follow me." When believers follow Jesus, they will be kept busy and less curious about others. He who knows the will of God for everybody else does not know the will of God for himself, for God does not tell us what his will is for others. It is not his will for me to know God's will for anyone else.

21:25 God has made known to us all we need to know about Jesus. What can be known about him would fill more books than we could ever read. His prayers alone would fill many a book, for he prayed many a night until the dawn of another day. And the words he spoke that have been given to us in part would fill many other volumes. His thought life alone would give us enough books to keep us going for a long time. But we do know enough to realize him as our Savior and Lord.

THE ACTS OF THE APOSTLES

Authorship, date, and background The Acts of the Apostles and Luke's Gospel were written by the same person. Luke has been identified with both books from the earliest days, and while neither book has any author's identification in the text, there is no reason for supposing the books were written by anyone else. The internal evidences clearly point to someone close to Paul, to one who was his co-laborer in the gospel. No other Pauline companion fits the facts as closely as Luke. The date for the book lies somewhere between A.D. 64 and 72. Tradition has it that Luke died shortly after Paul was executed and The Acts ends with Paul's imprisonment in Rome. The two years spent there gave Luke sufficient time to do his research work in tracing down what happened as the gospel was preached throughout the Roman Empire. There is good reason to believe that the Good News was preached in North Africa and in the regions to the east of Palestine and perhaps as far as India and maybe even China. Luke did not write about that aspect of the gospel's progress. He confined his attention to Palestine, Turkey, and the Greek and Roman areas.

In so short a book as The Acts of the Apostles it would be impossible to do more than give the briefest account of all that transpired following the ascension of Jesus Christ and the beginning of the church at Pentecost. So Luke's account is limited largely to the ministries of Peter and Paul. For this reason, some say the title could well be The Acts of Peter and Paul. Others have suggested it should be titled The Acts of the Holy Spirit. But this might tend to depreciate the historical aspect of the book, which is definitely a book of history. Still others have suggested it be called The Acts of the Church, which would then include many others who participated in the forward march and progress of the gospel. Taking all this into account, The Acts of the Apostles appears to be the appropriate title.

In these discussions it should be remembered that the ultimate author of all Scripture is the Holy Spirit, who selected and used the writers to accomplish the divine purpose. In the doing of this, while we have not been told everything that happened, we can know that what we are told is trustworthy and can be depended on theologically and factually. Moreover, in Luke's case he certainly knew by personal experience some of what he wrote about. He gathered information no doubt from such people as Silas, Titus, Timothy, Apollos, John Mark, Barnabas, and many others. The Holy Spirit aided him in the choice and selection of his material and kept him from saying that which is not true.

Characteristics and content Luke provides the link which connects the four Gospels with all of the other apostolic writings found in the New Testament. This book is really the bridge, the absence of which would leave us immeasurably poorer and in the dark about the earliest days of the church. Luke commences with the ascension, recording another statement of Jesus' command to take the gospel to the ends of the earth (Acts 1:8). Then comes Pentecost, which is the birthday of the church. Here it was that the disciples of Jesus received the power the Master had promised and were enabled to go forth preaching the Word and performing miracles to attest to the truth of what they proclaimed.

The sermons Luke records are strikingly similar in content. Again and again the core of the messages claims that Jesus Christ died for men's sins, rose again, and had been exalted in heaven at the throne of his Father. This Jesus, they claim, is the Lord, and Christ the Messiah, who is for Jew and Gentile alike. They urge men everywhere to repent, accept Christ by faith, be baptized, receive the gift of the Holy Spirit, and enjoy the promise of God of their participation in the new age which began at Pentecost and which would reach its consummation with the return of Jesus in righteousness to judge the world. The resurrection of Jesus lies at the heart of the apostolic Good News.

Luke also emphasizes the person and work of the Holy Spirit—the one who brings *conviction of sin, of righteousness, and of judgment*. He sends forth workers into the harvest field (see Acts 13). Sin is judged immediately in the early church to show men they cannot play fast and loose with God and with truth. Ananias and Sapphira are the first to experience the wrath of God for transgression. It is Peter who speaks of their sin as one in which they were lying to the Holy Spirit (5:3). Luke records how believers are filled with the Holy Spirit and this makes all the difference in their lives and ministry. Of Paul and Silas, Luke says they "were forbidden of the Holy Ghost [Spirit] to preach the word in Asia" (16:6).

This book comes to a conclusion at a time when the Roman Empire had been evangelized, churches established, elders and deacons selected, and the basic order of the church set up.

Outline

I. Planting the church in Jerusalem (1:1—8:3)
II. Church planting in Judea and Samaria (8:4—11:18)
III. Church planting among the Gentiles: Antioch and the Roman Empire (11:19—21:14)
IV. Paul's imprisonment: Jerusalem, Caesarea, and Rome (21:15—28:31)

I. PLANTING THE CHURCH IN JERUSALEM (1:1—8:3)

A. INTRODUCTION

1. The Background for Acts

1 THE former treatise have I made, O The-oph'i-lus, of all that Jesus
began both to do and teach,
2 Until the day in which he was taken up, after that he through the Holy
Ghost had given commandments unto the apostles whom he had chosen:
3 To whom also he shewed himself alive after his passion by many
infallible proofs, being seen of them forty days, and speaking of the things
pertaining to the kingdom of God:
4 And, being assembled together with *them*, commanded them that they
should not depart from Jerusalem, but wait for the promise of the Father,
which, *saith he*, ye have heard of me.
5 For John truly baptized with water; but ye shall be baptized with the
Holy Ghost not many days hence.

2. The Ascension of Jesus

6 When they therefore were come together, they asked of him, saying,
Lord, wilt thou at this time restore again the kingdom to Israel?
7 And he said unto them, It is not for you to know the times or the
seasons, which the Father hath put in his own power.
8 But ye shall receive power, after that the Holy Ghost is come upon you:
and ye shall be witnesses unto me both in Jerusalem, and in all Judæa, and
in Sa-ma'ri-a, and unto the uttermost part of the earth.
9 And when he had spoken these things, while they beheld, he was taken
up; and a cloud received him out of their sight.

☆**1:1** Lk 1:3
1:2 Mt 28:19, 20; Mk 16:19; Lk 24:49–51; Jn 20:22, 23; Acts 1:9–11, 22; Heb 1:3
☆**1:3** Mk 16:12, 14; Lk 24:33–36; Jn 20:19, 26; 21:1, 14; Acts 8:12; 10:41; 13:31; 19:8; 28:31; 1 Cor 15:5
1:4 Jn 14:16, 17, 26; Lk 24:49; Acts 2:33
☆**1:5** Joel 2:28, 29; Mt 3:11; Acts 2:4; 11:16
☆**1:6** Dan 7:27; Amos 9:11; 1 Cor 15:7
1:7 Deut 29:29; Mt 24:36; 1 Thess 5:1, 2
☆**1:8** Mt 28:19; Lk 24:48, 49; Jn 15:27; Acts 2:4; 8:1; Rom 10:18
☆**1:9**

1:1 *The former treatise,* i.e., "The Book of Luke." (See note on Luke 1:1.)

1:3 Christ remained on earth for forty days following his resurrection. He wanted (1) to verify his resurrection by many appearances, in order to silence those who would deny the miracle; (2) to instruct his disciples in the great truths of Scripture concerning his life and ministry; (3) to prevent false teachers and seducing spirits from subverting the faith of the apostles; and (4) to pave the way for the Holy Spirit's work of instruction and confirmation (John 14:26).

1:5 *with water,* or, "in water." *baptized with the Holy Ghost,* or, "baptized in the Holy Spirit."† This occurred shortly thereafter, according to Acts 2. There are differences of opinion as to whether this was a one-time event that marked the advent of the Spirit at Pentecost or whether it still happens today. Acts 2:4 says the disciples were all filled with the Spirit. If "filling" constitutes the baptism, then it is repeatable. If there is a difference between the baptism and the infilling of the Spirit, it would not be repeatable.

1:6 *wilt thou at this time* restore the kingdom to Israel? That is, "Will you make the nation of the Jews what it used to be under the kingly reigns of David and Solomon?"

1:8 This is the fifth statement of the Great Commission. It is also found in Matt. 28:18–20, Mark 16:15, Luke 24:46–49, and John 20:21. The mission of the church is to preach the gospel to every creature. When this is completed, Jesus Christ will return the second time in power and great glory.

1:9 The ascension occurred in the presence of the eleven apostles and two white-robed men (who may have been angels, or perhaps Moses and Elijah, who

1:10 Lk 24:4 Jn 20:12
1:11 Dan 7:13 Zech 14:4 Mt 16:27 Acts 3:21 1 Thess 1:10 4:16 Rev 1:7

10 And while they looked stedfastly toward heaven as he went up, behold,
two men stood by them in white apparel;
11 Which also said, Ye men of Galilee, why stand ye gazing up into
heaven? this same Jesus, which is taken up from you into heaven, shall so
come in like manner as ye have seen him go into heaven.

B. THE BEGINNINGS OF THE FIRST CHURCH

1. The Upper Room

1:12 Zech 14:4 Lk 24:50
1:13 Lk 22:12 Acts 12:12; 20:8 Jude 20
1:14 a) Mt 10:2–4 Mk 3:16–19 Lk 6:14–16 b) Mt 13:55 Lk 8:2, 3

12 Then returned they unto Jerusalem from the mount called Olivet, which
is from Jerusalem a sabbath day's journey.
13 And when they were come in, they went up into an upper room, where
abode both Peter, and James, and John, and Andrew, Philip, and Thomas,
Bartholomew, and Matthew, James *the son* of Al-phæ'us, and Simon Ze-
lo'tes, and Judas *the brother* of James.
14 These all continued with one accord in prayer and supplication, with
the women, and Mary the mother of Jesus, and with his brethren.

2. The Selection of Judas Iscariot's Successor

1:15☆
1:16 Ps 41:9 Jn 18:3
1:17 Jn 6:70, 71 Acts 1:24, 25 20:24; 21:19
1:18 Mt 26:14, 15 27:3–10
1:20 Ps 69:25; 109:8
1:21, 22 Mk 1:1–4 Acts 1:2; 2:32
1:24 1 Sam 16:7 Acts 6:6; 15:8
1:25 Acts 1:17 Rom 1:5
1:26☆ Lev 16:8 Josh 14:1, 2 1 Sam 14:41 Prov 16:33

15 ¶And in those days Peter stood up in the midst of the disciples, and
said, (the number of names together were about an hundred and twenty,)
16 Men *and* brethren, this scripture must needs have been fulfilled, which
the Holy Ghost by the mouth of David spake before concerning Judas,
which was guide to them that took Jesus.
17 For he was numbered with us, and had obtained part of this ministry.
18 Now this man purchased a field with the reward of iniquity; and falling
headlong, he burst asunder in the midst, and all his bowels gushed out.
19 And it was known unto all the dwellers at Jerusalem; insomuch as that
field is called in their proper tongue, A-cel'da-ma, that is to say, The field of
blood.
20 For it is written in the book of Psalms, Let his habitation be desolate,
and let no man dwell therein: and his bishoprick let another take.
21 Wherefore of these men which have companied with us all the time that
the Lord Jesus went in and out among us,
22 Beginning from the baptism of John, unto that same day that he was
taken up from us, must one be ordained to be a witness with us of his
resurrection.
23 And they appointed two, Joseph called Bar'sa-bas, who was surnamed
Justus, and Mat-thi'as.
24 And they prayed, and said, Thou, Lord, which knowest the hearts of all
men, shew whether of these two thou hast chosen,
25 That he may take part of this ministry and apostleship, from which
Judas by transgression fell, that he might go to his own place.
26 And they gave forth their lots; and the lot fell upon Mat-thi'as; and he
was numbered with the eleven apostles.

---

were with Jesus on the Mount of Transfiguration). They were gathered at the Mount of Olives near Bethany (Luke 24:50). 1:11 states Jesus "will come in the same way as you saw him go into heaven" (RSV). Christ's return will be personal and visible. He will come (1) "in *flaming fire with* his mighty angels" (2 Thess. 1:7, TLB); (2) "with all his saints" (1 Thess. 3:13); (3) "as a thief in the night" (1 Thess. 5:2; 2 Pet. 3:10; Rev. 16:15); (4) "in his glory" (Matt. 25:31); (5) "with the soul-stirring cry of the archangel and the great trumpet-call of God" (1 Thess. 4:16, TLB); and (6) unexpectedly (Mark 13:36).

1:15 Peter, in company with the one hundred and twenty, addresses the issue of Judas Iscariot, who now was dead. His death left only eleven of the twelve apostles. Why choose anyone to fill Judas' place? Because they knew the Scripture and fulfilled it. Psalm 109:8 says, "Let another take his office." They chose Matthias to replace Judas. Some think that Paul filled the vacant place, but that is suppositious.

1:26 *gave forth their lots,* i.e., "drew straws," or "threw dice."† *Matthias* was chosen to replace Judas Iscariot as an apostle. The selection was made by lot. The main function of the office of apostle was to

C. THE COMING OF THE HOLY SPIRIT
1. The Spirit's Descent

2 AND when the day of Pentecost was fully come, they were all with one
accord in one place.
2 And suddenly there came a sound from heaven as of a rushing mighty
wind, and it filled all the house where they were sitting.
3 And there appeared unto them cloven tongues like as of fire, and it sat
upon each of them.
4 And they were all filled with the Holy Ghost, and began to speak with
other tongues, as the Spirit gave them utterance.
5 And there were dwelling at Jerusalem Jews, devout men, out of every
nation under heaven.
6 Now when this was noised abroad, the multitude came together, and
were confounded, because that every man heard them speak in his own
language.
7 And they were all amazed and marvelled, saying one to another, Behold,
are not all these which speak Galilæans?
8 And how hear we every man in our own tongue, wherein we were born?
9 Par′thi-ans, and Medes, and E′lam-ites, and the dwellers in Mes-o-po-
ta′mi-a, and in Judæa, and Cap-pa-do′ci-a, in Pontus, and Asia,
10 Phryg′i-a, and Pam-phyl′i-a, in Egypt, and in the parts of Libya about
Cy-re′ne, and strangers of Rome, Jews and proselytes,
11 Cretes and Arabians, we do hear them speak in our tongues the
wonderful works of God.
12 And they were all amazed, and were in doubt, saying one to another,
What meaneth this?
13 Others mocking said, These men are full of new wine.

2. PETER'S FIRST SERMON

14 ¶But Peter, standing up with the eleven, lifted up his voice, and said
unto them, Ye men of Judæa, and all *ye* that dwell at Jerusalem, be this
known unto you, and hearken to my words:
15 For these are not drunken, as ye suppose, seeing it is *but* the third hour
of the day.
16 But this is that which was spoken by the prophet Jo′el;
17 And it shall come to pass in the last days, saith God, I will pour out of
my Spirit upon all flesh: and your sons and your daughters shall prophesy,

☆**2:1** Lev 23:15, 16; Deut 16:9, 10; Acts 1:14, 15; 20:16
2:2 Acts 4:31
☆**2:4** Mk 16:7; Acts 4:8, 31; 10:46; 13:9, 19:6; 1 Cor 12:10; 13:1; Eph 5:18
2:7 Mt 26:73; Acts 1:11
☆**2:8**
2:9 Acts 6:9; 19:10; 1 Pet 1:1
2:10 Ex 12:48; Mt 23:15; 27:32; Acts 13:13; 16:6
2:13 1 Cor 2:14; 14:23; Eph 5:18
2:16 Joel 2:28–32
☆**2:17** Isa 44:3; Ezek 11:10; 36:27; Zech 12:10; Acts 10:45

---

witness to Jesus' resurrection. Throughout the Book of Acts Christ's resurrection is emphasized (2:32; 3:15; 4:2, 10, 33; 5:30–32; 10:29–41; 13:30, 31). In their preaching, the apostles said that God had exalted the resurrected Christ and had enthroned him as Savior and Leader. It is significant to note the acceptance of the saving work of Christ by the Father, evidenced by Christ's ascension and appointment to the seat at the right hand of the Father.

2:1 *the day of Pentecost* marks the beginning of the Christian church. Pentecost was a miraculous event marked by (1) the suddenness of its coming; (2) the wind that filled the place and revealed the presence of the Holy Spirit; (3) the tongues of fire, signifying the preaching of the good news to all nations; and (4) the fire, which symbolized the power and zeal given to those who obeyed Christ in taking the gospel to the ends of the earth. Pentecost (Greek *pentekostē*), meaning "fiftieth day," was celebrated on the seventh day of Sivan (May-June), fifty days after the Passover. It was one of the three festivals at which all males were supposed to congregate. Pentecost was also known as the festival of weeks, the day of the first fruits and the festival of harvest. (See note on Lev. 23:15, 16.)

2:4 *with other tongues,* i.e., languages given to them by the Holy Spirit which they did not know themselves.

2:8 Some think the disciples spoke just one language and that the audience—composed of speakers of different languages—were given the gift of understanding the disciples' language. It seems clear enough, however, that the disciples were given the gift of speaking in the tongues of the other peoples present.

2:17 *the last days* began with the First Advent of Jesus Christ and will end with the Second Advent. How long this period will last is nowhere stated in Scripture. Whether we are now in the latter end of the last days is a question that cannot be answered dogmatically.

2:18
1 Cor 12:10
14:1
2:20
MT 24:29
2:21
Gen 4:26
Ps 55:16; 88:9
116:2, 4, 13, 17
145:18
Acts 9:14, 21
22:16
Rom 10:13
1 Cor 1:2
2 Tim 2:22
2:22
Jn 17:4
Acts 10:38
Heb 2:4
2:23☆
Acts 3:17, 18
4:28
1 Pet 1:11, 20
Rev 13:8
2:24
Acts 3:15; 10:40
17:31
Rom 4:24
1 Cor 6:14
2 Cor 4:14
Gal 1:1
Col 2:12
1 Pet 1:21
2:25–27
Ps 16:8–11
Acts 13:30–35
2:29
1 Kings 2:10
Neh 3:16
Acts 13:35, 36
2:30
2 Sam 7:12–14
Ps 89:3, 4
132:11
Lk 1:32
Rom 1:3
Eph 4:9, 10
2 Tim 2:8
2:31
Acts 13:35, 36
2:32
Acts 1:8
2:33
Lk 24:49
Jn 14:26
Acts 1:4, 8
5:31; 10:45
Eph 4:8
Phil 2:9
Heb 10:12
2:34☆
Ps 110:1
2:35
1 Cor 15:25
2:36
Lk 2:11
Acts 5:31
2:37
Zech 12:10
Acts 16:30
2:38☆
Mk 16:16
Lk 24:47
Acts 3:19; 5:31
8:12; 22:16

and your young men shall see visions, and your old men shall dream
dreams:
18 And on my servants and on my handmaidens I will pour out in those
days of my Spirit; and they shall prophesy:
19 And I will shew wonders in heaven above, and signs in the earth
beneath; blood, and fire, and vapour of smoke:
20 The sun shall be turned into darkness, and the moon into blood, before
that great and notable day of the Lord come:
21 And it shall come to pass, *that* whosoever shall call on the name of the
Lord shall be saved.
22 Ye men of Israel, hear these words; Jesus of Nazareth, a man approved
of God among you by miracles and wonders and signs, which God did by
him in the midst of you, as ye yourselves also know:
23 Him, being delivered by the determinate counsel and foreknowledge of
God, ye have taken, and by wicked hands have crucified and slain:
24 Whom God hath raised up, having loosed the pains of death: because it
was not possible that he should be holden of it.
25 For David speaketh concerning him, I foresaw the Lord always before
my face, for he is on my right hand, that I should not be moved:
26 Therefore did my heart rejoice, and my tongue was glad; moreover also
my flesh shall rest in hope:
27 Because thou wilt not leave my soul in hell, neither wilt thou suffer
thine Holy One to see corruption.
28 Thou hast made known to me the ways of life; thou shalt make me full
of joy with thy countenance.
29 Men *and* brethren, let me freely speak unto you of the patriarch David,
that he is both dead and buried, and his sepulchre is with us unto this day.
30 Therefore being a prophet, and knowing that God had sworn with an
oath to him, that of the fruit of his loins, according to the flesh, he would
raise up Christ to sit on his throne;
31 He seeing this before spake of the resurrection of Christ, that his soul
was not left in hell, neither his flesh did see corruption.
32 This Jesus hath God raised up, whereof we all are witnesses.
33 Therefore being by the right hand of God exalted, and having received
of the Father the promise of the Holy Ghost, he hath shed forth this, which
ye now see and hear.
34 For David is not ascended into the heavens: but he saith himself, The
LORD said unto my Lord, Sit thou on my right hand,
35 Until I make thy foes thy footstool.
36 Therefore let all the house of Israel know assuredly, that God hath
made that same Jesus, whom ye have crucified, both Lord and Christ.

3. Additions to the Church

37 ¶Now when they heard *this*, they were pricked in their heart, and said
unto Peter and to the rest of the apostles, Men *and* brethren, what shall we
do?
38 Then Peter said unto them, Repent, and be baptized every one of you in

2:23 *by wicked hands,* i.e., "by the hands of lawless *men" (RSV).*
2:34 David died and was buried and his body still lay in the grave. Thus the words quoted from David were not spoken about himself. He did not ascend into heaven to sit at the right hand of God. Since David was still entombed, this prophetic word applies to God's Son, Jesus Christ, and is the fulfillment of Ps. 110:1. Jesus is now exalted *by* God *to* God's right hand as the supreme ruler over the entire cosmos. This exaltation of Jesus is an integral part of the apostolic message; it should be part of the same message we preach today.
2:38 Water baptism upon profession of faith is commanded here, in Matt. 28:19, and elsewhere in the New Testament. It is not to be confused with the baptism of the Spirit, by which new converts are made members of

the name of Jesus Christ for the remission of sins, and ye shall receive the
gift of the Holy Ghost.
39 For the promise is unto you, and to your children, and to all that are
afar off, *even* as many as the Lord our God shall call.
40 And with many other words did he testify and exhort, saying, Save
yourselves from this untoward generation.
41 ¶Then they that gladly received his word were baptized: and the same
day there were added *unto them* about three thousand souls.
42 And they continued stedfastly in the apostles' doctrine and fellowship,
and in breaking of bread, and in prayers.

4. The Spirit at Work among the Believers

43 And fear came upon every soul: and many wonders and signs were
done by the apostles.
44 And all that believed were together, and had all things common;
45 And sold their possessions and goods, and parted them to all *men*, as
every man had need.
46 And they, continuing daily with one accord in the temple, and breaking
bread from house to house, did eat their meat with gladness and singleness
of heart,
47 Praising God, and having favour with all the people. And the Lord
added to the church daily such as should be saved.

D. THE GROWTH OF THE CHURCH AMID PERSECUTION
1. Peter's Second Sermon; the Healing of the Lame Beggar

3 NOW Peter and John went up together into the temple at the hour of
prayer, *being* the ninth *hour*.
2 And a certain man lame from his mother's womb was carried, whom
they laid daily at the gate of the temple which is called Beautiful, to ask
alms of them that entered into the temple;

2:39 Isa 44:3 Joel 2:32 Rom 9:8 Eph 2:13, 17
2:40 Phil 2:15
☆**2:41**
☆**2:42** Lk 24:30 Acts 2:46; 20:7 1 Cor 10:16 Heb 10:25 1 Jn 1:3
☆**2:43** Mk 16:17 Acts 2:22
2:44 Acts 4:32; 5:4
2:45 Isa 58:7 Acts 4:34–37 5:1, 2
2:46 Acts 2:42; 5:42 Rom 16:5 1 Cor 16:19 Col 4:5 Phm 2
☆**2:47** Acts 4:4; 6:7 Rom 14:18, 19

---

the body of Christ. Water baptism normally precedes admission to the fellowship of the church and is required by most denominations. Significant differences exist on almost every other aspect of water baptism. Some baptize infants; others practice believer's baptism only. Some sprinkle, some affuse, and some immerse. Some practice trine immersion on behalf of the Trinity. Some call baptism a sacrament, which conveys grace; others call it merely an ordinance. Some believe in baptismal regeneration, by which an infant upon baptism is born again on the basis of parents' faith; this is to be followed later by a confession of faith by the child who has reached the age of accountability. In accordance with Christ's command in Matt. 28:19 most baptisms, whether infant or adult, are performed in the name of the Father, the Son, and the Holy Spirit.

2:41 The "greater works" of the disciples, prophesied and promised by Jesus Christ in John 14:12, is now fulfilled. Peter, empowered by the Spirit, sees three thousand people respond to the gospel invitation. This was more than the total number of people who came to Christ during his own lifetime.

2:42 *in breaking of bread,* i.e., in the Eucharist, or the Lord's Supper, one of the two ordinances or sacraments of most churches.

2:43 *many wonders and signs.* Apparently the power of the Holy Spirit worked so effectively that many signs and wonders took place—the hearers then had corroborating evidence to support the spoken word of the disciples. This apparently casual statement should not obfuscate the fact that a complete record of these wonders would have required a book much larger than the entire New Testament.

2:47 *the church* (from the Greek word *ekklesia,* meaning the "called-out assembly," or, "congregation") comprises those who have been regenerated and baptized, and who make a credible profession of faith. Not all who profess Christ have truly been regenerated, but God knows the hearts of all men. Some who are not church members may have been born again. The word for "church" is used in the New Testament to refer both to local congregations and to the church universal (e.g., 1 Cor. 1:2; 2 Cor. 1:1; Gal. 1:2; Eph. 1:22). Dispensationalists distinguish between Israel and the church; others hold that the church is the true Israel. Eph. 3:5 appears to support the dispensationalist's view, for it says that the church which had its beginnings at Pentecost was a mystery hidden from the ages and only then made known to men. On the other hand, in the Greek, Acts 7:38 mentions Israel as the "church in the wilderness," which supports the other view. In any event, the Calvary event is something to which the Jews looked forward and to which the church since Pentecost looks back. The saints of both the Old and the New Testaments have been redeemed by what Christ did on Calvary's tree.

3 Who seeing Peter and John about to go into the temple asked an alms.
4 And Peter, fastening his eyes upon him with John, said, Look on us.
5 And he gave heed unto them, expecting to receive something of them.

3:6☆ Acts 4:10; 1 Pet 4:10

6 Then Peter said, Silver and gold have I none; but such as I have give I
thee: In the name of Jesus Christ of Nazareth rise up and walk.
7 And he took him by the right hand, and lifted *him* up: and immediately
his feet and ancle bones received strength.

3:8 Isa 35:6

8 And he leaping up stood, and walked, and entered with them into the
temple, walking, and leaping, and praising God.

3:9 Acts 4:16, 21

9 And all the people saw him walking and praising God:

3:10 Jn 9:8

10 And they knew that it was he which sat for alms at the Beautiful gate of
the temple: and they were filled with wonder and amazement at that which
had happened unto him.

3:11 Jn 10:22, 23; Acts 5:12

11 And as the lame man which was healed held Peter and John, all the
people ran together unto them in the porch that is called Solomon's, greatly
wondering.

3:12 2 Cor 3:5

12 ¶And when Peter saw *it*, he answered unto the people, Ye men of Israel,
why marvel ye at this? or why look ye so earnestly on us, as though by our
own power or holiness we had made this man to walk?

3:13 Mt 22:32; 27:2; Lk 23:4; Jn 17:1; Acts 5:30, 31; Phil 2:9–11

13 The God of Abraham, and of Isaac, and of Jacob, the God of our
fathers, hath glorified his Son Jesus; whom ye delivered up, and denied him
in the presence of Pilate, when he was determined to let *him* go.

3:14☆ Mt 27:20; Lk 23:17–25; Acts 7:52

14 But ye denied the Holy One and the Just, and desired a murderer to be
granted unto you;

3:15☆ Acts 2:24; 5:31, 32; Heb 2:10; 5:9

15 And killed the Prince of life, whom God hath raised from the dead;
whereof we are witnesses.

3:16 Acts 3:6

16 And his name through faith in his name hath made this man strong,
whom ye see and know: yea, the faith which is by him hath given him this
perfect soundness in the presence of you all.

3:17☆ Lk 23:34; Acts 13:27; 1 Cor 2:8; 1 Tim 1:13

17 And now, brethren, I wot that through ignorance ye did *it*, as *did* also
your rulers.

3:18 Ps 22; 41:9; 69:4, 21; Isa 50:6; 53:4–11; Zech 12:10; 13:7; 1 Pet 1:10

18 But those things, which God before had shewed by the mouth of all his
prophets, that Christ should suffer, he hath so fulfilled.

3:19☆ Acts 2:38; 26:20; 1 Thess 1:9, 10; Heb 4:1–16

19 ¶Repent ye therefore, and be converted, that your sins may be blotted
out, when the times of refreshing shall come from the presence of the Lord;
20 And he shall send Jesus Christ, which before was preached unto you:

3:21 Mt 17:11; Acts 1:11; Rom 8:21

21 Whom the heaven must receive until the times of restitution of all
things, which God hath spoken by the mouth of all his holy prophets since
the world began.

3:22☆ Deut 18:15, 18; Jn 1:20, 21; 7:40, 41, 52; Heb 3:2–6

22 For Moses truly said unto the fathers, A prophet shall the Lord your
God raise up unto you of your brethren, like unto me; him shall ye hear in
all things whatsoever he shall say unto you.

3:6 Peter and John had no alms to give the cripple. But they had something else they could give him which was more valuable than money. They had power in the name of Jesus, and by his warrant they could heal for Christ's glory.

3:14, 15 Peter forthrightly declares that the Jews of Jerusalem had Jesus in their power and handed him over to the Romans for execution. They cannot escape their responsibility nor shrug off their guilt. This does not mean we are to hold the Jews of our day responsible for what their forebears did. Anti-Semitism is not only a virulent disease; it breaches the second table of the law, which requires that we love our neighbors as ourselves, and our enemies as well. In any event Gentiles are equally at fault for the death of Jesus, since they too were and are sinners for whom salvation via the death of Christ is necessary.

3:17 Peter here gives his listeners and their leaders the benefit of the doubt—they may have crucified Jesus in ignorance. He hastens to inform them that a free pardon can be theirs by the death of Jesus; they must repent of their sins and believe on the very Messiah they executed.

3:19 Repentance followed by conversion results in (1) pardon and forgiveness of sins (Isa. 55:7); (2) the gift of the Holy Spirit (2:38).

3:22 *A prophet . . . like unto me,* i.e., "will raise up for you a prophet like me from among your own people" (NIV).

23 And it shall come to pass, *that* every soul, which will not hear that
prophet, shall be destroyed from among the people.

3:23 Deut 18:19

24 Yea, and all the prophets from Samuel and those that follow after, as
many as have spoken, have likewise foretold of these days.

3:24 Lk 24:27

25 Ye are the children of the prophets, and of the covenant which God
made with our fathers, saying unto Abraham, And in thy seed shall all the
kindreds of the earth be blessed.

3:25 Gen 12:3; 22:18 Rom 9:4–8 Gal 3:8, 9

26 Unto you first God, having raised up his Son Jesus, sent him to bless
you, in turning away every one of you from his iniquities.

3:26 Acts 13:46 Rom 1:16

2. Beginning of the Persecution
a. The Seizure of Peter and John

4 AND as they spake unto the people, the priests, and the captain of the
temple, and the Sad′du-cees, came upon them,

☆4:1 Lk 22:4 Acts 5:24

2 Being grieved that they taught the people, and preached through Jesus
the resurrection from the dead.

4:2 Acts 17:18; 23:8 Rom 10:9

3 And they laid hands on them, and put *them* in hold unto the next day:
for it was now eventide.

4:3 Acts 5:18

4 Howbeit many of them which heard the word believed; and the number
of the men was about five thousand.

4:4 Acts 4:21

b. Peter before the Jewish Council

5 ¶And it came to pass on the morrow, that their rulers, and elders, and
scribes,
6 And An′nas the high priest, and Cai′a-phas, and John, and Alexander,
and as many as were of the kindred of the high priest, were gathered
together at Jerusalem.

4:6 Mt 26:3 Lk 3:1, 2 Jn 11:49; 18:13

7 And when they had set them in the midst, they asked, By what power, or
by what name, have ye done this?

4:7 Mt 21:23

8 Then Peter, filled with the Holy Ghost, said unto them, Ye rulers of the
people, and elders of Israel,

☆4:8 Lk 12:1

9 If we this day be examined of the good deed done to the impotent man,
by what means he is made whole;
10 Be it known unto you all, and to all the people of Israel, that by the
name of Jesus Christ of Nazareth, whom ye crucified, whom God raised
from the dead, *even* by him doth this man stand here before you whole.

4:10 Acts 2:22, 24; 3:6

11 This is the stone which was set at nought of you builders, which is
become the head of the corner.

4:11 Ps 118:22 Isa 28:16 Mt 21:42 Rom 9:33

12 Neither is there salvation in any other: for there is none other name
under heaven given among men, whereby we must be saved.

4:12 Mt 1:21 Acts 10:43 Rom 3:24 1 Tim 2:5

c. The Release of Peter and John

13 ¶Now when they saw the boldness of Peter and John, and perceived
that they were unlearned and ignorant men, they marvelled; and they took
knowledge of them, that they had been with Jesus.

☆4:13 Mt 11:25 1 Cor 1:27

4:1 *the Sadducees* were members of a Jewish religious sect that denied resurrection.†

4:8 *filled.* The original Greek word translated "filled" here is in the aorist passive tense, which suggests Peter was given immediate inspiration by the Holy Spirit. This is the fulfillment of the promise of Jesus in Matt. 10:19, 20. We need not fear about what to say when we are forced to appear before kings and rulers. The same Holy Spirit will help us and give us the right words. In 6:5 the adjective "full" describes Stephen, who was "full of . . . the Holy Ghost." This betokens the abiding infilling of the Spirit in the believer who has met the conditions for securing that blessing.

4:13 *unlearned and ignorant men.* To the members of the Sanhedrin, the chief priests, elders, and scribes these Galileans were nonprofessional scholars and therefore looked down upon. Since they had no special training, their persuasive eloquence was most astonishing but fully in accord with the teaching office of the Holy Spirit and the promise of Christ (Luke 12:11, 12).

14 And beholding the man which was healed standing with them, they
could say nothing against it.
15 But when they had commanded them to go aside out of the council,
they conferred among themselves,
4:16 Jn 11:47; Acts 3:7–10
16 Saying, What shall we do to these men? for that indeed a notable
miracle hath been done by them *is* manifest to all them that dwell in
Jerusalem; and we cannot deny *it*.
4:17 Jn 15:20, 21
17 But that it spread no further among the people, let us straitly threaten
them, that they speak henceforth to no man in this name.
4:18 Act 5:28
18 And they called them, and commanded them not to speak at all nor
teach in the name of Jesus.
4:19☆ Acts 5:29
19 But Peter and John answered and said unto them, Whether it be right
in the sight of God to hearken unto you more than unto God, judge ye.
4:20☆ Acts 1:8; 1 Cor 9:16; 1 Jn 1:1
20 For we cannot but speak the things which we have seen and heard.
4:21 Mt 21:26; Lk 20:6; 22:2; Acts 3:7, 8
21 So when they had further threatened them, they let them go, finding
nothing how they might punish them, because of the people: for all *men*
glorified God for that which was done.
22 For the man was above forty years old, on whom this miracle of healing
was shewed.

d. Peter and John Return; the Holy Spirit Fills the Believers

23 ¶And being let go, they went to their own company, and reported all
that the chief priests and elders had said unto them.
4:24 Ex 20:11; Ps 103:1; 107:1; 146:6
24 And when they heard that, they lifted up their voice to God with one
accord, and said, Lord, thou *art* God, which hast made heaven, and earth,
and the sea, and all that in them is:
4:25, 26 Ps 2:1, 2
25 Who by the mouth of thy servant David hast said, Why did the heathen
rage, and the people imagine vain things?
26 The kings of the earth stood up, and the rulers were gathered together
against the Lord, and against his Christ.
4:27 Isa 61:1; Mt 20:19; Lk 23:12; Acts 3:13; Heb 7:26
27 For of a truth against thy holy child Jesus, whom thou hast anointed,
both Herod, and Pontius Pilate, with the Gentiles, and the people of Israel,
were gathered together,
4:28 Acts 2:23
28 For to do whatsoever thy hand and thy counsel determined before to be
done.
4:29 Ezek 2:6, 7; Eph 6:19; Phil 1:14; 2 Thess 3:1
29 And now, Lord, behold their threatenings: and grant unto thy servants,
that with all boldness they may speak thy word,
4:30 Acts 3:6, 16; 5:12
30 By stretching forth thine hand to heal; and that signs and wonders may
be done by the name of thy holy child Jesus.
4:31☆ Acts 2:2, 4; 16:26; Phil 1:14
31 ¶And when they had prayed, the place was shaken where they were
assembled together; and they were all filled with the Holy Ghost, and they
spake the word of God with boldness.
4:32☆ Acts 2:44; Rom 15:5; Phil 2:2; 1 Pet 3:8
32 And the multitude of them that believed were of one heart and of one
soul: neither said any *of them* that ought of the things which he possessed
was his own; but they had all things common.

4:19, 20 Peter and John were denied freedom of speech when they were banned from speaking the name of Jesus publicly. Being men of principle, they *refused to obey the ban*, for to do so would be to affront conscience. They said they would do what God commanded and what was right, regardless of the consequences. Few Christians today would be this daring, opening themselves to the loss of their lives.

4:31 As a result of this prayer meeting, the place was shaken and the disciples were filled with the Holy Spirit. This fresh infilling had to do with power for the discharge of their obligations to God. It was unrelated to their being sealed and indwelt by the Spirit; this had already occurred and was not repeatable. The new infusion of power enabled them to speak the Word of God with boldness.

4:32 *neither said any of them that aught of the things which he possessed was his own.* This passage does not support the notion that community of property was practiced in the early church. In every case the act of

[33]And with great power gave the apostles witness of the resurrection of
the Lord Jesus: and great grace was upon them all.
[34]Neither was there any among them that lacked: for as many as were
possessors of lands or houses sold them, and brought the prices of the
things that were sold,
[35]And laid *them* down at the apostles' feet: and distribution was made
unto every man according as he had need.
[36]And Joses, who by the apostles was surnamed Barnabas, (which is,
being interpreted, The son of consolation,) a Levite, *and* of the country of
Cyprus,
[37]Having land, sold *it*, and brought the money, and laid *it* at the apostles'
feet.

4:33 Lk 24:48; Acts 1:8; 1 Thess 1:5
4:34 Acts 2:45; Jas 1:27; 1 Jn 3:17
4:36 Acts 9:27; 11:19–30; 12:25; 13:1–4; 15:39
4:37 Prov 11:24, 25; Lk 12:33; 1 Tim 6:18, 19

3. Exercising Discipline in the Church

a. Ananias

5 BUT a certain man named An-a-ni′as, with Sap-phi′ra his wife, sold a
possession,
[2]And kept back *part* of the price, his wife also being privy *to it*, and
brought a certain part, and laid *it* at the apostles' feet.
[3]But Peter said, An-a-ni′as, why hath Satan filled thine heart to lie to the
Holy Ghost, and to keep back *part* of the price of the land?
[4]Whiles it remained, was it not thine own? and after it was sold, was it
not in thine own power? why hast thou conceived this thing in thine heart?
thou hast not lied unto men, but unto God.
[5]And An-a-ni′as hearing these words fell down, and gave up the ghost:
and great fear came on all them that heard these things.
[6]And the young men arose, wound him up, and carried *him* out, and
buried *him*.

5:2 Acts 4:37; 1 Tim 6:10
☆**5:3** Num 30:1, 2; Deut 23:21; Eccles 5:4; Isa 29:15
5:5 Ezek 11:13

b. Sapphira

[7]And it was about the space of three hours after, when his wife, not
knowing what was done, came in.
[8]And Peter answered unto her, Tell me whether ye sold the land for so
much? And she said, Yea, for so much.
[9]Then Peter said unto her, How is it that ye have agreed together to
tempt the Spirit of the Lord? behold, the feet of them which have buried thy
husband *are* at the door, and shall carry thee out.
[10]Then fell she down straightway at his feet, and yielded up the ghost:
and the young men came in, and found her dead, and, carrying *her* forth,
buried *her* by her husband.

☆**5:9** Deut 6:16; Mt 4:7; Lk 4:12; 1 Cor 10:9

---

selling property and giving the proceeds for the work of the church was voluntary. No one was required to do so and no coercion was applied. Peter clearly said that Ananias' property belonged to him, and once he sold it he was free to do as he pleased with the money. When money was given, it was used to help those in need. It was not shared among the saints. The donations were simply expressions of Christian love and concern. Any group of Christians has the right to engage in communal living, but they have no right to force anyone else to follow their pattern; nor do they have a biblical right to seize any property by law or by force. Scripture teaches the inalienable right to private property and ownership of the means of production.

5:3 *the Holy Ghost* is the third person of the Trinity. As God, he has all the attributes of deity; he is united with the Father and the Son and is equal to them. The Holy Spirit is (1) eternal (Heb. 9:14); (2) omniscient (1 Cor. 2:10); (3) omnipresent (Ps. 139:7–13); and (4) omnipotent (Luke 1:35; Rom. 15:19). The Holy Spirit authored Scripture, had a part in creation, and also participated in man's redemption. When Ananias lied to the apostles, he lied to the Holy Spirit. In 5:4 Peter declares that lying to the Holy Spirit is lying to God. Judgment begins first at the house of God. In 5:5 that judgment was executed—Ananias fell down and died.

5:9 *agreed together to tempt the Spirit of the Lord.* In effect Peter was asking them: "Did you think you could get away with this sin so that even the Holy Spirit would be unable to detect you? You have therefore tempted or challenged the Holy Spirit."

11 And great fear came upon all the church, and upon as many as heard
these things.

4. The First Persecution

a. The Great Growth of the Church

5:12 Mk 16:15–20; Jn 10:23; Acts 3:10; Heb 2:4
5:13 Jn 9:22, 23; 12:42; Acts 2:47
5:14 Acts 2:47; 11:24

12 ¶And by the hands of the apostles were many signs and wonders
wrought among the people; (and they were all with one accord in
Solomon's porch.
13 And of the rest durst no man join himself to them: but the people
magnified them.
14 And believers were the more added to the Lord, multitudes both of men
and women.)

5:15 Mt 9:21; 14:36; Acts 19:12

15 Insomuch that they brought forth the sick into the streets, and laid
them on beds and couches, that at the least the shadow of Peter passing by
might overshadow some of them.

5:16☆

16 There came also a multitude *out* of the cities round about unto
Jerusalem, bringing sick folks, and them which were vexed with unclean
spirits: and they were healed every one.

b. The Imprisonment of the Apostles

5:17 Acts 4:1, 2
5:18 Lk 21:12
5:19☆ Ps 34:7; Acts 12:7; 16:26; Heb 1:14
5:20 Jn 6:63, 68; 17:3; 1 Jn 5:11
5:21 Acts 4:5, 6

17 ¶Then the high priest rose up, and all they that were with him, (which
is the sect of the Sad'du-cees,) and were filled with indignation,
18 And laid their hands on the apostles, and put them in the common
prison.
19 But the angel of the Lord by night opened the prison doors, and
brought them forth, and said,
20 Go, stand and speak in the temple to the people all the words of this
life.
21 And when they heard *that,* they entered into the temple early in the
morning, and taught. But the high priest came, and they that were with
him, and called the council together, and all the senate of the children of
Israel, and sent to the prison to have them brought.
22 But when the officers came, and found them not in the prison, they
returned, and told,
23 Saying, The prison truly found we shut with all safety, and the keepers
standing without before the doors: but when we had opened, we found no
man within.
24 Now when the high priest and the captain of the temple and the chief
priests heard these things, they doubted of them whereunto this would
grow.
25 Then came one and told them, saying, Behold, the men whom ye put in
prison are standing in the temple, and teaching the people.

5:26 Mt 14:5; 21:26

26 Then went the captain with the officers, and brought them without
violence: for they feared the people, lest they should have been stoned.

5:16 *they were healed every one.* That there are *healings today cannot be denied.* What distinguished the work of the apostles is that *everyone* was healed. There are no healing meetings today in which all who come are healed. In fact very few are actually healed and sometimes many of those who are said to have been healed are not really cured. Christ had given his disciples the power to heal. That power, exercised under the aegis of the Holy Spirit, was freely used.

5:19 God's angel had the power to open prison doors to free the imprisoned followers of Jesus. This was not an act performed by a secret supporter of the apostles among the temple police, as some believe. It was a specific act of God and marks the intervention of divine activity into human affairs.

27 And when they had brought them, they set *them* before the council: and
the high priest asked them,
28 Saying, Did not we straitly command you that ye should not teach in
this name? and, behold, ye have filled Jerusalem with your doctrine, and
intend to bring this man's blood upon us.
29 ¶Then Peter and the *other* apostles answered and said, We ought to
obey God rather than men.
30 The God of our fathers raised up Jesus, whom ye slew and hanged on a
tree.
31 Him hath God exalted with his right hand *to be* a Prince and a Saviour,
for to give repentance to Israel, and forgiveness of sins.
32 And we are his witnesses of these things; and *so is* also the Holy Ghost,
whom God hath given to them that obey him.

c. Gamaliel's Advice and the Apostles' Release

33 ¶When they heard *that*, they were cut *to the heart*, and took counsel to
slay them.
34 Then stood there up one in the council, a Pharisee, named Ga-ma'li-el,
a doctor of the law, had in reputation among all the people, and
commanded to put the apostles forth a little space;
35 And said unto them, Ye men of Israel, take heed to yourselves what ye
intend to do as touching these men.
36 For before these days rose up Theu'das, boasting himself to be
somebody; to whom a number of men, about four hundred, joined
themselves: who was slain; and all, as many as obeyed him, were scattered,
and brought to nought.
37 After this man rose up Judas of Galilee in the days of the taxing, and
drew away much people after him: he also perished; and all, *even* as many
as obeyed him, were dispersed.
38 And now I say unto you, Refrain from these men, and let them alone:
for if this counsel or this work be of men, it will come to nought:
39 But if it be of God, ye cannot overthrow it; lest haply ye be found even
to fight against God.
40 And to him they agreed: and when they had called the apostles, and
beaten *them*, they commanded that they should not speak in the name of
Jesus, and let them go.
41 ¶And they departed from the presence of the council, rejoicing that
they were counted worthy to suffer shame for his name.
42 And daily in the temple, and in every house, they ceased not to teach
and preach Jesus Christ.

5:28 Mt 23:35; 27:25 Acts 2:23; 3:15 4:18; 7:52
5:29 Acts 4:19
5:30 Acts 10:39–41 1 Pet 2:24
5:31 Isa 9:6 Mt 1:21 Acts 2:33 Phil 2:9 Heb 2:10; 12:2 Rev 1:5
☆**5:32** Lk 24:28 Jn 15:26 Rom 8:16 Heb 2:4
5:33 Acts 2:37; 7:54
☆**5:34** Acts 22:3
☆**5:36** Acts 8:9
☆**5:37** Lk 2:1
5:38 Ps 127:1
5:39 Prov 21:30 Isa 46:9, 10 Mt 16:18 Acts 9:5 1 Cor 1:25
5:40 Mt 10:17 Mk 13:9
5:41 Mt 5:11, 12 Jn 15:20, 21 Rom 5:3 Phil 1:29 Heb 10:34 1 Pet 4:13, 14, 16
☆**5:42**

5:32 The disciples were possessed, indwelt, and filled with the Spirit in such a way that they became the *Spirit's organs of expression. Through them* the Spirit worked to accomplish the divine purpose. All believers are witnesses to God's mighty acts under the control and supervision of the Divine Witness, the Holy Spirit.
5:34 *Gamaliel* was a well-known teacher under whom Saul of Tarsus studied (22:3). He was an elder, a rabbi, belonging to the liberal group of Jewish teachers who followed the interpretations of Hillel, a deeply respected rabbi who died shortly before the time of Jesus.
5:36 *Theudas* led a revolt against the Roman authorities. Apparently, no other extant material refers to this event. However, Josephus, the Jewish historian, *does* speak of a revolt led by a man named Theudas (A.D. 44). Since the name was common, it may well be that two revolutionary leaders had the same name.
5:37 *Judas of Galilee* is mentioned by Josephus as a bandit in the days of King Herod. He led a revolt against the census being carried out by Quirinius in A.D. 6. (There is some question whether the Judas of 5:37 is the same person, but it is quite probable.) Judas was defeated, but his movement—the Zealots—pressed on. This revolutionary party was dedicated to overthrowing Roman power by force of arms.
5:42 Publicly and privately the apostles and disciples taught and preached despite the ban placed on those activities by the Jewish religious leaders. They had to obey God rather than men even when the men happened to be the religious leaders.

5. Choosing the First Deacons

6:1☆ Ex 18:17; Acts 2:47; 4:35; 1 Tim 5:3

6 AND in those days, when the number of the disciples was multiplied, there arose a murmuring of the Grecians against the Hebrews, because their widows were neglected in the daily ministration.

2 Then the twelve called the multitude of the disciples *unto them,* and said, It is not reason that we should leave the word of God, and serve tables.

6:3☆ Acts 2:4; Eph 5:18; 1 Tim 3:7, 8

3 Wherefore, brethren, look ye out among you seven men of honest report, full of the Holy Ghost and wisdom, whom we may appoint over this business.

6:4 Acts 1:14; 2:42

4 But we will give ourselves continually to prayer, and to the ministry of the word.

6:5☆ Acts 8:5; 21:8

5 ¶And the saying pleased the whole multitude: and they chose Stephen, a man full of faith and of the Holy Ghost, and Philip, and Proch′o-rus, and Ni-ca′nor, and Ti′mon, and Par′me-nas, and Nicolas a proselyte of Antioch:

6:6 Num 8:10; Acts 1:24; 13:3; 1 Tim 4:14; 2 Tim 1:6; Heb 6:2

6 Whom they set before the apostles: and when they had prayed, they laid *their* hands on them.

6:7 Jn 12:42; Acts 12:24; 19:20; 21:20; Col 1:6

7 And the word of God increased; and the number of the disciples multiplied in Jerusalem greatly; and a great company of the priests were obedient to the faith.

6. Stephen, the First Christian Martyr

a. Stephen Arrested

6:8☆ Jn 14:12

8 And Stephen, full of faith and power, did great wonders and miracles among the people.

6:9☆ Mt 27:32; Acts 2:10; 18:24; 21:39; 24:18

9 ¶Then there arose certain of the synagogue, which is called *the synagogue* of the Lib′er-tines, and Cy-re′ni-ans, and Alexandrians, and of them of Ci-li′ci-a and of Asia, disputing with Stephen.

6:10 Ex 4:12; Lk 21:15

10 And they were not able to resist the wisdom and the spirit by which he spake.

6:11 Mt 26:59

11 Then they suborned men, which said, We have heard him speak blasphemous words against Moses, and *against* God.

6:12 Lk 20:1; Acts 4:1

12 And they stirred up the people, and the elders, and the scribes, and came upon *him,* and caught him, and brought *him* to the council,

6:13☆ Mt 26:59; Acts 7:58; 21:28

13 And set up false witnesses, which said, This man ceaseth not to speak blasphemous words against this holy place, and the law:

6:14 Mt 26:60, 61; Jn 2:19–21

14 For we have heard him say, that this Jesus of Nazareth shall destroy this place, and shall change the customs which Moses delivered us.

6:1 The Hellenists and the Hebrews may be designated as follows: the Hellenists were Jews who spoke Greek and followed some of the Greek customs; the Hebrews were conservative Jews who spoke Hebrew (or Aramaic) and refused to keep Greek customs. The Hebrews probably were natives of Jerusalem. A certain tension between these diverse groups in the early church is not surprising.

6:3 Deacons were to be selected only if they met three qualifications: (1) they were to be men of good report; (2) they had to have the gift of wisdom; and (3) they had to be full of the Holy Spirit. The third qualification *was the most important. Obviously,* not all of the male believers in that day were Spirit-filled. If they had been, there would have been no need to specify this as a qualification. Since all the believers were sealed and indwelt, it follows that the Spirit's filling is something additional. More frequently than not, this infilling takes place in the lives of believers subsequent to their conversion, occurring when certain conditions have been met.

6:5 *Nicolas,* one of the first seven deacons, was a Gentile who came to Christ at Antioch. The church fathers thought he was the founder of the Nicolaitan sect, which practiced all kinds of wickedness. If this was so, his appointment to the role of deacon represented a marked departure from the kind of person he had been.

6:8 *full of faith and power,* i.e., he had strong faith, which was reinforced by the powerful presence of the Holy Spirit in his heart and life.

6:9 Synagogue. See note on 13:5.

6:13 Even religious leaders do not have the right to use wrongful means to attain what they think to be rightful ends. It is never right to induce witnesses to commit perjury, no matter how right the cause may be. In this case both the means and the issue at stake were contrary to justice.

15 And all that sat in the council, looking stedfastly on him, saw his face
as it had been the face of an angel.

b. Stephen's Own Defense

7 THEN said the high priest, Are these things so?
2 And he said, Men, brethren, and fathers, hearken; The God of
glory appeared unto our father Abraham, when he was in Mes-o-po-ta′-
mi-a, before he dwelt in Char′ran,
3 And said unto him, Get thee out of thy country, and from thy kindred,
and come into the land which I shall shew thee.
4 Then came he out of the land of the Chal-dæ′ans, and dwelt in
Char′ran: and from thence, when his father was dead, he removed him into
this land, wherein ye now dwell.
5 And he gave him none inheritance in it, no, not *so much as* to set his foot
on: yet he promised that he would give it to him for a possession, and to his
seed after him, when *as yet* he had no child.
6 And God spake on this wise, That his seed should sojourn in a strange
land; and that they should bring them into bondage, and entreat *them* evil
four hundred years.
7 And the nation to whom they shall be in bondage will I judge, said God:
and after that shall they come forth, and serve me in this place.
8 And he gave him the covenant of circumcision: and so *Abraham* begat
Isaac, and circumcised him the eighth day; and Isaac *begat* Jacob; and
Jacob *begat* the twelve patriarchs.
9 And the patriarchs, moved with envy, sold Joseph into Egypt: but God
was with him,
10 And delivered him out of all his afflictions, and gave him favour and
wisdom in the sight of Pharaoh king of Egypt; and he made him governor
over Egypt and all his house.
11 Now there came a dearth over all the land of Egypt and Cha′naan, and
great affliction: and our fathers found no sustenance.
12 But when Jacob heard that there was corn in Egypt, he sent out our
fathers first.
13 And at the second *time* Joseph was made known to his brethren; and
Joseph's kindred was made known unto Pharaoh.
14 Then sent Joseph, and called his father Jacob to *him*, and all his
kindred, threescore and fifteen souls.
15 So Jacob went down into Egypt, and died, he, and our fathers,
16 And were carried over into Sy′chem, and laid in the sepulchre that

6:15 Mt 28:3
☆**7:2** Gen 15:7
7:3 Gen 12:1
7:4 Gen 11:31; 12:4 Heb 11:8
7:5 Gen 12:7 13:15, 16 17:7, 8; 26:3
☆**7:6** Gen 15:13 Ex 12:40 Gal 3:17 1 Pet 2:11
7:7 Ex 3:12
7:8 Gen 17:9, 10 21:1, 2; 25:26 35:23–26 1 Chron 1:34 Mt 1:2
☆**7:9** Gen 37:4, 11, 28 39:2 Ps 105:17
7:10 Gen 42:6 Ps 37:23; 105:21
7:11 Gen 41:54
7:12 Gen 42:2
7:13 Gen 45:1–4
7:14 Gen 45:9; 46:27 Deut 10:22
7:15 Gen 49:33 Ex 1:6
☆**7:16** Gen 23:16

7:2ff Stephen's detailed defense of himself is broken off rather abruptly at verse 50. Evidently his enemies would not listen to him any further. Justice presupposes that the defendant has a right to state his case fully and fairly. In his discourse Stephen quotes from the Septuagint rather than from the Hebrew text of Scripture, just as we quote from English translations rather than from the Hebrew and the Greek originals.
7:6 *four hundred years.* Exod. 12:40 says 430 years. "Four hundred" may be a round number here. Rabbinical tradition reckoned 400 years from Isaac's birth to the Exodus. Paul's 430-year figure (Gal. 3:17) spans the divine promise to Abraham to the Exodus. Depending on the starting point, either figure is correct.
7:9 Joseph, Jacob's darling, was abused by his brethren, who sold him into slavery. So also was Christ, the Father's darling, abused by wicked men.
7:16 Stephen is supposed by some to have made a mistake here. In the Old Testament we read that Abraham purchased a field from Ephron the Hittite; it included what is called the Cave of Machpelah, where he buried Sarah and where he, Isaac, and Jacob were also buried (Gen. 23:17ff; 50:13). Jacob made a land purchase from the children of Hamor, Shechem's father, according to Gen. 33:19. Stephen's statement seems to contradict these facts. At least two explanations have been offered. Scofield argues that the field Jacob purchased was the same field Abraham had bought, but that the land had changed hands at least once before Jacob *repurchased* it. Dr. Daniel Whitby explains the apparent discrepancy this way: "Jacob went down into Egypt and died, he and our fathers; and (our fathers) were carried over into Sychem (Shechem); and he, that is, Jacob, was laid in the sepulchre that Abraham bought for a sum of money (Gen 33:16). (Or, they were laid there, that is, Abraham, Isaac, and

Abraham bought for a sum of money of the sons of Em'mor *the father* of
Sy'chem.
7:17, 18 17 But when the time of the promise drew nigh, which God had sworn to
Gen 15:13 Ex 1:7, 8 Abraham, the people grew and multiplied in Egypt.
18 Till another king arose, which knew not Joseph.
7:19☆ 19 The same dealt subtilly with our kindred, and evil entreated our fathers,
Ex 1:10, 15, 16 so that they cast out their young children, to the end they might not live.
7:20 20 In which time Moses was born, and was exceeding fair, and nourished
Ex 2:1, 2 Heb 11:23 up in his father's house three months:
21 And when he was cast out, Pharaoh's daughter took him up, and
nourished him for her own son.
7:22 22 And Moses was learned in all the wisdom of the Egyptians, and was
1 Kgs 4:30 mighty in words and in deeds.
7:23 23 And when he was full forty years old, it came into his heart to visit his
Ex 2:11 brethren the children of Israel.
7:24 24 And seeing one *of them* suffer wrong, he defended *him,* and avenged
Ex 2:12 him that was oppressed, and smote the Egyptian:
7:25☆ 25 For he supposed his brethren would have understood how that God by
his hand would deliver them: but they understood not.
26 And the next day he shewed himself unto them as they strove, and
would have set them at one again, saying, Sirs, ye are brethren; why do ye
wrong one to another?
7:27, 28 27 But he that did his neighbour wrong thrust him away, saying, Who
Ex 2:14 made thee a ruler and a judge over us?
28 Wilt thou kill me, as thou diddest the Egyptian yesterday?
7:29 29 Then fled Moses at this saying, and was a stranger in the land of Ma'di-
Ex 2:15 an, where he begat two sons.
7:30☆ 30 And when forty years were expired, there appeared to him in the
Ex 3:2 Deut 33:16 wilderness of mount Si'na an angel of the Lord in a flame of fire in a bush.
31 When Moses saw *it,* he wondered at the sight: and as he drew near to
behold *it,* the voice of the Lord came unto him,
7:32 32 *Saying,* I *am* the God of thy fathers, the God of Abraham, and the God
Ex 3:6 of Isaac, and the God of Jacob. Then Moses trembled, and durst not
behold.
7:33 33 Then said the Lord to him, Put off thy shoes from thy feet: for the place
Josh 5:15 where thou standest is holy ground.
7:34 34 I have seen, I have seen the affliction of my people which is in Egypt,
Ex 3:7, 10 and I have heard their groaning, and am come down to deliver them. And
now come, I will send thee into Egypt.
7:35 35 This Moses whom they refused, saying, Who made thee a ruler and a
Ex 14:19 Num 20:16 judge? the same did God send *to be* a ruler and a deliverer by the hand of
the angel which appeared to him in the bush.
7:36 36 He brought them out, after that he had shewed wonders and signs in
Ex 7:3; 12:40, 41 16:35 the land of Egypt, and in the Red sea, and in the wilderness forty years.

Jacob.) And they, namely, the other patriarchs, were buried in the sepulchre bought of the sons of Emmor (Hamor), the father of Sychem (Shechem)." (See also Gleason L. Archer's *Encyclopedia of Bible Difficulties,* Zondervan, 1982, pp. 379, 380.)

7:19 *dealt subtilly.* Egypt dealt with the Hebrews *cruelly and deceitfully.* No one serves himself wisely who deals deceitfully with others. Egypt found this out later when God destroyed the nation.

7:25 *they understood not.* Stephen was accused of blaspheming Moses (6:13, 14). He asks his listeners to look at what their fathers had done to Moses, whom they did not understand when he tried to deliver them from their enemies. He warns them to take heed that they do not reject the one whom God has now sent to deliver them from a worse Egypt. If they reject Stephen's word from God, they will suffer a worse punishment than did their forefathers who died in the wilderness and did not enter the promised land.

7:30ff Stephen shows how he favors Moses, and he quotes him with approbation. God called him and sent him to deliver Israel from Egypt. Israel refused to obey Moses and went so far as to make a golden calf. Stephen argues that their treatment of himself is similar to the treatment accorded Moses by their forefathers and thus they are guilty of the same kind of sin.

37 ¶This is that Moses, which said unto the children of Israel, A prophet
shall the Lord your God raise up unto you of your brethren, like unto me;
him shall ye hear.
38 This is he, that was in the church in the wilderness with the angel which
spake to him in the mount Si'na, and *with* our fathers: who received the
lively oracles to give unto us:
39 To whom our fathers would not obey, but thrust *him* from them, and in
their hearts turned back again into Egypt,
40 Saying unto Aaron, Make us gods to go before us: for *as for* this Moses,
which brought us out of the land of Egypt, we wot not what is become of
him.
41 And they made a calf in those days, and offered sacrifice unto the idol,
and rejoiced in the works of their own hands.
42 Then God turned, and gave them up to worship the host of heaven; as
it is written in the book of the prophets, O ye house of Israel, have ye
offered to me slain beasts and sacrifices *by the space of* forty years in the
wilderness?
43 Yea, ye took up the tabernacle of Mo'loch, and the star of your god
Rem'phan, figures which ye made to worship them: and I will carry you
away beyond Babylon.
44 Our fathers had the tabernacle of witness in the wilderness, as he had
appointed, speaking unto Moses, that he should make it according to the
fashion that he had seen.
45 Which also our fathers that came after brought in with Jesus into the
possession of the Gentiles, whom God drave out before the face of our
fathers, unto the days of David;
46 Who found favour before God, and desired to find a tabernacle for the
God of Jacob.
47 But Solomon built him an house.
48 Howbeit the most High dwelleth not in temples made with hands; as
saith the prophet,
49 Heaven *is* my throne, and earth *is* my footstool: what house will ye
build me? saith the Lord: or what *is* the place of my rest?
50 Hath not my hand made all these things?
51 ¶Ye stiffnecked and uncircumcised in heart and ears, ye do always
resist the Holy Ghost: as your fathers *did*, so *do* ye.
52 Which of the prophets have not your fathers persecuted? and they have
slain them which shewed before of the coming of the Just One; of whom ye
have been now the betrayers and murderers:

☆**7:37** Deut 18:15 Mt 17:5 Acts 3:22
7:38 Ex 19:2, 3, 17 20:1 Deut 32:47 Rom 3:2
7:39 Num 14:3
7:40 Ex 32:1, 23
7:42 Deut 17:2, 3 Josh 24:20 2 Kgs 17:16 Isa 63:10 Jer 19:13 Ezek 20:25 Amos 5:25–27 2 Thess 2:11
☆**7:43**
7:44 Ex 25:8, 40 Heb 8:5
7:45 Josh 3:13, 14 18:1; 22:19 2 Sam 7:6 1 Chron 17:5 21:29 2 Chron 1:3
7:46 2 Sam 7:1–14 1 Kgs 8:17 Ps 132:1–5
7:47 2 Sam 7:12, 13 1 Kgs 8:20
7:48 2 Chron 2:6 Isa 57:15 Mt 5:34 Eph 2:22 1 Pet 2:5
7:49, 50 Isa 66:1, 2
☆**7:51** Ex 32:9 Isa 48:4 Ezek 44:9
☆**7:52** 2 Chron 36:16 Mt 23:30–34 Acts 3:14 1 Thess 2:15

7:37 *like unto me,* i.e., "much like me." Jesus occupied the offices of prophet, priest, and king. Here he is the "Prophet" promised by Moses in Deut. 18:15. As prophet, he came to declare God's counsel and to reveal God's person. As God's spokesman, he pointed men to God the Father, indicating that all have sinned and all need a Savior. As priest (Heb. 8:1), he filled the office of the one who offers the sacrifice and who is the sacrifice (the Lamb of God). He entered the Holy of Holies as a priest and sprinkled the blood (his own) on the mercy seat of God. As king, he has inherited the throne of his father David. He who was rejected by the Jews and was given a crown of thorns, a reed, and a cross, has been raised from the dead and now "sits on the throne of the highest honor in heaven, next to God" (2:33, TLB). From there he shall someday come to judge the living and the dead as King of kings and Lord of lords (Rev 19:16), "and he shall reign for ever and ever" (Rev. 11:15).

7:43 *Moloch* and *Remphan* (or, "Rephan"). In Hebrew their names are *Sakkuth* and *Kaiwan,* the former a Canaanite deity, the latter believed to be an Egyptian god.

7:51 Stephen accused his listeners of resisting the Holy Spirit as their fathers had done. When the Jews in the Old Testament resisted the prophets, they were resisting the Holy Spirit, who guided the prophets. Whoever persecutes or silences those who speak under the inspiration of the Holy Spirit is guilty of the same sin.

7:52 Nothing Stephen said could have angered his listeners more than his accusation that they were betrayers and murderers of Jesus. Nothing angers unbelieving Jews today more than the accusation that such was the case. It is most unfortunate for anyone to speak of today's Jews as "Christ-slayers," unless he makes it clear that Jews and Gentiles are equally responsible for the death of Jesus.

7:53 Ex 20:1 Gal 3:19 Heb 2:2

53 Who have received the law by the disposition of angels, and have not
kept *it.*

c. Stephen Stoned to Death

54 ¶When they heard these things, they were cut to the heart, and they
gnashed on him with *their* teeth.

7:55 Mt 26:64 Mk 16:19 Acts 2:33, 34 5:31 Rom 8:34 Col 3:1 Heb 1:3, 13 8:1; 10:12 12:2 1 Pet 3:22

7:56 Mt 3:16 Heb 9:24

7:58☆ Lev 24:14–16 Deut 17:7

7:59 Ps 31:5 Lk 23:46

7:60 Mt 5:44 Lk 6:28; 23:34 Rev 14:13

55 But he, being full of the Holy Ghost, looked up stedfastly into heaven,
and saw the glory of God, and Jesus standing on the right hand of God,
56 And said, Behold, I see the heavens opened, and the Son of man
standing on the right hand of God.
57 Then they cried out with a loud voice, and stopped their ears, and ran
upon him with one accord,
58 And cast *him* out of the city, and stoned *him:* and the witnesses laid
down their clothes at a young man's feet, whose name was Saul.
59 And they stoned Stephen, calling upon *God,* and saying, Lord Jesus,
receive my spirit.
60 And he kneeled down, and cried with a loud voice, Lord, lay not this
sin to their charge. And when he had said this, he fell asleep.

d. The Flight of the Believers

8:1☆ Acts 7:58; 9:31 11:19

8 AND Saul was consenting unto his death. And at that time there was
a great persecution against the church which was at Jerusalem; and
they were all scattered abroad throughout the regions of Judæa and Sa-
ma'ri-a, except the apostles.

8:2☆ 2 Sam 3:31, 32

2 And devout men carried Stephen *to his burial,* and made great lamenta-
tion over him.

8:3 Acts 9:1, 22:4 26:10 1 Cor 15:9 Gal 1:13 Phil 3:6 1 Tim 1:13

3 As for Saul, he made havock of the church, entering into every house,
and haling man and women committed *them* to prison.

II. CHURCH PLANTING IN JUDEA AND SAMARIA (8:4—11:18)

A. PHILIP EVANGELIZING

1. Preaching at Samaria

8:4☆ Acts 11:19

4 Therefore they that were scattered abroad went every where preaching
the word.

8:5 Acts 6:5; 15:35

5 Then Philip went down to the city of Sa-ma'ri-a, and preached Christ
unto them.

7:58 *and stoned him.* The Mishnah (a division of the Talmud) relates that after a person was convicted and sentenced to die by stoning, he would be taken to the stoning place outside the court. Before the actual execution the victim was called upon to make a confession. As he got close to the stoning place, his garments were removed. Then one of the witnesses would push the accused into a twelve-foot-deep pit. If this did not kill the victim, a second witness would drop a large stone on his heart. If he still lived, he would then be stoned by all the members of the congregation of Israel. Saul (Paul) was present at Stephen's death; he approved of the stoning. According to 22:20 he kept the clothes of the executioners; he was determined not to forget his antipathy toward those who embraced the Christian faith.

8:1 God changed some names in the Old Testament: Abram became Abraham, Sarai became Sarah, Jacob became Israel. But God did not change the name of Saul to Paul. Saul was his Hebrew name; Paul was his Greek name (see 13:9).

8:2 *devout men.* It is not clear whether these were Christians who braved the persecution or whether they were godly and sympathetic Jews.†

8:4 *they,* i.e., "the believers." The primary mission of the church is to preach the good news. This mission can be accomplished by (1) evangelism through direct oral presentation or mass communication media; (2) medical missions, by which the healing of men's bodies opens the door to bringing healing to men's souls through gospel witnessing; (3) education, by which people interested in improving themselves can be reached by the gospel; and (4) literary work: the translation of the Bible, or parts of it, or the writing of books, articles, and tracts and their dissemination, by which men can come to know Christ as Savior.

6 And the people with one accord gave heed unto those things which
Philip spake, hearing and seeing the miracles which he did.
7 For unclean spirits, crying with loud voice, came out of many that were **8:7** Mt 10:1
possessed *with them:* and many taken with palsies, and that were lame, were Mk 16:17
healed. Lk 10:17
8 And there was great joy in that city. **8:8** Jn 4:40

2. The Winning of Simon the Sorcerer

9 But there was a certain man, called Simon, which beforetime in the same ☆**8:9** Acts 5:36; 13:6
city used sorcery, and bewitched the people of Sa-ma′ri-a, giving out that
himself was some great one:
10 To whom they all gave heed, from the least to the greatest, saying, This ☆**8:10**
man is the great power of God.
11 And to him they had regard, because that of long time he had
bewitched them with sorceries.
12 But when they believed Philip preaching the things concerning the **8:12** Acts 1:3; 2:38
kingdom of God, and the name of Jesus Christ, they were baptized, both
men and women.
13 Then Simon himself believed also: and when he was baptized, he ☆**8:13** Acts 19:11
continued with Philip, and wondered, beholding the miracles and signs
which were done.
14 Now when the apostles which were at Jerusalem heard that Sa-ma′ri-a **8:14** Acts 8:1
had received the word of God, they sent unto them Peter and John:
15 Who, when they were come down, prayed for them, that they might **8:15** Acts 2:38
receive the Holy Ghost: 19:2
16 (For as yet he was fallen upon none of them: only they were baptized in **8:16** Acts 10:48
the name of the Lord Jesus.)
17 Then laid they *their* hands on them, and they received the Holy Ghost. ☆**8:17** Acts 2:4
18 And when Simon saw that through laying on of the apostles' hands the
Holy Ghost was given, he offered them money,
19 Saying, Give me also this power, that on whomsoever I lay hands, he
may receive the Holy Ghost. **8:20** Mic 3:11, 12
20 But Peter said unto him, Thy money perish with thee, because thou hast Mt 10:8
thought that the gift of God may be purchased with money. Acts 2:38
21 Thou hast neither part nor lot in this matter: for thy heart is not right **8:21** Jer 17:9
in the sight of God. Eph 5:5

8:9ff *Simon,* a magician, was thought to manifest the power of God. Following his dubious conversion he sought to buy this power so that it could be conveyed to others by the laying on of his hands (8:19). No doubt he wanted this power to increase his authority and enlarge his prestige among men. He was severely rebuked by Peter, who urged upon him the necessity for repentance. The word "simony" (the crime of buying or selling ecclesiastical preferment) is derived from this incident.

8:10 *This man is the great power of God.* The Samaritans attributed to Simon the great power of God, when actually the power was from Satan. Thus, devils pass for deities. This sort of thing will be reproduced at the end of the age, according to Rev. 13:2–5.

8:13 A miracle has been defined as "an effect in nature not attributable to any of the recognized operations of nature, nor to the act of man, but indicative of a superhuman power, and serving as a sign or witness thereof; a wonderful work manifesting a power superior to the ordinary forces of nature." Miracles differ from providence, which has to do with preservation and government. God's providences are numerous; miracles are much rarer, for God does not do supernaturally what can be done naturally. Generally a person recovers from surgery by providence, not by miracle. While there may be miracles that occur in the pattern of providence, they are the exception. Many of the so-called miracles attested to by sincere Christians fall instead within the scope of God's providence. (See note on Prov. 16:33 for a definition of providence.) Miracles are so imbedded in Scripture that to take away the supernatural or miraculous would make Christianity nonsensical as well as unbelievable.

8:17 *they received the Holy Ghost.* The receiving of the Holy Spirit must have been accompanied by some sign or signs that impressed Simon the sorcerer. Whatever it was, he wanted it—whether for good or for bad reasons. He offered money if the apostles would give him the power to confer the Holy Spirit to others by laying on of his hands. He was wrong in supposing that it came from the laying on of hands.

8:22 Isa 55:7 Dan 4:27

22 Repent therefore of this thy wickedness, and pray God, if perhaps the
thought of thine heart may be forgiven thee.

8:23☆ Heb 12:15

23 For I perceive that thou art in the gall of bitterness, and *in* the bond of
iniquity.

8:24 Gen 20:7 Ex 8:8 Num 21:7 Job 42:8 Jas 5:16

24 Then answered Simon, and said, Pray ye to the Lord for me, that none
of these things which ye have spoken come upon me.
25 And they, when they had testified and preached the word of the Lord,
returned to Jerusalem, and preached the gospel in many villages of the Sa-
mar′i-tans.

3. The Winning of the Ethiopian Eunuch

8:26☆ Ps 91:11 Heb 1:14

26 And the angel of the Lord spake unto Philip, saying, Arise, and go
toward the south unto the way that goeth down from Jerusalem unto Ga′za,
which is desert.

8:27☆ 1 Kgs 8:41, 42 Ps 68:29 Isa 43:6, 53:7 56:3 Zeph 3:10

27 And he arose and went: and, behold, a man of E-thi-o′pi-a, an eunuch
of great authority under Can′da-ce queen of the E-thi-o′pi-ans, who had the
charge of all her treasure, and had come to Jerusalem for to worship,
28 Was returning, and sitting in his chariot read E-sai′as the prophet.

8:29☆

29 Then the Spirit said unto Philip, Go near, and join thyself to this
chariot.
30 And Philip ran thither to *him*, and heard him read the prophet E-sai′as,
and said, Understandest thou what thou readest?

8:31 2 Cor 3:14

31 And he said, How can I, except some man should guide me? And he
desired Philip that he would come up and sit with him.

8:32, 33☆ Isa 53:7, 8 Phil 2:7, 8

32 The place of the scripture which he read was this, He was led as a sheep
to the slaughter; and like a lamb dumb before his shearer, so opened he not
his mouth:
33 In his humiliation his judgment was taken away: and who shall declare
his generation? for his life is taken from the earth.
34 And the eunuch answered Philip, and said, I pray thee, of whom
speaketh the prophet this? of himself, or of some other man?

8:35 Lk 24:27 Acts 18:28

35 Then Philip opened his mouth, and began at the same scripture, and
preached unto him Jesus.
36 And as they went on *their* way, they came unto a certain water: and the
eunuch said, See, *here is* water; what doth hinder me to be baptized?

8:23 *thou art in the gall of bitterness,* i.e., he was odious to God, abominable to God, and the end of this estate would be as bitter as wormwood.

8:26ff Philip is directed first by an angel of God to start his journey toward the south. Then he is commanded by the Holy Spirit to join himself to the chariot of the Ethiopian eunuch (8:29). Neither the Spirit nor the angel was to explain the Scripture to the eunuch. This duty was reserved for the church, that is, the human followers of the Lamb. The eunuch was ripe fruit waiting to be harvested. It may be said that wherever and whenever anyone sincerely wants to know God, God will, one way or another, make himself known.

This passage illustrates what personal witnessing is all about. Christ has commanded the church to be a witnessing body. Every believer who is part of that body of Christ is called to be a witness; whoever fails this call *can become spiritually stagnant. All witnessing is to be* done through the instrumentality and power of the Holy Spirit. Philip's witness was marked by prayer, humility, obedience, enthusiasm, compassion, tact, holy boldness, guidance by the Spirit, and knowledge of the Word of God. He preached Jesus, he pressed for a decision, he followed the eunuch's commitment by water baptism, and joy attended his ministry. Love, loyalty, and gratitude to Christ constitute the motivation for personal witness.

8:27 The Ethiopian eunuch had gone to Jerusalem to worship in the temple as a proselyte. He came to Christ under the witness of Philip, and was the second Gentile convert to be mentioned by name in Acts. (Cf. note on 6:5 regarding Nicolas.)

8:29 Among other activities, the Holy Spirit (1) directs God's servants where, when, and what they are to do or preach (8:29; 10:19, 20; 16:6, 7; 1 Cor. 2:13); (2) chooses and commissions workers for service (13:2; 20:28); (3) teaches the church the truth about Jesus (John 14:26; 1 Cor. 12:3); (4) testifies to the Son and magnifies him (John 15:26; 16:14); (5) reproves sinners and convicts them of their guilt (John 16:8); and (6) communicates God's truth to men (1:16; 1 Pet. 1:11, 12; 2 Pet. 1:21). Believers may quench the Spirit or grieve him (Eph. 4:30; 1 Thess. 5:19).

8:33 *who shall declare his generation?* i.e., "who can express the wickedness of the people of his generation." Alternatively, "who will be able to speak of his posterity. . . ."†

37 And Philip said, If thou believest with all thine heart, thou mayest. And
he answered and said, I believe that Jesus Christ is the Son of God.
38 And he commanded the chariot to stand still: and they went down both
into the water, both Philip and the eunuch; and he baptized him.
39 And when they were come up out of the water, the Spirit of the Lord
caught away Philip, that the eunuch saw him no more: and he went on his
way rejoicing.
40 But Philip was found at A-zo′tus: and passing through he preached in
all the cities, till he came to Cæs-a-re′a.

☆**8:37** Mt 16:16; 28:19 Mk 16:16 Jn 6:69; 11:27 Rom 10:10
☆**8:39** 1 Kgs 18:12 2 Kgs 2:16 Ezek 3:12

B. THE CONVERSION OF PAUL OF TARSUS
1. Christ Confronts Paul on the Damascus Road

9 AND Saul, yet breathing out threatenings and slaughter against the
disciples of the Lord, went unto the high priest,
2 And desired of him letters to Damascus to the synagogues, that if he
found any of this way, whether they were men or women, he might bring
them bound unto Jerusalem.
3 And as he journeyed, he came near Damascus: and suddenly there
shined round about him a light from heaven:
4 And he fell to the earth, and heard a voice saying unto him, Saul, Saul,
why persecutest thou me?
5 And he said, Who art thou, Lord? And the Lord said, I am Jesus whom
thou persecutest: *it is* hard for thee to kick against the pricks.
6 And he trembling and astonished said, Lord, what wilt thou have me to
do? And the Lord *said* unto him, Arise, and go into the city, and it shall be
told thee what thou must do.
7 And the men which journeyed with him stood speechless, hearing a
voice, but seeing no man.
8 And Saul arose from the earth; and when his eyes were opened, he saw
no man: but they led him by the hand, and brought *him* into Damascus.
9 And he was three days without sight, and neither did eat nor drink.

9:1 Acts 8:3 Gal 1:13 1 Tim 1:13
☆**9:2** Acts 22:5, 26:10
9:3 Acts 22:6, 7 26:12, 13 1 Cor 15:8
☆**9:5** Acts 5:39
☆**9:6**
9:7 Dan 10:7 Acts 22:9; 26:14

2. Paul Baptized by Ananias

10 ¶And there was a certain disciple at Damascus, named An-a-ni′as; and
to him said the Lord in a vision, An-a-ni′as. And he said, Behold, I *am here*,
Lord.
11 And the Lord *said* unto him, Arise, and go into the street which is
called Straight, and inquire in the house of Judas for *one* called Saul of
Tarsus: for, behold, he prayeth,
12 And hath seen in a vision a man named An-a-ni′as coming in, and
putting *his* hand on him, that he might receive his sight.
13 Then An-a-ni′as answered, Lord, I have heard by many of this man,
how much evil he hath done to thy saints at Jerusalem:
14 And here he hath authority from the chief priests to bind all that call on
thy name.
15 But the Lord said unto him, Go thy way: for he is a chosen vessel unto

9:10 Acts 10:3; 11:5 12:9; 22:12
9:11 Acts 21:39
9:13 Acts 26:10
9:14 1 Cor 1:2
9:15 Acts 13:2 22:21; 26:1–18 Rom 1:1, 5 11:13 1 Cor 15:10 Gal 1:15, 16 2:7–9 Eph 3:7 1 Tim 2:7 2 Tim 1:11

8:37 The earliest manuscripts do not contain this verse.
8:39 Philip was miraculously transported by the Spirit of God from his place beside the eunuch to another destination. This would have provided the eunuch outward corroborating evidence that what had happened indeed proceeded from a miracle-working God.
9:2 *way.* In the Acts Christians were called the people of the "Way" (see also 19:9, 23; 24:14, 22). In 18:26 it is called "the way of God," and "the way of salvation" in 16:17. Jesus said, "I am the way" (John 14:6); by faith in him people become followers of the way.
9:5, 6 This is undoubtedly the point at which Paul received Christ and was regenerated, sealed, and indwelt by the Holy Spirit.

me, to bear my name before the Gentiles, and kings, and the children of
Israel:
9:16☆ Acts 20:23 21:11 — 16 For I will shew him how great things he must suffer for my name's sake.
2 Cor 11:23–27 — 17 And An-a-ni′as went his way, and entered into the house; and putting
9:17☆ — his hands on him said, Brother Saul, the Lord, *even* Jesus, that appeared
Acts 2:4; 13:52 — unto thee in the way as thou camest, hath sent me, that thou mightest
22:12, 13 — receive thy sight, and be filled with the Holy Ghost.
18 And immediately there fell from his eyes as it had been scales: and he
received sight forthwith, and arose, and was baptized.

3. Paul Preaches at Damascus

9:19 Acts 26:20 — 19 And when he had received meat, he was strengthened. Then was Saul
certain days with the disciples which were at Damascus.
20 And straightway he preached Christ in the synagogues, that he is the
Son of God.
9:21 Acts 8:3 — 21 But all that heard *him* were amazed, and said; Is not this he that
Gal 1:13 — destroyed them which called on this name in Jerusalem, and came hither
for that intent, that he might bring them bound unto the chief priests?
9:22 Acts 18:28 — 22 But Saul increased the more in strength, and confounded the Jews
which dwelt at Damascus, proving that this is very Christ.

4. Paul Escapes from the Jewish Leaders

9:23☆ Gal 1:17, 18 — 23 ¶And after that many days were fulfilled, the Jews took counsel to kill
him:
9:24 Acts 20:3; 23:12 — 24 But their laying await was known of Saul. And they watched the gates
25:3 — day and night to kill him.
2 Cor 11:32 **9:25** — 25 Then the disciples took him by night, and let *him* down by the wall in
Josh 2:15 1 Sam 19:12 — a basket.

5. Paul's Reception by the Jerusalem Church

9:26☆ Acts 22:17, 18 — 26 And when Saul was come to Jerusalem, he assayed to join himself to
the disciples: but they were all afraid of him, and believed not that he was
a disciple.
9:27 Acts 4:36 — 27 But Barnabas took him, and brought *him* to the apostles, and declared
11:24; 13:2 — unto them how he had seen the Lord in the way, and that he had spoken to
him, and how he had preached boldly at Damascus in the name of Jesus.
9:29 — 28 And he was with them coming in and going out at Jerusalem.
Acts 4:13 2 Cor 11:26 — 29 And he spake boldly in the name of the Lord Jesus, and disputed
Phil 1:14 Eph 6:19 — against the Grecians: but they went about to slay him.
9:30 — 30 *Which* when the brethren knew, they brought him down to Cæs-a-re′a,
Gal 1:21 — and sent him forth to Tarsus.
9:31☆ Acts 5:11; 8:1 — 31 Then had the churches rest throughout all Judæa and Galilee and Sa-

---

9:16 This prophetic word was fulfilled in the life and ministry of Paul. A partial description of Paul's sufferings is recorded in 2 Cor. 11. No believer can suppose that salvation guarantees exemption from suffering. As believers, we have only the certainty of grace to bear whatever God allows.

9:17 It is here, subsequent to his conversion, that Paul is filled with the Holy Spirit. His entire life from that moment forward indicates that, unlike men such as Samson, he never lost the fullness of the Spirit. Nothing is said here or elsewhere about Paul's speaking in tongues either at his conversion or when he was filled with the Spirit.

9:23ff Paul has long since left Damascus and is now in Nabataean Arabia. Apparently the Jews of the area and the local government were annoyed with him and with his persistent preaching of Jesus. These enemies sought to kill him; but Paul escaped. The city gates were guarded, so he could not pass through them. But he was in a house built on the city wall; this facilitated his escape. The disciples placed him in a large basket, tied a rope to its handle, then lowered Paul to the ground outside the wall.

9:26 *They were all* afraid of him because they feared that he might be putting on an act that was insincere, and then would entrap them and bring them to their death.

9:31 *churches.* In the original text, this word appears in the singular. There were a number of local congregations, but here Luke marks off the unity of all

ma'ri-a, and were edified; and walking in the fear of the Lord, and in the
comfort of the Holy Ghost, were multiplied.

C. PETER EVANGELIZING

1. Aeneas Miraculously Healed

32 ¶And it came to pass, as Peter passed throughout all *quarters*, he came
down also to the saints which dwelt at Lyd'da.
33 And there he found a certain man named Æ-ne'as, which had kept his
bed eight years, and was sick of the palsy.
34 And Peter said unto him, Æ-ne'as, Jesus Christ maketh thee whole:
arise, and make thy bed. And he arose immediately.
35 And all that dwelt at Lyd'da and Sa'ron saw him, and turned to the
Lord.

2. Dorcas (Tabitha) Miraculously Restored to Life

36 ¶Now there was at Joppa a certain disciple named Tabitha, which by
interpretation is called Dorcas: this woman was full of good works and
almsdeeds which she did.
37 And it came to pass in those days, that she was sick, and died: whom
when they had washed, they laid *her* in an upper chamber.
38 And forasmuch as Lyd'da was nigh to Joppa, and the disciples had
heard that Peter was there, they sent unto him two men, desiring *him* that
he would not delay to come to them.
39 Then Peter arose and went with them. When he was come, they brought
him into the upper chamber: and all the widows stood by him weeping, and
shewing the coats and garments which Dorcas made, while she was with
them.
40 But Peter put them all forth, and kneeled down, and prayed; and
turning *him* to the body said, Tabitha, arise. And she opened her eyes: and
when she saw Peter, she sat up.
41 And he gave her *his* hand, and lifted her up, and when he had called the
saints and widows, presented her alive.
42 And it was known throughout all Joppa; and many believed in the
Lord.
43 And it came to pass, that he tarried many days in Joppa with one
Simon a tanner.

3. The Salvation of Cornelius

a. Cornelius' Vision

10 THERE was a certain man in Cæs-a-re'a called Cornelius, a
centurion of the band called the Italian *band*,
2 A devout *man*, and one that feared God with all his house, which gave
much alms to the people, and prayed to God alway.

☆**9:32** Acts 8:14
☆**9:34** Mt 9:6; Jn 5:8; Acts 3:6; 4:10
9:35 Acts 11:21
9:36 Prov 31:31; 1 Tim 2:9, 10; 5:10; Tit 3:8; Jas 1:27
☆**9:38**
9:40 1 Kgs 17:19–23; 2 Kgs 4:32–36; Mt 9:25; Mk 5:41, 42; Jn 11:43
9:42 Jn 11:45; 12:11
9:43 2 Chron 2:16; Ezra 3:7; Jonah 1:3; Acts 10:5, 6
☆**10:1** Acts 8:40; 27:1
10:2 Gen 18:19; Josh 24:15

believers as members of the one body. This spiritual unity transcends all of our divisions; in the New Jerusalem those differences will have disappeared.

9:32 *he came down also to the saints,* i.e., "to visit and talk with them."

9:34 In this miracle Paul calls on the power of Jesus Christ and says, *Christ maketh thee whole.* During the time of Jesus and the early apostles miracles were abundant, just as they were with Moses in Egypt and during the times of Elijah and Elisha. Since then miracles have not totally disappeared, but they are fewer in number. At the end of the age, miracles both by Satan and believers may increase dramatically in number.

9:38ff Tabitha, who died, was known for her good works. Her Christian friends washed the body but did not bury it. Instead they sent two men to bring Peter back with them. He came and commanded her to rise from the dead. This she did. It was so eminent a miracle and the facts were so widely known that many came to believe in Jesus Christ. We should expect that the preaching of Jesus' resurrection should have equally good response from those who hear of that miracle.

10:1ff Cornelius, the Roman army officer, was the third Gentile convert mentioned in Acts. As the Holy Spirit fell upon Cornelius, his household, and his friends, a new phase began in the spread of the good news. Peter referred specifically to this later (15:7–9), but at the time a vision from God caused him to preach to a Gentile.

10:3☆ Ps 34:7; Acts 11:13; Heb 1:14
10:4 2 Chron 7:15; Ps 65:1, 2; 141:2; Prov 15:29; Heb 6:10; 13:16; Jas 5:16; 1 Pet 3:2; Rev 5:8; 8:4
10:6 Acts 9:43; 11:14

3 He saw in a vision evidently about the ninth hour of the day an angel of
God coming in to him, and saying unto him, Cornelius.
4 And when he looked on him, he was afraid, and said, What is it, Lord?
And he said unto him, Thy prayers and thine alms are come up for a
memorial before God.
5 And now send men to Joppa, and call for *one* Simon, whose surname is
Peter:
6 He lodgeth with one Simon a tanner, whose house is by the sea side: he
shall tell thee what thou oughtest to do.
7 And when the angel which spake unto Cornelius was departed, he called
two of his household servants, and a devout soldier of them that waited on
him continually;
8 And when he had declared all *these* things unto them, he sent them to
Joppa.

b. Peter's Trance

10:9 Ps 55:17; Acts 11:5
10:10☆
10:11 Ezek 1:1–3; Mt 3:16; Acts 7:56; Rev 19:11
10:12☆
10:14 Lev 11:4–7; 20:25; Deut 14:3–5; Ezek 4:14
10:15 Mt 15:11; Rom 14:14, 17, 20; 1 Cor 10:25; 1 Tim 4:4; Tit 1:15
10:16☆

9 ¶On the morrow, as they went on their journey, and drew nigh unto the
city, Peter went up upon the housetop to pray about the sixth hour:
10 And he became very hungry, and would have eaten: but while they
made ready, he fell into a trance,
11 And saw heaven opened, and a certain vessel descending unto him, as it
had been a great sheet knit at the four corners, and let down to the earth:
12 Wherein were all manner of fourfooted beasts of the earth, and wild
beasts, and creeping things, and fowls of the air.
13 And there came a voice to him, Rise, Peter; kill, and eat.
14 But Peter said, Not so, Lord; for I have never eaten any thing that is
common or unclean.
15 And the voice *spake* unto him again the second time, What God hath
cleansed, *that* call not thou common.
16 This was done thrice: and the vessel was received up again into heaven.

c. Cornelius Sends for Peter

17 Now while Peter doubted in himself what this vision which he had seen
should mean, behold, the men which were sent from Cornelius had made
inquiry for Simon's house, and stood before the gate,
18 And called, and asked whether Simon, which was surnamed Peter, were
lodged there.

10:3 Cornelius devotedly followed the Jewish way of life, except for circumcision. He was a devout God-fearer. God sent an angel so that this Gentile could know the Messiah. The angel appeared in a vision that disturbed Cornelius but supplied him with the information he needed in order to obtain eternal life.

10:10ff For Peter to go to the home of Cornelius, some sort of earthshaking revelation from God would be required. Jews did not enter Gentile homes even if the people in the house were God-fearing. Jewish orthodoxy dictated that no nonkosher food was to be consumed, and no Gentile observed the kosher rules. *To partake of anything that was nonkosher* was forbidden. Orthodox Jews today will not eat both meat and dairy products at the same meal. They have different sets of dishes for dairy and meat meals. And no animal is "clean" that is not killed according to kosher rules. It required a trance and a conversation with Jesus (Peter said, "Not so, Lord," which suggests that Jesus appeared to him and that Peter recognized his voice) to convince Peter to visit Cornelius.

10:12 The Scripture here does not say whether the animals, reptiles, and birds were all unclean or whether there was a mixture of both clean and unclean creatures. The latter is likely because the Jews regarded the Gentiles as unclean. God was to show that his grace was sufficient for both Jew and Gentile. What God declares to be clean, men are not to call unclean. In Christ there are only clean people.

10:16 *This was done thrice.* We are not told whether the trebling of the vision was done to assure Peter that this was certain and not to be disputed, or whether Peter said no to God twice and only after the third appearance of the vision was he willing to capitulate. God often has respect for our weakness; therefore, when a believer doubts the first call of God, he gives a second witness to assure that servant that it is of God and not of self.

19¶While Peter thought on the vision, the Spirit said unto him, Behold,
three men seek thee.
20Arise therefore, and get thee down, and go with them, doubting
nothing: for I have sent them.
21Then Peter went down to the men which were sent unto him from
Cornelius; and said, Behold, I am he whom ye seek: what *is* the cause
wherefore ye are come?
22And they said, Cornelius the centurion, a just man, and one that feareth
God, and of good report among all the nation of the Jews, was warned from
God by an holy angel to send for thee into his house, and to hear words of
thee.

d. Peter Visits Cornelius

23Then called he them in, and lodged *them*. And on the morrow Peter
went away with them, and certain brethren from Joppa accompanied him.
24And the morrow after they entered into Cæs-a-re′a. And Cornelius
waited for them, and had called together his kinsmen and near friends.
25And as Peter was coming in, Cornelius met him, and fell down at his
feet, and worshipped *him*.
26But Peter took him up, saying, Stand up; I myself also am a man.
27And as he talked with him, he went in, and found many that were come
together.
28And he said unto them, Ye know how that it is an unlawful thing for a
man that is a Jew to keep company, or come unto one of another nation;
but God hath shewed me that I should not call any man common or
unclean.
29Therefore came I *unto you* without gainsaying, as soon as I was sent for:
I ask therefore for what intent ye have sent for me?
30And Cornelius said, Four days ago I was fasting until this hour; and at
the ninth hour I prayed in my house, and, behold, a man stood before me
in bright clothing,
31And said, Cornelius, thy prayer is heard, and thine alms are had in
remembrance in the sight of God.
32Send therefore to Joppa, and call hither Simon, whose surname is
Peter; he is lodged in the house of *one* Simon a tanner by the sea side: who,
when he cometh, shall speak unto thee.
33Immediately therefore I sent to thee; and thou hast well done that thou
art come. Now therefore are we all here present before God, to hear all
things that are commanded thee of God.

e. Peter Leads Cornelius to Christ

34¶Then Peter opened *his* mouth, and said, Of a truth I perceive that God
is no respecter of persons:
35But in every nation he that feareth him, and worketh righteousness, is
accepted with him.
36The word which *God* sent unto the children of Israel, preaching peace
by Jesus Christ: (he is Lord of all:)

☆**10:19** Acts 8:29; 11:12
10:20 Mt 28:19; Mk 16:15; Acts 15:7
10:22 Acts 10:2
10:23 Acts 10:45; 11:12
10:24 Acts 8:40; 10:1
10:26 Lk 4:8; Acts 14:14; Col 2:18; Rev 19:10; 22:9
10:28 Jn 4:9; Acts 11:3; 15:9; Gal 2:12
10:30 Acts 10:3–6
10:31 Prov 14:31; Dan 10:12; Mt 6:4; 10:42; 25:40; Heb 6:10
☆**10:33**
10:34 Job 34:19; Rom 2:11; Gal 2:6; Eph 6:9; Col 3:11, 25; 1 Pet 1:17
10:35 Acts 15:9; Rom 2:6–15; 3:22; 10:12; 1 Cor 12:13; Gal 3:28; Eph 2:13; 3:6
10:36 Isa 57:19; Dan 7:14; Mt 28:18; Lk 1:79; Rom 5:1; 1 Cor 15:27; Eph 2:17; Col 1:20; 1 Pet 3:22; Rev 19:16

10:19 *Peter thought on the vision.* Any adequate knowledge of the Old Testament would have convinced Peter that God is the God of the Gentiles, too (see Isa. 42:6, 7). *the Spirit said unto him.* We do not know whether this was an audible voice or an inward persuasion of the Spirit. In any event, Peter obeyed the command and Cornelius became a Christian.

10:33 *are we all here present . . . to hear all things.* Cornelius, his kinsmen, and close friends were gathered together, prepared to listen to the Word of God. Surely no evangelist has ever had a more promising audience than this. The fields were truly ripe to harvest and only needed Peter to explain the way of salvation.

37 That word, *I say,* ye know, which was published throughout all Judæa, and began from Galilee, after the baptism which John preached;

10:38☆ Lk 4:18, 19; Jn 1:32; Col 2:9; Heb 1:9

38 How God anointed Jesus of Nazareth with the Holy Ghost and with power: who went about doing good, and healing all that were oppressed of the devil; for God was with him.

10:39 Lk 24:48

39 And we are witnesses of all things which he did both in the land of the Jews, and in Jerusalem; whom they slew and hanged on a tree:

10:40, 41 Jn 14:19–23; 15:27; 21:13

40 Him God raised up the third day, and shewed him openly;

41 Not to all the people, but unto witnesses chosen before of God, *even* to us, who did eat and drink with him after he rose from the dead.

10:42 Mt 28:19; Jn 5:22; Rom 14:9; 2 Cor 5:10; 2 Tim 4:1; 1 Pet 4:5

42 And he commanded us to preach unto the people, and to testify that it is he which was ordained of God *to be* the Judge of quick and dead.

10:43 Isa 53:11; Jer 31:34; Dan 9:24; Zech 13:1; Mal 4:2; Lk 24:27

43 To him give all the prophets witness, that through his name whosoever believeth in him shall receive remission of sins.

10:44☆ Acts 11:15; 15:8

44 ¶While Peter yet spake these words, the Holy Ghost fell on all them which heard the word.

f. Cornelius Is Baptized in Water

10:45 Acts 2:33

45 And they of the circumcision which believed were astonished, as many as came with Peter, because that on the Gentiles also was poured out the gift of the Holy Ghost.

10:46 Mk 16:17; Acts 2:4; 19:6

46 For they heard them speak with tongues, and magnify God. Then answered Peter,

10:47☆ Acts 8:36; 11:17; 15:8

47 Can any man forbid water, that these should not be baptized, which have received the Holy Ghost as well as we?

10:48 Acts 2:38; 8:16; 19:5

48 And he commanded them to be baptized in the name of the Lord. Then prayed they him to tarry certain days.

g. Peter Defends the Evangelization of Non-Jews

11:1☆

11 AND the apostles and brethren that were in Judæa heard that the Gentiles had also received the word of God.

11:2☆

2 And when Peter was come up to Jerusalem, they that were of the circumcision contended with him,

11:3 Mt 9:11; Acts 10:28; Gal 2:12

3 Saying, Thou wentest in to men uncircumcised, and didst eat with them.

11:4☆

4 But Peter rehearsed *the matter* from the beginning, and expounded *it* by order unto them, saying,

---

10:38 *God anointed Jesus of Nazareth with the Holy Ghost.* This is the fulfillment of Isa. 61:1ff. In his humanity Jesus was filled with the Spirit. He was anointed by the Spirit. So believers today need and can have the Spirit's anointing. (See 1 John 2:27 and 2 Cor. 1:21, 22.)

10:44 *the Holy Ghost fell on all them.* This may well be called the Gentile Pentecost. Peter's companions were amazed that the Holy Spirit fell on the Gentiles just as he had fallen on the Jews at Pentecost. They spoke with tongues and magnified God. This was enough to convince Peter that it was of God and that the Gentiles were fellow heirs with believing Jews in the kingdom.

10:47 *Here the converts were born again, sealed, and indwelt by the Spirit before they were baptized with water.* This incident has been quoted by those who do not hold the notion that baptismal regeneration is biblical. The proponents of baptismal regeneration use John 3:5 to support their case, for it says that a man must be "born of water and of the Spirit." The matter may be one of indifference and thus not fundamental to the Christian faith.

11:1 The Gentiles received the Word of God, believed on Jesus, and were baptized. But they were not circumcised. The first ecumenical council (Acts 15) had not yet taken place, so the circumcision question was open for discussion.

11:2 The early church was plagued by legalism, particularly as it related to circumcision. Paul addressed the question definitively in his letter to the Galatians.

11:4 Paul was suspect but Peter was not. Here he joins Paul in defending evangelizing the Gentiles without circumcising them. He recounts what happened to him in connection with the conversion of Cornelius. He testifies that the Holy Spirit had come upon those Gentiles; this validates his ministry and confirms the fact that the gospel was for Gentiles as well as for Jews.

5I was in the city of Joppa praying: and in a trance I saw a vision, A
certain vessel descend, as it had been a great sheet, let down from heaven
by four corners; and it came even to me:

11:5 Acts 10:9, 10

6Upon the which when I had fastened mine eyes, I considered, and saw
fourfooted beasts of the earth, and wild beasts, and creeping things, and
fowls of the air.
7And I heard a voice saying unto me, Arise, Peter; slay and eat.
8But I said, Not so, Lord: for nothing common or unclean hath at any
time entered into my mouth.

11:8 Ezek 4:14

9But the voice answered me again from heaven, What God hath cleansed,
that call not thou common.
10And this was done three times: and all were drawn up again into
heaven.
11And, behold, immediately there were three men already come unto the
house where I was, sent from Cæs-a-re′a unto me.
12And the spirit bade me go with them, nothing doubting. Moreover
these six brethren accompanied me, and we entered into the man's house:

11:12 Jn 16:13 Acts 10:23; 15:7

13And he shewed us how he had seen an angel in his house, which stood
and said unto him, Send men to Joppa, and call for Simon, whose surname
is Peter;

11:13 Acts 10:30

14Who shall tell thee words, whereby thou and all thy house shall be
saved.

11:14 Acts 10:2; 16:15 18:8 1 Cor 1:16

15And as I began to speak, the Holy Ghost fell on them, as on us at the
beginning.

11:15 Acts 2:4

16Then remembered I the word of the Lord, how that he said, John
indeed baptized with water; but ye shall be baptized with the Holy Ghost.

11:16 Isa 44:3 Joel 2:28 Mt 3:11 Jn 1:26, 33

17Forasmuch then as God gave them the like gift as *he did* unto us, who
believed on the Lord Jesus Christ; what was I, that I could withstand God?

11:17 Acts 10:47 15:8, 9

18When they heard these things, they held their peace, and glorified God,
saying, Then hath God also to the Gentiles granted repentance unto life.

11:18 Rom 10:12; 15:9

III. CHURCH PLANTING AMONG THE GENTILES: ANTIOCH AND THE ROMAN EMPIRE (11:19—21:14)

A. BARNABAS EVANGELIZING AT ANTIOCH

19¶Now they which were scattered abroad upon the persecution that
arose about Stephen travelled as far as Phe-ni′ce, and Cyprus, and Antioch,
preaching the word to none but unto the Jews only.

11:19 Acts 8:1; 13:1 14:25–27; 15:3

20And some of them were men of Cyprus and Cy-re′ne, which, when they
were come to Antioch, spake unto the Grecians, preaching the Lord Jesus.

11:20 Acts 6:1

21And the hand of the Lord was with them: and a great number believed,
and turned unto the Lord.

☆**11:21** Lk 1:66

22¶Then tidings of these things came unto the ears of the church which
was in Jerusalem: and they sent forth Barnabas, that he should go as far as
Antioch.

☆**11:22** Acts 9:27 13:43; 14:22, 23

11:21 *the hand of the Lord was with them.* Those who preached were not apostles, only ordinary ministers. Yet God was at work in them and through them, and multitudes believed. The same thing is true today for lay witnesses to Jesus Christ. Multitudes of sinners have come to know Christ by those who have never been ordained to the gospel ministry. God accomplishes what he wants however he is pleased to do so.

11:22 Barnabas went to Antioch at the direction of the church. The Holy Spirit directed them to send him on this journey, and he willingly accepted direction from the brethren. Ministers and evangelists do have a responsibility to a larger body of believers, to which they give an accounting and under whose direction they labor.

11:23 Deut 10:20; 1 Cor 15:58; Col 2:6

23 Who, when he came, and had seen the grace of God, was glad, and exhorted them all, that with purpose of heart they would cleave unto the Lord.

11:24 Acts 2:4, 47; 5:14

24 For he was a good man, and full of the Holy Ghost and of faith: and much people was added unto the Lord.

11:25 Acts 9:30

25 Then departed Barnabas to Tarsus, for to seek Saul:

11:26☆

26 And when he had found him, he brought him unto Antioch. And it came to pass, that a whole year they assembled themselves with the church, and taught much people. And the disciples were called Christians first in Antioch.

11:27☆ Acts 2:17; 13:1; 1 Cor 12:28; Eph 4:11

27 ¶And in these days came prophets from Jerusalem unto Antioch.

11:28☆ Acts 21:10

28 And there stood up one of them named Ag′a-bus, and signified by the spirit that there should be great dearth throughout all the world: which came to pass in the days of Claudius Cæsar.

11:29 Rom 15:25, 26; 1 Cor 16:1; 2 Cor 9:1; Gal 2:10

29 Then the disciples, every man according to his ability, determined to send relief unto the brethren which dwelt in Judæa:

11:30☆ 1 Pet 5:1

30 Which also they did, and sent it to the elders by the hands of Barnabas and Saul.

B. HEROD'S PERSECUTION

1. James Martyred; Peter Imprisoned

12:1☆ Mt 10:17

12 NOW about that time Herod the king stretched forth *his* hands to vex certain of the church.

12:2☆ Mt 4:21; 20:20–23; Mk 10:39

2 And he killed James the brother of John with the sword.

12:3 Ex 12:14, 15

3 And because he saw it pleased the Jews, he proceeded further to take Peter also. (Then were the days of unleavened bread.)

12:4 Jn 21:18

4 And when he had apprehended him, he put *him* in prison, and delivered *him* to four quaternions of soldiers to keep him; intending after Easter to bring him forth to the people.

12:5 2 Cor 1:11; Eph 6:18

5 Peter therefore was kept in prison: but prayer was made without ceasing of the church unto God for him.

11:26 This is the first instance in which believers are called Christians. The word appears only two other times in the New Testament (26:28; 1 Pet. 4:16). In Antioch the word may have been used as a slur.

11:27 This is the first mention of Christian prophets in the New Testament. John the Baptist and Jesus were called prophets. Besides Agabus (see also 21:10), mention is made of prophets in the church at Antioch (13:1). Judas and Silas are denominated prophets (15:32), and the four unmarried daughters of Philip the evangelist prophesied (21:9). Prophets are mentioned in 1 Cor. 12:28; 14:29, 37; Eph. 4:11. We do not know whether the prophets referred to in Eph. 2:20 and 3:5 are Old or New Testament prophets.

11:28 The gift of prophecy was not limited to the apostles. Here Agabus, who came from Jerusalem, prophesied the coming famine. He also predicted that Paul would be shackled and bound to be delivered to the Gentiles (21:10, 11). This was on the third missionary journey. The prediction was made at Caesarea. Tradition has it that Agabus was one of the Seventy and *that he was later martyred. Claudius* was the Roman emperor in A.D. 41–54. He was a nephew of the emperor Tiberius, and a grandson of Livia, the wife of Augustus. Agrippina, his last wife, was his niece. He adopted her son Nero, who became emperor.

11:30 The relief for the hungry in Judea was limited to the brethren in Christ. Obviously the small group of Christians could not send enough money to feed everyone who was suffering in the famine. Mercy begins with succoring those who belong to Jesus first. After that, one can help those who are outside the kingdom. *elders.* This is the first mention of elders in the New Testament church. Other references to elders in the Jerusalem church include 15:2–23; 16:4; and 21:18. Other references to elders include 14:23; 20:17. Outside of the Acts they are spoken of in 1 Tim. 4:14; 5:17–19; Titus 1:5; James 5:14; 1 Pet. 5:1, 5; 2 John 1; 3 John 1. Of their origin, nothing is said. Probably the office was taken from the Jewish pattern of elders in the synagogue with respect to name and function. (See note on Titus 1:5.)

12:1 *Herod* Agrippa I was a grandson of Herod the Great. He was born in 11 B.C., educated in Rome, and made tetrarch of Iturea, Trachonitis, and Gaulinitis by A.D. 37 by Gaius, the Roman emperor. Gaius also gave him the title of king. Then he was made ruler over Galilee and Perea and later Emperor Claudius extended his kingdom to include Judea and Samaria.

12:2 *he* killed James, i.e., "he killed the apostle James." James was the first of the apostles to suffer martyrdom. There is no answer to why God permitted James to die and Peter to live. The reason lies in the secret counsels of God. James' brother John, on the other hand, outlived all of the apostles.

2. Peter Delivered by the Angel

6 And when Herod would have brought him forth, the same night Peter
was sleeping between two soldiers, bound with two chains: and the keepers
before the door kept the prison.
7 And, behold, the angel of the Lord came upon *him*, and a light shined in **12:7**
the prison: and he smote Peter on the side, and raised him up, saying, Arise Acts 5:19; 21:33
up quickly. And his chains fell off from *his* hands. Heb 1:14
8 And the angel said unto him, Gird thyself, and bind on thy sandals. And
so he did. And he saith unto him, Cast thy garment about thee, and follow
me.
9 And he went out, and followed him; and wist not that it was true which **12:9**
was done by the angel; but thought he saw a vision. Ps 126:1 Acts 10:3
10 When they were past the first and the second ward, they came unto the ☆**12:10**
iron gate that leadeth unto the city; which opened to them of his own Acts 5:19; 16:26
accord: and they went out, and passed on through one street; and forthwith
the angel departed from him.
11 And when Peter was come to himself, he said, Now I know of a surety, **12:11**
that the Lord hath sent his angel, and hath delivered me out of the hand of Job 5:19 Ps 33:18, 19
Herod, and *from* all the expectation of the people of the Jews. 34:7; 97:10 Dan 3:28; 6:22 2 Pet 2:9

3. Peter's Account of His Deliverance

12 And when he had considered *the thing*, he came to the house of Mary **12:12**
the mother of John, whose surname was Mark; where many were gathered Acts 12:25; 13:5 15:37
together praying. Col 4:10 1 Pet 5:13
13 And as Peter knocked at the door of the gate, a damsel came to ☆**12:13**
hearken, named Rhoda.
14 And when she knew Peter's voice, she opened not the gate for gladness,
but ran in, and told how Peter stood before the gate.
15 And they said unto her, Thou art mad. But she constantly affirmed that **12:15**
it was even so. Then said they, It is his angel. Mt 18:10
16 But Peter continued knocking: and when they had opened *the door*, and
saw him, they were astonished.
17 But he, beckoning unto them with the hand to hold their peace, **12:17**
declared unto them how the Lord had brought him out of the prison. And Acts 15:35; 21:18
he said, Go shew these things unto James, and to the brethren. And he
departed, and went into another place.

4. Herod Executes the Guards

18 Now as soon as it was day, there was no small stir among the soldiers,
what was become of Peter.
19 And when Herod had sought for him, and found him not, he examined ☆**12:19**
the keepers, and commanded that *they* should be put to death. And he went Acts 8:40; 16:27
down from Judæa to Cæs-a-re′a, and *there* abode.

12:10 Skeptics who have trouble with miracles suppose that Peter was delivered by human hand. The Scripture, however, says plainly that the iron gate leading to the city opened of itself. It was not unlocked by human hand. This was surely a miraculous act.

12:13ff What a strange scene this is! Rhoda responds to Peter, who knocks at the gate. She recognizes the apostle's voice but refuses to open the gate. She runs to tell the others who are praying for Peter. The brethren now refuse to believe that their prayers have been answered; they tell Rhoda she is mad. They prefer to believe that he is dead and that an angel is making use of his name. They went to great lengths to do everything except believe that God had affirmatively answered their prayers. "Sometimes that which we most earnestly wish for we are most backward to believe."*

12:19 *found him not.* "In times of public danger, all believers have God for their hiding-place, which is such a secret, that there the ignorant world cannot find them; such strength that the impotent world cannot reach them."*

5. God's Judgment on Herod

20¶And Herod was highly displeased with them of Tyre and Si′don: but
they came with one accord to him, and, having made Blas′tus the king's
chamberlain their friend, desired peace; because their country was
nourished by the king's *country*.
21And upon a set day Herod, arrayed in royal apparel, sat upon his
throne, and made an oration unto them.
22And the people gave a shout, *saying*, *It is* the voice of a god, and not of
a man.
23And immediately the angel of the Lord smote him, because he gave not
God the glory: and he was eaten of worms, and gave up the ghost.
24¶But the word of God grew and multiplied.
25And Barnabas and Saul returned from Jerusalem, when they had
fulfilled *their* ministry, and took with them John, whose surname was Mark.

C. THE FIRST MISSIONARY JOURNEY

1. The Spirit Calls Paul and Barnabas

13 NOW there were in the church that was at Antioch certain prophets
and teachers; as Barnabas, and Simeon that was called Ni′ger, and
Lucius of Cy-re′ne, and Man′a-en, which had been brought up with Herod
the tetrarch, and Saul.
2As they ministered to the Lord, and fasted, the Holy Ghost said,
Separate me Barnabas and Saul for the work whereunto I have called them.
3And when they had fasted and prayed, and laid *their* hands on them,
they sent *them* away.

2. Evangelizing Cyprus

4¶So they, being sent forth by the Holy Ghost, departed unto Se-leu′ci-a;
and from thence they sailed to Cyprus.
5And when they were at Sal′a-mis, they preached the word of God in the
synagogues of the Jews: and they had also John to *their* minister.
6And when they had gone through the isle unto Pa′phos, they found a
certain sorcerer, a false prophet, a Jew, whose name *was* Bar-je′sus:
7Which was with the deputy of the country, Sergius Paulus, a prudent

12:23☆ Deut 28:58, 59; 1 Sam 25:37, 38; 2 Sam 24:16; 2 Kgs 19:35; Isa 42:8; 48:11; Dan 4:30–37; Rev 15:3, 4
12:24☆ Isa 55:11; Acts 6:7; 19:20
12:25 Acts 11:29, 30; 15:37
13:1☆ a) Acts 8:1; Rom 16:1; 1 Cor 1:2; 2 Cor 1:1; Rev 1:11; b) Acts 11:22; 14:26; Rom 16:21; Eph 4:11, 12
13:2☆ Rom 10:15; Gal 1:15; 2:7–9; Eph 3:7–9; 1 Tim 2:7; Heb 5:4
13:3 Acts 6:6
13:4 Acts 4:36
13:5☆ Acts 9:20; 12:25; Col 4:10; 1 Pet 5:13
13:6☆ Ex 7:11; Mt 7:15; Acts 8:9; 2 Tim 3:8

12:23 Josephus recounts a story about Herod Agrippa and an owl. Earlier in his life, when Tiberias had imprisoned him, he saw an owl in a tree. A fellow prisoner told him it was a good sign and that he would be freed shortly. He also said that if Herod ever saw the owl again, he would have only five days to live. When the angel of God smote Herod Agrippa, he lived five days before dying.

12:24 The more the church is persecuted, the more it grows by God's singular grace. For example, Israel in Egypt grew greatly. Here the death of James (which all knew about) multiplied the number of believers.

13:1 *teachers* as a distinct group are referred to here and in 1 Cor. 12:28, 29; Eph. 4:11; Heb. 5:12; James 3:1 ("masters"). Paul calls himself a teacher in 1 Tim. 2:7 and 2 Tim. 1:11. His teaching ministry is spoken of in 11:26; 15:35; 18:11; 20:20; 28:31.

13:2ff *The missionary call* for Paul and Barnabas came when the gathered people of God were worshipping and fasting. The Holy Spirit made his will known. The church laid hands on them and sent them away. Missionaries who are sent by a church and have not been called by the Spirit will fail miserably. Missionaries should be certain that the Spirit of God has called them and then look to the church to ratify the call and send them forth. Some missionary leaders declare that the recognition of the need constitutes a call. They assert that all Christians are called to live holy lives and to make disciples of all nations and that no one needs a special call to do what is already commanded.

13:5 *synagogues*, derived from the Greek *synagōgē*, a place where people gather together. The origins of the synagogue are hazy, but perhaps they can be traced to the fact that the dispersion of the Jews left them without a temple. Synagogues were established for the worship of God. The services included the reading and exposition of the Old Testament, prayer, praise, and thanksgiving. (See 13:15; 15:21; Matt. 6:5; Luke 4:16–21.) Jesus taught in synagogues and performed miracles for the members of the congregations (Matt. 4:23; 12:9, 10; Luke 4:16; 13:10–13). Paul usually resorted to the synagogues wherever he visited, telling worshippers about Jesus the Messiah.

13:6 The *Bar-jesus* of this verse is called "Elymas" in 13:8. These names represent the same person, but we do not know why both names were used. It may be that Bar-jesus gave himself the name or title of Elymas. We know he was an enemy of the gospel, for he had power

man; who called for Barnabas and Saul, and desired to hear the word of
God.
8 But El'y-mas the sorcerer (for so is his name by interpretation)
withstood them, seeking to turn away the deputy from the faith.
9 Then Saul, (who also *is called* Paul,) filled with the Holy Ghost, set his
eyes on him,
10 And said, O full of all subtilty and all mischief, *thou* child of the devil,
thou enemy of all righteousness, wilt thou not cease to pervert the right
ways of the Lord?
11 And now, behold, the hand of the Lord *is* upon thee, and thou shalt be
blind, not seeing the sun for a season. And immediately there fell on him a
mist and a darkness; and he went about seeking some to lead him by the
hand.
12 Then the deputy, when he saw what was done, believed, being
astonished at the doctrine of the Lord.

3. Evangelizing Perga and Antioch

13 Now when Paul and his company loosed from Pa'phos, they came to
Per'ga in Pam-phyl'i-a: and John departing from them returned to
Jerusalem.
14 ¶But when they departed from Per'ga, they came to Antioch in Pi-
sid'i-a, and went into the synagogue on the sabbath day, and sat down.
15 And after the reading of the law and the prophets the rulers of the
synagogue sent unto them, saying, *Ye* men *and* brethren, if ye have any
word of exhortation for the people, say on.
16 Then Paul stood up, and beckoning with *his* hand said, Men of Israel,
and ye that fear God, give audience.
17 The God of this people of Israel chose our fathers, and exalted the
people when they dwelt as strangers in the land of Egypt, and with an high
arm brought he them out of it.
18 And about the time of forty years suffered he their manners in the
wilderness.
19 And when he had destroyed seven nations in the land of Cha'naan, he
divided their land to them by lot.
20 And after that he gave *unto them* judges about the space of four
hundred and fifty years, until Samuel the prophet.
21 And afterward they desired a king: and God gave unto them Saul the
son of Cis, a man of the tribe of Benjamin, by the space of forty years.
22 And when he had removed him, he raised up unto them David to be
their king; to whom also he gave testimony, and said, I have found David
the *son* of Jesse, a man after mine own heart, which shall fulfil all my will.
23 Of this man's seed hath God according to *his* promise raised unto Israel
a Saviour, Jesus:
24 When John had first preached before his coming the baptism of
repentance to all the people of Israel.

13:9 Acts 2:4; 4:8
13:10 Mt 13:38; Jn 8:44; 2 Pet 2:15; 1 Jn 3:8
13:11 2 Kgs 6:18
☆**13:13** Acts 14:24, 25; 15:38
13:14 Acts 14:19, 21, 24
13:15 Lk 14:16; Acts 15:21; 2 Cor 3:14
13:16 Acts 10:2, 13:26
☆**13:17** Deut 7:6–8; Acts 7:36
13:18 Deut 1:31; 32:11, 12; Isa 46:3, 4; 63:9; Hos 11:3; Acts 7:36, 38
13:19, 20 Deut 7:1; Josh 19:51; Judg 2:16; 1 Kgs 6:1; Ps 78:55; Acts 3:24; 7:45
13:21 1 Sam 8:5; 10:1
13:22 1 Sam 13:14; 15:23, 26, 28; 16:1, 13; Ps 89:20; Hos 13:11
☆**13:23** 1 Sam 7:12; Isa 11:1; Lk 1:32; 2:11; Jn 4:42; Rom 1:3; 11:26
☆**13:24** Mk 1:1–14

---

with Sergius Paulus the proconsul. He thought that if Sergius Paulus became a Christian, he might lose his influence. Paul, filled with the Spirit, rebuked him and said he would be blinded. This happened immediately, and what Elymas feared then took place: Sergius Paulus became a Christian.

13:13 John Mark left Paul and Barnabas without giving them a reason or seeking their consent. This was to have repercussions later on in the relationship between Barnabas and Paul.

13:17 Since God chose Israel, these people were his favored subjects. Israel did not choose God. Rather they sinned against him again and again. David was made their king by God's choice, not theirs. And it was from his seed that the Messiah was to come.

13:23, 24 Jesus was raised up by God. He came from David's loins, and he was the Savior according to divine promise. Since many of the Jews believed that John the Baptist was a prophet, Paul injects him into the picture by speaking of his preaching of the need for repentance—which would have no meaning if people were living as they should. Nonetheless, John refused to dignify himself as that prophet which should come; rather, he pointed to the true prophet, Jesus Christ.

25 And as John fulfilled his course, he said, Whom think ye that I am? I
am not *he*. But, behold, there cometh one after me, whose shoes of *his* feet
I am not worthy to loose.
26 Men *and* brethren, children of the stock of Abraham, and whosoever
among you feareth God, to you is the word of this salvation sent.
27 For they that dwell at Jerusalem, and their rulers, because they knew
him not, nor yet the voices of the prophets which are read every sabbath
day, they have fulfilled *them* in condemning *him*.
28 And though they found no cause of death *in him*, yet desired they Pilate
that he should be slain.
29 And when they had fulfilled all that was written of him, they took *him*
down from the tree, and laid *him* in a sepulchre.
30 But God raised him from the dead:
31 And he was seen many days of them which came up with him from
Galilee to Jerusalem, who are his witnesses unto the people.
32 And we declare unto you glad tidings, how that the promise which was
made unto the fathers,
33 God hath fulfilled the same unto us their children, in that he hath raised
up Jesus again; as it is also written in the second psalm, Thou art my Son,
this day have I begotten thee.
34 And as concerning that he raised him up from the dead, *now* no more to
return to corruption, he said on this wise, I will give you the sure mercies of
David.
35 Wherefore he saith also in another *psalm*, Thou shalt not suffer thine
Holy One to see corruption.
36 For David, after he had served his own generation by the will of God,
fell on sleep, and was laid unto his fathers, and saw corruption:
37 But he, whom God raised again, saw no corruption.
38 ¶Be it known unto you therefore, men *and* brethren, that through this
man is preached unto you the forgiveness of sins:
39 And by him all that believe are justified from all things, from which ye
could not be justified by the law of Moses.
40 Beware therefore, lest that come upon you, which is spoken of in the
prophets;
41 Behold, ye despisers, and wonder, and perish: for I work a work in your
days, a work which ye shall in no wise believe, though a man declare it unto
you.
42 And when the Jews were gone out of the synagogue, the Gentiles
besought that these words might be preached to them the next sabbath.
43 Now when the congregation was broken up, many of the Jews and
religious proselytes followed Paul and Barnabas: who, speaking to them,
persuaded them to continue in the grace of God.
44 ¶And the next sabbath day came almost the whole city together to hear
the word of God.
45 But when the Jews saw the multitudes, they were filled with envy, and

13:25 Mt 3:11 Mk 1:7 Lk 3:16 Jn 1:26, 27
13:26 Acts 4:12; 13:46
13:27☆ Acts 3:17 1 Cor 2:8
13:28 Acts 3:14
13:29 Lk 23:52, 53 Act 5:30 26:22
13:30☆ Mt 28:6 Acts 2:24
13:31 Lk 24:48 Acts 1:11 1 Cor 15:5
13:32 Acts 26:6 Rom 1:2–4 9:4, 5 Gal 3:16
13:33 Ps 2:7 Heb 1:5; 5:5
13:34 Isa 55:3
13:35 Ps 16:10
13:36 1 Kgs 2:10 Ps 78:70–72 Acts 2:29
13:37 Acts 2:24 1 Cor 15:42
13:38☆ Jer 31:34 Col 1:13, 14
13:39 Isa 53:11 Rom 3:28; 10:4 Gal 2:16
13:41 Hab 1:5
13:43 Acts 11:23
13:45☆ Acts 14:2; 18:6 1 Thess 2:15, 16 Jude 10

13:27 The reason the Jews condemned Jesus was that they did not know him, i.e., recognize him as the Savior. They had the sound of the gospel but not the sense of it. The knew, read, and listened to the words of the prophets, but their hearts and eyes were so darkened that they made no sense of the Word of God. No one can make sense out of the Scriptures without the help of the Holy Spirit.

13:30 *God raised him from the dead.* David was dead and his body still lay in his tomb. But Jesus is alive, for God has resurrected him. It was not done in secret, for many saw him in his resurrection and witnessed to that truth. In verse 35 he shows that the resurrection was the promise of God. He preached the resurrection, for it is the main pillar by which the whole fabric of the gospel is supported and maintained.

13:38 Paul here draws the net of *salvation by imploring* his listeners to receive the forgiveness of their sins, which they will secure in and through Jesus Christ.

13:45, 46 The success of the preaching of Paul aroused the envy and hatred of some Jews, who contradicted all he said and went so far as to blas-

spake against those things which were spoken by Paul, contradicting and
blaspheming.
46Then Paul and Barnabas waxed bold, and said, It was necessary that
the word of God should first have been spoken to you: but seeing ye put it
from you, and judge yourselves unworthy of everlasting life, lo, we turn to
the Gentiles.
47For so hath the Lord commanded us, *saying*, I have set thee to be a
light of the Gentiles, that thou shouldest be for salvation unto the ends of
the earth.
48And when the Gentiles heard this, they were glad, and glorified the
word of the Lord: and as many as were ordained to eternal life believed.
49And the word of the Lord was published throughout all the region.
50But the Jews stirred up the devout and honourable women, and the
chief men of the city, and raised persecution against Paul and Barnabas,
and expelled them out of their coasts.
51But they shook off the dust of their feet against them, and came unto
I-co'ni-um.
52And the disciples were filled with joy, and with the Holy Ghost.

13:46 Deut 32:21; Mt 10:6; Acts 3:26; 9:20; 13:5; 18:6; 22:21; 28:28; Rom 1:16; 10:19
13:47 Isa 42:6; 49:6; Lk 2:32
☆**13:48** Rom 8:29, 30; Eph 1:4, 5, 11; 1 Pet 1:2
13:51 Mt 10:14; Lk 9:5; Acts 18:6; 2 Tim 3:11
13:52 1 Pet 1:8

4. Evangelizing Iconium

14 AND it came to pass in I-co'ni-um, that they went both together
into the synagogue of the Jews, and so spake, that a great multitude
both of the Jews and also of the Greeks believed.
2But the unbelieving Jews stirred up the Gentiles, and made their minds
evil affected against the brethren.
3Long time therefore abode they speaking boldly in the Lord, which gave
testimony unto the word of his grace, and granted signs and wonders to be
done by their hands.
4But the multitude of the city was divided: and part held with the Jews,
and part with the apostles.
5And when there was an assault made both of the Gentiles, and also of
the Jews with their rulers, to use *them* despitefully, and to stone them,
6They were ware of *it*, and fled unto Lys'tra and Der'be, cities of Ly-ca-
o'ni-a, and unto the region that lieth round about:
7And there they preached the gospel.

14:2 2 Tim 3:11
14:3 Mk 16:20; Rom 15:19; Heb 2:4
14:4 Acts 17:4, 5; 19:9, 28:24
14:5 Acts 14:19; 16:1; 1 Thess 2:14–16
☆**14:6**

5. Evangelizing Lystra

8¶And there sat a certain man at Lys'tra, impotent in his feet, being a
cripple from his mother's womb, who never had walked:

☆**14:8** Acts 3:2

---

pheme the name Paul preached. Paul and Barnabas offered the gospel first to the Jews. Their rejection encouraged them to preach the same gospel to the Gentiles. Strangely enough, these Jews judged themselves *"unworthy of everlasting life."*

13:48 *as many as were ordained to eternal life believed.* This Scripture has a predestinarian note attached to it. Some in the Arminian tradition have translated this: "as many as were disposed to eternal life believed." F. F. Bruce translates it in a predestinarian sense and argues against toning down the language. He says, "All, in fact, who had been enrolled for eternal life in the records of heaven" believed the gospel (*International Commentary on the New Testament*, Eerdmans, 1977, p. 283).

14:6 When Paul and Barnabas learned that the enemies of the gospel intended to do them bodily harm, they fled from Iconium to Lystra and Derbe. Instead of seeking martyrdom by remaining in Iconium, they prudently left the city. God did not intend for his people to seek martyrdom. They were to welcome it and submit to it when there was nothing they could do about it. In the will of God we are to preserve our lives as long as we can.

14:8 Here was an impotent man who could not walk or stand erect. He had been this way since birth. He differed from the one healed by Peter and John in Acts 3:2 inasmuch as this man had faith, whereas the first one expected nothing but alms, yet God graciously healed him. Paul had the gift of discernment by the Spirit and sensed the faith of the man herein described. He commanded him to do what he had never done before: stand up on his feet and walk. The miracle was immediate and soul-shaking.

9 The same heard Paul speak: who stedfastly beholding him, and
perceiving that he had faith to be healed,
14:10 Isa 35:6 Acts 3:8 — 10 Said with a loud voice, Stand upright on thy feet. And he leaped and
walked.
14:11 Acts 28:6 — 11 And when the people saw what Paul had done, they lifted up their
voices, saying in the speech of Ly-ca-o′ni-a, The gods are come down to us
in the likeness of men.
14:12☆ — 12 And they called Barnabas, Jupiter; and Paul, Mer-cu′ri-us, because he
was the chief speaker.
14:13 Dan 2:46 — 13 Then the priest of Jupiter, which was before their city, brought oxen
and garlands unto the gates, and would have done sacrifice with the people.
14 *Which* when the apostles, Barnabas and Paul, heard *of*, they rent their
clothes, and ran in among the people, crying out,
14:15 Ex 20:11 Deut 32:21 Jer 14:22 Mt 16:16 1 Thess 1:9 Rev 14:7; 19:10 — 15 And saying, Sirs, why do ye these things? We also are men of like
passions with you, and preach unto you that ye should turn from these
vanities unto the living God, which made heaven, and earth, and the sea,
and all things that are therein:
14:16 Ps 81:12 — 16 Who in times past suffered all nations to walk in their own ways.
14:17 Deut 11:14 Ps 65:10–12 147:8 Acts 17:27 Rom 1:19, 20 — 17 Nevertheless he left not himself without witness, in that he did good,
and gave us rain from heaven, and fruitful seasons, filling our hearts with
food and gladness.
18 And with these sayings scarce restrained they the people, that they had
not done sacrifice unto them.

6. The Return to Antioch

14:19☆ Acts 13:45 2 Cor 1:8; 11:25 2 Tim 3:11 — 19 ¶And there came thither *certain* Jews from Antioch and I-co′ni-um,
who persuaded the people, and, having stoned Paul, drew *him* out of the
city, supposing he had been dead.
14:20 Acts 14:6 — 20 Howbeit, as the disciples stood round about him, he rose up, and came
into the city: and the next day he departed with Barnabas to Der′be.
21 And when they had preached the gospel to that city, and had taught
many, they returned again to Lys′tra, and *to* I-co′ni-um, and Antioch,
14:22 Mt 10:38; 16:24 Jn 15:18 Rom 8:17 2 Tim 2:11; 3:12 — 22 Confirming the souls of the disciples, *and* exhorting them to continue in
the faith, and that we must through much tribulation enter into the
kingdom of God.
14:23 Tit 1:5 — 23 And when they had ordained them elders in every church, and had
prayed with fasting, they commended them to the Lord, on whom they
believed.
14:24 Acts 13:13, 14 — 24 And after they had passed throughout Pi-sid′i-a, they came to Pam-
phyl′i-a.
25 And when they had preached the word in Per′ga, they went down into
At-ta′li-a:
14:26 Acts 11:26 13:1–3 — 26 And thence sailed to Antioch, from whence they had been recom-
mended to the grace of God for the work which they fulfilled.

14:12 Barnabas and Paul are looked upon as gods, and sacrifices are about to be offered to them. They tear their clothes, repulsed by the insult this is to their God in heaven. They state plainly that they are just like other men (14:15). Their difference with these pagans lay in the fact that Barnabas and Paul were regenerated believers.

14:19 Here at Lystra Paul experienced stoning. He was to say later that he was stoned once (2 Cor. 11:25). It refers to this incident. He also said he bore branded on his body the marks of Jesus (Gal. 6:17), which also refers to the same incident. The ones who stoned him dragged him out of the city and left him for dead. The account has the earmarks of a miracle. We can well suppose that he really was dead and that God revived him, for he still had a ministry to perform.

See 2 Cor. 11—12 for Paul's sufferings. Paul prayed just as we do. He was given grace to bear what God called him to endure. He stands as a model for those who must suffer in the will of God, knowing that God loves them and will deliver them through death, if not before.

27 And when they were come, and had gathered the church together, they
rehearsed all that God had done with them, and how he had opened the
door of faith unto the Gentiles.
28 And there they abode long time with the disciples.

☆14:27 1 Cor 16:9; Col 4:3; Rev 3:8
☆14:28

D. THE COUNCIL AT JERUSALEM

1. The Problem of Circumcision

15 AND certain men which came down from Judæa taught the
brethren, *and said*, Except ye be circumcised after the manner of
Moses, ye cannot be saved.
2 When therefore Paul and Barnabas had no small dissension and
disputation with them, they determined that Paul and Barnabas, and
certain other of them, should go up to Jerusalem unto the apostles
and elders about this question.
3 And being brought on their way by the church, they passed through
Phe-ni'ce and Sa-ma'ri-a, declaring the conversion of the Gentiles: and they
caused great joy unto all the brethren.
4 And when they were come to Jerusalem, they were received of the
church, and *of* the apostles and elders, and they declared all things that
God had done with them.
5 But there rose up certain of the sect of the Pharisees which believed,
saying, That it was needful to circumcise them, and to command *them* to
keep the law of Moses.

☆15:1 Gen 17:9–11; Lev 12:3; Gal 5:2; Phil 3:2, 3
☆15:2 Gal 2:1–10
☆15:3 Acts 14:27
☆15:4
☆15:5 1 Cor 7:18; Gal 5:2–11

2. The Discussion by the Council

6 ¶And the apostles and elders came together for to consider of this
matter.
7 And when there had been much disputing, Peter rose up, and said unto
them, Men *and* brethren, ye know how that a good while ago God made
choice among us, that the Gentiles by my mouth should hear the word of
the gospel, and believe.
8 And God, which knoweth the hearts, bare them witness, giving them the
Holy Ghost, even as *he did* unto us;

☆15:6
15:7 Acts 10:19–29
15:8 1 Chron 28:9; Jer 17:10; Acts 10:44, 47; Heb 4:13

14:27, 28 Paul and his small band come back to Antioch of Pisidia from whence they had been sent on their missionary tour. They wish to report what had happened and to explain that God had opened the door of faith to the Gentiles. When God opens a door no man can shut it—surely not the powers of hell. Paul and his cohorts spend some time here in Antioch with friends they loved. At the same time, they are kept from enemies who wished to assault them.

15:1 The enemies of the gospel now catch up with Paul and Barnabas at Antioch. Coming from Jerusalem *they tell the believers that* Gentiles must be circumcised and keep the law of Moses. If they are not circumcised, they cannot be saved. It created no small dissension among the believers and for Paul and Barnabas.

15:2 Paul and Barnabas are appointed to go to Jerusalem to settle the question of circumcision and keeping the law in a conference with the apostles and elders of the church there. The case for the gospel would be strengthened if the apostles and elders in Jerusalem confirmed what Paul and Barnabas taught. It was generally agreed that the apostles and elders in Jerusalem were the ones who could best decide.

15:3 *conversion* represents a change from one state of affairs to another. Turning *from* something is to repent; turning *to* something is to exercise faith. Both are at work in conversion.

15:4, 5 Paul and Barnabas received a royal welcome in Jerusalem. They were embraced as brethren and shown love and friendship. Moreover, they gave a full report of what God had done on their missionary journey. Verse 5 makes it certain that Paul and Barnabas talked about circumcision in relation to Gentile believers because some who were Pharisees, and yet believers in Jesus, immediately challenged this view and insisted upon the necessity to circumcise all who believed on Jesus.

15:6ff Peter now addresses the assembly after there had been much debate. Again he witnesses that the Holy Spirit had come on Gentile believers who had not been circumcised. If by giving the Holy Spirit God showed he was satisfied they were believers without circumcision, why should the church not accept this? If they do not accept this fact, Peter indicates that they will offend God and the Gentile believers as well. Christ came to proclaim liberty to the captives, not bondage to the law.

15:9 Acts 10:43; Rom 10:11, 12
15:10 Mt 23:4; Gal 5:1
15:11 Rom 3:23, 24; 5:15; 2 Cor 13:14; Eph 1:7, 8; 2:8
15:12☆ Acts 14:27; 15:4
15:13☆ Acts 12:17
15:15 Isa 11:10; 54:1–5
15:16 Amos 9:11, 12
15:18 Isa 45:21
15:19 Acts 21:15
15:20 Gen 9:4; Ex 20:3, 4; Lev 3:17; Deut 12:16; Ezek 20:30; Dan 1:8; 1 Cor 8:7; 10:7; 1 Thess 4:3, 4
15:21 Acts 13:15
15:22☆ Acts 1:23; 15:27; 16:19; 17:4; 1 Thess 1:1; 1 Pet 5:12
15:23 Mt 4:24; Acts 6:9; 11:20; 15:41; Gal 1:21
15:24 Gal 1:7; 2:4; 5:12; Tit 1:10

9 And put no difference between us and them, purifying their hearts by faith.

10 Now therefore why tempt ye God, to put a yoke upon the neck of the disciples, which neither our fathers nor we were able to bear?

11 But we believe that through the grace of the Lord Jesus Christ we shall be saved, even as they.

12 ¶Then all the multitude kept silence, and gave audience to Barnabas and Paul, declaring what miracles and wonders God had wrought among the Gentiles by them.

13 ¶And after they had held their peace, James answered, saying, Men *and* brethren, hearken unto me:

14 Simeon hath declared how God at the first did visit the Gentiles, to take out of them a people for his name.

15 And to this agree the words of the prophets; as it is written,

16 After this I will return, and will build again the tabernacle of David, which is fallen down; and I will build again the ruins thereof, and I will set it up:

17 That the residue of men might seek after the Lord, and all the Gentiles, upon whom my name is called, saith the Lord, who doeth all these things.

18 Known unto God are all his works from the beginning of the world.

19 Wherefore my sentence is, that we trouble not them, which from among the Gentiles are turned to God:

20 But that we write unto them, that they abstain from pollutions of idols, and *from* fornication, and *from* things strangled, and *from* blood.

21 For Moses of old time hath in every city them that preach him, being read in the synagogues every sabbath day.

3. The Decision of the Council

22 Then pleased it the apostles and elders, with the whole church, to send chosen men of their own company to Antioch with Paul and Barnabas; *namely*, Judas surnamed Bar′sa-bas, and Silas, chief men among the brethren:

23 And they wrote *letters* by them after this manner; The apostles and elders and brethren *send* greeting unto the brethren which are of the Gentiles in Antioch and Syria and Ci-li′ci-a.

24 Forasmuch as we have heard, that certain which went out from us have troubled you with words, subverting your souls, saying, *Ye must* be circumcised, and keep the law: to whom we gave no *such* commandment:

15:12ff This passage indicates that some Jews felt there was no place for the Gentiles in the gospel economy. James indicates that the Old Testament prophets spoke of the Gentiles and God's interest in and concern for them. Paul stated that Gentile believers constitute the new Israel (see Gal. 3 and Rom. 9–11). Nonetheless, God still has an interest in Israel and promises that all Israel eventually will be saved (Rom. 11:26).

15:13ff Up to this point Paul, Barnabas, and Peter have had their say. All three are in agreement with each other that circumcision is not necessary for salvation. Now James enters the fray to speak on behalf of these brothers and to support their view about circumcision. When he speaks about "Simeon," he is talking about Peter. After giving scripture (Amos 9:11, 12) to support his view, James renders a definitive judgment that God does not wish to approve of, or insist on, circumcision as essential to salvation. But then James suggests that Gentiles stay away from idols, fornication, things strangled, and from blood. Even the Pharisee believers would have to be satisfied with this, for they read Moses and were loath to part with their traditions. So James made some allowance for their sensitivities until they had matured in the faith. Questions about idols and fornication are both clearly mentioned in the New Testament and they are to be avoided. The other matters belong to the area of the indifferent; they could be kept or not kept according to the light each individual has.

15:22 James had the agreement of the apostles, elders, and the whole church for the verdict he rendered. The Jerusalem leaders sent a delegation back to the Gentile believers in Antioch and Syria and Cilicia with a letter. Judas and Silas (Barsabbas), leading men from Jerusalem, brought the letter and thus supported the views of Paul and Barnabas. Most important of all, the letter contained the note that what the apostles and elders had agreed on was approved by the Holy Spirit (15:28).

[25]It seemed good unto us, being assembled with one accord, to send
chosen men unto you with our beloved Barnabas and Paul,
[26]Men that have hazarded their lives for the name of our Lord Jesus
Christ.
[27]We have sent therefore Judas and Silas, who shall also tell *you* the same
things by mouth.
[28]For it seemed good to the Holy Ghost, and to us, to lay upon you no
greater burden than these necessary things;
[29]That ye abstain from meats offered to idols, and from blood, and from
things strangled, and from fornication: from which if ye keep yourselves, ye
shall do well. Fare ye well.
[30]So when they were dismissed, they came to Antioch: and when they
had gathered the multitude together, they delivered the epistle:
[31] *Which* when they had read, they rejoiced for the consolation.
[32]And Judas and Silas, being prophets also themselves, exhorted the
brethren with many words, and confirmed *them.*
[33]And after they had tarried *there* a space, they were let go in peace from
the brethren unto the apostles.
[34]Notwithstanding it pleased Silas to abide there still.
[35]Paul also and Barnabas continued in Antioch, teaching and preaching
the word of the Lord, with many others also.

15:26 Acts 13:50; 14:19; 1 Cor 15:30; 2 Cor 11:23, 26
☆15:29 Lev 17:14; Acts 21:25; Rev 2:14
15:32 Acts 13:1

E. THE SECOND MISSIONARY JOURNEY
1. Turkey
a. The Disagreement between Paul and Barnabas

[36]¶And some days after Paul said unto Barnabas, Let us go again and
visit our brethren in every city where we have preached the word of the
Lord, *and see* how they do.
[37]And Barnabas determined to take with them John, whose surname was
Mark.
[38]But Paul thought not good to take him with them, who departed from
them from Pam-phyl′i-a, and went not with them to the work.
[39]And the contention was so sharp between them, that they departed
asunder one from the other: and so Barnabas took Mark, and sailed unto
Cyprus;
[40]And Paul chose Silas, and departed, being recommended by the
brethren unto the grace of God.
[41]And he went through Syria and Ci-li′ci-a, confirming the churches.

☆15:36 Acts 13:4, 13, 14, 51; 14:5, 6, 24–28
15:37 Acts 12:12; 13:5; Col 4:10; 2 Tim 4:11; Philem 24
15:38 Acts 13:13
15:39 Acts 4:36
15:40 Acts 15:22

b. Paul's Choice of Timothy to Assist Him

16 THEN came he to Der′be and Lys′tra: and, behold, a certain
disciple was there, named Ti-mo′the-us, the son of a certain woman,
which was a Jewess, and believed; but his father *was* a Greek:
[2]Which was well reported of by the brethren that were at Lys′tra and
I-co′ni-um.

16:1 Acts 14:5, 6; 19:22; Rom 16:21; 1 Cor 4:17; Phil 1:1; 2:19–22; 1 Thess 1:1; 3:2, 3; 1 Tim 1:2; 2 Tim 1:2, 5; 3:15

15:29 With the sending of this letter, the first ecumenical or church council ever held came to its conclusion. The Holy Spirit conveyed his will through the elders and deacons, who felt assured that he had spoken to them. Decisions made apart from such a conviction are often wrong. Scripture does not intimate or suggest that believers can go it alone, however sensible and prudent they think their conclusions to be. The Holy Spirit is both teacher and leader.

15:36ff Paul and Barnabas had a difference of opinion over John Mark. When they could not agree, they separated, Paul taking Silas with him and Barnabas taking John Mark. The solution for them to go their separate ways lays down a pattern for us when we are troubled by the same problem. Paul and Barnabas transcended their difficulties without resorting to acrimony or hostility. Later, Paul and John Mark worked together once more.

16:3☆ 1 Cor 9:20; Gal 2:3; 5:2
16:4 Acts 15:24–29
16:5 Acts 9:31; Col 2:2; Jude 20, 21

3 Him would Paul have to go forth with him; and took and circumcised
him because of the Jews which were in those quarters: for they knew all
that his father was a Greek.
4 And as they went through the cities, they delivered them the decrees for
to keep, that were ordained of the apostles and elders which were at
Jerusalem.
5 And so were the churches established in the faith, and increased in
number daily.

c. Paul's Macedonian Vision

16:6☆
16:7 Rom 8:9; Gal 2:20; Phil 1:19
16:8 2 Cor 2:12; 2 Tim 4:13
16:9 Num 12:6; Acts 10:3, 30; Rom 15:26; 18:5; 20:3
16:10☆

6 Now when they had gone throughout Phryg'i-a and the region of Ga-
la'tia, and were forbidden of the Holy Ghost to preach the word in Asia,
7 After they were come to Mys'i-a, they assayed to go into Bi-thyn'i-a: but
the Spirit suffered them not.
8 And they passing by Mys'i-a came down to Troas.
9 And a vision appeared to Paul in the night; There stood a man of
Macedonia, and prayed him, saying, Come over into Macedonia, and help
us.
10 And after he had seen the vision, immediately we endeavoured to go
into Macedonia, assuredly gathering that the Lord had called us for to
preach the gospel unto them.

2. Paul's Ministry in Macedonia

a. Evangelizing Philippi

16:11 Acts 20:5; 2 Cor 2:12; 2 Tim 4:13
16:12 Acts 20:6; Phil 1:1; 1 Thess 2:2
16:14 a) Rev 1:11; 2:18–29; b) Acts 13:43; 18:7
16:15 Acts 16:14
16:16 Lev 19:31; 20:6; Deut 18:10, 11; 1 Sam 28:3, 7, 8

11 Therefore loosing from Troas, we came with a straight course to Sam-o-
thra'ci-a, and the next *day* to Ne-ap'o-lis;
12 And from thence to Phi-lip'pi, which is the chief city of that part of
Macedonia, *and* a colony: and we were in that city abiding certain days.
13 And on the sabbath we went out of the city by a river side, where
prayer was wont to be made; and we sat down, and spake unto the women
which resorted *thither.*
14 ¶And a certain woman named Lyd'i-a, a seller of purple, of the city of
Thy-a-ti'ra, which worshipped God, heard *us:* whose heart the Lord
opened, that she attended unto the things which were spoken of Paul.
15 And when she was baptized, and her household, she besought *us,*
saying, If ye have judged me to be faithful to the Lord, come into my house,
and abide *there.* And she constrained us.
16 ¶And it came to pass, as we went to prayer, a certain damsel possessed
with a spirit of divination met us, which brought her masters much gain by
soothsaying:

16:3 Paul argued strongly that circumcision was no longer required (Gal. 2:3–5); yet here he had Timothy circumcised. Principle did not require that it be done, but expediency made it appropriate. Scripture does lay down the maxim that what is wrong in principle should never be done, however expedient it may appear to be. Many acts are not wrong in principle and may be done or not done, depending on the circumstances surrounding the situation. Paul, for example, said that eating meat offered to idols was legitimate, but he refrained from doing so because it offended the consciences of weaker brothers. Paul had Timothy submit to circumcision, but not because a failure to do so would be wrong in principle. It would have been inexpedient not to have him circumcised, because the progress of the gospel would have been set back and evangelization made more difficult.

16:6 The apostolic band was forbidden by the Holy Spirit to preach the Word in Asia. We do not know whether this was by way of inward persuasion of the Spirit or caused by external circumstances. Either way, they knew they were being led by the Spirit.

16:10 Here, for the first time, the word "we" becomes part of the narrative voice. This means that Luke, the author of the book, has joined himself to Paul in his ministry. He joined Paul in Troas and went with him to Philippi, but he left the party when they left Philippi (16:40). The other segment of Acts begins in Philippi six or seven years later (20:5) and continues through the remainder of the book.

17 The same followed Paul and us, and cried, saying, These men are the
servants of the most high God, which shew unto us the way of salvation.
18 And this did she many days. But Paul, being grieved, turned and said to
the spirit, I command thee in the name of Jesus Christ to come out of her.
And he came out the same hour.
19 ¶And when her masters saw that the hope of their gains was gone, they
caught Paul and Silas, and drew *them* into the marketplace unto the rulers,
20 And brought them to the magistrates, saying, These men, being Jews,
do exceedingly trouble our city,
21 And teach customs, which are not lawful for us to receive, neither to
observe, being Romans.
22 And the multitude rose up together against them: and the magistrates
rent off their clothes, and commanded to beat *them.*
23 And when they had laid many stripes upon them, they cast *them* into
prison, charging the jailor to keep them safely:
24 Who, having received such a charge, thrust them into the inner prison,
and made their feet fast in the stocks.
25 ¶And at midnight Paul and Silas prayed, and sang praises unto God:
and the prisoners heard them.
26 And suddenly there was a great earthquake, so that the foundations of
the prison were shaken: and immediately all the doors were opened, and
every one's bands were loosed.
27 And the keeper of the prison awaking out of his sleep, and seeing the
prison doors open, he drew out his sword, and would have killed himself,
supposing that the prisoners had been fled.
28 But Paul cried with a loud voice, saying, Do thyself no harm: for we are
all here.
29 Then he called for a light, and sprang in, and came trembling, and fell
down before Paul and Silas,
30 And brought them out, and said, Sirs, what must I do to be saved?
31 And they said, Believe on the Lord Jesus Christ, and thou shalt be
saved, and thy house.
32 And they spake unto him the word of the Lord, and to all that were in
his house.
33 And he took them the same hour of the night, and washed *their* stripes;
and was baptized, he and all his, straightway.
34 And when he had brought them into his house, he set meat before
them, and rejoiced, believing in God with all his house.
35 And when it was day, the magistrates sent the serjeants, saying, Let
those men go.
36 And the keeper of the prison told this saying to Paul, The magistrates
have sent to let you go: now therefore depart, and go in peace.
37 But Paul said unto them, They have beaten us openly uncondemned,

☆**16:18** Mk 1:25, 34 16:17
16:19 Mt 10:18 2 Cor 6:5
16:20, 21 Esth 3:8 Acts 16:12; 17:6
16:22 2 Cor 11:23 1 Thess 2:2
16:23 Lk 21:11
16:24 Jer 20:2; 29:26
16:25 Mt 5:10–12 Acts 5:41 Eph 5:19 Col 1:24 2 Tim 1:8
☆**16:26** Acts 5:19; 12:7, 10
16:27 Acts 12:19
16:30 Acts 2:37
16:31 Jn 3:16, 36 Acts 11:14 Rom 10:9
16:34 1 Sam 2:1, 2 1 Chron 16:10 Ps 119:111 Rom 5:2 1 Pet 1:8
☆**16:37** Mt 10:16 Acts 22:25–29

16:18 *Here Paul exorcises the demon who has inhab*ited the slave girl. He performed this action in the name of the Lord Jesus Christ, and it was successful. There are many instances recorded in the history of the Church in which demons have been exorcised. The infamous Salem witch trials in the American colonies point to the fact that the concept of demon possession can be abused, and innocent people can suffer. Nevertheless, this should not cause believers to suppose that all cases of demon possession are fraudulent.

16:26 Paul and Silas, jailed in Philippi, were beaten; their feet were put in stocks. Yet they prayed and sang praises to God. Suddenly there was a great earthquake. Critics like to suppose that this earthquake incident did not really happen and was arbitrarily concocted by Luke. But it was clearly a natural event occasioned by God's supernatural intervention. It occurred in the right place at the right time, accomplishing God's intended purpose to free his servants.

16:37 Paul did not hesitate to claim his rights as a Roman citizen. He demanded the protection of the law and got it. Christians should not refuse to use their rights to protect their persons. Whoever pays taxes and respects government is entitled to the rights common to all citizens.

being Romans, and have cast *us* into prison; and now do they thrust us out privily? nay verily; but let them come themselves and fetch us out.

16:38 Acts 22:29

38 And the serjeants told these words unto the magistrates: and they feared, when they heard that they were Romans.

39 And they came and besought them, and brought *them* out, and desired *them* to depart out of the city.

16:40 Acts 16:14, 15

40 And they went out of the prison, and entered into *the house of* Lyd'i-a: and when they had seen the brethren, they comforted them, and departed.

b. Evangelizing Thessalonica

17:1☆ Phil 4:16; 1 Thess 1:1; 2 Thess 1:1

17 NOW when they had passed through Am-phip'o-lis and Ap-ol-lo'ni-a, they came to Thes-sa-lo-ni'ca, where was a synagogue of the Jews:

17:2☆ Acts 9:20; 13:5, 14; 14:1; 17:10, 17; 19:8
17:3 Lk 24:26; Acts 3:18; 9:22; 18:5

2 And Paul, as his manner was, went in unto them, and three sabbath days reasoned with them out of the scriptures,

3 Opening and alleging, that Christ must needs have suffered, and risen again from the dead; and that this Jesus, whom I preach unto you, is Christ.

4 And some of them believed, and consorted with Paul and Silas; and of the devout Greeks a great multitude, and of the chief women not a few.

17:5☆ Rom 16:21

5 ¶But the Jews which believed not, moved with envy, took unto them certain lewd fellows of the baser sort, and gathered a company, and set all the city on an uproar, and assaulted the house of Jason, and sought to bring them out to the people.

17:6 Acts 16:20, 21

6 And when they found them not, they drew Jason and certain brethren unto the rulers of the city, crying, These that have turned the world upside down are come hither also;

17:7 Lk 23:2

7 Whom Jason hath received: and these all do contrary to the decrees of Cæsar, saying that there is another king, *one* Jesus.

8 And they troubled the people and the rulers of the city, when they heard these things.

9 And when they had taken security of Jason, and of the other, they let them go.

c. Evangelizing Berea

17:10 Acts 9:25

10 ¶And the brethren immediately sent away Paul and Silas by night unto Be-re'a: who coming *thither* went into the synagogue of the Jews.

17:11 Isa 34:16; Lk 16:29; Jn 5:39; Acts 26:22, 23

11 These were more noble than those in Thes-sa-lo-ni'ca, in that they received the word with all readiness of mind, and searched the scriptures daily, whether those things were so.

12 Therefore many of them believed; also of honourable women which were Greeks, and of men, not a few.

17:13☆ 1 Thess 2:15

13 But when the Jews of Thes-sa-lo-ni'ca had knowledge that the word of God was preached of Paul at Be-re'a, they came thither also, and stirred up the people.

17:1 *Thessalonica,* known now as Salonica.

17:2 Following his usual custom Paul went to the synagogue and preached the gospel for three weeks to the Jews, emphasizing the death and resurrection of Jesus, who was the promised Messiah. Paul also must have preached to Gentile idolators, for in 1 Thessalonians it says they turned from idols to God (1 Thess. 1:9). (The Jews had been cured of making and worshipping idols after the captivity.)

17:5ff Paul and Silas encounter severe persecution in Thessalonica. The unbelieving Jews used men of the basest sort to attack Christianity. They persecuted Paul's followers who, they claimed, were public enemies that presented a danger to the state. The people and the rulers of the city were upset. Paul and Silas practiced what Jesus taught: when you are persecuted in one place, go to another (Matt. 10:14). They fled from Thessalonica and went to Berea. They were well received, and many *Jews and Gentiles* believed.

17:13 The wicked Jewish opponents of Paul in Thessalonica learned what was happening in Berea. They sent an embassy to Berea to put out the light of the gospel and to warn the Jews there that Paul was a

14 And then immediately the brethren sent away Paul to go as it were to
the sea: but Silas and Ti-mo′the-us abode there still.
15 And they that conducted Paul brought him unto Athens: and receiving
a commandment unto Silas and Ti-mo′the-us for to come to him with all
speed, they departed.

3. Paul's Ministry in Greece
a. Evangelizing Athens

16 ¶Now while Paul waited for them at Athens, his spirit was stirred in
him, when he saw the city wholly given to idolatry.
17 Therefore disputed he in the synagogue with the Jews, and with the
devout persons, and in the market daily with them that met with him.
18 Then certain philosophers of the Ep-i-cu-re′ans, and of the Sto′icks,
encountered him. And some said, What will this babbler say? other some,
He seemeth to be a setter forth of strange gods: because he preached unto
them Jesus, and the resurrection.
19 And they took him, and brought him unto Ar-e-op′a-gus, saying, May
we know what this new doctrine, whereof thou speakest, *is?*
20 For thou bringest certain strange things to our ears: we would know
therefore what these things mean.
21 (For all the Athenians and strangers which were there spent their time
in nothing else, but either to tell, or to hear some new thing.)
22 ¶Then Paul stood in the midst of Mars' hill, and said, *Ye* men of
Athens, I perceive that in all things ye are too superstitious.
23 For as I passed by, and beheld your devotions, I found an altar with
this inscription, TO THE UNKNOWN GOD. Whom therefore ye igno-
rantly worship, him declare I unto you.
24 God that made the world and all things therein, seeing that he is Lord
of heaven and earth, dwelleth not in temples made with hands;
25 Neither is worshipped with men's hands, as though he needed any
thing, seeing he giveth to all life, and breath, and all things;
26 And hath made of one blood all nations of men for to dwell on all the
face of the earth, and hath determined the times before appointed, and the
bounds of their habitation;
27 That they should seek the Lord, if haply they might feel after him, and
find him, though he be not far from every one of us:
28 For in him we live, and move, and have our being; as certain also of
your own poets have said, For we are also his offspring.
29 Forasmuch then as we are the offspring of God, we ought not to think
that the Godhead is like unto gold, or silver, or stone, graven by art and
man's device.
30 And the times of this ignorance God winked at; but now commandeth
all men every where to repent:

17:14 Mt 10:23
17:15 Acts 18:5; 1 Thess 3:1
17:16 Acts 18:1
☆**17:18** 1 Cor 1:20–24; 4:10
17:19 Mk 1:27
17:23 Jn 4:22; 2 Thess 2:4
17:24 1 Kgs 8:27; Isa 42:5; Acts 7:48, 49; 14:15
17:25 Ps 50:10–12; Dan 4:35; Rom 11:36
☆**17:26** Deut 30:20; 32:8; Job 12:23; 14:5; Mal 2:10
17:27 Deut 4:7; Jer 23:23, 24; Acts 14:17; Rom 1:20
17:28 Job 12:10; Dan 5:23; Col 1:17–19; Heb 1:3
17:29 Isa 40:18–25; Rom 1:23
☆**17:30** Lk 24:47; Acts 14:16, 17; 26:20; Rom 3:25

deceiver. The tense situation was relieved when Paul's *friends took him to Athens. Silas and Timothy* were to join him in Athens. Timothy went by way of Thessalonica in order to bring word with him about the progress of the faith there. Paul wanted that information.

17:18 Epicurus (born 342 B.C.) was the founder of Epicurean philosophy. He lived in Athens the later years of his life. He taught that pleasure is the supreme good in life and that men should pursue it unabashedly. The *Stoicks* charged that this teaching led to sloth and sensuality; they also said Epicurus was an atheist. Stoicism was founded by Zeno (ca. 278 B.C.). It taught indifference to pain or pleasure as well as the need for the courage never to submit or yield. Paul's teaching cut across the teachings of both groups and appeared to them to be novel.

17:26 The entire human race has descended from Adam and Eve, our first parents. Since this is so, racism is in itself sinful. God makes no distinction based on the color of a man's skin; neither should the Christian. Racial intermarriage is not forbidden, nor is it wrong. It may be inexpedient, however, depending on the circumstances.

17:30 Repentance is essential to salvation. But repentance in and of itself does not save. It merely brings the sinner to a place where God's forgiving grace meets him. True repentance comprises five parts: (1) a change of mind (Matt. 21:28, 29); (2) genuine heart

17:31 Ps 96:13 / Jn 5:22, 27 / Acts 2:24; 10:42 / Rom 2:16; 4:25 / 1 Cor 15
17:32 Acts 17:18

31 Because he hath appointed a day, in the which he will judge the world
in righteousness by *that* man whom he hath ordained; *whereof* he hath given
assurance unto all *men,* in that he hath raised him from the dead.
32 ¶And when they heard of the resurrection of the dead, some mocked:
and others said, We will hear thee again of this *matter.*
33 So Paul departed from among them.
34 Howbeit certain men clave unto him, and believed: among the which
was Di-o-nys'i-us the Ar-e-op'a-gite, and a woman named Dam'a-ris, and
others with them.

b. Evangelizing Corinth

18:1☆ Acts 18:8 / 1 Cor 1:2 / 2 Cor 6:11
18:2 Acts 11:28 / 18:18, 25, 26 / Rom 16:3 / 1 Cor 16:19 / 2 Tim 4:19
18:3☆ Acts 20:34 / 1 Cor 4:12; 9:15 / 2 Cor 11:7 / 12:13 / 1 Thess 2:9 / 2 Thess 3:8
18:5 Acts 17:3 / 18:28
18:6 2 Sam 1:16 / Ezek 3:18, 19 / 33:4, 6, 8 / Mt 10:14 / 27:24, 25 / Acts 13:46 / 20:26; 28:26–28
18:7☆ Acts 16:14
18:8 1 Cor 1:2, 14 / 2 Cor 6:11
18:9☆
18:10 Isa 41:10 / Jer 1:18 / Mt 28:20 / 2 Tim 2:19

18 AFTER these things Paul departed from Athens, and came to
Corinth;
2 And found a certain Jew named Aq'ui-la, born in Pontus, lately come
from Italy, with his wife Priscilla; (because that Claudius had commanded
all Jews to depart from Rome:) and came unto them.
3 And because he was of the same craft, he abode with them, and
wrought: for by their occupation they were tentmakers.
4 And he reasoned in the synagogue every sabbath, and persuaded the
Jews and the Greeks.
5 And when Silas and Ti-mo'the-us were come from Macedonia, Paul was
pressed in the spirit, and testified to the Jews *that* Jesus *was* Christ.
6 And when they opposed themselves, and blasphemed, he shook *his*
raiment, and said unto them, Your blood *be* upon your own heads; I *am*
clean: from henceforth I will go unto the Gentiles.
7 ¶And he departed thence, and entered into a certain *man's* house,
named Justus, *one* that worshipped God, whose house joined hard to the
synagogue.
8 And Crispus, the chief ruler of the synagogue, believed on the Lord with
all his house; and many of the Co-rinth'i-ans hearing believed, and were
baptized.
9 Then spake the Lord to Paul in the night by a vision, Be not afraid, but
speak, and hold not thy peace:
10 For I am with thee, and no man shall set on thee to hurt thee: for I have
much people in this city.

---

sorrow for sin (Luke 18:9–14); (3) confession of sin (Luke 15:18; 18:13); (4) forsaking one's sins (Prov. 28:13; Isa. 55:7; John 8:11); and (5) turning to God as Savior and Lord (1 Thess. 1:9).

18:1ff Paul comes to Corinth after a rather bad experience in Athens. But Corinth is to be a better mission field. Multitudes will come to know Christ. Corinth was a very wicked city; in fact, "to Corinthianize" was a phrase used to denote how a city or people could become evil. Corinth was the least likely city to experience a spiritual awakening. But that makes no difference to God. His Word can break down the hardest heart and sweep away the strongest barrier. The Jews in Corinth, among whom one would suppose the gospel might have free recourse, turned against Paul. So he turned from them to the Gentiles and reaped a bountiful harvest. He met up with Aquila and Priscilla, who joined with him in preaching the gospel. Aquila had left Rome because Emperor Claudius Caesar banished all Jews from Rome, and Aquila was a Jew—a Christian Jew. At this period in the history of the church, Gentiles found it difficult to distinguish between a Jew and a Christian. Therefore they persecuted both Jews and Christians. Paul was joined by Silas and Timothy, but the Jews in Corinth resisted their preaching. So Paul turned to the Gentiles.

18:3 The highly educated Paul had been apprenticed as a leatherworker, here called a tentmaker. This enabled Paul to support himself; scribes and rabbis did not think it proper to receive payment for their teaching, so they practiced a trade in addition to their teaching of the law and their study. Rabbi Gamaliel III said: "An excellent thing is the study of the Torah combined with some secular occupation, for the labour demanded by them both puts sin out of one's mind. All study of the Torah which is not combined with work will ultimately be futile and lead to sin" (F. F. Bruce, *The Book of the Acts,* Eerdman's, 1954, p. 367).

18:7 When he leaves the Jews and the synagogue, Paul goes to the house of Titus ("Titius" in better manuscripts) Justis, who lives next door to the synagogue and is a Gentile believer. Then Crispus, the ruler of the synagogue, gets converted and many of the Corinthian Gentiles hear the Word of God, believe on Jesus Christ, and are baptized.

18:9–11 God visits Paul in a vision. He tells him that he has many people in Corinth. Their names were written in the book of life even before they knew it. God

11 And he continued *there* a year and six months, teaching the word of
God among them.
12 ¶And when Gal'li-o was the deputy of A-chai'a, the Jews made
insurrection with one accord against Paul, and brought him to the
judgment seat,

☆**18:12** Rom 15:26; 1 Thess 1:7; 2:16

13 Saying, This *fellow* persuadeth men to worship God contrary to the law.
14 And when Paul was now about to open *his* mouth, Gal'li-o said unto
the Jews, If it were a matter of wrong or wicked lewdness, O *ye* Jews, reason
would that I should bear with you:
15 But if it be a question of words and names, and *of* your law, look ye *to*
it; for I will be no judge of such *matters.*

18:15 Acts 23:29; 25:19

16 And he drave them from the judgment seat.
17 Then all the Greeks took Sos'the-nes, the chief ruler of the synagogue,
and beat *him* before the judgment seat. And Gal'li-o cared for none of those
things.

18:17 Acts 18:8; 1 Cor 1:1

4. Paul Revisits Antioch

18 ¶And Paul *after this* tarried *there* yet a good while, and then took his
leave of the brethren, and sailed thence into Syria, and with him Priscilla
and Aq'ui-la; having shorn *his* head in Cen'chre-a: for he had a vow.
19 And he came to Eph'e-sus, and left them there: but he himself entered
into the synagogue, and reasoned with the Jews.
20 When they desired *him* to tarry longer time with them, he consented
not;

18:18 Num 6:2, 18; Acts 18:2, 26; 21:24; Rom 16:1; 1 Cor 9:20

☆**18:19** Eph 1:1; Rev 1:11; 2:1

21 But bade them farewell, saying, I must by all means keep this feast that
cometh in Jerusalem: but I will return again unto you, if God will. And he
sailed from Eph'e-sus.

18:21 Acts 19:1; Jas 4:15

F. THE THIRD MISSIONARY JOURNEY

1. Visiting Galatia and Phrygia

22 And when he had landed at Cæs-a-re'a, and gone up, and saluted the
church, he went down to Antioch.

18:22 Acts 8:40; 11:19

23 And after he had spent some time *there,* he departed, and went over *all*
the country of Ga-la'tia and Phryg'i-a in order, strengthening all the
disciples.

18:23 Isa 35:3; Acts 16:6; Gal 1:2; 4:14

2. Evangelizing Ephesus

a. The Ministry of Apollos

24 ¶And a certain Jew named Apollos, born at Alexandria, an eloquent
man, *and* mighty in the scriptures, came to Eph'e-sus.

☆**18:24** Acts 19:1; 1 Cor 1:12; 4:1, 6; 16:12; Tit 3:13

---

promises Paul much fruit. He stays in Corinth for a year and a half, preaching and teaching the Word of God. **18:12** *Achaia* was a Roman province; Corinth was its capital. *Gallio, the proconsul, was appointed to his* position by Claudius, the emperor, in July of A.D. 51. Gallio was the brother of the famous philosopher Seneca. He was born in Spain and adopted by Lucius Junius Gallio, who trained him for government work. **18:19** *Ephesus.* Paul stopped at Ephesus for the first time at the end of his second missionary journey. He preached the gospel for a short while and went on to Antioch, which was his home base. The Holy Spirit had previously forbade him to preach in the Roman province of Asia, of which Ephesus was the capital. On his third missionary journey Paul went to Ephesus, where he spent three years (19:1; 20:1). Toward the end of his third missionary journey, he started for Jerusalem to celebrate Pentecost (20:16) and summoned the Ephesian elders to meet him at the seaport of Miletus, where he tearfully told them that he would see them no more (20:17–38).

18:24ff *Apollos* was a well taught, scholarly preacher. He was eloquent and knew the Old Testament Scriptures well. He may have been a disciple of John the Baptist. He believed Jesus was the Messiah and was zealously sharing this knowledge with others. But he was not fully informed concerning the Christian faith and knew little or nothing about the Holy Spirit. Apollos was baptized, as were the others in his company. Paul laid hands on them, they were filled with the Holy Spirit, and spoke in tongues (19:1–7).

18:25 Acts 18:2, 18; 19:3

25 This man was instructed in the way of the Lord; and being fervent in the spirit, he spake and taught diligently the things of the Lord, knowing only the baptism of John.

26 And he began to speak boldly in the synagogue: whom when Aq′ui-la and Priscilla had heard, they took him unto *them,* and expounded unto him the way of God more perfectly.

18:27 1 Cor 3:6

27 And when he was disposed to pass into A-chai′a, the brethren wrote, exhorting the disciples to receive him: who, when he was come, helped them much which had believed through grace:

18:28 Gen 49:10; Deut 18:15; Ps 22; Isa 7:14; 9:6; 53; Jer 23:5, 6; Dan 9:25, 26; Mic 5:2; Mal 3:1; Lk 24:27

28 For he mightily convinced the Jews, *and that* publickly, shewing by the scriptures that Jesus was Christ.

b. The Baptism of Converts

19:1☆ Acts 18:21

19 AND it came to pass, that, while Apollos was at Corinth, Paul having passed through the upper coasts came to Eph′e-sus: and finding certain disciples,

19:2☆ Jn 7:39; Acts 8:15, 16

2 He said unto them, Have ye received the Holy Ghost since ye believed? And they said unto him, We have not so much as heard whether there be any Holy Ghost.

19:3 Lk 7:29; Acts 18:25, 26

3 And he said unto them, Unto what then were ye baptized? And they said, Unto John's baptism.

19:4 Jn 1:7; Acts 1:5; 11:16; 13:24

4 Then said Paul, John verily baptized with the baptism of repentance, saying unto the people, that they should believe on him which should come after him, that is, on Christ Jesus.

19:5 Acts 8:12, 16; 10:48; Gal 3:27

5 When they heard *this,* they were baptized in the name of the Lord Jesus.

19:6 Acts 2:4; 10:46

6 And when Paul had laid *his* hands upon them, the Holy Ghost came on them; and they spake with tongues, and prophesied.

7 And all the men were about twelve.

c. Paul's Extended Ministry in the Synagogue and the Hall of Tyrannus

19:8 Acts 1:3; 28:23, 31

8 And he went into the synagogue, and spake boldly for the space of three months, disputing and persuading the things concerning the kingdom of God.

19:9☆

9 But when divers were hardened, and believed not, but spake evil of that way before the multitude, he departed from them, and separated the disciples, disputing daily in the school of one Ty-ran′nus.

19:10 Acts 16:6; 19:20, 22; 20:31

10 And this continued by the space of two years; so that all they which dwelt in Asia heard the word of the Lord Jesus, both Jews and Greeks.

d. Paul's Unusual Miracles

19:11 Mk 16:20

11 And God wrought special miracles by the hands of Paul:

19:12☆ 2 Kgs 4:29; Jn 14:12; Acts 5:15

12 So that from his body were brought unto the sick handkerchiefs or

---

19:1 Paul, now on his third and last missionary journey, comes to Ephesus. In this city was a temple to Diana, which was regarded as one of the seven wonders of the world. From Ephesus the gospel was to spread, and in this area the seven churches of the Apocalypse came into being. Along with Ephesus were included Smyrna, Laodicea, Pergamum, Sardis, Phila*delphia, and Thyatira.* The apostle John in The Revelation inscribed a letter to these seven churches (chapters 2 and 3).

19:2 Paul finds some believers in Ephesus and asks them whether they have received the Holy Spirit. Though they had never heard of the Holy Spirit, Paul regards them as true believers, for his question includes the phrase "since ye believed." They knew only of John's baptism. So they are now baptized and receive the gift of tongues. They also prophesied. It was a small company of believers—twelve in number.

19:9 The hall of Tyrannus, whose name means "tyrant," was probably a lecture hall or building for hire. Paul used this room or house regularly for a period of two years, where he was able to preach and speak without interference. He enjoyed a wide hearing in what was apparently a well situated and spacious accommodation.

19:12 Healings and exorcisms resulted from placing Paul's handkerchiefs or aprons upon the afflicted. The handkerchiefs and aprons were sweat rags that he tied

aprons, and the diseases departed from them, and the evil spirits went out
of them.
13 ¶Then certain of the vagabond Jews, exorcists, took upon them to call
over them which had evil spirits the name of the Lord Jesus, saying, We
adjure you by Jesus whom Paul preacheth.
14 And there were seven sons of *one* Sce'va, a Jew, *and* chief of the priests,
which did so.
15 And the evil spirit answered and said, Jesus I know, and Paul I know;
but who are ye?
16 And the man in whom the evil spirit was leaped on them, and overcame
them, and prevailed against them, so that they fled out of that house naked
and wounded.
17 And this was known to all the Jews and Greeks also dwelling at Eph'e-
sus; and fear fell on them all, and the name of the Lord Jesus was
magnified.
18 And many that believed came, and confessed, and shewed their deeds.
19 Many of them also which used curious arts brought their books
together, and burned them before all *men:* and they counted the price of
them, and found *it* fifty thousand *pieces* of silver.
20 So mightily grew the word of God and prevailed.

19:13 Mt 12:26–28 Mk 9:38, 39 Lk 9:49, 50 11:19
☆19:14
19:15 Mt 8:29 Mk 1:24 Lk 4:34 Acts 16:16–18 Jas 2:19
19:17 Lk 7:16 Acts 2:43 5:5, 11
19:18 Isa 30:22 Jer 3:13
19:20 Acts 6:7; 12:24 19:10

e. Paul's Future Plans

21 ¶After these things were ended, Paul purposed in the spirit, when he
had passed through Macedonia and A-chai'a, to go to Jerusalem, saying,
After I have been there, I must also see Rome.
22 So he sent into Macedonia two of them that ministered unto him, Ti-
mo'the-us and E-ras'tus; but he himself stayed in Asia for a season.

19:21 Acts 20:1, 22 23:11 Rom 15:24–26 1 Cor 16:5
19:22 Acts 16:9 Rom 16:23 2 Tim 4:20

f. Demetrius and the Ephesian Riot

23 And the same time there arose no small stir about that way.
24 For a certain *man* named De-me'tri-us, a silversmith, which made silver
shrines for Diana, brought no small gain unto the craftsmen;
25 Whom he called together with the workmen of like occupation, and
said, Sirs, ye know that by this craft we have our wealth.
26 Moreover ye see and hear, that not alone at Eph'e-sus, but almost
throughout all Asia, this Paul hath persuaded and turned away much
people, saying that they be no gods, which are made with hands:
27 So that not only this our craft is in danger to be set at nought; but also
that the temple of the great goddess Diana should be despised, and her

19:23 2 Cor 1:8
☆19:24 Acts 16:16, 19
19:25 1 Tim 6:10
19:26 1 Chron 16:26 Ps 115:4 Isa 44:10–20 46:7 Jer 16:20 Acts 17:29 1 Cor 8:4

around his head and waist while working at his trade. Several evangelists today advertise handkerchiefs for such use and money is asked for, but the materials have not come from the sweat of honest labor. The healings constituted a reminder of Jesus' miracles among people who touched the fringe of his cloak.

19:14ff *Sceva,* described as *chief of the priests,* could not have functioned in this capacity in Asia Minor. He may have exercised that office in Jerusalem, or he may have been a member of a high-priestly family or the head of one of the twenty-four courses of priests. His sons tried to exorcise demons by using the name of Jesus. Apparently these sons worked together, for in this incident the demon left them naked and wounded. Not having the authority of either Jesus or Paul, they failed miserably. As a result of their failure the true faith was forwarded, the church was revived, and believers who still practiced the occult gave up their magic books and burned them publicly. Truth prevailed over error.

19:24ff *Diana* (*Artemis* in the Greek text) was an Ephesian goddess. She should not be confused with the Greek virgin goddess Artemis (*Diana* in the Latin). The Ephesian Artemis was a fertility goddess whose worship went back for centuries. The temple at Ephesus was one of the seven wonders of the ancient world.

Demetrius, the silversmith, owed his living to the manufacture of idols to Diana. Paul was so successful that his business and that of other silversmiths was severely affected. Here, Demetrius gathers a mob and claims that Paul has hurt his business by persuading people not to worship Diana, and thus Diana is being despised and her greatness assailed. If her temple is set aside, Asia will lose its greatest prize, for her statue was supposed to have dropped down out of heaven.

magnificence should be destroyed, whom all Asia and the world worship-
peth.

19:28 Jer 50:38 Hab 2:18–20 Rev 13:4 **19:29** Acts 20:4; 27:2 Rom 16:23 1 Cor 1:14 Col 4:10 Philem 24 **19:30☆**

28 And when they heard *these sayings,* they were full of wrath, and cried
out, saying, Great *is* Diana of the E-phe′sians.
29 And the whole city was filled with confusion: and having caught Gaius
and Ar-is-tar′chus, men of Macedonia, Paul's companions in travel, they
rushed with one accord into the theatre.
30 And when Paul would have entered in unto the people, the disciples
suffered him not.
31 And certain of the chief of Asia, which were his friends, sent unto him,
desiring *him* that he would not adventure himself into the theatre.

19:32 Acts 21:34

32 Some therefore cried one thing, and some another: for the assembly
was confused; and the more part knew not wherefore they were come
together.

19:33 1 Tim 1:20 2 Tim 4:14

33 And they drew Alexander out of the multitude, the Jews putting him
forward. And Alexander beckoned with the hand, and would have made his
defence unto the people.
34 But when they knew that he was a Jew, all with one voice about the
space of two hours cried out, Great *is* Diana of the E-phe′sians.

19:35☆

35 And when the townclerk had appeased the people, he said, *Ye* men of
Eph′e-sus, what man is there that knoweth not how that the city of the
E-phe′sians is a worshipper of the great goddess Diana, and of the *image*
which fell down from Jupiter?
36 Seeing then that these things cannot be spoken against, ye ought to be
quiet, and to do nothing rashly.
37 For ye have brought hither these men, which are neither robbers of
churches, nor yet blasphemers of your goddess.
38 Wherefore if De-me′tri-us, and the craftsmen which are with him, have
a matter against any man, the law is open, and there are deputies: let them
implead one another.
39 But if ye inquire any thing concerning other matters, it shall be
determined in a lawful assembly.
40 For we are in danger to be called in question for this day's uproar, there
being no cause whereby we may give an account of this concourse.
41 And when he had thus spoken, he dismissed the assembly.

3. Paul Starts toward Jerusalem

a. Visiting Macedonia and Achaia en Route to Miletus

20:1☆ 1 Cor 16:5 2 Cor 7:5

20 AND after the uproar was ceased, Paul called unto *him* the
disciples, and embraced *them,* and departed for to go into Macedo-
nia.
2 And when he had gone over those parts, and had given them much
exhortation, he came into Greece,

19:30ff Paul wishes to enter the theater and speak to the crowd assembled there. His friends, the disciples, will not let him do this. The angry mob would probably tear him to bits. The Jews join the unbelieving Gentiles and appoint Alexander to speak against Paul. When the Ephesians note that he is a Jew, they will not hear him, for they know that both Jews and Christians are against their idol worship.

19:35 The town clerk brings order out of chaos. He warns the crowd that their conduct is irregular and constitutes a riot. He dismisses the assembly and the riot ends. Paul's personal ministry in Ephesus also ends.

20:1 Paul leaves Ephesus. He had spent more time there than in any other place where he had ministered. After this he never breaks any new ground in his evangelistic outreach. He simply returns to places where he previously has ministered. He did not leave Ephesus because he was frightened. He thought it was what he should do in the providence of God. Some think Paul wrote his first letter to the Corinthians before leaving Ephesus and that his description of fighting with beasts at Ephesus (1 Cor. 15:32) was an account of the riot involving the silversmiths and the goddess Diana. It was a tearful parting from friends whom he had grown to love and who loved him dearly. He went to Macedonia, visiting the churches at Philippi and Thessalonica.

3And *there* abode three months. And when the Jews laid wait for him, as
he was about to sail into Syria, he purposed to return through Macedonia.
4And there accompanied him into Asia Sop'a-ter of Be-re'a; and of the
Thes-sa-lo'ni-ans, Ar-is-tar'chus and Se-cun'dus; and Gaius of Der'be, and
Ti-mo'the-us; and of Asia, Tych'i-cus and Troph'i-mus.
5These going before tarried for us at Troas.
6And we sailed away from Phi-lip'pi after the days of unleavened bread,
and came unto them to Troas in five days; where we abode seven days.
7And upon the first *day* of the week, when the disciples came together to
break bread, Paul preached unto them, ready to depart on the morrow; and
continued his speech until midnight.
8And there were many lights in the upper chamber, where they were
gathered together.
9And there sat in a window a certain young man named Eu'ty-chus,
being fallen into a deep sleep: and as Paul was long preaching, he sunk
down with sleep, and fell down from the third loft, and was taken up dead.
10And Paul went down, and fell on him, and embracing *him* said, Trouble
not yourselves; for his life is in him.
11When he therefore was come up again, and had broken bread, and
eaten, and talked a long while, even till break of day, so he departed.
12And they brought the young man alive, and were not a little comforted.
13¶And we went before to ship, and sailed unto As'sos, there intending to
take in Paul: for so had he appointed, minding himself to go afoot.
14And when he met with us at As'sos, we took him in, and came to Mit-
y-le'ne.
15And we sailed thence, and came the next *day* over against Chi'os; and
the next *day* we arrived at Sa'mos, and tarried at Tro-gyl'li-um; and the
next *day* we came to Mi-le'tus.
16For Paul had determined to sail by Eph'e-sus, because he would not
spend the time in Asia: for he hasted, if it were possible for him, to be at
Jerusalem the day of Pentecost.

b. Paul's Meeting with the Ephesian Elders

17¶And from Mi-le'tus he sent to Eph'e-sus, and called the elders of the
church.
18And when they were come to him, he said unto them, Ye know, from
the first day that I came into Asia, after what manner I have been with you
at all seasons,
19Serving the Lord with all humility of mind, and with many tears, and
temptations, which befell me by the lying in wait of the Jews:
20*And* how I kept back nothing that was profitable *unto you,* but have
shewed you, and have taught you publickly, and from house to house,

20:3 Acts 9:24; 20:19; 23:12, 13; 2 Cor 11:26
20:4 Acts 16:1; 19:22, 29; 21:29; 27:2; Eph 6:21; Col 4:7, 10; 2 Tim 4:12, 20; Tit 3:12
20:6 Ex 23:15; 2 Cor 2:12; 2 Tim 4:13
☆**20:7** Acts 2:42; 1 Cor 10:16, 17; 11:20–34; 16:2; Rev 1:10
20:10 1 Kgs 17:21; 2 Kgs 4:34; Mt 9:23–25; Mk 5:39–42
20:15 Acts 21:4, 12; 24:17; 2 Tim 4:20
☆**20:16**
20:17 1 Tim 4:14
☆**20:18** Acts 18:19; 19:1, 10

20:7 Paul is now at Troas and Luke has rejoined him, *for the "we" section begins again. It took five days to* get to Troas by sea, and he remains in Troas for seven days. While there he preached a very long sermon the night before his departure. A man named Eutychus occupied a dangerous spot from which he listened to Paul. He fell fast asleep and fell to his death from his perch on the third loft. The incident distracted the assembly and interrupted Paul's discourse. An undaunted Paul embraced the dead body, which came to life. It was a miraculous display of the power and mercy of God.

20:16 Since Paul is anxious to celebrate Pentecost in Jerusalem, he decides to bypass Ephesus on the journey back to the holy city. The ship stops at Miletus and Paul sends a note to the Ephesian elders to visit with him at Miletus. The elders and their families come to Miletus to see him off to Jerusalem.

20:18 Paul speaks to his dear friends from Ephesus and tells them something about his preaching. It was plain, powerful, profitable, painstaking, faithful, catholic, and evangelical. He knows that sufferings will be his destiny in the days ahead, but he is under the compulsion of the Holy Spirit to continue his journey. He manifests holy courage and resolution, a holy contempt for his life, and a holy concern to finish his work. He will see these beloved friends no more in this life, but in the life which is yet to come.

20:21 Lk 24:47 Acts 2:38; 11:18, 26:20 **20:22** Acts 19:21 **20:23** Acts 9:16; 21:4, 11, 33 **20:24☆** Acts 21:13 Rom 8:35, 39 2 Cor 4:16 2 Tim 4:7 **20:25** Act 28:23, 31 **20:26** Acts 18:6 2 Cor 7:2 1 Thess 2:10 **20:28☆** Jn 21:15–17 1 Cor 12:28 Eph 1:7 Col 1:14 1 Tim 4:16 Heb 9:14 1 Pet 1:19; 5:2 Rev 5:9 **20:29** Ezek 22:27 Mt 7:15 Jn 10:10, 12 2 Pet 2:1 **20:30** 1 Jn 2:19 **20:31** Acts 19:10 **20:32** Jn 17:17 Acts 9:31; 26:18 Eph 1:18 Col 3:24 1 Pet 1:4; 2:2 **20:33☆** 1 Sam 12:3 1 Cor 9:12 2 Cor 7:2 11:8, 9; 12:17 **20:34** 1 Cor 4:12 1 Thess 2:9 2 Thess 3:8 **20:35** 2 Cor 8:9 1 Thess 4:11 5:14 Heb 13:1, 3 **20:36☆** **20:38** Acts 20:25

21 Testifying both to the Jews, and also to the Greeks, repentance toward
God, and faith toward our Lord Jesus Christ.
22 And now, behold, I go bound in the spirit unto Jerusalem, not knowing
the things that shall befall me there:
23 Save that the Holy Ghost witnesseth in every city, saying that bonds
and afflictions abide me.
24 But none of these things move me, neither count I my life dear unto
myself, so that I might finish my course with joy, and the ministry, which I
have received of the Lord Jesus, to testify the gospel of the grace of God.
25 And now, behold, I know that ye all, among whom I have gone
preaching the kingdom of God, shall see my face no more.
26 Wherefore I take you to record this day, that I *am* pure from the blood
of all *men*.
27 For I have not shunned to declare unto you all the counsel of God.
28 ¶Take heed therefore unto yourselves, and to all the flock, over the
which the Holy Ghost hath made you overseers, to feed the church of God,
which he hath purchased with his own blood.
29 For I know this, that after my departing shall grievous wolves enter in
among you, not sparing the flock.
30 Also of your own selves shall men arise, speaking perverse things, to
draw away disciples after them.
31 Therefore watch, and remember, that by the space of three years I
ceased not to warn every one night and day with tears.
32 And now, brethren, I commend you to God, and to the word of his
grace, which is able to build you up, and to give you an inheritance among
all them which are sanctified.
33 I have coveted no man's silver, or gold, or apparel.
34 Yea, ye yourselves know, that these hands have ministered unto my
necessities, and to them that were with me.
35 I have shewed you all things, how that so labouring ye ought to support
the weak, and to remember the words of the Lord Jesus, how he said, It is
more blessed to give than to receive.
36 ¶And when he had thus spoken, he kneeled down, and prayed with
them all.
37 And they all wept sore, and fell on Paul's neck, and kissed him,
38 Sorrowing most of all for the words which he spake, that they should
see his face no more. And they accompanied him unto the ship.

c. Paul Arrives at Caesarea

21 AND it came to pass, that after we were gotten from them, and had
launched, we came with a straight course unto Co'os, and the *day*
following unto Rhodes, and from thence unto Pat'a-ra:

20:24 At Iconium Paul had fled for his life. Here he states that he thinks nothing of his life and its value. Self-preservation is not important; doing the will of God is. He is under the control of the Spirit; although he knows what this will mean in the future, he is perfectly willing to suffer death for the cause of Christ with the assurance that, in this instance, it is in the will of God.
20:28 *the flock . . . the church.* The church is given several names in the New Testament, names descriptive of its function, position, and relation to Christ its head: (1) his body (Eph. 1:22, 23; Col. 1:24); (2) the flock of God (1 Pet. 5:2); (3) God's husbandry, God's building (1 Cor. 3:9); (4) God's temple (2 Cor. 6:16); and (5) the bride at the marriage supper of the Lamb (Rev. 21:9).
20:33 Without boasting, Paul commends himself as an example of indifference to the world. He never sought worldly wealth. He worked for a living while he preached. By his own work he earned enough to help others as well as himself. His apt conclusion is this: it is more blessed to give than to receive. He had received little and given much and was happy to do so.
20:36ff Paul and his friends weep together, pray together, embrace each other, and kiss each other. They bring him to the ship on which he will sail eastward to meet his date with destiny and finish his course.

[2]And finding a ship sailing over unto Phe-ni'cia, we went aboard, and set
forth.
[3]Now when we had discovered Cyprus, we left it on the left hand, and
sailed into Syria, and landed at Tyre: for there the ship was to unlade her
burden.
[4]And finding disciples, we tarried there seven days: who said to Paul
through the Spirit, that he should not go up to Jerusalem.
[5]And when we had accomplished those days, we departed and went our
way; and they all brought us on our way, with wives and children, till *we
were* out of the city: and we kneeled down on the shore, and prayed.
[6]And when we had taken our leave one of another, we took ship; and
they returned home again.
[7]And when we had finished *our* course from Tyre, we came to Ptol-e-
ma'is, and saluted the brethren, and abode with them one day.
[8]And the next *day* we that were of Paul's company departed, and came
unto Cæs-a-re'a: and we entered into the house of Philip the evangelist,
which was *one* of the seven; and abode with him.
[9]And the same man had four daughters, virgins, which did prophesy.
[10]And as we tarried *there* many days, there came down from Judæa a
certain prophet, named Ag'a-bus.
[11]And when he was come unto us, he took Paul's girdle, and bound his
own hands and feet, and said, Thus saith the Holy Ghost, So shall the Jews
at Jerusalem bind the man that owneth this girdle, and shall deliver *him*
into the hands of the Gentiles.
[12]And when we heard these things, both we, and they of that place,
besought him not to go up to Jerusalem.
[13]Then Paul answered, What mean ye to weep and to break mine heart?
for I am ready not to be bound only, but also to die at Jerusalem for the
name of the Lord Jesus.
[14]And when he would not be persuaded, we ceased, saying, The will of
the Lord be done.

21:4 Acts 20:23; 21:11
21:5 Acts 20:36
☆**21:8** Acts 6:3, 5; 8:26, 40; Eph 4:11
21:9 Joel 2:28; Acts 2:17
21:10 Acts 11:28
21:11 Acts 20:23, 21:3; Eph 6:20
☆**21:12**
21:13 Acts 20:24; 2 Cor 4:10; Col 1:24
21:14 Mt 26:42

IV. PAUL'S IMPRISONMENT: JERUSALEM, CAESAREA, AND ROME (21:15—28:31)

A. PAUL'S ARRIVAL IN JERUSALEM

[15]And after those days we took up our carriages, and went up to
Jerusalem.
[16]There went with us also *certain* of the disciples of Cæs-a-re'a, and
brought with them one Mna'son of Cyprus, an old disciple, with whom we
should lodge.
[17]And when we were come to Jerusalem, the brethren received us gladly.

☆**21:16**

21:8 *Philip.* This Philip was chosen to be a deacon (Acts 6:5). He also was an evangelist along with Stephen who was martyred. After Stephen's death Philip had great success preaching in Samaria. He was responsible for the conversion of the Ethiopian eunuch (Acts 8:26ff). When Paul stayed at his home, he was settled in Caesarea. He had four daughters who prophesied, i.e., they were female preachers. Philip introduced Christianity to northeast Africa and was the first one to overcome Jewish prejudice and to expand the boundaries of the church interracially via the admission of Gentiles to the faith.

21:12 Paul's companions and the saints at Caesarea, having heard the prophecy of Agabus, seek to keep Paul from going to Jerusalem. Paul, however, is fixed in his determination to go and refuses to be dissuaded by his friends. The advice and counsel of friends should never stop the believer from proceeding along the course laid out by the Holy Spirit. Faithful friends who have our interests at heart can hinder us from doing God's will, although their intentions are excellent from the human perspective. The human and the divine perspectives are not always in agreement.

21:16 *Mnason.* He was a friend of Paul mentioned only in this verse. He was a Cypriot, was probably Jewish, and as an early disciple was probably converted at Pentecost or shortly thereafter. His fidelity to the faith was exemplary and his hospitality in taking Paul and others into his home outstanding.

21:18 Acts 15:13 Gal 1:19 Jas 1:1

18 And the *day* following Paul went in with us unto James; and all the
elders were present.

21:19 Acts 20:24 Rom 15:18

19 And when he had saluted them, he declared particularly what things
God had wrought among the Gentiles by his ministry.

21:20☆ Acts 15:1, 5 Gal 3:10, 11

20 And when they heard *it,* they glorified the Lord, and said unto him,
Thou seest, brother, how many thousands of Jews there are which believe;
and they are all zealous of the law:

21:21 Acts 16:3 Gal 2:3

21 And they are informed of thee, that thou teachest all the Jews which are
among the Gentiles to forsake Moses, saying that they ought not to
circumcise *their* children, neither to walk after the customs.
22 What is it therefore? the multitude must needs come together: for they
will hear that thou art come.

21:23☆ Acts 18:18

23 Do therefore this that we say to thee: We have four men which have a
vow on them;

21:24☆ Num 6:2, 13–21 1 Cor 9:20

24 Them take, and purify thyself with them, and be at charges with them,
that they may shave *their* heads: and all may know that those things,
whereof they were informed concerning thee, are nothing; but *that* thou
thyself also walkest orderly, and keepest the law.

21:25 Acts 15:19–29

25 As touching the Gentiles which believe, we have written *and* concluded
that they observe no such thing, save only that they keep themselves from
things offered to idols, and from blood, and from strangled, and from
fornication.

B. PAUL'S DETENTION IN JERUSALEM
1. His Seizure

26 Then Paul took the men, and the next day purifying himself with them
entered into the temple, to signify the accomplishment of the days of
purification, until that an offering should be offered for every one of them.

21:27 Acts 24:18 26:21 Rom 8:35 2 Cor 4:9 2 Tim 3:12

27 And when the seven days were almost ended, the Jews which were of
Asia, when they saw him in the temple, stirred up all the people, and laid
hands on him,

21:28 Mt 5:11 Lk 6:22; 11:49 21:12; 23:2 Jn 15:10 Acts 6:13 16:20, 21; 17:6 24:5, 6 1 Cor 4:12

28 Crying out, Men of Israel, help: This is the man, that teacheth all *men*
every where against the people, and the law, and this place: and further
brought Greeks also into the temple, and hath polluted this holy place.

21:29☆ Acts 20:4 2 Tim 4:20

29 (For they had seen before with him in the city Troph'i-mus an
E-phe'sian, whom they supposed that Paul had brought into the temple.)
30 And all the city was moved, and the people ran together: and they took
Paul, and drew him out of the temple: and forthwith the doors were shut.
31 And as they went about to kill him, tidings came unto the chief captain
of the band, that all Jerusalem was in an uproar.

21:32 Acts 23:27

32 Who immediately took soldiers and centurions, and ran down unto
them: and when they saw the chief captain and the soldiers, they left
beating of Paul.

21:20 James and others play a mediating role. A number of Jewish believers are still functioning under the law and are unhappy with Paul who, they think, opposes the circumcision of their children and teaches that the customs they accepted should be abrogated. So James and the others ask Paul to show his allegiance to Moses and the law by going to the temple and showing himself publicly with four others who were ending their Nazarite vows. He agrees to do this.

21:23 See note to Num. 6:2 on vows.

21:24 If Paul did what James and others asked him to do, they felt it would appease the objectors by helping them to be free of any suspicion that they were opposed to following the ancient Jewish customs.

21:29 *Trophimus,* a Gentile Christian, accompanied Paul to Rome. As a Gentile he could enter the court of the Gentiles, but he could not go beyond the barrier separating it from the inner court of the temple. The penalty for doing so was death. Signs were posted in Greek and Latin to warn Gentiles to stay out. It was falsely reported that Paul had taken a Gentile into the inner court where the sacrifices were offered. The people were aroused and this occasioned the closing of the temple gates. The presence of the Gentile meant that the temple had been defiled (see 21:28, 30).

33 Then the chief captain came near, and took him, and commanded *him*
to be bound with two chains; and demanded who he was, and what he had
done.
34 And some cried one thing, some another, among the multitude: and
when he could not know the certainty for the tumult, he commanded him to
be carried into the castle.
35 And when he came upon the stairs, so it was, that he was borne of the
soldiers for the violence of the people.
36 For the multitude of the people followed after, crying, Away with him.

21:33 Acts 20:23; 28:20 Eph 6:20
21:36 Lk 23:18 Jn 19:15 Acts 22:22

2. His Defense of Himself

37 And as Paul was to be led into the castle, he said unto the chief captain,
May I speak unto thee? Who said, Canst thou speak Greek?
38 Art not thou that Egyptian, which before these days madest an uproar,
and leddest out into the wilderness four thousand men that were murder-
ers?
39 But Paul said, I am a man *which am* a Jew of Tarsus, *a city* in Ci-li′-
ci-a, a citizen of no mean city: and, I beseech thee, suffer me to speak unto
the people.
40 And when he had given him licence, Paul stood on the stairs, and
beckoned with the hand unto the people. And when there was made a great
silence, he spake unto *them* in the Hebrew tongue, saying,

☆**21:38**
21:39 Acts 9:11 2 Cor 11:22 Gal 3:5 1 Pet 3:15; 4:16
21:40 Acts 26:14

22 MEN, brethren, and fathers, hear ye my defence *which I make* now
unto you.
2 (And when they heard that he spake in the Hebrew tongue to them, they
kept the more silence: and he saith,)
3 I am verily a man *which am* a Jew, born in Tarsus, *a city* in Ci-li′ci-a, yet
brought up in this city at the feet of Ga-ma′li-el, *and* taught according to
the perfect manner of the law of the fathers, and was zealous toward God,
as ye all are this day.
4 And I persecuted this way unto the death, binding and delivering into
prisons both men and women.
5 As also the high priest doth bear me witness, and all the estate of the
elders: from whom also I received letters unto the brethren, and went to
Damascus, to bring them which were there bound unto Jerusalem, for to be
punished.
6 And it came to pass, that, as I made my journey, and was come nigh
unto Damascus about noon, suddenly there shone from heaven a great light
round about me.
7 And I fell unto the ground, and heard a voice saying unto me, Saul,
Saul, why persecutest thou me?
8 And I answered, Who art thou, Lord? And he said unto me, I am Jesus
of Nazareth, whom thou persecutest.
9 And they that were with me saw indeed the light, and were afraid; but
they heard not the voice of him that spake to me.
10 And I said, What shall I do, Lord? And the Lord said unto me, Arise,

☆**22:3** Acts 5:34–40 26:5 Rom 10:2 2 Cor 11:22 Gal 1:14 Phil 3:5
22:4 Acts 8:3 1 Tim 1:13
22:5 Acts 9:2, 3
22:6 Acts 9:3–8; 26:12, 13
☆**22:8** Acts 26:15
22:9 Dan 10:7 Acts 9:7, 26:13

21:38 Josephus, the Jewish historian, refers to this *Egyptian,* whose followers congregated on the Mount of Olives in A.D. 54 to watch the walls of Jerusalem fall. Felix routed the revolters, although the Egyptian himself escaped.

22:3 *Gamaliel.* See note concerning him in Acts 5:34.

22:8 Paul had not seen Jesus during his earthly ministry. But here he sees the resurrected Jesus, which was essential for one who held the office of an apostle. He saw him as one born out of due time (1 Cor. 15:8).

and go into Damascus; and there it shall be told thee of all things which are
appointed for thee to do.

22:11 Acts 9:8

11 And when I could not see for the glory of that light, being led by the
hand of them that were with me, I came into Damascus.

22:12, 13☆ Acts 9:10, 17, 18

12 And one An-a-ni'as, a devout man according to the law, having a good
report of all the Jews which dwelt *there,*
13 Came unto me, and stood, and said unto me, Brother Saul, receive thy
sight. And the same hour I looked up upon him.

22:14☆ Acts 3:13; 26:16 1 Cor 9:1; 15:8 Gal 1:12

14 And he said, The God of our fathers hath chosen thee, that thou
shouldest know his will, and see that Just One, and shouldest hear the voice
of his mouth.

22:15 Acts 26:16

15 For thou shalt be his witness unto all men of what thou hast seen and
heard.

22:16 Ps 116:13 Acts 2:38 Rom 10:13 1 Cor 6:11 Heb 10:22

16 And now why tarriest thou? arise, and be baptized, and wash away thy
sins, calling on the name of the Lord.
17 And it came to pass, that, when I was come again to Jerusalem, even
while I prayed in the temple, I was in a trance;
18 And saw him saying unto me, Make haste, and get thee quickly out of
Jerusalem: for they will not receive thy testimony concerning me.

22:19 Acts 8:3; 22:4; 26:11

19 And I said, Lord, they know that I imprisoned and beat in every
synagogue them that believed on thee:

22:20 Acts 7:58–8:1

20 And when the blood of thy martyr Stephen was shed, I also was
standing by, and consenting unto his death, and kept the raiment of them
that slew him.

22:21☆ Acts 13:2; 18:6 26:17 Rom 11:13 15:15, 16 Gal 2:7–9 1 Tim 2:7 2 Tim 1:11

21 And he said unto me, Depart: for I will send thee far hence unto the
Gentiles.
22 And they gave him audience unto this word, and *then* lifted up their
voices, and said, Away with such a *fellow* from the earth: for it is not fit that
he should live.

22:22 Acts 21:36 25:24

23 And as they cried out, and cast off *their* clothes, and threw dust into the
air,

22:24☆

24 The chief captain commanded him to be brought into the castle, and
bade that he should be examined by scourging; that he might know
wherefore they cried so against him.

22:25☆ Acts 16:37

25 And as they bound him with thongs, Paul said unto the centurion that
stood by, Is it lawful for you to scourge a man that is a Roman, and
uncondemned?
26 When the centurion heard *that,* he went and told the chief captain,
saying, Take heed what thou doest: for this man is a Roman.

22:12 *Ananias.* (See 9:17.) He was a believer whom God chose to minister to Paul while he was blind. Despite his fears he undertook the job with alacrity. Tradition has it that he was bishop of Damascus and one of the seventy. He died a martyr.

22:14 *that Just One.* Jesus is called "the Holy One and the Just" (Acts 3:14), "the Just One" (Acts 7:52), and "the righteous" (1 John 2:1). Since righteousness is an attribute of God, it is to be expected that Jesus Christ should be called *the righteous.*

22:21ff By referring to the Gentiles and claiming that God had commissioned him to preach to them, Paul *inflamed the mob more than ever. A riotous situation* prevailed.

22:24 The chief captain (tribune) now orders scourging for Paul, a dreadful and oftentimes fatal punishment given to criminals. He did not yet know that Paul was a Roman citizen.

22:25 Paul held Roman citizenship. If both parents were Roman citizens, the children were automatically Roman citizens. If the woman in a marriage was not a Roman citizen, the offspring were not citizens. People could become Roman citizens by manumission and by grant for services rendered (of various kinds). Roman citizens could not be scourged or put to death without the right of appeal to the emperor. Once an appeal was granted, no further action could be taken until the emperor had acted, although not all appeals to the emperor were granted. While waiting for his trial, the accused could be housed with a friend who *vouched for his appearance, kept in a common jail,* placed in the custody of a soldier to whom he was chained, or permitted to live in his own lodgings. It was a capital crime to claim Roman citizenship falsely. According to 25:11, Paul was permitted to make his appeal to Caesar.

27 Then the chief captain came, and said unto him, Tell me, art thou a
Roman? He said, Yea.
28 And the chief captain answered, With a great sum obtained I this
freedom. And Paul said, But I was *free* born.
29 Then straightway they departed from him which should have examined
him: and the chief captain also was afraid, after he knew that he was a
Roman, and because he had bound him.

22:29 Acts 16:38

3. His Appearance before the Jewish Council

30 On the morrow, because he would have known the certainty wherefore
he was accused of the Jews, he loosed him from *his* bands, and commanded
the chief priests and all their council to appear, and brought Paul down,
and set him before them.

23 AND Paul, earnestly beholding the council, said, Men *and* brethren, I have lived in all good conscience before God until this day.
2 And the high priest An-a-ni'as commanded them that stood by him to
smite him on the mouth.
3 Then said Paul unto him, God shall smite thee, *thou* whited wall: for
sittest thou to judge me after the law, and commandest me to be smitten
contrary to the law?
4 And they that stood by said, Revilest thou God's high priest?
5 Then said Paul, I wist not, brethren, that he was the high priest: for it is
written, Thou shalt not speak evil of the ruler of thy people.
6 But when Paul perceived that the one part were Sad'du-cees, and the
other Pharisees, he cried out in the council, Men *and* brethren, I am a
Pharisee, the son of a Pharisee: of the hope and resurrection of the dead I
am called in question.
7 And when he had so said, there arose a dissension between the Pharisees
and the Sad'du-cees: and the multitude was divided.
8 For the Sad'du-cees say that there is no resurrection, neither angel, nor
spirit: but the Pharisees confess both.
9 And there arose a great cry: and the scribes *that were* of the Pharisees'
part arose, and strove, saying, We find no evil in this man: but if a spirit or
an angel hath spoken to him, let us not fight against God.
10 And when there arose a great dissension, the chief captain, fearing lest
Paul should have been pulled in pieces of them, commanded the soldiers to
go down, and to take him by force from among them, and to bring *him* into
the castle.
11 And the night following the Lord stood by him, and said, Be of good
cheer, Paul: for as thou hast testified of me in Jerusalem, so must thou bear
witness also at Rome.

☆**23:1** 1 Cor 4:4; 2 Cor 1:12; 4:2; Heb 13:18
23:2 Jn 18:22; Acts 24:1
23:3 Lev 19:15; Ezek 13:10–15; Jn 7:51
23:5 Ex 22:28
☆**23:6** Phil 3:5
23:8 Mt 22:23; Mk 12:18; Lk 20:27; Acts 24:5
23:9 Prov 16:7; Jn 12:29; Acts 5:39; 22:7
☆**23:11** Ps 46:1; Isa 41:10; 43:2; Acts 18:9; 22:1–21; 27:23

23:1 *Paul now stands before the Sanhedrin* (see note to Matt. 26:59). With holy confidence, he is unafraid to stand before this august body and give a fair account of his conduct. When Paul affirms his innocence, the high priest (Ananias) orders him to be struck. Apparently "when he (Ananias) could charge him with no crime, he thought it was crime enough that he asserted his own innocence."* Under Roman law a prisoner was considered guilty until he could prove he was innocent. Later, under English common law, a man was innocent until proved guilty.

23:6 See notes to Matt. 3:7 on the Pharisees and Sadducees.

23:11 This is a supernatural visitation of the risen Lord to his servant. It was a fulfillment of Matt. 28:20, "I am with you alway." God's people are always to be cheerful despite unfortunate circumstances. Jesus here says, "be of good cheer," for those who trust the Savior have nothing to fear, not even death itself. Scripture speaks of four instances when the Lord appeared to Paul: (1) on the Damascus road (9:5; 22:8; 26:15); (2) on his first visit to Jerusalem (22:17, 18); (3) in Corinth (18:9, 10); and (4) on his last visit to Jerusalem (23:11).

C. PAUL'S INCARCERATION IN CAESAREA

23:12 12 And when it was day, certain of the Jews banded together, and bound
Acts 9:23 themselves under a curse, saying that they would neither eat nor drink till
they had killed Paul.
13 And they were more than forty which had made this conspiracy.
14 And they came to the chief priests and elders, and said, We have bound
ourselves under a great curse, that we will eat nothing until we have slain
Paul.
23:15 15 Now therefore ye with the council signify to the chief captain that he
Ps 37:32 bring him down unto you to morrow, as though ye would inquire something
more perfectly concerning him: and we, or ever he come near, are ready to
kill him.
23:16☆ 16 And when Paul's sister's son heard of their lying in wait, he went and
Job 5:12, 13 entered into the castle, and told Paul.
17 Then Paul called one of the centurions unto *him,* and said, Bring this
young man unto the chief captain: for he hath a certain thing to tell him.
18 So he took him, and brought *him* to the chief captain, and said, Paul the
prisoner called me unto *him,* and prayed me to bring this young man unto
thee, who hath something to say unto thee.
19 Then the chief captain took him by the hand, and went *with him* aside
privately, and asked *him,* What is that thou hast to tell me?
20 And he said, The Jews have agreed to desire thee that thou wouldest
bring down Paul to morrow into the council, as though they would inquire
somewhat of him more perfectly.
23:21 21 But do not thou yield unto them: for there lie in wait for him of them
Ps 10:9 more than forty men, which have bound themselves with an oath, that they
37:12, 13, 32 will neither eat nor drink till they have killed him: and now are they ready,
looking for a promise from thee.
22 So the chief captain *then* let the young man depart, and charged *him,*
See thou tell no man that thou hast shewed these things to me.
23 And he called unto *him* two centurions, saying, Make ready two
hundred soldiers to go to Cæs-a-re'a, and horsemen threescore and ten, and
spearmen two hundred, at the third hour of the night;
23:24☆ 24 And provide *them* beasts, that they may set Paul on, and bring *him* safe
unto Felix the governor.
25 And he wrote a letter after this manner:
26 Claudius Ly'si-as unto the most excellent governor Felix *sendeth*
greeting.
23:27 27 This man was taken of the Jews, and should have been killed of them:
Acts 21:33 22:25–29 then came I with an army, and rescued him, having understood that he was
a Roman.
23:28 28 And when I would have known the cause wherefore they accused him,
Acts 22:30 I brought him forth into their council:
23:29 29 Whom I perceived to be accused of questions of their law, but to have
Acts 18:15 25:19; 26:31 nothing laid to his charge worthy of death or of bonds.
28:18 23:30 30 And when it was told me how that the Jews laid wait for the man, I sent
Acts 24:8, 19 25:16 straightway to thee, and gave commandment to his accusers also to say
before thee what *they had* against him. Farewell.

23:16 Nowhere else in the Scriptures is any reference *made to Paul's relatives.* When his nephew learns of his uncle's predicament, he informs Paul, who then sends him to the chief captain (tribune) with the information.
23:24 *Felix* was the procurator of Judea who exercised military and civil authority over that region. His wife Drusilla was the youngest daughter of Herod Agrippa I; she left her husband Azizus, king of Emesa, for Felix, a Gentile (24:24). They lived in Caesarea. Felix was hated by the Jews; their rioting and charges against him resulted in his being recalled to Rome. His appointment had come from Claudius Caesar through his friendship with Pallas, who had the ear of Claudius. His procuratorship was confirmed by Nero. Before returning to Rome, Felix tried to win Jewish favor by leaving Paul in jail (24:27).

[31]Then the soldiers, as it was commanded them, took Paul, and brought
him by night to An-tip′a-tris.
[32]On the morrow they left the horsemen to go with him, and returned to
the castle:
[33]Who, when they came to Cæs-a-re′a, and delivered the epistle to the
governor, presented Paul also before him.
[34]And when the governor had read *the letter,* he asked of what province
he was. And when he understood that *he was* of Ci-li′ci-a;
[35]I will hear thee, said he, when thine accusers are also come. And he
commanded him to be kept in Herod's judgment hall.

23:33 Acts 8:40
23:34 Acts 21:39
☆**23:35** Acts 24:1, 19; 25:16

D. PAUL DEFENDING HIMSELF
1. Before Felix

24 AND after five days An-a-ni′as the high priest descended with the
elders, and *with* a certain orator *named* Ter-tul′lus, who informed
the governor against Paul.
[2]And when he was called forth, Ter-tul′lus began to accuse *him,* saying,
Seeing that by thee we enjoy great quietness, and that very worthy deeds
are done unto this nation by thy providence,
[3]We accept *it* always, and in all places, most noble Felix, with all
thankfulness.
[4]Notwithstanding, that I be not further tedious unto thee, I pray thee
that thou wouldest hear us of thy clemency a few words.
[5]For we have found this man *a* pestilent *fellow,* and a mover of sedition
among all the Jews throughout the world, and a ringleader of the sect of the
Nazarenes:
[6]Who also hath gone about to profane the temple: whom we took, and
would have judged according to our law.
[7]But the chief captain Ly′si-as came *upon us,* and with great violence took
him away out of our hands,
[8]Commanding his accusers to come unto thee: by examining of whom
thyself mayest take knowledge of all these things, whereof we accuse him.
[9]And the Jews also assented, saying that these things were so.
[10]Then Paul, after that the governor had beckoned unto him to speak,
answered, Forasmuch as I know that thou hast been of many years a judge
unto this nation, I do the more cheerfully answer for myself:
[11]Because that thou mayest understand, that there are yet but twelve days
since I went up to Jerusalem for to worship.
[12]And they neither found me in the temple disputing with any man,
neither raising up the people, neither in the synagogues, nor in the city:
[13]Neither can they prove the things whereof they now accuse me.
[14]But this I confess unto thee, that after the way which they call heresy,

☆**24:1** Acts 21:26, 27; 23:2, 24–30
☆**24:5** Mt 5:11; Lk 23:2; Jn 15:20; Acts 16:20, 21; 17:6; 24:14; 1 Thess 2:14–16; 2 Tim 3:2; 1 Pet 2:12, 19
☆**24:6** Jn 18:31; Acts 21:28
☆**24:7** Acts 21:33
☆**24:8** Acts 23:30
24:11 Acts 21:26, 27
24:12 Acts 15:8
24:13 Acts 15:7
☆**24:14** Lk 24:27; Acts 9:2; 26:22; 2 Tim 1:3

23:35 *Herod's judgment hall.* The palace built by Herod in Caesarea was now being used as the residence of the Roman procurators.
24:1ff *Tertullus* was a professional orator hired by the Jews to state their case against Paul. He was probably a Hellenistic Jew with a common Roman name. He tried to flatter Felix and then sought to show that Paul was an enemy of two elements Felix was assigned to protect—the public peace and the Jewish religion.
24:5 The charges against Paul by the Jews are enlarged by Tertullus, who says that Paul is guilty of sedition (i.e., he is an insurrectionist who wants to overthrow the control of Rome in and around Jerusalem). Tertullus does not say they *think* Paul is such a person. He assumes that he *is* such a person and thus condemns him before he is tried.
24:6b–8a Some early manuscripts do not include verses 6b–8a ("and would have judged according to our law. 7 But the chief captain Lysias came upon us, and with great violence took him away out of our hands, 8 commanding his accusers to come unto thee . . ."). See the margins of RSV and NIV.
24:8 Tertullus here alleges that the tribune, Lysias, is guilty of exceeding his authority when he seized Paul and thus prevented the Jews from trying him for a religious offense—that of profaning the temple.
24:14 *after the way,* i.e., "according to the Way which they call a sect" (RSV).

so worship I the God of my fathers, believing all things which are written in
the law and in the prophets:
15 And have hope toward God, which they themselves also allow, that
there shall be a resurrection of the dead, both of the just and unjust.
16 And herein do I exercise myself, to have always a conscience void of
offence toward God, and *toward* men.
17 Now after many years I came to bring alms to my nation, and offerings.
18 Whereupon certain Jews from Asia found me purified in the temple,
neither with multitude, nor with tumult.
19 Who ought to have been here before thee, and object, if they had ought
against me.
20 Or else let these same *here* say, if they have found any evil doing in me,
while I stood before the council,
21 Except it be for this one voice, that I cried standing among them,
Touching the resurrection of the dead I am called in question by you this
day.
22 And when Felix heard these things, having more perfect knowledge of
that way, he deferred them, and said, When Ly′si-as the chief captain shall
come down, I will know the uttermost of your matter.
23 And he commanded a centurion to keep Paul, and to let *him* have
liberty, and that he should forbid none of his acquaintance to minister or
come unto him.
24 And after certain days, when Felix came with his wife Dru-sil′la, which
was a Jewess, he sent for Paul, and heard him concerning the faith in
Christ.
25 And as he reasoned of righteousness, temperance, and judgment to
come, Felix trembled, and answered, Go thy way for this time; when I have
a convenient season, I will call for thee.
26 He hoped also that money should have been given him of Paul, that he
might loose him: wherefore he sent for him the oftener, and communed
with him.
27 But after two years Por′ci-us Fes′tus came into Felix′ room: and Felix,
willing to shew the Jews a pleasure, left Paul bound.

2. Before Festus

25 NOW when Fes′tus was come into the province, after three days he
ascended from Cæs-a-re′a to Jerusalem.
2 Then the high priest and the chief of the Jews informed him against
Paul, and besought him,
3 And desired favour against him, that he would send for him to
Jerusalem, laying wait in the way to kill him.

24:15 Dan 12:2 Mt 22:31, 32 Jn 5:28, 29 Acts 23:6 26:6–8 1 Thess 4:14 Rev 20:12
24:16 Acts 23:1
24:17 Acts 11:29 20:16 Rom 15:25–28 1 Cor 16:3 2 Cor 8:4
24:18☆ Acts 21:26, 27
24:19☆ Acts 23:30 25:16
24:21 Acts 23:6
24:22☆
24:23☆ Acts 27:3; 28:16
24:25 Acts 10:42 Gal 5:23 Tit 2:12 2 Pet 1:6
24:26 Acts 24:17
24:27☆ Acts 25:9, 24–27; 26:24
25:1☆
25:2☆ Acts 23:12–21 24:1

24:18, 19 Paul objects to the fact that the Jews from Asia, who have charged him with a crime, are not present to witness to their charge. This is palpably irregular and unfair.
24:22 Felix justly deferred action on Paul's case because Lysias was not present to testify. This was important because Tertullus had already accused Lysias of misconduct. Felix also was familiar with the *Way, and this had something to do with* the deferment.
24:23 Felix made sure that Paul would not run away, but he left him enough freedom so that his friends had access to him. This indicates that Felix did not regard the charges against Paul so grievous, for if he were an insurrectionist he would have put him in chains.
24:27 Justice was not speedy; Paul waits for two years. Meanwhile, Felix is replaced by Porcius Festus. The sad note is that Paul is left in prison without a trial.
25:1ff *Festus* replaced Felix as procurator of Judea (ca. A.D. 57–60). We know little about him except that he inherited a bad situation and tried to keep the Jews within bounds. Festus suggested that Paul stand trial before his own people. Paul's appeal to Caesar for trial was a welcome relief to Festus, who gladly allowed him his request. (Any Roman citizen had this right of appeal, but it had to be confirmed by the emperor.)
25:2 The law forbade lying. This did not deter the chief priests and leaders of the Jews from asking Festus to remit Paul to Jerusalem for trial when they intended to have him killed en route. For them, the end would justify the means.

4 But Fes′tus answered, that Paul should be kept at Cæs-a-re′a, and that
he himself would depart shortly *thither.*
5 Let them therefore, said he, which among you are able, go down with
me, and accuse this man, if there be any wickedness in him.
6 And when he had tarried among them more than ten days, he went
down unto Cæs-a-re′a; and the next day sitting on the judgment seat
commanded Paul to be brought.
7 And when he was come, the Jews which came down from Jerusalem
stood round about, and laid many and grievous complaints against Paul,
which they could not prove.

25:7 Esth 3:8; Acts 24:13, 27

8 While he answered for himself, Neither against the law of the Jews,
neither against the temple, nor yet against Cæsar, have I offended any thing
at all.

25:8 Acts 6:13; 24:12; 28:17; Rom 13:1–7

9 But Fes′tus, willing to do the Jews a pleasure, answered Paul, and said,
Wilt thou go up to Jerusalem, and there be judged of these things before
me?
10 Then said Paul, I stand at Cæsar's judgment seat, where I ought to be
judged: to the Jews have I done no wrong, as thou very well knowest.

25:10 Acts 25:21; 26:32

11 For if I be an offender, or have committed any thing worthy of death, I
refuse not to die: but if there be none of these things whereof these accuse
me, no man may deliver me unto them. I appeal unto Cæsar.

☆**25:11** Acts 23:11; 27:24; 28:19

12 Then Fes′tus, when he had conferred with the council, answered, Hast
thou appealed unto Cæsar? unto Cæsar shalt thou go.

3. Before Festus and Agrippa

13 And after certain days king A-grip′pa and Bernice came unto Cæs-a-
re′a to salute Fes′tus.

☆**25:13**

14 And when they had been there many days, Fes′tus declared Paul's
cause unto the king, saying, There is a certain man left in bonds by Felix:

25:14 Acts 24:27

15 About whom, when I was at Jerusalem, the chief priests and the elders
of the Jews informed *me,* desiring *to have* judgment against him.

25:15 Acts 25:2

16 To whom I answered, It is not the manner of the Romans to deliver any
man to die, before that he which is accused have the accusers face to face,
and have licence to answer for himself concerning the crime laid against
him.

25:16 Acts 23:30

17 Therefore, when they were come hither, without any delay on the
morrow I sat on the judgment seat, and commanded the man to be brought
forth.
18 Against whom when the accusers stood up, they brought none
accusation of such things as I supposed:

☆**25:18**

19 But had certain questions against him of their own superstition, and of
one Jesus, which was dead, whom Paul affirmed to be alive.
20 And because I doubted of such manner of questions, I asked *him*
whether he would go to Jerusalem, and there be judged of these matters.

☆**25:19** Acts 18:15; 23:29; 1 Cor 15:2–8

25:11 Paul was no objector to capital punishment, for he readily agreed that if he was guilty of the charges he was willing to be executed.

25:13 This *Agrippa* was Herod Agrippa II. He was seventeen when his father died. He sought (without success) to build up the kingdom and to reconcile Judaism and Hellenism. The apostle Paul appeared before him and his sister Bernice, of whom history has little good to say. In 26:28 we see the enigmatic statement made by Agrippa, which has been translated variously. The LB, for example, says: "With trivial proofs like these, you expect me to become a Christian?" The RSV says: "In a short time you think to make me a Christian!"

25:18, 19 Festus in his report to King Agrippa says the accusers "brought no accusations of such things as I supposed." He thought they would accuse him of a crime against the public peace, or of a property offense, or of a rebellion against the Roman government. They did not so do. And they did not accuse him of anything that properly belonged to the Roman courts for decision.

21 But when Paul had appealed to be reserved unto the hearing of
Augustus, I commanded him to be kept till I might send him to Cæsar.
22 Then A-grip′pa said unto Fes′tus, I would also hear the man myself. To
morrow, said he, thou shalt hear him.
23 And on the morrow, when A-grip′pa was come, and Bernice, with great
pomp, and was entered into the place of hearing, with the chief captains,
and principal men of the city, at Fes′tus' commandment Paul was brought
forth.
24 And Fes′tus said, King A-grip′pa, and all men which are here present
with us, ye see this man, about whom all the multitude of the Jews have
dealt with me, both at Jerusalem, and *also* here, crying that he ought not to
live any longer.
25 But when I found that he had committed nothing worthy of death, and
that he himself hath appealed to Augustus, I have determined to send him.
26 Of whom I have no certain thing to write unto my lord. Wherefore I
have brought him forth before you, and specially before thee, O king
A-grip′pa, that, after examination had, I might have somewhat to write.
27 For it seemeth to me unreasonable to send a prisoner, and not withal to
signify the crimes *laid* against him.

4. Before Agrippa

26 THEN A-grip′pa said unto Paul, Thou art permitted to speak for
thyself. Then Paul stretched forth the hand, and answered for
himself:
2 I think myself happy, king A-grip′pa, because I shall answer for myself
this day before thee touching all the things whereof I am accused of the
Jews:
3 Especially *because I know* thee to be expert in all customs and questions
which are among the Jews: wherefore I beseech thee to hear me patiently.
4 My manner of life from my youth, which was at the first among mine
own nation at Jerusalem, know all the Jews;
5 Which knew me from the beginning, if they would testify, that after the
most straitest sect of our religion I lived a Pharisee.
6 And now I stand and am judged for the hope of the promise made of
God unto our fathers:
7 Unto which *promise* our twelve tribes, instantly serving *God* day and
night, hope to come. For which hope's sake, king A-grip′pa, I am accused
of the Jews.
8 Why should it be thought a thing incredible with you, that God should
raise the dead?
9 I verily thought with myself, that I ought to do many things contrary to
the name of Jesus of Nazareth.
10 Which thing I also did in Jerusalem: and many of the saints did I shut
up in prison, having received authority from the chief priests; and when
they were put to death, I gave my voice against *them.*
11 And I punished them oft in every synagogue, and compelled *them* to

25:22 Acts 9:15
25:24 Acts 22:22
25:25 Acts 23:22
26:2 Acts 9:15
26:4 Phil 3:5
26:5 Acts 23:6 Gal 1:13, 14
26:6☆ Gen 3:15 22:18; 26:4 49:10 Deut 18:15 Isa 7:14; 9:6, 7 Jer 23:5, 6 33:14 Ezek 34:23 37:24 Dan 9:24 Mal 3:1; 4:2 Lk 24:27 Acts 13:32, 33 28:20
26:7 Phil 3:11
26:8☆ Dan 12:2
26:9 Jn 15:21; 16:2 1 Tim 1:13
26:10 Acts 8:3; 22:5
26:11☆ Acts 9:1; 22:19

26:6 *the hope of the promise* refers to the Messiah promised by God in the Scriptures (e.g., Gen. 22:18; *49:10).*

26:8 Paul's argument turns on the fact that, as a Pharisee, he believed in the resurrection of the dead, as did all the Pharisees. He said it was strange that Pharisees would object to his preaching what they all believed. From the viewpoint of the Pharisees, it is obvious that while they believed in resurrection, there was one resurrection they did not believe in—that of Jesus Christ. They refused to believe he was the Messiah.

26:11 *compelled them to blaspheme,* i.e., to say that Jesus was a deceiver, that he had deceived them, and that they now renounce him and admit they have no obligations to him. The Jews would not have thought this to be blasphemous, but all Christians would.

blaspheme; and being exceedingly mad against them, I persecuted *them*
even unto strange cities.
12 Whereupon as I went to Damascus with authority and commission
from the chief priests,
13 At midday, O king, I saw in the way a light from heaven, above the
brightness of the sun, shining round about me and them which journeyed
with me.
14 And when we were all fallen to the earth, I heard a voice speaking unto
me, and saying in the Hebrew tongue, Saul, Saul, why persecutest thou me?
it is hard for thee to kick against the pricks.
15 And I said, Who art thou, Lord? And he said, I am Jesus whom thou
persecutest.
16 But rise, and stand upon thy feet: for I have appeared unto thee for this
purpose, to make thee a minister and a witness both of these things which
thou hast seen, and of those things in the which I will appear unto thee;
17 Delivering thee from the people, and *from* the Gentiles, unto whom
now I send thee,
18 To open their eyes, *and* to turn *them* from darkness to light, and *from*
the power of Satan unto God, that they may receive forgiveness of sins, and
inheritance among them which are sanctified by faith that is in me.
19 Whereupon, O king A-grip′pa, I was not disobedient unto the heavenly
vision:
20 But shewed first unto them of Damascus, and at Jerusalem, and
throughout all the coasts of Judæa, and *then* to the Gentiles, that they
should repent and turn to God, and do works meet for repentance.
21 For these causes the Jews caught me in the temple, and went about to
kill *me.*
22 Having therefore obtained help of God, I continue unto this day,
witnessing both to small and great, saying none other things than those
which the prophets and Moses did say should come:
23 That Christ should suffer, *and* that he should be the first that should
rise from the dead, and should shew light unto the people, and to the
Gentiles.
24 And as he thus spake for himself, Fes′tus said with a loud voice, Paul,
thou art beside thyself; much learning doth make thee mad.
25 But he said, I am not mad, most noble Fes′tus; but speak forth the
words of truth and soberness.
26 For the king knoweth of these things, before whom also I speak freely:
for I am persuaded that none of these things are hidden from him; for this
thing was not done in a corner.
27 King A-grip′pa, believest thou the prophets? I know that thou believest.
28 Then A-grip′pa said unto Paul, Almost thou persuadest me to be a
Christian.
29 And Paul said, I would to God, that not only thou, but also all that
hear me this day, were both almost, and altogether such as I am, except
these bonds.

26:15 Acts 9:5; 22:8
26:16 Acts 22:15 Gal 1:12 Col 1:25 1 Tim 1:12
☆**26:17** Acts 13:46–48 22:21 Rom 11:13 15:16 Gal 1:15, 16 2:7–9 1 Tim 2:7 2 Tim 1:11
26:18 Isa 35:5; 42:6, 7 Lk 1:77, 79 Eph 1:11; 5:8 Col 1:13 1 Pet 2:9
26:20 Mt 3:8 Acts 9:20, 26 13:46
26:21 Acts 21:30
26:22 Jn 5:46 Rom 3:21, 22
26:23 Ps 2:7 6:8–11; 22 Isa 53:1–12 Lk 24:26, 27, 46, 47 Rom 1:3, 4 1 Cor 15:20 Col 1:18 Rev 1:5
☆**26:24** 1 Cor 1:23
26:26 Acts 26:3
☆**26:28**

26:17 Paul testifies to the spiritual protection he was given by God, who delivered him "from the people of the Jews and from the Gentiles"—those who spurned the gospel and hated the one who preached it.

26:24 *thou art beside thyself; much learning doth make thee mad,* i.e., Paul had cracked his brains by too much studying, for he was talking like a madman. Festus simply did not understand what Paul was saying. To him it was a riddle he could not unravel, and so he said it came from Paul's heated imagination.

26:28 Agrippa agreed that much of what Paul said made sense. His statement, "Almost thou persuadest me to become a Christian," may have been ironical and meant, "Do you really think that in such a short time you could convince me to become a Christian?" Others take it literally and think he was saying that he almost believed that Jesus Christ was the Messiah. If so, he was then one of the "almost persuaded," who stopped short of salvation by refusing to take Jesus Christ into his heart.

30 And when he had thus spoken, the king rose up, and the governor, and
Bernice, and they that sat with them:
26:31 Acts 23:9; 25:25
31 And when they were gone aside, they talked between themselves,
saying, This man doeth nothing worthy of death or of bonds.
26:32☆ Acts 25:11
32 Then said A-grip′pa unto Fes′tus, This man might have been set at
liberty, if he had not appealed unto Cæsar.

E. PAUL DISPATCHED TO ROME BY AGRIPPA
1. The Sea Voyage

27:1☆ Acts 25:12, 25
27 AND when it was determined that we should sail into Italy, they
delivered Paul and certain other prisoners unto *one* named Julius, a
centurion of Augustus' band.
27:2 Acts 19:29; 20:4 Col 4:10
2 And entering into a ship of Ad-ra-myt′ti-um, we launched, meaning to
sail by the coasts of Asia; *one* Ar-is-tar′chus, a Macedonian of Thes-sa-lo-
ni′ca, being with us.
27:3 Mt 11:21 Acts 24:23 27:43; 28:16
3 And the next *day* we touched at Si′don. And Julius courteously
entreated Paul, and gave *him* liberty to go unto his friends to refresh
himself.
4 And when we had launched from thence, we sailed under Cyprus,
because the winds were contrary.
5 And when we had sailed over the sea of Ci-li′ci-a and Pam-phyl′i-a, we
came to My′ra, *a city* of Ly′ci-a.
27:6 Acts 28:11
6 And there the centurion found a ship of Alexandria sailing into Italy;
and he put us therein.
7 And when we had sailed slowly many days, and scarce were come over
against Cni′dus, the wind not suffering us, we sailed under Crete, over
against Sal-mo′ne;
8 And, hardly passing it, came unto a place which is called The fair
havens; nigh whereunto was the city *of* La-se′a.
27:9☆
9 Now when much time was spent, and when sailing was now dangerous,
because the fast was now already past, Paul admonished *them*,
27:10 Amos 3:7
10 And said unto them, Sirs, I perceive that this voyage will be with hurt
and much damage, not only of the lading and ship, but also of our lives.
11 Nevertheless the centurion believed the master and the owner of the
ship, more than those things which were spoken by Paul.
12 And because the haven was not commodious to winter in, the more part
advised to depart thence also, if by any means they might attain to Phe-
ni′ce, *and there* to winter; *which is* an haven of Crete, and lieth toward the
south west and north west.
13 And when the south wind blew softly, supposing that they had
obtained *their* purpose, loosing *thence*, they sailed close by Crete.
27:14☆
14 But not long after there arose against it a tempestuous wind, called Eu-
roc′ly-don.
15 And when the ship was caught, and could not bear up into the wind, we
let *her* drive.

26:32 Perhaps Paul made a mistake in appealing to Caesar. Yet King Agrippa could have assumed that Paul's appeal came because of the great danger to himself. Once the king saw he was innocent, he should *have set him free by asking him* to reverse his request to appeal to Caesar. Paul might have been better advised to appeal to God in the first place rather than to Caesar.

27:1 A centurion commanded a hundred soldiers. This large number of men was assigned to assure that Paul got to Rome for trial. There were other prisoners, however, who made this trip along with Paul, and so the number of soldiers was by no means too large to guarantee the delivery of the prisoners to Rome.

27:9 *the fast* referred to here is the only one prescribed by the Mosaic law and occurred on the Day of Atonement (the tenth day of *Tishri—September/October*). If this incident took place in A.D. 59, the Day of Atonement was on or near October 5.

27:14 *Euroclydon,* apparently a compound word meaning a "northeaster," as the ASV and RSV have it. It was a threatening gale.

16 And running under a certain island which is called Clau'da, we had
much work to come by the boat:
17 Which when they had taken up, they used helps, undergirding the ship;
and, fearing lest they should fall into the quicksands, strake sail, and so
were driven.
18 And we being exceedingly tossed with a tempest, the next *day* they
lightened the ship;
19 And the third *day* we cast out with our own hands the tackling of the
ship.
20 And when neither sun nor stars in many days appeared, and no small
tempest lay on *us,* all hope that we should be saved was then taken away.
21 But after long abstinence Paul stood forth in the midst of them, and
said, Sirs, ye should have hearkened unto me, and not have loosed from
Crete, and to have gained this harm and loss.
22 And now I exhort you to be of good cheer: for there shall be no loss of
any man's life among you, but of the ship.
23 For there stood by me this night the angel of God, whose I am, and
whom I serve,
24 Saying, Fear not, Paul; thou must be brought before Cæsar: and, lo,
God hath given thee all them that sail with thee.
25 Wherefore, sirs, be of good cheer: for I believe God, that it shall be
even as it was told me.
26 Howbeit we must be cast upon a certain island.

2. The Shipwreck

27 But when the fourteenth night was come, as we were driven up and
down in A'dri-a, about midnight the shipmen deemed that they drew near
to some country;
28 And sounded, and found *it* twenty fathoms: and when they had gone a
little further, they sounded again, and found *it* fifteen fathoms.
29 Then fearing lest we should have fallen upon rocks, they cast four
anchors out of the stern, and wished for the day.
30 And as the shipmen were about to flee out of the ship, when they had
let down the boat into the sea, under colour as though they would have cast
anchors out of the foreship,
31 Paul said to the centurion and to the soldiers, Except these abide in the
ship, ye cannot be saved.
32 Then the soldiers cut off the ropes of the boat, and let her fall off.
33 And while the day was coming on, Paul besought *them* all to take meat,
saying, This day is the fourteenth day that ye have tarried and continued
fasting, having taken nothing.
34 Wherefore I pray you to take *some* meat: for this is for your health: for
there shall not an hair fall from the head of any of you.

☆**27:18** Jonah 1:5
27:21 Acts 27:10
☆**27:23** Acts 18:9; 23:11 27:44 2 Tim 4:17
27:24 Isa 41:10, 14 43:1, 2 Acts 19:21 23:11; 25:11
27:25 2 Chron 20:20 Lk 1:45 Rom 4:20 Heb 6:17
27:26 Acts 28:1
☆**27:28**
☆**27:30**
27:34 Mt 10:30 Lk 12:7; 21:18

27:18 "Any man will rather make shipwreck of his goods than of his life; but many will rather make *shipwreck of faith and a good conscience* than of their goods (1 Tim. 1:19)."*

27:23 God used angels on many occasions to bring messages to his servants. The angel assured Paul that the passengers on board the ship would all be saved if they followed his advice. We might well ask whether God still uses angels today when the canon of Scripture is closed and the revelation of God ended. There are many indications that on occasion God still sends angels to do his bidding among the people of God and among those whose hearts are inclined toward him and need help to find the Savior.

27:28 A fathom is six feet.

27:30 The sailors now think only of themselves in spite of the fact that the rule of sea always has been that sailors must look to the passengers first, even if they drown as a consequence. Paul intervenes and the soldiers cut the rope of the small boat they had lowered and into which they hoped to clamber and escape. Solomon wrote, "Confidence in an unfaithful man in time of trouble is like a broken tooth, and a foot out of joint" (Prov. 25:19).

27:35 Mt 14:19 Jn 6:11 1 Tim 4:4, 5
35 And when he had thus spoken, he took bread, and gave thanks to God
in presence of them all: and when he had broken *it,* he began to eat.
36 Then were they all of good cheer, and they also took *some* meat.
37 And we were in all in the ship two hundred threescore and sixteen
souls.
27:38☆ Jonah 1:5 Acts 27:18
38 And when they had eaten enough, they lightened the ship, and cast out
the wheat into the sea.
39 And when it was day, they knew not the land: but they discovered a
certain creek with a shore, into the which they were minded, if it were
possible, to thrust in the ship.
40 And when they had taken up the anchors, they committed *themselves*
unto the sea, and loosed the rudder bands, and hoised up the mainsail to
the wind, and made toward shore.
27:41 2 Cor 11:25
41 And falling into a place where two seas met, they ran the ship aground;
and the forepart stuck fast, and remained unmoveable, but the hinder part
was broken with the violence of the waves.
42 And the soldiers' counsel was to kill the prisoners, lest any of them
should swim out, and escape.
43 But the centurion, willing to save Paul, kept them from *their* purpose;
and commanded that they which could swim should cast *themselves* first
into the sea, and get to land:
27:44 Ps 107:30
44 And the rest, some on boards, and some on *broken pieces* of the ship.
And so it came to pass, that they escaped all safe to land.

3. Spending the Winter on Malta

28:1☆ Acts 27:26
28 AND when they were escaped, then they knew that the island was
called Mel'i-ta.
28:2☆
2 And the barbarous people shewed us no little kindness: for they kindled
a fire, and received us every one, because of the present rain, and because of
the cold.
3 And when Paul had gathered a bundle of sticks, and laid *them* on the
fire, there came a viper out of the heat, and fastened on his hand.
28:4☆ Lk 13:2, 4
4 And when the barbarians saw the *venomous* beast hang on his hand, they
said among themselves, No doubt this man is a murderer, whom, though he
hath escaped the sea, yet vengeance suffereth not to live.
28:5 Mk 16:18 Lk 10:19
5 And he shook off the beast into the fire, and felt no harm.
28:6 Acts 14:11
6 Howbeit they looked when he should have swollen, or fallen down dead
suddenly: but after they had looked a great while, and saw no harm come
to him, they changed their minds, and said that he was a god.
7 In the same quarters were possessions of the chief man of the island,
whose name was Publius; who received us, and lodged us three days
courteously.
28:8☆ Mk 5:23 Acts 19:11 1 Cor 12:9, 28 Jas 5:14
8 And it came to pass, that the father of Publius lay sick of a fever and of
a bloody flux: to whom Paul entered in, and prayed, and laid his hands on
him, and healed him.

27:38 Knowing that the ship was heading toward the beach, the mariners dropped overboard everything they could so that the ship would be lightened and be beached as far up on the shore as possible. But the ship was wrecked, and the passengers and crew had to make their way to shore as best they could. All escaped, as Paul said they would.

28:1ff The incident of the snake falls in line with Mark 16:18. Paul was doing the will of God and was under divine protection. The bystanders were understandably impressed, although Paul then had to remind them that he was no god. Paul's healing of the father of Publius, who had fever and dysentery, added to the excitement and provided corroborating evidence to the gospel.

28:2 *barbarous people,* i.e., people who spoke a tongue other than Greek.

28:4 *vengeance,* i.e., they thought that justice had caught up with Paul for some crime he had committed and therefore he was about to perish.

28:8 *a bloody flux.* This was dysentery.

9 So when this was done, others also, which had diseases in the island,
came, and were healed:
10 Who also honoured us with many honours; and when we departed,
they laded *us* with such things as were necessary.
11 And after three months we departed in a ship of Alexandria, which had ☆**28:11**
wintered in the isle, whose sign was Castor and Pollux. Acts 27:6
12 And landing at Syracuse, we tarried *there* three days.
13 And from thence we fetched a compass, and came to Rhe′gi-um: and ☆**28:13**
after one day the south wind blew, and we came the next day to Pu-te′o-li:
14 Where we found brethren, and were desired to tarry with them seven ☆**28:14**
days: and so we went toward Rome.
15 And from thence, when the brethren heard of us, they came to meet us
as far as Ap′pi-i fo′rum, and The three taverns: whom when Paul saw, he
thanked God, and took courage.

4. Paul's Arrival at Rome

16 And when we came to Rome, the centurion delivered the prisoners to **28:16**
the captain of the guard: but Paul was suffered to dwell by himself with a Acts 24:33; 27:3
soldier that kept him.
17 And it came to pass, that after three days Paul called the chief of the ☆**28:17**
Jews together: and when they were come together, he said unto them, Men Acts 24:12; 25:8
and brethren, though I have committed nothing against the people, or
customs of our fathers, yet was I delivered prisoner from Jerusalem into the
hands of the Romans.
18 Who, when they had examined me, would have let *me* go, because there **28:18**
was no cause of death in me. Acts 23:29
19 But when the Jews spake against *it,* I was constrained to appeal unto **28:19**
Cæsar; not that I had ought to accuse my nation of. Acts 25:11; 26:32
20 For this cause therefore have I called for you, to see *you,* and to speak **28:20**
with *you:* because that for the hope of Israel I am bound with this chain. Acts 26:6
21 And they said unto him, We neither received letters out of Judæa
concerning thee, neither any of the brethren that came shewed or spake any
harm of thee.
22 But we desire to hear of thee what thou thinkest: for as concerning this **28:22**
sect, we know that every where it is spoken against. Acts 24:14 1 Pet 2:12, 3:16 4:16
23 And when they had appointed him a day, there came many to him into
his lodging; to whom he expounded and testified the kingdom of God, ☆**28:23** Lk 24:27
persuading them concerning Jesus, both out of the law of Moses, and *out of* Acts 1:3; 23:11 28:31
the prophets, from morning till evening.
24 And some believed the things which were spoken, and some believed ☆**28:24**
not. Acts 14:4
25 And when they agreed not among themselves, they departed, after that **28:25–27**
Paul had spoken one word, Well spake the Holy Ghost by E-sai′as the Isa 6:9, 10
prophet unto our fathers, Jn 12:39, 40

28:11 The Roman soldiers and the prisoners had to wait for three months before another ship left Malta, which they boarded for Italy.

28:13, 14 The ship now disembarked the Romans, Paul, and the other prisoners at Puteoli. From there they had to make their journey to Rome on foot. Verse 14 indicates they stayed there for seven days. Believers in Christ greeted them, but we do not know how they had heard the gospel or when they had become Christians. God has his people everywhere, and we find them in the most unexpected places.

28:17 Paul now is in Rome. There are Jews there. Earlier Claudius Caesar had driven all Jews from Rome, but after his death a number of them returned to Rome. They did not have a synagogue or any place for public worship, so Paul calls the leadership together to explain his case before them. No one from Jerusalem had yet come to press charges against him.

28:23, 24 Paul the prisoner is still Paul the missionary; he is still keeping the faith and finishing his course. The results are the same as usual. Some believe and some do not. He worked from morning to evening, eagerly seeking to persuade them to accept the Christ who was spoken of in their own Scriptures.

28:26☆ [26]Saying, Go unto this people, and say, Hearing ye shall hear, and shall
not understand; and seeing ye shall see, and not perceive:
[27]For the heart of this people is waxed gross, and their ears are dull of
hearing, and their eyes have they closed; lest they should see with *their* eyes,
and hear with *their* ears, and understand with *their* heart, and should be
converted, and I should heal them.
28:28 [28]Be it known therefore unto you, that the salvation of God is sent unto
Ps 98:3 Lk 2:30–32 the Gentiles, and *that* they will hear it.
Acts 9:15; 13:26, 46 [29]And when he had said these words, the Jews departed, and had great
reasoning among themselves.
28:30☆ [30]And Paul dwelt two whole years in his own hired house, and received
all that came in unto him,
28:31 [31]Preaching the kingdom of God, and teaching those things which
Acts 20:25; 28:23 concern the Lord Jesus Christ, with all confidence, no man forbidding him.

28:26ff Paul affirms the fact that Isaiah's words were from the Holy Spirit, for the prophet had been under the control of the Spirit and got his message from the Spirit (see Isa. 6:9, 10). Paul then states that since the Jews have rejected the message of the gospel, God has turned to the Gentiles, who are willing to listen and to embrace the Lord Jesus. (Some ancient manuscripts do not include 28:29.)

28:30 How Paul supported himself we are not told. Whether it was from gifts he was given or work that he performed is not known. In our last view of him in Acts, Paul is still witnessing and speaking forth the word of truth. The book ends without telling us what happened to him. There are many things God has chosen not to disclose to us; only eternity will reveal them.

THE EPISTLE OF PAUL THE APOSTLE TO THE

ROMANS

Authorship, date, and background Romans was written by Paul about A.D. 56–57. He had completed his third missionary tour and was in Corinth where he composed the letter which was sent to Rome by Phoebe (16:1), who was a deaconess of the church of Cenchreae. The letter was addressed to friends, not to a church at Rome. Indeed, how the church at Rome got started is not known, although at Pentecost in Jerusalem there were visitors from that city who probably returned to Rome to proclaim the gospel and to spread the faith. At the time of the writing, there were more Gentile believers in Rome than there were Jewish converts. Paul was on his way to Jerusalem with funds for the saints, but he expected to visit Rome in the days ahead, something he had longed to do earlier but had been prevented from doing. He hoped to use Rome as the base of operations for a trip to Spain; he wanted it to be an urban missionary center like Antioch, Ephesus, and Philippi.

Apparently there were no gross theological errors to be corrected in the church at Rome. The letter was designed to set forth the Christian faith systematically and thus is comparable to Galatians; both are theological and didactic. Romans is notably lacking in data having to do with the end of the age (eschatology); rather, it consists of an exposition of foundational truths essential to a full-orbed gospel. This letter, by way of an introduction, was written for the purpose of opening the door for Paul's future visit which, unknown to him, would come in fetters and not in freedom, and would find its culmination in his execution. At this point, he yearned to visit his friends later, instruct them in the holy faith, and go from Rome to Spain for evangelistic outreach with their help and prayers.

Characteristics and content Paul presents, in orderly fashion, the essential elements of the gospel, having for its central motif the concept of salvation (justification) by faith alone without good works. The Good News is "the power of God unto salvation to everyone that believeth" (1:16). All need the Good News, for Jews and non-Jews are guilty before God. Jesus Christ is man's only hope; by his death and resurrection, through faith in him, heaven's doors are opened for redeemed men to enter in. The grace (that is, the favor) of God is freely offered. How it is obtained, what it involves, and what the consequences are, are spelled out by Paul. Law and grace are powerfully contrasted in Romans. Paul discusses the person and the work of the Holy Spirit. Believers are indwelt by the Spirit; the Spirit raised Jesus from the dead; believers are led by the Spirit, are aided by the Spirit in prayer, are the firstfruits of the Spirit and call God "Father" by the Spirit's witness. To believers there is given the assurance that "all things work together for good" (8:28). Our salvation is certain, for the Scriptures tell us that nothing can separate us from the love of God through Christ Jesus our Lord.

Chapters 9–11 constitute a parenthesis (an interruption of the line of thought to insert another idea) in which Paul deals with Israel and God's purpose for his people, a purpose which is certain to be executed because God is sovereign.

In chapter 12 Paul speaks about the Christian holistically, insisting that the true Christian life consists in the body's being given to God as a living sacrifice, and the mind's being renewed or transformed to reflect the mind of Christ. He orders Christians to be subject to governing authorities, in chapter 13, along with additional ethical teachings summed up in the second table of the Law which, when abbreviated, says you shall love your neighbor as you love yourself. Paul shares his future plans with his readers and closes the letter with commendations and a doxology. There has been some question about whether chapter 16 belongs to the letter, since one ancient manuscript has the benediction of 16:25–27 at the end of chapter 15. There is, however, no good reason for supposing it was not part of the original letter.

Outline

I. Introduction (1:1–17)
II. The world's need of salvation (1:18—3:20)
III. Salvation by faith (3:21—8:39)
IV. Israel in the plan of God (9:1—11:36)
V. Living the Christian life (12:1—15:13)
VI. The conclusion and postscript (15:14—16:27)

I. INTRODUCTION (1:1–17)

A. SALUTATION

1 PAUL, a servant of Jesus Christ, called *to be* an apostle, separated
unto the gospel of God,
[2](Which he had promised afore by his prophets in the holy scriptures,)
[3]Concerning his Son Jesus Christ our Lord, which was made of the seed
of David according to the flesh;
[4]And declared *to be* the Son of God with power, according to the spirit of
holiness, by the resurrection from the dead:
[5]By whom we have received grace and apostleship, for obedience to the
faith among all nations, for his name:
[6]Among whom are ye also the called of Jesus Christ:
[7]To all that be in Rome, beloved of God, called *to be* saints: Grace to you
and peace from God our Father, and the Lord Jesus Christ.

B. THANKSGIVING AND PRAYER

[8]First, I thank my God through Jesus Christ for you all, that your faith is
spoken of throughout the whole world.
[9]For God is my witness, whom I serve with my spirit in the gospel of his
Son, that without ceasing I make mention of you always in my prayers;
[10]Making request, if by any means now at length I might have a
prosperous journey by the will of God to come unto you.
[11]For I long to see you, that I may impart unto you some spiritual gift, to
the end ye may be established;
[12]That is, that I may be comforted together with you by the mutual faith
both of you and me.
[13]Now I would not have you ignorant, brethren, that oftentimes I
purposed to come unto you, (but was let hitherto,) that I might have some
fruit among you also, even as among other Gentiles.
[14]I am debtor both to the Greeks, and to the Barbarians; both to the
wise, and to the unwise.
[15]So, as much as in me is, I am ready to preach the gospel to you that are
at Rome also.

1:1☆ Acts 9:15; 13:2 1 Cor 1:1 2 Cor 1:1 Gal 1:15 1 Thess 2:2–9 1 Tim 1:11
1:2 Lk 1:70 Rom 3:21 Tit 1:2
1:3☆ Mt 1:1–17
1:4☆ Rom 8:11 Heb 9:13–15
1:5 Acts 9:15 Rom 16:26 Gal 1:16 Eph 3:8, 9
1:6 1 Cor 1:3 2 Cor 1:2 Gal 1:3 Eph 1:1, 2 Jude 1 Rev 17:14
1:7☆
1:8☆ Rom 16:19 Phil 1:3 1 Thess 1:8
1:9 Eph 1:16 Phil 1:3 1 Thess 1:2 2 Tim 1:3 Philem 4–7
1:10 Rom 15:32 Jas 4:15
1:11☆ Rom 15:29
1:13 Acts 19:21 Rom 15:22, 23 1 Thess 2:18
1:14 Ps 40:9 1 Cor 9:16
1:15 Rom 15:20

1:1 *a servant of Jesus Christ.* Paul and his evangelism team were, and all Christians should be, Christ's slaves (*douloi*). Paul distinguished them from hired servants (*misthios* or *diakonos*), who had certain rights. Hired servants were paid for their labor and were free to leave their employment. Slaves were not free nor did they have any privileges. They were never free to leave their slavery. Paul states that we are Christ's slaves and also slaves to each other as Christians (2 Cor. 4:5).

1:3, 4 Romans was written to explain the gospel, at the center of which is Jesus Christ. Paul witnesses to the human and the divine natures of Jesus. He calls him God's Son. He is born in the line of David according to the flesh (i.e., his humanity). He has risen from the dead and is the Lord Jesus Christ. The resurrection proved that he was the divine Son of God.

1:7 *saints, from the Greek hagioi, from hagios,* meaning "set apart," "separated to God," "holy." It is used of those who have been regenerated and indicates that the person so denominated is holy and a sanctified possession of the Lord, indwelt by the Holy Spirit. All believers—saints—should strive to become more and more like Jesus, even though perfection cannot be attained until after death. *God our Father.* God is the Creator of all men, but he is not the Father of all men. He is the Father only of those who believe. Nor are all men the children of God; only those who have been regenerated are God's children. There is no universal brotherhood of man. Men are divided into two classes—those who are in the family of God and those who are not. Jesus stated that unbelievers "are the children of your father the devil and you love to do the evil things he does" (John 8:44, TLB). When wicked men are born again, they are adopted into God's family; then God becomes their Father.

1:8 Paul thanks God through Jesus Christ for the Romans. We must not only pray to God for our friends; we must also praise him for them as well. Paul prays with constancy for the Romans, and with charity, adducing God as witness to his secret prayers.

1:11ff Paul wants to visit the Roman church to edify the people, comfort himself by their mutual faith with him, and discharge his obligation as an apostle to the Gentiles. His apostolic office made him a debtor both to the Greeks and the barbarians (i.e., to those who did not speak the same tongue as the Romans).

C. THEME

16 For I am not ashamed of the gospel of Christ: for it is the power of God
unto salvation to every one that believeth; to the Jew first, and also to the
Greek.
17 For therein is the righteousness of God revealed from faith to faith: as
it is written, The just shall live by faith.

☆**1:16** Acts 3:26; 1 Cor 1:18; 2 Tim 1:8–12
1:17 Hab 2:4; Jn 3:36; Rom 3:21; Gal 3:11; Phil 3:9; Heb 10:38

II. THE WORLD'S NEED OF SALVATION

A. THE GUILT OF THE NON-JEWS

18 For the wrath of God is revealed from heaven against all ungodliness
and unrighteousness of men, who hold the truth in unrighteousness;
19 Because that which may be known of God is manifest in them; for God
hath shewed *it* unto them.
20 For the invisible things of him from the creation of the world are clearly
seen, being understood by the things that are made, *even* his eternal power
and Godhead; so that they are without excuse:
21 Because that, when they knew God, they glorified *him* not as God,
neither were thankful; but became vain in their imaginations, and their
foolish heart was darkened.
22 Professing themselves to be wise, they became fools,
23 And changed the glory of the uncorruptible God into an image made
like to corruptible man, and to birds, and fourfooted beasts, and creeping
things.
24 Wherefore God also gave them up to uncleanness through the lusts of
their own hearts, to dishonour their own bodies between themselves:
25 Who changed the truth of God into a lie, and worshipped and served
the creature more than the Creator, who is blessed for ever. Amen.
26 For this cause God gave them up unto vile affections: for even their
women did change the natural use into that which is against nature:
27 And likewise also the men, leaving the natural use of the woman,
burned in their lust one toward another; men with men working that which
is unseemly, and receiving in themselves that recompence of their error
which was meet.
28 And even as they did not like to retain God in *their* knowledge, God
gave them over to a reprobate mind, to do those things which are not
convenient;

☆**1:18** Rom 5:9; Eph 5:6; Col 3:6
1:19 Jn 1:9; Acts 14:17
1:20 Ps 19:1; Acts 17:24
1:21 2 Kgs 17:15; Ps 106:13; Eph 4:17, 18
1:22 Jer 10:14; 1 Cor 1:20
1:23 Ps 106:20; Isa 40:18; Jer 2:11
☆**1:24** Lev 18:22; Ps 81:12; Acts 7:42; 1 Cor 6:18; Eph 4:19; 2 Thess 2:11; 1 Pet 4:3
1:25 Jer 13:25; Amos 2:4; 1 Thess 1:9; 1 Jn 5:20
1:26 1 Thess 4:5; Jude 1
1:27 Lev 18:22; 20:13; 1 Cor 6:9, 10
☆**1:28** Eph 5:4

1:16 *salvation,* from the Greek word *sōtēria,* meaning "safety" or "soundness." Included in the term "salvation" are other doctrinal components such as justification, regeneration, sanctification, glorification, redemption, propitiation, grace, and forgiveness. Salvation is (1) of the Lord (Ps. 37:39); (2) by and through the saving work of Jesus Christ (Acts 4:12; Gal. 1:4; Heb. 2:10; 5:9); and (3) not of works by men, lest they should boast (11:6; Eph. 2:9; 2 Tim. 1:9; Titus 3:5). Salvation is past, present, and future. Believers have been delivered from their guilt and the penalty of sin; they are now being delivered from the power of sin; they will at last be delivered from the presence of sin and conformed to the glorious image of God's sinless Son.

1:18ff Paul says that retrogression, not progression, occurred after the fall. Men turned from monotheism to polytheism. They turned from God to idols, from purity to adultery, fornication, and perverse sins against nature itself. At last God gave them up "to doing everything their evil minds could think of" (1:28, TLB). Bodies and minds that once were holy have become depraved with no hope of improvement apart from regeneration and sanctification. Evil men now call wrong right, yet they know what they do is wrong.

1:24 Paul says three times that "God gave them up": (1) he gave them up to using sexual relations in a wrong fashion, that is, fornication and adultery; (2) he gave them up to using sexual relations in a way that is *always* wrong, that is, through homosexual conduct; and (3) he gave them up to a debased and reprobate mind, so that they called evil good and defended those who did everything described in 1:24–32.

1:28ff The consequences of sin are (1) *degradation*—man's nature is corrupted, his desires polluted, his spiritual sight blinded, and his will set in opposition to God's will; (2) *condemnation*—this is the irrevocable law of God (3:19); and (3) *separation* from God, which is death (5:21; 6:23; Ezek. 18:4; Eph. 2:1).

29 Being filled with all unrighteousness, fornication, wickedness, covetous-
ness, maliciousness; full of envy, murder, debate, deceit, malignity;
whisperers,
1:30 2 Tim 3:2
30 Backbiters, haters of God, despiteful, proud, boasters, inventors of evil
things, disobedient to parents,
1:31 2 Tim 3:3
31 Without understanding, covenant breakers, without natural affection,
implacable, unmerciful:
1:32 Rom 6:21, 23
32 Who knowing the judgment of God, that they which commit such
things are worthy of death, not only do the same, but have pleasure in them
that do them.

B. THE DOOM OF THE CRITICS

2:1☆ 2 Sam 12:5–9 Mt 7:1
2 THEREFORE thou art inexcusable, O man, whosoever thou art that
judgest: for wherein thou judgest another, thou condemnest thyself;
for thou that judgest doest the same things.
2:2 2 Thess 1:6
2 But we are sure that the judgment of God is according to truth against
2:3 Prov 11:21
them which commit such things.
3 And thinkest thou this, O man, that judgest them which do such things,
2:4☆ Ex 34:5, 6 Rom 9:22, 23 11:22 Eph 1:7 2 Pet 3:9
and doest the same, that thou shalt escape the judgment of God?
4 Or despisest thou the riches of his goodness and forbearance and
longsuffering; not knowing that the goodness of God leadeth thee to
2:5 Ps 110:5 Jas 5:3
repentance?
5 But after thy hardness and impenitent heart treasurest up unto thyself
2:6 Mt 16:27
wrath against the day of wrath and revelation of the righteous judgment of
2:7 Mt 25:46 Lk 8:15 2 Cor 4:17 Heb 10:36 Jude 21 Rev 2:7
God;
6 Who will render to every man according to his deeds:
7 To them who by patient continuance in well doing seek for glory and
honour and immortality, eternal life:
2:8 Isa 3:11 2 Thess 2:12
8 But unto them that are contentious, and do not obey the truth, but obey
unrighteousness, indignation and wrath,
2:9 1 Pet 4:17
9 Tribulation and anguish, upon every soul of man that doeth evil, of the
2:10 1 Pet 1:7
Jew first, and also of the Gentile;
2:11 Job 34:19
10 But glory, honour, and peace, to every man that worketh good, to the
2:12–15☆ Mt 7:21–26 Jn 13:17 Acts 10:35 Jas 1:22
Jew first, and also to the Gentile:
11 For there is no respect of persons with God.
12 For as many as have sinned without law shall also perish without law:
and as many as have sinned in the law shall be judged by the law;

2:1 Paul has shown that the Gentiles are under sin and condemned. Now he shows that the Jews are also in the same predicament. They exhibit censoriousness and self-conceit by supposing that the Gentiles are guilty and they are not. Paul shows them that they are guilty too.

2:4ff The Jews are guilty of having slighted the goodness of God. They have provoked the wrath of God against them. Since God will judge men by their works and the works of the Jews are not in accord with obedience to the truth, God will bring ruin to the Jewish sinners, as well as to Gentile sinners. On the other hand, he will reward the righteous. God does not show partiality; he does not judge sinning Gentiles and excuse sinning Jews (2:11).

2:12–15 *The condition of those who die without ever* having heard of Christ is a serious theological problem. Scripture does seem to assign them to everlasting punishment on the basis of the light they have, however limited. Thus one who knows neither Christ nor the law (the Ten Commandments) still has the light of conscience or of nature. There is no biblical warrant for the belief that there is a second chance for those who have never heard. Once this life is over, the state of the dead is fixed finally and forever.

God gave Adam a conscience that was uncorrupted before he sinned. After his sin it was depraved and corrupted, but not totally erased. Conscience serves as a witness to truth (Prov. 20:27), but moral choice tells whether it has been obeyed (Josh. 24:15). A man's own conscience accuses him of sin (Gen. 42:21; 2 Sam. 24:10; Matt. 27:3), and it will condemn him when the books are opened. Every mouth will be silenced and God's judgments will be seen to be true and just (Rev. 20:12–15). The believer who is walking in the Spirit will repent of and confess any known sin. In this way it is possible to have a blameless conscience that is void of offense (9:1; 14:22; Acts 24:16). Conscience is educated and perfected by faith through the atoning sacrifice of Jesus Christ.

The law of God is the revealed expression of the will of God. That will is imperfectly manifested in conscience and perfectly in the Word of God, the Scripture. The Ten Commandments constitute the moral law

13 (For not the hearers of the law *are* just before God, but the doers of the
law shall be justified.
14 For when the Gentiles, which have not the law, do by nature the things
contained in the law, these, having not the law, are a law unto themselves:
15 Which shew the work of the law written in their hearts, their conscience
also bearing witness, and *their* thoughts the mean while accusing or else
excusing one another;)
16 In the day when God shall judge the secrets of men by Jesus Christ
according to my gospel.

C. THE GUILT OF THE JEWS (2:17—3:8)

17 Behold, thou art called a Jew, and restest in the law, and makest thy
boast of God,
18 And knowest *his* will, and approvest the things that are more excellent,
being instructed out of the law;
19 And art confident that thou thyself art a guide of the blind, a light of
them which are in darkness,
20 An instructor of the foolish, a teacher of babes, which hast the form of
knowledge and of the truth in the law.
21 Thou therefore which teachest another, teachest thou not thyself? thou
that preachest a man should not steal, dost thou steal?
22 Thou that sayest a man should not commit adultery, dost thou commit
adultery? thou that abhorrest idols, dost thou commit sacrilege?
23 Thou that makest thy boast of the law, through breaking the law
dishonourest thou God?
24 For the name of God is blasphemed among the Gentiles through you,
as it is written.
25 For circumcision verily profiteth, if thou keep the law: but if thou be a
breaker of the law, thy circumcision is made uncircumcision.
26 Therefore if the uncircumcision keep the righteousness of the law, shall
not his uncircumcision be counted for circumcision?
27 And shall not uncircumcision which is by nature, if it fulfil the law,
judge thee, who by the letter and circumcision dost transgress the law?
28 For he is not a Jew, which is one outwardly; neither *is that* circumci-
sion, which is outward in the flesh:
29 But he *is* a Jew, which is one inwardly; and circumcision *is that* of the
heart, in the spirit, *and* not in the letter; whose praise *is* not of men, but of
God.

3 WHAT advantage then hath the Jew? or what profit *is there* of
circumcision?

☆**2:16** Jn 5:22; Acts 10:42; Rom 16:25, 26; Rev 20:12
☆**2:17** Mic 3:11; Jn 8:41; Rom 9:6
2:18 Deut 4:8
2:19 Mt 15:14; Jn 9:39–41
2:20 2 Tim 3:5
2:21 Mt 23:3
2:22 Mal 3:8
2:23 Jn 5:45; Rom 9:4
2:24 2 Sam 12:14; Isa 52:5; Ezek 36:20
☆**2:25** Gal 5:3
2:26 Acts 10:34
2:27 Mt 12:41
2:28 Mt 3:9; Jn 8:39; Gal 6:15; Rev 2:9
2:29 Jn 1:47; Rom 7:6; 2 Cor 3:6; Phil 3:3; Col 2:11; 1 Pet 3:4
☆**3:1**

(Exod. 20:2–17; Deut. 5:6–21). The judicial and ceremonial laws of the Old Testament were given with a specific people in mind—the Jews—and for a specific period in their history. The moral law is timeless, for it concerns itself with the permanent relations of man with respect to marriage, sex, property, and filial obedience. Faith in Christ does not release anyone from the demands of God's law.

2:16 The Gentiles have the light of nature. The Jews have the light of nature and the light of the law. Now all men have the light of nature, the light of the law, and the light of the gospel. The more light men have, the greater their responsibility.

2:17ff The Jews had more knowledge or light than the Gentiles, but they sinned against their knowledge and their profession. They preached better in the pulpit than they lived outside of it. Their sins consisted in stealing, adultery, and sacrilege. This occasioned unbelievers to blaspheme the name of God.

2:25ff Paul agrees that circumcision has value if Jews keep the law. But if they are circumcised and then break the law, their circumcision is of no avail. Therefore the circumcised Jew is no better off than the uncircumcised Gentile if all he has is circumcision. True circumcision is of the heart, not of the flesh; it is spiritual and not literal.

3:1 The Jews do have some advantages over the Gentiles. To them was given the Old Testament, the oracles of God, in their own language. They had Moses and the prophets. They had the true means of salvation but not a monopoly of it. God had good news for the Gentiles too.

3:2 Deut 4:8; Ps 147:19; Acts 7:38
3:3☆ Num 23:18, 19
3:4 Job 40:8; Ps 51:4; 62:9; 116:11; Jn 3:33; Rom 10:16; 2 Tim 2:13; Heb 4:2
3:5☆ Rom 5:8; 7:7; Gal 3:15
3:6☆
3:7 Rom 9:19, 20
3:8 Rom 5:20
3:9☆ Rom 1:18–32; 2:1–29; Gal 3:21, 22
3:10 Ps 14:1–3; 53:1–4
3:13 Ps 5:9; 140:3
3:14 Ps 10:7
3:15 Prov 1:16; Isa 59:7
3:18 Ps 36:1
3:19 Rom 2:2, 12
3:20☆ Ps 143:2; Acts 13:39; Rom 4:15; 7:7; Gal 2:16; 3:11
3:21 Rom 1:2, 17; 9:30
3:22☆ Rom 4:16; 10:4, 12; Gal 2:16; Col 3:11; Heb 11:4; 1 Pet 1:10; 2 Pet 1:1

2 Much every way: chiefly, because that unto them were committed the
oracles of God.
3 For what if some did not believe? shall their unbelief make the faith of
God without effect?
4 God forbid: yea, let God be true, but every man a liar; as it is written,
That thou mightest be justified in thy sayings, and mightest overcome when
thou art judged.
5 But if our unrighteousness commend the righteousness of God, what
shall we say? *Is* God unrighteous who taketh vengeance? (I speak as a man)
6 God forbid: for then how shall God judge the world?
7 For if the truth of God hath more abounded through my lie unto his
glory; why yet am I also judged as a sinner?
8 And not *rather*, (as we be slanderously reported, and as some affirm that
we say,) Let us do evil, that good may come? whose damnation is just.

D. THE GUILT OF THE WHOLE WORLD

9 What then? are we better *than they?* No, in no wise: for we have before
proved both Jews and Gentiles, that they are all under sin;
10 As it is written, There is none righteous, no, not one:
11 There is none that understandeth, there is none that seeketh after God.
12 They are all gone out of the way, they are together become unprofit-
able; there is none that doeth good, no, not one.
13 Their throat *is* an open sepulchre; with their tongues they have used
deceit; the poison of asps *is* under their lips:
14 Whose mouth *is* full of cursing and bitterness:
15 Their feet *are* swift to shed blood:
16 Destruction and misery *are* in their ways:
17 And the way of peace have they not known:
18 There is no fear of God before their eyes.
19 Now we know that what things soever the law saith, it saith to them
who are under the law: that every mouth may be stopped, and all the world
may become guilty before God.
20 Therefore by the deeds of the law there shall no flesh be justified in his
sight: for by the law *is* the knowledge of sin.

III. SALVATION BY FAITH (3:21—8:39)

A. FAITH, THE MEDIUM OF SALVATION

21 But now the righteousness of God without the law is manifested, being
witnessed by the law and the prophets;
22 Even the righteousness of God *which is* by faith of Jesus Christ unto all
and upon all them that believe: for there is no difference:

3:3 Although the Jews were unfaithful this could neither annul what God said nor lead God to be unfaithful to himself or to his promises.

3:5, 6 The Jews thought something like this: if our sins serve to demonstrate God's justice, why should there be any punishment for sin? But if God were not to inflict punishment, then God could not judge anyone. But God will judge all, for all are under judgment for their *sins.*

3:9ff Here we learn that all men are guilty and corrupt—Jew and Gentile alike. There is none who does good. All are guilty of cruelty, cheating, and cursing. Their feet are swift to shed blood. There is no fear of God before their eyes. This is their depravity, and the whole world is guilty before God. There is no hope for anyone were it not for the good news Paul will announce later in this book.

3:20 God's moral law purposes to (1) demonstrate God's own moral perfection; (2) show man his guilt and take away all of his excuses; (3) provide a standard for the governing of human society; and (4) provide a guide for believers as to how their conduct will please and glorify God.

3:22 *righteousness*, as it pertains to man, refers to keeping God's will, law, and moral standards perfectly. This no man has ever done except Christ; therefore, no man has ever been truly righteous (3:10, 23). God imputes the perfect righteousness to all those who trust his Son by faith for eternal life. And the Holy Spirit empowers the believer so that he can live in accord

23 For all have sinned, and come short of the glory of God;
24 Being justified freely by his grace through the redemption that is in
Christ Jesus:
25 Whom God hath set forth *to be* a propitiation through faith in his
blood, to declare his righteousness for the remission of sins that are past,
through the forbearance of God;
26 To declare, *I say*, at this time his righteousness: that he might be just,
and the justifier of him which believeth in Jesus.
27 Where *is* boasting then? It is excluded. By what law? of works? Nay:
but by the law of faith.
28 Therefore we conclude that a man is justified by faith without the deeds
of the law.
29 *Is he* the God of the Jews only? *is he* not also of the Gentiles? Yes, of
the Gentiles also:
30 Seeing *it is* one God, which shall justify the circumcision by faith, and
uncircumcision through faith.
31 Do we then make void the law through faith? God forbid: yea, we
establish the law.

☆**3:23** Rom 3:9; Gal 3:21,22
3:24 Eph 1:7; 2:8; Heb 9:12; 1 Pet 1:18, 19
☆**3:25** Lev 16:15; Acts 17:30; Heb 9:13, 14; 1 Pet 1:19; 1 Jn 2:2; 4:10
☆**3:27** Rom 2:17; 4:2; 1 Cor 1:29; Eph 2:9
3:28 Acts 13:39; Gal 2:16; Tit 3:5
3:29 Rom 9:24; 10:12; 15:9; Gal 3:28
3:30 Rom 10:12; Gal 3:8, 9
3:31 Mt 5:17; Lk 20:16

B. THE ILLUSTRATION OF ABRAHAM: SAVED BY FAITH

4 WHAT shall we say then that Abraham our father, as pertaining to the
flesh, hath found?
2 For if Abraham were justified by works, he hath *whereof* to glory; but
not before God.
3 For what saith the scripture? Abraham believed God, and it was
counted unto him for righteousness.
4 Now to him that worketh is the reward not reckoned of grace, but of
debt.
5 But to him that worketh not, but believeth on him that justifieth the
ungodly, his faith is counted for righteousness.

☆**4:1**
4:2 1 Cor 1:31
4:3 Gen 15:6; Gal 3:6; Jas 2:23
4:4, 5 Josh 24:2; Acts 13:38, 39; Rom 11:6; Gal 2:16

---

with the will of God. Men become righteous by faith, which is the *means,* whereas justification is the *act* of God that makes men righteous. Righteousness is the *result* of the justification that comes from believing faith. Righteousness is also used as a term to stress one of God's attributes and carries with it the assurance about what God is, and that he will do what he has promised. It expresses God's own moral purity, contrasted with man's inherent sinfulness. Moreover, God's righteousness expresses itself in divine wrath or holy displeasure against all iniquity or unrighteousness.
3:23 Sin is the lack of conformity to the will of God, a violation of the moral law as written in the hearts of men and revealed in the Word of God. The Hebrew term for sin means "to deviate from the way"; the Greek term *indicates "a missing of the mark," or "a going* aside from." Sin could not exist unless there were a norm or standard against which the acts of men could be measured or judged. Sin exists both in overt acts and in the attitude of the heart. The overt act indicates the presence of heart sinfulness. Guilt, then, normally supposes the intention is present to do evil. Men often are unable to read the intentions of each other's hearts, but God knows the hearts of men infallibly (1 Chron. 28:9; Heb. 4:13). Moreover, all men, irrespective of race, color, or creed, are sinners. No one can escape sin's guilt. Jews and Gentiles alike are guilty (1:18; 3:23). Sin is universal (Isa. 53:6).
3:25 *propitiation.* Theologians have argued whether there is a difference between expiation and propitiation, both of which appear in the New Testament in connection with the sacrifice of Christ on Calvary. Here Paul uses the Greek word *hilastērion* (which also appears in Heb. 9:5, translated *"mercy seat"*). Some interpreters think expiation has to do with the ritual satisfaction offered for sins committed, and propitiation has to do with the person offended. Charles Hodge says the words are correlative terms: "The sinner, or his guilt, is expiated; God, or justice, is propitiated" (*Systematic Theology,* Eerdmans, Vol. 2, p. 478). In any event, God was satisfied and man was reconciled by Christ's atoning death.
3:27ff No one has any reason to boast, for the grace of God excludes the possibility of doing so. The law of faith also precludes boasting. God justifies the circumcision by faith and not by works, and he justifies the uncircumcision through faith. And faith does not break the law or make it of no use so that it has no meaning.
4:1ff The Jews regarded Abraham as their father, and rightly so. But Paul shows them that Abraham was not justified either by circumcision or by works. Abraham believed God and it was accounted to him for righteousness *before* he was circumcised. Thus circumcision followed his justification. Moreover faith of necessity excludes works, for if salvation is by works, then faith is not necessary.

4:6☆ 1 Cor 1:30; 2 Cor 5:19
4:7 Ps 32:1, 2
4:8 Ps 32:1, 2; 2 Cor 5:19
4:9 Gen 15:6; Rom 3:30
4:10 Gen 15:6; 17:10, 11
4:11☆ Gen 17:1–11; Lk 19:9; Jn 8:39; Rom 4:16
4:13☆ Gen 12:3; 17:4–6; 22:17, 18; Rom 9:8; Gal 3:16, 29
4:14 Gal 3:18
4:15 Rom 3:20, 7:7; 1 Cor 15:55, 56; Gal 3:10
4:16 Rom 9:8; Col 3:11
4:17 Gen 17:5; Isa 51:2; Jn 5:21; 1 Cor 1:28–30
4:18☆ Gen 15:5
4:19 Gen 17:17; 18:11; Heb 11:11, 12
4:22 Rom 4:3

6 Even as David also describeth the blessedness of the man, unto whom
God imputeth righteousness without works,
7 *Saying*, Blessed *are* they whose iniquities are forgiven, and whose sins
are covered.
8 Blessed *is* the man to whom the Lord will not impute sin.
9 *Cometh* this blessedness then upon the circumcision *only*, or upon the
uncircumcision also? for we say that faith was reckoned to Abraham for
righteousness.
10 How was it then reckoned? when he was in circumcision, or in
uncircumcision? Not in circumcision, but in uncircumcision.
11 And he received the sign of circumcision, a seal of the righteousness of
the faith which *he had yet* being uncircumcised: that he might be the father
of all them that believe, though they be not circumcised; that righteousness
might be imputed unto them also:
12 And the father of circumcision to them who are not of the circumcision
only, but who also walk in the steps of that faith of our father Abraham,
which *he had* being *yet* uncircumcised.
13 For the promise, that he should be the heir of the world, *was* not to
Abraham, or to his seed, through the law, but through the righteousness of
faith.
14 For if they which are of the law *be* heirs, faith is made void, and the
promise made of none effect:
15 Because the law worketh wrath: for where no law is, *there is* no
transgression.
16 Therefore *it is* of faith, that *it might be* by grace; to the end the promise
might be sure to all the seed; not to that only which is of the law, but to
that also which is of the faith of Abraham; who is the father of us all,
17 (As it is written, I have made thee a father of many nations,) before him
whom he believed, *even* God, who quickeneth the dead, and calleth those
things which be not as though they were.
18 Who against hope believed in hope, that he might become the father of
many nations, according to that which was spoken, So shall thy seed be.
19 And being not weak in faith, he considered not his own body now dead,
when he was about an hundred years old, neither yet the deadness of
Sarah's womb:
20 He staggered not at the promise of God through unbelief; but was
strong in faith, giving glory to God;
21 And being fully persuaded that, what he had promised, he was able also
to perform.
22 And therefore it was imputed to him for righteousness.

4:6 *the blessedness of the man.* When we trust Christ for salvation God reckons us to be righteous. In fact, he declares that we are righteous, not because we have any inherent righteousness, but because the righteousness of Christ is imputed to us. Christ bore the sinner's guilt and punishment (Isa. 53:5, 11; 2 Cor. 5:21; Gal. 3:13) and Christ's righteousness is laid to our account (1 Cor. 1:30; 2 Cor. 5:21; Phil. 3:9). Christ has taken our guilt and given us his righteousness.

4:11 *circumcision* was the seal of the Abrahamic covenant. Yet circumcision did not save. The Jews of Paul's day had all been circumcised, yet they were not saved. Abraham was saved before he was circumcised. In the New Testament, water baptism is the seal of the new covenant. But not all baptized people are saved, just as not all circumcised people were saved in Paul's time. Moreover, uncircumcised and unbaptized people can and do get to heaven. The dying thief was not baptized, yet he was with Jesus in paradise. None of this undermines the importance of water baptism so long as the implications are understood as propounded by Paul when he spoke about circumcision. Ultimately, faith alone determines the destiny of all.

4:13ff Abraham was justified before the law was given, and justification did not come through the law (which did not then exist) but through faith. What was true for Abraham was true for his descendants, and it is true for the Gentiles and all men here and now.

4:18 Abraham believed God in hope or even against hope. Sense, reason, and experience told him that the promise of a son by Sarah could not happen, but in spite of this he believed. He believed in hope, which arose from his belief in God's all-sufficiency and that he would and could do what he had promised. He staggered not at the promise of God through unbelief, and neither should any believer today.

23 Now it was not written for his sake alone, that it was imputed to him;
24 But for us also, to whom it shall be imputed, if we believe on him that
raised up Jesus our Lord from the dead;
25 Who was delivered for our offences, and was raised again for our
justification.

C. THE BLESSINGS OF SALVATION BY FAITH

5 THEREFORE being justified by faith, we have peace with God
through our Lord Jesus Christ:
2 By whom also we have access by faith into this grace wherein we stand,
and rejoice in hope of the glory of God.
3 And not only *so*, but we glory in tribulations also: knowing that
tribulation worketh patience;
4 And patience, experience; and experience, hope:
5 And hope maketh not ashamed; because the love of God is shed abroad
in our hearts by the Holy Ghost which is given unto us.
6 For when we were yet without strength, in due time Christ died for the
ungodly.
7 For scarcely for a righteous man will one die: yet peradventure for a
good man some would even dare to die.
8 But God commendeth his love toward us, in that, while we were yet
sinners, Christ died for us.
9 Much more then, being now justified by his blood, we shall be saved
from wrath through him.
10 For if, when we were enemies, we were reconciled to God by the death
of his Son, much more, being reconciled, we shall be saved by his life.
11 And not only *so*, but we also joy in God through our Lord Jesus Christ,
by whom we have now received the atonement.

D. ADAM AND DEATH VERSUS CHRIST AND LIFE

12 Wherefore, as by one man sin entered into the world, and death by sin;
and so death passed upon all men, for that all have sinned:

4:23 Acts 13:30 Rom 15:4 1 Cor 10:11 2 Tim 3:16
☆**4:25** Isa 53:5 Rom 8:32–34 1 Cor 15:12–20 2 Cor 5:15 Heb 9:28 1 Pet 1:21; 3:18
☆**5:1** Jn 16:33 Eph 2:14 Col 1:20
5:2 Eph 2:18; 3:12 Heb 3:6; 10:19
☆**5:3** Mt 5:11 Phil 2:17
5:5 2 Cor 1:22 Gal 4:6 Eph 1:13 Phil 1:20
5:6 Gal 2:20; 4:4 Eph 5:2
5:8 Jn 3:16; 15:13 1 Pet 3:18
☆**5:9** Rom 1:18 1 Thess 1:10 1 Jn 1:7
☆**5:10** Rom 8:34 2 Cor 5:18 Eph 2:3 Heb 7:25
☆**5:12** Gen 2:17 Ezek 18:4 Rom 6:23 1 Cor 15:21, 22, 56

4:25 *was raised again for our justification*, i.e., "rose again to make us right with God."† This phrase is theologically important here. The Greek word for justification—*dikaiōsis*—appears only twice in the New Testament, while the verb *dikaioō* ("to justify") appears almost forty times. Justification has to do with the believer's relationship to God through the imputation of the righteousness of Jesus Christ through his shed blood. Justification is outward, or forensic, in that the slate of justice is wiped clean. On the other hand, regeneration is subjective and internal. Both must take place for salvation to be genuine. Justification insures the believer that the penalty of sin has been paid and that the rewards assured to him by God are his portion forever. Justification is by grace and excludes works of all kinds (11:6; Gal. 2:16; 2:21; 3:10, 21; 5:3, 4; Eph. 2:8, 9; Phil. 3:9). Justification is more than a pardon, for a pardon cannot extinguish guilt. By the blood of Christ the demands of the law have been fully met and satisfied so that the believer's situation is just as though he had never sinned.

5:1 *peace.* Sin is the obstacle that makes for war between man and God. When sin is taken care of by faith in Christ and justification, the cause of the war is removed and peace begins. Every believer has made his peace with God through the blood of the cross. The war is ended, the enmity gone. Peace reigns in the heart.

5:3 *patience,* better translated "endurance." Endurance is a result of testing, of being tried and not being found wanting. Without suffering there is little possibility that endurance will be attained. And without endurance, character is not developed and hope—if it exists at all—is weak.

5:9, 10 We are justified by Christ's blood. Without the shedding of blood there is no remission of sin (Heb. 9:22). The life is in the blood, and the blood makes atonement for the soul (Lev. 17:11). We are also reconciled to God by Christ's death and saved by his life. We are reconciled by the humbled Christ and saved by the exalted Christ. The dying Christ was a testator who left us a legacy; the living Christ is the executor who dispenses it.

5:12ff In this passage Paul delineates two opposite states of existence: life versus death. In Adam there is sin and death; in Christ there is righteousness and life. In Christ, Adam's situation, which we have inherited, is reversed. Instead of death and condemnation there is justification and eternal life. The comparison is not precise, because grace far exceeds man's sin and condemnation. Some have interpreted 5:18 as teaching universalism, the doctrine that all men will be saved.

5:13
1 Jn 3:4
5:14☆
Hos 6:7
1 Cor 15:45
5:15☆
Isa 53:11
5:17
Gen 2:17
3:6, 19
1 Cor 15:21
5:18☆
Rom 4:25
Heb 2:9
5:19
Rom 11:32
Phil 2:8
5:20
Lk 7:47
Jn 15:22
Rom 3:20; 4:15
7:8
Gal 3:19
1 Tim 1:14
5:21☆
Jn 1:17
Rom 6:23
6:1☆
Rom 3:5, 8; 6:15
6:2☆
Rom 6:11; 7:4
Gal 6:14
Col 2:20; 3:3
1 Pet 2:24
6:3
Gal 3:27
6:4☆
1 Cor 6:14
2 Cor 5:17
Gal 6:15
Eph 4:22
Col 2:12; 3:10
1 Pet 4:1
6:5
Jn 14:19, 20
15:5
2 Cor 4:10
Phil 3:10

13(For until the law sin was in the world: but sin is not imputed when
there is no law.
14Nevertheless death reigned from Adam to Moses, even over them that
had not sinned after the similitude of Adam's transgression, who is the
figure of him that was to come.
15But not as the offence, so also *is* the free gift. For if through the offence
of one many be dead, much more the grace of God, and the gift by grace,
which is by one man, Jesus Christ, hath abounded unto many.
16And not as *it was* by one that sinned, *so is* the gift: for the judgment *was*
by one to condemnation, but the free gift *is* of many offences unto
justification.
17For if by one man's offence death reigned by one; much more they
which receive abundance of grace and of the gift of righteousness shall
reign in life by one, Jesus Christ.)
18Therefore as by the offence of one *judgment came* upon all men to
condemnation; even so by the righteousness of one *the free gift came* upon
all men unto justification of life.
19For as by one man's disobedience many were made sinners, so by the
obedience of one shall many be made righteous.
20Moreover the law entered, that the offence might abound. But where
sin abounded, grace did much more abound:
21That as sin hath reigned unto death, even so might grace reign through
righteousness unto eternal life by Jesus Christ our Lord.

E. THE NEW LIFE IN CHRIST
1. The New Life, No License to Sin

6 WHAT shall we say then? Shall we continue in sin, that grace may
abound?
2God forbid. How shall we, that are dead to sin, live any longer therein?
3Know ye not, that so many of us as were baptized into Jesus Christ were
baptized into his death?
4Therefore we are buried with him by baptism into death: that like as
Christ was raised up from the dead by the glory of the Father, even so we
also should walk in newness of life.
5For if we have been planted together in the likeness of his death, we
shall be also *in the likeness* of *his* resurrection:

But this interpretation takes the analogy and presses it beyond what Paul meant, by saying that as in Adam all men sinned and lost everything, so in Christ all men gain what they lost in Adam. Nevertheless, Paul does say that God's redemptive grace in Christ is freely offered to all and is certainly efficacious for those who believe.

5:14 Adam was our common father, the root and representative of all men. What he did may be said to have been done by us in him. By this one man sin entered the human race. Christ the mediator acted as a public person, a common agent, and the head of all the elect—inasmuch as he dealt with God by his redemption for all of us who are his people.

5:15 If guilt and wrath can be communicated, so can *grace and love. If there is power and efficacy in the sin* of man, there is greater power and efficacy in the righteousness and grace of Jesus Christ.

5:18 Adam's sin was disobedience. What he did was evil because it was forbidden by God. By God's judicial act we are made sinners along with Adam, for we are his posterity. The figure follows that through the obedience and the righteousness of Jesus Christ the many are made righteous. The free gift comes upon all who believe. The free gift is freely proffered to all.

5:21 By God's grace righteousness has been imputed for justification to all who believe and implanted in us for sanctification—and all of this through Jesus Christ our Lord.

6:1ff Some people suppose that the doctrine of grace releases men from the obligation to keep the law of God. This error is known as "antinomianism" (meaning "against the moral law") and leads to the conclusion that the more one sins, the more God's grace abounds. Paul refutes that view here (and in 3:8; 6:15–23) by showing that salvation includes deliverance from the power of sin and death, not continued bondage to it.

6:2 *dead to sin.* Death to sin should result in holiness of life. In this chapter Paul exhorts all believers to live a life of holiness.

6:4 We now are what we were not, and we now do what we did not because we have newness of life in Jesus Christ.

6 Knowing this, that our old man is crucified with *him*, that the body of
sin might be destroyed, that henceforth we should not serve sin.
7 For he that is dead is freed from sin.
8 Now if we be dead with Christ, we believe that we shall also live with
him:
9 Knowing that Christ being raised from the dead dieth no more; death
hath no more dominion over him.
10 For in that he died, he died unto sin once: but in that he liveth, he
liveth unto God.
11 Likewise reckon ye also yourselves to be dead indeed unto sin, but alive
unto God through Jesus Christ our Lord.

6:6 Rom 7:24; Gal 2:20; Col 2:11, 12
6:7 1 Pet 4:1
6:8 Jn 14:19; 2 Tim 2:11
6:9 Acts 2:24; Rev 1:17, 18
☆**6:11** Rom 7:4; Col 2:20; 3:3; 1 Pet 2:24

2. Justification, an Incentive to Holiness

12 Let not sin therefore reign in your mortal body, that ye should obey it
in the lusts thereof.
13 Neither yield ye your members *as* instruments of unrighteousness unto
sin: but yield yourselves unto God, as those that are alive from the dead,
and your members *as* instruments of righteousness unto God.
14 For sin shall not have dominion over you: for ye are not under the law,
but under grace.
15 What then? shall we sin, because we are not under the law, but under
grace? God forbid.
16 Know ye not, that to whom ye yield yourselves servants to obey, his
servants ye are to whom ye obey; whether of sin unto death, or of
obedience unto righteousness?
17 But God be thanked, that ye were the servants of sin, but ye have
obeyed from the heart that form of doctrine which was delivered you.
18 Being then made free from sin, ye became the servants of righteousness.
19 I speak after the manner of men because of the infirmity of your flesh:
for as ye have yielded your members servants to uncleanness and to
iniquity unto iniquity; even so now yield your members servants to
righteousness unto holiness.
20 For when ye were the servants of sin, ye were free from righteousness.
21 What fruit had ye then in those things whereof ye are now ashamed? for
the end of those things *is* death.
22 But now being made free from sin, and become servants to God, ye
have your fruit unto holiness, and the end everlasting life.
23 For the wages of sin *is* death; but the gift of God *is* eternal life through
Jesus Christ our Lord.

6:12 Eph 4:22
6:13 Rom 12:1; 2 Cor 5:14; Col 3:5
☆**6:14** Rom 7:4, 6; 8:2, 12; Gal 5:18; Tit 2:14
☆**6:16** Jn 8:34; 1 Cor 6:9, 15; 2 Pet 2:19
6:17 2 Tim 1:13
6:18 1 Cor 7:22; Gal 5:1; 1 Pet 2:16
6:19 Mt 6:24
6:21 Jer 12:13; Rom 1:32; 8:6; Gal 6:8
6:22 Jn 8:32; Rom 8:2; 1 Cor 7:22; 1 Pet 1:9; 2:16
☆**6:23** Mt 25:46; Jn 3:16; 4:10; 17:2; Rom 5:21; Gal 6:8

3. Married to Christ

7 KNOW ye not, brethren, (for I speak to them that know the law,) how
that the law hath dominion over a man as long as he liveth?
2 For the woman which hath an husband is bound by the law to *her*
husband so long as he liveth; but if the husband be dead, she is loosed from
the law of *her* husband.

7:2 Mt 19:5, 6; 1 Cor 7:39

6:11ff *alive unto God through Jesus Christ our Lord.* We have a new life in God, a new delight in him for whom we live, a yieldedness to him so that he may have from us the giving of our parts—eyes, ears, tongues, hands, and appetites—to him.

6:14 *sin shall not have dominion over you.* This glorious freedom in Christ means Christians can live victoriously. They can obey God, experience complete dedication, and enjoy God's grace, which makes such a life possible. Indeed, if there is no evidence of this new life in one who professes to be a Christian, the question may be rightly asked whether such a person has really been regenerated.

6:16 We are slaves to the master we obey. There are only two choices: God or Satan. Once a Christian has been delivered from obedience and slavery to Satan, he would be a fool to return to the slavery from which he has been gloriously delivered.

6:23 Sinners merit death as their wages. But saints do not merit eternal life. It is a free gift through Jesus Christ.

7:3 Mt 5:32 Mk 10:12 Lk 16:18 1 Cor 6:9 Heb 13:4

3 So then if, while *her* husband liveth, she be married to another man, she
shall be called an adulteress: but if her husband be dead, she is free from
that law; so that she is no adulteress, though she be married to another
man.

7:4☆ Rom 6:2 Gal 5:18 1 Pet 2:24

4 Wherefore, my brethren, ye also are become dead to the law by the body
of Christ; that ye should be married to another, *even* to him who is raised
from the dead, that we should bring forth fruit unto God.

7:5 Rom 6:21; 8:8 Gal 5:19–21

5 For when we were in the flesh, the motions of sins, which were by the
law, did work in our members to bring forth fruit unto death.

7:6 2 Cor 3:6 Gal 5:22 Phil 3:3

6 But now we are delivered from the law, that being dead wherein we were
held; that we should serve in newness of spirit, and not *in* the oldness of the
letter.

4. The Struggle against Sin

7:7☆ Ex 20:17 Rom 3:20 4:15; 5:20

7 What shall we say then? *Is* the law sin? God forbid. Nay, I had not
known sin, but by the law: for I had not known lust, except the law had
said, Thou shalt not covet.

7:8 Rom 3:20; 4:15 1 Cor 15:56

8 But sin, taking occasion by the commandment, wrought in me all
manner of concupiscence. For without the law sin *was* dead.
9 For I was alive without the law once: but when the commandment
came, sin revived, and I died.

7:10 Ezek 20:13 Rom 10:15 2 Cor 3:7 Gal 3:12

10 And the commandment, which *was ordained* to life, I found *to be* unto
death.
11 For sin, taking occasion by the commandment, deceived me, and by it
slew *me*.

7:11 Gen 3:13 **7:12**☆ Ps 19:8 1 Tim 1:8

12 Wherefore the law *is* holy, and the commandment holy, and just, and
good.

7:13☆

13 Was then that which is good made death unto me? God forbid. But sin,
that it might appear sin, working death in me by that which is good; that
sin by the commandment might become exceeding sinful.

7:14☆ Rom 3:9; 6:6 **7:15**☆ 1 Kgs 21:20–25 Gal 5:17

14 For we know that the law is spiritual: but I am carnal, sold under sin.
15 For that which I do I allow not: for what I would, that do I not; but
what I hate, that do I.

7:16 1 Tim 1:8

16 If then I do that which I would not, I consent unto the law that *it is*
good.

7:4 *married to another.* We were married to the law by our transgressions. But in salvation we have died to the law and been separated from bondage to Satan to bondage to God. Now we are married to Jesus Christ. As members of this new order, we are to demonstrate to the world what the new life in Christ is all about.

7:7ff The whole import of chapter 7 depends on whether Paul is speaking of life before or after conversion. The war Paul is experiencing in his own life leads some to believe he was emphasizing the acute sense of one's own sin and impotence, humanly speaking, to gain victory over it. Whatever the problem and however deep the sense of despair, Paul makes a sharp turnabout in chapter 8, which is the key to the life of victory. Paul, who cannot gain victory after the flesh, knows that victory is in Christ through the power of the Holy Spirit. Therefore, holiness is not only a possibility and a duty; it is our hope and it can be attained.

7:12 *the law is holy . . . just and good.* It is agreeable to the will of God, the lawgiver. It is consonant with the rules of justice, and it has for its grand design reaching men and aiding them to come to God and receive eternal life.

7:13 Sin perverts the law. The commandments, which were ordained to life and happiness, proved to be unto death. The same sun that softens wax, hardens clay.

7:14ff There are two things in this passage that seem quite paradoxical. On one hand, Paul is speaking about a convinced soul that is still unregenerate; on the other hand, he is talking about a renewed, sanctified soul still in a state of imperfection. When he speaks about someone "sold under sin" (7:14), it hardly seems to be a regenerate believer. When he speaks of those who delight in the law of God and serve the law of God (7:22, 25), it is difficult to think they are dead in trespasses and sin.

7:15 For the believer to say he has no sin is to lie (see 1 John 1:8). All believers do struggle in their hearts against the remainders of indwelling corruption. The truly regenerate person groans under these struggles, mourns over them, and hates sin in any form. But failure should not be the lot of believers, because Romans 8 refers to the possibility of a victorious life.

17 Now then it is no more I that do it, but sin that dwelleth in me.
18 For I know that in me (that is, in my flesh,) dwelleth no good thing: for
to will is present with me; but *how* to perform that which is good I find not.
19 For the good that I would I do not: but the evil which I would not, that
I do.
20 Now if I do that I would not, it is no more I that do it, but sin that
dwelleth in me.
21 I find then a law, that, when I would do good, evil is present with me.
22 For I delight in the law of God after the inward man:
23 But I see another law in my members, warring against the law of my
mind, and bringing me into captivity to the law of sin which is in my
members.
24 O wretched man that I am! who shall deliver me from the body of this
death?
25 I thank God through Jesus Christ our Lord. So then with the mind I
myself serve the law of God; but with the flesh the law of sin.

7:18 Gen 8:21 Jn 3:6 Rom 8:3
7:21 Rom 8:2
☆**7:22** Ps 1:2
7:23–25 Rom 8:2 1 Cor 15:57 Gal 5:17 Col 2:11 Jas 4:1 1 Pet 2:11
☆**7:25**

F. LIFE IN THE HOLY SPIRIT

1. Holiness, a Possibility and Duty

8 *THERE is* therefore now no condemnation to them which are in
Christ Jesus, who walk not after the flesh, but after the Spirit.
2 For the law of the Spirit of life in Christ Jesus hath made me free from
the law of sin and death.
3 For what the law could not do, in that it was weak through the flesh,
God sending his own Son in the likeness of sinful flesh, and for sin,
condemned sin in the flesh:
4 That the righteousness of the law might be fulfilled in us, who walk not
after the flesh, but after the Spirit.
5 For they that are after the flesh do mind the things of the flesh; but they
that are after the Spirit the things of the Spirit.
6 For to be carnally minded *is* death; but to be spiritually minded *is* life
and peace.
7 Because the carnal mind *is* enmity against God: for it is not subject to
the law of God, neither indeed can be.
8 So then they that are in the flesh cannot please God.
9 But ye are not in the flesh, but in the Spirit, if so be that the Spirit of
God dwell in you. Now if any man have not the Spirit of Christ, he is none
of his.
10 And if Christ *be* in you, the body *is* dead because of sin; but the Spirit
is life because of righteousness.

☆**8:1** Rom 8:30, 34
8:2 Jn 8:36 Rom 8:11 1 Cor 15:45 2 Cor 3:6 Gal 2:19; 5:1
8:3 Acts 13:39 2 Cor 5:21 Phil 2:7 Heb 2:14; 4:15 10:1
8:4 Gal 5:16, 25
8:5 Gal 5:19–22
☆**8:6** Gal 6:8
8:7 Jas 4:4
☆**8:9** Jn 14:17, 18, 23 1 Cor 3:16 Gal 4:6 Phil 1:19 1 Pet 1:11
☆**8:10** Jn 14:20; 15:5 17:23, 26 2 Cor 13:5 Gal 1:16 Eph 3:17 Col 1:26, 27

7:22 The regenerate man has a new mind, which delights in the law of God. He consents to it and struggles to serve or obey it. This is the flash point of *the struggle*.

7:25 In this struggle Paul reassures us that Christ is all-sufficient. In the midst of his complaint he begins to praise the One through whom God pities us, spares us, and pardons us.

8:1 All men deserve condemnation, but it will not be the ruin of believers. They have the unspeakable privilege of being among those to whom God says, "There is therefore no condemnation to those who are in Christ." Christ is the believers' advocate, who makes the removal of condemnation possible so that God is pleased with them.

8:6 *minded . . . minded.* There are two kinds of mind—the spiritual mind and the carnal mind. Each leads to a different end, either death or life and peace. Whoever has a spiritual mind does not walk after the flesh (8:1). Anyone who professes Christ and then walks after the flesh must ask himself two questions: (1) Am I truly regenerated? (2) If I am regenerated, how can I be sanctified so that my life corresponds to my claim to be a Christian? The end of regeneration is to live in the Spirit and not fulfill the demands of the flesh.

8:9 Whoever is regenerated is sealed by the Holy Spirit and indwelt by the same Spirit. Whoever does not have the Spirit, who was sent by the Father and the Son, does not have Christ and lives in a state of darkness and separation from God.

8:10 One of the benefits of regeneration is spiritual life, but the body is under the sentence of death. Believers

8:11☆ Rom 6:4, 5; 1 Cor 6:14; 15:45; 2 Cor 4:14
8:13☆ Gal 6:8; Col 3:5
8:14 Mt 5:9; Jn 1:12; 2 Cor 6:18; Gal 3:26; 1 Jn 3:1
8:15 Mk 14:36; Gal 4:5, 6; 2 Tim 1:7
8:16☆ Jn 3:6; 2 Cor 1:22; Eph 1:13; Tit 3:5
8:17☆ Acts 26:18; Gal 3:29; 4:7; Tit 3:7
8:18 2 Cor 4:17; Col 3:4; 1 Pet 1:6, 7
8:19 2 Pet 3:13; 1 Jn 3:2
8:20 Ps 39:5; Eccles 1:2
8:21 Acts 3:21; 2 Pet 3:13; Rev 21:1
8:22☆ Jer 12:4, 11
8:23 Lk 20:36; 2 Cor 1:22; 5:3–6; Phil 3:21
8:24☆ 2 Cor 5:7; 1 Thess 5:8; Heb 11:1
8:25 1 Thess 1:3
8:26☆ Zech 12:10; Jn 14:16; Rom 8:15, 16; 2 Cor 12:8

11 But if the Spirit of him that raised up Jesus from the dead dwell in you,
he that raised up Christ from the dead shall also quicken your mortal
bodies by his Spirit that dwelleth in you.
12 Therefore, brethren, we are debtors, not to the flesh, to live after the
flesh.
13 For if ye live after the flesh, ye shall die: but if ye through the Spirit do
mortify the deeds of the body, ye shall live.
14 For as many as are led by the Spirit of God, they are the sons of God.
15 For ye have not received the spirit of bondage again to fear; but ye
have received the Spirit of adoption, whereby we cry, Abba, Father.
16 The Spirit itself beareth witness with our spirit, that we are the children
of God:
17 And if children, then heirs; heirs of God, and joint-heirs with Christ; if
so be that we suffer with *him*, that we may be also glorified together.

2. The Glory to Come

18 For I reckon that the sufferings of this present time *are* not worthy *to be*
compared with the glory which shall be revealed in us.
19 For the earnest expectation of the creature waiteth for the manifesta-
tion of the sons of God.
20 For the creature was made subject to vanity, not willingly, but by
reason of him who hath subjected *the same* in hope,
21 Because the creature itself also shall be delivered from the bondage of
corruption into the glorious liberty of the children of God.
22 For we know that the whole creation groaneth and travaileth in pain
together until now.
23 And not only *they*, but ourselves also, which have the firstfruits of the
Spirit, even we ourselves groan within ourselves, waiting for the adoption,
to wit, the redemption of our body.
24 For we are saved by hope: but hope that is seen is not hope: for what
a man seeth, why doth he yet hope for?
25 But if we hope for that we see not, *then* do we with patience wait for *it*.
26 Likewise the Spirit also helpeth our infirmities: for we know not what

---

will die in the flesh but not in the spirit. Sin is the enemy of the body, but there is a future bodily resurrection in which the body will then become immortal. It will be reunited with the soul and clothed in glory (8:11).

8:11 It was the Holy Spirit who raised Christ from the dead. The same Spirit is the agent who gives life to sinners who are dead in their trespasses and raises them from their spiritual deadness.

8:13 Paul and James were in full agreement that the regenerated children of God must live differently. Faith without works is a dead faith, for true faith quickens those who have it, and their lives manifest that change by the way they think and live.

8:16 *The Spirit itself beareth witness with our spirit.* The world of the unregenerate cannot understand what is taught here. The great certainty of our salvation comes from the witness of the Holy Spirit with our spirits. Whoever has not experienced this cannot understand it. Converted believers can only seek to get them to try it for themselves by receiving Christ as Savior. *The children of God* are those who have received Christ and have been regenerated, for "to all who received him, he gave the right to become children of God" (John 1:12, TLB). No one by nature is a child of God, but sinners can become saints and be adopted into the family of God as sons and daughters via the new birth.

8:17 Believers are joint-heirs with Jesus Christ. He is their elder brother. All that belongs to him belongs also to those who are his brothers and sisters through redemption.

8:22 By his transgression Adam not only sold his descendants over to sin and death, but his act also brought the bondage of corruption to all nonhuman life and to nature itself. Fortunately, redemption is cosmic; all things will be reconstituted and no longer subject to vanity and corruption.

8:24 *hope* constitutes confidence in something that will surely come to pass. It is based on the reliable promises of God. The day of hope will arrive when what we hope for comes to pass. The lack of hope is sin, for it denies what God and Scripture affirm. Some believers have weak hope; others have strong hope. Hope is reinforced by reading the Word of God, by prayer, and by the infilling of the Holy Spirit.

8:26 Believers are imperfect in their prayer lives. They *do not know what to ask for nor how to pray.* The Spirit in the Word of God and in the believers' hearts helps. He teaches us how to pray, what to pray for, and engages in groanings which cannot be uttered. When the Spirit's strength is added to our weak power, we are unconquerable.

we should pray for as we ought: but the Spirit itself maketh intercession for
us with groanings which cannot be uttered.
27 And he that searcheth the hearts knoweth what *is* the mind of the
Spirit, because he maketh intercession for the saints according to *the will of*
God.
28 And we know that all things work together for good to them that love
God, to them who are the called according to *his* purpose.
29 For whom he did foreknow, he also did predestinate *to be* conformed to
the image of his Son, that he might be the firstborn among many brethren.
30 Moreover whom he did predestinate, them he also called: and whom he
called, them he also justified: and whom he justified, them he also glorified.

8:27 Rom 8:34; 1 Thess 2:4; 1 Jn 5:14
☆8:28 Gen 50:20; 2 Cor 4:17; Eph 1:11; 2 Tim 1:9
☆8:29 a) Jer 1:5; Rom 11:2; Eph 1:5; 2 Tim 2:19; 1 Pet 1:2; b) 1 Cor 15:49; Col 1:18; Heb 1:6; Rev 1:5
8:30 Rom 9:23, 24; 1 Cor 6:11; Eph 4:4

3. The Certainty of Salvation

31 What shall we then say to these things? If God *be* for us, who *can be*
against us?
32 He that spared not his own Son, but delivered him up for us all, how
shall he not with him also freely give us all things?
33 Who shall lay any thing to the charge of God's elect? *It is* God that
justifieth.
34 Who *is* he that condemneth? *It is* Christ that died, yea rather, that is
risen again, who is even at the right hand of God, who also maketh
intercession for us.
35 Who shall separate us from the love of Christ? *shall* tribulation, or
distress, or persecution, or famine, or nakedness, or peril, or sword?
36 As it is written, For thy sake we are killed all the day long; we are
accounted as sheep for the slaughter.
37 Nay, in all these things we are more than conquerors through him that
loved us.
38 For I am persuaded, that neither death, nor life, nor angels, nor
principalities, nor powers, nor things present, nor things to come,
39 Nor height, nor depth, nor any other creature, shall be able to separate
us from the love of God, which is in Christ Jesus our Lord.

8:31 Ps 118:6
8:32 Jn 3:16; Rom 4:25; 5:8
8:33 Isa 50:8, 9
8:34 Heb 7:25; 1 Jn 2:1
8:35 2 Cor 4:7–12
8:36 Ps 44:22
8:37 Jn 16:33; 1 Cor 15:57; 1 Jn 5:4
☆8:38 Jn 10:28; Col 3:3
☆8:39 Rom 5:3–8

IV. ISRAEL IN THE PLAN OF GOD (9:1—11:36)

A. ISRAEL'S UNBELIEF

9 I SAY the truth in Christ, I lie not, my conscience also bearing me
witness in the Holy Ghost,
2 That I have great heaviness and continual sorrow in my heart.

☆9:1–3 Ex 32:32; Rom 11:14

8:28 The statement *we know* is the basis of the believer's certainty. There are no ifs, ands, or buts about that certainty. It is an assured fact.
***8:29** he . . . did predestinate.* Predestination or preordination with respect to salvation is an act of God effected in accordance with his will. The attempt to undercut predestination by saying that foreknowledge conditions it (in the sense that God foresees what a man will do and then ordains that he do it) is inconsistent, for predestination loses all credible meaning. Maybe we should admit that we are faced with a mystery in which God works out his sovereign will so as to preserve a free will in man. Thus man may act freely to accept or reject Jesus Christ; though only the Holy Spirit can move him to accept it. At the same time, his response to God's grace is certain, foreknown, and foreordained in the mind and will of God.
8:38, 39 Paul fully and strongly knows that there is nothing living or dead, animate or inanimate, that can breach the believer's defense and separate him from the God to whom he is indissolubly attached by faith through Jesus Christ. This is the promise of God, who cannot lie and whose word cannot be broken by anyone or anything.
9:1ff Paul interrupts his argument and in chapters 9—11 speaks about Israel and its future. Beginning in chapter 12 Paul picks up where he left off at the end of chapter 8. We do well to temporarily skip the reading of chapters 9—11 and go right to chapter 12. Later, we can return to chapters 9—11. In this way we follow the discussion of Paul, for the "therefore" of 12:1 refers back to the mercies of God found in chapter 8.

9:3☆
3For I could wish that myself were accursed from Christ for my brethren,
my kinsmen according to the flesh:

9:4☆ Gen 17:2; Ex 4:22; 40:34; Deut 4:13; 7:6; Eph 2:12
4Who are Israelites; to whom *pertaineth* the adoption, and the glory, and
the covenants, and the giving of the law, and the service *of God*, and the
promises;

9:5☆ a) Rom 11:28; b) Jn 1:1, 14; Rom 1:3; Tit 2:13; 2 Pet 1:1; 1 Jn 5:20
5Whose *are* the fathers, and of whom as concerning the flesh Christ *came*,
who is over all, God blessed for ever. Amen.

B. GOD'S PROMISES CANNOT FAIL

9:6☆ Num 23:19; Rom 2:28; Gal 6:16
6Not as though the word of God hath taken none effect. For they *are* not
all Israel, which are of Israel:

9:7 Gen 21:12; Gal 4:23; Heb 11:17, 18
7Neither, because they are the seed of Abraham, *are they* all children:
but, In Isaac shall thy seed be called.
8That is, They which are the children of the flesh, these *are* not the

9:8 Rom 4:23; 8:14; Gal 3:29
children of God: but the children of the promise are counted for the seed.

9:9 Gen 18:10
9For this *is* the word of promise, At this time will I come, and Sarah shall
have a son.

9:10 Gen 25:21–23; Deut 21:15; Eph 1:4
10And not only *this;* but when Rebecca also had conceived by one, *even*
by our father Isaac;
11(For *the children* being not yet born, neither having done any good or
evil, that the purpose of God according to election might stand, not of
works, but of him that calleth;)
12It was said unto her, The elder shall serve the younger.

9:13☆ Mal 1:2, 3
13As it is written, Jacob have I loved, but Esau have I hated.

9:14 Deut 32:4; 2 Chron 19:7
14What shall we say then? *Is there* unrighteousness with God? God
forbid.

9:15 Ex 33:19
15For he saith to Moses, I will have mercy on whom I will have mercy,
and I will have compassion on whom I will have compassion.

9:16 Ps 115:3; Eph 2:8
16So then *it is* not of him that willeth, nor of him that runneth, but of
God that sheweth mercy.

9:17 Ex 9:16; Prov 16:4
17For the scripture saith unto Pharaoh, Even for this same purpose have
I raised thee up, that I might shew my power in thee, and that my name
might be declared throughout all the earth.

9:18 Ex 4:21; 14:4; Josh 11:20; Jn 12:40; Rom 11:7, 22–25
18Therefore hath he mercy on whom he will *have mercy*, and whom he
will he hardeneth.

C. GOD'S JUSTICE AND MERCY DEFENDED

9:19 Job 9:12
19Thou wilt say then unto me, Why doth he yet find fault? For who hath
resisted his will?

9:3 *I could wish,* i.e., he would if he could—but he knows that he cannot be accursed for the sake of Israel his people. So great is his affection for the children of Abraham that he would willingly lose eternal life if they could gain it by his losing it.

9:4 There is a certain irony in the fact that the Israelites had everything anyone could want given to them by God. In spite of that they rejected the very One who gave them so much; they sold their birthright for a mess of pottage.

9:5 *Christ . . . God blessed for ever.* According to the construction in the Greek, this is one of the clearest *verses in the Scriptures* that confirms the deity of Jesus Christ. He is God almighty, the second person of the holy Trinity.

9:6ff Paul marks the difference between those who belong to Israel by physical birth and those who are part of spiritual Israel. Not all who were born into Jewish families belonged to spiritual Israel. But all who share Father Abraham's faith in God, whether Jew or Gentile, are the real spiritual descendants of Abraham. Thus Gentile Christians are sons of Abraham.

9:13 *Jacob have I loved, but Esau have I hated.* Jacob was chosen by God to be Abraham's heir of promise through whom the Messiah should come. This was done while both were in their mother's womb and before either had done good or evil. Verse 11 makes it clear that the purpose of God stands "according to election." God called Mary to be the mother of the historical Jesus, and John the Baptist to be Christ's forerunner, and Jeremiah to be his prophet before any of them were conceived. In such things the purpose of God stands. The quotation here from Malachi about loving Jacob and hating Esau does not refer to them as individuals but to Israel, the descendants of Jacob, and to the Edomites, the descendants of Esau. The Edomites were hated by God for their sins against deity.

20 Nay but, O man, who art thou that repliest against God? Shall the thing
formed say to him that formed *it*, Why hast thou made me thus?
21 Hath not the potter power over the clay, of the same lump to make one
vessel unto honour, and another unto dishonour?
22 *What* if God, willing to shew *his* wrath, and to make his power known,
endured with much longsuffering the vessels of wrath fitted to destruction:
23 And that he might make known the riches of his glory on the vessels of
mercy, which he had afore prepared unto glory,
24 Even us, whom he hath called, not of the Jews only, but also of the
Gentiles?
25 As he saith also in O'see, I will call them my people, which were not my
people; and her beloved, which was not beloved.
26 And it shall come to pass, *that* in the place where it was said unto them,
Ye *are* not my people; there shall they be called the children of the living
God.
27 E-sai'as also crieth concerning Israel, Though the number of the
children of Israel be as the sand of the sea, a remnant shall be saved:
28 For he will finish the work, and cut *it* short in righteousness: because a
short work will the Lord make upon the earth.
29 And as E-sai'as said before, Except the Lord of Sab'a-oth had left us a
seed, we had been as Sod'o-ma, and been made like unto Go-mor'rha.
30 What shall we say then? That the Gentiles, which followed not after
righteousness, have attained to righteousness, even the righteousness which
is of faith.
31 But Israel, which followed after the law of righteousness, hath not
attained to the law of righteousness.
32 Wherefore? Because *they sought it* not by faith, but as it were by the
works of the law. For they stumbled at that stumblingstone;
33 As it is written, Behold, I lay in Sion a stumblingstone and rock of
offence: and whosoever believeth on him shall not be ashamed.

9:20 Isa 29:16; 45:9 64:8
☆**9:21** Jer 18:6 2 Tim 2:20
9:22 Prov 16:4 Rom 2:4 1 Thess 5:9
☆**9:23** Acts 9:15 Rom 8:29
9:24 Rom 3:29
9:25 Hos 2:23
9:26 Hos 1:10 1 Pet 2:10
9:27 Isa 10:22 Rom 11:5
9:28 Isa 28:22
9:29 Isa 1:9; 13:19 Lam 3:22
☆**9:30** Gal 2:16 3:24–26 Phil 3:9 Heb 11:7
9:31 Isa 51:1 Gal 5:4
9:32 Isa 8:14, 15 1 Pet 2:6–8
9:33 Ps 118:22 Isa 28:16 Mt 21:42 1 Pet 2:6–8

D. ISRAEL'S FALL, A RESULT OF UNBELIEF

10 BRETHREN, my heart's desire and prayer to God for Israel is,
that they might be saved.
2 For I bear them record that they have a zeal of God, but not according
to knowledge.
3 For they being ignorant of God's righteousness, and going about to
establish their own righteousness, have not submitted themselves unto the
righteousness of God.

10:2 Jn 16:2 Acts 21:20
☆**10:3** Rom 1:17 Phil 3:9 Heb 10:29

9:21 This verse must be understood within the larger context of all the teachings of Scripture about man's capability and responsibility. Man is not merely an impotent organism, an automaton void of responsibility for either his actions or his ultimate destiny. According to verse 16, the merciful God has freely opened the gate of life to all who would respond to the gospel invitation. Mercy has been extended to all; man, of his own volition, may take it or leave it.

9:23 Nothing required God to make salvation available to sinners. He owed them nothing; sinners owed him everything and they could not pay. By his free grace he offers life both to the Jew and to the Gentile, for both are under condemnation.

9:30ff The Gentiles did not follow after righteousness nor did they seek a remedy for their desperate condition. But God extended gospel benefits to them through faith, and they were made righteous. Contrariwise, the Jews followed after the law of righteousness and talked much about justification and holiness, but they did not attain them, for they did not obtain the righteousness they sought by their works. Christ, who was sent to remedy their condition, was rejected by them. He became a stumbling-block to them, a rock over which they tripped and fell flat on their faces. To them God has also extended the good news in the person of Jesus, to whom they must turn if they are to attain the righteousness they worked for and did not attain.

10:3 Self-righteousness undercuts God's own righteousness and inserts a spurious substitute in its place, a righteousness of man that gives him no standing in the sight of God (Isa. 64:6; Mark 10:18). It comes from the false view that man in himself is or can be righteous with God or can make himself righteous by his own efforts.

10:4 Gal 3:24
10:5 Lev 18:4, 5; Ezek 20:11, 13, 21; Rom 7:10
10:6 Deut 30:11–14
10:7 1 Cor 15:3, 4
10:8 Deut 30:14
10:9☆ Mt 10:32; Lk 12:8; Acts 2:24; 16:31; Rom 4:24
10:10☆
10:11 Isa 28:16
10:12 Acts 15:9; Eph 2:4–7
10:13☆ Joel 2:32; Acts 2:21
10:14 Acts 8:28–31; Tit 1:3
10:15☆ Isa 52:7; Rom 1:15; 15:20
10:16 Isa 53:1; Jn 12:38; Heb 4:2
10:17 Gal 3:2, 5; Col 3:16
10:18 Ps 19:4; Mt 24:14
10:19 Deut 32:21
10:20 Isa 65:1, 2
10:21 1 Sam 12:22; Jer 31:37

4 For Christ *is* the end of the law for righteousness to every one that
believeth.
5 For Moses describeth the righteousness which is of the law, That the
man which doeth those things shall live by them.
6 But the righteousness which is of faith speaketh on this wise, Say not in
thine heart, Who shall ascend into heaven? (that is, to bring Christ down
from above:)
7 Or, Who shall descend into the deep? (that is, to bring up Christ again
from the dead.)
8 But what saith it? The word is nigh thee, *even* in thy mouth, and in thy
heart: that is, the word of faith, which we preach;
9 That if thou shalt confess with thy mouth the Lord Jesus, and shalt
believe in thine heart that God hath raised him from the dead, thou shalt be
saved.
10 For with the heart man believeth unto righteousness; and with the
mouth confession is made unto salvation.
11 For the scripture saith, Whosoever believeth on him shall not be
ashamed.
12 For there is no difference between the Jew and the Greek: for the same
Lord over all is rich unto all that call upon him.
13 For whosoever shall call upon the name of the Lord shall be saved.
14 How then shall they call on him in whom they have not believed? and
how shall they believe in him of whom they have not heard? and how shall
they hear without a preacher?
15 And how shall they preach, except they be sent? as it is written, How
beautiful are the feet of them that preach the gospel of peace, and bring
glad tidings of good things!
16 But they have not all obeyed the gospel. For E-sai′as saith, Lord, who
hath believed our report?
17 So then faith *cometh* by hearing, and hearing by the word of God.
18 But I say, Have they not heard? Yes verily, their sound went into all the
earth, and their words unto the ends of the world.
19 But I say, Did not Israel know? First Moses saith, I will provoke you to
jealousy by *them that are* no people, *and* by a foolish nation I will anger
you.
20 But E-sai′as is very bold, and saith, I was found of them that sought me
not; I was made manifest unto them that asked not after me.
21 But to Israel he saith, All day long I have stretched forth my hands
unto a disobedient and gainsaying people.

E. GOD'S ULTIMATE PURPOSE FOR ISRAEL

1. The Rejection of Israel Not Total

11:1☆ 1 Sam 12:22; Jer 31:36, 37; 2 Cor 11:22; Phil 3:5

11 I SAY then, Hath God cast away his people? God forbid. For I also
am an Israelite, of the seed of Abraham, *of* the tribe of Benjamin.

10:9, 10 These two verses contain that which is basic and essential to salvation from sin. Whoever hears that Jesus is Lord, believes in his heart, and confesses him with his lips can be sure that he has eternal life. Whoever meets the conditions has the sure word from God that he is saved and has eternal life beginning in *the here and now.*

10:13 Theologians have long argued whether man has free choice. The problem has never been finally resolved. But this verse says that whoever calls on the name of the Lord shall be saved. Evangelism and missionary outreach have one main task: to cast a wide net and exhort whoever hears to come to Christ. Why some respond to the invitation and others do not is not the business of the evangelist or the missionary. That belongs to the secret counsels of God and is his responsibility.

10:15 *unless they are sent.* All believers are to pray that the Lord of the harvest shall send forth laborers into the harvest fields (Luke 10:2). And all believers should say in their hearts, "Here am I, Lord, send me," and then do what the Spirit says in response to this.

11:1ff *hath God cast away his people?* i.e., "Has God totally and finally rejected Israel?" or, "Are they all

2 God hath not cast away his people which he foreknew. Wot ye not what
the scripture saith of E-li′as? how he maketh intercession to God against
Israel, saying,
3 Lord, they have killed thy prophets, and digged down thine altars; and
I am left alone, and they seek my life.
4 But what saith the answer of God unto him? I have reserved to myself
seven thousand men, who have not bowed the knee to *the image of* Ba′al.
5 Even so then at this present time also there is a remnant according to
the election of grace.
6 And if by grace, then *is it* no more of works: otherwise grace is no more
grace. But if *it be* of works, then is it no more grace: otherwise work is no
more work.
7 What then? Israel hath not obtained that which he seeketh for; but the
election hath obtained it, and the rest were blinded
8 (According as it is written, God hath given them the spirit of slumber,
eyes that they should not see, and ears that they should not hear;) unto this
day.
9 And David saith, Let their table be made a snare, and a trap, and a
stumblingblock, and a recompence unto them:
10 Let their eyes be darkened, that they may not see, and bow down their
back alway.

11:2 1 Kgs 19:10
11:4 1 Kgs 19:18
11:5 2 Kgs 19:4; Rom 9:27
11:6 Rom 4:4, 5
☆**11:7** Mk 6:52; 2 Cor 3:14, 15
11:8 Deut 29:4; Isa 6:9–13; 29:10; Mt 13:14; Jn 12:40; Acts 28:26, 27
11:9 Ps 69:22
11:10 Ps 69:23

2. The Rejection of Israel Not Final

11 I say then, Have they stumbled that they should fall? God forbid: but
rather through their fall salvation *is come* unto the Gentiles, for to provoke
them to jealousy.
12 Now if the fall of them *be* the riches of the world, and the diminishing
of them the riches of the Gentiles; how much more their fulness?
13 For I speak to you Gentiles, inasmuch as I am the apostle of the
Gentiles, I magnify mine office:
14 If by any means I may provoke to emulation *them which are* my flesh,
and might save some of them.
15 For if the casting away of them *be* the reconciling of the world, what
shall the receiving *of them be*, but life from the dead?
16 For if the firstfruit *be* holy, the lump *is* also *holy:* and if the root *be* holy,
so *are* the branches.
17 And if some of the branches be broken off, and thou, being a wild olive

☆**11:11** Ezek 18:23; 33:11; Acts 18:6
11:12 Jer 30:3–9, 11; Zech 2:11
11:13 Acts 9:15
11:14 Rom 9:3; 1 Cor 9:20; 2 Tim 1:9
11:15 Lk 15:24, 32; Rom 5:11
☆**11:17** Jer 11:16; Eph 2:11–16

abandoned to wrath and ruin, and that eternal?'' Indeed many of them have been cast off, but not all. There is a remnant according to grace who will be saved (11:5). But their salvation shall be by grace without works (11:6). Both Jews and Gentiles come to God the same way: by faith alone.

People in the Reformed tradition hold that the church is the new Israel and thus do not distinguish Israel as uniquely different from the church. On the other hand, dispensationalism represents another school of biblical interpretation that is analogous in some ways to Calvinism and Arminianism. In general, dispensationalists hold to seven dispensations, or covenants. They say there are two peoples of God: Israel and the church. They are uniformly premillennial and generally believe in the secret, pretribulational rapture of the church. World evangelization will be completed by the Jews subsequent to the rapture of the church. They say that while all Scripture is written to us, not all Scripture is for us in this age. Many do not pray the Lord's Prayer. Hyperdispensationalists do not practice water baptism and distinguish between the gospel and the Pauline gospel of the grace of the Son of God. Nondispensationalists consider the saved of all ages to be members of the church, the body of Christ.

11:7 Some Jews came (and come) to know God in Christ. But those who spurn God's grace perish.

11:11 Paul preached to the Jews first. When they rejected the gospel, God ordered the apostles to preach to the Gentiles. In this sense Israel was responsible for the preaching of the gospel to the Gentiles. But it does not mean that had Israel accepted the gospel the Gentiles would have been left to themselves. Isaiah had prophesied that the good news was for the Gentiles as well as for the Jews (Isa. 49:6). This was repeated by Simeon at the presentation of Jesus (Luke 2:30–32).

11:17 Paul's use of the *olive tree* revolves around faith and unbelief. The Jews who were part of God's olive tree have been removed because of their unbelief; Gentiles who came from wild olive trees have been grafted into the stock of Israel because of their faith.

tree, wert graffed in among them, and with them partakest of the root and fatness of the olive tree;

11:18 Jn 4:22; 1 Cor 10:12

18 Boast not against the branches. But if thou boast, thou bearest not the root, but the root thee.

19 Thou wilt say then, The branches were broken off, that I might be graffed in.

11:20 Rom 12:16; Phil 2:12

20 Well; because of unbelief they were broken off, and thou standest by faith. Be not highminded, but fear:

21 For if God spared not the natural branches, *take heed* lest he also spare not thee.

11:22 Jn 15:2; Heb 3:6

22 Behold therefore the goodness and severity of God: on them which fell, severity; but toward thee, goodness, if thou continue in *his* goodness: otherwise thou also shalt be cut off.

11:23 2 Cor 3:14–16

23 And they also, if they abide not still in unbelief, shall be graffed in: for God is able to graff them in again.

24 For if thou wert cut out of the olive tree which is wild by nature, and wert graffed contrary to nature into a good olive tree: how much more shall these, which be the natural *branches*, be graffed into their own olive tree?

11:25☆ Lk 21:24; Rom 11:12; 16:25; Eph 3:3–6

25 For I would not, brethren, that ye should be ignorant of this mystery, lest ye should be wise in your own conceits; that blindness in part is happened to Israel, until the fulness of the Gentiles be come in.

11:26☆ Ps 14:7; Isa 59:20; Jer 3:18

26 And so all Israel shall be saved: as it is written, There shall come out of Sion the Deliverer, and shall turn away ungodliness from Jacob:

11:27 Jer 31:31; Heb 8:8; 10:16

27 For this *is* my covenant unto them, when I shall take away their sins.

11:28 Deut 7:8; 9:5; Rom 9:5

28 As concerning the gospel, *they are* enemies for your sakes: but as touching the election, *they are* beloved for the fathers' sakes.

11:29 Num 23:18–24; Heb 7:21

29 For the gifts and calling of God *are* without repentance.

30 For as ye in times past have not believed God, yet have now obtained mercy through their unbelief:

31 Even so have these also now not believed, that through your mercy they also may obtain mercy.

11:32 Rom 3:9; Gal 3:22

32 For God hath concluded them all in unbelief, that he might have mercy upon all.

11:33☆ Job 11:7; 15:8; Eph 3:8, 10; Col 2:3

33 O the depth of the riches both of the wisdom and knowledge of God! how unsearchable *are* his judgments, and his ways past finding out!

11:34 Isa 40:13; 1 Cor 2:16

34 For who hath known the mind of the Lord? or who hath been his counsellor?

11:35 Job 35:7; 41:11; Col 1:16

35 Or who hath first given to him, and it shall be recompensed unto him again?

11:36 Rom 16:27; 1 Cor 8:6; Eph 3:21; Heb 2:10; Jude 25; Rev 1:6

36 For of him, and through him, and to him, *are* all things: to whom *be* glory for ever. Amen.

Paul says that Jews who repent and return to God may be regrafted into the true tree. And Gentiles can be removed if they abandon their faith. Figures and analogies usually break down at some point and are not fully adequate to explain the truths at hand. The paradox of man's freedom and God's sovereign election remains. Believers must respond to this by *giving God thanks* and praise for his inscrutable ways.

11:25, 26 People are brought to God individually. Nowhere is God said to save nations as such. However, God did choose Israel and used that nation to be a channel for his purposes. But each Israelite was saved or lost depending upon his personal response to God's good news and provision for redemption. God's new Israel is made up of all the redeemed from every tribe, nation, kindred, and tongue. As TLB puts it ". . . some of the Jews have set themselves against the Gospel now, but this will last only until all of you Gentiles have come to Christ. . . . And then all Israel will be saved" (11:25, 26). This means that substantial numbers of the Jews will turn to God in Christ before the end of the age. They will be saved the same way everyone else is saved—by faith in Christ.

11:33 "The judgments of his [God's] hands, and the ways of his providence, are dark and mysterious, which therefore we must not pry into, but silently adore and acquiesce in."*

V. LIVING THE CHRISTIAN LIFE (12:1––15:13)

A. THE PLEA FOR CONSECRATION

12 I BESEECH you therefore, brethren, by the mercies of God, that ye
present your bodies a living sacrifice, holy, acceptable unto God,
which is your reasonable service.
2 And be not conformed to this world: but be ye transformed by the
renewing of your mind, that ye may prove what *is* that good, and
acceptable, and perfect, will of God.

B. THE USE OF GIFTS

3 For I say, through the grace given unto me, to every man that is among
you, not to think *of himself* more highly than he ought to think; but to think
soberly, according as God hath dealt to every man the measure of faith.
4 For as we have many members in one body, and all members have not
the same office:
5 So we, *being* many, are one body in Christ, and every one members one
of another.
6 Having then gifts differing according to the grace that is given to us,
whether prophecy, *let us prophesy* according to the proportion of faith;
7 Or ministry, *let us wait* on *our* ministering: or he that teacheth, on
teaching;
8 Or he that exhorteth, on exhortation: he that giveth, *let him do it* with
simplicity; he that ruleth, with diligence; he that sheweth mercy, with
cheerfulness.

C. PERSONAL RELATIONSHIPS

9 *Let* love be without dissimulation. Abhor that which is evil; cleave to
that which is good.
10 *Be* kindly affectioned one to another with brotherly love; in honour
preferring one another;
11 Not slothful in business; fervent in spirit; serving the Lord;
12 Rejoicing in hope; patient in tribulation; continuing instant in prayer;
13 Distributing to the necessity of saints; given to hospitality.
14 Bless them which persecute you: bless, and curse not.
15 Rejoice with them that do rejoice, and weep with them that weep.
16 *Be* of the same mind one toward another. Mind not high things, but
condescend to men of low estate. Be not wise in your own conceits.
17 Recompense to no man evil for evil. Provide things honest in the sight
of all men.

☆**12:1** Rom 6:12, 13; 1 Cor 6:18–20; Eph 4:1
12:2 Gal 1:4; Eph 4:23; Col 3:10; 1 Pet 1:14; 1 Jn 2:15
☆**12:3** 1 Cor 12:7; Phil 2:3–5; Eph 4:7
12:4, 5 1 Cor 10:17; 12:12–14; Eph 1:22, 23; 4:4, 12, 25
☆**12:6** 1 Cor 12:4, 10; 1 Pet 4:10, 11
12:7 1 Cor 12:8, 28
12:8 Acts 15:32; 20:27, 28; 1 Cor 14:3, 4; 1 Pet 5:2
12:9 Amos 5:15; 1 Tim 1:5
12:10 Jn 13:34; Phil 2:3, 4; 1 Thess 4:9; 2 Pet 1:7
☆**12:11** Acts 18:25; 20:19; Rev 3:15
12:12 Rom 5:2, 3; Heb 3:6; 10:32
12:13 Heb 6:10; 13:1–3
12:14 1 Pet 3:9
12:15 Job 30:25; Heb 13:3
12:16 Prov 3:7, 8; 2 Cor 13:11; Phil 2:2; 4:2
12:17 Prov 20:22; 24:29; 2 Cor 8:21

12:1ff In chapter 1 Paul speaks holistically about man. He says that man commits all kinds of sexual and other sins and does so because his mind has been corrupted. Thus he unifies mind and body, for the body merely expresses what is in the mind. Now in chapter 12 Paul ties body and mind together in the new relationship in Jesus Christ. He beseeches us to lay our bodies on the altar of sacrifice to God just as Abraham tied his son Isaac to the altar. Then he speaks about the renewal and metamorphosis of the mind.

12:3 *think of himself.* Every believer should have a good self-image based on the fact that he is a new creation in Christ Jesus. Some believers think of themselves as totally worthless; this is neurotic guilt. Others fall into the sin of thinking more highly of themselves than they ought. We should have a sober, realistic view of ourselves, a view that neither downgrades nor exalts ourselves beyond the truth.

12:6 God by his Spirit gives believers different gifts. They are not to be abused, misused, or unused. It is wrong to sit down and do nothing with the gifts of God. They are to be accepted realistically, used appropriately, and enjoyed thankfully.

12:11 A flat rendering of the Greek text would run as follows: "In zeal not slothful, Spirit burning, the Lord serving." The RSV speaks of being "aglow with the Spirit," the NIV says, "keep your spiritual fervor," and the KJV *fervent in spirit.* Spirit-filled believers will be aglow with the Spirit. Their lives will be in conformity to the will of God, bringing forth the fruit of the Spirit.

12:18☆ Mk 9:50
12:19 Deut 32:35
12:20 Prov 25:21; Mt 5:44
12:21☆ 1 Pet 2:21

18 If it be possible, as much as lieth in you, live peaceably with all men.
19 Dearly beloved, avenge not yourselves, but *rather* give place unto
wrath: for it is written, Vengeance *is* mine; I will repay, saith the Lord.
20 Therefore if thine enemy hunger, feed him; if he thirst, give him drink:
for in so doing thou shalt heap coals of fire on his head.
21 Be not overcome of evil, but overcome evil with good.

D. POLITICAL RELATIONSHIPS

13:1☆ Dan 2:21; 4:32; Jn 19:11; Tit 3:1
13:3 1 Pet 2:14
13:5 Eccles 8:2; 1 Pet 2:13
13:7 Mt 17:24, 25; 22:21; Lk 20:25

13 LET every soul be subject unto the higher powers. For there is no
power but of God: the powers that be are ordained of God.
2 Whosoever therefore resisteth the power, resisteth the ordinance of
God: and they that resist shall receive to themselves damnation.
3 For rulers are not a terror to good works, but to the evil. Wilt thou then
not be afraid of the power? do that which is good, and thou shalt have
praise of the same:
4 For he is the minister of God to thee for good. But if thou do that which
is evil, be afraid; for he beareth not the sword in vain: for he is the minister
of God, a revenger to *execute* wrath upon him that doeth evil.
5 Wherefore *ye* must needs be subject, not only for wrath, but also for
conscience sake.
6 For for this cause pay ye tribute also: for they are God's ministers,
attending continually upon this very thing.
7 Render therefore to all their dues: tribute to whom tribute *is due;*
custom to whom custom; fear to whom fear; honour to whom honour.

E. PUBLIC RELATIONSHIPS

13:8 Mt 7:12; 22:39; Jn 13:34; Jas 2:8
13:9☆ Ex 20:13–17; Lev 19:18; Gal 5:14; Col 3:14; Jas 2:8
13:10☆ Mt 22:39; Jn 13:34, 35; Gal 5:13, 14
13:11☆ 1 Cor 7:29; 1 Thess 5:6; Jas 5:8; 1 Pet 4:7; Rev 1:3

8 Owe no man any thing, but to love one another: for he that loveth
another hath fulfilled the law.
9 For this, Thou shalt not commit adultery, Thou shalt not kill, Thou
shalt not steal, Thou shalt not bear false witness, Thou shalt not covet; and
if *there be* any other commandment, it is briefly comprehended in this
saying, namely, Thou shalt love thy neighbour as thyself.
10 Love worketh no ill to his neighbour: therefore love *is* the fulfilling of
the law.
11 And that, knowing the time, that now *it is* high time to awake out of
sleep: for now *is* our salvation nearer than when we believed.

12:18 Christians are to endeavor to live peaceably with all men, believers and unbelievers. But peace at any price is not the rule here. One must not offend God or wound his conscience for the sake of keeping the peace.

12:21 "He that cannot quietly bear an injury is perfectly conquered by it."*

13:1ff Governments are ordained of God and are to be obeyed. They are to bear the sword and execute vengeance on evildoers; and they are entitled to gather taxes from the citizenry (13:1–7; 1 Pet. 2:13–17). The rights of governments are derived from the governed. A citizen should neither cringe before government nor be subservient to it. He is a patriot who should love his country; he is not a slave to it. Only as long as his God-given rights of religious and political liberty exist is he compelled to render government its taxes, import duties, and the like (13:7). When Caesar's laws require the Christian to break God's laws, he must resist Caesar and obey God.

13:9, 10 Scripture lays down at least three specific injunctions with respect to the law of love. They are: "love your neighbor as you love yourself" (TLB); do "no wrong to anyone" (TLB); and the Golden Rule: "Do for others what you want them to do for you" (Matt. 7:12, TLB). All of this, of course, is based upon the commandment to love God first. If the principles of love are employed, the relationships between men and nations will be improved and their disputes settled. (See note on 1 Cor. 10:23.)

13:11ff Here Paul proposes that believers should be motivated by their expectation of the return of the Lord. It is wrong to assume that this means Paul expected the imminent coming of Christ. Chapter 11 shows that he expected a long interval between the First and the Second Comings. But there is another important factor. There is a sense in which the Lord comes to each person in his own generation through physical death. Since death may occur at any time, and surely not more than a few decades ahead in Paul's own life, one should be ready and hard at work, for the night is coming when man shall work no more.

12 The night is far spent, the day is at hand: let us therefore cast off the
works of darkness, and let us put on the armour of light.
13 Let us walk honestly, as in the day; not in rioting and drunkenness, not
in chambering and wantonness, not in strife and envying.
14 But put ye on the Lord Jesus Christ, and make not provision for the
flesh, to *fulfil* the lusts *thereof.*

13:12, 13 Eph 5:11; 6:13 Phil 4:8 Col 3:5–10 1 Thess 5:8 Jas 3:14 1 Pet 4:7
13:14 Gal 5:16 1 Pet 2:11; 3:11

F. THE CHRISTIAN AND HIS CONSCIENCE
1. Warning against a Critical Spirit

14 HIM that is weak in the faith receive ye, *but* not to doubtful
disputations.
2 For one believeth that he may eat all things: another, who is weak,
eateth herbs.
3 Let not him that eateth despise him that eateth not; and let not him
which eateth not judge him that eateth: for God hath received him.
4 Who art thou that judgest another man's servant? to his own master he
standeth or falleth. Yea, he shall be holden up: for God is able to make him
stand.
5 One man esteemeth one day above another: another esteemeth every
day *alike.* Let every man be fully persuaded in his own mind.
6 He that regardeth the day, regardeth *it* unto the Lord; and he that
regardeth not the day, to the Lord he doth not regard *it.* He that eateth,
eateth to the Lord, for he giveth God thanks; and he that eateth not, to the
Lord he eateth not, and giveth God thanks.
7 For none of us liveth to himself, and no man dieth to himself.
8 For whether we live, we live unto the Lord; and whether we die, we die
unto the Lord: whether we live therefore, or die, we are the Lord's.
9 For to this end Christ both died, and rose, and revived, that he might be
Lord both of the dead and living.
10 But why dost thou judge thy brother? or why dost thou set at nought
thy brother? for we shall all stand before the judgment seat of Christ.
11 For it is written, *As* I live, saith the Lord, every knee shall bow to me,
and every tongue shall confess to God.
12 So then every one of us shall give account of himself to God.

14:1 1 Cor 9:22
☆**14:2** 1 Cor 10:25
14:3 Col 2:16
14:5 Rom 14:23 Gal 4:10
14:6 1 Cor 10:31 1 Tim 4:3
14:7 1 Cor 6:19 2 Cor 5:15 Gal 2:20
☆**14:8** Phil 1:20 1 Thess 5:10
14:9 Phil 2:11 Rev 1:18
14:10 Mt 25:31, 32 Rom 2:16 2 Cor 5:10
14:11 Isa 45:23
14:12 Mt 12:36

2. Warning against Being a Stumbling Block

13 Let us not therefore judge one another any more: but judge this rather,
that no man put a stumblingblock or an occasion to fall in *his* brother's
way.
14 I know, and am persuaded by the Lord Jesus, that *there is* nothing

14:13 Mt 7:1 1 Cor 8:9
☆**14:14** 1 Cor 8:7

14:2 The Romans were divided over the question of eating meats and vegetables or eating only vegetables. *This was a problem peculiar to this church* at that time. But there will always be differences of opinion about secondary matters for which there are no explicit instructions. We are to bear with one another and not make our own opinions a matter of faith and practice. Live and let live is a good injunction about such matters. See note to 14:8.

14:8 Biblical rules governing Christian conduct turn on two foci: general principles and specific injunctions. Among the general principles are the following: (1) we are to respect others (1 Thess. 4:11, 12); (2) we are to be fully pleasing to God (Col. 1:10); (3) we are to walk in the Spirit (Gal. 5:25); (4) we are to walk in newness of life (6:4); and (5) we are to walk worthy of our calling (Eph. 4:1). God's specific commands include (1) controling the body (1 Cor. 9:27); (2) forgiving those who wrong us (12:17–20); (3) subduing anger (Eph. 4:26; James 1:19); (4) having no fellowship with sinners (Ps. 1:1; 2 Thess. 3:6); and (5) living peaceably with all men (12:18; Heb. 12:14).

14:14 Paul teaches that no food is unclean in itself. Some Roman believers, for religious reasons, abstained from certain kinds of food, especially meat (14:2). Paul says they are weak or immature Christians and warns them not to pass judgment on those who have not followed their example (14:3, 4, 10), since they had eaten with thanksgiving to God. Paul commended those believers who were not bound by silly

unclean of itself: but to him that esteemeth any thing to be unclean, to him
it is unclean.
15 But if thy brother be grieved with *thy* meat, now walkest thou not
charitably. Destroy not him with thy meat, for whom Christ died.
16 Let not then your good be evil spoken of:
17 For the kingdom of God is not meat and drink; but righteousness, and
peace, and joy in the Holy Ghost.
18 For he that in these things serveth Christ *is* acceptable to God, and
approved of men.
19 Let us therefore follow after the things which make for peace, and
things wherewith one may edify another.
20 For meat destroy not the work of God. All things indeed *are* pure; but
it is evil for that man who eateth with offence.
21 *It is* good neither to eat flesh, nor to drink wine, nor *any thing* whereby
thy brother stumbleth, or is offended, or is made weak.
22 Hast thou faith? have *it* to thyself before God. Happy *is* he that
condemneth not himself in that thing which he alloweth.
23 And he that doubteth is damned if he eat, because *he eateth* not of
faith: for whatsoever *is* not of faith is sin.

3. Christ, Our Blessed Example

15 WE then that are strong ought to bear the infirmities of the weak,
and not to please ourselves.
2 Let every one of us please *his* neighbour for *his* good to edification.
3 For even Christ pleased not himself; but, as it is written, The reproaches
of them that reproached thee fell on me.
4 For whatsoever things were written aforetime were written for our
learning, that we through patience and comfort of the scriptures might have
hope.
5 Now the God of patience and consolation grant you to be likeminded
one toward another according to Christ Jesus:
6 That ye may with one mind *and* one mouth glorify God, even the Father
of our Lord Jesus Christ.
7 Wherefore receive ye one another, as Christ also received us to the glory
of God.
8 Now I say that Jesus Christ was a minister of the circumcision for the
truth of God, to confirm the promises *made* unto the fathers:
9 And that the Gentiles might glorify God for *his* mercy; as it is written,
For this cause I will confess to thee among the Gentiles, and sing unto thy
name.
10 And again he saith, Rejoice, ye Gentiles, with his people.
11 And again, Praise the Lord, all ye Gentiles; and laud him, all ye people.

14:15 1 Cor 8:11
14:16 1 Cor 10:29, 30; Tit 2:5
14:17 Rom 15:13; Gal 5:22
14:19 Ps 34:14
14:20 Acts 10:15; 1 Cor 8:9
14:21☆ 1 Cor 8:13
14:22 1 Jn 3:21
14:23☆
15:1, 2☆ Rom 14:1; 1 Cor 9:19, 22; 10:23, 24; Gal 6:2; Phil 2:4, 5
15:3 Ps 69:9
15:4 Rom 4:23; 2 Tim 3:16
15:5 1 Cor 1:10; 2 Cor 1:3, 4
15:6 Rev 1:6
15:7 Rom 5:2
15:8 Mt 15:24; Jn 1:11; Acts 3:25, 26; Rom 3:3, 4; 2 Cor 1:20
15:9 Ps 18:49; Jn 10:16; Rom 9:23
15:10 Deut 32:43
15:11 Ps 117:1

---

scruples while warning them not to despise their weaker brothers. He said the strong should not injure the weak by their example, for a weak brother who thought something impure would be injured in his *conscience if he ate of it.*

14:21 When it comes to decisions about personal conduct, three general rules will help us make proper choices: (1) zeal in doing those things about which all agree; (2) liberty in making choices in matters of indifference; and (3) deference toward those who are weak, tender, and easily influenced.

14:23 Where there is doubt about an activity, don't do it. This is a good principle to follow when we are uncertain as to whether we should or should not do something. Always give God the benefit of the doubt.

15:1, 2 Living "Christianly" includes putting up with the faults, failures, and finicky habits of other Christians who may be ill-taught, wrongly disposed, or stubbornly opinionated. Mature believers are to softly, meekly, and pleasingly humor their neighbors, so long as it does not require them to sin.

12 And again, E-sai'as saith, There shall be a root of Jesse, and he that
shall rise to reign over the Gentiles; in him shall the Gentiles trust.
13 Now the God of hope fill you with all joy and peace in believing, that
ye may abound in hope, through the power of the Holy Ghost.

VI. THE CONCLUSION AND POSTSCRIPT (15:14—16:27)

A. PAUL'S PERSONAL PLANS

14 And I myself also am persuaded of you, my brethren, that ye also are
full of goodness, filled with all knowledge, able also to admonish one
another.
15 Nevertheless, brethren, I have written the more boldly unto you in
some sort, as putting you in mind, because of the grace that is given to me
of God,
16 That I should be the minister of Jesus Christ to the Gentiles, minister-
ing the gospel of God, that the offering up of the Gentiles might be
acceptable, being sanctified by the Holy Ghost.
17 I have therefore whereof I may glory through Jesus Christ in those
things which pertain to God.
18 For I will not dare to speak of any of those things which Christ hath
not wrought by me, to make the Gentiles obedient, by word and deed,
19 Through mighty signs and wonders, by the power of the Spirit of God;
so that from Jerusalem, and round about unto Il-lyr'i-cum, I have fully
preached the gospel of Christ.
20 Yea, so have I strived to preach the gospel, not where Christ was
named, lest I should build upon another man's foundation:
21 But as it is written, To whom he was not spoken of, they shall see: and
they that have not heard shall understand.
22 For which cause also I have been much hindered from coming to you.
23 But now having no more place in these parts, and having a great desire
these many years to come unto you;
24 Whensoever I take my journey into Spain, I will come to you: for I trust
to see you in my journey, and to be brought on my way thitherward by you,
if first I be somewhat filled with your *company*.
25 But now I go unto Jerusalem to minister unto the saints.
26 For it hath pleased them of Macedonia and A-chai'a to make a certain
contribution for the poor saints which are at Jerusalem.
27 It hath pleased them verily; and their debtors they are. For if the
Gentiles have been made partakers of their spiritual things, their duty is
also to minister unto them in carnal things.
28 When therefore I have performed this, and have sealed to them this
fruit, I will come by you into Spain.
29 And I am sure that, when I come unto you, I shall come in the fulness
of the blessing of the gospel of Christ.

15:12 Isa 11:10 Rev 5:5; 22:16
☆**15:13** Rom 14:17
15:14 2 Pet 1:12 1 Jn 2:21
15:15, 16 Acts 9:15 Gal 1:15; 2:7–9 1 Tim 2:7
15:17 Phil 3:3
15:18 Acts 15:12; 21:19 Rom 1:5
☆**15:19** Acts 19:11 1 Cor 2:4 1 Thess 1:5
15:20 Rom 1:15 1 Cor 3:10 2 Cor 10:13, 15
15:21 Isa 52:14, 15
15:22 Rom 1:13 1 Thess 2:18
☆**15:23** Acts 19:21 Rom 1:10
15:24 Acts 15:3 Rom 1:12
15:25 Acts 19:21; 24:17
15:26 1 Cor 16:1, 5 2 Cor 8:1; 9:2
15:27 1 Cor 9:11
15:29 Acts 19:21 Rom 1:10, 11

15:13 Paul prays to the God of hope, who is the author of our hope. He entreats God to fill the Romans with joy and peace which spring out of hope, and he calls upon the Holy Spirit to enable his readers not simply to have hope but to abound in it and with it.

15:19 Paul did not hesitate to declare that he had performed signs and wonders, which had convinced skeptics and been helpful in bringing them to Christ. He said these miracles came from the Spirit's power.

15:23ff Paul wanted to visit Spain to preach the gospel, and he expected to stop over en route in Rome to edify the saints there. We have no record that he ever fulfilled this desire. But he did come to Rome under different circumstances. Before this was to take place, he had other important things to do. He had to go to Jerusalem with the offering taken by believers for the aid of the poor saints in that territory.

B. PAUL'S APPEAL FOR PRAYER

15:30☆ 2 Cor 1:11; Col 1:8; 4:12

30 Now I beseech you, brethren, for the Lord Jesus Christ's sake, and for
the love of the Spirit, that ye strive together with me in *your* prayers to God
for me;

15:31 2 Cor 8:4; 2 Thess 3:2
15:32 2 Cor 7:13; 2 Tim 1:16; Philem 7
15:33 Rom 16:20; Heb 13:20

31 That I may be delivered from them that do not believe in Judæa; and
that my service which *I have* for Jerusalem may be accepted of the saints;
32 That I may come unto you with joy by the will of God, and may with
you be refreshed.
33 Now the God of peace *be* with you all. Amen.

C. PRAISE AND GREETINGS

16:1☆ Acts 18:18
16:2 Phil 2:29; 3 Jn 5, 6
16:3☆ Acts 18:2, 3, 26; 1 Cor 16:19; 2 Tim 4:19
16:5 1 Cor 16:15, 19; Col 4:15; Philem 1, 2
16:7☆ Rom 16:11, 21; 2 Cor 11:23; Col 4:10; Philem 23
16:8☆
16:10 1 Cor 1:11
16:11 Rom 16:7, 21
16:13 Mk 15:21; Eph 1:4; 2 Jn 1
16:16 1 Thess 5:26; 1 Pet 5:14
16:17 Acts 15:1–29; 1 Cor 5:9; 2 Thess 3:6; 1 Tim 6:3; 2 Tim 3:5, 6; Tit 3:10; 2 Jn 10

16 I COMMEND unto you Phebe our sister, which is a servant of the
church which is at Cen′chre-a:
2 That ye receive her in the Lord, as becometh saints, and that ye assist
her in whatsoever business she hath need of you: for she hath been a
succourer of many, and of myself also.
3 Greet Priscilla and Aq′ui-la my helpers in Christ Jesus:
4 Who have for my life laid down their own necks: unto whom not only I
give thanks, but also all the churches of the Gentiles.
5 Likewise *greet* the church that is in their house. Salute my wellbeloved
E-pæn′e-tus, who is the firstfruits of A-chai′a unto Christ.
6 Greet Mary, who bestowed much labour on us.
7 Salute An-dro-ni′cus and Junia, my kinsmen, and my fellowprisoners,
who are of note among the apostles, who also were in Christ before me.
8 Greet Am′pli-as my beloved in the Lord.
9 Salute Ur′bane, our helper in Christ, and Sta′chys my beloved.
10 Salute A-pel′les approved in Christ. Salute them which are of Ar-is-to-
bu′lus' *household.*
11 Salute He-ro′di-on my kinsman. Greet them that be of the *household* of
Nar-cis′sus, which are in the Lord.
12 Salute Try-phe′na and Try-pho′sa, who labour in the Lord. Salute the
beloved Persis, which laboured much in the Lord.
13 Salute Rufus chosen in the Lord, and his mother and mine.
14 Salute A-syn′cri-tus, Phle′gon, Her′mas, Pat′ro-bas, Her′mes, and the
brethren which are with them.
15 Salute Phi-lol′o-gus, and Julia, Ne′re-us, and his sister, and O-lym′pas,
and all the saints which are with them.
16 Salute one another with an holy kiss. The churches of Christ salute you.
17 Now I beseech you, brethren, mark them which cause divisions and
offences contrary to the doctrine which ye have learned; and avoid them.

15:30 He who does not pray for himself and for others ought not expect others to pray for him. Paul entreats the Romans to pray for him, i.e., to join him in his own prayers for himself, and particularly that he might come to them in Rome. In 1:8 Paul prayed to God with thankfulness for the Roman saints whom he loved and cared for.

16:1 This is the Bible's only mention of *Phebe.* She is *called a deaconess. We may* assume from this the right and privilege for churches to have deaconesses although this passage does not indicate whether it was a definite office or simply social service to the community. Nowhere does Scripture set up the office of deaconess, but by inference this statement by Paul surely allows for such an office.

16:3 See note on 2 Tim. 4:19 for information on Priscilla and Aquila.

16:7 Andronicus and Junia were Paul's cousins. They had come to Christ before him. Some think they were husband and wife; others think they were both males. Since Paul mentions being in prision a number of times (2 Cor. 11:23), it appears that these fellow-believers were fellow-prisoners in one of those imprisonments.

16:8ff Paul had many good friends and close acquaintances. Their names dot the Scriptures even though we know little about many of them. Christians are privileged to make friends who are closer than brothers or sisters. Christians are "blood relatives" not according to the flesh but according to their common life and faith in Jesus Christ.

18 For they that are such serve not our Lord Jesus Christ, but their own
belly; and by good words and fair speeches deceive the hearts of the simple.
19 For your obedience is come abroad unto all *men*. I am glad therefore on
your behalf: but yet I would have you wise unto that which is good, and
simple concerning evil.
20 And the God of peace shall bruise Satan under your feet shortly. The
grace of our Lord Jesus Christ *be* with you. Amen.
21 Ti-mo′the-us my workfellow, and Lucius, and Jason, and So-sip′a-ter,
my kinsmen, salute you.
22 I Ter′tius, who wrote *this* epistle, salute you in the Lord.
23 Gaius mine host, and of the whole church, saluteth you. E-ras′tus the
chamberlain of the city saluteth you, and Quartus a brother.
24 The grace of our Lord Jesus Christ *be* with you all. Amen.

D. BENEDICTION

25 Now to him that is of power to stablish you according to my gospel,
and the preaching of Jesus Christ, according to the revelation of the
mystery, which was kept secret since the world began,
26 But now is made manifest, and by the scriptures of the prophets,
according to the commandment of the everlasting God, made known to all
nations for the obedience of faith:
27 To God only wise, *be* glory through Jesus Christ for ever. Amen.

16:18 Phil 3:19 Col 2:4 2 Pet 2:3
16:19 Mt 10:16
16:20 Gen 3:15
16:21 Acts 13:1; 16:1 17:5 1 Tim 1:2
☆**16:22** 1 Cor 16:21 Gal 6:11 Col 4:18 2 Thess 3:17 Philem 19
16:23 Acts 19:22 1 Cor 1:14
☆**16:24**
☆**16:25** 1 Cor 2:1, 7; 4:1 Eph 3:3–5 Col 1:27; 2:2 2 Tim 1:10 1 Pet 1:20
☆**16:26** Rom 1:2, 5
16:27 Rom 11:36

16:22 *Tertius* was either a secretary who wrote what Paul dictated or a scribe who copied from what may have been Paul's otherwise illegible handwriting.
16:24 This verse is not present in all the good early manuscripts. It was apparently added by later copyists, who repeated the second sentence of 16:20.
16:25, 26 Paul refers, no doubt, to some of his own writings, in which the mystery which was kept secret for many ages has been revealed and inscripturated. Apparently he knew of other New Testament prophetic writings that were extant at the time of this writing. The Holy Spirit saw to it that what God wanted known to men was put into written form, even as the Old Testament had been put down in writing for its own preservation and for the prevention of errors creeping into the life of Israel and the church.

THE FIRST EPISTLE OF PAUL THE APOSTLE TO THE
CORINTHIANS

Authorship, date, and background The Corinthian church was founded by Paul on his second missionary circuit (Acts 18:1). He was assisted in this task by Aquila and Priscilla, and later by Silas and Timothy. Paul went to Corinth from Athens where his ministry had not resulted in the founding of a church. His disappointment at Athens was softened by what happened at Corinth, where a strong and very gifted church came into being. It was largely a Gentile church, although Paul began his ministry in the synagogue and some Jews were converted. His ministry in the synagogue was brought to a halt when certain Jews appealed to Gallio the governor (proconsul) for help to stop the apostle who was persuading "men to worship God contrary to the law" (Acts 18:13). Gallio ruled in favor of Paul, who continued his evangelism in the home of Titus Justus (thought to be the Gaius of 1 Cor. 1:14 and Rom. 16:23), whose house was next door to the synagogue and to which he had gone before the trial. He spent the better part of two years in the city. Paul went from Corinth to Jerusalem via Ephesus, returning there after ministering in other parts of Turkey first. He was in Ephesus when he wrote his first letter to the church at Corinth. That letter has been lost, although some scholars believe that portions of it may be included in both First and Second Corinthians. Either through a personal visit or by a letter, Paul learned from those of the household of Chloe of some of the difficulties in the Corinthian church. Later Stephanas, Fortunatus, and Achaicus (16:17) brought a letter to the apostle from the church, in which a response to certain specific questions was requested of him. It was this combination of incidents which led to the writing of First Corinthians. It was probably written in the winter of A.D. 55 at the height of his Ephesian ministry.

Characteristics and content Corinth is a bustling metropolis, an important commercial and maritime city. It has a vile reputation for licentiousness and immorality of all sorts. The verb "corinthianize" means "to behave as they do in Corinth." Since most of the converts coming from this environment are unfamiliar with the Old Testament life style, they need instruction and help as they move from the ethical standards of paganism to those of the Christian life. Numerous problems beset these young believers. Thus Paul's letter addresses itself to specific difficulties in the church. The church is divided into warring factions. A case of flagrant immorality has arisen. Christians are suing each other. Marriage and divorce problems trouble the church. Paul's authority is being questioned. Food offered to idols as well as questions about the role of women, the Lord's Supper, spiritual gifts, and speaking in tongues continually plague the congregation. Above all, the bodily resurrection of Jesus from the dead is under assault. Paul addresses himself to these issues and in so doing lays down guidelines which remain for the instruction of the Church of Jesus Christ through the ages.

First Corinthians is marked by three outstanding segments, the absence of any one of which would leave the church markedly poorer. The first has to do with the eucharist (the Lord's Supper); here we find the earliest account of its celebration and the instruction of the apostle concerning it; the second is the great hymn of love in which Paul states that all of the other gifts of the Corinthian church shrink into insignificance if love is missing (chapter 13); and the third is the magnificent apologetic for the bodily resurrection of Jesus Christ, the truth or falsity of which establishes or undercuts the foundation of the Christian faith and thus becomes a theological touchstone of evangelical orthodoxy (chapter 15).

Outline

I. Prologue (1:1–9)
II. Dealing with factions (1:10—4:21)
III. Church discipline (5:1—6:20)
IV. Response to the Corinthian letter (7:1—15:58)
V. Epilogue (16:1–24)

I. PROLOGUE (1:1–9)

A. SALUTATION

1 PAUL, called *to be* an apostle of Jesus Christ through the will of God,
and Sos′the-nes *our* brother,
2 Unto the church of God which is at Corinth, to them that are sanctified
in Christ Jesus, called *to be* saints, with all that in every place call upon the
name of Jesus Christ our Lord, both theirs and ours:
3 Grace *be* unto you, and peace, from God our Father, and *from* the Lord
Jesus Christ.

B. THANKSGIVING

4 I thank my God always on your behalf, for the grace of God which is
given you by Jesus Christ;
5 That in every thing ye are enriched by him, in all utterance, and *in* all
knowledge;
6 Even as the testimony of Christ was confirmed in you:
7 So that ye come behind in no gift; waiting for the coming of our Lord
Jesus Christ:
8 Who shall also confirm you unto the end, *that ye may be* blameless in the
day of our Lord Jesus Christ.
9 God *is* faithful, by whom ye were called unto the fellowship of his Son
Jesus Christ our Lord.

II. DEALING WITH FACTIONS (1:10—4:21)

A. APPEAL FOR UNITY, NOT DIVISION

10 Now I beseech you, brethren, by the name of our Lord Jesus Christ,
that ye all speak the same thing, and *that* there be no divisions among you;
but *that* ye be perfectly joined together in the same mind and in the same
judgment.
11 For it hath been declared unto me of you, my brethren, by them *which*
are of the house of Chlo′e, that there are contentions among you.
12 Now this I say, that every one of you saith, I am of Paul; and I of
Apollos; and I of Ce′phas; and I of Christ.
13 Is Christ divided? was Paul crucified for you? or were ye baptized in the
name of Paul?
14 I thank God that I baptized none of you, but Crispus and Gaius;
15 Lest any should say that I had baptized in mine own name.
16 And I baptized also the household of Steph′a-nas: besides, I know not
whether I baptized any other.
17 For Christ sent me not to baptize, but to preach the gospel: not with
wisdom of words, lest the cross of Christ should be made of none effect.

☆**1:1** Acts 18:17 Rom 1:1
1:2 a) Acts 18:1 Rom 8:28 1 Cor 10:32 b) Acts 22:16 Rom 10:12, 13 2 Tim 2:22
1:3 Rom 1:7
☆**1:4, 5** Rom 15:14 2 Cor 8:7; 9:11 2 Tim 1:6–8
1:7 Lk 17:30 Rom 8:19, 23 Phil 3:20 2 Pet 3:12
1:8 Phil 1:6 1 Thess 5:23 2 Thess 3:3
1:9 Deut 7:9 1 Cor 10:13 1 Thess 5:23, 24 Heb 10:23 1 Jn 1:3
☆**1:10** Rom 12:16 1 Cor 11:18 Phil 1:27
1:12 Jn 1:42 Acts 18:24 1 Cor 3:4
1:13 Acts 2:38 Eph 4:5
☆**1:14** Acts 18:8 Rom 16:23
1:16 1 Cor 16:15
1:17 Acts 26:17 2 Cor 10:10 11:16

1:1 *Sosthenes.* The Sosthenes of Acts 18:17 was the successor to Crispus as ruler of the synagogue in Corinth. He was beaten by the mob before the tribunal subsequent to the dismissal of charges against Paul by Gallio. That Sosthenes may be the one spoken of here. In that event he had become a Christian. If it is not the same person, we do not know who he was.

1:5 The Corinthian church was especially gifted by the Holy Spirit with utterance and knowledge. Some have the ability to talk but have nothing to say. Some have something to say but are unable to say it. In Corinth the people had something to say and they had the gift of speech so that they could say it well. Gifts, however, sometimes bring problems. In this letter Paul had to address some of those problems.

1:10 Schism generally has to do with marginal matters, not those which are foundational to the Christian faith. Schism breaks the unity of the body and is condemned by God, for it is contrary to the divine will (1:13; 12:13; John 17:21–23). Schism usually exposes the existence of carnality among the brethren. Christ alludes to schism when he describes the house divided against itself. Believers are commanded to avoid fellowship with those who create dissension in the body (Rom. 16:17). When apostasy is involved, the situation is quite different. Apostates are to be excommunicated from the fellowship.

1:14 The Corinthians took great pride in who performed the rite of water baptism for them. They bragged that it was worth more if an apostle did it than if it were done by a person of lesser stature. Paul notes that he baptized only a few personally, for which he was happy because some placed a wrong construction on it.

B. THE WISDOM OF GOD VERSUS THE WISDOM OF MEN

18 For the preaching of the cross is to them that perish foolishness; but
unto us which are saved it is the power of God.
19 For it is written, I will destroy the wisdom of the wise, and will bring to
nothing the understanding of the prudent.
20 Where *is* the wise? where *is* the scribe? where *is* the disputer of this
world? hath not God made foolish the wisdom of this world?
21 For after that in the wisdom of God the world by wisdom knew not
God, it pleased God by the foolishness of preaching to save them that
believe.
22 For the Jews require a sign, and the Greeks seek after wisdom:
23 But we preach Christ crucified, unto the Jews a stumblingblock, and
unto the Greeks foolishness;
24 But unto them which are called, both Jews and Greeks, Christ the
power of God, and the wisdom of God.
25 Because the foolishness of God is wiser than men; and the weakness of
God is stronger than men.
26 For ye see your calling, brethren, how that not many wise men after the
flesh, not many mighty, not many noble, *are called:*
27 But God hath chosen the foolish things of the world to confound the
wise; and God hath chosen the weak things of the world to confound the
things which are mighty;
28 And base things of the world, and things which are despised, hath God
chosen, *yea,* and things which are not, to bring to nought things that are:
29 That no flesh should glory in his presence.
30 But of him are ye in Christ Jesus, who of God is made unto us wisdom,
and righteousness, and sanctification, and redemption:
31 That, according as it is written, He that glorieth, let him glory in the
Lord.

2 AND I, brethren, when I came to you, came not with excellency of
speech or of wisdom, declaring unto you the testimony of God.
2 For I determined not to know any thing among you, save Jesus Christ,
and him crucified.
3 And I was with you in weakness, and in fear, and in much trembling.
4 And my speech and my preaching *was* not with enticing words of man's
wisdom, but in demonstration of the Spirit and of power:
5 That your faith should not stand in the wisdom of men, but in the power
of God.

1:18 Acts 17:18 Rom 1:16 1 Cor 2:14 2 Cor 2:15, 16
1:19 Isa 29:14
1:20 Job 12:17 Isa 44:25 1 Cor 2:6
1:21 Lk 10:21
1:22☆ Mt 12:38 Lk 11:16
1:23☆ Isa 8:14, 15 Mt 11:6
1:24 Mt 11:19 Lk 7:35 Rom 1:4 Col 2:3
1:25 2 Cor 4:7; 13:4
1:26☆ Mt 11:25 Jn 7:48 1 Cor 2:8
1:27 Ps 8:2
1:28 Job 34:19 Rom 4:17 1 Cor 2:6 Heb 2:14
1:29 Eph 2:8–10
1:30☆ Rom 3:24; 8:1, 2 2 Cor 5:21 Eph 1:7
1:31 Jer 9:23, 24 2 Cor 10:17
2:1☆ 1 Cor 1:17 2 Cor 11:6
2:2 Gal 6:14 Phil 3:8
2:3 Acts 18:1 2 Cor 10:1 Gal 4:13
2:4 Rom 15:19 1 Cor 4:20
2:5 2 Cor 4:7; 6:7 12:9

1:22, 23 The Jews and the Greeks rejected Jesus but for different reasons. The Jews required a sign and Jesus brought none. The Messiah was to be a great temporal prince and Jesus was not that. Because he did not come according to their ideas, they rejected, despised, and hated him. The Greeks looked at Christ from the perspective of the wisdom of the world. They laughed at the idea of a crucified Savior and mocked unlearned and uneducated disciples who proclaimed Jesus as Redeemer. This sort of Savior neither suited *their taste nor satisfied their vanity,* so they rejected Jesus too. Paul preached a Jesus who was a stumbling-block to the Jews and folly or foolishness to the Greeks or Gentiles.

1:26 Queen Victoria said she thanked God for the letter M. The Scripture says that not *many* mighty are called to salvation. This left the door open for her to be saved. But if it had said "not *any* mighty," it would have left her out. Indeed not many mighty are called, but some of them are and in this she rejoiced.

1:30 George Whitefield preached often on the subject that Christ alone is our righteousness. This excludes works and rites, even circumcision and water baptism. Whoever wishes to boast of his salvation should boast of the righteousness he has in Christ.

2:1ff Paul affirms that he did not come to preach in wisdom or in greatness of speech. He wanted to know nothing among them save Jesus Christ and him crucified. He wanted to preach nothing *else. Christ is* the sum and substance of the gospel, the one and only subject of true gospel preaching. Paul wanted the believers' faith to stand on the power of God, not on the wisdom of men, which the Corinthians cherished.

C. TRUE WISDOM, THE GIFT OF THE HOLY SPIRIT

6 Howbeit we speak wisdom among them that are perfect: yet not the
wisdom of this world, nor of the princes of this world, that come to nought:
7 But we speak the wisdom of God in a mystery, *even* the hidden *wisdom*,
which God ordained before the world unto our glory:
8 Which none of the princes of this world knew: for had they known *it*,
they would not have crucified the Lord of glory.
9 But as it is written, Eye hath not seen, nor ear heard, neither have
entered into the heart of man, the things which God hath prepared for them
that love him.
10 But God hath revealed *them* unto us by his Spirit: for the Spirit
searcheth all things, yea, the deep things of God.
11 For what man knoweth the things of a man, save the spirit of man
which is in him? even so the things of God knoweth no man, but the Spirit
of God.
12 Now we have received, not the spirit of the world, but the spirit which
is of God; that we might know the things that are freely given to us of God.
13 Which things also we speak, not in the words which man's wisdom
teacheth, but which the Holy Ghost teacheth; comparing spiritual things
with spiritual.
14 But the natural man receiveth not the things of the Spirit of God: for
they are foolishness unto him: neither can he know *them*, because they are
spiritually discerned.
15 But he that is spiritual judgeth all things, yet he himself is judged of no
man.
16 For who hath known the mind of the Lord, that he may instruct him?
But we have the mind of Christ.

2:6 Eph 4:13; Heb 5:14; Jas 3:15
☆**2:7** Rom 8:29; 16:25; Eph 3:3–5; Col 2:2, 3; 2 Tim 1:9
2:8 Acts 13:27
2:9 Isa 64:4; 65:17
☆**2:10** Mt 11:25; 16:17; Jn 14:26; 15:26; 16:13–15; 1 Jn 2:27
2:11 Prov 20:27; Jer 17:9; Rom 11:33
2:12 Rom 8:15; 1 Cor 1:27
2:13 Mt 16:23; Rom 8:5; 2 Pet 1:20, 21
☆**2:14** Jn 14:17; Jude 19
2:15 Prov 28:5
2:16 Ps 25:14; Isa 40:13; Jer 23:18; Jn 15:15; Rom 11:34

3 AND I, brethren, could not speak unto you as unto spiritual, but as
unto carnal, *even* as unto babes in Christ.
2 I have fed you with milk, and not with meat: for hitherto ye were not
able *to bear it*, neither yet now are ye able.
3 For ye are yet carnal: for whereas *there is* among you envying, and
strife, and divisions, are ye not carnal, and walk as men?
4 For while one saith, I am of Paul; and another, I *am* of Apollos; are ye
not carnal?

☆**3:1** Gal 6:1; Eph 4:14
3:2 Heb 5:12–13; 1 Pet 2:2, 3
3:3 Rom 13:12–13; 1 Cor 1:10; 11:18
3:4 1 Cor 1:12

D. MINISTERS AS CO-WORKERS, NOT COMPETITORS

5 Who then is Paul, and who *is* Apollos, but ministers by whom ye
believed, even as the Lord gave to every man?

☆**3:5** Rom 12:3, 6; 2 Cor 6:4

2:7 *the hidden wisdom.* Paul was not opposed to right wisdom or wisdom as such. He did oppose human wisdom which always rejects divine wisdom, which defies and destroys human wisdom.

2:10ff *The natural man cannot understand* the true meaning of the Bible by himself. The Holy Spirit illumines men's minds so they can understand God's salvation. He also illumines the minds of believers so they can grasp the deeper truths of God's Word. Illumination is not to be confused with inspiration. The former has to do with heightening the powers of ordinary men. The latter is unique in that it was given only to the writers of Scripture: it was special, direct, and inerrant.

2:14 *the natural man,* or the unspiritual man (RSV). The Greek word here is *psychikos,* which indicates the natural, fallen man who is dead in trespasses and sins and has no hope because he is without God (Eph. 2:1, 12). He must be distinguished from the carnal man (*sarkikos*), who has been born again but is not wholly yielded to Christ and lives largely under the control of his fleshly nature.

3:1 Christians usually fall into one of two classes. They are either carnal or spiritual, that is, they are either babies or mature. The baby Christian lives a fleshly (*sarkinos*) life under the dominion of a self-pleasing propensity. He is not fully yielded to Christ as Lord and is not walking in full fellowship with God. He is not filled with the Spirit as he should be (Eph. 5:18), nor does his life reflect the fruit of the Spirit.

3:5–9 Paul argues that ministers, i.e., preachers of the gospel, are servants of God, not masters of men. They are only agents of God, not objects of faith in whom men should trust. God's servants are given different

3:6 Isa 55:10 Acts 18:4; 19:1
3:8 Ps 62:12 Rom 2:6 Rev 2:23; 22:12
3:9 Isa 61:3 Jn 15:1–5 Eph 2:20 Col 2:7 1 Pet 2:5
3:10☆ Rom 15:20 1 Pet 4:11
3:11 Isa 28:16 Mt 16:18 1 Pet 2:4
3:13 2 Tim 1:12, 18 4:8
3:14☆ 1 Cor 9:25 Gal 6:4
3:15 Jude 23
3:16☆ 2 Cor 6:16 Eph 2:21
3:17 Heb 3:1
3:18 Isa 5:21 1 Cor 8:2 Gal 6:3
3:19 Job 5:13 1 Cor 1:20
3:20 Ps 94:11
3:21☆ Rom 8:28, 32
3:22 Rom 8:38
3:23 Rom 14:8 1 Cor 11:3 Gal 3:29 Heb 1:3

6 I have planted, Apollos watered; but God gave the increase.
7 So then neither is he that planteth any thing, neither he that watereth;
but God that giveth the increase.
8 Now he that planteth and he that watereth are one: and every man shall
receive his own reward according to his own labour.
9 For we are labourers together with God: ye are God's husbandry, *ye are*
God's building.
10 According to the grace of God which is given unto me, as a wise
masterbuilder, I have laid the foundation, and another buildeth thereon.
But let every man take heed how he buildeth thereupon.
11 For other foundation can no man lay than that is laid, which is Jesus
Christ.
12 Now if any man build upon this foundation gold, silver, precious
stones, wood, hay, stubble;
13 Every man's work shall be made manifest: for the day shall declare it,
because it shall be revealed by fire; and the fire shall try every man's work
of what sort it is.
14 If any man's work abide which he hath built thereupon, he shall receive
a reward.
15 If any man's work shall be burned, he shall suffer loss: but he himself
shall be saved; yet so as by fire.
16 Know ye not that ye are the temple of God, and *that* the Spirit of God
dwelleth in you?
17 If any man defile the temple of God, him shall God destroy; for the
temple of God is holy, which *temple* ye are.
18 Let no man deceive himself. If any man among you seemeth to be wise
in this world, let him become a fool, that he may be wise.
19 For the wisdom of this world is foolishness with God. For it is written,
He taketh the wise in their own craftiness.
20 And again, The Lord knoweth the thoughts of the wise, that they are
vain.
21 Therefore let no man glory in men. For all things are yours;
22 Whether Paul, or Apollos, or Ce'phas, or the world, or life, or death, or
things present, or things to come; all are yours;
23 And ye are Christ's; and Christ *is* God's.

---

tasks: Paul planted, Apollos watered, but it was God who gave the increase (3:7). All glory be to God and none to men, not even to those who planted or watered. God's servants are not in competition with each other. Rather they are to be united in aim and purpose (3:8, 9).

3:10 *a wise master-builder,* i.e., a chief workman, not the designer, who is God. As God's workman he lays a foundation, and the only foundation for the Christian church is the unique faith in Jesus Christ himself. The foundation is not a system of truths (as important as that is) but a *person.* The end of all doctrine is to bring us to faith in the person of Jesus Christ.

3:14 Compare this with the note to 2 Cor. 5:10 on the judgment seat of Christ. Rewards have nothing whatever to do with salvation, which is attained by faith alone and springs from God's grace. Rewards are determined by God according to the works of the believer, performed from the moment of his regeneration. Some Christians will get to heaven with the smell of smoke on their garments because all of their works will be tested and burned up—they enter heaven empty-handed, as it were. The reward for works springs from God's grace in the sense that no works are perfect and all are lacking at some point. God mercifully accepts the intentions of the heart, as in the case of David, whose intention to build the temple was accepted as though he had done so (1 Kings 8:17–19). We are not to despise the reward (see Heb. 11:26); but the motivation for the reward should be the urge to glorify God, whether there is or is not any reward at all.

3:16 Our bodies are temples of the Holy Spirit. Just as God's Shekinah glory came into the Holy Place of the tabernacle in the wilderness and in the temple, so the Spirit indwells the bodies of believers. Since the believer's body is the Spirit's temple, he must not defile it in any way. A great incentive for living a life of holiness is that the Holy Spirit lives in the believer.

3:21 *let no man glory in men.* The ministry is a wonderful calling and institution. And faithful ministers are a blessing to church and people. Whoever pays to men a deference that belongs to God is in error, and whoever receives and permits that deference takes away from God the glory that belongs only to him.

E. THE APOSTLES AS EXAMPLES TO EMULATE

4 LET a man so account of us, as of the ministers of Christ, and
stewards of the mysteries of God.
2 Moreover it is required in stewards, that a man be found faithful.
3 But with me it is a very small thing that I should be judged of you, or of
man's judgment: yea, I judge not mine own self.
4 For I know nothing by myself; yet am I not hereby justified: but he that
judgeth me is the Lord.
5 Therefore judge nothing before the time, until the Lord come, who both
will bring to light the hidden things of darkness, and will make manifest the
counsels of the hearts: and then shall every man have praise of God.
6 And these things, brethren, I have in a figure transferred to myself and
to Apollos for your sakes; that ye might learn in us not to think *of men*
above that which is written, that no one of you be puffed up for one against
another.
7 For who maketh thee to differ *from another?* and what hast thou that
thou didst not receive? now if thou didst receive *it*, why dost thou glory, as
if thou hadst not received *it?*
8 Now ye are full, now ye are rich, ye have reigned as kings without us:
and I would to God ye did reign, that we also might reign with you.
9 For I think that God hath set forth us the apostles last, as it were
appointed to death: for we are made a spectacle unto the world, and to
angels, and to men.
10 We *are* fools for Christ's sake, but ye *are* wise in Christ; we *are* weak,
but ye *are* strong; ye *are* honourable, but we *are* despised.
11 Even unto this present hour we both hunger, and thirst, and are naked,
and are buffeted, and have no certain dwellingplace;
12 And labour, working with our own hands: being reviled, we bless;
being persecuted, we suffer it:
13 Being defamed, we intreat: we are made as the filth of the world, *and*
are the offscouring of all things unto this day.

F. PAUL'S WARNING AND COUNSEL

14 I write not these things to shame you, but as my beloved sons I warn
you.
15 For though ye have ten thousand instructors in Christ, yet *have ye* not
many fathers: for in Christ Jesus I have begotten you through the gospel.

☆**4:1** Rom 16:25–27; 1 Cor 2:1, 7; Eph 3:3–5
☆**4:2** Ps 143:1, 2; Lk 12:42–45; Acts 23:1; Rom 2:12, 13; 2 Cor 1:12
☆**4:4**
4:5 Mt 7:1; Rom 2:16, 29; 2 Cor 5:10; Rev 20:12
4:6 1 Cor 1:12, 31; 4:18
☆**4:7** Jn 3:27; Rom 12:3, 6; 1 Pet 4:10
4:8 Rev 3:17
☆**4:9** Ps 44:22; Rom 8:36; 2 Cor 4:11
4:10 1 Cor 1:18, 19; 2 Cor 11:19, 20; 13:9
4:11 Acts 23:2; Rom 8:35; 2 Cor 11:23–27
4:12 Mt 5:44; Acts 18:2, 3; 1 Tim 4:9, 10; 1 Pet 3:9
4:13 Lam 3:45
4:14 1 Cor 6:5; 15:34; 2 Cor 6:13; 12:14; 1 Thess 2:11; 1 Jn 2:1
4:15 Rom 15:20; Gal 4:19

4:1, 2 Paul is God's steward and so are all ministers of the gospel. The great requirement in their stewardship is for them to be found faithful, i.e., trustworthy. They must not lay down requirements for the laity that do not have God's approval. And they must feed them with the wholesome food of true doctrine and not with chaff.

4:4 Paul asserts that even though he may think himself to be without fault, and though he knows of no fault in him, yet he is not acquitted. God sees the heart and the inner thoughts and motivations that may be unknown to us but known to God. The day will come when even the hidden things will be brought to light and the purposes of the heart will be disclosed. Then every man shall receive God's verdict and either his commendation or disapproval.

4:7 The word for stewardship connotes the idea of household management. The steward manages but does not own what he manages; the true owner has a right to an accounting. A steward can misuse, abuse, or properly use what has been entrusted to him. Paul says, "All you have is from God" (TLB) who owns everything. David affirmed the same truth: "All things come of thee" (1 Chron. 29:14). Then David adds: "and of thine own have we given thee." Stewardship involves the use of our treasure, our time, and our talents. All come from God, all belong to God, and all are to be used for God's glory. Someday an accounting of stewardship will take place, according to Rom. 14:12.

4:9 *as it were appointed to death.* In this figure of speech Paul is speaking about the gladiatorial contests in the Roman amphitheatres. Men were exposed to fight with wild animals or to cut each other down. The victor was not freed but kept to fight another day; so at last even victors were slaughtered. In like figure, Paul and others like him are made a spectacle to the world. Paul also describes what they have suffered: they are weak, despised, hungry, thirsty, naked, buffeted, homeless, reviled, persecuted, defamed, and made the offscouring of all things.

16 Wherefore I beseech you, be ye followers of me.
17 For this cause have I sent unto you Ti-mo′the-us, who is my beloved
son, and faithful in the Lord, who shall bring you into remembrance of my
ways which be in Christ, as I teach every where in every church.
18 Now some are puffed up, as though I would not come to you.
19 But I will come to you shortly, if the Lord will, and will know, not the
speech of them which are puffed up, but the power.
20 For the kingdom of God *is* not in word, but in power.
21 What will ye? shall I come unto you with a rod, or in love, and *in* the
spirit of meekness?

III. CHURCH DISCIPLINE (5:1—6:20)

A. A CASE OF INCEST

5 IT is reported commonly *that there is* fornication among you, and such
fornication as is not so much as named among the Gentiles, that one
should have his father's wife.
2 And ye are puffed up, and have not rather mourned, that he that hath
done this deed might be taken away from among you.
3 For I verily, as absent in body, but present in spirit, have judged
already, as though I were present, *concerning* him that hath so done this
deed,
4 In the name of our Lord Jesus Christ, when ye are gathered together,
and my spirit, with the power of our Lord Jesus Christ,
5 To deliver such an one unto Satan for the destruction of the flesh, that
the spirit may be saved in the day of the Lord Jesus.

B. DISFELLOWSHIPPING THE SINNER

6 Your glorying *is* not good. Know ye not that a little leaven leaveneth the
whole lump?
7 Purge out therefore the old leaven, that ye may be a new lump, as ye are
unleavened. For even Christ our passover is sacrificed for us:
8 Therefore let us keep the feast, not with old leaven, neither with the
leaven of malice and wickedness; but with the unleavened *bread* of sincerity
and truth.

C. SOCIAL RELATIONS WITH EVIL PEOPLE FORBIDDEN

9 I wrote unto you in an epistle not to company with fornicators:
10 Yet not altogether with the fornicators of this world, or with the

4:16 1 Cor 11:1; Phil 3:17
4:17☆ Acts 16:1; 19:22; 1 Tim 1:2
4:19 Acts 19:21; 1 Cor 11:34; 16:5; 2 Cor 1:15
4:20 1 Thess 1:5
4:21☆ 2 Cor 1:23; 2:1
5:1☆ Lev 18:7, 8; Deut 27:20; 2 Cor 7:12; Eph 5:3
5:2 2 Cor 7:7–12
5:3, 4 Mt 18:15–18; Jn 20:23; 2 Cor 2:5–10; 13:3, 4
5:5☆ Acts 26:18; 1 Tim 1:20
5:6 Mt 13:33; 16:6, 11; Gal 5:9
5:7☆ Ex 12:21; Isa 53:7; Jn 1:29; 19:14; 1 Pet 1:19; Rev 5:6
5:8 Ex 12:15–19; Deut 16:3
5:9 2 Cor 6:14
5:10 Jn 17:15

4:17 No matter how interested and committed believers are, they need to be reminded constantly of things they are apt to forget. Paul is sending Timothy to them to remind them of the things Paul taught them and of his ways in Christ.
4:21 Paul gives the Corinthians a choice: either they must make things right so that he can come in a spirit of gentleness, or he will come with a heavy hand to censure sinners, chastise them, make them an example to others, and use his apostolic authority in a way he preferred not to do.
5:1 *The Corinthian church* was singularly gifted by God, but it was a church that had hangovers from earlier days when "to Corinthianize" meant to live an immoral life. The believers in this church were justified, but they were not yet sufficiently sanctified. One of the church members had his father's wife, that is, he had either married her while his father was still alive, or he was living with her as his concubine when his father was either alive or dead. The woman was not his mother; rather she was his step-mother. Paul said that even the heathen objected to such a mode of life and urged the church to practice discipline in this case.
5:5 *to deliver such a one unto Satan*. This was probably an extreme case, which required extreme measures. Paul would have this guilty party, by an act of extraordinary power, given over to Satan, not to destroy him, but to deliver him from his sin, even if it meant the destruction of his body. He wanted to be sure that his soul was saved.
5:7 Christ is called the *paschal* or *Passover lamb*, which is a fulfillment of the Old Testament type of the sacrificial lamb offered as an atoning sacrifice; this foreshadowed the advent of Christ and his sacrificial work on Calvary (see note to Exod. 12:11 on the Passover).

covetous, or extortioners, or with idolaters; for then must ye needs go out
of the world.
11 But now I have written unto you not to keep company, if any man that
is called a brother be a fornicator, or covetous, or an idolater, or a railer, or
a drunkard, or an extortioner; with such an one no not to eat.
12 For what have I to do to judge them also that are without? do not ye
judge them that are within?
13 But them that are without God judgeth. Therefore put away from
among yourselves that wicked person.

☆5:11 Mt 18:17; Rom 16:17; 2 Thess 3:6; 2 Jn 1:10
5:12 1 Tim 3:7
5:13 Eccles 12:14; Heb 13:4

D. LAWSUITS BEFORE UNBELIEVERS

6 DARE any of you, having a matter against another, go to law before
the unjust, and not before the saints?
2 Do ye not know that the saints shall judge the world? and if the world
shall be judged by you, are ye unworthy to judge the smallest matters?
3 Know ye not that we shall judge angels? how much more things that
pertain to this life?
4 If then ye have judgments of things pertaining to this life, set them to
judge who are least esteemed in the church.
5 I speak to your shame. Is it so, that there is not a wise man among you?
no, not one that shall be able to judge between his brethren?
6 But brother goeth to law with brother, and that before the unbelievers.
7 Now therefore there is utterly a fault among you, because ye go to law
one with another. Why do ye not rather take wrong? why do ye not rather
suffer yourselves to be defrauded?
8 Nay, ye do wrong, and defraud, and that *your* brethren.
9 Know ye not that the unrighteous shall not inherit the kingdom of God?
Be not deceived: neither fornicators, nor idolaters, nor adulterers, nor
effeminate, nor abusers of themselves with mankind,
10 Nor thieves, nor covetous, nor drunkards, nor revilers, nor extortioners,
shall inherit the kingdom of God.
11 And such were some of you: but ye are washed, but ye are sanctified,
but ye are justified in the name of the Lord Jesus, and by the Spirit of our
God.

6:1 Mt 18:15–17
☆6:2 Dan 7:18, 22; Lk 22:30; Rev 2:26; 20:4
6:3 2 Pet 2:4; Jude 6
6:5 1 Cor 4:14; 15:34
6:7 Prov 20:22; Mt 5:39; Rom 12:17; 1 Thess 5:15
6:8 1 Thess 4:6
6:9, 10 Isa 3:11; Acts 20:32; Gal 5:21; Eph 5:5
☆6:11 Acts 22:16; Rom 8:30; 1 Cor 1:2, 30; Heb 10:22

E. SEXUAL VIRTUE

12 All things are lawful unto me, but all things are not expedient: all
things are lawful for me, but I will not be brought under the power of any.

☆6:12 1 Cor 10:23

5:11 Paul laid down the dictum that believers should break fellowship with those who were guilty of sexual sins, greed, swindling, worship of idols, and drunkenness. He categorically said they were to be put out of the church. Evidently he regarded these sins as contagious and wished to keep the saints from being infected.

6:2ff Six times Paul uses the phrase "Do ye not know?" The Corinthians were so smart, so wise, so cocksure that Paul (ironically) wants to know why, if they are so wise, they do not know the things he is telling them. His teaching is plain: Christians are not to go to secular or civil courts to settle disputes among themselves. The church should act as mediator and the parties involved should accept its verdict. He hammers home the truth that recourse to law courts by Christians against one another is a sure sign of defeat in their Christian life and walk (6:7). It is better to suffer wrong or injury and leave it in the hands of God.

6:11 In justification God does something *for* the sinner. This has to do with his *standing* with God; he becomes righteous by the imputation of Christ's righteousness. In sanctification God does something *in* the believer; it has to do with *character* and *conduct*. Sanctification is the work of the triune God—Father, Son, and Holy Spirit (1 Thess. 5:23; Heb. 2:11; Rom. 15:16). In sanctification the believer puts off the old and puts on the new and is being conformed to the image of Jesus Christ (Rom. 6:11, 12; Col. 3:3–14; Rom. 8:28, 29; 1 Thess. 4:3).

6:12–20 Apparently the Corinthians agreed that adultery was wrong, but not fornication. As the appetite that demands food finds satisfaction by eating, so they may have thought that the sexual appetite of the unmarried can be satisfied by fornication. They may have misconstrued Paul's teaching about freedom or liberty to include the rightness of fornication. Paul corrects their error, showing that the sex act joins two bodies into a single relationship. To fornicate is immoral; it is a sin against the Holy Spirit, who dwells in the Christian's heart. God is to be gloried in all believers' bodies, and fornication does not do this.

6:13 Mt 15:17 Col 2:22 1 Thess 4:3
6:14 Acts 2:24 Rom 6:5 1 Cor 15:23 Eph 1:19, 20
6:16 Gen 2:24 Mt 19:5, 6
6:17 Jn 17:21 Rom 8:16 2 Cor 3:17 Eph 5:30
6:18 Rom 1:24 Eph 5:3 1 Thess 4:3, 4
6:19 Rom 14:7, 8 2 Cor 6:16
6:20 2 Cor 7:1 Gal 3:13 Heb 9:12 1 Pet 1:18, 19 Rev 5:9

13 Meats for the belly, and the belly for meats: but God shall destroy both it and them. Now the body *is* not for fornication, but for the Lord; and the Lord for the body.

14 And God hath both raised up the Lord, and will also raise up us by his own power.

15 Know ye not that your bodies are the members of Christ? shall I then take the members of Christ, and make *them* the members of an harlot? God forbid.

16 What? know ye not that he which is joined to an harlot is one body? for two, saith he, shall be one flesh.

17 But he that is joined unto the Lord is one spirit.

18 Flee fornication. Every sin that a man doeth is without the body; but he that committeth fornication sinneth against his own body.

19 What? know ye not that your body is the temple of the Holy Ghost *which is* in you, which ye have of God, and ye are not your own?

20 For ye are bought with a price: therefore glorify God in your body, and in your spirit, which are God's.

IV. RESPONSE TO THE CORINTHIAN LETTER (7:1—15:58)

A. MARRIAGE AND DIVORCE

1. True Marriage and Its Duties

7:1 1 Cor 7:8, 26
7:2☆ Prov 5:19
7:3 Ex 21:10 1 Pet 3:7
7:5☆ 1 Thess 3:5
7:6 2 Cor 8:8; 11:17
7:7☆ Mt 19:12 1 Cor 9:5; 12:11
7:9 1 Tim 5:14
7:10 Mal 2:14, 16 Mt 5:32; 19:5, 6 Mk 10:10–12 Lk 16:18

7 NOW concerning the things whereof ye wrote unto me: *It is* good for a man not to touch a woman.

2 Nevertheless, *to avoid* fornication, let every man have his own wife, and let every woman have her own husband.

3 Let the husband render unto the wife due benevolence: and likewise also the wife unto the husband.

4 The wife hath not power of her own body, but the husband: and likewise also the husband hath not power of his own body, but the wife.

5 Defraud ye not one the other, except *it be* with consent for a time, that ye may give yourselves to fasting and prayer; and come together again, that Satan tempt you not for your incontinency.

6 But I speak this by permission, *and* not of commandment.

7 For I would that all men were even as I myself. But every man hath his proper gift of God, one after this manner, and another after that.

8 I say therefore to the unmarried and widows, It is good for them if they abide even as I.

9 But if they cannot contain, let them marry: for it is better to marry than to burn.

10 And unto the married I command, *yet* not I, but the Lord, Let not the wife depart from *her* husband:

7:2 Marriage was intended to be a union of one man and one woman. Polygamy was not God's intention (Gen. 2:24; Mark 10:6–8). As Christ is the head of the body, so the husband is the head of the wife (Eph. 5:23). Husbands are to support, protect, and care for their wives. They are to (1) love their wives (Eph. 5:25); (2) be thoughtful of their needs (1 Pet. 3:7); (3) be *faithful to them (Mal. 2:14); and* (4) stay married (not divide except in the case of fornication, Matt. 19:3–9). A man's duty is first toward God, second toward his wife, and third toward his children.

7:5 Many a marriage has ended by the failure of one partner to render the conjugal due, that is, providing sexual satisfaction to the partner. Paul says it is legitimate for a married couple to interrupt this aspect of the marital bond for a season if there is agreement by both parties. But he advises them to come together lest Satan tempt one or both of the spouses to seek sexual satisfaction outside the marriage. Adultery for any reason is never condoned in Scripture.

7:7 The continuance of life requires marriage and propagation. Since most people do not have the gift of continence, they are to marry and have offspring. But God gives some of his people the gift of continence. For them the single state is in accord with the will of God. Paul wishes all of God's children had the gift he had, but acknowledges that for those who do not have his gift, it is better to marry than to burn with lust.

[11]But and if she depart, let her remain unmarried, or be reconciled to *her*
husband: and let not the husband put away *his* wife.

2. Mixed Marriages

[12]But to the rest speak I, not the Lord: If any brother hath a wife that
believeth not, and she be pleased to dwell with him, let him not put her
away.
[13]And the woman which hath an husband that believeth not, and if he be
pleased to dwell with her, let her not leave him.
[14]For the unbelieving husband is sanctified by the wife, and the
unbelieving wife is sanctified by the husband: else were your children
unclean; but now are they holy.
[15]But if the unbelieving depart, let him depart. A brother or a sister is not
under bondage in such *cases:* but God hath called us to peace.
[16]For what knowest thou, O wife, whether thou shalt save *thy* husband?
or how knowest thou, O man, whether thou shalt save *thy* wife?
[17]But as God hath distributed to every man, as the Lord hath called every
one, so let him walk. And so ordain I in all churches.
[18]Is any man called being circumcised? let him not become uncircum-
cised. Is any called in uncircumcision? let him not be circumcised.
[19]Circumcision is nothing, and uncircumcision is nothing, but the
keeping of the commandments of God.
[20]Let every man abide in the same calling wherein he was called.
[21]Art thou called *being* a servant? care not for it: but if thou mayest be
made free, use *it* rather.
[22]For he that is called in the Lord, *being* a servant, is the Lord's freeman:
likewise also he that is called, *being* free, is Christ's servant.
[23]Ye are bought with a price; be not ye the servants of men.
[24]Brethren, let every man, wherein he is called, therein abide with God.

7:12 2 Cor 11:17
7:14 Ezra 9:2; Mal 2:15
☆7:15
7:16 1 Pet 3:1
☆7:17 1 Cor 4:17; 11:16; 14:33; 2 Cor 8:18; 11:28
7:18 Acts 15:4–19; Gal 5:2
7:19 Rom 2:25; Gal 5:6; 6:15; Col 3:11; 1 Jn 2:3; 3:24
☆7:21 Gal 3:28
7:22 Gal 5:13; Eph 6:6; 1 Pet 2:16
7:23 Lev 25:42; 1 Cor 6:20; 1 Pet 1:18

3. Instructions to the Unmarried

[25]Now concerning virgins I have no commandment of the Lord: yet I
give my judgment, as one that hath obtained mercy of the Lord to be
faithful.
[26]I suppose therefore that this is good for the present distress, *I say,* that
it is good for a man so to be.
[27]Art thou bound unto a wife? seek not to be loosed. Art thou loosed
from a wife? seek not a wife.
[28]But and if thou marry, thou hast not sinned; and if a virgin marry, she

7:25 2 Cor 4:1
☆7:26 Lk 21:23

7:15 See note on Deut. 24:1 concerning divorce.
7:17 This verse might be better understood when translated: "Only, let every one lead the life which the Lord has assigned to him, and in which God has called him" (RSV). What was good for the apostle Paul may not be good for most believers, so far as marriage is concerned.
7:21 Freedom is better than slavery. Therefore, any slave would do well to obtain his freedom if he can. The free man can control the use of his time and is not under the dominion of another. He also has power over himself. Yet Paul does not condemn slavery per se, nor does he say it is wrong for a Christian to have slaves. The absence of explicit condemnation is the reason for differences of opinions among Christians on this issue. But the Scriptures implicitly indicate that slavery is not something to be endorsed by believers.
7:26 Paul was not a woman-hater, nor did he belittle marriage. He elevated it to the highest possible position. In this passage Paul did not say that bachelorhood is best for all men in all times. By way of advice, because God had not given a specific command, he thought it wise for those who had the gift of continence to remain single so as to devote themselves wholly to the service of God. The impending distress or *great dangers* to come might cause men to forswear Christ to save their wives and children from torture and death. Or his advice may have been based on the possibility of the imminent coming of the Lord. He was not binding all Christians by this statement so that one who marries would fall under his apostolic displeasure.

hath not sinned. Nevertheless such shall have trouble in the flesh: but I
spare you.
7:29 Rom 13:11; 1 Cor 7:31; 1 Pet 4:7
[29]But this I say, brethren, the time *is* short: it remaineth, that both they
that have wives be as though they had none;
[30]And they that weep, as though they wept not; and they that rejoice, as
though they rejoiced not; and they that buy, as though they possessed not;
7:31 Ps 39:6; Jas 4:14; 1 Jn 2:17
[31]And they that use this world, as not abusing *it:* for the fashion of this
world passeth away.
[32]But I would have you without carefulness. He that is unmarried careth
for the things that belong to the Lord, how he may please the Lord:
[33]But he that is married careth for the things that are of the world, how
he may please *his* wife.
7:34 Lk 10:40; 1 Tim 5:5
[34]There is difference *also* between a wife and a virgin. The unmarried
woman careth for the things of the Lord, that she may be holy both in body
and in spirit: but she that is married careth for the things of the world, how
she may please *her* husband.
7:35☆
[35]And this I speak for your own profit; not that I may cast a snare upon
you, but for that which is comely, and that ye may attend upon the Lord
without distraction.
[36]But if any man think that he behaveth himself uncomely toward his
virgin, if she pass the flower of *her* age, and need so require, let him do what
he will, he sinneth not: let them marry.
[37]Nevertheless he that standeth stedfast in his heart, having no necessity,
but hath power over his own will, and hath so decreed in his heart that he
will keep his virgin, doeth well.
7:38 Heb 13:4
[38]So then he that giveth *her* in marriage doeth well; but he that giveth *her*
not in marriage doeth better.

4. Advice to Widows

7:39 Rom 7:2; 2 Cor 6:14
[39]The wife is bound by the law as long as her husband liveth; but if her
husband be dead, she is at liberty to be married to whom she will; only in
the Lord.
7:40 1 Cor 7:6, 25
[40]But she is happier if she so abide, after my judgment: and I think also
that I have the Spirit of God.

B. FOOD SACRIFICED TO IDOLS

8:1☆ Acts 15:20; Rom 14:19
8 NOW as touching things offered unto idols, we know that we all have
knowledge. Knowledge puffeth up, but charity edifieth.
8:2 1 Cor 3:18; 13:8, 9; 1 Tim 6:4
[2]And if any man think that he knoweth any thing, he knoweth nothing
yet as he ought to know.
8:3 Ex 33:12; Gal 4:9; 2 Tim 2:19
[3]But if any man love God, the same is known of him.
8:4 Deut 4:39; Isa 44:8; Acts 15:20
[4]As concerning therefore the eating of those things that are offered in
sacrifice unto idols, we know that an idol *is* nothing in the world, and that
there is none other God but one.
8:5 Jn 10:34
[5]For though there be that are called gods, whether in heaven or in earth,
(as there be gods many, and lords many,)

7:35 Paul says in effect, "That condition of life is best for every man which is best for his soul, and keeps him *most clear of the cares* and snares of the world." But no rule can be laid down that will govern all cases, and no one else can determine for friends and neighbors what the best state of life is for them. That decision lies between the believer and Almighty God.

8:1ff In ancient Corinth parts of the animals sacrificed to idols found their way into the meat markets for sale to the public (see 10:25). Some Corinthian believers felt that eating meat of this kind was idolatrous, since the animal had been offered as a sacrifice to an idol. Paul said that idols were nothing; thus, eating meat offered to them was not wrong in itself. But since weaker consciences were offended by this act of eating, believers should abstain from food offered to idols for the sake of the weaker brother's conscience.

6 But to us *there is but* one God, the Father, of whom *are* all things, and
we in him; and one Lord Jesus Christ, by whom *are* all things, and we by
him.
7 Howbeit *there is* not in every man that knowledge: for some with
conscience of the idol unto this hour eat *it* as a thing offered unto an idol;
and their conscience being weak is defiled.
8 But meat commendeth us not to God: for neither, if we eat, are we the
better; neither, if we eat not, are we the worse.
9 But take heed lest by any means this liberty of yours become a
stumblingblock to them that are weak.
10 For if any man see thee which hast knowledge sit at meat in the idol's
temple, shall not the conscience of him which is weak be emboldened to eat
those things which are offered to idols;
11 And through thy knowledge shall the weak brother perish, for whom
Christ died?
12 But when ye sin so against the brethren, and wound their weak
conscience, ye sin against Christ.
13 Wherefore, if meat make my brother to offend, I will eat no flesh while
the world standeth, lest I make my brother to offend.

8:6 Mal 2:10 Jn 1:3 Acts 17:28 Rom 11:36 Eph 4:6 Phil 2:11 Col 1:16 Heb 1:2
8:7 Rom 14:14, 22 1 Cor 8:4
8:8 Rom 14:17
☆8:9 Rom 14:1, 13, 21 1 Cor 8:10 10:28 Gal 5:13
8:10 Acts 15:20
☆8:11 Rom 14:15, 20 1 Cor 8:4
8:12 Mt 18:6 Rom 14:20
8:13 Rom 14:21 1 Cor 10:32 2 Cor 6:3; 11:29

C. CHRISTIAN FREEDOM

1. The Christian's Rights

9 AM I not an apostle? am I not free? have I not seen Jesus Christ our
Lord? are not ye my work in the Lord?
2 If I be not an apostle unto others, yet doubtless I am to you: for the seal
of mine apostleship are ye in the Lord.
3 Mine answer to them that do examine me is this,
4 Have we not power to eat and to drink?
5 Have we not power to lead about a sister, a wife, as well as other
apostles, and *as* the brethren of the Lord, and Ce'phas?
6 Or I only and Barnabas, have not we power to forbear working?
7 Who goeth a warfare any time at his own charges? who planteth a
vineyard, and eateth not of the fruit thereof? or who feedeth a flock, and
eateth not of the milk of the flock?
8 Say I these things as a man? or saith not the law the same also?
9 For it is written in the law of Moses, Thou shalt not muzzle the mouth
of the ox that treadeth out the corn. Doth God take care for oxen?
10 Or saith he *it* altogether for our sakes? For our sakes, no doubt, *this* is
written: that he that ploweth should plow in hope; and that he that
thresheth in hope should be partaker of his hope.
11 If we have sown unto you spiritual things, *is it* a great thing if we shall
reap your carnal things?

☆9:1 Acts 9:3; 18:9 1 Cor 3:6; 4:15 15:8 1 Tim 2:7 2 Tim 1:11
9:2 2 Cor 3:2
☆9:3
9:4 2 Thess 3:9
9:5 Mt 8:14; 12:46 Mk 6:2, 3 Lk 6:15
9:6 2 Thess 3:8
9:7 Deut 20:6 Prov 27:18 1 Cor 3:6 2 Cor 10:4 2 Tim 4:7 1 Pet 5:2
9:9 Deut 25:4 1 Tim 5:18
9:10 Rom 4:23 2 Tim 2:6
9:11 Rom 15:27

8:9 See note to Acts 16:3 on principle vs. expediency.

8:11ff Paul so values the soul of a brother or sister that he will gladly deny himself even something that is legitimate for him, so that another's conscience is not troubled and then he stumbles in his faith.

9:1 Paul had served the Corinthians well and they owed their salvation to his faithful preaching. He was therefore deeply agitated when some questioned whether he was really an apostle. He says that these people who have come to Christ are a seal of his apostleship; to question him on this is base ingratitude toward one whose life was given to help them.

9:3ff Paul is reduced to defending the right of the ministry to receive wages for their services. A soldier of war cannot be expected to support himself when he serves in the army. Those who are benefited by his services are to support him. A shepherd has a right to milk his flock to live, and whoever tends a vineyard has a right to eat of its fruit. Paul uses Moses' words, "Thou shalt not muzzle the mouth of the ox that treadeth out the corn" (Deut. 25:4). If God cares enough for animals to let them feed from their labors, does he not also care for preachers, intending that their listeners should support them?

9:12 2 Cor 6:3; 11:7, 12

12 If others be partakers of *this* power over you, *are* not we rather?
Nevertheless we have not used this power; but suffer all things, lest we
should hinder the gospel of Christ.

9:13 Lev 6:16 Num 5:9, 10

13 Do ye not know that they which minister about holy things live *of the*
things of the temple? and they which wait at the altar are partakers with the
altar?

9:14☆ Mt 10:10 Lk 10:7 Gal 6:6 1 Tim 5:17

14 Even so hath the Lord ordained that they which preach the gospel
should live of the gospel.

2. Giving Up One's Rights

9:15 Acts 18:3; 20:33 2 Cor 11:8–10

15 But I have used none of these things: neither have I written these
things, that it should be so done unto me: for *it were* better for me to die,
than that any man should make my glorying void.

9:16 Acts 9:15 Rom 1:14

16 For though I preach the gospel, I have nothing to glory of: for necessity
is laid upon me; yea, woe is unto me, if I preach not the gospel!

9:17 Gal 2:7 Eph 3:1–8 Phil 1:16, 17 Col 1:25

17 For if I do this thing willingly, I have a reward: but if against my will,
a dispensation *of the gospel* is committed unto me.

9:18 2 Cor 11:7 12:13

18 What is my reward then? *Verily* that, when I preach the gospel, I may
make the gospel of Christ without charge, that I abuse not my power in the
gospel.

9:19☆ Gal 5:13

19 For though I be free from all *men*, yet have I made myself servant unto
all, that I might gain the more.

9:20 Acts 16:3 21:20–27 Rom 11:14

20 And unto the Jews I became as a Jew, that I might gain the Jews; to
them that are under the law, as under the law, that I might gain them that
are under the law;

9:21 Rom 2:8–11 Gal 3:2

21 To them that are without law, as without law, (being not without law to
God, but under the law to Christ,) that I might gain them that are without
law.

9:22 Rom 14:1; 15:1 1 Cor 10:33 2 Cor 11:29

22 To the weak became I as weak, that I might gain the weak: I am made
all things to all *men*, that I might by all means save some.
23 And this I do for the gospel's sake, that I might be partaker thereof
with *you*.

3. The Race the Christian Runs

9:24☆ Heb 12:1

24 Know ye not that they which run in a race run all, but one receiveth the
prize? So run, that ye may obtain.

9:25 1 Tim 6:12 2 Tim 2:5 Jas 1:12 1 Pet 5:4 Rev 2:10; 3:11

25 And every man that striveth for the mastery is temperate in all things.
Now they *do it* to obtain a corruptible crown; but we an incorruptible.

9:26 2 Tim 4:7, 8 Heb 12:1

26 I therefore so run, not as uncertainly; so fight I, not as one that beateth
the air:

9:27 2 Cor 13:5

27 But I keep under my body, and bring *it* into subjection: lest that by any
means, when I have preached to others, I myself should be a castaway.

9:14 Paul was unsalaried. He supported himself by tent-making. He could not be accused of ministering to make money. At the same time he vigorously insisted *that he and all other ministers* of the gospel are entitled to financial support from the people to whom they have ministered. Gal. 6:6 repeats what is taught here.

9:19ff Paul was free in Christ, that is, he was in bondage to none. Yet he surrendered his freedom in many instances so that he might win unbelievers to Christ. To the Jew he became a Jew. To those outside the law he became as one outside the law. To the weak he became weak. It is biblically permissible and methodologically sound to identify with people where they are and in what they do, so long as the Christian conscience is not defiled.

9:24 It was true that in the Isthmian games only the winner received the garland. But this is not so for Christians. We are encouraged to run, and all those who do will receive a crown. We cannot fail if we run well. All can be winners in God's race.

D. THE PERILS OF IDOLATRY
1. The Israelites in the Wilderness

10 MOREOVER, brethren, I would not that ye should be ignorant,
how that all our fathers were under the cloud, and all passed
through the sea;
2And were all baptized unto Moses in the cloud and in the sea;
3And did all eat the same spiritual meat;
4And did all drink the same spiritual drink: for they drank of that
spiritual Rock that followed them: and that Rock was Christ.
5But with many of them God was not well pleased: for they were
overthrown in the wilderness.
6Now these things were our examples, to the intent we should not lust
after evil things, as they also lusted.
7Neither be ye idolaters, as *were* some of them; as it is written, The
people sat down to eat and drink, and rose up to play.
8Neither let us commit fornication, as some of them committed, and fell
in one day three and twenty thousand.
9Neither let us tempt Christ, as some of them also tempted, and were
destroyed of serpents.
10Neither murmur ye, as some of them also murmured, and were
destroyed of the destroyer.
11Now all these things happened unto them for ensamples: and they are
written for our admonition, upon whom the ends of the world are come.
12Wherefore let him that thinketh he standeth take heed lest he fall.
13There hath no temptation taken you but such as is common to man:
but God *is* faithful, who will not suffer you to be tempted above that ye are
able; but will with the temptation also make a way to escape, that ye may
be able to bear *it*.

☆**10:1** Ex 13:21, 22; 14:15–22; Isa 63:11–13
☆**10:2** Rom 6:2, 3; 1 Cor 1:13; Gal 3:27
☆**10:3, 4** Ex 16:4, 13–15; 17:5, 6; Num 20:11; Ps 78:15; Jn 4:10; 6:32–58; 7:37; Rev 22:17
☆**10:5** Num 14:29, 37; 26:65; Heb 3:17; Jude 5
10:6 Num 11:4, 5, 34; Ps 106:14
10:7 Ex 32:4–19
☆**10:8** Num 25:1–9
10:9 Ex 17:2, 7; Num 21:6
☆**10:10** Num 16:3, 32, 41, 49; Rom 13:11; 15:4; Heb 10:25
10:11 Rom 4:23
10:12 Rom 11:20; 2 Pet 3:17
☆**10:13** 2 Pet 2:9

2. Idol Worship Forbidden

14Wherefore, my dearly beloved, flee from idolatry.
15I speak as to wise men; judge ye what I say.
16The cup of blessing which we bless, is it not the communion of the

10:14 1 Jn 5:21
10:16 Mt 26:26–29; Acts 2:42; 1 Cor 11:25–27

10:1–4 In verses 1–4 Paul, using Israel as an illustration, warns the Corinthians that God's covenant of grace, freely offered to all, does not mean that all will inherit the covenant promises. He argues that all God's benefits bestowed on Israel came from Christ whether they were aware of it or not. These benefits were granted to all Israel, both good and bad people. All were under the cloud and all were delivered from Egypt. The benefits had a spiritual character. The same spiritual principles that applied to the old dispensation apply to the new dispensation and thus to the Corinthians.

10:5 Although all of these Israelites experienced the outward, material blessing of God, God was not pleased with all of them. Most of these Israelites did not share the spiritual blessings of God. Virtually all of those who left Egypt died in the desert, never entering the promised land. Paul uses the illustration to warn the Corinthians that those who sin boldly against God will not inherit eternal life, even though they might identify themselves with those of the Christian faith.

10:8 This incident is popularly confused with the account in Num. 25:9 of the death of 24,000 at Baal-peor. It really refers to the golden calf plague of Exodus 32. In 1 Cor. 10:7 Paul quotes directly from Exodus 32:6, which ties the incident to the golden calf apostasy. The Exodus account gives us no number of the people who died. By the inspiration of the Spirit Paul gives us the number. The supposed contradiction between the 24,000 of Baal-peor and the 23,000 of 1 Cor. 10:8 does not exist. (See *Encyclopedia of Bible Difficulties* by Gleason L. Archer, Zondervan, 1982, pp. 141, 401.)

10:10 Murmuring, grumbling, and complaining are sins against God. They arise from bitter dislike of adverse circumstances—whether the result of sin or sent by God—to purify and to test us. We are told not to murmur, for God is provoked when we do so; and to do so is wrong and indefensible.

10:13 No believer who falls into sin will ever be able to say, "I could not help it; it wasn't my fault." We will never be tempted in ways and manners not common to all flesh. And there is no temptation that cannot be resisted or overcome. Therefore, believers who sin are always at fault and have no one to blame except themselves.

blood of Christ? The bread which we break, is it not the communion of the
body of Christ?
10:17 Rom 12:4, 5; 1 Cor 12:12, 13 — 17 For we *being* many are one bread, *and* one body: for we are all
partakers of that one bread.
10:18 Deut 12:17; Lev 7:15 — 18 Behold Israel after the flesh: are not they which eat of the sacrifices
partakers of the altar?
10:19 1 Cor 8:4 — 19 What say I then? that the idol is any thing, or that which is offered in
sacrifice to idols is any thing?
10:20 Deut 32:16, 17; Ps 106:36, 37; Gal 4:8; Rev 9:20 — 20 But *I say*, that the things which the Gentiles sacrifice, they sacrifice to
devils, and not to God: and I would not that ye should have fellowship with
devils.
10:21 Deut 32:38; Isa 65:11; 2 Cor 6:15 — 21 Ye cannot drink the cup of the Lord, and the cup of devils: ye cannot
be partakers of the Lord's table, and of the table of devils.
10:22 Deut 32:21; Ezek 22:14 — 22 Do we provoke the Lord to jealousy? are we stronger than he?

3. Freedom and the Weaker Brother's Conscience

10:23☆ Rom 14:19; 1 Cor 6:12 — 23 All things are lawful for me, but all things are not expedient: all things
are lawful for me, but all things edify not.
10:24 Rom 15:1, 2 — 24 Let no man seek his own, but every man another's *wealth*.
10:25 Acts 10:15; 1 Cor 8:7; 1 Tim 4:4 — 25 Whatsoever is sold in the shambles, *that* eat, asking no question for
conscience sake:
10:26 Ps 24:1; 105:12 — 26 For the earth *is* the Lord's, and the fulness thereof.
10:27 Lk 10:8, 9 — 27 If any of them that believe not bid you *to a feast*, and ye be disposed to
go; whatsoever is set before you, eat, asking no question for conscience
sake.
10:28 Rom 14:16; 1 Cor 8:7, 10 — 28 But if any man say unto you, This is offered in sacrifice unto idols, eat
not for his sake that shewed it, and for conscience sake: for the earth *is* the
Lord's, and the fulness thereof:
29 Conscience, I say, not thine own, but of the other: for why is my liberty
judged of another *man's* conscience?
30 For if I by grace be a partaker, why am I evil spoken of for that for
which I give thanks?
10:31☆ Mt 5:15, 16; Jn 15:8; Rom 14:6; Phil 1:11 — 31 Whether therefore ye eat, or drink, or whatsoever ye do, do all to the
glory of God.
10:32☆ Acts 24:16; 1 Cor 8:13 — 32 Give none offence, neither to the Jews, nor to the Gentiles, nor to the
church of God:
10:33☆ Rom 11:14; 15:1–2; 1 Cor 9:22; 13:1–8 — 33 Even as I please all *men* in all *things*, not seeking mine own profit, but
the *profit* of many, that they may be saved.

11:1 1 Cor 4:16 — **11** BE ye followers of me, even as I also *am* of Christ.

10:23 The law of love is basic to all human relationships. Happy, healthy, and wholesome relations must be based on love that is genuinely self-forgetful. The love of which Scripture speaks has to do with love for God and love for others. In the Christian's relationships *to men, two principles* govern his conduct: (1) whatever is stated to be wrong in principle, i.e., whatever is explicitly forbidden, must be shunned; (2) the principle of expediency governs all other decisions in relation to men. Anything that is questionable or has the appearance of evil or that may cause a weaker brother to take offense or stumble is to be avoided. In matters of expediency the believer foregoes that which he does not think to be wrong in principle but which he gives up out of love for God and his fellowman.

10:31–33 In verses 31 to 33 Paul lays down two principles by which we are to govern our choices: (1) do that which is for the glory of God; and (2) take care of the well-being of others. It is particularly important for us to note that Paul speaks here about glorifying God in the ordinary things of life. If we do this we will also glorify him in the spiritual and the extraordinary affairs of life. Nothing we think, say, or do should be exempted from the two principles adduced here.

E. WORSHIP SERVICES
1. A Head Covering for a Woman

2 Now I praise you, brethren, that ye remember me in all things, and keep ☆**11:2**
the ordinances, as I delivered *them* to you.
3 But I would have you know, that the head of every man is Christ; and **11:3** Gen 3:16
the head of the woman *is* the man; and the head of Christ *is* God. 1 Cor 3:23; 7:17
4 Every man praying or prophesying, having *his* head covered, dishonour- Gal 4:4 Eph 5:23
eth his head. Phil 2:7
5 But every woman that prayeth or prophesieth with *her* head uncovered ☆**11:5** Lk 2:36
dishonoureth her head: for that is even all one as if she were shaven. Acts 21:9
6 For if the woman be not covered, let her also be shorn: but if it be a **11:6** Num 5:18
shame for a woman to be shorn or shaven, let her be covered.
7 For a man indeed ought not to cover *his* head, forasmuch as he is the **11:7** Gen 1:26
image and glory of God: but the woman is the glory of the man. Jas 3:9
8 For the man is not of the woman; but the woman of the man. **11:8** Gen 2:21
9 Neither was the man created for the woman; but the woman for the 1 Tim 2:13
man. **11:9** Gen 2:18
10 For this cause ought the woman to have power on *her* head because of **11:10** Gen 24:65
the angels. 1 Pet 1:12
11 Nevertheless neither is the man without the woman, neither the woman **11:11** Gal 3:28
without the man, in the Lord.
12 For as the woman *is* of the man, even so *is* the man also by the woman; **11:12** Rom 11:36
but all things of God.
13 Judge in yourselves: is it comely that a woman pray unto God **11:13** Lk 12:57
uncovered?
14 Doth not even nature itself teach you, that, if a man have long hair, it
is a shame unto him?
15 But if a woman have long hair, it is a glory to her: for *her* hair is given
her for a covering.
16 But if any man seem to be contentious, we have no such custom, ☆**11:16** 1 Tim 6:4
neither the churches of God.

2. Communion Service Injunctions

17 Now in this that I declare *unto you* I praise *you* not, that ye come ☆**11:17**
together not for the better, but for the worse.

11:2 *the ordinances, as I delivered them to you,* i.e., "the traditions I taught you" (according to the Greek). Before the New Testament was written, these traditions were passed around by word of mouth. 1 Corinthians was written perhaps ten years earlier than any of the Gospels, or twenty years after Christ's ascension. Meanwhile, oral transmission of what Christ did and said was common. Paul declares that whatever traditions he passed on were true (2 Thess. 2:15—3:6). Inspiration by the Holy Spirit means that among all the traditions known in the early church, only those that were accurate and historical became part of the written Word of God, so that any tradition not found in Scripture is not binding on Christian conscience.

11:5 Evidently Paul is saying that it is permissible for a woman to pray or to prophesy publicly, but she is to have her head covered. Should this custom continue today or was it simply a cultural pattern which no longer should be practiced? In current discussions one fact is often overlooked. In this same segment of Scripture, men are commanded to have their heads uncovered. Few, if any, men wear hats in public worship. Thus there are two commands: one is for women to be covered and the other for men to be uncovered. Some churches have generally insisted that women be hatted; others have not. John Calvin regarded the matter as one of indifference. It was permissible for women to do either. Liberty at this point is important since at best it is a secondary matter.

11:16 The apostle concludes that since the wearing of a head covering for women was the common custom of the churches, women should follow that custom. He does not deal with the question whether this or other customs may be changed or how to make such changes.

11:17–22 The Lord's Supper in the early church was accompanied by a love feast. In this church the love feast degenerated into schism, disaffection, and disorder. Some of those who attended got drunk. Others refused to share what they brought with their poorer brothers and sisters. The poor were looked on with contempt and were treated insolently. Paul accuses them of treating the celebration of the Supper contemptuously by their scandalous conduct at the love feast. He judges them strongly and with great disapproval.

11:18, 19 1 Cor 1:10; 2 Pet 2:1; 1 Tim 4:1; 1 Jn 2:19

[18]For first of all, when ye come together in the church, I hear that there
be divisions among you; and I partly believe it.
[19]For there must be also heresies among you, that they which are
approved may be made manifest among you.
[20]When ye come together therefore into one place, *this* is not to eat the
Lord's supper.

11:21 Jude 12

[21]For in eating every one taketh before *other* his own supper: and one is
hungry, and another is drunken.

11:22 Lev 19:30; 1 Cor 10:32; Jas 2:6

[22]What? have ye not houses to eat and to drink in? or despise ye the
church of God, and shame them that have not? What shall I say to you?
shall I praise you in this? I praise *you* not.

11:23☆ Mt 26:26–28; Mk 14:22–24; Lk 22:17–20; 1 Cor 10:16; Gal 1:12
11:24☆

[23]For I have received of the Lord that which also I delivered unto you,
That the Lord Jesus the *same* night in which he was betrayed took bread:
[24]And when he had given thanks, he brake *it*, and said, Take, eat: this is
my body, which is broken for you: this do in remembrance of me.

11:25 Lk 22:20; 1 Cor 10:16; 2 Cor 3:6

[25]After the same manner also *he took* the cup, when he had supped,
saying, This cup is the new testament in my blood: this do ye, as oft as ye
drink *it*, in remembrance of me.

11:26 Acts 1:11; Rev 1:7

[26]For as often as ye eat this bread, and drink this cup, ye do shew the
Lord's death till he come.

11:27 Heb 10:29

[27]Wherefore whosoever shall eat this bread, and drink *this* cup of the
Lord, unworthily, shall be guilty of the body and blood of the Lord.

11:28☆ Mt 26:20–22; 2 Cor 13:5; Gal 6:4

[28]But let a man examine himself, and so let him eat of *that* bread, and
drink of *that* cup.
[29]For he that eateth and drinketh unworthily, eateth and drinketh
damnation to himself, not discerning the Lord's body.
[30]For this cause many *are* weak and sickly among you, and many sleep.

11:31 1 Jn 1:9; Rev 3:19
11:32 2 Sam 7:14; Job 5:17; Ps 94:12; Amos 3:2; Heb 12:5–7
11:34 1 Cor 4:19

[31]For if we would judge ourselves, we should not be judged.
[32]But when we are judged, we are chastened of the Lord, that we should
not be condemned with the world.
[33]Wherefore, my brethren, when ye come together to eat, tarry one for
another.
[34]And if any man hunger, let him eat at home; that ye come not together
unto condemnation. And the rest will I set in order when I come.

F. SPIRITUAL GIFTS AND THEIR USE

1. The Source and Diversity of the Gifts

12:1☆ 1 Cor 14:1
12:2 Isa 46:7; Hab 1:18, 19; 1 Thess 1:9; 1 Pet 4:3

12 NOW concerning spiritual *gifts*, brethren, I would not have you
ignorant.
[2]Ye know that ye were Gentiles, carried away unto these dumb idols,
even as ye were led.

11:23 The Lord's Supper was instituted without Paul's being there. How then can he instruct the church about its observance? He carefully points out that his knowledge about the celebration was given to him by divine revelation from Jesus Christ.

11:24 The Supper was a memorial remembrance of *Christ's redeeming work on Calvary*. They were to eat the bread and drink the cup and do so in a worthy manner. Various churches interpret the meaning of the bread and cup differently. Some believe in the real presence of Christ in the elements; others believe in his spiritual presence; and still others hold to his symbolic presence in the elements.

11:28ff Some Corinthians celebrated the Eucharist (the Lord's Supper) in an unworthy manner. Verse 30 indicates that God sent judgment upon them and many were ill because of their abuse of the Supper. Paul enjoins them and us to prove ourselves *before* we celebrate the Supper.

12:1 Many times the Scriptures speak to issues after the fact. Abuses creep in and correction must take place. The Corinthian church abounded in spiritual gifts, and abuses arose among people who were not yet mature in the faith and who had not advanced greatly in their sanctification. Paul needed to instruct them about spiritual gifts and their proper use.

3 Wherefore I give you to understand, that no man speaking by the Spirit
of God calleth Jesus accursed: and *that* no man can say that Jesus is the
Lord, but by the Holy Ghost.
4 Now there are diversities of gifts, but the same Spirit.
5 And there are differences of administrations, but the same Lord.
6 And there are diversities of operations, but it is the same God which
worketh all in all.
7 But the manifestation of the Spirit is given to every man to profit withal.
8 For to one is given by the Spirit the word of wisdom; to another the
word of knowledge by the same Spirit;
9 To another faith by the same Spirit; to another the gifts of healing by
the same Spirit;
10 To another the working of miracles; to another prophecy; to another
discerning of spirits; to another *divers* kinds of tongues; to another the
interpretation of tongues:
11 But all these worketh that one and the selfsame Spirit, dividing to every
man severally as he will.

☆**12:3** Mk 9:39 Jn 13:13 Rom 10:9 Phil 2:11 1 Jn 4:2
12:4 Rom 12:6 Eph 4:4 Heb 2:4
12:6 Eph 1:23
12:7 Rom 12:6 1 Cor 14:26 Eph 4:12
☆**12:8** 1 Cor 2:6, 11 2 Cor 8:7
12:9 Mt 17:19, 20 Mk 16:18
12:10 Acts 2:4 Rom 12:6 1 Cor 14:26–32 Gal 3:5 1 Jn 4:1
☆**12:11** Rom 12:6–8 1 Cor 7:7 Eph 4:7 Heb 2:4

2. The Functions of the Spirit's Gifts

12 For as the body is one, and hath many members, and all the members
of that one body, being many, are one body: so also *is* Christ.
13 For by one Spirit are we all baptized into one body, whether *we be* Jews
or Gentiles, whether *we be* bond or free; and have been all made to drink
into one Spirit.
14 For the body is not one member, but many.
15 If the foot shall say, Because I am not the hand, I am not of the body;
is it therefore not of the body?
16 And if the ear shall say, Because I am not the eye, I am not of the body;
is it therefore not of the body?
17 If the whole body *were* an eye, where *were* the hearing? If the whole
were hearing, where *were* the smelling?
18 But now hath God set the members every one of them in the body, as
it hath pleased him.
19 And if they were all one member, where *were* the body?
20 But now *are they* many members, yet but one body.
21 And the eye cannot say unto the hand, I have no need of thee: nor
again the head to the feet, I have no need of you.
22 Nay, much more those members of the body, which seem to be more
feeble, are necessary:

12:12 Rom 12:4 1 Cor 10:17 12:27
12:13 Jn 6:63; 7:37–39 Rom 6:5 Gal 3:27, 28 Eph 2:13–16, 18 Col 3:11
12:18 Rom 12:6 1 Cor 12:28

12:3 *no man speaking by the Spirit of God calleth Jesus accursed.* Jews and Gentiles blasphemed Jesus as an imposter, and angrily denounced him. Yet some Gentiles pretended to have inspiration, and some Jews were exorcists and magicians, claiming to work wonders by the Spirit of God. Paul says that those who blasphemed or disowned the Son of God could not do this if they were controlled by the Spirit. This means that those who blaspheme Christ do not have the Spirit and thus are pagans under the sentence of death by God unless and until they receive Christ and are given the gift of the Spirit.

12:8 Some say that the sign gifts (healing, tongues, miracles, etc.) ceased at the end of the apostolic age. Nowhere does Scripture affirm this notion. However, there are those who give the impression that these gifts abound. This is incorrect. In the Old and New Testaments healings were infrequent and occurred in only a few special instances (e.g., through Moses, Elijah and Elisha, Jesus, and the Apostles). However rare the sign gifts may be, they cannot be ruled out for this age; yet the temptation to exaggerate them must be avoided.

12:11 The Holy Spirit gives different gifts to different people. None of the gifts described in the preceding verses is given to all believers. The Corinthian church was specially enthralled with the gift of tongues. Paul carefully places that gift (*glōssōn*) in the lowest order of enumeration. When he says the Corinthians are to "covet earnestly the best gifts," he has in mind that there are more important gifts than speaking in tongues. Yet even then, believers who cherish any gifts and pray to receive them must remember that they are given according to God's will.

12:23☆
12:27 Rom 12:4, 5; 1 Cor 12:12; Eph 1:22, 23; 4:12; 5:23, 30; Col 1:24
12:28☆ Num 11:16, 17; Acts 13:1; Rom 12:6–8; Eph 2:20; 3:5; 4:11; 1 Tim 5:17; Heb 13:17
12:30☆
12:31 1 Cor 14:1–39

23 And those *members* of the body, which we think to be less honourable,
upon these we bestow more abundant honour; and our uncomely *parts* have
more abundant comeliness.
24 For our comely *parts* have no need: but God hath tempered the body
together, having given more abundant honour to that *part* which lacked:
25 That there should be no schism in the body; but *that* the members
should have the same care one for another.
26 And whether one member suffer, all the members suffer with it; or one
member be honoured, all the members rejoice with it.
27 Now ye are the body of Christ, and members in particular.
28 And God hath set some in the church, first apostles, secondarily
prophets, thirdly teachers, after that miracles, then gifts of healings, helps,
governments, diversities of tongues.
29 *Are* all apostles? *are* all prophets? *are* all teachers? *are* all workers of
miracles?
30 Have all the gifts of healing? do all speak with tongues? do all
interpret?
31 But covet earnestly the best gifts: and yet shew I unto you a more
excellent way.

3. The Superiority of Love

13:1☆ 1 Tim 1:5
13:2 Mk 17:20; Lk 17:6; 1 Cor 12:8–10
13:3 Mt 6:1, 2
13:4 1 Cor 4:6; 1 Pet 4:8
13:5 1 Cor 10:24; Phil 2:4; 4:8
13:6 Ps 10:3; Prov 10:12; Rom 1:32; 2 Thess 2:12; 2 Jn 4

13 THOUGH I speak with the tongues of men and of angels, and have
not charity, I am become *as* sounding brass, or a tinkling cymbal.
2 And though I have *the gift of* prophecy, and understand all mysteries,
and all knowledge; and though I have all faith, so that I could remove
mountains, and have not charity, I am nothing.
3 And though I bestow all my goods to feed *the poor*, and though I give
my body to be burned, and have not charity, it profiteth me nothing.
4 Charity suffereth long, *and* is kind; charity envieth not; charity vaunteth
not itself, is not puffed up,
5 Doth not behave itself unseemly, seeketh not her own, is not easily
provoked, thinketh no evil;
6 Rejoiceth not in iniquity, but rejoiceth in the truth;

12:23 The message is clearer if this verse in the latter part (*and our uncomely parts have more abundant comeliness*) is translated "and the parts that are unpresentable are treated with special modesty" (NIV). Nakedness is nowhere encouraged in the Scriptures. The parts of the body devoted to reproduction should be covered from common view.

12:28 God has given the church workmen whose functions vary but whose endowments enable the church to operate effectively. God also calls specific individuals to specific roles. In Eph. 4:11 Paul refers to these as gifts of *Christ* (apostles, prophets, evangelists, pastors and teachers). Here in 12:28 they are the gifts of *God*. In 12:8ff they are gifts given by the *Spirit*. Thus, the three persons of the Trinity give gifts by which chosen men can execute the offices of apostles, prophets, teachers, miracle workers, healing, helps, tongues, and the like. Every genuine call to an office carries with it the divine enablement to discharge the duties of the office.

12:30 The New Testament refers to the gift of tongues several times. At Pentecost one of the miracles that attested to the advent of the Spirit was the gift of tongues. The Holy Spirit gave them this gift, and the languages they spoke were known languages of the various peoples who had come from afar to Jerusalem for Pentecost. In 1 Cor. 12:20 the gift of tongues (expanded on in chapter 14) appears to be ecstatic utterances rather than known languages. Such tongues-speaking benefits the person who has the gift. Paul states that the use of tongues in the church must conform to certain requirements: (1) not more than two or three shall speak (14:27); (2) they must speak in order, one at a time (14:27); (3) women should be silent (14:34). The private, devotional use of tongues is an individual matter. Not all tongues-speaking is genuine. Some do not believe that speaking in tongues belongs to this present age. Tongues-speaking, however, cannot be ruled out as a matter of principle during this present age. Paul classifies tongues as a lesser gift (14:5). Speaking in tongues is not needed as a sign of regeneration or of sanctification.

13:1 *charity,* (*agapē*) translated as *love* elsewhere in the New Testament. Beginning with this verse Paul compares love with such gifts as tongues, prophecy, understanding of mysteries, knowledge, faith, and giving of one's goods to feed the poor; and Paul concludes that where love is lacking, none of these gifts will benefit a man or woman. Without love, whatever gifts anyone has will not keep him from being a dead instrument.

7 Beareth all things, believeth all things, hopeth all things, endureth all
things.
8 Charity never faileth: but whether *there be* prophecies, they shall fail;
whether *there be* tongues, they shall cease; whether *there be* knowledge, it
shall vanish away.
9 For we know in part, and we prophesy in part.
10 But when that which is perfect is come, then that which is in part shall
be done away.
11 When I was a child, I spake as a child, I understood as a child, I
thought as a child: but when I became a man, I put away childish things.
12 For now we see through a glass, darkly; but then face to face: now I
know in part; but then shall I know even as also I am known.
13 And now abideth faith, hope, charity, these three; but the greatest of
these *is* charity.

13:7 Gal 6:2
☆**13:8** 1 Cor 13:1, 2
13:9 1 Cor 8:2
13:10 Isa 60:19 Jer 31:34
13:12 2 Cor 3:18; 5:7 Phil 3:12 1 Jn 3:2
☆**13:13** Mt 22:37–39 Gal 5:6

4. Tongues Speaking and Prophecy
a. The Preeminence of Prophecy

14 FOLLOW after charity, and desire spiritual *gifts*, but rather that ye
may prophesy.
2 For he that speaketh in an *unknown* tongue speaketh not unto men, but
unto God: for no man understandeth *him;* howbeit in the spirit he speaketh
mysteries.
3 But he that prophesieth speaketh unto men *to* edification, and exhortation,
and comfort.
4 He that speaketh in an *unknown* tongue edifieth himself; but he that
prophesieth edifieth the church.
5 I would that ye all spake with tongues, but rather that ye prophesied: for
greater *is* he that prophesieth than he that speaketh with tongues, except he
interpret, that the church may receive edifying.
6 Now, brethren, if I come unto you speaking with tongues, what shall I
profit you, except I shall speak to you either by revelation, or by knowledge,
or by prophesying, or by doctrine?
7 And even things without life giving sound, whether pipe or harp, except
they give a distinction in the sounds, how shall it be known what is piped or
harped?
8 For if the trumpet give an uncertain sound, who shall prepare himself to
the battle?
9 So likewise ye, except ye utter by the tongue words easy to be
understood, how shall it be known what is spoken? for ye shall speak into
the air.

☆**14:1** Lev 19:18 Num 11:25 Mt 22:37–40 Mk 12:29–31 Rom 12:6 13:8–10 1 Cor 12:1 Gal 5:14 Eph 5:2 Col 3:14 1 Tim 1:5 Jas 2:8
14:2 Mk 16:17 Acts 2:4 10:46, 47; 19:6
14:3 Rom 14:19
☆**14:4** 1 Cor 12:10, 30 14:18, 19, 26–28
14:6 Rom 6:17 1 Cor 12:8; 13:2 Eph 1:16, 17
14:8 Num 10:9 Jer 4:19 Ezek 33:2–6 Joel 2:1

13:8 The statement that love will remain when prophecy, tongues, and knowledge have passed away cannot be used to support the notion that they passed away at the end of the apostolic age and therefore no longer exist. These things will cease when the need for them no longer exists, when Christ returns in glory and great power.

13:13 Faith, hope, and love are the three most important graces. But two of the three are temporal and are needed in this present life. Faith and hope will disappear when we get to heaven. But love will remain forever.

14:1 Paul elevated the gift of love above all other gifts, but he did not rule out or underestimate other gifts. Here in chapter 14 he "teaches them, among spiritual gifts, which they should prefer, and by what rules they should make comparisons."* Those who choose to rule out some of the spiritual gifts and retain others do the church an injustice. At the same time, some gifts are more useful and valuable than others and we need to follow Paul's order of importance when we seek for gifts from the Spirit.

14:4 Speaking in tongues is rewarding and helpful to the one who has this gift. But whoever has the gift of prophecy can do more than the one who uses tongues. The latter will edify the church, whereas the tongues speaker edifies only himself. Paul says that whatever usefulness a tongue may have for the people who speak that tongue, it is like gibberish to men of another language. They hear only sounds without sense. Prophecy is a better and more useful gift than tongues, so far as the congregation is concerned.

10 There are, it may be, so many kinds of voices in the world, and none of
them *is* without signification.
11 Therefore if I know not the meaning of the voice, I shall be unto him
that speaketh a barbarian, and he that speaketh *shall be* a barbarian unto
me.

14:12 Rom 14:19
14:13 1 Cor 12:10

12 Even so ye, forasmuch as ye are zealous of spiritual *gifts*, seek that ye
may excel to the edifying of the church.
13 Wherefore let him that speaketh in an *unknown* tongue pray that he
may interpret.
14 For if I pray in an *unknown* tongue, my spirit prayeth, but my
understanding is unfruitful.

14:15☆ Ps 47:6, 7; Eph 5:19; Col 3:16

15 What is it then? I will pray with the spirit, and I will pray with the
understanding also: I will sing with the spirit, and I will sing with the
understanding also.

14:16 1 Chron 16:36; Neh 5:13; 8:6; Ps 106:48

16 Else when thou shalt bless with the spirit, how shall he that occupieth
the room of the unlearned say Amen at thy giving of thanks, seeing he
understandeth not what thou sayest?

14:17 Rom 14:19
14:18☆

17 For thou verily givest thanks well, but the other is not edified.
18 I thank my God, I speak with tongues more than ye all:
19 Yet in the church I had rather speak five words with my understanding,
that *by my voice* I might teach others also, than ten thousand words in an
unknown tongue.

14:20 Mt 11:25; Rom 16:19; Eph 4:14; Heb 5:12
14:21 Isa 28:11; Jn 10:34

20 Brethren, be not children in understanding: howbeit in malice be ye
children, but in understanding be men.
21 In the law it is written, With *men of* other tongues and other lips will I
speak unto this people; and yet for all that will they not hear me, saith the
Lord.

14:22 1 Cor 14:1

22 Wherefore tongues are for a sign, not to them that believe, but to them
that believe not: but prophesying *serveth* not for them that believe not, but
for them which believe.

14:23 Acts 2:12, 13

23 If therefore the whole church be come together into one place, and all
speak with tongues, and there come in *those that are* unlearned, or
unbelievers, will they not say that ye are mad?

14:24 1 Cor 14:1

24 But if all prophesy, and there come in one that believeth not, or *one*
unlearned, he is convinced of all, he is judged of all:

14:25 Isa 45:14; Zech 8:23; Heb 4:12, 13

25 And thus are the secrets of his heart made manifest; and so falling
down on *his* face he will worship God, and report that God is in you of a
truth.

b. Regulating the Use of Spiritual Gifts

14:26☆ Rom 14:19; 1 Cor 12:8–10; 14:2–6; Eph 4:12, 13; 5:19

26 How is it then, brethren? when ye come together, every one of you hath
a psalm, hath a doctrine, hath a tongue, hath a revelation, hath an
interpretation. Let all things be done unto edifying.

14:15 He who prays in public should pray intelligibly, not in a tongue the people do not understand, nor in a language foreign to those who listen. He who hears a *sound void of meaning is not helped.*

14:18 The Corinthian church both valued and misused the gift of tongues. Paul was critical of the abuse and corrected the Corinthians. But he apparently thought they might bypass his criticism if he himself was not one who had the same gift; so he said, *I speak with tongues more than ye all.* Had he ruled out tongues in this age he surely would have said so to this church.

14:26 Paul here states that believers are given, by way of the Spirit's gifts, a psalm, a doctrine, a tongue, a revelation, or an interpretation. But they are not given for ostentation; they are given for edification. This rules out the misuse of these gifts. At the end of his discourse he lays down a second rule, that all things are to be done decently and in orderly fashion. Thus anything childish, ridiculous, or tumultuous is to be eschewed (14:40).

27 If any man speak in an *unknown* tongue, *let it be* by two, or at the most
by three, and *that* by course; and let one interpret.
28 But if there be no interpreter, let him keep silence in the church; and let
him speak to himself, and to God.
29 Let the prophets speak two or three, and let the other judge.
30 If *any thing* be revealed to another that sitteth by, let the first hold his
peace.
31 For ye may all prophesy one by one, that all may learn, and all may be
comforted.
32 And the spirits of the prophets are subject to the prophets.
33 For God is not *the author* of confusion, but of peace, as in all churches
of the saints.
34 Let your women keep silence in the churches: for it is not permitted
unto them to speak; but *they are commanded* to be under obedience, as also
saith the law.
35 And if they will learn any thing, let them ask their husbands at home:
for it is a shame for women to speak in the church.
36 What? came the word of God out from you? or came it unto you only?
37 If any man think himself to be a prophet, or spiritual, let him
acknowledge that the things that I write unto you are the commandments
of the Lord.
38 But if any man be ignorant, let him be ignorant.
39 Wherefore, brethren, covet to prophesy, and forbid not to speak with
tongues.
40 Let all things be done decently and in order.

G. THE RESURRECTION

1. The Resurrection, a Part of the Gospel

15 MOREOVER, brethren, I declare unto you the gospel which I
preached unto you, which also ye have received, and wherein ye
stand;
2 By which also ye are saved, if ye keep in memory what I preached unto
you, unless ye have believed in vain.
3 For I delivered unto you first of all that which I also received, how that
Christ died for our sins according to the scriptures;
4 And that he was buried, and that he rose again the third day according
to the scriptures:
5 And that he was seen of Ce′phas, then of the twelve:
6 After that he was seen of above five hundred brethren at once; of whom
the greater part remain unto this present, but some are fallen asleep.

14:27 1 Cor 12:10; 14:2, 5, 13; 1 Thess 5:20, 21
14:31 Rom 12:6
14:32 1 Jn 4:1
14:33 1 Cor 4:17; 7:17
☆**14:34** Gen 3:16; 1 Cor 11:3, 16; Eph 5:22; Col 3:18; 1 Tim 2:11; Tit 2:5; 1 Pet 3:1
☆**14:35**
14:36 Isa 2:3
☆**14:37** Lk 10:16; 1 Cor 2:15; 2 Cor 10:7; 1 Jn 4:6
14:39 1 Cor 12:31; 1 Thess 5:20
☆**15:1** Rom 2:16; 11:20; 1 Cor 4:15; 2 Cor 1:24
15:2 Rom 1:16; Gal 3:4
15:3 Gen 3:15; Isa 53:5; Lk 24:25–27; 1 Pet 2:24
☆**15:4** Ps 16:10; Isa 53:10; Lk 24:25–27
15:5 Mk 16:14; Lk 24:34, 35; Jn 20:19
15:6 Lk 24:13–31, 36; Jn 20:19, 26, 30; 21:1; Acts 1:3; 28:8–9, 16

14:34, 35 F. W. Grosheide in his *Commentary on the First Epistle to the Corinthians* (p. 342) observes that Paul in this pericope has given us "an absolute prohibition against women's speaking in the services." Albeit, Grosheide recognizes that they may have the gift of prophecy and tongues. The vexing question remains whether this prohibition is binding at all times and in all ages. Churches vary widely on this subject. Some ordain women to the gospel ministry, and others do not ordain women but permit them to speak in the worship services. In general, it may be said that very few churches adhere explicitly to what is taught by Paul in this segment of Scripture.

14:37ff The Spirit, when speaking to different people, cannot contradict himself by saying one thing to one person and something different to another. If anyone thinks the Spirit has told him something that is opposed to what the Spirit has told Paul, either Paul or the other person must be a false prophet.

15:1ff Paul reiterates the fundamental truths of the Christian faith: Christ died, was buried, and rose again the third day. The theological meaning of this statement is expanded elsewhere in the Pauline writings. No true gospel omits or devalues any part of Paul's definitive assertion.

15:4 The resurrection of Jesus from the dead distinguishes the Christian faith from all other ethnic religions and cults. None of them claims that their founder died and rose again in the same body. Buddha, Mohammed, Zoroaster, Confucius, Lao-Tze and the others are dead and gone. Jesus is said to be alive forevermore. Moreover, Paul's argument includes the fact that if Christ did not rise from the dead, the Christian faith has no foundation on which to rest.

7 After that, he was seen of James; then of all the apostles.
8 And last of all he was seen of me also, as of one born out of due time.
9 For I am the least of the apostles, that am not meet to be called an
apostle, because I persecuted the church of God.
10 But by the grace of God I am what I am: and his grace which *was*
bestowed upon me was not in vain; but I laboured more abundantly than
they all: yet not I, but the grace of God which was with me.
11 Therefore whether *it were* I or they, so we preach, and so ye believed.

2. No Resurrection, No Gospel

12 Now if Christ be preached that he rose from the dead, how say some
among you that there is no resurrection of the dead?
13 But if there be no resurrection of the dead, then is Christ not risen:
14 And if Christ be not risen, then *is* our preaching vain, and your faith *is*
also vain.
15 Yea, and we are found false witnesses of God; because we have testified
of God that he raised up Christ: whom he raised not up, if so be that the
dead rise not.
16 For if the dead rise not, then is not Christ raised:
17 And if Christ be not raised, your faith *is* vain; ye are yet in your sins.
18 Then they also which are fallen asleep in Christ are perished.
19 If in this life only we have hope in Christ, we are of all men most
miserable.

3. Christ's Resurrection Guarantees the Believer's Resurrection

20 But now is Christ risen from the dead, *and* become the firstfruits of
them that slept.
21 For since by man *came* death, by man *came* also the resurrection of the
dead.
22 For as in Adam all die, even so in Christ shall all be made alive.
23 But every man in his own order: Christ the firstfruits; afterward they
that are Christ's at his coming.
24 Then *cometh* the end, when he shall have delivered up the kingdom to
God, even the Father; when he shall have put down all rule and all
authority and power.
25 For he must reign, till he hath put all enemies under his feet.
26 The last enemy *that* shall be destroyed *is* death.
27 For he hath put all things under his feet. But when he saith, all things
are put under *him, it is* manifest that he is excepted, which did put all things
under him.

15:8 Acts 9:3–12; 1 Cor 9:1
15:9☆ Acts 8:3; 2 Cor 12:11; Eph 3:8
15:10 2 Cor 11:23; Gal 2:8; Eph 2:7; 1 Tim 4:10
15:12☆ Acts 17:32; 23:6–8; 2 Tim 2:18
15:13 1 Thess 4:14
15:17 Rom 4:25
15:18☆ 1 Thess 4:16; Rev 14:13
15:19 2 Tim 3:12
15:20 Acts 2:23–32; 26:23; Col 1:18; 1 Pet 1:3; Rev 1:5
15:21 Jn 11:25; Rom 5:12
15:22☆ Rom 5:14–18
15:23 1 Thess 4:15–17
15:24 Dan 7:14; Jn 17:2; 2 Cor 4:14
15:25 Ps 110:1; Mt 22:44; Heb 1:13
15:26 1 Cor 15:54, 55; 2 Tim 1:10; Heb 2:14; Rev 1:18; 20:14; 21:4
15:27 Ps 8:6; Mt 28:18; Eph 1:22; Heb 2:8; 1 Pet 3:22

15:9 Humility causes Paul to affirm that he is the least of the apostles, certainly the last of them. And he was not worthy, for he severely persecuted the church and did so with full knowledge of the Old Testament, which speaks of the Messiah, names the time of his coming, and affirms his deity. By ways of gifts, service to Christ, sufferings for the faith, and Christian graces he was in no sense inferior to any of the others. "A humble spirit, in the midst of high attainments, is a great ornament to any man; it sets his good qualities off to much greater advantage."*
15:12ff Paul's argument for the bodily resurrection of Jesus Christ is unassailable. If Christ arose, the Christian faith is real; if he didn't, the faith is nothing. A dead Christ means a dead and useless faith. And if the Christian hope does not avail beyond the grave, we have nothing to look forward to. If Jesus did not rise from the grave, we might as well eat, drink, and be merry—for there is no salvation.
15:18 This has reference to the physical body, which sleeps in the grave. But the spirits of the saints go to be with the Lord (Eccles. 12:11; Luke 24:36; Acts 7:59). They exist in a state of bliss (Luke 16:19ff), having joyful fellowship with Christ as they await their resurrection bodies (1 Thess. 4:13ff; Rev. 20:4–6).
15:22 Because of his sin the first Adam brought death to his descendants. The second man, the last Adam, brings life and immortality by his death for sin and his resurrection unto everlasting life. Jesus Christ brought death to death. Because he who did this lives, we also shall live forever.

28 And when all things shall be subdued unto him, then shall the Son also
himself be subject unto him that put all things under him, that God may be
all in all.

4. Practical Implications of the Resurrection

29 Else what shall they do which are baptized for the dead, if the dead rise
not at all? why are they then baptized for the dead?
30 And why stand we in jeopardy every hour?
31 I protest by your rejoicing which I have in Christ Jesus our Lord, I die
daily.
32 If after the manner of men I have fought with beasts at Eph'e-sus, what
advantageth it me, if the dead rise not? let us eat and drink; for to morrow
we die.
33 Be not deceived: evil communications corrupt good manners.
34 Awake to righteousness, and sin not; for some have not the knowledge
of God: I speak *this* to your shame.

5. The Character of the Resurrection Body

35 But some *man* will say, How are the dead raised up? and with what
body do they come?
36 *Thou* fool, that which thou sowest is not quickened, except it die:
37 And that which thou sowest, thou sowest not that body that shall be,
but bare grain, it may chance of wheat, or of some other *grain:*
38 But God giveth it a body as it hath pleased him, and to every seed his
own body.
39 All flesh *is* not the same flesh: but *there is* one *kind of* flesh of men,
another flesh of beasts, another of fishes, *and* another of birds.
40 *There are* also celestial bodies, and bodies terrestrial: but the glory of
the celestial *is* one, and the *glory* of the terrestrial *is* another.
41 *There is* one glory of the sun, and another glory of the moon, and
another glory of the stars: for *one* star differeth from *another* star in glory.
42 So also *is* the resurrection of the dead. It is sown in corruption; it is
raised in incorruption:
43 It is sown in dishonour; it is raised in glory: it is sown in weakness; it
is raised in power:
44 It is sown a natural body; it is raised a spiritual body. There is a natural
body, and there is a spiritual body.
45 And so it is written, The first man Adam was made a living soul; the
last Adam *was made* a quickening spirit.
46 Howbeit that *was* not first which is spiritual, but that which is natural;
and afterward that which is spiritual.

15:28 Jn 14:28; 1 Cor 3:23; 11:3; Eph 1:10; Phil 3:21
☆15:29
15:30 Rom 8:36; 2 Cor 11:26
15:31 2 Cor 4:10
15:32 Isa 22:13; Lk 12:19–21; 1 Cor 16:8; 2 Cor 1:8
15:34 Mt 22:29; Eph 5:14; 1 Cor 6:5; 1 Thess 4:5
15:35 Ezek 37:3
15:36 Jn 12:23, 24
15:38 Gen 1:11; Ps 104:14
☆15:42 Dan 12:3; Mt 13:43; 1 Cor 15:50
15:43 Phil 3:21; Col 3:4
☆15:45 Gen 2:7; Jn 5:21; Rom 8:2; 2 Cor 3:17; Col 3:4; 1 Pet 3:18

15:29 This verse is unclear in its meaning to us today. It must have been quite clear to the Corinthians. Some have used this verse to support the view that we can undergo water baptism for relatives long since dead and by vicarious baptism they will obtain the forgiveness of sins and inherit eternal life. This notion supposes that those who are saved in this manner do not exercise personal faith and this contradicts every scripture that speaks of justification by faith alone.
15:42 The bodies of all men are mortal. Christ's resurrected body was the same body that lay in the grave, with this exception—it became immortal. Mortality was the consequence of the fall of Adam. Immortality is the gift of God through the death and resurrection of Christ, whereby believers in the day of resurrection will regain all they lost in Adam and will live forever. The new or changed body will be perfect and incorruptible.
15:45 *the first man Adam . . . the last Adam.* God's covenant between himself and the first Adam was conditioned on Adam's perfect obedience. This was a covenant of works. When Adam sinned he broke the covenant and, as representative and progenitor of the whole human race, plunged the world into sin. Christ, the last Adam, kept the law of God perfectly, so that his works fulfilled the terms of the covenant. By his death he paid the penalty and set man free from the law of sin and of death. Even as guilt was imputed to the human race by Adam's sin, so righteousness is imputed to those who believe by Jesus Christ. Christ exercises a federal headship for believers, who stand absolved in him.

15:47 Gen 3:19; Jn 3:13, 31
15:48 Phil 3:20, 21
15:49 Gen 5:3; Rom 8:29; Phil 3:21; 1 Jn 3:2
15:50 Mt 16:17; Jn 3:3, 5

47 The first man *is* of the earth, earthy: the second man *is* the Lord from
heaven.
48 As *is* the earthy, such *are* they also that are earthy: and as *is* the
heavenly, such *are* they also that are heavenly.
49 And as we have borne the image of the earthy, we shall also bear the
image of the heavenly.
50 Now this I say, brethren, that flesh and blood cannot inherit the
kingdom of God; neither doth corruption inherit incorruption.

6. The Final Victory over Death

15:51☆ 2 Cor 5:2–4; Phil 3:21; 1 Thess 4:15, 16
15:52 Mt 24:31
15:53 2 Cor 5:4
15:54 Isa 25:8
15:55 Hos 13:14; Rom 4:15
15:57 Rom 7:23–25; 1 Jn 5:4
15:58☆ 2 Chron 15:7; 1 Cor 16:10; 2 Pet 3:14; Rev 22:12

51 Behold, I shew you a mystery; We shall not all sleep, but we shall all be
changed,
52 In a moment, in the twinkling of an eye, at the last trump: for the
trumpet shall sound, and the dead shall be raised incorruptible, and we
shall be changed.
53 For this corruptible must put on incorruption, and this mortal *must* put
on immortality.
54 So when this corruptible shall have put on incorruption, and this
mortal shall have put on immortality, then shall be brought to pass the
saying that is written, Death is swallowed up in victory.
55 O death, where *is* thy sting? O grave, where *is* thy victory?
56 The sting of death *is* sin; and the strength of sin *is* the law.
57 But thanks *be* to God, which giveth us the victory through our Lord
Jesus Christ.
58 Therefore, my beloved brethren, be ye stedfast, unmoveable, always
abounding in the work of the Lord, forasmuch as ye know that your labour
is not in vain in the Lord.

V. EPILOGUE (16:1–24)

A. THE COLLECTION FOR JERUSALEM

16:1 Acts 11:29; 24:17; Rom 15:26; 2 Cor 8:4; 9:1; Gal 2:10
16:2☆ Lk 24:1; Acts 20:7; Rev 1:10
16:3 2 Cor 8:19–21

16 NOW concerning the collection for the saints, as I have given order
to the churches of Ga-la'tia, even so do ye.
2 Upon the first *day* of the week let every one of you lay by him in store,
as *God* hath prospered him, that there be no gatherings when I come.
3 And when I come, whomsoever ye shall approve by *your* letters, them
will I send to bring your liberality unto Jerusalem.
4 And if it be meet that I go also, they shall go with me.

B. PAUL'S FUTURE PLANS

16:5☆ Acts 19:21; 1 Cor 4:19; 2 Cor 1:15, 16

5 Now I will come unto you, when I shall pass through Macedonia: for I
do pass through Macedonia.

15:51 This scripture unfolds a mystery now made known to the people of God. Not all believers will die in the flesh. Some will remain alive until the coming of the Lord Jesus Christ. Christ will catch them up into the clouds. They shall be miraculously changed or altered in their physical being in the twinkling of an eye (see *1 Thess. 4:13–18.*).

15:58 Believers are to be *steadfast, unmoveable and always abounding in the work of the Lord* because Jesus arose from the dead. Because he lives, believers also live—in time and in eternity. What they do, whether good or bad, has consequences in eternity as well as in time.

16:2 The principles for the use of money include (1) giving regularly—on the first day of the week or Lord's Day; (2) *every one of you*—including all believers; (3) giving proportionately—depending on "how much the Lord had helped you earn" (TLB); (4) preventive—don't wait so that a large sum must be raised suddenly. (See also note to Mal. 3:8.)

16:5 Paul expects to leave Asia and come to Achaia, where Corinth was located. He would stop for a season with the Corinthian believers, many of whom must have loved him tenderly. He indicates that he hopes they will assist him in expediting his future plans by way of encouragement and provision.

6 And it may be that I will abide, yea, and winter with you, that ye may
bring me on my journey whithersoever I go.
7 For I will not see you now by the way; but I trust to tarry a while with
you, if the Lord permit.
8 But I will tarry at Eph'e-sus until Pentecost.
9 For a great door and effectual is opened unto me, and *there are* many
adversaries.
10 Now if Ti-mo'the-us come, see that he may be with you without fear:
for he worketh the work of the Lord, as I also *do*.
11 Let no man therefore despise him: but conduct him forth in peace, that
he may come unto me: for I look for him with the brethren.
12 As touching *our* brother Apollos, I greatly desired him to come unto
you with the brethren: but his will was not at all to come at this time; but
he will come when he shall have convenient time.

C. CONCLUDING REMARKS AND BENEDICTION

13 Watch ye, stand fast in the faith, quit you like men, be strong.
14 Let all your things be done with charity.
15 I beseech you, brethren, (ye know the house of Steph'a-nas, that it is the
firstfruits of A-chai'a, and *that* they have addicted themselves to the
ministry of the saints,)
16 That ye submit yourselves unto such, and to every one that helpeth with
us, and laboureth.
17 I am glad of the coming of Steph'a-nas and For-tu-na'tus and A-cha'i-
cus: for that which was lacking on your part they have supplied.
18 For they have refreshed my spirit and yours: therefore acknowledge ye
them that are such.
19 The churches of Asia salute you. Aq'ui-la and Priscilla salute you much
in the Lord, with the church that is in their house.
20 All the brethren greet you. Greet ye one another with an holy kiss.
21 The salutation of *me* Paul with mine own hand.
22 If any man love not the Lord Jesus Christ, let him be A-nath'e-ma
Mar'an-a'tha.
23 The grace of our Lord Jesus Christ *be* with you.
24 My love *be* with you all in Christ Jesus. Amen.

16:6 Acts 15:3; 17:5 21:5
16:7 Acts 18:21
16:8 Acts 2:1
16:9 Acts 14:27 19:8–10 2 Cor 2:12
☆**16:10** Acts 16:1 Rom 16:21
16:11 1 Tim 4:12, 13
16:12 Acts 18:24 1 Cor 1:12 Tit 3:13
16:13 Mt 24:42 Phil 1:27; 4:1 1 Thess 3:7, 8 2 Thess 2:15
16:14 1 Cor 14:1
16:15 1 Cor 14:16
16:16 1 Thess 5:12, 13 Heb 13:17
☆**16:17** 2 Cor 11:9
16:18 Phil 2:25, 29, 30 Col 4:8
16:19 Rom 16:5 Philem 2 Rev 1:4, 11
16:21 Rom 16:22 Gal 6:11 Col 4:18 2 Thess 3:17 Philem 19
☆**16:22** Gal 1:8, 9 Heb 10:26 Jude 14, 15
16:23 Rom 16:20

16:10 Paul indicates that Timothy would come to Corinth before he does. He wants the church to receive him well, not despise him, and help him as he corrects the difficulties in the Corinthian church. He pleads that they will speed him on his way to rejoin the apostle. He especially hopes Timothy will come in peace, i.e., bring the good news that all is well in the church.

16:17 *Stephanas and Fortunatus and Achaicus* were the three members of a delegation that brought a letter from the Corinthian church (see 7:1) to Paul, who was then in Ephesus. Achaicus may have been a slave or ex-slave of the family of the conqueror of Achaia, namely L. Mummius. Fortunatus was a well-thought-of member of the Corinthian church, of whom we have no more definite knowledge. Stephanas was baptized by Paul. He and his family were the first converts of Achaia. The family was active in the ministry, i.e., their home was open for Christian worship, and hospitality was extended to traveling believers. All three members of the delegation were commended by Paul and recognized as co-laborers.

16:22 He who does not love the Lord Jesus is doomed. Let such a person be under the most weighty and awful curse. Paul writes, "let him be Anathema Maran-atha." An *anathema* is a ban or curse pronounced by ecclesiastical authority, and in this instance by no less than an apostle of Christ. *Maran-atha* is a Syriac word meaning "The Lord cometh."

THE SECOND EPISTLE OF PAUL THE APOSTLE TO THE
CORINTHIANS

Authorship, date, and background The letter known to us as 2 Corinthians was written by Paul in A.D. 56. It was probably composed in Macedonia and sent to Corinth. Paul had hoped his second letter to Corinth (1 Corinthians) would correct the problems of the young church. Instead, the situation deteriorated and the apostle was severely alienated from these believers. The pressures were both internal and external. Internally, someone in the congregation led a revolt against the apostle, a revolt which included other church members. Externally, a group of Jewish Christians came from Jerusalem claiming to represent the other apostles. They purported to bring with them information which undercut both the apostolic commission and the authority of Paul with the congregation (11:4, 5, 12, 13, 20–23). All of this, plus the fact that 1 Corinthians had not solved the problems, caused Paul to make a hasty journey to Corinth. He was rebuffed and humiliated (2:1; 12:14; 13:1). The situation worsened. Upon his return he wrote a third letter to Corinth (2:3, 4, 9; 7:8, 12). It was a "stern" communication delivered by Titus (7:6–8) who was instructed to return with a response as soon as possible. First Paul waited for Titus at Troas. Then he moved on to Macedonia where Titus came to tell him that the crisis was over; the Corinthian church had been reconciled to Paul.

Paul now wrote his fourth letter to the Corinthian church, a letter which we now have under the title of 2 Corinthians. Some scholars have claimed that chapters 10—13 are the third or "stern" letter which was incorporated into the fourth letter. But the manuscript evidence does not warrant this conclusion. We can only conclude that the third letter is no longer in existence.

Characteristics and content 2 Corinthians is not a theological treatise *per se*, nor does it have the systematic and ordered appearance characteristic of 1 Corinthians. In this second (Paul's fourth) letter, the apostle runs the gamut of human emotions: despair, joy, ecstatic elation, sarcasm, and even threats mark the progress of the epistle. One sees in it the deep currents of a pastor's sense of rejection by his beloved children whom he has brought to Christ, followed by a sense of relief and joy when the crisis is over and the dissidents have been reconciled to him. Even though the letter is after the fact, Paul makes a passionate and detailed response to the attacks leveled against his apostolic commission and authority. Later in the letter, he defends his authority in relation to his person.

Speaking biographically, Paul recounts his own background and with deep emotion rightfully boasts of his sufferings for the sake of Jesus. He glories in the sober reality that he supports himself and does not look to the churches for financial help. He rebukes the false teachers sharply who attacked his personhood, and discloses that God, who has given him an exalted state and ministry, has also given him a thorn in the flesh to keep him humble. The reader must ask himself the questions: "Did not the apostle pray to be delivered from the appalling experiences he suffered?" Why did God allow all of these dreadful circumstances to cloud the life of this servant? The answer comes through loud and clear in Paul's letter to the Romans, which was written later. There the apostle says for the comfort of believers in all ages who are called upon to suffer: "Nay, in all these things we are more than conquerers through him that loved us" (Rom 8:37).

Outline

I. Introduction (1:1–11)
II. Defense of the ministry (1:12—7:4)
III. Paul's reconciliation to the Corinthians (7:5–16)
IV. The grace of giving (8:1—9:15)
V. Paul champions his apostolic authority (10:1—13:10)
VI. Concluding exhortation and benediction (13:11–14)

I. INTRODUCTION (1:1–11)

A. SALUTATION

1 PAUL, an apostle of Jesus Christ by the will of God, and Timothy *our*
brother, unto the church of God which is at Corinth, with all the saints
which are in all A-chai′a:
2 Grace *be* to you and peace from God our Father, and *from* the Lord
Jesus Christ.

1:1 1 Cor 1:1; 2 Cor 1:19; Eph 1:1
☆**1:2** Rom 1:7

B. THANKSGIVING

3 Blessed *be* God, even the Father of our Lord Jesus Christ, the Father of
mercies, and the God of all comfort;
4 Who comforteth us in all our tribulation, that we may be able to
comfort them which are in any trouble, by the comfort wherewith we
ourselves are comforted of God.
5 For as the sufferings of Christ abound in us, so our consolation also
aboundeth by Christ.
6 And whether we be afflicted, *it is* for your consolation and salvation,
which is effectual in the enduring of the same sufferings which we also
suffer: or whether we be comforted, *it is* for your consolation and salvation.
7 And our hope of you *is* stedfast, knowing, that as ye are partakers of the
sufferings, so *shall ye be* also of the consolation.
8 For we would not, brethren, have you ignorant of our trouble which
came to us in Asia, that we were pressed out of measure, above strength,
insomuch that we despaired even of life:
9 But we had the sentence of death in ourselves, that we should not trust
in ourselves, but in God which raiseth the dead:
10 Who delivered us from so great a death, and doth deliver: in whom we
trust that he will yet deliver *us;*
11 Ye also helping together by prayer for us, that for the gift *bestowed*
upon us by the means of many persons thanks may be given by many on
our behalf.

☆**1:3** Ex 34:6; Eph 1:3; 1 Pet 1:3
1:4 Isa 51:12; 66:13; 2 Cor 7:6; 2 Thess 2:16
1:5 2 Cor 4:10; Phil 3:10; Col 1:24
1:6 2 Cor 4:15; 2 Tim 2:10; 4:10
1:7 Rom 8:17; 2 Tim 2:12
1:8 Acts 19:23; 1 Cor 16:9
1:9 Jer 17:5, 7
1:10 2 Pet 2:9
☆**1:11** Rom 15:30; 2 Cor 4:15; Phil 1:19; Philem 22

II. DEFENSE OF THE MINISTRY (1:12—7:4)

A. PAUL'S CURRENT ACTIVITIES

1. Why He Changed His Travel Plans

12 For our rejoicing is this, the testimony of our conscience, that in
simplicity and godly sincerity, not with fleshly wisdom, but by the grace of
God, we have had our conversation in the world, and more abundantly to
you-ward.

☆**1:12** Acts 23:1; 1 Cor 2:4; 2 Cor 2:17; 4:15

1:2 *the Lord Jesus Christ.* Jesus means "savior"; Christ means "the anointed one"; Lord means "master." For the believer Jesus is both Savior and Lord. But what does Lordship mean? It means that Jesus Christ has the undivided possession and control of the Christian who comes under that Lordship. One can be regenerated or born again without being under the Lordship of Christ. Jesus is Lord theologically, but he is not Lord in the Christian's experience until, by an act of will, the believer chooses to come under Christ's Lordship. This can happen at the time of conversion or subsequent to it.

1:3 *the Father of our Lord Jesus Christ.* God is the Father of Jesus Christ in his divine nature by eternal generation. He is the Father of the human Jesus by supernatural generation through the womb of the virgin Mary, who was impregnated by the Holy Spirit.

1:11 Paul here thanks the Corinthians for the help they have given him through their prayers. Other believers will also give thanks to God for the effectiveness of the Corinthian prayers. Paul assuredly believed that God does answer the petitions of his people.

1:12 This marks the beginning of Paul's defense of himself and of his actions for which he had been maligned by some. The criticisms against the apostle were that (1) he cared little for the church because he did not keep his promises about visiting that church; (2) he was no speaker, no leader, just a man of insignificant appearance who lacked spirituality; (3) he had a way of insinuating himself into favor with men and was deceitful; (4) he obtained money in underhanded ways because he accepted no money.

13 For we write none other things unto you, than what ye read or
acknowledge; and I trust ye shall acknowledge even to the end;

1:14 2 Cor 5:12; Phil 4:1; 1 Thess 2:19
14 As also ye have acknowledged us in part, that we are your rejoicing,
even as ye also *are* ours in the day of the Lord Jesus.

1:15 Rom 1:11, 12; 1 Cor 4:19
15 And in this confidence I was minded to come unto you before, that ye
might have a second benefit;

1:16 1 Cor 16:5
16 And to pass by you into Macedonia, and to come again out of
Macedonia unto you, and of you to be brought on my way toward Judæa.

1:17 2 Cor 10:2
17 When I therefore was thus minded, did I use lightness? or the things
that I purpose, do I purpose according to the flesh, that with me there
should be yea yea, and nay nay?
18 But *as* God *is* true, our word toward you was not yea and nay.

1:19 Ex 3:14; Mt 16:16; 26:63; Lk 1:35; Acts 9:20; 18:5; Heb 13:8
19 For the Son of God, Jesus Christ, who was preached among you by us,
even by me and Sil-va′nus and Ti-mo′the-us, was not yea and nay, but in
him was yea.

1:20 Rom 15:8, 9; Rev 3:14
20 For all the promises of God in him *are* yea, and in him Amen, unto the
glory of God by us.

1:21 1 Jn 2:20, 27
21 Now he which stablisheth us with you in Christ, and hath anointed us,
is God;

1:22☆ 2 Cor 5:5; Eph 1:13, 14; 4:30; 2 Tim 2:19; Rev 2:17
22 Who hath also sealed us, and given the earnest of the Spirit in our
hearts.

2. Why He Did Not Come to Corinth

1:23☆ 1 Cor 4:21
23 Moreover I call God for a record upon my soul, that to spare you I
came not as yet unto Corinth.

1:24 Rom 11:20; 1 Cor 15:1, 2
24 Not for that we have dominion over your faith, but are helpers of your
joy: for by faith ye stand.

2:1 1 Cor 4:21; 2 Cor 12:20
2 BUT I determined this with myself, that I would not come again to
you in heaviness.

2:2 2 Cor 7:8
2 For if I make you sorry, who is he then that maketh me glad, but the
same which is made sorry by me?
3 And I wrote this same unto you, lest, when I came, I should have sorrow
from them of whom I ought to rejoice; having confidence in you all, that
my joy is *the joy* of you all.

2:4☆ 2 Cor 2:9; 7:8, 9
4 For out of much affliction and anguish of heart I wrote unto you with
many tears; not that ye should be grieved, but that ye might know the love
which I have more abundantly unto you.

3. Forgiving the Penitent

2:5☆ 1 Cor 5:1–5; 2 Cor 7:11
5 But if any have caused grief, he hath not grieved me, but in part: that I
may not overcharge you all.

1:22 Paul here mentions two important truths about the work of the Holy Spirit. He seals every believer, i.e., all believers bear the mark of God upon them; and he indwells every believer so that they have the earnest (a token of what is to come, a pledge) of the Spirit in their hearts.

1:23 *Paul explains why* he did not come to Corinth earlier according to his promise. Thus he answered one of the objections against him (see note on 1:12). He wanted to spare them, for the time was not ripe for his visit.

2:4 Paul affirms his sorrow, joy, tears, sympathy, anguish, and love for the people of the Corinthian church. This answered the charge that he did not care for the Corinthians (see note on 1:12).

2:5–11 Here, certain principles emerge about dealing with those who need to be disciplined. They are as follows: (1) no church should fail to discipline offending members; (2) discipline is not a decision to be made by one man but by the whole church; (3) the purpose of discipline is not penal but seeks the reformation and reclamation of the offender; (4) a repentant brother or sister should receive forgiveness upon repentance and be treated with affection; (5) severity and lack of sympathy may drive the sinner to desperation and place him under the power of Satan.

[6]Sufficient to such a man *is* this punishment, which *was inflicted* of many. ☆2:6
[7]So that contrariwise ye *ought* rather to forgive *him*, and comfort *him*, lest 2:7 Gal 6:1
perhaps such a one should be swallowed up with overmuch sorrow. Eph 4:32
[8]Wherefore I beseech you that ye would confirm *your* love toward him.
[9]For to this end also did I write, that I might know the proof of you,
whether ye be obedient in all things.
[10]To whom ye forgive any thing, I *forgive* also: for if I forgave any thing, 2:10 1 Cor 5:4
to whom I forgave *it*, for your sakes *forgave I it* in the person of Christ;
[11]Lest Satan should get an advantage of us: for we are not ignorant of his 2:11 2 Cor 4:4; 11:3 1 Pet 5:8
devices.

B. A DEFENSE OF THE MINISTRY
1. The Nature of the Ministry
a. Triumphant

[12]Furthermore, when I came to Troas to *preach* Christ's gospel, and a ☆2:12 Acts 14:27 2 Cor 4:3; 10:14
door was opened unto me of the Lord,
[13]I had no rest in my spirit, because I found not Titus my brother: but 2:13 2 Cor 7:5, 6
taking my leave of them, I went from thence into Macedonia.
[14]Now thanks *be* unto God, which always causeth us to triumph in ☆2:14 Col 2:15
Christ, and maketh manifest the savour of his knowledge by us in every
place.
[15]For we are unto God a sweet savour of Christ, in them that are saved, ☆2:15 Eph 5:2
and in them that perish:
[16]To the one *we are* the savour of death unto death; and to the other the 2:16 Lk 2:34 Jn 9:39 2 Cor 3:5
savour of life unto life. And who *is* sufficient for these things?
[17]For we are not as many, which corrupt the word of God: but as of 2:17 2 Cor 4:2
sincerity, but as of God, in the sight of God speak we in Christ.

b. Commended

3 DO we begin again to commend ourselves? or need we, as some *others*, ☆3:1 Acts 18:27 2 Cor 5:12; 10:12
epistles of commendation to you, or *letters* of commendation from
you?
[2]Ye are our epistle written in our hearts, known and read of all men: ☆3:2 1 Cor 9:2
[3]*Forasmuch as ye are* manifestly declared to be the epistle of Christ 3:3 Ex 24:12 Ps 40:8 Prov 3:3 Jer 31:33 Ezek 36:26 1 Cor 3:5
ministered by us, written not with ink, but with the Spirit of the living God;
not in tables of stone, but in fleshy tables of the heart.

c. Glorious

[4]And such trust have we through Christ to God-ward:
[5]Not that we are sufficient of ourselves to think any thing as of ourselves; 3:5 Jn 15:5 1 Cor 15:10
but our sufficiency *is* of God;

2:6 Paul here is referring to the incestuous person who had been excommunicated for his sin. The punishment was effective, for he had repented. Paul orders the *church to restore this brother, release him from the* excommunication, and forgive him. They must renew and confirm their love for him.

2:12 Starting with this verse Paul engages in a systematic defense of his ministry. He answers the various charges leveled against him by those who were suspicious of him (see note on 1:12). We learn from this episode that the best of God's servants may be misunderstood, libeled, defamed, and their motives impugned. God delivers his servants in the midst of such experiences, not from them. Paul had to endure these things, and his prayers provided him with the power to be an overcomer in the midst of trials.

2:14 Paul asserts that God always causes us to triumph in Christ. On the surface this may not always appear to be true. The fact that saints have been persecuted, imprisoned, and murdered seems to belie this truth. But the records show that such people willingly and persistently endure these things with a heroism that defies understanding.

2:15 "Make me a captive, Lord,/And then I shall be free;/Force me to render up my sword,/And I shall conqueror be" (George Matheson).

3:1, 2 Some Jews who opposed Paul had come with letters from Jerusalem recommending them to the Corinthians. Paul apologizes for seeming to recommend himself but argues that the Corinthians themselves were his best letters written on his heart. He says, "Ye are our epistle."

3:6☆ Jer 31:31; Lk 22:20; Jn 6:63; Rom 2:27; 7:6; 8:2; Gal 3:10; Heb 8:6
3:7☆ Ex 34:29–35; Deut 9:10
3:8☆ Gal 3:5
3:9 Rom 1:17; 3:21
3:10, 11 Jn 17:10, 22; Heb 2:10
3:12 Eph 6:19; 1 Thess 2:2
3:13 Ex 34:33; Rom 10:4; Gal 3:23
3:14 Isa 6:10; Jn 12:40; Acts 13:15; Rom 11:7; 2 Cor 4:4
3:16☆ Isa 25:7; Rom 11:23; 1 Cor 2:10
3:17☆ Rom 8:9; 1 Cor 15:45; Gal 4:6; Phil 1:19
3:18 Rom 8:29; 2 Cor 4:4, 6; Col 3:10

6 Who also hath made us able ministers of the new testament; not of the
letter, but of the spirit: for the letter killeth, but the spirit giveth life.
7 But if the ministration of death, written *and* engraven in stones, was
glorious, so that the children of Israel could not stedfastly behold the face
of Moses for the glory of his countenance; which *glory* was to be done
away:
8 How shall not the ministration of the spirit be rather glorious?
9 For if the ministration of condemnation *be* glory, much more doth the
ministration of righteousness exceed in glory.
10 For even that which was made glorious had no glory in this respect, by
reason of the glory that excelleth.
11 For if that which is done away *was* glorious, much more that which
remaineth *is* glorious.
12 Seeing then that we have such hope, we use great plainness of speech:
13 And not as Moses, *which* put a vail over his face, that the children of
Israel could not stedfastly look to the end of that which is abolished:
14 But their minds were blinded: for until this day remaineth the same vail
untaken away in the reading of the old testament; which *vail* is done away
in Christ.
15 But even unto this day, when Moses is read, the vail is upon their heart.
16 Nevertheless when it shall turn to the Lord, the vail shall be taken
away.
17 Now the Lord is that Spirit: and where the Spirit of the Lord *is*, there
is liberty.
18 But we all, with open face beholding as in a glass the glory of the Lord,
are changed into the same image from glory to glory, *even* as by the Spirit
of the Lord.

2. The Sincerity of the Ministry

4:2☆ 2 Cor 2:17; 1 Thess 2:3, 5
4:3 Isa 6:9; 1 Cor 1:18; 2 Cor 3:14
4:4 Isa 6:10; Jn 1:18; 12:31, 40, 45; 14:9, 30; 16:11; 2 Cor 3:14; Eph 6:12; Col 1:15; Heb 1:3
4:5 1 Cor 9:19

4 THEREFORE seeing we have this ministry, as we have received
mercy, we faint not;
2 But have renounced the hidden things of dishonesty, not walking in
craftiness, nor handling the word of God deceitfully; but by manifestation
of the truth commending ourselves to every man's conscience in the sight of
God.
3 But if our gospel be hid, it is hid to them that are lost:
4 In whom the god of this world hath blinded the minds of them which
believe not, lest the light of the glorious gospel of Christ, who is the image
of God, should shine unto them.
5 For we preach not ourselves, but Christ Jesus the Lord; and ourselves
your servants for Jesus' sake.

3:6 Paul contrasts the old and the new covenants, betokened by the fact that under the new covenant the Holy Spirit has come in mighty power. Thus the ministry of men through the preaching of the gospel is accompanied by the ministry of the Spirit who produces life spiritual and life eternal as the fruit of the preaching.
3:7, 8 *Moses' face* shone with the brightness of the glory of God when he came off the mountain. Yet this was related to law. Now that the Spirit has come, the gospel by the Spirit has a greater and eternally enduring brightness and glory that outshines anything Moses ever experienced.
3:16, 17 A veil covered Moses' face. That veil is taken away in Jesus Christ. Having Christ produces liberty; bondage to the law and obedience to it is gone. The believer enters into a glorious freedom. The gospel is greater than the law, and now believers go from glory to glory (3:18).
4:2 Ministers of the gospel then and now can expect to be criticized as crafty adulterers of the Word of God, who are guilty of hidden works of darkness. Paul defends himself and his colleagues by asserting that God's work must be performed by good means suitable to a good end. The use of bad means for good ends is everywhere forbidden in the Scriptures.

6 For God, who commanded the light to shine out of darkness, hath
shined in our hearts, to *give* the light of the knowledge of the glory of God
in the face of Jesus Christ.

3. The Perseverance of the Ministry

7 But we have this treasure in earthen vessels, that the excellency of the
power may be of God, and not of us.
8 *We are* troubled on every side, yet not distressed; *we are* perplexed, but
not in despair;
9 Persecuted, but not forsaken; cast down, but not destroyed;
10 Always bearing about in the body the dying of the Lord Jesus, that the
life also of Jesus might be made manifest in our body.
11 For we which live are alway delivered unto death for Jesus' sake, that
the life also of Jesus might be made manifest in our mortal flesh.
12 So then death worketh in us, but life in you.
13 We having the same spirit of faith, according as it is written, I believed,
and therefore have I spoken; we also believe, and therefore speak;
14 Knowing that he which raised up the Lord Jesus shall raise up us also
by Jesus, and shall present *us* with you.
15 For all things *are* for your sakes, that the abundant grace might through
the thanksgiving of many redound to the glory of God.

4. The Boldness of the Ministry

16 For which cause we faint not; but though our outward man perish, yet
the inward *man* is renewed day by day.
17 For our light affliction, which is but for a moment, worketh for us a far
more exceeding *and* eternal weight of glory;
18 While we look not at the things which are seen, but at the things which
are not seen: for the things which are seen *are* temporal; but the things
which are not seen *are* eternal.

5 FOR we know that if our earthly house of *this* tabernacle were
dissolved, we have a building of God, an house not made with hands,
eternal in the heavens.
2 For in this we groan, earnestly desiring to be clothed upon with our
house which is from heaven:
3 If so be that being clothed we shall not be found naked.
4 For we that are in *this* tabernacle do groan, being burdened: not for that

☆**4:6** Gen 1:3; Ps 36:9; Jn 8:12; 12:46; Eph 5:8, 14; 1 Pet 2:9; 2 Pet 1:19
☆**4:7** 1 Cor 2:5; 2 Cor 5:1; 2 Tim 2:20
4:8 2 Cor 7:5
4:9 Jn 15:20; Rom 8:35, 36; Ps 37:24; 129:2; Prov 24:16
☆**4:10** Rom 8:17; 1 Cor 15:31; Gal 6:17; Phil 3:10; Col 1:24; 2 Tim 2:11; 1 Pet 4:13
☆**4:13** Ps 116:10
4:14 Acts 2:24; 1 Thess 2:19
4:15 2 Cor 1:6, 11
4:16 Eph 3:16; Col 3:10
☆**4:17** Rom 8:18; 1 Pet 1:6, 7
4:18 Rom 8:24; 2 Cor 5:7
☆**5:1** 1 Cor 15:47; 2 Cor 4:7; Phil 3:21; Heb 11:10; 2 Pet 1:13
5:2 Rom 8:23; 1 Cor 15:53
5:3 Rom 3:18
5:4 1 Cor 15:53, 54

4:6 Wherever God is not, there is darkness. But God is overcoming the darkness in the souls of men by bringing them *the light of the knowledge of the glory of God in the face of Jesus Christ.* Where there is no gospel there is no true light. Thus the church is to take Jesus, the light of the world, to the ends of the earth that men may not sit in darkness forever.

4:7 *Ministers are weak, but their God is strong.* The divine strength is demonstrated more through human weakness, so that the weaker the human vessel the stronger the power of God appears. All of God's people have a treasure in them which consists in the knowledge of the glory of God in the face of Jesus Christ.

4:10 Paul's sufferings constituted a continual process of death. They were gradually killing him and one day would kill him. He had the consolation and joy of knowing that he was sharing an experience with Jesus Christ, who had been subjected to a gradual dying until at last he went to the cross of Calvary.

4:13 It was faith that kept Paul from fainting. He quotes David, from whose words he gained strength and whose example he wished to imitate. Christians should be careful to leave behind them a good example for others' encouragement when they suffer.

4:17 Faith looks at life from the long view, not the short one. Afflictions are temporary and limited. The wise Christian looks at things unseen, which are eternal; and so he labors in this temporal world with the sure knowledge that what lies before him is infinitely greater than anything he dreamed of. Thus, whatever he suffers in this life means nothing in the light of eternity.

5:1ff Paul refers to the body as a tabernacle (or tent). At death the spirit is separated from this tent to await a heavenly body God has prepared for all of his people. Paul is anxious to inherit that new body so as to escape the bodiless state when he dies. He assures us that we have a realizable hope—for mortality will be swallowed up, and endless life in the new body will eventually come.

we would be unclothed, but clothed upon, that mortality might be
swallowed up of life.
5:5 5Now he that hath wrought us for the selfsame thing *is* God, who also
Rom 8:23 2 Cor 1:22 hath given unto us the earnest of the Spirit.
Eph 1:14 6Therefore *we are* always confident, knowing that, whilst we are at home
in the body, we are absent from the Lord:
5:7☆ 7(For we walk by faith, not by sight:)
1 Cor 13:12 **5:8** 8We are confident, *I say*, and willing rather to be absent from the body,
Phil 1:23 and to be present with the Lord.
9Wherefore we labour, that, whether present or absent, we may be
accepted of him.
5:10☆ 10For we must all appear before the judgment seat of Christ; that every
Mt 16:27 Acts 10:42 one may receive the things *done* in *his* body, according to that he hath done,
Rom 14:10 1 Cor 3:13–15 whether *it be* good or bad.
Eph 6:8 Rev 22:12

5. The Sanctions and Example of the Ministry

5:11☆ 11Knowing therefore the terror of the Lord, we persuade men; but we are
made manifest unto God; and I trust also are made manifest in your
consciences.
5:12 12For we commend not ourselves again unto you, but give you occasion
2 Cor 1:14; 3:1 to glory on our behalf, that ye may have somewhat to *answer* them which
glory in appearance, and not in heart.
13For whether we be beside ourselves, *it is* to God: or whether we be
sober, *it is* for your cause.
5:14☆ 14For the love of Christ constraineth us; because we thus judge, that if
Rom 5:15 Gal 2:20 one died for all, then were all dead:
5:15 15And *that* he died for all, that they which live should not henceforth live
Rom 14:7–9 1 Pet 4:2 unto themselves, but unto him which died for them, and rose again.
5:16 16Wherefore henceforth know we no man after the flesh: yea, though we
Mt 12:50 have known Christ after the flesh, yet now henceforth know we *him* no
5:17☆ more.
Isa 65:17 Gal 6:15 17Therefore if any man *be* in Christ, *he is* a new creature: old things are
Eph 4:24 Rev 21:5 passed away; behold, all things are become new.
5:18☆ Rom 5:10 18And all things *are* of God, who hath reconciled us to himself by Jesus
Col 1:20–22 Christ, and hath given to us the ministry of reconciliation;

5:7 *we walk by faith.* Faith is for this world and sight for the world to come. It is the Christian's duty to walk by faith until he comes to live by sight in eternity. The walk by faith provides courage (5:8) for all times and all circumstances.

5:10 Scripture speaks of two different and distinct judgments: one is the judgment seat of Christ, before which only believers stand and at which their works will be judged; the other is the judgment of the great white throne, at which only unbelievers will appear before being consigned forever to the lake of fire. The believer's judgment occurs at the coming of the Lord (see also 1 Cor. 4:5; 2 Tim. 4:8; Rev. 22:12). At this time (1) all believers must appear (Rom. 14:10; 2 Cor. 5:10); (2) each will give account of himself (Rom. 14:12); (3) the good deeds and the bad ones will be reviewed (5:10); (4) rewards will be determined *according to our* deeds (Rev. 22:12); (5) some will receive no reward but will be saved "yet so as by fire" (1 Cor. 3:12–15).

5:11 The apostle continues to defend himself against evil attacks. Some thought he was not what he claimed to be (see note on 1:12). Here he says that the terror of facing God in the judgment is the basis for the life he has lived. God knows what lies inside him and he does not fear standing before God. He hopes that what God knows about him the Corinthians would also know (in their consciences) to be true of him.

5:14 *the love of Christ constraineth us.* Paul is not saying that it is *his* love of (towards) Christ that directs him, although that is quite true; here he speaks of Christ's love toward him and his fellow-workers. That love, which motivated Christ to die on the cross, is the love that moves them and causes them to endure all things.

5:17 For man, the *new creature* means he has become "a brand new person" (TLB) in Jesus Christ by regeneration or the new birth (Eph. 2:10); for the universe, the "new creation" means a new heaven and a new earth (2 Pet. 3:13; Isa. 65:17; Rom. 8:20, 21).

5:18 *reconciled us to himself.* Reconciliation occurred (1) through the death of God's Son (Rom. 5:10; Col. 1:22) and through his blood on the cross (Col. 1:20; Eph. 2:16). Here and in Rom. 5 Paul uses reconciliation and justification as synonymous. Reconciliation is God's work, not man's; it is secured by faith, which grants to the recipient peace with God and immediate access to God (Eph. 2:16–18).

19To wit, that God was in Christ, reconciling the world unto himself, not
imputing their trespasses unto them; and hath committed unto us the word
of reconciliation.
20Now then we are ambassadors for Christ, as though God did beseech
you by us: we pray *you* in Christ's stead, be ye reconciled to God.
21For he hath made him *to be* sin for us, who knew no sin; that we might
be made the righteousness of God in him.

6 WE then, *as* workers together *with him*, beseech *you* also that ye receive
not the grace of God in vain.
2(For he saith, I have heard thee in a time accepted, and in the day of
salvation have I succoured thee: behold, now *is* the accepted time; behold,
now *is* the day of salvation.)
3Giving no offence in any thing, that the ministry be not blamed:
4But in all *things* approving ourselves as the ministers of God, in much
patience, in afflictions, in necessities, in distresses,
5In stripes, in imprisonments, in tumults, in labours, in watchings, in
fastings;
6By pureness, by knowledge, by longsuffering, by kindness, by the Holy
Ghost, by love unfeigned,
7By the word of truth, by the power of God, by the armour of
righteousness on the right hand and on the left,
8By honour and dishonour, by evil report and good report: as deceivers,
and *yet* true;
9As unknown, and *yet* well known; as dying, and, behold, we live; as
chastened, and not killed;
10As sorrowful, yet alway rejoicing; as poor, yet making many rich; as
having nothing, and *yet* possessing all things.

6. The Entreaty of the Ministry

11O *ye* Co-rinth'i-ans, our mouth is open unto you, our heart is enlarged.
12Ye are not straitened in us, but ye are straitened in your own bowels.
13Now for a recompence in the same, (I speak as unto *my* children,) be ye
also enlarged.
14Be ye not unequally yoked together with unbelievers: for what
fellowship hath righteousness with unrighteousness? and what communion
hath light with darkness?
15And what concord hath Christ with Be'li-al? or what part hath he that
believeth with an infidel?
16And what agreement hath the temple of God with idols? for ye are the
temple of the living God; as God hath said, I will dwell in them, and walk
in *them;* and I will be their God, and they shall be my people.

5:19 Isa 43:25; Rom 3:24; 4:28
5:20 Rom 5:10
5:21 Isa 53:6, 9; Jer 23:6; Dan 9:24; Rom 1:17; Gal 3:13; Heb 4:15; 7:26; 1 Pet 2:22
☆**6:1** 1 Cor 3:9; 2 Cor 5:20; Heb 12:15
6:2 Isa 49:8
6:3 1 Cor 8:9; 9:12
6:4 2 Cor 4:8; 11:23–28
6:5 Acts 16:23; 1 Cor 4:11
6:6 2 Cor 11:6
☆**6:7** 1 Cor 2:4; 2 Cor 2:17; 4:2; 10:4
☆**6:8** Mt 27:63; Rom 3:8; 1 Cor 4:10, 13; 2 Cor 4:2
6:9 Ps 118:18; Rom 8:36; 1 Cor 4:9; 2 Cor 1:8; 4:11
6:10 Acts 3:6; Rom 8:32; 1 Cor 3:21; 2 Cor 8:9
☆**6:11** 2 Cor 7:3
6:12 2 Cor 12:15
6:13 1 Cor 4:14
6:14 Deut 7:3; 22:10; Eph 5:6, 7; 1 Jn 1:6, 7
6:15 1 Cor 10:21
6:16 Ex 25:8; 29:45; Lev 26:12; Jer 31:33; Ezek 36:28; Zech 13:9; Jn 14:23; 1 Pet 2:5; Rev 21:3

6:1 *God is the Author of grace and he does the work* to make grace effective. Paul and all ministers and other workers cooperate with God by proclaiming what God has done. And they entreat men not to receive the grace of God in vain. Isaiah, whom Paul quotes, is saying that in due time God would hear the cry of those who called on him for help and he would deliver those who needed salvation. That time has now come in the gospel age via the ministry of Paul and the other evangelists.

6:7 "The godly man's arsenal" (TLB) consists of an offensive weapon, the sword (carried in the right hand), and a defensive weapon, a shield (carried in the left hand). See his description of the Christian's armor in Eph. 6:11, 13–17.

6:8 *as deceivers,* i.e., some had said that Paul and his company were imposters. In 6:9, 10 Paul cites his experiences and characteristics (and those of his friends) in order to rebut this charge.

6:11ff Paul appeals for sympathy. He says he is frank, candid, and open. He has revealed the secret springs of his actions. He has a large, broad heart; he says, in effect, "It is not in us you are cramped but in your own affections." He begs them to love him as he loves them. There should be room in their hearts for him.

6:17☆ Isa 52:11; Rev 18:4
6:18 Jer 31:1, 9; Hos 1:10; Rom 8:14; Rev 21:7

17 Wherefore come out from among them, and be ye separate, saith the
Lord, and touch not the unclean *thing;* and I will receive you,
18 And will be a Father unto you, and ye shall be my sons and daughters,
saith the Lord Almighty.

7:1☆ 1 Pet 1:22; 1 Jn 3:3
7:2☆ 2 Cor 6:12
7:3 2 Cor 6:11
7:4 1 Cor 1:4; 2 Cor 7:14; 8:24; 10:8; Phil 2:17

7 HAVING therefore these promises, dearly beloved, let us cleanse
ourselves from all filthiness of the flesh and spirit, perfecting holiness
in the fear of God.
2 Receive us; we have wronged no man, we have corrupted no man, we
have defrauded no man.
3 I speak not *this* to condemn *you:* for I have said before, that ye are in
our hearts to die and live with *you.*
4 Great *is* my boldness of speech toward you, great *is* my glorying of you:
I am filled with comfort, I am exceeding joyful in all our tribulation.

III. PAUL'S RECONCILIATION TO THE CORINTHIANS (7:5–16)

7:5 2 Cor 2:13; 4:8
7:6 2 Cor 2:13; 7:13; 2 Thess 2:16
7:8☆ 2 Cor 2:2–4
7:10 2 Sam 12:13; Jer 31:18–20; Mt 26:75; 27:4, 5
7:11 Jer 50:4, 5; Zech 12:10; 2 Cor 2:6

5 For, when we were come into Macedonia, our flesh had no rest, but we
were troubled on every side; without *were* fightings, within *were* fears.
6 Nevertheless God, that comforteth those that are cast down, comforted
us by the coming of Titus;
7 And not by his coming only, but by the consolation wherewith he was
comforted in you, when he told us your earnest desire, your mourning, your
fervent mind toward me; so that I rejoiced the more.
8 For though I made you sorry with a letter, I do not repent, though I did
repent: for I perceive that the same epistle hath made you sorry, though *it*
were but for a season.
9 Now I rejoice, not that ye were made sorry, but that ye sorrowed to
repentance: for ye were made sorry after a godly manner, that ye might
receive damage by us in nothing.
10 For godly sorrow worketh repentance to salvation not to be repented
of: but the sorrow of the world worketh death.
11 For behold this selfsame thing, that ye sorrowed after a godly sort,
what carefulness it wrought in you, yea, *what* clearing of yourselves, yea,
what indignation, yea, *what* fear, yea, *what* vehement desire, yea, *what* zeal,
yea, *what* revenge! In all *things* ye have approved yourselves to be clear in
this matter.

6:17 God commands his people to be separated from unbelievers and from the world. Like Christ, we are in the world but not of the world. Christians must shun compromising relationships with nonbelievers. They are not to marry unbelievers, nor are they to choose them for intimate companions, nor are they to have cordial fellowship with theological apostates. Separation is not only *from* something. Believers are to be separated *unto* God. Separation is not only from people but also from worldly attitudes and activities. The *maxim is: cling to what* is good; flee from what is evil.

7:1 This verse is the proper ending for 6:14–18. In the light of those precious promises it behooves believers to be cleansed from their sins by confession, restitution, and sorrow. They are to make holiness the one great desire of their hearts and press on toward the goal of being like Jesus Christ.

7:2ff "Make room for us in your hearts" (NASB) says Paul. We have wronged no man; we have neither corrupted nor destroyed anyone; we have taken advantage of no one. He stresses his confidence in the Corinthians and his pride in them, being overjoyed despite all the afflictions he and his friends have suffered.

7:8 In this verse and in 7:12 Paul speaks of a stern letter he had written to the church at Corinth. Many believe that this letter has been lost. Some hold that chapters 10–13 constitute this stern letter. The matter probably will never be fully resolved. The incident does make plain that Paul did not hesitate to take corrective action in the interest of a church whenever it was necessary.

12Wherefore, though I wrote unto you, *I did it* not for his cause that had
done the wrong, nor for his cause that suffered wrong, but that our care for
you in the sight of God might appear unto you.
13Therefore we were comforted in your comfort: yea, and exceedingly the
more joyed we for the joy of Titus, because his spirit was refreshed by you
all.
14For if I have boasted any thing to him of you, I am not ashamed; but
as we spake all things to you in truth, even so our boasting, which *I made*
before Titus, is found a truth.
15And his inward affection is more abundant toward you, whilst he
remembereth the obedience of you all, how with fear and trembling ye
received him.
16I rejoice therefore that I have confidence in you in all *things*.

☆7:12 1 Cor 5:1–5
7:13 Rom 15:32; 2 Cor 2:13; 7:6
7:15 2 Cor 2:9; Phil 2:12
7:16 2 Cor 2:3; 2 Thess 3:4; Philem 21

IV. THE GRACE OF GIVING (8:1—9:15)

A. THE MACEDONIAN EXAMPLE

8 MOREOVER, brethren, we do you to wit of the grace of God
bestowed on the churches of Macedonia;
2How that in a great trial of affliction the abundance of their joy and
their deep poverty abounded unto the riches of their liberality.
3For to *their* power, I bear record, yea, and beyond *their* power *they were*
willing of themselves;
4Praying us with much intreaty that we would receive the gift, and *take
upon us* the fellowship of the ministering to the saints.
5And *this they did*, not as we hoped, but first gave their own selves to the
Lord, and unto us by the will of God.
6Insomuch that we desired Titus, that as he had begun, so he would also
finish in you the same grace also.
7Therefore, as ye abound in every *thing, in* faith, and utterance, and
knowledge, and *in* all diligence, and *in* your love to us, *see* that ye abound
in this grace also.

B. THE EXAMPLE OF THE LORD JESUS

8I speak not by commandment, but by occasion of the forwardness of
others, and to prove the sincerity of your love.
9For ye know the grace of our Lord Jesus Christ, that, though he was

☆8:1 Acts 16:9
8:4 Acts 24:17; Rom 15:25; 1 Cor 16:1, 3
☆8:5 Mt 25:40; Heb 13:16
8:6 2 Cor 12:18
8:7 Prov 22:9; 28:27; Mt 19:21; Mk 10:21; Lk 18:22; 1 Cor 1:5; 12:13; 2 Cor 9:8
☆8:9 Mt 8:20; Lk 9:58; Phil 2:6, 7

7:12ff The earlier letter of Paul was written with the good desire to help the church, even though he may have appeared to be severe. His concern went far beyond the guilty brother to the church itself. The church must not have allowed the crime to go unnoticed or the scandal unheeded. Any church that refuses to exercise discipline by reproof and admonition will itself suffer serious loss, and its spiritual state will worsen. To endorse a misdeed is very bad; to refuse to deal with a misdeed is not much better. Churches suffer from the failure to act when they should, for they are guilty of refusing to do what they know they ought to do. This is institutional evil.

8:1 This section of Paul's letter (8:1—9:15) refers to the Macedonian offering taken for the relief of Christians in Jerusalem. Paul's care in the way the money was to be carried indicates his fiscal integrity and shows that the gift was designed to express the unity of the faith between Jew and Gentile. The principle of the fellowship of the one body of Christ that allows for no division is most important. The generosity of the new Macedonian converts is also significant. Salvation touched their pocketbooks as well as their souls.

8:5 *first gave their own selves to the Lord.* Believers ought to give themselves to the Lord; but not all do so. No one can do better for himself than to give himself to the Lord. Giving oneself includes all one has—for God to use and dispose of as he chooses. But the believer only gives back to God what belongs to him in the first place. Whatever anyone gives of his goods or services is of no account if that believer has not first given himself to God.

8:9 Paul urges the Corinthians to help the poor saints. He uses Christ as an illustration. Jesus became poor in two ways. First, he gave up his glory with the Father in heaven to become man. Second, he was literally poor in the things of this world. He was born into a poor family, lived a poor life, died in poverty, and was buried in a borrowed grave. Yet this demeaning of himself has worked to our advantage; for through his poverty we have acquired great riches—not only the riches of a new relationship to God but also the riches of heaven as joint heirs with Jesus Christ in his kingdom.

rich, yet for your sakes he became poor, that ye through his poverty might
be rich.

8:10 Prov 19:17; Mt 10:42; 1 Tim 6:18; Heb 13:16

10 And herein I give *my* advice: for this is expedient for you, who have
begun before, not only to do, but also to be forward a year ago.
11 Now therefore perform the doing *of it;* that as *there was* a readiness to
will, so *there may be* a performance also out of that which ye have.

8:12 Mk 12:43; 2 Cor 9:7

12 For if there be first a willing mind, *it is* accepted according to that a
man hath, *and* not according to that he hath not.
13 For *I mean* not that other men be eased, and ye burdened:

8:14 Acts 4:34, 35

14 But by an equality, *that* now at this time your abundance *may be a
supply* for their want, that their abundance also may be *a supply* for your
want: that there may be equality:

8:15 Ex 16:18

15 As it is written, He that *had gathered* much had nothing over; and he
that *had gathered* little had no lack.

C. THE ARRANGEMENTS FOR THE OFFERING

8:16 2 Cor 2:13, 14

16 But thanks *be* to God, which put the same earnest care into the heart of
Titus for you.

8:17 2 Cor 12:18

17 For indeed he accepted the exhortation; but being more forward, of his
own accord he went unto you.

8:18☆ 2 Cor 12:18

18 And we have sent with him the brother, whose praise *is* in the gospel
throughout all the churches;

8:19 Acts 14:23; 1 Cor 16:3

19 And not *that* only, but who was also chosen of the churches to travel
with us with this grace, which is administered by us to the glory of the same
Lord, and *declaration of* your ready mind:
20 Avoiding this, that no man should blame us in this abundance which is
administered by us:

8:21 Prov 3:4; Rom 12:17; Phil 4:8; 1 Pet 2:12

21 Providing for honest things, not only in the sight of the Lord, but also
in the sight of men.
22 And we have sent with them our brother, whom we have oftentimes
proved diligent in many things, but now much more diligent, upon the great
confidence which *I have* in you.

8:23☆ Phil 2:25

23 Whether *any do inquire* of Titus, *he is* my partner and fellowhelper
concerning you: or our brethren *be inquired of, they are* the messengers of
the churches, *and* the glory of Christ.

8:24 2 Cor 7:4

24 Wherefore shew ye to them, and before the churches, the proof of your
love, and of our boasting on your behalf.

D. THE ENCOURAGEMENT TO GIVE

9:1☆ Rom 15:26; 1 Cor 16:1; Gal 2:10; 1 Thess 4:9

9:2 2 Cor 8:6, 17

9 FOR as touching the ministering to the saints, it is superfluous for me
to write to you:
2 For I know the forwardness of your mind, for which I boast of you to

8:18 *whose praise is in the gospel throughout all the churches.* The RSV translates this clause as, "the brother who is famous among all the churches for his preaching of the gospel." The NIV has, "the brother who is praised by all the churches for his service to the gospel." We do not know who this brother was, although some have suggested it was Luke. Apparently he was well known, yet unnamed, and a splendid *evangelist. The rolls* of heaven are filled with unnamed warriors of the cross who are not known of men but are known of God.

8:23 Paul began his letter by identifying Timothy with himself. The very adding of his name to this letter gave him status. Now he makes reference to faithful Titus, who is leading a party to accept the Corinthian offering and bring it to the poor saints in Jerusalem. Paul does this deliberately, because Titus and the others (probably Luke and Apollos) have an unblemished reputation. Because Paul had nothing to do personally with the gift of money, no one could accuse him of personal interest or the desire for personal gain in this effort. He was avoiding all appearance of evil for the sake of weaker brothers' consciences.

9:1ff Paul tells the Corinthians that he has boasted of their liberality and their good intentions. He urges them to justify his confidence in them so that he and his coworkers will not be humiliated by any failure on the part of the Corinthians to fulfill the expectation created by the apostle's words.

them of Macedonia, that A-chai'a was ready a year ago; and your zeal hath
provoked very many.
3 Yet have I sent the brethren, lest our boasting of you should be in vain
in this behalf; that, as I said, ye may be ready:
4 Lest haply if they of Macedonia come with me, and find you unpre-
pared, we (that we say not, ye) should be ashamed in this same confident
boasting.
5 Therefore I thought it necessary to exhort the brethren, that they would
go before unto you, and make up beforehand your bounty, whereof ye had
notice before, that the same might be ready, as *a matter of* bounty, and not
as *of* covetousness.

9:3 1 Cor 16:2
☆**9:5** Gen 33:11

E. THE REWARD FOR LIBERALITY

6 But this *I say,* He which soweth sparingly shall reap also sparingly; and
he which soweth bountifully shall reap also bountifully.
7 Every man according as he purposeth in his heart, *so let him give;* not
grudgingly, or of necessity: for God loveth a cheerful giver.
8 And God *is* able to make all grace abound toward you; that ye, always
having all sufficiency in all *things,* may abound to every good work:
9 (As it is written, He hath dispersed abroad; he hath given to the poor:
his righteousness remaineth for ever.
10 Now he that ministereth seed to the sower both minister bread for *your*
food, and multiply your seed sown, and increase the fruits of your
righteousness;)
11 Being enriched in every thing to all bountifulness, which causeth
through us thanksgiving to God.
12 For the administration of this service not only supplieth the want of the
saints, but is abundant also by many thanksgivings unto God;
13 Whiles by the experiment of this ministration they glorify God for your
professed subjection unto the gospel of Christ, and for *your* liberal
distribution unto them, and unto all *men;*
14 And by their prayer for you, which long after you for the exceeding
grace of God in you.
15 Thanks *be* unto God for his unspeakable gift.

☆**9:6** Prov 11:24 19:17 Lk 6:38 Gal 6:7, 9
9:7 Ex 35:5 Deut 15:7–10 Rom 12:8 2 Cor 8:12
9:8 Prov 28:27 Phil 4:19
9:9 Ps 112:9
☆**9:10** Hos 10:12 Mt 6:1
9:11 2 Cor 1:11; 4:16
9:12 2 Cor 8:14
9:13 Mt 5:16 Heb 13:16
☆**9:15** Jas 1:17

V. PAUL CHAMPIONS HIS APOSTOLIC AUTHORITY (10:1—13:10)

A. HIS RESPONSE TO HIS ACCUSERS

1. He Is Neither Weak Nor Cowardly

10 NOW I Paul myself beseech you by the meekness and gentleness of
Christ, who in presence *am* base among you, but being absent am
bold toward you:

☆**10:1** 1 Cor 2:3 2 Cor 10:10

9:5ff Sometimes the Spirit gives individuals and churches the special gift of giving. Here we see the principles of giving outlined for us: (1) giving should be bountiful; (2) giving should be deliberate, i.e., by thought and design; (3) giving should be done cheerfully, not grudgingly or of necessity.

9:6 The more seed a farmer plants in his field, the more crops he will reap at harvest time. Paul applies this obvious principle to the spiritual realm of giving. Works of charity should be done carefully, to be sure; but the act of giving should be done liberally. God promises that those who share liberally of their means will also reap a generous harvest in the divine kingdom when the accounts are balanced and the rewards are handed out.

9:10 God graciously gives so much to us; therefore, we can give to others. Givers are never losers. God promises to enrich them in everything.

9:15 Some interpreters suppose that Paul here means the gift of grace given to the Corinthians, which made them able and willing to help the poor saints. Rather it appears to denote Jesus Christ as God's gift, a gift so great that it defies anyone's ability to express it with words.

10:1 Previously Paul uses the word "we" in this letter. Now he turns to the more personal word "I." He is speaking for himself. Because he wishes to avoid severity, he asks them not to give him any occasion that will require it.

10:2 1 Cor 4:18, 21; 2 Cor 1:17; 13:2

2 But I beseech *you,* that I may not be bold when I am present with that
confidence, wherewith I think to be bold against some, which think of us as
if we walked according to the flesh.
3 For though we walk in the flesh, we do not war after the flesh:

10:4☆ Jer 1:10; 1 Cor 9:7; Eph 6:13–17; 1 Thess 5:8
10:5 Isa 2:11; 1 Cor 1:19; 3:19

4 (For the weapons of our warfare *are* not carnal, but mighty through
God to the pulling down of strong holds;)
5 Casting down imaginations, and every high thing that exalteth itself
against the knowledge of God, and bringing into captivity every thought to
the obedience of Christ;

10:6 2 Cor 2:9; 7:15; 13:2

6 And having in a readiness to revenge all disobedience, when your
obedience is fulfilled.

10:7☆ Jn 7:24; 1 Cor 9:1; 14:37; 2 Cor 11:23; 1 Jn 4:6

7 Do ye look on things after the outward appearance? If any man trust to
himself that he is Christ's, let him of himself think this again, that, as he *is*
Christ's, even so *are* we Christ's.
8 For though I should boast somewhat more of our authority, which the
Lord hath given us for edification, and not for your destruction, I should
not be ashamed:
9 That I may not seem as if I would terrify you by letters.

10:10 1 Cor 1:17; 2:3; 2 Cor 11:6; Gal 4:13

10 For *his* letters, say they, *are* weighty and powerful; but *his* bodily
presence *is* weak, and *his* speech contemptible.
11 Let such an one think this, that, such as we are in word by letters when
we are absent, such *will we be* also in deed when we are present.

10:12 2 Cor 3:1; 5:12

12 For we dare not make ourselves of the number, or compare ourselves
with some that commend themselves: but they measuring themselves by
themselves, and comparing themselves among themselves, are not wise.

2. God Sets the Boundaries of His Ministry

10:13 Rom 12:3

13 But we will not boast of things without *our* measure, but according to
the measure of the rule which God hath distributed to us, a measure to
reach even unto you.

10:14 1 Cor 9:1

14 For we stretch not ourselves beyond *our measure*, as though we reached
not unto you: for we are come as far as to you also in *preaching* the gospel
of Christ:

10:15 Rom 15:20; 2 Thess 1:3
10:16 Acts 19:21
10:17☆ Jer 9:24; 1 Cor 1:31
10:18☆ Prov 27:2; Lk 18:10; Rom 2:29; 1 Cor 4:5

15 Not boasting of things without *our* measure, *that is,* of other men's
labours; but having hope, when your faith is increased, that we shall be
enlarged by you according to our rule abundantly,
16 To preach the gospel in the *regions* beyond you, *and* not to boast in
another man's line of things made ready to our hand.
17 But he that glorieth, let him glory in the Lord.
18 For not he that commendeth himself is approved, but whom the Lord
commendeth.

10:4 "The doctrines of the gospel and discipline of the church are the weapons of this warfare."* Because they are not carnal, outward force must never be used. Believers can depend on the power of truth, the humility of wisdom, and the persuasive power of the Holy Spirit to do the work.

10:7ff *Paul now reasons* with the Corinthians over against those who have despised him, maligned him, and judged him. He begs them not to judge the gift by the package in which it is wrapped. A man may be learned who has not learned Christ, and he may appear virtuous when he has no virtue in his heart. Paul is now back to using "we" so as to include his fellow-workers with him. Since Paul and they are also ministers of Christ, those who boast that they are ministers of Christ should allow for the fact that Paul and his workers are equally ministers. In Jesus' words, "He who is not against us is for us" (Mark 9:40; Luke 9:50).

10:17, 18 Let no one boast about himself. If we must boast, *let us boast of the Lord and glorify him* (Jer. 9:24). Ministers should be careful to give God all the glory for their work and success, for in and of themselves they are nothing. Whoever commends himself is not thereby commended; that is self-flattery. The man God commends has what counts most.

B. THE AUTHENTICATION OF HIS MINISTRY
1. By His Solicitude for the Corinthians

11 WOULD to God ye could bear with me a little in *my* folly: and
indeed bear with me.
2 For I am jealous over you with godly jealousy: for I have espoused you
to one husband, that I may present *you as* a chaste virgin to Christ.
3 But I fear, lest by any means, as the serpent beguiled Eve through his
subtilty, so your minds should be corrupted from the simplicity that is in
Christ.
4 For if he that cometh preacheth another Jesus, whom we have not
preached, or *if* ye receive another spirit, which ye have not received, or
another gospel, which ye have not accepted, ye might well bear with *him.*
5 For I suppose I was not a whit behind the very chiefest apostles.
6 But though *I be* rude in speech, yet not in knowledge; but we have been
throughly made manifest among you in all things.
7 Have I committed an offence in abasing myself that ye might be exalted,
because I have preached to you the gospel of God freely?
8 I robbed other churches, taking wages *of them,* to do you service.
9 And when I was present with you, and wanted, I was chargeable to no
man: for that which was lacking to me the brethren which came from
Macedonia supplied: and in all *things* I have kept myself from being
burdensome unto you, and *so* will I keep *myself.*
10 As the truth of Christ is in me, no man shall stop me of this boasting in
the regions of A-chai'a.
11 Wherefore? because I love you not? God knoweth.
12 But what I do, that I will do, that I may cut off occasion from them
which desire occasion; that wherein they glory, they may be found even as
we.
13 For such *are* false apostles, deceitful workers, transforming themselves
into the apostles of Christ.
14 And no marvel; for Satan himself is transformed into an angel of light.
15 Therefore *it is* no great thing if his ministers also be transformed as the
ministers of righteousness; whose end shall be according to their works.

☆**11:1** 2 Cor 5:13
11:2 Hos 2:19; 1 Cor 4:15; Gal 4:17; Eph 5:26; Col 1:28
☆**11:3** Gen 3:4; Jn 8:44; 1 Thess 3:5; 1 Tim 1:3; 4:1; 2 Pet 3:17; Jude 4; Rev 12:9
11:4 Rom 8:15; Gal 1:6–8
11:5 2 Cor 12:11; Gal 2:6
11:6 2 Cor 10:10; Eph 3:4
☆**11:7** Acts 18:3; 2 Cor 12:13
11:9 2 Cor 12:14
11:11 2 Cor 7:3; 12:15
☆**11:12** 1 Cor 9:12
☆**11:13** Gal 1:7; Rev 2:2
11:14 Rev 12:9
11:15 Rom 2:6; 3:8; Phil 3:19

2. By His Divine Credentials
a. The Necessity for His Boasting

16 I say again, Let no man think me a fool; if otherwise, yet as a fool
receive me, that I may boast myself a little.

☆**11:16**

11:1 Paul explains that he is bold in his statements, because he fears that the fidelity of his beloved Corinthians may be corrupted. He is jealous for their sake. He apologizes for the argument he is about to advance, but is forced to do so by his opponents. He does not relish controversy. His is a godly jealousy. (Elizabeth Barrett Browning's father loved her so much he would not permit her to marry, but she did. After that, he never opened her letters and refused to see her again. That's jealousy, but it is not godly jealousy.)
11:3 The Corinthian church, Paul fears, may be like Eve, who was taken in by Satan. So may this church be wooed away from its first allegiance to Christ and become unfaithful or adulterous, which is the greatest of sins for the church, the bride of Christ.
11:7 The Corinthians could never say Paul preached to them for the money they gave him. He was self-supporting, and any funds from others were given by "the brethren which came from Macedonia." He did claim in 1 Tim. 5:18 that "the labourer is worthy of his hire," but he never pressed the Corinthians for money to help himself.
11:12 We learn the real reason why Paul refused financial help from the Corinthians. Those who opposed him wanted money; indeed, they demanded it. He says, in effect, "Let them do as I do, preach for nothing." His enemies, who claimed equality with him, could not match him in this.
11:13 Beginning in the New Testament age there were counterfeit apostles who sought to give the impression they were like the true apostles of Jesus Christ. They were "as industrious and as generous in promoting error as the apostles were in preaching truth."* They sought as much to undermine the faith as true believers sought to establish it. What was true then is equally true today and will always be until the end of the age.
11:16ff Now Paul is about to boast about what he has suffered for the sake of Christ. He carefully notes that

11:17 2 Cor 7:4
17 That which I speak, I speak *it* not after the Lord, but as it were
foolishly, in this confidence of boasting.
11:18 Phil 3:3
18 Seeing that many glory after the flesh, I will glory also.
19 For ye suffer fools gladly, seeing ye *yourselves* are wise.
11:20 Gal 2:4; 4:9
20 For ye suffer, if a man bring you into bondage, if a man devour *you*, if
a man take *of you*, if a man exalt himself, if a man smite you on the face.

b. The Reason for His Boasting

11:21 2 Cor 10:10
21 I speak as concerning reproach, as though we had been weak. Howbeit
whereinsoever any is bold, (I speak foolishly,) I am bold also.
11:22 Acts 22:3; Rom 11:1; Phil 3:5
22 Are they Hebrews? so *am* I. Are they Israelites? so *am* I. Are they the
seed of Abraham? so *am* I.
11:23 Rom 8:36; 1 Cor 15:10; 16:23; 2 Cor 6:4, 5
23 Are they ministers of Christ? (I speak as a fool) I *am* more; in labours
more abundant, in stripes above measure, in prisons more frequent, in
deaths oft.
11:24☆ Deut 25:3
24 Of the Jews five times received I forty *stripes* save one.
11:25 Acts 14:19; 16:22; 27:41
25 Thrice was I beaten with rods, once was I stoned, thrice I suffered
shipwreck, a night and a day I have been in the deep;
11:26 Acts 9:23; 13:50; 14:5; 17:5; 19:23; 21:31; 23:10; Gal 2:4
26 *In* journeyings often, *in* perils of waters, *in* perils of robbers, *in* perils by
mine own countrymen, *in* perils by the heathen, *in* perils in the city, *in* perils
in the wilderness, *in* perils in the sea, *in* perils among false brethren;
11:27 1 Cor 4:11; 2 Cor 6:5; 1 Thess 2:9
27 In weariness and painfulness, in watchings often, in hunger and thirst,
in fastings often, in cold and nakedness.
11:28 Acts 20:18; Rom 1:14
28 Beside those things that are without, that which cometh upon me daily,
the care of all the churches.
11:29 1 Cor 9:22
29 Who is weak, and I am not weak? who is offended, and I burn not?
30 If I must needs glory, I will glory of the things which concern mine
infirmities.
11:31☆ Rom 9:5
31 The God and Father of our Lord Jesus Christ, which is blessed for
evermore, knoweth that I lie not.
11:32 Acts 9:24
32 In Damascus the governor under Ar'e-tas the king kept the city of the
Dam'as-cenes with a garrison, desirous to apprehend me:
11:33 Acts 9:25
33 And through a window in a basket was I let down by the wall, and
escaped his hands.

12:1 Gal 1:12
12 IT is not expedient for me doubtless to glory. I will come to visions
and revelations of the Lord.
12:2☆ Deut 10:14; Acts 22:17; Rom 16:7; 2 Cor 5:17; Gal 1:22
2 I knew a man in Christ above fourteen years ago, (whether in the body,
I cannot tell; or whether out of the body, I cannot tell: God knoweth;) such
an one caught up to the third heaven.

Jesus did not directly reveal to him that he should do this. He hopes they will not regard what he is about to do as folly. The circumstances of his case made this step necessary. Now we understand why it was that God allowed Paul to endure so much suffering. It was this suffering that made his case of being under the Lordship of Christ airtight. No one could accuse anyone who had suffered this much of being in the ministry for the sake of gaining money—for there were easier ways of making money than that. Only devotedness *to the living God could explain* why Paul lived and suffered as he did.

11:24 Paul was whipped five times. This shows that Paul subjected himself to synagogue discipline even though he was a Christian. Deut. 25:1–3 limited the beating to forty lashes by the whip. Lest a mistake be made, the Jews stopped at thirty-nine, so as not to break the law. Offenders were stripped of their clothes and bound to two pillars by their outstretched hands. The minister of the synagogue used a triple-thonged lash, and Scripture was read as the beating was given. The *Mishnah* says, "And he that smites, smites with his one hand with all his might."

11:31 So deeply moved is Paul that he calls upon God as his witness to the fact that he has told them the truth. He took, as it were, an oath that he would tell the truth, the whole truth, and nothing but the truth, so help him, God. This calls into the arena the omniscient God, who knows every thought, every intent, and every word that we have spoken or will speak in this life. And he never forgets any of them.

12:2 The word *heaven* (*ouranos*), used more than 275 times in the New Testament, has a variety of meanings. It is spoken of as God's dwelling place (1 Kings 8:30;

3 And I knew such a man, (whether in the body, or out of the body, I
cannot tell: God knoweth;)
4 How that he was caught up into paradise, and heard unspeakable words,
which it is not lawful for a man to utter.
5 Of such an one will I glory: yet of myself I will not glory, but in mine
infirmities.
6 For though I would desire to glory, I shall not be a fool; for I will say
the truth: but *now* I forbear, lest any man should think of me above that
which he seeth me *to be,* or *that* he heareth of me.
7 And lest I should be exalted above measure through the abundance of
the revelations, there was given to me a thorn in the flesh, the messenger of
Satan to buffet me, lest I should be exalted above measure.
8 For this thing I besought the Lord thrice, that it might depart from me.
9 And he said unto me, My grace is sufficient for thee: for my strength is
made perfect in weakness. Most gladly therefore will I rather glory in my
infirmities, that the power of Christ may rest upon me.
10 Therefore I take pleasure in infirmities, in reproaches, in necessities, in
persecutions, in distresses for Christ's sake: for when I am weak, then am I
strong.
11 I am become a fool in glorying; ye have compelled me: for I ought to
have been commended of you: for in nothing am I behind the very chiefest
apostles, though I be nothing.
12 Truly the signs of an apostle were wrought among you in all patience,
in signs, and wonders, and mighty deeds.
13 For what is it wherein ye were inferior to other churches, except *it be*
that I myself was not burdensome to you? forgive me this wrong.

C. PAUL'S PREPARATIONS FOR HIS VISIT
1. His Concern for Them

14 Behold, the third time I am ready to come to you; and I will not be
burdensome to you: for I seek not yours, but you: for the children ought
not to lay up for the parents, but the parents for the children.
15 And I will very gladly spend and be spent for you; though the more
abundantly I love you, the less I be loved.

12:4 Lk 23:43 Rev 2:7
12:5 1 Cor 2:3 2 Cor 11:30
12:6 2 Cor 10:8
☆**12:7** Job 2:7 Lk 13:16 Gal 4:13
☆**12:8** Mt 26:44
12:9 Eccles 7:18 Isa 40:29; 42:10 1 Cor 10:13 Eph 3:16 Phil 4:13 Heb 2:18 1 Pet 4:14 2 Pet 2:9
☆**12:10** Rom 5:3 2 Cor 7:4; 13:4
12:11 1 Cor 15:9, 10 2 Cor 11:15, 16 Gal 2:6
☆**12:12** Rom 15:18, 19 1 Cor 9:1, 2
12:13 1 Cor 1:7; 9:12, 18 2 Cor 11:7
12:14 1 Cor 4:14 9:19; 10:33 2 Cor 13:1
☆**12:15** 2 Cor 1:6; 6:12 11:11 1 Thess 2:8 Phil 2:17

Matt. 6:9), as God's throne (Isa. 66:1; also Acts 7:49), and as God's creation (Rev. 10:6). As the Mediator, Christ entered into heaven (Acts 3:21, 22; Heb. 6:19, 20; 9:11, 24). All the holy angels are in heaven (Matt. 18:10; 24:36), and all of the wicked are forever excluded from heaven (Gal. 5:21; Rev. 22:15). Believers are to lay up treasure in heaven (Matt. 6:20; Luke 12:33), and heaven holds the priceless gift of eternal life which the saints will inherit in the resurrection (1 Pet. 1:4).

12:7 Paul does not say specifically what his thorn in the flesh was. He prayed for its removal, but God declined. The thorn was a messenger from Satan, which means that God permitted Satan to do this even as he permitted Job to suffer under Satan's onslaught. But Satan was defeated, because the thorn made possible the exhibition of the surpassing grace of God. Paul's affliction brought glory to God and allowed Paul to experience the mighty power of God in his life.

12:8 Paul prayed three times (or the word *thrice* may simply mean *often*) that his thorn in the flesh might be removed. God answered his prayer by saying no. But God helped Paul by giving him a sufficiency of divine grace that he might bear the infirmity in a manner by which God would be glorified. No doubt the example in the life of Paul should assist us today when God, for our spiritual benefit, does not take away from us some of the physical burdens he has sent. So Paul and we can glory in our infirmities, knowing that God produces strength out of our weaknesses and disabilities.

12:10 For the sake of Christ, for whom he is willing to do anything and suffer anything, Paul proclaims his willingness to experience infirmities, reproaches, necessities, persecutions, and distresses. And so ought we who follow the same Master.

12:12 God gave the apostles outward, confirming, extraordinary indicators to show they were what they said they were and to keep their listeners from ever saying they were uninformed or there was no way they could tell whether the apostles were telling the truth. They had the power to perform "signs, and wonders, and mighty deeds." These were sufficient and beyond question, so that those who refused to heed their words and their works (which gave credence to their words) would have no defense in the day of judgment.

12:15 The love of Paul for the Corinthians did not abate; it increased more and more. He was willing to serve them and teach them, even if the more he loved them, the less they loved him.

12:16 2 Cor 11:9

[16]But be it so, I did not burden you: nevertheless, being crafty, I caught
you with guile.

12:17 2 Cor 7:2; 9:5
12:18 2 Cor 8:6, 18

[17]Did I make a gain of you by any of them whom I sent unto you?
[18]I desired Titus, and with *him* I sent a brother. Did Titus make a gain of
you? walked we not in the same spirit? *walked we* not in the same steps?

2. His Call to Repentance

12:19 Rom 9:1; 1 Cor 10:33; 2 Cor 5:12; 11:31
12:20☆ 1 Cor 4:21

[19]Again, think ye that we excuse ourselves unto you? we speak before
God in Christ: but *we do* all things, dearly beloved, for your edifying.
[20]For I fear, lest, when I come, I shall not find you such as I would, and
that I shall be found unto you such as ye would not: lest *there be* debates,
envyings, wraths, strifes, backbitings, whisperings, swellings, tumults:

12:21 1 Cor 5:1; 2 Cor 2:1, 4; Gal 5:19; Phil 3:18

[21]*And* lest, when I come again, my God will humble me among you, and
that I shall bewail many which have sinned already, and have not repented
of the uncleanness and fornication and lasciviousness which they have
committed.

13:1 Num 35:30; Deut 19:15; Acts 18:1; 2 Cor 2:1; 12:14
13:2☆ 2 Cor 1:23; 10:2; 12:21

13 THIS *is* the third *time* I am coming to you. In the mouth of two or
three witnesses shall every word be established.
[2]I told you before, and foretell you, as if I were present, the second time;
and being absent now I write to them which heretofore have sinned, and to
all other, that, if I come again, I will not spare:

13:3 Mt 10:20; 1 Cor 7:40; 9:2

[3]Since ye seek a proof of Christ speaking in me, which to you-ward is not
weak, but is mighty in you.

13:4 2 Cor 10:3, 4; Rom 1:4; 6:4; Phil 2:7, 8; 1 Pet 3:18

[4]For though he was crucified through weakness, yet he liveth by the
power of God. For we also are weak in him, but we shall live with him by
the power of God toward you.

3. His Promise if They Repent

13:5☆ Jn 14:20; 17:23, 26; Rom 8:10; 1 Cor 9:27; 11:28; Gal 4:19; Col 1:27
13:7 2 Cor 6:9

[5]Examine yourselves, whether ye be in the faith; prove your own selves.
Know ye not your own selves, how that Jesus Christ is in you, except ye be
reprobates?
[6]But I trust that ye shall know that we are not reprobates.
[7]Now I pray to God that ye do no evil; not that we should appear
approved, but that ye should do that which is honest, though we be as
reprobates.
[8]For we can do nothing against the truth, but for the truth.

13:9 1 Cor 4:10; Eph 4:12–16; 1 Thess 3:10
13:10 Tit 1:13

[9]For we are glad, when we are weak, and ye are strong: and this also we
wish, *even* your perfection.
[10]Therefore I write these things being absent, lest being present I should
use sharpness, according to the power which the Lord hath given me to
edification, and not to destruction.

12:20 Paul warns the Corinthians of his fears that the sinners among them may not repent and thus the problems may continue to persist. In that event he will come to reprove and rebuke them, and they will find *him not to be what they expected because they would* not be as he had expected and had hoped for.

13:2ff *I will not spare.* The apostle means business and speaks forthrightly. If he comes and finds things out of order, he will not spare anyone. He will do it so that they know Christ is speaking in him. This Jesus was crucified in weakness, and Paul preaches in weakness, without outward charisma or power. But both the Son of God and the apostle have the power of God working in and through them.

13:5 Paul's exhortation for the Corinthian Christians to examine themselves to be sure they are in the faith is important. There are people who make false professions of faith in Christ either deliberately or unwittingly. Paul would have such people and all of us today examine ourselves to be certain that we are not reprobates, but are firmly grounded on the true Rock, Jesus Christ, who is in us by faith.

VI. CONCLUDING EXHORTATION AND BENEDICTION (13:11–14)

11 Finally, brethren, farewell. Be perfect, be of good comfort, be of one
mind, live in peace; and the God of love and peace shall be with you.
12 Greet one another with an holy kiss.
13 All the saints salute you.
14 The grace of the Lord Jesus Christ, and the love of God, and the
communion of the Holy Ghost, *be* with you all. Amen.

☆**13:11** Rom 12:16; 15:33; 1 Cor 1:10; 1 Pet 3:8
13:13 Rom 5:5; 16:20; Phil 2:1
☆**13:14**

13:11 When the people of God are knit together in love, are living in peace, of one mind, and enduring their sufferings gracefully, they have the promise that the God of love and peace will be present among them.
13:14 Paul concludes this epistle with his trinitarian, apostolic benediction, in which he pronounces, not prays for, the grace of Christ, the love of the Father, and the communion of the Holy Spirit. The word "Trinity" does not appear in Scripture. However, Christianity has always been trinitarian. This doctrine asserts that God is one in essence, eternally subsisting in three persons, the Father, the Son, and the Holy Spirit. In Matt. 3:16, 17, at the baptism of Jesus, the Holy Spirit appears as a dove, and the Father's voice is heard; also in Matt. 28:19 the trinitarian baptismal formula is given (into the name of the Father and of the Son and of the Holy Spirit). Other biblical evidences for the Trinity can be found in Rom. 8:9; 1 Cor. 12:3–6; Eph. 4:4–6; 1 Pet. 1:2; Jude 20, 21; Rev. 1:4, 5. All three persons of the Trinity share the same divine attributes. Each has a unique office or work to do. God the Father sent Jesus the Son; God the Son died on Calvary's cross. The Father and the Son sent the Holy Spirit, who seals and indwells every believer. Salvation is the work of the Trinity (the Father, the Son, and the Holy Spirit), according to Titus 3:4–6 and 2 Thess. 2:13, 14.

THE EPISTLE OF PAUL THE APOSTLE TO THE

GALATIANS

Authorship, date, and background The apostle Paul was the author of the Galatian letter. His Damascus Road conversion experience occurred around A.D. 32. The letter was composed after he had been in the ministry fifteen or more years. He was known as the apostle to the Gentiles, that is, to the non-Jews. One of the great questions of that day had to do with the relationship of new converts to Judaism. The Old Testament clearly taught that salvation is by faith alone. But Judaism insisted on the necessity of circumcision and the keeping of the law as part of the salvatory process. Some Jewish Christians and non-Jews who had been circumcised and who followed the law insisted that faith alone was insufficient for salvation. Known as the Judaizers, they followed Paul as he evangelized, insisting that converts keep the law and be circumcised. This was true in the region of Galatia where Paul's ministry had been quite successful. Paul did not hesitate to accept the challenge, since salvation by faith alone was foundational to his understanding of the Good News. Any concession at this point would destroy the entire faith.

The dating of Galatians depends in large measure on the question of the destination of the letter—whether it was addressed to the Christians of South Galatia or North Galatia. Paul visited South Galatia on his first missionary expedition, and since the letter to the Galatians does not mention the first missionary council at Jerusalem, some suppose it was composed around A.D. 49 and sent to South Galatia. This would make it the earliest of Paul's writings. Others, however, date the letter A.D. 55–56, since Acts 16:6 and 18:23 specifically mention visits to Galatia by Paul on his second and third journeys, which occurred after the Jerusalem conference (Acts 15). Whether the letter was written in A.D. 49 or A.D. 55–56, as so many hold, is not of great importance, for the Pauline authorship is not in question and the contents of the letter have universal and enduring value. In any event, the books of Galatians and Romans constitute the most systematic theological presentation of the Good News with all of its implications. They are the most highly didactic (teaching) books in the New Testament, and all of the other letters in the New Testament must be understood in the light of these.

Characteristics and content Galatians has been called "the Magna Charta of spiritual emancipation" and was for Martin Luther what he called "my own little epistle." He said, "I have betrothed myself to it." For the apostle Paul the issue at stake is the most important one relating to his preaching of the gospel. At the heart of the controversy lies this question: "Is a man saved by faith alone or by a combination of faith plus works?" Stated another way, it involves a choice between faith or works, between grace or law. The Judaizers were saying that new believers should be circumcised and observe Jewish laws and customs, one of which was the refusal to eat with non-Jews (Gentiles). Paul rightly sees that the principle involved is of such magnitude that to compromise the issue will result in the loss of the true gospel and bring men into the bondage from which the same Good News is supposed to free them. He claims in Galatians that the gospel he knows has not come from men, but from God by way of direct revelation. "The tone of the book is warlike. It fairly crackles with indignation though it is not the anger of personal pique but of spiritual principle" (M. C. Tenney). Thus, Paul can say with vehemence and without apology or likelihood of change: men are justified (saved) by faith rather than by the works of the law. Anyone who mixes in works as a basis for salvation is preaching another gospel. And Paul places an anathema (a solemn ban or curse) on anyone who does this. In Galatians he summarizes the gospel he preaches. Later Paul will reaffirm and *expand the central* truths of Galatians in his letter to the Romans.

What Paul does not say is of equal importance, for there are some who *think that the* apostles James and Paul are in sharp disagreement. What Paul is saying is that men are saved by faith alone, but saving faith is always accompanied by good works; that is, the saved man produces the fruits of righteousness which are displayed in a transformed walk and a holy life. But works follow faith and salvation is by grace alone without works of any kind.

Outline

I. Introduction (1:1–10)
II. God's special revelation to Paul (1:11—2:21)
III. Right standing by faith discussed and depicted (3:1—4:31)
IV. The effect of Christian freedom (5:1—6:10)
V. Conclusion (6:11–18)

I. INTRODUCTION (1:1–10)

A. APOSTOLIC GREETING

1 PAUL, an apostle, (not of men, neither by man, but by Jesus Christ,
and God the Father, who raised him from the dead;)
2 And all the brethren which are with me, unto the churches of Ga-la'tia:
3 Grace *be* to you and peace from God the Father, and *from* our Lord
Jesus Christ,
4 Who gave himself for our sins, that he might deliver us from this present
evil world, according to the will of God and our Father:
5 To whom *be* glory for ever and ever. Amen.

B. THE REASON FOR THE LETTER

6 I marvel that ye are so soon removed from him that called you into the
grace of Christ unto another gospel:
7 Which is not another; but there be some that trouble you, and would
pervert the gospel of Christ.
8 But though we, or an angel from heaven, preach any other gospel unto
you than that which we have preached unto you, let him be accursed.
9 As we said before, so say I now again, If any *man* preach any other
gospel unto you than that ye have received, let him be accursed.
10 For do I now persuade men, or God? or do I seek to please men? for if
I yet pleased men, I should not be the servant of Christ.

☆**1:1, 2** Acts 20:24; 1 Cor 16:1; 2 Cor 1:1; Gal 1:11; Phil 4:21
1:3 Rom 1:7
☆**1:4** Isa 65:17; Jn 15:19; 17:14; Rom 4:25; Col 1:13; 1 Jn 2:2
1:5 Rom 11:36
☆**1:6** 2 Cor 11:4
1:7 Acts 15:1; Gal 5:10
☆**1:8** 2 Cor 11:14
1:9 Deut 4:2; 12:32; Prov 30:6; Rev 22:18
1:10 1 Thess 2:4

II. GOD'S SPECIAL REVELATION TO PAUL (1:11—2:21)

A. ITS DIVINE SOURCE

11 But I certify you, brethren, that the gospel which was preached of me is
not after man.
12 For I neither received it of man, neither was I taught *it*, but by the
revelation of Jesus Christ.

1:11 1 Cor 15:1–3
☆**1:12** 1 Cor 2:10; Gal 1:15, 16; Eph 3:3

1:1ff The three essential themes of this letter are included in the salutation: (1) Paul's apostolic authority; (2) the doctrine of justification by faith alone; and (3) the life believers should live, i.e., their sanctification, which always follows justification.

1:4 Jesus died to accomplish redemption for us. Three principles underlie what Jesus did on the cross: (1) the principle of "covering," by which the believer's sins are covered over by Christ's blood so that they are no longer seen by God (Rom. 4:7); (2) the principle of reconciliation through expiation, i.e., through the payment of the penalty for sin by Jesus Christ our sin-bearer, divine justice has been vindicated and the sinner brought back into fellowship with God (Eph. 2:16; Col. 1:20); (3) the principle of substitution, by which Jesus Christ died the death believers should have died, i.e., he took their place and died in their stead (2 Cor. 5:21; 1 Pet. 2:24).

1:6 Paul writes as one deeply moved by the possibility that his beloved Galatians have defected from grace. He pronounces an anathema and calls for radical surgery on those who argue in favor of circumcision (5:12). To him, insistence on circumcision as part of the salvatory process is a matter of life and death, for grace and works cannot be mixed.

1:8 *let him be accursed.* The Greek word used here is *anathema;* it speaks of an "object devoted to destruction." The word, in this sense, is used here and in Rom. 9:3; 1 Cor. 12:3; 16:22; and in Acts 23:12–14, where it refers to the curse that is to bring destruction. Traditionally, an anathema is a pronouncement against an individual by an ecclesiastical body, accompanied by excommunication.

1:12 Those who were the disciples of Jesus when he was on earth could say they had received their knowledge of the gospel by direct revelation. They

1:13 Acts 8:3; 9:21; 22:3–5; 26:4–11
1:14 Acts 26:3

13 For ye have heard of my conversation in time past in the Jews' religion,
how that beyond measure I persecuted the church of God, and wasted it:
14 And profited in the Jews' religion above many my equals in mine own
nation, being more exceedingly zealous of the traditions of my fathers.

1:15☆ Acts 9:15; 15:10; Eph 2:3
1:16☆ Rom 1:17; 8:3, 10; Gal 2:9, 20; Col 1:27
1:17 1 Jn 3:8

15 But when it pleased God, who separated me from my mother's womb,
and called *me* by his grace,
16 To reveal his Son in me, that I might preach him among the heathen;
immediately I conferred not with flesh and blood:
17 Neither went I up to Jerusalem to them which were apostles before me;
but I went into Arabia, and returned again unto Damascus.

B. ITS INDEPENDENCE FROM THE OTHER APOSTLES

1:18☆ Acts 9:26
1:19 Mt 13:55; Acts 12:17; 15:13; 21:18; 1 Cor 15:7; Gal 2:9, 12
1:23 Acts 9:20

18 Then after three years I went up to Jerusalem to see Peter, and abode
with him fifteen days.
19 But other of the apostles saw I none, save James the Lord's brother.
20 Now the things which I write unto you, behold, before God, I lie not.
21 Afterwards I came into the regions of Syria and Ci-li′ci-a;
22 And was unknown by face unto the churches of Judæa which were in
Christ:
23 But they had heard only, That he which persecuted us in times past
now preacheth the faith which once he destroyed.
24 And they glorified God in me.

C. PAUL'S ACCEPTANCE BY THE CHURCH

2:1 Acts 15:2–29
2:2 Gal 1:6
2:3☆ Acts 16:3
2:4 Gal 1:7; 4:3, 9; 5:1

2 THEN fourteen years after I went up again to Jerusalem with
Barnabas, and took Titus with *me* also.
2 And I went up by revelation, and communicated unto them that gospel
which I preach among the Gentiles, but privately to them which were of
reputation, lest by any means I should run, or had run, in vain.
3 But neither Titus, who was with me, being a Greek, was compelled to be
circumcised:
4 And that because of false brethren unawares brought in, who came in
privily to spy out our liberty which we have in Christ Jesus, that they might
bring us into bondage:

2:5 Gal 1:6; 2:14
2:6 Acts 10:34; Rom 2:11; 2 Cor 12:11; Gal 6:3
2:7☆ Acts 13:46
2:8☆ Acts 9:15; 13:2; 22:21; 26:17; 1 Cor 15:10; Col 1:29

5 To whom we gave place by subjection, no, not for an hour; that the
truth of the gospel might continue with you.
6 But of these who seemed to be somewhat, (whatsoever they were, it
maketh no matter to me: God accepteth no man's person:) for they who
seemed *to be somewhat* in conference added nothing to me:
7 But contrariwise, when they saw that the gospel of the uncircumcision
was committed unto me, as *the gospel* of the circumcision *was* unto Peter;
8 (For he that wrought effectually in Peter to the apostleship of the
circumcision, the same was mighty in me toward the Gentiles:)

---

received it directly from Jesus. Paul did not know or see Jesus in the flesh. Normally he would have received his knowledge of the gospel through other human beings, but Paul affirmed that he obtained his knowledge of the gospel directly from Jesus Christ through special revelation. He did not receive it from *men nor was he taught by men.* He was taught by the risen Lord who appeared to him and who instructed him. Jesus was the source of his apostolate. The call was from Jesus Christ and the Father.

1:15, 16 In the sovereignty of God, Paul was set apart by God for salvation and service before he was born. He was called by grace, which was effective in his conversion, at which time Christ was revealed *in* him, not simply *to* him.

1:18 Peter's name in Aramaic is *Cephas; Peter* is the Greek form. Both mean "rock." Many translations use the name Cephas.

2:3 Paul wanted to make it clear that the ceremonial law contributed nothing to salvation. He refused to have Titus, a non-Jew, *circumcised. Paul and Titus* worked together. This demonstrated to all that Paul was not afraid to own his doctrine that salvation is by faith alone—faith plus nothing.

2:7–9 Peter and Paul preached the same gospel. Paul was called to preach to the Gentiles; Peter to the Jews.

9 And when James, Ce'phas, and John, who seemed to be pillars,
perceived the grace that was given unto me, they gave to me and Barnabas
the right hands of fellowship; that we *should go* unto the heathen, and they
unto the circumcision.

2:9 Mt 16:18 Rom 1:5 Rev 21:14

10 Only *they would* that we should remember the poor; the same which I
also was forward to do.

2:10 Acts 11:30 24:17

D. HIS PUBLIC REBUKE OF PETER FOR HIS ERROR

11 But when Peter was come to Antioch, I withstood him to the face,
because he was to be blamed.

☆**2:11**

12 For before that certain came from James, he did eat with the Gentiles:
but when they were come, he withdrew and separated himself, fearing them
which were of the circumcision.

2:12 Acts 10:28; 11:2, 3

13 And the other Jews dissembled likewise with him; insomuch that
Barnabas also was carried away with their dissimulation.
14 But when I saw that they walked not uprightly according to the truth of
the gospel, I said unto Peter before *them* all, If thou, being a Jew, livest after
the manner of Gentiles, and not as do the Jews, why compellest thou the
Gentiles to live as do the Jews?

2:14 Acts 11:3

15 We *who are* Jews by nature, and not sinners of the Gentiles,
16 Knowing that a man is not justified by the works of the law, but by the
faith of Jesus Christ, even we have believed in Jesus Christ, that we might
be justified by the faith of Christ, and not by the works of the law: for by
the works of the law shall no flesh be justified.
17 But if, while we seek to be justified by Christ, we ourselves also are
found sinners, *is* therefore Christ the minister of sin? God forbid.
18 For if I build again the things which I destroyed, I make myself a
transgressor.

2:15 Acts 15:10 Eph 2:3 Phil 3:4
☆**2:16** Acts 13:39 Rom 1:17; 3:20 8:3 Heb 7:18
2:17 1 Jn 3:8

19 For I through the law am dead to the law, that I might live unto God.
20 I am crucified with Christ: nevertheless I live; yet not I, but Christ
liveth in me: and the life which I now live in the flesh I live by the faith of
the Son of God, who loved me, and gave himself for me.
21 I do not frustrate the grace of God: for if righteousness *come* by the
law, then Christ is dead in vain.

2:19 Rom 6:2, 14; 7:4 8:2 Heb 9:14
☆**2:20** Rom 6:6 2 Cor 5:15
2:21 Heb 7:11

III. RIGHT STANDING BY FAITH DISCUSSED AND DEPICTED (3:1—4:31)

A. THE GIFT OF THE SPIRIT BY FAITH

3 O FOOLISH Ga-la'tians, who hath bewitched you, that ye should not
obey the truth, before whose eyes Jesus Christ hath been evidently set
forth, crucified among you?

☆**3:1** 1 Cor 1:23 Gal 5:7

2:11 Peter was not rebuked by Paul because he was a heretic; rather, it was his failure to practice what he himself believed in principle. Peter never taught that a man can be saved by circumcision (see 2:14), but he refused to fellowship with uncircumcised Gentiles because he was being pressured to do so by circumcised Hebrew Christians. He probably did not wish to offend prospective Jewish converts. Paul said that his policy of expediency was really a surrender of a basic principle, namely, that salvation is purely of grace without obedience to the ritual law of Moses. We are to be concerned for weaker brothers' consciences, but when this leads to a betrayal of the gospel it is wrong. And Peter was wrong.

2:16 From beginning to end the believer's life depends on faith. Scripture provides illustrations of this truth as follows: the believer (1) lives by faith (2:20); (2) is kept by faith and stands firm through it (1 Pet. 1:5); (3) resists the devil and overcomes him by faith (1 Pet. 5:8, 9; Eph. 6:16); (4) walks by faith (2 Cor. 5:7—from the Greek, "for we walk through faith, not through appearance.")

2:20 Paul here employs amazing paradoxes concerning his relationship to Jesus Christ. He is dead to the law that he might live unto God. He is crucified, yet he lives. He is dead to the world and to the law, yet he is alive to God and Jesus Christ. He lives and yet not he. He is crucified with Christ and yet Christ lives in him. He lives in the flesh and yet lives by faith. This scripture is grand!

3:1–5 The Galatians had the cross of Christ preached to them. When they received Christ, they were given

3:2 Acts 2:38 Rom 10:17 2 This only would I learn of you, Received ye the Spirit by the works of
the law, or by the hearing of faith?
3:3 Gal 4:9 Heb 7:16 3 Are ye so foolish? having begun in the Spirit, are ye now made perfect
by the flesh?
3:4 2 Jn 8 4 Have ye suffered so many things in vain? if *it be* yet in vain.
3:5 Phil 1:19 5 He therefore that ministereth to you the Spirit, and worketh miracles
among you, *doeth he it* by the works of the law, or by the hearing of faith?

B. THE ILLUSTRATION OF ABRAHAM

3:6☆ Gen 15:6 Rom 4:3 6 Even as Abraham believed God, and it was accounted to him for
righteousness.
3:7 Jn 8:39 7 Know ye therefore that they which are of faith, the same are the children
of Abraham.
3:8 Gen 12:3 8 And the scripture, foreseeing that God would justify the heathen
through faith, preached before the gospel unto Abraham, *saying,* In thee
shall all nations be blessed.
9 So then they which be of faith are blessed with faithful Abraham.

C. FAITH ALONE SAVES

3:10☆ Deut 27:26 Jer 11:3 10 For as many as are of the works of the law are under the curse: for it is
written, Cursed *is* every one that continueth not in all things which are
written in the book of the law to do them.
3:11☆ Hab 2:4 11 But that no man is justified by the law in the sight of God, *it is* evident:
for, The just shall live by faith.
3:12 Lev 18:5 Rom 4:4; 11:6 12 And the law is not of faith: but, The man that doeth them shall live in
them.
3:13 Deut 21:23 13 Christ hath redeemed us from the curse of the law, being made a curse
for us: for it is written, Cursed *is* every one that hangeth on a tree:
3:14 Isa 44:3 Joel 2:28 Acts 2:33 Eph 1:13 14 That the blessing of Abraham might come on the Gentiles through
Jesus Christ; that we might receive the promise of the Spirit through faith.

D. GOD'S COVENANT WITH ABRAHAM

3:15 Heb 9:17 15 Brethren, I speak after the manner of men; Though *it be* but a man's
covenant, yet *if it be* confirmed, no man disannulleth, or addeth thereto.
3:16 Gen 22:17, 18 16 Now to Abraham and his seed were the promises made. He saith not,
And to seeds, as of many; but as of one, And to thy seed, which is Christ.
3:17 Ex 12:40 Rom 4:13, 14 17 And this I say, *that* the covenant, that was confirmed before of God in
Christ, the law, which was four hundred and thirty years after, cannot
disannul, that it should make the promise of none effect.
3:18 Rom 4:14 Heb 6:14 18 For if the inheritance *be* of the law, *it is* no more of promise: but God
gave *it* to Abraham by promise.

E. THE ROLE OF THE LAW

3:19 Ex 20:19 Deut 5:5; 33:2 Jn 15:22 Acts 7:53 1 Tim 1:9 Heb 2:2 19 Wherefore then *serveth* the law? It was added because of transgressions,
till the seed should come to whom the promise was made; *and it was*
ordained by angels in the hand of a mediator.

---

the Spirit by faith, not by the works of the law. Paul *warns them not to go back to the law when they had* started in the Spirit by faith, without the law.

3:6 For God's covenant with Abraham, see note to Gen. 12:2.

3:10 Men fall under the curse of God who has given us the law. No one has ever been able to keep the whole law of God, so all fall under the condemnation of God. The breaking of a single commandment makes men guilty of having broken the whole law of God. Men could be saved if they kept the whole law of God. But since all men sin and fall short of God's glory, another way had to be found if men were to be saved. Christ became a curse for us, and by faith in him believers are redeemed from the curse of the law.

3:11 See note to Hab. 2:4 for salvation by faith alone.

20 Now a mediator is not *a mediator* of one, but God is one.
21 *Is* the law then against the promises of God? God forbid: for if there
had been a law given which could have given life, verily righteousness
should have been by the law.
22 But the scripture hath concluded all under sin, that the promise by faith
of Jesus Christ might be given to them that believe.

F. THE PRIMACY OF FAITH OVER LAW

23 But before faith came, we were kept under the law, shut up unto the
faith which should afterwards be revealed.
24 Wherefore the law was our schoolmaster *to bring us* unto Christ, that we
might be justified by faith.
25 But after that faith is come, we are no longer under a schoolmaster.
26 For ye are all the children of God by faith in Christ Jesus.
27 For as many of you as have been baptized into Christ have put on
Christ.
28 There is neither Jew nor Greek, there is neither bond nor free, there is
neither male nor female: for ye are all one in Christ Jesus.
29 And if ye *be* Christ's, then are ye Abraham's seed, and heirs according
to the promise.

4 NOW I say, *That* the heir, as long as he is a child, differeth nothing
from a servant, though he be lord of all;
2 But is under tutors and governors until the time appointed of the father.
3 Even so we, when we were children, were in bondage under the elements
of the world:
4 But when the fulness of the time was come, God sent forth his Son,
made of a woman, made under the law,
5 To redeem them that were under the law, that we might receive the
adoption of sons.
6 And because ye are sons, God hath sent forth the Spirit of his Son into
your hearts, crying, Abba, Father.
7 Wherefore thou art no more a servant, but a son; and if a son, then an
heir of God through Christ.

3:20 1 Tim 2:5
3:22 Rom 11:32
☆**3:24** Mt 5:17
3:26 Jn 1:12; Rom 8:14, 15; Gal 4:5
3:27 Rom 6:3
☆**3:28** Jn 10:16; 17:21; 1 Cor 12:13; Col 3:10, 11
3:29 Gen 21:10; Rom 8:17; 9:7; Gal 3:16; 4:28; Heb 11:18
☆**4:1**
4:3 Col 2:8; Heb 9:10
4:4 Gen 3:15; Dan 9:24; Mt 5:17; Mk 1:15; Jn 1:14; Eph 1:10; Heb 2:14
☆**4:5** Mt 20:28; Jn 1:12; Rom 8:14, 15; Eph 1:5; 1 Pet 1:18
4:7 Rom 8:16, 17

3:24 God's law is good but it cannot save. It is designed to show man his deficiencies, but it cannot deliver him from them. It enlightens him but does not empower him. It reveals what he ought to be like and tells what he ought to do, but it cannot make him what he should be or give him strength to do what he knows he should. Salvation by keeping the law would be salvation by works, because God has ordained that salvation shall be of grace without works. Moreover, since no man can keep the law, works fall short with respect to saving efficacy.

3:28 *neither Jew nor Greek . . . neither male nor female.* All who believe are baptized into Christ; in him there are no distinctions. Jews and Gentiles can come to him with no distinction. So can male and female. So can black and white. So can slave and master. Earthly distinctions, however, do not disappear when salvation comes. But in heaven racial distinctions, national barriers, sexual discrimination, and all other biases will cease.

4:1 Paul now uses the illustration of a child under age to signify the Old Testament dispensation. It was an age of darkness and bondage when compared to the liberty and light under the gospel. In the fullness of time God put an end to the legal dispensation and brought in the gospel age; i.e., the old covenant gave way to the new covenant in Jesus Christ. Jesus came to redeem those who were under the law, which could not save.

4:5 *adoption* (*huiothesia,* "placing as a son") is a New Testament word used only by Paul and has legal connotations. Believers through the new birth are adopted into the family of God and made sons and daughters of God. It does not come from natural birth but by supernatural regeneration. Adoption has privileges and responsibilities attached to it because God has ordained that believers "should become like his Son" (Rom. 8:29, TLB). Among the privileges, adopted children (1) are objects of the Father's love (John 17:23); (2) bear God's image (Rom. 8:29; 2 Pet. 1:4); (3) are indwelt by God's Spirit (4:6); (4) have his name (1 John 3:1); (5) are disciplined and trained by God the Father (Heb. 12:5–11); and (6) are God's heirs who share his treasures (Rom. 8:17; 1 Pet. 1:4). God's sons and daughters are responsible to do the Father's will, embrace the Father's teaching, witness to the Father's love, and obey the Father's commandments.

G. THE BONDAGE OF LEGALISM

4:8 8 Howbeit then, when ye knew not God, ye did service unto them which
2 Chron 13:9 Rom 1:25 by nature are no gods.
1 Cor 8:4 Eph 2:12 9 But now, after that ye have known God, or rather are known of God,
1 Thess 1:9 how turn ye again to the weak and beggarly elements, whereunto ye desire
4:9 Col 2:20 again to be in bondage?
4:10 10 Ye observe days, and months, and times, and years.
Rom 14:5 Col 2:16 11 I am afraid of you, lest I have bestowed upon you labour in vain.
4:12 12 Brethren, I beseech you, be as I *am;* for I *am* as ye *are:* ye have not
Gal 6:14 injured me at all.
4:13☆ 13 Ye know how through infirmity of the flesh I preached the gospel unto
1 Cor 2:3 Gal 1:6 you at the first.
4:14 14 And my temptation which was in my flesh ye despised not, nor
Mt 10:40 1 Thess 2:13 rejected; but received me as an angel of God, *even* as Christ Jesus.
15 Where is then the blessedness ye spake of? for I bear you record, that,
if *it had been* possible, ye would have plucked out your own eyes, and have
given them to me.
4:16 16 Am I therefore become your enemy, because I tell you the truth?
Amos 5:10 4:17☆ 17 They zealously affect you, *but* not well; yea, they would exclude you,
Rom 10:2 that ye might affect them.
18 But *it is* good to be zealously affected always in *a* good *thing*, and not
only when I am present with you.
4:19 19 My little children, of whom I travail in birth again until Christ be
1 Cor 4:15 Eph 3:17; 4:13 formed in you,
20 I desire to be present with you now, and to change my voice; for I stand
in doubt of you.
4:21☆ 21 Tell me, ye that desire to be under the law, do ye not hear the law?
4:22 22 For it is written, that Abraham had two sons, the one by a bondmaid,
Gen 16:15; 21:2 the other by a freewoman.
4:23 23 But he *who was* of the bondwoman was born after the flesh; but he of
Gen 18:10 Rom 9:7, 8 the freewoman *was* by promise.
4:24 24 Which things are an allegory: for these are the two covenants; the one
Deut 32:2–4 from the mount Si′nai, which gendereth to bondage, which is A′gar.
25 For this A′gar is mount Si′nai in Arabia, and answereth to Jerusalem
which now is, and is in bondage with her children.
4:26 26 But Jerusalem which is above is free, which is the mother of us all.
Heb 12:22 Rev 3:12; 21:2 27 For it is written, Rejoice, *thou* barren that bearest not; break forth and
4:27 Isa 54:1 cry, thou that travailest not: for the desolate hath many more children than
she which hath an husband.
4:28 Rom 4:16 28 Now we, brethren, as Isaac was, are the children of promise.
Gal 3:29 4:29 29 But as then he that was born after the flesh persecuted him *that was*
Gen 21:9 *born* after the Spirit, even so *it is* now.

4:13 Nobody knows what Paul's bodily ailment was. Paul's only mention of it comes here and in 2 Cor. 12:7–10. We may suppose that it was chronic, recurrent, painful, and repulsive to others as well as humiliating to the apostle himself. Malaria, epilepsy, migraine, and ophthalmia have all been suggested.

4:17ff Paul here warns against the false teachers, the *Judaizers, who want to bring the* Galatians under the law from which they have been delivered. The Judaizers are more interested in themselves than in the Galatians, but they pretend to be interested in order to seduce them. So great is his concern for the Galatians that he says he travailed for them as a woman giving birth to a baby. They are his little children, and he continues to travail for them until Christ is fully formed in them. He has no ulterior motive and seeks nothing for himself.

4:21ff Paul illustrates the difference between those who trust Christ and those who trust the law. He mentions Isaac and Ishmael in an allegory. Ishmael represents Sinai and the law, which leads to bondage and death. He was the son of a bondwoman. But Isaac was the son of promise. He represents Jerusalem, which is free and has life. Christ is the true inheritor of the covenant made by God with Abraham and his seed. The son of the bondwoman shall not inherit what belongs to the son of the promise.

30 Nevertheless what saith the scripture? Cast out the bondwoman and
her son: for the son of the bondwoman shall not be heir with the son of the
freewoman.

4:30 Gen 21:10; Jn 8:35; Gal 3:8

31 So then, brethren, we are not children of the bondwoman, but of the
free.

IV. THE EFFECT OF CHRISTIAN FREEDOM (5:1—6:10)

A. THE CONSEQUENCES OF LEGALISM

5 STAND fast therefore in the liberty wherewith Christ hath made us
free, and be not entangled again with the yoke of bondage.

☆**5:1** Jn 8:32; Acts 15:10; Gal 2:4

2 Behold, I Paul say unto you, that if ye be circumcised, Christ shall profit
you nothing.

☆**5:2** Acts 15:1

3 For I testify again to every man that is circumcised, that he is a debtor
to do the whole law.

5:3 Gal 3:10

4 Christ is become of no effect unto you, whosoever of you are justified by
the law; ye are fallen from grace.

5:4 Heb 12:15

5 For we through the Spirit wait for the hope of righteousness by faith.

☆**5:5** Rom 8:23

6 For in Jesus Christ neither circumcision availeth any thing, nor
uncircumcision; but faith which worketh by love.

☆**5:6** Col 3:11; 1 Thess 1:3; Jas 2:18

7 Ye did run well; who did hinder you that ye should not obey the truth?

5:7 1 Cor 9:24

8 This persuasion *cometh* not of him that calleth you.

☆**5:8** Rom 8:28

9 A little leaven leaveneth the whole lump.

5:9 1 Cor 5:6

10 I have confidence in you through the Lord, that ye will be none
otherwise minded: but he that troubleth you shall bear his judgment,
whosoever he be.

5:10 Gal 1:7

11 And I, brethren, if I yet preach circumcision, why do I yet suffer
persecution? then is the offence of the cross ceased.

5:11 1 Cor 1:23; 15:30

12 I would they were even cut off which trouble you.

5:12 Acts 15:1; 1 Cor 5:13

B. DEFINITION OF FREEDOM

13 For, brethren, ye have been called unto liberty; only *use* not liberty for
an occasion to the flesh, but by love serve one another.

☆**5:13** 1 Pet 2:16

5:1 *Christ hath made us free.* This is Christian liberty obtained through Jesus' work (Col. 1:13; Gal. 4:3–5). True liberty consists in freedom from (1) the law (Rom. 7:6; 8:2); (2) the curse of the law (3:13); (3) the fear of death (Heb. 2:15); (4) sin (Rom. 6:7, 18); and (5) the Old Testament ceremonial laws (4:3; Col. 2:20). But liberty must not become license; we must not be antinomians. Liberty brings the believer by voluntary choice into total subjection to Jesus Christ, based upon what Jesus has done for him. The great freedom or liberty is to be found by the one who is in bondage to Jesus Christ, though this appears to be paradoxical.

5:2 The Judaizers said that one must be circumcised and keep the law in order to be saved. Paul here says that those who do this forfeit all rights in Jesus Christ. Christ will then profit them nothing. Jesus will not be the Savior of any who rely on something or anything other than himself.

5:5 *the hope of righteousness by faith.* The hope of righteousness is the happiness to be received in the world to come. But this must be qualified by two facts. This hope is ours by faith, not by the works of the law. No happiness can or will come to those who trust in the law. The second fact is that this belongs to us through the Spirit, who is the author of salvation, our teacher, and the wellspring from which our hope comes.

5:6 Paul here rules out circumcision from all consideration. If we are in Christ by faith, neither circumcision nor uncircumcision has any value. Therefore, circumcision is a matter of indifference. Christ is the end of the law, i.e., the law no longer has dominion over us. It is ended so far as salvation is concerned.

5:8 Paul adamantly insists that the call to return to the law and to circumcision did not come from the God who called them to himself. Such a call comes from Satan. Whatever does not have its foundation in Christ and in the Bible is not for any believer.

5:13, 14 Believers are called to liberty but they are not to make this an occasion to serve the passions of the flesh. We are freed from the curse of the law but not from the commandments of God. We are not free to do as we like but as God orders. Verse 14 comprehends the whole law in the believer's relationship to other people: we must love our neighbors as we love ourselves.

5:14 Lev 19:18 Jn 13:34 Rom 13:8

14 For all the law is fulfilled in one word, *even* in this; Thou shalt love thy
neighbour as thyself.
15 But if ye bite and devour one another, take heed that ye be not
consumed one of another.

C. FREEDOM IN PRACTICE

5:16 Rom 6:12; 8:4–6

16 *This* I say then, Walk in the Spirit, and ye shall not fulfil the lust of the
flesh.

5:17 Rom 7:15, 23

17 For the flesh lusteth against the Spirit, and the Spirit against the flesh:
and these are contrary the one to the other: so that ye cannot do the things
that ye would.

5:18 Rom 6:14; 8:14

18 But if ye be led of the Spirit, ye are not under the law.

5:19 Rom 13:12, 13 1 Cor 3:3 Jas 3:14

19 Now the works of the flesh are manifest, which are *these;* Adultery,
fornication, uncleanness, lasciviousness,
20 Idolatry, witchcraft, hatred, variance, emulations, wrath, strife, sedi-
tions, heresies,

5:21 1 Cor 6:9 Eph 5:5 Rev 22:15

21 Envyings, murders, drunkenness, revellings, and such like: of the which
I tell you before, as I have also told *you* in time past, that they which do
such things shall not inherit the kingdom of God.

5:22☆ Jas 3:17

22 But the fruit of the Spirit is love, joy, peace, longsuffering, gentleness,
goodness, faith,
23 Meekness, temperance: against such there is no law.

5:24 Rom 6:6 Gal 6:14 Col 3:9

24 And they that are Christ's have crucified the flesh with the affections
and lusts.

D. COUNSELS AND CAUTIONS

5:25☆ Gal 5:16

25 If we live in the Spirit, let us also walk in the Spirit.

5:26 Phil 2:3

26 Let us not be desirous of vain glory, provoking one another, envying
one another.

6:1 1 Cor 2:15; 7:5 Jms 5:19, 20 1 Jn 5:16

6 BRETHREN, if a man be overtaken in a fault, ye which are spiritual,
restore such an one in the spirit of meekness; considering thyself, lest
thou also be tempted.

6:2☆ Jn 13:14 Rom 15:1

2 Bear ye one another's burdens, and so fulfil the law of Christ.

6:3 Rom 12:3 1 Cor 3:18 2 Cor 3:5; 12:11

3 For if a man think himself to be something, when he is nothing, he
deceiveth himself.
4 But let every man prove his own work, and then shall he have rejoicing
in himself alone, and not in another.

6:5 Rom 14:12

5 For every man shall bear his own burden.

6:6☆ Rom 15:27 1 Cor 9:11, 14

6 Let him that is taught in the word communicate unto him that teacheth
in all good things.

6:7☆ Job 13:9 1 Cor 6:9 2 Cor 9:6

7 Be not deceived; God is not mocked: for whatsoever a man soweth, that
shall he also reap.

5:22 The true evidence of a holy life or the blessing of sanctification is seen when the fruit of the Spirit is manifested in the believer's life (5:22–26).

5:25 If Christians claim to have received the Spirit of Christ, the only way the world can tell is by the Christians' living a Spirit-filled life. Walking in the Spirit *is no more and no less than being filled with the Spirit.* This is the inheritance and the privilege of all believers who meet the conditions and claim the promise.

6:2 The law of Christ is the law of love. We fulfill this law when we bear one another's burdens, which means to comfort, counsel, and assist other believers as our circumstances allow. It obliges us to exercise mutual forbearance and to have a spirit of forgiveness, as well as sympathy.

6:6 Believers are here ordered to take good care of their ministers in the material things of life. Those who pray for their ministers, "Lord you keep him humble, we will keep him poor," do not understand this *scripture. There is a happy medium between poverty* and wealth.

6:7 There is a law of retribution written large in the universe. No one can escape it. We shall reap as we have sown. There will be a pay day. For those who have done well, there will be a reward; for those who have done evil, punishment.

8 For he that soweth to his flesh shall of the flesh reap corruption; but he
that soweth to the Spirit shall of the Spirit reap life everlasting.
9 And let us not be weary in well doing: for in due season we shall reap,
if we faint not.
10 As we have therefore opportunity, let us do good unto all *men*,
especially unto them who are of the household of faith.

6:8 Job 4:8 Hos 8:7 Rom 8:9–14 Jas 3:18
6:9 Mt 24:13 2 Thess 3:13
6:10 Jn 9:4 Eph 2:19 1 Tim 6:18 Heb 3:6

V. CONCLUSION (6:11–18)

A. FREEDOM AND THE CROSS

11 Ye see how large a letter I have written unto you with mine own hand.
12 As many as desire to make a fair shew in the flesh, they constrain you
to be circumcised; only lest they should suffer persecution for the cross of
Christ.
13 For neither they themselves who are circumcised keep the law; but
desire to have you circumcised, that they may glory in your flesh.
14 But God forbid that I should glory, save in the cross of our Lord Jesus
Christ, by whom the world is crucified unto me, and I unto the world.
15 For in Christ Jesus neither circumcision availeth any thing, nor
uncircumcision, but a new creature.
16 And as many as walk according to this rule, peace *be* on them, and
mercy, and upon the Israel of God.

6:11 1 Cor 16:21
6:12 Mt 23:27, 28 Acts 15:1 Gal 5:11 Phil 3:18
6:13 Rom 2:25
☆6:14 Rom 6:2, 3, 6 1 Cor 2:2 Gal 2:20 Col 2:20
☆6:15 2 Cor 5:17 Gal 5:6
6:16 Gal 3:7 Phil 3:3

B. THE PRICE OF LIBERTY

17 From henceforth let no man trouble me: for I bear in my body the
marks of the Lord Jesus.

6:17 2 Cor 1:5; 4:10 Col 1:24

C. THE BENEDICTION OF LIBERTY

18 Brethren, the grace of our Lord Jesus Christ *be* with your spirit. Amen.

6:18 Rom 16:20 2 Tim 4:22

6:14 The Judaizers gloried in the law and circumcision. Paul gloried in the cross of Christ. He desired to glory in nothing else. The cross was the ground of his hope. It was the doctrine he intended to preach, whatever the cost and however much he had to suffer.
6:15 *neither circumcision availeth any thing, nor uncircumcision, but a new creature.* True religion and salvation do not consist in circumcision or uncircumcision. Paul knows that people are neither helped nor hurt by circumcision unless they make it necessary to salvation. The only thing that counts is being a new creation through faith in Christ, whose merits are applied to our account and who justifies us before our God, with or without circumcision.

THE EPISTLE OF PAUL THE APOSTLE TO THE
EPHESIANS

Authorship, date, and background Ephesians is one of the four "prison epistles" which include also Colossians, Philippians, and Philemon. Since Paul was in prison a number of times, the question arises, which of the many imprisonments was the locale from which these letters were sent to their destinations. Despite the difference of opinion, Rome is the most likely city, and the date of writing is A.D. 60–61. Two of the other most important questions have to do with the authorship of Ephesians and the destinations for which the letter was intended.

Liberal scholars almost without exception think Paul did not write Ephesians. Conservatives have always thought he did. The case for non-Pauline authorship is tenuous at best. The weight of evidence falls in favor of Pauline authorship. Perhaps the most important fact is that the letter itself claims to be Pauline, for the salutation says: "Paul, an apostle" (1:1). Thus, to say Paul did not write the letter is to disregard what the Bible itself says. If what is said is not true, then the same principle can be applied elsewhere with great damage. To suppose that someone else would claim to be Paul, however high his motive, given the fact that God is the author of Scripture, is hardly acceptable. The principle that what the Bible says is true must lead to the conclusion that Paul indeed was the author of the letter.

Some of the ancient manuscripts leave out the phrase "at Ephesus," which raises the question to whom the letter was addressed. A number of conservative scholars say it was an "encyclical letter," by which is meant a letter intended for more than a single person or place. It probably was sent to a number of churches in Asia which included Ephesus, of course. Tychicus was Paul's messenger who brought the letter from Rome to Asia (Ausia) (6:21). Aristarchus, Epaphras, Luke, and Demas, as well as Mark, were with Paul at the time of writing. The letter represents Paul's maturest thinking about the church. It also overlaps at points with Colossians, which was written during the same period.

Characteristics and content Ephesians comes at a point in time when many new churches have come into being. Paul, no doubt, has given great thought to the nature of the church and the churches, and under the guidance of the Holy Spirit he writes something unique. In this letter he talks about the church as a universal phenomenon, whereas in his other letters he has written to local congregations. Ephesians presents an overview of God's plan of the ages. Paul speaks about the purpose of God from before the beginning of the world, and the certainty that the divine intention will be realized through Jesus Christ via the apostles, prophets, and the apostle Paul himself.

Paul develops the doctrine of the church. He calls the church "his body," that is, the body of Christ (1:23). He also proclaims that it is the bride or wife of Christ (5:22ff.) and the dwelling place (temple) of the Holy Spirit (2:19–22). Christ is the head over the church and all believers are members of the body. This church includes believers of all ages, even those yet to come into it. Believers hear the good news that there is something beyond this earthly sphere. They are related to the "heavenly places" (as in 1:3, 2:6, and 3:10) both as a present relationship and with the sure guarantee of its eternal nature when Christ's people shall reign and rule with him forever. This view of the church in relation to the heavenlies finds its fullest disclosure in Ephesians as a mystery (secret plan) now made manifest.

Ephesians also treats the work of the Holy Spirit in the lives of believers by way of summation. Herein we learn that believers are "sealed with that holy spirit of promise" (1:13); that Jew and Gentile may come to God the Father through the Holy Spirit (2:18); that the Father would grant us "according to the riches of his glory, to be strengthened with might by his Spirit in the inner man" (3:16); that the revelation of God's plan of the ages has come to apostles and prophets by the Holy Spirit (3:5); that we ought to, and therefore can, "be filled with the Spirit" (5:18); that believers should pray "always with all prayer and supplication in the Spirit" (6:18); and that they are to be careful that they don't "grieve the holy Spirit of God" by the way they live (4:30).

In Ephesians, believers are marked off as members of the new humanity, a worldwide family of redeemed sons and daughters who have peace with God and should be at peace with each other and rejoice in and make use of the unfathomable riches they have in Jesus Christ.

Outline

I. Introduction (1:1, 2)
II. Doctrinal teaching (1:3—3:21)
III. Exhortations for the church (4:1—6:20)
IV. Conclusion (6:21–23)

I. INTRODUCTION (1:1, 2)

1 PAUL, an apostle of Jesus Christ by the will of God, to the saints
which are at Eph'e-sus, and to the faithful in Christ Jesus:
2 Grace *be* to you, and peace, from God our Father, and *from* the Lord
Jesus Christ.

II. DOCTRINAL TEACHING (1:3—3:21)

A. PRAISE TO THE TRIUNE GOD

3 Blessed *be* the God and Father of our Lord Jesus Christ, who hath
blessed us with all spiritual blessings in heavenly *places* in Christ:
4 According as he hath chosen us in him before the foundation of the
world, that we should be holy and without blame before him in love:
5 Having predestinated us unto the adoption of children by Jesus Christ
to himself, according to the good pleasure of his will,
6 To the praise of the glory of his grace, wherein he hath made us accepted
in the beloved.
7 In whom we have redemption through his blood, the forgiveness of sins,
according to the riches of his grace;
8 Wherein he hath abounded toward us in all wisdom and prudence;
9 Having made known unto us the mystery of his will, according to his
good pleasure which he hath purposed in himself:
10 That in the dispensation of the fulness of times he might gather
together in one all things in Christ, both which are in heaven, and which are
on earth; *even* in him:
11 In whom also we have obtained an inheritance, being predestinated
according to the purpose of him who worketh all things after the counsel of
his own will:
12 That we should be to the praise of his glory, who first trusted in Christ.
13 In whom ye also *trusted*, after that ye heard the word of truth, the
gospel of your salvation: in whom also after that ye believed, ye were sealed
with that holy Spirit of promise,

1:1 Rom 1:1; 1 Cor 1:1; 2 Cor 1:1; Col 1:2
1:2 Rom 1:7; Tit 1:4
☆**1:3** Ps 72:17; Eph 1:20; 2:6
☆**1:4** Lk 1:75; 2 Thess 2:13; 1 Pet 1:2, 20
1:5 Jn 1:12; Rom 8:15, 29; Gal 4:5; Eph 1:11
1:6 Isa 43:21; Mt 3:17; 17:5; Rom 3:24; Col 1:13
☆**1:7** 1 Cor 6:20; Col 1:14; Heb 9:12; Rev 5:9
1:9 Col 1:26, 27; 2:2
1:10 Mk 1:15; Gal 4:4; Col 1:20
1:11 Isa 46:10; Rom 9:11; Eph 3:11
1:12 Eph 1:6, 14; Jas 1:18
☆**1:13** 2 Cor 1:22; Eph 4:30; Col 1:5

1:3 *in heavenly places* (or "the heavenlies," from the Greek *hoi epouranioi*) is to be found in 1:20; 2:6; 3:10; 6:12 in the Greek. It is the place where Christ now reigns, his sacrifice having been accepted by the Father. In this spiritual realm believers enjoy every spiritual blessing. In this unseen but real world the Christian wages his warfare against the malign forces of Satan (6:12).

1:4 The doctrine of election is taught in the Scriptures. It is the outworking of God's power to effect what he chooses. The New Testament uses the term "elect" (*eklektoi*) variously. We are elected or chosen (1) to good works (2:10); (2) to become like Jesus (Rom. 8:29); (3) to obtain eternal glory (Rom. 8:21); and (4) to be adopted as sons and daughters of God (1:5). When it comes to salvation, theologians have argued about election. Some say that if only those who are elected are saved, then Christ's redemption was limited. Others reply that the call to salvation is universal, so that it is the divine intention to save all men; therefore, the redemption is potentially efficacious for all men, even when all men do not accept Christ. The Scriptures teach that election is according to God's sovereign purpose (Rom. 9:10–13; Eph. 1:11) and that it is related to God's foreknowledge (Rom. 8:29). Scripture does not explicitly say what it is in the divine foreknowledge that determines his elective choice. Scripture indicates that man is a free moral agent and that God sovereignly works out all things according to his own good pleasure.

1:7 Redemption includes the following: (1) the forgiveness of sins (1:7; Col. 1:14); (2) justification or right standing with God (Rom. 3:24); (3) adoption into the family of God (Gal. 4:4, 5); and (4) purification (Titus 2:14).

1:13 Whoever receives Jesus Christ as Savior is sealed by the Holy Spirit of God. This sealing guarantees that we are his and that we will secure the full

1:14 Rom 8:23; 2 Cor 1:22; 5:5

14 Which is the earnest of our inheritance until the redemption of the
purchased possession, unto the praise of his glory.

B. PRAYER FOR THE EPHESIAN CHURCH

1:15 Col 1:4
1:16 Col 1:9
1:17 1 Cor 2:9–12
1:18 Acts 26:18; Eph 1:11; 4:4
1:19 Eph 3:7, 16; 6:10; Phil 3:21; Col 1:29
1:20 Acts 2:24
1:21 Phil 2:9
1:22☆ Mt 28:18; 1 Cor 15:27; Eph 4:15; Col 2:19; Heb 2:7
1:23 Eph 3:19; 4:10; Col 1:18; 2:9; 3:11

15 Wherefore I also, after I heard of your faith in the Lord Jesus, and love
unto all the saints,
16 Cease not to give thanks for you, making mention of you in my prayers,
17 That the God of our Lord Jesus Christ, the Father of glory, may give
unto you the spirit of wisdom and revelation in the knowledge of him:
18 The eyes of your understanding being enlightened; that ye may know
what is the hope of his calling, and what the riches of the glory of his
inheritance in the saints,
19 And what *is* the exceeding greatness of his power to us-ward who
believe, according to the working of his mighty power,
20 Which he wrought in Christ, when he raised him from the dead, and set
him at his own right hand in the heavenly *places,*
21 Far above all principality, and power, and might, and dominion, and
every name that is named, not only in this world, but also in that which is
to come:
22 And hath put all *things* under his feet, and gave him *to be* the head over
all *things* to the church,
23 Which is his body, the fulness of him that filleth all in all.

C. THE CREATION OF THE CHURCH

2:1 Jn 5:24; Eph 2:5; Col 2:13
2:2 Eph 5:6, 8; 6:10; 1 Jn 5:19
2:3 Ps 51:5; Gal 5:16; Tit 3:3
2:4 Jn 3:16; Rom 10:12; Eph 1:7
2:5 Rom 5:6; 6:4
2:6☆ Eph 1:3, 20; Col 2:12
2:7 Tit 3:4

2 AND you *hath he quickened,* who were dead in trespasses and sins;
2 Wherein in time past ye walked according to the course of this
world, according to the prince of the power of the air, the spirit that now
worketh in the children of disobedience:
3 Among whom also we all had our conversation in times past in the lusts
of our flesh, fulfilling the desires of the flesh and of the mind; and were by
nature the children of wrath, even as others.
4 But God, who is rich in mercy, for his great love wherewith he loved us,
5 Even when we were dead in sins, hath quickened us together with
Christ, (by grace ye are saved;)
6 And hath raised *us* up together, and made *us* sit together in heavenly
places in Christ Jesus:
7 That in the ages to come he might shew the exceeding riches of his grace
in *his* kindness toward us through Christ Jesus.

---

possession of that salvation when we die or at his coming if we remain alive. What the Spirit does, God does too. Thus in 2 Cor. 1:22 God seals us and gives us the earnest of the Spirit in our hearts. John 6:27 speaks about Christ as the One whom "God the Father sealed." At Christ's baptism the Spirit rested on him. In the case of the believer he is not only sealed by the Spirit, he is also indwelt by the same Spirit according to 1 Cor. 3:16 ("the Spirit of God dwelleth in you"). Every believer, then, is sealed and indwelt by the Spirit, and should be filled with the Spirit also (5:18).

1:22 The church universal includes all believers of past ages, *of the present age, and for all time to come* until the consummation of the ages. The church is the body of Christ. This is the mystical body known only to God and yet it is manifested in visible forms. Today there are many churches, including Roman Catholic, Russian Orthodox, Eastern Orthodox, Methodist, Presbyterian, Baptist, etc. There is little likelihood that all of the churches that call themselves Christian will ever become one undivided church, although some insist that the visible churches should become one visibly as well as spiritually. At any rate, many things can be said of Christ's church: (1) it was purchased with his blood (Acts 20:28); (2) all believers are baptized into the body which is the church (1 Cor. 12:13); (3) it is a spiritual organism with many members (1 Cor. 12:12); and (4) all members of the body, the church, are subject to Christ (5:24). The Scriptures uphold the unity of the church (John 17:11), but this is a spiritual unity that is independent of all ecclesiastical organizations. Unity must be based on a common deposit of truth. Unity at the expense of doctrinal purity is heretical; disunity when doctrinal purity exists is a scandal.

2:6 Believers are said to sit with Christ in the heavenly realms right now! They already share in Christ's royal status and his sovereign power. They work to advance

8 For by grace are ye saved through faith; and that not of yourselves: *it is*
the gift of God:
9 Not of works, lest any man should boast.
10 For we are his workmanship, created in Christ Jesus unto good works,
which God hath before ordained that we should walk in them.

D. UNION OF JEWISH AND GENTILE BELIEVERS

11 Wherefore remember, that ye *being* in time past Gentiles in the flesh,
who are called Uncircumcision by that which is called the Circumcision in
the flesh made by hands;
12 That at that time ye were without Christ, being aliens from the
commonwealth of Israel, and strangers from the covenants of promise,
having no hope, and without God in the world:
13 But now in Christ Jesus ye who sometimes were far off are made nigh
by the blood of Christ.
14 For he is our peace, who hath made both one, and hath broken down
the middle wall of partition *between us;*
15 Having abolished in his flesh the enmity, *even* the law of command-
ments *contained* in ordinances; for to make in himself of twain one new
man, *so* making peace;
16 And that he might reconcile both unto God in one body by the cross,
having slain the enmity thereby:
17 And came and preached peace to you which were afar off, and to them
that were nigh.
18 For through him we both have access by one Spirit unto the Father.
19 Now therefore ye are no more strangers and foreigners, but fellow-
citizens with the saints, and of the household of God;
20 And are built upon the foundation of the apostles and prophets, Jesus
Christ himself being the chief corner *stone;*
21 In whom all the building fitly framed together groweth unto an holy
temple in the Lord:
22 In whom ye also are builded together for an habitation of God through
the Spirit.

E. THE CALLING OF THE CHURCH

1. To Show Forth the Wisdom of God

3 FOR this cause I Paul, the prisoner of Jesus Christ for you Gentiles,
2 If ye have heard of the dispensation of the grace of God which is
given me to you-ward:

☆**2:8** Jn 4:10 Rom 4:16
2:9 Rom 3:20 2 Tim 1:9 Tit 3:5
2:11 Rom 2:28 Col 2:11
☆**2:12** Rom 9:4, 8 Gal 4:8 1 Thess 4:13
2:13 Acts 2:39 Col 1:20
2:14 Mic 5:5 1 Cor 12:13
2:15 2 Cor 5:17 Gal 3:28 Col 1:22; 2:14
2:16 Eph 4:4 Col 1:20
2:17 Isa 57:19 Zech 9:10 Acts 10:36
☆**2:18** Jn 14:6, 17–20 Eph 3:12; 4:4
☆**2:19** Eph 2:12
2:20 Ps 118:22 Isa 28:16 Mt 16:18; 21:42 1 Cor 3:11 Rev 21:14
2:21 1 Cor 3:16 Eph 4:15, 16
2:22 Jn 17:23 1 Pet 2:5
☆**3:1** Acts 21:33 26:17–18 2 Cor 1:6 2 Tim 2:10
3:2 Acts 9:15 Rom 16:25 Gal 2:7 Col 1:25

his kingdom by their worship, prayers, witness, and missionary outreach. Their life is hid with Christ in God (Col. 3:3), thus they are in the world but not of it. Their true homeland is the heavenly commonwealth (Phil. 3:20).

2:8 *and that not of yourselves,* or, "Salvation is not of yourselves."† It is secured by trusting, i.e., by faith alone (*sola fide*). This excludes any and all works of righteousness. True faith always has in it three elements: (1) knowledge, for no one is saved without knowing something (Rom. 10:17); (2) mental consent to the knowledge, i.e., one is convinced in his mind that the gospel is true; and (3) a volitional act of personal appropriation or laying hold of Christ—i.e., receiving Jesus Christ as one's Savior (John 1:12). The absence of any one of the three elements means the absence of true faith. Moreover, true faith is never alone; it is always accompanied by good works which are the fruit of faith. The absence of good works subsequent to salvation leaves open the question whether one has truly been regenerated.

2:12 *having no hope, and without God.* He who does not have God has no hope, and what worse condition could be the lot of anyone than to be without God? Moreover, to be without Christ is to be without God as well. These assertions deny the possibility that anyone can get to heaven through any other religion or by any other road. Christianity is the only true faith, and without it men are lost.

2:18, 19 Through Jesus Christ, in his name and by virtue of his atoning sacrifice, all believers have access or admission to the holy presence of Almighty God. They draw near by the Spirit. They are no longer aliens or strangers but fellow citizens with all the saints.

3:1 *I, Paul, a prisoner of Jesus Christ.* Paul is a prisoner for having preached Christ. He is not a

3:3 Rom 16:25; Gal 1:12; Eph 1:9; 3:4–9; Col 1:25–27
3 How that by revelation he made known unto me the mystery; (as I
wrote afore in few words,

3:4 1 Cor 4:1; 2 Cor 11:6
4 Whereby, when ye read, ye may understand my knowledge in the
mystery of Christ)

3:5☆ Eph 1:17
5 Which in other ages was not made known unto the sons of men, as it is
now revealed unto his holy apostles and prophets by the Spirit;

3:6 Gal 3:14; Eph 2:14–16
6 That the Gentiles should be fellowheirs, and of the same body, and
partakers of his promise in Christ by the gospel:

3:7 Rom 15:18; Col 1:23
7 Whereof I was made a minister, according to the gift of the grace of God
given unto me by the effectual working of his power.

3:8☆ 1 Cor 15:9; Col 2:2, 3, 9, 10
8 Unto me, who am less than the least of all saints, is this grace given, that
I should preach among the Gentiles the unsearchable riches of Christ;

3:9 1 Cor 2:7
9 And to make all *men* see what *is* the fellowship of the mystery, which
from the beginning of the world hath been hid in God, who created all
things by Jesus Christ:

3:10 Rom 11:33; 1 Cor 2:7; Eph 1:21; 6:12; 1 Pet 3:22
10 To the intent that now unto the principalities and powers in heavenly
places might be known by the church the manifold wisdom of God,

3:11 Eph 1:11
11 According to the eternal purpose which he purposed in Christ Jesus our
Lord:

3:12☆ Eph 2:18; Heb 4:16
12 In whom we have boldness and access with confidence by the faith of
him.

13 Wherefore I desire that ye faint not at my tribulations for you, which is
your glory.

2. To Enjoy the Resources of God

3:14 Phil 2:9, 10
14 For this cause I bow my knees unto the Father of our Lord Jesus
Christ,

15 Of whom the whole family in heaven and earth is named,

3:16 Phil 4:13, 19; Col 1:11
16 That he would grant you, according to the riches of his glory, to be
strengthened with might by his Spirit in the inner man;

3:17 Jn 14:23; Col 1:27; 2:7
17 That Christ may dwell in your hearts by faith; that ye, being rooted and
grounded in love,

3:18 Job 11:8, 9; Jn 1:16; Col 2:9, 10
18 May be able to comprehend with all saints what *is* the breadth, and
length, and depth, and height;

3:19 Eph 1:23; Col 2:10
19 And to know the love of Christ, which passeth knowledge, that ye
might be filled with all the fulness of God.

3:20☆ Eph 1:19, 20
20 Now unto him that is able to do exceeding abundantly above all that
we ask or think, according to the power that worketh in us,

3:21 1 Tim 1:17
21 Unto him *be* glory in the church by Christ Jesus throughout all ages,
world without end. Amen.

---

prisoner of men or of the devil. As Christ's servant, he has become Christ's prisoner. What higher glory could he have than to be a slave for the Savior's sake?

3:5 Paul asserts that the Jews and Gentiles are one body in Christ, thus they are fellow-heirs in the kingdom. It was no mystery that God intended to include Gentiles in the gospel benefits, but the Old *Testament did* not state what Paul here affirms. Revelation is progressive, and some things hidden in former ages are now made clear in the New Testament.

3:8 Paul magnifies his office as an apostle who is privileged to preach the gospel, and at the same time he humbly speaks of himself as less than the least of all the saints. Humility is a virtue less sought yet most needed by ministers of the good news.

3:12 Through Christ, justified and righteous sinners can come to God by faith, without fear. God will not reject those who come. He will receive them, hear them, and help them. Since the believers, as Christ's brothers, have the same Father as Jesus, they can confidently come to the Father through the Son.

3:20 God is *able* to do superabundantly above all we can ask or even think. He is also *willing* to do all of this for us as well. Some people have the power to do good but do not choose to use it. God can do great things and he chooses to do so. The God most Christians worship is too small. We need to understand that God is bigger than we can possibly imagine.

III. EXHORTATIONS FOR THE CHURCH (4:1—6:20)

A. UNITY IN DIVERSITY

4 I THEREFORE, the prisoner of the Lord, beseech you that ye walk worthy of the vocation wherewith ye are called,

2 With all lowliness and meekness, with longsuffering, forbearing one another in love;

3 Endeavouring to keep the unity of the Spirit in the bond of peace.

4 *There is* one body, and one Spirit, even as ye are called in one hope of your calling;

5 One Lord, one faith, one baptism,

6 One God and Father of all, who *is* above all, and through all, and in you all.

7 But unto every one of us is given grace according to the measure of the gift of Christ.

8 Wherefore he saith, When he ascended up on high, he led captivity captive, and gave gifts unto men.

9 (Now that he ascended, what is it but that he also descended first into the lower parts of the earth?

10 He that descended is the same also that ascended up far above all heavens, that he might fill all things.)

11 And he gave some, apostles; and some, prophets; and some, evangelists; and some, pastors and teachers;

12 For the perfecting of the saints, for the work of the ministry, for the edifying of the body of Christ:

13 Till we all come in the unity of the faith, and of the knowledge of the Son of God, unto a perfect man, unto the measure of the stature of the fulness of Christ:

14 That we *henceforth* be no more children, tossed to and fro, and carried about with every wind of doctrine, by the sleight of men, *and* cunning craftiness, whereby they lie in wait to deceive;

15 But speaking the truth in love, may grow up into him in all things, which is the head, *even* Christ:

16 From whom the whole body fitly joined together and compacted by that which every joint supplieth, according to the effectual working in the measure of every part, maketh increase of the body unto the edifying of itself in love.

B. MORAL STANDARDS

17 This I say therefore, and testify in the Lord, that ye henceforth walk not as other Gentiles walk, in the vanity of their mind,

4:1 Eph 2:10; Col 1:10
4:2 Gal 5:22; Col 3:12, 13
☆**4:3** Col 3:14
☆**4:4** Rom 12:5; 1 Cor 12:12, 13; Eph 2:16, 18
4:5 1 Cor 8:6; Heb 6:6
4:6 Ps 83:18; Mal 2:10; Rom 11:36
4:7 Rom 12:3; 1 Cor 12:7
4:8 Ps 68:18; Col 2:15
4:9 Jn 3:13; Acts 2:27; 1 Pet 3:18
4:10 Eph 1:23; 1 Tim 3:16; Heb 4:14: 8:1; 1 Pet 3:22
☆**4:11** 1 Cor 12:28
☆**4:12** 1 Cor 14:26
4:13 Eph 1:17; Col 2:2
☆**4:14** Mt 11:7; 1 Cor 14:20; Eph 6:11
4:15, 16 Col 2:19
☆**4:17** Jn 1:4, 5; Acts 17:30; 26:18; Rom 1:21; Eph 2:2; 1 Thess 4:5

4:3, 4 Paul says that believers constitute one body. And they are to be eager to keep the unity of that body. Unity, however, exists in the midst of diversity. Many people suppose that unity means uniformity and ecclesiastical oneness headed up by one leader in whom all authority is vested. But Christ is the Head of the church, and genuine unity can exist even though there may be many churches with varying ecclesiastical customs and practices. Many of the divisions in the church are of a theological nature, not of an ecclesiological sort, and the theological differences often conflict with the clearer teachings of the Scriptures.

4:11, 12 The visible church must have organization and leadership. Christ through the Holy Spirit provides the church with leaders: apostles, prophets, evangelists, pastors, and teachers. These have for their ministry the perfecting of the saints, which is to encourage believers, strengthen them, and equip them for the purpose of conforming them to the image of Christ.

4:14 Paul here emphasizes the importance of correct doctrine. Believers who are doctrinally ignorant can be easily led astray. Every Christian should be acquainted with the great doctrines of the faith. Some people say doctrine divides; love unites. Peace without right doctrinal agreement will destroy the foundations of the faith; right doctrine without love can be mere formalism. Right doctrine and love should go hand in hand.

4:17 Paul here uses the word *therefore* similar to the usage in Rom. 12:1. It functions as a causative. *Because* they now are Christians, therefore (i.e., of necessity) they must prove the rightness of this new relationship by their holy walk. Faith without works is dead faith. True faith always leads to a holy walk. Paul exhorts these brethren to show forth purity of heart and life.

18 Having the understanding darkened, being alienated from the life of
God through the ignorance that is in them, because of the blindness of their
heart:
19 Who being past feeling have given themselves over unto lasciviousness,
to work all uncleanness with greediness.
20 But ye have not so learned Christ;
21 If so be that ye have heard him, and have been taught by him, as the
truth is in Jesus:
22 That ye put off concerning the former conversation the old man, which
is corrupt according to the deceitful lusts;
23 And be renewed in the spirit of your mind;
24 And that ye put on the new man, which after God is created in
righteousness and true holiness.
25 Wherefore putting away lying, speak every man truth with his neigh-
bour: for we are members one of another.
26 Be ye angry, and sin not: let not the sun go down upon your wrath:
27 Neither give place to the devil.
28 Let him that stole steal no more: but rather let him labour, working
with *his* hands the thing which is good, that he may have to give to him that
needeth.
29 Let no corrupt communication proceed out of your mouth, but that
which is good to the use of edifying, that it may minister grace unto the
hearers.
30 And grieve not the holy Spirit of God, whereby ye are sealed unto the
day of redemption.
31 Let all bitterness, and wrath, and anger, and clamour, and evil
speaking, be put away from you, with all malice:
32 And be ye kind one to another, tenderhearted, forgiving one another,
even as God for Christ's sake hath forgiven you.

5 BE ye therefore followers of God, as dear children:
2 And walk in love, as Christ also hath loved us, and hath given
himself for us an offering and a sacrifice to God for a sweetsmelling savour.
3 But fornication, and all uncleanness, or covetousness, let it not be once
named among you, as becometh saints;
4 Neither filthiness, nor foolish talking, nor jesting, which are not
convenient: but rather giving of thanks.
5 For this ye know, that no whoremonger, nor unclean person, nor
covetous man, who is an idolater, hath any inheritance in the kingdom of
Christ and of God.
6 Let no man deceive you with vain words: for because of these things
cometh the wrath of God upon the children of disobedience.
7 Be not ye therefore partakers with them.
8 For ye were sometimes darkness, but now *are ye* light in the Lord: walk
as children of light:

4:19 Rom 1:24; Col 3:5
4:22 Rom 6:6; Col 3:8; Jas 1:21
4:23 Rom 12:2
4:24 2 Cor 5:17; Col 3:10
4:25☆ Zech 8:16; Rom 12:5; Col 3:9
4:27 Rom 12:19; Jas 4:7
4:28 1 Thess 4:11
4:29 Mt 12:34; Rom 14:19; Col 4:6
4:30☆ Isa 63:10; Eph 1:13; 1 Thess 5:19
4:31 Col 3:8; 1 Pet 2:1
4:32 Col 3:12, 13
5:1 Mt 5:45
5:2 Gen 8:21; Jn 13:34; 2 Cor 2:15
5:3☆ Col 3:5
5:4 Rom 1:28
5:5 1 Cor 6:9; Gal 5:21
5:6 Jer 29:8; Rom 1:18
5:8 Isa 9:2; Jn 8:12; Eph 2:2; 1 Jn 2:9

4:25 Lest the readers of the letter not know what Paul considers right conduct, he bans lying, anger, stealing, and corrupt use of the tongue. These must have been some of the common sins of the Ephesians; at any rate, most of the sins of Christians everywhere are comprehended by extension within this list.

4:30 The way this comes about is for the believer to go against the will of the Spirit who dwells in his heart. Lack of love, lying, uncleanness, or harshness are some of the sins that interrupt fellowship between him and Christ. Sinning incurs the loss of the Spirit's power and fullness. Paul also says not to quench the Holy Spirit (1 Thess. 5:19) and the writer of Hebrews says he is not to be outraged or insulted (Heb. 10:29).

5:3ff Those who wish to walk in love must shun fornication, all uncleanness, covetousness, filthiness, foolish talking, and jesting. Those who practice these things can expect only the wrath of God on them. He shuts the door of heaven to them. The Ephesian Christians are not to associate with such people (5:7). Moreover, he delights that although these new believers were once like these people who are in darkness, now these Christians have experienced the light of the gospel, and they are to walk as children of light.

9(For the fruit of the Spirit *is* in all goodness and righteousness and
truth;)
10Proving what is acceptable unto the Lord.
11And have no fellowship with the unfruitful works of darkness, but
rather reprove *them.*
12For it is a shame even to speak of those things which are done of them
in secret.
13But all things that are reproved are made manifest by the light: for
whatsoever doth make manifest is light.
14Wherefore he saith, Awake thou that sleepest, and arise from the dead,
and Christ shall give thee light.
15See then that ye walk circumspectly, not as fools, but as wise,
16Redeeming the time, because the days are evil.
17Wherefore be ye not unwise, but understanding what the will of the
Lord *is.*
18And be not drunk with wine, wherein is excess; but be filled with the
Spirit;
19Speaking to yourselves in psalms and hymns and spiritual songs,
singing and making melody in your heart to the Lord;
20Giving thanks always for all things unto God and the Father in the
name of our Lord Jesus Christ;
21Submitting yourselves one to another in the fear of God.

5:10 Phil 1:10
5:11 Lev 19:17; 1 Cor 5:9
5:13 Jn 3:20; Heb 4:13
5:14 Isa 26:19; 51:17; 52:1; 60:1; Jn 5:25; Rom 6:4, 5; 13:11
5:15 Col 4:5
5:17 1 Thess 4:3
☆**5:18** Prov 20:1; 23:31; Jn 7:37–39; 1 Cor 12:13
5:19 1 Cor 14:26; Col 3:16; Jas 5:13
5:20 Ps 34:1
5:21 1 Pet 5:5

C. THE CHRISTIAN HOME
1. Wives and Husbands

22Wives, submit yourselves unto your own husbands, as unto the Lord.
23For the husband is the head of the wife, even as Christ is the head of
the church: and he is the saviour of the body.
24Therefore as the church is subject unto Christ, so *let* the wives *be* to
their own husbands in every thing.
25Husbands, love your wives, even as Christ also loved the church, and
gave himself for it;
26That he might sanctify and cleanse it with the washing of water by the
word,
27That he might present it to himself a glorious church, not having spot,
or wrinkle, or any such thing; but that it should be holy and without
blemish.
28So ought men to love their wives as their own bodies. He that loveth his
wife loveth himself.
29For no man ever yet hated his own flesh; but nourisheth and cherisheth
it, even as the Lord the church:
30For we are members of his body, of his flesh, and of his bones.

☆**5:22** Gen 3:16
☆**5:23** 1 Cor 11:3
5:25 Eph 5:2
5:26 Jn 15:3; 17:17; Tit 3:5; Heb 10:22
5:27 Eph 1:4; Col 1:22; Rev 21:2
5:28 1 Pet 3:7
5:29 1 Cor 12:27
5:30 1 Cor 6:15

5:18 Every believer is sealed with the Holy Spirit, i.e., "marked . . . with a seal, the promised Holy Spirit" (1:13, 14, NIV) when born again or regenerated. But not all believers are spiritual Christians; some are carnal ("mere infants in Christ"), leading a defeated life (1 Cor. 3:1, NIV). "The mind of sinful man is death" (Rom. 8:6, NIV). Thus, a permanent carnal state is evidence of nonregeneration. Christian maturity or the Spirit-filled life is the objective for every believer. It can be attained by (1) meeting the first prerequisite for being filled—confessing all known sins (1 John 1:7–9; 2 Cor. 7:1); (2) giving oneself over to God by laying the life on the altar (Rom. 12:1; 6:13); (3) asking God to fill one's heart, believing he will fill those who confess their sins and surrender their lives to him (see Rom. 4:20–22); (4) embracing the promise that the Holy Spirit has filled them; and (5) going out to live as one who has been filled with the Holy Spirit. (See note to 1 Cor. 12:20.)

5:22 See note to Titus 2:4 on duties of wives to their husbands and children.

5:23ff This passage sets forth most clearly the teaching that the church is the bride of Christ. The idea of God's being married to his people is implicit in Hosea, who denounces the spiritual adultery of Israel. In the Revelation, John likens the New Jerusalem to a bride adorned for her husband. Jesus used the analogy of the bridegroom in his teachings (Matt. 25:1–13; Luke 5:34, 35; Matt. 9:15).

5:31 Gen 2:24

31 For this cause shall a man leave his father and mother, and shall be
joined unto his wife, and they two shall be one flesh.
32 This is a great mystery: but I speak concerning Christ and the church.

5:33 1 Pet 3:1, 2, 5

33 Nevertheless let every one of you in particular so love his wife even as
himself; and the wife *see* that she reverence *her* husband.

2. Children and Parents

6:1☆ Prov 23:22; Col 3:20 **6:2** Ex 20:12; Mt 15:4 **6:4** Col 3:21

6 CHILDREN, obey your parents in the Lord: for this is right.
2 Honour thy father and mother; (which is the first commandment
with promise;)
3 That it may be well with thee, and thou mayest live long on the earth.
4 And, ye fathers, provoke not your children to wrath: but bring them up
in the nurture and admonition of the Lord.

3. Slaves and Masters

6:5☆ Col 3:22; 1 Tim 6:1; Tit 2:9, 10 **6:6** Gal 1:10; Col 3:22, 23 **6:8** Rom 2:6; 2 Cor 5:10; Col 3:24 **6:9** Lev 25:43; Job 31:13, 14; Col 4:1

5 Servants, be obedient to them that are *your* masters according to the
flesh, with fear and trembling, in singleness of your heart, as unto Christ;
6 Not with eyeservice, as menpleasers; but as the servants of Christ, doing
the will of God from the heart;
7 With good will doing service, as to the Lord, and not to men:
8 Knowing that whatsoever good thing any man doeth, the same shall he
receive of the Lord, whether *he be* bond or free.
9 And, ye masters, do the same things unto them, forbearing threatening:
knowing that your Master also is in heaven; neither is there respect of
persons with him.

D. THE CHURCH AT WAR

6:10☆ 1 Cor 16:13; Eph 1:19; 2 Tim 2:1 **6:11** Rom 13:12; Eph 4:14; 1 Thess 5:8 **6:12**☆ Jn 12:31; 2 Cor 10:4; Eph 3:10; Col 1:13 **6:13** Jas 4:7 **6:14** Isa 11:5; 59:17; 1 Thess 5:8 **6:15** Isa 52:7

10 Finally, my brethren, be strong in the Lord, and in the power of his
might.
11 Put on the whole armour of God, that ye may be able to stand against
the wiles of the devil.
12 For we wrestle not against flesh and blood, but against principalities,
against powers, against the rulers of the darkness of this world, against
spiritual wickedness in high *places.*
13 Wherefore take unto you the whole armour of God, that ye may be able
to withstand in the evil day, and having done all, to stand.
14 Stand therefore, having your loins girt about with truth, and having on
the breastplate of righteousness;
15 And your feet shod with the preparation of the gospel of peace;

6:1 Children are enjoined to obey their parents. But when the orders of parents conflict with the laws of God, even children are not required to obey. Obedience is "in the Lord." If a parent orders a child to steal, lie, or cheat, this is contrary to the express will of God and cannot be complied with. (See also note on Ezek. 20:18.)

6:5ff A Christian slave has two masters: one is his earthly master and the other is his heavenly master, Jesus Christ. He must therefore serve his earthly master as though he is serving Christ, in singleness of heart, doing the will of God. Beginning at verse 9 Paul admonishes Christian masters to treat their slaves according to the rules of God, for both slaves and masters belong to the same Master, who shows no partiality in favor of or against either of them.

6:10ff God's children are soldiers; Jesus is the Commander; the cross is the banner. Satan is the great adversary. Here God indicates how the soldiers of the cross are to be armored and how they are to fight. The body is protected by God's armor. The head has its helmet too. The helmet and the shield are the defensive aspects to warfare. The believer also has a sword with which to conquer and overcome evil. Most of all he is to "put on the Lord Jesus Christ" (Rom. 13:14).

6:12 Satan is (1) God's mighty enemy who leads the *hosts of darkness (6:12); (2) "the chief of the devils,"* (Luke 11:15) whose number is legion (Luke 8:30); (3) a remarkably shrewd and cunning being (Rev. 12:9; 2 Cor. 11:3, 13–15); and (4) extremely wicked (1 John 3:8).

16 Above all, taking the shield of faith, wherewith ye shall be able to
quench all the fiery darts of the wicked.
17 And take the helmet of salvation, and the sword of the Spirit, which is
the word of God:
18 Praying always with all prayer and supplication in the Spirit, and
watching thereunto with all perseverance and supplication for all saints;
19 And for me, that utterance may be given unto me, that I may open my
mouth boldly, to make known the mystery of the gospel,
20 For which I am an ambassador in bonds: that therein I may speak
boldly, as I ought to speak.

6:16 1 Jn 5:4
6:17 Isa 59:17; Jn 6:63
1 Thess 5:8; Heb 4:12
☆**6:18** Lk 18:1; Rom 8:26; Phil 4:6; Col 4:2; 1 Tim 2:1
☆**6:19** Col 4:3, 4
6:20 1 Thess 2:2

IV. CONCLUSION (6:21–24)

21 But that ye also may know my affairs, *and* how I do, Tych'i-cus, a
beloved brother and faithful minister in the Lord, shall make known to you
all things:
22 Whom I have sent unto you for the same purpose, that ye might know
our affairs, and *that* he might comfort your hearts.
23 Peace *be* to the brethren, and love with faith, from God the Father and
the Lord Jesus Christ.
24 Grace *be* with all them that love our Lord Jesus Christ in sincerity.
Amen.

☆**6:21** Acts 20:4; 2 Tim 4:12; Tit 3:12
6:22 Col 4:7, 8
6:23 2 Thess 3:16

6:18 Prayer has its own precepts. Among them are: (1) pray to God the Father (Heb. 11:6); (2) pray in the name of Jesus (see John 14:6); (3) pray in the Spirit (6:18); (4) pray according to the will of God (1 John 5:14, 15); (5) pray in faith, believing (James 1:6; Eph. 3:20); (6) pray earnestly (Luke 6:12); (7) pray without display or hypocrisy (Matt. 6:5). Prayer also has its own order: (1) adoration of God; (2) thanksgiving; (3) confession of sin; (4) petition (for one's own needs); (5) intercession (for the needs of others).

6:19 Paul asks for prayer for himself. He does not ask them to pray for his physical deliverance from his bonds. Rather, he asks for boldness so that he may proclaim the gospel which has been entrusted to him. Implicit in this request is the truth that believers should share their faith whatever their temporal situation.

6:21 Tychicus was a good friend and able helper of Paul. When Paul was imprisoned, it was Tychicus who delivered letters to the Ephesians and to the Colossians. He encouraged these Christian believers and informed them concerning the welfare of the apostle. According to 2 Tim. 4:12 Paul sent Tychicus to Ephesus to minister there when Paul was in jail in Rome. Tychicus is described by Paul as a "beloved brother, and a faithful minister and fellow-servant of the Lord" (Col. 4:7).

THE EPISTLE OF PAUL THE APOSTLE TO THE
PHILIPPIANS

Authorship, date, and background Paul wrote this letter to the Philippians. This has been the universal view of the church across the centuries and there are no good reasons to question it. Philippians, Philemon, Ephesians, and Colossians constitute the "prison letters" of Paul. The letter was composed around A.D. 60–61 and the place from which it was written was Rome. Other cities such as Ephesus and Caesarea have been suggested, but there are no cogent reasons for ruling out Rome.

A special relationship developed between Paul and the Philippian church. He came to Philippi on his second missionary tour, believing that God had specifically called him and his co-laborers to work in Macedonia. Paul had a vision in which "he saw a man over in Macedonia, Greece, pleading with him, 'Come over here and help us.' " Paul took this vision to mean "God was sending us to preach the Good News there" (Acts 16:9, 10, TLB). When Paul came to Macedonia he left Asia for Europe. And many were the numbers of people converted and churches founded in Europe as a result of that vision and Paul's prompt response to it. There were few Jews in Philippi, not enough of them to form a synagogue. Thus it was to be a Gentile church, which had for its early members Lydia, the Roman jailer, and probably the demon-possessed slave girl whose deliverance brought about Paul's and Silas's beatings. Clement, Euodia, and Syntyche were won to Christ either at this time or later. When Paul departed from Philippi, Luke remained there to carry on the ministry.

The ties between Paul and this church were close and binding. Paul visited Philippi at the end of his third missionary tour, prior to spending the winter at Corinth (Acts 20:1–3; 2 Cor. 11:9). With the coming of spring he returned to Philippi where he spent the Passover season among these beloved friends (Acts 20:3, 6). Apparently letters were written to and received by Paul from the Philippians at various times. This letter is the most personal one of all the apostle wrote and which appear in Scripture. In it he was to speak about his personal life and his ambitions.

Characteristics and content Paul writes a letter to his beloved friends at Philippi who have assisted him materially in the spread of the gospel by their gifts for his work. "I rejoiced in the Lord greatly, that . . . your care of me hath flourished again" (4:10). Paul well knows that those who help him will be properly rewarded as though they themselves had preached the gospel to the people he has reached. He emphasizes the gospel (Good News) in this short letter by referring to it nine times. He speaks about the Philippians helping him in the spread of the gospel (1:5); his imprisonment furthering the gospel (1:12); the brethren being more bold to speak the Word (1:14); the Philippians "striving together for the faith of the gospel" (1:27); and his appreciation for the women who labored with him in the gospel (4:3).

The second refrain of this letter has to do with joy and rejoicing. Paul prayed for them with joy (1:4); he would continue to live for their joy (1:25); he urges them to unity to fulfill his joy (2:2); and he tells them, "Rejoice in the Lord alway and again I say, Rejoice" (4:4).

Paul speaks about advancing the faith in suffering as he faces death. He calls for the living of a holy life, using Jesus as our model, and states what the believers' Christian duties are. Along with exhortations, he mentions he will send Timothy and Epaphroditus to them. The latter has been sick unto death, but God has preserved him. He closes with the admonition that they always be full of joy (4:4) even as he thanks them for their gift and assures them in the closing chapter that God will give them peace (4:7), power (4:13), and provision (4:19).

Outline

I. Introduction (1:1–11)
II. News about himself (1:12–26)
III. Living the Christian life (1:27—2:18)
IV. Sending Timothy and Epaphroditus (2:19–30)
V. Instructions and exhortations (3:1—4:9)
VI. Thanksgiving for the Philippian gift (4:10–20)
VII. The concluding greeting and benediction (4:21–23)

I. INTRODUCTION (1:1–11)

A. THE APOSTOLIC GREETING

1 PAUL and Ti-mo'the-us, the servants of Jesus Christ, to all the saints
in Christ Jesus which are at Phi-lip'pi, with the bishops and deacons:
2 Grace *be* unto you, and peace, from God our Father, and *from* the Lord
Jesus Christ.

B. THANKSGIVING AND PRAYER

3 I thank my God upon every remembrance of you,
4 Always in every prayer of mine for you all making request with joy,
5 For your fellowship in the gospel from the first day until now;
6 Being confident of this very thing, that he which hath begun a good
work in you will perform *it* until the day of Jesus Christ:
7 Even as it is meet for me to think this of you all, because I have you in
my heart; inasmuch as both in my bonds, and in the defence and
confirmation of the gospel, ye all are partakers of my grace.
8 For God is my record, how greatly I long after you all in the bowels of
Jesus Christ.
9 And this I pray, that your love may abound yet more and more in
knowledge and *in* all judgment;
10 That ye may approve things that are excellent; that ye may be sincere
and without offence till the day of Christ;
11 Being filled with the fruits of righteousness, which are by Jesus Christ,
unto the glory and praise of God.

☆**1:1** Acts 16:1, 12; 2 Cor 1:1; Col 1:1; 1 Thess 1:1; 2 Thess 1:1; Philem 1
1:2 Rom 1:7
1:3 Rom 1:8; Col 1:3
1:4 Rom 1:9
1:5 2 Cor 8:1–5
☆**1:6** Jn 6:29; 1 Cor 1:8
1:7 2 Cor 7:3; Eph 3:1; 6:20; Col 4:3; 2 Tim 1:8
1:8 Rom 1:9
1:9 Col 1:9; 1 Thess 3:12; Philem 6
1:10 Rom 12:2; 1 Cor 1:8
1:11 Jn 15:4

II. NEWS ABOUT HIMSELF (1:12–26)

A. ADVANCING THE GOSPEL IN SUFFERING

12 But I would ye should understand, brethren, that the things *which
happened* unto me have fallen out rather unto the furtherance of the gospel;
13 So that my bonds in Christ are manifest in all the palace, and in all
other *places;*
14 And many of the brethren in the Lord, waxing confident by my bonds,
are much more bold to speak the word without fear.
15 Some indeed preach Christ even of envy and strife; and some also of
good will:
16 The one preach Christ of contention, not sincerely, supposing to add
affliction to my bonds:

☆**1:12** Lk 21:12, 13
☆**1:13** Acts 28:30, 31
1:14 Phil 1:20
☆**1:15** Phil 2:3

1:1 *bishops and deacons.* See footnotes to Titus 1:5 and 1 Tim. 3:8 for information on these offices.

1:6 The good work referred to here begins with regeneration and springs from the grace of God who quickens those who are dead in trespasses and sins and makes them alive in Jesus Christ. God who begins *this good work will not rest until the work is completed.* He intends to crown the work of his hands, but it will not be completely finished until the day of Jesus Christ—that is, the Second Advent when the Mediator's work will be fully completed.

1:12 Some might suppose that when a servant of God is put aside by imprisonment or laid on a shelf by accident or infirmity that God does not care for his servant and that this hinders God's work. Not so. Paul here affirms that even these apparent defeats and disasters would actually further the work of God and bring to pass the things God intended.

1:13 This was the praetorian guard, which was a select group of soldiers organized first by Augustus in 2 B.C. Numbering nine or ten thousand men, they were attached to the emperor's palace and to the palaces of provincial governors and procurators. The word here translated *palace* is *praitōrion* (from the Latin *praetorium*), and was used of Pilate's palace in Jerusalem (Matt. 27:27; Mark 15:16; John 18:28, 33; 19:9), and of the governor's official residence in Caesarea (cf. note to Acts 23:35).

1:15ff Paul suffered from false friends as well as from enemies. They considered themselves rivals of his and were envious of his apostleship and success. They supposed that they would add affliction to the bonds by which he was then bound. But his mind and heart are at ease for one reason: at least they preach Christ, whether from good or bad intentions. In verse 18 he says that he rejoices that Christ is preached. Let God judge the motivation that directs their actions.

1:17 1 Col 9:17

17 But the other of love, knowing that I am set for the defence of the gospel.

18 What then? notwithstanding, every way, whether in pretence, or in truth, Christ is preached; and I therein do rejoice, yea, and will rejoice.

B. FACING LIFE AND DEATH

1:19 Acts 16:7; Rom 8:9; 2 Cor 1:11
1:20☆ Rom 5:5; 14:8; 1 Cor 6:20; Eph 6:19
1:21 Gal 2:20; Col 1:27
1:22 Rom 1:13
1:23 2 Cor 5:8; 2 Tim 4:6
1:25 Phil 2:24

19 For I know that this shall turn to my salvation through your prayer, and the supply of the Spirit of Jesus Christ,

20 According to my earnest expectation and *my* hope, that in nothing I shall be ashamed, but *that* with all boldness, as always, *so* now also Christ shall be magnified in my body, whether *it be* by life, or by death.

21 For to me to live *is* Christ, and to die *is* gain.

22 But if I live in the flesh, this *is* the fruit of my labour: yet what I shall choose I wot not.

23 For I am in a strait betwixt two, having a desire to depart, and to be with Christ; which is far better:

24 Nevertheless to abide in the flesh *is* more needful for you.

25 And having this confidence, I know that I shall abide and continue with you all for your furtherance and joy of faith;

26 That your rejoicing may be more abundant in Jesus Christ for me by my coming to you again.

III. LIVING THE CHRISTIAN LIFE (1:27—2:18)

A. THE CALL TO A WORTHY LIFE

1:27☆ Acts 4:32; Phil 4:1, 2
1:28 Mt 10:28; Rom 8:17; 2 Tim 2:11; Heb 13:6
1:29 Mt 5:11, 12; Acts 5:41
1:30 Acts 16:19; Col 2:1; 1 Thess 2:2

27 Only let your conversation be as it becometh the gospel of Christ: that whether I come and see you, or else be absent, I may hear of your affairs, that ye stand fast in one spirit, with one mind striving together for the faith of the gospel;

28 And in nothing terrified by your adversaries: which is to them an evident token of perdition, but to you of salvation, and that of God.

29 For unto you it is given in the behalf of Christ, not only to believe on him, but also to suffer for his sake;

30 Having the same conflict which ye saw in me, and now hear *to be* in me.

B. JESUS, OUR MODEL

2:1 2 Cor 13:14; Col 3:12
2:2 1 Pet 3:8
2:3 Rom 12:10, 16; 1 Pet 5:5
2:4 Rom 15:1, 2; 1 Cor 10:24
2:5 Jn 13:15; 1 Pet 2:21
2:6 Isa 9:6; Jn 1:1, 2; 2 Cor 4:4; Col 1:15; 1 Tim 3:16; Heb 1:3

2 IF *there be* therefore any consolation in Christ, if any comfort of love, if any fellowship of the Spirit, if any bowels and mercies,

2 Fulfil ye my joy, that ye be likeminded, having the same love, *being* of one accord, of one mind.

3 *Let* nothing *be done* through strife or vainglory; but in lowliness of mind let each esteem other better than themselves.

4 Look not every man on his own things, but every man also on the things of others.

5 Let this mind be in you, which was also in Christ Jesus:

6 Who, being in the form of God, thought it not robbery to be equal with God:

1:20 Believers must affirm, as Paul did here, that the one objective in their lives is to glorify Christ even if this must be done by death. While we should never seek martyrdom, we should have a spirit of willingness to endure it, if it is the will of God.

1:27 *let your conversation be as it becometh the gospel of Christ,* i.e., "let your manner of life [how you live] be worthy of the gospel of Christ" (RSV). The gospel is demeaned when those who profess it do not live up to its standards of life.

7 But made himself of no reputation, and took upon him the form of a
servant, and was made in the likeness of men:
8 And being found in fashion as a man, he humbled himself, and became
obedient unto death, even the death of the cross.
9 Wherefore God also hath highly exalted him, and given him a name
which is above every name:
10 That at the name of Jesus every knee should bow, of *things* in heaven,
and *things* in earth, and *things* under the earth;
11 And *that* every tongue should confess that Jesus Christ *is* Lord, to the
glory of God the Father.

☆**2:7** Ps 22:6; Isa 53:3, 11; Ezek 34:23; Mt 20:28; Jn 1:14; Gal 4:4 **2:8** Heb 5:8; 12:2 **2:9** Eph 1:20, 21; Heb 1:4 **2:10** Isa 45:23; Rom 14:11 **2:11** Jn 13:13; Rom 14:9; Rev 5:13

C. OUR CHRISTIAN DUTIES

12 Wherefore, my beloved, as ye have always obeyed, not as in my
presence only, but now much more in my absence, work out your own
salvation with fear and trembling.
13 For it is God which worketh in you both to will and to do of *his* good
pleasure.
14 Do all things without murmurings and disputings:
15 That ye may be blameless and harmless, the sons of God, without
rebuke, in the midst of a crooked and perverse nation, among whom ye
shine as lights in the world;
16 Holding forth the word of life; that I may rejoice in the day of Christ,
that I have not run in vain, neither laboured in vain.
17 Yea, and if I be offered upon the sacrifice and service of your faith, I
joy, and rejoice with you all.
18 For the same cause also do ye joy, and rejoice with me.

☆**2:12** Phil 1:5 ☆**2:13** Rom 8:28; 1 Cor 12:6; Heb 13:20, 21 ☆**2:14** Rom 14:1; 1 Cor 10:10 **2:15** Mt 5:45; Jn 12:36; Eph 5:1 **2:16** Jn 6:63, 68; 1 Thess 2:19, 20 **2:17** Rom 15:16; Col 1:24

IV. SENDING TIMOTHY AND EPAPHRODITUS (2:19–30)

19 But I trust in the Lord Jesus to send Ti-mo'the-us shortly unto you, that
I also may be of good comfort, when I know your state.
20 For I have no man likeminded, who will naturally care for your state.
21 For all seek their own, not the things which are Jesus Christ's.
22 But ye know the proof of him, that, as a son with the father, he hath
served with me in the gospel.
23 Him therefore I hope to send presently, so soon as I shall see how it will
go with me.
24 But I trust in the Lord that I also myself shall come shortly.

☆**2:20** 1 Cor 16:10 **2:21** 1 Cor 10:24; 13:5 **2:22** 1 Cor 4:17; 1 Tim 1:2 **2:24** Phil 1:25

2:7 *Kenosis* (emptying) is a theological term applied to the incarnation of Christ. He "laid aside his mighty power and glory, taking the disguise of a slave and becoming like men" (TLB). This means that he divested himself of some things pertaining to his divine state, assuming human limitations such as being hungry and thirsty and requiring sleep. It was a self-assumed limitation consistent with being a true man. Thus Jesus was the God-man—having a truly human and a truly divine nature, i.e., two natures in one person without confusion. This is a great mystery and Scripture does not tell us all the details about the *kenosis.* (Cf. 2 Cor. 8:9; Matt. 27:46; Mark 13:32; John 17:4; Luke 2:40–52; Heb. 4:15; 5:7, 8.)

2:12, 13 Paul speaks of the sovereignty of God and the free agency of man. Man is to work, yet God is at work in man. Both the free agency of man and the sovereignty of God are expressed repeatedly in the Scriptures. The resolution of these two apparently contradictory ideas will take place at last in eternity when we see more clearly what is hazy to us now.

2:14 The Christian's testimony is beautified by an equable temper and proper behavior. Paul specifies two things here: (1) we should cheerfully do the will of God, not murmuring against it; and (2) we should not engage in useless disputes with fellow believers, because this destroys unity and impairs harmony.

2:20 Paul is sending Timothy to them to find out how they are faring. He takes time to praise his assistant by saying that he has been tried and proved to be good and true. He was as good a man as he seemed to be, and in his service for Christ he was acceptable to God and approved of men. Timothy cared for the Philippians more than he cared for himself.

2:25☆ Phil 4:18
2:29 Rom 16:2; 1 Cor 16:18; 1 Thess 5:12; 1 Tim 5:17
2:30 1 Cor 16:17
3:1☆ Phil 4:4
3:2 Ps 22:16, 20; Rom 2:28; Gal 5:2
3:3☆ Deut 30:6; Jn 4:21–24; Rom 2:29; 7:6; Col 2:11
3:5 Acts 22:3; 23:6; Rom 11:1; 2 Cor 11:22
3:6 Acts 8:3; 22:4; Rom 10:5; Gal 1:13
3:7☆ Mt 13:44; Lk 14:33
3:8 Isa 53:11; Jn 17:3; Eph 4:13; 2 Pet 3:18
3:9 Isa 64:6; Rom 1:17; 9:30; 10:3; Gal 2:16; 2 Pet 1:1
3:10 Jn 17:3; Rom 8:17, 29; Eph 1:19, 20; 1 Pet 4:13
3:11 Acts 26:8; 1 Cor 15:23
3:12 1 Cor 9:24; 1 Tim 6:12; Heb 12:23
3:13 Lk 9:62; 1 Cor 9:24; Heb 6:1

25 Yet I supposed it necessary to send to you E-paph-ro-di′tus, my
brother, and companion in labour, and fellowsoldier, but your messenger,
and he that ministered to my wants.
26 For he longed after you all, and was full of heaviness, because that ye
had heard that he had been sick.
27 For indeed he was sick nigh unto death: but God had mercy on him;
and not on him only, but on me also, lest I should have sorrow upon
sorrow.
28 I sent him therefore the more carefully, that, when ye see him again, ye
may rejoice, and that I may be the less sorrowful.
29 Receive him therefore in the Lord with all gladness; and hold such in
reputation:
30 Because for the work of Christ he was nigh unto death, not regarding
his life, to supply your lack of service toward me.

V. INSTRUCTIONS AND EXHORTATIONS (3:1—4:9)

A. PAUL'S OWN EXAMPLE

3 FINALLY, my brethren, rejoice in the Lord. To write the same things
to you, to me indeed *is* not grievous, but for you *it is* safe.
2 Beware of dogs, beware of evil workers, beware of the concision.
3 For we are the circumcision, which worship God in the spirit, and
rejoice in Christ Jesus, and have no confidence in the flesh.
4 Though I might also have confidence in the flesh. If any other man
thinketh that he hath whereof he might trust in the flesh, I more:
5 Circumcised the eighth day, of the stock of Israel, *of* the tribe of
Benjamin, an Hebrew of the Hebrews; as touching the law, a Pharisee;
6 Concerning zeal, persecuting the church; touching the righteousness
which is in the law, blameless.
7 But what things were gain to me, those I counted loss for Christ.
8 Yea doubtless, and I count all things *but* loss for the excellency of the
knowledge of Christ Jesus my Lord: for whom I have suffered the loss of all
things, and do count them *but* dung, that I may win Christ,
9 And be found in him, not having mine own righteousness, which is of
the law, but that which is through the faith of Christ, the righteousness
which is of God by faith:
10 That I may know him, and the power of his resurrection, and the
fellowship of his sufferings, being made conformable unto his death;
11 If by any means I might attain unto the resurrection of the dead.
12 Not as though I had already attained, either were already perfect: but I
follow after, if that I may apprehend that for which also I am apprehended
of Christ Jesus.
13 Brethren, I count not myself to have apprehended: but *this* one thing *I*

2:25ff Epaphroditus was a highly thought-of member of the Philippian church. He brought an offering to Paul from the church and was commissioned to stay with the apostle to help him. He became ill, probably from overextending himself to fulfill his ministry. Following a slow recovery, he was sent by Paul back to Philippi, being commended as a brother, fellow worker, and *fellow soldier*.

3:1 *rejoice in the Lord.* They were to be content with the interest they had in the Lord Jesus and the benefit they hoped for by his grace. The more we rejoice in Jesus, the more we will be desirous of serving him and the less likely will be the chance of falling away from him.

3:3 True circumcision is not of the flesh but of the spirit. True Christians worship in the spirit, rejoice in Jesus Christ, and have no confidence in the flesh (i.e., in carnal ordinances and outward performance).

3:7 Paul was a high-class Jew steeped in Judaism. He was a circumcised Hebrew of the Hebrews, a Benjaminite, a Pharisee, blameless under the law, and a persecutor of the people of the way. All these things he counted as worthless and useless when compared with what he had in Jesus Christ. Believers should say the same thing with regard to their fame, their fortune, their attainments, and their place in the community. These things are refuse when compared to their standing in Jesus Christ.

do, forgetting those things which are behind, and reaching forth unto those
things which are before,
14 I press toward the mark for the prize of the high calling of God in
Christ Jesus.
15 Let us therefore, as many as be perfect, be thus minded: and if in any
thing ye be otherwise minded, God shall reveal even this unto you.
16 Nevertheless, whereto we have already attained, let us walk by the same
rule, let us mind the same thing.

B. WARNING AGAINST ENEMIES

17 Brethren, be followers together of me, and mark them which walk so as
ye have us for an ensample.
18 (For many walk, of whom I have told you often, and now tell you even
weeping, *that they are* the enemies of the cross of Christ:
19 Whose end *is* destruction, whose God *is their* belly, and *whose* glory *is*
in their shame, who mind earthly things.)
20 For our conversation is in heaven; from whence also we look for the
Saviour, the Lord Jesus Christ:
21 Who shall change our vile body, that it may be fashioned like unto his
glorious body, according to the working whereby he is able even to subdue
all things unto himself.

C. WORDS OF ADMONITION AND PROMISE

4 THEREFORE, my brethren dearly beloved and longed for, my joy
and crown, so stand fast in the Lord, *my* dearly beloved.
2 I beseech Eu-o′di-as, and beseech Syn′ty-che, that they be of the same
mind in the Lord.
3 And I intreat thee also, true yokefellow, help those women which
laboured with me in the gospel, with Clement also, and *with* other my
fellowlabourers, whose names *are* in the book of life.
4 Rejoice in the Lord alway: *and* again I say, Rejoice.
5 Let your moderation be known unto all men. The Lord *is* at hand.
6 Be careful for nothing; but in every thing by prayer and supplication
with thanksgiving let your requests be made known unto God.
7 And the peace of God, which passeth all understanding, shall keep your
hearts and minds through Christ Jesus.
8 Finally, brethren, whatsoever things are true, whatsoever things *are*

3:14 2 Tim 4:7, 8; Heb 12:1
3:15 1 Cor 2:6; 14:20; Gal 5:10; Phil 1:9, 10
3:16 Gal 6:16
3:17 1 Cor 4:16; 1 Pet 5:3
3:18 Gal 6:14
☆**3:20** 1 Cor 1:7; Eph 2:16, 19; Col 3:1, 3; 1 Thess 1:10; 2 Tim 4:8; Tit 2:13
3:21 Isa 63:1; Mt 17:2; 28:18; 1 Cor 15:43–53; Eph 1:19; Col 3:4; Heb 7:25; 1 Jn 3:2
4:1 1 Cor 16:13; Phil 1:8
☆**4:2** Phil 2:2
☆**4:3** Ex 32:32; Dan 12:1; Lk 10:20; Rom 16:3; Rev 3:5; 20:12; 21:27
4:4 Rom 12:12; Phil 3:1
4:5 Heb 10:25, 37; Jas 5:8, 9; 1 Pet 4:7
☆**4:6** Ps 55:22; Prov 16:3; Mt 6:25; Lk 12:22; Eph 6:18; 1 Pet 5:7
4:7 Isa 26:3; Jn 14:27; Rom 5:1; Col 3:15
4:8 1 Thess 5:22

3:20 *Conversation* comes from the Greek word *politeuma,* which means citizenship. Thus the Christian has two citizenships; one is in heaven and the other on earth. The citizenship of the world (under the domination of Satan) is transitory; heavenly citizenship (under the rule of God) is eternal. We wait for the coming of the Lord's kingdom on earth and the triumph of the crucified One over principalities and powers.

4:2 Christians sometimes fall out with each other. Euodias and Syntyche, two female believers, were influential in the church at Philippi, where women were prominent. Paul wanted to bring them together again. He asks them to agree in the Lord. What the cause of the estrangement was we are not told; perhaps that is good, for we can adduce the common principle that anything that separates us from other believers should be reconciled as soon as possible, unless the issue at stake is one that cannot be compromised.

4:3 Clement alone is mentioned here. This indicates that he was esteemed by Paul, especially since the others are referred to as "the rest of my fellow workers" (NIV). From the context, Paul may have hoped that Clement would be the one to help Euodia and Syntyche reconcile their differences. All three of these people were held in respect by Paul as co-laborers in the gospel.

4:6 Prayerlessness brings nothing but anxiety and insecurity, whereas prayer with thanksgiving brings that peace that passes all human understanding. This peace is independent of outward circumstances, springing from the love of God for his people, who know that he will answer their prayers according to his will and for their good. To be anxious about nothing excludes everything; to pray about everything excludes nothing.

honest, whatsoever things *are* just, whatsoever things *are* pure, whatsoever
things *are* lovely, whatsoever things *are* of good report; if *there be* any
virtue, and if *there be* any praise, think on these things.
4:9 9 Those things, which ye have both learned, and received, and heard, and
Rom 15:33 seen in me, do: and the God of peace shall be with you.

VI. THANKSGIVING FOR THE PHILIPPIAN GIFT (4:10–20)

4:10 10 But I rejoiced in the Lord greatly, that now at the last your care of me
2 Cor 11:9 hath flourished again; wherein ye were also careful, but ye lacked
opportunity.
4:11 11 Not that I speak in respect of want: for I have learned, in whatsoever
1 Tim 6:6 state I am, *therewith* to be content.
4:12 12 I know both how to be abased, and I know how to abound: every where
1 Cor 4:11 2 Cor 11:9 and in all things I am instructed both to be full and to be hungry, both to
abound and to suffer need.
4:13☆ 13 I can do all things through Christ which strengtheneth me.
Jn 15:5 2 Cor 12:9 14 Notwithstanding ye have well done, that ye did communicate with my
4:14 Phil 1:7 affliction.
Heb 10:33, 34 **4:15** 15 Now ye Phi-lip'pi-ans know also, that in the beginning of the gospel,
Rom 15:26 2 Cor 11:8, 9 when I departed from Macedonia, no church communicated with me as
Phil 1:5 concerning giving and receiving, but ye only.
16 For even in Thes-sa-lo-ni'ca ye sent once and again unto my necessity.
4:17 17 Not because I desire a gift: but I desire fruit that may abound to your
Tit 3:14 account.
4:18 18 But I have all, and abound: I am full, having received of E-paph-ro-
2 Cor 9:12 Phil 2:25 di'tus the things *which were sent* from you, an odour of a sweet smell, a
Heb 13:16 sacrifice acceptable, wellpleasing to God.
4:19 19 But my God shall supply all your need according to his riches in glory
Ps 23:1 Prov 8:21 by Christ Jesus.
2 Cor 9:8 **4:20** 20 Now unto God and our Father *be* glory for ever and ever. Amen.
Rom 11:36 Gal 1:4

VII. THE CONCLUDING GREETING AND BENEDICTION (4:21–23)

4:21 Gal 1:2 21 Salute every saint in Christ Jesus. The brethren which are with me greet
4:22☆ 2 Cor 13:13 you.
4:23 Rom 16:20 22 All the saints salute you, chiefly they that are of Cæsar's household.
2 Tim 4:22 23 The grace of our Lord Jesus Christ *be* with you all. Amen.

4:13 Paul speaks of three great promises of God in this chapter. In verse 7 he mentions the *peace* of God that passes understanding; in this verse he speaks about the *power* of God by which we are enabled to do whatever God wants us to do; in verse 19 he mentions the *provision* of God that supplies every need.
4:22 *they that are of Caesar's household,* i.e., the Christian converts who belonged to the emperor's court. There were believers in the emperor's family, and these saints in high places were willing to join with Paul in sending greetings to their fellow Christians in Philippi. Man-made barriers are broken down when salvation comes.

THE EPISTLE OF PAUL THE APOSTLE TO THE

COLOSSIANS

Authorship, date, and background Colossians, like Ephesians, Philippians, and Philemon, was one of the "prison letters" of the apostle Paul. Caesarea, Ephesus, and Rome have been suggested as the places from which they were written. No good reason can be given for supposing it was other than Rome where Paul suffered imprisonment. The date for the composition of this letter is in the general time frame of A.D. 60–61. Similarities between Colossians and Ephesians have occasioned some to suppose that Colossians was written by someone other than Paul. However, such similarities should be expected when the two letters were sent to two different churches in different localities.

The town of Colosse was located in Turkey, not far from Laodicea and Hierapolis. It had been a thriving commercial city, but it declined as Hierapolis and Laodicea grew in importance. It was noted for its glossy black wool taken from sheep which grazed in the surrounding hills. Paul had never visited Colosse, although the church there was founded during the time of his Ephesian ministry. Since Epaphras was a native of this city in the Lycus Valley, it was probably he who preached there and started a church (see Acts 19:10; Col. 4:12). Philemon and his slave Onesimus came from that city, and Paul told Philemon to have a room ready for him when he visited Colosse as he hoped to do (Philemon 22). He also sent Philemon greetings from Epaphras, whom he identified as his fellow prisoner (Philemon 23).

The Colossian church had been deeply infiltrated by teachings foreign to the Christian faith. As a result, the people became syncretists who added to Christianity elements from non-Christian sources such as Gnosticism, paganism, and Judaic speculative philosophy. Some worshipped angelic powers, some said asceticism was essential to salvation, and still others had an inordinate liking for knowledge and wisdom of a secret sort. As a result of these practices and persuasions, the person and work of Jesus Christ were downgraded. These wrong customs in the church occasioned the writing of this letter by Paul, in which he set forth clearly and passionately the correct view of Jesus Christ and his preeminence.

Characteristics and content Paul's hymn or prayer of praise to Jesus Christ stands out in the Colossian letter (1:15–20). Whether Paul writes this himself, gets it from an earlier Christian liturgy, or whether it comes directly from the Holy Spirit makes no difference. However it came to be part of the letter, it clearly assigns to Jesus Christ expressions which belong to deity alone—that is, to God. Paul's superb and dazzling statement sums up his teaching about Jesus, when he says, "For in him dwelleth all the fulness of the Godhead bodily" (2:9). This is the Jesus he describes in chapter one as bearing "the image of the invisible God," as the One through whom all things were created, as the One who by his power holds everything together, as the Head of the body, the church . . . so "that in all things he might have the preeminence" (1:15–20).

Paul goes on to destroy the idea of a syncretistic faith by showing that Jesus and Jesus alone is all the believer needs, so that nothing can or should be added to what he has done and what he commands. He warns the Colossians against the wrong beliefs which have crept into their midst, even as he sweeps away the legalism to which they have become attached. Paul urges them to put off or do away with things which hinder them and to put on those things which mark them as true believers in Christ. He carefully delineates what the relationships should be between husbands and wives, parents and children, and masters and slaves.

The letter closes with exhortations, a commendation both of Tychicus and Onesimus, as well as greetings from Luke and Demas. He asks that they pass his letter on to the church at Laodicea, which suggests that that group faced similar problems. He also speaks of a letter he has written to Laodicea which is no longer extant.

Outline

I. Introduction (1:1–14)
II. Doctrinal concerns (1:15—2:23)
III. The new life versus the old life (3:1—4:6)
IV. Conclusion (4:7–18)

I. INTRODUCTION (1:1–14)

A. THE APOSTOLIC GREETING

1:1☆ 2 Cor 1:1 Eph 1:1

1 PAUL, an apostle of Jesus Christ by the will of God, and Ti-mo′the-us
our brother,

1:2 Rom 1:7

2 To the saints and faithful brethren in Christ which are at Co-los′se:
Grace *be* unto you, and peace, from God our Father and the Lord Jesus
Christ.

B. PAUL'S ALLELUIA FOR THE COLOSSIANS

1:3☆ Rom 1:8

3 We give thanks to God and the Father of our Lord Jesus Christ, praying
always for you,

1:4 Gal 5:6 Eph 1:15 Heb 6:10

4 Since we heard of your faith in Christ Jesus, and of the love *which ye*
have to all the saints,

1:5 Mt 5:12 Eph 1:13 2 Tim 4:8 1 Pet 1:4

5 For the hope which is laid up for you in heaven, whereof ye heard before
in the word of the truth of the gospel;

1:6 Mt 24:14 Jn 15:16 Rom 10:18 2 Cor 6:1 Eph 3:2 Col 1:23 Tit 2:11

6 Which is come unto you, as *it is* in all the world; and bringeth forth
fruit, as *it doth* also in you, since the day ye heard *of it*, and knew the grace
of God in truth:

1:7☆ Col 4:12, 13 Philem 23

7 As ye also learned of Ep′a-phras our dear fellowservant, who is for you
a faithful minister of Christ;
8 Who also declared unto us your love in the Spirit.

C. THE INTERCESSION FOR THE SAINTS

1:9☆ Rom 12:2 Eph 1:15–17

9 For this cause we also, since the day we heard *it*, do not cease to pray for
you, and to desire that ye might be filled with the knowledge of his will in
all wisdom and spiritual understanding;

1:10☆ Jn 15:16 Eph 4:1 1 Thess 2:12 4:1

10 That ye might walk worthy of the Lord unto all pleasing, being fruitful
in every good work, and increasing in the knowledge of God;

1:11 Acts 5:41 Eph 3:16, 20

11 Strengthened with all might, according to his glorious power, unto all
patience and longsuffering with joyfulness;

1:12 Acts 26:18 Eph 1:11; 5:20

12 Giving thanks unto the Father, which hath made us meet to be
partakers of the inheritance of the saints in light:

1:13☆ Acts 26:18 Heb 2:14, 15

13 Who hath delivered us from the power of darkness, and hath translated
us into the kingdom of his dear Son:

1:14 Eph 1:7

14 In whom we have redemption through his blood, *even* the forgiveness of
sins:

1:15☆ Jn 1:1, 18; 14:9 2 Cor 4:4 Phil 2:6 1 Tim 1:17 Heb 1:3 Rev 3:14

II. DOCTRINAL CONCERNS (1:15—2:23)

A. JESUS AND HIS GLORY

1:16 Jn 1:3 Heb 1:2 1 Pet 3:22

15 Who is the image of the invisible God, the firstborn of every creature:
16 For by him were all things created, that are in heaven, and that are in

---

1:1 In Philippians Paul calls himself a bond-slave of Jesus Christ. Here he calls himself an apostle. He had a divine call to that high office and he enjoyed three outward evidences that were seals of the apostleship: (1) he had seen the risen Christ; (2) he was an inspired witness to the resurrection of Jesus Christ; and (3) he had the gift of performing miracles.

1:3ff *Paul begins with a* prayer of thanksgiving for the three major graces manifested in the lives of the Colossians: (1) faith in Christ; (2) love of the brethren; (3) the hope laid up for them in heaven, elsewhere called the blessed hope (Titus 2:13).

1:7 *Epaphras* is mentioned here and in 4:12 and Philem. 23. He was a *dear fellow-servant,* i.e., "a faithful fellow-slave," according to Paul, and one who may have founded the church at Colosse. He suffered with Paul during part of his first Roman imprisonment and may have been imprisoned with him as an accomplice in the case. Paul paid him a high compliment when he called him a *faithful slave* (*doulos* in the Greek means *slave* over whom the master had the right of life and death).

1:9, 10 Paul prays for knowledge, which has for its end a worthy walk. Knowing and doing go hand in hand. Knowing is related to doctrine and doing to duty. Right actions always come from right thinking.

1:13 The church is the bride of Christ and Christ is the Bridegroom. Here Paul speaks about the believer's

earth, visible and invisible, whether *they be* thrones, or dominions, or
principalities, or powers: all things were created by him, and for him:
17 And he is before all things, and by him all things consist.
18 And he is the head of the body, the church: who is the beginning, the
firstborn from the dead; that in all *things* he might have the preeminence.
19 For it pleased *the Father* that in him should all fulness dwell;
20 And, having made peace through the blood of his cross, by him to
reconcile all things unto himself; by him, *I say*, whether *they be* things in
earth, or things in heaven.
21 And you, that were sometime alienated and enemies in *your* mind by
wicked works, yet now hath he reconciled
22 In the body of his flesh through death, to present you holy and
unblameable and unreproveable in his sight:
23 If ye continue in the faith grounded and settled, and *be* not moved
away from the hope of the gospel, which ye have heard, *and* which was
preached to every creature which is under heaven; whereof I Paul am made
a minister;

B. PAUL'S MINISTRY

24 Who now rejoice in my sufferings for you, and fill up that which is
behind of the afflictions of Christ in my flesh for his body's sake, which is
the church:
25 Whereof I am made a minister, according to the dispensation of God
which is given to me for you, to fulfil the word of God;
26 *Even* the mystery which hath been hid from ages and from generations,
but now is made manifest to his saints:
27 To whom God would make known what *is* the riches of the glory of this
mystery among the Gentiles; which is Christ in you, the hope of glory:
28 Whom we preach, warning every man, and teaching every man in all
wisdom; that we may present every man perfect in Christ Jesus:
29 Whereunto I also labour, striving according to his working, which
worketh in me mightily.

C. PAUL'S CONCERN FOR THE CHURCH

2 FOR I would that ye knew what great conflict I have for you, and *for*
them at La-od-i-ce'a, and *for* as many as have not seen my face in the
flesh;
2 That their hearts might be comforted, being knit together in love, and
unto all riches of the full assurance of understanding, to the acknowledge-
ment of the mystery of God, and of the Father, and of Christ;
3 In whom are hid all the treasures of wisdom and knowledge.
4 And this I say, lest any man should beguile you with enticing words.

1:17 Jn 1:1, 2; 8:58
1:18 Jn 17:5 Eph 1:22, 23 Heb 13:8 Rev 1:5
1:19 Jn 1:16 3:33, 34 Eph 1:23 Col 2:9
1:20 Rom 5:1 2 Cor 5:18 Eph 2:13, 14
1:21 Rom 5:10 2 Cor 5:18, 19 Eph 2:3, 12
☆**1:22** Rom 7:4 Eph 1:4; 5:27
1:23 Eph 3:17 Col 1:5, 6
1:24 Eph 1:22, 23 Phil 2:17; 3:10 2 Tim 1:8
1:25 Eph 3:2
☆**1:26** Eph 3:3
☆**1:27** Rom 8:10; 9:23, 24 Eph 3:8, 9, 16
1:28 Acts 20:31 Eph 4:13
1:29 1 Cor 15:10 Eph 1:19 Col 4:12
2:1 Col 4:12, 13 Rev 1:11
2:2 Mt 11:25–27 Eph 1:18, 19 Phil 3:8 Col 2:19 2 Pet 3:18
2:3 Isa 11:2 Rom 11:33 Eph 3:8
2:4 Rom 16:18

---

deliverance from the kingdom of darkness to the kingdom of God's dear Son. Christ is King and a king has a kingdom. Thus Scripture speaks about both church and kingdom with respect to Christ.

1:15ff In verses 15–20 Paul says that Christ is the Creator of all things in heaven and on earth. In different places in Scripture the creating work of the triune God is attributed to one or the other members of the Trinity. Thus Genesis 1:1 says that God created; Job declares, "The Spirit of God hath made me" (33:4).

1:22 God commands holiness and gives grace to make it possible. Some hold that it is possible to reach a state of sinless perfection; others hold that sinless perfection is not attainable in this life, but does come, upon death, through glorification. The former view maintains that the believer *cannot* sin, the latter that the Christian *must* sin. Perhaps the better way to express it is to say that the believer *can* sin yet he *does not have to.* In principle, every believer should be wholly yielded to God for his will and set apart for God's service.

1:26, 27 Christ takes up his abode in our hearts when we have been regenerated. This is union with Christ and includes two things: (1) we are members of his body and partakers of the divine nature (Eph. 3:17; Col. 1:27) as we feed on him (John 6:56) and as his Word abides in us (John 15:7); and (2) we grow in grace and fruitfulness as we abide in him (John 15:5ff).

2:5 1 Cor 5:7
5 For though I be absent in the flesh, yet am I with you in the spirit,
joying and beholding your order, and the stedfastness of your faith in
Christ.

2:6 Jn 1:12; Col 1:10
6 As ye have therefore received Christ Jesus the Lord, *so* walk ye in him:

2:7 Eph 2:20; 3:17; 4:21
7 Rooted and built up in him, and stablished in the faith, as ye have been
taught, abounding therein with thanksgiving.

D. THE ALL-SUFFICIENT CHRIST

2:8 Jer 29:8; Mt 15:2, 3; Col 2:20, 23; Heb 13:9
8 Beware lest any man spoil you through philosophy and vain deceit, after
the tradition of men, after the rudiments of the world, and not after Christ.

2:9 Isa 7:14; 9:6; Jn 1:14; Col 1:19
9 For in him dwelleth all the fulness of the Godhead bodily.

2:10 Eph 1:21; 3:19; 1 Pet 3:22
10 And ye are complete in him, which is the head of all principality and
power:

2:11☆ Jer 4:4
11 In whom also ye are circumcised with the circumcision made without
hands, in putting off the body of the sins of the flesh by the circumcision of
Christ:

2:12☆ Rom 6:4, 5; Eph 2:6
12 Buried with him in baptism, wherein also ye are risen with *him* through
the faith of the operation of God, who hath raised him from the dead.

2:13 Eph 2:1, 5
13 And you, being dead in your sins and the uncircumcision of your flesh,
hath he quickened together with him, having forgiven you all trespasses;

2:14 Eph 2:15; 1 Pet 2:24
14 Blotting out the handwriting of ordinances that was against us, which
was contrary to us, and took it out of the way, nailing it to his cross;

2:15 Isa 53:12; Jn 12:31; 2 Cor 2:14; Eph 4:8
15 *And* having spoiled principalities and powers, he made a shew of them
openly, triumphing over them in it.

E. ERRORS TO BE SHUNNED

2:16 1 Chron 23:31; Rom 14:3, 5; Gal 4:10
16 Let no man therefore judge you in meat, or in drink, or in respect of an
holyday, or of the new moon, or of the sabbath *days:*

2:17 Heb 8:5; 10:1
17 Which are a shadow of things to come; but the body *is* of Christ.
18 Let no man beguile you of your reward in a voluntary humility and
worshipping of angels, intruding into those things which he hath not seen,
vainly puffed up by his fleshly mind,

2:19 Eph 1:22, 23; 4:15, 16
19 And not holding the Head, from which all the body by joints and bands
having nourishment ministered, and knit together, increaseth with the
increase of God.

2:20☆ Rom 6:2; Gal 2:20; 4:9
20 Wherefore if ye be dead with Christ from the rudiments of the world,
why, as though living in the world, are ye subject to ordinances,
21 (Touch not; taste not; handle not;

2:22 Mt 15:9; 1 Cor 6:13
22 Which all are to perish with the using;) after the commandments and
doctrines of men?

2:23 1 Tim 4:3
23 Which things have indeed a shew of wisdom in will worship, and
humility, and neglecting of the body; not in any honour to the satisfying of
the flesh.

2:11, 12 These verses are used by those who practice infant baptism, to establish the dogma that baptism has replaced circumcision. Since infants were circumcised, so also should infants in the church age be baptized in water. Col. 2:12 in the Greek speaks of the believer being co-buried with him in baptism, which suggests immersion. But pedobaptists insist that this refers to the spiritual aspect of conversion and has nothing to say about the mode of baptism. Anti-pedobaptists think the connection made in Colossians between circumcision and baptism is merely spiritual and has nothing to say about who are the proper subjects for baptism. Every covenant made by God has a seal—e.g., the Noahic covenant was sealed by the sign of the rainbow; the covenant of grace has water baptism for its seal.

2:20 Here and in the book of Hebrews, Scripture makes plain that the ceremonial law with its "not eating, tasting, or even touching certain foods" (TLB) has forever been abolished. Under the New Covenant, the laws for blood sacrifices and the dietary proscriptions need not be followed any longer—now that Jesus has set us free. Peter needed a vision from God to be delivered from this bondage (Acts 10), and the Jerusalem conference in Acts 15 declared that circumcision was no longer binding.

III. THE NEW LIFE VERSUS THE OLD LIFE (3:1—4:6)

A. THE BELIEVER'S LIFE ROOTED IN CHRIST

3 IF ye then be risen with Christ, seek those things which are above,
where Christ sitteth on the right hand of God.
2 Set your affection on things above, not on things on the earth.
3 For ye are dead, and your life is hid with Christ in God.
4 When Christ, *who is* our life, shall appear, then shall ye also appear with
him in glory.

B. PUTTING OFF THE OLD MAN

5 Mortify therefore your members which are upon the earth; fornication,
uncleanness, inordinate affection, evil concupiscence, and covetousness,
which is idolatry:
6 For which things' sake the wrath of God cometh on the children of
disobedience:
7 In the which ye also walked some time, when ye lived in them.
8 But now ye also put off all these; anger, wrath, malice, blasphemy, filthy
communication out of your mouth.
9 Lie not one to another, seeing that ye have put off the old man with his
deeds;
10 And have put on the new *man*, which is renewed in knowledge after the
image of him that created him:
11 Where there is neither Greek nor Jew, circumcision nor uncircumcision,
Barbarian, Scyth'i-an, bond *nor* free: but Christ *is* all, and in all.

C. PUTTING ON THE NEW MAN

12 Put on therefore, as the elect of God, holy and beloved, bowels of
mercies, kindness, humbleness of mind, meekness, longsuffering;
13 Forbearing one another, and forgiving one another, if any man have a
quarrel against any: even as Christ forgave you, so also *do* ye.
14 And above all these things *put on* charity, which is the bond of
perfectness.
15 And let the peace of God rule in your hearts, to the which also ye are
called in one body; and be ye thankful.
16 Let the word of Christ dwell in you richly in all wisdom; teaching and
admonishing one another in psalms and hymns and spiritual songs, singing
with grace in your hearts to the Lord.
17 And whatsoever ye do in word or deed, *do* all in the name of the Lord
Jesus, giving thanks to God and the Father by him.

D. THE NEW LIFE AND THE CHRISTIAN FAMILY

18 Wives, submit yourselves unto your own husbands, as it is fit in the
Lord.

☆**3:1** Mt 6:33; Eph 2:6; Col 2:2
3:2 Phil 3:19, 20
☆**3:3** Gal 2:20
☆**3:4** 1 Cor 15:43; 1 Jn 3:2
3:5 Mk 7:21–23; Rom 8:13; Gal 5:19; Eph 5:3, 5
3:7 Eph 2:2
☆**3:8** Eph 4:22, 29; Jas 1:21
3:9 Lev 19:11; Eph 4:22, 25
3:10 Rom 8:29; 12:2; Eph 2:10; 4:24
3:11 Rom 10:12; 1 Cor 12:13; Gal 3:28
☆**3:12** Gal 5:22; Eph 4:2, 24; 1 Pet 1:2
3:13 Eph 4:32
3:14 Rom 13:8
3:15 Jn 14:27; 1 Cor 7:15; Eph 2:14–16; Phil 4:7
3:16 Jer 15:16; Rom 10:17; Eph 5:19; 2 Tim 3:15–17
3:17 1 Cor 10:31; Eph 5:20; 1 Thess 5:18
☆**3:18** Eph 5:22

3:1 *If ye then be risen with Christ.* The gospel message of the apostolic church stressed the resurrection of Christ as the climax of God's redemptive work. The apostles, in their preaching as recorded in Acts, continually emphasized the fact that Christ has risen from the dead. When Peter faced the Sanhedrin his main point was, "Jesus Christ . . . whom ye crucified . . . God raised from the dead . . ." (Acts 4:10).
3:3, 4 Paul here says much the same thing he says in Gal. 2:20. Christ is the believer's life, for he who was dead has been made alive in Jesus Christ. And Christ lives in every believer. All will appear with him in glory.
3:8 Sanctification involves putting off certain things as stated here. Then we are to put on other things as specified beginning with verse 12. When the sins of the flesh have been put to death, then the things of life can come alive. So long as we live in sin, we are void of sanctification.
3:12 If believers put off the sins of the flesh without putting on the good characteristics described in this verse, they will be of little use. We need to be properly clothed; and compassion, kindness, lowliness, meekness, and longsuffering are the best garments.
3:18ff Beginning here Paul repeats in abbreviated

3:19☆ Eph 5:25 — 19 Husbands, love *your* wives, and be not bitter against them.
3:20 Eph 6:1 — 20 Children, obey *your* parents in all things: for this is well pleasing unto
the Lord.
3:21 Eph 6:4 — 21 Fathers, provoke not your children *to anger*, lest they be discouraged.
3:22☆ Eph 6:5, 6 — 22 Servants, obey in all things *your* masters according to the flesh; not with
eyeservice, as menpleasers; but in singleness of heart, fearing God:
3:23 Eph 6:7 — 23 And whatsoever ye do, do *it* heartily, as to the Lord, and not unto men;
3:24 Eph 6:8 — 24 Knowing that of the Lord ye shall receive the reward of the inheritance:
for ye serve the Lord Christ.
3:25 Acts 10:34 — 25 But he that doeth wrong shall receive for the wrong which he hath
done: and there is no respect of persons.

4:1 Lev 19:13 Eph 6:9 — 4 MASTERS, give unto *your* servants that which is just and equal;
knowing that ye also have a Master in heaven.

E. THE COMMAND TO PRAY AND WITNESS

4:2☆ Lk 18:1 Acts 1:14 Eph 6:18 1 Thess 5:17 — 2 Continue in prayer, and watch in the same with thanksgiving;
3 Withal praying also for us, that God would open unto us a door of
utterance, to speak the mystery of Christ, for which I am also in bonds:
4:3☆ — 4 That I may make it manifest, as I ought to speak.
4:4 Eph 6:20 — 5 Walk in wisdom toward them that are without, redeeming the time.
4:5 Eph 5:15, 16 — 6 Let your speech *be* alway with grace, seasoned with salt, that ye may
4:6 Eccles 10:12 Eph 4:29 1 Pet 3:15 — know how ye ought to answer every man.

IV. CONCLUSION (4:7–18)

A. TYCHICUS AND ONESIMUS INTRODUCED

4:7☆ Acts 20:4 Eph 6:21, 22 — 7 All my state shall Tych′i-cus declare unto you, *who is* a beloved brother,
and a faithful minister and fellowservant in the Lord:
8 Whom I have sent unto you for the same purpose, that he might know
your estate, and comfort your hearts;
4:9 Philem 10 — 9 With O-nes′i-mus, a faithful and beloved brother, who is *one* of you.
They shall make known unto you all things which *are done* here.

4:10☆ Acts 12:12; 15:37 19:29; 20:4 27:2 2 Tim 4:11

B. GREETINGS FROM FRIENDS; INJUNCTIONS

10 Ar-is-tar′chus my fellowprisoner saluteth you, and Marcus, sister's son

---

form what he wrote to the church at Ephesus about husbands and wives, children and parents, and slaves and masters. There are still places on earth today where slavery exists. The principle laid down in Colossians is just as pertinent for those who are slaves today as for those who were slaves in Paul's day.

3:18, 19 Paul says that a wife is to submit to the authority of her husband. This recognizes that authority is essential to social and domestic order. Yet it is not unlimited, for a wife is not required to submit to anything that violates conscience or requires any action contrary to the will of God. A wife is protected by the command that a husband love his wife. Love makes tyranny, unkindness, selfishness, and cruelty impossible. *A wife has a right to support, sympathy, protection,* and happiness. "A wife need never fear to obey a husband of whose love she is sure."*

3:22 The Scriptures lay down three broad principles governing the relationships between employers and employees or servants and masters: (1) servants are to obey their masters and serve them well (3:22; Eph. 6:5–7; 1 Pet. 2:18–20); (2) masters are to treat their servants right (Eph. 6:9); and (3) masters and servants alike are servants of God. Capital and labor must include God in a triangular relationship in which both are responsible to the Creator.

4:2, 3 This verse may be connected with what precedes it about masters and servants. In that event, masters are to pray with their servants daily and to continue in prayer. This means they will be concerned about their souls as well as their bodies. Nothing is to divert them from praying and doing it with thanksgiving. In verse 3, Paul requests prayer for himself. This request must be seen in the light of 4:18 where he says, "Remember my bonds." Prisoners need prayer and more prayer, especially when they have been imprisoned for their faith in Christ.

4:7 See note to Eph. 6:21 for information about Tychicus.

4:10 See note to Philem. 24 on Aristarchus.

to Barnabas, (touching whom ye received commandments: if he come unto
you, receive him;)
[11]And Jesus, which is called Justus, who are of the circumcision. These
only *are my* fellowworkers unto the kingdom of God, which have been a
comfort unto me.
[12]Ep'a-phras, who is *one* of you, a servant of Christ, saluteth you, always
labouring fervently for you in prayers, that ye may stand perfect and
complete in all the will of God.
[13]For I bear him record, that he hath a great zeal for you, and them *that*
are in La-od-i-ce'a, and them in Hi-e-rap'o-lis.
[14]Luke, the beloved physician, and Demas, greet you.
[15]Salute the brethren which are in La-od-i-ce'a, and Nym'phas, and the
church which is in his house.
[16]And when this epistle is read among you, cause that it be read also in
the church of the La-od-i-ce'ans; and that ye likewise read the *epistle* from
La-od-i-ce'a.
[17]And say to Ar-chip'pus, Take heed to the ministry which thou hast
received in the Lord, that thou fulfil it.

4:11 Acts 11:2
☆**4:12** Col 1:7, 28
4:13 Col 2:1
4:14 2 Tim 4:10, 11; Philem 24
4:15 Rom 16:5; 1 Cor 16:19; Philem 2
4:16 1 Thess 5:27
☆**4:17** 2 Tim 4:5; Philem 2

C. PAUL'S CLOSING WORD

[18]The salutation by the hand of me Paul. Remember my bonds. Grace *be*
with you. Amen.

4:18 1 Cor 16:21; Heb 13:3

4:12 See note to Col. 1:7 about Epaphras.
4:17 Archippus is mentioned in Philem. 2. He was entrusted with some form of ministry and is encouraged by Paul to fulfill that ministry. This was hardly by way of reproof. Rather it came from concern for him to be all God wanted him to be. He was probably the son, or brother, of Philemon.

THE FIRST EPISTLE OF PAUL THE APOSTLE TO THE
THESSALONIANS

Authorship, date, and background The Apostle Paul, on his second missionary tour, visited Thessalonica (now known as Saloniki) around A.D. 49. He had walked from the city of Philippi to Thessalonica, along the Egnatian highway. He and his colleagues spent three Sabbaths in the synagogue at Thessalonica preaching the gospel. Apparently they then spent several months more in the city and established a church. Thessalonica, a free city, had been founded by Cassander. He named it for his wife, who was the half-sister of Alexander the Great. It was a flourishing seaport and a successful commercial center. In this pagan city, some Jews and a number of Gentiles came to faith in Jesus Christ. The Jews who did not respond to the gospel persecuted Paul, forcing him to flee the city (Acts 17:5ff.). He went to Berea, where the Jews willingly inquired into the truth of Paul's message.

When the reports of Paul's success became known in Thessalonica, the unbelieving Jews came to Berea to foment a riot. Paul left Berea and eventually arrived in Athens. Silas and Timothy remained in Berea to help the infant church. From Athens, Paul went to Corinth where he was to plant another church. While in Corinth, Timothy brought a report of certain happenings in the church at Thessalonica, a church about which the apostle was deeply concerned. He had planned to revisit the church, for he later wrote, "But we, brethren, being taken from you for a short time in presence, not in heart, endeavored the more abundantly to see your face with great desire. Wherefore we would have come unto you . . . but Satan hindered us" (2:17, 18).

1 and 2 Thessalonians were written within a short time of each other and Corinth was the city in which the letters were composed; the date was ca. A.D. 50–51. These two letters comprise the earliest epistles of Paul which are found in the New Testament. There are some who think Galatians may have been written earlier, but this seems unlikely. The Thessalonian church was in turmoil because of divisions between Jewish converts who were steeped in the traditions of the Old Testament so far as personal living and family life were concerned and the Gentile believers who had come out of paganism and were quite casual about sexual and other matters. It is possible that Paul may have received a letter from the Thessalonian church, and that his own letters to them may have been a result of such a communication.

Characteristics and content Paul writes to the Thessalonians to assure them of his love and to praise them for their steadfastness in standing up to the persecution which has come their way from the unbelieving Jews. He also wishes to correct certain errors which have crept into the infant church. He wishes to strengthen the believers for the future conflicts he knows they will experience. Since his own personhood has been attacked, he defends himself against the charges by affirming that his motivation was good and his conduct appropriate. He speaks about the great fundamentals of the Christian faith, one of which has to do with holy living. He wants the Thessalonians to separate themselves from the current flagrant immorality by which they are surrounded. The church members are also upset over the fate of Christians who depart this life prior to the coming of the Lord. Paul assures them that the dead in Christ will be raised to everlasting life at the coming of the Lord Jesus. He definitely teaches that the true church will be raptured or caught up in the air to be with Jesus, without saying whether this will happen before the great tribulation, in the middle of it, or after the church has gone through it. Other Scriptures must be adduced for further light on this point.

Paul instructs believers to be busy about the ordinary tasks of life since their expectation of the immediate return of Christ has caused them to grow careless about daily duties. He urges them to honor the elders who labored among them (5:12). He also cautions believers not to quench the Spirit and not despise those who prophesy (5:19, 20).

Outline

I. *Salutation (1:1)*
II. The character and reputation of the church (1:2–10)
III. The apostolic labors among them (2:1—3:13)
IV. Dealing with church problems (4:1—5:11)
V. Final exhortations and conclusion (5:12–28)

I. SALUTATION (1:1)

1 PAUL, and Sil-va'nus, and Ti-mo'the-us, unto the church of the Thes-
sa-lo'ni-ans *which is* in God the Father and *in* the Lord Jesus Christ:
Grace *be* unto you, and peace, from God our Father, and the Lord Jesus
Christ.

II. THE CHARACTER AND REPUTATION OF THE CHURCH (1:2–10)

2 We give thanks to God always for you all, making mention of you in our
prayers;
3 Remembering without ceasing your work of faith, and labour of love,
and patience of hope in our Lord Jesus Christ, in the sight of God and our
Father;
4 Knowing, brethren beloved, your election of God.
5 For our gospel came not unto you in word only, but also in power, and
in the Holy Ghost, and in much assurance; as ye know what manner of men
we were among you for your sake.
6 And ye became followers of us, and of the Lord, having received the
word in much affliction, with joy of the Holy Ghost:
7 So that ye were ensamples to all that believe in Macedonia and A-chai'a.
8 For from you sounded out the word of the Lord not only in Macedonia
and A-chai'a, but also in every place your faith to God-ward is spread
abroad; so that we need not to speak any thing.
9 For they themselves shew of us what manner of entering in we had unto
you, and how ye turned to God from idols to serve the living and true God;
10 And to wait for his Son from heaven, whom he raised from the dead,
even Jesus, which delivered us from the wrath to come.

III. THE APOSTOLIC LABORS AMONG THEM (2:1—3:13)

A. PAUL'S BEHAVIOR TOWARD THE CHURCH

2 FOR yourselves, brethren, know our entrance in unto you, that it was
not in vain:
2 But even after that we had suffered before, and were shamefully
entreated, as ye know, at Phi-lip'pi, we were bold in our God to speak unto
you the gospel of God with much contention.
3 For our exhortation *was* not of deceit, nor of uncleanness, nor in guile:
4 But as we were allowed of God to be put in trust with the gospel, even
so we speak; not as pleasing men, but God, which trieth our hearts.

☆**1:1** Jn 14:23; Rom 1:7; 2 Cor 1:19; 2 Thess 1:1; 1 Pet 5:12; 1 Jn 1:3
☆**1:2** Rom 1:9; 2 Thess 1:3
☆**1:3** Rom 8:25; Gal 5:6; 1 Thess 3:6; 2 Thess 1:11; Heb 6:10; Jas 2:17
1:4 Col 3:12; 2 Thess 2:13; 2 Pet 1:10
☆**1:5** Rom 15:19; 1 Cor 2:4; 2 Cor 6:6; Col 2:2; 1 Thess 2:10; 2 Thess 3:7
1:6 Acts 17:1–6; 1 Cor 4:16
1:8 Rom 1:8; 10:18; 2 Thess 3:1
1:9 Mt 16:16; 1 Cor 12:2; 1 Thess 2:1
1:10 Mt 16:27; Acts 1:11; Rom 2:7; 5:9; Phil 3:20; 1 Thess 5:9; Heb 9:28; 2 Pet 3:12; Rev 1:7
☆**2:1** 1 Thess 1:9
2:2 Acts 16:22; 17:2; Phil 1:30
2:3 2 Cor 4:2; 2 Pet 1:16
2:4 Prov 17:3; 1 Cor 7:25; 2 Cor 2:17; Gal 1:10; 1 Tim 1:11; Tit 1:3

1:1 In the Greek the Latinized name of Silas, *Silvanus,* appears. He is called Silas in Acts 15:22—18:5, and he is called Silvanus in 2 Cor. 1:19 and 1 Pet. 5:12. He was a trusted companion of Paul on his second missionary journey.

1:2, 3 Thanksgiving in prayer involves adoration or the worship of God. God is the object of our worship and praise. Thanksgiving is a great duty to be performed constantly. Paul here thanks God for three particulars about the Thessalonians: (1) their faith and their work of faith; (2) their love and their labor of love; (3) their hope and the patience of hope.

1:5ff Paul thanks God for three things: (1) the manner in which the gospel was preached—in the power of the Holy Spirit and with much assurance (1:5); (2) the way in which the gospel was received as evidenced by the conduct of the converts—they became imitators of the apostles and of the Lord (1:6); (3) the widespread report of the new faith and life of the converts among their neighbors—they became models for imitation by a wide circle of believers, an example to those in Macedonia and Achaia (1:7–10).

2:1ff Paul reminds the readers of the manner of his preaching among them. It was done (1) with courage and resolution (2:2); (2) with great simplicity and godly sincerity (2:3); (3) without either flattery or covetousness (2:5); (4) without ambition or vain-glory (2:6). What better model than this for those who preach the gospel today?

2:5 Acts 20:33
5 For neither at any time used we flattering words, as ye know, nor a cloak
of covetousness; God *is* witness:
2:6 Jn 5:41, 44
6 Nor of men sought we glory, neither of you, nor *yet* of others, when we
might have been burdensome, as the apostles of Christ.
2:7☆ 2 Tim 2:24
7 But we were gentle among you, even as a nurse cherisheth her children:
2:8 Rom 1:11; 15:29; 2 Cor 12:15
8 So being affectionately desirous of you, we were willing to have
imparted unto you, not the gospel of God only, but also our own souls,
because ye were dear unto us.
2:9☆ Acts 18:3; 2 Cor 11:9; 2 Thess 3:8
9 For ye remember, brethren, our labour and travail: for labouring night
and day, because we would not be chargeable unto any of you, we preached
unto you the gospel of God.
2:10 1 Thess 1:5
10 Ye *are* witnesses, and God *also*, how holily and justly and unblameably
we behaved ourselves among you that believe:
2:11 1 Cor 4:14
11 As ye know how we exhorted and comforted and charged every one of
you, as a father *doth* his children,
2:12 Eph 4:1; Col 1:10; 1 Pet 1:15
12 That ye would walk worthy of God, who hath called you unto his
kingdom and glory.

B. HOW THE CHURCH RECEIVED PAUL

2:13☆ Mt 10:40; Heb 4:2, 12
13 For this cause also thank we God without ceasing, because, when ye
received the word of God which ye heard of us, ye received *it* not *as* the
word of men, but as it is in truth, the word of God, which effectually
worketh also in you that believe.
2:14 Acts 17:5; 1 Thess 1:6; Heb 10:33
14 For ye, brethren, became followers of the churches of God which in
Judæa are in Christ Jesus: for ye also have suffered like things of your own
countrymen, even as they *have* of the Jews:
2:15 Mt 5:12; Lk 24:20; Acts 7:52
15 Who both killed the Lord Jesus, and their own prophets, and have
persecuted us; and they please not God, and are contrary to all men:
2:16 Lk 11:52; Acts 9:23; 13:50; 14:19; 17:5; 22:21
16 Forbidding us to speak to the Gentiles that they might be saved, to fill
up their sins alway: for the wrath is come upon them to the uttermost.

C. PAUL'S CONCERN FOR THE CHURCH

2:17 1 Cor 5:3; 1 Thess 3:10
17 But we, brethren, being taken from you for a short time in presence, not
in heart, endeavoured the more abundantly to see your face with great
desire.
2:18☆ Rom 1:13; 15:22
18 Wherefore we would have come unto you, even I Paul, once and again;
but Satan hindered us.
2:19 1 Cor 15:23; Phil 2:16; 1 Thess 3:13; Rev 1:7; 22:12
19 For what *is* our hope, or joy, or crown of rejoicing? *Are* not even ye in
the presence of our Lord Jesus Christ at his coming?
2:20 2 Cor 1:14
20 For ye are our glory and joy.

3:1☆ Acts 17:15
3 WHEREFORE when we could no longer forbear, we thought it good
to be left at Athens alone;

2:7ff Paul speaks of the manner of his conversation among them: (1) he was like a nurse to children (2:7); (2) he was ready to do them good (2:8); (3) he took no wages from them (2:9); (4) his behavior (and that of those who accompanied him) was devoid of scandal or offense (2:9); it was holy and unblameable (2:10). By word of mouth and by holiness of life they ministered to these people.
2:9 *Paul argued that the laborer is worthy of his hire;* yet here he makes it clear that he was willing to forego his rights, working night and day as a tentmaker so that the Thessalonians need not be concerned about his material welfare.
2:13 Paul testifies that the words he has written are the words of God and as such are true. See also 1 Cor. 14:37; Gal. 1:11, 12; 1 Cor. 11:23ff; 15:1–4.
2:18 *Satan hindered us.* It may be that human agencies were responsible for Paul's inability to do what he thought to be the will of God. If so, it still was caused by Satan, who works through human instrumentalities to obstruct and defeat the work of God.
3:1 Paul, Silas, and Timothy had to leave Thessalonica because of persecution. Now Paul sends Timothy to them to strengthen them in the faith and to exhort them. It was a high price to pay, because Timothy was so useful to him. But Paul was eager to find out what the situation was among these people he loved, and when he could bear the strain no longer, he sent Timothy to

2 And sent Ti-mo'the-us, our brother, and minister of God, and our
fellowlabourer in the gospel of Christ, to establish you, and to comfort you
concerning your faith:
3 That no man should be moved by these afflictions: for yourselves know
that we are appointed thereunto.

3:2 Jn 16:33; Acts 9:16; Rom 16:21; 2 Cor 1:19; Eph 3:13

4 For verily, when we were with you, we told you before that we should
suffer tribulation; even as it came to pass, and ye know.

3:4 1 Thess 2:14

5 For this cause, when I could no longer forbear, I sent to know your
faith, lest by some means the tempter have tempted you, and our labour be
in vain.

3:5 Mt 4:3; 1 Cor 7:5; 2 Cor 11:3

6 But now when Ti-mo'the-us came from you unto us, and brought us
good tidings of your faith and charity, and that ye have good remembrance
of us always, desiring greatly to see us, as we also *to see* you:
7 Therefore, brethren, we were comforted over you in all our affliction and
distress by your faith:

☆**3:6** Phil 1:8

8 For now we live, if ye stand fast in the Lord.
9 For what thanks can we render to God again for you, for all the joy
wherewith we joy for your sakes before our God;

3:8 Phil 4:1

10 Night and day praying exceedingly that we might see your face, and
might perfect that which is lacking in your faith?

3:10 2 Cor 13:9; 1 Thess 1:2, 3; 2 Tim 1:3

D. PAUL'S PRAYER FOR THE CHURCH

11 Now God himself and our Father, and our Lord Jesus Christ, direct our
way unto you.

3:11 2 Thess 3:5

12 And the Lord make you to increase and abound in love one toward
another, and toward all *men*, even as we *do* toward you:

3:12 Phil 1:9

13 To the end he may stablish your hearts unblameable in holiness before
God, even our Father, at the coming of our Lord Jesus Christ with all his
saints.

☆**3:13** Zech 14:5; 1 Cor 1:8; 1 Thess 2:19; 4:17; Jude 14; Rev 22:12

IV. DEALING WITH CHURCH PROBLEMS (4:1—5:11)

A. SEXUAL SIN FORBIDDEN

4 FURTHERMORE then we beseech you, brethren, and exhort *you* by
the Lord Jesus, that as ye have received of us how ye ought to walk and
to please God, *so* ye would abound more and more.
2 For ye know what commandments we gave you by the Lord Jesus.

☆**4:1** Eph 4:1; Col 1:10

3 For this is the will of God, *even* your sanctification, that ye should
abstain from fornication:
4 That every one of you should know how to possess his vessel in
sanctification and honour;

☆**4:3, 4** 1 Cor 6:18; 7:2; Eph 5:17; Heb 13:4; 1 Pet 3:7

5 Not in the lust of concupiscence, even as the Gentiles which know not
God:

4:5 Eph 2:12

---

find out how they were doing. This is an example of genuine pastoral concern for the children of God.

3:6ff To Paul's great satisfaction, Timothy returned to tell him that the Thessalonians were keeping the faith and continuing in their love of the apostle. He assures them that he is praying constantly for them. Those we give thanks for still need our prayers.

3:13 Paul says that the Lord will surely come in his glory, and when he comes the saints will come with him. Then the excellency as well as the necessity of holiness will appear, for without holiness no hearts will be established at that day. The saints, however, are blameless and need not fear that everlasting punishment that comes to those who lack this holiness and consequently true faith.

4:1 As in all his writing, Paul ties faith together with the transformed life by which true disciples of Jesus, through their deeds, demonstrate the reality of this conversion experience.

4:3, 4 It is God's will for us to be sanctified, which means holiness in the heart and purity in the body. Immorality among the believers troubled Paul. Its existence meant there was an absence of holiness in the heart. (See note to 1 Cor. 6:11 on sanctification.)

4:6 1 Cor 6:8; Heb 13:4 **4:7** Lev 11:44; 1 Pet 1:15 **4:8** Rom 5:5; 1 Jn 3:24

6 That no *man* go beyond and defraud his brother in *any* matter: because
that the Lord *is* the avenger of all such, as we also have forewarned you and
testified.
7 For God hath not called us unto uncleanness, but unto holiness.
8 He therefore that despiseth, despiseth not man, but God, who hath also
given unto us his holy Spirit.

B. HOW TO LIVE AMONG UNBELIEVERS

4:9☆ Jer 31:34; Jn 6:45; 13:34; 1 Jn 2:20, 27 **4:10** 1 Thess 3:12 **4:11** Eph 4:28; 2 Thess 3:11, 12

9 But as touching brotherly love ye need not that I write unto you: for ye
yourselves are taught of God to love one another.
10 And indeed ye do it toward all the brethren which are in all Macedo-
nia: but we beseech you, brethren, that ye increase more and more;
11 And that ye study to be quiet, and to do your own business, and to
work with your own hands, as we commanded you;
12 That ye may walk honestly toward them that are without, and *that* ye
may have lack of nothing.

C. THE CONDITION OF DEAD BELIEVERS

4:13☆ Lev 19:28; Deut 14:1, 2; Eph 2:12 **4:14** 1 Cor 15:18, 52 **4:15☆** 1 Cor 15:52 **4:16** Joel 2:11; Mt 24:30; Acts 1:11; 1 Cor 15:52; 2 Thess 1:7 **4:17** Dan 7:13; Acts 1:9; Rev 11:12; 21:3, 4

13 But I would not have you to be ignorant, brethren, concerning them
which are asleep, that ye sorrow not, even as others which have no hope.
14 For if we believe that Jesus died and rose again, even so them also
which sleep in Jesus will God bring with him.
15 For this we say unto you by the word of the Lord, that we which are
alive *and* remain unto the coming of the Lord shall not prevent them which
are asleep.
16 For the Lord himself shall descend from heaven with a shout, with the
voice of the archangel, and with the trump of God: and the dead in Christ
shall rise first:
17 Then we which are alive *and* remain shall be caught up together with
them in the clouds to meet the Lord in the air: and so shall we ever be with
the Lord.
18 Wherefore comfort one another with these words.

D. HOW TO WAIT FOR THE LORD'S COMING

5:1☆ Mt 24:3; Acts 1:7

5 BUT of the times and the seasons, brethren, ye have no need that I
write unto you.

4:9 See note to Rom. 13:9 on love.

4:13 *them which are asleep.* The Scriptures speak about those who are asleep in Jesus. At death they fell asleep. Does this mean that the dead in Christ are not conscious? The statement that we are asleep has primary reference to the body, which lies in the grave to await the resurrection morning. The spirit is separated from the body at death and goes to be with Jesus. The spirit is alive and awaits the reunion of itself with a resurrected body. There are some who teach what is called soul-sleep—i.e., those who die are as though they were asleep at night. They do not know anything and are at peace. The Scriptures support the view that the dead in Christ are present, in spirit, with Christ in glory as soon as they die.

4:15 *the coming of the Lord.* In this passage (verses 4–18) Paul is speaking about the *parousia.* The word in koine Greek means "coming—especially the visitation of royalty." The *parousia* of Jesus is related to the catching away of live believers and dead believers who are raised from their graves. It has been called by many the rapture of the church. There are three views commonly held about the rapture: (1) pretribulation rapturists believe that the church will be caught away into the air before the great tribulation begins; (2) midtribulation rapturists believe the church will be exposed to the wrath of men but will be caught away just before the second half of the tribulation when the wrath of God is poured out on mankind; (3) posttribulation rapturists believe the church will go through the tribulation but will be miraculously preserved by the power of God, as the children of Israel were preserved from the plagues in Egypt. The rapture will be marked by the cry of command or mighty shout of the Lord, the soul-stirring cry of the archangel, and the great trumpet call of God.

5:1 The Scriptures warn against setting any timetable for the consummation of the age, that is, the second coming of the Lord. Paul says Christ's coming will be like that of a thief in the night. Since no one knows

2 For yourselves know perfectly that the day of the Lord so cometh as a
thief in the night.
3 For when they shall say, Peace and safety; then sudden destruction
cometh upon them, as travail upon a woman with child; and they shall not
escape.
4 But ye, brethren, are not in darkness, that that day should overtake you
as a thief.
5 Ye are all the children of light, and the children of the day: we are not
of the night, nor of darkness.
6 Therefore let us not sleep, as *do* others; but let us watch and be sober.
7 For they that sleep sleep in the night; and they that be drunken are
drunken in the night.
8 But let us, who are of the day, be sober, putting on the breastplate of
faith and love; and for an helmet, the hope of salvation.
9 For God hath not appointed us to wrath, but to obtain salvation by our
Lord Jesus Christ,
10 Who died for us, that, whether we wake or sleep, we should live
together with him.
11 Wherefore comfort yourselves together, and edify one another, even as
also ye do.

5:2 2 Pet 3:10; Rev 3:3
5:3 Isa 26:17
5:4 Lk 21:34; 1 Jn 2:8
5:5 Jn 12:36; Acts 26:18; Eph 5:8
☆**5:6**
5:7 Acts 2:15
5:8 Isa 59:17; Rom 8:24; Eph 6:14, 17; 1 Pet 1:13
5:9 Rom 5:9; 2 Tim 2:19
5:10 Rom 14:9

V. FINAL EXHORTATIONS AND CONCLUSION (5:12–28)

12 And we beseech you, brethren, to know them which labour among you,
and are over you in the Lord, and admonish you;
13 And to esteem them very highly in love for their work's sake. *And* be at
peace among yourselves.
14 Now we exhort you, brethren, warn them that are unruly, comfort the
feebleminded, support the weak, be patient toward all *men*.
15 See that none render evil for evil unto any *man;* but ever follow that
which is good, both among yourselves, and to all *men*.
16 Rejoice evermore.
17 Pray without ceasing.
18 In every thing give thanks: for this is the will of God in Christ Jesus
concerning you.
19 Quench not the Spirit.
20 Despise not prophesyings.
21 Prove all things; hold fast that which is good.
22 Abstain from all appearance of evil.
23 And the very God of peace sanctify you wholly; and *I pray God* your
whole spirit and soul and body be preserved blameless unto the coming of
our Lord Jesus Christ.

5:12 Phil 2:29; Heb 13:17
5:14 Rom 14:1; 2 Thess 3:6
5:15 Lev 19:18; Prov 20:22; Rom 12:17; Gal 6:10
5:16 Phil 4:4
5:17 Lk 18:1; Eph 6:18; Col 4:2
☆**5:19** Eph 4:30; 2 Tim 1:6
5:20 1 Cor 14:1
5:21 1 Jn 4:1
☆**5:23** 1 Cor 1:8; Phil 4:9; 1 Thess 2:19; 2 Pet 3:14

---

when that coming will take place, believers are always to be ready (5:6–8; Matt. 24:42, 25:13; Mark 13:33–37; Luke 12:35–38).

5:6ff What should believers do while they wait for Christ's coming? They are to be watchful and sober; they are not to sleep or get drunk; they are to be temperate and moderate; they are to be armed with faith, hope, and love. The reason for all this is that they are not destined to experience the wrath of God but salvation. Therefore, live in the light of that expectation!

5:19 See the note to Eph. 4:30 where Paul says believers must not grieve the Holy Spirit. In Thessalonians Paul is saying something quite different. The Holy Spirit gives gifts to Christians such as speaking in tongues, prophecy, healing, etc. Believers can be unenthusiastic or overly enthusiastic about these gifts. The caution here is not to dampen or smother or quench the Spirit's gifts. They are to be employed for edifying (1 Cor. 14:26) and doing things decently and in order (4:11, 12; 1 Cor. 14:40).

5:23 Here Paul speaks about spirit, soul, and body. Theologians have wrestled with the question of whether man is trichotomous, i.e., made up of three parts, or dichotomous, i.e., made up of two parts. No final answer can be given. We do know that the Hebrews looked upon man as a unit, neither trichotomous nor dichotomous. In the Old Testament the words *flesh, heart, soul* (*nephesh*), and *spirit* (*ruach*) are used, but

5:24 1 Cor 1:9 Phil 2:13 1 Thess 2:12
5:27 Col 4:16
5:28 Rom 16:20

24 Faithful *is* he that calleth you, who also will do *it.*
25 Brethren, pray for us.
26 Greet all the brethren with an holy kiss.
27 I charge you by the Lord that this epistle be read unto all the holy
brethren.
28 The grace of our Lord Jesus Christ *be* with you. Amen.

nothing is said about whether man is the sum of the different parts. Scripture does say that man exists after death, at least for a time, as a disembodied person who is conscious and for whom pain and sufferings are realities (Luke 16:19ff; Phil. 1:23; Rev. 7:14–17). Progressive revelation means that some things that are indefinite in the Old Testament may well be more definite in the New.

THE SECOND EPISTLE OF PAUL THE APOSTLE TO THE

THESSALONIANS

Authorship, date, and background See the introduction to 1 Thessalonians. This second letter was written shortly after 1 Thessalonians by Paul at Corinth (A.D. 50–51). Paul had written the first letter to instruct believers about matters having to do with the second advent of the Lord Jesus. Apparently they misunderstood what he had said. He had emphasized the imminence of the Lord's coming. The results of that teaching were quite different from what the apostle expected. Instead of getting down to business as they waited for his coming, some of them thought that the day of the Lord had already started. Others thought he was coming so soon that they stopped work and waited idly. They had missed the point that Jesus will come as a thief in the night and at a time when men do not expect him. But no dates were set. As a consequence, Paul received disheartening news from Thessalonica about this situation. It occasioned the writing of the second letter to straighten them out.

One statement made by Paul seems to suggest that the Thessalonians had been led astray by wrong teaching from unauthentic sources. Paul alluded to this in his letter when he said, "Now we beseech you, brethren, by the coming of our Lord Jesus Christ, . . . that ye be not soon shaken in mind, or be troubled, neither by spirit, nor by word, nor by letter as from us, as that the day of Christ is at hand" (2:1, 2). The speed with which Paul wrote the second letter after having composed the first one a short time before indicates his deep concern for the believers, his distaste for the erroneous doctrine, and his pastoral heart which demanded immediate action on his part.

Characteristics and content It is not clear to believers today what some of the conditions are which will be a sign of the end of the age and the coming of the Lord. Paul's references certainly must have been clear to the Thessalonians, but they are less clear to us. He tells them that the day of the Lord has not started and it will not commence until after certain events occur. The first is the appearance of "the man of sin," who will cause many others to rebel against God. It is a period of sudden and rapidly accelerating apostasy from godliness.

Second, this will not occur until the removing or the stepping out of the way of the one who is holding him back. Who the hinderer is, Paul does not say. Some have thought this refers to the Holy Spirit, whose presence they think will be withdrawn, and if such an event were to occur, society would crumble because the restraining power of the Spirit would no longer hold things together. But this cannot be certain, and eminent commentators disagree. Believers had best be tentative in their efforts to identify the "hinderer."

Third, the evil one who will come is he "who opposeth and exalteth himself above all that is called God, or that is worshipped; so that he as God sitteth in the temple of God, shewing himself that he is God" (2:4). He is the one "whose coming is after the working of Satan with all power and signs and lying wonders" (2:9). Obviously this has not occurred at the time Paul writes his letter. Nor has it occurred at any time since then. Therefore it is still future. Until this happens, believers can know that any reports of the Lord's having come are untrue. Meanwhile they are to keep on doing the will of God as though Christ were to tarry for another thousand years. Yet they are to work as though he will come tonight.

Outline

I. Salutation (1:1, 2)
II. Personal matters (1:3–12)
III. The coming of the Lord (2:1–17)
IV. Final instructions (3:1–15)
V. Benediction and salutation (3:16–18)

I. SALUTATION (1:1, 2)

1:1☆ 2 Cor 1:19; 1 Thess 1:1
1:2 Rom 1:7

1 PAUL, and Sil-va'nus, and Ti-mo'the-us, unto the church of the Thes-
sa-lo'ni-ans in God our Father and the Lord Jesus Christ:
2 Grace unto you, and peace, from God our Father and the Lord Jesus
Christ.

II. PERSONAL MATTERS (1:3–12)

A. THANKSGIVING FOR THEIR GROWTH

1:3☆ Job 17:9; Ps 84:7; 1 Thess 1:2; 3:5, 10, 12
1:4☆ 2 Cor 7:14; 1 Thess 2:14

3 We are bound to thank God always for you, brethren, as it is meet,
because that your faith groweth exceedingly, and the charity of every one of
you all toward each other aboundeth;
4 So that we ourselves glory in you in the churches of God for your
patience and faith in all your persecutions and tribulations that ye endure:

B. THE GLORY THAT IS TO COME

1:5 2 Tim 2:12
1:6 Ex 23:22; Rev 6:10
1:7 Mk 8:38; 1 Thess 4:16; Rev 14:13
1:8☆ Ps 79:6; Rom 2:8; Heb 10:27
1:9 Deut 33:2; Isa 2:19; 1 Thess 5:3; 2 Thess 2:8
1:10 Jn 17:10; Eph 3:21

5 *Which is* a manifest token of the righteous judgment of God, that ye
may be counted worthy of the kingdom of God, for which ye also suffer:
6 Seeing *it is* a righteous thing with God to recompense tribulation to
them that trouble you;
7 And to you who are troubled rest with us, when the Lord Jesus shall be
revealed from heaven with his mighty angels,
8 In flaming fire taking vengeance on them that know not God, and that
obey not the gospel of our Lord Jesus Christ:
9 Who shall be punished with everlasting destruction from the presence of
the Lord, and from the glory of his power;
10 When he shall come to be glorified in his saints, and to be admired in
all them that believe (because our testimony among you was believed) in
that day.

C. PAUL'S PRAYER FOR THEM

1:11 Eph 4:1; 1 Thess 1:3
1:12 Phil 2:9

11 Wherefore also we pray always for you, that our God would count you
worthy of *this* calling, and fulfil all the good pleasure of *his* goodness, and
the work of faith with power:
12 That the name of our Lord Jesus Christ may be glorified in you, and ye
in him, according to the grace of our God and the Lord Jesus Christ.

III. THE COMING OF THE LORD (2:1–17)

A. EVENTS THAT PRECEDE HIS COMING

2:1 Mt 24:31; 1 Thess 2:19; 4:15–17

2 NOW we beseech you, brethren, by the coming of our Lord Jesus
Christ, and *by* our gathering together unto him,

1:1 See note on 1 Thess. 1:11.

1:3, 4 In 1 Thess. 1:3 Paul gave thanks for the faith, love, and patience of the Thessalonians. Here he gives thanks for the increase of these graces. Their faith grew exceedingly (1:3); their love to God and man abounded (1:3); and their patience increased in spite *of, or because of, their persecution* and tribulations (1:4).

1:8 The wrath of God is consistent with his holiness, righteousness, honor, and justice. Wrath means the imposition of penal judgment on sinners who have broken God's laws and is based upon God's love for his moral universe. Those who trample his moral law must pay for their wickedness. The wrath of God was satisfied by the death of Christ on Calvary for those who believe. God is angry with unbelief, apostasy, idolatry, and all wickedness. His justice is beyond man's understanding, and no mouth shall reply against him at last. Sometimes God's wrath is poured out on men and nations in time. Witness, for example, the destruction of Nineveh, Jerusalem, Rome, etc. But his wrath may also be delayed until the final moment, which may be denominated the "day of wrath" (Rev. 6:17; 11:18; 19:15).

[2]That ye be not soon shaken in mind, or be troubled, neither by spirit, nor by word, nor by letter as from us, as that the day of Christ is at hand.
[3]Let no man deceive you by any means: for *that day shall not come,* except there come a falling away first, and that man of sin be revealed, the son of perdition;
[4]Who opposeth and exalteth himself above all that is called God, or that is worshipped; so that he as God sitteth in the temple of God, shewing himself that he is God.
[5]Remember ye not, that, when I was yet with you, I told you these things?
[6]And now ye know what withholdeth that he might be revealed in his time.
[7]For the mystery of iniquity doth already work: only he who now letteth *will let,* until he be taken out of the way.
[8]And then shall that Wicked be revealed, whom the Lord shall consume with the spirit of his mouth, and shall destroy with the brightness of his coming:
[9]*Even him,* whose coming is after the working of Satan with all power and signs and lying wonders,
[10]And with all deceivableness of unrighteousness in them that perish; because they received not the love of the truth, that they might be saved.
[11]And for this cause God shall send them strong delusion, that they should believe a lie:
[12]That they all might be damned who believed not the truth, but had pleasure in unrighteousness.

2:2 2 Thess 2:15 3:17
☆**2:3** Dan 7:25 Jn 17:12 Eph 5:6 1 Tim 4:1 2 Tim 3:1
2:4 Isa 14:13 Dan 9:27; 11:31, 36 12:11 Mt 24:15 1 Cor 8:5, 6 Rev 13:5, 6
☆**2:7** Gen 6:3 1 Jn 4:3
2:8 Job 4:9 Isa 11:4 Mt 25:31 Heb 10:27 Rev 19:15
☆**2:9** Mt 24:24 Eph 2:2 Rev 13:13
2:10 2 Cor 4:3
☆**2:11** 1 Kgs 22:22, 23 Mt 24:5 Rom 1:24, 28
☆**2:12** Rom 1:32; 2:8

B. THANKSGIVING AND EXHORTATION

[13]But we are bound to give thanks alway to God for you, brethren beloved of the Lord, because God hath from the beginning chosen you to salvation through sanctification of the Spirit and belief of the truth:
[14]Whereunto he called you by our gospel, to the obtaining of the glory of our Lord Jesus Christ.
[15]Therefore, brethren, stand fast, and hold the traditions which ye have been taught, whether by word, or our epistle.

☆**2:13** Eph 1:4 1 Pet 1:2
2:14 Jn 17:22 Rom 8:29, 30 1 Thess 2:12
2:15 1 Cor 11:2; 16:13

2:3 Before the Second Advent of Christ certain events are prophesied as having occurred: (1) the gospel shall have been preached to all the world for a witness (Matt. 24:14); and (2) the great tribulation will have occurred, and the man of lawlessness (or sin) will rise for a short period of time. Wickedness will be unrestrained as the power of the Holy Spirit is lifted and great misfortune will be the lot of the human race. Prophetic references to this period include: Dan. 7:8ff; 9:27; Matt. 24:15; Rev. 13:2–10.

2:7 This verse does not indicate who the restrainer is who holds back lawlessness. Some have suggested it is the Holy Spirit, who will be removed from the scene at the end of the age. Others think he remains but lifts his restraining power, at which time wicked men will do what they had wanted to do but had been restrained from doing by the Holy Spirit. In any event the time is coming when restraints will be lifted; great evil will result because men will be free to do as they please.

2:9 See note to Exod. 8:7 for signs and wonders done by Satan.

2:11, 12 These verses proclaim the sins and the ruin of God's adversaries. Because they did not love truth, they did not believe it. And because they did not believe truth, they took great pleasure in their unrighteousness. God's grace toward them was withdrawn, and they were given over to Satan to be his deluded assistants. "God is just when he inflicts spiritual judgments here, and eternal judgments hereafter, upon those who have no love to the truths of the gospel, who do not believe them, nor live suitable to them, but indulge false doctrines in their minds, and wicked practices in their lives and conversations."* What they did agreed with what they believed; thus, they are numbered among the damned.

2:13ff These saints were chosen by God (i.e., elected by God) from the beginning (i.e., before the foundation of the world—Eph. 1:4). They were chosen to salvation and their call was made effectual by the inward operation of the Holy Spirit in their hearts. Paul exhorts them to stand fast and firm. They were taught the traditions by the apostles, for the oral Word of God was not yet committed to writing. Now that we have the written Word, we are not bound by traditions, unless they can be found in the written Word (i.e., the sacred writings).

2:16 Jn 3:16
16 Now our Lord Jesus Christ himself, and God, even our Father, which
hath loved us, and hath given *us* everlasting consolation and good hope
through grace,
2:17 1 Thess 3:2; 5:11
17 Comfort your hearts, and stablish you in every good word and work.

IV. FINAL INSTRUCTIONS (3:1–15)

A. TO PRAYER

3:1☆ 1 Thess 1:8; 5:25
3 FINALLY, brethren, pray for us, that the word of the Lord may have
free course, and be glorified, even as *it is* with you:
3:2 Rom 15:30, 31
2 And that we may be delivered from unreasonable and wicked men: for
all *men* have not faith.
3:3 Jn 17:15; 1 Cor 1:9; 2 Pet 2:9
3 But the Lord is faithful, who shall stablish you, and keep *you* from evil.
3:4 1 Thess 4:9, 10
4 And we have confidence in the Lord touching you, that ye both do and
will do the things which we command you.
3:5 1 Jn 4:16
5 And the Lord direct your hearts into the love of God, and into the
patient waiting for Christ.

B. TO HARD WORK

3:6☆ Rom 16:17; 1 Cor 5:4; 11:2; 1 Thess 5:14
6 Now we command you, brethren, in the name of our Lord Jesus Christ,
that ye withdraw yourselves from every brother that walketh disorderly,
and not after the tradition which he received of us.
7 For yourselves know how ye ought to follow us: for we behaved not
ourselves disorderly among you;
3:8 Acts 18:3; 1 Thess 2:9
8 Neither did we eat any man's bread for nought; but wrought with
labour and travail night and day, that we might not be chargeable to any of
you:
3:9 Mt 10:10; 1 Cor 9:4; 1 Tim 5:17; 1 Pet 5:3
9 Not because we have not power, but to make ourselves an ensample
unto you to follow us.
3:10☆ 1 Thess 4:11
10 For even when we were with you, this we commanded you, that if any
would not work, neither should he eat.
3:11 Isa 56:10; 1 Tim 5:13
11 For we hear that there are some which walk among you disorderly,
working not at all, but are busybodies.
3:12 Rom 12:11; 1 Thess 4:1, 11
12 Now them that are such we command and exhort by our Lord Jesus
Christ, that with quietness they work, and eat their own bread.
13 But ye, brethren, be not weary in well doing.
3:14☆ **3:15☆** Lev 19:17; Gal 6:1; 1 Thess 5:14
14 And if any man obey not our word by this epistle, note that man, and
have no company with him, that he may be ashamed.
15 Yet count *him* not as an enemy, but admonish *him* as a brother.

3:1 Paul asks the Thessalonians to pray for him and his small band. He always remembered them in his prayers and did not want them to forget him in their prayers. The communion of saints and the unity of the body are kept by praying together and by praying for each other when absent from each other. Moreover, it is the duty of believers to pray for their ministers, who need and should desire their prayers.

3:6 The church is told to break fellowship with those who walk in a disorderly manner. This includes those who have broken away from the tradition of Paul. In *verse 14 Paul commands the* Thessalonians not to fellowship with those who refuse to obey his instructions in this letter. Such persons are not to be looked upon as enemies, however. They are to be admonished.

3:10 *If any would not work, neither should he eat.* So commands the apostle Paul. He is not talking about people who through no fault of their own—such as unemployment or illness—are unable to work. Nor is he talking about people who would like to work but cannot find any work to do. Christians who succor the hungry should not use their largesse indiscriminately.

3:14, 15 Paul instructs the church as to how believers should respond to disorderly members of the congregation. There must first be sufficient evidence of their wrongdoing. Then the disorderly are to be admonished in a friendly fashion, with the expectation that they will mend their ways. If any continue in their wrong conduct, the true believers are to withdraw from such and not keep company with them. They are to hate their vices but love them, pray for them, and work toward their recovery and return to their church privileges as brethren.

V. BENEDICTION AND SALUTATION (3:16–18)

16 Now the Lord of peace himself give you peace always by all means. The
Lord *be* with you all.
17 The salutation of Paul with mine own hand, which is the token in every
epistle: so I write.
18 The grace of our Lord Jesus Christ *be* with you all. Amen.

☆**3:16**
Rom 15:33
3:17
1 Cor 16:21
Gal 6:11
Col 4:18
Philem 19
3:18
Rom 16:20

3:16 *The Lord be with you all.* This is all any believer needs to be both safe and happy. And all Christians can desire nothing better for themselves and their families and friends than to experience continually the gracious presence of the Lord with them and with their loved ones.

THE FIRST EPISTLE OF PAUL THE APOSTLE TO
TIMOTHY

Authorship, date, and background The three letters 1 Timothy, 2 Timothy, and Titus are known as the Pastorals. They were obviously written by the same person and around the same time. From the second century until the nineteenth century it was commonly accepted that the apostle Paul was the author of these letters. The dates of their writing, on this assumption, must have been before his traditional execution date, in the early A.D. sixties. Beginning in the nineteenth century, liberal scholars have attacked the Pauline authorship vigorously and have generally concluded that the letters were written after Paul's death; many have supposed they were written in the second century. Some say a disciple wrote the letters in the name of his teacher and that this involved no dishonesty since this was done occasionally in other connections in the secular world. Others think a later admirer of Paul put them in their present form with a view to preserving Pauline traditions and to sustain the impact of Paul's authority by attaching his name to them. Other scholars do not accept Pauline authorship on the grounds that the letters do not contain some things they insist Paul would have included if he had written them. They conveniently overlook the fact that the Holy Spirit is the divine author of Scripture and that he worked through human instrumentalities. Moreover, for critics to state what *must* have been included in order for these letters to be considered genuinely Pauline is to place themselves in a position of authority which belongs to the Holy Spirit and not to the critics.

It is quite correct that The Acts of the Apostles does not include some of the details of Paul's life and ministry mentioned in the Pastorals. But Pauline authorship would make it clear that Paul suffered two Roman imprisonments. Between the two, he was free to travel so that his mission with Titus to Crete, a winter spent at Nicopolis, and the period when he visited Asia Minor and left Trophimus ill at Miletus occurred subsequent to his release from the first Roman imprisonment. 2 Timothy, however, places him back in Rome as a prisoner awaiting his execution. If these details which are not recorded in The Acts of the Apostles were inventions of someone who wrote these letters in Paul's name, it throws open the whole question of biblical authority and truthfulness and calls into doubt the very gospel itself. Those who trust the Word of God can live comfortably with the claim of these letters that Paul is the author.

Characteristics and content Timothy, to whom this letter is addressed, was born in Lystra. His mother was Jewish, his father was a Greek. He had been raised in the Jewish faith, becoming a co-laborer with Paul in his early years. Paul had Timothy circumcised (Acts 16:3) not because circumcision was a necessity, but to avoid controversy, and in the larger interests of Timothy's ministry. Timothy was timid, not forceful, and appeared to be immature. He suffered from a weak stomach. Paul assigned him to a ministry at Ephesus. The letter was designed to encourage him and to strengthen him for that ministry. It was also designed to help the church members understand that he had the apostolic authority of Paul behind him, which was a badge of his authenticity. Paul was probably traveling at the time of the writing and was himself actively engaged in ministry. The church which Timothy pastored was troubled by some who were teaching wrong doctrine, fables, and myths (1:3).

The burden of the letter is to communicate to Timothy pastoral advice on the operation and conduct of a local congregation. In the course of doing this, Paul speaks about women at worship, the offices of bishop and deacon, the coming apostasy, and Timothy's relationships to widows, elders, backsliders, slaves, and lovers of money. Paul's concluding advice to Timothy is to flee from sin, follow righteousness, fight the good fight, and keep or fulfill the commandment of Jesus Christ.

Outline

I. Salutation (1:1, 2)
II. Church order and church officers (1:3—3:16)
III. Advice and exhortations to Timothy (4:1—6:19)
IV. Concluding salutation (6:20, 21)

I. SALUTATION (1:1, 2)

1 PAUL, an apostle of Jesus Christ by the commandment of God our
Saviour, and Lord Jesus Christ, *which is* our hope;
2 Unto Timothy, *my* own son in the faith: Grace, mercy, *and* peace, from
God our Father and Jesus Christ our Lord.

☆1:1 Gal 1:1, 2; Col 1:27; Tit 1:3; 3:4
1:2 Acts 16:1; 1 Cor 4:17; 2 Tim 1:2; Tit 1:4

II. CHURCH ORDER AND CHURCH OFFICERS (1:3—3:16)

A. TIMOTHY CHARGED TO CORRECT UNSOUND DOCTRINE

3 As I besought thee to abide still at Eph'e-sus, when I went into
Macedonia, that thou mightest charge some that they teach no other
doctrine,
4 Neither give heed to fables and endless genealogies, which minister
questions, rather than godly edifying which is in faith: *so do*.
5 Now the end of the commandment is charity out of a pure heart, and *of*
a good conscience, and *of* faith unfeigned:
6 From which some having swerved have turned aside unto vain jangling;
7 Desiring to be teachers of the law; understanding neither what they say,
nor whereof they affirm.
8 But we know that the law *is* good, if a man use it lawfully;
9 Knowing this, that the law is not made for a righteous man, but for the
lawless and disobedient, for the ungodly and for sinners, for unholy and
profane, for murderers of fathers and murderers of mothers, for manslay-
ers,
10 For whoremongers, for them that defile themselves with mankind, for
menstealers, for liars, for perjured persons, and if there be any other thing
that is contrary to sound doctrine;
11 According to the glorious gospel of the blessed God, which was
committed to my trust.

☆1:3, 4 Acts 19:1, 10; 20:1–3; Gal 1:6, 7; 1 Tim 4:7; 6:3, 4; Tit 3:9
1:5 Rom 13:8; Gal 5:14; 2 Tim 1:5; 2:22; 1 Pet 3:16
1:6 Tit 1:10
☆1:8 Rom 7:12, 16
☆1:9 Gal 3:19; Rev 21:8
☆1:10
1:11 2 Cor 4:4

B. PAUL'S PERSONAL TESTIMONY

12 And I thank Christ Jesus our Lord, who hath enabled me, for that he
counted me faithful, putting me into the ministry;
13 Who was before a blasphemer, and a persecutor, and injurious: but I
obtained mercy, because I did *it* ignorantly in unbelief.
14 And the grace of our Lord was exceeding abundant with faith and love
which is in Christ Jesus.
15 This *is* a faithful saying, and worthy of all acceptation, that Christ Jesus
came into the world to save sinners; of whom I am chief.

1:12 2 Cor 3:5, 6; Phil 4:13; Col 1:25
1:13 Lk 23:34; Acts 8:3; 26:9; 1 Cor 15:9
1:14 Lk 7:47; Rom 5:20; 2 Tim 1:13
1:15 Lk 19:10; Rom 5:8

1:1 Most of Paul's letters were addressed to churches. Four were sent to individuals: Timothy (two letters), Titus, and Philemon. All of these were ministers. Titus and Timothy were evangelists, a lesser order than that of apostle. The Scriptures speak of some prophets, some apostles, and some evangelists (Eph. 4:11). Timothy was Paul's own son in the faith, i.e., he was converted under the ministry of the apostle.

1:4 *fables* are false teachings. Some of these were dealt with by Paul in his letters. Further references are made to these things in 4:7; 2 Tim. 4:4; and Titus 1:14. They are called godless and silly and are the opposite of truth. Current myths include those that say that Jesus is not God, that he did not rise from the dead in the same body, and that his death was not substitutionary. 1 Tim. 1:4 and Titus 3:9 speak in the Greek about *endless genealogies*. We cannot be sure what these are. Some think they had to do with Gnosticism and the notion that someone lower than God through many creative acts was the one who created the world. In any event these notions created controversy and were to be avoided in order to prevent dissension in the church.

1:8 The law may be used rightly or wrongly. The Jews used the law to divide and to oppose the gospel of Jesus Christ. They set it up in opposition to justification by faith alone, which was wrong and wicked.

1:9, 10 The law does not exist primarily for the righteous but for sinners. Here Paul lists some notorious breaches of the law. Most of them are comprehended under the second table of the law, which pertains to love of one's neighbor. He specifically speaks of breaches of the fifth through the ninth commandments.

1:16 Eph 2:7
16 Howbeit for this cause I obtained mercy, that in me first Jesus Christ
might shew forth all longsuffering, for a pattern to them which should
hereafter believe on him to life everlasting.

1:17 Ps 10:16; Rom 11:36; Col 1:15; 1 Tim 6:15, 16
17 Now unto the King eternal, immortal, invisible, the only wise God, *be*
honour and glory for ever and ever. Amen.

C. PAUL CHARGES TIMOTHY TO BE FAITHFUL

1:18☆ 2 Cor 10:4
18 This charge I commit unto thee, son Timothy, according to the
prophecies which went before on thee, that thou by them mightest war a
good warfare;

1:19 1 Tim 6:12
19 Holding faith, and a good conscience; which some having put away
concerning faith have made shipwreck:

1:20☆ 1 Cor 5:5; 2 Tim 2:17; 4:14
20 Of whom is Hy-me-næ′us and Alexander; whom I have delivered unto
Satan, that they may learn not to blaspheme.

D. PUBLIC PRAYER

2:1 Eph 6:18
2 I EXHORT therefore, that, first of all, supplications, prayers, interces-
sions, *and* giving of thanks, be made for all men;

2:2 Jer 29:7; Rom 13:1
2 For kings, and *for* all that are in authority; that we may lead a quiet and
peaceable life in all godliness and honesty.

2:3 1 Tim 1:1
3 For this *is* good and acceptable in the sight of God our Saviour;

2:4 Jn 3:16; 1 Tim 4:10; 2 Tim 2:25; 2 Pet 3:9
4 Who will have all men to be saved, and to come unto the knowledge of
the truth.

2:5☆ Rom 8:35
5 For *there is* one God, and one mediator between God and men, the man
Christ Jesus;

2:6 Mt 20:28; Gal 4:4
6 Who gave himself a ransom for all, to be testified in due time.

2:7 Acts 9:15; 1 Cor 9:1; 2 Tim 1:1
7 Whereunto I am ordained a preacher, and an apostle, (I speak the truth
in Christ, *and* lie not;) a teacher of the Gentiles in faith and verity.

E. THE ROLE OF WOMEN

2:8 Ps 24:4; 63:4; Mal 1:11; Jn 4:21
8 I will therefore that men pray every where, lifting up holy hands,
without wrath and doubting.

2:9☆ 1 Pet 3:3
9 In like manner also, that women adorn themselves in modest apparel,
with shamefacedness and sobriety; not with broided hair, or gold, or pearls,
or costly array.
10 But (which becometh women professing godliness) with good works.

2:11 1 Cor 14:34
11 Let the woman learn in silence with all subjection.

2:12 Tit 2:5
12 But I suffer not a woman to teach, nor to usurp authority over the man,
but to be in silence.

2:13☆ Gen 2:7, 22
13 For Adam was first formed, then Eve.

1:18 The Christian life is a battle or warfare that lasts until death. It is directed against such enemies as (1) Satan (2 Cor. 2:11; Eph. 6:11, 12); (2) the flesh (Rom. 7:23; Gal. 5:17; 1 Pet. 2:11); (3) the world (John 16:33; 1 John 5:4, 5); and (4) death (1 Cor. 15:26; Heb. 2:14, 15). Believers are called upon to be (1) well armed (Eph. 6:14–18); (2) watchful (1 Pet. 5:8); (3) always exercising faith (1 Tim. 1:18, 19). Final victory is ours along with the rewards (Rom. 16:20; 2 Tim. 4:8; Rev. *2:17; 3:5; 21:7).*

1:20 *whom I have delivered to Satan,* (see 1 Cor. 5:5) means that remedial discipline had been applied by which they were probably excommunicated from the fellowship of the church.

2:5 A mediator or middleman is one who stands between two opposing parties. Christ is the mediator who stands between guilty men and God. By his blood Christ has broken down the wall of hostility between Jew and Gentile, God and sinful man (Eph. 2:14). We have direct and immediate access to God the Father through the mediator (Rom. 5:2; Eph. 2:18; 3:12). There is no other mediator and no hope without Christ (Acts 4:12). This scripture eliminates all angels, saints, priests, or relatives of Jesus himself; they have no validity whatever.

2:9 Good works are the best ornaments for a woman. Paul enjoins women not to dress immodestly or to wear expensive attire.

2:13 Some scholars disbelieve the historicity of Adam and Eve, but Paul testifies to his acceptance of Genesis 1—3 as literal and factual, not myth or saga.

14 And Adam was not deceived, but the woman being deceived was in the **2:14** Gen 3:6, 13
transgression.
15 Notwithstanding she shall be saved in childbearing, if they continue in **2:15** Gen 3:16
faith and charity and holiness with sobriety.

F. THE OFFICE OF BISHOP (OR OVERSEER)

3 THIS *is* a true saying, If a man desire the office of a bishop, he desireth ☆**3:1** Acts 20:28
a good work.
2 A bishop then must be blameless, the husband of one wife, vigilant, ☆**3:2** Tit 1:6, 8
sober, of good behaviour, given to hospitality, apt to teach;
3 Not given to wine, no striker, not greedy of filthy lucre; but patient, not **3:3** Tit 1:7
a brawler, not covetous;
4 One that ruleth well his own house, having his children in subjection **3:4** 1 Tim 3:12
with all gravity;
5 (For if a man know not how to rule his own house, how shall he take
care of the church of God?)
6 Not a novice, lest being lifted up with pride he fall into the condemna-
tion of the devil.
7 Moreover he must have a good report of them which are without; lest he **3:7** 2 Cor 8:21
fall into reproach and the snare of the devil. 2 Tim 2:26

G. THE OFFICE OF DEACON

8 Likewise *must* the deacons *be* grave, not doubletongued, not given to ☆**3:8** Phil 1:1
much wine, not greedy of filthy lucre;
9 Holding the mystery of the faith in a pure conscience. **3:9** 1 Tim 1:19
10 And let these also first be proved; then let them use the office of a
deacon, being *found* blameless.
11 Even so *must their* wives *be* grave, not slanderers, sober, faithful in all ☆**3:11**
things.
12 Let the deacons be the husbands of one wife, ruling their children and **3:12** 1 Tim 3:2, 4
their own houses well.
13 For they that have used the office of a deacon well purchase to **3:13** Mt 25:21
themselves a good degree, and great boldness in the faith which is in Christ
Jesus.
14 These things write I unto thee, hoping to come unto thee shortly:
15 But if I tarry long, that thou mayest know how thou oughtest to behave **3:15** Mt 16:16–18
thyself in the house of God, which is the church of the living God, the pillar Eph 2:21
and ground of the truth.

3:1ff It is no sin to entertain aspirations to attain the office of *bishop* (overseer), providing that the one who does this understands that it is a work, not a preferment. Whoever seeks this office with honor and advantage in mind is guilty of covetousness. The qualifications for the office are laid out in verses 2–7.
3:2 *the husband of one wife.* This has been taken by some to mean that a minister of the gospel should be married only once. Since the priests of the Old Testament were permitted to remarry after the death of a wife, there is no reason to suppose that the rule here is not the same. Paul seems to mean that no one should be an elder who has divorced his wife and married another woman, or who has more than one wife, that is, is a polygamist.
3:8 The New Testament prescribes two offices for the congregation: elders or bishops, and *deacons.* (See note to Titus 1:5 for the office of elders or bishops.) The diaconate was begun in Acts 6:1–6 for the purpose of freeing the apostles to preach the Word and to pray. Temporal affairs, such as caring for the poor, were entrusted to the deacons. The word *deacon* comes from the Greek *diakonos,* meaning "ministrant" or "one who serves." Deacons, like elders or bishops, were ordained by the laying on of hands. In Acts 6:3 and 1 Tim. 3:8–13 the qualifications are laid down for the office of deacon.
3:11 From the Greek it is impossible to say whether this verse applies to wives of deacons, or to deaconesses of the church. Rom. 16:1 specifically states that Phoebe was a deaconess. Thus the office is open to women.

3:16☆ Isa 7:14; Mt 4:11; Jn 1:14; Rom 1:3, 4; Acts 1:9; 1 Jn 4:2, 3; 5:6

16 And without controversy great is the mystery of godliness: God was
manifest in the flesh, justified in the Spirit, seen of angels, preached unto
the Gentiles, believed on in the world, received up into glory.

III. ADVICE AND EXHORTATIONS TO TIMOTHY (4:1—6:19)

A. ERRONEOUS DOCTRINE

4:1☆ Jn 16:13; 2 Thess 2:3; 2 Pet 2:1; 1 Jn 4:6
4:2 Eph 4:19

4 NOW the Spirit speaketh expressly, that in the latter times some shall
depart from the faith, giving heed to seducing spirits, and doctrines of
devils;
2 Speaking lies in hypocrisy; having their conscience seared with a hot
iron;

4:3☆ Prov 18:22; Col 2:16; Heb 13:4

3 Forbidding to marry, *and commanding* to abstain from meats, which
God hath created to be received with thanksgiving of them which believe
and know the truth.

4:4 1 Cor 10:26; Tit 1:15

4 For every creature of God *is* good, and nothing to be refused, if it be
received with thanksgiving:
5 For it is sanctified by the word of God and prayer.

B. RIGHT LIVING

4:6 2 Tim 3:14

6 If thou put the brethren in remembrance of these things, thou shalt be a
good minister of Jesus Christ, nourished up in the words of faith and of
good doctrine, whereunto thou hast attained.

4:7 1 Tim 1:4

7 But refuse profane and old wives' fables, and exercise thyself *rather* unto
godliness.

4:8☆ Col 2:23

8 For bodily exercise profiteth little: but godliness is profitable unto all
things, having promise of the life that now is, and of that which is to come.
9 This *is* a faithful saying and worthy of all acceptation.

4:10 1 Tim 2:4; 3:15

10 For therefore we both labour and suffer reproach, because we trust in
the living God, who is the Saviour of all men, specially of those that believe.

C. PREACHING AND TEACHING THE WORD

4:11 1 Tim 5:7
4:12 1 Cor 16:11; Tit 2:7
4:13 1 Tim 3:14
4:14☆ Acts 6:6; 1 Tim 1:8; 2 Tim 1:6

11 These things command and teach.
12 Let no man despise thy youth; but be thou an example of the believers,
in word, in conversation, in charity, in spirit, in faith, in purity.
13 Till I come, give attendance to reading, to exhortation, to doctrine.
14 Neglect not the gift that is in thee, which was given thee by prophecy,
with the laying on of the hands of the presbytery.
15 Meditate upon these things; give thyself wholly to them; that thy
profiting may appear to all.

4:16☆

16 Take heed unto thyself, and unto the doctrine; continue in them: for in
doing this thou shalt both save thyself, and them that hear thee.

3:16 See the notes to John 1:14 on Christ's incarnation and Phil. 2:7 on *kenosis.*
4:1 *in latter times.* We can suppose this to mean the end times preceding the return of Christ.
4:3 *forbidding to marry.* By this statement Paul clearly establishes the legitimacy of marriage; and since the letter is directed to Timothy, it also means that evangelists, as well as prophets and apostles, have the right to marry. Some, however, are given the gift of continence; for them the single state is the will of God.
4:8 *bodily exercise profiteth little.* By this Paul means that abstaining from such things as meat, marriage, and the like—thought by some to be acts of self-denial and mortification—are of little account if sin is not mortified. Godliness or a life of true holiness is far better than refusing to eat meat or to marry.
4:14 *neglect not the gift that is in thee.* Whoever neglects the gifts that God has given will discover that unused gifts wither.
4:16 Whoever is interested in saving souls must first see that his own soul is saved. The dangers of an unconverted minister cannot be overemphasized.

D. PAUL'S INSTRUCTIONS ABOUT:
1. Widows

5 REBUKE not an elder, but intreat *him* as a father; *and* the younger
men as brethren;
2 The elder women as mothers; the younger as sisters, with all purity.
3 Honour widows that are widows indeed.
4 But if any widow have children or nephews, let them learn first to shew
piety at home, and to requite their parents: for that is good and acceptable
before God.
5 Now she that is a widow indeed, and desolate, trusteth in God, and
continueth in supplications and prayers night and day.
6 But she that liveth in pleasure is dead while she liveth.
7 And these things give in charge, that they may be blameless.
8 But if any provide not for his own, and specially for those of his own
house, he hath denied the faith, and is worse than an infidel.
9 Let not a widow be taken into the number under threescore years old,
having been the wife of one man,
10 Well reported of for good works; if she have brought up children, if she
have lodged strangers, if she have washed the saints' feet, if she have
relieved the afflicted, if she have diligently followed every good work.
11 But the younger widows refuse: for when they have begun to wax
wanton against Christ, they will marry;
12 Having damnation, because they have cast off their first faith.
13 And withal they learn *to be* idle, wandering about from house to house;
and not only idle, but tattlers also and busybodies, speaking things which
they ought not.
14 I will therefore that the younger women marry, bear children, guide the
house, give none occasion to the adversary to speak reproachfully.
15 For some are already turned aside after Satan.
16 If any man or woman that believeth have widows, let them relieve
them, and let not the church be charged; that it may relieve them that are
widows indeed.

☆**5:1** Lev 19:32; Tit 2:2, 6
☆**5:3**
5:4 Mt 15:4; Eph 6:2; 1 Tim 2:3
5:5 Lk 2:37; 1 Pet 3:5
5:6 Jas 5:5
5:10 Gen 18:3, 4; Acts 9:36
5:12 Heb 6:4–6
5:13 2 Thess 3:11; Tit 1:11
5:14 1 Cor 7:9; 1 Tim 3:15; Tit 2:5
5:15 1 Tim 1:20
5:16 Ruth 2:18

2. Elders

17 Let the elders that rule well be counted worthy of double honour,
especially they who labour in the word and doctrine.
18 For the scripture saith, Thou shalt not muzzle the ox that treadeth out
the corn. And, The labourer *is* worthy of his reward.
19 Against an elder receive not an accusation, but before two or three
witnesses.
20 Them that sin rebuke before all, that others also may fear.

☆**5:17** Rom 12:8; Gal 6:6; 1 Thess 5:12
5:18 Deut 25:4; Lk 10:7
5:19 Mt 18:16
☆**5:20** Deut 13:11; 2 Cor 7:11; Eph 5:11

5:1 One of the works of the ministry is to rebuke. Paul cautions Timothy about how to perform this part of his ministry. Elder men in age or in office must be rebuked tenderly. Younger men must be spoken to as brothers in Christ, lovingly and tenderly. Older women must be approached as though they were Timothy's mother, and younger women as if they were his own sisters.

5:3ff Widows occupied an important place in the early church. They were financially helpless unless their children or grandchildren supported them. The churches made provision for widows but Paul wanted to be sure only the needy ones who had no other means of support were helped. He gave detailed instructions on this subject (5:3–16).

5:17 The work of the eldership is two-fold: to rule well and to labor in teaching the Word and doctrine. They are not to be lazy but to work zealously in this office to which they have been called by the Holy Spirit. Such servants of God are worthy of double honor—public esteem, and adequate maintenance so as to be provided for in material things.

5:20 If the sin or sins are public and done before men, the rebuke shall be as public as the transgressions. Censure of a minister may be insufficient for correction. Other steps would be suspension from the ministry, removal from the ministry by defrocking, that is, unordaining a man, and finally excommunication, which removes the offender from the communion of the church. Excommunication can be removed upon repentance of the malefactor, who will then be restored.

5:21 1 Tim 6:13
21 I charge *thee* before God, and the Lord Jesus Christ, and the elect
angels, that thou observe these things without preferring one before
another, doing nothing by partiality.
5:22 1 Tim 4:14
22 Lay hands suddenly on no man, neither be partaker of other men's
sins: keep thyself pure.
5:23☆ 1 Tim 3:8
23 Drink no longer water, but use a little wine for thy stomach's sake and
thine often infirmities.
5:24 Rev 14:13
24 Some men's sins are open beforehand, going before to judgment; and
some *men* they follow after.
25 Likewise also the good works *of some* are manifest beforehand; and
they that are otherwise cannot be hid.

3. Slaves

6:1☆ Tit 2:9
6 LET as many servants as are under the yoke count their own masters
worthy of all honour, that the name of God and *his* doctrine be not
blasphemed.
6:2 1 Tim 4:11
2 And they that have believing masters, let them not despise *them,* because
they are brethren; but rather do *them* service, because they are faithful and
beloved, partakers of the benefit. These things teach and exhort.

4. False Teachers and Lovers of Money

6:3 1 Tim 1:3, 10; Tit 1:1
3 If any man teach otherwise, and consent not to wholesome words, *even*
the words of our Lord Jesus Christ, and to the doctrine which is according
to godliness;
6:4 1 Cor 8:2; 1 Tim 1:4; 2 Tim 2:14
4 He is proud, knowing nothing, but doting about questions and strifes of
words, whereof cometh envy, strife, railings, evil surmisings,
6:5☆ Rom 16:17; 2 Tim 3:8; Tit 1:11
5 Perverse disputings of men of corrupt minds, and destitute of the truth,
supposing that gain is godliness: from such withdraw thyself.
6:6 Ps 37:16; Phil 4:11; 1 Tim 4:8
6 But godliness with contentment is great gain.
6:7 Job 1:21
7 For we brought nothing into *this* world, *and it is* certain we can carry
nothing out.
6:8 Prov 30:8; Heb 13:5
8 And having food and raiment let us be therewith content.
6:9 Mt 13:22
9 But they that will be rich fall into temptation and a snare, and *into* many
foolish and hurtful lusts, which drown men in destruction and perdition.
6:10☆
10 For the love of money is the root of all evil: which while some coveted

---

5:23 Evidently Paul was concerned about Timothy's health. He was not physically strong and was apparently troubled by stomach problems. Nothing is said here about healing. Many of God's servants have to bear physical infirmities from which they are not delivered in this life. Paul suggests that Timothy use a *little* wine, implying that he was a water drinker, which could have been the cause of his many stomach difficulties inasmuch as the water of that day (not to mention this day) was contaminated.

6:1 *as many servants as are under the yoke.* Paul is speaking about believers who are slaves (*douloi*). They are to honor, respect, and obey their masters. If they do not, then the name of the God they profess to *worship is defamed.* Paul had respect for the bond of civil law and did not militate against that law of slavery. The ethical implications of human slavery remained to be worked out later. In verse 2 Paul speaks about masters of Christian slaves who are also Christians. A Christian slave is not to use the excuse that he is his master's brother, and therefore need not be respectful.

6:5 *from such withdraw thyself.* This phrase is not found in RSV, NASB, and NIV because the words do not appear in the best manuscripts. What Timothy should do about the people described in verses 3–5 is therefore left unexpressed. At the very least, by implication, he should withdraw from such who are openly disobedient to the various commandments of God. Such people have corrupt minds. It is hardly likely that fellowship in the church should be continued with such people.

6:10 Money is neither good nor bad in itself. Nor is it wrong for the believer to be wealthy. But many people have even been turned away from God because of their love for money. It is called "the first step toward all kinds of sins." The love of money is related to covetousness. More crimes have been committed for money than for almost any other reason. Pride in riches is forbidden and the wealthy are "to use their money to do good." Being rich in good works is infinitely better than being wealthy yet poor in good works.

after, they have erred from the faith, and pierced themselves through with
many sorrows.

E. FIGHTING THE GOOD FIGHT

[11]But thou, O man of God, flee these things; and follow after righteous-
ness, godliness, faith, love, patience, meekness.
[12]Fight the good fight of faith, lay hold on eternal life, whereunto thou
art also called, and hast professed a good profession before many witnesses.
[13]I give thee charge in the sight of God, who quickeneth all things, and
before Christ Jesus, who before Pontius Pilate witnessed a good confession;
[14]That thou keep *this* commandment without spot, unrebukeable, until
the appearing of our Lord Jesus Christ:
[15]Which in his times he shall shew, *who is* the blessed and only Potentate,
the King of kings, and Lord of lords;
[16]Who only hath immortality, dwelling in the light which no man can
approach unto; whom no man hath seen, nor can see: to whom *be* honour
and power everlasting. Amen.

6:11 2 Tim 2:22
☆**6:12** Phil 3:12; 1 Tim 1:19; 2 Tim 2:2–4; 4:7
6:13 Jn 18:37
6:14 1 Thess 3:13; Tit 2:13
☆**6:15** Ps 136:3; 1 Tim 1:17; Rev 17:14; 19:16
6:16 Ex 33:20; 2 Chron 5:14; Ps 104:2; Jn 1:18; 5:26; 1 Tim 1:17; Jude 24; Rev 7:12

F. THE USE OF RICHES

[17]Charge them that are rich in this world, that they be not highminded,
nor trust in uncertain riches, but in the living God, who giveth us richly all
things to enjoy;
[18]That they do good, that they be rich in good works, ready to distribute,
willing to communicate;
[19]Laying up in store for themselves a good foundation against the time to
come, that they may lay hold on eternal life.

☆**6:17** Lk 12:20; Acts 14:17
6:19 Mt 6:20; 1 Tim 6:12

IV. CONCLUDING SALUTATION (6:20, 21)

[20]O Timothy, keep that which is committed to thy trust, avoiding profane
and vain babblings, and oppositions of science falsely so called:
[21]Which some professing have erred concerning the faith. Grace *be* with
thee. Amen.

6:20 2 Tim 2:16
6:21 1 Tim 1:19; 2 Tim 2:18

6:12 *a good profession before many witnesses,* i.e., the confession Timothy made in public at the time of his baptism.

6:15 Paul here and John in the Revelation use the phrase "King of kings and Lord of lords"—an expression Handel appropriated so magnificently in the Hallelujah Chorus of the *Messiah.*

6:17 The poor are not apt to be haughty. It is a temptation that plagues those who are rich. In the twinkling of an eye God can remove the riches of men by death, disaster, or some other means; whereas setting one's hope on God instead of riches assures such a person the blessing and enjoyment of God.

THE SECOND EPISTLE OF PAUL THE APOSTLE TO

TIMOTHY

Authorship, date, and background See the introduction to 1 Timothy. Paul had now come close to the end of his earthly pilgrimage. He was a prisoner at Rome. There he sat in prison where he wrote the last letter of his which we have in the Bible. We do not know whether he visited Spain between his first and second imprisonment. He did, however, stop at Crete, Corinth, Miletus, and Troas. The order of these stops is unknown. Evidently he was arrested suddenly and unexpectedly; his travel plans were interrupted. He had left books at Troas, hoping to return for them later, but he never did. He may have been arrested by the authorities either at Troas or Nicopolis. The reason for Paul's seizure is not stated. Some have suggested that it was due to the pique of Alexander the coppersmith, whom Paul mentions in 4:14 and who may be the same person talked about in Acts 19:33. It is possible that Alexander and his fellow tradesmen, whose businesses were hurt by the response of the people to the gospel, may have witnessed against Paul to the Roman authorities. Since Paul warned Timothy against Alexander, he must have been operating within the same general area where Timothy was located.

Characteristics and content 2 Timothy makes clear how intimate the relationship is between Paul and Timothy, whom he addresses as "my dearly beloved son." Paul speaks about Timothy's background and family, his ordination to the gospel ministry, and his own teaching ministry to this younger colleague. Paul mentions his constant prayers for Timothy, and his desire to draw Timothy closer to himself in his imprisonment. Whereas in his first Roman imprisonment he had other colleagues with him, he now seems to be isolated from them and in need of Christian fellowship and the presence of co-workers. He urgently desires to strengthen Timothy for the work he will have to undertake alone since Paul expects his own immediate death. He wants Timothy to approach the task as a soldier of Jesus Christ who is willing to lay down his life for the Lord and the faith. He admonishes Timothy to be a servant without a contentious spirit, helping people to understand the Christian faith.

Paul envisions difficult days to come. This prophetic statement has been partially fulfilled in some of the dark days in the history of the church, and will be one of the chief characteristics of the closing days of this age before the coming of the Lord Jesus. The only way by which the spirit of anti-Christ can be overcome, in that age and in any age, is by the knowledge and use of the holy Scriptures "which are able to make thee wise unto salvation through faith which is in Christ Jesus" (3:15). His final charge to Timothy (4:1–8) is a masterpiece. No one should consider the Christian ministry unless his life and outlook conform to the standard Paul lays down for that office.

Outline

I. Salutation (1:1, 2)
II. Exhortation to faithfulness and fervency (1:3—2:26)
III. Facing difficult times (3:1–17)
IV. Paul's last charge to Timothy (4:1–8)
V. Concluding instructions, greetings, and benediction (4:9–22)

I. SALUTATION (1:1, 2)

1:1 Jn 5:24; Tit 1:1, 2; 1 Jn 5:10, 11, 20
1:2 1 Tim 1:2; Tit 1:4

1 PAUL, an apostle of Jesus Christ by the will of God, according to the
promise of life which is in Christ Jesus,
2 To Timothy, *my* dearly beloved son: Grace, mercy, *and* peace, from God
the Father and Christ Jesus our Lord.

II. EXHORTATION TO FAITHFULNESS AND FERVENCY (1:3—2:26)

A. TIMOTHY'S GOOD BACKGROUND

3 I thank God, whom I serve from *my* forefathers with pure conscience,
that without ceasing I have remembrance of thee in my prayers night and
day;
4 Greatly desiring to see thee, being mindful of thy tears, that I may be
filled with joy;
5 When I call to remembrance the unfeigned faith that is in thee, which
dwelt first in thy grandmother Lois, and thy mother Eunice; and I am
persuaded that in thee also.
6 Wherefore I put thee in remembrance that thou stir up the gift of God,
which is in thee by the putting on of my hands.
7 For God hath not given us the spirit of fear; but of power, and of love,
and of a sound mind.

☆**1:3** Acts 23:1; 24:14 Rom 1:9
☆**1:4** Acts 20:37 2 Tim 4:9
☆**1:5** Acts 16:1
☆**1:6** Acts 8:18 1 Tim 4:14
1:7 Rom 8:15

B. A CHARGE TO GOSPEL FAITHFULNESS

8 Be not thou therefore ashamed of the testimony of our Lord, nor of me
his prisoner: but be thou partaker of the afflictions of the gospel according
to the power of God;
9 Who hath saved us, and called *us* with an holy calling, not according to
our works, but according to his own purpose and grace, which was given us
in Christ Jesus before the world began,
10 But is now made manifest by the appearing of our Saviour Jesus Christ,
who hath abolished death, and hath brought life and immortality to light
through the gospel:
11 Whereunto I am appointed a preacher, and an apostle, and a teacher of
the Gentiles.
12 For the which cause I also suffer these things: nevertheless I am not
ashamed: for I know whom I have believed, and am persuaded that he is
able to keep that which I have committed unto him against that day.
13 Hold fast the form of sound words, which thou hast heard of me, in
faith and love which is in Christ Jesus.
14 That good thing which was committed unto thee keep by the Holy
Ghost which dwelleth in us.
15 This thou knowest, that all they which are in Asia be turned away from
me; of whom are Phy-gel'lus and Her-mog'e-nes.

1:8 Rom 1:16 Eph 3:1 2 Tim 2:3
1:9 Rom 8:28–30 11:29 Eph 1:4; 2:9 1 Thess 4:7 Tit 3:5
1:10 1 Cor 15:54 Col 1:26 Tit 2:11 Heb 2:14
☆**1:11** 1 Tim 2:7
☆**1:12** 1 Tim 6:20 1 Pet 4:19
1:13 Rom 6:17 1 Tim 1:14 2 Tim 3:14 Heb 10:23
1:14 Rom 8:9, 11, 16 Gal 4:6
☆**1:15** 2 Tim 4:10

1:3 Paul remembered Timothy in his prayers night and day. He thanked God that he did this. God had put it into his heart to pray for Timothy, and thanks must be given for what God did, since all things must be performed for the divine glory. Prayer was Paul's constant business, and he never forgot his friends. If *the apostle had to spend so much time in prayer,* why should believers today suppose they can get along without much prayer?

1:4 *mindful of thy tears.* We do not know whether these tears were shed when Timothy and Paul parted (so that each could perform his ministry), or whether these were tears shed while Timothy was ministering and his heart was moved to tears. Godly ministers may have occasion to weep much over the spiritual condition of their parishioners.

1:5 Lois and Eunice, Timothy's grandmother and mother, were godly women who greatly influenced this young man. We know little about them except the role they played in leading Timothy to Christ. Faith can be communicated and family devotedness is not to be scoffed at. Multitudes of Christians were brought to Christ in their godly homes.

1:6 *stir up the gift of God,* i.e., stir it up like the fire under the embers. Extraordinary gifts were conferred on Timothy when Paul laid his hands on him. Paul did not have that gift within himself. It was done under the direction of God, who is the author of all gifts.

1:11, 12 Paul thought his cause, the preaching of the gospel, worth suffering for. "Good men often suffer many things for the best cause in the world."* *he is able to keep that which I have committed unto him.* Paul said, in effect, "I have lodged the great trust in the hands of the best trustee (i.e., God)."

1:15 This is the only mention of Phygelus and Hermogenes. Virtually nothing is known of them except that they were defectors who deserted Paul. This points up the truth that the church has always had those whose

1:16 2 Tim 4:19 Philem 7
[16]The Lord give mercy unto the house of On-e-siph'o-rus; for he oft
refreshed me, and was not ashamed of my chain:
[17]But, when he was in Rome, he sought me out very diligently, and found
me.
1:18 Heb 6:10
[18]The Lord grant unto him that he may find mercy of the Lord in that
day: and in how many things he ministered unto me at Eph'e-sus, thou
knowest very well.

C. A CHARGE TO FERVENCY AND ENDURANCE

2:1 Eph 3:16; 6:10 Col 1:11
2 THOU therefore, my son, be strong in the grace that is in Christ Jesus.
2:2 1 Cor 15:3–7 2 Tim 2:13
[2]And the things that thou hast heard of me among many witnesses,
the same commit thou to faithful men, who shall be able to teach others
also.
2:3☆ 1 Cor 9:7
[3]Thou therefore endure hardness, as a good soldier of Jesus Christ.
2:4 2 Pet 2:20
[4]No man that warreth entangleth himself with the affairs of *this* life; that
he may please him who hath chosen him to be a soldier.
2:5☆ 1 Cor 9:25
[5]And if a man also strive for masteries, *yet* is he not crowned, except he
strive lawfully.
2:6 1 Cor 9:7, 10
[6]The husbandman that laboureth must be first partaker of the fruits.
[7]Consider what I say; and the Lord give thee understanding in all things.
2:8 Acts 2:24; 13:33, 34 Rom 1:3, 4 1 Cor 15:4
[8]Remember that Jesus Christ of the seed of David was raised from the
dead according to my gospel:
[9]Wherein I suffer trouble, as an evil doer, *even* unto bonds; but the word
2:9 Phil 1:7
of God is not bound.
2:10 Col 1:24
[10]Therefore I endure all things for the elect's sakes, that they may also
obtain the salvation which is in Christ Jesus with eternal glory.
2:11 Rom 6:5, 8 1 Thess 5:10
[11]*It is* a faithful saying: For if we be dead with *him,* we shall also live with
him:
2:12☆ Mt 10:33 Rom 8:17 1 Pet 4:13
[12]If we suffer, we shall also reign with *him:* if we deny *him,* he also will
deny us:
2:13☆ Num 23:19 1 Cor 1:9
[13]If we believe not, *yet* he abideth faithful: he cannot deny himself.

D. PERSONAL CONDUCT

2:14 1 Tim 1:4; 6:4 Tit 3:9
[14]Of these things put *them* in remembrance, charging *them* before the
Lord that they strive not about words to no profit, *but* to the subverting of
the hearers.
2:15☆
[15]Study to shew thyself approved unto God, a workman that needeth not
to be ashamed, rightly dividing the word of truth.
[16]But shun profane *and* vain babblings: for they will increase unto more
ungodliness.

---

profession turned out to be false. This sort of person is to be distinguished from someone like Onesiphorus (1:16), who was a faithful and devout believer.

2:3 Christian soldiers (Paul uses a military term) fight under Christ's banner, "in his cause, and against his enemies, for he is the captain of our salvation (Heb. 2:10)."*

2:5 This verse might be translated this way: "If anyone wrestles, he is not crowned unless he wrestles law*fully," that is, according* to the rules of the game. Spiritual warfare must be conducted according to spiritual laws. Only the devil can cheat and operate unlawfully, but he cannot win the crown.

2:12, 13 Paul sets up two operating principles characteristic of Jesus. He is faithful to his promises and to his threatenings. We are warned that if we prove faithful, he will be faithful to us; if we prove faithless he still remains faithful, but he will institute judgment against us and refuse to affirm us before his Father. Christ cannot deny himself nor can he do what is inconsistent with his divine nature.

2:15 The quality of the Christian walk is related to one's knowledge and use of the Word of God. The reasons for studying the Word include the following: (1) it is, in part, the source of faith (Rom. 10:17); (2) it makes possible a holy life (Ps. 119:11); (3) it provides light and guidance (Ps. 119:105); (4) the Holy Spirit uses it to bring conviction of sin and to accomplish the work of sanctification (Eph. 6:17); and (5) it keeps the believer from error and provides a standard by which to measure the opinions of men (3:16, 17).

17 And their word will eat as doth a canker: of whom is Hy-me-næ'us and **2:17** 1 Tim 1:20
Phi-le'tus;
18 Who concerning the truth have erred, saying that the resurrection is ☆**2:18** 1 Cor 15:12–20
past already; and overthrow the faith of some.
19 Nevertheless the foundation of God standeth sure, having this seal, The ☆**2:19** Num 16:5
Lord knoweth them that are his. And, Let every one that nameth the name Nah 1:7
of Christ depart from iniquity. Jn 10:14
20 But in a great house there are not only vessels of gold and of silver, but **2:20** Rom 9:21
also of wood and of earth; and some to honour, and some to dishonour.
21 If a man therefore purge himself from these, he shall be a vessel unto **2:21** 2 Tim 3:17
honour, sanctified, and meet for the master's use, *and* prepared unto every
good work.
22 Flee also youthful lusts: but follow righteousness, faith, charity, peace, ☆**2:22** 1 Tim 6:11
with them that call on the Lord out of a pure heart.
23 But foolish and unlearned questions avoid, knowing that they do **2:23** 1 Tim 6:4
gender strifes. Tit 3:9
24 And the servant of the Lord must not strive; but be gentle unto all *men,* **2:24** 1 Tim 3:2, 3
apt to teach, patient, Tit 1:7–9
25 In meekness instructing those that oppose themselves; if God perad- **2:25** 1 Tim 2:4
venture will give them repentance to the acknowledging of the truth; Tit 3:2
26 And *that* they may recover themselves out of the snare of the devil, who 1 Pet 3:15 **2:26** Eph 4:27; 6:11
are taken captive by him at his will. 1 Tim 3:7

III. FACING DIFFICULT TIMES (3:1–17)

A. THE COMING APOSTASY

3 THIS know also, that in the last days perilous times shall come. ☆**3:1** 1 Tim 4:1
2 For men shall be lovers of their own selves, covetous, boasters, Jude 18 **3:2** Lk 16:14
proud, blasphemers, disobedient to parents, unthankful, unholy, Rom 1:30
3 Without natural affection, trucebreakers, false accusers, incontinent, 1 Tim 1:9
fierce, despisers of those that are good, **3:3** Rom 1:31
4 Traitors, heady, highminded, lovers of pleasures more than lovers of
God;
5 Having a form of godliness, but denying the power thereof: from such **3:5** 1 Tim 5:8
turn away.
6 For of this sort are they which creep into houses, and lead captive silly **3:6** Jude 4
women laden with sins, led away with divers lusts,

2:18 Scripture indicates there are different kinds of error. No Christian can say he entertains no error, for none can grasp the totality of truth. Some error springs from ignorance (Acts 19:1–6). Obviously when Christians disagree about baptism, church government, and the like, all of them cannot be correct. Someone is wrong. All believers should be ready to forsake error when truth is pointed out to them. Here Paul is talking about serious error which overthrows the faith of some. Even though the error was grave, Paul probably was not calling it apostasy. The Greek word for *apostasy* is found in Acts 21:21 and 2 Thess. 2:3, 4. Apostasy dissolves any relation one might have had with God in Jesus Christ. Normally, apostasy includes a denial of the deity of Christ or of his atoning work on Calvary (Phil. 3:18; 2 Pet. 2:1; 1 John 4:1–3). Descriptions of apostates are found in 2 Pet. 2:1–19 and in the book of Jude. They are to be dealt with forthrightly (2 John 10; Rom. 16:17, 18; 2 Tim. 3:9) when their views have been tested by Scripture. The end of the age will be marked by widespread departure from the faith (3:1–13).

2:19 *knoweth them that are his.* He knows them and owns them such that he will never lose them. This foundational truth stands sure, and believers can rest on this promise of God. God's purpose cannot be defeated.

2:22 *flee also youthful lusts.* With age, the attraction of youthful lusts will diminish—not necessarily because we have complete victory over them but because they tend to lose their appeal. But then the elderly will be overtaken by other temptations, such as concentration on financial security, ease, and comfort—all of which seem to have less attraction to the young and more to the old.

3:1 In the last days perilous times will come—not that the church will be free from these things until the last days. In the last days there will be a heightening of wickedness such as we do not presently see. It should not be cause for undue alarm, for it is a necessary precursor of the Second Advent of Jesus, which all believers desire above all else.

[7]Ever learning, and never able to come to the knowledge of the truth.
3:8☆ Ex 7:11
[8]Now as Jan′nes and Jam′bres withstood Moses, so do these also resist
the truth: men of corrupt minds, reprobate concerning the faith.
3:9 Ex 8:18; 9:11
[9]But they shall proceed no further: for their folly shall be manifest unto
all *men,* as theirs also was.

B. FOLLOWING PAUL'S OWN EXAMPLE

3:10 1 Tim 6:11
[10]But thou hast fully known my doctrine, manner of life, purpose, faith,
longsuffering, charity, patience,
3:11☆ Acts 13:14, 45, 50; 14:19 2 Cor 1:5; 11:23–27; 12:10
[11]Persecutions, afflictions, which came unto me at Antioch, at I-co′ni-um,
at Lys′tra; what persecutions I endured: but out of *them* all the Lord
delivered me.
3:12☆ Mt 16:24 Jn 15:20 Acts 14:22 1 Thess 3:3
[12]Yea, and all that will live godly in Christ Jesus shall suffer persecution.
[13]But evil men and seducers shall wax worse and worse, deceiving, and
being deceived.
3:14 2 Tim 1:13; 2:2
[14]But continue thou in the things which thou hast learned and hast been
assured of, knowing of whom thou hast learned *them;*
3:15 Jn 5:47; 20:30, 31 Rom 10:17
[15]And that from a child thou hast known the holy scriptures, which are
able to make thee wise unto salvation through faith which is in Christ Jesus.
3:16☆ Rom 15:4 2 Pet 1:20, 21
[16]All scripture *is* given by inspiration of God, and *is* profitable for
doctrine, for reproof, for correction, for instruction in righteousness:
3:17 1 Tim 6:11 2 Tim 2:21
[17]That the man of God may be perfect, throughly furnished unto all good
works.

IV. PAUL'S LAST CHARGE TO TIMOTHY (4:1–8)

4:1☆ Acts 10:42
4 I CHARGE *thee* therefore before God, and the Lord Jesus Christ, who
shall judge the quick and the dead at his appearing and his kingdom;
4:2 1 Tim 5:10 Tit 1:13
[2]Preach the word; be instant in season, out of season; reprove, rebuke,
exhort with all longsuffering and doctrine.
4:3 2 Tim 3:1
[3]For the time will come when they will not endure sound doctrine; but
after their own lusts shall they heap to themselves teachers, having itching
ears;
4:4 2 Thess 2:11 1 Tim 1:4
[4]And they shall turn away *their* ears from the truth, and shall be turned
unto fables.
4:5 Col 4:17 2 Tim 1:8
[5]But watch thou in all things, endure afflictions, do the work of an
evangelist, make full proof of thy ministry.

3:8 Jewish tradition has it that Jannes and Jambres were Egyptian magicians who opposed Moses before Pharaoh (Exod. 7:11; 9:11). Their names are found in ancient Jewish writings and in Christian apocryphal works.

3:11, 12 Paul did not speak of his sufferings and difficulties to deter believers from serving Christ. When we fully know and fully understand that believers will be subjected to afflictions and that God will sustain and deliver us from them all, we will take courage and pursue our calling with greater determination than ever before. Under persecutions believers grow stronger.

3:16 The Bible is "God-breathed" (Greek, *theopneustos*) or "God-inspired." God the Holy Spirit used men *to write Scripture (2 Pet. 1:20, 21).* From the earliest days the church has believed and taught that the Bible is free from all error in the whole and in the part. It is inerrant precisely because it was inspired by the Holy Spirit, even as Jesus was sinless because he was conceived by the same Spirit. The prophets, the apostles, and Jesus all taught that the Bible is the Word of God and can be trusted at all points. Inspiration is plenary and verbal, i.e., all of the Bible is inspired and inspiration extends to the very words of Scripture. A few think the Bible was dictated; most hold that the writers were free to use their own style and manner, but were superintended by the Spirit, who kept them from error. Both views hold that inerrancy pertains to the original manuscripts (the *autographa*), agreeing that ancient copyists made a few minor transmissional mistakes. Some believe that inerrancy is limited to matters of faith and practice and does not extend to historical and scientific phenomena. They think such errors in minor matters do not impair the essential message of the Bible, nor do they destroy Christian faith. Experience teaches, however, that limited inerrancy generally leads to unlimited errancy.

4:1 "The best of men have need to be awed into the discharge of their duty. The work of a minister is not an indifferent thing, but absolutely necessary. Woe be to him if he preach not the gospel."*

6For I am now ready to be offered, and the time of my departure is at
hand.
7I have fought a good fight, I have finished *my* course, I have kept the
faith:
8Henceforth there is laid up for me a crown of righteousness, which the
Lord, the righteous judge, shall give me at that day: and not to me only, but
unto all them also that love his appearing.

4:6 Phil 1:23
☆**4:7** 1 Cor 9:24–27; Phil 3:12–14; 1 Tim 6:12
☆**4:8** 1 Cor 9:25; Phil 3:11; Col 1:5; 2 Tim 1:12; Rev 2:10

V. CONCLUDING INSTRUCTIONS, GREETINGS, AND BENEDICTION (4:9–22)

9Do thy diligence to come shortly unto me:
10For Demas hath forsaken me, having loved this present world, and is
departed unto Thes-sa-lo-ni′ca; Cres′cens to Ga-la′tia, Titus unto Dal-
ma′tia.
11Only Luke is with me. Take Mark, and bring him with thee: for he is
profitable to me for the ministry.
12And Tych′i-cus have I sent to Eph′e-sus.
13The cloak that I left at Troas with Carpus, when thou comest, bring
with thee, and the books, *but* especially the parchments.
14Alexander the coppersmith did me much evil: the Lord reward him
according to his works:
15Of whom be thou ware also; for he hath greatly withstood our words.
16At my first answer no man stood with me, but all *men* forsook me: *I*
pray God that it may not be laid to their charge.
17Notwithstanding the Lord stood with me, and strengthened me; that by
me the preaching might be fully known, and *that* all the Gentiles might
hear: and I was delivered out of the mouth of the lion.
18And the Lord shall deliver me from every evil work, and will preserve
me unto his heavenly kingdom: to whom *be* glory for ever and ever. Amen.
19Salute Pris′ca and Aq′ui-la, and the household of On-e-siph′o-rus.
20E-ras′tus abode at Corinth: but Troph′i-mus have I left at Mi-le′tum
sick.
21Do thy diligence to come before winter. Eu-bu′lus greeteth thee and
Pu′dens, and Li′nus, and Clau′di-a, and all the brethren.
22The Lord Jesus Christ *be* with thy spirit. Grace *be* with you. Amen.

4:9 2 Tim 1:4
☆**4:10** Col 4:14; Philem 24; 1 Jn 2:15
4:11 Acts 12:25; 15:37–39; Col 4:10, 14
4:12 Acts 20:4; Eph 6:21
☆**4:14** 2 Sam 3:39; Rom 12:19
4:16 Acts 7:60; 1 Cor 13:5
4:17 Ps 22:21; Acts 9:15; 2 Tim 3:11; Tit 1:3
4:18 Ps 121:7; Rom 11:36
☆**4:19** Acts 18:2; 2 Tim 1:16
☆**4:20** Acts 19:22; 20:4, 15
☆**4:21** 2 Tim 4:9; Tit 3:12
4:22 Gal 6:18

4:7 The Christian life is a battle to be fought, a race to run, and a faith to keep.

4:8 The New Testament as a whole stresses the need for eager expectancy relative to the coming of the Lord Jesus at the end of history. They should (1) show their love for his coming by demonstrating it in their lives (4:8); (2) look or wait for his coming (Phil. 3:20; Titus 2:13; 1 Cor. 1:7; 1 Thess. 1:10); (3) be ready for his coming (Matt. 24:44; Luke 12:40); (4) wait patiently for his coming (James 5:7, 8); and (5) pray for his coming (Rev. 22:20).

4:10 How awful that anyone should have his name written indelibly into the sacred record that he so loved this present evil world that he forsook the calling of God for something menial and God-denying. Demas did this, to his everlasting shame.

4:14 Alexander the coppersmith (see Acts 19:33) wronged Paul. The apostle guarantees that he will smart for what he did—he will be rewarded "according to his works." Let all believers live consciously in the light of this truth that their works will be judged; they will be rewarded according to what they have done.

4:19 *Priscilla* was the wife of Aquila. They fled from Rome when Claudius expelled the Jews in A.D. 52. They returned to Rome later from Ephesus, where they were living when Paul wrote to Timothy here. They were true followers of Jesus Christ and personal, trustworthy friends of the apostle Paul.

4:20 *Erastus* is not identified here. The name appears in Acts 19:22 and Rom. 16:23. In the latter, the person is the city treasurer who is obviously some other individual. The Erastus of Acts could easily be the same person as the one spoken of in Timothy. For *Trophimus,* see the note to Acts 21:29 on this Gentile believer.

4:21 *Eubulus* was a leading church member in Rome. He sent greetings to Timothy via Paul. Nothing is known about *Pudens* except that he was a believer who sent greetings. *Linus* has been identified with one of the earliest bishops of Rome who bore the same name. *Claudia* may have been the wife of Pudens. In one extrabiblical reference she is called the mother or wife of Linus, the first bishop of Rome.

THE EPISTLE OF PAUL TO
TITUS

Authorship, date, and background See the introduction to 1 Timothy for the question of authorship and date. Titus and 1 and 2 Timothy constitute the Pastoral Letters written toward the end of Paul's life. The letter to Titus was written between that of 1 Timothy and 2 Timothy. Paul, together with Titus, ministered to the people of Crete. When he finished his ministry, he left Titus behind to solidify the work by establishing a church and correcting the errors which abounded among the converts. He intended to send Artemas or Tychicus to Crete. Upon the arrival of one or the other in Crete to replace Titus, Paul wanted Titus then to meet him at Nicopolis where he expected to spend the winter.

At the time Paul wrote to Titus, the gospel at Crete had not yet produced mature believers. The church was not properly organized and its members lived irregular lives. The older women were gossipy and overindulged in wine; the men were lazy and careless; the young women were not working hard enough and they were apt to neglect their families and be flirtatious. The Cretans failed to relate the gospel of grace to an earthly life of good works, something Paul was careful to maintain and insist on. Apparently the Cretans had a bad reputation, for Paul quoted one of their own who said: "The Cretans are always liars, evil beasts, slow bellies." And Paul affirmed, "this witness is true" (1:12, 13).

Titus, to whom this letter was addressed, was a long-time companion of Paul. He is named in 2 Corinthians, Galatians, and 2 Timothy, but not in The Acts of the Apostles. He was a Gentile who was not circumcised and whom Paul refused to have circumcised since, in this instance, it would have been a concession to the legalism which Paul was fighting. Titus was an ideal pastor and one to whom Paul could entrust the difficult mission among the Cretans.

Characteristics and content Paul calls Titus one "mine own son after the common faith" (1:4). Paul instructs him to come to Nicopolis to spend the winter with him (3:12). He says he left him in Crete to strengthen each of its churches and "to appoint elders in every city" (1:5). Paul has great confidence in Titus. The letter has been called "a model and manual for a pastor," for in it Paul counsels Titus on how to work out the problems of a difficult pastorate. Titus is more doctrinal than 1 Timothy. Two passages stand out particularly: 2:11–14 and 3:4–7. In them Paul speaks about the deity of Jesus Christ; his vicarious substitutionary atonement; the universality of salvation for all who receive Christ; salvation by faith without works; the coming of the Holy Spirit; sanctification; and God, who is the God of love and of grace. Especially important is Paul's reference to the return of Jesus to earth from heaven. Paul's emphasis on sound doctrine (that is, being strong in the true faith) indicates that there was a body of truth generally regarded as foundational to the Christian faith and that deviations from that norm are to be regarded seriously and disapproved vigorously (see 1:9, 13; 2:1, 2)

Outline

I. Salutation (1:1–4)
II. The appointment of elders (1:5–9)
III. Exposing false teachers (1:10–16)
IV. Teaching sound doctrine (2:1–15)
V. How Titus and his fellow believers should walk (3:1–11)
VI. Concluding observations and benediction (3:12–15)

I. SALUTATION (1:1–4)

1:1 1 Tim 2:4; 6:3 2 Tim 1:9; 2:25

1 PAUL, a servant of God, and an apostle of Jesus Christ, according to
the faith of God's elect, and the acknowledging of the truth which is
after godliness;

[2]In hope of eternal life, which God, that cannot lie, promised before the
world began;
[3]But hath in due times manifested his word through preaching, which is
committed unto me according to the commandment of God our Saviour;
[4]To Titus, *mine* own son after the common faith: Grace, mercy, *and*
peace, from God the Father and the Lord Jesus Christ our Saviour.

☆**1:2** 1 Tim 1:9; Tit 3:7
1:3 Acts 9:15; 1 Tim 1:1, 11; 2 Tim 4:17; Tit 2:10
1:4 2 Cor 2:13; Gal 2:3; 2 Tim 1:2; 2 Pet 1:2

II. THE APPOINTMENT OF ELDERS (1:5–9)

[5]For this cause left I thee in Crete, that thou shouldest set in order the
things that are wanting, and ordain elders in every city, as I had appointed
thee:
[6]If any be blameless, the husband of one wife, having faithful children
not accused of riot or unruly.
[7]For a bishop must be blameless, as the steward of God; not selfwilled,
not soon angry, not given to wine, no striker, not given to filthy lucre;
[8]But a lover of hospitality, a lover of good men, sober, just, holy,
temperate;
[9]Holding fast the faithful word as he hath been taught, that he may be
able by sound doctrine both to exhort and to convince the gainsayers.

☆**1:5** Acts 14:23
1:6 1 Tim 3:2–4
1:7 1 Cor 4:1, 2; 1 Tim 3:2, 3
1:8 1 Tim 3:2, 3
1:9 2 Thess 2:15

III. EXPOSING FALSE TEACHERS (1:10–16)

[10]For there are many unruly and vain talkers and deceivers, specially
they of the circumcision:
[11]Whose mouths must be stopped, who subvert whole houses, teaching
things which they ought not, for filthy lucre's sake.
[12]One of themselves, *even* a prophet of their own, said, The Cretians *are*
alway liars, evil beasts, slow bellies.
[13]This witness is true. Wherefore rebuke them sharply, that they may be
sound in the faith;
[14]Not giving heed to Jewish fables, and commandments of men, that turn
from the truth.
[15]Unto the pure all things *are* pure: but unto them that are defiled and
unbelieving *is* nothing pure; but even their mind and conscience is defiled.
[16]They profess that they know God; but in works they deny *him,* being
abominable, and disobedient, and unto every good work reprobate.

☆**1:10** Acts 15:1; 2 Cor 11:13; 1 Tim 1:6
1:11 1 Tim 5:13; 6:5
1:12 Acts 17:28
1:13 2 Cor 13:10; 1 Tim 5:20
1:14 Isa 29:13, 14; Mt 15:9; Col 2:22; 1 Tim 1:4; 2 Tim 4:4
1:15 Lk 11:39; Rom 14:14
1:16 Ezek 33:31; 1 Tim 5:8; 2 Tim 3:8; 1 Jn 2:4

1:2 *in hope of eternal life.* Hope is not wishful thinking. According to the Scriptures hope is based on the promises of God. He cannot lie. And eternal life was promised *before* the world began. Faith for the believer *does not rest on fallible reason or probable opinions* but on the infallible Word of God.

1:5 The words "elder" (Greek, *presbuteros*) and "bishop" (Greek, *episkopos*—"overseer") are used interchangeably in the New Testament. Paul does so in 1:5, 7. The plural eldership was common in the apostolic church. There is no record of a single bishop or elder in any New Testament church, although a single person, like Diotrephes, usurped controlling authority over a local church (3 John 9). The qualifications for the office are laid down in 1 Tim. 3:1–7 and Titus 1:5–9. The call comes from the Holy Spirit but must be ratified by the church, and hands were to be laid on the called one by the other elders (Acts 14:23; Titus 1:5). The Spirit's call also meant the endowment by the Spirit with the gifts necessary to discharge the duties of the office (1 Cor. 12:28; Eph. 4:11). The functions of the office include (1) rulership (1 Tim. 5:17, KJV); (2) preaching of the Word and keeping the people sound in the faith (1:9); (3) care for the flock, like a shepherd over his sheep (Acts 20:28; 1 Pet. 5:2).

1:10ff Titus is told by Paul to avoid or reject bad teachers who entertain false notions not in accord with the truth. He is to rebuke them sharply. Paul hopes they will be correctable, become sound in the faith, and no longer give heed to fables and the commandments of men which have no warrant in the Scriptures (1:14). Paul reinforces the unhappy fact that Epimenides, a Greek poet, accused his own people as infamously known for their falsehood and lying (1:12).

IV. TEACHING SOUND DOCTRINE (2:1–15)

2:1☆ 1 Tim 6:3; Tit 1:9
2:3 1 Pet 3:3, 4
2:4☆
2:5 Eph 5:22; Col 3:18; 1 Tim 5:14
2:7 1 Tim 4:12; 1 Pet 5:3
2:8 1 Pet 2:12
2:9 Eph 6:5
2:10 Tit 1:3
2:11 Jn 1:9; 1 Tim 2:4; 2 Tim 1:10
2:13☆ Isa 9:6; John 1:1; 20:28; Rom 9:5; 2 Pet 1:1; 1 Jn 5:20
2:14 Ex 19:5; Deut 7:6; 14:2; Ezek 37:23; Eph 2:10; 1 Pet 2:9; 1 Jn 1:7
2:15 1 Tim 4:12

2 BUT speak thou the things which become sound doctrine:
[2]That the aged men be sober, grave, temperate, sound in faith, in
charity, in patience.
[3]The aged women likewise, that *they be* in behaviour as becometh
holiness, not false accusers, not given to much wine, teachers of good
things;
[4]That they may teach the young women to be sober, to love their
husbands, to love their children,
[5]*To be* discreet, chaste, keepers at home, good, obedient to their own
husbands, that the word of God be not blasphemed.
[6]Young men likewise exhort to be sober minded.
[7]In all things shewing thyself a pattern of good works: in doctrine
shewing uncorruptness, gravity, sincerity,
[8]Sound speech, that cannot be condemned; that he that is of the contrary
part may be ashamed, having no evil thing to say of you.
[9]*Exhort* servants to be obedient unto their own masters, *and* to please
them well in all *things;* not answering again;
[10]Not purloining, but shewing all good fidelity; that they may adorn the
doctrine of God our Saviour in all things.
[11]For the grace of God that bringeth salvation hath appeared to all men,
[12]Teaching us that, denying ungodliness and worldly lusts, we should live
soberly, righteously, and godly, in this present world;
[13]Looking for that blessed hope, and the glorious appearing of the great
God and our Saviour Jesus Christ;
[14]Who gave himself for us, that he might redeem us from all iniquity, and
purify unto himself a peculiar people, zealous of good works.
[15]These things speak, and exhort, and rebuke with all authority. Let no
man despise thee.

V. HOW TITUS AND HIS FELLOW BELIEVERS SHOULD WALK (3:1–11)

3:1☆ Rom 13:1
3:2 Eph 4:31; 2 Tim 2:25

3 PUT them in mind to be subject to principalities and powers, to obey
magistrates, to be ready to every good work,
[2]To speak evil of no man, to be no brawlers, *but* gentle, shewing all
meekness unto all men.

2:1ff Paul commands Titus to preach and teach sound doctrine to old men, old women, young women (who will be taught by old ones), and young men too. But faith without works is dead. Titus must therefore do good works and thus be a model against whom no charges of hypocrisy can be leveled (2:7, 8). Titus also is charged to speak to servants, outlining to them their duties according to the biblical pattern (2:9, 10).

2:4 Wives have certain obligations to their husbands. Among them are (1) to love them (2:4); (2) to live with their husbands until death parts them (Rom. 7:2, 3); (3) *to obey or be submissive to their husbands* (2:5; Eph. 5:22); (4) to respect their husbands (Eph. 5:33); and (5) to respond to their husbands' sexual needs (1 Cor. 7:3–5).

2:13 The Greek speaks of the blessed hope and the epiphany (*epiphaneia*) or appearing of the Lord Jesus, in all of his glory, as the great God and Savior. (See NIV for proper translation, which correctly indicates that the Lord Jesus is both the great God and Savior.) The coming of the Lord is the church's blessed hope. But the blessed hope includes all of the events connected with the return of the Lord and cannot be limited to what is popularly called the rapture of the church. The first epiphany (see 2 Tim. 1:10) refers to the incarnation of Jesus; the second epiphany refers to his coming the second time in power and great glory.

3:1 Christians are to have respect for government and obey magistrates. This is to be understood with regard to matters that do not conflict with biblical teaching or go against conscience. Believers are not to be slanderers or brawlers. This does not mean that silence is the rule, for there are times when wicked men, whose conduct is opprobrious, need to be spoken to and against.

3 For we ourselves also were sometimes foolish, disobedient, deceived,
serving divers lusts and pleasures, living in malice and envy, hateful, *and*
hating one another.
4 But after that the kindness and love of God our Saviour toward man
appeared,
5 Not by works of righteousness which we have done, but according to his
mercy he saved us, by the washing of regeneration, and renewing of the
Holy Ghost;
6 Which he shed on us abundantly through Jesus Christ our Saviour;
7 That being justified by his grace, we should be made heirs according to
the hope of eternal life.
8 *This is* a faithful saying, and these things I will that thou affirm
constantly, that they which have believed in God might be careful to
maintain good works. These things are good and profitable unto men.
9 But avoid foolish questions, and genealogies, and contentions, and
strivings about the law; for they are unprofitable and vain.
10 A man that is an heretick after the first and second admonition reject;
11 Knowing that he that is such is subverted, and sinneth, being con-
demned of himself.

3:3 1 Cor 6:9–11
3:4 Rom 2:4; Tit 2:10, 11
☆**3:5** Jn 3:3, 5; Rom 3:20; 8:16; Gal 2:16; 4:6; Eph 2:9; 1 Pet 1:3
3:6 Joel 2:28; Jn 1:16; Rom 5:5
☆**3:7** Rom 8:17
3:8 Tit 3:14
3:9 1 Tim 1:4; 2 Tim 2:14, 16, 23
☆**3:10** Mt 18:15–17; Rom 16:2

VI. CONCLUDING OBSERVATIONS AND BENEDICTION (3:12–15)

12 When I shall send Artemas unto thee, or Tych'i-cus, be diligent to come
unto me to Ni-cop'o-lis: for I have determined there to winter.
13 Bring Zenas the lawyer and Apollos on their journey diligently, that
nothing be wanting unto them.
14 And let ours also learn to maintain good works for necessary uses, that
they be not unfruitful.
15 All that are with me salute thee. Greet them that love us in the faith.
Grace *be* with you all. Amen.

☆**3:12** Acts 20:4; 2 Tim 4:12, 21; Col 4:9
3:13 Acts 18:24
3:14 Rom 12:13; Phil 1:11; Tit 3:8; 2 Pet 1:8
3:15 Col 4:18

3:5 *the washing of regeneration* is inward and spiritual. Although it is expressed outwardly by the sign and seal of water baptism, this regeneration is the renewing work of the Holy Spirit in the new believer.

3:7 Christians are not only justified; they also have assurance from God concerning the many results and blessings of justification. Among them are (1) the assurance of salvation itself (Isa. 12:2; John 3:17; Acts 16:30, 31); (2) the certainty of eternal life (1 John 5:13); (3) peace with God (Rom. 5:1); (4) freedom from condemnation (Rom. 8:33, 34); (5) the guarantee of a glorious resurrection (Phil. 3:21); (6) the promise of a kingdom (Heb. 12:28); (7) the gift of a crown in heaven (2 Tim 4:7, 8); (8) joint-heirship with Jesus (3:7); (9) the assurance of glorification (Rom 8:30); (10) untold blessings (Rom. 5:1–12, which is a gold mine of truth).

3:10 Paul tells Titus how to deal with heretics. They are to be admonished once and again with the hope of bringing them back to the true faith. If and when this does not happen, they are to be cast out of the communion, and all believers should be warned to have nothing to do with them. The Greek word for heresy is *hairesis* and generally denotes "choice." It is used with various connotations in the New Testament. In Acts it simply means a party within a group and thus was neutral. In Paul's writing it has a negative connotation, implying schism, as in 1 Cor. 11:19, which speaks of divisions in the church that threaten the unity of the church. Peter used it to denote heretical doctrine (2 Pet. 2:1). The early church Fathers thought of it in connection with erroneous doctrine, no doubt from Peter's use of the word. In popular terminology today the word means doctrinal departure from orthodoxy, such as the denial of Christ's deity, the Trinity, the virgin birth, and the like.

3:12ff Paul is sending Artemas or Tychicus to replace Titus as resident minister. He also instructs Titus to help send Zenas and Apollos on their way with what they need. Titus himself is an evangelist and not a settled minister. So Paul wants him to rejoin him at Nicopolis to assist him in his labors.

THE EPISTLE OF PAUL TO
PHILEMON

Authorship, date, and background Philemon is the shortest of Paul's letters. It is one of the "prison letters" along with Philippians, Colossians, and Ephesians. It was written during the same period as the other letters and can be dated around A.D. 60–61. Paul wrote these letters while imprisoned in Rome. At that time, slavery was a recognized institution. Nowhere in the New Testament is there any specific injunction against it. Indeed, slavery was a common practice in the Old Testament and explicit Mosaic instructions were given concerning it. For example, the people of Israel were permitted to own non-Jewish slaves. In any case, even slaves had some rights and were protected by Jewish law. There is general agreement that the teaching of Jesus was responsible for doing away with slavery, since it was inconsistent with the Sermon on the Mount, and most certainly, so far as Christians were concerned, the Pauline teaching that there is neither slave nor free, neither male nor female, struck at the root of the system. Yet, in one form or another, slavery persists to this day in certain parts of the world.

The letter addressed to Philemon arose out of a situation in which his slave Onesimus had fled with some of his master's money or property. Apparently he came into contact with Paul, who brought him to salvation through Jesus Christ. What should Onesimus do now that he was a Christian, inasmuch as his master Philemon was a believer? Since salvation includes repentance and restitution, it was apparent that Onesimus could do nothing else than return to his master and reassume his role as a slave. Philemon had the right of life and death over Onesimus and could have had him executed for stealing his property and running away. It was against this background that the apostle Paul wrote not only to Philemon but also to the church which met in his home. This made the letter something more than a personal note to a friend. It brought the church into the picture and with it the moral suasion of other believers who would watch the decision Philemon was called upon to make.

Characteristics and content The letter centers on the motif of forgiveness. Onesimus had committed a crime and this was a sin against God too. Paul acknowledges that Onesimus was not much use to Philemon in the past (11), and makes it clear that he was also a thief, for he says: "If he hath wronged thee, or oweth thee aught, put that on my account" (18). He pleads for compassion and intercedes by saying he will pay it all back for Onesimus, which is nothing less than the biblical idea of substitution (18, 19). He notes that the relationship of Onesimus to Philemon has changed from that of a slave to "a beloved brother" (16). He pleads with Philemon to treat Onesimus kindly, to remember what Philemon owes to Paul, and he encourages him by saying, "Having confidence in thy obedience I wrote unto thee, knowing that thou wilt also do more than I say" (21). He really wants to retain Onesimus, but sends him back because it is the right thing to do. The letter breathes out Paul's unspoken hope that Philemon will set him free. By adding greetings from his other fellow workers, he lets Philemon know that they are also watching to see how he will react to the apostle's appeal.

Outline

I. Greeting and thanksgiving (1–7)
II. Plea for Onesimus (8–20)
III. Hopes, greetings, and benediction (21–25)

I. GREETING AND THANKSGIVING (1–7)

1:1☆ Eph 4:1; 2 Tim 1:8; Philem 9, 23, 24

1 PAUL, a prisoner of Jesus Christ, and Timothy our brother, unto Phi-
le'mon our dearly beloved, and fellowlabourer,

1:1 *Paul, a prisoner of Jesus Christ.* No one is distinguished simply because he is in jail, as Paul was when he wrote this letter. But being a prisoner for the true faith and for preaching the gospel is true glory.

2 And to *our* beloved Ap′phi-a, and Ar-chip′pus our fellowsoldier, and to the church in thy house:

☆1:2 Rom 16:5; 1 Cor 16:29; Phil 2:25; Col 4:17

3 Grace to you, and peace, from God our Father and the Lord Jesus Christ.

1:3 Rom 1:7

4 I thank my God, making mention of thee always in my prayers,

1:4 Rom 1:8, 9; 2 Thess 1:3

5 Hearing of thy love and faith, which thou hast toward the Lord Jesus, and toward all saints;

1:5 Eph 1:15

6 That the communication of thy faith may become effectual by the acknowledging of every good thing which is in you in Christ Jesus.

1:6 Phil 1:9

7 For we have great joy and consolation in thy love, because the bowels of the saints are refreshed by thee, brother.

1:7 2 Cor 7:13; 2 Tim 1:16

II. PLEA FOR ONESIMUS (8–20)

8 Wherefore, though I might be much bold in Christ to enjoin thee that which is convenient,

☆1:8 1 Thess 2:6

9 Yet for love's sake I rather beseech *thee,* being such an one as Paul the aged, and now also a prisoner of Jesus Christ.

☆1:9

10 I beseech thee for my son O-nes′i-mus, whom I have begotten in my bonds:

1:10 1 Cor 4:15; Gal 4:19; Col 4:9

11 Which in time past was to thee unprofitable, but now profitable to thee and to me:

12 Whom I have sent again: thou therefore receive him, that is, mine own bowels:

☆1:12

13 Whom I would have retained with me, that in thy stead he might have ministered unto me in the bonds of the gospel:

1:13 Phil 1:7; 2:30

14 But without thy mind would I do nothing; that thy benefit should not be as it were of necessity, but willingly.

1:14 2 Cor 9:7

15 For perhaps he therefore departed for a season, that thou shouldest receive him for ever;

☆1:15 Gen 45:5, 8; Rom 8:28

16 Not now as a servant, but above a servant, a brother beloved, specially to me, but how much more unto thee, both in the flesh, and in the Lord?

1:16 Mt 23:8; 1 Cor 7:22; Col 3:22

17 If thou count me therefore a partner, receive him as myself.

1:17 2 Cor 8:23

18 If he hath wronged thee, or oweth *thee* ought, put that on mine account;

19 I Paul have written *it* with mine own hand, I will repay *it:* albeit I do not say to thee how thou owest unto me even thine own self besides.

1:19 2 Thess 3:17

20 Yea, brother, let me have joy of thee in the Lord: refresh my bowels in the Lord.

1:2 Although this letter is entitled *Philemon,* Paul also *addressed Apphia, Aristarchus, and the church which* was in Philemon's house. No doubt Paul wanted these people to know what his request for Onesimus was, for Philemon would be under an added burden to accede to Paul's petition.

1:8 Paul asserts that Philemon is so noted for his Christian life and deeds that he is giving his friend another opportunity to demonstrate the reality of his faith and life in Christ by setting Onesimus free.

1:9 Paul could order Philemon to free Onesimus, but he prefers to plead his case on the basis of love, not commandment. He pictures himself as an aged saint in bonds whose load will be lightened if Philemon grants him his request.

1:12 Paul's appeal for Onesimus arises in part from the fact that this slave had found Christ under his ministry. Therefore he had more than an ordinary interest in his situation.

1:15 Onesimus was a runaway slave who was worthy of death for his deed. Paul argues that since he has found Christ, Onesimus would come back to Philemon not simply as a slave, but as a beloved brother in Christ. Since Onesimus had become born again, he and Philemon became brothers in Christ. Thus, for Philemon to treat Onesimus simply as a servant would be incongruent with his testimony as a Christian.

III. HOPES, GREETINGS, AND BENEDICTION (21–25)

1:21 2 Cor 7:16
1:22 Phil 1:24–26; 2:24
1:23☆ Col 1:7; 4:12
1:24☆ Acts 12:12; 19:29; 27:2; Col 4:10, 14; Philem 1
1:25 Gal 6:18; 2 Tim 4:22

21 Having confidence in thy obedience I wrote unto thee, knowing that
thou wilt also do more than I say.
22 But withal prepare me also a lodging: for I trust that through your
prayers I shall be given unto you.
23 There salute thee Ep'a-phras, my fellowprisoner in Christ Jesus;
24 Marcus, Ar-is-tar'chus, Demas, Lucas, my fellowlabourers.
25 The grace of our Lord Jesus Christ *be* with your spirit. Amen.

1:23 *Epaphras.* See note to Col. 1:7.
1:24 *Aristarchus,* one of Paul's followers from Thessalonica who may have been imprisoned with the apostle and martyred in Rome under Nero. *Demas,* spoken of by Paul in 2 Tim. 4:10 as having deserted him because he loved this present world. Tradition has it that he was an apostate from the faith.

THE EPISTLE OF PAUL THE APOSTLE TO THE

HEBREWS

Authorship, date, and background We do not know with any certainty who the author of Hebrews was. No name is given, nor does the letter supply details which would enable anyone to make a positive identification. For these reasons, a number of different people have been suggested as the author; for example, the apostle Paul, Barnabas, and Apollos. We do know that the letter was not written by Timothy, for the author names him as just having been released from jail. If he knew Timothy, he must have known Paul, and if Paul was the author of the book, he would hardly have spoken of Timothy as "brother" when he usually called him "son." Apparently the author was a Jew. He was familar with the Old Testament, was a man of literary skills, and was fully acquainted with the Old Testament of the Greek Septuagint.

The letter came from the second generation era of Christians (see 5:12, 13; 10:32). Since persecution was seen as imminent but had not yet come, and since the author wrote as though the temple was still standing, it appears that the letter can probably be dated before the sack of Jerusalem (A.D. 70), and after the death of Paul. That would make it the late sixties.

The book of Hebrews does not state to whom it was written. But a reconstruction of the history of the times leads to the conclusion that the Christian church was moving away from the synogogue, and that questions were being asked about the relation of the gospel to the new developments and about how Jesus Christ fit into the picture of the Old Testament sacrificial system. The gap between the Christian faith and Judaism would have been widened when Christ's prophetic word about the destruction of the temple was fulfilled. This, accompanied by the dispersion of the Jews along with the loss of their political state and the absence of the temple, would bring all sorts of questions into their minds. Indeed, there was a need for a book like Hebrews to explain more fully the plan of God and how Jesus Christ was the fulfillment of the Old Testament prophetic word.

Characteristics and content Hebrews centers around the use of the word "better." The Son, Jesus Christ, is better than the angels, whom the Jews greatly respected and feared. He is better than Moses, and his priesthood is better than that of Aaron, the founding father of the priesthood. Jesus is linked to the Melchizedek priesthood, which existed before the Aaronic priesthood, and to Father Abraham, who paid tithes to Melchizedek. Jesus is the center of the new covenant which is better than the old covenant, for the old one was temporary and the new one is eternal. Christ is the better sacrifice since the blood of bulls and goats could never take away sin forever. These sacrifices had to be repeated again and again. The sacrifice of Jesus, however, is a once-for-all sacrifice which never needs to be repeated. And it took away sin. Moreover, the writer shows that faith is the better way. No man can faultlessly keep the whole law of God. All the law can do is condemn men as Paul also says in Galatians. But faith is the excellent way in which God makes it possible for men to come to him for salvation and life everlasting. Nowhere else in the New Testament is the new covenant explained more fully. The atonement and its vicarious aspect is fully revealed in this treatment of the person and work of Christ.

Typology finds a large place in this letter. Here the reader finds how the Old Testament promises by way of type are finally and forever fulfilled in the New Testament in the person of Jesus. The author speaks of all three persons of the Trinity, the Father, the Son, and the Holy Spirit, in a way which advances this doctrine noticeably.

The author defines faith succinctly (11:1) and then illustrates it profusely in the lives of the Old Testament saints, all of whom were saved by faith and not by works. The roster of believers includes some whose works indeed were suspect but who, despite some of the actions they performed, nevertheless were saved by their faith. Deliverance is pictured as historical and miraculous interventions of God in some instances; in others, the deliverance came through death after great suffering. But whichever way it comes, the writer makes plain that deliverance is the end result of faith. He closes the letter with admonitions and sounds forth the divine promise of a kingdom which cannot be destroyed (12:28). In the last chapter, he reiterates the eternal nature of Jesus Christ who is the same yesterday, today, and forever (13:8), and concludes with the magnificent benediction in which Christ, the great Shepherd of the sheep, has risen from the dead, and the new and everlasting agreement between God and man by virtue of Christ's atonement on the cross is available to all who will come.

Outline

I. Jesus Christ, the better Messenger (1:1—2:18)
II. Jesus Christ, the better Apostle (3:1—4:13)
III. Jesus Christ, the better Priest (4:14—7:28)
IV. Christ's better covenant (8:1—9:28)
V. Christ's better sacrifice (10:1-39)
VI. Faith, the better way (11:1—12:29)
VII. Conclusion (13:1-25)

I. JESUS CHRIST, THE BETTER MESSENGER (1:1—2:18)

A. HIS QUALIFICATIONS

1:1☆ Num12:6-8
1:2 Ps 2:8; Jn 1:1, 3, 18; 8:25; 15:15; Col 1:16; Gal 4:4
1:3☆ Ps 110:1; Jn 14:9; 2 Cor 4:4; Col 1:15; Tit 2:14; Heb 8:1

1 GOD, who at sundry times and in divers manners spake in time past
unto the fathers by the prophets,
2 Hath in these last days spoken unto us by *his* Son, whom he hath
appointed heir of all things, by whom also he made the worlds;
3 Who being the brightness of *his* glory, and the express image of his
person, and upholding all things by the word of his power, when he had by
himself purged our sins, sat down on the right hand of the Majesty on high;

B. HIS SUPERIORITY TO ANGELS

1:4 Eph 1:21; Phil 2:9
1:5☆ a) Ps 2:7; Lk 20:36; Rom 1:4; Col 1:18; Rev 1:5; b) 2 Sam 7:14
1:6 Ps 89:27; 97:7
1:7 Ps 104:4
1:8, 9☆ Ps 45:6, 7
1:10-12 Ps 102:25-27

4 Being made so much better than the angels, as he hath by inheritance
obtained a more excellent name than they.
5 For unto which of the angels said he at any time, Thou art my Son, this
day have I begotten thee? And again, I will be to him a Father, and he shall
be to me a Son?
6 And again, when he bringeth in the firstbegotten into the world, he
saith, And let all the angels of God worship him.
7 And of the angels he saith, Who maketh his angels spirits, and his
ministers a flame of fire.
8 But unto the Son *he saith*, Thy throne, O God, *is* for ever and ever: a
sceptre of righteousness *is* the sceptre of thy kingdom.
9 Thou hast loved righteousness, and hated iniquity; therefore God, *even*
thy God, hath anointed thee with the oil of gladness above thy fellows.
10 And, Thou, Lord, in the beginning hast laid the foundation of the
earth; and the heavens are the works of thine hands:
11 They shall perish; but thou remainest; and they all shall wax old as
doth a garment;

1:1ff The opening verses of Hebrews contain as much or more specific theology as any book in the Bible. The seven great theological themes are (1) theism—God is affirmed as existing; (2) revelation—God spoke and unless he chose to do so we could never know him; (3) *incarnation—the Son became* flesh and dwelt among us; (4) creation—this is how all things came into being; (5) redemption—Christ by his mediatorship and atoning death made salvation possible; (6) ascension—the Lord Jesus has ascended into heaven and is seated at the right hand of the Father; (7) providence—he upholds all things by the word of his power.

1:3 *sat down.* See note to Heb. 10:12 for information on the meaning of this term.

1:5 Although angels are great in power and position, they are subject to Jesus Christ. No angel was ever called the Son of God. They worship and glorify the Father, the Son, and the Holy Spirit.

1:8, 9 Christ holds the sceptre of power and authority in his hand. He is king; he has a kingdom; and there are people over whom he reigns. This includes the angels. Peter says he has "gone into heaven, and is on the right hand of God; angels and authorities and powers being made subject to him" (1 Pet. 3:22).

[12]And as a vesture shalt thou fold them up, and they shall be changed:
but thou art the same, and thy years shall not fail.
[13]But to which of the angels said he at any time, Sit on my right hand,
until I make thine enemies thy footstool?
[14]Are they not all ministering spirits, sent forth to minister for them who
shall be heirs of salvation?

1:13 Ps 110:1; Mt 22:44
☆1:14 Ps 34:7; 91:11; Rom 8:17; Heb 2:3

C. THE DANGER OF REJECTING CHRIST

2 THEREFORE we ought to give the more earnest heed to the things
which we have heard, lest at any time we should let *them* slip.
[2]For if the word spoken by angels was stedfast, and every transgression
and disobedience received a just recompence of reward;
[3]How shall we escape, if we neglect so great salvation; which at the first
began to be spoken by the Lord, and was confirmed unto us by them that
heard *him*;
[4]God also bearing *them* witness, both with signs and wonders, and with
divers miracles, and gifts of the Holy Ghost, according to his own will?

☆2:1
☆2:2 Deut 5:5; 33:2; Acts 7:38, 53; Gal 3:19; Heb 1:1; 10:28
☆2:3 Isa 45:17; Heb 1:1, 2; 10:29; 12:25
2:4 Mk 6:14; 1 Cor 12:4, 11

D. THE INCARNATION

1. The Kingdom Is the Son's

[5]For unto the angels hath he not put in subjection the world to come,
whereof we speak.
[6]But one in a certain place testified, saying, What is man, that thou art
mindful of him? or the son of man, that thou visitest him?
[7]Thou madest him a little lower than the angels; thou crownedst him
with glory and honour, and didst set him over the works of thy hands:
[8]Thou hast put all things in subjection under his feet. For in that he put
all in subjection under him, he left nothing *that is* not put under him. But
now we see not yet all things put under him.
[9]But we see Jesus, who was made a little lower than the angels for the
suffering of death, crowned with glory and honour; that he by the grace of
God should taste death for every man.

2:5 Heb 6:5
2:6 Ps 8:4–6
☆2:8 1 Cor 15:27
☆2:9 Acts 2:33; Phil 2:6–9

2. The Son Is True Man

[10]For it became him, for whom *are* all things, and by whom *are* all things,
in bringing many sons unto glory, to make the captain of their salvation
perfect through sufferings.
[11]For both he that sanctifieth and they who are sanctified *are* all of one:
for which cause he is not ashamed to call them brethren,
[12]Saying, I will declare thy name unto my brethren, in the midst of the
church will I sing praise unto thee.

2:10 Lk 13:32; 24:46; Acts 3:15; Rom 11:36; Heb 5:9
☆2:11 Mt 28:10; Jn 20:17; Rom 8:29; Heb 10:10; 13:12
2:12 Ps 22:22

1:14 As to their nature angels are spirits, which means *they have no bodies. As to their work they are minister*ing spirits (i.e., they serve God and do his will). They are called to minister to those who are the heirs of salvation (i.e., they serve the people of God). "For he shall give his angels charge over thee" (Ps. 91:11).
2:1 *give the more earnest heed,* i.e., we are to heed them, prize them, hearken to them, read them, meditate on them, and mix faith with them.
2:2 *the word spoken by angels* refers to the law given to Israel on Mount Sinai. Angels were involved in the giving of the law, as indicated in Acts 7:38, 53 and Gal. 3:19, as well as Deut. 33:2.
2:3 The gospel is said to be "so great salvation." It reveals the Savior and shows us how we can be saved *from* sin and restored to holiness and happiness. Those who despise this great salvation are condemned already. The Lord Jesus was the first one who spoke the gospel plainly and clearly.
2:8 *all things in subjection under his feet.* This stupendous claim affirms Christ's sovereignty. It extends to everything, so that nothing is excluded from it.
2:9 *the suffering of death.* The cross was necessary to accomplish God's purpose of redeeming lost men. There was no other way by which men could be saved.
2:11 Union with Christ means that he and we are all brothers. He, as our elder brother, is not ashamed to call us brethren.

2:13 Isa 8:17, 18 Jn 17:6, 9 11, 12

[13]And again, I will put my trust in him. And again, Behold I and the
children which God hath given me.

3. The Son Is Our True Sacrifice

2:14☆ Jn 1:14 Rom 8:3 1 Cor 15:54, 55 2 Tim 1:10 1 Jn 3:8

[14]Forasmuch then as the children are partakers of flesh and blood, he
also himself likewise took part of the same; that through death he might
destroy him that had the power of death, that is, the devil;
[15]And deliver them who through fear of death were all their lifetime
subject to bondage.
[16]For verily he took not on *him the nature of* angels; but he took on *him*
the seed of Abraham.

2:17☆ Phil 2:7 Heb 3:1; 4:15 5:1 1 Jn 2:2 **2:18** Heb 4:15; 5:2

[17]Wherefore in all things it behoved him to be made like unto *his*
brethren, that he might be a merciful and faithful high priest in things
pertaining to God, to make reconciliation for the sins of the people.
[18]For in that he himself hath suffered being tempted, he is able to succour
them that are tempted.

II. JESUS CHRIST, THE BETTER APOSTLE (3:1—4:13)

A. SUPERIOR TO MOSES

3:1☆ Jn 17:3 Heb 2:17; 4:14 **3:2** Num 12:7, 8 **3:3** 2 Cor 3:7–11 **3:4** Jn 1:3, 4

3 WHEREFORE, holy brethren, partakers of the heavenly calling,
consider the Apostle and High Priest of our profession, Christ Jesus;
[2]Who was faithful to him that appointed him, as also Moses *was faithful*
in all his house.
[3]For this *man* was counted worthy of more glory than Moses, inasmuch
as he who hath builded the house hath more honour than the house.
[4]For every house is builded by some *man;* but he that built all things *is*
God.

3:5☆ Ex 14:31 Deut 18:15, 18 **3:6☆** a) Eph 2:19–22 1 Tim 3:15 1 Pet 2:5 b) Mt 10:22 Rom 11:22 Heb 6:11

[5]And Moses verily *was* faithful in all his house, as a servant, for a
testimony of those things which were to be spoken after;
[6]But Christ as a son over his own house; whose house are we, if we hold
fast the confidence and the rejoicing of the hope firm unto the end.

B. THE SUPERIORITY OF HIS REST

1. The Danger of Unbelief

3:7☆ 2 Sam 23:2 Ps 95:7, 8 Acts 1:16

[7]Wherefore (as the Holy Ghost saith, To day if ye will hear his voice,
[8]Harden not your hearts, as in the provocation, in the day of temptation
in the wilderness:

2:14 *himself likewise took part of the same,* i.e., Jesus Christ who is God became incarnate—possessing not the nature of angels, but the nature of men. He united his divine nature with human nature and became the God-man.

2:17 *making reconciliation for the sins* is translated elsewhere as "make expiation" or "propitiation" for our sins. It comes from the Greek word *hilaskomai,* which means "to propitiate," or "to make atonement." At Calvary Christ atoned for mankind's sins. His death accomplished at least three things: (1) our sins were covered (the Old Testament word *kaphar* means "to cover over," or "atone for"); (2) we were reconciled, *i.e., the broken relationship* was reestablished; (3) Jesus was our substitute, i.e., he stood in the sinner's place and paid the penalty for his sins. The shedding of blood was basic to the atonement. It was a once-for-all sacrifice; it becomes effective when claimed by faith; and it is illustrated in the Old Testament (Exod. 12:3–14; Lev. 16).

3:1 *consider . . . Christ Jesus.* The writer wants the "holy brethren" (i.e., those holy in principle through the new birth and holy in conduct and life), who have a heavenly calling, to think about the Apostle and High Priest of their profession. Unfortunately, the word "holy" has often been used as a term of opprobrium, such as Wesley's "Holy Club," "holier than thou," and "Holy Rollers."

3:5, 6 Moses was a servant in God's house; Jesus is the Son. The Jews always considered Moses. Let them now consider Christ who *made* the house of which Moses was only a member. The house is the church of God made up of all believers, and Christ is the master of that house as well as the maker of it.

3:7 What *the Psalmist said (Ps. 95:7), the Holy Spirit* said; conversely, what the Holy Spirit said, the Psalmist said. The Scripture is thus both human and divine. However, the ultimate author of Scripture is the Holy Spirit.

[9]When your fathers tempted me, proved me, and saw my works forty
years.
[10]Wherefore I was grieved with that generation, and said, They do alway
err in *their* heart; and they have not known my ways.
[11]So I sware in my wrath, They shall not enter into my rest.)
[12]Take heed, brethren, lest there be in any of you an evil heart of
unbelief, in departing from the living God.
[13]But exhort one another daily, while it is called To day; lest any of you
be hardened through the deceitfulness of sin.
[14]For we are made partakers of Christ, if we hold the beginning of our
confidence stedfast unto the end;
[15]While it is said, To day if ye will hear his voice, harden not your hearts,
as in the provocation.
[16]For some, when they had heard, did provoke: howbeit not all that came
out of Egypt by Moses.
[17]But with whom was he grieved forty years? *was it* not with them that
had sinned, whose carcases fell in the wilderness?
[18]And to whom sware he that they should not enter into his rest, but to
them that believed not?
[19]So we see that they could not enter in because of unbelief.

3:9 Ps 95:9; Acts 7:36
3:10 Ps 95:10
3:11 Ps 95:11
☆3:12
3:13 Eph 4:22
3:14 Heb 3:6
3:15 Ps 95:7
3:16 Deut 1:34, 35
☆3:17 1 Cor 10:5

2. The Promise of Christ's Rest

4 LET us therefore fear, lest, a promise being left *us* of entering into his
rest, any of you should seem to come short of it.
[2]For unto us was the gospel preached, as well as unto them: but the word
preached did not profit them, not being mixed with faith in them that heard
it.
[3]For we which have believed do enter into rest, as he said, As I have
sworn in my wrath, if they shall enter into my rest: although the works were
finished from the foundation of the world.
[4]For he spake in a certain place of the seventh *day* on this wise, And God
did rest the seventh day from all his works.
[5]And in this *place* again, If they shall enter into my rest.
[6]Seeing therefore it remaineth that some must enter therein, and they to
whom it was first preached entered not in because of unbelief:
[7]Again, he limiteth a certain day, saying in David, To day, after so long
a time; as it is said, To day if ye will hear his voice, harden not your hearts.
[8]For if Jesus had given them rest, then would he not afterward have
spoken of another day.
[9]There remaineth therefore a rest to the people of God.

☆4:2 1 Thess 2:13
4:3 Ps 95:11
4:4 Gen 2:2; Ex 31:17
4:6 Num 14:26–30; Heb 3:18
4:7 Ps 95:7
4:8 Josh 22:4
☆4:9

3:12 *Take heed.* This warning speaks about the kind of sin that kept the Israelite fathers from entering the land of Canaan. If the Israelites repudiated Moses, which they did, and were punished for it, how much more shall they be punished if they spurn Christ who is greater than Moses.

3:17ff *God is grieved only with those who sin against* him. As an example, he was grieved by the corporate sins of the whole nation of Israel. When divine patience is exhausted, judgment must fall. At the heart of all sin lies unbelief.

4:2 *gospel* comes from the Greek word *euaggelion,* meaning *good news, good tidings, good message.* In the New Testament the following expressions are representative ways of speaking about this good news: (1) good news of peace (Eph. 2:17); (2) the good news about God's mighty kindness and love (Acts 20:24); (3) the good news about the kingdom (Matt. 24:14); and (4) the everlasting good news (Rev. 14:6). On the basis of different usages, some have supposed there are different gospels. Such distinctions are unwarranted. In all ages men have been saved by the good news of salvation by faith—whether looking forward to Calvary or looking back to it. Abraham was saved by the good news (Gal. 3:8), just as everybody else in the New Testament age is saved. The bottom line of the good news is that the incarnate Son of God died and rose again for our justification.

4:9 *a rest for the people of God.* The first rest in Scripture came on the seventh day of the creative work of God, at which time he rested (Gen. 2:3). The second rest was the one promised to Israel in Canaan but into which they could not enter because of their unbelief (Heb. 4:2; Ps. 95:11). The third is the rest of Jesus. God fully entered into his rest after creation on the seventh day. Jesus entered into his rest and actually took possession of that rest when he had finished the work of redemption. Thus, the rest enjoyed by God the

4:10☆ Rev 14:13

10 For he that is entered into his rest, he also hath ceased from his own
works, as God *did* from his.

4:11 2 Pet 2:6

11 Let us labour therefore to enter into that rest, lest any man fall after the
same example of unbelief.

4:12 Isa 49:2; Jer 23:29; 1 Cor 14:24, 25; Eph 6:17; 1 Pet 1:23

12 For the word of God *is* quick, and powerful, and sharper than any
twoedged sword, piercing even to the dividing asunder of soul and spirit,
and of the joints and marrow, and *is* a discerner of the thoughts and intents
of the heart.

4:13 2 Chron 16:9; Jn 2:25

13 Neither is there any creature that is not manifest in his sight: but all
things *are* naked and opened unto the eyes of him with whom we have to
do.

III. JESUS CHRIST, THE BETTER PRIEST (4:14—7:28)

A. CHRIST, OUR HIGH PRIEST

4:14 Heb 2:17; 3:1

14 Seeing then that we have a great high priest, that is passed into the
heavens, Jesus the Son of God, let us hold fast *our* profession.

4:15☆ 2 Cor 5:21; Heb 2:17, 18; 1 Pet 2:22; 1 Jn 3:5

15 For we have not an high priest which cannot be touched with the
feeling of our infirmities; but was in all points tempted like as *we are*, *yet*
without sin.

4:16 Heb 7:19; 10:19, 22

16 Let us therefore come boldly unto the throne of grace, that we may
obtain mercy, and find grace to help in time of need.

B. CHRIST AFTER THE RANK OF MELCHIZEDEK

5:1☆ Lev 4:3; 9:7; Heb 2:17; 7:27; 8:3, 4

5 FOR every high priest taken from among men is ordained for men in
things *pertaining* to God, that he may offer both gifts and sacrifices for
sins:

5:2 Heb 2:18; 7:28

2 Who can have compassion on the ignorant, and on them that are out of
the way; for that he himself also is compassed with infirmity.

5:3 Heb 7:27; 9:7

3 And by reason hereof he ought, as for the people, so also for himself, to
offer for sins.

5:4☆ Ex 28:1; Num 16:40; 1 Sam 13:8–13

4 And no man taketh this honour unto himself, but he that is called of
God, as *was* Aaron.

5:5 Ps 2:7; Jn 8:54; Acts 13:33; Heb 1:5; Rev 1:5

5 So also Christ glorified not himself to be made an high priest; but he
that said unto him, Thou art my Son, to day have I begotten thee.

5:6 Ps 110:4

6 As he saith also in another *place*, Thou *art* a priest for ever after the
order of Mel-chis'e-dec.

Father and by Jesus Christ prefigure the believers' rest. As they have entered into their rest, we shall also enter ours.

4:10 True believers do not rely on their own works of righteousness by trying to keep the law. Believers in Christ and his righteousness enter into the grace of rest here and the glory of rest hereafter. Christ himself cannot give to unbelievers either spiritual or eternal rest. It remains only for the people of God.

4:15 Jesus was sinless. In order for anyone to be sinless, two things are required. The first concerns the person's inward motivations, for these determine one's conduct. The second has to do with the outward actions of a man. Sinlessness exists only when the *inward* motivations and the outward acts are perfect in *the sight of God. There must be inward and outward* conformity to what is holy and good. Jesus is the only human being who ever lived of whom it can be said that he exhibited an immaculate (or sinless) and absolutely holy life. The Scriptures bear witness to this in the following ways: (1) Jesus' own witness (John 8:46; see also John 8:29; 17:19); (2) the witness of others (Matt. 27:4; 27:19; Luke 23:41; John 18:38); (3) the witness of the apostles (2 Cor. 5:21; Heb. 4:15; 1 Pet. 2:21, 22; Heb. 7:26; 1 John 3:5).

5:1 The high priest was ordained by God to enter the office and to offer sacrifices for himself and for men. He was a sinner whose own transgressions were covered by the blood of bulls and goats first. Then he offered sacrifices for others. He functioned as a mediator between God and man. This high priest, though mortal and sinful, prefigured Jesus, the divine and sinless high priest whose own blood made atonement for the sins of men.

5:4ff Christ is our high priest, not after the order of Aaron but after the order of Melchizedek, who pre-*ceded Aaron. In the manner* of Christ's call and in the holiness of his person, he far surpassed Aaron, who was the first high priest of God to offer sacrifices in the tent in the wilderness. At every point and in all connections Christ is superior.

7Who in the days of his flesh, when he had offered up prayers and
supplications with strong crying and tears unto him that was able to save
him from death, and was heard in that he feared;
8Though he were a Son, yet learned he obedience by the things which he
suffered;
9And being made perfect, he became the author of eternal salvation unto
all them that obey him;
10Called of God an high priest after the order of Mel-chis'e-dec.

5:7 Ps 22:1–4; Mt 26:39, 53; Jn 17:1
☆**5:8** Phil 2:8; Heb 1:2
5:10 Heb 2:17; 6:20

C. LAYING HOLD OF CHRIST AND HIS SALVATION
1. Baby-Christians Reproved

11Of whom we have many things to say, and hard to be uttered, seeing ye
are dull of hearing.
12For when for the time ye ought to be teachers, ye have need that one
teach you again which *be* the first principles of the oracles of God; and are
become such as have need of milk, and not of strong meat.
13For every one that useth milk *is* unskilful in the word of righteousness:
for he is a babe.
14But strong meat belongeth to them that are of full age, *even* those who
by reason of use have their senses exercised to discern both good and evil.

☆**5:12** 1 Cor 3:1, 2
5:13 1 Cor 14:20; Eph 4:13, 14
5:14 1 Cor 2:6, 14

2. A Warning against Apostasy

6 THEREFORE leaving the principles of the doctrine of Christ, let us
go on unto perfection; not laying again the foundation of repentance
from dead works, and of faith toward God,
2Of the doctrine of baptisms, and of laying on of hands, and of
resurrection of the dead, and of eternal judgment.
3And this will we do, if God permit.
4For *it is* impossible for those who were once enlightened, and have
tasted of the heavenly gift, and were made partakers of the Holy Ghost,
5And have tasted the good word of God, and the powers of the world to
come,
6If they shall fall away, to renew them again unto repentance; seeing they
crucify to themselves the Son of God afresh, and put *him* to an open shame.

☆**6:1** Phil 3:13–16; Heb 5:12, 16
☆**6:2** Acts 6:6; 8:17; 17:31; 19:4; 24:25; Rom 2:16
6:3 1 Cor 4:19
☆**6:4** Mt 7:22; Jn 4:10; 6:32; Eph 2:8; Heb 10:26, 32; 2 Pet 2:20; 1 Jn 5:16
6:5 Heb 2:5; 1 Pet 2:3
6:6 Heb 10:26, 29

5:8 *learned he obedience by the things which he suffered.* Even though Christ was God's Son, he learned obedience in his humanity by the things he endured. In his passive obedience he always did the Father's will. Thus he did what the first Adam did not. He was tempted in all points as we are, yet he did not sin. He did all this in discharging his duty in the office of mediator, to which he had been appointed by covenant agreement with the Father.

5:12 *Believers need to be taught and taught again,* for they easily forget. Some are babies who need milk (i.e., to be spoken to in the plainest terms—precept upon precept, line upon line). God provides the kind of food each believer needs. But we are not to remain babies forever. It is a sin to be a baby when you should be an adult.

6:1, 2 The writer wants babes in Christ to grow up into maturity. To do this they must remember the following six foundational principles: (1) repentance from dead works; (2) faith toward God; (3) doctrine of baptism, which constitutes the seal of the sign of the covenant; (4) the laying on of hands in connection with the ordination of ministers, something which should be done only once; (5) the resurrection of the dead; (6) eternal judgment, which promises life to the righteous and separation from God to the unrighteous.

6:4ff Can a saved person lose his salvation? This is a question about which theologians have differed through the centuries. After the Reformation, Jacob Arminius, a Dutch theologian who opposed the teaching of John Calvin, said salvation can be lost; the Calvinists insisted on the security of the believer. Arminians hold that verses 4 and 5 here mean the person was truly born again and has lost his salvation. This much seems clear, however; logically verse 4 implies that if salvation were to be lost, it would be impossible for that one to be *born again,* lose it, and then be *born again* again. Whatever view is taken about the state of an apostate prior to his apostasy, the outcome is virtually the same. Whoever openly and consciously rejects Jesus Christ is unregenerate even if he seemed to have been saved earlier. The Arminian would say he had lost his salvation; the Calvinist that he never had it. Either way, the result is identical.

7 For the earth which drinketh in the rain that cometh oft upon it, and
bringeth forth herbs meet for them by whom it is dressed, receiveth blessing
from God:
8 But that which beareth thorns and briers *is* rejected, and *is* nigh unto
cursing; whose end *is* to be burned.

3. Encouragement of True Believers

9 But, beloved, we are persuaded better things of you, and things that
accompany salvation, though we thus speak.
10 For God *is* not unrighteous to forget your work and labour of love,
which ye have shewed toward his name, in that ye have ministered to the
saints, and do minister.
11 And we desire that every one of you do shew the same diligence to the
full assurance of hope unto the end:
12 That ye be not slothful, but followers of them who through faith and
patience inherit the promises.

6:10 Mt 10:42; 25:40 Jn 13:20 1 Thess 1:3
6:11☆ Col 2:2 Heb 3:6; 10:22
6:12 Heb 1:14; 10:36 13:7

4. The Certainty of the Covenant Promise

13 For when God made promise to Abraham, because he could swear by
no greater, he sware by himself,
14 Saying, Surely blessing I will bless thee, and multiplying I will multiply
thee.
15 And so, after he had patiently endured, he obtained the promise.
16 For men verily swear by the greater: and an oath for confirmation *is* to
them an end of all strife.
17 Wherein God, willing more abundantly to shew unto the heirs of
promise the immutability of his counsel, confirmed *it* by an oath:
18 That by two immutable things, in which *it was* impossible for God to
lie, we might have a strong consolation, who have fled for refuge to lay hold
upon the hope set before us:
19 Which *hope* we have as an anchor of the soul, both sure and stedfast,
and which entereth into that within the veil;
20 Whither the forerunner is for us entered, *even* Jesus, made an high
priest for ever after the order of Mel-chis′e-dec.

6:13 Gen 22:16 Gal 3:16
6:14 Gen 22:16–17
6:15 Gen 21:5
6:16 Ex 22:11 Gal 3:15
6:17☆ Ps 110:4 Rom 11:29 Heb 11:9
6:18 Tit 1:2 Heb 3:6; 12:1
6:19 Lev 16:15, 16 Ps 130:7 Heb 9:7
6:20 Heb 4:14; 5:6 9:24

D. CHRIST'S MELCHIZEDEK PRIESTHOOD BETTER THAN AARON'S

1. Melchizedek's Priesthood First

7 FOR this Mel-chis′e-dec, king of Salem, priest of the most high God,
who met Abraham returning from the slaughter of the kings, and
blessed him;

7:1☆ Gen 14:17–20 Ps 110:4 Heb 5:6, 10

6:11 *the full assurance of hope.* Some have strong hope; others have weak hope. We all need the full assurance of the hope we have and must be careful to promote that hope through the grace of God. Hope is based on faith, and some who had this hope have now inherited what they hoped for (6:12). We are to follow their example. How lovely are those Christians whose faith and hope are strong, vital, and challenging! We *are encouraged* to lay hold of the hope set before us (6:18), *which means it is available.* If we do not seize it, we have no one to blame except ourselves.

6:17 God, unlike humans, does not change. He is immutable or unchangeable. From eternity to eternity this is so. It is the foundation on which the faith of all believers rests. Whatever God promises to do, he does. His promise is sufficient. But it is reinforced by the divine oath made by himself and to himself, and this is unbreachable.

7:1–3 Apparently Melchizedek was a Canaanite king who reigned in Salem and who worshipped the true God. He, therefore, was a Gentile (and there may have been many of whom we have no knowledge) in the kingdom of God. He was raised up by God to be a type of Christ and was honored as such by Abraham. The expression "without father, without mother" (7:3) means no more than that Melchizedek's parentage has been kept hidden from us so he might typify Christ, who had no human father according to the flesh and no mother according to his deity.

2 To whom also Abraham gave a tenth part of all; first being by
interpretation King of righteousness, and after that also King of Salem,
which is, King of peace;
3 Without father, without mother, without descent, having neither
beginning of days, nor end of life; but made like unto the Son of God;
abideth a priest continually.
4 Now consider how great this man *was*, unto whom even the patriarch
Abraham gave the tenth of the spoils.
5 And verily they that are of the sons of Levi, who receive the office of the
priesthood, have a commandment to take tithes of the people according to
the law, that is, of their brethren, though they come out of the loins of
Abraham:
6 But he whose descent is not counted from them received tithes of
Abraham, and blessed him that had the promises.
7 And without all contradiction the less is blessed of the better.
8 And here men that die receive tithes; but there he *receiveth them*, of
whom it is witnessed that he liveth.
9 And as I may so say, Levi also, who receiveth tithes, payed tithes in
Abraham.
10 For he was yet in the loins of his father, when Mel-chis′e-dec met him.

2. Christ, the Eternal Priest according to Melchizedek

11 If therefore perfection were by the Le-vit′i-cal priesthood, (for under it
the people received the law,) what further need *was there* that another priest
should rise after the order of Mel-chis′e-dec, and not be called after the
order of Aaron?
12 For the priesthood being changed, there is made of necessity a change
also of the law.
13 For he of whom these things are spoken pertaineth to another tribe, of
which no man gave attendance at the altar.
14 For *it is* evident that our Lord sprang out of Juda; of which tribe Moses
spake nothing concerning priesthood.
15 And it is yet far more evident: for that after the similitude of Mel-
chis′e-dec there ariseth another priest,
16 Who is made, not after the law of a carnal commandment, but after the
power of an endless life.
17 For he testifieth, Thou *art* a priest for ever after the order of Mel-chis′e-
dec.
18 For there is verily a disannulling of the commandment going before for
the weakness and unprofitableness thereof.
19 For the law made nothing perfect, but the bringing in of a better hope
did; by the which we draw nigh unto God.

☆**7:4** Gen 14:20
7:5 Num 18:21, 26
7:6 Rom 4:13; Gal 3:16
7:8 Heb 5:6
☆**7:9**
7:11 Gal 2:21; Heb 7:17, 18
☆**7:12**
7:14 Gen 49:10; Isa 11:1; Mt 1:3; Lk 3:33; Rom 1:3; Rev 5:5
☆**7:17** Ps 110:4
7:18 Rom 8:3; Gal 4:9; Heb 7:11
7:19 Acts 13:39; Rom 3:20; 5:2; Gal 2:16; Heb 6:18; 9:9; 10:19–22

7:4 If Abraham paid tithes to Melchizedek, then he paid tithes to Jesus Christ who proceeds from Melchizedek. (See note to 7:9.)
7:9 Abraham paid tithes to Melchizedek. Levi paid tithes to him in the loins of his father Abraham, from whom he descended. He who was to take tithes from the people of Israel paid tithes himself. So the one to whom he paid tithes was superior to himself. And Christ is superior to Melchizedek, to whom Abraham and Levi paid tithes.
7:12 *the priesthood being changed . . . a change also of the law.* There was a change of the tribe of the priesthood, from Levi to Judah from whom came Jesus, our high priest. Levi and the law went together. Jesus and the gospel go hand in hand. The Old Testament priesthood was weak, imperfect, and could not save. Christ's priesthood is perfect, has power, and takes away sin. Gospel supersedes law.
7:17 The quotation from Psalm 110:4 comes from the lips of David. When he wrote this by the help of the Spirit, he would not have known that the author of Hebrews would appropriate it and claim it to be fulfilled in Jesus Christ, who came from the seed of David but whose priesthood sprang from Melchizedek.

3. Christ's One Time Sacrifice for Sin

20 And inasmuch as not without an oath *he was made priest:*

7:21☆ Num 23:19 Ps 110:4 Heb 7:28

21 (For those priests were made without an oath; but this with an oath by
him that said unto him, The Lord sware and will not repent, Thou *art* a
priest for ever after the order of Mel-chis′e-dec:)

7:22 Heb 8:6

22 By so much was Jesus made a surety of a better testament.
23 And they truly were many priests, because they were not suffered to
continue by reason of death:

7:24 Isa 9:6, 7 Jn 12:34 Rom 9:5 Rev 1:18

24 But this *man*, because he continueth ever, hath an unchangeable
priesthood.

7:25☆ Rom 8:34 1 Tim 2:5 1 Jn 2:1

25 Wherefore he is able also to save them to the uttermost that come unto
God by him, seeing he ever liveth to make intercession for them.

7:26☆ 2 Cor 5:21 Eph 1:20; 4:10 Heb 4:14 1 Pet 2:22

26 For such an high priest became us, *who is* holy, harmless, undefiled,
separate from sinners, and made higher than the heavens;

7:27 Lev 9:7 16:6, 11, 15 Rom 6:10 Eph 5:2 Heb 5:3; 9:7, 12

27 Who needeth not daily, as those high priests, to offer up sacrifice, first
for his own sins, and then for the people's: for this he did once, when he
offered up himself.

7:28☆ Heb 2:10; 5:1, 2

28 For the law maketh men high priests which have infirmity; but the
word of the oath, which was since the law, *maketh* the Son, who is
consecrated for evermore.

IV. CHRIST'S BETTER COVENANT (8:1—9:28)

A. THE OLD AND THE NEW

8:1☆ Col 3:1 Heb 1:3; 2:17

8 NOW of the things which we have spoken *this is* the sum: We have
such an high priest, who is set on the right hand of the throne of the
Majesty in the heavens;

8:2 Ex 33:7 Heb 9:11; 10:11

2 A minister of the sanctuary, and of the true tabernacle, which the Lord
pitched, and not man.

8:3 Eph 5:2 Heb 5:1

3 For every high priest is ordained to offer gifts and sacrifices: wherefore
it is of necessity that this man have somewhat also to offer.
4 For if he were on earth, he should not be a priest, seeing that there are
priests that offer gifts according to the law:

8:5 Ex 25:40 Col 2:17 Heb 9:23

5 Who serve unto the example and shadow of heavenly things, as Moses
was admonished of God when he was about to make the tabernacle: for,
See, saith he, *that* thou make all things according to the pattern shewed to
thee in the mount.

7:21 *The Lord swore and will not repent* informs us that the God of the covenant does that which is permanent and effective, not that which is temporary and provisional. The divine purposes will be fulfilled, men will be brought into fellowship with God, and their sins will be forgiven.

7:25 *is able to save them to the uttermost.* Jesus is the only solution to the sin problem. By faith in him even the vilest sinner can be saved.

7:26 Jesus Christ, as opposed to Levi and all the high priests who succeeded him in that office, is precisely the high priest sinners need. The Old Testament priests *were sinners; Christ is sinless.* He was free from actual sin. He was undefiled and thus never contributed to the sins of others. He was separate from sinners, in that he was born without original sin. And he is made higher than the heavens, even above the angels, because of his personal holiness and dignity.

7:28 Jesus, the Son, is God and as such shares the divine attributes, which include the following: (1) holiness (7:26; John 8:46; 2 Cor. 5:21); (2) eternalness (Micah 5:2; John 1:1; 8:58; 17:5, 24; Col. 1:17); (3) omnipotence (1:3; Rev. 1:8; Matt. 28:18); (4) omniscience (John 16:30; Matt. 9:4; John 6:64; see also John 2:24; 18:4; Col. 2:3); (5) immutability (1:11, 12; 13:8); (6) omnipresence (John 3:13; Matt. 28:20; see also Matt. 18:20; Eph. 1:23); (7) creative activity (Col. 1:16, 17; John 1:3; see also 1 Cor. 8:6; Heb. 1:8, 10); (8) power to forgive sins (Mark 2:5, 7, 9, 10; see also Luke 24:47; John 1:29; Acts 10:43; 1 John 1:7); (9) the right to be worshipped—he did not hesitate to accept the worship of men (Matt. 8:2; Phil. 2:10).

8:1 *who is set,* i.e., "who is seated." The priests always ministered standing. There were no seats in the tabernacle or temple. Christ's work is a finished work. He is seated, which means that his sacrifice was accepted by the Father. Nothing more needs to be added to what Christ has already done.

6 But now hath he obtained a more excellent ministry, by how much also
he is the mediator of a better covenant, which was established upon better
promises.

8:6 2 Cor 3:6 Heb 7:22

7 For if that first *covenant* had been faultless, then should no place have
been sought for the second.

8:7 Heb 7:11

8 For finding fault with them, he saith, Behold, the days come, saith the
Lord, when I will make a new covenant with the house of Israel and with
the house of Judah:

☆**8:8–11** Jer 31:31–34

9 Not according to the covenant that I made with their fathers in the day
when I took them by the hand to lead them out of the land of Egypt;
because they continued not in my covenant, and I regarded them not, saith
the Lord.

10 For this *is* the covenant that I will make with the house of Israel after
those days, saith the Lord; I will put my laws into their mind, and write
them in their hearts: and I will be to them a God, and they shall be to me
a people:

☆**8:10**

11 And they shall not teach every man his neighbour, and every man his
brother, saying, Know the Lord: for all shall know me, from the least to the
greatest.

8:11 Jn 6:45 1 Jn 2:27

12 For I will be merciful to their unrighteousness, and their sins and their
iniquities will I remember no more.

13 In that he saith, A new *covenant*, he hath made the first old. Now that
which decayeth and waxeth old *is* ready to vanish away.

8:13 Heb 12:24

B. CHRIST'S DEATH FULFILLS THE NEW COVENANT

9 THEN verily the first *covenant* had also ordinances of divine service,
and a worldly sanctuary.

2 For there was a tabernacle made; the first, wherein *was* the candlestick,
and the table, and the shewbread; which is called the sanctuary.

3 And after the second veil, the tabernacle which is called the Holiest of
all;

4 Which had the golden censer, and the ark of the covenant overlaid
round about with gold, wherein *was* the golden pot that had manna, and
Aaron's rod that budded, and the tables of the covenant;

9:1 Ex 25:8
☆**9:2** Ex 25:23, 31 26:1 Lev 24:5
9:3 Ex 26:31, 33, 40:3
☆**9:4** Ex 16:33 25:10, 16 30:1; 31:18 Num 17:10 Deut 10:2 2 Chron 5:10

8:8 The *new covenant* is superior to the old one. Under the old covenant believers were given symbols and types. Under the new covenant (or agreement) the historical person Jesus, who died and rose again, is the reality. Men put their trust in him. Moreover, believers now have the Holy Spirit, who takes up his residence in the hearts of the faithful. Israel misused the old agreement by falling into legalism, which included works and self-justification. Salvation, then and now, was and is by faith alone through God's free grace. By the old covenant sins were covered; now sins are removed. The benefits of the new covenant are secured by faith in Christ, which includes submitting to his Lordship. And this salvation is sealed by water baptism.

8:10ff Here we learn of the extraordinary provisions of the new covenant. God gave the law *to* the Israelites. He now puts his laws in the minds and on the hearts of those who believe in Christ. We were given minds to remember, hearts to love, consciences to recognize, courage to profess, and the power to put all these things required of us into practice. He is our God and we are his people, and our sins are remembered against us no more.

9:2 See note to Exod. 25:9 on the tabernacle. The *candlestick* provided light, for there were no windows in the tabernacle. It signifies God as light or Christ as the light of men, who are in darkness and need the light from God. The table and shewbread were useless without light. We come to Christ's table by his light and eat of the provision he has made for us, his people. In the light, we eat the bread of life.

9:4 *the golden censer.* Here the writer is speaking proleptically about the altar of incense, for it was historically stationed in front of the veil. He sees it now subsequent to Christ's atonement (at which time the veil was rent in two); now the altar of incense stands before the altar since the veil is gone. Nothing separates the believer from the Holy of Holies to which he, as a priest of God, has access. *the ark of the covenant,* which was overlaid with pure gold, typifies Christ's perfect obedience in which he fulfilled all righteousness. The golden pot contained manna, which when kept by men putrified but which was miraculously preserved in the pot by God. Aaron's rod typifies Christ our high priest, who died for our transgressions and rose for our justification.

9:5☆ Ex 25:18–20; Lev 16:2

5 And over it the cherubims of glory shadowing the mercyseat; of which
we cannot now speak particularly.
6 Now when these things were thus ordained, the priests went always into
the first tabernacle, accomplishing the service *of God.*

9:7 Ex 30:10; Lev 16:11; Num 15:25; Heb 5:3

7 But into the second *went* the high priest alone once every year, not
without blood, which he offered for himself, and *for* the errors of the
people:

9:8☆ Jn 14:6; Heb 10:20

8 The Holy Ghost this signifying, that the way into the holiest of all was
not yet made manifest, while as the first tabernacle was yet standing:

9:9☆ Gal 3:21, 22; Heb 5:1

9 Which *was* a figure for the time then present, in which were offered both
gifts and sacrifices, that could not make him that did the service perfect, as
pertaining to the conscience;

9:10☆ Lev 11:2, 25; Num 6:3; 19:7; Rom 14:17; Eph 2:15

10 *Which stood* only in meats and drinks, and divers washings, and carnal
ordinances, imposed *on them* until the time of reformation.

9:11☆ Mk 14:58; Heb 8:2; 9:24; 10:1

11 But Christ being come an high priest of good things to come, by a
greater and more perfect tabernacle, not made with hands, that is to say,
not of this building;

9:12 Lev 4:3; Dan 9:24; Zech 3:9; Heb 7:27

12 Neither by the blood of goats and calves, but by his own blood he
entered in once into the holy place, having obtained eternal redemption *for*
us.

9:13 Lev 16:14, 15; Num 19:2, 9

13 For if the blood of bulls and of goats, and the ashes of an heifer
sprinkling the unclean, sanctifieth to the purifying of the flesh:

9:14 Lk 1:74; Rom 1:4; 1 Cor 15:45; Eph 2:5; Heb 1:3; 6:1; 1 Pet 3:18; 1 Jn 1:7

14 How much more shall the blood of Christ, who through the eternal
Spirit offered himself without spot to God, purge your conscience from
dead works to serve the living God?

9:15 Rom 3:25; 1 Tim 2:5; Heb 3:1; 1 Pet 3:18

15 And for this cause he is the mediator of the new testament, that by
means of death, for the redemption of the transgressions *that were* under
the first testament, they which are called might receive the promise of
eternal inheritance.
16 For where a testament *is,* there must also of necessity be the death of
the testator.

9:17 Gal 3:15

17 For a testament *is* of force after men are dead: otherwise it is of no
strength at all while the testator liveth.
18 Whereupon neither the first *testament* was dedicated without blood.

9:18 Ex 24:6

19 For when Moses had spoken every precept to all the people according

9:19 Ex 24:5–8; Lev 14:4; Heb 1:1

to the law, he took the blood of calves and of goats, with water, and scarlet
wool, and hyssop, and sprinkled both the book, and all the people,

9:20 Ex 24:8; Mt 26:28

20 Saying, This *is* the blood of the testament which God hath enjoined
unto you.

9:21 Ex 29:12; Lev 8:15

21 Moreover he sprinkled with blood both the tabernacle, and all the
vessels of the ministry.

9:5 The cherubim represent the angels of God who rejoice in the merits and the work of Christ. They chant his eternal praises. They overshadow the mercy seat, which was also covered by pure gold. The mercy seat (or propitiatory cover) is the perfect type of Jesus Christ and his righteousness that provides a covering *for all of our sins.*

9:8–10 The Holy Spirit tells us that the Old Testament institutions were external, temporary arrangements imposed until the coming of Christ. We learn that the type leads to the antitype or the fulfillment, and the antitype exceeds the type in every way. The Old Testament priesthood was the type of which Christ is the antitype.

9:11ff Christ is our priest. The Jewish high priest ministered at the altar, a function he shared with other priests. But he alone entered into the Holy of Holies once a year with blood to make atonement for himself and for the sins of the people. Apart from Christ's priestly work, there is no salvation. Hebrews says that Christ is our mediator, the one who stands between us and a holy God. By his death Christ, in a once-for-all act, made atonement for our sins. Believers can approach God boldly through the only valid priest, Jesus Christ.

[22]And almost all things are by the law purged with blood; and without
shedding of blood is no remission.

☆**9:22** Lev 17:11

C. CHRIST'S DEATH, THE ONE TIME SACRIFICE

[23]*It was* therefore necessary that the patterns of things in the heavens
should be purified with these; but the heavenly things themselves with
better sacrifices than these.
[24]For Christ is not entered into the holy places made with hands, *which*
are the figures of the true; but into heaven itself, now to appear in the
presence of God for us:
[25]Nor yet that he should offer himself often, as the high priest entereth
into the holy place every year with blood of others;
[26]For then must he often have suffered since the foundation of the world:
but now once in the end of the world hath he appeared to put away sin by
the sacrifice of himself.
[27]And as it is appointed unto men once to die, but after this the
judgment:
[28]So Christ was once offered to bear the sins of many; and unto them
that look for him shall he appear the second time without sin unto
salvation.

9:23 Heb 8:5
9:24 Rom 8:34; Heb 6:20; 7:25; 8:2; 9:12; 1 Jn 2:1
9:25 Heb 9:2, 7
9:26 1 Cor 10:11; Eph 1:10; Heb 7:27; 10:10; 1 Pet 3:18
9:27 Gen 3:19; Eccles 3:20
☆**9:28** Mt 25:34; 26:28; Acts 1:11; Rom 5:15; 6:10; Tit 2:13; Heb 4:15; 5:19; 7:27; 1 Pet 2:24

V. CHRIST'S BETTER SACRIFICE (10:1–39)

A. CHRIST'S SACRIFICE COMPARED TO THE OLD SACRIFICES

10 FOR the law having a shadow of good things to come, *and* not the
very image of the things, can never with those sacrifices which they
offered year by year continually make the comers thereunto perfect.
[2]For then would they not have ceased to be offered? because that the
worshippers once purged should have had no more conscience of sins.
[3]But in those *sacrifices there is* a remembrance again *made* of sins every
year.
[4]For *it is* not possible that the blood of bulls and of goats should take
away sins.
[5]Wherefore when he cometh into the world, he saith, Sacrifice and
offering thou wouldest not, but a body hast thou prepared me:
[6]In burnt offerings and *sacrifices* for sin thou hast had no pleasure.
[7]Then said I, Lo, I come (in the volume of the book it is written of me,)
to do thy will, O God.

☆**10:1** Col 2:17; Heb 7:19; 8:5; 9:11
10:3 Lev 16:21; Heb 9:7
10:4 Mic 6:6; Heb 9:12
☆**10:5–7** Ps 40:6–8; 50:8; Isa 1:11; Jer 6:20; Amos 5:21

9:22 Men seek every other way of salvation except that which God offers. No one can be saved apart from the shedding of blood. It does not matter whether men like this method; they can do nothing but accept the way God decided to make salvation possible. Further, the work of Christ is far more important than the work of the Levitical priesthood. The priests offered the blood of animals; Christ offered his own blood. His is a far more important work, because the blood of bulls and goats could not bring salvation. Only the blood of Christ could do that. The sins of the Old Testament saints were remitted by virtue of the fact that the offering of the blood of bulls and goats was a type looking forward to the blood of Christ shed on the cross.

9:28 When Christ comes again many purposes in the plan of God will be consummated: (1) our salvation will be completed (9:28; 1 Pet. 1:5); (2) he will reign in heaven and on earth as absolute sovereign (Rev. 11:15); (3) he will destroy the power and the reign of death (1 Cor. 15:25, 26); (4) he will be admired and praised by all the saints (2 Thess. 1:10); (5) every dark and hidden thing will be revealed (1 Cor. 4:5); (6) the final judgment of the living and the dead will take place (John 5:22; 2 Tim. 4:1; Jude 15; Rev. 20:11–13); (7) the dead saints will rise first (1 Thess. 4:16); (8) the living saints will be caught up together with the risen dead saints in the clouds (1 Thess. 4:17); and (9) the man of sin (or lawlessness) will be destroyed (2 Thess. 2:8).

10:1 Law has been replaced by gospel. The law was a shadow of better things to come. In Christ we now have the substance of what was previously a shadow. The animals to be slain for the sacrifices could not offer themselves by consent. Christ gave himself voluntarily.

10:7 Christ came to do the Father's will. He was ready and willing to provide redemption; it was his delight to do this. In effect he said, "Let the curse fall on me."

8 Above when he said, Sacrifice and offering and burnt offerings and
offering for sin thou wouldest not, neither hadst pleasure *therein;* which are
offered by the law;
9 Then said he, Lo, I come to do thy will, O God. He taketh away the first,
that he may establish the second.
10 By the which will we are sanctified through the offering of the body of
Jesus Christ once *for all.*

10:10☆ Jn 17:19; Eph 5:26; Heb 7:27; 9:14, 28; 1 Pet 2:24

B. CHRIST'S ASCENSION, THE EVIDENCE OF HIS FINISHED WORK

11 And every priest standeth daily ministering and offering oftentimes the
same sacrifices, which can never take away sins:
12 But this man, after he had offered one sacrifice for sins for ever, sat
down on the right hand of God;
13 From henceforth expecting till his enemies be made his footstool.
14 For by one offering he hath perfected for ever them that are sanctified.
15 *Whereof* the Holy Ghost also is a witness to us: for after that he had
said before,
16 This *is* the covenant that I will make with them after those days, saith
the Lord, I will put my laws into their hearts, and in their minds will I write
them;
17 And their sins and iniquities will I remember no more.
18 Now where remission of these *is, there is* no more offering for sin.

10:11 Num 28:3; Heb 5:1
10:12☆ Col 3:1; Heb 1:3
10:13 Ps 110:1
10:15 Heb 3:7; 2 Pet 1:21
10:16, 17☆ Jer 31:33, 34

C. THE DANGER OF REJECTING CHRIST

1. Our Access and Boldness through the Blood of Christ

19 Having therefore, brethren, boldness to enter into the holiest by the
blood of Jesus,
20 By a new and living way, which he hath consecrated for us, through the
veil, that is to say, his flesh;
21 And *having* an high priest over the house of God;
22 Let us draw near with a true heart in full assurance of faith, having our
hearts sprinkled from an evil conscience, and our bodies washed with pure
water.
23 Let us hold fast the profession of *our* faith without wavering; (for he *is*
faithful that promised;)

10:19 Heb 9:25
10:20☆ Jn 10:9; 14:6; Heb 6:19; 9:8
10:21 1 Tim 3:15; Heb 2:17; 3:6
10:22 Ezek 36:25; 2 Cor 7:1; Eph 3:12; Jas 1:6; 1 Jn 3:21
10:23 1 Cor 1:9; 10:13; Heb 3:6

10:10 The words *we are sanctified* derive from a Greek word, *hagiasmos* (here *hagiasmenoi,* meaning "having been sanctified"), which comes from *hagios* ("holy"). The Oxford Dictionary defines sanctification as "the action of the Holy Ghost in sanctifying or making holy the believer, by the implanting within him of the Christian graces and the destruction of the sinful affections." The theologian Charles Hodge defines it as "the work of God's free grace, whereby we are renewed in the whole man after the image of God, and are enabled more and more to die unto sin and live unto righteousness" (*Systematic Theology,* III, part 3, p. 213, Eerdmans, 1981). Upon conversion the believer is set apart from the world as God's possession, and he is already wholly or perfectly sanctified in the sight of God in principle. But sanctification also involves a *process in which the believer dies more and more to* self and lives more and more to God.

10:12 Here and in Heb. 1:2 the expression *sat down* is used in connection with Christ's work for us. The tabernacle and the temple had no seats. The priests performed their work standing. This meant their work was never finished. The high priest entered the Holy of Holies year after year. The Aaronic priesthood never finished its work. However, when Christ atoned for our sins he entered the heavenly sanctuary with his blood and he was *seated* at the right hand of the Father—signifying the satisfaction of the Father for the work he did, and the fact that it is finished once and for all.

10:17 Our sins, when covered by the blood of Christ, are forgiven. They are (1) remembered no more (10:17); (2) put away by God (2 Sam. 12:13); (3) cast behind God's back (Isa. 38:17); (4) blotted out (Isa. 43:25); (5) cast into the depths of the sea (Mic. 7:19); and (6) removed as far as the east is from the west (Ps. 103:12).

10:20 *by a new and living way.* Salvation by the blood of Jesus is (1) the only way of salvation; (2) the new way—for it supersedes the old covenant and the law; and (3) the living way—for were we to come to God by any other way it would be death, not life. Salvation which gives life is made possible by the offering of the flesh of the Son of God in death. The veil, which partitioned off the Holy of Holies, has been rent; we can enter in. We are priests unto God by the new and living way.

24 And let us consider one another to provoke unto love and to good
works:

10:24 Tit 3:8

25 Not forsaking the assembling of ourselves together, as the manner of
some *is;* but exhorting *one another:* and so much the more, as ye see the day
approaching.

☆**10:25** Acts 2:42; Heb 3:13; 2 Pet 3:9

2. The Consequences of Rejection

26 For if we sin wilfully after that we have received the knowledge of the
truth, there remaineth no more sacrifice for sins,

☆**10:26** Num 15:30; 1 Tim 2:4; 2 Pet 2:20; 1 Jn 5:16

27 But a certain fearful looking for of judgment and fiery indignation,
which shall devour the adversaries.

10:27 Ezek 36:5

28 He that despised Moses' law died without mercy under two or three
witnesses:

10:28 Deut 17:2–5

29 Of how much sorer punishment, suppose ye, shall he be thought
worthy, who hath trodden under foot the Son of God, and hath counted the
blood of the covenant, wherewith he was sanctified, an unholy thing, and
hath done despite unto the Spirit of grace?

10:29 Mt 12:31; Jn 5:29; 1 Cor 11:29

30 For we know him that hath said, Vengeance *belongeth* unto me, I will
recompense, saith the Lord. And again, The Lord shall judge his people.

10:30 Deut 32:35, 36; Ps 50:4; 135:14

31 *It is* a fearful thing to fall into the hands of the living God.

10:31 Lk 12:5; 2 Cor 5:11

3. The Reward for Endurance

32 But call to remembrance the former days, in which, after ye were
illuminated, ye endured a great fight of afflictions;

10:32 Gal 3:4

33 Partly, whilst ye were made a gazingstock both by reproaches and
afflictions; and partly, whilst ye became companions of them that were so
used.

10:33 1 Cor 4:9; Phil 1:7; 1 Thess 2:14

34 For ye had compassion of me in my bonds, and took joyfully the
spoiling of your goods, knowing in yourselves that ye have in heaven a
better and an enduring substance.

10:34 Mt 5:12; Heb 13:3

35 Cast not away therefore your confidence, which hath great recompence
of reward.

☆**10:35**

36 For ye have need of patience, that, after ye have done the will of God,
ye might receive the promise.

10:36 Col 3:24; Heb 9:15

37 For yet a little while, and he that shall come will come, and will not
tarry.
38 Now the just shall live by faith: but if *any man* draw back, my soul shall
have no pleasure in him.

10:37, 38 Lk 18:8; Hab 2:3, 4

39 But we are not of them who draw back unto perdition; but of them that
believe to the saving of the soul.

10:25 The church is a community of believers who are commanded to come together for worship. They assemble also to celebrate the Lord's Supper, to baptize new believers, and to have fellowship one with another. The Word of God is to be preached, offerings gathered, and other activities included that are conducive to the edification of believers. All Christians should unite with a church and attend its services regularly.

10:26ff We are given good reasons why we should avoid apostasy: (1) because of what apostasy is—sinning willfully after we have received the truth; (2) because of the awful fate awaiting such people; (3) because of the execution of divine justice against those who broke the law of Moses and died at the hands of two or three witnesses; (4) because of God's vindictive judgment or vengeance upon sinners.

10:35 Believers are encouraged to persevere because of the recompense of the reward. God will liberally reward those who truly seek to follow him and obey his commandments. Sometimes the actions may be wanting, but if the desire is present, God will honor the sincere heart.

VI. FAITH, THE BETTER WAY (11:1—12:29)

A. DEFINITION AND EXAMPLES OF FAITH

1. Faith Defined

11:1☆ Rom 8:24; Heb 3:6, 14

11 NOW faith is the substance of things hoped for, the evidence of things not seen.

11:2 Heb 11:39

2 For by it the elders obtained a good report.

11:3 Gen 1:1–31; John 1:3; Rom 1:19, 20; 4:20; Heb 1:2

3 Through faith we understand that the worlds were framed by the word of God, so that things which are seen were not made of things which do appear.

2. The Examples of the Early Patriarchs

11:4☆ Gen 4:3–5

4 By faith Abel offered unto God a more excellent sacrifice than Cain, by which he obtained witness that he was righteous, God testifying of his gifts: and by it he being dead yet speaketh.

11:5☆

5 By faith E'noch was translated that he should not see death; and was not found, because God had translated him: for before his translation he had this testimony, that he pleased God.

11:6 Jn 3:18, 36; Heb 7:19; 10:19–22

6 But without faith *it is* impossible to please *him:* for he that cometh to God must believe that he is, and *that* he is a rewarder of them that diligently seek him.

11:7☆ Gen 6:13–22; Rom 3:22; Phil 3:9

7 By faith Noah, being warned of God of things not seen as yet, moved with fear, prepared an ark to the saving of his house; by the which he condemned the world, and became heir of the righteousness which is by faith.

3. The Example of Abraham and His Family

11:8☆ Gen 12:1–4

8 By faith Abraham, when he was called to go out into a place which he should after receive for an inheritance, obeyed; and he went out, not knowing whither he went.

11:9 Gen 12:8

9 By faith he sojourned in the land of promise, as *in* a strange country, dwelling in tabernacles with Isaac and Jacob, the heirs with him of the same promise:

11:10 Heb 11:16; 12:22; Rev 21:2

10 For he looked for a city which hath foundations, whose builder and maker *is* God.

11:11 Gen 17:19; 21:1–3

11 Through faith also Sara herself received strength to conceive seed, and was delivered of a child when she was past age, because she judged him faithful who had promised.

11:12 Gen 15:5; Rom 4:19

12 Therefore sprang there even of one, and him as good as dead, *so many* as the stars of the sky in multitude, and as the sand which is by the sea shore innumerable.

11:1 See note to Eph. 2:8 for a definition of faith.

11:4ff The saints named in this chapter may be divided into two classes: those whose names and exploits are mentioned and those whose names but not their exploits are stated. The account is also interesting both for those whose names are omitted and for some of those who are named. Adam, Elijah, and Elisha are not specifically named. Samson and Jephthah represent some who, humanly speaking, rank below some of the unnamed. Only two women are mentioned: Sarah and Rahab. All those mentioned are examples of people who had faith. By mentioning Abel first, the writer indicates that subsequent to Adam's fall God opened a new way of worship: it was to be done through animal sacrifices, which carry with them a confession of sin and of faith in a redeemer. (See note on Gen. 4:4.)

11:5 See note to Gen. 5:24 on the translation of Enoch.

11:7 Noah was given a divine revelation by God. He was faithful in communicating God's message to men. He was not very successful, for only his family entered the ark; all other listeners to his preaching were lost. As one in the evangelism business for a hundred and twenty years, he had perseverance.

11:8 A major component of Abraham's faith consisted in his going out without knowing where he was going. He had an implicit trust in God and lived as a sojourner who kept his eye on his true home, the heavenly Canaan.

[13]These all died in faith, not having received the promises, but having
seen them afar off, and were persuaded of *them*, and embraced *them*, and
confessed that they were strangers and pilgrims on the earth.
[14]For they that say such things declare plainly that they seek a country.
[15]And truly, if they had been mindful of that *country* from whence they
came out, they might have had opportunity to have returned.
[16]But now they desire a better *country*, that is, an heavenly: wherefore
God is not ashamed to be called their God: for he hath prepared for them
a city.
[17]By faith Abraham, when he was tried, offered up Isaac: and he that had
received the promises offered up his only begotten *son*,
[18]Of whom it was said, That in Isaac shall thy seed be called:
[19]Accounting that God *was* able to raise *him* up, even from the dead;
from whence also he received him in a figure.
[20]By faith Isaac blessed Jacob and Esau concerning things to come.
[21]By faith Jacob, when he was a dying, blessed both the sons of Joseph;
and worshipped, *leaning* upon the top of his staff.
[22]By faith Joseph, when he died, made mention of the departing of the
children of Israel; and gave commandment concerning his bones.

11:13 Gen 23:4; Mt 13:17; Jn 8:56; Heb 11:39
11:14 Heb 13:14
11:15 Gen 24:6
11:16 Gen 26:24; Ex 3:6, 15; Phil 3:20
11:17 Gen 22:1, 2; Jas 2:21
11:18 Gen 21:12
☆**11:19** Rom 4:21
11:20 Gen 27:27–29
☆**11:21** Gen 47:31; 48:5
11:22 Gen 50:24, 25; Ex 13:19

4. The Example of Moses

[23]By faith Moses, when he was born, was hid three months of his parents,
because they saw *he was* a proper child; and they were not afraid of the
king's commandment.
[24]By faith Moses, when he was come to years, refused to be called the son
of Pharaoh's daughter;
[25]Choosing rather to suffer affliction with the people of God, than to
enjoy the pleasures of sin for a season;
[26]Esteeming the reproach of Christ greater riches than the treasures in
Egypt: for he had respect unto the recompence of the reward.
[27]By faith he forsook Egypt, not fearing the wrath of the king: for he
endured, as seeing him who is invisible.
[28]Through faith he kept the passover, and the sprinkling of blood, lest he
that destroyed the firstborn should touch them.

11:23 Ex 1:16; 2:2
11:25 Ex 2:10–12; Ps 84:10
☆**11:27** Ex 10:28; 12:37; Heb 11:1
11:28 Ex 12:1–13, 21–30

5. The Example of the Israelites and Rahab

[29]By faith they passed through the Red sea as by dry *land:* which the
Egyptians assaying to do were drowned.
[30]By faith the walls of Jericho fell down, after they were compassed about
seven days.
[31]By faith the harlot Rahab perished not with them that believed not,
when she had received the spies with peace.

11:29 Ex 14:13–31
11:30 Josh 6:20
11:31 Josh 2:9; 6:23; Jas 2:25

11:19 Abraham was willing to offer Isaac and was kept from doing so by a command from God. He had faith to believe that if he did offer his son, God would raise Isaac from the dead. God did not ask of Abraham what he himself was not willing to do. He gave his only Son to die on the cross of Calvary.

11:21 Faith's greatest test comes when death approaches. We should finish this life in faith, even as Jacob did.

11:27 *he endured, as seeing him who is invisible.* God is spirit and thus has no parts and is not a material being. He is invisible to the eye of the body but not to the eye of faith. Idolaters make images of God because they lean on what can be seen. God is no less real because he is invisible. Moses saw God by faith and this enabled him to endure.

6. The Example of Judges and Prophets

11:32☆ Judg 4:6; 6:11; 11:1; 13:24; 1 Sam 1:20; 16:1
11:33☆ 1 Sam 17:34; Dan 6:22
11:34☆ Judg 7:18–21; 1 Sam 14:13; 1 Kgs 19:3; 2 Kgs 20:7; Job 42:10; Dan 3:25
11:35☆ 1 Kgs 17:22; 2 Kgs 4:35; Acts 22:25
11:36 Gen 39:20; Jer 20:2; 37:15
11:37 1 Kgs 19:10; 21:13; 2 Chron 24:21; Acts 7:58; 14:19
11:38 1 Kgs 18:4

32 And what shall I more say? for the time would fail me to tell of Ged′e-
on, and *of* Ba′rak, and *of* Samson, and *of* Jeph′tha-e; *of* David also, and
Samuel, and *of* the prophets:
33 Who through faith subdued kingdoms, wrought righteousness, obtained
promises, stopped the mouths of lions,
34 Quenched the violence of fire, escaped the edge of the sword, out of
weakness were made strong, waxed valiant in fight, turned to flight the
armies of the aliens.
35 Women received their dead raised to life again: and others were
tortured, not accepting deliverance; that they might obtain a better
resurrection:
36 And others had trial of *cruel* mockings and scourgings, yea, moreover of
bonds and imprisonment:
37 They were stoned, they were sawn asunder, were tempted, were slain
with the sword: they wandered about in sheepskins and goatskins; being
destitute, afflicted, tormented;
38 (Of whom the world was not worthy:) they wandered in deserts, and *in*
mountains, and *in* dens and caves of the earth.
39 And these all, having obtained a good report through faith, received not
the promise:

11:40 Rom 11:26; Rev 6:11

40 God having provided some better thing for us, that they without us
should not be made perfect.

B. THE EXERCISE OF FAITH

1. Jesus, Our Leader and Teacher

12:1☆ 1 Cor 9:24; Phil 3:12–14
12:2 Ps 110:1; 2 Cor 3:18; Heb 2:9, 10; 1 Pet 1:11

12 WHEREFORE seeing we also are compassed about with so great a
cloud of witnesses, let us lay aside every weight, and the sin which
doth so easily beset *us*, and let us run with patience the race that is set
before us,
2 Looking unto Jesus the author and finisher of *our* faith; who for the joy
that was set before him endured the cross, despising the shame, and is set
down at the right hand of the throne of God.

2. Faith Aided by God's Discipline

12:3 Jn 15:20
12:4☆ Heb 10:32
12:5 Job 5:17; Prov 3:11

3 For consider him that endured such contradiction of sinners against
himself, lest ye be wearied and faint in your minds.
4 Ye have not yet resisted unto blood, striving against sin.
5 And ye have forgotten the exhortation which speaketh unto you as unto
children, My son, despise not thou the chastening of the Lord, nor faint
when thou art rebuked of him:

11:32–35 In these verses the writer speaks of great deliverances that came to many saints who trusted in God. In verse 35, starting with the phrase *and others were tortured*, we learn of others who, for their faith, suffered greatly and found deliverance in death rather than in life. They were the martyrs for the faith and *were just as much in the will of God* as those who performed great exploits for God (11:32–34).

12:1ff The cloud of witnesses are (1) those who did great exploits by faith and (2) Jesus, the Redeemer. We are to live as they did and run the kind of race they ran, with patience and persistence. (See note on Rom. 14:8.)

12:4 The Scriptures indicate several ways by which temptation can be overcome: (1) resisting temptation in faith (Eph. 6:16; 1 Pet. 5:8, 9; Heb. 12:4); (2) guarding against temptation (Matt. 26:41); (3) employing the resources of prayer (Matt. 6:13); (4) not letting Satan use a believer as an instrument of evil (Rom. 14:13); (5) helping to restore a fallen brother who repents (Gal. 6:1). An erring brother can be brought back into fellowship with God by (1) applying the blood of Jesus for cleansing (1 John 1:7); (2) making confession of sin (1 John 1:9); and, in some cases, (3) making repayment or restitution (Luke 19:8, 9).

6 For whom the Lord loveth he chasteneth, and scourgeth every son
whom he receiveth.
7 If ye endure chastening, God dealeth with you as with sons; for what
son is he whom the father chasteneth not?
8 But if ye be without chastisement, whereof all are partakers, then are ye
bastards, and not sons.
9 Furthermore we have had fathers of our flesh which corrected *us*, and we
gave *them* reverence: shall we not much rather be in subjection unto the
Father of spirits, and live?
10 For they verily for a few days chastened *us* after their own pleasure; but
he for *our* profit, that *we* might be partakers of his holiness.
11 Now no chastening for the present seemeth to be joyous, but grievous:
nevertheless afterward it yieldeth the peaceable fruit of righteousness unto
them which are exercised thereby.

3. Believers Exhorted to Endure

12 Wherefore lift up the hands which hang down, and the feeble knees;
13 And make straight paths for your feet, lest that which is lame be turned
out of the way; but let it rather be healed.
14 Follow peace with all *men*, and holiness, without which no man shall
see the Lord:
15 Looking diligently lest any man fail of the grace of God; lest any root
of bitterness springing up trouble *you*, and thereby many be defiled;
16 Lest there *be* any fornicator, or profane person, as Esau, who for one
morsel of meat sold his birthright.
17 For ye know how that afterward, when he would have inherited the
blessing, he was rejected: for he found no place of repentance, though he
sought it carefully with tears.

4. The Danger of Refusing to Obey God

18 For ye are not come unto the mount that might be touched, and that
burned with fire, nor unto blackness, and darkness, and tempest,
19 And the sound of a trumpet, and the voice of words; which *voice* they
that heard intreated that the word should not be spoken to them any more:
20 (For they could not endure that which was commanded, And if so
much as a beast touch the mountain, it shall be stoned, or thrust through
with a dart:
21 And so terrible was the sight, *that* Moses said, I exceedingly fear and
quake:)
22 But ye are come unto mount Sion, and unto the city of the living God,
the heavenly Jerusalem, and to an innumerable company of angels,
23 To the general assembly and church of the firstborn, which are written
in heaven, and to God the Judge of all, and to the spirits of just men made
perfect,
24 And to Jesus the mediator of the new covenant, and to the blood of
sprinkling, that speaketh better *things* than *that of* Abel.

☆**12:6** Prov 3:12; Ps 94:12; Jas 1:12; Rev 3:19
12:7 Deut 8:5
12:8 1 Pet 5:9
12:9 Isa 38:16
12:10 2 Pet 1:4
12:11 1 Pet 1:6
12:12 Isa 35:3
12:13 Prov 4:26; Gal 6:1
12:14 Mt 5:8; Rom 6:22; 14:19
12:15 Deut 29:18; Heb 4:1
☆**12:16** Gen 25:33
12:17 Gen 27:34
12:18 Ex 19:12, 16
12:19 Ex 20:19; Deut 4:12
12:20 Ex 19:12
☆**12:22** Ps 68:17; Dan 7:10; Gal 4:26; Phil 3:20; Heb 11:10; Rev 3:12; 14:1; 21:2
12:23 Lk 10:20; Phil 3:12; Heb 2:12
12:24 Gen 4:10; Ex 24:8; Heb 9:19; 10:19

12:6ff The false notion is spread abroad: "come to Christ and all your problems will disappear." When we come to Christ our problems just begin. Satan goes after God's people in an effort to undo the work of Christ. God himself is determined that we will be perfect as the Son of God is perfect. And in order to make us like that, he must discipline us. Discipline is hard to bear, but afterwards "it yieldeth the peaceable fruit of righteousness."

12:16 For note on Esau, see Gen. 25:25.

12:22 *the city of the living God.* The city of man is being built all around the world today, but it is unsubstantial and fades away. When history ends we will live in the city of God, which is the New Jerusalem (see note to Rev. 21:2). Life began in the Garden of Eden; it will end in the city of God, whose builder and maker is God himself. What he builds can never be destroyed.

12:25☆ Num 16; Heb 1:1; 2:2; 3:12
12:26 Ex 19:18; Hag 2:6
12:27 Ps 102:26; Mt 24:35; 2 Pet 3:10
12:28 Dan 2:44
12:29 Ex 24:17; Deut 9:3; Isa 66:15; 2 Thess 1:7

[25]See that ye refuse not him that speaketh. For if they escaped not who
refused him that spake on earth, much more *shall not* we *escape*, if we turn
away from him that *speaketh* from heaven:
[26]Whose voice then shook the earth: but now he hath promised, saying,
Yet once more I shake not the earth only, but also heaven.
[27]And this *word*, Yet once more, signifieth the removing of those things
that are shaken, as of things that are made, that those things which cannot
be shaken may remain.
[28]Wherefore we receiving a kingdom which cannot be moved, let us have
grace, whereby we may serve God acceptably with reverence and godly
fear:
[29]For our God *is* a consuming fire.

VII. CONCLUSION (13:1–25)

A. GENERAL ADMONITIONS

13:1☆ Rom 12:10
13:2 Gen 18:1–3; Mt 25:35
13:3 Mt 25:36; Col 4:18; Heb 10:34
13:4☆ 1 Cor 7:38
13:5☆ Gen 28:15; Ps 37:25
13:6 Ps 118:6

13 LET brotherly love continue.
[2]Be not forgetful to entertain strangers: for thereby some have
entertained angels unawares.
[3]Remember them that are in bonds, as bound with them; *and* them which
suffer adversity, as being yourselves also in the body.
[4]Marriage *is* honourable in all, and the bed undefiled: but whoremongers
and adulterers God will judge.
[5]*Let your* conversation *be* without covetousness; *and be* content with such
things as ye have: for he hath said, I will never leave thee, nor forsake thee.
[6]So that we may boldly say, The Lord *is* my helper, and I will not fear
what man shall do unto me.

B. LIVING IN THE LIGHT OF ETERNITY

13:7☆ Heb 6:12
13:8☆ Jn 8:58; 1 Cor 1:24; 2 Cor 1:19, 20; Rev 1:4
13:9 Eph 4:14; Col 2:16
13:10 1 Cor 10:18
13:11 Lev 4:12, 21
13:12 Jn 19:17; Heb 9:12
13:13 1 Pet 4:14

[7]Remember them which have the rule over you, who have spoken unto
you the word of God: whose faith follow, considering the end of *their*
conversation.
[8]Jesus Christ the same yesterday, and to day, and for ever.
[9]Be not carried about with divers and strange doctrines. For *it is* a good
thing that the heart be established with grace; not with meats, which have
not profited them that have been occupied therein.
[10]We have an altar, whereof they have no right to eat which serve the
tabernacle.
[11]For the bodies of those beasts, whose blood is brought into the
sanctuary by the high priest for sin, are burned without the camp.
[12]Wherefore Jesus also, that he might sanctify the people with his own
blood, suffered without the gate.
[13]Let us go forth therefore unto him without the camp, bearing his
reproach.

12:25ff When God speaks he expects men to listen and to act appropriately. We know that those who did not obey in the old dispensation have not escaped. And we shall not escape, if we follow in their footsteps. Believers have received a kingdom (of grace and *glory), which is so firmly founded* that it can never be shaken and will stand for all eternity (12:28). Whoever believes in God through Jesus Christ must worship him acceptably, in reverence and with godly fear.

13:1ff If God be our God, how then shall we live? By demonstrating brotherly love, giving hospitality, exuding sympathy, living purely and chastely, avoiding immorality and adultery.

13:4 See note to 1 Cor. 7:25 on marriage.

13:5 The reason we can be content with little or nothing in this life is the promise of God, *I will never leave thee, nor forsake thee.* (See note to 1 Tim. 6:10 on money.)

13:7 Ministers are God's guides and governors. They minister the Word of God. We are to pray for them, attend to their teaching, and follow it as they faithfully expound it.

13:8 This scripture bears testimony to the immutability and eternity of Jesus Christ, who is God.

14 For here have we no continuing city, but we seek one to come.

13:14 Heb 10:34; 11:10

15 By him therefore let us offer the sacrifice of praise to God continually,
that is, the fruit of *our* lips giving thanks to his name.

13:15 Lev 7:12 Ps 50:14 1 Pet 2:5

16 But to do good and to communicate forget not: for with such sacrifices
God is well pleased.

17 Obey them that have the rule over you, and submit yourselves: for they
watch for your souls, as they that must give account, that they may do it
with joy, and not with grief: for that *is* unprofitable for you.

☆**13:17** Ezek 3:17 33:2, 7 Acts 20:28

C. PERSONAL REQUEST, BENEDICTION, AND GREETINGS

18 Pray for us: for we trust we have a good conscience, in all things willing
to live honestly.

13:18 Acts 24:16

19 But I beseech *you* the rather to do this, that I may be restored to you the
sooner.

13:19 Philem 22

20 Now the God of peace, that brought again from the dead our Lord
Jesus, that great shepherd of the sheep, through the blood of the everlasting
covenant,

☆**13:20** Isa 40:11 Ezek 31:23 37:24 Zech 9:11 Jn 10:11

21 Make you perfect in every good work to do his will, working in you that
which is wellpleasing in his sight, through Jesus Christ; to whom *be* glory
for ever and ever. Amen.

☆**13:21** Rom 11:36 Phil 2:13 1 Pet 5:10

22 And I beseech you, brethren, suffer the word of exhortation: for I have
written a letter unto you in few words.

☆**13:22**

23 Know ye that *our* brother Timothy is set at liberty; with whom, if he
come shortly, I will see you.

☆**13:23** Acts 16:1 1 Thess 3:2

24 Salute all them that have the rule over you, and all the saints. They of
Italy salute you.

25 Grace *be* with you all. Amen.

13:17 More specifically than in verse 7, the writer commands believers to submit to their leaders and to do so joyfully. This, of course, does not mean believers are to follow this injunction if the ministers are unfaithful to the Word of God.

13:20, 21 In this apostolic benediction God is called the God of peace, Jesus Christ is named the shepherd (see note on John 10:11) who was brought back from the dead, salvation is said to come through the blood of the everlasting covenant, and a prayer is offered for the perfection of the saints through the work of Jesus Christ. All glory be to the Savior!

13:22, 23 From verses like this some have assumed it was Paul who wrote this letter to the Hebrews. If he did, it would be the only letter he wrote without his superscription.

THE GENERAL EPISTLE OF
JAMES

Authorship, date, and background The letter of James opens with the statement "James, a servant of God and of the Lord Jesus Christ" (1:1). This immediately establishes the author as James, unless the letter is pseudepigraphic (a spurious work purporting to come from James), which it cannot be if the Bible is to be trusted. The James spoken of in the opening salutation is none other than the brother of the Lord Jesus. Some have asserted that James was really a cousin and that the word *brother* can be so understood. This is highly unlikely. Others think he was the son of Joseph by a former marriage, in which event he would have been Jesus' stepbrother. Most conservative protestants accept him as the son of Joseph and Mary and thus the half-brother of Jesus. He was converted after the resurrection of the Lord Jesus and became the leader of the church in Jerusalem. He was among those who waited for the coming of the Holy Spirit on the day of Pentecost (Acts 1:14).

The letter best fits the period between A.D. 45 and 50. The city of Jerusalem had not been seized and destroyed. Jews from around the Roman empire returned to Jerusalem for feast occasions so that addressing the letter to "the twelve tribes which were scattered abroad" indicates that they had been dispersed before the fall of Jerusalem so that the letter need not be dated after the fall. The letter was not intended for Gentile Christians per se. It was written to Jews who had become Christians and who knew the Old Testament and were keepers of the law. James himself, according to Galatians 2:12, was well known for his strict adherence to the law. At this time in the history of the church, Jewish Christians had not fully understood their freedom in Christ. Indeed at the Council at Jerusalem, the question of circumcision as part of the salvatory process for Gentile converts and the requirement to follow all the Jewish customs and ceremonies was considered (Acts 15:5). The result was to break the yoke of legalism and to set free both Gentiles and Jews.

James' letter was directed to Jews and had for its basic purpose setting forth ethical standards of the Christian life. It was, therefore, an intensely practical letter and did not delve too deeply into other aspects of theology.

Characteristics and content Many Bible students have supposed that what James said about faith and works differs substantively from what Paul said. It was because of this notion that Martin Luther, who so strongly taught salvation by faith alone without works, could call the letter of James "a strawy epistle." He missed the point that James' letter makes. Basically there is no difference between the teaching of Paul and James. Paul taught that we are saved by faith alone, but saving faith is never alone; it is always accompanied by good works. In other words, the product of saving faith is a life that shows forth the fruit of the new birth. James 2:24 says, "Ye see then how that by works a man is justified, and not by faith only." But when this statement is seen in the light of its context, James is only saying that the proof of real salvation is to be seen in the life of obedience, that is, of works commanded and ordained of God. James said, "Was not Abraham our father justified by works, when he had offered Isaac his son upon the altar?" (3:21). But Abraham had been saved long before he offered Isaac. Thus James can say, "Seest thou how faith wrought with his works, and by works was faith made perfect" (2:22). Thus it can be said that faith without works is dead, but it cannot be said that works of any kind are necessary to salvation or that works can save anyone.

The letter of James should be understood within its larger context because he lays down ethical precepts about other matters like lawsuits, relations between employers and employees, giving rich men special places in houses of worship, the use of the tongue, peacemaking, slander, and evil desires. The concluding chapter is rich in its promises about divine help for the sick when they are anointed with oil and prayed over. And the illustration of the prayer prowess of Elijah stands as a monumental challenge to Christians of all ages.

Outline

I. Living the Christian life (1:1–27)
II. Injunctions and reproofs (2:1—4:17)
III. The confidence of the saints (5:1–20)

I. LIVING THE CHRISTIAN LIFE (1:1–27)

A. SALUTATION

1 JAMES, a servant of God and of the Lord Jesus Christ, to the twelve
tribes which are scattered abroad, greeting.

B. VICTORY AMID TRIALS

2 My brethren, count it all joy when ye fall into divers temptations;
3 Knowing *this*, that the trying of your faith worketh patience.
4 But let patience have *her* perfect work, that ye may be perfect and entire,
wanting nothing.
5 If any of you lack wisdom, let him ask of God, that giveth to all *men*
liberally, and upbraideth not; and it shall be given him.
6 But let him ask in faith, nothing wavering. For he that wavereth is like a
wave of the sea driven with the wind and tossed.
7 For let not that man think that he shall receive any thing of the Lord.
8 A double minded man *is* unstable in all his ways.

C. THE PERILS OF WEALTH

9 Let the brother of low degree rejoice in that he is exalted:
10 But the rich, in that he is made low: because as the flower of the grass
he shall pass away.
11 For the sun is no sooner risen with a burning heat, but it withereth the
grass, and the flower thereof falleth, and the grace of the fashion of it
perisheth: so also shall the rich man fade away in his ways.

D. THE SOURCE OF SIN AND GOD'S GOODNESS

12 Blessed *is* the man that endureth temptation: for when he is tried, he
shall receive the crown of life, which the Lord hath promised to them that
love him.
13 Let no man say when he is tempted, I am tempted of God: for God
cannot be tempted with evil, neither tempteth he any man:
14 But every man is tempted, when he is drawn away of his own lust, and
enticed.
15 Then when lust hath conceived, it bringeth forth sin: and sin, when it is
finished, bringeth forth death.
16 Do not err, my beloved brethren.
17 Every good gift and every perfect gift is from above, and cometh down

☆**1:1**
Mt 10:3; 13:55
Mk 3:18
Lk 6:15
Jn 7:35
Acts 1:13; 2:5
12:17
1 Pet 1:1
☆**1:2**
Heb 11:36–38
1 Pet 1:6–8
1:3
Rom 2:7; 5:3–5
1:4
Jas 3:2
☆**1:5**
Prov 2:3–13
Isa 55:6, 7
Mt 7:7–11
Lk 11:9, 10
Jn 14:12, 13
Jas 3:17
1:6
Mt 21:22
Mk 11:22–24
1:9
Deut 15:7–11
Prov 17:5
Lk 14:11
1:10, 11
Isa 40:7
1 Pet 1:24
☆**1:12**
Job 5:17–19
Prov 3:11, 12
2 Tim 4:8
Heb 6:15
10:32–34
Jas 5:11
Rev 2:10; 3:11
☆**1:13**
Gen 22:1
Rom 9:19, 20
1:15
Isa 59:4
Mic 2:1, 2
Acts 5:1–3
1:16
1 Cor 6:9
☆**1:17**
Gen 1:1–5,
14–16
Num 23:18–24
Ps 19:1–8; 136:7
Rom 11:29
Heb 1:11, 12
13:8
Jas 3:15

1:1 James was a half brother of Jesus. He never mentions that. But he does call himself a servant, i.e., a bond-slave of Jesus who, after the Spirit, is very God. His epistle addresses the Jews of the dispersion, which includes both saved and lost Jews. James 5:1 is addressed particularly to unsaved Jews, who might not listen to what he says but who have the written record to remind them of his spoken word.
1:2 See note to Job 1:14 on the testing of Job.
1:5 Wisdom is the gift of God and should be prayed for. All can have it and as much as is needed. Anyone can come as often as he wishes and will receive what he asks for. And God does not reproach anyone who asks for wisdom. The prayer must be salted with faith.
1:12 The crown of life is promised to all who have the love of God reigning in their hearts. This crown is not reserved for great and eminent saints alone. The humblest believers are also entitled to it.

1:13ff The word for temptation (*peirazō*) is used two ways in the New Testament. In 1:2 and 1 Pet. 1:6 it means trials such as all Christians undergo simply because they are alive. In 1:13 it means solicitation to evil with the assurance that God never solicits man to sin. Thus no one can ever blame God for his sinful acts. Satan himself is the great temptor (1 Chron. 21:1; Matt. 4:1; John 13:2). 1:14–17 indicates that good comes from God, and evil from within man himself. God allows trials to mature and perfect his people. But God's people sometimes fall into sin because they are careless and ill-prepared to meet Satan's onslaughts. Christians are to pray for God to deliver them from the power of the evil one (Matt. 6:13).
1:17 God is the Author and Fountain of all good. The Father of lights is immutable and gives his people the light of reason, the light of learning, the light of revelation, and the light of faith.

from the Father of lights, with whom is no variableness, neither shadow of turning.

18 Of his own will begat he us with the word of truth, that we should be a kind of firstfruits of his creatures.

E. HEARING AND DOING

19 Wherefore, my beloved brethren, let every man be swift to hear, slow to speak, slow to wrath:

20 For the wrath of man worketh not the righteousness of God.

21 Wherefore lay apart all filthiness and superfluity of naughtiness, and receive with meekness the engrafted word, which is able to save your souls.

22 But be ye doers of the word, and not hearers only, deceiving your own selves.

23 For if any be a hearer of the word, and not a doer, he is like unto a man beholding his natural face in a glass:

24 For he beholdeth himself, and goeth his way, and straightway forgetteth what manner of man he was.

25 But whoso looketh into the perfect law of liberty, and continueth *therein*, he being not a forgetful hearer, but a doer of the work, this man shall be blessed in his deed.

26 If any man among you seem to be religious, and bridleth not his tongue, but deceiveth his own heart, this man's religion *is* vain.

27 Pure religion and undefiled before God and the Father is this, To visit the fatherless and widows in their affliction, *and* to keep himself unspotted from the world.

II. INJUNCTIONS AND REPROOFS (2:1—4:17)

A. RESPECT OF PERSONS

2 MY brethren, have not the faith of our Lord Jesus Christ, *the Lord* of glory, with respect of persons.

2 For if there come unto your assembly a man with a gold ring, in goodly apparel, and there come in also a poor man in vile raiment;

3 And ye have respect to him that weareth the gay clothing, and say unto him, Sit thou here in a good place; and say to the poor, Stand thou there, or sit here under my footstool:

4 Are ye not then partial in yourselves, and are become judges of evil thoughts?

5 Hearken, my beloved brethren, Hath not God chosen the poor of this world rich in faith, and heirs of the kingdom which he hath promised to them that love him?

6 But ye have despised the poor. Do not rich men oppress you, and draw you before the judgment seats?

7 Do not they blaspheme that worthy name by the which ye are called?

8 If ye fulfil the royal law according to the scripture, Thou shalt love thy neighbour as thyself, ye do well:

1:18 Jn 1:13; 1 Cor 15:20; 1 Pet 1:23; Rev 14:4
1:19☆ Prov 10:19; 14:29; 15:18; 16:32; 17:27, 28; 18:21; 19:11; Mt 5:22; Eph 4:26, 31; Jas 1:26
1:21 Isa 30:22; Jn 6:68; Rom 13:12, 13; Eph 4:22; Heb 4:2; 1 Pet 1:23
1:22 Mt 7:24; 12:50; 28:20; Lk 6:46–49; Jn 13:17
1:23 1 Cor 13:12
1:25 Jn 8:32, 36; 13:17; Rom 8:15; 2 Cor 3:17, 18; Gal 5:1; Jas 2:12; 1 Pet 2:16; Rev 14:13; 22:14
1:26☆ Prov 13:3; 21:23; Jas 1:19
1:27☆ Ex 22:22; Deut 14:29; 16:11, 14; 24:17–20; Job 29:12, 13; Rom 12:2; Col 3:1–3; Jas 4:4; 1 Jn 2:15–17
2:1☆ Lev 19:15; Deut 16:19; Ps 24:7–10; Prov 24:23; 28:21; 1 Cor 2:8
2:4 Jn 7:24
2:5 Prov 8:17–21; Mt 5:3; 11:6; Lk 6:20; 12:21; 1 Cor 1:27; 2 Cor 6:10
2:7 Acts 11:26; 1 Pet 4:16
2:8☆ Lev 19:18; Mt 7:12; Rom 13:8

1:19ff James says we are to be swift to hear. We are to hear the word eagerly and obey it carefully. Truth must be received in the heart and expressed in the life. Talk *and walk belong together.*

1:26, 27 The three tests of true faith include self-control, charity, and keeping oneself unspotted from the world.

2:1 All believers are one in Jesus Christ. Distinctions like male and female, Jew and Gentile, slave or free no longer apply. Scripture nowhere allows for distinctions among believers based on position, power, race, color, wealth, or popularity. It is sinful to show favoritism based on any of these.

2:8 Love here is called the royal law, for it comes from the King of kings. The second table of that law is to love one's neighbor. That means, "Ye shall do no unrighteousness in judgment: thou shalt not respect the person of the poor, nor honor the person of the mighty: but in righteousness shalt thou judge thy neighbor" (Lev. 19:15).

9 But if ye have respect to persons, ye commit sin, and are convinced of
the law as transgressors.
10 For whosoever shall keep the whole law, and yet offend in one *point*, he
is guilty of all.
11 For he that said, Do not commit adultery, said also, Do not kill. Now
if thou commit no adultery, yet if thou kill, thou art become a transgressor
of the law.
12 So speak ye, and so do, as they that shall be judged by the law of
liberty.
13 For he shall have judgment without mercy, that hath shewed no mercy;
and mercy rejoiceth against judgment.

B. THE DEADNESS OF FAITH WITHOUT WORKS

14 What *doth it* profit, my brethren, though a man say he hath faith, and
have not works? can faith save him?
15 If a brother or sister be naked, and destitute of daily food,
16 And one of you say unto them, Depart in peace, be *ye* warmed and
filled; notwithstanding ye give them not those things which are needful to
the body; what *doth it* profit?
17 Even so faith, if it hath not works, is dead, being alone.
18 Yea, a man may say, Thou hast faith, and I have works: shew me thy
faith without thy works, and I will shew thee my faith by my works.
19 Thou believest that there is one God; thou doest well: the devils also
believe, and tremble.
20 But wilt thou know, O vain man, that faith without works is dead?
21 Was not Abraham our father justified by works, when he had offered
Isaac his son upon the altar?
22 Seest thou how faith wrought with his works, and by works was faith
made perfect?
23 And the scripture was fulfilled which saith, Abraham believed God, and
it was imputed unto him for righteousness: and he was called the Friend of
God.
24 Ye see then how that by works a man is justified, and not by faith only.
25 Likewise also was not Rahab the harlot justified by works, when she
had received the messengers, and had sent *them* out another way?
26 For as the body without the spirit is dead, so faith without works is
dead also.

☆**2:10** Deut 27:26; Mt 5:18, 19; Gal 5:3
2:11 Ex 20:13, 14; Deut 5:17, 18; Mt 19:18
2:12 Jas 1:25
2:13 Mt 18:32–35
☆**2:14**
2:15 Mt 25:35, 36
2:16 1 Jn 3:17
2:17 Gal 5:6; Jas 2:14–16, 20, 26; 1 Pet 1:5–9
2:18 Mt 7:16; Rom 3:28
2:19 Deut 6:4; Isa 43:10; 44:6, 8; Mt 8:28, 29
2:20 Gal 5:6; Jas 2:14, 17, 26
☆**2:21** Gen 22:16–18
☆**2:22** Heb 11:17
2:23 Gen 15:6; Isa 41:8; Jn 15:13–15; Rom 4:3–5
2:25 Josh 2:4, 6, 15; Heb 11:31
2:26 Gal 5:6; Jas 2:14, 17, 20

2:10 James is saying here that a single sin, however small and insignificant, automatically causes the sinner to breach the whole law of God and brings him under God's condemnation as though he had sinned the greatest sin possible. The Scriptures do indeed indicate *that there are greater and lesser sins.* Qualitatively, any and all sin offends God equally; quantitatively, some sins are of lesser importance than others. Sin, whether considered quantitatively or qualitatively, is to be shunned.

2:14ff Some have supposed that James' and Paul's teachings about faith and works are at variance. Not so. James argues that while men are saved by faith alone, saving faith is never alone. It is always accompanied by good works. Thus he says that if one's life does not show forth any good works, it should be asked whether this person has genuine faith. True faith always produces outward evidences to demonstrate or prove that faith. Paul says the same thing in 2 Cor. 5:17. The regenerated man becomes "a brand new person inside . . ." (TLB). And he will act like one, so that a profession of faith cannot be considered valid if the so-called new believer's life remains unchanged.

2:21 The illustration James uses about Abraham and his offering of Isaac validates the principle that *works* follow regeneration; they do not accompany salvation or precede it. Works are the normal product of conversion. Abraham was justified by faith long before he offered Isaac on the altar.

2:22 George Whitefield said that salvation by faith alone "excludes works . . . from being any cause of our justification in the sight of God; but it requires good works as a proof of our having this righteousness imputed to us, and as a declarative evidence of our justification in the sight of men." This is precisely what James means here.

C. CONTROLLING THE TONGUE

3:1 Mt 23:8–10; Rom 2:17–24; Jas 1:26 **3:2** Jas 1:4 **3:3** Ps 32:9

3 MY brethren, be not many masters, knowing that we shall receive the
greater condemnation.
2 For in many things we offend all. If any man offend not in word, the
same *is* a perfect man, *and* able also to bridle the whole body.
3 Behold, we put bits in the horses' mouths, that they may obey us; and
we turn about their whole body.
4 Behold also the ships, which though *they be* so great, and *are* driven of
fierce winds, yet are they turned about with a very small helm, whitherso-
ever the governor listeth.

3:5 Prov 26:20 **3:6** Ps 120:3; Prov 6:12–19; 10:11; 16:27; Mt 15:11; Mk 7:15, 16 **3:7**☆ **3:8** Ps 140:3; Rom 3:13 **3:9**☆ Gen 1:26, 27; 5:1; 1 Cor 11:7 **3:12** Mt 7:16

5 Even so the tongue is a little member, and boasteth great things. Behold,
how great a matter a little fire kindleth!
6 And the tongue *is* a fire, a world of iniquity: so is the tongue among our
members, that it defileth the whole body, and setteth on fire the course of
nature; and it is set on fire of hell.
7 For every kind of beasts, and of birds, and of serpents, and of things in
the sea, is tamed, and hath been tamed of mankind:
8 But the tongue can no man tame; *it is* an unruly evil, full of deadly
poison.
9 Therewith bless we God, even the Father; and therewith curse we men,
which are made after the similitude of God.
10 Out of the same mouth proceedeth blessing and cursing. My brethren,
these things ought not so to be.
11 Doth a fountain send forth at the same place sweet *water* and bitter?
12 Can the fig tree, my brethren, bear olive berries? either a vine, figs? so
can no fountain both yield salt water and fresh.

D. RIGHT AND WRONG WISDOM

3:13 Jas 2:18 **3:14** Rom 13:13; Jas 3:16 **3:15**☆ Jas 1:17 **3:16** 1 Cor 3:3; Jas 3:14 **3:17** Lk 6:36; Rom 12:9–11, 18; 2 Cor 6:6; Phil 1:11; Heb 12:10, 11; Jas 2:13; 4:8; 1 Jn 3:18–20 **3:18** Prov 11:18; Mt 5:9

13 Who *is* a wise man and endued with knowledge among you? let him
shew out of a good conversation his works with meekness of wisdom.
14 But if ye have bitter envying and strife in your hearts, glory not, and lie
not against the truth.
15 This wisdom descendeth not from above, but *is* earthly, sensual,
devilish.
16 For where envying and strife *is*, there *is* confusion and every evil work.
17 But the wisdom that is from above is first pure, then peaceable, gentle,
and easy to be intreated, full of mercy and good fruits, without partiality,
and without hypocrisy.
18 And the fruit of righteousness is sown in peace of them that make
peace.

E. PRIDE, GREED, AND SLANDER

4:1 Rom 7:23

4 FROM whence *come* wars and fightings among you? *come they* not
hence, *even* of your lusts that war in your members?

3:7 All the animals, fish, and birds can be tamed but not the tongue—unless there is supernatural grace and *the help of the Almighty*. *God* tamed a great fish, which swallowed Jonah and ejected him according to the will of God. The lions in the den into which Daniel was cast had their mouths closed by God. And God tamed ravens to feed Elijah the prophet.

3:9 To use the same tongue that blesses God to curse men, slander them, and revile them is contradictory. A fountain cannot give forth both sweet and bitter water nor can a fig tree produce olives. Let the tongue glorify God.

3:15ff There are two kinds of wisdom. One comes from above and the other from below (i.e., from the devil). One can tell what kind of love he has by the fruit of his heart. Verses 17 and 18 describe the fruits of true wisdom.

2Ye lust, and have not: ye kill, and desire to have, and cannot obtain: ye
fight and war, yet ye have not, because ye ask not.
3Ye ask, and receive not, because ye ask amiss, that ye may consume *it*
upon your lusts.
4Ye adulterers and adulteresses, know ye not that the friendship of the
world is enmity with God? whosoever therefore will be a friend of the world
is the enemy of God.
5Do ye think that the scripture saith in vain, The spirit that dwelleth in us
lusteth to envy?
6But he giveth more grace. Wherefore he saith, God resisteth the proud,
but giveth grace unto the humble.
7Submit yourselves therefore to God. Resist the devil, and he will flee
from you.
8Draw nigh to God, and he will draw nigh to you. Cleanse *your* hands, *ye*
sinners; and purify *your* hearts, *ye* double minded.
9Be afflicted, and mourn, and weep: let your laughter be turned to
mourning, and *your* joy to heaviness.
10Humble yourselves in the sight of the Lord, and he shall lift you up.
11Speak not evil one of another, brethren. He that speaketh evil of *his*
brother, and judgeth his brother, speaketh evil of the law, and judgeth the
law: but if thou judge the law, thou art not a doer of the law, but a judge.
12There is one lawgiver, who is able to save and to destroy: who art thou
that judgest another?

F. REPRESSING OVERCONFIDENCE

13Go to now, ye that say, To day or to morrow we will go into such a city,
and continue there a year, and buy and sell, and get gain:
14Whereas ye know not what *shall be* on the morrow. For what *is* your
life? It is even a vapour, that appeareth for a little time, and then vanisheth
away.
15For that ye *ought* to say, If the Lord will, we shall live, and do this, or
that.
16But now ye rejoice in your boastings: all such rejoicing is evil.
17Therefore to him that knoweth to do good, and doeth *it* not, to him it is
sin.

III. THE CONFIDENCE OF THE SAINTS (5:1–20)

A. IN THE DOOM OF OPPRESSORS

5 GO to now, *ye* rich men, weep and howl for your miseries that shall
come upon *you*.
2Your riches are corrupted, and your garments are motheaten.
3Your gold and silver is cankered; and the rust of them shall be a witness
against you, and shall eat your flesh as it were fire. Ye have heaped treasure
together for the last days.

☆**4:2** Jas 5:6; 1 Jn 3:15
4:3 Ps 18:41; Jer 11:11; 1 Jn 3:22; 5:14
4:4 Isa 57:3; Ezek 16:32; Jn 15:19; Rom 8:7; 1 Jn 2:15
4:5 Num 11:29; 1 Cor 6:19; 2 Cor 6:16
4:6 Ps 138:6; Prov 3:34; 29:23; Mt 23:12; 1 Pet 5:5
4:7 2 Chron 30:8; Rom 14:11; Eph 5:21; 6:11, 12; 1 Pet 5:6, 8, 9
4:8 Ps 73:28; Isa 1:16; 55:6, 7; Zech 1:3; Mt 15:2; 1 Pet 3:21
4:9 Lk 6:25
☆**4:11** Mt 7:1; 2 Cor 12:20; Eph 4:31; 2 Tim 3:3; 1 Pet 2:1
4:12 Isa 33:22; Mt 10:28; Rom 2:1; 14:4, 13; Jas 5:9
4:13 Prov 27;1
4:14 Ps 102:3
☆**4:15** Acts 18:21
4:16 Isa 47:7, 8; 1 Cor 4:7, 8; 5:6
4:17 Lk 12:47, 48; Jn 9:41; Rom 2:17–23
☆**5:1** Prov 11:4, 28; Isa 13:6; Zeph 1:18; Mt 19:23, 24; Lk 6:24

4:2 Virtually all sins have their origin in covetousness. For example, Satan coveted the power of the Creator. Virtually all wars begin by one nation's coveting what another nation possesses. Judas Iscariot coveted money; as keeper of the common purse, he stole what was not his. The corruption found among people in public life is most frequently caused by the same sin.

4:11 See note to Exod. 23:1 on slander, which is mentioned here.

4:15 Believers should make all of their plans provisionally because no one knows what tomorrow will bring. What we plan to do is always contingent on the acts of God, which are unknown to us, for he has a secret design that we know only when it takes place.

5:1–6 Here James does not call those to whom he addresses himself as brethren. They are unbelieving Jews. He accuses them of covetousness, oppression, sensuality, voluptuousness, and persecution. He warns them that they face miseries, for their riches will rot, their gold and silver will rust, and they shall be eaten up as by fire. This is the end for wicked, unregenerate Jews who spurn the grace of God.

5:4 Ex 2:23, 24 Lev 19:13 Deut 24:14, 15 Ps 9:12 Jer 22:13
5:5 Lk 16:19
5:6☆ Jas 4:2
5:7☆ Deut 11:14 Mt 24:27 Lk 21:27 Gal 6:9 1 Thess 2:19 3:13 2 Pet 3:4–13
5:8 Ps 37:7 Rom 8:25; 13:11 Heb 10:25–37 1 Pet 4:7 Rev 22:20
5:9 Mt 24:33 1 Cor 4:5 Jas 4:12
5:10 2 Chron 36:16 Jer 2:30 Mt 5:11, 12
5:11 Ex 34:5, 6 Num 14:17, 18 Job 1:20–22 2:7–10 Ps 25:6, 7; 51:1 Rom 2:4
5:12 Mt 5:33–37 23:16–22
5:13 Ps 18:6; 95:2 105:2 Hos 6:1 Lk 22:44 Col 3:16, 17 Jas 5:10
5:14 Mk 6:13 Acts 14:23 Tit 1:5
5:15☆ Mt 21:22 Mk 16:18 Jas 1:6
5:16☆ a) Mt 3:6; 18:15–18 Acts 19:18, 19 b) 1 Thess 5:17 Heb 13:18
5:17☆ 1 Kgs 17:1–7 18:36–39

4 Behold, the hire of the labourers who have reaped down your fields,
which is of you kept back by fraud, crieth: and the cries of them which have
reaped are entered into the ears of the Lord of Sab'a-oth.
5 Ye have lived in pleasure on the earth, and been wanton; ye have
nourished your hearts, as in a day of slaughter.
6 Ye have condemned *and* killed the just; *and* he doth not resist you.

B. IN THE COMING OF THE LORD

7 Be patient therefore, brethren, unto the coming of the Lord. Behold, the
husbandman waiteth for the precious fruit of the earth, and hath long
patience for it, until he receive the early and latter rain.
8 Be ye also patient; stablish your hearts: for the coming of the Lord
draweth nigh.
9 Grudge not one against another, brethren, lest ye be condemned:
behold, the judge standeth before the door.
10 Take, my brethren, the prophets, who have spoken in the name of the
Lord, for an example of suffering affliction, and of patience.
11 Behold, we count them happy which endure. Ye have heard of the
patience of Job, and have seen the end of the Lord; that the Lord is very
pitiful, and of tender mercy.

C. IN TELLING THE TRUTH

12 But above all things, my brethren, swear not, neither by heaven, neither
by the earth, neither by any other oath: but let your yea be yea; and *your*
nay, nay; lest ye fall into condemnation.

D. IN PRAYER FOR THE SICK

13 Is any among you afflicted? let him pray. Is any merry? let him sing
psalms.
14 Is any sick among you? let him call for the elders of the church; and let
them pray over him, anointing him with oil in the name of the Lord:
15 And the prayer of faith shall save the sick, and the Lord shall raise him
up; and if he have committed sins, they shall be forgiven him.
16 Confess *your* faults one to another, and pray one for another, that ye
may be healed. The effectual fervent prayer of a righteous man availeth
much.
17 E-li'as was a man subject to like passions as we are, and he prayed

---

5:7ff Believing Jews are encouraged to be patient. The Lord is coming and the Judge is standing at the door. They should follow the pattern of Job, who suffered the loss of children, wealth, and health. But he triumphed in the end. So will believers who are steadfast in the faith.

5:15 Historical evidence confirms the fact that God does heal people miraculously. Here, James speaks about prayer offered in faith. God gives some the gift of faith to believe for healing, but this is not promised to all. Beyond this, there is the grace of faith, which has to do with specific promises God makes and which can *always be claimed by the believer.* When the gift of faith has not been given, the believer can and should pray for healing (even as he employs medical means, which are also the gift of God) and include the proviso, "if it be thy will." Paul prayed earnestly for healing, which God denied him for a special reason. It was not the will of God for him in that instance (see 2 Cor. 12:7–19).

5:16 Confessing sins to one another is a hazardous practice if those to whom we make the confession cannot keep secrets and are gossips. Sometimes we make confessions to relieve ourselves of the sense of guilt, yet we place the burden of that guilt on the one to whom we confess. Great care needs to be exercised as to when we do it and how we do it. Properly used, the admonition is valuable and has good therapeutic potential.

5:17 The example of Elijah and the answer to his prayer is given by way of encouragement to us—that our prayers can have equal power and bring about good results for us, for those we pray about, and for the nation in which we live. Nothing lies beyond the power of God to change, and prayer is the divinely ordained method to make God's power available to us concerning any and all things about which we have a godly concern.

earnestly that it might not rain: and it rained not on the earth by the space
of three years and six months.
18 And he prayed again, and the heaven gave rain, and the earth brought
forth her fruit.

☆5:19
Prov 19:27
Mt 18:15
1 Tim 6:10
2 Pet 3:17
☆5:20
Ps 32:1
Prov 11:30
1 Pet 4:8
1 Jn 5:16
Jude 22, 23

E. IN THE RETURN OF THE BACKSLIDER

19 Brethren, if any of you do err from the truth, and one convert him;
20 Let him know, that he which converteth the sinner from the error of his
way shall save a soul from death, and shall hide a multitude of sins.

5:19, 20 James is not talking about someone who has ceased to be a believer. Rather it refers to someone who has slipped into error in his daily life or in the practice of his faith. Believers should be concerned about the spiritual condition of a backslidden brother or sister. All believers are their brothers' keepers, and believers should engage in restoring brothers to the truth. It will save the backslider's soul "out of death," as the Greek has it.

THE FIRST EPISTLE GENERAL OF

PETER

Authorship, date, and background 1 Peter was written by the apostle Peter. This view has been challenged in the modern era even though it was the view of the church through the ages. Objections to Petrine authorship have been based on linguistic, theological, and historical considerations. However, Peter identified Silvanus as his secretary (amanuensis), and this could well explain anything which gives the appearance of being un-Petrine. Certainly the internal evidences clearly affirm the Petrine authorship of the letter, and his identification of John Mark's presence with him also attests to it. The whole letter gives the appearance of an eyewitness to the events described. Thus one can confidently insist that Peter was indeed the author.

Peter's greeting at the end of the letter from the church in Babylon has been generally understood to refer to Rome. There are evidences which confirm the opinion that Peter was martyred in Rome under Nero around A.D. 65–67. This does not mean that he founded the church at Rome, only that he was there at the end of his life. Thus the letter was written in Rome and sent to "the strangers . . . scattered throughout Pontus, Galatia, Cappadocia, Asia, and Bithynia" (1:1). Certainly many of them therefore were Jewish Christians who had been converted to Christ and were now among the dispersed. Other references in the letter suggest that at least a few of them were Gentile converts. Possibly Peter had preached to the people to whom he wrote the letter. This may be one reason for Paul's not having evangelized in some of these areas, since he sought to go where Christ had not been preached. Now persecution had come and would grow worse in the years ahead. The situation required some word from the apostle by way of comfort and encouragement. This came in the letter.

Characteristics and content The basic theme of 1 Peter is a lively hope in the midst of persecution and suffering. More than a dozen times Peter refers to persecution: ". . . ye greatly rejoice, though now for a season, if need be, ye are in heaviness through manifold temptations" (1:6); "for this is thankworthy, if a man for conscience toward God endure grief, suffering wrongfully (2:19); ". . . if ye suffer for righteousness sake, happy are ye" (3:14); "for it is better . . . that ye suffer for well doing, than for evil doing" (3:17); etc. These all indicate persecution then or in the future and Peter encourages them to meet it with the knowledge that victory would be theirs at last.

The letter clearly teaches the sovereignty of God both with respect to the choice of Jesus Christ as the slain Lamb from before the foundation of the world and these believers as chosen of God (1:2; 2:9). Suffering is part of the believer's identification with Christ and his suffering. This is a privilege and points to future joy and gladness. The repeated mention of Christ's suffering bears all the earmarks of one who was there when it happened. In staccato-like fashion, the apostle uses imperatives to tell believers what they are to do. Nowhere else in the New Testament letters will this be found to the same degree. Thus Peter says: be holy (1:15); be honest (2:12); obey every law (2:13); show respect for everyone (2:17); wives, be in subjection to your husbands (3:1); husbands, give honor to your wives (3:7); be of one mind (3:8); be sober, thoughtful men of prayer (4:7); rejoice (4:13); and, "let none of you suffer as a murderer, or as a thief, or as an evildoer, or as a busybody in other men's matters" (4:15).

Peter's conclusion fits in with his certainty that they will be persecuted. He says believers are to be careful to watch out for Satan's attacks and to stand firm when he does attack. They are to trust the Lord and know that other believers around the world are also being persecuted. But after they have suffered they can be absolutely certain that God will give them his eternal glory. He will perfect, establish, and strengthen them (5:10). Why then should Christians fear anything or anyone?

Outline

I. Salutation (1:1, 2)
II. The blessings of believers (1:3—2:10)
III. The conduct of believers (2:11—4:11)
IV. Constancy in suffering (4:12—5:11)
V. Conclusion and benediction (5:12–14)

I. SALUTATION (1:1, 2)

1 PETER, an apostle of Jesus Christ, to the strangers scattered through-
out Pontus, Ga-la'tia, Cap-pa-do'ci-a, Asia, and Bi-thyn'i-a,
2 Elect according to the foreknowledge of God the Father, through
sanctification of the Spirit, unto obedience and sprinkling of the blood of
Jesus Christ: Grace unto you, and peace, be multiplied.

II. THE BLESSINGS OF BELIEVERS (1:3—2:10)

A. THEIR PRESERVATION IN CHRIST

3 Blessed *be* the God and Father of our Lord Jesus Christ, which
according to his abundant mercy hath begotten us again unto a lively hope
by the resurrection of Jesus Christ from the dead,
4 To an inheritance incorruptible, and undefiled, and that fadeth not
away, reserved in heaven for you,
5 Who are kept by the power of God through faith unto salvation ready to
be revealed in the last time.
6 Wherein ye greatly rejoice, though now for a season, if need be, ye are in
heaviness through manifold temptations:
7 That the trial of your faith, being much more precious than of gold that
perisheth, though it be tried with fire, might be found unto praise and
honour and glory at the appearing of Jesus Christ:
8 Whom having not seen, ye love; in whom, though now ye see *him* not,
yet believing, ye rejoice with joy unspeakable and full of glory:
9 Receiving the end of your faith, *even* the salvation of *your* souls.
10 Of which salvation the prophets have inquired and searched diligently,
who prophesied of the grace *that should come* unto you:
11 Searching what, or what manner of time the Spirit of Christ which was
in them did signify, when it testified beforehand the sufferings of Christ,
and the glory that should follow.
12 Unto whom it was revealed, that not unto themselves, but unto us they
did minister the things, which are now reported unto you by them that have
preached the gospel unto you with the Holy Ghost sent down from heaven;
which things the angels desire to look into.

B. HOLY LIVING

13 Wherefore gird up the loins of your mind, be sober, and hope to the end
for the grace that is to be brought unto you at the revelation of Jesus
Christ;
14 As obedient children, not fashioning yourselves according to the former
lusts in your ignorance:
15 But as he which hath called you is holy, so be ye holy in all manner of
conversation;
16 Because it is written, Be ye holy; for I am holy.

1:1 Acts 2:9, 10; 6:9; 16:6, 7; 18:2; Gal 1:2; 2 Pet 1:1
☆**1:2** Rom 8:29, 30; 9:24, 25; 15:16; 2 Cor 13:14; Heb 9:19–22; 1 Pet 1:20; 2 Pet 1:2
1:3 1 Cor 15:20; Gal 6:16; 1 Thess 4:14; Tit 3:5; Jas 1:18; 1 Pet 1:13, 23; 1 Jn 3:3
1:4 Acts 20:32; Col 3:24; 2 Tim 4:8; Heb 11:16
1:5 Jn 10:28; Phil 4:7; 2 Thess 2:13; 1 Pet 4:13
1:6 Mt 5:12; Rom 5:2; Jas 1:2; 1 Pet 3:17; 4:12
1:7 Job 23:10; Prov 17:3; Isa 48:10; Mal 3:3; Jas 1:3
1:8 Jn 20:29; Eph 3:19; 1 Jn 4:2
1:10 Gen 49:10; Mt 13:17; 26:24; Lk 10:24; Col 3:4
1:11 Ps 22:6; Mt 26:24; Rom 8:9; 2 Pet 1:21
☆**1:12** Dan 12:9; Acts 2:2–4; Eph 3:10; Heb 11:39
1:13 Eph 6:14; 1 Thess 5:6; 1 Pet 4:7
1:14 Rom 12:2; Eph 4:18
1:15 1 Thess 4:7; Jas 3:13; 1 Jn 3:3
1:16 Lev 11:44, 45; 19:2

1:2 *Foreknowledge* simply means that God knows everything from eternity past. He knew who would be saved before creation began. Foreknowledge must be related to the doctrine of *election.* (See note to Eph. 1:4 on election and foreknowledge.) *sprinkling of the blood of Jesus Christ.* This verse speaks about cleansing by the blood that was sprinkled. In the Old Testament the blood was not only shed, it was sprinkled, which meant that the offerer received the benefit of the sacrifice. The sprinkled blood of Christ does four things for us: (1) we are justified (Rom. 5:19); (2) we have the seal of God's covenant promise, of which the Lord's Supper is a sign (Luke 22:20); (3) we are cleansed from all sin (1 John 1:7); and (4) we become citizens of the kingdom of heaven (Heb. 10:19).

1:12 The effectiveness of the ministries of God's people depends upon the Holy Spirit sent down from heaven by the Father and the ascended Lord Jesus Christ. The success of sharing the good news hinges on the operation of the Spirit and his blessing. The surest guarantee for a spiritually successful Christian life and ministry is unalterably connected with being filled with the Holy Spirit.

17 And if ye call on the Father, who without respect of persons judgeth
according to every man's work, pass the time of your sojourning *here* in
fear:
18 Forasmuch as ye know that ye were not redeemed with corruptible
things, *as* silver and gold, from your vain conversation *received* by tradition
from your fathers;
19 But with the precious blood of Christ, as of a lamb without blemish and
without spot:
20 Who verily was foreordained before the foundation of the world, but
was manifest in these last times for you,
21 Who by him do believe in God, that raised him up from the dead, and
gave him glory; that your faith and hope might be in God.
22 Seeing ye have purified your souls in obeying the truth through the
Spirit unto unfeigned love of the brethren, *see that ye* love one another with
a pure heart fervently:
23 Being born again, not of corruptible seed, but of incorruptible, by the
word of God, which liveth and abideth for ever.
24 For all flesh *is* as grass, and all the glory of man as the flower of grass.
The grass withereth, and the flower thereof falleth away:
25 But the word of the Lord endureth for ever. And this is the word which
by the gospel is preached unto you.

2 WHEREFORE laying aside all malice, and all guile, and hypocrisies,
and envies, and all evil speakings,
2 As newborn babes, desire the sincere milk of the word, that ye may grow
thereby:
3 If so be ye have tasted that the Lord *is* gracious.

C. CHRIST, THEIR SURE FOUNDATION

4 To whom coming, *as unto* a living stone, disallowed indeed of men, but
chosen of God, *and* precious,
5 Ye also, as lively stones, are built up a spiritual house, an holy
priesthood, to offer up spiritual sacrifices, acceptable to God by Jesus
Christ.
6 Wherefore also it is contained in the scripture, Behold, I lay in Sion a
chief corner stone, elect, precious: and he that believeth on him shall not be
confounded.

1:17 Deut 10:17 Ps 89:26 Jer 3:19 Mt 16:27 Heb 12:28 1 Pet 2:11
1:18☆ Isa 52:3 Ezek 20:18 Eph 4:17
1:19 Ex 12:5 Jn 1:29 Acts 20:28 Heb 9:14 1 Pet 1:2
1:20 Mt 25:34 Gal 4:4 2 Tim 1:9, 10 Heb 2:14; 9:26
1:21 Rom 4:24 Phil 2:9 1 Tim 3:16 Heb 2:9
1:22 Jn 13:34 Rom 12:10 Heb 13:1
1:23☆ Jn 1:13; 3:3 Heb 4:12 Jas 1:18 1 Jn 3:9
1:24 Isa 40:6–8
1:25 Isa 40:8 Lk 16:17 Heb 6:5
2:1 Eph 4:22, 25, 31 Jas 1:21; 4:11
2:2 Mt 18:3; 19:14 Lk 18:17 1 Cor 14:20 Eph 4:15 Heb 6:5
2:4 1 Pet 2:7
2:5☆ Isa 61:6; 66:21 Rom 15:16 Gal 6:10 Eph 2:21 1 Tim 3:15 Heb 13:12
2:6☆ Isa 28:16 Rom 9:32, 33 10:11 Eph 2:20

1:18 The word *redeemed* comes from the Greek *lutroō*, which means "to buy back from bondage" or "to redeem." The Greek noun *apolutrōsis* is translated "redemption." The need for being redeemed or brought back springs from our bondage to Satan and to sin (John 8:34; Rom. 6:17, 23). It is God who redeems us by his grace. God has done this through the meritorious death of Jesus Christ (1 Cor. 1:30; Gal. 3:13; 4:4, 5; Eph. 1:7; Titus 2:14). Redemption is past, present, and future. We have been redeemed; we are being redeemed; and we will be redeemed. The final redemption occurs when that which we have embraced *by faith becomes a historical* reality.

1:23 *being born again.* See note on John 3:3.

2:5 All those who are united to Christ by faith are priests unto God (see also 2:9; Rev. 1:6). Under the old covenant, believers required a priest to mediate between them and God at the altar. The high priest was their mediator in the Holy of Holies. Jesus Christ has become our high priest (Heb. 4:14; 5:10; 7:27; 9:11); we now may go directly to God through Jesus without any human mediator. This New Testament truth, the priesthood of *all* believers, includes both laity and clergy. The term "priest" (*hiereūs*) is never applied to an apostle or elder in any church except as he is part of this universal priesthood. From Luther's time onward this concept has been one of the great liberating impulses for all believers.

2:6 Paul says Christians are seated with Christ in the heavenly realms. This is positional and someday will be a physical reality. Believers constitute a heavenly commonwealth (Phil. 3:20); they are not of the world, although they continue to live in it for a while. Their real life is in heaven with Christ in God (Col. 3:1–3). Christians already share in Christ's royal status and authority, and they advance his kingdom through their prayers and missionary witness.

7 Unto you therefore which believe *he is* precious: but unto them which be
disobedient, the stone which the builders disallowed, the same is made the
head of the corner,
8 And a stone of stumbling, and a rock of offence, *even to them* which
stumble at the word, being disobedient: whereunto also they were
appointed.
9 But ye *are* a chosen generation, a royal priesthood, an holy nation, a
peculiar people; that ye should shew forth the praises of him who hath
called you out of darkness into his marvellous light:
10 Which in time past *were* not a people, but *are* now the people of God:
which had not obtained mercy, but now have obtained mercy.

2:7 Ps 118:22 Mt 21:42 Lk 2:34
2:8 Isa 8:14 Lk 2:34, 35 1 Cor 1:23 Gal 5:11
2:9 Ex 19:6 Deut 7:6; 10:15 Isa 43:20 Jn 17:19 Acts 26:18 1 Pet 2:5 Rev 1:6
2:10 Hos 1:10; 2:23 Rom 9:25; 10:19

III. THE CONDUCT OF BELIEVERS (2:11—4:11)

A. IN RELATION TO THE UNSAVED

11 Dearly beloved, I beseech *you* as strangers and pilgrims, abstain from
fleshly lusts, which war against the soul;
12 Having your conversation honest among the Gentiles: that, whereas
they speak against you as evildoers, they may by *your* good works, which
they shall behold, glorify God in the day of visitation.

☆**2:11** Lev 25:23 Rom 12:1; 13:14 Gal 5:16 Jas 4:1
2:12 Acts 28:22 2 Cor 8:21 Phil 2:15 Tit 2:8

B. IN RELATION TO THE STATE

13 Submit yourselves to every ordinance of man for the Lord's sake:
whether it be to the king, as supreme;
14 Or unto governors, as unto them that are sent by him for the
punishment of evildoers, and for the praise of them that do well.
15 For so is the will of God, that with well doing ye may put to silence the
ignorance of foolish men:
16 As free, and not using *your* liberty for a cloak of maliciousness, but as
the servants of God.
17 Honour all *men*. Love the brotherhood. Fear God. Honour the king.

2:13 Rom 13:1
2:14 Rom 13:3, 4
2:15 1 Pet 2:12; 3:17
2:16 Jn 8:32 1 Cor 7:22 Jas 1:25
☆**2:17** Prov 24:21 Mt 22:21 Rom 12:10; 13:7 1 Pet 1:22

C. SERVANTS IN RELATION TO MASTERS

18 Servants, *be* subject to *your* masters with all fear; not only to the good
and gentle, but also to the froward.
19 For this *is* thankworthy, if a man for conscience toward God endure
grief, suffering wrongfully.
20 For what glory *is it*, if, when ye be buffeted for your faults, ye shall take
it patiently? but if, when ye do well, and suffer *for it*, ye take it patiently,
this *is* acceptable with God.

2:18 Eph 6:5 Jas 3:17
2:20 1 Pet 3:14, 17

D. FOLLOWING THE EXAMPLE OF CHRIST

21 For even hereunto were ye called: because Christ also suffered for us,
leaving us an example, that ye should follow his steps:

2:21 Mt 11:29; 16:24 Acts 14:22 1 Pet 3:9, 18

2:11 *strangers and pilgrims.* "This world is not my home, I'm just apassing through." Believers are in the world but are not to be of the world. Their real world is heaven. As strangers they are pilgrims moving toward their true homes. They must never give in to or engage in the practice of those sins found in the countries through which they pass on their way to glory.

2:17 The brotherhood of man is a much abused concept. The Scriptures place some limitations on its use. Certainly all men are brothers in the sense that they have descended from Adam and Eve, their common ancestors. Yet the Scriptures speak of a brotherhood brought into being by regeneration and adoption into the family of God. Believers are related to God and to each other as children and heirs of God. Only believers are said to be children of God in the biblical sense; because of this, whoever owns the name of Christ is likewise their brother.

2:22☆ Isa 53:9; Jer 8:46; 2 Cor 5:21
2:23 Isa 53:7; Jer 8:48; Heb 12:3; 1 Pet 3:9
2:24☆ Isa 53:4, 5, 11; Acts 5:30; Rom 6:2; Heb 12:13; Jas 5:16
2:25 Isa 53:6; Jn 10:11; Heb 13:20; 1 Pet 5:4

22 Who did no sin, neither was guile found in his mouth:
23 Who, when he was reviled, reviled not again; when he suffered, he
threatened not; but committed *himself* to him that judgeth righteously:
24 Who his own self bare our sins in his own body on the tree, that we,
being dead to sins, should live unto righteousness: by whose stripes ye were
healed.
25 For ye were as sheep going astray; but are now returned unto the
Shepherd and Bishop of your souls.

E. IN THE RELATION OF A HUSBAND TO HIS WIFE

3:1 1 Cor 7:16; 9:19; Eph 5:22; 1 Pet 2:18; 3:7
3:3☆ Isa 3:16–24; 1 Tim 2:9
3:4 Ps 45:13; Rom 2:29; 7:22
3:5 1 Tim 5:5; 1 Pet 1:3
3:6 Gen 18:12
3:7 Mt 5:23, 24; 18:19; Eph 5:25; Col 3:19

3 LIKEWISE, ye wives, *be* in subjection to your own husbands; that, if
any obey not the word, they also may without the word be won by the
conversation of the wives;
2 While they behold your chaste conversation *coupled* with fear.
3 Whose adorning let it not be that outward *adorning* of plaiting the hair,
and of wearing of gold, or of putting on of apparel;
4 But *let it be* the hidden man of the heart, in that which is not corruptible,
even the ornament of a meek and quiet spirit, which is in the sight of God of
great price.
5 For after this manner in the old time the holy women also, who trusted
in God, adorned themselves, being in subjection unto their own husbands:
6 Even as Sara obeyed Abraham, calling him lord: whose daughters ye
are, as long as ye do well, and are not afraid with any amazement.
7 Likewise, ye husbands, dwell with *them* according to knowledge, giving
honour unto the wife, as unto the weaker vessel, and as being heirs together
of the grace of life; that your prayers be not hindered.

F. SUMMARY

3:8 Rom 12:16; Eph 4:32; Phil 2:3; 1 Pet 5:5
3:9 Mt 25:34–36; Lk 6:28; Rom 12:14, 17; Heb 6:14; 12:17; 1 Pet 2:21–23
3:10 Ps 34:12, 13
3:11 Ps 34:14
3:12 Ps 34:15, 16

8 Finally, *be ye* all of one mind, having compassion one of another, love as
brethren, *be* pitiful, *be* courteous:
9 Not rendering evil for evil, or railing for railing: but contrariwise
blessing; knowing that ye are thereunto called, that ye should inherit a
blessing.
10 For he that will love life, and see good days, let him refrain his tongue
from evil, and his lips that they speak no guile:
11 Let him eschew evil, and do good; let him seek peace, and ensue it.
12 For the eyes of the Lord *are* over the righteous, and his ears *are open*
unto their prayers: but the face of the Lord *is* against them that do evil.

2:22 If Jesus had sinned, (1) he could not have been the Son of God; (2) the Christian church could not have been correct in asserting his sinlessness for two thousand years; (3) he could not have been the prototype of perfect redeemed men; (4) he could not have been our sacrifice for sin (since he would have needed a sacrifice for his own sinfulness); (5) there could be no secure foundation on which to rest the Christian faith; and (6) there would be no ground for the existence of the church.

2:24 Christ was our vicarious or substitutionary sacrifice for sin. He actually bore our sins in his own body on the tree. Three principles are inherent in the plan of redemption: (1) men are lost and undone, separated from God because of their sins (Rom. 1:18; 3:19; 6:23); (2) the God of grace provided a substitute for the sinner in the person of his Son, to be our sin-bearer (Isa. 53:6; 2 Cor. 5:21); (3) the Father accepted the finished work of the Son, which secures for men the forgiveness of sins, resulting in peace and fellowship with God (Rom. 5:1, 6, 8, 10). Animal sacrifices under the old covenant had to be repeated because they were not permanent. Since the death of Christ no further sacrifices are needed. He has bridged the chasm that separated sinful men from a holy God.

3:3 The Bible does not prohibit the use of jewelry and other outward adornments. But there are principles which should be regarded seriously. True adornment consists in spiritual qualities of a gentle and peaceable nature. Modesty and circumspection are virtues. However, attitude of heart plus outward modesty in dress and adornment go together. While this verse speaks specifically to women, men are also to regard the advice earnestly.

G. CHRISTIANS UNDER PERSECUTION

13 And who *is* he that will harm you, if ye be followers of that which is
good?
14 But and if ye suffer for righteousness' sake, happy *are ye:* and be not
afraid of their terror, neither be troubled;
15 But sanctify the Lord God in your hearts: and *be* ready always to *give*
an answer to every man that asketh you a reason of the hope that is in you
with meekness and fear:
16 Having a good conscience; that, whereas they speak evil of you, as of
evildoers, they may be ashamed that falsely accuse your good conversation
in Christ.
17 For *it is* better, if the will of God be so, that ye suffer for well doing,
than for evil doing.
18 For Christ also hath once suffered for sins, the just for the unjust, that
he might bring us to God, being put to death in the flesh, but quickened by
the Spirit:
19 By which also he went and preached unto the spirits in prison;
20 Which sometime were disobedient, when once the longsuffering of God
waited in the days of Noah, while the ark was a preparing, wherein few,
that is, eight souls were saved by water.
21 The like figure whereunto *even* baptism doth also now save us (not the
putting away of the filth of the flesh, but the answer of a good conscience
toward God,) by the resurrection of Jesus Christ:
22 Who is gone into heaven, and is on the right hand of God; angels and
authorities and powers being made subject unto him.

H. TRAITS TO CULTIVATE

4 FORASMUCH then as Christ hath suffered for us in the flesh, arm
yourselves likewise with the same mind: for he that hath suffered in the
flesh hath ceased from sin;
2 That he no longer should live the rest of *his* time in the flesh to the lusts
of men, but to the will of God.
3 For the time past of *our* life may suffice us to have wrought the will of
the Gentiles, when we walked in lasciviousness, lusts, excess of wine,
revellings, banquetings, and abominable idolatries:
4 Wherein they think it strange that ye run not with *them* to the same
excess of riot, speaking evil of *you:*
5 Who shall give account to him that is ready to judge the quick and the
dead.

3:13 Prov 16:7
☆**3:14** Isa 8:12, 13 Jas 5:11
3:15 Col 4:6 2 Tim 2:25 1 Pet 1:3, 17
3:16 1 Tim 1:5 Heb 13:18 1 Pet 2:12; 3:21
3:17 1 Pet 2:20, 21 4:15, 19
3:18 Rom 5:2 1 Cor 15:45 Eph 3:12 Col 1:22 Heb 9:26 1 Pet 2:21; 4:6
☆**3:19** Isa 42:7; 61:1 1 Pet 4:6
3:20 Gen 6:3; 7:1 8:18 Acts 2:41 Rom 2:4 Heb 11:7 1 Pet 1:9, 22 2:25; 4:19
3:21 Acts 16:33 1 Tim 1:5 Tit 3:5 Heb 9:14 10:22; 13:18
3:22 Ps 110:1 Mk 16:19 Rom 8:38 Heb 1:6; 4:14 6:20
☆**4:1** Rom 6:7 Gal 2:20 Eph 6:13 Col 3:5 1 Pet 2:21
4:2 Rom 6:2, 11 Gal 2:20
4:3 Rom 13:13 1 Cor 12:2 Eph 2:2; 4:17
☆**4:4** Eph 5:18 1 Pet 3:16
4:5 Acts 10:42 17:31 Rom 14:10 2 Tim 4:1 Jas 5:9

3:14 *suffer for righteousness' sake.* Christians are called upon to do right even though that act entails suffering for them. This is particularly true in matters having to do with theological errors. Standing for the truth will always produce suffering, reproach, and character assassination. It is a great sin for good men to do nothing when error abounds and action is called for.

3:19 Some have interpreted this verse as meaning that during the time between his crucifixion and resurrection Christ preached to the lost in Hades (see note to Luke 10:15) so that they might have a second opportunity to be saved. This view runs quite contrary to other very explicit Scriptures that preclude the possibility of a second chance (e.g., Luke 16:25; Heb. 9:27). Others think this verse means that Christ was in Noah by the Holy Spirit when Noah preached to the doomed race of antediluvians.

4:1–3 Even as Christ died to save us, we are to die to sin by self-denial and mortification. Negatively, we are not to live in the flesh. Positively, we are to be conformed to the revealed will of God, which means that lasciviousness, lust, drunkenness, revelings, banquetings, and abominable idolatry will have lost their hold on us.

4:4 Wicked friends cannot understand the new life of converted comrades who have sloughed off the old habits of sin. They see the new life in Christ as irksome and tedious. For them such conduct is strange and incredible. Not infrequently they will make fun of their old friends as they seek to turn them back to their old ways.

4:6 1 Pet 3:19
4:7 Rom 13:11–13 Heb 9:26 Jas 5:8 1 Pet 1:13 2 Pet 3:9 1 Jn 2:18
4:8 Prov 10:12 1 Cor 13:4, 7 Jas 5:20 1 Pet 1:22
4:9 2 Cor 9:7 Phil 2:14 1 Tim 3:2 Heb 13:2
4:10 Rom 12:6–8 1 Cor 4:1
4:11 Acts 7:38 1 Cor 10:31 Eph 6:10
4:12☆ 1 Pet 1:6
4:13 Rom 8:17 2 Cor 1:5 Phil 3:10 2 Tim 2:12
4:14☆ Mt 5:11 Lk 6:22 Jn 15:21 2 Cor 4:10 Heb 11:26
4:15☆ 1 Thess 4:11 2 Thess 3:11 1 Tim 5:13
4:16 Acts 5:41; 28:22 Jas 2:7
4:17 Jer 25:29 Mal 3:5 Rom 2:9 2 Thess 1:8
4:18 Prov 11:31 Lk 23:31
4:19 Ps 31:5, 6
5:1☆ Lk 24:48 Acts 11:30 Heb 12:1 2 Jn 1 Rev 1:9
5:2 Jn 21:16 Acts 20:28 1 Tim 3:8 Philem 14
5:3 Ps 74:2 Ezek 34:4 Mt 20:25 Phil 3:17 2 Thess 3:9 Tit 2:7

6 For for this cause was the gospel preached also to them that are dead,
that they might be judged according to men in the flesh, but live according
to God in the spirit.
7 But the end of all things is at hand: be ye therefore sober, and watch
unto prayer.
8 And above all things have fervent charity among yourselves: for charity
shall cover the multitude of sins.
9 Use hospitality one to another without grudging.
10 As every man hath received the gift, *even so* minister the same one to
another, as good stewards of the manifold grace of God.
11 If any man speak, *let him speak* as the oracles of God; if any man
minister, *let him do it* as of the ability which God giveth: that God in all
things may be glorified through Jesus Christ, to whom be praise and
dominion for ever and ever. Amen.

IV. CONSTANCY IN SUFFERING (4:12—5:11)

A. THE COMMAND TO ENDURE

12 Beloved, think it not strange concerning the fiery trial which is to try
you, as though some strange thing happened unto you:
13 But rejoice, inasmuch as ye are partakers of Christ's sufferings; that,
when his glory shall be revealed, ye may be glad also with exceeding joy.
14 If ye be reproached for the name of Christ, happy *are ye;* for the spirit
of glory and of God resteth upon you: on their part he is evil spoken of, but
on your part he is glorified.
15 But let none of you suffer as a murderer, or *as* a thief, or *as* an evildoer,
or as a busybody in other men's matters.
16 Yet if *any man suffer* as a Christian, let him not be ashamed; but let him
glorify God on this behalf.
17 For the time *is come* that judgment must begin at the house of God:
and if *it* first *begin* at us, what shall the end *be* of them that obey not the
gospel of God?
18 And if the righteous scarcely be saved, where shall the ungodly and the
sinner appear?
19 Wherefore let them that suffer according to the will of God commit the
keeping of their souls *to him* in well doing, as unto a faithful Creator.

B. EXHORTATIONS TO VARIOUS GROUPS

5 THE elders which are among you I exhort, who am also an elder, and
a witness of the sufferings of Christ, and also a partaker of the glory
that shall be revealed:
2 Feed the flock of God which is among you, taking the oversight *thereof,*
not by constraint, but willingly; not for filthy lucre, but of a ready mind;
3 Neither as being lords over *God's* heritage, but being ensamples to the
flock.

4:12 *the fiery trial.* We are not told what the fiery trials are to which we will be subjected. It is a general statement that means each age has its particular problems, all of which are difficult to face and overcome. Believers should never be surprised that these trials come. The surprise would be if there were none. Trials test our faith in God and our human patience, strength, and sincerity.

4:15ff There is a kind of suffering that comes to the saints as a result of their own sins and shortcomings. But God also allows believers to suffer as part of his will for them. They are to be more concerned for their souls than for their bodies. Therefore they are to commit their souls to God and engage in that kind of life that is designed to glorify God. The faithful Creator will keep all his promises made to his beloved children.

5:1 See note to Titus 1:5 for information on elders.

4 And when the chief Shepherd shall appear, ye shall receive a crown of
glory that fadeth not away.
5 Likewise, ye younger, submit yourselves unto the elder. Yea, all *of you*
be subject one to another, and be clothed with humility: for God resisteth
the proud, and giveth grace to the humble.
6 Humble yourselves therefore under the mighty hand of God, that he
may exalt you in due time:
7 Casting all your care upon him; for he careth for you.
8 Be sober, be vigilant; because your adversary the devil, as a roaring lion,
walketh about, seeking whom he may devour:
9 Whom resist stedfast in the faith, knowing that the same afflictions are
accomplished in your brethren that are in the world.
10 But the God of all grace, who hath called us unto his eternal glory by
Christ Jesus, after that ye have suffered a while, make you perfect, stablish,
strengthen, settle *you.*
11 To him *be* glory and dominion for ever and ever. Amen.

V. CONCLUSION AND BENEDICTION (5:12–14)

12 By Sil-va'nus, a faithful brother unto you, as I suppose, I have written
briefly, exhorting, and testifying that this is the true grace of God wherein
ye stand.
13 The *church that is* at Babylon, elected together with *you,* saluteth you;
and *so doth* Marcus my son.
14 Greet ye one another with a kiss of charity. Peace *be* with you all that
are in Christ Jesus. Amen.

☆**5:4** 1 Cor 9:25 Heb 13:20, 21
☆**5:5** Prov 3:34 Isa 57:15 Lk 22:26 Eph 5:21 Jas 4:6
5:6 Jas 4:10
☆**5:7** Ps 37:5 Mt 6:25 Heb 13:5
☆**5:8** Job 1:7 Jas 4:7 1 Pet 1:13
5:9 Acts 14:22 Col 2:5 Heb 12:8 Jas 4:7
5:10 Rom 16:25 1 Cor 1:9 2 Cor 4:17 2 Thess 2:17 2 Tim 2:10 1 Pet 1:6; 4:10
5:11 Rom 11:36
☆**5:12** Acts 11:23 2 Cor 1:19 Heb 13:22
5:13 Acts 12:12
5:14 Rom 16:16 Eph 6:23

5:4 See note to John 10:11 on Christ, the Good Shepherd.

5:5 Humility solves most of life's problems. Pride will always abase the believer, for God and pride are at odds. God's grace will enable a believer to be humble, and he who is humble will be exalted sooner or later. The omnipotent God has the power and the will to put down the proud at his pleasure. Therefore no believer can lose anything by being humble.

5:7 Care, that is anxiety, is a great threat to peace of mind and constancy of Christian conduct. See note to Psalm 37:5 concerning the cure for anxiety.

5:8 Peter warns believers that Satan is ever busy seeking to destroy the work of God. Believers must resist Satan by being steadfast in the holy faith. If Satan did not exist and if he had no power to work harm to the people of God, this warning would have little or no meaning. Jesus called Satan the prince of this world. And Paul said he is "the prince of the power of the air, the spirit that now worketh in the children of disobedience" (Eph. 2:2). Thus we have the witness of Jesus, Peter, and Paul about the reality of Satan and the greatness of his power.

5:12 *Silvanus.* See note to 1 Thess. 1:1 for information about Silvanus. *The true grace of God wherein ye stand.* He wrote his letter to assure believers that the doctrine of salvation he taught is the true account of the grace of God. Therefore he earnestly exhorts them to stand fast in this grace.

THE SECOND EPISTLE GENERAL OF

PETER

Authorship, date, and background Five books of the New Testament were written to combat the rising tide of heresy. These short writings are 2 Peter, Jude, and 1, 2, and 3 John. All of them were composed after A.D. 60. Wherever truth exists, error always follows. This has been a fact in the history of the Christian church. By A.D. 60, false doctrines had crept into and were being propagated in the church. In the case of 2 Peter, the apostle chose to stress the need for believers to have true knowledge to offset error. Churches always need to be reminded of the truths on which their faith rests. It was against this background that Peter wrote this second letter to stimulate strong faith and to encourage believers that the expected soon coming of the Lord was no fantasy even though that coming was delayed beyond the time they had in mind for it.

The great problem surrounding 2 Peter has to do with the authorship. Liberal scholars almost without exception refuse to accept the Petrine authorship of the letter. They do so despite the claim of the letter itself that Peter was the author. The salutation says it was "Simon Peter" who was writing. The author spoke of his imminent homegoing and stated this was shown to him by the Lord Jesus (1:14). He claimed to have been with Jesus on the holy mountain during the transfiguration (1:17, 18). This was the second epistle he had written to them, harking back to 1 Peter which his readers had already received (3:1). He spoke about the apostle Paul as though he were still alive and called him a wise and beloved brother (3:15). To those who accept the Word of God at face value, all of this is sufficient to accept the Petrine authorship of the letter. The opinion that some unknown writer composed the letter and that it was written somewhere between A.D. 100 and 150, long after the death of Peter, would make the letter a forgery despite the excuse that such a conclusion is not necessary. There is an overlapping of portions of this letter with that of Jude, which was definitely written after Peter's death. The argument that Peter in his letter was indebted to Jude turns out to be quite the opposite; it was Jude who was indebted to 2 Peter instead. 2 Peter, then, was written at Rome and composed about A.D. 65–67, prior to Peter's death.

Characteristics and content This letter serves to remind believers of the unchanging nature of the gospel. It castigates the false teachers who bring in destructive heresies and indicates that heresy is usually accompanied by corrupt and immoral behavior on the part of those who spread it. Chapter two describes the kind of people these heretics are and the sort of lives they live. This section and the letter of Jude say the same things. Believers are warned to be pure and urged to grow in the grace and the knowledge of Jesus Christ. Peter emphasizes the certainty of punishment for unbelief even as God cast out the wicked angels from his presence and as he executed divine judgment upon evil men in Noah's time. Peter also presents Sodom and Gomorrah as well as Balaam as examples of cities and a man who suffered for their misdeeds.

Peter says that judgment is delayed so that men may repent. But he envisions a day when the earth and the heavens will be burned with fire at the judgment day and at that time all ungodly men will perish (3:7). In the place of the destroyed universe there will emerge "new heavens and a new earth, wherein dwelleth righteousness" (3:13). Thus his letter contains both the certain threat of judgment for the wicked and the sure promise of deliverance and happiness for those who believe in Jesus.

Outline

I. Salutation (1:1, 2)
II. Right knowledge (1:3–21)
III. False knowledge and false teachers (2:1–22)
IV. The coming of the Lord (3:1–18)

I. SALUTATION (1:1, 2)

1 SIMON Peter, a servant and an apostle of Jesus Christ, to them that
have obtained like precious faith with us through the righteousness of
God and our Saviour Jesus Christ:
2 Grace and peace be multiplied unto you through the knowledge of God,
and of Jesus our Lord,

II. RIGHT KNOWLEDGE (1:3–21)

A. THE GROWTH OF RIGHT KNOWLEDGE

3 According as his divine power hath given unto us all things that *pertain*
unto life and godliness, through the knowledge of him that hath called us to
glory and virtue:
4 Whereby are given unto us exceeding great and precious promises: that
by these ye might be partakers of the divine nature, having escaped the
corruption that is in the world through lust.
5 And beside this, giving all diligence, add to your faith virtue; and to
virtue knowledge;
6 And to knowledge temperance; and to temperance patience; and to
patience godliness;
7 And to godliness brotherly kindness; and to brotherly kindness charity.
8 For if these things be in you, and abound, they make *you that ye shall*
neither *be* barren nor unfruitful in the knowledge of our Lord Jesus Christ.
9 But he that lacketh these things is blind, and cannot see afar off, and
hath forgotten that he was purged from his old sins.
10 Wherefore the rather, brethren, give diligence to make your calling and
election sure: for if ye do these things, ye shall never fall:
11 For so an entrance shall be ministered unto you abundantly into the
everlasting kingdom of our Lord and Saviour Jesus Christ.

B. THE SOURCE OF RIGHT KNOWLEDGE

12 Wherefore I will not be negligent to put you always in remembrance of
these things, though ye know *them,* and be established in the present truth.
13 Yea, I think it meet, as long as I am in this tabernacle, to stir you up by
putting *you* in remembrance;
14 Knowing that shortly I must put off *this* my tabernacle, even as our
Lord Jesus Christ hath shewed me.
15 Moreover I will endeavour that ye may be able after my decease to have
these things always in remembrance.

☆**1:1**
Isa 12:2
Lk 1:47
Jn 1:1, 18; 20:28
Rom 1:1, 12
2 Cor 4:13
Eph 4:5
Tit 2:13
1 Pet 1:1, 7; 2:7
1:2
Num 6:24–26
Isa 53:11
1 Pet 1:2
2 Pet 3:18
1 Jn 5:20, 21
1:3
Mt 28:18
Jn 17:2
Rom 1:19
Eph 4:1, 4
1 Thess 2:12
2 Thess 2:14
☆**1:4**
Jas 1:27
2 Pet 3:9, 13
1 Jn 2:15, 16
1:5
1 Cor 14:20
Phil 4:8
Col 2:3
2 Pet 1:3; 3:18
1:6
Ps 37:7
Acts 24:25
1 Cor 9:25
Gal 5:22
1 Tim 2:2
2 Pet 1:3
1:7
Jn 13:34, 35
Rom 12:10
1 Pet 1:22
1:8
Jn 15:1–6
Col 1:10
2 Pet 1:3
1:9
2 Cor 4:3, 4
1 Jn 2:11
1:10
Mt 22:14
Rom 8:28–31
11:29
1 Thess 1:4
Jude 24
1:11
2 Tim 4:18
2 Pet 2:20
Rev 3:21
☆**1:12**
Rom 15:14, 15
Phil 3:1
Jude 5, 17
1:13, 14
Jn 13:36; 21:18,
19
2 Tim 4:6
2 Pet 1:12; 3:1

1:1 In the first epistle of Peter only the name Peter appears in the text (1 Pet. 1:1). Here we have *Simon Peter.* Simon was his given name by birth. The name Peter was given to him by Christ. He probably used the Jewish "Simon" here to show his Jewish Christian friends that he was no despiser of circumcision, for it was at his circumcision that the name Simon was given him.

1:4 *promises.* Scripture contains almost 5,000 different promises made by God for his people. Peter speaks of "all the other rich and wonderful blessings he promised," (TLB). Believers can claim with assurance any and all the promises of God, for what God promises he performs or fulfills. He always keeps his word. Paul says, "All the promises of God in him are yea, and in him Amen, unto the glory of God by us" (2 Cor. 1:20). *partakers of the divine nature.* By this Peter means that believers are renewed in the spirit of their mind, after the image of God, in knowledge, righteousness, and holiness (see Eph. 4:23, 24; Col. 3:10).

1:12 Ministers are to be good "remembrancers." They must remind their brothers and sisters what their beliefs are and what duties are expected of them. Given our humanness and the assaults of the wicked one, we tend to forget what we have learned and cease to do what we formerly did.

1:16☆ Mt 17:1–5; 28:18 Mk 13:26 Lk 9:28–32 Eph 4:14 1 Thess 2:19 1 Tim 1:4 2 Pet 2:3
1:17 Mt 17:5 Heb 1:3
1:19☆ Ps 119:105 Prov 6:23 Lk 1:78, 79 2 Cor 4:6 1 Pet 1:10–12 Rev 22:16
1:20 Rom 12:6 2 Pet 3:3
1:21 Jn 14:26 1 Cor 2:13 2 Tim 3:16
2:1☆ Deut 13:1–3 Jer 6:13 Mt 7:15 1 Cor 11:19 2 Cor 11:13 Gal 2:4; 5:20 1 Tim 4:1 Jude 4 Rev 6:10
2:2 Gen 19:5–8 Rom 2:24 1 Tim 6:1 2 Pet 2:7, 18
2:3 Deut 32:35 Rom 16:18 1 Tim 6:5 2 Pet 2:14 Jude 16
2:4☆ Gen 6:1–7 Job 4:18 Lk 8:31 Jn 8:44 1 Jn 3:8 Jude 6 Rev 20:1–3
2:5 Gen 6:13–22 Ezek 26:20 1 Pet 3:20 2 Pet 3:6

16 For we have not followed cunningly devised fables, when we made known unto you the power and coming of our Lord Jesus Christ, but were eyewitnesses of his majesty.

17 For he received from God the Father honour and glory, when there came such a voice to him from the excellent glory, This is my beloved Son, in whom I am well pleased.

18 And this voice which came from heaven we heard, when we were with him in the holy mount.

19 We have also a more sure word of prophecy; whereunto ye do well that ye take heed, as unto a light that shineth in a dark place, until the day dawn, and the day star arise in your hearts:

20 Knowing this first, that no prophecy of the scripture is of any private interpretation.

21 For the prophecy came not in old time by the will of man: but holy men of God spake *as they were* moved by the Holy Ghost.

III. FALSE KNOWLEDGE AND FALSE TEACHERS (2:1–22)

A. THE INVASION OF ERROR

2 BUT there were false prophets also among the people, even as there shall be false teachers among you, who privily shall bring in damnable heresies, even denying the Lord that bought them, and bring upon themselves swift destruction.

2 And many shall follow their pernicious ways; by reason of whom the way of truth shall be evil spoken of.

3 And through covetousness shall they with feigned words make merchandise of you: whose judgment now of a long time lingereth not, and their damnation slumbereth not.

B. THE PENALTY FOR ERROR

4 For if God spared not the angels that sinned, but cast *them* down to hell, and delivered *them* into chains of darkness, to be reserved unto judgment;

5 And spared not the old world, but saved Noah the eighth *person*, a preacher of righteousness, bringing in the flood upon the world of the ungodly;

1:16 There were many myths and fables abroad in Peter's day. The non-Christian religions were filled with them. Peter insists upon the historicity of the Christian faith. He offers an apologetic based upon the experience of himself and James and John, who were with the Lord Jesus Christ on the Mount of Transfiguration. They were eyewitnesses of his majesty. They heard God confirm the fact that Jesus was the divine Son to whom they should listen. Their inward convictions were supported by external corroborative events. See also note to Mark 9:2 regarding the Transfiguration.

1:19ff See note to 2 Tim. 3:16 on inspiration. Scripture is authoritative, i.e., it sits in judgment on us, not we on *it; it is revelatory, i.e., it tells us* what we cannot otherwise know; it is inspired, i.e., the Holy Spirit is the true author of Scripture; it is without error, a doctrine that springs from an authoritative, revelatory, and inspired Word of God. Here Peter carefully states that holy men of God were used to write the Scriptures. The Holy Spirit moved on them, in them, and through them so that what they delivered was the mind and the will of God. Prophecy did not come from men but from the Holy Spirit, who moved them to write what God wanted written. Thus it is the Word of God and the word of men, trustworthy in all of its parts.

2:1 We are assured that false teachers will arise in the church. They will teach damnable heresies and will do so under the cloak of so-called truth. They will deny the Lord who bought them, as do those who deny the deity of Jesus Christ. Many will follow false teachers, who will exploit them for their own ends. But swift destruction is promised to false teachers and, obviously, to those who embrace their erroneous doctrine.

2:4ff If God punished sinning angels, the world in Noah's day, and the people of Sodom and Gomorrah, who then can escape the wrath of God for his sins? Peter encourages believers by assuring them that even as God rescued Lot, so he will sustain and rescue faithful believers, who live in the midst of a sinful world.

6 And turning the cities of Sodom and Go-mor'rha into ashes condemned
them with an overthrow, making *them* an ensample unto those that after
should live ungodly;
7 And delivered just Lot, vexed with the filthy conversation of the wicked:
8 (For that righteous man dwelling among them, in seeing and hearing,
vexed *his* righteous soul from day to day with *their* unlawful deeds);
9 The Lord knoweth how to deliver the godly out of temptations, and to
reserve the unjust unto the day of judgment to be punished:
10 But chiefly them that walk after the flesh in the lust of uncleanness, and
despise government. Presumptuous *are they,* selfwilled, they are not afraid
to speak evil of dignities.
11 Whereas angels, which are greater in power and might, bring not railing
accusation against them before the Lord.

C. THE EARMARKS AND WORKS OF FALSE TEACHERS

12 But these, as natural brute beasts, made to be taken and destroyed,
speak evil of the things that they understand not; and shall utterly perish in
their own corruption;
13 And shall receive the reward of unrighteousness, *as* they that count it
pleasure to riot in the day time. Spots *they are* and blemishes, sporting
themselves with their own deceivings while they feast with you;
14 Having eyes full of adultery, and that cannot cease from sin; beguiling
unstable souls: an heart they have exercised with covetous practices; cursed
children:
15 Which have forsaken the right way, and are gone astray, following the
way of Ba'laam *the son* of Bo'sor, who loved the wages of unrighteousness;
16 But was rebuked for his iniquity: the dumb ass speaking with man's
voice forbad the madness of the prophet.
17 These are wells without water, clouds that are carried with a tempest: to
whom the mist of darkness is reserved for ever.
18 For when they speak great swelling *words* of vanity, they allure through
the lusts of the flesh, *through much* wantonness, those that were clean
escaped from them who live in error.
19 While they promise them liberty, they themselves are the servants of
corruption: for of whom a man is overcome, of the same is he brought in
bondage.
20 For if after they have escaped the pollutions of the world through the
knowledge of the Lord and Saviour Jesus Christ, they are again entangled
therein, and overcome, the latter end is worse with them than the
beginning.
21 For it had been better for them not to have known the way of
righteousness, than, after they have known *it,* to turn from the holy
commandment delivered unto them.
22 But it is happened unto them according to the true proverb, The dog *is
turned to his own vomit again;* and the sow that was washed to her
wallowing in the mire.

2:6 Gen 19:24, 25; Mt 10:15; 11:23; Rom 9:29; Jude 7
2:7 Gen 19:5, 16, 29; 2 Pet 3:17
2:9 Ps 34:17; Mt 10:15; 1 Cor 10:13; Jude 6; Rev 3:10
2:10 Ex 22:28; 2 Pet 3:3; Jude 8, 16, 18
☆**2:11** Jude 9
2:12 Jude 10
2:13 Rom 13:13; 1 Cor 11:21; Phil 3:19; 2 Pet 2:15
2:14 Eph 2:3; 2 Pet 2:18; 3:16
☆**2:15** Num 22:5–7, 17; Deut 23:4; Acts 13:10; 2 Pet 2:13; Jude 11; Rev 2:14
2:16 Num 22:21–28
2:17 Jude 12, 13
2:18 Acts 2:40; Eph 4:17–19; 2 Pet 2:2, 14, 20; Jude 16
2:19 Jn 8:34; Rom 6:16; Gal 5:13
2:20 Mt 12:43–45; Lk 11:26; 2 Tim 2:4; 2 Pet 1:2; 2:18
2:21 Ezek 18:24; 1 Tim 6:14; Heb 6:4; 10:26; Jas 4:17
2:22 Prov 26:11

2:11 The good angels who stand before the presence of God have a zeal for his honor and do not hesitate to accuse wicked men and angels before God. They bring their charges to God, not to other created beings, and so should we. Angels do not bring their complaints with reviling and rage, and neither should we. God, as Judge, will judge all wickedness and pronounce true and final judgment upon all who disobey him.

2:15 Balaamism is the way of compromise. Balaam used his God-given prophetic gift for personal advancement. He professed to be serving God, but he was advancing his own self-interest. This kind of person will experience divine condemnation sooner or later. (See also notes to Num. 22:5; Jude 11; Rev. 2:14.)

IV. THE COMING OF THE LORD (3:1–18)

A. THE PROMISE OF THAT COMING

3:1 Acts 3:21 Eph 3:5 2 Pet 1:13

3 THIS second epistle, beloved, I now write unto you; in *both* which I
stir up your pure minds by way of remembrance:
[2]That ye may be mindful of the words which were spoken before by the
holy prophets, and of the commandment of us the apostles of the Lord and
Saviour:

3:3☆ 1 Tim 4:1 2 Pet 2:10 Jude 18
3:4☆ Isa 5:19 Jer 17:15 Ezek 11:3 12:22, 27
3:5, 6☆ Gen 1:6, 9, 10 7:10–12 Ps 24:2; 136:6 Col 1:17 Heb 11:3 2 Pet 2:5

[3]Knowing this first, that there shall come in the last days scoffers,
walking after their own lusts,
[4]And saying, Where is the promise of his coming? for since the fathers
fell asleep, all things continue as *they were* from the beginning of the
creation.
[5]For this they willingly are ignorant of, that by the word of God the
heavens were of old, and the earth standing out of the water and in the
water:
[6]Whereby the world that then was, being overflowed with water,
perished:

3:7 Isa 66:15 Mt 10:15 1 Cor 3:13 2 Thess 1:8 Heb 12:29

[7]But the heavens and the earth, which are now, by the same word are
kept in store, reserved unto fire against the day of judgment and perdition
of ungodly men.

B. THE EVENTS CONNECTED WITH THAT COMING

3:8 Ps 90:4
3:9☆ Isa 30:18 Hab 2:3 Rom 2:4; 13:11 1 Tim 2:4 Rev 2:21
3:10☆ Isa 34:4 Mic 1:4 Mt 24:43 1 Cor 1:8 1 Thess 5:2 2 Pet 3:7 Rev 3:3

[8]But, beloved, be not ignorant of this one thing, that one day *is* with the
Lord as a thousand years, and a thousand years as one day.
[9]The Lord is not slack concerning his promise, as some men count
slackness; but is longsuffering to us-ward, not willing that any should
perish, but that all should come to repentance.
[10]But the day of the Lord will come as a thief in the night; in the which
the heavens shall pass away with a great noise, and the elements shall melt
with fervent heat, the earth also and the works that are therein shall be
burned up.

3:3 *scoffers.* These are people who live as they please, not as God pleases. They talk as they please, not as God pleases. They own no master except themselves and are a law to themselves. They seek to deliver God's people from what they think to be their foolish convictions and way of life.

3:4 *Where is the promise of his coming?* The longer Jesus tarries, the more unbelievers raise their voices to disclaim his Second Coming. Surely, they say, we should see signs of that coming if indeed he were coming. Robert Ingersoll, the atheist, who spoke to multiplied thousands of people, used to hold up his watch before the audience and challenge God: "If there is a God, let him strike me dead in one minute." When this did not happen he would offer this as evidence that there is no God. Similarly, many say, in effect, that if Jesus has not come yet, he is not coming. In verse 8 Peter speaks of the fact that a thousand years is as a day in the mind of God. Why then should finite minds think it strange that Jesus has not yet *returned?*

3:5ff Peter refers to the great deluge in which the world, except for the Noahic family, perished. This happened by the Word of God. The same powerful Word that made the world can also destroy the world. And what happened in Noah's day will, by the Word of God, result in the purgation of the heavens and the earth at the end of the age. The time of that coming event is unknown to men, who must remember that a thousand years are as a day to God.

3:9 The good news for sinful men is that Christ has delayed his coming. And he delays because he continues to reach out to sinful men that they may repent, be converted, and have their sins blotted out. When he does come, the day of opportunity will be foreclosed and the gates of heaven shut. Until then there still is room.

3:10 This phrase, *the day of the Lord,* appears in Acts 2:20; 1 Cor. 5:5, 1 Thess. 5:2. It refers to Christ's Second Advent. It reiterates what is found in the Old Testament prophets (Joel 2:1; Zeph. 1:7, for example). Of this advent three things can be said: (1) Christ's coming is certain, although the time is known to God alone (Mark 13:32); (2) Christ's coming will be sudden, unexpected, and with no advance warning (1 Thess. 5:1–3); (3) it will be a day of solemn judgment (Acts 17:31). In this verse "the day of the Lord" is spoken of in relation to the passing away of the heavens and the dissolving of the elements with fire. This statement, when looked at in conjunction with other eschatological passages, has led some to think "the day of the Lord" constitutes a period of time with at least a thousand years between its beginning and its termination.

11*Seeing* then *that* all these things shall be dissolved, what manner *of*
persons ought ye to be in *all* holy conversation and godliness,
12Looking for and hasting unto the coming of the day of God, wherein
the heavens being on fire shall be dissolved, and the elements shall melt
with fervent heat?
13Nevertheless we, according to his promise, look for new heavens and a
new earth, wherein dwelleth righteousness.

C. WATCHING WHILE WAITING FOR THAT COMING

14Wherefore, beloved, seeing that ye look for such things, be diligent that
ye may be found of him in peace, without spot, and blameless.
15And account *that* the longsuffering of our Lord *is* salvation; even as our
beloved brother Paul also according to the wisdom given unto him hath
written unto you;
16As also in all *his* epistles, speaking in them of these things; in which are
some things hard to be understood, which they that are unlearned and
unstable wrest, as *they do* also the other scriptures, unto their own
destruction.
17Ye therefore, beloved, seeing ye know *these things* before, beware lest ye
also, being led away with the error of the wicked, fall from your own
stedfastness.
18But grow in grace, and *in* the knowledge of our Lord and Saviour Jesus
Christ. To him *be* glory both now and for ever. Amen.

3:12 Ps 50:3; Isa 24:19; 34:4; 1 Cor 1:7; 2 Pet 3:7
☆**3:13** Isa 60:21; 64:17, 25; Rom 8:21; Rev 21:1, 27
3:14 Phil 2:15; Jas 1:27; 1 Pet 1:7
☆**3:15** Acts 9:17; Rom 2:4; 11:25, 26; 1 Cor 3:10; Eph 3:3; Col 1:25–27; Heb 5:11; 2 Pet 3:9
3:16 Isa 28:13; Heb 5:11; 2 Pet 3:2
3:17 1 Cor 10:12; Eph 4:14; 2 Pet 2:18; Rev 2:5
☆**3:18** Rom 11:36; 2 Tim 4:18; 2 Pet 1:2, 8; Rev 1:6

3:13 Peter exhorts the people of God to live lives of purity and godliness while they wait for the Lord's coming. They can wait because they have the promise of a new heavens and a new earth where righteousness prevails and sin is banished. This hope is based on the promise of God alone, and he cannot lie.

3:15 Peter speaks highly of Paul. He calls him a brother, a beloved friend, a man who has wisdom and whose writings are difficult for Jews to understand because what he says goes against the grain of what they have thought and entertained about certain critical matters. Paul indeed was maligned by the Jews, and unstable, unlearned men twisted his words to their own destruction.

3:18 What greater advice can be given than to grow in grace and in the knowledge of Jesus Christ, who is both Savior and Lord?

THE FIRST EPISTLE GENERAL OF
JOHN

Authorship, date, and background The authorship of 1 John as well as 2 and 3 John has been questioned because none of the letters names the author specifically. Most scholars agree that the same person wrote the three letters. Tradition has associated John, the son of Zebedee, with them. This is the same John who wrote the Gospel of John and later The Revelation on the Isle of Patmos. Conservative scholars have always agreed that these books were written by the apostle John. The dates for 1, 2, and 3 John have been set around A.D. 90, prior to the persecution by Domitian which resulted in John's banishment from Ephesus to Patmos in A.D. 95, followed by his return to Ephesus around A.D. 97. John died around the turn of the century.

The letters do not tell us much about whom they were written for. Undoubtedly they were intended for Ephesus and the surrounding area and were sent and read elsewhere at a later date whenever Christian communities were threatened by Gnosticism. We do know what the purpose of 1 John was. Gnosticism (meaning *knowledge*) had come in like a flood and was seriously challenging the Christian faith. Three errors lay at the heart of this heresy. The most important one had to do with the incarnation (God becoming man in Jesus Christ). Gnosticism could not reconcile Christ's deity with Jesus' humanity. So the real humanity of Jesus was submerged, making him, in effect, an incorporeal being. Cerinthus later said Jesus was an ordinary human being on whom the Logos (Word) came at his baptism and departed from him before his death on Calvary. Thus only the human Jesus died on the cross.

The second Gnostic error centered around human dualism. Christians had saved souls in sinful bodies. The soul was separated from the body, so that immorality and spiritual accommodation to evil were true of the body but not of the soul. The third error claimed that only those who had been initiated into Gnosticism and knew its secrets had the true light. 1 John was written to combat these serious errors which threatened the life of the Church.

Characteristics and content 1 John has no introduction, no author is named, no prayer of thanksgiving appears, and there is no concluding salutation. Largely because of these omissions the letter has been thought of as an encyclical or circular letter intended for wide circulation, perhaps to be read in all of the churches in the region. John writes in a homiletical tone and uses repetition and parallelisms for effect. It is quite apparent that he is a leader who has apostolic authority and does not hesitate to use it.

The letter is not organized as tightly as a book like Romans, yet three dominant ideas are set forth powerfully and dogmatically. The first is that God is light (1:5) in whom there is no darkness. The children of God are to walk in the light. To do less than this is to deny the light. The second idea is that God is life; that is, believers have eternal life through Jesus Christ which commences at conversion and continues forever. Believers are to live the life of God in Christ by the Holy Spirit who indwells each believer and teaches each one what is right (2:24–29). Third, God is love (4:8). John argues that whoever knows God must love because God is love. Whoever does not love does not have God. All believers are to dwell in love. All of these things are true because Jesus came in the flesh. Whoever does not believe what God has said about his Son calls God a liar (5:10, 11). The closing admonition is always appropriate: "Little children, keep yourselves from idols. Amen" (5:21).

Outline

I. Introduction (1:1–4)
II. Certainty through living in the light (1:5—2:29)
III. Certainty and abiding in love (3:1—4:21)
IV. Certainty through true faith (5:1–12)
V. Conclusion: the certainties of faith (5:13–21)

I. INTRODUCTION (1:1–4)

1 THAT which was from the beginning, which we have heard, which we
have seen with our eyes, which we have looked upon, and our hands
have handled, of the Word of life;
2 (For the life was manifested, and we have seen *it*, and bear witness, and
shew unto you that eternal life, which was with the Father, and was
manifested unto us;)
3 That which we have seen and heard declare we unto you, that ye also
may have fellowship with us: and truly our fellowship *is* with the Father,
and with his Son Jesus Christ.
4 And these things write we unto you, that your joy may be full.

II. CERTAINTY THROUGH LIVING IN THE LIGHT (1:5—2:29)

A. FELLOWSHIP WITH GOD

5 This then is the message which we have heard of him, and declare unto
you, that God is light, and in him is no darkness at all.
6 If we say that we have fellowship with him, and walk in darkness, we lie,
and do not the truth:
7 But if we walk in the light, as he is in the light, we have fellowship one
with another, and the blood of Jesus Christ his Son cleanseth us from all
sin.
8 If we say that we have no sin, we deceive ourselves, and the truth is not
in us.
9 If we confess our sins, he is faithful and just to forgive us *our* sins, and
to cleanse us from all unrighteousness.
10 If we say that we have not sinned, we make him a liar, and his word is
not in us.

2 MY little children, these things write I unto you, that ye sin not. And
if any man sin, we have an advocate with the Father, Jesus Christ the
righteous:
2 And he is the propitiation for our sins: and not for ours only, but also
for *the sins of* the whole world.
3 And hereby we do know that we know him, if we keep his command-
ments.

☆**1:1** Prov 8:22-31; Mic 5:2; Lk 24:39; Jn 1:1, 4, 14; 19:35; 2 Pet 1:16; 1 Jn 4:14; Rev 19:13
1:2 Jn 1:1–4; 19:35; 20:30, 31; 21:24, 25; Rom 16:26; 1 Tim 3:16; 1 Jn 2:25; 5:11, 13, 20
1:3 Jn 1:18; 8:16, 29, 38; 10:38; 14:9, 10; 17:3, 5, 21–24; 1 Cor 1:9; 2 Pet 1:16; 1 Jn 2:23, 24
1:4 Jn 15:11
1:5 Jn 1:9; 8:12; 12:35; 1 Tim 6:16; 1 Jn 3:11
1:6 Ps 5:4–6; Prov 4:18, 19; Jn 3:21; 2 Cor 6:14; 1 Jn 2:4, 11; 4:20
☆**1:7** Isa 2:5; Heb 9:14; Rev 7:14
1:8 Prov 20:9; Eccles 7:20; Jas 3:1, 2; 1 Jn 2:4
1:9 Ps 32:5; Prov 28:13; Heb 9:14; Rev 7:14
1:10 Prov 20:9
☆**2:1** Rom 8:34; 1 Tim 2:5; Heb 7:25; 9:24
2:2 Jn 1:29; 4:42; Rom 3:25; Heb 2:17; 1 Jn 4:10
2:3 1 Jn 3:22, 24; 5:3

1:1 Jesus was no spectre, no phantom, no invisible person. He was seen by John and others who were *eye-witnesses to his glory.* They touched him and knew that he was real. They heard him with their ears as he spoke the words of life. They looked upon him through the eye of the mind so that what they said about him was based on their discernment, their cogitation, and their convictions. The senses inform the mind and aid it in drawing conclusions. John therefore speaks about Jesus without mental reservation or equivocation of any kind.

1:7ff Christians do sin after they have been converted. Thus they must be cleansed from their sins day by day. John says three things about cleansing: (1) the blood of Christ is the means of cleansing (1:7); (2) the method of cleansing is confession of sin (1:9); (3) the measure of cleansing is that every wrong is cared for (1:9). The Scripture implies that confession must be made to God himself.

2:1 *we have an advocate with the Father.* The one who pleads for us is the *paraklētos,* literally, "the one called alongside in order to help." Christ is our advocate or Paraclete before the Father with respect to our sins. When believers sin, repent, and confess their transgressions, their advocate, Jesus Christ the righteous, pleads his blood in their behalf before the Father. His blood covers all their sins and brings them back into full fellowship with their Father in heaven. The same Greek word is used for the Holy Spirit four times in the Gospel of John and is there translated "Comforter."

4 He that saith, I know him, and keepeth not his commandments, is a liar,
and the truth is not in him.
5 But whoso keepeth his word, in him verily is the love of God perfected:
hereby know we that we are in him.
6 He that saith he abideth in him ought himself also so to walk, even as he
walked.

B. THE PROOF OF REAL LOVE

7 Brethren, I write no new commandment unto you, but an old command-
ment which ye had from the beginning. The old commandment is the word
which ye have heard from the beginning.
8 Again, a new commandment I write unto you, which thing is true in him
and in you: because the darkness is past, and the true light now shineth.
9 He that saith he is in the light, and hateth his brother, is in darkness
even until now.
10 He that loveth his brother abideth in the light, and there is none
occasion of stumbling in him.
11 But he that hateth his brother is in darkness, and walketh in darkness,
and knoweth not whither he goeth, because that darkness hath blinded his
eyes.
12 I write unto you, little children, because your sins are forgiven you for
his name's sake.
13 I write unto you, fathers, because ye have known him *that is* from the
beginning. I write unto you, young men, because ye have overcome the
wicked one. I write unto you, little children, because ye have known
the Father.
14 I have written unto you, fathers, because ye have known him *that is*
from the beginning. I have written unto you, young men, because ye are
strong, and the word of God abideth in you, and ye have overcome the
wicked one.
15 Love not the world, neither the things *that are* in the world. If any man
love the world, the love of the Father is not in him.
16 For all that *is* in the world, the lust of the flesh, and the lust of the eyes,
and the pride of life, is not of the Father, but is of the world.
17 And the world passeth away, and the lust thereof: but he that doeth the
will of God abideth for ever.

C. KEEPING THE TRUE FAITH

18 Little children, it is the last time: and as ye have heard that antichrist
shall come, even now are there many antichrists; whereby we know that it
is the last time.

2:4☆ 1 Jn 1:8
2:5 Jn 14:23; 1 Jn 2:3; 3:24; 4:12; 5:2
2:6 Mt 11:29; Jn 6:56, 57; 15:4; 1 Pet 2:21
2:7 Heb 6:9; 1 Jn 3:2, 11, 23; 2 Jn 5, 6
2:8 Jn 1:9; 13:34; Eph 5:8; 1 Thess 5:4
2:9☆
2:10 Jn 11:9; 1 Jn 3:10, 14
2:11 Jn 12:35; 2 Cor 4:4; 2 Pet 1:9; 1 Jn 2:9; 3:15
2:12 Lk 24:27; Acts 4:12; 1 Cor 6:11; 1 Jn 2:1
2:13 1 Jn 1:1; 4:4
2:14 Jer 31:33; Eph 6:10; 1 Jn 1:1; 1:10; 2:13
2:15 Mt 6:24; Rom 12:2; Jas 1:27; 4:4
2:16☆ Prov 27:20; Rom 13:14
2:17 Ps 125:1; Prov 10:25; 1 Cor 7:31
2:18☆ Mt 24:5, 24; Mk 13:22; Rom 13:11; 2 Thess 2:3; Heb 1:2; 1 Pet 4:7; 1 Jn 2:22; 4:1

2:4 John reiterates here the testimony of Paul and James about the relationship between faith and works. James said that faith without works is dead (James 2:17, 20, 26). Paul indicates that rewards will be based on our good and bad works (2 Cor. 5:10). John says here that whoever does not keep the commandments of Jesus is a liar and the truth is not in him. Thus faith in Christ without good works, or keeping the commandments, is not real.

2:9ff One of the firstfruits of the Spirit is love. He who *hates his brother is in darkness, and hatred is* disobedience to the great commandment that we should love one another. Whoever is loveless shows that his profession of faith cannot be genuine. Such a person cannot know where he is going, because hatred has blinded him.

2:16 John here defines man's three great weaknesses: the lust of the flesh, the lust of the eyes, and the pride of life. The first has to do with pleasure, by which bodily desires are satisfied; the second has to do with covetousness, which springs from the eye and has to do with the desire for riches and great possessions; the third has to do with worldly ambition, which is a vainglory that craves honor and applause.

2:18 The Bible distinguishes the *antichrist* from *antichrists* and *the spirit of antichrist* (4:3). Here John does not have in mind *the* antichrist, but those who make common cause with him and whose evil spirit they imitate. Since they deny the basic truths of the gospel they are called *antichrists.* (See also note to 4:3 for additional information.)

19 They went out from us, but they were not of us: for if they had been of
us, they would *no doubt* have continued with us: but *they went out*, that they
might be made manifest that they were not all of us.
20 But ye have an unction from the Holy One, and ye know all things.
21 I have not written unto you because ye know not the truth, but because
ye know it, and that no lie is of the truth.
22 Who is a liar but he that denieth that Jesus is the Christ? He is
antichrist, that denieth the Father and the Son.
23 Whosoever denieth the Son, the same hath not the Father: *[but] he that*
acknowledgeth the Son hath the Father also.
24 Let that therefore abide in you, which ye have heard from the
beginning. If that which ye have heard from the beginning shall remain in
you, ye also shall continue in the Son, and in the Father.
25 And this is the promise that he hath promised us, *even* eternal life.
26 These *things* have I written unto you concerning them that seduce you.
27 But the anointing which ye have received of him abideth in you, and ye
need not that any man teach you: but as the same anointing teacheth you of
all things, and is truth, and is no lie, and even as it hath taught you, ye shall
abide in him.
28 And now, little children, abide in him; that, when he shall appear, we
may have confidence, and not be ashamed before him at his coming.
29 If ye know that he is righteous, ye know that every one that doeth
righteousness is born of him.

III. CERTAINTY AND ABIDING IN LOVE (3:1—4:21)

A. LOVE DOES WHAT IS RIGHT

3 BEHOLD, what manner of love the Father hath bestowed upon us,
that we should be called the sons of God: therefore the world knoweth
us not, because it knew him not.
2 Beloved, now are we the sons of God, and it doth not yet appear what
we shall be: but we know that, when he shall appear, we shall be like him;
for we shall see him as he is.
3 And every man that hath this hope in him purifieth himself, even as he
is pure.
4 Whosoever committeth sin transgresseth also the law: for sin is the
transgression of the law.
5 And ye know that he was manifested to take away our sins; and in him
is no sin.
6 Whosoever abideth in him sinneth not: whosoever sinneth hath not seen
him, neither known him.
7 Little children, let no man deceive you: he that doeth righteousness is
righteous, even as he is righteous.

2:19 Mt 24:24; Acts 20:30; 1 Cor 11:19; 2 Tim 2:19
2:20 Prov 28:5; Mt 13:11; Jn 14:26; Acts 10:38; 2 Cor 1:21; 1 Jn 2:27
2:21 1 Jn 3:19
2:22 1 Jn 4:3
2:23 Jn 8:19; 16:3; 17:3; 1 Jn 4:15; 5:1
2:24 1 Jn 1:3; 2:7; 2 Jn 9
2:25 Jn 3:15; 6:40; 17:3
2:26 1 Jn 3:7; 2 Jn 7
☆**2:27** Jer 31:33; Jn 14:16, 26; 16:13; 1 Cor 2:10–12; 1 Thess 4:9; 1 Jn 2:20
2:28 Mk 8:38; Lk 17:30; Col 3:4; 1 Thess 2:19; 1 Jn 3:2, 21
2:29 1 Jn 3:7, 9; 4:7; 5:1, 4, 18
☆**3:1** Jn 1:11, 12; 17:26; Rom 8:16; Eph 1:4, 5
☆**3:2** Ps 17:15; Jn 17:24; Rom 8:19, 29; 1 Cor 15:49; 2 Cor 3:18; Col 3:10; 2 Pet 1:4
3:3 1 Thess 5:25; 1 Pet 1:7–9
3:5 Isa 53:1–12; Jn 1:29; 2 Cor 5:21; 1 Jn 3:8
3:6 1 Jn 3:9
3:7 1 Jn 2:1, 26, 29

2:27 Here John talks about *the anointing* that abides in believers and teaches them all things. By the Spirit believers have an inward witness and confirmation of the divine truth they have imbibed. The Spirit is the constant witness to Jesus Christ in the hearts of his people. He is each believer's indwelling teacher. And since the Spirit is truth, he can teach them only what is true, which includes all things necessary to our knowledge of God in Jesus Christ.

3:1 *be called the sons of God.* The word "sons" should be "children." God the Father has adopted all his children. Jesus Christ calls all believers his brethren and confers on them the power and dignity of the sons of God. By nature all men are heirs of sin and guilt, children of corruption. By grace God is not ashamed to be called our Father. The term "children of God" is reserved only for those who have come to Jesus Christ in faith for their salvation. Before this, believers were not the children of God. It is wrong in principle and in fact to call unbelievers the children of God. They are not and cannot be this until they are in Christ.

3:2 *we shall be like him,* i.e., like Jesus Christ. Only three people ever lived who had normal minds. They were Adam, Eve, and Jesus. The first two lost their normal minds. Only Jesus had a normal mind, and it is this that distinguished him in his humanity from all other men. The day is coming when believers will regain normal minds, which will then be sinless.

8 He that committeth sin is of the devil; for the devil sinneth from the beginning. For this purpose the Son of God was manifested, that he might destroy the works of the devil.

9 Whosoever is born of God doth not commit sin; for his seed remaineth in him: and he cannot sin, because he is born of God.

10 In this the children of God are manifest, and the children of the devil: whosoever doeth not righteousness is not of God, neither he that loveth not his brother.

B. LOVE SHARES ITSELF WITH OTHERS

11 For this is the message that ye heard from the beginning, that we should love one another.

12 Not as Cain, *who* was of that wicked one, and slew his brother. And wherefore slew he him? Because his own works were evil, and his brother's righteous.

13 Marvel not, my brethren, if the world hate you.

14 We know that we have passed from death unto life, because we love the brethren. He that loveth not *his* brother abideth in death.

15 Whosoever hateth his brother is a murderer: and ye know that no murderer hath eternal life abiding in him.

16 Hereby perceive we the love *of God*, because he laid down his life for us: and we ought to lay down *our* lives for the brethren.

17 But whoso hath this world's good, and seeth his brother have need, and shutteth up his bowels *of compassion* from him, how dwelleth the love of God in him?

18 My little children, let us not love in word, neither in tongue; but in deed and in truth.

19 And hereby we know that we are of the truth, and shall assure our hearts before him.

20 For if our heart condemn us, God is greater than our heart, and knoweth all things.

21 Beloved, if our heart condemn us not, *then* have we confidence toward God.

22 And whatsoever we ask, we receive of him, because we keep his commandments, and do those things that are pleasing in his sight.

23 And this is his commandment, That we should believe on the name of his Son Jesus Christ, and love one another, as he gave us commandment.

24 And he that keepeth his commandments dwelleth in him, and he in him. And hereby we know that he abideth in us, by the Spirit which he hath given us.

3:8 Gen 3:15; Mt 13:38; Jn 8:44; 16:11; 1 Jn 3:10
3:9 Jas 1:18; 1 Pet 1:3; 1 Jn 2:29; 3:6; 4:7; 5:1, 4, 18
3:10☆ Rom 13:8–14; Col 3:14; 1 Tim 1:5; 1 Jn 2:9; 4:8
3:11 Jn 13:34; 15:12; 1 Jn 1:5; 2:7; 2 John 5, 6
3:12 Gen 4:3–8; Prov 29:10
3:13 Jn 15:18; 17:14
3:14 Jn 5:24; 13:35
3:15☆ Mt 5:21, 22; Jn 8:44; Gal 5:21; Rev 21:8
3:16 Jn 3:16; 15:13; Rom 5:8; Eph 5:2, 25
3:17 Deut 15:7; Lk 3:11; Jas 2:15; 1 Jn 4:20
3:18☆ Rom 12:9; 1 Jn 3:7
3:19 Jn 18:37; 1 Jn 2:21
3:21 Heb 10:22
3:22☆ Job 22:26; Mt 21:22; Jn 8:29; 9:31; Heb 13:21; Jas 5:16
3:24 Ezek 37:27; Jn 17:21; Rom 8:9; 1 Thess 4:8; 1 Jn 2:3, 5, 27

3:10 John clearly states that unbelievers are children of the devil. Such children neglect true religion and give no place to God. They also have no use for the children of God, despising, hating, and persecuting them. This can be seen in the history of the church and in society today.

***3:15** John is not here speaking about the believer's relation to saved and unsaved people. He has in mind hatred toward a fellow-believer. Such a person commits "heart-murder" even though he or she does not kill the body of the person hated. Hatred is inconsistent with a true life in Christ; therefore, such a person does not have eternal life in him.*

3:18 John, like James, insists on the necessity for good works. Love is not simply a matter of lip service but should be seen and known in action and deed. To speak swelling words is nothing unless those words are accompanied by good works.

3:22 Those who have a good conscience toward God will not desire anything that is contrary to the honor and glory of God. They will depend on God, who will give them the good things they ask for. "No good thing will he withhold from them that walk uprightly" (Ps. 84:11).

C. LOVE TESTS EVERY MESSAGE

4 BELOVED, believe not every spirit, but try the spirits whether they
are of God: because many false prophets are gone out into the world.
2 Hereby know ye the Spirit of God: Every spirit that confesseth that
Jesus Christ is come in the flesh is of God:
3 And every spirit that confesseth not that Jesus Christ is come in the flesh
is not of God: and this is that *spirit* of antichrist, whereof ye have heard
that it should come; and even now already is it in the world.
4 Ye are of God, little children, and have overcome them: because greater
is he that is in you, than he that is in the world.
5 They are of the world: therefore speak they of the world, and the world
heareth them.
6 We are of God: he that knoweth God heareth us; he that is not of God
heareth not us. Hereby know we the spirit of truth, and the spirit of error.

D. LOVE'S SOURCE IS GOD

7 Beloved, let us love one another: for love is of God; and every one that
loveth is born of God, and knoweth God.
8 He that loveth not knoweth not God; for God is love.
9 In this was manifested the love of God toward us, because that God sent
his only begotten Son into the world, that we might live through him.
10 Herein is love, not that we loved God, but that he loved us, and sent his
Son *to be* the propitiation for our sins.
11 Beloved, if God so loved us, we ought also to love one another.
12 No man hath seen God at any time. If we love one another, God
dwelleth in us, and his love is perfected in us.
13 Hereby know we that we dwell in him, and he in us, because he hath
given us of his Spirit.
14 And we have seen and do testify that the Father sent the Son *to be* the
Saviour of the world.
15 Whosoever shall confess that Jesus is the Son of God, God dwelleth in
him, and he in God.
16 And we have known and believed the love that God hath to us. God is
love; and he that dwelleth in love dwelleth in God, and God in him.
17 Herein is our love made perfect, that we may have boldness in the day
of judgment: because as he is, so are we in this world.
18 There is no fear in love; but perfect love casteth out fear: because fear
hath torment. He that feareth is not made perfect in love.
19 We love him, because he first loved us.
20 If a man say, I love God, and hateth his brother, he is a liar: for he that

☆**4:1** Jer 29:8; 1 Cor 12:10; 1 Thess 5:20; 1 Jn 2:7, 18
4:2 1 Cor 12:3; 1 Jn 1:2; 2:23; 5:1
☆**4:3** 2 Thess 2:3–7; 1 Jn 2:22; 2 Jn 7
4:4 Jn 12:31; 14:30; Rom 8:31; 1 Jn 2:1, 13; 3:20
4:5 Jn 15:19; 17:14, 16
4:6 Jn 8:47; 10:27; 14:17; 1 Cor 14:37; 1 Tim 4:1
4:7 1 Jn 2:3, 29; 3:11; 5:1
4:8 Ex 34:4, 5; Mic 7:18
4:9 Jn 3:16
☆**4:10** Jn 15:16; Rom 5:8, 10; Tit 3:4, 5; 1 Jn 2:2
4:12 Jn 1:18; 14:23; 1 Tim 6:16
4:13 Jn 14:20; Rom 8:9; 1 Jn 3:24
4:14 Jn 1:14; 3:17; 4:42; 1 Jn 1:2; 2:2
4:15 Mt 16:16; Jn 6:69; Rom 10:9; 1 Jn 2:23, 24; 3:24; 5:5
4:17 Mt 10:15; Jas 2:13; 1 Jn 2:6; 3:1, 7, 16; 4:12
☆**4:18** Rom 8:15; 1 Jn 4:12
4:19 1 Jn 4:10
4:20 1 Pet 1:8; 1 Jn 1:6; 2:4, 9; 3:17; 4:12

4:1 Wherever the true exists, the false or counterfeit will always appear. We are to examine all claims that *are supposed to come from* the Spirit of God. Since John warns that many false prophets have gone out into the world, it is necessary to test the spirits whether they are from God. We test all things against the Holy Scriptures. Whatever is not in agreement with the Scriptures must be rejected.

4:3 John refers to "antichrist(s)" in 2:18, 22, and 4:3. Some of the people involved in this heresy had belonged to the Christian fellowship. Their error, for which they left the fellowship, was a denial of the reality of the incarnation, which was also a repudiation of the Father. The heresy was a direct result of Gnostic teaching. (See Introduction and note to 2:18).

4:10 God first loved us when we had no love for him. This love occasioned the giving of his Son to be the propitiation for our sins. God is love. That love is boundless, incomprehensible, mysterious, and unsearchable. "He that dwelleth in love dwelleth in God, and God in him" (4:16).

4:18 We need to make the distinction between "the fear of God" and "to be afraid of him." Fear as reverential trust toward the infinite Being is appropriate. But we do not need to be afraid of him, for this implies a sense of guilt for transgressions. Perhaps we might better say that he who walks according to the will of God has no dread in his heart. Perfect love casts out dread.

loveth not his brother whom he hath seen, how can he love God whom he
hath not seen?

4:21 Lev 19:18; Mt 5:43; 22:37; Jn 13:34; 1 Jn 3:11

21 And this commandment have we from him, That he who loveth God
love his brother also.

IV. CERTAINTY THROUGH TRUE FAITH (5:1–12)

A. VICTORY THROUGH TRUSTING CHRIST

5:1 Jn 1:11; 8:41, 42; 1 Jn 4:2, 15; 5:4, 18
5:2 1 Jn 2:5; 3:14
5:3☆ Mic 6:8; Mt 11:30; Jn 14:15; 1 Jn 2:3
5:4☆ Jn 1:13; 16:33; 1 Jn 2:13; 4:4; 5:1
5:5 1 Cor 15:57; 1 Jn 4:15; 5:1

5 WHOSOEVER believeth that Jesus is the Christ is born of God: and
every one that loveth him that begat loveth him also that is begotten of
him.
2 By this we know that we love the children of God, when we love God,
and keep his commandments.
3 For this is the love of God, that we keep his commandments: and his
commandments are not grievous.
4 For whatsoever is born of God overcometh the world: and this is the
victory that overcometh the world, *even* our faith.
5 Who is he that overcometh the world, but he that believeth that Jesus is
the Son of God?

B. TRUE LIFE THROUGH CHRIST

5:6☆ Hag 2:5; Mt 18:16; Jn 15:26; 19:34; Rev 19:11, 13
5:7, 8☆
5:9 Mt 3:16, 17; Jn 5:31–38; 8:18
5:10 Jn 3:18, 33; Rom 8:16; Gal 4:6; 1 Jn 1:10
5:11 Jn 1:4; 1 Jn 2:25; 4:9; 5:13, 20
5:12 Jn 3:15, 36; 5:24; 14:6; 17:2, 3

6 This is he that came by water and blood, *even* Jesus Christ; not by water
only, but by water and blood. And it is the Spirit that beareth witness,
because the Spirit is truth.
7 For there are three that bear record in heaven, the Father, the Word,
and the Holy Ghost: and these three are one.
8 And there are three that bear witness in earth, the spirit, and the water,
and the blood: and these three agree in one.
9 If we receive the witness of men, the witness of God is greater: for this
is the witness of God which he hath testified of his Son.
10 He that believeth on the Son of God hath the witness in himself: he
that believeth not God hath made him a liar; because he believeth not the
record that God gave of his Son.
11 And this is the record, that God hath given to us eternal life, and this
life is in his Son.
12 He that hath the Son hath life; *and* he that hath not the Son of God
hath not life.

V. CONCLUSION: THE CERTAINTIES OF FAITH (5:13–21)

5:13☆ Jn 20:31; 1 Jn 3:23; 5:11, 20

13 These things have I written unto you that believe on the name of the
Son of God; that ye may know that ye have eternal life, and that ye may
believe on the name of the Son of God.

5:3 *are not grievous,* i.e., "are not burdensome" or "are not heavy."
5:4 *overcometh the world.* We who are born *of* God are born *for* God. This makes possible the spiritual and intellectual conquest of the world. Faith is the means by which believers conquer.
5:6 *it is the Spirit that beareth witness, because the Spirit is truth.* The Holy Spirit, who is truth, witnesses to our hearts that Jesus is Lord and that the Bible is God's infallible Word. Indeed the words of the Scriptures were not "taught by human wisdom but taught by the Spirit" (1 Cor. 2:13). This is known as "the testimony of the Holy Spirit" (*testimonium spiritus sancti*).
5:7, 8 The earliest manuscripts do not contain the words: *in heaven, the Father, the Word, and the Holy Ghost: and these three are one.* 8. *And there are three who bear witness in earth.* The translators of RSV, NIV and NASB concurred. In his study Bible, Scofield said, "It is generally agreed that verse 7 has no real authority and has been inserted."
5:13 *that ye may know.* Some Christians do not have the assurance of faith and tend to stumble around blindly, lacking confidence in their salvation. John has written his epistle that all may know (i.e., be certain) that they have eternal life. Since what John says, God says, confidence in the Word of God assures the weakest of hearts and minds that all can know with certainty that they have eternal life.

[14]And this is the confidence that we have in him, that, if we ask any thing
according to his will, he heareth us:
[15]And if we know that he hear us, whatsoever we ask, we know that we
have the petitions that we desired of him.
[16]If any man see his brother sin a sin *which is* not unto death, he shall ask,
and he shall give him life for them that sin not unto death. There is a sin
unto death: I do not say that he shall pray for it.
[17]All unrighteousness is sin: and there is a sin not unto death.
[18]We know that whosoever is born of God sinneth not; but he that is
begotten of God keepeth himself, and that wicked one toucheth him not.
[19]*And* we know that we are of God, and the whole world lieth in
wickedness.
[20]And we know that the Son of God is come, and hath given us an
understanding, that we may know him that is true, and we are in him that
is true, *even* in his Son Jesus Christ. This is the true God, and eternal life.
[21]Little children, keep yourselves from idols. Amen.

☆**5:14, 15** Mt 7:7; Jn 14:13; 15:7; 1 Jn 3:21, 22
5:16 Num 15:30; Jer 7:16; 14:11; Mk 3:29; Heb 6:4; 10:26; Jas 5:15
5:17 1 Jn 2:1; 3:4
☆**5:18** Jn 10:28, 29; 1 Jn 2:13; 3:9
5:19 1 Jn 4:6
5:20 Isa 9:6; 54:5; Lk 24:45; Jn 1:1, 18; 14:20; 15:5; 17:3, 21, 23; 1 Jn 5:5, 10; Rev 3:7
5:21 1 Cor 10:7; 1 Thess 1:9

5:14, 15 These verses contain one of the greatest of all promises in the Scriptures. If we pray according to the will of God, God hears us. And if God hears us we can be absolutely certain that we will get what we have prayed for. We can discern the will of God from Scripture in many cases so that when we pray according to that Word we know that our prayers will be answered in the affirmative. The pattern stated here should be normative in prayers of petition and intercession. Prayers that have to do with adoration, thanksgiving, and confession of sin come under a different rubric.

5:18 *whosoever is born of God sinneth not.* This statement, as it stands, seems to contradict 1:8. The clause might better be translated as, "no one born of God makes sin the practice of his life." Whoever deliberately and with malicious forethought sins and keeps on sinning should ask himself whether he has really been born of God, for those who have been do not live this sort of life.

THE SECOND EPISTLE GENERAL OF
JOHN

Authorship, date, and background 2 John was written by "the elder," as was 3 John. The question of authorship depends upon identifying who "the elder" was. Studies of 1, 2, and 3 John clearly show that all were written by the same person. Some modern scholars do not think it was the apostle John. So far as the ancient church is concerned, it was said to be John, the son of Zebedee. Conservative scholars say with one voice that the Gospel of John and these three letters were all composed by the apostle. This letter and the other two were undoubtedly written in the city of Ephesus around A.D. 90.

John wrote the letter to "the elect lady," but whether this is the correct translation of the Greek remains an open question. It could be translated "the lady Eclecta," "the elect Cyria," or "the elect lady," depending upon whether the greeting is a proper name. Interpretation takes over at this point when the question is asked whether the apostle was writing to an individual or whether the term "lady" was a figurative expression applied to a church whose members could easily be called her "children." The problem has not been definitely resolved and no additional light has been thrown on the matter in recent years.

If the address of the letter is an open question, the content is not. To whomever it was addressed, the problem John spoke about leaves no doubt in the mind of the reader. False teachers had crept in and believers were being subverted. John not only warned them; he also wanted them to be vigilant so they would not be swept away by error. It was the Gnostic error (see introduction to 1 John) which was causing trouble.

Characteristics and content The church has been plagued by false doctrine through the ages. It always dilutes the witness of believers, brings ill effects to those who accept it, and results in decay and decline in the Christian's personal walk. The person of Jesus Christ is at issue here. The specific question is whether Jesus became a true human being with a body like ours (7). John stresses the doctrine of Christ and thereby makes plain that Christianity is based upon propositions which are forever true. A departure from the foundational truths of the faith produces shipwreck. John calls such departures wicked and forbids believers to invite such a heretic into their homes; nor is such a one to be encouraged in any way. It is always possible for someone to affirm faith in what he does not really believe. Thus, there were then and are now hypocrites among true believers. But we can be certain that whoever denies the truth cannot be a Christian. Whoever does not love is not a true believer, however much he professes faith in doctrine; a person who denies basic doctrinal truths is unsaved and neither will he love.

Outline

I. Salutation (1–3)
II. Apostolic injunctions (4–11)
III. Conclusion (12, 13)

I. SALUTATION (1–3)

1 THE elder unto the elect lady and her children, whom I love in the
truth; and not I only, but also all they that have known the truth;
2 For the truth's sake, which dwelleth in us, and shall be with us for ever.
3 Grace be with you, mercy, *and* peace, from God the Father, and from
the Lord Jesus Christ, the Son of the Father, in truth and love.

II. APOSTOLIC INJUNCTIONS (4–11)

4 I rejoiced greatly that I found of thy children walking in truth, as we
have received a commandment from the Father.
5 And now I beseech thee, lady, not as though I wrote a new command-
ment unto thee, but that which we had from the beginning, that we love one
another.
6 And this is love, that we walk after his commandments. This is the
commandment, That, as ye have heard from the beginning, ye should walk
in it.
7 For many deceivers are entered into the world, who confess not that
Jesus Christ is come in the flesh. This is a deceiver and an antichrist.
8 Look to yourselves, that we lose not those things which we have
wrought, but that we receive a full reward.
9 Whosoever transgresseth, and abideth not in the doctrine of Christ, hath
not God. He that abideth in the doctrine of Christ, he hath both the Father
and the Son.
10 If there come any unto you, and bring not this doctrine, receive him not
into *your* house, neither bid him God speed:
11 For he that biddeth him God speed is partaker of his evil deeds.

III. CONCLUSION (12, 13)

12 Having many things to write unto you, I would not *write* with paper
and ink: but I trust to come unto you, and speak face to face, that our joy
may be full.
13 The children of thy elect sister greet thee. Amen.

☆**1:1** 1 Pet 5:1; 2 Jn 13; 3 Jn 1
1:2 Jn 8:32; 14:16, 17; 2 Cor 4:7, 10; 1 Jn 1:8; 3:18
1:3 1 Tim 1:2
1:4 Phil 4:10; 1 Thess 2:19, 20; 3 Jn 3, 4
☆**1:5** Lev 19:18; Jn 13:34; 15:12; Eph 5:2; 1 Pet 1:22; 1 Jn 2:7, 8, 24; 3:14–18; 4:7–12, 20
1:6 Jn 14:15; 15:10, 14; Rom 13:8; 1 Jn 2:7; 4:7–12; 2 Jn 5
☆**1:7** Mt 24:11, 24; 1 Tim 4:1–5; 2 Pet 2:1–3; 1 Jn 2:18, 26; 4:1–3; Jude 4, 8–20
1:8 Mt 13:23; Phil 3:14; 4:1; Heb 10:35; 12:15
1:9 Jn 8:31; 15:7; 1 Jn 2:23, 24
☆**1:10** Rom 16:17; 1 Cor. 5:11; Tit 3:10
1:11 Ps 50:16–18; 1 Tim 5:22; Jude 23
☆**1:12** 1 Jn 1:4; 3 Jn 13, 14
1:13 2 Jn 1

1:1ff The elect lady was a person of eminent birth, education, and estate. Not all Christians were poor and uneducated. John rejoiced in her influence, particularly on her children (verse 4), who were walking in truth. They had the truth and they walked in it. The Greek word for *walking* has given us the English word "peripatetic," which means moving or traveling from place to place. Thus wherever these children went, they so lived that their faith could be seen by all.

1:5 John reiterates the truth that talk and walk go together. Love is to walk in the commandments of Jesus. When we obey his commandments we are walking in the faith.

1:7 An early gnostic heresy held that Jesus' body was not real flesh and blood; it was a purely spiritual body. This heresy has been called Docetism, and it is denounced by John, who affirms that Jesus came in the flesh and was a real human being composed of flesh and blood. Whoever affirms this heresy cannot be of God, and whoever is not of God is not a regenerate believer.

1:10 Those who deny the faith are destroyers of the soul. They are not to be welcomed into the home or the church, and no one should wish them Godspeed. Whoever does this becomes a partaker of the wicked one's deeds.

1:12 Some things are better said than written. John still could travel, so he hoped to see this sister shortly and speak at length with her.

THE THIRD EPISTLE GENERAL OF
JOHN

Authorship, date, and background Tradition has it that this letter, like those of 1 and 2 John, was written by the apostle John who also wrote the Gospel of John. Its form and vocabulary clearly indicate that the three letters of John were all written by the same person. The salutation identifies the author as "the elder," for the name of John does not appear in the Greek. Scholars in the liberal tradition do not accept the Johannine authorship and suggest a possible date after the death of the apostle. Assuming Johannine authorship, as conservatives always have, it was written sometime around A.D. 90. The absence of any reference to the Roman persecutions in any of the three letters by John suggests all were written before the Emperor Trajan's time and probably before the last years of Domitian, whose reign ended in A.D. 96.

3 John is less theological. It deals with administrative matters for local congregations. This letter was addressed to Gaius, who was a pastor or a leader in the church. But where the church was located is not stated. In those days, traveling prophets, evangelists, and teachers went from church to church. They were entertained by the churches to which they went and were helped on their way to the next station. It appears that Gaius knew Diotrephes, who is also mentioned in the letter. Gaius was a beloved and faithful servant of the Lord. Diotrephes, on the other hand, refused to help the traveling visitors, withstood the authority of the elder, and took occasion to speak against him. Moreover, those members of the congregation who wished to help the visiting preachers were put out of the church.

Characteristics and content John encourages faithful Gaius, who remains unknown to us although the name appears in Acts 19:29, 20:4, Romans 16:23 and 1 Corinthians 1:14. John evidently has authority over some of the churches and feels put upon by Diotrephes for his insubordination. He expects to visit the church and put things right. He commends Demetrius whose reputation is excellent and who clings to the truth. Implied in the letter is the Gnostic problem mentioned in 1 John, a heresy agitating the churches and destroying the true gospel. Beloved Gaius is urged not to let the evil influence of Diotrephes influence him. John emphasizes one aspect of the faith which is always pertinent to believers. He says, "he that doeth good is of God: but he that doeth evil hath not seen God" (11). The conclusion of the verse can apparently be applied to Diotrephes, whose insubordination may have been connected with a commitment to Gnosticism.

Outline

I. Introduction (1–4)
II. True workers encouraged (5–8)
III. Opponents of truth rebuked (9, 10)
IV. Commending a witness for truth (11, 12)
V. Conclusion (13, 14)

I. INTRODUCTION (1–4)

1:1 2 Jn 1; **1:2**☆; **1:3** 2 Jn 4; **1:4** 1 Cor 4:15; *Gal 4:19*; 1 Jn 2:1

1 THE elder unto the wellbeloved Gaius, whom I love in the truth.
[2]Beloved, I wish above all things that thou mayest prosper and be in
health, even as thy soul prospereth.
[3]For I rejoiced greatly, when the brethren came and testified of the truth
that is in thee, even as thou walkest in the truth.
[4]I have no greater joy than to hear that my children walk in truth.

1:2 John rejoiced that Gaius prospered in spiritual matters and wished for him to prosper equally in physical health. Grace and health are two of God's best gifts.

II. TRUE WORKERS ENCOURAGED (5–8)

5 Beloved, thou doest faithfully whatsoever thou doest to the brethren,
and to strangers;
6 Which have borne witness of thy charity before the church: whom if
thou bring forward on their journey after a godly sort, thou shalt do well:
7 Because that for his name's sake they went forth, taking nothing of the
Gentiles.
8 We therefore ought to receive such, that we might be fellowhelpers to
the truth.

1:5 Rom 12:13; Heb 13:2; 1 Pet 4:10, 11
☆**1:6** Col 1:10; 1 Thess 1:12
1:7 Mt 10:9–14; Mk 6:8–13; Lk 9:3–5; 10:4–11; Acts 20:33

III. OPPONENTS OF TRUTH REBUKED (9, 10)

9 I wrote unto the church: but Di-ot're-phes, who loveth to have the
preeminence among them, receiveth us not.
10 Wherefore, if I come, I will remember his deeds which he doeth, prating
against us with malicious words: and not content therewith, neither doth he
himself receive the brethren, and forbiddeth them that would, and casteth
them out of the church.

☆**1:9** Mt 19:30; 20:16; Mk 10:31; Lk 13:30; Phil 2:3
1:10 3 Jn 5

IV. COMMENDING A WITNESS FOR TRUTH (11, 12)

11 Beloved, follow not that which is evil, but that which is good. He that
doeth good is of God: but he that doeth evil hath not seen God.
12 De-me'tri-us hath good report of all *men*, and of the truth itself: yea,
and we *also* bear record; and ye know that our record is true.

1:11 Ps 34:14; 1 Cor 4:16; 11:1; 1 Jn 2:29; 3:6, 9
☆**1:12** Jn 19:35; 21:24; Acts 6:3; 1 Thess 4:12; 1 Tim 3:7

V. CONCLUSION (13, 14)

13 I had many things to write, but I will not with ink and pen write unto
thee:
14 But I trust I shall shortly see thee, and we shall speak face to face. Peace
be to thee. *Our* friends salute thee. Greet the friends by name.

☆**1:13** 2 Jn 12
☆**1:14** 2 Jn 12

1:6 Gaius was a man of faith, sincere in his religious convictions, devoted to God, charitable (which included concern for the poor), and a provider of hospitality to traveling evangelists. The brethren in his church testified to his goodness. He was a faithful servant of Jesus Christ.

1:9 Compared to Gaius, Diotrephes was a disaster. Apparently he was an officer and minister in the church who was proud and ambitious. He had no use for the apostle's authority and talked against him. He disfellowshipped people at will, and otherwise lacked the graces displayed by Gaius.

1:12 The third person mentioned by John is Demetrius. He was held in esteem by all good men. He was a firm believer in whom John had confidence. Therefore he could recommend him highly and claim that his testimony was true and should therefore be trusted.

1:13, 14 John stopped writing, since he expected to see these people in person shortly. He preferred that to pen and ink. He asked Gaius to greet the friends, which obviously excluded the enemies.

THE GENERAL EPISTLE OF

JUDE

Authorship, date, and background Jude was the brother of James (Jude 1), who was the moderator of the Jerusalem church. In Mark 6:3 both of them are called the brothers of Jesus. Jude, like James, came to know Jesus the Christ as Savior subsequent to the resurrection. He was not an important figure in the early church. His letter in its style, vocabulary, and terseness is similar to the one written by his brother James. He was not listed among the apostles. The date of the letter is important because parts of it are similar to 2 Peter, and verses 17, 18 are verbatim quotations from 2 Peter 3:3. This is important to note because the letter of Jude was written after the destruction of Jerusalem. Peter was already dead; therefore, Peter could not have copied from Jude. Jude must have copied from Peter, unless they both copied from another source. Liberal scholars uniformly suppose that Peter copied from Jude and therefore have concluded that the apostle Peter did not write 2 Peter; it was written, in their opinion, in the second century. They also think the letter combated a heresy more in keeping with second century history than first. But this is very difficult to substantiate. Evangelical scholars, and the church through the ages, have accepted Jude as the author.

Nothing in the letter indicates specifically for whom it was intended. It was probably composed outside of Palestine and was intended for the Jews of the Diaspora (that is, the Jews who had been dispersed) who had come to the knowledge of Jesus Christ and were associated with the church. Jude's illustrations from the Old Testament involving obscure figures and his use of extrabiblical quotations suggest that his readers were familiar with these literary sources commonly known to Jews. The heresy Jude was combating was somehow connected with Gnosticism, based on the opinion that the grace of God allowed for fleshly indulgence since body and spirit were regarded as separate and unrelated. This allowed them to indulge with abandon in all kinds of licentious conduct and other evils.

Characteristics and content Jude articulates the foundational truths of the Christian faith as though they are well established and unchanging. He addresses his readers as "beloved," and has for his purpose the need to urge them to "contend for the faith which was once delivered unto the saints" (3). In doing so, he presents them with the consequences which fall on those who depart from the faith. First he speaks about Israel which had been saved out of Egypt, and when they distrusted God he destroyed them (5). He recalls God's awful judgment on the fallen angels who have been chained up in prisons, waiting for the judgment day (6). As if this were not enough, he cites the judgment of God against Sodom and Gomorrah which were destroyed by fire and thus continue to be a warning to us (7). These are sobering illustrations and hard words.

Jude also uses illustrations of persons who experienced the wrath of God: Cain, Balaam, and Korah (11). He quotes with approval from the noncanonical book of Enoch about the coming of the Lord with his holy ones to render judgment and mete out punishment to the wicked; he also quotes from the Assumption of Moses about the dispute between Michael and Satan over the body of Moses. These quotations from extrabiblical sources simply illustrate the point Jude makes. They were undoubtedly books familiar to his readers. He warns his readers to be careful and assures them that God "is able to keep you from falling, and to present you faultless before the presence of his glory with exceeding joy" (24).

Outline

I. Introduction (1–4)
II. Warning against false teachers (5–16)
III. Exhortation to faithfulness (17–23)
IV. Benediction (24, 25)

I. INTRODUCTION (1–4)

1 JUDE, the servant of Jesus Christ, and brother of James, to them that
are sanctified by God the Father, and preserved in Jesus Christ, *and*
called:
2 Mercy unto you, and peace, and love, be multiplied.
3 Beloved, when I gave all diligence to write unto you of the common
salvation, it was needful for me to write unto you, and exhort *you* that ye
should earnestly contend for the faith which was once delivered unto the
saints.
4 For there are certain men crept in unawares, who were before of old
ordained to this condemnation, ungodly men, turning the grace of our God
into lasciviousness, and denying the only Lord God, and our Lord Jesus
Christ.

II. WARNING AGAINST FALSE TEACHERS (5–16)

5 I will therefore put you in remembrance, though ye once knew this, how
that the Lord, having saved the people out of the land of Egypt, afterward
destroyed them that believed not.
6 And the angels which kept not their first estate, but left their own
habitation, he hath reserved in everlasting chains under darkness unto the
judgment of the great day.
7 Even as Sodom and Go-mor'rha, and the cities about them in like
manner, giving themselves over to fornication, and going after strange flesh,
are set forth for an example, suffering the vengeance of eternal fire.
8 Likewise also these *filthy* dreamers defile the flesh, despise dominion,
and speak evil of dignities.
9 Yet Michael the archangel, when contending with the devil he disputed
about the body of Moses, durst not bring against him a railing accusation,
but said, The Lord rebuke thee.
10 But these speak evil of those things which they know not: but what they
know naturally, as brute beasts, in those things they corrupt themselves.
11 Woe unto them! for they have gone in the way of Cain, and ran greedily
after the error of Ba'laam for reward, and perished in the gainsaying of
Co're.

☆**1:1** Mt 13:55; 1 Thess 5:24
1:2 Gal 6:16; 1 Pet 1:2
☆**1:3** Acts 20:27; 1 Cor 15:3–9; 1 Tim 6:12; Tit 1:4; 2 Pet 3:1, 2; Jude 20
1:4 Rom 6:1–4; Gal 6:13; 2 Tim 3:6; 1 Pet 2:16; 2 Pet 2:1–4, 10, 18–22; 2 Jn 7
1:5 Ex 14:21–31; Num 14:20–24; Deut 2:14, 15; 1 Cor 10:5–10
☆**1:6** Mt 25:31, 41; Mk 8:38; 2 Pet 2:4, 9; Rev 12:9
1:7 Gen 19:24, 25; Lev 18:22; 20:13; Deut 23:17, 18; 29:23; Lk 16:23; 2 Pet 2:2, 6; Rev 20:15; 21:8
1:8 2 Pet 2:10; Jude 4
☆**1:9** Deut 34:6; Dan 10:13, 20, 21; 12:1; Zech 3:2; Rev 12:7
1:10 Phil 3:19; 2 Pet 2:12
☆**1:11** Gen 4:3–16; Num 16:1–35; 22:20–33; 26:5–11; 31:16; Hab 2:6–19; Mt 11:21; 23:13–33; 2 Pet 2:15, 16; 1 Jn 3:12; Rev 2:14

1:1 Jude chooses to name himself as the brother of James, who was a half brother of Jesus. Thus Jude was also a half brother of the Lord after the flesh. But he does not press his family claim; instead, he identifies himself as a servant of Jesus Christ—as must all who have been redeemed through the blood of Jesus Christ. *sanctified . . . and preserved.* Whoever perishes because of his sins must bear the blame. But whoever is sanctified and preserved must ascribe all of this to God and his grace. Sanctification is not the work of the believer. It belongs to God and his grace.

1:3 Error is dangerous, so those who have the common faith must contend for it earnestly. This must not be done furiously but lawfully. And scolding is not always the best way to defend truth. "Ungodly men raise scruples, start questions, cause divisions, widen breaches, merely to advance and promote their own selfish, ambitious, and covetous ends. This has been the plague of the church in all past ages, and . . . no age is, or will be, wholly free from such men and practices as long as time shall last."*

1:6 The angels referred to here were obviously sinless and unfallen at one time. They "abandoned their original rank and left their proper home."* They were expelled from heaven, consigned to "hell and chains of darkness" (2 Pet. 2:4) where they await the last judgment and their final punishment. They will be cast into the lake of fire with their leader, Satan (Matt. 25:41; Rev. 20:7–15).

1:9 The dispute over the body of Moses is recounted in the Jewish apocryphal book titled "The Assumption of Moses." According to some of the early church fathers, Satan tried to claim the body of Moses for two reasons: (1) that he, Satan, was the lord of matter, to which the angel replied that God is Lord of all, since he created matter; (2) that Moses was a murderer and therefore his body belonged to Satan; at which accusation the angel said, "The Lord rebuke thee," and Satan fled (cf. Zech. 3:2).

1:11 See 2 Pet. 2:15. In both Jude and Peter the error or the "way of Balaam" pertains to the desire and greed for money. This differs from what is stated in Rev. 2:14, which has to do with the teaching of Balaam.

1:12 Prov 25:14 Mt 15:13 1 Cor 11:20–22 Phil 3:19 1 Thess 5:6, 7 Jas 5:5 2 Pet 2:13
1:13 Isa 57:20 Phil 3:19 2 Pet 2:17 Jude 6 Rev 20:10; 21:8
1:14☆ Gen 5:18–24 Deut 33:2 1 Chron 1:1–4
1:15 2 Pet 2:6
1:16 Num 14:36–38 Deut 1:27, 28 Isa 29:24 1 Thess 4:3–8 Jas 1:14, 15 1 Pet 2:3, 10, 18 Jude 18
1:17 Heb 2:3 2 Pet 3:2
1:18 2 Pet 3:3 Jude 16
1:19 Prov 18:1 1 Cor 2:14
1:20☆ Acts 9:31 Rom 8:15, 26, 27 Eph 4:12, 17, 18; 6:18 Col 2:7 Jude 3
1:21 2 Tim 4:8 Tit 2:13 Heb 9:28
1:23 Amos 4:11 Rom 11:14 1 Cor 5:5 Rev 3:4
1:24, 25☆ Jn 10:28, 29 Rom 14:4; 16:25 2 Cor 4:14 Eph 3:20 1 Pet 4:13

12 These are spots in your feasts of charity, when they feast with you,
feeding themselves without fear: clouds *they are* without water, carried
about of winds; trees whose fruit withereth, without fruit, twice dead,
plucked up by the roots;
13 Raging waves of the sea, foaming out their own shame; wandering
stars, to whom is reserved the blackness of darkness for ever.
14 And E'noch also, the seventh from Adam, prophesied of these, saying,
Behold, the Lord cometh with ten thousands of his saints,
15 To execute judgment upon all, and to convince all that are ungodly
among them of all their ungodly deeds which they have ungodly com-
mitted, and of all their hard *speeches* which ungodly sinners have spoken
against him.
16 These are murmurers, complainers, walking after their own lusts; and
their mouth speaketh great swelling *words*, having men's persons in
admiration because of advantage.

III. EXHORTATION TO FAITHFULNESS (17–23)

17 But, beloved, remember ye the words which were spoken before of the
apostles of our Lord Jesus Christ;
18 How that they told you there should be mockers in the last time, who
should walk after their own ungodly lusts.
19 These be they who separate themselves, sensual, having not the Spirit.
20 But ye, beloved, building up yourselves on your most holy faith,
praying in the Holy Ghost,
21 Keep yourselves in the love of God, looking for the mercy of our Lord
Jesus Christ unto eternal life.
22 And of some have compassion, making a difference:
23 And others save with fear, pulling *them* out of the fire; hating even the
garment spotted by the flesh.

IV. BENEDICTION (24, 25)

24 Now unto him that is able to keep you from falling, and to present *you*
faultless before the presence of his glory with exceeding joy,
25 To the only wise God our Saviour, *be* glory and majesty, dominion and
power, both now and ever. Amen.

1:14 The phrase translated *the seventh from Adam* (i.e., seven generations after Adam) appears in Enoch 60:8. The noncanonical book of Enoch contains portions that can be dated from the beginning of the Christian era. It contains this statement: "And behold! He cometh with ten thousand of His Holy ones to execute judgment upon all, and to destroy all the ungodly: and to convict all flesh of all the works of their ungodliness which they have ungodly committed, and of all the hard things which ungodly sinners have spoken against Him."

1:20 *praying in the Holy Ghost.* We do this when we submit ourselves to the guidance and the teaching of the Holy Spirit. Faith, fervency, and importunity constitute the right spirit for prayer. Whenever we truly pray in the Holy Spirit, great results will come.

1:24, 25 God is willing and able to keep his people from falling. And of those given to Jesus by the Father, none shall be lost (John 6:39). Our faults may fill us with fears, but our Redeemer has undertaken to present us faultless; and we shall be so presented. This apostolic benediction is used by many ministers to conclude a service of worship.

THE REVELATION OF SAINT JOHN THE DIVINE

Authorship, date, and background The book of the Revelation closes the canon of Scripture. It is appropriately placed at the end of the New Testament. The closing of the canon means that there is no new revelation given to men by God. The Old and New Testaments are all there is. The next revelation will be the revealing of the Son of God from heaven when Jesus comes the second time.

The Revelation itself claims to have come from John. When all of the scholarly claims have been examined, it boils down to the conclusion that John, the son of Zebedee, the brother of James, and the author of the Gospel of John and the three letters of John, wrote the book. He was an apostle, an eyewitness, and an aged saint. The book itself was written during the time of the persecution by Domitian, which places it in the last decade of the first century (ca. A.D. 96).

John, the author, had been imprisoned on the isle of Patmos. The stated reason for his imprisonment was that he was exiled there for preaching "the word of God, and for the testimony of Jesus" (1:9). It must be remembered that he was an eyewitness who had been with Jesus throughout the days of his ministry on this earth. Christianity, which had been regarded as a cult under the umbrella of Judaism, no longer enjoyed this protection. It was regarded as a new religion, and the stubborn refusal of Christians to bow before the emperor, who set himself up as God, occasioned their persecution. Toleration was no longer possible. The church was placed on the defensive, a situation which was to continue until Constantine's day, when the church was victorious over paganism for a time.

The Revelation is the only completely apocalyptic book in the New Testament. As such, it discloses things otherwise hidden which could only be made known by revelation from God. As an apocalyptic work it is similar to that of Daniel in the Old Testament. As a book of prophecy, it majors on future events. It fits into the history of that day when Christians were inclined toward despair because of the persecution they suffered. Their despair was offset only by the expectation of being saved by divine intervention on their behalf. Times of persecution usually brought forth apocalyptic books and this was one of those times. The book itself followed this type of literature with strange dreams and visions of a symbolic nature; with celestial beings and demonic powers fighting against each other; with the assurance of the victory of right over wrong, which included the deliverance of the righteous and the judgment of the wicked.

Characteristics and content The big question about The Revelation is: What does it all mean? The first three chapters are plain enough. They include the prologue, the vision, the portrait, and the messages to the seven churches of Asia. These are historic churches. John evaluates their strengths and weaknesses and warns them that their candlesticks may be removed. Beginning with chapter four, John writes about the seven seals, the seven trumpets, the seven signs, and the seven bowls. These are followed by the advent of Christ the conqueror, the binding of Satan, the millennial reign of the Lord, the last rebellion, the final judgment, and the new heavens and the new earth. The consummation brings with it the total end of evil and the total victory of God and good forever and ever. The real problem has to do with interpretation. What do these things mean? There have been four schools of thought.

The *Preterist School* holds that all of The Revelation pertains only to the events of that day. Nothing in the book is futuristic; that is, it has no predictive prophecy. This view commends itself to liberal scholars who do not believe in the possibility of predictive prophecy to begin with.

The second is the *Idealist School,* which holds that the book simply gives us a picture of the struggle between good and evil characteristic of all ages. This school does not think the symbols can be attached to any real historical events. The emphasis is on ethical and spiritual truths, not on historical happenings. By spiritualizing the book, it dehistoricizes it so that there is no climax to history when Jesus comes to sit on a visible throne in all of his glory.

The third school is known as the *Historicist School,* which claims that the book discloses in broad outline form the future course of history from the descent of the Holy Spirit to the second coming of Jesus. Major events in history since the age of the apostles are made known through the symbols in the book. The advocates of this view are not agreed about the meaning of each symbol. The seven seals are thought to represent the division of the Roman empire and its dissolution; the coming of the locusts is thought to represent the invasions of Europe by the Muslims.

The fourth school is the *Futurist School,* which holds generally that the first three chapters of The Revelation are historical and the remaining portions of the book, beginning with chapter four, have to do with the period at the end of the age, known as the Great Tribulation. These events are regarded as literally as possible and are thought to be wholly future.

Broadly speaking, most Christians today adhere to one of three interpretations of eschatology, each of which is related to the understanding of Revelation chapter 20. The three views are known as the postmillennial, the amillennial, and the premillennial.

Postmillennialism teaches that Satan is bound during this present age. The church will progress and an earthly millennium will come, at the end of which Jesus Christ will return. This view presents an optimistic account of the triumph of righteousness quite at variance with the experience of history. It is a view held by few Christians in our time, although it was strongly held by many in bygone ages.

Amillennialism interprets Revelation 20 in such a way as to foreclose any possibility of a future thousand-year millennium after the coming of the Lord during which time peace will reign and righteousness will prevail. So far as the events connected with the end of this age are concerned, the amillennialist is much in agreement with the premillennialist. In this view, the coming of Christ will not bring in the millennium. History, as we know it, will end with the return of the Lord, when the final judgment will take place and the eternal age will begin.

The premillennialist believes the course of history moves inevitably toward the climax of the age, the rapture of the church, and the second advent of Jesus. The closing days of the age will witness the coming of the Great Tribulation such as the world has never seen. At the end of this period Jesus will come again. He will then establish his thousand-year (millennial) kingdom on earth which will be a period of enforced righteousness. Satan will be bound for the thousand-year reign and loosed at the end of that time to commence the final episode in the history of man. Christ will be triumphant; the Devil and his hosts, including the unsaved, will be consigned to the Lake of Fire, while the righteous saints will live and reign with Christ in the city of God, the new Jerusalem, which comes down from God out of heaven.

Fundamentalists almost without exception hold to the premillennial viewpoint; among evangelicals there are premillennialists and amillennialists; liberals who take the Bible seriously generally fall into the postmillennial camp, although there are a few orthodox believers who hold this view too. Other liberals have no use for millennialism of any kind. Material on the rapture of the church will be found in the commentary notes to the text.

Outline

I. The prologue (1:1–8)
II. The first vision (1:9—3:22)
III. The second vision (4:1—16:21)
IV. The third vision (17:1—21:8)
V. The fourth vision (21:9—22:5)
VI. The epilogue (22:6–21)

I. THE PROLOGUE (1:1–8)
A. THE REVELATION OF JESUS CHRIST

1 THE Revelation of Jesus Christ, which God gave unto him, to shew
unto his servants things which must shortly come to pass; and he sent
and signified *it* by his angel unto his servant John:
2 Who bare record of the word of God, and of the testimony of Jesus
Christ, and of all things that he saw.
3 Blessed *is* he that readeth, and they that hear the words of this prophecy,
and keep those things which are written therein: for the time *is* at hand.

B. THE SALUTATION

4 JOHN to the seven churches which are in Asia: Grace *be* unto you, and
peace, from him which is, and which was, and which is to come; and from
the seven Spirits which are before his throne;
5 And from Jesus Christ, *who is* the faithful witness, *and* the first begotten
of the dead, and the prince of the kings of the earth. Unto him that loved
us, and washed us from our sins in his own blood,
6 And hath made us kings and priests unto God and his Father; to him *be*
glory and dominion for ever and ever. Amen.
7 Behold, he cometh with clouds; and every eye shall see him, and they
also which pierced him: and all kindreds of the earth shall wail because of
him. Even so, Amen.
8 I am Alpha and Omega, the beginning and the ending, saith the Lord,
which is, and which was, and which is to come, the Almighty.

II. THE FIRST VISION (1:9—3:22)
A. THE VOICE AND THE VISION

9 I John, who also am your brother, and companion in tribulation, and in
the kingdom and patience of Jesus Christ, was in the isle that is called
Patmos, for the word of God, and for the testimony of Jesus Christ.
10 I was in the Spirit on the Lord's day, and heard behind me a great
voice, as of a trumpet,
11 Saying, I am Alpha and Omega, the first and the last: and, What thou
seest, write in a book, and send *it* unto the seven churches which are in
Asia; unto Eph′e-sus, and unto Smyrna, and unto Per′ga-mos, and unto
Thy-a-ti′ra, and unto Sardis, and unto Philadelphia, and unto La-od-i-ce′a.

☆**1:1** Dan 2:28–45; Jn 12:49; 17:8; Rev 22:6, 8, 16
☆**1:2** Rev 1:9; 12:17
☆**1:3** Lk 11:28; Rom 13:11; 1 Pet 4:7; Rev 3:11; 22:7, 10
☆**1:4** Ex 3:14; Ps 90:2; Isa 11:2; 43:13; Zech 3:9; 4:2–6; Jn 1:1, 2; 8:58; 1 Cor 12:4–13; Heb 1:10–13; Jas 1:17
1:5 Deut 7:8; 23:5; Zech 13:1; Rom 8:37; 1 Cor 15:20; Eph 1:20; Col 1:18; Heb 9:11–14; Rev 3:14; 17:14
1:6 Ex 19:6; Dan 4:34; Rom 11:36; 1 Tim 6:16; 1 Pet 2:5, 9; Jude 24, 25
1:7 Dan 7:13; Zech 12:10; Jn 19:36, 37; Heb 10:29
☆**1:8** Isa 41:4; 48:12; 2 Cor 6:18; Rev 21:6; 22:13
1:9 Rom 8:17; Phil 4:14; 2 Thess 3:5; Rev 1:6; 3:10
1:10 Acts 20:7; Rev 21:10
☆**1:11** Deut 31:19; Isa 30:8; Jer 30:2; Hab 2:2

1:1 *Revelation* differs from *inspiration.* Revelation is the self-disclosure of God and the revealing to men of that which they could not know by themselves. Some Scriptures were written by men who had immediate access to the information; some were passed down to them in written records or by word of mouth. The Revelation of John was given to him immediately. *Irrespective of the source of their information, whether* by oral tradition, written records, or revelation, the writers through inspiration by the Holy Spirit chose the right material and gave us a Bible free from all error in the whole and in the part. This view does not demand that those who copied the Bible were kept free from incidental, transcriptional errors, which have been corrected by textual criticism. Some hold there were incidental errors in the original manuscripts, but the churches through the ages, until recently, have believed in an inerrant Bible.

1:2 John was the recipient of the revelation. He received it from the angel, who was acting under the direction of Jesus Christ, who received the revelation from the Father. The Revelation is about Jesus and came from him as well.

1:3 This book is important, for it promises that those who read it are blessed, those who hear it are blessed, and those who keep the things written therein are blessed.

1:4 *which is, and which was, and which is to come.* The Father here is spoken of in terms of his eternal being. *the seven spirits* indicates the Holy Spirit in terms of his perfection and completeness. The number seven is used as a symbol for this.

1:8 *I am Alpha and Omega.* This has to do with God's almighty power, not his eternity of existence. All events are controlled by him: what was, is, and will come to pass.

1:11 The letters or messages to the seven churches refer to (1) literal churches in existence at the time John wrote; (2) conditions that existed in those and other churches of the age; (3) similar conditions in the

1:12 Ex 25:31–39 Zech 4:2–6 Rev 1:17, 20
1:13 Dan 10:5, 6 Rev 2:1; 14:14 15:6
1:14 Dan 7:9, 10 10:6 Mt 28:3 Rev 2:18; 19:12
1:15 Ezek 43:2 Dan 10:6 Rev 2:18; 14:2 19:6
1:16 Judg 5:31 Isa 49:2 Mt 17:2 Eph 6:17 Heb 4:12 Rev 1:20; 2:12 10:1; 19:15
1:17, 18 Isa 41:4 Ezek 1:27, 28 Dan 8:17, 18 10:8, 9, 17–19 Lk 24:5 Rev 2:8
1:19 Rev 1:11–16 4:1
1:20 Zech 4:2 Rom 11:25 Rev 1:4, 11, 16 2:1; 3:1

12 And I turned to see the voice that spake with me. And being turned, I saw seven golden candlesticks;

13 And in the midst of the seven candlesticks *one* like unto the Son of man, clothed with a garment down to the foot, and girt about the paps with a golden girdle.

14 His head and *his* hairs *were* white like wool, as white as snow; and his eyes *were* as a flame of fire;

15 And his feet like unto fine brass, as if they burned in a furnace; and his voice as the sound of many waters.

16 And he had in his right hand seven stars: and out of his mouth went a sharp twoedged sword: and his countenance *was* as the sun shineth in his strength.

17 And when I saw him, I fell at his feet as dead. And he laid his right hand upon me, saying unto me, Fear not; I am the first and the last:

18 *I am* he that liveth, and was dead; and, behold, I am alive for evermore, Amen; and have the keys of hell and of death.

19 Write the things which thou hast seen, and the things which are, and the things which shall be hereafter;

20 The mystery of the seven stars which thou sawest in my right hand, and the seven golden candlesticks. The seven stars are the angels of the seven churches: and the seven candlesticks which thou sawest are the seven churches.

B. THE MESSAGES TO THE SEVEN CHURCHES

1. The Message to Ephesus

2:1☆ Rev 1:11–16
2:2 Mt 7:23 2 Cor 11:13 1 Jn 4:1 Rev 2:19
2:3 Jn 15:21 Heb 12:1–13
2:4 Jer 2:2 Mt 24:12 Jas 2:14–16
2:5 Hos 14:1 Heb 10:32 Rev 1:20; 3:3, 19
2:6☆ Num 31:15, 16 Rev 2:15

2 UNTO the angel of the church of Eph′e-sus write; These things saith he that holdeth the seven stars in his right hand, who walketh in the midst of the seven golden candlesticks;

2 I know thy works, and thy labour, and thy patience, and how thou canst not bear them which are evil: and thou hast tried them which say they are apostles, and are not, and hast found them liars:

3 And hast borne, and hast patience, and for my name's sake hast laboured, and hast not fainted.

4 Nevertheless I have *somewhat* against thee, because thou hast left thy first love.

5 Remember therefore from whence thou art fallen, and repent, and do the first works; or else I will come unto thee quickly, and will remove thy candlestick out of his place, except thou repent.

6 But this thou hast, that thou hatest the deeds of the Nic-o-la′i-tanes, which I also hate.

---

church or churches of Jesus Christ in later ages. Some interpreters think the seven churches represent seven successive epochs of church history between the beginning and the end of the present age of the Holy Spirit. This view has serious defects, particularly since it identifies the Protestant Reformation with the Sardis church, which is said to be more dead than alive! (See 3:1.) While these letters may not be applied to particular periods in church history, it is true that during the *end times, there will be an* intensifying of the evils mentioned in these letters, particularly the lukewarmness, the nakedness, and shame of the Laodicean church.

2:1 *Ephesus* was one of the strategic centers of the Roman world. A church was established there. The city was in a state of decline for some centuries. It had once been a seaport, but silt from the river around which the city was built eventually left Ephesus seven miles from the Mediterranean Sea. The pagan temple was one of the wonders of the world. It was said to have been four times the size of Athens' Parthenon. It was destroyed when the Goths sacked Ephesus in A.D. 263. The Council of Ephesus convened in that city in A.D. 431. Today it is a vast archeological dig, being gradually uncovered to reveal the ancient splendor of a pagan metropolis.

2:6 The *Nicolaitans* were a heretical group tolerated by the church of Pergamum, but rejected by the church at Ephesus. They were antinomians who made license out of liberty. Early church fathers such as Irenaeus, Clement, and Tertullian wrote about their carnal living and their vices.

[7]He that hath an ear, let him hear what the Spirit saith unto the
churches; To him that overcometh will I give to eat of the tree of life, which
is in the midst of the paradise of God.

2:7 Gen 2:9; 3:22–24; Prov 3:18; 11:30; 13:12; Rev 22:2, 14

2. The Message to Smyrna

[8]And unto the angel of the church in Smyrna write; These things saith
the first and the last, which was dead, and is alive;
[9]I know thy works, and tribulation, and poverty, (but thou art rich) and
I know the blasphemy of them which say they are Jews, and are not, but *are*
the synagogue of Satan.
[10]Fear none of those things which thou shalt suffer: behold, the devil
shall cast *some* of you into prison, that ye may be tried; and ye shall have
tribulation ten days: be thou faithful unto death, and I will give thee a
crown of life.
[11]He that hath an ear, let him hear what the Spirit saith unto the
churches; He that overcometh shall not be hurt of the second death.

☆2:8 Rev 1:8, 11, 17, 18
2:9 Mt 4:10; Rom 2:17; 2 Cor 6:10; 8:9; Jas 2:5; Rev 1:9; 2:13, 24
2:10 Dan 1:12, 14; 3:16–18; 1 Cor 9:25; Jas 1:12; Rev 3:10; 12:11; 17:14
2:11 Rev 2:7, 29; 20:6, 14

3. The Message to Pergamos

[12]And to the angel of the church in Per′ga-mos write; These things saith
he which hath the sharp sword with two edges;
[13]I know thy works, and where thou dwellest, *even* where Satan's seat *is:*
and thou holdest fast my name, and hast not denied my faith, even in those
days wherein An′ti-pas *was* my faithful martyr, who was slain among you,
where Satan dwelleth.
[14]But I have a few things against thee, because thou hast there them that
hold the doctrine of Ba′laam, who taught Balac to cast a stumblingblock
before the children of Israel, to eat things sacrificed unto idols, and to
commit fornication.
[15]So hast thou also them that hold the doctrine of the Nic-o-la′i-tanes,
which thing I hate.
[16]Repent; or else I will come unto thee quickly, and will fight against
them with the sword of my mouth.
[17]He that hath an ear, let him hear what the Spirit saith unto the
churches; To him that overcometh will I give to eat of the hidden manna,
and will give him a white stone, and in the stone a new name written, which
no man knoweth saving he that receiveth *it.*

☆2:12 Rev 1:16; 2:16
2:13 Mt 4:10; Rev 14:12
☆2:14 Num 31:16; Acts 15:27–29; 1 Cor 6:13–20; 2 Pet 2:15; Rev 2:20
2:15 Rev 2:6
2:16 Acts 17:30, 31; Eph 6:17; 2 Thess 2:8; Rev 1:16; 2:5; 22:7
2:17 Isa 56:5; 62:2; 65:15; Prov 3:32; 14:10; Jn 6:49–58; Rev 2:7; 14:3; 19:12

2:8 *Smyrna* now is called Izmir and is the only one of the seven churches of Asia that is alive and flourishing today. It lies at the head of the gulf into which the *Hermus River flows. This seaport is still important and* is under the control of Turkey. Polycarp, the bishop of Smyrna, was martyred there in A.D. 155. How the Christian faith came into Smyrna is not known exactly. The city was the last to fall under the military advance of Islam. Wherever Islam gained control, the advance of the Christian faith was halted and reversed.

2:12 *Pergamos* (or Pergamum) was the capital city of the Roman province of Pergamum in Asia. It was a center for pagan worship. The imperial cult built around the Roman emperor required citizens to burn a pinch of incense at the foot of Caesar's statue. The Nicolaitans thought a little compromise would preserve the faith and keep the anti-Christian sentiment at a minimum. The apostles knew that no compromise was possible. To allow the pinch of incense to be offered before the emperor would lead to a landslide away from the true faith. They resisted it vigorously. Christianity and Caesarism faced off against each other to the death. Today Pergamum is an archeological ruin.

2:14 The teaching of Balaam should be distinguished from the way of Balaam or the error of Balaam (see 2 Pet. 2:15 and Jude 11). Balaam taught King Balak to entice Israel to worship idols, to marry his unbelieving subjects, and to partake of their ritual prostitution (Num. 31:15, 16). Multitudes of well-meaning Christians who have married unbelievers have lost their spirituality and have backslidden from the true faith.

4. The Message to Thyatira

18 And unto the angel of the church in Thy-a-ti′ra write; These things
saith the Son of God, who hath his eyes like unto a flame of fire, and his
feet *are* like fine brass;
19 I know thy works, and charity, and service, and faith, and thy patience,
and thy works; and the last *to be* more than the first.
20 Notwithstanding I have a few things against thee, because thou
sufferest that woman Jez′e-bel, which calleth herself a prophetess, to teach
and to seduce my servants to commit fornication, and to eat things
sacrificed unto idols.
21 And I gave her space to repent of her fornication; and she repented not.
22 Behold, I will cast her into a bed, and them that commit adultery with
her into great tribulation, except they repent of their deeds.
23 And I will kill her children with death; and all the churches shall know
that I am he which searcheth the reins and hearts: and I will give unto every
one of you according to your works.
24 But unto you I say, and unto the rest in Thy-a-ti′ra, as many as have
not this doctrine, and which have not known the depths of Satan, as they
speak; I will put upon you none other burden.
25 But that which ye have *already* hold fast till I come.
26 And he that overcometh, and keepeth my works unto the end, to him
will I give power over the nations:
27 And he shall rule them with a rod of iron; as the vessels of a potter shall
they be broken to shivers: even as I received of my Father.
28 And I will give him the morning star.
29 He that hath an ear, let him hear what the Spirit saith unto the
churches.

5. The Message to Sardis

3 AND unto the angel of the church in Sardis write; These things saith
he that hath the seven Spirits of God, and the seven stars; I know thy
works, that thou hast a name that thou livest, and art dead.
2 Be watchful, and strengthen the things which remain, that are ready to
die: for I have not found thy works perfect before God.
3 Remember therefore how thou hast received and heard, and hold fast,
and repent. If therefore thou shalt not watch, I will come on thee as a thief,
and thou shalt not know what hour I will come upon thee.

2:18☆ Rev 1:11, 14; 2:24
2:19 Rev 2:2
2:20☆ 1 Kgs 16:31; 2 Kgs 9:7; Acts 15:29; 1 Cor 10:20
2:21 Rom 2:4, 5; 2 Pet 3:9; Rev 9:20
2:22 Rev 17:2
2:23 Deut 13:11; 21:21; Ps 7:9; 26:2; 139:1; Jer 11:20; Mt 16:27; Lk 16:15; Rom 8:27
2:24 1 Cor 2:10; Rev 2:18; 3:11
2:25 Rev 3:11
2:26 Dan 7:22; Ps 2:8; Mt 10:22; 19:28; Lk 22:29, 30; 1 Cor 6:3, 4; Heb 3:6; Rev 2:7; 3:21; 20:4
2:27 Ps 2:8, 9; Isa 30:14; Rev 12:5
2:28 2 Pet 1:19; Rev 22:16
3:1☆ 1 Tim 5:6; Rev 1:4, 11, 16; 3:8, 15
3:2☆
3:3 Ezek 16:61–63; Mt 24:42, 43; 1 Thess 5:2–6; 1 Pet 3:10; Rev 2:5; 16:15

2:18 *Thyatira* was founded by Seleucus I, a general of Alexander, who located the city on a valley road between the Hermus and Caicus rivers. It was twenty miles southeast of Pergamum. It was a commercial center engaged in vigorous trade. The trade guilds were pagan in orientation and their social events were interlaced with pagan rituals, making it difficult for Christians to stay in business while refusing to participate in the social excesses. The Nicolaitans sought a compromise, but it was rejected by John, who demanded maintaining Christian principles. The modern city is known as Akhisar and has a small population.
2:20 *Jezebel's* teaching at Thyatira was the same as that of Balaam (2:14)—to practice immorality and eat food sacrificed to idols. These were sins of idolatry and immorality which commonly went together in pagan religions, in which sex indulgence was part of cult practices. We do not know whether this was a real Jezebel or simply a title applied to a woman whose life resembled that of Jezebel in the Old Testament (cf. 1 Kings 16:31; 2 Kings 9:22).
3:1 *Sardis* is associated with the name of Croesus, who brought wealth, prosperity, and doom to this ancient capital and royal seat. Under Roman auspices it became an administrative center of Roman Asia. The worship of Cybele along with the Caesar cult was prominent there. The temple of Artemis apparently was changed into a Christian place of assembly. The site is only an archeological dig today in an area beset by earthquakes. *he that hath the seven Spirits of God.* This refers to Jesus Christ, the anointed One, on whom the Holy Spirit abides in all his power and perfection, which is symbolized by the number seven.
3:2 This church manifests no fruit in the spiritual realm: sinners are not being saved, the church members are not being sanctified, and the needy are not being helped. The church members themselves are living sinful lives.

4 Thou hast a few names even in Sardis which have not defiled their
garments; and they shall walk with me in white: for they are worthy.
5 He that overcometh, the same shall be clothed in white raiment; and I
will not blot out his name out of the book of life, but I will confess his name
before my Father, and before his angels.
6 He that hath an ear, let him hear what the Spirit saith unto the churches.

3:4 Rev 3:5; 4:4; 6:11; 19:14
3:5 Ex 32:32; Deut 9:14; Ps 49:28; Mt 10:32; Lk 10:20; 12:8; Rev 13:8; 17:8; 20:12
3:6 Rev 2:7

6. The Message to Philadelphia

7 And to the angel of the church in Philadelphia write; These things saith
he that is holy, he that is true, he that hath the key of David, he that
openeth, and no man shutteth; and shutteth, and no man openeth;
8 I know thy works: behold, I have set before thee an open door, and no
man can shut it: for thou hast a little strength, and hast kept my word, and
hast not denied my name.
9 Behold, I will make them of the synagogue of Satan, which say they are
Jews, and are not, but do lie; behold, I will make them to come and worship
before thy feet, and to know that I have loved thee.
10 Because thou hast kept the word of my patience, I also will keep thee
from the hour of temptation, which shall come upon all the world, to try
them that dwell upon the earth.
11 Behold, I come quickly: hold that fast which thou hast, that no man
take thy crown.
12 Him that overcometh will I make a pillar in the temple of my God, and
he shall go no more out: and I will write upon him the name of my God,
and the name of the city of my God, *which is* new Jerusalem, which cometh
down out of heaven from my God: and *I will write upon him* my new name.
13 He that hath an ear, let him hear what the Spirit saith unto the
churches.

☆**3:7** Job 12:14; Isa 6:3; 22:22; Mt 16:19; Lk 1:32; Heb 7:26; 1 Jn 5:20
☆**3:8** Acts 14:27; Rev 2:13
3:9 Isa 43:4; 45:14; 49:23; 60:14; Zech 8:20–23; Acts 16:37–39; Rev 2:9
3:10 Jn 17:6; 2 Tim 2:12; 2 Pet 2:9; Rev 2:10; 3:8
3:11 Rev 2:10, 25; 22:7, 12, 20
3:12 1 Kgs 7:21; Jer 1:18; Ezek 48:35; Gal 4:26, 27; Eph 3:15; Heb 12:22; Rev 14:1, 21; 21:2; 22:4

7. The Message to Laodicea

14 And unto the angel of the church of the La-od-i-ce′ans write; These
things saith the Amen, the faithful and true witness, the beginning of the
creation of God;
15 I know thy works, that thou art neither cold nor hot: I would thou wert
cold or hot.
16 So then because thou art lukewarm, and neither cold nor hot, I will
spue thee out of my mouth.
17 Because thou sayest, I am rich, and increased with goods, and have
need of nothing; and knowest not that thou art wretched, and miserable,
and poor, and blind, and naked:

☆**3:14** Jn 1:3; 2 Cor 1:20; Col 1:15–18; Heb 13:8; Rev 1:5; 21:6
3:15 Rom 12:11; Rev 3:1
3:17 Hos 12:8; Zech 11:5; Mt 5:3; 1 Cor 4:8

3:7, 8 *Philadelphia,* a significant center of influence, was built on the fault line of a major volcanic area. It has disappeared into history. There was an active synagogue in the city whose members were intensely nationalistic and persecuted those who joined the Christian cult. Centuries later the Moslem advance found this conclave an "island of Christian civilization in the Turkish sea."*

No word of reproof is spoken to the church of Philadelphia. The church had great opportunities but it was small, uninfluential, and had little power. The saints were persecuted and further severe trials could be expected. Christ says he has the key of David (3:7) to open doors that no man can shut. The key symbolizes his rule and authority, which covers heaven and earth.

3:14 Laodicea became an important trading center during the period of the Roman supremacy. It was also a military outpost. Its wealth came from its famous black sheep and a poultice used in connection with diseases of the eye. The Christian faith in this center was intimately connected with the missionary interest and emphasis in the surrounding churches at Ephesus and Colosse. John's advice about the Laodecians' need to become poor, blind, and naked was based on his knowledge of their wealth, their woolen clothing, and the poultice for eye diseases—referred to in the phrase "anoint thine eyes with eye-salve." The site of the city is a ruins today.

3:18 Isa 55:1; 61:1, 10; Mt 13:44; 1 Cor 3:12, 13; 1 Pet 1:7; Rev 3:4; 16:15
3:19 Job 5:17; 1 Cor 11:32; Heb 12:6; Rev 2:5
3:20 Song 5:2; Mt 24:33; Lk 12:36; Jn 10:3; 14:23; Jas 5:9
3:21 Mt 19:28; 2 Tim 2:12; Rev 5:5; 6:2; 17:14; 20:4
3:22 Rev 2:7

18 I counsel thee to buy of me gold tried in the fire, that thou mayest be
rich; and white raiment, that thou mayest be clothed, and *that* the shame of
thy nakedness do not appear; and anoint thine eyes with eyesalve, that thou
mayest see.
19 As many as I love, I rebuke and chasten: be zealous therefore, and
repent.
20 Behold, I stand at the door, and knock: if any man hear my voice, and
open the door, I will come in to him, and will sup with him, and he with me.
21 To him that overcometh will I grant to sit with me in my throne, even
as I also overcame, and am set down with my Father in his throne.
22 He that hath an ear, let him hear what the Spirit saith unto the
churches.

III. THE SECOND VISION (4:1—16:21)

A. THE SCENE IN HEAVEN

1. Worship in Heaven

4:1☆ Ezek 1:1; Mt 3:16; Rev 1:10, 19; 11:12; 19:11
4:2☆ Isa 6:1; Ezek 1:26; Dan 7:9; Rev 1:10; 4:9
4:3☆ Ezek 1:28; 28:13; Rev 10:1; 21:11, 19, 20
4:4 Mt 19:28; 2 Tim 2:12; Rev 11:16; 20:4
4:5 Ex 25:31–39; Ps 18:13, 14; Joel 3:16; Zech 4:2–6; Rev 1:4; 5:6
4:6☆ Ezek 1:5–14; 10:12, 14; Rev 15:7; 19:4
4:7 Ezek 1:10; 10:21
4:8☆ Isa 6:3; 62:1, 6, 7; Acts 20:31; 1 Thess 2:9; Heb 13:8; Rev 1:4, 8
4:9 Ps 47:8; Dan 4:34; 12:7; Rev 4:2; 10:6; 15:7
4:10 Rev 4:4; 5:8, 14; 10:6; 11:16

4 AFTER this I looked, and, behold, a door *was* opened in heaven: and
the first voice which I heard *was* as it were of a trumpet talking with
me; which said, Come up hither, and I will shew thee things which must be
hereafter.
2 And immediately I was in the spirit: and, behold, a throne was set in
heaven, and *one* sat on the throne.
3 And he that sat was to look upon like a jasper and a sardine stone: and
there was a rainbow round about the throne, in sight like unto an emerald.
4 And round about the throne *were* four and twenty seats: and upon the
seats I saw four and twenty elders sitting, clothed in white raiment; and
they had on their heads crowns of gold.
5 And out of the throne proceeded lightnings and thunderings and voices:
and *there were* seven lamps of fire burning before the throne, which are the
seven Spirits of God.
6 And before the throne *there was* a sea of glass like unto crystal: and in
the midst of the throne, and round about the throne, *were* four beasts full of
eyes before and behind.
7 And the first beast *was* like a lion, and the second beast like a calf, and
the third beast had a face as a man, and the fourth beast *was* like a flying
eagle.
8 And the four beasts had each of them six wings about *him;* and *they*
were full of eyes within: and they rest not day and night, saying, Holy, holy,
holy, Lord God Almighty, which was, and is, and is to come.
9 And when those beasts give glory and honour and thanks to him that sat
on the throne, who liveth for ever and ever,
10 The four and twenty elders fall down before him that sat on the throne,
and worship him that liveth for ever and ever, and cast their crowns before
the throne, saying,

4:1 *Come up hither* is understood by some in the dispensational tradition to mean the pretribulation rapture of the church. It is hard to see how this verse supports that view since it was spoken to John, who *was then in the Spirit before the* throne. While it is true that the word for "church" is not used again until the end of the Revelation, the view is based on inference.
4:2, 3 The one seated on the throne is God Almighty, the God of Israel. The jasper stone may symbolize the holiness of God and the sardine stone (sardius or carnelian) God's divine wrath. The rainbow bespeaks the unfailing mercy of God.
4:6 *four beasts.* Commentators differ on the meaning of the four beasts. They may be angelic beings so described with animal-like comparisons denoting their strength (lion), their service (an ox), their intelligence (a man), and their speed (an eagle).
4:8 The praises of these creatures start with the holiness of God, go on to stress his omnipotence, and end with his eternity ("who was . . . is . . . and is to come"). All of the Revelation emphasizes the Second Advent and the consummation of history.

11 Thou art worthy, O Lord, to receive glory and honour and power: for
thou hast created all things, and for thy pleasure they are and were created.

2. The Book (Scroll) Opened and the Lamb Worshipped

5 AND I saw in the right hand of him that sat on the throne a book
written within and on the backside, sealed with seven seals.
2 And I saw a strong angel proclaiming with a loud voice, Who is worthy
to open the book, and to loose the seals thereof?
3 And no man in heaven, nor in earth, neither under the earth, was able to
open the book, neither to look thereon.
4 And I wept much, because no man was found worthy to open and to
read the book, neither to look thereon.
5 And one of the elders saith unto me, Weep not: behold, the Lion of the
tribe of Juda, the Root of David, hath prevailed to open the book, and to
loose the seven seals thereof.
6 And I beheld, and, lo, in the midst of the throne and of the four beasts,
and in the midst of the elders, stood a Lamb as it had been slain, having
seven horns and seven eyes, which are the seven Spirits of God sent forth
into all the earth.
7 And he came and took the book out of the right hand of him that sat
upon the throne.
8 And when he had taken the book, the four beasts and four *and* twenty
elders fell down before the Lamb, having every one of them harps, and
golden vials full of odours, which are the prayers of saints.
9 And they sung a new song, saying, Thou art worthy to take the book,
and to open the seals thereof: for thou wast slain, and hast redeemed us to
God by thy blood out of every kindred, and tongue, and people, and
nation;
10 And hast made us unto our God kings and priests: and we shall reign
on the earth.
11 And I beheld, and I heard the voice of many angels round about the
throne and the beasts and the elders: and the number of them was ten
thousand times ten thousand, and thousands of thousands;
12 Saying with a loud voice, Worthy is the Lamb that was slain to receive
power, and riches, and wisdom, and strength, and honour, and glory, and
blessing.

☆**4:11** Acts 14:15; 17:24–26; Rev 10:6
☆**5:1** Isa 29:11; Ezek 2:9; Dan 12:4; Rev 5:7
5:2 Rev 10:1; 18:21
5:3 Phil 2:10
☆**5:5** Gen 49:9; Isa 11:1, 10; Jer 31:16; Lk 7:13; 8:52; Jn 20:13; Heb 2:10; 7:14, 25; Rev 22:16
☆**5:6** Isa 53:7; Zech 3:9; 4:10; Dan 8:3; Acts 8:32; 1 Pet 1:19; Rev 1:4, 4:5
☆**5:8** Ps 141:2; Rev 4:4, 10; 5:6, 11; 8:3, 4; 14:2; 15:2
☆**5:9** 1 Cor 6:20; 1 Pet 2–6; Rev 4:11; 7:9; 14:3; 15:3, 4
☆**5:10** Ex 19:6; Dan 7:18, 27; 1 Pet 2:5–9; Rev 1:6; 3:21; 20:4
☆**5:11** Deut 33:2; Ps 68:17; Dan 7:10; Heb 12:22; Rev 4:4, 6
5:12 Zech 13:7; Mt 28:18; Jn 3:35, 36; Rev 1:6; 4:11

4:11 *Thou art worthy.* This phrase was used to salute the emperor in a triumphal procession. *O Lord* ("our Lord and God" in the RSV; "our Lord and our God" in the NASB) was added by Domitian in the cult of emperor worship. Any such use by men pales into insignificance when compared to its use for our God.
5:1 The scroll or book is in the hands of Christ. He has all authority in heaven and on earth. He rules throughout history to insure the continuance of the church and the establishment of God's kingdom everywhere. The scroll is written on both sides. There is no room for any additions. All the decrees of God are contained on the scroll, which outlines all that will transpire until the end of this present age. John did not know what is written on the scroll, for the testimony was sealed until Jesus Christ opened the scroll (5:5).
5:5 There are two allusions here to Old Testament Scriptures that have distinct messianic implication. One is Gen. 49:9, 10, which speaks of a lion's whelp and of the sceptre not departing from him "until Shiloh come." The other is from Isa. 11:1, "a shoot out of the stock of Jesse" ("a rod out of the stem of Jesse," KJV).
5:6 See note to 3:1 on the sevenfold Spirit of God.
5:8 See note to Exod. 30:1 for information on the incense offering.
5:9, 10 *sang a new song.* It is new, for it goes beyond creation to redemption and exalts Jesus Christ, who is worthy because (1) he was slaughtered (i.e., he paid it all for sinners on the cross of Calvary); (2) he has redeemed sinners by his shed blood; (3) he has redeemed people from every tribe, nation, kindred, and tongue (i.e., he is the universal Redeemer); (4) the saved are made priests and kings unto their God; (5) we shall reign on earth with him.
5:11ff In this oratorio or praise the participants are living creatures, elders, angels, and all creation. The worship is to God on his throne and to the Lamb that was slain; both are God Almighty. At the end the four creatures shout, "Amen," and the elders fall down and worship.

5:13 Ps 96:11–13; Isa 24:14; 42:10; Rom 11:36; Phil 2:10, 11

[13]And every creature which is in heaven, and on the earth, and under the
earth, and such as are in the sea, and all that are in them, heard I saying,
Blessing, and honour, and glory, and power, *be* unto him that sitteth upon
the throne, and unto the Lamb for ever and ever.

5:14 Rev 4:6, 10; 7:11, 12

[14]And the four beasts said, Amen. And the four *and* twenty elders fell
down and worshipped him that liveth for ever and ever.

B. THE SEVEN SEALS

1. The White Horse

6:1 Rev 5:1, 6

6 AND I saw when the Lamb opened one of the seals, and I heard, as it
were the noise of thunder, one of the four beasts saying, Come and see.

6:2☆ Zech 6:1–3; Rev 10:3, 4; 14:14; 19:11

[2]And I saw, and behold a white horse: and he that sat on him had a bow;
and a crown was given unto him: and he went forth conquering, and to
conquer.

2. The Red Horse

6:3 Rev 4:7

[3]And when he had opened the second seal, I heard the second beast say,
Come and see.

6:4 Zech 1:8; 6:2; Mt 10:34; Jn 19:11

[4]And there went out another horse *that was* red: and *power* was given to
him that sat thereon to take peace from the earth, and that they should kill
one another: and there was given unto him a great sword.

3. The Black Horse

6:5☆ Ezek 4:16; Zech 6:2; Rev 4:7

[5]And when he had opened the third seal, I heard the third beast say,
Come and see. And I beheld, and lo a black horse; and he that sat on him
had a pair of balances in his hand.

6:6☆

[6]And I heard a voice in the midst of the four beasts say, A measure of
wheat for a penny, and three measures of barley for a penny; and *see* thou
hurt not the oil and the wine.

4. The Pale Horse

6:7 Rev 4:7

[7]And when he had opened the fourth seal, I heard the voice of the fourth
beast say, Come and see.

6:8 Prov 5:5; Jer 15:2; Ezek 5:12, 17; 14:21; Hos 13:14; Zech 6:3; Mt 11:23; Rev 1:18; 20:14

[8]And I looked, and behold a pale horse: and his name that sat on him
was Death, and Hell followed with him. And Power was given unto them
over the fourth part of the earth, to kill with sword, and with hunger, and
with death, and with the beasts of the earth.

5. The Souls of the Martyrs

6:9☆ Ex 29:12; Lev 4:7; Jn 16:2; Phil 2:17; 2 Tim 4:6; Rev 12:17; 20:4

[9]And when he had opened the fifth seal, I saw under the altar the souls of
them that were slain for the word of God, and for the testimony which they
held:

6:2 The white horse represents peace, which comes and goes during the course of this present age. The peace disappears when the second horse of red appears *to take peace from the earth.* In other words, war follows peace.

6:5 The white horse spoke of peace; the red horse of war. Now the black horse bespeaks famine. It is followed by the pale horse, which represents death, for famine is always followed by death. In war the sword kills, in famine starvation kills; and pestilence usually erupts to kill as well.

6:6 *A measure of wheat for a penny, and three measures of barley for a penny.* The penny (denarius) equaled a day's wage.

6:9 The four horses give way to a scene in heaven where the souls of the martyrs who have died for the true faith cry out for vengeance against their murderers. Their martyrdom has given way to the blessedness of their heavenly rest.

10 And they cried with a loud voice, saying, How long, O Lord, holy and
true, dost thou not judge and avenge our blood on them that dwell on the
earth?
11 And white robes were given unto every one of them; and it was said
unto them, that they should rest yet for a little season, until their
fellowservants also and their brethren, that should be killed as they *were,*
should be fulfilled.

6:10 Ps 79:10; Zech 1:12; Lk 18:7; Rev 3:7, 10; 19:2
6:11 Dan 12:13; 2 Thess 1:7; Heb 4:9; 11:40; Rev 3:5; 14:13

6. The Signs in Heaven

12 And I beheld when he had opened the sixth seal, and, lo, there was a
great earthquake; and the sun became black as sackcloth of hair, and the
moon became as blood;
13 And the stars of heaven fell unto the earth, even as a fig tree casteth her
untimely figs, when she is shaken of a mighty wind.
14 And the heaven departed as a scroll when it is rolled together; and
every mountain and island were moved out of their places.
15 And the kings of the earth, and the great men, and the rich men, and
the chief captains, and the mighty men, and every bondman, and every free
man, hid themselves in the dens and in the rocks of the mountains;
16 And said to the mountains and rocks, Fall on us, and hide us from the
face of him that sitteth on the throne, and from the wrath of the Lamb:
17 For the great day of his wrath is come; and who shall be able to stand?

☆**6:12** Isa 50:3; Joel 2:10; Mt 24:29; Acts 21:19, 20; Rev 16:18
6:13 Isa 34:4; Rev 8:10; 9:1
6:14 Ps 102:26; Isa 34:4; Jer 3:23; 4:23–26; Heb 1:10–12; 2 Pet 3:10; Rev 16:20; 21:1
☆**6:15** Isa 2:10, 19, 21; Mic 7:17; Heb 11:38
6:16 Lk 23:30; 2 Thess 1:7–9
6:17 Ps 76:7; Isa 13:6; 63:4; Zeph 1:14; Mal 3:2

7. The Parenthesis or Interlude

a. God's Servants Sealed

7 AND after these things I saw four angels standing on the four corners
of the earth, holding the four winds of the earth, that the wind should
not blow on the earth, nor on the sea, nor on any tree.
2 And I saw another angel ascending from the east, having the seal of the
living God: and he cried with a loud voice to the four angels, to whom it
was given to hurt the earth and the sea,
3 Saying, Hurt not the earth, neither the sea, nor the trees, till we have
sealed the servants of our God in their foreheads.
4 And I heard the number of them which were sealed: *and there were*
sealed an hundred *and* forty *and* four thousand of all the tribes of the
children of Israel.
5 Of the tribe of Juda *were* sealed twelve thousand. Of the tribe of Reuben
were sealed twelve thousand. Of the tribe of Gad *were* sealed twelve
thousand.

☆**7:1** Jer 49:36; Zech 6:5; Mt 24:31
7:2 Rev 9:14
7:3 Ezek 9:4, 6; Dan 6:16; Eph 4:30; 2 Tim 2:19; Rev 14:1; 22:4
☆**7:4** Rev 9:16; 14:1, 3

6:12 What the details of this passage mean is difficult to determine. But what is clear is that the impenitent, which covers all classes of society, seek to escape their doom but cannot do so. The great day of the wrath of God has come against them. Who can stand?
6:15 *So great are the physical disturbances that men* now seek to escape, desiring the mountains and the rocks to fall on them. They fear the One who sits on the throne and the Lamb. God and Christ are again linked together in cosmic power. Seven kinds of people are mentioned: kings, great men, rich men, chief captains, mighty men, slaves, and free men. No class or segment of unbelieving society is untouched.
7:1ff Six of the seven seals have been opened in chapter six. Before the seventh seal is opened there is an interlude, after which the last seal will be opened. There are now four angels covering the four corners of the earth and holding the four winds. The judgment that is about to fall is universal; no one can escape except those who are believers and are made secure by God (7:3). The sealing comes before the judgment itself falls. The sealed are those chosen by God. The seal guarantees the preservation of those sealed against the judgment that falls on the unsealed.
7:4-8 *one hundred and forty-four thousand.* The tribe of Dan is omitted. The tribe of Manasseh takes Dan's place. Ephraim, the brother of Manasseh, is also omitted (both Manasseh and Ephraim were sons of Joseph and grandsons of Jacob). The omission is curious since Ephraim was one of the most significant of the Jewish tribes. The number, 144,000, is probably not an exact number. Some think it represents the complete number of Jews, known to and elected by God, who will come to Christ during the period of the Great Tribulation. The number 144,000 occurs also in 14:1, 3.

6 Of the tribe of A'ser *were* sealed twelve thousand. Of the tribe of
Neph'tha-lim *were* sealed twelve thousand. Of the tribe of Ma-nas'ses *were*
sealed twelve thousand.
7 Of the tribe of Simeon *were* sealed twelve thousand. Of the tribe of Levi
were sealed twelve thousand. Of the tribe of Is'sa-char *were* sealed twelve
thousand.
8 Of the tribe of Zab'u-lon *were* sealed twelve thousand. Of the tribe of
Joseph *were* sealed twelve thousand. Of the tribe of Benjamin *were* sealed
twelve thousand.

b. The Tribulation Saints

9 After this I beheld, and, lo, a great multitude, which no man could
number, of all nations, and kindreds, and people, and tongues, stood before
the throne, and before the Lamb, clothed with white robes, and palms in
their hands;
10 And cried with a loud voice, saying, Salvation to our God which sitteth
upon the throne, and unto the Lamb.
11 And all the angels stood round about the throne, and *about* the elders
and the four beasts, and fell before the throne on their faces, and
worshipped God,
12 Saying, Amen: Blessing, and glory, and wisdom, and thanksgiving, and
honour, and power, and might, *be* unto our God for ever and ever. Amen.
13 And one of the elders answered, saying unto me, What are these which
are arrayed in white robes? and whence came they?
14 And I said unto him, Sir, thou knowest. And he said to me, These are
they which came out of great tribulation, and have washed their robes, and
made them white in the blood of the Lamb.
15 Therefore are they before the throne of God, and serve him day and
night in his temple: and he that sitteth on the throne shall dwell among
them.
16 They shall hunger no more, neither thirst any more; neither shall the
sun light on them, nor any heat.
17 For the Lamb which is in the midst of the throne shall feed them, and
shall lead them unto living fountains of waters: and God shall wipe away
all tears from their eyes.

8. The Seventh Seal: the Silence in Heaven

8 AND when he had opened the seventh seal, there was silence in heaven
about the space of half an hour.

7:9☆ Gen 22:17 Lev 23:40 Isa 2:2, 3; 43:6 Rev 3:5; 6:11; 5:9
7:10 Isa 43:11 Hos 13:4 Rev 5:13; 12:10 19:1 22:3
7:11 Rev 4:4, 6, 10
7:12 Rev 5:12, 14
7:13 Acts 3:12 Rev 7:9
7:14☆ Isa 1:18 Zech 3:3–5 Mt 24:21 Heb 9:14 1 Jn 1:7 Rev 6:11; 22:14
7:15 Isa 4:5, 6 Ezek 37:27 1 Cor 3:16 Rev 4:9; 11:19 22:3
7:16 Isa 49:10 Mt 5:6 Lk 6:21 Jas 1:11
7:17 Ps 23:1–5 Isa 25:8; 35:10 Jn 4:14; 10:11 Acts 20:28 1 Pet 5:2 Rev 21:4, 6 22:1
8:1☆ Rev 5:1, 9 6:1–17

7:9ff Here the scene changes from earth to heaven. For the encouragement of God's people they are assured that their sacrifices are not in vain. After the tribulation has passed, there will be triumph and reward for God's faithful people. All the difficulties and martyrdoms of life are transitory; at last, they give way to victory and perfection.
7:14 The *great tribulation* is that period of time just prior to the return of the Lord Jesus, a time when great trials and afflictions will come to believers. Many interpreters hold that the people of God will be cruelly dealt with and numbers of them will be martyred. Many hold that the period of the great tribulation is to be divided into two segments. During the first half of that period, the wrath of man will be poured out on the earth. During the second half, the wrath of God will be poured out. Pretribulation rapturists believe that the church will be taken away before the wrath of man starts. Midtribulationists believe that the church will experience the wrath of man but will be taken away before the wrath of God is poured out. Posttribulationists hold that the church will go through the entire period of the tribulation; they will experience the wrath of man but be supernaturally kept from the wrath of God. None of these three views is *explicitly* taught in the Scriptures. We do well not to be dogmatic. What is clear from this passage is that some believers do suffer during some part of this period—whether they are those converted during the tribulation or they belonged to Christ before the tribulation period began.
8:1 The silence here means that there is an interruption for a short time. The contents of the seventh seal will be revealed shortly. But the end will not come until they have been made known. The seven trumpets and the seven bowls constitute the contents of the seventh seal.

2 And I saw the seven angels which stood before God; and to them were
given seven trumpets.
3 And another angel came and stood at the altar, having a golden censer;
and there was given unto him much incense, that he should offer *it* with the
prayers of all saints upon the golden altar which was before the throne.
4 And the smoke of the incense, *which came* with the prayers of the saints,
ascended up before God out of the angel's hand.
5 And the angel took the censer, and filled it with fire of the altar, and cast
it into the earth: and there were voices, and thunderings, and lightnings,
and an earthquake.

C. THE SEVEN TRUMPETS
1. Hail, Fire, and Blood

6 And the seven angels which had the seven trumpets prepared themselves
to sound.
7 The first angel sounded, and there followed hail and fire mingled with
blood, and they were cast upon the earth: and the third part of trees was
burnt up, and all green grass was burnt up.

2. The Sea Turned into Blood

8 And the second angel sounded, and as it were a great mountain burning
with fire was cast into the sea: and the third part of the sea became blood;
9 And the third part of the creatures which were in the sea, and had life,
died; and the third part of the ships were destroyed.

3. The Falling Star

10 And the third angel sounded, and there fell a great star from heaven,
burning as it were a lamp, and it fell upon the third part of the rivers, and
upon the fountains of waters;
11 And the name of the star is called Wormwood: and the third part of the
waters became wormwood; and many men died of the waters, because they
were made bitter.

4. Sun, Moon, and Stars Darkened

12 And the fourth angel sounded, and the third part of the sun was
smitten, and the third part of the moon, and the third part of the stars; so
as the third part of them was darkened, and the day shone not for a third
part of it, and the night likewise.
13 And I beheld, and heard an angel flying through the midst of heaven,
saying with a loud voice, Woe, woe, woe, to the inhabiters of the earth by
reason of the other voices of the trumpet of the three angels, which are yet
to sound!

8:2 Mt 18:10; 1 Cor 15:52
☆**8:3** Ex 30:1; Num 4:11; Amos 9:1; Eph 5:2; Heb 9:4; Rev 5:8; 6:9
☆**8:4** Ps 141:2
8:5 Lev 16:12; 1 Kgs 19:11; Ezek 10:2; Lk 12:49; Rev 16:18
☆**8:6**
☆**8:7** Ezek 38:22; Isa 28:2; Joel 2:30; Zech 13:8, 9; Mt 7:25–27; Rev 9:4
☆**8:8** Ex 7:17; Jer 51:25; Zech 13:8, 9; Rev 16:2
☆**8:9** Isa 2:16; Rev 8:7–12; 9:15, 18
☆**8:10** Isa 14:12; Rev 6:13; 9:1; 12:4; 16:4
☆**8:11** Ex 15:23; Jer 9:15; 23:15; Amos 5:7; 6:12; Heb 12:15; Rev 9:15
☆**8:12** Ex 10:21; Isa 13:10; Amos 8:9; Zech 13:8; Rev 16:8
☆**8:13** Rev 3:10; 9:12

8:3, 4 See note to Exod. 30:1 for information concerning the incense offering.
8:6 The meaning of the seven trumpets is plain. They constitute the divine judgments of Almighty God against sinful men in the world, before the return of Christ. These occur at the end of the age and are only partial. A third of the people of the earth are affected.
8:7 The first four sounding trumpets concern God's judgment on the natural elements: the earth, the sea, the rivers, and the heavenly bodies (including the stars, the sun, and the moon).
8:8, 9 The events connected with the trumpets' judgments seem to parallel some of those connected with God's judgments on the Egyptians just before Israel was delivered from its bondage to Pharaoh. The events connected with the second trumpet recall the first plague of God against Egypt when the Nile became blood.
8:10, 11 The events connected with the third trumpet are similar to the experience the Israelites had with the bitter waters of Marah (Exod. 15:23). But here the sweet waters are made bitter, whereas at Marah the bitter water was made sweet.
8:12, 13 The result of the fourth trumpet is like the ninth plague of God on Egypt, when darkness came. Here it is a partial judgment by way of warning, and not for destruction. Verse 13 warns that the remaining trumpets will bring more disaster and greater dread.

5. Opening of the Bottomless Pit

9 AND the fifth angel sounded, and I saw a star fall from heaven unto
the earth: and to him was given the key of the bottomless pit.
2 And he opened the bottomless pit; and there arose a smoke out of the
pit, as the smoke of a great furnace; and the sun and the air were darkened
by reason of the smoke of the pit.
3 And there came out of the smoke locusts upon the earth: and unto them
was given power, as the scorpions of the earth have power.
4 And it was commanded them that they should not hurt the grass of the
earth, neither any green thing, neither any tree; but only those men which
have not the seal of God in their foreheads.
5 And to them it was given that they should not kill them, but that they
should be tormented five months: and their torment *was* as the torment of
a scorpion, when he striketh a man.
6 And in those days shall men seek death, and shall not find it; and shall
desire to die, and death shall flee from them.
7 And the shapes of the locusts *were* like unto horses prepared unto
battle; and on their heads *were* as it were crowns like gold, and their faces
were as the faces of men.
8 And they had hair as the hair of women, and their teeth were as *the teeth*
of lions.
9 And they had breastplates, as it were breastplates of iron; and the sound
of their wings *was* as the sound of chariots of many horses running to
battle.
10 And they had tails like unto scorpions, and there were stings in their
tails: and their power *was* to hurt men five months.
11 And they had a king over them, *which is* the angel of the bottomless pit,
whose name in the Hebrew tongue *is* A-bad′don, but in the Greek tongue
hath *his* name A-pol′ly-on.
12 One woe is past; *and,* behold, there come two woes more hereafter.

6. The Four Angels Released

13 And the sixth angel sounded, and I heard a voice from the four horns of
the golden altar which is before God,
14 Saying to the sixth angel which had the trumpet, Loose the four angels
which are bound in the great river Eu-phra′tes.
15 And the four angels were loosed, which were prepared for an hour, and
a day, and a month, and a year, for to slay the third part of men.
16 And the number of the army of the horsemen *were* two hundred
thousand thousand: and I heard the number of them.
17 And thus I saw the horses in the vision, and them that sat on them,
having breastplates of fire, and of jacinth, and brimstone: and the heads of

9:1☆ Isa 14:12 Lk 8:31; 10:18 2 Thess 2:3–8 2 Tim 3:1–5 Rev 3:10; 8:10 17:8; 20:1
9:2 Gen 15:17; 19:28 Joel 2:2, 30
9:3 Ex 10:4, 5, 12–15 2 Chron 10:11, 14 Ezek 2:6 Rev 9:5, 7, 10
9:4☆ Ex 12:23 Ezek 9:4 Rev 6:6; 7:2, 3 8:7
9:5 2 Chron 10:11 Ezek 2:6
9:6 Job 3:21 Jer 8:3 Lk 10:19 Rev 6:16
9:7 Joel 2:4
9:8 Joel 1:6
9:9 Jer 47:3 Joel 2:5
9:10 Ezek 2:6
9:11 Job 26:6 Prov 15:11 Lk 8:31 Jn 12:31; 14:30 Eph 2:2 Rev 9:1
9:12 Rev 8:13; 11:14
9:13☆ Ex 30:2–10 Heb 9:24; 10:21 Rev 8:3
9:14 Gen 2:14; 15:18 Deut 1:7 Josh 1:4 2 Sam 8:3 Rev 7:1; 16:12
9:15 Rev 9:18; 20:7
9:16 Dan 7:10; 11:40 Rev 5:11; 7:4
9:17 Dan 8:2; 9:21

9:1 The fifth trumpet is sounded after an interruption by an angel who proclaims the three "woes," which introduce the last three trumpets (8:13). The resemblance between the items contained in the first four trumpets and to the things that happened to Egypt in Moses' day is noteworthy. The fifth trumpet makes this even clearer. Locusts come on the scene—differing *from the locust invasion* of Egypt in that they come from the bottomless pit. They torture but do not kill men, according to the divine command.

9:4 The locusts are commanded not to touch anyone who has the seal of God on his forehead. Thus the people of God are supernaturally preserved from this plague.

9:13 The sixth trumpet sounds and four destroying angels are released to do the bidding of God. They bring the retributive justice of God with them and execute divine judgment against unbelievers. The ruin and devastation of the invading horde mark this scene in which a third of mankind are killed and the remainder of men are warned about their impending judgment. The terrifying account of the angelic judgment does not cause impenitent men to change their ways or abandon their ungodly living. They refuse to repent. What is significant is the fact that what happens is said to come at a specific hour, day, month, and year. God's timetable is at work and nothing can hinder it or stop it from coming to pass.

the horses *were* as the heads of lions; and out of their mouths issued fire
and smoke and brimstone.
18 By these three was the third part of men killed, by the fire, and by the
smoke, and by the brimstone, which issued out of their mouths.
19 For their power is in their mouth, and in their tails: for their tails *were*
like unto serpents, and had heads, and with them they do hurt.
20 And the rest of the men which were not killed by these plagues yet
repented not of the works of their hands, that they should not worship
devils, and idols of gold, and silver, and brass, and stone, and of wood:
which neither can see, nor hear, nor walk:
21 Neither repented they of their murders, nor of their sorceries, nor of
their fornication, nor of their thefts.

7. The Second Interlude or Parenthesis
a. The Eating of the Little Book

10 AND I saw another mighty angel come down from heaven, clothed
with a cloud: and a rainbow *was* upon his head, and his face *was* as
it were the sun, and his feet as pillars of fire:
2 And he had in his hand a little book open: and he set his right foot upon
the sea, and *his* left *foot* on the earth,
3 And cried with a loud voice, as *when* a lion roareth: and when he had
cried, seven thunders uttered their voices.
4 And when the seven thunders had uttered their voices, I was about to
write: and I heard a voice from heaven saying unto me, Seal up those things
which the seven thunders uttered, and write them not.
5 And the angel which I saw stand upon the sea and upon the earth lifted
up his hand to heaven,
6 And sware by him that liveth for ever and ever, who created heaven, and
the things that therein are, and the earth, and the things that therein are,
and the sea, and the things which are therein, that there should be time no
longer:
7 But in the days of the voice of the seventh angel, when he shall begin to
sound, the mystery of God should be finished, as he hath declared to his
servants the prophets.
8 And the voice which I heard from heaven spake unto me again, and
said, Go *and* take the little book which is open in the hand of the angel
which standeth upon the sea and upon the earth.
9 And I went unto the angel, and said unto him, Give me the little book.
And he said unto me, Take *it,* and eat it up; and it shall make thy belly
bitter, but it shall be in thy mouth sweet as honey.
10 And I took the little book out of the angel's hand, and ate it up; and it
was in my mouth sweet as honey: and as soon as I had eaten it, my belly
was bitter.

9:20 Deut 4:28; Ps 115:4–7; 135:15–17; Dan 5:23; Mic 5:13; Acts 7:41; 1 Cor 10:20; Rev 2:21
☆**9:21** Rev 7:2
☆**10:1** Mt 17:2; Rev 1:15, 16; 4:3; 5:2; 18:1
10:2 Rev 10:8–10
10:3 Ps 29:3–9; Hos 11:10; Rev 4:5
☆**10:4** Dan 8:26; 12:4; Hab 2:2, 3; Rev 1:10; 22:10
10:5 Gen 14:22; Deut 32:40
10:6 Jer 10:10; Dan 12:7; Rev 4:9, 11; 16:17; 21:6
☆**10:7** Amos 3:7; Rev 11:15
☆**10:8** Rev 10:2
10:9 Jer 15:16; Ezek 2:8; 3:1–3

9:21 *The end of the age will be marked by persistent* impenitence by unbelievers and a refusal to heed the warnings conveyed to them through apocalyptic events of staggering magnitude.

10:1 Before the seventh seal was broken, there was an interlude. Now, before the seventh trumpet sounds, there is another interlude. In it John eats a small open book, which seems to indicate that more has been revealed to him than he is permitted to disclose. It is followed by the story of the two witnesses.

10:4 John is about to write what he has seen but is forbidden to do so. The seven thunders spoken of here are a mystery to us. Since they are sealed, it is useless for us to conjecture what they mean.

10:7 *the mystery of God.* This is something previously concealed from us but now to be revealed and made plain. It appears that this denotes the purpose of God to consummate history, solve the problems of men and nations, and bless the world by the fulfillment of God's redemptive purpose.

10:8ff Before the consummation there will be a time of great suffering for the people of God. The little scroll is to be eaten by John. It will taste sweet in his mouth, but it will be bitter in his stomach. However, this little scroll is not the end of God's revelation. There is still more to be given to John for his benefit and for ours.

10:11 Rev 5:9

[11]And he said unto me, Thou must prophesy again before many peoples,
and nations, and tongues, and kings.

b. The Two Witnesses

11:1☆ Zech 2:1; 1 Cor 3:16, 17; Gal 6:14–16; Rev 21:15
11:2 Isa 52:1; Ezek 40:17–20; Dan 7:25; 12:7; Lk 21:24; 2 Thess 2:3–12; Rev 12:6; 13:5
11:3☆ Gen 37:34; 1 Kgs 21:27; Neh 9:1; Esth 4:1; Rev 2:13; 12:6
11:4☆ Ps 52:8; Jer 11:16; Zech 4:3, 11, 14
11:5 2 Kgs 1:10–12; Jer 5:14; Zech 1:6; 2:8
11:6 Ex 7:19; 1 Kgs 17:1; Lk 4:25; Jas 5:17; Rev 8:8
11:7☆ Rev 13:1, 7
11:8 Ps 79:2, 3; Isa 1:9; Ezek 16:53–55; Amos 4:11; Rev 14:8; 16:9; 17:5, 18; 18:24
11:9 Ps 79:2
11:10 Neh 8:10; Esth 9:19, 22; Mt 10:22; Jn 7:7; Rev 13:8
11:11 Ezek 37:5, 9–14
11:12☆ 2 Kgs 2:11; Mt 17:1–9; Acts 1:9; Rev 4:1

11 AND there was given me a reed like unto a rod: and the angel
stood, saying, Rise, and measure the temple of God, and the altar,
and them that worship therein.
[2]But the court which is without the temple leave out, and measure it not;
for it is given unto the Gentiles: and the holy city shall they tread under
foot forty *and* two months.
[3]And I will give *power* unto my two witnesses, and they shall prophesy a
thousand two hundred *and* threescore days, clothed in sackcloth.
[4]These are the two olive trees, and the two candlesticks standing before
the God of the earth.
[5]And if any man will hurt them, fire proceedeth out of their mouth, and
devoureth their enemies: and if any man will hurt them, he must in this
manner be killed.
[6]These have power to shut heaven, that it rain not in the days of their
prophecy: and have power over waters to turn them to blood, and to smite
the earth with all plagues, as often as they will.
[7]And when they shall have finished their testimony, the beast that
ascendeth out of the bottomless pit shall make war against them, and shall
overcome them, and kill them.
[8]And their dead bodies *shall lie* in the street of the great city, which
spiritually is called Sodom and Egypt, where also our Lord was crucified.
[9]And they of the people and kindreds and tongues and nations shall see
their dead bodies three days and an half, and shall not suffer their dead
bodies to be put in graves.
[10]And they that dwell upon the earth shall rejoice over them, and make
merry, and shall send gifts one to another; because these two prophets
tormented them that dwelt on the earth.
[11]And after three days and an half the Spirit of life from God entered
into them, and they stood upon their feet; and great fear fell upon them
which saw them.
[12]And they heard a great voice from heaven saying unto them, Come up
hither. And they ascended up to heaven in a cloud; and their enemies
beheld them.

11:1ff Beginning here we learn that God's people will be empowered for witness and will bear a faithful testimony. Many of them will even seal their testimony with their blood. They will not be delivered *from* persecution and great difficulties; they will, however, be delivered from the evil one by their martyrdom, which will result in glorious resurrection to endless life.

11:3 The two witnesses are identified with Elijah and Moses. Their ministry is to prophesy for 1,260 days or three and a half years. Elijah kept the rain from falling for this length of time, and Moses called down the plagues on Egypt. These two people are named together in Mal. 4:4, 5 and they appeared at Christ's transfiguration (Mark 9:4).

11:4ff The two witnesses are called two olive trees and two candlesticks, or lampstands. The candlesticks get their oil for burning from the olive trees. God will sustain his witnesses in their labors, and if any oppose them, they have power to devour their enemies by a fire that comes out of their mouths. They can keep rains from falling, turn waters into blood, and let plagues loose among the peoples. This is so terrifying in its potential that one wonders how and why anyone would not hear their message, repent, and turn to God for forgiveness.

11:7 When the two witnesses have finished their work, and only then, can they be martyred by the beast that ascends out of the bottomless pit. Their bodies will lie in the streets of the great city that represents Sodom and Egypt. What will be true for the witnesses is true for God's people today. No one can take their lives from them unless and until they have finished the work God has entrusted to them.

11:12 *Come up hither*. Some who hold to a midtribulation rapture of the church think that event occurs at this time.

13 And the same hour was there a great earthquake, and the tenth part of
the city fell, and in the earthquake were slain of men seven thousand: and
the remnant were affrighted, and gave glory to the God of heaven.

14 The second woe is past; *and,* behold, the third woe cometh quickly.

15 And the seventh angel sounded; and there were great voices in heaven,
saying, The kingdoms of this world are become *the kingdoms* of our Lord,
and of his Christ; and he shall reign for ever and ever.

16 And the four and twenty elders, which sat before God on their seats,
fell upon their faces, and worshipped God,

17 Saying, We give thee thanks, O Lord God Almighty, which art, and
wast, and art to come; because thou hast taken to thee thy great power, and
hast reigned.

18 And the nations were angry, and thy wrath is come, and the time of the
dead, that they should be judged, and that thou shouldest give reward unto
thy servants the prophets, and to the saints, and them that fear thy name,
small and great; and shouldest destroy them which destroy the earth.

19 And the temple of God was opened in heaven, and there was seen in his
temple the ark of his testament: and there were lightnings, and voices, and
thunderings, and an earthquake, and great hail.

11:13 Jn 9:24; Rev 6:12; 16:9, 11, 18, 19
11:14 Rev 8:13; 9:12
☆**11:15** Dan 2:44; 7:14, 27; Mic 4:7; Lk 1:33; Acts 4:26; Rev 8:2; 10:7; 12:10; 16:17
11:16 Mt 19:28; Rev 4:4, 10
☆**11:17** Rev 1:8; 19:6
11:18 Ps 2:1; Dan 7:10; Acts 10:42; 2 Tim 4:1; 1 Pet 4:5; Rev 10:7; 13:16; 19:5; 20:12
☆**11:19** Heb 9:4; Rev 4:5; 15:5

D. THE SEVEN SIGNS

1. The Woman

12 AND there appeared a great wonder in heaven; a woman clothed
with the sun, and the moon under her feet, and upon her head a
crown of twelve stars:

2 And she being with child cried, travailing in birth, and pained to be
delivered.

☆**12:1** Song 6:10; Mt 24:30; Gal 4:26
12:2 Isa 26:17; 66:6-9; Mic 4:9, 10; Jn 16:21

2. The Dragon

3 And there appeared another wonder in heaven; and behold a great red
dragon, having seven heads and ten horns, and seven crowns upon his
heads.

4 And his tail drew the third part of the stars of heaven, and did cast them
to the earth: and the dragon stood before the woman which was ready to be
delivered, for to devour her child as soon as it was born.

12:3 Isa 27:1; Rev 13:1, 2; 17:3, 9, 12, 16
12:4 Ex 1:15, 16; Mt 2:16; Jn 8:44; 1 Pet 5:8; Rev 17:18

11:15ff While there will be much more to be told us by John, the seventh trumpet marks the climax of God's purpose, because the final goal will have been reached. His kingdom will have come on earth as it is in heaven. That which the people of God had longed and prayed for will now have come to pass. At the time the seventh seal was opened, it was followed by silence in heaven. When the seventh trumpet sounds, there are heard great voices from heaven chanting the praise of God. All creation will have been *bought* and *brought* back under the rule and reign of its rightful Lord and King. This reign of God and of his Christ shall be forever and forever.

11:17 *which art, and wast, and art to come.* The last four words are not present in the best manuscripts. This should read "who art and who wast" (see NASB and RSV). Those who sang here did not need to add, "who art to come" for he had now come and was there. Those who sang here look upon the universal and eternal reign of the King as already started.

11:19 The heavenly temple is opened and the ark of the covenant is now visible because God has consummated his work. It symbolizes the fact that we now have perfect access to God. We perceive his glory as we never perceived it before, and we understand the meaning of grace beyond anything we ever dreamed possible.

12:1 The woman arrayed or clothed with the sun and the moon under her feet represents the people of God. She is beset by the dragon, who is Satan, the arch-enemy of God and Christ. The male child represents the Lord Jesus Christ, who is to rule over the cosmos. The child is caught up to God and his throne. The woman flees into the wilderness. So we learn that God protects and keeps his people against the onslaughts of Satan. Verses 7–17 speak of the defeat of Satan, who is powerless against the Son of God. Yet his time has not come and he goes back to earth to persecute the people of God. But again he is ineffective because God protects his people as a whole, even though individual believers can be the victims of Satan's hatred and power.

3. The Man-Child

5 And she brought forth a man child, who was to rule all nations with a
rod of iron: and her child was caught up unto God, and *to* his throne.
6 And the woman fled into the wilderness, where she hath a place
prepared of God, that they should feed her there a thousand two hundred
and threescore days.

12:5 Ps 2:9 Isa 7:14 Mk 16:19 Rev 2:27; 19:15
12:6 Rev 11:3; 13:5 17:18

4. Michael, the Archangel

7 And there was war in heaven: Michael and his angels fought against the
dragon; and the dragon fought and his angels,
8 And prevailed not; neither was their place found any more in heaven.
9 And the great dragon was cast out, that old serpent, called the Devil,
and Satan, which deceiveth the whole world: he was cast out into the earth,
and his angels were cast out with him.
10 And I heard a loud voice saying in heaven, Now is come salvation, and
strength, and the kingdom of our God, and the power of his Christ: for the
accuser of our brethren is cast down, which accused them before our God
day and night.
11 And they overcame him by the blood of the Lamb, and by the word of
their testimony; and they loved not their lives unto the death.
12 Therefore rejoice, *ye* heavens, and ye that dwell in them. Woe to the
inhabiters of the earth and of the sea! for the devil is come down unto you,
having great wrath, because he knoweth that he hath but a short time.
13 And when the dragon saw that he was cast unto the earth, he
persecuted the woman which brought forth the man *child.*
14 And to the woman were given two wings of a great eagle, that she might
fly into the wilderness, into her place, where she is nourished for a time, and
times, and half a time, from the face of the serpent.
15 And the serpent cast out of his mouth water as a flood after the woman,
that he might cause her to be carried away of the flood.
16 And the earth helped the woman, and the earth opened her mouth, and
swallowed up the flood which the dragon cast out of his mouth.
17 And the dragon was wroth with the woman, and went to make war with
the remnant of her seed, which keep the commandments of God, and have
the testimony of Jesus Christ.

12:7☆ Dan 10:13; 12:1 Mt 4:11; 25:41 Jude 9 Rev 12:3
12:9☆ Gen 3:1 Isa 65:25 Zech 3:1, 2 Mt 4:10 Lk 10:18 2 Cor 11:3 Rev 12:3, 15 20:2–10
12:10 Job 1:6–11 Dan 2:44 Zech 3:1 Lk 22:31 Rev 7:10; 11:15
12:11 Lk 14:26 Rom 8:37 Rev 2:10; 6:9 7:14; 15:2
12:12 Ps 96:11 Isa 44:23 Rev 8:13; 10:6 12:9; 13:6; 18:20
12:13☆
12:14 Ex 19:4 Dan 7:25; 12:7 Rev 17:3, 18
12:15 Hos 5:10
12:17 Gen 3:15 Dan 7:23–26 Mt 28:20 1 Jn 2:3 Rev 1:2; 11:7 13:7; 14:12

5. The Beast from the Sea

13 AND I stood upon the sand of the sea, and saw a beast rise up out
of the sea, having seven heads and ten horns, and upon his horns
ten crowns, and upon his heads the name of blasphemy.

13:1☆ Dan 7:2–8 11:36 Hos 13:7 Rev 13:4, 12 17:12

12:7ff There is a great war in heaven. It is fought between Satan and the fallen angels who are opposed by Michael and the good angels. Satan is dethroned; he and his angels are cast down to earth. Satan's expulsion from heaven has come about by reason of the incarnation, the life, the death, and the resurrection *of Jesus Christ. He defeated the enemy.*

12:9 The precise time when this happened or happens is not clear. One thing is sure: in the struggle between God and Satan this malign spirit will be defeated because of Christ's victory at Calvary (John 12:31).

12:13ff Satan can no longer oppose Jesus Christ, for his power has been diminished. But Satan seeks to persecute the woman, who is given a refuge in the wilderness. The phrase "for a time, and times, and half a time" of verse 14 is a period of three and a half years prior to the time of Jesus' Second Advent. The wrath of Satan is directed against the church during this time.

13:1 The dragon of chapter 12 and the two beasts of chapter 13 constitute a trinity of evil. Under their awful assaults the saints of God experience persecution probably worse than anything suffered by God's people before. The trinity of evil is offset by the true Trinity of God—the Father, the Son, and the Holy Spirit—to whom be glory for their victory over the trinity of evil.

2 And the beast which I saw was like unto a leopard, and his feet were as
the feet of a bear, and his mouth as the mouth of a lion: and the dragon
gave him his power, and his seat, and great authority.
3 And I saw one of his heads as it were wounded to death; and his deadly
wound was healed: and all the world wondered after the beast.
4 And they worshipped the dragon which gave power unto the beast: and
they worshipped the beast, saying, Who *is* like unto the beast? who is able
to make war with him?
5 And there was given unto him a mouth speaking great things and
blasphemies; and power was given unto him to continue forty *and* two
months.
6 And he opened his mouth in blasphemy against God, to blaspheme his
name, and his tabernacle, and them that dwell in heaven.
7 And it was given unto him to make war with the saints, and to overcome
them: and power was given him over all kindreds, and tongues, and
nations.
8 And all that dwell upon the earth shall worship him, whose names are
not written in the book of life of the Lamb slain from the foundation of the
world.
9 If any man have an ear, let him hear.
10 He that leadeth into captivity shall go into captivity: he that killeth
with the sword must be killed with the sword. Here is the patience and the
faith of the saints.

6. The Beast from the Earth

11 And I beheld another beast coming up out of the earth; and he had two
horns like a lamb, and he spake as a dragon.
12 And he exerciseth all the power of the first beast before him, and
causeth the earth and them which dwell therein to worship the first beast,
whose deadly wound was healed.
13 And he doeth great wonders, so that he maketh fire come down from
heaven on the earth in the sight of men,
14 And deceiveth them that dwell on the earth by *the means of* those
miracles which he had power to do in the sight of the beast; saying to them
that dwell on the earth, that they should make an image to the beast, which
had the wound by a sword, and did live.
15 And he had power to give life unto the image of the beast, that the
image of the beast should both speak, and cause that as many as would not
worship the image of the beast should be killed.
16 And he causeth all, both small and great, rich and poor, free and bond,
to receive a mark in their right hand, or in their foreheads:
17 And that no man might buy or sell, save he that had the mark, or the
name of the beast, or the number of his name.

☆**13:2** Dan 7:4–6; Rev 2:13; 12:3
13:3 Ezek 30:24; Jn 12:19; 2 Thess 2:9–12; Rev 13:12, 14; 17:8
13:4 Ex 15:11; Rev 13:2, 12
13:5 Dan 7:8, 11, 20, 25; 11:36; 2 Thess 2:3; Rev 11:2
13:6 Rev 7:15; 12:12
13:7 Rev 5:9; 11:7
13:8 Ex 32:32; Dan 12:1; Lk 10:12, 15; Jn 1:29, 36; Eph 1:4; 1 Pet 1:19, 20; Rev 3:5; 5:6–13; 7:17; 17:8; 21:27
13:9 Rev 2:7
13:10 Gen 9:6; Isa 33:1; Jer 15:2; 43:11; Mt 26:52; Heb 6:12; Rev 14:12
☆**13:11** Dan 8:3; Rev 13:1, 4
13:12 2 Thess 2:4; Rev 14:9; 19:20
13:13 Ex 7:11; 19:9–11; Deut 13:1–4; 2 Kgs 1:10–14; Mt 24:24; 2 Thess 2:9; 2 Tim 3:8; Rev 11:15; 16:14; 19:20
13:14 2 Thess 2:9; Rev 12:9; 13:3, 8, 12
13:15 Dan 3:3; 7:20, 25; Jer 10:14; Rev 20:4
13:16 Ps 49:2; 1 Cor 12:13; Gal 3:28; Rev 14:9; 19:17, 18
13:17 Rev 14:9, 11; 15:2

13:2 The beast from the sea has ten horns and seven heads. On his horns are ten diadems. The beast represents the power of paganism, which is worldwide and has extensive control over the destinies of the nations. This beast has features common to a leopard, a bear, and a lion—the savageness and agility of a leopard, the overwhelming power of a bear, and the petrifying snarl of a lion. The dragon has given power to this beast so that men worship it. This beast exercises political power over the world.

13:11 The beast from the earth has two horns like a lamb and speaks like a dragon. The beast encourages men to worship the first beast. This second beast is called the false prophet. He performs what appear to be miraculous acts and is a religious rather than a civil power. The mark of his name is 666. The sphere of his work is in the religious, not the political, arena. In place of the Christian faith he would substitute worship of the first beast. The beast from the earth represents the antichrist, a false Christ who is at enmity with the true Christ while he pretends to be good.

18 Here is wisdom. Let him that hath understanding count the number of
the beast: for it is the number of a man; and his number *is* Six hundred
threescore *and* six.

7. The Lamb on Mount Zion

14 AND I looked, and, lo, a Lamb stood on the mount Sion, and with
him an hundred forty *and* four thousand, having his Father's name
written in their foreheads.
2 And I heard a voice from heaven, as the voice of many waters, and as
the voice of a great thunder: and I heard the voice of harpers harping with
their harps:
3 And they sung as it were a new song before the throne, and before the
four beasts, and the elders: and no man could learn that song but the
hundred *and* forty *and* four thousand, which were redeemed from the earth.
4 These are they which were not defiled with women; for they are virgins.
These are they which follow the Lamb whithersoever he goeth. These were
redeemed from among men, *being* the firstfruits unto God and to the Lamb.
5 And in their mouth was found no guile: for they are without fault before
the throne of God.

8. Interlude or Parenthesis: the Angelic Messages

6 And I saw another angel fly in the midst of heaven, having the
everlasting gospel to preach unto them that dwell on the earth, and to every
nation, and kindred, and tongue, and people,
7 Saying with a loud voice, Fear God, and give glory to him; for the hour
of his judgment is come: and worship him that made heaven, and earth,
and the sea, and the fountains of waters.
8 And there followed another angel, saying, Babylon is fallen, is fallen,
that great city, because she made all nations drink of the wine of the wrath
of her fornication.
9 And the third angel followed them, saying with a loud voice, If any man
worship the beast and his image, and receive *his* mark in his forehead, or in
his hand,

14:1☆ Ps 2:6; Dan 12:5; Amos 8:2; Heb 12:22; Rev 3:12; 5:6; 7:4
14:2 Rev 1:15; 5:8; 6:1
14:3 Ps 25:14; Mt 11:25–27; Rev 2:17; 4:4, 6; 5:9
14:4 Mt 19:12; 2 Cor 11:2; Eph 5:27; Heb 12:23; Jas 1:18; Rev 5:9; 7:13–17
14:5 Ps 32:2; Zeph 3:13; Heb 9:14; 1 Pet 2:22; Jude 24
14:6☆ Rev 5:9
14:7 Ps 124:8; Dan 8:19; Jn 5:25–29; Acts 14:15; Rev 4:11
14:8☆ Isa 21:8, 9; Jer 51:7, 8; Nah 3:19; Rev 16:19; 17:2–5; 18:2, 3, 10
14:9 Rev 13:14, 16

14:1 The number 144,000 is enigmatic. Commentators differ as to its meaning. Some think it is a figure of speech denoting the church represented by the 144,000. The statement that they have not defiled themselves with women is another point about which no one should be dogmatic. Some think the 144,000 are martyrs who have sealed their testimony with their blood. The event seems to be placed in heaven. The Lamb is present and so are some of the people of God. Since it follows hard on the emergence of the two beasts from the sea and earth, it may well depict the suffering of a persecuted church whose members have on their foreheads the mark of God rather than the number of the beast, 666.

14:6ff In the interlude between 14:1–5 and 14:14–20 three angels appear, each with a message. The first *angel, in line with the everlasting* gospel, speaks of God's mercy and justice, and announces that divine judgment is about to fall. The second angel (14:8) looks toward the doom of Babylon (see note to 14:8). The third angel speaks of the wrath of God directed against those who worship the beast and receive his mark on the forehead or the hand. The saints are called upon to endure. Those who endure unto death are designated as specially blessed (see 14:13).

14:8 *Babylon.* See 16:17–21 and 17:1–8. To identify Babylon here with any known city or nation with certainty is impossible. Widespread disagreement exists about this. Some identify Babylon with Jerusalem. Some think it to be an ecclesiastical system. The Reformers thought it to be the Roman papacy. Later expositors thought it to be apostate Christendom at the end of this age. The most favored identification of Babylon is with Rome, the capital of Italy, where the emperor of Rome resided when the Revelation was written. 17:4, 5 describes a woman arrayed in purple and scarlet, called Babylon the Great. In 17:18 it says, "This woman . . . represents the great city that rules over the kings of the earth." In 16:17–21 John sees Babylon about to be destroyed. In chapter 18 Babylon has fallen. Whatever the final identification, Babylon kills faithful Christians and seduces people under its dominion, sharing its wealth with the merchants of the earth, who in the end shall suffer with it. At last, "Babylon . . . shall be thrown away . . . and she shall disappear forever" (18:21, TLB).

10The same shall drink of the wine of the wrath of God, which is poured
out without mixture into the cup of his indignation; and he shall be
tormented with fire and brimstone in the presence of the holy angels, and in
the presence of the Lamb:
11And the smoke of their torment ascendeth up for ever and ever: and
they have no rest day nor night, who worship the beast and his image, and
whosoever receiveth the mark of his name.
12Here is the patience of the saints: here *are* they that keep the
commandments of God, and the faith of Jesus.
13And I heard a voice from heaven saying unto me, Write, Blessed *are* the
dead which die in the Lord from henceforth: Yea, saith the Spirit, that they
may rest from their labours; and their works do follow them.
14And I looked, and behold a white cloud, and upon the cloud *one* sat
like unto the Son of man, having on his head a golden crown, and in his
hand a sharp sickle.
15And another angel came out of the temple, crying with a loud voice to
him that sat on the cloud, Thrust in thy sickle, and reap: for the time is
come for thee to reap; for the harvest of the earth is ripe.
16And he that sat on the cloud thrust in his sickle on the earth; and the
earth was reaped.
17And another angel came out of the temple which is in heaven, he also
having a sharp sickle.
18And another angel came out from the altar, which had power over fire;
and cried with a loud cry to him that had the sharp sickle, saying, Thrust in
thy sharp sickle, and gather the clusters of the vine of the earth; for her
grapes are fully ripe.
19And the angel thrust in his sickle into the earth, and gathered the vine
of the earth, and cast *it* into the great winepress of the wrath of God.
20And the winepress was trodden without the city, and blood came out of
the winepress, even unto the horse bridles, by the space of a thousand *and*
six hundred furlongs.

E. THE SEVEN BOWLS

1. The Scene in Heaven

15 AND I saw another sign in heaven, great and marvellous, seven
angels having the seven last plagues; for in them is filled up the
wrath of God.
2And I saw as it were a sea of glass mingled with fire: and them that had
gotten the victory over the beast, and over his image, and over his mark,
and over the number of his name, stand on the sea of glass, having the
harps of God.
3And they sing the song of Moses the servant of God, and the song of the
Lamb, saying, Great and marvellous *are* thy works, Lord God Almighty;
just and true *are* thy ways, thou King of saints.

14:10 Ps 75:8; Jer 25:15; Ezek 38:22; Mk 8:38; 2 Thess 1:7; Rev 16:19; 19:20; 20:15; 21:8
14:11 Rev 13:17
14:12 Rev 2:13; 12:17; 13:10
14:13 Eccles 4:1, 2; Isa 57:1, 2; 2 Cor 5:8; Phil 1:21–23; 1 Tim 5:25; Heb 4:9; Rev 2:7; 6:11
☆**14:14** Ps 21:3; Ezek 1:26; Dan 7:13; Mt 17:5; Rev 1:13; 6:2
14:15 Jer 51:33; Joel 3:13; Mt 13:39–41; Mk 4:29; Rev 14:17; 15:6; 16:17
14:18 Joel 3:13; Rev 6:9; 8:3; 14:15
14:19 Deut 32:32, 33; Isa 63:2, 3; Rev 16:8; 19:15
14:20 Gen 49:11; Lam 1:15; Ezek 39:17–21; Heb 13:11, 12
☆**15:1** Lev 26:21; Dan 4:2, 3; 6:27; 12:6–12; Rev 14:10; 15:6; 16:1; 21:9
15:2 Rev 4:6; 5:8; 12:11
☆**15:3, 4** Ex 15:1; Deut 32:3; Ps 86:9; Jer 10:7; Dan 9:11; Rev 5:9; 14:7

14:14ff This segment is climactic. The church of God is to be delivered and the enemies of God are to be destroyed. There is a harvest and a vintage. The wheat and the tares have grown together. Now is the time for harvesting and separating the chaff from the wheat. The avenging angel uses his sickle to cut and gather the vintage to be thrown into the wine press, which is called the wrath of God. At last, the victory of God over his enemies will be fulfilled.

15:1 Chapters 15 and 16 constitute a surprise. Instead of ending with the victory of the Lamb, John goes back and recapitulates and enlarges on what he has already described. The seven bowls of wrath are the elements contained in the seventh seal. Seven angels with seven plagues will come upon unbelievers. The angels are dispatched by a voice from the temple telling them to go about their work.

15:3 *they sing.* These are the company of the redeemed. They stand by the sea of glass and have the harps of God in their hands. They sing the song of Moses and of the Lamb. This refers back to Moses and the deliverance of the Israelites from Egypt. The song of the Lamb indicates the completed redemption of God's people; it is the song of the church universal.

4 Who shall not fear thee, O Lord, and glorify thy name? for *thou* only *art*
holy: for all nations shall come and worship before thee; for thy judgments
are made manifest.

15:5☆ Lev 16:2 Num 1:50, 53 Mt 27:51 Heb 8:5 Rev 11:19 **15:6** Ex 28:5–8 Rev 1:13 14:5; 15:6 **15:7** Ps 75:8 1 Thess 1:9 Rev 4:6, 9 **15:8** Ex 19:18 1 Kgs 8:10 Isa 6:4 Rom 11:33

5 And after that I looked, and, behold, the temple of the tabernacle of the
testimony in heaven was opened:
6 And the seven angels came out of the temple, having the seven plagues,
clothed in pure and white linen, and having their breasts girded with golden
girdles.
7 And one of the four beasts gave unto the seven angels seven golden vials
full of the wrath of God, who liveth for ever and ever.
8 And the temple was filled with smoke from the glory of God, and from
his power; and no man was able to enter into the temple, till the seven
plagues of the seven angels were fulfilled.

2. The Judgments

a. The Sores on Men

16:1 Ps 79:6 Jer 10:25 Ezek 22:31 Zeph 3:8 Rev 11:19, 15:1 **16:2**☆ Ex 9:9–11 Deut 28:35 Lk 16:20–22 Rev 8:7 13:15–17

16 AND I heard a great voice out of the temple saying to the seven
angels, Go your ways, and pour out the vials of the wrath of God
upon the earth.
2 And the first went, and poured out his vial upon the earth; and there fell
a noisome and grievous sore upon the men which had the mark of the beast,
and *upon* them which worshipped his image.

b. Turning the Sea into Watery Blood

16:3 Ex 7:17–21 Ps 78:44 Rev 8:8, 9

3 And the second angel poured out his vial upon the sea; and it became as
the blood of a dead *man:* and every living soul died in the sea.

c. Rivers and Springs Become Blood

16:4 Ex 17:7 Rev 8:10; 11:16 **16:5**☆ Jn 17:25 Rev 1:4, 8; 4:8 6:10; 11:17 **16:6** Deut 32:42, 43 2 Kgs 24:4 Isa 49:26 Rev 17:6; 18:24 **16:7** Rev 1:8; 6:9 14:18 15:3; 19:2

4 And the third angel poured out his vial upon the rivers and fountains of
waters; and they became blood.
5 And I heard the angel of the waters say, Thou art righteous, O Lord,
which art, and wast, and shalt be, because thou hast judged thus.
6 For they have shed the blood of saints and prophets, and thou hast
given them blood to drink; for they are worthy.
7 And I heard another out of the altar say, Even so, Lord God Almighty,
true and righteous *are* thy judgments.

15:5ff The seven angels with the seven plagues emerge from the temple of God in heaven. The Scripture speaks of the tabernacle of the testimony, which refers to the law of God housed in the Holy of Holies. The seven angels have seven golden bowls full of the wrath of God. When they leave the temple, the smoke from the glory of God and from his power fills the temple so that no one can enter until the work of the seven angels is completed.

16:2 Six of the seven bowls (vials) are now poured out. *The seventh awaits the usual interval* (as previously seen) between the sixth and the seventh seal, and trumpet, and now the bowls. Some hold that the church has been removed and only tribulation saints (i.e., those who have come to salvation after the church has been raptured) and unbelievers are here. Whether these tribulation saints are part of the church or constitute a separate and special body is not explicitly stated in any event. Others hold that the church will go through the great tribulation but will be supernaturally preserved from the wrath of God, as the Israelites were preserved from the plagues in Egypt.

16:5ff In the narrative of the trumpets (8:6—11:15) there are no voices explaining the happenings. Here, when the third bowl of the wrath of God is poured out, two voices are heard: one is that of the angel of the waters and the other that of the prophets and martyrs whose intercessions have come to the altar of God (16:7). Both rejoice in this just judgment and proclaim the righteousness of the one who is and was. The "shalt be" of the KJV does not appear in the Greek text (see the correct rendering in the RSV or the NASB). Clearly it refers to Jesus Christ, who is to come.

d. The Blasting Heat of the Sun

8 And the fourth angel poured out his vial upon the sun; and power was
given unto him to scorch men with fire.
9 And men were scorched with great heat, and blasphemed the name of
God, which hath power over these plagues: and they repented not to give
him glory.

e. The Darkness

10 And the fifth angel poured out his vial upon the seat of the beast; and
his kingdom was full of darkness; and they gnawed their tongues for pain,
11 And blasphemed the God of heaven because of their pains and their
sores, and repented not of their deeds.

f. The Unclean Spirits

12 And the sixth angel poured out his vial upon the great river Eu-
phra'tes; and the water thereof was dried up, that the way of the kings of
the east might be prepared.
13 And I saw three unclean spirits like frogs *come* out of the mouth of the
dragon, and out of the mouth of the beast, and out of the mouth of the false
prophet.
14 For they are the spirits of devils, working miracles, *which* go forth unto
the kings of the earth and of the whole world, to gather them to the battle
of that great day of God Almighty.
15 Behold, I come as a thief. Blessed *is* he that watcheth, and keepeth his
garments, lest he walk naked, and they see his shame.
16 And he gathered them together into a place called in the Hebrew
tongue Ar-ma-ged'don.

g. The Great Earthquake

17 And the seventh angel poured out his vial into the air; and there came
a great voice out of the temple of heaven, from the throne, saying, It is
done.
18 And there were voices, and thunders, and lightnings; and there was a
great earthquake, such as was not since men were upon the earth, so mighty
an earthquake, *and* so great.
19 And the great city was divided into three parts, and the cities of the
nations fell: and great Babylon came in remembrance before God, to give
unto her the cup of the wine of the fierceness of his wrath.
20 And every island fled away, and the mountains were not found.
21 And there fell upon men a great hail out of heaven, *every stone* about
the weight of a talent: and men blasphemed God because of the plague of
the hail; for the plague thereof was exceeding great.

16:8 Rev 6:12
16:9 Isa 8:21; Jer 5:3; Dan 5:22, 23; 2 Cor 12:21; Rev 11:13
16:10 Ex 10:21; Mt 8:12; 1 Pet 2:17; Rev 8:12; 9:1, 2; 13:2
16:11 Rev 2:21
16:12 Isa 11:15; 41:2; Jer 51:36; Dan 11:43–45; Rev 9:13, 14
☆**16:13** Rev 12:3; 13:1, 11, 14; 19:20
16:14 1 Kgs 22:21–23; 1 Tim 4:1; Rev 6:17; 17:14; 19:19
16:15 Ezek 16:37; Hos 2:3; Lk 12:35–38; 1 Thess 5:2; 2 Pet 3:10; Rev 3:3, 18
☆**16:16** Judg 5:19; Zech 12:10, 11; Rev 19:19
☆**16:17** Dan 12:7–13; Jn 19:30; Rev 11:15; 21:6
16:18 Dan 12:1; Mt 24:21; Rev 4:5; 6:12
16:19 Rev 14:8, 10
16:20 Rev 6:14; 20:11
☆**16:21** Ex 9:18–25; Josh 10:11; Ezek 13:11, 13; Rev 11:19; 16:9

16:13ff After verse 12 there is the usual interruption between the sixth and seventh bowl, as there was for the seals and trumpets. It specifies that the nations of the earth are to be gathered together for the last and great battle of the age, the Battle of Armageddon. Then comes the seventh bowl.
16:16 Armageddon is the place where the last great battle of the age will be fought between good and evil, and it is also the name of the battle itself. Evil will be defeated and destroyed. God will triumph. Premillennialists believe that this triumph of Christ will bring about his thousand-year reign on earth and the binding of Satan. Amillennialists hold that this battle will be the beginning of the end of history and will be followed by the final judgments and the start of the new age. (Read 16:12–16 and see note on 2 Chron. 35:22 for location of Armageddon.)
16:17ff The seventh bowl is poured into the air. There follow cosmic judgments in which the great city is split into three parts, islands disappear, hail falls, lightning flashes, and the earth quakes.
16:21 Instead of repenting, wicked men blaspheme the name of God. Great calamities will not bring men to repentance unless the grace of God works repentance in their hearts. Whoever is not made better by God's judgments will become worse. And whoever is so hardened that he will not repent will experience utter destruction.

IV. THE THIRD VISION (17:1—21:8)

A. THE DESTRUCTION OF BABYLON

1. The Notorious Prostitute

17:1☆ Jer 51:13 Nah 3:4 Lk 9:30 Rev 17:5, 15 19:2; 21:9

17 AND there came one of the seven angels which had the seven vials,
and talked with me, saying unto me, Come hither; I will shew unto
thee the judgment of the great whore that sitteth upon many waters:

17:2 Jer 51:7–9 Rev 14:8; 17:8 18:3, 9

2 With whom the kings of the earth have committed fornication, and the
inhabitants of the earth have been made drunk with the wine of her
fornication.

17:3 Rev 1:10; 12:3, 6 13:1

3 So he carried me away in the spirit into the wilderness: and I saw a
woman sit upon a scarlet coloured beast, full of names of blasphemy,
having seven heads and ten horns.

17:4 Jer 51:7 Rev 14:8; 18:6 19:2

4 And the woman was arrayed in purple and scarlet colour, and decked
with gold and precious stones and pearls, having a golden cup in her hand
full of abominations and filthiness of her fornication:

17:5 2 Thess 2:7 Rev 16:19 17:2, 7

5 And upon her forehead *was* a name written, MYSTERY, BABYLON
THE GREAT, THE MOTHER OF HARLOTS AND ABOMINATIONS
OF THE EARTH.

17:6 Dan 7:21, 25 Hab 1:13 Rev 6:9; 12:11; 16:6

6 And I saw the woman drunken with the blood of the saints, and with the
blood of the martyrs of Jesus: and when I saw her, I wondered with great
admiration.

2. The Prostitute and the Beast Identified

17:7☆

7 And the angel said unto me, Wherefore didst thou marvel? I will tell
thee the mystery of the woman, and of the beast that carrieth her, which
hath the seven heads and ten horns.

17:8 Rev 11:7; 13:1–8, 12, 14

8 The beast that thou sawest was, and is not; and shall ascend out of the
bottomless pit, and go into perdition: and they that dwell on the earth shall
wonder, whose names were not written in the book of life from the
foundation of the world, when they behold the beast that was, and is not,
and yet is.

17:9 Rev 17:3

9 And here *is* the mind which hath wisdom. The seven heads are seven
mountains, on which the woman sitteth.

10 And there are seven kings: five are fallen, and one is, *and* the other is
not yet come; and when he cometh, he must continue a short space.

17:11☆ Rev 18:19

11 And the beast that was, and is not, even he is the eighth, and is of the
seven, and goeth into perdition.

17:12☆ Dan 7:20–22 Rev 17:16 18:10, 17, 19

12 And the ten horns which thou sawest are ten kings, which have received
no kingdom as yet; but receive power as kings one hour with the beast.

17:1 In chapters 17 and 18 John paints a picture that graphically describes Babylon and the beast. John states what the relationship of the one is to the other and announces the impending destruction of both. The great harlot is Babylon. This woman is drunk with the blood of the saints and martyrs. Many commentators think she represents imperial Rome, a city marked by idolatry, cruelty, and godlessness. She is a persecutor of the true faith.

17:7ff *Verses 7–18* describe the relationship between the woman and the beast. The beast has seven heads and ten horns. In verse 3 the woman was pictured as sitting on this beast. Here we discover the woman and the beast collaborating to rule the world. Babylon here appears to control even the beast. Then Babylon is destroyed by the beast. She is made naked and desolate, and her flesh is eaten and the city burned. The religious system is overthrown by the beast, who may well be the man of sin (or, lawlessness) spoken of by Paul in 2 Thess. 2:3, 4. If this is so, he will purpose to destroy all true religion and require all men to worship him.

17:11, 12 The number seven represents completeness and ten is the number of the world. It appears that seven here symbolizes the apostate religious hierarchy in league with the political power symbolized by the ten horns. After the apostate religious system has served the purpose of the beast, it will be cast down and destroyed by the beast, who has for his purpose the destruction of all religion, good or bad. The beast then demands that he be worshipped as God (see 2 Thess. 2:3, 4).

13 These have one mind, and shall give their power and strength unto the
beast.
14 These shall make war with the Lamb, and the Lamb shall overcome
them: for he is Lord of lords, and King of kings: and they that are with him
are called, and chosen, and faithful.
15 And he saith unto me, The waters which thou sawest, where the whore
sitteth, are peoples, and multitudes, and nations, and tongues.
16 And the ten horns which thou sawest upon the beast, these shall hate
the whore, and shall make her desolate and naked, and shall eat her flesh,
and burn her with fire.
17 For God hath put in their hearts to fulfil his will, and to agree, and give
their kingdom unto the beast, until the words of God shall be fulfilled.
18 And the woman which thou sawest is that great city, which reigneth
over the kings of the earth.

17:14 Mt 22:14; 1 Tim 6:15; 1 Pet 2:9; Rev 3:21; 16:14
17:15 Isa 8:7; Jer 47:2; Rev 13:7; 17:1
17:16 Jer 50:41, 42; Ezek 16:37; Dan 7:5; Rev 18:8, 19
☆**17:17** Rev 10:7; 17:13
17:18 Rev 11:8; 16:19

3. The Fall of Babylon Prophesied

18 AND after these things I saw another angel come down from
heaven, having great power; and the earth was lightened with his
glory.
2 And he cried mightily with a strong voice, saying, Babylon the great is
fallen, is fallen, and is become the habitation of devils, and the hold of
every foul spirit, and a cage of every unclean and hateful bird.
3 For all nations have drunk of the wine of the wrath of her fornication,
and the kings of the earth have committed fornication with her, and the
merchants of the earth are waxed rich through the abundance of her
delicacies.

☆**18:1** Ezek 43:2; Lk 17:24; 2 Thess 2:8; Rev 10:1
☆**18:2** Isa 13:19–22; 14:23; 21:8, 9; Jer 50:39; Rev 14:8
☆**18:3** Ezek 27:9–25; 1 Tim 5:11; Rev 17:2

4. The Call to Come out of Babylon

4 And I heard another voice from heaven, saying, Come out of her, my
people, that ye be not partakers of her sins, and that ye receive not of her
plagues.
5 For her sins have reached unto heaven, and God hath remembered her
iniquities.
6 Reward her even as she rewarded you, and double unto her double
according to her works: in the cup which she hath filled fill to her double.
7 How much she hath glorified herself, and lived deliciously, so much
torment and sorrow give her: for she saith in her heart, I sit a queen, and
am no widow, and shall see no sorrow.
8 Therefore shall her plagues come in one day, death, and mourning, and
famine; and she shall be utterly burned with fire: for strong *is* the Lord
God who judgeth her.

18:4 Gen 19:12, 13; Isa 52:11; Jer 51:6, 9, 45; 2 Cor 6:17
18:5 Jer 51:9; Jonah 1:2; Rev 16:19
☆**18:6** Ps 137:8; Jer 51:24; Rev 17:4
18:7 Isa 47:7, 8
18:8 Isa 47:9; Jer 50:31, 34; Rev 17:16

17:17 In the midst of this great evil, God is using wicked men to accomplish divine purposes. God has supreme power and control. All the forces of darkness on earth and hell are subject to him, as he directs events toward the consummation of all things.

18:1ff Babylon is about to fall. In verses 4–8 God calls for his people to flee the city. Its punishment is certain.

18:2, 3 Babylon is guilty of having corrupted the nations. Kings have shared in her wantonness and merchants have grown rich in their trade through her. She and all of them shall share her doom and be rewarded according to their works.

18:6 *double unto her double according to her works.* She is not to receive twice as much punishment as she deserves; rather, the extent of her punishment will be equal to the extent of her sin. God is not unjust even in punishment, and no one shall receive more than his sins deserve.

5. The World Mourns over Babylon

18:9☆ Ps 58:10; Jer 50:46; Ezek 26:16; Dan 4:14; Rev 17:2

9 And the kings of the earth, who have committed fornication and lived deliciously with her, shall bewail her, and lament for her, when they shall see the smoke of her burning,

18:10☆ Num 16:34; Amos 5:16; Rev 14:8

10 Standing afar off for the fear of her torment, saying, Alas, alas that great city Babylon, that mighty city! for in one hour is thy judgment come.

18:11☆ Ezek 27:27; Rev 18:3

11 And the merchants of the earth shall weep and mourn over her; for no man buyeth their merchandise any more:

12 The merchandise of gold, and silver, and precious stones, and of pearls, and fine linen, and purple, and silk, and scarlet, and all thyine wood, and all manner vessels of ivory, and all manner vessels of most precious wood, and of brass, and iron, and marble,

18:13 1 Tim 1:10

13 And cinnamon, and odours, and ointments, and frankincense, and wine, and oil, and fine flour, and wheat, and beasts, and sheep, and horses, and chariots, and slaves, and souls of men.

14 And the fruits that thy soul lusted after are departed from thee, and all things which were dainty and goodly are departed from thee, and thou shalt find them no more at all.

15 The merchants of these things, which were made rich by her, shall stand afar off for the fear of her torment, weeping and wailing,

18:16 Lk 16:19; Rev 17:4

16 And saying, Alas, alas, that great city, that was clothed in fine linen, and purple, and scarlet, and decked with gold, and precious stones, and pearls!

18:17☆ Isa 47:9; Ezek 27:27–36; Jonah 1:6; Rev 17:16

17 For in one hour so great riches is come to nought. And every shipmaster, and all the company in ships, and sailors, and as many as trade by sea, stood afar off,

18:18 Ezek 27:30, 32; Rev 13:4

18 And cried when they saw the smoke of her burning, saying, What *city is* like unto this great city!

18:19 Job 2:12; Ezek 27:30; Rev 18:3

19 And they cast dust on their heads, and cried, weeping and wailing, saying, Alas, alas, that great city, wherein were made rich all that had ships in the sea by reason of her costliness! for in one hour is she made desolate.

6. Heaven Rejoices over Babylon's Fate

18:20☆ Ps 96:11–13; Jer 51:48; Lk 11:49, 50; Eph 2:20; 3:5; Rev 6:10; 12:12; 19:2

20 Rejoice over her, *thou* heaven, and *ye* holy apostles and prophets; for God hath avenged you on her.

7. Babylon Doomed Forever

18:21☆ Jer 51:63, 64; Dan 11:19

21 And a mighty angel took up a stone like a great millstone, and cast *it* into the sea, saying, Thus with violence shall that great city Babylon be thrown down, and shall be found no more at all.

18:9, 10 The kings of the earth lament the fall of Babylon. They position themselves afar off, lest they share the same fate. They will share that fate, for there is no sign of repentance, only a dirge of woe for fallen Babylon.

18:11ff The merchants weep and mourn over the judgment against Babylon. It is purely selfish because they would have acres of unsold merchandise. Babylon *was their chief market, their patron; in a single hour* all is destroyed, their market perished.

18:17ff The third lamentation is heard from shipmasters whose maritime interests are impaired by the loss of Babylon. They looked on the smoke of her burning and cast dust in the air and on their heads in dismay and consternation.

18:20 While the whole world mourns the loss of Babylon, all heaven rejoices that judgment has come at last. There is a pay day some day, and that day has come for Babylon.

18:21–24 A mighty angel takes a huge millstone and drops it into the ocean. As that stone sinks to rise no more and be seen of no one forever, so shall this happen to Babylon. All music will have been stilled. All commerce will have ceased. All lights will have gone out. All marriage will have ceased. All that will be left is the bloodstains of the saints and the prophets who have been murdered. *The voice of the bridegroom and of the bride shall be heard no more,* i.e., there will no longer be any marriages, any more than music or commerce.

22 And the voice of harpers, and musicians, and of pipers, and trumpeters,
shall be heard no more at all in thee; and no craftsman, of whatsoever craft
he be, shall be found any more in thee; and the sound of a millstone shall be
heard no more at all in thee;

18:22 Isa 24:8 Ezek 26:13

23 And the light of a candle shall shine no more at all in thee; and the
voice of the bridegroom and of the bride shall be heard no more at all in
thee: for thy merchants were the great men of the earth; for by thy sorceries
were all nations deceived.

18:23 Prov 4:18, 19 24:20 Jer 7:34; 16:9 Nah 3:4

24 And in her was found the blood of prophets, and of saints, and of all
that were slain upon the earth.

18:24 Mt 23:34–36 Rev 16:6; 17:6

B. HEAVEN'S "ALLELUIA" OVER GOD'S JUDGMENT OF BABYLON

19 AND after these things I heard a great voice of much people in
heaven, saying, Alleluia; Salvation, and glory, and honour, and
power, unto the Lord our God:
2 For true and righteous *are* his judgments: for he hath judged the great
whore, which did corrupt the earth with her fornication, and hath avenged
the blood of his servants at her hand.
3 And again they said, Alleluia. And her smoke rose up for ever and ever.
4 And the four and twenty elders and the four beasts fell down and
worshipped God that sat on the throne, saying, Amen; Alleluia.
5 And a voice came out of the throne, saying, Praise our God, all ye his
servants, and ye that fear him, both small and great.
6 And I heard as it were the voice of a great multitude, and as the voice of
many waters, and as the voice of mighty thunderings, saying, Alleluia: for
the Lord God omnipotent reigneth.

☆**19:1** Ps 104:35 Jer 51:48 Jonah 2:9 Mt 6:13 Rev 4:11; 7:10 12:10
☆**19:2** Rev 6:10; 16:7 17:1; 18:20
19:3 Gen 19:28 Isa 34:10 Rev 4:4; 14:11
☆**19:4** Rev 4:10; 5:14
19:5 Ps 115:12, 13 134:1; 135:1 Rev 11:18
☆**19:6** Rev 11:15

7 Let us be glad and rejoice, and give honour to him: for the marriage of
the Lamb is come, and his wife hath made herself ready.
8 And to her was granted that she should be arrayed in fine linen, clean
and white: for the fine linen is the righteousness of saints.
9 And he saith unto me, Write, Blessed *are* they which are called unto the
marriage supper of the Lamb. And he saith unto me, These are the true
sayings of God.
10 And I fell at his feet to worship him. And he said unto me, See *thou do
it* not: I am thy fellowservant, and of thy brethren that have the testimony
of Jesus: worship God: for the testimony of Jesus is the spirit of prophecy.

☆**19:7** Ps 45:10–16 Hos 2:19, 20 Mt 25:1–10 Eph 5:25–32 Rev 21:2
19:8 Ps 45:13; 132:9 Rev 15:4, 6 19:14
19:9 Hab 2:2 Lk 14:15; 22:16 Rev 21:5; 22:6
19:10 Acts 10:26 Rev 22:8, 9

19:1ff In this segment of Scripture (from 19:1 to 19:8) there are four "Alleluias." The word means "Praise the Lord." Up to this point there has been music on earth and in heaven. But now the "Hallelujah Chorus" is sung. In all of the New Testament the word "Alleluia" *never appears until it is used in the Revelation.* The first two "Alleluias" are in celebration of the end of Babylon. The harlot has been judged (19:2) and the smoke goes up from her for ever and ever (19:3). (See notes on 19:4 and 6 concerning the third and fourth "Alleluias.")

19:2 There are at least four bases on which God renders judgment: (1) he judges according to truth—and there can be no concealment or deception because he is omniscient; (2) he makes no exceptions, i.e., none can escape the judicial verdict and he will give each one whatever his deeds deserve; (3) he is not moved by personal considerations, i.e., he treats everyone the same (Rom. 2:11) and no extenuating circumstances, personal heritage, or background makes any difference; (4) he judges the motives as well as the external conduct. Men behold the external act but cannot measure the internal motivation. All secret thoughts are known to him.

19:4 This is the third "Alleluia," sung by the twenty-four elders and the four living creatures.

19:6 The fourth "Alleluia" is sung in celebration of the marriage supper of the Lamb. This is the grand oratorio in which all the choirs of heaven join. It is the "voice of a great multitude" and the "voice of many waters and . . . mighty thunderings."

19:7 The marriage supper or the wedding banquet of the Lamb apparently precedes the Second Advent of Christ, since it is mentioned first. The saints attend the supper. This means the saved of all ages, including those who died in the faith, before and after Calvary.

C. THE OVERTHROW OF THE BEAST AND THE FALSE PROPHET

11 And I saw heaven opened, and behold a white horse; and he that sat
upon him *was* called Faithful and True, and in righteousness he doth judge
and make war.
12 His eyes *were* as a flame of fire, and on his head *were* many crowns; and
he had a name written, that no man knew, but he himself.
13 And he *was* clothed with a vesture dipped in blood: and his name is
called The Word of God.
14 And the armies *which were* in heaven followed him upon white horses,
clothed in fine linen, white and clean.
15 And out of his mouth goeth a sharp sword, that with it he should smite
the nations: and he shall rule them with a rod of iron: and he treadeth the
winepress of the fierceness and wrath of Almighty God.
16 And he hath on *his* vesture and on his thigh a name written, KING OF
KINGS, AND LORD OF LORDS.
17 And I saw an angel standing in the sun; and he cried with a loud voice,
saying to all the fowls that fly in the midst of heaven, Come and gather
yourselves together unto the supper of the great God;
18 That ye may eat the flesh of kings, and the flesh of captains, and the
flesh of mighty men, and the flesh of horses, and of them that sit on them,
and the flesh of all *men, both* free and bond, both small and great.
19 And I saw the beast, and the kings of the earth, and their armies,
gathered together to make war against him that sat on the horse, and
against his army.
20 And the beast was taken, and with him the false prophet that wrought
miracles before him, with which he deceived them that had received the
mark of the beast, and them that worshipped his image. These both were
cast alive into a lake of fire burning with brimstone.
21 And the remnant were slain with the sword of him that sat upon the
horse, which *sword* proceeded out of his mouth: and all the fowls were filled
with their flesh.

D. THE BINDING OF THE DEVIL

20 AND I saw an angel come down from heaven, having the key of the
bottomless pit and a great chain in his hand.
2 And he laid hold on the dragon, that old serpent, which is the Devil, and
Satan, and bound him a thousand years,

19:11 Isa 11:4; Jn 1:51; Rev 1:14; 3:14; 6:2
19:12 Gen 32:29; Isa 9:6; Lk 10:22; Rev 2:17
19:13☆ Isa 63:1–3; Jn 1:1, 14
19:14 Mt 28:3; Rev 3:4; 4:4
19:15 Isa 11:4; 63:3; 2 Thess 2:8; Rev 1:16; 2:27; 14:19, 20
19:16 Rev 2:17; 17:14
19:17 Isa 56:9; Jer 12:9; Ezek 39:17–20
19:19 Rev 13:1; 16:14, 16; 18:9
19:20 Dan 2:40–45; 7:7, 11–14; 2 Thess 2:8–11; Rev 13:11–16; 14:10; 20:10, 14, 15; 21:8
20:1 Lk 8:31; 2 Pet 2:4; Rev 1:18; 9:1
20:2☆ Gen 3:15; Isa 24:21, 22; 27:1; Rom 16:20; Heb 2:14; Rev 12:9

19:13 The Bible is the Word of God; Jesus is the Word of God incarnate. He comes as conquering Lord with a sharp sword to take vengeance on the enemies of God. The beast and the false prophet are taken captive and thrown alive into the lake of fire that burns with brimstone. In 20:2 Satan is bound for a thousand years. The people of God of all ages have nothing now to fear. The victory has been won, and God has triumphed over evil forever.

20:2 Generally, Christians have entertained one of three views regarding the millennium (which means a period of a thousand years—although some think it indicates a period of time rather than an exact number *of years). (1) Postmillennialism* looks for a thousand-year period of peace and plenty brought in by the church whereby the preached gospel conquers the world. At the end of the thousand years Christ will return to earth, at which time the new heaven and the new earth will be established and eternity will begin. St. Augustine was a great proponent of postmillennialism and many evangelical scholars a hundred years ago promoted the view. Very few Bible believers accept this view today, especially in the light of the decline of optimism about the human race. (2) Amillennialism says there can be no literal thousand-year earthly kingdom before or after the coming of the Lord which will mark the inauguration of the new heaven and the new earth and eternity. Some amillenarians hold that the thousand years of 20:2 constitute the period between the first and the second coming of Christ. (3) Premillennialism looks for the Second Coming of Christ, at which time the millennium will begin. At the end of that time, Satan (who has been bound for a thousand years) will be loosed and a great rebellion will be brought into being. Then Satan will be cast into the lake of fire forever. Before the coming of the Lord there will be the period of the great tribulation and at this point premillennialists differ. Some think the church will be raptured before the great tribulation begins; some hold it will be raptured at the end of the first half of that

3 And cast him into the bottomless pit, and shut him up, and set a seal
upon him, that he should deceive the nations no more, till the thousand
years should be fulfilled: and after that he must be loosed a little season.

E. THE THOUSAND YEAR REIGN

4 And I saw thrones, and they sat upon them, and judgment was given
unto them: and *I saw* the souls of them that were beheaded for the witness
of Jesus, and for the word of God, and which had not worshipped the beast,
neither his image, neither had received *his* mark upon their foreheads, or in
their hands; and they lived and reigned with Christ a thousand years.
5 But the rest of the dead lived not again until the thousand years were
finished. This *is* the first resurrection.
6 Blessed and holy *is* he that hath part in the first resurrection: on such
the second death hath no power, but they shall be priests of God and of
Christ, and shall reign with him a thousand years.

20:4 Dan 7:9, 18, 22, 27; Mt 19:28; 2 Tim 2:12; Rev 3:21; 6:9, 13
☆**20:5** Ezek 37:2–14; Lk 14:14; Jn 5:28, 29; Rom 11:15
20:6 1 Pet 2:9; Rev 1:6; 5:10; 20:14; 21:8

F. THE LAST REVOLT

7 And when the thousand years are expired, Satan shall be loosed out of
his prison,
8 And shall go out to deceive the nations which are in the four quarters of
the earth, Gog and Ma′gog, to gather them together to battle: the number
of whom *is* as the sand of the sea.
9 And they went up on the breadth of the earth, and compassed the camp
of the saints about, and the beloved city: and fire came down from God out
of heaven, and devoured them.
10 And the devil that deceived them was cast into the lake of fire and
brimstone, where the beast and the false prophet *are,* and shall be
tormented day and night for ever and ever.

20:7 Rev 20:2
20:8 Ezek 38:2; Heb 11:12; 1 Pet 5:8; Rev 16:14
20:9 Ps 87:2; Ezek 38:9, 22; 39:6; Lk 9:54; 17:29; 2 Thess 1:8; Heb 13:13
☆**20:10** Mt 25:41, 46; Rev 14:10; 19:20; 20:14, 15

---

period; others hold that the church will go through the great tribulation, at which time both the rapture and the Second Coming take place.

Amillennialism makes unnecessary the fulfillment of the Old Testament prophecies concerning Israel's restoration, the creation of a new temple, and a time of peace and prosperity for Abraham's seed. Differing views of the millennium do not constitute grounds for division, since all believe in the coming of the Lord and the establishment of his eternal kingdom. Perhaps a fourth eschatological scheme should be mentioned, one which none of the others take seriously. It holds that the Revelation simply portrays the perennial struggle between good and evil, so that neither the historical nor the geographical details have more than symbolical significance. (See also the note to Rom. 11:1 on dispensationalism for the distinction between Israel and the church.) Virtually all amillennialists hold that the church is the new Israel. This forecloses for them the need for any literal fulfillment of Old Testament prophecies for Israel.

20:5 Some commentators think this first resurrection includes only those martyrs mentioned in verse 4. They then participate in Christ's thousand-year reign, after which the general resurrection of the other dead takes place. Others understand the first resurrection to include *all* the righteous dead who will then reign with Christ for a thousand years, at the end of which time the second resurrection of the unbelieving dead will occur. This view is tied in with 1 Thess. 4, which speaks of the rapture. This latter view is, of course, part of the premillennial position. Whatever view one takes, there are problems, not fully resolved, having to do with Israel and the church.

20:10 Here Satan is cast into the lake of fire. Satan's existence cannot be denied. He apparently was one of God's holy angels, highest in the angelic hierarchy, who revolted against his Creator and fell. Many believe that the serpent of Gen. 3:1 was Satan. He tempted Jesus (Matt. 4:1; Luke 4:2). Paul called him "the prince of the power of the air" (Eph. 2:2). Jesus said he is "the prince of this world" (John 12:31). In chapter 20 Satan is bound for a thousand years, loosed at the end of that period, and then cast into the lake of fire to suffer consciously forever.

Some have challenged the doctrine of eternal conscious punishment either by assuming that all men will ultimately be saved or that unrepentant sinners will be annihilated and cease to exist. But the doctrine of eternal, conscious punishment is clearly indicated in the Scriptures by such expressions as (1) eternal fire (Matt. 25:41); (2) the fire never goes out (Mark 9:48); and (3) the lake that burns with fire and sulphur (21:8). Furthermore, the Greek term for the adjective "eternal" is the same, whether it modifies "life" or "death." The phrase *eis tous aiōnas tōn aiōnōn,* "unto the ages of the ages" is used for endless life and endless death (cf. 1:18; 11:15; 14:11; 20:10).

G. THE GREAT WHITE THRONE JUDGMENT

20:11☆ Dan 2:35 Rev 4:2; 6:14
20:12☆ Jer 17:10 Dan 7:10; 12:1 Rom 14:10–12 2 Cor 5:10 Rev 2:23 20:13, 15
20:13 Mt 16:27
20:14 1 Cor 15:26; 53 Rev 20:6, 10, 15
20:15 Rev 3:5; 20:12

11 And I saw a great white throne, and him that sat on it, from whose face the earth and the heaven fled away; and there was found no place for them.

12 And I saw the dead, small and great, stand before God; and the books were opened: and another book was opened, which is *the book* of life: and the dead were judged out of those things which were written in the books, according to their works.

13 And the sea gave up the dead which were in it; and death and hell delivered up the dead which were in them: and they were judged every man according to their works.

14 And death and hell were cast into the lake of fire. This is the second death.

15 And whosoever was not found written in the book of life was cast into the lake of fire.

H. THE NEW EARTH AND HEAVENS

21:1 Isa 65:17; 66:22 2 Pet 3:10, 13 Rev 20:11
21:2☆ Jer 31:23 Gal 4:26 Heb 11:10; 12:22 13:14
21:3 Lev 26:11 1 Kgs 8:27 Zech 13:9 2 Cor 6:16
21:4 Isa 25:8; 35:10 61:3 1 Cor 7:31 Rev 7:17
21:5☆ Isa 43:19 2 Cor 5:17 Heb 11:26, 27 Rev 22:6
21:6☆ Joel 3:18 Jn 4:14 Rev 1:8; 22:17
21:7 Rom 8:17, 32 Heb 8:10 Rev 2:7; 23:3
21:8 Deut 20:8 Judg 7:3 Mal 3:5 1 Cor 6:9, 10 Gal 5:19–21 Eph 5:5 Rev 2:11

21 AND I saw a new heaven and a new earth: for the first heaven and the first earth were passed away; and there was no more sea.

2 And I John saw the holy city, new Jerusalem, coming down from God out of heaven, prepared as a bride adorned for her husband.

3 And I heard a great voice out of heaven saying, Behold, the tabernacle of God *is* with men, and he will dwell with them, and they shall be his people, and God himself shall be with them, *and be* their God.

4 And God shall wipe away all tears from their eyes; and there shall be no more death, neither sorrow, nor crying, neither shall there be any more pain: for the former things are passed away.

5 And he that sat upon the throne said, Behold, I make all things new. And he said unto me, Write: for these words are true and faithful.

6 And he said unto me, It is done. I am Alpha and Omega, the beginning and the end. I will give unto him that is athirst of the fountain of the water of life freely.

7 He that overcometh shall inherit all things; and I will be his God, and he shall be my son.

8 But the fearful, and unbelieving, and the abominable, and murderers, and whoremongers, and sorcerers, and idolaters, and all liars, shall have their part in the lake which burneth with fire and brimstone: which is the second death.

20:11, 12 The last judgment, that of the great white throne, will take place, so many believe, at the end of the thousand years, at which time the wicked dead will be raised and then judged. The passage refers to books, one of which is the book of life. We do not know how many other books there are, but surely the book of works and the book of memory will be among them. Whoever does not have his name inscribed in the book of life will be cast into the lake of fire. There will be no appeal. Since one's works are included in the scrutiny, it gives substance to the notion that there are degrees of punishment for the wicked dead just as there are *degrees of reward for the righteous.*

21:2 The *holy city, new Jerusalem,* is the final abode of the saints. This eternal habitation becomes theirs after the judgment of the great white throne. This city comes down from God out of heaven, and its boundaries, structures, and inhabitants are all described. The description is only symbolic, but the saints can rest assured that the reality will defy description and meet the highest expectations of all who inhabit the city.

21:5 *I make all things new.* The cosmos was stained with the sin of Satan and of Adam. Following the victory of Jesus Christ, which is a cosmic victory, all residual elements of the fall are removed and the universe returns to its prefall perfection for eternity. The new age, timewise, is referred to by Jesus Christ in Matt. 19:28, where he says, "in the regeneration when the Son of man shall sit in the throne of his glory." This will occur after the Second Advent, when Satan will have been finally defeated.

21:6 I am the Alpha and Omega, the beginning and the *end.* The will and the power of God Almighty were the first cause of everything seen and unseen. Now the pleasure and the glory of the Creator, Sustainer, and Redeemer are fulfilled. Sinless perfection has come and God is all in all.

V. THE FOURTH VISION (21:9—22:5)

A. THE NEW CITY OF GOD

9And there came unto me one of the seven angels which had the seven
vials full of the seven last plagues, and talked with me, saying, Come hither,
I will shew thee the bride, the Lamb's wife.
10And he carried me away in the spirit to a great and high mountain, and
shewed me that great city, the holy Jerusalem, descending out of heaven
from God,
11Having the glory of God: and her light *was* like unto a stone most
precious, even like a jasper stone, clear as crystal;
12And had a wall great and high, *and* had twelve gates, and at the gates
twelve angels, and names written thereon, which are *the names* of the twelve
tribes of the children of Israel:
13On the east three gates; on the north three gates; on the south three
gates; and on the west three gates.
14And the wall of the city had twelve foundations, and in them the names
of the twelve apostles of the Lamb.

☆**21:9** Rev 21:2
21:10 Ezek 40:1, 2; Acts 8:39; 2 Cor 12:2–4; Rev 1:10; 17:3
21:11 Job 28:17; Isa 60:1; Ezek 48:35; Rev 4:3
21:12 Ezek 48:31–34; Rev 22:14
21:14 Eph 2:20; Heb 11:10

B. THE DIMENSIONS OF THE CITY

15And he that talked with me had a golden reed to measure the city, and
the gates thereof, and the wall thereof.
16And the city lieth foursquare, and the length is as large as the breadth:
and he measured the city with the reed, twelve thousand furlongs. The
length and the breadth and the height of it are equal.
17And he measured the wall thereof, an hundred *and* forty *and* four
cubits, *according to* the measure of a man, that is, of the angel.
18And the building of the wall of it was *of* jasper: and the city *was* pure
gold, like unto clear glass.
19And the foundations of the wall of the city *were* garnished with all
manner of precious stones. The first foundation was jasper; the second,
sapphire; the third, a chalcedony; the fourth, an emerald;
20The fifth, sardonyx; the sixth, sardius; the seventh, chrysolyte; the
eighth, beryl; the ninth, a topaz; the tenth, a chrysoprasus; the eleventh, a
jacinth; the twelfth, an amethyst.
21And the twelve gates *were* twelve pearls; every several gate was of one
pearl: and the street of the city *was* pure gold, as it were transparent glass.

21:15 Ezek 40:3; Zech 2:1, 3; Rev 11:1
21:17 Deut 3:11; Rev 13:18
21:18–20 Ex 28:15–21; Isa 54:11, 12; Rev 4:3, 6; 21:11, 21

C. THE LIGHT OF THE CITY

22And I saw no temple therein: for the Lord God Almighty and the
Lamb are the temple of it.
23And the city had no need of the sun, neither of the moon, to shine in it:
for the glory of God did lighten it, and the Lamb *is* the light thereof.
24And the nations of them which are saved shall walk in the light of it:
and the kings of the earth do bring their glory and honour into it.
25And the gates of it shall not be shut at all by day: for there shall be no
night there.
26And they shall bring the glory and honour of the nations into it.

☆**21:22** Ps 90:1; Jn 4:21–24; 17:23, 24; Rev 7:17; 14:4
☆**21:23** Isa 60:19, 20; Rev 21:25
21:24 Ps 72:10; Isa 60:3; 66:10–14; Zech 2:11; Rom 15:10–12
21:25 Isa 60:11, 20; Zech 14:7; Rev 22:5
21:26 Ps 72:10; Isa 49:23

21:9 *the bride, the Lamb's wife,* i.e., the church of God—at last triumphant, perfected, and glorious in holiness.
21:22, 23 The New Jerusalem needs neither the sun nor the moon to light it. Nor is there any temple. God and the Son are the temple and the light of the city. God is light and wherever God is, there is light—nothing else is needed.

21:27☆ Isa 52:1; Joel 3:17; Rev 3:5; 22:14, 15

27 And there shall in no wise enter into it any thing that defileth, neither
whatsoever worketh abomination, or *maketh* a lie: but they which are
written in the Lamb's book of life.

D. THE BLESSINGS OF THE CITY

22:1 Ps 36:8; 46:4; Ezek 47:1, 2; Zech 14:8; Jn 4:10–14; 7:37–39; Rev 7:17
22:2☆ Gen 2:9; Ezek 47:12; Lk 4:18; 1 Pet 2:24; Rev 2:7, 22:14
22:3 Zech 14:11; Rom 5:17; Rev 7:15
22:4 Mt 5:8; 1 Cor 13:12; 1 Jn 3:2; Rev 7:3, 14:1
22:5 Dan 7:18, 27; Zech 14:6, 7; Rev 21:23, 25

22 AND he shewed me a pure river of water of life, clear as crystal,
proceeding out of the throne of God and of the Lamb.
2 In the midst of the street of it, and on either side of the river, *was there*
the tree of life, which bare twelve *manner of* fruits, *and* yielded her fruit
every month: and the leaves of the tree *were* for the healing of the nations.
3 And there shall be no more curse: but the throne of God and of the
Lamb shall be in it; and his servants shall serve him:
4 And they shall see his face; and his name *shall be* in their foreheads.
5 And there shall be no night there; and they need no candle, neither light
of the sun; for the Lord God giveth them light: and they shall reign for ever
and ever.

VI. THE EPILOGUE (22:6–21)

A. THE TRUTH OF THE REVELATION

22:6, 7☆ Rev 1:3; 21:5; 22:12

6 And he said unto me, These sayings *are* faithful and true: and the Lord
God of the holy prophets sent his angel to shew unto his servants the things
which must shortly be done.
7 Behold, I come quickly: blessed *is* he that keepeth the sayings of the
prophecy of this book.

22:8 Rev 1:1–4
22:9 Rev 19:10

8 And I John saw these things, and heard *them.* And when I had heard
and seen, I fell down to worship before the feet of the angel which shewed
me these things.
9 Then saith he unto me, See *thou do it* not: for I am thy fellowservant,
and of thy brethren the prophets, and of them which keep the sayings of
this book: worship God.

B. THE EVILDOERS AND THE RIGHTEOUS CONTRASTED

22:10 Dan 12:4, 9; Rev 1:3
22:11☆ Ezek 3:27; Dan 12:10; 2 Tim 3:13
22:12 Isa 40:10; 62:11, 12; Mt 16:27; Rev 22:7
22:13☆ Isa 44:6; Rev 1:8, 17; 21:6

10 And he saith unto me, Seal not the sayings of the prophecy of this
book: for the time is at hand.
11 He that is unjust, let him be unjust still: and he which is filthy, let him
be filthy still: and he that is righteous, let him be righteous still: and he that
is holy, let him be holy still.
12 And, behold, I come quickly; and my reward *is* with me, to give every
man according as his work shall be.
13 I am Alpha and Omega, the beginning and the end, the first and the
last.

21:27 The city's residents comprise those whose names are written in the Lamb's book of life, and no others. In contrast, 21:8 characterizes those who are excluded from the city and who will be assigned to their final destiny in the lake of fire.

22:2 *the tree of life.* Adam could have but did not eat of the fruit of the tree of life. When he sinned he was no longer free to eat of the tree of life. Now at the end of the age in the new Jerusalem the tree of life is there for the people of God, who will eat of its fruit forever and live forever.

22:7 We are to read, understand, and obey the words of this prophecy.

22:11ff John states plainly that at the end of the age evil will be stronger than ever. Instead of turning to God, evildoers will flee from him even further. There is no word about universal salvation, but there is always the one invitation, even to the worst sinner, to come to Christ. Verse 17 is ever the open door for sinners.

22:13 The Revelation opens with Jesus portrayed as the Alpha and the Omega, and it closes with the same refrain. All of the book is about the reigning Christ who waits at the Father's right hand for that moment when he will come the second time in power and great glory.

14Blessed *are* they that do his commandments, that they may have right
to the tree of life, and may enter in through the gates into the city.
15For without *are* dogs, and sorcerers, and whoremongers, and murder-
ers, and idolaters, and whosoever loveth and maketh a lie.

C. THE INVITATION TO COME

16I Jesus have sent mine angel to testify unto you these things in the
churches. I am the root and the offspring of David, *and the bright and
morning star.*
17And the Spirit and the bride say, Come. And let him that heareth say,
Come. And let him that is athirst come. And whosoever will, let him take
the water of life freely.
18For I testify unto every man that heareth the words of the prophecy of
this book, If any man shall add unto these things, God shall add unto him
the plagues that are written in this book:
19And if any man shall take away from the words of the book of this
prophecy, God shall take away his part out of the book of life, and out of
the holy city, and *from* the things which are written in this book.
20He which testifieth these things saith, Surely I come quickly. Amen.
Even so, come, Lord Jesus.

D. THE BENEDICTION

21The grace of our Lord Jesus Christ *be* with you all. Amen.

☆**22:14** Rev 21:2, 12, 27
22:15 Deut 23:18; 1 Cor 6:9; Gal 5:19–21; Phil 3:2; Rev 21:8
22:16 Isa 11:1; Jer 23:5; Mt 1:1; 2:2; Rev 1:1; 2:28
22:17 Isa 55:1; Zech 8:21–23; Jn 7:37–39; Rev 2:7, 7:17; 21:2, 6, 9
☆**22:18** Deut 4:2; 12:32; Prov 30:5, 6; Eph 4:17; Rev 15:6–16; 22:7
22:19 Ex 32:33; Deut 4:2; Ps 69:28; Lk 11:52; Rev 3:5; 21:10—22:5
☆**22:20** 1 Thess 1:10; Heb 9:28; Rev 1:2; 22:7, 16
22:21 Rom 16:20

22:14 There are choices to be made. The time is short and no one should defer making the right choice, so that they may enjoy the right to the tree of life. Everlasting life or everlasting death is at stake.

22:18 John warns one and all about the dangers that can spring from tampering with the Word of God. This reference has to do with the Revelation. But by inference we can extend it to the totality of Scripture. For if it is wrong to tamper with the Revelation, which is God's Word, it is equally wrong to tamper with anything else that is the Word of God.

22:20 John expresses his fervent hope that Christ will come shortly as promised. The Revelation closes the Bible as Genesis opens it. The garden in which Adam lived and from which he was ejected because of his sin has been replaced by the new Jerusalem, where the inhabitants experience the regaining of the Paradise that Adam lost.

GUIDE TO
DAILY BIBLE READING

JANUARY
1☐ Gen 1, 2
2☐ Gen 3-5
3☐ Gen 6-9
4☐ Gen 10, 11
5☐ Gen 12-15
6☐ Gen 16-19
7☐ Gen 20-22
8☐ Job 1-4
9☐ Job 5-7
10☐ Job 8-10
11☐ Job 11-13
12☐ Job 14-17
13☐ Job 18-20
14☐ Job 21-24
15☐ Job 25-27
16☐ Job 28-31
17☐ Job 32-34
18☐ Job 35-37
19☐ Job 38-42
20☐ Gen 23-26
21☐ Gen 27-29
22☐ Gen 30-32
23☐ Gen 33-36
24☐ Gen 37-39
25☐ Gen 40-42
26☐ Gen 43-46
27☐ Gen 47-50
28☐ Ex 1-4
29☐ Ex 5-7
30☐ Ex 8-10
31☐ Ex 11-13

FEBRUARY
1☐ Ex 14-17
2☐ Ex 18-20
3☐ Ex 21-24
4☐ Ex 25-27
5☐ Ex 28-31
6☐ Ex 32-34
7☐ Ex 35-37
8☐ Ex 38-40
9☐ Lev 1-3
10☐ Lev 4-7
11☐ Lev 8-10
12☐ Lev 11-13
13☐ Lev 14-16
14☐ Lev 17-19
15☐ Lev 20-23
16☐ Lev 24-27
17☐ Num 1-3
18☐ Num 4-6
19☐ Num 7-10
20☐ Num 11-14
21☐ Num 15-17
22☐ Num 18-20
23☐ Num 21-24
24☐ Num 25-27
25☐ Num 28-30
26☐ Num 31-33
27☐ Num 34-36
28☐ Deut 1-3

MARCH
1☐ Deut 4-6
2☐ Deut 7-9
3☐ Deut 10-12
4☐ Deut 13-16
5☐ Deut 17-19
6☐ Deut 20-22
7☐ Deut 23-25
8☐ Deut 26-28
9☐ Deut 29-31
10☐ Deut 32-34
11☐ Josh 1-3; Ps. 91
12☐ Josh 4-6
13☐ Josh 7-9
14☐ Josh 10-12
15☐ Josh 13-15
16☐ Josh 16-18
17☐ Josh 19-21
18☐ Josh 22-24
19☐ Jud 1-4
20☐ Jud 5-8
21☐ Jud 9-12
22☐ Jud 13-15
23☐ Jud 16-18
24☐ Jud 19-21
25☐ Ruth 1-4
26☐ 1 Sam 1-3
27☐ 1 Sam 4-7
28☐ 1 Sam 8-10
29☐ 1 Sam 11-13
30☐ 1 Sam 14-16
31☐ 1 Sam 17-19; Ps. 23

APRIL
1☐ Ps 59; 1 Sam 20-21
2☐ Ps. 34, 56; 1 Sam 22
3☐ Ps 57, 142, 52
4☐ 1 Sam 23; Ps. 54, 63
5☐ 1 Sam 24-27
6☐ 1 Sam 28-31
7☐ 2 Sam 1-4
8☐ 2 Sam 5-7
9☐ Ps 30, 60; 2 Sam. 8
10☐ 2 Sam 9-12
11☐ Ps 51, 32
12☐ 2 Sam 13-15
13☐ Ps 3, 69; 2 Sam 16
14☐ 2 Sam 17-19
15☐ 2 Sam 20; Ps. 64, 70
16☐ 2 Sam 21, 22; Ps 18
17☐ 2 Sam 23, 24
18☐ Ps 4, 5
19☐ Ps 7-9
20☐ Ps 11-13
21☐ Ps 14-17
22☐ Ps 19-21
23☐ Ps 22, 24, 25
24☐ Ps 26-28
25☐ Ps 29, 31, 35
26☐ Ps 36-38
27☐ Ps 39-41
28☐ Ps 53, 55, 58
29☐ Ps 61, 62, 65
30☐ Ps 68, 72, 86

MAY
1☐ Ps 101, 103, 108
2☐ Ps 109, 110, 138
3☐ Ps 139-141
4☐ Ps 143-145
5☐ 1 Kin 1-4
6☐ Prov 1-3
7☐ Prov 4-7
8☐ Prov 8-11
9☐ Prov 12-14
10☐ Prov 15-18
11☐ Prov 19-21
12☐ Prov 22-24
13☐ Prov 25-28
14☐ Prov 29-31
15☐ Song of Sol 1-4
16☐ Song of Sol 5-8
17☐ 1 Kin 5-7
18☐ 1 Kin 8-11
19☐ Ecc 1-3
20☐ Ecc 4-6
21☐ Ecc 7-9
22☐ Ecc 10-12
23☐ 1 Kin 12-14
24☐ 1 Kin 15-17
25☐ 1 Kin 18-20
26☐ 1 Kin 21-22
27☐ 2 Kin 1-3
28☐ 2 Kin 4-6
29☐ 2 Kin 7-10
30☐ 2 Kin 11-14
31☐ Jonah 1-4

JUNE
1☐ Amos 1-3
2☐ Amos 4-6
3☐ Amos 7-9
4☐ 2 Kin 15-17
5☐ 2 Kin 18, 19
6☐ 2 Kin 20, 21
7☐ 2 Kin 22-25
8☐ Ps 1, 2, 10
9☐ Ps 33, 43, 66
10☐ Ps 67, 71, 89
11☐ Ps 92, 94
12☐ Ps 95-97
13☐ Ps 98-100
14☐ Ps 102, 104, 105
15☐ Ps 106, 111, 112
16☐ Ps 113-115
17☐ Ps 116-118
18☐ Ps 119
19☐ Ps 120-122
20☐ Ps 123-125
21☐ Ps 127-129
22☐ Ps 130-132
23☐ Ps 133-135
24☐ Ps 136, 146, 147
25☐ Ps 148-150
26☐ 1 Chron 1-3
27☐ 1 Chron 4-6
28☐ 1 Chron 7-9
29☐ 1 Chron 10-13
30☐ 1 Chron 14-16

JULY
1☐ Ps 42, 44, 45
2☐ Ps 46-48

3☐ Ps 49, 50, 73
4☐ Ps 85, 87, 88
5☐ 1 Chron 17-19
6☐ 1 Chron 20-23
7☐ 1 Chron 24-26
8☐ 1 Chron 27-29
9☐ 2 Chron 1-3
10☐ 2 Chron 4-6
11☐ 2 Chron 7-9
12☐ 2 Chron 10-13
13☐ 2 Chron 14-16
14☐ 2 Chron 17-19
15☐ 2 Chron 20, 21
16☐ Obad; 2 Chron 22
17☐ Joel 1-3
18☐ 2 Chron 23-25
19☐ 2 Chron 26; Is 1-3
20☐ Is 4-6
21☐ 2 Chron 27-29
22☐ 2 Chron 30-32
23☐ Is 7-9
24☐ Is 10-12
25☐ Is 13-15
26☐ Is 16-18
27☐ Is 19-21
28☐ Is 22-24
29☐ Is 25-27
30☐ Is 28-30
31☐ Is 31-33

AUGUST
1☐ Is 34-36
2☐ Is 37-39
3☐ Is 40-42
4☐ Is 43-45
5☐ Is 46-48
6☐ Is 49-51
7☐ Is 52-54
8☐ Is 55-57
9☐ Is 58-60
10☐ Is 61-63
11☐ Is 64-66
12☐ Hos 1-4
13☐ Hos 5-7
14☐ Hos 8-10
15☐ Hos 11-14
16☐ Micah 1-4
17☐ Micah 5-7
18☐ Nah 1-3
19☐ 2 Chron 33, 34
20☐ Zeph 1-3
21☐ 2 Chron 35; Hab 1-3
22☐ Jer 1-3
23☐ Jer 4-6
24☐ Jer 11, 12, 26
25☐ Jer 7-10
26☐ Jer 14-18
27☐ Jer 19, 20, 35, 36
28☐ Jer 45, 25, 46
29☐ Jer 47-49
30☐ Jer 13, 22-24
31☐ Jer 27-29

SEPTEMBER
1☐ Jer 50, 51, 30
2☐ Jer 31-33
3☐ Jer 21, 34, 37, 38
4☐ Jer 39, 52, 40
5☐ Jer 41-44
6☐ Lam 1-5
7☐ 2 Chron 36; Dan 1-3
8☐ Dan 4-6
9☐ Dan 7-9
10☐ Dan 10-12
11☐ Ps 137; Ezek 1-3
12☐ Ezek 4-7
13☐ Ezek 8-11
14☐ Ezek 12-14
15☐ Ezek 15-18
16☐ Ezek 19-21
17☐ Ezek 22-24
18☐ Ezek 25-27
19☐ Ezek 28-30
20☐ Ezek 31-33
21☐ Ezek 34-36
22☐ Ezek 37-39
23☐ Ezek 40-42
24☐ Ezek 43-45
25☐ Ezek 46-48
26☐ Ezra 1-4
27☐ Hag 1, 2
28☐ Zech 1-5
29☐ Zech 6-10
30☐ Zech 11-14

OCTOBER
1☐ Ps 74-76
2☐ Ps 77-79
3☐ Ps 80-82
4☐ Ps 83, 84, 90
5☐ Ps 107, 126
6☐ Ezra 5-7
7☐ Es 1-5
8☐ Es 6-10
9☐ Ezra 8-10
10☐ Neh 1-3
11☐ Neh 4-6
12☐ Neh 7-9
13☐ Neh 10-13
14☐ Mal 1-4

NEW TESTAMENT
15☐ Matt 1-4
16☐ Matt 5-8
17☐ Matt 9-12
18☐ Matt 13-16
19☐ Matt 17-20
20☐ Matt 21-24
21☐ Matt 25-28
22☐ Mk 1-4
23☐ Mk 5-8
24☐ Mk 9-12
25☐ Mk 13-16
26☐ Lk 1-4
27☐ Lk 5-8
28☐ Lk 9-12
29☐ Lk 13-16
30☐ Lk 17-20
31☐ Lk 21-24

NOVEMBER
1☐ John 1-3
2☐ John 4-6
3☐ John 7-10
4☐ John 11-13
5☐ John 14-17
6☐ John 18-21
7☐ Acts 1, 2
8☐ Acts 3-5
9☐ Acts 6-9
10☐ Acts 10-12
11☐ Acts 13, 14
12☐ James 1, 2
13☐ James 3-5
14☐ Acts 15; Gal 1-3
15☐ Gal 4-6
16☐ Acts 16; Phil 1-4
17☐ Acts 17; 1 Thes 1-5
18☐ 2 Thes 1-3
19☐ Acts 18; 1 Cor 1-4
20☐ 1 Cor 5-8
21☐ 1 Cor 9-12
22☐ 1 Cor 13-16
23☐ 2 Cor 1-3
24☐ 2 Cor 4-6
25☐ 2 Cor 7-9
26☐ 2 Cor 10-13
27☐ Acts 19, 20; Eph 1, 2
28☐ Eph 3-6
29☐ Rom 1-4
30☐ Rom 5-8

DECEMBER
1☐ Rom 9-12
2☐ Rom 13-16
3☐ Acts 21, 22
4☐ Acts 23-25
5☐ Acts 26-28
6☐ Col 1-4
7☐ Heb 1-4
8☐ Heb 5-7
9☐ Heb 8-10
10☐ Heb 11-13
11☐ Titus; Phm.
12☐ 1 Tim 1-3
13☐ 1 Tim 4-6
14☐ 2 Tim 1-4
15☐ 1 Peter 1, 2
16☐ 1 Peter 3-5
17☐ 2 Peter 1-3
18☐ 1 John 1, 2
19☐ 1 John 3-5
20☐ 2 & 3 John; Jude
21☐ Rev 1-3
22☐ Rev 4, 5
23☐ Rev 6-8
24☐ Rev 9, 10
25☐ Christmas Story (Lk 1, 2)
26☐ Rev 11, 12
27☐ Rev 13, 14
28☐ Rev 15, 16
29☐ Rev 17, 18
30☐ Rev 19, 20
31☐ Rev 21, 22

THE BIBLE

F. F. Bruce

THE word "Bible" is derived through Latin from the Greek word *biblia* ("books"), specifically the books that are acknowledged as canonical by the Christian church. The earliest Christian use of *ta biblia* ("the books") in this sense is said to be *2 Clement* 14:2 (c. A.D. 150): "the books and the apostles declare that the church . . . has existed from the beginning." *Cf.* Dn. 9:2, "I Daniel perceived in the books" where the reference is to the corpus of OT prophetic writings. Gk. *biblion* (of which *biblia* is the plural) is a diminutive of *biblos,* which in practice denotes any kind of written document, but originally one written on papyrus.

A term synonymous with "the Bible" is "the writings" or "the Scriptures" (Gk. *hai graphai, ta grammata*), frequently used in the NT to denote the OT documents in whole or in part; *cf.* Mt. 21:42, "Have you never read in the scriptures?" (*en tais graphais*); the parallel passage Mk. 12:10 has the singular, referring to the particular text quoted, "have you not read this scripture?" (*ten graphen tauten*); 2 Tim. 3:15, "the sacred writings" (*ta hiera grammata*), v. 16, "all scripture is inspired by God" (*pasa graphe theopneustos*). In 2 Pet. 3:16 "all" the letters of Paul are included along with "the other scriptures" (*tas loipas graphas*), by which the OT writings and probably also the Gospels are meant.*

I. CONTENT AND AUTHORITY

Among Christians, for whom the OT and NT together constitute the Bible, there is not complete agreement on their content. Some branches of the Syriac church do not include 2 Peter, 2 and 3 John, Jude, and Revelation in the NT. The Roman and Greek communions include a number of books in the OT in addition to those that make up the Hebrew Bible; these additional books formed part of the Christian Septuagint.

While they are included, along with one or two others, in the complete Protestant English Bible, the Church of England (like the Lutheran Church) follows Jerome in holding that they may be read "for example of life and instruction of manners; but yet doth it not apply them to establish any doctrine" (Article VI). Other Reformed Churches accord them no canonical status at all. The Ethiopic Bible includes *1 Enoch* and the book of *Jubilees.*

In the Roman, Greek, and other ancient communions the Bible, together with the living tradition of the church in some sense, constitutes the ultimate authority. In the churches of the Reformation, on the other hand, the Bible alone is the final court of appeal in matters of doctrine and practice. Thus Article VI of the Church of England affirms: "Holy Scripture containeth all things necessary to salvation; so that whatsoever is not read therein, nor may be proved thereby, is not to be required of any man, that it should be believed as an article of the Faith, or be thought requisite or necessary to salvation." To the same effect the *Westminster Confession of Faith* (1.2) lists the 39 books of the OT and the 27 of the NT as "all . . . given by inspiration of God, to be the rule of faith and life."

*Some of the following articles use special abbreviations for frequently used theological terms. Please see page xxx for a list of these terms with accompanying explanations.

II. THE TWO TESTAMENTS

The word "testament" in the designations "Old Testament" and "New Testament," given to the two divisions of the Bible, goes back through Latin *testamentum* to Gk. *diatheke,* which in most of its occurrences in the Greek Bible means "covenant" rather than "testament." In Jer. 31:31ff. a new covenant is foretold which will supersede that which Yahweh made with Israel in the wilderness (*cf.* Exod. 24:7f.). "In speaking of a new covenant, he treats the first as obsolete" (Heb. 8:13). The NT writers see the fulfillment of the prophecy of the new covenant in the new order inaugurated by the work of Christ; his own words of institution (1 Cor. 11:25) give the authority for this interpretation. The OT books, then, are so called because of their close association with the history of the "old covenant"; the NT books are so called because they are the foundation documents of the "new covenant." An approach to our common use of the term "Old Testament" appears in 2 Cor. 3:14, "in the reading of the old covenant," although Paul probably means the law, the basis of the old covenant, rather than the whole volume of Hebrew Scripture. The terms "Old Testament" and "New Testament" for the two collections of books came into general Christian use in the later part of the 2nd century; Tertullian rendered *diatheke* into Latin by *instrumentum* (a legal document) and also by *testamentum*; it was the latter word that survived—unfortunately, since the two parts of the Bible are not "testaments" in the ordinary sense of the term.

III. THE OLD TESTAMENT

In the Hebrew Bible the books are arranged in three divisions—the Law, the Prophets, and the Writings. The Law comprises the Pentateuch, the five "books of Moses." The Prophets fall into two subdivisions—the "Former Prophets," comprising Joshua, Judges, Samuel, and Kings, and the "Latter Prophets," comprising Isaiah, Jeremiah, Ezekiel, and "The Book of the Twelve Prophets." The Writings contain the rest of the books—first, Psalms, Proverbs, and Job; then the five "Scrolls," namely Canticles, Ruth, Lamentations, Ecclesiastes, and Esther; and finally Daniel, Ezra-Nehemiah, and Chronicles. The total is traditionally reckoned as 24, but these 24 correspond exactly to our common reckoning of 39, since in the latter reckoning the Minor Prophets are counted as 12 books, and Samuel, Kings, Chronicles, and Ezra-Nehemiah as two each. There were other ways of counting the same 24 books in antiquity; in one (attested by Josephus) the total was brought down to 22; in another (known to Jerome) it was raised to 27.

The origin of the arrangement of books in the Hebrew Bible cannot be traced; the threefold division is frequently believed to correspond to the three stages in which the books received canonical recognition, but there is no direct evidence for this.

In the LXX the books are arranged according to similarity of subject matter. The Pentateuch is followed by the historical books, these are followed by the books of poetry and wisdom, and these by the prophets. It is this order which, in its essential features, is perpetuated (*via* the Vulgate) in most Christian editions of the Bible. In some respects this order is truer to chronological sequence of the narrative contents than that of the Hebrew Bible; for example, Ruth appears immediately after Judges (since it records things that happened "in the days when the judges ruled"), and the work of the Chronicler appears in the order Chronicles, Ezra, Nehemiah.

The threefold division of the Hebrew Bible is reflected in the wording of Lk. 24:44 ("the law of Moses . . . the prophets . . . the psalms"); more commonly the NT refers to "the law and the prophets" (see Mt. 5:17, *etc.*) or "Moses and the prophets" (Lk. 16:29, *etc.*).

The divine revelation which the OT records was conveyed in two principal ways—by mighty works and prophetic words. These two modes of revelation are bound up indissolubly together. The acts of mercy and judgment by which the God of Israel made himself known to his covenant people would not have carried their proper message had they not been interpreted to them by the prophets—the "spokesmen" of God who received and communicated his word. For example, the events of the Exodus would not have acquired their abiding significance for the Israelites if Moses had not told them that in these events the God of their fathers was acting for their deliverance, in accordance with his ancient promises, so that they might henceforth be his people and he their God. On the other hand, Moses' words would have been fruitless apart from their vindication in the events of the Exodus. We may compare the similarly significant role of Samuel at the time of the Philistine menace, of the great 8th-century prophets when Assyria was sweeping all before her, of Jeremiah and Ezekiel when the kingdom of Judah came to an end, and so forth.

This interplay of mighty work and prophetic word in the OT explains why history and prophecy are so intermingled throughout its pages; it was no doubt some realization of this that led the Jews to include the chief historical books among the Prophets.

But not only do the OT writings record this progressive twofold revelation of God; they record at the same time men's response to God's revelation—a response sometimes obedient, too often disobedient. In this OT record of the response of those to whom the word of God came, the NT finds practical instruction for Christians; of the Israelites' rebellion in the wilderness and the disasters which ensued Paul writes: "these things happened to them as a warning, but they were written down for our instruction, upon whom the end of the ages has come" (1 Cor. 10:11).

As regards its place in the Christian Bible, the OT is preparatory in character: what "God . . . spoke of old to our fathers by the prophets" waited for its completion in the word which "in these last days" he has "spoken unto us by a Son" (Heb. 1:1). Yet the OT was the Bible which the apostles and other preachers of the gospel in the earliest days of Christianity took with them when they proclaimed Jesus as the divinely sent Messiah, Lord, and Saviour: they found in it clear witness to Christ (Jn. 5:39) and a plain setting forth of the way of salvation through faith in him (Rom. 3:21; 2 Tim. 3:15). For their use of the OT they had the authority and example of Christ himself; and the church ever since has done well when it has followed the precedent set by him and his apostles and recognized the OT as Christian scripture. "What was indispensable to the Redeemer must always be indispensable to the redeemed" (G. A. Smith).

IV. THE NEW TESTAMENT

The NT stands to the OT in the relation of fulfillment to promise. If the OT records what "God . . . spoke of old to our fathers by the prophets," the NT records that final word which he spoke in his Son, in which all the earlier revelation was summed up, confirmed, and transcended. The mighty works of the OT revelation culminate in the redemptive work of Christ; the words of the OT prophets receive their fulfillment in him. But he is not only God's crowning revelation to man; he is also man's perfect response to God—the high priest as well as the apostle of our confession (Heb. 3:1). If the OT records the witness of those who saw the day of Christ before it dawned, the NT records the witness of those who saw and heard him in the days of his flesh, and who came to know and proclaim the significance of his coming more fully, by the power of his Spirit, after his rising from the dead.

The NT has been accepted by the great majority of Christians, for the past 1,600 years, as comprising 27 books. These 27 fall naturally into four divisions: (1) the four Gospels, (2) the Acts of the Apostles, (3) 21 letters written by apostles and "apostolic men," (4) the Revelation. This order is not only logical, but roughly chronological so far as the subject matter of the documents is concerned; it does not correspond, however, to the order in which they were written.

The first NT documents to be written were the earlier Epistles of Paul. These (together, possibly, with the Epistle of James) were written between A.D. 48 and 60, before even the earliest of the Gospels was written. The four Gospels belong to the decades between 60 and 100, and it is to these decades too that all (or nearly all) the other NT writings are to be ascribed. Whereas the writing of the OT books was spread over a period of 1,000 years or more, the NT books were written within a century.

The NT writings were not gathered together in the form which we know immediately after they were penned. At first the individual Gospels had a local and independent existence in the constituencies for which they were originally composed. By the beginning of the second century, however, they were brought together and began to circulate as a fourfold record. When this happened, Acts was detached from Luke, with which it had formed one work in two volumes, and embarked on a separate but not unimportant career of its own.

Paul's letters were preserved at first by the communities or individuals to whom they were sent. But by the end of the first century there is evidence to suggest that his surviving correspondence began to be collected into a Pauline corpus, which quickly circulated among the churches—first a shorter corpus of 10 letters and soon afterwards a longer one of 13, enlarged by the inclusion of the 3 Pastoral Epistles. Within the Pauline corpus the letters appear to have been arranged not in chronological order but in descending order of length. This principle may still be recognized in the order found in most editions of the NT today: the letters to churches come before the letters to individuals, and within these two subdivisions they are arranged so that the longest comes first and the shortest last. (The only departure from this scheme is that Galatians comes before Ephesians, although Ephesians is slightly the longer of the two.)

With the Gospel collection and the Pauline corpus, and Acts to serve as a link between the two, we have the beginning of the NT Canon as we know it. The early church, which inherited the Hebrew Bible (or the Greek version of the LXX) as its sacred Scriptures, was not long in setting the new evangelic and apostolic writings alongside the Law and the Prophets, and in using them for the propagation and defense of the gospel and in Christian worship. Thus Justin Martyr, about the middle of the second century, describes how Christians in their Sunday meetings read "the memoirs of the apostles or the writings of the prophets" (*Apology* 1. 67). It was natural, then, that when Christianity spread among people who spoke other languages than Greek, the NT should be translated from Greek into those languages for the benefit of new converts. There were Latin and Syriac versions of the NT by A.D. 200, and a Coptic one within the following century.

V. THE MESSAGE OF THE BIBLE

The Bible has played, and continues to play, a notable part in the history of civilization. Many languages have been reduced to writing for the first time in order that the Bible, in whole or in part, might be translated into them in written form. And this is but a minor sample of the civilizing mission of the Bible in the world.

This civilizing mission is the direct effect of the central message of the Bible. It may be thought surprising that one should speak of a central message in a collection of writings that reflects the history of civilization in the Near East over several millennia. But a central message there is, and it is the recognition of this that has led to the common treatment of the Bible as a book, and not simply a collection of books—just as the Greek plural *biblia* ("books") *became the Latin singular biblia* ("the book").

The Bible's central message is the story of salvation, and throughout both Testaments three strands in this unfolding story can be distinguished: the bringer of salvation, the way of salvation, and the heirs of salvation. This could be reworded in terms of the covenant idea by saying that the central message of the Bible is God's covenant with men, and that the strands are the mediator of the covenant, the basis of the covenant, and the covenant people. God himself is the Saviour of his people; it is he who confirms his covenant mercy with them. The bringer of salvation, the Mediator of the covenant, is Jesus Christ, the Son of God. The way of salvation, the basis of the covenant, is God's grace, calling forth from his people a response of faith and obedience. The heirs of salvation, the covenant people, are the Israel of God, the church of God.

The continuity of the covenant people from the OT to the NT is obscured for the reader of the common English Bible because "church" is an exclusively NT word, and he naturally thinks of it as something which began in the NT period. But the reader of the Greek Bible was confronted by no new word when he found *ekklesia* in the NT; he had already met it in the LXX as one of the words used to denote Israel as the "assembly" of Yahweh. To be sure, it has a new and fuller meaning in the NT. Jesus said "I will build my church" (Mt. 16:18), for the old covenant people had to die with him in order to rise with him to new life—a new life in which national restrictions had disappeared. But he provides in himself the vital continuity between the old Israel and the new, and his faithful followers were both the righteous remnant of the old and the nucleus of the new. The Servant Lord and his servant people bind the two Testaments together.

The message of the Bible is God's message to man, communicated "in many and various ways" (Heb.1:1) and finally incarnated in Christ. Thus "the authority of the holy scripture, for which it ought to be believed and obeyed, dependeth not upon the testimony of any man or church, but wholly upon God (who is truth itself), the author thereof; and therefore it is to be received, because it is the word of God" (*Westminster Confession of Faith,* 1. 4).

THE BIBLE

AN OVERVIEW

William Kerr

UNIQUE among the books of the world is the Bible. The perennial best seller, the Bible is to the believer the Holy Scriptures, the Word of God. And the wayfaring man, though he be a fool, can find the way of salvation by reading it.

The word "Bible" means book, being derived from the smaller form of *biblios* which is *biblion* (a little book). The Bible is *the book* of books. The story of the death of Sir Walter Scott illustrates this. When dying, Scott, the possessor of a great library, called to his son: "Bring me the book!" "Which book?" asked the son. Sir Walter Scott replied, "There is only *one* book; it is the Bible." That this book so impressed him as did no other—is recorded in the poem he had already written:

Within that awful volume lies
The mystery of mysteries!
Happiest they of the human race
To whom their God has granted grace
To read, to fear, to hope, to pray,
To lift the latch, and force the way;
And better had they ne'er been born
Who read to doubt, or read to scorn.

The Bible is, indeed, the most unique of all books and its uniqueness may be seen from the following considerations:

1. *In its source,* the Bible comes *not* from any attempt by men to discover God and thus record their experiences with God. Those who hold this view say that these experiences are analyzed to determine those principles which are common to all of them. From these common characteristics of each experience a normative standard is derived by which to judge all religious experiences. Any authority which the Bible, therefore, has over mankind comes from this view of a common set of experiences. In this view, which is the view of Liberalism, man is the initiator in any revelation concerning God.

The Bible itself, however, states that God is the *source,* the initiator of revelation. "All Scripture is given by inspiration of God . . ." (2 Tim. 3:16). If man was to know anything about God, with any degree of assurance, then God must reveal himself—his nature, his claims upon men and his purpose, both in the history of mankind and in and for his own *among men.* His revelation is unfolded progressively in and through historical events. Beginning with our first parents in the Garden of Eden (Gen. 1-3), his purpose is made known as he unfolds redemptive history through a chosen individual—Abraham (Gen. 12—50), a chosen people—Israel (Exod.—Mal.) a chosen Redeemer—Christ (Matt.—John), a chosen Body—his church (Acts—Jude), and then is consummated in his kingdom (Rev. 20) and then his heavenly state (Rev. 21, 22).

2. *In its style.* The literary style of the Bible portrays a sublimity and unity that is startling. Men such as H. G. Wells have tried to duplicate it but have given up the attempts in hopeless frustration.

This is remarkable since the Bible was produced over a period of some fifteen centuries by a variety of authors. It consists of three different languages: Hebrew—the language of the bulk of the Old Testament; Aramaic—found in Ezra 4:8-6:18; 7:12-26; Daniel 2:4—7:28; Jeremiah 10:11; and Greek—the universal language of Christ's day and in which the entire New Testament was written. Also compounding this remarkability is the wide variety of backgrounds—from scholars to fishermen— among the human instruments God used to record his revelation.

But how could such unity of style be attained? The Bible itself gives the reason: "For the prophecy came not in the old time by the will of man: but holy men of God spake as they were moved by the Holy Ghost" (2 Pet. 1:21). The Holy Spirit was the real author of the Bible, and the variety of human instruments to produce it were under his guiding and guarding control (John 14:26; 15:26, 27; 16:12-15; 1 Cor. 2:7-12). Such an authorship is responsible for this unique literary style and the inability of any human author to duplicate it.

3. *In its supernatural authority and inspiration.* Because of the uniqueness of its source and style, there needs to be an explanation of why this book is superior to all other sacred books of competing religions that contend that they are authoritative for man.

Why is the Bible superior to all other sacred books and unique as a revelation of religious truth? Because it is divinely inspired. And inspiration is not accomplished in isolation. Several factors are related to it:

a. *Selection*: God did not simply use any human instrument to bring the Bible into existence. God selected special men with the right backgrounds and qualifications. For a book such as Genesis, with its opening chapters dealing with the creation of the universe, man, and history, he selected a man like Moses who "was learned in all the wisdom of the Egyptians" (Acts 7:22); a man like David—a mighty king and the sweet singer of Israel, to write the Psalms; and Isaiah, related to royalty, to pen the book that bears his name; a John—meditative, compassionate, devoted to God—to speak of God's love and the need for men to believe in Christ; a Paul—educated, brilliant, trained at Gamaliel's feet and the "University of Tarsus"—to write Romans and his other profound letters.

Without divine selection of special human instruments, there could be no supernaturally authoritative Bible.

b. *Revelation*: By his Holy Spirit, God revealed to these specially chosen instruments the truth—both known and unknown—that he wanted included in the Bible.

c. *Inspiration*: The Holy Spirit guarded and guided the human instruments so that the revealed truth God desired was recorded in a written record. Consequently, a number of factors were involved in a process which had to take into consideration such factors as the background, preparation, personality, and writing syle of the particular human author of the book. The significant fact then is the *result* of this act rather than the act itself. Hence, there is a confluence or flowing together of the influence of the Holy Spirit in his control over the human authors so that the Bible is an inspired record of divine revelation in the words of God in the languages, literary style, and personalities of the human authors.

Contrasting inspiration with revelation and defining the relationship between the two, one notes that revelation is a *process* that can be described as an *inflow* that *terminates* in the human author; inspiration is an *act* that *outflows* and *terminates* in a written record. It is, therefore, the record that is inspired rather than the human instruments. In all this the *Holy Spirit is the Agent, guiding,* controlling both process and act to give mankind an inspired Bible—a God-breathed book—unique among all sacred books of all religious systems because of its supernatural authority and inspiration.

d. *Transmission*: This facet of the Bible is not in the same category as those already discussed. While the Holy Spirit so guided and controlled revelation and inspiration that the Bible is infallible (does not tend to error) and inerrant (it is without error) in the original writings, he did not exercise the same kind of supervision over its transmission. And yet he exercised such a general oversight and supervision over the text that it is essentially today what it was when originally given.

That such a product is possible is the result of two basic factors: (1) the very careful preservation of the Old Testament text by the Jews who believed it to be the inspired Word of God—the very oracles of God (Rom. 3:2); and (2) the equally diligent efforts of scholars in textual criticism to compare the nearly 7,000 manuscripts of the Greek New Testament in order to arrive at as pure a text as possible.

God has carefully supervised the transmission of his Holy Word over the centuries so that today man has, in many cases in his own language, the reliable and authoritative Word of God.

The believer also can have the assurance that the Bible is the supernaturally authoritative and inspired record of God's revelation, as Paul says, by the inner witness of the Holy Spirit to his spirit (Rom. 8:14-16). The Westminster Confession expresses this same idea in these words: ". . . our full persuasion and assurance of the infallible truth and divine authority thereof, is from the inward work of the Holy Spirit, bearing witness by and with the word in our hearts."

4. *In its subject matter.* The subject matter and the method of its treatment mark the Bible as unique. No other sacred book, among religious faiths, discusses the concepts with which mankind is concerned in the same way and in such depth as does the Bible. The three fundamental questions that face every man are answered profoundly by the Bible: From whence did I come? Who am I? What is my destiny? Beginning with Genesis and running all the way through the book of Revelation, these questions are considered and answered: Man came by direct creation of God, was placed in a perfect paradise, and fell into sin. Then God declared man a sinner, corrupt and unable to please him; his heart is deceitful above all things and desperately wicked. Consequently, he cannot make himself right with God. Only God can redeem him and guarantee to him eternal life through saving grace by the death of his own Son. The promise of redemption begins in Genesis 3:15, "And I will put enmity between thee and the woman, and between thy seed and her seed; it shall bruise thy head, and thou shalt bruise his heel" (Gen. 3:15) and continues to its consummation in Rev. 22:17, "And the Spirit and the bride say, Come, and let him that heareth say, Come. And let him that is athirst come. And whosoever will, let him take the water of life freely." Many events, consuming centuries, take place between the time of man's creation and fall and the event of the cross—which provides man's redemption—and the revelation of God's final program when man's final destiny shall be settled— either a glorious heaven by faith in Christ or an eternal hell by rejecting God's provision of salvation (Rev. 20:14,15).

Many and varied are the subjects covered in this great drama of salvation answering man's profoundest questions: From whence did I come? From God's creative hand and made in God's image! Who am I? A sinner—corrupt and depraved, subject to the temptations and lusts and sins of this sinful nature but also the object of God's love! What is my destiny? As a believer— heaven; as an unbeliever—hell!

An anonymous writer has succinctly summarized that which makes the Bible the world's most unique book: "This Book contains the word of God, the state of man, the way of salvation, the doom of sinners, and the happiness of believers. Its doctrines are holy, its precepts are binding, its histories are truth, and its decisions are immutable. Read it to be wise, believe it to be safe, and practice it to be holy. It contains light to direct you, food to support you, and comfort to cheer you. It is the traveler's map, the pilgrim's staff, the pilot's compass, the soldier's sword, and the Christian's charter. Here paradise is restored, heaven opened, and the gates of hell disclosed. Christ is its grand object, our good its design, and the glory of God its end. It should fill the memory, rule the heart, and guide the feet. Read it slowly, frequently, prayerfully. It is a mine of wealth, a paradise of glory, and a river of pleasure. It is given in life, will be opened at the judgment, and be remembered forever. It involves the highest responsibility, will restore the greatest labor, and condemns all who trifle with its sacred contents."

5. *In its standard as authoritative and divine.* Many books of a religious nature relating to both the Old Testament and the New Testament were in existence but were not recognized as canonical and thus not included in the books that finally were collected and became what we know as the Bible today. Of course, as a result of the Council of Trent, following the Reformation, the Roman Catholic Church included those apocryphal books written during the time between Malachi and the Gospels. These books were called apocryphal or "hidden" because they were not properly related to the Old Testament. They were not automatically or genuinely scriptural. They just did not possess those characteristics nor meet the "standard" that would have given them equal status with the biblical books.

This standard was conformity to two principles which, if met, would give them canonicity and recognition as authoritative and divine. The word "canonicity" comes from the word "canon," which means a "rule" or "standard of measurement." Utilizing these principles: (a) that the book was written by a prophet or an apostle or by one who stood in a special relationship to such (e.g., Mark and his relationship to Peter and Luke in his relationship to Paul)—this principle then is known as prophetic witness or apostolic authority; (b) the inner witness of the Holy Spirit, by which the true believer has the basic conviction that the books of the Bible are indeed the very Word of God. This conviction becomes more and more settled in the believer's heart, and as he reads competing books that are not biblical, he rejects them. Anyone who is a believer today can utilize this process; by comparing noncanonical with the canonical books he can determine which books are God's Word and thus authoritative. These two principles have enabled God's people from the days of the Old and New Testament to know which books comprised God's Word. This explains why certain books were collected into what is called the Old Testament and certain books formed the New Testament. This also demonstrates that it was God and not man who determined the canonicity of the biblical books. God's people simply recognized the books as coming from the hand of an accredited messenger of God. The continued use by the church of these books—and only these books—from the time of the apostles on has simply recognized what God had already signified—that the books that constitute our Bible are the very Word of God.

A distinction needs to be made, however, between *canonicity* and *collection* of the biblical books. While no man nor church can make or pronounce a book to be canonical, yet it was the responsibility of the people to collect these canonical books and preserve them. Such collecting took place for both the Old and New Testament. The Old Testament seems to have been collected by the time of Ezra and "The Great Synagogue," according to some scholars. By the time of Christ, it appears evident that the thirty-nine books of the Old Testament in the English Old Testament today were already collected and certainly were canonical. And the twenty-seven books of the English New Testament were collected by the time of the Council of Carthage (A.D. 397).

6. *In its ability to satisfy the needs of mankind universally.* Wherever the Bible has gone and in whatever nations, culture, or people its message has been given, man has sensed the answer to his deepest needs. And today the Bible's circulation in a multitude of translations has been worldwide, making a portion of the Bible available to 97 percent of the world's population. In addition, the whole Bible has been translated into more than 285 languages, the complete New Testament into nearly 600 additional languages, and other portions into more than 900 languages.

THE BIBLE
GOD'S INSPIRED WORD
Harold Lindsell

CHRISTIANS believe that the Bible and the Bible alone is their sacred book. Christians believe that the Bible provides the answers to all the important questions men ask about themselves and about the world in which they live. For the Christian the Bible is the only true source of spiritual knowledge.

Whoever begins with the claim that the Bible is the only source of true spiritual knowledge must face an important question: "Is the Bible trustworthy?" If the Bible cannot be trusted, then its content cannot be regarded as certain. Therefore, we must ascertain whether or not the Bible is the Word of God. If it is, then it can be trusted; if it is not, it is not worthy of our trust.

The Bible itself claims to be the Word of God. It claims to have been written by God the Holy Spirit through human instrumentalities. Peter says, "For the prophecy came not in old time by the will of man: but holy men of God spake as they were moved by the Holy Ghost" (2 Pet. 1:21). The apostle Paul says, "For this cause also thank we God without ceasing, because, when ye received the word of God which ye heard of us, ye received it not as the word of men, but as it is in truth, the word of God, which effectually worketh also in you that believe" (1 Thess. 2:13). Of course, many other Scriptures convey the same idea.

The Bible, according to its own testimony, is the Word of God. As such, the Bible is (1) authoritative; (2) revelatory; (3) inspired; and (4) inerrant.

First, the Bible is authoritative. By this I mean that it is the absolute, preeminent standard. All the opinions of men must be tested against this standard. Man stands beneath the Bible, not above it. I may say this another way: human reason stands under divine revelation and is subject to it; reason is not above revelation.

Second, the Bible is revelatory, i.e., it unveils spiritual realities that could not be realized any other way. In no way could we learn about heaven, the immortality of the soul, the final judgment, or the nature of God without the Bible's revealing these things to us. Many people stood by the cross of Calvary and watched three men die. No bystander could know what the difference was between the death of Jesus Christ and the deaths of the other two men, except by revelation.

Third, the Bible is the inspired Word of God. By this I mean that holy men, under the guidance and superintendence of the Holy Spirit, wrote what God wanted written. While they themselves retained their own peculiar styles, they were inspired by God to use certain words—all of which were kept from historical or scientific error. This leads to the fourth matter: the Bible is inerrant.

We do not need to know where the authors of the Scriptures obtained their information. They may have drawn from firsthand experience; they may have gotten it from other written records; or they may have received special revelation from God— as in the case of the Revelation written by John and the details of future events recorded in the Book of Daniel.

We may now say that the Bible is the revelation of God to men, against which all human opinions may be tested. It is the source for all theological dogma, and no one should be asked to believe anything that cannot be found in or deduced from the written Word of God. Thus the Christian faith can be supported and defended as to its validity only to the extent that the source from which it springs is reliable. If the revelation of God in the Scriptures is not reliable, neither is Christianity. If the premise from which we start is false, then the conclusions we draw must also be false. And if we say that some parts of the Bible are true and other parts are not true, then we must leave it to imperfect mortals to determine which parts of the Bible can be trusted. This gives license to manifold differences of opinion and establishes men as the final arbiters of what we ought to believe. But I believe the Bible can be trusted in all of its parts because it does not contain error.

First, I believe the Bible to be wholly true because the prophets of the Old Testament claimed their utterances came from God. More than two thousand times the writers of the Old Testament used the phrase "thus saith the LORD," or a comparable expression. They claimed that what they said, God had said to them. If their claim is false, why should we believe their other teachings? Moreover, men like King David said such things as, "The Spirit of the Lord spake by me, and his word was in my tongue. The God of Israel said, the Rock of Israel spake to me . . ." (2 Sam. 23:2, 3). The Psalmist said, "Thy word have I hid in mine heart, that I might not sin against thee" (Ps. 119:11). In the same psalm we read: "For ever, O Lord, thy word is settled in heaven" (119:89). Whoever does not believe the claims of the Old Testament prophets does not believe what they witnessed to. And if that witness is false, then whatever else they said is also suspect and cannot be believed.

Second, we have the witness of the New Testament apostles about the inerrancy of the Old and New Testaments. Paul wrote, "For whatsoever things were written aforetime were written for our learning, that we through patience and comfort of the scriptures might have hope" (Rom. 15:4). Here he was speaking about the Old Testament; he said all things were written for our learning. What is untrue is not good for learning. Paul also gave us what is perhaps the greatest of all the apostolic sayings about the truthfulness of the Word of God: "All scripture is given by inspiration of God (Greek *theopneustos*—"God-breathed"), and is profitable for doctrine, for reproof, for correction, for instruction in righteousness: that the man of God may be perfect, thoroughly furnished unto all good works" (2 Tim. 3:16, 17). Every word of Scripture is included here. All of it is God-breathed, and all of it is profitable.

Third, we have the witness of the Lord Jesus Christ to the complete truthfulness of the Word of God. In John 10:35 Jesus said, "The scripture cannot be broken." Jesus understood the Scriptures to be inviolable and irrefragable. He said, "Think not I am come to destroy the law, or the prophets: I am not come to destroy, but to fulfil. For verily I say unto you, Till heaven and earth pass, one jot or one tittle shall in no wise pass from the law, till all be fulfilled" (Matt. 5:17, 18). Jesus also claimed that his works testified to the truth of his words (Jn. 10:37, 38). His miracles validate that claim. Whoever believes that Jesus is true must also believe that the Scriptures he certified are true in their totality.

The Holy Spirit is the fourth witness to the claim that the Bible is inerrant. He bears witness to our spirits that the Bible is true. He was the instrumental agent in connection with the two Words of God. Jesus is the Word of God incarnate and the Bible is the Word of God written. The Spirit is the divine author of Scripture, and the Spirit is the progenitor of the Incarnate Word of God. It was he who came upon the Virgin Mary so that what was conceived in her womb was the true Son of God. In both instances, a miracle was performed by the Spirit. The Spirit who was responsible for the incarnation of the sinless Son of God was also responsible for making possible the errorless Word of God written. When we speak of this errorless Word, we are talking about the autographs of Scripture, i.e., the Bible as it was first written in the Hebrew, the Aramaic, and the Greek. Minor copyists' errors exist in some of the texts that we have, but textual critics who have worked to establish the original text of Scripture have succeeded so well that, apart from a few minor exceptions, we rest assured that we have the genuine Word of God.

The fifth witness to the inerrancy of the Word of God is fulfilled prophecy. In many instances the Bible contains prophecies of what would happen in advance of the incidents themselves. There are more than forty prophecies about Jesus Christ, all of which have been fulfilled literally, except for those that have to do with the Second Advent. The Bible forecast what would happen to nations such as Damascus, Philistia, Tyre, Edom, Ammon, and Moab. It foretold the end of the Northern Kingdom of Israel and the Babylonian Captivity of Judah. It also prophesied the return of the remnant to the land at the end of the seventy-year captivity. Fulfilled prophecy gives us every reason to accept the complete truthfulness of the Bible.

A sixth reason for believing the Bible to be true is the evidence found by biblical archeologists. As ancient sites have been excavated, the historical reliability of the Bible has been demonstrated again and again. There is no evidence from archeology that any historical fact in the Bible is untrue. We need not fear the further work of the archeologist's spade. He should be encouraged to uncover more and more of the ruins of ancient cultures and civilizations. Such labors can only strengthen the fact that the Bible, on whatever subject it speaks, tells us the truth. It is not a textbook of chemistry, physics, biology, or astronomy, but when it speaks about these or any other subjects it does not lie.

The seventh reason we can trust the Bible is that it does what it claims it will do: it transforms lives. Millions of people have testified that their sins have been forgiven and that they have received the gift of eternal life. Their prayers have been answered; their deepest needs satisfied. Lives have been radically changed. Thieves steal no more, liars become honest, adulterers live holy lives, and covetous people lose their greed. Churches, schools, and hospitals have risen as proof of the salutary effect the gospel of Jesus Christ has had on multitudes.

God has spoken and has not stuttered in his speech. The Bible, his Word, is inspired, inerrant, and credible in its entirety.

INSPIRATION

J. I. Packer

THE word "inspiration" comes from Latin and English translations of *theopneustos* in 2 Tim. 3:16, which KJV rendered: "All Scripture is given by inspiration of God, and is profitable for doctrine, for reproof, for correction, for instruction in righteousness." "Inspired of God" in RSV is no improvement on KJV, for *theopneustos* means *out*-breathed rather than *in*-breathed by God—divinely *ex*-spired, rather than *in*-spired. In the last century Ewald and Cremer argued that the adjective bore an active sense, "breathing the Spirit", and Barth appears to agree (he glosses it as meaning not only "given and filled and ruled by the Spirit of God", but also "actively outbreaking and spreading abroad and making known the Spirit of God" [*Church Dogmatics,* I.2, E.T. 1956]); but B. B. Warfield showed decisively in 1900 that the sense of the word can only be passive. The thought is not of God as breathing out God, but of God as having breathed out Scripture. Paul's words mean, not that Scripture is inspiring (true though it is), but that Scripture is a divine product, and must be approached and estimated as such.

The "breath" or "spirit" of God in the Old Testament denotes the active outgoing of divine power, whether in creation (Ps. 33:6; Job 33:4; *cf.* Gen. 1:2; 2:7), preservation (Job 34:14), revelation to and through prophets (Isa. 48:16; 61:1; Mic. 3:8 Joel 2:28ff.), regeneration (Ezek. 36:27), or judgment (Isa. 30:28, 33). The New Testament reveals this divine "breath" (Gk. *pneuma*) to be a Person of the Godhead. God's "breath" (i.e. the Holy Spirit) produced Scripture, as a means to the conveyance of spiritual understanding. Whether we render *pasa graphe* as "the whole Scripture" or "every text", and whether we follow RSV or RV in construing the sentence (RV has "Every scripture inspired of God is also profitable . . .", which is a possible translation), Paul's meaning is clear beyond all doubt. He is affirming that all that comes in the category of Scripture, all that has a place among the "sacred writings" (*hiera grammata,* v. 15, RV), just because it is God-breathed, is profitable for the guiding of both faith and life.

On the basis of this Pauline text, English theology regularly uses the word "inspiration" to express the thought of the divine origin and quality of Holy Scripture. Actively, the noun denotes God's out-breathing operation which produced Scripture: passively, the inspiredness of the Scriptures so produced. The word is also used more generally of the divine influence which enabled the human organs of revelation—prophets, psalmists, wise men and apostles—to speak, as well as to write, the words of God.

I. THE IDEA OF BIBLICAL INSPIRATION

According to 2 Tim. 3:16, what is inspired is precisely the biblical writings. Inspiration is a work of God terminating, not in the men who were to write Scripture (as if, having given them an idea of what to say, God left them to themselves to find a way of saying it), but in the actual written product. It is Scripture—*graphe,* the written text—that is God-breathed. The essential idea here is that all Scripture has the same character as the prophets' sermons had, both when preached and when written (*cf.* 2 Pet. 1:19-21, on the divine origin of every "prophecy of the scripture"; see also Jer. 36; Isa. 8:16-20). That is to say, Scripture is not only man's word, the fruit of human thought, premeditation and art, but also, and equally, God's word, spoken through man's lips or written with man's pen. In other words, Scripture has a double authorship, and man is only the secondary author; the primary author, through whose initiative, prompting and enlightenment, and under whose superintendence, each human writer did his work, is God the Holy Spirit.

Revelation to the prophets was essentially verbal; often it had a visionary aspect, but even "revelation in visions is also verbal revelation" (L. Koehler, *Old Testament Theology*, E.T. 1957). Brunner has observed that in "the words of God which the Prophets proclaim as those which they have received directly from God, and have been commissioned to repeat, as they have received them . . . perhaps we may find the closest analogy to the meaning of the theory of verbal inspiration" (*Revelation and Reason*, 1946). Indeed we do; we find not merely an analogy to it, but the paradigm of it; and "theory" is the wrong word to use, for this is just the biblical doctrine itself. Biblical inspiration should be defined in the same theological terms as prophetic inspiration: namely, as the whole process (manifold, no doubt, in its psychological forms, as prophetic inspiration was) whereby God moved those men whom he had chosen and prepared (*cf.* Jer. 1:5; Gal. 1:15) to write exactly what he wanted written for the communication of saving knowledge to his people, and through them to the world. Biblical inspiration is thus verbal by its very nature; for it is of God-given words that the God-breathed Scriptures consist.

Thus, inspired Scripture is written revelation, just as the prophets' sermons were spoken revelation. The biblical record of God's self-disclosure in redemptive history is not merely human testimony to revelation, but is itself revelation. The inspiring of Scripture was an integral part in the revelatory process, for in Scripture God gave the church his saving work in history, and his own authoritative interpretation of its place in his eternal plan. "Thus saith the Lord" could be prefixed to each book of Scripture with no less propriety than it is (359 times, according to Koehler, *op.cit.*) to individual prophetic utterances which Scripture contains. Inspiration, therefore, guarantees the truth of all that the Bible asserts, just as the inspiration of the prophets guaranteed the truth of their representation of the mind of God. ("Truth" here denotes correspondence between the words of man and the thoughts of God, whether in the realm of fact or of meaning.) As truth from God, man's Creator and rightful King, biblical instruction, like prophetic oracles, carries divine authority.

II. BIBLICAL PRESENTATION

The idea of canonical Scripture, *i.e.* of a document or corpus of documents containing a permanent authoritative record of divine revelation, goes back to Moses' writing of God's law in the wilderness (Exod. 34:27ff.; Deut. 31:9ff., 24ff.). The truth of all statements, historical or theological, which Scripture makes, and their authority as words of God, are assumed without question or discussion in both Testaments. The Canon grew, but the concept of inspiration, which the idea of canonicity presupposes, was fully developed from the first, and is unchanged throughout the Bible. As there presented, it comprises two convictions.

1. *The words of Scripture are God's own words.* Old Testament passages identify the Mosaic law and the word of the prophets, both spoken and written, with God's own speech (*cf.* 1 Kings 22:8-16; Neh. 8; Ps. 119; Jer. 25:1-13; 36, *etc.*). New Testament writers view the Old Testament as a whole as "the oracles of God" (Rom. 3:2), prophetic in character (Rom. 16:26; *cf.* 1:2; 3:21), written by men who were moved and taught by the Holy Spirit (2 Pet. 1:21; *cf.* 1 Pet. 1:10-12). Christ and his apostles quote Old Testament texts, not merely as what, *e.g.*, Moses, David or Isaiah said (see Mark 7:10; 12:36; 7:6; Rom. 10:5; 11:9; 10:20 etc.), but also as what God said through these men (see Acts 4:25; 28:25, etc.), or sometimes simply as what "he" (God) says (*e.g.* 1 Cor. 6:16; Heb. 8:5, 8), or what the Holy Spirit says (Heb. 3:7; 10:15). Furthermore, Old Testament statements, not

made by God in their contexts, are quoted as utterances of God (Matt. 19:4ff.; Heb. 3:7; Acts 13:34, citing Gen. 2:24; Ps. 95:7; Isa. 55:2 respectively). Also, Paul refers to God's promise to Abraham and his threat to Pharaoh, both spoken long before the biblical record of them was written, as words which *Scripture* spoke to these two men (Gal. 3:8; Rom. 9:17); which shows how completely he equated the statements of Scripture with the utterance of God.

2. *Man's part in the producing of Scripture was merely to transmit what he had received.* Psychologically, from the standpoint of form, it is clear that the human writers contributed much to the making of Scripture—historical research, theological meditation, linguistic style, *etc.* Each biblical book is in one sense the literary creation of its author. But theologically, from the standpoint of content, the Bible regards the human writers as having contributed nothing, and Scripture as being entirely the creation of God. This conviction is rooted in the self-consciousness of the founders of biblical religion, all of whom claimed to utter—and, in the case of the prophets and apostles, to write—what were, in the most literal sense, the words of another: God himself. The prophets (among whom Moses must be numbered: Deut. 18:15; 34:10) professed that they spoke the words of Yahweh, setting before Israel what Yahweh had shown them (Jer. 1:7; Ezek. 2:7; Amos 3:7; *cf.* 1 Kings 22). Jesus of Nazareth professed that he spoke words given him by his Father (John 7:16; 12:49). The apostles taught and issued commands in Christ's name (2 Thess. 3:6), so claiming his authority and sanction (1 Cor. 14:37), and they maintained that both their matter and their words had been taught them by God's Spirit (1 Cor. 2:9-13; *cf.* Christ's promises, John 14:26; 15:26ff.; 16:13ff.). These are claims to inspiration. In the light of these claims, the evaluation of prophetic and apostolic writings as wholly God's word, in just the same way in which the two tables of the law, "written with the finger of God" (Exod. 24:12; 31:18; 32:16), were wholly God's word, naturally became part of the biblical faith.

Christ and the apostles bore striking witness to the fact of inspiration by their appeal to the authority of the Old Testament. In effect, they claimed the Jewish Scriptures as the Christian Bible: a body of literature bearing prophetic witness to Christ (John 5:39; Luke 24:25, 44; 2 Cor. 3:14ff.) and designed by God specially for the instruction of Christian believers (Rom. 15:4; 1 Cor. 10:11; 2 Tim. 3:14ff.; *cf.* the exposition of Ps. 95:7-11 in Heb. 3-4, and indeed the whole of Hebrews, in which every major point is made by appeal to Old Testament texts). Christ insisted that what was written in the Old Testament "cannot be broken" (John 10:35). He had not come, he told the Jews, to annul the law or the prophets (Matt. 5:17); if they thought he was doing that, they were mistaken. He had come to do the opposite—to bear witness to the divine authority of both by fulfilling them. The law stands for ever, because it is God's word (Matt. 5:18; Luke 16:17); the prophecies, particularly those concerning himself, must be fulfilled, for the same reason (Matt. 26:54; Luke 22:37; *cf* Mark 8:31; Luke 18:31). To Christ and his apostles, the appeal to Scripture was always decisive (*cf.* Matt 4:4, 7, 10; Rom. 12:19; 1 Pet. 1:16, *etc.*).

The freedom with which New Testament writers quote the Old Testament (following *LXX, Targums, or an ad hoc* rendering of the Hebrew, as best suits them) has been held to show that they did not believe in the inspiredness of the original words. But their interest was not in the words, as such, but in their meaning; and recent study has made it appear that these quotations are interpretative and expository—a mode of quotation well known among the Jews. The writers seek to indicate the true (*i.e.,* Christian) meaning and application of their text by the form in which they cite it. In most cases this meaning has evidently been reached by a strict application of clear-cut theological principles about the relation of Christ and the church to the Old Testament. (See C. H. Dodd, *According to the Scriptures,* 1952; K. Stendahl, *The School of St. Matthew,* 1954; R. V. G. Tasker, *The Old Testament in the New Testament,* 1954; E. E. Ellis, *Paul's Use of the Old Testament,* 1957).

III. THEOLOGICAL STATEMENT

In formulating the biblical idea of inspiration, it is desirable that four negative points be made.

1. The idea is not of mechanical dictation, or automatic writing, or any process which involved the suspending of the action of the human writer's mind. Such concepts of inspiration are found in the Talmud, Philo and the Fathers, but not in the Bible. The divine direction and control under which the biblical authors wrote was not a physical or psychological force, and it did not detract from, but rather heightened, the freedom, spontaneity and creativeness of their writing.

2. The fact that in inspiration God did not obliterate the personality, style, outlook and cultural conditioning of his penmen does not mean that his control of them was imperfect, or that they inevitably distorted the truth they had been given to convey in the process of writing it down. B. B. Warfield gently mocks the notion that when God wanted Paul's letters written "He was reduced to the necessity of going down to earth and painfully scrutinizing the men He found there, seeking anxiously for the one who, on the whole, promised best for His purpose; and then violently forcing the material He wished expressed through him, against his natural bent, and with as little loss from his recalcitrant characteristics as possible. Of course, nothing of the sort took place. If God wished to give His people a series of letters like Paul's, He prepared a Paul to write them, and the Paul He brought to the task was a Paul who spontaneously would write just such letters" (*The Inspiration and Authority of the Bible,* 1951).

3. Inspiredness is not a quality attaching to corruptions which intrude in the course of the transmission of the text, but only to the text as originally produced by the inspired writers. The acknowledgment of biblical inspiration thus makes more urgent the task of meticulous textual criticism, in order to eliminate such corruptions and ascertain what that original text was.

4. The inspiredness of biblical writing is not to be equated with the inspiredness of great literature, not even when (as often) the biblical writing is in fact great literature. The biblical idea of inspiration relates, not to the literary quality of what is written, but to its character as divine revelation in writing.

CHRONOLOGICAL TABLE OF ENGLISH VERSIONS OF THE BIBLE

J. H. Skilton

Date AD	*Version (italics=Catholic Version)*	*Translator*
ANGLO-SAXON VERSIONS		
Late 7th cent.	English verse (oral)	Caedmon
	John's Gospel, + ?	Bede
	Psalms; entire Bible?	Aldhelm (640-709)
	Anglo-Saxon Psalter glosses	
Late 9th cent.	Ten Commandments	Alfred the Great (849-901)
	Ex. 21-23	
	Acts 15	
	Scripture refs. in Gregory's "De Cura Pastorali"	
c.950	Anglo-Saxon gloss of the Lindisfarne Gospels	
	Anglo-Saxon gloss of the Rushworth Gospels	
11th cent.	Parts of the OT	Aelfric
	Four Gospels into continuous English text	
MIDDLE ENGLISH VERSIONS		
c.1300	Metric Psalter	
	Prose Psalter	Richard Rolle of Hampole c.1380-1383
	Wyclif Bible	Nicholas of Hereford and Wyclif (?)
	Revision of Wyclif's Bible	John Purvey
SIXTEENTH-CENTURY VERSIONS		
1525/6	NT	William Tyndale
1530	Pentateuch	Tyndale
1531	Jonah	Tyndale
	Isaiah	George Joye
1534	OT selections	Tyndale
	NT revision	
	Psalms	Joye
	Lamentations	
	Jeremiah	
	Song of Moses at the Red Sea	
	Revision (unauthorized) of Tyndale's NT	

Date AD	Version (*italics = Catholic Version*)	Translator
1535	NT revision	Tyndale
	First complete Bible in English	Miles Coverdale
1537	The Matthew Bible	John Rogers? ('Thomas Matthew')
1538	Parallel English-Latin NT (Vulgate)	Coverdale
1539	Revision of the Matthew Bible	Richard Taverner
	The Great Bible	Coverdale, for Thomas Cromwell
1540	2nd edition of the Great Bible	Preface by Archbp. Cranmer
1545	Revised Primer ("Primer of Henry VIII")	
1557	Geneva NT	William Whittingham
1560	Geneva Bible	Various (including Whittingham)
1568	The Bishops' Bible	Matthew Parker and others
1572	Revised folio edition of the Bishops' Bible	
1582	*Rheims NT*	*Gregory Martin, William Allen and others*

SEVENTEENTH-CENTURY VERSIONS

1609-1610	*Douay OT*	*Gregory Martin and others*
1611	Authorized (King James) Version	Fifty-four translators
1613	Revision of AV	
1616-1623	Pentateuch	Henry Ainsworth
	Song of Solomon	
	Psalms	

EIGHTEENTH-CENTURY VERSIONS

1718-1719	*NT*	*Cornelius Nary*
1729	Greek and English NT	William Mace
1730	NT	*Robert Witham*
1738	*Fifth edition of Rheims NT*	
1745	The Primitive NT	William Whiston
1749-1772	*Two rev. of Douay OT, five rev. of Rheims NT*	*Richard Challoner*
1755	Revision of AV	John Wesley
1764	NT	Richard Wynne
	Bible	Anthony Purver
1768	Liberal translation of the NT	E. Harwood
1770	NT	John Worsley
1783-1810	*Revisions of Rheims and Douay texts*	*Bernard MacMahon*

NINETEENTH-CENTURY VERSIONS

1822	Paul's Epistles	Thomas Belsham (Unitarian)
1832	*Paul's Epistles*	Charles Eyre (Unitarian)
1833	NT	Rodolphus Dickinson
1840	NT	Samuel Sharpe (Unitarian)
1849-1860	*Annotated revision of Douay-Rheims text*	*Bishop Francis Patrick Kenrick*

Date AD	Version (italics=Catholic Version)	Translator
1855	Gospels	Andrew Norton
1858	NT	Leicester Ambrose Sawyer
1862	OT & NT	Robert Young
1863	Gospels	G. W. Braineld
1869	NT	Henry Alford
	OT & NT	Robert Ainslie
1871	NT	J. N. Darby
1872	NT	J. B. Rotherham
1875	NT	Samuel Davidson
1881	Revised version of the AV NT	British & American companies
1882	Romans	Ferrar Fenton
1883	Paul's Epistles	Fenton
1885	RV complete Bible	British & American companies
1890	Bible	J. N. Darby
1895	Current English NT	Fenton

TWENTIETH-CENTURY VERSIONS

1898-1901	The Twentieth Century NT	Twenty lay scholars
1901	American Standard Edition (of RV)	American scholars
1903	Bible in Modern English	Fenton
	NT in Modern Speech	R. F. Weymouth
1913	NT	James Moffatt
1923	American translation of the NT	E. J. Goodspeed
	Riverside NT	W. G. Ballantine
1924	OT	Moffatt
	Centenary translation of the NT	Helen B. Montgomery
1927	American translation of the OT	A. R. Gordon, T. J. Meek, Leroy Waterman, J. M. Powis Smith
1935	*Westminster Version of the Sacred Scriptures, NT*	*Various Catholic scholars*
	Revision of Challoner's edition of the Rheims NT	*J. A. Carey*
1937	NT	C. B. Williams
	NT	*F. A. Spencer*
1941	The NT in Basic English	S. H. Hooke
	Revision of Challoner-Rheims NT	*Confraternity of Christian Doctrine*
1945	Berkeley Version of the NT	Gerrit Verkuyl
	NT (trans. from Vulgate)	*Monsignor R. A. Knox*
1946	Revision of American RV NT (RSV)	International Council of Religious Education
1947-1957	NT	J. B. Phillips
1948	The Letchworth Version (NT) in Modern English	T. F. & R. E. Ford
1949	Bible in Basic English	S. H. Hooke
	OT	*R. A. Knox*
1952	Entire RSV Bible	
	Plain English NT	C. K. Williams

Date AD	*Version (italics=Catholic Version)*	*Translator*
1954	*NT*	*J. A. Kleist & J. L. Lilly*
1955	Authentic NT	H. J. Schonfield
	Revision of Knox's OT	
1956-1959	Expanded Translation of the Greek NT	K. S. Wuest
1958	The Amplified NT	F. E. Siewert & Lockman Foundation
1959	The Berkeley Bible	Gerrit Verkuyl
1961	The New English Bible NT	Representatives of major British churches & Bible societies
1962	The Amplified OT (I)	F. E. Siewert & Lockman Foundation
1962-1971	The Living Bible	K. N. Taylor
1963	The NT in the Language of Today	W. F. Beck
	New American Standard Bible (rev. of the American RV)	Evangelical scholars
1964	The Amplified OT (II)	F. E. Siewert & Lockman Foundation
1965	*Catholic edition of RSV*	
1966	Today's English Version (Good News for Modern Man) NT	American Bible Society
	Jerusalem Bible	*Catholic scholars*
1968-9	New translation, NT	William Barclay
1969	The New Berkeley (Modern Language) Bible	Verkuyl
1970	The New English Bible OT	Representatives of major British churches, etc.
	The New American Bible	*Bishops' Committee of the Confraternity of Christian Doctrine*
1972	New International Version (NT)	Evangelical scholars & International Bible Society
1973	The Translator's NT	British & Foreign Bible Society
1976	Complete Good News Bible	American Bible Society
1979	New International Version Holy Bible	Evangelical scholars & International Bible Society

ENGLISH VERSIONS OF THE BIBLE

I. ANGLO-SAXON VERSIONS

The history of versions of the Bible in English has its beginnings in challenging obscurity and uncertainty in the Anglo-Saxon period of the English language. The Venerable Bede has supplied a fascinating account (*Ecclesiastical History* 4, ch. 24) of a heavenly endowment granted to the herdsman Caedmon in the latter part of the 7th century AD, which enabled him to sing in English verse the substance and the themes of Scripture. Caedmon was followed, according to Bede's testimony, by others who endeavoured to write religious verse. Although Bede does not quote any of Caedmon's poetry verbatim, he gives us the sense of the initial verses attributed to him, verses of stirring freshness and exaltation. Surviving Anglo-Saxon metrical treatments or paraphrases of biblical materials, whether or not they are to be connected with Caedmon, witness to an important means of disseminating knowledge of the Scriptures in that period.

To Bede himself has been attributed the translation of the Gospel according to John. His follower Cuthbert, in a letter on the death of his "father and master," relates that Bede completed his translation of the Fourth Gospel on the day of his death at the virtual moment of his departure. If Bede did translate the entire Bible or the greater part of it into English, as certain evidence might indicate, his work has regrettably not survived.

Aldhelm (640-709) has been credited with a translation of the Psalms and indeed of much, if not all, of the Bible into English; but no extant MS can with certainty be said to represent his work. The Vespasian Psalter, the oldest surviving Latin text of the Psalms with a gloss or interlinear translation of the individual words into Anglo-Saxon, cannot with any assurance be held to contain Aldhelm's work. This MS of the Psalter was succeeded by a considerable number of others with Anglo-Saxon glosses.

King Alfred the Great (849-901) introduced his *Code of Saxon Laws* with an abbreviated and rearranged English rendering of the Ten Commandments and portions in English of Exod. 21-23 and Acts 15. William of Malmesbury says that Alfred was at work on an English translation of the Psalms at the time of his death. There has been disagreement as to whether Alfred's work is represented by the prose rendering in English of the first fifty psalms in the Paris Psalter. His translation of Gregory's *De cura pastorali* involved, of course, translation of the Scripture references in the text.

Aelfric, an abbot at about the beginning of the 11 century, made translations or paraphrases of extensive parts of the OT text.

Two MSS of the Gospels in Latin with an Anglo-Saxon gloss have survived. One of them is the famous Lindisfarne Gospels (*c.* 700, with a gloss made *c.* 950). The other MS is the Rushworth Gospels, whose gloss is very much dependent on that of the Lindisfarne MS in Mark, Luke and John.

A noteworthy development in the Anglo-Saxon period was the competent translation of the four Gospels into a continuous English text, a text which is represented by six extant MSS.

II. MIDDLE ENGLISH VERSIONS

The development of a literature in Middle English begins in the closing part of the 12th century. About 1300 a metrical version of the Psalter appeared; it was followed by prose translations, one of which was the work of Richard Rolle of Hampole. Portions of the NT were also translated. The distinguishing achievement of the Middle English period, however, was the translation work associated with Wyclif (*c.* 1320-84) and the movement he represented. An earlier Wyclifite version was produced in the latter part of the 14th century *c.* 1380-3, a substantial portion of which was made by Nicholas of Hereford (from Genesis to Baruch 3:20) and the rest, including the NT, has been thought by some to have been made by Wyclif himself. Whatever may have been Wyclif's part in the actual work of translation, his zeal for the Scriptures and for making them accessible to the people in the English language must be credited with giving the impetus to this highly influential version. It was made from a Latin base and it clung to the original with some damage to English idiom and clarity, but it was a commendable new effort addressed to the needs of the present and facing towards the future. It was soon followed by a translation in smoother style which was quite probably made by John Purvey, a follower of Wyclif, with the assistance of others. The principles and procedures which were followed by Purvey were in many respects exemplary, and his revision was very influential. It was indeed finally superseded by the work of Tyndale and Coverdale in the 16th century, but its influence has been perpetuated through its successors.

III. WILLIAM TYNDALE

William Tyndale was the first to translate the NT directly from Greek into English. He received his MA degree at Oxford in 1515, the year before the appearance of Erasmus' Greek NT, the first printed NT in Greek actually to be published. Tyndale may have studied Greek at Cambridge. His zeal for making the Scriptures available in the vernacular is indicated in the story of his encounter with "a learned man" who expressed the judgment that we might better be without the laws of God than without those of the Pope. To him Tyndale expressed defiance of the Pope and his laws and said that if God would spare his life he would cause a ploughboy to know more of the Scripture than his learned adversary did. Finding England uncongenial to his desire to lay the NT plainly before the eyes of the people in their native language, he went to Hamburg. He was never to return to the land which was to enter into his labours and to be enriched by his dedication.

In completing his translation of the NT, Tyndale made use of the 1519 and 1522 editions of Erasmus' Greek NT. He consulted also Erasmus' Latin translation, Luther's German text and the Latin Vulgate. The printing of his NT was begun in 1525 in Cologne, but opposition forced him to flee to Worms with the sheets that had been printed. There before long (in 1525 or 1526) two editions were completed (one quarto, the other octavo) of 3,000 copies each. Virulent official opposition in England was so very successful in destroying copies of early issues of Tyndale's NT that there are only minimal remains today. Revised editions appeared in 1534 and 1535. Tyndale's NT, despite the opposition to it, could not be destroyed. The first printed English NT, the first made from the Greek, opened a new period in the history of the English Bible and made an ineradicable contribution to the English Bibles yet to come. The influence of the wording and structure of Tyndale's NT on the AV is immense, and the latter provides a continuing tribute to the simplicity, freshness, vitality and felicity of his work. Tyndale also published a translation of the Pentateuch in 1530, of Jonah in 1531 and of selections from the OT (published with his edition of the NT in 1534). An edition of the Pentateuch with a revised translation of Genesis was printed in 1534. There is good authority for believing that Tyndale translated an extensive additional section of the OT text, but before he could complete his translation of the Bible he suffered a martyr's death. In his OT work he used the Hebrew text. Among other works available to him were Luther's German translation, the Latin Vulgate and a Latin rendering by Pagninus. Like his version of the NT, Tyndale's faithful and vivid translation of books of the OT has been exceedingly influential. His dying prayer was that the Lord would open the eyes of the king of England.

George Joye also had a significant part in the development of the English Bible in Tyndale's day. He graduated from Cambridge in 1513, was later influenced by Lutheran doctrine, and found it necessary to seek refuge abroad *c.* 1527. He may have published a version of the Psalter in 1530, a version different from that which he published in 1534. He also published English translations of Isaiah (1531), of Jeremiah, Lamentations, and the Song of Moses at the Red Sea (1534), a revision of Tyndale's NT (1534) without Tyndale's authorization and with changes of which Tyndale did not approve. After Tyndale had issued his own revision of his NT in 1534, with selections from the OT, Joye published another edition of his NT, together with selections from the OT. He may also have published translations of Proverbs and Ecclesiastes. (See C. C. Butterworth, *The Literary Lineage of the King James Bible,* 1941, pp. 87ff).

IV. MILES COVERDALE

The first really notable name in the history of English Bible translation and revision in the period from Tyndale to the appearance of the KJV is that of Miles Coverdale, whose work benefited from an altered royal and ecclesiastical attitude. In 1535 Coverdale published a translation (which he had prepared on the Continent) of the entire Bible, the first full Bible to be printed in English. This version was given a dedication to Henry VIII. It was made from German and Latin versions and with the aid of translation made by Tyndale. A folio edition and a quarto edition appeared in 1537. The quarto edition asserts on its title-page that it was set forth with the king's most gracious licence. In 1538 Coverdale published an edition of the Latin Vulgate NT with an English translation in parallel columns. His capacity for beautiful rhythm and phrasing have made an enduring contribution to the great tradition of English Bible translation.

V. THE MATTHEW BIBLE

In 1537 there appeared a Bible whose title-page asserts that it was truly and purely translated into English by Thomas Matthew. This Bible has often been regarded as the work of one of Tyndale's followers, John Rogers, who regarded it as inexpedient to send it forth under his own name. It was virtually a compilation of Tyndale's and Coverdale's work with minor alterations. It was a fact of remarkable irony that a Bible which was substantially the work of Tyndale, who had been opposed by Henry VIII and the church, could now be dedicated to Henry and set forth with his most gracious licence! On the solicitation of Cranmer, the Archbishop of Canterbury, Thomas Cromwell secured Henry's authorization that this Bible would be allowed by his authority to be bought and read within the realm.

VI. *TAVERNER'S BIBLE*

Richard Taverner published in 1539 a revision of Matthew's Bible which introduced a number of improvements indicating some scholarly competence. It was not without influence on future versions, but has not generally been regarded as occupying a place in the main line of English versions of the Bible.

VII. THE GREAT BIBLE

In 1539 there appeared a Bible which was to exercise enormous influence on England and on the subsequent history of the English Bible. It was prepared by Coverdale on the invitation of Thomas Cromwell, and has therefore been called Cromwell's Bible. Because of its large size it has also been called the Great Bible. The second edition of April 1540 and later editions had a preface by Archbishop Cranmer, and consequently the version has frequently been referred to as Cranmer's Bible. But regardless of its multiple designations, it is really a revision of Matthew's Bible. It was authorized for distribution among the people and for the use of every church. Copies were obtained for the churches; people collected around them, and even disturbed church services with their reading and discussions. Three editions appeared in 1540 and three more in 1541. The Psalter of the Great Bible has been perpetuated in the Book of Common Prayer.

VIII. THE GENEVA BIBLE

In the last years of Henry VIII no new editions of the English Bible were produced, and the official attitude towards the use of the Scriptures changed. The Great Bible was not banned, as were Tyndale's and Coverdale's Bibles, but its use was limited. The new attitude was carried over into the field of Primers, which contained selections from the Scriptures. In 1545 a revised Primer, frequently referred to as the Primer of Henry VIII, was published, and the use of any other was forbidden. In the reign of Edward VI the climate again became favourable to the development and use of the Bible in English. Many editions of the older translations were published, but practically no new work was done. Sir John Cheke did prepare an independent translation of Matthew and the beginning of Mark made from the Greek in a style designed to be intelligible to the less cultured, which tried to avoid words of non-English origin, but his work was not in fact published until 1843.

The reign of Mary Tudor was of a quite different character from that of Edward. Bibles were taken from churches, and many Protestants suffered martyrdom. Some fled to the Continent. A group of such men in Geneva was responsible for the production of the Geneva Bible. First, however, a Geneva NT was published in 1557, prepared chiefly, it would seem, by William Whittingham. This NT employed the verse divisions which Stephanus had introduced into the fourth edition of his Greek NT in 1551. Italics were used to distinguish words introduced by the translator to clarify the meaning. Whittingham seems to have used as the foundation text for his praiseworthy revision a recently published edition of Tyndale's NT.

In 1558 Elizabeth's reign began, and again the official attitude towards the use of the Bible and towards its translators changed. Whittingham and others nevertheless continued in Geneva until they had completed the version of the Bible on which they had been working. This Geneva Bible, dedicated to Elizabeth, was published in 1560. It made an enormous contribution to the Authorized King James Version, and achieved a dominant popularity in the period 1570-1620. A very scholarly work, it drew upon the unique competence and assistance of the great and devoted men who were in Geneva at the time, and upon works in different languages which were available there. The OT section was a painstaking revision of that of the Great Bible with careful attention to the Hebrew; and for the NT it drew upon the Whittingham 1557 edition. Because of its use of "breeches" in Genesis 3:7 (a reading which, however, was not new), it became known as the "Breeches Bible." Verse divisions were employed throughout the entire Bible.

IX. THE BISHOPS' BIBLE

The Geneva Bible was more accurate than the Great Bible, but official endorsement was not transferred to it. Instead, the Archbishop of Canterbury, Matthew Parker, promoted a revision of the Great Bible, with much of the work done by bishops. This revision, of varying merit, and at points considerably influenced by the Geneva Bible, was published in a folio edition in 1568. It came to be known as the Bishops' Bible, and received ecclesiastical authorization. A slightly revised quarto edition appeared in 1569. A folio edition with an extensive revision of the NT sections was published in 1572. The Prayer Book version of the Psalms and the Bishops' Bible Psalter were printed in this edition in parallel columns. In following editions, except for that of 1585, only the Prayer Book Psalter was included. The 1572 revision had a substantial influence on the KJV.

X. THE RHEIMS-DOUAY VERSION

Roman Catholics, who during the reign of Elizabeth I had found refuge on the Continent, in 1582 brought forth in Rheims a NT which they hoped would counteract the influence of Protestant translations. This was the work of Gregory Martin, William Allen, and others of the English College in Rheims. Their reason for addressing themselves to this task was not that which actuated Protestant translators (*i.e.,* a zealous desire to make the Word of God accessible to all men in the vernacular), for in their preface they held that, on the contrary, the translation of the Bible into the "vulgar tongues" was not an absolute necessity, or even necessarily profitable. They based their translation on a Latin Vulgate basic text, but did give attention to the Greek, as is evidenced by their treatment of the definite article. They gave some attention also to previous works in English. Of set purpose they retained certain Latin words and followed their basic text closely, even, at times, to the point of sacrifice of intelligibility. For all this, they did provide a glossary to assist the English reader, and their work served to broaden the word-base on which the KJV was constructed. The OT was not published until 1609-10 at Douai, which was too late to exert much, if any, influence on the KJV. In style it was similar to the Rheims NT.

XI. THE AUTHORIZED KING JAMES VERSION

At the Hampton Court Conference in 1604 a proposal was made by Dr. John Reynolds, a Puritan and president of Corpus Christi College, Oxford, that a new translation of the Bible be made. This proposal, although not favoured by a majority of those present, did appeal to King James I, and resulted ultimately in the production of the KJV. The king wished to have a uniform translation made by the finest scholars in the two English universities, a translation to be reviewed by the bishops and the most learned men in the church, afterwards presented to the Privy Council, and finally ratified by his authority.

James appointed fifty-four learned men for the work of translation, and the translators were divided into six companies. Among other things, the revisers were to follow the Bishops' Bible, and were to modify it as slightly as the "truth of the original" or emphasis required; they were to retain the old ecclesiastical terms such as "church," and marginal notes were to be avoided except for certain non-controversial uses.

Further information about the principles and practices which were followed by the revisers is furnished in the preface, "The Translators to the Reader." The Scriptures are there acknowledged to be high and divine, full and perfect; and their translation into the vernacular is shown to be necessary. The revisers appreciated the excellent translation work that had been done before. They never designed to make a new translation or to change a bad one into a good one, but their aim was "to make a good one better, or out of many good ones, one principal good one, not justly to be excepted against." They sought not praise, but the truth.

They worked from the Hebrew text of the OT and from the Greek text of the NT. They did not labour with undue haste or hesitate to revise what they had done; but brought back to the anvil that which they had hammered. They consulted translators or commentators in various languages. When the text was not clear, they took account of diversity of signification and sense in the margin. They did not bind themselves to a uniformity of phrasing or an identity of words, but felt free to use synonyms. They avoided the obscurity of the Douay Bible with its Latinate element. Their desire was that the Bible speak like itself, that it be understood "euen of the very vulgar."

When the various companies had completed their work, twelve representatives chosen from among them revised the entire translation. After some further touching up, the version was ready for publication. There is no record of official ecclesiastical or royal authorization, but the words "appointed to be read in churches" appeared on the title-page of the first edition. Whether there was official formal authorization or not, the version immediately displaced the Bishops' Bible in the churches and in time gained a victory over the Geneva Bible in popular favour, although the latter continued in use privately for a long while. The KJV gathered to itself the virtues of the long and brilliant royal line of English Bible translations; it united high scholarship with Christian devotion and piety. It came into being at a time when the English language was vigorous and young, and its scholars had a remarkable mastery of the instrument which Providence had prepared for them. Their version has justifiably been called "the noblest monument of English prose." The stylistic dependence of the KJV on its predecessors has been sharply brought out by C. C. Butterworth in his work on *The Literary Lineage of the King James Bible,* 1941. Butterworth estimates in a study of selected passages that it is indebted to the earlier English translations of the Bible for about 60 percent of its text (pp. 230f.). The chief contributors were the Geneva Bible and the Geneva NT (about 19 percent), and Tyndale's translations, including the Matthew Bible (about 18 percent).

XII. FROM THE AUTHORIZED TO THE REVISED VERSION

It may be thought that with the appearance of the KJV the high point in the history of the English Bible was attained and that all else is anticlimactic. But the story of the English Bible after 1611 must not be neglected. In the case of the KJV itself, change and revision of an unofficial kind were introduced through the years. More than 300 changes are found in the 1613 edition. Very extensive modifications were introduced in editions published in the 18th century. Other English versions continued to be made. Henry Ainsworth from 1616 to 1623 published translations of the Pentateuch and the Song of Solomon, and his translation of these books and of the Psalms was published after his death. His work was animated by a desire for accurate rendering. Paraphrases became fairly numerous. Several significant contributions were made in the 18th century. William Mace published in 1729 a NT in Greek and English in which he attempted to take into account "the most Authentic Manuscripts" and to use the accepted colloquial style of his day. Translations made in the 18th century by Philip Doddridge (*Family Expositor, or, a Paraphrase and Version of the New Testament*), George Campbell (*Translation of the Gospels*), and James Macknight (*A New Literal Translation of all the Apostolical Epistles*) were utilized in a NT published in 1818. In 1745 William Whiston published his *Primitive New Testament,* which uses the text of the KJV, but modifies it in the interest of readings found in Codex Bezae, Codex Claromontanus and Codex Alexandrinus. John Wesley published in 1755 a revision of the KJV. Richard Wynne issued in 1764 *The New Testament, carefully collated with the Greek, corrected, divided and printed according to the subjects treated of.* Wynne sought to find a middle course between a literal rendering and loose paraphrase. Anthony Purver, a member of the Society of Friends, worked for thirty years on the translation of the Bible which he published in 1764. One of the most noteworthy of 18th-century efforts was that of E. Harwood, who published in 1768 his *Liberal Translation of the New Testament.* His use of an "elegant," literary, paraphrastic 18th-century style dates his work.

John Worsley made an effort to translate the NT from the Greek into the "Present Idiom of the English Tongue." He wished to remove from the text obsolete and hardly intelligible words, and to bring the translation closer to the original. His translation was published posthumously in 1770. Other versions which were published (or printed) in the late 18th century were those of Gilbert Wakefield, W. H. Roberts, Thomas Haweis, William Newcome, who utilized Griesbach's Greek text of 1774-5, Nathaniel Scarlett, assisted by certain other "men of piety and literature" (whose translation allows itself the freedom of arranging material in the form of a drama), and "J. M. Ray."

The 19th century brought forth translations of the Epistles of Paul by the Unitarians Thomas Belsham (1822) and Charles Eyre (1832), and of the entire NT by the Unitarian Samuel Sharpe (1840) from J. J. Griesbach's Greek text. In 1865 Sharpe published a revised text of the KJV of the OT. Rodolphus Dickinson in 1833 with indifferent success published a NT in which he attempted to improve on the style of the KJV. Among the literal translations of the 19th century, mention should be made of that of Robert Young in 1862. New textual information continued to be reflected in the English versions. "Herman Heinfetter" made use of the Vatican MS; G. W. Braineld took into account the texts of Griesbach, Lachmann, Tischendorf, Alford and Tregelles in his translation of the Gospels (1863); Robert Ainslie used the KJV in 1869, but modified it in the interest of readings favoured by Tischendorf; Samuel Davidson published in 1875 a translation of the NT from the text of Tischendorf; and J. B. Rotherham translated the NT from the text of Tregelles (1872).

Andrew Norton's new translation of the Gospels (1855) and Leicester Ambrose Sawyer's translation of the NT (1858) were efforts to use the style of their day. They have been credited with introducing the succession of the "modern-speech" versions of the 20th century (H. Pope, *English Versions of the Bible,* pp. 546f.). Various private revisions of the KJV were published in the 19th century.

XIII. ROMAN CATHOLIC VERSIONS IN THE 18TH AND 19TH CENTURIES

In the 18th century a number of Roman Catholic efforts were made to provide an improved English version. Cornelius Nary published in 1718 and 1719 a NT translated from the Latin Vulgate with attention given to the Greek and Hebrew idiom, in which he attempted to use intelligible, idiomatic English. Robert Witham also desired to make the text of the English NT intelligible to the contemporary reader. His version, translated from the Latin Vulgate, was published in 1730. In 1738 the fifth and lightly revised edition of the Rhemish NT appeared, more than a century after the fourth edition (1633). Richard Challoner, who has been credited with some of the editorial work on this fifth edition, later published two revisions of the Douay OT and five of the NT (1749-72), and provided a simpler, more idiomatic type of text, which continued in general use among English-speaking Roman Catholics until at least 1941. He was not averse to following the KJV when he approved its readings. The revisions made by Bernard MacMahon 1783-1810 had a considerable influence, especially in Ireland. Bishop Francis Patrick Kenrick from 1849 to 1860 published a revised text of the Rheims-Douay version with annotations.

XIV. THE REVISED VERSION

Conviction that a revision of the KJV had become necessary came to formal ecclesiastical expression in 1870, and a revision of the KJV was undertaken by the Convocation of Canterbury of the Church of England. Distinguished scholars, not all of whom were members of the Church of England, participated in the project. (See B. F. Westcott, *A General View of the History of the English Bible,* 1927, pp. 324f.) Among the general principles adopted, it was agreed that as few changes as possible were to be made in the text of the KJV consistent with faithfulness, and that such changes as were introduced should be expressed in the language of the KJV and its predecessors.

The initial meeting of the NT Company was held on 22 June 1870, in the Jerusalem Chamber of Westminster Abbey. This opening session was preceded by a communion service conducted by the Dean of Westminster in the Henry VII Chapel. Among those who were admitted to the Lord's table was a Unitarian member of the company. Strong protest was naturally aroused. From this inauspicious beginning the company entered upon more than ten years of labour. The assistance of American biblical scholars was sought; and two American companies, one for the OT and one for the NT, were formed. Exclusive copyright was given to the University Presses of Oxford and Cambridge; the American companies agreed not to publish an edition embodying their distinctive readings for fourteen years after the publication of the English RV; the University Presses promised to publish during that period an appendix listing readings preferred by the American companies which had not been accepted by the British revisers. On 17 May 1881 the RV of the NT was published in England, and the whole Bible was published on 19 May 1885. The textual theories of Westcott and Hort were manifest in the NT; the OT characteristically followed the Massoretic Text, and much effort was made to represent the original faithfully and accurately even in details. Where possible the revisers attempted consistently to represent a given word in the original by a given English word. Because of its accuracy the RV has proved very valuable for study purposes. Its style, however, has not generally been approved by those who have been captivated by the rhythm and the music of the KJV.

In 1901 the preferences of the American companies and other preferences of the surviving members of the committee were embodied in the text of an "American Standard Edition" of the Revised Bible. Among the changes which were introduced, the substitution of "Jehovah" for "LORD" and "GOD" (in small capitals) was unwelcome to many. A note on a Gk. word for "worship" was introduced in the NT, and at John 9:38 it took a form that called forth most necessary objection.

XV. SINCE THE REVISED VERSION

The RV did not succeed in displacing the KJV in the affections of the majority of Bible-readers, and they were furthermore unable to satisfy all of those who were persuaded of the need and desirability of revision. They did, however, break the way open to a remarkably prolific period of Bible translation work. Since 1881 there has been an unceasing flow of translations, or revisions of translations, of the NT, or the entire Bible, or of parts of the Bible. In the case of the NT new translations or revisions have been appearing on the average of more than one a year. Among them there has been a diversity in basic texts employed, in methods of translation, in language and style, and in theological viewpoint. The influence of the Greek text and of the principles of textual criticism advocated by Westcott and Hort has been strongly felt. The view that the Greek of the NT was in the main at least the popular, vernacular Greek of the 1st century and not the literary Greek of that time has encouraged translators to undertake versions in "everyday English." There has been a generally successful effort to achieve intelligibility and contemporaneity of expression. However, in the realm of felicity and grace of style the accomplishment has often been undistinguished. While devout and believing scholarship has been ably represented in this period, heterodoxy and rationalistic criticism have also been in evidence.

A number of the versions or revisions which have appeared since the time of the English RV might be given brief mention. Among the pioneers in the translation of the Scriptures into modern English was Ferrar Fenton, who published a translation of Romans "direct from the original Greek into modern English" in 1882 and a translation of the Epistles of Paul in 1883. His NT translated into "current English" appeared in 1895 and his *Bible in Modern English* in 1903. *The Twentieth Century New Testament,* the work of about twenty persons, was published from 1898 to 1901, and was subsequently issued in revised form. The *New Testament in Modern Speech,* R. F. Weymouth's much-used translation from the text of his *Resultant Greek Testament,* was posthumously published in 1903, with Ernest

Hampden-Cook as editor. James Moffatt issued *The Historical New Testament* in 1901, in which he attempted to arrange the writings of the NT in a conjectured order of "literary growth" and date of composition. In 1913 his new translation of the NT appeared. Its textual basis was mainly von Soden's Greek text. The clearly erroneous reading of the Sinaitic MS of the Old Syr. Version is followed at Matt. 1:16, and the reader is not assisted by any textual note (see J. G. Machen, *The Virgin Birth of Christ,* 1930, pp. 176ff.). Moffatt's translation of the OT was published in 1924. E. J. Goodspeed's "American" translation of the NT, based on the Greek text of Westcott and Hort and intended to be expressed in popular American idiom, appeared in 1923, and the "American" translation of the OT, prepared by A. R. Gordon, T. J. Meek, Leroy Waterman, and J. M. Powis Smith, appeared in 1927.

Attention should also be called to W. G. Ballantine's *Riverside New Testament* (1923); Helen B. Montgomery's *Centenary Translation of the New Testament* (1924); C. B. Williams' translation of the New Testament "in the language of the people" (1937), a version which attempts a precise rendering of Gk. verb forms; *The New Testament in Basic English* (1941) and *The Bible in Basic English* (1949); Gerrit Verkuyl's *Berkeley Version of the New Testament* (1945), the Berkeley Version of the entire Bible (1959), the OT section of which was prepared by a sizeable staff of translators, with Gerrit Verkuyl as editor-in-chief, and the *New Berkeley* or *Modern Language Bible* (1969); J. B. Phillips' translation of the NT (1947-57; one-volume edition, 1958), at times quite free and paraphrastic; *The Letchworth Version (of the NT) in Modern English,* by T. F. Ford and R. E. Ford (1948), a remarkably successful light revision of the KJV which conserves much of the stylistic beauty of its original; *The New World Translation of the Christian Greek Scriptures* (1950), a version prepared by the Jehovah's Witnesses; C. K. Williams' translation of the NT into a limited-vocabulary "Plain English" (1952); H. J. Schonfield's *Authentic New Testament* (1955); Kenneth S. Wuest's *Expanded Translation of the Greek New Testament* (1956-9); the *Amplified New Testament* (1958); W. F. Beck's New Testament in the Language of Today (1963); William Barclay's *New Translation* of the New Testament (1968-9); and *The Translator's New Testament* (1973).

Several Roman Catholic translations of special interest have appeared. The NT section of *The Westminster Version of the Sacred Scriptures,* which was completed in 1935 (1913-35), was translated from the Greek by various men working on individual assignments under general editors. It employs a solemn or "biblical" style with archaic forms. J. A. Carey issued a revision of the Challoner-Rheims NT in 1935. F. A. Spencer's translation of the NT from the Greek was published in 1937. In 1941 a revision of the Challoner-Rheims NT appeared in USA, prepared under the supervision of the Confraternity of Christian Doctrine by a large number of scholars. It was not bound by the official Clementine text of the Latin Vulgate, but its revisers were free to take account of critical editions. They succeeded in commendable measure in producing a version of clarity, simplicity and contemporary style.

Monsignor R. A. Knox published in 1945 a trial edition of a translation of the NT from the Vulgate and a slightly modified definitive edition in 1945, which was "authorized by the Archbishops and Bishops of England and Wales. It was accorded an official status along with the Rhemish version. Knox's translation of the OT from the Latin Vulgate was published in 1949 in two volumes "for private use only." A revision appeared in 1955 with hierarchical authorization. The translation of the NT by James A. Kleist and Joseph L. Lilly (1954) was made from the Greek. Kleist translated the Gospels from the text of Bover; Lilly translated the rest of the NT. The *Jerusalem Bible* (1966) is related to the French version *La Bible de Jerusalem,* though is not simply a translation of it. *The New American Bible* (1970), sponsored by the Bishops' Committee of the Confraternity of Christian Doctrine, represented a major translation effort. It was based on the original languages of Scripture or on what was held to be the oldest form of the text extant.

Several of the most widely used and most influential of recent versions remain to be mentioned. A committee-revision of the American RV, authorized by the International Council of Religious Education, was published in 1946 (NT, 1971), 1952 (entire Bible), 1965 (Catholic edition). This *Revised Standard Version* (RSV) differs considerably in important aspects from the KJV and RV. It lacks their confidence in the Massoretic Hebrew text, and in places indulges in critical conjectures; it allows itself more freedom in rendering its text than did the KJV and RV.

Another revision of the American RV, *The New American Standard Bible* (1963), prepared by evangelical scholars, is a close and faithful translation in a clear and readable style, which is admirable for study purposes. A further notable accomplishment by evangelicals is the *New International Version* (1978). It is a completely new translation into contemporary English, somewhat freer than is NASB. Very free in its rendering is the *New English Bible* (1961-1970), a version produced with the cooperation of representatives of the larger British churches (apart from the Roman Catholics), of the Oxford and Cambridge University Presses, and of the British and Foreign Bible Society and the National Bible Society of Scotland. Very extensively circulated have been the NT in *Today's English Version* or *Good News for Modern Man* (1966), followed by the complete *Good News Bible* (1976), prepared by the American Bible Society; and *The Living Bible* (1962-71), a paraphrase or thought-for-thought translation, prepared by Kenneth N. Taylor.

GUIDE TO THE ANCIENT MANUSCRIPTS

A Guide to Understanding Marginal Notes on Different Readings in the New Testament Manuscripts

P H I L I P W . C O M F O R T

INTRODUCTION

Nearly every reader of the English New Testament encounters marginal notes that make reference to the New Testament manuscripts—referred to variously as "the ancient manuscripts," "the authorities," or "the witnesses." Such marginal references are very significant, but most readers have no idea what they convey. The purpose of this reference guide is to provide the reader with a select listing of manuscripts for each New Testament verse or portion that has a variant reading cited in the margins of most standard New Testament versions. The list of manuscripts is purposely select; only the best and earliest Greek manuscripts are cited. The list usually does not include other ancient translations of the New Testament (e.g., Old Latin, Syriac, Coptic) or citations from the writings of the church fathers. The most important manuscripts are briefly described on the next page. The reader should be able, in a short time and with little effort, to become familiar with the most prominent Greek New Testament manuscripts. With this reference tool, the reader can directly observe which "authorities" support which readings.

Succinct comments are provided on some of the more critical readings, comments that explain the differences between various readings in the manuscripts and demonstrate why only one such reading was most probably the original wording of the author. This critical examination, known as textual criticism, seeks to recover the original wording of the Scriptures. What the New Testament authors originally wrote (called the autographs) were, in certain portions, corrupted by succeeding generations of copyists. Some of the textual corruption was intentional (usually for theological reasons) but some was unintentional (due to common transcriptional mistakes). For the most part, the tendency of the scribes who copied the New Testament was to add interpolations and harmonizations into the text. As a result, the text of the Greek New Testament grew and expanded, as when leaven is added into flour. For example, the word "Spirit" often was expanded to "Holy Spirit" (see John 7:39; Acts 6:3; 8:18; Rom. 15:19 in the following notes) and unusual titles of the Spirit were conformed to more usual appelations. Thus, in some manuscripts the title "the Spirit of the Lord" was changed to "the Holy Spirit" (Acts 5:9; 8:39; 2 Cor 3:17), "the Spirit of Jesus" to "the Spirit of the Lord" (Acts 16:7), "the Spirit of Christ" to "the Spirit" (1 Pet 1:11), "the Spirit of His Son" to "His Spirit" (Gal. 4:6), "the eternal Spirit" to "the Holy Spirit" (Heb. 9:14), and "the seven Spirits" to "spirits" (Rev. 1:4; 4:5; 5:6).

The history of the transmission of the text of the Greek New Testament is a record of expansion and corruption. Generally speaking, the later manuscripts (i.e., those after the sixth century) are more corrupt than the earlier ones. The textual critic, consequently, looks to the earlier manuscripts for a purer text. At the same time, he also searches for the reading which was most likely written by the author, the reading from which all other variants were derived. He must consider context, style, and theology. The context of a passage and an author's style can be quite revealing. And it is usually not too difficult to detect theological tampering. Scribes were fond of harmonizing the Gospels and of ameliorating difficult (if not obscure) theology. As a rule, the shorter and more difficult reading is probably the original. Of course, there are exceptions; therefore, each passage must be examined as a unique entity. It should also be added that knowledge of manuscripts must accompany every textual decision. For example, manuscripts of Alexandrian origin are usually more accurate than those from other derivations, and earlier manuscripts are generally more trustworthy than later ones.

The Greek text underlying the King James Version, popularly called the Textus Receptus, is a text which contains a vast culmination of textual corruption. (The Textus Receptus was compiled from manuscripts of the twelfth to the fifteenth centuries.) Although a minority of scholars have continued to defend the reliability of the Textus Receptus, most scholars (for the last 100 years) have been convinced, on the basis of both theory and praxis, that the *Textus Receptus* is corrupt—i.e., it does not adequately present the text written by the God-inspired, New Testament authors. By God's sovereignty, better and earlier manuscripts have been discovered since the time of the Textus Receptus (ca. 1600), and these manuscripts display a more accurate text. In the century prior to this one, Codex Alexandrinus, Codex Sinaiticus, Codex Vaticanus, and Codex Ephraemi Rescriptus (to name a few) provided scholars with a text of the New Testament dated between the fourth and fifth centuries. As a result, textual critics like Tischendorf, Tregelles, Westcott and Hort were able to compile editions of the Greek New Testament which far exceed the reliability of the Textus Receptus.

The recovery has continued in this century. Nearly ninety papyrus manuscripts containing portions of the New Testament have been discovered in this century, and several of these manuscripts are dated between A.D. 200–350. The Chester Beatty Papyri, including some of the earliest witnesses to the Gospels, Acts, Paul's Epistles, and Revelation (namely P45, P46, P47), and the Martin Bodmer Papyri, containing some of the earliest extant copies of Luke, John, 1& 2 Peter, and Jude (namely P66, P72, and P75), furnish for these portions of the

New Testament a text that is but one hundred to one hundred and fifty years removed from the autographs. These manuscripts have had great impact upon the formation of critical editions of the Greek New Testament in this century. The most useful, and probably the most accurate of these editions is the Nestle text (now called Nestle-Aland in the most recent edition, the 26th).

One of the primary reasons this century has witnessed so many new English versions of the New Testament is that new translations have been undertaken in order to reflect the fresh evidence discovered in earlier and better manuscripts. (This is explicitly stated in the introduction to the Revised Standard Version.) The more recent translations have the advantage of having access to the most up-to-date material. This is clearly evident, for example, in the New International Version. At any rate, there is something to learn from all the translations contained in this volume—and more specifically, from their marginal notes on various readings in the ancient manuscripts.

There has been an on-going recovery of the Greek New Testament, and the more recent translations reflect that restoration. At one point in the history of the Israelites the book of the law had been lost—until Hilkiah, the high priest, discovered it in the temple (see 2 Kings 22:8–13). The recovery of that book brought revival to God's people. We, in like manner, should be thankful that earlier and better manuscripts have been uncovered, manuscripts which attest to the pure, original words of God.

PRIMARY MANUSCRIPTS

name	*date* (AD)	*contents*	*location*	*published/ discovered*	*reliability*
Chester Beatty Papyrus I (P45)	250	portions of Mt, Mk, Lk, Jn, Acts	Beatty Museum Dublin, Ireland	1930 (Egypt)	fair
Chester Beatty Papyrus II (P46)	225	most of Paul's epistles, in this order: Rom, Heb, 1 Cor, 2 Cor, Eph, Gal, Phil, Col, 1 Thess	Beatty Museum & University of Michigan, Ann Arbor	1930 (Egypt)	excellent (close to B)
Bodmer Papyrus II (P66)	175	most of Jn	Bodmer Library Geneva, Switzerland	1956 (Egypt)	good
Bodmer Papyrus VII/VIII (P72)	3rd C.	Jude, 1 & 2 Peter	Bodmer Library	1959 (Egypt)	good
Bodmer Papyrus XIV/XV (P75)	200	most of Lk and Jn	Bodmer Library	1961 (Egypt)	excellent (close to B)
Codex Sinaiticus (א)	4th C.	all of the NT	British Museum London	1859 (by Tischendorf at St. Catherine's Monastery, Mt. Sinai)	good
Codex Alexandrinus (A)	450	nearly all of the NT	British Museum	1078 (given to the Patriarch of Alexandria)	poor in the Gospels, good in Acts & Epistles, excellent in Rev
Codex Vaticanus (B)	4th C.	all of NT except Heb 9:14 to the end (1, 2 Tim & Tit also missing)	Vatican Library Vatican City	in Vatican Library since at least 1475 but not published until 1904	excellent
Codes Ephraemi Rescriptus (C)	5th C.	all of NT except 2 Thess & 2 John & parts of other books	National Library Paris	owned by Catherine de Medici, given to library in late 16th C.	fair, excellent in Rev
Codex Bezae Cantabrigiensis *(D)*	late 5th C.	all four gospels in this order: Mt, Jn, Lk, Mk; Acts, 3 John	Cambridge Univ. Library	presented to Cambridge by Theodore Beza in 1581	idiosyncratic, varied—fair to poor
Codex Washingtonianius I (W)	late 4th C.	all four gospels in this order: Mt, Jn, Lk, Mk	Freer Museum of Smithsonian Institute, Washington, D.C.	1906 (Egypt)	varied, good in Lk 1–8, Jn 5–21, fair elsewhere

Two other important MSS which include extensive portions of the NT are: 1) 048, 5th C, containing portions of Acts and the Epistles, in the Vatican Library, and 2) 33, 9th C, containing most of the NT, in the National Library in Paris. Both MSS are quite reliable. Facsimiles of some of the manuscripts referred to in this Index can be seen in *The Illustrated Bible Dictionary* (Tyndale House Publishers). The illustrations are as follows: P13 (p. 628), P45 (pp. 952, 963, 1149, 1669), P46 (pp. 1146, 1218, 1347, 1547, 1557), P47 (p. 1337), P52 (pp. 582, 1542, cover of Vol. III), P66 (p. 802), P72 (p. 1206), P74 (p. 918), P75 (pp. 583, 919), א (p. 194), and A (p. 1545).

TERMINOLOGY USED IN MARGINS OF VARIOUS TRANSLATIONS

authority, authorities (used in RSV): authoritative copies of the Greek NT; synonym for manuscript(s), witness(es).

manuscript, manuscripts: handwritten copies of the Greek NT.

witness, witnesses (used in NEB): manuscripts that constitute evidence of authority for the Greek NT text.

(Note: all of the above terms can be used interchangeably.)

early or *ancient* authorities, manuscripts, and/or witnesses are those copies which are closest (chronologically) to the original writings (called autographs).

late authorities, manuscripts, and/or witnesses are those copies which are furthest (chronologically) from the autographs. For the most part, they are not as reliable as the early manuscripts.

ABBREVIATIONS USED IN THIS INDEX

P45	Chester Beatty Papyrus I
P46	Chester Beatty Papyrus II
P66	Bodmer Papyrus II
P72	Bodmer Papyrus VII/VIII
P75	Bodmer Papyrus XIV/XV
א	Codex Sinaiticus
A	Codex Alexandrinus
B	Codex Vaticanus
C	Codex Ephraemi Rescriptus
D	Codex Bezae/Claromontanus
W	Codex Washingtonianius I
vid	"as it seems": used to designate an apparent reading
c	indicates a corrector†
s	denotes a reading supplied by a later scribe
*	indicates hand of original scribe
mg	indicates a marginal note
om.	means "omit" (to be understood as "not present")
inc.	means "include" (i.e., "present")
ASV	American Standard Version
KJV	The King James Version
JB	The Jerusalem Bible
NASB	New American Standard Bible
NEB	New English Bible
NIV	New International Version
Phps	Phillips' Modern English NT
RSV	Revised Standard Version
TEV	Today's English Version
TLB	The Living Bible
LXX	Septuagint (Greek translation of the OT)
MS	manuscript
MSS	manuscripts
NT	New Testament
OT	Old Testament
NA^{26}	*Novum Testamentum Graece,* 26th edition, Nestle-Aland
TR	Textus Receptus
UBS^{3}	*The Greek New Testament,* 3rd edition, United Bible Societies
WH	*The New Testament in the Original Greek,* Westcott and Hort

† $א^{c}$ indicates the first corrector, $א^{a}$ a second corrector (6th & 7th century scribes from Caesarea)
B^{c} indicates the first corrector, B^{2} and B^{3} successive correctors—so also for Codex C.

The following pages contain citations of all the variant readings noted in the margins of the English translations. Each Greek word or phrase has been translated into English, and is then followed by a list of manuscripts that support each particular reading. The first word (or phrase) cited is most likely the original; the words that follow are secondary emendations. In this list a semicolon (;) demarcates each variant reading. If, however, two (or more) readings have equal or nearly equal claim to being original, the readings are separated with a double slash (//). In addition to the principle manuscripts, other important witnesses are included in certain portions. These are noted section by section and/or book by book.

GOSPELS

added MSS: L (8th C), Q (5th C), T (4th C)

MATTHEW

added MSS: P1 (3rd C), P21 (4th C), P25 (4th C), P37 (3rd C), P67 (200)

1:10 *Amos* א B C D 33: *Amon* L W

1:16 *Joseph, the husband of Mary of whom Jesus was born* P1 א B C L W 33; *Joseph, to whom was betrothed Mary, a virgin, who gave birth to Jesus* early Latin translations and a few later MSS; *Joseph, to whom Mary, a virgin, was betrothed, was the father of Jesus* one Syriac MS
The best MSS assert the Gospel's claim that Jesus was born of the virgin Mary; He was not the direct offspring of Joseph. In fact, this is attested to in every extant copy of the Greek NT. The one variant reading in the Sinaitic Syriac (the witness noted in NEB) cannot be taken seriously.

1:18 *Jesus Christ* P1 א C L 33: *Christ Jesus* B; *Jesus* W; *Christ* (or, *Messiah*) in some early translations

3:16 *opened* א* B; *opened to him* א^{b} C D^{s} L W 33

4:17 *Repent, for* א B C D L W 33; om. a few early translations

5:22 om. *without cause* P67^{vid} א* B; inc. א^{c} D L W 33

5:43 om. *bless those who curse you, do good to those who hate you* א B; inc. D L W 33

5:44 om. *treat you spitefully and* א B; inc. D L W 33 (probably taken from Lk 6:27, 28)

6:4, 6 om. *openly* א B D; inc. L W

6:13 om. *For thine is the kingdom and the power and the glory forever. Amen.* א B D; inc. L W 33
It is doubtful that Jesus ended His prayer with this doxology. If it had been original, no good reason can be found to explain its absence in א B D. The doxology was added by later scribes for liturgical purposes; it may have been modeled after 1 Chron 29:11, 12.

6:22 The one witness referred to in NEB is B.

7:13 inc. *gate* א^{b} B C L W 33; om. א*

8:10 *not even in Israel* B W; *with no one in Israel* א C L 33 (cf. Lk 7:9)

8:28 *Gadarenes* (א*) B C; *Gergesenes* א^{c} L W

9:4 *seeing* א C D L W 33; *knowing* B

9:14 *fast often* א^{b} C D L W 33 // *fast* א* B

9:34 inc. verse א B C L W 33; om. D

10:3 *Thaddaeus* א B; *Lebbaeus* D; *Lebbaeus called Thaddaeus* C L W 33

10:25 *Beelzebul* C D L W; *Beezebul* א B; *Beelzebub* in early translations

11:9 *Why then did you go out? To see a prophet?* א* B^{c} W // *What then did you go out to see? A prophet?* א^{c} B*^{vid} C D L 33

11:15 om. *to hear* B D; inc. א C L W 33

11:19 *works* א B* W // *children* B^{2} C D L 33
Since Lk 7:35 reads *children,* it is quite possible that the scribes of B^{2} et al changed *works* to *children.* There is no discernible reason why the change would have gone the other way, unless of course the word *works* seemed to make better sense to these copyists. Actually both readings are appropriate in this context, inasmuch as Wisdom, though momentarily jeered, is always proven correct by her future generations and/or future deeds. Though derided by their own generation, John the Baptist and the Son of Man were to be vindicated by successive generations.

12:24 *Beelzebul* P21 C D L W, *Beezebul* א B; *Beelzebub* in early translations

12:47 inc. verse א^{a} C D W 33; om. א* B L (probably due to homoeoteleuton—"like endings"—compare the similar wording in 12:46 and 12:47. A scribe could easily pass from 12:46 to 12:48.)

13:9, 43 om. *to hear* א* B L; inc. א^{c} C D W 33 (see Mk 4:9; Lk 8:8)

13:35 *the prophet* א^{a} B C D L W; *Isaiah the prophet* א* 33
The quotation comes from Ps 78:2, written by Asaph.

14:3 *his brother Philip's wife* א B C L W 33; *his brother's wife* D

14:24 *was many furlongs distant from the land* B // *was in the middle of the sea* א C D L W 33 (taken from Mk 6:47?)

14:30 *strong wind* B[2] C D L (W) // *wind* ℵ B* 33

15:6a *his father* ℵ B D; *father or his mother* C L W 33

15:6b *word* ℵ[a] B D; *law* ℵ*[,b] C; *commandment* L W 33

The original reading is most likely *word,* which was supplanted by *law,* then *commandment.* Jesus' reproof in this passage (Mt 15:1–9) is directed toward the Jews who had substituted their traditions for God's Word. As a case in point, Jesus cites a scripture (Exod 20:12) that they had supplanted with a man-made ordinance (see Mt 15:5), thus nullifying God's Word.

15:14 om. *of the blind* ℵ*[,b] B D // inc. ℵ[a] C L W 33

16:2b, 3 inc. verses C D L W 33 // om. ℵ B

Since these verses are absent in ℵ B, it could be ascertained that Matthew did not write them. Their presence in other MSS could be due to later assimilation—from Lk 12:54–56. However, it must be noted that the Matthew account is different from Luke's. And certain scholars have argued that the copyists of ℵ and B (both from Egypt) omitted these verses because the Egyptian red sky in the morning does not signify the advent of rain.

16:13 *that the Son of man is* ℵ B; *that I, the Son of man, am* C D L W

17:21 om. verse ℵ* B 33; inc. ℵ[b] C D L W

There is no good explanation as to why, if original, this verse would have been omitted in ℵ* B 33. On the contrary, it appears that it was added in later MSS as a harmonization to Mk 9:29.

17:22 *were gathering together* B; *abode* C (D) L W 33

18:11 om. verse ℵ B L* 33; inc. D W (probably taken from Mt 9:13; Lk 19:10)

18:14 *your Father* ℵ D[c] L W; *my Father* B 33

18:15 *sins against you* D L W 33 // *sins* ℵ B

19:9a *if a man divorces his wife, except for unchastity,* ℵ C[3] L (W); *if a man divorces his wife, except for unchastity, he makes her commit adultery* P25[vid?] B C* (see Mt 5:32)

19:9b *and marries another, he commits adultery* ℵ C[3] D L; *and he who marries a divorced woman commits adultery* (P25) (B) C* W (see Mt 5:32)

19:29a *mother or children* B // *mother or wife or children* ℵ C L W 33 (assimilated from Lk 18:29?)

19:29b *hundredfold* ℵ C D W 33; *manifold* B L

20:30 *Lord, Son of David* P45[vid] C W 33; *Jesus, Son of David* ℵ (see Mk 10:47; Lk 18:38); *Son of David* D

21:12 *temple* ℵ B L 33; *temple of God* C D W

21:44 inc. verse ℵ B C L W; om. D 33

This verse has been omitted in the Greek text of the NEB and bracketed in the Greek texts of WH, NA[26], and UBS[3] because it has been suspected as being an interpolation taken from Lk 20:18. But several scholars have pointed out that it would have been more natural to insert the verse after 21:42, not after 21:43. Besides, its inclusion has strong external testimony, and it is very appropriate in this context, because this verse, combining the prophecies of Isa 8:14, 15 and Dan 2:34, 35, 44, 45, depicts Christ as the Stone over which the Jews stumbled and were broken (cf. Rom 9:30–33; 1 Cor 1:23), and the Stone which will smash all kingdoms in the process of establishing God's kingdom (see Lk 21:43).

22:30 *angels* B D; *angels of God* ℵ L W

22:35 inc. *lawyer* ℵ B D L W 33; om. a few early translations

23:4 inc. *and hard to bear* B D[c] W 33; om. ℵ L

23:14 om. verse ℵ B D L 33; inc. W and a few early translations (an interpolation taken from Mk 12:40 or Lk 20:47, inserted in some MSS before 23:13 and in others after 23:13)

23:38 inc. *desolate* ℵ C D W 33; om. B L

Since the Jews rejected the Messiah, the temple was forsaken by God and left desolate. This is the idea contained in Jer 22:5, the source of Jesus' statement here. The temple abandoned by God (cf. Ezek 10) was eventually desolated (see Lk 21:20).

24:36 inc. *nor the Son* ℵ*[,b] B D; om. ℵ[a] L W 33

The words *nor the Son* were purposely excluded in several MSS because of the doctrinal problem they presented—i.e., how could the Son, if He was God, not know what the Father knows? The dilemma is solved when we realize that Jesus is here speaking as a man, in a position subordinate to the Father (see 1 Cor 11:3; 15:24).

25:1 *the bride* ℵ B L W 33; *the bride and the bridegroom* D and some early translations

26:20 *the twelve* P37[vid] P45[vid] B D; *the twelve disciples* ℵ A L W 33

26:28 *covenant* P37 P45[vid] ℵ B L 33; *new covenant* A C D

The covenant Jesus instituted through the shedding of his blood is indeed the new covenant, according to Lk 22:20 and 1 Cor 15:25. But here and in Mk 14:25 the best MSS read simply *covenant.*

27:16, 17 *Barabbas* ℵ A B D L W 33; *Jesus Barabbas* a few Caesarean MSS and translations

27:24 *innocent of the blood of this man* B D; *innocent of the blood of this righteous man* (or, *of the righteous blood of this man*) ℵ L W 33

27:35 The reading noted in NIV mg is supported by late Caesarean MSS and a few translations. However, it is clearly an assimilation from Jn 19:24.
27:49 om. *And another took a spear and pierced his side, and out came water and blood* A D W 33; inc. ℵ B C L
Although several good MSS contain the above expression, it probably was an early interpolation taken from Jn 19:34. If the expression had been an original part of Matthew's account, there is no good reason why it would have been omitted in later MSS.
28:6 *he lay* ℵ B 33; *the Lord lay* A C D L W

MARK

added MS: P88 (4th C)
1:1 inc. *Son of God* ℵ[a] A B D L W; om. ℵ*
The manuscript support for *Son of God* is impressive. Furthermore, it is quite likely that Mark chose to begin and conclude his narrative with the affirmation that Jesus is the Son of God (cf 1:1 and 15:39).
1:2 *in Isaiah the prophet* ℵ B D L; *in the prophets* A W
Mk 1:2, 3 is a composite quotation, taken first from Mal 3:1 and then from Isa 40:3. Isaiah is cited because it was customary for biblical writers to credit the more prominent prophet. In this light, it is easy to see why the first reading is original and the second an emendation.
1:4 *John came baptizing in the wilderness and preaching* A D W // *John the baptizer appeared in the wilderness, preaching* ℵ B L 33
1:29 *he left* ℵ A C L 33 // *they left* B D W
1:34 *knew him* ℵ* A D; *knew him to be Christ* ℵ[c] B L W 33[vid] (probably assimilated from Lk 4:41)
1:41 *being filled with compassion* ℵ A B C L W 33; *being angry* D; om. one Old Latin MS
2:16a *the scribes of the Pharisees* (P88) ℵ B L W 33; *the scribes and the Pharisees* A C D
2:16b *eat* ℵ B D W // *eat and drink* P88 A C L 33
2:22 inc. *but new wine is for fresh wineskins* P88 ℵ A B C L W 33; om. D and a few Old Latin MSS
3:14 inc. *whom he also named apostles* ℵ B C*[vid] W; om. C[2] L 33
3:16 inc. *so he appointed the twelve* ℵ B C*; om. L 33
3:32 *brothers* ℵ B C L W 33; *brothers and sisters* A D
5:1 *Gerasenes* ℵ* B D; *Gadarenes* A C; *Gergesenes* ℵ[c] L 33
5:36 *ignoring* (or, *overhearing*) ℵ B L W; *hearing* ℵ[a] A C D
6:3 *Is not this the carpenter, the son of Mary. . . ?* ℵ A B C D L W; *Is not this the son of the carpenter and Mary. . . ?* P45[vid] 33[vid]
Certain scribes evidently took offense at Jesus himself being called a carpenter, rather than just a son of a carpenter. These scribes emended the statement to read like Mt 13:55.
6:14 *some said* B (D) W; *he said* ℵ A C L 33
6:20 *greatly perplexed* ℵ B L (W); *did many things A C D 33*
7:3 *wash their hands with the fist* (lit.) A B (D) L 33; *wash their hands frequently* ℵ W; *wash their hands* a few MSS
7:4a *wash* (or, *immerse*) *themselves* A W 33 // *wash* (or, *immerse*) *it* L // *sprinkle themselves* ℵ B
7:4b *bronze vessels and beds* (or, *dining couches*) P45[vid] ℵ B L; *bronze vessels* A D W 33
7:6 *keep* ℵ A L 33 // *continue to keep* B // *establish* (or, *set up*) D W
7:16 om. verse ℵ B L; inc. A D W 33 (see Mk 4:9, 23)
7:24 *Tyre* D L W // *Tyre and Sidon* ℵ A B 33 (assimilated from Mt 15:2; Mk 7:31?)
8:10 *Dalmanutha* ℵ A B C L W 33; *Magedan* or *Magdala* in a few translations (D reads *Melegada*)
8:15 *Herod* ℵ A B C D L 33; *Herodians* P45 W
8:26 *do not go into the village* ℵ* B L W; *do not go and tell anyone in the village* A C 33; *do not tell anyone in the village* D
8:38a *me and my words* ℵ A B C D L 33; *me and mine* (i.e., my disciples) P45[vid] W
8:38b *when he comes in the glory of his Father with his holy angels* ℵ A B C D L 33; *when he comes in the glory of his Father and of the holy angels* P45 W
9:24 *cried out* P45 ℵ A* B C* L (W); *cried out with tears* A[2] C[3] D 33
9:29 *prayer* ℵ* B; *prayer and fasting* P45[vid] ℵ[b] A C D L W 33
The words *and fasting* are most likely an accretion which reflects an early obsession with ascetic practices (see also 1 Cor 7:5).
9:38 *a man casting out demons in your name* ℵ B C L; *a man casting out demons in your name who does not follow us* A D W
9:44, 46 om. verses ℵ B C L W (each verse is identical to 9:48); inc. verses A D
9:49 *for everyone will be salted with fire* ℵ B L W; *for every sacrifice will be salted with salt* D; *for everyone will be salted with fire, and every sacrifice will be salted with salt* A C
It seems that a marginal gloss (from Lev 2:13) found its way into the text as an addition (third

reading above) or as a replacement (second reading above)—see Metzger. But this difficult passage is hardly illuminated by Lev 2:13, for the statement in context (9:42–50) conveys the idea that all men need to be purified and preserved by the refining fire—the fire which, like salt, preserves and purifies a man's soul (see Isa 33:14; Mal 3:2; 1 Cor 3:13, 15; 1 Pet 1:7).

10:2 *Pharisees came and asked him* ℵ A B C L W; *they* [people] *asked him* (or, *he was asked*) D

10:7 inc. *and be joined to his wife* A C D W // om. ℵ B
Although the above clause is absent in ℵ and B, there are good reasons to support its originality: 1) "the two" in 10:8 refers back to the husband and wife, not the father and mother, 2) without the clause Gen 2:24 would not be quoted in full, 3) the clause could have been dropped from ℵ and B due to transcriptional oversight (Metzger).

10:24 om. *for those who trust riches* ℵ B; inc. A C (D) (W *a rich man*)

10:26 *said to him* ℵ B C; *said to each other* A D W

10:40 om. *by my Father* ℵ^{a} A B C D L W; inc. ℵ^{*,b}

11:19 *they went* A B W // *he went* ℵ C D

11:22 *have faith* (imperative) A B C L W 33*; *if you have faith* ℵ D 33^{c}

11:24 *have received* ℵ B C L W; *are receiving* A 33; *will receive* D

11:26 om. verse ℵ B L W; inc. A D (33) (taken from Mt 6:15)

12:23 *in the resurrection* ℵ B C* L; *in the resurrection therefore* C^{2} D W 33; *in the resurrection, when men rise* A

13:33 *watch* B D // *watch and pray* ℵ A C L W

14:24 *covenant* ℵ B C D L W; *new covenant* A and later MSS (assimilated from Lk 22:20; 1 Cor 11:25—see note on Mt 26:28)

14:30 inc. *twice* A B L; om. ℵ D W (see Mt 26:34; Lk 22:34; Jn 13:38)

14:39 *saying the same word(s)* (or, *thing*) ℵ A B C L W; om. D

14:65 om. *Who hit you?* ℵ A B C D L; inc. W 33 (taken from Mt 26:68; Lk 22:64)

14:68 om. *and the rooster crowed* ℵ B L W // inc. A C D 33

14:72a *the rooster crowed the second time* A B C^{2vid} D W 33; om. ℵ C^{*vid} L

14:72b inc. *twice* A B C^{2} L 33; om. ℵ C^{*vid} W (see Mt 26:75; Lk 22:61)

15:8 *came up* ℵ* B; *shouted* ℵ^{b} A C W 33
The two Greek words represented here look very much alike (ἀναβὰς/ἀναβοήσας); thus, they could easily be confused. The former is most probably the original.

15:28 om. verse ℵ A B C D; inc. L 33 (taken from Lk 22:37)

15:34 *why have You forsaken me?* ℵ (A) B C L 33; *why have You reproached (or, shamed) me?* D

15:39 *that thus he expired* ℵ B L; *that thus, crying out, he expired* A C W 33; *that he thus cried out and expired* D

15:44 *had been dead for some time* ℵ A C L 33; *had already died* B D W

16:1 inc. *Mary Magdalene, and Mary the mother of James and* ℵ A B C L W 33; om. (thus the reading, "When the Sabbath was over, Salome . . .") D

16:9–20 The ending of Mark according to all extant MSS has come to us in five basic forms:

1) The Gospel ends with 16:8—supported by ℵ and B, some early translations (Syriac, Coptic, Armenian, Georgian), and attested to by Clement, Origen, Eusebius, Jerome and a few others.
2) The Gospel ends with a short conclusion after 16:8—supported by one Old Latin, African MS (it^{k}), which reads:

But they reported briefly to Peter and those with him all that they had been told. And after this Jesus himself sent out by means of them, from east to west, the sacred and imperishable proclamation of eternal salvation. (See RSV mg and NEB mg.)

3) The Gospel ends with the short conclusion above (in it^{k}) plus verses 9–20—supported by L Ψ 099 0122 and a few other MSS.
4) The Gospel ends with 16:9–20—supported by A, C, D, 33, several later MSS, several early translations (Old Latin, Syriac, Coptic) and attested to by the Diatessaron, Irenaeus (born 202), Aphraates (337), and others.
5) The Gospel ends with 16:9–20, incorporating a longer addition after 16:14—supported by W and the testimony of Jerome about certain Greek MSS. The addition is as follows:

And they excused themselves saying, This age of lawlessness and unbelief is under Satan, who does not allow the truth and power of God to prevail over the unclean things of the spirits. Therefore, reveal thy righteousness now—thus they spoke to Christ. And Christ replied to them, The term of years of Satan's power has been fulfilled, but other terrible things draw near. And for those who have sinned I was delivered over to death, that they may return to the truth and sin no more, in order that they may inherit the spiritual and incorruptible glory of righteousness which is in heaven. (Translation by Metzger.)

Most scholars would not consider the additions in it^{k} (#2), L Ψ 099 0122 etc (#3), or W (#5) to have any serious claim to originality. But debate still continues about verses 9 through 20. Scholars have demonstrated that these verses are narratively incongruous with 16:1-8. (For example, 16:9 abruptly introduces a new subject, Jesus; whereas, in 16:8 it is the women. And 16:9 introduces Mary Magdalene as if she had not yet been introduced—but see 16:1.) The major consensus is that Mark did not write 16:9-20; it is the work of another writer (probably in the early second century) who provided an extended conclusion derived from various sources, including the other Gospels. Many have considered this appendage to be an authentic part of the NT canon because they believe that 1) Mark himself, for whatever reason, was not able to complete his Gospel and thus had to stop at verse 8, or 2) the autographed ending was permanently lost and thus needed to be replaced. Most readers would have to admit that it is quite unlikely that Mark would stop his Gospel so abruptly. How could the Gospel close on such a negative note of fear and bewilderment? Undoubtedly, Mark wrote more or intended to write more; but of such we have no record. Since the two earliest MSS conclude with verse 8,* we should accept this testimony—until more light can be shed on this textual problem.

* It should be noted that one other Greek MS concludes with verse 8, namely, Codex 304 (a twelfth century MS containing only Matthew and Mark, most likely transcribed in Rome). When this writer looked at this MS in the Bibliotheque Nationale in Paris, it was apparent that the copyist's exemplar did not contain the longer ending—for though the last leaf of the codex contains the last portion of Mark, the scribe had enough space to have written the longer ending if it was in his exemplar.

LUKE

added MSS: P4 (3rd C), 0171 (4th C), 0181 (4th/5th C)

1:28 om. *blessed are you among women* ℵ B L W; inc. A C D 33 (taken from 1:42 which has this phrase in all the MSS)

1:35 *born* ℵ A B C^{3} D L W; *born of you* C* 33

1:37 *no word from God will be impossible* (i.e., *will be void of power*—ASV) ℵ* B (D) L W; *for with God nothing will be impossible* ℵ^{c} A C 33
The first reading, as the more difficult, is more likely to have been written by Luke. As such, Gabriel's utterance to Mary indicates that what God had just spoken (or, promised) He was able to perform (see 1:28–36). The second reading demonstrates a probable change from παρὰ τοῦ θεοῦ πᾶν ῥῆμα to παρὰ τῷ θεῷ πᾶν ῥῆμα in which the word ῥῆμα becomes "thing" instead of "word." Scribes, recalling what God told Sarah in a similar circumstance, conformed Luke's words to Gen 18:14 LXX.

1:46 *Mary* ℵ A B C D L W 33; *Elizabeth* a few Old Latin MSS

1:66 *the hand of the Lord was with him* P4^{vid} ℵ A B C L W; *the hand of the Lord is with him* D

1:78 *the dayspring will visit us* P4^{vid} ℵ* B (L) W; *the dayspring has visited us* ℵ^{c} A C D 33
The change from the future tense to the aorist (past) is more probable than vice versa because the same verb is aorist in 1:68. But even though the verb is future, the expression in context indicates Christ's *first* advent, His visitation as the sunrising or dayspring from the heights. (Note: P4^{vid} is not listed in UBS^{3} or NA^{26} probably because the MS is very difficult to read in this place. Having examined the actual MS in Bibliotheque Nationale in Paris, this writer is fairly certain that the word in P4 is επι[σκεψεται ("will visit"), not επε[σκεψατο ("has visited") because the letter before the lacuna is a broken *iota,* not a broken *epsilon.*)

2:14 *peace on earth among men of His good pleasure* ℵ* A B* D W; *peace on earth, good pleasure* (or, *will*) *toward men* ℵ^{c} B^{3} L
One Greek letter (*sigma*) makes the difference: εὐδοκίας/εὐδοκία. The first reading has the best external support and is apparently a more difficult statement. While the second reading indicates that the birth of the Savior would bring peace on earth and would be a display of God's good pleasure toward mankind in general, the first reading suggests that the Savior's birth would bring peace to the men who were specifically pleasing to God (i.e., His elect).

3:22 *You are my beloved Son in whom I am well pleased* P4 ℵ A B L W 33; *You are my beloved Son; this day I have begotten you* D and a few Old Latin translations
The second reading (taken from Ps 2:7) is a manifest corruption, probably evolving from the Adoptionist heresy which was promoted by the Ebionites (Jewish Christians of the late first century—*probably from Qumran*) and was recorded in the Gospel of the Ebionites. They believed that Jesus, the son of Joseph and Mary, became God's Son at the time of His baptism by being joined to the eternal Christ through the Spirit. The prophetic proclamation in Ps 2:7 was orthodoxically applied by Paul to Christ's resurrection (see Acts 13:33), for in resurrection Jesus was manifestly designated and expressly glorified as God's divine Son (see also Rom 1:3, 4; Heb 1:5; 5:5).

3:32 *Sala* P4 ℵ* B; *Salmon* ℵ^{c} A D L 33
Here we see two spellings of one name.

3:33 *Amminadab, the son of Admin, the son of Arni* P4^{vid} ℵ^{c} L; *Amminadab, son of Aram* (or, *Ram*) A D 33 (see Mt 1:4)

4:44 *synagogues of Judea* P75 ℵ B C L W; *synagogues of Galilee* A D 33
The first reading, as the more difficult and better attested wording, is most likely original. Scribes

harmonized Luke's account to Mt 4:23; Mk 1:39 and/or fixed what they believed to be a contradiction of facts in Luke's record (Lk 4:14 and 5:1 indicate that Jesus was in Galilee). It should be noted, though, that scholars have pointed out that Luke sometimes used Judea to cover all of Palestine, which includes Galilee (see Lk 7:17; 23:5).

5:17a *and there were sitting by Pharisees and teachers of the law who were come out of every village* $\aleph^{a}$ A^{2} B C L W; *and there were sitting by Pharisees and teachers of the law. And they* (i.e., people) *had come out of every village* ℵ* (D) 33

5:17b *and the power of the Lord was with him to heal* ℵ B L W; *and the power of the Lord was present to heal them* A C D 33

5:39 *good* P4 ℵ B L W; *better* A C 33^{vid}

6:1 *sabbath* P4 $P75^{vid}$ ℵ B L W 33; *second first sabbath* (i.e., the second sabbath after the first) A C D

6:35 *expecting nothing in return* A B D 33; *despairing of on one* ℵ W

6:48 *because it was well built* $P75^{vid}$ ℵ B L W 33; *for it was founded upon the rock* A C D (taken from Mt 7:25); om. $P45^{vid}$

7:11 *soon afterward* P75 $\aleph^{c}$ A B L 33; *on the next day* ℵ* C D

7:39 *prophet* ℵ A B^{2} D L W 33; *the prophet* B*

By inserting the article, the scribe of B* attempted to make the Pharisee's statement incorporate the Messianic title, "the Prophet" (as in Deut 18:15; Jn 1:21; 6:14; 7:40). As it stands, the Pharisees were speaking of a prophet in general (see note on Jn 7:52).

8:3 *them* B D W // *him* ℵ A L 33

8:26 *Gerasenes* P75 B D; *Gergesenes* ℵ L; *Gadarenes* A W

8:43 *who had spent all her living on physicians* ℵ A C L W 33 // om. P75 B (D)

9:26 *me and my words* P45 $P75^{vid}$ ℵ A B C L W 33; *me* D

9:35 *my Son, the chosen One* P45 P75 ℵ B L; *my Son, the Beloved* A C* W 33 (taken from Mk 9:7; Lk 3:22); *my Son, the Beloved, in whom I am well pleased* C^{3} D (taken from Mt 17:5).

It is easier to see that the more unusual appelation (*my Son, the chosen One*) was changed to the more customary expressions, than vice versa. (See note on Jn 1:34.)

9:54 om. *as Elijah did* P45 P75 ℵ B L; inc. A C D W 33

9:55b om. P45 P75 ℵ A B C L W 33; inc. as following: *and he said, You do not know what manner of spirit you are of* D, other late MSS add even further *for the Son of Man came not to destroy men's lives but to save them*

9:62 *No one putting his hand to the plow and looking back* P75 ℵ A B C L W 0181 33; *No one who looks back as he sets his hand to the plow* $P45^{vid}$ D

10:1 *seventy-two* P75 B D 0181; *seventy* ℵ A C L W

10:17 *seventy-two* P45 P75 B D; *seventy* ℵ A C L W

10:21 *in the Holy Spirit* P75 ℵ B C L 33; *in the Spirit* (or, *in his spirit*) P45 A W

Since it appears that the first reading has better external support, Luke most likely said that Jesus rejoiced *in the Holy Spirit.* If the second reading were original, Jesus could have been rejoicing in the divine Spirit or in His spirit—the Greek can be taken either way.

10:22 om. *And turning to his disciples he said* P45 P75 ℵ B D L 33; inc. A C W (see 10:23)

10:42 *but one thing is needful* P45 P75 A $C^{*,3vid}$ W; *but few things are needful or only one* $\aleph^{c}$ (B) C^{2} L 33; some later MSS (including D and Old Latin) omit this clause and the preceeding one.

11:2a *Father* P75 ℵ B; *our Father in heaven* A C D W (taken from Mt 6:9)

11:2b *your kingdom come* P75 ℵ A B C W 33; *your name be sanctified upon us; your kingdom come* D; *your Holy Spirit come upon us and cleanse us* two late miniscules and cited by a few fathers

11:2c *your kingdom come* P75 B L; *Your kingdom come, your will be done on earth as in heaven* $\aleph^{a}$ A C D W 33 (taken from Mt 6:10)

11:4 *and lead us not into temptation* P75 $\aleph^{*,a}$ B L; *and lead us not into temptation but deliver us from the evil one* (or, *evil*) $\aleph^{c}$ A C D W 33 (taken from Mt 6:13)

In three of the above four citations (11:2a, c and 11:4) the secondary readings are evident interpolations, inserted by later scribes who wanted to harmonize Luke's account to Matthew's. If Luke's account of the Lord's prayer was originally the same as Matthew's, there is no good reason to explain why the scribes of P75, ℵ, and B would purposely disharmonize them. On the contrary, this is a classic example of the kind of textual harmonization scribes would apply to the Gospels. Luke's record demonstrates that the Lord's prayer was not monolithic (or should we say, formulaic), as it was made later for liturgical purposes.

11:11 om. *if his son asks for bread will give him a stone or* P45 P75 B; inc. (ℵ) A C D (L) 33 (taken from Mt 7:9)

11:13 *the Holy Spirit* P75 ℵ A B C W 33; *the good Spirit* P45 L; *good gifts* D; *good things* two ancient translations (see Mt 7:11)

11:15, 19 *Beelzeboul* P45 P75 A C D (L) W; *Beezeboul* ℵ B; *Beelzebub* a few early translations

11:23 *he who does not gather with me scatters* P45 (P75) $\aleph^{a}$ A B C* D W; *he who does not gather with me scatters me* $\aleph^{*,b}$ C^{2} L 33

11:25 *swept clean and put in order* P75 ℵ* A D W; *unoccupied, swept clean and put in order* ℵ[c] B C L 33 (taken from Mt 12:44)
11:33 *puts it in a hidden place* P45 P75 L // *puts it in a hidden place or under a bushel* ℵ A B C D W 33
11:42 *these things you ought to have done, without neglecting the others* P45 P75 ℵ A B C L W 33; om. D one Old Latin MS and Marcion
It is interesting to note that Marcion deleted this statement from his New Testament version. Since Marcion held the heretical belief that the God of the Old Testament (and that dispensation) was not the same as the God of the New Testament, he could not have Jesus telling the Pharisees to observe minute details of the Old Testament law.
12:14 *judge or arbitrate* P75 ℵ A B L 33; *judge* D
12:21 inc. verse P45 P75 ℵ A B L W 33; om. D; the addition referred to in NEB mg—a few late MSS
12:27 *how they grow; they neither toil nor spin* P45 P75 ℵ A B L W 33; *they neither spin nor weave* D
12:31 *His kingdom* ℵ B D* L; *God's kingdom* P45 A D[b] W 33
12:39 om. *he would have watched and* P75 ℵ* (D) // inc. ℵ[c] A B W 33 (see Mt 24:43)
13:19 *a tree* P75 ℵ B D L; *a great tree* P45 A W 33
14:5 *son or an ox* P45 P75 A B W; *donkey or an ox* ℵ L 33; *sheep or an ox* D
15:21 om. *make me like one of your hired men* P75 A L W; inc. ℵ B D 33[vid] (probably taken from Lk 15:19)
17:24 *the Son of man in his day* ℵ A L W // *the Son of man* P75 B D
17:36 om. verse P75 ℵ A B L W 33; inc. D (from Mt 24:40)
18:11 *The Pharisee stood and prayed these things with himself* P75 ℵ[c] B L T; *The Pharisee standing by himself prayed these things* A W 33[vid]; *The Pharisee stood and prayed these things privately* D; *The Pharisee stood and prayed these things* ℵ*
21:38 Concerning the note in NEB mg, see Jn 7:53—8:11.
22:16 *I shall not eat* P75[vid] ℵ A B L; *I shall no longer eat* D; *I shall never eat it again* C W
22:19b–20 inc. verses P75 ℵ A B C L T[vid] W; om. D and several Old Latin MSS
All the early and best MSS support the inclusion of verses 19b, 20, but the copyist of D omitted this portion in an attempt to conform Luke's account of the Lord's supper to the other Gospels—not realizing that the cup mentioned in 22:17 is the cup of the passover (see vv. 15, 16), not the cup of the new covenant. Following the traditional passover meal, Jesus instituted the supper first with the loaf (v. 19) and then with the cup (v. 20).
22:43, 44 om. verses P69[vid] P75 ℵ[a] B T W; inc. ℵ*,[b] D L
It seems doubtful that Luke wrote these verses; if so, then why is this portion missing in so many good early witnesses? These verses probably came from an oral tradition and were inserted in some copies of Luke at a very early date, for this portion was acknowledged by several early church fathers. But other church fathers indicated that these verses were lacking in many codices known to them (from *Expositor's Greek New Testament*). Furthermore, these verses are marked with asterisks or obeli in several later MSS, so indicating that certain scribes questioned their authenticity.
22:62 inc. verse P75 ℵ A B D L T W; om. 0171[vid] and several Old Latin MSS
23:17 om. verse P75 A B L T; inc. ℵ (D after 23:19) W (taken from Mt 27:25; Mk 15:6)
23:24 om. *Father, forgive them, for they do not know what they are doing* P75 ℵ[avid] B D* W // inc. ℵ*,[c] A C L 33
23:42 *come into your kingdom* P75 B L; *come in your kingdom* ℵ A C W
The first reading has better external support and is more appropriate in this context. The thief was not speaking about the Lord coming in his future kingdom—which is the meaning the second reading produces. The thief's request was urgent; the Lord's response respected that immediacy: "today you will be with me in paradise" (v. 43).
23:45 *the sun was eclipsed* (or, *the sun's light failed*) P75 ℵ B C*[vid] L; *the sun was darkened* A C[3] D W; om. 33
24:3 *body of the Lord Jesus* P75 ℵ A B C L W 33; *body* D and a few Old Latin MSS
24:6 inc. *He is not here but is risen* P75 ℵ A B (C) L (W); om. D and a few Old Latin MSS
24:12 inc. verse *P75 ℵ A B L W 33; om.* D and a few early translations
24:13 *sixty stadia* P75 A B D L W 33[vid]; *one hundred and sixty stadia* ℵ
24:32 inc. *within us* ℵ A L W 33 // om. P75 B D
24:36 inc. *and he said to them, Peace be with you* P75 ℵ A B L 33; om. D and a few Old Latin MSS
24:40 inc. verse P75 ℵ A B L W 33; om. D and some early translations
24:51 inc. *and was carried up into heaven* P75 ℵ[c] A B C L W 33; om. ℵ* D and some early translations
24:52 inc. *they worshipped him and returned to Jerusalem* P75 ℵ A B C L W 33; om. D and some early translations
It should be noted that Westcott and Hort thought D represented the original wording in Lk 24:3, 6, 12, 36, 40, 51, 52 (see above and also see 22:19b, 20). Calling the omissions in D "Western non-interpolations," they argued that all the other MSS incorporated interpolations. The WH text (1881)

affected the Nestle text in this regard and several English translations (see RSV, NEB). Most scholars today do not adhere to Westcott and Hort's theory of "Western non-interpolations." The manuscript evidence is stacked against D. P75 and W, both discovered in this century, add to the proof against D. The most recent Nestle text (the 26th edition, 1979) no longer adheres to the testimony of D; and this is reflected in the more recent English translations (see TEV, TLB, JB, NIV).

JOHN

added MSS: P5 (3rd C), P22 (3rd C), P36 (6th C), P60 (7th C), P63 (ca. 500), Q (5th C), 0125 (5th C) (remember P66 and P75—see Introduction)

Note: W^{s} in John chpts 1–5 indicates a text supplied by a later hand (7th C)

1:3–4 The variation in punctuation among the translations in verses 3 and 4 is basically a textual problem. The phrase *that which was created* has been placed with either verse 3 or verse 4 among different translations by means of punctuation. The earliest MSS (P66 P75* ℵ*A B) do not have any punctuation in these verses. P75 was later corrected, as was ℵ. In P75^{c} a punctuation mark was placed before the phrase (as in #1 below); in ℵ^{c} after it (as in #2 below):

1) . . . and without him was not anything created. That which was created in him was life. . . .

2) . . . and without him was not anything created that was created. In him was life. . . .

The majority of the early fathers exegeted Jn 1:3, 4 according to the phrasing in #1. The passage was taken to mean that all created things were "life" by virtue of being in Him. The statement was somehow supposed to affirm that the Word not only created the universe, He presently sustains it. Exegesis changed after some heretics used the passage to say that the Holy Spirit was a created thing. All the fathers then supported the phrasing in #2. Most exegesis has followed this up until the present, although some scholars (e.g., see Westcott's commentary on the Greek text of John) support #1. But the structure of #1 hardly makes sense, really strains the syntax, and runs contrary to the overall Johannine thought concerning *life* (ζωή). *Life,* according to John's presentation, is the divine, eternal life; it is not inherent in any man, let alone any creature. Life is in Christ and has always been in Him; it can be received by men only when they believe in Him.

1:18 *an only-begotten, God* (or, *a unique One, himself God*) P66 P75 ℵ B C* L 33; *the only-begotten Son* A C^{3} W^{s} and later MSS

The manuscript evidence for the first reading, *an only-begotten, God* (μονογενὴς θεὸς) is decidedly superior to the evidence for the second reading, *the only-begotten Son* (μονογενὴς υἱός). The papyrus MSS (P66 P75), the earliest and best uncial MSS (ℵ* B C* L) and some good early versions (Coptic and Syriac) support the first reading (hereafter referred to as —*God*). Some of the earliest church fathers (Irenaeus, Clement, Origen, Eusebius, Serapion, Basil, Didymus, Gregory-Nyssa, and Epiphanium) knew of the reading —*God.* Later MSS support the second reading (hereafter referred to as —*Son*), namely, A, C^{3}, W^{s}, and so on. Some early versions reflect the second reading (Old Latin and Syriac), and some early fathers knew of the reading (Irenaeus, Clement, Hippolytus, Alexander, Eusebius, Eastathius, Serapion, Julian, Basil, and Gregory-Nazianzus). From the above evidence, it is apparent that both —*God* and —*Son* were early readings because both were known to Irenaeus and Clement. However, the earliest witness to the reading —*Son* is it^{a} (A.D. 370), while the earliest manuscript witness to the reading —*God* is P66 (A.D. 150–175), followed by P75 (A.D. 200), B (A.D. 350), and ℵ (A.D. 375). The fact that P66 and P75, two of the earliest extant MSS, read—*God* has firmly secured this reading a place in the text of John.

The reading *a unique One, himself God* (or, *an Only-begotten, God*) also has very strong internal vigor. John begins the prologue (verses 1–18) by calling the Word *God* (1:1), and then he calls Him *an only-begotten* (1:14). In the last verse of the prologue, he combines the titles: *an Only-begotten, God.* This is a fine touch for culminating the prologue. Thus, 1:18 mirrors 1:1. In 1:1 we see that the Word, who is God's expression, is himself God; in 1:18 we see that the only-begotten, who is himself God, explains the Father. No one could know God the Father like one who was the One and Only, and was himself God, and was the closest to God's heart. He alone could explain the Father to mankind. One who is himself God can explain and express God.

Thus, we conclude that the reading *an only-begotten, God* has the strongest external and internal attestation. Scribes, uncomfortable with this unique title, changed it to the more usual appelation, *the only-begotten Son.*

1:34 *the Son of God P66 P75 ℵ^{c} A B C W^{s}* 33; *the* chosen One of God P5^{vid} ℵ*

Despite the fact that the first reading has, by far, earlier and more diverse testimony than the second one, it has been argued that the second reading is original because it is more likely that *chosen One* was changed to *Son* than vice versa. Furthermore, it has been urged that the title *chosen One* would add one more Messianic title to John chapter 1, while *Son* is repetitive. Jesus is called God (1:1, 18; cf Isa 9:6), Christ or Messiah (1:17, 41; cf Ps 2:2; Dan 9:25), the Son of God (1:14, 34, 49; cf

2 Sam 7:12–14; Ps 2:7), the Lamb of God (1:29, 36; cf Isa 53), the One predicted by Moses (1:45; cf Deut 18:18), the King of Israel (1:49; cf Ps 2:6; Zeph 3:15); and the Son of Man (1:51; cf Dan 7:13). If *chosen One of God* also came from the pen of John, there is yet another Messianic witness (see Isa 42:1). But since the external evidence so strongly favors *the Son of God,* the textual critic can not confidently declare *chosen One of God* to be what John wrote.

1:41 *first* P66 P75 ℵ A B (W^{s}); *early* some Old Latin MSS

3:13 *the Son of Man who is in heaven* A, many later MSS, and some early translations//*the Son of Man* P66 P75 ℵ B L W^{s} 33

Although the second reading has better testimony than the first, there is a good possibility that the first reading is genuine. It is difficult to discern why scribes would add the enigmatic clause, *who is in heaven*—when it was usually the custom of scribes to emend problematic expressions. In the context of Jn 3:13 the extra clause indicates that Jesus was bi-locating heaven and earth simultaneously ("no one has ascended into heaven but He who descended from heaven, the Son of Man who is in heaven"). This is startling, so startling that it was probably deleted from MSS at a very early date. But there is no absolute certainty about this hypothesis.

3:15 There is a textual discrepancy in this verse. Some MSS read *whoever believes may have eternal life in him* (P75 B W^{s}); others read *whoever believes in him may have eternal life* (P66 L); and still others read *whoever believes on him may have eternal life* (P63^{vid} ℵ). The first reading is most likely original.

3:31 inc. *is above all* (last words of the verse) P36^{vid} P66 ℵ^{c} B L W^{s} 33; om. A and later MSS

3:34 The best MSS (P36^{vid} P66 P75 P80^{vid} ℵ B^{2} C* L W^{s}) read *he gives the Spirit,* while inferior MSS (A C^{2} D) read *God gives the Spirit.* According to the best attested reading, the statement in Jn 3:34 could very well mean that Jesus gives the Spirit—and that, by means of speaking the words of God (see Jn 6:63 for a parallel statement). But the immediate context has led many exegetes to think that the verse speaks of God giving the immeasurable Spirit to His Son. Apparently several scribes thought the same, for they added the word *God.*

4:9 inc. *For Jews do not associate with Samaritans* (or it could be rendered, *For Jews do not use the same dishes Samaritans use*) P63 P66 P75 P76 ℵ^{a} A B C L W^{s} 33; om. ℵ* D

5:1 *a festival of the Jews* P66 P75 A B D W^{s}; *the festival of the Jews* ℵ C L 33

5:2 *Bethsaida* P66 P75 B W^{s}// *Bethzatha* ℵ 33 // *Bethesda* A C and many late MSS

5:3b, 4 om. verses P66 P75 ℵ B C* D W^{s} 0125 33; inc. A C^{3} and many later MSS

All modern translations omit verses 3b–4 and append a marginal note which explains that these verses are not found in the earliest and best MSS or that they are found in later MSS (see above). The words are spurious because 1) the best MSS do not include them; 2) the presence of special markings to designate the words as spurious in more than twenty Greek witnesses; 3) the presence of non-Johannine words; 4) the diversity of ways this portion was composed in those MSS which included it (see Metzger). Thus, we conclude that verses 3b, 4 were a later addition—probably added to explain the troubling of the water in verse 7.

5:44 *glory from the only One* (or, *unique One*) P66 P75 B W and some ancient translations; *glory from the only God* P63^{vid} ℵ A D L

Since *the only One* (τοῦ μόνου) is supported by so many good, early witnesses (including Origen), it seems highly probable that it is original. Later copyists thought that there must have been a lacuna, so they added *God* after *only.* Some have argued, though, that *God* (θεοῦ) was original, but it dropped out of the text of some MSS due to homoeoteleuton (TOYMONOYΘY). Although this is a possibility, it is a possibility for only one or two MSS, not ten or more—three of which (P66 P75 W) are quite reliable!

The expression τοῦ μόνου is a titular substantive—which could be written τοῦ Μόνου (see Edwin E. Abbot's *Johannine Grammar*). This title, which means "the only One" or "the unique One," perfectly suits this passage. Since the Jews were seeking to receive glory from one another, they had neglected to seek the glory which comes from the unique One, the only One who gives glory.

6:23a *however, boats from Tiberias* P75 B; *[but] other boats from Tiberias* A D L W 33

6:23b inc. *after the Lord had given thanks* P75 ℵ A B L W 33; om. D and some early translations

6:36 *seen me* P66 P75^{vid} B D L (T) W 33; *seen* ℵ A

7:8 *I am not yet going* P66 P75 B L T W // *I am not going* ℵ D and some early translations

7:37, 38 The careful reader will observe that these verses have been punctuated differently in the various translations. Most versions punctuate as follows: . . . *Jesus stood and cried, saying, If any man thirsts, let him come to me and drink. He who believes in me* . . . . But an alternative rendering is customarily given in the margin (see also NEB): *Jesus stood and cried, saying, If any man thirsts, let him come to me. And let him drink who believes in me. As the Scripture said, out of his innermost being shall flow rivers of living water.*

When we look at the two ways in which verses 37 and 38 have been punctuated, it should at once be evident that the first reading is natural and that the second reading is strained. Certain scholars, without any textual evidence, imposed the second kind of punctuation on the text in an attempt to make the scriptural declaration in verse 38 refer, not to the believer, but to Christ as the source from which the rivers of living water flow. Knowing that Christ was the antitype of the smitten Rock, such scholars wanted to make Christ appear to be the referent of "*his* innermost being," instead of the believer. As good as this reasoning may seem, there are three basic arguments against it. First, P66 and P75 are punctuated after *drink*; and as these are two of the earliest extant MSS which contain John, they very well may reflect the original intention of the author here. Second, to punctuate as does NEB et al is to strain the Greek grammar into a most harsh and awkward construction. Third, according to the historical and textual context of this passage, *verse 37* indicates, through allusion, that Christ, as the real fulfillment of the smitten Rock, is the source from which the believers may drink; whereas verse 38 indicates that the believer who drinks of Christ will also become a source from which the rivers of living water will flow. The Scripture the Lord referred to was not a particular OT verse, but the general tenor of Scripture which speaks of living waters flowing forth (see Isa 12:3; 44:3; 58:11; Ezek 47:1–12; Joel 3:18).

7:39 It should be noted that most translations follow a secondary textual variant in this verse. Whereas the best testimony (P66[c] P75 ℵ T W) affirms the reading *the Spirit was not yet* (or, *there was no Spirit as yet*—JB), inferior attestation (B and some early translations) displays an added word: *given—for the Spirit was not yet given.* Undoubtedly, scribes and early translators were attempting to fill out a bare expression and/or clarify a difficult statement. The declaration *the Spirit was not yet* (or, *there was no Spirit as yet*) probably appeared to such scribes as a contradiction to the fact that the Spirit already existed (see Jn 1:33). But the statement, in context, has nothing to do with whether or not the Spirit yet existed. Of course, the Spirit existed; but the Spirit about to be made available through the glorification of Jesus was not yet. In short, the Spirit of the glorified Jesus was not yet available for the believers to partake of. One could not yet actually come to Jesus and drink of Him until He was glorified and became spirit. Thus, when the copyists added the word *given* they clarified the matter of the Spirit's availability; but at the same time they obfuscated the fact that a new Spirit, the Spirit of the glorified Jesus, was about to come into existence. According to the text which has *given,* there is a sequence: Jesus would be glorified, and then the Spirit would be given. But when the text stands without *given,* it implies that there would be a union between the glorified Jesus and the Spirit.

7:52 It should be noted that one or perhaps two of the earliest MSS read *the Prophet* (see NIV mg), while all other MSS read *prophet.* P66 originally read *the prophet,* and P75 could very well have read the same. Indeed, the editors of *Papyrus Bodmer XV, Evangile de Jean chapters 1–15* (Victor Martin and Rudolphe Kasser) wrote ὁ προφήτης (*the Prophet*) in their transcription of the text, even though it appears that the lacuna could be supplied with either arthrous προφήτης or anarthrous. If *the prophet* is the original reading, the reference in this passage would clearly indicate the Messianic title, "the Prophet" (see Deut 18:15; Jn 1:21; 7:40). Undoubtedly the Pharisees had this particular Prophet in mind in their retort to Nicodemus—unless their statement meant something like this: "If, according to the Scriptures, not even a prophet comes out of Galilee, how much less the Christ?" From this perspective, *prophet* could have very well been what John wrote, as is indeed attested to by all other MSS.

7:53–8:11 om. verses P66 P75 ℵ A[vid] B C[vid] L T W; inc. D and many later MSS

The story of the adulterous woman in John 7:53–8:11 is one of the best examples of an addition coming into the text from an oral tradition. This story is not included in the best and earliest MSS. In fact, it is absent from all witnesses earlier than the ninth century, with the exception of a fifth-century Greek-Latin MS. No Greek church father comments on the passage prior to the twelfth century—until Euthymius Zigabenus, who himself declares that the accurate copies do not contain it. When this story is inserted in later MSS, it appears in different places: after Jn 7:52, after Lk 21:38, at the end of John, etc.; and when it does appear, it is often marked with obeli. The story is known to have been a piece of oral tradition first recorded in a Syriac version (syr[p]), circulated in the Western church, eventually finding its way into the Latin Vulgate and from there into later Greek texts, from which the Textus Receptus was derived (see Metzger).

There is enough external evidence to demonstrate that the pericope adulteress was not an original part of John's Gospel. Some internal evidence would make the case even stronger. E. C. Colwell has suggested that the pericope interrupts the two major ceremonies of the Feast of Tabernacles: the pouring out of the water over the rock in commemoration of the smitten rock, and the lighting of the lamps in commemoration of the pillar of light. (Note: the Festival of Tabernacles was also commonly called the Festival of Lights.) Colwell said, "The story does not fit the context because it interrupts the narrative. If this story is absent, then the great day of the Feast of Tabernacles is signalized by Jesus' twin declarations that he is the Water of Life and the Light of the World" (*What is the best New Testament?* pp. 81, 82). Though this argument is excellent, it is not sufficiently comprehensive for it does not deal with the connection between 7:40–52 and 8:12 which, excluding the pericope adulteress, must constitute a contiguous narrative.

In John 7:52 we read about the Pharisees' retort to Nicodemus' weak defense (on behalf of Jesus): "Are you also from Galilee? Search and look, that a prophet does not arise out of Galilee." Seemingly, the Lord did not respond to their confident assertions. Yet it seems odd that He would not because the Lord was usually quick to reply to the Pharisees. Indeed, in 7:28, 29, Jesus had countered their erroneous opinions concerning Him, as expressed in 7:27. Where is the response to 7:41, 42 and 52? (Both 7:41, 42 and 7:52 concern the matter of Christ's or the Prophet's place of origin. According to the Jews' estimation, the fact that Jesus came from Galilee annulled His claim.) When one reads 8:12 as directly following 7:52, it should be clear that the Lord was addressing the Pharisees who had so confidently denied His right to be a prophet, much less the Christ. The Pharisees may have been correct to say that the Scriptures never spoke about *a prophet* coming out of Galilee, but they did not recall those Scriptures which said that *a great light* would appear in Galilee. Surely, those Pharisees should have realized that the Lord's response in 8:12 echoed Isaiah 9:1, 2 (also cited in Matthew 4:15, 16). Compare the two:

Isa 9:1, 2 . . . the land of Zebulun, and the land of Naphtali . . . by the way of the sea, beyond the Jordan, the Galilee of the Gentiles, the people that walked in darkness have seen a great light: they that dwell in the land of the shadow of death, upon them has the light shined.

Jn 8:12 Again therefore Jesus spoke to them, saying, I am the light of the world: he that follows Me shall not walk in darkness, but shall have the light of life.

There are three parallel figures in these two passages: 1) "the light of the world" corresponds to "the great light," 2) the phrase "he who follows Me will not walk in darkness" and 3) the phrase "but shall have the light of life" is the positive antithesis to "those who dwelt in the land of the shadow of death." He is the great light who came to give life to all those who walked in darkness and dwelt in the land of the shadow of death. Instead of being under "the shadow of death" they could have "the light of life."

8:16 *the Father who sent me* P39 P66 P75 א^c B L T W; *He who sent me* א* D

8:25 The difference in translation of the second part of this verse in the various versions stems from an underlying textual discrepancy. The rendering, *what I have been telling you from the beginning* (or, *principally that which I also speak to you*) comes from P75 and B; whereas the rendering *why do I speak to you at all?* comes from early translations (Old Latin, Syriac, Coptic).
Because so many early Greek MSS did not leave any spaces between the words, it is difficult to determine if the text is to be read as ὅ τι (that which) or ὅτι (why). P75 and B have a space between ο and τι, but P66 does not. According to the context of the statement, either reading is possible. Disgusted with the Pharisees' query concerning His identity (see first part of the verse—Then they said to Him, "Who are you?"), Jesus could have retorted, "Why do I speak to you at all?" But the other reading is more meaningful, for it reveals that Jesus considered His identity to have been essentially or principally expressed in what He had said about Himself. J. N. Darby translated the phrase, "principally that which I also speak to you"—to which he appendaged an explanation: "in the principle and universality of what I am, i.e., his speech presented himself" (*New Translation*).

8:39 *you would be doing the works of Abraham* P75 א* B² D W; *do the works of Abraham* P66 B*

8:57 *and you have seen Abraham?* P66 א^c A B^c C D L W; *and Abraham has seen you?* P75 א*

9:35 *the Son of Man* P66 P75 א B D W; *the Son of God* A and later MSS

10:16 *they shall become one flock, one shepherd* P45 א^c B D L W 33; *they shall be one flock, one shepherd* P66 א* A

10:18 *takes* P66 א^c A D L W // *took* P45 א* B

10:29 *that which my Father has given Me is greater than all* B // *my Father, who has given them to me is greater than all* P66 P75^vid // *my Father, as to that which He has given Me, is greater than all* א D L W
Although the second reading makes perfectly good sense, there are several good reasons why the first reading may have been written by John. Unfortunately, it takes a lot of explanation, most of which is very technical, to substantiate this claim. It can be posited here, though, that the expression *that which my Father has given me* is common to John when speaking of that one collective entity of all believers given to the Son as a gift from the Father (see Jn 6:37, 39; 17:2, 24). Since this entity (which could be called the church) is invincible to the attack of the enemy (see 10:1, 5, 8, 10, 12), it could be said to be *greater than all* (i.e., all the enemies mentioned in John chapter 10).

11:25 inc. *and the life* P66 P75 א A B C D L W; om. P45^vid

12:8 inc. verse P66 P75^vid א A B (L) W; om. D and a few early translations

12:41 *because he saw His glory* P66 P75 א A B L; *when he saw His glory* D

13:10 *he who has been bathed needs only to wash his feet* (P66) B C* (L) W; *he who has been bathed does not need to wash* א
External evidence strongly supports the first reading, as does the context. It should be observed that two Greek verbs have been used in this verse to designate two different kinds of washing: 1) λούω means bathing, and 2) νίπτω, appearing in 13:5, 6, 8, and in the last part of 13:10, is used throughout the LXX and NT to indicate the washing of the extremeties (i.e., the hands and the feet). According to the customs of those times, once a person had bathed his body, he needed only

to wash his feet before partaking of a meal. Jesus was going around to all the disciples washing their feet until Peter protested. In response to Peter, the Lord appropriately used both words in order to advance a precious truth. As he who has been bathed is clean and therefore needs only to wash his feet daily, so he who has been bathed by the Lord (through initial salvation) needs only to wash himself day to day from the filth and defilement he accumulates by his contact with the world.

13:32 inc. *if God was glorified in him* ℵ^{c} A C^{2} // om. P66 ℵ* B C* D L W

14:4 *and where I go you know the way* P66^{c} ℵ B C* L W; *and where I go you know and the way you know* P66* A C^{3} D

14:7 *If you had known me, you would have known my Father also* A B C D^{b} L W; *If you have come to know me, you will know my Father also* P66 ℵ D

The first reading has the best external support and it is much more suitable to the context of John 14. Up to this point in John 14 Jesus has revealed the great truth that He is the unique way to the Father. Then He unveils the fact that He is the visible manifestation of the Father (see 14:8, 9). If the disciples were to realize that coming to dwell in the Son was equivalent to coming to dwell in the Father, they would have had to realize that the Son was the Father seen, the manifestation of the Father (see Jn 1:18; Col. 1:15; Heb. 1:2). If they had come to know (*ἐγνώκειτέ*) the Son, they should have perceived (*ἤδειτε*) the Father also. However, the compilers of UBS^{3} decided upon the second reading, which is translated in TEV: "Now that you have known me, you will know my Father also." But the entire context of this portion asserts the opposite. It is not that the disciples *will* come to know the Father as they have known the Son, but that they should have already known the Father as manifest in the Son. The Lord was reproving them, not promising them some future knowledge of the Father. If He was making a promise, how could the Lord say in the very next sentence: "And from now on you know Him and have seen Him."

14:14 inc. *me* P66 ℵ B W 33; om. A D L

14:17 *will be in you* P66^{c} P75^{vid} ℵ A D^{b} L Q; *is in you* P66* B D* W

In Jn 14:17 Jesus identifies the *Paraclete*; He is the Spirit of truth, (or, the Spirit of reality). The world cannot receive (or accept) this Spirit of truth because the world does not see Him or know Him. And then Jesus declares, *you know Him* [lit. *it*], *because He abides with you and will be in.* The translations differ here because of a textual problem. Some adhere to the Greek text as I have just cited it, but others adhere to another text which reads, *you know Him* [lit. *it*], *because He abides with you and is in you.* The manuscript evidence is partially inconclusive because so many early MSS (P66 P75 ℵ A B D W etc.) do not have an accent mark over *μενει*; thus, it could be understood as *μένει* (present tense—"he abides") or *μενεῖ* (future tense—"he will abide"). But the vast majority of later MSS read *μένει*, modern NT Greek editions have *μένει* in the text, and all the translations render it accordingly. The real problem is with the final verb: the verb *is* (*ἐστιν*) is supported by P66*, B, D*, W; the verb *will be* (*ἔσται*) is supported by P66^{c}, P75^{vid}, ℵ, a, D^{b}, L, Q. Since the textual evidence is nearly divided, we must look to the context to determine the most probable reading.

If the text originally had two present tense verbs, the statement could be taken to describe, proleptically, the twofold location of the Spirit in relationship to each believer. In other words, the Spirit is viewed in its future state as present *with* and *in* the believer. This is a possible meaning. But the original thought of John seems to be that 1) the Spirit embodied in Jesus was then and there abiding *with* the disciples, and 2) the same Spirit of Jesus would, in the future, be *in* the disciples. Quite simply the One who was *with* them would be *in* them. Notice the shift of pronouns from verse 17 to verse 18: "He [the Spirit] will be in you . . . *I* [the Son] am coming to you." And notice that further on, in verse 20, the Lord says "I in you." Compare this to verse 17 where Jesus said that the Spirit "shall be in you."

15:8 *so be my disciples* P66^{vid} B D L; *so will be my disciples* ℵ A

16:23 *whatever you ask the Father he will give it to you in my name* P5^{vid} ℵ B C* L; *whatever you ask the Father in my name he will give it to you* P22^{vid} A C^{3vid} D W

17:11, 12 *Keep them in the name which you have given me* P60^{vid} P66^{cvid} ℵ B C L W; *Keep in your name those whom you have given me* D

18:13–27 (verses in this order) P60 P66 ℵ A B C D L W; different order in a few early translations

19:29 *hyssop* all MSS except one; *javelin* 476 (an eleventh century MS)—adopted by NEB

19:35 It should be noted that the best attestation (P66^{vid} ℵ* B) supports the reading *that you also may continue to believe* (see TEV mg. 4th ed.). Other MSS (ℵ^{b} A D^{s} L W) read, *that you also may believe.* John always used the present subjunctive of *πιστεύω* (believe) when speaking about a continual believing, a believing which extends beyond the initial act of faith (see 1:7; 6:29; 13:19; *17:21; and 20:31). In this verse*, as well as in 20:31, John was certifying the trustworthiness of his testimony so that the readers (who were probably already believers) *may continue to believe* the veracity of the gospel (see note on Jn 20:31).

20:31 *that you may continue to believe that Jesus is the Christ* P66^{vid} ℵ* B; *that you may believe that Jesus is the Christ* ℵ^{b} A C D L W

The first reading (containing a present subjunctive of the verb *believe*) has earlier and better support than the second (containing an aorist subjunctive). Because the present subjunctive denotes continual action, it appears that John's Gospel was primarily addressed to those who already believed that Jesus was the Christ, the Son of God, yet needed to be encouraged to continue to believe. John was not necessarily appealing to unbelievers—that they might begin to believe in Jesus (which would be indicated by the aorist subjunctive); rather, John was inviting all men (whether believers or unbelievers) to enter into a continual experience of believing in Christ. The NEB translators, adhering to the first reading, translated this passage: "that you may hold to the faith that Jesus is the Christ, the Son of God."

Note: for further commentary on most of the above passages in John please see *A Study Guide to Translating The Gospel of John*, Philip W. Comfort, B.B.H. Distributors, a division of Baker Book House, 1985.

ACTS

added MSS: P41 (8th C), P74 (7th C), E (6th C), 0165 (5th C), 1739 (10th C)

2:37 *the rest of the apostles* P74vid ℵ A B C E; *apostles* D

2:38 It should be noted that several good MSS (P74 ℵ A E) read *baptized on* (from ἐπὶ) *the name of Jesus Christ* (i.e., baptism occured on the basis of confessing the name of Jesus Christ). Although this is the generally recognized original wording, all the translations adhere to the secondary reading (*in the name*) probably because the original makes for hard—if not impossible—English.

2:47 *And the Lord daily added to the fellowship those who were being saved* P74 ℵ A B C; *And the Lord daily added to the church those who were being saved* E 33 many late MSS
It is apparent that scribes of later MSS replaced the words *to the fellowship* (ἐπὶ τὸ αὐτό) with *to the church* (τῇ ἐκκλησίᾳ). (The scribe of D added the second phrase to the first.) Both expressions convey the same idea. ἐπὶ τὸ αὐτὸ literally means "toward the same thing (or, goal)," but in the early church it acquired a quasi-technical meaning which denoted the union of the Christian body (see Metzger). As such, ἐπὶ τὸ αὐτό could be rendered "in the fellowship" or "for the fellowship" (see Acts 1:15; 2:1; 2:47; 1 Cor 11:20; 14:23).

3:21 *his holy prophets from of old* (or, *from the beginning of the world*—NEB) P74vid ℵ* A B* D E; *his holy prophets* D Old Latin MSS

4:1 *priests* ℵ A D E 0165 33; *chief priests* B C

4:6 *John* P74 ℵ A B 0165 33; *Jonathan* D

4:10 om. *and no other* [name] P74 ℵ A B D 0165; inc. E

4:12 inc. *And there is salvation in no one else* P74vid ℵ A B E 0165 33; om. a few early translations and patristic citations

4:25 *who by the Holy Spirit,* [*even by*] *the mouth of our father David, Your servant, said* P74 ℵ A B E 33; *who by the mouth of our father David, Your servant, said* many late MSS; *who through the Holy Spirit speaking through the mouth of David Your servant, said* D
The Greek behind the first reading is difficult—but not impossible—to comprehend. The thought is that God spoke through the Holy Spirit and David's mouth as through one united mouthpiece. According to the Greek, David's mouth is in apposition to the Holy Spirit; this indicates that David's prophetic utterance was the same as the Holy Spirit's utterance.

7:46 *God of Jacob* ℵc A C E // *house of Jacob* P74 ℵ* B D
On one hand, the reading *house of Jacob* appears to be original because of better manuscript support; on the other hand, *God of Jacob* is certainly more congruent with the Scripture, for David was seeking a house for God to inhabit, as is clearly declared in Ps 132:5, the OT scripture cited here by Stephen.

8:18 *the Spirit* ℵ B; *the Holy Spirit* P45 P74 A C D E 33
Since scribes had a penchant for expanding titles that designate the divine Spirit (see Introduction) and since ℵ and B attest to the simpler expression (*the Spirit*), it seems fair to conclude that the second reading is a scribal expansion.

8:37 om. verse P45 P74 ℵ A B C 33vid; inc. E and late MSS
This verse (*And Philip said, If you believe with all your heart, you may. And he answered and said, I believe that Jesus Christ is the Son of God.*) did not appear in any Greek MSS until the sixth century. Evidently, it was an ecclesiastical formula (used for the baptismal ceremony) that found its way into the text.

10:19 *three men* P74 ℵ A C E 33; *two men* B; om. D

11:11 *we were* P74 ℵ A B D; *I was* P45 E 33

11:12 inc. *making no distinction* (i.e., distinction between Gentiles and Jews) (P74) ℵ A B E 33; *without doubting* later MSS; om. P45vid D

11:20 *Hellenists* B Db E; *Greeks* P74 ℵc A D*
The textual problem here is complicated by the fact that scholars are not in agreement as to what class of people *Hellenists* designates. Are they the Gentiles or the Greek-speaking Jews? The term appears only in Acts 6:1 (where it means Greek-speaking Jews); 9:29 (again, it probably designates

the Greek-speaking Jews); and here, 11:20. In this verse *Hellenists* can not mean Greek-speaking Jews because they are contrasted to the Jews of the previous verse. It is best to understand that these Hellenists are, broadly speaking, Greek-speaking people (see Metzger).

12:25 *Barnabas and Saul returned, having fulfilled their service in Jerusalem* (which is a better way to render and punctuate this portion that would normally be translated, *Barnabas and Saul, having fulfilled their service, returned to Jerusalem*) ℵ B; *Barnabas and Saul, having fulfilled their service, returned from Jerusalem* P74 A D 33

13:18 *cared for them* (lit. *carried them as a nurse*) P74 A C* E 33; *bore with them* (or, *put up with them*) ℵ B C^2 D

This textual problem involves a one–letter difference (ϕ/π) in two Greek words, ἐτροφοφόρησεν (*nourished*) and ἐτροποφόρησεν (*bore with*). The first word is more likely original for two reasons: 1) the first word comes from Deut 1:31 (LXX), the passage cited by Paul; and 2) in the context of 13:17–19, which contains a series of positive acts which God did for Israel, it would be incongruous to inject a disparaging word (as in the second reading).

13:33a *to us their children* C^3 E 33; *to our children* P74 ℵ A B C* D

13:33b *second psalm* P74 ℵ A B C E 33; *first psalm* D Old Latin MSS; *psalms* P45

The first and second psalms (as we know them in our English Bibles) were often counted as one psalm in the Hebrew text.

13:44 *the word of the Lord* P74 ℵ A B^3 // *the word of God* B* C E

15:18 *these things known from old* (or, *for ages*) ℵ B C 33; *these things—known to the Lord for ages is his work* P74 A D E

15:20a inc. *and from fornication* P74 ℵ A B C D E; om. P45

15:20b inc. *and from what is strangled* P45 P74 ℵ A B C E 33; om. D

15:20c *from blood* P45 P74 ℵ A B C E 33; *from blood and from doing to others what they would not like done to themselves* D

15:24 *went out and troubled you* P33 P74 A C E 33; *troubled you* ℵ* B

15:34 om. verse P74 ℵ A B E; inc. C 33 (and D adds *and Judas journeyed alone*)

16:6 *the Phrygian and Galatian region* P74 ℵ A B C D; *Phrygian and the region of Galatia* E L

16:7 It is unfortunate that a remarkable title of the Spirit has been veiled from English readers of the Bible for so long a time because the KJV followed an inferior text here. The earliest and best MSS read *the Spirit of Jesus* (P74 ℵ A B C^2 D E 33 1739). But this unique NT title was changed in certain MSS to *the Spirit of the Lord* (C*), in others to *the Holy Spirit* (Armenian MSS), and in many others to *the Spirit* (many late MSS). The TR adopted the last emendation, and subsequently the KJV does not have the appelation, *the Spirit of Jesus* (cf. Rom 8:9, "the Spirit of Christ" and Phil 1:19, "the Spirit of Jesus Christ").

16:12 A marginal note in the RSV tells the reader that the Greek text behind the translation *the leading city of the district* is uncertain. The scholarly debate concerning the uncertainty is complex; nevertheless, the reading *a leading city of the district of Macedonia* has good manuscript support (P74 ℵ A C 33) and makes good sense.

16:13 *where we thought there would be a place of prayer* A^2 B (C) 33; *where there was a place of prayer according to custom* (i.e., custom of the Jews) $A^{*vid?}$ E

Since there was no synagogue in this city, the Jews customarily met by a river for prayer (see Ezra 8:14, 21–23; Ps 137; Ezek 1:1; Dan 8:2).

16:32 *word of the Lord* P45 P74 $ℵ^c$ A C D E 33; *word of God* ℵ* B

16:36 *go in peace* $P45^{vid}$ P74 ℵ A B C E 33; om. D

17:4 *not a few of the leading women* P74 ℵ A B E; *not a few of the wives of the leading men* D

17:26 It should be noted that the translations differ in this verse due to an underlying textual variation. P74, ℵ, A, B, 33 read *made from one* (man or unnamed substance); while D and E read *made from one blood.* The first reading, undoubtedly original, can mean one man (see TLB, TEV, NIV) or one unidentifiable substance (called "stock" in JB, NEB) because the Greek word ἑνὸς can be either masculine or neuter. The scribes of D and E took the liberty to insert their own verbalization of what they thought that substance was—*blood* (see TR, KJV).

17:27 The translations differ in one place in this verse due to adopting various variant readings from among the MSS. The best MSS (P74 ℵ A B) read *seek God* (and so do most of the translations); E and later MSS read *seek the Lord* (as in TR, KJV); and D reads *seek the Deity* (as in JB). The first reading is most likely original; the second an emendation; the third is probably an assimilation taken from 17:29, in which τὸ θεῖον (*the Deity*) is the true word in all extant MSS.

17:28 *some of your own poets* ℵ A E 33^{vid}; *some of our own poets* P74 B; *some among you* D

The poet quoted by Paul was probably Aratus of Soli in Cilicia (315–240 B.C.) or perhaps Epimenides, a Cretan poet.

18:5 *occupied in the word* (or, *in preaching the word*) P74 ℵ A B D E 33; *pressed in spirit* many late MSS

18:7 *Titius Justus* P74 B* D^b // *Titus Justus* ℵ E 1739; *Justus* A B^3 D

18:25 *the things concerning Jesus* $P74^{vid}$ ℵ A B D E 33; *the things concerning the Lord* later MSS

18:26 *the way of God* P74 ℵ* A B; *the Way* D; *the way of the Lord* E
19:6 *in the lecture hall of Tyrannus* P74 ℵ A B; *in the lecture hall of Tyrannus from the fifth hour to the tenth* D and some early translations
19:20 *Thus, according to the might of the Lord the word grew and prevailed* ℵ* A B; *so the word of the Lord grew and prevailed mightily* P74 ℵ^{c}; *so the word of God grew and prevailed mightily* E
19:39 om. *about other matters* P74 B 33; inc. ℵ A D E
20:4 *Gaius of Derbe* P74 ℵ A B D^{c} E 33; *Gaius the Doberian* D*^{vid}
20:15 om. *remained at Trogyllim* P74 ℵ A B C E 33; inc. P41^{vid} D
20:28a *church of God* ℵ B; *church of the Lord* P74 A C* D E 33; *church of the Lord and God* C^{3}
20:28b *the blood of his own* (i.e., his own Son) P74 ℵ A B C D E 33; *his own blood* later MSS
Putting the above two citations together, the reading with the best possibility of being original is *the church of God which he has purchased with the blood of his Own.* The Greek expression underlying the words *his Own* (τοῦ ἰδίου) was used in Koine papyri as a term of endearment (see Moulton and Milligan's *The Vocabulary of the Greek New Testament*). Thus, God's Son, as dear to Him, is called *his Own*—as elsewhere He is called "the Beloved" (without the word "Son" following). However, it must be said that the verse, according to the Greek, can equally mean that God purchased the church with His own blood. The theological implication of this statement is startling, for it identifies the blood of Jesus with the blood of God and thus simultaneously identifies Jesus as God. Although this statement is true, the form in which it is conveyed is unusual (one does not usually think of God as having blood). For this reason certain scribes must have changed *church of God* to *church of the Lord.* The true text, however, tells us that God purchased the church through the blood of His own Son and/or through His own blood—this blood being one and the same.
21:1 om. *and Myra* P74 ℵ A B C E; inc. P41^{vid} D
21:22 *there must be a meeting of the church for all will hear* P74 ℵ A C^{2} D E 33 // *for they will hear* B C*
21:25 inc. *and from what is strangled* P74 ℵ A B C E; om. D
23:30 om. *farewell* P74^{vid} A B 33; inc. ℵ E
24:6b–8a om. verses P74 ℵ A B; inc. E 33
26:16 *bear witness both of the things wherein you have seen Me and of the things wherein I will appear to you* B C*$^{vid?}$ 1739; *bear witness both of the things you have seen and the things I will show you* P74 ℵ A C^{2} E
The difference between the second reading and the first is that the second omits the word *Me*—an unfortunate (probably accidental) omission. Paul's commission was clearly Christo-centric. Christ did not reveal a lot of things, a lot of items to Paul; He revealed Himself to Paul that Paul might preach Him, the unsearchably rich Christ, to the nations (see Eph 3:8). And again, Paul himself testified that God was pleased to reveal His Son in him (Gal 1:16).
27:16 *Cauda* P74 ℵ^{c} B // *Clauda* ℵ* A^{vid} L 33 (alternate spelling, same location)
28:29 om. verse P74^{vid} ℵ A B E 048 33; inc. later MSS

PAUL'S EPISTLES

added MSS: H (6th C), I (5th C), 1739 (10th C)

ROMANS

added MSS: P26 (ca. 600), 0220 (3rd C)
1:13 *I do not want you to be ignorant* P26^{vid} ℵ A B C D^{c}; *I do not suppose you are ignorant* D*
4:1 *say what Abraham, our forefather, discovered* ℵ^{*,c} A C*; *say what Abraham, our father, discovered* ℵ^{a} C^{3} D; *say about Abraham our forefather* B 1739
It appears that the manuscript evidence strongly favors the inclusion of the words *discovered* and *forefather.* In context, Paul was focusing not on Abraham himself but on what Abraham discovered—namely, justification by faith.
4:19 It should be noted that according to the TR and KJV, Abraham did not consider that his body was dead. This reading has inferior manuscript support (D 33 and later MSS) than the reading which indicates that he did consider his body already dead (ℵ A B C 1739).
5:1 *we have peace with God* ℵ^{a} B^{3} 0220^{vid}; *let us have peace with God* ℵ* A B* C D 33
One reading could have easily been confounded for the other because they differ by only one letter (ο/ω): ἔχομεν (*we have peace*) and ἔχωμεν (*let us have peace*). Nevertheless, the first reading is more attractive because the manuscript support is decent (note the support from 0220^{vid}, the earliest extant MS that contains this portion of Romans), and it seems more suitable to the context. Now that we are justified by faith, we have peace with God. It is an accomplished fact. The second

reading, although attractive due to its presence in some very good MSS, does not suit the context as well. Paul is probably not exhorting Christians to make peace with God; rather, he is informing them that peace with God has been attained for them through Christ's redemptive work (cf. 5:2, 5–11).

5:2 *access into this grace* B D 0220; *access by faith into this grace* ℵ A C 33 1739
Because the words *by faith* do not appear in B, D, 0220 and there is no good reason to account for them being deleted, it is reasonable to surmise that these words were added by other scribes (perhaps to continue the idea of faith from 5:1).

8:1 om. *who walk not according to the flesh but according to the Spirit* ℵ* B C^2 D* 1739; inc. A D^b (KJV, TR) (taken from Rom 8:4)

8:23 inc. *adoption as sons* (or, *sonship*) ℵ A B C 33 1739; om. P46^{vid} D

8:24 *[who] hopes for what he sees* P46 ℵ^c B C D 33 1739*; *[why] wait for what he sees* ℵ* A 1739^{mg}

8:28 *God works all things together for good* 46 A B // *He works all things together for good* (or, *everything works together for good*) ℵ C D 33 1739
Quite possibly, scribes added *God* in order to clarify an ambiguous subject—for the second reading, according to the Greek, can be rendered as either "He [i.e., God] works everything" or "everything works." In the context of Romans 8, it would seem that the subject is unquestionably *God*; He is the One who works all things together for the good of those who love Him and are called according to His purpose.

9:5 Although this verse has been punctuated in many ways in different translations, the punctuation basically functions to either conjoin the expression *who is over all, God, blessed forever* with *the Christ* or to separate it from *the Christ.* Depending upon which punctuation is employed, Christ is said to be God or not to be God. The difference is critical.
One of the following two renderings represents the original thought:

1) whose are the fathers, and from whom is the Christ according to the flesh, who *is* over all, God, blessed forever. Amen.
2) whose are the fathers, and from whom is the Christ according to the flesh. God, who is over all, *be* blessed forever. Amen.

In the first rendering, the comma following *flesh* signals that the following words constitute appositional expressions; hence, *the Christ* is 1) *over all,* 2) *God,* and 3) *blessed forever.* In the second rendering, the period following *flesh* separates *the Christ* from these expressions—which are, instead, turned into a sentence of their own by inserting a predicate: *God, who is over all, be blessed forever*!
The first rendering closely follows the syntax of the Greek; the second is asyndetic—it really strains the Greek. Nearly all the Greek fathers understood the expression *God over all* to describe Christ. (They, being Greeks, would be very sensitive to the sense of the Greek language.) And most of the early translations also joined *Christ* to *God.* The evidence in the NT MSS themselves is difficult to weigh because so much of the punctuation (especially in the early MSS) is sporadic and unsystematic (see Metzger). Several late MSS have a punctuation mark after *flesh,* but the mark may have been equivalent to the English comma, semi-colon, or period.
In conclusion, little can be offered to validify the second rendering, while much can be said to support the first. The language itself provides the strongest defense (*the Christ* is naturally and smoothly followed by the appositional expression, *who is over all, God, blessed forever.*) And so does the context. Paul would not abruptly, even sporadically, insert a praise to God the Father at the end of his enumeration of the divine privileges and promises given to the Jews. To the contrary, he was culminating that list with the greatest blessing of all—i.e., the Christ, who is God over all, blessed forever, would come from the Jewish race! How could the Jews then reject Him? This created anguish in Paul's heart, not joy or praise. How incongruous it would be, then, for him to praise God. Paul was grieved that the Jews rejected the greatest blessing—Christ Himself, who is God.

10:17 The KJV, based upon ℵ^c A D^{b,c} 33 (see TR), reads *the word of God,* instead of *the word of Christ* (or, *the preaching of Christ*) found in P46^{vid} ℵ* B C D* 1739. The *word of Christ* has been rendered as *the preaching of Christ* or *the message of Christ* in certain versions because the Greek term (ῥῆμα) underlying *word* designates specific utterance (in contrast to the Greek word, λόγος, which usually designates comprehensive expression—often in written form).

11:6b om. second sentence of verse (see KJV) P46 ℵ* A C D 1739; inc. B ℵ^c

11:17 *a partaker of the root, namely the riches,* (or simply, *the rich root*) *of the olive tree* ℵ* B C; *a partaker of the root and the riches of the olive tree* ℵ^c A D^{b,c} 33 1739; *a partaker of the riches of the olive tree* P46 D*

11:31 *they may receive mercy* P46^{vid} A D^{b,c} 1739; *they may now receive mercy* ℵ B D^{*,d}; *they may receive mercy later* 33

12:11 *serving the Lord* P46 ℵ A B D^{b,c} 33 1739; *meeting the demands of the hour* D*

14:10 The original wording in this verse is most likely *the judgment seat of God* (supported by ℵ* A B C

D 1739). It was changed at a very early date (2nd/3rd century) to *the judgment seat of Christ* (present in ℵ[c] C[2vid] 048 33, noted by Marcion, Polycarp, Tertullian, and Origen). The change was either 1) doctrinally motivated (i.e., it has been taught that Christians will stand before the judgment seat of Christ but not the judgment seat of God—which is taken to mean the great white throne in Rev 20:11), or 2) undertaken to conform Rom 14:10 to 2 Cor 5:10, or 3) both.

14:21 *stumble* ℵ[a] A C 048 1739; *stumble or be offended or be weakened* ℵ[c] B D

14:23 See note on 16:25–27.

15:19 The careful reader will notice that there are different titles for the divine Spirit in the different translations. This is because the MSS differ. P46 ℵ D[b] read *the Spirit of God*; B reads simply *the Spirit*; A D*[,c] 33 1739 read *the Holy Spirit.* Given the fact that scribes tended to expand divine titles (see Introduction), the reading in B is quite possibly original.

15:29 *the fulness of the blessing of Christ* P46 ℵ* A B C D 1739; *the fulness of the blessing of the gospel of Christ* ℵ[c] 33

15:33 See note on 16:25–27.

16:7 *Junia* ℵ A B C D 33 1739; *Julia* P46

16:15 *Julias* ℵ A B C[2] D 33 1739; *Junia* C*

16:20 inc. *the grace of our Lord Jesus be with you* P46 ℵ B; (A C 33 1739 add *Christ*); om. D

16:24 om. verse P46 P61[vid] ℵ A B C 1739; inc. D and later MSS

16:25–27 These verses have been placed in various spots in the book of Romans—as follows: 1) after 16:23 (P61[vid?] ℵ B C D 1739 and some early translations); 2) after 14:23 and 16:23 (A 33); 3) after 14:23 (L Ψ 0209[vid]); 4) after 15:33 (P46)

Scholars have entertained many opinions and conjectures concerning this textual problem, one too involved to recapitulate here. The simplest solution is to adhere to the best attestation among the witnesses; far and away, the first position indicated above has the best testimony.

1 CORINTHIANS

added MSS: P11 (7th C), P15 (3rd C), 088 (5th C)

1:4 *my God* ℵ[a] A C D 33; *God* ℵ* B

1:14 *I am thankful* ℵ* B 1739; *I thank God* ℵ[c] C D; *I thank my God* A 33

2:1 *mystery of God* P46[vid] ℵ* A C; *testimony of God* ℵ[c] B D 33 1739

NA[26] and UBS[3] site P46[vid?] in support of the first reading; the question mark follows "vid" because they are not certain P46 reads *mystery*. This writer examined the manuscript (at the University of Michigan) and saw that though there is a lacuna in this place, *mystery* is the word in P46. This could be determined because the Greek letter *eta* (H), though partially broken, is visible before the final four letters (PION). The one letter makes all the difference in determining whether the Greek word is MAPTYPION (*testimony*) or MYΣTHPION (*mystery*) because, in this case, the first four letters of either word were missing and the last four letters of both words are the same. If the middle letter was an *upsilon* (Y) the word had to be MAPTYPION (*testimony*); if the letter was *eta,* (H), then the word had to be MYΣTHPION (*mystery*). The word *mystery* suits the context of 1 Corinthians chapter one better than *testimony.* Christ is God's mystery (cf Col. 2:2), God's secret revealed to Paul and the believers by the Spirit.

3:17 *God will destroy* (or, *desecrate*) *him* P46 ℵ A B C; *God destroys* (or, *desecrates*) *him* D 33

5:5 *Lord* P46 B 1739; *Lord Jesus* ℵ; *Lord Jesus Christ* D; om A 33

7:5 It should be noted that the manuscript evidence (P11[vid] P46 ℵ* A B C D 33 1739) is decidedly against the inclusion of the words *fasting and* before *prayer* (as in TR, KJV). See note on Mk 9:29.

7:34 *and his interests are divided. And the unmarried woman or virgin* . . . P15 B (essentially P46 ℵ A 33 1739); *And there is a difference between the wife and the virgin* some early translations and later MSS

7:40 Two good MSS (P15 and 33) read *Spirit of Christ,* a more unusual title than *Spirit of God* and quite suitable to the context (see 7:10, 24). But however attractive the reading *Spirit of Christ* looks, its attestation is yet too slim—by comparison to *Spirit of God* (found in all other MSS)—to affirm its genuineness.

8:3 *loves God* P15 ℵ A B D 33 1739; *loves* P46

8:7 *being hitherto accustomed to idols* ℵ* A B 33 1739; *with conscience of* [toward] *the idols* ℵ[c] D

8:12 inc. *when it is weak* ℵ A B D 33 1739; om. P46

10:9 *Christ* P46 D 1739; *the Lord* ℵ B C 33; *God* A

It is far more likely that *Christ* was changed to *Lord* or *God* than that either of these two titles were changed to *Christ.* In the context of 1 Cor 10 it was very natural for Paul to say "let us not tempt Christ, as some of them did" because he saw the Lord God of the Old Testament as equal to Christ and he viewed Christ as being present with the Israelites in the wilderness. Since Christ was the spiritual Rock that accompanied them in their journeys (10:4), He was also the One that the Israelites were taunting. Furthermore, it was not uncommon for New Testament writers to name the

Old Testament God according to New Testament parlance and thus call Him (as here and Heb 11:26) "Christ," or even "Jesus" (see note on Jude 4).

10:28 om. *for the earth is the Lord's and the fulness thereof* א A B C D H* 33 1739; inc. H^{c} and later MSS

11:10 *authority* P46 א A B C D H 33 1739; *veil* some early translations

11:24 *my body which is for you* P46 א* A B C* 33 1739; *my body which is broken for you* א^{c} C^{3} D^{b,c}; *my body which is given for you* some early translations

13:3 *if I give my body that I may boast* P46 א A B 33 1739 // *if I give my body to be burned* C D L
According to the Greek there is but a one–letter difference between the first reading and the second (θ/χ): καυθήσωμαι (*that I may boast*) and καυχήσωμαι (*that I may be burned*). Good arguments for the authenticity of each of the readings have been advanced by scholars. Nevertheless, it seems that the first reading was written by Paul because it has earlier and better testimony and because martyrdom by burning was a phenomenon yet unknown to the original readers of this epistle.

14:38 *if anyone ignores* (or, *does not recognize*) *this, he himself is ignored* (or, *not recognized*) א* A^{*vid} 048 33 1739; *if anyone ignores this, let him ignore this*! P46 א^{c} A^{2} B D^{b,c}

15:49 *we shall also bear the image of the heavenly man* B I // *let us also bear the image of the heavenly man* 46 א A C D 1739

15:54 *when the perishable has been clothed with the imperishable, and the mortal with immortality* א^{c} B C^{2vid} D (33) 1739^{mg}; *when the mortal has been clothed with immortality* P46 א* 1739* 088

2 CORINTHIANS

1:6–7 The sequence of clauses as in RSV and NIV is supported by P46 א A C.

1:10 *and He will deliver* P46 א B C 33; *and He delivers* D^{c} 1739

1:11 *our* P46^{c} א A C D* 33 1739; *your* P46* B D^{c}

1:12 *holiness* P46 א* A B C 33 1739 // *simplicity* א^{c} D.
One word could have easily been confused with the other because the two words differ in only two letters ($\gamma\iota/\pi\lambda$): ἁγιότητι (*holiness*) and ἁπλότητι (*simplicity*).

1:15 *favor* א* A C 33 1739; *pleasure* א^{c} B L

3:2 *our hearts* P46 A B C D 1739; *your hearts* א 33

8:7 *your love for us* א C D 33; *our love for you* (or, *the love we have for you*) P46 B 1739

11:3 inc. *pure devotion* P46 א* B D* 33; om. א^{c} D^{c} H 1739

12:7 inc. *that I may not be overly exalted* P46 א^{c} B I^{vid} 1739; om. א* A D 33

GALATIANS

added MSS: P51 (ca. 400), 062 (5th C)

1:3 *God the Father and our Lord Jesus Christ* P46 P51^{vid} B D 1739; *God our Father and Lord Jesus Christ* א A 33

1:6 *grace of Christ* P51^{vid} א A B 33 1739; *grace of Christ Jesus* D; *grace* P46$^{vid?}$ H^{vid}
P46 might have very well read *grace of Christ* even though it is listed in critical texts as supporting the shorter reading (*grace*)—but note the question mark after "vid." When the actual MS was examined (in the University of Michigan library), it was evident to this writer that there was enough space in the lacuna (as consistent with the line lengths of other unfragmented lines on the same page) to fit the two more letters required to designate the words *of Christ* (XY = Χριστοῦ).

2:5 *to whom we did not yield for a moment* P46 א A B C D^{c} 1739; *to whom we did yield for a moment* D* and a few patristic citations

2:12a *certain men* א A B C D H^{vid} 33 1739; *a certain man* P46^{vid}

4:25 *Hagar is Mount Sinai in Arabia* A B D 062^{vid} 33; *Sinai is a mountain in Arabia* P46 א C 1739

4:28 *you* P46 B D* 33 1739 // *we* א A C D^{c} 062

5:21 om. *murder* P46 א B 33; inc. A C D 1739

EPHESIANS

added MS: P49 (3rd C)

1:1 om. *in Ephesus* P46 א* B* 1739; inc. א^{c} A B^{3} D 33
The absence of the words *in Ephesus* in the three best, earliest MSS (P46 א* B*) is strong proof that this phrase was not an original part of the text. Therefore, this epistle has been considered by many scholars to have been a kind of circular letter. Indeed, the character of this epistle affirms its universality; it contains that which Paul wanted all the churches to read (see 3:1–7), and it does not address particular local problems or situations, as in all of Paul's other epistles. But to all this, it should be added that the syntax of this verse, according to the Greek, would require that some locality be supplied. (Note that the expression preceeding *in Ephesus*, τοῖς ἁγίοις τοῖς οὖσιν,

requires a prepositional phrase designating a locality to complete the sense—see Rom 1:7; 1 Cor 1:2; 2 Cor 1:1; Phil 1:1 for parallel expressions.) It could have been that Paul left the name of the locality blank, so that it might be filled in later with the names of different localities as the epistle circulated. This epistle could have been the very same one that went to Laodicea and from there on to Colossae (see Col 4:16). Such an epistle probably first went to Ephesus, the leading city in Asia, and then circulated throughout the local churches.

1:14 *which* P46 A B 1739; *who* א D 33

1:15 inc. *your love* א^{c} D; om. P46 א* A B 33 1739

2:21 It should be noted that certain MSS (א* B D 33 1739*) read *every building,* while others read *all the building* (א^{a} A C 1739^{c}). If the first reading is original, it could be Paul meant that each local church was a building for God's habitation, fit together with all the other buildings to comprise one dwelling place for God (see NEB). But most commentators take the first and second reading to mean the same; they both identify the universal church, the unique habitation of God.

3:9 Translations differ in this verse due to adhering to one of two readings among the MSS: *to enlighten all men* (P46 א^{c} B C D 33) or *to bring to light* (א* A 1739). The first reading has better support from the MSS; and furthermore, it should be remembered that Paul had been commissioned by God to open the eyes of the nations that they might turn from darkness to light (Acts 26:17, 18).

5:9 The TR and KJV read *fruit of the Spirit* (supported by P46 D^{c} 1739^{mg}), whereas most other texts and translations read *fruit of the light* (attested to by P49 א A B D* 33 1739). The reading in the KJV is clearly secondary, for scribes would naturally change a less familiar expression to a more usual one than vice versa.

5:19 *spiritual songs* א A D 33 1739 // *songs* P46 B

PHILIPPIANS

added MS: P16 (late 3rd C)

3:3 *who worship by* (or, *in*) *the Spirit of God* א* A B C D^{c} 33 1739 // *who worship God in spirit* א^{c} D* // *who worship in spirit* P46

Because of its good external support the reading in א* A B C et al is listed first, but the other two readings, from an internal view, look as equally viable because it was typical for Paul to contrast the flesh of man with the human spirit (cf verses 2 and 3). The scribe of P46 wrote out the word for *spirit* (πνευμα) instead of using the usual abbreviation to denote a divine title (i.e., ΠΝΑ). In his way of thinking, the *spirit* mentioned here is probably the human spirit. (For futher information on this, see this writer's article in *The Bible Translator,* Jan. 1984.)

4:3 *the rest of my fellow workers* P46 א^{c} A B D I^{vid} 33 1739; *my fellow workers and the rest* P16^{vid} א*

4:16 *sent me help* א B 33 1739; *sent money for my needs* P46 A

4:22 The best MSS (P 46 א* A B D 33 1739) read *the grace of our Lord Jesus Christ be with your spirit,* not . . . *be with you all,* as in TR, KJV.

COLOSSIANS

1:7 *our behalf* P46 א* A B D; *your behalf* א^{c} C D^{c} 33 1739

1:12 *you* א B 1739; *us* A C D 33

1:14 om. *through his blood* P 46 א A B C D; inc. a few late MSS

2:2 *the mystery of God, Christ* P46 B; *the mystery of God, which is Christ* D; *the mystery of God the Father, Christ* A C; *the mystery of the Father, Christ* א* 048; *the mystery of God and of the Father and of Christ* א^{b} D^{c} and late MSS

The reading in P46 and B is most likely the one from which all the others varied. According to the Greek, *Christ* is an appositive to *the mystery of God,* which means *the mystery of God* is *Christ.* (The word *mystery* in Greek denotes a secret revealed only to the initiates; to the outsiders, the secret *is* veiled.) Christ is God's secret revealed to the believers.

3:6 om. *upon the sons of disobedience* P46 B // inc. א A C D^{vid} H I 33 1739 (taken from Eph 5:6?)

3:16 *God* P46^{vid} א A B C* D* 33 1739; *the Lord* C^{2} D^{c}

4:15 *Nympha and the church* (or, *meeting*) *in her house* B 1739; *Nympha and the church* (or, *meeting*) *in his house* D; *Nympha and the church* (or, *meeting*) *in their house* א A C 33

1 THESSALONIANS

added MSS: P65 (3rd C), 0226 (5th C)

2:7 *gentle* A C$^{2?}$ D^{c} 33 1739; *babes* P65 א B C* D* I

Although *babes* has better attestation than *gentle,* it is a dubious reading. Paul never refers to himself and the apostles as *babes*, and the verse itself makes it very evident that the Thessalonians were the babes Paul cared for as a nurse. Undoubtedly, the last letter (ν) of the Greek word preceeding *gentle* (ἤπιοι) was inadvertently duplicated and added to it, thus making the Greek word for *babes* (νήπιοι). One letter makes all the difference.

2:15 *the prophets* ℵ A B D* I 33 1739; *their own prophets* D^{c}

3:2 *brother and God's fellow worker* D* 33; *brother and fellow worker* B; *brother and God's servant* ℵ A 1739; *brother and servant of God and our fellow worker* D^{c}

5:4 *thief* ℵ D 0226^{vid} 33 1739; *thieves* A B

2 THESSALONIANS

2:3 *man of lawlessness* ℵ B 1739; *man of sin* A D L
The first reading is undoubtedly original; its external testimony is superior and its internal suitability is more congruous with this portion of 2 Thessalonians. A few verses later, Paul talks about the mystery of lawlessness (2:7) and again mentions the lawless one (2:8); in both instances all the MSS concur.

2:13 *God chose you from the beginning* ℵ D L // *God chose you as his firstfruits* B 33 1739
One reading could have been easily confounded for the other because there is only a one letter difference (ς/ν) between the two expressions in Greek: ἀπ' ἀρχῆς (*from beginning*) and ἀπαρχήν (*firstfruits*). (In the early MSS no space was left between words.) The first reading is attractive because it was customary for the New Testament writers (especially Paul) to speak of God choosing His elect from the very beginning, even before the foundation of the world (see Eph 1:4). The second reading is equally attractive because Paul was in the habit of calling the first converts (in certain geographical regions) "the firstfruits" (see Rom 16:5; 1 Cor 16:15). Nevertheless, most translations contain the first reading and note the second.

3:16 *peace at all times and in every way* ℵ A^{c} B D^{c}; *peace at all times and in every place* A* D* 33

1 TIMOTHY

added MS: 061 (5th C)

3:1 *the saying is trustworthy* ℵ A D 33 1739; *the saying is popular* D*

3:16 *He who was manifested in the flesh* ℵ* A*^{vid} C* 33; *God was manifested in the flesh* ℵ^{c} A^{2} C^{2} D^{c} L 1739; *which was manifested in the flesh* D
Few textual problems have occasioned as much stir and controversy as this one—especially in the nineteenth century. Many scholars entered the debate—and not without good reason, inasmuch as this verse pertains to the doctrine of incarnation. When the reading in the TR and KJV (*God was manifest in the flesh*) was challenged by another reading (*He who was manifest in the flesh*), some may have thought the doctrine of God becoming man was being undermined. Not so. The scholars who defended the reading with *He who* primarily did so because they realized that the second reading was a manifest corruption. In three MSS (ℵ A C) a later scribe changed ΟΣ (*He who*) to ΘΕΟΣ (*God*), and this can be done in Greek simply by placing a line through the middle of the omega in the word ΟΣ: ΘΣ, thus creating the standard abbreviation for ΘΕΟΣ (*God*). In the original text, the subject of the verse is simply *who*—which most translators render as *He* and which most commentators identify as Christ.

4:9 *strive* ℵ* A C 33; *suffer reproach* ℵ^{c} D L

5:16 *woman* (lit. *female believer*) ℵ A C 048 33 1739; *man* (lit. *male believer*) a few ancient translations; *man or woman* D L

6:7 om. *it is certain that* ℵ* A 048 061 33; inc. ℵ^{c} D L

2 TIMOTHY

2:14 *God* ℵ C I; *Lord* A D 048 1739

4:10 *Galatia* A D L 33; *Gallia* (Gaul) ℵ C

HEBREWS

added MS: P13 (late 3rd C)

1:8 *your kingdom* A D 33 1739; *his kingdom* P46 ℵ B
In this verse God is addressing His Son and calling him "God"; God the Father is speaking *to* God the Son, not *about* Him (see Ps 45:7). Thus, the first reading maintains the vocative voice.

1:12 inc. *like a garment* P46 ℵ A B (D) 1739; om. D^{c} 33 (as in LXX)

2:7 om. *and did set him over the works of your hands* P46 B D^{c} L // inc. ℵ A C D* 33 1739 (see Ps 8:6 LXX)

2:9 *by the grace of God he might taste death* P46 ℵ A B C D 33; *apart from God he might taste death* 1739* and several patristic citations

3:2 *in God's house* (or, *household*) P13 P46^{vid} B // *in all God's house* (or, *household*) ℵ A C D 33 1739 (see Num 12:17 LXX)

3:6 om. *firm to the end* P13 P46 B; inc. ℵ A C D 33 1739 (see 3:14)

4:2 *they were not united in faith with those who heard* P13 P46 A B C D* 33; *those who heard did not combine it* [*the word*] *with faith* ℵ
The first reading is most likely original because it has better external attestation and it is more difficult. According to the best MSS, the Greek word for *united* or *combine* agrees grammatically with *those who heard* (or, *the hearers*); the inferior attestation agrees with *the word.* Thus, this verse is not talking about combining, mixing, or mingling faith with the word; it is talking about the fact that the majority of the Israelites were not united in faith with those who heard the good news (i.e., Moses, Joshua, and Caleb). Moses, Joshua, and Caleb truly heard the word concerning the promise of entering the good land, and they believed it; but the Israelites did not share their faith.

6:2 *with instruction about baptisms* ℵ A C D I 33 1739; *of instruction about baptisms* P46 B

6:3 *we will do this* P46 ℵ B I^{vid} 33; *let us do this* A C

8:8 *finding fault with them said* ℵ* A D* I 33; *finding fault said to them* P46 ℵ^{c} B D^{c} 1739

8:11 *brother and fellow citizen* P46 ℵ A B D 33 1739; *brother and neighbor* later MSS

9:11 *of the good things that have come* P46 B D* 1739; *of the good things that are about to come* ℵ A D^{c} I^{vid} 33 (see 10:1)

10:1 *the law contains but a shadow of the good things to come, not the true form of the realities* ℵ A C D H^{vid} 33 1739; *the law contains but a shadow and likeness of the good things to come* P46

10:38 *my righteous one* P46 ℵ A H* 33^{vid}; *(the) righteous one* P13 (the MS referred to in NIV mg) D^{c} H^{c}

11:37 The Greek word underlying *they were tested* 1) is not in P46, 2) appears in A, D^{c}, 1739 after *they were sawn in two* (see RSV mg), and 3) is included in ℵ, 048, 33 after *they were stoned* (see NEB mg, NIV mg).

12:1 *clinging* (or, *entangling*) *sin* P13 ℵ A D 33; *distracting sin* P46 1739

13:21 *us* P46 ℵ A D 33 1739; *you* C and later MSS

JAMES

added MSS: P23 (early 3rd C), P74 (7th C)

1:17 *the Father of lights with whom there is no variation or shadow of turning* ℵ^{c} A C 1739 // ... *no variation which consists in the turning of the shadow* ℵ* B // ... *no variation or turning of the shadow* P23
Due to the complexity of the metaphor, different scribes attempted to clarify the sense, and it is not easy to determine which scribe emended what. The image seems to portray God as an unchanging orb of light—quite unlike the natural sun which, from our perspective, shifts and thus causes shadows. The reading in P23 could possibly evoke the image of an ancient sundial (which told time by the turning of the shadow). If so, James would be indicating that God is changeless *and* timeless. But the context appears to deal only with God's unchanging, steadfast nature.

2:3 *stand there or sit* A C* 33; *stand* [where you are] *or sit here* P74^{vid} ℵ; *stand* [where you are] *or sit there* B 1739

2:20 *useless* B C* 1739; *dead* ℵ A C^{2} 33 (see 2:17, 26); *empty* P74

4:5 The reading *the Spirit which He* [*God*] *made to dwell in us* is supported by P74, ℵ, A, B, 1739, while other MSS, mostly later, support the reading in TR, KJV: *the Spirit that dwells in us.*

1 PETER

(remember P72 for 1 and 2 Peter and Jude—see Introduction)

1:8 *seen* P72 ℵ B C 1739; *known* A and later MSS

1:11 Several scholars have pointed out that Codex Vaticanus (B) simply reads *Spirit*—against the testimony of all other MSS, which read *Spirit of Christ.* In spite of the overall excellence of B, this is a manifest emendation. The scribe probably found it difficult to believe that the Spirit of Christ could have indwelt the OT prophets, so he changed the text.

1:22 *pure heart* P72 ℵ* (*true heart* ℵ^{c}) C 33 1739 // *heart* A B

2:21 *suffered* P72 A B C^{vid} 33 1739; *died* ℵ (see 3:18)

3:15 The TR and KJV read *sanctify the Lord God in your hearts* (and this reading is supported by later MSS). But the best MSS (P72 ℵ A B C 33 1739) read *sanctify Christ as Lord in your hearts.*

3:18a *died* P72 ℵ A C^{vid} 33 1739; *suffered* B

3:18b *for sins* ℵ* B; *for our sins* C*^{vid}; *for sins on our behalf* P72 ℵ^{c} A C^{2vid} 33 1739

4:1 *Christ suffered in the flesh* P72 B C 1739; add *for us* ℵ^{c} A 33; add *for you* ℵ*

4:15 *the Spirit of glory and of God* P72 B; *the Spirit of glory and of power and of God* ℵ^{c} A 33 1739

5:2a inc. *overseeing* (or, *exercising the oversight*—RSV) P72 ℵ^{c} A 33 1739; om. ℵ* B

The testimony supporting the inclusion of the word *overseeing* is strong—both externally and internally. If the word were not originally in the text, it is difficult to explain why scribes would have added it. On the contrary, it is easy to see why the scribes of ℵ* and B omitted it. These scribes must have had the misconception that elders (*presbytery*—5:1) could not function as overseers. At that time in church history (4th century), the offices of elder and overseer (i.e., bishop) were differentiated. The overseer or bishop was elevated to a rank above an elder. This contradicts the teaching in the NT. Paul told the elders at Ephesus that the Holy Spirit had made them overseers (bishops) of the flock of God (Acts 20:17, 28). And here Peter charges the elders that they should shepherd the flock of God by overseeing it (i.e., by functioning as bishops). Thus, the function of an elder was to oversee the church. But this truth had become blurred with the passage of time, and undoubtedly was the cause for two fourth century scribes to alter the text (see Alford's *Greek Testament*).

5:2b inc. *as God would have you* P72 ℵ A 33 1739; om. B

5:10 *strengthen you* A B 0206; *strengthen, settle* (or, *establish*) *you* ℵ 1739; *establish you* P72

2 PETER

1:1 *Simon* P72 B // *Simeon* ℵ A 1739

1:3 *called us to His own glory and virtue* ℵ A C 33 1739 // *called us through* (or, *by*) *His own glory and virtue* P72 B

It is difficult to decide which of the two readings was written by Peter. Both have good support and both are true: God called us by means of His glory and virtue (perhaps, as expressed in Jesus Christ) to participate in His very own glory and virtue. It appears, though, that the first reading is more in harmony with the immediate context—especially verse 4, which indicates that we can participate in God's glory and virtue because we have become partakers of the divine nature.

1:21 *men moved* (lit. *borne along*) *by the Holy Spirit spoke from God* P72 B C 1739; *moved by the Holy Spirit holy men of God spoke* ℵ 33

The first reading has better attestation and is more suitable to the context. The second reading tells us that the prophets were *holy men of God* (ἅγιοι θεοῦ)—interesting but hardly significant. The first reading tells us the source from which the inspired men spoke—they spoke *from God* (ἀπὸ θεοῦ), as they were borne along by the Holy Spirit. This strengthens the statement made in the previous verse: "no prophecy of Scripture is of one's own interpretation"—i.e., the prophetic Word did not originate from any prophet's interpretation of what God spoke to them. They spoke what God spoke; they spoke from God without interpreting the message according to their own understanding or concept.

2:4 *chains* P72 33 1739 // *pits* ℵ A B C

2:13 *deceits* P72 ℵ A* C 33 // *lovefeasts* A^c B

The two words could have been easily confounded for one another: ἀπάταις (*deceits*), ἀγάπαις (*lovefeasts*).

3:10 *will be exposed* (or, *found out*, or *laid bare*) ℵ B 1739^txt; *will be burned* A 048 33 1739^mg; *will be found dissolved* P72

1 JOHN

1:4 *our joy* ℵ B // *your joy* A C^2vid 33 1739

2:20 *you all know* ℵ B // *you know everything* A C 33 1739

2:25 *us* ℵ A C 33 1739; *you* B

4:20 *cannot love* ℵ B 1739; *how can he love* A 048

5:7, 8 om. *in heaven; the Father, the Word, and the Holy Spirit, and these three are one. And there are three that testify on earth:* ℵ A B 048 33 1739 and all Greek MSS prior to the eleventh century, all early translations, all ancient Greek patristic citations; inc. a few late Greek miniscules (11th–15th centuries), a few Latin patristic citations

This famous—or infamous—passage, called "the heavenly witnesses," has been the object of much discussion. The passage is blatantly spurious. It came from a gloss on 1 Jn 5:8 which explained that the three elements (water, blood, and Spirit) symbolized the Trinity. This gloss, evidently, found its way into the text in the form quoted above. The passage has a Latin origin. Its first appearance was in the work of Priscillian, a fourth century Spanish heretic. It showed up in the writings of other Latin fathers from the fifth century onward, and it found its way into more and more copies of the Latin Vulgate. But "the heavenly witnesses" can not be found in any Greek MS prior to the eleventh century, and it was never cited by any Greek father. Erasmus did not include "the heavenly witnesses" in the first two editions of his Greek New Testement. He was criticized for this by defenders of the Latin Vulgate. Erasmus, in reply, said that he would include it if he could see it in any one Greek MS. In turn, a manuscript was especially produced to contain the passage. Erasmus kept his promise; he included it in the third edition. From there it became part of the TR and hence was translated in the KJV.

5:18 The difference in translations of this verse comes from an underlying textual variation. A* and B read *the one born of God keeps him,* while א, A^c 33, 1739 read *the one born of God keeps himself.* The first reading indicates that the Son of God, being *the One born of God,* keeps the believer from sin; the second reading indicates that the believer, as a son of God, keeps himself from sin. The first reading is preferable because 1) the first clause of this verse already mentions the believer who is born of God, 2) John consistently uses the perfect tense to describe the believer who has become a son of God (2:29; 3:9; 4:7; 5:1; 5:4; 5:18a) whereas here the aorist is used, and 3) there is little or no security in the fact that the believer must keep himself. Rather, it is the One begotten of God, the Son of God, who keeps each believer.

2 JOHN

added MS: 0232 (late 5th C.)

v.8 *you have worked for* א A 0232 33 1739; *we have worked for* B

JUDE

added MS: P78 (late 3rd C)

v.5 *Jesus delivered his people out of Egypt* A B 33 1739; *God, the Messiah, delivered his people out of Egypt* P72; *the Lord delivered his people out of Egypt* א C* L; *God delivered his people out of Egypt* C^2

It is quite probable that Jude wrote, *Jesus delivered his people out of Egypt.* This remarkable reading is found in A, B, 33, 1739, early Coptic MSS, Origen, and Bede. P72 also is an indirect witness to the reading with *Jesus* because it shows that the scribe had before him (in the exemplar) a Messianic name—whether Jesus or Christ. The reading with *Jesus* is the one from which all the other variants came because no good reason can be purported to explain why a reading with *God* or *Lord* would be changed to the unusual (even arresting) name, *Jesus.* Given the fact that Jude was writing from a NT perspective, a perspective that viewed Jesus as being Jehovah the Savior, it is not difficult to imagine that Jude would say that Jesus delivered the Israelites out of Egypt. Paul spoke of Christ as present with the Israelites in the wilderness (see 1 Cor 10:4 and note on 1 Cor 10:9), and the writer of Hebrews spoke of Christ as the reward Moses esteemed above the riches of Egypt (Heb 11:26). Some scholars have said that "Jesus" here (in Jude 5) indicates "Joshua" (e.g., see NEB mg), as in Heb. 4:8; but this is generally regarded as unlikely. Joshua led the Israelites into the good land, but not out of Egypt; and Joshua certainly did not "destroy those who did not believe" (Jude 5b).

v.22 *show mercy to those who have doubts* א B C^2 // *reprove* (or, *convince*) *those who have doubts* A C* 33 1739

v.23 *others save, snatching them out of the fire* א A (C adds *with fear*) 33 1739; *save them* (i.e., the ones who have doubts—v.22), *snatching them out of the fire* (P72 in a shortened form) B

REVELATION

added MSS: P18 (late 3rd C), P24 (4th C), P47 (3rd C), P (9th C), 046 (10th C), 051 (10th C), 0169 (4th C) (A and C are the two best witnesses in Revelation)

1:5 The TR and KJV read *washed us from our sins* (supported by P and other late MSS); whereas most modern translations read *freed us from our sins* (supported by P18 א^c A C). On the surface, *freed* appears to be more unnatural than *washed,* but the Greek word underlying *freed* means "destroy, put away, abolish." In freeing us from our sins, Jesus did away with them (cf Isa 40:2, LXX).

2:22 *bed* א C P 046; *prison* A; *furnace* one late MS (2071)—noted in NEB

12:18 *And he stood* P47 א A C; *And I stood* later MSS (connects with 13:1)

13:6 *blaspheming his name and his dwelling place, that is, those who dwell in heaven* א* A C 046^c; *blaspheming his name and his dwelling place and those who dwell in heaven* א^c P 046* 051; *blaspheming his name and his dwelling place in heaven* P47

The first reading has all the qualities of being original. It has the best external support (א* A C); it is the seemingly most difficult reading; and it is the reading from which the others deviated. According to the Greek syntax of this verse, the phrase *those who dwell* (lit. *tabernacle* or, *pitch their tent*) *in heaven* is in direct apposition to *his dwelling place* (lit. *tabernacle*). Thus, those who dwell in heaven are God's dwelling place in heaven; the people in heaven and the heavenly place are not two separate entities—as is indicated by the second reading. In the final chapters of

Revelation we learn that the New Jerusalem coming down out of heaven is equated with God's tabernacle—He tabernacles among men (22:1–3). Thus, God's dwelling place and God's people are seen as one entity. He dwells in His people and His people dwell in Him (see Rev 21:22).

13:7 inc. *Also it was allowed to make war on the saints and to conquer them* א 046 051; om. P47 A C P (most likely due to transcriptional oversight)

13:18 *666* P47 א A P 046 051 and almost all other MSS; *616* C and a few other MSS

14:13 *Yes, says the Spirit*... א[c] A C P 051; ... *says the Spirit* P47 א*

15:3 *King of the nations* א[a] A P 046 051 // *King of the ages* P47 א*,c C; *King of saints* late MSS

18:3 *have drunk of* P 051 // *have fallen by* (or, *have been ruined by*) א A C 046

19:13 *dipped* (or, *drenched*) *in blood* A 046 051; *sprinkled* (or, *spattered*) *with blood* א P

20:9 *out of heaven* A; *out of heaven from God* 046; *from God out of heaven* א[a]

21:3a *peoples* א A 046 // *people* P 051

21:3b *God Himself will be with them* [*and be*] *their God* (or better rendered, *God-with-them shall Himself be their God*) A; *God will be with them* [*and be*] *their God* P 051; *God Himself will be with them* א 046

The first reading is the best inasmuch as it has the best attestation (A, some early patristic citations, and a few early versions), and it is the most unusual. The appelation *God-with-them* (i.e., "Immanuel," see Isa 7:14; 8:8; Mt 1:23) may have seemed too extraordinary (in this context) to certain scribes, who therefore changed it to a simpler expression.

22:14 *wash their robes* א A; *do his commandments* 046 and later MSS

22:21a *grace be with all* A; *grace be with you all* a few witnesses; *grace be with the saints* א; *grace be with all the saints* 046 051

22:21b om. *Amen* A; inc. א 046 051

For those who desire additional commentary on the textual problems addressed in this index, see Bruce M. Metzger's work, *A Textual Commentary on the Greek New Testament* (New York: United Bible Societies, 1975).

A CHRONOLOGY OF THE OLD AND NEW TESTAMENTS

OLD TESTAMENT (B.C.)

2166	Abram born
2091	Abram enters Canaan
2066	Isaac born
2006	Jacob and Esau born
1991	Abraham dies
1929	Jacob flees to Haran
1915	Joseph born
1898	Joseph sold into slavery
1886	Isaac dies
1885	Joseph begins to rule in Egypt
1876	Jacob's family comes to Egypt
1859	Jacob dies
1805	Joseph dies
1526	Moses born
1446	Exodus from Egypt
1406	Israel enters Canaan
1375-1050	Judges' rule:
1367-1327	Othniel
1309-1229	Ehud
1209-1169	Deborah
1162-1122	Gideon
1105	**Samuel born**
1078-1072	Jepthath
1075-1055	Samson

UNITED KINGDOM

1050-1010	Saul's rule
1010-970	David's rule
970-930	Solomon's rule

DIVIDED KINGDOMS

Judah (Kings/**Prophets**)

930-913	Rehoboam
910-869	Asa
872-848	Jehoshaphat
855-840	**Obadiah**
853-841	Jehoram
841-835	Athaliah
835-796	Joash
810-750	**Joel**
792-740	Azzariah (Uzziah)
750-735	Jotham
742-687	**Micah**
740-681	**Isaiah**
735-715	Ahaz
715-686	Hezekiah

DIVIDED KINGDOMS cont.

Judah (Kings/**Prophets**)

697-642	Manasseh
664-612	**Nahum**
640-609	**Zephaniah**
640-609	Josiah
627-586	**Jeremiah**
609-598	Jehoiakim
605-589	**Habakkuk**
597	Jehoiachin
597-586	Zedekiah
c.587	**Obadiah**
586	Fall of Jerusalem

Israel (Kings/**Prophets**)

930-909	Jeroboam I
909-908	Nadab
908-886	Baasha
886-885	Elah
885	Zimri, Timri
885-874	Omri
875-848	**Elijah**
874-853	Ahab
852-841	Joram
848-797	**Elisha**
841-814	Jehu
814-798	Jehoahaz
798-782	Jehoash
793-753	Jeroboam II
785-775	**Jonah**
760-750	**Amos**
753-752	Zechariah
752	Shallum
752-742	Menahem
752-732	Pekah
750-715	**Hosea**
732-722	Hoshea
722	Fall of Northern Kingdom

Captivity

586	Babylonian Captivity
	Prophets in exile:
605-530	Daniel
593-571	Ezekiel

RECOVERY

538	First group returns with Zerubbabel
537	Rebuilding of Temple begins
520	**Haggai**
520-480	**Zechariah**
516	Rebuilding of Temple finished
458	Second group returns with Ezra
445	Nehemiah comes to Jerusalem, begins first governorship
440-430	**Malachi**
433	Nehemiah begins second governorship
432-6 B.C.	Between the Testaments

NEW TESTAMENT EVENTS

6/5 B.C.	Christ's birth
A.D. 6/7	Jesus in the temple
26	John the baptist begins his ministry
26/27	Christ is baptized, begins his ministry
30	Christ is crucified, resurrected, and enthroned
30	Pentecost
34/35	Paul's conversion
44	James, the apostle, is martyred
46-48	Paul's first missionary journey
49/50	Jerusalem council
50-52	Paul's second missionary journey
53-57	Paul's third missionary journey
59-62	Paul's imprisonment in Rome
67	Paul's second imprisonment
65-67	Peter martyred
68	Paul martyred
90-95	John exiled
c.100	John dies

NEW TESTAMENT BOOKS

45-50	James
49 or 56	Galatians
50's	Mark
50, 51	1 & 2 Thessalonians
55, 56	1 & 2 Corinthians
56/57	Romans
60	Luke
60's	Matthew
60/61	Colossians, Philemon, Ephesians
61/62	Philippians
63	1 Timothy
63	1 Peter
64-68	Hebrews
64-72	Acts
65	Titus
65-67	2 Peter
67	2 Timothy
70-80	Jude
85-90	John, Epistles of John
95	Revelation

THE HEBREW CALENDAR

Present-day†	*Post-exilic** (Pre-exilic)***	*Seasonal Description*	*Festivals*
JANUARY			
	SHEBAT	Almonds blossom	
FEBRUARY			
	ADAR	Citrus fruit harvest	Purim (Esther 9)
MARCH		Spring/latter rains	Passover (Exod 12:18)
	NISAN (ABIB)	Barley harvest Flax harvest	Unleavened Bread (Lev 23:6) Firstfruits (Lev 23:10ff)
APRIL			Late Passover (Num 9:10, 11)
	IYYAR (ZIV)	Dry season begins	
MAY			Pentecost (Lev 23:15ff)
	SIVAN		
JUNE		Early figs ripen	
	TAMMUZ	Grape harvest	
JULY			
	AB		
AUGUST		Olive harvest	
	ELUL		
SEPTEMBER		Dates and summer figs	Trumpets (Num 29:1)
	TISHRI (ETHANIM)	Early rains	Day of Atonement (Lev 16:29ff) Tabernacles (Lev 23:34)
OCTOBER			Solemn Assembly (Lev 23:36)
	MARCHESVAN (BUL)	Winter figs Plowing	
NOVEMBER			Dedication (John 10:22)
	CHISLEV		
DECEMBER		Sowing	
	TEBETH	Rains (Snow on high ground)	

Until c. 100 BC the Hebrew calendar was based on lunar months, which followed the Babylonian practice. The new year began in the spring (March/April) and accommodated the agricultural seasons. To maintain this a second twelfth month (Adar) or sixth month (Elul) was periodically added to control the beginning or 'return of the year' at the time of the spring equinox (1 Kings 20:26). There is no sure evidence that at the time of the final Judaean kingdom there was an administrative new year beginning in autumn (Tishri) at the time of the autumnal equinox ('the going out of the year', *cf.* Exod. 23:16). Some early names for months are known also from Phoenicia and reflect agricultural and seasonal changes such as Abib, 'ripening of corn' (Exod. 13:4). These names are given in parentheses. Festivals follow both agricultural and historical events. Most local references to the calendar would describe the seasons but in post-exilic times the Babylonian month names were followed.

*Post-exilic Name—Biblical References: Esther 3:7; Neh. 2:1 (Nisan); Esther 8:9 (Sivan); Neh. 6:15 (Elul): Neh. 1:1 (Chislev); Esther 2:16 (Tebeth); Zech. 1:7 (Shebat); Esther 3:7 (Adar)

***Pre-exilic Name—Biblical* References: Exod. 13:4; 23:15; 34:18: Deut. 16:1 (Abib); 1 Kings 6:1, 37 (Ziv); 1 Kings 8:2 (Ethanim); 1 Kings 6:38 (Bul)

†Note that each Hebrew month extends from the middle of the present-day month to the middle of the next month; thus, Shebat corresponds to January 15—February 15, etc.

WEIGHTS AND MEASURES IN THE BIBLE

Liquid Capacity

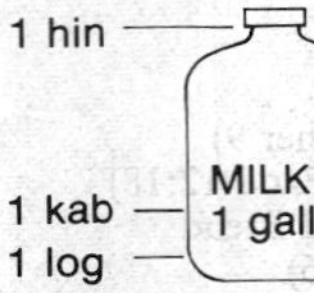

Measure	*System equivalent*	*Approximate equivalents Metric*	*U.S.*
log	$\frac{1}{12}$ hin	0.33 *l*	$\frac{1}{12}$ gal.
kab	4 logs $\frac{1}{3}$ hin	1.3 *l*	$\frac{1}{3}$ gal.
hin	12 logs 3 kabs	3.67 *l*	1 gal.
seah	6 kabs 2 hins	7.33 *l*	2 gal.
bath	3 seahs 6 hins	22 *l*	6 gal.
homer	10 baths 60 hins	220 *l*	60 gal.

Weight

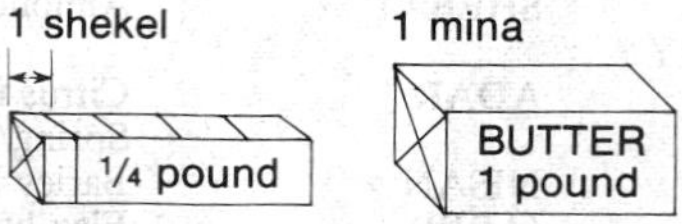

Measure	*System equivalent*	*Approximate equivalents Metric*	*U.S.*
gerah	$\frac{1}{20}$ shekel	0.5 g	$\frac{1}{50}$ oz.
beka	10 gerahs $\frac{1}{2}$ shekel	5 g	$\frac{3}{16}$ oz.
pim	$1\frac{1}{2}$ bekas $\frac{3}{4}$ shekel	7 g	$\frac{1}{4}$ oz.
shekel	2 bekas $1\frac{1}{2}$ pims	10 g	$\frac{1}{2}$ oz.
mina	75 pims 50 shekels	500 g	1 lb.
talent	60 minas 3000 shekels	30 kg	66 lbs.

Dry Capacity

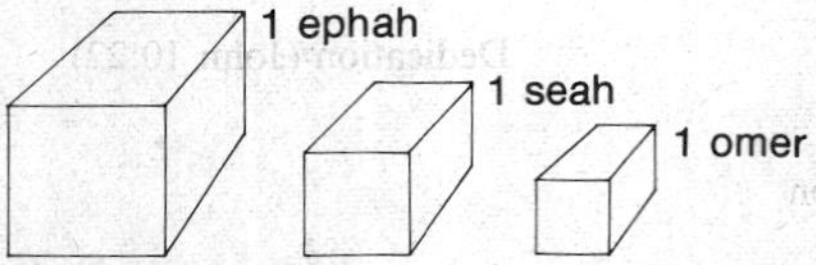

Measure	*System equivalent*	*Approximate equivalents Metric*	*U.S.*
log	$\frac{1}{4}$ kab	0.33 *l*	$20\frac{1}{2}$ cu. in.
kab	4 logs	1.2 *l*	73 cu. in.
omer	7 logs $1\frac{4}{5}$ kabs	2.4 *l*	$146\frac{1}{2}$ cu. in.
seah	$3\frac{1}{3}$ omers 6 kabs	7.3 *l*	$\frac{1}{4}$ cu. ft.
ephah	10 omers 3 seahs	22 *l*	$\frac{3}{4}$ cu. ft.
lethech	15 seahs 5 ephahs	110 *l*	$3\frac{3}{4}$ cu. ft.
homer	10 ephahs 2 lethech	220 *l*	$7\frac{3}{4}$ cu. ft.

Length

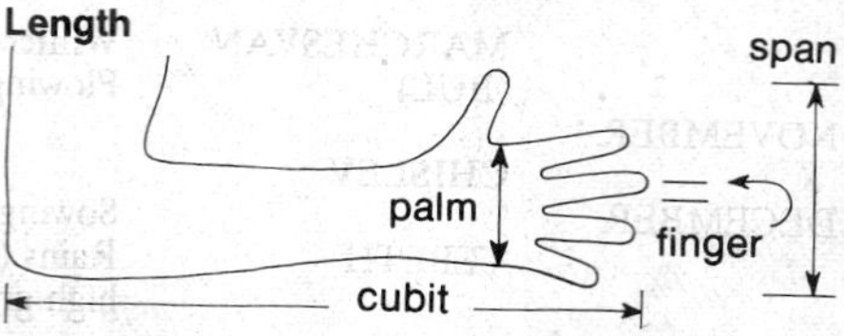

Measure	*System equivalent*	*Approximate equivalents Metric*	*U.S.*
finger (digit)	$\frac{1}{12}$ span	2 cm	$\frac{3}{4}$ in.
palm (hand-breadth)	4 fingers $\frac{1}{3}$ span	7.5 cm	3 in.
span	12 fingers 3 palms	22.25 cm	9 in.
gomedh	$3\frac{3}{4}$ palms $1\frac{1}{4}$ spans	30 cm	12 in.
cubit	6-7 palms 2 spans	44.5 cm	$17\frac{1}{2}$ in.
fathom	4 cubits 8 spans	2 m	2 yds.

HARMONY OF THE GOSPELS

Events Connected with the Birth and Childhood of our Lord
Time: about thirteen and a half years

	MATTHEW	MARK	LUKE	JOHN
Preface to Luke's gospel			1:1-4	
An angel appears to Zacharias. *Jerusalem*			1:5-25	
An angel appears to Mary. *Nazareth*			1:26-38	
Mary visits Elisabeth. *Juttah*			1:39-56	
Birth of John the Baptist. *Juttah*			1:57-80	
An angel appears to Joseph. *Nazareth*	1:18-25			
The birth of Jesus. *Bethlehem*			2:1-7	
An angel appears to the shepherds. *Near Bethlehem*			2:8-20	
The circumcision of Jesus, and his presentation in the temple. *Bethlehem. Jerusalem*			2:21-38	
The magi. *Jerusalem. Bethlehem*	2:1-12			
The flight into Egypt. Herod's cruelty. The return. *Bethlehem. Nazareth*	2:13-23		2:39, 40	
At twelve years of age Jesus goes to the Passover. *Jerusalem*			2:41-52	
Genealogies	1:1-17		3:23-38	

Announcement and Introduction of our Lord's Public Ministry
Time: about one year

	MATTHEW	MARK	LUKE	JOHN
The ministry of John the Baptist. *The desert. The Jordan*	3:1-12	1:1-8	3:1-18	
The baptism of Jesus. *The Jordan*	3:13-17	1:9-11	3:21-23	
The temptation. *Desert of Judea*	4:1-11	1:12, 13	4:1-13	
Preface to John's gospel				1:1-18
Testimony of John the Baptist to Jesus. *Bethabara beyond Jordan*				1:19-34
Jesus gains disciples. *The Jordan. Galilee?*				1:35-51
The marriage at Cana of Galilee				2:1-12

Our Lord's First Passover, and the Subsequent Transactions until the Second
Time: one year

	MATTHEW	MARK	LUKE	JOHN
At the Passover Jesus drives the traders out of the temple. *Jerusalem*				2:13-25
Our Lord's discourse with Nicodemus. *Jerusalem*				3:1-21
Jesus remains in Judea, and baptizes. Further testimony of John the Baptist				3:22-36
John's imprisonment	14:3-5	6:17-20	3:19, 20	
Jesus' departure into Galilee	4:12	1:14	4:14	4:1-3
Our Lord's discourse with the Samaritan woman. Many of the Samaritans believe on him. *Shechem* or *Neapolis*				4:4-12
Jesus teaches publicly *in Galilee*	4:17	1:14, 15	4:14, 15	1:43-45

	MATTHEW	MARK	LUKE	JOHN
Jesus again at Cana, where he heals the son of a nobleman lying ill at Capernaum. *Cana of Galilee*				4:46-54
Jesus at Nazareth: he is there rejected, and fixes his abode at Capernaum	4:13-16		4:10-31	
The call of Simon Peter and Andrew, and of James and John, with the miraculous draught of fishes. *Near Capernaum*	4:18-22	1:16-20	5:1-11	
The healing of the demoniac in the synagogue. *Capernaum*		1:21-28	4:31-37	
The healing of Peter's wife's mother, and many others. *Capernaum*	8:14-17	1:29-34	4:38-41	
Jesus with his disciples goes from Capernaum throughout Galilee	4:23-25	1:35-39	4:42-44	
The healing of a leper. *Galilee*	8:1-4	1:40-45	5:12-16	
The healing of a paralytic. *Capernaum*	9:2-8	2:1-12	5:17-26	
The call of Matthew. *Capernaum*	9:9	2:13, 14	5:27, 28	

Our Lord's Second Passover, and Subsequent Transactions until the Third.
Time: one year

	MATTHEW	MARK	LUKE	JOHN
The Pool of Bethesda; the healing of the infirm man; and our Lord's subsequent discourse. *Jerusalem*				5:1-47
The disciples pluck ears of grain on the Sabbath. *On the way to Galilee?*	12:1-8	2:23-28	6:1-5	
The healing of the withered hand on the Sabbath. *Galilee*	12:9-14	3:1-6	6:6-11	
Jesus arrives at the sea of Tiberias, and is followed by multitudes. *Lake of Galilee*	12:15-21	3:7-12		
Jesus withdraws to the mountain and chooses the Twelve; the multitudes follow him. *Near Capernaum*	10:1-4	3:13-19	6:12-19	
The sermon on the mount. *Near Capernaum*	5:1; 8:1		6:20-49	
The healing of the centurion's servant. *Capernaum*	8:5-13		7:1-10	
The raising of the widow's son. *Nain*			7:11-17	
John the Baptist in prison sends disciples to Jesus. *Galilee. Capernaum?*	11:2-19		7:18-35	
Reflections of Jesus on appealing to his mighty works. *Capernaum*	11:20-30			
While sitting at meat with a Pharisee, Jesus is anointed by a woman who had been a sinner. *Capernaum?*			7:36-50	
Jesus, with the Twelve, makes a second circuit in Galilee			8:1-3	
The healing of a demoniac. The scribes and Pharisees blaspheme. *Galilee*	12:22-37	3:19-30	11:14, 15, 17-23	
The scribes and Pharisees seek a sign. Our Lord's reflections. *Galilee*	12:38-45		11:16, 24-36	
The true disciples of Christ his nearest relatives. *Galilee*	12:46-50	3:31-35	8:19-21	
At a Pharisee's table, Jesus pronounces woes against the Pharisees and others. *Galilee*			11:37-54	
Jesus discourses *to his disciples and the multitude. Galilee*			12:1-59	
The slaughter of certain Galileans. Parable of the barren fig tree. *Galilee*			13:1-9	
Parable of the sower. *Lake of Galilee. Near Capernaum?*	13:1-23	4:1-25	8:4-18	

	MATTHEW	MARK	LUKE	JOHN
Parable of the tares. Other parables. *Near Capernaum?*	13:24-53	4:26-34		
Jesus directs to cross the lake. Incidents. The tempest stilled. *Lake of Galilee*	8:18-27	4:35-41	8:22-25 9:57-62	
The two demoniacs of Gadara. *Southeast coast of the lake of Galilee*	8:28-34; 9:1	5:1-21	8:26-40	
Levi's feast. *Capernaum*	9:10-17	2:15-22	5:29-39	
The raising of Jairus' daughter. The woman with a bloody flux. *Capernaum*	9:18-26	5:22-43		
Two blind men healed, and a dumb spirit cast out. *Capernaum*	9:27-34			
Jesus again at Nazareth, and again rejected	13:54-58	6:1-6		
A third circuit in Galilee. The Twelve instructed, and sent forth. *Galilee*	9:35-38 10:1-42; 11:1	6:6-13	9:1-6	
Herod holds Jesus to be John the Baptist, whom he had just before beheaded. *Galilee? Perea*	14:1-12	6:14-16, 21-29	9:7-9	
The Twelve return, and Jesus retires with them across the lake. Five thousand are fed. *Capernaum. Northeast coast of the lake of Galilee*	14:13-21	6:30-44	9:10-17	6:1-14
Jesus walks upon the water. *Lake of Galilee. Gennesareth*	14:22-36	6:45-56		6:15-21
Our Lord's discourse to the multitude in the synagogue at Capernaum. Many disciples turn back. Peter's profession of faith. *Capernaum*				6:22-71; 7:1

From Our Lord's Third Passover until His Final Departure From Galilee at the Festival of Tabernacles
Time: six months

	MATTHEW	MARK	LUKE	JOHN
Our Lord justifies his disciples for eating with unwashen hands. Pharisaic traditions. *Capernaum*	15:1-20	7:1-23		
The daughter of a Syrophenician woman is healed. *Region of Tyre and Sidon*	15:21-28	7:24-30		
A deaf and dumb man healed; also many others. Four thousand are fed. *The Decapolis*	15:29-39	7:31-37 8:1-9		
The Pharisees and Sadducees again require a sign. *Near Magdala*	15:39; 16:1-4	8:10-12		
The disciples cautioned against the leaven of the Pharisees, etc. *Northeast coast of the lake of Galilee.*	16:5-12	8:13-21		
A blind man healed. *Bethsaida (Julias)*		8:22-26		
Peter and the rest again profess their faith in Christ. *Region of Cesarea Philippi*	16:13-20	8:27-30	9:18-21	
Our Lord foretells his own death and resurrection, and the trials of his followers. *Region of Cesarea Philippi*	16:21-28	8:31-38; 9:1	9:22-27	
The transfiguration. Our Lord's subsequent discourse with the three disciples. *Region of Cesarea Philippi*	17:1-13	9:2-13	9:28-36	
The healing of a demoniac, whom the disciples could not heal. *Region of Cesarea Philippi*	17:14-21	9:14-29	9:37-43	
Jesus again foretells his own death and resurrection. *Galilee*	17:22, 23	9:30-32	9:43-45	
The tribute-money miraculously provided. *Capernaum*	17:24-27	9:33		
The disciples contend who should be the greatest. Jesus exhorts to humility, forbearance, and brotherly love. *Capernaum*	18:1-35	9:33-50	9:46-50	

	MATTHEW	MARK	LUKE	JOHN
The Seventy instructed and sent out. *Capernaum*			10:1-16	
Jesus goes up to the festival of tabernacles. His final departure from Galilee. Incidents in Samaria.			9:51-56	7:2-10
Ten lepers cleansed. *Samaria*			17:11-19	

The Festival of Tabernacles, and the Subsequent Transactions Until Our Lord's Arrival in Bethany, Six Days Before the Fourth Passover
Time: six months, less six days

	MATTHEW	MARK	LUKE	JOHN
Jesus at the festival of tabernacles. His public teaching. *Jerusalem*				7:11-53; 8:1
The woman taken in adultery. *Jerusalem*				8:2-11
Further public teaching of our Lord. He reproves the unbelieving Jews, and escapes from their hands. *Jerusalem*				8:12-59
A lawyer instructed. Love to our neighbor defined. Parable of the good Samaritan. *Near Jerusalem*			10:25-37	
Jesus in the house of Martha and Mary. *Bethany*			10:38-42	
The disciples again taught how to pray. *Near Jerusalem*			11:1-13	
The Seventy return. *Jerusalem*			10:17-24	
A man born blind is healed on the Sabbath. Our Lord's subsequent discourses. *Jerusalem*				9:1-41 10:1-21
Jesus in Jerusalem at the festival of dedication. He retires beyond Jordan. *Jerusalem. Bethabara beyond Jordan*				10:22-42
The raising of Lazarus. *Bethany*				11:1-46
The counsel of Caiaphas against Jesus. He retires from Jerusalem. *Jerusalem. Ephraim*				11:47-54
Jesus beyond Jordan is followed by multitudes. The healing of the infirm woman on the Sabbath. *Valley of Jordan. Perea*	19:1, 2	10:1	13:10-21	
Our Lord goes teaching and journeying towards Jerusalem. He is warned against Herod. *Perea*			13:22-35	
Our Lord dines with a chief Pharisee on the Sabbath. Incidents. *Perea*			14:1-24	
What is required of true disciples. *Perea*			14:25-35	
Parable of the lost sheep, etc. Parable of the prodigal son. *Perea*			15:1-32	
Parable of the unjust steward. *Perea*			16:1-13	
The Pharisee reproved. Parable of the rich man and Lazarus. *Perea*			16:14-31	
Jesus inculcates forbearance, faith, humility. *Perea*			17:1-10	
Christ's coming will be sudden. *Perea*			17:20-37	
Parables: the importunate widow; the Pharisee and publican. *Perea*			18:1-14	
Precepts respecting divorce. *Perea*	19:3-12	10:2-12		
Jesus receives and blesses little children. *Perea*	19:13-15	10:13-16	18:15-17	
The rich young man. Parable of the laborers in the vineyard. *Perea*	19:16-30 20:1-16	10:17-31	18:18-30	
Jesus a third time foretells his death and resurrection. *Perea*	20:17-19	10:32-34	18:31-34	
James and John present their ambitious request. *Perea*	20:20-28	10:35-45		
The healing of two blind men near Jericho	20:29-34	10:46-52	18:35-43 19:1	
The visit to Zaccheus. Parable of the ten pounds. *Jericho*			19:2-28	

	MATTHEW	MARK	LUKE	JOHN
Jesus arrives at Bethany six days before the Passover. *Bethany*				11:55-57 12:1, 9-11

Our Lord's Public Entry into Jerusalem, and the Subsequent Transactions before the Fourth Passover
Time: four days

	MATTHEW	MARK	LUKE	JOHN
Our Lord's public entry into Jerusalem. *Bethany. Jerusalem*	21:1-11, 14-17	11:1-11	19:29-44	12:12-19
The barren fig-tree. The cleansing of the temple. *Bethany. Jerusalem*	21:12, 13, 18, 19	11:12-19	19:45-48, 21:37, 38	
The barren fig-tree withers away. *Between Bethany and Jerusalem*	21:20-22	11:20-26		
Christ's authority questioned. Parable of the two sons. *Jerusalem*	21:23-32	11:27-33	20:1-8	
Parable of the wicked husbandmen. *Jerusalem*	21:33-46	12:1-12	20:9-19	
Parable of the marriage of the king's son. *Jerusalem*	22:1-14			
Insidious question of the Pharisees: tribute to Caesar. *Jerusalem*	22:15-22	12:13-17	20:20-26	
Insidious question of the Sadducees: the resurrection. *Jerusalem*	22:23-33	12:18-27	20:27-40	
A lawyer questions Jesus. The two great commandments. *Jerusalem*	22:34-40	12:28-34		
How is Christ the son of David? *Jerusalem*	22:41-46	12:35-37	20:41-44	
Warnings against the evil example of the scribes and Pharisees. *Jerusalem*	23:1-12	12:38, 39	20:45, 46	
Woes against the scribes and Pharisees. Lamentation over Jerusalem. *Jerusalem*	23:13-19	12:40	20:47	
The widow's mite. *Jerusalem*		12:41-44	21:1-4	
Certain Greeks desire to see Jesus. *Jerusalem*				12:20-36
Reflections upon the unbelief of the Jews. *Jerusalem*				12:37-50
Jesus, on taking leave of the temple, foretells its destruction, and the persecution of his disciples. *Jerusalem. Mount of Olives*	24:1-14	13:1-13	21:5-19	
The signs of Christ's coming to destroy Jerusalem, and to put an end to the Jewish state and dispensation. *Mount of Olives*	24:15-42	13:14-37	21:20-36	
Transition to Christ's final coming at the day of judgment. Exhortation to watchfulness. Parables: the ten virgins; the five talents. *Mount of Olives*	24:43-51 25:1-30			
Scenes of the judgment day. *Mount of Olives*	25:31-46			
The rulers conspire. The supper at Bethany. Treachery of Judas. *Jerusalem. Bethany*	26:1-16	14:1-11	22:1-6	12:2-8
Preparations for the Passover. *Bethany. Jerusalem*	26:17-19	14:12-16	22:7-13	

The Fourth Passover, Our Lord's Passion, and the Accompanying Events until the End of the Jewish Sabbath
Time: two days

	MATTHEW	MARK	LUKE	JOHN
The Passover meal. Contention among the Twelve. *Jerusalem*	26:20	14:17	22:14-18, 24-30	
Jesus washes the feet of his disciples. *Jerusalem*				13:1-20
Jesus points out the traitor. Judas withdraws. *Jerusalem*	26:21-25	14:18-21	22:21-23	13:21-35
Jesus foretells the fall of Peter, and the dispersion of the twelve. *Jerusalem*	26:31-35	14:27-31	22:31-38	13:36-38
The Lord's Supper. *Jerusalem*	26:26-29	14:22-25	22:19, 20	

	MATTHEW	MARK	LUKE	JOHN
Jesus comforts his disciples. The Holy Spirit promised. *Jerusalem*				14:1-31
Christ the true vine. His disciples hated by the world. *Jerusalem*				15:1-27
Persecution foretold. Further promise of the Holy Spirit. Prayer in the name of Christ. *Jerusalem*				16:1-33
Christ's last prayer with his disciples. *Jerusalem*				17:1-26
The agony in Gethsemane. *Mount of Olives*	26:30, 36-46	14:26, 32-42	22:39-46	18:1
Jesus betrayed and made prisoner. *Mount of Olives*	26:47-56	14:43-52	22:47-53	18:2-12
Jesus before Caiaphas. Peter thrice denies him. *Jerusalem*	26:57, 58, 69-75	14:53, 54, 66-72	22:54-62	18:13-18, 25-27
Jesus before Caiaphas and the Sanhedrin. He declares himself to be the Christ; is condemned and mocked. *Jerusalem*	26:59-68	11:56-65	22:63-71	18:19-24
The Sanhedrin lead Jesus away to Pilate. *Jerusalem*	27:1, 2	15:1-5	23:1-5	18:28-38
Christ before the governor. *Jerusalem*	27:11-14			
Jesus before Herod. *Jerusalem*			23:6-12	
Pilate seeks to release Jesus. The Jews demand Barabbas. *Jerusalem*	27:15-26	15:6-15	23:13-25	18:39, 40
Pilate delivers up Jesus to death. He is scourged and mocked. *Jerusalem*	27:26-30	15:15-19		19:1-3
Pilate again seeks to release Jesus. *Jerusalem*				19:4-16
Judas repents and hangs himself. *Jerusalem*	27:3-10			
Jesus is led away to be crucified. *Jerusalem*	27:31-34	15:20-23	23:26-33	19:16, 17
The crucifixion. *Jerusalem*	27:35-38	15:24-28	23:33, 34	19:18-24
The Jews mock at Jesus on the cross. He commends his mother to John. *Jerusalem*	27:39-44	15:29-32	23:35-37, 39-43	19:25-27
Darkness prevails. Christ expires on the cross. *Jerusalem*	27:45-50	15:33-37	23:44-46	19:28-30
The veil of the temple rent, and graves opened. Judgment of the centurion. The women at the cross. *Jerusalem*	27:51-56	15:38-41	23:45, 47-49	
The taking down from the cross. The burial. *Jerusalem*	27:57-61	15:42-47	23:50-56	19:31-42
The watch at the sepulchre. *Jerusalem*	27:62-66			

Our Lord's Resurrection, His Subsequent Appearances, and His Ascension
Time: forty days

	MATTHEW	MARK	LUKE	JOHN
The morning of the resurrection. *Jerusalem*	28:2-4	16:1		
Visit of the women to the sepulchre. Mary Magdalene returns. *Jerusalem*	28:1	16:2-4	24:1-3	20:1, 2
Vision of angels in the sepulchre. *Jerusalem*	28:5-7	16:5-7	24:4-8	
The women return to the city. Jesus meets them. *Jerusalem*	28:8-10	16:8	24:9-11	
Peter and John run to the sepulchre. *Jerusalem*			24:12	20:3-10
Our Lord is seen by Mary Magdalene at the sepulchre. *Jerusalem*		16:9-11		20:11-18
Report of the watch. *Jerusalem*	28:11-15			
Our Lord is seen by Peter. Then by two disciples on the way to Emmaus. *Jerusalem. Emmaus*		16:12, 13	24:13-35	
Jesus appears in the midst of the apostles, Thomas being absent. *Jerusalem*		16:14-18	24:36-49	20:19-23
Jesus appears in the midst of the apostles, Thomas being present. *Jerusalem*				20:24-29

	MATTHEW	MARK	LUKE	JOHN
The apostles go away into Galilee. Jesus shows himself to seven of them at the sea of Tiberias. *Galilee*	28:16			21:1-24
Jesus meets the apostles and over five hundred brothers on a mountain in Galilee. *Galilee*	28:16-20			
Our Lord is seen of James; then of all the apostles. *Jerusalem*				1 Cor. 15:6 1 Cor. 15:7; Acts 1:3-8
The ascension. *Bethany*		16:19, 20	24:50-53	
Conclusion of John's gospel				20:30, 31; 21:25

PARABLES OF CHRIST

Barren fig-tree	Luke 13:6-9
Beam and mote	Luke 6:41, 42
Blind leading the blind	Luke 6:39
Builder of a tower	Luke 14:28-30, 33
Children in the marketplace	Matt. 11:16-19
Children of bridechamber	Matt. 9:15; Mark 2:18.
Children's bread	Mark 7:27-29
Cloud and wind	Luke 12:54-57
Creditor and debtors	Luke 7:41-47
Door, and the hireling	John 10:7-16
Faithful and evil servants	Matt. 24:45-51
Fig-tree leafing	Matt. 24:32-34
Good Samaritan	Luke 10:30-37
Grain of Wheat	John 12:24
Good Shepherd	John 10:1-6
Great Supper	Luke 14:15-24
House divided against itself	Mark 3:25
Importunate friend	Luke 11:5-9
Importunate widow	Luke 18:1-8
Kingdom divided against itself	Mark 3:24
King going to war	Luke 14:31-33
King's marriage feast	Matt. 22:2-14
Laborers hired	Matt. 20:1-16
Leaven	Matt. 13:33; Luke 13:20, 21
Lighted candle	Mark 4:21; Luke 11:33-36
Lost piece of silver	Luke 15:8-10
Lost sheep	Luke 15:3-7; Matt. 18:12-14
Man of the house watching	Matt. 24:43
Man taking a far journey	Mark 13:34-37
Meats defiling not	Matt. 15:10-15
Men bidden to a feast	Luke 14:7-11
Mustard seed	Matt. 13:31, 32; Luke 13:19
Net cast into the sea	Matt. 13:47-50
New cloth and old garment	Matt. 9:16
New wine and old wineskins	Matt. 9:17
Pearl of great price	Matt. 13:45, 46
Pharisee and publican	Luke 18:9-14
Pounds	Luke 19:12-27
Prodigal son	Luke 15:11-32
Rich fool	Luke 12:16-21
Rich man and Lazarus	Luke 16:19-31
Savor of salt	Luke 14:34, 35
Seed growing secretly	Mark 4:26-29
Sheep fallen in a pit	Matt. 12:11, 12
Sower	Matt. 13:3-23; Luke 8:5, 11
Strong man armed	Mark 3:27; Luke 11:21
Talents	Matt. 25:14-30
Tares	Matt. 13:24-30, 36-43
Ten virgins	Matt. 25:1-13
Treasure hid in a field	Matt. 13:44
Tree and its fruit	Luke 6:43-45
Two sons	Matt. 21:28-32
Unclean spirit	Matt. 12:43
Unjust steward	Luke 16:1-8
Unmerciful servant	Matt. 18:23-35
Unprofitable servants	Luke 17:7-10
Vine and branches	John 15:1-5
Waiting servants	Luke 12:35-40
Wicked husbandmen	Matt. 21:33-45
Wind blowing where it wishes	John 3:8
Wise and foolish builders	Matt. 7:24-27
Wise householder	Matt. 13:51, 52
Wise steward	Luke 12:41-48
Woman in travail	John 16:21

MIRACLES OF CHRIST

	MATTHEW	MARK	LUKE	JOHN
Water turned into wine. *Galilee*				2:6-12
Nobleman's son healed. *Galilee*				4:46-54
First draught of fishes. *Capernaum*	4:18-22	1:16-20	5:1-11	
All manner of diseases healed.	4:23, 24	1:34	6:17-19	
Demoniac healed. *Capernaum*		1:21-28	4:31-37	
Peter's wife's mother healed. *Capernaum*	8:14-17	1:29-34	4:38-41	
Leper healed. *Galilee*	8:1-4	1:40-45	5:12-16	
Paralytic healed. *Capernaum*	9:2-8	2:1-12	5:17-26	
Impotent man healed. *Jerusalem*				5:5-9
Withered hand restored. *Galilee*	12:9-14	3:1-6	6:6-11	
Centurion's servant healed. *Capernaum*	8:5-13		7:1-10	
Raising the widow's son. *Nain*			7:11-17	
Cures before John's messengers.	11:4, 5		7:21	
Devil cast out. *Galilee*	12:22, 23		11:14, 15	
Tempest stilled. *Sea of Galilee*	8:23-27	4:35-41	8:22-25	
Two demoniacs healed. *Gadara*	8:27-32	5:1-15	8:26-35	
Jairus' daughter raised. *Capernaum*	9:23-26	5:35-42	8:49-55	
Issue of blood healed. *Capernaum*	9:20-22	5:25-34	8:43-48	
Two blind men healed. *Capernaum*	9:27-31			
A devil cast out, and dumb man cured. *Capernaum*	9:32, 33			
Many sick persons healed. *Capernaum*	14:14			
Feeding of the five thousand. *Capernaum*	14:15-21	6:34-44	9:12-17	6:1-13
Jesus walks upon the water. *Sea of Galilee*	14:24-27	6:45-51		6:19
Peter walking on the sea.	14:29			
Vessel's sudden arrival at the shore.				6:21
Syrophenician woman's daughter healed. *Tyre and Sidon*	15:21-28	7:24-30		
Deaf and dumb man healed. *Decapolis*		7:32-35		
Many sick healed. *Decapolis*	15:29-31			
The feeding of four thousand. *Decapolis*	15:32-39	8:1-9		
Blind man healed. *Bethsaida*		8:22-26		
Devil cast out. *Cesarea Philippi*	17:14-18	9:14-27	9:37-42	
Tribute money provided. *Capernaum*	17:24-27			
Ten lepers cleansed. *Samaria*			17:11-19	
Blind man healed on the Sabbath. *Jerusalem*				9:1-7
Raising of Lazarus. *Bethany*				11:17-44
Healing of the multitudes. *Beyond Jordan*	19:1, 2			
Woman healed of infirmity. *Perea*			13:10-13	
Dropsy cured. *Perea*			14:2-4	
Blind Bartimeus and one other healed. *Jericho*	20:29-34	10:46-52	18:35-43	
Fig-tree blighted. *Bethany*	21:17-20	11:12-14, 20		
Malchus' ear healed. *Mount of Olives*			22:50, 51	
Graves opened, and dead raised.	27:51-53			
Veil of the temple rent.		15:38	23:45	
Resurrection of Jesus.			24:1-6	
His appearance, the doors being shut. *Jerusalem*			24:36-40	20:19
Second draught of fishes. *Sea of Galilee*				21:3-7
His ascension. *Bethany*			24:50, 51	Acts 1:9
Paul's conversion.				Acts 9

OLD TESTAMENT
PROPHECIES
FULFILLED BY CHRIST
Harold Willmington

Old Testament Prediction	*Nature of the Prophecy*	*New Testament Fulfillment*
Isa. 7:14	Born of a virgin	Matt. 1:22,23
2 Sam. 7:11,12; Ps. 132:11; Isa. 9:6; 16:5; Jer. 23:5	Given the throne of David	Luke 1:31,32
Dan. 2:44; 7:14,27; Mic. 4:7	This throne to be an eternal throne	Luke 1:33
Isa. 7:14	To be called Emmanuel	Matt. 1:23
Isa. 40:3-5; Mal. 3:1	To have a forerunner	Luke 1:76-78; 3:3-6; Matt. 3:1-3
Mic. 5:2	To be born in Bethlehem	Matt. 2:5, 6
Ps. 72:10; Isa. 60:3,6,9	To be worshiped by wise men and presented with gifts	Matt. 2:11
Num. 24:8; Hos. 11:1	To be in Egypt for a season	Matt. 2:15
Jer. 31:15	Birthplace to suffer a massacre of infants	Matt. 2:17,18
Isa. 11:1	To be called a Nazarene	Matt. 2:23
Ps. 69:9; 119:139	To be zealous for the Father	John 2:16,17
Isa. 11:2; 61:1,2; Ps. 45:7	To be filled with God's Spirit	Luke 4:18,19
Isa. 53:4	To heal many	Matt. 8:16,17
Isa. 9:1,2; 42:1-3	To deal gently with the Gentiles	Matt 12:17-21; 4:13-16
Isa. 6:9,10	To speak in parables	Matt. 13:10-15
Isa. 53:3; Ps. 69:8	To be rejected by his own	John 1:11; 7:5
Zech. 9:9	To make a triumphal entry into Jerusalem	Matt. 21:4,5
Ps. 8:2	To be praised by little children	Matt. 21:16
Ps. 118:22,23	To be the rejected cornerstone	Matt. 21:42
Isa. 53:1	That his miracles would not be believed	John 12:37,38
Ps. 41:9; 55:12-14	To be betrayed by his friend for *thirty* pieces of silver	Matt. 26:14-16, 21-25
Isa. 53:3	To be a man of sorrows	Matt. 26:37,38
Zech. 13:7	To be forsaken by his disciples	Matt. 26:31,56
Isa. 50:6	To be scourged and spat upon	Matt. 26:67; 27:26
Zech. 11:12,13; Jer. 18:1-4; 19:1-4	His price money to be used to buy a potter's field	Matt. 27:9,10
Isa. 53:12	To be crucified between two thieves	Matt. 27:38
Ps. 69:21	To be given vinegar to drink	Matt. 27:34,48; John 19:28-30

Old Testament Prediction	*Nature of the Prophecy*	*New Testament Fulfillment*
Ps. 22:16; Zech. 12:10	To suffer the piercing of hands and feet	Mark 15:25; John 19:34,37; 20:25-27
Ps. 22:18	His garments to be parted and gambled for	Luke 23:34; John 19:23,24
Ps. 22:7,8	To be surrounded and ridiculed by his enemies	Matt. 27:39-44; Mark 15:29-32
Ps. 22:15	That he would thirst	John 19:28
Ps. 31:5	To commend his spirit to the Father	Luke 23:46
Ps. 34:20; Ex. 12:46; Num. 9:12	No bones to be broken	John 19:33-36
Zech. 12:10	To be stared at in death	John 19:37; Matt. 27:36
Isa. 53:9	To be buried with the rich	Matt. 27:57-60
Ps. 16:10	To be raised from the dead	Matt. 28:2-8
Ps. 24:7-10; Isa. 52:13	To ascend	Mark 16:19; Luke 24:51

INDEX
TO KEY THOUGHT COMMENTARY

This provides a listing of all the subjects discussed in the commentary notes. The reader can also use it to locate scriptures on each of the listed subjects.

INDEX

Proper Names with Pronunciation Guide

ă as in *sat* ā as in *gate* ĕ as in *get* ē as in *be* ĭ as in *hit* ī as in *ice* ŏ as in *got* ō as in *go* ŭ as in *fun* ū as in *use* er as in *herd* ah as in *hurrah* or as in *order* oo as in *soon* oi as in *oil* aw as in *saw* uh as u in *but*

Allammelech (uh·lăm′·mē·lĕk) Josh 19:24–26
Alexander (ăl′·ĕx·ăn′·der) Mk 15:21
Alexandria (ăl·ĕx·ăn′·drē·uh) Acts 18:24
Aliah (uh·lī′·uh) 1 Chron 1:51–54
Alian (uh·lī′·ăn) 1 Chron 1:40
Allon (ăl′·lŏn) 1 Chron 4:34–39
Almodad (ăl·mō′·dăd) Gen 10:26–30
Almon (ăl′·mŏn) Josh 21:17, 18
Almon-diblathaim (ăl′·mŏn·dĭb·luh·thā′·ĭm) Num 33:46
Alpha (ăl′·fah) Rev 1:8
Alphaeus (ăl·fē′·ŭs) Mt 10:2–4
Alush (ā′·lŭsh) Num 33:13
Alvah (ăl′·vuh) Gen 36:40–43
Alvan (ăl′·văn) Gen 36:23
Amad (ā′·măd) Josh 19:24–26
Amal (ā′·măl) 1 Chron 7:35
Amalek (ite) (ăm′·uh·lĕk) (ă·măl′·ē·kīt) Gen 36:10–12 (2 Sam 1:1)
Amana (uh·mă′·nuh) Song 4:8
Amariah (ăm·uh·rī′·uh) 1 Chron 6:4–15
Amasa (uh·mă′·suh) 2 Sam 17:25
Amasai (uh·mă′·sī) 1 Chron 6:25–27
Amashsai (uh·măsh′·sī) Neh 11:10–14
Amasiah (ăm·uh·sī′·uh) 2 Chron 17:16
Amaziah (ăm·uh·zī′·uh) 2 Kgs 14:1
Ami (ā′·mī) Ezra 2:55–57
Amittai (uh·mĭt′·tī) 2 Kgs 14:25
Ammah (ăm′·uh) 2 Sam 2:24
Ammi (ăm′·mī) Hos 2:1
Ammiel (ăm′·mĭ·ĕl) Num 13:3–15
Ammihud (ăm·mī′·hŭd) Num 1:2–15
Amminadab (ăm·mĭn′·uh·dăb) Ex 6:23
Ammizabad (ăm·mĭz′·uh·băd) 1 Chron 27:5, 6
Ammon (ites) (ăm′·ŏn) (īts) Judg 10:6 (Deut 2:20)
Amnon (ăm′·nŏn) 2 Sam 3:2
Amok (ā′·mŏk) Neh 12:1–7
Amon (ā′·mŏn) 2 Kgs 21:18
Amorite (ăm′·or·īt) Gen 10:15–19
Amos (ā′·mŏs) Amos 1:1
Amoz (ā′·mŏz) Isa 1:1
Amphipolis (ăm·fĭp′·ō·lĭs) Acts 17:1
Ampliatus (ăm·plĭ·ā′·tŭs) Rom 16:8
Amram (ăm′·răm) Ex 6:18
Amraphel (ăm′·rah·fĕl) Gen 14:1
Amzi (ăm′·zī) 1 Chron 6:44–47
Anab (ā′·năb) Josh 11:21
Anah (ăn′·uh) Gen 36:2, 3
Anaharath (uh·nā′·huh·răth) Josh 19:17–23
Anaiah (uh·nī′·uh) Neh 8:1–5
Anak (ā′·năk) Num 13:22
Anakim (ăn′·uh·kĭm) Deut 1:28
Anamim (ăn′·uh·mĭm) Gen 10:13, 14
Anammelech (uh·năm′·mē·lĕk) 2 Kgs 17:31
Anan (ā′·năn) Neh 10:14–27
Anani (uh·nā′·nī) 1 Chron 3:24
Ananiah (ăn·uh·nī′·uh) Neh 3:23
Ananias (ăn·uh·nī′·ŭs) Acts 5:1
Anath (ā′·năth) Judg 3:31
Anathoth (ăn′·uh·thŏth) Josh 21:17, 18
Andrew (ăn′·drū) Mk 1:29, 30
Andronicus (ăn·drŏn′·ĭ·kŭs) Rom 16:7
Anem (ā′·nĕm) 1 Chron 6:73
Aner (ā′·ner) Gen 14:13
Aniam (uh·nī′·ŭm) 1 Chron 7:19
Anim (ā′·nĭm) Josh 15:48–62
Anna (ăn′·uh) Lk 2:36, 37
Annas (ăn′·năs) Lk 3:1, 2
Antioch (ăn′·tĭ·ŏk) Acts 6:5
Antipas (ăn′·tĭ·păs) Rev 2:13
Antipatris (ăn·tĭp′·uh·trĭs) Acts 23:31
Anthothijah (ăn·thŭ·thī′·jah) 1 Chron 8:22–25
Anub (ā′·nŭb) 1 Chron 4:8
Apelles (uh·pĕl′·lēz) Rom 16:10
Aphek (ā′·fĕk) Josh 12:8–24
Aphekah (ă·fē′·kuh) Josh 15:48–62
Aphiah (uh·fī′·uh) 1 Sam 9:1
Aphik (ā′·fĭk) Judg 1:31, 32
Apollonia (ăp·uh·lō′·nĭ·uh) Acts 17:1
Apollos (uh·pŏl′·ŏs) Acts 18:24
Apollyon (uh·pŏl′·yŏn) Rev 9:11
Appa-im (ăp′·puh·ĭm) 1 Chron 2:30
Apphia (ăp′·fē·uh) Philem 2
Aquila (ă·kwĭ′·luh) Acts 18:2, 3
Ar (ahr) Num 21:27–30
Ara (ahr′·uh) 1 Chron 7:38
Arab (ā′·rŭb) Josh 15:48–62
Arabah (ahr′·uh·buh) Josh 18:18
Arabia (n) (uh·rā′·bē·uh) (n) Gal 1:17 (Ezek 27:19)
Arad (ahr′·ŭd) 1 Chron 8:15, 16
Arah (ahr′·uh) 1 Chron 7:39
Aram (ahr′·răm) Gen 10:22
Aramaean (ahr′·uh·mē′·ŭn) 1 Chron 7:14
Aran (ahr′·ŭn) Gen 36:28–30
Ararat (ahr′·ruh·răt) Gen 8:3, 4
Araunah (uh·raw′·nuh) 2 Sam 24:18
Arbath (ahr′·băth) 1 Chron 11:26–47
Archelaus (ahr′·kĕ·lā′·ŭs) Mt 2:22
Archippus (ahr·kĭp′·ŭs) Col 4:17
Ard (ites) (ahrd′) (īts) Gen 46:19–22 (Num 26:40)
Ardon (ahr′·dŏn) 1 Chron 2:18
Areli (te) (uh·rē′·lī) (t) Gen 46:16, 17 (Num 26:15–18)
Aretas (ăr′·ē·tās) 2 Cor 11:32
Argob (ahr′·gŭb) Deut 3:4
Aridai (ahr′·ĭ·dī) Esth 9:7–10
Aridatha (ahr·ĭ·dā′·thuh) Esth 9:7–10
Arieh (uh·rī′·ĕh) 2 Kgs 15:25
Ari-el (ahr′·ĭ·ĕl) Ezra 8:16
Arimathea (ăr·ĭ·muh·thē′·uh) Mt 27:57
Arioch (ahr′·ĭ·ŏk) Gen 14:1
Arisai (ahr′·ĭ·sī) Esth 9:7–10
Aristarchus (ăr·ĭs·tahr′·kŭs) Acts 19:29
Aristobulus (ăr·ĭs·tŏb′·ū·lŭs) Rom 16:10
Arkites (ahr′·kīts) Gen 10:15–19
Armageddon (ahr·muh·gĕd′·ŭn) Rev 16:16
Armoni (ahr·mō′·nī) 2 Sam 21:8
Arnan (ahr′·nŭn) 1 Chron 3:21, 22
Arnon (ahr′·nŏn) Num 21:13
Arod (ites) (ahr′·ŭd) (īts) Num 26:15–18
Arodi (uh·rō′·dī) Gen 46:16, 17
Aroer (uh·rō′·er) Deut 2:35, 36
Arpad (ahr′·păd) 2 Kgs 18:34
Arpachshad (ahr·păk′·shăd) Gen 10:22
Artaxerxes (ahr·tuh·zerk′·sēz) Ezra 4:17
Artemas (ahr′·tē·mŭs) Tit 3:12
Arubboth (uh·roo′·bŏth) 1 Kgs 4:10
Arumah (uh·roo′·muh) Judg 9:41
Arvad (ites) (ahr′·văd) (īts) Ezek 27:8 (Gen 10:15–19)
Arza (ahr′·zuh) 1 Kgs 16:9
Asa (ā′·suh) 1 Kgs 15:8
Asahel (ăs′·uh·hĕl) 2 Sam 2:18
Asaiah (uh·sā′·uh) 2 Kgs 22:12
Asaph (ā′·săf) 2 Kgs 18:37
Asarel (ăs′·uh·rĕl) 1 Chron 4:16
Asenath (ăs′·ē·năth) Gen 41:45
Ashan (ā·shŭn) Josh 15:37–44
Asharelah (ăsh·uh·rē′·luh) 1 Chron 25:2
Ashbel (ite) (ăsh′·bĕl) (īt) Gen 46:19–22 (Num 26:38–41)
Ashdod (ites) (ăsh′·dŏd) (īts) Josh 15:46 (Neh 4:7)
Asher (im) (ăsh′·er) (ĭm) Gen 30:13 (2 Chron 17:6)
Ashima (ăsh′·ĭ·muh) 2 Kgs 17:30
Ashkelon (ăsh′·kĕ·lŏn) Judg 1:18
Ashkenaz (ăsh′·kĕ·năz) Gen 10:3
Ashnah (ăsh′·nuh) Josh 15:33–36
Ashpenaz (ăsh′·pĕ·năz) Dan 1:3, 4
Ashtaroth (ăsh′·tuh·rŏth) Judg 2:12–14
Ashteroth-karnaim (ăsh′·tĕ·rŏth·kahr·nā′·ĭm) Gen 14:5, 6
Ashur (ăsh′·ŭr) 1 Chron 2:24
Ashvath (ăsh′·văth) 1 Chron 7:33
Asnah (ăs′·nuh) Ezra 2:43–54
Aspatha (ăs·pā′·thuh) Esth 9:7–10
Asriel (ăs′·rĭ·ĕl) Num 26:28–37
Asshur (im) (ăz′·shŭr) (ĭm) Gen 10:22 (Gen 25:3)
Assir (ăs′·ser) Ex 6:24
Assos (ă′·sŏs) Acts 20:13
Assyria (ns) (uh·sĭr′·ē·uh) (nz) Gen 10:11, 12 (Isa 10:12)
Asyncritus (uh·sĭn′·krĭ·tŭs) Rom 16:14
Atad (ā′·tăd) Gen 50:10
Atarah (ăt′·uh·ruh) 1 Chron 2:26
Ataroth (ăt′·uh·rŏth) Num 32:3, 4
Ater (ā′·ter) Ezra 2:3–35
Athach (ā′·thăk) 1 Sam 30:27–31
Athaiah (uh·thī′·uh) Neh 11:4–6
Athaliah (ăth·uh·lī′·uh) 2 Kgs 8:26
Athlai (ăth′·lī) Ezra 10:28
Athenians (uh·thē′·nē·uhnz) Acts 17:21
Athens (ăth′·ĕnz) Acts 17:15
Atroth-shophan (ăt′·rŏth·shō′·fŭn) Num 32:34–36
Attai (ăt′·tī) 1 Chron 2:34, 35
Attalia (ăt·tuh·lī′·uh) Acts 14:25
Augustus (uh·gŭs′·tŭs) Lk 2:1
Avith (ā′·vĭth) Gen 36:31–39
Avva (ă′·vuh) 2 Kgs 17:24
Avvim (ă′·vĭm) Josh 18:21–28
Azaliah (ăz·uh·lī′·uh) 2 Kgs 22:3, 4
Azaniah (ăz·uh·nī′·uh) Neh 10:9–13
Azarel (ăz′·uh·rĕl) Neh 12:35, 36
Azaz (ā′·zăz) 1 Chron 5:7, 8
Azaziah (ăz·uh·zī′·uh) 1 Chron 15:21
Azbuk (ăz′·bŭk) Neh 3:16
Azekah (uh·zē′·kuh) Josh 10:10
Azel (ā′·zĕl) 1 Chron 8:37
Azgad (ăz′·găd) Ezra 2:3–35
Aziel (ā′·zĭ·ĕl) 1 Chron 15:20
Aziza (uh·zī′·zuh) Ezra 10:27
Azmaveth (ăz′·muh·vĕth) 2 Sam 23:31

Azmon (ăz′·mŏn) Num 34:4
Aznoth-tabor (ăz′·nŏth·tā′·bor) Josh 19:34
Azor (ā′·zor) Mt 1:13
Azotus (uh·zō′·tŭs) Acts 8:40
Azrikam (ăz·rī′·kăm) 1 Chron 3:23
Azubah (uh·zoo′·buh) 1 Kgs 22:42
Azzan (ăz′·ŭn) Num 34:16–28
Azzur (ăz′·er) Neh 10:14–27
Baal (bā′·ŭl) Num 25:3
Baalah (bā′·uh·luh) Josh 15:10, 11
Baalath-beer (bā′·uh·lăth·bē′·er) Josh 19:8
Baal-berith (bā′·ŭl·bē′·rĭth) Judg 8:33
Baal-gad (bā′·ŭl·găd) Josh 11:17
Baal-hamon (bā′·ŭl·hā′·mŏn) Song 8:11
Baal-hanan (bā′·ŭl·hā′·nŭn) Gen 36:31–39
Baal-hazor (bā′·ŭl·hā′·zor) 2 Sam 13:23
Baal-hermon (bā′·ŭl·her′·mŏn) Judg 3:1–3
Baalis (bā′·uh·lĭs) Jer 40:13, 14
Baal-meon (bā′·ŭl·mē′·ŏn) Num 32:37, 38
Baal-peor (bā′·ŭl·pē′·or) Deut 4:3
Baal-perazim (bā′·ŭl·pĕ·rā′·zĭm) 2 Sam 5:20
Baal-shalishah (bā′·ŭl·shăl′·ĭ·shuh) 2 Kgs 4:42
Baal-tamar (bā′·ŭl·tā′·mahr) Judg 20:33
Baal-zebub (bā′·ŭl·zē′·bŭb) 2 Kgs 1:2
Baal-zephon (bā′·ŭl·zē′·fŏn) Ex 14:2
Baana (bā′·uh·nuh) 1 Kgs 4:8–19
Baanah (bā′·uh·nuh) 2 Sam 4:2, 3
Baara (bā′·uh·ruh) 1 Chron 8:8–10
Ba-aseiah (bā·uh·sē′·ĭ·uh) 1 Chron 6:39–43
Baasha (bā′·uh·shuh) 1 Kgs 15:16
Babel (bā′·bŭl) Gen 10:10
Babylon (bă′·bĭ·lŏn) Gen 11:2
Baharum (buh·hah′·rŭm) 1 Chron 11:26–47
Bahurim (buh·hū′·rĭm) 2 Sam 16:5
Bakbakkar (băk·băk′·kahr) 1 Chron 9:15, 16
Bakbuk (băk′·bŭk) Ezra 2:43–54
Bakbukiah (băk·boo·kī′·uh) Neh 11:15–17
Balaam (bā′·lŭm) Num 22:5, 6
Baladan (băl′·uh·dŭn) 2 Kgs 20:12
Balah (bā′·luh) Josh 19:2–7
Balak (bā′·lŭk) Num 22:2, 3
Bamah (bā′·muh) Ezek 20:29
Bamoth (bā′·mŏth) Num 21:19
Bamoth-baal (bā′·mŏth·bā′·ŭl) Josh 13:17
Bani (bā′·nī) 2 Sam 23:24–39
Barabbas (buh·răb′·ŭs) Mk 15:7
Barachel (bahr′·uh·kĕl) Job 32:2
Barachiah (bahr·uh·kī′·uh) Mt 23:35
Barak (bahr′·ŭk) Judg 4:6
Bariah (buh·rī′·uh) 1 Chron 3:21, 22
Bar-Jesus (bahr·jē′·sŭs) Acts 13:6, 7
Barkos (bahr′·kŏs) Ezra 2:43–54
Barnabas (bahr′·nuh·bŭs) Acts 9:27
Barsabbas (bahr·să′·bŭs) Acts 1:23
Bartholomew (bahr·thŏl′·uh·mū) Mt 10:2–4
Bartimaeus (bahr·tĭ·mā′·ŭs) Mk 10:46
Baruch (bahr·ook′) Jer 32:12
Barzillai (bahr·zĭl′·ī) 2 Sam 17:27
Basemath (bā′·suh·măth) Gen 26:34
Bashan (bā′·shŭn) Num 21:33
Bath-rabbim (băth′·răb′·bĭm) Song 7:4
Bath-sheba (băth·shē′·buh) 2 Sam 11:3
Bath-shua (băth·shoo′·uh) 1 Chron 3:5
Bavvai (bā′·vī) Neh 3:18
Bazlith (băz′·lĭth) Neh 7:46–56
Bazluth (băz′·lŭth) Ezra 2:43–54
Bealiah (bē·uh·lī′·uh) 1 Chron 12:3–7
Be-aloth (bē′·uh·lŏth) Josh 15:21–32
Bebai (bē′·bī) Ezra 8:2–14
Becher (ites) (bē′·ker) (īts) Gen 46:19–22 (Num 26:28–37)
Becorath (bē·cō′·răth) 1 Sam 9:1
Bedad (bē′·dăd) Gen 36:31–39
Bedeiah (bĕ·dī′·uh) Ezra 10:34–42
Beeliada (bē·ĕ·lī′·uh·duh) 1 Chron 14:4–7
Beelzebub (bē·ĕl′·zĕ·bŭb) Mt 12:24
Beer (bē′·ĕr) Num 21:16
Be-era (bē·ē′·ruh) 1 Chron 7:36, 37
Beerah (bē·ē′·ruh) 1 Chron 5:6
Be-eri (bē·ē′·rī) Gen 26:34
Beer-lahai-roi (bē′·ĕr·lah·hī′·roi) Gen 24:62
Be-eroth (bē·ĕr′·ŏth) Josh 9:17
Beer-sheba (bē′·ĕr·shē′·buh) Gen 21:31
Be-eshterah (bē·ĕsh·tē′·ruh) Josh 21:27
Bel (bĕl) Isa 46:1, 2
Bela (ites) (bē′·luh) (īts) Gen 14:2 (Num 26:38–41)
Belshazzar (bĕl·shăz′·zŭr) Dan 5:1
Benaiah (bĕ·nā′·ĭ·uh) 2 Sam 8:18
Benammi (bĕn·ăm′·mī) Gen 19:38
Bene-berek (bĕn·ē·bē′·răk) Josh 19:41–46
Bene-jaakan (bē′·nē·jā′·uh·kŭn) Num 33:15–37
Ben-hadad (bĕn·hā′·dăd) 1 Kgs 15:18
Ben-hail (bĕn·hā′·ĭl) 2 Chron 17:7–9
Ben-hanan (bĕn·hā′·nŭn) 1 Chron 4:20
Ben-hesed (bĕn·hē′·sĕd) 1 Kgs 4:8–19
Beninu (bē·nī′·noo) Neh 10:9–13
Benjamin (ite) (bĕn′·juh·mĭn) (īt) Gen 35:18 (Judg 3:15)
Beno (bē′·nō) 1 Chron 24:26, 27
Ben-oni (bĕn·ō′·nī) Gen 35:18
Ben-zoheth (bĕn·zō′·hĕth) 1 Chron 4:20
Beon (bē′·ŏn) Num 32:3, 4
Beor (bē′·or) Gen 36:31–39
Bera (bē′·ruh) Gen 14:2
Beracah (bĕr′·uh·kuh) 1 Chron 12:3–7
Berachiah (bĕr·ah·kī′·uh) 1 Chron 6:39–43
Beraiah (bĕ·rā′·ĭ·uh) 1 Chron 8:19–21
Beroea (bĕ·rē′·uh) Acts 17:10
Berechiah (bĕr·ĕ·kī′·uh) 1 Chron 3:19, 20
Bered (bē′·rĕd) Gen 16:14
Beri (ites) (bē′·rī) (īts) 1 Chron 7:36, 37 (Num 26:44–47)
Beriah (bē·rī′·uh) Gen 46:16, 17
Bernice (bĕr·nī′·sē) Acts 25:13
Berothah (bĕ·rō′·thuh) Ezek 47:16
Berothai (bĕ·rō′·thī) 2 Sam 8:8
Besai (bē′·sī) Ezra 2:43–54
Besodeiah (bĕs·uh·dē′·uh) Neh 3:6
Besor (bē′·sor) 1 Sam 30:9, 10
Betah (bē′·tuh) 2 Sam 8:8
Beten (bē′·tĕn) Josh 19:24–26
Beth-anath (bĕth·ā′·năth) Josh 19:35–39
Beth-anoth (bĕth·ā′·nŏth) Josh 15:48–62
Bethany (bĕth′·ă·nē) Mt 21:17
Beth-arabah (bĕth·ahr′·uh·buh) Josh 15:6
Beth-ashbea (bĕth·ăsh′·bē·uh) 1 Chron 4:21, 22
Beth-arbel (bĕth·ahr′·bĕl) Hos 10:14
Beth-aven (bĕth·ā′·vĕn) Josh 18:12
Beth-azmaveth (bĕth·ăz′·muh·vĕth) Neh 7:8–38
Beth-baal-meon (bĕth·bā′·ŭl·mē′·ŏn) Josh 13:17
Beth-barah (bĕth·bahr′·uh) Judg 7:24
Beth-biri (bĕth·bĭr′·ī) 1 Chron 4:31
Beth-car (bĕth′·kahr) 1 Sam 7:11
Beth-dagon (bĕth·dā′·gŏn) Josh 15:37–44
Beth-diblathaim (bĕth′·dĭb·luh·thā′·ĭm) Jer 48:22
Bethel (bĕth′·ĕl) Gen 12:8
Beth-emek (bĕth·ē′·mĕk) Josh 19:27
Bethesda (bĕth·ĕz′·duh) Jn 5:2
Beth-ezel (bĕth·ē′·zĕl) Mic 1:11
Beth-gader (bĕth·gā′·der) 1 Chron 2:51
Beth-gamul (bĕth·gā′·mŭl) Jer 48:23
Beth-haccerem (bĕth·hăk·ē′·rĕm) Neh 3:14
Beth-haram (bĕth·hā′·rŭm) 1 Chron 4:21, 22
Beth-haran (bĕth·hā′·rŭn) Num 32:34–35
Beth-hoglah (bĕth·hŏg′·luh) Josh 15:6
Beth-horon (bĕth·hō′·rŏn) Josh 10:10
Beth-jeshimoth (bĕth·jĕsh′·ĭ·mŏth) Num 33:49
Beth-le-aphrah (bĕth′·lĕ·ăf′·ruh) Mic 1:10
Beth-lebaoth (bĕth·lĕ·bā′·ŏth) Josh 19:2–7
Bethlehem (bĕth′·lĕ·hĕm) Gen 35:19
Beth-maacah (bĕth·mā′·uh·kuh) 2 Sam 20:14
Beth-marcaboth (bĕth·mahr′·kuh·bŏth) Josh 19:2–7
Beth-meon (bĕth·mē′·ŏn) Jer 48:23
Beth-nimrah (bĕth·nĭm′·ruh) Num 32:34–36
Beth-pelet (bĕth·pĕl′·ĕt) Josh 15:21–32
Beth-pazzez (bĕth·păz′·zĕz) Josh 19:17–23
Beth-peor (bĕth·pē′·or) Deut 3:29
Bethphage (bĕth′·fuh·gē) Mt 21:1
Bethrapha (bĕth·rā′·fuh) 1 Chron 4:11, 12
Beth-rehob (bĕth·rē′·hŏb) Judg 18:28
Bethsaida (bĕth·sā′·ĭ·duh) Mk 6:45
Beth-shan (bĕth·shăn) 1 Sam 31:10

Beth-shean (bĕth·shē′·ŭn) Josh 17:11
Beth-shemesh (bĕth·shē′·mĕsh) Josh 15:10, 11
Beth-shittah (bĕth·shĭt′·tuh) Judg 7:22
Beth-tappu-ah (bĕth·tăp′·pū·uh) Josh 15:48–62
Bethuel (bĕ·thū′·ĕl) Gen 22:20–23
Bethul (bĕ′·thūl) Josh 19:2–7
Beth-zur (bĕth·zoor) Josh 15:48–62
Betonim (bĕt′·ō·nĭm) Josh 13:26
Bezai (bē′·zī) Ezra 2:3–35
Bezalel (bĕz′·uh·lĕl) Ex 31:1, 2
Bezek (bē′·zĕk) Judg 1:4–6
Bezer (bē′·zer) Deut 4:43
Bichri (bĭk′·rī) 2 Sam 20:1
Bidkar (bĭd′·kahr) 2 Kgs 9:25
Bigtha (bĭg′·thuh) Esth 1:10
Bigthan (bĭg′·thăn) Esth 2:21
Bigthana (bĭg·thā′·nuh) Esth 6:2
Bigvai (bĭg′·vī) Ezra 2:2
Bildad (bĭl′·dăd) Job 2:11
Bile-am (bĭl′·ē·ăm) 1 Chron 6:70
Bilgah (bĭl′·guh) 1 Chron 24:7–18
Bilgai (bĭl′·gī) Neh 10:1–8
Bilhah (bĭl′·huh) Gen 29:29
Bilhan (bĭl′·hăn) Gen 36:27
Bilshan (bĭl′·shăn) Ezra 2:2
Bimhal (bĭm′·hŭl) 1 Chron 7:33
Bine-a (bĭn′·ē·uh) 1 Chron 8:37
Binnui (bĭn′·noo·ī) Ezra 8:33
Birsha (ber′·shuh) Gen 14:2
Birzaith (ber′·zā·ĭth) 1 Chron 7:31
Bishlam (bĭsh′·lŭm) Ezra 4:7
Bithynia (bĭ·thĭn′·ĭ·uh) Acts 16:7
Biziothiah (bĭz·ĭ·uh·thī′·uh) Josh 15:21–32
Biztha (bĭz′·thuh) Esth 1:10
Blastus (blăs′·tŭs) Acts 12:20
Boaz (bō′·ăz) Ruth 2:1
Bocheru (bō′·kĕ·roo) 1 Chron 8:38
Bochim (bō′·kĭm) Judg 2:1
Bohan (bō′·hăn) Josh 15:6
Borashan (bor·ăsh′·ŭn) 1 Sam 30:30
Bozez (bō′·zĕz) 1 Sam 14:4
Bozkath (bŏz′·kăth) Josh 15:37–44
Bozrah (bŏz′·ruh) Gen 36:31–39
Bukki (bŭk′·kī) Num 34:16–28
Bukkiah (bŭ·kī′·uh) 1 Chron 24:4, 5
Bunah (boo′·nuh) 1 Chron 2:25
Bunni (bŭn′·nī) Neh 9:4
Buz (bŭz) Gen 22:20–23
Buzi (te) (bŭz·ī) (t) Ezek 1:1–3 (Job 32:2)
Cabbon (kăb′·bŏn) Josh 15:37–44
Caesar (sē′·zahr) Mt 22:21
Caesarea (sĕs·uh·rē′·uh) Acts 8:40
Caesarea Philippi (sĕs·uh·rē′·uh fĭl′·ĭ·pī) Mt 16:13
Caiaphas (kā′·uh·fŭs) Jn 11:49
Cainan (kā·ī′·nŭn) Lk 3:23–38
Calah (kā′·luh) Gen 10:11, 12
Calcol (kăl′·kŏl) 1 Chron 2:6
Caleb (kā′·lĕb) Num 13:30
Calneh (kăl′·nĕh) Gen 10:10
Calno (kăl′·nō) Isa 10:9
Cana (kā′·nuh) Jn 2:1
Canaan (ites) (kā′·nŭn) (īts) Gen 12:5 (Gen 9:24, 25)
Candace (kăn·dā′·sē) Acts 8:27
Canneh (kăn′·nĕh) Ezek 27:23
Capernaum (kah·per′·nuh·ŭm) Mt 4:12, 13
Caphtor (kăf′·tor) Deut 2:23
Caphtorim (kăf′·tuh·rĭm) Gen 10:13, 14
Cappadocia (kăp·uh·dō′·sĭ·uh) Acts 2:9
Carkas (kahr′·kăs) Esth 1:10
Carchemish (kahr′·kĕ·mĭsh) Jer 46:2
Carmel (kahr′·mĕl) Josh 12:8–24
Carmi (kahr′·mī) Gen 46:8–14
Carpus (kahr′·pŭs) 2 Tim 4:13
Carshena (kahr·shē′·nuh) Esth 1:13–15
Casiphia (kăs·ĭ·fī′·uh) Ezra 8:17
Casluhim (kăs′·loo·hĭm) Gen 10:13, 14
Cenchrea (sĕn′·krē·uh) Acts 18:18
Chaldea (ns) (kăl·dē′·uh) (nz) Isa 47:1 (Job 1:17)
Chebar (kē′·bahr) Ezek 3:14, 15
Ched-or-laomer (kĕd′·or·luh·ō′·mer) Gen 14:4
Chelal (kē′·lăl) Ezra 10:30
Cheluhi (kĕl′·oo·hī) Ezra 10:35
Chelub (kē′·lŭb) 1 Chron 4:11, 12
Chelubai (kĕ·loo′·bī) 1 Chron 2:9
Chemosh (kē′·mōsh) Num 21:27–30
Chenaanah (kĕ·nā′·uh·nuh) 1 Kgs 22:11
Chenani (kĕ·nā′·nī) Neh 9:4
Chenaniah (kĕn·uh·nī′·uh) 1 Chron 15:22
Chephar-ammoni (kē′·fer·ăm′·muh·nī) Josh 18:21–28
Cheran (kē′·rŭn) Gen 36:26
Cherith (ites) (kē′·rĭth) (īts) 1 Kgs 17:3 (Ezek 25:16)
Chesalon (kĕs′·uh·lŏn) Josh 15:10, 11
Chesed (kē′·sĕd) Gen 22:20–23
Chesil (kē′·sĭl) Josh 15:21–32
Chesulloth (kĕ·sŭl′·lŏth) Josh 19:17–23
Chezib (kē′·zĭb) Gen 38:3–5
Chidon (kī′·dŏn) 1 Chron 13:9
Chileab (kĭl′·ē·ăb) 2 Sam 3:3
Chilion (kĭl′·ĭ·ŭn) Ruth 1:1
Chilmad (kĭl′·măd) Ezek 27:23
Chimham (kĭm′·hăm) 2 Sam 19:37
Chinnereth (kĭn′·ĕ·rĕth) Deut 3:17
Chinneroth (kĭn′·ĕ·rŏth) Josh 11:1
Chios (kī′·ŏs) Acts 20:15
Chislon (kĭs′·lŭn) Num 34:16–28
Chisloth-tabor (kĭs′·lŏth·tā′·bor) Josh 19:12
Chitlish (kĭt′·lĭsh) Josh 15:37–44
Chloe (klō′·ē) 1 Cor 1:11
Chorazin (kō·rā′·zĭn) Mt 11:21
Chuza (koo′·zuh) Lk 8:3
Cilicia (sĭ·lĭ′·sĭ·uh) Acts 15:23
Clauda (klawd′·uh) Acts 27:16
Claudia (klawd′·ĭ·uh) 2 Tim 4:21
Claudius (klawd′·dĭ·ŭs) Acts 11:28
Clement (klĕ′·mĕnt) Phil 4:3
Cleopas (klē′·uh·pŭs) Lk 24:18
Cnidus (nī′·dŭs) Acts 27:7, 8
Colhozeh (kŏl·hō′·zeh) Neh 3:15
Colosse (kō·lŏ′·sē) Col 1:2
Conaniah (kŏn·uh·nī′·uh) 2 Chron 35:9
Coniah (kō·nī′·uh) Jer 22:24, 25
Corinth (ians) (kor′·ĭnth) (kor·ĭn′·thĭ·ănz) Acts 19:1 (1 Cor 14:36)
Cornelius (kor·nē′·lĭ·ŭs) Acts 10:1
Cos (kŏs) Acts 21:1
Cosam (kō′·săm) Lk 3:23–38
Cozbi (kŏz′·bī) Num 25:15
Cozeba (kō·zē′·buh) 1 Chron 4:21, 22
Crescens (krĕs′·sĕnz) 2 Tim 4:10
Cretans (krĕt′·ŭnz) Acts 2:11
Crete (krēt) Acts 27:7, 8
Crispus (krĭs′·pŭs) Acts 18:8
Cun (koon) 1 Chron 18:8
Cush (ite) (kŭsh) (īt) Gen 10:6 (Num 12:1)
Cushan (koosh′·ăn) Hab 3:7
Cushan-rishathaim (koo′·shăn·rĭsh·uh·thā′·ĭm) Judg 3:8
Cuth (kŭth) 2 Kgs 17:30
Cuthah (kū′·thuh) 2 Kgs 17:24
Cyprus (sī′·prŭs) Acts 4:36
Cyrene (sī·rē′·nē) Mt 27:32
Cyrus (sī′·rŭs) 2 Chron 36:22, 23
Dabbasheth (dăb′·bĕ·shĕth) Josh 19:11
Daberath (dăb′·ĕ·răth) Josh 19:12
Dagon (dā′·gŏn) Judg 16:23, 24
Dalaiah (dĕ·lā′·uh) 1 Chron 3:24
Dalmanutha (dăl·muh·noo′·thuh) Mk 8:10
Dalmatia (dăl·mā′·shuh) 2 Tim 4:10
Dalphon (dăl′·fŏn) Esth 9:7–10
Damaris (dăm′·uh·rĭs) Acts 17:34
Damascus (dah·măs′·kŭs) Gen 15:2, 3
Dan-jaan (dăn′·jā·ăn) 2 Sam 24:6
Daniel (dăn′·ĭ·ĕl) Dan 1:6
Dannah (dăn′·nuh) Josh 15:48–62
Dara (dahr′·uh) 1 Chron 2:6
Darda (dahr′·duh) 1 Kgs 4:31
Darius (duh·rī′·ŭs) Ezra 4:4, 5
Darkon (dahr′·kŏn) Ezra 2:55–57
Dathan (dā′·thŭn) Num 16:1
David (dā′·vĭd) Ruth 4:18–22
Debir (dē′·ber) Josh 10:3
Deborah (dĕb′·or·uh) Judg 4:4
Decapolis (dĕ·căp′·ō·lĭs) Mk 5:20
Dedan (dē′·dăn) Gen 10:7
Delaiah (dĕ·lī′·uh) 1 Chron 24:7–18
Delilah (dĕ·lī′·luh) Judg 16:4
Demas (dē′·mŭs) Col 4:14
Demetrius (dĕ·mē′·trĭ·ŭs) Acts 19:24
Derbe (der′·bē) Acts 14:5, 6
Deuel (doo′·ĕl) Num 1:2–15
Deuteronomy (doo·ter·ŏn′·uh·mē)
Diana (dī·ăn′·uh) Acts 19:24
Diblaim (dĭb·lā′·ĭm) Hos 1:3
Dibon (dī′·bŏn) Num 21:27–30
Dibon-gad (dī′·bŏn·găd) Num 33:45
Dibri (dĭb′·rī) Lev 24:11
Diklah (dĭk′·luh) Gen 10:26–30
Dilean (dĭ′·lē·ŭn) Josh 15:37–44
Dimnah (dĭm′·nuh) Josh 21:34, 35
Dimonah (dĭ·mō′·nuh) Josh 15:21–32
Dinah (dī′·nuh) Gen 30:21
Dinhabah (dĭn′·huh·buh) Gen 36:31–39
Dionysius (dī·uh·nĭs′·ĭ·ŭs) Acts 17:34
Diotrephes (dī·ŏt′·rĕ·fēz) 3 Jn 9
Dishan (dī′·shăn) Gen 36:28–30
Dishon (dī′·shŏn) Gen 36:20, 21
Dizahab (dī′·zuh·hăb) Deut 1:1
Dodai (dō′·dī) 1 Chron 27:4
Dodanim (dō′·duh·nĭm) Gen 10:4
Dodavahu (dō·dăv′·uh·hū) 2 Chron 20:37
Dodo (dō′·dō) 2 Sam 23:9
Doeg (dō′·ĕg) 1 Sam 21:7
Dophkah (dŏf′·kuh) Num 33:12
Dorcas (dor′·kŭs) Acts 9:36
Dothan (dō′·thăn) Gen 37:17
Drusilla (droo·sĭl′·luh) Acts 24:24
Dumah (doo′·muh) Gen 25:12–15
Dura (dū′·ruh) Dan 3:1
Ebal (ē′·bŭl) Gen 36:23
Ebed (ē′·bĕd) Judg 9:26

Ebed-melech (ē'·bĕd·mĕl'·ĕk) Jer 38:7
Ebenezer (ĕ·bĕn·nē'·zer) 1 Sam 4:1
Eber (ē'·ber) Gen 10:21
Ebiasaph (ĕ·bī'·uh·săf) 1 Chron 6:22–24
Ecclesiastes (ē·klē·zē·ăs'·tēz)
Eden (ē'·dĕn) Gen 2:8
Eder (ē'·der) Gen 35:21
Edom (ites) (ē'·dŭm) (īts) Gen 25:30 (Gen 36:9)
Edre-i (ĕd'·rē·ī) Num 21:33
Eglah (ĕg'·luh) 2 Sam 3:5
Eglon (ĕg'·lŏn) Judg 3:12
Egypt (ian) (ē'·jĭpt) (ē·jĭp'·shŭn) Gen 12:10 (1 Sam 30:11, 12)
Ehi (ē'·hī) Gen 46:19–22
Ehud (ē'·hŭd) Judg 3:15
Eker (ē'·ker) 1 Chron 2:27
Ekron (ĕk'·rŏn) Josh 13:2–7
Elah (ē'·luh) Gen 36:40–43
Elam (ē'·lŭm) Gen 10:22
Elasah (ĕ·lā'·suh) Ezra 10:22
Elath (ē'·lăth) Deut 2:8
Eldaah (ĕl·dā'·uh) Gen 25:4
Eldad (ĕl'·dăd) Num 11:26
Ele-ad (ĕl'·ē·ăd) 1 Chron 7:20, 21
Eleadah (ĕl·ē·ā'·duh) 1 Chron 7:20, 21
Elealeh (ē'·lē·ā'·lē) Num 32:3, 4
Eleasah (ĕl·ē·ā'·suh) 1 Chron 8:37
Eleazar (ĕl·ē·ā'·zer) Ex 6:23
El-Elohe-Israel (ĕl·ĕl'·ō·hē·ĭs'·ruh·ĕl) Gen 33:20
Elhanan (ĕl·hā'·nŭn) 2 Sam 21:19
Eli (ē'·lī) 1 Sam 1:3
Eliab (ĕ·lī'·ŭb) Num 1:2–15
Eliada (ĕ·lī'·uh·duh) 2 Sam 5:14–16
Eliahba (ĕ·lī'·uh·buh) 2 Sam 23:24–39
Eliakim (ĕ·lī'·uh·kĭm) 2 Kgs 18:18
Eliam (ĕ·lī'·ŭm) 2 Sam 11:3
Eliasaph (ĕ·lī'·uh·săf) Num 1:2–15
Eliashib (ĕ·lī'·uh·shĭb) Neh 3:1
Eliathah (ĕ·lī'·uh·thuh) 1 Chron 25:4, 5
Elidad (ē·lī'·dăd) Num 34:16–28
Eliel (ĕ·lī'·ĕl) 1 Chron 5:24
Eli-enai (ĕl·ĭ·ē'·nī) 1 Chron 8:19–21
Eliezer (ĕ·lī·ē'·zer) Gen 15:2, 3
Eli-e-ho-enai (ĕl'·ĭ·ĕ·hō·ē'·nī) Ezra 8:4
Elihoreph (ĕl·ĭ·hor'·ĕf) 1 Kgs 4:1
Elihu (ĕ·lī'·hū) 1 Sam 1:1
Elijah (ĕ·lī'·jah) 1 Kgs 17:1
Elika (ĕ·lī'·kuh) 2 Sam 23:24–39
Elim (ē'·lĭm) Ex 15:27
Elimelech (ĕ·lĭm'·uh·lĕk) Ruth 1:1
Eli-o-enai (ĕl'·ĭ·ō·ē'·nī) 1 Chron 3:23
Eliphal (ĕ·lī'·făl) 1 Chron 11:26–47
Eliphaz (ĕ·lī'·făz) Gen 36:4
Eliphelet (ĕ·lĭf'·ĕ·lĕt) 1 Chron 3:6–8
Elisha (ĕ·lī'·shuh) 1 Kgs 19:16
Elishah (ĕ·lī'·shuh) Gen 10:4
Elishama (ĕ·lī'·shuh·muh) Num 1:2–15
Elishaphat (ĕ·lī'·shuh·făt) 2 Chron 23:1
Elisheba (ĕ·lī'·shĕ·buh) Ex 6:23
Eliud (ĕ·lī'·ŭd) Mt 1:14
Elizabeth (ĕ·lĭz'·uh·bĕth) Lk 1:5
Elizaphan (ĕ·lĭ·zā'·făn) Num 3:25–30
Elizur (ĕ·lī'·zer) Num 1:2–15
Elkanah (ĕl·kā'·nuh) Ex 6:24
Elkosh (ĕl'·kŏsh) Nah 1:1
Ellasar (ĕl·lah'·ser) Gen 14:1
Elmadam (ĕl·mā'·dŭm) Lk 3:23–38
Elna-am (ĕl·nā'·ŭm) 1 Chron 11:26–47
Elnathan (ĕl·nā'·thŭn) 2 Kgs 24:8, 9
Elon (ites) (ē'·lŏn) (īts) Gen 26:34 (Num 26:26, 27)
Elon-beth-hanan (ē'·lŏn·bĕth·hā'·nŭn) 1 Kgs 4:8–19
Eloth (ē'·lŏth) 1 Kgs 9:26
Elpaal (ĕl·pā'·ŭl) 1 Chron 8:11
El-paran (ĕl·pah'·rŭn) Gen 14:6
Elpelet (ĕl'·pĕ·lĕt) 1 Chron 14:4–7
Eltekeh (ĕl·tē'·kĕ) Josh 19:41–46
Eltekon (ĕl·tē'·kŏn) Josh 15:48–62
Eltolad (ĕl·tō'·lăd) Josh 15:21–32
Elul (ē'·lŭl) Neh 6:15
Eluzai (ĕ·loo'·zī) 1 Chron 12:3–7
Elymas (ĕl·ĭ'·mŭs) Acts 13:8
Elzabad (ĕl·zā'·băd) 1 Chron 12:8–13
Elzaphan (ĕl'·zuh·făn) Ex 6:22
Emek-kaziz (ē'·mĕk·kē'·zĭz) Josh 18:21–28
Emim (ē'·mĭm) Gen 14:5, 6
Emmanuel (ĕm·măn'·ū·ĕl) Mt 1:23
Emmaus (ĕ·mā'·ŭs) Lk 24:13
Enam (ē'·năm) Josh 15:33–36
Enan (ē'·năn) Num 1:2–15
Endor (ĕn'·dor) Josh 17:11
En-eglaim (ĕn·ĕg'·lā·ĭm) Ezek 47:10
En-gannim (ĕn·găn'·nĭm) Josh 15:33–36
En-gedi (ĕn·gĕ'·dī) Josh 15:48–62
En-haddah (ĕn·hăd'·uh) Josh 19:17–23
Enhazor (ĕn·hā'·zor) Josh 19:35–39
Enmishpat (ĕn·mĭsh'·păt) Gen 14:7
Enoch (ē'·nŏk) Gen 4:17
Enosh (ē'·nŏsh) Gen 4:26
En-rimmon (ĕn·rĭm'·mŏn) Neh 11:25–30
En-rogel (ĕn·rō'·gĕl) Josh 15:7
En-shemesh (ĕn·shĕ'·mĕsh) Josh 15:7
Epaenetus (ĕ·pē'·nĕ·tŭs) Rom 16:5
Epaphras (ĕp'·uh·frăs) Col 1:7
Epaphroditus (ĕp·ăf·rō·dī'·tŭs) Phil 2:25
Ephah (ē'·fuh) Gen 25:4
Ephai (ē'·fī) Jer 40:8
Epher (ē'·fer) Gen 25:4
Ephes-dammim (ē'·fĕz·dăm'·ĭm) 1 Sam 17:1
Ephesians (ĕ·fē'·shŭnz) Acts 19:28
Ephesus (ĕf'·ĕ·sŭs) Acts 18:19
Ephlal (ĕf'·lăl) 1 Chron 2:37
Ephod (ē'·fŏd) Num 34:16–28
Ephraim (ē'·fruh·ĭm) Gen 41:52
Ephrathah (ĕf'·ruh·thuh) 1 Chron 2:50
Ephrathites (ĕf'·ruh·thīts) Ruth 1:1
Ephron (ē'·frŭn) Gen 23:8
Epicureans (ĕp'·ĭ·kū·rē'·ănz) Acts 17:18
Eran (ē'·rŭn) Num 26:28–37
Erastus (ĕ·răs'·tŭs) Acts 19:22
Erech (ē'·rĕk) Gen 10:10
Eri (te) (ĕr'·ī) (t) Gen 46:16, 17
Esarhaddon (ē·sahr·hăd'·dŭn) 2 Kgs 19:37
Esau (ē'·saw) Gen 25:25
Eshan (ē'·shăn) Josh 15:48–62
Eshbaal (ĕsh·bā'·ŭl) 1 Chron 8:33
Eshban (ĕsh'·bŭn) Gen 36:26
Eshcol (ĕsh'·kŭl) Gen 14:13
Eshek (ē'·shĕk) 1 Chron 8:39
Eshtaol (ites) (ĕsh'·tā·ōl) (ĕsh·tā'·ō·līts) Josh 15:33–36 (1 Chron 2:53)
Eshtemoa (ĕsh·tĕ·mō'·uh) Josh 21:9–16
Eshtemoh (ĕsh'·tē·mō) Josh 15:48–62
Eshton (ĕsh'·tŭn) 1 Chron 4:11, 12
Esli (ĕs'·lī) Lk 3:23–38
Esther (ĕs'·ter) Esth 2:7
Etam (ē'·tăm) Judg 15:8
Etham (ē'·thŭm) Ex 13:20
Ethan (ē'·thŭn) 1 Kgs 4:31
Ethbaal (ĕth·bā'·ŭl) 1 Kgs 16:31
Ether (ē'·ther) Josh 15:37–44
Ethiopia (n) (ē·thē·ō'·pē·uh) (n) Num 12:1 (Jer 13:23)
Ethkazin (ĕth·kā'·zĭn) Josh 19:13
Ethnan (ĕth'·năn) 1 Chron 4:7
Ethni (ĕth'·nī) 1 Chron 6:39–43
Eubulus (ŭ'·bū·lŭs) 2 Tim 4:21
Eunice (ū'·nĭs) 2 Tim 1:5
Euodias (ū·ō'·dĭ·ŭs) Phil 4:2
Euphrates (ū·frā'·tēs) Gen 2:14
Eutychus (ū'·tĭ·kŭs) Acts 20:9
Evi (ē'·vī) Num 31:8
Evil-merodach (ē·vĭl·mer'·uh·dăk) 2 Kgs 25:27
Ezbai (ĕz'·bī) 1 Chron 11:26–47
Ezbon (ĕz'·bŭn) Gen 46:16, 17
Ezekiel (ĕ·zēk'·ĭ·ĕl) Ezek 1:1–3
Ezem (ē'·zĕm) 1 Chron 4:21–32
Ezer (ē'·zer) 1 Chron 4:3, 4
Ezion-geber (ē'·zĭ·ŏn·gē'·ber) Num 33:15–37
Eznite (ĕz'·nīt) 2 Sam 23:8
Ezra (ĕz'·rah) Ezra 7:1
Ezrahite (ĕz'·ruh·hīt) 1 Kgs 4:31
Ezri (ĕz'·rī) 1 Chron 27:26
Felix (fē'·lĭx) Acts 23:23, 24
Festus (fĕs'·tŭs) Acts 24:27
Fortunatus (for·tū·nā'·tŭs) 1 Cor 16:17
Gaal (gā'·ŭl) Judg 9:26
Gaash (gā'·ăsh) Josh 24:30
Gaba (gā'·buh) Josh 21:17, 18
Gabbai (găb'·bā·ī) Neh 11:7–9
Gabbatha (găb'·buh·thuh) Jn 19:13
Gabriel (gā'·brē·ĕl) Dan 8:16
Gad (găd) Gen 30:11
Gadarenes (găd'·uh·rēnz) Mt 8:28
Gaddi (găd'·dī) Num 13:3–15
Gaddiel (găd'·ĭ·ĕl) Num 13:3–15
Gadi (gā'·dī) 2 Kgs 15:14
Gaham (gā'·ŭm) Gen 22:24
Gahar (gā'·hahr) Ezra 2:43–54
Gaius (gā'·ĭ·ŭs) Acts 19:29
Galal (gā'·lăl) 1 Chron 9:15, 16
Galatia (ns) (guh·lā'·shuh) (nz) Acts 16:6 (Gal 3:1)
Galeed (găl·ē'·ĕd) Gen 31:47, 48
Galileans (găl·ĭ·lē'·unz) Jn 4:45
Galilee (găl'·ĭ·lē) Josh 20:7
Gallim (găl'·lĭm) 1 Sam 25:44
Gallio (găl'·ĭ·ō) Acts 18:12
Gamaliel (guh·mā'·lĭ·ĕl) Num 1:2–15
Gammad (gā'·măd) Ezek 27:11
Gamul (gā'·mool) 1 Chron 24:7–18
Gareb (gā'·rĕb) 2 Sam 23:24–39
Garmite (gahr'·mīt) 1 Chron 4:19
Gatam (gā'·tăm) Gen 36:10–12
Gath (găth) Josh 11:22
Gath-hepher (găth·hē'·fer) 2 Kgs 14:25
Gath-rimmon (găth·rĭm'·mŏn) Josh 19:41–46

Gaza (gah'·zun) Gen 10:15–19
Gazez (gā'·zĕz) 1 Chron 2:46
Gazzam (găz'·ŭm) Ezra 2:43–54
Geba (gē'·buh) Josh 18:21–28
Gebal (ite) (gē'·bŭl) (īt) Ps 83:7 (Josh 13:2–7)
Geber (gē'·ber) 1 Kgs 4:8–19
Gebim (gē'·bĭm) Isa 10:31
Gedaliah (gĕd·uh·lī'·uh) 2 Kgs 25:22
Geder (gē'·der) Josh 12:8–24
Gederah (gĕ·dē'·ruh) Josh 15:33–36
Gederoth (gĕ·dē'·rŏth) Josh 15:37–44
Gederothaim (gĕ·dē'·rŏth·ā'·ĭm) Josh 15:33–36
Gedor (gē'·dor) Josh 15:48–62
Gehazi (gĕ·hā'·zī) 2 Kgs 4:11, 12
Geliloth (gĕ·lī'·lŏth) Josh 18:17
Gemalli (gĕ·măl'·lī) Num 13:3–15
Gemariah (gĕm·uh·rī'·uh) Jer 29:3
Gennesaret (gĕn·nĕs'·uh·rĕt) Mt 14:34
Gentile (jĕn'·tīl) Deut 32:21
Genubath (gĕ·nū'·băth) 1 Kgs 11:20
Gera (gē'·ruh) Gen 46:19–22
Gerar (gē'·rahr) Gen 10:15–19
Gerizim (ger'·ĭ·zĭm) Deut 11:29
Gershom (ger'·shŭm) Ex 2:22
Geshan (gē'·shăn) 1 Chron 2:47
Geshem (gē'·shĕm) Neh 2:19
Geshur (ites) (gē·sher) (īts) 2 Sam 3:3 (Deut 3:14)
Gether (gē'·ther) Gen 10:23
Gethsemane (gĕth·sĕm'·uh·nē) Mt 26:36
Geuel (guh·ū'·ĕl) Num 13:3–15
Gezer (gē'·zer) Josh 10:33
Giah (gī'·uh) 2 Sam 2:24
Gibbar (gĭb'·ahr) Ezra 2:3–35
Gibbethon (gĭb'·buh·thŏn) Josh 19:41–46
Gibe-a (gĭb'·ē·uh) 1 Chron 2:48, 49
Gibe-ah (gĭb'·ē·uh) Josh 15:48–62
Gibeon (ites) (gĭb'·ē·ŭn) (īts) Josh 9:3–5 (2 Sam 21:1)
Giddalti (gĭd·ăl'·tī) 1 Chron 25:9–31
Giddel (gĭd'·ĕl) Ezra 2:43–54
Gideon (gĭd'·ē·ŭn) Judg 6:11
Gideoni (gĭd·ē·ō'·nī) Num 1:2–15
Gidom (gī'·dŭm) Judg 20:45
Gihon (gī'·hŏn) Gen 2:13
Gilalai (gĭl'·uh·lī) Neh 12:35, 36
Gilboa (gĭl·bō'·uh) 1 Sam 28:4
Gilead (ite) (gĭl'·ē·ăd) (īt) Gen 31:21
Gilgal (gĭl'·găl) Josh 4:19
Giloh (gī'·lō) Josh 15:48–62
Gimzo (gĭm'·zō) 2 Chron 28:17, 18
Ginath (gī'·năth) 1 Kgs 16:21
Ginnethoi (gĭn'·nuh·thoi) Neh 12:1
Ginnethon (gĭn'·nuh·thŏn) Neh 10:1
Girgashites (ger'·guh·shīts) 1 Chron 1:13–16
Girzites (ger'·zīts) 1 Sam 27:8
Gishpa (gĭsh'·pah) Neh 11:21
Gittaim (gĭt'·tā·ĭm) 2 Sam 4:2, 3
Gizon (gī'·zŭn) 1 Chron 11:26–47
Goah (gō'·uh) Jer 31:38, 39
Gob (gōb) 2 Sam 21:18
Gog (gŏg) 1 Chron 5:4
Golan (gō'·lăn) Deut 4:43
Golgotha (gŏl'·guh·thuh) Mt 27:33
Goliath (gō·lī'·ŭth) 1 Sam 17:4–7
Gomer (gō'·mer) Gen 10:2
Gomorrah (guh·mor'·uh) Gen 10:15–19
Goshen (gō'·shĕn) Gen 45:10
Gozan (gō'·zăn) 2 Kgs 17:6
Gudgodah (gŭd·gō'·duh) Deut 10:7
Guni (tes) (gū'·nī) (ts) Gen 46:23–25 (Num 26:48–50)
Gurbaal (ger·bā'·ŭl) 2 Chron 26:7
Haahashtari (hā'·uh·hăsh'·tuh·rī) 1 Chron 4:6
Habaiah (huh·bī'·uh) Ezra 2:61
Habakkuk (huh·băk'·kŭk) Hab 1:1
Habazziniah (huh·bă'·zĭn·ī·uh) Jer 35:3
Habor (hā'·bor) 2 Kgs 17:6
Hacaliah (hăk·uh·lī'·uh) Neh 1:1
Hachmon (hăk'·mŭn) 1 Chron 11:11
Hachmoni (hăk'·mŭn·ī) 1 Chron 27:32
Hadad (hā'·dăd) Gen 36:31–39
Hadadezer (hăd·uh·dē'·zer) 2 Sam 8:3
Hadad-rimmon (hā'·dăd·rĭm'·mŏn) Zech 12:11
Hadashah (huh·dăsh'·uh) Josh 15:37–44
Hadassah (huh·dăs'·suh) Esth 2:7
Hadid (hā'·dĭd) Ezra 2:3–35
Hadlai (hăd'·lī) 2 Chron 28:12
Hadoram (huh·dor'·ŭm) Gen 10:26–30
Hadrach (hăd'·răk) Zech 9:1
Ha-eleph (hă·ē'·lĕf) Josh 18:27
Hagab (hā'·găb) Ezra 2:43–54
Hagaba (hăg'·uh·buh) Neh 7:46–56
Hagar (hā'·gahr) Gen 16:1
Haggai (hăg'·gī) Hag 1:1
Haggi (hăg'·gī) Num 26:15–18
Haggiah (hăg·gī'·uh) 1 Chron 6:29, 30
Haggites (hăg·gīts) Num 26:15–18
Haggith (hăg'·gĭth) 2 Sam 3:4
Hagri (te) (hăg'·rī) (t) 1 Chron 11:26–47 (1 Chron 27:31)
Hakkatan (hăk'·kuh·tăn) Ezra 8:2–14
Hakkoz (hăk·kŏz) 1 Chron 24:7–18
Hakupha (huh·kū'·fuh) Ezra 2:43–54
Halah (hā'·luh) 2 Kgs 17:6
Halak (hā'·lăk) Josh 11:17
Halhul (hăl'·hŭl) Josh 15:48–62
Hali (hā'·lī) Josh 19:24–26
Hallohesh (hăl'·lō·hĕsh) Neh 10:14–27
Ham (hăm) Gen 9:18
Haman (hā'·mŭn) Esth 3:1
Hamathites (hā'·muh·thīts) Gen 10:15–19
Hamath-zobah (hā'·măth·zō'·buh) 2 Chron 8:3
Hammath (hăm'·măth) 1 Chron 2:55
Hammedatha (hăm·uh·dā'·thuh) Esth 3:1
Hammolecheth (hăm·ō'·luh·kĕth) 1 Chron 7:18
Hammon (hăm'·mŏn) Josh 19:28
Hammoth-dor (hăm'·ŏth·dor) Josh 21:32
Hamor (hā'·mor) Gen 33:19
Hammu-el (hăm'·ū·ĕl) 1 Chron 4:26
Hamul (ites) (hā'·mŭl) (īts) Gen 46:8–14 (Num 26:19–22)
Hamutal (huh·moo'·tăl) 2 Kgs 23:31, 32
Hanamel (hăn'·uh·mĕl) Jer 32:6, 7
Hanan (hā'·nŭn) 1 Chron 8:22–25
Hananel (huh·năn'·ĕl) Neh 3:1
Hanani (huh·nā'·nī) 2 Chron 16:7
Hananiah (hăn·uh·nī'·uh) 1 Chron 3:19, 20
Hanes (hā'·nēz) Isa 30:4
Hannah (hăn'·nuh) 1 Sam 1:2
Hannathon (hăn'·nuh·thŏn) Josh 19:14
Hanniel (hăn'·ĭ·ĕl) Num 34:16–28
Hanoch (ites) (hā'·nŭk) (īts) Gen 25:4 (Num 26:5–11)
Hanun (hā'·nŭn) 2 Sam 10:1
Hapharaim (hăf·uh·rā'·ĭm) Josh 19:17–23
Happizzez (hăp'·pĭz·zĕz) 1 Chron 24:7–18
Hara (hĕr'·uh) 1 Chron 5:26
Haradah (huh·rā'·duh) Num 33:15–37
Haran (hĕr'·ŭn) Gen 11:27
Harar (hăr'·ŭr) 2 Sam 23:11, 12
Harbona (hahr·bō'·nuh) Esth 7:9
Hareph (hahr'·ĕf) 1 Chron 2:51
Harhaiah (hahr·hī'·uh) Neh 3:8
Harhas (hahr'·hăs) 2 Kgs 22:14
Harhur (hahr'·her) Ezra 2:43–54
Harim (hā'·rĭm) 1 Chron 24:7–18
Hariph (hā'·rĭf) Neh 7:8–38
Harnepher (hahr·nĕ'·fer) 1 Chron 7:36, 37
Harod (hahr'·rŏd) Judg 7:1
Haroeh (huh·rō'·uh) 1 Chron 2:52
Harosheth-ha-goiim (huh·rō'·shĕth·huh·goi'·ĭm) Judg 4:2, 3
Harsha (hahr'·shuh) Ezra 2:43–54
Harum (hahr'·rŭm) 1 Chron 4:8
Harumaph (hahr·oo'·măf) Neh 3:10
Haruph (hahr'·ŭf) 1 Chron 12:3–7
Haruz (hā'·rŭz) 2 Kgs 21:19, 20
Hasadiah (hăs·uh·dī'·uh) 1 Chron 3:19, 20
Hashabiah (hăsh·uh·bī'·uh) 1 Chron 6:44–47
Hashabnah (huh·shăb'·nuh) Neh 10:14–27
Hashabneiah (hăsh·ăb·nī'·uh) Neh 3:10
Hash-baddanah (hăsh·băd'·duh·nuh) Neh 8:1–5
Hashem (hā'·shĕm) 1 Chron 11:26–47
Hashmonah (hăsh·mō'·nuh) Num 33:15–37
Hashubah (hă·shoo'·buh) 1 Chron 3:19, 20
Hashum (hā'·shŭm) Ezra 2:3–35
Hasrah (hăs'·ruh) 2 Chron 34:22
Hassenaah (hăs·suh·nā'·uh) Neh 3:3
Hassenuah (hăs·suh·noo'·uh) 1 Chron 9:7, 8
Hasshub (hā'·shŭb) 1 Chron 9:14
Hassophereth (hăs·sō'·fuh·rĕth) Ezra 2:55–57
Hasupha (huh·soo'·fuh) Ezra 2:43–54
Hathach (hā'·thăk) Esth 4:5
Hatipha (huh·tī'·fuh) Ezra 2:43–54
Hatita (huh·tī'·tuh) Ezra 2:40–42
Hattil (hăt'·tīl) Ezra 2:55–57
Hattush (hăt'·tŭsh) 1 Chron 3:21, 22
Hauran (haw'·rahn) Ezek 47:16
Havilah (hăv'·ĭ·luh) Gen 10:7
Havoth-jair (hăv'·ŏth·jā'·er) Num 32:41
Hazael (hăz'·uh·ĕl) 1 Kgs 19:15
Hazaiah (huh·zī'·uh) Neh 11:4–6

Hazanon-tamar (hăz'·uh·nŏn·tā'·mahr) Gen 14:7
Hazaraddar (hā'·zahr·ăd'·dŭr) Num 34:4
Hazar-enan (hā'·zahr·ē'·nŭn) Num 34:7–9
Hazar-gaddah (hā'·zahr·găd'·duh) Josh 15:21–32
Hazarmaveth (hā'·zahr·mā'·vĕth) Gen 10:26–30
Hazar-shual (hā'·zahr·shoo'·ŭl) Josh 15:21–32
Hazar-susah (hā'·zahr·soo'·suh) Josh 19:2–7
Hazar-susim (hā'·zahr·soo'·sĭm) 1 Chron 4:31
Hazer-hatticon (hā'·zer·hăt'·ĭ·kŏn) Ezek 47:16
Hazeroth (hă·zē'·rŏth) Num 11:35
Haziel (hā'·zĭ·ĕl) 1 Chron 23:8, 9
Hazo (hā'·zō) Gen 22:20–23
Hazor (hā'·zor) Josh 11:1
Hazor-hadattah (hā'·zor·huh·dăt'·tuh) Josh 15:21–32
Hazzelelponi (hăz'·zuh·lĕl·pō'·nī) 1 Chron 4:3, 4
Heber (ite) (hē'·ber) (īt) Judg 4:11 (Num 26:44–47)
Hebrew (hē'·broo) Gen 14:13
Hebron (ites) (hē'·brŭn) (īts) Gen 13:18 (Num 26:58, 59)
Hegai (hĕg'·ī) Esth 2:3
Helah (hē'·luh) 1 Chron 4:5
Helam (hē'·lŭm) 2 Sam 10:15, 16
Helbah (hĕl'·buh) Judg 1:31, 32
Helbon (hĕl'·bŭn) Ezek 27:18
Heldai (hĕl'·dī) 1 Chron 27:15
Heleb (hē'·lĕb) 2 Sam 23:24–29
Heled (hē'·lĕd) 1 Chron 11:26–47
Helek (ite) (hē'·lĕk) (īt) Num 26:28–37
Helem (hē'·lĕm) 1 Chron 7:35
Heleph (hē'·lĕf) Josh 19:34
Helez (hē'·lĕz) 2 Sam 23:24–39
Heli (hē'·lī) Lk 3:23–38
Helkath (hĕl'·kăth) Josh 19:24–26
Helon (hē'·lŏn) Num 1:2–15
Heman (hē'·mŭn) Gen 36:22
Hemdan (hĕm'·dŭn) Gen 36:26
Hena (hē'·nuh) 2 Kgs 18:34
Henadad (hĕn'·uh·dăd) Ezra 3:9
Hepher (ites) (hē'·fer) (īts) Josh 12:8–24 (Num 26:28–37)
Hephzibah (hĕf'·zĭ·buh) 2 Kgs 21:1
Heres (hē'·rēz) Judg 1:35
Heresh (hē'·rĕsh) 1 Chron 9:15, 16
Hereth (hē'·rĕth) 1 Sam 22:5
Hermas (her'·mŭs) Rom 16:14
Hermes (her'·mēz) Rom 16:14
Hermogenes (her·mŏj'·uh·nēz) 2 Tim 1:15
Hermon (her'·mŭn) Deut 3:8
Herod (hĕr'·ŭd) Mt 2:1
Herodians (hĕr·ō'·dĭ·ŭnz) Mt 22:16
Herodias (hĕr·ō'·dĭ·ŭs) Mt 14:3
Herodion (hĕr·ō'·dĭ·ŭn) Rom 16:11
Heshbon (hĕsh'·bŭn) Num 21:25, 26
Heshmon (hĕsh'·mŭn) Josh 15:21–32
Heth (hĕth) Gen 10:15–19
Hethlon (hĕth'·lŏn) Ezek 47:15
Hezekiah (hĕz·uh·kī'·uh) 2 Kgs 18:1
Hezir (hē'·zer) 1 Chron 24:7–18
Hezro (hĕz'·rō) 1 Chron 11:26–47
Hezron (ites) (hĕz'·rŭn) (īts) Gen 46:8–14 (Num 26:5–11)
Hiddai (hĭd'·dī) 2 Sam 23:24–39
Hiel (hī'·ĕl) 1 Kgs 16:34
Hierapolis (hī·er·ăp'·ō·lĭs) Col 4:13
Higgaion (hĭg'·ā·ĭ·ŭn) Ps 9:16
Hilen (hī'·lĕn) 1 Chron 6:58, 59
Hilkiah (hĭl·kī'·uh) 2 Kgs 18:37
Hillel (hĭl'·lĕl) Judg 12:13
Hinnom (hĭn'·nŭm) 2 Kgs 23:10
Hirah (hī'·ruh) Gen 38:1
Hiram (hī'·rŭm) 2 Sam 5:11
Hittites (hĭt'·tīts) Gen 15:19–21
Hivites (hĭv'·īts) Gen 10:15–19
Hizki (hĭz'·kī) 1 Chron 8:17, 18
Hobab (hō'·băb) Num 10:29
Hobah (hō'·buh) Gen 14:15
Hod (hŏd) 1 Chron 7:36, 37
Hodaviah (hŏd·uh·vī'·uh) 1 Chron 5:24
Hodesh (hō'·dĕsh) 1 Chron 8:8–10
Hodevah (hō'·duh·vuh) Neh 7:43–45
Hodiah (hō·dī'·uh) 1 Chron 4:19
Hoglah (hŏg'·luh) Num 26:28–37
Hoham (hō'·hăm) Josh 10:3
Holon (hō'·lŏn) Josh 15:48–62
Homam (hō'·măm) 1 Chron 1:38, 39
Hophni (hŏf'·nī) 1 Sam 1:3
Hophra (hŏf'·ruh) Jer 44:30
Horam (hō'·răm) Josh 10:33
Horeb (hō'·rĕb) Ex 3:1
Horem (hō'·rĕm) Josh 19:35–39
Hor-haggidgad (hor'·huh·gĭd'·găd) Num 33:15–37
Hori (tes) (hō'·rī) (ts) Gen 36:22 (Gen 14:5, 6)
Hormah (hor'·muh) Num 14:45
Horonaim (hor'·ō·nā'·ĭm) Isa 15:5
Horonite (hor'·ō·nīt) Neh 2:10
Hosah (hō'·zuh) Josh 19:29
Hosea (hō·zā'·uh) Hos 1:1
Hoshaiah (hō·shī'·uh) Neh 12:33
Hoshama (hŏsh'·uh·muh) 1 Chron 3:17, 18
Hotham (hō'·thăm) 1 Chron 7:32
Hothir (hō'·ther) 1 Chron 25:4, 5
Hukkok (hŭk'·kŏk) Josh 19:34
Hul (hool) Gen 10:23
Huldah (hŭl'·duh) 2 Kgs 22:14
Humtah (hŭm'·tuh) Josh 15:48–62
Hupham (ites) (hū'·făm) (īts) Num 26:38–41
Huppah (hŭp'·puh) 1 Chron 24:7–18
Huppim (hŭp'·pĭm) Gen 46:19–22
Hurai (hū'·rī) 1 Chron 11:26–47
Huramabi (hū'·rŭm·ā'·bī) 2 Chron 2:13
Huri (hū'·rī) 1 Chron 5:14
Hushah (hū'·shuh) 1 Chron 4:3, 4
Hushai (hū'·shī) 2 Sam 15:32
Husham (hū'·shŭm) Gen 36:31–39
Hushathite (hū'·shuh·thīt) 2 Sam 21:18
Hushim (hū'·shĭm) Gen 46:23–25
Hymenaeus (hī·mē·nē'·ŭs) 1 Tim 1:20
Ibhar (ĭb'·hahr) 2 Sam 5:14–16
Ible-am (ĭb'·lē·ŭm) Josh 17:11
Ibneiah (ĭb·nī'·uh) 1 Chron 9:7, 8
Ibnijah (ĭb·nī'·juh) 1 Chron 9:7, 8
Ibri (ĭb'·rī) 1 Chron 24:26, 27
Ibsam (ĭb'·sŭm) 1 Chron 7:2
Ibzan (ĭb'·zŭn) Judg 12:8
Ichabod (ĭk'·uh·bŏd) 1 Sam 4:21, 22
Iconium (ī·cō'·nĭ·ŭm) Acts 13:51
Idalah (ĭd'·uh·luh) Josh 19:15, 16
Idbash (ĭd'·băsh) 1 Chron 4:3, 4
Iddo (ĭd'·dō) 1 Chron 27:16–22
Igal (ī'·găl) Num 13:3–15
Igdaliah (ĭg·duh·lī'·uh) Jer 35:4
Ijon (ī'·jŏn) 1 Kgs 15:20
Ikkesh (ĭk'·kĕsh) 2 Sam 23:24–29
Ilai (ī'·lā) 1 Chron 11:26–47
Illyricum (ĭl·lĭr'·ĭ·kŭm) Rom 15:19
Imlah (ĭm'·luh) 2 Chron 18:6, 7
Immanuel (ĭm·măn'·ū·ĕl) Isa 7:14
Immer (ĭm'·mer) 1 Chron 9:12
Imna (ĭm'·nuh) 1 Chron 7:35
Imnah (ĭm'·nuh) 1 Chron 7:30
Imrah (ĭm'·ruh) 1 Chron 7:36, 37
Imri (ĭm'·rī) 1 Chron 9:4
India (ĭn'·dĭ·uh) Esth 1:1
Iphdeiah (ĭf·dē'·ĭ·uh) 1 Chron 8:22–25
Iphtah (ĭf'·tuh) Josh 15:37–44
Iphtahel (ĭf'·tuh·hĕl) Josh 19:14
Ir (ĭr) 1 Chron 7:12
Ira (ī'·ruh) 2 Sam 20:26
Irad (ī'·răd) Gen 4:18
Iram (ī'·rŭm) Gen 36:40–43
Iri (ī'·rī) 1 Chron 7:7
Irijah (ī·rī'·juh) Jer 37:13
Irnahash (ĭr·nā'·hăsh) 1 Chron 4:11, 12
Irpeel (ĭr·pē'·ĕl) Josh 18:21–28
Ir-shemesh (ĭr·shē'·mĕsh) Josh 19:41–46
Iru (ī'·roo) 1 Chron 4:15
Isaac (ī'·zŭk) Gen 17:19
Isaiah (ī·zā'·uh) Isa 1:1
Iscah (ĭz'·kuh) Gen 11:29
Iscariot (ĭs·kăr'·ĭ·ŏt) Mt 10:2–4
Ishbah (ĭsh'·buh) 1 Chron 4:17
Ishbak (ĭsh'·băk) Gen 25:1, 2
Ishbi-benob (ĭsh'·bĭ·bē'·nŏb) 2 Sam 21:16
Ish-bosheth (ĭsh·bō'·shĕth) 2 Sam 2:8
Ishhod (ĭsh'·hŏd) 1 Chron 7:18
Ishma (ĭsh'·muh) 1 Chron 4:3, 4
Ishmael (ite) (ĭsh'·muh·ĕl) (īt) Gen 16:9–12
Ishmaiah (ĭsh·mā'·ĭ·uh) 1 Chron 27:16–22
Ishmerai (ĭsh'·muh·rī) 1 Chron 8:17, 18
Ishpah (ĭsh'·puh) 1 Chron 8:15, 16
Ishpan (ĭsh'·păn) 1 Chron 8:22–25
Ishvah (ĭsh'·vuh) Gen 46:16, 17
Ishvi (ĭsh'·vī) 1 Sam 14:49
Ismachiah (ĭs·muh·kī'·uh) 2 Chron 31:12, 13
Israel (ites) (ĭs'·ruh·ĕl) (īts) Gen 32:28 (Ex 14:3)
Issachar (ĭs'·suh·kahr) Gen 30:18
Isshiah (ĭs·shī'·uh) 1 Chron 7:3
Isshijah (ĭs·shī'·juh) Ezra 10:31, 32
Ithai (ĭth'·ī) 1 Chron 11:26–47
Ithamar (ĭth'·uh·mahr) Ex 6:23
Ithi-el (ī'·thĭ·ĕl) Neh 11:7–9
Ithlah (ĭth'·luh) Josh 19:41–46
Ithmah (ĭth'·muh) 1 Chron 11:26–47
Ithnan (ĭth'·năn) Josh 15:21–32
Ithra (ĭth'·ruh) 2 Sam 17:25
Ithran (ĭth'·răn) Gen 36:26
Ithream (ĭth'·rē·ăm) 2 Sam 3:5
Ithrites (ĭth'·rīts) 1 Chron 2:53
Ittai (ĭt'·tī) 2 Sam 15:19, 20
Ituraea (ī·tū·rē'·uh) Lk 3:1
Ivvah (ĭv'·vuh) 2 Kgs 18:34
Iye-abarim (ī'·yē·ăb'·uh·rĭm) Num 21:11
Izhar (ĭz'·hăr) Ex 6:18
Izliah (ĭz·lī'·uh) 1 Chron 8:17, 18
Izrahiah (ĭz·ruh·hī'·uh) 1 Chron 7:3

Izri (ī′z·rī) 1 Chron 25:9–31
Izziah (ĭz·zī′·uh) Ezra 10:25
Jaakan (jā′·uh·kăn) 1 Chron 1:42
Jaala (jā′·uh·luh) Neh 7:57–59
Jaalah (jā′·uh·luh) Ezra 2:55–57
Jaareshiah (jā·ahr·uh·shī′·uh) 1 Chron 8:26, 27
Jaasu (jā·uh′·soo) Ezra 10:34–42
Ja-asiel (jā·uh·sī′·ĕl) 1 Chron 27:16–22
Ja-azaniah (jā·ăz·uh·nī′·uh) 2 Kgs 25:23
Ja-aziah (jā·uh·zī′·uh) 1 Chron 24:26, 27
Ja-aziel (juh·ā′·zī·ĕl) 1 Chron 15:18
Jabal (jā′·bŭl) Gen 4:20
Jabbok (jăb′·bŭk) Gen 32:22, 24
Jabesh (jā′·bĕsh) 2 Kgs 15:10
Jabesh-gilead (jā′·bĕsh·gĭl′·ē·ŭd) Judg 21:8, 9
Jabez (jā′·bēz) 1 Chron 4:9
Jabin (jā′·bĭn) Judg 4:2, 3
Jabneel (jăb′·nē·ĕl) Josh 15:10, 11
Jabneh (jăb′·nĕh) 2 Chron 26:6
Jacan (jā′·kŭn) 1 Chron 5:13
Jachin (ites) (jā′·kĭn) (īts) 1 Kgs 7:16–22 (Num 26:12–14)
Jacob (jā′·kŭb) Gen 25:26
Jada (jā′·duh) 1 Chron 2:28
Jaddai (jăd′·ī) Ezra 10:43
Jaddu-a (jăd′·oo·uh) Neh 10:14–27
Jadon (jā′·dŏn) Neh 3:7
Jael (jā′·ĕl) Judg 4:17
Jagur (jā′·ger) Josh 15:21–32
Jahath (jā′·hăth) 1 Chron 19–21
Jahaz (jā′·hăz) Num 21:23
Jahaziel (juh·hā′·zī·ĕl) 1 Chron 16:6
Jahdai (jah′·dī) 1 Chron 2:47
Jahdi-el (jah′·dī·ĕl) 1 Chron 5:24
Jahdo (jah′·dō) 1 Chron 5:14
Jahleel (ites) (jah′·lē·ĕl) (īts) Num 26:26, 27
Jahmai (jah′·mī) 1 Chron 7:2
Jahzah (jah′·zuh) 1 Chron 6:78, 79
Jahzeel (ites) (jah′·zē·ĕl) (īts) Gen 46:23–25 (Num 26:48–50)
Jahzeiah (jah·zē′·uh) Ezra 10:15
Jahzerah (jah′·zuh·ruh) 1 Chron 9:12
Jahzi-el (jăh′·zī·ĕl) 1 Chron 7:13
Jair (ite) (jā′·er) (īt) Num 32:41 (2 Sam 20:26)
Jairus (jā′·ī·rŭs) Mk 5:22
Jakeh (jā′·kĕh) Prov 30:1
Jakim (jā′·kĭm) 1 Chron 8:19–21
Jalam (jā′·lŭm) Gen 36:5
Jalon (jā′·lŭn) 1 Chron 4:17
Jambres (jăm′·brēz) 2 Tim 3:8
Jamin (ites) (jā′·mĭn) (īts) Gen 46:8–14 (Num 26:12–14)
Jamlech (jăm′·lĕk) 1 Chron 4:34–39
Jannai (jăn′·uh·ī) Lk 3:23–38
Jannes (jăn′·nēz) 2 Tim 3:8
Janoah (juh·nō′·uh) 2 Kgs 15:29
Japheth (jā′·fĕth) Gen 5:32
Japhia (juh·fī′·uh) Josh 19:12
Japhlet (jăf′·lĕt) 1 Chron 7:32
Japhletites (jăf′·luh·tītes) Josh 16:1–4
Jarah (jah′·ruh) 1 Chron 9:42
Jared (jah′·rŭd) Gen 5:15, 17
Jarha (jahr′·huh) *1 Chron 2:34, 35*
Jarib (jā′·rĭb) 1 Chron 4:24
Jarmuth (jahr′·mŭth) Josh 10:3
Jaroah (juh·rō′·uh) 1 Chron 5:14
Jashar (jā′·shŭr) Josh 10:13
Jashen (jā′·shŭn) 2 Sam 23:24–39
Jashobeam (juh·shō′·bē·ŭm) 1 Chron 11:11
Jashub (ites) (jăsh′·ŭb) (īts) Num 26:23–25
Jason (jā′·sŏn) Acts 17:5
Jathni-el (jăth′·nī·ĕl) 1 Chron 26:2, 3
Jattir (jăt′·ter) Josh 15:48–62
Javan (jā′·vŭn) Gen 10:2
Jazar (jā′·zŭr) Num 32:1
Jaziz (jā′·zīz) 1 Chron 27:31
Jearim (jē′·uh·rĭm) Josh 15:10, 11
Jeatherai (jē·ăth′·uh·rī) 1 Chron 6:19–21
Jeberechiah (jē·ber′·uh·kī′·uh) Isa 8:2
Jebus (jē′·bŭs) Judg 19:10
Jebusites (jĕb′·ū·sīts) Gen 15:19–21
Jechoniah (jĕk·ō·nī′·uh) Mt 1:11, 12
Jecoliah (jĕk·ōlī′·uh) 2 Chron 26:3
Jeconiah (jĕk·ō·nī′·uh) 1 Chron 3:16
Jedaiah (jĕ·dī′·uh) 1 Chron 4:34–39
Jedia-el (jĕ·dī′·uh·ĕl) 1 Chron 7:6
Jedidah (jĕ·dī′·duh) 2 Kgs 22:1
Jedidiah (jĕd·ĭ·dī′·uh) 2 Sam 12:25
Jeduthun (jĕ·doo′·thŭn) 1 Chron 16:38
Jegar-sahadutha (jē′·gŭr·sā·huh·dū′·thuh) Gen 31:47, 48
Jehallelel (jĕ·hăl′·luh·lĕl) 2 Chron 29:12–14
Jehdeiah (jĕ·dī′·uh) 1 Chron 24:20
Jehezkel (jĕ·hĕz′·kĕl) 1 Chron 24:7–18
Jehiah (jĕ·hī′·uh) 1 Chron 15:24
Jehiel (jĕ·hī′·ĕl) 1 Chron 15:18
Jehieli (jĕ·hī′·uh·lī) 1 Chron 26:20–22
Jehizkiah (jĕ·hĭz·kī′·uh) 2 Chron 28:12
Jehoaddah (jĕ·hō′·ăd·duh) 1 Chron 8:36
Jeho-addin (jē·hō′·ăd·dĭn) 2 Kgs 14:2
Jehoahaz (jĕ·hō′·uh·hăz) 2 Kgs 10:35
Jehohanan (jē′·hō·hā′·nŭn) 2 Chron 23:1
Jehoiachin (jĕ·hoi′·uh·kĭn) 2 Kgs 24:6
Jehoiada (jĕ·hoi′·uh·duh) 2 Sam 8:18
Jehoiakim (jĕ·hoi′·uh·kĭm) 2 Kgs 23:34
Jehoiarib (jĕ·hoi′·uh·rĭb) 1 Chron 9:10, 11
Jehonadab (jĕ·hŏn′·uh·dăb) 2 Kgs 10:15
Jehoram (jĕ·hō′·rŭm) 1 Kgs 22:50
Jehoshabeath (jĕ·hō·shăb′·ē·ăth) 2 Chron 22:11
Jehoshaphat (jĕ·hŏsh′·uh·făt) 1 Kgs 15:24
Jehosheba (jĕ·hŏsh′·uh·buh) 2 Kgs 11:2, 3
Jehovah (jĕ·hō′·vuh) Ex 6:2, 3
Jehovah-nissi (jĕ·hō′·vuh·nĭs′·sī) Ex 17:15, 16
Jehovah-Shammah (jĕ·hō′·vuh·shăm′·muh) Ezek 48:35
Jehozabad (jĕ·hō′·zuh·băd) 2 Kgs 12:21
Jehozadak (jĕ·hŏz′·uh·dăk) 1 Chron 6:4–15
Jehu (jē′·hū) 1 Kgs 16:1
Jehubbah (jĕ·hŭb′·buh) 1 Chron 7:34
Jehucal (jĕ·hū′·kăl) Jer 37:3
Jehud (jē′·hŭd) Josh 19:41–46
Jehudi (jĕ·hū′·dī) Jer 36:14, 15
Jeiel (jĕ·ī′·ĕl) 1 Chron 9:35–37
Jekabzeel (jĕ·kăb′·zē·ĕl) Neh 11:25–30
Jekameam (jĕk·uh·mē′·ŭm) 1 Chron 23:19
Jekamiah (jĕk·uh·mī′·uh) 1 Chron 2:41
Jekuthiel (jĕ·kū′·thī·ĕl) 1 Chron 4:18
Jemima (jĕ·mī′·muh) Job 42:13, 14
Jemuel (juh·mū′·ĕl) Gen 46:8–14
Jephthah (jĕf′·thuh) Judg 11:1
Jephunneh (juh·foon′·nuh) Num 13:3–15
Jerah (jē′·ruh) Gen 10:26–30
Jerahmeel (juh·rah′·mē·ĕl) 1 Chron 2:9
Jerahmeelites (juh·rah′·mē·ĕl·ītes) 1 Sam 30:27–31
Jered (jē′·rĕd) 1 Chron 4:18
Jeremai (jĕr′·uh·mī) Ezra 10:33
Jeremiah (jĕr′·uh·mī′·uh) Jer 1:1, 2
Jeremoth (jĕr′·uh·mŏth) 1 Chron 8:14
Jeriah (jĕ·rī′·uh) 1 Chron 23:19
Jeribai (jĕr′·ĭ·bī) 1 Chron 11:26–47
Jericho (jĕr′·ĭ·kō) Num 22:1
Jeri-el (jē′·rī·ĕl) 1 Chron 7:2
Jerijah (jĕ·rī′·juh) 1 Chron 26:31, 32
Jerimoth (jĕr′·ĭ·mŏth) 1 Chron 7:7
Jerioth (jĕr′·ĭ·ŏth) 1 Chron 2:18
Jeroboam (jĕr·uh·bō′·ŭm) 1 Kgs 11:26
Jeroham (jĕ·rō′·hăm) 1 Sam 1:1
Jerubbaal (jĕr·ŭb·bā′·ŭl) Judg 6:32
Jeruel (jĕ·roo′·ĕl) 2 Chron 20:16
Jerusalem (jĕ·roo′·suh·lĕm) Josh 10:1
Jerusha (jĕ·roo′·shuh) 2 Kgs 15:32, 33
Jerushah (jĕ·roo′·shuh) 2 Chron 27:1
Jeshaiah (jĕ·shā′·uh) 1 Chron 25:3
Jeshanah (jĕ·shā′·nuh) 2 Chron 13:18, 19
Jesharelah (jĕsh·uh·rē′·luh) 1 Chron 25:9–31
Jeshebe-ab (jĕ·shĕb′·ē·ŭb) 1 Chron 24:7–18
Jesher (jē′·sher) 1 Chron 2:18
Jeshishai (jĕ·shĭsh′·ī) 1 Chron 5:14
Jeshohaiah (jĕsh·ō·hā′·uh) 1 Chron 4:34–39
Jeshua (jĕsh′·oo·uh) Ezra 2:2
Jeshurun (jĕsh′·ū·rŭn) Deut 32:15
Jesimi-el (jĕ·sĭm′·ĭ·ĕl) 1 Chron 4:34–39
Jesse (jĕs′·sē) Ruth 4:16, 17
Jesus (jē′·zŭs) Mt 1:21
Jether (jē′·ther) Judg 8:20
Jetheth (jē′·thĕth) Gen 36:40–43
Jethro (jĕth′·rō) Ex 3:1
Jetur (jē′·ter) Gen 25:12–15
Jeuel (jĕ·oo′·ĕl) 1 Chron 9:6
Jeush (jē′·ŭsh) Gen 36:5
Jeuz (jē′·ŭz) 1 Chron 8:8–10
Jezaniah (jĕz·uh·nī′·uh) Jer 40:8
Jezebel (jĕz′·uh·bĕl) 1 Kgs 16:31
Jezer (ites) (jē′·zer) (īts) Gen 46:23–25 (Num 26:48–50)
Jezi-el (jē′·zī·ĕl) 1 Chron 12:3–7

Jezrahiah (jĕz·ruh·hī′·uh) Neh 12:42
Jezreel (jĕz′·rē·ĕl) 1 Chron 4:3, 4
Jidlaph (jĭd′·lăf) Gen 22:20–23
Joab (jō′·ăb) 2 Sam 2:13
Joah (jō′·uh) 2 Kgs 18:18
Joahaz (jō′·uh·hăz) 2 Chron 34:8
Joanna (jō·ăn′·nuh) Lk 8:3
Joash (jō′·ăsh) 2 Kgs 11:2, 3
Job (jōb) Job 1:1
Jobab (jō′·băb) Gen 10:26–30
Jochebed (jŏk′·uh·bĕd) Ex 6:20
Joed (jō′·ĕd) Neh 11:7–9
Joel (jō′·ĕl) Joel 1:1
Jo-elah (jō′·uh·luh) 1 Chron 12:3–7
Jo-ezer (jō·ē′·zer) Chron 12:3–7
Jogbehah (jŏg′·bē·hah) Num 32:34–36
Jogli (jŏg′·lī) Num 34:16–28
Joha (jō′·huh) 1 Chron 8:15, 16
Johanan (jō·hā′·nŭn) 2 Kgs 25:23
Joiada (joi′·uh·duh) Neh 12:10, 11
Joiakim (joi′·uh·kĭm) Neh 12:10, 11
Joiarib (joi′-uh-rĭb) Ezra 8:16
Jokim (jō′·kĭm) 1 Chron 4:21, 22
Jokde-am (jŏk′·dē·ăm) Josh 15:48–62
Jokme-am (jŏk′·mē·ăm) 1 Chron 6:66–69
Jokne-am (jŏk′·nē·ăm) Josh 12:8–24
Jokshan (jŏk′·shăn) Gen 25:1, 2
Joktan (jŏk′·tăn) Gen 10:25
Jokthe-el (jŏk′·thē·ĕl) Josh 15:37–44
Jonadab (jŏn′·uh·dăb) 2 Sam 13:3
Jonah (jō′·nuh) 2 Kgs 14:25
Jonam (jō′·nŭm) Lk 3:23–38
Jonathan (jŏn′·uh·thŭn) 1 Sam 13:2
Joppa (jŏp′·puh) 2 Chron 2:16
Jorah (jō′·ruh) Ezra 2:3–35
Jorai (jō′·rī) 1 Chron 5:13
Joram (jō′·răm) 2 Sam 8:10
Jordan (jor′·dăn) Gen 13:10
Jorim (jō′·rĭm) Lk 3:23–38
Jorke-am (jor′·kē·ăm) 1 Chron 2:44
Josedech (jō′-sĕ·dĕk) Hag 1:1
Joseph (jō′·sĕf) Gen 30:23, 24
Joshah (jō′·shuh) 1 Chron 4:34–39
Joshaphat (jŏsh′·uh·făt) 1 Chron 11:26–47
Joshaviah (jŏsh·uh·vī′·uh) 1 Chron 11:26–47
Joshbekashah (jŏsh·bĕ·kăsh′·uh) 1 Chron 25:4, 5
Joshua (jŏsh′·oo·uh) Num 14:6
Josiah (jō·sī′·uh) 2 Kgs 21:24
Josiphiah (jŏs·ĭ·fī′·uh) Ezra 8:2–14
Jotbah (jŏt′·buh) 2 Kgs 21:19, 20
Jotbathah (jŏt′·buh·thuh) Num 33:15–37
Jotham (jō′·thŭm) Judg 9:5
Jozabad (jŏz′·uh·băd) 1 Chron 12:20
Jozachar (jō′·zuh·kahr) 2 Kgs 12:21
Jozadak (jō′·zuh·dăk) Ezra 3:1, 2
Jubal (joo′·bŭl) Gen 4:21
Jucal (jū′·căl) Jer 38:1
Judah (joo′·duh) Gen 29:35
Judas (joo′·dŭs) Mt 10:2–4
Judea (joo·dē′·uh) Acts 1:8
Judith (joo′·dĭth) Gen 26:34
Julia (joo′·lĭ·uh) Rom 16:15
Julius (joo′·lĭ·ŭs) Acts 27:1
Junias (joo′·nĭ·ŭs) Rom 16:7
Jupiter (joo′·pĭ·ter) Acts 14:12
Jushab-hesed (joo′·shăb·hē′·sĕd) 1 Chron 3:19, 20
Justus (jŭs′·tŭs) Acts 1:23
Juttah (jŭt′·tuh) Josh 15:48–62
Kabul (kā′·bŭl) Josh 19:27
Kabzeel (kăb′·zē·ĕl) Josh 15:21–32
Kadesh (kā′·dĕsh) Gen 20:1
Kadesh-Barnea (kā′·dĕsh·bahr·nē′·uh) Num 34:4
Kadmi-el (kăd′·mĭ·ĕl) Ezra 3:9
Kadmonites (kăd′·muh·nīts) Gen 15:19–21
Kaiwan (kī′·wahn) Amos 5:25–27
Kallai (kăl′·lī) Neh 12:12–21
Kamon (kā′·mŏn) Judg 10:5
Kanah (kā′·nuh) Josh 19:28
Kareah (kuh·rē′·uh) Jer 40:8
Karka (kahr′·kuh) Josh 15:2–4
Karkor (kahr′·kor) Judg 8:10
Kartah (kahr′·tuh) Josh 21:34, 35
Kartan (kahr′·tŭn) Josh 21:32
Kattath (kăt′·tŭth) Josh 19:15, 16
Kedar (kē′·dahr) Gen 25:12–15
Kedemah (kĕd′·ĕ·muh) Gen 25:12–15
Kedemoth (kĕd′·ĕ·mŏth) Josh 13:18
Kedesh (kē′·dĕsh) Josh 12:8–24
Kehelathah (kē·hĕ·lā′·thuh) Num 33:15–37
Keilah (kē·ī′·luh) Josh 15:37–44
Kelaiah (kĕ·lā′·uh) Ezra 10:23
Kelita (kĕ·lī′·tuh) Neh 8:7, 8
Kemuel (kĕm′·ū·ĕl) Gen 22:20–23
Kenan (Cainan) (kē′·nŭn) Gen 5:12–14
Kenath (kē′·nŭth) Num 32:42
Kenaz (kē′·năz) Gen 36:10–12
Kenites (kĕn′·īts) Gen 15:19–21
Kenizzites (kĕn′·ĭz·zīts) Gen 15:19–21
Keren-happuch (ker′·ĕn·hăp′·pŭk) Job 42:13, 14
Keri-oth-hezron (ker′·ĭ·ŏth·hĕz′·rŭn) Josh 15:21–32
Keros (kē′·rŏs) Ezra 2:43–54
Keturah (kĕ·too′·ruh) Gen 25:1
Kezia (kĕ·zī′·uh) Job 42:13, 14
Kibroth-hattaavah (kĭb′·rŏth·huh·tā′·uh·vuh) Num 11:34
Kibza-im (kĭb′·zuh·ĭm) Josh 21:20–22
Kidron (kĭd′·rŭn) 2 Sam 15:23
Kinah (kī′·nuh) Josh 15:21–32
Kir (ker) 2 Kgs 16:9
Kir-hareseth (ker·hahr′·ĕ·sĕth) 2 Kgs 3:25
Kir-haresh (ker·hahr′·ĕsh) Isa 16:11
Kir-heres (ker·hē′·rĕs) Jer 48:31
Kiriathaim (ker′·ĭ·uh·thā′·ĭm) Jer 48:1
Kiriath-arba (ker′·ĭ·ăth·ahr′·buh) Gen 35:27
Kiriatharim (ker′·ĭ·ăth·ahr′·rĭm) Ezra 2:3–35
Kiriath-baal (ker′·ĭ·ăth·bā′·ŭl) Josh 15:48–62
Kiriath-huzoth (ker′·ĭ·ăth·hū′·zŏth) Num 22:39
Kiriath-jearim (ker′·ĭ·ăth·jē′·uh·rĭm) Josh 9:17
Kiriath-sannah (ker′·ĭ·ăth·săn′·nuh) Josh 15:48–62
Kiriath-sepher (ker′·ĭ·ăth·sē′·fer) Josh 15:15
Kish (kĭsh) 1 Sam 9:1
Kishi (kĭsh′·ī) 1 Chron 6:44–47
Kishion (kĭsh′·ĭ·ŭn) Josh 19:17–23
Kishon (kī′·shŏn) Ps 83:9
Kitron (kĭt′·rŏn) Judg 1:30
Kittim (kĭt′·tĭm) Gen 10:4
Koa (kō′·uh) Ezek 23:23
Kohath (kō′·hăth) Gen 46:8–14
Kolaiah (kō·lī′·uh) Neh 11:7–9
Korah (ites) (kor′·uh) (īts) Num 16:1 (1 Chron 9:19)
Kore (kō′·rē) 1 Chron 9:19
Koz (kŏz) 1 Chron 4:8
Kushaiah (kū·shā′·ĭ·uh) 1 Chron 15:17
Laadah (lā′·uh·duh) 1 Chron 4:21, 22
Laban (lā′·bŭn) Gen 24:29, 30
Lachish (lā′·kĭsh) Josh 10:3
Ladan (lā′·dŭn) 1 Chron 7:25–27
Lael (lā′·ĕl) Num 3:16–24
Lahad (lā′·hăd) 1 Chron 4:2
Lahman (lah′·măm) Josh 15:37–44
Lahmi (lah′·mī) 1 Chron 20:5
Laish (lā′·ĭsh) 1 Sam 25:44
Lakkum (lā′·kŭm) Josh 19:33
Lamech (lā′·mĕk) Gen 4:18
Laodicea (lā′·ō·dĭ·sē′·uh) Col 2:1
Lappidoth (lăp′·pĭ·dŏth) Judg 4:4
Lasea (luh·sē′·uh) Acts 27:7, 8
Lasha (lā′·shuh) Gen 10:15–19
Lasharon (lă·shahr′·ŏn) Josh 12:8–24
Lazarus (lăz′·uh·rŭs) Lk 16:20
Leah (lē′·uh) Gen 29:16
Lebanah (lĕ·bā′·nuh) Ezra 2:43–54
Lebanon (lĕ′·bah·nŭn) Deut 1:7
Lebaoth (lĕ·bā′·ŏth) Josh 15:21–32
Lebo-Hamath (lē′·bō·hā′·măth) Num 34:7–9
Lebonah (lĕ·bō′·nuh) Judg 21:19
Lecah (lē′·cuh) 1 Chron 4:21, 22
Lehabim (lĕ·hā′·bĭm) Gen 10:13, 14
Lehi (lē′·hī) Judg 15:9
Lemuel (lĕm′·ū·ĕl) Prov 31:1
Leshem (lē′·shĕm) Josh 19:47, 48
Letushim (lĕ·tū′·shĭm) Gen 25:3
Leummim (lĕ·ŭm′·mĭm) Gen 25:3
Levi (tes) (lē′·vī) (ts) Gen 29:34 (Ex 6:25)
Leviticus (lĕ·vĭt′·ĭ·kŭs)
Libnah (lĭb′·nuh) Num 33:15–37
Libni (tes) (lĭb′·nī) (ts) Ex 6:17 (Num 26:58, 59)
Libyans (lĭb′·yănz) 2 Chron 12:3
Likhi (lĭk′·hī) 1 Chron 7:19
Linus (lī′·nŭs) 2 Tim 4:21
Lo-Ammi (lō·ăm′·mī) Hos 1:9
Lod (lŏd) 1 Chron 8:12
Lo-debar (lō·dē′·bahr) 2 Sam 9:4
Lois (lō′·ĭs) 2 Tim 1:5
Lo-ruhamah (lō′·roo·hā′·muh) Hos 1:6
Lot (lŏt) Gen 11:27
Lotan (lō′·tăn) Gen 36:20, 21
Lucifer (loo′·sĭ·fer) Isa 14:12
Lucius (loo′·sĭ·ŭs) Acts 13:1
Lud (lood) Gen 10:22
Ludim (loo′·dĭm) Gen 10:13, 14
Luhith (lū′·hĭth) Isa 15:5
Luz (lŭz) Gen 28:19
Lycaonia (lĭk·ā·ō′·nĭ·uh) Acts 14:5, 6
Lycia (lĭ′·sĭ·uh) Acts 27:5
Lydda (lĭd′·duh) Acts 9:32
Lydia (lĭd′·ĭ·uh) Acts 16:14
Lysanias (lī·sā′·nĭ·ŭs) Lk 3:1
Lysias (lĭs′·ĭ·ŭs) Acts 23:26
Lystra (lĭs′·truh) Acts 14:5, 6
Maacah (mā′·uh·kuh) 2 Sam 3:3
Ma-acathites (mā·ăk′·uh·thīts) Deut 3:14
Ma-adai (mā′·uh·dā′·ī) Ezra 10:34–42
Ma-adiah (mā·uh·dī′·uh) Neh 12:1–7

Maai (mā'·ī) Neh 12:35, 36
Maarath (mā'·uh·răth) Josh 15:48–62
Ma-aseiah (mā·uh·sē'·uh) Ezra 10:16–19
Maasai (mā'·uh·sī) 1 Chron 9:12
Maath (mā'·ăth) Lk 3:23–38
Maaz (mā'·ăz) 1 Chron 2:27
Maaziah (mā·uh·zī'·uh) 1 Chron 24:7–18
Macedonia (măs·uh·dō'·nī·uh) Acts 16:9
Machbannai (măk'·băn·nī) 1 Chron 12:8–13
Machbenah (măk·bē'·nuh) 1 Chron 2:48, 49
Machi (mā'·kī) Num 13:3–15
Machir (ites) (mā'·ker) (īts) Gen 50:23 (Num 26:28–37)
Machnadebai (măk·năd'·uh·bī) Ezra 10:34–42
Machpelah (măk·pē'·luh) Gen 23:9
Madai (mā'·dī) Gen 10:2
Madmannah (măd·măn'·uh) Josh 15:21–32
Madmen (măd'·mĕn) Jer 48:2–4
Madmenah (măd·mē'·nuh) Isa 10:31
Madon (mā'·dŏn) Josh 11:1
Magbish (măg'·bĭsh) Ezra 2:3–35
Magadan (măg'·uh·dăn) Mt 15:39
Magdalene (măg'·duh·lēn) Mt 27:56
Magdiel (măg'·dī·ĕl) Gen 36:40–43
Magog (mā'·gŏg) Gen 10:2
Magpiash (măg'·pī·ăsh) Neh 10:14–27
Mahalaleel (muh·hā'·luh·lē'·ĕl) Lk 3:23–38
Mahalalel (muh·hā'·luh·lē'·ĕl) Gen 5:12–14
Mahalath (mă·hā'·lăth) Gen 28:9
Maharai (mā'·huh·rī) 2 Sam 23:24–39
Mahath (mā'·hăth) 1 Chron 6:33–38
Mahazi-oth (muh·hā'·zī·ōth) 1 Chron 25:4, 5
Maher-shalal-hash-baz (mā'·her·shăl'·ăl·hăsh·băz) Isa 8:1
Mahlah (mah'·luh) Num 26:28–37
Mahli (mah'·lī) 1 Chron 6:19–21
Mahlon (mah'·lŏn) Ruth 1:1, 2
Mahol (mā'·hŏl) 1 Kgs 4:31
Makaz (mā'·kăz) 1 Kgs 4:8–19
Makheloth (măk·hē'·lōth) Num 33:15–37
Makkedah (măk·kē'·duh) Josh 10:10
Malachi (măl'·uh·kī) Mal 1:1
Malcam (măl'·kŭm) 1 Chron 8:8–10
Malchi-el (ites) (măl'·kī·ĕl) (īts) Gen 46:16, 17 (Num 26:44–47)
Malchijah (măl·kī'·juh) 1 Chron 9:12
Malchiram (măl·kī'·rŭm) 1 Chron 3:17, 18
Malchishua (măl·kĭsh'·ū·uh) 1 Chron 8:33
Malchus (măl'·kŭs) Jn 18:10
Mallothi (măl·lō'·thī) 1 Chron 25:4, 5
Malluch (măl'·ŭk) 1 Chron 6:44–47
Malluchi (măl'·loo·kī) Neh 12:12–21
Mamre (măm'·rē) Gen 13:18
Manaen (măn'·uh·ĕn) Acts 13:1
Manahath (ites) (măn'·uh·hăth) (īts) Gen 36:23 (1 Chron 2:54)
Manasseh (muh·năs'·suh) Gen 41:51
Manoah (muh·nō'·uh) Judg 13:2, 3
Maon (ites) (mā'·ŏn) (īts) Josh 15:48–62 (Judg 10:12)
Mara (mahr'·uh) Ruth 1:20
Marah (mĕr'·uh) Ex 15:23
Mareal (măr'·ē·ăl) Josh 19:11
Mareshah (mah·rē'·shuh) Josh 15:37–44
Maroth (mā'·rŏth) Mic 1:12
Marsena (mahr·sē'·nuh) Esth 1:13–15
Mash (măsh) Gen 10:23
Mashal (mā'·shŭl) 1 Chron 6:74
Masrekah (măs·rē'·kuh) Gen 36:31–39
Massa (măs'·suh) Gen 25:12–15
Massah (măs'·suh) Ex 17:7
Mattattah (măt'·tŭt·tuh) Ezra 10:33
Matred (mā'·trĕd) Gen 36:31–39
Matrites (mā'·trīts) 1 Sam 10:21
Mattan (măt'·tăn) 2 Kgs 11:18
Mattanah (măt'·tuh·nuh) Num 21:17, 18
Mattaniah (măt·tuh·nī'·uh) 2 Kgs 24:17
Mattatha (măt'·tuh·thuh) Lk 3:23–38
Mattathias (măt·uh·thī'·ŭs) Lk 3:23–38
Mattenai (măt·tē'·nī) Ezra 10:33
Matthan (măt'·thŭn) Mt 1:15
Matthat (măt'·thăt) Lk 3:23–38
Matthew (mă'·thū) Mt 9:9
Matthias (mă·thī'·ŭs) Acts 1:23
Mattithiath (măt·tĭ·thī'·ăth) 1 Chron 9:31
Me-arah (mē·ahr'·uh) Josh 13:2–7
Meconah (mē·cō'·nuh) Neh 11:25–30
Mebunnai (mē·bŭn'·nī) 2 Sam 23:24–39
Mecherath (mē·kē'·rŭth) 1 Chron 11:26–47
Medad (mē'·dăd) Num 11:26
Medan (mē'·dăn) Gen 25:1, 2
Medeba (mĕd'·uh·buh) Num 21:27–30
Medes (mēdz) 2 Kgs 17:6
Media (mē'·dī·ah) Esth 10:2
Megiddo (mē·gĭd'·dō) Josh 12:8–24
Mehetabel (mē·hĕt'·uh·bĕl) Gen 36:31–39
Mehida (mē·hī'·duh) Ezra 2:43–54
Mehir (mē'·her) 1 Chron 4:11, 12
Meholath (muh·hō'·lŭth) 1 Sam 18:19
Mehujael (mē·hū'·juh·ĕl) Gen 4:18
Mehuman (mē·hoo'·mŭn) Esth 1:10
Me-jarkon (mē·jahr'·kŏn) Josh 19:41–46
Melatiah (mē·luh·tī'·uh) Neh 3:7
Melchi (mĕl'·kī) Lk 3:23–38
Melchizedek (mĕl·kĭz'·uh·dĕk) Gen 14:18
Melea (mē'·lē·ah) Lk 3:23–38
Melech (mē'·lĕk) 1 Chron 8:35
Memphis (mĕm'·fĭs) Hos 9:6
Memucan (mē·mū'·cŭn) Esth 1:13–15
Menahem (mĕn'·uh·hĕm) 2 Kgs 15:14
Mene (mĕ'·nā) Dan 5:24, 25
Menna (mĕn'·nuh) Lk 3:23–38
Menuhoth (mē·nū'·hŏth) 1 Chron 2:52
Meonenim (mē·ŏn'·ē·nĭm) Judg 9:37
Meonothai (mē·ō'·nuh·thī) 1 Chron 4:14
Mepha-ath (mēf'·uh·ăth) Josh 13:18
Mephibosheth (mē·fĭb'·ō·shĕth) 2 Sam 4:4
Merab (mē'·răb) 1 Sam 14:49
Meraiah (mē·rī'·uh) Neh 12:12–21
Meraioth (mē·rā'·ī·ŏth) 1 Chron 6:4–15
Merari (mē·rahr'·ī) Gen 46:8–14
Merathaim (mer·uh·thā'·ĭm) Jer 50:21
Mercury (mer'·kū·rē) Acts 14:12
Mered (mĕr'·ĕd) 1 Chron 4:17
Meremoth (mĕr'·ē·mŏth) Ezra 8:33
Meres (mē'·rēz) Esth 1:13–15
Meribah (mĕr'·ĭ·bah) Ex 17:7
Merib-baal (mer'·ĭb·bā'·ŭl) 1 Chron 8:34
Merodach-baladan (mer'·uh·dahk·băl'·uh·dŭn) 2 Kgs 20:12
Merom (mē'·rŏm) Josh 11:5
Meronoth (mē·rŏn'·ŏth) 1 Chron 27:30
Meroz (mē'·rŏz) Judg 5:23
Mesha (mē'·shuh) 2 Kgs 3:4
Meshach (mē'·shăk) Dan 1:7
Meshech (mē'·shĕk) Gen 10:2
Meshelemiah (mē·shĕl·ē·mī'·uh) 1 Chron 9:21
Meshezabel (mē·shĕz'·uh·bĕl) Neh 3:4
Meshillemith (mē·shĭl'·lē·mĭth) 1 Chron 9:12
Meshillemoth (mē·shĭl'·lē·mŏth) 2 Chron 28:12
Meshobab (mē·shō'·băb) 1 Chron 4:34–39
Meshullam (mē·shŭl'·lŭm) 2 Kgs 22:3, 4
Meshullemeth (mē·shŭl'·lē·mĕth) 2 Kgs 21:19, 20
Messiah (mē·sī'·uh) Jn 1:41
Methusael (mē·thū'·sā·ĕl) Gen 4:18
Methuselah (mē·thoo'·sē·luh) Gen 5:21–24
Me-unim (mē·oo'·nĭm) Neh 7:46–56
Mezahab (mē'·zuh·hăb) Gen 36:31–39
Mezoba (mē·zō'·buh) 1 Chron 11:26–47
Mibhar (mĭb'·hahr) 1 Chron 11:26–47
Mibsam (mĭb'·sŭm) Gen 25:12–15
Mibzar (mĭb'·zahr) Gen 36:40–43
Micah (mī'·cah) Judg 17:1
Micaiah (mī·kī'·uh) 1 Kgs 22:8
Michal (mī'·kŭl) 1 Sam 14:49
Michmas (mĭk'·măs) Ezra 2:3–35
Michmash (mĭk'·măsh) 1 Sam 13:2
Michmethath (mĭk·mē'·thăth) Josh 16:5, 6
Michri (mĭk'·rī) 1 Chron 9:7, 8
Middin (mĭd'·dĭn) Josh 15:48–62
Midian (ites) (mĭd'·ĭ·ŭn) (īts) Gen 25:1, 2 (Gen 37:28)
Migdal-el (mĭg'·dŭl·ĕl) Josh 19:35–39
Migdal-gad (mĭg'·dŭl·găd) Josh 15:37–44
Migdol (mĭg'·dŏl) Ex 14:2
Migron (mĭg'·rŏn) Isa 10:28, 29

Mijamin (mī′·juh·mĭn) 1 Chron 24:7–18
Mikloth (mĭk′·lŏth) 1 Chron 8:30–32
Mikneiah (mĭk·nē′·ĭ·uh) 1 Chron 15:18
Milalai (mĭl′·uh·lī) Neh 12:35, 36
Milcah (mĭl′·kuh) Gen 11:29
Milcom (mĭl′·kŭm) 1 Kgs 11:5
Miletus (mī·lē′·tŭs) Acts 20:15
Miniamin (mĭ·nī′·uh·mĭn) 2 Chron 31:14, 15
Minni (mĭn′·nī) Jer 51:27
Minnith (mĭn′·nĭth) Judg 11:33
Miriam (mĭr′·ē·ŭm) Ex 15:20
Mirmah (mer′·muh) 1 Chron 8:8–10
Misha-el (mĭsh′·uh·ĕl) Ex 6:22
Mishal (mī′·shŭl) Josh 21:30, 31
Misham (mī′·shŭm) 1 Chron 8:12
Mishma (mĭsh′·muh) Gen 25:12–15
Mishmannah (mĭsh·măn′·uh) 1 Chron 12:8–13
Mishraites (mĭsh′·ruh·īts) 1 Chron 2:53
Mispar (mĭs′·pahr) Ezra 2:2
Mispereth (mĭs′·pē·rĕth) Neh 7:7
Misrephoth-maim (mĭs′·rē·fŏth·mā′·ĭm) Josh 13:2–7
Mithkah (mĭth′·kuh) Num 33:15–37
Mithna (mĭth′·nuh) 1 Chron 11:26–47
Mithredath (mĭth′·rĕ·dăth) Ezra 1:8
Mitylene (mĭt·ĭ·lē′·nē) Acts 20:14
Mizar (mī′·zahr) Ps 42:6
Mizpah (mĭz′·pah) Gen 31:49
Mizraim (mĭz′·rā·ĭm) Gen 10:6
Mizzah (mĭz′·zuh) Gen 36:13, 14
Mnason (nā′·sŭn) Acts 21:16
Moab (ites) (mō′·ăb) (īts) Gen 19:37 (Deut 2:9)
Moadiah (mō·uh·dī′·uh) Neh 12:12–21
Moladah (mō′·luh·duh) Josh 15:21–32
Molech (mō′·lĕk) Lev 18:21
Molid (mō′·lĭd) 1 Chron 2:29
Morasthite (mō·răs′·thīt) Jer 26:18
Mordecai (mor′·dĕ·kī) Esth 2:5
Moreh (mō′·rĕh) Gen 12:6
Moresheth (mor′·ĕ·shĕth) Mic 1:1
Moriah (mō·rī′·uh) Gen 22:2
Moserah (mō·sē′·ruh) Deut 10:6
Moseroth (mō·sē′·rŏth) Num 33:15–37
Moza (mō′·zuh) 1 Chron 2:46
Mozah (mō′·zuh) Josh 18:21–28
Muppim (mŭp′·pĭm) Gen 46:19–22
Mushi (mū′·shī) Ex 6:19
Myra (mī′·ruh) Acts 27:5
Mysia (mĭ′·sĭ·uh) Acts 16:7
Naam (ites) (nā′·ŭm) (īts) *1 Chron 4:15 (Num 26:38–41)*
Naamah (nā′·uh·muh) 1 Kgs 14:21
Naaman (nā′·uh·măn) 2 Kgs 5:1
Naamathite (nā′·uh·muh·thīt) Job 2:11
Naarah (nā′·uh·ruh) 1 Chron 4:5
Naarai (nā′·uh·rī) 1 Chron 11:26–47
Naaran (nā′·uh·răn) 1 Chron 7:28
Nabal (nā′·băl) 1 Sam 25:3
Naboth (nā′·bŏth) 1 Kgs 21:1
Nacon (nā′·kŭn) 2 Sam 6:6
Nadab (nā′·dăb) Ex 6:23
Naggai (năg′·guh·ī) Lk 3:23–38
Nahalal (nā′·huh·lăl) Josh 21:34, 35
Nahaliel (nuh·hăl′·ĭ·ĕl) Num 21:19
Nahalol (nuh·hăl′·ŏl) Judg 1:30
Naham (nā′·hăm) 1 Chron 4:19
Nahamani (nā·hăm′·uh·nī) Neh 7:7
Naharai (nā′·huh·rī) 1 Chron 11:26–47
Nahash (nā′·hăsh) 1 Sam 11:1
Nahath (nā′·hăth) Gen 36:13, 14
Nahbi (năh′·bī) Num 13:13–15
Nahor (nā′·hor) Gen 11:22, 23
Nahshon (nah′·shŭn) Num 1:2–15
Nahum (nā′·hŭm) Nah 1:1
Nain (nā′·ĭn) Lk 7:11
Naioth (nī′·ŏth) 1 Sam 19:18
Naomi (nā·ō′·mē) Ruth 1:1, 2
Naphish (nā′·fĭsh) Gen 25:12–15
Naphtali (năf′·tuh·lī) Gen 30:8
Naphtuhim (năf′·too·hĭm) Gen 10:13, 14
Narcissus (nahr·sĭs′·ŭs) Rom 16:11
Nathan (nā′·thăn) 2 Sam 7:2
Nathanael (nuh·thăn′·ā·ĕl) Jn 1:45
Nathan-melech (nā′·thăn·mē′·lĕk) 2 Kgs 23:11
Nazarene (nă′·zuh·rēn) Mt 2:23
Nazareth (nă′·zuh·rĕth) Lk 1:26
Nazirite (nă′·zuh·rīt) Num 6:1, 2
Neah (nē′·uh) Josh 19:13
Neapolis (nē·ăp′·uh·lĭs) Acts 16:11
Neariah (nē·uh·rī′·uh) 1 Chron 3:21, 22
Nebai (nē′·bī) Neh 10:14–27
Nebaioth (nĕ·bā′·ĭ·ŏth) Gen 25:12–15
Neballat (nĕ·băl′·lăt) Neh 11:31–35
Nebat (nē′·băt) 1 Kgs 11:26
Nebo (nē′·bō) Deut 32:49
Nebuchadnezzar (nĕ′·boo·kŭd·nĕz′·zer) 2 Kgs 24:1
Nebuzaradan (nĕ·boo′·zuh·răd′·ŭn) 2 Kgs 25:8
Neco (nē′·cō) 2 Kgs 23:29
Necho (nē′·cō) Jer 46:2
Nedabiah (nĕd·uh·bī′·uh) 1 Chron 3:17, 18
Nehelam (nĕ·hĕl′·ŭm) Jer 29:24
Nehemiah (nē·hĕ·mī′·uh) Neh 1
Nehum (nē′·hŭm) Neh 7:7
Nehushta (nĕ·hŭsh′·tuh) 2 Kgs 24:8, 9
Neiel (nē·ī′·ĕl) Josh 19:27
Nekoda (nĕ·kō′·duh) Ezra 2:43–54
Nemu-el (ites) (nĕm′·ū·ĕl) (īts) Num 26:5–11 (Num 26:12–14)
Nepheg (nē′·fĕg) Ex 6:21
Nephisim (nĕ·fī′·sĭm) Ezra 2:43–54
Nephtoah (nĕf·tō′·uh) Josh 15:9
Nephushesim (nĕ·foosh′·ĕ·sĭm) Neh 7:46–56
Ner (ner) 1 Sam 14:50, 51
Nereus (nēr′·ĕ·ŭs) Rom 16:15
Nergal (ner′·găl) 2 Kgs 17:30
Nergal-sharezer (ner′·găl·shah·rē′·zer) Jer 39:3
Neri (nē′·rī) Lk 3:23–38
Neriah (nĕ·rī′·uh) Jer 32:12
Nethanel (nĕ·thăn′·ĕl) Num 1:2–15
Nethaniah (nĕth·uh·nī′·uh) 2 Kgs 25:23
Netophah (nĕ·tŏf′·uh) Ezra 2:3–35
Netophathites (nuh·tŏf′·uh·thīts) Neh 12:28
Neziah (nĕ·zī′·uh) Ezra 2:43–54
Nezib (nē′·zĭb) Josh 15:37–44
Nibhaz (nĭb′·hăz) 2 Kgs 17:31
Nibshan (nĭb′·shăn) Josh 15:48–62
Nicanor (nī·kā′·nor) Acts 6:5
Nicodemus (nĭk·uh·dē′·mŭs) Jn 3:1
Nicolaitans (nĭk·ō·lā′·ĭ·tăns) Rev 2:6
Nicolaus (nĭk·uh·lā′·ŭs) Acts 6:5
Nicopolis (nĭ·cŏp′·ō·lĭs) Tit 3:12
Nimrah (nĭm′·ruh) Num 32:3, 4
Nimrim (nĭm′·rĭm) Isa 15:6
Nimrod (nĭm′·rŏd) Gen 10:8
Nimshi (nĭm′·shī) 2 Kgs 9:2
Nineveh (nĭn′·ĕ·vuh) Gen 10:11, 12
Nisroch (nĭs′·rŏk) 2 Kgs 19:37
No-adiah (nō·uh·dī′·uh) Neh 6:14
Noah (nō′·uh) Num 26:28–37
Nob (nŏb) 1 Sam 21:1
Nobah (nō′·buh) Num 32:42
Nod (nŏd) Gen 4:16
Nodabites (nō′·dăb·īts) 1 Chron 5:19
Nogah (nō′·guh) 1 Chron 3:6–8
Nohah (nō′·huh) 1 Chron 8:1, 2
Nophah (nō′·fah) Num 21:27–30
Nun (nŭn) Ex 33:11
Nymphas (nĭm′·fŭs) Col 4:15
Obadiah (ō·buh·dī′·uh) Obad 1:1
Obal (ō′·bŭl) Gen 10:26–30
Obed (ō′·bĕd) Ruth 4:16, 17
Obed-edom (ō′·bĕd·ē′·dŭm) 2 Sam 6:10
Obil (ō′·bĭl) 1 Chron 27:30
Oboth (ō′·bŏth) Num 21:10
Ochran (ŏk′·rŭn) Num 1:2–15
Oded (ō′·dĕd) 2 Chron 15:1
Og (ŏg) Num 21:33
Ohad (ō′·hăd) Gen 46:8–14
Ohel (ō′·hĕl) 1 Chron 3:19, 20
Oholah (ō·hō′·luh) Ezek 23:4, 5
Oholiab (ō·hō′·lĭ·ăb) Ex 31:6
Oholibah (ō·hŏl′·ĭ·buh) Ezek 23:4, 5
Olympas (ō·lĭm′·pŭs) Rom 16:15
Omar (ō′·mahr) Gen 36:10–12
Omri (ŏm′·rī) 1 Kgs 16:15, 16
Onam (ō′·nŭm) Gen 36:23
Onan (ō′·nŭn) Gen 38:3–5
Onesimus (ō·nĕs′·ĭ·mŭs) Col 4:9
Onesiphorus (ŏn·ĕ·sĭf′·ō·rŭs) 2 Tim 1:16
Ono (ō′·nō) 1 Chron 8:12
Ophel (ō′·fĕl) Neh 3:26
Ophir (ō′·fer) Gen 10:26–30
Ophni (ŏf′·nī) Josh 18:21–28
Ophrah (ŏf′·ruh) 1 Chron 4:14
Oreb (or′·ĕb) Judg 7:25
Oren (ō′·rĕn) 1 Chron 2:25
Orion (ō·rī′·ŭn) Job 9:9
Orpah (or′·pah) Ruth 1:4, 5
Osnapper (ŏs·năp′·per) Ezra 4:10
Othni (ŏth′·nī) 1 Chron 26:6, 7
Othni-el (ŏth′·nĭ·ĕl) Josh 15:17
Ozem (ō′·zĕm) 1 Chron 2:15
Ozni (tes) (ŏz′·nī) (ts) Num 26:15–18
Paarai (pā′·uh·rī) 2 Sam 23:24–39
Paddan-Aram (păd′·dŭn·ahr′·ŭm) Gen 28:2
Padon (pā′·dŏn) Ezra 2:43–54
Pagiel (pā′·gĭ·ĕl) Num 1:2–15
Pahath-moab (pā′·hăth·mō′·ăb) Ezra 2:3–35
Pai (pā′·ī) 1 Chron 1:50
Palal (pā′·lăl) Neh 3:25
Pallu (ites) (păl′·oo) (īts) Ex 6:14 (Num 26:5–11)
Palti (păl′·tī) Num 13:3–15
Paltiel (păl′·tĭ·ĕl) Num 34:16–28

Pamphylia (păm·fĭl′·ĭ·uh) Acts 2:10
Paphos (pā′·fŏs) Acts 13:6, 7
Parah (pahr′·uh) Josh 18:21–28
Paran (pahr′·ŭn) Gen 21:20, 21
Parmashta (pahr·măsh′·tuh) Esth 9:7–10
Parmenas (pahr′·mē·nahs) Acts 6:5
Parnach (pahr′·năk) Num 34:16–28
Parosh (pā′·rŏsh) Ezra 2:3–35
Parshandatha (pahr·shŭn·dā′·thuh) Esth 9:7–10
Parsin (pahr′·sĭn) Dan 5:24, 25
Parthians (pahr′·thĭ·ŭnz) Acts 2:9
Paruah (puh·roo′·uh) 1 Kgs 4:8–19
Parvaim (pahr·vā′·ĭm) 2 Chron 3:6
Pasach (pā′·săk) 1 Chron 7:33
Pas-dammim (păs·dăm′·mĭm) 1 Chron 11:13
Paseah (puh·sē′·uh) 1 Chron 4:11, 12
Pashur (păsh′·er) Jer 20:1
Patara (păt′·uh·ruh) Acts 21:1
Pathros (păth′·rŏs) Ezek 29:14
Pathrusim (păth·roo′·sĭm) Gen 10:13, 14
Patmos (păt′·mŏs) Rev 1:9
Patrobas (păt·rō′·bŭs) Rom 16:14
Pau (pā′·uh) Gen 36:31–39
Pedahel (pĕ·dā′·ĕl) Num 34:16–28
Pedahzur (pĕ·dah′·zer) Num 2:3–31
Pedaiah (pĕ·dā′·uh) 1 Chron 27:16–22
Pekah (pē′·kuh) 2 Kgs 15:25
Pekahiah (pĕk·uh·hī′·uh) 2 Kgs 15:22
Pekod (pē′·kŏd) Jer 50:21
Pelaiah (pĕ·lā′·uh) 1 Chron 3:24
Pelaliah (pĕl·uh·lī′·uh) Neh 11:10–14
Pelatiah (pĕl·uh·tī′·uh) Ezek 11:1
Peleg (pē′·lĕg) Gen 10:25
Pelet (pē′·lĕt) 1 Chron 2:47
Peleth (ites) (pē′·lĕth) (īts) Num 16:1 (2 Sam 8:18)
Pelon (pĕl′·ŭn) 1 Chron 11:26–47
Peniel (pĕ·nī′·ĕl) Gen 32:30
Peninnah (pĕ·nĭn′·nuh) 1 Sam 1:2
Pentecost (pĕn′·tĕ·cŏst) Acts 2:1
Penuel (pĕ·nū′·ĕl) Judg 8:8
Peor (pē′·or) Num 23:28
Perazim (pĕ·rā′·zĭm) Isa 28:21
Peresh (pē′·rĕsh) 1 Chron 7:16
Perez (pĕr′·ĕz) 1 Chron 2:4
Perga (per′·guh) Acts 13:13
Pergamos (per′·guh·mŭs) Rev 1:11
Perida (pĕ·rī′·duh) Neh 7:57–59
Perizzites (pĕr′·ĭz·zīts) Gen 13:7
Persis (pĕr′·sĭs) Rom 16:12
Peruda (pĕ·roo′·duh) Ezra 2:55–57
Pethahiah (pĕth·uh·hī′·uh) 1 Chron 24:7–18
Pethor (pē′·thor) Num 22:5, 6
Pethuel (pĕ·thū′·ĕl) Joel 1:1
Pe-ullethai (pĕ·ŭl′·ĕ·thī) 1 Chron 26:4, 5
Phanuel (făn′·ū·ĕl) Lk 2:36, 37
Pharaoh (fĕr′·ō) Gen 12:15
Pharaoh-Neco (fĕr′·ō·nē′·kō) 2 Kgs 23:33
Pharisees (fĕr′·ĭ·sēz) Jn 3:1
Pharpar (fahr′·pahr) 2 Kgs 5:12
Phicol (fī′·cŏl) Gen 21:22
Philadelphia (fĭl·ah·dĕl′·fē·uh) Rev 1:11
Philemon (fĭ·lē′·mŭn) Philem 1
Philetus (fĭ·lē′·tŭs) 2 Tim 2:17
Philippi (ans) (fĭl′·ĭ·pī) (fĭ·lĭp′·ĭ·ănz) Acts 16:12 (Phil 4:15)
Philistines (fĭ·lĭs′·tĭns) Gen 21:34
Philologus (fĭ·lŏl′·uh·gŭs) Rom 16:15
Phinehas (fĭn′·ē·hŭs) Ex 6:25
Phlegon (flē′·gŏn) Rom 16:14
Phoebe (fē′·bē) Rom 16:1
Phoenicia (fē·nĭ′·sĭ·uh) Acts 11:19
Phrygia (frĭj·ĭ·uh) Acts 2:10
Phygellus (fĭ′·gĕ·lŭs) 2 Tim 1:15
Piha-hiroth (pī′·huh·hī′·rŏth) Ex 14:2
Pilate (pī′·lăt) Mt 27:2
Pildash (pĭl′·dăsh) Gen 22:20–23
Pilha (pĭl′·huh) Neh 10:14–27
Piltai (pĭl′·tī) Neh 12:12–21
Pinon (pī′·nŏn) Gen 36:40–43
Piram (pī′·rŭm) Josh 10:3
Pirathon (pĭr′·uh·thŏn) Judg 12:15
Pisgah (pĭz′·guh) Num 21:20
Pishon (pī′·shŏn) Gen 2:11, 12
Pisidia (pĭ·sĭd′·ĭ·uh) Acts 13:14
Pispa (pĭs′·pah) 1 Chron 7:38
Pithom (pī′·thŏm) Ex 1:11
Pithon (pī′·thŏn) 1 Chron 8:35
Pleiades (plē′·uh·dēz) Job 9:9
Pochereth-hazzebaim (pō′·kĕ·rĕth·hăz·ē·bā′·ĭm) Ezra 2:55–57
Pontius (Pilate) (pŏn′·tĭ·ŭs)
Pontus (pŏn′·tŭs) Acts 2:9
Poratha (pō·rā′·thuh) Esth 9:7–10
Porcius Festus (por′·sĭ·ŭs fĕs′·tŭs) Acts 24:27
Potiphar (pŏt′·ĭ·fŭr) Gen 37:36
Potiphera (pō·tĭ′·fĕ·ruh) Gen 41:45
Priscilla (prĭ·sĭl′·luh) Acts 18:2, 3
Prochorus (prŏk′·uh·rŭs) Acts 6:5
Ptolemais (tŏl·uh·mā′·ĭs) Acts 21:7
Puah (poo′·uh) Ex 1:15, 16
Publius (pŭb′·lĭ·ŭs) Acts 28:7
Pudens (pū′·dĕnz) 2 Tim 4:21
Pul (pool) 2 Kgs 15:19, 20
Punites (pū′·nīts) Num 26:23–25
Punon (pū′·nŏn) Num 33:42
Pur (poor) Esth 9:26
Purah (pū′·rah) Judg 7:10
Purim (poor′·ĭm) Esth 9:26
Put (poot) 1 Chron 1:5–9
Puteoli (pū·tē′·ō·lī) Acts 28:13
Puthites (pū′·thīts) 1 Chron 2:53
Puti-el (pū′·tĭ·ĕl) Ex 6:25
Puvah (pū′·vuh) Gen 46:8–14
Quartus (kwahr′·tŭs) Rom 16:23
Quirinius (kwĭ·rĭn′·ĭ·ŭs) Lk 2:2
Raamah (rā′·uh·muh) Gen 10:7
Ra-amiah (rā·uh·mī′·uh) Neh 7:7
Ra-amses (ruh·ăm′·sēz) Ex 1:11
Rabbah (răb′·buh) Josh 13:25
Rabbi (răb′·ī) Mt 23:7
Rabbith (răb′·bĭth) Josh 19:17–23
Racal (rā′·cŭl) 1 Sam 30:27–31
Rachel (rā′·chĕl) Gen 29:6
Raddai (răd′·dī) 1 Chron 2:14
Rahab (rā′·hăb) Josh 2:1
Raham (rā′·hăm) 1 Chron 2:44
Rakem (rā′·kĕm) 1 Chron 7:16
Rakkath (răk′·kăth) Josh 19:35–39
Rakkon (răk′·kŏn) Josh 19:41–46
Ramah (rā′·muh) Josh 18:21–28
Ramath (rā′·măth) 1 Chron 27:27
Ramathaim-zophim (rā·muh·thā′·ĭm·zō′·fĭm) 1 Sam 1:1
Ramath-mizpeh (rā′·măth·mĭz′·puh) Josh 13:26
Rameses (răm′·ĕ·sēz) Gen 47:11
Ramiah (ruh·mī′·uh) Ezra 10:25
Ramoth (rā′·mŏth) 1 Chron 6:73
Raphah (rā′·fah) 1 Chron 8:37
Raphu (rā′·fū) Num 13:3–15
Re-aiah (rē·ā′·uh) 1 Chron 4:2
Reba (rē′·buh) Num 31:8
Rebecca (rĕ·bĕk′·kah) Rom 9:10–13
Rebekah (rĕ·bĕk′·ah) Gen 22:20–23
Rechab (ites) (rē′·kăb) (īts) 2 Kgs 10:15 (Jer 35:2)
Rechah (rē′·kuh) 1 Chron 4:11, 12
Re-el-aiah (rē·ĕl·ā′·uh) Ezra 2:2
Regem (rē′·gĕm) 1 Chron 2:47
Regem-melech (rē′·gĕm·mĕl′·ĕk) Zech 7:2
Rehabiah (rē·huh·bī′·uh) 1 Chron 23:17
Rehob (rē′·hŏb) 2 Sam 8:3
Rehoboam (rē·huh·bō′·ŭm) 1 Kgs 11:43
Rehoboth-Ir (rĕ·hō′·bŏth·ĭr) Gen 10:11, 12
Rehum (rē′·hŭm) Ezra 4:8, 9
Rei (rē′·ī) 1 Kgs 1:8
Rekem (rē′·kĕm) Num 31:8
Remaliah (rĕm·uh·lī′·uh) 2 Kgs 15:25
Remeth (rē′·mĕth) Josh 19:17–23
Repha-el (rĕf′·uh·ĕl) 1 Chron 26:6, 7
Rephah (rē′·fuh) 1 Chron 7:25–27
Rephaiah (rĕf·ā′·uh) 1 Chron 3:21, 22
Rephaim (rĕf′·uh·ĭm) 2 Sam 5:18
Rephidim (rĕf′·ĭ·dĭm) Ex 17:1
Resen (rē′·sĕn) Gen 10:11, 12
Resheph (rē′·shĕf) 1 Chron 7:25–27
Reu (rē′·ū) Gen 11:18, 19
Reuben (roo′·bĕn) Gen 29:32
Reuel (roo′·ĕl) 1 Chron 9:7, 8
Reumah (rĕ·oo′·muh) Gen 22:24
Rezeph (rē′·zĕf) 2 Kgs 19:12
Rezin (rē′·zĭn) 2 Kgs 15:37
Rezon (rē′·zŏn) 1 Kgs 11:23
Rhegium (rē′·jĭ·ŭm) Acts 28:13
Rhesa (rē′·suh) Lk 3:23–38
Rhoda (rō′·duh) Acts 12:13
Rhodes (rōdz) Acts 21:1
Ribai (rī′·bī) 2 Sam 23:24–39
Riblah (rĭb′·luh) Num 34:10, 11
Rimmon (rĭm′·mŏn) 2 Sam 4:2, 3
Rimmon-parez (rĭm′·mŏn·pĕr′·ĕz) Num 33:15–37
Rinnah (rĭn′·nuh) 1 Chron 4:20
Riphath (rī′·făth) Gen 10:3
Rissah (rĭs′·suh) Num 33:15–37
Rithmah (rĭth′·muh) Num 33:15–37
Rizia (rĭ·zī′·uh) 1 Chron 7:39
Rizpah (rĭz′·puh) 2 Sam 3:7
Rogelim (rō′·guh·lĭm) 2 Sam 17:27
Rohgah (rō′·guh) 1 Chron 7:34
Romamti-ezer (rō·măm′·tĭ·ē′·zer) 1 Chron 25:4, 5
Rosh (rŏsh) Gen 46:21
Rufus (roo′·fŭs) Mk 15:19–22
Ruhamah (roo·hā′·muh) Hos 2:1
Rumah (roo′·muh) 2 Kgs 23:36, 37
Sabeans (suh·bē′·ŭnz) Job 1:14, 15
Sabtah (săb′·tuh) Gen 10:7
Sabteca (săb′·tē·kuh) Gen 10:7
Sacher (sā′·ker) 1 Chron 11:26–47
Sachia (suh·kī′·uh) 1 Chron 8:8–10
Sadducees (săd′·dū·sēz) Mt 16:1
Sakkuth (săk′·kŭth) Amos 5:25–27
Salamis (săl′·uh·mĭs) Acts 13:5
Salecah (săl′·ĕ·kuh) Deut 3:10
Salem (sā′·lĕm) Gen 14:18

Salim (sā′·lĭm) Jn 3:23, 24
Sallai (săl′·lī) Neh 11:7–9
Sallu (săl′·loo) 1 Chron 9:7
Salma (săl′·muh) 1 Chron 2:11
Salmone (săl·mō′·nē) Acts 27:7, 8
Salome (suh·lō′·mē) Mk 15:40
Salu (sah′·loo) Num 25:14
Samaria (suh·mĕr′·ĭ·uh) 1 Kgs 16:24
Samaritan (suh·mĕr′·ĭ·tŭn) Lk 10:33
Samgar-nebo (săm′·gahr·nē′·bō) Jer 39:3
Samlah (săm′·luh) Gen 36:31–39
Samos (sā′·mŏs) Acts 20:15
Samothrace (săm′·ō·thrās) Acts 16:11
Samson (săm′·sŏn) Judg 13:24
Samuel (săm′·ū·ĕl) 1 Sam 1:19, 20
Sanballat (săn·băl′·lăt) Neh 2:10
Sansannah (săn·săn′·nuh) Josh 15:21–32
Saph (săf) 2 Sam 21:18
Sapphira (să·fī′·ruh) Acts 5:1
Sarai (sahr′·ī) Gen 11:29
Saraph (sahr′·ăph) 1 Chron 4:21, 22
Sardis (săr′·dĭs) Rev 1:11
Sargon (săr′·gŏn) Isa 14:31
Sarid (sā′·rĭd) Josh 19:10
Sarsechim (sahr′·sĕ·kĭm) Jer 39:3
Sceva (sē′·vuh) Acts 19:14
Seba (sē′·buh) Gen 10:7
Sebam (sē′·băm) Num 32:3, 4
Secacah (sĕ·kā′·kah) Josh 15:48–62
Secu (sē′·kū) 1 Sam 19:22
Secundus (sĕ·kŭn′·dŭs) Acts 20:4
Segub (sē′·gŭb) 1 Kgs 16:34
Seir (sē′·er) Gen 14:5, 6
Seirah (sē·ī′·ruh) Judg 3:26
Sela (sē′·luh) Isa 16:1
Seled (sē′·lĕd) 1 Chron 2:30
Seleucia (sĕ·loo′·sĭ·uh) Acts 13:4
Semein (sĕm′·ē·ĭn) Lk 3:23–38
Senaah (sĕ·nā′·uh) Ezra 2:3–35
Seneh (sē′·nē) 1 Sam 14:4
Senir (sē′·ner) 1 Chron 5:23
Sennacherib (sĕn·năk′·ē·rĭb) 2 Kgs 18:13
Se-orim (sĕ·ō′·rĭm) 1 Chron 24:7–18
Sephar (sē′·fahr) Gen 10:26–30
Sepharvaim (sĕf′·ahr·vā′·ĭm) 2 Kgs 17:24
Serah (sē′·ruh) Gen 46:16, 17
Seraiah (sĕ·rā′·uh) 2 Sam 8:17
Sered (ites) (sē′·rĕd) (īts) Gen 46:8–14 (Num 26:26, 27)
Sergius (ser′·gĭ·ŭs) Acts 13:6, 7
Serug (sē′·rŭg) Gen 11:20, 21
Seth (sĕth) Gen 4:25
Sethur (sĕth′·er) Num 13:3–15
Sha-alabbin (shā·uh·lăb′·bĭn) Josh 19:41–46
Sha-albim (shā·ăl′·bĭm) Judg 1:35
Sha-albon (shā′·ăl·bŏn) 2 Sam 23:24–39
Shaalim (shā′·uh·lĭm) 1 Sam 9:4
Shaaph (shā′·ăf) 1 Chron 2:47
Shaaraim (shā·uh·rā′·ĭm) 1 Sam 17:52
Shaashgaz (shuh·ăsh′·găz) Esth 2:12–14
Shabbethai (shăb′·bē·thī) Ezra 10:15
Shadrach (shăd′·răk) Dan 1:7
Shagee (shā′·gē) 1 Chron 11:26–47
Shaharaim (shā·huh·rā′·ĭm) 1 Chron 8:8–10
Shahazumah (shuh-ha-zoo′·muh) Josh 19:17–23
Shalisha (shăl′·ĭ·shuh) 1 Sam 9:4
Shallecheth (shăl′·ĕ·kĕth) 1 Chron 26:16
Shallum (shăl′·lŭm) 2 Kgs 15:10
Shalmai (shăl′·mī) Neh 7:46–56
Shalman (shăl′·mŭn) Hos 10:14
Shalmaneser (shăl·mŭn·ē′·zer) 2 Kgs 17:3
Shama (shā′·muh) 1 Chron 11:26–47
Shamgar (shăm′·găr) Judg 3:31
Shamir (shā′·mer) 1 Chron 24:24, 25
Shamlai (shăm′·lī) Ezra 2:43–54
Shamma (shăm′·muh) 1 Chron 7:36, 37
Shammah (shăm′·muh) Gen 36:13, 14
Shammai (shăm′·mī) 1 Chron 2:28
Shammoth (shăm′·mŏth) 1 Chron 11:26–47
Shammu-a (shăm′·ū·uh) Num 13:3–15
Shamsherai (shăm′·shuh·rī) 1 Chron 8:26, 27
Shamuth (shăm′·ŭth) 1 Chron 27:8
Shapham (shā′·fŭm) 1 Chron 5:12
Shaphan (shā′·fŭn) 2 Kgs 22:3, 4
Shaphat (shā′·făt) Num 13:3–15
Shaphir (shā′·fer) Mic 1:11
Sharai (shā′·rī) Ezra 10:34–42
Sharar (shā′·rahr) 2 Sam 23:24–39
Sharezer (shuh·rē′·zer) 2 Kgs 19:37
Sharuhen (shuh·roo′·hĕn) Josh 19:2–7
Shashai (shā′·shī) Ezra 10:34–42
Shashak (shā′·shăk) 1 Chron 8:14
Shaul (ites) (shā′·ool) (īts) Gen 46:8–14 (Num 26:12–14)
Shaveh (shā′·vĕh) Gen 14:17
Shavsha (shăv′·shuh) 1 Chron 18:16
Sheal (shē′·ŭl) Ezra 10:29
She-alti-el (shē·ăl′·tĭ·ĕl) Ezra 3:1, 2
She-ariah (shē·uh·rī′·uh) 1 Chron 8:38
Shear-jashub (shē′·ahr·jăsh′·ŭb) Isa 7:3
Sheba (shē′·buh) Gen 25:3
Shebaniah (shĕb·uh·nī′·uh) 1 Chron 15:24
Sheber (shē′·ber) 1 Chron 2:48, 49
Shebnah (shĕb′·nuh) 2 Kgs 18:18
Shebuel (shĕ·bū′·ĕl) 1 Chron 23:16
Shecaniah (shĕk·uh·nī′·uh) 1 Chron 24:7–18
Shechem (ites) (shē′·kĕm) (īts) Gen 34:2 (Num 26:28–37)
Shedeur (shĕd′·ē·er) Num 1:2–15
Sheerah (shē′·ē·ruh) 1 Chron 7:24
Shehariah (shē·huh·rī′·uh) 1 Chron 8:26, 27
Shelah (shē′·luh) Gen 10:24
Shelanites (shē′·luh·nīts) Num 26:19–22
Shelemiah (shĕl·ē·mī′·uh) 1 Chron 26:14, 15
Sheleph (shē′·lĕf) Gen 10:26–30
Shelesh (shē′·lĕsh) 1 Chron 7:35
Shelomi (shĕ·lō′·mī) Num 34:16–28
Shelomith (shĕ·lō′·mĭth) Lev 24:11
Shelomoth (shĕ·lō′·mŏth) 1 Chron 23:8, 9
Shelumi-el (shĕ·loo′·mĭ·ĕl) Num 1:2–15
Shem (shĕm) Gen 5:32
Shema (shē′·muh) Josh 15:21–32
Shemaah (shĕ·mā′·uh) 1 Chron 12:3–7
Shemaiah (shĕ·mā′·uh) 1 Kgs 12:22
Shemariah (shĕm·uh·rī′·uh) 1 Chron 12:3–7
Shemeber (shĕm·ē′·ber) Gen 14:2
Shemed (shē′·mĕd) 1 Chron 8:12
Shemer (shē′·mer) 1 Kgs 16:24
Shemida (ites) (shĕ·mī′·duh) (īts) Num 26:28–37
Sheminith (shĕm′·ĭ·nĭth) 1 Chron 15:21
Shemiramoth (shĕ·mĭr′·uh·mŏth) 1 Chron 15:18
Shemuel (shĕ·mū′·ĕl) Num 34:16–28
Shenazzar (shĕn·ăz′·zahr) 1 Chron 3:17, 18
Shepham (shē′·fŭm) Num 34:10, 11
Shephatiah (shĕf·uh·tī′·uh) 2 Sam 3:4
Shepher (shē′·fer) Num 33:15–37
Shephi (shē′·fī) 1 Chron 1:40
Shepho (shē′·fō) Gen 36:23
Shephuphan (shĕ·foo′·fŭn) 1 Chron 8:3–5
Sherebiah (shĕr·ē·bī′·uh) Ezra 8:18
Sheresh (shē′·rĕsh) 1 Chron 7:16
Sheshai (shē′·shī) Josh 15:14
Sheshan (shē′·shăn) 1 Chron 2:31
Sheshbazzar (shĕsh·băz′·zŭr) Ezra 1:8
Sheth (shĕth) Num 24:15–19
Shethar (shē′·thahr) Esth 1:13–15
Shethar-bozenai (shē′·thahr·bŏz′·ē·nī) Ezra 5:3
Sheva (shē′·vuh) 2 Sam 20:25
Shibah (shī′·buh) Gen 26:33
Shibboleth (shĭb′·buh·lĕth) Judg 12:6
Shigionoth (shĭg·ĭ·ŏn′·ŏth) Hab 3:1
Shihor (shī′·hor) 1 Chron 13:5
Shihor-libnath (shī′·hor·lĭb′·năth) Josh 19:24–26
Shikkeron (shĭk′·ĕ·rŏn) Josh 15:10, 11
Shilhi (shĭl′·hī) 1 Kgs 22:42
Shilhim (shĭl′·hĭm) Josh 15:21–32
Shillem (shĭl′·lĕm) Gen 46:23–25
Shiloah (shī·lō′·uh) Isa 8:6
Shiloh (shī′·lō) Gen 49:10
Shilonite (shī′·luh·nīt) Neh 11:4–6
Shilshah (shĭl′·shuh) 1 Chron 7:36, 37
Shimea (shĭm′·ē·uh) 1 Chron 2:13
Shime-am (shĭm′·ē·ăm) 1 Chron 9:38
Shimeath (ites) (shĭm′·ē·ăth) (īts) 2 Kgs 12:21 (1 Chron 2:55)
Shime-i (shĭm′·ē·ī) Ex 6:17
Shime-on (shĭm′·ē·ŏn) Ezra 10:31, 32
Shimon (shī′·mŏn) 1 Chron 4:20
Shimrath (shĭm′·răth) 1 Chron 8:19–21
Shimri (shĭm′·rī) 1 Chron 4:34–39
Shimrith (shĭm′·rĭth) 2 Chron 24:26
Shimron (ites) (shĭm′·rŏn) (īts) Josh 11:1 (Num 26:23–25)

Shimron-meron (shĭm′·rŏn·mē′·rŏn) Josh 12:8–24
Shimshai (shĭm′·shī) Ezra 4:8, 9
Shinab (shī′·năb) Gen 14:2
Shinar (shī′·nahr) Gen 10:10
Shion (shī′·ŏn) Josh 19:17–23
Shiphi (shī′·fī) 1 Chron 4:34–39
Shiphrah (shĭf′·ruh) Ex 1:15, 16
Shiphtan (shĭf′·tăn) Num 34:16–28
Shisha (shī′·shuh) 1 Kgs 4:1–6
Shishak (shī′·shăk) 1 Kgs 11:40
Shitrai (shĭt′·rī) 1 Chron 27:29
Shiza (shī′·zuh) 1 Chron 11:26–47
Shoa (shō′·uh) Ezek 23:23
Shobab (shō′·băb) 2 Sam 5:14–16
Shobach (shō′·băk) 2 Sam 10:15, 16
Shobai (shō′·bī) Ezra 2:40–42
Shobal (shō′·bŭl) Gen 36:20, 21
Shobek (shō′·bĕk) Neh 10:14–27
Shobi (shō′·bī) 2 Sam 17:27
Shoham (shō′·hăm) 1 Chron 24:26, 27
Shomer (shō′·mer) 2 Kgs 12:21
Shophach (shō′·făk) 1 Chron 19:16
Shuah (shoo′·uh) Gen 25:1, 2
Shual (shoo′·ăl) 1 Chron 7:36, 37
Shuba-el (shoo′·buh·ĕl) 1 Chron 24:20
Shuham (ites) (shoo′·hăm) (īts) Num 26:42, 43
Shuhite (shoo′·hīt) Job 8:1
Shulammite (shoo′·luh·mīt) Song 6:13
Shumathites (shoo′·muh·thīts) 1 Chron 2:53
Shunammite (shoo′·nuh·mīt) 1 Kgs 2:17
Shunem (shoo′·nĕm) Josh 19:17–23
Shuni (tes) (shoo′·nī) (ts) Gen 46:16, 17 (Num 26:15–18)
Shuphamites (shoo′·fuh·mīts) Num 26:38–41
Shuppim (shŭp′·pĭm) 1 Chron 7:12
Shur (sher) Gen 16:7
Shushan (shoo′·shăn) Neh 1:1
Shuthelah (ites) (shoo′·thē·luh) (shoo′·thē·lā·hīts) Num 26:28–37
Sia (sī·uh) Neh 7:46–56
Siaha (sī′·uh·huh) Ezra 2:43–54
Sibbecai (sĭb′·ĕ·kī) 2 Sam 21:18
Sibboleth (sĭb′·buh·lĕth) Judg 12:6
Sibmah (sĭb′·muh) Josh 13:19
Sibraim (sĭb′·rā·ĭm) Ezek 47:16
Siddem (sĭd′·dĭm) Gen 14:3
Sidon (ians) (sī′·dŏn) (sī·dō′·nĭ·ănz) Josh 19:28 (Deut 3:9)
Sihn (sĭn) Ex 16:1
Sihon (sī′·hŭn) Num 21:21
Silas (sī′·lŭs) Acts 15:22
Silla (sĭl′·luh) 2 Kgs 12:20
Siloam (sī·lō′·um) Jn 9:7
Silvanus (sĭl·vā′·nŭs) 2 Cor 1:19
Simeon (sĭm′·ē·ŏn) Gen 29:33
Simon (sī′·mŏn) Mt 10:2–4
Sinai (sī′·nī) Ex 19:1
Siphmoth (sĭf′·mŏth) 1 Sam 30:26–31
Sippai (sĭp′·pī) 1 Chron 20:4
Sirah (sī′·ruh) 2 Sam 3:26
Sirion (ser′·ĭ·ŏn) *Deut 4:48*
Sisera (sĭs′·ĕ·ruh) Judg 4:2, 3
Sismai (sĭs′·mī) 1 Chron 2:40
Sithri (sĭth′·rī) Ex 6:22
Sitnah (sĭt′·nuh) Gen 26:21
Smyrna (smer′·nuh) Rev 1:11
Soco (sō′·kō) 2 Chron 11:5–10
Socoh (sō′·kō) Josh 15:33–36
Sodi (sō′·dī) Num 13:3–15
Sodom (sŏd′·ŏm) Gen 10:15–19
Solomon (sŏl′·ō·mŏn) 2 Sam 5:14–16
Sopater (sō′·puh·ter) Acts 20:4
Sorek (sō′·rĕk) Judg 16:4
Sosipater (sō·sĭp′·uh·ter) Rom 16:21
Sosthenes (sŏs′·thĕ·nēz) Acts 18:17
Sotai (sō′·tī) Ezra 2:55–57
Stachys (stā′·kĭs) Rom 16:9
Stephanas (stĕf′·uh·nŭs) 1 Cor 1:16
Stoic (stō′·ĭk) Acts 17:18
Suah (soo′·uh) 1 Chron 7:36, 37
Succoth (sŭk′·ŏth) Gen 33:17
Succoth-benoth (sŭk′·ŏth·bē′·nŏth) 2 Kgs 17:30
Suchathites (soo′·kuh·thīts) 1 Chron 2:55
Sukkiim (sŭk′·kī·ĭm) 2 Chron 12:3
Susa (sŭ′·suh) Ezra 4:8, 9
Susi (soo′·sī) Num 13:3–15
Sychar (sī′·kahr) Jn 4:5, 6
Syene (sī·ē′·nē) Ezek 29:10
Syntyche (sĭn′·tĭ·kē) Phil 4:2
Syria (sĭr′·ĭ·uh) Judg 10:6
Syrophenician (sī·rō·fē·nĭ′·sĭ·ŭn) Mk 7:26
Taanach (tā′·uh·năk) Josh 12:8–24
Taanath-shiloh (tā′·uh·năth·shī′·lō) Josh 16:5, 6
Tabbaoth (tăb·bā′·ŏth) Ezra 2:43–54
Tabbath (tăb′·băth) Judg 7:22
Tabe-el (tā′·bē·ĕl) Ezra 4:7
Taberah (tăb′·ē·ruh) Num 11:3
Tabitha (tăb′·ĭ·thuh) Acts 9:40
Tabor (tā′·bor) Josh 19:17–23
Tah-chemon (tah·kē′·mŏn) 2 Sam 23:8
Tahan (ites) (tā′·hăn) (īts) Num 26:28–37
Tahpanhes (tah′·păn·hēz) Jer 2:16
Tahpenes (tah′·pĕ·nēz) 1 Kgs 11:19
Tahash (tā′·hăsh) Gen 22:24
Tahath (tā′·hăth) 1 Chron 6:22–24
Tahre-a (tah′·rē·uh) 1 Chron 9:41
Tahtim-hodshi (tah′·tĭm·hŏd′·shī) 2 Sam 24:6
Talmai (tăl′·mī) Josh 15:14
Talmon (tăl′·mŏn) 1 Chron 9:17, 18
Tamar (tā′·mahr) Gen 38:6
Tammuz (tahm′·mooz) Ezek 8:14
Tanhumeth (tăn·huh′·mĕth) 2 Kgs 25:23
Taphath (tā′·făth) 1 Kgs 4:8–19
Tappuah (tăp·pū′·uh) 1 Chron 2:43
Taralah (tahr′·uh·luh) Josh 18:21–28
Tarea (tuh·rē′·uh) 1 Chron 8:35
Tarshish (tahr′·shĭsh) Gen 10:4
Tarsus (tahr′·sŭs) Acts 9:11
Tartak (tahr′·tăk) 2 Kgs 17:31
Tattenai (tăt′·tē·nī) Ezra 5:3
Tebah (tē′·buh) Gen 22:24
Tebaliah (tĕb·uh·lī′·uh) 1 Chron 26:11
Tehaphnehes (tē·hăf′·nĕ·hēz) Ezek *30:18*
Tehinnah (tē·hĭn′·nuh) 1 Chron 4:11, 12
Tekel (tĕk′·ĕl) Dan 5:24, 25
Tekoa (tē·kō′·uh) 1 Chron 2:24
Tel Abib (tĕl·ā′·bĭb) Ezek 3:14, 15
Telah (tē′·luh) 1 Chron 7:25–27
Telaim (tĕ·lā′·ĭm) 1 Sam 15:4
Telassar (tē·lăs′·ser) Isa 37:12
Telem (tē′·lĕm) Ezra 10:24
Tel-harsha (tĕl·hahr′·shuh) Ezra 2:59
Tel-melah (tĕl·mē′·luh) Ezra 2:59
Tema (tē′·muh) Gen 25:12–15
Temah (tē′·muh) Ezra 2:43–54
Teman (ites) (tē′·mŭn) (īts) Gen 36:10–12 (Gen 36:31–39)
Temeni (tē′·mē·nī) 1 Chron 4:6
Terah (tē′·ruh) Gen 11:24, 25
Teresh (tē′·rĕsh) Esth 2:21
Tertius (ter′·shŭs) Rom 16:22
Tertullus (tĕr·tŭl′·ŭs) Acts 24:1
Tetrarch (tē′·trahrk) Mt 14:1
Thaddaeus (thăd′·dē·ŭs) Mt 10:2–4
Thebez (thē′·bĕz) Judg 9:50
Theophilus (thē·ŏf′·ĭ·lŭs) Lk 1:1
Thessalonica (thĕs·suh·lō·nī′·kuh) Acts 17:1
Theudas (thū′·dŭs) Acts 5:36
Thummim (thŭm′·mĭm) Ex 28:30, 31
Thyatira (thī·uh·tī′·ruh) Acts 16:14
Tiberias (tī·bē′·rĭ·ŭs) Jn 6:1
Tiberius (tī·bē′·rĭ·ŭs) Lk 3:1
Tibhath (tĭb′·hăth) 1 Chron 18:8
Tibni (tĭb′·nī) 1 Kgs 16:21
Tidal (tī′·dăl) Gen 14:1
Tiglath-pileser (tĭg′·lăth·pī·lē′·zer) 2 Kgs 15:29
Tikvah (tĭk′·vuh) 2 Kgs 22:14
Tilgath-pilneser (tĭl′·găth·pĭl·nē′·zer) 1 Chron 5:6
Tilon (tī′·lŏn) 1 Chron 4:20
Timaeus (tĭ·mē′·ŭs) Mk 10:46
Timna (tĭm′·nah) Gen 36:10–12
Timnah (tĭm′·nah) Josh 15:10, 11
Timnath-heres (tĭm′·năth·hē′·rēz) Judg 2:7–9
Timnath-serah (tĭm′·năth·sē′·ruh) Josh 19:50
Timon (tī′·mŭn) Acts 6:5
Tiphsah (tĭf′·suh) 1 Kgs 4:24
Tiras (tī′·rŭs) Gen 10:2
Tirathites (tī′·ruh·thīts) 1 Chron 2:55
Tirhakah (ter·hā′·kuh) 2 Kgs 19:9
Tirhanah (tĭr′·huh·nuh) 1 Chron 2:48, 49
Tiri-a (tĭr′·ĭ·ă) 1 Chron 4:16
Tirzah (ter′·zuh) Num 36:11, 12
Tishbe (tĭsh′·bē) 1 Kgs 17:1
Titus (tī′·tŭs) Gal 2:3
Tiza (tī′·zuh) 1 Chron 11:26–47
Toah (tō′·uh) 1 Chron 6:33–38
Tob (tōb) Judg 11:3
Tobadonijah (tōb·ăd·ō·nī′·juh) 2 Chron 17:8
Tobiah (tō·bī′·uh) Ezra 2:60
Tobijah (tō·bī′·juh) 2 Chron 17:7–9
Tochen (tō′·kĕn) 1 Chron 4:32, 33
Togarmah (tō·gahr′·muh) Gen 10:3
Tohu (tō′·hū) 1 Sam 1:1
Toi (tō′·ī) 2 Sam 8:9
Tokhath (tŏk′·hăth) 2 Chron 34:22
Tola (ites) (tō′·luh) (īts) Gen 46:8–14 (Num 26:23–25)
Tolad (tō′·lăd) 1 Chron 4:29
Tophel (tō′·fĕl) Deut 1:1
Topheth (tō′·fĕth) 2 Kgs 23:10
Tou (tō′·uh) 1 Chron 18:9
Trachonitis (trăk·ō·nī′·tĭs) Lk 3:1
Troas (trō′·ăs) Acts 16:8
Trophimus (trŏf′·ĭ·mŭs) Acts 20:4

Tryphaena (trī·fē'·nuh) Rom 16:12
Tryphosa (trī·fō'·suh) Rom 16:12
Tubal (too'·bŭl) Gen 10:2
Tubal-cain (too'·bŭl·kān) Gen 4:22
Tychicus (tĭk'·ĭ·kŭs) Acts 20:4
Tyrannus (tī·răn'·ŭs) Acts 19:9
Tyre (tīr) Josh 19:29
Ucal (ū'·kŭl) Prov 30:1
Uel (ū'·ĕl) Ezra 10:34–42
Ulai (ū'·lī) Dan 8:2
Ulam (ū'·lăm) 1 Chron 7:16
Ulla (ŭl'·luh) 1 Chron 7:39
Ummah (ŭm'·muh) Josh 19:30, 31
Unni (ŭn'·nī) 1 Chron 15:18
Uphaz (ū'·făz) Jer 10:9
Ur (ūr) Gen 11:28
Urbanus (ūr·bā'·nŭs) Rom 16:9
Uri (ŭ'·rī) Ex 31:1, 2
Uriah (ū·rī'·uh) 2 Sam 11:3
Uriel (ū·rī'·ĕl) 1 Chron 6:22–24
Urim (ū'·rĭm) Ex 28:30, 31
Uthai (ū'·thī) 1 Chron 9:4
Uz (ŭz) Gen 10:23
Uzai (ū'·zī) Neh 3:25
Uzal (ū'·zŭl) Gen 10:26–30
Uzza (ŭ'·zuh) 2 Kgs 21:18
Uzzah (ŭ'·zuh) 2 Sam 6:3
Uzzen-sheerah (ŭz'·ŭn·shē'·ĕ·ruh) 1 Chron 7:24
Uzzi (ŭz'·zī) 1 Chron 6:4–15
Uzzia (ŭz·zī'·uh) 1 Chron 11:26–47
Uzziah (ŭz·zī'·uh) 2 Kgs 15:13
Uzziel (ŭz·zī'·ĕl) Ex 6:18
Vaizatha (vī·zā'·thuh) Esth 9:7–10
Vaniah (vuh·nī'·uh) Ezra 10:34–42
Vashti (văsh'·tī) Esth 1:9
Vophsi (vŏf'·sī) Num 13:3–15
Yiron (yī'·rŏn) Josh 19:35–39
Zaanan (zā'·uh·năn) Mic 1:11
Zaanannim (zā·uh·năn'·nĭm) Josh 19:33
Zaavan (zā'·uh·văn) Gen 36:27
Zabad (zā'·băd) 1 Chron 2:36
Zabbai (zăb'·bī) Ezra 10:28
Zabdi (zăb'·dī) Josh 7:1
Zabdiel (zăb'·dĭ·ĕl) Neh 11:10–14
Zabud (zā'·bŭd) 1 Kgs 4:1–6
Zaccai (zăk'·kī) Ezra 2:3–35
Zacchaeus (zăk·kē'·ŭs) Lk 19:1, 2
Zaccur (zăk'·ker) Num 13:3–15
Zadok (zā'·dŏk) 2 Sam 8:17
Zaham (zā'·hăm) 2 Chron 11:19
Zair (zā'·er) 2 Kgs 8:21
Zalaph (zā'·lăf) Neh 3:30
Zalmon (zăl'·mŏn) 2 Sam 23:24–29
Zalmonah (zăl·mō'·nuh) Num 33:41
Zalmunna (zăl·mŭn'·nuh) Judg 8:5
Zamzummim (zăm·zŭm'·mĭm) Deut 2:20
Zanoah (zuh·nō'·uh) Josh 15:33–36
Zaphon (zā'·fŏn) Josh 13:27, 28
Zarephath (zăr'·ĕ·făth) 1 Kgs 17:10
Zarethan (zahr'·uh·thăn) Josh 3:15, 16
Zattu (zā'·too) Ezra 2:3–35
Zaza (zā'·zuh) 1 Chron 2:33
Zebadiah (zĕb·uh·dī'·uh) 1 Chron 8:15, 16
Zebah (zē'·buh) Judg 8:5
Zebedee (zĕb'·uh·dē) Mt 4:21
Zebidah (zĕ·bī'·duh) 2 Kgs 23:36, 37
Zebina (zĕ·bī'·nuh) Ezra 10:43
Zeboiim (zĕ·boi'·ĭm) Gen 10:15–19
Zebul (zē'·bŭl) Judg 9:28
Zebulun (zĕb'·ū·lŭn) Gen 30:20
Zechariah (zĕk·uh·rī'·uh) 2 Chron 24:20
Zecher (zē'·ker) 1 Chron 8:30–32
Zedad (zē'·dăd) Num 34:7–9
Zedekiah (zĕd·uh·kī'·uh) 1 Kgs 22:11
Zeeb (zē'·ĕb) Judg 7:25
Zela (zē'·luh) Josh 18:21–28
Zelek (zē'·lĕk) 2 Sam 23:24–39
Zelophehad (zē·lŏf'·ĕ·hăd) Num 26:28–37
Zelzah (zĕl'·zuh) 1 Sam 10:2
Zemaraim (zĕm·uh·rā'·ĭm) 2 Chron 13:4
Zemarites (zĕm'·uh·rīts) Gen 10:15–19
Zemirah (zĕ·mī'·ruh) 1 Chron 7:8
Zenan (zē'·nŭn) Josh 15:37–44
Zenas (zē'·nŭs) Tit 3:13
Zephaniah (zĕf·uh·nī'·uh) 2 Kgs 25:18
Zephath (zē'·făth) Judg 1:17
Zephathah (zĕf'·uh·thuh) 2 Chron 14:9, 10
Zephi (zē'·fī) 1 Chron 1:36
Zepho (zē'·fō) Gen 36:10–12
Zephon (ites) (zē'·fŏn) (īts) Num 26:15–18
Zer (zer) Josh 19:35–39
Zerah (ites) (zē'·ruh) (hīts) Gen 38:30 (Num 26:12–14)
Zerahiah (zĕr·uh·hī'·uh) 1 Chron 6:4–15
Zered (zē'·rĕd) Deut 2:13
Zeredah (zĕr'·ĕ·duh) 1 Kgs 11:26
Zererath (zer'·ĕ·răth) Judg 7:22
Zeresh (zē'·rĕsh) Esth 5:10
Zereth (zē'·rĕth) 1 Chron 4:7
Zereth-shahar (zĕ'·rĕth·shā'·hahr) Josh 13:19
Zeri (zē'·rī) 1 Chron 25:3
Zeror (zē'·ror) 1 Sam 9:1
Zerubbabel (zĕ·rŭb'·buh·bĕl) Ezra 2:2
Zeruiah (zĕ·roo'·ĭ·uh) 1 Sam 26:5–7
Zetham (zē'·thŭm) 1 Chron 23:8, 9
Zethan (zē'·thŭn) 1 Chron 7:10
Zethar (zē'·thahr) Esth 1:10
Zia (zī'·uh) 1 Chron 5:13
Ziba (zī'·buh) 2 Sam 9:2
Zibeon (zĭb'·ē·ŏn) Gen 36:2, 3
Zibia (zĭb'·ĭ·uh) 1 Chron 8:8–10
Zibiah (zĭb'·ĭ·uh) 2 Kgs 12:1
Zichri (zĭk'·rī) 2 Chron 23:1
Ziddim (zĭd'·dĭm) Josh 19:35–39
Ziha (zī'·huh) Ezra 2:43–54
Ziklag (zĭk'·lăg) Josh 15:21–32
Zillah (zĭl'·luh) Gen 4:19
Zilpah (zĭl'·puh) Gen 29:24
Zille-thai (zĭl'·lĕ·thī) 1 Chron 8:19–21
Zimmah (zĭm'·muh) 1 Chron 6:19–21
Zimran (zĭm'·răn) Gen 25:1, 2
Zimri (zĭm'·rī) 1 Kgs 16:9
Zin (zĭn) Num 13:21
Zina (zī'·nuh) 1 Chron 23:10, 11
Zion (zī'·ŏn) 2 Sam 5:7
Zior (zī'·or) Josh 15:48–62
Ziph (zĭf) 1 Chron 4:16
Ziphah (zī'·fuh) 1 Chron 4:16
Ziphion (zĭf'·ĭ·ŏn) Gen 46:16, 17
Ziphron (zĭf'·rŏn) Num 34:7–9
Zippor (zĭp'·por) Num 22:2, 3
Zipporah (zĭp·pō'·ruh) Ex 2:21
Ziz (zĭz) 2 Chron 20:16
Ziza (zī'·zuh) 1 Chron 4:34–39
Zizah (zī'·zuh) 1 Chron 23:10, 11
Zoan (zō'·ăn) Num 13:22
Zoar (zō'·ahr) Gen 13:10
Zobah (zō'·buh) 1 Sam 14:47
Zobebah (zō·bē'·buh) 1 Chron 4:8
Zohar (zō'·hahr) Gen 25:9, 10
Zoheth (zō'·hĕth) 1 Chron 4:20
Zophah (zō'·fuh) 1 Chron 7:35
Zophai (zō'·fī) 1 Chron 6:25–27
Zophar (zō'·fahr) Job 2:11
Zophim (zō'·fĭm) Num 23:14
Zorah (zō'·ruh) Josh 19:41–46
Zorathite (zō'·ruh·thīt) 1 Chron 4:2
Zorites (zō'·rīts) 1 Chron 2:54
Zuar (zoo'·ahr) Num 1:2–15
Zuph (zŭf) 1 Sam 1:1
Zur (zer) Num 25:15
Zuriel (zū'·rĭ·ĕl) Num 3:31–35
Zuri-shaddai (zoo·rĭ·shăd'·dī) Num 1:2–15
Zuzim (zū'·zĭm) Gen 14:5, 6

KEY WORD
CONCORDANCE

PLAN OF THE WORK—This Concordance is based on Cruden's and contains 40,000 references. Meanings of words and references of minor importance are stated first; the others follow in the order of the Books. The *inflexions* and *derivatives* of a word, and *phrases* in which it occurs, are *grouped* under it alphabetically; and are in the first instance set out in full in *italic*, but afterwards abbreviated, the *phrases* being represented by a dash ("—"), to avoid repetition and facilitate comparison.

ABASE, make low, &c.
Job 40:11. every one proud *a.*
Isa 31:4. lion will not *a.* himself
Ezek 21:26. *a.* him that is high
Dan 4:37. walk in pride is able to *a.*
Matt 23:12. exalt himself shall be *abased*
2 Cor 11:7. offence in *abasing* myself
ABATED, waters were, Gen 8:3, 11.
Lev 27:18. *a.* from thy estimation
Deut 34:7. nor his natural force *a.*
Judg 8:3. their anger was *a.* towards
ABHOR, greatly hate and loathe.
Lev 26:11. my soul shall not *a.* you
15. if your soul *a.* my judgments
30. my soul shall *a.* you
44. neither will I *a.* them
Deut 23:7. not *a.* an Edomite
1 Sam 27:12. made his people to *a.* him
Job 30:10. they *a.* me, they flee
42:6. I *a.* myself, and repent
Ps 5:6. Lord will *a.* the bloody
119:163. I hate and *a.* lying
Jer 14:21. do not *a.* us for name's sake
Amos 5:10. they *a.* him that speaketh
6:8. I *a.* the excellency of Jacob
Mic 3:9. ye that *a.* judgment
Exod 5:21. made our savour *abhorred*
Lev 26:43. their soul *a.* my statutes
Deut 32:19. Lord saw it he *a.* them
1 Sam 2:17. men *a.* the offering
Job 19:19. my inward friends *a.* me
Ps 22:24. nor *a.* affliction of afflicted
89:38. hath cast off and *a.* anointed
106:40. he *a.* his own inheritance
Prov 22:14. *a.* of the Lord shall fall
Lam 2:7. Lord hath *a.* his sanctuary
Zech 11:8. their soul *a.* me
Rom 2:22. thou that *abhorrest* idols
Job 33:20. his life *abhorreth* bread
Ps 10:3. covetous whom the Lord *a.*
36:4. he *a.* not evil
107:18. their soul *a.* all manner of meat
Isa 49:7. him whom the nation *a.*
66:24. be an *abhorring* unto all flesh
ABIDE, continue, bear.
Exod 16:29. *a.* ye every man in his place
Num 35:25. *a.* to death of high priest
2 Sam 11:11. ark and Israel *a.* in tents
Ps 15:1. who shall *a.* in thy tabernacle
61:4. I will *a.* in tabernacle
61:7. he shall *a.* before God for ever
91:1. *a.* under shadow of Almighty
Prov 7:11. her feet *a.* not in her house
19:23. that hath it shall *a.* satisfied
Hos 3:3. shall *a.* for me many days
3:4. Israel shall *a.* without a king
Joel 2:11. terrible; who can *a.* it
Mal 3:2. who may *a.* the day of his
Matt 10:11. there *abide* till ye go thence
Luke 19:5. I must *a.* at thy house
24:29. *a.* with us the day is far spent
John 14:16. Comforter that he may *a.*
15:4. *a.* in me and I in you, 7.
10. ye shall *a.* in my love, *a.* in his
Acts 20:23. afflictions *a.* me
1 Cor 3:14. if any man's work *a.*
7:8. good for them if they *a.* even as I
20. every man *a.* in the same
24. is called therein *a.* with God
Phil 1:24. to *a.* in the flesh is needful
25. know that I shall *a.* with you
1 John 2:24. let that therefore *a.* in you
27. ye shall *a.* in him
28. little children *a.* in him
Ps 49:12. man in honour *abideth* not
55:19. even he that *a.* of old
Eccles 1:4. the earth *a.* for ever
John 3:36. wrath of God *a.* on him
8:35. servant *a.* not, Son *a.* for ever
12:24. except it die it *a.* alone
34. Christ *a.* for ever
15:5. he that *a.* in me bringeth forth
2 Tim 2:13. yet he *a.* faithful
1 Pet 1:23. word of God *a.* for ever
1 John 3:6. whoso *a.* in him sinneth not
24. hereby we know he *a.* in us
John 5:38. not his word *abiding* in you
1 John 3:15. no murderer hath eternal life *a.*
John 14:23. make our *abode* with
ABILITY, in strength, wealth, &c., Lev 27:8. Ezra 2:69. Neh 5:8. Dan 1:4.
Matt 25:15. to every man according to his several *a.*
Acts 11:29.
1 Pet 4:11. as of the *a.* God giveth
ABLE men, such as fear God, Exod 18:21.
Lev 14:22. such as he is *a.* to get
Deut 16:17. every man give as he is *a.*
2 Chron 20:6. none is *a.* to withstand
Dan 3:17. God is *a.* to deliver
4:37. walk in pride he is *a.* to abase
Matt 3:9. *God is a.* of these stones to raise up children, Luke 3:8.
9:28. believe ye I am *a.* to do this?
10:28. are not *a.* to kill the soul
19:12. he that is *a.* to receive it, let
Mark 4:33. as they were *a.* to hear
John 10:29. no man *a.* to pluck you

Rom 4:21. he was *a.* to perform
14:4. God is *a.* to make him stand
1 Cor 3:2. neither yet now are ye *a.*
10:13. tempted above that ye are *a.*
2 Cor 9:8. *a.* to make all grace abound
Phil 3:21. *a.* to subdue all to himself
2 Tim 1:12. *a.* to keep that which
3:15. Scriptures *a.* to make wise
Heb 2:18 *a.* to succour the tempted
ABLE, Heb 5:7. *able* to save him from death
7:25. *a.* to save to the uttermost
11:19. *a.* to raise him from dead
Eph 1:21. every *n.* that is named
Phil 2:9. a *n.* above every *n.*
James 1:21. *a.* to save your souls
4:12. *a.* to save and to destroy
Jude 24. *a.* to keep you from falling
ABOLISH, make to cease.
Isa 2:18. idols he shall utterly *a.*
51:6. righteousness shall not be *abolished*
Ezek 6:6. your works may be *a.*
2 Cor 3:13. to the end of that *a.*
Eph 2:15. having *a.* in his flesh
2 Tim 1:10. Jesus Christ hath *a.* death
ABOMINABLE, very hateful, Lev 7:21; 11:43; 18:30. Isa 14:19; 65:4. Jer 16:18.
1 Chron 21:6. king's word was *a.* to Joab
Job 15:16. how much more *a.* is man
Ps 14:1. have done *a.* works, 53:1.
Jer 44:4. do not this *a.* thing I hate
Nah 3:6. I will cast *a.* filth on thee
Titus 1:16. in works deny him being *a.*
1 Pet 4:3. walked in *a.* idolatries
Rev 21:8. unbelieving and *a.* shall
ABOMINATION, what is very filthy, hateful, and loathsome, as sin, Isa 66:3; idols, Exod 8:26.
Prov 6:16. seven things are an *a.* to Lord
11:1. a false balance is *a.* to the Lord
20. they of froward heart are *a.*
12:22. lying lips are *a.* to the Lord
15:8. sacrifice of wicked is an *a.*
26. thoughts of wicked are an *a.*
16:5. proud in heart is an *a.* to Lord, 3:32.
20:23. divers weights are an *a.* to the Lord
28:9. his prayer shall be *a.*
Isa 1:13. incense is an *a.* to me
Dan 11:31. *a.* that maketh *desolate*
12:11. Matt 24:15. Mark 13:14. a. of des.
Luke 16:15. is *a.* in the sight of God
2 Kings 21:2. *abominations* of heathen

Ezra 9:14. join people of these *a.*
Prov 26:25. seven *a.* in his heart
Jer 7:10. delivered to do all these *a.*
Ezek 16:2. cause Jerusalem to know her *a.* 20:4; 23:36.
18:13. hath done all these *a.* shall die
Dan 9:27. for the overspreading of *a.*
Rev 17:5. mother of harlots and *a.*
ABOUND, become very full, large, Prov 8:24.
Prov 28:20. faithful shall *a.* with blessings
Matt 24:12. because iniquity shall *a.*
Rom 5:20. offence might *a.* but where sin *a.* grace did much more *a.*
6:1. in sin that grace may *a.*
Phil 1:9. that your love may *a.* more
4:12. both to *a.* and to suffer need
17. fruit that may *a.* to your account
18. I have all and *a.*
1 Thess 3:12. the Lord make you *a.* in love
2 Pet 1:8. these things be in you and *a.*
Rom 3:7. truth of God hath more *a.*
Eph 1:8. hath *a.* toward us
1 Cor 15:58. always *abounding*
Col 2:7. *a.* therein with thanksgiving
ABOVE, higher, heaven, Exod 20:4.
John 3:31. cometh from *a.* is *a.* all
8:23. I am from *a.* ye are from beneath
John 19:11. power given thee from *a.*
Gal 4:26. Jerusalem which is *a.* is free
Eph 4:6. one God who is *a.* all
Col 3:1. seek things which are *a.*
2. set your affection on things *a.*
James 1:17. every perfect gift is from *a.*
3:15, 17. wisdom from *a.* is pure
ABSENT one from another, Gen 31:49. 2 Cor 10:1.
2 Cor 5:6. in body we are *a.* from the Lord
8. willing rather to be *a.* from the body
9. that whether present or *a.*
Col 2:5. though I be *a.* in the flesh
ABSTAIN from idols, Acts 15:20.
1 Thess 4:3. ye should *a.* from fornication
5:22. *a.* from all appearance of evil
1 Tim 4:3. commanding to *a.* from meats
1 Pet 2:11. *a.* from fleshly lusts
Abstinence from meats, Acts 27:21.
ABUNDANCE, great fulness, and plenty, Job 22:11; 38:34. Deut 33:19. 1 Chron 22:3, 4, 14, 15.
Deut 28:47. for the *a.* of all things
Eccles 5:10. he that loveth *a.* with

12. *a.* of rich not suffer him to sleep
Matt 12:34. out of *a.* of the heart the mouth speaketh, Luke 6:45.
13:12. shall have more *a.* 25:29.
Mark 12:44. cast in of their *a.*
Luke 12:15. life consisteth not in *a.*
2 Cor 8:2. *a.* of their joy abounded
12:7. through *a.* of revelations
ABUNDANT in goodness and truth, Exod 34:6. 2 Cor 4:15; 9:12.
2 Cor 11:23. in labours more *a.*
1 Tim 1:14. grace of Lord exceeding *a.*
1 Pet 1:3. his *a.* mercy hath
Job 12:6. God bringeth *abundantly*
Ps 36:8. shall be *a.* satisfied
Song of Sol 5:1. yea drink *a.* O beloved
Isa 55:7. he will *a.* pardon
John 10:10. might have life more *a.*
1 Cor 15:10. laboured more *a.* than all
Titus 3:6. shed on us *a.* through Jesus
2 Pet 1:11. entrance ministered *a.*
ABUSE not my power, 1 Cor 9:18.
1 Cor 7:31. use world as not *abusing* it
ACCEPT, receive kindly in favour, Gen 32:20. Acts 24:3.
Lev 26:41. *a.* punishment of iniquity, 43.
Deut 33:11. *a.* work of his hands
2 Sam 24:23. Lord thy God *a.* thee
Job 13:8. will ye *a.* his person, 10.
32:21. not *a.* any man's person
42:8. servant Job, him will I *a.*
Ps 119:108. *a.* freewill offerings
Prov 18:5. not good to *a.* person
Ezek 43:27. I will *a.* you, saith Lord
Mal 1:13. should I *a.* this of your
Gen 4:7. shalt thou not be *accepted*
19:21. *a.* thee concerning this thing
Luke 4:24. no prophet *a.* in his own
Acts 10:35. worketh righteousness is *a.*
2 Cor 5:9. we may be *a.* of him
6:2. heard thee in a time *a.* now is
Eph 1:6. made us *a.* in the beloved
Luke 20:21. neither *acceptest* thou
Job 34:19. *accepteth* not the person
Eccles 9:7. God now *a.* thy works
Hos 8:13. Lord *a.* them not
Gal 2:6. God *a.* no man's person
Heb 11:35. not *accepting* deliverance
Acceptable day of the Lord, Isa 58:5.
Ps 19:14. meditation of heart *a.*

Eccles 12:10. sought out *a.* words
Isa 49:8. in an *a.* time I heard thee
61:2. proclaim the *a.* year of the Lord, Luke 4:19.
Dan 4:27. let my counsel be *a.*
Rom 12:1. sacrifice holy *a.* to God
Eph 5:10. proving what is *a.* to Lord
Phil 4:18. sacrifice *acceptable* well-pleasing
1 Pet 2:5. *a.* to God by Jesus Christ
Heb 12:28. serve God *acceptably*
1 Tim 1:15. worthy of *acceptation*

ACCESS, admission through Christ, Rom 5:2. Eph 2:18; 3:12.

ACCOMPLISH, perform fully, finish, Lev 22:21. Job 14:6.
Ps 64:6. *a.* a diligent search
Isa 55:11. it shall *a.* that I please
Ezek 6:12. thus will I *a.* my fury
Dan 9:2. would *a.* seventy years
Luke 9:31. should *a.* at Jerusalem
Prov 13:19. desire *accomplished* is sweet to soul
Isa 40:2. her warfare is *a.* her sin
John 19:28. all things were now *a.*
1 Pet 5:9. same afflictions are *a.*
Heb 9:6. *accomplishing* service

ACCORD, hearty agreement, Acts 1:14; 2:1, 46; 4:24; 15:25.

ACCOUNT, reckoning, esteem.
Job 33:13. not *a.* of his matters
Ps 144:3. that thou makest *a.* of him
Eccles 7:27. one by one to find out *a.*
Matt 12:36. give *a.* in day of judgment
18:23. would take *a.* of his servants
Luke 16:2. give *a.* of stewardship
Rom 14:12. give *a.* of himself to God
Phil 4:17. fruit abound to your *a.*
Heb 13:17. as they that must give *a.*
1 Pet 4:5. shall give *a.* to him that
Ps 22:30. *accounted* to the Lord
Isa 2:22. wherein is he to be *a.* of
Luke 20:35. they which shall be *a.* worthy to obtain that world
21:36. *a.* worthy to escape
22:24. which should be *a.* greatest
Gal 3:6. *a.* to him for righteousness

ACCURSED, devoted to ruin
Deut 21:23. hanged is *a.* of God.
Josh 6:18. keep from the *a.* thing
Isa 65:20. one hundred years old shall be *a.*
Rom 9:3. wish myself *a.* from Christ
1 Cor 12:3. no man by Spirit calls Jesus *a.*
Gal 1:8, 9. preach other gospel be *a.*

ACCUSATION, Ezra 4:6. Matt 27:37. Luke 6:7; 19:8. John 18:29. Acts 25:18.
2 Pet 2:11. bring not a railing *a.* Jude 9.

ACCUSE, charge with crimes.
Prov 30:10. *a.* not servant to master
Luke 3:14. neither *a.* any falsely
John 5:45. that I will *a.* you to Father
1 Pet 3:16. falsely *a.* your good conversation
Titus 1:6. not *accused* of riot
Rev 12:10. *a.* them before our God, *accuser* of brethren is cast down
Acts 25:16. have *accusers* face to face
2 Tim 3:3. false *a.* Titus 2:3.
John 5:45. there is one that *accuseth*
Rom 2:15. thoughts *accusing* or

ACCUSTOMED to do evil, Jer 13:23.

ACKNOWLEDGE, own, confess.
Deut 33:9. neither did he *a.* his brethren
Ps 32:5. I *a.* my sin unto thee, and mine
51:3. I *a.* my transgression
Prov 3:6. in all thy ways *a.* him
Isa 33:13. ye that are near *a.* my might
63:16. though Israel *a.* us not
Jer 3:13. only *a.* thine iniquity
14:20. we *a.* our wickedness
Hos 5:15. till they *a.* their offence
1 Cor 16:18. *a.* them that are such
2 Tim 2:25. *acknowledging* the truth

ACKNOWLEDGE—Titus 1:1. *acknowledging* truth
Col 2:2. to the *acknowledgment* of the mystery of God and of the Father

ACQUAINT thyself with him, Job 22:21.
Ps 139:3. *acquainted* with my ways
Isa 53:3. man of sorrows, and *a.* with grief
Acquaintance, familiar friends or companions, Job 19:13; 42:11. Ps 31:11; 55:13; 88:8, 18.

ACQUIT, hold innocent, Job 10:14.
Nah 1:3. will not *a.* the wicked

ACTS of the Lord, Deut 11:3, 7.
Judg 5:11. rehearse righteous—
1 Sam 12:7. reason of all righteous—
Ps 106:2. utter mighty—
145:4, 6. speak of thy mighty *a.*
Isa 28:21. his *act* his strange *a.*
John 8:4. taken in adultery in very *a.*

ACTIONS weighted, 1 Sam 2:3.

ADAMANT, Ezek 3:9. Zech 7:12.

ADD fifth part, Lev 5:16; 6:5; 27:13, 15, 19, 27, 31.
Deut 4:2. shall not *a.* to word
29:19. *a.* drunkenness to thirst
Ps 69:27. *a.* iniquity to their iniquity
Prov 30:6. *a.* not unto his words
Isa 30:1. that they may *a.* sin to sin
Matt 6:27. *a.* one cubit, Luke 12:25.
Phil 1:16. *a.* affliction to bonds
2 Pet 1:5. *a.* to your faith virtue
Rev 22:18. if any man *a.* unto these things, God shall *a.* unto him
Deut 5:22. he *added* no more
1 Sam 12:19. *a.* to all our sins this evil
Jer 36:32. were *a.* many like words
45:3. Lord *a.* grief to my sorrow
Acts 2:41. were *a.* 3,000 souls
47. Lord *a.* to the church . . . saved
5:14. believers were the more *a.*
11:24. much people was *a.* to the Lord
Prov 10:22. *addeth* no sorrow with

ADDER, poisonous serpent, Gen 49:17. Ps 58:4; 91:13; 140:3. Prov 23:32. Isa 14:29.

ADDICTED, devoted, 1 Cor 16:15.

ADJURE, to charge under pain of God's curse, 1 Kings 22:16. 2 Chron 18:15. Matt 26:63. Mark 5:7. Acts 19:13. Josh 6:26. 1 Sam 14:24.

ADMINISTRATION, 1 Cor 12:5. 2 Cor 9:12; *administered,* 8:19, 20.

ADMIRATION, undue regard, Jude 16. or wonder and amazement, Rev 17:6.
2 Thess 1:10. *admired* in them that believe

ADMONISH, warn, reprove.
Rom 15:14. able to *a.* one another
1 Thess 5:12. over you and *a.* you
2 Thess 3:15. *a.* him as a brother
Eccles 4:13. foolish king will no more be *admonished*
12:12. by these be *a.*
Jer 42:19. know that I have *a.* you
Heb 8:5. as Moses was *a.* of God
Col 3:16. *admonishing* . . . in psalms
1 Cor 10:11. are written for our *admonition*
Eph 6:4. bring up in the nurture and *a.* of Lord
Titus 3:10. after first and second *a.* reject

ADOPTION, putting among God's children, Jer 3:19. 2 Cor 6:18.
Rom 8:15. received spirit of *a.*
23. *a.* redemption of our body
Gal 4:5. might receive *a.* of sons
Eph 1:5. unto *a.* of children

ADORN, deck out, Isa 61:10. Jer 31:4.
1 Tim 2:9. women *a.* in modest
Titus 2:10. *a.* the doctrine of God our
Jer 31:4. *adorned* with thy tabrets
Luke 21:5. *adorned* with goodly stones
1 Pet 3:5. holy women *a.* themselves
Rev 21:2. as bride *a.* for her husband

Isa 61:10. as bride *adorneth* herself
ADULTERER, put to death, Lev 20:10.
Job 24:15. eye of *a.* waits for twilight
Isa 57:3. seed of the *a.* and the
Jer 23:10. land is full of *adulterers*
9:2. Hos 7:4. they are all *a.*
Mal 3:5. I swift witness against *a.*
Heb 13:4. *a.* God will judge
James 4:4. ye *a.* and *adulteresses*
Prov 6:26. *adulteress* hunt for life
32. committeth *adultery* lacks
Matt 5:28. committed *a.* in his heart Mark 7:21.
2 Pet 2:14. having eyes full of *a.*
Matt 15:19. out of the heart proceed *adulteries,*
Prov 30:20. way of *adulterous* woman
Matt 12:39. *a.* generation seeketh a sign, 16:4. Mark 8:38.
ADVANTAGE hath the Jew, Rom 3:1.
2 Cor 2:11. lest Satan get an *a.*
Luke 9:25. what is a man *advantaged*?
ADVERSARY, opposer, enemy.
Exod 23:22. I will be an *a.* to thy *a.*
1 Kings 5:4. is neither *a.* nor evil
Job 31:35. my *a.* had written a book
Matt 5:25. agree with thine *a.*
1 Tim 5:14. give no occasion to *a.*
1 Pet 5:8. your *a.* the devil as a
1 Sam 2:10. *adversaries* of Lord broken
Lam 1:5. her *a.* are the chief
Luke 21:15. all your *a.* not be able
1 Cor 16:9. and there are many *a.*
Phil 1:28. and in nothing terrified by your *a.*
Heb 10:27. shall devour the *a.*
ADVERSITY, affliction, misery.
1 Sam 10:19. saved you out of *all a.*
2 Sam 4:9. redeemed my soul from—
2 Chron 15:6. God did vex with—
Ps 10:6. I shall never be in *a.*
31:7. thou hast known my soul in *a.*
94:13. give rest from days of *a.*
Prov 17:17. brother is born for *a.*
Eccles 7:14. in the day of *a.* consider
Isa 30:20. give you the bread of *a.*
ADVICE, Judg 19:30. 1 Sam 25:33. 2 Sam 19:43. Prov 20:18.
ADVOCATE with Father, 1 John 2:1.
AFAR off, Gen 22:4; 37:18. Ps *65:5; 138:6. proud he knoweth a.*
Ps 139:2. understandest thoughts *a.* off
Jer 23:23. not a God *a.*
Eph 2:17. preached peace to you *a.*
Heb 11:13. having seen promises *a.*
2 Pet 1:9. blind and cannot see *a.*
AFFAIRS, Ps 112:5. 2 Tim 2:4.
AFFECT, strive after, court.
Gal 4:17. they zealously *a.* you
18. good to be zealously *affected*
Lam 3:51. mine eye *affecteth* my heart.
Col 3:5. mortify inordinate *affection*
1 Thess 2:8. *affectionately* desirous
Rom 12:10. be kindly *affectioned*
1:26. them to vile *affections*
Gal 5:24. crucify flesh with *a.*
AFFINITY, relation by marriage, 1 Kings 3:1. 2 Chron 18:1. Ezra 9:14.
AFFLICT, grieve, trouble, Gen 15:13. Exod 1:11; 22:22.
Ezra 8:21. that we might *a.* ourselves
Lev 16:29, 31; 23:27, 32. Num 29:7; 30:13. shall *a.* your souls
Isa 58:5. day for man to *afflict* his soul Ps 18:27
Lam 3:33. doth not *a.* willingly
2 Sam 22:28. *afflicted* people thou wilt save.
Job 6:14. to *a.* pity should be showed
34:28. heareth the cry of the *a.*
Ps 22:24. not abhorred affliction of *a.*
119:67. before I was *a.* I went astray
71. it is good that I have been *a.*
75. thou in faithfulness hast *a.* me
107. I am *a.* very
140:12. wilt maintain cause of the *a.*
Prov 15:15. all days of *a.* are evil
Isa 49:13. he will have mercy on *a.*
53:4. smitten of God and *a.*
7. he was oppressed and *a.*
58:10. satisfy the *a.* soul
Mic 4:6. gather her I have *a.*
Exod 3:7. seen the *affliction* of my people
2 Kings 14:26. Lord saw *a.* of Israel
Job 5:6. *a.* cometh not forth of dust
36:8. holden in cords of *a.*
15. delivereth poor in his *a.*
21. this chosen rather than *a.*
Ps 25:18. look upon my *a.* and pain
107:10. bound in *a.* and iron
39. brought low through *a.*
119:92. should have perished in *a.*
Isa 48:10. chosen thee in furnace of *a.*
63:9. in all their *a.* he was afflicted
Hos 5:15. in their *a.* they will seek
Amos 6:6. not grieved for *a.* of Joseph
Obad 13. not looked on their *a.*
Nah 1:9. *a.* not rise the second time
Zech 1:15. helped forward the *a.*
2 Cor 4:17. our light *a.* which is
Phil 4:14. communicate with my *a.*
1 Thess 1:6. received word in much *a.*
Heb 11:25. choosing to suffer *a.*
James 1:27. visit fatherless and widows in *a.*
Ps 34:19. *afflictions* of righteous
132:1. remember David and all his *a.*
Acts 7:10. delivered him out of all *a.*
20:23. bonds and *a.* abide me
1 Thess 3:3. moved by these *a.*
2 Tim 1:8. partaker of *a.* of gospel
Heb 10:32. endured great fight of *a.*
1 Pet 5:9. the same *a.* accomplished
AFRAID, Lev 26:6. Num 12:8. Job 13:21. Ps 56:3; 119:120.
Not be *afraid,* Ps 56:11; 112:7. Isa 12:2. Matt 14:27. Mark 5:36. Luke 12:4. 1 Pet 3:6, 14. Heb 11:23.
AFRESH, crucify Son of God, Heb 6:6.
AGE is as nothing before thee, Ps 39:5.
Job 5:26. to grave in full *a.*
John 9:21. he is of *a.* ask him
Heb 5:14. meat to those of full *a.*
Titus 2:2, 3. *aged* men be sober
Ages, Eph 2:7; 3:5, 21.
Col 1:26. mystery hid from *a.*
AGREE together, Acts 5:9.
Matt 5:25. *a.* with thine adversary quickly
18:19. if two shall *a.* on earth
1 John 5:8. these three *a.* in one
Amos 3:3. can two walk except *agreed*
Isa 28:15. with hell at *agreement*
2 Cor 6:16. what *a.* hath temple . . . idols
ALIEN, stranger, Exod 18:3. Job 19:15. Ps 69:8; heathens, Deut 14:21. Isa 61:5. Lam 5:2. Heb 11:34.
Eph 2:12. *a.* from commonwealth
4:18. *alienated* from life of God
Col 1:21. were sometime *a.*
ALIVE, Gen 12:12. Num 22:33.
1 Sam 2:6. killeth and maketh *a.*
15:8. he took Agag *a.*
Luke 15:24. my son was dead and is *a.*
Rom 6:11. *a.* unto God through Jesus
13. as those *a.* from the dead
7:9. I was *a.* without the law once
1 Cor 15:22. in Christ all be made *a.*
1 Thess 4:15, 17. we *a.* and remain
Rev 1:18. I am *a.* for evermore
2:8. was dead and is *a.*
ALLEGING, prove by quoting, Acts 17:3.
ALLOW, deeds of fathers, Luke 11:48.
Acts 24:15. which themselves *a.*
Rom 7:15. that which I do I *a.* not
1 Thess 2:4. as we were *allowed* of God

Rom 14:22. in that which he *alloweth*
ALLURE, Hos 2:14. 2 Pet 2:18.
ALMIGHTY GOD, Gen 17:1; 28:3; 35:11; 43:14; 48:3. Exod 6:3. Num 24:4. Ruth 1:20. Ezek 1:24. 2 Cor 6:18. Rev 1:8; 4:8; 15:3; 16:14; 19:15; 21:22.
Job 21:15. what is the *Almighty*
22:25. *A.* shall be thy defence
27:10. delight himself in the *A.*
Ps 91:1. under shadow of *A.*
Rev 1:8. is to come, the *A.*
ALMOST all things, Heb 9:22.
Exod 17:4. *a.* ready to stone me
Ps 73:2. my feet were *a.* gone
94:17. soul had *a.* dwelt in silence
Prov 5:14. I was *a.* in all evil in the congregation
Acts 26:28. *a.* thou persuadest me to be a Christian
ALMS, Acts 3:2, 3; 24:17.
Matt 6:1. do not your *a.* before men
Luke 11:41. give *a.* of such things
12:33. sell that ye have, give *a.*
Acts 10:2. gave much *a.* to people
4. thine *a.* are come up for memorial
ALONE, Jacob left, Gen 32:24.
Gen 2:18. not good for man to be *a.*
Num 23:9. dwell *a.* Deut 33:28
Deut 32:12. Lord *a.* did lead him
Ps 136:4. *a.* doeth great wonders
Eccles 4:10. woe to him that is *a.*
Isa 5:8. that they may be placed *a.*
John 8:16. I am not *a.* 16:32.
17:20. neither pray I for these *a.*
Gal 6:4. rejoicing in himself *a.*
Exod 32:10. let me *a.* that my wrath
Hos 4:17. Ephraim is joined to idols, let him *a.*
Matt 15:14. let them *a.*
ALTAR, Gen 13:4; 26:25; 33:20. Exod 17:15; 20:24. Deut 7:5; 12:3. Josh 22:10.
altar to Lord, Gen 8:20; 12:7; 22:9; 35:1, 3. Exod 30:27; 40:10.
Judg 6:25. throw down *a.* of Baal
1 Kings 13:2. cried against *a.* O *a. a.*
Ps 26:6. so will I compass thine *a.*
43:4. then will I go to the *a.* of God
Matt 5:23. if thou bring gift to *a.*
24. leave there thy gift before the *a.*
Acts 17:23. found *a.* with inscription 1 Cor 9:13. they that wait at *a.* are partakers with *a.* 10:18. of the *a.*
Heb 13:10. we have an *a.* whereof
Rev 8:3; 9:13. the golden *a.*
ALWAY(S), Deut 5:29, Job 7:16.
Gen 6:3. Spirit not *a.* strive
Deut 14:23. learn to fear the Lord *a.*
1 Chron 16:15. mindful *a.* of covenant
Job 27:10. will he *a.* call on God
Job 32:9. great men are not *always* wise
Ps 9:18. needy not *a.* be forgotten
16:8. I set the Lord *a.* before me
Prov 5:19. ravished *a.* with her love
28:14. happy is man that feareth *a.*
Isa 57:16. neither will I be *a.* wroth
Matt 26:11. have poor *a.* with you
28:20. I am with you *a.* to the end
Luke 18:1. men ought *a.* to pray
John 8:29. I do *a.* things that please
Acts 10:2. Cornelius prayed God *a.*
2 Cor 6:10. yet *a.* rejoicing
Eph 6:18. praying *a.* with all prayer
Phil 4:4. rejoice in the Lord *a.*
Col 4:6. your speech be *a.* with grace
AMBASSADOR, Prov 13:17. Isa 33:7. 2 Cor 5:20. Eph 6:20.
AMEN, even so come, Rev 22:20.
2 Cor 1:20. promises of God in him *a.*
Rev 3:14. these things saith the *a.*
AMEND your ways, Jer 7:3, 5; 26:13.
Jer 35:15. *a.* your doings
AMISS, 2 Chron 6:37. Dan 3:29. Luke 23:41. James 4:3.
ANCHOR, Acts 27:30. Heb 6:19.
ANCIENT, wisdom is with, Job 12:12.
Dan 7:9. the *a.* of days did sit
Ps 119:100. I understand more than *ancients*
ANGEL, who redeemed me, Gen 48:16.
Gen 24:7. send his *a.* before thee
Exod 23:23. my *a.* shall go before thee
Angel of the Lord, Ps 34:7. Zech 12:8. Acts 5:19; 12:7, 23.
Isa 63:9. *a.* of his presence saved
Dan 3:28. sent his *a.* and delivered
6:22. sent his *a.* and shut lions' mouths
John 5:4. *a.* went down at a certain
Acts 6:15. his face as face of an *a.*
23:8. Sadducees say neither *a.* nor
Job 4:18. *angels* he charged with folly
Ps 8:5. a little lower than *a.*
68:17. chariots of God thousands *a.*
78:25. man did eat *a.* food
104:4. maketh his *a.* spirits
Matt 4:11. *a.* came and ministered
13:39. reapers are the *a.*
18:10. their *a.* behold face of my Father
24:31. send his *a.* with trumpet
36. no, not *a.* of heaven, Mark 13:32.
25:31. all holy *a.* with him
Mark 12:25. are as *a.* in heaven
Luke 20:36. equal unto the *a.*
Acts 7:53. the law by disposition of *a.*
1 Cor 6:3. we shall judge *a.*
Col 2:18. beguile worshipping of *a.*
2 Thess 1:7. with his mighty *a.*
1 Tim 3:16. seen of *a.* preached unto
Heb 2:16. took not the nature of *a.*
12:22. an innumerable company of *a.*
13:2. entertained *a.* unawares
1 Pet 1:12. *a.* desire to look into
2 Pet 2:11. *a.* which are greater in power & might, bring not railing
Jude 6. *a.* which kept not first estate
Rev 1:20. *a.* of seven churches
Angel of God, Gen 28:12; 32:1. Matt 22:30. Luke 12:8; 15:10. John 1:51.
ANGER, let not the *a.* of my lord wax hot, Exod 32:22.
Deut 29:24. meaneth heat of this *a.*
Josh 7:26. from fierceness of his *a.*
Job 9:13. if God will not withdraw *a.*
Ps 27:9. put not servant away in *a.*
Ps 30:5. his *anger* endureth but a moment
77:9. hath he in *a.* shut up
78:38. turned he his *a.* away
50. he made a way to his *a.*
85:4. cause *a.* towards us to cease
90:7. we are consumed by thine *a.*
11. who knoweth power of thine *a.*
103:9. keep *a.* for ever, Jer 3:5, 12.
Prov 15:1. grievous words stir up *a.*
Eccles 7:9. *a.* resteth in the bosom of fools
Hos 11:9. not execute mine *a.*
14:4. my *a.* is turned away from him
Mic 7:18. retaineth not *a.* for ever
Nah 1:6. who can abide his *a.*
Eph 4:31. let all *a.* be put away
Col 3:8. put off all these; *a.* wrath
Slow to anger, Neh 9:17. Ps 103:8. Joel 2:13. Jon 4:2. Nah 1:3. James 1:19.
Ps 106:32. they *angered* him at waters
Gen 18:30. let not Lord be *angry*
Deut 1:37. Lord was *a.* with me
9:20. Lord was *a.* with Aaron
1 Kings 11:9. Lord was *a.* with Solomon
Ps 2:12. kiss Son lest he be *a.*
7:11. God is *a.* with wicked every day
76:7. who stand when thou art *a.*
Prov 14:17. soon *a.* dealeth foolishly
22:24. no friendship with an *a.* man
29:22. *a.* man stirreth up strife
Eccles 7:9. be not hasty to be *a.*

Isa 12:1. though thou wast *a.* with
Jon 4:9. I do well to be *a.* even
Matt 5:22. whoso is *a.* with brother
Eph 4:26. be *a.* and sin not
Titus 1:7. bishop must not be soon *a.*
ANGUISH, excessive pain.
Gen 42:21. saw the *a.* of his soul
Exod 6:9. hearkened not for *a.* of spirit
Ps 119:143. trouble and *a.* take hold
Jer 6:24. *a.* taken hold of us
John 16:21. remember not *a.* for joy
Rom 2:9. tribulation and *a.* upon
ANOINT, with oil, to appoint, to qualify for office of king, priest, or prophet, Exod 28:41.
Dan 9:24. to *a.* the most holy
Amos 6:6. *a.* with chief ointments
Matt 6:17. when fastest *a.* thy head
Rev 3:18. *a.* eyes with eyesalve
1 Sam 2:10. exalt the horn of his *anointed*
24:6. seeing he is the *a.* of the Lord
1 Chron 16:22. touch not my *a.* Ps 105:15.
2 Chron 6:42. turn not away the face of thine *a.* Ps 132:10.
Ps 2:2. against the Lord and his *a.*
18:50. mercy to his *a.* to David, 2 Sam 22:51.
20:6. the Lord saveth his *a.*
28:8. Lord is saving strength of his *a.*
45:7. *a.* thee with oil of gladness
84:9. look upon face of thine *a.*
89:38. wroth with thine *a.*
132:17. ordained a lamp for mine *a.*
Zech 4:14. two *a.* that stand by the Lord
Hab 3:13. salvation with thine *a.*
Acts 4:27. Jesus whom thou hast *a.*
10:38. how God *a.* Jesus of Nazareth
2 Cor 1:21. who hath *a.* us is God
Ps 23:5. *anointest* my head with oil
1 John 2:27. same *anointing* teacheth you of all
James 5:14. *a.* him with oil
ANSWER of peace, Gen 41:16. Deut 20:11.
Prov 15:1. soft *a.* turneth wrath
16:1. *a.* of tongue is from the Lord
Job 19:16. gave me no *a.* Song of Sol 5:6.
Mic 3:7. there is no *answer* of God
Rom 11:4. what saith the *a.* of God
2 Tim 4:16. at my first a. no man
1 Pet 3:15. ready to give an *a.* to
21. the *a.* of a good conscience
Job 40:4. what shall I *a.* thee
Ps 102:2. *a.* me speedily
143:1. in thy faithfulness *a.* me
Prov 26:4, 5. *a.* fool according to his folly
Isa 14:32. what *a.* messengers
58:9. shalt thou call, and the Lord shall *a.*
66:4. when I called none did *a.*
Matt 25:37. then shall righteous *a.*
Luke 12:11. what thing ye shall *a.*
13:25. he shall *a.* I know you not
21:14. meditate not what to *a.*
2 Cor 5:12. somewhat to *a.* them
Col 4:6. know how to *a.* every man
Job 14:15. thou shalt call and I will *a.* & 13:22. Ps 91:15. Isa 65:24. Jer 33:3. Ezek 14:4, 7.
9:3. he cannot *a.* one
40:5. once have I spoken, but I will not *a.*
Ps 18:41. to Lord but he *answered* not
81:7. I *a.* thee in secret place
99:6. called on the Lord and he *a.*
Prov 18:23. rich *answereth* roughly
13. he that *a.* matter before hear
27:19. as in water face *a.* to face
Eccles 10:19. money *a.* all things
Titus 2:9. not *answering* again
ANT, Prov 6:6; 30:25.
ANTICHRIST, 1 John 2:18, 22. & 4:3. 2 John 7.
APART, Ps 4:3. Zech 12:12. James 1:21.
APOSTLE, *one sent forth* by Christ to preach the gospel, found and uphold churches, Rom 1:1. 1 Cor 12:28, especially the twelve eyewitnesses, Acts 1:21, 22.
Rom 11:13. I am *a.* of Gentiles
1 Cor 9:1. am I not an *a.*
15:9. not meet to be called an *a.*
2 Cor 12:12. signs of *a.* were wrought
Heb 3:1. consider *a.* and high priest
Matt 10:2. names of the twelve *apostles*
Luke 11:49. send prophets and *a.*
1 Cor 4:9. God hath set forth us *a.*
15:9. I am the least of the *a.*
2 Cor 11:13. false *a.*
Eph 2:20. built on foundation of *a.*
4:11. gave some *a.* some prophets
Rev 2:2. say they are *a.* and are not
18:20. holy *a.* and prophets, Eph 3:5.
21:14. names of twelve *a.* of the Lamb
Acts 1:25. part of this *apostleship*
Rom 1:5. received grace and *a.*
1 Cor 9:2. seal of my *a.* are ye
Gal 2:8. to *a.* of circumcision
APPAREL, Isa 63:1. Zeph 1:8. *1 Tim 2:9. 1* Pet 3:3. James 2:2.
APPEAR, Gen 1:9. Heb 11:3.
Exod 23:15. none shall *a.* before me empty, 34:20. Deut 16:16.
1 Sam 2:27. did I *a.* to house of thy father
2 Chron 1:7. did God *a.* to Solomon
Ps 42:2. when shall I *a.* before God
Isa 1:12. when ye *a.* before me who
66:5. shall *a.* to your joy, but they
Matt 6:16. may *a.* to men to fast
23:27. *a.* beautiful outward
Rom 7:13. sin that it might *a.* sin
2 Cor 5:10. we must all *a.* before the judgment seat of Christ.
Col 3:4. Christ *a.* ye also shall *a.*
1 Tim 4:15. thy profiting *a.* to all
Heb 9:24. to *appear* in the presence of God for us
28. *a.* second time without sin to
1 Pet 5:4. when chief shepherd *a.*
1 John 3:2. not yet *a.* what we shall
1 Sam 16:7. man looketh on outward *appearance,* but the Lord on heart
John 7:24. judge not according to *a.*
1 Thess 5:22. abstain from all *a.* of evil
Titus 2:11. grace *appeared* to all men
Heb 9:26. he *a.* to put away sin
2 Tim 1:10. manifest by *appearing* of Jesus
4:1. judge quick and dead at his *a.*
8. all them that love his *a.*
Titus 2:13. look for glorious *a.* of great God
1 Pet 1:7. unto praise at *a.* of Jesus
APPETITE, Prov 23:2. Isa 29:8.
APPLE of eye, Deut 32:10. Ps 17:8. Prov 7:2. Lam 2:18. Zech 2:8.
Apple tree, Song of Sol 2:3. & 8:5.
Apples, Prov 25:11. Song of Sol 2:5; 7:8.
APPLY heart to wisdom, &c., Ps 90:12. Prov 2:2; 22:17; 23:12. Eccles 7:25.
APPOINT me thy wages, and I, Gen 30:28.
Isa 61:3. *a.* to them that mourn in Zion
26:1. salvation will God *a.* for walls
Matt 24:51. *a.* his portion with hypocrites
Luke 22:29. I *a.* unto you a kingdom
Job 7:1. an *appointed* time to man
14:14. all the days of my *a.* time
30:23. to house *a.* for all living
Ps 79:11. preserve those *a.* to die
Jer 5:24. reserve *a.* weeks of harvest
Hab 2:3. vision is for an *a.* time
1 Thess 5:9. God not *a.* us to wrath
Heb 9:27. *a.* to men once to die
APPREHENDED, lay hold of, grasp, Phil 3:12, 13. Acts 12:4. 2 Cor 11:32.
APPROACH, come near to, marry.
Lev 18:6. *a.* to near of kin, 20:16.

Ps 65:4. blessed is the man whom thou choosest and causest to *a.*
Jer 30:21. engaged heart to *a.* to me
1 Tim 6:16. light to which none can *a.*
Isa 58:2. delight in *approaching* to God
Heb 10:25. as ye see day *a.*
APPROVE, prove, attest, test.
Ps 49:13. posterity *a.* their sayings
Phil 1:10. may *a.* things excellent
Acts 2:22. man *approved* of God
Rom 14:18. acceptable to God, *a.*
16:10. Apelles *a.* in Christ
1 Cor 11:19. *a.* be made manifest of men
Rom 2:18. *approvest* things excellent
Lam 3:36. to subvert the Lord *approveth* not
2 Cor 6:4. in all things *approving* ourselves
APT to teach, 1 Tim 3:2. 2 Tim 2:24.
ARE seven years, Gen 41:26, 27.
1 Cor 1:28. things which *a.* not
30. of him *a.* ye in Christ Jesus
8:6. of whom *a.* all things
Heb 2:10. for and by whom *a.* all
Rev 1:19. write things that *a.*
20. *a.* angels; *a.* seven churches
ARGUE, Job 6:25; 23:4.
ARIGHT, set not their heart, Ps 78:8.
Ps 50:23. ordereth his conversation *a.*
Jer 8:6. but they spake not *a.*
ARISE for our help, Ps 44:26.
1 Chron 22:16. *a.* and be doing
Ps 68:1. let God *a.* and enemies be
Amos 7:2. by whom shall Jacob *a.* 5.
Mic 7:8. when I fall I shall *a.*
Mal 4:2. Sun of righteousness *arise*
Ps 112:4. to upright *ariseth* light
Matt 13:21. persecution *a.* because
ARM of flesh with him, 2 Chron 32:8.
Exod 15:16. by greatness of thine *a.*
Job 40:9. hast thou an *a.* like God
Ps 44:3. own *a.* did not save them, 77:15.
89:13. hast a mighty *a.*
Isa 33:2. be thou their *a.* every
51:5. mine *a.* shall judge; on my *a.*
9. put on strength, O *a.* of the Lord
53:1. *a.* of Lord revealed, John 12:38.
62:8. Lord hath sworn by the *a.*
63:12. led them by his glorious *a.*
Acts 13:17. high *a.* brought he them
1 Pet 4:1. *a.* yourselves with same
Luke 11:21. strong man *armed* keepeth
His arm, Ps 98:1. Isa 40:10, 11; 59:16. Jer 17:5. Ezek 31:17. Zech 11:17. Luke 1:51.
Gen 49:24. *arms* of his hands made
Deut 33:27. underneath everlasting *a.*
ARMIES of living God, 1 Sam 17:26
Job 25:3. any number of his *a.*
Ps 44:9. goest not with our *a.* 60:10.
Song of Sol 6:13. company of two *a.*
Rev 19:14. *a.* in heaven followed
ARMOUR of light, Rom 13:12.
2 Cor 6:7. by *a.* of righteousness
Eph 6:11, 13, put on whole *a.* of God
ARRAY, order of battle, 2 Sam 10:9. Job 6:4. Jer 50:14.
ARRAY, to clothe, Esther 6:9. Job 40:10. Jer 43:12. Matt 6:29. 1 Tim 2:9. Rev 7:13; 17:4; 19:8.
ARROGANCY, 1 Sam 2:3. Prov 8:13. Isa 13:11.
ARROWS of the Almighty, Job 6:4.
2 Kings 13:17. *arrow* of Lord's deliverance
Ps 91:5. nor for *a.* that flieth by day
Lam 3:12. set me as a mark for *a.*
Deut 32:23. I will spend mine *arrows* upon
Ps 38:2. thine *a.* stick fast in me
45:5. thine *a.* are sharp in the heart
ASCEND into hill of Lord, Ps 24:3.
Ps 139:8. if I *a.* to heaven, Rom 10:6.
John 20:17. I *a.* to my Father and
Prov 30:4. who hath *ascended* into heaven
John 3:13. no man hath *a.* to heaven
Eph 4:8. when he *a.* up on high
Rev 8:4. smoke of incense *a.*
11:12. *a.* up to heaven in a cloud
Gen 28:12. angels *ascending* and descending, John 1:51. on Son of man
ASCRIBE greatness to God, Deut 32:3.
Job 36:3. *a.* righteousness to my Maker
ASHAMED to lift face, Ezra 9:6.
Gen 2:25. man and wife naked not *a.*
Ezek 16:61. remember ways and be *a.*
Mark 8:38. be *a.* of me and my word
Rom 1:16. I am not *a.* of the gospel
6:21. whereof ye are now *a.*
Not be ashamed, Ps 25:2; 119:6, 80. Isa 49:23. Rom 9:33. 2 Tim 2:15.
ASHES, Gen 18:27. Job 2:8; 13:12; 30:19; 42:6. Ps 102:9. Isa 44:20; 61:3. Jer 6:26. Ezek 28:18. Mal 4:3.
ASK the way to Zion, Jer 50:5.
Jer 6:16. *a.* for the old paths
Matt 7:7. *a.* and it shall be given
11. give good things to them that *a.* him
20:22. ye know not what ye *a.*
Luke 12:48. of him they will *a.* more
John 14:13, 14. whatsoever ye *a.* in my name, & 15:16; 16:23.
John 16:24. *asked* . . . *ask* and ye shall receive
Eph 3:20. above all that we *a.* or think
James 1:5. wisdom let him *a.* of God
6. let him *a.* in faith, not wavering
4:2, 3, because ye *a.* not; ye *a.* and receive not, because ye *a.* amiss
1 John 3:22. whatsoever we *a.* we receive
5:14, 15. *a.* according to his will
Matt 7:8. that *asketh* receiveth
ASLEEP, 1 Cor 15:6, 18. 1 Thess 4:13.
ASP, poisonous serpent, Deut 32:33. Job 20:14, 16. Isa 11:8. Rom 3:13.
ASS knows master's crib, Isa 1:3.
Zech 9:9. riding on an *a.* Matt 21:5. John 12:15.
ASSEMBLY of wicked, Ps 22:16.
Ps 89:7. God feared in the *a.* of saints
Heb 12:23. general *a.* of firstborn
Isa 4:5. create on her *assemblies* a cloud
Heb 10:25. forsake not *assembling*
ASSUAGE, Gen 8:1. Job 16:5, 6.
ASSURANCE, quiet confidence.
Isa 32:17. effect of righteousness *a.*
Col 2:2. riches of full *a.* of understanding
1 Thess 1:5. gospel came in much *a.*
Heb 6:11. to full *a.* of hope unto the end
1 John 3:19. of truth, and shall *assure* our hearts before him
ASTRAY, Ps 119. 176. Isa 53:6. Matt 18:12. Luke 15:4. 1 Pet 2:25.
ATHIRST, sore, called, Judg 15:18.
Rev 21:6. give to him *a.* of fountain
ATONEMENT (setting at one), pacifying, satisfaction for sin, Lev 16:11; 23:27, 28; 25:9. Exod 30:16. Num 8:19, 21; 16:46; 28:22.
ATTAIN to wise counsels, Prov 1:5.
Ps 139:6. high, I cannot *a.* unto it
Ezek 46:7. according as hand shall *a.*
Phil 3:11, 12. *a.* to resurrection of dead . . . not already *attained*
ATTEND to my cry, Ps 55:2; 61:1; 66:19; 86:6; 142:6.
Prov 4:1. *a.* to know understanding
20. *a.* to my words, 7:24.
Acts 16:14. she *attended* to things spoken
Attendance, 1 Kings 10:5. 1 Tim 4:13. Heb 7:13. Rom 13:6.

B

9:12. *b.* there come two woes more
11:14. *b.* third woe cometh quickly
21:5. *b.* I make all things new
Ps 33:13. Lord *beholdeth* all sons of men
James 1:24. he *b.* himself and goeth
Ps 119:37. turn eyes from *beholding* vanity
Prov 15:3. *b.* evil and good
2 Cor 3:18. open face *b.* as in glass
Col 2:5. joying and *b.* your order
James 1:23. like man *b.* natural face
BEING, Ps 104:33; 146:2. Acts 17:28.
BELIAL, *Heb.* worthlessness, Deut 13:13. Judg 19:22; 20:13. 1 Sam 1:16; 2:12; 10:27; 25:17, 25; 30:22. 2 Sam 16:7; 20:1; 23:6. 1 Kings 21:10, 13. 2 Chron 13:7. 2 Cor 6:15.
BELIEVE, Exod 4:1. Num 14:11; 20:12.
Deut 1:32. ye did not *b.* the Lord
2 Chron 20:20. *b.* Lord, *b.* prophets
Isa 7:9. not *b.* not established
Matt 9:28. *b.* ye that I am able
Mark 1:15. repent and *b.* the gospel
9:24. Lord, I *b.* help my unbelief
11:24. *b.* that ye receive them
Luke 8:13. for a while *b.* and
24:25. slow of heart to *b.* all
John 1:12. even to them that *b.*
6:69. we *b.* and are sure thou art Christ
John 7:39. that *b.* him should receive
8:24. if ye *b.* not I am he, ye die
11:27. I *b.* that thou art the Christ
40. if thou *b.* should see glory of God
42. may *b.* thou hast sent me
12:36. *b.* in the light while ye have
14:1. ye *b.* in God, *b.* also in me
17:20. pray for them who shall *b.*
20:31. written that ye might *b.*
Acts 8:37. I *b.* Jesus Christ is the Son
13:39. all that *b.* are justified
16:31. *b.* on Lord Jesus and be saved
Rom 3:22. on all them that *b.*
10:9. shalt *b.* in thine heart
14. how shall they *b.* on him
2 Cor 4:13. we *b.* and therefore speak
Phil 1:29. not only to *b.* but suffer
2 Thess 2:11. they should *b.* lie
1 Tim 4:10. especially those that *b.*
Heb 10:39. *b.* to saving of the soul
11:6. cometh to God must *b.* that he is
James 2:19. devils also b. and tremble
1 John 3:23. his comm . . . *b.* on Jesus Christ
Believe not, Isa 7:9. John 4:48; 8:24; 10:26; 12:39; 16:9; 20:25.
Rom 3:3. 2 Cor 4:4.
2 Tim 2:13. 1 John 4:1.
Gen 15:6. *believed* in Lord, and he counted Rom 4:3. Gal 3:6. James 2:23.
Ps 27:13. fainted unless I had *b.*
116:10. I *b.* therefore have I spoken
119:66. I *b.* thy commandments
Isa 53:1. who hath *b.* our report, John 12:38. Rom 10:16.
Jon 3:5. people of Nineveh *believed* God.
Matt 8:13. as thou hast *b.* so be it
21:32. publicans and harlots *b.* him
John 4:53. himself *b.* and his house
7:48. have any of the Pharisees *b.* on
17:8. have *b.* thou didst send me
Acts 4:32. that *b.* were of one heart
8:13. Simon *b.* and was baptized
11:21. great number *b.* and turned
13:48. were ordained to eternal life *b.*
Rom 4:18. against hope *b.* in hope
13:11. salvation nearer than when we *b.*
Eph 1:13. after ye *b.* ye were sealed
1 Tim 3:16. God was *b.* on in world
2 Tim 1:12. know whom I have *b.*
Believed not, Ps 78:22, 32; 106:24. Luke 24:41. Acts 9:26. Rom 10:14. 2 Thess 2:12. Heb 3:18. Jude 5.
Believers, Acts 5:14. 1 Tim 4:12.
Believest, Luke 1:20. John 1:50; 11:26; 14:10. James 2:19.
Acts 8:37. if thou *b.* with all thine heart
26:27. *b.* thou prophets? I know thou *b.*
Believeth, Job 15:22; 39:24.
Prov 14:15. simple *b.* every word
Isa 28:16. he that *b.* shall not make haste
Mark 9:23. all things possible to him that *b.*
16:16. he that *b.* shall be saved
John 3:15, 16. *b.* in him not perish
18. that *b.* not is condemned already
36. *b.* on Son hath everlasting life
5:24. *b.* on him that sent me
6:35. *b.* on me shall never thirst
40. seeth Son, and *b.* have everlasting life, 47.
7:38. that *b.* on me out of his belly shall flow
11:25. *b.* in me though he were dead
26. he that *b.* in me shall never *die*
12:44. *b.* in me, *b.* not on me, but
John 12:46. *b.* on me should not abide in darkness
14:12. *b.* on me the works that I do
Rom 1:16. power of God . . . to every that *b.*
3:26. justifier of him that *b.* in Jesus
4:5. worketh not, but *b.* on him
9:33. *b.* on him shall not be ashamed, 10:11.
10:4. end of the law for righteousness to every one that *b.*
14:2. one *b.* that he may eat all things
1 Cor 7:12. wife that *b.* not
13. husband that *b.* not
1 Cor 13:7. charity *b.* all
14:24. come in one that *b.* not
2 Cor 6:15. he that *b.* with infidel
1 Tim 5:16. that *b.* have widows
1 Pet 2:6. *b.* on him not confounded
1 John 5:1. whoso *b.* Jesus is Christ
5. overcometh world, but he that *b.*
10. he that *b.* on Son of God hath witness: *b.* not God hath made him a liar
John 20:27. be not faithless, but *believing*
31. that *b.* ye might have life
Acts 16:34. *b.* in God with all his house
Rom 15:13. all joy and peace in *b.*
1 Tim 6:2. that have *b.* masters
1 Pet 1:8. yet *b.* ye rejoice with joy
2 Thess 2:13. *belief* of the truth
BELLOWS are burnt, Jer 6:29.
BELLY, on *b.* shalt go, Gen 3:14.
Num 5:21. *b.* to swell and thigh rot
25:8. thrust them through the *b.*
Job 3:11. when I came out of *b.*
15:2. fill his *b.* with east wind
35. their *b.* prepareth deceit
Job 20:15. God cast them out of his *belly*
Ps 17:14. whose *b.* thou fillest with
22:10. art my God from mother's *b.*
44:25. our *b.* cleaveth to the earth
Isa 46:3. borne by me from the *b.*
Jon 1:17. *b.* of fish, Matt 12:40.
2:1. prayed to God out of fish's *b.*
2. out of the *b.* of hell cried I
Hab 3:16. my *b.* trembled that I
Luke 15:16. fill his *b.* with husks
John 7:38. out of his *b.* shall flow
1 Cor 6:13. meats for *b.* and *b.* for
Phil 3:19. whose god is their *b.*
Rev 10:9. make thy *b.* bitter
Titus 1:12. Cretians slow *bellies*
BELONG, Lev 27:24. Luke 23:7.
Gen 40:8. interpretations *b.* to God
Deut 29:29. secret things *b.* to Lord, things revealed *b.* to us and children
Ps 47:9. shields of earth *b.* to God
68:20. to God *b.* issues from death

Dan 9:9. to Lord *b.* mercies and forgivenesses
Mark 9:41. because ye *b.* to Christ
Luke 19:42. things that *b.* to thy peace
1 Cor 7:32. care for things *b.* to Lord
Ezra 10:4. this matter *belongeth* to
Ps 3:8. salvation *b.* to the Lord
62:11. power *b.* to God, 12. *b.* mercy
Dan 9:7. righteousness *b.* to thee
8. to us *b.* confusion of face
Heb 5:14. strong meat *b.* to them
BELOVED—another hated, Deut 21:15.
Neh 13:26. Solomon *b.* of his God
Ps 60:5. thy *b.* may be delivered
127:2. Lord giveth his *b.* sleep
Song of Sol 1:14. *my beloved,* 2:3, 9, 16, 17; 4:16. 5:2, 4–6, 8, 10, 16; 6:2, 3; 7:10, 13.
Isa 5:1. *my beloved* hath a vineyard in a fruitful
Song of Sol 5:9. thy *b.* more than another *b.*
Dan 10:11, 19. man, greatly *b.* 9:23.
Matt 3:17. this is my *b.* Son, 17:5.
Rom 9:25. *b.* which was not *b.*
11:28. *b.* for the fathers' sake
16:8. Amplias *b.* in the Lord
Eph 1:6. accepted in the *b.*
Col 3:12. elect of God and *b.*
4:14. Luke the *b.* physician
2 Pet 3:15. *b.* brother Paul
Rev 20:9. they compassed *b.* city
BEMOAN, Jer 15:5; 16:5; 22:10; 31:18; 48:17.
BEND bow, Ps 11:2; 64:3; 58:7; 7:12; 37:14. Lam 2:4; 3:12. Isa 5:28.
Jer 9:3. *b.* their tongues like a bow
Isa 60:14. afflicted thee come *bending*
Zech 9:13. I have *bent* Judah for me
BENEATH, Prov 15:24. John 8:23.
BENEFACTORS, Luke 22:25.
BENEFITS, loadeth us with Ps 68:19.
Ps 103:2. forget not all his *b.*
116:12. render to Lord for all his *b.*
BENEVOLENCE, due, 1 Cor 7:3.
BEREAVE soul of good, Eccles 4:8.
Jer 15:7. *b.* of children, 18:21. Gen 42:36; 43:14. Ezek 5:17; 36:12, 13, 14. Lam 1:20. Hos 9:12; 13:8.
BESEECH God to be gracious, Mal 1:9.
2 Cor 5:20. as though God did *b.*
BESET me behind and before, Ps 139:5.
Hos 7:2. own doings have *b.* them
Heb 12:1. sin which doth so easily *b.* us
BESIDE waters, Ps 23:2. Isa 32:20.
Song of Sol 1:8. feed kids *b.* shepherds' tents
Isa 56:8. *b.* those that are gathered
BESOM of destruction, Isa 14:23.
BESOUGHT the Lord, Deut 3:23.
2 Sam 12:16. 1 Kings 13:6.
2 Kings 13:4. 2 Chron 33:12. Ezra 8:23. 2 Cor 12:8.
BEST estate is vanity, Ps 39:5.
Luke 15:22. bring forth *b.* robe
1 Cor 12:31. covet earnestly *b.* gifts
BESTEAD, placed, hardly, Isa 8:21.
BESTOW a blessing, Exod 32:29.
Luke 12:17. room to *b.* my fruits
1 Cor 12:23. *b.* more abundant honour
13:3. *b.* all my goods to feed the poor
John 4:38. *bestowed* no labour
1 Cor 15:10. his grace *b.* on me
2 Cor 1:11. gift *b.* on us by means
8:1. grace of God *b.* on churches
Gal 4:11. lest *b.* labour in vain
1 John 3:1. love Father hath *b.* on us
BETIMES, 2 Chron 36:15. Job 8:5; 24:5. Prov 13:24. Gen 26:31.
BETRAY, Matt 24:10; 26:21. Mark 13:12; 14:18. Luke 22:4, 21. John 13:21.
BETROTH, Deut 28:30. Hos 2:19, 20.
BETTER than ten sons, 1 Sam 1:8.
Judg 8:2. gleanings *b.* than vintage
Prov 15:16. *b.* is little with fear of Lord
17. *b.* is a dinner of herbs with love
16:8. *b.* is a little with righteousness
16. much *b.* to get wisdom than gold
17:1. *b.* is dry morsel, and quietness
27:10. *b.* is a neighbour near than
Eccles 4:9. two are *b.* than one
13. *b.* is a poor and wise child than
7:1. *b.* is a good name than precious
2. *b.* to go to the house of mourning than house of feasting
3. *b.* is sorrow than laughter
5. *b.* to hear rebuke of the wise than
8. *b.* is the patient than proud in
9:16. wisdom is *b.* than strength
18. wisdom is *b.* than weapons of
Song of Sol 1:2. love *b.* than wine, 4:10.
Rom 3:9. are we *b.* than they
1 Cor 9:15. were *b.* for me to die
11:17. come not for the b. but worse
Phil 1:23. with Christ is far *b.*
2:3. esteem others *b.* than themselves
Heb 1:4. so much *b.* than angels
6:9. persuaded *b.* things of you
7:19. bringing in of a *b.* hope did
22. Jesus made a surety of a *b.* testament
8:6. mediator of a *b.* covenant
10:34. a *b.* and an enduring substance
11:16. desire a *b.* country
35. might obtain a *b.* resurrection
40. God provided some *b.* thing
12:24. blood speaketh *b.* than Abel
2 Pet 2:21. *b.* not to have known
BETWEEN thy seed and her, Gen 3:15.
1 Kings 3:9. discern *b.* good and bad
18:21. how long halt *b.* two opinions
1 Tim 2:5. one mediator *b.* God and men
BETWIXT Phil 1:23. In a strait *b.* two
BEWARE of men, Matt 10:17.
Matt 7:15. *b.* of false prophets
16:6. *b.* of leaven of Pharisees, 11. Mark 8:15.
Luke 12:15. *b.* of covetousness
Phil 3:2. *b.* of dogs, *b.* of evil workers
Col 2:8. *b.* lest any man spoil you
2 Pet 3:17. *b.* lest being led away
BEYOND, go, over-reach, 1 Thess 4:6.
BID, Matt 22:9; 23:3. Luke 14:10.
BIDE, not in unbelief, Rom 11:23.
BILL, Deut 24:1, 3. Isa 50:1. Jer 3:8. Mark 10:4. Luke 16:6, 7.
BILLOWS, Ps 42:7. Jon 2:3.
BIND sweet influences, Job 38:31.
Job 31:36. I would *b.* it as a crown
Ps 105:22. *b.* his princes at pleasure
149:8. to *b.* their kings with chains
Prov 3:3. *b.* them about thy neck
Isa 8:16. *b.* up testimony, seal law
Hos 6:1. smitten, and will *b.* us up
Matt 12:29. first *b.* strong man and
13:30. *b.* them in bundles to burn
16:19. thou shalt *b.* on earth, 18:18.
22:13. *b.* him hand and foot, and cast
Bindeth up, Job 5:18. Ps 147:3.
BIRD hasteth to snare, Prov 7:23.
Ps 124:7. soul is escaped as a *b.*
Eccles 10:20. *b.* of air tell the matter
Isa 46:11. ravenous *b.* from the east
Jer 12:9. heritage as a speckled *b.*
Birds, Gen 15:10; 40:17. Lev 14:4.
2 Sam 21:10. Ps 104:17. Eccles 9:12. Song of Sol 2:12. Isa 31:5.
Jer 5:27; 12:4, 9. Matt 8:20.
BIRTH, 2 Kings 19:3. Eccles 7:1. Isa 66:9. Ezek 16:3. Gal 4:19.
BIRTHDAY, Gen 40:20. Matt 14:6.
BIRTHRIGHT, Gen 25:31, 32, 33; 27:36; 43:33. 1 Chron 5:1. Heb 12:16.
BISHOP, 1 Tim 3:1, 2. Titus 1:7.
1 Pet 2:25. return to *b.* of souls
Phil 1:1. with *bishops* and deacons
BITE, Num 21:6, 8, 9. Eccles 10:8, 11. Jer 8:17. Amos 9:3. Hab 2:7.

Mic 3:5. prophets *b.* with their teeth
Gal 5:15. if ye *b.* and devour one another
Prov 23:32. at last it *biteth* like a serpent
BITTER, made their lives, Exod 1:14.
Exod 12:8. with *b.* herbs, Num 9:11.
Deut 32:24. devoured with *b.* destruction
32. their grapes of gall, clusters are *b.*
2 Kings 14:26. affliction was very *b.*
Job 3:20. life given to the *b.* in soul
13:26. write *b.* things against me
Ps 64:3. their arrows even *b.* words
Prov 27:7. every *b.* thing is sweet
Isa 5:20. woe them that put *b.* for sweet
Jer 2:19. evil thing and *b.* that
Col 3:19. be not *b.* against them
James 3:14. if ye have *b.* envying
Rev 8:11. because they were made *b.*
10:9. make thy belly *b.*
Judg 5:23. curse *bitterly* inhabitants
Isa 22:4. I will weep *b.* 33:7.
Ezek 27:30. shall cry *b.* Zeph 1:14.
Hos 12:14. provoked him most *b.*
Matt 26:75. wept *b.* Luke 22:62.
Bitterness of soul, 1 Sam 1:10.
1 Sam 15:32. *b.* of death is past
2 Sam 2:26. it will be *b.* in end
Prov 14:10. heart knows its own *b.*
Acts 8:23. in gall of *b.* and bond of
Rom 3:14. full of cursing and *b.*
Eph 4:31. let all *b.* be put away
Heb 12:15. root of *b.* springing up
BITTERN, Isa 14:23; 34:11.
BLACK, 1 Kings 18:45. Matt 5:36. Song of Sol 1:5. I am *b.* 6.
Blackness of darkness, Heb 12:18. Jude 13.
BLAME, Gen 43:9; 44:32. 2 Cor 8:20. Eph 1:4.
Blamed, 2 Cor 6:3. Gal 2:11.
Blameless, Gen 44:10. Josh 2:17. Judg 15:3. Matt 12:5. Phil 3:6. 1 Tim 5:7.
Luke 1:6. in ordinances of the Lord *b.*
1 Cor 1:8. be *blameless* in day of our Lord
1 Thess 5:23. be preserved *b.*
1 Tim 3:2. bishop must be *b.* Titus 1:6, 7.
10. office of deacon found *b.*
2 Pet 3:14. without spot and *b.*
BLASPHEME, revile God, &c.
Ps 74:10. enemy *b.* thy name
Mark 3:29. *b.* against Holy Ghost not forgiven
Acts 26:11. *compelled them to b.*
1 Tim 1:20. may learn not to *b.*
James 2:7. do they not *b.* that name
2 Kings 19:6. servants *blasphemed* me, Isa 37:6.
Ps 74:18. foolish people have *b.*
Isa 52:5. my name continually is *b.*
Rom 2:24. God is *b.* through you
1 Tim 6:1. name of God be not *b.*
Rev 16:9, 11, 21. *b.* God of heaven
Lev 24:16. *blasphemeth* put to death
Ps 44:16. voice of him that reproacheth and *b.*
Matt 9:3. scribes said this man *b.*
Luke 12:10. to him that *b.* against the Holy Ghost it shall not be forgiven
Blasphemer, 1 Tim 1:13. 2 Tim 3:2.
Blasphemy, 2 Kings 19:3. Isa 37:3. Matt 12:31. Mark 7:22. Col 3:8. Rev 2:9.
BLAST, Exod 15:8. 2 Sam 22:16. 2 Kings 19:7. Job 4:9. Isa 25:4.
Blasting, Deut 28:22. 1 Kings 8:37.
BLEMISH, your lamb shall be without, Exod 12:5; 29:1. Lev 1:3, 10; 4:23.
Dan 1:4. children in whom was no *b.*
Eph 5:27. church holy, without *b.*
1 Pet 1:19. as a lamb without *b.*
BLESS them that *b.* thee, Gen 12:3.
Gen 22:17. in blessing I will *b.* thee
Exod 23:25. *b.* thy bread and water
24:1. pleased Lord to *b.* Israel
Num 6:24. Lord *b.* and keep thee
Ps 5:12. wilt *b.* the righteous
28:9. *b.* thine inheritance and feed
29:11. will *b.* his people with peace
67:1. be merciful to us and *b.* us
115:13. he will *b.* them that fear
132:15. I will abundantly *b.* her
134:3. the Lord *b.* thee out of Zion
Hag 2:19. from this day will I *b.*
Acts 3:26. sent him to *b.* you
Rom 12:14. *b.* them that persecute
1 Cor 4:12. being reviled we *b.*
Bless the Lord, Deut 8:10. Judg 5:9. Ps 16:7; 26:12; 34:1; 103:1, 21, 22; 104:1, 35.
Bless thee, Ps 63:4; 145:2, 10. Gen 12:2.
Gen 1:22. God *blessed* them and
2:3. God *b.* the seventh day
Exod 20:11. the Lord *b.* the sabbath
Ps 33:12. *b.* whose God is the Lord
Prov 10:7. memory of the just is *b.*
Matt 13:16. *b.* are eyes, Luke 10:23.
24:46. *b.* is that servant whom *his lord when he,* Luke 12:37, 38.
Mark 10:16. in his arms and *b.* them
Luke 1:28, 42. *b.* art thou among women
45. *b.* is she that believed
48. all generations shall call me *b.*
Acts 20:35. it is more *b.* to give
Rom 1:25. Creator *b.* for ever, 9:5. 2 Cor 11:31. Eph 1:3. 1 Pet 1:3.
1 Tim 1:11. glorious gospel of the *b.* God
6:15. *b.* and only potentate
John 12:13. *b.* is he that cometh in
Rev 14:13. *b. are* dead which die in the Lord
Prov 8:32. *b. are they* that keep my ways
Isa 30:18.—that wait for him
b. are they Matt 5:3–11.—poor in spirit—mourn—meek—hunger and thirst—merciful—pure in heart—peacemakers—persecuted—when men revile you, Luke 6:20–22.
Luke 11:28.—that hear the word
John 20:29.—that have not seen, and
Rom 4:7.—whose iniquities are forgiven
Rev 19:9.—called to marriage supper
22:14.—that do his commandments
Num 24:9. *blessed is he* that blesseth
Ps 32:1.—whose transgression is
41:1.—that considereth the poor
Dan 12:12.—that waiteth and cometh
Matt 11:6.—not offended in me
21:9.—cometh in the name of the Lord, 23:39. Mark 11:9. Luke 13:35.
Rev 1:3.—readeth this prophecy
20:6.—part in first resurrection
22:7.—keepeth the sayings of this book
Ps 1:1. *b. is the man* that walketh not in the counsel of the ungodly
32:2.—to whom the Lord imputeth
34:8.—that trusteth in him, 84:12.
65:4.—whom thou choosest
84:5.—whose strength is in thee
94:12.—whom thou chastenest
112:1.—*that* feareth the Lord
Prov 8:34. *b. is the man that* heareth me,
Isa 56:2.—doeth this, and son
Jer 17:7.—trusteth in the Lord
James 1:12.—endureth temptation
Blessedness, Rom 4:6, 9. Gal 4:15.
Gen 12:2. thou shalt be a *blessing*
27:36. he hath taken away my *b.*
28:4. give thee *b.* of Abraham
Deut 11:26. set before you a *b.* and a curse, 30:19. James 3:9, 10.
23:5. turned curse into *b.* Neh 13:2.
Neh 9:5. exalted above all *b.*
Job 29:13. *b.* of him ready to perish
Ps 3:8. thy *b.* is upon thy people
109:17. delighted not in *b.*
129:8. the *b.* of Lord be upon you

Isa 65:8. destroy it not, a *b.* is in it
Joel 2:14. leave a *b.* behind him
1 Cor 10:16. cup of *b.* which we *bless*
Gal 3:14. *b.* of Abraham come on Gentiles
Blessings, Gen 49:25, 26. Josh 8:34. Ps 21:3. Prov 10:6; 28:20. Mal 2:2. Eph 1:3.
BLIND, Exod 4:11. Lev 21:18.
Job 29:15. I was eyes to the *b.*
Ps 146.8. openeth the eyes of the *b.*
Isa 42:7. to open the *b.* eyes, 18.
19. who is *b.* but my servant
43:8. bring the *b.* people that have eyes
Matt 11:5. *b.* receive sight, Luke 7:21, 22.
23:16. woe to you *b.* guides, 24.
Luke 4:18. recovery of sight to *b.*
2 Pet 1:9. lacketh these things is *b.*
Rev 3:17. thou art *b.* and naked
John 12:40. *blinded* their eyes.
Rom 11:7. the rest were *b.*
2 Cor 4:4. god of this world *b.* the minds
1 John 2:11. darkness *b.* his eyes
BLOOD of grapes, Gen 49:11; of Abel, Gen 4:10, 11.
Job 16:18. cover thou not my *b.* let
Ps 9:12. maketh inquisition for *b.*
72:14. precious their *b.* in his sight
Isa 26:21. earth shall disclose her *b.*
Ezek 3:18. his *b.* will I require
9:9. land is full of *b.* and city full
16:6. polluted in thine own *b.*
Mic 3:10. they build up Zion with *blood*
Matt 26:28. *b.* of new testament, Mark 14:24. Luke 22:20. 1 Cor 11:25.
27:8. field of *b.* Acts 1:19.
25. his *b.* be on us and on our children
Luke 13:1. whose *b.* Pilate mingled
22:44. as it were great drops of *b.*
John 1:13. born not of *b.* nor of flesh
6:54. drinketh my *b.* hath eternal life
55. my *b.* is drink indeed
56. drinketh my *b.* dwelleth in me
Acts 17:26. made of one *b.* all nations
18:6. your *b.* be on your own heads
20:26. pure from the *b.* of *all* men
28. hath purchased with his own *b.*
Rom 3:25. through faith in his *b.*
1 Cor 11:27. guilty of body and *b.*
Col 1:20. peace through *b.* of cross
Eph 1:7. redemption through his *b.* even forgiveness of sins, Col 1:14.
Heb 9:20. the *b.* of the testament
10:19. into holiest by *b.* of Jesus
12:4. ye have not yet resisted unto *b.*
24. *b.* of sprinkling that speaketh
1 Pet 1:2. sprinkling of *b.* of Jesus
19. with precious *b.* of Christ
1 John 1:7. *b.* . . . cleanseth from all sin
5:6. came by water and *b.*
Rev 1:5. washed us in his own *b.*
6:10. dost thou not avenge our *b.*
8:7. hail and fire mingled with *b.*
16:6. shed *b.* . . . given them *b.* to drink
17:6. drunken with the *b.* of saints
Blood-guiltiness, Ps 51:14.
Bloody, Exod 4:25, 26. Ps 5:6; 55:23.
BLOSSOM, man's rod, Num 17:5.
Isa 5:24. their *b.* shall go up as dust
27:6. Israel shall *b.* and bud
35:1. the desert shall *b.* as the rose
2. it shall *b.* abundantly and rejoice
Hab 3:17. the fig tree shall not *b.*
Ezek 7:10. rod hath *blossomed*
BLOT, Job 31:7. Prov 9:7.
Exod 32:32, 33. *b.* me out of thy book, Num 5:23. Ps 69:28. Rev 3:5.
Blot out their name or remembrance, Deut 9:14; 25:19; 29:20. 2 Kings 14:27. Ps 109:13.
Blot out sin, transgression, iniquity, Neh 4:5. Ps 51:1, 9; 109:14. Isa 43:25; 44:22. Jer 18:23. Acts 3:19.
Col 2:14. *blotting* out handwriting
BLOW on my garden, Song of Sol 4:16.
Hag 1:9. I did *b.* upon it
John 3:8. wind *bloweth* where it listeth
BLUSH to lift up my face, Ezra 9:6.
Jer 6:15. neither could they *b.* 8:12.
BOAST, Ps 10:3; 34:2; 49:6; 52:1. Prov 20:14; 25:14. James 3:5.
1 Kings 20:11. *b.* as he that putteth it off
Prov 27:1. *b.* not of tomorrow
Rom 11:18. *b.* not against the branches, but if thou *b.* thou bearest not the root
Eph 2:9. not of works lest any *b.*
Rom 1:30. proud *boasters,* 2 Tim 3:2.
Boasting, Acts 5:36. Rom 3:27.
James 4:16. now ye rejoice in your *boastings*
BODY of heaven, Exod 24:10.
Job 19:26. worms destroy this *b.*
Matt 6:22. *b.* full of light, Luke 11:34.
10:28. that kill the *b.* Luke 12:4.
26:26. this is my *b.* 1 Cor 11:24.
John 2:21. of the temple of his *b.*
Rom 6:6. *b.* of sin be destroyed
Rom 7:4. dead to law by the *body* of Christ
24. me from the *b.* of this death
8:10. *b.* is dead because of sin
13. do mortify deeds of the *b.*
23. the redemption of our *b.*
1 Cor 5:3. absent in *b.* present in spirit
6:18. every sin is without the *b.* but
19. *b.* temple of Holy Ghost
7:4. wife not power of own *b.*
9:27. I keep under my *b.* and bring
10:16. communion of *b.* of Christ
11:29. not discerning the Lord's *b.*
12:14. the *b.* is not one member
27. ye are the *b.* of Christ
15:44. sown natural *b.* raised spiritual *b.*
2 Cor 5:6. home in *b.* absent from Lord
8. to be absent from the *b.*
10. receive things done in *b.*
12:2. whether in *b.* or out I cannot
Eph 3:6. fellow heirs of the same *b.*
4:12. for edifying the *b.* of Christ
5:23. he is the saviour of the *b.*
Phil 1:20. Christ magnified in my *b.*
3:21. shall change our vile *b.*
Col 1:18. head of the *b.* the church
2:11. putting off the *b.* of sins of flesh
2:23. neglecting of the *b.*
Heb 10:5. a *b.* hast thou prepared
James 3:6. tongue defileth whole *b.*
Jude 9. disputed about *b.* of Moses
Heb 13:3. being also in the *b.*
1 Pet 2:24. in his own *b.*
Deut 28:11, 18, 53. fruit of the *b.* 30:9. Ps 132:11. Mic 6:7.
Rom 8:11. quicken your mortal *bodies*
12:1. present your *b.* a living sacrifice
1 Cor 6:15. *b.* members of Christ
Eph 5:28. love wives as their own *b.*
Heb 10:22. *b.* washed with pure water
Luke 3:22. Holy Ghost in a *bodily* shape
2 Cor 10:10. his *b.* presence is weak
Col 2:9. the fulness of Godhead *b.*
1 Tim 4:8. *b.* exercise profiteth little
BOLD as a lion, Prov 28:1.
2 Cor 10:1. being absent am *b.*
11:21. if any is *b.* I am *b.* also
Phil 1:14. are much more *b.* to speak
Mark 15:43. went *boldly* unto Pilate
Heb 4:16. come *b.* to throne of grace
2 Cor 7:4. my *boldness* of speech
Eph 3:12. in whom we have *b.* and
Heb 10:19. *b.* to enter into the holiest
1 John 4:17. *b.* in day of judgment
BOND of the covenant, Ezek 20:37.
Job 12:18. looseth *b.* of kings

Eph 4:3. unity of Spirit in *b.* of peace, charity *b.* of perfectness, Col 3:14.
1 Cor 12:13. *bond and free,* Gal 3:28. Eph 6:8. Col 3:11. Rev 6:15; 13:16; 19:18.
Ps 116:16. hast loosed my *bonds*
Acts 20:23. *b.* and afflictions abide me
23:29. worthy of death or of *b.*
Eph 6:20. I am an ambassador in *b.*
Phil 1:16. to add affliction to my *b.*
Col 4:18. remember my *b.*
2 Tim 2:9. suffer trouble even unto *b.*
Philem 10. have begotten in my *b.*
Heb 10:34. compassion in my *b.*
11:36. trial of *b.* and imprisonments
Exod 13:3. house of *bondage,* 20:2.
1:14. their lives bitter with hard *b.*
2:23. sighed by reason of the *b.*
Rom 8:15. spirit of *b.* again to fear
1 Cor 7:15. sister is not under *bondage*
Gal 4:24. Sinai gendereth to *b.*
5:1. entangled with the yoke of *b.*
Bondwoman, Gen 21:10. Gal 4:23, 30.
BONE of my bone, and flesh of my flesh, Gen 2:23; 29:14. Judg 9:2. 2 Sam 5:1; 19:13. 1 Chron 11:1.
Exod 12:46. not break of *b.* of it
John 19:36. *b.* of him not be broken
Ps 51:8. *bones* thou hast broken may
Eccles 11:5. how the *b.* grow in the
Ezek 37:1. valley full of dry *b.* 3, 4, 5, 7. resurrection of *b.*
Matt 23:27. full of dead men's *b.*
His bones, Ps 34:20. Eph 5:30. Job 20:11. Prov 12:4.
Ps 6:2. heal me, *my bones* are vexed
22:14. all—out of joint, 17. I may tell all—
32:3.—waxed old through my roaring
35:10.—shall say, Lord, who is like
38:3. neither rest to—because of my sin
102:3.—are burnt as an hearth
5.—cleave to my skin
BOOK, Gen 5:1. Esther 6:1.
Exod 32:32. blot me out of *b.*
Job 19:23. O that they were printed in a *b.*
Ps 40:7. volume of *b.* Heb 10:7.
56:8. tears, are they not in thy *b.*
139:16. in *b.* members are written
Book of life, Phil 4:3. Rev 3:5; *13:8; 17:8; 20:12, 15; 21:27; 22:19.*
Books, Eccles 12:12. Dan 7:10; 9:2. John 21:25. 2 Tim 4:13. Rev 20:12.
BOOTHS, Lev 23:42, 43. Neh 8:14.
BORDER of his garment, Mark 6:56.
BORN to trouble, man is, Job 5:7.
Job 14:1. *b.* of a woman, 15:14; 25:4. Matt 11:11. Luke 7:28.
Ps 58:3. go astray as soon as *b.*
87:4. this man was *b.* there, 6.
Prov 17:17. brother *b.* for adversity
Eccles 3:2. a time to be *b.* and die
Isa 9:6. unto us a child is *b.* a son
66:8. shall a nation be *b.* at once
Matt 11:11. them *b.* of women
26:24. better if he had not been *b.*
1:13. *born of God,* 1 John 3:9; 4:7; 5:1, 4, 18.
John 3:3, 5, 7. *b.* again
4. can man be *b.* when old
5. *b.* of water and of the Spirit
6. *b.* of flesh is flesh; *b.* of Spirit is
Rom 9:11. children being not yet *b.*
1 Cor 15:8. one *b.* out of due time
Gal 4:23. he *b.* after the flesh, 29.
1 Pet 2:2. as new *b.* babes desire milk of
Jer 15:10. *borne* me a man of strife
BORROW, Deut 15:6; 28:12.
Exod 22:14. *b.* of his neighbour, 3:22; 11:2; 12:35.
Matt 5:42. would *b.* of thee turn not away
Prov 22:7. *borrower* is servant to lender
Isa 24:2. as with lender so with *b.*
BOSOM, Gen 16:5. Exod 4:6.
Num 11:12. carry them in *b.* as a
Deut 13:6. wife of thy *b.* 28:54, 56.
Ps 35:13. prayer returned to own *b.*
74:11. pluck thy hand out of thy *b.*
89:50. how I do bear in my *b.*
Prov 5:20. why embrace the *b.* of a
17:23. gift out of *b.* to pervert, 21:14.
19:24. hideth hands in *b.* 26:15.
Eccles 7:9. anger resteth in *b.* of fools
Isa 40:11. carry them in his *b.*
Isa 65:6, 7. recompense into their *bosom.* Ps 79:12. Jer 32:18.
Mic 7:5. her that lieth in thy *b.*
Luke 6:38. men give into your *b.*
16:22. carried into Abraham's *b.* 23.
John 13:23. leaning on Jesus' *b.*
BOTH, Gen 2:25; 3:7; 19:36.
Zech 6:13. peace between *b.*
Eph 2:14. our peace made *b.* one
16. that he might reconcile *b.* to God
BOTTLE, Gen 21:14, 15, 19.
Ps 56:8. put my tears into thy *b.*
119:83. I am like a *b.* in the smoke
Jer 13:12. every *b.* filled with wine
Job 38:37. stay *bottles* of heaven
Matt 9:17. new wine into old *b.*
Mark 2:22. new wine into new *b.*
BOUGHT, Gen 17:12, 13; 33:19.
Deut 32:6. is not he thy father that *b.* thee?
Matt 13:46. sold all and *b.* it
1 Cor 6:20. *b.* with a price, 7:23.
2 Pet 2:1. denying the Lord that *b.* them
BOUND Isaac, Gen 22:9.
Job 36:8. if they be *b.* in fetters
Ps 107:10. being *b.* in affliction
Prov 22:15. foolishness *b.* in heart
Isa 61:1. opening of prison to them that are *b.*
Matt 16:19. whatsoever ye bind on earth shall be *b.* in heaven, 18:18.
Acts 20:22. I go *b.* in the spirit
21:13. ready not to be *b.* only, but
Rom 7:2. wife is *b.* to her husband, 1 Cor 7:39.
1 Cor 7:27. *b.* to a wife, seek not
2 Tim 2:9. the word of God is not *b.*
Heb 13:3. in bonds as *b.* with them
Isa 1:6. not closed or *bound up*
Ezek 30:21. not—to be healed
34:4. neither have ye—the broken
Hos 13:12. iniquity of Ephraim is—
BOUNTY, 1 Kings 10:13. 2 Cor 9:5.
Prov 22:9. *bountiful* eye be blessed
Ps 13:6. dealt *bountifully* with me, 116:7; 119:17; 142:7.
BOW in the clouds, Gen 9:13, 14, 16.
Gen 49:24. his *b.* abode in strength
Josh 24:12. not with sword nor *b.*
2 Sam 1:18. teach children use of *b.*
Ps 7:12. hath bent his *b.* and made
11:2. lo, wicked bend their *b.*
44:6. I will not trust in my *b.*
78:57. turned aside like deceitful *b.*
Jer 9:3. bend tongue like *b.* for lies
Lam 2:4. bent his *b.* like an enemy
3:12. bent his *b.* and set me as a mark
Hos 1:5. break the *b.* of Israel
7. I will not save them by *b.*
7:16. turned like a deceitful *b.*
1 Sam 2:4. Ps 37:15. *bows,* 64:3; 78:9. Jer 51:56.
Bow down thine ear, 2 Kings 19:16. Ps 31:2; 86:1. Prov 22:17.
Job 31:10. let others—upon her
Ps 95:6. let us worship and—
Gen 23:12. Abraham *bowed down* himself before the people, 27:29.
Judg 7:5, 6.—on knees to drink
Ps 38:6. I am—greatly, I go mourning
145:14. raiseth up all that be—146.8.
Isa 2:11. haughtiness of men—17.

BOWELS did yearn, Gen 43:30. 1 Kings 3:26. 2 Chron 21:15, 18.
Ps 71:6. took out of mother's *b.*
Isa 63:15. the sounding of thy *b.*
Jer 4:19. my *bowels* my *b.* I am pained
31:20. my *b.* are troubled for him, Lam 1:20; 2:11. Song of Sol 5:4.
Acts 1:18. all his *b.* gushed out
2 Cor 6:12. straitened in your own *b.*
Phil 1:8. I long after you in the *b.* of Christ
Col 3:12. put on *b.* of mercies
Philem 7. *b.* of saints refreshed
20. refresh my *b.* in the Lord
1 John 3:17. shutteth up *b.* of compassion
BOWL, Num 7:85. Eccles 12:6. Zech 4:2, 3; 9:15; 14:20.
BRAKE the tables, Exod 32:19; 34:1.
1 Sam 4:18. Eli *b.* his neck and died
1 Kings 19:11. wind *b.* in pieces rocks
2 Kings 11:18. *b.* Baal's image, 10:27.
23:14. *b.* the images, 2 Chron 31:1.
Job 29:17. *b.* the jaws of the wicked
Ps 76:3. *b.* the arrows of the bow
105:16. *b.* the whole staff of bread
107:14. *b.* their bands in sunder
Jer 31:32. my covenant they *b.* Ezek 17:16.
Dan 2:1. his sleep *b.* from him
6:24. *b.* all their bones to pieces
Matt 14:19. blessed bread and *b.* and gave, 15:36; 26:26. Mark 6:41; 8:6; 14:22. Luke 9:16; 22:19; 24:30. 1 Cor 11:24.
Mark 14:3. she *b.* box and poured
Break down images—altars of Baal, 2 Kings 10:27; 11:18. 2 Chron 14:3; 23:17; 34:4.—wall of Jerusalem, 2 Kings 14:13; 25:10. 2 Chron 25:23; 36:19. Jer 39:8; 52:14.—houses of Sodomites—high places—altars—altar of Bethel, 2 Kings 23:7, 8, 12, 15.
BRAMBLE, Judg 9:14. Luke 6:44.
BRANCH, with clusters of grapes, Num 13:23. Isa 17:9; 18:5.
Job 14:7. tender *b.* thereof not cease
18:16. shall his *b.* be cut off
Prov 11:28. righteous flourish as *b.*
Isa 4:2. *b.* of the Lord be beautiful
9:14. cut off b. and rush, 19:15.
14:19. cast out like an abominable *b.*
25:5. *b.* of terrible be brought low
60:21. *b.* of my planting, 61:3.
Jer 23:5. to David righteous *b.*
Ezek 8:17. they put *b.* to their nose
Zech 3:8. bring forth my servant *b.*
6:12. behold man whose name is *b.*
Mal 4:1. leave neither root nor *b.*
Matt 24:32. when *b.* is yet tender
John 15:4. *b.* cannot bear fruit of itself
6. cast forth as a *b.* and is withered
Lev 23:40. take *branches* of palm-trees, Neh 8:15. John 12:13.
Job 15:30. flame shall dry up his *b.*
Ps 80:11. sent her *b.* unto the river
104:12. fowls sing among the *b.*
Isa 16:8. her *b.* are stretched out
17:6. four or five in outmost fruitful *b.*
18:5. take and cut down *b.* 27:10.
Jer 11:16. the *b.* of it are broken, Ezek 17:6, 7; 19:10, 11, 14.
Dan 4:14. hew down tree, cut off *b.*
Hos 14:6. his *b.* spread as olive
Zech 4:12. what be these two olive *b.*
John 15:5. I am vine, ye are the *b.*
Rom 11:16. if root be holy, so are *b.*
17. if some of the *b.* be broken off
18. boast not against the *b.*
21. God spared not natural *b.* 24.
BRAND, Judg 15:5. Zech 3:2.
BRASEN, Num 16:39. 2 Kings 18:4; 25:13. 2 Chron 6:13. Jer 1:18; 15:20; 52:20. Mark 7:4.
BRASS, Gen 4:22. Dan 5:4.
Num 21:9. made serpent of *b.*
Deut 8:9. out of hills mayest dig *b.*
28:23. the heaven shall be *b.*
Job 6:12. or is my flesh *b.*
41:27. he esteemeth *b.* as rotten wood
Ps 107:16. broken the gates of *b.*
Isa 48:4. thy neck iron, and brow *b.*
Dan 2:32. belly and thighs of *b.*
Zech 6:1. were mountains of *b.*
1 Cor 13:1. as sounding *b.* and
Rev 1:15. feet like fine *b.* 2:18.
BRAWLER, 1 Tim 3:3. Titus 3:2.
Prov 21:9; 25:24. *brawling* woman
BREACH be upon thee, Gen 38:29.
Num 14:34. know my *b.* of promise
Judg 21:15. Lord made *b.* in tribes
2 Sam 6:8. Lord made *b.* on Uzzah
Job 16:14. breaketh *b.* upon *b.*
Ps 106:23. Moses stood in the *b.*
Isa 30:13. this iniquity shall be as *b.*
58:12. called the repairer of the *b.*
Lam 2:13. thy *b.* is great like the sea
Ps 60:2. heal *breaches* thereof
BREAD shall be fat, Gen 49:20.
Exod 16:4. I will rain *b.* from heaven
23:25. he will bless thy *b.* and water
Lev 21:6. *b.* of their God they offer
Num 14:9. they are *b.* for us
21:5. soul loatheth this light *b.*
Deut 8:3. not live by *b.* only, Matt 4:4.
Ruth 1:6. visited his people giving *b.*
1 Sam 2:5. hired themselves for *b.*
25:11. take my *b.* and my water
1 Kings 18:4. fed them with *b.* and water
Neh 5:14. not eaten *b.* of governor, 18.
9:15. gavest them *b.* from heaven
Ps 37:25. nor his seed begging *b.*
78:20. can he give *b.* also
80:5. feedest them with *b.* of tears
102:9. I have eaten ashes like *b.*
132:15. satisfy her poor with *b.*
Prov 9:17. *b.* eaten in secret is pleasant
20:17. *b.* of deceit is sweet
22:9. giveth of his *b.* to the poor
31:27. she eateth not *b.* of idleness
Eccles 9:11. neither yet *b.* to the wise
11:1. cast thy *b.* upon the waters
Isa 3:1. away whole stay of *b.* 7.
30:20. Lord give you *b.* of adversity
55:2. money for that which is not *b.*
10. give seed to sower, *b.* to eater
58:7. deal thy *b.* to the hungry
Lam 4:4. the young children ask *b.*
Ezek 18:7. hath given *b.* to hungry
Hos 2:5. give me my *b.* and water
Amos 4:6. want of *b.* in all your places
Mal 1:7. ye offer polluted *b.* on mine
Matt 4:3. these stones be made *b.*
4. not live by *b.* alone, Luke 4:4.
6:11. this day our daily *b.*
7:9. son ask *b.* will he give a stone, Luke 11:11.
15:26. meet to take the children's *b.*
26:26. took *b.* and blessed it
Mark 8:4. satisfy these men with *b.*
Luke 7:33. neither eating *b.* nor
15:17. servants have *b.* enough
24:35. known in breaking of *b.*
John 6:32. Moses gave you not that *b.*
33. the *b.* of God is he that cometh
34. evermore give us this *b.*
John 6:35. I am the *bread* of life, 48. true *b.* 32.
50. this is the b. that cometh down
13:18. he that eateth *b.* with me
Acts 2:42. breaking *b.* and in prayer
46. breaking *b.* from house to house
20:7. came together to break *b.*
27:35. he took *b.* and gave thanks
1 Cor 10:16. *b.* we break is it not
17. we many are one *b.* and one body

11:26. as often as ye eat this *b.*
27.
2 Cor 9:10. minister *b.* for your food
Deut 16:3. *bread of affliction,* 1 Kings 22:27. 2 Chron 18:26. Isa 30:20.
Gen 3:19. *shall eat bread,* 28:20. Ps 14:4; 127:2. Prov 25:21. Eccles 9:7. Mark 7:5. Luke 14:15. 1 Cor 11:26. 2 Thess 3:12.
1 Sam 2:36. *piece of bread,* Prov 6:26; 28:21. Jer 37:21. Ezek 13:19.
Lev 26:26. *break staff of bread,* Ps 105:16. Ezek 4:16; 5:16; 14:13.
Gen 19:3. *unleavened bread,* Exod 12:8, 15, 17, 18, 20;13:6, 7. Mark 14:12. Luke 22:7. Acts 12:3; 20:6. 1 Cor 5:8.
BREAK, Gen 19:9. Exod 34:13.
Ezra 9:14. again *b.* commandments
Ps 2:3. let us *b.* their bands asunder
9. shalt *b.* them with a rod of iron
10:15. *b.* thou arm of the wicked
58:6. *b.* their teeth in their mouth
89:31. if they *b.* my statutes
34. my covenant will I not *b.* nor
Song of Sol 2:17. till the day *b.* 4:6.
Isa 38:13. as a lion so will he *b.* all
42:3. bruised reed not *b.* Matt 12:20.
Jer 14:21. *b.* not covenant with us
15:12. shall iron *b.* northern iron
33:20. *b.* my covenant
Ezek 4:16. *b.* of bread, 5:16; 14:13. Ps 105:16.
17:15. *b.* covenant and be delivered
Hos 1:5. *b.* the bow of Israel, 2:18.
Zech 11:10. might *b.* my covenant
Matt 5:19. *b.* one of least commandments
Acts 21:13. mean ye to *b.* my heart?
1 Cor 10:16. bread which we *b.*
Exod 23:24. *break down,* Deut 7:5. Ps 74:6. Eccles 3:3. Jer 31:28; 45:4. Hos 10:2.
Exod 19:22, 24. *break forth,* Isa 55:12. Jer 1:14. Gal 4:27.
Isa 14:7. *break forth into singing,* 44:23; 49:13; 54:1; 55:12; 52:9.
Exod 22:6. *break out,* Isa 35:6. Hos 4:2. Amos 5:6.
Job 19:2. *break in pieces,* 34:24. Ps 72:4; 94:5. Isa 45:2. Jer 51:20, 21, 22. Dan 2:40, 44; 7:23.
Exod 19:21, 24. *break through,* and gaze
Matt 6:19, 20. *thieves—and steal*
Jer 4:3. *break up* fallow ground, Hos 10:12.
Gen 32:26. let me go, day *breaketh*
Job 9:17. he *b.* me with a tempest
Ps 29:5. voice of Lord *b.* cedars
46:9. *b.* the bow and cutteth spear
119:20. my soul *b.* for the longing
Prov 25:15. a soft tongue *b.* the bone
Eccles 10:8. *b.* a hedge, a serpent
Jer 19:11. as one *b.* a potter's vessel
23:29. like a hammer that *b.* rocks
Luke 24:35. known of them in *breaking* of bread
Acts 2:42. *b.* of bread, 46.
Rom 2:23. through *b.* law dishonourest thou God?
BREAST, John 13:25. lying on Jesus' *b.* 21:20.
Isa 60:16. suck the *b.* of kings, 49:23.
Lam 4:3. sea monsters draw out the *breast*
Breasts, Gen 49:25.
Job 3:12. why *b.* that I should suck
21:24. his *b.* are full of milk
Ps 22:9. I was upon my mother's *b.*
Prov 5:19. let her *b.* satisfy thee at
Song of Sol 1:13. all night between my *b.*
4:5. thy *b.* are like two roes, 7:3.
7:7. thy *b.* to clusters of grapes, 8.
8:1. sucked the *b.* of my mother
8. a little sister, and she hath no *b.*
10. I am a wall, and my *b.* like towers
Isa 28:9. weaned and drawn from *b.*
66:11. satisfied with *b.* of her consolation
Ezek 16:7. thy *b.* are fashioned
23:3. there were their *b.* pressed
8. and they bruised the *b.* of her virginity, and poured
Hos 2:2. adulteries from between her *b.*
9:14. miscarrying womb and dry *b.*
Joel 2:16. gather those that suck *b.*
Luke 23:48. smote *b.* and returned
Rev 15:6. *b.* girded with golden
Exod 28:4. *breastplate,* Rev 9:9, 17.
Eph 6:14. *b.* of righteousness
1 Thess 5:8. *b.* of faith and love
BREATH of life, Gen 2:7; 6:17; 7:15, 22. Isa 2:22. Hab 2:19.
Job 12:10. in whose hands is *b.* of all
15:30. by *b.* of his mouth
17:1. my *b.* is corrupt, my days are extinct
33:4. *b.* of Almighty given me life
34:14. if he gather his spirit and *b.*
37:10. by the *b.* of God frost is given
41:21. his *b.* kindleth coals
Ps 33:6. made by *b.* of his mouth
104:29. thou takest away their *b.*
135:17. neither any *b.* in mouths
146:4. *b.* goeth forth, he returneth
Eccles 3:19. they have all one *b.*
Isa 2:22. whose *b.* is in his nostrils
11:4. with *b.* of his lips slay wicked
30:28. his *b.* an overflowing stream
33. the *b.* of the Lord doth kindle it
33:11. your *b.* as fire shall devour you
42:5. giveth *b.* unto the people
Jer 10:14. no *b.* in them, 51:17.
Lam 4:20. the *b.* of our nostrils
Dan 5:23. in whose hand thy *b.* is
Acts 17:25. giveth to all life and *b.*
Ps 27:12. *breathe* out cruelty
Ezek 37:9. come *b.* upon these slain
John 20:22. he *breathed* on them
Acts 9:1. *breathing* out slaughter
BREECHES, linen, Exod 28:42; 39:28. Lev 6:10; 16:4. Ezek 44:18.
BREED, abundantly, Gen 8:17.
Deut 32:14. rams of *b.* of Bashan
Exod 16:20. *bred* worms and stank
Zeph 2:9. *breeding* of nettles
BRETHREN, we be, Gen 13:8.
Gen 19:7. *b.* do not so wickedly
24:27. led me to house of my master's *b.*
42:3. Joseph's ten *b.* went to buy corn
6. *b.* bowed down themselves
45:16. Joseph's *b.* are come
49:5. Simeon and Levi are *b.*
26. separate from *b.* Deut 33:16.
50:15. Joseph's *b.* saw their father was dead
Num 27:4. give possession among *b.* 7.
10. if no *b.* . . . to his father's *b.* 11.
Deut 17:20. be not lifted up above *b.*
25:5. if *b.* dwell together
33:9. neither did he acknowledge his *brethren*
Deut 24. let him be acceptable to his *brethren*
Josh 6:23. Rahab and *b.*
Judg 9:1. Abimelech . . . mother's *b.* 3.
2 Kings 10:13. we are *b.* of Ahaziah
1 Chron 4:9. more honourable than his *b.*
5:2. prevailed above his *b.*
12:2. Saul's *b.* of Benjamin
26:7. *b.* were strong men
1 Chron 27:18. Elihu of *b.* of David
2 Chron 21:2. Jehoram and his *b.*
22:8. Jehu found *b.* of Ahaziah
Job 6:15. my *b.* dealt deceitfully
19:13. put my *b.* far from me
Ps 22:22. declare thy name unto my *b.*
69:8. become a stranger to my *b.*
Ps 122:8. for *b.* and companions' sakes
133:1. for *b.* to dwell in unity

Prov 6:19. soweth discord among *b.*
17:2. part of inheritance of *b.*
Hos 13:15. fruitful among his *b.*
Matt 4:18. Jesus saw two *b.* 21.
12:48. who are my *b.*
19:29. forsaken houses, or *b.* or sisters
20:24. moved against the two *b.*
22:25. seven *b.* . . . married a wife. Mark 12:20.
23:8. all ye are *b.* Acts 7:26.
25:40. the least of these my *b.*
28:10. go tell my *b.* that they go
Mark 10:29. left house or *b.* Luke 18:29.
Luke 14:26. hate not *b.* own life also
16:28. for I have five *b.*
21:16. betrayed by *b.*
John 7:5. neither did his *b.* believe
20:17. go to my *b.* and say, I ascend
Acts 6:3. *b.* look ye out seven men
7:26. sirs, ye are *b.* why do ye
9:30. when the *b.* knew
10:23. certain *b.* from Joppa
11:12. these six *b.* accompanied me
29. send relief to the *b.*
12:17. shew these things to James and *b.*
14:2. evil affected against *b.*
15:3. caused great joy to all the *b.*
22. chief among *b.* 23. greeting to *b.*
32. exhort *b.* with many words
40. by *b.* unto the grace of God
17:6. drew Jason and certain *b.*
10. *b.* sent away Paul and Silas, 14.
18:18. Paul took leave of *b.*
27. *b.* wrote exhorting the disciples
20:32. now *b.* I commend you to God
23:6. men and *b.* I am a Pharisee
Rom 8:29. the firstborn among many *b.*
9:3. accursed from Christ for my *b.*
1 Cor 6:5. to judge between his *b.*
8:12. sin against the *b.*
15:6. seen of above five hundred *b.* at once
Gal 2:4. false *b.* unawares brought in
1 Tim 4:6. put *b.* in remembrance
5:1. entreat the younger as *b.*
Heb 2:11. is not ashamed to call *them b.*
1 Pet 1:22. unfeigned love of the *b.*
3:8. love as *b.* be pitiful, courteous
1 John 3:14. because we love the *b.*
16. to lay down our lives for the *b.*
3 John 10. neither doth receive the *b.*
Gen 27:29. *thy brethren,* 48:22; 49:8. Deut 15:7; 18:15. 1 Sam 17:18. Matt 12:47. Mark 3:32. Luke 8:20; 14:12; 22:32.
Jer 12:6.—have dealt treacherously
Rev 19:10. I am of—22:9.
1 Kings 12:24. *your brethren,* 2 Chron 30:7, 9; 35:6.
Neh 4:14. fight for—your sons
Isa 66:5. *your brethren* that hated you
Acts 3:22. raise up of—prophet like unto me, 7:37. Deut 18:15.

BRIBES, 1 Sam 8:3. Amos 5:12.
1 Sam 12:3. have I received any *b.*
Ps 26:10. right hand full of *b.*
Isa 33:15. hands from holding *b.*
Job 15:34. tabernacles of *bribery*

BRICK, Gen 11:3. Exod 1:14; 5:7, 8, 14, 16, 18, 19. Isa 9:10; 65:3.
1 Sam 12:31. *brick-kiln,* Jer 43:9. Nah 3:14.

BRIDE, doth clothe with an ornament, Isa 49:18.
Isa 61:10. as a *b.* adorneth herself
Jer 2:32. can a *b.* forget her attire
Joel 2:16. *b.* go out of her closet
John 3:29. hath *b.* is the bridegroom
Rev 21:2. as *b.* adorned for husband
9. I will shew thee *b.* Lamb's wife
Matt 9:15. *bride-chamber,* Mark 2:19.

BRIDEGROOM, Joel 2:16. John 2:9.
Ps 19:5. as *b.* coming out of chamber
Isa 61:10. as a *b.* decketh himself
62:5. as a *b.* rejoiceth over the bride
Jer 7:34. cease voice of *b.* and bride, 16:9; 25:10; 33:11. Rev 18:23.
Matt 9:15. as long as the *b.* is with them, Mark 2:19, 20. Luke 5:34.
Matt 25:1. went forth to meet *b.* 6.
John 3:29. friend of *b.* rejoiceth

BRIDLE for the ass, Prov 26:3.
Job 30:11. let loose the *b.*
Ps 32:9. mouth held with *b.*
39:1. I will keep my mouth as with a *b.*
Isa 37:29. put my *b.* in thy lips, 30:28. 2 Kings 19:28. Rev 14:20.
James 3:2. able to *b.* the whole body
1:26. *bridleth* not his tongue

BRIEFLY, Rom 13:9. 1 Pet 5:12.

BRIERS, Judg 8:7, 16. Isa 7:23, 24, 25; 32:13. Heb 6:8. Mic 7:4.
Isa 5:6. come up *b.* and thorns
9:18. wickedness . . . shall devour *b.* 10:17.
27:4. set *b.* against me in battle
55:13. instead of *b.* shall come up myrtle
Ezek 2:6. though *b.* and thorns be
28:24. no more a pricking *b.* unto

BRIGANDINE, coat of mail, Jer 46:4. put on *b.* 51:3. lifteth self in *b.*

BRIGHT, Lev 13:2. *b.* spot, 2, 4, 19, 23, 24–26, 38, 39.
Job 37:11. *b.* cloud, 21.
Song of Sol 5:14. *b.* ivory
Jer 51:11. make *b.* the arrows
Ezek 1:13. fire was *b.* and out of
21:15. sword made *b.* it is
Nah 3:3. *b.* sword and glittering
Zech 10:1. the Lord shall make *b.* clouds
Matt 17:5. a *b.* cloud overshadowed
Luke 11:36. *b.* shining of a candle
Acts 10:30. a man stood in *b.* clothing
Rev 22:16. *b.* and morning star
Brightness, 2 Sam 22:13. Ezek 1:4, 27, 28; 8:2; 28:7, 17.
Job 31:26. beheld moon walking in *b.*
Isa 59:9. we wait for *b.* but walk
Ezek 10:4. full of the *b.* of Lord's glory
28:7. they shall defile thy *b.*
Dan 4:36. honour and *b.* returned
12:3. *b.* firmament
Amos 5:20. even very dark and no *b.* in it?
Hab 3:4. and his *b.* was as the light
Acts 26:13. a light above *b.* of sun
2 Thess 2:8. Lord with *b.* of his coming
Heb 1:3. being the *b.* of his glory

BRIM, Josh 3:15. 1 Kings 7:26. 2 Chron 4:2, 5. John 2:7.

BRIMSTONE, Gen 19:24. Lord rained on Sodom and Gomorrah *b.* Luke 17:29.
Deut 29:23. the whole land thereof is *b.*
Ps 11:6. rain snares, fire, and *b.*
Isa 30:33. breath of L. like a stream of *b.*
34:9. dust thereof into *b.*, land burning
Ezek 38:22. great hailstones, fire, and *b.*
Rev 9:17, 18. issued fire and *b.*
19:20. cast into a lake of fire and *b.* 20:10.

BRING a flood, Gen 6:17.
Josh 23:15. *b.* upon you all the evil
1 Kings 8:32. to *b.* his way on his head
Job 14:4. who can *b.* a clean thing
33:30. to *b.* back his soul from pit
Ps 60:9. who *b.* me into strong city
Eccles 11:9. God will *b.* thee into judgment, 12:14. Job 30:23.
Song of Sol 8:2. *b.* thee to my mother's house
Isa 1:13. *b.* no more vain oblations
43:5. I will *b.* thy seed from east
6. *b.* my sons from afar, 60:9.
46:13. I *b.* near my righteousness
66:9. *b.* to birth and not *b.* forth
Hos 2:14. allure and *b.* her into wilderness

Zeph 3:5. every morning *b.* his judgment
Luke 2:10. I *b.* you good tidings
8:14. *b.* no fruit to perfection
John 14:26. *b.* all to remembrance
Acts 5:28. *b.* this man's blood on us
1 Cor 1:28. *b.* to nought things that are
4:5. *b.* to light the hidden things
1 Thess 4:14. God will *b.* with him
1 Pet 3:18. that he might *b.* us to God
Gen 1:11, 20, 24. *bring forth,* 3:16. Matt 1:21. Job 39:1. Exod 3:10.
2 Kings 19:3. there is not strength to—
Job 15:35. they conceive mischief and—vanity.—iniquity, Isa 59:4.
Ps 37:6. he shall—thy righteousness
92:14. they shall still—fruit in old age
Prov 27:1. knowest not what a day may—
Isa 41:21.—your strong reasons
42:1.—judgment to the Gentiles, 3.
66:8. shall earth be made to—in one day?
Zeph 2:2. before the decree—
Mark 4:20.—fruit some thirtyfold
Luke 3:8.—fruits worthy of repentance
8:15. heard word—fruit with patience
John 15:2. that it may—more fruit
Ps 1:3. *bringeth forth* fruit in his season
Hos 10:1. Israel . . . —fruit to himself
Matt 3:10. bring not forth good fruit, 7:19; 12:35. Luke 6:43.
John 12:24. if it die it bring much fruit
James 1:15. bring sin bring death
BROAD, Num 16:38, 39. Nah 2:4. Matt 23:5.
Job 36:16. out of strait into *b.* place
Ps 119:96. commandment is exceeding *b.*
Isa 33:21. Lord . . . a place of *b.* rivers
Matt 7:13. *b.* is way to destruction
BROKEN my covenant, Gen 17:14. Ps 55:20. Isa 24:5; 33:8; 36:6. Jer 11:10; 33:21. Ezek 44:7.
Ps 34:18. nigh them of *b.* heart
44:19. sore *b.* us in place of dragons
51:8. bones thou hast *b.* rejoice
17. *b.* spirit, *b.* and contrite heart
147:3. healeth the *b.* in heart
Prov 17:22. *a b. spirit drieth bones*
Eccles 4:12. a threefold cord not *b.*
Isa 61:1. bind *b.* hearted, Luke 4:18.
Jer 2:13. hewed out *b.* cisterns
Jer 5:5. these have altogether *broken* the yoke
Dan 2:42. partly strong and partly *b.*
Hos 5:11. Ephraim *b.* in judgment
Matt 21:44. fall on stone shall be *b.*
BROOK, Num 13:23. Deut 2:13.
Ps 110:7. drink of the *b.* in the way
Job 20:17. *brooks* of honey and butter
Isa 19:6. *b.* of defence be emptied
BROTHER, for adversity, Prov 17:17.
Prov 18:19. a *b.* offended is harder
24. a friend that sticketh closer than a *b.*
27:10. neighbour near, than *b.* far
Jer 9:4. trust not in any *b.* for
Matt 10:21. *b.* shall deliver up *b.* to death, Mark 13:12. Mic 7:2.
Acts 9:17. *b.* Saul receive thy sight
1 Cor 5:11. *b.* be a fornicator or
7:15. *b.* or sister is not in bondage
8:11. shall the weak *b.* perish
1 Thess 4:6. no man defraud his *b.*
2 Thess 3:15. admonish him as a *b.*
James 1:9. let *b.* of low degree rejoice
Ps 35:14. *my brother,* Song of Sol 8:1. Matt 12:50; 18:21. 1 Cor 8:13.
Ps 50:20. *thy brother,* Matt 5:23, 24; 18:15. Rom 14:10, 15.
Gen 45:4. *your brother,* Rev 1:9.
Zech 11:14. *brotherhood,* 1 Pet 2:17.
Amos 1:9. *brotherly* covenant
Rom 12:10. affectioned with *b.* love
1 Thess 4:9. as touching *b.* love, ye
Heb 13:1. let *b.* love continue
2 Pet 1:7. to godliness *b.* kindness
BROUGHT me hitherto, 2 Sam 7:18.
Neh 4:15. God *b.* counsel to nought
9:33. thou art just in all that is *b.* on us
Ps 45:14. be *b.* unto the king in raiment
79:8. mercies prevent us: we are *b.* very low
106:43. *b.* low for their iniquities
107:39. *b.* low through oppression
Isa 1:2. nourished *b.* up children
Matt 10:18. *b.* before governors, Mark 13:9.
Luke 12:16. ground of a rich man *b.* forth
1 Cor 6:12. not be *b.* under power
Gal 2:4. false brethren unawares *b.* in
1 Tim 6:7. *b.* nothing into world
Ps 107:12. *brought down,* Matt 11:23.
Deut 33:14. *brought forth,* Ps 18:19. & 90:2. Isa 66:7. James 5:18.
BRUISE thy head . . . thou his heel, Gen 3:15.
Isa 53:10. it pleased the Lord to *b.* him.
Rom 16:20. God of peace *b.* Satan
2 Kings 18:21. trustest staff of *bruised* reed
Isa 42:3. *b.* reed, Matt 12:20.
53:5. He was *b.* for our iniquities
Ezek 23:3. *b.* teats, 21.
Luke 4:18. set at liberty the *b.*
Isa 1:6. wounds, *bruises* and putrifying
BRUIT, report, Jer 10:22. Nah 3:19.
BRUTISH man knoweth not, Ps 92:6.
Ps 94:8. understand ye *b.* among people
Prov 12:1. that hateth reproof is *b.*
Jer 10:14. *b.* in knowledge, 51:17.
BUCKET, nations as drop of a, Isa 40:15.
Num 24:7. water out of his *buckets*
BUCKLER, 1 Chron 5:18, &c., Job 15:26. runneth upon . . . his *bucklers*
Song of Sol 4:4. a thousand *b.*
BUD, horn to, Ps 132:17. Ezek 29:21.
BUFFET, 2 Cor 12:7.—ED, Matt 26:67. 1 Cor 4:11. 1 Pet 2:20.
BUILD walls of Jerusalem, Ps 51:18.
Ps 102:16. Lord shall *b.* up Zion
Ps 127:1. except the Lord *build* the house
Eccles 3:3. break down and a time to *b.* up
Mic 3:10. they *b.* up Zion with blood
Acts 20:32. grace, which is able to *b.* you up
Heb 11:10. *builder* and maker is God
Ps 118:22. stone which the *builders* refused is become head, Matt 21:42. Mark 12:10. Luke 20:17. Acts 4:11. 1 Pet 2:7.
1 Cor 3:10. as a wise *master builder,*
Josh 6:26. cursed *buildeth* this city
Prov 14:1. every wise woman *b.* her house
Jer 22:13. woe to him that *b.* house
Amos 9:6 *b.* his stories in heaven
Hab 2:12. *b.* a town with blood
1 Cor 3:10. another *b.* thereon
9. God's husbandry, ye are God's *building*
2 Cor 5:1. we have a *b.* of God, an house
Eph 2:21. all the b. fitly framed
Job 22:23. return shalt be *built* up
Ps 89:2. mercy be *b.* up for ever
Matt 7:24. *b.* his house on a rock
Eph 2:20. ye are *b.* on foundation of

Heb 3:4. he that *b.* all things is God
1 Pet 2:5. *b.* up a spiritual house
BULLS (foes) compassed me, Ps 22:12.
Ps 50:13. will I eat the flesh of *b.*
68:30. rebuke the multitude of *b.*
Heb 9:13. if *blood of b.* and goats
10:4. the—cannot take away sins
Ps 69:31. then *bullock* with horns
Jer 31:18. as a *b.* unaccustomed to yoke
Ps 51:19. offer *bullocks* on thy altar
Isa 1:11. delight not in blood of *b.*
BULRUSHES, Exod 2:3. Isa 18:2; 58:5.
BULWARKS, Ps 48:13. Isa 26:1.
BUNDLE, Gen 42:35. Acts 28:3.
1 Sam 25:29. bound in the *b.* of life
Matt 13:30. tares in *bundles* to burn
BURDEN, 2 Kings 5:17; 8:9.
Exod 18:22. shall bear the *b.* with thee, Num 11:17.
23:5. ass lying under his *b.*
Deut 1:12. how can I bear your *b.*
2 Sam 15:33. thou shalt be a *b.* unto
19:35. servant be yet *b.* to my lord
2 Kings 5:17. given two mules' *b.* of earth?
9:25. the Lord laid this *b.* upon him
2 Chron 35:3 not be *b.* on shoulders
Neh 13:19. no *b.* brought in on sabbath day, Jer 17:21, 22, 24, 27.
Job 7:20. so that I am a *b.* to myself
Ps 38:4. a *b.* they are too heavy for me
55:22. cast thy *b.* upon the Lord
81:6. I removed his shoulder from *b.*
Eccles 12:5. grasshopper shall be a *b.*
Isa 9:4. thou hast broken the yoke of his *b.*
30:27. the *b.* thereof is heavy: his lips full
Zeph 3:18. reproach of it was a *b.*
Zeph 12:3. that *b.* themselves with
Matt 11:30. my yoke easy, my *b.* is light
Acts 15:28. no greater *b.* than necessary
2 Cor 12:16. But be it so, I did not *b.* you
Gal 6:5. every man bear his own *b.*
Rev 2:24. put on you no other *b.*
Isa 13:1. *b.* threatening of heavy judgments, 14:28; 15. 1; 17:1; 19:1; 21:1, 11; 22:1; 23:1. Ezek 12:10. Nah 1:1. Hab 1:1. Zech 9:1. 12:1.
Mal 1:1 *b.* of the word of the Lord
2 Cor 5:4. we groan being *burdened*
8:13. not others eased and ye *b.*
Gen 49:14. *burdens,* Exod 1:11; 2:11; 5:4.
Isa 58:6. to undo the heavy *b.* and let the
Lam 2:14. seen for thee false *b.*
Matt 23:4. bind heavy *burdens.* Luke 11:46.
Gal 6:2. bear one another's *b.* and fulfil
Zeph 12:3. Jerusalem *burdensome,* 2 Cor 11:9; 12:13, 14. 1 Thess 2:6
BURN upon altar, Exod 29:13, 18, 25. Lev 1:9, 15; 2:2; 3:5, 11, 16; 5:12; 6:15; 9:17.
Gen 44:18. let not thine anger *b.*
Deut 32:22. shall *b.* to lowest hell
Isa 27:4. go through them and *b.*
Mal 4:1. day cometh shall *b.* as an oven
Luke 3:17. chaff he will *b.* with fire
24:32. did not our heart *b.* within us?
1 Cor 7:9. better marry than *b.* Rom 1:27.
2 Cor 11:29. who is offended and I *b.* not?
Exod 3:2. the bush *burned* with fire
Deut 9:15. the mount *b.* with fire
1 Cor 3:15. if man's work *b.* . . . himself saved
13:3. though I give my body to *b.* and
Heb 6:8. whose end is to be *b.*
12:18. not come to the mount that *b.*
Ps 46:9. *burneth* the chariot, 83:14—a wood
Isa 9:18. wickedness *b.* Prov 16:27.
Rev 21:8. lake which *b.* with fire
Gen 15:17. *burning* lamp, Rev 4:5.
Jer 20:9. his word *b.* fire shut up in bones
Ezek 1:13. *b.* coals forth at feet, Hab 3:5.
Luke 12:35. loins girded, your lights *b.*
John 5:35. a *b.* and a shining light
Exod 21:25. *b.* for *b.*, wound for wound
Deut 28:22. smite thee with extreme *b.*
2 Chron 16:14. a *b.* (burial); no *b.* 21:19. Jer 34:5.
Isa 3:24. *b.* instead of beauty
4:4. spirit of judgment and *b.* Matt 3:11.
Amos 4:11. firebrand out of *b.*
Isa 33:14. shall dwell with everlasting *burnings*
b. incense, Aaron & sons, 1 Chron *23:13. Korah, &c., Num 16:35.* Jeroboam, 1 Kings 13:1. Uzziah, 2 Chron 26:16. Zacharias, Luke 1:9. people, 1 Kings 22:43. Isa 65:7.—to idols, Hos 2:13; 4:13. Hab 1:16. Jer 7:9; 44:17. Amaziah, 2 Chron 25:14. Ahaz, 28:3.
Gen 8:20. *burnt-offerings,* Deut 12:6.
Hos 6:6. mercy, obey, contrition, justice, more than—, 1 Sam 15:22. Ps 51:17. Isa 1:11. Mic 6:8. Jer 7:21.
Mark 12:33. love neighbour more than—
Heb 10:6. in—for sin . . . no pleasure
Ps 74:8. *burned up* all the synagogues
Isa 64:11. our beautiful house is—
Matt 22:7. destroyed and—their city
2 Pet 3:10. earth and works . . . shall be—
BURST thy bands, Jer 2:20.
Jer 5:5. yoke and *b.* bonds, 30:8.
Prov 3:10. presses shall *b.* out = run over
Mark 2:22. new wine *b.* bottles, Job 32:19.
Acts 1:18. he *b.* asunder in midst
BURY dead out of my sight, Gen 23:4.
Gen 49:29 *b.* me with my fathers
Ps 79:3. there was none to *b.* them
Matt 8:21. first to go and *b.* my father
22. let the dead *b.* their dead, Luke 9:60.
Rom 6:4. *buried* with him by baptism, Col 2:12.
1 Cor 15:4. he was *b.* and rose again
Gen 23:4. a possession of a *burying* place
47:30. bury me in their *b.* place
2 Chron 26:23 *burial,* Acts 8:2.
Eccles 6:3. that he have no *b.*
Isa 14:20. not joined with them in *b.*
Jer 22:19. buried with the *b.* of an ass
BUSH, in the, Deut 33:16. Mark 12:26. Luke 20:37. angel—, Exod 3:2. Acts 7:35.
BUSHEL, Matt 5:15. Luke 11:33.
BUSHY & black locks, Song of Sol 5:11.
BUSINESS, Gen 39:11. Deut 24:5.
Ps 107:23. do *b.* in great waters
Dan 8:27. the king's *b.* Esther 3:9.
Luke 2:49. must be about my Father's *b.*
Rom 12:11. not slothful in *b.*; fervent
1 Thess 4:11. study to do your own *b.*
BUTTER, 2 Sam 17:29 *b.* and milk, Gen 18:8.
Deut 32:14. Judg 5:25. Prov 30:33.
Job 20:17. the brooks of honey and *b.*
Ps 55:21. words were smoother than *b.*
Isa 7:15. b. and honey shall he eat, 22.
BUY the truth, sell it not, Prov 23:23.
Isa 55:1 *b.* and eat, yea, *b.* wine
James 4:13 *b.* and sell, and get gain
Rev 3:18. I counsel thee to *b.* gold
13:17. no man *b.* or sell, save . . . mark
Prov 20:14. it is naught saith *buyer*
Isa 24:2. as with *b.* so with seller

Ezek 7:12. let not the *b.* rejoice, nor
Matt 13:44. selleth all and *buyeth* that field
Rev 18:11. no man *b.* their merchandise
BY and BY, immediately, Matt 13:21. Mark 6:25. Luke 17:7; 21:9.
BYWORD, song and, Job 17:6; 30:9.
1 Kings 9:7. Israel shall be a *b.*
Ps 44:14. makest us a *b.*, Deut 28:37.

C

CAGE, Jer 5:27; (Babylon) Rev 18:2.
CAKE . . . tumbled into host, Judg 7:13.
1 Kings 17:12. I have not a *c.* but meal
Hos 7:8. Ephraim a *c.* not turned
Cakes, Gen 18:6. Judg 6:19. 2 Sam 6:19.
Lev 24:5. bake twelve *c.* (shewbread)
Jer 7:18. make *c.* to queen of heaven
CALAMITY at hand, Deut 32:35.
Job 6:2. my *c.* laid in the balances
Ps 18:18. prevented me in day of my *c.*
Prov 1:26. I will laugh at your *c.*
19:13. a foolish son is the *c.* of his father
27:10. nor go to brother's house in *c.*
Jer 18:17. back not face in the day of *c.*
46:21. day of their *c.* is come, 48:16; 49:8, 32. Ezek 35:5. Obad 13.
Ps 57:1. until *calamities* be overpast
141:5. my prayer shall be in their *c.*
Prov 17:5. glad at *c.* not unpunished
CALDRONS, 1 Sam 2:14. Job 41:20. Ezek 11:3, 7, 11. Mic 3:3. Jer 52:18, 19.
CALF, Gen 18:7. Lev 9:2. Job 21:10. Ps 29:6. Isa 27:10. Rev 4:7.
Exod 32:4. made a molten *c.*, 20. Deut 9:16. Neh 9:18. Ps 106:19.
Isa 11:6. *c.* and young lion together
Jer 34:18. *c.* in twain and passed between
Hos 8:5. thy *c.* O Samaria, hath cast thee
Luke 15:23. bring the fatted *c.*
1 Kings 12:28. made two *calves* of gold
Hos 14:2. we will render the *c.* of our lips
Mic 6:6. come with *c.* of a year *old*
Mal 4:2. grow up as *c.* of the stall
Heb 9:12. blood of goats and *c.*, 19.
CALKERS, Gebal, wise men thy, Ezek 27:9.

CALL them what Adam would, Gen 2:19.
Gen 24:57. we will *c.* the damsel
30:13. *c.* me blessed, Prov 31:28.
Deut 4:7. nigh as God in all we *c.* . . . for
26. I *c.* heaven and earth to witness, 30:19.
1 Sam 3:6. for thou didst *c.* me
1 Kings 8:52. in all they *c.* for to thee
Job 5:1. *Call* now if there be any to answer
13:22. *c.* thou, I will answer, 14:15.
27:10. will he always *c.* upon God
Ps 4:1. hear me when I *c.* O God
14:4. they *c.* not upon the Lord, 53:4.
49:11. *c.* lands after their names
77:6. I *c.* to remembrance my song
80:18. quicken us and we will *c.* on thy
86:5. plenteous in mercy to all that *c.*
145:18. nigh to all that *c.* upon him
Prov 1:28. then shall *c.* I will not answer
Isa 5:20. woe that *c.* evil good and
22:12. day the Lord did *c.* to weeping
58:9. thou *c.* and Lord will answer
65:24. before they *c.* I will answer
Jer 25:29. *c.* for a sword upon all
29:12. shall ye *c.* and I will hearken
Joel 2:32. whosoever shall *c.* on Lord
Jon 1:6. arise, *c.* upon thy God
Zech 13:9. shall *c.* upon thy name
Mal 3:12. all nations shall *c.* you blessed
15. and now we *c.* the proud happy
Matt 9:13. I am not come to *c.* righteous
22:3. *c.* them that were bidden
23:9. *c.* no man your father on earth
Luke 1:48. all generations *c.* me blessed
6:46. why *c.* ye me Lord, Lord and
14:12, 13. *c.* not friends . . . *c.* poor
John 4:16. *c.* thy husband and come
13:13. ye *c.* me Master and Lord
15:15. I *c.* you not servants, but friends
Acts 2:39. as many as the Lord shall *c.*
24:14. after the way they *c.* heresy
Rom 9:25. I *will c.* them my people
10:12. rich in mercy to all that *c.* on him
2 Cor 1:23. I *c.* God for a record on my
Heb 2:11. not ashamed to *c.* brethren

James 5:14. *c.* for the elders of church
1 Pet 1:17. if ye *c.* on the Father
Call on the name of the Lord, Gen 4:26; 12:8; 13:4; 21:33; 26:25.
1 Kings 18:24. 2 Kings 5:11. Ps 116:4, 13, 17. Joel 2:32. Zeph 3:9. Acts 2:21. Rom 10:13. 1 Cor 1:2.
I will call unto, or, *on the Lord,* 1 Sam 12:17. 2 Sam 22:4. Ps 18:3; 55:16; 86:7.
Call upon me, Ps 50:15; 91:15. Prov 1:28. Jer 29:12.
Gen 21:17. angel of God *called* to Hagar
22:11. angel of Lord *c.* to Abraham, 15.
Exod 3:4. God *c.* him out of the bush
Judg 15:18. athirst, and *c.* on the Lord
2 Kings 8:1. Lord hath *c.* for a famine
1 Chron 4:10. Jabez *c.* on the God of Israel
21:26. David *c.* on Lord and he answered
Ps 17:6. I have *c.* upon thee, 31:17.
18:6. in my distress I *c.* upon the Lord
79:6. not *c.* on thy name, Jer 10:25.
88:9. I have *c.* daily upon thee
118:5. I *c.* on the Lord in my distress
Prov 1:24. I have *c.* and ye refused
Song of Sol 5:6. I *c.* him, he gave no answer
Isa 41:2. who *c.* him to his foot
42:6. I the Lord *c.* thee in righteousness
43:1. I have *c.* thee, 22. thou not *c.*
48:1. *c.* by the name of Israel, 45:4.
49:1. the Lord *c.* me from the womb
50:2. when I *c.* was none to answer
51:2. I *c.* him alone, and blessed him
61:3. might be *c.* trees of righteousness
62:4. thou shalt be *c.* Hephzibah
65:12. I *c.* ye not answer, Jer 7:13.
Lam 1:19. I *c.* for my lovers, they
3:55. I *c.* upon thy name, O Lord
Hos 11:1. I *c.* my son out of Egypt
Amos 7:4. the Lord *called* to contend by fire
Hag 1:11. I *c.* drought on the land
Mark 14:72. Peter *c.* to mind the word
Luke 15:19. not worthy to be *c.* thy son
John 1:48. before that Philip *c.* thee
10:35. if he *c.* them gods to whom
John 15:15. but I have *c.* you friends

Acts 9:21. destroy them which *c.* on this name
41. when he had *c.* the saints
10:23, 24. *c.* in . . . *c.* together his kinsmen
11:26. disciples were *c.* Christians first
13:2. for work whereto I *c.* them
15:17. on whom my name is *c.*
19:40. *c.* in question, 23:6. I am, 24:21.
Rom 1:1. *c.* to be an apostle, 1 Cor 1:1.
6. *c.* of Jesus Christ, 7. *c.* to be saints
2:17. art *c.* a Jew and restest in the law
8:28. the *c.* according to his purpose
30. predestinate, them he also *c.*
9:24. whom he *c.*, not of Jews only
1 Cor 1:9. faithful . . . were *c.*
26. not many wise, not many noble are *c.*
5:11. if any man *c.* a brother be
7:17. as the Lord hath *c.* every one, so let
18. *c.* circumcised? 21. *c.* servant?
24. every man wherein . . . *c.* abide with God
15:9. not meet to be *c.* an apostle
Gal 1:6. *c.* you into grace of Christ
15. God who *c.* me by his grace
5:13. ye have been *c.* to liberty; only use not
Eph 2:11. who are *c.* uncircumcision
4:4. are *c.* in one hope of your calling
Col 3:15. peace of God to which ye are *c.*
1 Thess 2:12. God . . . *c.* you unto kingdom
4:7. God hath not *c.* us to uncleanness
2 Thess 2:4. above all that is *c.* God
14. he *c.* you by our gospel to the obtaining
1 Tim 6:12. life, whereunto thou art *c.*
2 Tim 1:9. *c.* us with holy calling
Heb 3:13. exhort while it is *c.* to day
5:4. *c.* of God, as was Aaron
11:16. not ashamed to be *c.* their God
24. be *c.* the son of Pharaoh's daughter
James 2:7. name by the which ye are *c.*
1 Pet 1:15. as he that *c.* you is holy
2:9. who *c.* you out of darkness
21. suffer . . . for even hereunto were ye *c.*
5:10. God *c.* us to his eternal glory
2 Pet 1:3. *c.* us to glory and virtue
1 John 3:1. we should be *c.* sons of God
Jude 1. preserved in Christ Jesus and *c.*
Rev 17:14. with him *c.* and chosen
19:9. are *c.* unto the marriage supper
2 Chron 7:14. *called by my name,* Isa 43:7; 65:1. Jer 7:10, 11, 14, 30; 25:29; 32:34; 34:15. Amos 9:12.
1 Kings 8:43. *called by thy name,* 2 Chron 6:33. Isa 4:1; 43:1; 45:4; 63:19. Jer 14:9; 15:16. Dan 9:18, 19.
1 Kings 8:43. do all stranger *calleth* for
Ps 42:7. deep *c.* unto deep at the noise
147:4. *c.* them by name, Isa 40:26.
Isa 59:4. none *c.* for justice nor for truth
64:7. none that *c.* upon thy name
Hos 7:7. none among them that *c.*
Amos 5:8. that *c.* for waters of the sea
Luke 15:6 *c.* together his friends, 9.
John 10:3. he *c.* his own sheep by name
Rom 4:17. *c.* things which be not as though
9:11. not of works but of him that *c.*
Gal 5:8. persuasion not of him that *c.*
1 Thess 5:24. faithful is he that *c.*
Rom 11:29. the gifts and *calling* of God
1 Cor 1:26. ye see your *calling* brethren
7:20. let every man abide in the same *c.*
Eph 1:18. know what is the hope of his *c.*
4:4. called in one hope of your *c.*
Phil 3:14. prize of the high *c.* of God
2 Thess 1:11. count worthy of this *c.*
2 Tim 1:9. and called us with an holy *c.*
Heb 3:1. partakers of the heavenly *c.*
2 Pet 1:10. make your *c.* and election
Isa 41:4. *c.* the generations from
Matt 11:16. sitting and *c.* their fellows
Mark 11:21. Peter *c.* to remembrance
Acts 7:59. stoned Stephen *c.* on God
22:16. *c.* on name of Lord
1 Pet 3:6. obeyed Abraham *c.* him lord
CALM, Ps 107:29. Jon 1:11. great *c.*, Matt 8:26. Mark 4:39. Luke 8:24.
CALVE (cow), Job 21:10. (hinds), 39:1. Ps 29:9. Jer 14:5. See *Calf.*
CAME (of Christ), Matt 10:28. John 1:11; 8:14, 42; 18:37. Rom 9:5. 1 Tim 1:15. 1 John 5:6.
John 1:17. grace and truth *c.* by Jesus Christ
Came again, spirit, Judg 15:19. 1 Sam 30:12. soul, 1 Kings 17:22. Luke 8:55.
Came down, 2 Kings 1:10, 12, 14. 2 Chron 7:1, 3. Lam 1:9. John 3:13; 6:38, 41, 51, 58. Rev 20:9.
Came forth, Num 11:20. Judg 14:14. Eccles 5:15. Zech 10:4.
John 16:28. I—from the Father
Came upon, God's Spirit, Num 24:2. Judg 3:10; fear, 2 Chron 14:14. wrath, Ps 78:31.
2 Kings 24:3. Dan 4:28.
CAMEL, Gen 30:43. Lev 11:4.
Matt 3:4. raiment of *c.*'s hair, Mark 1:6.
19:24. it is easier for a *c.* to go through
23:24. strain at gnat, and swallow *c.*
CAMP, Ex 32:17; 36:6.
Exod 14:19. angel went before the *c.*
16:13. quails came up and covered the *c.*
Num 11:26. prophesied in the *c.*
31. let the quails fall by the *c.*
Deut 23:14. Lord walketh in midst of *c.* therefore shall thy *c.* be holy
Judg 13:25. began to move him in *c.*
Heb 13:13. go unto him without the *c.*
Rev 20:9. compassed the *c.* of saints
CAN we find such a one, Gen 41:38.
Deut 1:12. how *c.* I alone bear your
32:39. neither is there any that *c.* deliver
2 Sam 7:20. what *c.* David say more
2 Chron 1:10. who *c.* judge this people
Esther 8:6. how *c.* I endure
Job 8:11. *c.* the rush grow without mire
25:4. how *c.* man be justified with God?
34:29. who then *c.* make trouble?
Eccles 4:11. *c.* one be warm alone
Isa 49:15. *c.* woman forget sucking child
Jer 2:32. *c.* maid forget her ornaments
Ezek 22:14. *c.* thine heart endure
37:3. *c.* these bones live?
Amos 3:3. *c.* two walk together except
Matt 12:34. how *c.* ye speak good things?
19:25. who then *c.* be saved?
Mark 2:7. who *c.* forgive sins but God?
19. *c.* children of bridechamber fast
3:27. no man *c.* enter a strong man's
10:38. *c.* ye drink of the cup that I
John 3:4. how *c.* man be born when old?
9. how *c.* these things be, Luke 1:34.
5:19. Son *c.* do nothing of himself, 30.
6:44. no man *c.* come to me except
John 6:60. an hard saying, who *can* hear it?

9:4. night cometh, when no man *c.* work
14:5. how *c.* we know the way?
15:4. no more *c.* ye, except ye abide
1 Cor 12:3. no man *c.* say that Jesus is Lord
2 Chron 13:8. *c.* do nothing against the truth
1 Tim 6:7. we *c.* carry nothing out
Heb 10:11. *c.* never take away sins
James 2:14. not works? *c.* faith save him?
Cannot, Gen 32:12 *c.* be numbered for multitude, 1 Kings 3:8. Hos 1:10.
Num 23:20. blessed, I *c.* reverse it
Josh 24:19. ye *c.* serve the Lord; for he
1 Sam 12:21. things which *c.* profit
1 Kings 8:27. heaven of heavens *c.* contain thee, 2 Chron 6:18.
Ezra 9:15. we *c.* stand before thee
Job 9:3. he *c.* answer him one of a
12:14. he breaketh down and it *c.* be
14:5. appointed his bounds that he *c.* pass
28:15. it *c.* be gotten for gold, neither
36:18. a great ransom *c.* deliver thee
Ps 40:5. *c.* be reckoned up in order
77:4. I am so troubled that I *c.* speak
93:1. world established, that it *c.* be
139:6. too high, I *c.* attain unto it
Isa 38:18. the grave *c.* praise thee
44:18. they *c.* see; they *c.* understand
20. he *c.* deliver his soul, nor say, Is there
45:20. pray unto a god that *c.* save
56:11. shepherds that *c.* understand
59:1. neither his ear heavy, that it *c.*
Jer 4:19. I *c.* hold my peace, because
6:10. are uncircumcised, they *c.*
7:8. ye trust in lying words that *c.*
14:9. as a mighty man that *c.* save
18:6. *c.* I do with you as this potter?
29:17. I like the vile figs that *c.* be
33:22. the host of heaven *c.* be
Lam 3:7. hath hedged me, that I *c.* get
Matt 6:24. ye *c.* serve God and *mammon*
7:18. a good tree *c.* bring forth evil fruit
19:11. all men *c.* receive this saying
26:53. thinkest thou I *c.* now pray to
27:42. himself he *c.* save, Mark 15:31.
Luke 14:26. *c.* be my disciple, 27, 33.
John 3:3. *c.* see (5. enter) kingdom of God
7:34. thither *c.* come, 8:21; 13:33.
8:43. because ye *c.* hear my word
14:17. whom the world *c.* receive
15:4. branch *c.* bear fruit of itself
16:12. things to say, ye *c.* bear now
Acts 4:20. we *c.* but speak the things
5:39. if it be of God ye *c.* overthrow it
Rom 8:8 that are in the flesh *c.* please God
26. with groanings which *c.* be uttered
1 Cor 10:21. ye *c.* drink cup of the Lord
15:50. flesh and blood *c.* inherit kingdom
2 Cor 12:2. body or out of body I *c.* tell
Gal 5:17. ye *c.* do the things that ye
2 Tim 2:13. he *c.* deny himself
Titus 1:2. God who *c.* lie promised
2:8. sound speech *c.* be condemned
Heb 4:15. high priest which *c.* be
9:5. we *c.* now speak particularly
12:27. things which *c.* be shaken
28. kingdom that *c.* be moved
James 1:13. God *c.* be tempted with evil
1 John 3:9. he *c.* sin because born of God
Canst, Exod 33:20. thou *c.* not see my face
Deut 28:27. thou *c.* not be healed
Job 11:7. *c.* thou . . . find God?
Job 11:8. what *canst* thou do? what *c.* thou
Matt 8:2. if thou wilt, thou *c.* make
Mark 9:22. if thou *c.* do any thing have
John 3:8. *c.* not tell whence it cometh
13:36. thou *c.* not follow me now
CANDLE shall be put out, Job 18:6; 21:17. Prov 24:20. *See* Jer 25:10.
Job 29:3. when his *c.* shined on my head
Ps 18:28. the Lord will light my *c.*
Prov 20:27. spirit of man is *c.* of Lord
31:18. her *c.* goeth not out by night
Matt 5:15. do men light a *c.* and put it, Mark 4:21. Luke 8:16; 11:33.
Luke 15:8. *light c.* and sweep the house
Rev 18:23. light of *c.* shine no more
22:5. they need no *c.* neither light
Zeph 1:12. search Jerusalem with *candles*
Exod 25:31. *candlestick,* 37:17, 20. Lev 24:4. Num 8:2. 2 Kings 4:10. Dan 5:5.
Zech 4:2. behold a *c.* all of gold
Rev 2:5. I will remove thy *c.* out of his
1:20. seven *candlesticks* are the seven churches
CANKER, 2 Tim 2:17. James 5:3.
CAPTAIN, Num 2:3; 14:4.
Josh 5:14, 15. *c.* of the Lord's host
2 Chron 13:12. God himself is our *c.*
Heb 2:10. *c.* of their salvation perfect
CAPTIVE, Gen 14:14; 34:29.
Judg 5:12. lead thy captivity *c.*
Isa 49:24. or lawful *c.* be delivered
51:14. *c.* exile hasteneth to be loosed
Jer 22:12. die whither they led him *c.*
Amos 7:11. Israel be led away *c.*
2 Tim 2:26. taken *c.* by him at will
3:6. lead *c.* silly women laden with
Deut 30:3. Lord will turn thy *captivity*
Job 42:10. the Lord turned *c.* of Job
Ps 14:7. Lord bringeth back the *c.*
68:18. lead *c.* captive, Eph 4:8.
78:61. delivered his strength into *c.*
126:1. turned again the *c.* of Zion
4. turn again our *c.* as streams in south
Jer 15:2. such as are for *c.* to *c.*
29:14. I will turn away your *c.*
30:3. bring again *c.* of my people, 32:44; 33:26; 34:22; 42:12.
Hos 6:11. returned *c.* of my people
Zeph 2:7. Lord turn away their *c.*
Rom 7:23. bringing me to *c.* of sin
2 Cor 10:5. bringing into *c.* every
Rev 13:10. leadeth into *c.* go into *c.*
CARCASE, Num 14:29. Matt 24:28.
CARE, Luke 10:40. 1 Cor 7:21.
Matt 13:22. *c.* of this world choke
1 Cor 9:9. doth God take *c.* for oxen
2 Cor 11:28. *c.* of all the churches
1 Tim 3:5. how shall he take *c.* of
1 Pet 5:7. casting all your *c.* on him
Ps 142:4. no man *cared* for my soul
John 12:6. not that he *c.* for the poor
2 Kings 4:13. *careful* (anxious) for us
Jer 17:8. not *c.* in year of drought
Dan 3:16. not *c.* to answer thee
Luke 10:41. Martha art *c.* and troubled

Phil 4:6. be *c.* for nothing; but by
10. were *c.* but ye lacked opportunity
Titus 3:8. *c.* to maintain good works
Isa 32:9. *careless* daughters, 10, 11
Matt 22:16. *carest* not, Mark 4:38.
Deut 11:12. land thy God *careth* for
John 10:13. hireling *c.* not for the sheep
1 Cor 7:32. unmarried *c.* for things of Lord, married *c.* for things of the world
1 Pet 5:7. *care* on him; for he *careth*
CARNAL, sold under sin, Rom 7:14.
Rom 8:7. *c.* mind is enmity against God
15:27. minister to them in *c.* things
1 Cor 3:1. not speak but as to *c.*
9:11. is . . . if we reap your *c.* things?
2 Cor 10:4. our weapons are not *c.*
Heb 7:16. law of a *c.* commandment
9:10. *c.* ordinances imposed on them
Rom 8:6. to be *carnally* minded is death
CARPENTER, 2 Sam 5:11. Isa 41:7. Jer 24:1. four *c.* Zech 1:20
Matt 13:55. *carpenter's son,* Mark 6:3.
CARRY us not up hence, Exod 33:15.
Num 11:12. *c.* them in thy bosom
Eccles 10:20. bird of the air shall *c.* voice
Isa 40:11. *c.* lambs in his bosom
46:4. even to hoar hairs will I *c.* you
Luke 10:4. *c.* neither purse nor scrip
John 21:18. *c.* thee whither thou
1 Tim 6:7. we can *c.* nothing out
Luke 16:22. *carried* by the angels into
Eph 4:14. *c. about* with every wind
Heb 13:9. —with divers doctrines
Rev 17:3. *c.* me away in the spirit, 21:10.
CART is pressed full, Amos 2:13.
CASE (state), Exod 5:19. Ps 144:15.
CAST law behind backs, Neh 9:26.
Ps 22:10. *c.* upon thee from womb
55:22. *c.* thy burden on the Lord
Prov 1:14. *c.* in thy lot among us
16:33. the lot is *c.* into the lap
Eccles 11:1. *c.* thy bread upon the waters
Isa 2:20. man *c.* his idols of silver
38:17. hast *c.* all my sins behind thy back
Ezek 25:35. *c.* me behind thy back
Dan 3:20. *c.* into fiery furnace
Jon 2:4. I am *c.* out of thy sight
Mic 7:19. *c.* all their sins into the sea
Nah 3:6. *c.* abominable filth on thee
Mal 3:11. vine shall not *c.* her fruit
Matt 3:10. *c.* into fire, 7:19. Luke 3:9.
5:25. thou be *c.* into prison
29, 30. *c.* it from thee . . . *c.* into hell, 18:9.
7:6. neither *c.* pearls before swine
13:42. *c.* them into a furnace, 50.
18:30. went and *c.* him into prison
22:13. *c.* him into outer darkness
25:30. *c.* unprofitable servant into
Mark 11:23. be thou *c.* into the sea
12:44. she of her want *c.* in all, Luke 21:4.
Luke 1:29. she *c.* in her mind what
12:5. fear him . . . power to *c.* into hell
58. lest the officer *c.* thee into prison
John. 8:7. let him first *c.* a stone at her
Acts. 16:23. they *c.* them into prison
Rev 2:10. devil *c.* some into prison
22. I will *c.* her into a bed, and them
20:3. *c.* him into the . . . pit
Lev 26:44. I will not *cast away*
2 Sam 1:21. shield is vilely—
Job 8:20. God will not—perfect man
Ps 2:3. let us—their cords from us
Isa 41:9. I will not *c.* thee *a.*
Ezek 18:31. —all your transgressions
Rom 11:1. hath God—his people, 2.
Heb 10:35. *c.* not *a.* your confidence
1 Cor 9:27. myself a— (disqualified)
Job 22:29. when men are *cast down* then
Ps 37:24. though he fall . . . not be utterly—
42:5. why art thou—11; 43:5.
2 Cor 4:9. —but not destroyed
7:6. comforteth those that are—
Ps 44:9. hast *cast off,* 23. *c. us* not *off* forever, 77:7. will the Lord—for ever
71:9. c. me not off in the time of old age
89:38. thou hast—and abhorred, thou
94:14. the Lord will not—his people
Jer 31:37. I will—all the seed of Israel
Lam 3:31. the Lord will not—for ever
Rom 13:12. let us—works of darkness
1 Tim 5:12. they—their first faith
Gen 21:10. *cast out* this bondwoman and her son, Gal 4:30.
Exod 34:24. I will—the nations before thee
Lev 18:24. which I—before thee
Deut 7:1. —many nations before thee
Ps 78:55. he—heathen also before them
80:8. —the heathen and planted it
Isa 14:19. thou art—of thy grave
26:19. the earth shall—the dead
58:7. poor that are—to thy house
66:5. *c.* you out for my name's sake
Jer 7:15. I will *c.* you out (Judah), 15:1.
16:13. I will *c.* you out of this land
Matt 7:5. *c.* beam out of thine own eye
8:12. children of the kingdom shall be—
12:24. —devils but by Beelzebub
21:12. —them that sold and bought
Mark 9:28. why could not we *c.* him out?
12:8. *c.* him out of the vineyard
16:9. had—(of M. Magdalene) seven devils
17. in my name shall they—devils
Luke 6:22. —your name as evil.
John 6:37. that cometh in no wise—
12:31. prince of this world be—
Rev 12:9. and the great dragon was—
Ps 73:18. thou *castedst* them down
Job 15:4. thou *castest* off fear
Ps 50:17. *c.* my words behind thee
Job 21:10. cow *casteth* not her calf
Ps 147:6. *c.* the wicked to the ground
Jer 6:7. so she *c.* out wickedness
Matt 9:34. he *c.* out devils through Beelzebub. Mark 3:22. Luke 11:15.
1 John 4:18. perfect love *c.* out fear
3 John 10. *c.* them out of the church
Job 6:21. ye see my *casting* down
Rom 11:15. if the *c.* away of them be
2 Cor 10:5. *c.* down imaginations
1 Pet 5:7. *c.* all your care upon him
CASTOR and Pollux, Acts 28:11.
CATCH every man his wife, Judg 21:21.
Ps 10:9. he lieth in wait to *c.* the poor
35:8. his net . . . hid *c.* himself
109.11. let the extortioner *c.* all he hath
Jer 5:26. they set a trap, they *c.* men
Mark 12:13. they *c.* him in his words
Luke 5:10. henceforth thou shalt *c.* men
CATTLE on a thousand hills mine, Ps 50:10.

Ps 104:14. grass to grow for the *c.*
Ezek 34:17. I judge between *c.* and *c.*
John 4:12. drank thereof and his *c.*
CAUGHT and kissed him, Prov 7:13.
John 21:3. that night they *c.* nothing
Acts 8:39. Spirit of Lord *c.* away Philip
2 Cor 12:4 *c.* up into paradise
1 Thess 4:17. *c.* up together with
Rev 12:5. her child was *c.* up unto God
CAUL, *i.e.* net, Isa 3:18. Hos 13:8.
CAUSE of both before judges, Exod 22:9.
Exod 23:2. not speak in a *c.* to decline
3. not countenance a poor man in his *c.*
6. nor wrest judgment of thy poor in *c.*
Deut 1:17. *c.* too hard for you bring
Job 5:8. to God would I commit my *c.*
Ps 9:4. maintained my right and *cause*
35:23. awake unto my *c.* my God, 27.
Prov 18:17. that is first in his own *c.*
25:9. debate thy *c.* with thy neighbour
Eccles 7:10. what is *c.* . . . former days
Isa 51:22. pleadeth *c.* of his people
Jer 5:28. *c.* of the fatherless, 22:16.
Lam 3:36. to subvert a man in his *c.*
Matt 19:3. put away wife for every *c.*
2 Cor 4:16. for which *c.* we faint not
5:13. if we be sober it is for your *c.*
Exod 9:16. *for this cause,* Matt 19:5. Eph 5:31. John 12:27; 18:37. Rom 1:26; 13:6. 1 Cor 11:30.
1 Tim 1:16. —I obtained mercy
Ps 119:161. *without cause,* Prov 3:30. Matt 5:22. John 15:25.
Job 6:24. *c.* me to understand
Ps 10:17. wilt *c.* thine ear to hear
85:4. *c.* thine anger towards us to cease
143:8. *c.* me to know the way . . . walk
Isa 3:12. lead thee, *c.* to err, 9:16.
58:14. I will *c.* thee to ride on high
66:9. birth and not *c.* to bring forth
Jer 3:12. not *c.* my anger to fall
7:3. *c.* you to dwell in this place, 7.
15:4. *c.* them to be removed into all
11. *c.* the enemy to treat thee well
18:2. I will *c.* thee to hear my words
32:37. I will *c.* them to dwell safely
Lam 3:32. though he *c.* grief, yet he
Ezek 36:27. *c.* to walk in statutes
37:5. *c.* breath to enter into you
Dan 9:17. *c.* thy face to shine upon thy
Prov 7:21. fair speech *caused*
26:2. the curse *causeless* shall not
10:5. a son *causeth* shame, 17:2; 19:26.
18:18. the lot *c.* contentions to cease
19:27. cease instruction that *c.* to err
Matt 5:32. *c.* her to commit adultery
2 Cor 2:14. always *c.* us to triumph
CAVE, a stone lay on it, John 11:38.
Gen 19:30. Lot dwelt in a *c.*, he and
23:19. buried Sarah his wife in the *c.*
25:9. buried Abraham in the *c.*
49:29. bury me with my fathers in the *c.*
Josh 10:16. hid themselves in a *c.*
Isa 2:19. go to *caves* for fear of the Lord
Ezek 33:27. they that be in the *c.* shall die of pestilence
Heb 11:38. wandered in *c.* of the earth
CEASE, day and night not, Gen 8:22.
Neh 6:3. why should the work *c.*
Job 3:17. there wicked *c.* from troubling
Ps 37:8. *c.* from anger and wrath
46:9. he maketh wars to *c.* unto end
Prov 19:27. *c.* to hear instruction
23:4. *c.* from thine own wisdom
Acts 13:10. wilt thou not *c.* to pervert
1 Cor 13:8. tongues, they shall *c.*
Eph 1:16. *c.* not to give thanks for
Col 1:9. *c.* not to pray for you
2 Pet 2:14. that cannot *c.* from sin
Ps 12:1. the godly man *ceaseth*
Prov 26:20. where no talebearer, strife *c.*
1 Thess 5:17. pray without *ceasing,* 2:13. 1 Sam 12:23. Acts 12:5. Rom 1:9. 2 Tim 1:3.
CEDAR wood, Lev 14:4. Num 19:6.
2 Kings 14:9. thistle sent to *c.* in Lebanon
Ps 29:5. voice of the Lord breaketh *c.*
92:12. grow like a *c.* in Lebanon
Song of Sol 1:17. beams of our house are *c.*
Ezek 17:3. great eagle took highest branch of *c.*
Ezek 31:3. the Assyrian was a *cedar* in Lebanon
Song of Sol 5:15. countenance excellent as *cedars*
Isa 9:10. we will change them into *c.*
CELEBRATE, death cannot, Isa 38:18.
CELESTIAL, 1 Cor 15:40.
CHAFF, storm carries away, Job 21:18. Ps 1:4; 35:5. Isa 17:13; 29:5; 41:16. of summer threshing, Dan 2:35. flame consumeth, Isa 5:24. Hos 13:3. he will burn, Luke 3:17.
Isa 33:11. ye shall conceive *c.*
Jer 23:28. what is the *c.* to the wheat
Zeph 2:2. before the day pass as *c.*
Matt 3:12. burn up *c.* in unquenchable
CHAIN-S, gold, Gen 41:42. Dan 5:7. (partition by) 1 Kings 6:21. camel's, Judg 8:26. silver, Isa 40:19.
Ps 73:6. pride . . . as *c.*
Prov 1:9. (parent's) ornament of grace and *c.*
Isa 3:19. Lord will take away thy *c.*
Ezek 16:11. I put a *c.* on thy neck
(Captive's), make a *c.* Ezek 7:23 *c.* heavy, Lam 3:7. *See* Isa 45:14. Jer 40:4. Ezek 19:4. Mark 5:3. Rev 20:1.
Ps 149:8. to bind their kings with *c.*
Acts 12:7. Peter's *c.* fell from his hands
28:20. Israel I am bound with this *c.*
2 Tim 1:16. was not ashamed of my *c.*
2 Pet 2:4. delivered into *c.* of darkness
Jude 6. reserved in everlasting *c.*
CHALDEANS (*wise men* or Magi), Dan 2:2, &c (people), Job 1:17. Isa 48:20. Jer 38:2, &c. Dan 9:1.
Isa 43:14. *C.* whose cry is in the ships
Ezek 23:14. images of the *C.* portrayed
CHAMBER, Ps 19:5. Joel 2:16.
Gen 43:30. Joseph entered *c.* and wept
Dan 6:10. windows in *c.* toward Jerusalem
Job 9:9. maketh *chambers*
Ps 104:3. beams of *c.* in the waters
Prov 7:27. going down to the *c.* of death
Song of Sol 1:4. the king brought me to his *c.*
Isa 26:20. enter into *c.* and shut door
Matt 24:26. he is in the secret *c.*
CHANCE, happens, 1 Sam 6:9. Eccles 9:11. by *c.*, 2 Sam 1:6. Luke 10:31.
CHANGE, of raiment, Judg 14:12, 13. Zech 3:4. *changeable,* Isa 3:22.
Job 14:14. wait till my *c.* come
Prov 24:21. with them given to *c.*
Job 17:12. *c.* night into day
Ps 102:26. as a vesture *c.* them, Heb 1:12.
Jer 13:23. can Ethiopian *c.* his skin
Dan 7:25. think to *c.* times, laws
Mal 3:6. I am the Lord, I *c.* not
Rom 1:26. women did *c.* the natural

Phil 3:21. Christ shall *c.* our vile bodies
Heb 7:12. of necessity a *c.* of law
Dan 3:27. were coats *changed,* Job 30:18.
Rom 1:23. *c.* the glory of God into
25. *c.* the truth of God into a lie
2 Cor 3:18. *c.* into the same image
Job 10:17. *changes* and war are against me
Ps 55:19. they have no *c.* therefore
15:4. sweareth to his hurt and *changeth* not
Dan 2:21. he *c.* times and seasons
CHANT to sound of viol, Amos 6:5.
CHAPEL, it is the king's Amos 7:13.
CHARGE, Gen 26:5; 28:6. Exod 6:13.
Ps 91:11. give his angels *c.* over thee, Matt 4:6. Luke 4:10.
Ps 35:11. to my *c.* things I knew not
Acts 7:60. lay not to their *c.* 2 Tim 4:16.
Acts 16:24. received such a *charge,* thrust into prison
23:29. nothing laid to his *c.* worthy
Rom 8:33. lay to *c.* of God's elect
1 Cor 9:18. make gospel without *c.*
1 Tim 1:18. this *c.* I commit to thee
6:13. I give thee *c.* in the sight of God
Song of Sol 2:7. I *c.* you, O daughters of Jerusalem, 3:5; 5:8; 8:4.
1 Tim 6:17. *c.* them that are rich
Job 1:22. nor *charged* God foolishly
4:18. *c.* his angels with folly, 15:15.
Luke 9:21; Matt 12:16. *c.* not make known
1 Thess 2:11. *c.* every one as a father
Chargeable, 2 Sam 13:25. Neh 5:15. 2 Cor 11:9. 1 Thess 2:9. 2 Thess 3:8.
CHARIOT, (Joseph), Gen 41:43. (Pharaoh), Exod 14:6; 15:4. Song of Sol 1:9.
Exod 14:25. and took off their *c.* wheels
2 Kings 2:11, *c.* of fire. 13:14, *c.* of Israel.
Ps 104:3. who maketh the clouds *his c.*
Acts 8:28. sitting in *c.* read Esaias
Josh 17:16. *chariots* of iron, Judg 1:19.
1 Sam 8:11. king take sons for his *c.*
2 Sam 8:4. David reserved . . . for a hundred *c.*
1 Kings 10:26. Solomon's *c.,* Song of Sol 3:9.
6:17. mountain full of *c.* and horses
18:24. trust on Egypt for *c.,* Isa 31:1.
Ps 20:7. some trust in *c.,* Isa 22:18.
68:17. the *c.* of God are twenty thousand
Song of Sol 6:12. like the *c.* of Amminadib
Isa 21:7. saw *c.* of asses
Hab 3:8. didst ride upon thine horses, and thy *c.* of salvation
Zech 6:1. four *c.* between two mountains
Rev 9:9. sound of wings as of *c.*
Chariot cities (Solomon's), 2 Chron 1:14; 8:6; 9:25.
CHARITY edifieth, 1 Cor 8:1.
1 Cor 13:2, have not *c.* I am nothing. 4, *c.* suffereth long. 8, *c.* never faileth
13. faith, hope, *c.* . . . but the greatest is *c.*
Col 3:14. above all these things put on *c.*
1 Thess 3:6. tidings of your faith and *c.*
2 Thess 1:3. *c.* of every one aboundeth
1 Tim 1:5. end of commandment is *c.*
2:15. if they continue in faith and *c.*
4:12. be thou an example in *c.*
2 Tim 2:22. follow righteousness, faith, *c.*
3:10. known my doctrine, faith, *c.*
Titus 2:2. aged men be sound in *c.*
3 John 6. borne witness of thy *c.*
1 Pet 4:8. fervent *c.* . . . *c.* shall cover sins
5:14. greet one another with a kiss of *c.*
2 Pet 1:7. to brotherly kindness, *c.*
Jude 12. these are spots in your feasts of *c.*
Rev 2:19. I know thy works and *c.*
Rom 14:15. walkest not *charitably*
CHARMED, not, Jer 8:17. *charmers,* Deut 18:11. Ps 58:5. Isa 19:3.
CHASTE virgin, 2 Cor 11:2.
Titus 2:5, young women discreet, *c.*
1 Pet 3:2. your *c.* conversation, with
CHASTEN . . . rod of men, 2 Sam 7:14.
Ps 6:1. neither *c.* me in thy, 38:1.
Prov 19:18. *c.* son while there is hope
Dan 10:12. to *c.* thyself before God
Rev 3:19. as many as I love, I *c.*
Ps 69:10. chastened soul with fasting
118:18. the Lord hath *c.* me sore
1 Cor 11:32. *chastened* that we be not condemned
2 Cor 6:9. as *c.* and not killed
Heb 12:10. fathers for few days *c.* us
Ps 94:12. blessed whom thou *chastenest*
Deut 8:5. as man *chasteneth* his son
Prov 13:24. loveth him *chasteneth* betimes
Heb 12:6. whom the Lord loveth he *c.*
Job 5:17. despise not thou *chastening* of the Lord, Prov 3:11. Heb 12:5.
Isa 26:16. when *c.* was upon them
Heb 12:7. if *c.,* God dealeth as with sons
11. no *c.* for present seemeth joyous
CHASTISE you seven times, Lev 26:28.
Deut 22:18. the elders shall *c.* him
Hos 7:12. *c.* as congregation heard
10:10. my desire that I should *c.* them
Luke 23:16. *c.* and release him, 22.
Job 34:31. I have borne *chastisement* I will not
Isa 53:5. *c.* of our peace was upon him
Jer 30:14. with the *c.* of a cruel one
Heb 12:8. without *c.* then are ye bastards
CHATTER like a crane, Isa 38:14.
CHEEK, smite on, 1 Kings 22:24. Job 16:10—judge, Mic 5:1.—right *c.,* Matt 5:39.—one *c.,* Luke 6:29.
Song of Sol 1:10. *cheeks* comely rows of jewels
5:13. his *c.* are as a bed of spices
CHEER, Deut 24:5. Eccles 11:9.
Judg 9:13. wine which *cheereth* Ps 104.15.
Be of good c., Paul, Acts 23:11; 27:22, 25. son—thy sins be forgiven, Matt 9:2.—it is I, 14:27.—; I have overcome the world, John 16:33.
Cheerful feasts, Zech 8:19 *c.* giver, 2 Cor 9:7. merry heart . . . *c.* countenance, Prov 15:13.—*ness,* Rom 12:8.
Acts 24:10. *cheerfully* answer for
CHERISHETH, as Lord the church, Eph 5:29. as a nurse *c.* children, 1 Thess 2:7.
CHERUBIMS, between, 1 Sam 4:4. 2 Sam 6:2. 2 Kings 19:15. 1 Chron 13:6. Ps 80:1; 99:1. Isa 37:16. Ezek 10:7.
CHICKENS, hen gathereth, Matt 23:37.
CHIDE, not always, Ps 103:9.
CHIEF fathers, Num 31:26, &c *c.* house, Josh 22:14, &c *c.* men, 1 Chron 7:3, &c *c.* priest, 2 Kings 25:18, &c *c.* priests, Matt 16:21, &c
c. of ways of God, Job 40:19. strength, Ps 78:51.—nations, Jer 31:7. Amos 6:1.—Asia *(Asiarchs),* Acts 19:31.
Matt 20:27. whoso will be *c.* among you
Luke 22:26. is *c.,* as he that serveth
Eph 2:20. *c.* corner stone, 1 Pet 2:6.
1 Tim 1:15. sinners, of whom I am *c.*
Song of Sol 5:10. the *chiefest* among ten thousand

CHILD (Isaac), Gen 18:13. (Joseph), 37:30. goodly *c.* (Moses), Exod 2:2. Heb 11:23. (Samson), Judg 13:5. (Obed), Ruth 4:16, the *c.* Samuel, 1 Sam 2:21. (Bathsheba's), 2 Sam 12:14. (Jeroboam's), 1 Kings 14:3. (widow's), 1 Kings 17:21. Luke 7:12. (John Baptist), Luke 1:66. (JESUS) the young *c.*, Matt 2:8. thy holy *c.*, Acts 4:27. (possessed), Mark 9:21. (nobleman's), John 4:49.
Ps 131:2. quieted as a *c.* weaned
Prov 20:11. a *c.* known by his doings
22:6. train up a *c.* in the way he, 15.
Eccles 4:13. better . . . wise *c.* than king
10:16. woe when thy king is a *c.* Isa 3:4.
Isa 7:16. before *c.* knows to, 8:4.
9:6. for unto us a *c.* is born
Jer 31:20. Ephraim is he a pleasant *c.*?
Hos 11:1. when Israel was a *c.* I loved
Luke 2:34. this *c.* is set for the fall
Gal 4:1. heir, as . . . is a *c.*, differs nothing
Rev 12:5. *c.* to rule with a rod of iron. *See* Isa 11:8. *c.* . . . a hundred years old, 65:20.
1 Tim 2:15. saved in *childbearing,* if
1 Sam 12:2. *childhood,* Eccles 11:10.
1 Cor 13:11. put away *childish* things
Gen 15:2. *childless,* Jer 22:30. Luke 20:28.
Child of hell, Matt 23:15. Acts 13:10.
Little c., I know not, 1 Kings 3:7. *See* Jer 1:6—shall lead, Isa 11:6. receive one—, Matt 18:5. Luke 9:48. receive kingdom of God as—, Luke 18:17. suffer *l. children,* Matt 19:14, &c. *See* John 13:33. 1 John 2:1; 4:4. Gal 4:19.
2 Sam 12:16. David besought God for *c.*
1 Kings 3:25. divide living *c.* in two
2 Kings 5:14. flesh like a *c.* Job 33:25.
No child, Deut 25:5. 2 Sam 6:23.
Only c., Judg 11:34. Luke 9:38. *first c.,* Jer 4:31. *c. of old age* (Sarah's), Gen 21:2. Heb 11:11. (Jacob's), Gen 44:20. (Shunammite's), 2 Kings 4:16. (Elisabeth's), Luke 1:7.
CHILDREN, Gen 3:16. in sorrow bring *c.*
Gen 18:19. command *c.* and household after him, Deut 6:7. *See* Josh 4:6, 21. 2 Sam 1:18. Ps 78:5.
Gen 30:1. give me c. or else I die
Exod 20:5. iniquity of fathers upon the *c.*
13:15. all firstborn . . . *c.* I redeem. Num 3:45, Levites instead of all the firstborn . . . *c.*
Lev 25:45. *c.* of strangers, 1 Kings 9:20. Isa 2:6.
Num 14:33. your *c.* shall wander 40 years
Deut 32:5. their spot is not spot of his *c.*
24:16. fathers not (die) for *c.* nor *c.* for fathers, 2 Kings 14:6. Jer 31:30.
1 Kings 2:4. if *c.* heed, . . . shall not fail, Ps 89:30.
2 Kings 2:24. two she bears tare forty-two *c.*
17:31. Sepharvites burnt *c.* (= pass through fire to Molech). *See* 2 Chron 28:3; 33:6. Isa 57:5. Mic 6:7. Ezek 16:21; 23:39.
Ezra 2:55. *c.* of Solomon servants, 1 Kings 9:20.
Ps 17:14. are full of *c.* *See* Ps 127:5.
69:8. an alien to my mother's *c.*
72:4. he shall save the *c.* of needy
82:6. gods; all of you are *c.* of Most High
Prov 17:6. glory of *c.* are their fathers
20:7. just, his *c.* blessed after him
31:28. her *c.* rise and call her blessed
Isa 1:2. I brought up *c.* and they rebelled
8:18. I and *c.* whom Lord hath, Heb 2:13.
54:13. great shall be the peace of thy *c.*
Jer 3:14. backsliding *c.*, wise to evil
7:18. *c.* gather wood, . . . queen of heaven
Dan 5:13. *c.* of captivity, Ezra 4:1.
Mal 4:6. turn the hearts of fathers to *c.*
Matt 2:18. Rachel weeping for *c.*, Jer 31:15.
5:45. *c. of* Father in heaven. 8:12,—kingdom
9:15, bridechamber. 11:19,—wisdom
15:26, *c.* bread; 21:15, *c.* crying Hosanna
Luke 6:35. *c.* of the Highest
7:32, *c.* in marketplace. 11:7, in bed
16:8. *c.* of this world, 20:34. 1 Cor 1:26.
Acts 3:25. ye are the *c.* of the prophets
Rom 8:17. if *c.* then heirs, . . . of God
9:8. *c.* of promise, Gal 4:28. Acts 2:39.
9:26. there shall be called *c.* of living God
1 Cor 14:20. in malice be ye *c.* in understanding
2 Cor 12:14. *c.* not lay up for parents
Gal 4:3. *when c. were in* bondage, 31.
Eph 1:5, adoption of *c.* 2:3, *c.* of wrath
2:2. *c.* of disobedience, 5:6. Col 3:6.
4:14. no more *c.* tossed with every wind
5:1, as dear *c.* 1 Pet 1:14, as obedient *c.*
6:1. *c.* obey your parents, Col 3:20.
4. fathers provoke not *c.*, Col 3:21.
1 Thess 5:5. *c.* of light, day, not of night
1 Tim 5:4. *c.* shew piety at home
Heb 2:14. as *c.* partakers flesh, He also
Heb 12:5. exhortation as unto *children.* My son. *See* Ps 128:3; 147:13. Isa 54:13. Lam 4:4. Nah 3:10. Matt 23:31, 37.
Children of the East, Gen 29:1. Judg 6:3; 7:12; 8:10. wisdom of—,1 Kings 4:30.
Children of God, peacemakers, Matt 5:9.—*c.* of resurrection, Luke 20:36. gather—, John 11:52. witness we are—, Rom 8:16. liberty of—, 8:21. *c.* of flesh not—, Rom 9:8. all—by faith in Christ Jesus, Gal 3:26.—manifest, 1 John 3:10. we love—, 5:2. *c. of light,* John 12:36. Eph 5:8.
Children of Israel, Gen 50:25, &c—increased, Exod 1:7,—as sand, 1 Kings 4:20, *see* Gen 22:17. Hos 1:10. Neh 9:23 I will dwell among—, Exod 29:45. 1 Kings 6:13.—my servants, Lev 25:55, atonement money of—.Exod 30:16.—(10 tribes) and Judah shall come together, Jer 50:4. Hos 1:11.—days without king, 3:4 as *c.* of Ethiopians unto me, O—, Amos 9:7.
Children of men, fairer than, Ps 17:14. hearts of—before Lord, Prov 15:11.
Children to Abraham, Matt 3:9. *See* John 8:39. seed of Abraham not all—, Rom 9:7. *c.* of faith . . . are—, Gal 3:7.
Children's children (sin visited on), Exod 34:7. (mercy until), Jer 2:9. Ps 103:17. *see* thy —, 128:6.—crown of old men, Prov 17:6.
CHOKE, Matt 13:7. Mark 4:19. Luke 8:14. Mark 5:13. herd ran . . . and were *choked* Luke 8:33.
CHOOSE, Num 17:5. man's rod whom I *c.*
Deut 12:5. place Lord God shall *c.*, 17:10.
17:15. set king over thee . . . Lord God *c.*
30:19. life and death, . . . therefore *c.*
Josh 24:15. *c.* whom ye will serve
2 Sam 24:12. *c.* thee one of them
Neh 9:7. Lord God didst *c.* Abraham
Ps 65:4. blessed is the man whom thou *c.*
Prov 1:29. did not *c.* fear of the Lord
Isa 7:15. refuse evil and *c.* good, 16.
14:1. the Lord will yet *c.* Israel, 49:7.
56:4. *c.* the things that please me
Zech 1:17. I shall yet *c.* Jerusalem
Phil 1:22. what I shall *c.* I wot not

Heb 11:25. *choosing* affliction with people
Luke 6:13. *chose* twelve . . . named apostles
Gen 13:11. Lot *c.* plain of
Judg 10:14. the gods, . . . ye have *chosen*
1 Sam 16:8. neither hath the Lord *c.* this
1 Kings 8:48. city thou hast *c.*, Ps 132:13.
Job 36:21. iniquity *c.* rather than affliction
Prov 16:16. rather . . . *c.* than silver, 22:1.
Isa 58:5. is it such a fast that I have *c.*? 6.
Jer 8:3. death shall be *c.* rather than
33:24. two families *c.* cast off?
49:19. who is a *c.* man that, 50:44.
Matt 20:16. many called, few *c.* 22:14.
Mark 13:20. elect's sake . . . he hath *c.*
Luke 10:42. Mary hath *c.* that good part
23:35. Christ the *c.* of God,
John 15:16. have not *c.* me, . . . I you
Acts 9:15. *c.* vessel to me, 22:14.
1 Pet 2:4. *c.* of God; 9. a *c.* generation
Rev 17:14. called, and *c.* and faithful
1 Cor 1:27. God *hath c.* the foolish
Eph 1:4. —us in him before foundation
2 Chron 6:6. *I have chosen,* Isa 42. I. (Matt 12:18). Zerub . . . signet—Hag 2:23.
Ps 119:30. —way of truth; 173—precept
Isa 44:1. Israel, whom—, 41:9; 43:10.
48:10. —thee in furnace of affliction
John 13:18. I know whom—, 15:16, 19.
My chosen, Isa 43:20; 65:15. Jacob *his c.*, Ps 105:6, 43; 135:4. Isa 41:8.
CHRIST should be born, Matt 2:4.
Matt 16:16. thou art the *C.* the Son
23:8. one is your master, even *C.*, 10.
Mark 9:41. because ye belong to *C.*
Luke 2:26. not die before seeing *C.*
4:41. the devils knew he was *C.*
24:26. ought not *C.* to have *suffered*
46. it behoved *C.* to suffer and rise
John 4:25. Messias . . . which is called *C.*
7:26. that this is the very *C.*
27. when *C.* cometh, no man knoweth
41. shall *C.* come out of Galilee?
42. *C.* cometh of the seed of David
12:34. that *C.* abideth for ever: and how
Acts 8:5. Philip preached *C.* to (Samaria)
Rom 5:6. *C.* died for the ungodly
8. while yet sinners, *C.* died for us
8.9. have not the Spirit of *C.*, he is none of
10. if *C.* be in you, the body is dead
15:3. for *C.* pleased not himself; but
1 Cor 1:24. *C.* the power of God and
3:23. ye are *C.*'s, and *C.* is God's
5:7. *C.* our passover is sacrificed
15:14. if *C.* be not risen, . . . our preaching vain
16. if dead rise not, *C.* not raised
2 Cor 6:15. what concord *C.* with Belial
Gal 2:20. crucified with *C.*: *C.* liveth
3:13. *C.* hath redeemed us from curse
4:19. travail till *C.* be formed in you
Eph 2:12. ye were without *C.*, aliens
3:17. that *C.* dwell in your hearts
4:20. ye have not so learned *C.*, if so
5:14. dead, and *C.* shall give thee light
23. wife, as *C.* is head of the church; *see also* 24, 25, 32.
6:5. in singleness of heart, as unto *C.*
Phil 1:21. to me to live is *C.* and to die
3:8. all . . . but dung, that I may win *C.*
4:13. I can do all things through *C.*
Col 1:27. *C.* in you hope of glory
Rom 8:1. no condemnation . . . in *C. Jesus*
2. the law of the spirit of life in—
1 Cor 1:30. but of him are ye in—
2:2. not . . . you, save—and him crucified
2 Cor 13:5. know ye not—is in you?
Gal 3:28. ye are all one in—, 26.
5:6. in—neither circumcision nor uncircumcision
Eph 2:10. created in—unto good works
Phil 2:11. confess that—is Lord
3:3. rejoice in—no confidence in flesh
12. for which I am apprehended of—
Col 2:6. received—the Lord, 3:24.
1 Tim 1:15. —came into world to save
2 *Tim* 2:3. as a good soldier of—
3:12. will live godly in—shall suffer
Heb 13:8. —the same yesterday and to day
Rom 12:5. many, one body *in Christ*
1 Cor 15:18. fallen asleep—are perished
19. if in this life only we have hope—
2 Cor 5:17. if man be—new creature
19. God was—reconciling the world
12:2. I knew a man—above fourteen years
Gal 1:22. churches which were—
Phil 1:13. so that my bonds—are manifest in all the palace
2:1. if there be any consolation—if any
Col 1:2. saints and faithful—, Eph 1:1.
1 Thess 4:16. the dead—shall rise first
John 1:25. *that Christ,* 6:69.
Matt 16:20. *the Christ,* 26:63. Mark 8:29; 14:61. Luke 3:15; 9:20; 22:67. John 1:20, 41; 3:28; 4:29, 42; 7:41; 10:24; 11:27; 20:31
1 John 2:22; 5:1.
John 11:27. I believe that thou art *the Christ*
Rom 6:8. if we be dead *with Christ*
8:17. heirs of God and joint heirs—
Gal 2:20. I am crucified— . . . I live
Eph 2:5. quickened us together—
Phil 1:23. desire to depart and be—
Col 2:20. if ye be dead—from rudiments
3:3. dead, and your life is hid—in God
Rev 20:4. souls . . . reigned—a thousand years
Acts 26:28. almost . . . to be a *Christian*
11:26. *Christians* first at Antioch
CHURCH, Acts 14:27; 15:3, 1 Cor 4:17; 14:4, 23. 3 John 9.
Matt 16:18. this rock I will build my *c.*
18:17. tell it to *c.*: neglect to hear *c.*
Acts 2:47. the Lord added to *c.* daily
5:11. great fear came on all the *c.*
8:1. great persecution against the *c.*
11:26. assembled themselves with the *c.*
15:22. pleased elders, with the whole *c.*
1 Cor 14:4. that *c.* receive edifying
16:19. *c.* in their house, Col 4:15.
Eph 1:22. head over all . . . to the *c.*
3:10. known by *c.* . . . wisdom of God
5:24. as *c.* is subject unto Christ
25. as Christ loved the *c.* and gave
27. present to himself a glorious *c.*
32. I speak concerning Christ and the *c.*
Phil 3:6. . . . zeal, persecuting the *c.*
4:15. no *c.* communicated with me
Col 1:18. head of the body, the *c.*
24. for his body's sake, which is the *c.*

1 Tim 5:16. let not *c.* be charged
Heb 12:23. assembly and *c.* of firstborn
3 John 6. witness of charity before *c.*
Acts 7:38. *in the church,* 13:1. 1 Cor 6:4; 11:18; 12:28; 14:19, &c Eph 3:21. Col 4:16. *the church of God,* Acts 20:28. 1 Cor 1:2; 10:32; 15:9. 2 Cor 1:1. Gal 1:13. 1 Tim 3:5.
9:31. *churches rest,* 15:41. confirming the *c.*
16:5. so the *c.* established in faith
Rom 16:16. *c.* of Christ salute you
1 Cor 7:17. and so ordain I in all *c.*
14:33. as in all *c.* of the saints
34. women keep silence in the *c.*
1 Thess 2:14. followers of *c.* . . . in Judaea
2 Thess 1:4. we . . . glory in you in the *c.*
Rev 1:4. seven *c.* which are in Asia
2:7. &c. hear what the Spirit . . . to *c.*
22:16. testify these things in the *c.*
CHURL, Isa 32:5, 7.—*ish,* 1 Sam 25:3.
CIRCUIT, 1 Sam 7:16. Job 22:14. Ps 19:6.
CIRCUMCISE the flesh, Gen 17:11.
Deut 30:6. Lord will *c.* thy heart, 10:16.
Josh 5:2. *c.* again Israel, 4. Josh did *c.*
Jer 4:4. *c.* yourselves to the Lord
Gen 17:10. every male shall be *circumcised,* 14, 23, 26. Phil 3:5.
21:4. Abraham *c.* Isaac eight days old
Jer 9:25. punish all *c.* with uncircumcised
Acts 15:1. except *c.* cannot be saved
24. ye must be *c.* and keep the law
16:3. *c.* him because of the Jews
Gal 2:3. neither compelled to be *c.*
Col 2:11. in whom also ye are *c.*
John 7:22. Moses gave *circumcision*
Acts 7:8. God gave covenant of *c.*
Rom 2:25. *c.* profiteth if thou keep law
29. *c.* is that of the heart, in the spirit
3:1. what profit is there of *c.*? Much
30. which shall testify *c.* by faith
Rom 4:9. cometh this blessedness on *circumcision* only?
11. he received the sign of *c.*
15:8. Christ was minister of the *c.*
1 Cor 7:19. *c.* is nothing, but the keeping
Gal 2:7. gospel of *c.* unto Peter
5:6. neither *c.* availeth nor uncircumcision, 6:15.
Phil 3:3. we are *c.* which worship
Col 2:11. with *c.* . . . without hands
Titus 1:10. deceivers, specially of *c.*
CIRCUMSPECT, Exod 23:13. see that ye walk *circumspectly,* Eph 5:15.
CISTERN, 2 Kings 18:31. Prov 5:15. Jer 2:13. hewed *cisterns,* broken *c.*
CITY (of Cain), Gen 4:17. *see* 11:4. a *little c.* Gen 19:20. *see* Eccles 9:14.
Ps 48:2. *c.* of great King, Matt 5:35.
107.4. they found no *c.* to dwell in
127.1. except the Lord keep the *c.*
Prov 16:32. ruleth his spirit . . . taketh *c.*
Lam 1:1. How doth *c.* sit solitary
Song of Sol 3:2. I will go about the *c.* in
Isa 1:21. faithful *c.* become a harlot
22:2. a tumultuous *c.*, a joyous *c.*
25:2, *c.* an heap 26:1, a strong *c.*
33:20. look on Zion, *c.* of our solemnities
62:12. sought out, a *c.* not forsaken
Jer 3:14. take you one of a *c.*, two of a
29:7. seek peace of the *c.* (Babylon)
Amos 4:7. I rain on one *c.* not on
Zeph 2:15. this is the rejoicing *c.*
Zech 8:3. shall be called *c.* of truth
Matt 5:14. *c.* on hill cannot be hid
9:1. his own *c.* (Capernaum), *see* 4:13.
Luke 10:8. whatsoever *c.* ye enter
12. tolerable for Sodom than for that *c.*
19:41. he beheld the *c.* and wept over it
Heb 11:10. he looked for a *c.* which
16. he hath prepared for them a *c.*
12:22. to the *c.* of the living God
13:14. have here no continuing *c.*
Rev 3:12. name of the *c.* of my God
21:18. *c.* was pure gold, 23. no sun
Neh 11:1, 18. *holy city,* Isa 48:2; 52:1. Dan 9:24. Matt 4:5; 27:53. Rev 11:2; 21:2; 22:19.
Num 35:15. *c. of refuge,* Josh 21:13.
Luke 19:17. authority over ten *cities*
Rev 16:19. the *c.* of the nations fell
Luke 15:15. *citizen,* 19:14. Acts 21:39.
Eph 2:19. fellow *citizens* with the saints
CLAMOUR, Eph 4:31. Prov 9:13.
CLAY, Job 10:9; 13:12; 33:6. vessel of *c.*, Jer 18:4, *see* 2 Cor 4:7.
Job 4:19, houses of *c.* 38:14, it is turned as *c.* to the seal
Isa 41:25. on . . . as the potter treadeth *c.*
64:8. we are the *c.*, thou our potter, 45:9. Jer 18:6. Rom 9:21.
Jer 43:9. hide them in the *c.* in kiln
Dan 2:33. feet part of iron, part of *c.*
John 9:6. *c.* of spittle and anointed
Clay ground, 1 Kings 7:46. 2 Chron 4:17.
CLEAN beasts, Gen 7:2; 8:20.
Lev 10:10. between unclean and *c.* 11:47. Ezek 22:26; 44:23.
Job 14:4. who bring *c.* out of unclean, 15:14.
25:4. can he be *c.* . . . born of a woman
Ps 19:9. the fear of the Lord is *c.*
Prov 16:2. ways of man are *c.* in his own
Isa 1:16. wash you, make you *c.*; put
52:11. be ye *c.* that bear the vessels
Jer 13:27. wilt thou not be made *c.*
Ezek 36:25. sprinkle *c.* water, be *c.*
Matt 8:3. I will, be thou *clean,* Luke 5:13.
23:25. make *c.* outside of, Luke 11:39.
Luke 11:41. all things are *c.* to you
John 13:11. said he, Ye are not all *c.*
Rev 19:8. fine line, *c.* and white
Job 17:9. *clean hands,* Ps 24:4.
Ps 51:10. *clean heart,* 73:1.
18:24. *cleanness* of my hands in his sight
Amos 4:6. *c.* of teeth in all cities
Ps 19:12. *cleanse* me from secret faults
51:2. *c.* me from my sin
119:9. shall a young man *c.* his way
Jer 33:8. I will *c.* them from all sin
Ezek 36:25. from idols will I *c.* you
Matt 10:8. heal sick, *c.* the lepers
2 Cor 7:1. let us *c.* ourselves from
Eph 5:26. *c.* with washing of water
James 4:8. *c.* your hands, ye sinners
2 Chron 30:19. though not *cleansed* accor.
Ps 73:13. I have *c.* my heart in vain
Ezek 36:33. *c.* you from all iniquities
Matt 11:5. the lepers are *c.*
Luke 17:17. were there not ten *c.*?
Acts 10:15. what God hath *c.*, 11:9.
1 John 1:7. blood of Jesus Christ *cleanseth* us from all sin
CLEAR the guilty, Exod 34:7.
Ps 51:4. be *c.* when thou judgest
Song of Sol 6:10. looketh *c.* as the sun

Zech 14:6. light shall not be *c.* nor dark
CLEAVE to his wife, Gen 2:24. Matt 19:5.
Mark 10:7. Eph 5:31.
Deut 4:4. ye did *c.* to the Lord, 10:20; 11:22; 13:4; 30:20. Josh 22:5; 23:8.
Ps 137:6. tongue *c.* to the roof of my mouth
Rom 12:9. *c.* to that which is good
Ps 22:15. tongue *cleaveth* to my jaws
44:25. our belly *c.* unto the earth, 119:25.
CLIMB, 1 Sam 14:13. Joel 2:7. Luke 19:4.
Amos 9:2. though *c.* up to heaven
John 10:1. *climbeth* up some other way
CLOAK, Matt 5:40, &c. 2 Tim 4:13.
Isa 59:17. clad with zeal as a *c.*
John 15:22. have no *c.* for their sin
1 Pet 2:16. liberty *c.* of maliciousness
CLOSET, Joel 2:16. Matt 6:6.
CLOTHE, God *c.* grass, Matt 6:30.
Gen 3:21. Lord God . . . skins and *clothed*
Job 10:11. *c.* me with skin and flesh
Ps 35:26. be *c.* with shame, 132:18.
104:1. *c.* with honour and majesty
109:18. he *c.* himself with cursing
132:9. priests be *c.* with righteousness
Isa 61:10. *c.* with garments of salvation
Ezek 16:10. I *c.* thee with broidered
Zeph 1:8. *c.* with strange apparel
Zech 3:3. Joshua *c.* with filthy
Matt 11:8. *c.* in soft raiment, Luke 7:25.
25:36. naked, and ye *c.* me, 38.
2 Cor 5:2. desiring to be *c.* upon with
4. not unclothed, but *c.* upon
1 Pet 5:5 be *c.* with humility: for
Rev 3:5. be *c.* with white raiment
12:1. a woman *c.* with the sun
19:13. *c.* in vesture dipped in blood
14. *c.* in fine linen, clean and white
Job 22:6. *clothing,* 24:7. long, Mark 12:38. bright, Acts 10:30. gay, James 2:3.
Ps 45:13. her c. is of wrought gold
Prov 31:25. strength and honour her *c.*
Isa 59:17. garment of vengeance for *c.*
Matt 7:15, in sheep's *c.* 11:8, soft *c.*
CLOUD, Gen 9:13. Exod 14:20.
Exod 19:9. Lord said, I come in thick *c.*
Isa 44:22. blotted out as a thick *cloud*
1 Cor 10:1. our fathers were under the *c.*
Heb 12:1. so great a *c.* of witnesses
Rev 11:12. ascended up to heaven in a *c.*
Judg 5:4. *clouds* dropped water
2 Sam 23:4. a morning without *c.*
Ps 36:5. faithfulness reacheth to *c.*
57:10. thy truth unto the *c.* 108:4.
104:3. who maketh *c.* his chariot
Eccles 11:4. regardeth the *c.* shall not reap
Matt 24:30. coming in the *c.* of heaven, 26:64. Mark 13:26; 14:62.
1 Thess 4:17. caught up in *c.*, to meet
2 Pet 2:17. *c.* carried with a tempest
Jude 12. *c.* without water, carried about
Rev 1:7. he cometh with *c.*
CLOVEN, Deut 14:7. tongues, Acts 2:3
COAL, 2 Sam 14:7. Isa 6:6; 47:14. Lam 4:8. Ps 18:8, 12; 120:4; 140:10.
Job 41:21. his breath kindleth *coals*
Prov 6:28. can one go upon hot *c.*
25:22. heap *c.* of fire on his head, Rom 12:20.
26:21. as *c.* are to burning *c.*
Song of Sol 8:6. *c.* thereof are *c.* of fire. *See* 1 Kings 19:6 Isa 44:12, 19. Hab 3:5.
John 18:18. a fire of *c.* 21.9.
COAT, Gen 3:21; 37:3. Exod 28:4.
Song of Sol 5:3. put off *c.*; how put it on
John 19:23. the *c.* was without seam
21:7. Peter girt his fisher's *c.*
Matt 10:10. neither two *coats,* Mark 6:9.
Luke 3:11. he that hath two *c.* let him
Acts 9:39. *c.* and garments Dorcas
COLD, Gen 8:22. Job 24:7; 37:9.
Matt 24:12. the love of many shall wax *c.*
Rev 3:15. neither *c.* nor hot, 16.
COLLECTION, 1 Cor 16:1. Rom 15:26.
COME not to their secret, Gen 49:6.
Exod 20:24. where my name, I will *c.*
1 Sam 17:45. I *c.* to thee in name of
1 Chron 29:14. all things *c.* of *thee,* 12.
Job 22:21. (so) good shall *c.* unto thee
38:11. hitherto shalt thou *c.*, but no
Ps 40:7. lo I *c.*: in the volume, Heb 10:9.
65:2. to thee shall all flesh *c.*
Eccles 9:2. all things *c.* alike to all
Song of Sol 4:16. wind, *c.* thou south
Isa 1:18. *c.* let us reason together saith Lord
35:4. your God will *c.* and save you
55:1. *c.* ye to the waters, John 7:37.
3. incline your ear, and *c.* unto me
Jer 3:22. we *c.* to thee for thou art Lord
Hos 6:1. *C.* let us return unto the Lord
Mic 6:6. wherewith shall I *c.* before
Hab 2:3. it will surely *c.* it will not tarry
Mal 3:1. Lord suddenly *c.* to his temple
4:6. lest I *c.* and smite the earth
Matt 8:11. *c.* from east and west
11:3. art thou he that should *c.* or look we, Luke 7:19, 20. Gen 49:10.
28. *c.* unto me all ye that labour and
16:24. if any man will *c.* after me
17:10. say scribes Elias must first *c.*
22:4. all things ready, *c.* to marriage
Luke 7:8. I say *c.* and he cometh
14:20. married a wife, I cannot *c.*
John 1:39. *c.* and see, 46; 4:29. Rev 6:1, 3, 5, 7; 17:1; 21:9.
5:40. ye will not *c.* to me, that ye
6:44. no man can *c.* to me, except
7:37. if any man thirst, let him *c.*
14:18. not leave you, I will *c.* to
Acts 1:11. this Jesus shall so *c.* as
Acts 16:9. *come* over into . . . and help us
1 Cor 11:26. shew Lord's death till he *c.*
2 Cor 6:17. *c.* out from among them
1 Tim 4:8. promise of the life to *c.*
Heb 4:16. *c.* boldly unto the throne of
7:25. save them that *c.* to God by him
10:37. he that shall *c.* will *c.*
Rev 18:4. *c.* out of her, my people
22:17. the Spirit and the bride say, *c.*
Ps 118:26. *cometh* in name of the Lord
Isa 63:1. who is this that *c.* from Edom
Matt 3:11. he that *c.* after me is
Luke 6:47. whoso *c.*, heareth, doeth, is
John 3:31. he that *c.* from above
6:35. *c.* to me shall never hunger
37. *c.* to me, I will in no wise cast out
45. hath learned of Father *c.* unto me
Heb 11:6. that *c.* to God must believe
James 1:17. gift *c.* down from the Father
Heb 10:1. make the *comers* perfect
Ps 19:5. as bridegroom *coming* out
121:8. the Lord shall preserve thy *c.* in

Mal 3:2. who may abide day of his *c.*
Matt 24:3. what the sign of thy *c.* 27.
John 1:27. *c.* after me is preferred before
1 Cor 1:7. waiting for the *c.* of our
15:23. that are Christ's at his *c.*
1 Thess 2:19. presence of Jesus Christ at his *c.*, 3:13; 5:23.
1 Pet 2:4. to whom *c.* as to a living stone
2 Pet 1:16. power and *c.* of L.
3:12. hasting unto *c.* of day of God
1 Thess 4:15. *coming of the Lord,* 2 Thess 2:1. James 5:7, 8 [CAME.]
COMELY, 1 Sam 16:18. Job 41:12
Ps 33:1. praise is *c.* (becoming), 147:1.
Prov 30:29. yea, four are *c.* in going
Song of Sol 1:5, black but *c.* 10, cheeks *c.*
6:4. art *c.* as Jerusalem, Jer 6:2.
1 Cor 7:35, which is *c.* 12:24, *c.* parts
Isa 53:2. no form nor *comeliness*
Ezek. 16:14. perfect through my *c.*
COMFORT in affliction, Ps 119:50.
Matt 9:22. be of good *c.*, Mark 10:49.
Acts 9:31. walking in *c.* of Holy Ghost
1 Cor 14:3. to exhortation and *c.*
2 Cor 7:4. am filled with *c.* Phil 2:1, *c.* of love
Col 4:11. these only . . . a *c.* to me
Gen 5:29. this shall *c.* us
Job 7:13. my bed shall *c.* me, . . . then
Ps 23:4. thy rod and staff *c.*
Song of Sol 2:5. *c.* with apples. Judg 19:5, bread
Isa 40:1. 1 *c.* ye *c.* ye my people
51:3. Lord shall *c.* Zion, Zech 1:17.
61:2. to *c.* all that mourn, Matt 5:4.
Jer 31:13. I will *c.* and make them
Lam 1:2. she hath none to *c.* her, 21.
2 Cor 1:4. be able to *c.* them . . . by *c.*
1 Thess 4:18. *c.* one another with these
5:11. *c.* selves together, and edify one
14. *c.* feeble minded, support weak
2 Thess 2:17. Lord Jesus *c.* your hearts and
Isa 40:2. *comfortably,* Hos 2:14. 2 Sam 19:7. 2 Chron 30:22; 32:6.
Gen 24:67. Isaac was *comforted*
37:35. *refused to be c.*, Ps 77:2. *Jer 31:15. Ra(c)hel weeping*—, Matt 2:18.
Isa 49:13. Lord hath *c.* his people
54:11. tossed with tempest, not *c.*
Luke 16:25. he is *c.*, thou tormented

Rom 1:12. *c.* . . . by mutual faith both
1 Cor 14:31. one by one all be *c.*
2 Cor 1:4. wherewith we are *c.* of God
7:13. we were *c.* in your comfort
1 Thess 3:7. *comforted* over you by your faith
Job 16:2. *comforters.* Ps 69:20, no *c.*
Isa 51:12. I am he that *comforteth*
John 14:18. not leave *comfortless*
Ps 94:19. *comforts,* Isa 57:18.
COMMAND, Gen 49:33. 2 Chron 8:14.
Gen 18:19. Abraham will *c.* his children
Deut 28:8. Lord *c.* blessing, Lev 25:21.
Ps 42:8. Lord will *c.* his lovingkindness
Isa 45:11. work of my hands, *c.* me
Matt 4:3. *c.* these stones be made bread
John 15:14. if ye do whatsoever I *c.*
1 Cor 7:10. unto the married I *c.*
1 Tim 4:11. these things *c.* and teach
Ps 111:9. *commanded* his covenant
119:4. *c.* us to keep thy precepts
133:3. *c.* blessing, even life for ever
148:5. Lord *c.* and they were created
Matt 28:20. whatsoever I have *c.* you
2 Cor 4:6. God who *c.* the light to
Heb 12:20. not endure that which was *c.*
Lam 3:37. when the Lord *commandeth*
Mark 1:27, *c.* spirits. Job 9:7, *c.* sun
Acts 17:30. now *c.* all men to repent
1 Tim 4:3. *commanding* to abstain from meats, which God
Num 23:20. *commandment* to bless and
Ps 119:96. thy *c.* is exceeding broad
Prov 6:23. the *c.* a lamp; and law light
8:29. waters not pass his *c.*, Job 38:11.
Hos 5:11. willingly walked after the *c.*
Matt 22:38. is the first and great *c.*
Mark 7:9. reject *c.* of God, Matt 15:6.
John 10:18. this *c.* I received of my Father
12:50. his *c.* is life everlasting
13:34. a new *c.* give I unto you
15:12. this is my *c.* that ye love one
Rom 7:8. sin taking occasion by the *c.*
9. when the *c.* came, sin revived
1 Tim 1:5. end of the *c.* is charity
Heb 7:16. not after law of carnal *c.*

2 Pet 2:21. turn from the holy *c.*
1 John 2:7. and old *c.* which ye had, 8.
3:23. this is his *c.* that we believe
Exod 34:28. wrote ten *commandments*
Ps 111:7. all his *c.* are sure, 119:86.
112:1. delight greatly in his *c.*, 119:47.
119.6. I have respect unto all thy *c.*
19. hide not thy *c.* from me
21. which do err from thy *c.*
35. make me to go in the path of thy *c.*
48. thy *c.* which I have loved
66. I have believed thy *c.*
73. give understanding to learn thy *c.*
127, I love thy *c.* 131, I longed for thy *c.*
143, thy *c.* . . . my delights. 151, thy *c.* truth
172. all thy *c.* are righteousness
Matt 15:9. for doctrines *c.* of men
22:40. on these two *c.* hang all the law
Mark 10:19. knowest the *c.*, Luke 18:20.
Luke 1:6. walking in all the *c.* of Lord
Col 2:22. subject . . . after *c.* of men
1 John 3:24. keepeth his *c.* dwelleth
2 John 6. love . . . we walk after his *c.*
Num 15:40. *do all,—these,—my,—his, c.* Deut 6:25; 15:5; 28:1, 15; 19:9; 27:10; 30:8. 1 Chron 28:7. Neh 10:29. Ps 103:18, 20; 111:10. Rev 22:14.
COMMEND, Gen 12:15. Rom 16:1. *c.* selves, 2 Cor 3:1; 5:12; 10:12.
Luke 23:46. to thy hands I *c.* my spirit
Rom 3:5. if our unrighteousness *c.*
Acts 14:23. *commended* them to Lord on
Rom 5:8. God *commendeth* his love
1 Cor 8:8. meat *c.* us not to God
2 Cor 10:18. not he that *c.* self is approved
3:1. epistles of *commendation*
COMMISSION, Ezra 8:36. Acts 26:12.
COMMIT adultery, thou shalt not, Exod 20:14.
Deut 5:18. Matt 5:27; 19:18. Rom 13:9. Lev 5:17. Luke 18:20.
Gen 39:8, 22. *c.* (give in charge)
Job 5:8. to God would I *c.* my cause
Ps 31:5. to thy hand I *c.* my spirit
37.5. *c.* way (Prov. 16:3. *c.* works) to Lord
Luke 12:48. *c.* things worthy of stripes
16:11. who *c.* to . . . riches?
John 2:24. not *c.* himself to them
Rom 1:32. *c.* such things are worthy
1 Tim 1:18. this charge I *c.* unto

1 Pet 4:19. *c.* keeping of their souls
1 John 3:9. born of God not *c.* sin
Luke 12:48. *committed* much . . . ask
John 5:22. *c.* all judgment to the Son
1 Tim 1:11. gospel *c.* to my trust, 1 Cor 9:17. 2 Cor 5:19. Titus 1:3. Gal 2:7.
2 Tim 1:12. which I have *c.* to him
1 Pet 2:23. *c.* himself to him that
Jude 15. which they have ungodly *c.*
Ps 10:14. poor *committeth* himself
John 8:34. who *c.* sin is servant of sin
1 John 3:8. who *c.* sin is of the devil
COMMON, Num 16:29. *c.* bread, 1 Sam 21:4, 5. Jer 31:5. the *c.* people, Lev 4:27. Mark 12:37. Ezek 23:42.
Acts 2:44. had all things *c.*, 4:32.
10:15. God cleansed call not *c.* (unclean)
1 Cor 10:13. temptation *c.* to man
Titus 1:4. *c.* faith. Jude 3, *c.* salvation
Matt 28:15. *commonly,* 1 Cor 5:1.
Eph 2:12. *commonwealth* of Israel
COMMUNE with, heart, Ps 4:4. another, Luke 6:11. (of God), Exod 25:22.
COMMUNICATE to him that teacheth in all good tings, Gal 6:6.
Phil 4:14. *c.* with (share) my affliction
1 Tim 6:18. distribute, willing to *c.*
Heb 13:16. and to *c.* forget not
Gal 2:2. *communicated* that gospel
Phil 4:15. no church *c.* with me in
Eph 4:29. let no corrupt *communication,* Col 3:8.
Luke 24:17. what manner of *communications* are
1 Cor 15:33. evil *c.* . . . good manners
10:16. is it not the *communion* of the blood of Christ? *c.* of body of Christ?
2 Cor 6:14. what *c.* light with darkness?
13:14. *c.* of the Holy Ghost be with you
COMPACT(ED), Ps 122:3. Eph 4:16.
COMPANY (caravan), Gen 32:8, 21.
Ps 55:14. to the house of God in *c.*
Prov 29:3. keepeth *c.* with harlots
Song of Sol 6:13. as it were the *c.* of two armies
Acts 4:23, own *c.* 6:7, *c.* of priests
Rom 15:24. first filled with your *c.*
1 Cor 5:11. not to keep *c.*, if any
2 Thess 3:14. have no *c.* with him
Heb 12:22. an innumerable *c.* of angels
Ps 119:63. I am a *companion* of all
Prov 13:20. *c.* of fools shall be destroyed
Mal 2:14. thy *c.* and wife of covenant
Phil 2:25. Epaphroditus my *c.* in labour
Rev 1:9. your *c.* in tribulation
Ps 45:14. virgins, *companions* that
122:8. for my *c.* sakes . . . Peace be
Isa 1:23. thy princes *c.* of thieves
COMPARE God, Isa 40:18; 46:5.
2 Cor 10:12. *c.* ourselves . . . *c.* themselves
Ps 89:6. who in heaven be *compared*
Prov 3:15. not *c.* to wisdom, 8:11.
Song of Sol 1:9. *c.* my love to company
Rom 8:18. not worthy to be *c.*
1 Cor 2:13. *comparing* spiritual things with
COMPASS, circle, Exod 27:5; 38:4. *fetch a c.* 2 Sam 5:23. 2 Kings 3:9. Acts 28:13.
Ps 5:12. with favour *c.* him as with
26:6. innocency: so will I *c.* thy altar
32:10. mercy shall *c.* him about
Isa 50:11. *c.* yourselves with sparks
Jer 31:22. a woman shall *c.* a man
Hab 1:4. wicked doth *c.* the righteous
Matt 23:15. ye *c.* sea and land to
Ps 18:4. sorrow *compassed* me, 116:3.
118:10, 12. all nations *c.* me about
Jon 2:3. floods *c.* me about, 5.
Ps 139:3. thou *compassest* my path
73:6. pride *compasseth* them
Hos 11:12. Ephraim *c.* me with lies
COMPASSION, give them, 1 Kings 8:50. *See* 2 Chron 30:9.
Ps 78:38. (God) full of *c.* 86:15; 111:4; 112:4; 145:8; *bowels of c.*, 1 John 3:17. *moved with c.* (Jesus), Matt 9:36; 14:14. Mark 1:41. the lord—, Matt 18:27.
Zech 7:9. and shew mercy and c.
Deut 30:3. Lord turn captivity and *have c.*
Jer 12:15. return and—, Mic 7:19.
Lam 3:32. cause grief, yet will he—
Matt 15:32. I—on multitude, Mark 8:2.
Mark 9:22. canst do any thing—on us
Rom 9:15. will—on whom I will—
Heb 5:2. who can—on ignorant
10:34,—*of* me in bonds. 1 Pet 3:8,—one of another. Jude 22,—of some
Exod 2:6. babe wept. And she *had c.*
Matt 20:34. two blind men . . . Jesus—
Mark 5:19. friends, tell how Lord—on
Luke 7:13. Lord—and said, Weep not
15:20. off, father saw him, and—
Lam 3:22. his *compassions* fail not
COMPEL to, go a mile, Matt 5:41. —bear cross, Mark 15:21. —come in, Luke 14:23.
2 Chron 21:11. fornication and *compelled* Judah
Acts 26:11. I *c.* them to blaspheme
2 Cor 12:11. I am a fool ye *c.* me
Gal 2:3. not *c.* to be circumcised
14. *compellest* Gentiles to live as Jews
COMPLAIN, Job 7:11; 9:27; 23:2.
Lam 3:39. why doth a living man *c.*
Num 11:1. *complainers,* Jude 16.
Ps 144:14. *complaining* in streets
COMPLETE in him, Col 2:10; 4:12.
COMPREHEND, things we cannot, Job 37:5; *c.* with saints, Eph 3:18 darkness *comprehended* not, John 1:5.
Isa 40:12, *c.* dust. Rom 13:9, briefly *c.*
CONCEAL his blood, Gen 37:26.
Job 6:10. not *c.* words of Holy One, 27:11.
Prov 11:13, faithful *c.* 12:23, prudent *c.*
Ps 40:10 not *concealed* thy lovingkindness
CONCEIT, in own, Prov. 18:11; 26:5; 28:11, Rom 11:25; 12:16.
CONCEIVE, Gen 30:38. Luke 1:31.
Job 15:35. they *c.* mischief, Isa 59:4.
Ps 51:5. in sin did my mother *c.* me
Isa 7:14. a virgin shall *c.* and bear a son
33:11, *c.* chaff. 59:13, *c.* falsehood
Heb 11:11. through faith Sara *c.*
Num 11:12. *conceived* all this people?
Job 3:3. there is a man child *conceived*
Ps 7:14. hath *c.* mischief, and brought forth falsehood
Jer 49:30. *c.* a purpose against you
Matt 1:20. *c.* in her is of the Holy Ghost
Luke 1:36. Elisabeth . . . *c.* a son in old age
2:21. Jesus so named before *c.*
Acts 5:4. why hast thou *c.* in thy heart
James 1:15. lust hath *c.* it bringeth
CONCISION (a term of contempt = circumcision), Phil 3:2.

CONCLUDED (shut up) in unbelief, Rom 11:32. Gal 3:22. *c.* all under sin
Acts 21:25. *c.* that they observe no
Eccles 12:13. *conclusion* of the matter
CONCORD, 2 Cor 6:15. what *c.* hath Christ
CONCUBINE, Judg 19:1. 2 Sam 16:21. 1 Chron 1:32. 1 Kings 11:3. Dan 5:2.
CONCUPISCENCE, sinful lust, Rom 7:8. Col 3:5. 1 Thess 4:5.
CONDEMN the land in, 2 Chron 36:3.
Job 9:20. my own mouth shall *c.* me
10:2. I will say to God, do not *c.* me
Ps 37:33. nor *c.* him when judged
94:21. *c.* innocent blood, Matt 12:7.
Isa 50:9. Lord will help me, who shall *c.*?
Matt 12:41. this generation and shall *c.* it
Luke 6:37. *c.* not and ye shall not be *c.*
John 3:17. sent not Son to *c.* world
8:11. neither do I *c.* thee, go and sin no
Luke 23:40. in same *condemnation*
John 3:19. this is the *c.*, that light is
5:24. shall not come into *c.* but is
Rom 8:1. no *c.* to them . . . in Christ Jesus
5:16. judgment by one to *c.*, but free
2 Cor 3:9. the ministration of *c.*
1 Tim 3:6. fall into *c.* of the devil
James 3:1. receive the greater *c.*
5:12. swear not, lest ye fall into *c.*
Jude 4. of old ordained to this *c.*
Matt 12:37. by thy words thou shalt be *condemned*
Rom 8:3. for sin, *c.* sin in the flesh
1 Cor 11:32. not be *c.* with world
Titus 2:8. sound speech cannot be *c.*
Prov 17:15. *condemneth* just . . . abomination
Rom 8:34. who is he that *c.*? It is Christ
14:22. Happy is he he that *c.* not himself in
CONDESCEND to men, Rom 12:16.
CONFESS, Lev 5:5. Neh 1:6.
Lev 26:40. if they *c.*, 1 Kings 8:33, 35.
Ps 32:5. I will *c.* . . . and thou forgavest
Matt 10:32. shall c. me before men
Luke 12:8. him will I *c.*, Rev 3:5.
Rom 10:9. *c.* with thy mouth Lord Jesus;
James 5:16. *c.* your faults . . . and pray
1 John 1:9. if we *c.* our sins, he is faithful
4:15. *c.* Jesus is Son of God, 4:2, 3. 2 John 7.
Heb 11:13. *confessed,* John 1:20.
Prov 28:13. *confesseth* and forsaketh
Matt 3:6. in Jordan *confessing* sins
Josh 7:19. *confession,* 2 Chron 30:22. Ezra 10:11. Dan 9:4, 20.
Rom 10:10. *c.* is made to salvation
1 Tim 6:13. witnessed a good *c.*
CONFIDENCE, gold, my, Job 31:24.
Ps 65:5. *c.* of all ends of the earth
118:8. *c.* in man, Jer 2:37.
Prov 3:26. Lord be thy *c.*, 14:26.
Jer 48:13. Israel ashamed of *c.* (idols)
Ezek 29:16. no more the *c.* of Israel
Mic 7:5. put no *c.* in guide, Prov 25:19.
Eph 3:12. in whom we have access with *c.*
Phil 3:3. we have no *c.* in the flesh
Heb 3:6. if we hold fast the *confidence,* 14.
1 John 3:21. *c.* toward God, 2:28; 5:14.
Confident, 2 Cor 5:6. Phil 1:6.
CONFIRM feeble knees, Isa 35:3.
Dan 9:27. shall *c.* the covenant
Rom 15:8. *c.* the promises, Heb 6:17.
1 Cor 1:8. shall *c.* you to the end
2 Cor 2:8. *c.* your love toward him
Isa 44:26. *confirmeth* word of servant, Mark 16:20.
CONFLICT, Phil 1:30. Col 2:1.
CONFORMED to image, Rom 8:29.
Rom 12:2. be not *c.* to this world
CONFOUND language, Gen 11:7.
Jer 1:17. lest I *c.* thee before them
1 Cor 1:27. foolish things to *c.* wise
Ps 97:7. *confounded* that serve images
Jer 17:18. not be *c.*, Ps 69:6.
Ezek 16:52. *c.* and bear shame, 54.
Mic 3:7. diviners *c.* 7:16. nations be *c.*
Acts 2:6. multitude *c.* 9:22. *c.* the Jews
1 Pet 2:6. believeth shall not be *c.*
Ezra 9:7. *confusion* of face, Dan 9:7.
Ps 44:15. my *c.* is continually before
71:1. let me never be put to *c.*, 70:2.
Isa 24:10. city of c. 41:29. images are *c.*
1 Cor 14:33. God is not author of *c.*
CONGREGATION, assembly, people; tabernacle *of c.* Exod 27:21. &c.; tent—Exod 40:2; mount—Isa 14:13.
C. of Israel (especially under Moses and Joshua; frequently in Chronicles); rulers of *c.* Exod 16:22; elders of *c.* Lev 4:15; Judg 21:16; chief of *c.* Num 4:34; 250 princes famous in *c.*, men of renown, 16:2; 1:16. *see Josh 9:15; 22:30; chief fathers of c.* Num 31:26; *whole c.* Exod 16:2. Judg 21:13.
Num 14:27. this evil *c.* (generally of Exod.)
Lam 1:10. heathen not enter *c.*, Neh 13:1.
Ps 22:25. the great *c.*, 35:18; 40:9.
Mic 2:5. cast a cord by lot in *c.*
Ps 26:12. *congregations,* 68:26; 74:4.
CONIES, Ps 104:18. Prov 30:26.
CONQUER, conquering and to, Rev 6:2.
Rom 8:37. more than *conquerors*
CONSCIENCE, John 8:9. 1 Cor 8:7.
Acts 24:16. a *c.* void of offence
Rom 2:15. *c.* bearing witness, 9:1.
13:5. not . . . , for *c.* sake, 1 Cor 10:28.
2 Cor 1:12. testimony of our *c.*
1 Tim 3:9. in pure *c.*, 2 Tim 1:3.
4:2. having their *c.* seared with hot
Titus 1:15. their mind and *c.* is defiled
Heb 9:14. purge *c.* from dead works
10:2. *c.* of sins; 1 Cor 8:7. *c.* of idol
Acts 23:1. *good conscience,* 1 Tim 1:5, 19. Heb 13:18. 1 Pet 3:21.
CONSENT, Gen 34:15. with one *c.* Ps 83:5.
Luke 14:18. by *c.* Hos 6:9.
Prov 1:10. entice thee, *c.* thou not
Rom 7:16. I *c.* to law . . . good
1 Tim 6:3. if *c.* not to wholesome
Ps 50:18. *consentedst* with a thief
Acts 8:1. *consenting,* 22:20. Rom 7:16.
CONSIDER in thy heart, Deut 4:39.
Deut 32:29. O that . . . *c.* their latter end
1 Sam 12:24. *c.* how great things he
Ps 8:3. when I *c.* thy heavens
Eccles 7:13. *c.* work of God, Job 37:14.
Isa 1:3. my people doth not *c.*
5:12. neither *c.* operation of his hands
Hag 1:5. saith the Lord, *c.* your ways, 2:15.
Matt 6:28. *c.* the lilies, Luke 12:27.
2 Tim 2:7. *consider* what I say, and Lord give
Heb 3:1. *c.* Apostle and High Priest
10:24. *c.* one another to provoke to
12:3. *c.* him that endured such
Job 1:8. hast *considered* my servant, 2:3.
Ps 31:7. hast *c.* my trouble, 9:13.
77:5. have *c.* days of old, the years

Mark 6:52. *c.* not the miracle of loaves . . .
Rom 4:19. *c.* not his own body dead
Matt 7:3. *considerest* not the beam
Ps 41:1. blessed . . . *considereth* the poor
CONSIST, Col 1:17. Luke 12:15.
CONSOLATION, son of, Acts 4:36; 15:31.
Luke 2:25. waiting for *c.* of Israel
6:24. woe rich, have received your *c.*
Rom 15:5. God of *c.* grant you to
2 Cor 1:5. our *c.* aboundeth by Christ
Phil 2:1. if therefore any *c.* in Christ
Heb 6:18. might have a strong *c.*
Job 15:11. *consolations,* Isa 66:11.
CONSTRAIN, Gal 6:12. Acts 16:15.
2 Cor 5:14. for the love of Christ *constraineth*
1 Pet 5:2. not by *constraint,* but willingly
CONSUME, Deut 5:25; 7:16; 28:38.
Exod 33:3. lest I *c.* thee in the way
Ps 78:33. their days did he *c.* in vanity
Ezek 4:17. *c.* for iniquity, Ps 37:20.
2 Thess 2:8. Lord shall *c.* with the spirit of
James 4:3. *c.* it upon your lusts
Exod 3:2. bush was not *consumed*
Ps 90:7. we are *c.* by thine anger
119.139. my zeal hath *c.* me, because
Prov 5:11. thy flesh and body are *c.*
Lam 3:22. of the Lord's mercies not *c.*
Gal 5:15. not *c.* one of another
Deut 4:24. Lord *consuming* fire, Heb 12:29.
Lev 26:16. *consumption,* Deut 28:22. Isa 10:22, 23; 28:22.
CONTAIN, John 2:6. Rom 2:14.
1 Kings 8:27. heaven of heavens cannot *c.*
John 21:25. world not *c.* the books
1 Cor 7:9. if cannot *c.*, let them marry
CONTEMN God, wicked, Ps 10:13.
Ezek 21:13. if sword *c.* the rod, 10.
Ps 15:4. a vile person is *contemned*
123:3. we are filled with *contempt*
Dan 12:2. awake to shame and everlasting *c.*
Mal 1:7. table of the Lord *contemptible*
2:9. have I made you *c.* before all
2 Cor 10:10. weak, his speech *c.*
CONTEND, Deut 2:9. Job 9:3; 13:8.
Isa 49:25. I will *c.* with them that *c.*
50:8. *c.* with me. 57:16. not *c.* for ever
Jer 12:5. wearied thee, then how canst thou *c.* with horses?
Amos 7:4. the Lord God called to *c.* by fire
Jude 3. earnestly *c.* for the faith
Job 40:2. *contendeth* with the Almighty
Hab 1:3. *contention,* Acts 15:39. sharp *c.* Phil 1:16. preach Christ of *c.* 1 Thess 2:2.
Prov 13:10. by pride cometh *c.*, 22:10.
17:14. water, leave off *c.* before it be
18:6. A fool's lips enter into *c.*, and
Jer 15:10. borne me a man of *c.* to
Contentions, Prov 18:18. of wife, 19:13. *See* 23:29. 1 Cor 1:11. Titus 3:9.
Prov 21:19. *contentious* woman, 27:15. man, 26:21. Rom 2:8. 1 Cor 11:16.
CONTENT, Josh 7:7. Prov 6:35.
Phil 4:11. state . . . therewith to be *c.*
1 Tim 6:8. food and raiment let us be *c.*
Heb 13:5. be *c.* with Luke 3:14 wages
1 Tim 6:6. godliness with *contentment*
CONTINUAL burnt offering, Exod 29:42. bread, Num 4:7. stroke, Isa 14:6.
Rom 9:2. *c.* sorrow in my heart
Gen 6:5. heart was only evil *continually*
Exod 28:30. upon his heart before the Lord *c.*
Ps 34:1. his praise *c.* in my mouth
52:1. goodness of God endureth *c.*
71:3. habitation whereto I may *c.* resort
14. I will hope *c.* 73:23. *c.* with thee
Prov 6:21. bind *c.* upon thine heart
Isa 58:11. the Lord shall guide thee *c.*
Hos 12:6. turn and wait on thy God *c.*
Acts 6:4. give ourselves *c.* to prayer
Heb 13:15. sacrifice of praise to God *c.*
Ps 139:16. *continuance,* Rom 2:7.
CONTINUE, Matt 15:32. Acts 26:22.
1 Sam 12:14. *c.* following the Lord
Ps 36:10. O *c.* thy lovingkindness
102:28. children of servants shall *c.*
119:91. *c.* according to thine ordinances
John 8:31. *c.* in my word. 15:9.—love
Acts 13:43. to *c.* in the grace of God
14:22. to *c.* in the faith, 1 Tim 2:15.
Rom 6:1. shall we *c.* in sin that grace
Col 1:23. if ye *c.* in faith grounded
4:2. *c.* in prayer, and watch in same with
1 Tim 4:16. doctrine; *c.* in them: for
2 Tim 3:14. *c.* thou in things learned
Heb 13:1. let brotherly love *c.*
Rev 13:5. to *c.* forty-two months
Neh 5:16. *continued,* Dan 1:21.
Luke 6:12. *c.* all night in prayer
22:28. *c.* with me in my temptations
Acts 1:14. *c.* with one accord in prayer
2:42. *c.* stedfastly in apostles' doctrine
20:7. *c.* speech till midnight
Heb 8:9. *c.* not in my covenant
1 John 2:19. would have *c.* with us
Gal 3:10. that *continueth* not in all things
1 Tim 5:5. *c.* in supplication and prayer
Heb 7:24. this man, because he *c.* ever
James 1:25. law of liberty, and *c.*
Continuing, Jer 30:23. in prayer, Rom 12:12.
Acts 2:46. *c.* city Heb 13:14.
CONTRADICT-ING-ION, Acts 13:45. Heb 7:7. *c.* of sinners, 12:3.
CONTRARY, Ezek 16:34. walk *c.* Lev 26:21. *c.* wind, Matt 14:24. Acts 27:4.
Acts 18:13 *c.* to the law, 17:7; 23:3.
26:9. things *c.* to the name of Jesus
Rom 11:24. grafted *c.* to nature
Gal 5:17. Spirit against flesh: and . . . are *c.*
Col 2:14. of ordinances *c.* to us
1 Thess 2:15. not God, and are *c.* to all men
1 Tim 1:10. is *c.* to sound doctrine
CONTRITE heart, or spirit, Ps 34:18; 51:17. Isa 57:15; 66:2.
CONTROVERSY, Deut 17:8; 21:5; 25:1. 2 Chron 19:8. Ezek 44:24. Isa 34:8. Lord hath a *c.* Jer 25:31. Hos 4:1; 12:2. Mic 6:2.
1 Tim 3:16. without *c.* great is the
CONVENIENT, Acts 24:25. Philem 8.
Prov 30:8. feed with food *c.* for me
Rom 1:28. over to do things not *c.*
Eph 5:4. talking and jesting not *c.*
CONVERSATION (manner of life), Gal 1:13. Eph 2:3; 4:22. 2 Cor 1:12.
Ps 37:14. such as be of upright *c.*
50:23. ordereth his *c.* aright will I
Phil 1:27. *c.* be as becometh the gospel
3:20. our *c.* (citizenship) is in heaven
1 Tim 4:12. an example of believers in *c.*

Heb 13:5. *c.* without covetousness
James 3:13. shew out of good *conversation* works
1 Pet 1:15. holy in all manner of *c.*
2:12. *c.* honest among the Gentiles
3:1. won by *c.* of the wives. 2. chaste *c.*
16. accuse your good *c.* in Christ
2 Pet 2:7. filthy *c.* 3:11. in all holy *c.*

CONVERSION of Gentiles, Acts 15:3.

CONVERT, Isa 1:27. and be healed, 6:10.
James 5:19. err, and one *c.* him, 20.
Ps 51:13. sinners be *converted* to thee
Isa 60:5. abundance of sea, *c.* to thee
Matt 13:15. be *c.* and I heal, Mark 4:12.
18:3. except *c.* and become as children
Luke 22:32. when *c.* strengthen brethren
Acts 3:19. be *c.* and your sins blotted out

CONVINCE, refute, Job 32:12. Titus 1:9. convict, James 2:9. 1 Cor 14:24, &c.
John 8:46 (who) *convinceth* me of sin?

CORD, Josh 2:15. Ps 118:27. Jer 10:20. Mic 2:5. small *c.* John 2:15.
Job 30:11. loosed my *c.* (tent-*c.* life)
Eccles 4:12. threefold *c.* not quickly broken
Job 36:8. *cords* of affliction
Ps 2:3. away their *c.* 129:4. cut *c.*
Prov 5:22. *c.* of sins. Isa 5:18.—vanity
Isa 54:2. lengthen thy *c.*, strengthen
Hos 11:4. *c.* of a man, bands of love

CORN, Gen 41:49. Deut 7:13. Neh 13:5.
Deut 25:4. not muzzle ox that treadeth out *c.*, 1 Cor 9:9. 1 Tim 5:18.
Josh 5:11. eat of old *c.* of land, 12.
Job 5:26. as a shock of *c.* cometh in
Ps 65:9. thou preparest them *c.*, 13.
72:16. handful of *c.* in the earth
78:24. given them *c.* of heaven to eat
Isa 62:8. no more give *c.* to enemies
Ezek 36:29. call for *c.* and increase
Hos 2:8. I gave her *c.* . . . 9. I take my *c.*
10:11. heifer . . . loveth to tread out *c.*
Zech 9:17. how great. . . ! c. shall
Matt 12:1. to pluck the *c.* [EAR.]
John 12:24. *c.* of wheat, Mark 4:28.

CORNER, Lev 19:9. 2 Kings 11:11.
Lev 19:27. mar *c.* Jer 9:26. utmost *c.*
Prov 21:9. dwell in *c.*, Amos 3:12.
Isa 30:20. teachers removed into *c.*
Zech 10:4. out of him came forth the *c.*
Matt 6:5. pray in *c.* of streets, Prov 7:8.
21:42. *head of c.*, Acts 4:11.
Job 38:6. *c. stone,* Ps 118:22; 144:12. Isa 28:16. 1 Pet 2:6. Eph 2:20.

CORRECT son, Prov 29:17; 23:13.
Ps 39:11. with rebukes dost *c.* man
94:10. chastiseth heathen . . . shall not he *c.*?
Jer 2:19. own wickedness *c.* thee
10:24. *c.* me, 30:11. in measure, 46:28.
Heb 12:9. fathers of . . . *corrected* us, 11.
Job 5:17. happy man . . . God *correcteth*
Prov 3:12. whom the Lord loveth he *c.*
Job 37:13. whether for *correction*
Prov 3:11. but be not weary of his *c.*
22:15. rod of *c.* shall drive foolishness
Hab 1:12. established them for *c.*
2 Tim 3:16. Scripture profitable for *c.*

CORRUPT, Job 17:1. Ps 38:5.
Ps 14:1. they are *c.*, 53:1; 73:8.
Matt 6:19. moth and rust doth *c.*, 20.
7:17. *c.* tree, 12:33. tree *c.* and fruit *c.*
1 Cor 15:33. evil communications *c.*
2 Cor 2:17. not as many which *c.* word
Eph 4:22. the old man which is *c.*
1 Tim 6:5. of *c.* minds, 2 Tim 3:8.
Jude 10. in those they *corrupt* themselves
Exod 32:7. thy people *corrupted* selves, Judg 2:19.
Hos 9:9. have deeply *c.* themselves
Mal 2:8. ye have *c.* covenant of Levi
2 Cor 7:2. we have *c.* no man
1 Cor 9:25. *corruptible,* 15:53. 1 Pet 1:18, 23.
Job 17:14. *corruption,* Ps 16:10; 49:9. Isa 38:17. Dan 10:8. Jon 2:6. Acts 2:31; 13:34. Rom 8:21. 1 Cor 15:42. Gal 6:8. 2 Pet 1:4; 2:19. mount of *c.* 2 Kings 23:13.

COST, Luke 14:28. king's, 2 Sam 19:42. *c.* nothing, 24:24. 1 Chron 21:24.

COUNCIL, the Hebrew, Ps 68:27. 2 Chron 28:14 *(Sanhedrin)* Matt 5:22; 10:17; 26:59. Mark 15:1. Acts 4:5, 15, &c.

COUNSEL, ask of God, Num 27:21, references Num 31:16 *c.* of Balaam, 2 Pet 2:15.
1 Kings 12:8. *c.* of old men
Job 5:13. *c.* of froward carried headlong
12:13. Lord hath *c.* and understanding
21:16. *c.* of wicked far from me, 22:18.
Job 38:2. who is this that darkeneth *c.*? 42:3.
Ps 1:1. *c.* of ungodly. 14:6. *c.* of poor
33:10. *c.* of Lord stands for ever, Prov 19:21. Isa 46:10; in my *c.* Jer 23:22.
55:14. sweet *c.* 83:3. taken crafty *c.*
Prov 1:25. set at nought all my *c.*
8:14. *c.* is mine and sound wisdom
11:14. where no *c.* is the people fall
20:18. purpose established by *c.*
21:30. no wisdom . . . nor *c.* against the Lord
24:6. by wise *c.* make war, in multitude
27:9. sweetness . . . friend by hearty *c.*
Isa 11:2. spirit of *c.* and might
28:29. Lord . . . wonderful in *c.*, Jer 32:19.
40:14. with whom took he *c.*, Rom 11:34.
Zech 6:13. *c.* of peace between them
Luke 7:30. rejected *c.* of God against
Acts 2:23. by the determinate *c.*, 4:28.
5:38. if this *c.* be of men it will come
20:27. declare to you al the *c.* of God
Eph 1:11. after the *c.* of his own will
Ezra 4:5. *counsellor(s),* 2 Sam 15:12. 1 Chron 26:14; 27:33. Mark 15:43. 2 Chron 22:3. Job 3:14; 12:17. Dan 3:24.
Ps 119:24. thy testimonies are my *c.*
Prov 11:14. in multitude of *c.* safety
Isa 1:26. restore *c.* as at beginning
9:6. called Wonderful, *C.*, the mighty God

COUNT, Exod 12:4. Lev 23:15.
Num 23:10. who *c.* dust of Jacob, Gen 15:5.
Job 31:4. doth not he *c.* all my steps
Ps 139:18. if I *c.* them . . . more than
Acts 20:24. neither *c.* I my life dear
Phil 3:7, 8. I *c.* all things loss for Christ
13. I *c.* not to have apprehended
James 1:2. *c.* it all joy when ye fall
Gen 15:6. *counted* to him for righteousness, Ps 106:31. Rom 4:3.
Isa 40:17. *c.* to him less than nothing
Hos 8:12. law *c.* as a strange thing
Luke 21:36. *(ac) c. worthy* to escape, Acts 5:41. —suffer. 2 Thess 1:5.—of kingdom. 1 Tim 5:17.—double honour.

Heb 3:3.—more glory. 10:29. *c.* blood of covenant unholy
COUNTENANCE, Gen 4:5; 31:2.
Num 6:26. Lord lift up his *c.* on thee
1 Sam 1:18. her *c.* was no more sad
16:7. look not on his *c.* or height
Neh 2:2. why is thy *c.* sad, Eccles 7:3.
Job 29:24. light of my *c.*, Ps 4:6.
Ps 90:8. secret sins in the light of thy *c.*
Song of Sol 2:14. let me see thy *c.*
Matt 6:16. as hypocrites of a sad *countenance*
Acts 2:28. full of joy with thy *c.*
COUNTRY, far, Matt 21:33; 25:14. Mark 12:1. Luke 15:13; 19:12; 20:9. Prov 25:25.
Heb 11:14. declare plainly they seek a *c.*
16. they desire a better *c.* . . . an heavenly
2 Cor 11:26. *countrymen,* 1 Thess 2:14.
COURAGE, Josh 2:11. Acts 28:15.
Num 13:20. be of good *c.*, Deut 31:6. Josh 1:6; 10:25; 23:6. 2 Sam 10:12; 13:28. 1 Chron 22:13; 28:20. Ezra 10:4. Ps 27:14; 31:24. Isa 41:6.
COURSE(S), 1 Chron 23:6. 1 Cor 14:27.
Acts 20:24. finish my *c.* with joy
Eph 2:2. according to the *c.* of this world
2 Thess 3:1. word may have free *c.* and
2 Tim 4:7. finished my *c.*, Acts 13:25.
James 3:6. the *c.* of nature, Ps 82:5.
COURT, Exod 27:9. Isa 34:13.
Amos 7:13. Bethel . . . it is the king's *c.*
Rev 11:2. *c.* without the temple leave
Ps 65:4. dwell *in thy c.* 84:10. day—is
100:4. enter his *c.* with praise
Isa 1:12. who required, to tread my *c.*
62:9. drink it in *c.* of my holiness
1 Pet 3:8. be pitiful, be *courteous*
Acts 27:3. *courteously,* 28:7.
COVENANT, God's with Noah, Gen 9:9. Abram, 15:18. Israel, Exod 6:4. David, 2 Sam 23:5. Hag 2:23.
Gen 9:12 (bow) token of the *c.*
17:11. (circumcision)—13. in your flesh
Exod 2:24. God remembered his *c.*
24:7. book of *c.* 34:28. words of *c.*
Num 10:33. ark of *c.* Deut. 9:15. tables of *c.*
25:13. *c.* of everlasting priesthood
Judg 2:1. never break *c.* with you
1 Chron 16:15. mindful of his *c.*, Ps 105:8.
Job 31:1. I made a *c.* with mine eyes
Ps 25:14. fear him . . . shew them *c.*
50:5. made a *c.* with me by sacrifice
74:20. Have respect to the *c.*: for the
89:3. *c.* with my chosen . . . sworn to David
132:12. if thy children keep my *c.*
Prov 2:17. forgetteth *c.* of her God
Isa 28:15. your *c.* with death, 18.
42:6. give thee for a *c.* of people
54:10. nor *c.* of my peace be removed
55:3. everlasting *c.*, sure mercies of David
Jer 14:21. break not *c.* with us
31:31. I make a new *c.* with Israel
50:5. to the Lord in a perpetual *c.*
Ezek 20:37. bring into the bond of *c.*
Dan 9:27. confirm *c.* with many for one
Hos 6:7. have transgressed the *c.*
10:4. swearing falsely in making *c.*
Mal 2:4. *c.* with Levi, 14. wife of *c.*
Luke 1:72. to remember his holy *c.*
Acts 3:25. ye the children of the *c.*
Rom 9:4. adoption, and glory and *c.*
Heb 8:6. the mediator of a better *c.*, 7, 9.
C. breakers, Ps 55:20. Rom 1:31.
Gen 9:16. *everlasting covenant,* 17:7. Lev 24:8. 2 Sam 23:5. 1 Chron 16:17. Ps 105:10. Isa 24:5; 55:3; 61:8. Jer 32:40. Ezek 16:60; 37:26. Heb 13:20.
Gen 17:9, 10. *keep, keepest, keepeth covenant,* Exod 19:5. Deut 7:9, 12; 29:9; 33:9. 1 Kings 8:23; 11:11. 2 Chron 6:14. Neh 1:5; 9:32. Ps 25:10; 103:18; 132:12. Dan 9:4.
Gen 15:18. the Lord *made* a *c.* Exod 34:27. Deut 5:2. 2 Kings 23:3. Job 31:1.
Jer 31:31. *new c.*, Heb 8:8, 13; 12:24.
Gen 9:15. *remember covenant,* Exod 6:5. Lev 26:42, 45. Ps 105:8; 106:45. Ezek 16:60. Amos 1:9. Luke 1:72.
Lev 2:13. *c. of salt,* Num 18:19. 2 Chron 13:5.
Deut 17:2. *transgressed the c.* Josh 7:11, 15; 23:16. Judg 2:20. 2 Kings 18:12. Jer 34:18. Hos 6:7; 8:1.
Eph 2:12. *covenants* of promise
COVER, locusts, Exod 10:5. vail, 40:3.
Exod 21:33. dig a pit and not *c.* it
33:22. I will *c.* thee with my hand
Deut 33:12. Lord shall *c.* him all day
1 Sam 24:3. *c.* his feet, Judg 3:24.
Job 16:18. O earth *c.* not my blood
Ps 91:4. *c.* thee with his feathers
Isa 11:9. as the waters *c.* sea, Hab 2:14.
58:7. naked that thou *c.* him
Hos 10:8. *c.* us, Luke 23:30. Rev 6:16.
1 Cor 11:7. man ought not to *c.* his head
1 Pet 4:8. charity shall *c.* multitude of sins
Job 31:33. if I *covered* my transgressions
Ps 32:1. whose sin is *c.*, Rom 4:7.
Lam 3:44. *c.* thyself with a cloud
Ps 104:2. *coverest* thyself with light
73:6. violence *covereth* them as a garment
Prov 10:12. Hatred . . . love *c.* all sins
Isa 28:20. *covering,* 1 Cor 11:15
4:6. *covert,* 16:4; 32:2. Ps 61:4. Jer 25:38.
COVET, Exod 20:17. Mic 2:2.
1 Cor 12:31. *c.* earnestly the best gifts
14:39. *c.* to prophesy and forbid not
Acts 20:33. *coveted,* 1 Tim 6:10.
Prov 21:26. *coveteth,* Hab 2:9.
Ps 10:3. wicked blesseth the *covetous*
Luke 16:14. Pharisees who were *c.*
1 Cor 5:10. not company . . . with *c.*, 11
6:10. nor *c.* inherit kingdom of God
1 Tim 3:3. bishop must not be *c.*
2 Tim 3:2. in last days *c.*, boasters
2 Pet 2:14. exercised with *c.* practices
Exod 18:21. hating *covetousness*
Ps 119:36. incline my heart to thy testimonies and not to *c.*
Ezek 33:31. heart goeth after their *c.*
Luke 12:15 beware of *c.*: for man's
Col 3:5. *c.* which is idolatry, Eph 5:5.
Heb 13:5. conversation without *c.*
CRAFT, Dan 8:25. Mark 14:1. Acts 18:3; 19:25; *craftsman,* Rev 18:22.
Job 5:12. disappoint devices of *crafty*
15:5. choosest tongue of the *c.*
5:13. *craftiness,* 1 Cor 3:19. Luke 20:23. 2 Cor 4:2. Eph 4:14.
CREATE, Gen 1:1, &c. Deut 4:32.
Ps 51:10. *c.* in me a clean heart
Isa 4:5. *c.* on every dwellingplace
45:7. I form light and *c.* darkness
57:19. I *c.* the fruit of the lips, peace
65:18. rejoice in what I *c.*: I *c.*. Jerusalem
Ps 102:18. people which shall be *created*
104:30. forth thy spirit, they are *c.*
Isa 43:7. I have *c.* him for my glory
Jer 31:22. *c.* new thing in the earth

D

77:2. in the—I sought the Lord, *see* 86:7.
Isa 37:3. This *d.* is a—and of rebuke, and of blasphemy
Ezek 7:7. time is come,—is near
Nah 1:7. Lord is good, a strong hold in—
Hab 3:16. I might rest in—
Zeph 1:15. a—distress, desolation
Job 8:9. *days* on earth as a shadow
14:1. of few *d.* and full of trouble
32:7. *d.* should speak, and multitude
Ps 90:12. teach us to number our *d.*
Prov 3:16. length of *d.* is in right
Eccles 7:10. former *d.* better than
11:8. remember *d.* of darkness; many
12:1. while the evil *d.* come not
Jer 2:32. forgotten me *d.* without
Gal 4:10. observe *d.*, months, and years
Eph 5:16. because the *days* are evil
1 Pet 3:10. love life and see good *d.*
Gen 49:1. *last days,* Isa 2:2. Mic 4:1. Acts 2:17. 2 Tim 3:1. Heb 1:2. James 5:3. 2 Pet 3:3.
Num 24:14. *latter days,* Deut 31:29. Jer 23:20; 30:24. Dan 10:14. Hos 3:5.
Job 10:20, *my days,* 17:1, 11.
7:6. —are swifter than a shuttle
16. let me alone,—are vanity
Ps 39:4. to know end, and measure of—
102:3. —are consumed like smoke
11. —like shadow, 23. shortened—
Isa 39:8. peace and truth in—
Jer 20:18. —are consumed with shame
Job 9:33. *daysman,* or umpire
38:12. *dayspring,* Luke 1:78.
2 Pet 1:19. *day star* arise in your hearts
Ps 61:8. *daily* perform my vows
Prov 8:34. watching *d.* at my gates
Isa 58:2. seek me *d.* and delight in
Acts 2:47. added to church *d.* . . . saved
Heb 3:13. exhort one another *d.*
DEACON, Phil 1:1. 1 Tim 3:8, &c.
DEAD, Gen 20:3; 23:3.
Num 16:48. stood between *d.* and living
1 Sam 24:14. after a *d.* dog, . . . flea
Ps 88:10. shall *d.* arise and praise
115:17. the *d.* praise not the Lord
Eccles 9:5. the *d.* know not any thing
10:1. *d.* flies cause the ointment to
Matt 8:22. let the *d.* bury their *d.*
22:32. not God of *d.* but of living, 31.
Luke 8:52. she is not *d.* but sleepeth
John 5:25. *d.* hear voice of Son of God
11:25. though *d.* yet shall he live
Rom 6:8. *d.* with Christ, 11. *d.* to sin
Gal 2:19. I through law *d.* to the law
Eph 2:1. who were *d.* in trespasses
Col 2:13. being *d.* in your sins
1 Thess 4:16. *d.* in Christ rise first
2 Tim 2:11. *d.* with him, we shall live
Heb 11:4. being *d.* yet speaketh
Rev 14:13. blessed are *d.* . . . . in the Lord
Ps 17:9. *deadly,* James 3:8. Rev 13:3.
DEAF, Exod 4:11. Ps 38:13. Isa 29:18; 35:5. Mic 7:16. Mark 7:32.
Lev 19:14. thou shalt not curse the *d.*
Isa 42:18. hear, ye *d.* and look, ye blind
19. or *d.* as my messenger that I sent?
43:8. and the *d.* people that have ears
Matt 11:5. *d.* hear, dead are raised, Mark 7:37.
DEATH, Gen 21:16. Exod 10:17.
Num 23:10. let me die *d.* of the righteous
Deut 30:15. set before you life and *d.*
Ps 6:5. in *d.* no remembrance of thee
68:20. to Lord belong issues from *d.*
73:4. have no bands in their *d.*: but
89:48. liveth and shall not see *d.*
116:15. precious . . . Lord is *d.* of saints
118:18. not given me over to *d.*
Prov 2:18. her house inclineth to *d.*
8:36. all they that hate me love *d.*
18:21. *d.* and life in power of tongue
Eccles 7:26. more bitter than *d.* woman
8:8. no man . . . hath power in the day of *d.*
Isa 25:8. swallow up *d.* in victory
28:15. We . . . made covenant with *d.*
38:18. *d.* cannot celebrate thee
Jer 8:3. *d.* chosen rather than life
21:8. I set before you way of life, way of *d.*
Hos 13:14. O *d.* I will be thy plagues
Matt 16:28. not taste of *d.*, Luke 9:27.
Matt 26:38. sorrowful even unto *death*
John 5:24. from *d.* to life, 1 John 3:14.
8:51. he shall *never see d.*, 52.
12:33. what *d.* he should die, 21:19.
Acts 2:24. loosed the pains of *d.*
Rom 5:12. sin entered, and *d.* by sin
6:5. planted in the likeness of his *d.*
9. *d.* hath no more dominion over
21. for the end of those things is *d.*
7:5. to bring forth fruit unto *d.*
8:2. free from law of sin and *d.*
6. for to be carnally minded is *d.*
38. *d.* nor life shall separate us from
1 Cor 3:22. or life, or *d.*, or things
11:26. ye shew Lord's *d.* till he come
15:21. by man came *d.*, by man also
54. *d.* is swallowed up in victory
55. O *d.* where is thy sting, Hos 13:14.
56. sting of *d.* is sin, and strength
2 Cor 1:9. sentence of *d.* in ourselves
10. deliver from so great a *d.*, and doth
2:16. to one . . . savour of *d.* unto *d.*
4:11. delivered to *d.* for Jesus' sake
12. *d.* worketh in us, but life in you
Phil 2:8. obedient to *d.* . . . the *d.* of cross
Heb 2:9. taste *d.* for every man
15. through fear of *d.* are subject to
11:5. should not see *d.*, Luke 2:26.
James 1:15. sin finished bringeth *d.*
1 Pet 3:18. put to *d.* in the flesh
1 John 5:16. a sin unto *d.*, 17. not—
Rev 1:18. I have the keys of hell and *d.*
2:10. be faithful unto *d.* and I will
20:6. on such second *d.* hath no power
21:4. there shall be no more *d.* nor
DEBATE, (plead) Prov 25:9. Isa 27:8. (contention) Isa 58:4. Rom 1:29. 2 Cor 12:20.
DEBT, Rom 4:4. Matt 6:12; 18:27. Ezek 18:7. *debtor,* Gal 5:3. Rom 1:14; 8:12; 15:27. Luke 7:41. Matt 6:12.
DECEASE, Luke 9:31. 2 Pet 1:15.
DECEIT, Jer 5:27; 9:6, 8.
Ps 72:14. redeem soul from *d.*
101:7. worketh *d.* shall not dwell
Prov 20:17. bread of *d.* is sweet to man
Isa 53:9. any *d.* in his mouth
Jer 8:5. they hold fast *d.* and refuse
Col 2:8. spoil through vain *d.*
Ps 35:20. *deceitful,* 109:2. Prov 11:18; 14:25; 23:3; 27:6.
5:6. abhor bloody and *d.* man
55:23. *d.* men shall not live half their days
78:57. turn like a d. bow, Hos 7:16.
52:4. Mic 6:12. Zeph 3:13.
Jer 17:9. heart *d.* above all things
Eph 4:22. according to the *d.* lusts
Ps 24:4. *deceitfully,* Jer 48:10. Job 13:7. 2 Cor 4:2.

Matt 13:22. *deceitfulness* of riches
DECEIVE, 2 Kings 4:28; 18:29.
Prov 24:28. *d.* not with thy lips
Matt 24:4. take heed no man *d.* you
24:24. if possible *d.* the very elect
1 Cor 3:18. let no man *d.* himself
1 John 1:8. if we say . . . no sin, we *d.* ourselves
Deut 11:16. heart be not *deceived*
Job 12:16. *d.* and the deceiver are
Isa 44:20. a *d.* heart hath turned
Jer 20:7. O Lord, thou hast *d.* me
Ezek 14:9. if prophet be *d.*, I Lord *d.*
Obad 3. thy pride hath *d.* thee
Rom 7:11. sin *d.* me, and by it slew me
1 Tim 2:14. Adam was not *d.* but
2 Tim 3:13. *deceiving* and being *d.*
Gen 27:12. Mal 1:14. *deceiver,* Matt 27:63. 2 John 7. 2 Cor 6:8. Titus 1:10.
Prov 26:19. *deceiveth,* Rev 12:9.
Gal 6:3. when nothing, *d.* himself
James 1:26. *d.* his own heart, 22.
DECENTLY, 1 Cor 14:40.
DECLARE (make known), Gen 41:24. Isa 42:9.
Ps 22:22. I will *d.* thy name unto brethren
38:18. I will *d.* my iniquity and
50:16. what hast . . . to do to *d.* my statutes
78:6. may *d.* them to their children
145:4. shall *d.* thy mighty acts
Isa 3:9. they *d.* their sin as Sodom
53:8. who shall *d.* his generation
Acts 17:23. worship, him *d.* I unto
20:27. not shunned to *d.* all counsel
Rom 3:25. to *d.* his righteousness
Heb 11:14. say such things *d.* plainly
1 John 1:3. seen and heard *d.* we
Rom 1:4. *declared* to be the Son of God
Amos 4:13. *declareth* to man his thought
DECLINE, swerve, Deut 17:11. Ps 44:18.
DECREE, 2 Chron 30:5. of Nebuchadnezzar, Dan 3:29. Cyrus, Ezra 5:13. Darius, 6:1. Artaxerxes, 7:21. Ahasuerus (Xerxes), Esther 3:15. *Esther,* 9:32. Augustus, Luke 2:1.
Ps 2:7. I will declare the *d.*
Prov 8:15. by me . . . princes *d.* justice
Jer 5:22. bound of sea by a perpetual *d.* Prov 8:29. *See* Ps 148:6. Job 28:26.
Dan 4:17. *d.* of the watchers. *See* 24.
Zeph 2:2. before the *d.* bring forth
Isa 10:22. *decreed,* 1 Cor 7:37.
10:1. *decrees,* Acts 16:4; 17:7.

DEDICATE, Deut 20:5. 2 Sam 8:11. 1 Chron 26:20, 26, 27. Ezek 44:29.
Num 7:84. *dedication,* 2 Chron 7:9. Ezra 6:16, 17. Neh 12:27. John 10:22.
DEED, Judg 19:30. 2 Sam 12:14.
Rom 15:18. obedient by word and *d.*
Col 3:17. whatsoever ye do in word or *d.*
1 John 3:18. love in *d.* and in truth
Ps 28:4. give them according to their *deeds,* Jer 25:14. Rom 2:6. *See* Luke 23:41. 2 Cor 5:10.
Neh 13:14. wipe not out my good *d.*
John 3:19. because their *d.* were evil
Rom 3:20. by *d.* of law no flesh justified
8:13. mortify *d.* of body, Col 3:9.
2 John 11. partaker of his evil *d.*
DEEP, Gen 1:2; 7:11. Job 38:30.
Ps 36:6. thy judgments a great *d.*
42:7. *d.* calleth unto *d.* at the noise
1 Cor 2:10. yea, the *d.* things of God
2 Cor 11:25. I have been in the *d.*
Isa 31:6. *deeply* revolted, Hos 9:9.
Mark 8:12. sighed *d.* in spirit
DEFAME, 1 Cor 4:13. Jer 20:10.
DEFENCE, 2 Chron 11:5. Isa 19:6.
Num 14:9. their *d.* is departed
Job 22:25. the Almighty shall be thy *d.*
Ps 7:10; 59:9. God is my *d.*, 16, 17; 62:2, 6; 89:18; 94:22.
Eccles 7:12. wisdom is a *d.*, money is a *d.*
Isa 4:5. on all the glory shall be *d.*
33:16. place of *d.* the munitions of
DEFER, Isa 48:9. Prov 13:12; 19:11.
D. not, Eccles 5:4. Dan 9:19.
DEFILE land, Lev 18:25. Isa 24:5.
Dan 1:8. would not *d.* himself
Matt 15:18. they *d.* the man, 20.
1 Cor 3:17. if any *d.* temple of God
Mark 7:2. *defiled* hands, *see* Song of Sol 5:3.
Titus 1:15. mind and conscience is *defiled*
Heb 12:15. (by) bitterness many *d.*
Rev 3:4. have not *d.* their garments
21:27. not enter any thing that *defileth*
DEFRAUD, Lev 19:13. *See* Mark 10:19.
1 Sam 12:3. whom have I *defrauded?* 2 Cor 7:2.
1 Cor 6:7. law . . . why not rather be *d.*
DELAY, Exod 32:1. not *d.* 22:29. Acts 9:38.
Ps 119:60. I *delayed* not to keep
Matt 24:48. my lord *delayeth* coming

DELICATE, (dainty), Jer 51:34 (luxurious),
Deut 28:56. Isa 47:1. Jer 6:2. Mic 1:16. *delicately,* 1 Sam 15:32. Prov 29:21. Lam 4:5. Luke 7:25.
DELIGHT, Ps 1:2. his *d.* is in the law of God, 119:92.
16:3. saints in whom is all my *d.*
40:8. I *d.* to do thy will, O my God
94:19. thy comforts *d.* my soul
Prov 11:1. just weight *his d.* 20. upright—. 15:8. prayer of upright—
Song of Sol 2:3. under his shadow with *d.*
Isa 1:11. I *d.* not in blood of bullocks
Jer 9:24. in these things I *d.* saith Lord
Gen 34:19. *delight* in Jacob's daughter
Num 14:8. If Lord—us, then he will bring
Deut 10:15. Lord had a—thy fathers
1 Sam 15:22. hath Lord as great—offerings
2 Sam 24:3. Why doth the king—this thing?
Job 22:26. thy—the Almighty, 27:10.
Isa 55:2. eat . . . good let your soul—
58:2. take—approaching to God
Rom 7:22. I—law of God . . . but see
2 Sam 22:20. *delighted in* me. 1 Kings 10:9.
Esther 2:14. except the king—her, that
Ps 22:8. deliver him, seeking he—him
109:17. he *d. not in* blessing, so let
Esther 6:6. king *delighteth* to honour,
Ps 147:10. he *d.* not in strength of horse
Prov 3:12. as father son in whom he *d.*
Isa 42:1. elect in whom my soul *d.*
62:4. Hephzibah, Lord *d.* in thee
Mic 7:18. because he *d.* in mercy
Prov 8:31. my *delights* with sons of men
Song of Sol 7:6. how pleasant, O love, for *d.*
Mal 3:12. ye shall be a *delightsome* land
DELIVER, Exod 3:8; 5:18.
Job 5:19. *d.* thee in six troubles
10:7. none can *d.* out of thy hand
Ps 33:19. to *d.* their soul from death
50:15. I will *d.* thee, and thou, 91:15.
56:13. wilt thou not *d.* my feet
74:19. *d.* not the soul of thy turtle
Eccles 8:8. shall wickedness *d.* those
Ezek 14:14. should *d.* but own souls
34:10. I will *d.* my flock from their mouth

Dan 3:17. our God is able to *d.* us
Hos 11:8. how shall I *d.* thee, Israel
Rom 7:24. shall *d.* me from body
1 Cor 5:5. to *d.* such a one to Satan
2 Tim 4:18. Lord shall *d.* me from
Heb 2:15. *d.* them who through fear
2 Pet 2:9. Lord knows to *d.* godly
Prov 28:26. walketh wisely shall be *delivered*
Isa 38:17. love to soul, *d.* it from pit
49:24, 25. prey . . . lawful captive *d.*?
Jer 7:10. *d.* to do all abominations
Ezek 3:19. hast *d.* thy soul, 21; 33:9.
Dan 12:1. thy people shall be *d.*
Joel 2:32. call on name of Lord . . . be *d.*
Mic 4:10. Babylon, there shalt thou be *d.*
Matt 11:27. all *d.* to me of my Father
Acts 2:23. *d.* by determinate counsel
Rom 4:25. who was *delivered* for our offences
7:6. now we are *d.* from the law, that
8:32. (God) *d.* him up for us all
2 Cor 1:10. who *d.* us from so great a death, and doth *d.*, and will *d.* us
4:11. *d.* to death for Jesus' sake
1 Thess 1:10. *d.* us from wrath to come
1 Tim 1:20. whom I have *d.* to Satan
Jude 3. faith once *d.* to the saints
2 Kings 5:1. given *deliverance.* 13:17. 2 Chron 12:7. Esther 4:14. Ps 32:7; 44:4. Joel 2:32. Obad 17. Luke 4:18.
Gen 45:7. *great deliverance,* Judg 15:18. 1 Chron 11:14. Ps 18:50.
Ezra 9:13. given us such *d.* as this
Heb 11:35. tortured, not accepting *d.*
DELUSION, 2 Thess 2:11. Isa 66:4.
DEMAND (requirement), Dan 4:17.
DEMONSTRATION, 1 Cor 2:4.
DEN, Job 37:8. Ps 104:22. (refuge) Judg 6:2. Heb 11:38. Rev 6:15.
Jer 9:11. *den of dragons,* 10:22.
Ps 10:9. *den of lions,* Song of Sol 4:8. Dan 6:7, 24. Amos 3:4. Nah 2:12.
Jer 7:11. *den of robbers*
Matt 21:13. Mark 11:17. *den of thieves*
DENY, 1 Kings 2:16. Job 8:18.
Prov 30:9. lest I be full, and *d.* thee
Matt 10:33. shall *d.* me before men
16:24. let him *d.* himself and take up
26:34. before the cock crow thou shalt *d.* me, 75. Mark 14:30, 72.
Matt 26:35. I not *d.* thee, Mark 14:31.
2 Tim 2:12, if we *d.* him, he will *d.* us
Titus 1:16. but in works they *d.* him
1 Tim 5:8. hath *denied* the faith
Rev 2:13. hast not *d.* my faith
Titus 2:12. *denying* ungodliness and worldly
2 Pet 2:1. *d.* Lord that bought them
DEPART from us, Job 21:14; 22:17.
Hos 9:12. woe when I *d.*, Judg 16:20.
Matt 7:23. *d.* from me, ye that work
25:41. *d.* from me, ye cursed, into
Luke 2:29. lettest thy servant *d.* in peace
5:8. *d.* from me . . . a sinful man, O Lord
Phil 1:23. having a desire to *d.* and
1 Tim 4:1. some shall *d.* from faith
Ps 18:21. not wickedly *departed* from my God, 119:102. 2 Sam 22:22.
D. from evil, Ps 34:14; 37:27. Prov 3:7; 13:19; 14:16; 16:6, 17. to—is understanding, Job 28:28.
Isa 59:15. that—makes himself prey
Acts 20:29. after my *departing,* wolves
Heb 3:12. unbelief, in *d.* from living God
2 Tim 4:6. *departure,* Ezek 26:18.
DEPTH, Job 28:14; 38:16. Prov 8:27. Matt 18:6. Mark 4:5.
Rom 8:39. height nor *d.* . . . separate us
Eph 3:18. breadth, length, *d.*, height
Exod 15:5, 8. *depths,* Ps 68:22; 71:20; 130:1. Prov 3:20; 9:18.
Mic 7:19. cast sins into *d.* of sea
Rev 2:24. have not known *d.* of Satan
DERISION, Job 30:1. Ps 2:4; 44:13; 59:8; 119:51. Jer 20:7, 8.
DESCEND (God), Exod 19:18; 33:9.
Ps 49:17. glory not *d.* after him
Isa 5:14. rejoiceth shall *d.* into it
1 Thess 4:16. Lord *d.* from heaven
Gen 28:12. angels of God ascending and *descending,* John 1:51.
Matt 3:16. the Spirit of God *d.*, Mark 1:10. John 1:32, 33.
DESERT (described), Jer 2:6;—(arid, *see* Jer 17:6.). *desert* blossom as the rose, Isa 35:1. make rivers in *d.* 35:6; 43:19. set in *d.* fir tree, 41:19. *d.* like garden of Lord, 51:3. (trackless) in *d.* highway, Isa 40:3. *see* Matt 3:3. towers in *d.*, wells, 2 Chron 26:10.
Mark 1:45. Jesus . . . was without in *d. place*
Luke 1:80. in *deserts* till day of shewing
Heb 11:38. wandered in *d.* and mountains
D. of the sea (Babylonia), Isa 21:1.
D. (Heb. pasture ground) *of Wanderings,* Exod 3:1; 5:3. (described) Jer 2:6. *see* Ps 78:40, &c. John 6:31.
Wild beasts of d. Isa 13:21, &c. asses in *d.* Job 24:5. owl of *d.* Ps 102:6. foxes in *d.* Ezek 13:4.
DESIRE, whole, 2 Chron 15:15. Deut 18:6.
Gen 3:16. *d.* shall be to thy husband
Exod 34:24. nor any man *d.* thy land
Neh 1:11. who *d.* to fear thy name
Job 14:15. wilt have a *d.* to the work of
21:14. we *d.* not knowledge of thy ways
Ps 38:9. all my *d.* is, 2 Sam 23:5.
145:16. satisfieth *d.* of every living thing
Prov 10:24. *d.* of righteous granted
11:23. *d.* of righteous is only good
13:19. *d.* accomplished is sweet
Eccles 12:5. *d.* fail because man goeth
Isa 26:8. *d.* of our souls is to thy name
Hag 2:7. the *d.* of all nations shall
Luke 22:15. with *d.* I have desired
James 4:2. *d.* . . . and cannot obtain
Rev 9:6. *d.* to die, and death shall flee
Ps 19:10. more to be *desired* are
27:4. one thing have I *d.* of the Lord
Isa 26:9. with my soul have I *d.* thee
Jer 17:16. neither have I *d.* woeful day
Hos 6:6. I *d.* mercy, not sacrifice
Ps 37:4. give *desires* of thine heart
Eph 2:3. fulfilling *d.* of the flesh
Ps 51:6. thou *desirest* truth in the
16. thou *d.* not sacrifice, else would
Job 7:2. servant earnestly *desireth*
Ps 34:12. what man *d.* life and loveth
68:16. hill which God *d.* to dwell in
Prov 12:12. wicked *d.* net of evil men
13:4. soul of sluggard *d.* and hath not
21:10. soul of wicked *d.* evil.
DESOLATE, 2 Sam 13:20. Job 15:28; 16:7. Ps 25:16. Isa 49:21; 54:1. Matt 23:38. Rev 17:16.
Isa 49:6. *desolations,* 61:4. Jer 25:9, 12. Ezek 35:9. Dan 9:2, 18, 26.
DESPAIR, 2 Cor 4:8; 1:8. Eccles 2:20.
Job 6:26. *desperate,* Isa 17:11.
Jer 17:9. *desperately* wicked

DESPISE my statutes, Lev 26:15.
1 Sam 2:30. that *d.* me be lightly
Job 5:17. *d.* not the chastening of the Almightly, Prov 3:11.
Ps 102:17. will not *d.* their prayer
Prov 23:22. *d.* not mother when old
Amos 5:21. I *d.* your feast days
Matt 6:24. hold to one, and *d.* the other
Rom 14:3. *d.* him that eateth not
1 Tim 4:12. no man *d.* thy youth
Gen 16:4. mistress was *despised* in
2 Sam 6:16. she *d.* him in her heart
Prov 12:9. is *d.* and hath a servant
Isa 53:3. he is *d.* and rejected, Ps 22:6.
Zech 4:10. who *d.* day of small things
Luke 18:9. righteous and *d.* others
Heb 10:28. that *d.* Moses' law died
Acts 13:41. *despisers,* 2 Tim 3:3.
Rom 2:4. *despisest* riches of goodness
Job 36:5. God *despiseth* not any
Prov 11:12. void of wisdom *d.* his neighbour; 14:21. that—sinneth
13:13. whoso *d.* the word shall be destroyed: but he
15:32. refuseth instruction *d.* his soul
19:16. he that *d.* his ways shall die
30:17. eye . . . *d.* to obey his mother
Isa 33:15. *d.* gain of oppression
Luke 10:16. *d.* you, *d.* me *d.* him
1 Thess 4:8. *d.* not man but God
Heb 12:2. *despising* the shame
10:29. done *despite* to the Spirit of grace
DESTROY, Sodom, Gen 19:13.
Ps 101:8. I will *d.* the wicked of land
Prov 1:32. prosperity of fools *d.*
Eccles 7:16. why shouldest *d.* thyself
Matt 5:17. not come to *d.* but to
21:41. miserably *d.* those wicked men
John 2:19. *d.* this temple, and I
Rom 14:15. *d.* not him with thy meat
20. for meat *d.* not work of God
1 Cor 3:17. defile temple of God shall God *d.*
6:13. God shall *d.* both it and them
James 4:12. able to save and to *d.*
1 John 3:8. might *d.* works of the devil
Hos 4:6. *destroyed* for lack of knowledge
13:9. Israel, thou hast *d.* thyself
2 Cor 4:9. cast down, but not *d.*
Job 15:21. *destroyer,* Ps 17:4. Prov 28:24. Jer 4:7. 1 Cor 10:10.
Shall be destroyed, Esther 4:14. wicked, Ps 37:38; 92:7. Prov 13:20; 29:1. Aven, Hos 10:8. death, 1 Cor 15:26.
Dan 2:44. kingdom . . . never be *d.*
Deut 7:23. *destruction,* 32:24.
Job 5:22. at *d.* and famine shall laugh
26:6. *d.* before him hath no covering
31:23. *d.* from God was a terror to me
Ps 90:3. thou turnest man to *d.*
91:6. *d.* that wasteth at noonday
Prov 10:29. *d.* shall be to workers of iniquity, 21:15. Job 21:30; 31:3.
15:11. Hell and *d.* are before the Lord
16:18. pride goeth before *d.*
18:12. before *d.* . . . heart is haughty
27:20. hell and *d.* are never full
Jer 4:20. *d.* upon *d.* is cried, for
Hos 13:14. O grave, I will be thy *d.*
Matt 7:13. the way, that leadeth to *d.*
Rom 3:16. *d.* and misery are in their ways
1 Cor 5:5. for the *d.* of the flesh
2 Cor 10:8 not for your *d.*, 13:10.
1 Thess 5:3. sudden *d.* cometh on them
2 Pet 2:1. bring on selves swift *d.*
3:16. wrest . . . scriptures to their own *d.*
DETERMINED, 2 Chron 25:16. Job 14:5. Isa 10:23; 28:22. Dan 9:24. Acts 2:23; 4:28; 17:26. 1 Cor 2:2.
DETESTABLE, Deut 7:26. Jer 16:18. Ezek 5:11; 7:20; 11:18; 37:23.
DEVICE, Eccles 9:10. Job 5:12. Ps 33:10. Prov 1:31; 12:2; 14:17; 19:21. Jer 18:11, 12, 18. 2 Cor 2:11.
DEVIL, Matt 4:5; 8:16; 9:32.
Matt 4:1. to be tempted of the *d.*
13:39. the enemy that sowed is the *d.*
John 6:70. twelve, and one of you is a *d.*
7:20. thou hast a *d.*, 8:48.
8:44. of your father the *d.*, Acts 13:10.
13:2. *d.* having now put into, *see* 27.
Eph 4:27. neither give place to *d.*
1 Tim 3:6. fall into condemnation of *devil*
2 Tim 2:26. recover out of snare of *d.*
James 4:7. resist *d.* and he will *flee*
1 Pet 5:8. your adversary the *d.*
1 John 3:8. to destroy the works of *d.*
10. children of God and children of *d.*
Rev 2:10. the *d.* shall cast some of
Lev 17:7. sacrifice to *devils,* Deut 32:17.
2 Chron 11:15. priests for *d.* (satyrs)
Ps 106:37. sacrificed their sons to *d.*
Matt 4:24. which were possessed with *d.*, 8:16, 28:33. Luke 4:41; 8:36.
10:8. raise the dead, cast out *d.*
Mark 16:9. cast . . . seven *d.*, Luke 8:2.
Luke 10:17. even *d.* are subject to us
1 Tim 4:1. heed to . . . doctrines of *d.*
James 2:19. *d.* believe and tremble
DEVISE not evil against, Prov 3:29.
Prov 14:22. do they not err that *d.* evil
Jer 18:18. *d.* devices against Jeremiah
Mic 2:1. woe to them that *d.* iniquity
Prov 16:9. a man's heart *deviseth* his ways
DEVOTED, Lev 27:21, 28. Num 18:14.
Ps 119:38. servant is *d.* to thy fear
Acts 17:23. I beheld your *devotions*
DEVOUR, Gen 49:27. Isa 1:7; 9:12.
Prov 30:14. to *d.* the poor off the earth
Matt 23:14. ye *d.* widows' houses
2 Cor 11:20. if a man *d.* you
Gal 5:15. if ye bite and *d.* one another
Heb 10:27. which *d.* the adversaries
1 Pet 5:8. seeking whom he may *d.*
Isa 24:6. curse *devoured* the earth
Jer 3:24. shame hath *d.* the labour
50:17. Israel the king of Assyria hath *d.*
Hos 7:7. *d.* judges. 9. *d.* strength
Mal 3:11. I will rebuke *devourer*
Exod 24:17. *devouring fire,* Isa 29:6; 30:27, 30; 33:14. *d.* words, Ps 52:4.
DEVOUT, Luke 2:25. Acts 2:5; 8:2; 10:2, 7; 13:50. women, 17:4, 17; 22:12.
DEW, Gen 27:28. distil as, Deut 32:2. of youth, Ps 110:3. of herbs, Isa 26:19.
Hos 6:4. goodness is as the early *d.*
14:5. I will be as *d.* to Israel
Mic 5:7. Jacob . . . as *d.* from Lord
DIADEM, Job 29:14. Isa 28:5; 62:3.
DIAL of Ahaz, 2 Kings 20:11. Isa 38:8.
DIE, Gen 6:17. Exod 20:19. Num 16:29.
Gen 2:17. thou shalt surely *d.*, 20:7. 1 Sam 14:44; 22:16. 1 Kings 2:37, 42. Jer 26:8. Ezek 3:18; 33:8, 14.
Gen 3:4. ye shall not surely *d.*
Job 14:14. if a man *d.* shall he live again?
Ps 82:7. but ye shall *d.* like men
Prov 23:13. if . . . rod, he shall not *d.*
Eccles 3:2. time to *d.* 7:17. why *d.* before
Isa 22:13. to-morrow we shall *d.*

Jer 31:30. *d.* for his own iniquity, 33:8.
18:31. why will ye *d.* O . . . Israel, 33:11.
Jon 4:3. better to *d.* than live
Matt 26:35. though I should *d.* with thee
Luke 20:36. neither can *d.* any more
John 8:21. ye shall *d.* in your sins, 24.
11:50. expedient that one *d.* for people
Rom 14:8. we *d.* we *d.* unto the Lord
1 Cor 9:15. better for me to *d.* than
Phil 1:21. to live is Christ, to *d.* gain
Heb 9:27. appointed for men once to *d.*
Rev 3:2. that are ready to *d.*
Rom 5:6. Christ *died* for the ungodly
8. while yet sinners, Christ *d.* for us
Rom 6:10. for in that he *died* he *d.* unto sin
7.9. command, came, sin revived and I *d.*
14:9. to this end Christ *d.* and rose
1 Cor 15:3. Christ *d.* for our sins
2 Cor 5:15. he *d.* for all, that they
1 Thess 5:10. who *d.* for us that whether
Heb 11:13. these all *d.* in faith, not
Rom 6:9. being raised . . . *dieth* no more
14:7. no man *d.* to himself
2 Cor 4:10. *dying,* 6:9. Heb 11:21.

DIFFER, who maketh to, 1 Cor 4:7.
1 Cor 15:41. star *d.* Rom 12:6. gifts *d.*
Lev 10:10. *difference,* Jude 22.
Acts 15:9. no *d.* Rom 3:22; 10:12.

DILIGENCE, do thy, 2 Tim 4:9, 21.
Prov 4:23. keep thy heart with all *d.*
2 Pet 1:5. *give d.* Luke 12:58. Jude 3.
10.—to make . . . election sure
Rom 12:8. ruleth, with *d.* 2 Cor 8:7. abound in all *d.*
Deut 19:18. *diligent,* Josh 22:5.
Prov 10:4. hand of *d.* maketh rich
12:24. hand of *d.* shall bear rule
13:4. soul of *d.* shall be made fat
Prov 21:5. thoughts of *d.* tend to plenty
Ps 64:6. *d.* search, 77:6. *d.* inquisition. Deut 19:18.
Prov 22:29. man *d.* in his business, 27:23.
2 Cor 8:22. (Titus) proved *d.,* more *d.*
2 Pet 3:14. be d. to be found of him
Exod 15:26. if *diligently* hearken to, Deut 28:1. Jer 17:24. Zech 6:15.
Deut 4:9. keep thy soul *d.* . . . forget
6:17. *d.* keep the commandments, Ps 119:4.
Ps 37:10. *d.* consider, Jer 2:10.
Luke 15:8. *d.* seek. Heb 11:6.—him
Heb 12:15. looking *d.* lest . . . fail of
1 Pet 1:10. prophets searched *d.* what

DIM, Moses' eye not *d.* Deut 34:7.
Isa 8:22. *dimness* of anguish, Job 17:7.

DIMINISH, Deut 4:2. &c. Prov 13:11.
Rom 11:12.—*ing* of them riches of Gentiles

DINNER, Prov 15:17. Luke 14:12.

DIP, Ruth 2:14. John 13:26. Ps 68:23.

DIRECT, Eccles 10:10. Isa 45:13.
Ps 5:3. will I *d.* my prayer to thee
Prov 3:6. he shall *d.* thy paths
Isa 61:8. I will *d.* their work in truth
Jer 10:23. man that walketh to *d.* his steps
Ps 119:5. my ways were *directed* to keep
Isa 40:13. who hath *d.* the Spirit of Lord
Prov 16:9. a man's heart deviseth his way: the Lord *directeth* his steps

DISCERN, Eccles 8:5. 2 Sam 14:17. *see* 1 Kings 3:9, 11. spiritually, 1 Cor 2:14.
Mal 3:18. *d.* between righteous and
Heb 5:14. to *d.* both good and evil
1 Cor 11:29. not *discerning* Lord's body
12:10. to another *d.* of spirits

DISCHARGE, in war. Eccles 8:8.

DISCIPLE, John 9:28; 19:38.
Matt 10:24. *d.* is not above his master
42. cup of water in the name of a *d.*
Luke 14:26. if . . . he cannot be my *d.*
Acts 21:16. an old *d.* with whom
John 8:31. then are ye my *disciples* indeed

DISCORD, soweth, Prov 6:14, 19.

DISCRETION, Ps 112:5. Prov 1:4; 2:11; 3:21. without *d.* 11:22; 19:11. to *d.* Isa 28:26. heavens by *d.* Jer 10:12.

DISEASE, Ps 38:7. Eccles 6:2. healing *d.* Matt 4:23, &c.; 10:1.
2 Chron 16:12, in his *d.* (Asa) sought not Lord
Diseases of Egypt, Exod 15:26.
Ps 103:3. who healeth all thy *diseases*
John 6:2. miracles . . . on . . . *diseased*

DISFIGURE faces, Matt 6:16.

DISGRACE not throne, Jer 14:21.

DISHONOUR, Ezra 4:14. Prov 6:33.
Ps 35:26. clothed with *d.* 71:13.
Rom 1:24. to *d.* their own bodies
1 Cor 15:43. it is sown in *d.* it is raised
2 Cor 6:8. approving . . . by honour and *d.*
Mic 7:6. son *dishonoureth* his father, Matt 10:35.

DISINHERIT (Israel), Num 14:12.

DISOBEDIENCE, 2 Cor 10:6. children of *d.* Eph 2:2; 5:6. Col 3:6
Rom 5:19. by one man's *d.* many
Heb 2:2. if every *d.* received just

DISOBEDIENT, 1 Kings 13:26. Neh 9:26.
Luke 1:17. *d.* to wisdom of the just
Rom 1:30. *d.* to parents, 2 Tim 3:2.
1 Tim 1:9. law made for lawless and *d.,*
Titus 1:16. in works deny him being . . . *d.*
1 Pet 3:20. which sometimes were *d.* Titus 3:3.

DISORDERLY, 2 Thess 3:6, 7, 11.

DISPENSATION, a, 1 Cor 9:17. Eph 3:2. Col 1:25. *d.* of fulness, Eph 1:10.

DISPERSED the (Jews), Isa 11:12. Esther 3:8. Zeph 3:10. John 7:35.

DISPLEASED, Gen 38:10. 2 Sam 11:27. 1 Chron 21:7. Zech 1:2, 15. Isa 59:15. Mark 10:14. 1 Kings 1:6. Ps 60:1.
Deut 9:19. *displeasure,* Ps 2:5; 6:1; 38:1.

DISPOSING is of the Lord, Prov 16:33.
Acts 7:53. *disposition* of angels

DISPUTE, Job 23:7. Mark 9:33. Acts 6:9; 9:29; 17:17; 19:8, 9.
Rom 14:1. doubtful *disputations*

DISQUIETED, Ps 39:6; 42:5, 11.

DISSEMBLE, Josh 7:11. Jer 42:20. Gal 2:13. Ps 26:4. Prov 26:24.
Rom 12:9. *dissimulation,* Gal 2:13.

DISSENSION, Acts 15:2; 23:7, 10.

DISSOLVED, Ps 75:3. Isa 24:19. 2 Cor 5:1. 2 Pet 3:11. Job 30:22.

DISTINCTLY, read law, Neh 8:8.

DISTRACT, Ps 88:15. 1 Cor 7:35.

DISTRESS, this, Gen 42:21. Neh 9:37. *d.* of nations, Luke 21:25.
Gen 35:3. answered in day of my *d.*
2 Sam 22:7, in my *d.* I called on the Lord, Ps 18:6; 118:5; 120:1.
1 Kings 1:29. redeemed soul out of *d.*
Ps 4:1. enlarged me when in *d.*
Prov 1:27. when *d.* and anguish cometh
Isa 25:4. strength to needy in *d.*
Zeph 1:15. day of trouble and *d.* 17.
Rom 8:35. from love of Christ? shall . . . *d.*
Gen 32:7. *distressed.* 2 Chron 28:20. *d.* Ahaz. 2 Sam 1:26. I am *d.* for thee
Ezek 30:16. Noph have distresses: 2 Cor 6:4. approve in *d.:* 12:10. pleasure—: Ps 25:17; 107:6 &c. out of *d.*

DISTRIBUTE, to poor, Luke 18:22; ready to, 1 Tim 6:18. to saints, Rom 12:13.
Job 21:17. God *distributeth* sorrows in anger

Deut 32:33. *dragons,* Job 30:29. Ps 44:19; 74:13; 148:7. Isa 13:22; 34:13; 43:20. Jer 9:11; 14:6. Mic 1:8. Mal 1:3.
DRAW, Gen 24:44. city, 2 Sam 17:13.
Job 21:33. every man *d.* after him
Ps 28:3. *d.* me not with wicked
Song of Sol 1:4. *d.* me, we will run after thee
Isa 5:18. woe that *d.* iniquity with cords
John 6:44. except the Father . . . *d.* him
Heb 10:38. if any man *d.* back, 39.
Ps 73:28. good for me to *d.* near God
Eccles 12:1. years *d.* nigh when thou . . . say
Isa 29:13. *d.* near me with their mouth
Heb 7:19. by which we *d.* nigh to God
James 4:8. *d.* nigh to God, he will *d.*
Jer 31:3. with lovingkindness have I *drawn* thee
Ps 18:16. *drew* me out of waters, Exod 2:10.
Hos 11:4. *d.* them with cords of a man
DREAD, Gen 9:2. Exod 15:16. Job 13:11.
Deut 1:29. *d.* not, 1 Chron 22:13.
2:25. I put *d.* of thee on nations
Isa 8:13. let him be your *d.* Job 13:11.
Gen 28:17. how *dreadful* is this place
Dan 9:4. great and *d.* God
Mal 1:14. my name is *d.* among
4:5. great and *d.* day of the Lord
DREAM (Joseph), Gen 37:5; 40:5; 41:7.
Gen 20:3. God came to Abimelech in a *d.*
28:12. (Jacob) *d.* 31:11. angel to Jacob in *d.*
Num 12:6. I speak to prophet in *d.*
Job 20:8. fly away as a *d.* Ps 73:20.
33:15. in a *d.* in a vision of the night
Ps 126:1. we were like them that *d.*
Eccles 5:3. *d.* cometh through . . . business
Isa 29:7. fight against Ariel be as *d.*
Jer 23:28. who hath a *d.* . . . tell a *d.*
Dan 2:28. thy *d.* 4:8. told *d.* 7:1. had *d.*
Matt 1:20. angel appeared in a *d.*
2:12. warned of God in a *d.*, 13, 19, 22.
27:19. suffered many things in a *d.*
Acts 2:17. old men *d. dreams,* Joel 2:28.
Eccles 5:7. in multitude of *d.* . . . vanities
Dreamer (law of), Deut 13:1. Jer 27:9.

DRINK, Exod 15:24; 32:20. Judg 7:5.
Job 21:20. *d.* of wrath of the Almighty
Ps 36:8. *d.* of river of . . . pleasures
60:3. *d.* wine of astonishment, Jer 25:15.
69:21. vinegar to *d. See* Ruth 2:14.
80:5. givest them tears to *d.*
110:7. *d.* of the brook in the way
Prov 4:17. *d.* the wine of violence
5:15. *d.* out of own cistern, 2 Kings 18:31.
Song of Sol 5:1. *d.*, yea, *d.* abundantly
Isa 22:13. let us eat and *d.* 1 Cor 15:32.
65:13. my servants shall *d.* but ye
Hos 4:18. their *d.* is sour: they have
Amos 4:1. say to masters, Bring, and let us *d.*
Matt 10:42. *d.* to one of these little ones
20:22. able to *d.* of cup, Mark 10:38.
25:35. thirsty, and ye gave me *d.*, 37, 42.
26:27. *d.* ye all of it
29. not *d.* henceforth, 42. except I *d.* it
27:34. gave him vinegar to *d.*
John 6:55. my blood is *d.* indeed
7:37. come to me and *d.* Isa 55:1.
Rom 12:20. enemy thirst give *d.* Prov 25:21.
14:17. kingdom of God is not *d.*
1 Cor 10:4. did all *d.* same spiritual *d.*
21. cannot *d.* the cup of Lord and devils
11:25. as often as ye *d.* it in remembrance
Lev 10:9. not *d.* wine nor *strong drink,* Judg 13:4. 1 Sam 1:15. Luke 1:15.
Prov 20:1; 31:4. nor for princes—
31:5. lest they *d.* and forget the law
Isa 5:11. follow—22. mingle—
28:7. priest and prophet erred through—
Mic 2:11. prophesy to them of—
Job 15:16. *drinketh* iniquity like water
John 6:54. *d.* my blood . . . eternal life
1 Cor 11:29. eateth and *d.* unworthily
Heb 6:7. earth which *d.* in rain
Rev 17:2. *drunk* with wine of fornication
Deut 21:20. glutton and *drunkard*
Prov 23:21. *d.* and glutton shall come to poverty
26:9. as thorn to hand of *d.*, so parable
Isa 24:20. earth shall reel like a *d.*
1 Cor 5:11. with railer of *d.* . . . not eat

Ps 69:12. *drunkards,* Isa 28:1, 3. Joel 1:5. Nah 1:10. 1 Cor 6:10.
Job 12:25. stagger like a *drunken* man, Ps 107:27. Jer 23:9. Isa 19:14.
Isa 29:9. *d.*, . . . not with wine, 51:21.
1 Cor 11:21. one is hungry, another *d.*
1 Thess 5:7. be *d.* are *d.* in the night
Deut 29:19. *drunkenness,* Eccles 10:17. Jer 13:13. Ezek 23:33. Luke 21:34. Rom 13:13. Gal 5:21.
DROP, Deut 33:28. Judg 5:4. Ps 68:8.
Ps 65:11. thy paths *d.* fatness, 12.
Prov 5:3. *d.* as honeycomb, Song of Sol 4:11.
Isa 40:15. nations as a *d.* of a bucket
Song of Sol 5:5. my hands *dropped* myrrh
Prov 19:13. continual *dropping,* 27:15.
Drops, he maketh small, Job 36:27. *d. of* dew, 38:28.—night, Song of Sol 5:5.—blood, Luke 22:44.
DROSS, Ps 119:119. Isa 1:25. Ezek 22:18.
DROWN, Song of Sol 8:7. 1 Tim 6:9.
DROWSINESS clothe, Prov 23:21.
DRY, Judg 6:37. Job 13:25. Prov 17:1. Isa 44:3. Jer 4:11. *d.* tree, Isa 56:3. Ezek 17:24; 37:2. Hos 9:14.
DUE, Lev 10:13. Deut 18:3.
1 Chron 15:13. sought him not after *d.* order
Prov 3:27. withhold not good . . . is *d.*
Matt 18:34. pay all that was *d.*
Luke 23:41. we receive *d.* reward . . . but
Rom 13:7. tribute to whom tribute is *d.*
Ps 104:27. meat in *due season,* 145:15. Matt 24:45. Luke 12:42.
Prov 15:23. a word in—how good is
Eccles 10:17. eat in—for strength
Gal 6:9. in—we shall reap, if we
Deut 32:35. foot slide in *due time*
1 Cor 15:8. as one born out of—
1 Tim 2:6. to be testified in—
Titus 1:3. hath in—manifested . . . word
DULL of hearing, Matt 13:15. Heb 5:11.
DUMB, Ezek 3:26, &c. Luke 1:20.
Ps 38:13. I was as a *d.* man, 39:2, 9.
Prov 31:8. open thy mouth for *d.*
Isa 35:6. tongue of *d.* to sing
53:7. as sheep before shearers is *d.*
56:10. watchmen are all *d.* dogs
D. idols, Hab 2:18. 1 Cor 12:2. *devil,* Matt 9:33; 12:22. Mark 9:25. *d.* ass, 2 Pet 2:16.
DUNG of solemn feasts, Mal 2:3.
Phil 3:8. I count them but *d.*
Dunghill, 1 Sam 2:8. Isa 25:10. Luke 14:35.

DURABLE riches, Prov 8:18.
Isa 23:18. merchandise . . . for *d.* clothing
DUST, Exod 8:17. Job 28:6; 39:14. *d.* thou art and to *d.* shalt return, Gen 3:19. Job 10:9; 34:15. Ps 104:29. Eccles 3:20; 12:7. sleep in *d.* Dan 12:2. Job 17:16.
D. before wind, Ps 18:42. Isa 29:5; 41:2.
Cast d. 2 Sam 16:13. Acts 22:23.—on head, Josh 7:6. Job 2:12.
Exalt out of d. 1 Sam 2:8. 1 Kings 16:2. Ps 113:7.
Lay in d. Ps 7:5. *see* Job 16:15. Ps 72:9. Isa 26:29. Lam 3:29. Amos 2:7. Rev 18:19.
Number as d. (Abraham's seed), Gen 13:16. 28:14. *d.* of Jacob, Num 23:10. 2 Chron 1:9. *see* Isa 29:5. gold—, Job 22:24. Zech 9:3. flesh—Ps 78:27.
Serpent of d. Deut 32:24. Isa 65:25.
Small as d. Ps 18:42. stamp—Deut 9:21. 2 Kings 23:12. (metaph.), 2 Sam 22:43. 2 Kings 13:7.
Gen 18:27. am but *d.* and *ashes*
Job 30:19. become like—, 42:6. repent in—Deut 28:24. make rain *d. See* Isa 5:24.
Ps 22:15. brought me into *d.* of death
30:9. shall the *d.* praise thee
Ps 102:14. thy servants . . . favor *dust* thereof
103:14. remembereth that we are *d.*
Matt 10:14. shake off *d.* Acts 13:51.
DUTY (rights) of marriage, Exod 21:10.
2 Chron 8:14. as *d.* of every day required
Eccles 12:13. this is the whole *d.* of man
Luke 17:10. which was our *d.* to do
DWELL in holy hill, Ps 15:1. Isa 33:16.
Ps 23:6. *d.* in house of Lord for ever, 27:4.
84:10. than to *d.* in tents of wickedness
120:5. that I *d.* in tents of Kedar
132:14. here will I *d.* for I desired
Isa 33:14. who *d.* with devouring fire
Rom 8:9. Spirit of God *d.* in you, 1 Cor 3:16.
2 Cor 6:16. I will *d.* in them, Ezek 43:7.
Eph 3:17. that Christ may *d.* in hearts
Col 1:19. that in *him should all* fulness *d.*
3:16. let the word of Christ *d.* in you richly
1 John 4:13. know that we *d.* in him
Rev 21:3. he will *d.* with them, and
John 6:56. *dwelleth* in me, and I in him
14:10. Father that *d.* in me, he doeth
17. Spirit of truth; . . . *d.* with you
Acts 7:48. *d.* not in temples, 17:24.
Rom 7:17. sin that *d.* in me, 20.
18. in my flesh *d.* no good thing
Col 2:9. in Christ *d.* all fulness of Godhead
2 Tim 1:14. Holy Ghost which *d.* in us
James 4:5. spirit which *d.* in us lusteth
2 Pet 3:13. wherein *d.* righteousness
1 John 3:17. how *d.* the love of God in him
4:12. God *d.* in us, and his love is
15. confesseth Jesus is Son of God, God *d.* in him, 16. *d.* in love, *d.* in God
2 John 2. truth's sake which *d.* in us
1 Tim 6:16. *dwelling* in light
Heb 11:9. *d.* in tabernacles with Isaac
2 Pet 2:8. that righteous (Lot) *d.* among them
Ps 87:2. more than all *dwellings* of Jacob
John 1:14. Word made flesh and *dwelt*
Acts 13:17. *d.* as strangers in Egypt
2 Tim 1:5. faith *d.* first in grandmother

E

EAGLE, Deut 28:49. as swift as the *e.* flieth Ezek 17:3. *See* Hab 1:8. Hos 8:1.
32:11. as *e.* stirreth nest, beareth
Job 9:26. *e.* hasteth to prey, Matt 24:28.
39:27. mount as *e.* Isa 40:31.
Ps 103:5. renewed like *e.*
Prov 30:19. too wonderful . . . way of *e.* in air
Jer 49:16. nest high as *e.* Obad 4.
Mic 1:16. enlarge thy baldness as *e.*
Rev 4:7. (beast), Ezek 10:14. Dan 7:4. *See* Lev 11:13. Prov 23:5. Dan 4:33.
12:14. woman wings of great *e.*
Exod 19:4. bare on *eagles'* wings
2 Sam 1:23. swifter than *eagles,* Jer 4:13.
Prov 30:17. young *e.* eat it, Job 39:30.
Lam 4:19. persecutors swifter than *e.*
EAR, bore his, Exod 21:6. Deut 15:17.
Exod 29:20. blood on tip of *e.* Lev 8:23.
2 Kings 19:16. bow down *e.* Ps 31:2; 86:1.
2 Chron 6:40. *e.* attent, Ps 130:2. Neh 1:6.
Job 4:12. mine *e.* received a little thereof
12:11. Doth not *e.* try words, 34:3.
36:10. God openeth man's *e.* 15; 33:16.
42:5. heard of thee by hearing of *e.*
Ps 94:9. He that planted the *e.* shall
Prov 15:31. *e.* that heareth reproof
20:12. The hearing *e.* and seeing eye
25:12. wise reprover on an obedient *e.*
Isa 48:8. time thine *ear* was not opened
50:5. Lord God hath opened mine *e.*, and
Jer 6:10. *e.* uncircumcised, Acts 7:51.
Amos 3:12. As shepherd . . . piece of an *e.*
Luke 12:3. spoken in *e.* 22:50. (Malchus)
1 Cor 2:9. nor *e.* heard; 12:16. if *e.* say
Give ear (to prayer), Ps 5:1; 17:1; 39:12; 54:2; 55:1; 80:1; 86:6; 141:1.—O heavens, Deut 32:1. Isa 1:2.—O princes, Judg 5:3.—O my people, Ps 78:1. *See* Isa 1:10; 51:4;—careless daughter, 32:9—house of king, Hos 5:1.—all inhabitants of world, Ps 49:1. Isa 8:9—of land, Joel 1:2. *See* 2 Chron 24:19. Neh 9:30.
Ps 17:6. *incline ear* (to prayer), 71:2; 88:2; 102:2; 116:2. Isa 37:17. Dan 9:18.
45:10.—, forget. 49:4.—to parable
78:1.—to words of my mouth, 4:20.
Isa 55:3.—and come unto me: hear
Jer 7:24; 11:8. *nor inclined their ear,* 17:23; 25:4; 35:15; 44:5.
Stop e. adder, Ps 58:4.—at (poor's) cry, *see* Isa 33:15. Zech 7:11. *e.* of deaf shall be unstopped, Isa 35:5.
Deut 29:4. eyes to see and *ears* to hear
2 Sam 7:22. heard with *e.* Job 28:22. Ps 44:1.
22:7. my cry into his *e.* James 5:4.
Job 15:21. a dreadful sound in his *e.*
33:16. God openeth (man's) *e.* 36:10, 15.
Ps 34:15. his *e.* open to cry, 1 Pet 3:12.
40:6. my *e.* hast thou opened
115:16. (idols) *have e. and hear not.* (Judah)—, Jer 5:21.
Isa 6:10. make *e.* heavy, Matt 13:15. *See* Acts 28:27. Rom 11:8; Isa 59:1. Lord's *e.* not heavy that it cannot hear
32:3. *e.* of hearers shall hearken
43:8. deaf . . . have *e.* Jer 5:21. Ezek 12:2.
Matt 11:15. *e.* to hear, let him hear, 13:9, 43. Rev 2:7; 3:6; 13:9.
13:16. blessed your *e.*, . . . they hear
Mark 7:33. Jesus put his fingers into *e.*
8:18. having *e.* hear ye not?
Luke 9:44. let sayings sink into your *e. See* Prov 26:17. Eccles 1:8. Ezek 23:25.
2 Chron 6:40. *thine ear(s)* be attent to
Ps 10:17. cause—to hear

Prov 23:12. apply—to words of knowledge
Isa 30:21.—shall hear a word behind
Ezek 3:10. hear with—40:4; 44:5.
EAR (of corn), in the, Exod 9:31. Mark 4:28. green *e.* Lev 2:14; 23:14. *See* 2 Kings 4:42. cut off tops of *e.* Job 24:24. reap, gathereth *e.* Isa 17:5.
EAR, to plough (*aro*), Deut 21:4. 1 Sam 8:12. Isa 30:24.
Earing time, Exod 34:21. Gen 45:6.
EARLY, Gen 19:2, 27. John 18:28; 20:1.
Ps 46:5. God shall help her and that right *e.*
57:8. will awake *e.* 108:2.
90:14. satisfy us *e.* with thy mercy
Prov 1:28. seek me *e.* and not find
8:17. that seek me *e.* shall find me
Isa 26:9. with spirit I seek thee *e.*
Jer 7:13, &c. *rising up e.* and speaking; 11:7.—and protesting; 7:25; 26:5, &c.
2 Chron 36:15.—and sending; Jer 32:33.—& teaching
Hos 5:15. in affliction will seek me *e.*
James 5:7. receive *e.* and latter rain
EARNEST (pledge) of Spirit, 2 Cor 1:22; 5:5.
Eph 1:14. *e.* of inheritance
Rom 8:19. *e.* expectation of, Phil 1:20.
2 Cor 7:7. told us of your *e.* desire
Heb 2:1. more *earnest* heed
Job 7:2. servant *earnestly* desireth shadow
Jer 11:7. I *e.* protested to fathers
Mic 7:3. do evil with both hands *e.*
Luke 22:44. in agony, prayed more *e.*
1 Cor 12:31. covet *e.* the best gifts
2 Cor 5:2. in this we groan, *e.* desiring
James 5:17. prayed *e.* it might not rain
Jude 3. ye should *e.* contend for the faith
EARNETH wages, Hag 1:6.
EARRING, Gen 24:47; 35:4. Exod 32:2; 35:22. Num 31:50. Judg 8:24. Job 42:11. Hos 2:13. Ezek 16:12.
EARTH corrupt, Gen 6:11, 12, 13.
Gen 11:1. whole *e.* of one language
41:47. *e.* brought forth by handfuls
Exod 9:29. *e.* is the Lord's, Deut 10:14. Ps 24:1. 1 Cor 10:26, 28.
Num 16:32. *e.* opened her *mouth, 26:10. Deut 11:6. Ps 106:*17. Rev 12:16.
Deut 28:23. *e.* under thee be iron
32:1. hear O *e.* words of my mouth
Judg 5:4. *e.* trembleth and heavens
1 Sam 2:8. pillars of *e.* are Lord's
1 Chron 16:31. let *e.* rejoice, Ps 96:11.
Job 9:6. shaketh *e.* out of her place
11:9. longer than *e.*, broader than sea
16:18. O *e.* cover not blood, Gen 4:10.
26:7. and hangeth *e.* upon nothing
30:8. base men, viler than the *e.*
38:4. I laid the foundations of the *e.*
Ps 33:5. *e.* is full of the goodness of Lord
65:9. visitest the *e.* and waterest it
67:6. *e.* shall increase, 85:12.
78:69. like *e.* established for ever
89:11. heaven and *e.* are thine
97:4. *e.* saw and trembled, 2 Sam 22:8.
104:24. *e. is full of* thy riches; Isa 6:3. whole *e.*—thy glory, Ps 72:19.
115:16. *e.* given to children of men
139:15. in lowest parts of the *e.*
Prov 25:3. heaven for height and *e.* for depth
Eccles 1:4. *e.* abideth for ever
Isa 11:4. smite *e.* with rod of mouth
9. *e.* full of knowledge of Lord, Hab 2:14.
13:13. *e.* shall remove out of her place
24:1. Lord maketh the *e.* empty
4. *e.* mourneth and fadeth, 33:9.
5. *e.* is defiled. 19. *e.* is utterly broken down
20. *e.* shall reel to and fro like a drunkard
26:19. *e.* shall cast out the dead
66:1. *e.* is my footstool, where is
Jer 22:29. O *e. e. e.* hear word of the Lord
Ezek 34:27. *e.* shall yield increase
43:2. the *e.* shined with his glory
Hos 2:22. *e.* shall hear the corn, and
Hab 3:3. and *e.* was full of his praise
Matt 13:5. stony ground . . . not much *e.*
John 3:31. he that is of *e.* is earthly
Heb 6:7. *e.* which drinketh in rain
Ps 67:2. way be known *upon earth*
73:25. none—I desire beside thee
Eccles 5:2. God is in heaven and thou—
7:20. not a just man—sinneth not
10:7. princes walking as servants—
Luke 5:24. Son of man power—to forgive
Col 3:5. mortify members—
Earthen, Lev 6:28. Jer 19:1; 32:14. Lam 4:2. 2 Cor 4:7. *earthly,* John 3:12, 31. 2 Cor 5:1. Phil 3:19.
James 3:15. *earthy,* 1 Cor 15:47.
Earthquake, 1 Kings 19:11, 12. Isa 29:6. Amos 1:1. Zech 14:5. Matt 24:7; 27:54.
Rev 8:5; 11:19. *A great earthquake,* Matt 28:2. Acts 16:26. Rev 6:12; 16:8.
EASE, Job 12:5; 16:12; 21:23. Ps 25:13; 123:4. Deut 28:65. Isa 32:9, 11. Jer 46:27; 48:11. Ezek 23:42. Amos 6:1. Zech 1:15.
Isa 1:24. I will *e.* me of adversaries
Luke 12:19. take thine *e.* and be merry
Matt 9:5. *easier,* 19:24. Luke 16:17.
Heb 12:1. sin which doth so *easily* beset us
Prov 14:6. knowledge is *easy* to him
Matt 11:30. my yoke is *e.* . . . my burden light
1 Cor 14:9. words *e.* to be understood
James 3:17. gentle, *e.* to be entreated
EAST, Gen 28:14. Matt 2:1. Ps 103.12.
Isa 43:5. bring thy seed from the *e.*
Matt 8:11. many shall come from the *e.*
Gen 41:6. *east wind,* Exod 14:21. Ps 48:7. Isa 27:8. Hos 13:15. Hab 1:9.
Children of the e. Judg 6:3. Gen 29:1.
EAT, Gen 2:16. of every tree . . . freely *e.*
Gen 2:17. of tree of knowledge thou shalt not *e.*
3:14. *e.* dust. 17. in sorrow *e.* 18. *e.* herb of field. 19. in sweat of thy face *e.* bread
18:8. angels, . . . did *e. See* Luke 24:43.
27:4. savoury meat, . . . that I may *e.*
Exod 10:5. (locusts), Joel 1:4. Amos 7:2.
12:48. no uncircumcised shall *e.* thereof
16:35. Israel did *e.* manna 40 years, until
Lev 6:29, &c. All the males . . . priests *e.* . . . it is *most holy;* (*viz.,* meat offering, 2:3; 6:18. shewbread, 24:9. *e. the holy* thing, 22;14.) *See* Deut 18:1. 1 Sam 2:36.
21:22. (priest) *e.* bread of his God, both of *most holy & holy. See* Ezra 2:63. Ezek 42:13.
7:21. (offerer) *e.* of the flesh of peace offering, 22:30. *e.* sin offering in the holy place, 10:17. Ezek 44:29. Hos 8:13.
8:31. *e.* . . . at door of the tabernacle; 10:13. *e. in* the holy place. 14.—a clean place. Num 18:31.—every place
11:2. beasts which ye shall *e.* [CLEAN.]
22. *e.* locusts. *See* Matt 3:4.
19:25. planted . . . in fifth year *e.* the fruit
26:38. land *e.* you up, Num 13:32.
Num 6:3. Nazarite . . . neither *e.* grapes

11:5. fish we *e.* in Egypt, melons, leeks
Deut 4:28. gods which neither *e.* nor
14:21. shall not *e.* anything that dieth
23. *e.* before Lord God tithe, firstlings
28:55. *e.* children, 2 Kings 6:29. Lam 2:20. Ezek 5:10. *e.* sons, Lev 26:29.
32:38. gods, . . . *e.* the fat of their sacrifices
2 Sam 9:13, *e.* at the king's table, 19:42. 1 Kings 2:7. 2 Kings 25:29. Dan 1:8.
1 Kings 13:9. *e.* no bread, drink no water
19:5. angel touched . . . said, Arise and *e.*
21:23. dogs shall *e.* Jezebel, 14:11.
2 Kings 4:43. an hundred men? . . . *e.* and leave
Neh 8:10. *e.* the fat, drink the sweet
Job 1:4. feasted, and called for their three sisters to *e.* and drink
Ps 22:26. meek shall *e.* and be satisfied
53:4. *e.* up my people as bread, 14:4.
78:25. did *e.* angels' food, John 6:31.
106:28. They . . . *ate* sacrifices of dead
128:2. *e.* the labour of thine hands. *See* Eccles 2:24; 3:13; 5:18, &c. Isa 62:9.
Prov 1:31. *e.* the fruit of their own way
13:2. *e.* good by fruit of mouth, 18:21.
25:16. honey? *e.* so much as sufficient
Eccles 9:7. *e.* with joy . . . God accepteth
Song of Sol 5:1. *e.*, O friends; drink, yea
Isa 1:19. if obedient ye shall *e.*
Isa 3:10. righteous *eat* of doings, Ps 128:2.
4:1. we will *e.* our own bread, only let
7:15. butter and honey shall he *e.* 22.
9:20. *e.* his own arm. Jer 19:9. *e.* friend's flesh (for hunger) [CHILDREN.]
11:7. and the lion shall *e.* straw, 65:25.
30:24. young asses *e.* clean provender
37:30. *e.* this year such as groweth of itself
51:8. worm shall *e.* them as wool
55:1. buy and *e.*; yea, come buy
2. *e.* that is good, let your soul delight
61:6. ye shall *e.* the riches of the Gentiles
65:4. which *e.* swine's flesh, 66:17.
13. my servants shall *e.* but ye, 22.
Jer 15:16. words . . . I did *e.* Ezek 3:1.
Ezek 4:9. bread . . . 390 days *e.* thereof
13. Israel *e.* defiled bread among Gentiles
16. *e.* by weight, with care, 12:18.
22:9. *e.* upon the mountains, 18:11.
Dan 1:12. let them give us pulse to *e.*
4:33. did *e.* grass as oxen, Ps 106:20.
Hos 4:10. *e.* and not have enough
Amos 7:12. there *e.* bread, and phophesy
9:14. gardens, and *e.* fruit, Jer 29:5.
Mic 3:3. *e.* the flesh of my people
Zech 7:6. did not ye *e.* for yourselves?
Matt 6:25. no thought what ye shall *e.*
26:26. Jesus said, Take *e.* this is my body, Mark 14:22. 1 Cor 11:24, 26, 28.
Mark 1:6. *e.* locusts and wild honey
7:5. *e.* bread with unwashen hands
28. dogs *e.* of children's crumbs
Luke 10:8. *e.* things set before you
15:23. let us *e.*, and be merry
22:30. ye may *e.* and drink at my table
John 4:31. Master *e.* 32. I have meat to *e.*
6:26. because ye did *e.* of the loaves
53. except ye *e.* the flesh of Son of man
Acts 2:46. did *e.* . . . with gladness
1 Cor 5:11. with such, no not to *e.*
8:7. some . . . *e.* as a thing offered to an idol
8. neither if we *e.* are we the better
10:31. whether ye *e.* . . . do all to glory of God
2 Thess 3:10. if not work, neither *e.*
James 5:3. rust . . . *e.* your flesh as fire
Rev 2:7. overcometh . . . *e.* tree of life
10:9–11. *e.* little book . . . prophesy again
17:16. shall *e.* her flesh, and burn
E. blood, Gen 9:4. flesh with life . . . blood shall ye not *e.*, *see* Lev 17:14. a perpetual statute *e.* neither fat nor blood, *see* Lev 3:17; 17:12. Acts 15:29. *e. with the blood,* 1 Sam 14:32. Ezek 33:25.
E. of sacrifice (idolatrous), 1 Cor 8:4. Rev 2:14. call to—Exod 34:15. Num 25:2. *e.* upon mountains, Ezek 18:6; 22:9—*e.* bread, Gen 31:54. *e.* bread before God, Exod 18:12; 24:11. Deut 12:7. Ezek 44:3.
1 Chron 29:22. *e.* flesh, Deut 12:27. Jer 7:21. to the high place to *e.*, 1 Sam 9:13.
Deut 26:14. not *eaten* in mourning
Ps 69:9. zeal of [for] thine house hath *e.* me up, John 2:17. Ps 119:139.
Prov 9:17. bread *e.* in secret is pleasant
Hos 10:13. having *e.* fruit of lies
Matt 14:21. *e.* were 5,000; 15:38.—4,000
Luke 13:26. *e.* . . . in thy presence
Acts 12:23. (Herod) was *e.* of worms
Judg 14:14. out of *eater* came forth meat
Isa 55:10. seed to the sower, bread to *e.*
Nah 3:12. fall into the mouth of the *e.*
Eccles 4:5. fool . . . *eateth* his own flesh
Matt 9:11. why *eateth* your master with publicans and sinners, Luke 15:2.
John 6:54. whoso *e.* my flesh and drinketh
58. he that *e.* this bread shall live
Rom 14:6. he that *e. e.* to Lord; he that *e.* not, to the Lord he *e.* not
14:20. for that man who *e.* with offence
1 Cor 11:29. *e.* unworthily, *e.* damnation
1 Sam 30:16. *eating* and drinking, and dancing, Exod 32:6. 1 Cor 10:7.
Matt 11:18. John came neither *e.* nor drinking. 19. Son of man came *e.*
24:38. were *e.* and drinking, Luke 17:27.
26:26. as they were *e.* Jesus took
EDIFY (build up), Rom 14:19. 1 Thess 5:11. 1 Cor 8:1; 10:23; 14:17. Acts 9:31.
Rom 15:2. please neighbour . . . to *edification*
1 Cor 14:3. speak unto men to *e.*
2 Cor 10:8. authority, for *e.* 13:10.
1 Cor 14:12. may excel to *edifying*
2 Cor 12:19. we do all for your *e.*
Eph 4:12. for the *e.* of the body of Christ
16. increase of body to the *e.* in love
29. but that which is good to the use of *e.*
1 Tim 1:4. questions rather than godly *e.*
EFFECT of every vision, Ezek 12:23.
Isa 32:17. *e.* of righteousness quietness
Matt 15:6. commdt. of God *of none effect*
Mark 7:13. making word of God—
Rom 3:3. unbelief make faith of God without *e.*
9:6. word of God had taken none *e.*
1 Cor 1:17. lest cross of Christ be made—
Gal 5:4. Christ is become of no *e.* to you
1 Cor 16:9. great door and *effectual*

2 Cor 1:6. which is *e.* in enduring
Eph 3:7. *e.* working of his power
Philem 6. faith may become *e.* by
James 5:16. *e.* fervent prayer of righteous
Gal 2:8. *effectually,* 1 Thess 2:13.
EFFEMINATE, 1 Cor 6:9.
EGG, Deut 22:6. Job 6:6; 39:14. Isa 10:14; 59:5. Jer 17:11. Luke 11:12.
ELDER, Gen 10:21. 2 John 1:3. 3 John 1.
Gen 25:23. *e.* serve younger, Rom 9:12.
1 Tim 5:1. rebuke not an *e.* but entreat
2. entreat *e.* women as mothers
1 Pet 5:1. *elders,* who am also an *e.*
5. younger submit yourselves to *e.*
Deut 32:7. ask *e.* they will tell thee
Ezra 10:8. according to counsel of *e.*
Joel 2:16. assemble *e.* Ps 107:32.
Acts 14:23. ordained *e.* in every church
15:23. *e.* and brethren send greeting
20:17. Ephesus, called *e.* of church
1 Tim 5:17. *e.* rule well be counted
Titus 1:5. ordain *e.* in every city
Heb 11:2. *e.* obtained good report
James 5:14. sick . . . call for *e.* of church
Rev 4:4. four and twenty *e.* sitting, 5:6; 11:16; 19:4; 7:11; 14:3.
ELECT, *chosen, choice one.*
Isa 42:1. *e.* in whom my soul delighteth
65:9. mine *e.* shall inherit it . . . dwell there
Matt 24:22. for *e.*'s sake days shortened
24. if possible deceive the very *e.*
31. gather his *e.* from the four winds
Luke 18:7. God avenge his own *e.*
Rom 8:33. to the charge of God's *e.*
Col 3:12. put on as the *e.* of God
1 Tim 5:21. before the *e.* angels
2 Tim 2:10. I endure all things for *e.*'s sake
Titus 1:1. according to faith of God's *e.*
1 Pet 1:2. *e.* according to foreknowledge of God
1 Pet 2:6. corner stone, *elect,* precious
2 John 1. *e.* lady. 13. *e.* sister
1 Pet 5:13. church *elected* with you
Rom 9:11. purpose . . . *according to election*
11:5. remnant according to the *e.* of grace
7. the *e.* hath obtained, the rest blinded
1 Thess 1:4. knowing . . . your *e.* of God

2 Pet 1:10. make your calling and *e.* sure
ELEMENTS (rudiments), Gal 4:9.
ELOQUENT, Exod 4:10. Acts 18:24.
EMPTY pit, Gen 37:24. ears, 41:27. pitchers, Judg 7:16. 2 Kings 4:3.
Exod 23:15. none appear before me *e.* 34:20. Deut 16:16.
Deut 15:13. go away *e.* Gen 31:42.
2 Sam 1:22. sword returned not *e.*
Hos 10:1. Israel is an *e.* vine
Luke 1:53. sent *e.* away, Mark 12:3.
Isa 34:11. stones of *emptiness*
EMULATION, (rivalry) Rom 11:14. (envy) Gal 5:20.
ENCHANTMENT, Lev 19:26. Num 23:23. Eccles 10:11. Isa 47:9.
END of all flesh is come, Gen 6:13.
Deut 32:20. see what their *e.* shall be
Ps 37:37. the *e.* of that man is peace
39:4. make sure to know mine *e.*
73:17. then undertsood I their *e.*
102:27. and thy years shall have no *e.*
119:96. seen an *e.* of all perfection
Prov 5:4. her *e.* is bitter as wormwood
Eccles 4:8. there is no *e.* of his labour
7:2. mourning, . . . for that is the *e.* of all
8. the *e.* is better than the beginning
Isa 9:7. of his government shall be no *e.*
Jer 5:31. what will ye do in the *e.*
17:11. days, and at his *e.* shall be a fool
31:17. and there is hope in thine *e.*
Lam 4:18. our *e.* is come, our *e.* is near, Ezek 7:2, 6. Amos 8:2.
Ezek 21:25. when iniquity have an *e.*
Dan 8:19. at time appointed the *e.*
Hab 2:3. at the *e.* if shall speak
Matt 13:39. harvest is *e.* of world
24:3. what . . . sign of the *e.* of world
6. but the *e.* is not yet, Luke 21:9.
Rom 6:21. the *e.* of those things is death
22. ye have . . . and the *e.* everlasting life
14:9. to this *e.* Christ both died and rose
1 Tim 1:5. *e.* of commandment is charity
Heb 6:8. whose *e.* is to be *burned*
16. oath . . . to them an *e.* of all strife
7:3. beginning of days, nor *e.* of life
James 5:11. seen the *e.* of the Lord

1 Pet 1:9. receiving the *e.* of your faith
4:7. the *e.* of all things is at hand
17. *e.* of those that obey not the gospel
Rev 21:6. beginning and *e.* 22:13; 1:8. 1 Sam 3:12.
Jer 4:27. *make a full end,* 5:10, 18; 30:11. Ezek 11:13.
Num 23:10. *last end,* Jer 12:4. Lam 1:9. Dan 8:19.
Deut 8:16. *latter end,* 32:29. Job 42:12. Prov 19:20. 2 Pet 2:20.
Ps 119:33. *unto the end,* Dan 6:26. Matt 24:13; 28:20. John 13:1. 1 Cor 1:8. Heb 3:6, 14; 6:11. Rev 2:26.
1 Tim 1:4. *endless,* Heb 7:16.
Ps 22:27. *ends* of the world remember
67:7. *all ends of earth* shall fear him, Zech 9:10.
98:3.—have seen the salvation, Isa 52:10.
Prov 17:24. eyes of fool in—
Isa 45:22. be ye saved—, Acts 13:47.
1 Cor 10:11. *ends of the world* are come
ENDUED, Gen 30:20. 2 Chron 2:12, 13. Luke 24:49. James 3:13.
ENDURE, Job 8:15; 31:23.
Gen 33:14. as children are able to *e.*
Ps 30:5. weeping may *e.* for a night
102:26. they shall perish, but thou shalt *e.*
Prov 27:24. crown *e.* to every generation
Ezek 22:14. can thine heart *e.* or
Mark 4:17. no root, and *e.* but for a time
13:13. that shall *e.* unto end shall
2 Tim 2:3. *e.* hardness as a soldier
10. *e.* all things for the elect's sake
4:5. watch thou, *e.* afflictions, do the
Heb 12:7. if ye *e.* chastening, God
James 5:11. we count happy which *e.*
Ps 81:15. should have *endured* for ever
Rom 9:22. *e.* with much longsuffering
2 Tim 3:11. what persecutions I *e.*
Heb 6:15. patiently *e.* he obtained
11:27. *e.* as seeing him who is invisible
12:2. *e.* cross. 3. *e.* contradiction
Ps 30:5. his anger *endureth* but a
100:5. his truth *e.* to all generations
145:13. thy dominion *e.* throughout
Matt 10:22. that *e.* to end shall be saved, 24:13. Mark 13:13.
John 6:27. meat which *e.* unto life
1 Cor 13:7. charity *e.* all things
James 1:12. blessed man that *e.* temptation

Gen 26:14. Philistines *envied* (Isaac); 30:1. Rachel *e.* Leah; 37:11. brethren *e.* (Joseph); Ps 106:16. they *e.* Moses
Eccles 4:4. work, for this a man is *e.*
1 Pet 2:1. laying aside all *envies*
Num 11:29. *enviest* thou for my sake
Ps 37:1. *envious,* 73:3. Prov 24:1, 19.
Rom 13:13. not in strife and *envying*
1 Cor 3:3. *e.* and strife, and divisions
Gal 5:26. not . . . *e.* one another
2 Cor 12:20. debates, *envyings* Gal 5:21.
EPHOD, Exod 39:2. Judg 8:27; 17:5. 1 Sam 2:18; 21:9; 23:9; 30:7. 2 Sam 6:14. Hos 3:4.
EPISTLE, Acts 15:30; 23:33. Rom 16:22. 1 Cor 5:9. 2 Cor 7:8. Col 4:16. 1 Thess 5:27. 2 Thess 2:15; 3:14, 17. 2 Pet 3:1.
2 Cor 3:2. *e.* written in our hearts
1. *epistles,* 2 Pet 3:16. (Paul's)
EQUAL, Job 28:17, 19. Ps 17:2; 55:13. Prov 26:7. Lam 2:13.
Isa 40:25. to whom make me *e.* 46:5.
Ezek 18:25. way of the Lord is not *e.*
Matt 20:12. made them *e.* to us
Luke 20:36. (not) die . . . *e.* to the angels
John 5:18. making himself *e. with God*
Phil 2:6. thought not robbery to be—
Col 4:1. master, give . . . just and *e.*
Rev 21:16. breadth, and height *e.*
Gal 1:14. *equals;* 2 Cor 8:14. *equality*
EQUITY, dost establish, Ps 99:4.
Ps 98:9. judge people with *e.*
Prov 1:3. wisdom, justice, judgment, *e.*
17:26. nor to strike princes for *e.*
Eccles 2:21. labour is in widsom, knowledge, *e.*
Isa 11:4. reprove with *e.* for meek
59:14. truth fallen, *e.* cannot enter
Mic 3:9. princes that pervert all *e.*
Mal 2:6. Levi walked with me in *e.*
ERR, 2 Chron 33:9. Isa 19:14.
Ps 95:10. do *e.* in heart, Heb 3:10.
119:21. *err* from thy commandments
Prov 14:22. not *e.* that devise evil
Isa 9:16. the leaders cause to *e.* 3:12.
30:28. bridle . . . causing them to *e.*
35:8. *wayfaring men . . . shall not e.*
Isa 63:17. why made us to *e.* from thy
Jer 23:13. prophet *caused to e.* 32.
Hos 4:12. spirit of whoredom—
Mic 3:5. prophets make people *e.*
Matt 22:29. *e.* not knowing scripture
James 5:19. if any of you *e.* from truth
Num 15:22. and if ye have *erred* . . . offer.
1 Sam 26:21. I . . . have *e.* exceedingly
Job 6:24. understand wherein I have *e.*
Ps 119:110. I *e.* not from thy precepts
Isa 28:7. priest and prophet have *e.* through strong drink
1 Tim 6:10. have *e.* from the faith
21. *e.* concerning the faith, 2 Tim 2:18.
Prov 10:17. *erreth,* Ezek 45:20.
2 Sam 6:7. *error,* Job 19:4. Eccles 5:6; 10:5. Dan 6:4.
Isa 32:6. utter *e.* against the Lord
Dan 6:4. neither was any *e.* found
Rom 1:27. recompence of their *e.*
James 5:20. sinner from the *e.* of his way
2 Pet 2:18. them who live in *e.*
1 John 4:6. know we . . . the spirit of *e.*
Jude 11. after the *e.* of Balaam
Ps 19:12. who understand his *errors*
Jer 10:15. vanity and work of *e.* 51:18.
Heb 9:7. for the *e.* of the people
ERRAND, Judg 3:19. 2 Kings 9:5.
ESCAPE, Gen 19:17, 22; 32:8.
Ezra 9:8. leave a remnant to *e.*
Esther 4:13. think not that thou shalt *e.*
Job11:20. but (wicked) shall not *e.*
Ps 56:7. shall they *e.* by iniquity
71:2. deliver me and cause me to *e.*
141:10. let the wicked fall . . . whilst I *e.*
Prov 19:5. that speaketh lies shall not *e.*
Eccles 7:26. pleaseth God shall *e.* her
Isa 20:6. we flee for help . . . how shall we *e.*
Jer 11:11. evil . . . shall not be able to *e.*
Ezek 17:15. shall he *e.* that doeth
Matt 23:33. *e.* the damnation of hell
Luke 21:36. accounted worthy to *e.*
Rom 2:3. *e.*the judgment of God
1 Cor 10:13. temptation . . . a way to *e.*
1 Thess 5:3. they shall not *e.*
Heb 2:3. how shall we *e.* if we neglect
Ezra 9:15. we remain yet *escaped*
Job 1:15, 16, 17, 19. I only am *e.* to tell
Ps 124:7. our soul is *e.* as a bird out of snare
Isa 45:20. *e.* of the nations
John 10:39. he *e.* out of their hand
Heb 12:25. *e.*not who refused him
2 Pet 1:4. *e.* corruption of world, 2:20.
2:18. allure those that were clean *e.*
ESCHEW evil, Job 1:8. 1 Pet 3:11.
ESPOUSALS, Song of Sol 3:11. Jer 2:2.
Matt 1:18. *espoused,* 2 Cor 11:2.
ESTABLISH, STABLISH, Num 30:13. 1 Kings 15:4. Deut 28:9. Job 36:7.
Gen 9:9. *e.* my covenant, 17:7, 19, 21. Exod 6:4. Lev 26:9. Deut 8:18. Ezek 16:60. *e.* an everlasting covenant
1 Sam 1:23. the Lord *e.* his word
2 Sam 7:12. I will *e.* his kingdom, 13.
2 Chron 9:8. God loved Israel to *e.* them
7:18. *S.* throne of kingdom, 1 Chron 17:12.
Ps 7:9. but *e.* the just, 48:8.
89:2. thy faithfulness shalt thou *e.* in heaven
4. David . . . thy seed will I *e.* for ever
Ps 90:17. *establish* the work of our hands, . . . *e.* thou
99:4. thou dost *e.* equity
119:38. *s.* thy word to thy servant
Prov 15:25. *e.* the border of the widow
Isa 9:7. order it, and to *e.* it with judgment
49:8. give thee for a . . . to *e.* the earth
62:7. no rest till he *e.* Jerusalem
Rom 3:31. yea, we *e.* the law
10:3. to *e.* their own righteousness
16:25. that is of power to *s.* you
1 Thess 3:13. *e.* your hearts, James 5:8.
2 Thess 2:17. *s.* in every good word
1 Pet 5:10. God of all grace *s.* you
Gen 41:32. the thing is *established*
Exod 15:17. which thy hands have *e.*
Ps 40:2. upon a rock, he *e.* my goings
78:5. he *e.* a testimony in Jacob
93:1. the world is *s.* 2. thy throne is *e.*
119:90. hast *e.* the earth, and it abideth
Prov 3:19. (Lord) . . . *e.* heavens, Ps 148:6.
4:26. ponder . . . let all thy ways be *e.*
12:3. man not be *e.* by wickedness
16:12. throne is *e.* by righteousness
20:18. every purpose is *e.* by counsel
Isa 7:9. if ye will not believe . . . not be *e.*
16:5. in mercy shall the throne be *e.*
Jer 10:12. *e.* the world by wisdom, 51:15.
Hab 1:12. *e.* them for correction

Matt 18:16. of two or three witnesses every word may be *e.* 2 Cor 13:1.
Acts 16:5. so were the churches *e.*
Rom 1:11. to the end ye may be *e.*
Col 2:7. built up in him, and . . . *s.* in faith
Heb 8:6. *e.* upon better promises
13:9. that the heart be *e.* with grace
2 Pet 1:12. *e.* in the present truth
Lev 25:30. *shall be established,* Deut 19:15. Ps 89:21. 2 Cor 13:1.
2 Chron 20:20. believe in God, so ye—
Job 22:28. decree a thing and it—
Ps 102:28. their seed—before thee
Prov 12:19. lip of truth—for ever
25:5. throne—in righteousness, 29:14.
Isa 2:2. the Lord's house—, Mic 4:1.
54:14. in righteousness thou—
Jer 30:20. their congregation—before me
Prov 29:4. king by . . . *establisheth* the land
Hab 2:12. woe to him that *s.* a city
2 Cor 1:21. *s.* us with you is God.
ESTATE, STATE, Gen 43:7. Esther 1:7, 19.
Ps 39:5. man at his best *s.* is vanity
136:23. remembered us in low *e.*
Prov 27:23. know *e.* of thy flocks
Matt 12:45. last *s.* is worse, Luke 11:26.
Luke 1:48. low *e.* of his handmaiden
Phil 4:11. in whatsoever *e.* . . . content
Jude 6. angels that kept not their first *e.*
ESTEEM, Job 36:19. Isa 29:16, 17.
Ps 119:128. I *e.* all thy precepts
Isa 53:4. we did *e.* him stricken of God
Phil 2:3. *e.* each other better than
1 Thess 5:13. *e.* them highly in love
Deut 32:15. and lightly *esteemed* the rock of his salvation
1 Sam 2:30. they that despise me shall be lightly *e.*
Job 23:12. *e.* the words of his mouth
Luke 16:15. is highly *e.* among men
Rom 14:5. *esteemeth* one day above
14. to him that *e.* it, it is unclean
Heb 11:26. *esteeming* reproach of Christ
ESTRANGED, Job 19:13. Jer 19:4.
Ps 58:3. wicked are *e.* from the womb
Ps 78:30. not *estranged* from their lusts
Ezek 14:5. they are all *e.* from me
ETERNAL God thy refuge, Deut 33:27.
Isa 60:15. make thee an *e.* excellency
Mark 3:29. danger of *e.* damnation
Rom 1:20. even his *e.* power
2 Cor 4:17. exceeding and *e.* weight of
18. the things which are not seen are *e.*
5:1. a house . . . hands, *e.* in the heavens
Eph 3:11. according to the *e.* purpose
1 Tim 1:17. to the King *e.* . . . be honour
2 Tim 2:10. salvation . . . with *e.* glory
Heb 5:9. author of *e.* salvation unto all
9:12. obtained *e.* redemption for us
14. through *e.* Spirit; 15. *e.* inheritance
1 Pet 5:10. *e.* glory; Jude 7. of *e.* fire
Matt 19:16. that I may have *eternal life,* Mark 10:17. Luke 10:25.
25:46. the righteous (shall go) into—
Mark 10:30. and in the world to come—
John 3:15. should not perish but have—
4:36. wages, gathereth fruit unto—
6:54. blood hath—and I will raise him up
68. we go? thou hast the words of—
10:28. and I give unto them—17:2.
12:25. hateth his life . . . shall keep it unto—
17:3. this is—to know the only true God
Acts 13:48. ordained to—believed
Rom 2:7. glory, honour, immortality, and . . .—
6:23. the gift of God is—through Jesus
1 Tim 6:12. lay hold on—19.
Titus 1:2. in hope of—which God
3:7. heirs according to the hope of—
1 John 1:2.—which was with the Father
3:15. ye know that no murderer hath—
5:11. record, . . . God hath given—in his Son
13. that ye may know that ye have—20.
Jude 21. looking for the mercy . . . unto—
ETERNITY, that inhabiteth, Isa 57:15.
EUNUCH, 2 Kings 9:32; 20:18.
Isa 56:3. neither *e.* say, I am a dry tree
Matt 19:12. some *e.* born . . . made *e.* . . . selves *e.*
Acts 8:27. *e.* of great authority, 39.
EVEN balance, Job 31:6.
Ps 26:12. my foot standeth in an *e.* place
Song of Sol 4:2. flock of sheep that are *e.* shorn
Luke 19:44. lay thee *e.* with the ground
EVEN or EVENING, Gen 1:5, &c.; 19:1. (between the evenings) Exod 12:6, 18.
1 Kings 18:29. at *e.* sacrifice, Ezra 9:4, 5. Ps 141:2. Dan 9:21.
Hab 1:8. horses more fierce than *e.* wolves, Zeph 3:3.
Zech 14:7. at *e.* time it shall be light
EVENT, Eccles 2:14; 9:2, 3.
EVER, a long time, constantly, eternally, Josh 4:7; 14:9.
Deut 19:9. to walk *e.* in his way
Ps 5:11. let them *e.* shout for joy
25:15. my eyes *e.* towards the Lord
37:26. he is *e.* merciful and lendeth
51:3. and my sin is *e.* before me
Luke 15:31. son, thou art *e.* with me
John 8:35. in house son abideth *e.*
1 Thess 4:17. shall we *e.* be with the Lord
5:15. *e.* follow that which is good
2 Tim 3:7. *e.* learning, and never able to
Heb 7:24. this man continueth *e.*
25. he *e.* liveth to make intercession
Jude 25. to God be glory now and *e.*
Gen 3:22. and eat and live *for ever*
Deut 32:40. and say, I live—
Josh 4:24. fear the Lord your God—
1 Kings 10:9. Lord loved Israel—
1 Kings 11:39. afflict seed of David, but not—
Ps 9:7. Lord shall endure—102:12.
12:7. thou will preserve them—
22:26. your heart shall live—
23:6. dwell in house of the Lord—61:4.
30:12. give thanks to thee—52:9.
33:11. counsel of the Lord standeth—
37:18. their inheritance shall be—
49:9. he should still live—
73:26. God the strength . . . and my portion—
74:19. forget not congregation of poor—
81:15. their time should have endured—
92:7. that they shall be destroyed—
103:9. (the Lord) will not keep his anger—
105:8. remember . . . covenant—111:9.
119:111. thy testimonies as heritage—
146:6. which keepeth truth—
Prov 27:24. riches are not—
Eccles 1:4. the earth abideth—
Isa 26:4. trust in the Lord—for in Lord
32:17. quietness and assurance—

40:8. the word of our God shall stand—
57:16. I will not contend—Gen 6:3.
Jer 3:5. will he reserve anger—12.
32:39. that they may fear me—
Lam 3:31. the Lord will not cast off—
Mic 7:18. retaineth not his anger—
Zech 1:5. prophets, do they live—
John 6:51. if any eat . . . shall live—58.
Rom 1:25. the Creator who is blessed—
9:5. (Christ) is over all, God blessed—
2 Cor 9:9. his righteousness remaineth—
Heb 13:8. Jesus Christ, same . . . and—
1 Pet 1:23. the word of God abideth—
25. word of the Lord endureth—Isa 40:8.
1 John 2:17. doeth will of God abideth—
Exod 15:18. Lord reigneth *for ever and ever*
1 Chron 16:36. blessed be God—29:10. Neh 9:5. Dan 2:20.
Ps 10:16. the Lord is king—
45:6. thy throne, O God, is—Heb 1:8.
48:14. this God is our God—52:8.
111:8. commandments stand fast—
119:44. I will keep thy law—
145:1. I will bless thy name—2, 21.
Mic 4:5. walk in the name of . . . God—
Gal 1:5. to whom be glory—Rom 11:36.
Phil 4:20. 1 Tim 1:17. Heb 13:21. 1 Pet 4:11. Rev 1:6, &c.
Rev 4:9. who liveth—Dan 4:34; 12:7.

EVERLASTING hills, Gen 49:26.
Gen 17:8. Canaan, an *e.* possession, 48:4.
21:33. called on the name of Lord, *e.* God
Exod 40:15. *e.* priesthood, Num 25:13.
Deut 33:27. underneath are *e.* arms
Ps 24:7. lifted up ye *e.* doors
41:13. blessed be God from *e.* to *e.*
90:2. from *e.* to *e.* thou art, 106:48.
103:17. mercy of Lord from *e.* to *e.* 100:5.
112:6. righteous in *e.* remembrance
139:24. lead me in the way *e.*
145:13. *e.* kingdom, Dan 4:3.
Prov 10:25. righteous is an *e.* *foundation*
Isa 9:6. The mighty God, the *e.* Father
26:4. in the Lord Jehovah is *e.* strength
33:14. who dwell with *e.* burnings
35:10. songs of *e.* joy, 51:11; 61:7.
40:28. the *e.* God . . . fainteth not
45:17. Israel saved with *e.* salvation
55:13. to the Lord for a name, an *e.* sign
56:5. an *e.* name, 63:12; from *e.* 16.
60:19. the Lord shall be an *e.* light, 20.
Jer 10:10. true . . . living God, *e.* King
Jer 20:11. *everlasting* confusion never forgotten
23:40. *e.* reproach. 31:3. with *e.* love
Dan 4:34. *e.* dominion, 7:14.
Mic 5:2. goings forth of old, from *e.*
Hab 1:12. art thou not from *e.*, 3:6. *e.* mountains scattered;
Matt 18:8. cast into *e.* fire, 25:41.
25:46. shall go into *e.* punishment
Luke 16:9. receive into *e.* habitations
2 Thess 1:9. punished with *e.* destruction
1 Tim 6:16. to whom be . . . power *e.*
2 Pet 1:11. *e.* kingdom of Lord Jesus Christ
Jude 6. reserved in *e.* chains
Rev 14:6. having the *e.* gospel
Dan 12:2. awake to *everlasting life*
Matt 19:29. shall inherit—
Luke 18:30. in world to come—
John 3:16. not perish but have—36.
4:14. well of water springing up into—
5:24. that heareth my word hath—
6:27. meat which endureth to—
40. whoso believeth may have—47.
12:50. his commandment is—
Acts 13:46. yourselves unworthy of—
Rom 6:22. ye have . . . and the end—
Gal 6:8. shall of the Spirit reap—
1 Tim 1:16. believe on him to—

EVERMORE, Ps 16:11, &c. John 6:34. 2 Cor 11:31. 1 Thess 5:16. Rev 1:18.

EVERY imagination evil, Gen 6:5.
Ps 32:6. for this *e.* one . . . godly pray
119:101. *e.* evil way. 104. *e.* false way, 128.
Prov 2:9. understand *e.* good path
14:15. simple believeth *e.* word
15:3. eyes of Lord are in *e.* place
Eccles 3:1. a time to *e.* purpose
Isa 45:23. *e.* knee shall bow, *e. tongue* swear, Rom 14:11. Phil 2:11.
2 Tim 2:21. *e.* good (4:18. *e.* evil) work
Heb 12:1. let us lay aside *e.* weight
1 John 4:1. believe not *e.* spirit

EVIDENCE, Jer 32:10. Heb 11:1.
Evidently (visibly), Acts 10:3. Gal 3:1.

EVIL, Gen 2:9, 17; 3:5, 22.
Deut 29:21. I will separate him to *e.*
30:15. life and good, death and *e.*
Josh 24:15. if it seem *e.* to you
Job 2:10. shall we not receive *e.*
5:19. there shall no *e.* touch thee
30:26. looked for good *e.* came
Ps 23:4. I will fear no *e.* for thou
34:21. *e.* shall slay the wicked
51:4. have done this *e.* in thy sight
52:3. lovest *e.* more than good
91:10. no *e.* shall befall thee
97:10. ye that love the Lord, hate *e.*
Prov 5:14. I was almost in all *e.*
12:21. no *e.* shall happen to just
15:3. beholding the *e.* and the good
31:12. will do him good and not *e.*
Eccles 5:13. sore *e.*, riches kept to hurt
9:3. heart of . . . men is full of *e.*
Isa 5:20. call *e.* good, and good *e.*
7:15. know to refuse the *e.* 16.
45:7. I make peace and create *e.*
57:1. taken away from the *e.* to come
59:7. feet run to *e.* and make haste
Jer 17:17. art my hope in day of *e.*
18:11. I frame *e.* against you,
29:11. thoughts of peace and not of *e.*
44:27. I will watch over them for *e.*
Lam 3:38. proceedeth not *e.* and good
Ezek 7:5. an *e.* an only *e.* is come
Dan 9:12. on us a great *evil,* 13, 14.
Amos 3:6. shall there be *e.* in a city
5:14. seek good and not *e.*
9:4. set eyes on them for *e.*
Hab 1:13. purer eyes than to behold *e.*
Matt 5:11. all manner of *e.* against you
6:34. sufficient to the day is *e.* thereof
Rom 2:9. on every soul that doeth *e.*
7:19. *e.* which I would not that I do
21. I would do good *e.* is present with me
12:17. recompense to no man *e.* for *e.*
21. be not overcome of *e.* but overcome *e.*
1 Cor 13:5. charity thinketh no *e.*
1 Thess 5:15. none render *e.* for *e.* 1 Pet 3:9.
22. abstain from all appearance of *e.*
1 Tim 6:10. love of money is the root of all *e.*
Titus 3:2. to speak *e.* of no man

EXPECTATION, Luke 3:15. Acts 12:11.
Ps 9:18. *e.* of poor shall not perish
62:5. on God; for my *e.* is from him
Prov 10:28.. *e. of wicked* shall perish, 11:7.
11:23.—is wrath
23:18. *e.* shall not be cut off, 24:14.
Isa 20:5. be ashamed of their *e.* 6.
Rom 8:19. *e.* of creature waiteth
Phil 1:20. according to earnest *e.*
Jer 29:11. give you an *expected* end
EXPEDIENT that one man die for the people, John 11:50; 18:14.
John 16:7. *e.* for you that I go away
1 Cor 6:12. all things not *e.* 10:23.
12:1. it is not *e.* for me to glory
EXPERIENCE, Gen 30:27. Rom 5:4.
2 Cor 9:13. by the *experiment* of
EXPERT in war, 1 Chron 12:33. Song of Sol 3:8. Jer 50:9. in customs, Acts 26:3.
EXPOUNDED, riddle, Judg 14:19. he *e.* Mark 4:34. Luke 24:27. Peter *e.* Acts 11:4. Aq. & Pris. *e.* 18:26. Paul *e.* 28:23.
EXPRESSLY, Ezek 1:3. 1 Tim 4:1.
EXTEND mercy, Ezra 7:28; 9:9.
Ps 109:12. *e.* peace like a river, Isa 66:12.
Ps 16:2. my goodness *extendeth* not to thee
EXTINCT, Job 17:1. Isa 43:17.
EXTOL (God), Ps 30:1; 66:17; 68:4; 145:1. Isa 52:13. Dan 4:37.
EXTORTION, Ezek 22:12. Matt 23:25.
Ps 109:11. *Extortioner,* Isa 16:4. Luke 18:11. 1 Cor 5:10, 11; 6:10.
EXTREME, Deut 28:22. Job 35:15.
EYE for *e.* Exod 21:24. Matt 5:38.
Deut 32:10. apple of *e.* Ps 17:8.
Job 24:15. no *e.* shall see me
Ps 33:18. the *e.* of the Lord on them
Prov 20:12. the seeing *e.* Lord hath
Eccles 1:8. the *e.* not satisfied, 4:8.
Isa 64:4. neither *e.* seen, 1 Cor 2:9.
Jer 13:17. mine *e.* shall weep sore, because
Matt 6:22. light of body is the *e.* Luke 11:34.
18:9. if thine *e.* offend thee, 5:29.
Rev 1:7. every *e.* shall see him
Prov 23:6. *evil eye,* 28:22. Matt 6:23; 20:15. Mark 7:22. Luke 11:34.
Job 16:16. *eyelids,* 41:18. Ps *11:4; 132:4. Prov 4:25; 6:4, 25; 30:13.* Jer 9:18.
Rev 3:18. *eyesalve;* Eph 6:6. *eyeservice,* Col 3:22.
2 Sam 22:25. *eyesight,* Ps 18:24.
Luke 1:2. *eyewitnesses,* 2 Pet 1:16.
Gen 3:5. your *eyes* shall be opened
Job 10:4. hast thou *e.* of flesh
Ps 15:4. in whose *e.* a vile person
145:15. *e.* of all wait on thee
Eccles 2:14. wise man's *e.* in his head
11:7. pleasant for *e.* to behold sun
Isa 3:16. walk with . . wanton *e.*
29:18. *e.* of blind see out of obscurity
32:3. *e.* of them that see shall not dim
Isa 35:5. *eyes* of blind shall be opened, 42:7.
43:8. blind people that have *e.*
Jer 5:21. have *e.* and see not, Isa 42:20.
Hab 1:13. purer *e.* than to behold
Zech 3:9. on one stone seven *e.*
Matt 13:16. blessed are your *e.* for
18:9. having two *e.* to be cast into hell fire
Mark 8:18. having *e.* see ye not
Luke 4:20. *e.* of all were fastened on him
10:23. blessed are the *e.* which see
John 9:6. anointed *e.* of blind man
Rom 11:8. *e.* that they should not
Eph 1:18. *e.* of your understanding
Heb 4:13. all open unto *e.* of him
2 Pet 2:14. *e.* full of adultery
1 John 2:16. lust of the *e.* and pride
Rev 1:14. his *e.* as fire, 2:18; 19:12.
3:18. anoint *e.* 4:6, full of *e.* 8.
Deut 13:18. right in the *eyes of the Lord,* 1 Kings 15:5, 11; 22:43.
Gen 6:8. Noah found grace in the—
1 Sam 26:24. my life be set by in—
2 Sam 15:25. find favour in—
2 Chron 16:9.—run to and fro, Zech 4:10.
Ps 34:15.—on righteous, 1 Pet 3:12.
Prov 5:21. ways of man before—
15:3.—are in every place beholding
22:12.—preserve knowledge
Isa 49:5. shall I be glorious in—
Amos 9:8.—on the sinful kingdom
Ps 25:15. *mine eyes* ever towards Lord
101:6.—shall be upon the faithful
119:148.—prevent the night watches
141:8.—are unto thee, O God
Isa 1:15. I will hide—from you
65:12. did evil before—66:4.
Jer 9:1. Oh that—were a fountain of tears
14:17.—run down with tears
24:6. I will set—upon them for good
Amos 9:4. I will set—on them for evil
Luke 2:30.—have seen thy salvation
Ps 123:2. *our eyes* wait on the Lord
Matt 20:33. that—may be opened
1 John 1:1. which we have seen with—
Deut 12:8. right *in his own eyes,* Judg 17:6; 21:25.
Job 32:1. he was righteous—
Neh 6:16. cast down *in their own eyes*
Ps 139:16. *thine eyes* did see my substance
Prov 23:5. set—on that which is not
Isa 30:20.—shall see thy teachers
Jer 5:3. are not—upon the truth
Ezek 24:16. take away the desire of—25.

F

FABLES, 1 Tim 1:4; 4:7. 2 Tim 4:4. Titus 1:14. 2 Pet 1:16.
FACE, Gen 3:19; 16:8.
Lev 19:32. honour the *f.* of old man
Num 6:25. Lord make his *f.* shine, Ps 31:16; 67:1; 80:3; 119:135. Dan 9:17.
2 Chron 6:42. turn not *f.* Ps 132:10.
Ps 17:15. behold thy *f.* in righteousness
84:9. behold the *f.* of anointed, 132:10.
Ezek 1:10. *f.* of a man, Rev 4:7.
Hos 5:5. testify to his *f.* 7:10.
Matt 11:10. my messenger before thy *f.* Mark 1:2. Luke 7:27; 9:52.
Acts 2:25. Lord always before my *f.*
1 Cor 13:12. but then *f.* to *f.*
2 Cor 3:18. with open *f.* beholding
James 1:23. his natural *f.* in a glass
FADE, we all *f.* as a leaf, Isa 64:6.
James 1:11. rich man *f.* away in his ways
1 Pet 1:4. inheritance that *fadeth* not away
1 Pet 5:4. crown of glory that *fadeth* not away
FAIL, Deut 28:32. Job 11:20.
Deut 31:6. Lord will not *f.* nor forsake, 8. Josh 1:5. 1 Chron 28:20.
Ps 12:1. faithful *f.* from among men
77:8. doth his promise *f.* for evermore
Lam 3:22. his compassions *f.* not
Luke 16:9. ye *f.* they may receive you
17. one tittle of law to *f.* Matt 5:18.
22:32. prayed that thy faith *f.* not
Heb 12:15. lest any *f.* of the grace
Song of Sol 5:6. soul *failed* when he spake

Ps 31:10. my strength *faileth,* 38:10; 71:9. heart *f.* 40:12. spirit *f.* 143:7.
Luke 12:33. treasure in heaven that *f.* not
1 Cor 13:8. charity never *f.*
Deut 28:65. shall give *failing* of eyes
Luke 21:26. men's hearts *f.* them
FAINT, Deut 25:18. Judg 8:4, 5.
Isa 1:5. head is sick, whole heart *f.*
40:29. he giveth power to the *f.*
30. youths shall *f.* and be weary
31. wait on Lord shall walk and not *f.*
2 Cor 4:1. received mercy we *f.* not, 16.
Gal 6:9. shall reap if we *f.* not
Heb 12:5. nor *f.* when rebuked of
Ps 27:13. *fainted* unless I believed
Rev 2:3. hast laboured and not *f.*
Ps 84:2. soul *fainteth* for courts of Lord 119:81—for thy salvation
Isa 40:28. God the Creator *f.* not
FAIR, Gen 6:2; 12:11; 24:16.
Prov 7:21. *f.* speech, Rom 16:18.
Song of Sol 1:15. behold thou art *f.* 4:1, &c.
Jer 12:6. they speak *f.* words
Acts 7:20. Moses was exceeding *f.*
Gal 6:12. desire to make *f.* shew in
Ps 45:2. *fairer* than children of men
Dan 1:15. their countenance *f.*
FAITH, Acts 3:16; 13:8.
Deut 32:20. children in whom is no *f.*
Matt 6:30. clothe you, O ye of little *f.* 8:26; 16:8; 14:31. Luke 12:28.
8:10. not found so great *f.* Luke 7:9.
17:20. *f.* as a grain of mustard seed
21:21. have *f.* and doubt not
23:23. omitted judgment, mercy, and *f.*
Mark 4:40. how is it ye have no *f.*
Luke 17:5. Lord, increase our *f.*
6. if ye had *f.* ye might say to this
18:8. shall (Son) find *f.* on the earth
Acts 3:16. the *f.* which is by him
6:5. Stephen, a man full of *f.* & Holy Ghost
7. company of priests obedient to *f.*
11:24. good man, full of Holy Ghost and of *f.*
14:9. that he had *f.* to be healed
16:5. churches established in the *f.*
20:21. *f.* toward our Lord Jesus Christ
Rom 1:5. for obedience to the *f.*
17. righteousness of God revealed from *f.* to *f.* . . . The just shall live by *f.*
3:3. make *f.* of God without effect
27. of works? Nay, but by the law of *f.*
4:5. his *f.* is counted for righteousness
11. circumcision, a seal of righteousness of the *f.* 12. *f.* of Abraham, 16.
13. through the righteousness of *f.*
14. if of law be heirs, *f.* is made void
10:8. the word of *f.* which we preach
10:17. *f.* cometh by hearing, and hearing
12:3. God dealt every man measure of *f.*
6. according to the proportion of *f.*
14:22. hast thou *f.*? have it to . . . God
Rom 16:26. nations for the obedience of *faith*
1 Cor 12:9. *f.* by the same spirit
13:2. though I have all *f.* to remove
13. now abideth *f.*, hope, charity
2 Cor 4:13. having the same Spirit of *f.*
Gal 1:23. preacheth the *f.* which
3:2. Spirit by the hearing of *f.* 5.
12. the law is not of *f.* but the man
23. before *f.* came, we were under the law
25. after that *f.* is come, we are no
5:6. but *f.* which worketh by love
22. but the fruit of the Spirit is . . . *f.*
Eph 4:5. one Lord, one *f.*, one baptism
6:16. above all taking the shield of *f.*
23. love with *f.* from God the Father
Phil 1:25. abide for your joy of *f.*
27. striving together for *f.* of the gospel
1 Thess 1:3. remember your work of *f.*
5:8. putting on the breastplate of *f.*
2 Thess 1:4. glory for your *f.* 11. fulfil work of *f.* 3:2. for all men have not *f.*
1 Tim 1:5. charity out of *f.* unfeigned
14. exceeding abundant with *f.*
3:9. holding the mystery of *f.*
4:1. in last days some shall depart from the *f.*
6. nourished up in the words of *f.*
5:8. denied *f.* 12. cast off first *f.*
6:12. fight the good fight of *f.*
2 Tim 1:5. unfeigned *f.* that is in thee
2:18. overthrow the *f.* of some
22. follow righteousness, *f.*, charity
3:8. reprobate concerning the *f.*
10. fully known my doctrine, manner of life, *f.*
4:7. fought a good fight, . . . kept the *f.*
Titus 1:1. according to the *f.* of God's elect
Heb 4:2. not being mixed with *f.*
6:1. dead works and of *f.* toward God
10:22. draw near in assurance of *f.*
23. hold fast the profession of our *f.*
11:1. *f.* substance of things hoped for
6. without *f.* impossible to please God
12:2. Jesus the finisher of our *f.*
13:7. whose *f.* follow, considering
James 2:1. have not *f.* of Lord Jesus
17. *f.* if it hath not works, is dead, 26.
18. hast *f.* and I works; shew me thy *f.*
22. *f.* wrought with his works; by works *f.* made perfect
5:15. prayer of *f.* shall save
2 Pet 1:1. like precious *f.* with us
1 John 5:4. overcometh world, even our *f.*
Jude 3. contend earnestly for the *f.*
20. building up yourselves on holy *f.*
Rev 2:13. hast not denied my *f.*
19. I know thy works and *f.*
13:10. here is the *f.* of the saints
14:12. which keep the *f.* of Jesus
Hab 2:4. just shall live *by faith,* Rom 1:17. Gal 3:11. Heb 10:38.
Acts 15:9. purifying their hearts—
26:18. are sanctified—that is in me
Rom 1:12. comforted *by* mutual *f.*
3:22. righteousness—of Christ
28. conclude a man is justified—
30. God, which shall justify circumcision—and uncircumcision through *f.*
5:1. being justified—we have peace
2. have access—Eph 3:12.
Rom 9:32. not—but by the works of the law
11:20. Thou standest—Be not highminded
2 Cor 1:24. of your joy; for—ye stand
5:7. we walk—and not by sight
Gal 2:16. not justified, but—3:24.
20. I live—of the Son of God
Gal 3:22. the promise *by faith* of Jesus Christ be given
26. children of God—in Jesus Christ
5:5. for hope of righteousness—
Eph 3:17. Christ dwell in your hearts—
Phil 3:9. righteousness through *f.*
Heb 11:4. —Abel, 5.—Enoch, &c.
7. heir of righteousness which is—
James 2:24. justified by works, not—
Rom 4:19. not weak *in faith*
20. strong—giving glory to God
1 Cor 16:13. stand fast—quit you
2 Cor 8:7. ye abound—and utterance
13:5. examine whether ye be—
Col 1:23. if ye continue—grounded

1 Tim 1:2. Timothy, my own son—
4. godly edifying which is—
2:7. teacher of the Gentiles—
15. if they continue—and charity
3:13. purchase great boldness—
2 Tim 1:13.—and love . . . in Christ Jesus
Titus 1:13. that they may be sound—2:2.
3:15. greet them that love us—
Heb 11:13. these died—not having
James 1:6. ask—nothing wavering
2:5. poor, rich—heirs of kingdom
1 Pet 5:9. whom resist, stedfast—
Matt 9:2. J., *their faith,* Mark 2:5. Luke 5:20.
Acts 3:16. *through faith* in his name
Rom 3:25. propitiation—in his blood
Gal 3:8. God would justify the heathen—
14. receive promise of Spirit—
Eph 2:8. by grace ye are saved—
Col 2:12.—of the operation of God
2 Tim 3:15. salvation—in Jesus
Heb 6:12.—and patience inherit promises
11:3.—we understand the worlds
28.—Moses kept the passover
33.—subdued kingdoms, &c.
39. obtained a good report—2.
1 Pet 1:5. kept by power of God—
Matt 9:22. *thy faith* hath made thee whole, Luke 8:48; 17:19.
15:28. O woman, great is—be it unto
Luke 7:50.—hath saved thee, 18:42.
22:32. I have prayed that—fail not
Philem 6. communication of—
James 2:18. shew me—without thy works
Luke 8:25. where is *your faith?*
Rom 1:8.—is spoken of through
1 Cor 2:5. that—not stand in wisdom
15:14. —is also vain, 17.
2 Cor 1:24. not . . . have dominion over—
10:15. when—is increased, we
Eph 1:15. heard of—in the Lord Jesus, Col 1:4.
Phil 2:17. sacrifice and service of—
Col 2:5. beholding stedfastness of—
1 Thess 1:8.—to God-ward is spread
3:2. comfort you concerning—
5. I sent to know—lest the tempter
6. brought us good tidings of—
7. comforted in affliction by—
10. perfect that which is lacking in—
2 Thess 1:3.—growth exceedingly
James 1:3. trying of—worketh patience
1 Pet 1:7. trial of—being precious
1:9. receiving the end of *your faith*
1:21. that—and hope might be in God
2 Pet 1:5. add to—virtue, and to virtue
Matt 17:17. O *faithless* and perverse generation, Mark 9:19. Luke 9:41.
John 20:27. be not *f.* but believing

FAITHFUL, 1 Sam 2:35; 22:14. 2 Sam 20:19. Neh 13:13. Dan 6:4. 1 Tim 6:2. 1 Pet 5:12.
Num 12:7. *faithful* in all my house
Heb 3:2, 5. Moses *f.* in all his house
Deut 7:9. He is God, the *f.* God keepeth covenant
Neh 7:2. a *f.* man, and feared God
9:8. foundest (Abraham's) heart *f.*
Ps 12:1. *f.* fail from among men
31:23. Lord preserveth the *f.*
89:37. as a *f.* witness in heaven
101:6. mine eyes be upon *f.* of the land
119:86. thy commandments are *f.*
Prov 11:13. He that is of a *f.* spirit
13:17. a *f.* ambassador is health
14:5. a *f.* witness will not lie
20:6. a *f.* man who can find?
27:6. *f.* are the wounds of a friend
28:20. *f.* man abound with blessings
Isa 1:21. the *f.* city become an harlot
26. city of righteousness, *f.* city
8:2. I took *f.* witnesses to record
49:7. Lord is *f.* Holy One of Israel
Jer 42:5. the Lord be a *f.* witness
Hos 11:12. Judah is *f.* with saints
Matt 25:21. well done . . . *f.* servant
23. *f.* in a few things, Luke 19:17.
Luke 12:42. who is that *f.* steward
16:10. *f.* in least is *f.* also in much
12. not *f.* in what is another man's
Acts 16:15. judged me *f.* to the Lord
1 Cor 1:9. God is *f.* by whom ye
4:2. required in stewards, a man *f.*
17. Timothy who is *f.* in the Lord
10:13. God is *f.* who will not suffer
Eph 1:1. *f.* in Christ Jesus, Col 1:2.
6:21. *f.* minister, Col 1:7; 4:7, 9.
1 Thess 5:24. *f.* is he that calleth
2 Thess 3:3. but the Lord is *f.*, who
1 Tim 1:12. for he counted me *f.*
15. a *f.* saying and worthy of all acceptation, 4:9. 2 Tim 2:11. Titus 3:8.
3:11. wives grave, . . . sober, *f.* in all
2 Tim 2:2. same commit to *f.* men
13. abideth *f.*: he cannot deny himself
Titus 1:6. one wife, having *f.* children
9. holding fast the *f.* word as taught
Heb 2:17. might be a merciful and *f.* high priest
10:23. *f.* is he that promised, 11:11.
1 Pet 4:19. as unto a *f.* Creator
1 John 1:9. he is *f.* and just to forgive
Rev 1:5. *f.* and true witness, 3:14.
17:14. they are chosen and *f.*
21:5. words are true and *f.* 22:6.
1 Sam 26:23. render every man his . . . *faithfulness*
Ps 5:9. no *f.* in their mouth
36:5. thy *f.* reacheth to the clouds
40:10. I have declared thy *f.* *See* 89:1.
88:11. or thy *f.* in destruction?
89:1. make known thy *f.* to all generations
5. praise thy *f.* in the congregation
8. who is like to thy *f.* round about thee
24. my *f.* shall be with him (David)
33. no suffer my *f.* to fail
92:2. to shew forth thy *f.* every night
119:75. thou in *f.* hast afflicted me
90. thy *faithfulness* is unto all generations
143:1. in thy *f.* answer me, and in thy
Isa 11:5. *f.* the girdle of his reins
Lam 3:23. great is thy *f.*
Hos 2:20. I will betroth thee to me in *f.*

FALL, Num 11:31; 14:29, 32.
Gen 45:24. *f.* not out by the way
2 Sam 24:14. *f.* into the hand of Lord
Ps 37:24. though he *f.* he shall not
45:5. whereby people *f.* under thee
Ps 141:10. let wicked *fall* into their own nets
145:14. the Lord upholdeth all that *f.*
Prov 11:5. wicked *f.* by own wickedness
24:16. wicked shall *f.* into mischief
26:27. diggeth pit shall *f.* in, Eccles 10:8.
28:14. hardeneth his heart shall *f.*
Eccles 4:10. if they *f.* one will lift up
Isa 8:15. many shall stumble and *f.*
Dan 11:35. them of understanding shall *f.*
Hos 10:8. and to the hills, *f.* on us, Luke 23:30. Rev 6:16.
Mic 7:8. rejoice not when I *f.*
Matt 7:27. great was the *f.* of it
10:29. sparrow not *f.* on the ground

15:14. blind lead blind, both *f.* into ditch
Luke 2:34. set for *f.* and rising of many
Rom 11:11. stumbled that they should *f.* . . . through their *f.* salvation is come
14:13. occasion to *f.* in his brother's
1 Cor 10:12. take heed lest he *f.*
1 Tim 3:6. *f.* into condemnation of devil
6:9. will be rich *f.* into temptation
Heb 4:11. *f.* after the same example
10:31. fearful to *f.* into hands of living God
James 1:2. when ye *f.* into divers
2 Pet 1:10. if ye do these . . . shall never *f.*
3:17. lest ye *f.* from stedfastness
Heb 6:6. impossible if . . . *fall away* to renew
Ps 16:6. *fallen* in pleasant places
Hos 14:1. thou hast *f.* by thine iniquity
Gal 5:4. justified . . . ye are *f.* from grace
Rev 2:5. remember whence thou art *f.*
Prov 24:16. just man *falleth* seven times
Rom 14:4. to his own master he *f.*
Ps 56:13. wilt not deliver (116:8. hast delivered) my feet from *falling*
2 Thess 2:3. there come a *f.* away first
Jude 24. able to keep you from *f.*
FALLOW, Jer 4:3. Hos 10:12.
FALSE, Jer 14:14; 37:14.
Exod 23:1. not raise a *f.* report
7. keep thee far from a *f.* matter
Ps 119:104. hate every *f.* way, 128.
Prov 11:1. *f.* balance abomination, 20:23.
Jer 14:14. prophesy to you a *f.* vision
23:32. against them that prophesy *f.* dreams
Zech 8:17. love no *f.* oath
Mal 3:5. witness against *f.* swearers
Matt 24:24. *f.* Christs, *f.* prophets
2 Cor 11:13. *f.* apostles, *f.* brethren
Gal 2:4. *f.* teachers, 2 Pet 2:1.
2 Tim 3:3. *f.* accusers, Titus 2:3.
Ps 119:118. their deceit is *falsehood*
144:8. whose right hand is a . . . of *f.*
Isa 57:4. are ye not . . . a seed of *f.*
59:13. from the heart words of *f.*
Jer 10:14. molten image is *f.* 51:17.
Lev 6:3. sweareth *falsely,* Jer 7:9.
19:12. swear by my name *f.* Jer 5:2.
Ps 44:17. not dealt *f.* in covenant
Jer 6:13. every one dealeth *f.* 8:10.
Zech 5:4. house of him that sweareth *f.*
Matt 5:11. evil against you *f.* for
Luke 3:14. neither accuse any *f.*
1 Pet 3:16. be ashamed that *f.* accuse
Matt 7:15. *false prophets,* 24:11, 24. Luke 6:26. 2 Pet 2:1. 1 John 4:1.
Exod 20:16. *false witness,* Deut 5:20; 19:16. Prov 6:19; 12:17; 14:5; 19:5, 9; 21:28; 25:18; Matt 15:19; 19:18. Rom 13:9. 1 Cor 15:15.
FAMILIAR, Job 19:14. Ps 41:9. Lev 19:31; 20:6, 27. Isa 8:19.
FAMILY, Gen 10:5. Lev 20:5.
Zech 12:12. mourn, every *f.* apart
Eph 3:15. whole *f.* in heaven are named
Ps 68:6. setteth the solitary in *families*
Amos 3:2. known of all the *f.* of the earth
FAMINE, Gen 12:10; 41:27.
Job 5:20. in *f.* he shall redeem thee
Ps 33:19. keep them alive in *f.*
37:19. in the days of *f.* be satisfied
Ezek 5:16. evil arrows of *f.* 6:11.
Amos 8:11. not a *f.* of bread
FAMISH, Gen 41:55. Prov 10:3. Isa 5:13. Zeph 2:11.
FAN, Isa 41:16. Jer 4:11; 51:2. Matt 3:12. Luke 3:17.
FAR, Exod 8:28. Neh 4:19.
Exod 23:7. keep thee *f.* from a false matter
Ps 73:27. *f.* from thee shall perish
Mark 12:34. not *f.* from the kingdom
Eph 2:13. were *f.* off made nigh by
Phil 1:23. to be with Christ . . . is *f.* better
FARTHING, Matt 5:26; 10:29.
FASHION, 1 Cor 7:31. Phil 2:8.
Job 10:8. thy hands . . . *fashioned* me, Ps 119:73.
Ps 139:16. in continuance were *f.*
Ezek 16:7. thy breasts are *f.*
Phil 3:21. be *f.* like his glorious body
Ps 33:15. he *fashioneth* their hearts
1 Pet 1:14. not *fashioning* yourselves
FAST, 2 Sam 12:21. Esther 4:16.
Isa 58:4. ye *f.* for strife; shall not *f.* as
Jer 14:12. when they *f.* I will not hear
Zech 7:5. did ye at all *f.* unto me
Matt 6:16. ye *f.* be not as hypocrites, *see* 18.
9:14. why do we *f.* but thy disciples *f.* not, 18. Luke 5:33.
15. can children of bride-chamber *f.* . . . shall they *f.* Mark 2:19, 20. Luke 5:34, 35.
Luke 18:12. I *f.* twice in the week
1 Kings 21:9. saying, proclaim a *f.* 12. 2 Chron 20:3. Ezra 8:21. Isa 58:3, 5, 6. Jer 36:9. Joel 1:14; 2:15. Jon 3:5. Zech 8:19. Acts 27:9.
Judg 20:26. *fasted* that day, 1 Sam 7:6.
2 Sam 1:12. wept and *f.* till even
12:16. David *f.* and lay all night on
Ezra 8:23. we *f.* and besought the Lord
Isa 58:3. why have we *f.* and thou
Matt 4:2. when he had *f.* forty days
Acts 13:2, 3. ministered to Lord, *f.* and prayed
Neh 9:1. assembled with *fasting*
Esther 4:3. Jews *f.* and weeping, 9:31.
Ps 109:24. my knees weak through *f.*
Jer 36:6. read the roll on *f.* day
Dan 6:18. king passed the night *f.*
9:3. to seek by prayer and supplication with *f.*
Joel 2:12. turn ye to me with *f.*
Matt 15:32. not send them away *f.*
Acts 10:30. was *f.* till this hour
14:23. ordained elders, prayed with *f.*
1 Cor 7:5. give yourselves to *f.*
Luke 2:37. with *fastings* and prayers night and day
2 Cor 6:5. in *f.* (often, 11:27.)
FASTENED, Job 38:6. Eccles 12:11. Isa 22:25. Luke 4:20.
FAT is Lord's, Lev 3:16; 4:8.
Prov 11:25. liberal soul shall be made *f.*
13:4. soul of the diligent shall be made *f.*
15:30. good report maketh bones *f.*
28:25. trust in the Lord shall be made *f.*
Isa 25:6. *f.* things full of marrow
11:6. *fatling,* Matt 22:4.
Job 36:16. be set on table . . . be full of *fatness*
Ps 36:8. satisfied with *f.* of thy house
63:5. satisfied with marrow and *f.*
Ps 65:11. and thy paths drop *fatness*
Isa 55:2. let your soul delight in *f.*
Jer 31:14. satiate the soul of priests with *f.*
Rom 11:17. root and *f.* of the olive-tree
FATHER, Gen 2:24; 4:20, 21.
Gen 17:4. be a *f.* of many nations
Num 11:12. as *f.* beareth sucking child
2 Sam 7:14. I will be his *f.* Heb 1:5.
Job 29:16. I was a *f.* to the poor
31:18. brought up with me as with a *f.*
38:28. hath the rain a *f.* or who
Ps 68:5. a *f.* of fatherless . . . is God
103:13. as a *f.* pitieth his children
Isa 9:6. the everlasting *F.,* prince of
Jer 31:9. I am a *f.* to Israel and
Mal 1:6. if I be a *f.* where is my honour
2:10. Have we not all one *f.*?
John 5:19. what he seeth the *F.* do

20. the *F.* loveth the Son, 3:35.
21. as *F.* raiseth dead and quickeneth
22. *F.* judgeth no man but hath . . . the Son
26. as *F.* hath life in himself; so Son
8:18. *F.* . . . beareth witness of me
29. *F.* hath not left me alone
16:32. I am not alone, *F.* is with me
Acts 1:4. wait for the promise of the *F.*
7. times . . . *F.* put in his own power
Rom 4:11. the *f.* of all that believe
12. *f.* of circumcision, 16. the *f.* of us all
17. made thee a *f.* of many nations
1 Cor 8:6. *F.* of whom are all things
2 Cor 1:3. God and *F.* of our Lord, *F.* of mercies, Eph 1:3, 1 Pet 1:3. *F.* of glory, Eph 1:17.
6:18. I will be a *F.* to you and ye
1 Tim 5:1. intreat him as a *f.*
Heb 1:5. I will be to him a *F.* and
12:9. subjection to the *F.* of spirits
James 1:17. gift . . . from the *F.* of lights
John 5:17. *my Father* worketh and I
10:30. I and—are one; 14:20. I am in—, 10; 28.—is greater
Ezek 16:45. *your father* an Amorite
Matt 5:16. glorify—in heaven
23:9. call no man—on earth
John 8:41. ye do the deeds of—. . . . said . . . We have one *F.*, even God
20:17. I ascend to my *F.* and—
Exod 15:2. my *f.*'s God, and I will exalt
Neh 9:16. *our fathers* dealt proudly
Ps 22:4.—trusted in thee
39:12. sojourner, as all my *f.* were
Lam 5:7.—have sinned . . . and we
Acts 15:10.—nor we able to bear
Exod 22:22. not afflict . . . the *fatherless*
Deut 10:18. execute judgment of *f.*
Ps 10:14. thou helper of the *f.*
68:5. a father of the *f.* . . . is God
146:9. (Lord) relieveth the *f.* and widow
Isa 1:17. judge the *f.*, plead for widow
Hos 14:3. in thee the *f.* findeth mercy
James 1:27. visit the *f.* in affliction

FAULT, Gen 41:9. Exod 5:16.
Matt 18:15. if trespass, tell him his *f.*
Luke 23:4. I find no *f.* in him, 14. John 18:38; 19:4, 6.
1 Cor 6:7. utterly a *f.* among you
Gal 6:1. if a man be overtaken in a *f.*
Ps 19:12. cleanse thou me from secret *faults*
1 Pet 2:20. if when . . . buffeted for your *f.*
Jude 24. to present you *faultless*

FAVOUR, Gen 39:21. Deut 33:23.
1 Sam 2:26. Samuel in *f.* with the Lord
Job 10:12. granted me life and *f.*
Ps 5:12. with *favour* wilt thou compass
30:5. in his *f.* is life; weeping may endure
Prov 31:30. *f.* is deceitful, beauty vain
Luke 2:52. in *f.* with God and man
Ps 41:11. know thou *favourest* me

FEAR, Gen 9:2. Exod 15:16.
Ps 53:5. in *f.* where no *f.* was
90:11. according to thy *f.* so is wrath
119:38. servant devoted to thy *f.*
120. flesh trembleth for *f.* of thee
Prov 1:26. mock when *f.* cometh
29:25. *f.* of man bringeth a snare
Isa 8:12. *f.* not their *f.* nor be afraid
29:13. their *f.* toward me is taught
63:17. hardened our heart from thy *f.*
Jer 32:40. put my *f.* in their hearts
Mal 1:6. if master where is my *f.*
Rom 13:7. render *f.* to whom *f.*
2 Tim 1:7. spirit of *f.* but of power
Heb 2:15. who through *f.* of death
12:28. with reverence and godly *f.*
1 Pet 1:17. time of sojourning here in *f.*
1 John 4:18. no *f.* in love, love casteth out *f.*
Gen 20:11. *fear of God* not in this place
2 Sam 23:3. ruleth men just, ruling in—
Neh 5:15. so did not I because of—
Ps 36:1. no—before eyes, Rom 3:18.
2 Cor 7:1. perfecting holiness in—
Job 28:28. *fear of the Lord,* that is
Ps 19:9.—is clean, enduring for ever
34:11. children, I will teach you—
Prov 1:29. they did not choose—
8:13.—is to hate evil
10:27.—prolongeth days
14:26. in—is strong confidence
15:33.—is instruction of wisdom
16:6. by—men depart from evil
19:23.—tendeth to life; satisfied
22:4. by—are riches, honour, life
23:17. be thou in—all day long
Isa 33:6.—is his treasure
Acts 9:31. walking in—and comfort
Ps 2:11. *with fear,* Phil 2:12.
Deut 4:10. learn to *f.* me
5:29. such a heart that would *f.* me
28:58. mayest *f.* this glorious name
1 Chron 16:30. *f.* before him all earth
2 Chron 6:31. that they may *f.* thee, 33.
Neh 1:11. servants, desire to *f.* thy name
Ps 23:4. I will *f.* no evil, for thou
31:19. goodness laid up for those that *f.*
61:5. heritage of them that *f.* thy name
86:11. unite my heart to *f.* thy name
Jer 10:7. who would not *f.* thee
32:39. heart that may *f.* me for ever
Luke 12:5. *f.*, him, which . . . cast into hell, Matt 10:28.
Rom 8:15. not received spirit of bondage again to *f.*
11:20. be not highminded, but *f.*
Heb 4:1. *f.* lest promise being left
12:21. Moses said, I exceedingly *f.*
Rev 2:10. *f.* none of those things
11:18. saints and them that *f.* thy name
Gen 42:18. this do and live, for I *fear God*
Exod 18:21. such as—men of truth
Ps 66:16. come and hear, all that—
Eccles 5:7. vanities, *f.* thou God
8:12. shall be well with them that—
12:13.—keep his commandments
Job 37:24. therefore men do *fear him*
Ps 25:14. secret of the Lord is with *them that fear him*
33:18. eye of the Lord upon—
Ps 85:9. salvation nigh to *them that fear him*
103:13. as father, so Lord pitieth—
17. mercy everlasting upon—
147:11. The Lord taketh pleasure in—
Luke 1:50. his mercy on—from generation
Deut 6:2. mightest *fear the Lord*
13. thou shalt—thy God, 10:20.
24.—our God for our good always
10:12.—thy God to walk in his ways
14:23. learn to—thy God, 17:19; 31:12, 13.
Josh 4:24. ye might—your God
24:14. therefore—serve in sincerity
1 Sam 12:14. if ye will—and serve
24. only—and serve him in truth
1 Kings 18:12. thy servant did—2 Kings 4:1.
2 Kings 17:28. how they should—
Ps 15:4. be honoureth them that—
22:23. ye that—trust in him, 115:11.
33:8. let all the earth—
115:13. he will bless them that—

118:4. let them that—say, his mercy
135:20. ye that—bless the Lord
Prov 3:7.—and depart from evil
24:21. my son—and meddle not
Jer 5:24. let us—that giveth rain
26:19. did not he—and besought Lord
Hos 3:5. and shall—and his goodness
Jon 1:9. I—the God of heaven
Gen 15:1. *fear not,* I am thy shield
Num 14:9. Lord is with us—them
Deut 1:21.—neither be discouraged, 31:8. Josh 8:1; 10:25.
Ps 56:4. I will not f. what flesh can do, 118:6. Heb 13:6.
Isa 41:10.—for I am with thee, I will help thee, 13; 43:5.
Jer 5:22. f. ye not me, saith the Lord
30:10.—O my servant Jacob, 46:27, 28.
Matt 10:28.—them that kill the body
Luke 12:32.—little flock
Exod 1:17. midwives *feared* God, 21.
14:31. people f. Lord and believed
1 Sam 12:18. all people greatly f. Lord
Neh 7:2. Hanani f. God above many
Job 1:1. that f. God and eschewed evil
Ps 76:7. thou art to be f.
89:7. God is greatly to be f. in the
96:4. Lord is to be f. above all gods
Mal 3:16. they that f. the Lord spake often
Acts 10:2. one that f. God
Heb 5:7. was heard in that he f.
Gen 22:12. that thou *fearest* God
Job 1:8. that *feareth* God, 2:3.
Prov 28:14. happy man that f. alway
Acts 10:22. one that f. God and of good report
35. that f. God and worketh righteousness
13:26. whosoever among you f. God
Ps 25:12. what man is he that *feareth the Lord*
112:1. blessed is the man that—
Isa 50:10. who among you—
Exod 15:11. *fearful* in praises
Matt 8:26. why are ye f. Mark 4:40.
Heb 10:27. *certain f. looking* for of
31. f. thing to fall into hands of the living God
Rev 21:8. f. and unbelieving shall have their part
Ps 139:14. I am *fearfully* and wonderfully made
55:5. *fearfulness* and trembling
Isa 33:14. f. hath surprised hypocrites
FEAST, Gen 19:3; 21:8.
Prov 15:15. merry heart continual f.
Eccles 10:19. f. is made for laughter
Isa 25:6. Lord make to all a f. of
1 Cor 5:8. let us keep f., not with
FEEBLE, Gen 30:42. Job 4:4.
Ps 105:37. not one f. person among
Isa 35:3. confirm f. knees
Zech 12:8. he that is f. shall be as David
1 Thess 5:14. comfort the f. minded
Heb 12:12. lift up the f. knees
FEED, *fed,* Gen 25:30; 30:36.
Ps 28:9. f. them and lift them up
37:3. verily thou shall be f.
49:14. death shall f. on them
Prov 10:21. lips of righteous f. many
Isa 58:14. f. thee with heritage of Jacob
Jer 3:15. pastors f. you with knowledge
Acts 20:28. to f. the church of God
1 Cor 13:3. give my goods to f. poor
3:2. I have f. you with milk, and
Prov 30:8. f. me with food convenient
Song of Sol 1:8. f. kids beside shepherds' tents
Mic 7:14. f. thy people with thy rod
John 21:15. f. my lambs, f. my sheep, 16, 17.
Rom 12:20. enemy hunger, f. him
1 Pet 5:2. f. flock of God among
Isa 44:20. he *feedeth* on ashes
Song of Sol 2:16. he f. among lilies, 6:3.
Hos 12:1. Ephraim f. on wind
1 Cor 9:7. who f. a flock and eateth not
FEEL, *feeling,* Gen 27:12. Acts 17:27. Eph 4:19. Heb 4:15.
FEET, Gen 18:4; 19:2; 49:10.
1 Sam 2:9. keep f. of his saints
Neh 9:21. their f. swelled not
Job 12:5. is ready to slip with his f.
29:15. eyes to blind, f. to lame
Ps 73:2. my f. were almost gone
116:8. delivered my f. from falling
119:101. refrained my f. from every evil
105. thy word is a lamp to my f.
Prov 4:26. ponder path of thy f.
Isa 59:7. their f. run to evil, and
Luke 1:79. guide our f. into way of
Eph 6:15. f. shod with preparation
Heb 12:13. straight paths for your f.
Rev 11:11. they stood upon their f.
FEIGNED, 1 Sam 21:13. Ps 17:1. 2 Pet 2:3. *feignedly,* Jer 3:10.
FELLOW, Gen 19:9. Exod 2:13.
Eccles 4:10. if they fall, one will lift up his f.
Acts 24:5. a pestilent f. 22:22.
Rom 16:7. my kinsmen and f. prisoners
2 Cor 8:23. my f. helper, 3 John 8.
Eph 2:19. f. citizens, 3:6. f. heirs
Col 1:7. f. servant, 4:7. Rev 6:11; 19:10; 22:9.
4:10. Aristarchus my f. prisoner
Phil 2:25. f. soldier, Philem 2.
4:3. Philem 1, 24. f. labourers, 1 Thess 3:2.
Ps 45:7. oil of gladness above *fellows,* Heb 1:9.
94:20. have *fellowship* with thee
Acts 2:42. continued . . . apostles' doctrine and f.
1 Cor 1:9. called to f. of Jesus Christ
10:20. should have f. with devils
2 Cor 6:14. what f. hath righteousness with unrighteousness
8:4. f. of ministering to saints
Gal 2:9. gave us right hands of f.
Eph 5:11. no f. with works of
Phil 1:5. for your f. in the gospel
2:1. if there be any f. of the spirit
3:10. may know him and f. of his sufferings
1 John 1:3. f. with us . . . our f. with Father
6. if we say we have f. with him
FERVENT in spirit, Acts 18:25.
Rom 12:11. f. in spirit, serving Lord
2 Cor 7:7. f. mind toward me
James 5:16. *fervent* prayer of righteous
1 Pet 4:8. have f. charity among
2 Pet 3:10. melt with f. heat, 12.
Col 4:12. Epaphras always labouring *fervently* for you in prayers
1 Pet 1:22. love one another f.
FEW, Gen 29:20. Ps 105:12.
Matt 7:14. way to life, f. that find it
20:16. many called, f. chosen, 22:14.
1 Pet 3:20. f. . . . eight souls saved
Rev 2:14. I have f. things against
3:4. thou hast a f. names in Sardis
FIDELITY, all good, Titus 2:10.
FIERCENESS of anger, Deut 13:17. Josh 7:26. 2 Kings 23:26. Job 4:9; 10:16; 39:24; 41:10. Ps 85:3. Jer 25:38. Hos 11:9.
FIERY law, Deut 33:2.
Num 21:6. f. serpents, 8. Deut 8:15.
Ps 21:9. make them as a f. oven
Eph 6:16. quench f. darts of wicked
Heb 10:27. f. indignation . . . devour
1 Pet 4:12. not strange the f. trial
FIGHT, 1 Sam 17:20. Exod 14:14.
Acts 5:39. found to f. against God
23:9. let us not f. against God
1 Tim 6:12. f. the good f. of faith
2 Tim 4:7. I have fought a good f.
Heb 10:32. a great f. of afflictions
FIGS, Gen 3:7. Isa 34:4; 38:21.
Jer 24:2. good f., vile f. 29:17.
Matt 7:16. gather f. of thistles?

1 Cor 12:15. if *f.* say, because I am not
Heb 10:29. trodden under *f.* Son of God
FORBEAR, Exod 23:5. 1 Cor 9:6.
Rom 2:4. goodness and *forbearance,* 3:25.
FORBID, Mark 10:14. Luke 18:16; 6:29. Acts 24:23; 28:31.
1 Thess 2:16. *forbidding* to speak to Gentiles
1 Tim 4:3. *f.* to marry
FORCE, Matt 11:12. Heb 9:17.
Isa 60:5. *forces* of Gentiles shall come, 11.
Job 6:25. how *forcible* right words
FOREFATHERS, 2 Tim 1:3. Jer 11:10.
FOREHEAD, Exod 28:38. Lev 13:41.
Jer 3:3. thou hast a whore's *f.*
Ezek 3:8. thy *f.* strong against their *foreheads*
Rev 7:3. sealed in their *f.* 9:4.
14:1. Father's name written in *f.* 22:4.
FOREIGNERS, Exod 12:45. Deut 15:3. Obad 11. Eph 2:19.
FOREKNOW, Rom 8:29; 11:2.
Acts 2:23. *foreknowledge* of God, 1 Pet 1:2.
FOREORDAINED, 1 Pet 1:20.
FORESEETH, Prov 22:3; 27:12.
FOREWARN, Luke 12:5.
FORGAT Lord, Judg 3:7. 1 Sam 12:9.
Ps 78:11. *f.* his works and wonders, 106:13.
Lam 3:17. I *f.* prosperity
Hos 2:13. *f.* me, saith the Lord
Deut 9:7. remember and *forget* not
Job 8:13. paths of all that *f.* God
Ps 45:10. *f.* thine own people, and
50:22. consider this, ye that *f.* God
103:2. *f.* not all his benefits
119:16. will not *f.* thy words, 83, 93, 109, 141, 153, 176.
Prov 3:1. my son *f.* not my law
Isa 49:15. woman *f.* sucking child
Jer 2:32. can a maid *forget* ornaments
Heb 6:10. God not unrighteous to *f.* your labour of love
13:16. to do good and to communicate *f.* not
2. be not *forgetful* to entertain
Ps 44:24. *forgettest* our affliction
9:12. he *forgetteth* not the city of humble
Prov 2:17. *f.* covenant of her God
James 1:24. *f.* what manner of man
Phil 3:13. *forgetting* those things
Ps 10:11. God hath *forgotten*
42:9. why hast thou *f.* me
77:9. hath God *f.* to be gracious
119:61. I have not f. thy law
Isa 17:10. *f.* God of thy salvation
49:14. Zion said, my Lord hath *f.* me
Jer 2:32. my people have *f.* me
3:21. have *f.* their God, Deut 32:18.
50:5. covenant that shall not be *f.*
Heb 12:5. *f.* the exhortation
FORGAVE their iniquity, Ps 78:38.
Matt 18:27. *f.* him the debt, 32.
Luke 7:42. frankly *f.* them both
43. love most, to whom *f.* most
Col 3:13. as Christ *f.* you, also do
Ps 32:5. *forgavest* the iniquity of
99:8. thou wast a God that *f.* them
Exod 32:32. *forgive* their sin
Ps 86:5. thou art . . . ready to *f.*
Isa 2:9. therefore *f.* them not
Jer 31:34. I *f.* their iniquity, 36:3.
Matt 6:12. *f.* us our debts, as we *f.*
14. if ye *f.* men, 15. if you *f.* not
9:6. Son of man hath power on earth to *f.*
Luke 6:37. *f.* and ye shall be forgiven
17:3. if he repent, *f.* him, 4.
23:34. Father, *f.* them, they know not
2 Cor 2:10. to whom ye *f.* any thing
1 John 1:9. faithful to *f.* us our sins
Ps 32:1. transgression is *forgiven*
85:2. *f.* the iniquity of thy people
Isa 33:24. people *f.* their iniquity
Luke 7:47. to whom little is *f.* loveth
Rom 4:7. blessed . . . whose iniquities *f.*
Eph 4:32. as God hath *f.* you, Col 3:13.
James 5:15. if he have . . . sins, they shall be *f.*
1 John 2:12. your sins are *f.* you
Acts 5:31. repentance to Israel and *forgiveness*
26:18. may receive *f.* of sins by faith
Col 1:14. redemption, even *f.* sins
Dan 9:9. to Lord belong mercies and *forgivenesses*
Ps 103:3. *forgiveth* thine iniquities
Exod 34:7. *forgiving* iniquity, transgression, sin, Num 14:18. Mic 7:18.
Eph 4:32. *f.* one another, Col 3:13.
FORM, Gen 1:2. 1 Sam 28:14.
Isa 53:2. hath no *f.* nor comeliness
Rom 2:20. hast *f.* of knowledge
6:17. obeyed that *f.* of doctrine
Phil 2:6. who being in *f.* of God
7. took upon him the *f.* of a servant
2 Tim 1:13. hold *f.* of sound words
3:5. having the *f.* of godliness
Isa 45:7. *f.* light and create darkness
Ps 94:9. that *formed* the eye shall he not see?
Prov 26:10. God that *f.* all things
Isa 27:11. *f.* them shew no favour
43:21. this people I *f.* for myself
44:2. *f.* thee from womb
54:17. no weapon *f.* against thee shall prosper
Rom 9:20. thing *f.* say to him that *f.*
Gal 4:19. till Christ be *f.* in you
Isa 10:16. the *former* of all things, 51:19.
Zech 12:1. *formeth* spirit of man within
FORNICATION, 2 Chron 21:11. Isa 23:17. Ezek 16:15, 26, 29.
John 8:41. we be not born of *f.*
Acts 15:20. abstain from *f.* 21:25.
Rom 1:29. filled with *f.*, wickedness
1 Cor 5:1. there is *f.* among you
6:13. body not for *f.* 18. flee *f.*
7:2. to avoid *f.* have own wife
10:8. neither let us commit *f.*
2 Cor 12:21. not repented of their *f.*
Gal 5:19. works of flesh, adultery, *f.*
Eph 5:3. *f.* and all uncleanness
Col 3:5. mortify . . . *f.* uncleanness
1 Thess 4:3. should abstain from *f.*
Jude 7. giving themselves to *f.*
Rev 2:14. and to commit *f.* 20, 21. I gave her space to repent her *f.*
9:21. neither repented of their *f.*
14:8. of the wine of her *f.* 17:2.
Rev 17:4. filthiness of her *f.*
18:3. committed *f.* with her, 9.
19:2. did corrupt earth with her *f.*
Ezek16:15. *fornications,* Matt 15:19.
1 Cor 5:9–11. *fornicators,* 6:9. Heb 12:16.
FORSAKE, Deut 12:19; 31:16.
Deut 4:31. (Lord thy God) will not *f.* thee, 31:6, 8. 1 Chron 28:20. Heb 13:5.
Josh 1:5. I will not fail thee nor *f.* thee, Isa 41:17; 42:16.
1 Sam 12:22. Lord will not *f.* his people, 1 Kings 6:13.
8:57. let him not leave nor *f.* us
Ps 27:10. when father and mother *f.*
94:14. neither will he *f.* inheritance
Isa 55:7. let the wicked *f.* his way
Jer 17:13. that *f.* thee be ashamed
Jon 2:8. *f.* their own mercy
Ps 71:11. God hath *forsaken* him
22:1. My God, my God, why hast thou *f.* me, Matt 27:46.
Isa 49:14. the Lord hath *f.* me
54:7. for a small moment have I *f.* thee
Jer 2:13. *f.* me the fountain, 17:13.
Matt 19:27. we have *f.* all, 29. houses or brethren, or sisters, &c.
2 Cor 4:9. persecuted but not *f.*
Prov 2:17. *forsaketh* guide of youth
28:12. confesseth and *f.* shall find
Deut 32:15. *forsook* God which made him
Ps 119:87. I *f.* not thy precepts
2 Tim 4:16. all men *f.* me

FORTRESS and rock, Lord is my, 2 Sam 22:2. Ps 18:2; 31:3; 71:3; 91:2; 144:2. Jer 16:19.
FOUND, Gen 26:19; 31:37.
Eccles 7:27. this have I *f.* that, 29.
Song of Sol 3:1. I *f.* him not, 4. I *f.* him
Isa 55:6. seek Lord while he may be *f.*
65:1. *f.* of them that sought me not
Ezek 22:30. I sought a man *f.* none
Dan 5:27. weighed and *f.* wanting
2 Pet 3:14. be *f.* of him in peace
Matt 7:25. *founded* on a rock, Ps 24:2. Prov 3:19. Isa 14:32.
Job 4:19. whose *foundation* is in dust
Prov 10:25. righteous is an everlasting *f.*
Isa 28:16. I lay in Zion a sure *f.*
Rom 15:20. build on another man's *f.*
1 Cor 3:10. laid *f.* 12. build on this *f.*
Eph 2:20. built on *f.* of prophets
1 Tim 6:19. lay up good *f.* for time
2 Tim 2:19. *f.* of God standeth sure
Ps 11:3. if *foundations* be destroyed
Heb 11:10. a city which hath *f.*
Rev 21:14. the city hath twelve *foundations*
Matt 13:35. *foundation of the world,* 25:34. John 17:24. Eph 1:4. 1 Pet 1:20. Rev 13:8; 17:8. Ps 104:5. Prov 8:29. Isa 51:13, 16.
FOUNTAIN, Gen 7:11. Deut 8:7.
Deut 33:28. *f.* of Jacob on a land
Ps 36:9. with thee is *f.* of life
68:26. bless Lord from *f.* of Israel
Prov 5:18. let thy *f.* be blessed
13:14. law of wise is a *f.* of life
14:27. fear of the Lord is a *f.* of life
Eccles 12:6. a pitcher broken at the *f.*
Song of Sol 4:12. *f.* sealed, 15. *f.* of gardens
Jer 2:13. forsaken me, the *f.* of living waters
9:1. that my eyes were a *f.* of tears
Joel 3:18. a *f.* out of house of Lord
Zech 13:1. a *f.* opened for house
James 3:12. can *f.* both yield salt
Rev 21:6. give *f.* of life freely, *22:17.*
FOXES, Judg 15:4. Ps 63:10. Song of Sol 2:15. Lam 5:18. Ezek 13:4. Matt 8:20. Luke 13:32.
FRAGMENTS, Matt 14:20. Mark 6:43; 8:19, 20. John 6:12, 13.
FRAIL I am, Ps 39:4.
FRAME, Ps 103:14. Isa 29:16. Jer 18:11. Eph 2:21. Heb 11:3.
FREE, Exod 21:2. Lev 19:20.
2 Chron 29:31. as many as were of a *f.* heart
Ps 51:12. uphold with thy *f.* spirit
88:5. *f.* among the dead, like slain
John 8:32. truth shall make you *f.*
36. if Son make *f.* shall be *f.* indeed
Rom 5:15. so also is *f.* gift, 16, 18.
1 Cor 7:22. the Lord's *f.* man
Gal 3:28. bond nor *f.* Col 3:11.
2 Thess 3:1. word of Lord may have *f.* course
1 Pet 2:16. *f.* and not using liberty
Hos 14:4. I will love them *freely*
Matt 10:8. *f.* ye have received, *f.* give
Rom 3:24. justified *f.* by his grace
8:32. with him *f.* give us all things
1 Cor 2:12. things *f.* given us of God
Rev 21:6. fountain of water of life *f.* 22:17.
FRET, Ps 37:1, 7, 8. Prov 24:19.
Ezek 16:43. hast *fretted* me in all
Prov 19:3. his heart *fretteth* against Lord
FRIEND, Jer 6:21. Hos 3:1.
Exod 33:11. as a man speaketh to his *f.*
Deut 13:6. *f.* which is as his own soul
2 Sam 16:17. is this kindness to thy *f.*
2 Chron 20:7. Abraham thy *f.* Isa 41:8. James 2:23.
Prov 17:17. *f.* loveth at all times
18:24. a *f.* closer than a brother
27:10. own *f.* father's forsake not
Song of Sol 5:16. this is my beloved, . . . *f.*
Mic 7:5. trust ye not in a *f.* . . .
Prov 18:24. hath *friends* shew himself friendly
John 15:13. lay down life for his *f.*
14. ye are my *f.* if, 15. called you *f.*
Prov 22:24. make no *friendship* with angry man
James 4:4. of the world is enmity with God
FROWARD, Job 5:13. 1 Pet 2:18.
Deut 32:30. a very *f.* generation
Ps 18:26. with *f.* wilt shew thyself *f.*
101:4. *f.* heart shall depart from
Prov 4:24. *f.* mouth, 6:12; 8:13.
10:31. *f.* tongue, 11:20. *f.* heart, 17:20.
Isa 57:17. went on *frowardly*
Prov 6:14. *frowardness* is in his heart
FRUIT, Gen 4:3. Lev 19:24.
Gen 30:2. *withheld f.* of the womb
Exod 21:22. hurt so that *f.* depart
2 Kings 19:30. bear *fruit* upward, Isa 37:31.
Ps 92:14. shall bring forth *f.* in old age
127:3. *f.* of womb is his reward
Prov 11:30. *f.* of righteous tree of life
Song of Sol 2:3. his *f.* was sweet to taste
Isa 3:10. eat the *f.* of their doings
27:9. all the *f.* to take away sin
57:19. create *f.* of the lips
Hos 10:1. empty vine bringeth *f.* to himself
Mic 6:7. *f.* of body for sin of my soul
Matt 7:17. good tree good *f.* 21:19.
12:33. *f.* good; tree known by his *f.*
26:29. not drink of *f.* of vine till
Luke 1:42. blessed is *f.* of thy womb
John 4:36. gathereth *f.* to life eternal
15:2. branch beareth not *f.* he taketh away; beareth *f.* he purgeth it
Rom 6:21. what *f.* 22. *f.* to holiness
7:4. should bring forth *f.* unto God
15:28. have sealed to them this *f.*
Gal 5:22. *f.* of Spirit is love
Eph 5:9. *f.* of Spirit is in all goodness
Phil 4:17. desire *f.* that may abound
Heb 12:11. peaceable *f.* of righteousness
James 3:18. *f.* of righteousness sown
Rev 22:2. yielded *f.* every month
Song of Sol 4:13. pleasant *fruits,* 6:11. *f.* of valley
7:13. all manner of pleasant *f.*
Matt 3:8. *f.* meet for repentance
2 Cor 9:10. increase *f.* of righteousness
Phil 1:11. filled with *f.* of righteousness
James 3:17. full of mercy and good *f.*
FRUSTRATE, Isa 44:25. Gal 2:21.
FULL, Gen 15:16. Exod 16:3, 8.
Deut 34:9. (Joshua) *f.* of spirit of wisdom
Ruth 1:21. went out *f.* . . . home empty
1 Sam 2:5. that were *f.* have hired
Job 5:26. come to grave in *f.* age
Ps 17:14. are *f.* of children
Prov 27:7. *f.* soul loatheth honeycomb
30:9. lest I be *f.* and deny thee
Luke 4:1. Jesus *f.* of the Holy Ghost
6:25. woe to you that are *f.*
John 1:14. the Word was made flesh, *f.* of grace and truth
Phil 4:12. know both to be *f.* and
Col 2:2. riches of *f.* assurance
2 Tim 4:5. *f.* proof of thy ministry
Heb 6:11. to *f.* assurance of hope
10:22. near in *f.* assurance of faith
Gen 29:27. *fulfil,* Exod 23:26.
Ps 145:19. *f.* the desire of them
Matt 3:15. us to *f.* all righteousness
Acts 13:22. which shall *f.* all my will
Gal 5:16. shall not *f.* lust of flesh
6:2. bear burden and so *f.* law of Christ

Phil 2:2. ye my joy, that ye be
Col 4:17. ministry . . . that thou *f.* it
James 2:8. if ye *f.* the royal law
Rev 17:17. put in their hearts to *f.* his will
Luke 21:24. till times of . . . be *fulfilled*
Gal 5:14. law is *f.* in one word
Eph 2:3. *fulfilling* desires of flesh, mind
Job 20:22. in *fulness* of sufficiency
John 1:16. of his *f.* have received
Rom 11:25. till *f.* of Gentiles become
15:29. *f.* of blessing of the Gospel
Gal 4:4. when *f.* of time was come
Eph 1:10. dispensation of *f.* of times
23. *f.* of him that filleth all in all
3:19. filled with the *f.* of God
4:13. to the stature of *f.* of Christ
Col 1:19. in him should all *f.* dwell
Col 2:9. all the *fulness* of the Godhead

FURNACE, Deut 4:20. Jer 11:4. Ps 12:6.
Isa 31:9; 48:10. Dan 3:6, 11. Matt 13:42, 50. Rev 1:15.

FURNISHED, Deut 15:14. Prov 9:2.
2 Tim 3:17. throughly *f.* to all good works

FURY is not in me, Isa 27:4.
Isa 59:18. repay *f.* to his adversaries
Jer 6:11. am full of *f.* of the Lord
10:25. pour out thy *f.* on heathen

G

GAIN, Prov 3:14. Job 22:3.
Isa 33:15. despiseth *g.* of oppressions
Phil 1:21. to live is Christ, to die is *g.*
1 Tim 6:5. supposing *g.* godliness, 6. godliness with contentment is great *g.*
Matt 16:26. if he *g.* world
1 Cor 9:19. servant to all, that I might *g.*
Job 27:8. hope of hypocrite though he hath *gained*
Matt 18:15. thou hast *g.* thy brother
Luke 19:16. thy pound hath *g.* ten
Titus 1:9. convince *gainsayers*
Acts 10:29. *gainsaying,* Rom 10:21. *g.* people
Jude 11. perished in the *g.* of Core

GALL, Job 16:13; 20:14, 25.
Deut 29:18. root beareth *g.* and wormwood
Ps 69:21. gave me g. for meat, Matt 27:34. g. to drink
Jer 8:14. given us water of *g.* 9:15.
Lam 3:19. remembering . . . wormwood and *g.*
Acts 8:23. in the *g.* of bitterness

GAP, to stand in, Ezek 22:30.

GARDEN, Gen 2:15; 3:23; 13:10.
Song of Sol 4:12. a *g.* enclosed is my sister
16. blow on my *g.* 5:1; 6:2, 11.
Jer 31:12. soul as a watered *g.* Isa 58:11.

GARMENT, Josh 7:21. Ezra 9:3.
Job 37:17. thy *garments* are warm
Ps 22:18. part my *g.* among them
Isa 9:5. and *g.* rolled in blood
59:17. put on *g.* of vengeance
Joel 2:13. rend your hearts not *g.*
Matt 21:8. spread their *g.* in way
Acts 9:39. coats and *g.* Dorcas made
Rev 3:4. have not defiled their *g.*
16:15. watcheth and keepeth his *g.*

GATE, Gen 19:1; 34:20, 24.
Gen 22:17. possess *g.* of his enemies
28:17. house of God, *g.* of heaven
Job 29:7. I went to *g.* prepared
Ps 118:20. this *g.* of the Lord
Matt 7:13. enter strait *g.* Luke 13:24.
Heb 13:12. suffered without the *g.*
Ps 9:13. up from *gates* of death
24:7. lift up heads, O *g.* 9. Isa 26:2.
100:4. enter his *g.* with thanksgiving
118:19. open to me *g.* of righteousness
Isa 38:10. go to *g.* of the grave
Matt 16:18. *g.* of hell not prevail

GATHER thee from all nations, Deut 30:3. Neh 1:9. Jer 29:14.
Ps 26:9. *g.* not my soul with sinners
Zeph 3:18. *g.* them that are sorrowful
Matt 3:12. *g.* his wheat into garner
7:16. do men *g.* grapes of thorns
Eph 1:10. *g.* in one all things in Christ
Matt 23:37. *gathered* thy children as hen *g.*
John 4:36. *gathereth* fruit unto life eternal

GAVE, Gen 14:20. Exod 11:3.
Ps 81:12. *g.* them up unto their own hearts' lust
Isa 42:24. *gave* Jacob for a spoil
John 1:12. *g.* power to become sons
3:16. God *g.* his only begotten Son
1 Cor 3:6. God *g.* the increase, 7.
2 Cor 8:5. first *g.* themselves to Lord
Gal 1:4. who *g.* himself for our sins
2:20. *g.* himself for me, Titus 2:14.
Eph 4:8. *g.* gifts unto men, 11. *g.* some apostles
1 Tim 2:6. g. himself a ransom for all
Ps 21:4. asked life of thee, thou *gavest* it
John 17:4. work thou *g.* 22. glory thou *g.* 6. (men) thou *g.* me, 12; 18:9. *g.* me, lost none

GENEALOGIES, 1 Tim 1:4. Titus 3:9.

GENERATION, Gen 2:4; 6:9.
Deut 32:5. perverse and crooked *g.*
20. a very froward *g.* in whom
Ps 14:5. God is in *g.* of righteous
22:30. accounted to Lord for a *g.*
24:6. this is *g.* of them that seek
102:18. written for the *g.* to come
112:2. *g.* of upright shall be blessed
145:4. one *g.* shall praise thy works
Matt 3:7. ye *g.* of vipers, 12:34; 23:33.
Acts 13:36. had served his own *g.*
1 Pet 2:9. chosen *g.* royal priesthood
Ps 33:11. thoughts . . . to all *generations*
45:17. name remembered in all *g.*
72:5. fear thee . . . throughout all *g.*
79:13. shew forth thy praise to all *g.*
89:4. build thy throne to all *g.*
90:1. our dwelling place in all *g.*
100:5. his truth endureth to all *g.*
102:24. thy years are throughout all *g.*
119:90. thy faithfulness is to all *g.*
145:13. dominion endureth to all *g.*
Col 1:26. mystery hid from ages and *g.*

GENTILES, Gen 10:5. Jer 4:7.
Isa 11:10. to it shall *g.* seek, 42:6. a light of *g.* 49:6. Luke 2:32. Acts 13:47.
60:3. *g.* shall come to thy light
62:2. *g.* shall see thy righteousness
Matt 6:32. after these things do the *g.* seek
Luke 21:24. trodden of *g.* till times of *g.*
John 7:35. dispersed among *g.*, teach *g.*
Acts 13:46. we turn to the *g.*
14:27. opened door of faith unto *g.*
Rom 2:14. *g.* which have not law
3:29. is he not also God of *g.?* yea
11:25. till fulness of *g.* be come
15:10. rejoice, ye *g.*, with his people
12. reign over *g.*; in him shall *g.* trust, Matt 12:21.
Eph 3:6. be fellowheirs, 8. preach among *g.*
1 Tim 2:7. teacher of *g.* 2 Tim 1:11.
3:16. God in flesh, preached to the *g.*

GENTLE among you, 1 Thess 2:7.
2 Tim 2:24. servant of Lord must be *g.*
Titus 3:2. be *g.* shewing all meekness
James 3:17. wisdom from above is *g.*
1 Pet 2:18. not only to the *g.* but to

Ps 18:35. thy *gentleness* made me great
2 Cor. 10:1. by the meekness *g.* of Christ
Gal 5:22. fruit of Spirit is longsuffering, *g.*
Isa 40:11. *gently* lead those with young
GIFT, 1 Cor 1:7; 7:7.
Exod 23:8. take no *g.* for a *g.*—blindeth the wise, Deut 16:19. 2 Chron 19:7.
Prov 17:8. *g.* is a precious stone, 23.
18:16. a man's *g.* maketh room for
21:14. *g.* in secret pacifieth anger
Eccles 7:7. a *g.* destroyeth the heart
John 4:10. if thou knewest *g.* of God
Rom 6:23. *g.* of god is eternal life
Eph 2:8. it is the *gift* of God
Phil 4:17. not because I desire a *g.*
1 Tim 4:14. neglect not the *g.* that
Heb 6:4. tasted of heavenly *g.*
Ps 68:18. received *gifts* for men
Matt 7:11. good *g.* to your children
Rom 11:29. for *g.* and calling of God
Eph 4:8. captivity captive gave *g.* to men
GIRD with strength, Ps 18:32.
1 Pet 1:13. *g.* up loins of mind
Ps 30:11. *girded* me with gladness
Luke 12:35. let your loins be *g.*
Eph 6:14. loins *girt* with truth
Isa 11:5. *girdle,* Matt 3:4. Rev 1:13; 15:6.
GIVE, Gen 12:7; 30:31.
1 Kings 3:5. ask what I shall *g.* thee
Ps 2:8. I shall *g.* thee the heathen
29:11. Lord will *g.* strength to his
84:11. Lord will *g.* grace and glory
104:27. mayest *g.* them their meat
109:4. I *g.* myself to prayer
Jer 17:10. to *g.* every man according to his works, 32:19. Rev 22:12.
Hos 11:8. how shall I *g.* thee up
Luke 6:38. *g.* and it shall be given
John 10:28. I *g.* to them eternal life
Acts 3:6. such as I have *g.* I thee
20:35. more blessed to *g.* than to receive
Rom 8:32. freely *g.* us all
Eph 4:28. have to *g.* to him that needeth
1 Tim 4:15. *g.* thyself wholly to them
2 Sam 22:50. *give thanks,* 1 Chron 16:8, 34, 35, 41. Neh 12:24. Ps 35:18; 79:13; 92:1; 105:1; 107:1; 118:1; 136:1.
Ps 6:5. in grave who shall—to thee
30:4.—at the remembrance of his holiness, 97:12.
119:62. at midnight I will rise to—
Eph 1:16, &c. cease not to—for you
1 Thess 5:18. in every thing—Phil 4:6.
Matt 13:12. to him shall be *given*
11. it is *g.* to you to know mysteries
Luke 12:48. to whomsoever much is *g.*
Rom 11:35. hath first *g.* to him
1 Cor 2:12. know things freely *g.* of God
2 Cor 9:7. God loveth cheerful *giver*
Ps 37:21. righteous . . . mercy and *giveth*
Prov 28:27. he that *g.* to poor shall
Isa 40:29. *g.* power to the faint
42:5. *g.* breath to people on earth
1 Tim 6:17. *g.* us richly all things
James 1:5. *g.* to all men liberally
GLAD, my heart is, Ps 16:9.
Ps 31:7. I will be *g.* and rejoice in
64:10. righteous shall be *g.* in Lord
104:34. I will be *g.* in the Lord
122:1. *g.* when they said, Luke 15:32.
Mark 6:20. heard him *gladly,* 12:37.
Luke 8:40. people *g.* received him
Acts 2:41. that *g.* received his word
2 Cor 12:15. I will very *g.* spend
Ps 4:7. put *gladness* in my heart
30:11. hast girded me with *g.*
45:7. anointed with oil of *g.* Heb 1:9.
51:8. make me to hear joy and *g.*
100:2. serve the Lord with *g.*
106:5. rejoice in *g.* of thy nation
Isa 35:10. obtain joy and *g.* 51:11.
Acts 2:46. eat their meat with *g.*
14:17. filling our hearts with food and *g.*
GLASS, we see through, 1 Cor 13:12.
2 Cor 3:18. beholding as in a *g.*
James 1:23. beholding natural face in *g.*
Rev 4:6. a sea of *g.* 15:2.
Rev 21:18. the city pure gold like clear *glass*
GLOOMINESS, Joel 2:2. Zeph 1:15.
GLORY, Gen 31:1. Ps 49:16.
1 Sam 4:21. *g.* departed from Israel
1 Chron 29:11. the power and *g.* Matt 6:13.
Ps 8:5. crowned him with *g.* and honour, Heb 2:7.
73:24. afterward receive me to *g.*
89:17. art the *g.* of their strength
145:11. speak of *g.* of thy kingdom
Prov 3:35. the wise shall inherit *g.*
16:31. hoary head is a crown of *g.*
25:27. to search their own *g.* is not *g.*
Isa 4:5. upon all the *g.* shall be a defence
23:9. Lord purposed it, to stain pride of all *g.*
24:16. heard songs, even *g.* to the righteous
28:5. Lord shall be for a crown of *g.*
Jer 2:11. changed their *g.* Ps 106:20.
Ezek 20:6. the *g.* of all lands, 15.
Hos 4:7. change their *g.* into shame
Hag 2:7. I will fill this house with *g.*
9. *g.* of this latter house greater
Zech 2:5. I will be a wall of fire, *g.*
8. after the *g.* hath he sent me
6:13. build temple and bear the *g.*
Matt 6:2. may have *g.* of men
Luke 2:14. *g.* to God in the highest
32. light of Gentiles, *g.* of thy people
John 1:14. his *g.*, *g.* as of only begotten Son
17:22. *g.* which thou gavest me I have
Rom 2:7. seek *g.* honour, immortality
11:36. to whom be *g.* for ever, Gal 1:5. 2 Tim 4:18. Heb 13:21.
16:27. God only wise be *g.* through Christ
1 Cor 11:7. (man) is image and *g.* of God.
15:43. sown in dishonour, raised in *g.*
2 Cor 3:18. changed . . . from *g.* to *g.*
4:17. eternal weight of *g.*
Eph 1:6. praise of *g.* of his grace
3:21. to him be *g.* in the church
13. my tribulation for you is your *g.*
Phil 3:19. whose *g.* is in their shame
Col 1:27. Christ in you hope of *g.*
3:4. appear with him in *g.*
1 Thess 2:12. called you to his kingdom and *g.*
20. ye are our *g.* and joy, 19.
1 Tim 3:16. received up into *g.*
1 Pet 1:8. joy unspeakable, full of *g.*
11. the sufferings of Christ, *g.* follow, 21.
4:13. his *g.* be revealed, 14. spirit of *g.*
5:1. partaker of *g.* to be revealed
4. ye shall receive a crown of *g.*
10. called us to eternal *g.* by Christ
2 Pet 1:3. called us to *g.* and virtue
17. came a voice from excellent *g.*
Rev 4:11. worthy to receive *g.* 5:12. Rom 16:27. 1 Tim 1:17. 1 Pet 5:11. Jude 25.
Ps 19:1. *glory of God,* Prov 25:2. Acts 7:55. Rom 3:23; 5:2. 1 Cor 10:31; 11:7. 2 Cor 4:6. Rev 21:11.
Exod 16:7. *glory of the Lord,* Num 14:21. 1 Kings 8:11. Ps

104:31; 138:5. Isa 35:2; 40:5; 60:1. Ezek 1:28; 3:12, 23; 43:5; 44:4. Luke 2:9. 2 Cor 3:18.
Ps 29:9. *his glory,* 49:17; 72:19; 113:4; 148:13. Prov 19:11. Isa 6:3. Hab 3:3. Matt 6:29; 19:28; 25:31. John 2:11. Rom 9:23. Eph 1:12; 3:16. Heb 1:3.
Job 29:20. *my glory,* Ps 16:9; 30:12; 57:8; 108:1. Isa 42:8; 43:7; 48:11; 60:7; 66:18. John 8:50; 17:24.
Exod 33:18. *thy glory.* Ps 8:1; 63:2. Isa 60:19; 63:15. Jer 14:21.
1 Chron 16:10. *glory* ye in his holy name
Ps 64:10. upright in heart shall *glory*
Isa 41:16. shalt *g.* in Holy One of
45:25. seed of Israel be justified, and *g.*
Rom 4:2. hath whereof to *g.* but not
5:3. we *g.* in tribulations also
2 Cor 5:12. to *g.* on our behalf . . . them which *g.* in appearance, not in heart
11:18. many *g.* after the flesh, I *g.* also
12:1. it is not expedient for me to *g.*
9. will I rather *g.* in my infirmities
Gal 6:14. God forbid I should *g.* save
1 Cor 5:6. *glorying,* 9:15. 2 Cor 7:4; 12:11.
Lev 10:3. before all I will be *glorified*
John 7:39. Jesus was not yet *g.*
12:23. the hour is come that the Son of man should be *g.*
15:8. herein is my Father *g.*
17:10. all mine are thine, I am *g.*
Acts 3:13. God of our fathers hath *g.* his Son
4:21. all men *g.* God for that which was done
Rom 1:21. they *g.* him not as God
Gal 1:24. they *g.* God in me
2 Thess 1:10. be *g.* in his saints
3:1. word have free course and be *g.*
Heb 5:5. even Christ *g.* not himself
Rev 18:7. how she hath *g.* herself
Ps 50:23. whoso offereth praise *glorifieth*
Isa 25:3. strong people *glorify* thee
60:7. I will *g.* house of my glory
Matt 5:16. *g.* your Father in heaven
John 12:28. Father, *g.* thy name
17:1. *g.* thy Son that Son *g.* thee
5. *g.* thou me . . . with the glory
21:19. by what death he should *g.* God
1 Cor 6:20. *g.* God *in your body and*
1 Pet 2:12. *g.* God in day of visitation
Rev 15:4. who shall not fear thee, and *g.*
Exod 15:6. *glorious* in power
11. who is like thee, *g.* in holiness
Deut 28:58. fear this *g.* and fearful name
1 Chron 29:13. praise thy *g.* name
Ps 45:13. king's daughter all *g.* within
66:2. make his praise *g.*
72:19. blessed be his *g.* name, Neh 9:5.
87:3. *g.* things spoken of thee, O city of God
111:3. his work is honourable and *g.*
145:5. speak of *g.* honour of thy
12. the *g.* majesty of his kingdom
Isa 4:2. branch of Lord shall be *g.*
11:10. his rest shall be *g.*
22:23. be for a *g.* throne to his father's house
30:30. cause his *g.* voice to be heard
49:5. I be *g.* in eyes of the Lord
60:13. make the place of my feet *g.*
63:12. his *g.* arm, 14. a *g.* name
Jer 17:12. a *g.* high throne from
Rom 8:21. *g.* liberty of children of God
2 Cor 3:7. ministration *g.* 8, 10, 11.
4:4. light of *g.* Gospel should shine
Eph 5:27. present to himself *g.* church
Phil 3:21. vile body . . . like his *g.* body
Col 1:11. according to his *g.* power
1 Tim 1:11. according to the *g.* gospel of
Titus 2:13. looking for *g.* appearing
Exod 15:1. *gloriously,* Isa 24:23.
GLUTTON, Deut 21:20. Prov 23:21.
Matt 11:19. *gluttonous,* Luke 7:34.
GNASH, Job 16:9. Ps 35:16; 37:12; 112:10. Lam 2:16. Mark 9:18.
Matt 8:12. *gnashing of teeth,* 13:42, 50; 22:13; 24:51; 25:30. Luke 13:28.
GNAT, strain at *g.*, swallow camel, Matt 23:24.
GNAW, Zeph 3:3. Rev 16:10.
GO, Judg 6:14. 1 Sam 12:21. Matt 8:9. Luke 10:37. John 6:68.
Job 10:21. *I go,* Ps 39:13; 139:7. Matt 21:30. John 7:33; 8:14, 21, 22; 13:33; 16:5.
Exod 4:23. *let my people go,* 5:1.
Gen 32:26. *not let go,* Exod 3:19. Job 27:6. Song of Sol 3:4.
Exod 23:23. *shall go,* 32:34; 33:14. Acts 25:12.
1 Sam 12:21. *should go,* Prov 22:6.
Judg 11:35. *go back,* Ps 80:18.
Num 22:18. go beyond, 1 Thess 4:6.
Gen 45:1. *go out,* Ps 60:10. Isa 52:11; 55:12. Jer 51:45. Ezek 46:9. Matt 25:6. John 10:9. 1 Cor 5:10.
Deut 4:40. *go well* with thee, 5:16; 19:13. Prov 11:10; 30:29.
Job 34:21. seeth all his *goings*
Ps 17:5. hold up my *g.* in thy paths
40:2. set my feet . . . established my *g.*
68:24. seen thy *g.*, O God, in sanctuary
Prov 5:21. he pondereth all his *g.*
20:24. man's *g.* are of the Lord
Mic 5:2. whose *g.* are of old, from
GOAT, Lev 3:12; 16:8, 21, 22.
Isa 1:11. delight not in blood of . . . *goats*
Ezek 34:17. judge between rams and *g.*
Zech 10:3. I punished the *g.*
Matt 25:32, 33. set *g.* on his left hand
Heb 9:12. blood of *g.* 13, 19; 10:4.
GOD, and *gods* for *men* representing God, Exod 4:16; 7:1; 22:28. Ps 82:1, 6.
John 10:34; for *idols* put in God's place, Deut 32:21. Judg 6:31, and 140 other places; for devil, god of this world, 2 Cor 4:4; and for the true God about 3,120 times
Gen 17:1. I am Almighty *G.* Job 36:5. Isa 9:6; 10:21. Jer 32:18.
7. a *G.* to thee and thy seed, Exod 6:7.
21:33. everlasting *G.* Ps 90:2. Isa 40:28. Rom 16:26.
Exod 8:10. none like Lord our *G.* 1 Kings 8:23. Ps 35:10; 86:8; 89:6.
18:11. Lord is greater than all *gods*
Deut 10:17. *G. of gods,* Josh 22:22. Dan 2:47. Ps 136:2.
32:39. there is no *g.* with me, 1 Kings 8:23. 2 Kings 5:15. 2 Chron 6:14; 32:15. Isa 43:10; 44:6, 8; 45:5, &c.
Job 33:12. *G.* is greater than man
Ps 18:31. who is *G.* save the Lord, 86:10.
Mic 7:18. who a *G.* like thee
Matt 6:24. cannot serve *G.* and mammon
19:17. none good but one, that is *G.*
Mark 12:32. there is one *G.* and none other
John 17:3. only true *G.* 1 John 5:20.
Acts 7:2. *G.* of glory appeared to Abraham
Rom 3:4. *G.* forbid: yea, let *G.* be true
8:31. if *G.* be for us, who against
9:5. over all, *G.* blessed for ever
15:5. *G.* of patience, 13. *G.* of hope
1 Cor 15:28. that *G.* may be all in all
2 Cor 1:3. *G.* of all comfort
2 Thess 2:4. above all called *G.* Dan 11:36.
1 Tim 3:16. *G.* manifest in flesh
1 Pet 5:10. *G.* of all grace
1 John 4:12. no man seen *G.* John 1:18.
Deut 10:17. *great G.* 2 Sam 7:22. 2 Chron 2:5. Job 36:26. Neh 1:5. Prov 26:10. Jer 32:18, 19.

Dan 9:4. Titus 2:13. Rev 19:17.
Deut 5:26. *living G.* Josh 3:10. 1 Sam 17:26, 36. 2 Kings 19:4, 16; and 22 other places
Exod 34:6. *G. merciful,* Deut 4:31. 2 Chron 30:9.
Neh 9:31. Ps 116:5. Jon 4:2.
Gen 49:24. *mighty G.* Deut 7:21; 10:17. Neh 9:32. Job 36:5. Ps 50:1; 132:2, 5. Isa 9:6; 10:21. Jer 32:18. Hab 1:12.
2 Chron 15:3. *true G.* Jer 10:10. John 17:3. 1 Thess 1:9. 1 John 5:20.
Gen 39:9. wickedness and sin *against G.* Num 21:5. Ps 78:19. Hos 13:16. Acts 5:39; 23:9. Rom 8:7; 9:20. Rev 13:6. Dan 11:36.
Ps 42:2. *before God,* 56:13; 61:7; 68:3. Eccles 2:26. Luke 1:6. Rom 2:13; 3:19. 1 Tim 5:21. James 1:27. Rev 3:2.
John 9:16. *of God,* Acts 5:39. Rom 9:16. 1 Cor 1:30; 11:12. 2 Cor 3:5; 5:18. Phil 1:28. 1 John 3:10; 4:1, 3, 6; 5:19. 3 John 11.
Exod 2:23. *(un)to God,* Ps 43:4. Eccles 12:7. Isa 58:2. Lam 3:41. John 13:3. Heb 7:25; 11:6; 12:23. 1 Pet 3:18; 4:6. Rev 5:9; 12:5.
Gen 5:22. *with God,* 24; 6:9; 32:28. Exod 19:17. 1 Sam 14:45. 2 Sam 23:5. Job 9:2; 25:4. Ps 78:8. Hos 11:12. John 5:18. Phil 2:6.
Gen 28:21. *my God,* Exod 15:2. Ps 22:1; 31:14; 91:2; 118:28. Hos 2:23. Zech 13:9. John 20:17, 28, and about 120 other places
Exod 5:8. *our God,* Deut 31:17; 32:3. Josh 24:18. 2 Sam 22:32. Ps 67:6, and 180 other places
Exod 20:2. *thy God,* 5, 7, 10, 12. Ps 50:7; 81:10, and 340 other places
2 Chron 36:23. *God of heaven,* Ezra 5:11; 6:10; 7:12, 23. Neh 1:4; 2:4. Ps 136:26. Dan 2:18, 19, 44. Jon 1:9. Rev 11:13; 16:11.
Exod 24:10. *God of Israel,* Num 16:9. Josh 7:19; 13:33; 22:16, 24; 24:23. Judg 11:23. Ruth 2:12. Isa 41:17. Jer 31:1. Ezek 8:4. Matt 15:31.
Rom 15:33. *God of peace,* 16:20. 2 Cor 13:11. 1 Thess 5:23. Heb 13:20.
Ps 24:5. *God of his salvation, of our salvation,* 65:5; 68:19, 20; 79:9; 85:4; 95:1.
Acts 17:29. *Godhead,* Rom 1:20. Col 2:9.

GODLY, Ps 4:3; 12:1; 32:6. Mal 2:15. 2 Pet 2:9. 3 John 6.
2 Cor 1:12. in simplicity and *g.* sincerity
7:9. sorrow after a *g.* manner, 10, 11.
Titus 2:12. live soberly, righteously and *g.*
Heb 12:28. with reverence and *g.* fear
1 Tim 2:2. quiet life in all *godliness,* 10; 3:16; 6:3, 5, 11. 2 Tim 3:5.
4:7. exercise thyself to *g.* 6:11.
8. *g.* is profitable to all things
6:3. doctrine according to *g.* Titus 1:1.
6. *g.* with contentment is great gain
2 Tim 3:5. having a form of *g.* but
2 Pet 1:3. all that pertain to life and *g.*
6. to patience *g.* 7. to *g.* brotherly kindness
3:11. . . . in all holy conversation and *g.*

GOLD, Gen 2:11; 13:2. Isa 2:7.
Job 23:10. I shall come forth as *g.*
31:24. if I made *g.* my hope, fine *g.*
Ps 19:10. more desired than *g.,* yea
119:127. love . . . above *g.,* yea, fine *g.* 72.
Prov 8:19. my fruit is better than *g.*
Isa 13:12. man more precious than fine *g.*
Zech 13:9. try them as *g.*
1 Cor 3:12. build on this foundation, *g.*
1 Tim 2:9. modest apparel . . . not *g.* 1 Pet 3:3.
1 Pet 1:7. trial of faith more precious than *g.*
Rev 3:18. buy of me *g.* tried in the fire

GOOD, Deut 6:24; 10:13.
Gen 1:31. every thing was very *good*
2:18. not *g.* for man to be alone
32:12. thou saidst, I will do thee *g.*
50:20. God meant it unto *g.*
2 Kings 20:19. *g.* is word of Lord, Isa 39:8.
Ps 34:8. taste and see that Lord is *g.*
73:1. truly God is *g.* to Israel
86:5. Lord, art *g.,* ready to forgive
106:5. may see the *g.* of thy chosen
145:9. Lord is *g.* to all, 136:1.
Lam 3:25. Lord *g.* to them that wait
Mic 6:8. shrewed thee what is *g.*
Matt 19:17. Why callest thou me *g.*? . . . none *g.*
Rom 3:8. do evil that *g.* may come
7:18. how to perform . . . *g.* I find not
1 Thess 5:15. follow that which is *g.* 3 John 11.
Neh 2:18. hand for this *good work*
Matt 26:10. wrought a—on me
John 10:33. a—we stone thee not
2 Cor 9:8. abound to every—
Phil 1:6. begun a—will finish it
Col 1:10. fruitful in every—
2 Thess 2:17. establish you in every—
1 Tim 5:10. followed every—
Titus 1:16. to every—reprobate
3:1. ready to every—
Heb 13:21. perfect in every—
John 10:32. many *good works* I shewed you
Acts 9:36. Dorcas was full of—
Rom 13:3. not a terror to—
Eph 2:10. created in Christ Jesus to—
1 Tim 2:10. (women professing godliness) with—
5:10. reported of for—
25. the—of some are manifest
Titus 3:8. careful to maintain—14.
Heb 10:24. provoke to love and—
1 Pet 2:12. may by your—which
Exod 33:19. make my *goodness* pass
34:6. God abundant in *g.* and truth
2 Chron 6:41. let saints rejoice in *g.*
Neh 9:25. delight themselves in *g.*
35. not served thee in thy great *g.*
Ps 16:2. my *g.* extendeth not to
23:6. *g.* and mercy shall follow me
27:13. believed to see *g.* of Lord
31:19. how great is thy *g.* Zech 9:17.
33:5. earth full of *g.* of Lord, 145:7.
52:1. the *g.* of God endureth
65:4. satisfied with *g.* of thy house
11. crownest the year with thy *g.*
Isa 63:7. great *g.* bestowed on Israel
Hos 3:5. fear the Lord and his *g.*
Rom 2:4. *g.* of God leadeth to repentance
11:22. behold the *g.* and severity of God
Eph 5:9. fruit of Spirit in all *g.* Gal 5:22.

GOSPEL, Mark 1:1, 15; 8:35.
Matt 4:23. preaching *g.* of kingdom
Mark 16:15. preach *g.* to every creature
Acts 20:24. *g.* of grace of God
Rom 1:1. *g.* of God, 15:16. 1 Tim 1:11.
1 Cor 1:17. but to preach the *g.*
4:15. begotten you through the *g.*
2 Cor 4:3. if our *g.* hid, 4. glorious *g.*
11:4. another *g.* which ye, Gal 1:6.
Eph 1:13. *g.* of salvation, 6:15. *g.* of peace
Phil 1:5. fellowship in the *g.*
27. as becometh the *g.* . . . striving for faith of *g.*
Col 1:5. truth of *g.* Gal 2:5.
1 Thess 1:5. our *g.* came in power
Heb 4:2. unto us was *g.* preached
1 Pet 4:6. *g.* was preached to dead
Rev 14:6. everlasting *g.* to preach

GOVERNMENT, Isa 9:6, 7; 22:21. 1 Cor 12:28. 2 Pet 2:10.

GRACE, Ezra 9:8. Esther 2:17.
Ps 84:11. Lord will give *g.* and glory
Prov 3:34. *g.* to lowly, James 4:6.

Zech 4:7. with shoutings, crying, *g. g.* to it
12:10. spirit of *g.* and supplications
Acts 18:27. which had believed through *g.*
Rom 3:24. justified freely by his *g.*
5:20. *g.* did much more abound
6:14. not under law, but *g.*
11:5. according to the election of *g.*
6. if by *g.* then not of works, otherwise *g.* no more *g.*
2 Cor 12:9. my *g.* sufficient for thee
Eph 2:5. by *g.* ye are saved, 8.
7. shew exceeding riches of his *g.* 1:7.
4:29. minister *g.* to the hearers
Titus 3:7. justified by his *g.*
Heb 4:16. come boldly to the throne of *g.*
13:9. heart be established with *g.*
1 Pet 3:7. heirs of the *g.* of life
5:5. and giveth *g.* to the humble
2 Pet 3:18. grow in *g.* and knowledge
Rom 1:7. *grace and peace* to you
Luke 2:40. *grace of God,* Acts 11:23; 13:43; 14:3, 26; 15:40; 20:24, 32. Rom 5:15. 1 Cor 1:4; 3:10; 15:10. Eph 3:2, 7. Heb 2:9; 12:15.
2 Cor 1:12. by—our conversation
6:1. receive not—in vain
8:1. of—bestowed on churches
9:14. for the exceeding—in you
Gal 2:21. I do not frustrate—
Col 1:6. knew—in truth
1 Pet 4:10. stewards of manifold—
5:12. this the true—wherein ye stand
Jude 4. turning—into lasciviousness
Acts 15:11. *grace of our Lord Jesus Christ,* Rom 16:20, 24. 1 Cor 16:23. 2 Cor 8:9; 13:14. Gal 6:18. Phil 4:23. 1 Thess 5:28. 2 Thess 3:18. Philem 25.
Rev 22:21.—be with you all
Gen 43:29. God be *gracious* to thee
Exod 22:27. I will hear, for I am *g.* 33.
19. I will be *g.* to whom I will be *g.*
34:6. Lord God merciful and *g.* 2 Chron 30:9. Neh 9:17, 31. Ps 103:8; 116:5; 145:8. Joel 2:13.
Num 6:25. Lord be *g.* 2 Sam 12:22.
Job 33:24. then he is *g.* to him
Ps 77:9. hath God forgotten to be *g.*
86:15. compassion and *g.* 78:38; 111:4; 112:4.
Amos 5:15. may be, Lord will be *g.*
Jon 4:2. knew thou art a *g.* God
Mal 1:9. beseech God . . . *be g. Isa 33:2.*
1 Pet 2:3. if ye have tasted that Lord is *g.*
Gen 33:5. *graciously,* 11. Ps 119:29.
Hos 14:2. receive us *g.*

GRANT, Job 10:12. Prov 10:24. Rom 15:5. Eph 3:16. 2 Tim 1:18. Rev 3:21.
GRAPES, of gall, Deut 32:32.
Song of Sol 2:13. the tender *g.* 7:7. clusters of *g.*
Isa 5:4. wild *g.* Ezek 18:2. sour *g.*
Mic 7:1. *g.* gleanings of vintage
GRASS, Ps 37:2; 90:5; 92:7; 102:4, 11. Isa 44:4; 51:12.
Ps 103:15. as for may his days like *g.*
Isa 40:6. all flesh is *g.* 7, 8. 1 Pet 1:24. James 1:10, 11.
Matt 6:30. if God so clothe the *g.*
Rev 8:7. green *g.* 9:4. not hurt *g.*
GRAVE, 1 Kings 2:9; 14:13.
1 Sam 2:6. Lord bringeth down to *g.*
Job 5:26. come to thy *grave* in full age
14:13. hide me in the *g.* 17:1, 13.
Ps 6:5. in *g.* who shall give thanks
Prov 1:12. swallow alive, as the *g.*
Eccles 9:10. nor wisdom in the *g.*
Isa 38:18. *g.* cannot praise
Hos 13:14. the power of the *g.* O *g.* I will be thy
1 Cor 15:55. O *g.* where is thy victory
GRAVEN with an iron pen, Job 19:24.
Isa 49:16. have *g.* thee on the palms
Jer 17:1. sin *g.* upon table of heart
GREAT, Gen 12:2; 30:8.
Deut 29:24. *g.* anger, 2 Chron 34:21.
1 Sam 6:9. *great evil,* Neh 13:27. Eccles 2:21. Jer 44:7. Dan 9:12.
Ps 47:2. *great king,* 48:2; 95:3. Mal 1:14. Matt 5:35.
Job 32:9. *great men,* Jer 5:5.
Exod 32:11. *great power,* Neh 1:10. Job 23:6. Ps 147:5. Nah 1:3. Acts 4:33; 8:10. Rev 11:17.
Exod 32:21. *so great,* Deut 4:7, 8. 1 Kings 3:9. Ps 77:13; 103:11. Matt 8:10; 15:33. 2 Cor 1:10. Heb 2:3; 12:1. Rev 16:18; 18:17.
Job 5:9. *great things,* 9:10; 37:5. Jer 45:5. Hos 8:12. Luke 1:49.
Gen 6:5. *great wickedness,* 39:9. Job 22:5. Joel 3:13. 2 Chron 28:13.
Job 33:12. God is *greater* than man
Matt 12:42. *g.* than Solomon is here
John 1:50. see *g.* things than these
4:12. art thou *g.* than, 8:53.
10:29. my Father . . . is *g.* than all, 14:28. *g.* than I
1 Cor 14:5. g. is he that prophesieth
1 John 4:4. *g.* he that is in you, 3:20. God *g.* than our heart
5:9. witness of God is *g.*
1 Sam 30:6. David was *greatly* distressed

2 Sam 24:10. I have sinned *g.* in that I
1 Kings 18:3. Obadiah feared the Lord *g.*
1 Chron 16:25. great is Lord and *g.* to be praised, Ps 48:1; 96:4; 145:3.
2 Chron 33:12. humbled himself *g.*
Job 3:25. thing I *g.* feared is come
Ps 28:7. my heart *g.* rejoiceth
89:7. God is *g.* to be feared in the assembly
116:10. I was *g.* afflicted
Dan 9:23. O man, *g.* beloved, 10:11, 19.
Mark 12:27. ye do *g.* err
Exod 15:7. *greatness* of thy excellency
Num 14:19. pardon (spare me, Neh 13:22.) according to the *g.* of thy mercy
Deut 32:3. ascribe ye *g.* to our God
Ps 66:3. *g.* of thy power, 79:11. Eph 1:19.
145:3. his *g.* unsearchable, 6.
Isa 63:1. travelling in *g.* of strength
GREEDY, of gain, Prov 1:19; 15:27.
Isa 56:11. they are *g.* dogs, never
1 Tim 3:3. not *g.* of filthy lucre, 8.
Eph 4:19. work uncleanness with *greediness*
GRIEF, Isa 53:3, 4, 10. Heb 13:17.
Lam 3:33. nor *grieve* children of men
Gen 6:6. *grieved* him at his heart
Judg 10:16. his soul was *g.* for misery
Ps 95:10. forty years long was I *g.*
119:158. I beheld transgressors and was *g.*
139:21. *g.* with those that rise up
Isa 54:6. woman forsaken and *g.*
Jer 5:3. stricken, they have not *g.*
Amos 6:6. not *g.* for (Joseph's) affliction
Mark 3:5. *g.* for hardness of hearts
Rom 14:15. if brother be *g.* with thy meat
Ps 10:5. ways are always *grievous*
Matt 23:4. burdens *grievous* to be borne
Acts 20:29. shall *g.* wolves enter
1 John 5:3. his commandments are not *g.*
Matt 8:6. *grievously* tormented, 15:22.
GRIND the faces of poor, Isa 3:15.
Matt 21:44. it will *g.* him to powder
Eccles 12:3. *grinders* cease because few, 4.
GROAN earnestly, 2 Cor 5:2, 4.
John 11:33. (Jesus) *groaned* in spirit
Rom 8:22. whole creation *groaneth*
Ps 6:6. weary with my *groaning*
38:9. my *g.* is not hid from thee
102:20. to hear the *g.* of prisoner
Rom 8:26. *groanings* which cannot be uttered

H

HAPPY am I, for the daughters, Gen 30:13.
Deut 33:29. *h.* art thou, O Israel
1 Kings 10:8. *h.* are thy men, *h.* these
Job 5:17. *h.* the man whom God correcteth
Ps 127:5. *h.* the man who hath his quiver
128:2. *h.* shalt thou be, and be well
144:15. *h.* people whose God is Lord
146:5. *h.* is he that hath God of Jacob
Prov 3:13. *h.* the man that findeth wisdom, 18.
14:21. that hath mercy on poor, *h.* is he
16:20. who trusteth in Lord, *h.* is he
28:14. *h.* is man that feareth alway
29:18. he that keepeth law, *h.* is he
Mal 3:15. we call the proud *h.*
John 13:17. *h.* ye if ye do them
Rom 14:22. *h.* he that condemneth not
1 Pet 3:14. suffer for righteousness' sake, *h.* are ye
4:14. reproached for the name of Christ, *h.* are ye
1 Cor 7:40. *happier* if she so abide
HARD, Gen 35:16, 17. Exod 1:14; 18:26. 2 Sam 13:2. Ps 88:7.
Gen 18:14. any thing too *h.* for the Lord
2 Kings 2:10. thou hast asked a *h.* thing
Ps 60:3. shewed thy people *h.* things
Prov 13:15. way of transgressors is *h.*
Jer 32:17. nothing too *h.* for thee, 27.
Mark 10:24. how *h.* for them . . . riches
Acts 9:5. *h.* for thee to kick, 26:14.
2 Pet 3:16. things *h.* to be understood
Jude 15. of all their *h.* speeches
HARDEN, Exod 4:21. Deut 15:7. Josh 11:20. Job 6:10; 39:16.
Heb 3:8. *h.* not hearts as in the provocation, 15; 4:7. Ps 95:8.
Job 9:4. *hardened* himself against (God)
Isa 63:17. *h.* our heart from thy fear
Mark 6:52. their heart was *h.* 3:5.
Heb 3:13. *h.* through deceitfulness
Prov 21:29. *hardeneth* face, 28:14. *h.* heart
29:1. he . . . reproved *h.* his neck shall be destroyed
Prov 18:19. brother offended *harder* . . . won
Jer 5:3. made faces *h.* than a *rock*
Ezek 3:9. forehead *h.* than flint
Matt 19:8. *hardness* of your hearts
Mark 3:5. grieved for the *h.* of their
Rom 2:5. after thy *h.* and impenitent
2 Tim 2:3. endure *h.* as a good soldier
HARLOT
Gen 34:31. Josh 2:1. Judg 11:1. Prov 7:10. Isa 1:21; 23:15.
Jer 2:20. play the *h.* 3:1, 6, 8. Ezek 16:15, 16, 41. Hos 2:5; 4:15.
1 Cor 6:16. joined to *h.* is one body
Heb 11:31. by faith *h.* Rahab
James 2:25. Rahab *h.* justified by works
Matt 21:31. *harlots* into kingdom of God before, 32.
Rev 17:5. mother of *h.*
HARM, Gen 31:52. Acts 28:5.
1 Chron 16:22. do my prophets no *harm.* Ps 105:15. Prov 3:30. Jer 39:12.
1 Pet 3:13. who is he that will *h.* you
Matt 10:16. *harmless,* Phil 2:15.
HARVEST, Gen 8:22; 30:14.
Exod 34:21. in *h.* thou shalt rest
Isa 9:3. according to joy in *h.*
Jer 5:24. appointed weeks of *h.*
8:20. *h.* is past, summer is ended
51:33. time of *h.* come, Joel 3:13.
Matt 9:37. *h.* plenteous, 38. pray ye the Lord of the *h.*
13:39. *h.* is the end of the world
Rev 14:15. *h.* of earth is ripe
HASTE, Exod 12:11, 33. Isa 52:12.
Ps 31:22. I said in my *h.* 116:11.
38:22. make *h.* help me, 40:13; 70:1, 5; 71:12; 141:1.
119:60. I made *h.* and delayed not
Song of Sol 8:14. make *h.*, my beloved
Isa 28:16. believeth shall not make *h.*
49:17. thy children shall make *h.*
Ps 16:4. *hasten* after another god
Isa 5:19. let him make speed and *h.*
60:22. I the Lord will *h.* it in his time
Jer 1:12. I will *h.* my word
Prov 20:21. inheritance may be gotten *hastily*
14:29. *hasty* of spirit, Eccles 7:9.
29:20. *h.* in words? more hope of fool
HATE, Gen 24:60. Deut 21:15.
Lev 19:17. shall not *h.* thy brother
Deut 7:10. repayeth them that *h.*
Ps 68:1. let them that *h.* him flee
97:10. ye that love the Lord, *h.* evil
119:104. I *h.* every false way, 128.
113. I *h.* vain thoughts, 163. *h.* lying
139:21. do not I *h.* them that *h.*
Prov 8:13. fear of Lord is to *h.* evil
36. all they that *h.* me love death
Jer 44:4. abominable thing that I *h.*
Amos 5:10. they *h.* him that
15. *h.* the evil, and love the good
Luke 14:26. and *h.* not his father
Rom 7:15. what I *h.* that do I
1 John 3:13. marvel not if world *h.*
Rev 2:6. *h.* deeds, which I *h.* 15.
17:16. these shall *h.* the whore
Prov 1:29. they *hated* knowledge
5:12. how have I *h.* instruction
Isa 66:5. your brethren that *h.* you
Mal 1:3. I *h.* Essau, Rom 9:13.
Matt 10:22 &c. shall be *h.* of all men
Luke 19:14. his citizens *h.* him
John 15:24. *h.* me and my Father, 18.
Eph 5:29. no man *h.* his own flesh
Titus 3:3. *hateful* and *h.* one another
Jude 23. *h.* garment spotted by flesh
Rom 1:30. backbiters, *haters* of God
Ps 5:5. *hatest* workers of iniquity
50:17. seeing thou *h.* instruction
Exod 23:5. ass of him that *hateth*
Prov 13:24. spareth rod, *h.* his son
John 12:25. *h.* his life in this world
1 John 2:9. *h.* his brother is in darkness, 11; 3:15; 4:20.
Exod 18:21. men of truth, *hating* covetousness
HAUGHTY, my heart not, Ps 131:1.
Prov 16:18. *h.* spirit before fall, 18:12.
21:24. proud and *h.* scorner dealeth
Zeph 3:11. no more be *h.* because
Isa 2:11. *haughtiness,* 17; 13:11; 16:6.
HEAD, Gen 2:10; 40:13.
Gen 3:15. it shall bruise thy *h.* and
Gen 49:26. blessings on Joseph's *head* Deut 33:16
Ezra 9:6. iniquity increased over *h.*
Ps 38:4. iniquities gone over my *h.*
Prov 16:31. hoary *h.* is a crown of
20:29. beauty of old men is gray *h.*
Eccles 2:14. wise man's eyes are in *h.*
9:8. let thy *h.* lack no ointment
Song of Sol 5:2. my *h.* is filled with dew
11. his *h.* is as most fine gold
Isa 1:5. whole *h.* is sick and heart
6. from sole of foot even unto *h.*
Jer 9:1. Oh that my *h.* were waters
48:37. every *h.* shall be bald
Ezek 9:10. their way on *h.* 16:43.
Dan 2:28. visions of thy *h.* on bed
38. thou art this *h.* of gold, 32.
Zech 4:7. bring forth *h.* stone
Matt 8:20. not where to lay his *h.*
14:8. give me *h.* of John Baptist
Rom 12:20. coals of fire on *h.* Prov 25:22.
Eph 1:22. gave him to be *h.* over all
4:15. which is the *h.* even Christ

5:23. husb. *h.* of wife, Christ *h.* of the church
Col 1:18. he is *h.* of the body, 2:19.
Rev 19:12. on his *h.* many crowns
Ps 24:7. lift up your *heads,* 9.
Isa 35:10. everlasting joy on *h.* 51:11.
Luke 21:28. lift up your *h.*
Rev 13:1. seven *h.* and ten horns
Job 5:13. *headlong,* Luke 4:29. Acts 1:18.
2 Tim 3:4. *heady,* highminded.
HEAL her now, O God, Num 12:13.
Deut 32:39. I wound, and I *h.*
2 Chron 7:14. and will *h.* their land
Ps 6:2. *h.* me, for my bones are
41:4. *h.* my soul, for I have sinned
Isa 57:18. seen his ways and will *h.* him
Jer 3:22. *h.* your backslidings, Hos 14:4.
17:14. *h.* me, and I shall be *h.*
Hos 6:1. hath torn and he will *h.* us
Luke 4:18. *h.* the brokenhearted
23. will say, Physician, *h.* thyself
John 12:40. converted and I should *h.*
2 Chron 30:20. (Lord) *healed* the people
Ps 30:2. I cried . . . and thou hast *h.*
Isa 6:10. convert and be *h.* Acts 28:27.
53:5. with his stripes we are *h.* 1 Pet 2:24.
Jer 6:14. *h.* hurt of daughter, 8:11.
15:18. wound . . . which refuseth to be *h.*
Hos 7:1. I would have *h.* Israel
Matt 4:24. and he *h.* them, 12:15; 14:14.
Heb 12:13. let it rather be *h.*
James 5:16. pray that ye may be *h.*
Rev 13:3. his deadly wound was *h.*
Exod 15:26. I the Lord that *healeth* thee
Ps 103:3. who *h.* all thy diseases
147:3. he *h.* the broken in heart
Isa 30:26. *h.* stroke of their wound
Jer 14:19. looked for time of *healing*
30:13. thou hast no *h.* medicine
Mal 4:2. with *h.* in his wings
Matt 4:23. *h.* all manner of sickness
1 Cor 12:9. to another the gifts of *h.*
Rev 22:2. leaves were for *h.* nations
Ps 42:11. *health* of countenance, 43:5.
Prov 3:8. shall be *h.* to thy navel
12:18. the tongue of the wise is *h.*
Jer 8:15. looked for a time of *h.*
30:17. I will restore *h.* and heal
HEAP coals, Prov 25:22. Rom 12:20.
Deut 32:23. I will *h.* mischiefs upon
Job 36:13. hypocrites . . . *h.* up wrath
2 Tim 4:3. *h.* to themselves teachers
James 5:3. ye have *heaped* treasure
Ps 39:6. he *heapeth* up riches, and
Judg 15:16. *heaps* upon *h.* with the
HEAR, Gen 21:6; 23:6.
Deut 30:17. if thou wilt not *h.*
1 Kings 8:30. *h.* in heaven thy dwelling
2 Kings 19:16. bow thine ear, and *h.*
2 Chron 6:21. *h.* from thy dwelling
Job 5:27. *h.* it and know it for good
Ps 4:1. *h.* my prayer, 39:12; 54:2; 51:8; 84:8; 102:1; 143:1. Dan 9:17, 19.
4:3. Lord will *h.* 17:6; 145:19. Zech 10:6.
10:17. thou wilt cause thine ear to *h.*
59:7. who, say they, doth *h.*
66:16. come and *h.* all ye that
115:6. they have ears, but *h.* not
Prov 19:27. cease to *h.* instruction
Eccles 5:1. be more ready to *h.* than
Song of Sol 2:14. let me *h.* thy voice, 8:13.
Isa 1:2. *h.* O heavens, and give ear
6:10. lest they *h.* with ears, Deut 29:4.
55:3. *h.* and your soul shall live
Matt 10:27. what ye *h.* in the ear
13:17. to *h.* those things which ye *h.*
17:5. this is my beloved Son, . . . *h.* ye him
18:17. if he neglect to *h.* them
Mark 4:24. take heed what ye *h.*
33. spake word . . . as they were able to *h.*
Luke 8:18. take heed how ye *h.*
John 5:25. they that *h.* shall live
Acts 10:33. to *h.* all things that are commanded
James 1:19. every man be swift to *h.*
Rev 3:20. if any *h.* my voice, and open
Exod 2:24. God *heard* their groaning
Ps 6:9. Lord hath *h.* supplication
10:17. hast *h.* desire of humble, 34:6.
34:4. I sought the Lord, and he *h.*
61:5. thou hast *h.* my vows, 116:1.
66:19. verily God hath *h.* me, 18:6.
118:21. I will praise thee, for thou hast *h.* me
120:1. I cried to Lord, and he *h.*
Isa 40:28. hast thou not *h.* that God
Jer 8:6. I hearkened and *h.*
Jon 2:2. I cried to Lord and he *h.*
Mal 3:16. Lord hearkened and *h.*
Matt 6:7. be *h.* for much speaking
Luke 1:13. thy prayer is *h.* and thy
John 3:32. what he hath seen and *h.*
8:6. wrote as though he *h.* them not
Rom 10:14. of whom they have not *h.*
1 Cor 2:9. eye not seen nor ear *h.*
Phil 4:9. things learned and received and *h.*
Heb 4:2. with faith in them that *h.*
5:7. was *h.* in that he feared
James 5:11. ye have *h.* of patience of Job
Rev 3:3. how thou hast received and *h.*
Exod 3:7. *I have heard* their cry
6:5.—the groaning, Acts 7:34.
16:12.—the murmurings, Num 14:27.
Job 42:5.—of thee by the hearing
Isa 49:8. in an acceptable time—
Jer 31:18.—Ephraim bemoaning
James 1:25. not a forgetful *hearer* but a doer
Rom 2:13. not *hearers* of the law just
Eph 4:29. minister grace to the *h.*
James 1:22. doers of word, not *h.*
Ps 65:2. O thou that *hearest* prayer
John 11:42. I knew thou *h.* me
1 Sam 3:9. speak, thy servant *heareth*
Prov 8:34. blessed the man that *h.* me
Matt 7:24. whoso *h.* these sayings
Luke 10:16. he that *h.* you *h.* me
John 9:31. God *h.* not sinners, but
1 John 5:14. ask according to his will he *heareth*
Rev 22:17. let him that *h.* say, Come
Job 42:5. of thee by *hearing* of ear
Prov 20:12. the *h.* ear, and seeing
28:9. turneth away his ear from *h.*
Rom 10:17. faith cometh by *h.* and *h.* by
Heb 5:11. seeing ye are dull of *h.*
2 Pet 2:8. in seeing and *h.* vexed his
HEARKEN to the Lord, Deut 28:15.
Deut 28:1. if thou *h.* diligently, 30:10.
1 Sam 15:22. to *h.* better than fat of rams
Ps 103:20. angels *h.* to voice of his word
Isa 46:12. *h.* unto me, ye stouthearted
51:1. *h.* unto me, ye that follow
55:2. *h.* diligently unto me, eat
HEART, Exod 28:30; 35:5.
1 Sam 1:13. she spake in her *h.* only
10:9. God gave him another *h.*
16:7. but the Lord looketh on the *h.*
24:5. David's *h.* smote him because

1 Chron 16:10. let the *h.* of them rejoice that seek the Lord, Ps 105:3.
22:19. set *h.* . . . Lord your God
2 Chron 17:6. *h.* lifted up in Lord's ways
30:19. prepareth his *h.* to seek God
Ps 22:26. your *h.* life for ever, 69:32.
37:31. law of his God is in his *h.*
51:17. broken and contrite *h.* Isa 66:2.
64:6. inward thought . . . and *h.* deep
78:37. their *h.* was not right with
Prov 4:23. keep thy *h.* with diligence
10:20. *h.* of wicked is little worth
14:10. *h.* knoweth own bitterness
16:9. a man's *h.* deviseth his way
27:19. (answereth) *h.* of man to man
Eccles 7:4. *h.* of wise is in house of mourning
10:2. wise man's *h.* at his right hand, a fool's *h.* at his left
Song of Sol 3:11. day of gladness of his *h.*
Isa 6:10. make *h.* of this people fat
57:15. to revive the *h.* of contrite
Jer 11:20. triest reins and *h.* 17:10.
12:11. no man layeth it to *h.* Isa 42:25.
17:9. *h.* is deceitful above all things
24:7. I will give them an *h.* to know
32:39. give them one *h.* Ezek 11:19.
Lam 3:41. lift up our *h.* with hands
Ezek 11:19. take stony *h.*, give *h.* of flesh
18:31. make you a new *h.*
36:26. new *h.*, take stony *h.*, give *h.*
Joel 2:13. rend your *h.* not garments
Mal 4:6. turn *h.* of fathers
Matt 6:21. there will your *h.* be also
12:35. of good treasure of *h.* Luke 6:45.
15:19. out of *h.* proceed evil thoughts, Mark 7:21.
Luke 2:19. pondered them in *h.* 51.
24:25. O fools, slow of *h.* to believe
32. did not our *h.* burn within us
John 14:1. let not *h.* be troubled, 27.
Acts 5:33. were cut to the *h.* 7:54.
11:23. with purpose of *h.* cleave to
13:22. found man after mine own *h.*
Rom 10:10. with *h.* man believeth
1 Cor 2:9. *nor entered into h. of man*
2 Cor 3:3. in fleshy tables of the *h.*
1 Pet 3:4. in hidden man of *h.*
1 John 3:20. if *h.* condemn us, God

Deut 11:13. serve him *with all your h.* and soul, Josh 22:5. 1 Sam 12:20,—
Jer 29:13. search for me—
Deut 6:5. love God *with all thy h.* and soul, 30:6. Matt 22:37. Mark 12:30. Luke 10:27.
26:16. keep and do them—and soul
Prov 3:5. trust in Lord—
Deut 30:2. (re)turn to Lord *with all thy h.* and soul, 10.
2 Kings 23:25. *(his h.).* Joel 2:12. *(your h.).*
1 Kings 2:4. walk bef. me *with all their h.* and soul
8:48. return to thee—and soul
2 Chron 15:12. seek God of their fathers—and soul
15:15. sworn—
22:9. sought Lord *with all his h.* 31:21. did it—
Zeph 3:14. sing . . rejoice *with all the h.*
Ps 86:12. praise thee *with all my heart*
45:1. *my heart* is inditing a good
57:7.—is fixed, O God, 108:1.
61:2. when—is overwhelmed
73:26. my flesh and—faileth, but
84:2.—and my flesh crieth for the
109:22.—is wounded within me
131:1. Lord—is not haughty, nor
Song of Sol 5:2. I sleep, but—waketh
Jer 3:15. give pastors according to—
Hos 11:8.—is turned within me
2 Kings 20:3. and with *perfect heart,* 2 Chron 19:9.
1 Chron 28:9. serve him with—29.
2 Chron 16:9. toward him whose—
Ps 101:2. within my house with a—
24:4. clean hands and *pure heart*
Matt 5:8. blessed are the pure in *h.*
1 Tim 1:5. charity out of a—
2 Tim 2:22. call on Lord out of—
1 Pet 1:22. love with—fervently
Ps 9:1. praise thee, O Lord, *with my whole heart,* 111:1; 138:1.
119:2. seek him—10.—have I sought
34. observe it—58. thy favour—69. keep thy precepts—
Jer 3:10. not turned unto me with whole *h.*
Col 3:23. do it *heartily* as to Lord
HEATH, Jer 17:6; 48:6.
HEATHEN, Lev 25:44; 26:45.
Ps 2:1. why do the *h.* rage, Acts 4:25.
2:8. give them the *h.* for
Gal 3:8. justify *h.* through faith
HEAVEN of *h.* cannot contain thee, 1 Kings 8:27. 2 Chron 2:6; 6:18.
Ps 103:11. as h. is high above the
115:16. *h.* even heavens are Lord's
Prov 25:3. *h.* for height, and earth
Isa 66:1. *h.* is my throne, Acts 7:49.

Jer 31:37. if *h.* can be measured
Hag 1:10. *h.* is stayed from dew
Luke 15:18. sinned against *h.* 21.
John 1:51. see *h.* open and angels
Acts 3:21. the *h.* must receive him
Ps 73:25. whom have I *in heaven*
Eccles 5:2. God is—thou upon earth
Heb 10:34. have—better substance
1 Pet 1:4. inheritance reserved—
Ps 8:3. when I consider *thy heavens*
19:1. *the heavens* declare the glory of God
89:11.—are thine, and earth also
Isa 65:17. I create new *heavens* and a new earth, 66:22. Rev 21:1.
2 Cor 5:1. a house eternal in the *h.*
Eph 4:10. ascended far above all *h.*
2 Pet 3:12. *h.* being on fire shall be dissolved
Matt 6:14. *heavenly* Father, 26, 32; 15:13; 18:35. Luke 11:13.
John 3:12. if I tell you of *h.* things
1 Cor 15:48. as is *h.* such the *h.* 49.
Eph 1:3. in *h.* places, 20; 2:6; 3:10.
2 Tim 4:18. unto his *h.* kingdom
Heb 3:1. partakers of *h.* calling
HEAVY, Num 11:14. Job 33:7.
Prov 31:6. wine to those of *h.* hearts
Isa 6:10. make their ears *h.* lest
Isa 58:6. to undo the *heavy* burden
Matt 11:28. that labour and are *h.* laden
23:4. bind *h.* burdens and grievous
Ps 69:20. I am full of *heaviness*
119:28. my soul melteth for *h.*
Prov 12:25. *h.* in heart maketh it stoop
14:13. end of that mirth is *h.*
Rom 9:2. I have great *h.* and sorrow
1 Pet 1:6. in *h.* through . . . temptations
HEDGE, Job 1:10. Prov 15:19. Isa 5:5. Hos 2:6. Job 3:23. Lam 3:7.
HEED, 2 Sam 20:10. 2 Kings 10:31.
Deut 2:4. take good *h.* to yourselves, 4:15.
Josh 22:5. take diligent *h.* to do the
Ps 119:9. by taking *h.* thereto
Jer 18:18. not give *h.* to any of his
HEEL, his, shalt bruise, Gen 3:15.
Ps 41:9. lifted *h.* against me, John 13:18.
Hos 12:3. he took his brother by *h.*
Ps 49:5. iniquity of *heels* shall compass
HEIFER, Num 19:2. Jer 46:20; 48:34. Hos 4:16; 10:11. Heb 9:13.

HEIR, Gen 15:4; 21:10.
Jer 49:1. hath Israel no sons . . . no *h.*
Rom 4:13. (Abraham) should be *h.* of the world through faith
Gal 4:7. if a son, then an *h.* of God
Heb 1:2. whom God appointed *h.*
11:7. became *h.* of righteousness
Rom 8:17. *heirs* of God, joint *h.* with Christ
Gal 3:29. if ye be Christ's then Abraham's seed and *h.* according to the promise
Eph 3:6. Gentiles should be fellow *h.*
Heb 6:17. willing to shew *h.* of promise
1 Pet 3:7. *h.* together of grace of
HELD, Ps 94:18. Song of Sol 3:4.
HELL, Matt 18:9. Mark 9:43, 45.
Deut 32:22. shall burn to lowest *h.*
2 Sam 22:6. the sorrows of *h.*
Job 11:8. it is deeper than *h.*; what
26:6. *h.* is naked before him and
Ps 9:17. wicked be turned into *h.*
16:10. not leave soul in *h.* Acts 2:27.
55:15. let them go down quick into *h.*
86:13. delivered soul from lowest *h.*
139:8. make my bed in *h.* thou art
Prov 5:5. her steps take hold on *h.*
7:27. her house is the way to *h.*
9:18. her guests are in depths of *h.*
15:11. *h.* and destruction before the Lord
24. that he may depart from *h.*
23:14. shalt deliver his soul from *h.*
27:20. *h.* and destruction are never
Isa 5:14. *h.* hath enlarged herself
14:9. *h.* from beneath is moved to
15. thou shalt be brought down to *h.*
57:9. debase thyself even to *h.*
Ezek 31:16, 17; 32:21, 27.
Amos 9:2. though they dig into *h.*
Jon 2:2. out of belly of *h.* cried I
Hab 2:5. enlargeths his desire as *h.*
Matt 5:22. be in danger of *h.* fire
29. body, eye, &c., be cast into *h.* 30.
10:28. destroy soul and body in *h.*
11:23. brought down to *h.* Luke 10:15.
16:18. gates of *h.* shall not prevail
23:15. twofold more the child of *h.*
Luke 12:5. power to cast into *h.*
16:23. in *h.* he lift up his eyes
Acts 2:31. his soul not left in *h.* 27.
James 3:6. tongue set on fire of *h.*
2 Pet 2:4. cast them down to *h.*
Rev 1:18. have keys of *h.* and
Rev 6:8. Death, and *Hell* followed with
20:13. death and *h.* delivered up dead
14. death and *h.* were cast into lake
HELMET, 1 Sam 17:5. 2 Chron 26:14.
Eph 6:17. take the *h.* of salvation
1 Thess 5:8. an *h.*, hope of salvation
HELP meet for him, Gen 2:18.
Deut 33:29. Lord, shield of thy *h.*
Jude 5:23. came not to *h.* of Lord
Ps 27:9. thou hast been my *h.*
33:20. he is our *h.* and shield
40:17. my *h.* and deliverer, 70:5.
46:1. God a very present *h.* in trouble
60:11. vain is *h.* of man, 108:12.
71:12. my God, make haste for my *h.*
89:19. laid *h.* on one that is mighty
115:9. Lord is *h.* and shield, 10:11.
124:8. our *h.* is in name of Lord
Hos 13:9. but in me is thy *h.*
Acts 26:22. having obtained *h.* of God
2 Chron 14:11. nothing with thee to *h.*
Ps 40:13. make haste to *h.* me, 70:1.
Isa 41:10. I will *h.* thee, 13, 14; 44:2.
63:5. I looked and there was none to *h.*
Acts 16:9. come to Macedonia, and *h.* us
Heb 4:16. find grace to *h.* in time
1 Sam 7:12. hitherto the Lord *helped* us
Isa 49:8. in day of salvation I *h.*
Zech 1:15. *h.* forward affliction
Acts 18:27. *h.* them much which believed
Rev 12:16. the earth *h.* the woman
Ps 10:14. art the *helper* of the fatherless
Job 9:13. proud *helpers* do stoop
2 Cor 1:24. (we) are *h.* of your joy
3 John 8. fellow *h.* to the truth
Rom 8:26. Spirit *helpeth* our infirmities
1 Cor 12:28. *helps,* governments
HEM, Matt 9:20; 14:36.
HEN, Matt 23:37. Luke 13:34.
HERESY, Acts 24:14. 1 Cor 11:19. Gal 5:20. 2 Pet 2:1.
HERITAGE appointed by God, Job 20:29.
Ps 16:6. I have a goodly *h.*
61:5. *h.* of those that fear thy name
119:111. testimonies taken as *h.* for
Isa 54:17. *h.* of Lord's servants, 58:14.
Jer 3:19. goodly *h.* of the hosts
Joel 2:17. give not thine *h.* to reproach, 3:2.
1 Pet 5:3. not as lords over God's *h.*
HEW tables of stone, Exod 34:1. Deut 12:3.
Jer 2:13. *hewed* out cisterns
Hos 6:5. I *h.* them by prophets
Matt 3:10. *hewn* down, 7:19. Luke 3:9.
HID themselves, Gen 3:8.
Ps 119:11. word have I *h.* in heart
Matt 10:26. and *h.* that shall not be
11:25. *h.* from wise, Luke 10:21.
2 Cor 4:3. if gospel be *h.* it is *h.* to
Col 2:3. in whom are *h.* all treasures
3:3. your life is *h.* with Christ
1 Cor 4:5. bring to light *hidden* things
1 Pet 3:4. the *h.* man of heart
Rev 2:17. give the *h.* manna
Gen 18:17. shall I *hide* from Abraham
Job 33:17. and *h.* pride from man
Ps 17:8. *h.* me under the shadow
27:5. in time of trouble he shall *h.*
30:7. didst *h.* thy face and I was troubled
31:20. shalt *h.* them in the secret of thy presence
51:9. *h.* thy face from my sins
Isa 26:20. *h.* thyself for a little
James 5:20. *h.* a multitude of sins, 1 Pet 4:8.
Rev 6:16. *h.* us from face of him
Job 13:24. why *hidest* thou thy face, Ps 30:7; 44:24; 88:14; 143:7.
Isa 45:15. thou art a God that *h.* thyself
Job 34:29. when he *hideth* his face
42:3. who is he that *h.* counsel
Ps 139:12. darkness *h.* not from
Isa 8:17. I will wait on Lord that *h.*
Hab 3:4. *hiding* of his power
Ps 32:7. *h.* place, 119:114, Isa 32:2.
HIGH, Deut 12:2. &c. places . . . upon *h.* mountains
Deut 26:19. make thee *h.* above all
1 Kings 9:8. at this house which is *h.*
1 Chron 17:17. man of *h.* degree
Job 11:8. *h.* as heaven, what canst
Ps 49:2. both low and *h.*, rich and
89:13. strong hand, and *h.* is right hand
97:9. Lord art *h.* above all, 113:4.
103:11. as heaven is *h.* above earth
131:1. or in things too *h.* for me
138:6. though Lord be *h.* yet hath
Eccles 12:5. afraid of that which is *h.*
Isa 57:15. I dwell in *h.* and holy place
Ezek 21:26. abase him that is *h.*
Rom 12:16. mind not *h.* things
2 Cor 10:5. every *h.* thing that exalteth itself against knowledge of God

Matt 13:57. prophet is not without *h.* save in his own country, Mark 6:4. John 4:44.
John 5:41. I receive not *h.* from men
Rom 2:7. in well doing seek glory, *h.*
9:21. one vessel to *h.* another, 2 Tim 2:20.
12:10. in *h.* preferring one another
2 Cor 6:8. by *h.* and dishonour, by evil report
Heb 5:4. taketh this *h.* to himself
1 Pet 1:7. found unto praise and *h.*
3:7. *h.* to wife as weaker vessel
1 Sam 2:30. that *h.* me I will *h.*
15:30. *h.* me before elders . . . and Israel
Prov 3:9. *h.* Lord with substance
Isa 29:13. with their lips do *h.* me
John 5:23. *h.* Son as they *h.* Father
12:26. serve me, him will my Father *h.*
1 Pet 2:17. *h.* all men, 1 Tim 5:3. *h.* widows
Heb 13:4. marriage is *honourable*
Ps 15:4. *honoureth* them that fear
Matt 15:8. *h.* me with lips, Mark 7:6.
HOOF, Exod 10:26. Lev 11:3–7. Judg 5:22. Isa 5:28. Mic 4:13.
HOOK, Exod 26:32. Job 41:1. Ezek 29:4. Matt 17:27. *pruninghooks,* Isa 2:4; 18:5.
HOPE in Israel concerning this, Ezra 10:2.
Job 11:20. *h.* shall be as giving up ghost
Ps 78:7. might set their *h.* in God
Prov 10:28. *h.* of righteous shall be gladness
11:7. *h.* of unjust men perisheth
14:32. righteous hath *h.* in his death
19:18. chasten thy son while there is *h.*
26:12. more *h.* of a fool, 29:20.
Isa 57:10. saidst thou not, There is no *h.* Jer 2:25; 18:12. Ezek 37:11.
Jer 14:8. the *h.* of Israel, Acts 28:20.
17:7. blessed whose *h.* the Lord is
50:7. the *h.* of their fathers
Lam 3:29. if there be *h.*
Hos 2:15. valley of Achor for door of *h.*
Joel 3:16. Lord will be the *h.* of his people
Zech 9:12. turn to the strong hold, ye prisoners of *h.*
Acts 24:15. have *h.* towards God
Rom 5:4. experience (worketh) *h.*
5. *h.* not ashamed
8:24. we are saved by *h.*: but *h.* that is seen is not *h.*
15:4. comfort of scriptures, have *h.*
1 Cor 9:10. that ploweth . . . plow in *h.* and that thresheth in *h.* . . . partaker of his *h.*
13:13. now abideth faith, *h.*, charity
15:19. if in this life only . . . *h.* in Christ
Gal 5:5. wait for *h.* of righteousness
Eph 2:12. no *h.* and without God
Col 1:23. not moved away from *h.* of Gospel, 27. Christ . . . the *h.* of glory
1 Thess 4:13. sorrow not as others which have no *h.*
5:8. for helmet, the *h.* of salvation
1 Tim 1:1. Jesus Christ who is our *h.*
Titus 2:13. looking for that blessed *h.*
Heb 6:11. to full assurance of *hope*
19. which *h.* we have as an anchor
1 Pet 1:3. begotten again to lively *h.*
3:15. asketh a reason of *h.* in you
1 John 3:3. every man that hath this *h.*
Ps 16:9. my flesh shall rest *in hope*
Rom 4:18. against *h.* believed—
5:2. rejoice—of glory of God, 12:12.
Titus 1:2.—eternal life God promised
Job 17:15. where is now *my hope*
31:24. if I have made gold—
Ps 39:7.—is in thee, 71:5; Jer 17:17.
22:9. didst make me *hope* on mother's
33:18. . . . *h.* in his mercy, 22; 147:11.
42:5. *h.* thou in God, for, 11; 43:5.
119:49. thou hast caused me to *h.*
81. I *h.* in thy word, 114; 130:5.
Lam 3:26. good that a man should *h.*
Rom 8:25. if *h.* for that we see not
1 Pet 1:13. be sober and *h.* to end
Ps 119:43. *I have hoped* in thy judgments 74, 147,—in thy word. 166,—for thy salvation
Heb 11:1. faith is the substance of things *hoped for*
1 Cor 13:7. charity . . . *hopeth* all things
Luke 6:35. lend, *hoping* for nothing
HORN of my salvation, Ps 18:2.
1 Sam 2:1, my *h.* is exalted in the Lord, 10.
Ps 92:10. my *h.* as *h.* of unicorn
148:14. he exalteth the *h.* of his
Mic 4:13. I will make thy *h.* iron
Rev 13:1. beast having ten *horns,* 17:3, 7.
5:6. lamb having seven *h.*
HORRIBLE, Ps 11:6; 40:2. Jer *5:30; 18:13; 23:14.* Hos 6:10. Jer 2:12. Ezek 32:10.
HORROR, Gen 15:12. Job 18:20. Ps 55:5; 119:53. Ezek 7:18.
HORSE and rider thrown, Exod 15:21.
Ps 32:9. be ye not as *h.* or mule
33:17. *h.* is a vain thing for safety
147:10. delighteth not in the strength of the *h.*
24 8:6. as *h.* rusheth into battle
Eccles 10:7. have seen servants on *horses*
Jer 12:5. canst thou contend with *h.*
Hos 14:3. we will not ride upon *h.*
Zech 1:8; 6:2, 3, 6. *h.* red, white, black & Rev 6:2, 4, 5, 8; 9:17.
HOSPITALITY, Rom 12:13. 1 Tim 3:2. Titus 1:8. 1 Pet 4:9.
HOST, Luke 10:35. Rom 16:23. Ps 27:3; 33:16; 103:21; 108:11; 148:2. Isa 40:26. Luke 2:13. Jer 3:19.
HOT, Ps 38:1; 39:3. Prov 6:28. Hos 7:7. 1 Tim 4:2. Rev 3:15.
HOUR, Dan 3:6, 15; 4:33.
Matt 10:19. given you in that same *h.*
24:36. day and *h.* knoweth no man
25:13. know neither day nor *h.*
Luke 12:12. Holy Ghost shall teach you that same *h.*
22:53. this is your *h.* and power of darkness
John 2:4. mine *h.* is not yet come
4:23. *h.* cometh, and now is, 5:25.
7:30. *h.* was not yet come, 8:20.
Rev 3:3. not know what *h.* I come
10. keep from the *h.* of temptation
17:12. power as kings one *h.* with
18:10. in one *h.* is thy judgment
HOUSE, Exod 20:17. Lev 14:36.
Exod 12:30. not a *h.* where . . . not one dead
Job 21:28. where is the *h.* of prince
30:23. *h.* appointed for all living
Prov 3:33. curse of Lord is in *h.* of
7:27. her *h.* is the way to hell
Prov 12:7. *house* of the righteous shall stand
Eccles 7:2. go to the *h.* of mourning than *h.* of feasting
12:3. when keepers of *h.* tremble
Song of Sol 2:4. brought me to the banqueting *h.*
Isa 5:8. woe to them that join *h.* to *h.*
60:7. I will glorify the *h.* of my
64:11. our holy and beautiful *h.*
Matt 10:13. if the *h.* be worthy
12:25. a *h.* divided, Luke 11:17.
23:38. *h.* left desolate, Luke 13:35; Jer 12:7.
Luke 12:3. proclaimed on *h.*tops
John 14:2. in my Father's *h.* are
Rom 16:5. church in their *h.*
1 Cor 16:19. Col 4:15. Philem 2.
2 Tim 1:16. mercy to *h.* of Onesiphorus
Heb 3:3. who built *h.* more honour than *h.*
2 John 10. receive him not to your *h.*

Ps 105:21. him lord of all *his house*
112:3. wealth and riches shall be in—
Acts 10:2. feared God with all—
16:34. believing in God with all—
Heb 3:2. faithful in all—5, 6.
John 4:53. believed and his *whole house*
1 Tim 5:8. specially for those of his own *h.*
Josh 24:15. as for me and *my house*
2 Sam 23:5. although—not so with God
Ps 101:2. will walk within—with
Matt 12:44. will return to—Luke 11:24.
Acts 16:15. judged me faithful . . . come into—
Deut 6:7. when thou sittest in *thine house*
Ps 26:8. I loved habitation of—
36:8. satisfied with fatness of—65:4.
Isa 38:1. set—in order, for thou
Acts 11:14. thou and all—saved, 16:31.
Gen 28:17. *house of God* or *Lord,* Ps 23:6; 27:4; 42:4; 55:14. Eccles 5:1. Isa 2:3. Mic 4:2. 1 Tim 3:15. 1 Pet 4:17. Exod 23:19. Josh 6:24, and about 100 other places.
Job 4:19. dwell in *houses* of clay
Ps 49:11. *h.* shall continue for ever
Prov 19:14. *h.* and riches are inheritance of fathers
Matt 11:8. wear soft clothing are in king's *h.*
19:29. forsaken *h.*, brethren, Mark 10:29.
23:14. devour widows' *h.* Luke 20:47.
Luke 16:4. may receive me into their *h.*
1 Cor 11:12. have ye not *h.* to eat . . . in
1 Tim 3:12. ruling . . . own *h.* well
2 Tim 3:6. creep into *h.* and lead
Titus 1:11. subvert whole *h.* teaching things which they ought not
Acts 16:15. baptized and her whole *household*
Gal 6:10. *h.* of faith
Eph 2:19. *h.* of God
Matt 13:52. like *householder,* 20:1.
HOW long, Ps 6:3; 13:1; 74:9; 79:5; 80:4; 89:46. Isa 6:11. Jer 4:14. Dan 8:13; 12:6. Matt 17:17. Luke *9:41. Rev 6:10.*
Job 15:16. *how much more,* Prov 21:27. Matt 7:11. Luke 12:24, 28. Heb 9:14.
Matt 18:21; 12:37. *how oft,* Luke 13:34. Job 21:17. Ps 78:40.
HUMBLE person, save, Job 22:29.
Ps 9:12. forgetteth not the cry of the *h.*
10:12. forget not the *h.*
17. desire of the *h.*
34:2. *h.* shall hear thereof, and be
Prov 16:19. to be of an *h.* spirit
Isa 57:15. of contrite and *h.* spirit, to revive the spirit of *h.*
Exod 10:3. thou refuse to *h.* thyself
Deut 8:2. to *h.* thee, and prove, 3:16.
2 Chron 7:14. shall *h.* themselves
34:27. didst *h.* thyself before God
Prov 6:3. *humble* thyself, make sure thy friend
Jer 13:18. *h.* yourselves
Matt 18:4. whosoever *h.* himself shall be exalted, 23:12. Luke 14:11; 18:14.
2 Cor 12:21. my God will *h.* me
James 4:6. giveth grace to *h.* 1 Pet 5:5.
4:10. *h.* yourselves in the sight of Lord
1 Pet 5:6. *h.* yourselves under the mighty hand of God
Lev 26:41. if uncircumcised hearts be *humbled*
2 Kings 22:19. hast *h.* thyself before the Lord
2 Chron 12:6. princes . . . and king *h.* themselves
12. he *h.* himself, 32:26; 33:12.
33:23. *h.* not himself before Lord, 36:12.
Ps 35:13. I *h.* my soul with fasting
Isa 2:11. lofty looks of man shall be *h.*, 9:17.
5:15. mighty man shall be *h.* and eyes of the lofty shall be *h.*
10:33. haughty shall be *h.*
Jer 44:10. they are not *h.* unto this day
Lam 3:20. my soul is *h.* in me
Dan 5:22. hast not *h.* thy heart
Phil 2:8. *h.* himself and became obedient
Deut 21:14. *humbled her,* 22. 24, 29. Ezek 22:10, 11.
Col 3:12. put on *humbleness* of mind
Ps 113:6. Lord who *humbleth* himself to behold
Mic 6:8. walk *humbly* with thy God
Prov 22:4. by *humility* are riches and honour, 15:33; 18:12.
Acts 20:19. serving Lord with all *h.*
Col 2:18. in a voluntary *h.* 23.
1 Pet 5:5. be clothed with *h.*
HUNGER, Exod 16:3. Deut 28:48.
Ps 34:10. young lions . . . suffer *h.*
Prov 19:15. idle soul shall suffer *h.*
Lam 4:9. sword better than slain with *h.*
Deut 8:3. suffered thee to h.
Isa 49:10. shall not *h.* nor *thirst,* Rev 7:16.
Matt 5:6. blessed are they which do *h.*
Luke 6:21. blessed are ye that *h.* now
25. woe to you that are full, ye shall *h.*
John 6:35. cometh to me shall never *h.*
Rom 12:20. if thine enemy *h.* feed
1 Cor 4:11. we both *h.* and thirst
11:34. if any man *h.* let him eat at
Ps 107:9. filleth the *hungry* soul with goodness
146:7. God giveth food to the *h.*
Prov 25:21. if enemy be *h.* give him
27:7. to the *h.* soul every bitter thing is sweet
Isa 58:7. to deal thy bread to the *h.*
10. if thou draw out thy soul to the *h.*
65:13. shall eat; but ye shall be *h.*
Ezek 18:7. given bread to the *h.* 16.
Luke 1:53. filled the *h.* with good things
Phil 4:12. how to be full and to be *h.*
HUNT, 1 Sam 26:20. Job 38:39.
Ps 140:11. evil shall *h.* the violent
Job 10:16. thou *huntest* me as a fierce lion
HURT, Gen 4:23; 26:29.
Josh 24:20. will turn and do you *h.*
Ps 15:4. sweareth to his own *h.*
Eccles 5:13. riches . . . to their *h.*
Jer 6:14. healed *h.* of the daughter, 8:11, 21.
Rev 2:11. shall not be *h.* of second death
6:6. *h.* not the oil and wine, 7:3; 9:4.
Ezra 4:15. *hurtful,* Ps 144:10.
1 Tim 6:9. fall into foolish and *h.* lusts
HUSBAND, Gen 3:6, 16; 29:32.
Exod 4:25. bloody *h.* art thou to me, 26.
Isa 54:5. thy Maker is thine *h.*
Mark 10:12. if a woman put away her *h.*
John 4:17. I have no *h.*
1 Cor 7:14. unbelieving *husband* is sanctified by
34. careth how she may please *h.*
2 Cor 11:2. espoused you to one *h.*
Eph 5:23. the *h.* is the head of wife, 24.
33. the wife reverence her *h.*
John 4:18. thou hast had five *husbands*
1 Cor 14:35. let them ask *h.* at home
Eph 5:22. wives, submit to your *h.*
25. *h.*, love wives, as Christ, Col 3:19.
Col 3:18. wives, submit to your *h.*
1 Pet 3:1. subject to their own *h.*
7. ye h., dwell with them according to knowledge
HUSBANDMAN, my Father is the, John 15:1.
James 5:7. *h.* waiteth for precious fruit
1 Cor 3:9. ye are God's *husbandry*
HYMN, Matt 26:30. Eph 5:19. Col 3:16.
HYPOCRISY, Isa 32:6. Matt 23:28. Mark 12:15. Luke 12:1. 1 Tim 4:2. James 3:17. 1 Pet 2:1.

Matt 7:5. *hypocrite,* Luke 6:42; 13:15.
Job 8:13. the *h's.* hope shall perish
20:5. joy of *h.* for a moment
27:8. what is the hope of the *h.*
Isa 9:17. every one is a *h.* and evil
Matt 6:2. *hypocrites,* 5, 16; 15:7; 16:3; 23:13, 14, 15, 23.
Job 15:34. congregation of *h.* shall be desolate
Isa 33:14. fearfulness hath surprised *h.*
Matt 24:51. appoint him portion with *h.*

I

IDLE, they be, Exod 5:8, 17.
Prov 19:15. an *i.* soul shall suffer
Matt 12:36. every *i.* word that men shall speak
20:6. why stand ye all day *i.*
Luke 24:11. words seemed as *i.* tales
Prov 31:27. *idleness,* Eccles 10:18. Ezek 16:49.
IDOL, 2 Chron 15:16; 33:7.
Isa 66:3. as if he blessed an *i.*
Zech 11:17. woe to the *i.* shepherd
1 Cor 8:4. an *i.* is nothing in world
Ps 96:5. gods of nations are *idols*
Isa 2:8. land is full of *i.*; they worship the work of their own hands
Jer 50:38. they are mad upon *i.*
Hos 4:17. Ephraim is joined to *i.*
Acts 15:20. abstain from pollutions of *i.*
Rom 2:22. thou that abhorrest *i.*
1 Cor 8:1. touching things offered to *i.*
1 John 5:21. keep yourselves from *i.*
Rev 2:14. eat things sacrificed to *i.*
9:20. not worship devils and *i.* of gold
1 Cor 5:10, 11. *idolater,* 6:9; 10:7. Eph 5:5. Rev 21:8; 22:15.
1 Sam 15:23. stubbornness as iniquity and *idolatry*
1 Pet 4:3. walked in . . . abominable *idolatries*
Acts 17:16. city wholly given to *i.*
1 Cor 10:14. dearly beloved, flee from *i.*
Gal 5:20. *i.*, witchcraft, hatred
Col 3:5. covetousness, which is *i.*
IGNORANCE, sin through, Lev 4:2, 13, 22, 27. Num 15:24, 25. Acts 3:17.
Acts 17:30. this *i.* God winked at
Eph 4:18. alienated from God through *i.*
Isa 63:16. though Abraham be *ignorant of*
Rom 10:3. *i.* of God's righteousness
1 Cor 14:38. if man be *i.* let him be *i.*
Heb 5:2. can have compassion on *i.*

Acts 17:23. *ignorantly,* 1 Tim 1:13.
ILLUMINATED, Heb 10:32.
IMAGE, Lev 26:1. Dan 2:31.
Gen 1:26. let us make man in our *i.* 27; 5:1; 9:6. Col 3:10.
5:3. Adam begat son . . . after his *i.*
Ps 73:20. thou shalt despise their *i.*
Matt 22:20. whose is this *i.* and superscription, Luke 20:24.
Rom 8:29. conformed to *i.* of Son
1 Cor 15:49. have borne *i.* of earthy shall also bear *i.* of heavenly
2 Cor 4:4. Christ is *i.* of God, Col 1:15.
Heb 1:3. express *i.* of his person
Rev 13:14. make an *i.* to the beast
Exod 23:24. break down *images,* 34:13.
IMAGINE, Ps 2:1. Nah 1:9. Zech 7:10; 8:17. Acts 4:25.
Gen 6:5. every *imagination* of the thoughts . . . was evil, 8:21. Deut 29:19. Prov 6:18. Lam 3:60, 61. Rom 1:21. 2 Cor 10:5.
IMMEDIATELY, Mark 4:15. Acts 12:23.
IMMORTAL, invisible, 1 Tim 1:17.
Rom 2:7. seek for glory, honour, *immortality*
1 Cor 15:53. this mortal put on *i.*
2 Tim 1:10. brought life and *i.* to light
IMMUTABLE Heb 6:17, 18.
IMPENITENT heart, Rom 2:5.
IMPERIOUS whorish woman, Ezek 16:30.
IMPLACABLE, Rom 1:31.
IMPORTUNITY, Luke 11:8.
IMPOSSIBLE, Matt 17:20; 19:26.
Luke 1:37. with God nothing shall be *i.*
17:1. it is *i.* but offences will come
Heb 6:4. *i.* for those once enlightened
18. in two things it was *i.* for God to
11:6. without faith it is *i.* to please
IMPUDENT, Prov 7:13. Ezek 2:4.
IMPUTE, 1 Sam 22:15. Lev 7:18; 17:4.
Rom 4:11. righteousness might be *imputed*
22. *i.* to him for righteousness, 24.
5:13. sin is not *i.* when there is no law
James 2:23. *i.* unto him for righteousness
Ps 32:2. Lord *imputeth* not iniquity
Rom 4:6. *i.* righteousness without
2 Cor 5:19. not *imputing* trespasses
IN Christ, Acts 24:24. Rom 12:5. 1 Cor 1:2, 30; 3:1; 15:18, 22. 2 Cor 1:21; 2:14; 3:14; 5:17, 19; 12:2. Gal 1:22. Eph 1:1, 3, 10, 12, 20; 2:6, 10, 13. Phil 1:1, 13; 2:1, 5; 3:14. Col 1:2, 4.
1 Thess 1:1. *in God,* John 3:21. Col 3:3.
Gen 15:6. *in the Lord,* Ps 4:5; 31:24; 34:2; 35:9; 37:4, 7. Isa 45:17, 24, 25. Jer 3:23. Zech 12:5. 1 Cor 1:31; 4:17; 7:22, 39. Eph 2:21; 6:10. Phil 4:2, 4. Col 3:18; 4:7, 17. 1 Thess 5:12. Philem 16:20. Rev 14:13.
INCLINE heart, Josh 24:23. Judg 9:3. 1 Kings 8:58. Ps 119:36, 112; 141:4.
Ps 78:1. *incline,* 40:1; 116:2. Prov 2:2; 5:13. Jer 7:24, 26; 11:8; 17:23; 25:4; 34:14; 35:15; 44:5. Isa 55:3.
INCLOSED, Ps 17:10; 22:16. Song of Sol 4:12; 8:9. Lam 3:9.
INCONTINENT, 1 Cor 7:5. 2 Tim 3:3.
INCORRUPTIBLE(UN-) God, Rom 1:23.
1 Cor 9:25. but we an *i.* (crown)
15:52. dead shall be raised *i.*
1 Pet 1:4. to an inheritance *i.*
23. not of corruptible seed, but of *i.*
1 Cor 15:42, 50, 53, 54. *incorruption*
INCREASE, Lev 19:25; 25:7.
Lev 25:36. take no usury of him nor *i.*, 37.
Num 32:14. risen up . . . an *i.* of sinful men
Deut 16:15. bless thee in all thine *increase*
Ps 67:6. earth yield her *i.*, 85:12.
Isa 9:7. of the *i.* of his government
Ezek 18:8. neither taken any *i.*, 13, 17.
1 Cor 3:6. I planted . . . God gave *i.*, 7.
Col 2:19. increaseth with *i.* of God
Ps 62:10. if riches *i.* set not heart
Prov 1:5. wise will *i.* learning, 9:9.
Eccles 5:11. when goods *i.* they are
Isa 29:19. meek shall *i.* their joy
Luke 17:5. Lord, *i.* our faith
John 3:30. he must *i.* but I decrease
1 Thess 3:12. Lord make you to *i.*
2 Tim 2:16. *i.* to more ungodliness
Ezra 9:6. iniquities are *increased*
Isa 9:3. multiplied nation, not *i.* joy
Luke 2:52. Jesus *i.* in wisdom and
Acts 6:7. the word of God *i.* and the
Rev 3:17. I am rich and *i.* with goods
Eccles 1:18. *increaseth* knowledge, *i.* sorrow
Col 2:19. whole body . . . *i.* with increase of God
1 Chron 11:9. David went on *increasing*
Col 1:10. *i.* in knowledge of God
INCURABLE wound, Job 34:6. Jer 15:18. Mic 1:9.
Jer 30:12. *i.* bruise. 15, *i.* sorrow

INDEED, 1 Kings 8:27. 1 Chron 4:10. Matt 3:11. John 1:47; 4:42; 6:55; 8:31, 36. 1 Tim 5:3, 5. 1 Pet 2:4.
INDIGNATION, Neh 4:1. Esther 5:9. Ps 69:24; 78:49; 102:10.
Isa 10:5. staff in their hand is mine *i.*
Mic 7:9. I will bear the *i.* of Lord
Nah 1:6. who can stand before his *i.*
Matt 20:24. moved with *i.*
26:8. when disciples saw it, they had *i.*
Rom 2:8. *i.* and wrath, tribulation
2 Cor 7:11. yea, what *i.*, yea, what
Heb 10:27. fiery *i.* which shall devour
Rev 14:10. poured into cup of his *i.*
INDITING a good matter, Ps 45:1.
INEXCUSABLE, O man, Rom 2:1.
INFALLIBLE proofs, Acts 1:3.
INFANT, 1 Sam 15:3. Job 3:16. Isa 65:20. Hos 13:16. Luke 18:15.
INFIDEL, 2 Cor 6:15. 1 Tim 5:8.
INFINITE iniquities, Job 22:5.
Ps 147:5. his understanding is *i.*
Nah 3:9. her strength, and it was *i.*
INFIRMITY, this is my *i.*, Ps 77:10.
Prov 18:14. spirit of man will sustain *i.*
Heb 5:2. himself is compassed with *i.*, 7:28.
Matt 8:17. himself took our *infirmities*
Rom 8:26. the Spirit helpeth our *i.*
2 Cor 12:9. glory in my *i.*
10. pleasure in *i.*
1 Tim 5:23. wine for . . . and thine often *i.*
Heb 4:15. with the feeling of our *i.*
INFLAME (EN-) them, Isa 5:11; 57:5.
INFLICTED punishment, 2 Cor 2:6.
INFLUENCES of Pleiades, Job 38:31.
INHABIT, Prov 10:30. Isa 65:21, 22.
Ps 22:3. *inhabitest* the praise of Israel
Isa 57:15. lofty One that *inhabiteth*
INHERIT, Gen *15:8. Ps 82:8.*
1 Sam 2:8. make them *i.* throne of glory
Ps 25:13. his seed shall *i.* earth
37:11. the meek shall *i.* the earth, Matt 5:5.
29. the righteous shall *i.* land, Isa 60:21.
82:8. O God, thou shalt *i.* all nations
Prov 3:35. wise shall *i.* glory; but
8:21. that love me to *i.* substance
Matt 25:34. *i.* kingdom prepared for you
Mark 10:17. what shall I do that I may *inherit* eternal life, Luke 10:25; 18:18.
1 Cor 6:9. unrighteous shall not *inherit the kingdom of God*
15:50. flesh and blood cannot—
Gal 5:21. do such things shall not—
Heb 6:12. through faith . . . *i.* promises
1 Pet 3:9. that ye should *i.* blessing
Rev 21:7. overcometh shall *i.* all things
Num 18:20. I am thy part and thine *inheritance,* Deut 10:9; 18:2. Ezek 44:28.
Deut 4:20. a people of *inheritance,* 9:26, 29; 32:9. 1 Kings 8:36. Ps 28:9; 33:12; 68:9; 74:2; 78:62, 71; 79:1; 94:14; 106:5, 40. Isa 19:25. Jer 10:16; 51:19.
Ps 16:5. Lord is portion of mine *i.*
Prov 19:14. riches are *i.* of fathers
Eccles 7:11. wisdom is good with an *i.*
Acts 20:32. *i.* among . . . sanctified, 26:18.
Eph 1:11. in whom we obtained an *i.*
14. earnest of our *i.*
5:5. any *i.* in the kingdom of Christ
Col 1:12. partakers of *i.* of saints
3:24. shall receive the reward of *i.*
Heb 9:15. the promise of eternal *i.*
1 Pet 1:4. to an *i.* incorruptible
INIQUITY, Gen 15:16; 19:15.
Exod 20:5. visiting *i.* of the fathers on children, 34:7. Num 14:18. Deut 5:9.
34:7. forgiving *i.* and transgression
Lev 26:41. accept the punishment of their *i.*, 43.
Num 23:21. hath not beheld *i.* in Jacob
Job 4:8. they that plow *i.* . . . reap same
5:16. *i.* stoppeth mouth, Ps 107:42.
15:16. man which drinketh *i.* like water
22:23. put away *i.* far from thy tabernacles
34:32. if I have done *i.* I will do no
Ps 32:5. mine *i.* have I not hid . . . and thou forgavest the *i.* of my sin
39:11. with rebukes dost correct man for *i.*
51:5. behold, I was shapen in *i.*
66:18. if I regard *i.* in my heart
69:27. add *i.* unto their *i.*
119:3. they also do no *i.*: they walk
133. let not any *i.* have dominion
Eccles 3:16. place of righteousness there *i.* was
Isa 1:4. people laden with *i.*, a seed
5:18. woe to them that draw *i.* with
27:9. by this shall *i.* of Jacob be purged
33:24. people shall be forgiven their *i.*
53:6. Lord laid on him the *i.* of us all
57:17. for *i.* of his covetousness
59:3. defiled . . . your fingers with *i.*
Jer 2:5. what *i.* have fathers found
3:13. only acknowledge thine *i.*
31:30. every one shall die for his own *i.*
50:20. *i.* of Israel be sought for
Ezek 3:18. he shall die in his *i.*, 19; 18:18; 33:8.
18:30. so *i.* shall not be your ruin
Dan 9:24. make reconciliation for *i.*
Hos 14:2. take away all *i.* and
Mic 7:18. a God . . . that pardoneth *i.*
Hab 1:13. thou . . . canst not look on *i.*
Matt 7:23. depart from me, ye that work *i.*
24:12. because *i.* shall abound
Acts 8:23. in gall . . . and bond of *i.*
Rom 6:19. uncleanness and to *i.* to *i.*
1 Cor 13:6. (charity) rejoiceth not in *i.*
2 Thess 2:7. mystery of *i.* doth already work
2 Tim 2:19. nameth . . . Christ depart from *i.*
Titus 2:14. he might redeem us from all *i.*
James 3:6. tongue is a fire, a word of *i.*
Ps 18:23. *mine iniquity,* 25:11; 32:5; 38:18; 51:2.
Job 34:22. *workers of iniquity,* Ps 5:5; 6:8; 14:4; 92:7. Prov 10:29; 21:15. Luke 13:27.
Lev 16:21. confess over him all *iniquities*
26:39. pine in their iniquity and *i.* of their fathers
Ezra 9:6. our *i.* are increased
13. punished less than our *i.* deserve
Neh 9:2. confessed *i.* of fathers
Job 13:26. to possess *i.* of my youth
Ps 38:4. mine *i.* are gone over my head
40:12. mine *i.* have taken hold upon
51:9. hide thy face . . . sins, blot out my *i.*
65:3. *i.* prevail against me: as for
79:8. remember not . . . former *i.*
90:8. thou hast set our *i.* before thee
107:17. fools, because of . . . *i.*, are afflicted
130:3. if thou, Lord, mark *i.*
8. he shall redeem Israel from all *i.*
Prov 5:22. his own *i.* shall take the wicked
Isa 43:24. hast wearied me with thine *i.*
Jer 14:7. our *i.* testify against us
Dan 4:27. break off . . . thine *i.* by shewing
Mic 7:19. he will subdue our *i.* and

Acts 3:26. bless you in turning . . . from *i.*
Rom 4:7. blessed are they whose *i.* forgiven
Rev 18:5. God remembered her *i.*
Isa 53:11. he shall bear *their iniquity(ies)*
Jer 33:8. I will cleanse them from all—and I will pardon all—
Ezek 43:10. may be ashamed of—
Heb 8:12. their sins and—will I remember no more, 10:17.
Num 14:34. ye bear *your iniquities*
Isa 50:1. for—have ye sold yourselves
59:2.—have separated you and God
Jer 5:25.—turned away these things
Ezek 24:23. ye shall pine away for—
36:31. lothe yourselves . . . for—
33. I shall have cleansed you from all—
Amos 3:2. I will punish you for all—
INJURED me, have not, Gal 4:12.
1 Tim 1:13. a persecutor and *injurious*
INK, 2 John 12. 3 John 13.
INNER, 1 Kings 6:27. Eph 3:16.
INNOCENT, Ps 19:13. Prov 28:20.
Gen 20:5. On . . . *innocency* of my hands
Ps 26:6. wash my hands in *i.*, 73:13.
Dan 6:22. before him *i.* found in me
Hos 8:5. how long ere they attain *i.*
INNUMERABLE, Job 21:33. Ps 40:12. Luke 12:1. Heb 11:12; 12:22.
INORDINATE, Ezek 23:11. Col 3:5.
INQUIRE after iniquity, Job 10:6.
Ps 27:4. to *i.* in his temple
Eccles 7:10. thou dost not *i.* wisely
Isa 21:12. if ye will *i. i.* ye: return
Ps 78:34. returned and *inquired* early after God
Ezek 36:37. I will yet for this be *i.* of by the house of Israel
Zeph 1:6. have not sought Lord, nor *i.* for him
Matt 2:7. Herod . . . *i.* of them diligently
1 Pet 1:10. of which salvation prophets *i.*
Judg 20:27. *inquired of Lord,* 1 Sam 23:2, 4; 30:8. 2 Sam 2:1; 5:19, 23; 21:1. Jer 21:2.
Prov 20:25. after vows to make *inquiry*
INQUISITION, Deut 19:18. Ps 9:12.
INSCRIPTION to unknown God, *Acts 17:23.*
INSPIRATION, Job 32:8. 2 Tim 3:16.
INSTANT, Isa 29:5; 30:13. Jer 18:7. Rom 12:12. 2 Tim 4:2. Acts 12:5.
Luke 7:4. besought him *instantly*
Acts 26:7. *i.* serving God day and
INSTRUCT, Deut 4:36; 32:10.
Neh 9:20. thy good spirit to *i.* them
Job 40:2. contendeth with Almighty *i.* him
Ps 16:7. my reins *i.* me in the night
Song of Sol 8:2. mother's house who would *i.* me
Isa 28:26. his God doth *i.* him
1 Cor 2:16. Lord that he may *i.* him
Isa 8:11. Lord . . . *instructed* me that I
Phil 4:12. in all things I am *i.* both
Job 33:16. sealeth their *instruction*
Ps 50:17. hatest *i.* and castest my
Prov 4:13. take fast hold of *i.*
5:12. how have I hated *i.* and
19:27. cease to hear *i.* that causeth
23:12. apply thine heart to *i.* and
2 Tim 3:16. profitable for . . . *i.* in
Rom 2:20. an *instructor* of foolish
1 Cor 4:15. ten thousand *instructors* in Christ
INSTRUMENTS of cruelty, Gen 49:5.
Ps 7:13. prepared for him *i.* of death
Rom 6:13. neither yield members *i.* of unrighteousness . . . but . . . *i.* of righteousness
Isa 32:7. the *i.* also of the churl are evil
INTEGRITY of my heart, Gen 20:5.
Job 2:3. still he holdeth fast his *i.*
27:5. I will not remove mine *i.*
Ps 7:8. according to my *i.* that is
25:21. let *i.* and uprightness preserve me
26:1. I have walked in mine *i.*
Prov 11:3. *i.* of upright shall guide
INTERCESSION, Jer 7:16; 27:18.
Isa 53:12. bare the sin of many, and made *i.* for the transgressors
Rom 8:26. Spirit maketh *i.* for us, 27.
34. who also maketh *i.* for us
11:2. (Elias) maketh *i.* to God against Israel
Heb 7:25. he ever liveth to make *i.*
Isa 59:16. there was no *intercessor*
INTERMEDDLE, Prov 14:10; 18:1.
INTERPRETATION, Gen 40:5; 41:11. Judg 7:15. Dan 2:4, 7, 36. 1 Cor 12:10; 14:26. 2 Pet 1:20.
Job 33:23. *interpreter,* one among a thousand
INTRUDING into things, Col 2:18.
INVENT, Amos 6:5. Rom 1:30.
Ps 99:8. tookest vengeance of their *inventions*
106:29. provoked him with their *i.*
39. went a whoring with their *i.*
Prov 8:12. find out witty *i.*
Eccles 7:29. men sought many *i.*
INVISIBLE, Rom 1:20. Col 1:15, 16. 1 Tim 1:17. Heb 11:27.
INWARD friends abhorred me, Job 19:19.
Ps 5:9. *inward part,* 51:6. Prov 20:27. Jer 31:33. Luke 11:39.
Rom 7:22. *inward man,* 2 Cor 4:16.
Ps 62:4. curse *inwardly*
Matt 7:15. *i.* . . . ravening wolves
Rom 2:29. he is a Jew which is one *i.*
IRON sharpeneth iron, Prov 27:17.
Eccles 10:10. if the *i.* be blunt, put to
Isa 48:4. neck is an *i.* sinew, and
Jer 15:12. shall *i.* break northern *i.*
Dan 2:33. legs of *i.*, his feet part *i.*
4:23. even with a bank of *i.* and
5:23. thou hast praised the gods of silver, and gold, of brass, *i.*
1 Tim 4:2. conscience seared with a hot *i.*
ISSUES from death, Ps 68:20.
Prov 4:23. out of (heart) are the *i.* of life
ITCHING ears, 2 Tim 4:3.
IVORY, 1 Kings 10:18; 22:39. Ps 45:8. Song of Sol 5:14; 7:4. Ezek 27:6. Amos 3:15; 6:4. Rev 18:12.

J

JEALOUS God, I am a, Exod 20:5; 34:14. Deut 5:9; 6:15. Josh 24:19.
Ezek 39:25. be *j.* for my holy name
Joel 2:18. will Lord be *j.* for his land
Nah 1:2. God is *j.* and the Lord
Zech 1:14. I am *j.* for Jerusalem, 8:2.
2 Cor 11:2. *j.* over you with godly *jealousy*
Deut 29:20. (Lord's) *j.* shall smoke
Ps 79:5. shall thy *j.* burn like fire
Prov 6:34. *j.* is the rage of a man
Song of Sol 8:6. *j.* is cruel as the grave
Rom 10:19. provoke them to *j.* 11:11.
1 Cor 10:22. we provoke Lord to *j.*
JEHOVAH. This name is translated LORD (in capitals) about 2,000 times. (See *Index.*)
JERUSALEM, for the church, Isa 24:23; 62:1; 66:10, 13. Jer 3:17. Joel 2:32; 3:16, 17. Zech 12:10; 8:22. Gal 4:25, 26. Heb 12:22. Rev 3:12; 21:2. (See *Index.*)
JESHURUN, *i.e.* Israel, Deut 32:15; 33:5, 26. Isa 44:2.
JESUS, or Joshua, Acts 7:45. Heb 4:8.
JESUS the Saviour of men, Matt 1:21; 2:1; 8:29; 14:1; 27:37. 1 Cor 12:3. 2 Cor 4:5. Eph 4:21. Heb 2:9; 12:2.

Rev 22:16, and about 650 other places. (See *Index.*)
JEWS first, and also Greeks, Rom 1:16; 2:9, 10.
Rom 2:28, 29. not a *J.* which. is one outwardly, but a *J.* which. is one inwardly
10:12. no difference between *J.* and Greek
1 Cor 9:20. to Jew I became as a *J.*
Gal 3:28. neither *J.* nor Greek, Col 3:11.
Rev 2:9. say they are *Jews* and are not, 3:9.
JOIN, Exod 1:10. Ezra 9:14.
Prov 11:21. hand *j.* in hand, 16:5.
Isa 5:8. woe to them that *j.* house to house
Jer 50:5. let us *j.* ourselves to Lord
Acts 5:13. durst no man *j.* himself
Hos 4:17. Ephraim is *joined* to idols
Num 25:3. Israel *j.* himself to Baal-Peor, Ps 106:28.
Eccles 9:4. for him that is *j.* to living there is hope
Zech 2:11. nations shall be *j.* to Lord
Matt 19:6. what God hath *j.* let not
1 Cor 1:10. be perfectly *j.* together
Eph 5:31. shall be *j.* to his wife
Col 2:19. all body by *joints* and bands
Heb 4:12. dividing asunder of . . . *j.*
JOURNEY, Num 9:13. Rom 1:10.
JOY, 1 Chron 12:40. 2 Chron 20:27.
Neh 8:10. *j.* of Lord your strength
Esther 8:17. Jews had *j.* and gladness
Job 20:5. *j.* of the hypocrite but for
Ps 16:11. thy presence is fulness of *j.*
43:4. God my exceeding *j.*
51:8. make me hear *j.* and gladness
12. restore to me *j.* of thy salvation
126:5. that sow in tears shall reap in *j.*
Eccles 9:7. eat thy bread with *j.*
Isa 9:3. hast not increased the *j.*: they *j.* . . . according to *j.* in harvest
12:3. with *j.* shall ye draw water out
35:10. with songs and everlasting *j.* . . . shall obtain *j.* and gladness
61:3. give them the oil of *j.* for mourning
7. everlasting *j.* shall be to them
66:5. he shall appear to your *j.*
Zeph 3:17. (Lord) will *j.* over thee with singing
Matt 2:10. rejoiced with great *j.*
13:20. hear the word, and with *j.*
Luke 1:44. babe leaped in womb for *j.*
15:7. *j.* shall be in heaven over one
John 15:11. your *joy* might be full, 16:24.
16:20. your sorrow be turned into *j.*
22. your *j.* no man taketh from you
17:13. my *j.* fulfilled in themselves
Acts 20:24. finish my course with *j.*
Rom 15:13. fill you with all *j.* and peace
2 Cor 1:24. we . . . are helpers of your *j.*
2:3. my *j.* is the *j.* of you all
Gal 5:22. fruit of the Spirit is love, *j.*
Phil 4:1. brethren . . . my *j.* and crown
1 Thess 1:6. receive word with *j.* of
Heb 12:2. who for the *j.* set before
James 1:2. count it all *j.* when ye
1 Pet 1:8. rejoice with *j.* unspeakable
4:13. be glad with exceeding *j.*
1 John 1:4. write we that your *j.* may be full
Ezra 6:22. Lord made them *joyful*
Ps 35:9. my soul shall be *j.* in Lord
63:5. I will praise thee with *j.* lips
89:15. people that know the *j.* sound
Eccles 7:14. in day of prosperity be *j.*
Isa 56:7. make them *j.* in my house
61:10. my soul shall be *j.* in God
2 Cor 7:4. exceeding *j.* in all our
Eccles 9:9. live *joyfully* with the wife
Heb 10:34. took *j.* spoiling of goods
Deut 28:47. servedst not Lord . . . with *joyfulness*
Col 1:11. longsuffering with *j*
2:5. *joying* and beholding your
Heb 12:11. no chastening . . . seemeth to be *joyous*
JUDGE, Deut 17:9; 25:2.
Gen 18:25. shall not the *J.* of earth
Exod 2:14. who made thee . . . *j.*, Acts 7:27.
1 Sam 2:25. the *j.* shall *j.* him; but
Isa 33:22. Lord is our *j.* . . . lawgiver
Ps 68:5. father of fatherless and *j.* of widows
75:7. God is the *j.*: he putteth down, 50:6.
Luke 12:14. *who made me a j.* over
Acts 10:42. to be the *J.* of quick and dead
2 Tim 4:8. Lord the righteous *J.*
Heb 12:23. are come to God the *J.*
James 5:9. the *J.* standeth before the door
Gen 16:5. Lord *j.* between me and thee, 1 Sam 24:12.
Deut 32:36. the Lord shall *j.* his people, Ps 135:14. Heb 10:30.
Ps 7:8. Lord shall *j.* the people: *j.* me
9:8. Lord shall *j.* world in righteousness, 96:13; 98:9. Acts 17:31.
Mic 3:11. heads thereof *j.* for reward
Matt 7:1. *j.* not, that ye be not judged
John 5:30. as I hear I *j.* and my
12:47. I came not to *j.* the world
Acts 23:3. sittest thou to *j.* me
Rom 2:16. when God shall *j.* secrets of men
3:6. then how shall God *j.* the world
14:10. why dost thou *j.* thy brother
1 Cor 4:3. I *j.* not mine own self
5. *j.* nothing before the time
6:3. know ye not that we shall *j.* angels
11:31. if we would *j.* ourselves, we
14:29. let prophets speak, . . . other *j.*
Col 2:16. let no man *j.* you in meat
2 Tim 4:1. who shall *j.* the quick and the dead, 1 Pet 4:5.
James 4:11. if thou *j.* the law
Ps 51:4. *judgest,* Rom 14:4. James 4:12.
7:11. God *judgeth* the righteous
58:11. he is a God that *j.* in earth
1 Cor 2:15. but he that is spiritual *j.* all things
4:4. he that *j.* me is the Lord
Matt 19:28. *judging* twelve tribes, Luke 22:30.
Deut 1:17. not respect persons in *j.*
Deut 1:17. the *judgment* is God's
Ps 1:5. ungodly not stand in the *j.*
9:16. Lord is known by the *j.* he executeth
101:1. I will sing of mercy and *j.*
143:2. enter not into *j.* with thy servant
149:9. to execute upon them the *j.*
Prov 21:15. it is joy to just to do *j.*
29:26. ever man's *j.* cometh from Lord
Eccles 11:9. but know thou . . . God will bring thee into *j.*, 12:14.
Isa 1:27. Zion shall be redeemed with *j.*
28:17. *j.* also will I lay to the line
30:18. Lord is a God of *j.*, Job 35:14.
42:1. he shall bring *j.* to Gentiles
53:8. he was taken from prison and *j.*
61:8. I the Lord love *j.*
Jer 5:1. if there be any that executeth *j.*
8:7. people know not the *j.* of Lord
10:24. correct me, but with *j.*; not in
Dan 4:37. all whose . . . ways *j.*
7:22. and *j.* was given to the saints
Hos 12:6. keep mercy and *j.*, wait on

Amos 5:7. who turn *j.* to wormwood
24. let *j.* run down as waters, and
Matt 5:21. be in danger of *j.*, 22.
12:20. till he send *j.* unto victory
John 5:27. given him authority to execute *j.*
9:39. for *j.* I am come into the world
16:8. reprove the world of sin . . . and *j.*
Acts 24:25. reasoned of . . . *j.* to come
Rom 5:18. *j.* came on all men
14:10. must all stand before *j.* seat
1 Pet 4:17. *j.* begin at house of God
Jude 15. execute *j.* on all
Rev 17:1. shew thee *j.* of great whore
Ps 19:9. *judgments* of Lord are true
36:6. thy *j.* are a great deep
119:75. I know, O Lord, that thy *j.* are right
108. O Lord, teach me thy *j.*
120. am afraid of thy *j.*
Isa 26:8. in way of thy *j.* . . . we waited
26:9. when thy *j.* are in the earth
Jer 12:1. let me talk with thee of thy *j.*
Rom 11:33. how unsearchable his *j.*

JUST man, Noah was, Gen 6:9.
Lev 19:36. *j.* balance, *j.* weights, &c., Deut 25:15. Ezek 45:10.
Deut 16:20. that which is *j.* shalt thou follow
32:4. a God of truth . . . *j.* and right is he
2 Sam 23:3. he that ruleth men must be *j.*
Neh 9:33. art *j.* in all that is brought upon us
Prov 4:18. path of *j.* is as shining
10:6. blessings are on head of *j.*
11:1. but a *j.* weight is his delight
12:21. no evil shall happen to *j.*
17:26. to punish the *j.* is not good
18:17. in his own cause seemeth *j.*
20:7. the *j.* man walketh in his integrity
24:16. *j.* man falleth seven times
Eccles 7:15. there is a *j.* man that perisheth in his righteousness
20. there is not a *j.* man on earth
8:14. be *j.* men, to whom it happeneth
Isa 26:7. way of *j.* is uprightness; thou dost weigh the path of the *j.*
45:21. no God beside me; a *j.* God
Ezek 18:9. he is *j.*, he shall live
Hab 2:4. *j.* shall live by his faith, Rom 1:17. Gal 3:11. Heb 10:38.
Zeph 3:5. the *j.* Lord is in the midst
Luke 15:7. more than over ninety-nine *j.* persons
20:20. who should feign themselves *j.*
John 5:30. my judgment is *j.*
Acts 7:52. shewed before the coming of *Just* One, 22:14.
24:15. resurrection . . . both of *j.* and
Rom 2:13. not hearers of law are *j.*
3:26. he might be *j.* and justifier
7:12. commandment holy, *j.*, and
Phil 4:8. whatsoever things are *j.*
Col 4:1. give . . . that which is *j.* and
Heb 2:2. received a *j.* recompence
12:23. spirits of *j.* men made perfect
1 Pet 3:18. once suffered for sins, *j.* for the
Rev 15:3. *j.* and true are thy ways
Mic 6:8. to do *justly,* and love
Luke 23:41. we indeed *j.*, for we
1 Thess 2:10. how holily and *j.* we behaved
Gen 18:19. to do *justice* and
Job 37:23. excellent in power, and in judgment, and in plenty of *j.*
Ps 89:14. *j.* and judgment are the habitation of thy throne
Prov 8:15. by me . . . princes decree *j.*
Jer 31:23. O habitation of *j.*, 50:7.

JUSTIFY not the wicked, Exod 23:7.
Deut 25:1. they shall *j.* the righteous
Job 9:20. if I *j.* myself, mine own mouth
27:5. God forbid that I should *j.*
33:32. speak, for I desire to *j.* thee
Isa 5:23. them which *j.* the wicked
53:11. shall my servant *j.* many
Luke 10:29. he, willing to *j.* himself
16:15. ye are they which *j.* yourselves before men
Rom 3:30. God shall *j.* circumcision
Gal 3:8. God would *j.* heathen
Rom 4:25. raised for our *justification*
5:16. gift is of many offences unto *j.*
Job 11:2. should a man full of talk be *justified*
13:18. I know that I shall be *j.*
25:4. how can man be *j.* with God?
32:2. he *j.* himself rather than God
Ps 51:4. mightest be *j.* when thou speakest
Isa 43:9. that they may be *j.*, 26.
45:25. in Lord shall the seed of Israel be *j.*
Jer 3:11. hath *j.* herself more than Judah
Ezek 16:51. thou . . . hast *j.* thy sisters in all thine *abominations*, 52.
Matt 11:19. wisdom is *j.* of children, Luke 7:35.
12:37. by thy words thou shalt be *j.*
Luke 7:29. *j.* God, being baptized of
Rom 2:13. doers of law shall be *j.*
3:4. thou mightest be *j.* in thy sayings
20. there shall no flesh be *j.* in his
24. being *j.* freely by his grace
28. man is *j.* by faith without deeds
4:2. if Abraham were *j.* by works
5:1. being *j.* by faith, we have
9. being now *j.* by his blood, we shall be saved
8:30. whom he *j.* them he also
1 Cor 4:4. yet am I not hereby *j.*
6:11. ye are *j.* in name of the Lord
Gal 2:16. not *j.* by works of law . . . we might be *j.* by faith of Christ, 17.
3:11. no man is *j.* by the law
24. that we might be *j.* by faith
5:4. *j.* by law, ye are fallen from grace
1 Tim 3:16. God . . . in flesh, *j.* in spirit
Titus 3:7. that being *j.* by his grace
James 2:21. Abraham *j.* by works when
25. was not Rahab the harlot *j.* by works
Rom 3:28. the *justifier* of him that
Prov 17:15. he that *justifieth* wicked
Isa 50:8. he is near that *j.* me
Rom 4:5. him that *justifieth* the ungodly
8:33. it is God that *j.*
1 Kings 8:32. *justifying* the righteous, 2 Chron 6:23.

K

KEEP, Gen 2:15; 33:9.
Gen 18:19. *k.* the way of the Lord
28:15. I am with thee and will *k.* thee
20. if God will be with me, and *k.* me
Exod 23:7. *k.* thee far from a false matter
20. I send an angel to *k.* thee in
Num 6:24. Lord bless thee and *k.* thee
Deut 23:9. *k.* thee from every wicked
29:9. *k.* words of this covenant
1 Sam 2:9. he will *k.* the feet of his
1 Chron 4:10. thou wouldest *k.* me
Ps 25:10. to such as *k.* his covenant, 103:18.
20. *k.* my soul, 17:8. *k.* me as apple of eye
39:1. *k.* my mouth with a bridle
89:28. my mercy will I *k.* for him
91:11. angels to *k.* thee in all thy ways
106:3. blessed are they that *k.* judgment
119:2. *k.* his testimonies, 88, 129, 146. *k.* thy precepts, 4, 63, 69, 100. *k.* his statutes, 33. *k.* his

word and law, 17, 34, 57, 101, 136.
127:1. except the Lord *k.* the city
140:4. *k.* me, O Lord, from hands of wicked
141:3. *k.* the door of my lips
Eccles 5:1. *k.* thy foot when thou goest
Isa 26:3. thou wilt *k.* him in perfect
Jer 3:12. I will not *k.* anger for ever
Hos 12:6. *k.* mercy and judgment
Mic 7:5. *k.* the doors of thy mouth
Mal 2:7. priest's lips should *k.* knowledge
Luke 11:28. hear word of God and *k.* it
1 Cor 5:8. let us *k.* the feast, not
11. not to *k.* company with such
9:27. I *k.* under my body, and
Eph 4:3. endeavouring to *k.* unity
Phil 4:7. peace of God shall *k.* your
2 Thess 3:3. Lord shall stablish you and *k.* you
1 Tim 5:22. *k.* thyself pure
6:20. *k.* that which is committed
2 Tim 1:12. able to *k.* that which I have
14. that good thing which was committed to thee, *k.* by Holy Ghost
James 1:27. *k.* himself unspotted
2:10. *k.* whole law, yet offend in one
Jude 21. *k.* yourselves in love of God
24. that is able to *k.* you from
Rev 1:3. blessed . . . that hear . . . and *k.*
3:10. I will *k.* thee from the hour of
22:9. them which *k.* sayings
Lev 26:3. *keep* my *commandments*
Deut 6:17. diligently—, 11:1, 22.
13:4.—his—and obey his voice, 11:8.
Ps 119:60. I delayed not to—thy—
Prov 4:4.—my—and live, 7:2.
Eccles 12:13. fear God, and—his—
Matt 19:17. if thou wilt enter into life—the—
John 14:15. if ye love me—my—
1 John 2:3. we know that we know him, if we—his—
5:3. this is the love of God that we—his—
Rev 14:12. here are they that—the—
Judg 3:19. *keep silence,* Ps 50:21. Eccles 3:7. Isa 41:1. Lam 2:10. Amos 5:13. Hab 2:20. 1 Cor 14:28, 34.
Ps 35:22. *k. not s.* 50:3; 83:1. Isa 62:6; 65:6.
1 Kings 8:23. who *keepest* covenant and mercy, 2 Chron 6:14. Neh 9:32.
Ps 121:3. he that *keepeth* thee will not slumber
146:6. which *k.* truth for ever
Prov 13:3. he that *k.* his mouth *k.* his life
29:18. he that *k.* the law, happy is he
1 John 5:18. that is begotten of God *k.* himself
Rev 16:15. blessed is he that . . . *k.* his garments
22:7. blessed is he that *k.* . . . this prophecy
Exod 34:7. *keeping* mercy for thousands
Ps 19:11. in *k.* of them is great reward
Dan 9:4. *k.* the covenant and mercy
1 Pet 4:19. commit *k.* of their souls
Ps 121:5. the Lord is thy *keeper*
Song of Sol 1:6. made me *k.* of vineyards
Eccles 12:3. when *keepers* of house shall
5:7. *k.* took away my veil from me
Titus 2:5. chaste, *k.* at home
Deut 32:10. *kept* them as the apple of eye
33:9. and *k.* thy covenant
Josh 14:10. Lord hath *k.* me alive
2 Sam 22:22. *k.* ways of Lord, Ps 18:21.
Ps 18:23. *k.* myself from mine iniquity
Job 23:11. his way have I *k.* and
Ps 17:4. *k.* me from paths of the
30:3. *k.* me alive, that I should not go
Song of Sol 1:6. mine own vineyard not *k.*
Matt 19:20. all these things have I *k.* from my youth
Luke 2:19. Mary *k.* all these things, and pondered them, 51.
John 15:20. if they have *k.* my sayings
17:6. they have *k.* thy word
12. that thou gavest me I have *k.*
Rom 16:25. *k.* secret since the world
2 Tim 4:7. I have *k.* the faith
1 Pet 1:5. *k.* by the power of God
Rev 3:8. hast *k.* my word, and not
KEY of house of David, Isa 22:22. Rev 3:7.
Rev 9:1. *k.* of the bottomless pit, 20:1.
Matt 16:19. *keys* of the kingdom of heaven
Rev 1:18. I have *k.* of hell
KICK, Deut 32:15. 1 Sam 2:29. Acts 9:5; 26:14.
KID, Isa 11:6. Luke 15:29.
Song of Sol 1:8. feed *kids* beside shepherds'
KILL, thou shalt not, Exod 20:13.
Eccles 3:3. time to *k.* and a time to heal
Matt 10:28. fear not them which *k.* body, but are not able to *k.* soul
Mark 3:4. lawful to save life, or *k.*
1 Kings 21:19. hast thou *killed* and
Ps 44:22. are we *k.* all day long, Rom 8:36.
Luke 12:5. after he hath *k.* hath power
Acts 3:15. *k.* the Prince of life
2 Cor 6:9. as chastened, not *k.*
1 Thess 2:15. *k.* Lord Jesus and . . . prophets
Rev 13:10. that *k.* with sword must be *k.*
1 Sam 2:6. the Lord *killeth* and maketh
John 16:2. who *k.* you will think he doeth
2 Cor 3:6. letter *k.* . . . spirit giveth life
KIND, Gen 1:11. 2 Chron 10:7.
Luke 6:35. he is *k.* to unthankful
1 Cor 13:4. charity suffereth long and is *k.*
1 Sam 20:14. while yet I live shew me the *kindness* of the Lord
2 Sam 9:3. may shew the *k.* of God
16:17. is this thy *k.* to thy friend
Neh 9:17. a God . . . slow to anger and of great *k.* Joel 2:13. Jon 4:2.
Ps 117:2. his merciful *k.* is great
141:5. let righteous smite me; it shall be a *k.*
Prov 19:22. the desire of a man is his *k.*
31:26. in her tongue is law of *k.*
Isa 54:8. with everlasting *k.* will I have mercy
10. my *k.* shall not depart from thee
Jer 2:2. I remember thee, the *kindness* of
Col 3:12. put on bowels of mercies, *k.*
2 Pet 1:7. to godliness brotherly *k.*, to brotherly *k.* charity
Ps 36:7. how excellent is thy *lovingkindness*
10. O continue thy—unto them
63:3. thy—is better than life
103:4. who crowneth thee with—
Isa 63:7. I will mention the—of Lord
Jer 9:24. the Lord which exercise—
31:3. with—have I drawn thee
32:18. thou shewest—to thousands
Hos 2:19. I will betroth thee . . . in—
Ps 25:5. remember . . . thy *lovingkindness*
KINDLE, Prov 26:21. Isa 10:16.
Isa 30:33. breath of Lord . . . doth *k.* it
Hos 11:8. my repentings are *kindled*
2 Sam 22:9. coals *k.* by it, Ps 18:8.
Ps 2:12. when his wrath is *k.* but a
Isa 50:11. walk in . . . sparks that ye have *k.*
Luke 12:49. fire on earth, what . . . if it be already *k.*?
KING, Gen 14:18; 36:31.
Job 18:14. bring him to *k.* of terrors
Ps 10:16. Lord is *K.* for ever and
24:7. *K.* of glory shall come in, 9, 10.
33:16. no *k.* saved by multitude of
47:7. God is *K.* of all the earth, 6.
74:12. God is my *k.* 5:2; 44:4.

Prov 30:31. a *k.* against whom is no
Eccles 5:9. *k.* himself is served by the field
8:4. where word of *k.* is there is power
Song of Sol 1:4. *k.* brought me into his chambers
12. while the *k.* sitteth at his table
7:5. the *k.* is held in the galleries
Isa 32:1. a *k.* shall reign in righteousness
33:22. Lord is our lawgiver . . . our *k.*
43:15. Creator of Israel, your *K.*
Hos 3:5. seek Lord their God and David their *k.*
7:5. in day of our *k.* the princes
13:11. I gave thee a *k.* in mine anger
Zech 9:9. behold, thy *K.* cometh
Luke 23:2. he himself is Christ, a *k.*
John 6:15. by force to make him *k.*
1 Tim 1:17. now unto the *K.* eternal
6:15. *K.* of kings, and Lord of lords, Rev 17:14; 19:16.
1 Pet 2:17. fear God, honour *k.*
Rev 15:3. just and true . . . *K.* of saints
Ps 76:12. terrible to *kings* of earth, 72:11.
102:15. *k.* of earth thy glory, Isa 62:2.
144:10. that giveth salvation to *k.*
149:8. to bind their *k.* with chains
Prov 8:15. by me *k.* reign, and
Hos 8:4. they set up *k.* but not by
Matt 11:8. soft clothing in *k.s'* houses
Luke 22:25. *k.* of Gentiles exercise
1 Cor 4:8. reigned as *k.* without us
1 Tim 2:2. giving of thanks . . . for *k.* and all
Rev 1:6. made us *k.* and priests to God, 5:10.
Exod 19:6. be a *kingdom* of priests, and an
1 Sam 10:25. Samuel told people manner of the *k.*
1 Chron 29:11. thine is the *k.*, O Lord, Matt 6:13.
Ps 22:28. for the *k.* is the Lord's
Dan 2:44. in days of these kings shall God of heaven set up a *k.*
4:17. the most High ruleth in *k.* of men, 25, 32.
7:27. whose *k.* is everlasting *k.*, 14.
Matt 12:25. every *k.* divided against itself
13:19. heareth the word of the *k.*
38. good seed are the children of *k.*
25:34. inherit k. prepared for you
Mark 11:10. blessed be the *k.* of our father David
Luke 12:32. Father's good pleasure to give you the *kingdom*
19:12. to receive for himself a *k.*
22:29. I appoint unto you a *k.*, as my Father appointed to me
John 18:36. my *k.* is not of this world
1 Cor 15:24. delivered up *k.* to God
Col 1:13. translated us into the *k.* of
2 Tim 4:18. preserve me to his heavenly *k.*
James 2:5. rich in faith, heirs of *k.*
2 Pet 1:11. an entrance . . . into everlasting *k.* of our Lord and Saviour
Rev 1:9. in *k.* and patience of Jesus
17:17. to give their *k.* to the beast
Matt 6:33. *kingdom of God,* 12:28; 21:43. Mark 1:15; 10:14, 15; 12:34; 15:43. Luke 4:43; 6:20; 9:62; 10:9, 11; 13:29; 17:20, 21; 18:16, 17, 29; 21:31.
John 3:3. except a man be born again, he cannot see—, 5.
Rom 14:17.—is not meat and drink
1 Cor 4:20.—is not in word, but
6:9. unrighteous shall not inherit—
Eph 5:5. hath any inheritance in—
2 Thess 1:5. be counted worthy of—
Rev 12:10. salvation and strength and—
Matt 3:2. *kingdom of heaven,* 4:17; 10:7; 5:3, 10, 19, 20; 7:21; 8:11; 11:11, 12; 13:11, 24, 31, 52; 16:19; 18:1, 3, 23; 20:1; 22:2; 23:13; 25:1, 14.
Rev 11:15. the *kingdoms* of this world are *k.* of our Lord
KISS the Son, lest he be angry, Ps 2:12.
Song of Sol 1:2. let him *k.* me with the kisses
Rom 16:16. salute one another with an holy *k.*
1 Pet 5:14. greet . . . with *k.* of charity
Ps 85:10. righteousness and peace have *kissed* each other
Luke 7:38. *k.* his feet and anointed
Prov 27:6. *kisses* of an enemy are deceitful
KNEES, Gen 30:3; 41:43.
Job 4:4. feeble *k.* Isa 35:3. Heb 12:12.
Isa 45:23. to God every *k.* shall bow, Rom 14:11. Phil 2:10. Matt 27:29. Eph 3:14.
Nah 2:10. *k.* smite together, Dan 5:6.
KNIFE, Prov 23:2; 30:14.
KNIT, 1 Sam 18:1. Col 2:2, 19.
KNOCK, Matt 7:7. Rev 3:20.
KNOW, Gen 3:7; 4:1; 42:7.
Gen 28:16. Lord in this place, I *knew* it not
Deut 34:10. whom Lord *k.* face to face
Jer 1:5. before I formed thee . . . I *k.*
Matt 7:23. I never *k.* you: depart ye
Rom 1:21. *k.* God they glorified him not
1 John 3:1. because it *k.* him not
John 4:10. if thou *knewest* the gift of God
Deut 8:2. to *know* what was in thy
Josh 22:22. Israel he shall *k.*
1 Sam 3:7. Samuel did not yet *k.* Lord
1 Kings 8:38. shall *k.* every man plague of . . . heart
1 Chron 28:9. *k.* thou the God of
Job 5:27. *k.* thou it for thy good
8:9. for we are but of yesterday, and *k.* nothing
13:23. make me to *k.* my transgression
22:13. how doth God *k.* Ps 73:11.
Ps 4:3. *k.* that Lord doth set apart the godly
9:10. that *k.* thy name will trust in
46:10. be still, and *k.* that I am God
51:6. thou shalt make me to *k.* wisdom
73:16. when I thought to *k.* this
139:23. *k.* my heart . . . *k.* my
Eccles 11:9. *k.* thou that for all these things God will bring thee into judgment
Isa 58:2. they seek me daily and delight to *k.*
Jer 17:9. heart deceitful . . . , who can *know* it
22:16. was not this to *k.* me, saith Lord
24:7. I will give them a heart to *k.*
31:34. *k.* the Lord, for they shall all *k.* me
44:28. shall *k.* whose words shall
Ezek 2:5. shall *k.* that there . . . prophet hath, 33:33.
Hos 2:20. in faithfulness, and thou shalt *k.* Lord
Mic 3:1. is it not for you to *k.* judgment
Matt 6:3. let not left hand *k.* what
7:11. *k.* how to give good gifts, Luke 11:13.
John 4:42. we *k.* this is the Christ
7:17. he shall *k.* of the doctrine
10:4. sheep follow him, for they *k.*
14. and *k.* my sheep and am known
13:7. knowest not now, but thou shalt *k.* 17. if ye *k.* these things, happy are. 35. by this shall all men *k.* that ye are my disciples
Acts 1:7. it is not for you to *k.* the times
1 Cor 2:14. neither can he *k.* them
4:19. and will *k.* not speech of them, but power
8:2. knoweth nothing as he ought to *k.*
Eph 3:19. to *k.* love of Christ
Titus 1:16. profess they *k.* God, but

Exod 4:14. *I know,* Job 9:2, 28; 13:18.
Gen 18:19.—him that he will command
22:12. now—that thou fearest God
2 Kings 19:27.—thy abode and thy
Job 19:25.—my Redeemer liveth
Ps 41:11. by this—thou favourest
Jer 10:23.—that way of man is not in himself
29:11.—thoughts that I think, saith Lord
Matt 25:12.—you not, Luke 13:25, 27.
John 13:18. *I know* whom I have chosen
Acts 26:27.—that thou believest
Rom 7:18.—that in me, that is in my
1 Cor 4:4. for—nothing by myself
13:12. now—in part; but then shall—
Phil 4:12.—how to be abased
2 Tim 1:12.—whom I have believed
1 John 2:4. he that saith—him, and keepeth
Rev 2:2.—thy works, 9, 13, 19; 3:1, 8, 15.
Hos 6:3. *we know,* 8:2. John 4:22. 1 Cor 2:12. 1 John 2:3, 5.
John 16:30. *thou knowest* all things
21:15, 16.—all things—I love thee
Ps 1:6. Lord *knoweth* the way of
94:11. Lord *k.* thoughts of man are
103:14. he *k.* our frame, that we
138:6. the proud he *k.* afar off
139:14. my soul *k.* right well
Eccles 9:1. no man *k.* either love or
Isa 1:3. ox *k.* his owner, and ass his
Jer 8:7. stork *k.* her appointed times
Zeph 3:5. the unjust *k.* no shame
Matt 6:8. Father *k.* things ye have need of
24:36. of that day and hour *k.* no man
2 Tim 2:19. Lord *k.* them that are his
2 Pet 2:9. Lord *k.* how to deliver
1 John 3:1. the world *k.* us not
Rev 2:17. a name which no man *k.*
Ps 9:16. Lord *known* by judgment
31:7. hast *k.* my soul in *adversities*
67:2. that thy way may be *k.* on earth
Isa 45:4. thou hast not *k.* me, 5.
Matt 10:26. there is nothing hid that shall not be *k.*, Luke 8:17; 12:2.
Luke 19:42. if thou hadst *k.* . . . in this
Acts 15:18. *k.* to God are all his works
Rom 1:19. that which may be *k.* of God
7:7. I had not *k.* sin but by the law

1 Cor 8:3. the same is *k.* of, 13:12.
Gal 4:9. *k.* God, or rather are *k.* of God
2 Tim 3:15. from a child thou hast *k.*
Rev 2:24. have not *known* the depths of Satan
Gen 2:17. *knowledge* of good and evil
1 Sam 2:3. the Lord is a God of *k.*
Ps 19:2. night unto night sheweth *k.*
73:11. is there *k.* in the Most High
139:6. such *k.* is too wonderful
Prov 8:12. I find out *k.* of witty inventions
9:10. *k.* of the holy is understanding
14:6. *k.* is easy to him that understandeth
19:2. that the soul be without *k.* is not good
30:3. nor have the *k.* of holy
Eccles 9:10. there is no . . . device nor *k.*
Isa 28:9. whom shall he teach *k.*
53:11. by his *k.* shall my righteous
Jer 3:15. pastors . . . feed you with *k.*
Dan 12:4. and *k.* shall be increased
Hos 4:6. are destroyed for lack of *k.*
Hab 2:14. earth filled with *k.* of the glory of God, Isa 11:9.
Mal 2:7. priest's lips should keep *k.*
Rom 2:20. a teacher . . . hast form of *k.*
3:20. for by the law is *k.* of sin
10:2. a zeal of God, but not according to *k.*
1 Cor 8:1. all have *k.* *K.* puffeth up
Eph 3:19. love of Christ which passeth *k.*
Phil 3:8. loss for excellency of the *k.* of
Col 2:3. treasures of wisdom and *k.*
3:10. renewed in *k.* after image of
1 Pet 3:7. dwell with them according to *k.*
2 Pet 1:5. and to virtue *k.* and to *k.*
3:18. grow in grace and in *k.* of Lord and Saviour Jesus Christ

L

LABOUR, Gen 31:42; 35:16.
Ps 90:10. yet is their strength *l.*
104:23. man goeth to his . . . *l.* till even
128:2. thou shalt eat the *l.* of thine
Prov 14:23. in all *l.* there is profit
Eccles 1:8. all things are full of *l.*
4:8. yet is there no end of all his *l.*
Isa 55:2. ye spend your *l.* for that which
John 4:38. no *l.* . . . their labours

1 Cor 15:58. your *l.* is not in vain in
1 Thess 1:3. work of faith, *l.* of love
Prov 23:4. *l.* not to be rich; cease
Matt 11:28. come unto me all ye that *l.* and are heavy laden
John 6:27. *l.* not for the meat that
1 Thess 5:12. know them which *l.*
Heb 4:11. let us *l.* to enter into
Isa 49:4. I have *laboured* in vain
John 4:38. other men *l.* and ye
1 Cor 15:10. I *l.* more abundantly
Phil 2:16. I have not run in vain, neither *l.* in vain
Luke 10:7. the *labourer* is worthy of his hire, 1 Tim 5:18.
Matt 9:37. but *labourers* are few, Luke 10:2.
1 Cor 3:9. *l.* together with God
Prov 16:26. he that *laboureth, l.* for
Eccles 5:12. sleep of *labouring* man is sweet
Col 4:12. Epaphras . . . *l.* fervently . . . in prayers
Rev 14:13. dead . . . may rest from *labours*
LACK, Hos 4:6. Matt 19:20. 2 Cor 11:9. 1 Thess 3:10. James 1:5.
LADEN with iniquity, Isa 1:4.
Matt 11:28. labour and heavy *l.*
LADY of kingdoms, Isa 47:5.
Isa 47:7. I shall be a *l.* for ever
2 John 1. unto the elect *l.*
Esther 1:18. *ladies* of Persia
Judg 5:29. her wise *l.* answered her
LAMB, Exod 12:3.
Gen 22:7. where is *l.* for a burnt offering
8. God will provide himself a *l.*
2 Sam 12:3. had nothing save one little ewe *l.*
Isa 11:6. wolf shall dwell with *l.*
53:7. brought as *l.* to slaughter
John 1:29. behold the *L.* of God, 36.
1 Pet 1:19. as a *l.* without blemish
Rev 5:12. worthy is *L.* that was slain
7:14. washed their robes, and made them white in blood of the *L.,* 12:11.
17. *L.* in the midst of the throne shall feed them
13:8. *L.* slain from foundation
John 21:15. Jesus said to Peter, Feed my *lambs*
LAME, Lev 21:18. Mal 1:8, 13.
Job 29:15. eyes to blind, feet to *l.*
Prov 26:7. legs of *l.* are not equal
Isa 35:6. shall the *l.* man leap as an hart
Heb 12:13. lest . . . *l.* be turned out of way
LAMP, Gen 15:17. Exod 27:20. 1 Kings 15:4. Matt 25:1, 3, 4, 7, 8.
2 Sam 22:29. thou art my *l.* O Lord
Job 12:5. is as a *l.* despised . . . of him
Ps 119:105. thy word a *l.* to my feet

132:17. I have ordained a *l.* for mine
Prov 6:23. the commandment is a *l.*
13:9. *l.* of wicked shall be put out
Isa 62:1. salvation as *l.* that burneth
Exod 25:37. *seven lamps,* 37:23. Num 8:2. Zech 4:2. Rev 4:5.
LAND, Eccles 10:16, 17. Isa 5:30.
Deut 19:14. not remove *landmark,* 27:17. Job 24:2. Prov 22:28; 23:10.
LANGUAGE, Gen 11:1. Neh 13:24. Ps 81:5. Isa 19:18. Zeph 3:9.
LANGUISH, Isa 24:4. Ps 41:3.
LASCIVIOUSNESS, Mark 7:22. 2 Cor 12:21. Gal 5:19. Eph 4:19. 1 Pet 4:3.
Jude 4. turning grace of God into *l.*
LAST end be like his, Num 23:10.
Lam 1:9. she remembered not *l.* end
Luke 11:26. *l.* state . . . is worse than first
1 Pet 1:5. *last time,* 20. 1 John 2:18.
Jude 18. should be mockers in the—
LATTER day, Job 19:25. *l.* end, Prov 19:20. *l.* house, Hag 2:9. *l.* time, 1 Tim 4:1. 2 Tim 3:1.
LAUGH, Gen 17:17; 18:12, 15.
Job 5:22. at destruction . . . thou shalt *l.*
Ps 2:4. he that sitteth in heavens shall *l.*
37:13. Lord shall *l.* at him
52:6. righteous shall see and fear and *l.*
Prov 1:26. I will *l.* at your calamity
Luke 6:21. blessed . . . that weep . . . ye shall *l.*
25. woe to you that *l.* . . . ye shall mourn
Job 8:21. till he fill thy mouth with *laughing*
Ps 126:2. mouth filled with *laughter*
Prov 14:13. in *l.* heart is sorrowful
Eccles 2:2. I said of *l.*, It is mad
7:3. sorrow is better than *l.*
James 4:9. let *l.* be turned to mourning
LAW, Gen 47:26. Prov 28:4.
Deut 33:2. from right hand went a fiery *l.*
Neh 8:7. caused people to understand *l.*
10:28. separated from people . . . to *l.* of God
Job 22:22. receive . . . *l.* from his mouth
Ps 19:7. *l.* of the Lord is perfect
37:31. *l.* of his God is in his heart
78:5. he . . . appointed a *l.* in Israel, 10.
119:72. *l.* of thy mouth is better
Prov 6:23. *l.* is light, 13:14. *l.* of wise
7:2. keep my *l.* as apple of thine eye
Prov 28:9. turneth away his ear from hearing *law*
29:18. keepeth the *l.* happy is he
Isa 2:3. shall go forth *l.*, Mic 4:2.
8:16. seal the *l.* among my disciples
20. to the *l.* and the testimony
42:21. magnify the *l.* and make it
51:7. people in whose heart is my *l.*
Jer 18:18. *l.* not perish from priest
31:33. I will put *l.* in inward parts
Hos 8:12. written to him great things of *l.*
Mal 2:7. they should seek *l.* at his mouth
Luke 16:16. *l.* and prophets were until John
John 1:17. *l.* was given by Moses
19:7. we have a *l.* and by our *l.* he
Acts 13:39. not justified by the *l.* of Moses
Rom 2:12. sinned without *l.* perish without *l.*
13. not hearers of *l.* . . . but doers of *l.*
14. having not *l.* a *l.* to themselves
3:20. by deeds of *l.* shall no flesh be justified, for by the *l.* is the
31. do we made void *l.*? . . . we establish the *l.*
4:15. *l.* worketh wrath; where no *l.*
5:13. sin is not imputed where no *l.*
7:7. had not known sin but by *l.*
8. for without the *l.* sin was dead
9. I was alive without the *l.* once
12. the *l.* is holy, just, and good
14. *l.* is spiritual, but I am carnal
22. I delight in the *l.* of God
23. *l.* in my members warring against *l.* of my mind
8:2. *l.* of Spirit . . . made me free from *l.* of sin
Rom 10:5. righteousness of *l.*, 9:31. Phil 3:9.
1 Cor 6:1. Dare any of you . . . go to *l.*
6:7. brother goeth to *l.* with brother
Gal 2:16. man not justified by works of the *l.* . . . by works of *l.* no flesh justified
19. I through the *l.* am dead to *l.*
3:10. of works of *l.* are under curse
12. the *l.* is not of faith, but the
13. Christ redeemed us from curse of *l.*
5:23. love, faith, against such is no *l.*
1 Tim 1:8. the *l.* is good, if a man use
9. that *l.* is not made for righteous
Heb 7:19. *l.* made nothing perfect
James 1:25. looketh into perfect *l.*
1 John 3:4. *sin* transgresseth the *l.* . . . sin is the transgression of *l.*
Neh 9:26. cast *thy law* behind their backs
Ps 40:8.—is within my heart
94:12. teachest him out of—
119:70. I delight in—77, 92, 174.
18. wondrous things out of—
97. how I love—113, 163, 165, 167.
Ezek 18:5. do that is *lawful* and right, 33:14, 19.
1 Cor 6:12. all things *l.* to me, 10:23.
Isa 33:22. Lord is *lawgiver,* James 4:12.
LAY, Gen 19:33, 35. Job 29:19.
Eccles 7:2. the living will *l.* it to heart
Isa 28:16. I *l.* in Zion . . . a tried stone
Mal 2:2. ye do not *l.* it to heart
Matt 8:20. hath not where to *l.* his head
Acts 7:60. *l.* not this sin to their charge
15:28. *l.* on you no greater burden
Heb 12:1. *l.* aside every weight
James 1:21. *l.* apart all filthiness and superfluity of, 1 Pet 2:1.
John 10:15. *lay down life,* 13:37; 15:13. 1 John 3:16.
1 Tim 5:22. *lay hands,* Heb 6:2.
6:12. *lay hold* on eternal life
Heb 6:18.—on hope set before us
Matt 6:20. *lay up* for yourselves
Ps 62:9. to be *laid* in the balance
89:19. I *l.* help on one that is
Isa 53:6. Lord hath *laid* on him the iniquity of us all
1 Cor 3:10. I have *l.* foundation, 11.
1 Sam 21:12. David *laid up* words
Ps 31:19. thy goodness . . . —for them
Song of Sol 7:13. pleasant fruits . . . —for thee
Luke 1:66.—in their hearts
12:19. much goods—for many years
Col 1:5. hope which is—for you
2 Tim 4:8.—for me a crown of
Job 21:19. God *layeth* up his iniquity
Prov 2:7. *l.* up wisdom, 26:24. *l.* up deceit
Isa 56:2. blessed is the man . . . that *l.* hold on it
57:1. no man *l.* it to heart, 42:25.
Jer 12:11. land desolate; no man *l.* it to heart
Heb 6:1. not *laying* again foundation
1 Tim 6:19. *l.* up . . . a good foundation
LEAD, Exod 15:10. Job 19:24. Zech 5:7, 8. Gen 33:14. Exod 13:21.
Ps 5:8. *lead me* . . . in thy righteousness
25:5.—in thy truth, 27.11.—in a plain path
61:2.—to rock higher than I
139:24.—in the way everlasting
Song of Sol 8:2. I would *l.* thee . . . to my mother's house
Isa 11:6. a little child shall *l.* them
40:11. gently *l.* those with young
Matt 15:14. blind *l.* blind, Luke 6:39.
1 Tim 2:2. may *l.* a quiet . . . life
Rev 7:17. Lamb . . . shall *l.* them to

Isa 55:4. *leader* to people, 9:16.
Ps 23:2. *leadeth* me beside still waters
Matt 7:13. broad is way that *l.* to
7:14. straight is the gate and narrow is the way that *l.* to life
John 10:3. calleth sheep and *l.* them out
Gen 24:27. *Lord led, leddest, leadest, leadeth,* 48. Exod 13:18; 15:13. Deut 8:2; 29:5; 32:10, 12. Neh 9:12. Ps 77:20; 80:1; 78:14, 53; 106:9; 136:16; 107:7. Isa 48:21; 63:13, 14. Jer 2:6, 17.
Rom 8:14. *led by Spirit,* Gal 5:18.
LEAF, Job 13:25. Ezek 47:12. Rev 22:2.
LEAGUE with stones, Job 5:23.
LEAN not unto thine own understanding, Prov 3:5.
Job 8:15. he shall *l.* upon his house
Mic 3:11. yet will they *l.* on Lord
Song of Sol 8:5. *leaning* on her beloved
John 13:23. *l.* on Jesus' bosom, 21:20.
LEANNESS, Job 16:8. Ps 106:15. Isa 10:16. Isa 24:16. my *l.*, my *l.*, woe
LEAP, Song of Sol 2:8. Isa 35:6. Zeph 1:9.
6:23. rejoice and *l.* for joy
Luke 1:41. the babe *leaped* in her womb
LEARN to fear me, Deut 4:10; 5:1; 14:23; 31:12, 13.
Ps 119:71. might *l.* thy statutes, 73.
Prov 22:25. lest thou *l.* his ways
Isa 1:17. *l.* to do well, seek
26:10. yet will he not *l.* righteousness
Jer 10:2. *l.* not way of the heathen
Matt 9:13. *l.* what that meaneth
11:29. *l.* of me, for I am meek
Titus 3:14. also *l.* to maintain good
Rev 14:3. no man could *l.* that song
Ps 106:35. *learned* their works
Isa 50:4. given me tongue of the *l.*
John 6:45. hath *l.* of Father cometh unto me
Acts 7:22. Moses was *l.* in all wisdom
Eph 4:20. ye have not so *l.* Christ
Heb 5:8. though a Son, yet *l.* he
Acts 26:24. much *learning* doth make thee mad
Rom 15:4. were written for our *l.*
2 Tim 3:7. ever *l.*, never able to
LEAST of thy mercies, Gen 32:10.
Jer 31:34. shall know me from *least* of them
Luke 16:10. faithful in . . . *l.* is faithful
1 Cor 6:4. judge who are *l.* esteemed
15:9. I am *l.* of the apostles
Eph 3:8. less than *l.* of all saints

LEAVE father and mother and cleave to wife, Gen 2:24. Matt 19:5. Mark 10:7. Eph 5:31.
1 Kings 8:57. let him not *l.* us, nor
27:9. *l.* me not, neither forsake me
Matt 5:24. *l.* there thy gift before
23:23. and not to *l.* other undone
John 14:18. will not *l.* you comfortless
27. peace I *l.* with you, my peace
Heb 13:5. I will never *l.* thee, nor forsake
LEAVEN, Exod 12:15. Lev 2:11.
Matt 13:33. kingdom of heaven is like *l.* 16:6. beware of *l.* of Pharisees, Luke 12:1. 1 Cor 5:7, 8. purge out the old *l.* of
1 Cor 5:6. a little *l.* leaveneth whole lump, Gal 5:9.
LEES, Isa 25:6. Jer 48:11. Zeph 1:12.
LEGS, Ps 147:10. Prov 26:7.
LEND, Exod 22:25. Deut 23:19, 20.
Ps 37:26. merciful and *lendeth,* 112:5.
Prov 19:17. giveth to the poor *l.* to Lord
22:7. borrower is servant to *lender*
1 Sam 1:28. I have *lent* him to Lord
Jer 15:10. neither *l.* on usury, nor
LEOPARD, Song of Sol 4:8. Isa 11:6. Jer 5:6; 13:23. Hos 13:7. Hab 1:8.
LESS, Ezra 9:13. Job 11:6. Isa 40:17. Heb 7:7. Eph 3:8. Gen 32:10.
LETTER, Rom 7:6. 2 Cor 3:6.
LETTEST, -TETH, Luke 2:29. 2 Thess 2:7.
LEVIATHAN, Job 41:1. Ps 74:14.
LIBERAL, Prov 11:25. Isa 32:5, 8. 2 Cor 9:13.
1 Cor 16:3. *liberality,* 2 Cor 8:2.
James 1:5. ask of God that giveth to all men *liberally*
LIBERTY, Lev 25:10. Jer 34:8.
Ps 119:45. I will walk at *l.* for I seek
Isa 61:1. anointed me to . . . proclaim *l.*
Luke 4:18. to set at *l.* the bruised
Rom 8:21. *l.* of the children of God
Gal 5:1. stand fast in *l.* wherewith
13. use not *l.* for an occasion to
James 1:25. but whoso looketh into perfect law of *l.*
2:12. be judged by the law of *l.*
LIE, Lev 6:3; 19:11. Job 11:3.
Ps 62:9. men of high degree are a *l.*
2 Thess 2:11. they should believe a *l.*
Num 23:19. God is not a man, that he should *l.*, neither son of man
Isa 63:8. children that will not *l.*
Hab 2:3. it shall speak and not *l.*
Col 3:9. *l.* not one to another, Eph 4:25.
Titus 1:2. God that cannot *l.* hath promised

Heb 6:18. impossible for God to *l.*
Ps 58:3. wicked go astray . . . speaking *lies*
101:7. that telleth *l.* shall not tarry
Hos 11:12. compasseth me with *l.*
1 Tim 4:2. speaking *l.* in hypocrisy
John 8:44. he is a *liar* and the father
Rom 3:4. let God be true, every man a *l.*
1 John 1:10. we make him a *l.*, 5:10.
2:4. keepeth not commandments is a *l.*
Ps 116:11. I said . . ., All men are *liars*
Isa 44:25. frustrateth tokens of *l.*
Titus 1:12. the Cretians are always *l.*
Rev 2:2. tried . . . and found them *l.*
Ps 119:29. remove . . . way of *lying*
163:1. hate and abhor *l.* but love thy law
Prov 12:19. *l.* tongue but for a moment
Jer 7:4. trust ye not in *l.* words, saying
Hos 4:2. by swearing and *lying* . . . they
Jon 2:8. observe *l.* vanities
LIFE, Gen 2:7, 9; 42:15; 44:30.
Deut 30:15. set before thee . . . *l.* and good
32:47. not a vain thing . . . it is your *l.*
1 Sam 25:29. soul of my Lord shall be bound in the bundle of *l.*
Job 10:12. granted me *l.* and favour
Ps 16:11. shew me the path of *l.*
21:4. asked *l.* of thee and thou gavest
36:9. with thee is the fountain of *l.*
63:3. lovingkindness better than *l.*
66:9. God holdeth our soul in *l.*
91:16. with long *l.* will I satisfy
Prov 8:35. whoso findeth me findeth *l.*
15:24. way of *l.* is above to the wise
18:21. death and *l.* in power of tongue
Isa 57:10. hast found *l.* of thy hand
Matt 6:25. take no thought for your *l.*
John 1:4. in him was *l.* and *l.* was light of
3:36. believeth on Son hath everlasting *l.*
5:40. not come to me, that ye might have *l.*
6:35. I am the bread of *l.* 48. everlasting *l.*, 40, 47.
51. my flesh I give for *l.* of world
63. words I speak unto you are spirit and *l.*
8:12. he that followeth me . . . shall have light of *l.*
10:10. I am come that they might have *l.*

11:25. I am the resurrection and the *l.*
John 14:6. I am the way, the truth, and the *l.*
Rom 5:17. reign in *l.* by Jesus Christ, 21.
8:2. law of Spirit of *l.* in Christ Jesus hath
6. to be spiritually minded is *l.* and
2 Cor 2:16. the savour of *l.* unto *l.*
3:6. letter killeth, spirit giveth *l.*
4:11. *l.* of Jesus might be manifest
5:4. mortality swallowed up of *l.*
Gal 2:20. the *l.* I now live in flesh
Eph 4:18. alienated from *l.* of God
Col 3:3. your *l.* is hid with Christ
4. when Christ our *l.* shall appear
1 Tim 2:2. a peaceable *l.* in all godliness
4:8. having promise of the *l.* that
2 Tim 1:10. brought *l.* and immortality to light
2 Pet 1:3. that pertain to *l.* and
1 John 5:12. that hath Son hath *l.* . . . that hath not Son hath not *l.*
Job 2:4. all man hath will he give for *his life*
Matt 10:39. findeth—shall lose it, and loseth—for my sake shall find
20:28. Son of man came . . . to give—a ransom for many
Rom 5:10. being reconciled shall be saved by—1 Kings 19:3, Elijah went for—
4. O Lord, take away *my life,* 14.
Ps 26:9. gather not . . .—with bloody men
27:1. *l.* the Lord is the strength of—
Jon 2:6. brought up—from corruption
John 10:15. I lay down—for sheep, 13:37.
Acts 20:24. neither count I—dear
Ps 17:14. *this life,* Luke 8:14; 21:34. Acts 5:20. 1 Cor 6:3; 15:19.
Prov 4:10. hear . . . and the years of *thy life*
Jer 39:18. —shall be for a prey, 45:5.
Prov 10:16. tendeth *(un) to life,* 11:19; 19:23. Matt 7:14. John 5:24. Acts 11:18. Rom 7:10. Heb 11:35. 1 John 3:14.
LIFT *up* his countenance upon thee, Num 6:26.
Ps 4:6. Lord—light of countenance
7:6. Lord—thyself because of rage
24:7. —ye gates,—ye doors, and
25:1. to thee I—my soul, 86:4.
75:4. —not the horn, 5.
121:1. —mine eyes, 123:1.
Eccles 4:10. one will—his fellow
Isa 33:10. I will be exalted . . . I *lift up* myself
42:2. he shall not cry, nor—. . . voice
Jer 7:16. neither—cry nor prayer, 11:14.
Lam 3:41. let us—our hearts with
Heb 12:12. —hands . . . and feeble knees
James 4:10. Lord . . . shall *l.* you up
2 Chron 17:6. heart *lifted up* in ways of the Lord
83:2. they that hate thee—the head
102:10. thou hast—and cast me down
Isa 26:11. Lord, when thy hand is—
Hab 2:4. his soul which is—is not upright
John 3:14. so must Son of man be—
8:28. when ye have—Son of man
12:32. if I be—will draw all men, 34.
Ps 3:3. my glory and *lifter up* of
Prov 2:3. *liftest up* voice for understanding
Ps 141:2. *lifting up* of hands, 1 Tim 2:8.
LIGHT, Num 21:5. Deut 27:16. Judg 9:4. 1 Kings 16:31. Ezek 8:17; 22:7.
Isa 49:6. it is a *l.* thing thou shouldest be my servant
Zeph 3:4. her prophets *l.* and
Matt 11:30. my yoke easy, my burden *l.*
2 Cor 4:17. our *l.* affliction which is but for a moment
Ps 62:9. they are altogether *lighter* than vanity
Jer 3:9. *lightness* of whoredom, 23:32.
LIGHT, Gen 1:3, 4, 5, 16; 44:3.
Job 18:5. *l.* of the wicked put out
25:3. on whom doth not his *l.* arise
33:30. enlightened with *l.* of living
Ps 4:6. life up *l.* of thy countenance
36:9. in thy *l.* shall we see *l.*
43:3. O send out thy *l.* and thy truth
90:8. our secret sins in *l.* of thy countenance
97:11. *l.* is sown for the righteous
104:2. coverest thyself with *l.* as a
112:4. to the upright ariseth *l.* in
119:105. thy word is . . . *l.* to my path
Prov 4:18. path of the just is as shining *l.*
6:23. law is *l.* and reproofs . . . are way
15:30. *l.* of the eyes rejoiceth the
Eccles 11:7. *l.* is sweet and a pleasant
Isa 5:20. darkness for *l.* and *l.* for
30. the l. is darkened, Job 10:22.
8:20. because there is no *l.* in them
9:2. walked . . . have seen a great *l.*
Isa 30:26. *l.* of moon as *l.* of sun, *l.* of
42:6. keep thee, and give thee for a *l.*
45:7. I form *l.* and create darkness
50:10. walketh in darkness and hath no *l.*
58:8. thy *l.* break forth as morning
60:1. shine; for thy *l.* is come, 19, 20.
Zech 14:6. *l.* shall not be clear nor
7. evening time it shall be *l.*
Matt 5:14. ye are the *l.* of the world
16. let your *l.* so shine before men
Luke 2:32. *l.* to lighten Gentiles
16:8. children of world wiser than the children of *l.*
John 1:4. the life was the *l.* of men
7. (John) came to bear witness of *l.*, 8.
9. true *l.* that lighteth every man
3:19. loved darkness rather than *l.*
20. cometh not to *l.* 21. cometh to *l.*
5:35. (John) a burning and a shining *l.*
8:12. I am the *l.* of the world; he that followeth me . . . shall have *l.* of life
12:35, 36. walk while ye have the *l.*
Acts 13:47. I have set thee for a *l.*
26:18. turn them from darkness to *l.*
Rom 13:12. put on the armour of *l.*
2 Cor 4:4. lest *l.* of . . . Gospel . . . should shine
6:14. what communion hath *l.* with darkness
Eph 5:8. walk as children of *l.*
14. awake . . . Christ shall give thee *l.*
1 Thess 5:5. ye are the children of *light*
1 Pet 2:9. called . . . to his marvellous *l.*
1 John 1:5. God is *l.* and in him is
Rev 21:23. Lamb is *l.* thereof, 11.
Ps 136:7. *lights,* Ezek 32:8. Luke 12:35. Phil 2:15. James 1:17.
2 Sam 22:29. *lighten,* Ezra 9:8. Ps 13:3; 34:5. Rev 21:23.
Exod 19:16. *lightning,* Ps 18:14. Matt 28:3; 24:27. Luke 10:18.
LIKE men, quit you, 1 Cor 16:13.
Heb 2:17. be made *l.* his brethren
1 John 3:2. we shall be *l.* him
Gen 1:26. after our *likeness*
5:3. Adam . . . begat a son in his own *l.*
Ps 17:15. satisfied when I awake with thy *l.*
Rom 6:5. *l.* of his death . . . *l.* of resurrection
8:3. in *l.* of sinful flesh, Phil 2:7.
LILY, Song of Sol 2:1, 2, 16; 4:5; 5:13; 6:2, 3; 7:2. Hos 14:5. Matt 6:28.
LINE upon *l.*, *l.* upon *l.* Isa 28:10, 13.

Isa 28:17. judgment will I lay to *l.*
34:11. stretch out on it *l.* of confusion
2 Cor 10:16. not to boast in another man's *l.* of things
Ps 16:6. *lines* are fallen unto me
LINGER, Gen 19:16. 2 Pet 2:3.
LION, Gen 49:9. Judg 14:5, 18. Job 4:10, 11; 10:16; 28:8. Ps 7:2; 10:9; 17:12; 22:13. Isa 38:13.
Prov 22:13. there is a *l.* without, 26:13.
28:1. righteous are bold as a *l.*
Isa 11:6. calf and young *l.*, 7; 65:25.
35:9. no *l.* shall be there, nor
Ezek 1:10. face of a *l.* 10:14. Rev 4:7.
Hos 5:14. be as young *l.*, Lam 3:10.
2 Tim 4:17. out of mouth of the *l.*
1 Pet 5:8. the devil as a roaring *l.*
Rev 5:5. *L.* of the tribe of Juda
LIPS, Exod 6:12, 30. Prov 16:10.
Ps 12:3. cut off all flattering *l.*
4. our *l.* are our own
17:1, not feigned *l.* 31:18, lying *l.*, 120:2. Prov 10:18; 12:22; 17:4, 7. Isa 59:3.
63:5. praise thee with joyful *l.*
Prov 10:21. *l.* of the righteous feed
26:23. burning *l.* and wicked heart
Song of Sol 7:9. *l.* of those that are asleep to speak
Isa 6:5. man of unclean *l.* . . . people of unclean *l.*
57:19. I create the fruit of the *l.*
Mal 2:7. priest's *l.* should keep knowledge
Ps 51:15. open thou *my lips*
63:3. —shall praise thee, 71:23.
141:3. keep the door of—
17:4. *thy lips,* 34:13; 45:2.
LITTLE, Ezra 9:8. Neh 9:32.
Ps 2:12. when his wrath is kindled but a *l.*
8:5. a *l.* lower than the angels, Heb 2:7.
37:16. a *l.* that a righteous man hath
Prov 6:10. *l.* sleep, *l.* slumber, 24:33.
15:16. better is *l.* with fear, 16:8.
Isa 28:10. here a *l.* and there a *l.*, 13.
54:8. in a *l.* wrath I hid my face
Ezek 11:16. will I be to them as a *l.* sanctuary
Matt 6:30. O ye of *l.* faith, 8:26; 14:31; 16:8.
Luke 12:32. fear not, *l.* flock, *it* is
19:17. been faithful in a very *l.*
1 Tim 4:8. bodily exercise profiteth *l.*
Rev 3:8. hast *l.* strength, and kept
LIVE, Gen 3:22; 17:18.
Lev 18:5. if a man do, he shall *l.*, Neh 9:29. Ezek 3:21; 18:9; 33:13, 15, 16, 19. Rom 10:5. Gal 3:12.
Deut 32:40. *live(th) for ever,* 1 Kings 1:31. Neh 2:3. Ps 22:26; 49:9. Dan 2:4; 3:9; 5:10; 6:21. Zech 1:5. John 6:51, 58. Rev 4:9; 5:14; 10:6; 15:7.
Job 14:14. if a man die, shall he *live*
Ps 55:23. bloody . . . men shall not *l.* out half
63:4. bless thee while I *l.*, 146:2.
118:17. I shall not die, but *l.* and
Isa 38:16. men *l.* . . . make me to *l.*
55:3. hear, and your soul shall *l.*
Ezek 16:6. I said, when thou wast in thy blood, *L.*; yea, I said unto thee . . ., *L.*
18:32. turn yourselves and *l.*, 33:11.
Hab 2:4. just *l.* by faith, Rom 1:17, &c.
Matt 4:4. man shall not *l.* by bread alone but by every word, Deut 8:3.
John 14:19. because I *l.* ye shall *l.*
Acts 17:28. in him we *l.* and move
Rom 8:13. if ye *l.* after the flesh, ye
14:8. whether we *l.*, we *l.* unto Lord
1 Cor 9:14. they which preach the Gospel *l.* of
2 Cor 5:15. which *l.* should not *l.* to themselves
6:9. as dying, and behold we *l.*
13:11. be of one mind, *l.* in peace
Gal 2:20. life I *l.* I *l.* by faith of Son of God
5:25. if we *l.* in Spirit, walk in
Phil 1:21. to *l.* is Christ, 22.
2 Tim 3:12. all that will *l.* godly in
Titus 2:12. we should *l.* soberly, righteously
Heb 13:18. willing to *l.* honestly
1 Pet 2:24. should *l.* to righteousness
1 John 4:9. that we might *l.* through
Acts 23:1. *lived* in all good conscience
James 5:5. ye have *l.* in pleasure
Rev 18:9. *l.* deliciously, Luke 7:25.
Job 19:25. my Redeemer *liveth*
Rom 6:10. in that he *l.*, he *l.* unto God
1 Tim 5:6. *l.* in pleasure dead while she *l.*
Heb 7:25. he ever *l.* to make intercession
Rev 1:18. he that *l.* and was dead
Acts 7:38. received *lively* oracles
1 Pet 1:3. begotten again to a *l.* hope
2:5. ye, as *l.* stones, are built up a
1 John 3:16. *lives,* Rev 12:11.
Eccles 7:2. *living* will lay it to heart
Isa 38:19. the *l.*, the *l.* shall praise
Jer 2:13. (Lord) fountain of *l.* waters
Matt 22:32. not God of dead, but of *l.*
John 7:38. flow rivers of *l.* water
Rom 12:1. your bodies a *l.* sacrifice
14:9. Lord both of dead and *l.*
1 Cor 15:45. first man Adam made a *l.* soul
Heb 10:20. by a new and *l.* way
1 Pet 2:4. coming as to a *l.* stone
Rev 7:17. lead them to *l.* fountains
LOAD, Ps 68:19. Isa 46:1.
LO(A)THE themselves for evil, Ezek 6:9; 16:5; 20:43; 36:31.
Num 21:5. soul *loatheth,* Prov 27:7.
Ps 38:7. *loathsome* disease
LOFTY eyes, Ps 131:1. Prov 30:13.
Isa 2:11. *l.* looks humbled, 5:15.
57:15. *l.* One that inhabiteth
LOINS girt, Prov 31:17. Isa 11:5. Luke 12:35. Eph 6:14. 1 Pet 1:13.
LONG, Ps 91:16. Eccles 12:5. Matt 23:14. Luke 18:7. James 5:7.
Exod 34:6. Lord God, *longsuffering,* Num 14:18. Ps 86:15. Jer 15:15. Rom 2:4; 9:22. 1 Tim 1:16. 1 Pet 3:20. 2 Pet 3:9, 15.
Gal 5:22. fruit of Spirit is . . . *l.*, Eph 4:2. Col 1:11; 3:12. 2 Tim 3:10; 4:2.
LONG Job 3:21; 6:8. Rom 1:11.
Ps 119:40. *I have longed* after thy precepts
131. —for thy commandments
174. —for thy salvation
Ps 63:1. my flesh *longeth* for thee
84:2. my soul *l.* . . . for courts of Lord
107:9. he satisfieth the *longing* soul
119:20. my soul breaketh for the *l.*
LOOK, Gen 13:14. Exod 10:10.
Isa 8:17. wait upon Lord . . . and I will *l.*
45:22. *l.* unto me and be saved
66:2. to this man will I *l.*
Mic 7:7. I will *l.* unto the Lord
Luke 7:19. do we *l.* for another, 20.
2 Cor 4:18. we *l.* not at things seen
Phil 2:4. *l.* not every man on his own
3:20. heaven, from whence also we *l.* for
Heb 9:28. to them that *l.* for him
1 Pet 1:12. angels desire to *l.* into
Gen 29:32. the Lord *looked* on my affliction, Exod 2:25; 3:7; 4:31. Deut 26:7.
Ps 34:5. they *l.* to him and were lightened
Song of Sol 1:6. *l.* not upon me, because I am black, because the sun hath *l.* upon me
Isa 5:7. he *l.* for judgment
22:11. ye have not *l.* to the maker of
64:3. didst terrible things we *l.* not for
Jer 8:15. we *l.* for peace, but, 14:19.
Hag 1:9. ye *l.* for much, and it
Luke 2:38. *l.* for redemption in Israel
22:61. the Lord *l.* on Peter

Heb 11:10. *l.* for a city . . . builder . . . is God
1 John 1:1. that which we have *l.* on
1 Sam 16:7. man *looketh* on outward appearance, but Lord *l.* on the heart
Ps 33:13. the Lord *l.* from heaven, 14:2.
Prov 14:15. prudent man *l.* well to his goings, 31:27.
Song of Sol 2:9. *l.* forth at the windows, 6:10.
Matt 5:28. *l.* on a woman to lust
24:50. come in a day he *l.* not for
James 1:25. *l.* into perfect law of
Isa 38:14. mine eyes fail with *looking* upward
Luke 9:62. no man . . . *l.* back is fit for kingdom of God
Titus 2:13. *l.* for that blessed hope
Heb 10:27. a certain fearful *l.* for
12:2. *l.* to Jesus, the author and
2 Pet 3:12. *l.* for . . . day of God
Jude 21. *l.* for the mercy of our Lord
Ps 18:27. wilt bring down high *looks*

LOOSE, Deut 25:9. Josh 5:15.
Ps 102:20. to *l.* those appointed to death
Eccles 12:6. or ever the silver cord be *loosed*
Acts 2:24. *l.* pains of death
1 Cor 7:27. bound to a wife? seek not to be *l.* Art thou *l.* . . . ? seek not a wife
Ps 146:7. the Lord *looseth* the prisoners

LORD, ascribed to God, Gen 28:16. Exod 5:2. 1 Cor 12:5; in about 300 other texts; and to man, Gen 18:12; 23:11. Isa 26:13. 1 Cor 8:5. 1 Pet 5:3, and in about 14 other places.
Exod 34:6. *L.*, the *L.* God, merciful
Deut 4:35. *L.* is God, 39. 1 Kings 18:39.
6:4. *L.* our God is one *L.*, 10.
10:17. *L.* of *l.*, Dan 2:47. 1 Tim 6:15. Rev 17:14; 19:16.
Neh 9:6. art *L.* alone, Isa 37:20.
Ps 118:27. God is the *L.*, 100:3.
Mark 2:28. Son of man is *L.* of sabbath
Acts 2:36. made . . . Jesus . . . *L.* and Christ
Rom 10:12. for the same *L.* over all is rich unto all, Acts 10:36.
14:9. *L.* of the dead and of the living
1 Cor 2:8. *L.* of glory
8:6. one God, one *L.* Jesus Christ
15:47. *L.* from heaven
Eph 4:5. one *L.*, one faith, one baptism
Gen 15:6. he believed *in the Lord*
1 Sam 2:1. heart rejoiced—Ps 32:11; 33:1; 35:9; 97:12; 104:34. Isa 41:*16; 61:10. Joel 2:23. Hab 3:18.* Zech 10:7. Phil 3:1; 4:4.
2 Kings 18:5. trust—Ps 4:5; 11:1; 31:6; 32:10; 37:3; 115:9, 10, 11; 118:8; 125:1. Prov 3:5; 16:20; 28:25; 29:25. Isa 26:4.
Zeph 3:2. she trusted not—
Ps 31:24. hope—130:7; 131:3.
34:2. soul make her boast—
37:4. delight thyself—7. rest—
Isa 45:17. Israel shall be saved—
24.—have I righteousness
45:25.—all seed of Israel be justified
Rom 16:12. labour—1 Cor 15:58.
1 Thess 5:12. over you—Col 4:7, 17.
Rev 14:13. blessed are dead which die—

LOSE, Eccles 3:6. Prov 23:8. Matt 10:39, 42; 16:26. John 6:39. 2 John 8.
Luke 15:4. having an hundred sheep, if he *l.* one
1 Cor 3:15. *loss,* Phil 3:7, 8.
Ps 119:176. astray like *lost* sheep
Ezek 37:11. our hope is *l.*, we are cut
Matt 5:13. if salt have *l.* his savour
10:6. to the *l.* sheep of . . . Israel, 15:24.
18:11. save that which was *l.*, Luke 19:10.
Luke 15:32. thy brother was *l.* and is found
2 Cor 4:3. gospel be hid, hid to them that are *l.*

LOT, Lev 16:8, 9, 10. Josh 15:1.
1 Sam 14:41. perfect *l.*, 42.
Ps 16:5. thou maintainest my *l.*
125:3. rod of wicked not rest on *l.* of righteous
Prov 16:33. the *l.* is cast into lap
18:18. *l.* causeth contentions to cease
Acts 1:26. the *l.* fell on Matthias
Ps 22:18. cast *lots* upon my vesture, Matt 27:35. Mark 15:24.

LOVE, Gen 27:4. 2 Sam 13:15.
2 Sam 1:26. passing the *l.* of women
Eccles 9:1. no man knoweth either *l.*
Song of Sol 2:5. I am sick of *l.*, 5:8.
8:6. *l.* is strong as death
Jer 2:2. remember the *l.* of thine espousals
31:3. loved thee with everlasting *l.*
Ezek 16:8. thy time was time of *l.*
33:31. their mouth they shew much *l.*
Matt 24:12. *l.* of many shall wax cold
John 15:9. continue ye in my *l.*, 10.
13. greater *l.* hath no man than this
Rom 8:35. who shall separate us from the *l.* of Christ, 39.
12:9. let *l.* be without dissimulation
13:10. *l.* is the fulfilling of the law
15:30. Christ's sake, and *l.* of Spirit
2 Cor 5:14. *l.* of Christ constraineth
Gal 5:6. faith which worketh by *l.*
13. by *l.* serve one another
22. fruit of the Spirit is *l.*, joy, peace
1 Thess 1:3. your labour of *l.*, Heb 6:10.
5:8. breastplate of faith and *l.*
2 Thess 2:10. received not *l.* of truth
Heb 13:1. let brotherly *l.* continue
1 John 3:1. what manner of *l.* Father bestowed on us
4:7. *l.* is of God. 8, 16, God is *l.*
4:9. manifested the *l.* of God
18. there is no fear in *l.* . . perfect *l.*
21. who loveth God *l.* his brother
Rev 2:4. thou hast left thy first *l.*
Song of Sol 7:12. there I will give thee my *loves*
Eph 1:4. without blame before him *in love*
3:17. grounded—4:2. forbearing one another—
Eph 4:15. speaking truth *in love,* 16.
5:2. walk—as Christ hath loved
Col 2:2. knit together—and
1 Thess 3:12. abound—
5:13. esteem very highly—
Luke 11:42. *love of God,* John 5:42.
Rom 5:5.—is shed abroad in our
2 Cor 13:14.— . . . be with you all
2 Thess 3:5. direct your hearts into—
1 John 2:5. in him is—perfected
3:16. perceive we—
4:9. in this was manifested—towards
5:3. this is the—that we keep his commandments
Deut 7:7. his *love,* Zeph 3:17. Ps 91:14. Isa 63:9. John 15:10. Rom 5:8.
Lev 19:18. thou shalt *l.* thy neighbour as thyself, 34. Matt 19:19; 22:39. Rom 13:8. Gal 5:14. James 2:8.
Deut 6:5. shalt *l.* Lord thy God with all thy heart, Matt 22:37. Mark 12:30. Luke 10:27.
Deut 10:12. to fear the Lord . . . and to *l.*
Ps 31:23. *l.* Lord, all ye his saints
145:20. Lord preserveth them that *l.* him
Song of Sol 1:4. the upright *l.* thee
Zech 8:19. *l.* the truth and peace
Matt 5:44. *l.* your enemies, bless
John 13:34. *l.* one another, 15:12, 17. Rom 13:8. 1 John 3:11, 23; 4:7, 11, 12. 1 Pet 1:22.
14:23. if a man *l.* me . . . my Father will *l.* him
1 Cor 16:22. if any man *l.* not Lord
Eph 5:25. *l.* your wives, Col 3:19.
2 Tim 4:8. all . . . that *l.* his appearing
1 Pet 1:8. having not seen, ye *l.*
2:17. *l.* brotherhood, 3:8.
1 John 2:15. *l.* not world . . . if any *l.* world, *l.* of Father not in him
4:19. we *l.* him because he first loved us, 7–12, 16.

Ps 116:1. *I love* Lord because, 18:1.
119:97. how—thy law, 113, 119, 127, 159, 163, 167; 26:8.
2 John 1. whom—in the truth, and
Rev 3:19. as many as—I rebuke
Deut 7:8. because the Lord *loved* you, 33:3.
1 Sam 18:1. *l.* (David) as his own soul, 20:17.
2 Sam12:24. and he called his name Solomon: and the Lord *l.* him.
1 Kings 3:3. Solomon *l.* the Lord
10:9. the Lord *l.* Israel
Hos 11:1. Israel was a child, then I *l.* him
Mark 10:21. Jesus beholding him, *l.* him
Luke 7:47. sins forgiven, she *l.* much
2 Tim 4:10. *l.* this present world
Heb 1:9. hast *l.* righteousness and
John 3:16. God so *l.* the world that
19. men *l.* darkness rather than
12:43. *l.* the praise of men more
13:1. having *l.* his own . . . he *l.* them
23. one of his disciples whom Jesus *l.*, 19:26; 20:2; 21:7, 20.
14:28. if ye *l.* me, ye would rejoice
15:9. as my Father *l.* me, so have I *l.*
16:27. Father loveth you because ye *l.* me
17:23. hast *l.* them as thou hast *l.* me
26. wherewith thou hast *l.* me
Rom 8:37. conquerors through him that *l.* us
9:13. Jacob I *l.*, Esau I hated, Mal 1:2.
Gal 2:20. Son of God, who *l.* me
Eph 2:4. great love wherewith he *l.* us
5:2. walk in love, as Christ *l.* us
25. love wives as Christ *l.* church
2 Thess 2:16. God, even our Father . . . *l.* us
2 Pet 2:15. *l.* wages of unrighteousness
1 John 4:10. not that we *loved* God, but he *l.* us
Rev 1:5. unto him that *l.* us and washed us from our sins in his own blood
12:11. *l.* not their lives unto death
Ps 146:8. the Lord *loveth* the righteous
Prov 3:12. whom the Lord *l.* he correcteth, Heb 12:6.
17:17. a friend *l.* at all times
21:17. he that *l.* pleasure shall be poor
Song of Sol 1:7. whom my soul *l.*, 3:1, 4.
Matt 10:37. *l.* father or mother more
John 3:35. Father *l.* the Son, 5:20.
2 Cor 9:7. God *l.* a cheerful giver
3 John 9. *l.* to have preeminence
Rev 22:15. whosoever *l.* and maketh a lie

2 Sam 1:23. *lovely,* Song of Sol 5:16. Ezek 33:32. Phil 4:8.
Ps 88:18. *lover,* Titus 1:8. Ps 38:11. Hos 2:5. 2 Tim 3:2, 4.
LOW, Deut 28:43. Ezek 17:24.
Job 40:12. look on every one that is proud and bring him *l.*
Ps 49:2. both *l.* and high, rich and
136:23. remembered us in our *l.* estate
Prov 29:23. man's pride shall bring him *l.*
Isa 26:5. the lofty city, he layeth it *l.*, 25:12.
32:19. city shall be *l.* in a *l.* place
Luke 1:48. he hath regarded the *l.* estate
52. exalted them of *l.* degree, Job 5:11. Ezek 21:26. James 1:9, 10.
3:5. every mountain and hill shall be brought *l.*
Ps 63:9. *lower* parts of the earth, 139:15. Isa 44:23. Eph 4:9.
Eph 4:2. *lowliness,* Phil 2:3.
138:6. yet hath he respect to *lowly*
Prov 3:34. he giveth grace unto *l.*
11:2. with *l.* is wisdom
Matt 11:29. learn of me, I am meek and *l.*
LUCRE, filthy, 1 Tim 3:3, 8. Titus 1:7. 1 Pet 5:2.
LUKEWARM, thou art, Rev 3:16.
LUMP, Isa 38:21. Rom 9:21; 11:16. 1 Cor 5:6, 7. Gal 5:9.
LUST, Exod 15:9. Ps 78:18. James 4:2.
Ps 81:12. up to their own hearts' *l.*
Matt 5:28. looketh on woman to *l.*
Rom 7:7. I had not known *l.* except the law
1 Cor 10:6. not *l.* after evil things
Gal 5:16. shall not fulfil *l.* of flesh
1 Thess 4:5. not in the *l.* of concupiscence
1 John 2:16. *l.* of the flesh, and *l.* of
Gal 5:17. flesh *lusteth* against Spirit
Mark 4:19. *lusts* of other things
John 8:44. *l.* of your father ye will do
Rom 6:12. should obey it in the *l.*
13:14. for the flesh, to fulfil the *l.*
24. crucified flesh with affections and *l.*
1 Tim 6:9. foolish and hurtful *l.*
2 Tim 2:22. flee youthful *l.*: but follow
3:6. laden with sins, led away with divers *l.*
Titus 2:12. denying ungodliness and worldly *l.*
3:3. divers *l.* and pleasures
James 4:3. consume it on your *l.*
1 Pet 2:11. abstain from fleshly *l.*
4:2. no longer live to the *l.* of men
2 Pet 3:3. walking after own *l.*, Jude 16, 18.

M

MAD, Deut 28:34. 1 Sam 21:13.
Jer 50:38. they are *m.* upon idols
Hos 9:7. prophet is a fool, spiritual man is *m.*
John 10:20. he hath a devil and is *m.*
Acts 26:11. exceedingly *mad* against
24. much learning doth make thee *m.*
Deut 28:28. *madness,* Eccles 1:17; 2:12; 9:3; 10:13. Zech 12:4. Luke 6:11. 2 Pet 2:16.
MADE, Exod 2:14. 2 Sam 13:6.
Ps 104:24. in wisdom hast thou *m.* them all
139:14. I am . . . wonderfully *m.*
Prov 16:4. Lord *m.* all things for
John 1:3. all things were *m.* by him
Rom 1:3. Christ, *m.* of the seed of David
20. being understood by things that are *m.*
1 Cor 1:30. Christ . . . who of God is *m.* unto us
9:22. *m.* all things to all men
Gal 4:4. *m.* of a woman, *m.* under law
Phil 2:7. *m.* in the likeness of men
MAGNIFY, Josh 3:7. 1 Chron 29:25.
Job 7:17. man, that thou shouldest *m.*
Ps 34:3. *m.* the Lord with me
69:30. *m.* him with thanksgiving
Isa 42:21. *m.* the law, and make it
Luke 1:46. my soul doth *m.* Lord
Acts 10:46. spake with tongues, *m.* God
Gen 19:19. *magnified* thy mercy
2 Sam 7:26. let thy name be *m.* for
Ps 35:27. let Lord be *m.*, 40:16; 70:4.
138:2. hast *m.* thy word above
Acts 19:17. name of Lord Jesus was *m.*
Phil 1:20. Christ be *m.* in my body
MAID, Gen 16:2. Deut 22:14. Job 31:1. Jer 2:32. Amos 2:7. Zech 9:17.
MAJESTY, Dan 4:30, 36; 5:18, 19. Job 40:10. Ps 21:5; 45:3, 4.
1 Chron 29:11. thine, O Lord, is . . . *m.*
Ps 29:4. voice of Lord is full of *m.*
93:1. (Lord) is clothed with *m.*, 104:1.
145:5. honour of thy *m.*
12. glorious *m.* of his kingdom
Isa 2:10. for glory of his *m.*, 19, 21.
Heb 1:3. right hand of *M.* on high
8:1. throne of *M.* in heavens
2 Pet 1:16. eyewitnesses of his *m.*
Jude 25. to only wise God . . . be glory and *m.*
MAINTAIN my cause, 1 Kings 8:45. Ps 9:4; 140:12. Job 13:15.
Titus 3:8. careful to *m.* good works, 14.
Ps 16:5. thou *maintainest* my lot

MAKE, Gen 1:26; 3:6, 21. Deut 32:35. 1 Cor 4:5. 1 Sam 20:38.
Job 4:17. more pure than *maker*?
32:22. my *m.* would soon take me
35:10. where is God my *m.*
36:3. ascribe righteousness to my *m.*
Prov 14:31. reproacheth his *m.*, 17:5.
22:2. Lord is the *m.* of them all
Isa 17:7. day shall man look to his *m.*
22:11. ye have not looked to *m.* thereof
45:9. woe to him striveth with *m.*
51:13. forgettest the Lord thy *m.*
54:5. thy *m.* is thy husband; the
Heb 11:10. builder and *m.* is God
MALE and female, Gen 1:27. Num 5:3. Mal 1:14. Matt 19:4. Gal 3:28.
MALICE, leaven of, 1 Cor 5:8.
1 Cor 14:20. in *m.* be children, but in
Eph 4:31. put away . . . with all *m.* Col 3:8. 1 Pet 2:1.
Titus 3:3. living in *m.* and envy
MAMMON, Matt 6:24. Luke 16:9.
MAN, Gen 1:26, 27. 2 Kings 9:11.
Job 4:17. shall . . . *m.* be more just than God?
7:17. what is *m.* thou shouldest be mindful of him
11:12. vain *m.* would be wise
14:1. *m.* born of woman is of few days
Job 15:14. What is *man,* that he should be clean?
25:4. How can *m.* be justified with God?
6. much less *m.* that is a worm
Ps 8:4. what is *m.* that thou art mindful
10:18. *m.* of earth may no more oppress
25:12. what *m.* is he that feareth Lord
49:12. *m.* being in honour abideth not
90:3. thou turnest *m.* to destruction
104:23. *m.* goeth forth to his work
118:6. not fear; what can *m.* do
144:3. what is *m.* that thou takest knowledge of him; or son of *m.*
Prov 20:24. *m.'s* goings are of Lord
Eccles 6:10. it is known that it is *m.*
7:29. God made *m.* upright, but
12:5. *m.* goeth to his long home
Isa 2:22. cease ye from *m.* whose
Zech 13:7. awake against the *m.* that
Matt 4:4. *m.* shall not live by bread
26:72. I know not the m., 74.
John 7:46. never *m.* spake like this *m.*
Rom 6:6. old *m.* crucified with him
7:22. delight in law of God after inward *m.*
1 Cor 2:11. what *m.* knoweth the things of a *m.* save the spirit of *m.*
14. natural *m.* receiveth not things
11:8. *m.* not of woman, but woman of *m.*
15:47. first *m.* is of the earth earthy; second *m.*
2 Cor 4:16. though outward *m.* perish, yet inward *m.* is renewed
Eph 4:22. put off . . . the old *m.* which
24. put on new *m.*, Col 3:9, 10.
1 Pet 3:4. be the hidden *m.* of heart
Exod 15:3. Lord is *a man* of war
Num 23:19. God is not—that he
Isa 47:3. I will not meet thee as—
53:3. —of sorrows and acquainted
Jer 15:10. borne me—of strife and
31:22. a woman shall compass—
Matt 8:9. I am—under authority
16:26. what shall—give in exchange
John 3:3. except—be born again, 5.
Acts 10:26. I myself also am—
2 Cor 12:2. I knew—in Christ, 3.
Phil 2:8. in fashion as—he humbled
Matt 16:24. *if any man,* John 6:51; 7:17, 37. Rom 8:9. 2 Cor 5:17. Gal 1:9. Rev 22:19.
Ps 39:5. *every man,* Prov 19:6. Mic 4:4; 7:2. Gal 6:4. Col 1:28. Heb 2:9.
87:4. *this man,* Isa 66:2. Mic 5:5. Luke 19:14. John 7:46. James 1:26.
Prov 1:5. *a wise man* will hear
9:8. rebuke—and he will love thee
14:16.—feareth and departeth
Eccles 2:14.—eyes are in his head
10:2.—heart is at his right hand
Jer 9:23. let not—glory in wisdom
James 3:13. who is—and endued with
Deut 33:1. *man of God,* Judg 13:6, 8. 2 Kings 1:9, 13. 1 Tim 6:11. 2 Tim 3:17.
MANDRAKES, Gen 30:14. Song of Sol 7:13.
MANIFEST, Eccles 3:18. 1 Cor 15:27.
John 14:21. *m.* myself to him, 22.
1 Cor 4:5. make *m.* counsels of hearts
Gal 5:19. works of the flesh are *m.*
1 Tim 3:16. God was *m.* in the flesh
1 John 3:10. in this children of God are *m.*
Mark 4:22. nothing hid . . . not be *manifested*
John 2:11. *m.* forth his glory, and his
17:6. I have *m.* thy name unto men
1 John 3:5. was *m.* to take away sin, 8.
4:9. in this was *m.* the love of God
Luke 8:17. *made manifest,* John 3:21. 1 Cor 3:13. 2 Cor 4:10; 5:11. Eph 5:13.
Rom 8:19. *manifestations* of sons of God
1 Cor 12:7. *m.* of the Spirit is given
MANIFOLD mercies, Neh 9:19, 27.
Ps 104:24. how *m.* are thy works
Amos 5:12. I know your *m.* transgressions
Luke 18:30. *m.* more in this present
Eph 3:10. known by the church *m.* wisdom of God
1 Pet 1:6. in heaviness through *m.* temptations
4:10. as good stewards of *m.* grace of God
MANNA, Exod 16:15. Num 11:6. Deut 8:3, 16. Josh 5:12. Neh 9:20. Ps 78:24. John 6:31, 49, 58.
Rev 2:17. give to eat of hidden *m.*
MANNER, 1 Sam 8:9, 11. Isa 5:17. Jer 22:21. 1 Thess 1:5, 9. 1 John 3:1. *manners,* 2 Kings 17:34. Acts 13:18. 1 Cor 15:33. Lev 20:23. Heb 1:1.
MANSIONS in my Father's house, John 14:2.
MARK, set me as a, Job 7:20; 16:12. Lam 3:12.
Ezek 9:4. set *m.* on the foreheads, Rev 13:16, 17; 14:9; 19:20.
Phil 3:14. I press toward the *m.*
Ps 37:37. *m.* perfect man
130:3. if thou shouldest *m.* iniquity, Job 10:14. Jer 2:22.
Rom 16:17. *m.* them which cause divisions
Gal 6:17. bear in my body *marks*
MARRIAGE, MARRIED, MARRY, Gen 38:8. Deut 25:5.
Matt 22:2. king made a *m.* for his son
25:10. that were ready went into *m.*
John 2:1. there was a *m.* in Cana, 2.
Heb 13:4. *m.* is honourable in all
Rev 19:7. *m.* of Lamb is come, 9.
Jer 3:14. I am *married* to you, saith Lord
Luke 14:20. I have *m.* a wife, and
Isa 62:5. as a young man *marrieth* a virgin
1 Cor 7:9. better to *marry* than to burn
1 Tim 4:3. forbidding to *m.* and
5:14. that younger women *m.* and
MARROW, to bones, Prov 3:8.
Job 21:24. bones moistened with *m.*
Ps 63:5. soul is satisfied as with *m.*
Isa 25:6. feast of fat things full of *m.*
Heb 4:12. dividing . . . joints and *m.*
MARTYR, Acts 22:20. Rev 2:13; 17:6.

Prov 10:7. *m.* of the just is blessed
Eccles 9:5. *m.* of them is forgotten
Isa 26:14. made all their *m.* to perish
1 Cor 15:2. if ye keep in *m.* what I
Exod 3:15. my *memorial* to all generations
13:9. be for *m.* between thine eyes
17:14. write this for a *m.* in book
Hos 12:5. God of hosts; Lord is his *m.*
Matt 26:13. be told for a *m.* of her
Acts 10:4. alms are come up for a *m.* before God

MEN, Gen 32:28; 42:11.
Ps 9:20. know themselves to be but *m.*
17:14. *m.* which are thy hand
82:7. ye shall die like *m.* and fall
Eccles 12:3. strong *m.* shall bow
Isa 31:3. Egyptians are *m.*, not God, Ezek 28:2.
Hos 6:7. they like *m.* have transgressed
Matt 7:12. ye would that *m.* should do to you
Eph 6:6. *m.* pleasers, Col 3:22. 1 Thess 2:4.

MENSTRUOUS, Isa 30:22. Lam 1:17. Ezek 18:6. come near a *m.* woman

MENTION, Exod 23:13. Job 28:18.
Ps 71:16. make *m.* of thy righteousness
Isa 26:13. by thee only will we make *m.* of
62:6. ye that make *m.* of the Lord
Rom 1:9. make *m.* of you in my prayers, Eph 1:16. 1 Thess 1:2. Philem 4.

MERCHANT, Hos 12:7. Matt 13:45.
Isa 23:18. *merchandise* . . . be holiness, Matt 22:5. John 2:16. 2 Pet 2:3.

MERCY, Gen 19:19; 39:21.
Exod 34:7. keep *m.* for thousands, Deut 7:9. 1 Kings 8:23. Neh 1:5; 9:32. Dan 9:4.
Num 14:18. Lord is . . . of great *m.*
Ps 23:6. goodness and *m.* shall follow
25:10. all paths of Lord are *m.* and
33:18. them that hope in his *m.*, 147:11.
52:8. I trust in the *m.* of God
57:3. God shall send forth his *m.*
66:20. not turned away . . . his *m.*
69:13. in multitude of thy *m.*, 16.
86:5. plenteous in *m.* to all, 103:8.
101:1. I will sing of *m.* and
103:17. *m. of the Lord is from everlasting*
106:1. *his m. endureth for ever,* 107:1; 118:1; 136:1–26. 1 Chron 16:34, 41. 2 Chron 5:13; 7:3, 6; 20:21. Ezra 3:11. Jer 33:11.
Prov 16:6. by *m.* and truth iniquity is purged
20:28. *m.* and truth preserve king
Hos 6:6. I desired *m.* and not sacrifice
10:12. reap in *m.* 12:6. keep *m.*
14:3. in thee fatherless findeth *m.*
Jon 2:8. they . . . forsake their own *m.*
Mic 6:8. to do justly, and love *m.*
7:18. because he delighteth in *m.*
20. and the *m.* to Abraham
Luke 1:50. *m.* is on them that fear
78. through tender *m.* of our God
Rom 9:23. on vessels of *m.* prepared
15. *m.* on whom I will have *m.*
11:31. through your *m.* they obtain *m.*
15:9. might glorify God for his *m.*
2 Cor 4:1. as we have received *m.*
1 Tim 1:13. I obtained *m.* because I did it ignorantly, 2. grace, *m.*, and peace, Titus 1:4. 2 John 3. Jude 2.
2 Tim 1:18. that he may find *m.* in
Heb 4:16. we may obtain *m.* and
James 2:13. shall have judgment without *m.* that shewed no *m.*; and *m.* rejoiceth
3:17. full of *m.* and good
5:11. Lord is very pitiful and of tender *m.*
Gen 32:10. not worthy of least of all the *mercies*
1 Chron 21:13. great are his *m.*
Isa 55:3. sure *m.* of David, Acts 13:34.
Dan 9:9. to the Lord our God belong *m.* and
Rom 12:1. I beseech you by *m.* of God
2 Cor 1:3. Father of *m.* and God of
Col 3:12. put on bowels of *m.*
Ps 25:6. *tender mercies,* 40:11; 51:1; 77:9; 79:8; 103:4; 119:77, 156; 145:9.
Prov 12:10. —of wicked are cruel
Gen 19:19. *thy mercy(ies),* Num 14:19. Neh 13:22. Ps 5:7; 6:4; 13:5; 25:7; 31:7, 16; 33:22; 36:5; 44:26; 57:10; 85:7; 86:13; 90:14; 94:18; 108:4; 119:64; 143:12.
Exod 34:6. Lord God *merciful* and gracious, 2 Chron 30:9. Neh 9:17, 31. Ps 103:8. Joel 2:13. Jon 4:2.
Ps 18:25. with *m.* thou wilt shew thyself *m.*
37:26. he is ever *m.* and lendeth
117:2. his *m.* kindness
Isa 57:1. *m.* men are taken away
Jer 3:12. *I am m.,* saith the Lord
Matt 5:7. blessed are the *m.*
Luke 6:36. be . . . *m.*, as your Father also is *m.*
Heb 2:17. a *m.* and faithful high priest
8:12. I will be *m.* to their unrighteousness

MERRY, be, Luke 12:19; 15:23–32.
James 5:13. is any *m.*? let him sing
Isa 24:7. *merryhearted,* Prov 17:22. Eccles 9:7. Prov 15:13.

MESSAGE from God, Judg 3:20. Hag 1:13. 1 John 1:5; 3:11.
Job 33:23. if there be a *messenger*
Isa 42:19. who is blind or deaf, as my *m.*
Mal 2:7. he is the *m.* of the Lord
Isa 14:32. one answer *messengers* of nation
44:26. that performeth counsel of his *m.*

MESSIAH(IAS), Dan 9:25, 26. John 1:41; 4:25.

MIDST, Ps 22:14; 46:5; 110:2. Prov 4:21. Isa 4:4; 41:18. Ezek 43:7, 9. Joel 2:27. Zeph 3:5, 12, 15, 17. Phil 2:15. Rev 1:13; 5:6.
Rev 7:17. Lamb in *m.* of the throne shall feed them

MIGHT, Gen 49:3. Num 14:13.
Deut 6:5. love Lord with all thy . . . *m.*
2 Kings 23:25. turned to Lord with *m.*
2 Chron 20:12. no *m.* against this great company
Ps 76:5. none of men of *m.* found
145:6. men speak of the *m.* of thy terrible acts
Eccles 9:10. findeth to do, do it with thy *m.*
Isa 40:29. to them that have no *m.*
Zech 4:6. not by *m.* . . . but by Spirit
Eph 3:16. strengthened with *m.*
6:10. be strong . . . in power of his *m.*
Col 1:11. strengthened with all *m.*
Deut 7:23. with *mighty* destruction
10:17. a great God, a *m.* and a
Judg 5:23. help of Lord against the *m.*
Ps 24:8. Lord strong and *m.*, . . . *m.* in battle
Isa 5:22. *m.* to drink wine, men of
Jer 32:19. great in counsel, *m.* in work
1 Cor 1:26. not many *m.* are called
2 Cor 10:4. weapons . . . but *m.* through God
Ps 93:4. Lord on high is *mightier*
Acts 18:28. *mightily,* Col 1:29.
19:20. so *m.* grew word of God

MILK, Gen 18:8; 49:12.
Job 10:10. hast poured me out as *m.*
Song of Sol 4:11. and *m.* under thy tongue
5:1. drunk my wine with my *m.*
Isa 55:1. buy wine and *m.* without
Joel 3:18. the hills shall flow with *m.*
Heb 5:12. such as have need of *m.*
1 Pet 2:2. desire sincere *m.* of word

20:24. none of these things *m.* me
Ps 15:5. never be *moved,* 21:7; 46:5; 55:22; 62:2, 6; 66:9; 112:6; 121:3. Prov 12:3.
Col 1:23. be not *m.* away from hope
1 Thess 3:3. no man be *m.* by these
Heb 12:28. kingdom which cannot be *m.*
2 Pet 1:21. spake as . . . *m.* by the Holy Ghost
Rom 7:5. when in flesh, *motions* of sins
MOURN, Neh 8:9. Job 5:11.
Isa 61:2. to comfort all that *m.*
Matt 5:4. blessed are they that *m.*
James 4:9. be afflicted and *m.* and
Matt 11:17. we have *mourned* unto you
1 Cor 5:2. and have not rather *m.*
Eccles 12:5. *mourners* go about streets
Isa 57:18. restore comforts to him and to his *m.*
Ps 30:11. turned . . . my *mourning* to dancing
Isa 61:3. to give . . . the oil of joy for *m.*
Jer 9:17. call for the *m.* women
31:13. I will turn their *m.* into joy
Joel 2:12. with fasting and with weeping and with *m.*
James 4:9. laughter be turned to *m.*
MOUTH of babes and sucklings, Ps 8:2. Matt 21:16.
Ps 37:30. *m.* of righteous speaketh wisdom
Prov 10:14. *m.* of foolish is near destruction
10:31. *m.* of just bringeth forth wisdom
12:6. *m.* of upright shall deliver
14:3. in *m.* of fools is a rod of pride
15:2. *m.* of fools poureth out foolishness
18:7. a fool's *m.* is his destruction
22:14. *m.* of strange women is a pit
Lam 3:38. out of *m.* of the Most High proceedeth not evil and good
Matt 12:34. out of abundance of heart *m.* speaketh
Luke 21:15. will give you a *m.* and
Rom 10:10. with the *m.* confession is made
Lam 3:29. putteth *his mouth* in dust
Mal 2:7. they should seek law at—
Ps 17:3. *my mouth* not transgress
39:1. I will keep—with a bridle
49:3.—shall speak of wisdom
51:15.—shall shew thy praise, 63:5.
71:15.—shall shew thy righteousness
Eph 6:19. that I may open—boldly
Ps 81:10. open *thy mouth* wide
103:5. who satisfieth—with good
Prov 31:8. open—for the dumb in
Eccles 5:6. suffer not—to cause thy flesh
MULTITUDE, Gen 16:10; 28:3. Exod 12:38; 23:2. Num 11:4.
Job 32:7. *m.* of years should teach wisdom
Ps 5:7. in *m.* of thy mercy
10. cast out in *m.* of their transgressions
33:16. no king saved by the *m.* of
51:1. according unto the *m.* of thy tender mercies, 106:7, 45.
94:19. in the *m.* of my thoughts
Prov 10:19. in *m.* of words wanteth not sin
11:14. in *m.* of counsellors safety, 15:22; 24:6.
Eccles 5:3. *m.* of business, . . . *m.* of words
James 5:20. hide *m.* of sins, 1 Pet 4:8.
MURDER, Rom 1:29. Matt 15:19. Gal 5:21. Rev 9:21.
Job 24:14. *murderer* rising with light
John 8:44. (devil) was a *m.* from the
Hos 9:13. bring forth children to *m.*
1 Pet 4:15. none suffer as a *m.*
MURMUR, Deut 1:27. Ps 106:25. Jude 16. Exod 16:7. Phil 2:14.
MUSE, Ps 39:3; 143:5.
MUSIC, Lam 3:63. Amos 6:5.
MUSTARD seed, Matt 13:31; 17:20.
MUZZLE, Eccles 25:4. 1 Cor 9:9. 1 Tim 5:18.
MYSTERY of kingdom, Mark 4:11.
Rom 11:25. not . . . be ignorant of *m.*
16:25. according to revelation of *m.*
1 Cor 2:7. wisdom of God in a *m.*
Eph 1:9. made known *m.* of, 3:3.
3:4. my knowledge in *m.* of Christ
9. fellowship of the *m.*
6:19. make known *m.* of gospel
Col 1:26. *m.* which hath been hid
27. glory of this *m.* among Gentiles
2:2. acknowledgment of *m.* of God
4:3. open a door to speak *m.* of Christ
2 Thess 2:7. *m.* of iniquity doth
1 Tim 3:9. holding *m.* of the faith
16. great is the *m.* of godliness
Rev 1:20. write the *m.* of seven stars
10:7. m. of God should be finished
1 Cor 4:1. stewards of the *mysteries* of God
13:2. prophecy and understand all *m.*
14:2. in the spirit he speaketh *m.*

N

NAIL, Judg 4:21; 5:26.
Isa 22:23. fasten him as a *n.* in a
Zech 10:4. out of him came the *n.*
Eccles 12:11. *nails* fastened by the masters
NAKED, Gen 2:25; 3:7, 11.
Exod 32:25. when Moses saw the people were *n.*
2 Chron 28:19. he made Judah *naked*
Job 1:21. *n.* came I out of my mother's womb
Matt 25:36. *n.* and ye clothed me, 38.
1 Cor 4:11. we hunger and thirst and are *n.*
2 Cor 5:3. clothed we shall not be found *n.*
Heb 4:13. all things are *n.* and open
Rev 16:15. keepeth his garments, lest he walk *n.*
NAME, Exod 34:14. Lev 18:21.
Ps 20:1. the *n.* of God of Jacob
109:13. let their *n.* be blotted
Prov 10:7. the *n.* of the wicked shall rot
22:1. a good *n.* is rather to be chosen than great riches
Eccles 7:1. good *n.* better than precious ointment
Isa 55:13. shall be to the Lord for *n.*
56:5. a *n.* better than of sons and
62:2. thou shalt be called by new *n.*
Jer 13:11. for a people, and for a *n.*
32:20. made thee *n.* as at this day
33:9. shall be to me a *n.* of joy, a
Mic 4:5. walk in the *n.* of the Lord
Matt 10:41. receive prophet in *n.* of
Luke 6:22. cast out your *n.* as evil
Rom 2:24. *n.* of God is blasphemed
Eph 1:21. every *n.* that is named
Phil 2:9. a *n.* above every *n.*
Col 3:17. do all in the *n.* of Lord
2 Tim 2:19. that nameth *n.* of Christ
Heb 1:4. obtained more excellent *n.*
1 Pet 4:14. reproached for *n.* of Christ
1 John 3:23. believe on *n.* of Son, 5:13.
Rev 2:17. new *n.* written, which no man
3:1. thou hast a *n.* that thou livest
12. write on him the *n.* of my God, and the *n.* of the city of my God . . . and will write upon him my new *n.*
14:1. his Father's *n.* written in their foreheads, 22:4.
Ps 76:1. *his name* is great in Israel
72:17.—shall endure for ever
106:8. he saved them for—'s sake
Prov 30:3. what is—and what is his

Isa 9:6.—shall be called Wonderful
Zech 14:9. shall be one Lord and—one
John 20:31. ye might have life through—
Rev 3:5. confess—before my father
13:17. or the number of—15:2.
Exod 23:21. *my name* is in him
3:15. and this is—for ever,
Isa 48:9. for—'s sake I defer anger
Ezek 20:9. wrought for—sake, 14, 22.
Mal 1:14.—is dreadful among the
2:2. lay it to heart, to give glory to—
Matt 10:22. hated of all for—'s sake
John14:13. ask in—15:16; 16:23, 26.
16:24. asked nothing in—
Acts 9:15. a chosen vessel to bear—
Rev 2:3. for—'s sake hast laboured, and
13. holdest fast—3:8. not denied—
2 Chron 14:11. in *thy name* we go
Ps 8:1. how excellent is—in all, 9.
48:10. according to—so is thy
75:1.—is near, thy wondrous works declare
138:2. praise—. . . thy word above all—
Song of Sol 1:3.—is as ointment poured
Isa 26:8. desire of our soul is to—
64:7. none that calleth on—
Jer 14:7. do it for—'s sake, 21. Josh 7:9. Ps 79:9. Dan 9:6.
Mic 6:9. man of wisdom shall see—
John 17:12. I kept them in—26.
Exod 23:13. no mention of the *name(s)* of other gods, Deut 12:3. Ps 16:4.
28:12. Aaron bear their *n.* before Lord
Ps 49:11. call lands after their *names*
Luke 10:20. *n.* written in heaven
Rev 3:4. hast a few *n.* in Sardis

NARROW, 1 Kings 6:4. Prov 23:27. Isa 28:20; 49:19. Matt 7:14.

NATION, Gen 15:14; 21:13.
Gen 20:4. wilt slay a righteous *n.*
Num 14:12. make of thee a greater *n.*
2 Sam 7:23. what one *n.* . . . is like thy people
Ps 33:12. blessed is *n.* whose God is Lord
147:20. not dealt so with any *n.*
Isa 1:4. Ah sinful *n.*, a people laden
2:4. *n.* shall not lift sword against *n.*
49:7. him whom the *n.* abhorreth
66:8. shall a *n.* be born at once
Matt 24:7. *n.* rise against *n.*, Mark 13:8.
Luke 7:5. he loveth our *n.* and he hath built
Acts 10:35. in every *n.* he that feareth (God)
Rom 10:19. by a foolish *n.* I will
Phil 2:15. in midst of a crooked . . . *n.*
1 Pet 2:9. ye are an holy *n.*, Exod 19:6.
Rev 5:9. redeemed us . . . out of every *n.*
Gen 10:32. *nations,* 17:4, 6, 16.
Ps 9:20. *n.* may know themselves
113:4. Lord high above all *n.*
Isa 2:2. all *n.* shall flow unto it
40:17. *n.* before him are as nothing
55:5. *n.* that knew thee not shall
Jer 4:2. *n.* shall bless themselves in
Zech 2:11. many *n.* be joined to Lord
Matt 25:32. before him be gathered all *n.*
Acts 14:16. suffered all *n.* to walk in
Rev 21:24. *n.* of them that are saved

NATURE, Rom 2:27. James 3:6.
Rom 1:26. that which is against *n.*
2:14. do by *n.* things contained in
1 Cor 11:14. doth not *n.* itself teach
Gal 4:8. them which by *n.* are no gods
Eph 2:3. by *n.* the children of wrath
Heb 2:16. took not on him *n.* of angels
2 Pet 1:4. partakers of divine *n.*
Deut 34:7. *natural(ly),* Rom 1:26, 27, 31; 11:21, 24. 1 Cor 2:14; 15:44, 46. Phil 2:20. 2 Tim 3:3. James 1:23. 2 Pet 2:12. Jude 10.

NAUGHT, it is, saith the buyer, Prov 20:14.
James 1:21. superfluity of *naughtiness*
1 Sam 17:28. the *n.* of thine heart

NEAR, Ps 119:151; 148:14. Isa 55:6; 57:19. Jer 12:2.

NECESSARY, Job 23:12. Acts 13:46; 15: 28. Titus 3:14. Heb 9:23.
Rom 12:13. *necessity(ies),* Acts 20:34. 1 Cor 9:16. 2 Cor 6:4; 9:7; 12:10. Philem 14. Heb 9:16.

NECK, Song of Sol 1:10. Isa 48:4. Rom 16:4.
Acts 15:10. yoke on *n.* of disciples
2 Kings 17:14. hardened their *necks,* Neh 9:16, 17, 29. Jer 7:26; 19:15.

NEED of all these things, Matt 6:32.
Matt 9:12. they that are whole *n.* not
Luke 15:7. just persons which *n.* no repentance
Heb 4:16. grace to help in time of *n.*
1 Pet 1:6. if *n.* be, ye are in heaviness
1 John 2:27. *n.* not that any man
Rev 3:17. rich . . . and have *n.* of nothing
21:23. the city had no *n.* of sin
22:5. and they *n.* no candle
Eph 4:28. give to him that *needeth*
Luke 10:42. one thing is *needful*
Ps 9:18. *needy* not alway forgotten
72:12. he shall deliver the *n.*
113:7. lifteth *n.* out of dunghill
Isa 14:30. *n.* shall lie down in safety

NEGLECT to hear, Matt 18:17.
1 Tim 4:14. *n.* not the gift that is in thee
Heb 2:3. if we *n.* so great salvation

NEIGH, Jer 5:8; 8:16; 13:27.

NEIGHBOUR, Exod 3:22; 11:2.
Exod 20:16. not bear false witness against thy *n.* Deut 5:20.
Lev 19:13. thou shalt not defraud thy *n.*
17. thou shalt in any wise rebuke thy *n.*
18. shalt love thy *n.* as thyself, Matt 19:19; 22:39. Rom 13:9. Gal 5:14. James 2:8.
Ps 15:3. nor doeth evil to his *n.*
Prov 27:10. better is a *n.* that is near
Jer 31:34. teach no more every man his *n.*
Luke 10:29. who is my *n.*, 36.
Rom 13:10. love worketh no ill to his *n.*
15:2. let every one of us please his *n.*

NEST, Job 29:18. Ps 84:3. Prov 27:8. Isa 10:14. Hab 2:9. Matt 8:20.

NET, Job 18:8; 19:6. Ps 9:15; 25:15; 31:4; 35:7, 8; 57:6; 66:11. Isa 51:20. Hab 1:15, 16. Matt 13:47. Ps 141:10. Eccles 7:26.

NEW, Lord make *n.* thing, Num 16:30.
Judg 5:8. chose *n.* gods, Deut 32:17.
Eccles 1:9. and there is no *n.* thing under the sun, 10.
Isa 65:17. *n.* heavens and a *n.* earth, 66:22. 2 Pet 3:13. Rev 21:1.
Jer 31:22. created a *n.* thing in earth
Ezek 11:19. a *n.* spirit within you, 36:26.
Matt 9:16. putteth *n.* cloth unto an old garment
17. neither put *n.* wine in old bottles
13:52. bringeth forth . . . things *n.* and old
Mark 1:27. what *n.* doctrine is this, Acts 17:19.
John 13:34. a *n.* commandment I give unto you, 1 John 2:7, 8.
Acts 17:21. to hear some *n.* thing
1 Cor 5:7. that ye may be a *n.* lump
2 Cor 5:17. if any man be in Christ, he is a *n.* creature; behold, all things are become *n.*
Gal 6:15. neither circumcision nor uncircumcision, but a *n.* creature

Eph 4:24. put on *n.* man, Col 3:10.
1 Pet 2:2. as *n.*born babes desire
Rev 2:17. a *n.* name written, which no man knoweth, 3:12. Isa 62:2.
5:9. sung a *n.* song, 14:3. Ps 33:3. Isa 42:10.
Rom 6:4. should walk in *newness* of life
7:6. we should serve in *n.* of spirit
NIGH, Lev 25:49. Num 24:17.
Deut 4:7. who hath God so *n.* unto
30:14. word is very *n.* to thee, Rom 10:8.
Ps 34:18. Lord is *n.* them of broken heart
145:18. Lord is *n.* them that call on
Matt 15:8. draweth *n.* unto me with their mouth
Eph 2:13. made *n.* by blood of Christ
17. peace to . . . them that were *n.*
NIGHT, Gen 1:5, 14; 26:24.
Exod 12:42. this is that *n.* of the Lord
Ps 19:2. *n.* unto *n.* sheweth knowledge
30:5. weeping may endure for a *n.*
139:11. *n.* shall be light about me
Isa 21:11. Watchman, what of *n.*?
Jer 14:8. turneth aside to tarry for a *n.*
Luke 6:12. continued all *n.* in prayer
12:20. this *n.* thy soul be required
John 9:4. *n.* cometh when no man
Rom 13:12. *n.* is far spent; day is at hand
Rev 21:25. shall be no *n.* there, 22:5.
Ps 134:1. *by night,* Song of Sol 3:1. John 3:2; 7:50; 19:39.
Job 35:10. giveth songs *in the night*
Ps 16:7. instruct me—seasons
42:8.—his song shall be with me
Ps 77:6. I call to remembrance my song—
119:55. I have remembered thy name . . .—
Isa 30:29. ye shall have a song as—
59:10. stumble at noonday as—
John 11:10. if a man walk—he stumbleth
1 Thess 5:7. sleep—and . . . are drunken—
NOBLE, Ezra 4:10. Esther 6:9. Jer 2:21. Acts 17:11.
1 Cor 1:26. not many *n.* are called
Exod 24:11. *nobles,* Num 21:18.
Neh 13:17. contended with *n.* of *Judah*
Ps 149:8. bind . . . their *n.* with fetters
Prov 8:16. by me princes rule, and *n.*
Eccles 10:17. when thy king is son of *n.*
Luke 19:12. *nobleman,* John 4:46, 49.
NOISOME, Ps 91:3. Rev 16:2.
NOSE, Prov 30:33. Isa 65:5.
Isa 2:22. breath in *nostrils,* Lam 4:20.
NOTHING, Gen 11:6. Exod 9:4; 12:10. Num 6:4; 16:26. Josh 11:15.
2 Sam 24:24. which doth cost me *n.*
1 Kings 8:9. *n.* in ark save the two tables
Neh 8:10. send to them for whom *n.* is prepared
Job 6:21. for now ye are *n.*
8:9. of yesterday, and know *n.*
26:7. hangeth earth on *n.*
34:9. it profiteth a man *n.*
Ps 17:3. tried me, and shalt find *n.*
49:17. when he dieth, shall carry *n.* away
119:165. *n.* shall offend them
Prov 13:4. sluggard desireth and hath *n.*
7. maketh himself rich, yet hath *n.*
Isa 40:17. nations before him as *n.*
Jer 10:24. lest thou bring me to *n.*
Lam 1:12. is it *n.* to you, all ye that
Luke 1:37. with God *n.* shall be impossible
John 14:30. prince of this world . . . hath *n.* in me
15:5. without me ye can do *n.*
1 Cor 1:19. bring to *n.* understanding
13:2. I am *n.*, 2 Cor 12:11.
2 Cor 6:10. having *n.* yet possessing all
1 Tim 6:7. we brought *n.* into world
NOUGHT, Gen 29:15. Deut 13:17.
Isa 41:12. shall be as nothing and as a thing of *n.*
49:4. I have spent my strength for *n.*
52:3. sold yourselves for *n.*, Ps 44:12.
Amos 6:13. rejoice in a thing of *n.*
Luke 23:11. Herod . . . set him at *n.*
Acts 19:27. in danger to be set at *n.*
Rom 14:10. why dost thou set at *n.* thy brother
NOVICE, not a, lest, 1 Tim 3:6.
NUMBER our days, Ps 90:12.
Isa 65:12. I will *n.* you to the sword
Rev 7:9. multitude no man could *n.*
13:17. the *n.* of his name, 18.
Isa 53:12. *numbered* with transgressors
Hos *1:10. children of Israel* as sand of the sea which cannot be . . . *n.*, Jer 33:22.
Job 14:16. thou *numberest* my steps
Ps 71:15. I know not the *numbers*
NURSE, 1 Thess 2:7. Isa 49:23.

O

OATH, Gen 24:8; 26:3, 28.
1 Sam 14:26. people feared the *o.*
2 Sam 21:7. Lord's *o.*, that was between
2 Chron 15:15. all Judah rejoiced at *o.*
Eccles 8:2. in regard of *o.* of God
Ezek 16:59. despised the *o.*, 17:18, 19.
Luke 1:73. *o.* which he sware to our
Heb 6:16. *oath* for confirmation is . . . end
James 5:12. swear not by heaven, neither by earth, neither by any other *o.*
OBEY, Gen 27:8. Exod 5:2.
Deut 11:27, 28. blessing if ye *o.* . . . and a curse if ye will not *o.* commandments
13:4. keep his commandments and *o.* his voice
Josh 24:24. his voice will we *o.*
1 Sam 12:14. serve him and *o.* his voice
15:22. to *o.* is better than sacrifice
Jer 7:23. *o.* my voice, 11:4, 7.
Acts 5:29. ought to *o.* God rather than men
Rom 2:8. contentious, and do not *o.* truth
6:16. servants ye are to whom ye *o.*
Eph 6:1. children, *o.* your parents in Lord, Col 3:20.
Col 3:22. servants, *o.* in all things
2 Thess 1:8. that *o.* not the gospel
3:14. if any man *o.* not our word
Titus 3:1. in mind to . . . *o.* magistrates
Heb 5:9. salvation to all them that *o.*
13:17. *o.* them that have rule over
1 Pet 3:1. if any *o.* not the word
Rom 6:17. *obeyed* from heart that
1 Pet 3:6. Sarah *o.* Abraham
Isa 50:10. *obeyeth* voice, Jer 11:3.
1 Pet 1:22. purified your souls in *obeying* truth
Rom 1:5. received grace . . . for *obedience*
5:19. by *o.* of one many made righteous
16:19. your *o.* is come abroad
26. made known to all nations for *o.* of faith
1 Cor 14:34. (women) are commanded to be under *o.*
2 Cor 7:15. he remembereth the *o.* of you
10:5. every thought to *o.* of Christ
6. when your *o.* is fulfilled
Heb 5:8. learned *o.* by things suffered
1 Pet 1:2. sanctification of spirit to *o.*

Exod 24:7. all Lord said will we do, and be *obedient*
Num 27:20. children of Israel may be *o.*
Deut 4:30. turn and be *o.* to his voice
8:20. perish; because ye would not be *o.* to voice
2 Sam 22:45. strangers . . . shall be *o.*
Prov 25:12. so is wise reprover upon an *o.* ear
Isa 1:19. if ye be . . . *o.* ye shall eat the
42:24. neither were they *o.* to his law
Acts 6:7. priests were *o.* to the faith
Rom 15:18. to make Gentiles *o.* by word
2 Cor 2:9. whether ye be *o.* in all
Eph 6:5. servants, be *o.* to . . . masters
Phil 2:8. he became *o.* unto death
Titus 2:9. exhort servants to be *o.*
1 Pet 1:14. as *o.* children, not
OBSCURITY, Isa 29:18; 58:10.
OBSERVE, Exod 12:17; 34:11.
Ps 107:43. who is wise and will *o.*
119:34. *o.* it with my whole heart
Prov 23:26. let thine eyes *o.* my ways
Jon 2:8. that *o.* lying vanities
Matt 28:20. teaching them to *o.* all things
Gal 4:10. ye *o.* days and months
Luke 17:20. not with *observation*
Exod 12:42. a night to be much *observed*
Mark 6:20. Herod feared John and *o.*
10:20. all these I *o.* from my youth
OBSTINATE, Deut 2:30. Isa 48:4.
OBTAIN favour of Lord, Prov 8:35.
Isa 35:10. *o.* joy and gladness, 51:11.
Luke 20:35. worthy to *o.* that world
1 Cor 9:24. so run, that ye may *o.*
Heb 4:16. may *o.* mercy and find
11:35. might *o.* better resurrection
James 4:2. ye desire to have, and cannot *o.*
Hos 2:23. her that had not *obtained* mercy
Acts 26:22. having *obtained* help of God
Rom *11:7. the* election hath *o.* it
Eph 1:11. we have *o.* inheritance
1 Tim 1:13. I *o.* mercy, because, 16.
Heb 1:4. *o.* a more excellent name
6:15. endured, he *o.* the promise
8:6. *o.* a more excellent ministry
9:12. *o.* eternal redemption for us
OCCASION, Gen 43:18. Judg 14:4.
2 Sam 12:14. given great *o.* to enemies
Jer 2:24. in her *o.* who can turn
Rom 7:8. *o.* by commandment, 11.
14:13. *o.* to fall in brother's way
2 Cor 11:12. I may cut off *o.* . . . desire *o.*
Gal 5:13. use not liberty for *o.* to the flesh
1 Tim 5:14. give none *o.* to adversary
1 John 2:10. none *o.* of stumbling
Job 33:10. he findeth *occasions* against me
OCCUPY, Luke 19:13. Heb 13:9.
ODOUR, Phil 4:18. Rev 5:8.
OFFENCE, 1 Sam 25:31. Isa 8:14.
Matt 16:23. thou art an *o.* unto me
18:7. woe . . . because of offences! for offences must come; woe . . . by whom the *o.* cometh
Acts 24:16. conscience void of *o.*
Rom 5:15. not as *o.* so is free gift
17. by one man's *o.* death reigned
9:33. rock of *o.*, 1 Pet 2:8. Isa 8:14.
14:20. for him that eateth with *o.*
2 Cor 6:3. giving no *o.* in any thing
11:7. have I committed an *o.*
Gal 5:11. then is *o.* of cross ceased
Phil 1:10. without *o.* till day of Christ
Eccles 10:4. yielding pacifieth great *offences*
Rom 4:25. delivered for our *o.* and
16:17. cause divisions and *o.*
OFFEND, not any more, Job 34:31.
Ps 73:15. *o.* against generation
119:165. nothing shall *o.* them
Jer 2:3. all that devour him shall *o.*
50:7. we *o.* not because they have
Hos 4:15. harlot, yet let not Judah *o.*
Matt 5:29. if right eye *o.* thee, 30.
13:41. gather out . . . all things that *o.*
17:27. yet lest we should *o.* them, go
18:6. whoso shall *o.* one of these little ones, 8, 9. if hand, foot, eye *o.*, Mark 9:43–47.
James 2:10. *o.* in one point is guilty
3:2. in many things we *o.* all
Prov 18:19. brother *offended* is harder to be won
Matt 11:6. blessed . . . not be *o.* in
26:33. though all be *o.* . . . I never be *o.* Mark 14:27.
Mark 4:17. immediately they are *o.*
Rom 14:21. brother . . . *o.* or is made weak
2 Cor 11:29. who is *o.* and I burn not
Isa 29:21. make a man *offender* for
OFFER, Gen 31:54. Lev 1:3.
Matt 5:24. then come and *o.* thy gift
Heb 13:15. *o.* the sacrifice of praise
Rev 8:3. *o.* it with prayers of saints
Phil 2:17. *offered* upon the sacrifice and service
2 Tim 4:6. I am now ready to be *o.*
Heb 9:14. *o.* himself without spot
28. Christ was once *o.* to bear sins
11:4. by faith Abel *o.* to God
17. Abraham . . . *o.* up Isaac
Ps 50:23. whoso *offereth* praise glorifieth
Eph 5:2. an *offering* to God for us
Heb 10:5. sacrifice and *o.* thou wouldest not
14. by one *o.* he hath perfected for ever
OFFSCOURING, Lam 3:45.
1 Cor 4:13. we are the *o.* of all things
OFFSPRING, Acts 17:28. Rev 22:16.
OFTEN reproved hardeneth, Prov 29:1.
Mal 3:16. spake *o.* one to another
Matt 23:37. how *o.* would I have gathered
1 Cor 11:26. as *o.* as ye eat this bread
Phil 3:18. of whom I have told you *o.*
Heb 9:25. should offer himself *o.*
OIL, Gen 28:18. Exod 25:6.
Ps 45:7. with *o.* of gladness, Heb 1:9.
89:20. with my holy *o.* I have
92:10. be anointed with fresh *o.* 23:5.
104:15. *o.* to make his face shine
141:5. it shall be an excellent *o.*
Isa 61:3. *o.* of joy for mourning
Mic 6:7. will Lord be pleased with . . . rivers of *o.*
Matt 25:3. foolish . . . took no *o.* with them
4. wise took *o.* in their vessels
8. give us of your *o.*; for our lamps
Luke 7:46. head with *o.* didst not anoint
10:34. pouring in *o.* and wine
OINTMENT, Ps 133:2. Prov 27:9, 16. Eccles 7:1; 10:1. Song of Sol 1:3. Isa 1:6. Amos 6:6. Matt 26:7, 9, 12. Mark 14:3. Luke 7:37, 46. John 12:5.
OLD, Gen 5:32; 18:12, 13.
Ps 37:25. been young, and now am *o.*
Prov 22:6. when he is *o.* he will not
Jer 6:16. ask for the *o.* paths
1 Cor 5:7. purge out the *o.* leaven
2 Cor 5:17. *o.* things are passed away
2 Pet 1:9. purged from his *o.* sins
Gen 25:8. *old age,* Judg 8:32. Job 30:2. Ps 71:9; 92:14. Isa 46:4.

OVERTAKE, Exod 15:9. Amos 9:13. Hos 2:7. Gal 6:1.
1 Thess 5:4.
OVERTHROW, Deut 12:3; 29:23. Job 12:19. Ps 140:4, 11. Prov 13:6; 21:12. Amos 4:11. Acts 5:39. 2 Tim 2:18.
OVERTURN, Ezek 21:27. Job 9:5; 12:15; 28:9; 34:25.
OVERWHELMED, Ps 55:5; 61:2; 77:3; 124:4; 142:3; 143:4.
OVER WISE, neither make thyself, Eccles 7:16.
OWE, Rom 13:8. Matt 18:24, 28.
OWL, Job 30:29. Ps 102:6. Isa 13:21; 34:11, 15; 43:20. Mic 1:8.
OWN, Deut 24:16. Judg 7:2.
John 1:11. his *o*. . . . *o*. received him not
1 Cor 6:19. ye are not your *o*.
10:24. let no man seek his *o*.
Phil 2:4. look not every man on his *o*. things
OX knoweth his owner, Isa 1:3; 11:7. Prov 7:22; 14:4; 15:17.
Ps 144:14. *oxen,* Isa 22:13. Matt 22:4. Luke 14:19. John 2:14. 1 Cor 9:9.

P

PACIFY, Esther 7:10. Prov 16:14.
Prov 21:14. gift in secret *pacifieth*
Eccles 10:4. yielding *p*. great offences
PAIN, Isa 21:3; 26:18; 66:7. Jer 6:24. Mic 4:10. Rev 21:4.
Ps 55:4. my heart is sore *pained,* Isa 23:5. Jer 4:19. Joel 2:6.
Rev 12:2. travailing in birth and *p*.
Ps 73:16. *painfulness,* 2 Cor 11:27.
116:3. *pains* of hell gat hold on me
Acts 2:24. loosed the *p*. of death
PAINTED, 2 Kings 9:30. Jer 4:30; 22:14. Ezek 23:40.
PALACE, 1 Chron 29:19. Ps 45:8, 15. Song of Sol 8:9. Isa 25:2. Phil 1:13.
PALM tree, Ps 92:12. Song of Sol 7:7.
PANT, Amos 2:7. Ps 38:10; 42:1; 119:131. Isa 21:4.
PARABLE, Ps 49:4; 78:2. Prov 26:7, 9. Ezek 20:49. Mic 2:4. Matt 13:3. Luke 5:36; 13:6; 21:29.
PARADISE, (Eden) Gen 2:15. (heaven) Luke 23:43. 2 Cor 12:4. Rev 2:7.
PARCHMENTS, 2 Tim 4:13.
PARDON our iniquity, Exod 34:9.
Exod 23:21. he will not *p*. your transgressions
Num 14:19. *p*. iniquity of people
1 Sam 15:25. *p*. my sin, 2 Kings 5:18.
2 Kings 24:4. which the Lord would not *p*.
2 Chron 30:18. the good Lord *p*.
Neh 9:17. a God ready to *p*.
Job 7:21. why dost thou not *p*. my transgression
Ps 25:11. for name's sake . . . *p*. my iniquity
Isa 55:7. God . . . will abundantly *p*.
Jer 5:7. how shall I *p*. thee for this
33:8. I will *p*. all their iniquities
50:20. I will *p*. them whom I reserve
Isa 40:2. cry . . . that her iniquity is *pardoned*
Mic 7:18. God like thee that *pardoneth*
PARENTS, Luke 2:27; 8:56.
Matt 10:21. children rise up against their *p*., Mark 13:12.
Luke 18:29. no man hath left house, or *p*.
21:16. ye shall be betrayed both by *p*.
Rom 1:30. disobedient to *p*., 2 Tim 3:2.
2 Cor 12:14. children ought not to lay up for *p*., but *p*. for children
1 Tim 5:4. learn to requite their *p*.
PART, it shall be thy, Exod 29:26.
Num 18:20. thy *p*. and inheritance
Ps 5:9. inward *p*. is wickedness
118:7. Lord taketh my *p*. with them
Luke 10:42. Mary hath chosen that good *p*.
Acts 8:21. neither *p*. nor lot in this
1 Cor 13:9. know in *p*. and prophesy in *p*., 10.
PARTAKER with adulterers, Ps 50:18.
1 Cor 9:10. should be *p*. of his hope
10:30. if I by grace be a *p*. why am I
1 Tim 5:22. be not *p*. of other men's sins
1 Pet 5:1. a *p*. of the glory . . . revealed
2 John 11. is *p*. of his evil deeds
Rom 15:27. *partakers* of their spiritual
1 Cor 9:13. wait at altar *p*. with altar
10:17. *p*. of that one bread
21. *p*. of Lord's table
Eph 5:7. be not *p*. with
Heb 3:14. for we are made *p*. of Christ
6:4. and were made *p*. of the Holy Ghost
12:10. might be *p*. of his holiness
PARTIAL, Mal 2:9. James 2:4.
1 Tim 5:21. *partiality,* James 3:17.
PASS, Exod 33:19. Ezek 20:37. Zeph 2:2. Zech 3:4. 2 Pet 3:10.
Mark 14:35. Jesus prayed that . . . the hour might *p*. from him
Luke 16:17. easier for heaven and earth to *p*. than one tittle of law to fail
John 5:24. is *passed* from death to life
Isa 43:2. when thou *passest* through the waters I will be with thee
Mic 7:18. *passeth* by transgression of remnant of this heritage
1 Cor 7:31. fashion of this world *p*.
Phil 4:7. peace of God *p*. all understanding
1 John 2:17. world *p*. away and lust
PASSION, Acts 1:3; 14:15.
PASSOVER, Exod 12:11. Deut 16:2. Josh 5:11. 2 Chron 30:15; 35:1, 11. Heb 11:28.
1 Cor 5:7. Christ our *p*. is sacrificed
PASTORS, Jer 3:15; 17:16.
Eph 4:11. and some, *p*. and teachers
PASTURE, Ps 23:2; 95:7. Isa 30:23; 49:9. Ezek 34:14, 18. John 10:9.
Ps 74:1. sheep of thy *p*., 79:13. his *p*., 100:3.
PATH, Num 22:24. Job 28:7.
Ps 16:11. wilt shew me *p*. of life
27:11. lead me in a plain *p*.
119:35. go in *p*. of thy commandments
139:3. thou compassest my *p*.
Prov 4:18. *p*. of just is as shining light
26. ponder the *p*. of thy feet
5:6. lest thou ponder the *p*. of life
Isa 26:7. thou dost weigh *p*. of just
Ps 17:4. kept me from the *paths* of destroyer
5. hold up my goings in thy *p*.
25:10. all *p*. of the Lord are mercy
65:11. and thy *p*. drop fatness
Prov 3:17. all her *p*. are peace
Isa 59:7. destruction are in their *p*.
8. they have made them crooked *p*.
Hos 2:6. shall not find her *p*.
Matt 3:3. make his *p*. straight, Isa 40:3.
Heb 12:13. make straight *p*. for feet
PATIENCE with me, Matt 18:26, 29.
Luke 8:15. bring forth fruit with *p*.
21:19. in your *p*. possess ye your souls
Rom 5:3. tribulation worketh *p*.
15:4. that we through *p*. . . . might have hope
5. God of *p*. . . . grant you to be likeminded
2 Cor 12:12. wrought among you in all *p*.
Col 1:11. strengthened . . . unto all *p*.
1 Thess 1:3. *p*. of hope in our Lord
2 Thess 1:4. for your *p*. and faith
1 Tim 6:11. follow after . . . *p*., meekness
2 Tim 3:10. faith, longsuffering, charity, *p*.
Titus 2:2. sound in faith, charity, *p*.
Heb 6:12. though faith and *p*. inherit promises
10:36. have need of *p*., that after
12:1. run with *p*. race that is set before us
James 1:3. trying of your faith worketh *p*.

4. let *p.* have her perfect work
5:10. prophets . . . for an example of . . . *p.*
11. ye have heard of the *p.* of Job
2 Pet 1:6. to temperance *p.*; to *p.*
Rev 1:9. brother in the . . *p.* of Jesus
2:2. I know thy . . . *p.* 3. hast *p.*
13:10. here is *p.* of saints, 14:12.
Eccles 7:8. the *patient* in spirit better than the proud
Rom 2:7. by *p.* continuance in well doing
12:12. *p.* in tribulation, instant in
2 Thess 3:5. *p.* waiting for Christ
1 Tim 3:3. not greedy of filthy lucre, but *p.*
2 Tim 2:24. gentle . . . apt to teach, *p.*
James 5:7. *p.* . . . unto coming of Lord
Ps 37:7. wait *patiently* for (Lord), 40:1.
Heb 6:15. after he had *p.* endured
1 Pet 2:20. ye be buffeted . . . take it *p.*
PATRIARCH, Acts 2:29; 7:8. Heb 7:4.
PATRIMONY, his, Deut 18:8.
PATTERN, 1 Tim 1:16. Titus 2:7. Ezek 43:10. Heb 8:5; 9:23.
PAVILION, Ps 27:5; 31:20; 18:11. 1 Kings 20:12, 16. Jer 43:10.
PAY, Matt 18:28. Ps 37:21.
PEACE, Lev 26:6. Num 6:26.
Job 22:21. acquaint thyself . . . and be at *p.*
Ps 34:14. seek *p.* and pursue it
37:37. the end of that man is *p.*
85:8. he will speak *p.* unto his people
119:165. great *p.* have they which love
120:6. hateth *p.* 7. I am for *p.*
122:6. pray for *p.* of Jerusalem
125:5. *p.* shall be upon Israel, 128:6.
Prov 16:7. his enemies to be at *peace*
Isa 9:6. everlasting Father, Prince of *p.*
26:3. keep him in perfect *p.*
27:5. that he may make *p.* with me; and he shall make *p.* with me
45:7. I make *p.* and create evil
48:18. had thy *p.* been as a river
22. there is no *p.* . . . to the wicked, 57:21.
57:19. *p.*, *p.* to him that is far off
59:8. way of *p.* they know not, Rom 3:17.
60:17. will make thy officers *p.*
66:12. extend *p.* to her like a river
Jer 6:14. saying *p.*, *p.*, when there is no *p.*, 8:11. Ezek 13:10. 2 Kings 9:18, 22.
8:15. looked for *p.* but no good came
29:7. seek *p.* of the city . . . for *in the p. thereof shall* ye have *p.*
11. thoughts of *p.* and not of evil
Mic 5:5. this man shall be the *p.*
Zech 8:19. love the truth and *p.*
Matt 10:34. I came not to send *p.*
Mark 9:50. have *p.* one with another
Luke 2:14. on earth *p.*, good will towards
29. lettest thou thy servant depart in *p.*
19:42. things that belong to thy *p.*
John 14:27. *p.* I leave with you; my *p.* I give
16:33. in me ye might have *p.*
Rom 5:1. we have *p.* with God through Jesus Christ
8:6. spiritually minded is life and *p.*
14:17. kingdom of God is . . . righteousness, *p.*
1 Cor 7:15. God hath called us to *p.*
2 Cor 13:11. live in *p.*, and God of . . . *p.*
Gal 5:22. fruit of Spirit is love, joy, *p.*
Eph 2:14. he is our *p.* 15. making *p.*
Phil 4:7. the *p.* of God, Col 3:15.
1 Thess 5:13. at *p.* among yourselves
Heb 12:14. follow *p.* with all men
James 3:18. righteousness sown in *p.*
1 Pet 3:11. let him seek *p.* and ensue
2 Pet 3:14. found of him in *p.*
1 Tim 2:2. lead a quiet and *peaceable life*
James 3:17. is first pure, then *p.*
Rom 12:18. live *peaceably* with all
Matt 5:9. blessed are the *peacemakers*
PEARL of great price, Matt 13:46.
Matt 7:6. cast not *pearls* before swine
Rev 21:21. gates were twelve *p.*
PECULIAR treasure to me, Exod 19:5.
Ps 135:4. Israel for his *p.* treasure
Eccles 2:8. *p.* treasure of kings
Deut 14:2. chosen thee to be a *p.* people, 26:18. Titus 2:14. 1 Pet 2:9.
PEN of iron, Job 19:24. Jer 17:1.
Ps 45:1. the *p.* of a ready writer
PENURY, Prov 14:23. Luke 21:4.
PEOPLE, Gen 27:29. Exod 6:7.
Ps 144:15. happy is that *p.* whose God
148:14. Israel a *p.* near unto him
Isa 1:4. a *p.* laden with iniquity
10:6. against the *p.* of my wrath
27:11. a *p.* of no understanding
34:5. upon the *p.* of my curse
Hos 4:9. like *p.*, like priest
1 Pet 2:10. in time past were not *p.*
Ps 100:3. we are *his people* and sheep of his
Matt 1:21. Jesus shall save—from their sins
Rom 11:2. God hath not cast away—
Ps 50:7. hear, O *my people,* and
81:11.—would not hearken, 8:13.
Isa 19:25. blessed by Egypt—, and Assyria
26:20. come—enter thou into thy chambers
63:8. they are—that will not lie
Jer 30:22. ye shall be *my people* and I will be 24:7; 31:33; 32:38. Ezek 11:20; 36:28; 37:27. Zech 2:11; 8:8; 13:9. 2 Cor 6:16.
Hos 1:9. ye are not—, 10. it was said to them, ye are not—, ye are
Heb 4:9. *p.* of God, 11:25. 1 Pet 2:10.
PERCEIVE, Deut 29:4. 1 John 3:16.
PERDITION, John 17:12. Phil 1:28. 2 Thess 2:3. 1 Tim 6:9. Heb 10:39. 2 Pet 3:7. Rev 17:8, 11.
PERFECT, Deut 25:15. Ps 18:32.
Gen 6:9. Noah was a just man and *p.*
17:1. walk before me, and be *p.*
Deut 18:13. shalt be *p.* with . . . God
2 Sam 22:31. his way is *p.*, Ps 18:30.
Job 1:1. man *p.* and upright, 8; 2:3.
Ps 19:7. law of the Lord is *p.*
37:37. mark the *p.* man, and behold
Matt 5:48. *p.* as your Father . . . is *p.*
19:21. if . . . be *p.* go and sell
1 Cor 2:6. among them that are *p.*
2 Cor 12:9. strength made *p.* in weakness
13:11. be *p.*, be of good comfort
Eph 4:13. a *p.* man, unto the measure of . . . Christ
Phil 3:12. not as though . . . already *p.*
Col 1:28. present every man *p.* in Christ
4:12. may stand *p.* and complete
2 Tim 3:17. man of God may be *p.*
Heb 2:10. captain of salvation *p.*
7:19. the law made nothing *p.*
12:23. spirits of just men made *p.*
13:21. make you *p.* in every good work
James 1:4. let patience have her *p.* work, that ye may be *p.*
17. good gift and every *p.* gift is from above
1 John 4:18. *p.* love casteth out fear
Rev 3:2. not found thy works *p.*
2 Cor 7:1. *perfecting* holiness in fear of God
Eph 4:12. for the *p.* of the saints
Job 11:7. find out Almighty to *perfection*
Ps 119:96. have seen an end of all *p.*
Luke 8:14. bring no fruit to *p.*
2 Cor 13:9. we wish, even your *p.*
Heb 6:1. let us go on unto *p.*
PERFORM, Gen 26:3. Ruth 3:13.
Job 5:12. hands cannot *p.* enterprise
Ps 119:106. have sworn and will *p.* it
112. inclined heart to *p.* statutes
Isa 9:7. zeal of Lord of hosts will *p.*
44:28. shall *p.* all my pleasure

Mic 7:20. thou wilt *p.* truth to Jacob
Rom 4:21. promised, was able to *p.*
7:18. how to *p.* that which is good
Phil 1:6. it to day of Jesus Christ
Neh 9:8. hast *performed* thy words
Isa 10:12. Lord *p.* his whole work
Jer 51:29. purpose of Lord shall be *p.*
Ps 57:2. God that *performeth* all things
Isa 44:26. *p.* counsel of messengers
PERILOUS times, 2 Tim 3:1.
PERISH, Gen 41:36. Lev 26:38.
Num 17:12. we die, we *p.*, we all *p.*
Esther 4:16. I will go in . . . if I *p.*, I *p.*
Ps 2:12. ye *p.* from the way, when
Prov 29:18. no vision, the people *p.*
Matt 8:25. Lord, save us, we *p.*, Luke 8:24.
John 3:15. believeth in him should not *p.*
16. should not *p.* but have everlasting life
10:28. they shall never *p.*
1 Cor 8:11. the weak *p.* for whom Christ died
2 Pet 3:9. not willing that any *p.*
Ps 119:92. have *perished* in my affliction
PERMIT, if Lord, 1 Cor 16:7. Heb 6:3. 1 Cor 7:6. by *permission,* not
PERNICIOUS ways, 2 Pet 2:2.
PERPETUAL, Jer 50:5; 51:39, 57.
PERPLEXED, 2 Cor 4:8. Isa 22:5.
PERSECUTE me, Ps 7:1; 31:15.
Job 19:22. why *p.* me as God, 28.
Ps 10:2. wicked . . . doth *p.* the poor
35:6. let angel of the Lord *p.* them
83:15. *p.* them with thy tempest
Matt 5:11. blessed are ye when men . . . *p.* you
44. pray for them that . . . *p.* you
10:23. when they *p.* you in this city
Rom 12:14. bless them which *p.*
Ps 109:16. *persecuted* the poor
119:161. princes *p.* me without cause
143:3. the enemy hath *p.* my soul
John 15:20. if they *p.* me they will *p.* you
Acts 22:4. *I p. this way to* death, 7, 8.
26:11. I *p.* them to strange cities, 14.
1 Cor 4:12. being *p.* we suffer it
15:9. because I *p.* the church of God
2 Cor 4:9. *p.* but not forsaken, cast
Gal 1:13. I *p.* the church of God
4:29. *p.* him born after the Spirit
Acts 9:4. why *persecutest* thou me? 22:7.
2 Tim 3:12. live godly . . . shall suffer *persecution*
1 Tim 1:13. who was . . . a *persecutor*
PERSEVERANCE, watching, Eph 6:18.
PERSON, Lev 19:15.
Mal 1:8. will he accept thy *p.*
Matt 22:16. regardest not *p.* of men
Heb 1:3. express image of his *p.*
Acts 10:34. God is no respecter of *persons,* Deut 10:17. Gal 2:6. Eph 6:9. Col 3:25. 1 Pet 1:17.
2 Pet 3:11. what manner of *p.* ought
Jude 16. men's *p.* in admiration
PERSUADE we men, 2 Cor 5:11.
Gal 1:10. do I *p.* men, or God
Acts 13:43. *persuaded* to continue
21:14. when he would not be *p.*
Rom 8:38. I am *p.* that neither death
Heb 6:9. are *p.* better things of you
11:13. having seen them . . . were *p.*
Gal 5:8. this *persuasion* cometh
PERTAIN, Lev 7:20. 1 Cor 6:3, 4. Rom 9:4. Heb 2:17; 5:1; 9:9. 2 Pet 1:3.
Acts 1:3. *pertaining* to kingdom of God
PERVERSE, Num 22:32. Deut 32:5. Job 6:30. Prov 4:24; 12:8; 14:2; 17:20. Isa 19:14. Matt 17:17. Acts 20:30. Phil 2:15. 1 Tim 6:5.
PERVERT judgment, Deut 24:17; 16:19. 1 Sam 8:3. Job 8:3; 34:12. Prov 17:23; 31:5. Mic 3:9.
Acts 13:10. not cease to *p.* right
Job 33:27. *perverted* that which was right
Jer 3:21. they have *p.* their way
Luke 23:2. this fellow *perverting* the nation
PESTILENCE, 2 Sam 24:15. 1 Kings 8:37. Ps 78:50; 91:3. Jer 14:12. Ezek 5:12. Amos 4:10. Hab 3:5. Matt 24:7.
Acts 24:5. this man a *pestilent* fellow
PETITION, 1 Sam 1:17. Esther 5:6.
Ps 20:5. *petitions,* 1 John 5:15.
PHILOSOPHY, Col 2:8.
PHYLACTERIES, Matt 23:5.
PHYSICIAN of no value, Job 13:4.
Jer 8:22. is there no *p.* there
Matt 9:12. that be whole need not *p.*
Luke 4:23. say . . . *P.*, heal thyself
Col 4:14. Luke the beloved *p.*
PIECE of bread, Prov 6:26; 28:21.
Matt 9:16. putteth *p.* of new cloth
Luke 14:18. bought a *piece* of ground
PIERCE, Num 24:8. 2 Kings 18:21.
Luke 2:35. sword shall *p.* through thy
Ps 22:16. they *pierced* my hands
1 Tim 6:10. *p.* themselves through
Rev 1:7. they also which *p.* him
Heb 4:12. *piercing* even to dividing
PIETY at home, 1 Tim 5:4.
PILGRIMS, Heb 11:13. 1 Pet 2:11. *pilgrimage,* Gen 47:9. Exod 6:4. Ps 119:54.
PILLAR of salt, Gen 19:26.
Exod 13:21. by day in *p.* of cloud . . . by night in *p.* of fire, Num 12:5; 14:14. Deut 31:15. Neh 9:12. Ps 99:7.
Isa 19:19. *p.* at the border thereof
Jer 1:18. I made thee an iron *p.*
1 Tim 3:15. *p.* and ground of truth
Rev 3:12. make a *p.* in temple
Job 9:6. *pillars* thereof tremble
26:11. the *p.* of heaven tremble
Ps 75:3. I bear up the *p.* of it
Prov 9:1. hath hewn out her seven *p.*
Song of Sol 3:6. *p.* of smoke
5:15. his legs are as *p.* of marble
3:10. made the *p.* thereof of silver
PILLOW, Gen 28:11. Ezek 13:18.
PINE, Lev 26:39. Ezek 24:23.
PIPE, Zech 4:2, 12. Matt 11:17.
PIT, Gen 14:10; 37:20.
Exod 21:33. if a man dig a *p.*, 34.
Job 33:24. deliver him from . . . the *p.*
Ps 9:15. sunk down in *p.* they had made
28:1. go down to the *p.* 30:3; 88:4; 143:7. Prov 1:12. Isa 38:18.
40:2. out of an horrible *p.*
55:23. *p.* of destruction
Prov 22:14. strange women a deep *p.*
23:27. strange women is a narrow *p.*
Isa 38:17. from the *p.* of corruption
51:1. *p.* whence ye are digged
Zech 9:11. sent prisoners out of *p.*
Rev 9:1. key of bottomless *p.*, 20:1.
Ps 119:85. proud digged *pits* for me
Jer 14:3. to *p.* and found no water
PITY, Deut 7:16; 13:8; 19:13.
Job 6:14. *p.* should be shewed
19:21. have *p.* on me, have *p.*
Isa 63:9. in his *p.* he redeemed
Ezek 36:21. had *p.* for my holy name
Matt 18:33. even as I had *p.* on thee
Ps 103:13. as a father *pitieth* his children, so the Lord *p.* them that
James 5:11. *pitiful,* 1 Pet 3:8.
PLACE, Exod 3:5. Deut 12:5, 14.
Ps 26:8. *p.* where thine honour
32:7. art my hiding *p.*, 119:114.
90:1. Lord, thou hast been our dwelling *p.*
Prov 15:3. eyes of Lord are in every *p.*
Isa 66:1. where is the *p.* of my rest, 18:4.
Hos 5:15. will go and return to my *p.*

John 8:37. my word hath no *p.* in
11:48. take away both our *p.* and
Rom 12:19. avenge not, but give *p.*
1 Cor 4:11. no certain dwelling *p.*
11:20. ye come together into one *p.*
Eph 4:27. neither give *p.* to devil
Rev 12:6. hath *p.* prepared of God
Job 7:10. neither shall *his place* know him any more, 20:9.
Ps 37:10. diligently consider— and
Isa 26:21. Lord cometh out of—
Acts 1:25. might go to—
Ps 16:6. lines fallen unto me in pleasant *places*
Isa 40:4. rough *p.* plain
Eph 1:3. *heavenly places,* 20; 2:6; 3:10.
6:12. *high p.*, Hab 3:19. Amos 4:13. Hos 10:8. Prov 8:2; 9:14.
PLAGUE, 1 Kings 8:37, 38. Ps 89:23. *plagues,* Hos 13:14. Rev 16:9; 18:4, 8; 22:18.
PLAIN man, Jacob was a, Gen 25:27.
Ps 27:11. lead me in a *p.* path
Prov 8:9. (words) are all *p.* to him
Zech 4:7. thou shalt become a *p.*
John 16:29. now speakest thou *plainly*
2 Cor 3:12. we use great *plainness*
PLAISTER, Lev 14:42. Isa 38:21.
PLAIT, Matt 27:29. 1 Pet 3:3.
PLANT, Gen 2:5. Job 14:9.
Jer 2:21. turned into degenerate *p.* of a strange
18:9. concerning a kingdom, to . . . *p.*
24:6. *p.* them and not pluck, 42:10.
Ezek 34:29. raise . . . a *p.* of renown
1:3. a tree *planted* by rivers
92:13. *p.* in the house of the Lord
Isa 40:24. yea, they shall not be *p.*
Jer 2:21. I *p.* thee a noble vine
17:8. as a tree *p.* by the waters
Matt 15:13. my heavenly Father hath not *p.*
21:33. *p.* a vineyard and hedged it
Rom 6:5. we have been *p.* together
1 Cor 3:6. I have *p.*, Apollos watered
9:7. who *planteth* a vineyard and eateth not
Isa 60:21. the branch of my *planting*
61:3. trees of righteousness, the *p.* of the Lord
Ps 128:3. children like olive *plants,* 144:12.
PLAY, *Exod 32:6. 2 Sam 2:14; 10:12.* Ezek 33:32. 1 Cor 10:7.
PLEAD for Baal, Judg 6:31.
Job 13:19. who will *p.* with me, 9:19.
16:21. might *p.* for man with God
23:6. will he *p.* against me with great power
Isa 1:17. *p.* for the widow
43:26. let us *p.* together
66:16. by fire and sword will Lord *p.*
Jer 2:29. wherefore will ye *p.* with me
12:1. righteous art thou, Lord, when I *p.*
25:31. he will *p.* with all flesh
Hos 2:2. *p.* with your mother, *p.*
Joel 3:2. I will *p.* for them there with my people
PLEASE, 2 Sam 7:29. Job 6:9.
Ps 69:31. this also shall *p.* the Lord
Prov 16:7. when man's ways *p.* Lord
Isa 55:11. accomplish that which I *p.*
56:4. choose the things that *p.* me
Rom 8:8. that are in flesh cannot *p.* God
15:1. bear . . . and not *p.* ourselves
2. let every one of us *p.* his neighbour
1 Cor 7:32. how he may *p.* the Lord
10:33. I *p.* men in all things
Gal 1:10. do I seek to *p.* men
1 Thess 4:1. how . . . to walk, and to *p.* him
Heb 11:6. without faith it is impossible to *p.* him
Ps 115:3. God hath done whatsoever he *pleased,* 135:6.
Isa 42:21. Lord is well *p.* for his
53:10. it *p.* the Lord to bruise him
Mic 6:7. will the Lord be *p.* with
Matt 3:17. . . . Son, in whom I am well *p.*, 17:5.
Rom 15:3. Christ *p.* not himself
Col 1:19. *p.* the Father that in him
Heb 11:5. (Enoch) *p.* God
13:16. with such sacrifices God is well *p.*
Eccles 7:26. whoso *pleaseth* God shall escape
8:3. he doeth whatsoever *p.* him
Phil 4:18. a sacrifice well *pleasing*
Col 1:10. worthy of Lord unto all *p.*
1 Thess 2:4. not as *pleasing* men, but God, Eph 6:6. Col 3:22. (menpleasers)
Heb 13:21. working that is well*p.*
1 John 3:22. do things *p.* in his sight
Gen 2:9. *pleasant,* 3:6. Mic 2:9.
2 Sam 1:23. Saul and Jonathan were . . . *p.*
Ps 16:6. lines fallen to me in *p.* places
133:1. how *p.* for brethren to dwell
Prov 2:10. knowledge is *p.* to *soul*
5:19. as a loving hind and *p.* roe
9:17. bread eaten in secret is *p.*
Eccles 11:7. *p.* for eyes to behold the sun
Song of Sol 1:16. thou art fair, yea, *p.*
4:13. *p.* fruits, 16; 7:13.
7:6. how *p.* art thou, O love, for delights
Jer 31:20. Ephraim . . . is he a *p.* child
Prov 3:17. ways of *pleasantness*
Gen 18:12. shall I have *pleasure*
1 Chron 29:17. *p.* in uprightness
Ps 5:4. not a God that hath *p.* in
35:27. hath *p.* in prosperity of his
51:18. do good in thy good *p.* unto Zion
102:14. servants take *p.* in her stones
103:21. ministers of his that do his *p.*
147:11. Lord taketh *p.* in them
Prov 21:17. he that loveth *p.* shall be poor
Eccles 5:4. for he hath no *p.* in fools
12:1. say, I have no *p.* in them
Isa 44:28. shall perform all my *p.*
53:10. *p.* of Lord shall prosper in
Jer 22:28. vessel wherein is no *p.*, Hos 8:8.
Ezek 18:32. no *p.* in death of, 33:11.
Mal 1:10. I have no *p.* in you, saith the Lord
Luke 12:32. it is your Father's good *p.*
2 Cor 12:10. I take *p.* in infirmities
Eph 1:5. according to the good *p.* of
Phil 2:13. and to do of his good *p.*
2 Thess 1:11. fulfil all good *p.* of
Heb 10:38. my soul shall have no *p.*
12:10. chastened us after their own *p.*
Rev 4:11. for thy *p.* they . . . were created
Ps 16:11. at thy right hand *pleasures* for evermore
36:8. drink of the river of thy *p.*
2 Tim 3:4. lovers of *p.* more than . . . God
Titus 3:3. serving divers lusts and *p.*
Heb 11:25. than to enjoy *p.* of sin
PLEDGE, Exod 22:26. Deut 24:6.
PLEIADES, Job 9:9; 38:31.
PLENTY, Job 37:23. Prov 3:10.
Ps 86:5. *plenteous* in mercy, 103:8.
130:7. with him is *p.* redemption
Matt 9:37. harvest is *p.* but labourers
PLOUGH, PLOW, Deut 22:10. Prov 20:4.
Luke 9:62. having put his hand to the *plough*
Job 4:8. they that *plow* iniquity, and
Isa 28:24. doth plowman *p.* all day
Judg 14:18. *plowed* with my heifer
Ps 129:3. plowers *p.* on my back
Jer 26:18. Zion shall be *p.* like a field, Mic 3:12.
Hos 10:13. ye have *p.* wickedness
1 Cor 9:10. *ploweth* should *p.* in hope
Prov 21:4. *plowing* of wicked is sin

Amos 9:13. *plowman,* Isa 61:5.
Isa 2:4. *plowshares,* Joel 3:10. Mic 4:3.
PLUCK out, Ps 25:15; 52:5; 74:11. Amos 4:11. Zech 3:2. Matt 5:29; 18:9. John 10:28, 29. Gal 4:15.
2 Chron 7:20. *pluck up,* Jer 12:17; 18:7; 31:28, 40. Dan 11:4. Jude 12.
Ezra 9:3. *pluck off,* Job 29:17. Isa 50:6. Ezek 23:34. Mic 3:2.
POISON, Deut 32:24, 33. Job 6:4; 20:16. Ps 58:4; 140:3. Rom 3:13. James 3:8.
POLLUTE, Num 18:32. Ezek 7:21. Mic 2:10. Zeph 3:1. Mal 1:7, 12.
Acts 15:20. *pollutions,* 2 Pet 2:20.
PONDER path of feet, Prov 4:26.
Luke 2:19. *pondered* them in her heart
Prov 21:2. Lord *pondereth* the hearts, 24:12.
POOR may eat, Exod 23:11.
Exod 30:15. the *p.* shall not give less
Lev 19:15. not respect person of *p.*
Deut 15:11. for the *p.* shall never cease out
1 Sam 2:7. Lord maketh *p.* and
8. raiseth *p.* out of dust, Ps 113:7.
Job 5:16. the *p.* hath hope
36:15. deliver *p.* in affliction
Ps 10:14. *p.* committeth himself to thee
69:33. the Lord heareth the *p.* and
72:4. he shall judge the *p.*, 2, 13.
132:15. satisfy her *p.* with bread
140:12. Lord will maintain . . . right of *p.*
Prov 13:7. there is that maketh himself *p.*
14:20. *p.* is hated of his neighbour
31. oppresseth *p.* reproacheth his Maker: he that honoureth him hath mercy on *p.*
19:4. *p.* is separated from his neighbour
7. all brethren of the *p.* do hate him
22:22. rob not *p.* because he is *p.*, neither oppress
30:9. lest I be *p.* and steal
Isa 14:32. *p.* of his people shall trust
29:19. *p.* among men shall rejoice
41:17. when the *p.* and needy seek water
58:7. bring *p.* that are cast out to thy house
66:2. that is *p.* and of a contrite
Jer 5:4. surely these are *p.*
Amos 2:6. sold *p.* for pair of shoes, 8:6.
Zeph 3:12. an afflicted and *p.* people
Zech 11:11. *p.* of flock waited on me
Matt 5:3. blessed are the *p.* in spirit
11:5. *p.* have gospel preached to
26:11. have *p.* always with you, John 12:8.
Luke 6:20. blessed be ye *p.*: for yours is the
2 Cor 6:10. as *p.*, yet making many rich
8:9. for your sakes he became *p.*
9:9. he hath given to *p.*, Ps 112:9.
Gal 2:10. we should remember the *p.*
James 2:5. God chosen *p.* of this world
Rev 3:17. knowest not thou art wretched, and miserable and *p.*
PORTION, Deut 21:17; 33:21.
Deut 32:9. Lord's *p.* is his people
2 Kings 2:9. double *p.* of thy spirit
Job 24:18. their *p.* is cursed in earth
26:14. how little a *p.* is heard
31:2. what *p.* of God is from above
Ps 16:5. Lord is *p.* of my inheritance
17:14. have their *p.* in this life
63:10. shall be a *p.* for foxes
73:26. God is my *p.* for ever, 119:57.
142:5. art my *p.* in land of living
Eccles 11:2. give *p.* to seven and to
Isa 53:12. divide him a *p.* with the
61:7. they shall rejoice in their *p.*
Jer 10:16. the *p.* of Jacob not like them, 51:19.
Hab 1:16. by them their *p.* is fat
Zech 2:12. Lord shall inherit Judah his *p.*
Neh 8:10. send *portions,* Esther 9:19, 22.
POSSESS, Gen 22:17. Judg 11:24.
Job 7:3. made to *p.* months of vanity
13:26. *p.* iniquities of my youth
Luke 21:19. in patience *p.* your souls
1 Thess 4:4. know how to *p.* vessel
Ps 139:13. hast *possessed* my reins
Prov 8:22. Lord *p.* me in beginning
Isa 63:18. people of thy holiness *p.* it a little
1 Cor 7:30. as though they *possessed* not
2 Cor 6:10. as having nothing yet *possessing* all
Eph 1:14. purchased *possession*
Gen 14:19. God, *possessor* of heaven
POSSIBLE, all things with God, Matt 19:26.
Matt 24:24. if *p.* shall deceive the very elect
Mark 9:23. all things *p.* to him that
14:36. Father, all things are *p.* to thee
Luke 18:27. impossible with men *p.* with God
Rom 12:18. if *p.* . . . live peaceably
Heb 10:4. not *p.* that blood of bulls
POSTERITY, Gen 45:7. Ps 49:13.
POT, Exod 16:33. Ps 68:13; 81:6. Jer 1:13. Zech 14:21.
Job 2:8. *potsherd,* Ps 22:15. Prov 26:23. Isa 45:9.
Isa 29:16. *potter,* 64:8. Jer 18:6. Lam 4:2. Rom 9:21. Rev 2:27.
POTENTATE, blessed, 1 Tim 6:15.
POUND, Luke 19:13. John 19:39.
POUR, Job 36:27. Lev 14:18, 41.
Ps 62:8. *p.* out your heart
79:6. *p.* out thy wrath on heathen, 69:24. Jer 10:25. Zeph 3:8.
Prov 1:23. I will *p.* out my Spirit
Isa 44:3. *p.* water on him that is thirsty
Lam 2:19. *p.* thine heart like water
Rev 16:1, 17. *p.* vials of God's wrath
Job 10:10. *poured* me out as milk
30:16. my soul *p.* out in me, Ps 42:4.
Ps 45:2. grace is *p.* into thy lips
Song of Sol 1:3. name is as ointment *p.*
Isa 32:15. till Spirit be *p.* on us from high
53:12. *p.* out his soul unto death
Jer 7:20. my fury shall be *p.* out, 42:18; 44:6. Isa 42:25. Ezek 7:8; 14:19; 20:8, 13, 21; 30:15.
Job 12:21. *poureth* contempt on princes, Ps 107:40.
16:20. mine eye *p.* out tears
POVERTY, Gen 45:11. Prov 11:24.
Prov 6:11. so shall *p.* come, 24:34.
10:15. destruction of the poor is their *p.*
20:13. love not sleep lest thou come to *p.*
30:8. give me neither *p.* nor riches
2 Cor 8:2. their deep *p.* abounded
9. ye through his *p.* might be rich
Rev 2:9. I know thy works . . . and *p.*
POWDER, Exod 32:20. Deut 28:24. 2 Kings 23:15. Song of Sol 3:6. Matt 21:44.
POWER, as a prince, Gen 32:28.
Gen 49:3. dignity and excellency of *p.*
Deut 8:18. giveth *p.* to get wealth
32:36. when he seeth that their *p.* is gone
2 Sam 22:33. God is my strength and *p.*
1 Chron 29:11. thine is the *p.* and
Ezra 8:22. *p.* and wrath is against
Job 26:2. him that is without *p.*
14. thunder of his *p.* who can
Ps 62:11. *p.* belongeth unto God
Prov 3:27. when it is in *p.* of hand
18:21. death and life in *p.* of tongue
Isa 40:29. he giveth *p.* to the faint
Eccles 8:4. where word of king is, there is *p.*
8:8. no man that hath *p.* over the spirit to

Jer 10:12. made earth by his *p.*, 51:15.
Hos 12:3. by strength he had *p.* with God
Mic 3:8. I am full of *p.* by the Spirit
Hab 1:11. imputing *p.* to his God
3:4. there was the hiding of his *p.*
Zech 4:6. not by might, nor by *p.*
Matt 9:6. *p.* on earth to forgive sins
8. glorified God which had given such *p.*
22:29. not knowing scriptures nor *p.* of God
28:18. all *p.* is given unto me in heaven and
Mark 9:1. kingdom of God come with *power*
Luke 1:35. *p.* of the Highest shall
5:17. *p.* of the Lord to heal them
22:53. this is your hour and *p.* of
24:49. till ye be endued with *p.*
John 1:12. gave he *p.* to become
10:18. *p.* to lay it down and *p.* to
17:2. given him *p.* over all flesh
19:10. *p.* to crucify, . . . *p.* to release
Acts 26:18. turn them from the *p.* of
Rom 1:16. gospel is *p.* of God to
20. his eternal *p.* and Godhead, 4.
9:22. to make his *p.* known
13:1. there is no *p.* but of God
1 Cor 1:24. Christ the *p.* of God, 18.
2:4. demonstration of Spirit and *p.*
4:19. not speech of them . . . but the *p.*
5:4. gathered together with the *p.* of our Lord
6:12. not be brought under *p.* of
9:4. have we not *p.* to eat and
2 Cor 4:7. excellency of *p.* may be
13:10. according to the *p.* . . . Lord hath given
Eph 1:19. exceeding greatness of his *p.*
2:2. prince of the *p.* of air
Phil 3:10. know *p.* of his resurrection
Col 1:11. according to his glorious *p.*
13. delivered from the *p.* of darkness
2 Thess 1:9. the glory of his *p.*
2 Tim 1:7. Spirit of *p.* and of love
3:5. form of godliness, denying *p.*
Heb 1:3. upholding all things by word of his *p.*
2:14. destroy him that had the *p.* of death
1 Pet 1:5. kept by *p.* of God through faith
2 Pet 1:3. his divine p. hath given
Rev 2:26. will give *p.* over nations
4:11. worthy to receive . . . *p.*, 5:13; 7:12; 19:1. 1 Tim 6:16. Jude 25.
11:3. *p.* to my two witnesses
17. taken to thee thy great *p.*
12:10. now is come . . . *p.* of his Christ
16:9. hath *p.* over these plagues
Exod 15:6. *in power,* Job 37:23. Nah 1:3. 1 Cor 4:20; 15:43. Eph 6:10.
Ps 63:2. *thy power,* 110:3; 145:11.
29:4. *powerful,* Heb 4:12.
Eph 6:12. principalities, *powers,* 1:21. Col 1:16; 2:10, 15. 1 Pet 3:22.
Heb 6:5. tasted good word of God and *p.* of
PRAISE, Judg 5:3. Ps 7:17.
Deut 10:21. he is thy *p.* and thy God
Neh 9:5. above all blessing and *p.*
Ps 22:25. my *p.* shall be of thee
33:1. *p.* is comely for upright, 147:1.
65:1. *p.* waiteth for thee, O God
109:1. hold not peace, God of my *p.*
Prov 27:21. so is a man to his *p.*
Isa 60:18. walls Salvation and thy gates *p.*
62:7. Jerusalem a *p.* in the earth
Jer 13:11. for a *p.* and for a glory
17:14. art my *p.* 26. sacrifices of *p.*
Hab 3:3. earth was full of his *p.*
John 12:43. loved *p.* of men more than *p.* of God
Rom 2:29. whose *p.* is not of men
Eph 1:6. *p.* of glory of his grace, 12.
Phil 4:8. if there be any *p.*, think on
Heb 13:15. offer sacrifice of *p.*
1 Pet 2:14. *p.* of them that do well
Exod 15:11. *praises,* Ps 22:3; 78:4; 149:6. Isa 60:6; 63:7. 1 Pet 2:9.
Ps 30:9. shall dust *praise* thee, 12.
42:5. shall *p.* him for help, 11; 43:5.
63:3. my lips shall *p.* thee
88:10. shall the dead arise and *p.*, 115:17.
119:164. seven times a day do I *praise*
145:10. all thy works *p.* thee
Prov 27:2. let another *p.* thee, not
31:31. her own works *p.* her in gates
Isa 38:18. the grave cannot *p.* thee
19. the living shall *p.* thee as I do
Joel 2:26. eat in plenty . . . and *p.* . . . Lord
Ps 9:1. *I will praise thee,* 111:1; 138:1; 35:18; 52:9; 56:4; 118:21; 119:7; 139:14. Isa 12:1.
2 Sam 22:4. worthy to be *praised*
1 Chron 16:25. greatly to be *p.*, Ps 48:1; 72:15; 96:4; 145:3.
2 Chron 5:13. *praising,* Ezra 3:11. Ps 84:4. Luke 2:13, 20. Acts 2:47.
PRATING, Prov 10:8, 10. 3 John 10.
PRAY for thee, and thou shalt live, Gen 20:7.
1 Sam 7:5. I will *p.* for you to Lord, 12:19.
2 Sam 7:27. found in his heart to *p.* this
Job 21:15. profit we have if we *p.*
42:8. my servant Job shall *p.* for
Ps 5:2. my God: to thee will I *p.*
55:17. morning and noon will I *p.*
122:6. *p.* for the peace of Jerusalem
Jer 7:16. *p.* not for this people, 11:14; 14:11.
Matt 5:44. *p.* for them which despitefully
26:41. watch and *p.* that ye enter not
Mark 11:24. things ye desire when ye *p.*
Luke 11:1. teach us to *p.*, as John
16:27. I *p.* thee therefore, father
18:1. men ought always to *p.*
21:36. watch ye and *p.* always
John 16:26. I will *p.* the Father for
17:9. I *p.* for them: I *p.* not
20. neither *p.* I for these alone
Acts 8:22. *p.* God, if perhaps, 24.
10:9. Peter went on housetop to *p.*
Rom 8:26. know not what we should *p.* for
1 Cor 14:15. I will *p.* with spirit, 14.
2 Cor 5:20. *p.* you in Christ's stead
Col 1:9. do not cease to *p.* for you
1 Thess 5:17. *p.* without ceasing
25. *p.* for us, 2 Thess 3:1. Heb 13:18.
1 Tim 2:8. that men *p.* every where
James 5:13. any afflicted? let him *p.*
16. *p.* one for another, Eph 6:18.
Luke 22:32. I have *prayed* for thee
44. in agony he *p.* more earnestly
Acts 10:2. gave much alms to people and *p.* to God
20:36. (Paul) *p.* with them all
James 5:17. (Elias) *p.* . . . that it might not rain
Acts 9:11. behold, he *prayeth*
Dan 9:20. *praying,* 1 Cor 11:4.
1 Thess 3:10. night and day *p.*
1 Kings 8:45. hear in heaven their *prayer*
28. respect to *p.* of servant
38. what *p.* and supplication
2 Sam 7:27. to pray this *p.* to thee
Neh 1:6. mayest hear *p.* of servant
4:9. we made our *p.* to our God
Job 15:4. restrainest *p.* before God
Ps 65:2. thou that hearest *p.*, to
102:17. he will regard *p.* of destitute, and not despise their *p.*
109:4. I give myself to *p.*
Prov 15:8. *p.* of the upright is his
29. Lord heareth *p.* of righteous

Job 31:37. as a *p.* would I go near
Isa 9:6. everlasting Father, *P.* of peace
Ezek 34:24. my servant David, a *p.* among them, 37:24, 25; 44:3; 45:7; 46:10, 16. Dan 9:25.
Dan 10:21. Michael your *p.*
12:1. Michael . . . the great *p.*
Hos 3:4. many days without a *p.*
John 12:31. now shall *prince* of this world
14:30. *p.* of this world cometh and hath
16:11. *p.* of this world judged
Acts 3:15. ye killed the *P.* of life
5:31. to be a *P.* and a Saviour
Eph 2:2. *p.* of the power of the air
Rev 1:5. Jesus . . . *p.* of kings of earth
Job 12:19. leadeth *princes* away
21. poureth contempt on *p.*, Ps 107:40.
34:19. that accepteth not persons of *p.*
Ps 45:16. thou mayest make *p.* in earth
76:12. he shall cut off spirit of *p.*
82:7. shall fall like one of the *p.*
118:9. than to put confidence in *p.*
119:23. *p.* did sit and speak against me
161. *p.* persecuted me without cause
Prov 8:15. *p.* decree justice, 16.
17:26. not good, nor to strike *p.* for equity
28:2. many are the *p.* thereof
31:4. nor for *p.* strong drink
Isa 3:4. give children to be their *p.*
Hos 7:5. *p.* made him sick with . . . wine
8:4. made *p.* and I knew it not
Matt 20:25. *p.* of Gentiles exercise
1 Cor 2:6. not wisdom of . . . *p.* of this world
Prov 4:7. wisdom is the *principal* thing
principality(ies), Jer 13:18.—*and power(s),* Eph 1:21; 6:12. Col 2:10, 15. Rom 8:38. Titus 3:1.
Heb 5:12. *principles,* 6:1.
PRISON, Gen 39:20. Eccles 4:14.
Isa 42:7. bring out prisoners from *p.*
53:8. he was taken from *p.*
61:1. opening of *p.* to them that are bound
Matt 5:25. and thou be cast into *p.*
18:30. cast into *p.* till he should pay
25:36. I was in *p.* and ye came, 43.
1 Pet 3:19. preached to spirits in *p.*
Rev 2:10. devil cast some of you into *p.*
Ps 79:11. sighing of *prisoner* come
102:20. to hear the groaning of *p.*
Eph 4:1. I *p.* of Lord beseech you, 3:1.

Ps 69:33. Lord despiseth not his *prisoners*
146:7. the Lord looseth the *p.*
Zech 9:11. send forth thy *p.* out of
12. turn to stronghold, ye *p.* of hope
Luke 21:12. *prisons,* 2 Cor 11:23.
PRIVATE, 2 Pet 1:20. Gal 2:2.
PRIVY, Deut 23:1. Acts 5:2.
Ps 10:8. *privily,* 11:2; 101:5. Acts 16:37. Gal 2:4. 2 Pet 2:1.
PRIZE, 1 Cor 9:24. Phil 3:14.
PROCEED, 2 Sam 7:12. Jer 30:21.
Isa 29:14. I will *p.* to do a marvellous work
51:4. a law shall *p.* from me
Jer 9:3. they *p.* from evil to evil
Matt 15:19. out of heart *p.* evil thoughts
Eph 4:29. no corrupt communication *p.* out of
2 Tim 3:9. they shall *p.* no further
Luke 4:22. the gracious words which *proceeded* out of his mouth
John 8:42. I *p.* forth and came from God
Gen 24:50. thing *proceedeth* from Lord
Deut 8:3. by every word that *p.* out of the mouth of God, Matt 4:4. Luke 4:4.
1 Sam 24:13. wickedness *p.* from the wicked
Lam 3:38. of mouth of most High *p.* not evil
John 15:26. Spirit of truth, which *p.*
James 3:10. out of mouth *p.* blessing
Rev 11:5. fire *p.* out of their mouth
PROCLAIM, Lev 23:2. Deut 20:10.
Exod 33:19. I will *p.* the name of the Lord
Prov 20:6. men *p.* every one his own goodness
Isa 61:2. to *proclaim* the acceptable year of Lord
Exod 34:6. Lord passed . . . and *proclaimed*
Prov 12:23. the heart of folls *proclaimeth* foolishness
PROCURED, Jer 2:17; 4:18.
PROFANE not name of Lord, Lev 18:21; 19:12; 20:3; 21:6; 22:9, 15.
Neh 13:17. *p.* sabbath, Matt 12:5.
Ezek 22:26. put not difference between holy and *p.*
1 Tim 1:9. law is for unholy and *p.*
4:7. refuse *p.* and old wives' fables
6:20. avoiding *p.* and vain babblings
Heb 12:16. fornicator or *p.* person
Ezek 22:8. thou . . . hast *profaned* my sabbaths
Mal 1:12. have *p.* it, in that ye say
2:11. Judah *p.* holiness of the Lord
10. *profaning* covenant of our fathers

PROFESS, Deut 26:3. Titus 1:16.
1 Tim 6:12. *profession,* 13. Heb 3:1; 4:14; 10:23.
PROFIT, Prov 14:23. Eccles 7:11. Jer 16:19. 2 Tim 2:14. Heb 12:10.
1 Sam 12:21. *not profit,* Job 33:27; 34:9. Prov 10:2; 11:4. Isa 30:5; 44:9, 10; 57:12. Jer 2:8, 11; 7:8; 23:32. John 6:63. 1 Cor 13:3. Gal 5:2. Heb 4:2. James 2:14.
Job 22:2. *profitable,* Eccles 10:10. Acts 20:20. 1 Tim 4:8. 2 Tim 3:16. Titus 3:8. Philem 11.
1 Tim 4:15. thy *profiting* appear
PROLONG thy days, Deut 4:26, 40; 5:16, 33; 6:2; 11:9; 17:20; 22:7; 30:18; 32:47. Prov 10:27; 28:16. Eccles 8:13. Isa 53:10.
PROMISE, Num 14:34. Neh 5:12.
Ps 77:8. doth his *p.* fail for evermore
Luke 24:49. the *p.* of my Father, Acts 1:4.
Rom 4:16. *p.* might be sure to all
9:8. children of *p.*, 9. Gal 4:28.
Eph 1:13. with that holy Spirit of *p.*
6:2. the first commandment with *p.*
1 Tim 4:8. *p.* of the life, 2 Tim 1:1.
Heb 4:1. lest a *p.* being left us of
6:17. willing to shew to heirs of *p.*, 11:9.
9:15. receive *p.* of eternal inheritance
2 Pet 3:4. where is the *p.* of his coming?
1 John 2:25. the *p.* that he promised us, even eternal life, Luke 1:72. Rom 1:2; 4:21. Titus 1:2. Heb 10:23; 11:11; 12:26.
Rom 9:4. pertaineth the *promises*
15:8. confirm *p.* made to fathers
2 Cor 1:20. all *p.* of God are yea
7:1. having these *p.* . . . let us cleanse ourselves
Gal 3:21. is the law against the *p.*
Heb 6:12. inherit *p.* 8:6. better *p.*
11:17. he that had received *p.*
2 Pet 1:4. precious *p.*
PROMOTION, Ps 75:6. Prov 3:35.
PROOF, Acts 1:3. 2 Cor 2:9; 8:24.
PROPER, 1 Chron 29:3. Heb 11:23.
PROPHECY, 1 Cor 12:10. 1 Tim 4:14; 1:18. 2 Pet 1:19, 20. Rev 1:3; 11:6; 19:10; 22:7, 10, 18, 19.
1 Kings 22:8. not *prophesy* good, 18.
Isa 30:10. *p.* not right things *p.* deceits
Joel 2:28. thy sons and thy daughters shall *p.*
Amos 2:12. *p.* not
3:8. Lord spoken, who can but *p.*?
1 Cor 13:9. we *p.* in part
14:1. but rather that ye may *p.*
31. for ye may all *p.* one by one
39. covet to *p.* and forbid not to
Rev 10:11. thou must *p.* again before many

Ezra 6:14. *prophesying,* 1 Cor 11:4; 14:6, 22. 1 Thess 5:20.
Num 11:25. *prophesied* and did not cease
Jer 23:21. I have not spoken to them, yet they *prophesied*
Matt 7:22. have we not *p.* in thy name
11:13. the prophets . . . *p.* until John
John 11:51. *p.* that Jesus should die
1 Pet 1:10. prophets *p.* of the grace
Jude 14. Enoch . . . also *p.* of these
PROPHET, Gen 20:7. he is a *p.* and shall pray for thee
Exod 7:1. and Aaron thy brother shall be thy *p.*
Deut 18:15. raise up unto thee a *p.*
18. raise them up a *p.* from among
2 Kings 5:13. if the *p.* had bid thee
Ezek 33:33. *p.* hath been among them
Hos 9:7. *p.* is a fool, the spiritual man
12:13. by a *p.* was he preserved
Matt 10:41. he that receiveth a *p.* in the name of a *p.* shall receive a *p.*'s reward
13:57. a *p.* is not without honour
Luke 7:28. there is not a greater *p.*
13:33. a *p.* perish out of Jerusalem
24:19. *p.* mighty in deed and word
John 7:40, this is the *P.*, 1:21; 6:14.
52. out of Galilee ariseth no *p.*
Acts 3:22. a *p.* shall the Lord raise
23. will not hear *p.* shall be destroyed
Titus 1:12. a *p.* of their own, said
2 Pet 2:16. ass . . . forbade madness of *p.*
Num 11:29. all Lord's people *prophets*
Ps 105:15. do my *p.* no harm
Jer 5:13. the *p.* shall become wind
23:26. are *p.* of the deceit of their
Lam 2:14. *p.* have seen vain and foolish things
Hos 6:5. I hewed them by the *p.*
Mic 3:11. *p.* divine for money
Zeph 3:4. her *p.* are light and treacherous
Matt 5:17. come to destroy the law, or *p.*
7:12. this is the law and the *p.*
13:17. many *p.* . . . have desired
22:40. on these hang all the law and *p.*
23:34. I send you *p.* and wise men
Luke 1:70. spake by mouth of his holy *p.*, Acts 3:18. 2 Pet 1:20, 21.
6:23. so did their fathers to *p.*
16:29. they have Moses and the *p.*
31. if they hear not Moses and the *p.*
24:25. to believe all that *p.* have spoken, 27.
Luke 24:44. written in the . . . *p.* concerning me
John 8:52. Abraham is dead, and the *p.*
Acts 3:25. ye are children of the *p.*
10:43. to him give all the *p.* witness
13:27. knew him not nor yet voices of the *p.*
26:27. believest thou the *p.*?
22. things which the *p.* and Moses
Rom 1:2. which he had promised afore by his *p.* in holy scriptures
3:21. witnessed by the law and *p.*
1 Cor 12:28. secondarily *p.*, 29.
14:32. spirits of *p.* are subject to *p.*
Eph 2:20. are built upon the foundation of the apostles and *p.*
1 Thess 2:15. who killed Lord Jesus and their own *p.*
Heb 1:1. God . . . spake to fathers by *p.*
James 5:10. take . . . *p.* . . . for example
Rev 18:20. rejoice, ye apostles and *p.*
22:6. Lord God of holy *p.* sent his
9. and of thy brethren the *p.*
PROPITIATION, Rom 3:25. 1 John 2:2; 4:10.
PROPORTION of faith, Rom 12:6.
PROSELYTE, Matt 23:15. Acts 2:10; 6:5; 13:43.
PROSPER, Gen 24:40. Neh 1:11.
Gen 39:3. Lord made all that he did to *p.*, 23.
Deut 29:9. *p.* in all ye do, Josh 1:7.
Job 12:6. tabernacles of robbers *p.*
Ps 1:3. whatsoever he doeth shall *prosper*
122:6. they shall *p.* that love thee
Isa 53:10. pleasure of Lord shall *p.*
54:17. no weapon against thee shall *p.*
55:11. shall *p.* in the thing whereto
Jer 12:1. Wherefore doth the way of the wicked *p.*?
23:5. a King shall reign and *p.*
1 Cor 16:2. God hath *prospered* him
3 John 2. *p.* . . . as thy soul *prospereth*
Job 36:11. spend days in *prosperity*
1 Kings 10:7. thy wisdom and *p.*
Ps 30:6. in my *p.* I said I shall never
73.3. when I saw *p.* of the *wicked*
118:25. O Lord, I beseech thee, send now *p.*
122:7. *p.* be in thy palaces, 35:27.
Prov 1:32. *p.* of fools shall destroy them
Eccles 7:14. in day of *p.* be joyful
Jer 22:21. I spake to thee in thy *p.*
Gen 24:21. journey *prosperous,* Josh 1:8. Ps 45:4. Rom 1:10.
PROTEST, Gen 43:3. 1 Sam 8:9. Jer 11:7. Zech 3:6. 1 Cor 15:31.
PROUD, Job 9:13; 26:12; 38:11; 40:11, 12. Ps 12:3.
Ps 40:4. respecteth not the *p.* nor
138:6. the *p.* he knoweth afar off
Prov 6:17. *p.* look and lying tongue
21:4. high look and *p.* heart, 28:25.
Eccles 7:8. patient is better than *p.*
Mal 3:15. we call the *p.* happy
Luke 1:51. the *p.* in imagination
James 4:6. God resisteth *p.* 1 Pet 5:5.
Exod 18:11. wherein they dealt *proudly*
1 Sam 2:3. talk no more so exceeding *p.*
Neh 9:10. knowest they dealt *p.*, 16.
Ps 17:10. they speak *p.*, 31:18.
Isa 3:5. child behave *p.* against ancient
PROVE them, Exod 16:4. Deut 8:16.
Exod 20:20. God is come to *p.* you
Deut 33:8. holy one . . . thou didst *p.* at
1 Kings 10:1. she came to *p.* him
Job 9:20. mouth shall *p.* me preverse
Ps 26:2. examine me, O Lord, *p.* me
Mal 3:10. *p.* me now herewith
Rom 12:2. *p.* what is . . . will of God
2 Cor 8:8. to *p.* the sincerity of your love
13:5. *p.* your own selves, know
Gal 6:4. let every man *p.* his work
1 Thess 5:21. *p.* all things; hold fast
Ps 17:3. thou hast *proved* mine heart
66:10. thou, O God, hast *p.* us as
95:9. *p.* me, and saw, Heb 3:9.
Deut 13:3. the Lord *proveth* you, 8:2, 16.
Acts 9:22. *proving,* Eph 5:10.
PROVERB and a byword, Deut 28:37. 1 Kings 9:7. Jer 24:9. Ezek 14:8.
Ps 69:11. I became a *p.* to them
Eccles 12:9. he set in order many *p.*, 1 Kings 4:32. Prov 1:1; 10:1; 25:1.
Isa 14:4. thou shalt take up this *p.* against
John 16:25. spoken in *p.* 29. no *p.*
2 Pet 2:22. according to true *p.*
PROVIDE, Exod 18:21. Acts 23:24.
Gen 22:8. God will *p.* himself a lamb
Ps 78:20. can he *p.* flesh for people
Matt 10:9. *p.* neither gold nor silver

Luke 12:33. *p.* bags which wax not old
Rom 12:17. *p.* things honest in sight
Job 38:41. *provideth* raven his food
Prov 6:8. *p.* her meat in summer
1 Tim 5:8. if any *p.* not for his own
Ps 132:15. *provision,* Rom 13:14.
PROVOKE him not, Exod 23:21.
Num 14:11. how long will this people *p.* me
Deut 31:20. *provoke* me, and break my
Ps 78:40. how oft did they *p.* him
Isa 3:8. to *p.* the eyes of his glory
Jer 7:19. do they *p.* me to anger . . . do they not *p.* themselves to
44:8. ye *p.* me to wrath with your
Luke 11:53. to *p.* him to speak of
Rom 10:19. *p.* to jealousy, 11:11, 14.
1 Cor 10:22. do we *p.* Lord to jealousy
Heb 3:16. when they heard, did *p.*
10:24. to *p.* unto love and good works
Num 16:30. these men have *provoked* the Lord
14:23. neither any of them that *p.* me
Deut 9:8. ye *p.* Lord to wrath, 22.
1 Kings 14:22. *p.* him to jealousy
2 Kings 23:26. that Manasseh *p.* him
1 Chron 21:1. Satan . . . *p.* David
Ezra 5:12. our fathers had *p.* God to
Ps 78:56. and *p.* the most high
106:7. *p.* him . . . at the Red sea
33. because they *p.* his Spirit
43. they *p.* him with their counsel
Zech 8:14. when your fathers *p.* me
2 Cor 9:2. your zeal hath *p.* many
Isa 65:3. a people that *provoketh* me to anger
Deut 32:19. *provoking,* 1 Kings 14:15; 16:7. Ps 78:17. Gal 5:26.
PRUDENT in matters, 1 Sam 16:18.
Prov 12:16. a *p.* man covereth shame
23. *p.* man concealeth knowledge
13:16. *p. man dealeth with* knowledge
14:8. wisdom of *p.* is to understand
15. *p.* man looketh
18. *p.* are crowned with knowledge
15:5. he that regardeth reproof is *p.*
16:21. wise in heart shall be called *p.*
18:15. heart of *p.* getteth knowledge
19:14. a *p.* wife is from the Lord
22:3. a *p.* man forseeth the evil, 27:12.
Isa 5:21. woe to them that are . . . *p.* in
Hos 14:9. who is *p.* and he shall
Matt 11:25. hid from wise and *p.*
1 Cor 1:19. I will bring to nothing the understanding of the *p.*
2 Chron 2:12. endued with *prudence* and understanding, Prov 8:12. Eph 1:8.
Isa 52:13. my servant shall deal *prudently*
PSALM, 1 Chron 16:7. Ps 81:2; 98:5. Acts 13:33. 1 Cor 14:26.
1 Chron 16:9. sing *psalms* to him, Ps 105:2.
Ps 95:2. joyful noise unto him with *p.*
Eph 5:19. speaking to yourselves in *p.*
James 5:13. merry? let him sing *p.*
PUBLICAN, Matt 18:17. Luke 18:13.
Matt 5:46. do not even the *publicans* the same, 47.
11:19. a friend of *p.* and sinners
21:31. *p.* and harlots go into kingdom of God
32. *p.* and harlots believed him
Luke 3:12. came also *p.* to be baptized
7:29. the *p.* justified God
PUBLISH name of Lord, Deut 32:3.
2 Sam 1:20. *p.* it not in the streets
Ps 26:7. *p.* with voice of thanksgiving
Acts 13:49. word of the Lord was *published*
Isa 52:7. feet of him that . . . *publisheth* peace, that *p.* salvation
Jer 4:15. a voice . . . *p.* affliction
PUFFED up, 1 Cor 4:6, 19; 5:2; 8:1; 13:4. Col 2:18.
PULL out, Ps 31:4. Jer 12:3. Matt 7:4. Luke 14:5. Jude 23. *pull down,* Isa 22:19. Jer 1:10; 18:7; 24:6; 42:10. Luke 12:18. 2 Cor 10:4.
Lam 3:11. *pull in pieces,* Acts 23:10.
Ezek 17:9. *pull up,* Amos 9:15.
Zech 7:11. *pulled* away shoulder
PULPIT of wood, Neh 8:4.
PUNISH, seven times, Lev 26:18, 24.
Isa 10:12. *p.* fruit of the stout heart
13:11. I will *p.* the world for their
Jer 9:25. *p.* all circumcised with
Hos 4:14. I will not p. daughters
12:2. will *p.* Jacob according *to*
Ezra 9:13. *p.* us less than we deserve
2 Thess 1:9. be *punished* with everlasting destruction
2 Pet 2:9. reserve unjust . . . to be *p.*
Gen 4:13. my *punishment* is greater
Lev 26:41. accept *p.* of their iniquity
Lam 3:39. complain . . . for *p.* of sins
Amos 1:3. not turn away the *p.*, 13.
Matt 25:46. go into everlasting *p.*
2 Cor 2:6. sufficient to such a man is this *p.*
Heb 10:29. of how much sorer *p.*
1 Pet 2:14. sent by him, for the *p.* of
PURCHASED, Ps 74:2. Acts 8:20; 20:28. Eph 1:14. 1 Tim 3:13.
PURE, Exod 27:20; 30:23, 34.
2 Sam 22:27. with the *p.* thou wilt shew thyself *p.*, Ps 18:26.
Job 4:17. man can be more *p.* than his Maker
25:5. stars are not *p.* in his sight
Ps 12:6. words of the Lord are *p.*
19:8. commandment of Lord is *p.*, 119:140.
24:4. clean hands and a *p.* heart
Prov 15:26. words of *p.* are pleasant
30:5. every word of God is *p.*, Ps 119:140.
30:12. generation *p.* in own eyes
Zeph 3:9. turn to people *p.* language
Acts 20:26. I am *p.* from blood of all
Rom 14:20. all things indeed are *p.*
Phil 4:8. whatsoever things are *p.*
1 Tim 3:9. faith in a *p.* conscience
5:22. keep thyself *p.*
Titus 1:15. to the *p.* all things are *p.*
Heb 10:22. washed with *p.* water
James 1:27. *p.* religion and undefiled
3:17. wisdom from above is first *p.*
2 Pet 3:1. stir up your *p.* minds
Isa 1:25. *purely* purge away dross
Job 22:30. by *pureness,* 2 Cor 6:6.
Hab 1:13. of *purer* eyes than to
1 Tim 4:12. *purity,* 5:2.
PURGE me with hyssop, Ps 51:7.
Ps 65:3. transgressions, thou shalt *p.*
79:9. *p.* away our sins for thy name's
Mal 3:3. purify and *p.* them as gold
Matt 3:12. throughly *p.* his floor
1 Cor 5:7. *p.* the old leaven
2 Tim 2:21. if a man *p.* himself
Heb 9:14. *p.* your conscience from
Isa 6:7. iniquity is taken, and sin *purged*
27:9. shall the iniquity of Jacob be *p.*
Heb 1:3. had by himself *p.* our sins
2 Pet 1:9. he was p. from old sins
PURIFY sons of Levi, Mal 3:3.
Titus 2:14. *p.* unto himself a peculiar
James 4:8. *p.* your hearts, ye double
Ps 12:6. silver . . . *purified* seven times
Dan 12:10. many shall be *p.*
1 Pet 1:22. *p.* your souls in obeying
Mal 3:3. sit as a . . . *purifier* of silver

1 John 3:3. *purifieth* himself, as he
Acts 15:9. *purifying* their hearts by
Heb 9:13. sanctifieth to *p.* of flesh
PURPOSE, Jer 6:20; 49:30.
Job 33:17. withdraw man from his *p.*
Prov 20:18. every *purpose* is established
Eccles 3:17. a time for every *p.*, 8:6.
Isa 14:26. the *p.* that is purposed
Jer 51:29. *p.* of Lord shall be performed
Acts 11:23. with *p.* of heart cleave
Rom 8:28. called according to his *p.*
Eph 1:11. according to *p.* of him
3:11. the eternal *p.* . . . in Christ
2 Tim 1:9. according to his own *p.*
1 John 3:8. for this *p.* the Son of God
Eph 1:9. mystery . . . which he *p.* in himself, 3:11.
PURSE, Prov 1:14. Matt 10:9.
PURSUE, Gen 35:5. Deut 28:22.
Exod 15:9. the enemy said, I will *p.*
Job 13:25. wilt thou *p.* dry stubble
Ps 34:14. seek peace and *p.* it
Prov 11:19. that *pursueth* evil, *p.* it
PUT, Gen 2:8; 3:15, 22.
Neh 2:12. what God *p.* in heart, 7:5. Ezra 7:27. Rev 17:17.
3:5. nobles *p.* not their necks to the work of their Lord
Job 4:18. he *p.* no trust in his servants
38:36. hath *p.* wisdom in inward parts
Ps 4:7. hast *p.* gladness in my heart
8:6. *p.* all things under his feet
9:20. *p.* them in fear, that they may
Eccles 10:10. *p.* to more strength
Song of Sol 5:3. *p.* off my coat, how shall I *p.* it on?
Isa 5:20. woe to them that *p.* darkness for light, *p.* bitter for sweet
42:1. I have *p.* my Spirit upon him
43:26. *p.* me in remembrance
63:11. who *p.* his Holy Spirit
Jer 31:33. *p.* my law in their inward parts
32:40. I will *p.* my fear in hearts
Ezek 11:19. *p.* a new spirit within you
36:27. I will *p.* my Spirit in you, 26.
Mic 7:5. *p.* not confidence in guide
Matt 5:15. *p.* it under a bushel
19:6. let no man *p.* asunder
Luke 1:52. *p. down mighty from*
Acts 1:7. Father hath *p.* in his own power
15:9. *p.* no difference between us
Eph 4:22. *p.* off . . . old man, Col 3:9.
2 Pet 1:14. *p.* off this tabernacle
Gen 28:20. God . . . give . . . raiment to *put on*
Job 29:14. I—righteousness and it
Isa 51:9. awake,—strength, arm of Lord
59:17. for he—righteousness as a breastplate,—garments of
Matt 6:25. nor for body, what ye shall—
Rom 13:12.—armour of light
14.—Lord Jesus Christ
Gal 3:27. baptized into Christ have—Christ
Eph 4:24.—the new man, Col 3:10.
6:11.—whole armour of God
Col 3:12.—. . . bowels of mercies
14. above all things—charity
1 Chron 5:20. *put trust* in, Ps 4:5; 7:1; 9:10; 56:4; 146:3. Prov 28:25; 29:25. Isa 57:13. Jer 39:18. Heb 2:13.
Num 22:38. word that God *putteth* in my mouth
Job 15:15. he *p.* no trust in saints
Ps 15:5. that *p.* not out his money,
75:7. God *p.* down one, and setteth
Song of Sol 2:13. *p.* forth green figs
Lam 3:29. he *p.* his mouth in dust
Mal 2:16. he hateth *putting* away
Eph 4:25. *p.* away lying, speak
Col 2:11. in *p.* off the body of sins
1 Thess 5:8. *p.* on breastplate of faith
1 Pet 3:3. wearing of gold or *p.* on of
21. not *p.* away of the filth of the flesh

Q

QUAILS, Exod 16:13. Num 11:31.
QUAKE, Exod 19:18. Matt 27:51.
Ezek 12:18. *quaking,* Dan 10:7.
QUARREL, Lev 26:25. Col 3:13.
QUEEN, 1 Kings 10:1; 15:13. Ps 45:9. Song of Sol 6:8. Jer 44:17, 25. Rev 18:7.
Matt 12:42. *q.* of the south rise up
QUENCH my coal, 2 Sam 14:7.
2 Sam 21:17. that thou *q.* not light
Song of Sol 8:7. many waters cannot *q.* love
Isa 42:3. smoking flax shall he not *q.*
Eph 6:16. to *q.* fiery darts of wicked
1 Thess 5:19. *q.* not the Spirit
Mark 9:43. fire that never shall be *quenched,* 44, 46, 48.
QUESTION, Mark 12:34. 1 Cor 10:25.
1 Kings 10:1. questions, Luke 2:46. 1 Tim 1:4; 6:4. 2 Tim 2:23.
QUICK, Num 16:30. Ps 55:15.
Isa 11:3. of *q.* understanding in fear
Acts 10:42. Judge of *q.* and dead
2 Tim 4:1. who shall judge *q.* and dead
Ps 71:20. *quicken* me again and
80:18. *q.* us, and we will call on thy name
119:25. *q.* thou me according to thy word
37. *q.* thou me in thy way
40. *q.* me in thy righteousness
149. *q.* me according to thy judgment
Rom 8:11. *q.* your mortal bodies
Ps 119:50. thy word hath *quickened* me
Col 2:13, *q.* together with him
1 Pet 3:18. but *q.* by the Spirit
John 5:21. Son *quickeneth* whom he will
6:63. it is the Spirit that *q.*
1 Cor 15:45. last Adam was made a *quickening* spirit
QUICKLY, Exod 32:8. Deut 11:17.
Eccles 4:12. threefold cord is not *q.* broken
Matt 5:25. agree with thine adversary *q.*
Rev 3:11. behold, I come *q.*, 22:7, 12, 20.
QUIET, Judg 18:27. Job 3:13, 26.
Eccles 9:17. words of wise heard in *q.*
Isa 7:4. take heed and be *q.*, fear not
1 Thess 4:11. study to be *q.* and to
1 Tim 2:2. lead a *q.* and peaceable
1 Pet 3:4. ornament of a meek and *q.* spirit
1 Chron 22:9. *quietness,* Job 20:20.
Job 34:29. when he giveth *q.* who
Eccles 4:6. better is a handful with *q.*
Isa 30:15. in *q.* and confidence shall be your strength
32:17. effect of righteousness shall be *q.*
2 Thess 3:12. exhort that with *q.* they work
QUIT you like men, 1 Sam 4:9. 1 Cor 16:13.
QUIVER full of them, Ps 127:5.
Isa 49:2. in his *q.* hath he hid me
Jer 5:16. *q.* is as an open sepulchre

R

RABBI, Matt 23:7, 8. *Rabboni,* John 20:16.
RACE, Ps 19:5. Eccles 9:11. 1 Cor 9:24. Heb 12:1.
RAGE, 2 Kings 5:12. 2 Chron 16:10.
2 Chron 28:9. ye have slain them in a *r.*
Prov 6:34. jealousy is *r.* of a man
29:9. whether he *r.* or laugh is no
Ps 46:6. the heathen *raged*
Prov 14:16. the fool *rageth*
Ps 89:9. rulest the *raging* of sea
Prov 20:1. mocker, strong drink is *r.*
Jude 13. *r.* waves of sea, foaming

RAGS, Prov 23:21. Isa 64:6.
RAILER, or drunkard, 1 Cor 5:11.
1 Pet 3:9. *railing,* 1 Tim 6:4.
2 Pet 2:11. *r.* accusation, Jude 9.
RAIMENT to put on, Gen 28:20.
Exod 21:10. *r.* not diminished
Deut 8:4. thy *r.* waxed not old upon
24:17. not take widow's *r.* to
Zech 3:4. clothe thee with change of *r.*
Matt 6:25. body more than *r.*, 28.
11:8. man clothed in soft *r.*
17:2. his *r.* was white as the light
1 Tim 6:8. having food and *r.* let
Rev 3:5. clothed in white *r.*, 18; 4:4.
RAIN in due season, Lev 26:4. Deut 11:14; 28:12.
Deut 32:2. my doctrine drop as *r.*
2 Sam 23:4. clear shining after *r.*
1 Kings 8:35. no *r.* because they have sinned
2 Chron 7:13. that there be no *r.*
Job 5:10. who giveth *r.* on the earth
28:26. he made a decree for the *r.*
Ps 68:9. didst send a plentiful *r.*
72:6. he shall come down like *r.*
147:8. who prepareth *r.* for earth
Prov 16:15. his favour is as cloud of latter *r.*
Eccles 12:2. nor clouds return after *r.*
Song of Sol 2:11. winter is past; *r.* is over
Isa 4:6. covert from storm and *r.*
5:6. clouds that they *r.* no *r.* upon
55:10. as *r.* cometh down from
Jer 5:24. fear Lord our God, that giveth *r.*
Amos 4:7. witholden *r.* from you
Zech 10:1. ask of the Lord *r.*
14:17. upon them shall be no *r.*
Matt 5:45. sendeth *r.* on the just
Heb 6:7. earth which drinketh in *r.*
James 5:18. prayed again, heaven gave *r.*
Job 38:26. cause it to *r.* on earth
Ps 11:6. on wicked he shall *r.* snares
Hos 10:12. till he *r.* righteousness
Ps 78:27. he *rained* flesh upon
Ezek 22:24. land not cleansed, nor *r.* upon
RAISE, Deut 18:15, 18. 2 Sam 12:11.
Isa 44:26. *r.* up decayed places
58:12. *r.* up foundations of many
Hos 6:2. third day he will *r.* us up
Amos 9:11. I will *r.* up tabernacle of
John 6:40. I will *r.* him up at last day
Exod 9:16. *raised* thee up to shew . . . my power
Matt 11:5. deaf hear, dead are *r.*
Luke 1:69. *r.* up an horn of salvation
Rom 4:25. *r.* again for our justification
6:4. as Christ was *r.* from the dead, 8:11.
1 Cor 6:14. God hath *r.* up the Lord
2 Cor 4:14. he which *r.* up the Lord Jesus, shall raise us also by Jesus
Eph 113:2:6. hath *r.* us up together
Ps 113:7. he *raiseth* up poor out of dust
145:14. *r.* up those that are bowed down
RANSOM of life, Exod 21:30.
Exod 30:12. give every man a *r.* for
Job 33:24. I have found *r.*
36:18. great *r.* cannot deliver thee
Ps 49:7. nor give to God a *r.* for
Prov 6:35. he will not regard any *r.*
13:8. *r.*of man's life are his riches
21:18. wicked shall be a *r.* for righteous
Isa 43:3. I gave Egypt for thy *r.*
Matt 20:28. to give his life a *r.* for
1 Tim 2:6. gave himself a *r.* for all
Isa 35:10. *ransomed,* 51:10. Jer 31:11.
RASH, Eccles 5:2. Isa 32:4.
RAVISHED, Prov 5:19. Song of Sol 4:9.
REACH, Gen 11:4. John 20:27.
Ps 36:5. faithfulness *reacheth* to clouds
Phil 3:13. *reaching* forth to those things
READ in audience, Exod 24:7.
Deut 17:19. *r.* therein all . . . his life
Neh 13:1. *r.* in the book of Moses
Acts 15:21. *r.* in synagogues every
2 Cor 3:2. known and *r.* of all men
1 Thess 5:27. epistle be *r.*, Col 4:16.
Acts 8:30. understandest thou what thou *readest?*
Rev 1:3. blessed is he that *readeth*
Neh 8:8. *reading,* 1 Tim 4:13.
READY to pardon, a God, Neh 9:17.
Ps 45:1. tongue is pen of *r.* writer
Eccles 5:1. more *r.* to hear, than
Matt 24:44. be ye also *r.*, Luke 12:40.
Mark 14:38. spirit is *r.* but the flesh
Acts 21:13. *r.* not to be bound only
1 Tim 6:18. do good, *r.* to distribute
2 Tim 4:6. now *r.* to be offered
Titus 3:1. *r.* to every good work
Rev 3:2. strengthen things . . . *r.* to die
Acts 17:11. *readiness,* 2 Cor 10:6.
REAP the harvest, Lev 19:9.
Hos 10:12. *r.* in mercy
Matt 6:26. sow not, neither do they *r.*, Luke 12:24.
1 Cor 9:11. a great thing if we *r.*
Gal 6:7. man soweth, that shall he also *r.*
8. soweth to flesh . . . *r.* corruption; . . . soweth to Spirit . . . *r.* life everlasting
9. shall *r.* if we faint not
Hos 10:13. plowed wickedness, ye have *reaped* iniquity
Rev 14:16. the earth was *r.*, 15.
Matt 13:39. *reapers* are angels, 30.
John 4:36. he that *reapeth* receiveth
REASON, Prov 26:16. Dan 4:36.
1 Pet 3:15. asketh a *r.* of the hope
Rom 12:1. your *reasonable* service
Acts 24:25. as he *reasoned* of righteousness
Isa 41:21. bring forth your strong *reasons*
REBEL not against Lord, Num 14:9. Josh 22:19.
Job 24:13. of those that *r.* against the light
Neh 9:26. *rebelled* against thee, Ps 5:10.
Isa 63:10. *r.* and vexed his holy Spirit
1 Sam 15:23. *rebellion* as sin of witchcraft
Deut 9:7. been *rebellious* against Lord, 24.
Isa 30:9. this is a *r.* people, lying
50:5. I was not *r.* neither turned away
65:2. spread my hands . . . to a *r.* people, 1:23.
Jer 4:17. hath been *r.*
5:23. this people hath a revolting and *r.* heart
Ezek 2:5, 8. *r. house,* 3:9, 26; 12:2, 3; 17:12. 24:3; 44:6.
Num 20:10. hear now, ye *rebels*
Ezek 20:38. purge out from you the *r.*
REBUKE thy neighbour, Lev 19:17.
2 Kings 19:3. a day of trouble, *r.* and blasphemy
Ps 6:1. *r.* me not in thine anger, nor
Prov 9:8. *r.* a wise man, he will love
27:5. open *r.* is better than secret love
Zech 3:2. Lord said to Satan, The Lord *r.* thee
Matt 16:22. Peter . . . began to *r.* him
Luke 17:3. if thy brother trespass . . . *r.* him
Phil 2:15. sons of God, without *r.*
1 Tim 5:1. *r.* not an elder, entreat
20. them that sin *r.* before all
Titus 1:13. *r.* them sharply, 2:15.
Heb 12:5. nor faint when *rebuked*
Ps 39:11. thou with *rebukes* dost correct
Amos 5:10. hate him that *rebuketh* in gate
RECEIVE good and not evil, Job 2:10.
Job 22:22. *r.* I pray thee the law from his mouth
Ps 6:9. the Lord will *r.* my prayer
Ps 49:15. he shall *receive* me

73:24. guide me . . . and afterward *r.* me
75:2. when I shall *r.* congregation
Matt 10:41. *r.* a prophet's reward
18:5. *r.* one such little child in my name
19:11. all men cannot *r.* this saying
21:22. ask, believing, ye shall *r.*
Mark 4:16. heard the word, *r.* it with gladness
11:24. believe that ye *r.* them
Luke 16:9. may *r.* you into everlasting
John 3:27. man can *r.* nothing except
5:44. which *r.* honour one of
16:24. ask, and ye shall *r.*, that your joy
Acts 2:38. shall *r.* gift of Holy Ghost
7:59. Lord Jesus, *r.* my spirit
10:43. whosoever believeth shall *r.* remission of sins
20:35. more blessed to give than to *r.*
26:18. may *r.* forgiveness of sins
Rom 14:1. him that is weak in faith *r.* ye
1 Cor 3:8. every man *r.* his own reward
2 Cor 5:10. may *r.* things done in the body
6:1. *r.* not grace of God in vain
Gal 3:14. *r.* promise of the Spirit
Eph 6:8. same shall he *r.* of the Lord
Col 3:24. *r.* reward of inheritance
James 1:21. *r.* with meekness the engrafted word
3:1. *r.* greater condemnation
1 Pet 5:4. shall *r.* a crown of glory
1 John 3:22. whatsoever we ask, we *r.*
2 John 8. we *r.* a full reward
Job 4:12. mine ear *received* a little
Ps 68:18. thou hast *r.* gifts for men
Matt 10:8. freely ye have *r.*, freely give
Luke 6:24. ye have *r.* your consolation
John 1:11. own *r.* him not, 12.
Acts 8:17. they *r.* the Holy Ghost
17:11. *r.* the word with all readiness
20:24. which I *r.* of Lord, 1 Cor 11:23.
Rom 5:11. by whom we have *r.* atonement
8:15. have *r.* the spirit of adoption
14:3. him that eateth, for God hath *r.* him
15:7. receive ye one another, as Christ also *r.* us
1 Tim 3:16. *r.* into glory, Mark 16:19.
4:3. meats which God hath created to be *r.*
Heb 11:13. not having *r.* promises
Luke 16:25. *receivedst* thy good things
Jer 7:28. nor *receiveth* correction
Matt 7:8. every one that asketh *r.*
10:40. he that *r.* you *r.* me, and he that *r.* me *r.* him that sent me
John 3:32. no man *r.* his testimony
12:48. rejecteth me, and *r.* not my words
1 Cor 2:14. natural man *r.* not things
Phil 4:15. in giving and *receiving*
Heb 12:28. we *r.* a kingdom
1 Pet 1:9. *r.* the end of your faith
RECKON(ED), Ps 40:5. Isa 38:13. Luke 22:37. Rom 4:4, 9, 10; 6:11; 8:18.
RECOMPEN(C)SE, Prov 12:14. Isa 35:4.
Deut 32:35. to me belongeth vengeance and *r.*
Job 15:31. vanity shall be his *r.*
Jer 25:14. *r.* them . . . their deeds, Hos 12:2.
Luke 14:14. they cannot *r.* thee
Rom 12:17. *r.* to no man evil for evil
Isa 66:6. render *r.* to his enemies, 59:18.
Hos 9:7. the days of *r.* are come
Luke 14:12. lest a *r.* be made, 14.
Heb 2:2. disobedience received just *r.* of reward
10:35. confidence, which hath great *r.* of
11:26. he had respect unto *r.* of
2 Sam 22:21. according to cleanness of my hands hath he *recompensed* me
Prov 11:31. the righteous shall be *recompensed*
Jer 18:20. shall evil be *r.* for good
Rom 11:35. it shall be *r.* to him
Isa 34:8. it is the year of *recompences* for Zion
Jer 51:56. the Lord God of *r.* shall
RECONCILE with blood, Lev 6:30.
Col 1:20. to *r.* all things to himself
Matt 5:24. be *reconciled* to thy brother
Rom 5:10. when we were enemies we were *r.*
2 Cor 5:18. God, who hath *r.* us to himself
20. we pray you . . . , be ye *r.* to God.
Lev 8:15. to make *reconciliation,* 2 Chron 29:24. Ezek 45:15, 17. Dan 9:24.
2 Cor 5:18. given to us ministry of *r.*
19. committed to us the word of *r.*
Heb 2:17. to make *r.* for sins of people
2 Cor 5:19. God was in Christ *reconciling* world
RECORD my name, Exod 20:24.
Deut 30:19. I call heaven and earth to *r.* this day, 31:28.
Job 16:19. my witness . . . and my *r.*
John 1:32. bare *r.* 8:13, 14; 12:17; 19:35. Rom 10:2. Gal 4:15.
2 Cor 1:23. I call God for a *r.*, Phil 1:8.
1 John 5:7. three bear *r.* in heaven
Rev 1:2. bare *r.* of the word of God
RECOVER strength, Ps 39:13.
Hos 2:9. I will *r.* my wool and flax
2 Tim 2:26. may *r.* themselves
Jer 8:22. is not . . . my people *recovered*
Luke 4:18. *recovering* of sight to
RED, Ps 75:8. Isa 1:18; 27:2; 63:2. Zech 1:8; 6:2. Rev 6:4; 12:3.
REDEEM with a stretched out arm, Exod 6:6.
2 Sam 7:23. Israel whom God went to *r.*
Job 5:20. in famine he shall *r.* thee
Ps 49:15. God will *r.* my soul from power
130:8. *r.* Israel from all his iniquities
Hos 13:14. I will *r.* them from death
Titus 2:14. might *r.* us from all iniquity
Gen 48:16. angel which *redeemed* me
2 Sam 4:9. *r.* my soul out of adversity
Ps 136:24. *r.* us from our enemies, 31:5.
Isa 1:27. Zion shall be *r.* with judgment
52:3. shall be *r.* without money, 9.
63:9. in his love and in his pity he *r.* them, 4.
Luke 1:68. visited and *r.* his people
24:21. which should have *r.* Israel
Gal 3:13. Christ hath *r.* us from the curse of the law
1 Pet 1:18. not *r.* with corruptible
Rev 5:9. hast *r.* us to God by thy blood
14:4. these were *r.* from among men
Job 19:25. I know that my *redeemer* liveth
Ps 19:14. my strength and my *r.*
Prov 23:11. their *r.* is mighty
Isa 63:16. our father and *r.* 48:17.
Jer 50:34. *R.* is strong, Isa 49:26.
Ps 34:22. the Lord *redeemeth* the soul of his servants
103:4. who *r.* thy life from destruction, 72:14.
Eph 5:16. *redeeming* time, Col 4:5.
Lev 25:24. *redemption,* Num 3:49.
Ps 49:8. *r.* of their soul is precious
111:9. he sent *r.* unto his people
Luke 2:38. looked for *r.* in Jerusalem
21:28. your *r.* draweth nigh
Rom 3:24. through *r.* that is in Christ Jesus
8:23. waiting for the *r.* of our body
1 Cor 1:30. Christ . . . made unto us . . . *r.*

RELIGION, Acts 26:5. Gal 1:13, 14.
James 1:27. pure *r.* and undefiled, 26.
Acts 13:43. *religious,* James 1:26.
REMAIN, 1 Thess 4:15. Rev 3:2. Eccles 2:9. Lam 5:19. John 1:33.
Ps 76:10. *remainder* of wrath
John 9:41. your sin *remaineth*
2 Cor 9:9. righteousness *r.* for ever
Heb 4:9. *r.* a rest to people of God
1 John 3:9. his seed *r.* in him
REMEDY, 2 Chron 36:16. Prov 6:15; 29:1.
REMEMBER, Gen 40:23. Neh 1:8.
Gen 9:16. look upon it that I may *r.*
Exod 13:3. *r.* this day . . . ye came out of Egypt
Deut 5:15. *r.* thou wast a servant
7:18. shalt well *r.* what Lord . . . did
8:18. thou shalt *r.* Lord thy God
9:7. *r.* . . . how thou provokedst Lord
2 Kings 20:3. *r.* how I walked before
Ps 20:7. we will *r.* name of Lord
25:6. *r.* . . . mercies, 7. *r.* not sins
74:2. *r.* thy congregation, 18.
79:8. not against us former iniquities, Isa 64:9. Jer 14:10. Hos 8:13.
89:47. *r.* how short my time is
119:49. *r.* word unto thy servant
132:1. *r.* David and all his afflictions
Eccles 12:1. *r.* now thy Creator in days of
Song of Sol 1:4. we will *r.* thy love more
Isa 43:25. I will not *r.* thy sins
46:8. *r.* this, shew yourselves men
Jer 31:20. I do earnestly *r.* him still
Ezek 16:61. shalt *r.* thy ways
36:31. shall ye *r.* your own evil ways
Mic 6:5. *r.* what Balak . . . consulted
Hab 3:2. in wrath *r.* mercy
Luke 1:72. to *r.* his holy covenant
17:32. *r.* Lot's wife, Gen 19:26.
Gal 2:10. that we should *r.* the poor
Col 4:18. *r.* my bonds
Heb 8:12. iniquities will I *r.* no more
13:3. *r.* them that are in bonds
Neh 13:14. *r. me,* 22, 31. Ps 25:7; 106:4. Luke 23:42.
Ps 63:6. *I remember,* 143:5.
Jer 2:2. for—thee, the kindness of thy youth
Lev 26:42. *I will remember* my covenant, 45. Ezek 16:60.
Ps 77:11.—the works of the Lord
Jer 31:34.—their sin no more
Gen 8:1. God *remembered* Noah
19:29. God *r.* Abraham and sent
30:22. God *r.* Rachel, 1 Sam 1:19.
Exod 2:24. and God *r.* his covenant with Abraham, 6:5.
Num 10:9. shall be *r.* before Lord
Ps 77:3. I *r.* God and was troubled
78:39. he *r.* they were but flesh
98:3. hath *r.* his mercy and truth
119:52. I *r.* thy judgments of old
55. I have *r.* thy name, O Lord, in the night
136:23. who *r.* us in our low estate
137:1. we wept when we *r.* Zion
Matt 26:75. Peter *r.* word of Jesus
Luke 24:8. they *r.* his words, and
John 2:17. disciples *r.* it was written
Rev 18:5. God hath *r.* her iniquities
Lam 1:9. she *remembereth* not her last end
3:19. *remembering,* 1 Thess 1:3.
1 Kings 17:18. call my sin to *remembrance*
Ps 6:5. in death is no *r.* of
Isa 26:8. and to the *remembrance* of thee
Lam 3:20. my soul hath them still in *r.*
Mal 3:16. a book of *r.* was written
Luke 1:54. he hath holpen . . . Israel in *r.*
22:19. this do in *r.*, 1 Cor 11:24, 25.
John 14:26. bring all things to your *r.*
Acts 10:31. thine alms are had in *r.*
2 Tim 1:6. put in *r.*, 2:14. 2 Pet 1:12; 3:1. Jude 5.
Rev 16:19. Babylon came in *r.*
REMIT sins, they shall, John 20:23.
Matt 26:28. *remission of sins,* Mark 1:4. Luke 1:77; 3:3; 24:47. Acts 2:38; 10:43. Rom 3:25. Heb 9:22; 10:18.
REMNANT, Lev 2:3. Deut 3:11.
2 Kings 19:4. lift up thy prayer for the *r.*
Ezra 9:8. leave us a *r.* to escape
Isa 1:9. left unto us a very small *r.*
10:21. a *r.* shall return, 22.
Jer 23:3. I will gather *r.* of my flock
Ezek 6:8. yet will I leave a *r.*
Rom 9:27. a *r.* shall be saved, 11:5.
REMOVE thy stroke, Ps 39:10.
Ps 119:22. *r.* from me reproach and
29. *r.* from me the way of lying
Prov 4:27. *r.* thy foot from evil
30:8. *r.* far from me vanity and lies
Eccles 11:10. *r.* sorrow from thy heart
Matt 17:20. *r.* hence and it shall *r.*
Luke 22:42. if thou be willing *r. this cup*
Rev 2:5. I will *r.* thy candlestick
Ps 103:12. so far hath he *removed* our transgressions from us
Prov 10:30. righteous shall never be *r.*
Isa 30:20. shall not thy teachers be *r.*
Ezek 36:17. uncleanness of a *r.* woman
REND heavens and come, Isa 64:1.
Joel 2:13. *r.* your heart and not your garments
Jer 4:30. though thou *rentest* thy face
RENDER vengeance, Deut 32:41, 43.
2 Chron 6:30. *r.* to every man according to his ways
Job 33:26. he will *r.* to man his righteousness
34:11. work of a man shall he *r.* to
Ps 116:12. what shall I *r.* to Lord
Prov 26:16. seven men that can *r.* a reason
Hos 14:2. *r.* the calves of our lips
Matt 22:21. *r.* to Cæsar the things
Rom 13:7. *r.* to all their dues
1 Thess 5:15. that none *r.* evil for evil, 3:9.
RENEW right spirit in me, Ps 51:10.
Isa 40:31. they that wait up on Lord shall *r.* . . . strength
Heb 6:6. *r.* them to repentance
Ps 103:5. thy youth is *renewed* like
2 Cor 4:16. inward man is *r.* day by day
Eph 4:23. be *r.* in spirit of your mind
Ps 104:30. *renewest* face of earth
Rom 12:2. *renewing,* Titus 3:5.
RENOUNCED hidden things, 2 Cor 4:2.
RENOWN, Ezek 34:29; 39:13.
Isa 14:20. *renowned,* Ezek 23:23.
REPAIRER of breaches, Isa 58:12.
REPAY, Job 21:21; 41:11.
Deut 7:10. he will *r.* him to his face
Isa 59:18. according to their deeds . . . he will *r.*
Rom 12:19. I will *r.*, saith the Lord
Prov 13:21. to righteous good shall be *repayed*
REPENT of this evil, Exod 32:12.
Num 23:19. neither son of man . . . *r.*
Deut 32:36. Lord shall . . . *r.* himself
1 Kings 8:47. *r.* and make supplication
Job 42:6. I abhor myself and *r.* in dust
Ps 90:13. let it *r.* thee concerning
135:14. will *r.* himself concerning
Jer 18:8. I will *repent* of evil I thought
Ezek 14:6. *r.* and turn yourselves, 18:30.
Jon 3:9. if God will turn and *r.*
Matt 3:2. *r.* ye, for the kingdom of heaven is at hand, 4:17.
Mark 1:15. *r.* and believe gospel
6:12. preached that men should *r.*
Luke 13:3. except ye *r.* ye shall all likewise perish, 5.

Isa 57:2. he shall *r.* in their beds
20. like the troubled sea, when it cannot *r.*
Hab 3:16. I might *r.* in day of trouble
Rev 14:13. dead . . . in the Lord . . . *r.* from
Rom 2:17. art called a Jew, and *restest* in
Prov 14:33. wisdom *resteth,* Job 24:23.
Eccles 7:9. anger *r.* in bosom of fools
1 Pet 4:14. spirit of . . . God *r.* upon you
Num 10:33. *resting place,* 2 Chron 6:41. Prov 24:15. Isa 32:18. Jer 50:6.
RESTORE, Ps 51:12; 23:3; 69:4. Isa 58:12. Luke 19:8. Gal 6:1
Exod 22:3. *restitution,* Acts 3:21.
RESTRAIN, 1 Sam 3:13. Job 15:4. Ps 76:10. Isa 63:15.
RESURRECTION, Matt 22:23, 28, 30. Acts 23:8. 1 Cor 15:12. Heb 6:2.
Luke 20:36. and are the children of God, being children of the *r.*
John 5:29. done good to *r.* of life . . . done evil to *r.* of damnation
11:25. I am the *r.* and the life
Acts 17:18. preached unto them Jesus and the *r.*
24:15. there shall be a *r.* of dead
Rom 6:5. in likeness of his *r.*
Phil 3:10. power of *r.* 11. attain *r.*
Heb 11:35. might obtain a better *r.*
Rev 20:5. this is the first *r.* 6.
RETAIN, Job 2:9. John 20:23. Prov 3:18; 11:16. Eccles 8:8. Rom 1:28.
Mic 7:18. *retaineth* not his anger
RETURN, to the dust, Gen 3:19.
1 Kings 8:48. *r.* to thee with all their heart
Job 1:21. naked shall I *r.* thither
Ps 73:10. his people *r.* hither
116:7. *r.* unto thy rest, O my soul
Eccles 12:7. dust shall *r.* to the earth
Song of Sol 6:13. *r.*, *r.*, O Shulamite; *r.*, *r.*
Isa 10:21. remnant shall *r.* . . . to . . . God, 22.
35:10. ransomed of lord shall *r.*, 51:11.
55:11. (my word) shall not *r.* unto me void
Jer 3:12. *r.*, backsliding Israel, 14, 22.
4:1. if thou wilt *r.* . . . *r.* unto me
5:3. they refused to *r.*, 8:5. Hos 11:5.
15:19. if thou *r.* . . . let them *r.* . . . but *r.* not thou
Hos 2:7. *r.* to my first husband
5:15. I will go and *r.* to my place
7:16. they r., but not to Most High
11:9. not *r.* to destroy Ephraim
Mal 3:7. *r.* to me, and I will *r.* to
18. then shall ye *r.* and
Ps 35:13. my prayer *returned* into my bosom
78:34. they *r.* and inquired early after God
Amos 4:6. have ye not *r.* to me, 8–11.
1 Pet 2:25. are *r.* unto Shepherd
Isa 30:15. in *returning* find rest
Deut 30:2. *return to the Lord,* 1 Sam 7:3. Isa 55:7. Hos 6:1; 3:5; 7:10; 14:1, 7.
REVEAL, Prov 11:13. Dan 2:19.
Job 20:27. heaven shall *r.* his iniquity
Gal 1:16. pleased God . . . to *r.* his Son
Deut 29:29. things which are *revealed*
Isa 22:14. it was *r.* in mine ears
53:1. to whom is arm of Lord *r.*?
Matt 10:26. covered that shall not be *r.*
11:25. hid . . . from wise . . . , *r.* them to babes
16:17. flesh and blood hath not *r.*
Rom 1:17. righteousness of God *r.*
8:18. glory which shall be *r.* in us
1 Cor 2:10. God hath *r.* them to us
2 Thess 1:7. when Lord Jesus shall be *r.*
2:3. falling away . . . man of sin be *r.*
Amos 3:7. *revealeth* his secret to his servants
Rom 2:5. *revelation,* 16:25. Gal 1:12. Eph 1:17; 3:3. 1 Pet 1:13. 2 Cor 12:1. Rev 1:1.
REVELLINGS, Gal 5:21. 1 Pet 4:3.
REVENGE, Jer 15:15. 2 Cor 7:11; 10:6. Nah 1:2.
Num 35:19. *revenger,* Rom 13:4.
Ps 79:10. by the *revenging* of the blood of thy servants
REVERENCE my sanctuary, Lev 19:30.
Ps 89:7. to be had in *r.* of all them
Eph 5:33. wife see that she *r.* her
Heb 12:28. serve God acceptably with *r.*
Ps 111:9. and *reverend* is his name
REVILE, Exod 22:28. Matt 5:11.
1 Cor 4:12. being *reviled* we bless
1 Pet 2:23. when he was *r.*, *r.* not
1 Cor 6:10. nor *revilers* . . . inherit the
Isa 51:7. *revilings,* Zeph 2:8.
REVIVE us again, Ps 85:6.
Isa 57:15. to *r.* the spirit of the humble, to *r.* heart of contrite
Hos 6:2. after two days will he *r.* us
14:7. they shall *r.* as the corn, and
Rom 7:9. sin *revived* and I died
14:9. Christ both died and rose, and *r.*
REVOLT more and more, Isa 1:5.
Isa 31:6. children of Israel have deeply *revolted*
Jer 5:23. this people hath a *revolting* and a rebellious heart
6:28. *revolters,* Hos 5:2; 9:15.
REWARD, exceeding great, Gen 15:1.
Deut 10:17. God . . . nor taketh *r.*, Ps 15:5.
Ps 19:11. in keeping them is great *r.*
58:11. there is a *r.* for righteous
127:3. fruit of the womb is his *r.*
Prov 11:18. righteousness shall be a sure *r.*
Isa 3:11. *r.* of his hands shall be
Mic 7:3. the judge asketh for a *r.*
Matt 5:12. great is your *r.* in heaven
6:2. verily . . . they have their *r.*
4. thy Father . . . shall *r.* thee openly
10:41. shall receive a prophet's *r.*
Rom 4:4. is the *r.* not reckoned of
1 Cor 3:8. shall receive his own *r.*
Col 2:18. no man beguile you of your *r.*
3:24. receive the *r.* of inheritance
1 Tim 5:18. labourer is worthy of his *r.*
2 Tim 4:14. Lord *r.* him according
Heb 2:2. just recompence of *r.*
2 John 8. we receive a full *r.*
Rev 22:12. I come quickly; and my *r.* is with
18:6. *r.* her as she *rewarded* you
Ps 103:10. nor *r.* us according to our iniquities
Isa 3:9. have *r.* evil to themselves
Heb 11:6. *rewarder* of them that
Ps 31:23. plentifully *rewardeth* proud
RICH, Gen 13:2; 14:23. Exod 30:15.
Prov 10:4. hand of diligent maketh *r.*
22. blessing of the Lord, it maketh *r.*
14:20. *r.* hath many friends
18:11. *r.* man's wealth is his strong city, 10:15.
Prov 22:2. *rich* and poor meet together
23:4. labour not to be *r.*
28:11. *r.* man wise in his own conceit
20. that maketh haste to be *r.* shall not
Eccles 5:12. abundance of *r.* will not suffer
10:20. curse not *r.* in thy bedchamber
Jer 9:23. let not *r.* man glory in his
Matt 19:23. *r.* man shall hardly enter
Luke 1:53. *r.* he hath sent empty away
6:24. woe unto you that are *r.*
16:1. certain *r.* man which had
18:23. sorrowful: for he was very *r.*
2 Cor 6:10. as poor yet making many *r.*
8:9. though he was *r.* yet . . . he became poor
Eph 2:4. God who is *r.* in mercy
1 Tim 6:9. they that will be *r.* fall
17. charge them that are *r.* in this
18. that they be *r.* in good works
James 2:5. poor of this world *r.* in faith

15:2. walketh uprightly and worketh *r.*
85:10. *r.* and peace have kissed
97:2. *r.* and judgment are habitation
106:3. he that doeth *r.* at all times
Prov 10:2. *r.* delivereth from death, 11:4.
11:5. *r.* of perfect shall direct his way
6. *r.* of upright shall deliver them
18. to him that soweth *r.* a sure
19. as *r.* tendeth to life; so he that
12:28. in the way of *r.* is life
13:6. *r.* keepeth him that is upright in way
14:34. *r.* exalteth a nation: but sin
15:9. he loveth him that followeth *r.*
16:12. the throne is established by *r.*
31. if it be found in the way of *r.*
Isa 11:5. *r.* shall be the girdle of his loins
26:9. inhabitants of world will learn *r.*
28:17. judgment . . . to line and *r.* to the plummet
32:17. work of *r.* shall be peace
45:24. in the Lord have I *r.* and
46:12. that are far from *r.*
13. I bring near my *r.*; it shall not
54:17. their *r.* is of me, saith Lord
61:3. trees of *r.*, planting of Lord
10. covered me with robe of *r.*
64:5. that rejoiceth and worketh *r.*
Jer 23:6. be called Lord our *R.*, 33:16.
Dan 4:27. break off thy sins by *r.*
9:7. O Lord, *r.* belongeth unto thee
24. to bring in everlasting *r.*
12:3. they that turn many to *r.* (shall shine) as the stars
Zeph 2:3. seek *r.*, seek meekness
Mal 4:2. Sun of *r.* arise with healing
Matt 3:15. it becometh us to fulfil all *r.*
5:6. which do hunger and thirst after *r.*
20. except your *r.* exceed the *r.* of
21:32. John came . . . in the way of *r.*
Luke 1:75. in holiness and *r.* before
John 16:8. reprove world of sin, of *r.*
Acts 10:35. he that . . . worketh *r.* is accepted
13:10. thou enemy of all *r.*
Rom 1:17. therein is the *r.* of God revealed
3:22. even *r.* of God which is by *faith of*
4:6. man to whom God imputeth *r.*
5:18. by *r.* of one the free gift came to all
21. grace reign through *r.* to eternal
6:13. members as instruments of *r.*
19. servants to *r.* unto holiness, 18.
8:4. that the *r.* of the law might
9:30. have attained to *r.*, even *r.*, 31.
10:3. ignorant of God's *r.* . . . establish their own *r.*, have not submitted themselves unto the *r.* of God. 4. Christ is end of law for *r.* 6 *r.* which is of faith.
10. with heart man believeth to *r.*
14:17. kingdom of God is . . . *r.*, peace
1 Cor 1:30. made unto us wisdom and *r.*
15:34. awake to *r.* and sin not
2 Cor 5:21. the *r.* of God in him
6:7. armour of *r.* on right hand
9:10. increase the fruits of your *r.*
11:15. ministers . . . transformed as ministers of *r.*
Gal 2:21. if *righteousness* come by the law, then
Eph 6:14. having on breastplate of *r.*
Phil 1:11. being filled with fruits of *r.*
3:6. touching *r.* which is in the law blameless
9. not mine own *r.* but the *r.* which is of God
1 Tim 6:11. follow after *r.*, 2 Tim 2:22.
Heb 12:11. peaceable fruit of *r.*
James 1:20. man worketh not *r.* of God
3:18. fruit of *r.* is sown in peace
1 Pet 3:14. if ye suffer for *r.*' sake happy
2 Pet 1:1. through the *r.* of God and our
3:13. new earth, wherein dwelleth *r.*
1 John 2:29. that doeth *r.* is born
Rev 19:8. fine linen is the *r.* of saints
Gen 15:6. counted it to him for *r.*, Ps 106:31. Rom 4:3, 5, 9, 22. Gal 3:6.
1 Kings 8:32. *his righteousness,* Job 33:26. Ps 50:6. Ezek 3:20. Matt 6:33. Rom 3:25. 2 Cor 9:9.
Ps 17:15. *in righteousness,* Hos 10:12. Acts 17:31. Eph 4:24. Rev 19:11. *with righteousness,* Ps 96:13; 98:9.
Deut 9:5. *thy righteousness,* Job 35:8. Ps 35:28; 40:10; 51:14; 89:16; 119:142. Isa 57:12; 58:8; 62:2.
Isa 64:6. *all our righteousnesses,* Ezek 33:13. Dan 9:18.

RIGOUR, Exod 1:13. Lev 25:43, 53.

RIOT, Titus 1:6. 1 Pet 4:4. 2 Pet 2:13.
Rom 13:13. *rioting*
Prov 23:20. riotous, 28:7. Luke 15:13.

RIPE fruit, Exod 22:29. Num 18:13. Mic 7:1. Jer 24:2. *r.* figs, Hos 9:10. Nah 3:12.
Gen 40:10. *ripe grapes,* Num 13:20. Isa 18:5. Joel 3:13.
Rev 14:15. harvest of the earth is *r.*

RISE, Song of Sol 3:2. Isa 14:21; 24:20; 26:14; 33:10; 43:17; 54:17; 58:10. 1 Thess 4:16.
Prov 30:31. *rising,* Luke 2:34.

RIVER, Exod 1:22; 4:9. Job 40:23. Ps 36:8; 46:4; 65:9. Isa 48:18; 66:12. Rev 22:1, 2.
Job 20:17. *rivers,* 29:6. Ps 119:136. Prov 5:16; 21:1. Isa 32:2; 33:21. Mic 6:7. John 7:38.

ROAR, Isa 42:13. Jer 25:30. Hos 11:10. Joel 3:16. Amos 1:2.

ROB, Lev 19:13. Prov 22:22.
Isa 42:22. a people *robbed* and
2 Cor 11:8. I *r.* other churches
Job 5:5. the *robber* swalloweth up, 18:9.
John 10:1. that climbeth up some other way is a thief and a *r.*
Ps 62:10. *robbery,* Prov 21:7. Isa 61:8. Amos 3:10. Phil 2:6.

ROBE, Isa 61:10. Rev 7:9, 13, 14.

ROCK, Exod 17:6. Num 20:8, 11. Deut 32:4, 13, 15, 18, 30, 31.
Ps 18:2. Lord is my *r.*, 92:15.
31:3. thou art my *r.* and my fortress, 2; 71:3.
61:2. lead me to the *r.* that is higher than
62:2. he only is my *r.*, 6.
89:26. my father . . . and *r.* of my salvation
94:22. God is the *r.* of my refuge
Matt 7:24. wise man, which built his house on a *r.*
16:18. on this *r.* I will build my church
1 Cor 10:4. that *R.* was Christ
Rev 6:16. said to . . . *rocks,* Fall on us

ROD, Exod 4:4, 20. Num 17:2, 8.
Ps 23:4. thy *r.* and staff they comfort
125:3. *r.* of wicked shall not
Prov 13:24. spareth his *r.* hateth his son
23:14. thou shalt beat him with *r.*
29:15. *r.* and reproof give wisdom
Ezek 20:37. cause to pass under *r.*, Lev 27:32.
Mic 6:9. hear ye the *rod* and who hath
7:14. feed thy people with thy *r.*
Rev 2:27. rule with *r.* of iron, 12:5. 19:15.

ROOM, Prov 18:16. Luke 14:22.

ROOT, Job 5:3; 31:12. Ps 52:5.
Deut 29:18. a *r.* that beareth gall
Job 19:28. seeing *r.* of the matter
Isa 11:10. there shall be *r.* of Jesse
37:31. take *r.* downwards, 27:6.
Matt 3:10. axe is laid to *r.* of trees
13:6. because they had no *r.*
Luke 17:6. be thou plucked up by *r.*
Rom 11:16. if *r.* be holy, so are the
1 Tim 6:10. love of money is *r.* of
Matt 15:13. planted . . . shall be *rooted* up

Eph 3:17. being *r.* and grounded in love
Col 2:7. *r.* and built up in him
ROSE, Song of Sol 2:1. Isa 35:1.
ROYAL diadem in hand of thy God, Isa 62:3.
James 2:8. if ye fulfil *r.* law
1 Pet 2:9. ye are . . . a *r.* priesthood
RUBIES, price of wisdom is above, Job 28:18. Prov 3:15; 8:11; 31:10.
RUDDY, Song of Sol 5:10. Lam 4:7.
RUDIMENTS, Col 2:8, 20.
RULE, Esther 9:1. Prov 17:2; 19:10.
Prov 25:28. no *r.* over his own spirit
Gal 6:16. walk according to this *r.*
Phil 3:16. let us walk by same *r.*
Heb 13:7. which have *r.* over you, 17.
Col 3:15. let the peace of God *r.* in
1 Tim 3:5. how to *r.* his own house
5:17. elders that *r.* well be counted worthy
Rev 12:5. man child who was to *r.* all
Mic 5:2. is to be *ruler* in Israel
Matt 25:21. make thee *r.* over many
Rom 13:3. *rulers* are not a terror to
Eph 6:12. *r.* of darkness of this world
Ps 103:19. his kingdom *ruleth* over all
Prov 16:23. he that *r.* his spirit than
Hos 11:12. Judah yet *r.* with God
RUN, Gen 49:22. Lev 15:3. 1 Sam 8:11. Ps 19:5. Eccles 1:7. *forerunner,* Heb 6:20.
2 Chron 16:9. eyes of the Lord *r.*
Ps 119:32. I will *r.* way of thy commandments
Song of Sol 1:4. draw me, we will *r.* after
Isa 40:31. shall *r.* and not be weary
Dan 12:4. many shall *r.* to and fro
Gal 2:2. *r.* in vain, 5:7. did *r.* well
Heb 12:1. *r.* with patience the race
1 Pet 4:4. *r.* not with them to same excess of
Ps 23:5. my cup *runneth* over
Rom 9:16. nor of him that *r.*, but

S

SABBATH holy, Exod 16:23, 29; 20:8–11; 31:14. Acts 13:42; 18:4.
Lev 23:3. seventh day is *s.* of rest
Neh 9:14. madest known . . . thy holy *s.*
13:18. bring more wrath . . . by profaning *s.*
Isa 56:2. keepeth *s.* from polluting it, 6.
58:13. call *s.* a delight, holy of the Lord
Matt 12:5. priests in the temple profane *s.*
28:1. end of *s.* as it began to dawn
Lev 19:3. *my sabbaths,* 30; 26:2. Isa 56:4. Ezek 20:12, 13; 22:8, 26; 23:38; 44:24; 46:3.
Deut 5:12. *sabbath day,* Neh 13:22. Jer 17:21. Acts 15:21. Col 2:16.
SACKCLOTH, Gen 37:34. Job 16:15. Ps 30:11; 35:13. Isa 22:12. Rev 11:3.
SACRIFICE, Gen 31:54. Exod 8:25.
1 Sam 2:29. wherefore kick ye at my *s.*
3:14. Eli's house shall not purged with *s.*
15:22. to obey is better than *s.*
Ps 50:5. made covenant with me by *s.*
107:22. *s.* the sacrifices of thanksgiving, 116:17.
141:2. lifting up of my hands as evening *s.*
Prov 15:8. *s.* of wicked is abomination
21:3. justice . . . more acceptable to Lord than *s.*
Eccles 5:1. than to give *s.* of fools
Dan 8:11. daily *s.* was taken away
9:27. cause *s.* and oblation to cease
11:31. take away daily *s.*, 12:11.
Hos 6:6. desired mercy and not *s.*, Matt 9:13; 12:7.
Mark 9:49. every *s.* be salted with
Rom 12:1. present your bodies a living *s.*
Eph 5:2. *s.* to God for a sweetsmelling
Phil 2:17. offered on *s.* and service of your faith
4:18. a *s.* acceptable, well pleasing to God
Heb 9:26. put away sin by *s.* of
1 Cor 5:7. Christ our passover is *sacrificed*
Ps 4:5. offer *sacrifices* of righteousness
51:17. *s.* of God are a broken spirit
Heb 13:15. *s.* of praise, 16. with such *s.*
1 Pet 2:5. priesthood, to offer up *s.*
SACRILEGE, commit, Rom 2:22.
SAD, 1 Sam 1:18. Ezek 13:22. Mark 10:22. Eccles 7:3. by *sadness* of countenance heart is
SAFE, Ps 119:117. Prov 18:10; 29:25.
Job 5:4. *safety,* 11. Ps 4:8; 12:5; 33:17. Prov 11:14; 21:31.
SAINTS, Ps 52:9; 79:2; 89:5.
Ps 106:16. envied . . . Aaron *saint* of Lord
Deut 33:2. came with ten thousands of *saints,* Jude 14.
3. all his *s.* are in thy hand
1 Sam 2:9. he will keep feet of his *s.*
Job 15:15. he putteth no trust in his *s.*
Ps 16:3. goodness extendeth . . . to *s.*
50:5. gather my *s.* together unto me
97:10. he preserveth souls of his *s.*
116:15. in sight of Lord is death of his *s.*
Prov 2:8. preserveth way of his *s.*
Dan 7:18. *s.* of most High shall take kingdom, 27.
Hos 11:12. and is faithful with the *s.*
Zech 14:5. Lord shall come, and all *s.*
Rom 1:7. called to be *s.* 1 Cor 1:2. 2 Cor 1:1. Eph 1:1. Col 1:2, 4, 12, 26.
8:27. intercession for *s.*, Eph 6:18.
12:13. necessity of *s.*, 2 Cor 9:12.
15:25. minister to *s.*, 26, 31. 1 Cor 16:1. 2 Cor 8:4; 9:1. Heb 6:10.
1 Cor 6:2. *s.* shall judge the world
Eph 3:8. less than the least of all *s.*
1 Thess 3:13. coming of . . . Jesus . . . with all his *s.*
2 Thess 1:10. to be glorified in his *s.*
Rev 5:8. prayers of the *s.*, 8:3, 4.
11:18. reward to thy servants the prophets and . . . *s.*
13:7. to make war with the *s.*
14:12. here is the patience of the *s.*
15:3. just and true are thy ways, thou King of *s.*
16:6. blood of *s.*, 17:6; 18:24.
19:8. fine linen is righteousness of *s.*
20:9. compassed the camp of the *s.*
SALT, Gen 19:26. Lev 2:13. Matt 5:13. Mark 9:49, 50. Col 4:6.
SALVATION, Ps 14:7; 53:6.
Exod 14:13. stand still and see *s.* of Lord, 2 Chron 20:17.
Ps 3:8. *s.* belongeth to Lord
37:39. *s.* of righteous is of Lord
50:23. I will shew him *s.* of God, 96:2.
68:20. God is the God of *s.*, 65:5.
85:9. his *s.* is nigh them that fear him
119:155. *s.* is far from the wicked
Ps 132:16. clothe her priests with *salvation*
149:4. (Lord) will beautify meek with *s.*
Isa 25:9. we will . . . rejoice in his *s.*, 12:3.
26:1. *s.* will God appoint for walls
33:2. be our *s.* 6. strength of *s.*
45:17. Israel shall be saved . . . with everlasting *s.*
46:13. I will place *s.* in Zion for
52:10. earth shall see *s.* of our God
59:16. arm brought *s.* unto me, 63:5.
17. for an helmet of *s.*, Eph 6:17.

60:18. call thy walls *S.*, thy gates
61:10. clothed me with garments of *s.*
62:1. *s.* as a lamp
Jer 3:23. in vain is *s.* hoped for from hills . . . ; God is *s.* of Israel
Lam 3:26. quietly wait for *s.* of Lord
Jon 2:9. *s.* is of the Lord
Hab 3:8. ride on . . . thy chariots of *s.*
Zech 9:9. he is just and having *s.*
Luke 19:9. is *s.* come to this house
John 4:22. *s.* is of the Jews
Acts 4:12. neither is there *s.* in any
13:26. word of *s.* sent, 47. be for *s.*
Rom 1:16. it is the power of God to *s.*
11:11. through their fall *s.* is come
13:11. now is our *s.* nearer than
2 Cor 1:6. for your . . . *s.* 6:2. day of *s.*
Phil 2:12. work out your own *s.* with
1 Thess 5:8. hope of *s.* 9. to obtain *s.*
2 Thess 2:13. hath chosen you to *s.*
2 Tim 2:10. to obtain *s.* which is in Christ
3:15. scriptures . . . able to make thee wise unto *s.*
Titus 2:11. grace of God that bringeth *s.*
Heb 1:14. who shall be heirs of *s.*
2:3. escape if we neglect so great *s.*
5:9. became author of eternal *s.*
6:9. things that accompany *s.*
9:28. appear the second time without sin unto *s.*
1 Pet 1:5. kept . . . through faith to *s.*
Jude 3. write unto you of common *s.*
Rev 7:10. *S.* to our God, 12:10; 19:1.
Exod 15:2. (God) is become *my salvation,* Job 13:16. Ps 18:2; 25:5; 27:1; 38:22; 51:14; 62:7; 88:1; 118:14. Isa 12:2. Mic 7:7. Hab 3:18.
Ps 89:26. rock of—140:7. strength of—56:1.
2 Sam 23:5. this is all—
Isa 46:13.—shall not tarry, 49:6; 51:5, 6, 8.
Gen 49:18. *thy salvation,* 1 Sam 2:1. Ps 9:14; 13:5; 20:5; 18:35; 21:1, 5; 35:3; 40:10, 16; 51:12; 69:13, 29; 70:4; 71:15; 85:7; 106:4; 119:41, 81, 123, 166, 174. Isa 17:10; 62:11. Luke 2:30.
SAME, Ps 102:27. Heb 13:8. Rom 10:12. 1 Cor 12:4, 5, 6. Eph 4:10.
SANCTIFY, Exod 13:2; 19:10.
Exod 31:13. I am the Lord that doth *s.*
Lev 20:7. *s.* yourselves therefore and be ye holy
Isa 8:13. *s.* the Lord of hosts himself
Ezek 38:23. I magnify myself and *s.* myself
Joel 1:14. *s.* a fast, 2:15.
2:16. *s.* the congregation
John 17:17. *s.* them through thy truth
19. for their sakes I *s.* myself
1 Thess 5:23. God of peace *s.* you
Heb 13:12. that he might *s.* people
1 Pet 3:15. *s.* Lord God in your hearts
Gen 2:3. blessed seventh day and *sanctified* it
Lev 10:3. I will be *s.* in them that
Deut 32:51. ye *s.* me not in midst of
Job 1:5. Job sent and *s.* them and
Isa 5:16. God that is holy shall be *s.*
Jer 1:5. before thou camest . . . I *s.* thee
Ezek 20:41. be *sanctified* in you before the heathen, 28:22, 25; 38:16; 39:27.
John 10:36. him whom Father hath *s.*
Acts 20:32. inheritance among all them which are *s.*, 26:18.
Rom 15:16. offering of Gentiles . . . *s.*
1 Cor 1:2. *s.* in Christ Jesus
6:11. ye are washed, but ye are *s.*
7:14. unbelieving husband is *s.* by the wife
1 Tim 4:5. *s.* by word of God and prayer
Heb 2:11. they who are *s.* are all of one
10:14. perfected for ever them that are *s.*
Matt 23:17. temple that *sanctifieth*
1 Cor 1:30. *sanctification,* 1 Thess 4:3, 4. 2 Thess 2:13. 1 Pet 1:2.
SANCTUARY, Ps 63:2; 73:17. Isa 8:14. Ezek 11:16. Dan 9:17. Heb 9:2.
SAND, Gen 22:17; 32:12. Job 6:3; 29:18. Isa 10:22. Matt 7:26.
SATAN provoked David, 1 Chron 21:1.
Job 1:6. *S.* came also among, 2:1.
Ps 109:6. let *S.* stand at his right
Matt 4:10. get thee hence, *S.*, 16:23.
Luke 10:18. I beheld *S.* as lightning
22:3. entered *S.* into Judas
Acts 26:18. turn from power of *S.*
Rom 16:20. God of peace shall bruise *S.*
1 Cor 5:5. deliver such an one to *S.*
7:5. *S.* tempt you not for your incontinency
2 Cor 2:11. lest *S.* should get an advantage
11:14. *S.* is transformed into angel
12:7. messenger of *S.* to buffet me
1 Tim 1:20. I have delivered to *S.*
Rev 2:9. synagogue of *S.*
24. have not known the depths of *S.*
SATIATE, Jer 31:14, 25; 46:10.
SATISFY, Job 38:27. Prov 6:30.
Ps 90:14. O *s.* us early with thy mercy
91:16. with long life will I *s.* him
103:5. who *s.* thy mouth with good
107:9. he *s.* the longing soul
132:15. will *s.* her poor with bread
Prov 5:19. breasts *s.* thee at all times
Isa 55:2. labour for that which *s.* not
Ps 17:15. *satisfied* with thy likeness
22:26. meek shall eat and be *s.*
63:5. soul shall be *s.* as with
65:4. *s.* with goodness of thy house
Prov 14:14. good man shall be *s.* from himself
27:20. eyes of man are never *s.*
30:15. are three things never *s.*
Eccles 5:10. loveth silver shall not be *s.*
Isa 9:20. eat . . . and they shall not be *s.*, Mic 6:14.
53:11. see travail of his soul and be *s.*
66:11. be *s.* with breasts of her consolations
Jer 31:14. people shall be *s.* with my goodness
Ezek 16:28. yet couldest not be *s.*
Hab 2:5. and cannot be *s.*
Num 35:31. shall take no *satisfaction* for life of a murderer, 32.
SAVE your lives, preserve, Gen 45:7.
Gen 50:20. people alive, to *s.* much
Job 22:29. he shall *s.* the humble
Ps 18:27. wilt *s.* afflicted people
69:35. God will *s.* Zion and build the
72:4. he shall *s.* children of needy
13. and shall *s.* the souls of needy
86:2. *s.* thy servant that trusteth
16. *s.* son of thine handmaid
109:31. those that condemn to *s.* him from
118:25. *s.* now; I beseech thee, O Lord
145:19. hear their cry and will *s.* them
Prov 20:22. wait on Lord, he shall *s.* thee
Isa 35:4. (God) will come and *save* you
45:20. cannot *s.*, 59:1. Jer 14:9.
Ezek 18:27. shall *s.* his soul, 3:18.
36:29. *s.* you from all your uncleanness, 37:23.
Zeph 3:17. Lord . . . is mighty; he will *s.*
19. *s.* her that halteth
Zech 8:7. I will *s.* my people, 9:16; 10:6.
Matt 1:21. *s.* his people from their sins

16:25. whosoever will *s.* his life shall lose
18:11. Son of man is come to *s.* that which was lost, Luke 19:10.
Mark 3:4. is it lawful . . . to *s.* life or to
John 12:47. not to judge world but to *s.* world
Acts 2:40. *s.* yourselves from this . . . generation
1 Cor 1:21. by foolishness of preaching to *s.* them that believe
9:22. that I might by all means *s.* some
1 Tim 1:15. to *s.* sinners, of
Heb 7:25. able to *s.* them to the uttermost
James 1:21. word which is able to *s.*
2:14. can faith *s.* him?
5:15. prayer of faith shall *s.* sick
20. converteth a sinner . . . shall *s.* soul
Jude 23. others *s.* with fear, pulling
Ps 6:4. *save me,* 55:16; 57:3; 119:94. Jer 17:14. John 12:27.
Isa 25:9. *save us,* 33:22; 37:20. Hos 14:3. Matt 8:25. 1 Pet 3:21.
Ps 44:7. thou hast *saved* us from our enemies
106:8. *s.* them for his name's sake
Isa 45:22. look unto me and be ye *s.*
Jer 8:20. we are not *s.*
Jer 4:14. that thou mayest be *s.*
Matt 19:25. who then can be *s.*? Luke 18:26.
Luke 1:71. be *s.* from our enemies
7:50. thy faith hath *s.* thee, 18:42.
23:35. he *s.* others, let him save himself
John 3:17. world through him might be *s.*
Acts 2:47. Lord added . . . daily such as should be *s.*
4:12. none other name whereby we must be *s.*
16:30. what must I do to be *s.*?
Rom 8:24. we are *s.* by hope
10:1. prayer . . . for Israel is that they might be *s.*
1 Cor 1:18. to us which are *s.* it is
5:5. spirit may be *s.* in day of Lord
Eph 2:5. by grace ye are *s.*, 8.
Titus 3:5. according to his mercy he *s.* us
1 Pet 4:18. righteous scarcely be s.
Rev 21:24. nations which are *s.*
Ps 80:3. *shall be saved,* 7, 19. Isa 45:17; 64:5. Jer 23:6; 30:7. Matt 10:22; 24:13. Mark 16:16. Acts 16:31. Rom 5:10; 11:26. 1 Tim 2:15.
2 Sam 22:3. God . . . my refuge, my *Saviour*
2 Kings 13:5. Lord gave Israel a *s.*, Neh 9:27.
Isa 43:3. I am thy *S.*, 49:26; 60:16.
11. beside me there is no *S.,* Hos 13:4.
45:15. God of Israel, the *S.,* Jer 14:8.
Obad 21. *saviours* shall come up on . . . Zion
Luke 1:47. spirit rejoiced in God my *S.*
2:11. to you is born . . . a *S.* which is
Acts 5:31. him God exalted . . . to be . . . *S.*
Eph 5:23. (Christ) is the *s.* of body
1 Tim 4:10. who is the *s.* of all men
1:1. God our *S.,* Titus 1:4; 2:10, 13; 3:4, 6. 2 Pet 1:1, 11. Jude 25.
2 Pet 2:20. knowledge of the Lord and *S.*
SAVOUR, sweet, Gen 8:21. Exod 29:18. Lev 1:9; 2:9; 3:16.
Song of Sol 1:3. of *s.* of thy good ointments
2 Cor 2:14. the *s.* of his knowledge
15. are to God a sweet *s.* of Christ
Eph 5:2. sacrifice to God for a sweetsmelling *savour*
Matt 16:23, *savourest* not things, . . . of God
SAY, Matt 3:9; 5:22, 28, 32, 34, 39, 44; 7:22; 23:3. 1 Cor 12:3.
SCARCELY, Rom 5:7. 1 Pet 4:18.
SCATTER them in Israel, Gen 49:7.
Num 10:35. let thine enemies be *scattered*
Matt 9:36. *s.* abroad as sheep, Ezek 34:5.
Luke 1:51. *s.* proud in imagination
Prov 11:24. that *scattereth* and yet
SCEPTRE not depart from Judah, Gen 49:10.
Num 24:17. *S.* shall rise out of Israel
Ps 45:6. the *s.* of thy kingdom is a right *s.* Heb 1:8.
Zech 10:11. *s.* of Egypt shall depart
SCHISM, 1 Cor 1:10; 12:25.
SCHOLAR, 1 Chron 25:8. Mal 2:12.
Gal 3:24. law was our *schoolmaster*
SCOFFERS, Hab 1:10. 2 Pet 3:3.
SCORN, Job 16:20. Ps 44:13.
Prov 9:8. reprove not a *scorner*
14:6. a *s.* seeketh wisdom and
15:12. *s.* loveth not one that reproveth
1:22. *scorners* delight in scorning
19:29. judgments are prepared for *s.*
9:12. if thou *scornest* thou shalt bear it
Ps 1:1. *scornful,* Prov 29:8. Isa 28:14.
SCORPIONS, 2 Chron 10:11. Ezek 2:6.
SCOURGE of the tongue, Job 5:21.
Isa 28:15. overflowing *s.*, 18.
Heb 12:6. Lord . . . *scourgeth* every son
SCRIPTURE of truth, Dan 10:21.
2 Tim 3:16. all *s.* is given by inspiration
2 Pet 1:20. no prophecy of *s.* is of
Matt 22:29. ye err, not knowing *scriptures*
John 5:39. search *s.*, Acts 17:11; 18:24.
Rom 15:4. through comfort of *s.*
2 Tim 3:15. from a child known holy *s.*
2 Pet 3:16. wrest, as they do also other *s.*
SEA, Ps 33:7; 72:8. Prov 8:29. Isa 48:18; 57:20. Zech 9:10. Rev 4:6; 10:2; 15:2; 21:1.
SEAL upon thine heart, Song of Sol 8:6.
John 3:33. set to his *s.* that God is
Rom 4:11. *s.* of the righteousness
1 Cor 9:2. *s.* of my apostleship are ye
Rev 7:2. angel . . . having *s.* of living God
Job 14:17. my transgression is *sealed* up
Song of Sol 4:12. spring shut up, fountain *s.*
John 6:27. hath God the Father *s.*
2 Cor 1:22. who hath *s.* us and
Eph 1:13. ye were *s.* with that Holy Spirit
Rev 5:1. a book *s.* with seven seals
7:3. *s.* the servants of our God
4. were *s.* an hundred and forty and four
SEARCH out resting place, Num 10:33.
Ps 139:23. *s.* me, O God, and know
Prov 25:27. men to *s.* their own glory is
Jer 17:10. I the Lord *s.* the heart
29:13. when ye shall *s.* for me with
Zeph 1:12. *s.* Jerusalem with candles
John 5:39. *s.* scriptures
Acts 17:11. these *searched* the scriptures daily
Job 10:6. that *searchest* after my sin
Prov 2:4. *s.* for her as for hid treasure
1 Chron 28:9. the Lord *searcheth* all hearts
Prov 18:17. neighbour cometh and *s.*
1 Cor 2:10. Spirit *s.* . . . deep things of God
Rev 2:23. I am he which *s.* the reins
SEARED with hot iron, 1 Tim 4:2.
SEASON, Gen 40:4. Exod 13:10.
Ps 1:3. bringeth forth his fruit in his *s.*
Isa 50:4. to speak a word in *s.*
Luke 4:13. departed from him for a *season*
John 5:35. willing for a *s.* to rejoice
2 Tim 4:2. instant in *s.*, out of *s.*
Heb 11:25. pleasures of sin for a *s.*
1 Pet 1:6. for a *s.* . . . ye are in heaviness

Col 4:6. let speech be *seasoned* with
Acts 1:7. to know the times or *seasons*
14:17. gave us rain . . . and fruitful *s.*
1 Thess 5:1. of times and *s.* brethren ye have
SECRET, Gen 49:6. Job 40:13.
Job 29:4. *s.* of God was on my tabernacle, 15:8.
Ps 25:14. *s.* of Lord is with them that
27:5. in *s.* of his tabernacle he will
139:15. when I was made in *s.*
Prov 3:32. his *s.* is with righteous
9:17. bread eaten in *s.* is pleasant
Amos 3:7. revealeth his *s.* to his servants
Matt 6:4. alms in *s.* . . . Father seeth
John 18:20. in *s.* have I said nothing
19:38. *secretly* for fear of Jews
Job 11:6. shew thee *secrets* of wisdom
Ps 44:21. he knoweth the *s.* of heart
Prov 11:13. talebearer revealeth *s.*, 20:19.
Dan 2:28. a God . . . that revealeth *s.*
Rom 2:16. God shall judge *s.*
SECT, Acts 24:5; 26:5; 28:22.
SEDUCE, Ezek 13:10. Mark 13:22.
2 Tim 3:13. *seducers—ing,* 1 Tim 4:1.
SEE, Ps 34:8. Matt 5:8. John 16:22. 1 John 3:2. Rev 1:7; 22:4.
Matt 6:1. before men to be *seen* of
13:17. desired to see . . . and have not *s.*
23:5. their works they do to be *s.* of men
John 1:18. no man hath *s.* God at any time
14:9. he that hath *s.* me hath *s.* the Father
20:29. thou hast *s.* me . . . blessed are they that have not *s.*, and yet have believed
2 Cor 4:18. look not at things . . . *s.* but
1 Tim 6:16. whom no man hath *s.*
Heb 11:1. evidence of things not *s.*
1 Pet 1:8. whom not having *s.* ye love
1 John 1:1. that which we have *s.* and
4:12. no man hath *s.* God at any time
John 12:45. he that *seeth* me *s.* him that
14:17. because it *s.* him not, 19.
SEED, Gen 1:11; 17:7; 38:9.
Ps 126:6. bearing precious *s.*
Eccles 11:6. in morning sow thy *s.*
Isa 55:10. give *s.* to the sower
Matt 13:38. good *s.* are children of
Luke 8:11. the *s.* is word of God
1 John 3:9. his *s.* remaineth in him
Ps 37:28. *s.* of wicked shall be cut off
69:36. *s.* of his servants shall inherit it
Prov 11:21. *s.* of righteous shall be
Isa 1:4. sinful nation, . . . *s.* of evildoers
45:25. all *s.* of Israel be justified
53:10. see his *s.*, prolong his days
Mal 2:15. he might seek a godly *s.*
Rom 9:8. children of promise counted for *s.*
29. except Lord of Sabaoth had left us a *s.*
Gal 3:16. not to *seeds,* but to thy *s.*
SEEK, Ezra 8:21. Job 5:8. Ps 10:15.
Deut 4:29. if thou *s.* him with all thy heart, 1 Chron 28:9. 2 Chron 15:2. Jer 29:13.
Ezra 8:22. on them for good that *s.*
Ps 9:10. not forsake them that *s.*
63:1. my God, early will I *s.* thee
69:32. heart shall live that *s.* God
119:2. blessed are they that *s.* him
176. *s.* thy servant, for I do not forget
Prov 8:17. that *s.* me early shall find
Song of Sol 3:2. *s.* him whom my soul loveth
Isa 26:9. with my spirit . . . will I *seek* thee
45:19. I said not. . . . *s.* me in vain
Jer 29:13. ye shall *s.* me and find
Amos 5:4. *s.* ye me, ye shall live, 6:8.
Zeph 2:3. *s.* Lord, . . . *s.* righteousness, *s.* meekness
Mal 2:7. *s.* the law
15. that he might *s.* a godly seed
Matt 6:33. *s.* ye first the kingdom of God
7:7. *s.* and ye shall find, 8. Deut 4:29.
Luke 13:24. many will *s.* to enter in
19:10. *s.* and to save that which was lost, Matt 18:11.
John 8:21. ye shall *s.* me and
Rom 2:7. *s.* for glory, honour
1 Cor 10:24. let no man *s.* his own but
Phil 2:21. all *s.* their own, not . . . Jesus Christ's
Col 3:1. *s.* those things which are above
1 Pet 3:11. *s.* peace, and ensue it
John 4:23. Father *seeketh* such to worship
1 Cor 13:5. charity *s.* not her own
1 Pet 5:8. *seeking* whom he may devour
SEEM, Gen 27:12. Deut 25:3.
1 Cor 11:16. if any man *s.* to be *contentious*
Heb 4:1. lest any of you *s.* to come short
James 1:26. if any . . . *s.* to be religious
Luke 8:18. even that which he *seemeth* to
1 Cor 3:18. if any man . . . *s.* to be wise in
Heb 12:11. no chastening . . . *s.* to be joyous
SELL me thy birthright, Gen 25:31.
Prov 23:23. buy truth and *s.* it not
Matt 19:21. go, and *s.* that thou hast
13:44. he . . . *selleth* all that he hath and buyeth
SENATORS, Ps 105:22.
SEND help from the sanctuary, Ps 20:2.
Ps 43:3. O *s.* out thy light and
57:3. he shall *s.* from heaven and
Matt 9:38. *s.* forth labourers into
John 14:26. whom the Father will *s.*
16:7. if I depart I will *s.* him unto
2 Thess 2:11. *s.* them strong delusion
SENSE, Neh 8:8. Heb 5:14.
James 3:15. *sensual,* Jude 19.
SENTENCE, Deut 17:9. Dan 5:12.
Prov 16:10. a divine *s.* is in lips of
Eccles 8:11. because *s.* is not executed
2 Cor 1:9. we had *s.* of death in
SEPARATE, Gen 13:9. Exod 33:16.
Gen 49:26. was *s.* from his brethren, Deut 33:16.
Deut 29:21. Lord shall *s.* him
Acts 13:2. *s.* me Barnabas and Saul
Rom 8:35. who shall *s.* us from love of Christ, 39.
2 Cor 6:17. be ye *s.*, saith the Lord
Heb 7:26. holy, harmless, . . . *s.* from sinners
Isa 59:2. iniquities have *separated*
Acts 19:9. departed from them and *s.* the disciples
Gal 1:15. who *s.* me from my mother's womb
SERAPHIMS, Isa 6:2, 6.
SERPENT, Gen 3:1, 13; 49:17.
Prov 23:32. at last it biteth like a *serpent,*
Matt 7:10. will he give him a *s.*?
John 3:14. as Moses lifted up *s.* in
2 Cor 11:3. as the *s.* beguiled Eve
Rev 12:9. that old *s.*, called the Devil
Num 21:6. Lord sent fiery *serpents,* 8, 9.
Matt 10:16. be ye wise as *s.*, harmless as
SERVE Lord with all thy heart, Deut 10:12, 20; 11:13. Josh 22:5. 1 Sam 12:20.
Deut 13:4. shall *s.* him, and cleave
Josh 24:14. fear the Lord, *s.* him
15. choose you this day whom ye will *s.* . . . me and my house, we will *s.* the Lord
1 Chron 28:9. *s.* him with a perfect
Job 21:15. Almighty that we should *s.* him
Ps 2:11. *s.* Lord with fear, rejoice

Matt 6:24. no man can *serve* two masters; ye cannot *s.* God and mammon
Luke 1:74. *s.* him without fear in
12:37. will come forth and *s.* them
John 12:26. if any man *s.* me let him
Acts 6:2. leave word of God and *s.* tables
27:23. whose I am, and whom I *s.*
Rom 1:9. whom I *s.* with my spirit
7:6. *s.* in newness of spirit
25. with the mind I myself *s.* law of God
16:18. they *s.* not Lord Jesus Christ
Col 3:24. ye *s.* Lord Christ
Gal 5:13. by love *s.* one another
1 Thess 1:9. to *s.* living God, Heb 9:14.
Heb 12:28. may *s.* God acceptably
Rev 7:15. *s.* him day and night in
Isa 24:2. with *servant* so with his master
42:1. behold my *s.*, 49:3; 52:13.
Matt 20:27. be chief . . . let him be your *s.*
25:21. well done, good and faithful *s.*, 23.
John 8:34. committeth sin is *s.* of sin
13:16. *s.* not greater than lord, 15:20.
1 Cor 7:21. art thou called, being *s.*?
9:19. have I made myself *s.* to all
Gal 1:10. if I yet pleased men . . . not *s.* of Christ
Phil 2:7. took on him form of a *s.*
2 Tim 2:24. *s.* of Lord must not
Ezra 5:11. *servants* of the God of heaven, Dan 3:26. Acts 16:17. 1 Pet 2:16. Rev 7:3.
Rom 6:16. yield yourselves *s.* to obey; his *s.* ye are to whom
17. ye were the *s.* of sin
18. ye became *s.* of righteousness
1 Cor 7:23. be not ye the *s.* of men
Phil 1:1. the *s.* of Jesus Christ
2 Pet 2:19. *s.* of corruption
Rev 22:3. his *s.* shall serve him
Rom 12:1. your reasonable *service*
Jer 22:13. useth neighbour's *s.*
Luke 10:40. Martha cumbered about much *serving*
Acts 20:19. *s.* Lord with all humility
26:7. twelve tribes instantly *s.* God
Rom 12:11. fervent in spirit; *s.* Lord
Titus 3:3. *s.* divers lusts and pleasures
SET, Ps 2:6; 4:3; 12:5; 16:8; 54:3; 75:7; 113:8. Prov 1:25. Song of Sol 8:6. Rom 3:25. Col 3:2.
SETTLE, Luke 21:14. 1 Pet 5:10.
Col 1:23. in faith grounded and *settled*
SEVERITY, goodness and, Rom 11:22.

SHADE, Lord is thy, Ps 121:5.
SHADOW, our days are as a, 1 Chron 29:15. Eccles 8:13; 6:12. Job 8:9. Ps 107:10; 109:23; 144:4.
Ps 17:8. me under the *s.* of thy wings, 36:7; 57:1; 63:7.
Song of Sol 2:3. I sat under his *s.*
Isa 4:6. for a *s.* in day, 25:4; 32:2.
49:2. in *s.* of his hand hath he hid
Acts 5:15. *s.* of Peter might overshadow
James 1:17. no variableness, neither *s.* of
Jer 6:4. *shadows* of evening are stretched
SHAKE heaven and earth, Hag 2:6, 21.
Hag 2:7. I will *s.* all nations and
Matt 10:14. *s.* off the dust of your feet
11:7. a reed *shaken* with the wind
Luke 6:38. good measure, *s.* together
Heb 12:27. things which cannot be *s.*
Ps 44:14. *shaking,* Isa 17:6; 24:13; 30:32. Ezek 37:7; 38:19.
SHAME, 1 Sam 20:34. 2 Sam 13:13.
Exod 32:25. made them naked to their *s.*
Ps 119:31. put me not to *s.*, 69:7.
Prov 3:35. *shame* shall be the promotion of fools, 9:7; 10:5; 11:2; 13:5, 18; 14:35; 17:2; 18:13; 19:26; 25:8; 29:15. Isa 22:18.
Isa 50:6. I hid not my face from *s.*
Hos 4:7. change their glory to *s.*, Ps 4:2.
Zeph 3:5. the unjust knoweth no *s.*
Acts 5:41. worthy to suffer *s.* for his
Heb 12:2. endured cross, despising *s.*
Rev 3:18. *s.* of thy nakedness do not
16:15. naked, and they see his *s.*
1 Tim 2:9. *shamefacedness*
SHAPE, Luke 3:22. John 5:37. Ps 51:5.
SHARP, Isa 41:15; 49:2. Rev 1:16.
Job 16:9. *sharpeneth,* Prov 27:17.
Mic 7:4. *sharper* than, Heb 4:12.
Judg 8:1. *sharply,* Titus 1:13.
2 Cor 13:10. should use *sharpness*
SHED for many for remission Matt 26:28.
Rom 5:5. love of God is *s.* abroad
Titus 3:6. Holy Ghost which he *s.* on us
SHEEP, Ps 49:14; 74:1; 78:52.
Ps 44:22. *s.* for slaughter, Rom 8:36.
79:13. *s.* of thy pasture, 95:7; 100:3.
119:176. gone astray like lost *s.*
Isa 53:6. like *s.* have gone astray
Zech 13:7. smite shepherd, and *s.* shall

Matt 9:36. as *s.* having no shepherd
10:6. to lost *s.* of house of Israel, 15:24.
18:12. If a man have an hundred *s.*
25:32. divideth his *s.* from goats, 33.
John 10:2–16. the *s.* 27. my *s.*
21:15. feed my lambs. 16–17. feed my *s.*
1 Pet 2:24. were as *s.* going astray
SHEPHERD, Gen 46:34; 49:24. Exod 2:17, 19.
Num 27:17. as sheep that have no *s.* 1 Kings 22:17. Mark 6:34
Ps 23:1. the Lord is my *s.*
80:1. give ear, O *S.* of Israel
Ezek 34:5. were scattered because there is no *s.*
12. *s.* seeketh out his flock
23. set up one *s.* . . . even my servant David
37:24. they all shall have one *s.*
Zech 13:7. awake, O sword, against my *s.*
John 10:11. I am the good *s.*; the good *s.* giveth his life, 14.
Heb 13:20. Lord Jesus, that great *s.*
1 Pet 2:25. returned to *S.* of souls
5:4. when the chief *S.* shall appear
Song of Sol 1:8. feed kids before *shepherds'* tents
Ezek 34:2. prophesy against *s.* . . . woe to the *s.*
7. ye *s.*, hear the word of the Lord
Mic 5:5. raise against him seven *s.*
SHEW, Ps 39:6. Luke 20:47. Col 2:23.
Ps 4:6. who will *s.* us any good?
16:11. thou wilt *s.* me path of life
91:16. I will *s.* him my salvation
92:15. to *s.* that Lord is upright
1 Cor 11:26. *s.* Lord's death
1 Pet 2:9. *s.* forth the praises of him
Rev 22:6. sent his angel to *s.* to his servants
John 5:20. loveth Son, and *sheweth*
Titus 2:7. *shewing* thyself a pattern of good works
SHIELD and great reward, Gen 15:1.
Deut 33:29. Lord the *s.* of thy help
Ps 3:3. thou, O Lord art a *s.* for me, 28:7.
18:35. the *s.* of thy salvation
33:20. he is our help and our *s.*
59:11. bring them down, O Lord our *s.*, 84:9.
115:9, 10, 11. their help and their *s.*
Eph 6:16. taking the *s.* of faith
SHINE, Job 22:28; 36:32; 37:15.
Num 6:25. Lord make his face *s.*
Job 10:3. *s.* on counsel of wicked
Ps 31:16. face to *shine* up on thy servant, 119:135.
Eccles 8:1. man's wisdom maketh his face *s.*

Matt 5:16. let your light so *s.* before
13:43. righteous *s.* forth as the sun
2 Cor 4:6. God, who commanded light to *s.*
Phil 2:15. among whom ye *s.* as
SHIPWRECK, 1 Tim 1:19.
2 Cor 11:25. thrice I suffered *s.*
SHORT, is Lord's hand waxed, Num 11:23.
Ps 89:47. remember how *s.* my time is
Rom 3:23. and come *s.* of glory of God
Ps 102:23. *shortened* my days, 89:45.
Isa 50:2. is my hand *s.*
Matt 24:22. except those days be *s.* Mark 13:20. Prov 10:27.
SHOUT, Num 23:21. Isa 12:6; 42:11; 44:23. Zeph 3:14. Zech 9:9.
Ps 47:5. God is gone up with a *s.*
1 Thess 4:16. Lord shall descend with a *s.*
SHRINES, Acts 19:24.
SHUT up, or left, Deut 32:36.
1 Sam 6:10. *s.* up their calves at home
Matt 23:13. ye *s.* up the kingdom of
Gal 3:23. *s.* up unto the faith which
Rev 3:7. that openeth, and no man *shutteth,* Isa 22:22.
SICK of love, Song of Sol 2:5; 5:8.
Isa 1:5. whole head is *s.* and whole heart
John 11:1. man was *s.* named Lazarus, 2, 3, 4, 6.
James 5:14. is any *s.* . . .? let him call the elders 15. prayer of faith shall save the *s.*
1 Cor 11:30. are weak and *sickly*
Exod 23:25. I will take *sickness* away
Matt 8:17. bare our *sicknesses*
SIFT, Isa 30:28. Amos 9:9. Luke 22:31.
SIGHT, Exod 3:3. 2 Cor 5:7.
SIGN (token), Gen 9:12, 13; 17:11. Exod 4:17. Isa 8:18. Rom 15:19.
Rom 4:11. received the *s.* of circumcision
Jer 22:24. *signet,* Hag 2:23.
SILENT in darkness, 1 Sam 2:9.
Ps 28:1. be not *s.* to me, 30:12.
31:18. *silence,* 32:3; 35:22; 50:3, 21; 83:1; 94:17. Jer 8:14. Amos 5:13; 8:3. 1 Cor 14:34. 1 Tim 2:11, 12. 1 Pet 2:15. Rev 8:1.
SILLY, Job 5:2. 2 Tim 3:6.
SIMPLE, Prov 1:4, 22, 32; 7:7; 8:5; 9:4, 13; 19:25; 21:11.
Ps 19:7. testimony . . . sure, making wise the *s.*
116:6. Lord preserveth the *s.*
119:130. understanding to the *s.*
Prov 14:15. *s.* believeth every word, 18.
Rom 16:18. *deceive the hearts of the s.*
19. but *s.* concerning evil
SIN lieth at the door, Gen 4:7.
Job 10:6. thou . . . searchest after my *s.*
Ps 4:4. stand in awe and *s.* not
32:1. blessed is he . . . whose *s.* is covered
5. I acknowledged my *s.* unto thee
38:18. I will be sorry for my *s.*
51:3. my *s.* is ever before me
5. in *s.* did my mother conceive me
Prov 14:34. *s.* is a reproach to any
Isa 30:1. that they may add *s.* to *s.*
53:10. make his soul an offering for *s.*
12. and he bare the *s.* of many
John 1:29. taketh away *s.* of the world
5:14. *s.* no more lest a worse thing
Rom 5:12. by one man *s.* entered world, and death by *s.*
6:14. *s.* shall not have dominion
7:9. *s.* revived, and I died, 8:10.
13. but *s.*, that it might appear *s.*
14. I am carnal, sold under *sin*
17. *s.* that dwelleth in me
25. with the flesh the law of *s.*
8:2. made me free from the law of *s.*
2 Cor 5:21. made him to be *s.* for us, who knew no *s.*
Eph 4:26. be ye angry and *s.* not
James 1:15. lust bringeth forth *s.*, and *s.*
1 Pet 2:22. who did no *s.*, neither
1 John 1:8. if we say we have no *s.*
2:1. ye *s.* not; if any man *s.* we have
3:9. he cannot *s.* because he is born of God
5:16. there is *s.* unto death
Ps 19:13. keep . . . from presumptuous *sins*
Isa 43:25. not remember thy *s.*, 44:22.
Ezek 33:16. none of his *s.* . . . shall be mentioned
Dan 9:24. finish transgression make end of *s.*
1 Tim 5:22. neither . . . partaker of other men's *s.*
2 Tim 3:6. silly women laden with *s.*
1 John 2:2. propitiation for our *s.* . . . also for *s.* of the whole world
Ps 69:5. *my sins,* 51:9. Isa 38:17.
79:9. *our sins,* 90:8; 103:10. Isa 59:12. Dan 9:16. Gal 1:4. 1 Cor 15:3. Heb 1:3. 1 Pet 2:24. Rev 1:5.
Matt 1:21. *their sins,* Rom 11:27. Heb 8:12; 10:17. Num 16:26.
Isa 59:2. *your sins,* Jer 5:25. John 8:21. 1 Cor 15:17. Josh 24:19.
Exod 32:33. whosoever hath *sinned* . . . will I
Job 1:22. in all this Job *s.* not
Lam 1:8. Jerusalem grievously *s.*
Rom 2:12. many as *s.* without law
3:23. all have s. and come short
1 John 1:10. if we say we have not *s.*
Exod 9:27. *I have sinned,* Num 22:34. Josh 7:20. 1 Sam 15:24, 30. 2 Sam 12:13; 24:10. Job 7:20; 33:27. Ps 41:4; 51:4. Mic 7:9. Matt 27:4. Luke 15:18, 21.
Judg 10:10. *we have sinned,* 1 Sam 7:6. Ps 106:6. Isa 42:24; 64:5. Jer 3:25; 8:14; 14:7, 20. Lam 5:16. Dan 9:5, 8, 11, 15.
Prov 8:36. but he that *sinneth* against me wrongeth his own soul
Eccles 7:20. not just man . . . doeth good, *s.* not
Ezek 18:4. soul that *s.* it shall die
1 John 5:18. born of God *s.* not
Eccles 7:26. the *sinner* shall be taken
9:18. one *s.* destroyeth much good
Luke 15:7. joy in heaven over one *s.* that
18:13. God be merciful to me a *s.*
James 5:20. converteth the *s.* from
1 Pet 4:18. where shall *s.* appear
Gen 13:13. *sinners* before the Lord
Ps 1:1. nor standeth in way of *s.*
25:8. therefore will he teach *s.* in the way
Isa 33:14. the *s.* in Zion are afraid
Matt 9:13. I am not come to call righteous, but *s.*
Luke 13:2. *s.* above all Galilaeans, 4.
John 9:31. God heareth not *s.*
Rom 5:8. while we were yet *s.* Christ died for us
19. by one man's disobedience many . . . *s.*
Gal 2:15. Jews . . . and not *s.* of the Gentiles
1 Tim 1:15. Jesus came into world to save *s.*
Heb 7:26. holy . . . separate from *s.*
James 4:8. cleanse your hands, ye *s.*
Jude 15. ungodly *s.* have spoken
Num 32:14. *sinful,* Isa 1:4. Luke 5:8. Rom 7:13; 8:3.
SINCERE, Phil 1:10, 16. 1 Pet 2:2.
Josh 24:14. serve him in *sincerity*
1 Cor 5:8. unleavened bread of *s.*
2 Cor 1:12. in simplicity and godly *s.* we have
8:8. to prove the *s.* of your love
Eph 6:24. that love Lord Jesus in *sincerity*
Titus 2:7. shewing uncorruptness, gravity, *s.*
SINEW, Isa 48:4. Job 10:11.
SING to the Lord, Exod 15:21. 1 Chron 16:23. Ps 30:4; 68:32; 81:1; 95:1; 96:1, 2; 98:1; 147:7; 149:1. Isa 12:5; Eph 5:19.
Exod 15:1. *I will s.*, Judg 5:3. Ps 13:6; 57:7, 9; 59:16, 17; 101:1; 104:33; 144:9. Isa 5:1. 1 Cor 14:15.
Job 29:13. *s. for joy,* Isa 65:14.
Ps 9:11. *s. praise(s),* 18:49; 27:6; 30:12; 47:6, 7; 68:4; 75:9; 92:1; 108:1, 3; 135:3; 146:2; 147:1; 149:3.
Ps 145:7. *s.* of thy righteousness
Prov 29:6. the righteous doth *s.* and

Isa 35:6. and the tongue of the dumb *s.*
1 Cor 14:15. I will *s.* with the spirit
James 5:13. is any merry? let him *s.*
SINGLE eye, Matt 6:22. Luke 11:34.
Acts 2:46. *singleness* of heart, Eph 6:5. Col 3:22.
SINK, Ps 2:14. Luke 9:44.
SISTER, Song of Sol 4:9; 5:1; 8:8.
SITUATION, 2 Kings 2:19. Ps 48:2.
SKIN, Job 2:4; 10:11; 19:26. Jer 13:23. sheep*s.* and goat*s.*, Heb 11:37.
SKIP, Ps 29:6; 114:4. Song of Sol 2:8.
SLACK, Deut 7:10. Prov 10:4. Hab 1:4. Zeph 3:16. 2 Pet 3:9.
SLAY, Job 13:15. Ps 139:19. Lev 14:13.
Eph 2:16. having *slain* the enmity
Rev 5:9. wast *s.* and hast redeemed
13:8. Lamb *s.* from foundation of
SLEEP, deep, Gen 2:21; 15:12. 1 Sam 26:12. Job 4:13. Ps 76:7. Prov 19:15. Isa 29:10.
Ps 90:5. they are as a *s.*: in morning
127:2. he giveth his beloved *s.*
132:4. will not give *s.* to mine eyes
Prov 3:24. thy *s.* shall be sweet
6:4. give not *s.* to thine eyes, nor
20:13. love not *s.* lest thou come to poverty
Eccles 5:12. *s.* of labouring man is sweet . . . but abundance of rich will not suffer him to *s.*
Jer 31:26. my *s.* was sweet to me
51:39. *s.* a perpetual *s.*, 57.
Luke 9:32. were heavy with *s.*
Rom 13:11. time to awake out of *s.*
Song of Sol 5:2. I *s.* but my heart waketh
1 Cor 11:30. for this cause . . . many *s.*
15:51. we shall not all *s.* but shall
1 Thess 4:14. them which *s.* in Jesus
5:6. let us not *s.* as others; but
7. they that *s. s.* in the night
10. whether we wake or *s.* should
Eph 5:14. awake, thou that *sleepest*
Ps 3:5. laid me down and *slept,* 4:8.
76:5. they have *s.* their sleep
1 Cor 15:20. firstfruits of them that *s.*
SLIDE, Deut 32:35. Ps 26:1; 37:31. Jer 8:5. Hos 4:16.
SLIGHTLY, Jer 6:14; 8:11.
SLING, 1 Sam 25:29. Jer 10:18.
SLIP, Ps 17:5; 18:36; 38:16; 94:18. Heb 2:1.
slippery, Ps 35:6; 73:18. Jer 23:12.
SLOTHFUL under tribute, Prov 12:24.
Prov 12:27. *s.* man roasteth not that which he
15:19. way of *s.* man is as hedge of thorns
18:9. *s.* is brother to . . . greater waster
21:25. desire of the *s.* killeth him
24:30. I went by the field of the *s.*
26:14. as door turneth on hinges, so doth *s.*
Heb 6:12. be not *s.* but followers of
Prov 19:15. *slothfulness* casteth into a deep sleep
SLOW to anger, Neh 9:17.
Luke 24:25. fools, *slow* of heart to
James 1:19. swift to hear, *s.* to speak, *s.* to wrath. Prov 14:29.
SLUGGARD, go to ant, Prov 6:6.
Prov 6:9. how long wilt sleep, O *s.*
13:4. the soul of the *s.* desireth
20:4. *s.* will not plow by reason
26:16. *s.* is wiser in his own conceit
SLUMBER, Ps 132:4. Rom 11:8.
Matt 25:5. they all *slumbered* and
2 Pet 2:3. their damnation *slumbereth* not
SMITE, Lord shall, Deut 28:22.
Ps 141:5. let the righteous *s.* me
Jer 18:18. let us *s.* him with tongue
Matt 5:39. *s.* thee on thy right cheek
John 18:23. why *smitest* thou me
Isa 53:4. him *smitten* of God
Hos 6:1. hath *s.* and he will bind
SMOKE, Gen 19:28. Exod 19:18.
Deut 29:20. his jealousy shall *s.*
Ps 74:1. why doth thine anger *s.*
Rev 14:11. *s.* of their torment ascendeth
Isa 42:3. *smoking* flax, Matt 12:20.
SMOOTH, Gen 27:11, 16. Isa 30:10.
Ps 55:21. *smoother,* Prov 5:3.
SNARE, Exod 23:33. Judg 2:3.
Ps 69:22. let their table become a *s.*, Rom 11:9.
91:3. deliver thee from the *s.* of
119:110. wicked laid a *s.* for me
124:7. *s.* is broken, and we are escaped
Prov 29:25. fear of man bringeth a *s.*
2 Tim 2:26. out of the *s.* of devil
Ps 9:16. *snared,* Prov 6:2; 12:13. Eccles 9:12. Isa 8:15; 28:13; 42:22.
11:6. on wicked he will rain *snares*
18:5. *s.* of death prevented me
Prov 13:14. depart from *s.* of death
SNOW, as, Ps 51:7; 68:14. Isa 1:18. Dan 7:9. Matt 28:3. Rev 1:14.
SNUFFED, Mal 1:13. Jer 2:24.
SOAP, Jer 2:22. Mal 3:2.
SOBER . . . for your cause, 2 Cor 5:13.
1 Thess 5:6. let us watch and be *s.*, 8.
1 Tim 3:2. bishop must be . . . vigilant, *s.*
11. wives be grave, not slanderers, *s.*
Titus 1:8. *s.*, just, holy, temperate
2:2. aged men be *s.*, grave
4. teach young women to be *s.*
1 Pet 1:13. gird up loins of your mind, be *s.*
4:7. be ye therefore *s.* and watch unto prayer
5:8. be *s.*, be vigilant
Rom 12:3. but to think *soberly*
Titus 2:12. teaching us that we should live *s.*
Acts 26:25. words of truth and *soberness*
1 Tim 2:9. *sobriety,* 15.
SOFT, God maketh my heart, Job 23:16.
Prov 15:1. *s.* answer turneth away
25:15. *s.* tongue breaketh the bone
Matt 11:8. man clothed in *s.* raiment
SOJOURN, Gen 12:10. Ps 120:5.
Lev 25:23. *sojourners* with me, 1 Chron 29:15. Ps 39:12.
Exod 12:40. *sojourning,* 1 Pet 1:17.
SOLD thyself to work evil, 1 Kings 21:20.
2 Kings 17:17. *s.* themselves to do evil
Rom 7:14. I am carnal, *s.* under sin
SOLDIER of Jesus Christ, 2 Tim 2:3, 4.
SON, 2 Sam 18:33; 19:4.
Ps 2:12. kiss the *S.* lest he be angry
Prov 10:1. a wise *s.* . . . a foolish *s.*, 15:20.
Mal 3:17. as a man spareth his own *s.*
Matt 11:27. no man knoweth the *S.*
17:5. this is my beloved *S.*, 3:17.
Luke 10:6. if *son* of peace be there
John 1:18. only begotten *S.*, 3:16, 18, 35.
5:21. *S.* quickeneth whom he will
23. men should honour the *S.*
8:35. but the *S.* abideth ever
36. if the *S.* shall make you free
Rom 8:3. sending his own *S.* in, 32.
Gal 4:7. if *s.* then an heir of God
Heb 5:8. though he were a *S.* yet learned he
1 John 2:22. antichrist that denieth . . . *S.*, 23.
5:11. eternal life, and this life is in his *S.*
12. hath *S.* hath life, hath not *S.* hath not life
Matt 21:37. *his Son,* Acts 3:13. Rom 1:3, 9; 5:10; 8:29, 32. 1 Cor 1:9. Gal 1:16; 4:4, 6. 1 Thess 1:10. Heb 1:2. 1 John 1:7; 3:23; 4:9, 10, 14; 5:9, 10, 11, 20.
Luke 15:19. *thy son,* John 17:1; 19:26.
Dan 3:25. *the Son of God,* Matt 4:3; 16:16. and 41 other places
Num 23:19. *Son of man,* Job 25:6. Ps 8:4; 80:17; 144:3. Dan 7:13. Ezekiel is so called about 90, and Christ about 84 times

Ps 144:12. that our *sons* may be as plants
Song of Sol 2:3. so is my beloved among *s.*
Mal 3:3. purify *s.* of Levi
Mark 3:17. Boanerges, . . . *s.* of thunder
1 Cor 4:14. as my beloved *s.* I warn
Gal 4:6. because ye are *s.* God sent Spirit of his
Heb 2:10. bringing many *s.* to glory
12:7. God dealeth with you as with *s.*
Gen 6:2. *sons of God,* Job 1:6; 2:1; 38:7. Hos 1:10. John 1:12. Rom 8:14, 19. Phil 2:15. 1 John 3:1, 2.
SONG to the Lord, Exod 15:1. Num 21:17.
Exod 15:2. Lord is my . . . *s.,* Ps 118:14. Isa 12:2.
Job 30:9. I am their *s.,* Ps 69:12.
Ezek 33:32. as a very lovely *s.*
Rev 14:3. no man could learn that *s.*
15:3. sing *s.* of Moses . . . of Lamb
Ps 33:3. sing a *new song,* 40:3; 96:1; 144:9; 149:1. Isa 42:10. Rev 5:9.
Job 35:10. giveth *songs* in the night, Ps 42:8; 77:6. Isa 30:29.
Ps 32:7. compass . . . with *s.* of deliverance
119:54. *s.* in house of my pilgrimage
Eph 5:19. speaking in . . . spiritual *s.*
SOON as they be born, Ps 58:3.
Prov 14:17. *s.* angry dealeth foolishly
Gal 1:6. so *s.* removed . . . to another gospel
2 Thess 2:2. not *s.* shaken
SORCERER, Acts 13:6, 8; 8:9, 11.
Jer 27:9. *sorcerers,* Mal 3:5. Rev 21:8.
SORE, 2 Chron 6:28. Job 5:18.
Heb 10:29. much *sorer* punishment
Isa 1:6. and putrifying *sores*
SORRY, Ps 38:18. 2 Cor 2:2; 7:8.
Ps 90:10. labour and *sorrow*
Prov 15:13. by *s.* of heart spirit is broken
Eccles 1:18. increaseth knowledge increaseth *s.*
7:3. *s.* is better than laughter
Isa 35:10. *s.* and sighing shall flee away, 51:11.
50:11. ye shall lie down in *s.*
Lam 1:12. if there be any *s.* like unto my *s.*
John 16:6. *s.* hath filled your heart
20. your *s.* shall be turned into joy
2 Cor 2:7. swallowed up with overmuch *s.*
7:10. godly *s.* worketh repentance to salvation: but *s. of world worketh death, 9.*
Phil 2:27. should have *s.* upon *s.*
1 Thess 4:13. *s.* not, as others which have no hope
Rev 21:4. no more death, neither *s.*
2 Cor 7:9. *sorrowed,* Jer 31:12.
Job 6:7. are as my *sorrowful* meat
Prov 14:13. in laughter heart is *sorrowful*
Jer 31:25. replenished *s.* soul, Ps 69:29
Zeph 3:18. gather them that are *s.*
Matt 19:22. young man . . . went way *s.*
26:22, 38. my soul is exceeding *s.*
Luke 2:48. *sorrowing,* Acts 20:38.
Ps 18:4. *sorrows* of death compassed me, 116:3.
5. the *s.* of hell compassed me
127:2. it is vain . . . to eat bread of *s.*
Isa 53:3. man of *s.* 4. carried our *s.*
Matt 24:8. beginning of *s.*
1 Tim 6:10. and pierced through with many *s.*
SORT, 2 Cor 7:11. 3 John 6.
SOUGHT the Lord, Exod 33:7. 2 Chron 14:7.
Ps 34:4. I *s.* Lord, and he heard
111:2. *s.* out of all them that have
119:10. with my whole heart have I *s.* thee
Eccles 7:29. *s.* out many inventions
Isa 62:12. be called *S.* out, a city
65:1. found of them that *s.* me not
Rom 9:32. *s.* it not by faith, but by
2 Chron 16:12. *s.* not to Lord, Zeph 1:6.
1 Chron 15:13. *sought him,* 2 Chron 14:7; 15:4. Ps 78:34. Song of Sol 3:1, 2; 5:6. Jer 8:2; 26:21.
SOUL abhor my judgments, Lev 26:15, 43.
Deut 11:13. serve him with . . . all *s.*
13:3. love the Lord with all . . . your *s.,* Josh 22:5. 1 Kings 2:4. Mark 12:33.
1 Sam 18:1. *s.* of Jonathan knit with *s.* of David
1 Kings 8:48. return with all their . . . *s.*
1 Chron 22:19. set your . . . *s.* to seek Lord
Ps 19:7. law of Lord is perfect, converting *s.*
34:22. Lord redeemeth *s.* of his servants
49:8. redemption of their *s.* is precious
74:19. deliver not the *s.* of thy turtledove
107:9. filleth the hungry *s.*
Prov 10:3. not suffer *s.* of righteous
19:2. that *s.* be without knowledge it is not good
27:7. full *s.* loatheth honeycomb
Isa 55:2. let your *s.* delight in fatness
55:3. hear and your *s.* shall live
58:10. and satisfy the afflicted *s.*
Jer 31:25. I have satiated weary *s.,* 12, 14.
38:16. Lord liveth, that made us this *s.*
Matt 10:28. not able to kill *s.*
Rom 13:1. let every *s.* be subject to
1 Thess 5:23. *s.* and body be preserved
Heb 4:12. piercing even to dividing . . . of *s.*
10:39. believe to saying of the *s.*
Exod 30:12. ransom for *his soul*
Judg 10:16.—was grieved for misery
2 Kings 23:25. turned to Lord . . . with all—
Job 27:8. when God taketh away—
Hab 2:4.—lifted up is not upright
Matt 16:26. gain whole world, and lose—
Ps 16:10. not leave *my soul* in hell
31:7. hast known—in adversities
35:3. say to—I am thy salvation
9.—shall be joyful in the Lord
42:5, 11. why cast down, O—, 43:5.
62:1.—waiteth upon God, 5.
63:1.—thirsteth for thee, my flesh
8.—followeth hard after thee
Isa 26:9. with—have I desired thee, 8.
61:10.—shall be joyful in my God
Luke 1:46.—doth magnify the Lord
John 12:27.—troubled, Matt 26:38.
Ps 33:20. *our soul,* 44:25; 66:9; 123:4; 124:4. Isa 26:8.
Deut 13:6. *own soul,* 1 Sam 18:1; 20:17. Ps 22:29. Prov 8:36; 11:17; 15:32; 19:8, 16; 6:32; 20:2; 29:24. Mark 8:36. Luke 2:35.
Deut 4:9. *with all thy soul,* 6:5; 10:12; 30:6. Matt 22:37.
Ezek 3:19. delivered *thy soul,* 21; 33:9.
Luke 12:20. this night—shall be
3 John 2. be in health even as—prospereth
Prov 11:30. that winneth *souls* is wise
Isa 57:16. spirit fail . . . and *s.* which I
Ezek 14:14. should deliver but their own *s.*
1 Pet 4:19. commit keeping of their *s.* to him
2 Pet 2:14. beguiling unstable *s.*
Rev 6:9. *s.* of slain 20:4. *s.* of beheaded
Luke 21:19. *your souls,* Josh 23:14. Jer 6:16; 26:19. Matt 11:29. Heb 13:17. 1 Pet 1:9, 22; 2:25.
SOUND, dreadful, Job 15:21.
Ps 47:5. Lord with *s.* of a trumpet
89:15. people that know joyful *s.*
119:80. let my heart be *s.* in thy statutes
Prov 2:7. *s.* wisdom, 3:21; 8:14.
Eccles 12:4. *s.* of the grinding is low
Amos 6:5. that chant to *s.* of viol
Rom 10:18. *s.* went into all the earth
1 Tim 1:10. contrary to *s.* doctrine, 2 Tim 4:3.

2 Tim 1:7. *s.* mind, 13. *s.* words
Titus 1:9; 2:1, *s.* doctrine. 2:2, *s.* in faith
Isa 63:15. *sounding* of bowels, 16:11.
Ps 38:3, 7. no *soundness.* Isa 1:6.
SOW that was washed, 2 Pet 2:22.
SOW wickedness reap same, Job 4:8.
Ps 126:5. *s.* in tears shall reap in joy
Eccles 11:4. observeth wind shall not *s.*
Jer 4:3. *s.* not among thorns
Obad 27. I will *s.* the house of Israel
Hos 10:12. *s.* to yourselves in righteousness, reap
Mic 6:15. thou shalt *s.* but . . . not reap
Matt 13:3. sower went forth to *s.*
Luke 12:24. the ravens; for they neither *s.* nor
19:22. reaping that I did not *s.*
Isa 55:10. seed to *sower,* 2 Cor 9:10.
Prov 11:18. *soweth* righteousness
22:8. *s.* iniquity shall reap vanity
John 4:37. one *s.*, another reapeth
2 Cor 9:6. *s.* sparingly . . . *s.* bountifully
Gal 6:7. whatsoever a man *s.*, that shall, 8.
Ps 97:11. light is *sown* for righteous
Hos 8:7. *s.* wind, they shall reap whirlwind
1 Cor 9:11. have *s.* to you spiritual things
15:42. it is *s.* in corruption
43. *s.* in dishonour . . . *s.* in weakness
2 Cor 9:10. multiply your seed *s.*
James 3:18. fruit of righteousness *s.* in peace
SPARE all the place, Gen 18:26.
Neh 13:22. *s.* me according to . . . thy mercy
Ps 39:13. *s.* me that I may recover
Joel 2:17. *s.* thy people O Lord and give not
Mal 3:17. I will *s.* them, as a man *spareth*
Rom 8:32. *spared* not his own Son
11:21. if God *s.* not the natural
2 Pet 2:4. God *s.* not angels that sinned
Prov 13:24. he that *spareth* rod
SPARKS, Job 5:7. Isa 50:11.
SPARROW, Ps 102:7. Matt 10:29.
SPEAK against Moses, Num 12:8.
Gen 18:27. taken on me to *s.* to Lord
Exod 4:14. I know he (Aaron) can *s.* well
34:35. went in to *s.* with him
1 Sam 3:9. *S.*, Lord, for thy servant heareth, 10.
Ps 85:8. he will *s.* peace to his people
Isa 50:4. how to *s.* a word in season
Jer 18:7. at what instant I shall *s.*, 9.
Matt 10:19. how or what ye shall *s.*
Luke 6:26. when all men *s.* well of
John 3:11. we *s.* that we do know
Acts 4:20. cannot but *s.* things we
1 Cor 1:10. ye all *speak* the same thing
Titus 3:2. to *s.* evil of no man
James 1:19. swift to hear, slow to *s.*
2 Pet 2:10. *s.* evil of dignities, Jude 8.
Jude 10. *s.* evil of things which they
Matt 12:32. *speaketh* a word against Son of man
34. out of abundance of heart mouth *s.*
Heb 11:4. he being dead yet *s.*
12:24. *s.* better things than that of Abel
12:25. refuse not him that *s.*
Isa 45:19. *I speak,* 63:1. John 4:26; 7:17; 8:26, 28, 38; 12:50. Rom 3:5; 6:19. 1 Tim 2:7.
58:13. nor *speaking* thine own words
65:24. while they are *s.* I will hear, 58:9.
Dan 9:20. whiles I was *s.* and
Matt 6:7. shall be heard for their much *s.*
Eph 4:15. *s.* the truth in love
31. evil *s.* be put away, 1 Pet 2:1.
5:19. *s.* to yourselves in psalms
1 Tim 4:2. *s.* lies in hypocrisy, Ps 58:3.
Rev 13:5. a mouth *s.* great things
Gen 11:1. earth was of one *speech*
Matt 26:73. thy *s.* bewrayeth thee
1 Cor 2:1. not with excellency of *s.*
2 Cor 3:12. use great plainness of *s.*
10:10. his *s.* contemptible
Col 4:6. let your *s.* be always with grace
Titus 2:8. sound *s.*, that cannot be condemned
Jude 15. of all their hard *speeches*
Rom 16:18. by fair *s.* deceive hearts
Matt 22:12. he was *speechless*
SPECTACLE to angels, 1 Cor 4:9.
SPEED, Gen 24:12. 2 John 10:11.
Ezra 7:21. *speedily,* 26. Ps 31:2; 79:8. Eccles 8:11. Luke 18:8.
SPEND their days in wealth, Job 21:13.
Ps 90:9. *s.* our years as a tale that
Isa 55:2. *s.* money for that which is
49:4. have *spent* my strength for
Rom 13:12. night is far *s.*
2 Cor 12:15. spend and be *s.*
SPICES, Song of Sol 4:10, 14, 16; 8:14.
SPIDER, Prov 30:28. Job 8:14. Isa 59:5.
SPIKENARD, Song of Sol 1:12; 4:13, 14.
SPIRIT made willing, Exod 35:21.
Num 11:17. take of *s.* which is on
14:24. Caleb had another *s.* with
2 Kings 2:9. double portion of thy *s.*
Ezra 1:5. whose *s.* God raised
Neh 9:20. gavest also thy good *s.* to instruct
Job 26:13. by his *s.* he garnished the
32:18. the *s.* within constraineth me
Ps 31:5. to thine hand I committ my *s.*
32:2. in whose *s.* there is no guile
34:18. a contrite *s.*, Isa 57:15; 66:2.
51:10. renew a right *s.* within me
11. take not thy holy *s.* from me
12. uphold me with thy free *s.*
17. a broken *s.*, Prov 17:22.
76:12. he shall cut off *s.* of princes
78:8. *s.* was not stedfast with God
139:7. whither should I go from thy *s.*?
142:3. my *s.* was overwhelmed, 143:4.
143:7. *s.* faileth. 10. thy *s.* is good
Prov 14:29. hasty of *s.* exalteth folly
15:13. by sorrow of heart *s.* is broken
16:18. a haughty *s.* before a fall
32. he that ruleth his *s.* (is better) than he
18:14. a wounded *s.* who can bear?
20:27. *s.* of man is candle of Lord
Eccles 3:21. who knoweth *s.* of man
8:8. no power over *s.* to retain *s.*
12:7. the *spirit* shall return to God
Isa 32:15. until *s.* be poured upon us
34:16. his *s.* it hath gathered them
57:15. to revive the *s.* of the humble
16. for the *s.* fail before me
61:3. garment of praise for *s.* of
Mic 2:11. walking in *s.* and falsehood
Zech 12:1. formeth *s.* of man within
12:10. *s.* of grace and supplication
Matt 22:43. David in *s.* call him Lord
26:41. *s.* is willing, but flesh weak
Luke 1:80. (John) waxed strong in *s.*
2:27. came by the *S.* into temple
8:55. *s.* came again and she arose
9:55. know not what manner of *s.* ye are
24:39. *s.* hath not flesh and bones
John 3:5. born of water and of *s.*
6. that which is born of the *S.* is *s.*
4:24. God is a *S.* 23. worship Father in *s.*
6:63. it is the *s.* that quickeneth; the words I speak . . . are *s.* and life
Acts 6:10. not able to resist the . . . *s.*

16:7. the *S.* suffered them not
17:16. (Paul's) *s.* was stirred in him
18:5. Paul was pressed in *s.* and
Rom 8:1. not after flesh, but after *S.*, 4.
2. *S.* of life in Christ Jesus made
9. if any have not *S.* of Christ, he
13. if ye through *S.* mortify deeds
15. *s.* of bondage, *S.* of adoption
16. *S.* beareth witness with our *s.*
1 Cor 2:10. *S.* searcheth all things
5:3. present in *s.* 5. *s.* may be saved
6:17. joined unto Lord is one *s.*
12:13. by one *S* . . . baptized . . . drink into one *S.*
2 Cor 3:3. written with *S.* of living God
6. not of letter but *s.* . . . *s.* giveth life
17. *S.* of Lord is, there is liberty
7:1. from filthiness of flesh and *s.*
Gal 3:3. begun in *S.* are ye now perfect
4:6. sent forth *S.* of his Son into your hearts
5:17. flesh lusteth against *S.* and *S.* against flesh
18. if led of *S.* ye are not under law
22. fruit of *S.* is love, joy, peace
25. if we live in *S.* let us walk in *S.*
6:18. the grace of our Lord Jesus Christ be with your *s.*, 2 Tim 4:22.
Eph 1:13. with holy *S.* of promise
4:4. there is one body and one *S.*
23. be renewed in *s.* of your mind
5:9. fruit of *S.* is in all goodness
6:18. praying always . . . in *S.*, Jude 20.
Col 2:5. am I with you in the *s.*
1 Thess 5:23. whole *s.* be preserved
Heb 4:12. dividing asunder of soul and *s.*
9:14. through eternal *s.* offered
James 4:5. *s.* that dwelleth in us
1 Pet 3:4. ornament of a meek and quiet *s.*
18. in flesh, but quickened by the *S.*
1 John 4:1. believe not every *s.*
Jude 19. sensual, not having the *S.*
Rev 1:10. I was in the *S.* on Lord's day
11:11. *S.* of life from God entered
14:13. yea, saith the *S.*, that they
Gen 6:3. *my spirit,* Job 10:12. Ps 31:5; 77:6. Isa 38:16. Ezek 36:27. Zech 4:6. Luke 1:47; 23:46. Acts 7:59. Rom 1:9. 1 Cor 14:14.
Gen 1:2. *Spirit of God,* Exod 31:3. 2 Chron 15:1. Job 33:4. Ezek 11:24. Matt 3:16; 12:28. Rom 8:9, 14; 15:19. 1 Cor 2:11, 14; 3:16; 6:11; 12:3. 2 Cor 3:3. Eph 4:30. 1 Pet 4:14. 1 John 4:2.
Isa 11:2. *spirit* of Lord, *s.* of wisdom, *s.* of counsel, *s.* of knowledge, Eph 1:17.
Zech 13:2. unclean *s.*, Matt 12:43.
Num 16:22. God of *spirits.* of all flesh, 27:16.
Prov 16:2. Lord weigheth the *s.*
Matt 10:1. *unclean spirits,* Acts 5:16; 8:7. Rev 16:13, 14.
Luke 10:20. rejoice not that the *s.* are subject to you
1 Cor 14:32. *s.* of the prophets are subject
Heb 12:23. to *s.* of just men made
1 Pet 3:19. preached to *s.* in prison
1 John 4:1. believe not every *spirit* but try *s.*
Hos 9:7. the *spiritual* man is mad
Rom 1:11. impart unto you some *s.* gift
7:14. law is *s.*, but I am carnal
15:27. partakers of their *s.* things
1 Cor 2:13. comparing *s.* things with *s.*
15. he that is *s.* judgeth all things
3:1. not speak unto you as unto *s.*
9:11. have sown to you *s.* things
10:3. did all eat the same *s.* meat
4. same *s.* drink . . . *S.* rock that followed
15:44. it is raised a *s.* body
Gal 6:1. ye which are *s.* restore
Eph 1:3. blessed us with all *s.* blessings
5:19. speaking in . . . *s.* songs, Col 3:16.
6:12. wrestle against . . . *s.* wickedness
1 Pet 2:5. built up *s.* house
Rom 8:6. to be *spiritually* minded
1 Cor 2:14. because they are *s.* discerned
Rev 11:8. which *s.* is called Sodom and Egypt
SPITE, Ps 10:14. Matt 22:6.
SPITTING, Isa 50:6. Luke 18:32.
SPOIL, Gen 49:27. Ps 68:12.
Isa 53:12. divide *s.* with the strong
Matt 12:29. he will *s.* his house
Col 2:8. beware lest any man *s.* you
Exod 12:36. *spoiled* the Egyptians
Col 2:15. having *s.* principalities
Heb 10:34. took joyfully *spoiling* of
SPOT, without, Num 19:2; 28:3, 9. Job 11:15. 1 Tim 6:14. Heb 9:14. 1 Pet 1:19. 2 Pet 3:14.
Deut 32:5. *s.* is not *s.* of his children
Song of Sol 4:7. there is no *s.* in thee
Jer 13:23. *spots,* Jude 12, 23.
SPREAD, Job 9:8. Isa 25:11; 37:14. Jer 43:10. Lam 1:17. *Ezek 16:8.*
SPRING, Ps 85:11. Matt 13:5, 7.
Ps 65:10. *springing,* John 4:14. Heb 12:15.
SPRINKLE, Lev 14:7; 16:14.
Isa 52:15. shall he *s.* many nations
Ezek 36:25. will I *s.* clean water on
Heb 10:22. hearts *sprinkled* from an evil
12:24. to blood of *sprinkling*
1 Pet 1:2. *s.* of the blood of Jesus Christ
SPUE thee out of my mouth, Rev 3:16. Hab 2:16. Lev 18:28. Jer 25:27.
SPY, Num 13:16. Josh 2:1. Gal 2:4.
STABILITY of times, Isa 33:6.
STAFF, Gen 32:10. Zech 11:10.
Ps 23:4. thy rod and thy *s.* they comfort me
Isa 3:1. stay and *s.* . . . of bread
9:4. broken . . . *s.* of his shoulder, 14:5.
10:5. *s.* in their hand is mine indignation
STAGGER, Ps 107:27. Rom 4:20.
STAIN, Isa 23:9; 63:3.
STAKES, Isa 33:30; 54:2.
STAMMER, Isa 28:11; 33:19; 32:4.
STAND, Ezek 29:7. Exod 9:11.
Job 19:25. *s.* at latter day up on earth
Ps 76:7. who may *s.* in thy sight
Ps 130:3. Lord who shall *stand*?
Prov 19:21. the counsel of the Lord, that shall *s.*
Isa 46:10. my counsel shall *s.*
Mal 3:2. who shall *s.* when he appeareth?
Matt 12:25. house divided . . . shall not *s.*
Rom 5:2. this grace wherein we *s.*
2 Cor 1:24. by faith ye *s.*, Rom 11:20.
1 Pet 5:12. grace of God wherein ye *s.*
Rev 3:20. I *s.* at the door and knock
Nah 1:6. *stand before,* 1 Sam 6:20. Luke 21:36. Rom 14:10. Rev 20:12.
1 Cor 16:13. *stand fast* in the faith
Gal 5:1.—in liberty wherewith Christ hath made us free
Phil 1:27.—in one spirit
4:1.—in the Lord, dearly beloved
1 Thess 3:8. we live, if ye—in Lord
2 Thess 2:15.—and hold traditions
Ps 1:5. *stand in,* 4:4; 24:3.
Exod 14:13. *stand still,* see salvation, 2 Chron 20:17. Josh 10:12. Zech 11:16.
Ps 1:1. *standeth,* 26:12; 33:11. Prov 8:2. Song of Sol 2:9. Isa 3:13.
Rom 14:4. to his own master he *s.* or falleth
1 Cor 10:12. thinketh he *s.* take heed
2 Tim 2:19. foundation of God *s.*
James 5:9. the Judge *s.* before the door
STAR, Num 24:17. Matt 2:2.
Judg 5:20. the *stars* in their courses
Job 25:5. *s.* are not pure in his sight

38:7. the morning *s.* sang together
Dan 12:3. shall shine as *s.* for ever
Rev 12:1. on her head crown of twelve *s.*
STATURE, Matt 6:27. Eph 4:13.
STATUTES and laws, Neh 9:14.
Ps 19:8. *s.* of the Lord are right
Ezek 20:24. had despised my *s.*, 25.
33:15. walk in *s.* of life without . . . iniquity
Mic 6:16. the *s.* of Omri are kept
Exod 15:26. *his statutes,* Deut 6:17. 2 Kings 17:15. Ps 18:22; 105:45.
1 Chron 29:19. *thy statutes,* Ps 119:12, 16, 23, 26, 33, 54, 64, 68, 71, 117.
STAY, Ps 18:18. Song of Sol 2:5. Isa 10:20; 26:3; 27:8; 48:2; 50:10.
STEAD, INSTEAD, Gen 4:25; 22:13.
Gen 30:2. Jacob said, Am I in God's *s.*?
Prov 11:8. wicked cometh in his *s.*
2 Cor 5:20. pray you in Christ's *s.*
STEAL, Exod 20:15. Lev 19:11.
Prov 6:30. is he *s.* to satisfy his soul
Jer 23:30. I am against prophets, saith the Lord, that *s.* my words
Matt 6:19. thieves break through and *s.*
27:64. lest his disciples . . . *s.* him away
Eph 4:28. that *stole* steal no more
Prov 9:17. *stolen* waters are sweet
STEDFAST, Job 11:15. Dan 6:26.
Ps 78:8. spirit not *s.* with God, 37.
1 Cor 15:58. be ye *s.*, unmoveable
Heb 3:14. hold . . . confidence *s.* to the end
1 Pet 5:9. whom resist *s.* in faith
Col 2:5. *stedfastness* of your faith
2 Pet 3:17. fall from your own *s.*
STEPS, Exod 20:26. Ps 18:36.
Ps 37:23. *s.* of good man are ordered
31. none of his *s.* shall slide
119:133. order my *s.* in thy word
Prov 16:9. but Lord directeth his *s.*
Jer 10:23. not in man . . . to direct his *s.*
Rom 4:12. walk in *s.* of that faith
1 Pet 2:21. ye should follow his *s.*
STEWARD, Luke 12:42; 16:2. 1 Cor 4:1. Titus 1:7. 1 Pet 4:10.
STIFF neck, Deut 31:27. Jer 17:23.
2 Chron 36:13. he *stiffeneth* his neck
Exod 32:9. *stiffnecked* people, 33:3, 5; 34:9. Deut 9:6, 13; 10:16.
Acts 7:51.—and uncircumcised in heart

STILL, Exod 15:16. Ps 8:2; 139:18.
Ps 4:4. be *s.*, Jer 47:6. Mark 4:39.
46:10. be *s.* and know that I am God
83:1. be not *s.*, O God
Isa 30:7. their strength is to sit *s.*
Ps 65:7. *stilleth* noise of seas, 89:9.
STING, 1 Cor 15:55, 56. Rev 9:10.
Prov 23:32. *stingeth* like an adder
STINK, Ps 38:5. Isa 3:24.
STIR up, Num 24:9. Job 17:8.
Ps 35:23. *s.* up thyself, awake, 80:2.
78:38. did not *s.* up all his wrath
Song of Sol 2:7. that ye *s.* not, 3:5; 8:4.
2 Tim 1:6. *s.* up gift of God that is
STONE of Israel, Gen 49:24.
Ps 118:22. *s.* which the builders refused
Isa 8:14. *s.* of strumbling, Rom 9:32, 33.
28:16. a *s.*, a tried *s.*, a precious corner *s.*
Dan 2:34. *s.* cut out without hands
Hab 2:11. *s.* shall cry out of wall
Zech 3:9. on one *s.* shall be seven eyes
Matt 7:9. ask bread, will he give him *s.*?
1 Pet 2:4. living *s.* 6. chief corner *s.*
Matt 3:9. God is able of these *stones* to raise up
Luke 19:40. *s.* would immediately cry
Ezek 11:19. *stony,* Matt 13:5.
STOOP, Job 9:13. Prov 12:25. Mark 1:7.
STORE, 1 Cor 16:2. 1 Tim 6:19. Luke 12:24. *storehouse,* Ps 33:7.
STORM, Ps 55:8; 83:15.
Ps 107:29. he maketh the *s.* a calm
Isa 4:6. covert from the *s.* 25:4. refuge from the *s.*
Nah 1:3. Lord hath his way in . . . the *s.*
Mark 4:27. a great *s.*, Luke 8:23.
Ps 148:8. *stormy* wind fulfilling his word
STOUT hearted, Ps 76:5. Isa 46:12.
Isa 10:12. punish fruit of *s.* heart
Dan 7:20. whose look was more *s.*
Mal 3:13. words have been *s.* against me
Isa 9:9. say in pride and *stoutness* of heart
STRAIGHT, Josh 6:5. Jer 31:9.
Ps 5:8. thy way *s.* before my face
Eccles 1:15. crooked cannot be made *s.*
7:31. who can make that *s.*
Isa 40:3. make *s.* in the desert a highway for our
4. crooked made *s.* 45:2. Luke 3:5.
Luke 3:4. way of Lord, make his paths *s.*
Heb 12:13. make *s.* paths for your feet

STRAIN at a gnat, Matt 23:24.
STRAIT, 2 Sam 24:14. Job 20:22; 36:16. Isa 49:20. Phil 1:23.
Matt 7:13. enter in at the *s.* gate, 14.
Mic 2:7. is the spirit of Lord *straitened*?
Luke 12:50. how am I *s.* till it be
2 Cor 6:12. not *s.* in us, but ye are *s.* in
STRANGE, Exod 21:8; 30:9. Lev 10:1. Ps 81:9. Jer 2:21. Luke 5:26. Heb 11:9. 1 Pet 4:12. Jude 7.
Isa 28:21. do his *s.* work . . . his *s.* act
Hos 8:12. they were counted as a *s.* thing
Zeph 1:8. clothed with *s.* apparel
Heb 13:9. about with divers and *s.* doctrines
1 Pet 4:4. think it *s.* that ye run not
Judg 11:2. *strange women,* Prov 2:16; 5:3, 20; 6:24; 20:16; 23:27; 27:13. Ezra 10:2, 11.
Gen 23:4. *stranger* and sojourner, Ps 39:12; 119:19. 1 Chron 29:15.
Jer 14:8. shouldest thou be as a *s.*
Matt 25:35. I was a *s.* and ye took
Luke 17:18. not found . . . save this *s.*
John 10:5. a *s.* will they not follow
Ps 105:12. very few and *strangers*
146:9. the Lord preserveth the *s.*
Eph 2:19. are no more *s.* and foreigners
Heb 11:13. confessed they were *s.*
13:2. be not forgetful to entertain *s.*, for thereby
1 Pet 2:11. beseech you as *s.* and
STRANGLED, Acts 15:20, 29; 21:25.
Job 7:15. soul chooseth *strangling*
STREAM, Isa 30:33; 66:12. Dan 7:10. Amos 5:24. Luke 6:48.
Ps 46:4. *streams,* 126:4. Song of Sol 4:15. Isa 30:25; 33:21; 35:6.
STREET, Rev 11:8; 21:21; 22:2.
Prov 1:20. *streets,* Song of Sol 3:2. Luke 14:21.
STRENGTH, Gen 49:24. Exod 13:3.
Exod 15:2. the Lord is my *s.*, Ps 18:2; 28:7; 118:14. Isa 12:2.
1 Sam 2:9. by *s.* shall no man prevail
15:29. the *S.* of Israel will not lie
Job 9:19. if I speak of *s.* lo, he is
12:13. with him is wisdom and *s.*, 16.
Ps 18:32. girded me with *s.*, 39.
27:1. the Lord is the *s.* of my life
29:11. Lord will give *s.* to his people
33:16. mighty man not delivered by much *s.*
39:13. spare me that I recover *s.*
46:1. God is our refuge and *s.*, 81:1.
68:35. God of Israel . . . giveth *s.* and power

28:7. err in vision, *s.* in judgment
1 Pet 2:8. which *s.* at the word
Rom 9:32. they *stumbled* at that stumblingstone
John 11:9. walk in the day he *stumbleth* not
Rom 14:21. whereby thy brother *s.*
Isa 8:14. *stumbling,* 1 John 2:10. 1 Pet 2:8. Rom 9:32.
Lev 19:14. *stumblingblock,* Isa 57:14. Jer 6:21. Ezek 3:20; 7:19; 14:3, 4, 7. Rom 11:9; 14:13. 1 Cor 1:23; 8:9. Rev 2:14.
stumblingstone, Rom 9:32, 33.
SUBDUE our iniquities, Mic 7:19.
Phil 3:21. able to *s.* all things
Heb 11:33. through faith *subdued*
SUBJECT, devils are, Luke 10:17, 20.
Rom 8:7. not *s.* to law of God
20. creature made *s.* to vanity
13:1. every soul be *s.* to higher powers, 5.
1 Cor 14:32. spirits of prophets *s.* to
15:28. Son . . . shall be *s.* to him that
Eph 5:24. as church is *s.* to Christ
Heb 2:15. all lifetime *s.* to bondage
James 5:17. Elias was a man *s.* to like passions
1 Pet 2:18. servants be *s.* to your masters
5:5. all of you be *s.* one to another
1 Cor 9:27. *subjection,* 1 Tim 2:11; 3:4. Heb 2:5, 8; 12:9. 1 Pet 3:1, 5.
SUBMIT, Gen 16:9. Ps 18:44; 66:3; 68:30; 81:15.
1 Cor 16:16. *submit yourselves,* Eph 5:21, 22. Col 3:18. Heb 13:17. James 4:7. 1 Pet 2:13; 5:5.
Rom 10:3. have not *submitted* unto the righteousness of God
SUBSCRIBE, Isa 44:5. Jer 32:44.
SUBSTANCE, Gen 7:4; 15:14.
Deut 33:11. bless, Lord, his *s.*
Job 30:22. and dissolvest my *s.*
Ps 139:15. my *s.* was not hid from thee, 16.
Prov 3:9. honour Lord with thy *s.*
Hos 12:8. I have found me out *s.*
Luke 8:3. ministered to him of their *s.*
Heb 10:34. a better and an enduring *s.*
11:1. faith is *s.* of things hoped for
SUBTIL, Gen 3:1. Prov 7:10.
Acts 13:10. *subtilty,* 2 Cor 11:3. Prov 1:4.
SUBVERT, Lam 3:36. Titus 1:11; 3:11.
Acts 15:24. *subverting,* 2 Tim 2:14.
SUCK, Gen 21:7. Deut 32:13; 33:19.
Job 20:16. he shall *suck* poison of asps
Isa 60:16. *s.* milk of Gentiles
Matt 24:19. woe to them . . . that give *s.*
Luke 23:29. paps which never gave *s.*
11:27. blessed are paps thou has *sucked*
Isa 11:8. *sucking* child, 49:15. Lam 4:4.
Ps 8:2. *suckling,* Lam 2:11.
SUDDEN, Prov 3:25. 1 Thess 5:3.
SUFFER, Exod 12:23. Lev 19:17.
Ps 55:22. never *s.* righteous to be moved
89:33. nor *s.* my faithfulness to fail
121:3. not *s.* thy foot to be moved
Prov 10:3. not *s.* soul of righteous to famish
Matt 16:21. he must . . . *s.* many things
17:17. how long shall I *s.* you?
19:14. *s.* little children . . . to come to me
1 Cor 4:12. being persecuted, we *s.*
10:13. God will not *s.* you to be tempted
Phil 1:29. but also to *s.* for his sake
2 Tim 2:12. if we *s.* we shall also reign
Heb 11:25. choosing rather to *s.* affliction
13:22. *s.* the word of exhortation
1 Pet 4:15. none of you *s.* as a murderer
19. that *s.* according to will of God
Ps 105:14. he *suffered* no man to do them wrong, 1 Chron 16:21.
Acts 14:16. *s.* all nations to walk in their own ways
16:7. the Spirit *s.* them not
Phil 3:8. for whom I *s.* loss of all
Heb 5:8. learned . . . by things which he *s.*
1 Pet 2:21. Christ *s.* for us, leaving
5:10. after that ye have *s.* a while
Matt 11:12. *suffereth,* 1 Cor 13:4.
Rom 8:18. *sufferings,* 2 Cor 1:5, 6. Phil 3:10. Col 1:24. Heb 2:10. 1 Pet 1:11; 4:13; 5:1.
SUFFICE, 1 Pet 4:3. John 14:8.
Job 20:22. *sufficiency,* 2 Cor 3:5; 9:8.
Matt 6:34. *sufficient* to day is evil
2 Cor 2:16. who is *s.* for these things?
3:5. not that we are *s.* of ourselves
12:8. my grace is *s.* for thee
SUM, Ps 139:17. Ezek 28:12. Heb 8:1.
SUMMER and winter not cease, Gen 8:22.
Ps 74:17. hast made *s.* and winter
Prov 6:8. provideth her meat in *s.*
10:5. that gathereth in *s.* is a wise son
Isa 18:6. fowls shall *s.* upon them
Zech 14:8. in *s.* and in winter shall it be
SUMPTUOUSLY, fared, Luke 16:19.
SUN, stand thou still, Josh 10:12.
Ps 19:4. he set a tabernacle for *s.*
74:16. prepared the light and *s.*
104:19. *s.* knoweth his going down
121:6. *s.* shall not smite thee by day, Isa 49:10.
136:8. *s.* to rule day, Gen 1:16.
Song of Sol 1:6. because *s.* looked on me
6:10. fair as moon, clear as the *s.*
Isa 30:26. light of the *s.* shall be sevenfold
60:19. *s.* shall be no more thy light by day
20. thy *s.* shall no more go down
Jer 31:35. giveth *s.* for a light by day
Mal 4:2. *S.* of righteousness arise
Matt 5:45. his *s.* to rise on evil and
13:43. shine forth as *s.* in the kingdom of
1 Cor 15:41. there is one glory of *s.*
Eph 4:26. let not *s.* go down upon
Rev 10:1. his face as *s.*, 1:16. Matt 17:2.
7:16. neither shall the *s.* light on them
21:23. city had no need of the *s.*, 22:5.
SUP, Luke 17:8. Rev 3:20. Hab 1:9.
Luke 14:16. made a great *supper*
1 Cor 11:20. the Lord's *s.*, Luke 22:20.
Rev 19:9. to marriage *s.* of Lamb
SUPERFLUITY of naughtiness, James 1:21.
SUPERSTITION, Acts 25:19; 17:22.
SUPPLICATION, 1 Kings 8:28; 9:3. Job 8:5; 9:15. Ps 6:9; 30:8; 55:1; 142:1; 119:170. Dan 6:11; 9:20. Hos 12:4. Zech 12:10. Eph 6:18. Phil 4:6. 1 Tim 2:1; 5:5. Heb 5:7.
SUPPLY of Spirit of Jesus, Phil 1:19.
Phil 4:19. my God shall *s.* all your need
2 Cor 9:12. *supplieth,* Eph 4:16.
SUPPORT the weak, Acts 20:35. 1 Thess 5:14.
SUPREME, 1 Pet 2:13.
SURE, Gen 23:17. 1 Sam 25:28.
2 Sam 23:5. covenant, ordered . . . and *s.*
Ps 19:7. testimony of the Lord is *s.*
93:5. thy testimonies are very *s.*
111:7. all his commandments are *s.*
Prov 11:15. that hateth suretiship is *s.*
18. righteousness shall be *s.* reward
Isa 22:23, 25. fasten him as a nail in a *s.* place
28:16. I lay in Zion . . . a *s.* foundation
33:16. his waters shall be *s.*
55:3. *s.* mercies of David, Acts 13:34.
John 6:69. we are *s.* thou art that Christ
Rom 4:16. promise might be *s.* to all

2 Tim 2:19. foundation of God standeth *s.*
2 Pet 1:10. calling and election *s.*
19. a more *s.* word of prophecy
SURETY for servant, Ps 119:122.
Heb 7:22. Jesus made *s.* of better
SURFEITING, Luke 21:34.
SURPRISED hypocrites, Isa 33:14.
SUSTAIN, Ps 55:22. Prov 18:14.
Ps 3:5. *sustained,* Isa 59:16.
SWALLOW, Ps 84:3. Jer 8:7.
Isa 25:8. will *s.* up death in victory
Matt 23:24. strain at a gnat, *s.* a camel
Exod 15:12. earth *swallowed,* Num 16:32.
2 Cor 2:7. be *s.* with overmuch sorrow
5:4. mortality be *s.* up of life
SWEAR, Num 30:2. Deut 6:13.
Isa 45:23. every tongue shall *s.*
65:16. shall *s.* by the God of truth
Jer 4:2. shalt *s.*, The Lord liveth, 12:16.
Zeph 1:5. *s.* by Lord . . . *s.* by Malcham
Matt 5:34. *s.* not at all, James 5:12.
Mal 3:5. swift witness against . . . false *swearers*
Ps 15:4. *sweareth* to his own hurt
Eccles 9:2. that *s.* as he that feareth
Zech 5:3. every one that *s.* shall be cut off
Jer 23:10. because of *swearing* land mourneth
Hos 4:2. by *s.* and lying . . . they break
10:4. *s.* falsely in making a covenant
SWEAT, Gen 3:19. Luke 22:44.
SWEET, Job 20:12. Ps 55:14.
Ps 104:34. my meditation of him shall be *s.*
119:103. how *s.* are thy words unto my taste
Prov 3:24. thy sleep shall be *s.*, Jer 31:26.
9:17. stolen waters are *s.*, 20:17.
27:7. to hungry soul every bitter thing is *s.*
Eccles 5:12. sleep of labouring man is *s.*
Song of Sol 2:3. his fruit was *s.* to my taste
14. *s.* is thy voice and thy countenance
5:16. his mouth is most *s.*
Isa 5:20. put bitter for *s.* and *s.* for bitter
Phil 4:18. odour of a *s.* smell
Rev 10:9. in thy mouth *s.* as honey
Ps 19:10. *sweeter* also than honey, 119:103.
Judg 14:14. *sweetness,* Prov 16:21; 27:9.
SWELLING, Jer 12:5. 2 Pet 2:18.
SWIFT, Deut 28:49. Job 9:26.
Eccles 9:11. the race is not to the *s.*
Rom 3:15. s. to shed blood, Prov 6:18.
James 1:19. *swift* to hear, slow to speak
2 Pet 2:1. bring on themselves *s.* destruction
Job 7:6. days *swifter* than a shuttle, 9:25.
Ps 147:15. *swiftly,* Joel 3:4.
SWIM, 2 Kings 6:6. Ps 6:6. Ezek 47:5.
SWORD, Exod 32:27. Lev 26:6, 25.
Gen 3:24. cherubims and a flaming *s.*
Judg 7:20. *s.* of Lord and Gideon
2 Sam 12:10. *s.* shall never depart
Ps 17:13. from wicked which is thy *s.*
Song of Sol 3:8. every man hath his *s.* on
Jer 9:16. I will send a *s.* after them
15:2. such as are for *s.* to the *s.*, 43:11.
Ezek 21:13. what if *s.* contemn even the rod
Zech 11:17. *s.* shall be upon his arm
Matt 10:34. not to send peace, but *s.*
Luke 2:35. a *s.* shall pierce through
Rom 13:4. he beareth not *s.* in vain
Eph 6:17. *s.* of Spirit which is word of God
Heb 4:12. sharper than any twoedged *s.*
Rev 1:16. sharp twoedged *s.*, 19:15.
Ps 55:21. *swords,* 59:7. Prov 30:14. Isa 2:4. Ezek 32:27. Joel 3:10.
SWORN by myself, Gen 22:16.
Ps 24:4. not *s.* deceitfully
119:106. I have *s.* and I will perform
SYNAGOGUE, Ps 74:8. Matt 6:5; 23:6. Luke 7:5. John 9:22; 18:20. Acts 15:21. Rev 2:9; 3:9.

T

TABERNACLE, Exod 26:1; 29:43.
Job 5:24. thy *t.* shall be in peace
Ps 15:1. who shall abide in thy *t.*?
Prov 14:11. *t.* of upright shall flourish
Isa 33:20. a *t.* that shall not be taken down
Amos 9:11. raise *t.* of David, Acts 15:16.
2 Cor 5:1. if our earthly house of this *t.*
4. we that are in this *t.* do groan
Heb 8:2. minister of sanctuary and the true *t.*
2 Pet 1:13. I am in this *t.*
14. knowing I must put off this my *t.*
Rev 21:3. the *t.* of God is with men
Job 12:6. *tabernacles* of robbers
Ps 84:1. how amiable are thy t.
118:15. salvation is in the *t.* of the
Heb 11:9. dwelling in *t.* with Isaac and
TABLE, Exod 25:23. Job 36:16.
Ps 23:5. preparest a *t.* before me
69:22. let their *t.* become a snare
128:3. olive plants round thy *t.*
Prov 3:3. write them on *t.* of heart
Song of Sol 1:12. while king sitteth at his *t.*
Jer 17:1. sin . . . is graven on *t.* of their heart
Mal 1:7. *t.* of Lord is contemptible
Matt 15:27. crumbs . . . from their masters' *t.*
1 Cor 10:21. partakers of Lord's *t.*
Deut 10:4. *tables,* 5. Heb 9:4. 2 Chron 4:8, 19. Isa 28:8. Ezek 40:41.
Hab 2:2. make it plain upon *t.*
Acts 6:2. leave word of God and serve *t.*
2 Cor 3:3. not in *t.* of stone, but fleshy *t.*
TAKE you for a people, Exod 6:7.
Exod 20:7. not *t.* name of the Lord in vain
34:9. *t.* us for thine inheritance
Ps 27:10. the Lord will *t.* me up
51:11. *t.* not thy holy spirit from me
116:13. I will *t.* cup of salvation
119:43. *t.* not the word of truth out
Hos 14:2. *t.* with you words . . . *t.* away all
Matt 16:24. *take* up his cross and follow
18:16. *t.* with thee one or two more
23. would *t.* account of his servants
20:14. *T.*, that is thine and go thy
26:26. Jesus said *T.*, eat, 1 Cor 11:24.
Luke 12:19. *t.* thine ease, eat, drink
John 10:17. that I might *t.* it again, 18.
Eph 6:13. *t.* . . . whole armour of God, 17.
Rev 3:11. that no man *t.* thy crown
Exod 23:25. *take away,* Josh 7:13. 2 Sam 24:10. 1 Chron 17:13. Job 7:21; 32:22; 36:18. Ps 58:9. Isa 58:9. Jer 15:15. Hos 1:6; 4:11; 14:2. Amos 4:2. Mal 2:3. Luke 17:31. John 11:39. 1 John 3:5. Rev 22:19.
Deut 4:9. *take heed,* 11:16; 27:9. 2 Chron 19:6. Ps 39:1. Isa 7:4. Mal 2:15. Matt 6:1; 16:6; 18:10; 24:4. Mark 4:24; 13:33. Luke 8:18; 12:15. 1 Cor 10:12. Col 4:17. Heb 3:12. 2 Pet 1:19.
Deut 32:41. *take hold,* Ps 69:24. Isa 27:5; 56:4; 64:7. Zech 1:6.
Ps 83:3. *taken* crafty counsel
119:111. thy testimonies have I *t.*
Isa 53:8. he was *t.* from prison and
Lam 4:20. the anointed . . . was *t.* in their pits
Matt 21:43. kingdom of God *t.* from
24:40. one shall be *t.*, the other left
Mark 4:25. shall be *t.* even that which he hath

Acts 1:9. he was *t.* up, 11:22.
2 Tim 2:26. *t.* captive by him
Isa 6:7. thy iniquity is *taken away*
16:10. gladness is—and joy out of
57:1. and merciful men are—
Luke 10:42. good part not be—from
2 Cor 3:16. turneth to Lord, veil shall be—
Ps 40:12. my iniquities have *taken hold*
119:143. trouble and anguish have—of me
Prov 1:19. *taketh away,* John 1:29; 15:2.
John 16:22. your joy no man *taketh from* you
Ps 119:9. by *taking* heed thereto
Matt 6:27. which of you by *t.* thought can
Rom 7:8, 11. sin *t.* occasion
Eph 6:16. above all *t.* shield of faith
TALE, Ps 90:9. Ezek 22:9. Luke 24:11.
Lev 19:16. *talebearer,* Prov 11:13; 18:8; 20:19; 26:20, 22.
TALENTS, Matt 18:24; 25:15, 25.
TALK of them when thou, Deut 6:7.
1 Sam 2:3. *t.* no more so exceeding proudly
Job 13:7. and *t.* deceitfully for him
Ps 71:24. my tongue shall *t.* righteousness
105:2. *t.* ye of all his wondrous works
145:11. speak of glory of thy kingdom and *t.* of thy
Jer 12:1. *t.* with thee of thy judgments
John 14:30. I will not *t.* much with
Titus 1:10. unruly and vain *talkers*
Ps 37:30. his tongue *talketh* of judgment
Eph 5:4. foolish *talking*
TAME, Mark 5:4. James 3:7, 8.
TARRY, 1 Chron 19:5. 2 Kings 14:10.
Ps 101:7. telleth lies shall not *t.* in my sight
Prov 23:30. that *t.* long at wine
Jer 14:8. turneth aside to *t.* for a night
Hab 2:3. though it *t.* wait for it
Matt 26:38. *t.* ye here and watch
John 21:22. that he *t.* till I come
1 Cor 11:33. *t.* one for another
Ps 68:12. she that *tarried* at home
Matt 25:5. bridegroom *t.*, they *all slumbered*
Luke 2:43. child Jesus *t.* behind in
Ps 40:17. make no *tarrying,* 70:5.
TASTE, Exod 16:31. 1 Sam 14:43.
Job 6:6. is there any *t.* in white of an egg?
Ps 34:8. O *taste* and see that the Lord is good
Song of Sol 2:3. his fruit was sweet to my *t.*
Jer 48:11. his *t.* remained in him
Matt 16:28. shall not *t.* of death
Luke 14:24. shall *t.* of my supper
John 8:52. keep my saying shall never *t.* death
Col 2:21. touch not, *t.* not, handle not
Heb 2:9. *t.* death for every man
6:4. have *tasted* of the heavenly gift
1 Pet 2:3. if ye have *t.* that Lord is gracious
TATTLERS, 1 Tim 5:13.
TEACH, Exod 4:12. Lev 10:11.
Deut 4:9. *t.* them thy sons, 6:7; 11:19.
33:10. shall *t.* Jacob thy judgments
1 Sam 12:23. *t.* you good . . . way, 1 Kings 8:36.
2 Chron 17:7. to *t.* in cities of Judah
Job 21:22. shall any *t.* God
Ps 25:8. *t.* sinners in the way
34:11. *t.* you fear of Lord, 32:8.
51:13. *t.* transgressors thy ways
90:12. so *t.* us to number our days
Isa 2:3. *t.* us of his ways, Mic 4:2.
Jer 31:34. *t.* no more every man his neighbour
Matt 28:19. go ye therefore and *t.* all nations
John 9:34. and dost thou *t.* us?
14:26. (Holy Ghost) shall *t.* you all
1 Cor 4:17. as I *t.* every where in every church
1 Tim 2:12. I suffer not a woman to *t.*
3:2. a bishop must be . . . given to hospitality, apt to *t.*
2 Tim 2:2. faithful men . . . able to *t.*
Heb 5:12. have need that one *t.* you
1 John 2:27. need not that any man *t.* you
Job 34:32. that which I see not *teach* thou *me*
teach me, Ps 25:5.—thy paths, 4.—thy way, 27:11; 86:11.—thy statutes, 119:12, 26, 64, 68, 124, 135.—good judgment, 66.—thy judgments, 108.—to do thy will, 143:10.
Hab 2:18. *teacher,* John 3:2. Rom 2:20. 1 Tim 2:7. 2 Tim 1:11.
Ps 119:99. *teachers,* Isa 30:20.
2 Tim 4:3. heap to themselves *t.*
Titus 2:3. be *t.* of good things
Heb 5:12. ought to be *t.* ye need
Ps 94:12. *teachest* him out of thy law
Matt 22:16. *t.* way of God in truth
Rom 2:21. *t.* another, *t.* thou not thyself
Job 36:22. who *teacheth* like him
35:11. who *t.* us more than beasts
Ps 18:34. *t.* my hands to war, 144:1.
Isa 48:17. Lord thy God which *t.* thee to profit
1 Cor 2:13. words which man's wisdom *t.* but which the Holy Ghost *t.*
1 John 2:27. same anointing *t.* you
2 Chron 15:3. a *teaching* priest
Matt 15:9. *t.* for doctrines the commandments
28:20. *t.* them to observe all things
Col 1:28. *t.* every man in all wisdom
Titus 2:12. *t.* us that denying ungodliness
2 Chron 30:22. *taught* good knowledge
Ps 71:17. hast *t.* me from my youth
Eccles 12:9. he still *t.* people knowledge
Isa 54:13. children shall be *t.* of Lord
John 6:45. shall be all *t.* of God
Acts 20:20. *t.* you publickly and from
Gal 6:6. let him that is *t.* in the word
1 Thess 4:9. yourselves are *t.* of God
TEAR, Ps 50:22. Hos 5:14. Job 16:9.
TEARS, Job 16:20. Ps 6:6. Isa 38:5.
Ps 56:8. put thou my *t.* in thy bottle, 39:12.
80:5. feedest them with bread of *t.*
126:5. they that sow in *t.* shall
Isa 25:8. wipe away all *t.* from off
Jer 9:1. mine eyes were a fountain of *tears*
Luke 7:38. to wash his feet with *t.*
Acts 20:19. *t.* and temptations, 31.
2 Cor 2:4. I wrote unto you with many *t.*
2 Tim 1:4. being mindful of thy *t.*
Heb 5:7. with strong crying and *t.*
Rev 7:17. wipe all *t.* from their eyes, 21:4.
TEATS, Isa 32:12. Ezek 23:3, 21.
TEETH white with milk, Gen 49:12.
Job 4:10. *t.* broken, Ps 3:7; 58:6.
Song of Sol 4:2. *t.* like a flock of sheep, 6:6.
Jer 31:29. *t.* set on edge, Ezek 18:2.
Amos 4:6. cleanness of *t.* in all cities
Matt 8:12. weeping and gnashing of *t.*, 22:13; 24:51; 25:30. Ps 112:10.
TELL it not in Gath, 2 Sam 1:20.
Ps 48:13. *t.* it to the generation following
Prov 30:4. name, if thou canst *t.*
Matt 8:4. see thou *t.* no man, 16:20.
18:15. go and *t.* him his fault
John 3:8. not *t.* whence it cometh
4:25. when he is come he will *t.* us all
8:14. ye cannot *t.* whence I come
2 Cor 12:2. in the body, I cannot *t.* . . . out of the body, I cannot *t.*, 3.
Gal 4:16. because I *t.* you the truth
Phil 3:18. now *t.* you even weeping

1 Cor 8:2. if any man *t.* that he knoweth
Gal 6:3. if a man *t.* himself to be something
Eph 3:20. above all that we ask or *t.*
Phil 4:8. *t.* on these things
Gen 50:20. *thought* evil against me
Ps 48:9. we have *t.* of thy lovingkindness
119:59. I *t.* on my ways and turned
Mal 3:16. and that *t.* on his name
Mark 14:72. when he *t.* thereon he wept
1 Cor 13:11. I *t.* as a child, but when
Phil 2:6. being in the form of God, *t.* it not robbery to be equal with God.
Ps 139:2. understandest my *t.* afar
Prov 24:9. the *t.* of foolishness is sin
Eccles 10:20. curse not king, no not in thy *t.*
Matt 6:25. take no *t.* for your life, Luke 12:22.
6:34. take no *t.* for the morrow
Mark 13:11. take no *t.* beforehand
2 Cor 10:5. bringing into captivity every *t.*
Ps 50:21. thou *thoughtest* that I was
Gen 6:5. imagination of *thoughts*
Judg 5:15. were great *t.* of heart
1 Chron 28:9. Lord understandeth . . . the *t.*
29:18. keep this for ever in imagination of *t.*
Ps 10:4. God is not in all his *t.*
33:11. the *t.* of his heart to all
40:5. many are . . . thy *t.* which are to us-ward
94:11. Lord knoweth the *t.* of man
19. in multitude of my *t.* within me
139:17. how precious are thy *t.* to me
23. try me and know my *t.*
Prov 12:5. *t.* of righteous are right
15:26. *t.* of wicked are abomination
Prov 16:3. thy *t.* shall be established
Isa 55:7. the unrighteous man his *t.*
8. my *t.* are not your *t.*
59:7. their *t.* are *t.* of iniquity
66:18. I know their works and their *t.*
Jer 4:14. how long shall thy vain *t.*
Mic 4:12. know not *t.* of the Lord
Matt 15:19. out of heart proceed evil *t.*
Luke 2:35. the *t.* of many hearts
Rom 2:15. their *t.* . . . else accusing or excusing
1 Cor 3:20. the Lord knoweth the *t.* of the wise
Heb 4:12. a discerner of the *t.* and
James 2:4. become judges of evil *thoughts*
THIRST, Deut 28:48; 29:19.
Isa 49:10. shall not hunger nor *t.*
Matt 5:6. blessed are they which do hunger and *t.* after righteousness
John 4:14. shall never *t.*, 6:35.
7:37. if any man *t.*, let him come unto me
Rom 12:20. if he *t.* give him drink
Rev 7:16. neither *t.* any more
Ps 42:2. my soul *thirsteth* for God
Isa 55:1. Ho, every one that *t.*
THORNS in your sides, Num 33:55. Judg 2:3. Gen 3:18.
Josh 23:13. and *t.* in your eyes
2 Sam 23:6. as *t.* thrust away
Jer 4:3. sow not among *t.*
12:13. sown wheat, but shall reap *t.*
Matt 7:16. do men gather grapes of *t.*?
13:7. some fell among *t.*, 22.
THREATENING, Eph 6:9. Acts 4:29; 9:1. 1 Pet 2:23.
THREE, 2 Sam 24:12. Prov 30:15, 18, 21, 29. Amos 1:3, 13; 2:1. 1 Cor 14:27. 1 John 5:7, 8. Rev 16:13.
THRESH, Isa 21:10; 41:15. Jer 51:33. Mic 4:13. Hab 3:12. 1 Cor 9:10.
Lev 26:5. and your *threshing* shall reach unto the vintage
2 Sam 24:18. *threshingfloor,* 21, 24.
THROAT an open sepulchre, Ps 5:9.
Ps 69:3. weary of my crying, my *t.* is dried
Prov 23:2. put a knife to thy *t.*
THRONE, Lord's is in heaven, Ps 11:4.
Ps 94:20. *t.* of iniquity have fellowship
Prov 25:5. *t.* shall be established in righteousness
Jer 14:21. do not disgrace *t.* of thy glory
Lam 5:19. thy *t.* from generation to
Dan 7:9. his *t.* was like fiery flame
Matt 19:28. shall sit in *t.* of his glory, ye shall sit on twelve thrones
25:31. shall sit on *t.* of his glory
Heb 4:16. boldly to the *t.* of grace
Rev 3:21. sit with me in my *t.* . . . with my Father in his *t.*
20:11. a great white *t.*
22:3. *t.* of God and Lamb shall be in it
Job 26:9. *his throne,* Ps 89:29, 44; 97:2; 103:19. Prov 20:28; 25:5. Dan 7:9. Zech 6:13.
Isa 22:23. *glorious throne,* Jer 17:12.
Ps 45:6. *thy throne,* 89:4, 14. Heb 1:8.
THRUST, Exod 11:1. Job 32:13. Luke 13:28. John 20:25. Acts 16:37.
THUNDER, Job 26:14; 40:9. Ps 29:3; 81:7. Mark 3:17.
Rev 4:5. *thunderings,* 8:5; 10:3; 11:19; 16:18; 19:6.
TIDINGS, evil, Exod 33:4. Ps 112:7.
Luke 1:19. shew thee glad *t.*, 8:1. Acts 13:32. Rom 10:15.
TIME when thou mayest be found, Ps 32:6.
Ps 37:19. evil *t.* 41:1. *t.* of trouble
69:13. acceptable *t.*, Isa 49:8. 2 Cor 6:2.
Ps 89:47. remember how short my *t.* is
Eccles 3:1–8. *a t.* to every purpose—to be born—to die—to plant—to pluck up—to kill—to heal—to break down—to build up—to weep—to laugh—to mourn—to dance—to cast away—to gather—to embrace—to refrain—to get—to lose—to keep—to cast away—to rend—to sew—to keep silence—to speak—to love—to hate—of war—of peace
9:11. *t.* and chance happeneth to them all
Ezek 16:8. thy *t.* was the *t.* of love
Dan 7:25. till a *time* and times
12:7. for a *t.*, times, and a half, Rev 12:14.
Amos 5:13. evil *t.*, Mic 2:3.
Luke 19:44. knewest not *t.* of thy visitation
John 7:6. my *t.* is not yet come: your *t.*
Acts 17:21. spent their *t.* in nothing else
Rom 13:11. high *t.* to awake out of
2 Cor 6:2. now is the accepted *t.*
Eph 5:16. redeeming the *t.*, Col 4:5.
1 Pet 1:17. pass *t.* of your sojourning
Rev 10:6. there should be *t.* no longer
Ps 31:15. my *times* are in thy hand
Luke 21:24. till *t.* of the Gentiles
Acts 1:7. not for you to know the *t.*
3:19. *t.* of refreshing shall come, 21.
17:26. determined *t.* before appointed
1 Tim 4:1. in latter *t.* some shall
2 Tim 3:1. in last days perilous *t.*
Ps 34:1. bless the Lord *at all times*
62:8. trust in him—
106:3. that doeth righteousness—
119:20. longing . . . unto thy judgments—
Prov 5:19. let her breasts satisfy thee—
17:17. a friend loveth—
TIN, Num 31:22. Isa 1:25. Ezek 22:18.
TITHES, Gen 14:20. Mal 3:8. Amos 4:4. Matt 23:23. Luke 18:12.
TITTLE pass from the law, Matt 5:18.
TOGETHER, Ps 2:2. Prov 22:2.
Rom 8:28. all things work *t.* for good

1 Cor 3:9. labourers *t.* with God
2 Cor 6:1. as workers *t.* with him
Eph 2:5. quickened us *t.* with Christ
6. raised us up *t.* and made us sit *t.* in Christ
TOKEN of covenant, Gen 9:12, 13; 17:11.
Ps 86:17. shew me *t.* for good
Phil 1:28. evident *t.* of perdition
2 Thess 1:5. *t.* of righteous judgment
Ps 65:8. they . . . are afraid at thy *tokens*
135:9. who sent *t.* and wonders
TONGUE, Exod 11:7. Josh 10:21.
Job 5:21. be hid from scourge of *t.*
20:12. hide it under his *t.*
Ps 34:13. keep thy *t.* from evil
Prov 10:20. *t.* of just is as choice silver
12:18. *t.* of wise is health, 31:26.
15:4. wholesome *t.* is a tree of life
18:21. death and life are in power of *t.*
21:6. getting of treasures by a lying *t.*
23. keepeth his *t.* keepeth his soul
25:15. a soft *t.* breaketh the bone
Isa 30:27. his *t.* as a devouring fire
50:4. the Lord hath given me *t.* of learned
Jer 9:5. taught their *t.* to speak lies
James 1:26. and bridleth not his *t.*
3:5. *t.* is a little member
8. the *t.* can no man tame
1 Pet 3:10. refrain his *t.* from evil
Ps 35:28. *my tongue,* 39:1; 45:1; 51:14; 71:24; 119:172; 137:6; 139:4. Acts 2:26.
Ps 31:20. *tongues,* 55:9. Mark 16:17. Acts 19:6. 1 Cor 12:10, 28.
1 Cor 14:23. and all speak with *t.*
TOOK me out of the womb, Ps 22:9.
Phil 2:7. *t.* on him form of servant
Heb 10:34. *t.* joyfully the spoiling of
TOPHET, Isa 30:33. Jer 7:31, 32.
TORCH, Zech 12:6. Nah 2:3, 4.
TORMENT us before time, Matt 8:29.
Luke 16:28. come to this place of *t.*
Rev 18:7. so much *t.* and sorrow
14:11. smoke of their *t.* ascendeth
Luke 16:24. I am *tormented* in this
Heb 11:37. destitute, afflicted, *tormented*
TORN, Hos 6:1. Mal 1:13. Mark 1:26.
TOSS, Isa 22:18. *Jer 5:22. James 1:6.*
Ps 109:23. I am *tossed* up and down
Eph 4:14. children *t.* to and fro
TOUCH not mine anointed, Ps 105:15.
Job 5:19. in seven there shall no evil *t.*
Isa 52:11. *t.* no unclean thing
Matt 9:21. may but *t.* his garment
14:36. only *t.* hem of his garment
Mark 10:13. children . . . that he should *t.*
Luke 11:46. *t.* not the burdens with
John 20:17. *t.* me not, for I am not
1 Cor 7:1. good for a man not to *t.* a woman
2 Cor 6:17. *t.* not the unclean thing
Col 2:21. *t.* not, taste not, handle not
1 Sam 10:26. there went with him a band of men whose hearts God had *touched*
Job 19:21. hand of God hath *t.* me
Zech 2:8. he that *toucheth* you *t.* apple of his eye
1 John 5:18. wicked one *t.* him not
TOWER, God is a high, Ps 144:2.
Ps 61:3. strong *t.*, Prov 18:10.
Song of Sol 4:4. thy neck like the *t.* of David
7:4. *t.* of ivory . . . *t.* of Lebanon
Isa 5:2. built a *t.*, Matt 21:33.
TRADITION, Matt 15:3. Gal 1:14. Col 2:8. 2 Thess 2:15; 3:6. 1 Pet 1:18.
TRAIN, Prov 22:6. Isa 6:1.
TRAITOR, Luke 6:16. 2 Tim 3:4.
TRAMPLE, Isa 63:3. Matt 7:6.
TRANCE, Num 24:4. Acts 10:10; 11:5; 22:17. *See* 2 Cor 12:2, 3, 4.
TRANQUILLITY, Dan 4:27.
TRANSFIGURED, Matt 17:2. Mark 9:2.
TRANSFORMED, Rom 12:2. 2 Cor 11:14, 15.
TRANSGRESS the commandment of the Lord, Num 14:41.
1 Sam 2:24. make the Lord's people to *t.*
2 Chron 24:20. why *t.* ye the commandments of the Lord?
Neh 1:8. if ye *t.* I will scatter you
Ps 17:3. my mouth shall not *t.*
25:3. be ashamed which *t.* without
Prov 28:21. for . . . bread that man will *t.*
Amos 4:4. come to Bethel and *t.*
Matt 15:2. why do thy disciples *t.*?
Rom 2:27. and circumcision dost *t.* law
Deut 26:13. not *transgressed* thy commandments
Josh 7:11. hath *t.* my covenant, Judg 2:20.
Isa 43:27. teachers have *t.* against
Jer 2:8. pastors also *t.* against me
Lam 3:42. we have *t.* and *rebelled*
Ezek 2:3. they and their fathers have *t.*
Dan 9:11. all Israel have *t.* thy law
Hos 6:7. men have *t.* the covenant
Hab 2:5. he *transgresseth* by wine
1 John 3:4. whosoever committeth sin *t.*
Ps 59:13. in *transgressing* and lying against Lord
Exod 34:7. forgiving iniquity, *transgression,* and sin
Num 14:18. forgiving iniquity and *t.*
1 Chron 10:13. Saul died for his *t.*
Job 13:23. make me to know my *t.*
Ps 19:13. innocent from the great *t.*
32:1. blessed he whose *t.* is forgiven
89:32. I will visit their *t.* with rod
107:17. fools because of *t.* are afflicted
Prov 17:9. that covereth *t.* seeketh love
Isa 53:8. for the *t.* of my people was he stricken
58:1. shew my people their *t.*
20. them that turn from *t.* in Jacob
Dan 9:24. to finish *t.* and make an end
Amos 4:4. at Gilgal multiply *transgression*
Mic 3:8. to declare to Jacob his *t.*
6:7. shall I give my firstborn for my *t.*
Rom 4:15. where no law is, there is no *t.*
1 John 3:4. sin is the *t.* of the law
Exod 23:21. not pardon your *transgressions*
Lev 16:21. all their *t.* in all their sins
Josh 24:19. will not forgive your *t.*
Job 31:33. I covered my *t.* as Adam
Ps 25:7. remember not . . . nor my *t.*
32:5. I said, I will confess my *t.*
39:8. deliver me from all my *t.*
51:1. blot out my *t.*
3. I acknowledge my *t.* and my sin is ever before me
103:12. so far hath he removed our *t.*
Isa 43:25. I am he that blotteth out thy *t.*
44:22. blotted out as a thick cloud thy *t.*
53:5. he was wounded for our *t.*
59:12. our *t.* are multiplied before thee
Ezek 18:31. cast away from you all your *t.*
Heb 9:15. for the redemption of *t.*
Isa 48:8. called a *transgressor* from the womb
James 2:11. if thou kill, thou art become a *t.* of the law
Ps 51:13. teach *transgressors* thy ways
59:5. be not merciful to any wicked *t.*
119:158. I beheld *t.* and was grieved
Prov 13:15. the way of *t.* is hard

Job 5:6. neither doth *t.* spring out
7. man is born to *t.* as sparks fly
14:1. man . . . is of few days and full of *t.*
Ps 9:9. a refuge in times of *t.*
27:5. in time of *t.* he shall hide me
37:39. their strength in time of *t.*
46:1. a very present help in *t.*
60:11. give us help from *t.*
91:15. I will be with him in *t.*
119:143. *t.* and anguish have taken
143:11. bring my soul out of *t.*
Prov 11:8. righteous delivered out of *t.*
Isa 26:16. Lord, in *t.* have they visited
33:2. our salvation also in time of *t.*
Jer 8:15. time of health, and behold *t.*
14:8. saviour thereof in time of *t.*
19. for time of healing, and behold *t.*
Dan 12:1. there shall be a time of *t.*
1 Cor 7:28. shall have *t.* in the flesh
Exod 14:24. Lord *troubled* the host of Egypt
Ps 30:7. hide thy face, and I was *t.*
77:3. I remembered God, and was *t.*
Isa 57:20. wicked are like the *t.* sea
John 5:4. an angel . . . *t.* the water
12:27. now is my soul *t.*
14:1. let not your heart be *t.*, 27.
2 Thess 1:7. to you who are *t.* rest
Ps 25:17. *troubles* of my heart are enlarged
34:17. deliver them out of all their *t.*
71:20. shewed me great and sore *t.*
88:3. my soul is full of *t.*
Job 23:16. Almighty *troubleth* me
1 Kings 18:17. thou he that *t.* Israel
Prov 11:17. cruel *t.* his own flesh
29. he that *t.* his own house
Luke 18:5. because this widow *t.* me
Gal 5:10. he that *t.* you shall bear
Job 3:17. the wicked cease from *troubling*
John 5:4. after *t.* of the water
TRUCE breakers, 2 Tim 3:3.
TRUE, Gen 42:11. 2 Sam 7:28.
Ps 19:9. judgments of Lord are *t.*
119:160. thy word is *t.* from beginning
Prov 14:25. *t.* witness delivereth souls
Ezek 18:8. *t.* judgment, Zech 7:9.
Matt 22:16. we know thou art *t.*
Luke 16:11. commit to your *trust t. riches*
John 1:9. that was the *t.* light
4:23. *t.* worshippers worship the Father in spirit
6:32. giveth you *t.* bread from heaven
7:28. but he that sent me is *t.*
15:1. I am the *t.* vine, and my Father
2 Cor 1:18. as God is *t.* our word to
6:8. as deceivers and yet *t.*
Phil 4:8. whatsoever things are *t.*
1 John 5:20. may know him that is *t.*
Rev 3:7. saith he that is *t.*
14. the faithful and *t.* witness
19:11. was called Faithful and *T.*
TRUMP, 1 Cor 15:52. 1 Thess 4:16.
TRUMPET, Exod 19:16. Ps 81:3.
Isa 27:13. great *t.* shall be blown
58:1. lift up thy voice like a *t.*
Matt 6:2. do not sound a *t.* before thee
Num 10:2. *trumpets,* Josh 6:4. Ps 98:6. Rev 8:6.
TRUST in him, 1 Chron 5:20.
Job 4:18. put no *t.* in his servants, 15:15.
8:14. whose *t.* shall be a spider's web
Ps 4:5. put your *t.* in the Lord
9:10. that know thy name will put their *t.*
40:4. blessed . . . that maketh the Lord his *t.*
71:5. thou art my *t.* from my youth
Prov 22:19. thy *t.* may be in Lord
Job 13:15. though he slay me, yet will I *t.*
Ps 37:3. *t.* in Lord, and do good
5. *t.* also in him; he shall bring it to pass
40. he shall . . . save them because they *t.*
55:23. but I will *t.* in thee
62:8. *t.* in him at all times, ye
115:9, 10, 11. *t.* in the Lord
118:8. it is better to *t.* in Lord, 9.
119:42. for I *t.* in thy word
125:1. they that *t.* in Lord shall
Isa 26:4. *t.* ye in the Lord for ever
50:10. *t.* in the name of the Lord
Jer 7:4. *t.* ye not in lying words
9:4. and *t.* ye not in any brother
Mic 7:5. *t.* ye not in a friend
Mark 10:24. hard for them that *t.* in riches
2 Cor 1:9. should not *t.* in ourselves
Phil 3:4. he might *t.* in flesh
Ps 22:4. our fathers *trusted* in thee
28:7. my heart *t.* in him, and I am
52:7. *t.* in abundance of his riches
Luke 18:9. which *t.* in themselves
Ps 32:10. that *trusteth* in Lord, mercy
34:8. blessed is man that *t.* in him
57:1. be merciful . . . for my soul *t.* in thee
84:12. blessed is man that *t.* in thee
86:2. save thy servant that t. in thee
Jer 17:5. cursed be man that *t.* in man
7. blessed is man that *t.* in Lord
1 Tim 5:5. widow indeed and desolate *t.* in God
Ps 112:7. his heart is fixed, *trusting*
TRUTH, Gen 24:27. Exod 18:21.
Exod 34:6. abundant in goodness and *t.*
Deut 32:4. a God of *t.* and without
Ps 15:2. speaketh *t.* in his heart
25:10. paths of Lord are mercy and *t.*
51:6. desirest *t.* in inward parts
91:4. his *t.* shall be thy shield
117:2. *t.* of Lord endureth for ever
Ps 119:30. I have chosen the way of *truth*
142. righteousness, and thy law is *t.*
151. all thy commandments are *t.*
Prov 12:19. lip of *t.* shall be established
16:6. by mercy and *t.* iniquity is purged
23:23. buy the *t.* and sell it not
Isa 59:14. *t.* is fallen in the street
Jer 4:2. swear, The Lord liveth, in *t.*
Dan 4:37. all whose works are *t.*
Zech 8:16. speak every man *t.* to his
John 1:14. full of grace and *t.*, 17.
8:32. know the *t.*, and the *t.* shall
14:6. I am the way, the *t.*, and life
17. Spirit of *t.* 16:13. guide you into all *t.*
17:17. thy word is *t.*
19. sanctified through the *t.*
18:37. bear witness to *t.* 38. what is *t.*?
Acts 26:25. words of *t.* and soberness
Rom 1:18. hold *t.* in unrighteousness
25. changed the *t.* of God into a lie
2:2. judgment of God is according to *t.*
1 Cor 5:8. bread of sincerity and *t.*
2 Cor 13:8. do nothing against *t.*
Gal 3:1. should not obey the *t.*, 5:7.
Eph 4:15. speaking *t.* in love, 25.
21. taught by him, as *t.* is in Jesus
5:9. fruit of the Spirit is in all . . . *t.*
6:14. having your loins girt about with *t.*
2 Thess 2:10. received not love of *t.*
1 Tim 3:15. pillar and ground of *t.*
6:5. destitute of the *t.*
2 Tim 2:18. who concerning the *t.* have erred
25. to the acknowledging of the *t.*
3:7. never able to come to knowledge of the t.
8. do these also resist the *t.*
4:4. turn away their ears from *t.*
James 3:14. lie not against the *t.*
1 Pet 1:22. purified your souls in obeying *t.*
2 Pet 1:12. established in present *t.*

1 John 1:8. and the *t.* is not in us
5:6. because the Spirit is *t.*
Josh 24:14. *in truth,* 1 Sam 12:24. Ps 145:18. Jer 4:2. John 4:24. 1 Thess 2:13. 1 John 3:18. 2 John 4.
Ps 25:5. *thy truth,* 26:3; 43:3; 108:4. John 17:17.
TRY, Judg 7:4. Job 12:11. Jer 6:27.
2 Chron 32:31. God left him, to *t.* him
Job 7:18. visit him . . . and *t.* him every moment
Ps 11:4. his eyelids *t.* children of men
139:23. *t.* me, and know my thoughts
Jer 9:7. will melt them, and *t.* them
Lam 3:40. search and *t.* our ways
Dan 11:35. some . . . shall fall, to *t.* them
Zech 13:9. will *t.* them as gold is tried
1 Cor 3:13. fire shall *t.* every man's work
1 Pet 4:12. fiery trial which is to *t.*
1 John 4:1. *t.* the spirits whether
Rev 3:10. to *t.* them which dwell on the earth
2 Sam 22:31. word of Lord is *tried,* Ps 18:30.
Ps 12:6. words of Lord are pure . . . as silver *t.* in
17:3. *t.* me, 66:10. *t.* us as silver is *t.*
105:19. word of the Lord *t.* him
Dan 12:10. many shall be purified . . . and *t.*
Heb 11:17. Abraham, when he was *t.*
James 1:12. when he is *t.* he shall receive the crown of life
1 Pet 1:7. though it be *t.* with fire
Rev 2:2. hast *t.* them which say they are apostles
10. into prison, that ye may be *t.*
3:18. buy of me gold *t.* in the fire
1 Chron 29:17. I know . . . thou *triest*
Jer 11:20. that *t.* the reins and heart
Ps 7:9. the righteous God *trieth* the heart, Prov 17:3.
11:5. Lord *t.* the righteous
1 Thess 2:4. pleasing . . . God, which *t.* hearts
James 1:3. *trying* of your faith
TUMULT, Ps 65:7. 2 Cor 12:20.
TURN from their sin, 1 Kings 8:35.
2 Kings 17:13. t. ye from your evil ways
Prov 1:23. *t.* you at my reproof
Song of Sol 2:17. *t.*, my beloved, be thou
Isa 31:6. *t.* ye not unto him from
Jer 18:8. if that nation . . . *t.* from their evil
31:18. *t.* thou me and I shall be turned
Lam 5:21. *t.* us unto thee, O Lord, and we shall be turned
Ezek 3:19. *t.* not from his wickedness
18:32. *t.* yourselves and live, 33:9, 11; 14:6. Hos 12:6. Joel 2:12. Zech 9:12.
Zech 1:3. *t.* to me, . . . and I will *t.* to you
Acts 26:18. *t.* them from darkness
20. should repent, and *t.* to God
2 Pet 2:21. to *t.* from holy commandment
2 Chron 30:6. *turn again,* Ps 60:1; 80:3, 7, 19; 85:8. Lam 3:40. Mic 7:19. Zech 10:9. Gal 4:9.
1 Sam 12:20. *turn aside,* Ps 40:4. Isa 30:11. Lam 3:35. Amos 2:7; 5:12.
Ps 119:37. *turn away,* 39. Song of Sol 6:5. Isa 58:13. 2 Tim 3:5. Heb 12:25.
Deut 4:30. *turn (un)to Lord,* 30:10. 2 Chron 15:4. Ps 22:27. Lam 3:40. Hos 14:2. Joel 2:13. Luke 1:16. 2 Cor 3:16.
Ps 9:17. wicked be *turned* into hell
30:11. *t.* for me my mourning into dancing
119:59. *t.* my feet to thy testimonies
Isa 53:6. *t.* every one to his own way
Jer 2:27. *t.* their back to me, 32:33.
8:6. every one *t.* to his course
Hos 7:8. Ephraim is a cake not *t.*
John 16:20. sorrow shall be *t.* to joy
1 Thess 1:9. *t.* to God from idols
James 4:9. laughter be *t.* to mourning
2 Pet 2:22. dog is *t.* to his own vomit
Deut 9:12. *turned aside,* Ps 78:57. Isa 44:20. 1 Tim 1:6; 5:15.
1 Kings 11:3. *turned away,* Ps 78:38. Jer 5:25. *turned not away,* Ps 66:20. Isa 5:25; 9:12; 10:4.
Ps 44:18. *turned back,* 78:9, 41. Isa 42:17. Jer 4:8. Zeph 1:6.
Job 15:13. *turnest,* Ps 90:3.
Ps 146:9. way of wicked he *turneth* upside down
Prov 15:1. soft answer *t.* away wrath
Isa 9:13. the people *t.* not unto him
Jer 14:8. *t.* aside to tarry for a night
James 1:17. neither shadow of *turning*
Jude 4. t. grace of God into lasciviousness
TURTLE(DOVES), Lev 1:14; 5:7, 11; 12:6. Ps 74:19. Song of Sol 2:12. Jer 8:7.
TUTORS, Gal 4:2.
TWAIN, Matt 5:41; 19:5. Eph 2:15.
TWICE, Gen 41:32. Exod 16:22. Num 20:11. 1 Kings 11:9. Job 33:14; 40:5. Ps 62:11. Mark 14:30.
Luke 18:12. I fast *t.* in the week
TWINKLING, 1 Cor 15:52.

U

UNACCUSTOMED, Jer 31:18.
UNADVISEDLY, Ps 106:33.
UNAWARES, Deut 4:42. Ps 35:8. Luke 21:34. Heb 13:2. Jude 4.
UNBELIEF, did not many mighty works there because of, Matt 13:58.
Mark 6:6. marvelled because of their *u.*
9:24. I believe; help thou mine *u.*
16:14. upbraided them with their *u.*
Rom 4:20. staggered not . . . through *u.*
11:20. because of *u.* they were broken off
32. hath concluded them all in *u.*
1 Tim 1:13. I did it ignorantly in *u.*
Heb 3:12. in any of you an evil heart of *u.*
UNBELIEVERS, Luke 12:46. 1 Cor 6:6; 14:23. 2 Cor 6:14.
UNBELIEVING, Acts 14:2. 1 Cor 7:14, 15. Titus 1:15. Rev 21:8.
UNBLAMEABLE, Col 1:22. 1 Thess 3:13.
1 Thess 2:10. *unblameably* we behaved
UNCERTAIN, 1 Cor 14:8. 1 Tim 6:17.
UNCIRCUMCISED, Exod 6:12, 30. Jer 6:10; 9:25, 26. Acts 7:51.
UNCIRCUMCISION, Rom 2:25, 26, 27; 3:30; 4:10. 1 Cor 7:18, 19. Gal 2:7; 5:6; 6:15. Col 2:13; 3:11.
UNCLEAN, Lev 5:2; 11:4, 26; 13:15. Num 19:19.
Lev 10:10. difference between *u.* and clean, Ezek 22:26.
Isa 6:5. I am a man of *u.* lips
Lam 4:15. depart ye; it is *u.*
Ezek 44:23. discern between *u.* and clean
Hag 2:13. if one . . . *u.* by a dead body touch . . . these, shall it be *u.*?
Rom 14:14. is nothing *u.* of itself
1 Cor 7:14. else were your children *u.*
Eph 5:5. no *u.* person hath . . . inheritance
Num 5:19. *uncleanness,* Ezra 9:11.
Matt 23:27. are within full of . . . all *u.*
Rom 6:19. members servants to *u.*
Eph 4:19. all *u.* with greediness
5:3. all *u.* let it not once be named
1 Thess 4:7. hath not called us to *u.*
Ezek 36:29. save you from all . . . *uncleannesses*
UNCLOTHED, 2 Cor 5:4.
UNCOMELY, 1 Cor 7:36; 12:23.
UNCONDEMNED, Acts 16:37; 22:25.
UNCORRUPTNESS, Titus 2:7.
UNCOVER, Lev 18:18. 1 Cor 11:5, 13.

V

Eph 2:2. in time past ye *w.*, Col 3:7.
1 Pet 4:3. we *w.* in lasciviousness
Rom 14:15. *walkest* thou not charitably
Ps 15:2. he that *walketh* uprightly
39:6. every man *w.* in a vain shew
Mic 2:7. do good to him that *w.* uprightly
2 Thess 3:6. brother that *w.* disorderly
1 Pet 5:8. devil . . . *w.* about seeking
Rev 2:1. *w.* in midst of seven golden
Gen 3:8. voice of Lord God *walking* in
Isa 57:2. in his uprightness
Jer 6:28. revolters *w.* with slanders
Mic 2:11. if man *w.* in spirit and falsehood
Luke 1:6. *w.* in all commandments
Acts 9:31. *w.* in the fear of the Lord
2 Cor 4:2. not *w.* in craftiness
2 Pet 3:3. *w.* after their own lusts, Jude 16.
2 John 4. thy children *w.* in truth
WALL, Ps 62:3. Prov 18:11. Song of Sol 2:9; 8:9, 10. Isa 26:1; 60:18.
WANDER, Num 14:33. Ps 119:10.
Lam 4:14. *wandered,* Heb 11:37.
Prov 21:16. *wandereth,* 27:8.
1 Tim 5:13. *wandering,* Jude 13.
Ps 56:8. tellest my *wanderings*
WANT, Deut 28:48. Job 31:19.
Ps 23:1. the Lord . . . I shall not *w.*
34:9. no *w.* to them that fear him, 10.
2 Cor 8:14. a supply for your *w.*
Phil 4:11. not that I speak in respect of *w.*
WANTONNESS, Rom 13:13. 2 Pet 2:18.
WAR, Exod 13:17; 17:16. Ps 27:3.
Job 10:7. changes and *w.* are against
Ps 18:34. teacheth my hands to *w.*, 144:1.
120:7. I am for peace . . . they are for *w.*
Prov 20:18. with good advice make *w.*
Eccles 8:8. is no discharge in that *w.*
Isa 2:4. neither . . . learn *w.* any more, Mic 4:3.
Mic 3:5. prepare *w.* against
2 Cor 10:3. we do not *w.* after flesh
1 Tim 1:18. *w.* a good warfare
1 Pet 2:11. fleshly lusts which *w.*
Rev 11:7. beast . . . shall make *w.*
12:7. there was *w.* in heaven
17:14. these shall make *w.* with the Lamb
19:11. in righteousness doth he . . . make w.
Num 21:14. in book of *wars* of Lord
Ps 46:9. he maketh *w.* to cease
Matt 24:6. hear of *w.* and rumours of *w.*
James 4:1. from whence come *w.* and
2 Tim 2:4. no man that *warreth*
Isa 37:8. *warring,* Rom 7:23.
WARFARE, Isa 40:2. 1 Cor 9:7. 2 Cor 10:4. 1 Tim 1:18.
WARN, 2 Chron 19:10. Acts 10:22.
Ezek 3:19. if thou *w.* the wicked
33:3. blow trumpet, *w.* people, 9.
Acts 20:31. I ceased not to *w.*
1 Cor 4:14. my beloved sons I *w.* you
1 Thess 5:14. *w.* them that are unruly
Ps 19:11. by them is they servant *warned*
Matt 3:7. who hath *w.* you to flee
Heb 11:7. Noah being *w.* of God
Jer 6:10. to whom I give *warning*
Col 1:28. Christ . . . whom we preach, *w.*
WASH, Lev 6:27; 14:9; 15:16.
Job 9:30. if I *w.* myself with snow water
Ps 26:6. *w.* my hands in innocency
51:2. *w.* me throughly from mine iniquity
7. *w.* me and I shall be whiter than
58:10. he shall *w.* his feet in blood
Isa 1:16. *w.* you, make you clean
Jer 2:22. thou *w.* thee with nitre
4:14. *w.* thy heart from wickedness
Luke 7:38. to *w.* his feet with tears
John 13:5. began to *wash* disciples' feet
8:1. *w.* thee not, thou hast no part
14. ought to *w.* one another's feet
Acts 22:16. be baptized and *w.* away
Job 29:6. when I *washed* my steps
Song of Sol 5:3. I have *w.* my feet
Isa 4:4. *w.* away filth of daughters
Ezek 16:4. neither wast thou *w.* in
Heb 10:22. *w.* with pure water
Rev 1:5. *w.* us from our sins in his own blood
7:14. *w.* their robes, and made them white in
Eph 5:26. *washing,* Titus 3:5
WASTE, Ps 80:13. Matt 26:8
Luke 15:13. *wasted,* 16:1. Gal 1:13.
Prov 18:9. *waster,* Isa 54:16.
Job 14:10. *wasteth,* Prov 19:26.
Isa 59:7. *wasting* and destruction, 60:18.
WATCH, Neh 4:9. Job 7:12.
Job 14:16. dost thou not *w.* over my sin?
Ps 102:7. I *w.* and am as a sparrow
130:6. they that *w.* for morning
141:3. set a *w.*, O Lord, before my mouth
Jer 44:27. *w.* over them for evil
Matt 24:42. *w.* therefore, for ye know not, 25:13.
Mark 13:33. take ye heed, *w.* and pray, 37.
1 Cor 16:13. *w.* ye, stand fast in the
Col 4:2. *w.* in the same with thanksgiving
1 Thess 5:6. let us *w.* and be sober
2 Tim 4:5. *w.* thou in all things
Heb 13:17. they *w.* for your souls
1 Pet 4:7. be sober, *w.* unto prayer
Rev 3:3. if therefore thou shalt not *w.* I will
Jer 31:28. like as I have *watched* over them
20:10. familiars *w.* for my halting
Matt 24:43. he would have *w.*
Ps 63:6. *watches,* 119:148. Lam 2:19.
37:32. the wicked *watcheth* the
Ezek 7:6. the end is come; it *w.* for
Rev 16:15. blessed is he that *w.* and
3:2. be *watchful* and strengthen
Prov 8:34. *watching* daily at my gates
Eph 6:18. *w.* with all perseverance
2 Cor 6:5. in *watchings,* 11:27.
Isa 21:11. *watchman,* Ezek 3:17; 33:7.
Song of Sol 3:3. *watchmen,* 5:7. Isa 52:8; 56:10; 62:6. Jer 31:6.
WATER, Gen 49:4. Exod 12:9; 17:6.
2 Sam 14:14. we are as *w.* split
Job 15:16. drinketh iniquity like *w.*
Ps 22:14. I am poured out like *w.*
Isa 12:3. draw *w.* out of wells of salvation
27:3. I will *w.* it every moment
30:20. give you . . . *w.* of affliction
41:17. when poor and needy seek *w.* and there
44:3. pour *w.* on him that is thirsty
58:11. shalt be like . . . a spring of *w.*
Lam 1:16. eye runneth down with *w.*, 3:48.
Ezek 36:25. sprinkle clean *w.*
Amos 8:11. nor a thirst for *w.*
Matt 3:11. I indeed baptize you with *w.*
10:42. cup of cold *w.* only in name of a
Luke 16:24. dip tip of his finger in *w.*
John 3:5. except a man be born of *w.*
23. baptized because there was much *w.*
4:14. shall be in him a well of *w.*
John 7:38. flow rivers of living *w.*
19:34. came there out blood and *w.*
Acts 8:38. went down both into *w.*
10:47. can any man forbid *w.* that these
Eph 5:26. cleanse it with washing of *w.*
1 John 5:6. he that came by *w.*

8. three bear witness in earth, spirit, *w.*, and
Jude 12. clouds they are without *w.*
Rev 21:6. fountain of *water* of life, 22:1.
22:17. take the *w.* of life freely
Isa 58:11. like a *watered* garden, Jer 31:12.
1 Cor 3:6. I have planted, Apollos *w.*, 7.
Ps 23:2. leadeth me beside still *waters*
124:4. *w.* had overwhelmed us, 5.
Prov 5:15. drink *w.* out of thine own cistern, and running *w.* out of thine own well
9:17. solen *w.* are sweet
Eccles 11:1. cast thy bread upon *w.*
Song of Sol 4:15. a well of living *w.*
Isa 32:20. blessed are ye that sow beside all *w.*
33:16. bread . . . given him; his *w.* shall be sure
35:6. in wilderness shall *w.* break forth
43:20. I give *w.* in the wilderness
54:9. this is as *w.* of Noah unto me
58:11. a spring of water, whose *w.* fail not
Jer 2:13. fountain of living *w.*, 17:13.
9:1. O that my head were *w.*
Hab 2:14. as *w.* cover the sea, Isa 11:9.
Zech 14:8. living *w.* shall go out from Jerusalem, *w.*, 14:2; 19:6. Ezek 47:1.
Rev 1:15. sound of many
7:17. lead them unto iiving fountains of *w.*
Ps 42:7. noise of thy *waterspouts*
WAVERING, Heb 10:23. James 1:6.
WAX, Exod 32:10, 11, 22. Ps 22:14; 68:2; 97:5. Matt 24:12. Luke 12:33. 1 Tim 5:11. 2 Tim 3:13.
WAY, Exod 13:21; 23:20; 32:8.
1 Sam 12:23. teach you good and right *w.*
1 Kings 2:2. I go *w.* of all the earth
Ezra 8:21. seek of him a right *w.*
Ps 1:6. *w.* of righteous . . . *w.* of ungodly
2:12. and ye perish from the *w.*
49:13. this their *w.* is their folly
67:2. that thy *w.* may be known
78:50. made a *w.* to his anger
119:30. I have chosen *w.* of truth
32. run *w.* of thy commandments
Prov 2:8. Lord preserveth the *w.* of his saints
10:29. *w.* of the Lord is strength
14:12. a *w.* which seemeth right
15:9. *w.* of wicked is abomination
24. *w.* of life is above to the wise
Eccles 11:5. knowest not what is *w.* of spirit
Isa 26:7. *w.* of just is uprightness, 8.
30:21. this is the *w.* walk ye in it
35:8. a *w.* . . . called The *w.* of holiness
43:19. make a *w.* in wilderness, 16.
59:8. *w.* of peace they know not
Jer 6:16. where is the good *w.* and
10:23. *w.* of man is not in himself
21:8. the *w.* of life and *w.* of death
32:39. give them one heart and one *w.*
50:5. shall ask the *w.* to Zion
Matt 7:13. broad is *w.* . . . to destruction
John 1:23. straight the *w.* of Lord
14:4. *w.* ye know. 6. I am the *w.*
Acts 16:17. shew unto us *w.* of salvation
18:25. instructed in *w.* of Lord, 26.
1 Cor 10:13. make a *w.* to escape
12:31. shew I unto you a more excellent *w.*
2 Pet 2:2. the *w.* of truth shall be evil spoken of
1 Kings 8:32. bring *his way* on his head
Job 17:9. righteous shall hold on—
Ps 18:30. as for God—is perfect
37:23. delighteth in—34. and keep—
119:9. shall a young man cleanse—
Prov 14:8. prudent is to understand—
16:9. man's heart deviseth—
Isa 55:7. let the wicked forsake—
Ps 25:8. teach sinners *in the way*
119:14. I rejoiced—of thy testimonies
Ps 139:24. lead me *in the way* everlasting
Isa 26:8.—of thy judgments . . . we waited
Matt 5:25. whiles thou art—with him
21:32. John came—of righteousness
Luke 1:79. guide our feet—of peace
Job 40:19. he is chief of *ways* of God
Ps 84:5. in whose heart are *w.* of
Prov 3:17. Her *w.* are *w.* of pleasantness
5:21. *w.* of man are before eyes of the Lord
16:2. *w.* of man are clean in his
7. when a man's *w.* please Lord
Jer 7:3. amend your *w.* and your doings
Lam 1:4. the *w.* of Zion do mourn
3:40. let us search and try our *w.*
Deut 32:4. *his ways,* Ps 145:17. Isa 2:3. Mic 4:2. Rom 11:33.
Ps 119:5. *my ways,* 26, 59, 168; 139:3; 39:1. Prov 23:26. Isa 55:8. *highways,* 49:11.
Prov 14:14. *own way(s),* Isa 53:6; 58:13; 66:3. Ezek 36:31, 32.
Job 21:14. *thy ways,* Ps 25:4; 91:11; 119:15. Prov 4:26. Isa 63:17. Ezek 16:61. Dan 5:23. Rev 15:3.
Isa 35:8. *wayfaring,* Jer 14:8.
WEAK, 2 Chron 15:7. Job 4:3. Ps 6:2.
Isa 35:3. strengthen ye the *w.* hands
Ezek 16:30. how *w.* is thy heart
Matt 26:41. the flesh is *w.*, Mark 14:38.
Rom 4:19. and being not *w.* in faith
14:1. him that is *w.* in the faith receive
1 Cor 4:10. we are *w.* but ye are strong
9:22. to the *w.* became I as *w.*
11:30. for this cause many are *w.* and sickly
12:10. I am *w.* then am I strong
1 Thess 5:14. support the *w.*
Isa 14:12. *weaken,* Ps 102:23. Job 12:21.
2 Sam 3:1. *weaker,* 1 Pet 3:7.
1 Cor 1:25. *weakness,* 2:3; 15:43. 2 Cor 12:9; 13:4. Heb 11:34.
WEALTH, Gen 34:29. Deut 8:17.
Deut 8:18. giveth thee power to get *w.*
Job 21:13. spend their days in *w.*
Ps 49:6. that trust in their *w.*
10. and leave their *w.* to others
112:3. *w.* and riches shall be in his
Prov 10:15. rich man's *w.* is his strong city, 18:11.
13:11. *w.* gotten by vanity shall be
22. *w.* of the sinner is laid up for
19:4. *w.* maketh many friends
1 Cor 10:24. but every man another's *w.*
WEANED, Ps 131:2. Isa 11:8; 28:9.
WEAPON, Deut 23:13. Neh 4:17. Job 20:24. Isa 13:5; 54:17. 2 Cor 10:4.
WEARY of my life, Gen 27:46.
Job 3:17. there the *w.* be at rest
10:1. soul is *w.* of life, Jer 4:31.
Prov 3:11. nor be *w.* of his correction
Isa 7:13. *w.* men, will ye *w.* my God
40:28. Lord . . . fainteth not, neither is *w.*
31. shall run and not be *w.*
50:4. speak a word in season to him that is *w.*
Jer 6:11. *w.* with holding in
9:5. *w.* themselves to commit
20:9. I was *w.* with forbearing
31:25. I have satiated the *w.* soul
Gal 6:9. not be *w.* in welldoing. 2 Thess 3:13.
Isa 43:24. *wearied,* 57:10. Jer 12:5. Ezek 24:12. Mic 6:3. Mal 2:17. John 4:6. Heb 12:3.
Eccles 12:12. *weariness,* Mal 1:13.
Job 7:3. *wearisome* nights
WEB, Job 8:14. Isa 59:5, 6.
WEDDING, Matt 22:3, 8, 11. Luke 14:8.
WEEK, Dan 9:27. Matt 28:1. Luke 18:12. Acts 20:7. 1 Cor 16:2.
Jer 5:24. *weeks,* Dan 9:24–26; 10:2.
WEEP, Job 30:25. Isa 30:19; 33:7. Jer 9:1; 13:17. Joel 2:17.
Luke 6:21. blessed are ye that *w.*
23:28. *w.* not for me, but *w.* for
Rom 12:15. *w.* with them that *w.*

1 Cor 7:30. that *w.* as though they wept not
James 5:1. rich men, *w.* and howl
1 Sam 1:8. why *weepest* thou, John 20:13, 15.
Ps 126:6. he that goeth forth and *weepeth*
Lam 1:2. she *w.* sore in the night
Ps 30:5. *weeping* may endure for a night
Isa 22:12. Lord God of hosts call to *w.* and
Joel 2:12. turn ye even to me with . . . *w.*
Mal 2:13. covering altar of Lord with *w.*
Matt 8:12. *w.* and gnashing of teeth, 22:13; 24:51; 25:30.

WEIGH the path of the just, Isa 26:7.
Job 31:6. let me be *weighed* in an even balance
Dan 5:27. art *w.* in the balances
Prov 16:2. Lord weigheth spirits
11:1. just *weight* in his delight
16:11. just *w.* and balance are the Lord's
2 Cor 4:17. eternal *w.* of glory
Heb 12:1. let us lay aside every *w.*
Matt 23:23. omitted *weightier* matters
Lev 19:36. just *weights*
Deut 25:13. divers *w.*, Prov 20:10, 23.

WELL, Ps 84:6. Prov 5:15; 10:11. Song of Sol 4:15. Isa 12:3. John 4:14. 2 Pet 2:17.
Gen 4:7. if thou doest *well,* shalt
Exod 1:20. God dealt *w.* with midwives
Ps 119:65. hast dealt *w.* with thy servant
128:2. it shall be *w.* with thee
Eccles 8:12. it shall be *w.* with them
Isa 3:10. shall be *w.* with him
Rom 2:7. *well doing,* Gal 6:9. 2 Thess 3:13. 1 Pet 2:15; 3:17; 4:19.

WENT, Ps 42:4; 119:67. Matt 21:30.

WEPT, Neh 1:4. Ps 69:10. Hos 12:4. Matt 26:75. Luke 19:41. John 11:35.

WHEAT, Ps 81:16. Prov 27:22. Song of Sol 7:2.
Jer 12:13. they have sown *w.*
Amos 8:5. we may set forth *w.*
Matt 3:12. gather his *w.* into the garner
Luke 22:31. may sift you as *w.*
John 12:24. except a corn of *w.* fall

WHEEL, Ps 83:13. Prov 20:26.
Ezek 1:16. *w.* in middle of *w.* 10:10.
10:13. it was cried unto them, O *w.*
Exod 14:25. *wheels,* Judg 5:28. Ezek 1:16; 10:9, 12, 13. Dan 7:9. Nah 3:2.

WHET, Deut 32:41. Ps 7:12; 64:3.

WHISPERER, Prov 16:28.

WHIT, 1 Sam 3:18. John 7:23. 2 Cor 11:5.

WHITE, Lev 13:3, 4. Num 12:10.
Job 6:6. any taste in *w.* of an egg
Ps 68:14. *w.* as snow, Dan 7:9.
Eccles 9:8. thy garments be always *w.*
Song of Sol 5:10. my beloved is *w.* and
Isa 1:18. sins . . . shall be *w.* as snow
Dan 11:35. to purge and to make them *w.*
12:10. many shall be purified and made *w.*
Matt 17:2. his raiment was *w.*, 28:3.
Rev 2:17. give him a *w.* stone
3:4. walk with me in *w.* (raiment), 5, 18; 4:4; 7:9; 13; 15:6; 19:8, 14.
Matt 23:27. *whited,* Acts 23:3.
Ps 51:7. *whiter* than snow, Lam 4:7.

WHOLE, Ps 9:1; 119:10. Isa 54:5. Mic 4:13. Zech 4:14. Matt 9:21. 1 John 2:2; 5:19.
Job 5:18. he woundeth and his hands make *whole*
Mark 5:34. thy faith hath made thee *w.*, 10:52.
John 5:4. *w.* of whatsoever disease
6. wilt thou be made *w.* 14. thou art made *w.*
Acts 9:34. Christ maketh thee *w.*
Prov 15:4. *wholesome,* 1 Tim 6:3.
Num 32:11. *wholly,* Deut 1:36. Jer 46:28. 1 Thess 5:23. 1 Tim 4:15.

WHORE, Lev 19:29; 21:7, 9. Deut 22:21; 23:17, 18. Prov 23:27. Ezek 16:28. Rev 17:1, 16.
Jer 3:9. *whoredom,* Ezek 16:26. Hos 2:2, 4; 4:11, 12; 5:3, 4.
Eph 5:5. *whoremonger,* 1 Tim 1:10. Heb 13:4. Rev 21:8; 22:15.

WICKED, Exod 23:7. Deut 15:9; 25:1.
Gen 18:25. slay the righteous with *w.*
1 Sam 2:9. the *w.* shall be silent in
Job 21:30. *w.* is reserved to the day
Ps 7:11. God is angry with the *w.*
9:17. *w.* shall be turned into hell
11:6. on *w.* he shall rain snares
58:3. *w.* are estranged from womb
119:155. salvation is far from the *w.*
145:20. all *w.* will he destroy, 147:6.
Prov 11:5. *w.* shall fall by his own
21:12. God overthroweth the *w.*
28:1. *w.* flee when no man pursueth
Eccles 7:17. be not overmuch *w.*
Isa 55:7. let the *w.* forsake his way
Jer 17:9. heart is deceitful and desperately *w.*
25:31. he will give . . . *w.* to the sword
Ezek 3:18. warn the *w.*, 33:8, 9, 11.
Dan 12:10. *w.* shall do *wickedly*
Gen 19:7. do not so *w.*, Neh 9:33.
1 Sam 12:25. if ye shall still do *w.*
Job 13:7. will ye speak *w.* for God?
Ps 18:21. have not *w.* departed
Gen 6:5. God saw that the *wickedness*
39:9. how can I do this great *w.*
1 Sam 24:13. *w.* proceedeth from the wicked
Job 4:8. and sow *w.* shall reap same
Ps 7:9. *w.* of wicked come to an end
45:7. righteousness, and hatest *w.*
Prov 8:7. *w.* is an abomination to my lips
10:2. treasures of *w.* profit nothing
Eccles 8:8. neither shall *w.* deliver
Isa 9:18. *w.* burneth as the fire
Jer 2:19. thine own *w.* shall correct
4:14. O Jerusalem, wash thy heart from *w.*
14:20. we acknowledge, O Lord, our *w.*
Hos 10:13. ye have plowed *w.*
Acts 8:22. repent therefore of this thy *w.*
1 John 4:19. whole world lieth in *w.*

WIDE, Deut 15:8, 11. Ps 35:21; 81:10. Prov 13:3. Matt 7:13.

WIDOW, Mark 12:42. 1 Tim 5:5. Deut 10:18. Ps 146:9. Luke 18:3, 5.
Ps 68:5. *widows,* Jer 49:11. Matt 23:14. 1 Tim 5:3. James 1:27.

WIFE, Exod 20:17. Lev 21:13.
Prov 5:18. rejoice with *w.* of youth
18:22. findeth a *w.* findeth a good
19:14. a prudent *w.* is from Lord
Eccles 9:9. live joyfully with the *w.*
Mal 2:15. against *w.* of his youth
Luke 17:32. remember Lot's *w.*
Eph 5:33. every one . . . love his *w.* even as
Rev 19:7. his *w.* hath made herself ready
21:9. the bride, the Lamb's *w.*
1 Cor 7:29. *wives,* Eph 5:25, 28. Col 3:18, 19. 1 Tim 3:11. 1 Pet 3:1.

WILDERNESS, Deut 32:10. Prov 21:19. Song of Sol 3:6; 8:5. Isa 35:1, 6; 41:18; 19; 42:11; 43:19, 20. Rev 12:6.

WILES, Num 25:18. Eph 6:11.

WILL, Lev 1:3; 19:5; 22:19.
Deut 33:16. the good *w.* of him that
Matt 7:21. doeth *w.* of my Father, 12:50.
John 1:13. *w.* of flesh, nor of *w.* of man
4:34. my meat is to do *w.* of him that
6:40. this is the *w.* of him that sent
Acts 21:14. the *w.* of the Lord be done
22:14. *his will,* John 7:17. Rom 2:18. Eph 1:5, 9. Col 1:9. 2 Tim 2:26. Heb 13:21. 1 John 5:14. Rev 17:17.
Luke 22:42. *my will,* Acts 13:22.

John 5:30. *own will,* 6:38. Eph 1:11. Heb 2:4. James 1:18.
Ps 40:8. *thy will,* 143:10. Matt 6:10; 26:42. Heb 10:7, 9.
Ezra 7:18. *will of God,* Mark 3:35. Rom 1:10; 8:27; 12:2. 1 Cor 1:1. 2 Cor 8:5. Gal 1:4. Eph 1:1; 6:6. Col 1:1; 4:12. 1 Thess 4:3. Heb 10:36. 1 Pet 4:2, 19. 1 John 2:17.
John 15:7. ask what ye *w.* and it
17:24. I *w.* that they also, whom thou hast
Rom 7:18. to *w.* is present with me
9:18. on whom he *w.* have mercy
Phil 2:13. worketh both to *w.* and to do
Rev 22:17. whosoever *w.* let him
Heb 10:26. if we sin *wilfully*
Rom 9:16. not of him that *willeth*
Exod 35:5. whosoever is of a *willing* heart
22. as many as were *w.* hearted.
1 Chron 28:9. serve him with a perfect heart and with a *w.* mind
Ps 110:3. thy people shall be *w.*
Matt 26:41. spirit is indeed *w.* but the flesh
Luke 22:42. if thou be *w.*, remove this cup
John 5:35. *w.* for a season to rejoice
2 Cor 5:8. *w.* rather to be absent
1 Tim 6:18. *w.* to communicate
Heb 13:18. in all things *w.* to live
2 Pet 3:9. not *w.* that any should perish
Judg 5:2. *willingly* offered, 9.
Lam 3:33. he doth not afflict *w.*
Hos 5:11. he *w.* walked after
1 Pet 5:2. not by constraint, but *w.*
Col 2:23. wisdom in *will worship*
WILLOWS, Lev 23:40. Isa 44:4.
WIN, that I may, Phil 3:8.
Prov 11:30. *winneth* souls is wise
WIND, Job 7:7; 30:15. Ps 103:16.
Ps 135:7. he bringeth the *w.* out of
Prov 11:29. inherit *w.* 27:16 hideth *w.*
Eccles 11:4. he that observeth the *w.*
Isa 26:18. have . . . brought forth *w.*
27:8. he stayeth his rough *w.* in
Jer 5:13. prophets shall become *w.*
10:13. *w.* out of his treasures, 51:16.
Hos 8:7. sown *w.* 12:1. feedeth on *w.*
John 3:8. *w.* bloweth where it listeth
Eph 4:14. about with every *w.* of
2 Kings 2:11. *whirlwind,* Prov 1:27; 10:25. Isa 66:15. Hos 8:7; 13:3. Nah 1:3. Hab 3:14. Zech 7:14; 9:14.
Ezek 37:9. *winds,* Matt 8:26. Luke 8:25.
WINDOWS, Gen 7:11. Eccles 12:3. Song of Sol 2:9. Isa 60:8. Jer 9:21.
WINE that maketh glad the heart, Ps 104:15.
Prov 20:1. *w.* is a mocker
21:17. loveth *w.* shall not be rich
23:31. look not thou upon the *w.* when it is red
31:6. and *w.* to those that be of heavy heart
Song of Sol 1:2. love is better than *wine,* 4.
Isa 5:11. till *w.* inflame them
12. pipe and *w.* are in their feasts
28:7. they have erred through *w.*
55:1. buy *w.* and milk, Song of Sol 5:1.
Hos 2:9. and my *w.* in the season
3:1. look to other gods, and love flagons of *w.*
Hab 2:5. he transgresseth by *w.*
Eph 5:18. be not drunk with *w.*
1 Tim 3:3. not given to *w.*, 8. Titus 1:7.
5:23. use a little *w.* for thy stomach's sake
Prov 23:20. *winebibber,* Matt 11:19.
Isa 25:6. *wines* on the lees well refined
WINGS of the God of Israel, Ruth 2:12.
Ps 17:8. hide me under shadow of thy *w.*, 36:7; 57:1; 61:4; 91:4.
18:10. on *w.* of wind, 2 Sam 22:11.
Prov 23:5. riches certainly make themselves *w.*
Isa 6:2. seraphims, each one had six *w.*
Mal 4:2. with healing in his *w.*
WINK, Job 15:12. Ps 35:19. Prov 6:13; 10:10. Acts 17:30.
WINTER, Song of Sol 2:11. Zech 14:8.
WISE, Gen 41:39. Exod 23:8. Deut 16:19.
Job 11:12. vain man would be *w.*
32:9. great men are not always *w.*
Ps 2:10. be *w.* . . . , O ye kings; be instructed
19:7. making *w.* the simple
107:43. whoso is *w.* and will observe
Prov 3:7. be not *w.* in thine own eyes
3:35. the *w.* shall inherit glory
13:20. walketh with *w.* men shall be *w.*
26:12. a man *w.* in his own conceit
Eccles 7:4. heart of *w.* is in house of
9:1. the *w.* and their work are in hand of God
Isa 5:21. are *w.* in their own eyes
Jer 4:22. they are *w.* to do evil
Dan 12:3. *w.* shall shine as brightness
Hos 14:9. who is *w.* and he shall
Matt 10:16. be ye therefore *w.* as serpents
11:25. hid these things from the *w.*
Rom 1:22. professing themselves to be *w.*
16:19. be *w.* to that which is good
1 Cor 3:18. seemeth to be *w.* in this world
4:10. but ye are *w.* in Christ
Eph 5:15. not as fools but as *w.*
Matt 10:42. *in no wise* lose his reward
Luke 18:17. shall—enter therein
John 6:37. cometh to me I will—cast out
Rev 21:27. shall—enter into it
Deut 4:6. this is your *wisdom*
1 Kings 4:29. God gave Solomon *w.*, 5:12.
Job 28:28. fear of Lord, that is *w.*
Prov 4:5. get *w.*, get understanding
7. *w.* is the principal thing, ch. 8.
16:16. better is it to get *w.* than gold
19:8. he that getteth *w.* loveth his own soul
23:4. cease from thine own *w.*
23. buy truth . . . also *w.*, and instruction
Eccles 1:18. in much *w.* is much grief
8:1. a man's *w.* maketh his face
Matt 11:19. *w.* is justified of her
1 Cor 1:17. not with *w.* of words
24. Christ the . . . *w.* of God, Luke 11:49.
30. who of God is made unto us *w.*
2:6. we speak *w.* among them that are perfect
3:19. *w.* of this world is foolishness
2 Cor 1:12. not with fleshly *w.*
Col 1:9. in all *w.* and spiritual understanding
James 1:5. if any of you lack *w.* let him ask of God
3:17. *w.* from above is first pure, then peaceable
Rev 5:12. worthy is the Lamb to receive *w.*
13:18. here is *w.*, 17:9.
Ps 111:10. *of wisdom,* Prov 9:10; 10:21. Mic 6:9. Col 2:3. James 3:13.
64:9. *wisely,* 101:2. Eccles 7:10.
1 Kings 4:31. *wiser,* Job 35:11. Ps 119:98. Luke 16:8. 1 Cor 1:25.
WITCH, Exod 22:18. Deut 18:10.
1 Sam 15:23. *witchcraft,* Gal 5:20.
WITHDRAW, Job 9:13; 33:17. Prov 25:17. Song of Sol 5:6. 2 Thess 3:6. 1 Tim 6:5.
WITHHOLD not they mercies, Ps 40:11.
Ps 84:11. no good thing will he *w.*
Prov 3:27. *w.* no good from them
23:13. *w.* not correction from child
Job 42:2. *withholden,* Jer 5:25.
Prov 11:24, 26. *withholdeth,* 2 Thess 2:6.
Gen 20:6. *withheld,* 22:12. Job 31:16.
WITHIN, Ps 40:8; 45:13. Matt 3:9; 23:26. Mark 7:21. 2 Cor 7:5. Rev 5:1.
WITHOUT, Prov 1:20; 24:27. 1 Cor 5:12. 2 Cor 7:5. Col 4:5. Rev 22:15.
WITHSTAND, Eccles 4:12. Eph 6:13.
Acts 11:17. that I could *w.* God
Gal 2:11. *withstood,* 2 Tim 4:15.

WITNESS, Gen 31:44, 48. Lev 5:1.
Num 35:30. one *w.* shall not testify, Deut 17:6; 19:15. 2 Cor 13:1.
Judg 11:10. Lord be *w.*, 1 Sam 12:5. Jer 42:5; 29:23. Mic 1:2. Mal 2:14.
Job 16:19. my *w.* is in heaven
Ps 89:37. as a faithful *w.* in heaven
Isa 55:4. him for a *w.* to the people
Mal 3:4. I will be a swift *w.* against
John 3:11. ye receive not our *w.*
5:36. greater *w.*
5:37. Father . . . borne *w.* of me
Acts 14:17. left not himself without *w.*
1 John 5:10. that believeth on Son of God hath *w.*
Rev 1:5. Christ, who is the faithful *w.*, 3:14.
20:4. beheaded for *w.* of Jesus
Deut 17:6. two or three *witnesses,* 19:15. 2 Cor 13:1. Matt 18:16. Heb 10:28. 1 Tim 5:19. Num 35:30.
Josh 24:22. *w.* against yourselves
Isa 43:10. my *w.*, saith the Lord, 12; 44:8.
1 Thess 2:10. ye are *w.* and God also
1 Tim 6:12. a good profession before many *w.*
Heb 12:1. so great a cloud of *w.*
Rev 11:3. power to my two *w.*
WIZARDS, Lev 19:31; 20:6. Isa 8:19.
WOLF, Isa 11:6; 65:25. Jer 5:6.
Ezek 22:27. *wolves,* Hab 1:8. Zeph 3:3. Matt 7:15; 10:16. Acts 20:29.
WOMAN, Gen 2:23; 3:15. Lev 18:22, 23; 20:13. Num 30:3.
Prov 11:16. gracious *w.* retaineth honour
Ps 48:6. pain as of a *w.* in travail, Isa 13:8; 21:3; 26:17; 42:14. Jer 4:31; 6:24; 13:21; 22:23; 30:6; 31:8; 48:41; 49:22, 24; 50:43.
Prov 12:4. a virtuous *w.* is a crown
14:1. every wise *w.* buildeth her house
31:10. who can find a virtuous *w.*?
30. *w.* that feareth Lord, she shall be praised
Eccles 7:26. *w.* whose heart is snares
28. *w.* among all have I not found
Isa 49:15. can *w.* forget her sucking child
54:6. called thee as a *w.* forsaken
Jer 31:22. *w.* shall compass a man
Matt 5:28. looketh on a *w.* to lust
John 2:4. *w.*, what have I to do *with*
8:3. brought unto him a *w.* taken in adultery
19:26. *w.*, behold thy son
Rom 1:27. the natural use of *w.*
1 Cor 11:7. *w.* is the glory of man
Gal 4:4. sent forth his Son, made of a *woman*
1 Tim 2:11. let *w.* learn in silence with
12. I suffer not *w.* to teach
Rev 12:1. *w.* clothed with sun, 6:16.
17:18. *w.* which thou sawest is that great city
Judg 5:24. blessed above *women* shall Jael
Prov 31:3. give not thy strength to *w.*
Song of Sol 1:8. fairest among *w.*, 5:9; 6:1.
Isa 3:12. *w.* rule over them
32:11. tremble, ye *w.* that are at ease
Jer 9:17. call for the mourning *w.*
Lam 4:10. *w.* have sodden their own children
Matt 11:11. among them that are born of *w.*
Luke 1:28. blessed art thou among *w.*
Rom 1:26. *w.* did change the natural use
1 Cor 14:34. let *w.* keep silence
1 Tim 2:9. *w.* adorn themselves in modest apparel
5:14. that the younger *w.* marry
2 Tim 3:6. lead captive silly *w.*
1 Pet 3:5. in the old time holy *w.*
Rev 14:4. were not defiled with *w.*
WOMB, Gen 25:23; 29:31.
Gen 49:25. blessings . . . of the *w.*
Ps 22:9. took me out of the *w.*
10. I was cast upon thee from *w.*
127:3. fruit of the *w.* is his reward
Ps 139:13. covered me in my mother's *w.*
Eccles 11:5. how the bones do grow in the *w.*
Isa 44:2. (Lord) formed thee from *w.*
66:9. to bring forth, and shut *w.*
Hos 9:14. give them a miscarrying *w.*
Luke 1:42. blessed is fruit of thy *w.*
11:27. blessed is *w.* that bare thee
23:29. blessed are *wombs* that never
WONDER, Deut 13:1; 28:46. Ps 71:7. Isa 29:14. Rev 12:1.
Acts 13:41. *w.* and perish, Hab 1:5.
Zech 3:8. they are men *wondered* at
Isa 59:16. *w.* was no intercessor
Luke 4:22. *w.* at the gracious words
Deut 28:59. thy plagues *wonderful*
Job 42:3. things too *w.* for me
Ps 119:129. thy testimonies are *w.*
139:6. such knowledge is too *w.*
Prov 30:18. three things which are too *w.* for
Isa 9:6. his name shall be called *W.*
25:1. thou hast done *w.* things
Jer 5:30. a *w.* and horrible thing is committed
Ps 139:14. *wonderfully,* Lam 1:9.
Exod 3:20. *wonders,* 7:3; 15:11.
Job 9:10. God doeth *w.*, Ps 77:11, 14.
Ps 78:11. forgat . . . his *w.*, Neh 9:17.
88:10. wilt thou shew *w.* to the dead?
136:4. who alone doeth great *w.*
Dan 12:6. how long . . . to end of these *w.*?
Joel 2:30. shew *w.* in heavens, Acts 2:19.
John 4:48. except ye see signs and *w.*
Acts 2:43. many *w.* and signs were done, 6:8.
Rom 15:19. mighty signs and *w.*
Rev 13:13. he doeth great *w.*
Job 37:14. *wondrous* works, Ps 26:7; 71:17; 75:1; 78:32; 105:2; 106:22; 119:27; 145:5.
Ps 72:18. *w.* things, 86:10; 119:18.
Judg 13:19. *wondrously,* Joel 2:26.
WOOD, hay, stubble, 1 Cor 3:12.
2 Tim 2:20. also of *w.* and of earth
WORD, Num 23:5. Deut 4:2.
Deut 8:3. every *w.* . . . of God, Matt 4:4.
30:14. *w.* is very nigh, Rom 10:8.
Ps 68:11. the Lord gave the *w.*
119:49. remember the *w.* to thy servant
Prov 15:23. *w.* spoken in due season
25:11. a *w.* fitly spoken is like apples
Isa 29:21. an offender for a *word*
30:21. shall hear a *w.* behind thee
44:26. confirmeth *w.* of his servant
50:4. how to speak a *w.* in season
Jer 5:13. the *w.* is not in them
Matt 8:8. speak the *w.* only and my
12:36. every idle *w.* that men
Luke 4:26. what a *w.* is this
John 1:1. in beginning was the *W.*
14. the *W.* was made flesh
15:3. ye are clean through the *w.*
Acts 13:15. any *w.* of exhortation
26. to you is *w.* of this salvation sent
17:11. the *w.* with all readiness
20:32. and to the *w.* of his grace
1 Cor 4:20. kingdom of God is not in *w.*
Gal 6:6. taught in *w.* communicate
Eph 5:26. washing of water by *w.*
Col 3:16. let *w.* of Christ dwell in
17. whatsoever ye do in *w.* or deed
2 Thess 2:17. stablish you in every good *w.*
3:14. if any obey not our *w.*
1 Tim 5:17. labour in *w.* and doctrine
Titus 1:9. holding fast the faithful *w.*
Heb 4:2. the *w.* preached did not

5:13. is unskilful in *w.* of righteousness
13:22. suffer the *w.* of exhortation
James 1:21. receive with meekness the engrafted *w.*
3:2. if any man offend not in *w.*
1 Pet 3:1. if any obey not the *w.*
2 Pet 1:19. sure *w.* of prophecy
1 John 1:1. hands have handled of the *W.*
Rev 3:10. kept *w.* of my patience
12:11. overcame by *w.* of their testimony
Ps 130:5. in *his word* do I hope, 119:81.
147:19. sheweth—unto Jacob
Jer 20:9.—was in mine heart as fire
John 5:38. have not—abiding in you
Acts 2:41. that gladly received—
John 8:31. *my word,* 43. Rev 3:8.
Isa 8:20. *this word,* Rom 9:9.
Ps 119:11. *thy word* have I hid in mine heart
50. for—hath quickened me
105.—is a lamp unto my feet
140.—is very pure. 160.—is true
138:2. magnified—above all thy
Jer 15:16.—was unto me joy and
John 17:6. they have kept—17.—is truth
Prov 30:5. *word of God,* Isa 40:8. Mark 7:13. Rom 10:17. 1 Thess 2:13. Heb 4:12; 6:5. 1 Pet 1:23. Rev 19:13.
2 Kings 20:19. *word of the Lord,* Ps 18:30; 33:4. 2 Thess 3:1. 1 Pet 1:25.
Ps 119:43. *word of truth,* 2 Cor 6:7. Eph 1:13. Col 1:5. 2 Tim 2:15. James 1:18.
Job 23:12. esteemed *words* of his mouth
Prov 15:26. *w.* of the pure are pleasant *w.*
19:7. he pursueth them with *w.*
22:17. bow down thine car, hear *w.*
Eccles 10:12. the *w.* of a wise man's mouth
12:10. to find out acceptable *w.*
11. *w.* of the wise are as goads
Jer 7:4. trust ye not in lying *w.*
44:28. know whose *w.* shall stand
Dan 7:25. speak great *w.* against most High
Josh 6:5. slain them by *w.* of my mouth
14:2. take with you *w.*
Zech 1:13. good *w.* and comfortable *w.*
Matt 26:44. prayed third time, saying same *w.*
Luke 4:22. the gracious w. which proceeded out of his mouth
Acts 7:22. (Moses) . . . mighty in *w.* and
15:24. troubled you with *w.*, 18:15.
20:35. remember the *words* of Lord
26:25. speak forth the *w.* of truth and soberness
1 Cor 2:4. not with enticing *w.* of
2 Tim 1:13. hold fast form of sound *w.*
2:14. strive not about *w.* to no profit
Rev 1:3. hear *w.* of this prophecy, 22:18.
Ps 50:17. *my words,* Isa 51:16; 59:21. Jer 5:14. Mic 2:7. Mark 8:38; 13:31. John 5:47; 15:7.
1 Thess 4:18. *these words,* Rev 21:5.
Ps 119:103. *thy words,* 130, 139. Prov 23:8. Eccles 5:2. Ezek 33:21. Matt 12:37.
WORK, Gen 2:3. Exod 20:10; 31:14.
Deut 33:11. accept *w.* of his hands
Job1:10. blessed the *w.* of his hands
10:3. despise the *w.* of thine hands
14:15. a desire to *w.* of thine hands
36:9. he sheweth them their *w.*
Ps 8:3. heavens, *w.* of thy fingers
9:16. wicked is snared in *w.*
101:3. I hate the *w.* of them that
143:5. muse on *w.* of thy hands
Eccles 8:14. according to *w.* of the wicked
8:17. I beheld all the *w.* of God
12:14. God shall bring every *w.* into judgment
Isa 10:12. performed his whole *w.*
28:21. do his *w.*, his strange *w.*
29:16. shall *w.* say of him that
45:11. concerning *w.* of my hands
49:4. my *w.* with my God
64:8. we all are the *w.* of thy hand
Jer 10:15. vainty and *w.* of errors
18:3. potter wrought a *w.* on the
John 17:4. finished *w.* which thou gavest
Acts 5:38. if this *w.* be of men
13:2. for the *w.* whereto I have called
Rom 2:15. shew *w.* of law written
11:6. otherwise *w.* is no more *w.*
1 Cor 3:13. every man's *w.* shall be made
9:1. are not ye my *w.* in the Lord?
Eph 4:12. for *w.* of the ministry
2 Thess 1:11. *w.* of faith with power
2:17. stablish you in every good *w.*
2 Tim 4:5. do *w.* of an evangelist
James 1:4. let patience have her perfect *w.*
25. doer of the *w.* this man shall be blessed
1 Pet 1:17. judgeth according to every man's *w.*
Ps 104:23. *his work,* 62:12; 111:3. Prov 24:29. Isa 40:10. Job 36:24.
90:16. *thy work,* 92:4. Prov 24:27. Jer 31:16. Hab 3:2.
Exod 32:16. *work of God,* Ps 64:9. Eccles 7:13; 8:17. John 6:29. Rom 14:20.
Ps 28:5. *work of the Lord,* Isa 5:12. Jer 48:10. 1 Cor 15:58; 16:10.
17:4. concerning *works* of men
92:4. triumph in *w.* of thy hands
111:7. *w.* of his hands are verity
138:8. forsake not *w.* of thine own hands
Prov 31:31. let her own *w.* praise
Isa 26:12. wrought all our *w.* in us
Dan 4:37. all whose *w.* are truth
John 5:20. shew him greater *w.*
10:32. of those *w.* do ye stone me?
38. believe the *w.*
14:11. believe me for the very *w.* sake
12. greater *w.* than these shall he do
Acts 26:20. *w.* meet for repentance
Rom 3:27. by what law? of *w.*? nay: but by the law of faith
4:6. God imputeth righteousness without *w.*
9:11. not of *w.* but of him that calleth
32. but as it were by *w.* of the law
Rom 11:6. then is it no more of *works*
Gal 2:16. by *w.* of law no flesh be
3:10. as many as are of the *w.* of the law
5:19. *w.* of the flesh are manifest
Eph 2:9. not of *w.* 10. to good *w.*
5:11. unfruitful *w.* of darkness
Col 1:21. enemies in your mind by wicked *w.*
1 Thess 5:13. esteem them . . . for their *w's.* sake
2 Tim 1:9. not according to our *w.*
Titus 1:16. in *w.* they deny him
3:5. not by *w.* or righteousness which
Heb 6:1. repentance from dead *w.*
9:14. conscience from dead *w.*
James 2:14. and have not *w.*
21. justified by *w.*, 24, 25.
22. by *w.* was faith made perfect
1 John 3:8. he might destroy *w.* of
Rev 9:20. repented not of the *w.* of
18:6. according to her *w.*, 20:12, 13.
Ps 33:4. *his works,* 78:11; 103:22; 104:31; 107:15, 22; 145:9, 17. Dan 9:14. Acts 15:18. Heb 4:10.
Ps 106:35. *their works,* Isa 66:18. Jon 3:10. Matt 23:3, 5. 2 Cor 11:15. Rev 14:13; 20:12, 13.
Deut 15:10. *thy works,* Ps 66:3; 73:28; 92:5; 104:24; 143:5. Prov 16:3. Eccles 9:7. Rev 2:13.
Ps 40:5. *wonderful works,* 78:4; 107:8; 111:4. Matt 7:22. Acts 2:11.
Job 37:14. *works of God,* Ps 66:5; 78:7. Eccles 11:5. John 6:28; 9:3.
Ps 46:8. *w.* of the Lord, 111:2.
1 Sam 14:6. the Lord will *work* for us
Ps 119:126. time for thee, O Lord, to *w.*
Isa 43:13. I will *w.* and who shall

John 6:28. might *w.* works of God
9:4. I must *w.* the works of him
1 Thess 4:11. to *w.* with your hands
2 Thess 2:7. iniquity doth already *w.*
3:10. if any would not *w.*, neither should he eat
Prov 11:18. wicked *worketh* a deceitful *w.*
Isa 64:5. meetest him that . . . *w.* righteousness
John 5:17. my Father *w.* hitherto, and I *w.*
Acts 10:35. that *w.* righteousness is
Rom 4:4. to him that *w.* is reward
1 Cor 12:6. same God which *w.* all
2 Cor 4:17. *w.* for us a far more
Gal 5:6. faith which *w.* by love
Eph 1:11. *w.* all things according
Phil 2:13. it is God which *w.* in you
1 Thess 2:13. effectually *w.* also in you
Isa 28:29. excellent in *working*
Rom 7:13. sin *w.* death in me
Eph 1:19. according to *w.* of his mighty
3:7. by effectual *w.* of his power
4:28. *w.* with his hands the thing
Phil 3:21. according to *w.* whereby
2 Thess 3:11. *w.* not at all, but are
Heb 13:21. *w.* in you that which is well pleasing
2 Cor 6:1. *workers,* 11:13. Phil 3:2.
Job 31:3. *workers of iniquity,* 34:8, 22. Ps 5:5; 6:8; 28:3; 125:5; 141:9. Prov 10:29; 21:15.
Matt 10:10. *workman,* 2 Tim 2:15.
Exod 31:3. *workmanship,* Eph 2:10.

WORLD, 1 Sam 2:8. 1 Chron 16:30.
Ps 17:14. from men of the *w.*
24. I *w.* and they that dwell therein, 9:8. Nah 1:5.
50:12. *w.* is mine and the fulness
Eccles 3:11. hath set *w.* in their heart
Isa 26:9. inhabitants of *w.* will learn
Jer 10:12. established the *w.* by his wisdom, 51:15. Ps 93:1; 96:10.
Matt 16:26. what is a man profited if he shall gain the whole *world* and lose his own soul? Mark 8:36.
18:7. woe to *w.* because of offences
24:3. what shall be . . . the end of *w.*
Mark 16:15. go ye into all the *w.* and
Luke 20:35. worthy to obtain that *w.*
John 1:29. Lamb of God which taketh away sin of *w.*
3:16. God so loved the *w.* that he gave
17. *w.* through him might be saved
7:7. the *w.* cannot hate you, but
12:47. not to judge *w.* but to save *w.*
14:17. whom *w.* cannot receive
19. *w.* seeth me no more; but ye
31. *w.* may know that I love the Father
15:18. if the *w.* hate you, ye know that it hated
19. chosen you out of the *w.*, therefore the *w.*
16:28. I leave *w.* and go to the Father
17:9. I pray not for the *w.*
11. I am no more in the *w.*, but these
John 17:16. not of *w.*, even as I am not of *w.*
17:18. thou hast sent me into the *w.*
23. *w.* may know that thou hast sent
Rom 3:19. all the *w.* may become guilty
1 Cor 1:21. *w.* by wisdom knew not
Gal 6:14. *w.* is crucified unto me
Col 1:6. as it is in all *w.*; and bringeth
Titus 1:2. promised before *w.* began
Heb 2:5. *w.* to come, 6:5.
11:38. the *w.* was not worthy
1 John 2:2. propitiation . . . for sins of the *w.*
17. *w.* passeth away and the lust
3:1. the *w.* knoweth us not
4:5. they are of the *w.* therefore speak they of the *w.* and the *w.* heareth them
5:19. whole *w.* lieth in wickedness
Rev 3:10. temptation shall come on all *w.*
13:3. all *w.* wondered after beast
Matt 12:32. *this world,* John 8:23; 13:1. Rom 12:2. 1 Tim 6:7.
Heb 1:2. he made the *worlds*
11:3. the *w.* were framed by him

WORM, Exod 16:20. Isa 51:8.
Job 25:6. man that is a *w.*
Ps 22:6. I am a *w.* and no man
Isa 41:14. fear not, thou *w.* Jacob, and ye men of Israel
66:24. their *w.* shall not die, Mark 9:44, 48.
Job 19:26. *worms* destroy body, Acts 12:23.

WORMWOOD, Deut 29:18. Prov 5:4. Lam 3:15, 19. Amos 5:7. Rev 8:11.

WORSE, Gen 19:9. Jer 7:26. Matt 12:45. John 5:14. 1 Cor 8:8; 11:17. 2 Tim 3:13. 2 Pet 2:20.

WORSHIP the Lord in beauty of holiness, 1 Chron 16:29. Ps 29:2; 66:4; 96:9; 45:11; 95:6; 99:5. Matt 4:10.
Matt 15:9. in vain do they *w.* me
John 4:24. *w.* him must *w.* him in spirit
Acts 17:23. whom therefore ye ignorantly *w.*
24:14. so *w.* I the God of my fathers
Rev 3:9. *w.* before thy feet
13:12. causeth earth . . . to *w.* first beast
19:10. to *w.* God, 22:9.
Exod 4:31. *worshipped,* 32:8. Jer 1:16. 1 Chron 29:20. Rom 1:25. 2 Thess 2:4. Rev 5:14; 7:11; 11:16; 13:4.

WORTH, Job 24:25. Prov 10:20.
Gen 32:10. I am not *worthy* of least
Matt 8:8. I am not *w.* . . . under my roof
10:10. workman is *w.* of his meat
13. if house be *w.* let your peace
22:8. which were bidden were not *w.*
Luke 3:8. fruits *worthy* of repentance
7:4. *w.* for whom he should do this
10:7. labourer is *w.* of his hire
15:19. no more *w.* to be called thy son, 21.
20:35. counted *w.* to obtain
21:36. *w.* to escape all these things
Acts 5:41. counted *w.* to suffer shame
Rom 8:18. not *w.* to be compared
Eph 4:1. walk *w.* of the vocation
1 Thess 2:12. walk *w.* of God, who
2 Thess 1:5. *w.* of the kingdom of God
11. God would count you *w.* of this calling
1 Tim 1:15. *w.* of all acceptation, 4:9.
5:18. labourer is *w.* of his reward
6:1. count their masters *w.* of all honour
Heb 3:3. *w.* of more glory than Moses
10:29. of how much sorer punishment shall he be thought *w.*
Rev 3:4. in white, for they are *worthy*
5:12. *w.* is the Lamb that was slain
16:6. blood to drink; for they are *w.*

WOULD God, Exod 16:3. Num 11:29. Acts 26:29. 1 Cor 4:8. 2 Cor 11:1.
Ps 81:11. Israel *w.* none of me
Prov 1:25. *w.* none of my reproof
30. they *w.* none of my counsel
Matt 7:12. whatsoever ye *w.* that men should do
Rom 7:15. what I *w.*, that I do not, 19.
Gal 5:17. cannot do the things ye *w.*
Rev 3:15. I *w.* thou wert cold or hot
Neh 9:30. *would not,* Isa 30:15. Matt 18:30; 23:30, 37. Rom 11:25.

WOUND, Exod 21:25. Prov 6:33. Jer 10:19; 15:18; 30:12, 14. Mic 1:9.
Deut 32:39. I *wound* and I heal
1 Cor 8:12. *w.* their weak conscience
Rev 13:3. his deadly *w.* healed, 14.
Ps 69:26. *wounded,* 109:22. Song of Sol 5:7.

Prov 18:14. a *w.* spirit who can bear?
Isa 53:5. *w.* for our transgressions
Job 5:18. he *woundeth* and his hands
Prov 27:6. *wounds,* Isa 1:6. Jer 30:17.

WRATH, Gen 49:7. Exod 32:10, 11.
Num 16:46. *w.* gone out from Lord
Deut 32:27. feared *w.* of the enemy
Neh 13:18. bring more *w.* on Israel
Job 5:2. *w.* killeth the foolish man
Ps 76:10. *w.* of man shall praise thee
Isa 54:8. in a little *w.* I hid my face
Hab 3:2. in *w.* remember mercy
Matt 3:7. flee from *w.* to come
Rom 2:5. treasurest up . . . *w.* against day of *w.*
5:9. saved from *w.* through him
12:19. give place unto *w.*
13:5. not only for *w.* but also for conscience
Eph 2:3. by nature children of *w.*
4:26. let not sun go down on your *w.*
1 Thess 1:10. delivered us from *w.* to come
5:9. not appointed us to *w.*
1 Tim 2:8. holy hands without *w.*
Heb 11:27. not fearing *w.* of king
James 1:19. slow to speak, slow to *w.*
20. *w.* of man worketh not righteousness of God
Rev 6:16. from *w.* of Lamb
14:8. wine of *w.* of her fornication, 18:3.
Ezra 8:22. *his wrath,* Ps 2:5, 12; 78:38. Jer 7:29; 10:10. Rev 6:17.
Num 25:11. *my wrath,* Ps 95:11. Isa 10:6; 60:10. Ezek 7:14. Hos 5:10.
Ps 38:1. *thy wrath,* 85:3; 88:7, 16; 89:46; 90:9, 11; 102:10.
89:38. *wrath,* Isa 54:9; 57:17.

WREST, Exod 23:2. 2 Pet 3:16.

WRESTLE, Gen 32:24, 25. Eph 6:12.

WRETCHED, Rom 7:24. Rev 3:17.

WRINKLE, Job 16:8. Eph 5:27.

WRITE, Exod 34:1, 27. Deut 27:3. Isa 8:1. Jer 30:2. Hab 2:2.
Deut 6:9. *w.* them upon the posts
Prov 3:3. *w.* them on table of thine heart, 7:3.
1 John 2:1. little children, these things *w.* I unto you that ye sin not, 12.
7. I *w.* no new commandment unto you
8. a new commandment I *w.* unto you
13. I *w.* unto you, fathers . . . I *w.* to you, young men . . . I *w.* to you, little children
Ps 69:28. not be *written* with the
102:18. be *w.* for the generation
Prov 22:20. have not I *w.* to thee
Eccles 12:10. that which was *w.*
1 Cor 10:11. *w.* for our admonition
2 Cor 3:2. epistle *w.* in our hearts
3. *w.* not with ink but with the Spirit
Heb 12:23. are *w.* in heaven, Luke 10:20.
1 John 2:14. I have *w.* to you, fathers . . . I have *w.* to you, young men
21. I have not *w.* unto you because ye
26. these things have I *w.* unto you

WRONG, Ps 105:14. Jer 22:3, 13.
1 Cor 6:7. why do ye not rather take *w.*, 8.
Col 3:25. he that doeth *w.* shall receive
2 Cor 7:2. *wronged,* Philem 18.
Prov 8:36. *wrongeth* his own soul

WROUGHT, 1 Sam 6:6; 14:45.
Ps 139:15. curiously *w.*
Isa 26:12. *w.* all our works in us
Ezek 20:9. I *w.* for my name's sake, 22.
John 3:21. that they are *w.* in God
Rom 7:8. *w.* in me all manner of concupiscence
2 Cor 5:5. that hath *w.* us for selfsame thing is God
1 Pet 4:3. have *w.* will of Gentiles

Y

YEA, yea, nay, nay, Matt 5:37.
2 Cor 1:18. *y.* and nay, 20. *y.* and in him amen

YEAR, acceptable, Isa 61:2. Luke 4:19.
Isa 63:4. *y.* of my redeemed is come
Jer 11:23. *y.* of their visitation, 23:12; 48:44.
Job 10:5. thy *years* as man's days
Ps 90:4. a thousand *y.* in thy sight
2 Pet 3:8. a thousand *y.* as one day
Rev 20:2. bound him a thousand *y.*, 3.

YESTERDAY, Job 8:9. Heb 13:8.

YIELD yourselves, 2 Chron 30:8.
Ps 67:6. earth *y.* her increase, 85:12.
Rom 6:13. neither *y.* ye your members as instruments . . . but *y.* yourselves
Rom 6:16. whom ye *yield* yourselves
19. *yielded* members servants
Heb 12:11. *yieldeth* peaceable fruit

YOKE, Deut 28:48. 1 Kings 12:4.
Isa 9:4. broken the *y.* of his burden
10:27. the *y.* shall be destroyed
Lam 1:14. *y.* of my transgressions
Matt 11:29. take my *y.* upon you
11:30. my *y.* is easy and my burden is light
Gal 5:1. *y.* of bondage, Acts 15:10.
2 Cor 6:14. be ye not unequally *yoked*

YOU only have I known, Amos 3:2.
Luke 10:16. despiseth *y.* despiseth me
13:28. and *y.* yourselves thrust out
2 Cor 12:14. I seek not yours but *y.*
Eph 2:1. *y.* hath he quickened
Col 1:21. *y.* that were sometime alienated and enemies in your mind
Luke 6:20. *yours* is the kingdom of God

YOUNG, I have been, Ps 37:25.
Isa 40:11. gently lead those that are with *y.*
1 Tim 5:1. and the *younger* men
14. I will therefore that *y.* women marry
1 Pet 5:5. ye *y.* submit yourselves to elder
Gen 8:21. the imagination of man is evil from his *youth*
1 Kings 18:12. fear the Lord from my *y.*
Job 13:26. possess iniquities of my *y.*
Ps 25:7. sins of my *y.*
Eccles 11:9. Rejoice, O young man, in thy *y.*
10. childhood and *y.* are vanity
Jer 2:2. the kindness of thy *y.*
1 Tim 4:12. let no man despise thy *y.*
2 Tim 2:22. flee *youthful* lusts
Prov 7:7. *youths,* Isa 40:30.

Z

ZEAL for Lord, 2 Kings 10:16.
Ps 69:9. the *z.* of thine house hath
119:139. my *z.* hath consumed me
Isa 9:7. *z.* of the Lord of hosts will perform
59:17. and was clad with *z.* as a cloak
63:15. where is thy *z.* and thy strength
Rom 10:2. they have a *z.* of God
Phil 3:6. concerning *z.*, persecuting
Num 25:13. was *zealous* for his God
Acts 22:3. and was *z.* toward God as
Titus 2:14. people *z.* of good works
Rev 3:19. be *z.* therefore and repent
Gal 4:18. *zealously* affected always in a

ZION, 2 Sam 5:7. 1 Kings 8:1. for Jerusalem, temple, or church, 2 Kings 19:31. Ps 2:6; 9:11; 14:7; 48:2, 11, 12; 146:10; 147:12. Isa 1:27; 2:3; 60:14; 62:1

PLACE NAME INDEX TO THE MAPS

Each place name in the alphabetical index is followed by the letter-number coordinates at which it is located, and then by the number of the map on which it can be found.

Example:	NAME	COORDINATES	MAP NUMBER
	Babylonia	E8	2

P 1
Books of the Bible in the Lands of the Bible
ITALY
Acts 21–28
Romans
Hebrews (?)
MACEDONIA
Philippians
1 and 2 Thessalonians
GREECE
1 and 2 Corinthians
Jude (?)
ACHAIA
Acts 15–18
PATMOS
The Revelation
CRETE
Titus
ASIA
Acts 18–21
Ephesians
Colossians
1 and 2 Timothy
Philemon
1, 2 and 3 John (?)
BITHYNIA/PONTUS
James (?)
1 and 2 Peter
GALATIA
Acts 13–15
Galatians
1 and 2 Peter
CAPPADOCIA
1 and 2 Peter
Black Sea
Caspian Sea
Mediterranean Sea
Tigris River
Euphrates River
MESOPOTAMIA
Genesis 12
ASSYRIA
Jonah
Nahum
PERSIA
Nehemiah 1,2
Esther
SYRIA
Acts 11–13
BABYLON
Ezekiel
Daniel
CHALDEA
Genesis 1–11
THE HOLY LAND
Genesis 12–38
Joshua
Judges
Ruth
1 and 2 Samuel
1 and 2 Kings
1 and 2 Chronicles
Psalms
Proverbs
Ecclesiastes
Song of Solomon
Matthew
Mark
Luke
John
Acts 1–11
ISRAEL
Hosea
Amos
JUDAH
MOAB
Deuteronomy
Job
EDOM
Obadiah
EGYPT
Genesis 39–50
Exodus 1–13
Ezra
Nehemiah 3–13
Isaiah
Jeremiah
Lamentations
Joel
Micah
Habakkuk
Zephaniah
Haggai
Zechariah
Malachi
Numbers
MT. SINAI
Exodus 14–40
Leviticus
Nile River
Red Sea
Persian Gulf
NORTH
(?) = Location uncertain
= Modern boundary
= Disputed boundary
0 200 400 Miles
0 200 400 600 Kilometers
Size of Bible lands compared to the United States
© 1980 Tyndale House Publishers, Inc.
A B C D E
3 4 5 6 7 8
40° 56° 32° 24° 8° 48°

Relation of Bible lands to the world

The Flow of Bible History
Numbers on the map show specific events in chronological order, and the arrows indicate general direction of movement.
Caspian Sea
Soviet Union
Turkey
MOUNTAINS OF ARARAT
2 Landing of Noah's Ark
Tigris River
MESOPOTAMIA
5 God's covenant with Abram
12 Israel scattered
17
Iran
MEDIA
ASSYRIA
SYRIA
Euphrates River
Iraq
Lebanon
Syria
BABYLONIA
14 Cyrus frees Jews
3 Tower of Babel
PERSIA
ISRAEL
Judah captive 70 years 13
1 Man's beginnings (?)
16 Christ and the Apostles
6 11 Conquest, Judges, Kings
CHALDEA
7 15 Jerusalem rebuilt
4 Call of Abram
MOAB
JUDAH
ARABIA
Jordan
Kuwait
EDOM
10 40 years of wandering
Saudi Arabia
Persian Gulf
9 MOUNT SINAI Moses receives Law
(?) = Location uncertain
= Modern boundary
= Disputed boundary
Iraq = Modern country name
0 200 400 Miles
0 200 400 Kilometers
Red Sea
© 1980 Tyndale House Publishers, Inc.

MAP
Old Testament Events
○ Cities of refuge (Thought to be less than half-day walk from any location) Numbers 35
• Other cities
(?) Location uncertain
0 10 20 Miles
0 10 20 Kilometers
NORTH
Mediterranean Sea
Zarephath
Dan (Laish)
Kedesh
300 miles to Haran
Jacob works for Laban; marries Leah and Rachel
Hazor
Sea of Chinnereth
Golan
Mount Carmel
Elijah's contest with Baal's prophets
Mount Tabor
Deborah and Barak defeat Sisera
Kishon River
Shunem
Elisha raises boy to life
Edrei
Gideon defeats Midianites
Mount Gilboa
Saul and Jonathan slain
Ramoth-gilead
Canaanites
Dothan
Joseph sold into slavery
Brook Cherith
Ravens feed Elijah
Jabesh-gilead
Samaria
Shechem
Law read between two mountains
Jordan River
Mahanaim
Absalom killed
Jabbok River
Peniel
Jacob wrestles angel
Joppa
Shiloh
Ammonites
Aijalon Valley
Jacob's ladder vision
Ophrah
Bethel
Ai
Rabbah
Mizpah
Achan's sin causes defeat
Gilgal
Beth-Horon
Sun stands still for Joshua
Jericho
Walls collapse
Gibeah
Heshbon
Bezer
Jerusalem
Melchizedek blesses Abram at Salem
Abraham offers Isaac at Mount Moriah
Elah Valley
David and Goliath
Bethlehem
Ruth marries Boaz
Mount Nebo
Moses dies
Jahaz
Adullam
David hides from Saul
Philistines
Amorites
Hebron
Salt Sea
Gaza
Samson destroys temple
Arnon River
Ziklag
Egypt
Jacob's family settles in Goshen
Beersheba
Esau gives Jacob his birthright
Moabites
Hormah
Amalekites
Sodom (?)
Sodom and Gomorrah destroyed
Edomites
Zoar
Brook Zered
© 1980 Tyndale House Publishers, Inc.
1 2 3 4 5
A B C D E F G H
35° 35°30′ 36° 34°30′ 33° 32°30′ 32° 31°30′ 31°

MAP 4

Jerusalem: Events in Jesus' Life

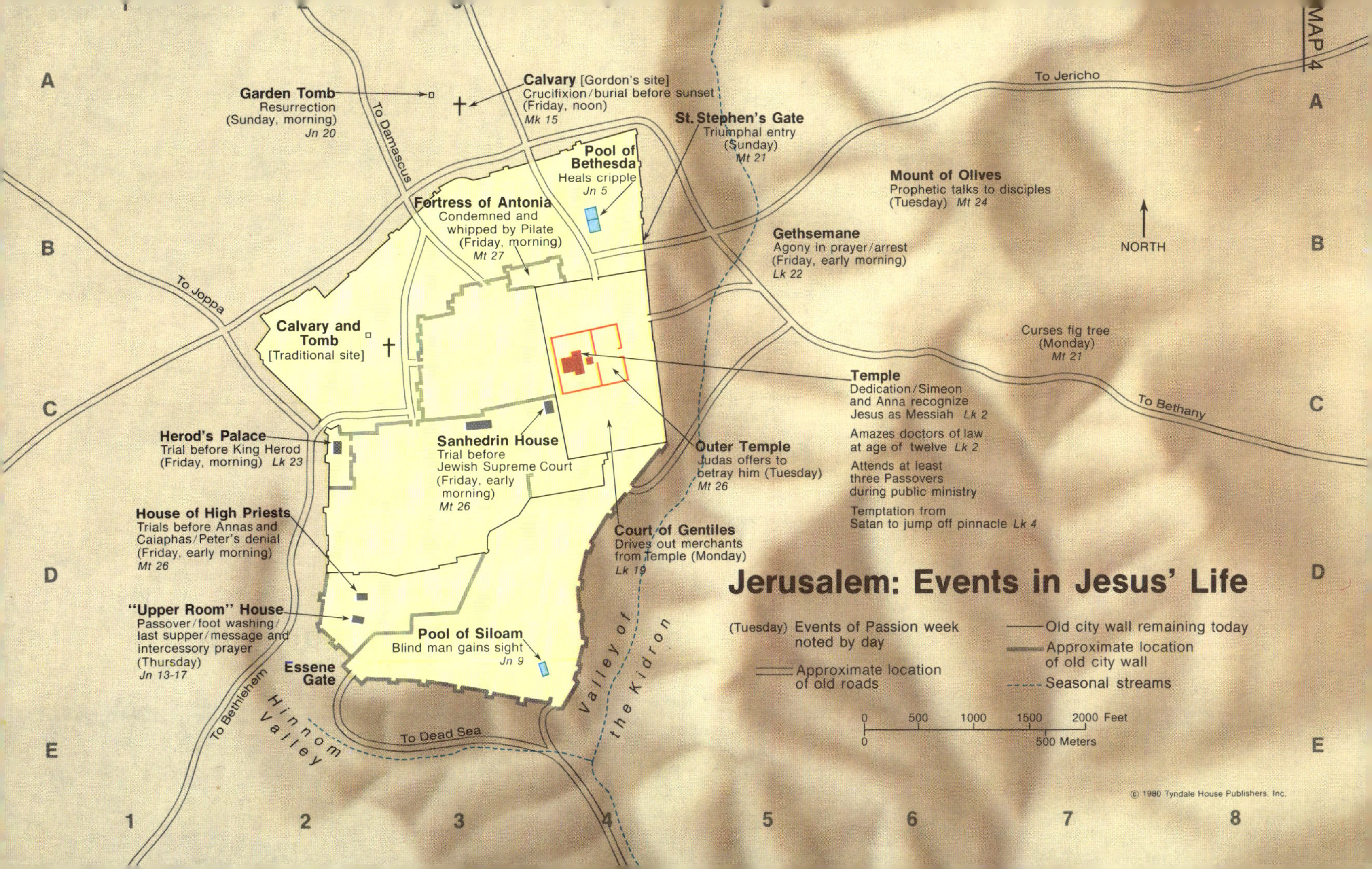

The Life of Christ
Events shown on map are numbered in chronological order beginning with Christ's birth in Bethlehem and ending with the ascension:
47 Ascension Acts 1
1
2
3
4
5
6
7
8
A
B
C
D
E
34°30′
35°
35°30′
36°
33°30′
33°
32°30′
Sidon
Zarephath
Damascus
Syria
Mount Hermon
35 Transfiguration (possible site) Lk 9
Tyre
30 Syrophoenician girl healed Mk 7
Caesarea-Philippi
34 Testimony of Peter: "You are the Messiah!" Lk 9
13 Settles here Mt 4
16 Heals centurion's servant Mt 8
18 Pharisees' opposition Mk 3
22 Raises Jairus' daughter Mk 5
24 Sends the Twelve Lk 9
29 Bread of Life sermon Jn 6
Chorazin
Capernaum
Bethsaida
26 Feeding of 5000 Jn 6
33 Heals blind man Mk 8
Gennesaret
28 Many miracles Mk 6
8 Turns water to wine Jn 2
11 Heals official's son Jn 4
Cana
Dalmanutha
32 Jews demand a sign Mk 8
Sea of Galilee
Tiberias
21 Heals Gadarene demoniac Mt 8
15 Appoints the Twelve Lk 6
Sermon on the Mount Mt 5-7
46 Great commission Mt 28
19 Parables of kingdom Mk 4
20 Stills storm Mk 4
27 Walks on water Mk 6
31 Feeding of 4000 Mk 8
Nazareth
4 Childhood Mt 2
12 Rejection Lk 4
23 Rejection Mk 6
Galilee
Gadara
Nain
17 Raises widow's son Lk 7
Caesarea
36 Ten lepers healed Lk 17
Decapolis
Mediterranean Sea
M

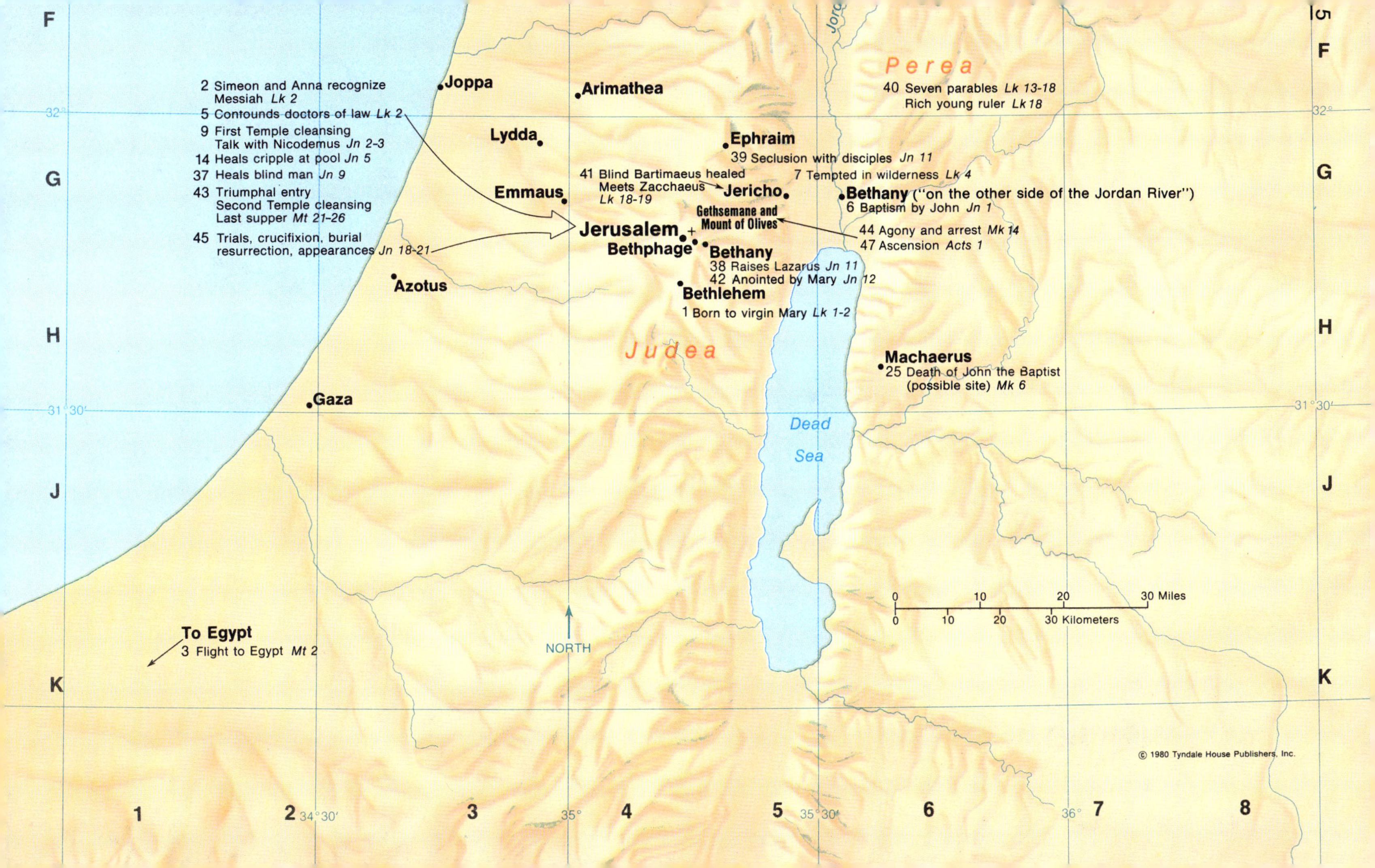
5
Perea
40 Seven parables Lk 13-18
Rich young ruler Lk 18
2 Simeon and Anna recognize Messiah Lk 2
5 Contounds doctors of law Lk 2
9 First Temple cleansing
Talk with Nicodemus Jn 2-3
14 Heals cripple at pool Jn 5
37 Heals blind man Jn 9
43 Triumphal entry
Second Temple cleansing
Last supper Mt 21-26
45 Trials, crucifixion, burial resurrection, appearances Jn 18-21
Joppa
Arimathea
Lydda
Emmaus
Azotus
Gaza
Ephraim
39 Seclusion with disciples Jn 11
7 Tempted in wilderness Lk 4
41 Blind Bartimaeus healed
Meets Zacchaeus
Lk 18-19
Jericho
Bethany ("on the other side of the Jordan River")
6 Baptism by John Jn 1
Gethsemane and Mount of Olives
44 Agony and arrest Mk 14
47 Ascension Acts 1
Jerusalem
Bethphage
Bethany
38 Raises Lazarus Jn 11
42 Anointed by Mary Jn 12
Bethlehem
1 Born to virgin Mary Lk 1-2
Judea
Machaerus
25 Death of John the Baptist (possible site) Mk 6
Dead Sea
To Egypt
3 Flight to Egypt Mt 2
NORTH
0 10 20 30 Miles
0 10 20 30 Kilometers
32°
31°30′
34°30′
35°
35°30′
36°
F G H J K
1 2 3 4 5 6 7 8

The Early Church

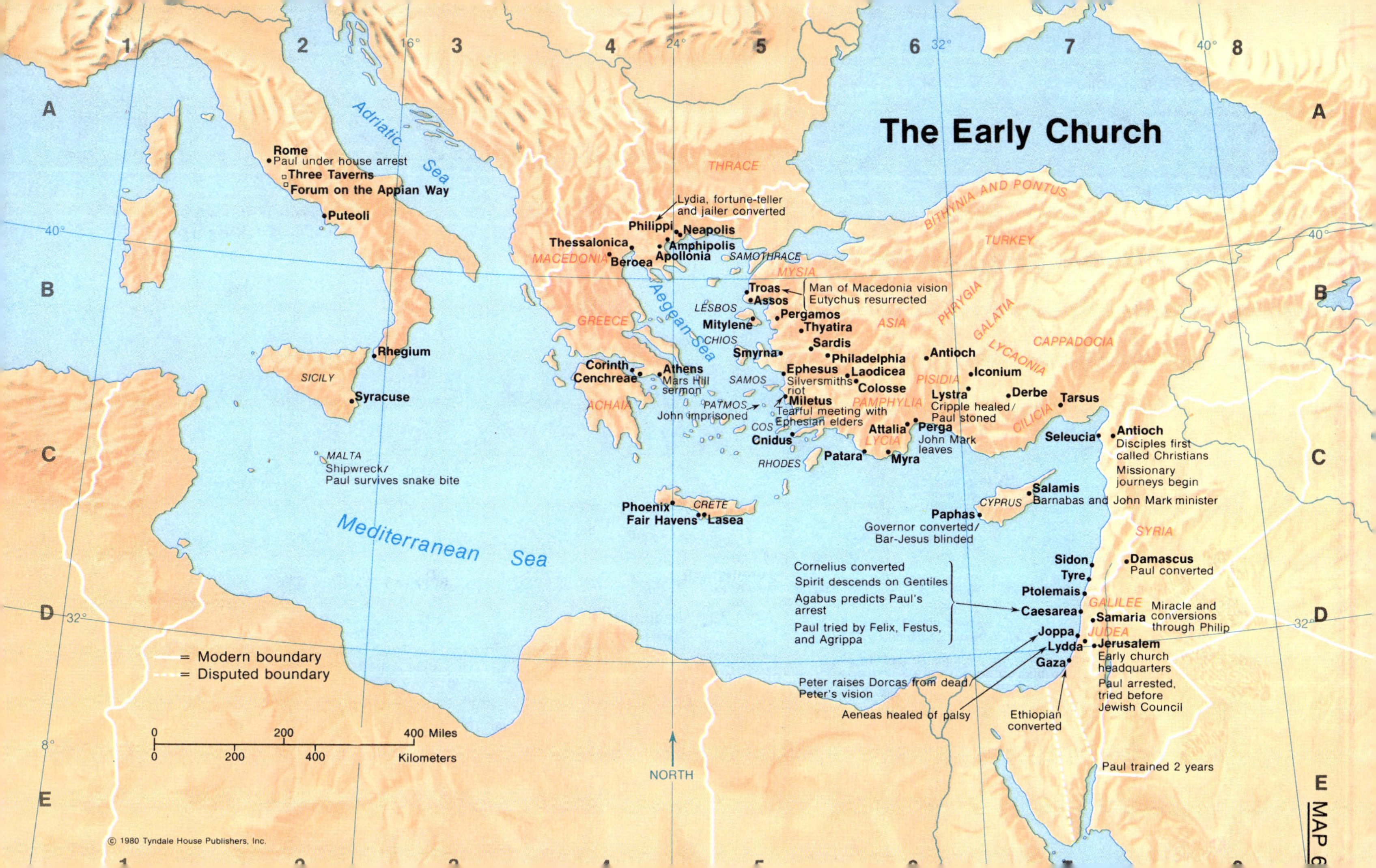